THE READER'S DIGEST · OXFORD

Wordfinder

THE READER'S DIGEST · OXFORD

Wordfinder

Edited by
SARA TULLOCH

CLARENDON PRESS · OXFORD ·

This edition of
THE READER'S DIGEST OXFORD COMPLETE WORDFINDER
was commissioned by The Reader's Digest Association Limited, London

Published by

The Reader's Digest Association Limited
Berkeley Square House
Berkeley Square
London WIX 6AB

In conjunction with

Oxford University Press
Walton Street
Oxford OX2 6DP

Reprinted 1996

ISBN 0 276 42101 9

Printed and bound in Italy by Rotolito Lombarda, Milan

Project team

Editor-in-chief
Sara Tulloch

Consultant editor
Robert Ilson

Senior editor
Judith Pearsall

Sub-editors
Michael Proffitt, David Shirt,
Catherine Soanes, Maurice Waite

Assistant editors
Julia Elliott, Anne Knight,
Rachel Unsworth, Jonathan Wetton

Editorial assistants
Christine Cowley, Louise Jones,
Susan Vickers

Data capture & validation
Pam Marjara, Kay Pepler, Anne Whear

Critical readers
Alan Buckley, Hazel Clarke,
Jonathan Jones, Helen McCurdy,
Elaine Pollard, Trish Stableford

Pronunciations
Judith Scott, Susan Wilkin

Additional specialist help
Patrick Hanks, John Kahn, Jeremy Marshall,
David Munro, John Simpson, Della Thompson,
Freda Thornton, and Edmund Weiner

Contents

Preface

The publication of this *Wordfinder* brings to a fruitful conclusion a stimulating collaboration between Reader's Digest and Oxford University Press; it also marks the beginning of an exciting new era in the preparation of lexical reference books. The *Wordfinder* combines the information one would expect to find in a conventional dictionary and a thesaurus in a single volume; moreover, the complete marrying of the two parts into an integrated whole has meant that every meaning for which synonyms are offered has been reappraised. This single analysis of the language, treating meanings and related words side by side, has produced a book which offers the reader an abundance of information about words, accessible from a number of different points but presented clearly in a fully integrated format.

Many people deserve thanks for their contribution to this project; those involved in the editorial work are listed as part of the project team. I would also like to thank Robin Hosie and Paul Middleton from Reader's Digest; Bill Ramson, Joan Hughes, and the late Harriet Michell for help with Australianisms; and, last but not least, Consultant Editor Dr Robert Ilson for his superhuman efforts in reading and commenting on the entire text.

SKT

Oxford, 1993

How to use this book

A great deal of the information given in the *Wordfinder* entries is self-explanatory, but if you need help in understanding any part of an entry, start here by looking at the 'entry maps'. In the sample entries, the various types of information are numbered (❶❷❸ etc.); find the number preceding whatever is puzzling you, then match it up with the numbers round the edges of the entries. The notes against these numbers will tell you which type of dictionary information you are looking at.

A Defining sections

❶ **Headword** introduces a new entry

❷ **Pronunciation** in oblique strokes / /

❸ **Part(s) of speech** in *italic* type

New part of speech signalled by a bullet •

❹ **Variant spellings** in **bold** type

❺ **Inflected forms** in **bold** type

❻ **Sense letters and numbers** in **bold** type subdivide meanings

Definitions explain meaning

❼ **Grammar notes** give constructional information

❶**adviser** ❷/ədvízer/ ❸*n.* (also ❾*disp.* ❹**advisor**) ❻**1** a person who advises, esp. one appointed to do so and regularly consulted. **2** *US* a person who advises students on education, careers, etc. ¶ The disputed form *advisor* is prob. influenced by the adj. *advisory*.
■ **1** counsellor, mentor, guide, counsel, consultant, confidant(e), director, *Law amicus curiae.*

brief /breef/ *adj., n., & v.* • *adj.* **1** of short duration; fleeting. **2** concise in expression. **3** abrupt, brusque (❽*was rather brief with me*). **4** scanty; lacking in substance (*wearing a brief skirt*). • *n.* **1** ❼(*in pl.*) **a** women's brief pants. **b** men's brief underpants. **2** *Law* **a** a summary of the facts and legal points of a case drawn up for counsel. **b** a piece of work for a barrister. **3** instructions given for a task, operation, etc. (orig. a bombing plan given to an aircrew). **4** ❾*RC Ch.* a letter from the Pope to a person or community on a matter of discipline. **5** ❾*US* a short account or summary; a synopsis. • *v.tr.* **1** *Brit. Law* instruct (a barrister) by brief. **2** instruct (an employee, a participant, etc.) in preparation for a task; inform or instruct thoroughly in advance (*briefed him for the interview*) (cf. DEBRIEF). ❿⓫□ **be brief** use few words. **hold a brief for 1** argue in favour of. **2** be retained as counsel for. **in brief** in short. **watching brief 1** a brief held by a barrister following a case for a client not directly involved. **2** a state of interest maintained in a proceeding not directly or immediately concerning one. ⓬□□ **briefly** *adv.* **briefness** *n.* ⓭[ME f. AF *bref*, OF *brief*, f. L *brevis* short]
■ *adj.* **1** short, momentary, short-lived; flying, brisk, hasty, speedy, swift; transitory, fleeting, transient, evanescent, passing. **2** short, concise, thumbnail, succinct, compact, to the point, laconic, terse, summary, compendious. **3** curt, abrupt, terse, short, blunt, brusque, direct . . .

broadcast /bráwdkaast/ *v., n., adj., & adv.* • *v.* (*past* ❺**broadcast** or **broadcasted**; *past part.* **broadcast**) **1** *tr.* **a** transmit (programmes or information) by radio or television. **b** disseminate (information) widely. **2** *intr.* undertake or take part in a radio or television transmission. **3** *tr.* scatter (seed etc.) over a large area, esp. by hand. • *n.* a radio or television programme or transmission. • *adj.* **1** transmitted by radio or television. **2 a** scatter widely. **b** (of information etc.) widely disseminated. • *adv.* over a large area. □□ **broadcaster** *n.* **broadcasting** *n.* [BROAD + ⓯CAST *past part.*]
■ *v.* **1 a** air, transmit, relay; radio; screen, televise, telecast. **b** announce, advertise, circulate, publish, proclaim, pronounce; put *or* give out, report; disseminate. **3** sow . . .

❽ **Examples** in *italic* type in brackets ( )

❾ **Usage labels** in *italic* type show restricted use

Further notes on usage signalled by ¶

❿ ⓫ **Phrase list** signalled by □ gives idioms, phrases, compounds

⓬ **Derivative list** signalled by □□ gives regularly derived forms

⓭ **Etymology** (word history) in square brackets [ ]

⓯ **Cross-references** in SMALL CAPITALS to other headwords or *italic* type to phrases etc.

Finding your way round an entry

Further information is to be found in the correspondingly numbered paragraphs on pp. xii-xix. For example, if you want to know more about how usage labels work in defining sections, look at paragraph A9 on p. xiv; if you want to understand synonym ordering, look at paragraphs B6, 7, and 8 on p. xviii, and so on.

B Synonym sections

❶ Synonyms
introduced by a black box ■

❷ Content
of synonym sections:
a synonyms,
b cross-references, or
c both

❸ Part(s) of speech
in *italic* type

New part of speech
signalled by a bullet •

❹ Forms
in brackets ( )

❺ Sense numbers and letters
refer back to defined meanings

❻ ❼ Ordering
of synonyms

❼ Punctuation
is significant

brief /breef/ *adj.*, *n.*, & *v.* • *adj.* **1** of short duration; fleeting. **2** concise in expression. **3** abrupt, brusque (*was rather brief with me*). **4** scanty; lacking in substance (*wearing a brief skirt*). • *n.* **1** (in *pl.*) **a** women's brief pants. **b** men's brief underpants. **2** *Law* **a** a summary of the facts and legal points of a case drawn up for counsel. **b** a piece of work for a barrister. **3** instructions given for a task, operation, etc. (orig. a bombing plan given to an aircrew). **4** *RC Ch.* a letter from the Pope to a person or community on a matter of discipline. **5** *US* a short account or summary; a synopsis. • *v.tr.* **1** *Brit. Law* instruct (a barrister) by brief. **2** instruct (an employee, a participant, etc.) in preparation for a task; inform or instruct thoroughly in advance (*briefed him for the interview*) (cf. DEBRIEF). □ **be brief** use few words. **hold a brief for 1** argue in favour of. **2** be retained as counsel for. **in brief** in short. **watching brief 1** a brief held by a barrister following a case for a client not directly involved. **2** a state of interest maintained in a proceeding not directly or immediately concerning one. □□ **briefly** *adv.* **briefness** *n.* [ME f. AF *bref*, OF *brief*, f. L *brevis* short]

❶■ ❸*adj.* ❺**1** ❷a❻short, momentary, short-lived ❼; flying, brisk, hasty, speedy, swift; transitory, fleeting, transient, evanescent, passing. **2** short, concise, thumbnail, succinct, compact, to the point, laconic, terse, summary, compendious. **3** curt, abrupt, terse, short, blunt, brusque, direct, unceremonious. **4** ❷bsee SCANTY. ❸• *n.* **1** ❹(*briefs*) pants, knickers, bikini briefs, G-string; underpants, boxer shorts, ❾*US* shorts, *propr.* Y-fronts. **3** instructions, guideline(s), directive(s), orders, directions. **5** summary, outline, digest, précis, résumé, *aperçu*, abstract, abridgement, synopsis. • *v.* **2** coach, instruct, train, drill, prime, prepare, make *or* get ready; advise, inform, apprise, acquaint, put in the picture, *colloq.* fill in, put a person wise. ❿⓫□ **hold a brief for 1** ⓭see ADVOCATE *v.* **in brief** in short, briefly, concisely, in sum, in summary, to sum up, succinctly, in a word, to cut a long story short, in a nutshell. ⓬□□ ❷c**briefly** momentarily, for a few moments *or* seconds *or* minutes, fleetingly, hurriedly, hastily, quickly; ⓭see also *in brief* above.

addictive /ədíktiv/ *adj.* (of a drug, habit, etc.) causing addiction or dependence.
■ ❷ahabit-forming, compulsive, obsessive, (❽*of a drug*) hard.

abash /əbásh/ *v.tr.* (usu. as **abashed** *adj.*) embarrass, disconcert. □□ **abashment** *n.* [ME f. OF *esbaïr* (*es-* = A-[4] 3, *baïr* astound or *baer* yawn)]
■ ❹(**abashed**) ⓭see *embarrassed* (EMBARRASS 1b).

❽ Explanations
in *italic* type

❾ Usage labels
in *italic* type show restricted use

❿ ⓫ Synonym phrase list
signalled by □

⓬ Synonym derivative list
signalled by □□

⓭ Cross-references
in the synonym sections

Visual Cues
Look out for the symbols which act as signposts

/ / **pronunciation**
• **part of speech**
□ **phrase list**
□□ **derivative list**
■ **synonym section**
SMALL CAPITALS **cross-references**

A Detailed explanation of defining sections

1 Headword

The headword is printed in bold roman type, or in bold italic type if the word is not naturalized in English and is usually found in italics in printed matter:

adumbrate /áddumbrayt/ *v.tr.* **1** indicate faintly. **2** represent in outline. **3** foreshadow, typify. **4** overshadow. □□ **adumbration** /-bráysh'n/ *n.* **adumbrative** /ədúmbrətiv/ *adj.* [L *adumbrare* (as AD-, *umbrare* f. *umbra* shade)]

ad valorem /ád vəlórem/ *adv.* & *adj.* (of taxes) in proportion to the estimated value of the goods concerned. [L, = according to the value]

Headwords are arranged in letter-by-letter alphabetical order.

Different words that are spelt the same way (homographs) are distinguished by raised numerals:

brig[1] /brig/ *n.* **1** a two-masted square-rigged ship, with an additional lower fore-and-aft sail on the gaff and a boom to the mainmast. **2** *US* a prison, esp. on a warship. [abbr. of BRIGANTINE]
■ **2** see PRISON *n.* 1.

brig[2] /brig/ *n. Sc.* & *N.Engl.* var. of BRIDGE[1].

2 Pronunciation

Guidance on the pronunciation of a headword will be found in most cases immediately after the headword, enclosed in oblique strokes / /. In some cases, more than one pronunciation is given: that given first is always the preferred pronunciation; if the variant is preceded by the label *disp.*, this indicates that some people disapprove of the variant or consider it incorrect. Guidance on the pronunciation of words printed in bold type within an entry (for example, in the derivatives list) is limited to cases in which the headword pronunciation would be of no help in establishing the correct pronunciation of the derivative.

The *Wordfinder* uses a simple respelling system to represent pronunciation. This is meant to be self-explanatory and easily readable by the lay person without constant recourse to a table of special characters. The system includes only one letter that is not found in the English alphabet: the character ə is used to represent the short neutral vowel called *schwa*, to which many unstressed vowels in English are reduced in normal speech. This vowel sounds something like the sound *er* or *uh* used by some people when hesitating; it is the sound of the initial *a* in words such as *abode* or *attract*, the *o* of *confide*, the *e* of *condiment*, etc. For speakers of Southern English 'received pronunciation' it is also the sound of the last syllable of words like *father* or *insular*, the first and last syllables of *particular*, and so on. This is represented as /ər/ in the transcriptions, since speakers of some varieties of English (Scottish and American, for instance) pronounce the *r* which follows the vowel.

The respelling system also uses a number of accents and diacritics over letters: an acute accent shows a stressed syllable. The macron (¯) is used over certain vowels to show that they are pronounced as long vowels, e.g. o͞o (the vowel sound in *food*), or diphthongs, e.g. ī (the vowel sound in *bright*). A breve mark (˘) shows that a sound is to be pronounced as a short vowel, e.g. o͝o (the vowel in *book* and *put*). An underline character is used to link certain consonants, e.g. to distinguish th (the sound at the beginning of *thin*) from t͟h (the sound at the beginning of *then*). An apostrophe (') is used between consonants in such words as *organization* to show that some speakers articulate the final syllable without a true vowel sound between 'sh' and 'n'.

For a full explanation of every sound's representation in the respelling system, please see the *Key to the pronunciations* on pp. xx–xxi.

3 Part of Speech

The grammatical identity of words as noun, verb, adjective, and so on, is given for all headwords and derivatives, and for compounds and phrases when necessary to aid clarity. The same part-of-speech label is used for groups of more than one word when the group has the function of that part of speech, e.g. *ad hoc*, *Parthian shot*.

When a headword has more than one part of speech, a list is given at the beginning of the entry, and the treatment of the successive parts of speech (in the same order as the list) is introduced by a bullet in each case:

accidental /áksidént'l/ *adj.* & *n.* ● *adj.* **1** happening by chance, unintentionally, or unexpectedly. **2** not essential to a conception; subsidiary. ● *n.* **1** *Mus.* a sign indicating a momentary departure from the key signature by raising or lowering a note. **2** something not essential to a conception. □□ **accidentally** *adv.* [ME f. LL *accidentalis* (as ACCIDENT)]

The standard part-of-speech names are used, and the following additional explanations should be noted:

- Nouns used attributively are designated *attrib.* when their function is not fully adjectival (e.g. *model* in a *model student*; *the student is very model* is not acceptable usage).
- Adjectives are labelled *attrib.* (= attributive) when they are normally placed before the word they modify (e.g. *undue* in *without undue effort*), and *predic.* (= predicative) when they normally occur (usually after a verb) in the predicate of a sentence (e.g. *afraid* in *he was afraid*). When an adjective can occur either attributively or predicatively, the designation *adj.* is used on its own.

- The designation *absol.* (= absolute) refers to uses of transitive verbs with an object implied but not stated (as in *smoking kills* and *let me explain*).
- The designation 'in *comb.*' (= in combination), or 'also in *comb.*', refers to uses of words (especially adjectives and nouns) as an element joined by a hyphen to another word, as with *crested* (which often appears in forms such as *red-crested, large-crested*) or *footer* (as *six-footer*).

4 Variants

Variant spellings are given before the definition; in all such cases the form given as the headword is the preferred form. Variant forms are also given at their own places in the dictionary when these are three or more entries away from the main form:

amir /əmeer/ *n.* (also **ameer**) the title of some Arab rulers. [Arab. *'amīr* commander f. *amara* command: cf. EMIR]
ameer var. of AMIR.

Variant spellings given at the beginning of an entry normally apply to the whole entry, including any phrases and undefined derivatives.

When variants apply only to certain functions or senses of a word, these are given in brackets at the relevant point in the entry:

burden /búrd'n/ *n.* & *v.* • *n.* **1** a load, esp. a heavy one. **2** an oppressive duty, obligation, expense, emotion, etc. **3** the bearing of loads (*beast of burden*). **4** (also *archaic* **burthen** /búrthən/) a ship's carrying-capacity, tonnage. **5 a** the refrain or chorus of a song. **b** the chief theme or gist of a speech, book, poem, etc. • *v.tr.* load with a burden; encumber, oppress.

Words that are normally spelt with a capital initial are given in this form as the headword; when they are in some senses spelt with a small initial and in others with a capital initial this is indicated by repetition of the full word in the appropriate form within the entry.

Variant American spellings are indicated by the designation *US*. These variants are often found in American use in addition to or instead of the main forms given:

amoeba /əmeebə/ *n.* (*US* **ameba**) (*pl.* **amoebas** or **amoebae** /-bee/) any usu. aquatic protozoan of the genus *Amoeba*, esp. *A. proteus*, capable of changing shape. ▫▫ **amoebic** *adj.* **amoeboid** *adj.* [mod.L f. Gk *amoibē* change]

Pronunciation of variants is given when this differs significantly from the pronunciation of the headword.

abatis /ábbətiss/ *n.* (also **abattis** /əbáttiss/) (*pl.* same or **abatises, abattises**) *hist.* a defence made of felled trees with the boughs pointing outwards. ▫▫ **abatised** *adj.* [F f. *abatre* fell: see ABATE]

5 Inflection

Inflection of words (i.e. plurals, past tenses, etc.) is given after the part of speech concerned:

broadcast /bráwdkaast/ *v., n., adj.,* & *adv.* • *v.* (*past* **broadcast** or **broadcasted**; *past part.* **broadcast**) **1** *tr.* **a** transmit (programmes or information) by radio or television. **b** disseminate (information) widely. **2** *intr.* undertake or take part in a radio or television transmission. **3** *tr.* scatter (seed etc.) over a large area, esp. by hand . . .

The forms given are normally those in use in British English. Variant American forms are identified by the label *US*; these variants are often found in American use in addition to or instead of the main forms given.

Pronunciation of inflected forms is given when this differs significantly from the pronunciation of the headword. The designation '*pronunc.* same' denotes that the pronunciation, despite a change of form, is the same as that of the headword.

In general, the inflection of nouns, verbs, adjectives, and adverbs is given when it is irregular (as described further below) or when, though regular, it causes difficulty (as with forms such as *budgeted, coos,* and *taxis*).

Plurals of nouns

Nouns that form their plural regularly by adding *-s* (or *-es* when they end in *-s, -x, -z, -sh,* or soft *-ch*) receive no comment. Other plural forms are given, notably:

- nouns endings in *-i* or *-o*.
- nouns ending in *-y*.
- nouns ending in Latinate forms such as *-a* and *-um*.
- nouns with more than one plural form, e.g. *fish* and *aquarium*.
- nouns with plurals involving a change in the stem, e.g. *foot, feet*.
- nouns with a plural form identical to the singular form, e.g. *sheep*.
- nouns in *-ful*, e.g. *handful*.

Forms of verbs

The following forms are regarded as regular:

- third person singular present forms adding *-s* to the stem (or *-es* to stems ending in *-s, -x, -z, -sh,* or soft *-ch*).
- past tenses and past participles adding *-ed* to the stem, dropping a final silent *-e* (e.g. *changed, danced*).
- present participles adding *-ing* to the stem, dropping a final silent *-e* (e.g. *changing, dancing*).

Other forms are given, notably:

- doubling of a final consonant, e.g. *bat, batted, batting*.
- strong and irregular forms involving a change in the stem, e.g. *come, came, come,* and *go, went, gone*.
- irregular inflections of borrowed words, e.g. *samba'd*.

Comparative and Superlative of Adjectives and Adverbs

Words of one syllable adding *-er* or *-est* and those ending in silent *-e* dropping the *-e* (e.g. *braver, bravest*) are regarded as regular. Most one-syllable words have these forms, but participial adjectives (e.g. *pleased*) do not.

Those that double a final consonant (e.g. *hot, hotter, hottest*) are given, as are two-syllable words that have comparative and superlative forms in *-er* and *-est* (of which very many are forms ending in *-y*, e.g. *lucky, luckier, luckiest*), and their negative forms (e.g. *unluckier, unluckiest*).

It should be noted that specification of these forms indicates only that they are available; it is usually also possible to form comparatives with *more* and superlatives with *most* (as in *more lucky, most unlucky*), which is the standard way of proceeding with adjectives and adverbs that do not admit of inflection.

Adjectives in -able formed from Transitive Verbs

These are given as derivatives when there is sufficient

evidence of their currency; in general they are formed as follows:

- verbs drop silent final *-e* except after *c* and *g* (e.g. *movable* but *changeable*).
- verbs of more than one syllable ending in *-y* (preceded by a consonant or *qu*) change *y* to *i* (e.g. *enviable*, *undeniable*).
- a final consonant is often doubled as in normal inflection (e.g. *conferrable*, *regrettable*).

6 Definition

Definitions are listed in a numbered sequence in order of comparative familiarity and importance, with the most current and important senses first.

They are subdivided into lettered senses (a, b, etc.) when these are closely related or call for collective treatment.

Definitions may include both multi-item paraphrases and single-item synonyms. A comma is generally used between synonyms, as in the definition of sense 3 of *impossible*: 'outrageous, intolerable'. A semicolon is generally used before and after paraphrases. For example, the definition of sense 2 of *impossible* reads 'not easy; not convenient; not easily believable'; that of *incommunicative* reads 'not communicative; taciturn'.

7 Grammar notes

Definitions are often accompanied by explanations in brackets of how the word or phrase in question is used in context. Often, the comment refers to words that usually follow (foll. by) or precede (prec. by) the word being explained. For example, at *bridle*:

... consisting of buckled leather straps, a metal bit, and reins. **b** a restraining device or influence (*put a bridle on your tongue*). **2** *Naut.* a mooring-cable. **3** *Physiol.* a ligament checking the motion of a part. ● *v.* **1** *tr.* put a bridle on (a horse etc.). **2** *tr.* bring under control; curb. **3** *intr.* (often foll. by *at* or *up at*) express offence, resentment, etc., esp. by throwing up the head and drawing in the chin. □ **bridle-path** (or **-road** or **-way**) a rough path or road fit only for riders or walkers, not vehicles. [OE *brīdel*]

The formula (foll. by *to* + infin.) means that the word is followed by a normal infinitive with *to*, as after *want* in *wanted to leave* and after *ready* in *ready to burst*.

The formula (foll. by *that* + clause) indicates the routine addition of a clause with *that*, as after *say* in *said that it was late* or after *warn* in *warned her that she was being followed*. (For the omission of *that*, as in *said it was late*, see the usage note in the entry for *that*.)

'*pres. part.*' and '*verbal noun*' denote verbal forms in *-ing* that function as adjectives and nouns respectively, as in *set him laughing* and *tired of asking*.

8 Illustrative examples

Many examples of words in use are given to support, and in some cases supplement, the definitions. These appear in italics in brackets. They are meant to amplify meaning and (especially when following a grammatical point) illustrate how the word is used in context.

(*See examples in the 'map' of articles on p. x.*)

9 Usage

If the use of a word is restricted in any way, this is indicated by any of various labels printed in italics, as follows:

Geographical

Brit. indicates that the use is found chiefly in British English (and often also in Australian and New Zealand English, and in other parts of the Commonwealth) but not in American English.

US indicates that the use is found chiefly in American English (often including Canada and also in Australian and New Zealand English) but not in British English except as a conscious Americanism.

Other geographical designations (e.g. *Austral.*, *NZ*, *S.Afr.*) restrict uses to the areas named.

These usage labels should be distinguished from comments of the type '(in the UK)' or '(in the US)' preceding definitions, which denote that the thing defined is associated with the country named. For example, *Pentagon* is a US institution, but the term is not restricted to American English.

Register

Levels of usage, or registers, are indicated as follows:

- *formal* indicates uses that are normally restricted to formal (esp. written) English, e.g. *commence*.
- *colloq.* (= colloquial) indicates a use that is normally restricted to informal (esp. spoken) English.
- *sl.* (= slang) indicates a use of the most informal kind, unsuited to written English and often restricted to a particular social group, while *coarse sl.* is used to show that an expression is regarded as vulgar or unacceptable even in spoken use in most social contexts.
- *archaic* indicates a word that is restricted to special contexts such as legal or religious use, or is used for special effect.
- *literary* indicates a word or use that is found chiefly in literature.
- *poet.* (= poetic) indicates uses confined to poetry or other contexts with romantic connotations.
- *joc.* (= jocular) indicates uses that are intended to be humorous or playful.
- *derog.* (= derogatory) denotes uses that are intentionally disparaging.
- *offens.* (= offensive) denotes uses that cause offence, whether intentionally or not.
- *disp.* (= disputed) indicates a use that is disputed or controversial. Often this is enough to alert the user to a danger or difficulty; when further explanation is needed a usage note (see below) is used as well or instead. Many uses labelled *disp.* are also treated more fully in Appendix 2, 'Some points of English Usage'.
- *hist.* (= historical) denotes a word or use that is confined to historical reference, normally because the thing referred to no longer exists.
- *propr.* (= proprietary) denotes a term that has the status of a trade mark (see the Note on Proprietary Status, p. xxiv).

Subject

The many subject labels, e.g. *Law*, *Math.*, *Naut.*, show that a word or sense is current only in a particular field of activity, and is not in general use.

Usage Notes

These are added to give extra information not central to the definition, and to explain points of grammar and usage. They are introduced by the symbol ¶. The purpose of these notes is not to prescribe usage but to alert the user to a difficulty or controversy attached to particular uses. Appendix 2 is devoted to the most important points of difficulty in English usage.

10 Phrases and idioms

These are listed (together with compounds) in alphabetical order after the treatment of the main senses, introduced by the symbol □. The words, *a*, *the*, *one*, and *person* do not count for purposes of alphabetical order.

They are normally defined under the earliest important word in the phrase, except when a later word is more clearly the key word or is the common word in a phrase with variants (in which case a cross-reference often appears at the entry for the earliest word).

11 Compounds

Compound terms forming one word (e.g. *bathroom*) are listed as main entries; those consisting of two or more words (e.g. *chain reaction*) or joined by a hyphen (e.g. *chain-gang*) are entered as phrases under the first word or occasionally as main entries.

12 Derivatives

Words formed by adding a suffix to another word are in many cases listed at the end of the entry for the main word, introduced by the symbol □□. In this position they are not defined since they can be understood from the sense of the main word and that given at the suffix concerned.

When further definition is called for they are given main entries in their own right (e.g. *changeable*).

For derivative words used in combination (e.g. *-crested* in *red-crested*), see 3 above.

13 Etymology

The user is also referred to Appendix 1, 'The History of English'.

A brief account of the etymology, or origin, of words is given in square brackets at the end of entries. It is not given for compound words of obvious formation (such as *bathroom* and *jellyfish*), for routinely formed derivatives (such as *changeable*, *muddy*, and *seller*), or for words consisting of clearly identified elements already explained (such as *Anglo-Saxon*, *overrun*, and many words in *in-*, *re-*, *un-*, etc.). It is not always given for every word of a set sharing the same basic origin (such as the group *proprietary* to *propriety*). Noteworthy features, such as an origin in Old English, are however always given.

More detailed information can be found in the *Oxford Dictionary of English Etymology* (ed. C. T. Onions et al., 1966) and the *Concise Oxford Dictionary of English Etymology* (ed. T. F. Hoad, 1986).

The immediate source language is given first. Forms in other languages are not given if they are exactly or nearly the same as the English form given in the headword.

Words of Germanic origin are described as 'f. Gmc' or 'f. WG' (West Germanic) as appropriate; unrecorded or postulated forms are not normally given.

OE (Old English) is used for words that are known to have been used before AD 1150, and ME (Middle English) for words traceable to the period 1150–1500 (no distinction being made between early and late Middle English).

Words of Romance origin are referred to their immediate source, usually F (French) or OF (Old French before 1400), and then to earlier sources when known.

AF (Anglo-French) denotes a variety of French current in England in the Middle Ages after the Norman Conquest.

Rmc (Romance) denotes the vernacular descendants of Latin that are the source of French, Spanish, Italian, etc. Romanic forms are almost always of the 'unrecorded' or 'postulated' kind, and are not specified except to clarify a significant change of form. Often the formula 'ult. f. L' etc. (ultimately from Latin etc.) is used to indicate that the route from Latin is via Romanic forms.

(Latin) denotes classical Latin up to about AD 200; OL (Old Latin) Latin before about 75 BC; LL (Late Latin) Latin of about 200–600; med.L (medieval Latin) Latin of about 600–1500; mod.L (modern Latin) Latin in use (mainly for technical purposes) since about 1500.

Similar divisions for 'late', 'medieval', and 'modern' are made for Greek.

Many English words have corresponding forms in both French and Latin, and it cannot always be established which was the immediate source. In such cases the formula 'F or L' is used (e.g. *section* ... F *section* or L *sectio*); in these cases the Latin form is the source of the French word and (either directly or indirectly) of the English word.

Some words are derived from languages which are not in wide enough use for them to be included as entries in the dictionary. These languages are listed below by regions; further information about them can be found in encyclopedias and other reference books.

- Those spoken in **America** are Aleut (related to Inuit), Surinam Negro (a Creole based on English), and the following American Indian languages: Abnaki, Araucan, Aymará, Chinook, Creek, Dakota, Fox, Galibi, Hopi, Miskito, Narragansett, Nootka, Ojibwa, Paiute, Penobscot, Renape, and Taino.
- Those spoken in **Africa** are Bangi, Fiot, Foulah, Khoisan, Kongo, Lingala, Mandingo, Mbuba, Mende, Nguni, Temne, and Twi.
- Those spoken in **Asia** are Ambonese (spoken in Indonesia), Assamese (in India), Batti (in Tibet), Maldive (in the Maldive Islands), Mishmi (in India), Sundanese (in Indonesia), and Tungus (in Siberia).
- Tongan is a Polynesian language.

When the origin of a word cannot be reliably established, the forms 'orig. unkn.' (=origin unknown) and 'orig. uncert.' (= origin uncertain) are used, even if frequently canvassed speculative derivations exist (as with *gremlin* and *pommy*). In these cases the century of the first recorded occurrence of the word in English is given.

An equals sign (=) precedes words in other languages that are parallel formations from a common source (cognates) rather than sources of the English word.

14 Prefixes, suffixes, and combining forms

A large selection of these is given in the main body of the text; prefixes are given in the form **ex-**, **re-**, etc., and suffixes in the form **-ion**, **-ness**, etc. These entries should be consulted to explain the many routinely formed derivatives given at the end of entries (see 12 above).

Combining forms (e.g. *bio-*, *-graphy*) are semantically significant elements that can be attached to words or elements as explained in the usage note at the entry for *combine*.

The pronunciation given for a prefix, suffix, or combining form is an approximate one for purposes of articulating and (in some cases) identifying the headword; pronunciation and stress may change considerably when they form part of a word.

15 Cross-references

Cross-references in defining sections are introduced in any of a number of ways, as follows:

- '=' denotes that the meaning of the item at which the cross-reference occurs is the same as that of the item referred to.
- 'see' indicates that the information sought will be found at the point referred to, and is widely used in the phrase sections of entries to deal with items that can be located at any of a number of words included in a phrase or idiom (see also 10 above).
- 'see also' indicates that further information can be found at the point referred to.
- 'cf.' denotes an item related or relevant to the one being consulted, and the reference often completes or clarifies the exact meaning of the item being treated.
- 'opp.' refers to a word or sense that is opposite to the one being treated, and again often completes or clarifies the sense.
- References of the kind '*pl.* of' (= plural of), '*past* of' (= past tense of), etc., are given at entries for inflections and other related forms.

Cross-references introduced in any of these ways appear in small capitals if the reference is to a main headword, and in italics if the reference is to a compound, idiom, or phrase within an entry.

References in italics to compounds and defined phrases and idioms are to the entry for the first word unless another is specified.

B Detailed explanation of synonym sections

1 Distribution and signalling of synonym sections

Synonyms are offered at over a third of the entries in this book, covering in all over 23,000 lexical items. The categories for which no synonyms are normally offered include the following:

- highly technical vocabulary, especially nouns in technical use only (e.g. *eosinophil*, *habeas corpus*, *organzine*, *spirochaete*, *trochoid*);
- words for which there are no true synonyms (e.g. *abbot*, *pannier*, *rectangle*);
- headwords that treat word-forming elements such as prefixes, suffixes, and combining forms (e.g. *ad-*, *hyper-*, *un-*, *-acious*, *-ling*, *-ness*);
- headwords that are abbreviations made up of initial capitals (e.g. *CPU*, *DSO*, *LPG*, *VSO*), and most other abbreviations;
- headwords providing only a cross-reference for a variant spelling of another headword (e.g. *disk*, *eon*, *inclosure*);
- most headwords that are labelled *archaic* in all their uses (e.g. *grimalkin*, *hitherward*, *whilom*);
- words and meanings that are labelled *coarse sl.* in their defining sections.

Outside these categories an attempt has been made to provide at least one full synonym list for each semantic group, together with cross-references to the full list from the most important words within the group. In general, nouns that are normally used in literal senses and have developed no metaphorical or extended uses are less likely to have synonyms than adjectives, adverbs, and verbs. Even if no synonyms are offered at the headword you first look up, it may be worth also looking up the keyword(s) used in its definition, where synonyms or related words could be used. Other ways of finding extra synonyms include looking up the items in synonym sections (which may have synonym sections of their own), and considering the synonyms of related items: as Laurence Urdang has pointed out, users 'can easily find synonyms for, say, *abdication* by making nouns out of the verbs listed under *abdicate*'. In the book, this is illustrated by using the synonyms listed, for example, under the word *savage* in order to create a set of synonyms for *savagely*. Moreover, extra information about the synonyms themselves can be found in the defining sections, for in this book the synonym sections and the defining sections complement each other.

A synonym section is always signalled by the symbol ■; the headword itself is never repeated. Readers will also notice that the synonym sections are set out with a ragged right-hand margin, contrasting with the justified setting of the defining sections; this is designed to aid orientation on the page.

2 Content of synonym sections

A synonym section may consist of one or more lists of synonyms, one or more cross-references to synonym sections under other headwords, or a mixture of the two. A synonym list may also be supplemented by a 'see also' reference to another list.

All cross-references in synonym sections are to the appropriate sense(s) of the *synonym section* of another entry, not to its defining section. For a full explanation of the cross-reference styles used in the synonym sections, see 13 below.

3 Parts of speech in synonym sections

The full list of parts of speech included in the entry is not repeated at the beginning of the synonym paragraph. Only those parts of speech for which synonyms are offered are mentioned again in the synonym paragraph; where more than one part of speech has synonyms, the bullet cue is used as a visual separator between the part-of-speech sections, but not before the first part of speech.

Parts of speech are mentioned within the phrases or derivatives list of a synonym section only when this is necessary to distinguish between synonyms for a single compound or phrase that may have different grammatical functions according to context. In these cases the bullet separator is not used, but the synonym lists for the different parts of speech are labelled with their part of speech in brackets.

4 Forms of synonyms

If the synonyms offered are only substitutable in context for any form other than the exact form of the headword, the altered form for which the synonyms substitute is given in brackets at the beginning of the synonym list. The type-style of the bracketed form follows as closely as possible the information given in the appropriate sense of the defining section. For example, in the entry for *bag*, sense 2a of the synonym section offers a list of synonyms for the headword in the sense of 'a piece of luggage'; after the semicolon there is an italicized note in brackets '(*bags*)', corresponding to the grammar note in the defining section '(usu. in *pl.*)', followed by synonyms for the plural use *bags* in the collective sense of 'luggage'. Senses 3 and 4 of the noun are used only in the plural, so the whole synonym list for each of these is preceded by '(*bags*)':

bag /bag/ *n.* & *v.* ● *n.* **1** a receptacle of flexible material with an opening at the top. **2 a** (usu. in *pl.*) a piece of luggage (*put the bags in the boot*). **b** a woman's handbag. **3** (in *pl.*;

usu. foll. by *of*) *colloq.* a large amount; plenty (*bags of time*). **4** (in *pl.*) *Brit. colloq.* trousers. **5** *sl. derog.* a woman, esp. regarded as unattractive or unpleasant. **6** an animal's sac containing poison, honey, etc. **7** an amount of game . . .

■ *n.* **1** sack, shopping bag, string bag, plastic bag, *Austral.* port, *Brit.* carrier bag, carrier, *dial.* poke, *usu. hist.* reticule. **2 a** valise, satchel, grip, suitcase, case, overnight bag, vanity case, carry-on luggage *or* bag, Gladstone bag, carpet-bag, portmanteau; briefcase, attaché case, dispatch-box, dispatch-case, *Austral.* port, *US sl.* keister; (*bags*) baggage, luggage, gear, belongings. **b** handbag, evening bag, clutch bag, shoulder-bag, wallet, *US* pocketbook, purse. **3** (*bags*) see LOT *n.* 1. **4** (*bags*) see TROUSERS.

In the case of verbs with grammar notes, an alternative form with a following particle is often given in brackets to show that the synonyms substitute for the phrase rather than the headword alone:

consist /kənsɪst/ *v.intr.* **1** (foll. by *of*) be composed; have specified ingredients or elements. **2** (foll. by *in*, *of*) have its essential features as specified (*its beauty consists in the use of colour*). **3** (usu. foll. by *with*) harmonize; be consistent. [L *consistere* exist (as COM-, *sistere* stop)]

■ **1** (*consist of*) contain, comprise, be composed of, include, have in it.

Forms that are given in bold type in the defining section are repeated in bold type in brackets in the synonym section if the synonyms offered are for that form; for example, the adjective *impoverished* is treated under the verb *to impoverish* by the grammar note '(often as **impoverished** *adj.*)' at the beginning of the entry. In the synonym section, a cross-reference is given for the verb in each of its senses, followed by a list of synonyms for the adjective *impoverished*, in each case introduced by '(**impoverished**)' to show that the synonyms are for this different form.

5 Synonym sense numbering

The sense numbering of synonym sections follows the pattern of the defining section of the entry, so that readers can easily see which synonyms are appropriate to which meanings of the headword. However, it is not the practice to give synonyms for every sense represented in the defining section, and in some cases it is less repetitious to give a list of synonyms for a number of senses together. Sense numbering in the synonym section may therefore take the form of a list of numbers (and sometimes also letters), as, for example, **1a, 2b, 3d**, or show a range of senses to which the synonyms apply, as **1–3, 2–5**, etc. Wherever a single list of synonyms covers all the meanings explained in the defining section, sense numbers are dispensed with and the synonym list is simply introduced by the synonym cue ■.

6 Arrangement of synonyms

Within a synonym sense, the synonyms are arranged in conceptual groups separated by semicolons. Each 'branch' of meaning has its own group, within which the synonyms are organized loosely in order of association, with labelled synonyms (see 9 below) in their own sequence at the end of the group.

This means that the synonyms which are semantically and stylistically closest to each other are also physically close to each other on the page. For each sense the list of synonyms begins with those closest in meaning to it; then come those less close to it in meaning. In each list of synonyms a comma separates items that are virtually synonyms of each other; a semicolon separates items that are less close to each other in meaning. Sometimes the division is a grammatical rather than a semantic one; for example, synonyms for a meaning of a verb that is labelled both for transitive and intransitive uses in the defining section may have first a group of synonyms that substitute for both types of context, then synonyms limited to one or the other use in their own group(s) after a semicolon.

7 Punctuation and style of synonym lists

Synonyms may be single words or phrases. The individual synonyms within a group are separated by commas, while a new group (and resetting of the label sequence) is signalled by a semicolon within synonym sections. Readers should note the difference in this use of the semicolon from that employed in defining sections (where it introduces a separate piece of defining text with a different nuance of meaning from the part of the definition that precedes it).

Brackets are sometimes used in synonym lists. Their principal use is to show optional parts of a synonym or phrase, e.g. for single-word synonyms, 'content(ed)' (indicating that both 'content' and 'contented' are appropriate synonyms); for phrases, '(have *or* take a) zizz' (indicating that the simple verb 'zizz' has phrasal variants 'have a zizz' and 'take a zizz'), etc.

Explanatory matter in italic type is discussed at 8 below. All synonym text is printed in roman type with the exception of unassimilated foreign words that are normally printed in italic in English contexts; these words (which at their own defining sections have the headword printed in bold italic type) are printed in light italic type in synonym sections.

8 Explanations in synonym lists

Sometimes it is necessary to provide further explanatory text in a synonym list; these are given in italic type to differentiate them from the synonyms themselves. Grammatical notes are explained at 4 above and usage labels at 9 below. Apart from these categories of explanatory matter, the reader will find that the word *or* is frequently used in phrasal synonyms to introduce a variant without repeating the whole phrase, e.g. 'make public *or* known' (expandable to 'make public' and 'make known'), 'not worth anything *or* a straw *or* a rap' ('not worth anything', 'not worth a straw', 'not worth a rap'), etc.

Occasionally it is necessary to limit the application of a synonym to a narrower field than that implied by the definition of the headword. For example, in the entry *habit*, the compound *habit-forming* is defined as 'causing addiction'. The corresponding synonym list reads 'addictive, compulsive, (*of a drug*) hard; see also *obsessive* (OBSESS)', indicating that the synonyms 'addictive' and 'compulsive' may be used of habit-forming substances in general and of activities etc. that may cause dependence, whereas the synonym 'hard' may only be applied to a habit-forming drug.

9 Usage labels in synonym lists

The same range of subject, regional, and register labels is used in synonym sections as in defining sections: for a full explanation of their meaning, please see 9 on p. xiv above.

In synonym sections, the labels are entirely printed in italic type (e.g. 'esp. *US*' becomes '*esp. US*'). Labelled synonyms have their own sequence at the end of the unlabelled group (which means that if, for example, you were looking for synonyms of a slang word, you would find the neutral synonyms before those that also are limited to a particular subject, regional variety, or style of language).

The label precedes the synonym or group of synonyms to which it applies and applies to all synonyms listed up to the next label, semicolon, or full stop (whichever comes first). The order of precedence of the labels themselves is:

(i) subject (only) in alphabetical order, e.g. *Archaeol.*, *Biol.*, *Law*;

(ii) region (only) in alphabetical order of the main label (with labels qualified by '*esp.*' preceding the main label and those followed by '*and*' and '*or*' following), e.g. *esp. Austral.*, *Austral.*, *Austral. & NZ*, *Brit.*, *NZ*, *S.Afr.*, *US*;

(iii) combinations of region and subject, e.g. *Brit. Law* fit in after the appropriate regional label on its own;

(iv) register (only) in alphabetical order, e.g. *archaic*, *colloq.*, *disp.*, *hist.*, *sl.*;

(v) combinations of register and region fit in after the appropriate register label on its own, e.g. *colloq.*, *Austral. colloq.*, *Brit. colloq.*, *US colloq.*, *sl.*, *Austral. sl.*, *Brit. sl.*, *US sl.*

10 Synonyms of phrases

Phrase lists in synonym sections are introduced by the same symbol, □, as is used in the defining section. Those phrases for which synonyms are being offered are shown in bold, followed by their part of speech (if needed: see 3 above), sense number (if needed: see 5 above), and synonyms and/or cross-references. The synonyms of phrases may, of course, include single words as well as other phrases.

11 Synonyms of compounds

The explanation of synonym phrase lists also applies to compounds, which are listed in a single alphabetical sequence with the phrases.

12 Synonyms of derivatives

Synonym derivative lists are introduced by the same symbol, □□, as is used in the defining section. Those derivatives for which synonyms are being offered are shown in bold, followed by their part of speech (if needed: see 3 above), synonyms and/or cross-references.

13 Synonym cross-references

Essentially the same conventions are used for cross-references in synonym sections as for cross-references elsewhere in the text, with the exception that, when referring to a derivative in a synonym section, the derivative itself is given in italic type, followed by the main headword under which this will be found, in small capitals inside round brackets, e.g. 'see *elasticity* (ELASTIC)'.

It should be noted that cross-references in synonym sections are to the *synonym section* of the appropriate entry, not to its defining section. Only such information (in the way of parts of speech, sense numbers, etc.) is given as is necessary to enable the reader to find the correct synonym list.

Key to the pronunciations

This book uses a simple respelling system to show how each headword is pronounced. As far as possible the phonetic symbols follow the letters of the English alphabet and special symbols have been kept to a minimum.

a, á	*as in*	**pat** /pat/, **pattern** /páttərn/
aa, áa	*as in*	**palm** /paam/, **rather** /ráat͟hər/, **maharaja** /maáhəraájə/
aar, áar	*as in*	**farm** /faarm/, **farmer** /fáarmər/
air, áir	*as in*	**fair** /fair/, **mayor** /mair/, **share** /shair/, **heir** /air/, **footwear** /fo͝otwair/, **fairy** /fáiri/
árr	*as in*	**carry** /kárri/, **barrier** /bárriər/
aw, áw	*as in*	**law** /law/, **caught** /kawt/, **thought** /thawt/, **caution** /káwsh'n/, **lawful** /láwfo͝ol/
awr, áwr	*as in*	**warm** /wawrm/, **warning** /wáwrning/
ay, áy	*as in*	**day** /day/, **raid** /rayd/, **made** /mayd/, **prey** /pray/, **gauge** /gayj/, **reign** /rayn/, **daily** /dáyli/, **graceful** /gráysfo͝ol/
b, bb	*as in*	**bay** /bay/, **bubble** /búbb'l/
ch	*as in*	**church** /church/, **itch** /ich/, **picture** /píkchər/, **cello** /chéllō/
d, dd	*as in*	**dog** /dog/, **sudden** /súdd'n/
e, é	*as in*	**men** /men/, **said** /sed/, **mellow** /méllō/, **many** /ménni/, **jealous** /jélləss/
ee, ée	*as in*	**feet** /feet/, **leave** /leev/, **siege** /seej/, **receive** /riséev/, **recent** /réess'nt/
eer, éer	*as in*	**hear** /heer/, **here** /heer/, **deer** /deer/, **weird** /weerd/, **hearing** /héering/, **merely** /méerli/, **souvenir** /so͞ovənéer/
er, ér	*as in*	**fern** /fern/, **prefer** /prifér/, **early** /érli/
érr	*as in*	**ferry** /férri/, **burial** /bérriəl/
ə	*as in*	**along** /əlóng/, **soda** /sṓdə/, **pollen** /póllən/, **lemon** /lémmən/, **suppose** /səpṓz/, **serious** /séeriəss/
ər	*as in*	**parade** /pəráyd/, **bitter** /bíttər/, **nuclear** /nyo͞okliər/
f, ff	*as in*	**fit** /fit/, **telephone** /téllifōn/, **tough** /tuf/, **coffee** /kóffi/, **sapphire** /sáffīr/
g, gg	*as in*	**get** /get/, **ghost** /gōst/, **exhaust** /igzáwst/, **struggle** /strúgg'l/
h	*as in*	**head** /hed/, **behave** /biháyv/
i, í	*as in*	**pin** /pin/, **little** /litt'l/, **guild** /gild/, **media** /méediə/, **decide** /disī́d/, **activity** /aktívviti/, **women** /wímmin/, **busy** /bízzi/, **gymnast** /jímnast/
ī, ī́	*as in*	**time** /tīm/, **fight** /fīt/, **guide** /gīd/, **buy** /bī/, **writing** /rī́ting/, **dial** /dī́əl/, **sky** /skī/
īr, ī́r	*as in*	**fire** /fīr/, **choir** /kwīr/, **desire** /dizī́r/, **thyroid** /thī́royd/
írr	*as in*	**lyrics** /lírriks/, **delirious** /dilírriəss/
j	*as in*	**judge** /juj/, **carriage** /kárrij/, **soldier** /sṓljər/
k, kk	*as in*	**kick** /kik/, **coat** /kōt/, **mix** /miks/, **chaos** /káyoss/, **school** /sko͞ol/, **pocket** /pókkit/
k͟h	*as in*	**loch** /lok͟h/, **verligte** /fairlík͟htə/
l, ll	*as in*	**like** /līk/, **lily** /lílli/
'l	*as in*	**bottle** /bótt'l/, **candle** /kánd'l/
m, mm	*as in*	**may** /may/, **hammer** /hámmər/
'm	*as in*	**chasm** /kázz'm/, **idealism** /idéeəliz'm/
n, nn	*as in*	**nun** /nun/, **runner** /rúnnər/
N	*as in*	**en route** /ON ro͞ot/, **thé dansant** /táy DONSÓN/ (used to show that the preceding vowel is nasalized)
'n	*as in*	**wooden** /wo͝odd'n/, **button** /bútt'n/
ng	*as in*	**sing** /sing/, **sink** /singk/
ngg	*as in*	**single** /síngg'l/, **anger** /ánggər/
o, ó	*as in*	**rob** /rob/, **robin** /róbbin/, **cough** /kof/, **restaurant** /réstəront/
ō, ṓ	*as in*	**go** /gō/, **boat** /bōt/, **show** /shō/, **toe** /tō/, **hotel** /hōtél/, **motion** /mṓsh'n/, **rainbow** /ráynbō/, **chateau** /sháttō/
ö, ö́	*as in*	**colonel** /kö́n'l/, **jeu** /z͟hö/, **chauffeuse** /shōfö́z/
oo	*as in*	**unite** /yoonī́t/, **speculate** /spékyoolayt/ (used to indicate that the value of the vowel may be long, like o͞o, or short, like o͝o)
o͝o, ó͝o	*as in*	**wood** /wo͝od/, **could** /ko͝od/, **push** /po͝osh/, **football** /fó͝otbawl/, **sugar** /shó͝oggər/
o͞o, ó͞o	*as in*	**food** /fo͞od/, **few** /fyo͞o/, **do** /do͞o/, **blue** /blo͞o/, **music** /myó͞ozik/, **review** /rivyó͞o/
oor, óor	*as in*	**tour** /toor/, **cure** /kyoor/, **jury** /jóori/
or, ór	*as in*	**door** /dor/, **four** /for/, **corner** /kórnər/

órr	*as in*	**sorry** /sórri/, **corridor** /kórridor/, **warrior** /wórriər/
ör, ṓr	*as in*	**fleur-de-lys** /flṓrdəleé/, **voyeur** /vwaayṓr/
ow, ów	*as in*	**mouse** /mowss/, **coward** /kówərd/
owr, ówr	*as in*	**hour** /owr/, **powerful** /pówrfŏŏl/
oy, óy	*as in*	**boy** /boy/, **noisy** /nóyzi/
p, pp	*as in*	**pit** /pit/, **supper** /súppər/
r, rr	*as in*	**run** /run/, **fur** /fur/, **spirit** /spírrit/
s, ss	*as in*	**sit** /sit/, **messy** /méssi/, **centre** /séntər/, **scent** /sent/, **accent** /áksənt/, **fix** /fiks/, **pizza** /peétsə/
sh	*as in*	**shut** /shut/, **social** /sṓsh'l/, **partial** /paársh'l/, **passion** /pásh'n/, **action** /áksh'n/, **machine** /məsheén/, **niche** /neesh/
t, tt	*as in*	**taste** /tayst/, **butter** /búttər/
th	*as in*	**thin** /thin/, **truth** /trōōth/
<u>th</u>	*as in*	**then** /<u>th</u>en/, **mother** /mú<u>th</u>ər/
u, ú	*as in*	**cut** /kut/, **blood** /blud/, **money** /múnni/, **enough** /inúf/
ur, úr	*as in*	**curl** /kurl/, **curtain** /kúrt'n/, **journey** /júrni/
úrr	*as in*	**hurry** /húrri/, **worry** /wúrri/
v, vv	*as in*	**vet** /vet/, **civil** /sívvil/
w	*as in*	**way** /way/, **quick** /kwik/
y	*as in*	**yet** /yet/, **million** /mílyən/, **queue** /kyōō/, **accuse** /əkyṓōz/, **tortilla** /torteéyə/, **junker** /yṓōngkər/
z, zz	*as in*	**zero** /zeérō/, **phrase** /frayz/, **lenses** /lénziz/, **examine** /igzámmin/, **cousin** /kúzz'n/, **fuzzy** /fúzzi/, **xylem** /zílem/
<u>zh</u>	*as in*	**measure** / mé<u>zh</u>ər/, **massage** /mássaa<u>zh</u>/, **jabot** /<u>zh</u>ábbō/, **vision** /ví<u>zh</u>'n/

Hyphen

As an aid to correct pronunciation a hyphen is used within a pronunciation entry to avoid confusion, for example to distinguish between *t* followed by *h* and *th*, or *s* followed by *h* and *sh*, etc.:

gatehouse /gáyt-howss/, **mishap** /miss-hap/

or where two or more vowels appearing together would be unclear, for example:

intuition /intyoo-ísh'n/, **vehicle** /veé-ik'l/

More than one acceptable pronunciation may be given, with commas between the variants, for example:

suit /sōōt, syōōt/

If the pronunciations of a word differ only in part then the syllable or syllables affected are shown as follows:

bedroom /bédroom, -rŏŏm/,
grandmother /gránmu<u>th</u>ər, gránd-/

The same principle applies to derivative forms that are given within the main entry, for example:

complete /kəmpleét/, **completion** /-pleésh'n/

Stress

The mark ˊ that appears over the vowel symbol in words of more than one syllable indicates the part of the word which carries the stress. Where a word has two or more stress markers then the main stress may vary according to the context in which a word is used, for example:

afternoon /aáftərnṓōn/

In the phrase 'afternoon tea' the main stress falls on the first syllable /aáftər-/ but in the phrase 'all afternoon' the main stress falls on the last syllable /-nṓōn/.

The stress on some words can vary according to the speaker's preference, for example:

television /téllivízh'n/

In the phrase 'on television' it is acceptable for the main stress to fall on either the first or the third syllable /téllivi<u>zh</u>'n/ or /televí<u>zh</u>'n/.

Abbreviations used in this book

Some abbreviations (especially of language-names) occur only in etymologies. Others may appear in italics. Abbreviations in general use (such as etc., i.e., and those for books of the Bible) are explained in the dictionary text itself.

abbr.	abbreviation
ablat.	ablative
absol.	absolute(ly)
acc.	according
accus.	accusative
adj.	adjective
adv.	adverb
Aeron.	Aeronautics
AF	Anglo-French
Afr.	Africa African
Afrik.	Afrikaans
Akkad.	Akkadian
AL	Anglo-Latin
alt.	alteration
Amer.	America American
Anat.	Anatomy
anc.	ancient
Anglo-Ind.	Anglo-Indian
Anthropol.	Anthropology
Antiq.	Antiquities Antiquity
app.	apparently
Arab.	Arabic
Aram.	Aramaic
arbitr.	arbitrary arbitrarily
Archaeol.	Archaeology
Archit.	Architecture
Arith.	Arithmetic
assim.	assimilated
assoc.	associated association
Assyr.	Assyrian
Astrol.	Astrology
Astron.	Astronomy
Astronaut.	Astronautics
attrib.	attributive(ly)
attrib.adj.	attributive adjective
augment.	augmentative
Austral.	Australia Australian
aux.	auxiliary
back-form.	back-formation
Bibl.	Biblical
Bibliog.	Bibliography
Biochem.	Biochemistry
Biol.	Biology
Bot.	Botany
Braz.	Brazil Brazilian
Bret.	Breton
Brit.	British in British use
Bulg.	Bulgarian
Burm.	Burmese
Byz.	Byzantine
c.	century
c.	*circa*
Can.	Canada Canadian
Cat.	Catalan
Celt.	Celtic
Ch.	Church
Chem.	Chemistry
Chin.	Chinese
Cinematog.	Cinematography
class.	classical
coarse sl.	coarse slang
cogn.	cognate
collect.	collective(ly)
colloq.	colloquial(ly)
comb.	combination; combining
compar.	comparative
compl.	complement
Conchol.	Conchology
conj.	conjunction
conn.	connected
constr.	construction
contr.	contraction
Corn.	Cornish
corresp.	corresponding
corrupt.	corruption
Criminol.	Criminology
Crystallog.	Crystallography
Da.	Danish
decl.	declension
def.	definite
Demog.	Demography
demons.	demonstrative
demons.adj.	demonstrative adjective
demons.pron.	demonstrative pronoun
deriv.	derivative
derog.	derogatory
dial.	dialect
different.	differentiated
dimin.	diminutive
disp.	disputed (use or pronunciation)
dissim.	dissimilated
distrib.	distributive
Du.	Dutch
E	English
Eccl.	Ecclesiastical
Ecol.	Ecology
Econ.	Economics
EFris.	East Frisian
Egypt.	Egyptian
E.Ind.	East Indian, of the East Indies
Electr.	Electricity
elem.	elementary
ellipt.	elliptical(ly)
emphat.	emphatic(ally)
Engin.	Engineering
Engl.	England; English
Entomol.	Entomology
erron.	erroneous(ly)
esp.	especial(ly)
etym.	etymology
euphem.	euphemism
Eur.	Europe, European
ex.	example
exc.	except
exclam.	exclamation
F	French
f.	from
fam.	familiar
fem.	feminine
fig.	figurative(ly)
Finn.	Finnish
Flem.	Flemish
foll.	followed, following
form.	formation
Fr.	French
Frank.	Frankish
frequent.	frequentative(ly)

G	German
Gael.	Gaelic
Gallo-Rom.	Gallo-Roman
gen.	general
genit.	genitive
Geog.	Geography
Geol.	Geology
Geom.	Geometry
Ger.	German
Gk	Greek
Gk Hist.	Greek History
Gmc	Germanic
Goth.	Gothic
Gram.	Grammar
Heb.	Hebrew
Hind.	Hindustani
Hist.	History
hist.	with historical reference
Horol.	Horology
Hort.	Horticulture
Hung.	Hungarian
Icel.	Icelandic
IE	Indo-European
illit.	illiterate
imit.	imitative
immed.	immediate(ly)
imper.	imperative
impers.	impersonal
incept.	inceptive
incl.	including; inclusive
Ind.	of the subcontinent comprising India, Pakistan, and Bangladesh
ind.	indirect
indecl.	indeclinable
indef.	indefinite
infin.	infinitive
infl.	influence(d)
instr.	instrumental (case)
int.	interjection
interrog.	interrogative(ly)
interrog.adj.	interrogative adjective
interrog.pron.	interrogative pronoun
intr.	intransitive
Ir.	Irish (language or usage)
iron.	ironical(ly)
irreg.	irregular(ly)
It.	Italian
Jap.	Japan, Japanese
Jav.	Javanese
joc.	jocular(ly)
L	Latin
lang.	language
LG	Low German
LHeb.	Late Hebrew
lit.	literal(ly)
LL	Late Latin
M	Middle (with languages)
masc.	masculine
Math.	Mathematics
MDa.	Middle Danish
MDu.	Middle Dutch
ME	Middle English
Mech.	Mechanics
Med.	Medicine
med.	medieval
med.L	medieval Latin
metaph.	metaphorical
metath.	metathesis
Meteorol.	Meteorology
Mex.	Mexican
MFlem.	Middle Flemish
MHG	Middle High German
Mil.	Military
Mineral.	Mineralogy
mistransl.	mistranslation
MLG	Middle Low German
mod.	modern
mod.L	modern Latin
MSw.	Middle Swedish
Mus.	Music
Mythol.	Mythology
n.	noun
N.Amer.	North America, North American
Nat.	National
Naut.	Nautical
neg.	negative(ly)
N.Engl.	North of England
neut.	neuter
Norm.	Norman
north.	northern
Norw.	Norwegian
n.pl.	noun plural
num.	numeral
NZ	New Zealand
O	Old (with languages)
obj.	object; objective
OBret.	Old Breton
OBrit.	Old British
obs.	obsolete
Obstet.	Obstetrics
OBulg.	Old Bulgarian
occas.	occasional(ly)
OCelt.	Old Celtic
ODa.	Old Danish
ODu.	Old Dutch
OE	Old English
OF	Old French
offens.	offensive
OFrank.	Old Frankish
OFris.	Old Frisian
OGael.	Old Gaelic
OHG	Old High German
OIcel.	Old Icelandic
OIr.	Old Irish
OIt.	Old Italian
OL	Old Latin
OLG	Old Low German
ON	Old Norse
ONF	Old Norman French
ONorw.	Old Norwegian
OPers.	Old Persian
OPort.	Old Portuguese
opp.	(as) opposed (to); opposite (of)
OProv.	Old Provençal
orig.	origin; original(ly)
Ornithol.	Ornithology
OS	Old Saxon
OScand.	Old Scandinavian
OSlav.	Old Slavonic
OSp.	Old Spanish
OSw.	Old Swedish
Palaeog.	Palaeography
Parl.	Parliament; Parliamentary
part.	participle
past part.	past participle
Pathol.	Pathology
pejor.	pejorative
perf.	perfect (tense)
perh.	perhaps
Pers.	Persian
pers.	person(al)
Peruv.	Peruvian
Pharm.	Pharmacy; Pharmacology
Philol.	Philology
Philos.	Philosophy
Phoen.	Phoenician
Phonet.	Phonetics
Photog.	Photography
phr.	phrase
Phrenol.	Phrenology
Physiol.	Physiology
pl.	plural
poet.	poetical
Pol.	Polish
Polit.	Politics
pop.	popular, not technical
pop.L.	popular Latin, informal spoken Latin
Port.	Portuguese
poss.	possessive
poss.pron.	possessive pronoun
prec.	preceded, preceding
predic.	predicate; predicative(ly)

Abbreviations

predic.adj.	predicative adjective
prep.	preposition
pres.part.	present participle
prob.	probable, probably
pron.	pronoun
pronunc.	pronunciation
propr.	proprietary term
Prov.	Provençal
Psychol.	Psychology
RC Ch.	Roman Catholic Church
redupl.	reduplicated
ref.	reference
refl.	reflexive(ly)
rel.	related; relative
rel.adj.	relative adjective
Relig.	Religion
rel.pron.	relative pronoun
repr.	representing
Rhet.	Rhetoric
rhet.	rhetorical(ly)
Rmc	Romanic
Rom.	Roman
Rom.Hist.	Roman History
Russ.	Russian
S.Afr.	South Africa, South African
S.Amer.	South America, South American

Sc.	Scottish
Scand.	Scandinavia, Scandinavian
Sci.	Science
Shakesp.	Shakespeare
sing.	singular
Sinh.	Sinhalese
Skr.	Sanskrit
sl.	slang
Slav.	Slavonic
Sociol.	Sociology
Sp.	Spanish
spec.	special(ly)
Stock Exch.	Stock Exchange
subj.	subject; subjunctive
superl.	superlative
Sw.	Swedish
syll.	syllable
symb.	symbol
syn.	synonym
techn.	technical(ly)
Telev.	Television
Teut.	Teutonic
Theatr.	Theatre, Theatrical
Theol.	Theology
tr.	transitive
transf.	in transferred sense
transl.	translation

Turk.	Turkish
Typog.	Typography
ult.	ultimate(ly)
uncert.	uncertain
unexpl.	unexplained
univ.	university
unkn.	unknown
US	American, in American use
usu.	usual(ly)
v.	verb
var.	variant(s)
v.aux.	auxiliary verb
Vet.	Veterinary
v.intr.	intransitive verb
voc.	vocative
v.refl.	reflexive verb
v.tr.	transitive verb
WFris.	West Frisian
WG	West Germanic
W.Ind.	West Indian, of the West Indies
WS	West Saxon
WSlav.	West Slavonic
Zool.	Zoology

Note on proprietary status

This book includes some words which are, or are asserted to be, proprietary names or trade marks. Their inclusion does not imply that they have acquired for legal purposes a non-proprietary or general significance, nor is any other judgement implied concerning their legal status. In cases where the editor has some evidence that a word is used as a proprietary name or trade mark this is indicated by the designation *propr.*, but no judgement concerning the legal status of such words is made or implied thereby.

THE READER'S DIGEST · OXFORD

Wordfinder

Aa

A[1] /ay/ *n.* (also **a**) (*pl.* **As** or **A's**) **1** the first letter of the alphabet. **2** *Mus.* the sixth note of the diatonic scale of C major. **3** the first hypothetical person or example. **4** the highest class or category (of roads, academic marks, etc.). **5** (usu. **a**) *Algebra* the first known quantity. **6** a human blood type of the ABO system. □ **A1** /áy wún/ *n. Naut.* a first-class vessel in Lloyd's Register of Shipping. ● *adj.* **1** *Naut.* (of a ship) first-class. **2** *colloq.* excellent, first-rate. **A1, A2,** etc. the standard European paper sizes, each half the previous one, e.g. A4 = 297 x 210 mm, A5 = 210 x 148 mm. **from A to B** from one place to another (*a means of getting from A to B*). **from A to Z** over the entire range, completely.

■ □ **A1** (*adj.*) **2** see *first-rate adj.* **from A to Z** see *completely* (COMPLETE).

A[2] /ay/ *abbr.* (also **A.**) **1** *Brit.* (of films) classified as suitable for an adult audience but not necessarily for children. ¶ Now replaced by *PG*. **2** = A LEVEL. **3** ampere(s). **4** answer. **5** Associate of. **6** atomic (energy etc.).

a[1] /ə, ay/ *adj.* (also **an** before a vowel) (called the indefinite article) **1** (as an unemphatic substitute) one, some, any. **2** one like (*a Judas*). **3** one single (*not a thing in sight*). **4** the same (*all of a size*). **5** in, to, or for each (*twice a year*; *£20 a man*; *seven a side*). [weakening of OE *ān* one; sense 5 orig. = A[2]]

a[2] /ə/ *prep.* (usu. as *prefix*) **1** to, towards (*ashore*; *aside*). **2** (with verb in pres. part. or infin.) in the process of; in a specified state (*a-hunting*; *a-wandering*; *abuzz*; *aflutter*). **3** on (*afire*; *afoot*). **4** in (*nowadays*). [weakening of OE prep. *an, on* (see ON)]

a[3] *abbr.* atto-.

Å *abbr.* ångström(s).

a-[1] /ay, a/ *prefix* not, without (*amoral*; *agnostic*; *apetalous*). [Gk *a-*, or L f. Gk, or F f. L f. Gk]

a-[2] /ə/ *prefix* implying motion onward or away, adding intensity to verbs of motion (*arise*; *awake*). [OE *a-*, orig. *ar-*]

a-[3] /ə/ *prefix* to, at, or into a state (*adroit*; *agree*; *amass*; *avenge*). [ME *a-* (= OF prefix *a-*), (f. F) f. L *ad-* to, at]

a-[4] /ə/ *prefix* **1** from, away (*abridge*). **2** of (*akin*; *anew*). **3** out, utterly (*abash*; *affray*). **4** in, on, engaged in, etc. (see A[2]). [sense 1 f. ME *a-*, OF *a-*, f. L *ab*; sense 2 f. ME *a-* f. OE *of* prep.; sense 3 f. ME, AF *a-* = OF *e-*, *es-* f. L *ex*]

a-[5] /ə, a/ *prefix* assim. form of AD- before *sc, sp, st*.

-a[1] /ə/ *suffix* forming nouns from Greek, Latin, and Romanic feminine singular, esp.: **1** ancient or Latinized modern names of animals and plants (*amoeba*; *campanula*). **2** oxides (*alumina*). **3** geographical names (*Africa*). **4** ancient or Latinized modern feminine names (*Lydia*; *Hilda*).

-a[2] /ə/ *suffix* forming plural nouns from Greek and Latin neuter plural, esp. names (often from modern Latin) of zoological groups (*phenomena*; *Carnivora*).

-a[3] /ə/ *suffix colloq.* **1** of (*kinda*; *coupla*). **2** have (*mighta*; *coulda*). **3** to (*oughta*).

AA *abbr.* **1** Automobile Association. **2** Alcoholics Anonymous. **3** *Mil.* anti-aircraft. **4** *Brit.* (of films) classified as suitable for persons of over 14 years. ¶ Now replaced by *PG*.

AAA *abbr.* **1** (in the UK) Amateur Athletic Association. **2** American Automobile Association. **3** Australian Automobile Association. **4** anti-aircraft artillery.

A. & M. *abbr.* (Hymns) Ancient and Modern.

A. & R. *abbr.* **1** artists and recording. **2** artists and repertoire.

aardvark /aárdvaark/ *n.* a nocturnal mammal of southern Africa, *Orycteropus afer*, with a tubular snout and a long extendible tongue, that feeds on termites. Also called *ant-bear, earth-hog*. [Afrik. f. *aarde* earth + *vark* pig]

aardwolf /aárdwoolf/ *n.* (*pl.* **aardwolves** /-woolvz/) an African mammal, *Proteles cristatus*, of the hyena family, with grey fur and black stripes, that feeds on insects. [Afrik. f. *aarde* earth + *wolf* wolf]

Aaron's beard /áirənz/ *n.* any of several plants, esp. rose of Sharon (*Hypericum calycinum*). [ref. to Ps. 133:2]

Aaron's rod /áirənz/ *n.* any of several tall plants, esp. the great mullein (*Verbascum thapsus*). [ref. to Num. 17:8]

A'asia *abbr.* Australasia.

aasvogel /aásfōg'l/ *n.* a vulture. [Afrik. f. *aas* carrion + *vogel* bird]

AAU *abbr. US* Amateur Athletic Union.

AB[1] /áybeé/ *n.* a human blood type of the ABO system.

AB[2] *abbr.* **1** able rating or seaman. **2** *US* Bachelor of Arts. [sense 1 f. *able-bodied*; sense 2 f. L *Artium Baccalaureus*]

ab- /əb, ab/ *prefix* off, away, from (*abduct*; *abnormal*; *abuse*). [F or L]

aba /ábbə/ *n.* (also **abba, abaya** /əbáy-yə, əbī́-yə/) a sleeveless outer garment worn by Arabs. [Arab. *'abā'*]

abaca /ábbəkə/ *n.* **1** Manila hemp. **2** the plant, *Musa textilis*, yielding this. [Sp. *abacá*]

aback /əbák/ *adv.* **1** *archaic* backwards, behind. **2** *Naut.* (of a sail) pressed against the mast by a head wind. □ **take aback 1** surprise, disconcert (*your request took me aback*; *I was greatly taken aback by the news*). **2** (as **taken aback**) (of a ship) with the sails pressed against the mast by a head wind. [OE *on bæc* (as A[2], BACK)]

■ □ **take aback 1** astound, astonish, surprise, startle, shock, stun, stagger, dumbfound, confound, nonplus, stupefy, *colloq.* floor, flabbergast, knock sideways, *sl.* knock out; disconcert, puzzle, mystify.

abacus /ábbəkəss/ *n.* (*pl.* **abacuses**) **1** an oblong frame with rows of wires or grooves along which beads are slid, used for calculating. **2** *Archit.* the flat slab on top of a capital, supporting the architrave. [L f. Gk *abax abakos* slab, drawing-board, f. Heb. *'ābāḳ* dust]

■ **1** see CALCULATOR.

Abaddon /əbádd'n/ *n.* **1** hell. **2** the Devil (Rev. 9:11). [Heb., =destruction]

abaft /əbaáft/ *adv.* & *prep. Naut.* ● *adv.* in the stern half of a ship. ● *prep.* nearer the stern than; aft of. [A[2] + *-baft* f. OE *beæftan* f. *be* BY + *æftan* behind]

abalone /ábbəlōni/ *n.* any mollusc of the genus *Haliotis*, with a shallow ear-shaped shell having respiratory holes, and lined with mother-of-pearl, e.g. the ormer. [Amer. Sp. *abulón*]

abandon /əbándən/ *v.* & *n.* ● *v.tr.* **1** give up completely or before completion (*abandoned hope*; *abandoned the game*). **2 a** forsake or desert (a person or a post of responsibility). **b**

leave or desert (a motor vehicle, ship, building, etc.). **3 a** give up to another's control or mercy. **b** *refl.* yield oneself completely to a passion or impulse. ● *n.* lack of inhibition or restraint; reckless freedom of manner. ▫▫ **abandoner** *n.* **abandonment** *n.* [ME f. OF *abandoner* f. *à bandon* under control ult. f. LL *bannus, -um* BAN]

■ *v.* **1** give up *or* over, relinquish, renounce, leave, quit, abort; withdraw from, pull out of, discontinue, forgo, drop, scrap, scrub, shelve, abstain from, bury, climb down from, *Austral.* give away, *sl.* jack in. **2 a** desert, forsake, leave behind, get out of, abdicate; jilt, walk *or* run out on, throw over, cast off *or* aside, turn one's back on, leave in the lurch, discard, drop, renege, jettison, throw overboard, give over; *colloq.* dump, *sl.* ditch. **b** leave, desert, evacuate, quit, depart from, go away from. **3** give up *or* over, yield (up), surrender, renounce, deliver (up), resign, cede, concede, let go. ● *n.* recklessness, lack of restraint *or* self-control, uninhibitedness, unrestraint, intemperance, dissipation, profligacy, dissolution, debauchery, wantonness, licentiousness.

abandoned /əbándənd/ *adj.* **1 a** (of a person or animal) deserted, forsaken (*an abandoned child*). **b** (of a building, vehicle, etc.) left empty or unused (*an abandoned cottage*; *an abandoned ship*). **2** (of a person or behaviour) unrestrained, profligate.

■ **1 a** forsaken, deserted, neglected, rejected, shunned, castaway, jilted, forlorn, dropped, outcast, lonely, lonesome, *predic.* left alone, cast-off, cast aside, out of it; stray. **b** deserted, desolate, derelict, uninhabited, vacant, discarded, disused, *predic.* thrown *or* cast aside *or* away, left behind *or* empty *or* unused. **2** unrestrained, uncontrolled, uninhibited, unconstrained, profligate, licentious, unprincipled, disreputable, loose, wanton, debauched, wild, dissolute, dissipated; depraved, lewd, impure, unchaste, promiscuous, lascivious; incorrigible, reprobate, immoral, amoral.

abase /əbáyss/ *v.tr.* & *refl.* humiliate or degrade (another person or oneself). ▫▫ **abasement** *n.* [ME f. OF *abaissier* (as A-[3], *baissier* to lower ult. f. LL *bassus* short of stature): infl. by BASE[2]]

■ see DEGRADE 2.

abash /əbásh/ *v.tr.* (usu. as **abashed** *adj.*) embarrass, disconcert. ▫▫ **abashment** *n.* [ME f. OF *esbaïr* (*es-* = A-[4] 3, *baïr* astound or *baer* yawn)]

■ (**abashed**) see *embarrassed* (EMBARRASS 1b).

abate /əbáyt/ *v.* **1** *tr.* & *intr.* make or become less strong, severe, intense, etc. **2** *tr. Law* **a** quash (a writ or action). **b** put an end to (a nuisance). ▫▫ **abatement** *n.* [ME f. OF *abatre* f. Rmc (as A-[3], L *batt(u)ere* beat)]

■ **1** see REDUCE 1, WANE *v.*

abatis /ábbətiss/ *n.* (also **abattis** /əbáttiss/) (*pl.* same or **abatises, abattises**) *hist.* a defence made of felled trees with the boughs pointing outwards. ▫▫ **abatised** *adj.* [F f. *abatre* fell: see ABATE]

abattoir /ábbətwaar/ *n.* a slaughterhouse. [F (as ABATIS, -ORY[1])]

abaxial /abáksiəl/ *adj. Bot.* facing away from the stem of a plant, esp. of the lower surface of a leaf (cf. ADAXIAL). [AB- + AXIAL]

abaya (also **abba**) var. of ABA.

abbacy /ábbəsi/ *n.* (*pl.* **-ies**) the office, jurisdiction, or period of office of an abbot or abbess. [ME f. eccl.L *abbacia* f. *abbat-* ABBOT]

Abbasid /əbássid/ *n.* & *adj.* ● *n.* a member of a dynasty of caliphs ruling in Baghdad 750–1258. ● *adj.* of this dynasty. [*Abbas*, Muhammad's uncle d. 652]

abbatial /əbáysh'l/ *adj.* of an abbey, abbot, or abbess. [F *abbatial* or med.L *abbatialis* (as ABBOT)]

abbé /ábbay/ *n.* (in France) an abbot; a man entitled to wear ecclesiastical dress. [F f. eccl.L *abbas abbatis* ABBOT]

abbess /ábbiss/ *n.* a woman who is the head of certain communities of nuns. [ME f. OF *abbesse* f. eccl.L *abbatissa* (as ABBOT)]

Abbevillian /abvílliən/ *n.* & *adj.* ● *n.* the culture of the earliest palaeolithic period in Europe. ● *adj.* of this culture. [F *Abbevillien* f. *Abbeville* in N. France]

abbey /ábbi/ *n.* (*pl.* **-eys**) **1** the building(s) occupied by a community of monks or nuns. **2** the community itself. **3** a church or house that was once an abbey. [ME f. OF *abbeie* etc. f. med.L *abbatia* ABBACY]

abbot /ábbət/ *n.* a man who is the head of an abbey of monks. ▫▫ **abbotship** *n.* [OE *abbod* f. eccl.L *abbas -atis* f. Gk *abbas* father f. Aram. *'abbā*]

abbreviate /əbreéviayt/ *v.tr.* shorten, esp. represent (a word etc.) by a part of it. [ME f. LL *abbreviare* shorten f. *brevis* short: cf. ABRIDGE]

■ shorten, compress, telescope, contract, truncate, trim, reduce, curtail, cut (off), cut down *or* short, clip, condense, abridge, abstract, précis, digest, epitomize, summarize, synopsize.

abbreviation /əbreéviáysh'n/ *n.* **1** an abbreviated form, esp. a shortened form of a word or phrase. **2** the process or result of abbreviating.

■ initialism, acronym, symbol; abridgement, contraction, précis, summary, abstract, synopsis, digest, epitome.

ABC[1] /áybeesee/ *n.* **1** the alphabet. **2** the rudiments of any subject. **3** an alphabetical guide.

ABC[2] *abbr.* **1** Australian Broadcasting Corporation. **2** American Broadcasting Company.

abdicate /ábdikayt/ *v.tr.* **1** (usu. *absol.*) give up or renounce (the throne). **2** renounce (a responsibility, duty, etc.). ▫▫ **abdication** /ábdikáysh'n/ *n.* **abdicator** *n.* [L *abdicare abdicat-* (as AB-, *dicare* declare)]

■ give up, renounce, surrender, yield, disclaim, relinquish, vacate, resign (from), quit, waive, disown; (*absol.*) step down; see also ABANDON *v.* 2a. ▫▫ **abdication** see RESIGNATION 1.

abdomen /ábdəmən/ *n.* **1** the part of the body containing the stomach, bowels, reproductive organs, etc. **2** *Zool.* the hinder part of an insect, crustacean, spider, etc. ▫▫ **abdominal** /əbdómmin'l/ *adj.* **abdominally** /abdómminəli/ *adv.* [L]

abduct /əbdúkt/ *v.tr.* **1** carry off or kidnap (a person) illegally by force or deception. **2** (of a muscle etc.) draw (a limb etc.) away from the middle line of the body. ▫▫ **abduction** *n.* **abductor** *n.* [L *abducere abduct-* (as AB-, *ducere* draw)]

■ **1** kidnap, carry off, make off with, seize, snatch, grab, nab, take (away), spirit away *or* off. ▫▫ **abduction** kidnap(ping), carrying-off, seizure, capture.

abeam /əbeém/ *adv.* **1** on a line at right angles to a ship's or an aircraft's length. **2** (foll. by *of*) opposite the middle of (a ship etc.). [A[2] + BEAM]

abed /əbéd/ *adv. archaic* in bed. [OE (as A[2], BED)]

abele /əbeél, áyb'l/ *n.* the white poplar, *Populus alba*. [Du. *abeel* f. OF *abel*, *aubel* ult. f. L *albus* white]

abelia /əbeéliə/ *n.* any shrub of the genus *Abelia*, esp. *A. grandiflora*. [Clarke *Abel*, Engl. botanist d. 1826]

Aberdeen Angus /ábbərdeen ánggəss/ *n.* **1** an animal of a Scottish breed of hornless black beef cattle. **2** this breed. [*Aberdeen* in Scotland, *Angus* former Scottish county]

Aberdonian /ábbərdṓniən/ *adj.* & *n.* ● *adj.* of Aberdeen. ● *n.* a native or citizen of Aberdeen. [med.L *Aberdonia*]

aberrant /əbérrənt/ *adj.* **1** esp. *Biol.* diverging from the normal type. **2** departing from an accepted standard. ▫▫ **aberrance** *n.* **aberrancy** *n.* [L *aberrare aberrant-* (as AB-, *errare* stray)]

■ see ABNORMAL. ▫▫ **aberrance, aberrancy** see ABNORMALITY 1.

aberration /ábbəráysh'n/ *n.* **1** a departure from what is normal or accepted or regarded as right. **2** a moral or mental lapse. **3** *Biol.* deviation from a normal type. **4** *Optics* the failure of rays to converge at one focus because of a defect in a lens or mirror. **5** *Astron.* the apparent displacement of a celestial body, meteor, etc., caused by the observer's velocity. ▫▫ **aberrational** *adj.* [L *aberratio* (as ABERRANT)]

■ **1–3** see ABNORMALITY 1.

abet /əbét/ *v.tr.* (**abetted, abetting**) (usu. in **aid and abet**) encourage or assist (an offender or offence). □□ **abetment** *n.* [ME f. OF *abeter* f. *à* to + *beter* BAIT[1]]
■ encourage, urge, instigate, prompt, incite, provoke, egg on, prod, goad, spur; aid, help, assist, support, back (up); endorse, second, sanction, countenance, connive at *or* with, cooperate in; further, advance, promote, uphold.

abetter /əbéttər/ *n.* (also **abettor**) one who abets.
■ see ACCESSORY 3, ACCOMPLICE.

abeyance /əbáyənss/ *n.* (usu. prec. by *in, into*) a state of temporary disuse or suspension. □□ **abeyant** *adj.* [AF *abeiance* f. OF *abeer* f. *à* to + *beer* f. med.L *batare* gape]
■ see PAUSE *n.*; (*in abeyance*) pending, abeyant, reserved, in reserve, shelved, pushed *or* shoved *or* shunted aside, postponed, deferred, put off, suspended, on the shelf, in the deep-freeze, in cold storage, in limbo; temporarily inactive, dormant, latent, on hold, tabled, laid on the table, *colloq.* on ice, on the back burner, hanging fire.
□□ **abeyant** see *in abeyance* (ABEYANCE) above.

abhor /əbhór/ *v.tr.* (**abhorred, abhorring**) detest; regard with disgust and hatred. □□ **abhorrer** *n.* [ME f. F *abhorrer* or f. L *abhorrēre* (as AB-, *horrēre* shudder)]
■ hate, loathe, detest, abominate, execrate; regard *or* view with horror *or* dread *or* fright *or* repugnance *or* loathing *or* disgust *or* hatred, despise, shudder at, recoil *or* shrink from, be *or* stand aghast at, have no use for; *literary* contemn.

abhorrence /əbhórrənss/ *n.* **1** disgust; detestation. **2** a detested thing.
■ **1** detestation, hatred, loathing, contempt, execration, abomination, disgust, horror, dread, repugnance.
2 abomination.

abhorrent /əbhórrənt/ *adj.* **1** (often foll. by *to*) (of conduct etc.) inspiring disgust, repugnant; hateful, detestable. **2** (foll. by *to*) not in accordance with; strongly conflicting with (*abhorrent to the spirit of the law*). **3** *archaic* (foll. by *from*) inconsistent with.
■ **1** hateful, detestable, abominable, contemptible, odious, loathsome, horrid, heinous, hideous, awful, execrable, repugnant, vile; repulsive, repellent, revolting, offensive, disgusting, distasteful, disagreeable, horrifying, frightful, obnoxious, *sl.* yucky. **2** (*abhorrent to*) against, in conflict with, contrary to, opposed to, averse to, resistant to, remote *or* distant from.

abide /əbī́d/ *v.* (*past* **abided** or rarely **abode** /əbṓd/) **1** *tr.* (usu. in *neg.* or *interrog.*) tolerate, endure (*can't abide him*). **2** *intr.* (foll. by *by*) **a** act in accordance with (*abide by the rules*). **b** remain faithful to (a promise). **3** *intr. archaic* **a** remain, continue. **b** dwell. **4** *tr. archaic* sustain, endure. □□ **abidance** *n.* [OE *ābīdan* (as A-[2], *bidan* BIDE)]
■ **1** stand, endure, tolerate, suffer, support, bear, put up with, stomach, accept, *literary* brook. **2** (*abide by*) comply with, observe, obey, heed, follow, fulfil, conform to, stick to *or* with, keep to, consent to, agree to, acknowledge, submit to, remain true to, stand by, adhere to, hold to.
3 a remain, stay, continue, stop, linger, rest, *archaic or literary* tarry. **b** live, stay, reside, sojourn, *archaic or dial.* bide, *literary* dwell.

abiding /əbī́ding/ *adj.* enduring, permanent (*an abiding sense of loss*). □□ **abidingly** *adv.*
■ lasting, permanent, constant, steadfast, everlasting, unending, eternal, enduring, indestructible, timeless; unchanging, (hard and) fast, fixed, firm, immutable, changeless, invariable.

ability /əbílliti/ *n.* (*pl.* **-ies**) **1** (often foll. by *to* + infin.) capacity or power (*has the ability to write songs*). **2** cleverness, talent; mental power (*a person of great ability*; *has many abilities*). [ME f. OF *ablete* f. L *habilitas -tatis* f. *habilis* able]
■ **1** capacity, power, adeptness, aptitude, facility, faculty, knack, proficiency, strength, competence. **2** talent(s), skill(s), gift(s), faculties; genius, cleverness, capacity, wit, qualification, skilfulness, capability, flair, adroitness, *savoir faire*, know-how.

-ability /əbílliti/ *suffix* forming nouns of quality from, or corresponding to, adjectives in *-able* (*capability*; *vulnerability*). [F *-abilité* or L *-abilitas*: cf. -ITY]

ab initio /áb inishiō/ *adv.* from the beginning. [L]
■ see *primarily* (PRIMARY).

abiogenesis /áybīōjénnisiss/ *n.* **1** the formation of living organisms from non-living substances. **2** the supposed spontaneous generation of living organisms. □□ **abiogenic** *adj.* [A-[1] + Gk *bios* life + GENESIS]

abject /ábjekt/ *adj.* **1** miserable, wretched. **2** degraded, self-abasing, humble. **3** despicable. □□ **abjectly** *adv.* **abjectness** *n.* [ME f. L *abjectus* past part. of *abicere* (as AB-, *jacere* throw)]
■ **1** see MISERABLE. **2** see SERVILE. **3** see LOW[1] *adj.* 11.

abjection /əbjéksh'n/ *n.* a state of misery or degradation. [ME f. OF *abjection* or L *abjectio* (as ABJECT)]
■ see MISERY 1.

abjure /əbjóor/ *v.tr.* **1** renounce on oath (an opinion, cause, claim, etc.). **2** swear perpetual absence from (one's country etc.). □□ **abjuration** /ábjooráysh'n/ *n.* [L *abjurare* (as AB-, *jurare* swear)]
■ **1** see RENOUNCE 1.

ablation /abláysh'n/ *n.* **1** the surgical removal of body tissue. **2** *Geol.* the wasting or erosion of a glacier, iceberg, or rock by melting or the action of water. **3** *Astronaut.* the evaporation or melting of part of the outer surface of a spacecraft through heating by friction with the atmosphere. □□ **ablate** *v.tr.* [F *ablation* or LL *ablatio* f. L *ablat-* (as AB-, *lat-* past part. stem of *ferre* carry)]

ablative /áblətiv/ *n.* & *adj. Gram.* ● *n.* the case (esp. in Latin) of nouns and pronouns (and words in grammatical agreement with them) indicating an agent, instrument, or location. ● *adj.* of or in the ablative. □ **ablative absolute** an absolute construction in Latin with a noun and participle or adjective in the ablative case (see ABSOLUTE). [ME f. OF *ablatif -ive* or L *ablativus* (as ABLATION)]

ablaut /áblowt/ *n.* a change of vowel in related words or forms, esp. in Indo-European languages, arising from differences of accent and stress in the parent language, e.g. in *sing, sang, sung*. [G]

ablaze /əbláyz/ *predic.adj.* & *adv.* **1** on fire (*set it ablaze*; *the house was ablaze*). **2** (often foll. by *with*) glittering, glowing, radiant. **3** (often foll. by *with*) greatly excited.
■ *adj.* **1** aflame, afire, burning, on fire, in flames, alight, blazing, fiery. **2** lit up, alight, brilliantly *or* brightly lit, glittering, sparkling, gleaming, aglow, glowing, bright, brilliant, luminous, illuminated, radiant. **3** see FERVENT 1.

able /áyb'l/ *adj.* (**abler, ablest**) **1** (often foll. by *to* + infin.; used esp. in *is able, will be able, was able*, etc., replacing tenses of *can*) having the capacity or power (*was not able to come*). **2** having great ability; clever, skilful. □ **able-bodied** fit, healthy. **able-bodied rating** (or **seaman**) *Naut.* one able to perform all duties. [ME f. OF *hable, able* f. L *habilis* handy f. *habēre* to hold]
■ **1** (*able to*) capable of, qualified to, competent to, equal to, up to, fit to, free to, prepared to. **2** talented, capable, competent, clever, brainy, knowledgeable, quick, skilled, masterful, masterly, adept, skilful, proficient, gifted, superior, expert, adroit, deft, accomplished.
□ **able-bodied** see FIT[1] *adj.* 2.

-able /əb'l/ *suffix* forming adjectives meaning: **1** that may or must be (*eatable*; *forgivable*; *payable*). **2** that can be made the subject of (*dutiable*; *objectionable*). **3** that is relevant to or in accordance with (*fashionable*; *seasonable*). **4** (with active sense, in earlier word-formations) that may (*comfortable*; *suitable*). [F *-able* or L *-abilis* forming verbal adjectives f. verbs of first conjugation]

abled /áyb'ld/ *adj.* having a full range of physical and mental abilities; able-bodied. □ **differently** (or **otherly**) **abled** *euphem.* disabled.
■ see FIT[1] *adj.* 2.

ableism /áybəliz'm/ *n.* (also **ablism, ablebodiedism**) discrimination in favour of the able-bodied.

abloom /əblōōm/ *predic.adj.* blooming; in flower.

ablush /əblúsh/ *predic.adj.* blushing.

ablution /əblōōsh'n/ *n.* (usu. in *pl.*) **1** the ceremonial washing of parts of the body or sacred vessels etc. **2** *colloq.* the ordinary washing of the body. **3** a building containing washing-places etc. in a camp, ship, etc. ▫▫ **ablutionary** *adj.* [ME f. OF *ablution* or L *ablutio* (as AB-, *lutio* f. *luere lut-* wash)]

ably /áybli/ *adv.* capably, cleverly, competently.
■ see WELL[1] *adv.* 3.

-ably /əbli/ *suffix* forming adverbs corresponding to adjectives in *-able.*

ABM *abbr.* anti-ballistic missile.

abnegate /ábnigayt/ *v.tr.* **1** give up or deny oneself (a pleasure etc.). **2** renounce or reject (a right or belief). ▫▫ **abnegator** *n.* [L *abnegare abnegat-* (as AB-, *negare* deny)]

abnegation /ábnigáysh'n/ *n.* **1** denial; the rejection or renunciation of a doctrine. **2** = SELF-ABNEGATION. [OF *abnegation* or LL *abnegatio* (as ABNEGATE)]

abnormal /abnórm'l/ *adj.* **1** deviating from what is normal or usual; exceptional. **2** relating to or dealing with what is abnormal (*abnormal psychology*). ▫▫ **abnormally** *adv.* [earlier and F *anormal, anomal* f. Gk *anōmalos* ANOMALOUS, assoc. with L *abnormis*: see ABNORMITY]
■ **1** peculiar, unusual, odd, strange, curious, unconventional, divergent, exceptional, unnatural, extraordinary, singular, weird, eccentric, bizarre, quirky, wayward, anomalous, aberrant, queer, freakish, deformed, perverse, deviant, deviating, irregular, offbeat, *colloq.* oddball, kinky, way-out, *sl.* bent.

abnormality /ábnormálliti/ *n.* (*pl.* **-ies**) **1 a** an abnormal quality, occurrence, etc. **b** the state of being abnormal. **2** a physical irregularity.
■ **1** oddity, peculiarity, irregularity, curiosity, deviation, aberration, idiosyncrasy, freak, perversion; nonconformity, unconformity, unusualness, singularity, eccentricity, oddness, queerness, unconventionality, uncommonness. **2** distortion, irregularity, malformation, deformity, anomaly.

abnormity /abnórmiti/ *n.* (*pl.* **-ies**) **1** an abnormality or irregularity. **2** a monstrosity. [L *abnormis* (as AB-, *normis* f. *norma* rule)]
■ **1** see ABNORMALITY 1.

Abo /ábbō/ *n.* & *adj.* (also **abo**) *Austral. sl. offens.* ● *n.* (*pl.* **Abos**) an Aborigine. ● *adj.* Aboriginal. [abbr.]

aboard /əbórd/ *adv.* & *prep.* **1** on or into (a ship, aircraft, train, etc.). **2** alongside. ▫ **all aboard!** a call that warns of the imminent departure of a ship, train, etc. [ME f. A[2] + BOARD & F *à bord*]

abode[1] /əbṓd/ *n.* **1** a dwelling-place; one's home. **2** *archaic* a stay or sojourn. [verbal noun of ABIDE: cf. *ride, rode, road*]
■ **1** residence, house, home, domicile, habitat, habitation, seat, quarters, rooms, lodging(s), place, accommodation, *Mil.* billet; *colloq.* pad, *Brit. colloq.* digs, diggings, *formal* dwelling(-place).

abode[2] *past* of ABIDE.

abolish /əbóllish/ *v.tr.* put an end to the existence or practice of (esp. a custom or institution). ▫▫ **abolishable** *adj.* **abolisher** *n.* **abolishment** *n.* [ME f. F *abolir* f. L *abolēre* destroy]
■ eliminate, end, put an end to, terminate, stop, *colloq.* knock on the head; destroy, annihilate, annul, set aside, (make) void, demolish, do away with, dispense with, nullify, repeal, revoke, cancel, rescind, abrogate, vitiate, obliterate, blot out, liquidate, stamp out, quash, extinguish, erase, delete, expunge, eradicate, extirpate, uproot; *Brit. colloq.* chop; *literary* deracinate.

abolition /ábbəlísh'n/ *n.* **1** the act or process of abolishing or being abolished. **2** an instance of this. [F *abolition* or L *abolitio* (as ABOLISH)]
■ elimination, end, ending, termination, abolishment, repeal, removal, rescindment, rescission, annulment, abrogation, nullification, repudiation, cancellation; vitiation, obliteration, eradication, dissolution, destruction, annihilation, liquidation, erasure, extirpation.

abolitionist /ábbəlíshənist/ *n.* one who favours the abolition of a practice or institution, esp. of capital punishment or (formerly) of Negro slavery. ▫▫ **abolitionism** *n.*

abomasum /ábbəmáysəm/ *n.* (*pl.* **abomasa** /-sə/) the fourth stomach of a ruminant. [mod.L f. AB- + OMASUM]

A-bomb /áybom/ *n.* = *atomic bomb.* [*A* (for ATOMIC) + BOMB]

abominable /əbómminəb'l/ *adj.* **1** detestable; loathsome; morally reprehensible. **2** *colloq.* very bad or unpleasant (*abominable weather*). ▫ **Abominable Snowman** an unidentified manlike or bearlike animal said to exist in the Himalayas; a yeti. ▫▫ **abominably** *adv.* [ME f. OF f. L *abominabilis* f. *abominari* deprecate (as AB-, *ominari* f. OMEN)]
■ **1** offensive, repugnant, repulsive, vile, monstrous, outrageous, loathsome, odious, execrable, detestable, reprehensible, despicable, base, disgusting, revolting, nauseous, nauseating, sickening, gruesome, foul, abhorrent, horrid, deplorable; see also EVIL *adj.* 1. **2** atrocious, distasteful, unpleasant, disagreeable, horrible, desperate, woeful, miserable, *colloq.* terrible, dreadful, awful, lousy, shocking, frightful, wicked, beastly, abysmal, *Brit. colloq.* chronic, *sl.* yucky.

abominate /əbómminayt/ *v.tr.* detest, loathe. ▫▫ **abominator** *n.* [L *abominari* (as ABOMINABLE)]
■ see DETEST.

abomination /əbómmináysh'n/ *n.* **1** loathing. **2** an odious or degrading habit or act. **3** (often foll. by *to*) an object of disgust. [ME f. OF (as ABOMINATE)]
■ **1** see REVULSION 1.

aboral /abórəl/ *adj.* away from or opposite the mouth. [AB- + ORAL]

aboriginal /ábbəríjin'l/ *adj.* & *n.* ● *adj.* **1** (of races and natural phenomena) inhabiting or existing in a land from the earliest times or from before the arrival of colonists. **2** (usu. **Aboriginal**) of the Australian Aborigines. ● *n.* **1** an aboriginal inhabitant. **2** (usu. **Aboriginal**) an aboriginal inhabitant of Australia. ▫▫ **Aboriginality** /-nálliti/ *n.* **aboriginally** *adv.* [as ABORIGINE + -AL]
■ *adj.* **1** see NATIVE *adj.* 2, 5. ● *n.* **1** native, aborigine, local, autochthon. **2** *Austral.* Aborigine, bushman, *Austral. sl. offens.* Abo.

aborigine /ábbəríjini/ *n.* (usu. in *pl.*) **1** an aboriginal inhabitant. **2** (usu. **Aborigine**) an aboriginal inhabitant of Australia. **3** an aboriginal plant or animal. [back-form. f. pl. *aborigines* f. L, prob. f. phr. *ab origine* from the beginning]
■ see ABORIGINAL *n.*

abort /əbórt/ *v.* & *n.* ● *v.* **1** *intr.* **a** (of a woman) undergo abortion; miscarry. **b** (of a foetus) suffer abortion. **2** *tr.* **a** effect the abortion of (a foetus). **b** effect abortion in (a mother). **3 a** *tr.* cause to end fruitlessly or prematurely; stop in the early stages. **b** *intr.* end unsuccessfully or prematurely. **4 a** *tr.* abandon or terminate (a space flight or other technical project) before its completion, usu. because of a fault. **b** *intr.* terminate or fail to complete such an undertaking. **5** *Biol.* **a** *intr.* (of an organism) remain undeveloped; shrink away. **b** *tr.* cause to do this. ● *n.* **1** a prematurely terminated space flight or other undertaking. **2** the termination of such an undertaking. [L *aboriri* miscarry (as AB-, *oriri ort-* be born)]
■ *v.* **1** see MISCARRY. **3a, 4a** see PREVENT 1, TERMINATE 1, 2. **3b, 4b** see FAIL *v.* 1, 2a, MISCARRY.

abortifacient /əbórtifáysh'nt/ *adj.* & *n.* ● *adj.* effecting abortion. ● *n.* a drug or other agent that effects abortion.

abortion /əbórsh'n/ *n.* **1** the expulsion of a foetus (naturally or esp. by medical induction) from the womb before it is able to survive independently, esp. in the first 28 weeks of a human pregnancy. **2** a stunted or deformed creature or

thing. **3** the failure of a project or an action. **4** *Biol.* the arrest of the development of an organ. [L *abortio* (as ABORT)]
▪ **1** miscarriage, termination. **2** see MONSTER 3, 4. **3** see MISCARRIAGE 2.

abortionist /əbórshənist/ *n.* **1** a person who carries out abortions, esp. illegally. **2** a person who favours the legalization of abortion.

abortive /əbórtiv/ *adj.* **1** fruitless, unsuccessful, unfinished. **2** resulting in abortion. **3** *Biol.* (of an organ etc.) rudimentary; arrested in development. ▫▫ **abortively** *adv.* [ME f. OF *abortif -ive* f. L *abortivus* (as ABORT)]
▪ **1** see UNSUCCESSFUL.

ABO system /áybee-ṓ/ *n.* a system of four types (A, AB, B, and O) by which human blood may be classified, based on the presence or absence of certain inherited antigens.

aboulia /əbo͞oliə/ *n.* (also **abulia**) the loss of will-power as a mental disorder. ▫▫ **aboulic** *adj.* [Gk *a-* not + *boulē* will]

abound /əbównd/ *v.intr.* **1** be plentiful. **2** (foll. by *in*, *with*) be rich; teem or be infested. [ME f. OF *abunder* etc. f. L *abundare* overflow (as AB-, *undare* f. *unda* wave)]
▪ **1** prevail, thrive, flourish, be prolific *or* plentiful, proliferate. **2** (*abound in*, *abound with*) be well supplied *or* furnished with, be crowded *or* packed *or* crammed *or* filled *or* jammed with, be abundant *or* rich in, teem *or* swarm *or* throng with, be infested with, overflow with, *colloq.* be jam-packed *or* stuffed with.

about /əbówt/ *prep.* & *adv.* ● *prep.* **1 a** on the subject of; in connection with (*a book about birds*; *what are you talking about?*; *argued about money*). **b** relating to (*something funny about this*). **c** in relation to (*symmetry about a plane*). **d** so as to affect (*can do nothing about it*; *what are you going to do about it?*). **2** at a time near to (*come about four*). **3 a** in, round, surrounding (*wandered about the town*; *a scarf about her neck*). **b** all round from a centre (*look about you*). **4** here and there in; at points throughout (*toys lying about the house*). **5** at a point or points near to (*fighting going on about us*). **6** carried with (*have no money about me*). **7** occupied with (*what are you about?*). ● *adv.* **1 a** approximately (*costs about a pound*; *is about right*). **b** *colloq.* used to indicate understatement (*just about had enough*; *it's about time they came*). **2** here and there; at points nearby (*a lot of flu about*; *I've seen him about recently*). **3** all round; in every direction (*look about*; *wandered about*; *scattered all about*). **4** on the move; in action (*out and about*). **5** in partial rotation or alteration from a given position (*the wrong way about*). **6** in rotation or succession (*turn and turn about*). **7** *Naut.* on or to the opposite tack (*go about*; *put about*). ▫ **be about to** be on the point of (doing something) (*was about to laugh*). [OE *onbūtan* (*on* = A[2], *būtan* BUT[1])]
▪ *prep.* **1 a, b, d** concerning, concerned *or* connected *or* dealing with, on, involving, in *or* with reference to, in *or* with regard to, regarding, affecting, in the matter of, on the subject of, in connection with, with respect to, respecting, relative to, relating to, apropos, *archaic or Sc. or US* anent, *literary* touching. **2** around, round about, close to, *archaic or dial.* nigh on. **3** round, around, surrounding, encircling, encompassing, enfolding, enveloping, all round, round about, in, all over. **5** around, all round, near (to), nearby, adjacent to, beside, alongside, close by *or* to, adjacent to, *archaic or dial.* nigh. **6** with, on, on one's person, in one's possession. ● *adv.* **1 a** approximately, around, nearly, roughly, more or less, almost, close to *or* upon, in the region of, in the neighbourhood of, something like, . . . or so; *US colloq.* in the ballpark of. **b** really, honestly, *archaic or rhet.* wellnigh. **2** around, close by, nearby; in the area *or* vicinity, round about; going on *or* around, in the air, abroad. **3** (all) round, around, all over, on every side, to and fro, up and down, back and forth, here and there, far and wide, hither and thither, helter-skelter, *US colloq.* every which way, *literary* & *dial.* hither and yon. **5** round, up. **6** round, again. ▫ **be about to** be just going to, be on the point *or* verge *or* brink of, be preparing to; be within an ace of.

about-face /əbówtfáyss/ *n.*, *v.*, & *int.* ● *n.* & *v.intr.* = ABOUT-TURN *n.* & *v.* ● *int.* = ABOUT TURN *int.*

about-turn /əbówt-túrn/ *n.*, *v.*, & *int.* ● *n.* **1** a turn made so as to face the opposite direction. **2** a change of opinion or policy etc. ● *v.intr.* make an about-turn. ● *int.* (**about turn**) *Mil.* a command to make an about-turn. [orig. as int.]
▪ *n.* **1, 2** about-face, volte-face, reversal, reverse, turn-about, turn-(a)round, U-turn. **2** change of heart *or* tune, (complete) switch.

above /əbúv/ *prep.*, *adv.*, *adj.*, & *n.* ● *prep.* **1** over; on the top of; higher (vertically, up a slope or stream etc.) than; over the surface of (*head above water*; *above the din*). **2** more than (*above twenty people*; *above average*). **3** higher in rank, position, importance, etc., than (*thwarted by those above him*). **4 a** too great or good for (*above one's station*; *is not above cheating at cards*). **b** beyond the reach of; not affected by (*above my understanding*; *above suspicion*). **5** *archaic* to an earlier time than (*not traced above the third century*). ● *adv.* **1** at or to a higher point; overhead (*the floor above*; *the clouds above*). **2 a** upstairs (*lives above*). **b** upstream. **3** (of a text reference) further back on a page or in a book (*as noted above*). **4** on the upper side (*looks similar above and below*). **5** in addition (*over and above*). **6** *rhet.* in heaven (*Lord above!*). ● *adj.* mentioned earlier; preceding (*the above argument*). ● *n.* (prec. by *the*) what is mentioned above (*the above shows*). ▫ **above all** most of all, more than anything else. **above-board** *adj.* & *adv.* without concealment; fair or fairly; open or openly. **above ground** alive. **above one's head** see HEAD. **above oneself** conceited, arrogant. [A[2] + OE *bufan* f. *be* = BY + *ufan* above]
▪ *prep.* **1** on, on (the) top of, upon, over, atop, higher than. **2** over, more than, exceeding, in excess of, beyond, greater than, surpassing. **4 b** beyond, insusceptible to, unaffected by, not subject to, not liable to, out of reach of, not open to, not susceptible *or* vulnerable *or* exposed to, not in danger of, superior to. ● *adv.* **1** overhead, on high, aloft, in the sky, *esp. poet.* in the heavens. **2 a** upstairs. **b** upstream. **3** earlier, before, previously, formerly, further back. **4** on (the) top, on the front. ● *adj.* earlier, former, previous, prior. ● *adj.* & *n.* preceding, above-mentioned, aforementioned, above-stated, aforestated, above-named. ▫ **above all** before *or* beyond everything, first *or* most of all, chiefly, primarily, in the first place, mainly, principally, especially, essentially, at bottom. **above-board** open, candid, fair, frank, straight, direct, honourable, straightforward, forthright, guileless, undeceiving, artless, ingenuous, undeceptive, undeceitful, straight from the shoulder; respectable, honest, genuine, sincere, *colloq.* on the level, upfront; openly, candidly, fairly, freely, publicly, frankly, straightforwardly, plainly, for all to see, (out) in the open, in plain *or* full view.

ab ovo /ab ṓvō/ *adv.* from the very beginning. [L, = from the egg]

Abp. *abbr.* Archbishop.

abracadabra /ábrəkədábrə/ *int.* & *n.* ● *int.* a supposedly magic word used by conjurors in performing a trick. ● *n.* **1** a spell or charm. **2** jargon or gibberish. [a mystical word engraved and used as a charm: L f. Gk]

abrade /əbráyd/ *v.tr.* scrape or wear away (skin, rock, etc.) by rubbing. ▫▫ **abrader** *n.* [L f. *radere ras-* scrape]
▪ see ERODE, SCRAPE *v.* 3b.

abrasion /əbráyzh'n/ *n.* **1** the scraping or wearing away (of skin, rock, etc.). **2** a damaged area resulting from this. [L *abrasio* (as ABRADE)]
▪ **1** see EROSION. **2** see SCRAPE *n.* 2.

abrasive /əbráysiv/ *adj.* & *n.* ● *adj.* **1 a** tending to rub or graze. **b** capable of polishing by rubbing or grinding. **2** harsh or hurtful in manner. ● *n.* an abrasive substance. [as ABRADE + -IVE]
▪ **1** see *gritty* (GRIT). **2** see ABRUPT 2.

abreact /ábriákt/ *v.tr.* *Psychol.* release (an emotion) by abreaction. [back-form. f. ABREACTION]

abreaction /ábriáksh'n/ *n. Psychol.* the free expression and consequent release of a previously repressed emotion. ▫▫ **abreactive** *adj.* [AB- + REACTION after G *Abreagierung*]

abreast /əbrést/ *adv.* **1** side by side and facing the same way. **2 a** (often foll. by *with*) up to date. **b** (foll. by *of*) well-informed (*abreast of all the changes*). [ME f. A² + BREAST]

abridge /əbríj/ *v.tr.* **1** shorten (a book, film, etc.) by using fewer words or making deletions. **2** curtail (liberty). ▫▫ **abridgeable** *adj.* **abridger** *n.* [ME f. OF *abreg(i)er* f. LL *abbreviare* ABBREVIATE]

■ **1** shorten, reduce, condense, abbreviate, cut (back *or* down *or* off *or* short), trim, clip, curtail, pare down, contract, compress, telescope, digest, summarize, epitomize, abstract, précis, synopsize. **2** curtail.

abridgement /əbríjmənt/ *n.* (also **abridgment**) **1 a** a shortened version, esp. of a book; an abstract. **b** the process of producing this. **2** a curtailment (of rights). [F *abrégement* (as ABRIDGE)]

■ **1 a** digest, condensation, epitome, compendium, concise edition *or* version, cut edition *or* version; synopsis, abstract, summary, précis, outline, résumé. **b** reduction, abbreviation, condensation, contraction, truncation. **2** curtailment.

abroad /əbráwd/ *adv.* **1** in or to a foreign country or countries. **2** over a wide area; in different directions; everywhere (*scatter abroad*). **3** at large; freely moving about; in circulation (*there is a rumour abroad*). **4** *archaic* in or into the open; out of doors. **5** *archaic* wide of the mark; erring. ▫ **from abroad** from another country. [ME f. A² + BROAD]

■ **1** overseas, in *or* to foreign lands *or* parts, out of the country. **2** about, around, everywhere, all over, broadly, widely, at large, near and far, far and wide, extensively, publicly, *colloq.* here, there, and everywhere, *US colloq.* every which way. **3** at large, about, in circulation, spread around, in the air. **4** outside, out, out of doors, away, out and about. ▫ **from abroad** foreign, non-native, exotic, alien; imported.

abrogate /ábrəgayt/ *v.tr.* repeal, annul, or abolish (a law or custom). ▫▫ **abrogation** /ábrəgáysh'n/ *n.* **abrogator** *n.* [L *abrogare* (as AB-, *rogare* propose a law)]

■ see REPEAL *v.*

abrupt /əbrúpt/ *adj.* **1** sudden and unexpected; hasty (*his abrupt departure*). **2** (of speech, manner, etc.) uneven; lacking continuity; curt. **3** steep, precipitous. **4** *Bot.* truncated. **5** *Geol.* (of strata) suddenly appearing at the surface. ▫▫ **abruptly** *adv.* **abruptness** *n.* [L *abruptus* past part. of *abrumpere* (as AB-, *rumpere* break)]

■ **1** sudden, hasty, quick, precipitate, immediate, summary, snap, rapid, swift; unexpected, unannounced, unplanned, unforeseen, unanticipated, impetuous. **2** broken, uneven, jerky, discontinuous, disconnected, irregular, inelegant; curt, short, brusque, blunt, terse, sharp, bluff, gruff, abrasive, offhand, uncivil, moody, rude, short- *or* quick-tempered, discourteous, impolite, unceremonious, ungracious, snappish, snappy. **3** precipitous, steep, sheer, sudden, sharp; declivitous, acclivitous. ▫▫ **abruptly** see *suddenly* (SUDDEN). **abruptness** see SPEED *n.* 1.

ABS *abbr.* anti-lock brake (or braking) system.

abs- /əbs, abs/ *prefix* = AB-. [var. of L *ab-* used before *c, q, t*]

abscess /ábsiss/ *n.* a swollen area accumulating pus within a body tissue. ▫▫ **abscessed** *adj.* [L *abscessus* a going away (as AB-, *cedere cess-* go)]

■ see ULCER 1.

abscisic acid /absízik/ *n.* a plant hormone which promotes leaf detachment and bud dormancy and inhibits germination. [L *abscis-* past part. stem of *abscindere* (as AB-, *scindere* to cut)]

abscissa /əbsíssə/ *n.* (*pl.* **abscissae** /-see/ or **abscissas**) *Math.* **1** (in a system of coordinates) the shortest distance from a point to the vertical or *y*-axis, measured parallel to the horizontal or *x*-axis; the Cartesian *x*-coordinate of a point (cf. ORDINATE). **2** the part of a line between a fixed point on it and an ordinate drawn to it from any other point. [mod.L *abscissa (linea)* fem. past part. of *abscindere abscis-* (as AB-, *scindere* cut)]

abscission /əbsízh'n/ *n.* **1** the act or an instance of cutting off. **2** *Bot.* the natural detachment of leaves, branches, flowers, etc. [L *abscissio* (as ABSCISSA)]

abscond /əbskónd/ *v.intr.* depart hurriedly and furtively, esp. unlawfully or to avoid arrest. ▫▫ **absconder** *n.* [L *abscondere* (as AB-, *condere* stow)]

■ see DEPART 1, FLEE 1.

abseil /ábsayl, -zeel/ *v.* & *n. Mountaineering* ● *v.intr.* descend a steep rock-face by using a doubled rope coiled round the body and fixed at a higher point. ● *n.* a descent made by abseiling. [G *abseilen* f. *ab* down + *Seil* rope]

absence /ábs'nss/ *n.* **1** the state of being away from a place or person. **2** the time or duration of being away. **3** (foll. by *of*) the non-existence or lack of. ▫ **absence of mind** inattentiveness. [ME f. OF f. L *absentia* (as ABSENT)]

■ **1, 2** non-attendance, non-appearance, truancy; leave, holiday. **3** lack, want, deficiency, non-existence, unavailability; insufficiency, scantiness, exiguousness, exiguity, paucity, scarcity, dearth, poverty.

absent *adj.* & *v.* ● *adj.* /ábs'nt/ **1 a** not present. **b** (foll. by *from*) not present at or in. **2** not existing. **3** inattentive to the matter in hand. ● *v.refl.* /əbsént/ **1** stay away. **2** withdraw. ▫▫ **absently** *adv.* (in sense 3 of *adj.*). [ME ult. f. L *absent-* pres. part. of *abesse* be absent]

■ *adj.* **1** out, off, elsewhere, not present, not here, away, on leave, on holiday, missing, gone, truant, *colloq.* AWOL. **2** missing, lacking, non-existent, wanting, deficient. **3** see ABSENT-MINDED. ● *v.* (*absent oneself*) **1** keep *or* stay away. **2** withdraw, retire, take one's leave, remove oneself, slip away, take oneself off. ▫▫ **absently** see *absent-mindedly* (ABSENT-MINDED).

absentee /ábsəntée/ *n.* a person not present, esp. one who is absent from work or school. ▫ **absentee landlord** a landlord who lets a property while living elsewhere.

■ see TRUANT *n.*

absenteeism /ábsəntée-iz'm/ *n.* the practice of absenting oneself from work or school etc., esp. frequently or illicitly.

■ truancy, malingering, *Brit. sl.* skiving (off).

absent-minded /ábs'ntmíndid/ *adj.* habitually forgetful or inattentive; with one's mind on other things. ▫▫ **absent-mindedly** *adv.* **absent-mindedness** *n.*

■ forgetful, preoccupied, inattentive, absorbed, unmindful, absent, withdrawn, careless, unheeding, heedless, unheedful, inadvertent; distracted, abstracted, day-dreaming, in a brown study, in the clouds, unaware, oblivious, in a trance, *distrait*, mooning, far-away, star-gazing, wool-gathering. ▫▫ **absent-mindedly** absently, vaguely, inattentively, forgetfully, distractedly, unthinkingly, carelessly, abstractedly, obliviously, in a brown study, with one's head in the clouds. **absent-mindedness** forgetfulness, obliviousness, carelessness, heedlessness, inattentiveness, unawareness, lack of awareness, blankness, vacantness, abstraction.

absinth /ábsinth/ *n.* **1** a shrubby plant, *Artemisia absinthium*, or its essence. Also called WORMWOOD. **2** (usu. **absinthe**) a green aniseed-flavoured potent liqueur based on wormwood and turning milky when water is added. [F *absinthe* f. L *absinthium* f. Gk *apsinthion*]

absit omen /ábsit ṓmen/ *int.* may what is threatened not become fact. [L, = may this (evil) omen be absent]

absolute /ábsəlo͞ot, -lyo͞ot/ *adj.* & *n.* ● *adj.* **1** complete, utter, perfect (*an absolute fool*; *absolute bliss*). **2** unconditional, unlimited (*absolute authority*). **3** despotic; ruling arbitrarily or with unrestricted power (*an absolute monarch*). **4** (of a standard or other concept) universally valid; not admitting exceptions; not relative or comparative. **5** *Gram.* **a** (of a construction) syntactically independent of the rest of the sentence, as in *dinner being over, we left the table*; *let us toss for it, loser to pay*. **b** (of an adjective or transitive verb) used or usable without an expressed noun or object (e.g. *the deaf, guns kill*). **6** (of a legal decree etc.) final. ● *n. Philos.* **1**

a value, standard, etc., which is objective and universally valid, not subjective or relative. **2** (prec. by *the*) **a** *Philos.* that which can exist without being related to anything else. **b** *Theol.* ultimate reality; God. □ **absolute alcohol** *Chem.* ethanol free from water or other impurities. **absolute magnitude** the magnitude, i.e. brightness, of a celestial body as seen at a standard distance of 10 parsecs (opp. *apparent magnitude*). **absolute majority 1** a majority over all others combined. **2** more than half. **absolute pitch** *Mus.* **1** the ability to recognize the pitch of a note or produce any given note. **2** a fixed standard of pitch defined by the rate of vibration. **absolute temperature** one measured from absolute zero. **absolute zero** a theoretical lowest possible temperature, at which the particles whose motion constitutes heat would be minimal, calculated as –273.15 °C (or 0 °K). □□ **absoluteness** *n.* [ME f. L *absolutus* past part.: see ABSOLVE]

■ *adj.* **1** perfect, complete, utter, unmitigated, categorical, unqualified, total, outright, sheer, out-and-out, all-out, veritable, downright, genuine, unmistakable, rank, pure, real, thorough, thoroughgoing, consummate, entire, unreserved, flawless, faultless, unadulterated, unmixed, unalloyed, undiluted. **2** unconditional, unlimited, limitless, unconditioned, untrammelled, unrestrained, unrestricted, unconstrained; total. **3** unrestrained, unconstrained, arbitrary, despotic, dictatorial, totalitarian, supreme, almighty, autocratic, tyrannical, autarchic, authoritarian. **4** positive, certain, sure, unambiguous, clear, fixed, definite, definitive, decided, categorical, unequivocal, conclusive, universal, infallible, unquestionable, indubitable, authoritative, incontrovertible, inevitable, stark, uncompromised.

absolutely /ábsəlo͞otli, -lyo͞otli/ *adv.* **1** completely, utterly, perfectly (*absolutely marvellous*; *he absolutely denies it*). **2** independently; in an absolute sense (*God exists absolutely*). **3** (foll. by *neg.*) (no or none) at all (*absolutely no chance of winning*; *absolutely nowhere*). **4** *colloq.* in actual fact; positively (*it absolutely exploded*). **5** *Gram.* in an absolute way, esp. (of a verb) without a stated object. **6** *colloq.* (used in reply) quite so; yes.

■ **1** totally, utterly, completely, perfectly, entirely, fully, quite, altogether, wholly; unqualifiedly, unconditionally, unreservedly, unequivocally, unquestionably, positively, manifestly, definitely, really, genuinely, decidedly, surely, truly, certainly, categorically. **3** (*absolutely no* or *none*) no . . . whatever *or* whatsoever *or* at all, none whatever *or* whatsoever *or* at all. **6** quite so, yes, certainly, assuredly, positively, definitely, of course, naturally, indubitably, without a doubt, (yes) indeed, to be sure, right you are, *colloq.* you bet, I'll say, sure, OK, *US colloq.* sure thing.

absolution /ábsəlo͞osh'n, -lyo͞osh'n/ *n.* **1** a formal release from guilt, obligation, or punishment. **2** an ecclesiastical declaration of forgiveness of sins. **3** a remission of penance. **4** forgiveness. [ME f. OF f. L *absolutio -onis* (as ABSOLVE)]

■ **1, 4** see FORGIVENESS 1, PARDON *n.* 1.

absolutism /ábsəlo͞otiz'm, -lyo͞otiz'm/ *n.* the acceptance of or belief in absolute principles in political, philosophical, ethical or theological matters. □□ **absolutist** *n.* & *adj.*

absolve /əbzólv/ *v.tr.* **1** (often foll. by *from*, *of*) **a** set or pronounce free from blame or obligation etc. **b** acquit; pronounce not guilty. **2** pardon or give absolution for (a sin etc.). □□ **absolver** *n.* [L *absolvere* (as AB-, *solvere solut-* loosen)]

■ see FORGIVE, PARDON *v.*

absorb /əbsórb, -zórb/ *v.tr.* **1** include or incorporate as part of itself or oneself (*the country successfully absorbed its immigrants*). **2** take in; suck up (liquid, heat, knowledge, etc.) (*she quickly absorbed all she was taught*). **3** reduce the effect or intensity of; deal easily with (an impact, sound, difficulty, etc.). **4** consume (income, time, resources, etc.) (*his debts absorbed half his income*). **5** engross the attention of (*television absorbs them completely*). □□ **absorbable** *adj.* **absorbability** /-bəbílliti/ *n.* **absorber** *n.* [ME f. F *absorber* or L *absorbēre absorpt-* (as AB-, *sorbēre* suck in)]

■ **1** see INCLUDE 1. **2** see SOAK *v.* 3. **5** see OCCUPY 6.

absorbed /əbsórbd, -zórbd/ *adj.* intensely engaged or interested (*he was absorbed in his work*). □□ **absorbedly** /-bidli/ *adv.*

■ engrossed, involved, lost, wrapped up, deep, occupied, interested, engaged, immersed, buried, preoccupied, rapt, in a brown study.

absorbent /əbsórb'nt, -zórb'nt/ *adj.* & *n.* ● *adj.* having a tendency to absorb (esp. liquids). ● *n.* **1** an absorbent substance. **2** any of the vessels in plants and animals (e.g. root tips) that absorb nutriment. □□ **absorbency** *n.* [L *absorbent-* f. *absorbēre* ABSORB]

absorbing /əbsórbing, -zórbing/ *adj.* engrossing; intensely interesting. □□ **absorbingly** *adv.*

■ engrossing, engaging, interesting, riveting, captivating, fascinating, spellbinding, gripping.

absorption /əbsórpsh'n, -zórpsh'n/ *n.* **1** the process or action of absorbing or being absorbed. **2** disappearance through incorporation into something else. **3** mental engrossment. □□ **absorptive** *adj.* [L *absorptio* (as ABSORB)]

abstain /əbstáyn/ *v.intr.* **1 a** (usu. foll. by *from*) restrain oneself; refrain from indulging in (*abstained from cakes and sweets*; *abstained from mentioning it*). **b** refrain from drinking alcohol. **2** formally decline to use one's vote. □□ **abstainer** *n.* [ME f. AF *astener* f. OF *abstenir* f. L *abstinēre abstent-* (as AB-, *tenēre* hold)]

■ **1 a** (*abstain from*) see LEAVE[1] *v.* 9a, REFRAIN[1].

abstemious /abstéemiəss/ *adj.* (of a person, habit, etc.) moderate, not self-indulgent, esp. in eating and drinking. □□ **abstemiously** *adv.* **abstemiousness** *n.* [L *abstemius* (as AB-, *temetum* strong drink)]

■ see TEMPERATE 4.

abstention /əbsténsh'n/ *n.* the act or an instance of abstaining, esp. from voting. [F *abstention* or LL *abstentio -onis* (as ABSTAIN)]

abstinence /ábstinənss/ *n.* **1** the act of abstaining, esp. from food or alcohol. **2** the habit of abstaining from pleasure, food, etc. [ME f. OF f. L *abstinentia* (as ABSTINENT)]

■ see SELF-DENIAL, TEMPERANCE 2.

abstinent /ábstinənt/ *adj.* practising abstinence. □□ **abstinently** *adv.* [ME f. OF f. L (as ABSTAIN)]

■ see TEMPERATE 4.

abstract *adj.*, *v.*, & *n.* ● *adj.* /ábstrakt/ **1 a** to do with or existing in thought rather than matter, or in theory rather than practice; not tangible or concrete (*abstract questions rarely concerned him*). **b** (of a word, esp. a noun) denoting a quality or condition or intangible thing rather than a concrete object. **2** (of art) achieving its effect by grouping shapes and colours in satisfying patterns rather than by the recognizable representation of physical reality. ● *v.* /əbstrákt/ **1** *tr.* (often foll. by *from*) take out of; extract; remove. **2 a** *tr.* summarize (an article, book, etc.). **b** *intr.* do this as an occupation. **3** *tr.* & *refl.* (often foll. by *from*) disengage (a person's attention etc.); distract. **4** *tr.* (foll. by *from*) consider abstractly or separately from something else. **5** *tr. euphem.* steal. ● *n.* /ábstrakt/ **1** a summary or statement of the contents of a book etc. **2** an abstract work of art. **3** an abstraction or abstract term. □ **abstract expressionism** a development of abstract art which aims at a subjective emotional expression of an ideal rather than a picture of a physical object. **in the abstract** in theory rather than in practice. □□ **abstractly** /ábstraktli/ *adv.* **abstractor** /əbstráktər/ *n.* (in sense 2 of *v.*). [ME f. OF *abstract* or L *abstractus* past part. of *abstrahere* (as AB-, *trahere* draw)]

■ *adj.* **1 a** theoretical, unapplied, pure, notional, ideational, conceptual, metaphysical, transcendental, unpractical, intellectual, academic, noetic; intangible.
2 non-representational. ● *v.* **1** extract, take out *or* away, remove, draw out. **2** epitomize, abbreviate, digest, summarize, précis, condense, compress, shorten, abridge, cut (down), synopsize, telescope. **4** see DISSOCIATE. **5** see STEAL *v.* 1. ● *n.* **1** summary, epitome,

synopsis, essence, digest, condensation, survey, conspectus, extract, abridgement; outline, précis, résumé; *Law* brief. **2** abstraction.

abstracted /əbstráktid/ *adj.* inattentive to the matter in hand; preoccupied. □□ **abstractedly** *adv.*
■ see INATTENTIVE.

abstraction /əbstráksh'n/ *n.* **1** the act or an instance of abstracting or taking away. **2 a** an abstract or visionary idea. **b** the formation of abstract ideas. **3 a** abstract qualities (esp. in art). **b** an abstract work of art. **4** absent-mindedness. [F *abstraction* or L *abstractio* (as ABSTRACT)]
■ **1** see DEDUCTION 1a. **4** see *absent-mindedness* (ABSENT-MINDED).

abstractionism /əbstrákshəniz'm/ *n.* **1** the principles and practice of abstract art. **2** the pursuit or cult of abstract ideas. □□ **abstractionist** *n.*

abstruse /əbstrŏŏss/ *adj.* hard to understand; obscure; profound. □□ **abstrusely** *adv.* **abstruseness** *n.* [F *abstruse* or L *abstrusus* (as AB-, *trusus* past part. of *trudere* push)]
■ see PROFOUND *adj.* 1b.

absurd /əbsúrd/ *adj.* **1** (of an idea, suggestion, etc.) wildly unreasonable, illogical, or inappropriate. **2** (of a person) unreasonable or ridiculous in manner. **3** (of a thing) ludicrous, incongruous (*an absurd hat*; *the situation was becoming absurd*). □□ **absurdly** *adv.* **absurdness** *n.* [F *absurde* or L *absurdus* (as AB-, *surdus* deaf, dull)]
■ ridiculous, silly, nonsensical, senseless, outlandish, preposterous, farcical, mad, stupid, foolish, idiotic, imbecilic, imbecile, moronic, childish, asinine, senseless, illogical, irrational, unreasoned, unreasonable, incongruous, inappropriate, paradoxical, unsound, meaningless; laughable, ludicrous, risible, inane, *colloq.* crazy, *esp. Brit. colloq.* daft, *sl.* nutty, nuts, batty, *sl.* kooky. □□ **absurdly** see MADLY 1. **absurdness** see ABSURDITY 1, 2.

absurdity /əbsúrditi/ *n.* (*pl.* **-ies**) **1** wild inappropriateness or incongruity. **2** extreme unreasonableness. **3** an absurd statement or act. [F *absurdité* or LL *absurditas* (as ABSURD)]
■ **1, 2** folly, silliness, ridiculousness, foolishness, ludicrousness, nonsense, senselessness, meaninglessness, illogicality, peculiarity, irrationality, unreasonableness, incongruity, stupidity, *colloq.* craziness, *sl.* nuttiness, *esp. Brit. colloq.* daftness. **3** paradox, self-contradiction, fallacy; stupidity, idiocy.

ABTA /ábtə/ *abbr.* Association of British Travel Agents.

abulia var. of ABOULIA.

abundance /əbúndənss/ *n.* **1** a very great quantity, usu. considered to be more than enough. **2** wealth, affluence. **3** wealth of emotion (*abundance of heart*). **4** a call in solo whist undertaking to make nine tricks. [ME f. OF *abundance* f. L *abundantia* (as ABUNDANT)]
■ **1** overflow, superfluity, over-abundance, superabundance, excess, surplus, too much, oversupply, glut, satiety, over-sufficiency; plethora, quantities, wealth, amplitude, ampleness, cornucopia, copiousness, profusion, mine, flush, cut-and-come-again, *literary* plenitude; *colloq.* pile, stack, heap, mountain, *Brit. colloq.* lashings; (*in abundance*) à gogo, galore. **2** see RICHES.

abundant /əbúndənt/ *adj.* **1** existing or available in large quantities; plentiful. **2** (foll. by *in*) having an abundance of (*a country abundant in fruit*). □□ **abundantly** *adv.* [ME f. L (as ABOUND)]
■ **1** plentiful, overflowing, ample, generous, copious, lavish, liberal, opulent, rich, luxuriant, over-sufficient, superabundant, profuse, inexhaustible, replete, full, bountiful, *colloq.* wall-to-wall, *poet.* bounteous, plenteous. **2** (*abundant in*) abounding in, full of, filled *or* replete with, rich in, teeming with, overflowing *or* spilling over *or* well-supplied *or* well-furnished *or* well-stocked *or* bristling with, *colloq.* jam-packed *or* stuffed with. □□ **abundantly** plentifully, copiously, prolifically, amply, generously, lavishly; absolutely, completely, very, quite.

abuse *v.* & *n.* ● *v.tr.* /əbyŏŏz/ **1 a** use to bad effect or for a bad purpose; misuse (*abused his position of power*). **b** take (a drug) for a purpose other than a therapeutic one; be addicted to (a substance). **2** insult verbally. **3** maltreat, assault (esp. sexually). ● *n.* /əbyŏŏss/ **1 a** incorrect or improper use (*the abuse of power*). **b** an instance of this. **2** insulting language (*a torrent of abuse*). **3** unjust or corrupt practice. **4** maltreatment of a person (*child abuse*). □□ **abused** /əbyŏŏzd/ *adj.* **abuser** /əbyŏŏzər/ *n.* [ME f. OF *abus* (n.), *abuser* (v.) f. L *abusus*, *abuti* (as AB-, *uti us-* USE)]
■ *v.* **1 a** misuse, take advantage of, misemploy, pervert, misapply, exploit. **b** take, use, be addicted to *or* dependent on, *sl.* do. **2** malign, insult, call a person names, revile, censure, upbraid, assail, berate, rebuke, scold, reproach, disparage, traduce, defame, swear at, curse (at), execrate, calumniate, slander, libel, decry, deprecate, vilify, bespatter, blackguard, rail at *or* against, rubbish, *colloq.* lambaste, *literary* objurgate, *Brit. sl.* rot, *esp. US sl.* dump on. **3** maltreat, ill-use, injure, wrong, hurt, mistreat, walk (all) over, molest, ill-treat, strafe, treat like dirt, *colloq.* manhandle; assault, beat (up), batter, hit, thrash, knock about *or* around, damage; rape, violate, *euphem.* interfere with. ● *n.* **1** misuse, misusage, misemployment, perversion, misapplication, misappropriation; catachresis, solecism, anacoluthon, abusiveness; addiction, dependence, use (*of drugs etc.*). **2** revilement, mud-slinging, reviling, execration, vituperation, malediction, imprecation, tongue-lashing, calumny, calumniation, vilification, obloquy, scurrility, invective, maligning, upbraiding, berating, scolding, (bad) language, name-calling, unparliamentary language, *literary* objurgation, *sl.* verbal, slagging (off). **3** injustice, unjustness, wrong, wrongdoing, fault, corruption, misdeed. **4** maltreatment, ill-treatment, ill use, molestation; battering, battery, beating; rape, violation. □□ **abused** misused, maltreated, ill-treated, mistreated, battered, beaten, molested, hurt; raped, violated. **abuser** maltreater, wife *or* husband *or* baby *or* child batterer, (child) molester; addict, dependent, user.

abusive /əbyŏŏssiv/ *adj.* **1** using or containing insulting language. **2** (of language) insulting. **3** involving or given to physical abuse. □□ **abusively** *adv.* **abusiveness** *n.*
■ **1, 2** insulting, scurrilous, vituperative, calumnious, calumniatory, offensive, slanderous, libellous, defamatory, censorious, opprobrious, disparaging, deprecatory, depreciatory, derogatory, pejorative, derisory, derisive, reviling, vilifying; profane, rude, foul, vulgar, obscene, vile. **3** brutal, cruel, injurious, hurtful, harmful, destructive; perverted, exploitive, exploitative, exploitatory. □□ **abusiveness** see ABUSE *n.* 2.

abut /əbút/ *v.* (**abutted**, **abutting**) **1** *intr.* (foll. by *on*) (of estates, countries, etc.) adjoin (another). **2** *intr.* (foll. by *on*, *against*) (of part of a building) touch or lean upon (another) with a projecting end or point (*the shed abutted on the side of the house*). **3** *tr.* abut on. [OF *abouter* (BUTT[1]) and AL *abuttare* f. OF *but* end]
■ see BORDER *v.* 3a.

abutment /əbútmənt/ *n.* **1** the lateral supporting structure of a bridge, arch, etc. **2** the point of junction between such a support and the thing supported.

abutter /əbúttər/ *n.* *Law* the owner of an adjoining property.

abuzz /əbúz/ *adv.* & *adj.* in a 'buzz' (see BUZZ *n.* 3); in a state of excitement or activity.

abysmal /əbízm'l/ *adj.* **1** *colloq.* extremely bad (*abysmal weather*; *the standard is abysmal*). **2** profound, utter (*abysmal ignorance*). □□ **abysmally** *adv.* [archaic or poet. *abysm* = ABYSS, f. OF *abi(s)me* f. med.L *abysmus*]
■ **1** awful, appalling, dreadful, terrible, abominable, fearful, wretched, foul, egregious, *colloq.* lousy, dire, vile. **2** abyssal, bottomless, profound, unfathomable, unfathomed; utter, complete, perfect, absolute, incredible, astounding. □□ **abysmally** see BADLY 1.

abyss /əbíss/ *n.* **1** a deep or seemingly bottomless chasm. **2 a** an immeasurable depth (*abyss of despair*). **b** a catastrophic situation as contemplated or feared (*his loss brought him a step nearer the abyss*). **3** (prec. by *the*) primal chaos, hell. [ME f. LL *abyssus* f. Gk *abussos* bottomless (as A-[1], *bussos* depth)]

■ **1** deep, gulf, (yawning) chasm, (gaping) void, (impenetrable *or* unfathomable *or* bottomless) depths. **2 a** see DEPTH 5a. **b** see CATASTROPHE 3. **3** see HELL 1.

abyssal /əbíss'l/ *adj.* **1** at or of the ocean depths or floor. **2** *Geol.* plutonic.

AC *abbr.* **1** (also **ac**) alternating current. **2** *Brit.* aircraftman. **3** before Christ. **4** Companion of the Order of Australia. [sense 3 f. L *ante Christum*]

Ac *symb. Chem.* the element actinium.

ac- /ək/ *prefix* assim. form of AD- before *c*, *k*, *q*.

a/c *abbr.* account. [*account current*: see ACCOUNT *n.* 2, 3]

-ac /ak/ *suffix* forming adjectives which are often also (or only) used as nouns (*cardiac*; *maniac*) (see also -ACAL). [F *-aque* or L *-acus* or Gk *-akos* adj. suffix]

acacia /əkáyshə/ *n.* **1** any tree of the genus *Acacia*, with yellow or white flowers, esp. *A. senegal* yielding gum arabic. **2** (also **false acacia**) the locust tree, *Robinia pseudoacacia*, grown for ornament. [L f. Gk *akakia*]

academe /ákkədeem/ *n.* **1 a** the world of learning. **b** universities collectively. **2** *literary* a college or university. □ **grove** (or **groves) of Academe** a university environment. [Gk *Akadēmos* (see ACADEMY): used by Shakesp. (*Love's Labour's Lost* I. i. 13) and Milton (*Paradise Regained* iv. 244)]

academia /ákkədeémiə/ *n.* the academic world; scholastic life. [mod.L: see ACADEMY]

academic /ákkədémmik/ *adj.* & *n.* ● *adj.* **1 a** scholarly; to do with learning. **b** of or relating to a scholarly institution (*academic dress*). **2** abstract; theoretical; not of practical relevance. **3** *Art* conventional, over-formal. **4 a** of or concerning Plato's philosophy. **b** sceptical. ● *n.* a teacher or scholar in a university or institute of higher education. □ **academic year** a period of nearly a year reckoned from the time of the main student intake, usu. from the beginning of the autumn term to the end of the summer term. □□ **academically** *adv.* [F *académique* or L *academicus* (as ACADEMY)]

■ *adj.* **1** scholastic, collegiate, academical, educational. **a** scholarly, learned, lettered, erudite, intellectual, high-brow, cerebral, well-read, studious, bookish. **2** abstract, theoretical, hypothetical, conjectural, speculative; ivory-tower, visionary, idealistic; impractical, unrealistic, unpractical, doctrinaire. ● *n.* lecturer, teacher, tutor, professor, reader, fellow, doctor, don, *US* instructor; intellectual, scholar, researcher, *usu. derog.* bluestocking.

academical /ákkədémmik'l/ *adj.* & *n.* ● *adj.* belonging to a college or university. ● *n.* (in *pl.*) university costume.

■ *adj.* see ACADEMIC *adj.* 1.

academician /əkáddəmísh'n/ *n.* a member of an Academy, esp. of the Royal Academy of Arts, the Académie française, or the Russian Academy of Sciences. [F *académicien* (as ACADEMIC)]

academicism /ákkədémmisiz'm/ *n.* (also **academism** /əkáddəmiz'm/) academic principles or their application in art.

academy /əkáddəmi/ *n.* (*pl.* **-ies**) **1 a** a place of study or training in a special field (*military academy*; *academy of dance*). **b** *hist.* a place of study. **2** (usu. **Academy**) a society or institution of distinguished scholars, artists, scientists, etc. (*Royal Academy*). **3** *Sc.* a secondary school. **4 a** Plato's followers or philosophical system. **b** the garden near Athens where Plato taught. [F *académie* or L *academia* f. Gk *akadēmeia* f. *Akadēmos* the hero after whom Plato's garden was named]

Acadian /əkáydiən/ *n.* & *adj.* ● *n.* **1** a native or inhabitant of Acadia in Nova Scotia, esp. a French-speaking descendant of the early French settlers in Canada. **2** a descendant of French-speaking Nova Scotian immigrants in Louisiana. ● *adj.* of or relating to Acadians. [F *Acadie* Nova Scotia]

-acal /ək'l/ *suffix* forming adjectives, often used to distinguish them from nouns in *-ac* (*heliacal*; *maniacal*).

acanthus /əkánthəss/ *n.* **1** any herbaceous plant or shrub of the genus *Acanthus*, with spiny leaves. **2** *Archit.* a conventionalized representation of an acanthus leaf, used esp. as a decoration for Corinthian column capitals. [L f. Gk *akanthos* f. *akantha* thorn perh. f. *akē* sharp point]

a cappella /aá kəpéllə/ *adj.* & *adv.* (also **alla cappella** /állə/) *Mus.* (of choral music) unaccompanied. [It., = in church style]

acaricide /əkárrisīd/ *n.* a preparation for destroying mites.

acarid /ákkərid/ *n.* any small arachnid of the order Acarina, including mites and ticks. [mod.L *acarida* f. *acarus* f. Gk *akari* mite]

acarpous /əkaárpəss/ *adj. Bot.* (of a plant etc.) without fruit or that does not produce fruit. [A-[1] + Gk *karpos* fruit]

ACAS /áykass/ *abbr.* (in the UK) Advisory, Conciliation, and Arbitration Service.

Accadian var. of AKKADIAN.

accede /akseéd/ *v.intr.* (often foll. by *to*) **1** take office, esp. become monarch. **2** assent or agree (*acceded to the proposal*). **3** (foll. by *to*) formally subscribe to a treaty or other agreement. [ME f. L *accedere* (as AC-, *cedere cess-* go)]

■ **2, 3** see AGREE 2, 4, 5.

accelerando /əksélləråndō, əchél-/ *adv.*, *adj.*, & *n. Mus.* ● *adv.* & *adj.* with a gradual increase of speed. ● *n.* (*pl.* **accelerandos** or **accelerandi** /-di/) a passage performed accelerando. [It.]

accelerate /əksélərayt/ *v.* **1** *intr.* **a** (of a moving body, esp. a vehicle) move or begin to move more quickly; increase speed. **b** (of a process) happen or reach completion more quickly. **2** *tr.* **a** cause to increase speed. **b** cause (a process) to happen more quickly. [L *accelerare* (as AC-, *celerare* f. *celer* swift)]

■ see QUICKEN 1, HURRY 1.

acceleration /əksélləráysh'n/ *n.* **1** the process or act of accelerating or being accelerated. **2** an instance of this. **3** (of a vehicle etc.) the capacity to gain speed (*the car has good acceleration*). **4** *Physics* the rate of change of velocity measured in terms of a unit of time. [F *accélération* or L *acceleratio* (as ACCELERATE)]

accelerative /əksélləratiʋ/ *adj.* tending to increase speed; quickening.

accelerator /əksélləraytər/ *n.* **1** a device for increasing speed, esp. the pedal that controls the speed of a vehicle's engine. **2** *Physics* an apparatus for imparting high speeds to charged particles. **3** *Chem.* a substance that speeds up a chemical reaction.

accelerometer /əkséllərómmitər/ *n.* an instrument for measuring acceleration esp. of rockets. [ACCELERATE + -METER]

accent *n.* & *v.* ● *n.* /áks'nt, -sent/ **1** a particular mode of pronunciation, esp. one associated with a particular region or group (*Liverpool accent*; *German accent*; *upper-class accent*). **2** prominence given to a syllable by stress or pitch. **3** a mark on a letter or word to indicate pitch, stress, or the quality of a vowel. **4** a distinctive feature or emphasis (*an accent on comfort*). **5** *Mus.* emphasis on a particular note or chord. ● *v.tr.* /aksént/ **1** pronounce with an accent; emphasize (a word or syllable). **2** write or print accents on (words etc.). **3** accentuate. **4** *Mus.* play (a note etc.) with an accent. □□ **accentual** /akséntyooəl/ *adj.* [L *accentus* (as AC-, *cantus* song) repr. Gk *prosōidia* (PROSODY), or through F *accent*, *accenter*]

■ *n.* **1** pronunciation, articulation, intonation, speech pattern, inflection. **2, 4** emphasis, stress, force, prominence, accentuation, weight; intensity, inflection; cadence, beat. **3** diacritic, (diacritical) mark, accent mark. ● *v.* **1, 3** accentuate, emphasize, stress, lay stress on, give prominence *or* weight to, place *or* put emphasis on, mark, underline, underscore, distinguish, highlight, focus on, spotlight, set off *or* apart.

accentor /akséntər/ *n.* any bird of the genus *Prunella*, e.g. the hedge sparrow. [med.L *accentor* f. L *ad* to + *cantor* singer]

accentuate /akséntyoo-ayt/ *v.tr.* emphasize; make prominent. □□ **accentuation** /akséntyoo-áysh'n/ *n.* [med.L *accentuare accentuat-* (as ACCENT)]

▪ see ACCENT *v.*

accept /əksépt/ *v.tr.* **1** (also *absol.*) consent to receive (a thing offered). **2** (also *absol.*) give an affirmative answer to (an offer or proposal). **3** regard favourably; treat as welcome (*her mother-in-law never accepted her*). **4 a** believe, receive (an opinion, explanation, etc.) as adequate or valid. **b** be prepared to subscribe to (a belief, philosophy, etc.). **5** receive as suitable (*the hotel accepts traveller's cheques; the machine only accepts tokens*). **6 a** tolerate; submit to (*accepted the umpire's decision*). **b** (often foll. by *that* + clause) be willing to believe (*we accept that you meant well*). **7** undertake (an office or responsibility). **8** agree to meet (a draft or bill of exchange). □ **accepted opinion** one generally held to be correct. □□ **accepter** *n.* [ME f. OF *accepter* or L *acceptare* f. *accipere* (as AC-, *capere* take)]

▪ **1** receive, take, be the recipient of. **2** accede *or* agree *or* say yes *or* assent *or* consent to, acknowledge, admit *or* allow that, recognize; (*absol.*) assent, consent, accede, agree, say yes. **3** be favourably disposed towards, favour, embrace, understand, warm to; receive, welcome, take in, be hospitable to. **4** see BELIEVE 1. **5** take, allow, permit; do, deal in. **6 a** submit to, tolerate, reconcile oneself to, resign oneself to, go along with, put up with, live with; suffer, undergo, experience, stand, withstand, stomach, endure, bear, allow, take, *literary* brook. **7** assume, undertake, take on *or* up, agree to bear.

acceptable /əkséptəb'l/ *adj.* **1 a** worthy of being accepted. **b** pleasing, welcome. **2** adequate, satisfactory. **3** tolerable (*an acceptable risk*). □□ **acceptability** /əkséptəbílliti/ *n.* **acceptableness** *n.* **acceptably** *adv.* [ME f. OF f. LL *acceptabilis* (as ACCEPT)]

▪ **1 a** worthy, deserving, suitable, appropriate, apt; competent, able, commendable. **b** agreeable, pleasing, welcome, satisfying, delightful, pleasant. **2** satisfactory, adequate, tolerable, all right, not (too) bad, fair, middling, respectable, sufficient, admissible, passable, *colloq.* OK, okay. **3** reasonable, tolerable, understandable, allowable. □□ **acceptability** suitability, aptness, acceptableness, worthiness; reasonableness, appropriateness, tolerableness, tolerability, bearableness, bearability. **acceptableness** see *acceptability* above. **acceptably** adequately, satisfactorily, reasonably, passably, tolerably, bearably; allowably.

acceptance /əkséptənss/ *n.* **1** willingness to receive (a gift, payment, duty, etc.). **2** an affirmative answer to an invitation or proposal. **3** (often foll. by *of*) a willingness to accept (conditions, a circumstance, etc.). **4 a** approval, belief (*found wide acceptance*). **b** willingness or ability to tolerate. **5 a** agreement to meet a bill of exchange. **b** a bill so accepted. [F f. *accepter* (as ACCEPT)]

▪ **3** see CONSENT *n.* **4 a** see APPROVAL. **b** see RESIGNATION 3.

acceptant /əkséptənt/ *adj.* (foll. by *of*) willingly accepting. [F (as ACCEPTANCE)]

acceptation /ákseptáysh'n/ *n.* a particular sense, or the generally recognized meaning, of a word or phrase. [ME f. OF f. med.L *acceptatio* (as ACCEPT)]

acceptor /əkséptər/ *n.* **1** *Commerce* a person who accepts a bill. **2** *Physics* an atom or molecule able to receive an extra electron, esp. an impurity in a semiconductor. **3** *Chem.* a molecule or ion etc. to which electrons are donated in the formation of a bond. **4** *Electr.* a circuit able to accept a given frequency.

access /áksess/ *n.* & *v.* ● *n.* **1** a way of approaching or reaching or entering (*a building with rear access*). **2 a** (often foll. by *to*) the right or opportunity to reach or use or visit; admittance (*has access to secret files; was granted access to the prisoner*). **b** the condition of being readily approached; accessibility. **3** (often foll. by *of*) an attack or outburst (*an access of anger*). **4** (*attrib.*) *Brit.* (of broadcasting) allowed to minority or special-interest groups to undertake (*access television*). ● *v.tr.* **1** *Computing* gain access to (data, a file, etc.). **2** accession. □ **access road** a road giving access only to the properties along it. **access time** *Computing* the time taken to retrieve data from storage. [ME f. OF *acces* or L *accessus* f. *accedere* (as AC-, *cedere cess-* go)]

▪ *n.* **2 a** see ADMISSION 2a, ADMITTANCE. **3** see OUTBURST.

accessary var. of ACCESSORY.

accessible /əkséssib'l/ *adj.* (often foll. by *to*) **1** that can readily be reached, entered, or used. **2** (of a person) readily available (esp. to subordinates). **3** (in a form) easy to understand. □□ **accessibility** /əksésibílliti/ *n.* **accessibly** *adv.* [F *accessible* or LL *accessibilis* (as ACCEDE)]

▪ **1** open, available, attainable, obtainable, reachable, at *or* to hand, handy, at one's fingertips, within (arm's) reach, *colloq.* get-at-able. **2** approachable, accommodating, available, obtainable, on hand. **3** simple, understandable, comprehensible.

accession /əksésh'n/ *n.* & *v.* ● *n.* **1** entering upon an office (esp. the throne) or a condition (as manhood). **2** (often foll. by *to*) a thing added (e.g. a book to a library); increase, addition. **3** *Law* the incorporation of one item of property in another. **4** assent; the formal acceptance of a treaty etc. ● *v.tr.* record the addition of (a new item) to a library or museum. [F *accession* or L *accessio -onis* (as ACCEDE)]

▪ *n.* **1** see SUCCESSION 2b.

accessorize /əkséssərīz/ *v.tr.* provide (a costume etc.) with accessories.

▪ see ORNAMENT *v.*

accessory /əkséssəri/ *n.* & *adj.* (also **accessary**) ● *n.* (*pl.* **-ies**) **1** an additional or extra thing. **2** (usu. in *pl.*) **a** a small attachment or fitting. **b** a small item of (esp. a woman's) dress (e.g. shoes, gloves, handbag). **3** (often foll. by *to*) a person who helps in or knows the details of an (esp. illegal) act, without taking part in it. ● *adj.* additional; contributing or aiding in a minor way; dispensable. □ **accessory before** (or **after) the fact** a person who incites (or assists) another to commit a crime. □□ **accessorial** /áksesóriəl/ *adj.* [med.L *accessorius* (as ACCEDE)]

▪ *n.* **1** extra, addition, adjunct, attachment, add-on, component, frill, doodah, *US* doodad. **2** (*accessories*) extras, bits and bobs *or* pieces, trappings, frills, trimmings, trim, adornments, *colloq.* bells and whistles. **3** accomplice, helper, assistant, confederate, colleague, abetter, aide, collaborator, co-conspirator, conspirator, fellow-criminal, associate *or* partner in crime. ● *adj.* extra, subordinate, auxiliary, additional, ancillary, supplemental, supplementary, secondary; see also DISPENSABLE.

acciaccatura /əchákkətoorə/ *n. Mus.* a grace-note performed as quickly as possible before an essential note of a melody. [It.]

accidence /áksid'nss/ *n.* the part of grammar that deals with the variable parts or inflections of words. [med.L sense of L *accidentia* (transl. Gk *parepomena*) neut. pl. of *accidens* (as ACCIDENT)]

accident /áksid'nt/ *n.* **1** an event that is without apparent cause, or is unexpected (*their early arrival was just an accident*). **2** an unfortunate event, esp. one causing physical harm or damage, brought about unintentionally. **3** occurrence of things by chance; the working of fortune (*accident accounts for much in life*). **4** *colloq.* an occurrence of involuntary urination or defecation. **5** an irregularity in structure. □ **accident-prone** (of a person) subject to frequent accidents. **by accident** unintentionally. [ME f. OF f. LL *accidens* f. L *accidere* (as AC-, *cadere* fall)]

▪ **1, 3** chance, coincidence, fortune, luck, fortuity, fluke; serendipity. **2** mishap, misfortune, mischance, misadventure, bit of bad luck, blunder, mistake; casualty, disaster, catastrophe, calamity; crash, collision, *colloq.* smash-up, pile-up; *Brit. sl.* prang. □ **by accident** accidentally, by chance, fortuitously, unintentionally, inadvertently, unwittingly, by mistake, unknowingly, unexpectedly.

accidental /áksidént'l/ *adj.* & *n.* ● *adj.* **1** happening by chance, unintentionally, or unexpectedly. **2** not essential to a conception; subsidiary. ● *n.* **1** *Mus.* a sign indicating a momentary departure from the key signature by raising or lowering a note. **2** something not essential to a conception. □□ **accidentally** *adv.* [ME f. LL *accidentalis* (as ACCIDENT)]
■ *adj.* **1** chance, fortuitous, lucky, unlucky, serendipitous, incidental; undesigned, unpremeditated, uncalculated, unintended, unintentional, unwitting, inadvertent; unexpected, unplanned, unlooked-for, unforeseen, unanticipated, adventitious; casual, random, fluky. **2** see INCIDENTAL *adj.* 1a, b. ● *n.* **2** incidental, inessential, extra, addition. □□ **accidentally** see *by accident* (ACCIDENT).

accidie /áksidee/ *n.* laziness, sloth, apathy. [ME f. AF *accidie* f. OF *accide* f. med.L *accidia*]

acclaim /əkláym/ *v.* & *n.* ● *v.tr.* **1** welcome or applaud enthusiastically; praise publicly. **2** (foll. by compl.) hail as (*acclaimed him king*; *was acclaimed the winner*). ● *n.* **1** applause; welcome; public praise. **2** a shout of acclaim. □□ **acclaimer** *n.* [ME f. L *acclamare* (as AC-, *clamare* shout: spelling assim. to *claim*)]
■ *v.* **1** see PRAISE *v.* 1. ● *n.* **1** see PRAISE *n.*

acclamation /ákləmáysh'n/ *n.* **1** loud and eager assent to a proposal. **2** (usu. in *pl.*) shouting in a person's honour. **3** the act or process of acclaiming. □ **by acclamation** *US Polit.* (elected) unanimously and without ballot. [L *acclamatio* (as ACCLAIM)]
■ **3** see PRAISE *n.*

acclimate /áklimayt, əklī́-/ *v.tr.* *US* acclimatize. [F *acclimater* f. *à* to + *climat* CLIMATE]
■ (*acclimate to*) see ACCUSTOM.

acclimation /áklimáysh'n/ *n.* esp. *US* acclimatization. [irreg. f. ACCLIMATE]
■ see ACCOMMODATION 3, ORIENTATION 3.

acclimatize /əklī́mətīz/ *v.* (also **-ise**) **1** *tr.* accustom to a new climate or to new conditions. **2** *intr.* become acclimatized. □□ **acclimatization** /-záysh'n/ *n.* [F *acclimater*: see ACCLIMATE]
■ **1** see ACCUSTOM. **2** see ADJUST 5. □□ **acclimatization** see ACCOMMODATION 3, ORIENTATION 3.

acclivity /əklívviti/ *n.* (*pl.* **-ies**) an upward slope. □□ **acclivitous** *adj.* [L *acclivitas* f. *acclivis* (as AC-, *clivis* f. *clivus* slope)]
■ see RISE *n.* 2.

accolade /ákkəláyd/ *n.* **1** the awarding of praise; an acknowledgement of merit. **2** a touch made with a sword at the bestowing of a knighthood. [F f. Prov. *acolada* (as AC-, L *collum* neck)]
■ **1** see HONOUR *n.* 1, PRAISE *n.*

accommodate /əkómmədayt/ *v.tr.* **1** provide lodging or room for (*the flat accommodates three people*). **2** adapt, harmonize, reconcile (*must accommodate ourselves to new surroundings*; *cannot accommodate your needs to mine*). **3 a** do a service or favour to; oblige (a person). **b** (foll. by *with*) supply (a person) with. [L *accommodare* (as AC-, *commodus* fitting)]
■ **1** put up, house, lodge, shelter, quarter, *Mil.* billet; hold, admit, have capacity for, carry, seat, sleep, contain. **2** (*accommodate a thing to*) harmonize with, make consistent with, reconcile to, adapt to, fit to *or* with, adjust to; (*accommodate oneself to*) become accustomed *or* acclimatized to, get used to, adapt to, adjust to. **3 a** suit, oblige, do a person a favour, favour, convenience, serve; aid, assist. **b** equip, supply, provide, furnish.

accommodating /əkómmədayting/ *adj.* obliging, compliant. □□ **accommodatingly** *adv.*
■ obliging, cooperative, helpful, hospitable; considerate, conciliatory, easy to deal with, adaptable, pliant, yielding, compliant, polite, friendly, accessible, complaisant, kind, kindly.

accommodation /əkómmədáysh'n/ *n.* **1** (in *sing.* or *US* in *pl.*) lodgings; a place to live. **2 a** an adjustment or adaptation to suit a special or different purpose. **b** a convenient arrangement; a settlement or compromise. **3** the act or process of accommodating or being accommodated. **4** (in *pl.*) *US* a seat in a vehicle etc. □ **accommodation address** an address used on letters to a person who is unable or unwilling to give a permanent address. **accommodation bill** a bill to raise money on credit. **accommodation ladder** a ladder up the side of a ship from a small boat. **accommodation road** a road for access to a place not on a public road. [F *accommodation* or L *accommodatio -onis* (as ACCOMMODATE)]
■ **1** lodging(s), room(s), quarters, shelter, housing, house, home, residence, domicile, abode, *Mil.* billet, *colloq.* pad, *Brit. colloq.* digs, diggings, *formal* dwelling(-place). **2 a** adaptation, adjustment, modification, change, alteration, conformation. **b** settlement, treaty, compromise, arrangement, terms, contract, deal; loan, (financial) assistance *or* aid, grant, grant-in-aid. **3** see sense 2a above; *also* conformity, orientation, acclimatization, *esp. US* acclimation. **4** (*accommodations*) seats, places.

accompaniment /əkúmpənimənt/ *n.* **1** *Mus.* an instrumental or orchestral part supporting or partnering a solo instrument, voice, or group. **2** an accompanying thing; an appendage. [F *accompagnement* (as ACCOMPANY)]

accompanist /əkúmpənist/ *n.* (also **accompanyist** /-ni-ist/) a person who provides a musical accompaniment.

accompany /əkúmpəni/ *v.tr.* (**-ies, -ied**) **1** go with; escort, attend. **2** (usu. in *passive*; foll. by *with, by*) **a** be done or found with; supplement (*speech accompanied with gestures*). **b** have as a result (*pills accompanied by side-effects*). **3** *Mus.* support or partner with accompaniment. [ME f. F *accompagner* f. *à* to + OF *compaing* COMPANION[1]: assim. to COMPANY]
■ **1** attend, escort, chaperon, go (along) with, keep a person *or* thing company, usher, guide, conduct, squire; *Naut.* convoy. **2** go (along) with, come with, occur with, be associated with, belong with, go together with, be linked with, be an adjunct to, be part of.

accomplice /əkúmpliss, əkóm-/ *n.* a partner or helper, esp. in a crime or wrongdoing. [ME and F *complice* (prob. by assoc. with ACCOMPANY), f. LL *complex complicis* confederate: cf. COMPLICATE]
■ accessory, partner in crime, confederate; participator, henchman, collaborator, conspirator, co-conspirator, abetter, fellow-criminal; ally, partner, helper, aide, right-hand man *or* woman, assistant, associate, colleague, fellow, *colloq.* sidekick, *US* cohort, *Austral. sl.* ram.

accomplish /əkúmplish, əkóm-/ *v.tr.* perform; complete; succeed in doing. □□ **accomplishable** *adj.* [ME f. OF *acomplir* f. L *complēre* COMPLETE]
■ fulfil, perform, achieve, carry out, execute, bring about, produce, carry off, do, complete, carry through, finish, conclude, effect, effectuate, bring off, pull off, bring to an end, conclude, wind up, end; attain, reach, gain; *colloq.* knock off, swing, *sl.* hack.

accomplished /əkúmplisht, əkóm-/ *adj.* clever, skilled; well trained or educated.
■ clever, consummate, expert, masterly, masterful, capable, competent, adept, skilful, proficient, practised, polished, gifted, talented, skilled, professional; qualified, well-trained, well-educated, experienced, *joc.* complete.

accomplishment /əkúmplishmənt, əkóm-/ *n.* **1** the fulfilment or completion (of a task etc.). **2** an acquired skill, esp. a social one. **3** a thing done or achieved.
■ **1** fulfilment, consummation, completion, realization, attainment, achievement, conclusion. **2** skill, talent, gift, ability. **3** achievement, attainment, acquirement, coup, feat, deed, act, stroke, exploit, triumph, *tour de force*.

accord /əkórd/ *v.* & *n.* ● *v.* **1** *intr.* (often foll. by *with*) (esp. of a thing) be in harmony; be consistent. **2** *tr.* **a** grant (permission, a request, etc.). **b** give (a welcome etc.). ● *n.* **1**

agreement, consent. **2** harmony or harmonious correspondence in pitch, tone, colour, etc. **3** a formal treaty or agreement. □ **in accord** of one mind, united; in harmony. **of one's own accord** on one's own initiative; voluntarily. **with one accord** unanimously; in a united way. [ME f. OF *acord, acorder* f. L *cor cordis* heart]

▪ *v.* **1** agree, harmonize, concur, be at one, correspond, be in harmony *or* accord, be consistent, go (together), coincide, conform, chime (in), *US colloq.* jibe. **2 a** see GIVE *v.* 4. **b** see EXTEND 5. ● *n.* **1** agreement, consent, unanimity, concord, harmony, mutual understanding, conformity, accordance, unison, rapport, concert. **2** agreement, harmony, sympathy, congruence, concord, concordance. **3** agreement, treaty, pact, compact, contract. □ **in accord** see UNITED 3. **of one's own accord** see *voluntarily* (VOLUNTARY). **with one accord** unanimously, uniformly, with one voice, in unison, unitedly, solidly, as one man, *US Polit.* by acclamation.

accordance /əkórd'nss/ *n.* harmony, agreement. □ **in accordance with** in a manner corresponding to (*we acted in accordance with your wishes*). [ME f. OF *acordance* (as ACCORD)]

▪ see ACCORD *n.* 2.

accordant /əkórd'nt/ *adj.* (often foll. by *with*) in tune; agreeing. □□ **accordantly** *adv.* [ME f. OF *acordant* (as ACCORD)]

▪ see CONSISTENT 1.

according /əkórding/ *adv.* **1** (foll. by *to*) **a** as stated by or in (*according to my sister; according to their statement*). **b** in a manner corresponding to; in proportion to (*he lives according to his principles*). **2** (foll. by *as* + clause) in a manner or to a degree that varies as (*he pays according as he is able*).

▪ **1** (*according to*) **a** on the authority of, in conformity *or* agreement with, as said *or* stated *or* believed *or* maintained by. **b** by, in keeping *or* line *or* step *or* conformity *or* harmony *or* agreement with, in proportion to.

accordingly /əkórdingli/ *adv.* **1** as suggested or required by the (stated) circumstances (*silence is vital so please act accordingly*). **2** consequently, therefore (*accordingly, he left the room*).

▪ **1** correspondingly, in accordance, suitably, in conformity, appropriately, compliantly. **2** hence, therefore, consequently, (and) so, that being so *or* the case, *formal* thus, in consequence whereof.

accordion /əkórdiən/ *n.* a portable musical instrument with reeds blown by bellows and played by means of keys and buttons. □ **accordion pleat, wall,** etc. one folding like the bellows of an accordion. □□ **accordionist** *n.* [G *Akkordion* f. It. *accordare* to tune]

accost /əkóst/ *v.tr.* **1** approach and address (a person), esp. boldly. **2** (of a prostitute) solicit. [F *accoster* f. It. *accostare* ult. f. L *costa* rib: see COAST]

▪ **1** see ADDRESS *v.* 3, HAIL² *v.* 1, 2. **2** see PROPOSITION *v.*

accouchement /ákkōōshmóɴ/ *n.* **1** childbirth. **2** the period of childbirth. [F f. *accoucher* act as midwife]

accoucheur /ákkōōshőr/ *n.* a male midwife. [F (as ACCOUCHEMENT)]

account /əkównt/ *n.* & *v.* ● *n.* **1** a narration or description (*gave a long account of the ordeal*). **2 a** an arrangement or facility at a bank or building society etc. for commercial or financial transactions, esp. for depositing and withdrawing money (*opened an account*). **b** the assets credited by such an arrangement (*has a large account; paid the money into her account*). **c** an arrangement at a shop for buying goods on credit (*has an account at the newsagent's*). **3 a** (often in *pl.*) a record or statement of money, goods, or services received or expended, with the balance (*firms must keep detailed accounts*). **b** (in *pl.*) the practice of accounting or reckoning (*is good at accounts*). **4** a statement of the administration of money in trust (*demand an account*). **5** the period during which transactions take place on a stock exchange; the period from one account day to the next. **6** counting, reckoning. **7** estimation, importance; consideration. ● *v.tr.* (foll. by *to be* or compl.) consider, regard as (*account it a misfortune; account him wise; account him to be guilty*). ¶ Use with *as* (*we accounted him as wise*) is considered incorrect. □ **account day** a day of periodic settlement of stock exchange accounts. **account for 1** serve as or provide an explanation or reason for (*that accounts for their misbehaviour*). **2 a** give a reckoning of or answer for (money etc. entrusted). **b** answer for (one's conduct). **3** succeed in killing, destroying, disposing of, or defeating. **4** supply or make up a specified amount or proportion of (*rent accounts for 50% of expenditure*). **account rendered** a bill which has been sent but is not yet paid. **by all accounts** in everyone's opinion. **call to account** require an explanation from (a person). **give a good** (or **bad**) **account of oneself** make a favourable (or unfavourable) impression; be successful (or unsuccessful). **keep account of** keep a record of; follow closely. **leave out of account** fail or decline to consider. **money of account** denominations of money used in reckoning, but not current as coins. **of no account** unimportant. **of some account** important. **on account 1** (of goods) to be paid for later. **2** (of money) in part payment. **on account of** because of. **on no account** under no circumstances; certainly not. **on one's own account** for one's own purposes; at one's own risk. **settle** (or **square**) **accounts with 1** receive or pay money etc. owed to. **2** have revenge on. **take account of** (or **take into account**) consider along with other factors (*took their age into account*). **turn to account** (or **good account**) turn to one's advantage. [ME f. OF *acont, aconter* (as AC-, *conter* COUNT¹)]

▪ *n.* **1** explanation, narration, narrative, statement, description, report, version, relation, recital, commentary; history, chronicle, story, sketch, tale. **3 a** books, (financial) statement; invoice, bill, *US colloq.* tab. **b** (*accounts*) accounting, accountancy, bookkeeping. **6** counting, reckoning, calculation, computation; enumeration. **7** consideration, use, worth, importance, import, consequence, note, value, merit; standing, significance, estimation, esteem. ● *v.* regard as, consider, count (as), view as, look upon as, rate (as), judge. □ **account for 1** explain, serve as an explanation, justify. **2 b** give *or* render a reckoning for, answer for, make plausible *or* believable *or* understandable, justify, excuse, explain (away), vindicate. **3** kill, destroy, do away with, dispose of, defeat. **4** make up, supply, constitute, form, *disp.* comprise. **of no account** unimportant, insignificant, paltry, inconsequential, trifling, trivial, negligible, non-essential, inessential, minor, nugatory, *colloq.* piddling. **of some account** see IMPORTANT 1. **on account 1** on credit, *colloq.* on tick, on tab; *Brit.* on the slate. **on account of** see OWING 2. **on no account** see *by no means* (MEANS). **settle** (or **square**) **accounts with 2** see REVENGE *v.* 1, 2. **take account of** (or **take into account**) notice, take note of, consider, take into consideration, allow for. **turn to account** (or **good account**) turn to one's advantage *or* benefit *or* profit; benefit *or* profit from.

accountable /əkówntəb'l/ *adj.* **1** responsible; required to account for (one's conduct) (*accountable for one's actions*). **2** explicable, understandable. □□ **accountability** /-billiti/ *n.* **accountableness** *n.* **accountably** *adv.*

▪ **1** answerable, responsible, liable, chargeable. **2** explicable, understandable, explainable, interpretable, comprehensible, decipherable. □□ **accountability, accountableness** answerability, responsibility, liability, culpability, accountableness. **accountably** understandably, discernibly, clearly.

accountancy /əkówntənsi/ *n.* the profession or duties of an accountant.

accountant /əkówntənt/ *n.* a professional keeper or inspector of accounts. [legal F f. pres. part. of OF *aconter* ACCOUNT]

▪ see BOOKKEEPER.

accounting /əkównting/ *n.* **1** the process of or skill in keeping and verifying accounts. **2** in senses of ACCOUNT *v.*

▪ **1** see ACCOUNT *n.* 3b.

accoutre /əkōōtər/ *v.tr.* (*US* **accouter**) (usu. as **accoutred** *adj.*) attire, equip, esp. with a special costume. [F *accoutrer* f. OF *acoustrer* (as A-^{3}, *cousture* sewing: cf. SUTURE)]
■ see EQUIP.

accoutrement /əkōōtrəmənt, -tərmənt/ *n.* (*US* **accouterment** /-tərmənt/) (usu. in *pl.*) **1** equipment, trappings. **2** *Mil.* a soldier's outfit other than weapons and garments. [F (as ACCOUTRE)]
■ (*accoutrements*) see EQUIPMENT.

accredit /əkréddit/ *v.tr.* (**accredited, accrediting**) **1** (foll. by *to*) attribute (a saying etc.) to (a person). **2** (foll. by *with*) credit (a person) with (a saying etc.). **3** (usu. foll. by *to* or *at*) send (an ambassador etc.) with credentials; recommend by documents as an envoy (*was accredited to the sovereign*). **4** gain belief or influence for or make credible (an adviser, a statement, etc.). □□ **accreditation** /-táysh'n/ *n.* [F *accréditer* (as AC-, *crédit* CREDIT)]
■ **1** see ATTRIBUTE *v.* **3** see DELEGATE *v.* 2. **4** see CONFIRM 1, 2.

accredited /əkrédditid/ *adj.* **1** (of a person or organization) officially recognized. **2** (of a belief) generally accepted; orthodox. **3** (of cattle, milk, etc.) having guaranteed quality.
■ **1** see OFFICIAL *adj.* 3, 4.

accrete /əkréet/ *v.* **1** *intr.* grow together or into one. **2** *intr.* (often foll. by *to*) form round or on, as round a nucleus. **3** *tr.* attract (such additions). [L *accrescere* (as AC-, *crescere cret-* grow)]

accretion /əkréesh'n/ *n.* **1** growth by organic enlargement. **2 a** the growing of separate things into one. **b** the product of such growing. **3 a** extraneous matter added to anything. **b** the adhesion of this. **4** *Law* **a** = ACCESSION. **b** the increase of a legacy etc. by the share of a failing co-legatee. □□ **accretive** *adj.* [L *accretio* (as ACCRETE)]

accrue /əkrōō/ *v.intr.* (**accrues, accrued, accruing**) (often foll. by *to*) come as a natural increase or advantage, esp. financial. □□ **accrual** *n.* **accrued** *adj.* **accruement** *n.* [ME f. AF *acru(e)*, past part. of *acreistre* increase f. L *accrescere* ACCRETE]

acculturate /əkúlchərayt/ *v.* **1** *intr.* adapt to or adopt a different culture. **2** *tr.* cause to do this. □□ **acculturation** /-ráysh'n/ *n.* **acculturative** /-rətiv/ *adj.*
■ □□ **acculturative** see ADAPTABLE 1.

accumulate /əkyōōmyoolayt/ *v.* **1** *tr.* **a** acquire an increasing number or quantity of; heap up. **b** produce or acquire (a resulting whole) in this way. **2** *intr.* grow numerous or considerable; form an increasing mass or quantity. [L *accumulare* (as AC-, *cumulus* heap)]
■ **1** collect, gather, amass, mass, pile *or* heap up, aggregate, cumulate; assemble, store, stock, hoard, stockpile, put *or* lay away. **2** collect, pile up.

accumulation /əkyōōmyooláysh'n/ *n.* **1** the act or process of accumulating or being accumulated. **2** an accumulated mass. **3** the growth of capital by continued interest. [L *accumulatio* (as ACCUMULATE)]
■ **1** collecting, amassing, gathering, accretion, accruement, aggregation, piling *or* heaping *or* building up; growth, increase, build-up. **2** heap, pile, mass, mound, stack, mountain, collection, hoard, store, stockpile, stock, aggregation, assemblage, *colloq.* stash.

accumulative /əkyōōmyoolətiv/ *adj.* **1** arising from accumulation; cumulative (*accumulative evidence*). **2** arranged so as to accumulate. **3** acquisitive; given to hoarding. □□ **accumulatively** *adv.*

accumulator /əkyōōmyoolaytər/ *n.* **1** *Brit.* a rechargeable electric cell. **2** a bet placed on a sequence of events, the winnings and stake from each being placed on the next. **3** a register in a computer used to contain the results of an operation. **4** a person who accumulates things.
■ **4** see COLLECTOR.

accuracy /ákyoorəsi/ *n.* exactness or precision, esp. arising from careful effort.
■ exactness, correctness, accurateness, exactitude, precision, preciseness.

accurate /ákyoorət/ *adj.* **1** careful, precise; lacking errors. **2** conforming exactly with a qualitative standard, physical or quantitative target, etc. □□ **accurately** *adv.* **accurateness** *n.* [L *accuratus* done carefully, past part. of *accurare* (as AC-, *cura* care)]
■ careful, precise, meticulous, nice, with an eye to *or* for detail, scrupulous, conscientious; exact, correct, perfect, true, right, truthful, faithful, unerring, on target, faultless, flawless, defectless, error-free, *Brit. colloq.* spot *or* bang on (target), *formal* veracious. □□ **accurately** see EXACTLY 1, TRULY 4.

accursed /əkúrsid, əkúrst/ *adj.* (*archaic* **accurst** /əkúrst/) **1** lying under a curse; ill-fated. **2** *colloq.* detestable, annoying. [past part. of *accurse*, f. A-^{2} + CURSE]
■ **1** see *doomed* (DOOM *v.* 2). **2** see DAMNABLE.

accusal /əkyōōz'l/ *n.* accusation.
■ see ACCUSATION.

accusation /ákyoozáysh'n/ *n.* **1** the act or process of accusing or being accused. **2** a statement charging a person with an offence or crime. [ME f. OF f. L *accusatio -onis* (as ACCUSE)]
■ accusal, charge, allegation, indictment, citation, arraignment, complaint; imputation, incrimination, denunciation, impeachment; reproach, reproof; *Brit. Law* plaint, *US Law* complaint.

accusative /əkyōōzətiv/ *n.* & *adj.* *Gram.* ● *n.* the case of nouns, pronouns, and adjectives, expressing the object of an action or the goal of motion. ● *adj.* of or in this case. □□ **accusatival** /-tīv'l/ *adj.* **accusatively** *adv.* [ME f. OF *accusatif -ive* or L (*casus*) *accusativus*, transl. Gk (*ptōsis*) *aitiatikē*]

accusatorial /əkyōōzətóriəl/ *adj.* *Law* (of proceedings) involving accusation by a prosecutor and a verdict reached by an impartial judge or jury (opp. INQUISITORIAL). [L *accusatorius* (as ACCUSE)]

accusatory /əkyōōzətəri/ *adj.* (of language, manner, etc.) of or implying accusation.

accuse /əkyōōz/ *v.tr.* **1** (foll. by *of*) charge (a person etc.) with a fault or crime; indict (*accused them of murder*; *was accused of stealing a car*). **2** lay the blame on. □ **the accused** the person or persons charged with a crime. □□ **accuser** *n.* **accusingly** *adv.* [ME *acuse* f. OF *ac(c)user* f. L *accusare* (as AC-, CAUSE)]
■ **1** (*accuse of*) charge with, indict *or* impeach *or* arraign for, incriminate in, *Law* implead in, cite for, *archaic* delate of. **2** blame, censure, hold responsible *or* accountable, charge, denounce, lay a thing at the door of, call to account, call down, *colloq.* stick *or* pin a thing on, point the finger at, *sl.* put the finger on. □□ **accuser** prosecutor, indicter, informer, *Law* plaintiff, prosecution, *archaic* delator. **accusingly** censoriously.

accustom /əkústəm/ *v.tr.* & *refl.* (foll. by *to*) make (a person or thing or oneself) used to (*the army accustomed him to discipline*; *was accustomed to their strange ways*). [ME f. OF *acostumer* (as AD-, *costume* CUSTOM)]
■ (*accustom to*) familiarize with, make *or* become familiar with, acquaint with, habituate to, inure to, train to, season to; adapt to, acclimatize to, make *or* get *or* become used to, *US* acclimate to.

accustomed /əkústəmd/ *adj.* **1** (usu. foll. by *to*) used to (*accustomed to hard work*). **2** customary, usual.
■ **1** (*accustomed to*) used *or* inured *or* habituated *or* acclimatized to, familiar *or* acquainted with. **2** customary, habitual, usual, traditional, normal, regular, set, routine, mundane, ordinary, familiar, wonted, common, *colloq.* common or garden.

ace /ayss/ *n.* & *adj.* ● *n.* **1 a** a playing-card, domino, etc., with a single spot and generally having the value 'one' or in card-games the highest value in each suit. **b** a single spot on a playing-card etc. **2 a** a person who excels in some activity. **b** *Aeron.* a pilot who has shot down many enemy aircraft. **3 a** (in lawn tennis) a service too good for the opponent to return. **b** a point scored in this way. ● *adj.* *sl.* excellent. □

ace up one's sleeve (*US* **in the hole**) something effective kept in reserve. **play one's ace** use one's best resource. **within an ace of** on the verge of. [ME f. OF f. L *as* unity, AS[2]]

■ *n.* **2 a** see EXPERT *n.* ● *adj.* see SUPERLATIVE *adj.*

-acea /áyshə/ *suffix* forming the plural names of orders and classes of animals (*Crustacea*) (cf. -ACEAN). [neut. pl. of L adj. suffix *-aceus* of the nature of]

-aceae /áysi-ee/ *suffix* forming the plural names of families of plants (*Rosaceae*). [fem. pl. of L adj. suffix *-aceus* of the nature of]

-acean /áysh'n/ *suffix* **1** forming adjectives, = -ACEOUS. **2** forming nouns as the sing. of names in *-acea* (*crustacean*). [L *-aceus*: see -ACEA]

acedia /əseédiə/ *n.* = ACCIDIE. [LL *acedia* f. Gk *akēdia* listlessness]

acellular /aysélyoolər/ *adj. Biol.* **1** having no cells; not consisting of cells. **2** (esp. of protozoa) consisting of one cell only; unicellular.

-aceous /áyshəss/ *suffix* forming adjectives, esp. from nouns in *-acea, -aceae* (*herbaceous*; *rosaceous*). [L *-aceus*: see -ACEA]

acephalous /əséffələss, əkéf-/ *adj.* **1** headless. **2** having no chief. **3** *Zool.* having no part of the body specially organized as a head. **4** *Bot.* with a head aborted or cut off. **5** *Prosody* lacking a syllable or syllables in the first foot. [med.L *acephalus* f. Gk *akephalos* headless (as A-[1], *kephalē* head)]

acerb /əsérb/ *adj.* = ACERBIC.

acerbic /əsérbik/ *adj.* **1** astringently sour; harsh-tasting. **2** bitter in speech, manner, or temper. □□ **acerbically** *adv.* **acerbity** *n.* (*pl.* **-ies**). [L *acerbus* sour-tasting]

■ **1** see TART[3] 1. **2** see TART[3] 2.

acetabulum /àssitábyooləm/ *n.* (*pl.* **acetabula** /-lə/) *Zool.* **1** the socket for the head of the thigh-bone, or of the leg in insects. **2** a cup-shaped sucker of various organisms, including tapeworms and cuttlefish. [ME f. L, = vinegar cup f. *acetum* vinegar + *-abulum* dimin. of *-abrum* holder]

acetal /ássital/ *n. Chem.* any of a class of organic compounds formed by the condensation of two alcohol molecules with an aldehyde molecule. [as ACETIC + -AL]

acetaldehyde /àssitáldihīd/ *n.* a colourless volatile liquid aldehyde. Also called ETHANAL. ¶ Chem. formula: CH_3CHO. [ACETIC + ALDEHYDE]

acetate /ássitayt/ *n.* **1** a salt or ester of acetic acid, esp. the cellulose ester used to make textiles, gramophone records, etc. Also called ETHANOATE. **2** a fabric made from cellulose acetate. □ **acetate fibre** (or **silk**) fibre (or silk) made artificially from cellulose acetate. [ACETIC + -ATE[1] 2]

acetic /əseétik/ *adj.* of or like vinegar. □ **acetic acid** the clear liquid acid that gives vinegar its characteristic taste: also called ETHANOATE. ¶ Chem. formula: CH_3COOH. [F *acétique* f. L *acetum* vinegar]

aceto- /ássitō/ *comb. form Chem.* acetic, acetyl.

acetone /ássitōn/ *n.* a colourless volatile liquid ketone valuable as a solvent of organic compounds esp. paints, varnishes, etc. Also called PROPANONE. ¶ Chem. formula: CH_3COCH_3. [ACETO- + -ONE]

acetous /ássitəss/ *adj.* **1** having the qualities of vinegar. **2** producing vinegar. **3** sour. [LL *acetosus* sour (as ACETIC)]

acetyl /ássitil, -tīl/ *n. Chem.* the univalent radical of acetic acid. ¶ Chem. formula: CH_3CO-. □ **acetyl silk** = *acetate silk*. [ACETIC + -YL]

acetylcholine /àssitīlkóleen, àssitīl-/ *n.* a compound serving to transmit impulses from nerve fibres. [ACETYL + CHOLINE]

acetylene /əséttileen/ *n.* a colourless hydrocarbon gas, burning with a bright flame, used esp. in welding and formerly in lighting. Also called ETHYNE. ¶ Chem. formula: C_2H_2. [ACETIC + -YL + -ENE]

acetylide /əséttilīd/ *n.* any of a class of salts formed from acetylene and a metal.

acetylsalicylic acid /àssitīlsàllisíllik/ *n.* = ASPIRIN. [ACETYL + SALICYLIC ACID]

Achaean /əkeéən/ *adj.* & *n.* ● *adj.* **1** of or relating to Achaea in ancient Greece. **2** *literary* (esp. in Homeric contexts) Greek. ● *n.* **1** an inhabitant of Achaea. **2** *literary* (usu. in *pl.*) a Greek. [L *Achaeus* f. Gk *Akhaios*]

Achaemenid /əkeémənid/ *adj.* & *n.* (also **Achaemenian** /àkkimeéniən/) ● *adj.* of or relating to the dynasty ruling in Persia from Cyrus I to Darius III (553–330 BC). ● *n.* a member of this dynasty. [L *Achaemenius* f. Gk *Akhaimenēs*, ancestor of the dynasty]

acharnement /àshaarnmóɴ/ *n.* **1** bloodthirsty fury; ferocity. **2** gusto. [F]

ache /ayk/ *n.* & *v.* ● *n.* **1** a continuous or prolonged dull pain. **2** mental distress. ● *v.intr.* **1** suffer from or be the source of an ache (*I ached all over*; *my left leg ached*). **2** (foll. by *to* + infin.) desire greatly (*we ached to be at home again*). □□ **achingly** *adv.* [ME f. OE *æce*, *acan*]

■ *n.* **1** pain, pang, throbbing, pounding, smarting, soreness; discomfort. **2** pang, pain; sorrow, grief, distress; longing, yearning, craving. ● *v.* **1** hurt, pain, smart, throb, pound, be sore *or* painful, sting. **2** yearn, long, hunger, hanker, pine; crave.

achene /əkeén/ *n. Bot.* a small dry one-seeded fruit that does not open to liberate the seed (e.g. a strawberry pip). [mod.L *achaenium* (as A-[1], Gk *khainō* gape)]

Acheulian /əshōōliən/ *adj.* & *n.* (also **Acheulean**) ● *adj.* of the palaeolithic period in Europe etc. following the Abbevillian and preceding the Mousterian. ● *n.* the culture of this period. [F *acheuléen* f. St-*Acheul* in N. France, where remains of it were found]

achieve /əcheév/ *v.tr.* **1 a** reach or attain by effort (*achieved victory*). **b** acquire, gain, earn (*achieved notoriety*). **2** accomplish or carry out (a feat or task). **3** *absol.* be successful; attain a desired level of performance. □□ **achievable** *adj.* **achiever** *n.* [ME f. OF *achever* f. *a chief* to a head]

■ **1** attain, reach, gain, get, manage, acquire, earn, win, obtain, accomplish, carry off, bring *or* pull off. **2** accomplish, carry out, execute, succeed in, complete, do, fulfil, bring off *or* about; realize, effect, effectuate, engineer, produce. **3** succeed, triumph, ride high, come through, perform (well), prosper, get ahead, give a good account of oneself, flourish, make a hit, *colloq.* go places, make it, click. □□ **achievable** see POSSIBLE *adj.* 2. **achiever** high-flyer, success story, *colloq.* golden boy *or* girl, whiz-kid, whiz, *esp. US colloq.* hotshot.

achievement /əcheévmənt/ *n.* **1** something achieved; an instance of achieving. **2** the act or process of achieving. **3** *Psychol.* performance in a standardized test. **4** *Heraldry* **a** an escutcheon with adjuncts, or bearing, esp. in memory of a distinguished feat. **b** = HATCHMENT.

■ **1** see ACCOMPLISHMENT 3, ACT *n.* 1. **2** see CONSUMMATION 1.

achillea /àkkileéə/ *n.* any plant of the genus *Achillea*, comprising hardy perennial, usu. aromatic plants with flower-heads (often white or yellow) usu. in corymbs. [L f. Gk *Akhilleios* a plant supposed to have been used medicinally by Achilles]

Achilles heel /əkílleez/ *n.* a person's weak or vulnerable point. [L *Achilles* f. Gk *Akhilleus*, a hero in the *Iliad*, invulnerable except in the heel]

■ see WEAKNESS 2.

Achilles tendon /əkílleez/ *n.* the tendon connecting the heel with the calf muscles.

achiral /aykīrəl/ *adj. Chem.* (of a crystal or molecule) not chiral.

achromat /ákrōmat/ *n.* a lens made achromatic by correction.

achromatic /àkrōmáttik/ *adj. Optics* **1** that transmits light without separating it into constituent colours (*achromatic lens*). **2** without colour (*achromatic fringe*). □□ **achromatically** *adv.* **achromaticity** /əkrōmətíssiti/ *n.* **achromatism** /əkrōmətiz'm/ *n.* [F *achromatique* f. Gk *akhromatos* (as A-[1], CHROMATIC)]

achy /áyki/ *adj.* (**achier**, **achiest**) full of or suffering from aches.

■ see PAINFUL 1, 2.

acid /ássid/ *n.* & *adj.* ● *n.* **1** *Chem.* **a** any of a class of substances that liberate hydrogen ions in water, are usu. sour and corrosive, turn litmus red, and have a pH of less than 7. **b** any compound or atom donating protons. **2** (in general use) any sour substance. **3** *sl.* the drug LSD. ● *adj.* **1** sharp-tasting, sour. **2** biting, sharp (*an acid wit*). **3** *Chem.* having the essential properties of an acid. **4** *Geol.* containing much silica. **5** (of a colour) intense, bright. □ **acid drop** *Brit.* a kind of sweet with a sharp taste. **acid-head** *sl.* a user of the drug LSD. **acid house** a kind of synthesized music with a simple repetitive beat, often associated with the taking of hallucinogenic drugs. **acid radical** one formed by the removal of hydrogen ions from an acid. **acid rain** acid formed in the atmosphere esp. from industrial waste gases and falling with rain. **acid test 1** a severe or conclusive test. **2** a test in which acid is used to test for gold etc. **put the acid on** *Austral. sl.* seek to extract a loan or favour etc. from. □□ **acidic** /əsíddik/ *adj.* **acidimeter** /ássidímmitər/ *n.* **acidimetry** /ássidímmitri/ *n.* **acidly** *adv.* **acidness** *n.* [F *acide* or L *acidus* f. *acēre* be sour]

■ *adj.* **1** see TART[3] 1. **2** see TART[3] 2.

acidify /əsíddifī/ *v.tr.* & *intr.* (**-ies**, **-ied**) make or become acid. □□ **acidification** /-fikáysh'n/ *n.*

acidity /əsídditi/ *n.* (*pl.* **-ies**) an acid quality or state, esp. an excessively acid condition of the stomach.

acidosis /ássidṓsiss/ *n.* an over-acid condition of the body fluids or tissues. □□ **acidotic** /-dóttik/ *adj.*

acidulate /əsídyoolayt/ *v.tr.* make somewhat acid. □□ **acidulation** /-láysh'n/ *n.* [L *acidulus* dimin. of *acidus* sour]

acidulous /əsídyooləss/ *adj.* somewhat acid.

■ see TART[3].

acinus /ássinəss/ *n.* (*pl.* **acini** /-nī/) **1** any of the small elements that make up a compound fruit of the blackberry, raspberry, etc. **2** the seed of a grape or berry. **3** *Anat.* **a** any multicellular gland with saclike secreting ducts. **b** the terminus of a duct in such a gland. [L, = berry, kernel]

-acious /áyshəss/ *suffix* forming adjectives meaning 'inclined to, full of' (*vivacious*; *pugnacious*; *voracious*; *capacious*). [L *-ax -acis*, added chiefly to verbal stems to form adjectives + -OUS]

-acity /ássiti/ *suffix* forming nouns of quality or state corresponding to adjectives in *-acious*. [F *-acité* or L *-acitas -tatis*]

ack-ack /ákkák/ *adj.* & *n.* *colloq.* ● *adj.* anti-aircraft. ● *n.* an anti-aircraft gun etc. [formerly signallers' name for the letters *AA*]

ackee /ákkee/ *n.* (also **akee**) **1** a tropical tree, *Blighia sapida*. **2** its fruit, edible when cooked. [Kru *ākee*]

ack emma /ak émmə/ *adv.* & *n.* *Brit. colloq.* = A.M. [formerly signallers' name for the letters *AM*]

acknowledge /əknóllij/ *v.tr.* **1 a** recognize; accept; admit the truth of (*acknowledged the failure of the plan*). **b** (often foll. by *to be* + compl.) recognize as (*acknowledged it to be a great success*). **c** (often foll. by *that* + clause or *to* + infin.) admit that something is so (*acknowledged that he was wrong*; *acknowledged him to be wrong*). **2** confirm the receipt of (*acknowledged her letter*). **3 a** show that one has noticed (*acknowledged my arrival with a grunt*). **b** express appreciation of (a service etc.). **4** own; recognize the validity of (*the acknowledged king*). □□ **acknowledgeable** *adj.* [obs. KNOWLEDGE *v.* after obs. *acknow* (as A-[4], KNOW), or f. obs. noun *acknowledge*]

■ **1** admit, accept, confess to, own up to, allow (for), concede, recognize, accede to, acquiesce in, homologate, own, grant. **2** answer, reply to, respond to, react to. **3 a** greet, mark, note, observe, salute, honour. **b** thank a person for, give thanks for, honour, reward, celebrate. **4** own, grant, accept. □□ **acknowledgeable** admittable, confessable; answerable; rewardable.

acknowledgement /əknóllijmənt/ *n.* (also **acknowledgment**) **1** the act or an instance of acknowledging. **2 a** a thing given or done in return for a service etc. **b** a letter confirming receipt of something. **3** (usu. in *pl.*) an author's statement of indebtedness to others.

■ **1** admission, confession, avowal, assent, affirmation, endorsement, confirmation, approval, acceptance; greeting, salutation, honouring, recognition. **2 a** reward, tribute, (show of) appreciation, honouring, thanks, thank you. **b** recognition, reply, response, answer; receipt.

aclinic line /əklínnik/ *n.* = *magnetic equator*. [Gk *aklinēs* (as A-[1], *klinō* bend)]

acme /ákmi/ *n.* the highest point or period (of achievement, success, etc.); the peak of perfection (*displayed the acme of good taste*). [Gk, = highest point]

■ climax, culmination; peak, apex, top, height(s), high point, summit, pinnacle, zenith, ne plus ultra.

acne /ákni/ *n.* a skin condition, usu. of the face, characterized by red pimples. □□ **acned** *adj.* [mod.L f. erron. Gk *aknas* for *akmas* accus. pl. of *akmē* facial eruption: cf. ACME]

■ see SPOT *n.* 1c.

acolyte /ákkəlīt/ *n.* **1** a person assisting a priest in a service or procession. **2** an assistant; a beginner. [ME f. OF *acolyt* or eccl.L *acolytus* f. Gk *akolouthos* follower]

■ **2** see ASSISTANT 1, APPRENTICE *n.*

aconite /ákkənīt/ *n.* **1 a** any poisonous plant of the genus *Aconitum*, esp. monkshood or wolfsbane. **b** the drug obtained from this. Also called ACONITINE. **2** (in full **winter aconite**) any ranunculaceous plant of the genus *Eranthis*, with yellow flowers. □□ **aconitic** /-níttik/ *adj. Chem.* [F *aconit* or L *aconitum* f. Gk *akoniton*]

aconitine /əkónniteen/ *n.* *Pharm.* a poisonous alkaloid obtained from the aconite plant.

acorn /áykorn/ *n.* the fruit of the oak, with a smooth nut in a rough cuplike base. □ **acorn barnacle** a multivalve marine cirriped, *Balanus balanoides*, living on rocks. **acorn worm** any marine wormlike animal of the phylum Hemichordata, having a proboscis and gill slits, and inhabiting seashores. [OE *æcern*, rel. to *æcer* ACRE, later assoc. with OAK and CORN[1]]

acotyledon /əkóttileéd'n/ *n.* a plant with no distinct seed-leaves. □□ **acotyledonous** *adj.* [mod.L *acotyledones* pl. (as A-[1], COTYLEDON)]

acoustic /əkóostik/ *adj.* & *n.* ● *adj.* **1** relating to sound or the sense of hearing. **2** (of a musical instrument, gramophone, or recording) not having electrical amplification (*acoustic guitar*). **3** (of building materials) used for soundproofing or modifying sound. **4** *Mil.* (of a mine) that can be exploded by sound waves transmitted under water. ● *n.* **1** (usu. in *pl.*) the properties or qualities (esp. of a room or hall etc.) in transmitting sound (*good acoustics*; *a poor acoustic*). **2** (in *pl.*; usu. treated as *sing.*) the science of sound (*acoustics is not widely taught*). □ **acoustic coupler** *Computing* a modem which converts digital signals into audible signals and vice versa, so that the former can be transmitted and received over telephone lines. □□ **acoustical** *adj.* **acoustically** *adv.* [Gk *akoustikos* f. *akouō* hear]

acoustician /ákkoostísh'n/ *n.* an expert in acoustics.

acquaint /əkwáynt/ *v.tr.* & *refl.* (usu. foll. by *with*) make (a person or oneself) aware of or familiar with (*acquaint me with the facts*). □ **be acquainted with** have personal knowledge of (a person or thing); have made the acquaintance of (a person). [ME f. OF *acointier* f. LL *accognitare* (as AC-, *cognoscere cognit-* come to know)]

■ (*acquaint with*) familiarize with, inform of *or* about, make aware of, verse in, tell of *or* about, apprise of, advise of, notify of, introduce to, *colloq.* fill in on, *Brit. sl.* gen up on. □ **be acquainted with** be familiar with *or* aware of *or* informed of *or* knowledgeable of *or* conversant with; know, be on speaking terms with.

acquaintance /əkwáyntənss/ *n.* **1** (usu. foll. by *with*) slight knowledge (of a person or thing). **2** the fact or process of being acquainted (*our acquaintance lasted a year*). **3** a person one knows slightly. □ **make a person's acquaintance** first meet or introduce oneself to another person; come to know. □□ **acquaintanceship** *n.* [ME f. OF *acointance* (as ACQUAINT)]

■ **1** familiarity, knowledge, acquaintanceship,

understanding, awareness; experience. **2** association, friendship, acquaintanceship, companionship, relationship. **3** associate, fellow, colleague, companion, nodding acquaintance. □ **make a person's acquaintance** introduce oneself to, make oneself known to, meet; come *or* get to know, become friendly *or* familiar with. □□ **acquaintanceship** see ACQUAINTANCE 1, 2 above.

acquiesce /ákwi-éss/ *v.intr.* **1** agree, esp. tacitly. **2** raise no objection. **3** (foll. by *in*) accept (an arrangement etc.). □□ **acquiescence** *n.* **acquiescent** *adj.* [L *acquiescere* (as AC-, *quiescere* rest)]
■ **1** see AGREE 1. **2** see AGREE 2. **3** see AGREE 4, 5.
□□ **acquiescent** see YIELDING 1.

acquire /əkwír/ *v.tr.* **1** gain by and for oneself; obtain. **2** come into possession of (*acquired fame*; *acquired much property*). □ **acquired characteristic** *Biol.* a characteristic caused by the environment, not inherited. **acquired immune deficiency syndrome** *Med.* see AIDS. **acquired taste 1** a liking gained by experience. **2** the object of such a liking. □□ **acquirable** *adj.* [ME f. OF *aquerre* ult. f. L *acquirere* (as AC-, *quaerere* seek)]
■ **1** get, obtain, gain, win, earn, make, take, procure, secure, get *or* lay one's hands on, get hold of, pull in, gather; buy, purchase. **2** come by *or* into, receive, come into possession of, amass, pick up; inherit. □□ **aquirable** obtainable, gettable, procurable, securable, winnable, gainable.

acquirement /əkwírmənt/ *n.* **1** something acquired, esp. a mental attainment. **2** the act or an instance of acquiring.
■ **1** see ACCOMPLISHMENT 3. **2** see ACQUISITION 2.

acquisition /ákwizish'n/ *n.* **1** something acquired, esp. if regarded as useful. **2** the act or an instance of acquiring. [L *acquisitio* (as ACQUIRE)]
■ **1** possession(s), belongings, property, purchase; object. **2** gain, acquirement, procurement, purchase, inheritance.

acquisitive /əkwízzitiv/ *adj.* keen to acquire things; avaricious; materialistic. □□ **acquisitively** *adv.* **acquisitiveness** *n.* [F *acquisitive* or LL *acquisitivus* (as ACQUIRE)]
■ see *avaricious* (AVARICE). □□ **acquisitiveness** see AVARICE.

acquit /əkwít/ *v.* (**acquitted, acquitting**) **1** *tr.* (often foll. by *of*) declare (a person) not guilty (*were acquitted of the offence*). **2** *refl.* **a** conduct oneself or perform in a specified way (*we acquitted ourselves well*). **b** (foll. by *of*) discharge (a duty or responsibility). [ME f. OF *aquiter* f. med.L *acquitare* pay a debt (as AC-, QUIT)]
■ **1** see FORGIVE 1. **2** see CONDUCT *v.* 5.

acquittal /əkwítt'l/ *n.* **1** the process of freeing or being freed from a charge, esp. by a judgement of not guilty. **2** performance of a duty.

acquittance /əkwítt'nss/ *n.* **1** payment of or release from a debt. **2** a written receipt attesting settlement of a debt. [ME f. OF *aquitance* (as ACQUIT)]

acre /áykər/ *n.* **1** a measure of land, 4,840 sq. yds., 0.405 ha. **2** a piece of land; a field. **3** (in *pl.*) a large area. □□ **acred** *adj.* (also in *comb.*). [OE *æcer* f. Gmc]

acreage /áykərij/ *n.* **1** a number of acres. **2** an extent of land.
■ **2** see AREA 1.

acrid /ákrid/ *adj.* (**acrider, acridest**) **1** bitterly pungent; irritating; corrosive. **2** bitter in temper or manner. □□ **acridity** /əkrídditi/ *n.* **acridly** *adv.* [irreg. f. L *acer acris* keen + -ID[1], prob. after *acid*]
■ **1** see BITTER *adj.* 1, TART[3] 1. **2** see TART[3] 2.

acridine /ákrideen/ *n.* a colourless crystalline compound used in the manufacture of dyes and drugs. [ACRID + -INE[4]]

acriflavine /ákrifláyvin, -veen/ *n.* a reddish powder used as an antiseptic. [irreg. f. ACRIDINE + FLAVINE]

acrimonious /ákrimṓniəss/ *adj.* bitter in manner or temper. □□ **acrimoniously** *adv.* [F *acrimonieux, -euse* f. med.L *acrimoniosus* f. L *acrimonia* ACRIMONY]
■ see TART[3] 2.

acrimony /ákriməni/ *n.* (*pl.* **-ies**) bitterness of temper or manner; ill feeling. [F *acrimonie* or L *acrimonia* pungency (as ACRID)]
■ see ANIMOSITY.

acrobat /ákrəbat/ *n.* **1** a performer of spectacular gymnastic feats. **2** a person noted for constant change of mind, allegiance, etc. □□ **acrobatic** /ákrəbáttik/ *adj.* **acrobatically** /ákrəbáttikəli/ *adv.* [F *acrobate* f. Gk *akrobatēs* f. *akron* summit + *bainō* walk]

acrobatics /ákrəbáttiks/ *n.pl.* **1** acrobatic feats. **2** (as *sing.*) the art of performing these. **3** a skill requiring ingenuity (*mental acrobatics*).

acrogen /ákrəjən/ *n. Bot.* any non-flowering plant having a perennial stem with the growing point at its apex, e.g. a fern or moss. □□ **acrogenous** /əkrójinəss/ *adj.* [Gk *akron* tip + -GEN]

acromegaly /ákrəméggəli/ *n. Med.* the abnormal growth of the hands, feet, and face, caused by excessive activity of the pituitary gland. □□ **acromegalic** /-migállik/ *adj.* [F *acromégalie* f. Gk *akron* extremity + *megas megal-* great]

acronym /ákrənim/ *n.* a word, usu. pronounced as such, formed from the initial letters of other words (e.g. *Ernie*, *laser*, *Nato*). [Gk *akron* end + *-onum-* = *onoma* name]

acropetal /əkróppit'l/ *adj. Bot.* developing from below upwards. □□ **acropetally** *adv.* [Gk *akron* tip + L *petere* seek]

acrophobia /ákrəfṓbiə/ *n. Psychol.* an abnormal dread of heights. □□ **acrophobic** *adj.* [Gk *akron* peak + -PHOBIA]

acropolis /əkróppəliss/ *n.* **1** a citadel or upper fortified part of an ancient Greek city. **2** (**Acropolis**) the ancient citadel at Athens. [Gk *akropolis* f. *akron* summit + *polis* city]

across /əkróss/ *prep.* & *adv.* ● *prep.* **1** to or on the other side of (*walked across the road*; *lives across the river*). **2** from one side to another side of (*the cover stretched across the opening*; *a bridge across the river*). **3** at or forming an angle (esp. a right angle) with (*deep cuts across his legs*). ● *adv.* **1** to or on the other side (*ran across*; *shall soon be across*). **2** from one side to another (*a blanket stretched across*). **3** forming a cross (*with cuts across*). **4** (of a crossword clue or answer) read horizontally (*cannot do nine across*). □ **across the board** general; generally; applying to all. [ME f. OF *a croix, en croix*, later regarded as f. A[2] + CROSS]
■ *prep.* **1, 2** see OVER *prep.* 3, 4. ● *adv.* **1, 2** see OVER *adv.* 4.

acrostic /əkróstik/ *n.* **1** a poem or other composition in which certain letters in each line form a word or words. **2** a word-puzzle constructed in this way. □ **double acrostic** one using the first and last letters of each line. **single acrostic** one using the first letter only. **triple acrostic** one using the first, middle, and last letters. [F *acrostiche* or Gk *akrostikhis* f. *akron* end + *stikhos* row, line of verse, assim. to -IC]

acrylic /əkríllik/ *adj.* & *n.* ● *adj.* **1** of material made with a synthetic polymer derived from acrylic acid. **2** *Chem.* of or derived from acrylic acid. ● *n.* an acrylic fibre. □ **acrylic acid** a pungent liquid organic acid. ¶ Chem. formula: $C_3H_4O_2$. **acrylic resin** any of various transparent colourless polymers of acrylic acid. [*acrolein* f. L *acer acris* pungent + *olēre* to smell + -IN + -YL + -IC]

ACT *abbr.* Australian Capital Territory.

act /akt/ *n.* & *v.* ● *n.* **1** something done; a deed; an action. **2** the process of doing something (*caught in the act*). **3 a** a piece of entertainment, usu. one of a series in a programme. **b** the performer(s) of this. **4** a pretence; behaviour intended to deceive or impress (*it was all an act*). **5** a main division of a play or opera. **6 a** a written ordinance of a parliament or other legislative body. **b** a document attesting a legal transaction. **7** (often in *pl.*) the recorded decisions or proceedings of a committee, an academic body, etc. **8** (**Acts**) (in full **Acts of the Apostles**) the New Testament book relating the growth of the early Church. ● *v.* **1** *intr.* behave (*see how they act under stress*). **2** *intr.* perform actions or functions; operate effectively; take action (*act as referee*; *the* *brakes failed to act; we must act quickly*). **3** *intr.* (also foll. by *on*) exert energy or influence (*the medicine soon began to act; alcohol acts on the brain*). **4** *intr.* **a** perform a part in a play, film, etc. **b** pretend. **5** *tr.* **a** perform the part of (*acted Othello; acts the fool*). **b** perform (a play etc.). **c** portray (an incident) by actions. **d** feign (*we acted indifference*). □ **act for** be the (esp. legal) representative of. **act of God** the operation of uncontrollable natural forces. **act of grace** a privilege or concession that cannot be claimed as a right. **act on** (or **upon**) perform or carry out; put into operation (*acted on my advice*). **act out 1** translate (ideas etc.) into action. **2** *Psychol.* represent (one's subconscious desires etc.) in action. **3** perform (a drama). **act up** *colloq.* misbehave; give trouble (*my car is acting up again*). **get one's act together** *sl.* become properly organized; make preparations for an undertaking etc. **get into** (or **in on**) **the act** *sl.* become a participant (esp. for profit). **put on an act** *colloq.* carry out a pretence. □□ **actable** *adj.* (in sense 5 of *v.*). **actability** /áktəbílliti/ *n.* (in sense 5 of *v.*). [ME ult. f. L *agere act-* do]

■ *n.* **1** deed, action, undertaking, operation, step, move; feat, exploit; accomplishment, achievement. **2** see PERFORMANCE 1. **3 a** performance, show, skit, stand, routine, turn, sketch, *sl.* shtick. **b** see CAST *n.* 6. **4** performance, pretence, posture, pose, stance, feigning, front, fake, dissimulation, show, sham, trick, deception, hoax, affectation. **6** bill, law, decree, edict, statute, order, ordinance, command, mandate, resolution, measure, enactment. ● *v.* **1** behave (oneself), carry on, deport oneself, conduct oneself, bear oneself, carry oneself, *literary* comport oneself. **3** take effect, work, operate, function, be effective *or* efficacious, perform. **4 a** perform, appear. **b** feign, pretend, counterfeit, fake, dissemble, make believe, sham, simulate, dissimulate, posture, pose. **5 a** portray, play, be, represent, impersonate, personify, take *or* play the part *or* role of, personate. **b** put on, do, play, act out. **d** pretend, feign, profess, make a show *or* pretence of, give the impression of, affect, put on an act *or* air of, simulate. □ **act for** see REPRESENT 10. **act on** see DEAL[1] *v.* 1. **act out** see ACT *v.* 5b above. **act up** see MISBEHAVE. **get one's act together** pull oneself together, rally oneself, *Brit. colloq.* pull one's socks up; hurry up, *colloq.* get moving, get a move on. **put on an act** see ACT *v.* 4b above. □□ **actable** performable, playable, portrayable.

ACTH *abbr. Med.* adrenocorticotrophic hormone.

acting /ákting/ *n.* & *attrib. adj.* ● *n.* **1** the art or occupation of performing parts in plays, films, etc. **2** in senses of ACT *v.* ● *attrib.adj.* serving temporarily or on behalf of another or others (*acting manager; Acting Captain*).

■ *attrib. adj.* see TEMPORARY *adj.*

actinia /aktínniə/ *n.* (*pl.* **actiniae** /-ni-ee/) any sea anemone, esp. of the genus *Actinia*. [mod.L f. Gk *aktis -inos* ray]

actinide /áktinīd/ *n.* (also **actinoid** /áktinoyd/) *Chem.* any of the series of 15 radioactive elements having increasing atomic numbers from actinium to lawrencium. □ **actinide series** this series of elements. [ACTINIUM + -IDE as in *lanthanide*]

actinism /áktiniz'm/ *n.* the property of short-wave radiation that produces chemical changes, as in photography. □□ **actinic** /aktínnik/ *adj.* [Gk *aktis -inos* ray]

actinium /aktínniəm/ *n. Chem.* a radioactive metallic element of the actinide series, occurring naturally in pitchblende. ¶ Symb.: **Ac**.

actinoid var. of ACTINIDE.

actinometer /áktinómmitər/ *n.* an instrument for measuring the intensity of radiation, esp. ultraviolet radiation. [Gk *aktis -tinos* ray + -METER]

actinomorphic /áktinəmórfik/ *adj. Biol.* radially symmetrical. [as ACTINOMETER + Gk *morphē* form]

actinomycete /áktinōmīseet/ *n.* any of the usu. non-motile filamentous anaerobic bacteria of the order Actinomycetales. [as ACTINOMORPHIC + *-mycetes* f. Gk *mukēs -ētos* mushroom]

action /áksh'n/ *n.* & *v.* ● *n.* **1** the fact or process of doing or acting (*demanded action; put ideas into action*). **2** forcefulness or energy as a characteristic (*a woman of action*). **3** the exertion of energy or influence (*the action of acid on metal*). **4** something done; a deed or act (*not aware of his own actions*). **5 a** a series of events represented in a story, play, etc. **b** *sl.* exciting activity (*arrived late and missed the action; want some action*). **6 a** armed conflict; fighting (*killed in action*). **b** an occurrence of this, esp. a minor military engagement. **7 a** the way in which a machine, instrument, etc. works (*explain the action of an air pump*). **b** the mechanism that makes a machine, instrument, etc. (e.g. a musical instrument, a gun, etc.) work. **c** the mode or style of movement of an animal or human (usu. described in some way) (*a runner with good action*). **8** a legal process; a lawsuit (*bring an action*). **9** (in *imper.*) a word of command to begin, esp. used by a film director etc. ● *v.tr.* bring a legal action against. □ **action committee** (or **group** etc.) a body formed to take active steps, esp. in politics. **action-packed** full of action or excitement. **action painting** an aspect of abstract expressionism with paint applied by the artist's random or spontaneous gestures. **action point** a proposal for action, esp. arising from a discussion etc. **action replay** a playback of part of a television broadcast, esp. a sporting event, often in slow motion. **action stations** positions taken up by troops etc. ready for battle. **go into action** start work. **out of action** not working. **take action** begin to act (esp. energetically in protest). [ME f. OF f. L *actio -onis* (as ACT)]

■ *n.* **1** activity, performance, movement, motion; operation, execution, enactment, practice. **2** forcefulness, energy, liveliness, vim, vigour, spirit, vitality, go, animation, *colloq.* get-up-and-go, *US sl.* feistiness; enterprise, initiative. **3** influence, effect, power, force, strength; effectiveness, activity, performance, reaction. **4** deed, act, undertaking, operation, feat, exertion; (*actions*) behaviour, conduct, deportment, demeanour, ways, manner(s). **5 b** excitement, interest, adventure, thrills (and spills). **6 a** fighting, combat, conflict; battle, war. **b** fight, battle, engagement, encounter, clash, fray, sortie, skirmish, affray. **7 a, b** see MOVEMENT 2, MECHANISM 1. **8** lawsuit, suit, litigation, proceeding, process, case; remedy. ● *v.* proceed against, institute proceedings against. □ **out of action** see DEFUNCT 1, 2.

actionable /ákshənəb'l/ *adj.* giving cause for legal action. □□ **actionably** *adv.*

■ see ILLEGAL 2.

activate /áktivayt/ *v.tr.* **1** make active; bring into action. **2** *Chem.* cause reaction in; excite (a substance, molecules, etc.). **3** *Physics* make radioactive. □ **activated carbon** carbon, esp. charcoal, treated to increase its adsorptive power. **activated sludge** aerated sewage containing aerobic bacteria. □□ **activation** /-váysh'n/ *n.* **activator** *n.*

■ **1** move, actuate, set in motion, get started, energize, get *or* set going, start, initiate, switch *or* turn on, trigger, bring into play, motivate, rouse, arouse, prompt, stimulate, stir, mobilize, animate, impel, galvanize. □□ **activation** operation, movement, actuation, ignition. **activator** initiator, starter.

active /áktiv/ *adj.* & *n.* ● *adj.* **1 a** consisting in or marked by action; energetic; diligent (*leads an active life; an active helper*). **b** able to move about or accomplish practical tasks (*infirmity made him less active*). **2** working, operative (*an active volcano*). **3** originating action; not merely passive or inert (*active support; active ingredients*). **4** radioactive. **5** *Gram.* designating the voice that attributes the action of a verb to the person or thing from which it logically proceeds (e.g. of the verbs in *guns kill; we saw him*). ● *n. Gram.* the active form or voice of a verb. □ **active birth** childbirth during which the mother is encouraged to remain as active as possible. **active carbon** = *activated carbon* (see ACTIVATE). **active citizen** a person who takes an active role in the community through crime prevention etc. **active list** *Mil.* a list of officers available for service. **active**

service service in the armed forces during a war. ▫▫ **actively** *adv.* **activeness** *n.* [ME f. OF *actif -ive* or L *activus* (as ACT *v.*)]

■ *adj.* **1 a** strenuous, vigorous, full, dynamic, physical, hectic; diligent, tireless, industrious, hard-working, untiring; energetic, lively, hyperactive, animated, busy, brisk, bustling, occupied, on the move, *colloq.* on the go. **b** agile, spry, nimble, quick, sprightly. **2, 3** effective, efficacious, effectual, working, functioning, operative, potent, influential; powerful.

activism /áktiviz'm/ *n.* a policy of vigorous action in a cause, esp. in politics. ▫▫ **activist** *n.*

activity /aktívviti/ *n.* (*pl.* **-ies**) **1 a** the condition of being active or moving about. **b** the exertion of energy; vigorous action. **2** (often in *pl.*) a particular occupation or pursuit (*outdoor activities*). **3** = RADIOACTIVITY. [F *activité* or LL *activitas* (as ACTIVE)]

■ **1** action, movement, motion, operation, function, work(ing); liveliness, busyness, (hustle and) bustle; exertion, vigour, vim, energy, effort. **2** pursuit, occupation, vocation, work, employment, function, operation, job, labour, endeavour, enterprise, project, undertaking, venture, interest.

actor /áktər/ *n.* **1** the performer of a part in a play, film, etc. **2** a person whose profession is performing such parts. [L, = doer, actor (as ACT, -OR[1])]

■ **1** see PLAYER 3.

actress /áktriss/ *n.* a female actor.

■ see PLAYER 3.

actual /ákchooəl, áktyooəl/ *adj.* (usu. *attrib.*) **1** existing in fact; real (often as distinct from ideal). **2** existing now; current. ¶ Redundant use, as in *tell me the actual facts*, is *disp.*, but common. ▫▫ **actualize** *v.tr.* (also **-ise**). **actualization** /-līzáysh'n/ *n.* [ME f. OF *actuel* f. LL *actualis* f. *agere* ACT]

■ **1** real, genuine, factual, true (to life), authentic, verifiable, manifest, realized, realistic, tangible, physical, hard, solid. **2** existing, existent, present, current, extant. ▫▫ **actualize** see REALIZE 4. **actualization** see *realization* 2 (REALIZE).

actuality /ákchoo-álliti, áktyoo-/ *n.* (*pl.* **-ies**) **1** reality; what is the case. **2** (in *pl.*) existing conditions. [ME f. OF *actualité* entity or med.L *actualitas* (as ACTUAL)]

■ **1** see CASE[1] 2, 9, REALITY 1.

actually /ákchooəli, áktyoo-/ *adv.* **1** as a fact, really (*I asked for ten, but actually got nine*). **2** as a matter of fact, even (strange as it may seem) (*he actually refused!*). **3** at present; for the time being.

■ **1** really, in reality, in fact, in actuality, in point of fact, as a matter of fact, truly, literally, *literary* in truth. **2** even, as a matter of fact, strange as it may seem, *colloq.* believe it or not. **3** at (the) present (time), for the time being, currently, (just) now.

actuary /ákchooəri, áktyoo-/ *n.* (*pl.* **-ies**) an expert in statistics, esp. one who calculates insurance risks and premiums. ▫▫ **actuarial** /-choo-áiriəl, -tyoo-áiriəl/ *adj.* **actuarially** /-choo-áiriəli, -tyoo-áiriəli/ *adv.* [L *actuarius* bookkeeper f. *actus* past part. of *agere* ACT]

actuate /ákchoo-ayt, áktyoo-/ *v.tr.* **1** communicate motion to (a machine etc.). **2** cause the operation of (an electrical device etc.). **3** cause (a person) to act. ▫▫ **actuation** /-áysh'n/ *n.* **actuator** *n.* [med.L *actuare* f. L *actus*: see ACTUAL]

■ see ACTIVATE.

acuity /əkyóō-iti/ *n.* sharpness, acuteness (of a needle, senses, understanding). [F *acuité* or med.L *acuitas* f. *acuere* sharpen: see ACUTE]

aculeate /əkyóōliət/ *adj.* **1** *Zool.* having a sting. **2** *Bot.* prickly. **3** pointed, incisive. [L *aculeatus* f. *aculeus* sting, dimin. of *acus* needle]

acumen /ákyoomən, əkyóōmən/ *n.* keen insight or discernment, penetration. [L *acumen -minis* anything sharp f. *acuere* sharpen: see ACUTE]

■ see DISCRIMINATION 2, 3, *profundity* (PROFOUND).

acuminate /əkyóōminət/ *adj. Biol.* tapering to a point. [L *acuminatus* pointed (as ACUMEN)]

acupressure /ákyoopreshər/ *n.* a form of therapy in which symptoms are relieved by applying pressure with the thumbs or fingers to specific points on the body. [alt. of ACUPUNCTURE]

acupuncture /ákyoopungkchər/ *n.* a method (orig. Chinese) of treating various conditions by pricking the skin or tissues with needles. ▫▫ **acupuncturist** *n.* [L *acu* with a needle + PUNCTURE]

acushla /əkóōshlə/ *n. Ir.* darling. [Ir. *a cuisle* O pulse (of my heart)!]

acutance /əkyóōt'nss/ *n.* sharpness of a photographic or printed image; a measure of this. [ACUTE + -ANCE]

acute /əkyóōt/ *adj.* & *n.* ● *adj.* (**acuter, acutest**) **1 a** (of senses etc.) keen, penetrating. **b** (of pain) intense, severe; sharp or stabbing rather than dull, aching, or throbbing. **2** shrewd, perceptive (*an acute critic*). **3** (of a disease) coming sharply to a crisis; severe, not chronic. **4** (of a difficulty or controversy) critical, serious. **5 a** (of an angle) less than 90°. **b** sharp, pointed. **6** (of a sound) high, shrill. ● *n.* = *acute accent.* ▫ **acute accent** a mark (´) placed over letters in some languages to show quality, vowel length, pronunciation (e.g. *maté*), etc. **acute rheumatism** *Med.* = *rheumatic fever.* ▫▫ **acutely** *adv.* **acuteness** *n.* [L *acutus* past part. of *acuere* sharpen f. *acus* needle]

■ *adj.* **1 a** keen, sharp, penetrating, sensitive, discriminating, exquisite, fine, fine-honed. **b** sharp, cutting, intense, keen, severe, violent, excruciating, exquisite, fierce, shooting, stabbing, piercing, sudden. **2** keen, sharp-witted, shrewd, clever, ingenious, astute, quick, sharp, canny, bright, incisive, discerning, perceptive, perspicacious, intelligent, penetrating, insightful, percipient, wise, sensitive, subtle, discriminating; alert, aware, on the qui vive, *colloq.* on the ball. **3** severe, intense, critical, dangerous, grave, serious, life-threatening. **4** see SERIOUS 2, 3, 7. **5 b** sharp, pointed, narrow. ▫▫ **acutely** see *severely* (SEVERE), VERY *adv.* **acuteness** see GRAVITY 3a, *penetration* (PENETRATE).

ACW *abbr. Brit.* (preceding a name) Aircraftwoman.

-acy /əsi/ *suffix* forming nouns of state or quality (*accuracy*; *piracy*; *supremacy*), or an instance of it (*conspiracy*; *fallacy*) (see also -CRACY). [a branch of the suffix -CY from or after F *-acie* or L *-acia* or *-atia* or Gk *-ateia*]

acyl /ássil, -īl/ *n. Chem.* the univalent radical of an organic acid. [G (as ACID, -YL)]

AD *abbr.* (of a date) of the Christian era. ¶ Strictly, AD should precede a date (e.g. AD 410), but uses such as *the tenth century* AD are well established. [*Anno Domini*, 'in the year of the Lord']

ad /ad/ *n. colloq.* an advertisement. [abbr.]

■ see ADVERTISEMENT 1.

ad- /əd, ad/ *prefix* (also **a-** before *sc*, *sp*, *st*, **ac-** before *c*, *k*, *q*, **af-** before *f*, **ag-** before *g*, **al-** before *l*, **an-** before *n*, **ap-** before *p*, **ar-** before *r*, **as-** before *s*, **at-** before *t*) **1** with the sense of motion or direction to, reduction or change into, addition, adherence, increase, or intensification. **2** formed by assimilation of other prefixes (*accurse*; *admiral*; *advance*; *affray*). [(sense 1) (through OF *a-*) f. L *ad* to: (sense 2) *a-* repr. various prefixes other than *ad-*]

-ad[1] /əd, ad/ *suffix* forming nouns: **1** in collective numerals (*myriad*; *triad*). **2** in fem. patronymics (*Dryad*). **3** in names of poems and similar compositions (*Iliad*; *Dunciad*; *jeremiad*). [Gk *-as -ada*]

-ad[2] /əd/ *suffix* forming nouns (*ballad*; *salad*) (cf. -ADE[1]). [F *-ade*]

adage /áddij/ *n.* a traditional maxim, a proverb. [F f. L *adagium* (as AD-, root of *aio* say)]

■ see MAXIM.

adagio /ədaázhiō/ *adv., adj.,* & *n. Mus.* ● *adv.* & *adj.* in slow time. ● *n.* (*pl.* **-os**) an adagio movement or passage. [It.]

Adam[1] /áddəm/ *n.* the first man, in the Biblical and Koranic traditions. □ **Adam's ale** water. **Adam's apple** a projection of the thyroid cartilage of the larynx, esp. as prominent in men. **not know a person from Adam** be unable to recognize the person in question. [Heb. *'ādām* man]

Adam[2] /áddəm/ *adj.* of the style of architecture, furniture, and design created by the Scottish brothers Robert and James Adam (18th c.).

adamant /áddəmənt/ *adj.* & *n.* ● *adj.* stubbornly resolute; resistant to persuasion. ● *n. archaic* diamond or other hard substance. □□ **adamance** *n.* **adamantine** /-mántīn/ *adj.* **adamantly** *adv.* [OF *adamaunt* f. L *adamas adamant-* untameable f. Gk (as A-[1], *damaō* to tame)]

■ *adj.* see RESOLUTE.

adapt /ədápt/ *v.* **1** *tr.* **a** (foll. by *to*) fit, adjust (one thing to another). **b** (foll. by *to, for*) make suitable for a purpose. **c** alter or modify (esp. a text). **d** arrange for broadcasting etc. **2** *intr.* & *refl.* (usu. foll. by *to*) become adjusted to new conditions. □□ **adaptive** *adj.* **adaptively** *adv.* [F *adapter* f. L *adaptare* (as AD-, *aptare* f. *aptus* fit)]

■ **1 a** (*adapt to*) fit to *or* with, adjust to, align to, coordinate with, attune to. **b** gear, suit, fit (out), adjust, make suitable, tailor, design, fashion, equip, outfit, get *or* make ready, prepare, revamp, regulate; qualify. **c, d** edit, rewrite, modify, alter, change, revise, correct, amend, emend, reword, restyle, convert, remodel, reshape, rework, remould, shape, fashion, polish, touch up, retouch, arrange. **2** (*adapt oneself to*) adjust (oneself) to, accommodate *or* accustom *or* acclimatize *or* habituate *or* inure *or* orient *or* orientate oneself to, get used to, *US* acclimate oneself to; comply with, conform to *or* with, follow, observe, respect.

adaptable /ədáptəb'l/ *adj.* **1** able to adapt oneself to new conditions. **2** that can be adapted. □□ **adaptability** /-bílliti/ *n.* **adaptably** *adv.*

■ **1** flexible, versatile, cooperative, amenable; acculturative, obliging, accommodating, compliant, tractable. **2** modifiable, alterable, changeable, adjustable; pliable, pliant, tractable, malleable, ductile. □□ **adaptability** see *flexibility* (FLEXIBLE).

adaptation /áddaptáysh'n/ *n.* **1** the act or process of adapting or being adapted. **2** a thing that has been adapted. **3** *Biol.* the process by which an organism or species becomes suited to its environment. [F f. LL *adaptatio -onis* (as ADAPT)]

■ **1** modification, change, adjustment, accommodation, customization, conversion. **2** modification, adjustment, conversion, alteration; see also VERSION 2, 3.

adaptor /ədáptər/ *n.* (also **adapter**) **1** a device for making equipment compatible. **2** a device for connecting several electrical plugs to one socket. **3** a person who adapts.

adaxial /adáksiəl/ *adj. Bot.* facing toward the stem of a plant, esp. of the upper side of a leaf (cf. ABAXIAL). [AD- + AXIAL]

ADC *abbr.* **1** aide-de-camp. **2** analogue-digital converter.

add /ad/ *v.tr.* **1** join (one thing to another) as an increase or supplement (*add your efforts to mine; add insult to injury*). **2** put together (two or more numbers) to find a number denoting their combined value. **3** say in addition (*added a remark; added that I was wrong; 'What's more, I don't like it,' he added*). □ **add in** include. **add-on** something added to an existing object or quantity. **add to** increase; be a further item among (*this adds to our difficulties*). **add up 1** find the total of. **2** (foll. by *to*) amount to; constitute (*adds up to a disaster*). **3** *colloq.* make sense; be understandable. □□ **added** *adj.* [ME f. L *addere* (as AD-, *dare* put)]

■ **1** join, unite, aggregate, combine, annex, attach, affix, append, tack on, *archaic* adjoin. **2** add up, total, sum (up), combine, count up, reckon (up), tot (up). **3** continue, go on. □ **add to** increase, enlarge, amplify, augment, supplement, complement; extend, expand, lengthen. **add up 1** see ADD 2 above. **2** amount to, constitute, be equivalent to, signify, mean. **3** make sense, hang together, cohere, be coherent *or* understandable, tie in. □□ **added** see EXTRA *adj.*

addax /áddaks/ *n.* a large antelope, *Addax nasomaculatus*, of North Africa, with twisted horns. [L f. an African word]

addendum /ədéndəm/ *n.* (*pl.* **addenda** /-də/) **1** a thing (usu. something omitted) to be added, esp. (in *pl.*) as additional matter at the end of a book. **2** an appendix; an addition. [L, gerundive of *addere* ADD]

■ see ADDITION 2.

adder /áddər/ *n.* any of various small venomous snakes, esp. the common viper, *Vipera berus*, the only poisonous snake in Great Britain. □ **adder's tongue** any fern of the genus *Ophioglossum*. [OE *nædre*: *n* lost in ME by wrong division of *a naddre*: cf. APRON, AUGER, UMPIRE]

addict *v.* & *n.* ● *v.tr.* & *refl.* /ədíkt/ (usu. foll. by *to*) devote or apply habitually or compulsively; make addicted. ● *n.* /áddikt/ **1** a person addicted to a habit, esp. one dependent on a (specified) drug (*drug addict; heroin addict*). **2** *colloq.* an enthusiastic devotee of a sport or pastime (*film addict*). [L *addicere* assign (as AD-, *dicere dict-* say)]

■ *v.* (*be(come) addicted*) be(come) dependent, *sl.* be(come) hooked, have a monkey on one's back. ● *n.* **1** (habitual) user, drug addict, drug abuser, *colloq.* druggy, freak, tripper, pill-popper, *sl.* junkie, doper, head, hype, pot-head, acid-head, mainliner, *US sl.* hophead. **2** devotee, aficionado, fan, admirer, follower, adherent, supporter, enthusiast, hound, energumen, *colloq.* buff, maniac, *sl.* nut, freak, fiend, groupie.

addicted /ədíktid/ *adj.* (foll. by *to*) **1** dependent on as a habit; unable to do without (*addicted to heroin; addicted to smoking*). **2** devoted (*addicted to football*).

■ (*addicted to*) **1** dependent on, *sl.* hooked on. **2** see KEEN[1] 2.

addiction /ədíksh'n/ *n.* the fact or process of being addicted, esp. the condition of taking a drug habitually and being unable to give it up without incurring adverse effects. [L *addictio*: see ADDICT]

■ see HABIT *n.* 2, 5.

addictive /ədíktiv/ *adj.* (of a drug, habit, etc.) causing addiction or dependence.

■ habit-forming, compulsive, obsessive, (*of a drug*) hard.

Addison's disease /áddis'nz/ *n.* a disease characterized by progressive anaemia and debility and brown discoloration of the skin. [T. *Addison*, Engl. physician d. 1860, who first recognized it]

addition /ədísh'n/ *n.* **1** the act or process of adding or being added. **2** a person or thing added (*a useful addition to the team*). □ **in addition** moreover, furthermore, as well. **in addition to** as well as, as something added to. [ME f. OF *addition* or f. L *additio* (as ADD)]

■ **1** increase, augmentation, union, combination, attachment, annexation, extension; reckoning, calculation, computation. **2** addendum, appendix, appendage, supplement, increment; extra, add-on; annexe, extension, wing. □ **in addition** moreover, furthermore, additionally, to boot, in *or* into the bargain, too, also, as well, *archaic* withal. **in addition to** as well as, besides, beyond, over and above, on top of.

additional /ədíshən'l/ *adj.* added, extra, supplementary. □□ **additionally** *adv.*

■ see EXTRA *adj.*

additive /ádditiv/ *n.* & *adj.* ● *n.* a thing added, esp. a substance added to another so as to give it specific qualities (*food additive*). ● *adj.* **1** characterized by addition (*additive process*). **2** to be added. [LL *additivus* (as ADD)]

addle /ádd'l/ *v.* & *adj.* ● *v.* **1** *tr.* muddle, confuse. **2** *intr.* (of an egg) become addled. ● *adj.* **1** muddled, unsound (*addle-brained; addle-head*). **2** empty, vain. **3** (of an egg) addled. [OE *adela* filth, used as adj., then as verb]

addled /ádd'ld/ *adj.* **1** (of an egg) rotten, producing no chick. **2** muddled. [ADDLE *adj.*, assim. to past part. form]

address /ədréss/ *n.* & *v.* ● *n.* **1 a** the place where a person lives or an organization is situated. **b** particulars of this, esp. for postal purposes. **c** *Computing* the location of an item of stored information. **2** a discourse delivered to an audience. **3** skill, dexterity, readiness. **4** (in *pl.*) a courteous

approach, courtship (*pay one's addresses to*). **5** *archaic* manner in conversation. ● *v.tr.* **1** write directions for delivery (esp. the name and address of the intended recipient) on (an envelope, packet, etc.). **2** direct in speech or writing (remarks, a protest, etc.). **3** speak or write to, esp. formally (*addressed the audience; asked me how to address a duke*). **4** direct one's attention to. **5** *Golf* take aim at or prepare to hit (the ball). □ **address oneself to 1** speak or write to. **2** attend to. □□ **addresser** *n.* [ME f. OF *adresser* ult. f. L (as AD-, *directus* DIRECT): (n.) perh. f. F *adresse*]
■ *n.* **1 a** location, whereabouts, position, site, situation. **2** speech, talk, oration, lecture, paper, declaration; sermon, *literary* discourse. ● *v.* **2** direct, send, post, mail; aim, focus, level, point, train, turn. **3** speak *or* talk *or* write to, deliver *or* give a speech to, present a paper to, lecture; greet, hail, accost, approach, salute, introduce oneself to, address oneself to. **4** focus on, aim at, turn to, concentrate on, converge on, zero in on; come *or* get to grips with. □ **address oneself to 1** see ADDRESS *v.* 3 above. **2** devote *or* direct *or* apply oneself to, take care of, occupy oneself with, concentrate on, concern oneself with; see also ADDRESS *v.* 4 above, ATTEND 4.

addressee /ádreseé/ *n.* the person to whom something (esp. a letter) is addressed.

Addressograph /ədréssəgraaf/ *n. propr.* a machine for printing addresses on envelopes.

adduce /ədyóoss/ *v.tr.* cite as an instance or as proof or evidence. □□ **adducible** *adj.* [L *adducere adduct-* (as AD-, *ducere* lead)]

adduct /ədúkt/ *v.tr.* draw towards a middle line, esp. draw (a limb) towards the middle line of the body. □□ **adduction** *n.*

adductor /ədúktər/ *n.* (in full **adductor muscle**) any muscle that moves one part of the body towards another or towards the middle line of the body.

-ade[1] /ayd/ *suffix* forming nouns: **1** an action done (*blockade; tirade*). **2** the body concerned in an action or process (*cavalcade*). **3** the product or result of a material or action (*arcade; lemonade; masquerade*). [from or after F *-ade* f. Prov., Sp., or Port. *-ada* or It. *-ata* f. L *-ata* fem. sing. past part. of verbs in *-are*]

-ade[2] /ayd/ *suffix* forming nouns (*decade*) (cf. -AD[1]). [F *-ade* f. Gk *-as -ada*]

-ade[3] /ayd/ *suffix* forming nouns: **1** = -ADE[1] (*brocade*). **2** a person concerned (*renegade*). [Sp. or Port. *-ado*, masc. form of *-ada*: see -ADE[1]]

adenine /áddəneen/ *n.* a purine derivative found in all living tissue as a component base of DNA or RNA. [G *Adenin* formed as ADENOIDS: see -INE[4]]

adenoids /áddinoydz/ *n.pl. Med.* a mass of enlarged lymphatic tissue between the back of the nose and the throat, often hindering speaking and breathing in the young. □□ **adenoidal** /-nóyd'l/ *adj.* **adenoidally** /-nóydəli/ *adv.* [Gk *adēn -enos* gland + -OID]

adenoma /áddinṓmə/ *n.* (*pl.* **adenomas** or **adenomata** /-mətə/) a glandlike benign tumour. [mod.L f. Gk *adēn* gland + -OMA]

adenosine /ədénnəseen/ *n.* a nucleoside of adenine and ribose present in all living tissue in a combined form (see ADP, AMP, ATP). [ADENINE + RIBOSE]

adept /áddept, ədépt/ *adj.* & *n.* ● *adj.* (foll. by *at, in*) thoroughly proficient. ● *n.* a skilled performer; an expert. □□ **adeptly** *adv.* **adeptness** *n.* [L *adeptus* past part. of *adipisci* attain]
■ *adj.* versed, proficient, skilled, well-skilled, expert, accomplished, talented, skilful, adroit, dexterous, able, masterful, masterly, polished. ● *n.* expert, master, specialist, authority, proficient, old hand, *esp. Brit. colloq.* dab hand, whiz, *US colloq.* maven. □□ **adeptly** see WELL[1] *adv.* 3. **adeptness** see *proficiency* (PROFICIENT).

adequate /áddikwət/ *adj.* **1** sufficient, satisfactory. **2** (foll. by *to*) proportionate. **3** barely sufficient. □□ **adequacy** *n.* **adequately** *adv.* [L *adaequatus* past part. of *adaequare* make equal (as AD-, *aequus* equal)]
■ sufficient, enough; satisfactory, fitting, fitted, equal, suitable, proper, qualified, competent, good enough, up to par, *colloq.* up to snuff; passable, fair, fair to middling, middling, average, tolerable, (barely) acceptable, (barely) satisfactory, all right, not (at all) bad, so so, *comme ci comme ça*, *colloq.* OK, not that *or* too bad, no great shakes. □□ **adequacy** see *fitness* (FIT[1]). **adequately** see FAIRLY 2.

à deux /aa dṓ/ *adv.* & *adj.* **1** for two. **2** between two. [F]

ad fin. /ad fín/ *abbr.* at or near the end. [L *ad finem*]

adhere /ədheér/ *v.intr.* **1** (usu. foll. by *to*) (of a substance) stick fast to a surface, another substance, etc. **2** (foll. by *to*) behave according to; follow in detail (*adhered to our plan*). **3** (foll. by *to*) give support or allegiance. [F *adhérer* or L *adhaerēre* (as AD-, *haerēre haes-* stick)]
■ **1** see STICK[2] 4. **2** (*adhere to*) see FOLLOW 5.

adherent /ədheérənt/ *n.* & *adj.* ● *n.* **1** a supporter of a party, person, etc. **2** a devotee of an activity. ● *adj.* **1** (foll. by *to*) faithfully observing a rule etc. **2** (often foll. by *to*) (of a substance) sticking fast. □□ **adherence** *n.* [F *adhérent* (as ADHERE)]
■ *n.* **1** see SUPPORTER. **2** see FOLLOWER. □□ **adherence** see DEDICATION 1.

adhesion /ədheézh'n/ *n.* **1** the act or process of adhering. **2** the capacity of a substance to stick fast. **3** *Med.* an unnatural union of surfaces due to inflammation. **4** the maintenance of contact between the wheels of a vehicle and the road. **5** the giving of support or allegiance. ¶ More common in physical senses (e.g. *the glue has good adhesion*), with *adherence* used in abstract senses (e.g. *adherence to principles*). [F *adhésion* or L *adhaesio* (as ADHERE)]
■ **2** see *tenacity* (TENACIOUS). **4** see TRACTION 3. **5** see DEVOTION 1.

adhesive /ədheéssiv/ *adj.* & *n.* ● *adj.* sticky, enabling surfaces or substances to adhere to one another. ● *n.* an adhesive substance, esp. one used to stick other substances together. □□ **adhesively** *adv.* **adhesiveness** *n.* [F *adhésif -ive* (as ADHERE)]
■ *adj.* see STICKY *adj.* 1. ● *n.* see GLUE *n.*

adhibit /ədhíbbit/ *v.tr.* (**adhibited, adhibiting**) **1** affix. **2** apply or administer (a remedy). □□ **adhibition** /ádhibísh'n/ *n.* [L *adhibēre adhibit-* (as AD-, *habēre* have)]

ad hoc /ád hók/ *adv.* & *adj.* for a particular (usu. exclusive) purpose (*an ad hoc appointment*). [L, = to this]

ad hominem /ad hómminem/ *adv.* & *adj.* **1** relating to or associated with a particular person. **2** (of an argument) appealing to the emotions and not to reason. [L, = to the person]

adiabatic /áydīəbáttik/ *adj.* & *n. Physics* ● *adj.* **1** impassable to heat. **2** occurring without heat entering or leaving the system. ● *n.* a curve or formula for adiabatic phenomena. □□ **adiabatically** *adv.* [Gk *adiabatos* impassable (as A-[1], *diabainō* pass)]

adiantum /áddiántəm/ *n.* **1** any fern of the genus *Adiantum*, e.g. maidenhair. **2** (in general use) a spleenwort. [L f. Gk *adianton* maidenhair (as A-[1], *diantos* wettable)]

adieu /ədyóō/ *int.* & *n.* ● *int.* goodbye. ● *n.* (*pl.* **adieus** or **adieux** /ədyóōz/) a goodbye. [ME f. OF f. *à* to + *Dieu* God]

ad infinitum /ad infinītəm/ *adv.* without limit; for ever. [L]

ad interim /ad íntərim/ *adv.* & *adj.* for the meantime. [L]

adios /áddióss/ *int.* goodbye. [Sp. *adiós* f. *a* to + *Dios* God]

adipocere /áddipəseer/ *n.* a greyish fatty or soapy substance generated in dead bodies subjected to moisture. [F *adipocire* f. L *adeps adipis* fat + F *cire* wax f. L *cera*]

adipose /áddipōz/ *adj.* of or characterized by fat; fatty. □ **adipose tissue** fatty connective tissue in animals. □□ **adiposity** /-póssiti/ *n.* [mod.L *adiposus* f. *adeps adipis* fat]

adit /áddit/ *n.* **1** a horizontal entrance or passage in a mine. **2** a means of approach. [L *aditus* (as AD-, *itus* f. *ire it-* go)]

Adivasi /áddivaàssi/ *n.* (*pl.* **Adivasis**) a member of the aboriginal tribal peoples of India. [Hindi *adinivāsī* original inhabitant]

Adj. *abbr.* (preceding a name) Adjutant.

adjacent /əjáys'nt/ *adj.* (often foll. by *to*) lying near or adjoining. □□ **adjacency** *n.* [ME f. L *adjacēre* (as AD-, *jacēre* lie)]
■ see *adjoining* (ADJOIN 1).

adjective /ájiktiv/ *n.* & *adj.* ● *n.* a word or phrase naming an attribute, added to or grammatically related to a noun to modify it or describe it. ● *adj.* additional; not standing by itself; dependent. □□ **adjectival** /ájiktī́v'l/ *adj.* **adjectivally** /ájiktī́vəli/ *adv.* [ME f. OF *adjectif -ive* ult. f. L *adjicere adject-* (as AD-, *jacere* throw)]

adjoin /əjóyn/ *v.tr.* **1** (often as **adjoining** *adj.*) be next to and joined with. **2** *archaic* = ADD 1. [ME f. OF *ajoindre, ajoign-* f. L *adjungere adjunct-* (as AD-, *jungere* join)]
■ **1** see BORDER *v.* 3a; (**adjoining**) neighbouring, contiguous, adjacent, abutting, bordering, next.

adjourn /əjúrn/ *v.* **1** *tr.* **a** put off; postpone. **b** break off (a meeting, discussion, etc.) with the intention of resuming later. **2** *intr.* of persons at a meeting: **a** break off proceedings and disperse. **b** (foll. by *to*) transfer the meeting to another place. [ME f. OF *ajorner* (as AD-, *jorn* day ult. f. L *diurnus* DIURNAL): cf. JOURNAL, JOURNEY]
■ **1 a** see POSTPONE. **b** see DISSOLVE *v.* 3a.

adjournment /əjúrnmənt/ *n.* adjourning or being adjourned. □ **adjournment debate** a debate in the House of Commons on the motion that the House be adjourned, used as an opportunity for raising various matters.

adjudge /əjúj/ *v.tr.* **1** adjudicate (a matter). **2** (often foll. by *that* + clause, or *to* + infin.) pronounce judicially. **3** (foll. by *to*) award judicially. **4** *archaic* condemn. □□ **adjudgement** *n.* (also **adjudgment**). [ME f. OF *ajuger* f. L *adjudicare*: see ADJUDICATE]

adjudicate /əjōōdikayt/ *v.* **1** *intr.* act as judge in a competition, court, tribunal, etc. **2** *tr.* **a** decide judicially regarding (a claim etc.). **b** (foll. by *to be* + compl.) pronounce (*was adjudicated to be bankrupt*). □□ **adjudication** /-káysh'n/ *n.* **adjudicative** *adj.* **adjudicator** *n.* [L *adjudicare* (as AD-, *judicare* f. *judex -icis* judge)]
■ **1** see JUDGE *v.* 5b. **2 a** see JUDGE *v.* 1a, 3.

adjunct /ájungkt/ *n.* **1** (foll. by *to, of*) a subordinate or incidental thing. **2** an assistant; a subordinate person, esp. one with temporary appointment only. **3** *Gram.* a word or phrase used to explain or amplify the predicate, subject, etc. □□ **adjunctive** /əjúngktiv/ *adj.* **adjunctively** /əjúngktivli/ *adv.* [L *adjunctus*: see ADJOIN]
■ **1** see ACCESSORY *n.* 1, EXTENSION 4. **2** see ASSISTANT 2.

adjure /əjoor/ *v.tr.* (usu. foll. by *to* + infin.) charge or request (a person) solemnly or earnestly, esp. under oath. □□ **adjuration** /ájooráysh'n/ *n.* **adjuratory** /-rətəri/ *adj.* [ME f. L *adjurare* (as AD-, *jurare* swear) in LL sense 'put a person to an oath']

adjust /əjúst/ *v.* **1** *tr.* **a** arrange; put in the correct order or position. **b** regulate, esp. by a small amount. **2** *tr.* (usu. foll. by *to*) make suitable. **3** *tr.* harmonize (discrepancies). **4** *tr.* assess (loss or damages). **5** *intr.* (usu. foll. by *to*) make oneself suited to; become familiar with (*adjust to one's surroundings*). □□ **adjustable** *adj.* **adjustability** /əjústəbílliti/ *n.* **adjuster** *n.* **adjustment** *n.* [F *adjuster* f. OF *ajoster* ult. f. L *juxta* near]
■ **1** put in (working) order, put *or* set to rights, (fine-)tune, fix, arrange, rearrange, reset, set, reposition, change, alter, modify, regulate, calibrate; repair. **2** see ADAPT 1b. **3** set right, arrange, settle, harmonize, reconcile, resolve, set *or* put to rights; redress, rectify, correct, patch up. **4** see EVALUATE 1. **5** (*adjust to*) adapt to, accommodate oneself to, accustom oneself to, familiarize oneself with, inure oneself to; get used to, acclimatize to, reconcile oneself to, *US* acclimate to. □□ **adjustable** see ADAPTABLE 2. **adjustability** see *flexibility* (FLEXIBLE). **adjustment** alteration, setting, regulation, correction, calibration, tuning; arrangement, coordination, alignment, harmonization.

adjutant /ájoot'nt/ *n.* **1 a** *Mil.* an officer who assists superior officers by communicating orders, conducting correspondence, etc. **b** an assistant. **2** (in full **adjutant bird**) a giant Indian stork. □ **Adjutant-General** a high-ranking Army administrative officer. □□ **adjutancy** *n.* [L *adjutare* frequent. of *adjuvare*: see ADJUVANT]

adjuvant /ájoov'nt/ *adj.* & *n.* ● *adj.* helpful, auxiliary. ● *n.* an adjuvant person or thing. [F *adjuvant* or L *adjuvare* (as AD-, *juvare jut-* help)]

Adlerian /adleériən/ *adj.* of or relating to A. Adler, Austrian psychologist d. 1937, or his system of psychology.

ad lib /ád líb/ *v.*, *adj.*, *adv.*, & *n.* ● *v.intr.* (**ad libbed**, **ad libbing**) speak or perform without formal preparation; improvise. ● *adj.* improvised. ● *adv.* as one pleases, to any desired extent. ● *n.* something spoken or played extempore. [abbr. of AD LIBITUM]
■ *v.* see IMPROVISE 1. ● *adj.* see EXTEMPORANEOUS.

ad libitum /ad líbbitəm/ *adv.* = AD LIB *adv.* [L, = according to pleasure]

ad litem /ad lī́tem/ *adj.* (of a guardian etc.) appointed for a lawsuit. [L]

Adm. *abbr.* (preceding a name) Admiral.

adman /ádman/ *n.* (*pl.* **admen**) *colloq.* a person who produces advertisements commercially.

admass /ádmass/ *n.* esp. *Brit.* the section of the community that is regarded as readily influenced by advertising and mass communication.

admeasure /ədmé<u>zh</u>ər/ *v.tr.* apportion; assign in due shares. □□ **admeasurement** *n.* [ME f. OF *amesurer* f. med.L *admensurare* (as AD-, MEASURE)]

admin /ádmin/ *n. colloq.* administration. [abbr.]

adminicle /ədmínnik'l/ *n.* **1** a thing that helps. **2** (in Scottish law) collateral evidence of the contents of a missing document. □□ **adminicular** /ádminíkyoolər/ *adj.* [L *adminiculum* prop]

administer /ədmínnistər/ *v.* **1** *tr.* attend to the running of (business affairs etc.); manage. **2** *tr.* **a** be responsible for the implementation of (the law, justice, punishment, etc.). **b** *Eccl.* give out, or perform the rites of (a sacrament). **c** (usu. foll. by *to*) direct the taking of (an oath). **3** *tr.* **a** provide, apply (a remedy). **b** give, deliver (a rebuke). **4** *intr.* act as administrator. □□ **administrable** *adj.* [ME f. OF *aministrer* f. L *administrare* (as AD-, MINISTER)]
■ **1** administrate, manage, control, run, direct, conduct, superintend, supervise, oversee, preside over, head, look after. **2 a** execute, carry out, discharge, deal out, dispense; apply, implement. **3 a** dispense, apply, supply, furnish, give (out), provide (with), distribute, deliver, deal, hand out, *literary* mete out. **b** see DELIVER 7. □□ **administrable** manageable, controllable; executable, dischargeable, dispensable.

administrate /ədmínnistrayt/ *v.tr.* & *intr.* administer (esp. business affairs); act as an administrator. [L *administrare* (as ADMINISTER)]
■ see ADMINISTER 1.

administration /ədmínnistráysh'n/ *n.* **1** management of a business. **2** the management of public affairs; government. **3** the government in power; the ministry. **4** *US* a President's period of office. **5** *Law* the management of another person's estate. **6** (foll. by *of*) **a** the administering of justice, an oath, etc. **b** application of remedies. [ME f. OF *administration* or L *administratio* (as ADMINISTRATE)]
■ **1** management, direction, conduct, supervision, oversight, superintendence, regulation, charge, *colloq.* admin. **2, 3** authority, management, ministry, government, leadership, *derog.* regime. **4** presidency, term, office, rule. **6** dispensation, provision, delivery, distribution, application.

administrative /ədmínnistrətiv/ *adj.* concerning or relating to the management of affairs. □□ **administratively** *adv.* [F *administratif -ive* or L *administrativus* (as ADMINISTRATION)]

administrator /ədmínnistraytər/ *n.* **1** a person who administers a business or public affairs. **2** a person capable of organizing (*is no administrator*). **3** *Law* a person appointed to manage the estate of a person who has died intestate. **4** a person who performs official duties in some sphere, e.g. in religion or justice. ▫▫ **administratorship** *n.* **administratrix** *n.* [L (as ADMINISTER)]

admirable /ádmərəb'l/ *adj.* **1** deserving admiration. **2** excellent. ▫▫ **admirably** *adv.* [F f. L *admirabilis* (as ADMIRE)]

■ **1** see PRAISEWORTHY. **2** wonderful, awe-inspiring, excellent, estimable, splendid, superb, marvellous, superior, first-rate, first-class, of the first water, fine, *colloq.* top-drawer, ripsnorting, A1, smashing, magic; see also GREAT *adj.* 5. ▫▫ **admirably** marvellously, wonderfully, superbly, excellently, splendidly, very *or* really well.

admiral /ádmərəl/ *n.* **1 a** the commander-in-chief of a country's navy. **b** a naval officer of high rank, the commander of a fleet or squadron. **c** (**Admiral**) an admiral of the second grade. **2** any of various butterflies (*red admiral*; *white admiral*). ▫ **Admiral of the Fleet** an admiral of the first grade. **Fleet Admiral** *US* = *Admiral of the Fleet*. ▫▫ **admiralship** *n.* [ME f. OF *a(d)mira(i)l* etc. f. med.L *a(d)miralis* etc., f. Arab. *'amīr* commander (cf. AMIR), assoc. with ADMIRABLE]

Admiralty /ádmərəlti/ *n.* (*pl.* **-ies**) **1** (*hist.* except in titles) (in the UK) the department administering the Royal Navy. **2** (**admiralty**) *Law* trial and decision of maritime questions and offences. ▫ **Admiralty Board** *hist.* a committee of the Ministry of Defence superintending the Royal Navy. [ME f. OF *admiral(i)té* (as ADMIRAL)]

admiration /ádmiráysh'n/ *n.* **1** pleased contemplation. **2** respect, warm approval. **3** an object of this (*was the admiration of the whole town*). [F *admiration* or L *admiratio* (as ADMIRE)]

■ **1** wonder, awe, delight, pleasure. **2** esteem, (high) regard, appreciation, respect, approval, high opinion, approbation. **3** focus *or* centre of attention, delight, sensation, cynosure.

admire /ədmír/ *v.tr.* **1** regard with approval, respect, or satisfaction. **2** express one's admiration of. [F *admirer* or L *admirari* (as AD-, *mirari* wonder at)]

■ **1** respect, approve of, esteem, regard *or* rate highly, look up to, revere, idolize, venerate, worship. **2** wonder at, delight in, *literary* marvel (at).

admirer /ədmírər/ *n.* **1** a woman's suitor. **2** a person who admires, esp. a devotee of an able or famous person.

■ **1** beau, suitor, wooer; lover, sweetheart, boyfriend, darling, *poet.* swain. **2** devotee, aficionado, fan, supporter, enthusiast, adorer, adherent, follower, idolator, *sl.* groupie, wannabe.

admiring /ədmíring/ *adj.* showing or feeling admiration (*an admiring follower*; *admiring glances*). ▫▫ **admiringly** *adv.*

admissible /ədmíssib'l/ *adj.* **1** (of an idea or plan) worth accepting or considering. **2** *Law* allowable as evidence. **3** (foll. by *to*) capable of being admitted. ▫▫ **admissibility** /-billiti/ *n.* [F *admissible* or med.L *admissibilis* (as ADMIT)]

■ see PERMISSIBLE.

admission /ədmísh'n/ *n.* **1** an acknowledgement (*admission of error*; *admission that he was wrong*). **2 a** the process or right of entering or being admitted. **b** a charge for this (*admission is £5*). **3** a person admitted to a hospital. ¶ Has more general application in senses of ADMIT than *admittance*. [ME f. L *admissio* (as ADMIT)]

■ **1** acknowledgement, confession, concession, avowal, allowance, profession, declaration, disclosure, affirmation, divulgence, divulgement, revelation. **2 a** access, admittance, entrée, entry, entrance; reception, acceptance, appointment, institution, induction, installation, investiture. **b** ticket, (entry *or* entrance) fee, tariff, charge.

admit /ədmít/ *v.* (**admitted, admitting**) **1** *tr.* **a** (often foll. by *to be*, or *that* + clause) acknowledge; recognize as true. **b** accept as valid or true. **2** *intr.* **a** (foll. by *to*) acknowledge responsibility for (a deed, fault, etc.). **b** (foll. by *of*) allow for something to exist, have influence, etc. **3** *tr.* **a** allow (a person) entrance or access. **b** allow (a person) to be a member of (a class, group, etc.) or to share in (a privilege etc.). **c** (of a hospital etc.) bring in (a person) for residential treatment. **4** *tr.* (of an enclosed space) have room for; accommodate. **5** *intr.* (foll. by *of*) allow as possible. ▫▫ **admittable** *adj.* [ME f. L *admittere admiss-* (as AD-, *mittere* send)]

■ **1** acknowledge, accept, concede, allow, grant, recognize, take cognizance of, *formal* aver. **2 a** (*admit to*) confess, own (up to); concede, divulge, reveal, acknowledge, declare. **b** (*admit of*) allow, permit, grant, tolerate, *literary* brook. **3** let in, allow to enter, give access to, take *or* allow in; accept, receive. **4** accommodate, hold, receive, embrace.

admittance /ədmítt'nss/ *n.* **1** the right or process of admitting or being admitted, usu. to a place (*no admittance except on business*). **2** *Electr.* the reciprocal of impedance. ¶ A more formal and technical word than *admission*.

■ **1** leave *or* permission to enter, entry, admission, entrance, access, entrée.

admittedly /ədmíttidli/ *adv.* as an acknowledged fact (*admittedly there are problems*).

admix /admíks/ *v.* **1** *tr.* & *intr.* (foll. by *with*) mingle. **2** *tr.* add as an ingredient.

admixture /admíks-chər/ *n.* **1** a thing added, esp. a minor ingredient. **2** the act of adding this. [L *admixtus* past part. of *admiscēre* (as AD-, *miscēre* mix)]

admonish /ədmónnish/ *v.tr.* **1** reprove. **2** (foll. by *to* + infin., or *that* + clause) urge. **3** give advice to. **4** (foll. by *of*) warn. ▫▫ **admonishment** *n.* **admonition** /ádmənísh'n/ *n.* **admonitory** *adj.* [ME f. OF *amonester* ult. f. L *admonēre* (as AD-, *monēre monit-* warn)]

■ **1** see REPRIMAND *v.* **2** see URGE *v.* 2. **3** see ADVISE 1, 2. **4** see WARN.

ad nauseam /ad náwziam, -siam/ *adv.* to an excessive or disgusting degree. [L, = to sickness]

adnominal /adnómmin'l/ *adj.* *Gram.* attached to a noun. [L *adnomen -minis* (added name)]

ado /ədóō/ *n.* fuss, busy activity; trouble, difficulty. ▫ **without more ado** immediately. [orig. in *much ado* = much to do, f. north. ME *at do* (= to do) f. ON *at* AT as sign of infin. + DO[1]]

-ado /aadō/ *suffix* forming nouns (*desperado*) (cf. -ADE[3]). [Sp. or Port. *-ado* f. L *-atus* past part. of verbs in *-are*]

adobe /ədóbi, ədób/ *n.* **1** an unburnt sun-dried brick. **2** the clay used for making such bricks. [Sp. f. Arab.]

adolescent /áddəléss'nt/ *adj.* & *n.* ● *adj.* between childhood and adulthood. ● *n.* an adolescent person. ▫▫ **adolescence** *n.* [ME f. OF f. L *adolescere* grow up]

■ *adj.* teenage(d), young, youthful, maturing, pubescent; immature, callow, puerile, juvenile, jejune. ● *n.* teenager, juvenile, minor, stripling, youngster, teen, *colloq.* teeny-bopper, kid; see also YOUTH 4. ▫▫ **adolescence** puberty, teenage years, the awkward age.

Adonis /ədóniss/ *n.* a handsome young man. ▫ **Adonis blue** a kind of butterfly, *Lysandra bellargus*. [the name of a youth loved by Venus: L f. Gk f. Phoen. *adōn* lord]

adopt /ədópt/ *v.tr.* **1** take (a person) into a relationship, esp. another's child as one's own. **2** choose to follow (a course of action etc.). **3** take over (an idea etc.) from another person. **4** choose as a candidate for office. **5** *Brit.* (of a local authority) accept responsibility for the maintenance of (a road etc.). **6** accept; formally approve (a report, accounts, etc.). ▫▫ **adoption** *n.* [F *adopter* or L *adoptare* (as AD-, *optare* choose)]

■ **1** take (in), accept, take *or* accept as one's own. **2, 4** choose, select, take on, assume, embrace. **3** take (up *or* on *or* over), espouse; arrogate, appropriate. **6** see ACCEPT 2.

adoptive /ədóptiv/ *adj.* due to adoption (*adoptive son; adoptive father*). □□ **adoptively** *adv.* [ME f. OF *adoptif -ive* f. L *adoptivus* (as ADOPT)]

adorable /ədórəb'l/ *adj.* **1** deserving adoration. **2** *colloq.* delightful, charming. □□ **adorably** *adv.* [F f. L *adorabilis* (as ADORE)]
■ **1** lovable, wonderful, estimable, honourable, praiseworthy; beloved, loved, cherished, prized. **2** delightful, appealing, attractive, charming, lovely, enchanting, gorgeous, captivating, fetching; darling, sweet, dear, *US* cunning, *Brit. colloq.* dinky, *esp. US colloq.* cute. □□ **adorably** delightfully, charmingly, enchantingly, gorgeously, attractively.

adore /ədór/ *v.tr.* **1** regard with honour and deep affection. **2 a** worship as divine. **b** *RC Ch.* offer reverence to (the Host etc.). **3** *colloq.* like very much. □□ **adoration** /áddəráysh'n/ *n.* **adoring** *adj.* **adoringly** *adv.* [ME f. OF *aourer* f. L *adorare* worship (as AD-, *orare* speak, pray)]
■ **1** esteem, honour, respect, admire; love, idolize, dote on. **2 a** worship, venerate, reverence, revere, exalt; hallow. **3** cherish, fancy, revere, adulate; carry the *or* a torch for; be mad on *or* about, be addicted to, be crazy about; *colloq.* love, be in love with, be hooked on, have a crush on. □□ **adoration** see LOVE *n.* 1, REVERENCE *n.*

adorer /ədórər/ *n.* **1** a worshipper. **2** an ardent admirer.

adorn /ədórn/ *v.tr.* **1** add beauty or lustre to; be an ornament to. **2** furnish with ornaments; decorate. □□ **adornment** *n.* [ME f. OF *ao(u)rner* f. L *adornare* (as AD-, *ornare* furnish, deck)]
■ see EMBELLISH 1.

ADP *abbr.* **1** adenosine diphosphate. **2** automatic data processing.

ad personam /ád pərsṓnam/ *adv.* & *adj.* ● *adv.* to the person. ● *adj.* personal. [L]

ad rem /ad rém/ *adv.* & *adj.* to the point; to the purpose. [L, = to the matter]

adrenal /ədreén'l/ *adj.* & *n.* ● *adj.* **1** at or near the kidneys. **2** of the adrenal glands. ● *n.* (in full **adrenal gland**) either of two ductless glands above the kidneys, secreting adrenalin. [AD- + RENAL]

adrenalin /ədrénnəlin/ *n.* (also **adrenaline**) **1** a hormone secreted by the adrenal glands, affecting circulation and muscular action, and causing excitement and stimulation. **2** the same substance obtained from animals or by synthesis, used as a stimulant.

adrenocorticotrophic hormone /ədreénəkórtikətróffik/ *n.* (also **adrenocorticotropic** /-tróppik/) a hormone secreted by the pituitary gland and stimulating the adrenal glands. ¶ Abbr.: **ACTH**. [ADRENAL + CORTEX + -TROPHIC, -TROPIC]

adrenocorticotrophin /ədreénəkórtikətróffin/ *n.* = ADRENOCORTICOTROPHIC HORMONE. [ADRENOCORTICOTROPHIC (HORMONE) + -IN]

adrift /ədríft/ *adv.* & *predic.adj.* **1** drifting. **2** at the mercy of circumstances. **3** *colloq.* **a** unfastened. **b** out of touch. **c** absent without leave. **d** (often foll. by *of*) failing to reach a target. **e** out of order. **f** ill-informed. [A² + DRIFT]

adroit /ədróyt/ *adj.* dexterous, skilful. □□ **adroitly** *adv.* **adroitness** *n.* [F f. *à droit* according to right]
■ see SKILFUL.

adsorb /ədsórb/ *v.tr.* (usu. of a solid) hold (molecules of a gas or liquid or solute) to its surface, causing a thin film to form. □□ **adsorbable** *adj.* **adsorbent** *adj.* & *n.* **adsorption** *n.* (also **adsorbtion**). [AD-, after ABSORB]

adsorbate /ədsórbayt/ *n.* a substance adsorbed.

adsuki var. of ADZUKI.

adulate /ádyoolayt/ *v.tr.* flatter obsequiously. □□ **adulation** /-láysh'n/ *n.* **adulator** *n.* **adulatory** *adj.* [L *adulari adulat-* fawn on]
■ see IDOLIZE.

adult /áddult, ədúlt/ *adj.* & *n.* ● *adj.* **1** mature, grown-up. **2 a** of or for adults (*adult education*). **b** *euphem.* sexually explicit; indecent (*adult films*). ● *n.* **1** an adult person. **2** *Law* a person who has reached the age of majority. □□ **adulthood** *n.* **adultly** *adv.* [L *adultus* past part. of *adolescere* grow up: cf. ADOLESCENT]
■ *adj.* **1** mature, grown(-up), full-grown, matured, of age, having reached the age of discretion. **2 b** see INDECENT. ● *n.* **1** grown-up. □□ **adulthood** see *maturity* (MATURE). **adultly** maturely, sensibly.

adulterant /ədúltərənt/ *adj.* & *n.* ● *adj.* used in adulterating. ● *n.* an adulterant substance.

adulterate *v.* & *adj.* ● *v.tr.* /ədúltərayt/ debase (esp. foods) by adding other or inferior substances. ● *adj.* /ədúltərət/ spurious, debased, counterfeit. □□ **adulteration** /-ráysh'n/ *n.* **adulterator** *n.* [L *adulterare adulterat-* corrupt]
■ *v.* falsify, corrupt, alloy, debase, spoil, water (down), weaken, dilute, bastardize, contaminate, pollute, taint, doctor, *US* cut. ● *adj.* see SPURIOUS. □□ **adulteration** see *pollution* (POLLUTE).

adulterer /ədúltərər/ *n.* (*fem.* **adulteress** /-tərISS/) a person who commits adultery. [obs. *adulter* (v.) f. OF *avoutrer* f. L *adulterare*: see ADULTERATE]

adulterine /ədúltərīn/ *adj.* **1** illegal, unlicensed. **2** spurious. **3** born of adultery. [L *adulterinus* f. *adulter*: see ADULTERY]

adulterous /ədúltərəss/ *adj.* of or involved in adultery. □□ **adulterously** *adv.* [ME f. *adulter*: see ADULTERER]

adultery /ədúltəri/ *n.* voluntary sexual intercourse between a married person and a person (married or not) other than his or her spouse. [ME f. OF *avoutrie* etc. f. *avoutre* adulterer f. L *adulter*, assim. to L *adulterium*]

adumbrate /áddumbrayt/ *v.tr.* **1** indicate faintly. **2** represent in outline. **3** foreshadow, typify. **4** overshadow. □□ **adumbration** /-bráysh'n/ *n.* **adumbrative** /ədúmbrətiv/ *adj.* [L *adumbrare* (as AD-, *umbrare* f. *umbra* shade)]

ad valorem /ád vəlórem/ *adv.* & *adj.* (of taxes) in proportion to the estimated value of the goods concerned. [L, = according to the value]

advance /ədvaánss/ *v.*, *n.*, & *adj.* ● *v.* **1** *tr.* & *intr.* move or put forward. **2** *intr.* make progress. **3** *tr.* **a** pay (money) before it is due. **b** lend (money). **4** *tr.* give active support to; promote (a person, cause, or plan). **5** *tr.* put forward (a claim or suggestion). **6** *tr.* cause (an event) to occur at an earlier date (*advanced the meeting three hours*). **7** *tr.* raise (a price). **8** *intr.* rise (in price). **9** *tr.* (as **advanced** *adj.*) **a** far on in progress (*the work is well advanced*). **b** ahead of the times (*advanced ideas*). ● *n.* **1** an act of going forward. **2** progress. **3** a payment made before the due time. **4** a loan. **5** (esp. in *pl.*; often foll. by *to*) an amorous or friendly approach. **6** a rise in price. ● *attrib.adj.* done or supplied beforehand (*advance warning; advance copy*). □ **advanced** (or **advanced supplementary**) **level** (in the UK) a GCE examination of a standard higher than ordinary level and GCSE. **advance guard** a body of soldiers preceding the main body of an army. **advance on** approach threateningly. **in advance** ahead in place or time. □□ **advancer** *n.* [ME f. OF *avancer* f. LL *abante* in front f. L *ab* away + *ante* before: (n.) partly through F *avance*]
■ *v.* **1, 2** move, move *or* put *or* push *or* go forward(s), move *or* send on(ward), go *or* push *or* press on, proceed, get ahead, make progress, gain ground, forge ahead, continue, keep going; move up, promote, be promoted, rise. **3** prepay; lend, loan. **4** support, further, promote, forward, help, aid, abet, assist; benefit, improve; contribute to. **5** see *put forward* (PUT¹). **6** bring forward. **7** see RAISE *v.* 3. **8** see RISE *v.* 7. **9** (**advanced**) **a** well-ahead, far on; nearing completion, nearly finished. **b** see PROGRESSIVE *adj.* 3. ● *n.* **1, 2** progress, progression, forward movement, development; headway; improvement, betterment, furtherance; breakthrough, step forward. **3, 4** prepayment, deposit; loan. **5** see APPROACH *n.* 4. **6** rise, increase, appreciation, gain, addition, *esp. US* hike. □ **advance guard** avant-garde; see also SPEARHEAD *n.* **in advance** beforehand, ahead (of time), before, previously, early, earlier; in front, ahead, beyond.

advancement /ədvaánsmənt/ *n.* the promotion of a person, cause, or plan. [ME f. F *avancement* f. *avancer* (as ADVANCE)]
■ see *promotion* (PROMOTE).

advantage /ədvaántij/ *n.* & *v.* ● *n.* **1** a beneficial feature; a favourable circumstance. **2** benefit, profit (*is not to your advantage*). **3** (often foll. by *over*) a better position; superiority in a particular respect. **4** (in lawn tennis) the next point won after deuce. ● *v.tr.* **1** be beneficial or favourable to. **2** further, promote. □ **have the advantage of** be in a better position in some respect than. **take advantage of 1** make good use of (a favourable circumstance). **2** exploit or outwit (a person), esp. unfairly. **3** *euphem.* seduce. **to advantage** in a way which exhibits the merits (*was seen to advantage*). **turn to advantage** benefit from. □□ **advantageous** /ádvəntáyjəss/ *adj.* **advantageously** /ádvəntáyjəsli/ *adv.* [ME f. OF *avantage*, *avantager* f. *avant* in front f. LL *abante*: see ADVANCE]

■ *n.* **1, 3** strength, benefit, feature, attraction, selling-point, asset, plus, bonus, added extra, convenience, improvement, boon, appeal, pull, beauty; superiority, upper hand, dominance, edge, head start, odds on one's side, trump (card); sway; *archaic* vantage. **2** gain, profit, benefit, interest, betterment, advancement; use, usefulness, utility, help, service. ● *v.* **1, 2** see BENEFIT *v.* 1. □ **take advantage of 1** see PROFIT *v.* 2. **2** see EXPLOIT *v.* **3** see SEDUCE 1. **to advantage** in a good light, (more) favourably, advantageously. **turn to advantage** see PROFIT *v.* 2. □□ **advantageous** profitable, worthwhile, gainful, opportune, beneficial, helpful, favourable, propitious, useful, valuable. **advantageously** see *favourably* (FAVOURABLE).

advection /ədvéksh'n/ *n. Meteorol.* transfer of heat by the horizontal flow of air. □□ **advective** *adj.* [L *advectio* f. *advehere* (as AD-, *vehere vect-* carry)]

Advent /ádvent/ *n.* **1** the season before Christmas, including the four preceding Sundays. **2** the coming or second coming of Christ. **3** (**advent**) the arrival of esp. an important person or thing. □ **Advent calendar** *Brit.* a calendar for Advent, usu. of card with flaps to open each day revealing a picture or scene. **Advent Sunday** the first Sunday in Advent. [OE f. OF *advent*, *auvent* f. L *adventus* arrival f. *advenire* (as AD-, *venire vent-* come)]

■ **3** see ARRIVAL 1.

Adventist /ádventist/ *n.* a member of a Christian sect that believes in the imminent second coming of Christ. □□ **Adventism** *n.*

adventitious /ádventíshəss/ *adj.* **1** accidental, casual. **2** added from outside. **3** *Biol.* formed accidentally or under unusual conditions. **4** *Law* (of property) coming from a stranger or by collateral succession rather than directly. □□ **adventitiously** *adv.* [L *adventicius* (as ADVENT)]

adventure /ədvénchər/ *n.* & *v.* ● *n.* **1** an unusual and exciting experience. **2** a daring enterprise; a hazardous activity. **3** enterprise (*the spirit of adventure*). **4** a commercial speculation. ● *v.intr.* **1** (often foll. by *into*, *upon*) dare to go or come. **2** (foll. by *on*, *upon*) dare to undertake. **3** incur risk; engage in adventure. □ **adventure playground** a playground where children are provided with functional materials for climbing on, building with, etc. □□ **adventuresome** *adj.* [ME f. OF *aventure*, *aventurer* f. L *adventurus* about to happen (as ADVENT)]

■ *n.* **1** experience, incident, event, occurrence, happening, episode. **2** exploit, escapade, affair, undertaking, feat, deed, enterprise; danger, peril, risk. **3** enterprise. **4** speculation, hazard, chance, risk, venture, enterprise. ● *v.* **1** (*adventure into* or *upon*) venture into *or* upon, brave. **2, 3** try one's luck (on *or* at), take a risk (on), gamble (on), wager (on), bet (on), *Brit. colloq.* punt (on); dare. □□ **adventuresome** see ADVENTUROUS 1.

adventurer /ədvénchərər/ *n.* (*fem.* **adventuress** /-chəriss/) **1** a person who seeks adventure, esp. for personal gain or enjoyment. **2** a financial speculator. [F *aventurier* (as ADVENTURE)]

■ **1** adventuress, soldier of fortune, swashbuckler, hero, heroine, daredevil. **2** speculator, punter, opportunist; adventuress, *colloq.* fortune-hunter, *sl.* gold-digger.

adventurism /ədvénchəriz'm/ *n.* a tendency to take risks, esp. in foreign policy. □□ **adventurist** *n.*

adventurous /ədvénchərəss/ *adj.* **1** rash, venturesome; enterprising. **2** characterized by adventures. □□ **adventurously** *adv.* **adventurousness** *n.* [ME f. OF *aventuros* (as ADVENTURE)]

■ **1** daring, bold, venturesome, adventuresome, audacious, fearless, intrepid, enterprising, undaunted, dauntless, unafraid, brave, courageous, valiant, heroic; rash, reckless, devil-may-care, foolhardy, hazardous, risky, daredevil, *literary* temerarious. **2** see EVENTFUL. □□ **adventurously** daringly, boldly, intrepidly, enterprisingly, fearlessly, undauntedly, dauntlessly, bravely, valiantly. **adventurousness** see DARING *n.*

adverb /ádverb/ *n.* a word or phrase that modifies or qualifies another word (esp. an adjective, verb, or other adverb) or a word-group, expressing a relation of place, time, circumstance, manner, cause, degree, etc. (e.g. *gently*, *quite*, *then*, *there*). □□ **adverbial** /ədvérbiəl/ *adj.* [F *adverbe* or L *adverbium* (as AD-, VERB)]

adversarial /ádvərsáiriəl/ *adj.* **1** involving conflict or opposition. **2** opposed, hostile. [ADVERSARY + -IAL]

■ **2** see ADVERSARY *adj.*

adversary /ádvərsəri/ *n.* & *adj.* ● *n.* (*pl.* **-ies**) **1** an enemy. **2** an opponent in a sport or game; an antagonist. ● *adj.* opposed, antagonistic. [ME f. OF *adversarie* f. L *adversarius* f. *adversus*: see ADVERSE]

■ *n.* **1** enemy, opponent, antagonist; opposition, other side, *esp. poet. or formal* foe. **2** opponent, antagonist, competitor, rival, challenger, contender; opposition, other side, competition. ● *adj.* opposed, hostile, antagonistic, competitive, adversarial.

adversative /ədvérsətiv/ *adj.* (of words etc.) expressing opposition or antithesis. □□ **adversatively** *adv.* [F *adversatif -ive* or LL *adversativus* f. *adversari* oppose f. *adversus*: see ADVERSE]

adverse /ádverss/ *adj.* (often foll. by *to*) **1** contrary, hostile. **2** hurtful, injurious. □□ **adversely** *adv.* **adverseness** *n.* [ME f. OF *advers* f. L *adversus* past part. of *advertere* (as AD-, *vertere vers-* turn)]

■ **1** see HOSTILE 2. **2** see INJURIOUS 1.

adversity /ədvérsiti/ *n.* (*pl.* **-ies**) **1** the condition of adverse fortune. **2** a misfortune. [ME f. OF *adversité* f. L *adversitas -tatis* (as ADVERSE)]

■ **1** see MISFORTUNE 1. **2** see MISFORTUNE 2.

advert[1] /ádvert/ *n. Brit. colloq.* an advertisement. [abbr.]

■ see ADVERTISEMENT 1.

advert[2] /ədvért/ *v.intr.* (foll. by *to*) *literary* refer in speaking or writing. [ME f. OF *avertir* f. L *advertere*: see ADVERSE]

■ see REFER 7, 8.

advertise /ádvərtīz/ *v.* **1** *tr.* draw attention to or describe favourably (goods or services) in a public medium to promote sales. **2** *tr.* make generally or publicly known. **3** *intr.* (foll. by *for*) seek by public notice, esp. in a newspaper. **4** *tr.* (usu. foll. by *of*, or *that* + clause) notify. □□ **advertiser** *n.* [ME f. OF *avertir* (stem *advertiss-*): see ADVERT[2]]

■ **1, 2** see PUBLICIZE. **4** see NOTIFY 2.

advertisement /ədvértismənt, -tizmənt/ *n.* **1** a public notice or announcement, esp. one advertising goods or services in newspapers, on posters, or in broadcasts. **2** the act or process of advertising. **3** *archaic* a notice to readers in a book etc. [earlier *avert-* f. F *avertissement* (as ADVERTISE)]

■ **1** notice, handbill, blurb, broadside, bill, circular, junk mail, mailshot, jingle, brochure, poster, placard, classified advertisement, commercial, spot, puff, *esp. US* announcement, *US* flyer, *colloq.* ad, plug, *Brit. colloq.* advert. **2** advertising, promotion, marketing; publicity; propaganda, ballyhoo, *colloq.* promo, plugging, boost, *sl.* hype.

advice /ədvīss/ *n.* **1** words given or offered as an opinion or recommendation about future action or behaviour. **2** information given; news. **3** formal notice of a transaction. **4** (in *pl.*) communications from a distance. □ **take advice 1**

obtain advice, esp. from an expert. **2** act according to advice given. [ME f. OF *avis* f. L *ad* to + *visum* past part. of *vidēre* see]
■ **1** counsel, guidance, recommendation, suggestion, tip, hint, opinion, view; warning, admonition. **2** information, news, intelligence, notice, notification; communication.

advisable /ədvízəb'l/ *adj.* **1** (of a course of action etc.) to be recommended. **2** expedient. □□ **advisability** /-bílliti/ *n.* **advisably** *adv.*
■ recommendable, expedient, prudent, practical, sensible, sound, seemly, well, judicious, wise, intelligent, smart, proper, politic. □□ **advisability** see *prudence* (PRUDENT).

advise /ədvíz/ *v.* **1** *tr.* (also *absol.*) give advice to. **2** *tr.* recommend; offer as advice (*they advise caution*; *advised me to rest*). **3** *tr.* (usu. foll. by *of*, or *that* + clause) inform, notify. **4** *intr.* (foll. by *with*) *US* consult. [ME f. OF *aviser* f. L *ad* to + *visare* frequent. of *vidēre* see]
■ **1, 2** counsel, guide, take under one's wing, direct, steer; caution, admonish, warn; recommend, suggest, commend, tell; urge, exhort, encourage, *archaic* rede. **3** tell, notify, announce to, inform, apprise, make known to, intimate to, give news *or* word to, acquaint, *colloq.* let on to.

advised /ədvízd/ *adj.* **1** judicious (*well-advised*). **2** deliberate, considered. □□ **advisedly** /-zidli/ *adv.*

adviser /ədvízər/ *n.* (also *disp.* **advisor**) **1** a person who advises, esp. one appointed to do so and regularly consulted. **2** *US* a person who advises students on education, careers, etc. ¶ The disputed form *advisor* is prob. influenced by the adj. *advisory*.
■ **1** counsellor, mentor, guide, counsel, consultant, confidant(e), director, *Law amicus curiae*.

advisory /ədvízəri/ *adj.* & *n.* ● *adj.* **1** giving advice; constituted to give advice (*an advisory body*). **2** consisting in giving advice. ● *n.* (*pl.* **-ies**) *US* an advisory statement, esp. a bulletin about bad weather.
■ *adj.* consultative, counselling, hortatory, hortative, admonitory, *literary* monitory. ● *n.* bulletin, notice, warning, admonition, announcement, prediction.

advocaat /ádvəkaat/ *n.* a liqueur of eggs, sugar, and brandy. [Du., = ADVOCATE (being orig. an advocate's drink)]

advocacy /ádvəkəsi/ *n.* **1** (usu. foll. by *of*) verbal support or argument for a cause, policy, etc. **2** the function of an advocate. [ME f. OF *a(d)vocacie* f. med.L *advocatia* (as ADVOCATE)]

advocate *n.* & *v.* ● *n.* /ádvəkət/ **1** (foll. by *of*) a person who supports or speaks in favour. **2** a person who pleads for another. **3 a** a professional pleader in a court of justice. **b** *Sc.* a barrister. ● *v.tr.* /ádvəkayt/ **1** recommend or support by argument (a cause, policy, etc.). **2** plead for, defend. □□ **advocateship** *n.* **advocatory** /ádvəkaytəri/ *adj.* [ME f. OF *avocat* f. L *advocatus* past part. of *advocare* (as AD-, *vocare* call)]
■ *n.* **1** supporter, champion, apostle, backer, upholder, second, exponent, proponent, patron, defender, apologist, *disp.* protagonist. **2, 3** lawyer, counsel, counsellor; intercessor; *Brit.* barrister, solicitor, *US* attorney, counselor-at-law. ● *v.* support, champion, back, endorse, uphold, defend, recommend, stand behind *or* by, second, favour, speak *or* plead *or* argue for *or* in favour of, hold a brief for; urge; preach, teach.

advowson /ədvówz'n/ *n. Brit. Eccl.* (in ecclesiastical law) the right of recommending a member of the clergy for a vacant benefice, or of making the appointment. [ME f. AF *a(d)voweson* f. OF *avoeson* f. L *advocatio -onis* (as ADVOCATE)]

advt. *abbr.* advertisement.

adytum /ádditəm/ *n.* (*pl.* **adyta** /-tə/) the innermost part of an ancient temple. [L f. Gk *aduton* neut. of *adutos* impenetrable (as A-[1], *duō* enter)]

adze /adz/ *n.* & *v.* (*US* **adz**) ● *n.* a tool for cutting away the surface of wood, like an axe with an arched blade at right angles to the handle. ● *v.tr.* dress or cut with an adze. [OE *adesa*]

adzuki /ədzóoki/ *n.* (also **adsuki, azuki**) **1** an annual leguminous plant, *Vigna angularis*, native to China and Japan. **2** the small round dark red edible bean of this plant. [Jap. *azuki*]

-ae /ee/ *suffix* forming plural nouns, used in names of animal and plant families, tribes, etc. (*Felidae*; *Rosaceae*) and instead of *-as* in the plural of many non-naturalized or unfamiliar nouns in *-a* derived from Latin or Greek (*larvae*; *actiniae*). [pl. *-ae* of L nouns in *-a* or pl. *-ai* of some Gk nouns]

aedile /éedīl/ *n.* either of a pair of Roman magistrates who administered public works, maintenance of roads, public games, the corn-supply, etc. □□ **aedileship** *n.* [L *aedilis* concerned with buildings f. *aedes* building]

AEEU *abbrev.* Amalgamated Engineering and Electrical Union.

aegis /éejiss/ *n.* a protection; an impregnable defence. □ **under the aegis of** under the auspices of. [L f. Gk *aigis* mythical shield of Zeus or Athene]
■ see AUSPICE 1.

aegrotat /éegrōtat/ *n. Brit.* **1** a certificate that a university student is too ill to attend an examination. **2** an examination pass awarded in such circumstances. [L, = is sick f. *aeger* sick]

-aemia /éemiə/ *comb. form* (also **-haemia** /héemiə/, *US* **-emia**, **-hemia** /héemiə/) forming nouns denoting that a substance is (esp. excessively) present in the blood (*bacteriaemia*; *pyaemia*). [mod.L f. Gk *-aimia* f. *haima* blood]

aeolian /ee-ṓliən/ *adj.* (*US* **eolian**) wind-borne. □ **aeolian harp** a stringed instrument or toy that produces musical sounds when the wind passes through it. [L *Aeolius* f. *Aeolus* god of the winds f. Gk *Aiolos*]

Aeolian mode /ee-ṓliən/ *n. Mus.* the mode represented by the natural diatonic scale A–A. [L *Aeolius* f. *Aeolis* in Asia Minor f. Gk *Aiolis*]

aeon /ée-on/ *n.* (also **eon**) **1** a very long or indefinite period. **2** an age of the universe. **3** *Astron.* a thousand million years. **4** an eternity. **5** *Philos.* (in Neoplatonism, Platonism, and Gnosticism) a power existing from eternity, an emanation or phase of the supreme deity. [eccl.L f. Gk *aiōn* age]
■ **1** see AGE *n.* 2a.

aerate /áirayt/ *v.tr.* **1** charge (a liquid) with a gas, esp. carbon dioxide, e.g. to produce effervescence. **2** expose to the mechanical or chemical action of the air. □□ **aeration** /-ráysh'n/ *n.* **aerator** *n.* [L *aer* AIR + -ATE[3], after F *aérer*]

aerenchyma /árrənkīmə/ *n. Bot.* a soft plant tissue containing air spaces found esp. in many aquatic plants. [Gk *aēr* air + *egkhuma* infusion]

aerial /áiriəl/ *n.* & *adj.* ● *n.* a metal rod, wire, or other structure by which signals are transmitted or received as part of a radio or television transmission or receiving system. ● *adj.* **1** by or from or involving aircraft (*aerial navigation*; *aerial photography*). **2 a** existing, moving, or happening in the air. **b** of or in the atmosphere, atmospheric. **3 a** thin as air, ethereal. **b** immaterial, imaginary. **c** of air, gaseous. □□ **aeriality** /-riálliti/ *n.* **aerially** *adv.* [L *aerius* f. Gk *aerios* f. *aēr* air]

aerialist /áiriəlist/ *n.* a high-wire or trapeze artist.

aerie var. of EYRIE.

aeriform /áiriform/ *adj.* **1** of the form of air; gaseous. **2** unsubstantial, unreal. [L *aer* AIR + -FORM]

aero- /áirō/ *comb. form* **1** air. **2** aircraft. [Gk *aero-* f. *aēr* air]

aerobatics /áirəbáttiks/ *n.pl.* **1** feats of expert and usu. spectacular flying and manoeuvring of aircraft. **2** (as *sing.*) a performance of these. [AERO- + ACROBATICS]

aerobe /áirōb/ *n.* a micro-organism usu. growing in the presence of air, or needing air for growth. [F *aérobie* (as AERO-, Gk *bios* life)]

aerobic /airṓbik/ *adj.* **1** of or relating to aerobics. **2** of or relating to aerobes.

aerobics /airṓbiks/ *n.pl.* vigorous exercises designed to increase the body's oxygen intake.

aerobiology /áirəbīólləji/ *n.* the study of airborne micro-organisms, pollen, spores, etc., esp. as agents of infection.

aerodrome /áirədrōm/ *n. Brit.* a small airport or airfield. ¶ Now largely replaced by *airfield* and *airport*.

aerodynamics /áirōdīnámmiks/ *n.pl.* (usu. treated as *sing.*) the study of the interaction between the air and solid bodies moving through it. ▫▫ **aerodynamic** *adj.* **aerodynamically** *adv.* **aerodynamicist** *n.*

aero-engine /áirō-enjin/ *n.* an engine used to power an aircraft.

aerofoil /áirəfoyl/ *n. Brit.* a structure with curved surfaces (e.g. a wing, fin, or tailplane) designed to give lift in flight.

aerogramme /áirəgram/ *n.* (also **aerogram**) an air letter in the form of a single sheet that is folded and sealed.

aerolite /áirəlīt/ *n.* a stony meteorite.

aerology /airólləji/ *n.* the study of the upper levels of the atmosphere. ▫▫ **aerological** /áirəlójik'l/ *adj.*

aeronautics /áirōnáwtiks/ *n.pl.* (usu. treated as *sing.*) the science or practice of motion or travel in the air. ▫▫ **aeronautic** *adj.* **aeronautical** *adj.* [mod.L *aeronautica* (as AERO-, NAUTICAL)]

aeronomy /airónnəmi/ *n.* the science of the upper atmosphere.

aeroplane /áirəplayn/ *n.* esp. *Brit.* a powered heavier-than-air flying vehicle with fixed wings. [F *aéroplane* (as AERO-, PLANE[1])]
■ see PLANE[1] 3.

aerosol /áirəsol/ *n.* **1 a** a container used to hold a substance packed under pressure with a device for releasing it as a fine spray. **b** the releasing device. **c** the substance contained in an aerosol. **2** a system of colloidal particles dispersed in a gas (e.g. fog or smoke). [AERO- + SOL[2]]
■ **1 a, b** see SPRAY[1] *n.* 3.

aerospace /áirōspayss/ *n.* **1** the earth's atmosphere and outer space. **2** the technology of aviation in this region.

aerotrain /áirōtrayn/ *n.* a train that is supported on an air-cushion and guided by a track. [F *aérotrain* (as AERO-, TRAIN)]

aeruginous /eeróōjinəss/ *adj.* of the nature or colour of verdigris. [L *aeruginosus* f. *aerugo -inis* verdigris f. *aes aeris* bronze]

Aesculapian /éeskyooláypiən/ *adj.* of or relating to medicine or physicians. [L *Aesculapius* f. Gk *Asklēpios* god of medicine]

aesthete /éess-theet/ *n.* (*US* **esthete**) a person who has or professes to have a special appreciation of beauty. [Gk *aisthētēs* one who perceives, or f. AESTHETIC]
■ connoisseur, art-lover, lover of beauty.

aesthetic /eess-théttik/ *adj.* & *n.* (*US* **esthetic**) ● *adj.* **1** concerned with beauty or the appreciation of beauty. **2** having such appreciation; sensitive to beauty. **3** in accordance with the principles of good taste. ● *n.* **1** (in *pl.*) the philosophy of the beautiful, esp. in art. **2** a set of principles of good taste and the appreciation of beauty. ▫▫ **aesthetically** *adv.* **aestheticism** /-tisiz'm/ *n.* [Gk *aisthētikos* f. *aisthanomai* perceive]
■ *adj.* **1** artistic, *colloq.* arty. **2** sensitive, artistic, refined, discriminating, cultivated, cultured; *colloq.* arty. **3** artistic, tasteful, beautiful, in good *or* excellent taste; elegant, polished, refined, cultured. ▫▫ **aesthetically** artistically; sensitively, tastefully, beautifully, elegantly. **aestheticism** beauty; sensitivity, tastefulness, artistry, elegance.

aestival /éstiv'l, estī́v'l, eestī́v'l/ *adj.* (*US* **estival**) *formal* belonging to or appearing in summer. [ME f. OF *estival* f. L *aestivalis* f. *aestivus* f. *aestus* heat]

aestivate /éstivayt, éess-/ *v.intr.* (*US* **estivate**) **1** *Zool.* spend the summer or dry season in a state of torpor. **2** *formal* pass the summer. [L *aestivare aestivat-*]

aestivation /éstiváysh'n, éess-/ *n.* (*US* **estivation**) **1** *Bot.* the arrangement of petals in a flower-bud before it opens (cf. VERNATION). **2** *Zool.* spending the summer or dry season in a state of torpor.

aet. *abbr.* (also **aetat.**) *aetatis.*

aetatis /eetaátiss, ī-/ *adj.* of or at the age of.

aether var. of ETHER 2, 3.

aetiology /éetiólləji/ *n.* (*US* **etiology**) **1** the assignment of a cause or reason. **2** the philosophy of causation. **3** *Med.* the science of the causes of disease. ▫▫ **aetiologic** /-tiəlójik/ *adj.* **aetiological** /-tiəlójik'l/ *adj.* **aetiologically** /-tiəlójikəli/ *adv.* [LL *aetiologia* f. Gk *aitiologia* f. *aitia* cause]

AEU *abbr.* (in the UK) Amalgamated Engineering Union.

AEU(TASS) *abbr.* Technical, Administrative, and Supervisory Section of the AEU.

AF *abbr.* audio frequency.

af- /əf/ *prefix* assim. form of AD- before *f.*

afar /əfaár/ *adv.* at or to a distance. ▫ **from afar** from a distance. [ME f. A-[2], A-[4] + FAR]

AFC *abbr.* **1** (in the UK) Air Force Cross. **2** Association Football Club.

AFDCS *abbr.* (in the UK) Association of First Division Civil Servants (cf. FDA).

affable /áffəb'l/ *adj.* **1** (of a person) approachable and friendly. **2** kind and courteous, esp. to inferiors. ▫▫ **affability** /-bílliti/ *n.* **affably** *adv.* [F f. L *affabilis* f. *affari* (as AD-, *fari* speak)]
■ see FRIENDLY *adj.* 1.

affair /əfáir/ *n.* **1** a concern; a business; a matter to be attended to (*that is my affair*). **2 a** a celebrated or notorious happening or sequence of events. **b** *colloq.* a noteworthy thing or event (*was a puzzling affair*). **3** = *love affair.* **4** (in *pl.*) **a** ordinary pursuits of life. **b** business dealings. **c** public matters (*current affairs*). [ME f. AF *afere* f. OF *afaire* f. *à faire* to do: cf. ADO]
■ **1** business, concern, interest, area. **2 b** event, occasion, episode, business, occurrence, happening, proceeding, incident, experience, operation. **3** *affaire*, love affair, amour, romance, fling, liaison, relationship, flirtation, *affaire de cœur*, *archaic* intrigue, *Brit. sl.* carry-on. **4** (*affairs*) **a, b** concerns, undertakings, activity, activities, interests, matters, business, dealings; transactions, operation(s), finances, ventures, enterprise(s). **c** topics, issues, matters, concerns.

affaire /afáir/ *n.* (also **affaire de cœur** /afáir də kőr/) a love affair. [F]

affairé /afáiray/ *adj.* busy; involved. [F]

affect[1] /əfékt/ *v.tr.* **1 a** produce an effect on. **b** (of a disease etc.) attack (*his liver is affected*). **2** move; touch the feelings of (*affected me deeply*). ¶ Often confused with *effect*, which as a verb means 'bring about; accomplish'. ▫▫ **affecting** *adj.* **affectingly** *adv.* [F *affecter* or L *afficere affect-* influence (as AD-, *facere* do)]
■ **1 a** influence, act *or* play *or* work on; sway, change, transform, modify, alter. **b** attack, act upon, damage, lay hold of, strike. **2** move, stir, impress, touch, strike; perturb, upset, disturb, trouble, agitate, bother.

affect[2] /əfékt/ *v.tr.* **1** pretend to have or feel (*affected indifference*). **2** (foll. by *to* + infin.) pretend. **3** assume the character or manner of; pose as (*affect the freethinker*). **4** make a show of liking or using (*she affects fancy hats*). [F *affecter* or L *affectare* aim at, frequent. of *afficere* (as AFFECT[1])]
■ **1** assume, adopt, put on, pretend, feign, sham, fake, counterfeit. **3** see POSE[1] *v.* 2. **4** choose, select; use, wear, adopt.

affect[3] /áffekt/ *n. Psychol.* a feeling, emotion, or desire, esp. as leading to action. [G *Affekt* f. L *affectus* disposition f. *afficere* (as AFFECT[1])]

affectation /áffektáysh'n/ *n.* **1** an assumed or contrived manner of behaviour, esp. in order to impress. **2** (foll. by *of*) a studied display. **3** pretence. [F *affectation* or L *affectatio* (as AFFECT[2])]
■ **1** affectedness, pretentiousness, pretension, airs (and graces), artificiality, insincerity, posturing, *Austral.* & *NZ sl.* guiver. **2, 3** pose, false display, act, show, front, façade; pretence, pretension.

affected /əféktid/ *adj.* **1** in senses of AFFECT[1], AFFECT[2]. **2** artificially assumed or displayed; pretended (*an affected air of innocence*). **3** (of a person) full of affectation; artificial. **4** (prec. by adv.; often foll. by *towards*) disposed, inclined. ▫▫ **affectedly** *adv.* **affectedness** *n.*

■ **1** (AFFECT[1]) attacked, seized, afflicted, diseased, gripped, laid hold of, *archaic* stricken; moved, touched, stirred, distressed, troubled, upset, hurt; influenced, swayed, impressed, struck, played *or* worked *or* acted upon; altered, modified, changed, transformed. **2** unnatural, artificial, specious, stilted, stiff, studied, awkward, non-natural, contrived, overstudied, mannered, euphuistic; pretended, simulated, hollow, assumed, feigned, fake, false, counterfeit, synthetic, spurious, sham, bogus, *colloq.* phoney. **3** pretentious, pompous, insincere, artificial, high-sounding, theatrical, mincing, minikin, chichi, niminy-piminy, lackadaisical, *colloq.* la-di-da. **4** see *inclined* (INCLINE *v.*).

affection /əféksh'n/ *n.* **1** (often foll. by *for*, *towards*) goodwill; fond or kindly feeling. **2** a disease; a diseased condition. **3** a mental state; an emotion. **4** a mental disposition. **5** the act or process of affecting or being affected. ▫▫ **affectional** *adj.* (in sense 3). **affectionally** *adv.* [ME f. OF f. L *affectio -onis* (as AFFECT[1])]

■ **1** goodwill, (high) regard, liking, fondness, fond *or* kindly feeling, (loving) attachment, tenderness, warmth, love. **2** see ILLNESS.

affectionate /əfékshənət/ *adj.* loving, fond; showing love or tenderness. ▫▫ **affectionately** *adv.* [F *affectionné* or med.L *affectionatus* (as AFFECTION)]

■ fond, loving, tender, caring, devoted, doting, warm, warm-hearted, tender-hearted. ▫▫ **affectionately** see *fondly* (FOND).

affective /əféktiv/ *adj.* **1** concerning the affections; emotional. **2** *Psychol.* relating to affects. ▫▫ **affectivity** /áffektívviti/ *n.* [F *affectif -ive* f. LL *affectivus* (as AFFECT[1])]

■ **1** see EMOTIONAL 4.

affenpinscher /áffənpinshər/ *n.* **1** a dog of a small breed resembling the griffon. **2** this breed. [G f. *Affe* monkey + *Pinscher* terrier]

afferent /áffərənt/ *adj. Physiol.* conducting inwards or towards (*afferent nerves; afferent vessels*) (opp. EFFERENT). [L *afferre* (as AD-, *ferre* bring)]

affiance /əfíənss/ *v.tr.* (usu. in *passive*) *literary* promise solemnly to give (a person) in marriage. [ME f. OF *afiancer* f. med.L *affidare* (as AD-, *fidus* trusty)]

affidavit /áffidáyvit/ *n.* a written statement confirmed by oath, for use as evidence in court. [med.L, = has stated on oath, f. *affidare*: see AFFIANCE]

affiliate *v.* & *n.* ● *v.* /əfílliayt/ **1** *tr.* (usu. in *passive*; foll. by *to*, *with*) attach or connect (a person or society) with a larger organization. **2** *tr.* (of an institution) adopt (persons as members, societies as branches). **3** *intr.* **a** (foll. by *to*) associate oneself with a society. **b** (foll. by *with*) associate oneself with a political party. ● *n.* /əfílliayt, -liət/ an affiliated person or organization. [med.L *affiliare* adopt (as AD-, *filius* son]

■ *v.* **1, 2** associate; attach, connect, combine, unite, join.

affiliation /əfílliáysh'n/ *n.* the act or process of affiliating or being affiliated. ▫ **affiliation order** *Brit.* a legal order that the man judged to be the father of an illegitimate child must help to support it. [F f. med.L *affiliatio* f. *affiliare*: see AFFILIATE]

■ see ASSOCIATION 2–4.

affined /əfínd/ *adj.* related, connected. [*affine* (adj.) f. L *affinis* related: see AFFINITY]

affinity /əfínniti/ *n.* (*pl.* **-ies**) **1** (often foll. by *between*, or *disp. to*, *for*) a spontaneous or natural liking for or attraction to a person or thing. **2** relationship, esp. by marriage. **3** resemblance in structure between animals, plants, or languages. **4** a similarity of character suggesting a relationship. **5** *Chem.* the tendency of certain substances to combine with others. [ME f. OF *afinité* f. L *affinitas -tatis* f. *affinis* related, lit. bordering on (as AD- + *finis* border)]

■ **1** friendliness, fondness, liking, taste, penchant, partiality, attractiveness, attraction, rapport, sympathy, agreement. **2–4** relationship, kinship, closeness, alliance, connection, affiliation, association, link, tie, interconnection, correspondence; similarity, similitude, resemblance; conformity.

affirm /əfúrm/ *v.* **1** *tr.* assert strongly; state as a fact. **2** *intr.* **a** *Law* make an affirmation. **b** make a formal declaration. **3** *tr. Law* confirm, ratify (a judgement). ▫▫ **affirmatory** *adj.* **affirmer** *n.* [ME f. OF *afermer* f. L *affirmare* (as AD-, *firmus* strong)]

■ **1** see DECLARE 3. **2 b** see DECLARE 1, 2.

affirmation /áffərmáysh'n/ *n.* **1** the act or process of affirming or being affirmed. **2** *Law* a solemn declaration by a person who conscientiously declines to take an oath. [F *affirmation* or L *affirmatio* (as AFFIRM)]

■ **1** see DECLARATION 1, 2a.

affirmative /əfúrmətiv/ *adj.* & *n.* ● *adj.* **1** affirming; asserting that a thing is so. **2** (of a vote) expressing approval. ● *n.* **1** an affirmative statement, reply, or word. **2** (prec. by *the*) a positive or affirming position. ▫ **affirmative action** esp. *US* action favouring those who often suffer from discrimination. **in the affirmative** with affirmative effect; so as to accept or agree to a proposal; yes (*the answer was in the affirmative*). ▫▫ **affirmatively** *adv.* [ME f. OF *affirmatif -ive* f. LL *affirmativus* (as AFFIRM)]

■ *adj.* **2** see FAVOURABLE 1b.

affix *v.* & *n.* ● *v.tr.* /əfíks/ **1** (usu. foll. by *to*, *on*) attach, fasten. **2** add in writing (a signature or postscript). **3** impress (a seal or stamp). ● *n.* /áffiks/ **1** an appendage; an addition. **2** *Gram.* an addition or element placed at the beginning (*prefix*) or end (*suffix*) of a root, stem, or word, or in the body of a word (*infix*), to modify its meaning. ▫▫ **affixture** /əfíks-chər/ *n.* [F *affixer*, *affixe* or med.L *affixare* frequent. of L *affigere* (as AD-, *figere fix-* fix)]

afflatus /əfláytəss/ *n.* a divine creative impulse; inspiration. [L f. *afflare* (as AD-, *flare flat-* to blow)]

afflict /əflíkt/ *v.tr.* inflict bodily or mental suffering on. ▫ **afflicted with** suffering from. ▫▫ **afflictive** *adj.* [ME f. L *afflictare*, or *afflict-* past part. stem of *affligere* (as AD-, *fligere flict-* dash)]

■ affect, bother, distress, oppress, trouble, torment, plague, disturb, agitate; weaken, enfeeble, debilitate, incapacitate, *archaic* ail.

affliction /əflíksh'n/ *n.* **1** physical or mental distress, esp. pain or illness. **2** a cause of this. [ME f. OF f. L *afflictio -onis* (as AFFLICT)]

■ **1** hardship, misery, misfortune, distress, ordeal, trial, tribulation, adversity, suffering, trouble, illness, agony, pain, grief, torment, torture, wretchedness, *archaic or literary* woe. **2** curse, calamity, catastrophe, disaster, plague, scourge, tribulation, trouble, sea of troubles; see also ILLNESS 1.

affluence /áflooənss/ *n.* an abundant supply of money, commodities, etc.; wealth. [ME f. F f. L *affluentia* f. *affluere*: see AFFLUENT]

■ see WEALTH 1, 2.

affluent /áflooənt/ *adj.* & *n.* ● *adj.* **1** wealthy, rich. **2** abundant. **3** flowing freely or copiously. ● *n.* a tributary stream. ▫ **affluent society** a society in which material wealth is widely distributed. ▫▫ **affluently** *adv.* [ME f. OF f. L *affluere* (as AD-, *fluere flux-* flow)]

■ *adj.* **1** see WEALTHY. **2** see ABUNDANT 1.

afflux /áfluks/ *n.* a flow towards a point; an influx. [med.L *affluxus* f. L *affluere*: see AFFLUENT]

afford /əfórd/ *v.tr.* **1** (prec. by *can* or *be able to*; often foll. by *to* + infin.) **a** have enough money, means, time, etc., for; be able to spare (*can afford £50; could not afford a holiday; can we afford to buy a new television?*). **b** be in a position to do something (esp. without risk of adverse consequences) (*can't afford to let him think so*). **2** yield a supply of. **3** provide (*affords a view of the sea*). ▫▫ **affordable** *adj.* **affordability** /-dəbílliti/ *n.* [ME f. OE *geforthian* promote (as Y-, FORTH), assim. to words in AF-]

■ **1 a** have the *or* sufficient means, be able *or* rich enough, manage, find the means *or* money, *colloq.* have the wherewithal; bear *or* meet the expense of, pay for. **2** yield, give, supply, produce, provide, furnish, grant, offer; give forth. **3** see PROVIDE 1. □□ **affordable** reasonably priced, inexpensive; reasonable, fair, acceptable, within reason, economical, cheap.

afforest /əfórrist/ *v.tr.* **1** convert into forest. **2** plant with trees. □□ **afforestation** /-stáysh'n/ *n.* [med.L *afforestare* (as AD-, *foresta* FOREST)]

affranchise /əfránchīz/ *v.tr.* release from servitude or an obligation. [OF *afranchir* (as ENFRANCHISE, with prefix A-[3])]

affray /əfráy/ *n.* a breach of the peace by fighting or rioting in public. [ME f. AF *afrayer* (v.) f. OF *esfreer* f. Rmc]

affricate /áfrikət/ *n. Phonet.* a combination of a plosive with an immediately following fricative or spirant, e.g. *ch.* [L *affricare* (as AD-, *fricare* rub)]

affront /əfrúnt/ *n.* & *v.* ● *n.* an open insult (*feel it an affront; offer an affront to*). ● *v.tr.* **1** insult openly. **2** offend the modesty or self-respect of. **3** face, confront. [ME f. OF *afronter* slap in the face, insult, ult. f. L *frons frontis* face]
■ *n.* see INSULT *n.* 1. ● *v.* **1** see INSULT *v.* 1. **2** see INSULT *v.* 2.

Afghan /áfgan/ *n.* & *adj.* ● *n.* **1 a** a native or national of Afghanistan. **b** a person of Afghan descent. **2** the official language of Afghanistan (also called PASHTO). **3** (**afghan**) a knitted and sewn woollen blanket or shawl. **4** (in full **Afghan coat**) a kind of sheepskin coat with the skin outside and usu. with a shaggy border. ● *adj.* of or relating to Afghanistan or its people or language. □ **Afghan hound** a tall hunting dog with long silky hair. [Pashto *afghānī*]

Afghani /afgaáni/ *n.* (*pl.* **Afghanis**) the chief monetary unit of Afghanistan. [Pashto]

aficionado /əfíssyənaádō/ *n.* (*pl.* **-os**) a devotee of a sport or pastime (orig. of bullfighting). [Sp.]

afield /əféeld/ *adv.* **1** away from home; to or at a distance (esp. *far afield*). **2** in the field. [OE (as A[2], FIELD)]

afire /əfír/ *adv.* & *predic.adj.* **1** on fire. **2** intensely roused or excited.

aflame /əfláym/ *adv.* & *predic.adj.* **1** in flames. **2** = AFIRE 2.

aflatoxin /áflətoksin/ *n. Chem.* any of several related toxic compounds produced by the fungus *Aspergillus flavus*, which cause tissue damage and cancer. [*Aspergillus* + *flavus* + TOXIN]

afloat /əflṓt/ *adv.* & *predic.adj.* **1** floating in water or air. **2** at sea; on board ship. **3** out of debt or difficulty. **4** in general circulation; current. **5** full of or covered with a liquid. **6** in full swing. [OE (as A[2], FLOAT)]

AFM *abbr.* (in the UK) Air Force Medal.

afoot /əfŏŏt/ *adv.* & *predic.adj.* **1** in operation; progressing. **2** astir; on the move.

afore /əfór/ *prep.* & *adv. archaic* before; previously; in front (of). [OE *onforan* (as A[2], FORE)]

afore- /əfór/ *comb. form* before, previously (*aforementioned; aforesaid*).

aforethought /əfórthawt/ *adj.* premeditated (following a noun: *malice aforethought*).

a fortiori /áy fortiórī/ *adv.* & *adj.* with a yet stronger reason (than a conclusion already accepted); more conclusively. [L]

afoul /əfówl/ *adv.* foul. □ **run afoul of** run foul of.
■ □ **run afoul of** run foul of, become entangled with, be in trouble *or* conflict with, be at odds with.

afraid /əfráyd/ *predic.adj.* **1** (often foll. by *of*, or *that* or *lest* + clause) alarmed, frightened. **2** (foll. by *to* + infin.) unwilling or reluctant for fear of the consequences (*was afraid to go in*). □ **be afraid** (foll. by *that* + clause) *colloq.* admit or declare with (real or politely simulated) regret (*I'm afraid there's none left*). [ME, past part. of obs. *affray* (v.) f. AF *afrayer* f. OF *esfreer*]
■ fearful, frightened, scared, alarmed, intimidated, apprehensive, lily-livered, white-livered, terrified, panic-stricken, faint-hearted, weak-kneed, timid, timorous, hesitant, unwilling, reluctant, nervous, anxious, jittery, on edge, edgy, jumpy; cowardly, pusillanimous, craven, *colloq.* yellow, chicken. □ **be afraid** be sorry *or* unhappy *or* regretful *or* apologetic *or* rueful; regret (to say), admit.

afreet /áfreet/ *n.* (also **afrit**) a demon in Muslim mythology. [Arab. *'ifrīt*]

afresh /əfrésh/ *adv.* anew; with a fresh beginning. [A-[2] + FRESH]

African /áfrikən/ *n.* & *adj.* ● *n.* **1** a native of Africa (esp. a dark-skinned person). **2** a person of African descent. ● *adj.* of or relating to Africa. □ **African American** an American citizen of African origin or descent. **African-American** of or relating to American Blacks. **African elephant** the elephant, *Loxodonta africana*, of Africa, which is larger than the Indian elephant. **African violet** a saintpaulia, *Saintpaulia ionantha*, with heart-shaped velvety leaves and blue, purple, or pink flowers. [L *Africanus*]

Africana /áfrikaánə/ *n.pl.* things connected with Africa.

Africander /áfrikándər/ *n.* (also **Afrikander**) one of a S. African breed of sheep or longhorn cattle. [Afrik. *Afrikaander* alt. of Du. *Afrikaner* after *Hollander* etc.]

Afrikaans /áfrikaánss/ *n.* the language of the Afrikaner people developed from Cape Dutch, an official language of the Republic of South Africa. [Du., = African]

Afrikander var. of AFRICANDER.

Afrikaner /áfrikaánər/ *n.* **1** an Afrikaans-speaking White person in S. Africa, esp. one of Dutch descent. **2** *Bot.* a S. African species of *Gladiolus* or *Homoglossum*. [Afrik., formed as AFRICANDER]

afrit var. of AFREET.

Afro /áfrō/ *adj.* & *n.* ● *adj.* (of a hairstyle) long and bushy, as naturally grown by some Blacks. ● *n.* (*pl.* **-os**) an Afro hairstyle. [AFRO-, or abbr. of AFRICAN]

Afro- /áfrō/ *comb. form* African (*Afro-Asian*). [L *Afer Afr-* African]

Afro-American /áfrōəmérrikən/ *adj.* & *n.* ● *adj.* of or relating to American Blacks or their culture. ● *n.* an American Black.

Afro-Caribbean /áfrōkárribéeən, -kəríbbiən/ *n.* & *adj.* ● *n.* a person of African descent in or from the Caribbean. ● *adj.* of or relating to the Afro-Caribbeans or their culture.

afrormosia /áfrormṓziə/ *n.* **1** an African tree, *Pericopsis* (formerly *Afrormosia*) *elata*, yielding a hard wood resembling teak and used for furniture. **2** this wood. [mod.L f. AFRO- + *Ormosia* genus of trees]

aft /aaft/ *adv. Naut.* & *Aeron.* at or towards the stern or tail. [prob. f. ME *baft*: see ABAFT]

after /aáftər/ *prep., conj., adv.,* & *adj.* ● *prep.* **1 a** following in time; later than (*after six months; after midnight; day after day*). **b** *US* in specifying time (*a quarter after eight*). **2** (with causal force) in view of (something that happened shortly before) (*after your behaviour tonight what do you expect?*). **3** (with concessive force) in spite of (*after all my efforts I'm no better off*). **4** behind (*shut the door after you*). **5** in pursuit or quest of (*run after them; inquire after him; hanker after it; is after a job*). **6** about, concerning (*asked after her; asked after her health*). **7** in allusion to (*named him William after the prince*). **8** in imitation of (a person, word, etc.) (*a painting after Rubens; 'aesthete' is formed after 'athlete'*). **9** next in importance to (*the best book on the subject after mine*). **10** according to (*after a fashion*). ● *conj.* in or at a time later than that when (*left after they arrived*). ● *adv.* **1** later in time (*soon after; a week after*). **2** behind in place (*followed on after; look before and after*). ● *adj.* **1** later, following (*in after years*). **2** *Naut.* nearer the stern (*after cabins; after mast; after-peak*). □ **after all 1** in spite of all that has happened or has been said etc. (*after all, what does it matter?*). **2** in spite of one's exertions, expectations, etc. (*they tried for an hour and failed after all; so you have come after all!*). **after-care** care of a patient after a stay in hospital or of a person on release from prison. **after-damp** choking gas left after an explosion of firedamp in a mine. **after-effect**

an effect that follows after an interval or after the primary action of something. **after-image** an image retained by a sense-organ, esp. the eye, and producing a sensation after the cessation of the stimulus. **after one's own heart** see HEART. **after-taste** a taste remaining or recurring after eating or drinking. **after you** a formula used in offering precedence. [OE *æfter* f. Gmc]

afterbirth /aaftərburth/ *n. Med.* the placenta and foetal membranes discharged from the womb after childbirth.

afterburner /aaftərburnər/ *n.* an auxiliary burner in a jet engine to increase thrust.

afterglow /aaftərglō/ *n.* a light or radiance remaining after its source has disappeared or been removed.

afterlife /aaftərlīf/ *n.* **1** *Relig.* life after death. **2** life at a later time.

aftermarket /aaftərmaarkit/ *n.* **1** a market in spare parts and components. **2** *US Stock Exch.* a market in shares after their original issue.

aftermath /aaftərmath, -maath/ *n.* **1** consequences; after-effects (*the aftermath of war*). **2** new grass growing after mowing or after a harvest. [AFTER *adj.* + *math* mowing f. OE *mæth* f. Gmc]

■ **1** see OUTCOME.

aftermost /aaftərmōst/ *adj.* **1** last. **2** *Naut.* furthest aft. [AFTER *adj.* + -MOST]

afternoon /aaftərnōōn/ *n.* & *int.* ● *n.* **1** the time from noon or lunch-time to evening (*this afternoon*; *during the afternoon*; *afternoon tea*). **2** this time spent in a particular way (*had a lazy afternoon*). **3** a time compared with this, esp. the later part of something (*the afternoon of life*). ● *int.* = *good afternoon* (see GOOD *adj.* 14).

afterpains /aaftərpaynz/ *n.pl.* pains caused by contraction of the womb after childbirth.

afters /aaftərz/ *n.pl. Brit. colloq.* the course following the main course of a meal.

■ see DESSERT.

aftershave /aaftərshayv/ *n.* an astringent lotion for use after shaving.

aftershock /aaftərshok/ *n.* a lesser shock following the main shock of an earthquake.

afterthought /aaftərthawt/ *n.* an item or thing that is thought of or added later.

afterwards /aaftərwərdz/ *adv.* (*US* **afterward**) later, subsequently. [OE *æftanwearde* adj. f. *æftan* AFT + -WARD]

■ see *subsequently* (SUBSEQUENT).

afterword /aaftərwurd/ *n.* concluding remarks in a book, esp. by a person other than its author.

Ag *symb. Chem.* the element silver. [L *argentum*]

ag- /əg/ *prefix* assim. form of AD- before *g*.

Aga /aagə/ *n. propr.* a type of heavy heat-retaining cooking stove or range burning solid fuel or powered by gas, oil, or electricity and intended for continuous heating. [Sw. f. Svenska *A*ktienbolaget *Ga*s*a*ckumulator (Swedish Gas Accumulator Company), the original manufacturer]

aga /aagə/ *n.* (in Muslim countries, esp. under the Ottoman Empire) a commander, a chief. □ **Aga Khan** the spiritual leader of the Ismaili Muslims. [Turk. *ağa* master]

again /əgáyn, əgén/ *adv.* **1** another time; once more. **2** as in a previous position or condition (*back again*; *home again*; *quite well again*). **3** in addition (*as much again*; *half as many again*). **4** further, besides (*again, what about the children?*). **5** on the other hand (*I might, and again I might not*). □ **again and again** repeatedly. [orig. a northern form of ME *ayen* etc., f. OE *ongēan*, *ongægn*, etc., f. Gmc]

■ **1** see OVER *adv.* 7b. **3** see EXTRA *adv.* 2.

against /əgáynst, əgénst/ *prep.* **1** in opposition to (*fight against the invaders*; *am against hanging*; *arson is against the law*). **2** into collision or in contact with (*ran against a rock*; *lean against the wall*; *up against a problem*). **3** to the disadvantage of (*his age is against him*). **4** in contrast to (*against a dark background*; *99 as against 102 yesterday*). **5** in anticipation of or preparation for (*against his coming*; *against a rainy day*; *protected against the cold*; *warned against pickpockets*). **6** as a compensating factor to (*income against expenditure*). **7** in return for (*issued against payment of the fee*). □ **against the clock** see CLOCK[1] 3. **against the grain** see GRAIN. **against time** see TIME. [ME *ayenes* etc. f. *ayen* AGAIN + *-t* as in *amongst*: see AMONG]

■ **1, 4** opposed to, anti, averse to, resistant towards.

agama /ággəmə/ *n.* any Old World lizard of the genus *Agama*. [Carib]

agamic /əgámmik/ *adj.* characterized by the absence of sexual reproduction. [as AGAMOUS + -IC]

agamogenesis /ággəməjénnisiss/ *n. Biol.* asexual reproduction. □□ **agamogenetic** /-jinéttik/ *adj.* [as AGAMOUS + Gk *genesis* birth]

agamous /ággəməss/ *adj. Biol.* without (distinguishable) sexual organs. [LL *agamus* f. Gk *agamos* (as A-[1], *gamos* marriage)]

agapanthus /ággəpánthəss/ *n.* any African plant of the genus *Agapanthus*, esp. the ornamental African lily, with blue or white flowers. [mod.L f. Gk *agapē* love + *anthos* flower]

agape[1] /əgáyp/ *adv.* & *predic.adj.* gaping, open-mouthed, esp. with wonder or expectation.

agape[2] /ággəpay/ *n.* **1** a Christian feast in token of fellowship, esp. one held by early Christians in commemoration of the Last Supper. **2** *Theol.* Christian love, esp. as distinct from erotic love. [Gk, = brotherly love]

agar /áygaar/ *n.* (also **agar-agar** /áygaaráygaar/) a gelatinous substance obtained from any of various kinds of red seaweed and used in food, microbiological media, etc. [Malay]

agaric /ággərik/ *n.* any fungus of the family Agaricaceae, with cap and stalk, including the common edible mushroom. [L *agaricum* f. Gk *agarikon*]

agate /ággət/ *n.* **1** any of several varieties of hard usu. streaked chalcedony. **2** a coloured toy marble resembling this. [F *agate*, *-the*, f. L *achates* f. Gk *akhatēs*]

agave /əgáyvi/ *n.* any plant of the genus *Agave*, with rosettes of narrow spiny leaves, and tall inflorescences, e.g. the American aloe. [L f. Gk *Agauē*, proper name in myth f. *agauos* illustrious]

agaze /əgáyz/ *adv.* gazing.

age /ayj/ *n.* & *v.* ● *n.* **1 a** the length of time that a person or thing has existed or is likely to exist. **b** a particular point in or part of one's life, often as a qualification (*old age*; *voting age*). **2 a** *colloq.* (often in *pl.*) a long time (*took an age to answer*; *have been waiting for ages*). **b** a distinct period of the past (*golden age*; *Bronze age*; *Middle Ages*). **c** *Geol.* a period of time. **d** a generation. **3** the latter part of life; old age (*the peevishness of age*). ● *v.* (*pres. part.* **ageing, aging**) **1** *intr.* show signs of advancing age (*has aged a lot recently*). **2** *intr.* grow old. **3** *intr.* mature. **4** *tr.* cause or allow to age. □ **age-long** lasting for a very long time. **age of consent** see CONSENT. **age of discretion** see DISCRETION. **age-old** having existed for a very long time. **come of age** reach adult status (esp. in Law at 18, formerly 21). **of age** old enough, of adult status. **over age 1** old enough. **2** too old. **under age** not old enough, esp. not yet of adult status. [ME f. OF ult. f. L *aetas -atis* age]

■ *n.* **1 a** lifetime, duration, (length of) existence; life-span, period. **b** period, time, point; see also STAGE *n.* 1. **2 a** long time, aeon; years, weeks, months, *colloq.* for ever, donkey's years, *sl.* yonks. **b** era, epoch, period, time(s), day(s), *Hinduism* & *Buddhism* kalpa. **3** old age, later *or* declining years, senescence; senility, dotage; *archaic or poet.* eld. ● *v.* **1, 2** grow *or* get *or* become old(er), get on (in years), senesce; decline. **3, 4** mature, ripen, mellow. □ **age-long** see EVERLASTING *adj.* **age of consent** maturity, years *or* age of discretion; majority, adulthood, seniority. **age-old** see ANCIENT[1] *adj.* 2. **come of age** see MATURE *v.* 1a, c.

-age /ij/ *suffix* forming nouns denoting: **1** an action (*breakage*; *spillage*). **2** a condition or function (*bondage*; *a peerage*). **3** an aggregate or number of (*coverage*; *the peerage*; *acreage*). **4** fees payable for; the cost of using (*postage*). **5** the product of an action (*dosage*; *wreckage*). **6** a place; an abode (*anchorage*; *orphanage*; *parsonage*). [OF ult. f. L *-aticum* neut. of adj. suffix *-aticus* -ATIC]

aged *adj.* **1** /ayjd/ **a** of the age of (*aged ten*). **b** that has been subjected to ageing. **c** (of a horse) over six years old. **2** /áyjid/ having lived long; old.
■ **1 b** mature(d), ripe(ned), mellow(ed). **2** old, elderly, superannuated, ancient, grey, decrepit, hoary, advanced in years, immemorial, old as the hills, having *or* with one foot in the grave, *colloq.* over the hill, antediluvian.

ageing /áyjing/ *n.* (also **aging**) **1** growing old. **2** giving the appearance of advancing age. **3** a change of properties occurring in some metals after heat treatment or cold working.

ageism /áyjiz'm/ *n.* (also **agism**) prejudice or discrimination on the grounds of age. □□ **ageist** *adj.* & *n.* (also **agist**).

ageless /áyjliss/ *adj.* **1** never growing or appearing old or outmoded. **2** eternal, timeless.
■ **2** see TIMELESS.

agency /áyjənsi/ *n.* (*pl.* **-ies**) **1 a** the business or establishment of an agent (*employment agency*). **b** the function of an agent. **2 a** active operation; action (*free agency*). **b** intervening action; means (*fertilized by the agency of insects*). **c** action personified (*an invisible agency*). **3** a specialized department of the United Nations. [med.L *agentia* f. L *agere* do]
■ **1 a** see BUSINESS 8. **2 a** activity, action, working(s), operation, performance, energy. **b** means, medium, instrumentality, ways and means, way, channel(s); intervention, intercession, intermediation, hand(s); operation, mechanism, force, power.

agenda /əjéndə/ *n.* **1** (*pl.* **agendas**) **a** a list of items of business to be considered at a meeting. **b** a series of things to be done. **2** (as *pl.*) **a** items to be considered. **b** things to be done. ¶ Now very common as a countable noun in sense 1 (cf. DATA, MEDIA). [L, neut. pl. of gerundive of *agere* do]
■ **1 a** see LIST[1] *n.* 1.

agent /áyjənt/ *n.* **1 a** a person who acts for another in business, politics, etc. (*estate agent*; *insurance agent*). **b** a spy. **2 a** a person or thing that exerts power or produces an effect. **b** the cause of a natural force or effect on matter (*oxidizing agent*). **c** such a force or effect. □ **agent-general** a representative of an Australian State or Canadian province, usu. in London. □□ **agential** /əjénsh'l/ *adj.* [L *agent-* part. stem of *agere* do]
■ **1 a** representative, intermediary, mediator, go-between, middleman, broker, negotiator, proxy, emissary, delegate, spokesman, spokeswoman, spokesperson, deputy, substitute, surrogate, advocate, envoy, messenger, factor, dealer. **b** secret *or* undercover *or* double agent, spy, informer, emissary; FBI *or* CIA *or* MI6 *or* KGB agent, *apparatchik*, fifth-columnist, Mata Hari, *archaic* lurcher, *colloq.* mole, G-man, *hist.* beagle, *sl.* spook. **2 a** see INFLUENCE *n.* **b** factor, agency, cause, means, medium, channel, force, instrument, power, vehicle, ingredient. □□ **agential** instrumental, causal, influential; mediating, intermediary.

agent provocateur /aázhon prəvókkətőr/ *n.* (*pl.* ***agents provocateurs*** *pronunc.* same) a person employed to detect suspected offenders by tempting them to overt self-incriminating action. [F, = provocative agent]

agglomerate *v.*, *n.*, & *adj.* ● *v.tr.* & *intr.* /əglómmərayt/ **1** collect into a mass. **2** accumulate in a disorderly way. ● *n.* /əglómmərət/ **1** a mass or collection of things. **2** *Geol.* a mass of large volcanic fragments bonded under heat (cf. CONGLOMERATE). ● *adj.* /əglómmərət/ collected into a mass. □□ **agglomeration** /-ráysh'n/ *n.* **agglomerative** /əglómmərətiv/ *adj.* [L *agglomerare* (as AD-, *glomerare* f. *glomus -meris* ball)]

agglutinate /əglőőtinayt/ *v.* **1** *tr.* unite as with glue. **2** *tr.* & *intr.* *Biol.* cause or undergo adhesion (of bacteria, erythrocytes, etc.). **3** *tr.* (of language) combine (simple words) without change of form to express compound ideas. □□ **agglutination** /-náysh'n/ *n.* **agglutinative** /əglőőtinətiv/ *adj.* [L *agglutinare* (as AD-, *glutinare* f. *gluten -tinis* glue)]

agglutinin /əglőőtinin/ *n.* *Biol.* a substance or antibody causing agglutination. [AGGLUTINATE + -IN]

aggrandize /əgrándīz/ *v.tr.* (also **-ise**) **1** increase the power, rank, or wealth of (a person or State). **2** cause to appear greater than is the case. □□ **aggrandizement** /-dizmənt/ *n.* **aggrandizer** *n.* [F *agrandir* (stem *agrandiss-*), prob. f. It. *aggrandire* f. L *grandis* large: assim. to verbs in -IZE]

aggravate /ágrəvayt/ *v.tr.* **1** increase the gravity of (an illness, offence, etc.). **2** *disp.* annoy, exasperate (a person). □□ **aggravation** /-váysh'n/ *n.* [L *aggravare aggravat-* make heavy f. *gravis* heavy]
■ **1** worsen, intensify, exacerbate, heighten, magnify, increase, inflame. **2** exasperate, frustrate, infuriate, irritate, irk, nettle, vex, annoy, pique, rankle; harass, hector, goad, bother; anger, incense, madden; get on a person's nerves, rub up the wrong way, *colloq.* peeve, needle, rile, niggle, wind up, get across, get a person's goat, *Brit. sl.* give *or* cause a person aggro.
□□ **aggravation** see ANNOYANCE.

aggregate *n.*, *adj.*, & *v.* ● *n.* /ágrigət/ **1** a collection of, or the total of, disparate elements. **2** pieces of crushed stone, gravel, etc. used in making concrete. **3 a** *Geol.* a mass of minerals formed into solid rock. **b** a mass of particles. ● *adj.* /ágrigət/ **1** (of disparate elements) collected into one mass. **2** constituted by the collection of many units into one body. **3** *Bot.* **a** (of fruit) formed from several carpels derived from the same flower (e.g. raspberry). **b** (of a species) closely related. ● *v.* /ágrigayt/ **1** *tr.* & *intr.* collect together; combine into one mass. **2** *tr.* *colloq.* amount to (a specified total). **3** *tr.* unite (*was aggregated to the group*). □ **in the aggregate** as a whole. □□ **aggregation** /-gáysh'n/ *n.* **aggregative** /ágrigaytiv/ *adj.* [L *aggregare aggregat-* herd together (as AD-, *grex gregis* flock)]
■ *n.* **1** see TOTAL *n.*, MASS[1] *n.* 1, 2. ● *v.* **1** see AMASS. **3** see ADD 1, UNITE 1, 5.

aggression /əgrésh'n/ *n.* **1** the act or practice of attacking without provocation, esp. beginning a quarrel or war. **2** an unprovoked attack. **3** self-assertiveness; forcefulness. **4** *Psychol.* hostile or destructive tendency or behaviour. [F *agression* or L *aggressio* attack f. *aggredi aggress-* (as AD-, *gradi* walk)]
■ **1** aggressiveness, hostility, belligerence, belligerency, combativeness, bellicosity, pugnacity, *Brit. sl.* aggro. **2** attack, assault, onslaught, invasion, encroachment. **3** (self-)assertion, (self-)assertiveness, forcefulness, boldness.

aggressive /əgréssiv/ *adj.* **1** of a person: **a** given to aggression; openly hostile. **b** forceful; self-assertive. **2** (of an act) offensive, hostile. **3** of aggression. □□ **aggressively** *adv.* **aggressiveness** *n.*
■ **1 a** combative, antagonistic, warlike, martial, belligerent, bellicose, truculent, pugnacious, quarrelsome, disputatious, litigious; hostile, unfriendly. **b** forward, (self-)assertive, forceful, bold, brash, loud, pushing, pushful, *colloq.* pushy, *US sl.* feisty. **2** offensive, hostile, unfriendly, threatening, provocative, combative. □□ **aggressively** forcefully, assertively, belligerently, quarrelsomely, disputatiously; antagonistically, hostilely, threateningly, combatively, pugnaciously, truculently, angrily. **aggressiveness** see AGGRESSION 1.

aggressor /əgréssər/ *n.* a person who attacks without provocation. [L (as AGGRESSION)]
■ assailant, attacker, assaulter; instigator, initiator, provoker; belligerent, enemy, adversary, *esp. poet. or formal* foe.

aggrieved /əgreévd/ *adj.* having a grievance. □□ **aggrievedly** /-vidli/ *adv.* [ME, past part. of *aggrieve* f. OF *agrever* make heavier (as AD-, GRIEVE[1])]

aggro /ágrō/ *n.* *Brit. sl.* **1** aggressive troublemaking. **2** trouble, difficulty. [abbr. of AGGRAVATION (see AGGRAVATE) or AGGRESSION]
■ **1** see TROUBLE *n.* 5, 6. **2** see TROUBLE *n.* 1.

aghast /əgaást/ *adj.* (usu. *predic.*; often foll. by *at*) filled with dismay or consternation. [ME, past part. of obs. *agast*, *gast* frighten: see GHASTLY]

agile /ájīl/ *adj.* quick-moving, nimble, active. □□ **agilely** *adv.* **agility** /əjílliti/ *n.* [F f. L *agilis* f. *agere* do]
■ nimble, quick, quick-moving, brisk, swift, active, lively, lithe, limber, spry, sprightly; dexterous, resourceful; keen, sharp, alert, acute. □□ **agility** see DEXTERITY 2.

agin /əgín/ *prep. colloq.* or *dial.* against. [corrupt. of AGAINST or synonymous *again* obs. prep.]

aging var. of AGEING.

agio /ájiō/ *n.* (*pl.* **agios**) **1** the percentage charged on the exchange of one currency, or one form of money, into another more valuable. **2** the excess value of one currency over another. **3** money-exchange business. [It. *aggio*]

agism var. of AGEISM.

agitate /ájitayt/ *v.* **1** *tr.* (often as **agitated** *adj.*) disturb or excite (a person or feelings). **2** *intr.* (often foll. by *for*, *against*) stir up interest or concern, esp. publicly (*agitated for tax reform*). **3** *tr.* shake or move, esp. briskly. □□ **agitatedly** *adv.* [L *agitare agitat-* frequent. of *agere* drive]
■ **1** excite, arouse, rouse, move, perturb, disturb, stir up, disquiet, fluster, ruffle, disconcert, discomfit, discompose, unsettle, upset, rock, unnerve, bother, shake (up), *colloq.* rattle, *US joc.* discombobulate; (**agitated**) excited, aroused, roused, *etc.*; nervous, jittery, jumpy, uneasy, ill at ease, fidgety. **2** push, press, campaign, fight, work; (*agitate for*) promote. **3** stir (up), churn, disturb, shake (up), roil, jolt, convulse.

agitation /ájitáysh'n/ *n.* **1** the act or process of agitating or being agitated. **2** mental anxiety or concern. [F *agitation* or L *agitatio* (as AGITATE)]
■ **1** shaking, disturbance, churning, stirring, turbulence, convulsion; rabble-rousing, provocation, stirring up, incitement, trouble; excitement, arousal, stimulation, over-stimulation, commotion, ferment. **2** see ANXIETY 1, 2.

agitato /ájitaátō/ *adv.* & *adj. Mus.* in an agitated manner. [It.]

agitator /ájitaytər/ *n.* **1** a person who agitates, esp. publicly for a cause etc. **2** an apparatus for shaking or mixing liquid etc. [L (as AGITATE)]
■ **1** activist, rabble-rouser, incendiary, militant, *agent provocateur*, insurrectionist, troublemaker, demagogue, firebrand. **2** mixer, blender, churn, beater, whisk; (food) processor.

agitprop /ájitprop, ág-/ *n.* the dissemination of Communist political propaganda, esp. in plays, films, books, etc. [Russ. (as AGITATION, PROPAGANDA)]

aglet /áglit/ *n.* **1** a metal tag attached to each end of a shoelace etc. **2** = AIGUILLETTE. [ME f. F *aiguillette* small needle, ult. f. L *acus* needle]

agley /əgláy, əgleé/ *adv. Sc.* askew, awry. [A[2] + Sc. *gley* squint]

aglow /əglṓ/ *adv.* & *adj.* ● *adv.* glowingly. ● *predic.adj.* glowing.

AGM *abbr.* annual general meeting.

agma /ágmə/ *n.* **1** the sound represented by the symbol /ng/. **2** this symbol. [Gk, lit. 'fragment']

agnail /ágnayl/ *n.* **1** a piece of torn skin at the root of a fingernail. **2** the soreness resulting from this. [OE *angnægl* f. *nægl* NAIL *n.* 2a: cf. HANGNAIL]

agnate /ágnayt/ *adj.* & *n.* ● *adj.* **1** descended esp. by male line from the same male ancestor (cf. COGNATE). **2** descended from the same forefather; of the same clan or nation. **3** of the same nature; akin. ● *n.* one who is descended esp. by male line from the same male ancestor. □□ **agnatic** /-náttik/ *adj.* **agnation** /-náysh'n/ *n.* [L *agnatus* f. *ad* to + *gnasci* be born f. stem *gen-* beget]

agnosia /agnṓsiə/ *n. Med.* the loss of the ability to interpret sensations. [mod.L f. Gk *agnōsia* ignorance]

agnostic /agnóstik/ *n.* & *adj.* ● *n.* a person who believes that nothing is known, or can be known, of the existence or nature of God or of anything beyond material phenomena. ● *adj.* of or relating to agnostics. □□ **agnosticism** *n.* [A-[1] + GNOSTIC]
■ *n.* see NON-BELIEVER.

Agnus Dei /ágnŏŏss dáyee/ *n.* **1** a figure of a lamb bearing a cross or flag, as an emblem of Christ. **2** the part of the Roman Catholic mass beginning with the words 'Lamb of God'. [L, = lamb of God]

ago /əgṓ/ *adv.* earlier, before the present (*ten years ago*; *long ago*). ¶ Note the construction *it is ten years ago that* (not *since*) *I saw them.* [ME (*ago*, *agone*), past part. of obs. *ago* (v.) (as A-[2], GO[1])]

agog /əgóg/ *adv.* & *adj.* ● *adv.* eagerly, expectantly. ● *predic. adj.* eager, expectant. [F *en gogues* f. *en* in + pl. of *gogue* fun]
■ *adv.* eagerly, expectantly, avidly, keenly, with bated breath, impatiently, breathlessly. ● *predic.adj.* eager, avid, keen, enthusiastic, expectant, waiting, itching, impatient, breathless, anxious, on tenterhooks, on the edge of one's seat, on pins and needles.

à gogo /əgṓgō/ *adv.* in abundance (*whisky à gogo*). [F]

agonic /əgónnik/ *adj.* having or forming no angle. □ **agonic line** a line passing through the two poles, along which a magnetic needle points directly north or south. [Gk *agōnios* without angle (as A-[1], *gōnia* angle)]

agonistic /ággənístik/ *adj.* polemical, combative. □□ **agonistically** *adv.* [LL *agonisticus* f. Gk *agōnistikos* f. *agōnistēs* contestant f. *agōn* contest]

agonize /ággənīz/ *v.* (also **-ise**) **1** *intr.* (often foll. by *over*) undergo (esp. mental) anguish; suffer agony. **2** *tr.* (often as **agonizing** *adj.*) cause agony or mental anguish to. **3** *tr.* (as **agonized** *adj.*) expressing agony (*an agonized look*). **4** *intr.* struggle, contend. □□ **agonizingly** *adv.* [F *agoniser* or LL *agonizare* f. Gk *agōnizomai* contend f. *agōn* contest]
■ **1** see WORRY *v.* 1. **2** see TORMENT *v.* 1; (**agonizing**) painful, distressful, distressing, harrowing, torturous, racking, excruciating.

agony /ággəni/ *n.* (*pl.* **-ies**) **1** extreme mental or physical suffering. **2** a severe struggle. □ **agony aunt** *colloq.* a person (esp. a woman) who answers letters in an agony column. **agony column** *colloq.* **1** a column in a newspaper or magazine offering personal advice to readers who write in. **2** = *personal column.* **agony uncle** *colloq.* the male equivalent of an agony aunt. [ME f. OF *agonie* or LL f. Gk *agōnia* f. *agōn* contest]
■ **1** anguish, trouble, distress, suffering, misery, wretchedness, pain, pangs, torment, hurt, throes, torture, affliction, *archaic or literary* woe. **2** see STRUGGLE *n.* 1, 3.

agoraphobe /ággərəfōb/ *n.* a person who suffers from agoraphobia.

agoraphobia /ággərəfṓbiə/ *n. Psychol.* an abnormal fear of open spaces or public places. □□ **agoraphobic** *adj.* & *n.* [mod.L f. Gk *agora* place of assembly, market-place + -PHOBIA]

agouti /əgŏŏti/ *n.* (also **aguti**) (*pl.* **agoutis**) any burrowing rodent of the genus *Dasyprocta* or *Myoprocta* of Central and S. America, related to the guinea-pig. [F *agouti* or Sp. *aguti* f. Tupi *aguti*]

AGR *abbr.* advanced gas-cooled (nuclear) reactor.

agrarian /əgráiriən/ *adj.* & *n.* ● *adj.* **1** of or relating to the land or its cultivation. **2** relating to landed property. ● *n.* a person who advocates a redistribution of landed property. [L *agrarius* f. *ager agri* field]

agree /əgreé/ *v.* (**agrees**, **agreed**, **agreeing**) **1** *intr.* hold a similar opinion (*I agree with you about that*; *they agreed that it would rain*). **2** *intr.* (often foll. by *to*, or *to* + infin.) consent (*agreed to the arrangement*; *agreed to go*). **3** *intr.* (often foll. by *with*) **a** become or be in harmony. **b** suit; be good for (*caviar didn't agree with him*). **c** *Gram.* have the same number, gender, case, or person as. **4** *tr.* reach agreement about (*agreed a price*). **5** *tr.* consent to or approve of (terms, a proposal, etc.). **6** *tr.* bring (things, esp. accounts) into harmony. **7** *intr.* (foll. by *on*) decide by mutual consent (*agreed on a compromise*). □ **agree to differ** leave a difference of opinion etc. unresolved. **be agreed** have reached the same opinion. [ME f. OF *agreer* ult. f. L *gratus* pleasing]

■ **1** concur, see eye to eye, be as one man, be at one, understand each other *or* one another, acquiesce, consent, assent; concede, grant, admit, allow, accept. **2** consent, acquiesce, approve, accede, assent. **3 a** concur, conform, come *or* go *or* blend together, coincide, be consonant, be in harmony *or* accord, correspond, harmonize, chime, accord, tally, match, *US colloq.* jibe. **b** suit, go well, prove suitable, assort. **4, 5** acquiesce in, assent to, approve, accept, accede to; consent to, approve of. **6** harmonize, adjust. **7** see SETTLE[1] 5–7, 8b.

agreeable /əgreéəb'l/ *adj.* **1** (often foll. by *to*) pleasing. **2** (often foll. by *to*) (of a person) willing to agree (*was agreeable to going*). **3** (foll. by *to*) conformable. □□ **agreeability** *n.* **agreeableness** *n.* **agreeably** *adv.* [ME f. OF *agreable* f. *agreer* AGREE]

■ **1** pleasing, pleasant, enjoyable, pleasurable, favourable, delightful, satisfying, satisfactory, good, nice, acceptable, appealing; to one's liking *or* taste *or* fancy. **2** in favour, willing, consenting, acquiescent, compliant, in agreement *or* accord, concurring, amenable, sympathetic, well-disposed; accommodating. □□ **agreeably** see *willingly* (WILLING), *favourably* (FAVOURABLE).

agreement /əgreémənt/ *n.* **1** the act of agreeing; the holding of the same opinion. **2** mutual understanding. **3** an arrangement between parties as to a course of action etc. **4** *Gram.* having the same number, gender, case, or person. **5** mutual conformity of things; harmony. [ME f. OF (as AGREE)]

■ **1, 2** concord, accord, concordance, accordance, consensus, harmony, compatibility, unity, concurrence, unanimity, understanding. **3** understanding, arrangement, covenant, treaty, pact, accord, compact, settlement, concordat, contract, bargain, capitulation, *colloq.* deal. **5** see HARMONY 3.

agribusiness /ágribizniss/ *n.* **1** agriculture conducted on strictly commercial principles, esp. using advanced technology. **2** an organization engaged in this. **3** the group of industries dealing with the produce of, and services to, farming. □□ **agribusinessman** /-bíznismən/ *n.* (*pl.* **-men**). [AGRICULTURE + BUSINESS]

agriculture /ágrikulchər/ *n.* the science or practice of cultivating the soil and rearing animals. □□ **agricultural** /-kúlchərəl/ *adj.* **agriculturalist** /-kúlchərəlist/ *n.* **agriculturally** /-kúlchərəli/ *adv.* **agriculturist** /-kúlchərist/ *n.* [F *agriculture* or L *agricultura* f. *ager agri* field + *cultura* CULTURE]

agrimony /ágriməni/ *n.* (*pl.* **-ies**) any perennial plant of the genus *Agrimonia*, esp. *A. eupatoria* with small yellow flowers. [ME f. OF *aigremoine* f. L *agrimonia* alt. of *argemonia* f. Gk *argemōnē* poppy]

agro- /ágrō/ *comb. form* agricultural (*agro-climatic*; *agro-ecological*). [Gk *agros* field]

agrochemical /ágrōkémmik'l/ *n.* a chemical used in agriculture.

agronomy /əgrónnəmi/ *n.* the science of soil management and crop production. □□ **agronomic** /ágrənómmik/ *adj.* **agronomical** /ágrənómmik'l/ *adj.* **agronomically** /ágrənómmikəli/ *adv.* **agronomist** *n.* [F *agronomie* f. *agronome* agriculturist f. Gk *agros* field + *-nomos* f. *nemō* arrange]

aground /əgrównd/ *predic.adj.* & *adv.* (of a ship) on or on to the bottom of shallow water (*be aground*; *run aground*). [ME f. A[2] + GROUND[1]]

ague /áygyoo/ *n.* **1** *hist.* a malarial fever, with cold, hot, and sweating stages. **2** a shivering fit. □□ **agued** *adj.* **aguish** *adj.* [ME f. OF f. med.L *acuta (febris)* acute (fever)]

aguti var. of AGOUTI.

AH *abbr.* in the year of the Hegira (AD 622); of the Muslim era. [L *anno Hegirae*]

ah /aa/ *int.* expressing surprise, pleasure, sudden realization, resignation, etc. ¶ The sense depends much on intonation. [ME f. OF *a*]

aha /aahaá, əhaá/ *int.* expressing surprise, triumph, mockery, irony, etc. ¶ The sense depends much on intonation. [ME f. AH + HA]

ahead /əhéd/ *adv.* **1** further forward in space or time. **2** in the lead; further advanced (*ahead on points*). **3** in the line of one's forward motion (*roadworks ahead*). **4** straight forwards. □ **ahead of 1** further forward or advanced than. **2** in the line of the forward motion of. **3** prior to. [orig. *Naut.*, f. A[2] + HEAD]

■ **1** at the front, in front, in advance, in the lead *or* vanguard, up ahead, before, to the fore. **2** winning, in the lead, in front. **4** onward(s), forward(s), on, straight (on). □ **ahead of 1** in front of, in advance of, before; beating, defeating, winning over, outdoing, routing, surpassing. **3** see BEFORE *prep.* 2.

ahem /əhém, əhém/ (not usu. clearly articulated) *int.* used to attract attention, gain time, or express disapproval. [lengthened form of HEM[2]]

ahimsa /əhímsaa/ *n.* (in the Hindu, Buddhist, and Jainist tradition) respect for all living things and avoidance of violence towards others both in thought and deed. [Skr. f. *a* without + *himsa* injury]

ahoy /əhóy/ *int. Naut.* a call used in hailing. [AH + HOY[1]]

à huis clos /áa wee klṓ/ *adv.* in private. [F, = with closed doors]

AI *abbr.* **1** artificial insemination. **2** artificial intelligence.

ai /áa-i/ *n.* (*pl.* **ais**) the three-toed sloth of S. America, of the genus *Bradypus*. [Tupi *ai*, repr. its cry]

AID *abbr.* artificial insemination by donor.

aid /ayd/ *n.* & *v.* ● *n.* **1** help. **2** financial or material help, esp. given by one country to another. **3** a material source of help (*teaching aid*). **4** a person or thing that helps. **5** *hist.* a grant of subsidy or tax to a king. ● *v.tr.* **1** (often foll. by *to* + infin.) help. **2** promote or encourage (*sleep will aid recovery*). □ **in aid of** in support of. **what's this** (or **all this**) **in aid of?** *colloq.* what is the purpose of this? [ME f. OF *aïde*, *aïdier*, ult. f. L *adjuvare* (as AD-, *juvare jut-* help)]

■ *n.* **1** help, support, assistance, backing, relief, benefit, service, succour, comfort. **2** funding, subsidy, subvention, grant-money, grant, grant-in-aid, relief money, donation; bursary, scholarship. **3** see EQUIPMENT. **4** see AIDE, AUXILIARY *n.* ● *v.* **1** help, support, assist, facilitate, back, abet, uphold, promote; succour, relieve, subsidize. **2** see PROMOTE 2.

-aid /ayd/ *comb. form* denoting an organization or event that raises money for charity (*school aid*). [20th c.: orig. in *Band Aid*, rock musicians campaigning for famine relief]

aide /ayd/ *n.* **1** an aide-de-camp. **2** esp. *US* an assistant. **3** an unqualified assistant to a social worker. [abbr.]

■ **1, 2** aide-de-camp; aid, assistant, helper, help, helpmate, coadjutor; good *or* strong right arm, right hand, right-hand man *or* woman; colleague, partner, ally, comrade, comrade-in-arms, man Friday, girl Friday, *US* cohort, *colloq.* sidekick.

aide-de-camp /áyd-dəkóɴ/ *n.* (*pl.* **aides-de-camp** *pronunc.* same) an officer acting as a confidential assistant to a senior officer. [F]

aide-mémoire /áydmemwaár/ *n.* (*pl.* ***aides-mémoire*** *pronunc.* same) **1 a** an aid to the memory. **b** a book or document meant to aid the memory. **2** *Diplomacy* a memorandum. [F f. *aider* to help + *mémoire* memory]

Aids /aydz/ *n.* (also **AIDS**) acquired immune deficiency syndrome, an often fatal syndrome caused by a virus transmitted in the blood, marked by severe loss of resistance to infection. □ **Aids-related complex** the symptoms of a person affected with the Aids virus without necessarily developing the disease. [abbr.]

aigrette /áygret, aygrét/ *n.* **1** an egret. **2** its white plume. **3** a tuft of feathers or hair. **4** a spray of gems or similar ornament. [F]

aiguille /aygwéel/ *n.* a sharp peak of rock, esp. in the Alps. [F: see AGLET]

aiguillette /áygwilét/ *n.* a tagged point hanging from the shoulder on the breast of some uniforms. [F: see AGLET]

AIH *abbr.* artificial insemination by husband.

aikido /īkidō/ *n.* a Japanese form of self-defence making use of the attacker's own movements without causing injury. [Jap. f. *ai* mutual + *ki* mind + *dō* way]

ail /ayl/ *v.* **1** *tr. archaic* (only in 3rd person interrog. or indefinite constructions) trouble or afflict in mind or body (*what ails him?*). **2** *intr.* (usu. **be ailing**) be ill. [OE *egl(i)an* f. *egle* troublesome]

■ **1** trouble, afflict, affect, bother, distress, upset, worry, make ill *or* sick, pain, hurt. **2** suffer, be *or* feel ill *or* poorly *or* unwell *or* indisposed *or* off colour, decline, feel strange *or* wretched, be out of sorts, *colloq.* feel rough, *Austral. colloq.* be not too clever, *Brit. colloq.* be a bit off, *esp. US* be sick.

ailanthus /aylánthəss/ *n.* a tall deciduous tree of the genus *Ailanthus*, esp. *A. altissima*, native to China and Australasia. [mod.L *ailantus* f. Ambonese *aylanto*]

aileron /áyləron/ *n.* a hinged surface in the trailing edge of an aeroplane wing, used to control lateral balance. [F, dimin. of *aile* wing f. L *ala*]

ailing /áyling/ *adj.* **1** ill, esp. chronically. **2** in poor condition.

■ **1** see ILL *adj.* 1.

ailment /áylmənt/ *n.* an illness, esp. a minor one.

■ illness, sickness, affliction, affection, disease, disorder, indisposition, malady, complaint, condition, infection, trouble, *sl.* bug; disability, infirmity; malaise, queasiness, nausea.

aim /aym/ *v.* & *n.* ● *v.* **1** *intr.* (foll. by *at* + verbal noun, or *to* + infin.) intend or try (*aim at winning*; *aim to win*). **2** *tr.* (usu. foll. by *at*) direct or point (a weapon, remark, etc.). **3** *intr.* take aim. **4** *intr.* (foll. by *at*, *for*) seek to attain or achieve. ● *n.* **1** a purpose, a design, an object aimed at. **2** the directing of a weapon, missile, etc., at an object. □ **take aim** direct a weapon etc. at an object. [ME f. OF ult. f. L *aestimare* reckon]

■ *v.* **1, 4** (*aim at*, *aim for*) focus on, try for, strive for, have designs on, aspire to, plan on, set one's sights on; (*aim to*) seek to, intend to, plan to, mean to, propose to, strive to, try to, wish to, want to. **2** direct, point, focus, train, level. ● *n.* **1** purpose, goal, design, ambition, desire, aspiration, object, end, objective, target, intent, intention, plan. □ **take aim** aim; (*take aim at*) draw a bead on, zero in on, focus on.

aimless /áymliss/ *adj.* without aim or purpose. □□ **aimlessly** *adv.* **aimlessness** *n.*

■ purposeless, pointless, undirected, erratic, haphazard, random, vagrant, wayward; wanton, frivolous. □□ **aimlessly** pointlessly, purposelessly, erratically, unsystematically, haphazardly, randomly.

ain't /aynt/ *contr. colloq.* **1** am not; are not; is not (*you ain't doing it right*; *she ain't nice*). **2** has not; have not (*we ain't seen him*). ¶ Usually regarded as an uneducated use, and unacceptable in spoken and written English, except to represent dialect speech. [contr. of *are not*]

air /air/ *n.* & *v.* ● *n.* **1** an invisible gaseous substance surrounding the earth, a mixture mainly of oxygen and nitrogen. **2 a** the earth's atmosphere. **b** the free or unconfined space in the atmosphere (*birds of the air*; *in the open air*). **c** the atmosphere as a place where aircraft operate. **3 a** a distinctive impression or characteristic (*an air of absurdity*). **b** one's manner or bearing, esp. a confident one (*with a triumphant air*; *does things with an air*). **c** (esp. in *pl.*) an affected manner; pretentiousness (*gave himself airs*; *airs and graces*). **4** *Mus.* a tune or melody; a melodious composition. **5** a breeze or light wind. ● *v.tr.* **1** warm (washed laundry) to remove damp, esp. at a fire or in a heated cupboard. **2** expose (a room etc.) to the open air; ventilate. **3** express publicly (an opinion, grievance, etc.). **4** parade; show ostentatiously (esp. qualities). **5** *refl.* go out in the fresh air. □ **air bag** a safety device that fills with air on impact to protect the occupants of a vehicle in a collision. **air-bed** an inflatable mattress. **air bladder** a bladder or sac filled with air in fish or some plants (cf. *swim-bladder*). **air brake 1** a brake worked by air pressure. **2** a movable flap or other device on an aircraft to reduce its speed. **air-brick** a brick perforated with small holes for ventilation. **air-bridge** a portable bridge or walkway put against an aircraft door. **Air Chief Marshal** an RAF officer of high rank, below Marshal of the RAF and above Air Marshal. **Air Commodore** an RAF officer next above Group Captain. **air-conditioned** (of a room, building, etc.) equipped with air-conditioning. **air-conditioner** an air-conditioning apparatus. **air-conditioning 1** a system for regulating the humidity, ventilation, and temperature in a building. **2** the apparatus for this. **air-cooled** cooled by means of a current of air. **air corridor** = CORRIDOR 4. **air-cushion 1** an inflatable cushion. **2** the layer of air supporting a hovercraft or similar vehicle. **air force** a branch of the armed forces concerned with fighting or defence in the air. **air hostess** a stewardess in a passenger aircraft. **air lane** a path or course regularly used by aircraft (cf. LANE 4). **air letter** a sheet of light paper forming a letter for sending by airmail. **air line** a pipe supplying air, esp. to a diver. **Air Marshal** an RAF officer of high rank, below Air Chief Marshal and above Air Vice-Marshal. **Air Officer** any RAF officer above the rank of Group Captain. **air plant** a plant growing naturally without soil. **air pocket** an apparent vacuum in the air causing an aircraft to drop suddenly. **air power** the ability to defend and attack by means of aircraft, missiles, etc. **air pump** a device for pumping air into or out of a vessel. **air raid** an attack by aircraft. **air rifle** a rifle using compressed air to propel pellets. **air sac** an extension of the lungs in birds or the tracheae in insects. **air-sea rescue** rescue from the sea by aircraft. **air speed** the speed of an aircraft relative to the air through which it is moving. **air terminal** a building in a city or town to which passengers report and which serves as a base for transport to and from an airport. **air time** time allotted for a broadcast. **air-to-air** from one aircraft to another in flight. **air traffic controller** an airport official who controls air traffic by giving radio instructions to pilots concerning route, altitude, take-off, and landing. **Air Vice-Marshal** an RAF officer of high rank, just below Air Marshal. **air waves** *colloq.* radio waves used in broadcasting. **by air** by aircraft; in an aircraft. **in the air** (of opinions, feelings, etc.) prevalent; gaining currency. **on** (or **off**) **the air** in (or not in) the process of broadcasting. **take the air** go out of doors. **tread** (or **walk**) **on air** feel elated. **up in the air** (of projects etc.) uncertain, not decided. [ME f. F and L f. Gk *aēr*]

■ *n.* **3 a** atmosphere, ambience, aura, climate, feeling, sense, mood, impression, quality. **b** manner, style, appearance, aura, attitude, demeanour, aspect, feeling, bearing, look, quality, flavour, *literary* mien. **c** (*airs*) pretension(s), pretence, pretentiousness, show, affectedness, affectation, posing; haughtiness, hauteur, arrogance, superiority, superciliousness. **4** melody, tune, song, music, ditty, strain. **5** breeze, current, draught, breath, puff, whiff, waft, wafting, wind, *literary* zephyr. ● *v.* **2** ventilate, freshen, refresh, aerate. **3** publish, broadcast, circulate, publicize, make public *or* known, disseminate, vent, reveal, expose, disclose, divulge, express, declare. **4** show off, parade, display, exhibit, flaunt; boast of, brag about, *colloq.* talk big about, *US* & *Austral. colloq.* blow about, *literary* vaunt. □ **by air** by aircraft, *esp. Brit.* by aeroplane *or US* airplane, *colloq.* by plane; by airmail. **in the air** see ABOUT *adv.* 2. **take the air** go out, go for a walk *or* stroll, get some fresh air. **tread** (or **walk**) **on air** be elated; (see ELATE 1). **up in the air** see UNCERTAIN 1.

airbase /áirbayss/ *n.* a base for the operation of military aircraft.
airborne /áirborn/ *adj.* **1** transported by air. **2** (of aircraft) in the air after taking off.
airbrush /áirbrush/ *n.* & *v.* ● *n.* an artist's device for spraying paint by means of compressed air. ● *v.tr.* paint with an airbrush.
Airbus /áirbuss/ *n. propr.* a passenger aircraft serving routes of relatively short distance.
aircraft /áirkraaft/ *n.* (*pl.* same) a machine capable of flight, esp. an aeroplane or helicopter. □ **aircraft-carrier** a warship that carries and serves as a base for aeroplanes.
aircraftman /áirkraaftmən/ *n.* (*pl.* **-men**) the lowest rank in the RAF.
aircraftwoman /áirkraaftwŏŏmmən/ *n.* (*pl.* **-women**) the lowest rank in the WRAF.
aircrew /áirkrōō/ *n.* **1** the crew manning an aircraft. **2** (*pl.* **aircrew**) a member of such a crew.
Airedale /áirdayl/ *n.* **1** a large terrier of a rough-coated breed. **2** this breed. [*Airedale* in Yorkshire]
airer /áirər/ *n.* a frame or stand for airing or drying clothes etc.
airfield /áirfeeld/ *n.* an area of land where aircraft take off and land, are maintained, etc.
airfoil /áirfoyl/ *n. US* = AEROFOIL. [AIR + FOIL²]
airframe /áirfraym/ *n.* the body of an aircraft as distinct from its engine(s).
airfreight /áirfrayt/ *n.* & *v.* ● *n.* cargo carried by an aircraft. ● *v.tr.* transport by air.
airglow /áirglō/ *n.* radiation from the upper atmosphere, detectable at night.
airgun /áirgun/ *n.* a gun using compressed air to propel pellets.
airhead /áirhed/ *n.* **1** *Mil.* a forward base for aircraft in enemy territory. **2** esp. *US sl.* a silly or foolish person.
airing /áiring/ *n.* **1** exposure to fresh air, esp. for exercise or an excursion. **2** exposure (of laundry etc.) to warm air. **3** public expression of an opinion etc. (*the idea will get an airing at tomorrow's meeting*).
airless /áirliss/ *adj.* **1** stuffy; not ventilated. **2** without wind or breeze; still. □□ **airlessness** *n.*
■ **1** see STUFFY 1.
airlift /áirlift/ *n.* & *v.* ● *n.* the transport of troops and supplies by air, esp. in a blockade or other emergency. ● *v.tr.* transport in this way.
airline /áirlīn/ *n.* an organization providing a regular public service of air transport on one or more routes.
airliner /áirlīnər/ *n.* a large passenger aircraft.
■ see PLANE¹ *n.* 3.
airlock /áirlok/ *n.* **1** a stoppage of the flow in a pump or pipe, caused by an air bubble. **2** a compartment with controlled pressure and parallel sets of doors, to permit movement between areas at different pressures.
airmail /áirmayl/ *n.* & *v.* ● *n.* **1** a system of transporting mail by air. **2** mail carried by air. ● *v.tr.* send by airmail.
airman /áirmən/ *n.* (*pl.* **-men**) **1** a pilot or member of the crew of an aircraft, esp. in an air force. **2** a member of the RAF below commissioned rank.
airmiss /áirmiss/ *n.* a circumstance in which two or more aircraft in flight on different routes are less than a prescribed distance apart.
airmobile /áirmōbīl/ *adj.* (of troops) that can be moved about by air.
airplane /áirplayn/ *n. US* = AEROPLANE.
airplay /áirplay/ *n.* broadcasting (of recorded music).
airport /áirport/ *n.* a complex of runways and buildings for the take-off, landing, and maintenance of civil aircraft, with facilities for passengers.
airscrew /áirskrōō/ *n. Brit.* an aircraft propeller.
airship /áirship/ *n.* a power-driven aircraft that is lighter than air.
airsick /áirsik/ *adj.* affected with nausea due to travel in an aircraft. □□ **airsickness** *n.*
airside /áirsīd/ *n.*, *adj.*, & *adv.* (designating, to, or towards) the sections of an airport to which only passengers and airport personnel have admittance.
airspace /áirspayss/ *n.* the air available to aircraft to fly in, esp. the part subject to the jurisdiction of a particular country.
airstrip /áirstrip/ *n.* a strip of ground suitable for the take-off and landing of aircraft.
airtight /áirtīt/ *adj.* not allowing air to pass through.
■ see TIGHT *adj.* 4.
airway /áirway/ *n.* **1 a** a recognized route followed by aircraft. **b** (often in *pl.*) = AIRLINE. **2** a ventilating passage in a mine. **3** *Med.* (often in *pl.*) the passage(s) through which air passes into the lungs.
airwoman /áirwŏŏmmən/ *n.* (*pl.* **-women**) **1** a woman pilot or member of the crew of an aircraft, esp. in an air force. **2** a member of the WRAF below commissioned rank.
airworthy /áirwurthi/ *adj.* (of an aircraft) fit to fly.
airy /áiri/ *adj.* (**airier, airiest**) **1** well-ventilated, breezy. **2** flippant, superficial. **3 a** light as air. **b** graceful, delicate. **4** insubstantial, ethereal, immaterial. □ **airy-fairy** *colloq.* unrealistic, impractical, foolishly idealistic. □□ **airily** *adv.* **airiness** *n.*
■ **1** see BREEZY 1. **2** see BREEZY 3. **3 b** see DELICATE 1a. **4** see IMMATERIAL 2.
aisle /īl/ *n.* **1** part of a church, esp. one parallel to and divided by pillars from the nave, choir, or transept. **2** a passage between rows of pews, seats, etc. □□ **aisled** *adj.* [ME *ele*, *ile* f. OF *ele* f. L *ala* wing: confused with *island* and F *aile* wing]
ait /ayt/ *n.* (also **eyot**) *Brit.* a small island, esp. in a river. [OE *iggath* etc. f. *īeg* ISLAND + dimin. suffix]
aitch /aych/ *n.* the name of the letter H. □ **drop one's aitches** fail to pronounce the initial *h* in words. [OF *ache*]
aitchbone /áychbōn/ *n.* **1** the buttock or rump bone. **2** a cut of beef lying over this. [ME *nage-*, *nache-bone* buttock, ult. f. L *natis*, *-es* buttock(s): for loss of *n* cf. ADDER, APRON]
ajar¹ /əjaar/ *adv.* & *predic.adj.* (of a door) slightly open. [A² + obs. *char* f. OE *cerr* a turn]
■ see OPEN *adj.* 1–4, 13, 20.
ajar² /əjaar/ *adv.* out of harmony. [A² + JAR²]
AK *abbr. US* Alaska (in official postal use).
a.k.a. *abbr.* also known as.
akee var. of ACKEE.
akela /aakáylə/ *n.* the adult leader of a group of Cub Scouts. [name of the leader of a wolf-pack in Kipling's *Jungle Book*]
akimbo /əkímbō/ *adv.* (of the arms) with hands on the hips and elbows turned outwards. [ME *in kenebowe*, prob. f. ON]
akin /əkín/ *predic.adj.* **1** related by blood. **2** (often foll. by *to*) of similar or kindred character. [A-⁴ + KIN]
■ **1** see KIN *adj.* **2** kindred; see also ALIKE *adj.*; (*akin to*) related to, allied *or* connected *or* affiliated to *or* with, associated with, germane to, like, similar to.
Akkadian /əkáydiən/ (also **Accadian**) *adj.* & *n. hist.* ● *adj.* of Akkad in ancient Babylonia. ● *n.* **1** the Semitic language of Akkad. **2** an inhabitant of Akkad.
akvavit var. of AQUAVIT.
AL *abbr. US* Alabama (in official postal use).
Al *symb. Chem.* the element aluminium.
al- /al, əl/ *prefix* assim. form of AD- before *-l*.
-al /əl/ *suffix* **1** forming adjectives meaning 'relating to, of the kind of': **a** from Latin or Greek words (*central*; *regimental*; *colossal*; *tropical*) (cf. -IAL, -ICAL). **b** from English nouns (*tidal*). **2** forming nouns, esp. of verbal action (*animal*; *rival*; *arrival*; *proposal*; *trial*). [sense 1 f. F *-el* or L *-alis* adj. suffix rel. to *-aris* (-AR¹); sense 2 f. F *-aille* or f. (or after) L *-alis* etc. used as noun]
Ala. *abbr.* Alabama.

à la /aa laa/ *prep.* after the manner of (*à la russe*). [F, f. À LA MODE]

alabaster /álləbaastər, -bastər/ *n.* & *adj.* ● *n.* a translucent usu. white form of gypsum, often carved into ornaments. ● *adj.* **1** of alabaster. **2** like alabaster in whiteness or smoothness. □□ **alabastrine** /-baastrin, -bástrin, -īn/ *adj.* [ME f. OF *alabastre* f. L *alabaster*, *-trum*, f. Gk *alabast(r)os*]

à la carte /aa laa kaart/ *adv.* & *adj.* ordered as separately priced item(s) from a menu, not as part of a set meal. [F]

alack /əlák/ *int.* (also **alack-a-day** /əlákkəday/) *archaic* an expression of regret or surprise. [prob. f. AH + LACK]

alacrity /əlákriti/ *n.* briskness or cheerful readiness. [L *alacritas* f. *alacer* brisk]
▪ see DISPATCH *n.* 4.

Aladdin's cave /əláddinz/ *n.* a place of great riches. [*Aladdin* in the *Arabian Nights' Entertainments*]

Aladdin's lamp /əláddinz/ *n.* a talisman enabling its holder to gratify any wish.

à la mode /aa laa mōd/ *adv.* & *adj.* **1** in fashion; fashionable. **2 a** (of beef) braised in wine. **b** *US* served with ice-cream. [F, = in the fashion]
▪ **1** see FASHIONABLE 1, 2.

alar /áylər/ *adj.* **1** relating to wings. **2** winglike or wing-shaped. **3** axillary. [L *alaris* f. *ala* wing]

alarm /əlaarm/ *n.* & *v.* ● *n.* **1** a warning of danger etc. (*gave the alarm*). **2 a** a warning sound or device (*the burglar alarm was set off accidentally*). **b** = *alarm clock*. **3** frightened expectation of danger or difficulty (*were filled with alarm*). ● *v.tr.* **1** frighten or disturb. **2** arouse to a sense of danger. □ **alarm clock** a clock with a device that can be made to sound at the time set in advance. [ME f. OF *alarme* f. It. *allarme* f. *all'arme!* to arms]
▪ *n.* **1** warning, alert, danger-signal, distress-signal. **2 a** tocsin, bell, gong, siren, whistle, horn; red *or* warning light; call. **3** fear, fright, apprehension, dismay, trepidation, terror, dread, anxiety, *angst*, excitement, panic, consternation, distress, nervousness, uneasiness, concern, discomfort. ● *v.* **1** frighten, scare, daunt, startle, terrify, panic; unnerve, dismay, disturb, upset. **2** alert, warn, rouse, put on the alert.

alarming /əlaarming/ *adj.* disturbing, frightening. □□ **alarmingly** *adv.*
▪ see *frightening* (FRIGHTEN).

alarmist /əlaarmist/ *n.* & *adj.* ● *n.* a person given to spreading needless alarm. ● *adj.* creating needless alarm. □□ **alarmism** *n.*

alarum /əlaarəm/ *n. archaic* = ALARM. □ **alarums and excursions** *joc.* confused noise and bustle.

Alas. *abbr.* Alaska.

alas /əláss, əlaass/ *int.* an expression of grief, pity, or concern. [ME f. OF *a las(se)* f. *a* ah + *las(se)* f. L *lassus* weary]

Alaska /əláskə/ *n.* □ **baked Alaska** sponge cake and ice-cream in a meringue covering. [name of a State of the US]

alate /áylayt/ *adj.* having wings or winglike appendages. [L *alatus* f. *ala* wing]

alb /alb/ *n.* a white vestment reaching to the feet, worn by some Christian priests at church ceremonies. [OE *albe* f. eccl.L *alba* fem. of L *albus* white]

albacore /álbəkor/ *n.* **1** a long-finned tunny, *Thunnus alalunga*. Also called GERMON. **2** any of various other related fish. [Port. *albacor*, *-cora*, f. Arab. *al* the + *bakr* young camel or *bakūr* premature, precocious]

Albanian /albáyniən/ *n.* & *adj.* ● *n.* **1 a** a native or national of Albania in SE Europe. **b** a person of Albanian descent. **2** the language of Albania. ● *adj.* of or relating to Albania or its people or language.

albata /albaatə/ *n.* German silver; an alloy of nickel, copper, and zinc. [L *albata* whitened f. *albus* white]

albatross /álbətross/ *n.* **1 a** any long-winged stout-bodied bird of the family Diomedeidae related to petrels, inhabiting the Pacific and Southern Oceans. **b** a source of frustration or guilt; an encumbrance. **2** *Brit. Golf* a score of three strokes under par at any hole. [alt. (after L *albus* white) of 17th-c. *alcatras*, applied to various sea-birds, f. Sp. and Port. *alcatraz*, var. of Port. *alcatruz* f. Arab. *alḳādūs* the pitcher]

albedo /albeedō/ *n.* (*pl.* **-os**) the proportion of light or radiation reflected by a surface, esp. of a planet or moon. [eccl.L, = whiteness, f. L *albus* white]

albeit /awlbee-it/ *conj. literary* though (*he tried, albeit without success*).

albert /álbərt/ *n.* a watch-chain with a bar at one end for attaching to a buttonhole. [Prince *Albert*, consort of Queen Victoria, d. 1861]

albescent /albéss'nt/ *adj.* growing or shading into white. [L *albescere albescent-* f. *albus* white]

Albigenses /álbijénseez/ *n.pl.* the members of a heretic sect in S. France in the 12th–13th c. □□ **Albigensian** *adj.* [L f. *Albi* in S. France]

albino /albeenō/ *n.* (*pl.* **-os**) **1** a person or animal having a congenital absence of pigment in the skin and hair (which are white), and the eyes (which are usu. pink). **2** a plant lacking normal colouring. □□ **albinism** /álbiniz'm/ *n.* **albinotic** /álbinóttik/ *adj.* [Sp. & Port. (orig. of White Negroes) f. *albo* L f. *albus* white + *-ino* = -INE[1]]

Albion /álbiən/ *n.* (also **perfidious Albion**) Britain or England. [OE f. L f. Celt. *Albio* (unrecorded): F *la perfide Albion* with ref. to alleged treachery to other nations]

albite /álbīt/ *n. Mineral.* a feldspar, usu. white, rich in sodium. [L *albus* white + -ITE[1]]

album /álbəm/ *n.* **1** a blank book for the insertion of photographs, stamps, etc. **2 a** a long-playing gramophone record. **b** a set of these. [L, = a blank tablet, neut. of *albus* white]

albumen /álbyoomin/ *n.* **1** egg-white. **2** *Bot.* the substance found between the skin and germ of many seeds, usu. the edible part; = ENDOSPERM. [L *albumen -minis* white of egg f. *albus* white]

albumin /álbyoomin/ *n.* any of a class of water-soluble proteins found in egg-white, milk, blood, etc. □□ **albuminous** /albyoominəss/ *adj.* [F *albumine* f. L *albumin-*: see ALBUMEN]

albuminoid /albyoominoyd/ *n.* = SCLEROPROTEIN.

albuminuria /álbyoominyooriə/ *n.* the presence of albumin in the urine, usu. as a symptom of kidney disease.

alburnum /albúrnəm/ *n.* = SAPWOOD. [L f. *albus* white]

alcahest var. of ALKAHEST.

alcaic /alkáyik/ *adj.* & *n.* ● *adj.* of the verse metre invented by Alcaeus, lyric poet of Mytilene *c.*600 BC, occurring in four-line stanzas. ● *n.* (in *pl.*) alcaic verses. [LL *alcaicus* f. Gk *alkaikos* f. *Alkaios* Alcaeus]

alcalde /aalkaalday/ *n.* a magistrate or mayor in a Spanish, Portuguese, or Latin American town. [Sp. f. Arab. *al-ḳāḍī* the judge: see CADI]

alchemy /álkəmi/ *n.* (*pl.* **-ies**) **1** the medieval forerunner of chemistry, esp. seeking to turn base metals into gold or silver. **2** a miraculous transformation or the means of achieving this. □□ **alchemic** /alkémmik/ *adj.* **alchemical** /alkémmik'l/ *adj.* **alchemist** *n.* **alchemize** *v.tr.* (also **-ise**). [ME f. OF *alkemie*, *alkamie* f. med.L *alchimia*, *-emia*, f. Arab. *alkīmiyā'* f. *al* the + *kīmiyā'* f. Gk *khēmia*, *-meia* art of transmuting metals]

alcheringa /álchəringgə/ *n.* (in the mythology of some Australian Aboriginals) the 'golden age' when the first ancestors were created. [Aboriginal, = dream-time]

alcohol /álkəhol/ *n.* **1** (in full **ethyl alcohol**) a colourless volatile inflammable liquid forming the intoxicating element in wine, beer, spirits, etc., and also used as a solvent, as fuel, etc. Also called ETHANOL. ¶ Chem. formula: C_2H_5OH. **2** any liquor containing this. **3** *Chem.* any of a large class of organic compounds that contain one or more hydroxyl groups attached to carbon atoms. [F or med.L f. Arab. *al-kuḥl* f. *al* the + *kuḥl* KOHL]
▪ **2** spirits, liquor, (strong) drink, *colloq.* booze, fire-water, *Austral.* & *NZ colloq.* grog, *US colloq.* hooch, *sl.* gut-rot, rot-gut, hard stuff, moonshine, *esp. US sl.* lush.

alcoholic /álkəhóllik/ *adj.* & *n.* ● *adj.* of, relating to, containing, or caused by alcohol. ● *n.* a person suffering from alcoholism.
■ *adj.* intoxicating, intoxicant, inebriating. ● *n.* drunkard, drunk, dipsomaniac, sot, drinker, winebibber, serious *or* hard *or* problem drinker, tippler, *archaic or literary* toper, *colloq.* barfly, soak, boozer, dipso, *sl.* wino, *Austral. sl.* metho, plonko, *Austral.* & *NZ sl.* hophead, *esp. US sl.* lush.

alcoholism /álkəholiz'm/ *n.* **1** an addiction to the consumption of alcoholic liquor. **2** the diseased condition resulting from this. [mod.L *alcoholismus* (as ALCOHOL)]

alcoholometer /álkəholómmitər/ *n.* an instrument for measuring alcoholic concentration. □□ **alcoholometry** *n.*

alcove /álkōv/ *n.* a recess, esp. in the wall of a room or of a garden. [F f. Sp. *alcoba* f. Arab. *al-ḳubba* f. *al* the + *ḳubba* vault]
■ see RECESS *n.* 1.

aldehyde /áldihīd/ *n. Chem.* any of a class of compounds formed by the oxidation of alcohols (and containing the group -CHO). □□ **aldehydic** /áldihídik/ *adj.* [abbr. of mod.L *alcohol dehydrogenatum* alcohol deprived of hydrogen]

al dente /al dénti/ *adj.* (of pasta etc.) cooked so as to be still firm when bitten. [It., lit. 'to the tooth']

alder /áwldər/ *n.* any tree of the genus *Alnus*, related to the birch, with catkins and toothed leaves. □ **alder buckthorn** a shrub, *Frangula alnus*, related to the buckthorn. [OE *alor*, *aler*, rel. to L *alnus*, with euphonic *d*]

alderman /áwldərmən/ *n.* (*pl.* **-men**) **1** esp. *hist.* a co-opted member of an English county or borough council, next in dignity to the Mayor. **2** *US* & *Austral.* the elected governor of a city. □□ **aldermanic** /-mánnik/ *adj.* **aldermanship** *n.* [OE *aldor* patriarch f. *ald* old + MAN]

Aldis lamp /áwldiss/ *n.* a hand lamp for signalling in Morse code. [A. C. W. *Aldis*, its inventor]

aldrin /áldrin/ *n.* a white crystalline chlorinated hydrocarbon used as an insecticide. [K. *Alder*, Ger. chemist d. 1958 + -IN]

ale /ayl/ *n.* beer (now usu. as a trade word). [OE *alu*, = ON *öl*]

aleatoric /áyliətórrik/ *adj.* **1** depending on the throw of a die or on chance. **2** *Mus.* & *Art* involving random choice by a performer or artist. [L *aleatorius aleator* dice-player f. *alea* die]

aleatory /áyliətəri/ *adj.* = ALEATORIC. [as ALEATORIC]

alec /állik/ *n.* (also **aleck**) *Austral. sl.* a stupid person. [shortening of SMART ALEC]
■ see FOOL[1] *n.* 1.

alee /əlée/ *adv.* & *predic.adj.* **1** on the lee or sheltered side of a ship. **2** to leeward. [ME, f. A[2] + LEE]

alehouse /áylhowss/ *n. hist.* a tavern.

alembic /əlémbik/ *n.* **1** *hist.* an apparatus formerly used in distilling. **2** a means of refining or extracting. [ME f. OF f. med.L *alembicus* f. Arab. *al-'anbīḳ* f. *al* the + *'anbīḳ* still f. Gk *ambix*, *-ikos* cup, cap of a still]

aleph /áalef/ *n.* the first letter of the Hebrew alphabet. [Heb. *'ālep̄*, lit. 'ox']

alert /əlért/ *adj.*, *n.*, & *v.* ● *adj.* **1** watchful or vigilant; ready to take action. **2** nimble (esp. of mental faculties); attentive. ● *n.* **1** a warning call or alarm. **2 a** warning of an air raid. **b** the duration of this. ● *v.tr.* (often foll. by *to*) make alert; warn (*were alerted to the danger*). □ **on the alert** on the lookout against danger or attack. □□ **alertly** *adv.* **alertness** *n.* [F *alerte* f. It. *all' erta* to the watch-tower]
■ *adj.* **1** awake, wide awake, watchful, vigilant, attentive, heedful, wary, cautious, aware, observant, open-eyed, on one's toes, on one's guard, *colloq.* on the ball. **2** active, nimble, lively, agile, quick, spry, sprightly, vivacious, alive; attentive, *colloq.* all there, with it, bright-eyed and bushy-tailed, *sl.* fly. ● *n.* **1** alarm, warning, signal, call, siren, danger-signal, distress-signal. ● *v.* warn, caution, alarm, forewarn; (*alert to*) advise of, notify of, point out. □ **on the alert** on the qui vive, on guard, on the lookout, watchful, on one's toes. □□ **alertness** see VIGILANCE, INTELLIGENCE 1b.

-ales /áyleez/ *suffix* forming the plural names of orders of plants (*Rosales*). [pl. of L adj. suffix *-alis*: see -AL]

aleuron /əlyóorən/ *n.* (also **aleurone** /-rōn/) *Biochem.* a protein found as granules in the seeds of plants etc. [Gk *aleuron* flour]

A level /ay/ *n. Brit.* = *advanced level* (see ADVANCE).

alewife /áylwīf/ *n.* (*pl.* **alewives**) *US* any of several species of fish allied to the herring. [corrupt. of 17th-c. *aloofe*: orig. uncert.]

alexanders /álligzáandərz/ *n.* an umbelliferous plant, *Smyrnium olusatrum*, formerly used in salads but superseded by celery. [OE f. med.L *alexandrum*]

Alexander technique /álligzáandər/ *n.* a system of body awareness designed to promote well-being by ensuring minimum effort in maintaining postures and carrying out movements. [F. M. *Alexander*, physiotherapist d. 1955]

Alexandrian /álligzáandriən/ *adj.* **1** of or characteristic of Alexandria in Egypt. **2 a** belonging to or akin to the schools of literature and philosophy of Alexandria. **b** (of a writer) derivative or imitative; fond of recondite learning.

alexandrine /álligzándrīn/ *adj.* & *n.* ● *adj.* (of a line of verse) having six iambic feet. ● *n.* an alexandrine line. [F *alexandrin* f. *Alexandre* Alexander (the Great), the subject of an Old French poem in this metre]

alexandrite /álligzándrīt/ *n. Mineral.* a green variety of chrysoberyl. [Tsar *Alexander* I of Russia + -ITE[1]]

alexia /əléksiə/ *n.* the inability to see words or to read, caused by a condition of the brain. [mod.L, A-[1] + Gk *lexis* speech f. *legein* to speak, confused with L *legere* to read]

alfalfa /alfálfə/ *n.* a leguminous plant, *Medicago sativa*, with clover-like leaves and flowers used for fodder. Also called LUCERNE. [Sp. f. Arab. *al-fasfaṣa*, a green fodder]

alfresco /alfréskō/ *adv.* & *adj.* in the open air (*we lunched alfresco*; *an alfresco lunch*). [It. *al fresco* in the fresh (air)]

alga /álgə/ *n.* (*pl.* **algae** /áljee, álgee/) (usu. in *pl.*) a non-flowering stemless water-plant, esp. seaweed and phytoplankton. □□ **algal** *adj.* **algoid** *adj.* [L]

algebra /áljibrə/ *n.* **1** the branch of mathematics that uses letters and other general symbols to represent numbers and quantities in formulae and equations. **2** a system of this based on given axioms (*linear algebra*; *the algebra of logic*). □□ **algebraic** /áljibráyik/ *adj.* **algebraical** /áljibráyik'l/ *adj.* **algebraically** /áljibráyikəli/ *adv.* **algebraist** /áljibráyist/ *n.* [It. & Sp. & med.L, f. Arab. *al-jabr* f. *al* the + *jabr* reunion of broken parts f. *jabara* reunite]

-algia /áljə/ *comb. form Med.* denoting pain in a part specified by the first element (*neuralgia*). □□ **-algic** *comb. form* forming adjectives. [Gk f. *algos* pain]

algicide /álgisīd/ *n.* a preparation for destroying algae.

algid /áljid/ *adj. Med.* cold, chilly. □□ **algidity** /aljídditi/ *n.* [L *algidus* f. *algēre* be cold]

alginate /áljinayt/ *n.* a salt or ester of alginic acid. [ALGA + -IN + -ATE[1]]

alginic acid /aljínnik/ *n.* an insoluble carbohydrate found (chiefly as salts) in many brown seaweeds. [ALGA + -IN + -IC]

algoid see ALGA.

Algol /álgol/ *n.* a high-level computer programming language. [ALGORITHMIC (see ALGORITHM) + LANGUAGE]

algolagnia /álgəlágniə/ *n.* sexual pleasure got from inflicting pain on oneself or others; masochism or sadism. □□ **algolagnic** *adj.* & *n.* [mod.L f. G *Algolagnie* f. Gk *algos* pain + *lagneia* lust]

algology /algólləji/ *n.* the study of algae. □□ **algological** /-gəlójik'l/ *adj.* **algologist** *n.*

Algonquian /algóngkwiən/ *adj.* & *n.* (also **Algonkian** /-kiən/) ● *adj.* of or relating to a large group of N. American Indian tribes. ● *n.* **1** a member of any of these tribes. **2** any of the languages or dialects used by them. [*Algonquin* N. Amer. tribal name + -IAN]

algorithm /álgərithəm/ *n.* (also **algorism** /álgəriz'm/) **1** *Math.* a process or set of rules used for calculation or problem-solving, esp. with a computer. **2** the Arabic or decimal notation of numbers. ▫▫ **algorithmic** /álgəríthmik/ *adj.* [*algorism* ME ult. f. Pers. *al-Kuwārizmī* 9th-c. mathematician: *algorithm* infl. by Gk *arithmos* number (cf. F *algorithme*)]

alguacil /álgwəsíl/ *n.* (also **alguazil** /-zíl/) **1** a mounted official at a bullfight. **2** a constable or an officer of justice in Spain or Spanish-speaking countries. [Sp. f. Arab. *al-wazīr* f. *al* the + *wazir*: see VIZIER]

alias /áyliəss/ *adv.* & *n.* ● *adv.* also named or known as. ● *n.* a false or assumed name. [L, = at another time, otherwise]

■ *n.* see PSEUDONYM.

alibi /állibī/ *n.* & *v.* (*pl.* **alibis**) ● *n.* **1** a claim, or the evidence supporting it, that when an alleged act took place one was elsewhere. **2** *disp.* an excuse of any kind; a pretext or justification. ● *v.* (**alibis, alibied, alibiing**) *colloq.* **1** *tr.* provide an alibi or offer an excuse for (a person). **2** *intr.* provide an alibi. [L, = elsewhere]

■ *n.* excuse, explanation; justification, reason; *colloq.* story, side of the story, line. ● *v.* excuse, explain, justify; give an explanation *or* excuse.

alicyclic /állisíklik/ *adj. Chem.* of, denoting, or relating to organic compounds combining a cyclic structure with aliphatic properties, e.g. cyclohexane. [G *alicyclisch* (as ALIPHATIC, CYCLIC)]

alidade /állidayd/ *n. Surveying* & *Astron.* an instrument for determining directions or measuring angles. [F f. med.L f. Arab. *al- 'iḍāda* the revolving radius f. *'aḍud* upper arm]

alien /áyliən/ *adj.* & *n.* ● *adj.* **1 a** (often foll. by *to*) unfamiliar; not in accordance or harmony; unfriendly, hostile; unacceptable or repugnant (*army discipline was alien to him*; *struck an alien note*). **b** (often foll. by *to* or *from*) different or separated. **2** foreign; from a foreign country (*help from alien powers*). **3** of or relating to beings supposedly from other worlds. **4** *Bot.* (of a plant) introduced from elsewhere and naturalized in its new home. ● *n.* **1** a foreigner, esp. one who is not a naturalized citizen of the country where he or she is living. **2** a being supposedly from another world. **3** *Bot.* an alien plant. ▫▫ **alienness** *n.* [ME f. OF f. L *alienus* belonging to another (*alius*)]

■ *adj.* **1 a** foreign, strange, odd, weird, bizarre, peculiar, abnormal; exotic, remote, outlandish, unfamiliar, unknown, unrelated, unconnected; see also UNACCEPTABLE, HOSTILE 2. **b** different, separate(d), unlike, unalike, dissimilar, differing. **2** see FOREIGN 1. **3** extraterrestrial, unearthly. ● *n.* **1** foreigner, stranger, denizen, outlander, outsider, non-native, immigrant, newcomer. **2** extraterrestrial, ET; Martian.

alienable /áyliənəb'l/ *adj. Law* able to be transferred to new ownership. ▫▫ **alienability** /-bílliti/ *n.*

alienage /áyliənij/ *n.* the state or condition of being an alien.

alienate /áyliənayt/ *v.tr.* **1 a** cause (a person) to become unfriendly or hostile. **b** (often foll. by *from*) cause (a person) to feel isolated or estranged from (friends, society, etc.). **2** transfer ownership of (property) to another person etc. ▫▫ **alienator** *n.* [ME f. L *alienare alienat-* (as ALIEN)]

■ **1** estrange, isolate, detach, distance, put at a distance; antagonize; (*alienate from*) turn away from, wean away from.

alienation /áyliənáysh'n/ *n.* **1** the act or result of alienating. **2** (*Theatr.* **alienation effect**) a dramatic effect whereby an audience remains objective, not identifying with the characters or action of a play.

alienist /áyliənist/ *n. US* a psychiatrist, esp. a legal adviser on psychiatric problems. [F *aliéniste* (as ALIEN)]

aliform /áyliform/ *adj.* wing-shaped. [mod.L *aliformis* f. L *ala* wing: see -FORM]

alight[1] /əlít/ *v.intr.* **1 a** (often foll. by *from*) descend from a vehicle. **b** dismount from a horse. **2** descend and settle; come to earth from the air. **3** (foll. by *on*) find by chance; notice. [OE *ālīhtan* (as A-[2], *līhtan* LIGHT[2] *v.*)]

■ **1 a** see DISEMBARK.

alight[2] /əlít/ *predic.adj.* **1** on fire; burning (*they set the old shed alight*; *is the fire still alight?*). **2** lighted up; excited (*eyes alight with expectation*). [ME, prob. f. phr. *on a light* (= lighted) *fire*]

■ **1** see ABLAZE *adj.* 1. **2** see ABLAZE 2, FERVENT 1.

align /əlín/ *v.tr.* **1** put in a straight line or bring into line (*three books were neatly aligned on the shelf*). **2** esp. *Polit.* (usu. foll. by *with*) bring (oneself etc.) into agreement or alliance with (a cause, policy, political party, etc.). ▫▫ **alignment** *n.* [F *aligner* f. phr. *à ligne* into line: see LINE[1]]

alike /əlík/ *adj.* & *adv.* ● *adj.* (usu. *predic.*) similar, like one another; indistinguishable. ● *adv.* in a similar way or manner (*all were treated alike*). [ME f. OE *gelīc* and ON *glíkr* (LIKE[1])]

■ *adj.* similar, akin, resembling *or* like one another, akin to one another, similar to one another, showing *or* exhibiting a resemblance, much of a muchness; agnate, allied, related; indistinguishable, identical, undifferentiated, like two peas in a pod; (like) Tweedledum and Tweedledee. ● *adv.* in like manner, in the same manner *or* way, similarly, the same, equally, uniformly, identically.

aliment /állimənt/ *n. formal* **1** food. **2** support or mental sustenance. ▫▫ **alimental** /álliméntʼl/ *adj.* [ME f. F *aliment* or L *alimentum* f. *alere* nourish]

alimentary /álliméntəri, -tri/ *adj.* of, relating to, or providing nourishment or sustenance. ▫ **alimentary canal** *Anat.* the passage along which food is passed from the mouth to the anus during digestion. [L *alimentarius* (as ALIMENT)]

alimentation /állimentáysh'n/ *n.* **1** nourishment; feeding. **2** maintenance, support; supplying with the necessities of life. [F *alimentation* or med.L *alimentatio* f. *alimentare* (as ALIMENT)]

alimony /álliməni/ *n.* the money payable by a man to his wife or former wife or by a woman to her husband or former husband after they are separated or divorced. ¶ In UK use replaced by *maintenance*. [L *alimonia* nutriment f. *alere* nourish]

■ maintenance.

A-line /áylīn/ *adj.* (of a garment) having a narrow waist or shoulders and somewhat flared skirt.

aliphatic /állifáttik/ *adj. Chem.* of, denoting, or relating to organic compounds in which carbon atoms form open chains, not aromatic rings. [Gk *aleiphar -atos* fat]

aliquot /állikwot/ *adj.* & *n.* ● *adj.* (of a part or portion) contained by the whole an integral or whole number of times (*4 is an aliquot part of 12*). ● *n.* **1** an aliquot part; an integral factor. **2** (in general use) any known fraction of a whole; a sample. [F *aliquote* f. L *aliquot* some, so many]

alive /əlív/ *adj.* (usu. *predic.*) **1** (of a person, animal, plant, etc.) living, not dead. **2 a** (of a thing) existing; continuing; in operation or action (*kept his interest alive*). **b** under discussion; provoking interest (*the topic is still very much alive today*). **3** (of a person or animal) lively, active. **4** charged with an electric current; connected to a source of electricity. **5** (foll. by *to*) aware of; alert or responsive to. **6** (foll. by *with*) **a** swarming or teeming with. **b** full of. ▫ **alive and kicking** *colloq.* very active; lively. **alive and well** still alive or active (esp. despite contrary assumptions or rumours). ▫▫ **aliveness** *n.* [OE *on līfe* (as A[2], LIFE)]

■ **1** living, live, breathing, *archaic* quick, *joc.* in the land of the living, among the living. **2** in operation *or* action; existing, continuing, in existence; discussed, under discussion, on the agenda. **3** alert, active, lively, vivacious, vibrant, quick, spirited, animated, brisk, spry, sprightly, vigorous, energetic, dynamic, vitalized, *colloq.* alive and kicking. **5** (*alive to*) sensitive *or* alert *or* responsive to, aware *or* conscious *or* mindful of, in touch with, cognizant *or* apprised of, *colloq.* wise to. **6 a** astir, teeming, swarming, thronging, crowded, packed, buzzing, crawling, jumping, bustling, humming, *colloq.*

lousy. □ **alive and kicking** *colloq.* full of beans, full of pep *or* go *or* life, full of vim and vigour; see also ALIVE 3 above.

alizarin /əlízzərin/ *n.* **1** the red colouring matter of madder root, used in dyeing. **2** (*attrib.*) (of a dye) derived from or similar to this pigment. [F *alizarine* f. *alizari* madder f. Arab. *al-ʿiṣara* pressed juice f. *ʿaṣara* to press fruit]

alkahest /álkəhest/ *n.* (also **alcahest**) the universal solvent sought by alchemists. [sham Arab., prob. invented by Paracelsus]

alkali /álkəlī/ *n.* (*pl.* **alkalis**) **1 a** any of a class of substances that liberate hydroxide ions in water, usu. form caustic or corrosive solutions, turn litmus blue, and have a pH of more than 7, e.g. caustic soda. **b** any other substance with similar but weaker properties, e.g. sodium carbonate. **2** *Chem.* any substance that reacts with or neutralizes hydrogen ions. □ **alkali metals** any of the univalent group of metals, lithium, sodium, potassium, rubidium, and caesium, whose hydroxides are alkalis. □□ **alkalimeter** /álkəlímmitər/ *n.* **alkalimetry** /álkəlímmitri/ *n.* [ME f. med.L, f. Arab. *al-ḳalī* calcined ashes f. *ḳala* fry]

alkaline /álkəlīn/ *adj.* of, relating to, or having the nature of an alkali; rich in alkali. □ **alkaline earth 1** any of the bivalent group of metals, beryllium, magnesium, calcium, strontium, barium, and radium. **2** an oxide of the lime group. □□ **alkalinity** /álkəlínniti/ *n.*

alkaloid /álkəloyd/ *n.* any of a series of nitrogenous organic compounds of plant origin, many of which are used as drugs, e.g. morphine, quinine. [G (as ALKALI)]

alkalosis /álkəlṓsiss/ *n. Med.* an excessive alkaline condition of the body fluids or tissues.

alkane /álkayn/ *n. Chem.* any of a series of saturated aliphatic hydrocarbons having the general formula C_nH_{2n+2}, including methane, ethane, and propane. [ALKYL + -ANE[2]]

alkanet /álkənet/ *n.* **1 a** any plant of the genus *Alkanna*, esp. *A. tinctoria*, yielding a red dye from its roots. **b** the dye itself. **2** any of various similar plants. [ME f. Sp. *alcaneta* dimin. of *alcana* f. Arab. *al-ḥinnāʾ* the henna shrub]

alkene /álkeen/ *n. Chem.* any of a series of unsaturated aliphatic hydrocarbons containing a double bond and having the general formula C_nH_{2n}, including ethylene and propene. [ALKYL + -ENE]

alkyd /álkid/ *n.* any of the group of synthetic resins derived from various alcohols and acids. [ALKYL + ACID]

alkyl /álkīl, -kil/ *n.* (in full **alkyl radical**) *Chem.* any radical derived from an alkane by the removal of a hydrogen atom. [G *Alkohol* ALCOHOL + -YL]

alkylate /álkilayt/ *v.tr. Chem.* introduce an alkyl radical into (a compound).

alkyne /álkīn/ *n. Chem.* any of a series of unsaturated aliphatic hydrocarbons containing a triple bond and having the general formula $C_n H_{2n-2}$, including acetylene. [ALKYL + -YNE]

all /awl/ *adj.*, *n.*, & *adv.* ● *adj.* **1 a** the whole amount, quantity, or extent of (*waited all day*; *all his life*; *we all know why*; *take it all*). **b** (with *pl.*) the entire number of (*all the others left*; *all ten men*; *the children are all boys*; *film stars all*). **2** any whatever (*beyond all doubt*). **3** greatest possible (*with all speed*). ● *n.* **1 a** all the persons or things concerned (*all were present*; *all were thrown away*). **b** everything (*all is lost*; *that is all*). **2** (foll. by *of*) **a** the whole of (*take all of it*). **b** every one of (*all of us*). **c** *colloq.* as much as (*all of six feet tall*). **d** *colloq.* affected by; in a state of (*all of a dither*). **3** one's whole strength or resources (prec. by *my*, *your*, etc.). **4** (in games) on both sides (*two goals all*). ¶ Widely used with *of* in sense 2a, b, esp. when followed by a pronoun or by a noun implying a number of persons or things, as in *all of the children are here*. However, use with mass nouns (as in *all of the bread*) is often avoided. ● *adv.* **1 a** entirely, quite (*dressed all in black*; *all round the room*; *the all-important thing*). **b** as an intensifier (*a book all about ships*; *stop all this grumbling*). **2** *colloq.* very (*went all shy*). **3** (foll. by *the* + compar.) **a** by so much; to that extent (*if they go, all the better*). **b** in the full degree to be expected (*that makes it all the worse*). □ **all along** all the time (*he was joking all along*). **all-American 1** representing the whole of (or only) America or the US. **2** truly American (*all-American boy*). **all and sundry** everyone. **all-around** *US* = *all-round*. **All Blacks** *colloq.* the New Zealand international Rugby Union football team. **all but** very nearly (*it was all but impossible*; *he was all but drowned*). **all-clear** a signal that danger or difficulty is over. **All Fools' Day** 1 April. **all for** *colloq.* strongly in favour of. **All Hallows** see HALLOW. **all-important** crucial; vitally important. **all in** *colloq.* exhausted. **all-in** (*attrib.*) inclusive of all. **all in all** everything considered. **all-in wrestling** wrestling with few or no restrictions. **all manner of** see MANNER. **all of a sudden** see SUDDEN. **all one** (or **the same**) (usu. foll. by *to*) a matter of indifference (*it's all one to me*). **all out** involving all one's strength; at full speed (also (with hyphen) *attrib.*: *an all-out effort*). **all over 1** completely finished. **2** in or on all parts of (esp. the body) (*went hot and cold all over*; *mud all over the carpet*). **3** *colloq.* typically (*that is you all over*). **4** *sl.* effusively attentive to (a person). **all-purpose** suitable for many uses. **all right** (*predic.*) **1** satisfactory; safe and sound; in good condition. **2** satisfactorily, as desired (*it worked out all right*). **3 a** an interjection expressing consent or assent to a proposal or order. **b** as an intensifier (*that's the one all right*). **all-right** *attrib.adj. colloq.* fine, acceptable (*an all-right guy*). **all round 1** in all respects (*a good performance all round*). **2** for each person (*he bought drinks all round*). **all-round** (*attrib.*) (of a person) versatile. **all-rounder** *Brit.* a versatile person. **All Saints' Day** 1 Nov. **all the same** nevertheless, in spite of this (*he was innocent but was punished all the same*). **all set** *colloq.* ready to start. **All Souls' Day** 2 Nov. **all there** *colloq.* mentally alert. **all-time** (of a record etc.) hitherto unsurpassed. **all the time** see TIME. **all together** all at once; all in one place or in a group (*they came all together*) (cf. ALTOGETHER). **all told** in all. **all-up weight** the total weight of an aircraft with passengers, cargo, etc., when airborne. **all very well** *colloq.* an expression used to reject or to imply scepticism about a favourable or consoling remark. **all the way** the whole distance; completely. **at all** (with *neg.* or *interrog.*) in any way; to any extent (*did not swim at all*; *did you like it at all?*). **be all up with** see UP. **in all** in total number; altogether (*there were 10 people in all*). **on all fours** see FOUR. **one and all** everyone. [OE *all*, *eall*, prob. f. Gmc]

■ *n.* **1 a** see EVERYONE, EVERYTHING 1. **b** see EVERYTHING 1. **2 a** see WHOLE *n.* 2. □ **all and sundry** see EVERYONE. **all but** see NEARLY 1. **all-important** see IMPORTANT 1. **all in** see *exhausted* (EXHAUST *v.* 2). **all-in** see INCLUSIVE 3. **all in all** see *on the whole* (WHOLE). **all out** see BREAKNECK, THOROUGH 1. **all over 2** see EVERYWHERE. **all-purpose** see VERSATILE 2. **all right 1** see SATISFACTORILY 1. **2** see OK *adv.* **all-right** see SATISFACTORY 1. **all-round** see VERSATILE 1. **all the same** see NEVERTHELESS. **all set** see READY *adj.* 1, 2. **all there** see ALERT *adj.* 2. **all together** see *at one time* 2 (TIME). **all the way** see *hook, line and sinker*, WIDE *adv.* 2. **at all** see SCARCELY 2. **in all** see ALTOGETHER 3. **one and all** see EVERYONE.

alla breve /állə bráyvay/ *n. Mus.* a time signature indicating 2 or 4 minim beats in a bar. [It., = at the BREVE]

alla cappella var. of A CAPPELLA.

Allah /állə/ *n.* the name of God among Arabs and Muslims. [Arab. *ʾallāh* contr. of *al-ʾilāh* f. *al* the + *ilāh* god]

allantois /əlántō-iss/ *n.* (*pl.* **allantoides** /álləntṓ-ideez/) *Zool.* one of several membranes that develop in embryonic reptiles, birds, or mammals. □□ **allantoic** /álləntṓ-ik/ *adj.* [mod.L f. Gk *allantoeidēs* sausage-shaped]

allay /əláy/ *v.tr.* **1** diminish (fear, suspicion, etc.). **2** relieve or alleviate (pain, hunger, etc.). [OE *ālecgan* (as A-[2], LAY[1])]

■ **2** see RELIEVE 2.

allegation /álligáysh'n/ *n.* **1** an assertion, esp. an unproved one. **2** the act or an instance of alleging. [ME f. F *allégation* or L *allegatio* f. *allegare* allege]

■ assertion, avowal, asseveration, claim, declaration,

deposition; charge, accusation, indictment, statement, complaint.

allege /əléj/ *v.tr.* **1** (often foll. by *that* + clause, or *to* + infin.) declare to be the case, esp. without proof. **2** advance as an argument or excuse. □□ **alleged** *adj.* [ME f. AF *alegier*, OF *esligier* clear at law; confused in sense with L *allegare*: see ALLEGATION]

▪ declare, claim, profess, state, assert, charge, hold, affirm, avow, asseverate, *formal* aver; maintain, contend, report, say. □□ **alleged** claimed, avowed, professed, ostensible, stated; purported, so-called, suspected, supposed, assumed, presumed, reputed; hypothetical, conjectural.

allegedly /əléjidli/ *adv.* as is alleged or said to be the case.

allegiance /əléejənss/ *n.* **1** loyalty (to a person or cause etc.). **2** the duty of a subject to his or her sovereign or government. [ME f. AF f. OF *ligeance* (as LIEGE): perh. assoc. with ALLIANCE]

▪ see LOYALTY.

allegorical /álligórrik'l/ *adj.* (also **allegoric** /-rik/) consisting of or relating to allegory; by means of allegory. □□ **allegorically** *adv.*

allegorize /álligərīz/ *v.tr.* (also **-ise**) treat as or by means of an allegory. □□ **allegorization** /-záysh'n/ *n.*

allegory /álligəri/ *n.* (*pl.* **-ies**) **1** a story, play, poem, picture, etc., in which the meaning or message is represented symbolically. **2** the use of such symbols. **3** a symbol. □□ **allegorist** *n.* [ME f. OF *allegorie* f. L *allegoria* f. Gk *allēgoria* f. *allos* other + *-agoria* speaking]

allegretto /álligréttō/ *adv.*, *adj.*, & *n.* *Mus.* ● *adv.* & *adj.* in a fairly brisk tempo. ● *n.* (*pl.* **-os**) an allegretto passage or movement. [It., dimin. of ALLEGRO]

allegro /əláygrō, əlég-/ *adv.*, *adj.*, & *n.* *Mus.* ● *adv.* & *adj.* in a brisk tempo. ● *n.* (*pl.* **-os**) an allegro passage or movement. [It., = lively, gay]

allele /álleel/ *n.* (also **allel** /állel/) one of the (usu. two) alternative forms of a gene. □□ **allelic** /əléelik/ *adj.* [G *Allel*, abbr. of ALLELOMORPH]

allelomorph /əléeləmorf/ *n.* = ALLELE. □□ **allelomorphic** /-mórfik/ *adj.* [Gk *allēl-* one another + *morphē* form]

alleluia /álliloṓyə/ *int.* & *n.* (also **alleluya**, **hallelujah** /hál-/) ● *int.* God be praised. ● *n.* **1** praise to God. **2** a song of praise to God. **3** *RC Ch.* the part of the mass including this. [ME f. eccl.L f. (Septuagint) Gk *allēlouia* f. Heb. *hall^e lûyāh* praise ye the Lord]

allemande /álmoND/ *n.* **1** **a** the name of several German dances. **b** the music for any of these, esp. as a movement of a suite. **2** a figure in a country dance. [F, = German (dance)]

Allen key /állən/ *n. propr.* a spanner designed to fit into and turn an Allen screw. [*Allen*, name of the US manufacturer]

Allen screw /állən/ *n. propr.* a screw with a hexagonal socket in the head.

allergen /állərjən/ *n.* any substance that causes an allergic reaction. □□ **allergenic** /állərjénnik/ *adj.* [ALLERGY + -GEN]

allergic /əlérjik/ *adj.* **1** (foll. by *to*) **a** having an allergy to. **b** *colloq.* having a strong dislike for (a person or thing). **2** caused by or relating to an allergy.

allergy /állərji/ *n.* (*pl.* **-ies**) **1** *Med.* a condition of reacting adversely to certain substances, esp. particular foods, pollen, fur, or dust. **2** *colloq.* an antipathy. □□ **allergist** *n.* [G *Allergie*, after *Energie* ENERGY, f. Gk *allos* other]

alleviate /əléeviayt/ *v.tr.* lessen or make less severe (pain, suffering, etc.). □□ **alleviation** /-áysh'n/ *n.* **alleviative** /əléeviətiv/ *adj.* **alleviator** *n.* **alleviatory** /əléeviətəri/ *adj.* [LL *alleviare* lighten f. L *allevare* (as AD-, *levare* raise)]

▪ see EASE *v.* 1a, 2a.

alley[1] /álli/ *n.* (*pl.* **-eys**) **1** (also **alley-way**) **a** a narrow street. **b** a narrow passageway, esp. between or behind buildings. **2** a path or walk in a park or garden. **3** an enclosure for skittles, bowling, etc. **4** (in lawn tennis) either of the two side strips of a doubles court. □ **alley cat** a stray town cat often mangy or half wild. **up** (or **right up**) **one's alley** (or **street**) see STREET. [ME f. OF *alee* walking, passage f. *aler* go f. L *ambulare* walk]

alley[2] var. of ALLY[2].

alliaceous /álliáyshəss/ *adj.* **1** of or relating to the genus *Allium*. **2** tasting or smelling like onion or garlic. [mod.L *alliaceus* f. L *allium* garlic]

alliance /əlī́ənss/ *n.* **1** **a** union or agreement to cooperate, esp. of States by treaty or families by marriage. **b** the parties involved. **2** (**Alliance**) a political party formed by the allying of separate parties. **3** a relationship resulting from an affinity in nature or qualities etc. (*the old alliance between logic and metaphysics*). **4** *Bot.* a group of allied families. [ME f. OF *aliance* (as ALLY[1])]

▪ **1** union, confederation, federation, league, association, coalition, affiliation; axis, pact, connection, bond. **3** affinity, connection, marriage, closeness; see also KINSHIP 2.

allied /állīd/ *adj.* **1** **a** united or associated in an alliance. **b** (**Allied**) of or relating to Britain and her allies in the wars of 1914–18 or 1939–45. **2** connected or related (*studied medicine and allied subjects*).

alligator /álligaytər/ *n.* **1** a large reptile of the crocodile family native to the Americas and China, with upper teeth that lie outside the lower teeth and a head broader and shorter than that of the crocodile. **2** (in general use) any of several large members of the crocodile family. **3** **a** the skin of such an animal or material resembling it. **b** (in *pl.*) shoes of this. □ **alligator clip** a clip with teeth for gripping. **alligator pear** an avocado. **alligator tortoise** a large freshwater snapping turtle. [Sp. *el lagarto* the lizard f. L *lacerta*]

alliterate /əlíttərayt/ *v.* **1** *intr.* **a** contain alliteration. **b** use alliteration in speech or writing. **2** *tr.* **a** construct (a phrase etc.) with alliteration. **b** speak or pronounce with alliteration. □□ **alliterative** /əlíttərətiv/ *adj.* [back-form. f. ALLITERATION]

alliteration /əlíttəráysh'n/ *n.* the occurrence of the same letter or sound at the beginning of adjacent or closely connected words (e.g. *cool, calm, and collected*). [mod.L *alliteratio* (as AD-, *littera* letter)]

allium /álliəm/ *n.* any plant of the genus *Allium*, usu. bulbous and strong smelling, e.g. onion and garlic. [L, = garlic]

allo- /állō, əló/ *comb. form* other (*allophone*; *allogamy*). [Gk *allos* other]

allocate /álləkayt/ *v.tr.* (usu. foll. by *to*) assign or devote to (a purpose, person, or place). □□ **allocable** /álləkəb'l/ *adj.* **allocation** /álləkáysh'n/ *n.* **allocator** *n.* [med.L *allocare* f. *locus* place]

▪ see ALLOT, ALLOW 2, ASSIGN 1a.

allocution /álləkyoṓsh'n/ *n.* formal or hortatory speech or manner of address. [L *allocutio* f. *alloqui allocut-* speak to]

allogamy /əlóggəmi/ *n.* *Bot.* cross-fertilization in plants. [ALLO- + Gk *-gamia* f. *gamos* marriage]

allomorph /álləmorf/ *n.* *Linguistics* any of two or more alternative forms of a morpheme. □□ **allomorphic** /álləmórfik/ *adj.* [ALLO- + MORPHEME]

allopath /álləpath/ *n.* one who practises allopathy. [F *allopathe* back-form. f. *allopathie* = ALLOPATHY]

allopathy /əlóppəthi/ *n.* the treatment of disease by conventional means, i.e. with drugs having opposite effects to the symptoms (cf. HOMOEOPATHY). □□ **allopathic** /álləpáthik/ *adj.* **allopathist** *n.* [G *Allopathie* (as ALLO-, -PATHY)]

allophone /álləfōn/ *n.* *Linguistics* any of the variant sounds forming a single phoneme. □□ **allophonic** /álləfónnik/ *adj.* [ALLO- + PHONEME]

allot /əlót/ *v.tr.* (**allotted**, **allotting**) **1** give or apportion to (a person) as a share or task; distribute officially to (*they allotted us each a pair of boots*; *the men were allotted duties*). **2** (foll. by *to*) give or distribute officially (*a sum was allotted to each charity*). [OF *aloter* f. *a* to + LOT]

▪ apportion, allocate, allow, assign, give, hand, deal,

earmark for; (*allot to*) divide among(st), share (out) among(st), distribute to, hand *or* deal out to, parcel *or* dole out to, deal (out) to, dispense to.

allotment /əlótmənt/ *n.* **1** a small piece of land rented (usu. from a local authority) for cultivation. **2** a share allotted. **3** the action of allotting.
■ **1** garden plot, kitchen garden, patch, tract, plot. **2** share, apportionment, ration, portion, quota, lot, allowance, measure. **3** see DISTRIBUTION 1, 2a.

allotrope /állətrōp/ *n.* any of two or more different physical forms in which an element can exist (*graphite, charcoal, and diamond are all allotropes of carbon*). [back-form. f. ALLOTROPY]

allotropy /əlótrəpi/ *n.* the existence of two or more different physical forms of a chemical element. □□ **allotropic** /állətróppik/ *adj.* **allotropical** /állətróppik'l/ *adj.* [Gk *allotropos* of another form f. *allos* different + *tropos* manner f. *trepō* to turn]

allottee /əlotée/ *n.* a person to whom something is allotted.

allow /əlów/ *v.* **1** *tr.* permit (a practice, a person to do something, a thing to happen, etc.) (*smoking is not allowed; we allowed them to speak*). **2** *tr.* give or provide; permit (a person) to have (a limited quantity or sum) (*we were allowed £500 a year*). **3** *tr.* provide or set aside for a purpose; add or deduct in consideration of something (*allow 10% for inflation*). **4** *tr.* **a** admit, agree, concede (*he allowed that it was so; 'You know best,' he allowed*). **b** *US* state; be of the opinion. **5** *refl.* permit oneself, indulge oneself in (conduct) (*allowed herself to be persuaded; allowed myself a few angry words*). **6** *intr.* (foll. by *of*) admit of. **7** *intr.* (foll. by *for*) take into consideration or account; make addition or deduction corresponding to (*allowing for wastage*). □□ **allowable** *adj.* **allowably** *adv.* [ME, orig. = 'praise', f. OF *alouer* f. L *allaudare* to praise, and med.L *allocare* to place]
■ **1** agree to, permit, give leave *or* permission for, authorize, admit, entertain, consent to, give the go-ahead *or colloq.* green light to; tolerate, suffer, stand (for), sanction, countenance, consider, put up with, *literary* brook; (*allow to*) let. **2** give, let have, grant, allot, allocate, assign, approve; provide *or* furnish with. **3** make allowance(s) *or* concession(s) for, set apart *or* aside, put aside, take into account *or* consideration; add (in), include; deduct, take away, exclude. **4 a** agree, acknowledge, admit, grant, concede, own, confess. **5** permit oneself, give oneself, grant oneself; (*allow oneself to*) let oneself. **7** see CONSIDER 4. □□ **allowable** see PERMISSIBLE. **allowably** see *acceptably* (ACCEPTABLE).

allowance /əlówənss/ *n.* & *v.* ● *n.* **1** an amount or sum allowed to a person, esp. regularly for a stated purpose. **2** an amount allowed in reckoning. **3** a deduction or discount (*an allowance on your old cooker*). **4** (foll. by *of*) tolerance of. ● *v.tr.* **1** make an allowance to (a person). **2** supply in limited quantities. □ **make allowances** (often foll. by *for*) **1** take into consideration (mitigating circumstances) (*made allowances for his demented state*). **2** look with tolerance upon, make excuses for (a person, bad behaviour, etc.). [ME f. OF *alouance* (as ALLOW)]
■ *n.* **1** stipend, grant, dole, pin *or* pocket money, perquisite, quota, ration; remittance, remuneration; pension, annuity, quarterage, per diem. **3** deduction, discount, reduction, rebate, payment, recompense, compensation, remuneration, reimbursement, remittal; tare; *hist.* tret. **4** tolerance, toleration, sufferance, concession, sanction, support, approval. □ **make allowances** (*make allowances for*) **1** take into consideration *or* account, consider, bear in mind, have regard for. **2** be patient *or* tolerant with, excuse, make concessions for.

allowedly /əlówidli/ *adv.* as is generally allowed or acknowledged.

alloy /álloy, əlóy/ *n.* & *v.* ● *n.* **1** a mixture of two or more chemical elements, at least one of which is a metal, e.g. brass (a mixture of copper and zinc). **2** an inferior metal mixed esp. with gold or silver. ● *v.tr.* **1** mix (metals). **2** debase (a pure substance) by admixture. **3** moderate. [F *aloi* (n.), *aloyer* (v.) f. OF *aloier*, *aleier* combine f. L *alligare* bind]
■ *n.* **1** mixture, mix, combination, compound, composite, blend, amalgam. **2** admixture. ● *v.* **1** see MIX *v.* 1, 3. **2** contaminate, pollute, adulterate, debase, diminish, impair, vitiate. **3** change, modify, temper, alter, moderate, reduce, diminish.

allseed /áwlseed/ *n.* any of various plants producing much seed, esp. *Radiola linoides*.

allspice /áwlspīss/ *n.* **1** the aromatic spice obtained from the ground berry of the pimento plant, *Pimenta dioica*. **2** the berry of this. **3** any of various other aromatic shrubs.

allude /əlóód, əlyóód/ *v.intr.* (foll. by *to*) **1** refer, esp. indirectly, covertly, or briefly to. **2** *disp.* mention. [L *alludere* (as AD-, *ludere lus-* play)]
■ **1** see REFER 7, 8.

allure /əlyóor/ *v.* & *n.* ● *v.tr.* attract, charm, or fascinate. ● *n.* attractiveness, personal charm, fascination. □□ **allurement** *n.* **alluring** *adj.* **alluringly** *adv.* [ME f. OF *alurer* attract (as AD-, *luere* LURE *v.* 1)]
■ *v.* see ATTRACT 2, CAPTIVATE. ● *n.* see CHARM *n.* 1a, b.

allusion /əlóózh'n, əlyóó-/ *n.* (often foll. by *to*) a reference, esp. a covert, passing, or indirect one. ¶ Often confused with *illusion*. [F *allusion* or LL *allusio* (as ALLUDE)]
■ see REFERENCE *n.* 3b.

allusive /əlóóssiv, əlyóó-/ *adj.* **1** (often foll. by *to*) containing an allusion. **2** containing many allusions. □□ **allusively** *adv.* **allusiveness** *n.*

alluvial /əlóóviəl/ *adj.* & *n.* ● *adj.* of or relating to alluvium. ● *n.* alluvium, esp. containing a precious metal.

alluvion /əlóóviən/ *n.* **1** the wash of the sea against the shore, or of a river against its banks. **2 a** a large overflow of water. **b** matter deposited by this, esp. alluvium. **3** the formation of new land by the movement of the sea or of a river. [F f. L *alluvio -onis* f. *luere* wash]

alluvium /əlóóviəm/ *n.* (*pl.* **alluvia** /-viə/ or **alluviums**) a deposit of usu. fine fertile soil left during a time of flood, esp. in a river valley or delta. [L neut. of *alluvius* adj. f. *luere* wash]

ally[1] /állī/ *n.* & *v.* ● *n.* (*pl.* **-ies**) **1** a State formally cooperating or united with another for a special purpose, esp. by a treaty. **2** a person or organization that cooperates with or helps another. ● *v.tr.* /also əlī́/ (**-ies, -ied**) (often foll. by *with*) combine or unite in alliance. [ME f. OF *al(e)ier* f. L *alligare* bind: cf. ALLOY]

ally[2] /álli/ *n.* (also **alley**) (*pl.* **-ies** or **-eys**) a choice playing-marble made of marble, alabaster, or glass. [perh. dimin. of ALABASTER]

-ally /əli/ *suffix* forming adverbs from adjectives in *-al* (cf. -AL, -LY[2], -ICALLY).

allyl /állil, -līl/ *n. Chem.* the unsaturated univalent radical $CH_2{=}CH{-}CH_2{\cdot}$. [L *allium* garlic + -YL]

almacantar var. of ALMUCANTAR.

Alma Mater /álmə maátər, máytər/ *n.* the university, school, or college one attends or attended. [L, = bounteous mother]

almanac /áwlmənak, ól-/ *n.* (also **almanack**) an annual calendar of months and days, usu. with astronomical data and other information. [ME f. med.L *almanac(h)* f. Gk *almenikhiaka*]

almandine /álməndeen, -dīn/ *n.* a kind of garnet with a violet tint. [F, alt. of obs. *alabandine* f. med.L *alabandina* f. *Alabanda*, ancient city in Asia Minor]

almighty /áwlmīti/ *adj.* & *adv.* ● *adj.* **1** having complete power; omnipotent. **2** (**the Almighty**) God. **3** *sl.* very great (*an almighty crash*). ● *adv. sl.* extremely; very much. [OE *ælmihtig* (as ALL, MIGHTY)]

almond /aámənd/ *n.* **1** the oval nutlike seed (kernel) of the stone-fruit from the tree *Prunus dulcis*, of which there are sweet and bitter varieties. **2** the tree itself, of the rose family and allied to the peach and plum. □ **almond eyes** narrow almond-shaped eyes. **almond oil** the oil expressed from the seed (esp. the bitter variety), used for toilet preparations, flavouring, and medicinal purposes. **almond paste** = MARZIPAN. [ME f. OF *alemande* etc. f. med.L *amandula* f. L *amygdala* f. Gk *amugdalē*: assoc. with words in AL-]

almoner /aámənər/ *n.* **1** *Brit.* a social worker attached to a hospital and seeing to the after-care of patients. ¶ Now usu. called *medical social worker*. **2** *hist.* an official distributor of alms. [ME f. AF *aumoner*, OF *aumonier*, ult. f. med.L *eleēmosynarius* (as ALMS)]

almost /áwlmōst/ *adv.* all but; very nearly. [OE *ælmǣst* for the most part (as ALL, MOST)]

■ nearly, (just) about, practically, virtually, bordering on, on the brink of, verging on, on the verge of, more or less, little short of, not quite, all but, *archaic* near, *archaic or rhet.* wellnigh, *colloq.* damn(ed) near.

alms /aamz/ *n.pl. hist.* the charitable donation of money or food to the poor. [OE *ælmysse*, *-messe*, f. Gmc ult. f. Gk *eleēmosunē* compassionateness f. *eleēmōn* (adj.) f. *eleos* compassion]

almshouse /aámz-howss/ *n. hist.* a house founded by charity for the poor.

almucantar /álməkántər/ *n.* (also **almacantar**) *Astron.* a line of constant altitude above the horizon. [ME f. med.L *almucantarath* or F *almucantara* etc., f. Arab. *almuḳanṭarāt* sundial f. *ḳanṭara* arch]

aloe /állō/ *n.* **1** any plant of the genus *Aloe*, usu. having toothed fleshy leaves. **2** (in *pl.*) (in full **bitter aloes**) a strong laxative obtained from the bitter juice of various species of aloe. **3** (also **American aloe**) an agave native to Central America. [OE *al(e)we* f. L *aloē* f. Gk]

aloetic /állō-éttik/ *adj.* & *n.* ● *adj.* of or relating to an aloe. ● *n.* a medicine containing aloes. [Gk *aloē* aloe, on the false analogy of *diuretic* etc.]

aloft /əlóft/ *predic.adj.* & *adv.* **1** high up; overhead. **2** upwards. [ME f. ON *á lopt(i)* f. *á* in, on, to + *lopt* air: cf. LIFT, LOFT]

■ **1** high up, above, overhead, (up) in the air, in flight, up (above), on high. **2** upwards, up, heavenwards, skywards.

alogical /áylójik'l/ *adj.* **1** not logical. **2** opposed to logic.

alone /əlṓn/ *predic.adj.* & *adv.* **1 a** without others present (*they wanted to be alone*; *the tree stood alone*). **b** without others' help (*succeeded alone*). **c** lonely and wretched (*felt alone*). **2** (often foll. by *in*) standing by oneself in an opinion, quality, etc. (*was alone in thinking this*). **3** only, exclusively (*you alone can help me*). □ **go it alone** act by oneself without assistance. □□ **aloneness** *n.* [ME f. ALL + ONE]

■ **1 a** unaccompanied, unescorted, solitar(il)y, by oneself *or* itself, on one's *or* its own, by *or* on one's lonesome, solo, solus, unattended, isolated, *sl.* on one's jack, on one's Jack Jones, *Austral. sl.* on one's pat, *Brit. sl.* on one's tod. **b** unassisted, unaided, unhelped, single-handed; by oneself *or* itself, single-handedly, independently, individually, personally, off one's own bat, under one's own steam. **c** lonely, wretched, friendless, abandoned, forsaken, desolate, remote, deserted. **2** unique, on one's own, without parallel; unequalled, unparalleled, nonpareil, unrivalled, unsurpassed, without equal, untypical, peerless, matchless. **3** only, solely, exclusively; simply, just, merely. □ **go it alone** act independently *or* by oneself, do it off one's own bat, do it under one's own steam. □□ **aloneness** see *loneliness* (LONELY), SOLITUDE 1.

along /əlóng/ *prep.* & *adv.* ● *prep.* **1** from one end to the other end of (*a handkerchief with lace along the edge*). **2** on or through any part of the length of (*was walking along the road*). **3** beside or through the length of (*shelves stood along the wall*). ● *adv.* **1** onward; into a more advanced state (*come along*; *getting along nicely*). **2** at or to a particular place; arriving (*I'll be along soon*). **3** in company with a person, esp. oneself (*bring a book along*). **4** beside or through part or the whole length of a thing. □ **along with** in addition to; together with. [OE *andlang* f. WG, rel. to LONG[1]]

alongshore /əlóngshór/ *adv.* along or by the shore.

alongside /əlóngsīd/ *adv.* & *prep.* ● *adv.* at or to the side (of a ship, pier, etc.). ● *prep.* close to the side of; next to. □ **alongside of** side by side with; together or simultaneously with.

■ *prep.* see BESIDE 1.

aloof /əlóōf/ *adj.* & *adv.* ● *adj.* distant, unsympathetic. ● *adv.* away, apart (*he kept aloof from his colleagues*). □□ **aloofly** *adv.* **aloofness** *n.* [orig. Naut., f. A[2] + LUFF]

■ *adj.* distant, remote, cold, cool, chilly, unresponsive, undemonstrative, reserved, indifferent, unapproachable, indrawn, withdrawn; unsympathetic, haughty, superior, supercilious, standoffish, antisocial, unsociable, unfriendly, unsocial, *colloq.* offish, stuck-up. ● *adv.* apart, away, at a distance, separate, at arm's length. □□ **aloofness** see DISTANCE *n.* 4.

alopecia /álləpeéshə/ *n. Med.* the absence (complete or partial) of hair from areas of the body where it normally grows; baldness. [L f. Gk *alōpekia* fox-mange f. *alōpēx* fox]

aloud /əlówd/ *adv.* **1** audibly; not silently or in a whisper. **2** *archaic* loudly. [A[2] + LOUD]

alow /əlṓ/ *adv.* & *predic.adj. Naut.* in or into the lower part of a ship. [A[2] + LOW[1]]

alp /alp/ *n.* **1 a** a high mountain. **b** (**the Alps**) the high range of mountains in Switzerland and adjoining countries. **2** (in Switzerland) pasture-land on a mountainside. [orig. pl., f. F f. L *Alpes* f. Gk *Alpeis*]

alpaca /alpákkə/ *n.* **1** a S. American mammal, *Lama pacos*, related to the llama, with long shaggy hair. **2** the wool from the animal. **3** fabric made from the wool, with or without other fibres. [Sp. f. Aymará or Quechua]

alpargata /álpaargaátə/ *n.* a light canvas shoe with a plaited fibre sole; an espadrille. [Sp.]

alpenhorn /álpənhorn/ *n.* a long wooden horn used by Alpine herdsmen to call their cattle. [G, = Alp-horn]

alpenstock /álpənstok/ *n.* a long iron-tipped staff used in hillwalking. [G, = Alp-stick]

alpha /álfə/ *n.* **1** the first letter of the Greek alphabet (A, α). **2** a first-class mark given for a piece of work or in an examination. **3** *Astron.* the chief star in a constellation. □ **alpha and omega** the beginning and the end; the most important features. **alpha particle** (or **ray**) a helium nucleus emitted by a radioactive substance, orig. regarded as a ray. [ME f. L f. Gk]

alphabet /álfəbet/ *n.* **1** the set of letters used in writing a language (*the Russian alphabet*). **2** a set of symbols or signs representing letters. [LL *alphabetum* f. Gk *alpha*, *bēta*, the first two letters of the alphabet]

alphabetical /álfəbéttik'l/ *adj.* (also **alphabetic** /-béttik/) **1** of or relating to an alphabet. **2** in the order of the letters of the alphabet. □□ **alphabetically** *adv.*

alphabetize /álfəbətīz/ *v.tr.* (also **-ise**) arrange (words, names, etc.) in alphabetical order. □□ **alphabetization** /-záysh'n/ *n.*

alphanumeric /álfənyooмérrik/ *adj.* (also **alphameric** /álfəmérrik/, **alphanumerical**) containing both alphabetical and numerical symbols. [ALPHABETIC (see ALPHABETICAL) + NUMERICAL]

alpine /álpīn/ *adj.* & *n.* ● *adj.* **1 a** of or relating to high mountains. **b** growing or found on high mountains. **2** (**Alpine**) of or relating to the Alps. ● *n.* a plant native or suited to mountain districts. [L *Alpinus*: see ALP]

Alpinist /álpinist/ *n.* (also **alpinist**) a climber of high mountains, esp. the Alps. [F *alpiniste* (as ALPINE; see -IST)]

already /awlréddi/ *adv.* **1** before the time in question (*I knew that already*). **2** as early or as soon as this (*already at the age of six*). [ALL *adv.* + READY]

alright /awlrīt/ *adj.*, *adv.*, & *int. disp.* = *all right*.

Alsatian /alsáysh'n/ *n.* **1 a** a large dog of a breed used as guard dogs etc. **b** this breed (also called *German shepherd dog*). **2** a native of Alsace, a region of E. France. [*Alsatia* (= Alsace) + -AN]

alsike /álsik/ *n.* a species of clover, *Trifolium hybridum*. [*Alsike* in Sweden]

also /áwlsō/ *adv.* in addition; likewise; besides. □ **also-ran 1** a horse or dog etc. not among the winners in a race. **2** an undistinguished person. [OE *alswā* (as ALL *adv.*, SO[1])]
■ see *in addition* (ADDITION).

Alta. *abbr.* Alberta.

altar /áwltər, ól-/ *n.* **1** a table or flat-topped block, often of stone, for sacrifice or offering to a deity. **2** a Communion-table. □ **altar boy** a boy who serves as a priest's assistant in a service. **lead to the altar** marry (a woman). [OE *altar* -*er*, Gmc adoption of LL *altar*, *altarium* f. L *altaria* (pl.) burnt offerings, altar, prob. rel. to *adolēre* burn in sacrifice]

altarpiece /áwltərpeess, ól-/ *n.* a piece of art, esp. a painting, set above or behind an altar.

altazimuth /altázzimәth/ *n.* an instrument for measuring the altitude and azimuth of celestial bodies. [ALTITUDE + AZIMUTH]

alter /áwltər, ól-/ *v.* **1** *tr.* & *intr.* make or become different; change. **2** *tr.* *US* & *Austral.* castrate or spay. □□ **alterable** *adj.* **alteration** /-ráysh'n/ *n.* [ME f. OF *alterer* f. LL *alterare* f. L *alter* other]
■ **1** change, revise, modify, vary, transform; adjust, adapt, convert, remodel, restyle, refashion, remould, revamp; correct, amend, emend. **2** neuter, castrate, spay, desex, doctor, fix, geld, *US* & *Austral.* mark. □□ **alterable** see CHANGEABLE 2. **alteration** change, modification, shift, switch, revision, amendment, emendation, transformation; adjustment, adaptation, conversion, remodelling, reworking; correction.

alterative /áwltərәtiv, ól-/ *adj.* & *n.* ● *adj.* **1** tending to alter. **2** (of a medicine) that alters bodily processes. ● *n.* an alterative medicine or treatment. [ME f. med.L *alterativus* (as ALTER)]

altercate /áwltərkayt, ól-/ *v.intr.* (often foll. by *with*) dispute hotly; wrangle. □□ **altercation** /-káysh'n/ *n.* [L *altercari altercat-*]
■ see ARGUE 1.

alter ego /áltər éegō, áwltər, éggō/ *n.* (*pl.* ***alter egos***) **1** an intimate and trusted friend. **2** a person's secondary or alternative personality. [L, = other self]

alternate *v.*, *adj.*, & *n.* ● *v.* /áwltərnayt, ól-/ **1** *intr.* (often foll. by *with*) (of two things) succeed each other by turns (*rain and sunshine alternated*; *elation alternated with depression*). **2** *intr.* (foll. by *between*) change repeatedly (between two conditions) (*the patient alternated between hot and cold fevers*). **3** *tr.* (often foll. by *with*) cause (two things) to succeed each other by turns (*the band alternated fast and slow tunes*; *we alternated criticism with reassurance*). ● *adj.* /awltérnәt, ol-/ **1** (with noun in *pl.*) every other (*comes on alternate days*). **2** (of things of two kinds) each following and succeeded by one of the other kind (*alternate joy and misery*). **3** (of a sequence etc.) consisting of alternate things. **4** *Bot.* (of leaves etc.) placed alternately on the two sides of the stem. **5** *US* = ALTERNATIVE. ● *n.* /awltérnәt, ol-/ esp. *US* something or someone that is an alternative; a deputy or substitute. □ **alternate angles** two angles, not adjoining one another, that are formed on opposite sides of a line that intersects two other lines. **alternating current** an electric current that reverses its direction at regular intervals. □□ **alternately** /awltérnәtli, ol-/ *adv.* [L *alternatus* past part. of *alternare* do things by turns f. *alternus* every other f. *alter* other]
■ *v.* **1** succeed *or* follow each other, be in alternation *or* succession *or* rotation; be interspersed. **2** see OSCILLATE. **3** rotate, exchange, interchange, switch (round), take in turn *or* by turns, intersperse. ● *adj.* **1** every other, every second. **2** successive, alternating, rotating, in rotation. **5** alternative, second, (an)other, additional, substitute. ● *n.* alternative, second (choice), substitute, deputy, delegate, proxy, representative, relief, reserve, stand-in, stand-by, backup, understudy, *Austral.* offsider, *US* pinch-hitter. □□ **alternately** by turns, reciprocally, in rotation.

alternation /áwltərnáysh'n, ól-/ *n.* the action or result of alternating. □ **alternation of generations** reproduction by alternate processes, e.g. sexual and asexual.
■ rotation; interspersion, exchange, interchange, substitution.

alternative /awltérnәtiv, ol-/ *adj.* & *n.* ● *adj.* **1** (of one or more things) available or usable instead of another (*an alternative route*). ¶ Use with reference to more than two options (e.g. *many alternative methods*) is common, and acceptable. **2** (of two things) mutually exclusive. **3** of or relating to practices that offer a substitute for the conventional ones (*alternative medicine*; *alternative theatre*). ● *n.* **1** any of two or more possibilities. **2** the freedom or opportunity to choose between two or more things (*I had no alternative but to go*). □ **the alternative society** a group of people dissociating themselves from conventional society and its values. □□ **alternatively** *adv.* [F *alternatif* -*ive* or med.L *alternativus* (as ALTERNATE)]
■ *adj.* **1** second, (an)other, additional, substitute, *US* alternate. **3** see DIFFERENT 3. ● *n.* **1** see ALTERNATE *n.* **2** see CHOICE 4, OPTION 1, 2.

alternator /áwltərnaytər, ól-/ *n.* a dynamo that generates an alternating current.

althorn /ált-horn/ *n.* *Mus.* an instrument of the saxhorn family, esp. the alto or tenor saxhorn in E flat. [G f. *alt* high f. L *altus* + HORN]

although /awlthṓ/ *conj.* = THOUGH *conj.* 1–3. [ME f. ALL *adv.* + THOUGH]

altimeter /áltimeetər/ *n.* an instrument for showing height above sea or ground level, esp. one fitted to an aircraft. [L *altus* high + -METER]

altitude /áltityood/ *n.* **1** the height of an object in relation to a given point, esp. sea level or the horizon. **2** *Geom.* the length of the perpendicular from a vertex to the opposite side of a figure. **3** a high or exalted position (*a social altitude*). □ **altitude sickness** a sickness experienced at high altitudes. □□ **altitudinal** /áltityóodin'l/ *adj.* [ME f. L *altitudo* f. *altus* high]
■ **1** height, elevation, level.

alto /áltō/ *n.* (*pl.* **-os**) **1** = CONTRALTO. **2 a** the highest adult male singing-voice, above tenor. **b** a singer with this voice. **c** a part written for it. **3 a** (*attrib.*) denoting the member of a family of instruments pitched second- or third-highest. **b** an alto instrument, esp. an alto saxophone. □ **alto clef** a clef placing middle C on the middle line of the staff, used chiefly for viola music. [It. *alto* (*canto*) high (singing)]

altocumulus /áltōkyóomyooləss/ *n.* (*pl.* **altocumuli** /-lī/) *Meteorol.* a cloud formation at medium altitude consisting of rounded masses with a level base. [mod.L f. L *altus* high + CUMULUS]

altogether /áwltәgéthәr/ *adv.* **1** totally, completely (*you are altogether wrong*). **2** on the whole (*altogether it had been a good day*). **3** in total (*there are six bedrooms altogether*). ¶ Note that *all together* is used to mean 'all at once' or 'all in one place', as in *there are six bedrooms all together*. □ **in the altogether** *colloq.* naked. [ME f. ALL + TOGETHER]
■ **1** entirely, utterly, completely, wholly, totally, fully, in all respects, absolutely, perfectly, quite. **2** on the whole, by and large, in the main, generally, for the most part, on balance; (all) in all. **3** in total, in all, all included. □ **in the altogether** see NAKED 1.

alto-relievo /áltō-rileévō/ *n.* (also **alto-rilievo** /áltō-rilyáyvō/) (*pl.* **-os**) *Sculpture* **1** a form of relief in which the sculptured shapes stand out from the background to at least half their actual depth. **2** a sculpture characterized by this. [ALTO + RELIEVO]

altostratus /áltōstráytәss, -straátәss/ *n.* (*pl.* **altostrati** /-tī/) a continuous and uniformly flat cloud formation at medium altitude. [mod.L f. L *altus* high + STRATUS]

altricial /altrísh'l/ *adj.* & *n.* ● *adj.* (of a bird) whose young require care and feeding by the parents after hatching. ● *n.*

an altricial bird (cf. PRAECOCIAL). [L *altrix altricis* (fem.) nourisher f. *altor* f. *alere altus* nourish]

altruism /áltroo-iz'm/ *n.* **1** regard for others as a principle of action. **2** unselfishness; concern for other people. ▫▫ **altruist** *n.* **altruistic** /áltroo-ístik/ *adj.* **altruistically** /áltroo-ístikəli/ *adv.* [F *altruisme* f. It. *altrui* somebody else (infl. by L *alter* other)]

■ **2** selflessness, self-sacrifice, unselfishness, philanthropy, beneficence, generosity, charity, charitableness, humanitarianism, humaneness, benevolence, largesse, humanity, public-spiritedness. ▫▫ **altruist** see *philanthropist* (PHILANTHROPY). **altruistic** see SELFLESS.

alum /álləm/ *n.* **1** a double sulphate of aluminium and potassium. **2** any of a group of compounds of double sulphates of a monovalent metal (or group) and a trivalent metal. [ME f. OF f. L *alumen aluminis*]

alumina /əloōminə/ *n.* the compound aluminium oxide occurring naturally as corundum and emery. [L *alumen* alum, after *soda* etc.]

aluminium /ályoomínniəm/ *n.* (*US* **aluminum** /əloōminəm/) a silvery light and malleable metallic element resistant to tarnishing by air. ¶ Symb.: **Al.** ▫ **aluminium bronze** an alloy of copper and aluminium. [*aluminium*, alt. (after *sodium* etc.) f. *aluminum*, earlier *alumium* f. ALUM + -IUM]

aluminize /əloōminīz/ *v.tr.* (also **-ise**) coat with aluminium. ▫▫ **aluminization** /-záysh'n/ *n.*

alumnus /əlúmnəss/ *n.* (*pl.* **alumni** /-nī/; *fem.* **alumna**, *pl.* **alumnae** /-nee/) a former pupil or student. [L, = nursling, pupil f. *alere* nourish]

alveolar /alveéələr, álviṓlər/ *adj.* **1** of an alveolus. **2** *Phonet.* (of a consonant) pronounced with the tip of the tongue in contact with the ridge of the upper teeth, e.g. *n, s, t.* [ALVEOLUS + -AR[1]]

alveolus /alveéələss, álviṓləss/ *n.* (*pl.* **alveoli** /-lī/ **1** a small cavity, pit, or hollow. **2** any of the many tiny air sacs of the lungs which allow for rapid gaseous exchange. **3** the bony socket for the root of a tooth. **4** the cell of a honeycomb. ▫▫ **alveolate** *adj.* [L dimin. of *alveus* cavity]

always /áwlwayz/ *adv.* **1** at all times; on all occasions (*they are always late*). **2** whatever the circumstances (*I can always sleep on the floor*). **3** repeatedly; often (*they are always complaining*). **4** for ever, for all time (*I am with you always*). [ME, prob. distrib. genit. f. ALL + WAY + -'S[1]]

■ **1** at all times, again and again, on all occasions, every *or* each time, each and every time, without exception, *archaic* aye. **2** in any case *or* event, as a last resort, if necessary. **3** repeatedly, usually; see also OFTEN. **4** for ever, continually, ever, perpetually; unceasingly, unendingly, eternally, evermore, ever after, everlastingly, for all time, till the end of time, in perpetuity, *archaic* for aye.

alyssum /állisəm/ *n.* any plant of the genus *Alyssum*, widely cultivated and usu. having yellow or white flowers. [L f. Gk *alusson*]

Alzheimer's disease /álts-hīmərz/ *n.* a serious disorder of the brain manifesting itself in premature senility. [A. *Alzheimer*, Ger. neurologist d. 1915]

AM *abbr.* **1** amplitude modulation. **2** *US* Master of Arts. **3** Member of the Order of Australia. [(sense 2) L *artium Magister*]

Am *symb. Chem.* the element americium.

am *1st person sing. present* of BE.

a.m. *abbr.* before noon. [L *ante meridiem*]

amadavat /ámmədəvát/ *n.* (also **avadavat** /ávvə-/) either of two small brightly coloured S. Asian waxbills, the green *Amandava formosa* or esp. the red *A. amandava.* [*Ahmadabad* in India]

amadou /ámmədoō/ *n.* a spongy and combustible tinder prepared from dry fungi. [F f. mod.Prov., lit. = lover (because quickly kindled) f. L (as AMATEUR)]

amah /áamə/ *n.* (in the Far East and India) a nursemaid or maid. [Port. *ama* nurse]

amalgam /əmálgəm/ *n.* **1** a mixture or blend. **2** an alloy of mercury with one or more other metals, used esp. in dentistry. [ME f. F *amalgame* or med.L *amalgama* f. Gk *malagma* an emollient]

■ **1** mixture, blend, combination, alloy, mix, composite, admixture, amalgamation, compound.

amalgamate /əmálgəmayt/ *v.* **1** *tr.* & *intr.* combine or unite to form one structure, organization, etc. **2** *intr.* (of metals) alloy with mercury. ▫▫ **amalgamation** /-máysh'n/ *n.* [med.L *amalgamare amalgamat-* (as AMALGAM)]

■ **1** blend, combine, unite, mix, join, merge, fuse; consolidate, compound, integrate, put together, marry. ▫▫ **amalgamation** blend, fusion, alloy, combination, mix(ture), amalgam, composite, compound, union, unification, marriage, consolidation, coalescence, integration, merger.

amanuensis /əmányoo-énsiss/ *n.* (*pl.* **amanuenses** /-seez/) **1** a person who writes from dictation or copies manuscripts. **2** a literary assistant. [L f. (*servus*) *a manu* secretary + *-ensis* belonging to]

amaranth /ámməranth/ *n.* **1** any plant of the genus *Amaranthus*, usu. having small green, red, or purple tinted flowers, e.g. prince's feather and pigweed. **2** an imaginary flower that never fades. **3** a purple colour. ▫▫ **amaranthine** /ámməránthīn/ *adj.* [F *amarante* or mod.L *amaranthus* f. L f. Gk *amarantos* everlasting f. *a-* not + *marainō* wither, alt. after *polyanthus* etc.]

amaryllis /ámmərílliss/ *n.* **1** a plant genus with a single species, *Amaryllis belladonna*, a bulbous lily-like plant native to S. Africa with white or rose-pink flowers (also called *belladonna lily*). **2** any of various related plants formerly of this genus now transferred to other genera, notably *Hippeastrum.* [L f. Gk *Amarullis*, name of a country girl]

amass /əmáss/ *v.tr.* **1** gather or heap together. **2** accumulate (esp. riches). ▫▫ **amasser** *n.* **amassment** *n.* [F *amasser* or med.L *amassare* ult. f. L *massa* MASS[1]]

■ accumulate, mass, pile *or* heap *or* rack up, collect, gather (together), assemble, muster, aggregate, cumulate, stock *or* store up, put away, stockpile, hoard, set aside.

amateur /ámmətər/ *n.* & *adj.* ● *n.* **1 a** a person who engages in a pursuit (e.g. an art or sport) as a pastime rather than a profession. **b** *derog.* a person who does something unskilfully, in the manner of an amateur rather than a professional. **2** (foll. by *of*) a person who is fond of (a thing). ● *adj.* for or done by amateurs; amateurish, unskilful (*amateur athletics*; *did an amateur job*). ▫▫ **amateurism** *n.* [F f. It. *amatore* f. L *amator -oris* lover f. *amare* love]

■ *n.* **1** layman, non-professional, non-specialist; tiro; dabbler, dilettante, tinkerer. ● *adj.* lay, non-professional, non-specialist, untrained, unpaid; dilettante, amateurish, unprofessional, unskilled, inexpert, inept, incompetent, unskilful, clumsy, mediocre, inferior, bungling, second-rate, sloppy, shoddy, poor. ▫▫ **amateurism** unprofessionalism, dilettantism, inexpertness; ineptitude, incompetence; mediocrity, inferiority, sloppiness, shoddiness.

amateurish /ámmətərish/ *adj.* characteristic of an amateur, esp. unskilful or inexperienced. ▫▫ **amateurishly** *adv.* **amateurishness** *n.*

amatory /ámmətəri/ *adj.* of or relating to sexual love or desire. [L *amatorius* f. *amare* love]

amaurosis /ámmərṓsiss/ *n.* the partial or total loss of sight, from disease of the optic nerve, retina, spinal cord, or brain. ▫▫ **amaurotic** /-róttik/ *adj.* [mod.L f. Gk f. *amauroō* darken f. *amauros* dim]

amaze /əmáyz/ *v.tr.* (often foll. by *at*, or *that* + clause, or *to* + infin.) surprise greatly; overwhelm with wonder (*am amazed at your indifference*; *was amazed to find them alive*). ▫▫ **amazement** *n.* **amazing** *adj.* **amazingly** *adv.* **amazingness** *n.* [ME f. OE *āmasod* past part. of *āmasian*, of uncert. orig.]

■ astound, astonish, surprise, awe, stun, stagger, take

aback, dumbfound, confound, nonplus, stupefy, *colloq.* floor, flabbergast, knock sideways, *sl.* knock out; (*be amazed*) be thunderstruck *or* dumbstruck, *sl.* be gobsmacked. □□ **amazement** astonishment, surprise, awe, wonder, wonderment, stupefaction. **amazing** astonishing, astounding, awe-inspiring, surprising, remarkable, extraordinary, spectacular, stupendous, marvellous, fabulous, wonderful, staggering, prodigious, awesome, far-out, *colloq.* incredible, stunning, *US & Austral. sl.* unreal. **amazingly** astonishingly, astoundingly, surprisingly, remarkably, extraordinarily, marvellously, spectacularly, stupendously, fabulously, prodigiously, unexpectedly, *colloq.* incredibly, stunningly, like nobody's business.

Amazon /ámməz'n/ *n.* **1** a member of a mythical race of female warriors in Scythia and elsewhere. **2** (**amazon**) a very tall, strong, or athletic woman. □□ **Amazonian** /ámməzṓniən/ *adj.* [ME f. L f. Gk: expl. by the Greeks as 'breastless' (as if A-[1] + *mazos* breast), but prob. of foreign orig.]

ambassador /ambássədər/ *n.* **1** an accredited diplomat sent by a State on a mission to, or as its permanent representative in, a foreign country. **2** a representative or promoter of a specified thing (*an ambassador of peace*). □ **ambassador-at-large** *US* an ambassador with special duties, not appointed to a particular country. □□ **ambassadorial** /ámbasədóriəl/ *adj.* **ambassadorship** *n.* [ME f. F *ambassadeur* f. It. *ambasciator*, ult. f. L *ambactus* servant]
■ **1, 2** envoy, delegate, emissary, minister, plenipotentiary, diplomat, *archaic* legate; agent, deputy, representative, (papal) nuncio, High Commissioner; messenger, herald. □□ **ambassadorial** ministerial, diplomatic, plenipotentiary, agential.

ambassadress /ambássədriss/ *n.* **1** a female ambassador. **2** an ambassador's wife.

ambatch /ámbach/ *n.* an African tree, *Aeschynomene elaphroxylon*, with very light spongy wood. [Ethiopic]

amber /ámbər/ *n.* & *adj.* ● *n.* **1 a** a yellowish translucent fossilized resin deriving from extinct (esp. coniferous) trees and used in jewellery. **b** the honey-yellow colour of this. **2** a yellow traffic-light meaning caution, showing between red for 'stop' and green for 'go'. ● *adj.* made of or coloured like amber. [ME f. OF *ambre* f. Arab. *'anbar* ambergris, amber]

ambergris /ámbərgriss, -greess/ *n.* a strong-smelling waxlike secretion of the intestine of the sperm whale, found floating in tropical seas and used in perfume manufacture. [ME f. OF *ambre gris* grey AMBER]

amberjack /ámbərjak/ *n. US* any large brightly-coloured marine fish of the genus *Seriola* found in tropical and subtropical Atlantic waters.

ambiance var. of AMBIENCE.

ambidextrous /ámbidékstrəss/ *adj.* (also **ambidexterous**) **1** able to use the right and left hands equally well. **2** working skilfully in more than one medium. □□ **ambidexterity** /-stérriti/ *n.* **ambidextrously** *adv.* **ambidextrousness** *n.* [LL *ambidexter* f. *ambi-* on both sides + *dexter* right-handed]

ambience /ámbiənss/ *n.* (also **ambiance**) the surroundings or atmosphere of a place. [AMBIENT + -ENCE or F *ambiance*]
■ see ATMOSPHERE 2a.

ambient /ámbiənt/ *adj.* surrounding. [F *ambiant* or L *ambiens -entis* pres. part. of *ambire* go round]

ambiguity /ámbigyṓō-iti/ *n.* (*pl.* **-ies**) **1 a** a double meaning which is either deliberate or caused by inexactness of expression. **b** an example of this. **2** an expression able to be interpreted in more than one way (e.g. *dogs must be carried*). [ME f. OF *ambiguité* or L *ambiguitas* (as AMBIGUOUS)]
■ **1 a** equivocalness, equivocality, ambiguousness, equivocacy, amphibology; vagueness, indistinctness, uncertainty, indefiniteness, imprecision, inexactness, inexactitude, inconclusiveness; equivocation, double-talk, double-speak, word-play. **b** pun, equivoque, equivocation, *double entendre*, amphibology, play on words, quibble, paronomasia.

ambiguous /ambígyooəss/ *adj.* **1** having an obscure or double meaning. **2** difficult to classify. □□ **ambiguously** *adv.* **ambiguousness** *n.* [L *ambiguus* doubtful f. *ambigere* f. *ambi-* both ways + *agere* drive]
■ equivocal, obscure, indistinct, inconclusive, vague, unclear, indefinite, indeterminate, inexact, uncertain, undefined, misty, foggy; cryptic, enigmatic(al), mysterious, Delphic, Delphian, oracular, puzzling, confusing, misleading, confusable; unreliable, undependable. □□ **ambiguously** equivocally; see also *vaguely* (VAGUE). **ambiguousness** see AMBIGUITY 1a.

ambisonics /ámbisónniks/ *n.pl.* a system of high-fidelity sound reproduction designed to reproduce the directional and acoustic properties of the sound source using two or more channels. [L *ambi-* on both sides + SONIC]

ambit /ámbit/ *n.* **1** the scope, extent, or bounds of something. **2** precincts or environs. [ME f. L *ambitus* circuit f. *ambire*: see AMBIENT]
■ see RANGE *n.* 1.

ambition /ambísh'n/ *n.* **1** (often foll. by *to* + infin.) the determination to achieve success or distinction, usu. in a chosen field. **2** the object of this determination. **3** aggressive self-seeking or self-centredness. [ME f. OF f. L *ambitio -onis* f. *ambire ambit-* canvass for votes: see AMBIENT]
■ **1** drive, enterprise, energy, initiative, push, vigour, enthusiasm, determination, motivation, zeal, eagerness, keenness, *colloq.* get-up-and-go. **2** goal, object, aim, end, aspiration, hope, desire, dream, objective, intent, wish, purpose. **3** *arrivisme*, pushiness, self-seeking.

ambitious /ambíshəss/ *adj.* **1 a** full of ambition. **b** showing ambition (*an ambitious attempt*). **2** (foll. by *of*, or *to* + infin.) strongly determined. □□ **ambitiously** *adv.* **ambitiousness** *n.* [ME f. OF *ambitieux* f. L *ambitiosus* (as AMBITION)]
■ **1 a** energetic, enterprising, go-ahead, vigorous, zealous, keen, enthusiastic, eager, aspiring, determined, (highly) motivated, high-flying, pushing, *colloq.* pushy, go-getting; greedy, avaricious, overzealous, overambitious, self-seeking. **b** enterprising, grandiose, *colloq.* big. **2** see DETERMINED 1. □□ **ambitiousness** see DRIVE *n.* 2a.

ambivalence /ambívvələnss/ *n.* (also **ambivalency** /-lənsi/) the coexistence in one person's mind of opposing feelings, esp. love and hate, in a single context. □□ **ambivalent** *adj.* **ambivalently** *adv.* [G *Ambivalenz* f. L *ambo* both, after *equivalence*, *-ency*]

ambivert /ámbivert/ *n. Psychol.* a person who fluctuates between being an introvert and an extrovert. □□ **ambiversion** /-vérsh'n/ *n.* [L *ambi-* on both sides + *-vert* f. L *vertere* to turn, after EXTROVERT, INTROVERT]

amble /ámb'l/ *v.* & *n.* ● *v.intr.* **1** move at an easy pace, in a way suggesting an ambling horse. **2** (of a horse etc.) move by lifting the two feet on one side together. **3** ride an ambling horse; ride at an easy pace. ● *n.* an easy pace; the gait of an ambling horse. [ME f. OF *ambler* f. L *ambulare* walk]
■ *v.* **1** see STROLL *v.*

amblyopia /ámbliṓpiə/ *n.* dimness of vision without obvious defect or change in the eye. □□ **amblyopic** /-lióppik/ *adj.* [Gk f. *ambluōpos* (adj.) f. *amblus* dull + *ōps*, *ōpos* eye]

ambo /ámbō/ *n.* (*pl.* **-os** or **ambones** /-bṓneez/) a stand for reading lessons in an early Christian church etc. [med.L f. Gk *ambōn* rim (in med.Gk = pulpit)]

amboyna /ambóynə/ *n.* the decorative wood of the SE Asian tree *Pterocarpus indicus*. [*Amboyna* Island in Indonesia]

ambrosia /ambrṓziə, -zhyə/ *n.* **1** (in Greek and Roman mythology) the food of the gods; the elixir of life. **2** anything very pleasing to taste or smell. **3** the food of certain bees and beetles. □□ **ambrosial** *adj.* **ambrosian** *adj.* [L f. Gk, = elixir of life f. *ambrotos* immortal]

ambry var. of AUMBRY.

ambulance /ámbyooləns/ *n.* **1** a vehicle specially equipped for conveying the sick or injured to and from hospital, esp. in emergencies. **2** a mobile hospital following an army. [F (as AMBULANT)]

ambulant /ámbyoolənt/ *adj. Med.* **1** (of a patient) able to walk about; not confined to bed. **2** (of treatment) not confining a patient to bed. [L *ambulare ambulant-* walk]
■ **1** see MOBILE *adj.* 1, 3.

ambulatory /ámbyoolətəri/ *adj.* & *n.* ● *adj.* **1** = AMBULANT. **2** of or adapted for walking. **3 a** movable. **b** not permanent. ● *n.* (*pl.* **-ies**) a place for walking, esp. an aisle or cloister in a church or monastery. [L *ambulatorius* f. *ambulare* walk]
■ *adj.* **3 a** see MOVABLE *adj.* 1.

ambuscade /ámbəskáyd/ *n.* & *v.* ● *n.* an ambush. ● *v.* **1** *tr.* attack by means of an ambush. **2** *intr.* lie in ambush. **3** *tr.* conceal in an ambush. [F *embuscade* f. It. *imboscata* or Sp. *emboscada* f. L *imboscare*: see AMBUSH, -ADE[1]]

ambush /ámbo͝osh/ *n.* & *v.* ● *n.* **1** a surprise attack by persons (e.g. troops) in a concealed position. **2 a** the concealment of troops etc. to make such an attack. **b** the place where they are concealed. **c** the troops etc. concealed. ● *v.tr.* **1** attack by means of an ambush. **2** lie in wait for. [ME f. OF *embusche*, *embuschier*, f. a Rmc form = 'put in a wood': rel. to BUSH[1]]
■ *n.* **1** trap, ambuscade. ● *v.* **1** trap, waylay, ensnare, entrap, ambuscade, intercept, jump, *US* bushwhack. **2** lie in wait for, lay wait for, *US* bushwhack.

ameba *US* var. of AMOEBA.

ameer var. of AMIR.

ameliorate /əméeliərayt/ *v.tr.* & *intr. formal* make or become better; improve. ◻◻ **amelioration** /-ráysh'n/ *n.* **ameliorative** *adj.* **ameliorator** *n.* [alt. of MELIORATE after F *améliorer*]
■ see IMPROVE 1a.

amen /aámén, áy-/ *int.* & *n.* ● *int.* **1** uttered at the end of a prayer or hymn etc., meaning 'so be it'. **2** (foll. by *to*) expressing agreement or assent (*amen to that*). ● *n.* an utterance of 'amen' (sense 1). [ME f. eccl.L f. Gk f. Heb. *'āmēn* certainly]

amenable /əméenəb'l/ *adj.* **1** responsive, tractable. **2** (often foll. by *to*) (of a person) responsible to law. **3** (foll. by *to*) (of a thing) subject or liable. ◻◻ **amenability** /-bílliti/ *n.* **amenableness** *n.* **amenably** *adv.* [AF (Law) f. F *amener* bring to f. *a-* to + *mener* bring f. LL *minare* drive animals f. L *minari* threaten]
■ **1** see TRACTABLE 1.

amend /əménd/ *v.tr.* **1** make minor improvements in (a text or a written proposal). **2** correct an error or errors in (a document). **3** make better; improve. ¶ Often confused with *emend*, a more technical word used in the context of textual correction. ◻◻ **amendable** *adj.* **amender** *n.* [ME f. OF *amender* ult. f. L *emendare* EMEND]
■ **1** enhance, revise, edit, refine, polish (up), improve. **2** correct, emend, rectify, put *or* set to rights, right, fix, revise, *Printing* read. **3** reform, mend, change for the better, improve, (make) better, *formal* ameliorate, *literary* meliorate. ◻◻ **amendable** correctable, emendable, rectifiable, rightable.

amende honorable /əmónd onoraáb'l/ *n.* (*pl.* ***amendes honorables*** *pronunc.* same) a public or open apology, often with some form of reparation. [F, = honourable reparation]

amendment /əméndmənt/ *n.* **1** a minor improvement in a document (esp. a legal or statutory one). **2** an article added to the US Constitution. [AMEND + -MENT]
■ **1** correction, emendation, change, alteration, modification, adjustment, insertion, rectification, revision, reform, enhancement, improvement, *formal* amelioration.

amends /əméndz/ *n.* ◻ **make amends** (often foll. by *for*) compensate or make up (for). [ME f. OF *amendes* penalties, fine, pl. of *amende* reparation f. *amender* AMEND]
■ ◻ **make amends** (*make amends for*) make reparation *or* restitution for, atone for, compensate for, expiate, repair, make good; (*make amends to*) make it up to, pay, repay, recompense, indemnify, redress, remedy, requite.

amenity /əméeniti, əmén-/ *n.* (*pl.* **-ies**) **1** (usu. in *pl.*) a pleasant or useful feature. **2** pleasantness (of a place, person, etc.). ◻ **amenity-bed** *Brit.* a bed available in a hospital to give more privacy for a small payment. [ME f. OF *amenité* or L *amoenitas* f. *amoenus* pleasant]

amenorrhoea /ayménnəréeə/ *n.* (*US* **amenorrhea**) *Med.* an abnormal absence of menstruation. [A-[1] + MENO- + Gk *-rrhoia* f. *rheō* flow]

ament /əmént/ *n.* (also **amentum** /-təm/) (*pl.* **aments** or **amenta** /-tə/) a catkin. [L, = thong]

amentia /əménshə/ *n. Med.* severe congenital mental deficiency. [L f. *amens ament-* mad (as A-[1], *mens* mind)]

amerce /əmérss/ *v.tr.* **1** *Law* punish by fine. **2** punish arbitrarily. ◻◻ **amercement** *n.* **amerciable** /-siəb'l/ *adj.* [ME *amercy* f. AF *amercier* f. *a* at + *merci* MERCY]

American /əmérrikən/ *adj.* & *n.* ● *adj.* **1** of, relating to, or characteristic of the United States or its inhabitants. **2** (usu. in *comb.*) of or relating to the continents of America (*Latin-American*). ● *n.* **1** a native or citizen of the United States. **2** (usu. in *comb.*) a native or inhabitant of the continents of America (*North Americans*). **3** the English language as it is used in the United States. ◻ **American dream** the traditional ideals of the American people, such as equality, democracy, and material prosperity. **American football** a kind of football played with an oval ball, evolved from Rugby football. **American Indian** see INDIAN. [mod.L *Americanus* f. *America* f. Latinized name of *Amerigo* Vespucci, It. navigator d. 1512]

Americana /əmérrikaánə/ *n.pl.* things connected with America, esp. with the United States.

Americanism /əmérrikəniz'm/ *n.* **1 a** a word, sense, or phrase peculiar to or originating from the United States. **b** a thing or feature characteristic of or peculiar to the United States. **2** attachment to or sympathy for the United States.

Americanize /əmérrikənīz/ *v.* (also **-ise**) **1** *tr.* **a** make American in character. **b** naturalize as an American. **2** *intr.* become American in character. ◻◻ **Americanization** /-záysh'n/ *n.*

americium /ámməríssiəm, -ríshiəm/ *n. Chem.* an artificially made transuranic radioactive metallic element. ¶ Symb.: **Am.** [*America* (where first made) + -IUM]

Amerind /ámmərind/ *adj.* & *n.* (also **Amerindian** /ámmərindiən/) = *American Indian* (see INDIAN). ◻◻ **Amerindic** /-ríndik/ *adj.* [portmanteau word]

amethyst /ámmithist/ *n.* a precious stone of a violet or purple variety of quartz. ◻◻ **amethystine** /-thísteen/ *adj.* [ME f. OF *ametiste* f. L *amethystus* f. Gk *amethustos* not drunken, the stone being supposed to prevent intoxication]

Amharic /amhárrik/ *n.* & *adj.* ● *n.* the official and commercial language of Ethiopia. ● *adj.* of this language. [*Amhara*, Ethiopian province + -IC]

amiable /áymiəb'l/ *adj.* friendly and pleasant in temperament; likeable. ◻◻ **amiability** /áymiəbílliti/ *n.* **amiableness** *n.* **amiably** *adv.* [ME f. OF f. LL *amicabilis* amicable: confused with F *aimable* lovable]
■ friendly, likeable, amicable, agreeable, cordial, congenial, genial, affable, pleasant, obliging, winsome, winning, tractable, approachable, benign, well-disposed; warm, kindly, kind, good-natured, good-hearted, kind-hearted, affectionate.

amianthus /ámmiánthəss/ *n.* (also **amiantus** /-təss/) any fine silky-fibred variety of asbestos. [L f. Gk *amiantos* undefiled f. *a-* not + *miainō* defile, i.e. purified by fire, being incombustible: for *-h-* cf. AMARANTH]

amicable /ámmikəb'l/ *adj.* showing or done in a friendly spirit (*an amicable meeting*). ◻◻ **amicability** /-bílliti/ *n.* **amicableness** *n.* **amicably** *adv.* [LL *amicabilis* f. *amicus* friend]
■ friendly, amiable, congenial, harmonious, brotherly,

kind-hearted; warm, courteous, cordial, polite, civil, pleasant; peaceful, peaceable.

amice[1] /ámmiss/ *n.* a white linen cloth worn on the neck and shoulders by a priest celebrating the Eucharist. [ME f. med.L *amicia*, *-sia* (earlier *amit* f. OF), f. L *amictus* outer garment]

amice[2] /ámmiss/ *n.* a cap, hood, or cape worn by members of certain religious orders. [ME f. OF *aumusse* f. med.L *almucia* etc., of unkn. orig.]

amicus curiae /ameékōōss kyoóri-ee/ *n.* (*pl.* ***amici curiae*** /ameékī/) *Law* an impartial adviser in a court of law. [mod.L, = friend of the court]

amid /əmíd/ *prep.* (also **amidst** /əmídst/) **1** in the middle of. **2** in the course of. [ME *amidde(s)* f. OE *on* ON + MID[1]]
▪ **1** in the middle *or* midst *or* centre *or* thick of, amongst, among, *poet.* mid, midst; surrounded by. **2** in the middle of, during, in the course of.

amide /áymīd, ám-/ *n. Chem.* a compound formed from ammonia by replacement of one (or sometimes more than one) hydrogen atom by a metal or an acyl radical. [AMMONIA + -IDE]

amidships /əmídships/ *adv.* (*US* **amidship**) in or into the middle of a ship. [MIDSHIP after AMID]

amidst var. of AMID.

amigo /ameégō/ *n.* (*pl.* ***-os***) esp. *US colloq.* (often as a form of address) a friend or comrade, esp. in Spanish-speaking areas. [Sp.]

amine /áymeen, ám-/ *n. Chem.* a compound formed from ammonia by replacement of one or more hydrogen atoms by an organic radical or radicals. [AMMONIA + -INE[4]]

amino /əmeénō/ *n.* (*attrib.*) *Chem.* of, relating to, or containing the monovalent group $-NH_2$. [AMINE]

amino acid /əmeénō/ *n. Biochem.* any of a group of organic compounds containing both the carboxyl (COOH) and amino (NH_2) group, occurring naturally in plant and animal tissues and forming the basic constituents of proteins. [AMINE + ACID]

amir /əmeér/ *n.* (also **ameer**) the title of some Arab rulers. [Arab. *'amīr* commander f. *amara* command: cf. EMIR]

Amish /aámish, áy-/ *adj.* belonging to a strict US Mennonite sect. [prob. f. G *Amisch* f. J. *Amen* 17th-c. Swiss preacher]

amiss /əmíss/ *predic.adj.* & *adv.* ● *predic.adj.* wrong; out of order; faulty (*knew something was amiss*). ● *adv.* wrong; wrongly; inappropriately (*everything went amiss*). ▫ **take amiss** be offended by (*took my words amiss*). [ME prob. f. ON *á mis* so as to miss f. *á* on + *mis* rel. to MISS[1]]
▪ *predic. adj.* wrong, at fault, awry, out of order, out of kilter, faulty, defective; untoward, astray, erroneous, fallacious, confused, incorrect, off. ● *adv.* wrong(ly), awry, badly, poorly, imperfectly, incorrectly; inopportunely, unfavourably, unpropitiously; inappropriately, out of place *or* turn, inopportunely, unsuitably, improperly. ▫ **take amiss** (also *take it amiss*) be offended (by), take offence (at), take (it) the wrong way, mistake, misinterpret, misunderstand.

amitosis /ámmitṓsiss/ *n. Biol.* a form of nuclear division that does not involve mitosis. [A-[1] + MITOSIS]

amitriptyline /ámmitríptileen/ *n. Pharm.* an antidepressant drug that has a mild tranquillizing action. [AMINE + TRI- + *heptyl* (see HEPTANE) + -INE[4]]

amity /ámmiti/ *n.* friendship; friendly relations. [ME f. OF *amitié* ult. f. L *amicus* friend]
▪ see FRIENDSHIP 1.

ammeter /ámmitər/ *n.* an instrument for measuring electric current in amperes. [AMPERE + -METER]

ammo /ámmō/ *n. colloq.* ammunition. [abbr.]

ammonia /əmṓniə/ *n.* **1** a colourless strongly alkaline gas with a characteristic pungent smell. ¶ Chem. formula: NH_3. **2** (in full **ammonia water**) (in general use) a solution of ammonia gas in water. [mod.L f. SAL AMMONIAC]

ammoniacal /ámmənī́ək'l/ *adj.* of, relating to, or containing ammonia or sal ammoniac. [ME *ammoniac* f. OF (*arm-*, *amm-*) f. L f. Gk *ammōniakos* of Ammon (cf. SAL AMMONIAC) + -AL]

ammoniated /əmṓniaytid/ *adj.* combined or treated with ammonia.

ammonite /ámmənīt/ *n.* any extinct cephalopod mollusc of the order Ammonoidea, with a flat coiled spiral shell found as a fossil. [mod.L *ammonites*, after med.L *cornu Ammonis*, = L *Ammonis cornu* (Pliny), horn of (Jupiter) Ammon]

ammonium /əmṓniəm/ *n.* the univalent ion NH_4^+, formed from ammonia. [mod.L (as AMMONIA)]

ammunition /ámyoonísh'n/ *n.* **1** a supply of projectiles (esp. bullets, shells, and grenades). **2** points used or usable to advantage in an argument. [obs. F *amunition*, corrupt. of (*la*) *munition* (the) MUNITION]
▪ **2** see FUEL *n.* 4.

amnesia /amneéziə/ *n.* a partial or total loss of memory. ▫▫ **amnesiac** /-ziak/ *n.* **amnesic** *adj.* & *n.* [mod.L f. Gk, = forgetfulness]

amnesty /ámnisti/ *n.* & *v.* ● *n.* (*pl.* **-ies**) a general pardon, esp. for political offences. ● *v.tr.* (**-ies**, **-ied**) grant an amnesty to. ▫ **Amnesty International** an independent international organization in support of human rights, esp. for prisoners of conscience. [F *amnestie* or L f. Gk *amnēstia* oblivion]
▪ *n.* see PARDON *n.* ● *v.* see PARDON *v.*

amniocentesis /ámniōsenteéssiss/ *n.* (*pl.* **amniocenteses** /-seez/) *Med.* the sampling of amniotic fluid by insertion of a hollow needle to determine the condition of an embryo. [AMNION + Gk *kentēsis* pricking f. *kentō* to prick]

amnion /ámniən/ *n.* (*pl.* **amnia**) *Zool.* & *Physiol.* the innermost membrane that encloses the embryo of a reptile, bird, or mammal. ▫▫ **amniotic** /ámniόttik/ *adj.* [Gk, = caul (dimin. of *amnos* lamb)]

amoeba /əmeébə/ *n.* (*US* **ameba**) (*pl.* **amoebas** or **amoebae** /-bee/) any usu. aquatic protozoan of the genus *Amoeba*, esp. *A. proteus*, capable of changing shape. ▫▫ **amoebic** *adj.* **amoeboid** *adj.* [mod.L f. Gk *amoibē* change]

amok /əmók/ *adv.* (also **amuck** /əmúk/) ▫ **run amok** run about wildly in an uncontrollable violent rage. [Malay *amok* rushing in a frenzy]

among /əmúng/ *prep.* (also **amongst** /əmúngst/) **1** surrounded by; in the company of (*lived among the trees*; *be among friends*). **2** in the number of (*among us were those who disagreed*). **3** an example of; in the class or category of (*is among the richest men alive*). **4 a** between; within the limits of (collectively or distributively); shared by (*had £5 among us*; *divide it among you*). **b** by the joint action or from the joint resources of (*among us we can manage it*). **5** with one another; by the reciprocal action of (*was decided among the participants*; *talked among themselves*). **6** as distinguished from; pre-eminent in the category of (*she is one among many*). [OE *ongemang* f. *on* ON + *gemang* assemblage (cf. MINGLE): *-st* = adverbial genitive *-s* + *-t* as in AGAINST]
▪ **1** amid, amidst, in the midst *or* middle *or* centre of, surrounded by, in the company of, *poet.* mid, midst. **3** one of, an example of. **4 a** to each *or* all (of), between. **6** out of, from.

amontillado /əmóntilaádō/ *n.* (*pl.* **-os**) a medium dry sherry. [Sp. f. *Montilla* in Spain + *-ado* = -ATE[2]]

amoral /áymórrəl/ *adj.* **1** not concerned with or outside the scope of morality (cf. IMMORAL). **2** having no moral principles. ▫▫ **amoralism** *n.* **amoralist** *n.* **amorality** /-rálliti/ *n.*

amoretto /ámmoréttō/ *n.* (*pl.* ***amoretti*** /-ti/) a Cupid. [It., dimin. of *amore* love f. L (as AMOUR)]

amorist /ámmərist/ *n.* a person who professes or writes of (esp. sexual) love. [L *amor* or F *amour* + -IST]

amoroso[1] /ámmərṓsō/ *adv.* & *adj. Mus.* in a loving or tender manner. [It.]

amoroso[2] /ámmərṓsō/ *n.* (*pl.* **-os**) a full rich type of sherry. [Sp., = amorous]

amorous /ámmərəss/ *adj.* **1** showing, feeling, or inclined to sexual love. **2** of or relating to sexual love. ▫▫ **amorously**

adv. **amorousness** *n.* [ME f. OF f. med.L *amorosus* f. L *amor* love]
■ see PASSIONATE.

amorphous /əmórfəss/ *adj.* **1** shapeless. **2** vague, ill-organized. **3** *Mineral.* & *Chem.* non-crystalline; having neither definite form nor structure. □□ **amorphously** *adv.* **amorphousness** *n.* [med.L *amorphus* f. Gk *amorphos* shapeless f. *a-* not + *morphē* form]
■ **1** see SHAPELESS. **2** see VAGUE 1.

amortize /əmórtīz/ *v.tr.* (also **-ise**) *Commerce* **1** gradually extinguish (a debt) by money regularly put aside. **2** gradually write off the initial cost of (assets). **3** transfer (land) to a corporation in mortmain. □□ **amortization** /-záysh'n/ *n.* [ME f. OF *amortir* (stem *amortiss-*) ult. f. L *ad* to + *mors mort-* death]

amount /əmównt/ *n.* & *v.* ● *n.* **1** a quantity, esp. the total of a thing or things in number, size, value, extent, etc. (*a large amount of money*; *came to a considerable amount*). **2** the full effect or significance. ● *v.intr.* (foll. by *to*) **1** be equivalent to in number, size, significance, etc. (*amounted to £100*; *amounted to a disaster*). **2** (of a person) develop into, become (*might one day amount to something*). □ **any amount of** a great deal of. **no amount of** not even the greatest possible amount of. [ME f. OF *amunter* f. *amont* upward, lit. uphill, f. L *ad montem*]
■ *n.* **1** quantity, extent, volume, mass, expanse, area, bulk, quantum, portion; number, total, aggregate. **2** see SIGNIFICANCE 2. ● *v.* (*amount to*) **1** add up to, total, aggregate, come (up) to; be equivalent *or* equal to. **2** become, develop into, be capable of. □ **any amount of** see LOT *n.* 1.

amour /əmóor/ *n.* a love affair, esp. a secret one. [F, = love, f. L *amor amoris*]
■ see *love affair*.

amour propre /amóor própra/ *n.* self-respect. [F]
■ see SELF-RESPECT.

AMP *abbr.* adenosine monophosphate.

amp[1] /amp/ *n. Electr.* an ampere. [abbr.]

amp[2] /amp/ *n. colloq.* an amplifier. [abbr.]

ampelopsis /ámpilópsiss/ *n.* (*pl.* same) any plant of the genus *Ampelopsis* or *Parthenocissus*, usu. a climber supporting itself by twining tendrils, e.g. Virginia creeper. [mod.L f. Gk *ampelos* vine + *opsis* appearance]

amperage /ámpərij/ *n. Electr.* the strength of an electric current in amperes.

ampere /ámpair/ *n. Electr.* the SI base unit of electric current. ¶ Symb.: **A**. [A. M. *Ampère*, Fr. physicist d. 1836]

ampersand /ámpərsand/ *n.* the sign & (= *and*). [corrupt. of *and per se and* ('&' by itself is 'and')]

amphetamine /amféttəmin, -meen/ *n.* a synthetic drug used esp. as a stimulant. [abbr. of chemical name *a*lpha-*m*ethyl *phe*nethyl*amine*]

amphi- /ámfi/ *comb. form* **1** both. **2** of both kinds. **3** on both sides. **4** around. [Gk]

amphibian /amfíbbiən/ *adj.* & *n.* ● *adj.* **1** living both on land and in water. **2** *Zool.* of or relating to the class Amphibia. **3** (of a vehicle) able to operate on land and water. ● *n.* **1** *Zool.* any vertebrate of the class Amphibia, with a life history of an aquatic gill-breathing larval stage followed by a terrestrial lung-breathing adult stage, including frogs, toads, newts, and salamanders. **2** (in general use) a creature living both on land and in water. **3** an amphibian vehicle.

amphibious /amfíbbiəss/ *adj.* **1** living both on land and in water. **2** of or relating to or suited for both land and water. **3** *Mil.* **a** (of a military operation) involving forces landed from the sea. **b** (of forces) trained for such operations. **4** having a twofold nature; occupying two positions. □□ **amphibiously** *adv.*

amphibology /ámfibólləji/ *n.* (*pl.* **-ies**) **1** a quibble. **2** an ambiguous wording. [ME f. OF *amphibologie* f. LL *amphibologia* for L f. Gk *amphibolia* ambiguity]
■ see AMBIGUITY 1.

amphimixis /ámfimíksiss/ *n. Biol.* true sexual reproduction with the fusion of gametes from two individuals (cf. APOMIXIS). □□ **amphimictic** *adj.* [mod.L, formed as AMPHI- + Gk *mixis* mingling]

amphioxus /ámfióksəss/ *n.* any lancelet of the genus *Branchiostoma* (formerly *Amphioxus*). [mod.L, formed as AMPHI- + Gk *oxus* sharp]

amphipathic /ámfipáthik/ *adj. Chem.* **1** of a substance or molecule that has both a hydrophilic and a hydrophobic part. **2** consisting of such parts. [AMPHI- + Gk *pathikos* (as PATHOS)]

amphipod /ámfipod/ *n.* any crustacean of the largely marine order Amphipoda, having a laterally compressed abdomen with two kinds of limb, e.g. the freshwater shrimp (*Gammarus pulex*). [AMPHI- + Gk *pous podos* foot]

amphiprostyle /amfíprəstīl/ *n.* & *adj.* ● *n.* a classical building with a portico at each end. ● *adj.* of or in this style. [L *amphiprostylus* f. Gk *amphiprostulos* (as AMPHI-, *prostulos* PROSTYLE)]

amphisbaena /ámfisbeénə/ *n.* **1** *Mythol.* & *poet.* a fabulous serpent with a head at each end. **2** *Zool.* any burrowing wormlike lizard of the family Amphisbaena, having no apparent division of head from body making both ends look similar. [ME f. L f. Gk *amphisbaina* f. *amphis* both ways + *bainō* go]

amphitheatre /ámfitheeətər/ *n.* (*US* **amphitheater**) **1** a round, usu. unroofed building with tiers of seats surrounding a central space. **2** a semicircular gallery in a theatre. **3** a large circular hollow. **4** the scene of a contest. [L *amphitheatrum* f. Gk *amphitheatron* (as AMPHI-, THEATRE)]

amphora /ámfərə/ *n.* (*pl.* **amphorae** /-ree/ or **amphoras**) a Greek or Roman vessel with two handles and a narrow neck. [L f. Gk *amphoreus*]

amphoteric /ámfətérrik/ *adj. Chem.* able to react as a base and an acid. [Gk *amphoteros* compar. of *amphō* both]

ampicillin /ámpisíllin/ *n. Pharm.* a semi-synthetic penicillin used esp. in treating infections of the urinary and respiratory tracts. [*am*ino + *penicillin*]

ample /ámp'l/ *adj.* (**ampler**, **amplest**) **1 a** plentiful, abundant, extensive. **b** *euphem.* (esp. of a person) large, stout. **2** enough or more than enough. □□ **ampleness** *n.* **amply** *adv.* [F f. L *amplus*]
■ **1 a** abundant, full, complete, plentiful, copious, generous, substantial, lavish; extensive, wide-ranging, broad, expansive, great, large; liberal, unsparing, unstinted, unstinting. **b** see STOUT *adj.* 1. **2** sufficient, adequate, enough, satisfactory. □□ **ampleness** see ABUNDANCE 1. **amply** to a great extent, largely, extensively, fully, completely, abundantly, broadly, copiously; well, liberally, unstintingly, generously, richly, substantially, lavishly; sufficiently, adequately, satisfactorily.

amplifier /ámplifīər/ *n.* an electronic device for increasing the strength of electrical signals, esp. for conversion into sound in radio etc. equipment.

amplify /ámplifī/ *v.* (**-ies**, **-ied**) **1** *tr.* increase the volume or strength of (sound, electrical signals, etc.). **2** *tr.* enlarge upon or add detail to (a story etc.). **3** *intr.* expand what is said or written. □□ **amplification** /-fikáysh'n/ *n.* [ME f. OF *amplifier* f. L *amplificare* (as AMPLE, -FY)]
■ **1** magnify, increase, add to, augment, make larger *or* greater *or* louder *or* bigger, supplement, *colloq.* boost; broaden, widen, extend, enlarge (on). **2** enlarge (on), elaborate (on), expand (on), develop, expound on, stretch, lengthen, broaden, widen, extend, detail, expatiate on, embellish, embroider, overstate, exaggerate. **3** elaborate, go into detail, explain, exaggerate, expatiate. □□ **amplification** see *elaboration* (ELABORATE), INCREASE *n.* 1, 2.

amplitude /ámplityood/ *n.* **1 a** *Physics* the maximum extent of a vibration or oscillation from the position of equilibrium.

b *Electr.* the maximum departure of the value of an alternating current or wave from the average value. **2 a** spaciousness, breadth; wide range. **b** abundance. □ **amplitude modulation** *Electr.* **1** the modulation of a wave by variation of its amplitude. **2** the system using such modulation. [F *amplitude* or L *amplitudo* (as AMPLE)]
■ **2 a** see BREADTH 1, 3. **b** see ABUNDANCE 1.

ampoule /ámpōōl/ *n.* a small capsule in which measured quantities of liquids or solids, esp. for injecting, are sealed ready for use. [F f. L AMPULLA]

ampster /ámstər/ *n.* (also **amster**) *Austral. sl.* the accomplice of a sideshow operator who acts as a purchaser in an attempt to persuade others to follow his example. [f. *Amsterdam*, rhyming sl. for RAM *n.* 6]

ampulla /ampŏŏllə/ *n.* (*pl.* **ampullae** /-lee/) **1 a** a Roman globular flask with two handles. **b** a vessel for sacred uses. **2** *Anat.* the dilated end of a vessel or duct. [L]

amputate /ámpyootayt/ *v.tr.* cut off by surgical operation (a part of the body, esp. a limb), usu. because of injury or disease. □□ **amputation** /-táysh'n/ *n.* **amputator** *n.* [L *amputare* f. *amb-* about + *putare* prune]

amputee /ámpyootée/ *n.* a person who has lost a limb etc. by amputation.

amtrac /ámtrak/ *n.* (also **amtrak**) *US* an amphibious tracked vehicle used for landing assault troops on a shore. [*am*phibious + *trac*tor]

amu *abbr.* atomic mass unit.

amuck var. of AMOK.

amulet /ámyoolit/ *n.* **1** an ornament or small piece of jewellery worn as a charm against evil. **2** something which is thought to give such protection. [L *amuletum*, of unkn. orig.]
■ charm, talisman, good-luck piece, periapt, phylactery, ju-ju, *Austral.* churinga; toadstone, horseshoe, rabbit's foot.

amuse /əmyŏŏz/ *v.* **1** *tr.* cause (a person) to laugh or smile. **2** *tr.* & *refl.* (often foll. by *with, by*) interest or occupy; keep (a person) entertained. □□ **amusing** *adj.* **amusingly** *adv.* [ME f. OF *amuser* cause to muse (see MUSE[2]) f. causal *a* to + *muser* stare]
■ **1** make laugh *or* smile, delight, tickle, cheer, *colloq.* get. **2** divert, entertain, please, beguile, interest, occupy, distract. □□ **amusing** see ENTERTAINING.

amusement /əmyŏŏzmənt/ *n.* **1** something that amuses, esp. a pleasant diversion, game, or pastime. **2 a** the state of being amused. **b** the act of amusing. **3** a mechanical device (e.g. a roundabout) for entertainment at a fairground etc. □ **amusement arcade** *Brit.* an indoor area for entertainment with automatic game-machines. [F f. *amuser*: see AMUSE, -MENT]
■ **1** entertainment, diversion, divertissement, recreation, distraction, pastime, activity, game, sport, joke, *colloq.* lark. **2** entertainment, diversion, recreation, pleasure, relaxation, distraction, beguilement, enjoyment, fun (and games), play, gaiety, jollity, sport, beer and skittles; mirth.

amygdaloid /əmígdəloyd/ *adj.* shaped like an almond. □ **amygdaloid nucleus** a roughly almond-shaped mass of grey matter deep inside each cerebral hemisphere, associated with the sense of smell. [L *amygdala* f. Gk *amugdalē* almond]

amyl /áymīl, ámmil/ *n.* (used *attrib.*) *Chem.* the monovalent group C_5H_{11}-, derived from pentane. Also called PENTYL. [L *amylum* starch, from which oil containing it was distilled]

amylase /ámmilayz/ *n. Biochem.* any of several enzymes that convert starch and glycogen into simple sugars. [AMYL + -ASE]

amylopsin /ámmilópsin/ *n. Biochem.* an enzyme of the pancreas that converts starch into maltose. [AMYL after *pepsin*]

Amytal /ámmital/ *n. propr.* a name for amylobarbitone, a barbiturate drug used as a sedative and a hypnotic. [chem. name *amylethyl barbituric acid*]

an /an, ən/ *adj.* the form of the indefinite article (see A[1]) used before words beginning with a vowel sound (*an egg*; *an hour*; *an MP*). ¶ Now less often used before aspirated words beginning with *h* and stressed on a syllable other than the first (so *a hotel*, not *an hotel*).

an-[1] /ən, an/ *prefix* not, without (*anarchy*) (cf. A-[1]). [Gk *an-*]

an-[2] /ən, an/ assim. form of AD- before *n.*

-an /ən/ *suffix* (also **-ean, -ian**) forming adjectives and nouns, esp. from names of places, systems, zoological classes or orders, and founders (*Mexican*; *Anglican*; *crustacean*; *European*; *Lutheran*; *Georgian*; *theologian*). [ult. f. L adj. endings *-(i)anus, -aeus*: cf. Gk *-aios, -eios*]

ana /áanə/ *n.* **1** (as *pl.*) anecdotes or literary gossip about a person. **2** (as *sing.*) a collection of a person's memorable sayings. [= -ANA]

ana- /ánnə/ *prefix* (usu. **an-** before a vowel) **1** up (*anadromous*). **2** back (*anamnesis*). **3** again (*anabaptism*). [Gk *ana* up]

-ana /áanə/ *suffix* forming plural nouns meaning 'things associated with' (*Victoriana*; *Americana*). [neut. pl. of L adj. ending *-anus*]

Anabaptism /ánnəbáptiz'm/ *n.* the doctrine that baptism should only be administered to believing adults. □□ **Anabaptist** *n.* [eccl.L *anabaptismus* f. Gk *anabaptismos* (as ANA-, BAPTISM)]

anabas /ánnəbass/ *n.* any of the freshwater fish of the climbing perch family native to Asia and Africa, esp. the genus *Anabas*, able to breathe air and move on land. [mod.L f. Gk past part. of *anabainō* walk up]

anabasis /ənábbəsiss/ *n.* (*pl.* **anabases** /-seez/) **1** the march of the younger Cyrus into Asia in 401 BC as narrated by Xenophon in his work *Anabasis*. **2** a military up-country march. [Gk, = ascent f. *anabainō* (as ANA-, *bainō* go)]

anabatic /ánnəbáttik/ *adj. Meteorol.* (of a wind) caused by air flowing upwards (cf. KATABATIC). [Gk *anabatikos* ascending (as ANABASIS)]

anabiosis /ánnəbīósiss/ *n.* (*pl.* **anabioses** /-seez/) revival after apparent death. □□ **anabiotic** /-bīóttik/ *adj.* [med.L f. Gk *anabiōsis* f. *anabioō* return to life]

anabolic /ánnəbóllik/ *adj. Biochem.* of or relating to anabolism. □ **anabolic steroid** any of a group of synthetic steroid hormones used to increase muscle size.

anabolism /ənábbəliz'm/ *n. Biochem.* the synthesis of complex molecules in living organisms from simpler ones together with the storage of energy; constructive metabolism (opp. CATABOLISM). [Gk *anabolē* ascent (as ANA-, *ballō* throw)]

anabranch /ánnəbraanch/ *n.* esp. *Austral.* a stream that leaves a river and re-enters it lower down. [ANASTOMOSE + BRANCH]

anachronic /ánnəkrónnik/ *adj.* **1** out of date. **2** involving anachronism. [ANACHRONISM after *synchronic* etc.]
■ **1** see *old-fashioned*.

anachronism /ənákrəniz'm/ *n.* **1 a** the attribution of a custom, event, etc., to a period to which it does not belong. **b** a thing attributed in this way. **2 a** anything out of harmony with its period. **b** an old-fashioned or out-of-date person or thing. □□ **anachronistic** /-nístik/ *adj.* **anachronistically** /-nístikəli/ *adv.* [F *anachronisme* or Gk *anakhronismos* (as ANA-, *khronos* time)]
■ **1** misdating, misapplication, prochronism, parachronism. **2 b** (old) fogy, conservative, *colloq.* stick-in-the-mud, geriatric, *sl.* fuddy-duddy, square, back number; dodo, *colloq.* fossil, *derog.* museum piece, troglodyte. □□ **anachronistic** see *old-fashioned*.

anacoluthon /ánnəkəlŏŏthon/ *n.* (*pl.* **anacolutha** /-thə/) a sentence or construction which lacks grammatical sequence (e.g. *while in the garden the door banged shut*). □□ **anacoluthic** *adj.* [LL f. Gk *anakolouthon* (as AN-[1], *akolouthos* following)]

anaconda /ánnəkóndə/ *n.* a large non-poisonous snake living mainly in water or in trees that kills its prey by constriction. [alt. of *anacondaia* f. Sinh. *henakandayā* whip-snake f. *hena* lightning + *kanda* stem: orig. of a snake in Sri Lanka]

anacreontic /ənákriόntik/ *n.* & *adj.* ● *n.* a poem written after the manner of Anacreon, a Greek lyric poet (d. 478 BC). ● *adj.* **1** after the manner of Anacreon. **2** convivial and amatory in tone. [LL *anacreonticus* f. Gk *Anakreōn*]

anacrusis /ánnəkrόόssiss/ *n.* (*pl.* **anacruses** /-seez/) **1** (in poetry) an unstressed syllable at the beginning of a verse. **2** *Mus.* an unstressed note or notes before the first bar-line. [Gk *anakrousis* (as ANA-, *krousis* f. *krouō* strike)]

anadromous /ənádrəməss/ *adj.* (of a fish, e.g. the salmon) that swims up a river from the sea to spawn (opp. CATADROMOUS). [Gk *anadromos* (as ANA-, *dromos* running)]

anaemia /əne͞emiə/ *n.* (*US* **anemia**) a deficiency in the blood, usu. of red cells or their haemoglobin, resulting in pallor and weariness. □ **pernicious anaemia** a defective formation of red blood cells through a lack of vitamin B_{12} or folic acid. [mod.L f. Gk *anaimia* (as AN-[1], -AEMIA)]

anaemic /əne͞emik/ *adj.* (*US* **anemic**) **1** relating to or suffering from anaemia. **2** pale; lacking in vitality.
■ **2** see PALE[1] *adj.* 1, 4, WEAK 2.

anaerobe /ánnərōb, ənáirōb/ *n.* an organism that grows without air, or requires oxygen-free conditions to live. □□ **anaerobic** /ánnairṓbik/ *adj.* [F *anaérobie* formed as AN-[1] + AEROBE]

anaesthesia /ánniss-the͞eziə/ *n.* (*US* **anesthesia**) the absence of sensation, esp. artificially induced insensitivity to pain usu. achieved by the administration of gases or the injection of drugs. □□ **anaesthesiology** /-ziόlləji/ *n.* [mod.L f. Gk *anaisthēsia* (as AN-[1], *aisthēsis* sensation)]

anaesthetic /ánniss-théttik/ *adj.* & *n.* (*US* **anesthetic**) ● *n.* a substance that produces insensibility to pain etc. ● *adj.* producing partial or complete insensibility to pain etc. □ **general anaesthetic** an anaesthetic that affects the whole body, usu. with loss of consciousness. **local anaesthetic** an anaesthetic that affects a restricted area of the body. [Gk *anaisthētos* insensible (as ANAESTHESIA)]
■ *n.* see PAINKILLER. ● *adj.* see NARCOTIC *adj.*

anaesthetist /əne͞ess-thətist/ *n.* a specialist in the administration of anaesthetics.

anaesthetize /əne͞ess-thətīz/ *v.tr.* (also **-ise**, *US* **anesthetize**) **1** administer an anaesthetic to. **2** deprive of physical or mental sensation. □□ **anaesthetization** /-záysh'n/ *n.*
■ **2** see NUMB *v.*

anaglyph /ánnəglif/ *n.* **1** *Photog.* a composite stereoscopic photograph printed in superimposed complementary colours. **2** an embossed object cut in low relief. □□ **anaglyphic** /-glíffik/ *adj.* [Gk *anagluphē* (as ANA-, *gluphē* f. *gluphō* carve)]

anaglypta /ánnəgliptə/ *n.* a type of thick embossed wallpaper, usu. for painting over. [L *anaglypta* work in bas-relief: cf. ANAGLYPH]

anagram /ánnəgram/ *n.* a word or phrase formed by transposing the letters of another word or phrase. □□ **anagrammatic** /-grəmáttik/ *adj.* **anagrammatical** /-grəmáttik'l/ *adj.* **anagrammatize** /-grámmətīz/ *v.tr.* (also **-ise**). [F *anagramme* or mod.L *anagramma* f. Gk ANA- + *gramma -atos* letter: cf. -GRAM]

anal /áyn'l/ *adj.* relating to or situated near the anus. □ **anal retentive** (of a person) excessively orderly and fussy (supposedly owing to aspects of toilet-training in infancy). □□ **anally** *adv.* [mod.L *analis* (as ANUS)]

analects /ánnəlekts/ *n.pl.* (also **analecta** /ánnəléktə/) a collection of short literary extracts. [L f. Gk *analekta* things gathered f. *analegō* pick up]

analeptic /ánnəléptik/ *adj.* & *n.* ● *adj.* (of a drug etc.) restorative. ● *n.* a restorative medicine or drug. [Gk *analēptikos* f. *analambanō* take back]

analgesia /ánnalje͞eziə, -siə/ *n.* the absence or relief of pain. [mod.L f. Gk, = painlessness]

analgesic /ánnalje͞ezik, -sik/ *adj.* & *n.* ● *adj.* relieving pain. ● *n.* an analgesic drug.
■ *n.* see PAINKILLER.

analog *US* var. of ANALOGUE.

analogize /ənáləjīz/ *v.* (also **-ise**) **1** *tr.* represent or explain by analogy. **2** *intr.* use analogy.

analogous /ənálləgəss/ *adj.* (usu. foll. by *to*) partially similar or parallel; showing analogy. □□ **analogously** *adv.* [L *analogus* f. Gk *analogos* proportionate]
■ see LIKE[1] *adj.* 1a.

analogue /ánnəlog/ *n.* (*US* **analog**) **1** an analogous or parallel thing. **2** (*attrib.*) (usu. **analog**) (of a computer or electronic process) using physical variables, e.g. voltage, weight, or length, to represent numbers (cf. DIGITAL). [F f. Gk *analogon* neut. adj.: see ANALOGOUS]
■ **1** see METAPHOR 2, PARALLEL *n.* 1.

analogy /ənálləji/ *n.* (*pl.* **-ies**) **1** (usu. foll. by *to*, *with*, *between*) correspondence or partial similarity. **2** *Logic* a process of arguing from similarity in known respects to similarity in other respects. **3** *Philol.* the imitation of existing words in forming inflections or constructions of others, without the existence of corresponding intermediate stages. **4** *Biol.* the resemblance of function between organs essentially different. **5** = ANALOGUE 1. □□ **analogical** /ánnəlόjik'l/ *adj.* **analogically** /ánnəlόjikəli/ *adv.* [F *analogie* or L *analogia* proportion f. Gk (as ANALOGOUS)]
■ **1** see METAPHOR. **5** see METAPHOR, PARALLEL *n.*

analysand /ənállisand/ *n.* a person undergoing psychoanalysis.

analyse /ánnəlīz/ *v.tr.* (*US* **analyze**) **1** examine in detail the constitution or structure of. **2 a** *Chem.* ascertain the constituents of (a sample of a mixture or compound). **b** take apart; break (something) down into its constituent parts. **3** find or show the essence or structure of (a book, music, etc.). **4** *Gram.* resolve (a sentence) into its grammatical elements. **5** psychoanalyse. □□ **analysable** *adj.* **analyser** *n.* [obs. *analyse* (n.) or F *analyser* f. *analyse* (n.) f. med.L ANALYSIS]
■ **1** examine, investigate, study, scrutinize, enquire *or* look into, dissect. **2 b** take apart *or* to pieces, separate, dissect, break down, anatomize. **3** interpret, assess, evaluate, critique, criticize, review. **5** psychoanalyse, give therapy to, put in therapy, *colloq.* psych.

analysis /ənállisiss/ *n.* (*pl.* **analyses** /-seez/) **1 a** a detailed examination of the elements or structure of a substance etc. **b** a statement of the result of this. **2 a** *Chem.* the determination of the constituent parts of a mixture or compound. **b** the act or process of breaking something down into its constituent parts. **3** psychoanalysis. **4** *Math.* the use of algebra and calculus in problem-solving. **5** *Cricket* a statement of the performance of a bowler, usu. giving the numbers of overs and maiden overs bowled, runs conceded, and wickets taken. □ **in the final** (or **last** or **ultimate**) **analysis** after all due consideration; in the end. [med.L f. Gk *analusis* (as ANA-, *luō* set free)]
■ **1** examination, investigation, study, scrutiny, enquiry, inquiry, dissection, anatomy, assessment; interpretation, criticism, critique; review. **2** assay, breakdown, division. **3** see THERAPY 2. □ **in the final** (or **last** or **ultimate**) **analysis** see *ultimately* (ULTIMATE).

analyst /ánnəlist/ *n.* **1** a person skilled in (esp. chemical) analysis. **2** a psychoanalyst. [F *analyste*]

analytic /ánnəlíttik/ *adj.* **1** of or relating to analysis. **2** *Philol.* analytical. **3** *Logic* (of a statement etc.) such that its denial is self-contradictory; true by definition (see SYNTHETIC). [LL f. Gk *analutikos* (as ANALYSIS)]

analytical /ánnəlíttik'l/ *adj.* **1** using analytic methods. **2** *Philol.* using separate words instead of inflections (cf. SYNTHETIC). □ **analytical geometry** geometry using co-ordinates. □□ **analytically** *adv.*

analyze *US* var. of ANALYSE.

anamnesis /ánnəmne͞essiss/ *n.* (*pl.* **anamneses** /-seez/) **1** recollection (esp. of a supposed previous existence). **2** a patient's account of his or her medical history. **3** *Eccl.* the part of the anaphora recalling the Passion, Resurrection, and Ascension of Christ. [Gk, = remembrance]

anandrous /ənándrəss/ *adj.* *Bot.* having no stamens. [Gk *anandros* without males f. *an-* not + *anēr andros* male]

Anangu /áanaangoo/ *n.* (*pl.* same) *Austral.* an Aborigine, esp. one from Central Australia. [Western Desert language, =person]

anapaest /ánnəpeest/ *n.* (*US* **anapest**) *Prosody* a foot consisting of two short or unstressed syllables followed by one long or stressed syllable. □□ **anapaestic** /-péestik/ *adj.* [L *anapaestus* f. Gk *anapaistos* reversed (because the reverse of a dactyl)]

anaphase /ánnəfayz/ *n. Biol.* the stage of meiotic or mitotic cell division when the chromosomes move away from one another to opposite poles of the spindle. [ANA- + PHASE]

anaphora /ənáffərə/ *n.* **1** *Rhet.* the repetition of a word or phrase at the beginning of successive clauses. **2** *Gram.* the use of a word referring to or replacing a word used earlier in a sentence, to avoid repetition (e.g. *do* in *I like it and so do they*). **3** *Eccl.* the part of the Eucharist which contains the consecration, anamnesis, and communion. □□ **anaphoric** /ánnəfórrik/ *adj.* [L f. Gk, = repetition (as ANA-, *pherō* to bear)]

anaphrodisiac /anáfrədízziak/ *adj.* & *n.* ● *adj.* tending to reduce sexual desire. ● *n.* an anaphrodisiac drug.

anaphylaxis /ánnəfiláksiss/ *n.* (*pl.* **anaphylaxes** /-seez/) *Med.* hypersensitivity of tissues to a dose of antigen, as a reaction against a previous dose. □□ **anaphylactic** *adj.* [mod.L f. F *anaphylaxie* (as ANA- + Gk *phulaxis* guarding)]

anaptyxis /ánnəptiksiss/ *n.* (*pl.* **anaptyxes** /-seez/) *Phonet.* the insertion of a vowel between two consonants to aid pronunciation (as in *went thataway*). □□ **anaptyctic** *adj.* [mod.L f. Gk *anaptuxis* (as ANA-, *ptussō* fold)]

anarchism /ánnərkiz'm/ *n.* the doctrine that all government should be abolished. [F *anarchisme* (as ANARCHY)]

anarchist /ánnərkist/ *n.* an advocate of anarchism or of political disorder. □□ **anarchistic** /-kístik/ *adj.* [F *anarchiste* (as ANARCHY)]

anarchy /ánnərki/ *n.* **1** disorder, esp. political or social. **2** lack of government in a society. □□ **anarchic** /ənaárkik/ *adj.* **anarchical** /ənaárkik'l/ *adj.* **anarchically** /ənaárkikəli/ *adv.* [med.L f. Gk *anarkhia* (as AN-[1], *arkhē* rule)]

anastigmat /ənástigmat/ *n.* a lens or lens-system made free from astigmatism by correction. [G f. *anastigmatisch* ANASTIGMATIC]

anastigmatic /ánnəstigmáttik/ *adj.* free from astigmatism.

anastomose /ənástəmōz/ *v.intr.* link by anastomosis. [F *anastomoser* (as ANASTOMOSIS)]

anastomosis /ənástəmṓsiss/ *n.* (*pl.* **anastomoses** /-seez/) a cross-connection of arteries, branches, rivers, etc. [mod.L f. Gk f. *anastomoō* furnish with a mouth (as ANA-, *stoma* mouth)]

anastrophe /ənástrəfi/ *n. Rhet.* the inversion of the usual order of words or clauses. [Gk *anastrophē* turning back (as ANA-, *strephō* to turn)]

anathema /ənáthəmə/ *n.* (*pl.* **anathemas**) **1** a detested thing or person (*is anathema to me*). **2 a** a curse of the Church, excommunicating a person or denouncing a doctrine. **b** a cursed thing or person. **c** a strong curse. [eccl.L, = excommunicated person, excommunication, f. Gk *anathema* thing devoted, (later) accursed thing, f. *anatithēmi* set up]
■ **1** see HATEFUL.

anathematize /ənáthəmətīz/ *v.tr.* & *intr.* (also **-ise**) curse. [F *anathématiser* f. L *anathematīzāre* f. Gk *anathematizo* (as ANATHEMA)]
■ see CURSE *v.* 1a.

anatomical /ánnətómmik'l/ *adj.* **1** of or relating to anatomy. **2** structural. □□ **anatomically** *adv.* [F *anatomique* or LL *anatomicus* (as ANATOMY)]

anatomist /ənáttəmist/ *n.* a person skilled in anatomy. [F *anatomiste* or med.L *anatomista* (as ANATOMIZE)]

anatomize /ənáttəmīz/ *v.tr.* (also **-ise**) **1** examine in detail. **2** dissect. [F *anatomiser* or med.L *anatomizare* f. *anatomia* (as ANATOMY)]
■ see ANALYSE 2b.

anatomy /ənáttəmi/ *n.* (*pl.* **-ies**) **1** the science of the bodily structure of animals and plants. **2** this structure. **3** *colloq.* a human body. **4** analysis. **5** the dissection of the human body, animals, or plants. [F *anatomie* or LL *anatomia* f. Gk (as ANA-, -TOMY)]
■ **2** see FORM *n.* 1a. **3** see FORM *n.* 1b, BODY *n.* 1.

anatta (also **anatto**) var. of ANNATTO.

ANC *abbr.* African National Congress.

-ance /ənss/ *suffix* forming nouns expressing: **1** a quality or state or an instance of one (*arrogance*; *protuberance*; *relevance*; *resemblance*). **2** an action (*assistance*; *furtherance*; *penance*). [from or after F *-ance* f. L *-antia*, *-entia* (cf. -ENCE) f. pres. part. stem *-ant-*, *-ent-*]

ancestor /ánsestər/ *n.* (*fem.* **ancestress** /-striss/) **1** any (esp. remote) person from whom one is descended. **2** an early type of animal or plant from which others have evolved. **3** an early prototype or forerunner (*ancestor of the computer*). [ME f. OF *ancestre* f. L *antecessor -oris* f. *antecedere* (as ANTE-, *cedere cess-* go)]
■ **1** forebear, forefather, progenitor, primogenitor, predecessor, grandam, *archaic* grandsire. **3** forerunner, precursor, antecedent, progenitor; prototype, archetype; harbinger.

ancestral /ansésträl/ *adj.* belonging to or inherited from one's ancestors. [F *ancestrel* (as ANCESTOR)]

ancestry /ánsestri/ *n.* (*pl.* **-ies**) **1** one's (esp. remote) family descent. **2** one's ancestors collectively. [ME alt. of OF *ancesserie* (as ANCESTOR)]

anchor /ángkər/ *n.* & *v.* ● *n.* **1** a heavy metal weight used to moor a ship to the sea-bottom or a balloon to the ground. **2** a thing affording stability. **3** a source of confidence. **4** (in full **anchorman, anchorperson, anchorwoman**) a person who plays a vital part, as the end member of a tug-of-war team, the compère of a broadcast programme, etc. ● *v.* **1** *tr.* secure (a ship or balloon) by means of an anchor. **2** *tr.* fix firmly. **3** *intr.* cast anchor. **4** *intr.* be moored by means of an anchor. □ **anchor-plate** a heavy piece of timber or metal, e.g. as support for suspension-bridge cables. **at anchor** moored by means of an anchor. **cast** (or **come to**) **anchor** let the anchor down. **weigh anchor** take the anchor up. [OE *ancor* f. L *anchora* f. Gk *agkura*]
■ *n.* **1** mooring, sheet anchor. **2** mainstay, support, stabilizer, sheet anchor, holdfast; hold, grasp, grip. **4** presenter, announcer, newsreader, newscaster, reporter, broadcaster; master of ceremonies, MC, *colloq.* emcee. ● *v.* **1, 2** attach, affix, secure, moor, fix, fasten, make fast; pin, rivet, glue. **3, 4** drop *or* cast anchor, harbour, moor, be moored, be at anchor.

anchorage /ángkərij/ *n.* **1** a place where a ship may be anchored. **2** the act of anchoring or lying at anchor. **3** anything dependable.

anchorite /ángkərīt/ *n.* (also **anchoret** /-rit/) (*fem.* **anchoress** /-riss/) **1** a hermit; a religious recluse. **2** a person of secluded habits. □□ **anchoretic** /-réttik/ *adj.* **anchoritic** /-ríttik/ *adj.* [ME f. med.L *anc(h)orita*, eccl.L *anchoreta* f. eccl.Gk *anakhōrētēs* f. *anakhōreō* retire]

anchorman /ángkərmən/ *n.* (*pl.* **-men**) **1** a person who coordinates activities, esp. as compère in a broadcast. **2** a person who plays a crucial part, esp. at the back of a tug-of-war team or as the last runner in a relay race.
■ **1** see ANCHOR *n.* 4.

anchoveta /ánchəvéttə/ *n.* a small Pacific anchovy caught for use as bait or to make fish-meal. [Sp., dimin. of *anchova*: cf. ANCHOVY]

anchovy /ánchəvi, anchṓvi/ *n.* (*pl.* **-ies**) any of various small silvery fish of the herring family usu. preserved in salt and oil and having a strong taste. □ **anchovy pear** a W. Indian fruit like a mango. **anchovy toast** toast spread with paste made from anchovies. [Sp. & Port. *ancho(v)a*, of uncert. orig.]

anchusa /ankyóozə, anchóozə/ *n.* any plant of the genus *Anchusa*, akin to borage. [L f. Gk *agkhousa*]

anchylose var. of ANKYLOSE.

anchylosis var. of ANKYLOSIS.

ancien régime /onsyáɴ rezhéem/ *n.* (*pl.* ***anciens régimes*** *pronunc.* same) **1** the political and social system in France before the Revolution of 1789. **2** any superseded regime. [F, = old rule]

ancient[1] /áynsh'nt/ *adj.* & *n.* ● *adj.* **1** of long ago. **2** having lived or existed long. ● *n. archaic* an old man. □ **ancient history 1** the history of the ancient civilizations of the Mediterranean area and the Near East before the fall of the Western Roman Empire in 476. **2** something already long familiar. **ancient lights** a window that a neighbour may not deprive of light by building. **ancient monument** *Brit.* an old building etc. preserved usu. under Government control. **the ancients** the people of ancient times, esp. the Greeks and Romans. □□ **ancientness** *n.* [ME f. AF *auncien* f. OF *ancien*, ult. f. L *ante* before]

■ *adj.* **1** old, archaic, antique, bygone, past, former, earlier, antediluvian, primitive, prehistoric, primeval, primordial, immemorial, *archaic* olden. **2** old, time-worn, aged, ageing, age-old, obsolescent, antiquated, antique, elderly, venerable, grey, hoary, superannuated, obsolete, fossil, fossilized, *colloq.* antediluvian. ● *n.* Methuselah, *archaic* greybeard.

ancient[2] /áynsh'nt/ *n. archaic* = ENSIGN. [corrupt. of form *ensyne* etc. by assoc. with *ancien* = ANCIENT[1]]

anciently /áynsh'ntli/ *adv.* long ago.

ancillary /ansílləri/ *adj.* & *n.* ● *adj.* **1** (of a person, activity, or service) providing essential support to a central service or industry, esp. the medical service. **2** (often foll. by *to*) subordinate, subservient. ● *n.* (*pl.* **-ies**) **1** an ancillary worker. **2** something which is ancillary; an auxiliary or accessory. [L *ancillaris* f. *ancilla* maidservant]

■ *adj.* see AUXILIARY *adj.* ● *n.* see AUXILIARY *n.*

ancon /ángkən/ *n.* (*pl.* **-es** /angkṓneez/) *Archit.* **1** a console, usu. of two volutes, supporting or appearing to support a cornice. **2** each of a pair of projections on either side of a block of stone etc. for lifting or repositioning. [L f. Gk *agkōn* elbow]

-ancy /ənsi/ *suffix* forming nouns denoting a quality (*constancy*; *relevancy*) or state (*expectancy*; *infancy*) (cf. -ANCE). [from or after L *-antia*: cf. -ENCY]

and /and, ənd/ *conj.* **1 a** connecting words, clauses, or sentences, that are to be taken jointly (*cakes and buns*; *white and brown bread*; *buy and sell*; *two hundred and forty*). **b** implying progression (*better and better*). **c** implying causation (*do that and I'll hit you*; *she hit him and he cried*). **d** implying great duration (*he cried and cried*). **e** implying a great number (*miles and miles*). **f** implying addition (*two and two are four*). **g** implying variety (*there are books and books*). **h** implying succession (*walking two and two*). **2** *colloq.* to (*try and open it*). **3** in relation to (*Britain and the EEC*). □ **and/or** either or both of two stated possibilities (usually restricted to legal and commercial use). [OE *and*]

-and /and/ *suffix* forming nouns meaning 'a person or thing to be treated in a specified way' (*ordinand*). [L gerundive ending *-andus*]

andante /andánti/ *adv.*, *adj.*, & *n. Mus.* ● *adv.* & *adj.* in a moderately slow tempo. ● *n.* an andante passage or movement. [It., part. of *andare* go]

andantino /ándantéenō/ *adv.*, *adj.*, & *n. Mus.* ● *adv.* & *adj.* rather quicker (orig. slower) than andante. ● *n.* (*pl.* **-os**) an andantino passage or movement. [It., dimin. of ANDANTE]

andesite /ándizīt/ *n.* a fine-grained brown or greyish intermediate volcanic rock. [*Andes* mountain chain in S. America + -ITE[1]]

andiron /ándīrn/ *n.* a metal stand (usu. one of a pair) for supporting burning wood in a fireplace; a firedog. [ME f. OF *andier*, of unkn. orig.: assim. to IRON]

androecium /andréessiəm/ *n.* (*pl.* **androecia** /-siə/) *Bot.* the stamens taken collectively. [mod.L f. Gk *andro-* male + *oikion* house]

androgen /ándrəjən/ *n.* a male sex hormone or other substance capable of developing and maintaining certain male sexual characteristics. □□ **androgenic** /-jénnik/ *adj.* [Gk *andro-* male + -GEN]

androgyne /ándrəjīn/ *adj.* & *n.* ● *adj.* hermaphrodite. ● *n.* a hermaphrodite person. [OF *androgyne* or L *androgynus* f. Gk *androgunos* (*anēr andros* male, *gunē* woman)]

androgynous /andrójinəss/ *adj.* **1** hermaphrodite. **2** *Bot.* with stamens and pistils in the same flower or inflorescence.

androgyny /andrójini/ *n.* hermaphroditism.

android /ándroyd/ *n.* a robot with a human appearance. [Gk *andro-* male, man + -OID]

-androus /ándrəss/ *comb. form Bot.* forming adjectives meaning 'having specified male organs or stamens' (*monandrous*). [mod.L f. Gk *-andros* f. *anēr andros* male + -OUS]

-ane[1] /ayn/ *suffix* var. of -AN; usu. with distinction of sense (*germane*; *humane*; *urbane*) but sometimes with no corresponding form in *-an* (*mundane*).

-ane[2] /ayn/ *suffix Chem.* forming names of paraffins and other saturated hydrocarbons (*methane*; *propane*). [after *-ene*, *-ine*, etc.]

anecdotage /ánnikdōtij/ *n.* **1** *joc.* garrulous old age. **2** anecdotes. [ANECDOTE + -AGE: sense 1 after DOTAGE]

anecdote /ánnikdōt/ *n.* a short account (or painting etc.) of an entertaining or interesting incident. □□ **anecdotal** /-dṓt'l/ *adj.* **anecdotalist** /-dṓtəlist/ *n.* **anecdotic** /-dóttik/ *adj.* **anecdotist** *n.* [F *anecdote* or mod.L f. Gk *anekdota* things unpublished (as AN-[1], *ekdotos* f. *ekdidōmi* publish)]

■ see STORY 1.

anechoic /ánnikṓ-ik/ *adj.* free from echo.

anele /ənéel/ *v.tr. archaic* anoint, esp. in extreme unction. [ME f. AN-[1] + *elien* f. OE *ele* f. L *oleum* oil]

anemia *US* var. of ANAEMIA.

anemic *US* var. of ANAEMIC.

anemograph /ənémməgraaf/ *n.* an instrument for recording on paper the direction and force of the wind. □□ **anemographic** /-gráffik/ *adj.* [Gk *anemos* wind + -GRAPH[1]]

anemometer /ánnimómmitər/ *n.* an instrument for measuring the force of the wind. [Gk *anemos* wind + -METER]

anemometry /ánnimómmitri/ *n.* the measurement of the force of the wind. □□ **anemometric** /-məmétrik/ *adj.* [Gk *anemos* wind + -METRY]

anemone /ənémməni/ *n.* **1** any plant of the genus *Anemone*, akin to the buttercup, with flowers of various vivid colours. **2** = PASQUE-FLOWER. [L f. Gk *anemōnē* wind-flower f. *anemos* wind]

anemophilous /ánnimóffiləss/ *adj.* wind-pollinated. [Gk *anemos* wind + *-philous* (see -PHILIA)]

anent /ənént/ *prep. archaic* or *Sc.* or *US* concerning. [OE *on efen* on a level with]

-aneous /áyniəss/ *suffix* forming adjectives (*cutaneous*; *miscellaneous*). [L *-aneus* + -OUS]

aneroid /ánnəroyd/ *adj.* & *n.* ● *adj.* (of a barometer) that measures air-pressure by its action on the elastic lid of an evacuated box, not by the height of a column of fluid. ● *n.* an aneroid barometer. [F *anéroïde* f. Gk *a-* not + *nēros* water]

anesthesia etc. *US* var. of ANAESTHESIA etc.

aneurin /ənyóorin, ányoorin/ *n.* = THIAMINE. [*a*nti + poly*neur*itis + vitam*in*]

aneurysm /ányooriz'm/ *n.* (also **aneurism**) an excessive localized enlargement of an artery. □□ **aneurysmal** /-rízm'l/ *adj.* (also **aneurismal**). [Gk *aneurusma* f. *aneurunō* widen out f. *eurus* wide]

anew /ənyóo/ *adv.* **1** again. **2** in a different way. [ME, f. A-[4] + NEW]

anfractuosity /ánfraktyoo-óssiti/ *n.* **1** circuitousness. **2** intricacy. [F *anfractuosité* f. LL *anfractuosus* f. L *anfractus* a bending]

anfractuous /anfráktyooəss/ *adj.* winding, sinuous; roundabout, circuitous. [f. late L *anfractuosus*, f. L *anfractus* a bending]

angary /ánggəri/ *n. Law* the right of a belligerent (subject to compensation for loss) to seize or destroy neutral property under military necessity. [F *angarie* ult. f. Gk *aggareia* f. *aggaros* courier]

angel /áynjəl/ *n.* **1 a** an attendant or messenger of God. **b** a conventional representation of this in human form with wings. **c** an attendant spirit (*evil angel*; *guardian angel*). **d** a member of the lowest order of the ninefold celestial hierarchy (see ORDER). **2 a** a very virtuous person. **b** an obliging person (*be an angel and answer the door*). **3** an old English coin bearing the figure of the archangel Michael piercing the dragon. **4** *sl.* a financial backer of an enterprise, esp. in the theatre. **5** an unexplained radar echo. □ **angel cake** a very light sponge cake. **angel dust** *sl.* the hallucinogenic drug phencyclidine hydrochloride. **angel-fish** any of various fish, esp. *Pterophyllum scalare*, with large dorsal and ventral fins. **angel-shark** = MONKFISH 2. **angels-on-horseback** a savoury of oysters wrapped in slices of bacon. [ME f. OF *angele* f. eccl.L *angelus* f. Gk *aggelos* messenger]

angelic /anjéllik/ *adj.* **1** like or relating to angels. **2** having characteristics attributed to angels, esp. sublime beauty or innocence. □□ **angelical** *adj.* **angelically** *adv.* [ME f. F *angélique* or LL *angelicus* f. Gk *aggelikos* (as ANGEL)]

angelica /anjéllikə/ *n.* **1** an aromatic umbelliferous plant, *Angelica archangelica*, used in cooking and medicine. **2** its candied stalks. [med.L (*herba*) *angelica* angelic herb]

angelus /ánjiləss/ *n.* **1** a Roman Catholic devotion commemorating the Incarnation, said at morning, noon, and sunset. **2** a bell rung to announce this. [opening words *Angelus domini* (L, = the angel of the Lord)]

anger /ánggər/ *n.* & *v.* ● *n.* extreme or passionate displeasure. ● *v.tr.* make angry; enrage. [ME f. ON *angr* grief, *angra* vex]

■ *n.* rage, fury, pique, spleen, *colloq.* dander, *literary* wrath, ire, *poet. or archaic* choler; antagonism, irritation, vexation, indignation, displeasure, ill *or* bad feeling, annoyance, irritability, resentment, outrage. ● *v.* enrage, infuriate, madden, pique, incense, make a person's hackles rise, make a person's blood boil, rile, gall, empurple; annoy, irritate, vex, nettle, displease, exasperate, provoke, get *or* put a person's back up, *US* mad.

Angevin /ánjivin/ *n.* & *adj.* ● *n.* **1** a native or inhabitant of Anjou. **2** a Plantagenet, esp. any of the English kings from Henry II to John. ● *adj.* **1** of Anjou. **2** of the Plantagenets. [F]

angina /anjīnə/ *n.* **1** an attack of intense constricting pain often causing suffocation. **2** (in full **angina pectoris** /péktəriss/) pain in the chest brought on by exertion, owing to an inadequate blood supply to the heart. [L, = spasm of the chest f. *angina* quinsy f. Gk *agkhonē* strangling]

angioma /ánjiōmə/ *n.* (*pl.* **angiomata** /-mətə/) a tumour produced by the dilatation or new formation of blood-vessels. [mod.L f. Gk *aggeion* vessel]

angiosperm /ánjiəsperm/ *n.* any plant producing flowers and reproducing by seeds enclosed within a carpel, including herbaceous plants, herbs, shrubs, grasses and most trees (opp. GYMNOSPERM). □□ **angiospermous** /ánjiəspérməss/ *adj.* [Gk *aggeion* vessel + *sperma* seed]

Angle /ángg'l/ *n.* (usu. in *pl.*) a member of a tribe from Schleswig that settled in Eastern Britain in the 5th c. □□ **Anglian** *adj.* [L *Anglus* f. Gmc (OE *Engle*: cf. ENGLISH) f. *Angul* a district of Schleswig (now in N. Germany) (as ANGLE[2])]

angle[1] /ángg'l/ *n.* & *v.* ● *n.* **1 a** the space between two meeting lines or surfaces. **b** the inclination of two lines or surfaces to each other. **2 a** a corner. **b** a sharp projection. **3 a** the direction from which a photograph etc. is taken. **b** the aspect from which a matter is considered. ● *v.* **1** *tr.* & *intr.* move or place obliquely; point in a particular direction. **2** *tr.* present (information) from a particular point of view (*was angled in favour of the victim*). □ **angle brackets** brackets in the form < > (see BRACKET *n.* 3). **angle-iron** a piece of iron or steel with an L-shaped cross-section, used to strengthen a framework. **angle of repose** the angle beyond which an inclined body will not support another on its surface by friction. [ME f. OF *angle* or f. L *angulus*]

■ *n.* **1 b** slant, inclination. **2** bend, corner, intersection, cusp, point, apex, tip; sharp end, projection, protrusion. **3** direction, slant, point of view, aspect, viewpoint, standpoint, approach, position, side, perspective, bias. ● *v.* **1** slant, bend, point, direct, aim. **2** see SLANT *v.* 3.

angle[2] /ángg'l/ *v.* & *n.* ● *v.intr.* **1** (often foll. by *for*) fish with hook and line. **2** (foll. by *for*) seek an objective by devious or calculated means (*angled for a pay rise*). ● *n. archaic* a fish-hook. [OE *angul*]

■ *v.* **2** (*angle for*) fish (for); look *or* hope for, seek, be *or* go after, try *or* aim for, hunt for.

angled /ángg'ld/ *adj.* **1** placed at an angle to something else. **2** presented to suit a particular point of view. **3** having an angle.

angler /ángglər/ *n.* **1** a person who fishes with a hook and line. **2** = *angler-fish*. □ **angler-fish** any of various fishes that prey upon small fish, attracting them by filaments arising from the dorsal fin: also called *frog-fish* (see FROG[1]).

Anglican /ángglikən/ *adj.* & *n.* ● *adj.* of or relating to the Church of England or any Church in communion with it. ● *n.* a member of an Anglican Church. □□ **Anglicanism** *n.* [med.L *Anglicanus* (Magna Carta) f. *Anglicus* (Bede) f. *Anglus* ANGLE]

anglice /ánglisi/ *adv.* in English. [med.L]

Anglicism /ánglisiz'm/ *n.* **1** a peculiarly English word or custom. **2** Englishness. **3** preference for what is English. [L *Anglicus* (see ANGLICAN) + -ISM]

Anglicize /ánglisīz/ *v.tr.* (also **-ise**) make English in form or character.

Anglist /ángglist/ *n.* a student of or scholar in English language or literature. □□ **Anglistics** /-glístiks/ *n.* [G f. L *Anglus* English]

Anglo /ángglō/ *n.* (*pl.* **-os**) *US* a person of British or northern-European origin. [abbr. of ANGLO-SAXON]

Anglo- /ángglō/ *comb. form* **1** English (*Anglo-Catholic*). **2** of English origin (*an Anglo-American*). **3** English or British and (*an Anglo-American agreement*). [f. mod.L f. L *Anglus* English]

Anglo-Catholic /ángglōkáthəlik, -káthlik/ *adj.* & *n.* ● *adj.* of a High Church Anglican group which emphasizes its Catholic tradition. ● *n.* a member of this group.

Anglocentric /ángglōséntrik/ *adj.* centred on or considered in terms of England.

Anglo-French /ángglōfrénch/ *adj.* & *n.* ● *adj.* **1** English (or British) and French. **2** of Anglo-French. ● *n.* the French language as retained and separately developed in England after the Norman Conquest.

Anglo-Indian /ángglō-indiən/ *adj.* & *n.* ● *adj.* **1** of or relating to England and India. **2 a** of British descent or birth but living or having lived long in India. **b** of mixed British and Indian parentage. **3** (of a word) adopted into English from an Indian language. ● *n.* an Anglo-Indian person.

Anglo-Latin /ángglōláttin/ *adj.* & *n.* ● *adj.* of Latin as used in medieval England. ● *n.* this form of Latin.

Anglomania /ángglōmáyniə/ *n.* excessive admiration of English customs.

Anglo-Norman /ángglōnórmən/ *adj.* & *n.* ● *adj.* **1** English and Norman. **2** of the Normans in England after the Norman Conquest. **3** of the dialect of French used by them. ● *n.* the Anglo-Norman dialect.

Anglophile /ángglōfīl/ *n.* & *adj.* (also **Anglophil** /-fil/) ● *n.* a person who is fond of or greatly admires England or the English. ● *adj.* being or characteristic of an Anglophile.

Anglophobe /ángglōfōb/ *n.* & *adj.* ● *n.* a person who greatly hates or fears England or the English. ● *adj.* being or characteristic of an Anglophobe.

Anglophobia /ángglōfōbiə/ *n.* intense hatred or fear of England or the English.

anglophone /ánggləfōn/ *adj.* & *n.* ● *adj.* English-speaking. ● *n.* an English-speaking person. [ANGLO-, after FRANCOPHONE]

Anglo-Saxon /ánggləsáks'n/ *adj.* & *n.* ● *adj.* **1** of the English Saxons (as distinct from the Old Saxons of the continent, and from the Angles) before the Norman Conquest. **2** of the Old English people as a whole before the Norman Conquest. **3** of English descent. ● *n.* **1** an Anglo-Saxon person. **2** the Old English language. **3 a** *colloq.* plain (esp. crude) English. **b** *US* the modern English language. [mod.L *Anglo-Saxones*, med.L *Angli Saxones* after OE *Angulseaxe*, *-an*]

angora /anggórə/ *n.* **1** a fabric made from the hair of the angora goat or rabbit. **2** a long-haired variety of cat, goat, or rabbit. □ **angora wool** a mixture of sheep's wool and angora rabbit hair. [*Angora* (Ankara) in Turkey]

angostura /ánggəstyŏŏrə/ *n.* (in full **angostura bark**) an aromatic bitter bark used as a flavouring, and formerly used as a tonic and to reduce fever. □ **Angostura Bitters** *propr.* a kind of tonic first made in Angostura. [*Angostura*, a town in Venezuela on the Orinoco, now Ciudad Bolívar]

angry /ánggri/ *adj.* (**angrier**, **angriest**) **1** feeling or showing anger; extremely displeased or resentful. **2** (of a wound, sore, etc.) inflamed, painful. **3** suggesting or seeming to show anger (*an angry sky*). □□ **angrily** *adv.* [ME, f. ANGER + -Y[1]]

■ **1** enraged, furious, irate, ireful, piqued, incensed, infuriated, fuming; irritated, annoyed, vexed, cross, provoked, indignant, exasperated, hot under the collar, in a bad *or* foul temper *or* mood, out of temper, up in arms, in high dudgeon, as cross as two sticks, *archaic* wroth, *colloq.* livid, on the warpath, (all) steamed up, mad, ratty, fit to be tied, *Austral.* & *NZ colloq.* crook, *literary* wrathful, *Austral.* & *NZ sl.* ropeable, snaky. **2** inflamed, irritated, sore, smarting, painful, stinging. **3** black, louring, dark, savage, glowering. □□ **angrily** furiously, irately, crossly, hotly, in high dudgeon, *literary* wrathfully; gloweringly, blackly, darkly, savagely.

angst /angst/ *n.* **1** anxiety. **2** a feeling of guilt or remorse. [G]

■ **1** see ANXIETY 1, 2.

angstrom /ángstrəm/ *n.* (also **ångström** /óngstrom/) a unit of length equal to 10^{-10} metre. ¶ Symb.: Å. [A.J. *Ångström*, Swedish physicist d. 1874]

anguine /ánggwin/ *adj.* of or resembling a snake. [L *anguinus* f. *anguis* snake]

anguish /ánggwish/ *n.* & *v.* ● *n.* severe misery or mental suffering. ● *v.tr.* (often as **anguished** *adj.*) cause to suffer physical or mental pain. [ME f. OF *anguisse* choking f. L *angustia* tightness f. *angustus* narrow]

■ *n.* suffering, pain, *angst*, distress, agony, torment, torture, anxiety, misery, throe, heartache, grief, *archaic or literary* woe, *archaic or poet.* bale. ● *v.* disturb, upset, distress, afflict, trouble; torment, torture.

anguished /ánggwisht/ *adj.* suffering or expressing anguish. [past part. of *anguish* (v.) f. OF *anguissier* f. eccl.L *angustiare* to distress, formed as ANGUISH]

■ see *worried* (WORRY *v.* 4).

angular /ánggyoolər/ *adj.* **1 a** having angles or sharp corners. **b** (of a person) having sharp features; lean and bony. **c** awkward in manner. **2** forming an angle. **3** measured by angle (*angular distance*). □ **angular momentum** the quantity of rotation of a body, the product of its moment of inertia and angular velocity. **angular velocity** the rate of change of angular position of a rotating body. □□ **angularity** /-lárriti/ *n.* **angularly** *adv.* [L *angularis* f. *angulus* ANGLE[1]]

anhedral /anheédrəl/ *n.* & *adj.* *Aeron.* ● *n.* the angle between wing and horizontal when the wing is inclined downwards. ● *adj.* of or having an anhedral. [AN-[1] + *-hedral* (see -HEDRON)]

anhydride /anhīdrīd/ *n.* *Chem.* a substance obtained by removing the elements of water from a compound, esp. from an acid. [as ANHYDROUS + -IDE]

anhydrite /anhīdrīt/ *n.* a naturally occurring usu. rock-forming anhydrous mineral form of calcium sulphate. [as ANHYDROUS + -ITE[1] 2]

anhydrous /anhīdrəss/ *adj.* *Chem.* without water, esp. water of crystallization. [Gk *anudros* (as AN-[1], *hudōr* water)]

aniline /ánnileen, -lin, -līn/ *n.* a colourless oily liquid, used in the manufacture of dyes, drugs, and plastics. □ **aniline dye 1** any of numerous dyes made from aniline. **2** any synthetic dye. [G *Anilin* f. *Anil* indigo (from which it was orig. obtained), ult. f. Arab. *an-nīl*]

anima /ánnimə/ *n.* *Psychol.* **1** the inner personality (opp. PERSONA). **2** Jung's term for the feminine part of a man's personality (opp. ANIMUS). [L, = mind, soul]

animadvert /ánnimadvért/ *v.intr.* (foll. by *on*) criticize, censure (conduct, a fault, etc.). □□ **animadversion** *n.* [L *animadvertere* f. *animus* mind + *advertere* (as AD-, *vertere vers-* turn)]

animal /ánnim'l/ *n.* & *adj.* ● *n.* **1** a living organism which feeds on organic matter, usu. one with specialized sense-organs and nervous system, and able to respond rapidly to stimuli. **2** such an organism other than man. **3** a brutish or uncivilized person. **4** *colloq.* a person or thing of any kind (*there is no such animal*). ● *adj.* **1** characteristic of animals. **2** of animals as distinct from vegetables (*animal charcoal*). **3** characteristic of the physical needs of animals; carnal, sensual. □ **animal husbandry** the science of breeding and caring for farm animals. **animal magnetism** *hist.* mesmerism. **animal rights** (a movement upholding) the natural right of animals to live free from human exploitation. **animal spirits** natural exuberance. [L f. *animale* neut. of *animalis* having breath f. *anima* breath]

■ *n.* **1** creature, (sentient) being, organism, living thing. **3** beast, brute, barbarian, savage, monster. ● *adj.* **1** zoological, biological. **3** physical, fleshly, sensual, gross, coarse, unrefined, uncultured, uncultivated, rude, carnal, crude, bestial, beastlike, subhuman. □ **animal spirits** see *exuberance* (EXUBERANT).

animalcule /ánnimálkyōōl/ *n.* *archaic* a microscopic animal. □□ **animalcular** *adj.* [mod.L *animalculum* (as ANIMAL, -CULE)]

animalism /ánniməliz'm/ *n.* **1** the nature and activity of animals. **2** the belief that humans are not superior to other animals. **3** concern with physical matters; sensuality.

animality /ánnimálliti/ *n.* **1** the animal world. **2** the nature or behaviour of animals. [F *animalité* f. *animal* (adj.)]

animalize /ánniməlīz/ *v.tr.* (also **-ise**) **1** make (a person) bestial; sensualize. **2** convert to animal substance. □□ **animalization** /-záysh'n/ *n.*

animate *adj.* & *v.* ● *adj.* /ánnimət/ **1** having life. **2** lively. ● *v.tr.* /ánnimayt/ **1** enliven, make lively. **2** give life to. **3** inspire, actuate. **4** encourage. [L *animatus* past part. of *animare* give life to f. *anima* life, soul]

■ *adj.* **1** alive, living, animated, moving, breathing, *archaic* quick. **2** lively, spirited, vivacious, animated, vigorous. ● *v.* **1, 2** activate, enliven, invigorate, stimulate, inspirit, excite, stir, vitalize, spark, vivify, revitalize, energize, breathe life into, ginger up. **3, 4** inspire, inspirit, stimulate, actuate, move, motivate, incite, rouse, arouse, excite, fire (up), ginger up, encourage, spur (on *or* onwards).

animated /ánnimaytid/ *adj.* **1** lively, vigorous. **2** having life. **3** (of a film etc.) using techniques of animation. □□ **animatedly** *adv.* **animator** *n.* (in sense 3).

■ **1** lively, alive, quick, spirited, active, vivacious, energetic, vigorous, excited, ebullient, enthusiastic, dynamic, vibrant, ardent, enlivened, passionate, impassioned, fervent, animate. **2** see ANIMATE *adj.* 1. □□ **animatedly** see *vigorously* (VIGOROUS). **animator** cartoonist.

animation /ánnimáysh'n/ *n.* **1** vivacity, ardour. **2** the state of being alive. **3** *Cinematog.* the technique of filming successive drawings or positions of puppets to create an illusion of movement when the film is shown as a sequence.

■ **1** vivacity, vivaciousness, spirit, spiritedness, vitality, dash, *élan*, zest, verve, liveliness, exhilaration, energy, go, dynamism, enthusiasm, eagerness, excitement, vigour, *colloq.* pep; fire, ardour, fervour, feeling, zeal, intensity, ardency.

animé /ánnimay/ *n.* any of various resins, esp. a W. Indian resin used in making varnish. [F, of uncert. orig.]

animism /ánnimiz'm/ *n.* **1** the attribution of a living soul to plants, inanimate objects, and natural phenomena. **2** the belief in a supernatural power that organizes and animates the material universe. □□ **animist** *n.* **animistic** /-místik/ *adj.* [L *anima* life, soul + -ISM]

animosity /ánnimóssiti/ *n.* (*pl.* **-ies**) a spirit or feeling of strong hostility. [ME f. OF *animosité* or LL *animositas* f. *animosus* spirited, formed as ANIMUS]

■ hostility, antagonism, antipathy, ill will, bad *or* ill feeling, malevolence, enmity, hatred, animus, loathing, detestation, contempt; bad *or* ill blood, malice, bitterness, acrimony, resentment, rancour.

animus /ánniməss/ *n.* **1** a display of animosity. **2** ill feeling. **3** a motivating spirit or feeling. **4** *Psychol.* Jung's term for the masculine part of a woman's personality (opp. ANIMA). [L, = spirit, mind]

anion /ánnīən/ *n.* a negatively charged ion; an ion that is attracted to the anode in electrolysis (opp. CATION). [ANA- + ION]

anionic /ánnīónnik/ *adj.* **1** of an anion or anions. **2** having an active anion.

anise /ánniss/ *n.* an umbelliferous plant, *Pimpinella anisum*, having aromatic seeds (see ANISEED). [ME f. OF *anis* f. L f. Gk *anison* anise, dill]

aniseed /ánniseed/ *n.* the seed of the anise, used to flavour liqueurs and sweets. [ME f. ANISE + SEED]

anisette /ánnizétt/ *n.* a liqueur flavoured with aniseed. [F, dimin. of *anis* ANISE]

anisotropic /ánnīsətróppik/ *adj.* having physical properties that are different in different directions, e.g. the strength of wood along the grain differing from that across the grain (opp. ISOTROPIC). □□ **anisotropically** *adv.* **anisotropy** /-sótrəpi/ *n.* [AN-[1] + ISOTROPIC]

ankh /angk/ *n.* a device consisting of a looped bar with a shorter crossbar, used in ancient Egypt as a symbol of life. [Egypt., = life, soul]

ankle /ángk'l/ *n.* & *v.* ● *n.* **1** the joint connecting the foot with the leg. **2** the part of the leg between this and the calf. ● *v.intr. sl.* walk. □ **ankle-biter** *Austral. colloq.* a child. **ankle-bone** a bone forming the ankle. **ankle sock** a short sock just covering the ankle. [ME f. ON *ankul-* (unrecorded) f. Gmc: rel. to ANGLE[1]]

■ □ **ankle-biter** see CHILD 1a.

anklet /ángklit/ *n.* an ornament or fetter worn round the ankle. [ANKLE + -LET, after BRACELET]

ankylose /ángkilōz/ *v.tr.* & *intr.* (also **anchylose**) (of bones or a joint) stiffen or unite by ankylosis. [back-form. f. ANKYLOSIS after *anastomose* etc.]

ankylosis /ángkilṓsiss/ *n.* (also **anchylosis**) **1** the abnormal stiffening and immobility of a joint by fusion of the bones. **2** such fusion. □□ **ankylotic** *adj.* [mod.L f. Gk *agkulōsis* f. *agkuloō* crook]

anna /ánnə/ *n.* a former monetary unit of India and Pakistan, one-sixteenth of a rupee. [Hind. *ānā*]

annal /ánn'l/ *n.* **1** the annals of one year. **2** a record of one item in a chronicle. [back-form. f. ANNALS]

annalist /ánnəlist/ *n.* a writer of annals. □□ **annalistic** /-lístik/ *adj.* **annalistically** /-lístikəli/ *adv.*

annals /ánn'lz/ *n.pl.* **1** a narrative of events year by year. **2** historical records. [F *annales* or L *annales* (*libri*) yearly (books) f. *annus* year]

annates /ánnayts/ *n.pl. RC Ch.* the first year's revenue of a see or benefice, paid to the Pope. [F *annate* f. med.L *annata* year's proceeds f. *annus* year]

annatto /ənáttō/ *n.* (also **anatta** /-tə/, **anatto**) an orange-red dye from the pulp of a tropical fruit, used for colouring foods. [Carib name of the fruit-tree]

anneal /əneél/ *v.* & *n.* ● *v.tr.* **1** heat (metal or glass) and allow it to cool slowly, esp. to toughen it. **2** toughen. ● *n.* treatment by annealing. □□ **annealer** *n.* [OE *onǣlan* f. *on* + *ǣlan* burn, bake f. *āl* fire]

annectent /ənéktənt/ *adj. Biol.* connecting (*annectent link*). [L *annectere annectent-* bind (as ANNEX)]

annelid /ánnəlid/ *n.* any segmented worm of the phylum Annelida, e.g. earthworms, lugworms, etc. [F *annélide* or mod.L *annelida* (pl.) f. F *annelés* ringed animals f. OF *anel* ring f. L *anellus* dimin. of *anulus* ring]

annelidan /ənéllid'n/ *adj.* & *n.* ● *adj.* of the annelids. ● *n.* an annelid.

annex /anéks/ *v.tr.* **1 a** add as a subordinate part. **b** (often foll. by *to*) append to a book etc. **2** incorporate (territory of another) into one's own. **3** add as a condition or consequence. **4** *colloq.* take without right. □□ **annexation** /-sáysh'n/ *n.* [ME f. OF *annexer* f. L *annectere* (as AN-[2], *nectere nex-* bind)]

■ **1** see ADD 1. **2** see CONQUER 1a. **3** see TACK[1] *v.* 3. **4** see APPROPRIATE *v.* 1.

annexe /ánneks/ *n.* (also **annex**) **1** a separate or added building, esp. for extra accommodation. **2** an addition to a document. [F *annexe* f. L *annexum* past part. of *annectere* bind: see ANNEX]

■ **1** extension, addition; wing. **2** see ADDITION 2.

annihilate /ənī́əlayt, ənī́-il-/ *v.tr.* **1** completely destroy. **2** defeat utterly; make insignificant or powerless. □□ **annihilator** *n.* [LL *annihilare* (as AN-[2], *nihil* nothing)]

■ **1** see DESTROY 1, 2. **2** see DEFEAT *v.* 1.

annihilation /ənī́əláysh'n, ənī́-il-/ *n.* **1** the act or process of annihilating. **2** *Physics* the conversion of a particle and an antiparticle into radiation. [F *annihilation* or LL *annihilatio* (as ANNIHILATE)]

anniversary /ánnivérsəri/ *n.* (*pl.* **-ies**) **1** the date on which an event took place in a previous year. **2** the celebration of this. [ME f. L *anniversarius* f. *annus* year + *versus* turned]

Anno Domini /ánnō dómminī/ *adv.* & *n.* ● *adv.* in the year of our Lord, in the year of the Christian era. ● *n. colloq.* advancing age (*suffering from Anno Domini*). [L, = in the year of the Lord]

annotate /ánnōtayt/ *v.tr.* add explanatory notes to (a book, document, etc.). □□ **annotatable** *adj.* **annotation** /-táysh'n/ *n.* **annotative** *adj.* **annotator** *n.* [L *annotare* (as AD-, *nota* mark)]

■ see GLOSS[2] *v.* 1a.

announce /ənówns/ *v.tr.* **1** (often foll. by *that*) make publicly known. **2** make known the arrival or imminence of (a guest, dinner, etc.). **3** make known (without words) to the senses or the mind; be a sign of. [ME f. OF *annoncer* f. L *annuntiare* (as AD-, *nuntius* messenger)]

■ **1** proclaim, make public, make known, set forth, put out, publish, advertise, publicize, promulgate, broadcast, herald, bill, *formal* put forth; circulate; reveal, disclose, divulge, declare, state, assert, affirm, asseverate, confirm, *formal* aver. **2** introduce, present, make known. **3** intimate, suggest, hint at, signal; foretell, betoken, augur, portend, presage, harbinger, herald, proclaim; precede.

announcement /ənównsmənt/ *n.* **1** the action of announcing; something announced. **2** an official communication or statement. **3** (esp. *US*) an advertisement or other piece of promotional material.

■ **1** declaration, pronouncement, proclamation, statement, annunciation, rescript; notification, notice, word. **2** report, bulletin, communiqué, disclosure. **3** see ADVERTISEMENT 1.

announcer /ənównsər/ *n.* a person who announces, esp. introducing programmes in broadcasting.

■ presenter, anchor, anchorman, anchorperson,

anchorwoman, newsreader, newscaster, reporter, broadcaster; master of ceremonies, MC, *colloq.* emcee.

annoy /ənóy/ *v.tr.* **1** cause slight anger or mental distress to. **2** (in *passive*) be somewhat angry (*am annoyed with you*; *was annoyed at my remarks*). **3** molest; harass repeatedly. □□ **annoyer** *n.* **annoying** *adj.* [ME f. OF *anuier, anui, anoi*, etc., ult. f. L *in odio* hateful]

■ **1** irritate, bother, irk, vex, nettle, spite, get on a person's nerves, exasperate, provoke, rile, madden, get *or* put a person's back up, *US* ride, *colloq.* peeve, get across, get in a person's hair, *Brit. colloq.* get on a person's wick, *disp.* aggravate, *sl.* get up a person's nose, ballyrag. **3** pester, harass, harry, badger, keep on at, nag, plague, molest, bedevil, *colloq.* needle, hassle, get under a person's skin, *sl.* bug. □□ **annoying** irritating, maddening, infuriating, irksome, vexing, vexatious, exasperating, galling, grating, bothersome, pestilential, *colloq.* pestilent, *US colloq.* pesky, *disp.* aggravating, *Austral. sl.* on the nose.

annoyance /ənóyənss/ *n.* **1** the action of annoying or the state of being annoyed; irritation, vexation. **2** something that annoys, a nuisance.

■ **1** irritation, bother, vexation, exasperation, pique, *colloq.* botheration, *disp.* aggravation, *Brit. sl.* aggro. **2** nuisance, pest, irritant, bore, *colloq.* pain, bind, pain in the neck, *disp.* aggravation, *esp. US sl.* pain in the butt.

annual /ányooəl/ *adj.* & *n.* ● *adj.* **1** reckoned by the year. **2** occurring every year. **3** living or lasting for one year. ● *n.* **1** a book etc. published once a year; a yearbook. **2** a plant that lives only for a year or less. □ **annual general meeting** a yearly meeting of members or shareholders, esp. for holding elections and reporting on the year's events. **annual ring** a ring in the cross-section of a plant, esp. a tree, produced by one year's growth. □□ **annually** *adv.* [ME f. OF *annuel* f. LL *annualis* f. L *annalis* f. *annus* year]

■ *adj.* **2** yearly, once-a-year, regular.

annualized /ányooəlīzd/ *adj.* (of rates of interest, inflation, etc.) calculated on an annual basis, as a projection from figures obtained for a shorter period.

annuitant /ənyóō-it'nt/ *n.* a person who holds or receives an annuity. [ANNUITY + -ANT, by assim. to *accountant* etc.]

annuity /ənyóō-iti/ *n.* (*pl.* **-ies**) **1** a yearly grant or allowance. **2** an investment of money entitling the investor to a series of equal annual sums. **3** a sum payable in respect of a particular year. [ME f. F *annuité* f. med.L *annuitas -tatis* f. L *annuus* yearly (as ANNUAL)]

■ **1** see ALLOWANCE *n.* 1.

annul /ənúl/ *v.tr.* (**annulled, annulling**) **1** declare (a marriage etc.) invalid. **2** cancel, abolish. □□ **annulment** *n.* [ME f. OF *anuller* f. LL *annullare* (as AD-, *nullus* none)]

■ **2** see CANCEL *v.* 4.

annular /ányoolər/ *adj.* ring-shaped; forming a ring. □ **annular eclipse** an eclipse of the sun in which the moon leaves a ring of sunlight visible round it. □□ **annularly** *adv.* [F *annulaire* or L *annularis* f. *an(n)ulus* ring]

annulate /ányoolət/ *adj.* having rings; marked with or formed of rings. □□ **annulation** /-láysh'n/ *n.* [L *annulatus* (as ANNULUS)]

annulet /ányoolit/ *n.* **1** *Archit.* a small fillet or band encircling a column. **2** a small ring. [L *annulus* ring + -ET[1]]

annulus /ányooləss/ *n.* (*pl.* **annuli** /-lī/) esp. *Math.* & *Biol.* a ring. [L *an(n)ulus*]

annunciate /ənúnsiayt/ *v.tr.* **1** proclaim. **2** indicate as coming or ready. [LL *annunciare* f. L *annuntiare annuntiat-* announce]

annunciation /ənúnsiáysh'n/ *n.* **1** (**Annunciation**) **a** the announcing of the Incarnation, made by the angel Gabriel to Mary, related in Luke 1:26-38. **b** the festival commemorating this (Lady Day) on 25 March. **2 a** the act or process of announcing. **b** an announcement. [ME f. OF *annonciation* f. LL *annuntiatio -onis* (as ANNUNCIATE)]

annunciator /ənúnsiaytər/ *n.* **1** a device giving an audible or visible indication of which of several electrical circuits has been activated, of the position of a train, etc. **2** an announcer. [LL *annuntiator* (as ANNUNCIATE)]

annus mirabilis /ánnəss miraábiliss/ *n.* a remarkable or auspicious year. [mod.L, = wonderful year]

anoa /ənṓə/ *n.* any of several small deerlike water buffalo of the genus *Bubalus*, native to Sulawesi. [name in Sulawesi]

anode /ánnōd/ *n. Electr.* **1** the positive electrode in an electrolytic cell or electronic valve or tube. **2** the negative terminal of a primary cell such as a battery (opp. CATHODE). □ **anode ray** a beam of particles emitted from the anode of a high-vacuum tube. □□ **anodal** *adj.* **anodic** /ənóddik/ *adj.* [Gk *anodos* way up f. *ana* up + *hodos* way]

anodize /ánnədīz/ *v.tr.* (also **-ise**) coat (a metal, esp. aluminium) with a protective oxide layer by electrolysis. □□ **anodizer** *n.* [ANODE + -IZE]

anodyne /ánnədīn/ *adj.* & *n.* ● *adj.* **1** able to relieve pain. **2** mentally soothing. ● *n.* an anodyne drug or medicine. [L *anodynus* f. Gk *anōdunos* painless (as AN-[1], *odunē* pain)]

■ *n.* see PAINKILLER.

anoesis /ánnō-éessiss/ *n. Psychol.* consciousness with sensation but without thought. □□ **anoetic** /-éttik/ *adj.* [A-[1] + Gk *noēsis* understanding]

anoint /ənóynt/ *v.tr.* **1** apply oil or ointment to, esp. as a religious ceremony (e.g. at baptism, or the consecration of a priest or king, or in ministering to the sick). **2** (usu. foll. by *with*) smear, rub. □□ **anointer** *n.* [ME f. AF *anoint* (adj.) f. OF *enoint* past part. of *enoindre* f. L *inungere* (as IN-[2], *ungere unct-* smear with oil)]

anomalistic /ənómməlístik/ *adj. Astron.* of the anomaly or angular distance of a planet from its perihelion. □ **anomalistic month** a month measured between successive perigees of the moon. **anomalistic year** a year measured between successive perihelia of the earth.

anomalous /ənómmələss/ *adj.* having an irregular or deviant feature; abnormal. □□ **anomalously** *adv.* **anomalousness** *n.* [LL *anomalus* f. Gk *anōmalos* (as AN-[1], *homalos* even)]

■ see ABNORMAL.

anomalure /ənómməlyoor/ *n.* any of the squirrel-like rodents of the family Anomaluridae, having tails with rough overlapping scales on the underside. [mod.L *anomalurus* f. Gk *anōmalos* ANOMALOUS + *oura* tail]

anomaly /ənómməli/ *n.* (*pl.* **-ies**) **1** an anomalous circumstance or thing; an irregularity. **2** irregularity of motion, behaviour, etc. **3** *Astron.* the angular distance of a planet or satellite from its last perihelion or perigee. [L f. Gk *anōmalia* f. *anōmalos* ANOMALOUS]

■ **1** see ODDITY 1. **2** see ODDITY 3.

anomy /ánnəmi/ *n.* (also **anomie**) lack of the usual social or ethical standards in an individual or group. □□ **anomic** /ənómmik/ *adj.* [Gk *anomia* f. *anomos* lawless: *-ie* f. F]

anon /ənón/ *adv. archaic* or *literary* soon, shortly (*will say more of this anon*). [OE *on ān* into one, *on āne* in one]

anon. /ənón/ *abbr.* anonymous; an anonymous author.

anonym /ánnənim/ *n.* **1** an anonymous person or publication. **2** a pseudonym. [F *anonyme* f. Gk *anōnumos*: see ANONYMOUS]

anonymous /ənónniməss/ *adj.* **1** of unknown name. **2** of unknown or undeclared source or authorship. **3** without character; featureless, impersonal. □□ **anonymity** /ánnənímmiti/ *n.* **anonymously** *adv.* [LL *anonymus* f. Gk *anōnumos* nameless (as AN-[1], *onoma* name)]

■ **1** see NAMELESS 1, 3, 5.

anopheles /ənóffileez/ *n.* any of various mosquitoes of the genus *Anopheles*, many of which are carriers of the malarial parasite. [mod.L f. Gk *anōphelēs* unprofitable]

anorak /ánnərak/ *n.* a waterproof jacket of cloth or plastic, usu. with a hood, of a kind orig. used in polar regions. [Greenland Eskimo *anoraq*]

anorectic var. of ANOREXIC.

anorexia /ánnəréksiə/ *n.* **1** a lack or loss of appetite for food. **2** (in full **anorexia nervosa** /nervṓsə/) a psychological illness, esp. in young women, characterized by an obsessive desire to lose weight by refusing to eat. [LL f. Gk f. *an-* not + *orexis* appetite]

anorexic /ánnəréksik/ *adj.* & *n.* (also **anorectic** /-réktik/) ● *adj.* **1** involving, producing, or characterized by a lack of appetite, esp. in anorexia nervosa. **2** *colloq.* extremely thin. ● *n.* **1** an anorexic agent. **2** a person with anorexia. [F *anoréxique*; *anorectic* f. Gk *anorektos* without appetite (as ANOREXIA)]

anosmia /anózmiə/ *n.* the loss of the sense of smell. ▫▫ **anosmic** *adj.* [LL f. Gk f. *an-* not + *osmē* smell]

another /ənúthər/ *adj.* & *pron.* ● *adj.* **1** an additional; one more (*have another cake; after another six months*). **2** a person like or comparable to (*another Callas*). **3** a different (*quite another matter*). **4** some or any other (*will not do another man's work*). ● *pron.* **1** an additional one (*have another*). **2** a different one (*take this book away and bring me another*). **3** some or any other one (*I love another*). **4** *Brit.* an unnamed additional party to a legal action (*X versus Y and another*). **5** (also **A. N. Other** /áy en úthər/) a player unnamed or not yet selected. ▫ **another place** *Brit.* the other House of Parliament (used in the Commons to refer to the Lords, and vice versa). **such another** another of the same sort. [ME f. AN + OTHER]

anothery /ənúthəri/ *n.* (also **anotherie**) *Austral. colloq.* another one (*I'll have anothery*).

anovulant /anóvyoolənt/ *n.* & *adj. Pharm.* ● *n.* a drug preventing ovulation. ● *adj.* preventing ovulation. [AN-[1] + *ovulation* (see OVULATE) + -ANT]

anoxia /ənóksiə/ *n. Med.* an absence or deficiency of oxygen reaching the tissues; severe hypoxia. ▫▫ **anoxic** *adj.* [mod.L, formed as AN-[1] + OXYGEN + -IA[1]]

anschluss /ánshlŏŏss/ *n.* a unification, esp. the annexation of Austria by Germany in 1938. [G f. *anschliessen* join]

anserine /ánsərīn/ *adj.* **1** of or like a goose. **2** silly. [L *anserinus* f. *anser* goose]

■ **2** see SILLY *adj.* 1.

answer /aánsər/ *n.* & *v.* ● *n.* **1** something said or done to deal with or in reaction to a question, statement, or circumstance. **2** the solution to a problem. ● *v.* **1** *tr.* make an answer to (*answer me; answer my question*). **2** *intr.* (often foll. by *to*) make an answer. **3** *tr.* respond to the summons or signal of (*answer the door; answer the telephone*). **4** *tr.* be satisfactory for (a purpose or need). **5** *intr.* **a** (foll. by *for, to*) be responsible (*you will answer to me for your conduct*). **b** (foll. by *for*) vouch (for a person, conduct, etc.). **6** *intr.* (foll. by *to*) correspond, esp. to a description. **7** *intr.* be satisfactory or successful. ▫ **answer back** answer a rebuke etc. impudently. **answering machine** a tape recorder which supplies a recorded answer to a telephone call. **answering service** a business that receives and answers telephone calls for its clients. **answer to the name of** be called. [OE *andswaru, andswarian* f. Gmc, = swear against (charge)]

■ *n.* **1** reply, response, rejoinder, retort, riposte, reaction, explanation, *sl.* comeback; *Law* defence, counter-statement, plea, rejoinder, surrejoinder, rebutter, surrebutter. **2** solution, explanation, explication; key. ● *v.* **1** reply to, respond to. **2** reply, respond; (make a) retort, riposte. **4** satisfy, fulfil, suffice for, meet, suit, serve, fit, fill, conform to, correlate with. **5** be accountable *or* responsible *or* answerable; (*answer for*) take *or* accept the blame for; take *or* undertake responsibility for, suffer the consequences of; vouch for, sponsor, support, guarantee the conduct of. **6** see CORRESPOND 1. ▫ **answer back** talk back. **answer to the name of** be named *or* called.

answerable /aánsərəb'l/ *adj.* **1** (usu. foll. by *to, for*) responsible (*answerable to them for any accident*). **2** that can be answered. ▫▫ **answerability** /-bílliti/ *n.*

■ **1** see RESPONSIBLE 1, 2.

answerphone /aánsərfōn/ *n.* a telephone answering machine.

ant /ant/ *n.* any small insect of a widely distributed hymenopterous family, living in complex social colonies, wingless (except for adults in the mating season), and proverbial for industry. ▫ **ant-bear** = AARDVARK. **ant** (or **ant's**) **eggs** pupae of ants. **ant-lion** any of various dragonfly-like insects. **have ants in one's pants** *colloq.* be fidgety, be restless. **white ant** = TERMITE. [OE *ǣmet(t)e, ēmete* (see EMMET) f. WG]

ant- /ant/ assim. form of ANTI- before a vowel or *h* (*Antarctic*).

-ant /ənt/ *suffix* **1** forming adjectives denoting attribution of an action (*pendant; repentant*) or state (*arrogant; expectant*). **2** forming nouns denoting an agent (*assistant; celebrant; deodorant*). [F *-ant* or L *-ant-, -ent-*, pres. part. stem of verbs: cf. -ENT]

antacid /antássid/ *n.* & *adj.* ● *n.* a substance that prevents or corrects acidity esp. in the stomach. ● *adj.* having these properties.

antagonism /antággəniz'm/ *n.* active opposition or hostility. [F *antagonisme* (as ANTAGONIST)]

■ opposition, animosity, enmity, rancour, hostility, antipathy; conflict, rivalry, discord, dissension, friction, strife; contention.

antagonist /antággənist/ *n.* **1** an opponent or adversary. **2** *Biol.* a substance or organ that partially or completely opposes the action of another. ▫▫ **antagonistic** /-nístik/ *adj.* **antagonistically** /-nístikəli/ *adv.* [F *antagoniste* or LL *antagonista* f. Gk *antagōnistēs* (as ANTAGONIZE)]

■ **1** adversary, opponent, enemy, contender, competitor, *esp. poet. or formal* foe; *collect.* competition, opposition, other side. ▫▫ **antagonistic** see HOSTILE 2.

antagonize /antággənīz/ *v.tr.* (also **-ise**) **1** evoke hostility or opposition or enmity in. **2** (of one force etc.) counteract or tend to neutralize (another). ▫▫ **antagonization** /-záysh'n/ *n.* [Gk *antagōnizomai* (as ANTI-, *agōnizomai* f. *agōn* contest)]

■ **1** see ALIENATE 1.

antalkali /antálkəlī/ *n.* (*pl.* **antalkalis**) any substance that counteracts an alkali.

Antarctic /antaárktik/ *adj.* & *n.* ● *adj.* of the south polar regions. ● *n.* this region. ▫ **Antarctic Circle** the parallel of latitude 66° 32′ S., forming an imaginary line round this region. [ME f. OF *antartique* or L *antarcticus* f. Gk *antarktikos* (as ANTI-, *arktikos* ARCTIC)]

ante /ánti/ *n.* & *v.* ● *n.* **1** a stake put up by a player in poker etc. before receiving cards. **2** an amount to be paid in advance. ● *v.tr.* (**antes, anted**) **1** put up as an ante. **2** *US* **a** bet, stake. **b** (foll. by *up*) pay. [L, = before]

ante- /ánti/ *prefix* forming nouns and adjectives meaning 'before, preceding' (*ante-room; antenatal; ante-post*). [L *ante* (prep. & adv.), = before]

anteater /ánteetər/ *n.* any of various mammals feeding on ants and termites, e.g. a tamandua.

ante-bellum /ántibélləm/ *adj.* occurring or existing before a particular war, esp. the US Civil War. [L f. *ante* before + *bellum* war]

antecedent /ántiseéd'nt/ *n.* & *adj.* ● *n.* **1** a preceding thing or circumstance. **2** *Gram.* a word, phrase, clause, or sentence, to which another word (esp. a relative pronoun, usu. following) refers. **3** (in *pl.*) past history, esp. of a person. **4** *Logic* the statement contained in the 'if' clause of a conditional proposition. ● *adj.* **1** (often foll. by *to*) previous. **2** presumptive, a priori. ▫▫ **antecedence** *n.* **antecedently** *adv.* [ME f. F *antecedent* or L *antecedere* (as ANTE-, *cedere* go)]

■ *n.* **1** see ANCESTOR 3, ROOT[1] *n.* 5a, 6. ● *adj.* **1** see PREVIOUS *adj.* 1.

antechamber /ántichaymbər/ *n.* a small room leading to a main one. [earlier *anti-*, f. F *antichambre* f. It. *anticamera* (as ANTE-, CHAMBER)]

antechapel /ántichapp'l/ *n.* the outer part at the west end of a college chapel.

antedate /antidáyt/ *v.* & *n.* ● *v.tr.* **1** exist or occur at a date earlier than. **2** assign an earlier date to (a document, event,

etc.), esp. one earlier than its actual date. ● *n.* a date earlier than the actual one.
■ *v.* **1** see PRECEDE 1a.

antediluvian /ántidilōōviən, -lyōōviən/ *adj.* **1** of or belonging to the time before the Biblical Flood. **2** *colloq.* very old or out of date. [ANTE- + L *diluvium* DELUGE + -AN]

antelope /ántilōp/ *n.* (*pl.* same or **antelopes**) **1** any of various deerlike ruminants of the family Bovidae, esp. abundant in Africa and typically tall, slender, graceful, and swift-moving with smooth hair and upward-pointing horns, e.g. gazelles, gnus, kudus, and impala. **2** leather made from the skin of any of these. [ME f. OF *antelop* or f. med.L *ant(h)alopus* f. late Gk *antholops*, of unkn. orig.]

antenatal /ántináyt'l/ *adj.* **1** existing or occurring before birth. **2** relating to the period of pregnancy.

antenna /anténnə/ *n.* (*pl.* **antennae** /-nee/) **1** *Zool.* one of a pair of mobile appendages on the heads of insects, crustaceans, etc., sensitive to touch and taste; a feeler. **2** (*pl.* **antennas**) = AERIAL *n.* □□ **antennal** *adj.* (in sense 1). **antennary** *adj.* (in sense 1). [L, = sail-yard]
■ **1** feeler, tentacle, palp.

antenuptial /ántinúpsh'l/ *adj.* existing or occurring before marriage. □ **antenuptial contract** *S.Afr.* a contract between two persons intending to marry each other, setting out the terms and conditions of their marriage. [LL *antenuptialis* (as ANTE-, NUPTIAL)]

antependium /ántipéndiəm/ *n.* (*pl.* **antependia** /-diə/) a veil or hanging for the front of an altar. [med.L (as ANTE-, *pendēre* hang)]

antepenult /ántipinúlt/ *n.* the last syllable but two in a word. [abbr. of LL *antepaenultimus* (as ANTE-, *paenultimus* PENULT)]

antepenultimate /ántipinúltimət/ *adj.* & *n.* ● *adj.* last but two. ● *n.* anything that is last but two.

ante-post /ántipōst/ *adj. Brit.* (of betting) done at odds determined at the time of betting, in advance of the event concerned. [ANTE- + POST[1]]

anterior /anteeriər/ *adj.* **1** nearer the front. **2** (often foll. by *to*) earlier, prior. □□ **anteriority** /-riórriti/ *n.* **anteriorly** *adv.* [F *antérieur* or L *anterior* f. *ante* before]
■ **1** see FRONT *attrib.adj.* **2** see FOREGOING.

ante-room /ántiroōm, -rŏŏm/ *n.* **1** a small room leading to a main one. **2** *Mil.* a sitting-room in an officers' mess.

antheap /ánt-heep/ *n.* = ANTHILL.

anthelion /antheeliən/ *n.* (*pl.* **anthelia** /-liə/) a luminous halo projected on a cloud or fog-bank opposite to the sun. [Gk, neut. of *anthēlios* opposite to the sun (as ANTI-, *hēlios* sun)]

anthelmintic /ánthelmíntik/ (also **anthelminthic** /-thik/) *n.* & *adj.* ● *n.* any drug or agent used to destroy parasitic, esp. intestinal, worms, e.g. tapeworms, roundworms, and flukes. ● *adj.* having the power to eliminate or destroy parasitic worms. [ANTI- + Gk *helmins helminthos* worm]

anthem /ánthəm/ *n.* **1** an elaborate choral composition usu. based on a passage of scripture for (esp. Anglican) church use. **2** a solemn hymn of praise etc., esp. = *national anthem.* **3** a composition sung antiphonally. [OE *antefn*, *antifne* f. LL *antiphona* ANTIPHON]

anthemion /antheemiən/ *n.* (*pl.* **anthemia** /-miə/) a flower-like ornament used in art. [Gk, = flower]

anther /ánthər/ *n. Bot.* the apical portion of a stamen containing pollen. □□ **antheral** *adj.* [F *anthère* or mod.L *anthera*, in L 'medicine extracted from flowers' f. Gk *anthēra* flowery, fem. adj. f. *anthos* flower]

antheridium /ánthəríddiəm/ *n.* (*pl.* **antheridia** /-diə/) *Bot.* the male sex organ of algae, mosses, ferns, etc. [mod.L f. *anthera* (as ANTHER) + Gk *-idion* dimin. suffix]

anthill /ánt-hil/ *n.* **1** a moundlike nest built by ants or termites. **2** a community teeming with people.

anthologize /anthólləjīz/ *v.tr.* & *intr.* (also **-ise**) compile or include in an anthology.

anthology /anthólləji/ *n.* (*pl.* **-ies**) a published collection of passages from literature (esp. poems), songs, reproductions of paintings, etc. □□ **anthologist** *n.* [F *anthologie* or med.L f. Gk *anthologia* f. *anthos* flower + *-logia* collection f. *legō* gather]
■ see COLLECTION 2.

anthozoan /ánthəzṓən/ *n.* & *adj.* ● *n.* any of the sessile marine coelenterates of the class Anthozoa, including sea anemones and corals. ● *adj.* of or relating to this class. [mod.L *Anthozoa* f. Gk *anthos* flower + *zōia* animals]

anthracene /ánthrəseen/ *n.* a colourless crystalline aromatic hydrocarbon obtained by the distillation of crude oils and used in the manufacture of chemicals. [Gk *anthrax -akos* coal + -ENE]

anthracite /ánthrəsīt/ *n.* coal of a hard variety burning with little flame and smoke. □□ **anthracitic** /-síttik/ *adj.* [Gk *anthrakitis* a kind of coal (as ANTHRACENE)]

anthrax /ánthraks/ *n.* a disease of sheep and cattle transmissible to humans. [LL f. Gk, = carbuncle]

anthropo- /ánthrəpō/ *comb. form* human, mankind. [Gk *anthrōpos* human being]

anthropocentric /ánthrəpōséntrik/ *adj.* regarding mankind as the centre of existence. □□ **anthropocentrically** *adv.* **anthropocentrism** *n.*

anthropogenesis /ánthrəpōjénnisiss/ *n.* = ANTHROPOGENY.

anthropogeny /ánthrəpójini/ *n.* the study of the origin of man. □□ **anthropogenic** /ánthrəpōjénnik/ *adj.*

anthropoid /ánthrəpoyd/ *adj.* & *n.* ● *adj.* **1** resembling a human being in form. **2** *colloq.* (of a person) apelike. ● *n.* a being that is human in form only, esp. an anthropoid ape. [Gk *anthrōpoeidēs* (as ANTHROPO-, -OID)]

anthropology /ánthrəpólləji/ *n.* **1** the study of mankind, esp. of its societies and customs. **2** the study of the structure and evolution of man as an animal. □□ **anthropological** /-pəlójik'l/ *adj.* **anthropologist** *n.*

anthropometry /ánthrəpómmitri/ *n.* the scientific study of the measurements of the human body. □□ **anthropometric** /-pəmétrik/ *adj.*

anthropomorphic /ánthrəpəmórfik/ *adj.* of or characterized by anthropomorphism. □□ **anthropomorphically** *adv.* [as ANTHROPOMORPHOUS + -IC]

anthropomorphism /ánthrəpəmórfiz'm/ *n.* the attribution of a human form or personality to a god, animal, or thing. □□ **anthropomorphize** *v.tr.*

anthropomorphous /ánthrəpəmórfəss/ *adj.* human in form. [Gk *anthrōpomorphos* (as ANTHROPO-, *morphē* form)]

anthroponymy /ánthrəpónnimi/ *n.* the study of personal names. [ANTHROPO- + Gk *ōnumia* f. *onoma* name: cf. TOPONYMY]

anthropophagy /ánthrəpóffəji/ *n.* cannibalism. □□ **anthropophagous** *adj.* [Gk *anthrōpophagia* (as ANTHROPO-, *phagō* eat)]

anthroposophy /ánthrəpóssəfi/ *n.* a movement inaugurated by Rudolf Steiner (1861–1925) to develop the faculty of cognition and the realization of spiritual reality. [ANTHROPO- + Gk *sophia* wisdom f. *sophos* wise]

anti /ánti/ *prep.* & *n.* ● *prep.* (also *absol.*) opposed to (*is anti everything*; *seems to be rather anti*). ● *n.* (*pl.* **antis**) a person opposed to a particular policy etc. [ANTI-]
■ *prep.* see AVERSE.

anti- /ánti/ *prefix* (also **ant-** before a vowel or *h*) forming nouns and adjectives meaning: **1** opposed to; against (*antivivisectionism*). **2** preventing (*antiscorbutic*). **3** the opposite of (*anticlimax*). **4** rival (*antipope*). **5** unlike the conventional form (*anti-hero*; *anti-novel*). **6** *Physics* the antiparticle of a specified particle (*antineutrino*; *antiproton*). [from or after Gk *anti-* against]

anti-abortion /ántiəbórsh'n/ *adj.* opposing abortion. □□ **anti-abortionist** *n.*

anti-aircraft /ántiáirkraaft/ *adj.* (of a gun, missile, etc.) used to attack enemy aircraft.

antiar /ántiaar/ *n.* = UPAS 1a, 2. [Jav. *antjar*]

antibiosis /ántibīṓsiss/ *n.* an antagonistic association between two organisms (esp. micro-organisms), in which one is adversely affected (cf. SYMBIOSIS). [mod.L f. F *antibiose* (as ANTI-, SYMBIOSIS)]

antibiotic /ántibīóttik/ *n.* & *adj. Pharm.* ● *n.* any of various substances (e.g. penicillin) produced by micro-organisms or made synthetically, that can inhibit or destroy susceptible micro-organisms. ● *adj.* functioning as an antibiotic. [F *antibiotique* (as ANTI-, Gk *biōtikos* fit for life f. *bios* life)]

antibody /ántiboddi/ *n.* (*pl.* **-ies**) any of various blood proteins produced in response to and then counteracting antigens. [transl. of G *Antikörper* (as ANTI-, *Körper* body)]

antic /ántik/ *n.* & *adj.* ● *n.* **1** (usu. in *pl.*) absurd or foolish behaviour. **2** an absurd or silly action. ● *adj. archaic* grotesque, bizarre. [It. *antico* ANTIQUE, used as = grotesque]
■ *n.* **2** see CAPER[1] *n.* 2a.

anticathode /ántikáthōd/ *n.* the target (or anode) of an X-ray tube on which the electrons from the cathode impinge and from which X-rays are emitted.

Antichrist /ántikrīst/ *n.* **1** an arch-enemy of Christ. **2** a postulated personal opponent of Christ expected by the early Church to appear before the end of the world. [ME f. OF *antecrist* f. eccl.L *antichristus* f. Gk *antikhristos* (as ANTI-, *Khristos* CHRIST)]

antichristian /ántikrístiən, -kríss-chən/ *adj.* **1** opposed to Christianity. **2** concerning the Antichrist.

anticipate /antíssipayt/ *v.tr.* **1** deal with or use before the proper time. **2** *disp.* expect, foresee; regard as probable (*did not anticipate any difficulty*). **3** forestall (a person or thing). **4** look forward to. ▫▫ **anticipative** *adj.* **anticipator** *n.* **anticipatory** *adj.* [L *anticipare* f. *anti-* for ANTE- + *-cipare* f. *capere* take]
■ **2** foretell, forecast, predict, prophesy, foretaste, foresee, see, expect; bank *or* reckon *or* count on. **3** forestall, pre-empt, intercept, head off, preclude, obviate, prevent, be beforehand with; nullify. **4** look forward to, prepare for, wait for, await. ▫▫ **anticipative, anticipatory** pre-emptive, forward-looking, interceptive, preclusive, preventative, preventive, precautionary; see also EXPECTANT *adj.* 1.

anticipation /antíssipáysh'n/ *n.* **1** the act or process of anticipating. **2** *Mus.* the introduction beforehand of part of a chord which is about to follow. [F *anticipation* or L *anticipatio* (as ANTICIPATE)]
■ **1** expectation, expectancy; hope; foreknowledge, precognition, presentiment; foreboding; compare ANTICIPATE.

anticlerical /ántiklérrik'l/ *adj.* & *n.* ● *adj.* opposed to the influence of the clergy, esp. in politics. ● *n.* an anticlerical person. ▫▫ **anticlericalism** *n.*

anticlimax /ántiklīmaks/ *n.* a trivial conclusion to something significant or impressive, esp. where a climax was expected. ▫▫ **anticlimactic** /-máktik/ *adj.* **anticlimactically** /-máktikəli/ *adv.*
■ see NON-EVENT.

anticline /ántiklīn/ *n. Geol.* a ridge or fold of stratified rock in which the strata slope down from the crest (opp. SYNCLINE). ▫▫ **anticlinal** /-klīn'l/ *adj.* [ANTI- + Gk *klinō* lean, after INCLINE]

anticlockwise /ántiklókwīz/ *adv.* & *adj.* ● *adv.* in a curve opposite in direction to the movement of the hands of a clock. ● *adj.* moving anticlockwise.

anticoagulant /ántikō-ágyoolənt/ *n.* & *adj.* ● *n.* any drug or agent that retards or inhibits coagulation, esp. of the blood. ● *adj.* retarding or inhibiting coagulation.

anticodon /ántikōdon/ *n. Biochem.* a sequence of three nucleotides forming a unit of genetic code in a transfer RNA molecule that corresponds to a complementary codon in messenger RNA.

anticonvulsant /ántikənvúls'nt/ *n.* & *adj.* ● *n.* any drug or agent that prevents or reduces the severity of convulsions, esp. epileptic fits. ● *adj.* preventing or reducing convulsions.

anticyclone /ántisīklōn/ *n.* a system of winds rotating outwards from an area of high barometric pressure, producing fine weather. ▫▫ **anticyclonic** /-klónnik/ *adj.*

antidepressant /ántidipréss'nt/ *n.* & *adj.* ● *n.* any drug or agent that alleviates depression. ● *adj.* alleviating depression.

antidiuretic hormone /ántidīyoorétik/ *n.* = VASOPRESSIN. [ANTI- + DIURETIC]

antidote /ántidōt/ *n.* **1** a medicine etc. taken or given to counteract poison. **2** anything that counteracts something unpleasant or evil. ▫▫ **antidotal** *adj.* [F *antidote* or L *antidotum* f. Gk *antidoton* neut. of *antidotos* given against (as ANTI- + stem of *didonai* give)]
■ **1** antitoxin, antiserum, antivenene, counterirritant; cure, remedy. **2** countermeasure, corrective, correction, remedy, cure, solution; (counter)balance. ▫▫ **antidotal** antitoxic; counteractive, corrective, remedial.

antifreeze /ántifreez/ *n.* a substance (usu. ethylene glycol) added to water to lower its freezing-point, esp. in the radiator of a motor vehicle.

anti-g /ántijeé/ *adj.* (of clothing for an astronaut etc.) designed to counteract the effects of high acceleration. [ANTI- + *g* symb. for acceleration due to gravity]

antigen /ántijən/ *n.* a foreign substance (e.g. toxin) which causes the body to produce antibodies. ▫▫ **antigenic** /-jénnik/ *adj.* [G (as ANTIBODY, -GEN)]

anti-gravity /ántigrávviti/ *n. Physics* a hypothetical force opposing gravity.

anti-hero /ántiheerō/ *n.* (*pl.* **-oes**) a central character in a story or drama who noticeably lacks conventional heroic attributes.

antihistamine /ántihístəmin, -meen/ *n.* a substance that counteracts the effects of histamine, used esp. in the treatment of allergies.

antiknock /ántinók/ *n.* a substance added to motor fuel to prevent premature combustion.

anti-lock /ántilók/ *n.* & *attrib. adj.* (of brakes) set up so as to prevent locking and skidding when applied suddenly.

antilog /ántilog/ *n. colloq.* = ANTILOGARITHM. [abbr.]

antilogarithm /ántilóggərithəm/ *n.* the number to which a logarithm belongs (*100 is the common antilogarithm of 2*).

antilogy /antílləji/ *n.* (*pl.* **-ies**) a contradiction in terms. [F *antilogie* f. Gk *antilogia* (as ANTI-, -LOGY)]

antimacassar /ántiməkássər/ *n.* a covering put over furniture, esp. over the back of a chair, as a protection from grease in the hair or as an ornament. [ANTI- + MACASSAR]

antimatter /ántimattər/ *n. Physics* matter composed solely of antiparticles.

antimetabolite /ántimitábbəlīt/ *n. Pharm.* a drug that interferes with the normal metabolic processes within cells, usu. by combining with enzymes.

antimony /ántiməni/ *n. Chem.* a brittle silvery-white metallic element used esp. in alloys. ¶ Symb.: **Sb**. ▫▫ **antimonial** /-mōniəl/ *adj.* **antimonic** /-mōnik/ *adj.* **antimonious** /-mōniəss/ *adj.* [ME f. med.L *antimonium* (11th c.), of unkn. orig.]

antinode /ántinōd/ *n. Physics* the position of maximum displacement in a standing wave system.

antinomian /ántinōmiən/ *adj.* & *n.* ● *adj.* of or relating to the view that Christians are released from the obligation of observing the moral law. ● *n.* (**Antinomian**) *hist.* a person who holds this view. ▫▫ **antinomianism** *n.* [med.L *Antinomi*, name of a sect in Germany (1535) alleged to hold this view (as ANTI-, Gk *nomos* law)]

antinomy /antínnəmi/ *n.* (*pl.* **-ies**) **1** a contradiction between two beliefs or conclusions that are in themselves reasonable; a paradox. **2** a conflict between two laws or authorities. [L *antinomia* f. Gk (as ANTI-, *nomos* law)]

antinovel /ántinovv'l/ *n.* a novel in which the conventions of the form are studiously avoided.

anti-nuclear /ántinyóokliər/ *adj.* opposed to the development of nuclear weapons or nuclear power.

antioxidant /ántióksid'nt/ *n.* an agent that inhibits oxidation, esp. used to reduce deterioration of products stored in air.

antiparticle /ántipaartik'l/ *n. Physics* an elementary particle having the same mass as a given particle but opposite electric or magnetic properties.

antipasto /ántipaástō, -pástō/ *n.* (*pl.* **-os** or **antipasti** /-ti/) an hors-d'œuvre, esp. in an Italian meal. [It.]
■ see HORS-D'ŒUVRE.

antipathetic /ántipəthéttik/ *adj.* (usu. foll. by *to*) having a strong aversion or natural opposition. □□ **antipathetical** *adj.* **antipathetically** *adv.* [as ANTIPATHY after PATHETIC]
■ see AVERSE.

antipathic /ántipáthik/ *adj.* of a contrary nature or character.

antipathy /antíppəthi/ *n.* (*pl.* **-ies**) (often foll. by *to, for, between*) a strong or deep-seated aversion or dislike. [F *antipathie* or L *antipathia* f. Gk *antipatheia* f. *antipathēs* opposed in feeling (as ANTI-, *pathos -eos* feeling)]
■ see AVERSION 1.

anti-personnel /ántipérsənél/ *adj.* (of a bomb, mine, etc.) designed to kill or injure people rather than to damage buildings or equipment.

antiperspirant /ántipérspirənt/ *n.* & *adj.* ● *n.* a substance applied to the skin to prevent or reduce perspiration. ● *adj.* that acts as an antiperspirant.

antiphlogistic /ántifləjístik/ *n.* & *adj.* ● *n.* any drug or agent that alleviates or reduces inflammation. ● *adj.* alleviating or reducing inflammation.

antiphon /ántif'n/ *n.* **1** a hymn or psalm, the parts of which are sung or recited alternately by two groups. **2** a versicle or phrase from this. **3** a sentence sung or recited before or after a psalm or canticle. **4** a response. [eccl.L *antiphona* f. Gk (as ANTI-, *phōnē* sound)]

antiphonal /antíffən'l/ *adj.* & *n.* ● *adj.* **1** sung or recited alternately by two groups. **2** responsive, answering. ● *n.* a collection of antiphons. □□ **antiphonally** *adv.*

antiphonary /antíffənəri/ *n.* (*pl.* **-ies**) a book of antiphons. [eccl.L *antiphonarium* (as ANTIPHON)]

antiphony /antíffəni/ *n.* (*pl.* **-ies**) **1** antiphonal singing or chanting. **2** a response or echo.

antipode /ántipōd/ *n.* (usu. foll. by *of, to*) the exact opposite. [see ANTIPODES]

antipodes /antíppədeez/ *n.pl.* **1 a** (also **Antipodes**) a place diametrically opposite to another, esp. Australasia as the region on the opposite side of the earth to Europe. **b** places diametrically opposite to each other. **2** (usu. foll. by *of, to*) the exact opposite. □□ **antipodal** *adj.* **antipodean** /-deéən/ *adj.* & *n.* [F or LL f. Gk *antipodes* having the feet opposite (as ANTI-, *pous podos* foot)]

antipole /ántipōl/ *n.* **1** the direct opposite. **2** the opposite pole.

antipope /ántipōp/ *n.* a person set up as pope in opposition to one (held by others to be) canonically chosen. [F *antipape* f. med.L *antipapa*, assim. to POPE[1]]

antiproton /ántiprṓton/ *n. Physics* the negatively charged antiparticle of a proton.

antipruritic /ántiprooríttik/ *adj.* & *n.* ● *adj.* relieving itching. ● *n.* an antipruritic drug or agent. [ANTI- + PRURITUS + -IC]

antipyretic /ántipīréttik/ *adj.* & *n.* ● *adj.* preventing or reducing fever. ● *n.* an antipyretic drug or agent.

antiquarian /ántikwáiriən/ *adj.* & *n.* ● *adj.* **1** of or dealing in antiques or rare books. **2** of the study of antiquities. ● *n.* an antiquary. □□ **antiquarianism** *n.* [see ANTIQUARY]

antiquary /ántikwəri/ *n.* (*pl.* **-ies**) a student or collector of antiques or antiquities. [L *antiquarius* f. *antiquus* ancient]

antiquated /ántikwaytid/ *adj.* old-fashioned; out of date. [eccl.L *antiquare antiquat-* make old]
■ old, old-fashioned, outmoded, *passé*, out of date, dated, archaic, obsolescent, antique, obsolete, quaint, *colloq.* old hat, medieval, antediluvian; primitive; extinct.

antique /anteék/ *n.*, *adj.*, & *v.* ● *n.* an object of considerable age, esp. an item of furniture or the decorative arts having a high value. ● *adj.* **1** of or existing from an early date. **2** old-fashioned, archaic. **3** of ancient times. ● *v.tr.* (**antiques, antiqued, antiquing**) give an antique appearance to (furniture etc.) by artificial means. [F *antique* or L *antiquus, anticus* former, ancient f. *ante* before]
■ *n.* collectible, collector's item, bibelot, *objet d'art*, object or article of virtu, heirloom, curio, rarity, treasure. ● *adj.* **1** old, age-old, ancient, historic(al), time-worn. **2** old-fashioned, archaic, antiquated, outmoded, *passé*, out of date, dated, obsolete. **3** see ANCIENT[1] *adj.* 1.

antiquity /antíkwiti/ *n.* (*pl.* **-ies**) **1** ancient times, esp. the period before the Middle Ages. **2** great age (*a city of great antiquity*). **3** (usu. in *pl.*) physical remains or relics from ancient times, esp. buildings and works of art. **4** (in *pl.*) customs, events, etc., of ancient times. **5** the people of ancient times regarded collectively. [ME f. OF *antiquité* f. L *antiquitas -tatis* f. *antiquus*: see ANTIQUE]
■ **1** see HISTORY 2c.

antiracism /ántiráysiz'm/ *n.* the policy or practice of opposing racism and promoting racial tolerance. □□ **antiracist** *n.* & *adj.*

antirrhinum /ántirī́nəm/ *n.* any plant of the genus *Antirrhinum*, esp. the snapdragon. [L f. Gk *antirrhinon* f. *anti* counterfeiting + *rhis rhinos* nose (from the resemblance of the flower to an animal's snout)]

antiscorbutic /ántiskorbyóótik/ *adj.* & *n.* ● *adj.* preventing or curing scurvy. ● *n.* an antiscorbutic agent or drug.

anti-Semite /ántiseémīt, -sémmīt/ *n.* a person hostile to or prejudiced against Jews. □□ **anti-Semitic** /-simíttik/ *adj.* **anti-Semitism** /-sémmitiz'm/ *n.*

antisepsis /ántisépsiss/ *n.* the process of using antiseptics to eliminate undesirable micro-organisms such as bacteria, viruses, and fungi that cause disease. [mod.L (as ANTI-, SEPSIS)]

antiseptic /ántiséptik/ *adj.* & *n.* ● *adj.* **1** counteracting sepsis esp. by preventing the growth of disease-causing micro-organisms. **2** sterile or free from contamination. **3** lacking character. ● *n.* an antiseptic agent. □□ **antiseptically** *adv.*
■ *adj.* **2** see STERILE 3. ● *n.* see DISINFECTANT *n.*

antiserum /ántiseerəm/ *n.* (*pl.* **antisera** /-rə/) a blood serum containing antibodies against specific antigens, injected to treat or protect against specific diseases.

antisocial /ántisṓsh'l/ *adj.* **1** opposed or contrary to normal social instincts or practices. **2** not sociable. **3** opposed or harmful to the existing social order.
■ **2** see UNSOCIAL.

antistatic /ántistáttik/ *adj.* that counteracts the effects of static electricity.

antistrophe /antístrəfi/ *n.* the second section of an ancient Greek choral ode or of one division of it (see STROPHE). [LL f. Gk *antistrophē* f. *antistrephō* turn against]

antitetanus /ántitéttənəss/ *adj.* effective against tetanus.

antithesis /antíthisiss/ *n.* (*pl.* **antitheses** /-seez/) **1** (foll. by *of, to*) the direct opposite. **2** (usu. foll. by *of, between*) contrast or opposition between two things. **3** a contrast of ideas expressed by parallelism of strongly contrasted words. [LL f. Gk *antitithēmi* set against (as ANTI-, *tithēmi* place)]
■ **1** see OPPOSITE *n.*

antithetical /ántithéttik'l/ *adj.* (also **antithetic**) **1** contrasted, opposite. **2** connected with, containing, or using antithesis. □□ **antithetically** *adv.* [Gk *antithetikos* (as ANTITHESIS)]

antitoxin /ántitóksin/ *n.* an antibody that counteracts a toxin. □□ **antitoxic** *adj.*

antitrades /ántitráydz/ *n.pl.* winds that blow in the opposite direction to (and usu. above) a trade wind.

antitrust /ántitrúst/ *adj. US* (of a law etc.) opposed to or controlling trusts or other monopolies.

antitype /ántitīp/ *n.* **1** that which is represented by a type or symbol. **2** a person or thing of the opposite type. □□ **antitypical** /-típpik'l/ *adj.* [Gk *antitupos* corresponding as an impression to the die (as ANTI-, *tupos* stamp)]

antivenene /ántivineén/ *n.* (also **antivenin** /-vénnin/) an antiserum containing antibodies against specific poisons in the venom of esp. snakes, spiders, scorpions, etc. [ANTI- + L *venenum* poison + -ENE, -IN]

antiviral /antivīrəl/ *adj.* effective against viruses.

antivivisectionism /antivívvisékshəniz'm/ *n.* opposition to vivisection. ▫▫ **antivivisectionist** *n.*

antler /ántlər/ *n.* **1** each of the branched horns of a stag or other (usu. male) deer. **2** a branch of this. ▫▫ **antlered** *adj.* [ME f. AF, var. of OF *antoillier*, of unkn. orig.]

antonomasia /ántənəmáyziə/ *n.* **1** the substitution of an epithet or title etc. for a proper name (e.g. *the Maid of Orleans* for Joan of Arc, *his Grace* for an archbishop). **2** the use of a proper name to express a general idea (e.g. *a Scrooge* for a miser). [L f. Gk f. *antonomazō* name instead (as ANTI-, + *onoma* name)]

antonym /ántənim/ *n.* a word opposite in meaning to another in the same language (e.g. *bad* and *good*) (opp. SYNONYM). ▫▫ **antonymous** /antónniməss/ *adj.* [F *antonyme* (as ANTI-, SYNONYM)]

antrum /ántrəm/ *n.* (*pl.* **antra** /-trə/) *Anat.* a natural chamber or cavity in the body, esp. in a bone. ▫▫ **antral** *adj.* [L f. Gk *antron* cave]

antsy /ántsi/ *adj. US colloq.* irritated, impatient; fidgety, restless. [*ants*, pl. of ANT + -Y[1]]
▪ see ANXIOUS 1.

anuran /ənyóorən/ *n.* & *adj.* ● *n.* any tailless amphibian of the order Anura, including frogs and toads. ● *adj.* of or relating to this order. [mod.L *Anura* (AN-[1] + Gk *oura* tail)]

anus /áynəss/ *n. Anat.* the excretory opening at the end of the alimentary canal. [L]

anvil /ánvil/ *n.* **1** a block (usu. of iron) with a flat top, concave sides, and often a pointed end, on which metals are worked in forging. **2** *Anat.* a bone of the ear; the incus. [OE *anfilte* etc.]

anxiety /angzīəti/ *n.* (*pl.* **-ies**) **1** the state of being anxious. **2** concern about an imminent danger, difficulty, etc. **3** (foll. by *for*, or *to* + infin.) anxious desire. **4** a thing that causes anxiety (*my greatest anxiety is that I shall fall ill*). **5** *Psychol.* a nervous disorder characterized by a state of excessive uneasiness. [F *anxieté* or L *anxietas -tatis* (as ANXIOUS)]
▪ **1, 2** solicitude, concern, uneasiness, disquiet, nervousness, worry, dread, *angst*, agitation, apprehension, foreboding; neurosis, depression; see also STRESS *n.* 2. **3** desire, longing, yearning, ache, avidity, concern; appetite, hunger, thirst. **4** see WORRY *n.* 1.

anxious /ángkshəss/ *adj.* **1** troubled; uneasy in the mind. **2** causing or marked by anxiety (*an anxious moment*). **3** (foll. by *for*, or *to* + infin.) earnestly or uneasily wanting or trying (*anxious to please*; *anxious for you to succeed*). ▫▫ **anxiously** *adv.* **anxiousness** *n.* [L *anxius* f. *angere* choke]
▪ **1** troubled, uneasy, disquieted, uncertain, apprehensive, depressed, neurotic; solicitous, concerned, worried, distressed, disturbed, nervous, tense, fretful, on edge, restless, edgy, perturbed, upset, *US colloq.* antsy; wary, cautious, careful, watchful. **3** desirous, eager, keen, enthusiastic, ardent, avid, yearning, longing, aching, impatient. ▫▫ **anxiousness** see ANXIETY 1, 2.

any /énni/ *adj.*, *pron.*, & *adv.* ● *adj.* **1** (with *interrog.*, *neg.*, or conditional expressed or implied) **a** one, no matter which, of several (*cannot find any answer*). **b** some, no matter how much or many or of what sort (*if any books arrive*; *have you any sugar?*). **2** a minimal amount of (*hardly any difference*). **3** whichever is chosen (*any fool knows that*). **4 a** an appreciable or significant (*did not stay for any length of time*). **b** a very large (*has any amount of money*). ● *pron.* **1** any one (*did not know any of them*). **2** any number (*are any of them yours?*). **3** any amount (*is there any left?*). ● *adv.* (usu. with *neg.* or *interrog.*) at all, in some degree (*is that any good?*; *do not make it any larger*; *without being any the wiser*). ▫ **any more** to any further extent (*don't like you any more*). **any time** *colloq.* at any time. **any time** (or **day** or **minute** etc.) **now** *colloq.* at any time in the near future. **not having any** *colloq.* unwilling to participate. [OE *ǣnig* f. Gmc (as ONE, -Y[1])]

anybody /énniboddi/ *n.* & *pron.* **1 a** a person, no matter who. **b** a person of any kind. **c** whatever person is chosen. **2** a person of importance (*are you anybody?*). ▫ **anybody's** (of a contest) evenly balanced (*it was anybody's game*). **anybody's guess** see GUESS.

anyhow /énnihow/ *adv.* **1** anyway. **2** in a disorderly manner or state (*does his work anyhow*; *things are all anyhow*).
▪ **1** see HOWEVER 1a, 2.

anyone /énniwun/ *pron.* anybody. ¶ Written as two words to imply a numerical sense, as in *any one of us can do it*.
▪ see ONE *pron.* 1, 2.

anyplace /énniplayss/ *adv. US* anywhere.

anything /énnithing/ *pron.* **1** a thing, no matter which. **2** a thing of any kind. **3** whatever thing is chosen. ▫ **anything but** not at all (*was anything but honest*). **like anything** *colloq.* with great vigour, intensity, etc.

anyway /énniway/ *adv.* **1** in any way or manner. **2** at any rate. **3** in any case. **4** to resume (*anyway, as I was saying*).
▪ **2, 3** see *at any rate* (RATE[1]).

anywhere /énniwair/ *adv.* & *pron.* ● *adv.* in or to any place. ● *pron.* any place (*anywhere will do*).

anywise /énniwīz/ *adv. archaic* in any manner. [OE *on ǣnige wīsan* in any wise]

Anzac /ánzak/ *n.* **1** a soldier in the Australian and New Zealand Army Corps (1914–18). **2** any person, esp. a member of the armed services, from Australia or New Zealand. ▫ **Anzac Day** 25 April, commemorating the Anzac landing at Gallipoli in 1915. [acronym]

Anzus /ánzəss/ *n.* (also **ANZUS**) Australia, New Zealand, and the US, as an alliance for the Pacific area.

AO *abbr.* Officer of the Order of Australia.

AOB *abbr.* any other business.

A-OK *abbr. US colloq.* excellent; in good order. [*a*ll systems *OK*]

aorist /áirist/ *n.* & *adj. Gram.* ● *n.* an unqualified past tense of a verb (esp. in Greek), without reference to duration or completion. ● *adj.* of or designating this tense. ▫▫ **aoristic** /airístik/ *adj.* [Gk *aoristos* indefinite f. *a-* not + *horizō* define, limit]

aorta /ayórtə/ *n.* (*pl.* **aortas**) the main artery, giving rise to the arterial network through which oxygenated blood is supplied to the body from the heart. ▫▫ **aortic** *adj.* [Gk *aortē* f. *a(e)irō* raise]

à outrance /aa ōōtronss/ *adv.* **1** to the death. **2** to the bitter end. [F, = to the utmost]

ap-[1] /ap/ *prefix* assim. form of AD- before *p*.

ap-[2] /ap/ *prefix* assim. form of APO- before a vowel or *h*.

apace /əpáyss/ *adv. literary* swiftly, quickly. [OF *à pas* at (a considerable) pace]

Apache /əpáchi/ *n.* **1** a member of a N. American Indian tribe. **2** (**apache**) (/əpásh/) a violent street ruffian, orig. in Paris. [Mex. Sp.]

apanage var. of APPANAGE.

apart /əpaárt/ *adv.* **1** separately; not together (*stand apart from the crowd*). **2** into pieces (*came apart in my hands*). **3 a** to or on one side. **b** out of consideration (placed after noun: *joking apart*). **4** to or at a distance. ▫ **apart from 1** excepting; not considering. **2** in addition to (*apart from roses we grow irises*). [ME f. OF f. *à* to + *part* side]
▪ **1** separately, individually, singly, alone, independently. **2** to *or* into pieces, to bits, in two *or archaic* twain, *literary* asunder. **3 a** aside, to one side, by oneself *or* itself, at a distance, separate, separately. **b** aside. ▫ **apart from 1** except (for), excepting, separately from, besides, but (for), bar, not including, excluding, not counting, *US* aside from. **2** see BESIDES *prep.*

apartheid /əpaártayt/ *n.* **1** (esp. in S. Africa) a policy or system of segregation or discrimination on grounds of race. **2** segregation in other contexts. [Afrik. (as APART, -HOOD)]

apartment /əpaártmənt/ *n.* **1** (in *pl.*) a suite of rooms, usu. furnished and rented. **2** a single room in a house. **3** *US* a flat. ▫ **apartment house** *US* a block of flats. [F *appartement* f. It. *appartamento* f. *appartare* to separate f. *a parte* apart]

■ **3** see FLAT[2] *n.*

apathetic /áppəthéttik/ *adj.* having or showing no emotion or interest. ▫▫ **apathetically** *adv.* [APATHY, after PATHETIC]

■ see UNMOVED 3.

apathy /áppəthi/ *n.* (often foll. by *towards*) lack of interest or feeling; indifference. [F *apathie* f. L *apathia* f. Gk *apatheia* f. *apathēs* without feeling f. *a-* not + *pathos* suffering]

■ see INDIFFERENCE 1.

apatite /áppətīt/ *n.* a naturally occurring crystalline mineral of calcium phosphate and fluoride, used in the manufacture of fertilizers. [G *Apatit* f. Gk *apatē* deceit (from its deceptive forms)]

ape /ayp/ *n.* & *v.* ● *n.* **1** any of the various primates of the family Pongidae characterized by the absence of a tail, e.g. the gorilla, chimpanzee, orang-utan, or gibbon. **2** (in general use) any monkey. **3 a** an imitator. **b** an apelike person. ● *v.tr.* imitate, mimic. ▫ **ape-man** (*pl.* **-men**) any of various apelike primates held to be forerunners of present-day man. **go ape** *sl.* become crazy. **naked ape** present-day man. [OE *apa* f. Gmc]

■ *n.* **1, 2** monkey, simian, primate. ● *v.* see IMITATE 2.

aperçu /áppersyōō/ *n.* **1** a summary or survey. **2** an insight. [F, past part. of *apercevoir* perceive]

aperient /əpeériənt/ *adj.* & *n.* ● *adj.* laxative. ● *n.* a laxative medicine. [L *aperire aperient-* to open]

■ *adj.* see PURGATIVE *adj.* 2. ● *n.* see PURGATIVE *n.* 2.

aperiodic /áypeerióddik/ *adj.* **1** not periodic; irregular. **2** *Physics* (of a potentially oscillating or vibrating system, e.g. an instrument with a pointer) that is adequately damped to prevent oscillation or vibration. **3** (of an oscillation or vibration) without a regular period. ▫▫ **aperiodicity** /-riədíssiti/ *n.*

aperitif /əpérriteéf/ *n.* an alcoholic drink taken before a meal to stimulate the appetite. [F *apéritif* f. med.L *aperitivus* f. L *aperire* to open]

aperture /áppərtyoor/ *n.* **1** an opening; a gap. **2** a space through which light passes in an optical or photographic instrument, esp. a variable space in a camera. [L *apertura* (as APERITIF)]

■ **1** opening, space, gap, cleft, chink, crevice, crack, fissure, hole, chasm.

apery /áypəri/ *n.* (*pl.* **-ies**) **1** mimicry. **2** an ape-house.

■ **1** see IMITATION *n.* 1.

apetalous /aypéttələss/ *adj. Bot.* (of flowers) having no petals. [mod.L *apetalus* f. Gk *apetalos* leafless f. *a-* not + *petalon* leaf]

APEX /áypeks/ *abbr.* Association of Professional, Executive, Clerical, and Computer Staff.

Apex /áypeks/ *n.* (also **APEX**) (often *attrib.*) a system of reduced fares for scheduled airline flights when paid for before a certain period in advance of departure. [*A*dvance *P*urchase *Ex*cursion]

apex /áypeks/ *n.* (*pl.* **apexes** or **apices** /áypiseez/) **1** the highest point. **2** a climax; a high point of achievement etc. **3** the vertex of a triangle or cone. **4** a tip or pointed end. [L, = peak, tip]

■ **1, 3, 4** see VERTEX, TIP[1] *n.* 1. **2** see ACME.

apfelstrudel /ápfəlstrōōd'l/ *n.* a confection of flaky pastry filled with spiced apple. [G f. *Apfel* apple + STRUDEL]

aphaeresis /əfeérisiss/ *n.* (*pl.* **aphaereses** /-seez/) the omission of a letter or syllable at the beginning of a word as a morphological development (e.g. in the derivation of *adder*). [LL f. Gk *aphairesis* (as APO-, *haireō* take)]

aphasia /əfáyziə/ *n. Med.* the loss of ability to understand or express speech, owing to brain damage. ▫▫ **aphasic** *adj.* & *n.* [mod.L f. Gk f. *aphatos* speechless f. *a-* not + *pha-* speak]

aphelion /ap-heéliən, əfeéliən/ *n.* (*pl.* **aphelia** /-liə/) the point in a body's orbit where it is furthest from the sun (opp. PERIHELION). ¶ Symb.: **Q**. [Graecized f. mod.L *aphelium* f. Gk *aph' hēliou* from the sun]

aphesis /áffisiss/ *n.* (*pl.* **apheses** /-seez/) the gradual loss of an unstressed vowel at the beginning of a word (e.g. of *e* from *esquire* to form *squire*). ▫▫ **aphetic** /əféttik/ *adj.* **aphetically** /əféttikəli/ *adv.* [Gk, = letting go (as APO-, *hiēmi* send)]

aphid /áyfid/ *n.* any small homopterous insect which feeds by sucking sap from leaves, stems, or roots of plants; a plant-louse. [back-form. f. *aphides*: see APHIS]

aphis /áyfiss/ *n.* (*pl.* **aphides** /áyfideez/) an aphid, esp. of the genus *Aphis* including the greenfly. [mod.L (Linnaeus) f. Gk (1523), perh. a misreading of *koris* bug]

aphonia /əfṓniə/ *n.* (also **aphony** /áffəni/) *Med.* the loss or absence of the voice through a disease of the larynx or mouth. [mod.L *aphonia* f. Gk f. *aphōnos* voiceless f. *a-* not + *phōnē* voice]

aphorism /áffəriz'm/ *n.* **1** a short pithy maxim. **2** a brief statement of a principle. ▫▫ **aphorist** *n.* **aphoristic** /-rístik/ *adj.* **aphoristically** /-rístikəli/ *adv.* **aphorize** *v.intr.* (also **-ise**). [F *aphorisme* or LL f. Gk *aphorismos* definition f. *aphorizō* (as APO-, *horos* boundary)]

■ **1** see MAXIM.

aphrodisiac /áfrədízziak/ *adj.* & *n.* ● *adj.* that arouses sexual desire. ● *n.* an aphrodisiac drug. [Gk *aphrodisiakos* f. *aphrodisios* f. *Aphroditē* Gk goddess of love]

■ *adj.* see EROTIC.

aphyllous /əfílləss/ *adj. Bot.* (of plants) having no leaves. [mod.L f. Gk *aphullos* f. *a-* not + *phullon* leaf]

apian /áypiən/ *adj.* of or relating to bees. [L *apianus* f. *apis* bee]

apiary /áypiəri/ *n.* (*pl.* **-ies**) a place where bees are kept. ▫▫ **apiarist** *n.* [L *apiarium* f. *apis* bee]

apical /áypik'l, áp-/ *adj.* of, at, or forming an apex. ▫▫ **apically** *adv.* [L *apex apicis*: see APEX]

apices *pl.* of APEX.

apiculture /áypikulchər/ *n.* bee-keeping. ▫▫ **apicultural** /-kúlchərəl/ *adj.* **apiculturist** /-kúlchərist/ *n.* [L *apis* bee, after AGRICULTURE]

apiece /əpeéss/ *adv.* for each one; severally (*had five pounds apiece*). [A[2] + PIECE]

apish /áypish/ *adj.* **1** of or like an ape. **2** silly; affected. ▫▫ **apishly** *adv.* **apishness** *n.*

■ **2** see SILLY *adj.* 1.

aplanat /áplənat/ *n.* a reflecting or refracting surface made aplanatic by correction. [G]

aplanatic /áplənáttik/ *adj.* (of a reflecting or refracting surface) free from spherical aberration. [Gk *aplanētos* free from error f. *a-* not + *planaō* wander]

aplasia /əpláyziə/ *n. Med.* total or partial failure of development of an organ or tissue. ▫▫ **aplastic** /əplástik/ *adj.* [mod.L f. Gk f. *a-* not + *plasis* formation]

aplenty /əplénti/ *adv.* in plenty.

■ see GALORE.

aplomb /əplóm/ *n.* assurance; self-confidence. [F, = perpendicularity, f. *à plomb* according to a plummet]

■ see ASSURANCE 5a.

apnoea /apneéə/ *n.* (*US* **apnea**) *Med.* a temporary cessation of breathing. [mod.L f. Gk *apnoia* f. *apnous* breathless]

apo- /áppə/ *prefix* **1** away from (*apogee*). **2** separate (*apocarpous*). [Gk *apo* from, away, un-, quite]

Apoc. *abbr.* **1** Apocalypse (New Testament). **2** Apocrypha.

apocalypse /əpókkəlips/ *n.* **1** (**the Apocalypse**) Revelation, the last book of the New Testament, recounting a divine revelation to St John. **2** a revelation, esp. of the end of the world. **3** a grand or violent event resembling those described in the Apocalypse. [ME f. OF ult. f. Gk *apokalupsis* f. *apokaluptō* uncover, reveal]

apocalyptic /əpókkəlíptik/ *adj.* **1** of or resembling the Apocalypse. **2** revelatory, prophetic. ▫▫ **apocalyptically** *adv.* [Gk *apokaluptikos* (as APOCALYPSE)]

apocarpous /áppəkaárpəss/ *adj. Bot.* (of ovaries) having distinct carpels not joined together (opp. SYNCARPOUS). [APO- + Gk *karpos* fruit]

apochromat /áppəkrəmat/ *n.* a lens or lens-system that reduces spherical and chromatic aberrations. ▫▫ **apochromatic** /-máttik/ *adj.* [APO- + CHROMATIC]

apocope /əpókkəpi/ *n.* the omission of a letter or letters at the end of a word as a morphological development (e.g. in the derivation of *curio*). [LL f. Gk *apokopē* (as APO-, *koptō* cut)]

Apocr. *abbr.* Apocrypha.

apocrine /áppəkrīn, -krin/ *adj. Biol.* (of a multicellular gland, e.g. the mammary gland) releasing some cytoplasm when secreting. [APO- + Gk *krinō* to separate]

Apocrypha /əpókrifə/ *n.pl.* **1** the books included in the Septuagint and Vulgate versions of the Old Testament but not in the Hebrew Bible. ¶ Modern Bibles sometimes include them in the Old Testament or as an appendix, and sometimes omit them. **2** (**apocrypha**) writings or reports not considered genuine. [ME f. eccl.L *apocrypha* (*scripta*) hidden writings f. Gk *apokruphos* f. *apokruptō* hide away]

apocryphal /əpókrif'l/ *adj.* **1** of doubtful authenticity (orig. of some early Christian texts resembling those of the New Testament). **2** invented, mythical (*an apocryphal story*). **3** of or belonging to the Apocrypha.
■ **2** see FICTITIOUS 1.

apodal /áppəd'l/ *adj.* **1** without (or with undeveloped) feet. **2** (of fish) without ventral fins. [*apod* apodal creature f. Gk *apous* footless f. *a-* not + *pous podos* foot]

apodictic /áppədíktik/ *adj.* (also **apodeictic** /-dīktik/) **1** clearly established. **2** of clear demonstration. [L *apodicticus* f. Gk *apodeiktikos* (as APO-, *deiknumi* show)]

apodosis /əpóddəsiss/ *n.* (*pl.* **apodoses** /-seez/) the main (consequent) clause of a conditional sentence (e.g. *I would agree* in *if you asked me I would agree*). [LL f. Gk f. *apodidōmi* give back (as APO-, *didōmi* give)]

apogee /áppəjee/ *n.* **1** the point in a celestial body's orbit where it is furthest from the earth (opp. PERIGEE). **2** the most distant or highest point. ▫▫ **apogean** /áppəjéeən/ *adj.* [F *apogée* or mod.L *apogaeum* f. Gk *apogeion* away from earth (as APO-, *gē* earth)]

apolitical /áypəlíttik'l/ *adj.* not interested in or concerned with politics.

Apollonian /áppəlṓniən/ *adj.* **1** of or relating to Apollo, the Greek and Roman sun-god, patron of music and poetry. **2** orderly, rational, self-disciplined. [L *Apollonius* f. Gk *Apollōnios*]

apologetic /əpólləjéttik/ *adj.* & *n.* ● *adj.* **1** regretfully acknowledging or excusing an offence or failure. **2** diffident. **3** of reasoned defence or vindication. ● *n.* (usu. in *pl.*) a reasoned defence, esp. of Christianity. ▫▫ **apologetically** *adv.* [F *apologétique* f. LL *apologeticus* f. Gk *apologētikos* f. *apologeomai* speak in defence]
■ *adj.* **1** regretful, sorry, contrite, remorseful, penitent, rueful, repentant, conscience-stricken. **2** diffident, retiring, meek, self-effacing, modest, unassuming, reticent, hesitant, shy, timid, cowering.
▫▫ **apologetically** contritely, sorrily, remorsefully, regretfully, penitently; diffidently, self-effacingly, meekly, shyly, timidly, reticently, hesitantly, modestly.

apologia /áppəlṓjiə/ *n.* a formal defence of one's opinions or conduct. [L: see APOLOGY]

apologist /əpólləjist/ *n.* a person who defends something by argument. [F *apologiste* f. Gk *apologizomai* render account f. *apologos* account]

apologize /əpólləjīz/ *v.intr.* (also **-ise**) **1** (often foll. by *for*) make an apology for an offence or failure; express regret. **2** (foll by *for*) seek to explain or justify. [Gk *apologizomai*: see APOLOGIST]
■ **1** beg *or* ask pardon, express regret(s), say sorry, make an apology. **2** (*apologize for*) make *or* give excuses *or* explanation(s) for, defend, justify, vindicate.

apologue /áppəlog/ *n.* a moral fable. [F *apologue* or L *apologus* f. Gk *apologos* story (as APO-, *logos* discourse)]

apology /əpólləji/ *n.* (*pl.* **-ies**) **1** a regretful acknowledgement of an offence or failure. **2** an assurance that no offence was intended. **3** an explanation or defence. **4** (foll. by *for*) a poor or scanty specimen of (*this apology for a letter*). [F *apologie* or LL *apologia* f. Gk (as APOLOGETIC)]
■ **1** see EXCUSE *n.* 1, 2. **3** see EXCUSE *n.* 1, 2, DEFENCE 4a. **4** excuse, farce, mockery, travesty.

apolune /áppəloōn/ *n.* the point in a body's lunar orbit where it is furthest from the moon's centre (opp. PERILUNE). [APO- + L *luna* moon, after *apogee*]

apomixis /áppəmíksiss/ *n.* (*pl.* **apomixes** /-seez/) *Biol.* a form of asexual reproduction (cf. AMPHIMIXIS). ▫▫ **apomictic** *adj.* [mod.L, formed as APO- + Gk *mixis* mingling]

apophthegm /áppəthem, áppəf-them/ *n.* (*US* **apothegm**) a terse saying or maxim, an aphorism. ▫▫ **apophthegmatic** /-thegmáttik/ *adj.* [F *apophthegme* or mod.L *apothegma* f. Gk *apophthegma -matos* f. *apophtheggomai* speak out]

apoplectic /áppəpléktik/ *adj.* **1** of, causing, suffering, or liable to apoplexy. **2** *colloq.* enraged. ▫▫ **apoplectically** *adv.* [F *apoplectique* or LL *apoplecticus* f. Gk *apoplēktikos* f. *apoplēssō* strike completely (as APO-, *plēssō* strike)]

apoplexy /áppəpleksi/ *n.* a sudden loss of consciousness, voluntary movement, and sensation caused by blockage or rupture of a brain artery; a stroke. [ME f. OF *apoplexie* f. LL *apoplexia* f. Gk *apoplēxia* (as APOPLECTIC)]

aposematic /áppəsimáttik/ *adj. Zool.* (of coloration, markings, etc.) serving to warn or repel. [APO- + Gk *sēma sēmatos* sign]

apostasy /əpóstəsi/ *n.* (*pl.* **-ies**) **1** renunciation of a belief or faith, esp. religious. **2** abandonment of principles or of a party. **3** an instance of apostasy. [ME f. eccl.L f. NT Gk *apostasia* f. *apostasis* defection (as APO-, *stat-* stand)]
■ **2, 3** see SECESSION.

apostate /əpóstayt/ *n.* & *adj.* ● *n.* a person who renounces a former belief, adherence, etc. ● *adj.* engaged in apostasy. ▫▫ **apostatical** /áppəstáttik'l/ *adj.* [ME f. OF *apostate* or eccl.L *apostata* f. Gk *apostatēs* deserter (as APOSTASY)]
■ *n.* see RENEGADE *n.* ● *adj.* see DISLOYAL.

apostatize /əpóstətīz/ *v.intr.* (also **-ise**) renounce a former belief, adherence, etc. [med.L *apostatizare* f. *apostata*: see APOSTATE]
■ see SECEDE.

a posteriori /áy postérriórī/ *adj.* & *adv.* ● *adj.* (of reasoning) inductive, empirical; proceeding from effects to causes. ● *adv.* inductively, empirically; from effects to causes (opp. A PRIORI). [L, = from what comes after]

apostle /əpóss'l/ *n.* **1** (**Apostle**) **a** any of the chosen twelve sent out to preach the Christian Gospel. **b** the first successful Christian missionary in a country or to a people. **2** a leader or outstanding figure, esp. of a reform movement (*apostle of temperance*). **3** a messenger or representative. ▫ **apostle-bird** any of various Australian birds, forming flocks of about a dozen. **Apostles' Creed** an early form of the Christian creed, ascribed to the Apostles. ▫▫ **apostleship** *n.* [OE *apostol* f. eccl.L *apostolus* f. Gk *apostolos* messenger (as APO-, *stellō* send forth)]
■ **2** see ADVOCATE *n.* 1.

apostolate /əpóstələt/ *n.* **1** the position or authority of an Apostle. **2** leadership in reform. [eccl.L *apostolatus* (as APOSTLE)]

apostolic /áppəstóllik/ *adj.* **1** of or relating to the Apostles. **2** of the Pope regarded as the successor of St Peter. **3** of the character of an Apostle. ▫ **Apostolic Fathers** the Christian leaders immediately succeeding the Apostles. **apostolic succession** the uninterrupted transmission of spiritual authority from the Apostles through successive popes and bishops. [F *apostolique* or eccl.L *apostolicus* f. Gk *apostolikos* (as APOSTLE)]

apostrophe[1] /əpóstrəfi/ *n.* a punctuation mark used to indicate: **1** the omission of letters or numbers (e.g. *can't*; *he's*; *1 Jan. '92*). **2** the possessive case (e.g. *Harry's book*; *boys' coats*). [F *apostrophe* or LL *apostrophus* f. Gk *apostrophos* accent of elision f. *apostrephō* turn away (as APO-, *strephō* turn)]

apostrophe[2] /əpóstrəfi/ *n.* an exclamatory passage in a speech or poem, addressed to a person (often dead or absent) or thing (often personified). ▫▫ **apostrophize** *v.tr.* & *intr.* (also **-ise**). [L f. Gk, lit. 'turning away' (as APOSTROPHE[1])]

apothecary /əpóthəkəri/ *n.* (*pl.* **-ies**) *archaic* a chemist licensed to dispense medicines and drugs. ▫ **apothecaries' measure** (or **weight**) *Brit.* units of weight and liquid volume formerly used in pharmacy. ¶ 12 ounces = one pound; 20 fluid ounces = one pint. [ME f. OF *apotecaire* f. LL *apothecarius* f. L *apotheca* f. Gk *apothēkē* storehouse]
▪ see PHARMACIST.

apothegm *US* var. of APOPHTHEGM.

apothem /áppəthem/ *n. Geom.* a line from the centre of a regular polygon at right angles to any of its sides. [Gk *apotithēmi* put aside (as APO-, *tithēmi* place)]

apotheosis /əpóthiṓsiss/ *n.* (*pl.* **apotheoses** /-seez/) **1** elevation to divine status; deification. **2** a glorification of a thing; a sublime example (*apotheosis of the dance*). **3** a deified ideal. [eccl.L f. Gk *apotheoō* make a god of (as APO-, *theos* god)]

apotheosize /əpóthiəsīz/ *v.tr.* (also **-ise**) **1** make divine; deify. **2** idealize, glorify.

apotropaic /àppətrəpáyik/ *adj.* supposedly having the power to avert an evil influence or bad luck. [Gk *apotropaios* (as APO-, *trepō* turn)]

appal /əpáwl/ *v.tr.* (*US* **appall**) (**appalled, appalling**) **1** greatly dismay or horrify. **2** (as **appalling** *adj.*) *colloq.* shocking, unpleasant; bad. ▫▫ **appallingly** *adv.* [ME f. OF *apalir* grow pale]
▪ **1** dismay, shock, horrify, alarm, outrage, scandalize; revolt, disgust, repel, repulse, sicken, offend. **2** (**appalling**) see ATROCIOUS 1. ▫▫ **appallingly** horrifically, shockingly, outrageously; badly, terribly, awfully, horrendously, atrociously, abysmally, dreadfully.

Appaloosa /àppəlṓōssə/ *n.* **1** a horse of a N. American breed having dark spots on a light background. **2** this breed. [*Opelousa* in Louisiana, or *Palouse*, a river in Idaho]

appanage /áppənij/ *n.* (also **apanage**) **1** provision for the maintenance of the younger children of kings etc. **2** a perquisite. **3** a natural accompaniment or attribute. [F ult. f. med.L *appanare* endow with the means of subsistence (as APO-, *panis* bread)]
▪ see PERQUISITE.

apparat /áppəraát/ *n.* the administrative system of a Communist party, esp. in a Communist country. [Russ. f. G, = apparatus]

apparatchik /áppəraátchik/ *n.* (*pl.* ***apparatchiks*** or ***apparatchiki*** /-kee/) **1 a** a member of a Communist *apparat*. **b** a Communist agent or spy. **2 a** a member of a political party in any country who executes policy; a jealous functionary. **b** an official of a public or private organization. [Russ.: see APPARAT]

apparatus /àppəráytəss/ *n.* **1** the equipment needed for a particular purpose or function, esp. scientific or technical. **2** a political or other complex organization. **3** *Anat.* the organs used to perform a particular process. **4** (in full **apparatus criticus**) a collection of variants and annotations accompanying a printed text and usu. appearing below it. [L f. *apparare apparat-* make ready for]
▪ **1** equipment, gear, gadgetry, paraphernalia, tackle, machinery; requisites, tools, instruments, utensils, implements; machine, appliance, gadget, device, outfit, *derog.* or *joc.* contraption.

apparel /əpárrəl/ *n.* & *v.* ● *n.* **1** *formal* clothing, dress. **2** embroidered ornamentation on some ecclesiastical vestments. ● *v.tr.* (**apparelled, apparelling**; *US* **appareled, appareling**) *archaic* clothe. [ME *aparailen* (v.) f. OF *apareillier* f. Rmc *appariculare* (unrecorded) make equal or fit, ult. f. L *par* equal]
▪ *n.* **1** clothing, clothes, dress, garments, outfit, *archaic* raiment, *colloq.* gear, glad rags, *formal* attire, *sl.* duds, threads. ● *v.* see CLOTHE 1.

apparent /əpárrənt/ *adj.* **1** readily visible or perceivable. **2** seeming. ▫ **apparent horizon** see HORIZON 1b. **apparent magnitude** the magnitude, i.e. brightness, of a celestial body as seen from the earth (opp. *absolute magnitude*). **apparent time** solar time (see SOLAR *adj.*). ▫▫ **apparently** *adv.* [ME f. OF *aparant* f. L (as APPEAR)]
▪ **1** evident, plain, clear, obvious, patent, unmistakable; conspicuous, marked, manifest, visible, perceivable, discernible. **2** seeming, ostensible, superficial, surface, outward; see also PROFESSED 2. ▫▫ **apparently** evidently, plainly, clearly, obviously, patently, manifestly, demonstrably; seemingly, ostensibly, superficially, outwardly, on the face of it, to all (outward) appearances; purportedly, allegedly, professedly.

apparition /àppərísh'n/ *n.* a sudden or dramatic appearance, esp. of a ghost or phantom; a visible ghost. [ME f. F *apparition* or f. L *apparitio* attendance (as APPEAR)]
▪ see PHANTOM *n.* 1.

appeal /əpéel/ *v.* & *n.* ● *v.* **1** *intr.* make an earnest or formal request; plead (*appealed for calm*; *appealed to us not to leave*). **2** *intr.* (usu. foll. by *to*) be attractive or of interest; be pleasing. **3** *intr.* (foll. by *to*) resort to or cite for support. **4** *Law* **a** *intr.* (often foll. by *to*) apply (to a higher court) for a reconsideration of the decision of a lower court. **b** *tr.* refer to a higher court to review (a case). **c** *intr.* (foll. by *against*) apply to a higher court to reconsider (a verdict or sentence). **5** *intr. Cricket* call on the umpire for a decision on whether a batsman is out. ● *n.* **1** the act or an instance of appealing. **2** a formal or urgent request for public support, esp. financial, for a cause. **3** *Law* the referral of a case to a higher court. **4** attractiveness; appealing quality (*sex appeal*). ▫▫ **appealer** *n.* [ME f. OF *apel*, *apeler* f. L *appellare* to address]
▪ *v.* **1** plead, supplicate, solicit, petition, pray, beg, cry; (*appeal to*) entreat, beseech, implore, invoke, ask, request. **2** be attractive *or* alluring *or* of interest; (*appeal to*) attract, allure, please, charm, fascinate, interest. **3** see RESORT *v.* 1. ● *n.* **1** entreaty, call, clamour, request, supplication, solicitation, petition, plea, application, suit, SOS, *cri de cœur*, cry (from the heart), prayer. **3** referral. **4** attraction, attractiveness, allurement, allure, (personal) charm, charisma, lure, fascination, interest, draw, pull.

appealable /əpéeləb'l/ *adj. Law* (of a case) that can be referred to a higher court for review.

appealing /əpéeling/ *adj.* attractive, likeable. ▫▫ **appealingly** *adv.*
▪ see ATTRACTIVE 1.

appear /əpéer/ *v.intr.* **1** become or be visible. **2** be evident (*a new problem then appeared*). **3** seem; have the appearance of being (*appeared unwell*; *you appear to be right*). **4** present oneself publicly or formally, esp. on stage or as the accused or counsel in a lawcourt. **5** be published (*it appeared in the papers*; *a new edition will appear*). [ME f. OF *apareir* f. L *apparēre apparit-* come in sight]
▪ **1** come forth, become visible *or* manifest, put in an appearance, show oneself *or* itself, arrive, show up. **2** materialize, surface, emerge, rise, arise, come up, enter (into) the picture, turn up, arrive, come, crop *or* show up, be revealed, become plain, show oneself *or* itself, manifest oneself *or* itself. **3** see SEEM. **4** (*appear as*) play, perform *or* act *or* take the part *or* role of. **5** be published, come out; become available.

appearance /əpéerənss/ *n.* **1** the act or an instance of appearing. **2** an outward form as perceived (whether correctly or not), esp. visually (*smarten up one's appearance*; *gives the appearance of trying hard*). **3** a semblance. ▫ **keep up appearances** maintain an impression or pretence of virtue, affluence, etc. **make** (or **put in**) **an appearance** be present, esp. briefly. **to all appearances** as far as can be seen; apparently. [ME f. OF *aparance*, *-ence* f. LL *apparentia* (as APPEAR, -ENCE)]
▪ **1** arrival, advent, coming, emergence, debut; presence; publication; compare APPEAR. **2** aspect, look(s), form; air, demeanour, *literary* mien; bearing, manner. **3** semblance,

show, hint, indication, suggestion; illusion; pretence. □ **to all appearances** see *apparently* (APPARENT).

appease /əpéez/ *v.tr.* **1** make calm or quiet, esp. conciliate (a potential aggressor) by making concessions. **2** satisfy (an appetite, scruples). □□ **appeasement** *n.* **appeaser** *n.* [ME f. AF *apeser*, OF *apaisier* f. *à* to + *pais* PEACE]

■ **1** see CALM *v.* **2** meet, comply with, answer, serve; see also FULFIL 4.

appellant /əpéllənt/ *n. Law* a person who appeals to a higher court. [ME f. F (as APPEAL, -ANT)]

■ see *supplicant n.* (SUPPLICATE).

appellate /əpéllət/ *adj. Law* (esp. of a court) concerned with or dealing with appeals. [L *appellatus* (as APPEAL, -ATE[2])]

appellation /ápplàysh'n/ *n. formal* a name or title; nomenclature. [ME f. OF f. L *appellatio -onis* (as APPEAL, -ATION)]

■ see NAME *n.* 1, 2.

appellative /əpéllətiv/ *adj.* **1** naming. **2** *Gram.* (of a noun) that designates a class; common. [LL *appellativus* (as APPEAL, -ATIVE)]

append /əpénd/ *v.tr.* (usu. foll. by *to*) attach, affix, add, esp. to a written document etc. [L *appendere* hang]

■ see TACK[1] *v.* 3.

appendage /əpéndij/ *n.* **1** something attached; an addition. **2** *Zool.* a leg or other projecting part of an arthropod.

■ **1** see ATTACHMENT 1.

appendant /əpéndənt/ *adj.* & *n.* ● *adj.* (usu. foll. by *to*) attached in a subordinate capacity. ● *n.* an appendant person or thing. [OF *apendant* f. *apendre* formed as APPEND, -ANT]

appendectomy /áppendéktəmi/ *n.* (also **appendicectomy** /-diséktəmi/) (*pl.* **-ies**) the surgical removal of the appendix. [APPENDIX + -ECTOMY]

appendicitis /əpéndisítiss/ *n.* inflammation of the appendix. [APPENDIX + -ITIS]

appendix /əpéndiks/ *n.* (*pl.* **appendices** /-diseez/; **appendixes**) **1** (in full **vermiform appendix**) *Anat.* a small outgrowth of tissue forming a tube-shaped sac attached to the lower end of the large intestine. **2** subsidiary matter at the end of a book or document. [L *appendix -icis* f. *appendere* APPEND]

■ **2** see ADDITION 2.

apperceive /ápparseév/ *v.tr.* **1** be conscious of perceiving. **2** *Psychol.* compare (a perception) to previously held ideas so as to extract meaning from it. □□ **apperception** /-sépsh'n/ *n.* **apperceptive** /-séptiv/ *adj.* [ME (in obs. sense 'observe') f. OF *aperceveir* ult. f. L *percipere* PERCEIVE]

appertain /áppərtáyn/ *v.intr.* (foll. by *to*) **1** relate. **2** belong as a possession or right. **3** be appropriate. [ME f. OF *apertenir* f. LL *appertinēre* f. *pertinēre* PERTAIN]

■ **1** see RELATE 4.

appetence /áppit'nss/ *n.* (also **appetency** /-tənsi/) (foll. by *for*) longing or desire. [F *appétence* or L *appetentia* f. *appetere* seek after]

■ see APPETITE 2.

appetite /áppitīt/ *n.* **1** a natural desire to satisfy bodily needs, esp. for food or sexual activity. **2** (usu. foll. by *for*) an inclination or desire. □□ **appetitive** /əpéttitiv/ *adj.* [ME f. OF *apetit* f. L *appetitus* f. *appetere* seek after]

■ **1** see HUNGER *n.* 2. **2** desire, inclination, proclivity, tendency, disposition, bent, preference, liking, predilection, zest, fondness, love, zeal, enthusiasm, taste; craving, hunger, thirst, keenness, hankering, yearning, longing, passion, demand; appetence.

appetizer /áppitīzər/ *n.* (also **-iser**) a small amount, esp. of food or drink, to stimulate an appetite. [*appetize* (back-form. f. APPETIZING)]

■ see HORS-D'ŒUVRE.

appetizing /áppitīzing/ *adj.* (also **-ising**) stimulating an appetite, esp. for food. □□ **appetizingly** *adv.* [F *appétissant* irreg. f. *appétit*, formed as APPETITE]

■ see TEMPTING.

applaud /əpláwd/ *v.* **1** *intr.* express strong approval or praise, esp. by clapping. **2** *tr.* express approval of (a person or action). [L *applaudere applaus-* clap hands]

■ **1** approve, express approval *or* approbation, clap, cheer. **2** clap, cheer, *colloq.* give a person a (big) hand, *US sl.* root for; express approval *or* approbation of, praise, hail, acclaim, sing the praises of, extol, congratulate, compliment, pay tribute *or* homage to; eulogize, commend, laud.

applause /əpláwz/ *n.* **1** an expression of approbation, esp. from an audience etc. by clapping. **2** emphatic approval. [med.L *applausus* (as APPLAUD)]

■ **1** clapping, (standing) ovation, plaudit; cheering, cheers, hurrah, salvo, *Brit.* Kentish fire. **2** acclamation, acclaim, congratulation, éclat, approval, commendation, approbation, praise, extolment, plaudit(s), *colloq.* kudos, *formal* laudation.

apple /ápp'l/ *n.* **1** the fruit of a tree of the genus *Malus*, rounded in form and with a crisp flesh. **2** the tree bearing this. □ **apple of one's eye** a cherished person or thing. **apple-pie bed** a bed made (as a joke) with the sheets folded short, so that the legs cannot be accommodated. **apple-pie order** perfect order; extreme neatness. **she's apples** *Austral. sl.* everything is fine. **upset the apple-cart** spoil careful plans. [OE *æppel* f. Gmc]

applejack /ápp'ljak/ *n. US* a spirit distilled from fermented apple juice. [APPLE + JACK[1]]

appliance /əplíənss/ *n.* a device or piece of equipment used for a specific task. [APPLY + -ANCE]

■ see DEVICE 1a.

applicable /áplikəb'l, əplíkkəb'l/ *adj.* (often foll. by *to*) **1** that may be applied. **2** having reference; appropriate. □□ **applicability** /-bílliti/ *n.* **applicably** *adv.* [OF *applicable* or med.L *applicabilis* (as APPLY, -ABLE)]

■ **2** fit, fitting, suitable, suited, appropriate, proper, apropos, befitting, pertinent, apt, germane, right, seemly, relevant, apposite. □□ **applicability** see *relevance* (RELEVANT).

applicant /áplikənt/ *n.* a person who applies for something, esp. a post. [APPLICATION + -ANT]

■ candidate, job-seeker, job-hunter; applier, auditioner, petitioner, solicitor, requester.

application /áplikáysh'n/ *n.* **1** the act or an instance of applying, esp. medicinal ointment to the skin. **2** a formal request, usu. in writing, for employment, membership, etc. **3 a** relevance. **b** the use to which something can or should be put. **4** sustained or concentrated effort; diligence. [ME f. F f. L *applicatio -onis* (as APPLY, -ATION)]

■ **1** administration, rubbing in, putting on. **2** request, solicitation; appeal, petition, submission, claim. **3 a** relevance, relevancy, reference, pertinence, germaneness, appositeness, aptness, importance; bearing. **b** use, purpose, function, employment, utilization, practice, operation. **4** attention, diligence, industriousness, industry, effort, perseverance, persistence, assiduity, assiduousness, devotion, dedication, commitment, attentiveness, *colloq.* guts.

applicator /áplikaytər/ *n.* a device for applying a substance to a surface, esp. the skin. [APPLICATION + -OR[1]]

applied /əplíd/ *adj.* (of a subject of study) put to practical use as opposed to being theoretical (cf. PURE *adj.* 10). □ **applied mathematics** see MATHEMATICS.

■ see PRACTICAL 1.

appliqué /apléekay/ *n.*, *adj.*, & *v.* ● *n.* ornamental work in which fabric is cut out and attached, usu. sewn, to the surface of another fabric to form pictures or patterns. ● *adj.* executed in appliqué. ● *v.tr.* (**appliqués, appliquéd, appliquéing**) decorate with appliqué; make using appliqué technique. [F, past part. of *appliquer* apply f. L *applicare*: see APPLY]

apply /əplí/ *v.* (**-ies, -ied**) **1** *intr.* (often foll. by *for*, *to*, or *to* + infin.) make a formal request for something to be done, given, etc. (*apply for a job*; *apply for help to the governors*; *applied to be sent overseas*). **2** *intr.* have relevance (*does not apply in this case*). **3** *tr.* **a** make use of as relevant or suitable; employ (*apply the rules*). **b** operate (*apply the handbrake*). **4** *tr.* (often foll. by *to*) **a** put or spread on (*applied the ointment* *to the cut*). **b** administer (*applied the remedy*; *applied common sense to the problem*). **5** *refl.* (often foll. by *to*) devote oneself (*applied myself to the task*). ▫▫ **applier** *n.* [ME f. OF *aplier* f. L *applicare* fold, fasten to]

■ **1** make application, register, bid, put in; audition; (*apply for*) seek, go after, appeal for; (*apply to*) petition, solicit, appeal to, request. **2** have bearing, be relevant, pertain; (*apply to*) involve, include, suit; bear on, refer to, appertain to, relate to. **3 a** use, utilize, employ, put to use, administer, implement, exercise, execute, practise, carry out. **b** engage, operate, put *or* turn on, activate, work. **4 a** administer, rub in *or* on, spread in *or* on; put, place, fix, set. **b** administer, direct. **5** devote, dedicate, commit, give, address; (*apply oneself*) focus, concentrate, pay attention, attend, buckle *or* knuckle down, *sl.* get stuck in; (*apply oneself to*) work at, do.

appoggiatura /əpójətoórə/ *n. Mus.* a grace-note performed before an essential note of a melody and normally taking half its time-value. [It.]

appoint /əpóynt/ *v.tr.* **1** assign a post or office to (*appoint him governor*; *appoint him to govern*; *appointed to the post*). **2** (often foll. by *for*) fix, decide on (a time, place, etc.) (*Wednesday was appointed for the meeting*; *8.30 was the appointed time*). **3** prescribe; ordain (*Holy Writ appointed by the Church*). **4** *Law* **a** (also *absol.*) declare the destination of (property etc.). **b** declare (a person) as having an interest in property etc. (*Jones was appointed in the will*). **5** (as **appointed** *adj.*) equipped, furnished (*a badly appointed hotel*). ▫▫ **appointee** /-teé/ *n.* **appointer** *n.* **appointive** *adj. US* [ME f. OF *apointer* f. *à point* to a point]

■ **1** name, designate, nominate, elect, *Mil.* detail; assign, delegate, commission; select, choose. **2** fix, set, settle, determine, decide on, ordain, authorize, establish, destine, arrange, assign, prescribe, decree. **5** (**appointed**) equipped, fitted out, furnished, decorated, presented, *colloq.* done out. ▫▫ **appointee** see APPOINTMENT 2b.

appointment /əpóyntmənt/ *n.* **1** an arrangement to meet at a specific time and place. **2 a** a post or office available for applicants, or recently filled (*took up the appointment on Monday*). **b** a person appointed. **c** the act or an instance of appointing, esp. to a post. **3** (usu. in *pl.*) **a** furniture, fittings. **b** equipment. [ME f. OF *apointement* (as APPOINT, -MENT)]

■ **1** meeting, rendezvous, engagement; time, slot; assignation, *archaic* tryst, *colloq.* date. **2 a** job, position, post, situation, office, place, assignment, *colloq.* berth. **b** appointee, choice, successful candidate. **c** nomination, election; assignment, designation; selection, choice. **3** (*appointments*) see FITTING *n.*

apport /əpórt/ *n.* **1** the production of material objects by supposedly occult means at a seance. **2** an object so produced. [ME (in obs. senses), f. OF *aport* f. *aporter* f. *à* to + *porter* bring]

apportion /əpórsh'n/ *v.tr.* (often foll. by *to*) share out; assign as a share. ▫▫ **apportionable** *adj.* **apportionment** *n.* [F *apportionner* or f. med.L *apportionare* (as AD-, PORTION)]

■ see ASSIGN *v.* 1a.

apposite /áppəzit/ *adj.* (often foll. by *to*) **1** apt; well chosen. **2** well expressed. ▫▫ **appositely** *adv.* **appositeness** *n.* [L *appositus* past part. of *apponere* (as AD-, *ponere* put)]

■ see APPLICABLE 2.

apposition /áppəzísh'n/ *n.* **1** placing side by side; juxtaposition. **2** *Gram.* the placing of a word next to another, esp. the addition of one noun to another, in order to qualify or explain the first (e.g. *William the Conqueror*; *my friend Sue*). ▫▫ **appositional** *adj.* [ME f. F *apposition* or f. LL *appositio* (as APPOSITE, -ITION)]

appraisal /əpráyz'l/ *n.* the act or an instance of appraising.

■ see *evaluation* (EVALUATE), PRICE *n.* 1b, SURVEY *n.* 1, 3.

appraise /əpráyz/ *v.tr.* **1** estimate the value or quality of (*appraised her skills*). **2** (esp. of an official valuer) set a price on; value. ▫▫ **appraisable** *adj.* **appraiser** *n.* **appraisive** *adj.* [APPRIZE by assim. to PRAISE]

■ **1** evaluate, assess, value.

appreciable /əpreéshəb'l/ *adj.* large enough to be noticed; significant; considerable (*appreciable progress has been made*). ▫▫ **appreciably** *adv.* [F f. *apprécier* (as APPRECIATE)]

■ see CONSIDERABLE 1, 2.

appreciate /əpreéshiayt, -siayt/ *v.* **1** *tr.* **a** esteem highly; value. **b** be grateful for (*we appreciate your sympathy*). **c** be sensitive to (*appreciate the nuances*). **2** *tr.* (often foll. by *that* + clause) understand; recognize (*I appreciate that I may be wrong*). **3 a** *intr.* (of property etc.) rise in value. **b** *tr.* raise in value. ▫▫ **appreciative** /-shətiv/ *adj.* **appreciatively** /-shətivli/ *adv.* **appreciativeness** /-shətivniss/ *n.* **appreciator** *n.* **appreciatory** /-shyətəri/ *adj.* [LL *appretiare* appraise (as AD-, *pretium* price)]

■ **1 a** value, find worthwhile *or* valuable, esteem, cherish, admire, rate *or* regard highly, think highly *or* much *or* well of, prize, treasure, respect. **b** be grateful *or* thankful for. **c** be sensitive to, perceive, detect, discern, recognize, feel. **2** understand, comprehend, recognize, realize, perceive, know, be aware *or* cognizant *or* conscious (of) *or* that. **3 a** increase *or* rise *or* gain in value *or* worth, go up, rise. ▫▫ **appreciative, appreciatory** understanding, aware, cognizant, perceptive; see also THANKFUL. **appreciatively** in appreciation *or* recognition *or* admiration, respectfully; thankfully, gratefully. **appreciativeness** see APPRECIATION 1, SENSITIVITY.

appreciation /əpreéshiáysh'n, -siáysh'n/ *n.* **1** favourable or grateful recognition. **2** an estimation or judgement; sensitive understanding of or reaction to (*a quick appreciation of the problem*). **3** an increase in value. **4** a (usu. favourable) review of a book, film, etc. [F f. LL *appretiatio -onis* (as APPRECIATE, -ATION)]

■ **1** gratitude, thankfulness, gratefulness, thanks; acknowledgement, recognition. **2** estimation, evaluation, judgement, assessment, valuation, appraisal; understanding, comprehension, perception, recognition, detection, knowledge, awareness, realization. **3** increase, rise, advance, growth, escalation, enhancement, gain. **4** review, critique, notice; tribute, acknowledgement, *formal* laudation.

apprehend /áprihénd/ *v.tr.* **1** understand, perceive (*apprehend your meaning*). **2** seize, arrest (*apprehended the criminal*). **3** anticipate with uneasiness or fear (*apprehending the results*). [F *appréhender* or L *apprehendere* (as AD-, *prehendere prehens-* lay hold of)]

■ **1** see PERCEIVE 1, 2. **2** see ARREST *v.* 1a. **3** see DREAD *v.*

apprehensible /áprihénsib'l/ *adj.* capable of being apprehended by the senses or the intellect (*an apprehensible theory*; *an apprehensible change in her expression*). ▫▫ **apprehensibility** /-bílliti/ *n.* [LL *apprehensibilis* (as APPREHEND, -IBLE)]

■ see SENSIBLE 1, 3, INTELLIGIBLE 1.

apprehension /áprihénsh'n/ *n.* **1** uneasiness; dread. **2** understanding, grasp. **3** arrest, capture (*apprehension of the suspect*). **4** an idea; a conception. [F *appréhension* or LL *apprehensio* (as APPREHEND, -ION)]

■ **1** see DREAD *n.* 1. **2** see UNDERSTANDING 1, 2. **3** see ARREST *n.* 1. **4** see IDEA 1, 2a, b.

apprehensive /áprihénsiv/ *adj.* **1** (often foll. by *of*, *for*) uneasily fearful; dreading. **2** relating to perception by the senses or the intellect. **3** *archaic* perceptive; intelligent. ▫▫ **apprehensively** *adv.* **apprehensiveness** *n.* [F *appréhensif* or med.L *apprehensivus* (as APPREHEND, -IVE)]

■ **1** see FEARFUL 1.

apprentice /əpréntiss/ *n.* & *v.* ● *n.* **1** a person who is learning a trade by being employed in it for an agreed period at low wages. **2** a beginner; a novice. ● *v.tr.* (usu. foll. by *to*) engage or bind as an apprentice (*was apprenticed to a builder*). ▫▫ **apprenticeship** *n.* [ME f. OF *aprentis* f. *apprendre* learn (as APPREHEND), after words in *-tis*, *-tif*, f. L *-tivus*: see -IVE]

■ *n.* trainee, novice, probationer, tiro, learner, starter, beginner, acolyte, greenhorn, tenderfoot, neophyte, noviciate, *US* cub, punk, *Austral. colloq.* jackaroo, *sl.* rookie. ● *v.* article, contract, bind, tie, *hist.* indenture; (*be apprenticed to*) be enrolled *or* employed *or* taken on by. □□ **apprenticeship** training, probation, noviciate, *hist.* indentureship.

apprise /əprīz/ *v.tr.* inform. □ **be apprised of** be aware of. [F *appris -ise* past part. of *apprendre* learn, teach (as APPREHEND)]

■ see INFORM 1. □ **be apprised of** be aware *or* conscious *or* cognizant *or* sensible of, be sensitive *or* awake *or* alert to, be informed *or* seized of, *colloq.* be wise to.

apprize /əprīz/ *v.tr. archaic* **1** esteem highly. **2** appraise. [ME f. OF *aprisier* f. *à* to + *pris* PRICE]

appro /áprō/ *n. Brit. colloq.* □ **on appro** = *on approval* (see APPROVAL). [abbr. of *approval* or *approbation*]

approach /əprṓch/ *v.* & *n.* ● *v.* **1** *tr.* come near or nearer to (a place or time). **2** *intr.* come near or nearer in space or time (*the hour approaches*). **3** *tr.* make a tentative proposal or suggestion to (*approached me about a loan*). **4** *tr.* **a** be similar in character, quality, etc., to (*doesn't approach her for artistic skill*). **b** approximate to (*a population approaching 5 million*). **5** *tr.* attempt to influence or bribe. **6** *tr.* set about, tackle (a task etc.). **7** *intr. Golf* play an approach shot. **8** *intr. Aeron.* prepare to land. **9** *tr. archaic* bring near. ● *n.* **1** an act or means of approaching (*made an approach*; *an approach lined with trees*). **2** an approximation (*an approach to an apology*). **3** a way of dealing with a person or thing (*needs a new approach*). **4** (usu. in *pl.*) a sexual advance. **5** *Golf* a stroke from the fairway to the green. **6** *Aeron.* the final part of a flight before landing. **7** *Bridge* a bidding method with a gradual advance to a final contract. □ **approach road** *Brit.* a road by which traffic enters a motorway. [ME f. OF *aproch(i)er* f. eccl.L *appropiare* draw near (as AD-, *propius* compar. of *prope* near)]

■ *v.* **1, 2** near, draw *or* come near *or* nearer *or* close *or* closer (to), *archaic or dial.* come nigh. **2** advance, creep up *or* on, loom. **3** make a proposal to, make advances *or* overtures to, proposition, sound out, *Brit. colloq.* chat up. **4 a** see COMPARE *v.* 3, 4. **b** approximate to, near, nearly equal *or* reach, come close to. **6** see TACKLE *v.* 1. ● *n.* **1** access, entrance, passage, way, path, drive, driveway, course; entry, advance, advancement. **3** method, procedure, *modus operandi*, way, technique, style, manner; attitude, angle, point of view, viewpoint, standpoint, position. **4** (*approaches*) advances, overtures, attentions, proposal, proposition, suit. □ **approach road** *Brit.* slip-road.

approachable /əprṓchəb'l/ *adj.* **1** friendly; easy to talk to. **2** able to be approached. □□ **approachability** /-billiti/ *n.*

■ **1** see FRIENDLY *adj.* 1. **2** see ACCESSIBLE 2.

approbate /áprəbayt/ *v.tr. US* approve formally; sanction. [ME f. L *approbare* (as AD-, *probare* test f. *probus* good)]

approbation /áprəbáysh'n/ *n.* approval, consent. □□ **approbative** /áprəbaytiv/ *adj.* **approbatory** *adj.* [ME f. OF f. L *approbatio -onis* (as APPROBATE, -ATION)]

■ see APPROVAL.

appropriate *adj.* & *v.* ● *adj.* /əprṓpriət/ (often foll. by *to*, *for*) **1** suitable or proper. **2** *formal* belonging or particular. ● *v.tr.* /əprṓpriayt/ **1** take possession of, esp. without authority. **2** devote (money etc.) to special purposes. □□ **appropriately** *adv.* **appropriateness** *n.* **appropriation** /-áysh'n/ *n.* **appropriator** /-aytər/ *n.* [LL *appropriatus* past part. of *appropriare* (as AD-, *proprius* own)]

■ *adj.* **1** suitable, apt, fitting, fit, proper, right, deserved, becoming, befitting, seemly, suited, apropos, correct, germane, pertinent, happy, felicitous, *archaic* meet. ● *v.* **1** take (over), seize, expropriate, usurp, commandeer, arrogate, impound; steal, pilfer, filch, carry away, snatch, thieve, make off with, *colloq.* lift, bag, swipe, snaffle, walk off with, *euphem.* abstract, *formal or joc.* purloin, *sl.* pinch, hook, knock off, snitch, *rhyming sl.* half-inch, *Brit. sl.* nick, whip, bone, crib, *US sl.* glom, knock down, nip. **2** set aside *or* apart, devote, assign, earmark, allot, apportion. □□ **appropriately** fittingly, aptly, suitably, properly, correctly, rightly, becomingly, befittingly, deservedly, meetly. **appropriateness** see *fitness* (FIT[1]), *relevance* (RELEVANT). **appropriation** see SEIZURE 1, THEFT.

approval /əpróov'l/ *n.* **1** the act of approving. **2** an instance of this; consent; a favourable opinion (*with your approval*; *looked at him with approval*). □ **on approval** (of goods supplied) to be returned if not satisfactory.

■ sanction, approbation, blessing, consent, agreement, backing, concurrence; endorsement, acceptance, imprimatur, seal of approval, affirmation, éclat, confirmation, mandate, authorization; licence, leave, permission, rubber stamp, go-ahead, thumbs up, *colloq.* OK, okay, green light.

approve /əpróov/ *v.* **1** *tr.* confirm; sanction (*approved his application*). **2** *intr.* give or have a favourable opinion. **3** *tr.* commend (*approved the new hat*). **4** *tr. archaic* (usu. *refl.*) demonstrate oneself to be (*approved himself a coward*). □ **approved school** *hist.* a residential place of training for young offenders. **approve of 1** pronounce or consider good or satisfactory; commend. **2** agree to. □□ **approver** *n.* **approvingly** *adv.* [ME f. OF *aprover* f. L (as APPROBATE)]

■ **1, 3** confirm, affirm, support, ratify, uphold, subscribe to, second, give the stamp of approval to, approve of, *US* approbate; allow, carry, countenance, condone, permit, sanction, authorize, endorse, commend, put one's imprimatur on, agree (to), accept, assent to, go along with, give the go-ahead *or* one's blessing to, rubber-stamp, *colloq.* OK, okay, give the green light to. □ **approved school** see BORSTAL. **approve of 1** sanction, commend, consider fair *or* good *or* right, think highly of, esteem, value, give one's blessing to, accept, favour, respect, have regard for, be partial to, like. **2** see APPROVE 1, 3 above.

approx. *abbr.* **1** approximate. **2** approximately.

approximate *adj.* & *v.* ● *adj.* /əpróksimət/ **1** fairly correct or accurate; near to the actual (*the approximate time of arrival*; *an approximate guess*). **2** near or next (*your approximate neighbour*). ● *v.tr.* & *intr.* /əpróksimayt/ (often foll. by *to*) bring or come near (esp. in quality, number, etc.), but not exactly (*approximates to the truth*; *approximates the amount required*). □□ **approximately** /-mətli/ *adv.* **approximation** /-máysh'n/ *n.* [LL *approximatus* past part. of *approximare* (as AD-, *proximus* very near)]

■ *adj.* **1** rough, inexact, loose, imprecise, estimated; (*attrib.*) *US colloq.* ballpark. ● *v.* near, approach, come close to, verge *or* border on; resemble, look *or* seem like; simulate. □□ **approximately** approaching; nearly, almost, close to, about, around, more or less, give or take a few, in the region of, roughly, generally, *US colloq.* in the ballpark of, in the right ballpark. **approximation** guess, (rough) estimate, estimation, rounding up *or* down, *US colloq.* ballpark figure; approach.

appurtenance /əpúrtinənss/ *n.* (usu. in *pl.*) a belonging; an appendage; an accessory. [ME f. AF *apurtenaunce*, OF *apertenance* (as APPERTAIN, -ANCE)]

■ see EQUIPMENT.

appurtenant /əpúrtinənt/ *adj.* (often foll. by *to*) belonging or appertaining; pertinent. [ME f. OF *apartenant* pres. part. (as APPERTAIN)]

APR *abbr.* annual or annualized percentage rate (esp. of interest on loans or credit).

Apr. *abbr.* April.

après-ski /áprayskee/ *n.* & *adj.* ● *n.* the evening, esp. its social activities, following a day's skiing. ● *attrib.adj.* (of clothes, drinks, etc.) appropriate to social activities following skiing. [F]

apricot /áyprikot/ *n.* & *adj.* ● *n.* **1 a** a juicy soft fruit, smaller than a peach, of an orange-yellow colour. **b** the tree, *Prunus armeniaca*, bearing it. **2** the ripe fruit's orange-yellow colour. ● *adj.* orange-yellow (*apricot dress*). [Port. *albricoque* or Sp. *albaricoque* f. Arab. *al* the + *barḳuḳ* f. late Gk *praikokion* f. L *praecoquum* var. of *praecox* early-ripe: *apri-* after L *apricus* ripe, *-cot* by assim. to F *abricot*]

April /áypril/ *n.* the fourth month of the year. □ **April Fool** a person successfully tricked on 1 April. **April Fool's** (or **Fools') Day** 1 April. [ME f. L *Aprilis*]

a priori /áy priórī/ *adj.* & *adv.* ● *adj.* **1** (of reasoning) deductive; proceeding from causes to effects (opp. A POSTERIORI). **2** (of concepts, knowledge, etc.) logically independent of experience; not derived from experience (opp. EMPIRICAL). **3** not submitted to critical investigation (*an a priori conjecture*). ● *adv.* **1** in an a priori manner. **2** as far as one knows; presumptively. □□ **apriorism** /aypríəriz'm/ *n.* [L, = from what is before]

apron /áyprən/ *n.* **1 a** a garment covering and protecting the front of a person's clothes, either from chest or waist level, and tied at the back. **b** official clothing of this kind (*bishop's apron*). **c** anything resembling an apron in shape or function. **2** *Theatr.* the part of a stage in front of the curtain. **3** the hard-surfaced area on an airfield used for manoeuvring or loading aircraft. **4** an endless conveyor belt. □ **tied to a person's apron-strings** dominated by or dependent on that person (usu. a woman). □□ **aproned** *adj.* **apronful** *n.* (*pl.* **-fuls**). [ME *naperon* etc. f. OF dimin. of *nape* table-cloth f. L *mappa*: for loss of *n* cf. ADDER]

apropos /áprəpō/ *adj.*, *adv.*, & *prep.* ● *adj.* to the point or purpose; appropriate (*his comment was apropos*). ● *adv.* **1** appropriately (*spoke apropos*). **2** (*absol.*) by the way; incidentally (*apropos, she's not going*). ● *prep.* in respect of; concerning. [F *à propos* f. *à* to + *propos* PURPOSE]
■ *adj.* see APPROPRIATE *adj.* ● *prep.* see CONCERNING.

apse /aps/ *n.* **1** a large semicircular or polygonal recess, arched or with a domed roof, esp. at the eastern end of a church. **2** = APSIS. □□ **apsidal** /ápsid'l/ *adj.* [L APSIS]

apsis /ápsiss/ *n.* (*pl.* **apsides** /-sideez/) either of two points on the orbit of a planet or satellite that are nearest to or furthest from the body round which it moves. □□ **apsidal** *adj.* [L f. Gk (*h*)*apsis*, *-idos* arch, vault]

APT *abbr.* (in the UK) Advanced Passenger Train.

apt /apt/ *adj.* **1** appropriate, suitable. **2** (foll. by *to* + infin.) having a tendency (*apt to lose his temper*). **3** clever; quick to learn (*an apt pupil*; *apt at the work*). □□ **aptly** *adv.* **aptness** *n.* [ME f. L *aptus* fitted, past part. of *apere* fasten]
■ **1** see APPROPRIATE *adj.* **2** see PRONE 2. **3** see QUICK *adj.* 4. □□ **aptness** see APTITUDE 2.

apterous /áptərəss/ *adj.* **1** *Zool.* (of insects) without wings. **2** *Bot.* (of seeds or fruits) having no winglike expansions. [Gk *apteros* f. *a-* not + *pteron* wing]

apteryx /áptəriks/ *n.* = KIWI. [mod.L f. Gk *a-* not + *pterux* wing]

aptitude /áptityōōd/ *n.* **1** a natural propensity or talent (*shows an aptitude for drawing*). **2** ability or fitness, esp. to acquire a particular skill. [F f. LL *aptitudo -inis* (as APT, -TUDE)]
■ **1** talent, gift, ability, capability, facility, faculty, flair; tendency, propensity, disposition, predilection, bent, proclivity. **2** fitness, suitability, appropriateness, relevance, applicability, suitableness, aptness; quick-wittedness, intelligence.

aqua /ákwə/ *n.* the colour aquamarine. [abbr.]

aquaculture /ákwəkulchər/ *n.* the cultivation or rearing of aquatic plants or animals. [L *aqua* water + CULTURE, after *agriculture*]

aqua fortis /ákwə fórtiss/ *n. Chem.* nitric acid. [L, = strong water]

aqualung /ákwəlung/ *n.* & *v.* (*US propr.* **Aqua-Lung**) ● *n.* a portable breathing-apparatus for divers, consisting of cylinders of compressed air strapped on the back, feeding air automatically through a mask or mouthpiece. ● *v.intr.* use an aqualung. [L *aqua* water + LUNG]

aquamarine /ákwəməréen/ *n.* **1** a light bluish-green beryl. **2** its colour. [L *aqua marina* sea water]

aquanaut /ákwənawt/ *n.* an underwater swimmer or explorer. [L *aqua* water + Gk *nautēs* sailor]

aquaplane /ákwəplayn/ *n.* & *v.* ● *n.* a board for riding on the water, pulled by a speedboat. ● *v.intr.* **1** ride on an aquaplane. **2** (of a vehicle) glide uncontrollably on the wet surface of a road. [L *aqua* water + PLANE[1]]

aqua regia /ákwə réejiə/ *n. Chem.* a mixture of concentrated nitric and hydrochloric acids, a highly corrosive liquid attacking many substances unaffected by other reagents. [L, = royal water]

aquarelle /ákwərél/ *n.* a painting in thin, usu. transparent water-colours. [F f. It. *acquarella* water-colour, dimin. of *acqua* f. L *aqua* water]

aquarium /əkwáiriəm/ *n.* (*pl.* **aquariums** or **aquaria** /-riə/) an artificial environment designed for keeping live aquatic plants and animals for study or exhibition, esp. a tank of water with transparent sides. [neut. of L *aquarius* of water (*aqua*) after *vivarium*]

Aquarius /əkwáiriəss/ *n.* **1** a constellation, traditionally regarded as contained in the figure of a water-carrier. **2 a** the eleventh sign of the zodiac (the Water-carrier). **b** a person born when the sun is in this sign. □□ **Aquarian** *adj.* & *n.* [ME f. L (as AQUARIUM)]

aquatic /əkwáttik/ *adj.* & *n.* ● *adj.* **1** growing or living in or near water. **2** (of a sport) played in or on water. ● *n.* **1** an aquatic plant or animal. **2** (in *pl.*) aquatic sports. [ME f. F *aquatique* or L *aquaticus* f. *aqua* water]

aquatint /ákwətint/ *n.* **1** a print resembling a water-colour, produced from a copper plate etched with nitric acid. **2** the process of producing this. [F *aquatinte* f. It. *acqua tinta* coloured water]

aquavit /ákwəvit, -veet/ (also **akvavit** /ákvə-/) *n.* an alcoholic spirit made from potatoes etc. [Scand.]

aqua vitae /ákwə véetī/ *n.* a strong alcoholic spirit, esp. brandy. [L = water of life]

aqueduct /ákwidukt/ *n.* **1** an artificial channel for conveying water, esp. in the form of a bridge supported by tall columns across a valley. **2** *Physiol.* a small canal, esp. in the head of mammals. [L *aquae ductus* conduit f. *aqua* water + *ducere duct-* to lead]

aqueous /áykwiəss/ *adj.* **1** of, containing, or like water. **2** *Geol.* produced by water (*aqueous rocks*). □ **aqueous humour** *Anat.* the clear fluid in the eye between the lens and the cornea. [med.L *aqueus* f. L *aqua* water]
■ **1** see FLUID *adj.* 1.

aquifer /ákwifər/ *n. Geol.* a layer of rock or soil able to hold or transmit much water. [L *aqui-* f. *aqua* water + *-fer* bearing f. *ferre* bear]

aquilegia /ákwiléejə/ *n.* any (often blue-flowered) plant of the genus *Aquilegia*. Also called COLUMBINE. [mod. use of a med.L word: orig. unkn.]

aquiline /ákwilīn/ *adj.* **1** of or like an eagle. **2** (of a nose) curved like an eagle's beak. [L *aquilinus* f. *aquila* eagle]

AR *abbr.* **1** *US* Arkansas (in official postal use). **2** Autonomous Republic.

Ar *symb. Chem.* the element argon.

ar- /ər/ *prefix* assim. form of AD- before *r*.

-ar[1] /ər/ *suffix* **1** forming adjectives (*angular*; *linear*; *nuclear*; *titular*). **2** forming nouns (*scholar*). [OF *-aire* or *-ier* or L *-aris*]

-ar[2] /ər/ *suffix* forming nouns (*pillar*). [F *-er* or L *-ar*, *-are*, neut. of *-aris*]

-ar[3] /ər/ *suffix* forming nouns (*bursar*; *exemplar*; *mortar*; *vicar*). [OF *-aire* or *-ier* or L *-arius*, *-arium*]

-ar[4] /ər/ *suffix* assim. form of -ER[1], -OR[1] (*liar*; *pedlar*).

ARA *abbr.* Associate of the Royal Academy.

Arab /árrəb/ *n.* & *adj.* ● *n.* **1** a member of a Semitic people inhabiting originally Saudi Arabia and the neighbouring countries, now the Middle East generally. **2** a horse of a breed orig. native to Arabia. ● *adj.* of Arabia or the Arabs (esp. with ethnic reference). [F *Arabe* f. L *Arabs Arabis* f. Gk *Araps -abos* f. Arab. *'arab*]

arabesque /árrəbésk/ *n.* **1** *Ballet* a posture with one leg extended horizontally backwards, torso extended forwards, and arms outstretched. **2** a design of intertwined leaves, scrolls, etc. **3** *Mus.* a florid melodic section or composition. [F f. It. *arabesco* f. *arabo* Arab]

Arabian /əráybiən/ *adj.* & *n.* ● *adj.* of or relating to Arabia (esp. with geographical reference) (*the Arabian desert*). ● *n.* a native of Arabia. ¶ Now less common than *Arab* in this sense. □ **Arabian camel** a domesticated camel, *Camelus dromedarius*, native to the deserts of N. Africa and the Near East, with one hump: also called DROMEDARY. [ME f. OF *arabi* prob. f. Arab. *'arabī*, or f. L *Arabus*, *Arabius* f. Gk *Arabios*]

Arabic /árrəbik/ *n.* & *adj.* ● *n.* the Semitic language of the Arabs, now spoken in much of N. Africa and the Middle East. ● *adj.* of or relating to Arabia (esp. with reference to language or literature). □ **arabic numeral** any of the numerals 0, 1, 2, 3, 4, 5, 6, 7, 8, and 9 (cf. *roman numeral*). [ME f. OF *arabic* f. L *arabicus* f. Gk *arabikos*]

arabis /árrəbiss/ *n.* any plant of the genus *Arabis*, low-growing with toothed leaves and usu. white flowers. Also called *rock cress* (see ROCK[1]), *wall-cress*. [med.L f. Gk, = Arabian]

Arabist /árrəbist/ *n.* a student of Arabic civilization, language, etc.

arable /árrəb'l/ *adj.* & *n.* ● *adj.* **1** (of land) ploughed, or suitable for ploughing and crop production. **2** (of crops) that can be grown on arable land. ● *n.* arable land or crops. [F *arable* or L *arabilis* f. *arare* to plough]

■ *n.* see FARM *n.* 1.

Araby /árrəbi/ *n. poet.* Arabia. [OF *Arabie* f. L *Arabia* f. Gk]

arachnid /əráknid/ *n.* any arthropod of the class Arachnida, having four pairs of walking legs and characterized by simple eyes, e.g. scorpions, spiders, mites, and ticks. □□ **arachnidan** *adj.* & *n.* [F *arachnide* or mod.L *arachnida* f. Gk *arakhnē* spider]

arachnoid /əráknoyd/ *n.* & *adj.* ● *n. Anat.* (in full **arachnoid membrane**) one of the three membranes (see MENINX) that surround the brain and spinal cord of vertebrates. ● *adj. Bot.* covered with long cobweb-like hairs. [mod.L *arachnoides* f. Gk *arakhnoeidēs* like a cobweb f. *arakhnē*: see ARACHNID]

arachnophobia /əráknəfṓbiə/ *n.* an abnormal fear of spiders. □□ **arachnophobe** /əráknəfōb/ *n.* [mod. L. f. Gk *arakhnē* spider + -PHOBIA]

arak var. of ARRACK.

Araldite /árrəldīt/ *n. propr.* an epoxy resin used as a strong heatproof cement to mend china, plastic, etc. [20th c.: orig. uncert.]

Aramaic /árrəmáyik/ *n.* & *adj.* ● *n.* a branch of the Semitic family of languages, esp. the language of Syria used as a lingua franca in the Near East from the sixth century BC, later dividing into varieties one of which included Syriac and Mandaean. ● *adj.* of or in Aramaic. [L *Aramaeus* f. Gk *Aramaios* of Aram (bibl. name of Syria)]

arational /áyráshən'l/ *adj.* that does not purport to be rational.

araucaria /árrawkáiriə/ *n.* any evergreen conifer of the genus *Araucaria*, e.g. the monkey-puzzle tree. [mod.L f. *Arauco*, name of a province in Chile]

arb /aarb/ *n. colloq.* = ARBITRAGEUR.

arbalest /aárbəlest/ *n.* (also **arblast** /aárblaast/) *hist.* a crossbow with a mechanism for drawing the string. [OE *arblast* f. OF *arbaleste* f. LL *arcubalista* f. *arcus* bow + BALLISTA]

arbiter /aárbitər/ *n.* (*fem.* **arbitress** /-triss/) **1 a** an arbitrator in a dispute. **b** a judge; an authority (*arbiter of taste*). **2** (often foll. by *of*) a person who has entire control of something. □ **arbiter elegantiarum** (or **elegantiae**) /éllegántiaárəm, éllegánshi-ee/ a judge of artistic taste and etiquette. [L]

■ **1 a** see JUDGE *n.* 2, *negotiator* (NEGOTIATE). **b** see JUDGE *n.* 3b, AUTHORITY 3c.

arbitrage /aárbitraazh, -trij/ *n.* the buying and selling of stocks or bills of exchange to take advantage of varying prices in different markets. [F f. *arbitrer* (as ARBITRATE)]

arbitrageur /aárbitraazhṓr/ *n.* (also **arbitrager** /aárbitrijər/) a person who engages in arbitrage. [F]

arbitral /aárbitrəl/ *adj.* concerning arbitration. [F *arbitral* or LL *arbitralis*: see ARBITER]

arbitrament /aarbítrəmənt/ *n.* **1** the deciding of a dispute by an arbiter. **2** an authoritative decision made by an arbiter. [ME f. OF *arbitrement* f. med.L *arbitramentum* (as ARBITRATE, -MENT)]

■ **1** see SETTLEMENT 3.

arbitrary /aárbitrəri, -tri/ *adj.* **1** based on or derived from uninformed opinion or random choice; capricious. **2** despotic. □□ **arbitrarily** *adv.* **arbitrariness** *n.* [L *arbitrarius* or F *arbitraire* (as ARBITER, -ARY[1])]

■ **1** capricious, erratic, uncertain, inconsistent, unpredictable, whimsical, irrational, varying, chance, random, subjective, unreasoned. **2** absolute, tyrannical, despotic, authoritarian, tyrannous, imperious, magisterial, summary, peremptory, autocratic, dogmatic, uncompromising, inconsiderate, high-handed, dictatorial. □□ **arbitrarily** inconsistently, despotically, tyrannically, tyrannously, autocratically, imperiously, magisterially, dictatorially, dogmatically; see also *at random* (RANDOM). **arbitrariness** inconsistency, irrationality, randomness; see also TYRANNY.

arbitrate /aárbitrayt/ *v.tr.* & *intr.* decide by arbitration. [L *arbitrari* judge]

■ see DECIDE 2b, JUDGE *v.* 5b.

arbitration /aárbitráysh'n/ *n.* the settlement of a dispute by an arbitrator. [ME f. OF f. L *arbitratio -onis* (as ARBITER, -ATION)]

■ see SETTLEMENT 3.

arbitrator /aárbitraytər/ *n.* a person appointed to settle a dispute; an arbiter. □□ **arbitratorship** *n.* [ME f. LL (as ARBITRATION, -OR[1])]

■ see JUDGE *n.* 2, *negotiator* (NEGOTIATE).

arbitress see ARBITER.

arblast var. of ARBALEST.

arbor[1] /aárbər/ *n.* **1** an axle or spindle on which something revolves. **2** *US* a device holding a tool in a lathe etc. [F *arbre* tree, axis, f. L *arbor*: refashioned on L]

arbor[2] *US* var. of ARBOUR.

arboraceous /aárbəráyshəss/ *adj.* **1** treelike. **2** wooded. [L *arbor* tree + -ACEOUS]

Arbor Day /aárbər/ *n.* a day dedicated annually to public tree-planting in the US, Australia, and other countries. [L *arbor* tree]

arboreal /aarbóriəl/ *adj.* of, living in, or connected with trees. [L *arboreus* f. *arbor* tree]

arboreous /aarbóriəss/ *adj.* **1** wooded. **2** arboreal.

arborescent /aárbəréss'nt/ *adj.* treelike in growth or general appearance. □□ **arborescence** *n.* [L *arborescere* grow into a tree (*arbor*)]

arboretum /aárbəreétəm/ *n.* (*pl.* **arboretums** or **arboreta** /-tə/) a botanical garden devoted to trees. [L f. *arbor* tree]

arboriculture /aárbərikulchər/ *n.* the cultivation of trees and shrubs. □□ **arboricultural** /-kúlchərəl/ *adj.* **arboriculturist** /-kúlchərist/ *n.* [L *arbor -oris* tree, after *agriculture*]

arborization /aárbərīzáysh'n/ *n.* (also **-isation**) a treelike arrangement esp. in anatomy.

arbor vitae /aárbər veétī, vī́ti/ *n.* any of the evergreen conifers of the genus *Thuja*, native to N. Asia and N. America, usu. of pyramidal habit with flattened shoots bearing scale-leaves. [L, = tree of life]

arbour /aárbər/ *n.* (*US* **arbor**) a shady garden alcove with the sides and roof formed by trees or climbing plants; a bower. □□ **arboured** *adj.* [ME f. AF *erber* f. OF *erbier* f. *erbe* herb f. L *herba*: phonetic change to *ar-* assisted by assoc. with L *arbor* tree]

arbutus /aarbyṓōtəss/ *n.* any evergreen ericaceous tree o- shrub of the genus *Arbutus*, having white or pink clus- of flowers and strawberry-like berries. Also c-

strawberry-tree. □ **trailing arbutus** *US* the mayflower, *Epigaea repens.* [L]

ARC *abbr.* **1** (in the UK) Agricultural Research Council. **2** Aids-related complex.

arc /aark/ *n.* & *v.* ● *n.* **1** part of the circumference of a circle or any other curve. **2** *Electr.* a luminous discharge between two electrodes. ● *v.intr.* (**arced** /aarkt/; **arcing** /aárking/) form an arc. □ **arc lamp** (or **light**) a light source using an electric arc. **arc welding** a method of using an electric arc to melt metals to be welded. [ME f. OF f. L *arcus* bow, curve]

arcade /aarkáyd/ *n.* **1** a passage with an arched roof. **2** any covered walk, esp. with shops along one or both sides. **3** *Archit.* a series of arches supporting or set along a wall. □□ **arcaded** *adj.* [F f. Prov. *arcada* or It. *arcata* f. Rmc: rel. to ARCH[1]]

Arcadian /aarkáydiən/ *n.* & *adj.* ● *n.* an idealized peasant or country dweller, esp. in poetry. ● *adj.* simple and poetically rural. □□ **Arcadianism** *n.* [L *Arcadius* f. Gk *Arkadia* mountain district in Peloponnese]

Arcady /aárkədi/ *n. poet.* an ideal rustic paradise. [Gk *Arkadia*: see ARCADIAN]

arcane /aarkáyn/ *adj.* mysterious, secret; understood by few. □□ **arcanely** *adv.* [F *arcane* or L *arcanus* f. *arcēre* shut up f. *arca* chest]

■ see MYSTERIOUS.

arcanum /aarkáynəm/ *n.* (*pl.* **arcana** /-nə/) (usu. in *pl.*) a mystery; a profound secret. [L neut. of *arcanus*: see ARCANE]

■ see MYSTERY 1.

arch[1] /aarch/ *n.* & *v.* ● *n.* **1 a** a curved structure as an opening or a support for a bridge, roof, floor, etc. **b** an arch used in building as an ornament. **2** any arch-shaped curve, e.g. as on the inner side of the foot, the eyebrows, etc. ● *v.* **1** *tr.* provide with or form into an arch. **2** *tr.* span like an arch. **3** *intr.* form an arch. [ME f. OF *arche* ult. f. L *arcus* arc]

arch[2] /aarch/ *adj.* self-consciously or affectedly playful or teasing. □□ **archly** *adv.* **archness** *n.* [ARCH-, orig. in *arch rogue* etc.]

arch- /aarch/ *comb. form* **1** chief, superior (*archbishop*; *archdiocese*; *archduke*). **2** pre-eminent of its kind (esp. in unfavourable senses) (*arch-enemy*). [OE *arce-* or OF *arche-*, ult. f. Gk *arkhos* chief]

■ **2** chief, principal, prime, primary, pre-eminent, foremost, first, greatest, major.

Archaean /aarkéeən/ *adj.* & *n.* (*US* **Archean**) ● *adj.* of or relating to the earlier part of the Precambrian era. ● *n.* this time. [Gk *arkhaios* ancient f. *arkhē* beginning]

archaeology /aárkióllәji/ *n.* (*US* **archeology**) the study of human history and prehistory through the excavation of sites and the analysis of physical remains. □□ **archaeologic** /-kiəlójik/ *adj.* **archaeological** /-kiəlójik'l/ *adj.* **archaeologist** *n.* **archaeologize** *v.intr.* (also **-ise**). [mod.L *archaeologia* f. Gk *arkhaiologia* ancient history (as ARCHAEAN, -LOGY)]

archaeopteryx /aárkióptəriks/ *n.* the oldest known fossil bird, *Archaeopteryx lithographica*, with teeth, feathers, and a reptilian tail. [Gk *arkhaios* ancient + *pterux* wing]

archaic /aarkáyik/ *adj.* **1 a** antiquated. **b** (of a word etc.) no longer in ordinary use, though retained for special purposes. **2** primitive. **3** of an early period of art or culture, esp. the 7th–6th c. BC in Greece. □□ **archaically** *adv.* [F *archaïque* f. Gk *arkhaïkos* (as ARCHAEAN)]

■ **1** see ANTIQUATED, OBSOLETE. **2, 3** see ANCIENT[1] *adj.* 1.

archaism /aárkayiz'm/ *n.* **1** the retention or imitation of the old or obsolete, esp. in language or art. **2** an archaic word or expression. □□ **archaist** *n.* **archaistic** /-ístik/ *adj.* [mod.L f. Gk *arkhaïsmos* f. *arkhaïzō* (as ARCHAIZE, -ISM)]

archaize /aárkayīz/ *v.* (also **-ise**) **1** *intr.* imitate the archaic. **2** *tr.* make (a work of art, literature, etc.) imitate the archaic. [Gk *arkhaïzō* be old-fashioned f. *arkhaios* ancient]

archangel /aárkaynjəl/ *n.* **1** an angel of the highest rank. **2** a member of the eighth order of the nine ranks of heavenly beings (see ORDER). □□ **archangelic** /-anjéllik/ *adj.* [OE f. AF *archangele* f. eccl.L *archangelus* f. eccl.Gk *arkhaggelos* (as ARCH-, ANGEL)]

archbishop /aárchbíshəp/ *n.* the chief bishop of a province. [OE (as ARCH-, BISHOP)]

archbishopric /aárchbíshəprik/ *n.* the office or diocese of an archbishop. [OE (as ARCH-, BISHOPRIC)]

archdeacon /aárchdéekən/ *n.* **1** an Anglican cleric ranking below a bishop. **2** a member of the clergy of similar rank in other Churches. □□ **archdeaconry** *n.* (*pl.* **-ies**). **archdeaconship** *n.* [OE *arce-*, *ercediacon*, f. eccl.L *archidiaconus* f. eccl.Gk *arkhidiakonos* (as ARCH-, DEACON)]

■ □□ **archdeaconry, archdeaconship** archidiaconate.

archdiocese /aárchdíəsiss/ *n.* the diocese of an archbishop. □□ **archdiocesan** /aáchdīóssis'n/ *adj.*

archduke /aárchdyóók/ *n.* (*fem.* **archduchess** /-dúchiss/) *hist.* the chief duke (esp. as the title of a son of the Emperor of Austria). □□ **archducal** *adj.* **archduchy** /-dúchi/ *n.* (*pl.* **-ies**). [OF *archeduc* f. med.L *archidux -ducis* (as ARCH-, DUKE)]

Archean *US* var. of ARCHAEAN.

archegonium /aárkigṓniəm/ *n.* (*pl.* **archegonia** /-iə/) *Bot.* the female sex organ in mosses, ferns, conifers, etc. [L, dimin. of Gk *arkhegonos* f. *arkhe-* chief + *gonos* race]

arch-enemy /aárchénnəmi/ *n.* (*pl.* **-ies**) **1** a chief enemy. **2** the Devil.

archeology *US* var. of ARCHAEOLOGY.

archer /aárchər/ *n.* **1** a person who shoots with a bow and arrows. **2** (**the Archer**) the zodiacal sign or constellation Sagittarius. □ **archer-fish** a SE Asian fish that catches flying insects by shooting water at them from its mouth. [AF f. OF *archier* ult. f. L *arcus* bow]

archery /aárchəri/ *n.* shooting with a bow and arrows, esp. as a sport. [OF *archerie* f. *archier* (as ARCHER, -ERY)]

archetype /aárkitīp/ *n.* **1 a** an original model; a prototype. **b** a typical specimen. **2** (in Jungian psychology) a primitive mental image inherited from man's earliest ancestors, and supposed to be present in the collective unconscious. **3** a recurrent symbol or motif in literature, art, etc. □□ **archetypal** /-tīp'l/ *adj.* **archetypical** /-típpik'l/ *adj.* [L *archetypum* f. Gk *arkhetupon* (as ARCH-, *tupos* stamp)]

■ **1 a** see PROTOTYPE 1.

archidiaconal /aárkidīákkən'l/ *adj.* of or relating to an archdeacon. □□ **archidiaconate** /-nət, -nayt/ *n.* [med.L *archidiaconalis* (as ARCH-, DIACONAL)]

■ □□ **archidiaconate** archdeaconry, archdeaconship.

archiepiscopal /aárki-ipískəp'l/ *adj.* of or relating to an archbishop. □□ **archiepiscopate** /-pət, -payt/ *n.* [eccl.L *archiepiscopus* f. Gk *arkhiepiskopos* archbishop]

archil var. of ORCHIL.

archimandrite /aárkimándrīt/ *n.* **1** the superior of a large monastery or group of monasteries in the Orthodox Church. **2** an honorary title given to a monastic priest. [F *archimandrite* or eccl.L *archimandrita* f. eccl. Gk *arkhimandritēs* (as ARCH-, *mandra* monastery)]

Archimedean /aárkiméediən/ *adj.* of or associated with the Greek mathematician Archimedes (d. 212 BC). □ **Archimedean screw** a device of ancient origin for raising water by means of a spiral inside a tube.

Archimedes' principle /aárkiméedeez/ *n.* the law that a body totally or partially immersed in a fluid is subject to an upward force equal in magnitude to the weight of fluid it displaces.

archipelago /aárkipélləgō/ *n.* (*pl.* **-os** or **-oes**) **1** a group of islands. **2** a sea with many islands. [It. *arcipelago* f. Gk *arkhi-* chief + *pelagos* sea (orig. = the Aegean Sea)]

architect /aárkitekt/ *n.* **1** a designer who prepares plans for buildings, ships, etc., and supervises their construction. **2** (foll. by *of*) a person who brings about a specified thing (*the architect of his own fortune*). [F *architecte* f. It. *architetto*, or L *architectus* f. Gk *arkhitektōn* (as ARCH-, *tektōn* builder)]

■ **1** see DESIGNER 1. **2** see AUTHOR *n.* 2.

architectonic /aárkitektónnik/ *adj.* & *n.* ● *adj.* **1** of or relating to architecture or architects. **2** of or relating to the systematization of knowledge. ● *n.* (in *pl.*; usu. treated as *sing.*) **1** the scientific study of architecture. **2** the study of the systematization of knowledge. [L *architectonicus* f. Gk *arkhitektonikos* (as ARCHITECT)]

architecture /aárkitekchər/ *n.* **1** the art or science of designing and constructing buildings. **2** the style of a building as regards design and construction. **3** buildings or other structures collectively. □□ **architectural** /-tékchərəl/ *adj.* **architecturally** /-tékchərəli/ *adv.* [F *architecture* or L *architectura* f. *architectus* (as ARCHITECT)]

architrave /aárkitrayv/ *n.* **1** (in classical architecture) a main beam resting across the tops of columns. **2** the moulded frame around a doorway or window. **3** a moulding round the exterior of an arch. [F f. It. (as ARCH-, *trave* f. L *trabs trabis* beam)]

archive /aárkīv/ *n.* & *v.* ● *n.* (usu. in *pl.*) **1** a collection of esp. public or corporate documents or records. **2** the place where these are kept. ● *v.tr.* **1** place or store in an archive. **2** *Computing* transfer (data) to a less frequently used file, e.g. from disc to tape. □□ **archival** /aarkī́v'l/ *adj.* [F *archives* (pl.) f. L *archi(v)a* f. Gk *arkheia* public records f. *arkhē* government]

■ *n.* **1** see CHRONICLE *n.* ● *v.* **1** see CHRONICLE *v.*

archivist /aárkivist/ *n.* a person who maintains and is in charge of archives.

archivolt /aárkivōlt/ *n.* **1** a band of mouldings round the lower curve of an arch. **2** the lower curve itself from impost to impost of the columns. [F *archivolte* or It. *archivolto* (as ARC, VAULT)]

archlute /aárchlōōt, -lyōōt/ *n.* a bass lute with an extended neck and unstopped bass strings. [F *archiluth* (as ARCH-, LUTE[1])]

archon /aárkən, aárkon/ *n.* each of the nine chief magistrates in ancient Athens. □□ **archonship** *n.* [Gk *arkhōn* ruler, = pres. part. of *arkhō* rule]

archway /aárchway/ *n.* **1** a vaulted passage. **2** an arched entrance.

Arctic /aárktik/ *adj.* & *n.* ● *adj.* **1** of the north polar regions. **2** (**arctic**) *colloq.* (esp. of weather) very cold. ● *n.* **1** the Arctic regions. **2** (**arctic**) *US* a thick waterproof overshoe. □ **Arctic Circle** the parallel of latitude 66° 33′ N, forming an imaginary line round this region. [ME f. OF *artique* f. L *ar(c)ticus* f. Gk *arktikos* f. *arktos* bear, Ursa Major]

■ *adj.* **2** see POLAR 6.

arcuate /aárkyooət/ *adj.* shaped like a bow; curved. [L *arcuatus* past part. of *arcuare* curve f. *arcus* bow, curve]

arcus senilis /aárkōōss seneéliss/ *n.* a narrow opaque band commonly encircling the cornea in old age. [L, lit. 'senile bow']

-ard /ərd/ *suffix* **1** forming nouns in depreciatory senses (*drunkard*; *sluggard*). **2** forming nouns in other senses (*bollard*; *Spaniard*; *wizard*). [ME & OF f. G *-hard* hardy (in proper names)]

ardent /aárd'nt/ *adj.* **1** eager, zealous; (of persons or feelings) fervent, passionate. **2** burning. □□ **ardency** *n.* **ardently** *adv.* [ME f. OF *ardant* f. L *ardens -entis* f. *ardēre* burn]

■ **1** eager, intense, zealous, keen, enthusiastic, fervent, fervid, passionate, avid, fierce, impassioned, hot, burning, warm, *literary* perfervid; earnest, sincere, deep. □□ **ardency** see ARDOUR, DEVOTION 1.

ardour /aárdər/ (*US* **ardor**) *n.* zeal, burning enthusiasm, passion. [ME f. OF f. L *ardor -oris* f. *ardēre* burn]

■ desire, zeal, fervency, ardency, burning desire, fervour, passion, full-heartedness, heat, warmth; enthusiasm, animation, eagerness, keenness.

arduous /aárdyooəss/ *adj.* **1** (of a task etc.) hard to achieve or overcome; difficult, laborious. **2** (of an action etc.) energetic, strenuous. □□ **arduously** *adv.* **arduousness** *n.* [L *arduus* steep, difficult]

■ laborious, difficult, hard, tough, strenuous, energetic, onerous, burdensome, back-breaking, painful; tiring, exhausting, wearisome, fatiguing, taxing, gruelling, trying, formidable. □□ **arduously** see HARD *adv.* 1. **arduousness** see DIFFICULTY 1.

are[1] *2nd sing. present* & *1st, 2nd, 3rd pl. present* of BE.

are[2] /aar/ *n.* a metric unit of measure, equal to 100 square metres. [F f. L AREA]

area /áiriə/ *n.* **1** the extent or measure of a surface (*over a large area*; *3 acres in area*; *the area of a triangle*). **2** a region or tract (*the southern area*). **3** a space allocated for a specific purpose (*dining area*; *camping area*). **4** the scope or range of an activity or study. **5** *US* a space below ground level in front of the basement of a building. **6** (prec. by *the*) *Football* = *penalty area*. □□ **areal** *adj.* [L, = vacant piece of level ground]

■ **1** extent, limit, compass, size, space, square footage, acreage; measure. **2** region, tract, territory, district, zone, stretch; section, quarter, precinct, *arrondissement*, neighbourhood, locality, *Law* bailiwick, *US* block. **3** space, room, ground, zone. **4** scope, range, compass, margin, sphere; section, part; subject. **5** court, courtyard, enclosure, close, yard.

areaway /áiriəway/ *n.* *US* = AREA 5.

areca /árrikə, əreékə/ *n.* any tropical palm of the genus *Areca*, native to Asia. □ **areca nut** the astringent seed of a species of areca, *A. catechu*: also called *betel-nut*. [Port. f. Malayalam *áḍekka*]

areg *pl.* of ERG[2].

arena /əreénə/ *n.* **1** the central part of an amphitheatre etc., where contests take place. **2** a scene of conflict; a sphere of action or discussion. □ **arena stage** a stage situated with the audience all round it. [L *(h)arena* sand, sand-strewn place of combat]

arenaceous /árrináyshəss/ *adj.* **1** (of rocks) containing sand; having a sandy texture. **2** sandlike. **3** (of plants) growing in sand. [L *arenaceus* (as ARENA, -ACEOUS)]

aren't /aarnt/ *contr.* **1** are not. **2** (in *interrog.*) am not (*aren't I coming too?*).

areola /areéələ/ *n.* (*pl.* **areolae** /-lee/) **1** *Anat.* a circular pigmented area, esp. that surrounding a nipple. **2** any of the spaces between lines on a surface, e.g. of a leaf or an insect's wing. □□ **areolar** *adj.* [L, dimin. of *area* AREA]

arête /arét/ *n.* a sharp mountain ridge. [F f. L *arista* ear of corn, fishbone, spine]

argali /aárgəli/ *n.* (*pl.* same) a large Asiatic wild sheep, *Ovis ammon*, with massive horns. [Mongol]

argent /aárjənt/ *n.* & *adj.* *Heraldry* silver; silvery white. [F f. L *argentum*]

argentiferous /aárjəntíffərəss/ *adj.* containing natural deposits of silver. [L *argentum* + -FEROUS]

Argentine /aárjəntīn, -teen/ *adj.* & *n.* (also **Argentinian** /-tínniən/) ● *adj.* of or relating to Argentina in S. America. ● *n.* **1** a native or national of Argentina. **2** a person of Argentine descent. □ **the Argentine** Argentina. [Sp. *Argentina* (as ARGENTINE)]

argentine /aárjəntīn/ *adj.* of silver; silvery. [F *argentin* f. *argent* silver]

argil /aárjil/ *n.* clay, esp. that used in pottery. □□ **argillaceous** *adj.* [F *argille* f. L *argilla* f. Gk *argillos* f. *argos* white]

arginine /aárjineen, -nīn/ *n.* an amino acid present in many animal proteins and an essential nutrient in the vertebrate diet. [G *Arginin*, of uncert. orig.]

Argive /aárgīv/ *adj.* & *n.* ● *adj.* **1** of Argos in ancient Greece. **2** *literary* (esp. in Homeric contexts) Greek. ● *n.* **1** a citizen of Argos. **2** *literary* (usu. in *pl.*) a Greek. [L *Argivus* f. Gk *Argeios*]

argol /aárgol/ *n.* crude potassium hydrogen tartrate. [ME f. AF *argoile*, of unkn. orig.]

argon /aárgon/ *n.* *Chem.* an inert gaseous element, of the noble gas group and forming almost 1% of the earth's atmosphere. ¶ Symb.: **Ar**. [Gk, neut. of *argos* idle f. *a-* not + *ergon* work]

argosy /áargəsi/ *n.* (*pl.* **-ies**) *poet.* a large merchant ship, orig. esp. from Ragusa (now Dubrovnik) or Venice. [prob. It. *Ragusea* (*nave*) Ragusan (vessel)]

argot /áargō/ *n.* the jargon of a group or class, formerly esp. of criminals. [F: orig. unkn.]

▪ see JARGON[1] 1, 2.

arguable /áargyooəb'l/ *adj.* **1** that may be argued or reasonably proposed. **2** reasonable; supported by argument. □□ **arguably** *adv.*

▪ **2** see REASONABLE 2.

argue /áargyoo/ *v.* (**argues, argued, arguing**) **1** *intr.* (often foll. by *with*, *about*, etc.) exchange views or opinions, especially heatedly or contentiously (with a person). **2** *tr.* & *intr.* (often foll. by *that* + clause) indicate; maintain by reasoning. **3** *intr.* (foll. by *for*, *against*) reason (*argued against joining*). **4** *tr.* treat by reasoning (*argue the point*). **5** *tr.* (foll. by *into*, *out of*) persuade (*argued me into going*). □ **argue the toss** *colloq.* dispute a decision or choice already made. □□ **arguer** *n.* [ME f. OF *arguer* f. L *argutari* prattle, frequent. of *arguere* make clear, prove, accuse]

▪ **1** bicker, wrangle, quarrel, squabble, spar, fight, debate, discuss, reason, dispute, disagree, remonstrate, altercate, *colloq.* row, scrap, *US colloq.* spat. **2** reason, assert, hold, maintain, claim, contend; indicate, suggest, signify, show, prove, demonstrate, establish. **3** reason, make *or* put a case, speak, plead. **4** see DEBATE *v.* 1. **5** persuade, talk, prevail (up)on, convince; dissuade; see also COAX.

argufy /áargyoofī/ *v.intr.* (**-ies, -ied**) *colloq.* argue excessively or tediously. [fanciful f. ARGUE: cf. SPEECHIFY]

argument /áargyoomənt/ *n.* **1** an exchange of views, esp. a contentious or prolonged one. **2** (often foll. by *for*, *against*) a reason advanced; a reasoning process (*an argument for abolition*). **3** a summary of the subject-matter or line of reasoning of a book. **4** *Math.* an independent variable determining the value of a function. [ME f. OF f. L *argumentum* f. *arguere* (as ARGUE, -MENT)]

▪ **1** debate, dispute, disagreement, quarrel, controversy, polemic, wrangle, squabble, tiff, altercation; conflict, fight, fracas, affray, fray, skirmish, Donnybrook, feud, falling out, *colloq.* row, scrap, miff, run-in, *Brit. colloq.* barney, *US colloq.* spat, *Sc. sl.* rammy. **2** (line of) reasoning, case, assertion, contention, plea, claim, pleading; defence; reason, explanation, excuse, justification, rationalization, vindication. **3** line (of reasoning), thread; see also THEME 1.

argumentation /áargyoomentáysh'n/ *n.* **1** methodical reasoning. **2** debate or argument. [F f. L *argumentatio* f. *argumentari* (as ARGUMENT, -ATION)]

▪ **2** see DEBATE *n.* 2.

argumentative /áargyooméntətiv/ *adj.* **1** fond of arguing; quarrelsome. **2** using methodical reasoning. □□ **argumentatively** *adv.* **argumentativeness** *n.* [F *argumentatif -ive* or LL *argumentativus* (as ARGUMENT, -ATIVE)]

▪ **1** quarrelsome, cantankerous, contentious, disputatious, belligerent, combative, pugnacious, disagreeable, contrary; litigious.

Argus /áargəss/ *n.* **1** a watchful guardian. **2** an Asiatic pheasant having markings on its tail resembling eyes. **3** a butterfly having markings resembling eyes. □ **Argus-eyed** vigilant. [ME f. L f. Gk *Argos* mythical person with a hundred eyes]

▪ □ **Argus-eyed** see VIGILANT.

argute /aargyóot/ *adj. literary* **1** sharp or shrewd. **2** (of sounds) shrill. □□ **argutely** *adv.* [ME f. L *argutus* past part. of *arguere*: see ARGUE]

argy-bargy /áarjibáarji/ *n.* & *v. joc.* ● *n.* (*pl.* **-ies**) a dispute or wrangle. ● *v.intr.* (**-ies, -ied**) quarrel, esp. loudly. [orig. Sc.]

aria /áariə/ *n. Mus.* a long accompanied song for solo voice in an opera, oratorio, etc. [It.]

Arian /áiriən/ *n.* & *adj.* ● *n.* an adherent of the doctrine of Arius of Alexandria (4th c.), who denied the divinity of Christ. ● *adj.* of or concerning this doctrine. □□ **Arianism** *n.*

-arian /áiriən/ *suffix* forming adjectives and nouns meaning '(one) concerned with or believing in' (*agrarian*; *antiquarian*; *humanitarian*; *vegetarian*). [L *-arius* (see -ARY[1])]

arid /árrid/ *adj.* **1 a** (of ground, climate, etc.) dry, parched. **b** too dry to support vegetation; barren. **2** uninteresting (*arid verse*). □□ **aridity** /ərídditi/ *n.* **aridly** *adv.* **aridness** *n.* [F *aride* or L *aridus* f. *arēre* be dry]

▪ **1 a** see DRY *adj.* 1c. **2** see BORING, DRY *adj.* 3b.

Aries /áireez/ *n.* (*pl.* same) **1** a constellation, traditionally regarded as contained in the figure of a ram. **2 a** the first sign of the zodiac (the Ram). **b** a person born when the sun is in this sign. □□ **Arian** /-riən/ *adj.* & *n.* [ME f. L, = ram]

aright /ərīt/ *adv.* rightly. [OE (as A[2], RIGHT)]

aril /árril/ *n. Bot.* an extra seed-covering, often coloured and hairy or fleshy, e.g. the red fleshy cup around a yew seed. □□ **arillate** *adj.* [mod.L *arillus*: cf. med.L *arilli* dried grape-stones]

-arious /áiriəss/ *suffix* forming adjectives (*gregarious*; *vicarious*). [L *-arius* (see -ARY[1]) + -OUS]

arise /ərīz/ *v.intr.* (*past* **arose** /ərōz/; *past part.* **arisen** /arízz'n/) **1** begin to exist; originate. **2** (usu. foll. by *from*, *out of*) result (*accidents can arise from carelessness*). **3** come to one's notice; emerge (*the question of payment arose*). **4** esp. *archaic* & *poet.* rise. [OE *ārīsan* (as A-[2], RISE)]

▪ **1** spring up, begin, start (up *or* off), originate, come up, come into existence, *formal* commence. **2** see DERIVE 2. **3** come up, be brought up, be mentioned, emerge, surface, *colloq.* crop up. **4** rise, get up, stand up, get to one's feet; wake up, get out of bed, awake, waken; be resurrected, be raised.

arisings /ərīzingz/ *n.pl.* materials forming the secondary or waste products of industrial operations.

aristocracy /árristókrəsi/ *n.* (*pl.* **-ies**) **1 a** the highest class in society; the nobility. **b** the nobility as a ruling class. **2 a** government by the nobility or a privileged group. **b** a State governed in this way. **3** (often foll. by *of*) the best representatives or upper echelons (*aristocracy of intellect*; *aristocracy of labour*). [F *aristocratie* f. Gk *aristokratia* f. *aristos* best + *kratia* (as -CRACY)]

aristocrat /árristəkrat/ *n.* a member of the nobility. [F *aristocrate* (as ARISTOCRATIC)]

▪ see NOBLE *n.*

aristocratic /árristəkráttik/ *adj.* **1** of or relating to the aristocracy. **2 a** distinguished in manners or bearing. **b** grand; stylish. □□ **aristocratically** *adv.* [F *aristocratique* f. Gk *aristokratikos* (as ARISTOCRACY)]

▪ **1** see NOBLE *adj.* 1. **2** see NOBLE *adj.* 3, 4.

Aristotelian /árristətéeliən/ *n.* & *adj.* ● *n.* a disciple or student of the Greek philosopher Aristotle (d. 322 BC). ● *adj.* of or concerning Aristotle or his ideas.

Arita /əréetə/ *n.* (usu. *attrib.*) a type of Japanese porcelain characterized by asymmetric decoration. [*Arita* in Japan]

arithmetic *n.* & *adj.* ● *n.* /əríthmətik/ **1 a** the science of numbers. **b** one's knowledge of this (*have improved my arithmetic*). **2** the use of numbers; computation (*a problem involving arithmetic*). ● *adj.* /árrithméttik/ (also **arithmetical** /-méttik'l/) of or concerning arithmetic. □ **arithmetic mean** the central number in an arithmetic progression. **arithmetic progression 1** an increase or decrease by a constant quantity (e.g. 1, 2, 3, 4, etc., 9, 7, 5, 3, etc.). **2** a sequence of numbers showing this. □□ **arithmetician** /əríthmətísh'n/ *n.* [ME f. OF *arismetique* f. L *arithmetica* f. Gk *arithmētikē* (*tekhnē*) art of counting f. *arithmos* number]

-arium /áiriəm/ *suffix* forming nouns usu. denoting a place (*aquarium*; *planetarium*). [L, neut. of adjs. in *-arius*: see -ARY[1]]

Ariz. *abbr.* Arizona.

Ark. *abbr.* Arkansas.

ark /aark/ *n.* **1** = NOAH'S ARK 1. **2** *archaic* a chest or box. □ **Ark of the Covenant** (or **Testimony**) a chest or cupboard containing the scrolls or tables of Jewish Law. **out of the ark** *colloq.* very antiquated. [OE *ærc* f. L *arca* chest]

arm[1] /aarm/ *n.* **1** each of the upper limbs of the human body from the shoulder to the hand. **2 a** the forelimb of an animal. **b** the flexible limb of an invertebrate animal (e.g. an octopus). **3 a** the sleeve of a garment. **b** the side part of a chair etc., used to support a sitter's arm. **c** a thing resembling an arm in branching from a main stem (*an arm of the sea*). **d** a large branch of a tree. **4** a control; a means of reaching (*arm of the law*). □ **an arm and a leg** a large sum of money. **arm in arm** (of two or more persons) with arms linked. **arm-twisting** *colloq.* (persuasion by) the use of physical force or moral pressure. **arm-wrestling** a trial of strength in which each party tries to force the other's arm down on to a table on which their elbows rest. **as long as your** (or **my**) **arm** *colloq.* very long. **at arm's length 1** as far as an arm can reach. **2** far enough to avoid undue familiarity. **in arms** (of a baby) too young to walk. **in a person's arms** embraced. **on one's arm** supported by one's arm. **under one's arm** between the arm and the body. **within arm's reach** reachable without moving one's position. **with open arms** cordially. □□ **armful** *n.* (*pl.* **-fuls**). **armless** *adj.* [OE f. Gmc]

▪ **3 d** see BRANCH *n.* 1. □ **arm-twisting** see FORCE[1] *n.* 2, PRESSURE *n.* 4.

arm[2] /aarm/ *n.* & *v.* ● *n.* **1** (usu. in *pl.*) **a** a weapon. **b** = FIREARM. **2** (in *pl.*) the military profession. **3** a branch of the military (e.g. infantry, cavalry, artillery, etc.). **4** (in *pl.*) heraldic devices (*coat of arms*). ● *v.tr.* & *refl.* **1** supply with weapons. **2** supply with tools or other requisites or advantages (*armed with the truth*). **3** make (a bomb etc.) able to explode. □ **arms control** international disarmament or arms limitation, esp. by mutual agreement. **arms race** a contest for superiority in nuclear weapons, esp. between East and West. **in arms** armed. **lay down one's arms** cease fighting. **take up arms** begin fighting. **under arms** ready for war or battle. **up in arms** (usu. foll. by *against*, *about*) actively rebelling. □□ **armless** *adj.* [ME f. OF *armes* (pl.), *armer*, f. L *arma* arms, fittings]

▪ *n.* **1** see HARDWARE 2. **4** (*arms*) see SYMBOL *n.*

armada /aarmaádə/ *n.* a fleet of warships, esp. that sent by Spain against England in 1588. [Sp. f. Rmc *armata* army]

armadillo /áarmədíllō/ *n.* (*pl.* **-os**) any nocturnal insect-eating mammal of the family Dasypodidae, native to Central and S. America, with large claws for digging and a body covered in bony plates, often rolling itself into a ball when threatened. [Sp. dimin. of *armado* armed man f. L *armatus* past part. of *armare* ARM[2]]

Armageddon /áarməgédd'n/ *n.* **1 a** (in the New Testament) the last battle between good and evil before the Day of Judgement. **b** the place where this will be fought. **2** a bloody battle or struggle on a huge scale. [Gk f. Heb. *har megiddōn* hill of Megiddo: see Rev. 16:16]

armament /áarməmənt/ *n.* **1** (often in *pl.*) military weapons and equipment, esp. guns on a warship. **2** the process of equipping for war. **3** a force equipped for war. [L *armamentum* (as ARM[2], -MENT)]

▪ **1** see HARDWARE 2.

armamentarium /áarməmentáiriəm/ *n.* (*pl.* **armamentaria** /-riə/) **1** a set of medical equipment or drugs. **2** the resources available to a person engaged in a task. [L, = arsenal]

armature /áarmətyoor/ *n.* **1 a** the rotating coil or coils of a dynamo or electric motor. **b** any moving part of an electrical machine in which a voltage is induced by a magnetic field. **2** a piece of soft iron placed in contact with the poles of a horseshoe magnet to preserve its power. Also called KEEPER. **3** *Biol.* the protective covering of an animal or plant. **4** a metal framework on which a sculpture is moulded with clay or similar material. **5** *archaic* arms; armour. [F f. L *armatura* armour (as ARM[2], -URE)]

armband /áarmband/ *n.* a band worn around the upper arm to hold up a shirtsleeve or as a form of identification etc.

armchair *n.* /áarmcháir/ **1** a comfortable, usu. upholstered, chair with side supports for the arms. **2** (*attrib.*) theoretical rather than active or practical (*an armchair critic*).

Armenian /aarmeéniən/ *n.* & *adj.* ● *n.* **1 a** a native of Armenia, an ancient kingdom and modern republic in the Caucasus. **b** a person of Armenian descent. **2** the language of Armenia. ● *adj.* of or relating to Armenia, its language, or the Christian Church established there *c.*300.

armhole /áarmhōl/ *n.* each of two holes in a garment through which the arms are put, usu. into a sleeve.

armiger /áarmijər/ *n.* a person entitled to heraldic arms. □□ **armigerous** /-míjərəss/ *adj.* [L, = bearing arms, f. *arma* arms + *gerere* bear]

armillary /aarmíllәri/ *adj.* relating to bracelets. □ **armillary sphere** *hist.* a representation of the celestial globe constructed from metal rings and showing the equator, the tropics, etc. [mod.L *armillaris* f. L *armilla* bracelet]

Arminian /aarmínniən/ *adj.* & *n.* ● *adj.* relating to the doctrine of Arminius, a Dutch Protestant theologian (d. 1609), who opposed the views of Calvin, esp. on predestination. ● *n.* an adherent of this doctrine. □□ **Arminianism** *n.*

armistice /áarmistiss/ *n.* a stopping of hostilities by common agreement of the opposing sides; a truce. □ **Armistice Day** the anniversary of the armistice of 11 Nov. 1918 (cf. *Remembrance Sunday*). [F *armistice* or mod.L *armistitium*, f. *arma* arms (ARM[2]) + *-stitium* stoppage]

▪ see TRUCE.

armlet /áarmlit/ *n.* **1** a band worn round the arm. **2** a small inlet of the sea, or branch of a river.

armor *n. US* var. of ARMOUR.

armorer *n. US* var. of ARMOURER.

armory[1] /áarməri/ *n.* (*pl.* **-ies**) heraldry. □□ **armorial** /aarmóriəl/ *adj.* [OF *armoierie*: see ARMOURY]

armory[2] *US* var. of ARMOURY.

armour /áarmər/ *n.* & *v.* (*US* **armor**) ● *n.* **1** a defensive covering, usu. of metal, formerly worn to protect the body in fighting. **2 a** (in full **armour-plate**) a protective metal covering for an armed vehicle, ship, etc. **b** armoured fighting vehicles collectively. **3** a protective covering or shell on certain animals and plants. **4** heraldic devices. ● *v.tr.* (usu. as **armoured** *adj.*) provide with a protective covering, and often with guns (*armoured car; armoured train*). [ME f. OF *armure* f. L *armatura*: see ARMATURE]

armourer /áarmərər/ *n.* (*US* **armorer**) **1** a maker or repairer of arms or armour. **2** an official in charge of a ship's or a regiment's arms. [AF *armurer*, OF *-urier* (as ARMOUR, -ER[5])]

armoury /áarməri/ *n.* (*US* **armory**) (*pl.* **-ies**) **1** a place where arms are kept; an arsenal. **2** an array of weapons, defensive resources, usable material, etc. **3** *US* a place where arms are manufactured. [ME f. OF *armoirie*, *armoierie* f. *armoier* to blazon f. *arme* ARM[2]: assim. to ARMOUR]

armpit /áarmpit/ *n.* **1** the hollow under the arm at the shoulder. **2** *US colloq.* a place or part considered disgusting or contemptible (*the armpit of the world*).

armrest /áarmrest/ *n.* = ARM[1] 3b.

army /áarmi/ *n.* (*pl.* **-ies**) **1** an organized force armed for fighting on land. **2** (prec. by *the*) the military profession. **3** (often foll. by *of*) a very large number (*an army of locusts; an army of helpers*). **4** an organized body regarded as fighting for a particular cause (*Salvation Army*). □ **army ant** any ant of the subfamily Dorylinae, foraging in large groups. **Army List** *Brit.* an official list of commissioned officers. **army worm** any of various moth or fly larvae occurring in destructive swarms. [ME f. OF *armee* f. Rmc *armata* fem. past part. of *armare* arm]

▪ **1** troops, soldiers, armed forces; legion, *archaic* host. **2** see MILITARY *n.* **3** see HOST[1].

arnica /áarnikə/ *n.* **1** any composite plant of the genus *Arnica*, having erect stems bearing yellow daisy-like flower heads, e.g. mountain tobacco. **2** a medicine prepared from this, used for bruises etc. [mod.L: orig. unkn.]

aroid /áiroyd/ *adj.* of or relating to the family Araceae, including arums. [ARUM + -OID]

aroma /ərṓmə/ *n.* **1** a fragrance; a distinctive and pleasing smell, often of food. **2** a subtle pervasive quality. [L f. Gk *arōma -atos* spice]
■ **1** smell, odour, fragrance, scent, perfume, bouquet, redolence, *archaic* savour. **2** aura, atmosphere, flavour, character, redolence, savour, hint, suggestion.

aromatherapy /ərṓməthérrəpi/ *n.* the use of plant extracts and essential oils in massage. □□ **aromatherapeutic** /-pyōōtik/ *adj.* **aromatherapist** *n.*

aromatic /árrəmáttik/ *adj.* & *n.* ● *adj.* **1** fragrant, spicy; (of a smell) pleasantly pungent. **2** *Chem.* of organic compounds having an unsaturated ring, esp. containing a benzene ring. ● *n.* an aromatic substance. □□ **aromatically** *adv.* **aromaticity** /árrəmətíssiti/ *n.* [ME f. OF *aromatique* f. LL *aromaticus* f. Gk *arōmatikos* (as AROMA, -IC)]
■ *adj.* **1** fragrant, spicy, pungent, perfumy, perfumed, sweet-smelling, balmy. □□ **aromaticity** see FRAGRANCE 2.

aromatize /ərṓmətīz/ *v.tr. Chem.* convert (a compound) into an aromatic structure. □□ **aromatization** /-záysh'n/ *n.*

arose *past* of ARISE.

around /ərównd/ *adv.* & *prep.* ● *adv.* **1** on every side; all round; round about. **2** in various places; here and there; at random (*fool around; shop around*). **3** *colloq.* **a** in existence; available (*has been around for weeks*). **b** near at hand (*it's good to have you around*). **4** approximately (*around 400 people attended*). ● *prep.* **1** on or along the circuit of. **2** on every side of; enveloping. **3** here and there; in or near (*chairs around the room*). **4 a** *US* (and increasingly *Brit.*) round (*the church around the corner*). **b** (of amount, time, etc.) about; at a time near to (*come around four o'clock; happened around June*). □ **have been around** *colloq.* be widely experienced. [A[2] + ROUND]
■ *adv.* **1** all round *or* about, everywhere, in every direction, on all sides *or* every side, round about, all over. **2** round, about, all about, everywhere, all over, back and forth, up and down, to and fro, here and there, hither and thither, far and wide, *literary* & *dial.* hither and yon; at random. **3** see ABOUT *adv.* 2, AVAILABLE 2. ● *prep.* **1** on, along. **2** round, about, surrounding, encompassing, enveloping, encircling, on all sides of, in all directions from, enclosing. **4 b** about, (at) approximately, (at) roughly, (at) nearly, (at) almost, *circa*; sometime in *or* during. □ **have been around** know the ropes *or* set-up, know one's stuff, be an old hand, *esp. Brit. colloq.* be a dab hand.

arouse /ərówz/ *v.tr.* **1** induce; call into existence (esp. a feeling, emotion, etc.). **2** awake from sleep. **3** stir into activity. **4** stimulate sexually. □□ **arousable** *adj.* **arousal** *n.* **arouser** *n.* [A-[2] + ROUSE]
■ **1** initiate, excite, stir up, call forth, stimulate, kindle, awaken, induce, summon up, spark (off), provoke, encourage, inspire, foster, foment. **2** awaken, raise (up), wake up, waken, rouse, revive, stir (up). **3** rouse, activate, stir up, animate, enliven, vivify, quicken, impassion, move. **4** excite, stimulate, *colloq.* turn on. □□ **arousal** excitement, stimulation, incitement, encouragement, fomentation, awakening, revival; activation, animation, enlivenment, vivification. **arouser** stimulator, inciter, encourager, fomenter, reviver, animator; stimulus, inspiration.

arpeggio /aarpéjiō/ *n.* (*pl.* **-os**) *Mus.* the notes of a chord played in succession, either ascending or descending. [It. f. *arpeggiare* play the harp f. *arpa* harp]

arquebus var. of HARQUEBUS.

arr. *abbr.* **1** *Mus.* arranged by. **2** arrives.

arrack /árrək/ *n.* (also **arak** /əràk/) an alcoholic spirit, esp. distilled from coco sap or rice. [Arab. *'araḳ* sweat, alcoholic spirit from grapes or dates]

arraign /əráyn/ *v.tr.* **1** indict before a tribunal; accuse. **2** find fault with; call into question (an action or statement). □□ **arraignment** *n.* [ME f. AF *arainer* f. OF *araisnier* (ult. as AD-, L *ratio -onis* reason, discourse)]
■ **1** see INDICT.

arrange /əráynj/ *v.* **1** *tr.* put into the required order; classify. **2** *tr.* plan or provide for; cause to occur (*arranged a meeting*). **3** *tr.* settle beforehand the order or manner of. **4** *intr.* take measures; form plans; give instructions (*arrange to be there at eight; arranged for a taxi to come; will you arrange about the cake?*). **5** *intr.* come to an agreement (*arranged with her to meet later*). **6** *tr.* **a** *Mus.* adapt (a composition) for performance with instruments or voices other than those originally specified. **b** adapt (a play etc.) for broadcasting. **7** *tr.* settle (a dispute etc.). □□ **arrangeable** *adj.* **arranger** *n.* (esp. in sense 6). [ME f. OF *arangier* f. *à* to + *rangier* RANGE]
■ **1** classify, (put in) order, dispose, array, organize, sort (out), systematize, methodize, marshal, group, set up, rank, line up, align, position. **2, 3** settle, convene, plan, set (up), organize, fix, call, prearrange; predetermine, decide on, prepare, determine, map out; orchestrate, choreograph. **5** agree, consent. **6 a** orchestrate, score, adapt, transcribe. **b** see ADAPT 1c, d. □□ **arranger** organizer, planner, settler, convener, orchestrator; transcriber, adapter.

arrangement /əráynjmənt/ *n.* **1** the act or process of arranging or being arranged. **2** the condition of being arranged; the manner in which a thing is arranged. **3** something arranged. **4** (in *pl.*) plans, measures (*make your own arrangements*). **5** *Mus.* a composition arranged for performance by different instruments or voices (see ARRANGE 6a). **6** settlement of a dispute etc. [F (as ARRANGE, -MENT)]
■ **1–3** classification, ordering, organization, grouping, disposition, structuring, planning, groundwork; configuration, combination, construction; order, array, display, structure, alignment, line-up, set-up. **4** (*arrangements*) preparations, plans, measures, programme, schedule, itinerary. **5** orchestration, instrumentation, adaptation, transcription; interpretation, version. **6** settlement, agreement, terms, plan, contract, covenant, compact.

arrant /árrənt/ *attrib.adj.* downright, utter, notorious (*arrant liar; arrant nonsense*). □□ **arrantly** *adv.* [ME, var. of ERRANT, orig. in phrases like *arrant* (= outlawed, roving) *thief*]
■ see BLATANT 1.

arras /árrəss/ *n. hist.* a rich tapestry, often hung on the walls of a room, or to conceal an alcove. [*Arras*, a town in NE France famous for the fabric]

array /əráy/ *n.* & *v.* ● *n.* **1** an imposing or well-ordered series or display. **2** an ordered arrangement, esp. of troops (*battle array*). **3** *poet.* an outfit or dress (*in fine array*). **4 a** *Math.* an arrangement of quantities or symbols in rows and columns; a matrix. **b** *Computing* an ordered set of related elements. **5** *Law* a list of jurors empanelled. ● *v.tr.* **1** deck, adorn. **2** set in order; marshal (forces). **3** *Law* empanel (a jury). [ME f. AF *araier*, OF *areer* ult. f. a Gmc root, = prepare]
■ *n.* **1** see DISPLAY *n.* 2. **2** see ARRANGEMENT 1–3. ● *v.* **1** see DRESS *v.* 1a, 3. **2** see ARRANGE 1.

arrears /əreérz/ *n.pl.* an amount still outstanding or uncompleted, esp. work undone or a debt unpaid. □ **in arrears** (or **arrear**) behindhand, esp. in payment. □□ **arrearage** *n.* [ME (orig. as adv.) f. OF *arere* f. med.L *adretro* (as AD-, *retro* backwards): first used in phr. *in arrear*]

arrest /ərést/ *v.* & *n.* ● *v.tr.* **1 a** seize (a person) and take into custody, esp. by legal authority. **b** seize (a ship) by legal authority. **2** stop or check (esp. a process or moving thing). **3 a** attract (a person's attention). **b** attract the attention of (a person). ● *n.* **1** the act of arresting or being arrested, esp. the legal seizure of a person. **2** a stoppage or check (*cardiac arrest*). □ **arrest of judgement** *Law* the staying of proceedings, notwithstanding a verdict, on the grounds of a material irregularity in the course of the trial. **under arrest** in custody, deprived of liberty. □□ **arresting** *adj.* **arrestingly** *adv.* [ME f. OF *arester* ult. f. L *restare* remain, stop]
■ *v.* **1 a** catch, capture, seize, apprehend, take (in), take

into custody *or* charge, pick up, detain, collar, *colloq.* run *or* pull in, *esp. US colloq.* bust, *sl.* nab, pinch, lag, *Brit. sl.* nick, cop. **2** stop, halt, check, stall, retard, slow, forestall, hold up, detain, delay, hinder, restrain, obstruct, block, interrupt, freeze, abort. **3 a** attract, draw, catch, get hold of, secure. ● *n.* **1** seizure, capture, apprehension, detention, restraint, *esp. US colloq.* bust, *Brit. sl.* cop. **2** stop, stoppage, check, cessation; retardation, slowness; blockage, obstruction; abortion. □ **under arrest** in custody, under legal restraint, in the hands of the law, imprisoned, arrested. □□ **arresting** striking, shocking, remarkable, impressive, electrifying, extraordinary, surprising, dazzling, *colloq.* stunning.

arrestable /əréstəb'l/ *adj.* **1** susceptible of arrest. **2** *Law* (esp. of an offence) such that the offender may be arrested without a warrant.

arrester /əréstər/ *n.* (also **arrestor**) a device, esp. on an aircraft carrier, for slowing an aircraft by means of a hook and cable after landing.

arrestment /əréstmənt/ *n.* esp. *Sc.* attachment of property for the satisfaction of a debt.

arrière-pensée /áryairponsáy/ *n.* **1** an undisclosed motive. **2** a mental reservation. [F, = behind thought]
■ **1** see MOTIVE *n.*

arris /árriss/ *n. Archit.* a sharp edge formed by the meeting of two flat or curved surfaces. [corrupt. f. F *areste*, mod. ARÊTE]

arrival /ərī́v'l/ *n.* **1 a** the act of arriving. **b** an appearance on the scene. **2** a person or thing that has arrived. □ **new arrival** *colloq.* a newborn child. [ME f. AF *arrivaille* (as ARRIVE, -AL)]
■ **1** coming, advent, appearance, entry, entrance, incoming; dawn; beginning, *formal* commencement. **2** newcomer; immigrant; traveller, passenger; tourist; migrant.

arrive /ərī́v/ *v.intr.* (often foll. by *at, in*) **1** reach a destination; come to the end of a journey or a specified part of a journey (*arrived in Tibet*; *arrived at the station*; *arrived late*). **2** (foll. by *at*) reach (a conclusion, decision, etc.). **3** *colloq.* establish one's reputation or position. **4** *colloq.* (of a child) be born. **5** (of a thing) be brought (*the flowers have arrived*). **6** (of a time) come (*her birthday arrived at last*). [ME f. OF *ariver*, ult. as AD- + L *ripa* shore]
■ **1** come, make one's *or* its appearance, come on the scene, appear, show, turn up, draw *or* pull *or* roll *or* walk in, check in, *colloq.* show *or* roll up, blow in, fetch up; (*arrive at*) make, hit, reach. **2** (*arrive at*) come *or* get to, reach, attain (to), hit, make. **3** succeed, be successful, prosper, get ahead (in the world), reach the top, establish oneself, come through, *colloq.* make it, make the grade, get somewhere, get there.

arrivisme /árreeveéez'm/ *n.* ambitious or ruthlessly self-seeking behaviour.

arriviste /árreeveést/ *n.* an ambitious or ruthlessly self-seeking person. [F f. *arriver* f. OF (as ARRIVE, -IST)]
■ see UPSTART *n.*

arrogant /árrəgənt/ *adj.* (of a person, attitude, etc.) aggressively assertive or presumptuous; overbearing. □□ **arrogance** *n.* **arrogantly** *adv.* [ME f. OF (as ARROGATE, -ANT)]
■ presumptuous, assuming, (self-)assertive, conceited, egotistical, pompous, superior, bumptious, hubristic; haughty, overbearing, imperious, high-handed, overweening, disdainful, opinionated, contemptuous, scornful, snobbish, supercilious, lofty, swaggering, cavalier, *colloq.* uppity, high and mighty, snotty, jumped-up, *esp. Brit. colloq.* uppish, *esp. Brit. sl.* toffee-nosed. □□ **arrogance** self-assertion, impertinence, insolence, presumption, nerve, effrontery, presumptuousness, opinionatedness, self-importance, conceit, egotism, hauteur, haughtiness, loftiness, pride, hubris, pompousness, pomposity, pretension, pretentiousness, bluster, snobbery, snobbishness, *colloq.* snottiness, *sl.* gall, *Brit. sl.* side.

arrogate /árrəgayt/ *v.tr.* **1** (often foll. by *to* oneself) claim (power, responsibility, etc.) without justification. **2** (often foll. by *to*) attribute unjustly (to a person). □□ **arrogation** /-gáysh'n/ *n.* [L *arrogare arrogat-* (as AD-, *rogare* ask)]
■ **1** see TAKE *v.* 2.

arrondissement /aróndeesmón/ *n.* **1** a subdivision of a French department, for local government administration purposes. **2** an administrative district of a large city, esp. Paris. [F]
■ see AREA 2.

arrow /árrō/ *n.* **1** a sharp pointed wooden or metal stick shot from a bow as a weapon. **2** a drawn or printed etc. representation of an arrow indicating a direction; a pointer. □ **arrow-grass** a marsh plant of the genus *Triglochin.* **arrow worm** = CHAETOGNATH. **broad arrow** *Brit.* a mark formerly used on British prison clothing and other government stores. □□ **arrowy** *adj.* [OE *ar(e)we* f. ON *ör* f. Gmc]
■ **1** see BOLT[1] *n.* 5. **2** see POINTER 1.

arrowhead /árrōhed/ *n.* **1** the pointed end of an arrow. **2** a water-plant, *Sagittaria sagittaria*, with arrow-shaped leaves. **3** a decorative device resembling an arrowhead.

arrowroot /árrō-rōōt/ *n.* a plant of the family Marantaceae from which a starch is prepared and used for nutritional and medicinal purposes.

arroyo /əróyō/ *n.* (*pl.* **-os**) *US* **1** a brook or stream. **2** a gully. [Sp.]

arse /aarss/ *n.* & *v.* (*US* **ass** /ass/) *coarse sl.* ● *n.* the buttocks. ● *v.intr.* (usu. foll. by *about, around*) play the fool. □ **arse-hole 1** the anus. **2** *offens.* a term of contempt for a person. **arse-kisser** = *arse-licker.* **arse-kissing** *n.* & *adj.* = *arse-licking.* **arse-licker** a toady. **arse-licking** *n.* & *adj.* obsequious(ness) for the purpose of gaining favour; toadying. ¶ Usually considered a taboo word. [OE *ærs*]

arsenal /aársən'l/ *n.* **1** a store of weapons. **2** a government establishment for the storage and manufacture of weapons and ammunition. **3** resources of anything compared with weapons (e.g. abuse), regarded collectively. [obs. F *arsenal* or It. *arzanale* f. Arab. *dārṣināʻa* f. *dār* house + *sināʻa* art, industry f. *ṣanáa* fabricate]

arsenic *n.* & *adj.* ● *n.* /aársənik/ **1** a non-scientific name for arsenic trioxide, a highly poisonous white powdery substance used in weed-killers, rat poison, etc. **2** *Chem.* a brittle semi-metallic element, used in semiconductors and alloys. ¶ Symb.: **As.** ● *adj.* /aarsénnik/ **1** of or concerning arsenic. **2** *Chem.* containing arsenic with a valency of five. □ **red arsenic** = REALGAR. **white arsenic** = sense 1. □□ **arsenious** /aarseéniəss/ *adj.* [ME f. OF f. L *arsenicum* f. Gk *arsenikon* yellow orpiment, identified with *arsenikos* male, but in fact f. Arab. *al-zarnīḵ* f. *al* the + *zarnīḵ* orpiment f. Pers. f. *zar* gold]

arsenical /aarsénnik'l/ *adj.* & *n.* ● *adj.* of or containing arsenic. ● *n.* a drug containing arsenic.

arsine /aárseen/ *n. Chem.* arsenic trihydride, a colourless poisonous gas smelling slightly of garlic. [ARSENIC after *amine*]

arsis /aársiss/ *n.* (*pl.* **arses** /-seez/) a stressed syllable or part of a metrical foot in Greek or Latin verse (opp. THESIS). [ME f. LL f. Gk, = lifting f. *airō* raise]

arson /aárs'n/ *n.* the act of maliciously setting fire to property. □□ **arsonist** *n.* [legal AF, OF, f. med.L *arsio -onis* f. L *ardēre ars-* burn]

arsphenamine /aarsfénnəmin, -meen/ *n.* a drug formerly used in the treatment of syphilis and parasitic diseases. [ARSENIC + PHENYL + AMINE]

art[1] /aart/ *n.* **1 a** human creative skill or its application. **b** work exhibiting this. **2 a** (in *pl.*; prec. by *the*) the various branches of creative activity concerned with the production of imaginative designs, sounds, or ideas, e.g. painting, music, writing, considered collectively. **b** any one of these branches. **3** creative activity, esp. painting and drawing, resulting in visual representation (*interested in music but not art*). **4** human skill or workmanship as opposed to the work of nature (*art and nature had combined to make her a great beauty*). **5** (often foll. by *of*) a skill, aptitude, or knack (*the art of writing clearly; keeping people happy is quite an art*). **6** (in *pl.*; usu. prec. by *the*) those branches of learning (esp. languages, literature, and history) associated with creative skill as opposed to scientific, technical, or vocational skills. **7** crafty or wily behaviour; an instance of this. □ **art and mystery** any of the special skills or techniques in a specified area. **art deco** /dékkō/ the predominant decorative art style of the period 1910–30, characterized by precise and boldly delineated geometric motifs, shapes, and strong colours. **art form 1** any medium of artistic expression. **2** an established form of composition (e.g. the novel, sonata, sonnet, etc.). **art nouveau** /áar nōōvō/ a European art style of the late 19th century characterized by flowing lines and natural organic forms. **art paper** smooth-coated high-quality paper. **arts and crafts** decorative design and handicraft. [ME f. OF f. L *ars artis*]

■ **1** creativity, creativeness, creative power(s), artistry, inventiveness, imagination, imaginativeness; creation. **2, 3** visual art(s). **4** skill, skilfulness, ingenuity, talent, artistry, craftsmanship, workmanship; knowledge, expertise; craft, technique, adroitness, dexterity, know-how. **5** skill, talent, craft, knack, aptitude, faculty, technique. **6** (*the arts*) humanities, non-sciences; letters, belles-lettres, fine arts, aesthetics, literae humaniores. **7** trickery, craftiness, cunning, wiliness, slyness, guile, deceit, duplicity, artfulness, cleverness, astuteness; wile, scheme, stratagem, artifice, subterfuge, trick, deception, dodge, manoeuvre.

art[2] /aart/ *archaic* or *dial. 2nd sing. present* of BE.

art. /aart/ *abbr.* article.

artefact /áartifakt/ *n.* (also **artifact**) **1** a product of human art and workmanship. **2** *Archaeol.* a product of prehistoric or aboriginal workmanship as distinguished from a similar object naturally produced. **3** *Biol.* etc. a feature not naturally present, introduced during preparation or investigation (e.g. as in the preparation of a slide). □□ **artefactual** *adj.* (in senses 1 and 2). [L *arte* (ablat. of *ars* art) + *factum* (neut. past part. of *facere* make)]

■ **1** product, commodity, item, article, object.

artel /aartél/ *n.* an association of craftsmen, peasants, etc., in the former USSR. [Russ.]

arterial /aartéeriəl/ *adj.* **1** of or relating to an artery (*arterial blood*). **2** (esp. of a road) main, important, esp. linking large cities or towns. [F *artériel* f. *artère* artery]

arterialize /aartéeriəlīz/ *v.tr.* (also **-ise**) **1** convert venous into arterial (blood) by reoxygenation esp. in the lungs. **2** provide with an arterial system. □□ **arterialization** /-záysh'n/ *n.*

arteriole /aartéeriōl/ *n.* a small branch of an artery leading into capillaries. [F *artériole*, dimin. of *artère* ARTERY]

arteriosclerosis /aartéeriōskleerṓsiss/ *n.* the loss of elasticity and thickening of the walls of the arteries, esp. in old age; hardening of the arteries. □□ **arteriosclerotic** /-róttik/ *adj.* [ARTERY + SCLEROSIS]

artery /áartəri/ *n.* (*pl.* **-ies**) **1** any of the muscular-walled tubes forming part of the blood circulation system of the body, carrying oxygen-enriched blood from the heart (cf. VEIN). **2** a main road or railway line. □□ **arteritis** /-rī́tiss/ *n.* [ME f. L *arteria* f. Gk *artēria* prob. f. *airō* raise]

artesian well /aartéeziən, -zh'n/ *n.* a well bored perpendicularly, esp. through rock, into water-bearing strata lying at an angle, so that natural pressure produces a constant supply of water with little or no pumping. [F. *artésien* f. *Artois*, an old French province]

artful /áartfōōl/ *adj.* **1** (of a person or action) crafty, deceitful. **2** skilful, clever. □□ **artfully** *adv.* **artfulness** *n.*

■ **1** scheming, wily, sly, cunning, foxy, crafty, deceitful, underhand, underhanded, double-dealing, guileful, disingenuous. **2** ingenious, clever, astute, shrewd, dexterous, skilful. □□ **artfully** see *astutely* (ASTUTE). **artfulness** see ART[1] 7, ARTIFICE 2a.

arthritis /aarthrī́tiss/ *n.* inflammation of a joint or joints. □□ **arthritic** /-thríttik/ *adj.* & *n.* [L f. Gk f. *arthron* joint]

arthropod /áarthrəpod/ *n. Zool.* any invertebrate animal of the phylum Arthropoda, with a segmented body, jointed limbs, and an external skeleton, e.g. an insect, spider, or crustacean. [Gk *arthron* joint + *pous podos* foot]

Arthurian /aarthyóoriən/ *adj.* relating to or associated with King Arthur, the legendary British ruler, or his court.

artichoke /áartichōk/ *n.* **1** a European plant, *Cynara scolymus*, allied to the thistle. **2** (in full **globe artichoke**) the flower-head of the artichoke, the bracts of which have edible bases (see also JERUSALEM ARTICHOKE). [It. *articiocco* f. Arab. *al-ḵaršūfa*]

article /áartik'l/ *n.* & *v.* ● *n.* **1** (often in *pl.*) an item or commodity, usu. not further distinguished (*a collection of odd articles*). **2** a non-fictional essay, esp. one included with others in a newspaper, magazine, journal, etc. **3 a** a particular part (*an article of faith*). **b** a separate clause or portion of any document (*articles of apprenticeship*). **4** *Gram.* the definite or indefinite article. ● *v.tr.* bind by articles of apprenticeship. □ **definite article** *Gram.* the word (*the* in English) preceding a noun and implying a specific or known instance (as in *the book on the table*; *the art of government*; *the famous public school in Berkshire*). **indefinite article** *Gram.* the word (e.g. *a*, *an*, *some* in English) preceding a noun and implying lack of specificity (as in *bought me a book*; *government is an art*; *went to a public school*). **the Thirty-nine Articles** a set of beliefs affirmed by the ministers of the Church of England. [ME f. OF f. L *articulus* dimin. of *artus* joint]

■ *n.* **1** see THING 2, 3, ITEM 1, 2. **2** see ESSAY *n.* 1. **3** see ITEM *n.* 1, 2. ● *v.* see APPRENTICE *v.*

articular /aartíkyoolər/ *adj.* of or relating to the joints. [ME f. L *articularis* (as ARTICLE, -AR[1])]

articulate *adj.* & *v.* ● *adj.* /aartíkyoolət/ **1** able to speak fluently and coherently. **2** (of sound or speech) having clearly distinguishable parts. **3** having joints. ● *v.* /aartíkyoolayt/ **1** *tr.* **a** pronounce (words, syllables, etc.) clearly and distinctly. **b** express (an idea etc.) coherently. **2** *intr.* speak distinctly (*was quite unable to articulate*). **3** *tr.* (usu. in *passive*) connect by joints. **4** *tr.* mark with apparent joints. **5** *intr.* (often foll. by *with*) form a joint. □ **articulated lorry** *Brit.* a lorry consisting of two or more sections connected by a flexible joint. □□ **articulacy** *n.* **articulately** *adv.* **articulateness** *n.* **articulator** *n.* [L *articulatus* (as ARTICLE, -ATE[2])]

■ *adj.* **1** see FLUENT, COHERENT. **3** articulated, jointed, hinged. ● *v.* **1 a** see ENUNCIATE 1, PRONOUNCE 1. **b** see EXPRESS[1] 1, 2.

articulation /aartíkyooláysh'n/ *n.* **1 a** the act of speaking. **b** articulate utterance; speech. **2 a** the act or a mode of jointing. **b** a joint. [F *articulation* or L *articulatio* f. *articulare* joint (as ARTICLE, -ATION)]

artifact var. of ARTEFACT.

artifice /áartifiss/ *n.* **1** a clever device; a contrivance. **2 a** cunning. **b** an instance of this. **3** skill, dexterity. **4** the products of human skill; man-made objects. [F f. L *artificium* f. *ars artis* art, *-ficium* making f. *facere* make]

■ **1** stratagem, device, manoeuvre, trick, contrivance, wile, ruse, subterfuge, expedient, dodge. **2 a** cunning, trickery, craft, craftiness, artfulness, guile, duplicity, deception, chicanery, underhandedness, shrewdness, slyness, wiliness, trickiness. **3** see DEXTERITY 1.

artificer /aartíffisər/ *n.* **1** an inventor. **2** a craftsman. **3** a skilled mechanic in the armed forces. [ME f. AF, prob. alt. of OF *artificien*]

artificial /áartifish'l/ *adj.* **1** produced by human art or effort rather than originating naturally (*an artificial lake*). **2** not real; imitation, fake (*artificial flowers*). **3** affected, insincere (*an artificial smile*). □ **artificial insemination** the injection of semen into the vagina or uterus other than by sexual intercourse. **artificial intelligence** the application of computers to areas normally regarded as requiring human intelligence. **artificial kidney** an apparatus that performs the functions of the human kidney (outside the body), when one or both organs are damaged. **artificial respiration** the restoration or initiation of breathing by manual or mechanical or mouth-to-mouth methods. **artificial silk** rayon. □□ **artificiality** /-shiálliti/ *n.* **artificially** *adv.* [ME f. OF *artificiel* or L *artificialis* (as ARTIFICE, -AL)]

■ **1, 2** synthetic, man-made, manufactured, fabricated; imitation, simulated, plastic; made-up, concocted, bogus, fake, sham, false, counterfeit, *colloq.* phoney. **3** affected, unnatural, forced, pretended, high-sounding, feigned, synthetic, assumed, contrived, factitious; insincere, sham, false, meretricious, hollow, faked, *colloq.* phoney. □□ **artificiality** see AFFECTATION 1.

artillery /aartílləri/ *n.* (*pl.* **-ies**) **1** large-calibre guns used in warfare on land. **2** a branch of the armed forces that uses these. □□ **artillerist** *n.* [ME f. OF *artillerie* f. *artiller* alt. of *atillier*, *atirier* equip, arm]

artilleryman /aartílləriman/ *n.* (*pl.* **-men**) a member of the artillery.

artisan /aártizán/ *n.* **1** a skilled (esp. manual) worker. **2** a mechanic. □□ **artisanship** *n.* [F f. It. *artigiano*, ult. f. L *artitus* past part. of *artire* instruct in the arts]

■ **1** see WORKER.

artist /aártist/ *n.* **1** a painter. **2** a person who practises any of the arts. **3** an artiste. **4** a person who works with the dedication and attributes associated with an artist (*an artist in crime*). **5** *colloq.* a devotee; a habitual practiser of a specified (usu. reprehensible) activity (*con artist*). □□ **artistry** *n.* [F *artiste* f. It. *artista* (as ART[1], -IST)]

■ **1, 2** see DESIGNER 1. **4, 5** see SPECIALIST 2. □□ **artistry** see SKILL.

artiste /aartéest/ *n.* a professional performer, esp. a singer or dancer. [F: see ARTIST]

■ see *performer* (PERFORM).

artistic /aartístik/ *adj.* **1** having natural skill in art. **2** made or done with art. **3** of art or artists. □□ **artistically** *adv.*

■ **1** see CREATIVE.

artless /aártliss/ *adj.* **1** guileless, ingenuous. **2** not resulting from or displaying art. **3** clumsy. □□ **artlessly** *adv.* **artlessness** *n.*

■ **1** innocent, sincere, guileless, ingenuous, true, natural, open, genuine, simple, direct, candid, frank, honest, straightforward, above-board, uncomplicated, undevious, undeceptive, *US colloq.* on the up and up; unassuming, unaffected, unpretentious, naïve, unsophisticated, plain, ordinary, humble. **2** unartistic, unimaginative, uncreative, talentless. **3** clumsy, inept, unskilled, untalented, unskilful, awkward, bungling, unpractised, inexperienced, inexpert, primitive, unproficient, incompetent, crude.

artwork /aártwurk/ *n.* the illustrations in a printed work.

■ see ILLUSTRATION 1.

arty /aárti/ *adj.* (**artier, artiest**) *colloq.* pretentiously or affectedly artistic. □ **arty-crafty** quaintly artistic; (of furniture etc.) seeking stylistic effect rather than usefulness or comfort. □□ **artiness** *n.*

arum /áirəm/ *n.* any plant of the genus *Arum*, usu. stemless with arrow-shaped leaves, e.g. lords and ladies. □ **arum lily** a tall lily-like plant, *Zantedeschia aethiopica*, with white spathe and spadix. [L f. Gk *aron*]

arvo /aárvō/ *n. Austral. sl.* afternoon. [abbr.]

-ary[1] /əri/ *suffix* **1** forming adjectives (*budgetary*; *contrary*; *primary*; *unitary*). **2** forming nouns (*dictionary*; *fritillary*; *granary*; *January*). [F *-aire* or L *-arius* 'connected with']

-ary[2] /əri/ *suffix* forming adjectives (*military*). [F *-aire* or f. L *-aris* 'belonging to']

Aryan /áiriən/ *n.* & *adj.* ● *n.* **1** a member of the peoples speaking any of the languages of the Indo-European (esp. Indo-Iranian) family. **2** the parent language of this family. **3** *improperly* (in Nazi ideology) a Caucasian not of Jewish descent. ● *adj.* of or relating to Aryan or the Aryans. [Skr. *āryas* noble]

aryl /árrīl, árril/ *n. Chem.* any radical derived from or related to an aromatic hydrocarbon by removal of a hydrogen atom. [G *Aryl* (as AROMATIC, -YL)]

AS *abbr.* Anglo-Saxon.

As *symb. Chem.* the element arsenic.

as[1] /az, unstressed əz/ *adv.*, *conj.*, & *pron.* ● *adv.* & *conj.* (*adv.* as antecedent in main sentence; *conj.* in relative clause expressed or implied) . . . to the extent to which . . . is or does etc. (*I am as tall as he*; *am as tall as he is*; *am not so tall as he*; (*colloq.*) *am as tall as him*; *as many as six*; *as recently as last week*; *it is not as easy as you think*). ● *conj.* (with relative clause expressed or implied) **1** (with antecedent *so*) expressing result or purpose (*came early so as to meet us*; *we so arranged matters as to avoid a long wait*; *so good as to exceed all hopes*). **2** (with antecedent adverb omitted) having concessive force (*good as it is* = although it is good; *try as he might* = although he might try). **3** (without antecedent adverb) **a** in the manner in which (*do as you like*; *was regarded as a mistake*; *they rose as one man*). **b** in the capacity or form of (*I speak as your friend*; *Olivier as Hamlet*; *as a matter of fact*). **c** during or at the time that (*came up as I was speaking*; *fell just as I reached the door*). **d** for the reason that; seeing that (*as you are here, we can talk*). **e** for instance (*cathedral cities, as York*). ● *rel.pron.* (with verb of relative clause expressed or implied) **1** that, who, which (*I had the same trouble as you*; *he is a writer, as is his wife*; *such money as you have*; *such countries as France*). **2** (with sentence as antecedent) a fact that (*he lost, as you know*). □ **as and when** to the extent and at the time that (*I'll do it as and when I want to*). **as for** with regard to (*as for you, I think you are wrong*). **as from** on and after (a specified date). **as if** (or **though**) as would be the case if (*acts as if he were in charge*; *as if you didn't know!*; *looks as though we've won*). **as it is** (or **as is**) in the existing circumstances or state. **as it were** in a way; to a certain extent (*he is, as it were, infatuated*). **as long as** see LONG[1]. **as much** see MUCH. **as of 1** = *as from*. **2** as at (a specified time). **as per** see PER. **as regards** see REGARD. **as soon as** see SOON. **as such** see SUCH. **as though** see *as if*. **as to** with respect to; concerning (*said nothing as to money*; *as to you, I think you are wrong*). **as was** in the previously existing circumstances or state. **as well** see WELL[1]. **as yet** until now or a particular time in the past (usu. with *neg.* and with implied reserve about the future: *have received no news as yet*). [reduced form of OE *alswá* ALSO]

as[2] /ass/ *n.* (*pl.* **asses**) a Roman copper coin. [L]

as- /əss/ *prefix* assim. form of AD- before *s*.

ASA *abbr.* **1** Amateur Swimming Association. **2** American Standards Association.

asafoetida /àssəféetidə, -féttidə/ *n.* (*US* **asafetida**) a resinous plant gum with a fetid ammoniac smell, formerly used in medicine, now as a herbal remedy and in Indian cooking. [ME f. med.L f. *asa* f. Pers. *azā* mastic + *fetida* (as FETID)]

a.s.a.p. *abbr.* as soon as possible.

asbestos /azbéstoss, as-/ *n.* **1** a fibrous silicate mineral that is incombustible. **2** this used as a heat-resistant or insulating material. □□ **asbestine** /-tin/ *adj.* [ME f. OF *albeston*, ult. f. Gk *asbestos* unquenchable f. *a-* not + *sbestos* f. *sbennumi* quench]

asbestosis /ázbestṓsiss, ás-/ *n.* a lung disease resulting from the inhalation of asbestos particles.

ascarid /áskərid/ *n.* (also **ascaris** /-riss/) a parasitic nematode worm of the genus *Ascaris*, e.g. the intestinal roundworm of mankind and other vertebrates. [mod.L *ascaris* f. Gk *askaris*]

ascend /əsénd/ *v.* **1** *intr.* move upwards; rise. **2** *intr.* **a** slope upwards. **b** lie along an ascending slope. **3** *tr.* climb; go up. **4** *intr.* rise in rank or status. **5** *tr.* mount upon. **6** *intr.* (of sound) rise in pitch. **7** *tr.* go along (a river) to its source. **8** *intr. Printing* (of a letter) have part projecting upwards. □ **ascend the throne** become king or queen. [ME f. L *ascendere* (as AD-, *scandere* climb)]

■ **1** see *go up* 1. **2 a** see RISE *v.* 2. **3** see CLIMB *v.* 1. **4** see RISE *v.* 9. **5** mount, climb *or* get *or* clamber (up) on; scale.

ascendancy /əséndənsi/ *n.* (also **ascendency**) (often foll. by *over*) a superior or dominant condition or position.
■ see SUPREMACY 1.

ascendant /əséndənt/ *adj.* & *n.* ● *adj.* **1** rising. **2** *Astron.* rising towards the zenith. **3** *Astrol.* just above the eastern horizon. **4** predominant. ● *n. Astrol.* the point of the sun's apparent path that is ascendant at a given time (*Aries in the ascendant*). □ **in the ascendant 1** supreme or dominating. **2** rising; gaining power or authority. [ME f. OF f. L (as ASCEND, -ANT)]
■ *adj.* **4** see PREDOMINANT 1.

ascender /əséndər/ *n.* **1 a** a part of a letter that extends above the main part (as in *b* and *d*). **b** a letter having this. **2** a person or thing that ascends.

ascension /əsénsh'n/ *n.* **1** the act or an instance of ascending. **2** (**Ascension**) the ascent of Christ into heaven on the fortieth day after the Resurrection. □ **Ascension Day** the Thursday on which this is celebrated annually. **right ascension** *Astron.* longitude measured along the celestial equator. □□ **ascensional** *adj.* [ME f. OF f. L *ascensio -onis* (as ASCEND, -ION)]

Ascensiontide /əsénsh'ntīd/ *n.* the period of ten days from Ascension Day to Whitsun Eve.

ascent /əsént/ *n.* **1** the act or an instance of ascending. **2 a** an upward movement or rise. **b** advancement or progress (*the ascent of man*). **3** a way by which one may ascend; an upward slope. [ASCEND, after *descent*]

ascertain /ássərtáyn/ *v.tr.* **1** find out as a definite fact. **2** get to know. □□ **ascertainable** *adj.* **ascertainment** *n.* [ME f. OF *acertener*, stem *acertain-* f. *à* to + CERTAIN]
■ **1** see DETERMINE 1. **2** see LEARN 5.

ascesis /əséessiss/ *n.* the practice of self-discipline. [Gk *askēsis* training f. *askeō* exercise]

ascetic /əséttik/ *n.* & *adj.* ● *n.* a person who practises severe self-discipline and abstains from all forms of pleasure, esp. for religious or spiritual reasons. ● *adj.* relating to or characteristic of ascetics or asceticism; abstaining from pleasure. □□ **ascetically** *adv.* **asceticism** /-tisiz'm/ *n.* [med.L *asceticus* or Gk *askētikos* f. *askētēs* monk f. *askeō* exercise]
■ *adj.* see SPARTAN *adj.*

ascidian /əsíddiən/ *n. Zool.* any tunicate animal of the class Ascidiacea, often found in colonies, the adults sedentary on rocks or seaweeds, e.g. the sea squirt. [mod.L *Ascidia* f. Gk *askidion* dimin. of *askos* wineskin]

ASCII /áski/ *abbr. Computing* American Standard Code for Information Interchange.

ascites /əsīteez/ *n.* (*pl.* same) *Med.* the accumulation of fluid in the abdominal cavity causing swelling. [ME f. LL f. Gk f. *askitēs* f. *askos* wineskin]

ascorbic acid /əskórbik/ *n.* a vitamin found in citrus fruits and green vegetables, essential in maintaining healthy connective tissue, a deficiency of which results in scurvy. Also called *vitamin C*.

ascribe /əskrīb/ *v.tr.* (usu. foll. by *to*) **1** attribute or impute (*ascribes his well-being to a sound constitution*). **2** regard as belonging. □□ **ascribable** *adj.* [ME f. L *ascribere* (as AD-, *scribere script-* write)]
■ see ATTRIBUTE *v.*

ascription /əskrípsh'n/ *n.* **1** the act or an instance of ascribing. **2** a preacher's words ascribing praise to God at the end of a sermon. [L *ascriptio -onis* (as ASCRIBE)]

asdic /ázdik/ *n.* an early form of echo-sounder. [initials of *A*llied *S*ubmarine *D*etection *I*nvestigation *C*ommittee]

-ase /ayz/ *suffix Biochem.* forming the name of an enzyme (*amylase*). [DIASTASE]

ASEAN /ássiən/ *abbr.* Association of South East Asian Nations.

asepsis /aysépsiss/ *n.* **1** the absence of harmful bacteria, viruses, or other micro-organisms. **2** a method of achieving asepsis in surgery.

aseptic /ayséptik/ *adj.* **1** free from contamination caused by harmful bacteria, viruses, or other micro-organisms. **2** (of a wound, instrument, or dressing) surgically sterile or sterilized. **3** (of a surgical method etc.) aiming at the elimination of harmful micro-organisms, rather than counteraction (cf. ANTISEPTIC).
■ **2** see STERILE 3.

asexual /áyséksyooəl, -sékshooəl/ *adj. Biol.* **1** without sex or sexual organs. **2** (of reproduction) not involving the fusion of gametes. **3** without sexuality. □□ **asexuality** /-séksyoo-álliti, -sékshoo-álliti/ *n.* **asexually** *adv.*

ASH /ash/ *abbr.* Action on Smoking and Health.

ash[1] /ash/ *n.* **1** (often in *pl.*) the powdery residue left after the burning of any substance. **2** (*pl.*) the remains of the human body after cremation or disintegration. **3** (**the Ashes**) *Cricket* a trophy competed for regularly by Australia and England. **4** ashlike material thrown out by a volcano. □ **ash blonde 1** a very pale blonde colour. **2** a person with hair of this colour. **Ash Wednesday** the first day of Lent (from the custom of marking the foreheads of penitents with ashes on that day). [OE *æsce*]

ash[2] /ash/ *n.* **1** any forest-tree of the genus *Fraxinus*, with silver-grey bark, compound leaves, and hard, tough, pale wood. **2** its wood. **3** an Old English runic letter, = æ (named from a word of which it was the first letter). □ **ash-key** the winged seed of the ash-tree, growing in clusters resembling keys. **ash-plant** a sapling from an ash-tree, used as a walking-stick etc. [OE *æsc* f. Gmc]

ashamed /əsháymd/ *adj.* (usu. *predic.*) **1** (often foll. by *of* (= with regard to), *for* (= on account of), or *to* + infin.) embarrassed or disconcerted by shame (*ashamed of his aunt*; *ashamed of having lied*; *ashamed for you*; *ashamed to be seen with him*). **2** (foll. by *to* + infin.) hesitant, reluctant (but usu. not actually refusing or declining) (*am ashamed to admit that I was wrong*). □□ **ashamedly** /-midli/ *adv.* [OE *āscamod* past part. of *āscamian* feel shame (as A-[2], SHAME)]
■ **1** embarrassed, conscience-stricken, remorseful, abashed, disconcerted, humiliated, chagrined, mortified, blushing, shamefaced, sheepish, red-faced. **2** afraid, sorry.

ashbin /áshbin/ *n.* a receptacle for the disposal of ashes.

ashcan /áshkan/ *n. US* a dustbin.

ashen[1] /ásh'n/ *adj.* **1** of or resembling ashes. **2** ash-coloured; grey or pale.
■ **2** see PALE[1] *adj.* 1, 2.

ashen[2] /ásh'n/ *adj.* **1** of or relating to the ash-tree. **2** *archaic* made of ash wood.

ashet /áshit/ *n. Sc.* & *NZ* a large plate or dish. [F *assiette*]

Ashkenazi /áshkənaázi/ *n.* (*pl.* **Ashkenazim** /-zim/) **1** an East European Jew. **2** a Jew of East European ancestry (cf. SEPHARDI). □□ **Ashkenazic** *adj.* [mod.Heb., f. *Ashkenaz* (Gen. 10:3)]

ashlar /áshlər/ *n.* **1** a large square-cut stone used in building. **2** masonry made of ashlars. **3** such masonry used as a facing on a rough rubble or brick wall. [ME f. OF *aisselier* f. L *axilla* dimin. of *axis* board]

ashlaring /áshləring/ *n.* **1** ashlar masonry. **2** the short upright boarding in a garret which cuts off the acute angle between the roof and the floor.

ashore /əshór/ *adv.* towards or on the shore or land (*sailed ashore*; *stayed ashore*).

ashpan /áshpan/ *n.* a tray under a grate to catch the ash.

ashram /áshrəm/ *n. Ind.* a place of religious retreat for Hindus; a hermitage. [Skr. *āshrama* hermitage]

ashtray /áshtray/ *n.* a small receptacle for cigarette ash, stubs, etc.

ashy /áshi/ *adj.* (**ashier, ashiest**) **1** = ASHEN[1]. **2** covered with ashes.

Asian /áysh'n, -zh'n/ *n.* & *adj.* ● *n.* **1** a native of Asia. **2** a person of Asian descent. ● *adj.* of or relating to Asia or its people, customs, or languages. [L *Asianus* f. Gk *Asianos* f. *Asia*]

Asiatic /áyshiáttik, áyzi-/ *n.* & *adj.* ● *n. offens.* an Asian. ● *adj.* Asian. [L *Asiaticus* f. Gk *Asiatikos*]

A-side /áysīd/ *n.* the side of a gramophone record regarded as the main one.

aside /əsī́d/ *adv.* & *n.* ● *adv.* **1** to or on one side; away. **2** out of consideration (placed after noun: *joking aside*). ● *n.* **1** words spoken in a play for the audience to hear, but supposed not to be heard by the other characters. **2** an incidental remark. □ **aside from** *US* apart from. **set aside** **1** put to one side. **2** keep for a special purpose or future use. **3** reject or disregard. **4** annul. **5** remove (land) from agricultural production for fallow, forestry, or other use. **take aside** engage (a person) esp. for a private conversation. [orig. *on side*: see A[2]]

■ *adv.* see APART 3. □ **aside from** see *apart from* 1. **set aside** annul, cancel, nullify, declare *or* render null and void, reverse, repudiate, abrogate, quash, overturn, overrule, discard.

asinine /ássinīn/ *adj.* **1** stupid. **2** of or concerning asses; like an ass. □□ **asininity** /-nínniti/ *n.* [L *asininus* f. *asinus* ass]

■ **1** see STUPID *adj.* 1, 5.

-asis /əsiss/ *suffix* (usu. as **-iasis**) forming the names of diseases (*psoriasis*; *satyriasis*). [L f. Gk *-asis* in nouns of state f. verbs in *-aō*]

ask /aask/ *v.* **1** *tr.* call for an answer to or about (*ask her about it*; *ask him his name*; *ask a question of him*). **2** *tr.* seek to obtain from another person (*ask a favour of*; *ask to be allowed*). **3** *tr.* (usu. foll. by *out* or *over*, or *to* (a function etc.)) invite; request the company of (*must ask them over*; *asked her to dinner*). **4** *intr.* (foll. by *for*) **a** seek to obtain, meet, or be directed to (*ask for a donation*; *ask for the post office*; *asking for you*). **b** invite, provoke (trouble etc.) by one's behaviour; bring upon oneself (*they were asking for all they got*). **5** *tr. archaic* require (a thing). □ **ask after** inquire about (esp. a person). **ask for it** *sl.* invite trouble. **asking price** the price of an object set by the seller. **ask me another** *colloq.* I do not know. **for the asking** (obtainable) for nothing. **I ask you!** an exclamation of disgust, surprise, etc. **if you ask me** *colloq.* in my opinion. □□ **asker** *n.* [OE *āscian* etc. f. WG]

■ **1** question, interrogate, quiz; inquire of, enquire of. **2** request, beg, seek, demand, apply *or* appeal *or* solicit *or* petition *or* plead for; beseech, pray, entreat, implore. **3** invite, summon, *archaic or literary* bid. **4** (*ask for*) **a** request, demand, seek, beg, beg *or* apply *or* appeal for, seek, petition *or* plead *or* pray for. **b** invite, attract, encourage, provoke, court, promote, bring upon oneself. □ **ask after** inquire after *or* about, enquire after *or* about. **ask me another** I don't know, I haven't a clue, it beats me, *colloq.* dunno, I haven't the faintest *or* foggiest (idea), no idea, search me, I wouldn't know. **for the asking** see FREE *adv.* 2. **if you ask me** see PERSONALLY 2.

askance /əskánss, -skáanss/ *adv.* (also **askant** /-skánt, -skáant/) sideways or squinting. □ **look askance at** regard with suspicion or disapproval. [16th c.: orig. unkn.]

askari /askáari/ *n.* (*pl.* same or **askaris**) an East African soldier or policeman. [Arab. *ʽaskarī* soldier]

askew /əskyóo/ *adv.* & *predic.adj.* ● *adv.* obliquely; awry. ● *predic.adj.* oblique; awry. [A[2] + SKEW]

■ *adv.* awry, obliquely, aslant, crookedly, *Sc.* agley. ● *predic.adj.* awry, bent, oblique, crooked, one-sided, lopsided, off-centre.

aslant /əsláant/ *adv.* & *prep.* ● *adv.* obliquely or at a slant. ● *prep.* obliquely across (*lay aslant the path*).

asleep /əsléep/ *predic.adj.* & *adv.* **1 a** in or into a state of sleep (*he fell asleep*). **b** inactive, inattentive (*the nation is asleep*). **2** (of a limb etc.) numb. **3** *euphem.* dead.

■ **1 b** see UNPREPARED. **2** see NUMB *adj.*

Aslef /ázlef/ *abbr.* (in the UK) Associated Society of Locomotive Engineers and Firemen.

aslope /əslṓp/ *adv.* & *predic.adj.* sloping; crosswise. [ME: orig. uncert.]

ASM *abbr.* air-to-surface missile.

asocial /áysṓsh'l/ *adj.* **1** not social; antisocial. **2** *colloq.* inconsiderate of or hostile to others.

asp /asp/ *n.* **1** a small viper, *Vipera aspis*, native to Southern Europe, resembling the adder. **2** a small venomous snake, *Naja haje*, native to North Africa and Arabia. [ME f. OF *aspe* or L *aspis* f. Gk]

asparagus /əspárrəgəss/ *n.* **1** any plant of the genus *Asparagus*. **2** one species of this, *A. officinalis*, with edible young shoots and leaves; this as food. □ **asparagus fern** a decorative plant, *Asparagus setaceus*. [L f. Gk *asparagos*]

aspartame /əspáartaym/ *n.* a very sweet low-calorie substance used as a sweetener instead of sugar or saccharin. [chem. name *1-methyl N*-L-*aspartyl*-L-*phenylalanine*, f. *aspartic acid* (invented name)]

aspect /áspekt/ *n.* **1 a** a particular component or feature of a matter (*only one aspect of the problem*). **b** a particular way in which a matter may be considered. **2 a** a facial expression; a look (*a cheerful aspect*). **b** the appearance of a person or thing, esp. as presented to the mind of the viewer (*has a frightening aspect*). **3** the side of a building or location facing a particular direction (*southern aspect*). **4** *Gram.* a verbal category or form expressing inception, duration, or completion. **5** *Astrol.* the relative position of planets etc. measured by angular distance. □ **aspect ratio** **1** *Aeron.* the ratio of the span to the mean chord of an aerofoil. **2** *Telev.* the ratio of picture width to height. □□ **aspectual** /aspéktyooəl/ *adj.* (in sense 4). [ME f. L *aspectus* f. *adspicere adspect-* look at (as AD-, *specere* look)]

■ **1 a** part, component, constituent, ingredient, feature, attribute, characteristic, quality, detail, bit, facet, side, manifestation, element. **b** viewpoint, point of view, position, standpoint, approach, side, angle, perspective; light, interpretation. **2 a** look, expression, face. **b** appearance, look(s), complexion, face, countenance; bearing, manner, air, *literary* mien. **3** perspective, prospect, outlook, orientation.

aspen /áspən/ *n.* a poplar tree, *Populus tremula*, with especially tremulous leaves. [earlier name *asp* f. OE *æspe* + -EN[2] forming adj. taken as noun]

asperity /əspérriti/ *n.* (*pl.* **-ies**) **1** harshness or sharpness of temper or tone. **2** roughness. **3** a rough excrescence. [ME f. OF *asperité* or L *asperitas* f. *asper* rough]

■ **1** see *bitterness* (BITTER).

asperse /əspérss/ *v.tr.* (often foll. by *with*) attack the reputation of; calumniate. □□ **aspersive** *adj.* [ME, = besprinkle, f. L *aspergere aspers-* (as AD-, *spargere* sprinkle)]

■ see DISCREDIT *v.* 1.

aspersion /əspérsh'n/ *n.* a slander, a false insinuation. □ **cast aspersions on** attack the reputation or integrity of. [L *aspersio* (as ASPERSE, -ION)]

■ slander, libel, false insinuation, calumny, imputation, allegation, detraction, slur, obloquy, defamation, disparagement. □ **cast aspersions on** see BLACKEN 2.

asphalt /ásfalt/ *n.* & *v.* ● *n.* **1** a dark bituminous pitch occurring naturally or made from petroleum. **2** a mixture of this with sand, gravel, etc., for surfacing roads etc. ● *v.tr.* surface with asphalt. □□ **asphalter** *n.* **asphaltic** /-fáltik/ *adj.* [ME, ult. f. LL *asphalton*, *-um*, f. Gk *asphalton*]

asphodel /ásfədel/ *n.* **1** any plant of the genus *Asphodelus*, of the lily family. **2** *poet.* an immortal flower growing in Elysium. [L *asphodelus* f. Gk *asphodelos*: cf. DAFFODIL]

asphyxia /asfíksiə/ *n.* a lack of oxygen in the blood, causing unconsciousness or death; suffocation. □□ **asphyxial** *adj.* **asphyxiant** *adj.* & *n.* [mod.L f. Gk *asphuxia* f. *a-* not + *sphuxis* pulse]

asphyxiate /asfíksiayt/ *v.tr.* cause (a person) to have asphyxia; suffocate. □□ **asphyxiation** /-áysh'n/ *n.* **asphyxiator** *n.*

■ see SMOTHER *v.* 1.

aspic /áspik/ *n.* a savoury meat jelly used as a garnish or to contain game, eggs, etc. [F, = ASP, from the colours of the jelly (compared to those of the asp)]

aspidistra /áspidistrə/ *n.* a foliage plant of the genus *Aspidistra*, with broad tapering leaves, often grown as a house-plant. [mod.L f. Gk *aspis -idos* shield (from the shape of the leaves)]

aspirant /áspirənt, əspī́rənt/ *adj.* & *n.* (usu. foll. by *to, after, for*) ● *adj.* aspiring. ● *n.* a person who aspires. [F *aspirant* or f. L *aspirant-* (as ASPIRE, -ANT)]

aspirate /áspirət/ *adj., n., & v. Phonet.* ● *adj.* **1** pronounced with an exhalation of breath. **2** blended with the sound of *h*. ● *n.* **1** a consonant pronounced in this way. **2** the sound of *h*. ● *v.* /also áspiráyt/ **1 a** *tr.* pronounce with a breath. **b** *intr.* make the sound of *h*. **2** *tr.* draw (fluid) by suction from a vessel or cavity. [L *aspiratus* past part. of *aspirare*: see ASPIRE]

aspiration /áspiráysh'n/ *n.* **1** a strong desire to achieve an end; an ambition. **2** the act or process of drawing breath. **3** the action of aspirating. [ME f. OF *aspiration* or L *aspiratio* (as ASPIRATE, -ATION)]

▪ **1** ambition, aim, goal, objective, end, purpose, intention, plan, scheme; desire, longing, yearning, craving, hankering, wish, dream, hope.

aspirator /áspiraytər/ *n.* an apparatus for aspirating fluid. [L *aspirare* (as ASPIRATE, -OR[1])]

aspire /əspī́r/ *v.intr.* (usu. foll. by *to* or *after*, or *to* + infin.) **1** have ambition or strong desire. **2** *poet.* rise high. [ME f. F *aspirer* or L *aspirare* f. *ad* to + *spirare* breathe]

▪ **1** desire, hope, long, wish, aim, yearn; (*aspire to*) dream of, hanker after, have designs on, set one's sights on, go after.

aspirin /áspriN/ *n.* (*pl.* same or **aspirins**) **1** a white powder, acetylsalicylic acid, used to relieve pain and reduce fever. **2** a tablet of this. [G, formed as ACETYL + *spiraeic* (= salicylic) *acid* + -IN]

asquint /əskwínt/ *predic.adj.* & *adv.* (usu. *look asquint*). **1** to one side; from the corner of an eye. **2** with a squint. [ME perh. f. Du. *schuinte* slant]

ass[1] /ass/ *n.* & *v.* ● *n.* **1 a** either of two kinds of four-legged long-eared mammal of the horse genus *Equus*, *E. africanus* of Africa and *E. hemionus* of Asia. **b** (in general use) a donkey. **2** a stupid person. ● *v.intr. sl.* (foll. by *about, around*) act the fool. □ **asses' bridge** = PONS ASINORUM. **make an ass of** make (a person) look absurd or foolish. [OE *assa* thr. OCelt. f. L *asinus*]

▪ *n.* **2** see DOLT.

ass[2] /ass/ *n. US* var. of ARSE.

assagai var. of ASSEGAI.

assai /así/ *adv. Mus.* very (*adagio assai*). [It.]

assail /əsáyl/ *v.tr.* **1** make a strong or concerted attack on. **2** make a resolute start on (a task). **3** make a strong or constant verbal attack on (*was assailed with angry questions*). □□ **assailable** *adj.* [ME f. OF *asaill-* stressed stem of *asalir* f. med.L *assalire* f. L *assilire* (as AD-, *salire salt-* leap)]

▪ **1** see ATTACK *v.* 1. **2** see ATTACK *v.* 5.

assailant /əsáylənt/ *n.* a person who attacks another physically or verbally. [F (as ASSAIL)]

▪ attacker, assaulter, mugger, aggressor; enemy, adversary, antagonist, opponent, *esp. poet. or formal* foe; detractor, critic.

assassin /əsássin/ *n.* **1** a killer, esp. of a political or religious leader. **2** *hist.* any of a group of Muslim fanatics sent on murder missions in the time of the Crusades. [F *assassin* or f. med.L *assassinus* f. Arab. *ḥaššāš* hashish-eater]

▪ **1** see KILLER 1.

assassinate /əsássinayt/ *v.tr.* kill (esp. a political or religious leader) for political or religious motives. □□ **assassination** /-náysh'n/ *n.* **assassinator** *n.* [med.L *assassinare* f. *assassinus*: see ASSASSIN]

▪ see KILL[1] *v.* 1.

assault /əsáwlt, əsólt/ *n.* & *v.* ● *n.* **1** a violent physical or verbal attack. **2 a** *Law* an act that threatens physical harm to a person (whether or not actual harm is done). **b** *euphem.* an act of rape. **3** (*attrib.*) relating to or used in an assault (*assault craft*; *assault troops*). **4** a vigorous start made to a lengthy or difficult task. **5** a final rush on a fortified place, esp. at the end of a prolonged attack. ● *v.tr.* **1** make an assault on. **2** *euphem.* rape. □ **assault and battery** *Law* a threatening act that results in physical harm done to a person. **assault course** an obstacle course used in training soldiers etc. □□ **assaulter** *n.* **assaultive** *adj.* [ME f. OF *asaut, assauter* ult. f. L (*salire salt-* leap)]

▪ *n.* **1, 5** attack, beating, battering, hold-up, mugging, *Law* battery; onslaught, onset, charge, offensive, blitzkrieg, strike, raid, incursion, sortie, invasion, rush, *colloq.* blitz. **2 b** rape, sexual assault, violation, molestation. **4** see ATTEMPT *n.* ● *v.* **1** attack, assail, set *or* fall *or* descend upon, pounce upon, storm, come at, beset, charge, rush, lay into; beat (up), batter, harm, hit, strike, punch, *archaic or literary* smite; mug. **2** rape, violate, molest, sexually assault. □□ **assaulter** see AGGRESSOR.

assay /əsáy, ássay/ *n.* & *v.* ● *n.* **1** the testing of a metal or ore to determine its ingredients and quality. **2** *Chem.* etc. the determination of the content or strength of a substance. ● *v.* **1** *tr.* make an assay of (a metal or ore). **2** *tr. Chem.* etc. perform a concentration on (a substance). **3** *tr.* show (content) on being assayed. **4** *intr.* make an assay. **5** *tr. archaic* attempt. □ **Assay Office** an establishment which awards hallmarks. □□ **assayer** *n.* [ME f. OF *assaier, assai*, var. of *essayer, essai*: see ESSAY]

▪ *v.* **5** see ATTEMPT *v.*

assegai /ássigī/ *n.* (also **assagai** /ássəgī/) a slender iron-tipped spear of hard wood, esp. as used by S. African peoples. [obs. F *azagaie* or Port. *azagaia* f. Arab. *az-zaġāyah* f. *al* the + *zaġāyah* spear]

assemblage /əsémblij/ *n.* **1** the act or an instance of bringing or coming together. **2** a collection of things or gathering of people. **3 a** the act or an instance of fitting together. **b** an object made of pieces fitted together. **4** a work of art made by grouping found or unrelated objects.

▪ **1, 2** see ASSEMBLY 1, 2a. **3** see FABRICATION 1.

assemble /əsémb'l/ *v.* **1** *tr.* & *intr.* gather together; collect. **2** *tr.* arrange in order. **3** *tr.* esp. *Mech.* fit together the parts of. [ME f. OF *asembler* ult. f. L *ad* to + *simul* together]

▪ **1** convene, gather, meet, call *or* get *or* meet together, summon, muster, marshal, rally, levy, round up, collect, congregate, forgather, *formal* convoke; accumulate, amass, collect, bring *or* group *or* lump together, pile *or* heap up, compile, join *or* draw together, aggregate. **2** see ARRANGE 1. **3** construct, put together, erect, set up, fit *or* join *or* piece together, connect, fabricate, manufacture, make.

assembler /əsémblər/ *n.* **1** a person who assembles a machine or its parts. **2** *Computing* **a** a program for converting instructions written in low-level symbolic code into machine code. **b** the low-level symbolic code itself; an assembly language.

assembly /əsémbli/ *n.* (*pl.* **-ies**) **1** the act or an instance of assembling or gathering together. **2 a** a group of persons gathered together, esp. as a deliberative body or a legislative council. **b** a gathering of the entire membership of a school. **3** the assembling of a machine or structure or its parts. **4** *Mil.* a call to assemble, given by drum or bugle. □ **assembly language** *Computing* the low-level symbolic code converted by an assembler. **assembly line** machinery arranged in stages by which a product is progressively assembled. **assembly room** (or **shop**) a place where a machine or its components are assembled. **assembly rooms** public rooms in which meetings or social functions are held. [ME f. OF *asemblee* fem. past part. of *asembler*: see ASSEMBLE]

▪ **1, 2a** gathering, group, meeting, assemblage, collection, body, circle, company, congregation, flock, crowd, audience, throng, multitude, host; convocation, council, convention, congress, association, caucus, committee, conclave; diet, synod. **3** construction, putting *or* fitting *or* joining *or* piecing together, fabrication, manufacture, making. □ **assembly rooms** see CHAMBER 1a.

assent /əsént/ *v.* & *n.* ● *v.intr.* (usu. foll. by *to*) **1** express agreement (*assented to my view*). **2** consent (*assented to my request*). ● *n.* **1** mental or inward acceptance or agreement (*a nod of assent*). **2** consent or sanction, esp. official. □ **royal**

assent assent of the sovereign to a bill passed by Parliament. ▫▫ **assenter** *n.* (also **assentor**). [ME f. OF *asenter, as(s)ente* ult. f. L *assentari* (*ad* to, *sentire* think)]
▪ *v.* **1** see AGREE 1. **2** see AGREE 2, 4, 5. ● *n.* **1** see CONSENT *n.* **2** see CONSENT *n.*, SANCTION *n.* 1.

assentient /əsénsh'nt, -shiənt/ *adj.* & *n.* ● *adj.* assenting. ● *n.* a person who assents. [L *assentire* (as ASSENT, -ENT)]

assert /əsért/ *v.* **1** *tr.* declare; state clearly (*assert one's beliefs; assert that it is so*). **2** *refl.* insist on one's rights or opinions; demand recognition. **3** *tr.* vindicate a claim to (*assert one's rights*). ▫▫ **assertor** *n.* [L *asserere* (as AD-, *serere sert-* join)]
▪ **1** see DECLARE 3.

assertion /əsérsh'n/ *n.* **1** a declaration; a forthright statement. **2** the act or an instance of asserting. **3** (also **self-assertion**) insistence on the recognition of one's rights or claims. [ME f. F *assertion* or L *assertio* (as ASSERT, -ION)]
▪ **1, 2** statement, declaration, claim, affirmation, contention, asseveration, averment, avowal, announcement, pronouncement, allegation, attestation, *Law* affidavit, deposition. **3** insistence, proclamation, representation, affirmation, confirmation; see also *assertiveness* (ASSERTIVE).

assertive /əsértiv/ *adj.* **1** tending to assert oneself; forthright, positive. **2** dogmatic. ▫▫ **assertively** *adv.* **assertiveness** *n.*
▪ **1** declaratory, affirmative, asseverative; forthright, definite, certain, sure, positive, confident, firm, emphatic, bold; aggressive, insistent, forceful. **2** dogmatic, self-assertive, doctrinaire, domineering, opinionated, peremptory, bumptious, pushful, officious, *colloq.* bossy, pushy. ▫▫ **assertively** forcefully, boldly, firmly, confidently, insistently, positively, emphatically; dogmatically, domineeringly, *colloq.* bossily, pushily; see also *aggressively* (AGGRESSIVE). **assertiveness** forcefulness, boldness, firmness, forthrightness, (self-)assertion, self-assertiveness, dogmatism.

asses *pl.* of AS², ASS¹, ASS².

assess /əséss/ *v.tr.* **1 a** estimate the size or quality of. **b** estimate the value of (a property) for taxation. **2 a** (usu. foll. by *on*) fix the amount of (a tax etc.) and impose it on a person or community. **b** (usu. foll. by *in, at*) fine or tax (a person, community, etc.) in or at a specific amount (*assessed them at £100*). ▫▫ **assessable** *adj.* **assessment** *n.* [ME f. F *assesser* f. L *assidēre* (as AD-, *sedēre* sit)]
▪ **1** see ESTIMATE *v.* 2–4. **2** see TAX *v.* 1. ▫▫ **assessment** see MEASUREMENT 1, REVIEW *n.* 1.

assessor /əséssər/ *n.* **1** a person who assesses taxes or estimates the value of property for taxation or insurance purposes. **2** a person called upon to advise a judge, committee of inquiry, etc., on technical questions. ▫▫ **assessorial** /ássesóriəl/ *adj.* [ME f. OF *assessour* f. L *assessor -oris* assistant-judge (as ASSESS, -OR¹): sense 1 f. med.L]

asset /ásset/ *n.* **1 a** a useful or valuable quality. **b** a person or thing possessing such a quality or qualities (*is an asset to the firm*). **2** (usu. in *pl.*) **a** property and possessions, esp. regarded as having value in meeting debts, commitments, etc. **b** any possession having value. ▫ **asset-stripping** *Commerce* the practice of taking over a company and selling off its assets to make a profit. [*assets* (taken as pl.), f. AF *asetz* f. OF *asez* enough, ult. f. L *ad* to + *satis* enough]
▪ **1 a** talent, strength, advantage, resource, benefit, attraction, selling-point, appeal. **b** see PLUS *n.* 3. **2 a** (*assets*) property, resources, possessions, holdings, effects, capital, means, valuables, money, wealth.

asseverate /əsévvərayt/ *v.tr.* declare solemnly. ▫▫ **asseveration** /-ráysh'n/ *n.* **asseverative** /-rətiv/ *adj.* [L *asseverare* (as AD-, *severus* serious)]
▪ see ATTEST 1, 3.

assibilate /əsíbbilayt/ *v.tr. Phonet.* **1** pronounce (a sound) as a sibilant or affricate ending in a sibilant. **2** alter (a syllable) to become this. ▫▫ **assibilation** /-láysh'n/ *n.* [L *assibilare* (as AD-, *sibilare* hiss)]

assiduity /ássidyóō-iti/ *n.* (*pl.* **-ies**) **1** constant or close attention to what one is doing. **2** (usu. in *pl.*) constant attentions to another person. [L *assiduitas* (as ASSIDUOUS, -ITY)]
▪ **1** see APPLICATION 4.

assiduous /əsídyooəss/ *adj.* **1** persevering, hard-working. **2** attending closely. ▫▫ **assiduously** *adv.* **assiduousness** *n.* [L *assiduus* (as ASSESS)]
▪ see DILIGENT. ▫▫ **assiduousness** see APPLICATION 4.

assign /əsī́n/ *v.* & *n.* ● *v.tr.* **1** (usu. foll. by *to*) **a** allot as a share or responsibility. **b** appoint to a position, task, etc. **2** fix (a time, place, etc.) for a specific purpose. **3** (foll. by *to*) ascribe or refer to (a reason, date, etc.) (*assigned the manuscript to 1832*). **4** (foll. by *to*) transfer formally (esp. personal property) to (another). ● *n.* a person to whom property or rights are legally transferred. ▫▫ **assignable** *adj.* **assigner** *n.* **assignor** *n.* (in sense 4 of v.). [ME f. OF *asi(g)ner* f. L *assignare* mark out to (as AD-, *signum* sign)]
▪ *v.* **1 a** allot, allocate, apportion, consign, appropriate, distribute, give (out), grant, hand (out), deal (out), dispense. **b** appoint, designate, order; name, delegate, nominate, attach. **2** fix (on), set apart *or* aside, settle on, determine on, allot, appoint, authorize, designate, ordain, prescribe, specify; choose, select. **3** attribute, ascribe, refer, accredit, put down, impute. ▫▫ **assignable** attributable, ascribable, imputable.

assignation /assignáysh'n/ *n.* **1 a** an appointment to meet. **b** a secret appointment, esp. between illicit lovers. **2** the act or an instance of assigning or being assigned. [ME f. OF f. L *assignatio -onis* (as ASSIGN, -ATION)]
▪ **1** see APPOINTMENT 1.

assignee /ássīnée/ *n.* **1** a person appointed to act for another. **2** an assign. [ME f. OF *assigné* past part. of *assigner* ASSIGN]

assignment /əsī́nmənt/ *n.* **1** something assigned, esp. a task allotted to a person. **2** the act or an instance of assigning or being assigned. **3 a** a legal transfer. **b** the document effecting this. [ME f. OF *assignement* f. med.L *assignamentum* (as ASSIGN, -MENT)]
▪ **1** task, obligation, responsibility, chore, duty, position, post, charge, job, mission, commission; lesson, homework. **2** allotment, allocation, apportionment, distribution, dispensation; appointment, designation, nomination, delegation; attribution, specification, ascription.

assimilate /əsímmilayt/ *v.* **1** *tr.* **a** absorb and digest (food etc.) into the body. **b** absorb (information etc.) into the mind. **c** absorb (people) into a larger group. **2** *tr.* (usu. foll. by *to, with*) make like; cause to resemble. **3** *tr. Phonet.* make (a sound) more like another in the same or next word. **4** *intr.* be absorbed into the body, mind, or a larger group. ▫▫ **assimilable** *adj.* **assimilation** /-láysh'n/ *n.* **assimilative** *adj.* **assimilator** *n.* **assimilatory** /-lətəri/ *adj.* [ME f. L *assimilare* (as AD-, *similis* like)]
▪ **1 b** see DIGEST *v.* 2.

assist /əsíst/ *v.* & *n.* ● *v.* **1** *tr.* (often foll. by *in* + verbal noun) help (a person, process, etc.) (*assisted them in running the playgroup*). **2** *intr.* (often foll. by *in, at*) attend or be present (*assisted in the ceremony*). ● *n. US* **1** an act of helping. **2** *Baseball* etc. a player's action of helping to put out an opponent, score a goal, etc. ▫▫ **assistance** *n.* **assister** *n.* [ME f. F *assister* f. L *assistere* take one's stand by (as AD-, *sistere* take one's stand)]
▪ *v.* **1** aid, help, support, work for *or* with, lend *or* give a hand, back (up), succour; further, promote, abet, advance, benefit, facilitate. **2** take part, have *or* take a hand, be present, attend, be in attendance. ▫▫ **assistance** help, aid, support, succour; backing, reinforcement, relief, benefit.

assistant /əsístənt/ *n.* **1** a helper. **2** (often *attrib.*) a person who assists, esp. as a subordinate in a particular job or role. **3** = *shop assistant.* [ME *assistent* f. med.L *assistens assistent-* present (as ASSIST, -ANT, -ENT)]
▪ **1** helper, mate, aide, right-hand man *or* woman, acolyte, amanuensis, PA, girl *or* man Friday, *Austral. colloq.* offsider; aide-de-camp, adjutant; see also ACCOMPLICE.

2 deputy, subordinate, subsidiary, auxiliary, underling, *colloq.* vice.

assize /əsīz/ *n.* (usu. in *pl.*) *hist.* a court sitting at intervals in each county of England and Wales to administer the civil and criminal law. ¶ In 1972 the civil jurisdiction of assizes was transferred to the High Court and the criminal jurisdiction to the Crown Court. [ME f. OF *as(s)ise*, fem. past part. of *aseeir* sit at, f. L *assidēre*: cf. ASSESS]

Assoc. *abbr.* (as part of a title) Association.

associable /əsōshəb'l/ *adj.* (usu. foll. by *with*) capable of being connected in thought. □□ **associability** /-bílliti/ *n.* [F f. *associer* (as ASSOCIATE, -ABLE)]

associate *v.*, *n.*, & *adj.* ● *v.* /əsōshiayt, əsōsi-/ **1** *tr.* connect in the mind (*associate holly with Christmas*). **2** *tr.* join or combine. **3** *refl.* make oneself a partner; declare oneself in agreement (*associate myself in your endeavour*; *did not want to associate ourselves with the plan*). **4** *intr.* combine for a common purpose. **5** *intr.* (usu. foll. by *with*) meet frequently or have dealings; be friends. ● *n.* /əsōshiət, əsōsi-/ **1** a business partner or colleague. **2** a friend or companion. **3** a subordinate member of a body, institute, etc. **4** a thing connected with another. ● *adj.* /əsōshiət, əsōsi-/ **1** joined in companionship, function, or dignity. **2** allied; in the same group or category. **3** of less than full status (*associate member*). □□ **associateship** /əsōshiətship, əsōsi-/ *n.* **associator** /əsōshiaytər, əsōsi-/ *n.* **associatory** /əsōshiətəri, əsōsi-/ *adj.* [E f. L *associatus* past part. of *associare* (as AD-, *socius* sharing, allied)]

■ *v.* **1** link, connect, make a connection between; affiliate, relate. **2** ally, join (up *or* together), unite, combine, couple, confederate, conjoin. **3** (*associate oneself*) ally, align, affiliate, connect, link. **4** unite, join (up *or* together), join ranks *or* forces, make a combined effort. **5** (*associate with*) see, be seen with, socialize *or* fraternize with, mix *or* mingle with, go (out *or* about *or* around) with, consort with, have to do with, hang about *or* around with, *colloq.* pal up with, *sl.* hang out with, *Austral. sl.* track with. ● *n.* **1** colleague, partner, fellow, fellow-worker, workmate, co-worker, comrade, *Brit. colloq.* oppo.; see also ACCOMPLICE. **2** comrade, companion, friend, mate, confidant(e), *colloq.* pal, *esp. US colloq.* buddy. **3** junior member. ● *adj.* **2** allied, affiliate, affiliated, associated; sister, related, connected. **3** subsidiary, secondary; deputy, auxiliary, supplementary, accessory.

association /əsōsiáysh'n/ *n.* **1** a group of people organized for a joint purpose; a society. **2** the act or an instance of associating. **3** fellowship; human contact or cooperation. **4** a mental connection between ideas. **5** *Chem.* a loose aggregation of molecules. **6** *Ecol.* a group of associated plants. □ **Association Football** *Brit.* football played by sides of 11 with a round ball which may not be handled during play except by the goalkeepers. □□ **associational** *adj.* [F *association* or med.L *associatio* (as ASSOCIATE, -ATION)]

■ **1** society, organization, confederation, confederacy, federation, league, union, alliance, guild, coalition, group; syndicate, combine, consortium, cooperative. **2** combination, alliance, marriage, union, amalgamation, integration, coalition, confederation. **3** fellowship, companionship, intimacy, friendship, amity, camaraderie, comradeship, relationship, liaison; affiliation, alliance, connection, contact, partnership, cooperation. **4** connection, interconnection, link, affiliation, relationship, bond, tie, thread, linkage, conjunction, correspondence.

associative /əsōshiətiv, əsōsi-/ *adj.* **1** of or involving association. **2** *Math.* & *Computing* involving the condition that a group of quantities connected by operators (see OPERATOR 4) gives the same result whatever their grouping, as long as their order remains the same, e.g. $(a \times b) \times c = a \times (b \times c)$.

assonance /ássənənss/ *n.* the resemblance of sound between two syllables in nearby words, arising from the rhyming of two or more accented vowels, but not consonants, or the use of identical consonants with different vowels, e.g. *sonnet*, *porridge*, and *killed*, *cold*, *culled*. □□ **assonant** *adj.* **assonate** /-nayt/ *v.intr.* [F f. L *assonare* respond to (as AD-, *sonus* sound)]

assort /əsórt/ *v.* **1** *tr.* (usu. foll. by *with*) classify or arrange in groups. **2** *intr.* suit; fit into; harmonize with (usu. *assort ill* or *well with*). [OF *assorter* f. *à* to + *sorte* SORT]

■ **1** see CATEGORIZE.

assortative /əsórtətiv/ *adj.* assorting. □ **assortative mating** *Biol.* selective mating based on the similarity of the partners' characteristics etc.

assorted /əsórtid/ *adj.* **1** of various sorts put together; miscellaneous. **2** sorted into groups. **3** matched (*ill-assorted*; *poorly assorted*).

■ **1** see MISCELLANEOUS.

assortment /əsórtmənt/ *n.* a set of various sorts of things or people put together; a mixed collection.

■ collection, mixture, miscellany, jumble, medley, *mélange*, array, agglomeration, conglomeration, group, grouping, lot, farrago, hotchpotch, olio, variety, pot-pourri, salmagundi, gallimaufry, mishmash, mixed bag *or* bunch.

ASSR *abbr. hist.* Autonomous Soviet Socialist Republic.

Asst. *abbr.* Assistant.

assuage /əswáyj/ *v.tr.* **1** calm or soothe (a person, pain, etc.). **2** appease or relieve (an appetite or desire). □□ **assuagement** *n.* **assuager** *n.* [ME f. OF *as(s)ouagier* ult. f. L *suavis* sweet]

■ **1** see STILL[1] *v.* **2** see SLAKE.

assume /əsyōōm/ *v.tr.* **1** (usu. foll. by *that* + clause) take or accept as being true, without proof, for the purpose of argument or action. **2** simulate or pretend (ignorance etc.). **3** undertake (an office or duty). **4** take or put on oneself or itself (an aspect, attribute, etc.) (*the problem assumed immense proportions*). **5** (usu. foll. by *to*) arrogate, usurp, or seize (credit, power, etc.) (*assumed to himself the right of veto*). □□ **assumable** *adj.* **assumedly** /-midli/ *adv.* [ME f. L *assumere* (as AD-, *sumere sumpt-* take)]

■ **1** presume, suppose, believe, fancy, expect, think, presuppose, take it (for granted *or* as read), accept; surmise, guess. **2** pretend, feign, simulate, affect, fake, counterfeit; profess. **3** take over *or* up, take control of, undertake, accept, adopt; arrogate, claim, appropriate. **4** take on *or* upon oneself *or* itself, don, adopt, acquire. **5** see *take over*.

assumed /əsyōōmd/ *adj.* **1** false, adopted (*went under an assumed name*). **2** supposed, accepted (*assumed income*).

■ **1** sham, false, feigned, affected, adopted, counterfeit, simulated, pretend, spurious, bogus, fake; pseudonymous, made-up, *colloq.* phoney. **2** presumed, supposed, accepted, expected, presupposed, taken (for granted); hypothetical, theoretical, suppositional.

assuming /əsyōōming/ *adj.* (of a person) taking too much for granted; arrogant, presumptuous.

■ see ARROGANT.

assumption /əsúmpsh'n/ *n.* **1** the act or an instance of assuming. **2 a** the act or an instance of accepting without proof. **b** a thing assumed in this way. **3** arrogance. **4** (**Assumption**) **a** the reception of the Virgin Mary bodily into heaven, according to Roman Catholic doctrine. **b** the feast in honour of this (15 August). [ME f. OF *asompsion* or L *assumptio* (as ASSUME, -ION)]

■ **1, 2** see PRESUMPTION 2. **3** see PRESUMPTION 1.

assumptive /əsúmptiv/ *adj.* **1** taken for granted. **2** arrogant. [L *assumptivus* (as ASSUME, -IVE)]

assurance /əshóorənss/ *n.* **1** a positive declaration that a thing is true. **2** a solemn promise or guarantee. **3** insurance, esp. life insurance. **4** certainty. **5 a** self-confidence. **b** impudence. [ME f. OF *aseürance* f. *aseürer* (as ASSURE, -ANCE)]

■ **1** see DECLARATION 2a. **2** promise, pledge, guarantee, word (of honour), oath, vow, warranty, undertaking, commitment, bond, surety. **3** (life) insurance, indemnity.

4 certainty, sureness, positiveness, fixedness, definiteness, assuredness, certitude, conviction, *archaic* surety. **5 a** self-confidence, self-reliance, confidence, steadiness, intrepidity, self-possession, poise, aplomb, coolness, control, self-control, resolve, *colloq.* gumption; conviction. **b** audacity, impudence, presumption, boldness, brazenness, nerve, cheek, effrontery, insolence, impertinence, *colloq.* brass, *sl.* gall, chutzpah.

assure /əshóor/ *v.tr.* **1** (often foll. by *of*) **a** make (a person) sure; convince (*assured him of my sincerity*). **b** tell (a person) confidently (*assured him the bus went to Westminster*). **2 a** make certain of; ensure the happening etc. of (*will assure her success*). **b** make safe (against overthrow etc.). **3** confirm, encourage. **4** insure (esp. a life). **5** (as **assured** *adj.*) **a** guaranteed. **b** self-confident. □ **rest assured** remain confident. □□ **assurable** *adj.* **assurer** *n.* [ME f. OF *aseürer* ult. f. L *securus* safe, SECURE]

■ **1 a** convince, persuade, reassure. **b** promise, reassure; assert *or* affirm *or* state *or* asseverate to, *archaic or literary* avouch to, *formal* aver to. **2** ensure, confirm, secure, stabilize, settle, establish, certify, guarantee, make safe, make sure, make certain; see also PROTECT. **3** confirm, encourage, inspirit, hearten. **4** insure, indemnify. **5** (**assured**) **a** guaranteed, warranted, certain, sure, inevitable, definite, firm, fixed, confirmed, *colloq.* sure-fire. **b** see CONFIDENT *adj.* 1. □□ **assurable** insurable, warrantable. **assurer** insurer, guarantor, warranter, indemnifier.

assuredly /əshóoridli/ *adv.* certainly.
■ see *undoubtedly* (UNDOUBTED).

assuredness /əshóoridniss, əshóordniss/ *n.* certainty, (self-)assurance.

Assyrian /əsírriən/ *n.* & *adj. hist.* ● *n.* **1** an inhabitant of Assyria, an ancient kingdom in Mesopotamia. **2** the Semitic language of Assyria. ● *adj.* of or relating to Assyria. [L *Assyrius* f. Gk *Assurios* of Assyria]

Assyriology /əsírrióllǝji/ *n.* the study of the language, history, and antiquities of Assyria. □□ **Assyriologist** *n.*

AST *abbr.* Atlantic Standard Time.

astable /áystáyb'l/ *adj.* **1** not stable. **2** *Electr.* of or relating to a circuit which oscillates spontaneously between unstable states.

astatic /áystáttik/ *adj.* **1** not static; unstable or unsteady. **2** *Physics* not tending to keep one position or direction. □ **astatic galvanometer** one in which the effect of the earth's magnetic field on the meter needle is greatly reduced. [Gk *astatos* unstable f. *a-* not + *sta-* stand]

astatine /ástəteen/ *n. Chem.* a radioactive element, the heaviest of the halogens, which occurs naturally and can be artificially made by nuclear bombardment of bismuth. ¶ Symb.: **At**. [formed as ASTATIC + -INE[4]]

aster /ástər/ *n.* any composite plant of the genus *Aster*, with bright daisy-like flowers, e.g. the Michaelmas daisy. □ **China aster** a related plant, *Callistephus chinensis*, cultivated for its bright and showy flowers. [L f. Gk *astēr* star]

-aster /ástər/ *suffix* **1** forming nouns denoting poor quality (*criticaster*; *poetaster*). **2** *Bot.* denoting incomplete resemblance (*oleaster*; *pinaster*). [L]

asterisk /ástərisk/ *n.* & *v.* ● *n.* a symbol (*) used in printing and writing to mark words etc. for reference, to stand for omitted matter, etc. ● *v.tr.* mark with an asterisk. [ME f. LL *asteriscus* f. Gk *asteriskos* dimin. (as ASTER)]

asterism /ástəriz'm/ *n.* **1** a cluster of stars. **2** a group of three asterisks (⁂) calling attention to following text. [Gk *asterismos* (as ASTER, -ISM)]

astern /əstérn/ *adv. Naut.* & *Aeron.* (often foll. by *of*) **1** aft; away to the rear. **2** backwards. [A[2] + STERN[2]]

asteroid /ástəroyd/ *n.* **1** any of the minor planets revolving round the sun, mainly between the orbits of Mars and Jupiter. **2** *Zool.* a starfish. □□ **asteroidal** /ástəróyd'l/ *adj.* [Gk *asteroeidēs* (as ASTER, -OID)]

asthenia /ass-theéniə/ *n. Med.* loss of strength; debility. [mod.L f. Gk *astheneia* f. *asthenēs* weak]

asthenic /ass-thénnik/ *adj.* & *n.* ● *adj.* **1** of lean or long-limbed build. **2** *Med.* of or characterized by asthenia. ● *n.* a lean long-limbed person.

asthma /ásmə/ *n.* a usu. allergic respiratory disease, often with paroxysms of difficult breathing. [ME f. Gk *asthma -matos* f. *azō* breathe hard]

asthmatic /asmáttik/ *adj.* & *n.* ● *adj.* relating to or suffering from asthma. ● *n.* a person suffering from asthma. □□ **asthmatically** *adv.* [L *asthmaticus* f. Gk *asthmatikos* (as ASTHMA, -IC)]

Asti /ásti/ *n.* (*pl.* **Astis**) an Italian white wine. □ **Asti spumante** /spoománti/ a sparkling form of this. [*Asti* in Piedmont]

astigmatism /əstígmətiz'm/ *n.* a defect in the eye or in a lens resulting in distorted images, as light rays are prevented from meeting at a common focus. □□ **astigmatic** /ástigmáttik/ *adj.* [A-[1] + Gk *stigma -matos* point]

astilbe /əstílbi/ *n.* any plant of the genus *Astilbe*, with plumelike heads of tiny white or red flowers. [mod.L f. Gk *a-* not + *stilbē* fem. of *stilbos* glittering, from the inconspicuous (individual) flowers]

astir /əstúr/ *predic.adj.* & *adv.* **1** in motion. **2** awake and out of bed (*astir early*; *already astir*). **3** excited. [A[2] + STIR[1] *n.*]

astonish /əstónnish/ *v.tr.* amaze; surprise greatly. □□ **astonishing** *adj.* **astonishingly** *adv.* **astonishment** *n.* [obs. *astone* f. OF *estoner* f. Gallo-Roman: see -ISH[2]]

■ amaze, surprise, shock, astound, stun, stagger, take aback, dumbfound, stupefy, daze, *colloq.* flabbergast, bowl over, floor, knock sideways, *sl.* knock out. □□ **astonishing** see *amazing* (AMAZE). **astonishingly** see *amazingly* (AMAZE). **astonishment** amazement, surprise, shock, awe, stupefaction, wonder, wonderment.

astound /əstównd/ *v.tr.* shock with alarm or surprise; amaze. □□ **astounding** *adj.* **astoundingly** *adv.* [obs. *astound* (adj.) = *astoned* past part. of obs. *astone*: see ASTONISH]

■ amaze, surprise, shock, astonish, stun, stagger, take aback, dumbfound, stupefy, bewilder, overwhelm, daze, *colloq.* flabbergast, bowl over, floor, knock sideways, *sl.* knock out. □□ **astounding** see *amazing* (AMAZE). **astoundingly** see *amazingly* (AMAZE).

astraddle /əstrádd'l/ *adv.* & *predic.adj.* in a straddling position.

astragal /ástrəg'l/ *n. Archit.* a small semicircular moulding round the top or bottom of a column. [ASTRAGALUS]

astragalus /əstrággələss/ *n.* (*pl.* **-li** /-lī/) **1** *Anat.* = TALUS[1]. **2** *Bot.* a leguminous plant of the genus *Astragalus*, e.g. the milk-vetch. [L f. Gk *astragalos* ankle-bone, moulding, a plant]

astrakhan /ástrəkán/ *n.* **1** the dark curly fleece of young lambs from Astrakhan. **2** a cloth imitating astrakhan. [*Astrakhan* in Russia]

astral /ástrəl/ *adj.* **1** of or connected with the stars. **2** consisting of stars; starry. **3** *Theosophy* relating to or arising from a supposed ethereal existence, esp. of a counterpart of the body, associated with oneself in life and surviving after death. [LL *astralis* f. *astrum* star]

astray /əstráy/ *adv.* & *predic.adj.* **1** in or into error or sin (esp. *lead astray*). **2** out of the right way. □ **go astray** be lost or mislaid. [ME f. OF *estraié* past part. of *estraier* ult. f. L *extra* out of bounds + *vagari* wander]

■ **1** (*lead astray*) lead on, mislead, misguide, misdirect, deceive; fool, decoy, hoodwink, *colloq.* bamboozle.

astride /əstrī́d/ *adv.* & *prep.* ● *adv.* **1** (often foll. by *of*) with a leg on each side. **2** with legs apart. ● *prep.* with a leg on each side of; extending across.

astringent /əstrínjənt/ *adj.* & *n.* ● *adj.* **1** causing the contraction of body tissues. **2** checking bleeding. **3** severe, austere. ● *n.* an astringent substance or drug. □□ **astringency** *n.* **astringently** *adv.* [F f. L *astringere* (as AD-, *stringere* bind)]

■ *adj.* **2** styptic. **3** see KEEN[1] 4.

astro- /ástrō/ *comb. form* **1** relating to the stars or celestial bodies. **2** relating to outer space. [Gk f. *astron* star]

astrochemistry /ástrōkémmistri/ *n.* the study of molecules and radicals in interstellar space.

astrodome /ástrədōm/ *n.* a domed window in an aircraft for astronomical observations.

astrohatch /ástrəhach/ *n.* = ASTRODOME.

astrolabe /ástrəlayb/ *n.* an instrument, usu. consisting of a disc and pointer, formerly used to make astronomical measurements, esp. of the altitudes of celestial bodies, and as an aid in navigation. [ME f. OF *astrelabe* f. med.L *astrolabium* f. Gk *astrolabon*, neut. of *astrolabos* star-taking]

astrology /əstróllәji/ *n.* the study of the movements and relative positions of celestial bodies interpreted as an influence on human affairs. □□ **astrologer** *n.* **astrological** /ástrəlójik'l/ *adj.* **astrologist** *n.* [ME f. OF *astrologie* f. L *astrologia* f. Gk (as ASTRO-, -LOGY)]

astronaut /ástrənawt/ *n.* a person who is trained to travel in a spacecraft. □□ **astronautical** /-náwtik'l/ *adj.* [ASTRO-, after *aeronaut*]

astronautics /ástrənáwtiks/ *n.* the science of space travel.

astronomical /ástrənómmik'l/ *adj.* (also **astronomic**) **1** of or relating to astronomy. **2** extremely large; too large to contemplate. □ **astronomical unit** a unit of measurement in astronomy equal to the mean distance from the centre of the earth to the centre of the sun, 1.496 x 10^{11} metres or 92.9 million miles. **astronomical year** see YEAR *n.* 1. □□ **astronomically** *adv.* [L *astronomicus* f. Gk *astronomikos*]
■ **2** see INFINITE *adj.* 1–3.

astronomy /əstrónnəmi/ *n.* the scientific study of celestial bodies. □□ **astronomer** *n.* [ME f. OF *astronomie* f. L f. Gk *astronomia* f. *astronomos* (adj.) star-arranging f. *nemō* arrange]

astrophysics /ástrōfízziks/ *n.* a branch of astronomy concerned with the physics and chemistry of celestial bodies. □□ **astrophysical** *adj.* **astrophysicist** /-zisist/ *n.*

Astroturf /ástrōturf/ *n. propr.* an artificial grass surface, esp. for sports fields. [*Astro*dome, name of a sports stadium in Texas where it was first used, + TURF]

astute /əstyóot/ *adj.* **1** shrewd; sagacious. **2** crafty. □□ **astutely** *adv.* **astuteness** *n.* [obs. F *astut* or L *astutus* f. *astus* craft]
■ **1** sharp, keen, perceptive, observant, shrewd, alert, quick, quick-witted, sage, sagacious, wise, intelligent, insightful, perspicacious, penetrating, discerning, knowledgeable, *colloq.* on the ball. **2** shrewd, subtle, clever, ingenious, adroit, wily, cunning, calculating, canny, crafty, artful, arch, sly, foxy, guileful, underhand, underhanded. □□ **astutely** perceptively, insightfully, perspicaciously, penetratingly, adroitly; shrewdly, sagaciously; artfully; craftily. **astuteness** shrewdness, subtleness, adroitness, sharpness, keenness, perceptiveness, perspicacity, discernment, alertness, quick-wittedness, sagacity; artfulness; see also ART[1] 7.

asunder /əsúndər/ *adv. literary* apart. [OE *on sundran* into pieces: cf. SUNDER]
■ see APART 2.

asylum /əsíləm/ *n.* **1** sanctuary; protection, esp. for those pursued by the law (*seek asylum*). **2** *hist.* any of various kinds of institution offering shelter and support to distressed or destitute individuals, esp. the mentally ill. □ **political asylum** protection given by a State to a political refugee from another country. [ME f. L f. Gk *asulon* refuge f. *a-* not + *sulon* right of seizure]
■ **1** see SANCTUARY 4, 5a. **2** see HOME *n.* 4.

asymmetry /aysímmitri/ *n.* lack of symmetry. □□ **asymmetric** /-métrik/ *adj.* **asymmetrical** /-métrik'l/ *adj.* **asymmetrically** /-métrikəli/ *adv.* [Gk *asummetria* (as A-[1], SYMMETRY)]
■ see DISPROPORTION.

asymptomatic /aysímptəmáttik/ *adj.* producing or showing no symptoms.

asymptote /ássimptōt/ *n.* a line that continually approaches a given curve but does not meet it at a finite distance. □□ **asymptotic** /-tóttik/ *adj.* **asymptotically** /-tóttikəli/ *adv.* [mod.L *asymptota* (*linea* line) f. Gk *asumptōtos* not falling together f. *a-* not + *sun* together + *ptōtos* falling f. *piptō* fall]

asynchronous /aysíngkrənəss/ *adj.* not synchronous. □□ **asynchronously** *adv.*

asyndeton /əsíndit'n/ *n.* (*pl.* **asyndeta** /-tə/) the omission of a conjunction. □□ **asyndetic** /ássindéttik/ *adj.* [mod.L f. Gk *asundeton* (neut. adj.) f. *a-* not + *sundetos* bound together]

At *symb. Chem.* the element astatine.

at /at, *unstressed* ət/ *prep.* **1** expressing position, exact or approximate (*wait at the corner*; *at the top of the hill*; *met at Bath*; *is at school*; *at a distance*). **2** expressing a point in time (*see you at three*; *went at dawn*). **3** expressing a point in a scale or range (*at boiling-point*; *at his best*). **4** expressing engagement or concern in a state or activity (*at war*; *at work*; *at odds*). **5** expressing a value or rate (*sell at £10 each*). **6 a** with or with reference to; in terms of (*at a disadvantage*; *annoyed at losing*; *good at cricket*; *play at fighting*; *sick at heart*; *came at a run*; *at short notice*; *work at it*). **b** by means of (*starts at a touch*; *drank it at a gulp*). **7** expressing: **a** motion towards (*arrived at the station*; *went at them*). **b** aim towards or pursuit of (physically or conceptually) (*aim at the target*; *work at a solution*; *guess at the truth*; *laughed at us*; *has been at the milk again*). □ **at all** see ALL. **at hand** see HAND. **at home** see HOME. **at it 1** engaged in an activity; working hard. **2** *colloq.* repeating a habitual (usu. disapproved of) activity (*found them at it again*). **at once** see ONCE. **at that** moreover (*found one, and a good one at that*). **at times** see TIME. **where it's at** *sl.* the fashionable scene or activity. [OE *æt*, rel. to L *ad* to]

at- /ət/ *prefix* assim. form of AD- before *t*.

Atabrine var. of ATEBRIN.

ataractic /áttəráktik/ *adj.* & *n.* (also **ataraxic** /-ráksik/) ● *adj.* calming or tranquillizing. ● *n.* a tranquillizing drug. [Gk *ataraktos* calm: cf. ATARAXY]

ataraxy /áttəraksi/ *n.* (also **ataraxia** /-ráksiə/) calmness or tranquillity; imperturbability. [F *ataraxie* f. Gk *ataraxia* impassiveness]

atavism /áttəviz'm/ *n.* **1** a resemblance to remote ancestors rather than to parents in plants or animals. **2** reversion to an earlier type. □□ **atavistic** /-vístik/ *adj.* **atavistically** /-vístikəli/ *adv.* [F *atavisme* f. L *atavus* great-grandfather's grandfather]

ataxy /ətáksi/ *n.* (also **ataxia** /-siə/) *Med.* the loss of full control of bodily movements. □□ **ataxic** *adj.* [mod.L *ataxia* f. Gk f. *a-* not + *taxis* order]

ATC *abbr. Brit.* **1** air traffic control. **2** Air Training Corps.

ate *past* of EAT.

-ate[1] /ət, ayt/ *suffix* **1** forming nouns denoting: **a** status or office (*doctorate*; *episcopate*). **b** state or function (*curate*; *magistrate*; *mandate*). **2** *Chem.* forming nouns denoting the salt of an acid with a corresponding name ending in *-ic* (*chlorate*; *nitrate*). **3** forming nouns denoting a group (*electorate*). **4** *Chem.* forming nouns denoting a product (*condensate*; *filtrate*). [from or after OF *-at* or *é(e)* or f. L *-atus* noun or past part.: cf. -ATE[2]]

-ate[2] /ət, ayt/ *suffix* **1** forming adjectives and nouns (*associate*; *delegate*; *duplicate*; *separate*). **2** forming adjectives from Latin or English nouns and adjectives (*cordate*; *insensate*; *Italianate*). [from or after (F *-é* f.) L *-atus* past part. of verbs in *-are*]

-ate[3] /ayt/ *suffix* forming verbs (*associate*; *duplicate*; *fascinate*; *hyphenate*; *separate*). [from or after (F *-er* f.) L *-are* (past part. *-atus*): cf. -ATE[2]]

Atebrin /áttəbrin/ *n.* (also **Atabrine** /-breen/) *propr.* = QUINACRINE. [-ATE[1] 2 + BRINE]

atelier /ətélliay, áttəlyay/ *n.* a workshop or studio, esp. of an artist or designer. [F]

a tempo /aa témpō/ *adv. Mus.* in the previous tempo. [It., lit. 'in time']

Athanasian Creed /àthənáysh'n/ *n.* an affirmation of Christian faith formerly thought to have been drawn up by Athanasius, bishop of Alexandria d. 373.

atheism /áythi-iz'm/ *n.* the theory or belief that God does not exist. □□ **atheist** *n.* **atheistic** /-ístik/ *adj.* **atheistical** /-ístik'l/ *adj.* [F *athéisme* f. Gk *atheos* without God f. *a-* not + *theos* god]

■ □□ **atheist** see NON-BELIEVER.

atheling /áthəling/ *n. hist.* a prince or lord in Anglo-Saxon England. [OE *ætheling* = OHG *ediling* f. WG: see -ING[3]]

athematic /áthimáttik/ *adj.* **1** *Mus.* not based on the use of themes. **2** *Gram.* (of a verb-form) having a suffix attached to the stem without a correcting (thematic) vowel.

athenaeum /áthinéeəm/ *n.* (*US* **atheneum**) **1** an institution for literary or scientific study. **2** a library. [LL *Athenaeum* f. Gk *Athēnaion* temple of Athene (used as a place of teaching)]

Athenian /əthéeniən/ *n.* & *adj.* ● *n.* a native or inhabitant of ancient or modern Athens. ● *adj.* of or relating to Athens. [L *Atheniensis* f. *Athenae* f. Gk *Athēnai* Athens, principal city of Greece]

atherosclerosis /áthərōskleerṓsiss/ *n.* a form of arteriosclerosis characterized by the degeneration of the arteries because of the build-up of fatty deposits. □□ **atherosclerotic** /-róttik/ *adj.* [G *Atherosklerose* f. Gk *athērē* groats + SCLEROSIS]

athirst /əthúrst/ *predic.adj. poet.* **1** (usu. foll. by *for*) eager (*athirst for knowledge*). **2** thirsty. [OE *ofthyrst* for *ofthyrsted* past part. of *ofthyrstan* be thirsty]

athlete /áthleet/ *n.* **1** a skilled performer in physical exercises, esp. in track and field events. **2** a healthy person with natural athletic ability. □ **athlete's foot** a fungal foot condition affecting esp. the skin between the toes. [L *athleta* f. Gk *athlētēs* f. *athleō* contend for a prize (*athlon*)]

athletic /athléttik/ *adj.* **1** of or relating to athletes or athletics (*an athletic competition*). **2** muscular or physically powerful. □□ **athletically** *adv.* **athleticism** /-tisiz'm/ *n.* [F *athlétique* or L *athleticus* f. Gk *athlētikos* (as ATHLETE, -IC)]

athletics /athléttiks/ *n.pl.* (usu. treated as *sing.*) **1 a** physical exercises, esp. track and field events. **b** the practice of these. **2** *US* physical sports and games of any kind.

athwart /əthwáwrt/ *adv.* & *prep.* ● *adv.* **1** across from side to side (usu. obliquely). **2** perversely or in opposition. ● *prep.* **1** from side to side of. **2** in opposition to. [A[2] + THWART]

-atic /áttik/ *suffix* forming adjectives and nouns (*aquatic*; *fanatic*; *idiomatic*). [F *-atique* or L *-aticus*, often ult. f. Gk *-atikos*]

atilt /ətílt/ *adv.* tilted and nearly falling. [A[2] + TILT]

-ation /áysh'n/ *suffix* **1** forming nouns denoting an action or an instance of it (*alteration*; *flirtation*; *hesitation*). **2** forming nouns denoting a result or product of action (*plantation*; *starvation*; *vexation*) (see also -FICATION). [from or after F *-ation* or L *-atio -ationis* f. verbs in *-are*: see -ION]

-ative /ətiv, aytiv/ *suffix* forming adjectives denoting a characteristic or propensity (*authoritative*; *imitative*; *pejorative*; *qualitative*; *talkative*). [from or after F *-atif -ative* or f. L *-ativus* f. past part. stem *-at-* of verbs in *-are* + *-ivus* (see -IVE): cf. -ATIC]

Atlantean /ətlántiən/ *adj. literary* of or like Atlas, esp. in physical strength. [L *Atlanteus* (as ATLAS)]

atlantes /ətlánteez/ *n.pl. Archit.* male figures carved in stone and used as columns to support the entablature of a Greek or Greek-style building. [Gk, pl. of *Atlas*: see ATLAS]

Atlantic /ətlántik/ *n.* & *adj.* ● *n.* the ocean between Europe and Africa to the east, and America to the west. ● *adj.* of or adjoining the Atlantic. □ **Atlantic Time** the standard time used in the most eastern parts of Canada and Central America. [ME f. L *Atlanticus* f. Gk *Atlantikos* (as ATLAS, -IC): orig. of the Atlas Mountains, then of the sea near the W. African coast]

atlas /átləss/ *n.* **1** a book of maps or charts. **2** *Anat.* the cervical vertebra of the backbone articulating with the skull at the neck. [L f. Gk *Atlas -antos* a Titan who held up the pillars of the universe, whose picture appeared at the beginning of early atlases]

atm *abbr. Physics* atmosphere(s).

atman /aátmən/ *n. Hinduism* **1** the real self. **2** the supreme spiritual principle. [Skr. *ātmán* essence, breath]

atmosphere /átməsfeer/ *n.* **1 a** the envelope of gases surrounding the earth, any other planet, or any substance. **b** the air in any particular place, esp. if unpleasant. **2 a** the pervading tone or mood of a place or situation, esp. with reference to the feelings or emotions evoked. **b** the feelings or emotions evoked by a work of art, a piece of music, etc. **3** *Physics* a unit of pressure equal to mean atmospheric pressure at sea level, 101,325 pascals. ¶ Abbr.: **atm.** □□ **atmospheric** /-férrik/ *adj.* **atmospherical** /-férrik'l/ *adj.* **atmospherically** /-férrikəli/ *adv.* [mod.L *atmosphaera* f. Gk *atmos* vapour: see SPHERE]

■ **1** air, gases, heaven(s), sky, ether. **2 a** air, ambience, environment, climate, mood, feeling, aura, feel, sense, spirit, tone, quality, *colloq.* vibes. □□ **atmospheric, atmospherical** aerial, meteorological; aural, auric. **atmospherically** meteorologically, climatically, environmentally.

atmospherics /átməsférriks/ *n.pl.* **1** electrical disturbance in the atmosphere, esp. caused by lightning. **2** interference with telecommunications caused by this.

atoll /áttol/ *n.* a ring-shaped coral reef enclosing a lagoon. [Maldive *atolu*]

atom /áttəm/ *n.* **1 a** the smallest particle of a chemical element that can take part in a chemical reaction. **b** this particle as a source of nuclear energy. **2** (usu. with *neg.*) the least portion of a thing or quality (*not an atom of pity*). □ **atom bomb** a bomb involving the release of energy by nuclear fission = *fission bomb*. **atom-smasher** *colloq.* = ACCELERATOR 2. [ME f. OF *atome* f. L *atomus* f. Gk *atomos* indivisible]

■ **1 a** particle, molecule. **2** see PARTICLE 2.

atomic /ətómmik/ *adj.* **1** concerned with or using atomic energy or atomic bombs. **2** of or relating to an atom or atoms. □ **atomic bomb** = *atom bomb*. **atomic clock** a clock in which the periodic process (time scale) is regulated by the vibrations of an atomic or molecular system, such as caesium or ammonia. **atomic energy** nuclear energy. **atomic mass** the mass of an atom measured in atomic mass units. **atomic mass unit** a unit of mass used to express atomic and molecular weights that is equal to one twelfth of the mass of an atom of carbon-12. ¶ Abbr.: **amu. atomic number** the number of protons in the nucleus of an atom, which is characteristic of a chemical element and determines its place in the periodic table. ¶ Symb.: Z. **atomic particle** any one of the particles of which an atom is constituted. **atomic philosophy** atomism. **atomic physics** the branch of physics concerned with the structure of the atom and the characteristics of the elementary particles of which it is composed. **atomic pile** a nuclear reactor. **atomic power** nuclear power. **atomic spectrum** the emission or absorption spectrum arising from electron transitions inside an atom and characteristic of the element. **atomic structure** the structure of an atom as being a central positively charged nucleus surrounded by negatively charged orbiting electrons. **atomic theory 1** the concept of an atom as being composed of elementary particles. **2** the theory that all matter is made up of small indivisible particles called atoms, and that the atoms of any one element are identical in all respects but differ from those of other elements and only unite to form compounds in fixed proportions. **3** *Philos.* atomism. **atomic warfare** warfare involving the use of atom bombs. **atomic weight** = *relative atomic mass*. □□ **atomically** *adv.* [mod.L *atomicus* (as ATOM, -IC)]

■ **1** see NUCLEAR.

atomicity /áttəmíssiti/ *n.* **1** the number of atoms in the molecules of an element. **2** the state or fact of being composed of atoms.

atomism /áttəmiz'm/ *n. Philos.* **1** the theory that all matter consists of tiny individual particles. **2** *Psychol.* the theory that mental states are made up of elementary units. ◻◻ **atomist** *n.* **atomistic** /-místik/ *adj.*

atomize /áttəmīz/ *v.tr.* (also **-ise**) **1** reduce to atoms or fine particles. **2** fragment or divide into small units. ◻◻ **atomization** /-záysh'n/ *n.*

■ break apart, fragment; separate, disperse, scatter.

atomizer /áttəmīzər/ *n.* (also **-iser**) an instrument for emitting liquids as a fine spray.

atomy /áttəmi/ *n.* (*pl.* **-ies**) *archaic* **1** a skeleton. **2** an emaciated body. [ANATOMY taken as *an atomy*]

atonal /áytṓn'l/ *adj. Mus.* not written in any key or mode. ◻◻ **atonality** /-nálliti/ *n.*

atone /ətṓn/ *v.intr.* (usu. foll. by *for*) make amends; expiate for (a wrong). [back-form. f. ATONEMENT]

■ make amends, pay, repay, answer, compensate; (*atone for*) expiate, make up for, make good, remedy, redress, redeem, condone, *Law* purge.

atonement /ətṓnmənt/ *n.* **1** expiation; reparation for a wrong or injury. **2** the reconciliation of God and man. ◻ **the Atonement** the expiation by Christ of mankind's sin. **Day of Atonement** the most solemn religious fast of the Jewish year, eight days after the Jewish New Year. [*at one* + -MENT, after med.L *adunamentum* and earlier *onement* f. obs. *one* (v.) unite]

■ **1** expiation, reparation, repayment, compensation, satisfaction, payment, restitution, recompense, propitiation.

atonic /ətónnik/ *adj.* **1** without accent or stress. **2** *Med.* lacking bodily tone. ◻◻ **atony** /áttəni/ *n.*

atop /ətóp/ *adv.* & *prep.* ● *adv.* (often foll. by *of*) on the top. ● *prep.* on the top of.

■ *prep.* see ABOVE *prep.* 1.

-ator /áytər/ *suffix* forming agent nouns, usu. from Latin words (sometimes via French) (*agitator*; *creator*; *equator*; *escalator*). See also -OR[1]. [L *-ator*]

-atory /ətəri/ *suffix* forming adjectives meaning 'relating to or involving (a verbal action)' (*amatory*; *explanatory*; *predatory*). See also -ORY[2]. [L *-atorius*]

ATP *abbr.* adenosine triphosphate.

atrabilious /átrəbílyəss/ *adj. literary* melancholy; ill-tempered. [L *atra bilis* black bile, transl. Gk *melagkholia* MELANCHOLY]

atrium /áytriəm/ *n.* (*pl.* **atriums** or **atria** /-triə/) **1 a** the central court of an ancient Roman house. **b** a usu. skylit central court rising through several storeys with galleries and rooms opening off at each level. **c** esp. *US* (in a modern house) a central hall or glazed court with rooms opening off it. **2** *Anat.* a cavity in the body, esp. one of the two upper cavities of the heart, receiving blood from the veins. ◻◻ **atrial** *adj.* [L]

atrocious /ətrṓshəss/ *adj.* **1** very bad or unpleasant (*atrocious weather*; *their manners were atrocious*). **2** extremely savage or wicked (*atrocious cruelty*). ◻◻ **atrociously** *adv.* **atrociousness** *n.* [L *atrox -ocis* cruel]

■ **1** bad, disagreeable, unpleasant, horrible, objectionable, woeful, horrendous, *colloq.* awful, terrible, appalling, dreadful, abysmal, lousy, horrid, frightful, desperate, hellish, ghastly, beastly, *Brit. colloq.* chronic, *sl.* rotten. **2** cruel, wicked, iniquitous, villainous, fiendish, execrable, appalling, abominable, monstrous, inhuman, savage, barbaric, brutal, barbarous, heinous, dreadful, flagrant, flagitious, gruesome, grisly, ghastly, unspeakable, horrifying, horrible, awful, infernal, satanic, hellish.

atrocity /ətróssiti/ *n.* (*pl.* **-ies**) **1** an extremely wicked or cruel act, esp. one involving physical violence or injury. **2** extreme wickedness. [F *atrocité* or L *atrocitas* (as ATROCIOUS, -ITY)]

■ **1** outrage, crime, villainy, offence, violation, evil, enormity. **2** enormity, wickedness, flagitiousness, iniquity, infamy, cruelty, heinousness, horror, horribleness, evil, inhumanity, barbarity, savagery, monstrousness, brutality.

atrophy /átrəfi/ *v.* & *n.* ● *v.* (**-ies, -ied**) **1** *intr.* waste away through undernourishment, ageing, or lack of use; become emaciated. **2** *tr.* cause to atrophy. ● *n.* the process of atrophying; emaciation. [F *atrophie* or LL *atrophia* f. Gk f. *a-* not + *trophē* food]

■ *v.* see WASTE *v.* 4.

atropine /átrəpeen, -pin/ *n.* a poisonous alkaloid found in deadly nightshade, used in medicine to treat renal and biliary colic etc. [mod.L *Atropa belladonna* deadly nightshade f. Gk *Atropos* inflexible, the name of one of the Fates]

attach /ətách/ *v.* **1** *tr.* fasten, affix, join. **2** *tr.* (in *passive*; foll. by *to*) be very fond of or devoted to (*am deeply attached to her*). **3** *tr.* attribute, assign (some function, quality, or characteristic) (*can you attach a name to it?*; *attaches great importance to it*). **4 a** *tr.* include, enclose (*attach no conditions to the agreement*; *attach particulars*). **b** *intr.* (foll. by *to*) be an attribute or characteristic (*great prestige attaches to the job*). **5** *refl.* (usu. foll. by *to*) (of a thing) adhere; (of a person) join, take part (*the sticky stamps attached themselves to his fingers*; *climbers attached themselves to the expedition*). **6** *tr.* appoint for special or temporary duties. **7** *tr. Law* seize (a person or property) by legal authority. ◻◻ **attachable** *adj.* **attacher** *n.* [ME f. OF *estachier* fasten f. Gmc: in Law sense thr. OF *atachier*]

■ **1** fasten, join, connect, secure, fix, affix, unite. **2** (*be attached to*) be fond of, be devoted *or* close *or* attracted to, love, adore, dote on, have a liking *or* fondness *or* penchant for, be affectionate towards, be partial to, *sl.* be hooked on; like. **3** ascribe, assign, attribute, apply, associate, connect; fix, affix, pin, put, place. **4 a** see INCLUDE 1. **b** (*attach to*) see ACCOMPANY 2. **5** adhere, stick, *literary* cleave; see also JOIN *v.* 3, 4. **6** appoint, assign, affiliate, enlist, engage; transfer, *Brit.* second. **7** seize, lay hold of, take into custody, confiscate, appropriate, commandeer, take possession of, impound. ◻◻ **attachable** joinable, connectable, securable, fixable; attributable, assignable, ascribable.

attaché /ətáshay/ *n.* a person appointed to an ambassador's staff, usu. with a special sphere of activity (*military attaché*; *press attaché*). ◻ **attaché case** a small flat rectangular case for carrying documents etc. [F, past part. of *attacher*: see ATTACH]

attached /ətácht/ *adj.* **1** fixed, connected, enclosed. **2** (of a person) involved in a long-term relationship, esp. engagement or marriage.

■ **1** connected, joined, (af)fixed, secured, enclosed. **2** spoken for, married, unavailable, engaged, betrothed, *literary* affianced.

attachment /ətáchmənt/ *n.* **1** a thing attached or to be attached, esp. to a machine, device, etc., for a special function. **2** affection, devotion. **3** a means of attaching. **4** the act of attaching or the state of being attached. **5** legal seizure. **6** a temporary position in, or secondment to, an organization. [ME f. F *attachement* f. *attacher* (as ATTACH, -MENT)]

■ **1** affixture, fixture; adjunct, addition, accessory, device, appliance, (added) extra, accoutrement, appendage, part, gadget; ornament, decoration. **2** affection, devotion, liking, fondness, warmth, regard, fidelity, faithfulness, affinity, friendliness, loyalty, admiration, tenderness, partiality, friendship, love. **3** see FASTENING, BOND *n.* 2a. **4** linkage, connection. **5** see SEIZURE 1. **6** assignment, posting, appointment, *Brit.* secondment.

attack /əták/ *v.* & *n.* ● *v.* **1** *tr.* act against with (esp. armed) force. **2** *tr.* seek to hurt or defeat. **3** *tr.* criticize adversely. **4** *tr.* act harmfully upon (*a virus attacking the nervous system*). **5** *tr.* vigorously apply oneself to; begin work on (*attacked his meal with gusto*). **6** *intr.* make an attack. **7** *intr.* be in a mode of attack. ● *n.* **1** the act or process of attacking. **2 a** an offensive operation or mode of behaviour. **b** severe criticism. **3** *Mus.* the action or manner of beginning a piece, passage, etc. **4** gusto, vigour. **5** a sudden occurrence of an illness. **6** a

player or players seeking to score goals etc. ▫▫ **attacker** *n.* [F *attaque, attaquer* f. It. *attacco* attack, *attaccare* ATTACH]
■ *v.* **1** assail, assault, fall *or* set *or* pounce (up)on, lay into, beset, throw oneself on *or* upon; charge, rush, raid, strike (at), storm; engage (in battle), fight; mug, jump; *colloq.* weigh into. **3** criticize, censure, berate, come down on, have a go at, rap, abuse, revile, inveigh against, denounce, condemn, malign, denigrate, decry, flay, disparage, deprecate, vilify, *US* bad-mouth, *colloq.* lay into, lambaste, put down, jump on, slate, bitch (about), *sl.* take to the cleaners, knock, slag (off), slam, *Austral. sl.* bag, *esp. US sl.* dump on, *US sl.* bomb. **4** affect, afflict, harm, damage, injure, infect, invade, destroy; waste, devour, eat, erode, corrode, decompose, dissolve. **5** launch into, embark on *or* upon, set off *or* out on, get going on, begin, start (off), *Austral. & NZ sl.* hoe into; approach, undertake. **6** charge, pounce; engage in battle, fight. ● *n.* **1** assault, bombardment, onset, offensive, onslaught, incursion, raid, charge, strike, blitzkrieg, inroad, invasion; destruction, wasting, erosion, corrosion. **2 b** criticism, censure, abuse, denunciation, condemnation, revilement, denigration, decrial, disparagement, deprecation, vilification. **4** gusto, vigour. **5** seizure, spell, spasm, paroxysm; fit, bout, outbreak, outburst, eruption, flare-up. ▫▫ **attacker** see AGGRESSOR.

attain /ətáyn/ *v.* **1** *tr.* arrive at; reach (a goal etc.). **2** *tr.* gain, accomplish (an aim, distinction, etc.). **3** *intr.* (foll. by *to*) arrive at by conscious development or effort. ▫▫ **attainable** *adj.* **attainability** /-nəbílliti/ *n.* **attainableness** *n.* [ME f. AF *atain-, atein-*, OF *ataign-* stem of *ataindre* f. L *attingere* (as AD-, *tangere* touch)]
■ **1** see REACH *v.* 5, 7. **2** see GAIN *v.* 1. **3** (*attain to*) see ARRIVE 2.

attainder /ətáyndər/ *n. hist.* the forfeiture of land and civil rights suffered as a consequence of a sentence of death for treason or felony. ▫ **act** (or **bill) of attainder** an item of legislation inflicting attainder without judicial process. [ME f. AF, = OF *ateindre* ATTAIN used as noun: see -ER[6]]

attainment /ətáynmənt/ *n.* **1** (often in *pl.*) something attained or achieved; an accomplishment. **2** the act or an instance of attaining.
■ **1** see ACCOMPLISHMENT 3. **2** see ACCOMPLISHMENT 1.

attaint /ətáynt/ *v.tr.* **1** *hist.* subject to attainder. **2 a** (of disease etc.) strike, affect. **b** taint. [ME f. obs. *attaint* (adj.) f. OF *ataint, ateint* past part. formed as ATTAIN: confused in meaning with TAINT]

attar /áttaar/ *n.* (also **otto** /óttō/) a fragrant essential oil, esp. from rose-petals. [Pers. *ʿaṭar* f. Arab. f. *ʿiṭr* perfume]

attempt /ətémpt/ *v.* & *n.* ● *v.tr.* (often foll. by *to* + infin.) seek to achieve, complete, or master (a task, action, challenge, etc.) (*attempted the exercise; attempted to explain; attempted Everest*). ● *n.* (often foll. by *at, on*, or *to* + infin.) an act of attempting; an endeavour (*made an attempt at winning; an attempt to succeed; an attempt on his life*). ▫ **attempt the life of** *archaic* try to kill. ▫▫ **attemptable** *adj.* [OF *attempter* f. L *attemptare* (as AD-, *temptare* TEMPT)]
■ *v.* try, undertake, take on, venture, *archaic* assay, *colloq.* have *or* take a crack at, have a go *or* shot *or* stab at, *formal* essay; (*attempt to*) endeavour *or* strive *or* struggle *or* make an effort to. ● *n.* endeavour, try, effort, undertaking, attack, assault, *colloq.* crack, go, shot, stab, bid, whirl, *formal* essay, *sl.* bash.

attend /əténd/ *v.* **1** *tr.* **a** be present at (*attended the meeting*). **b** go regularly to (*attends the local school*). **2** *intr.* **a** be present (*many members failed to attend*). **b** be present in a serving capacity; wait. **3 a** *tr.* escort, accompany (*the king was attended by soldiers*). **b** *intr.* (foll. by *on*) wait on; serve. **4** *intr.* **a** (usu. foll. by *to*) turn or apply one's mind; focus one's attention (*attend to what I am saying; was not attending*). **b** (foll. by *to*) deal with, take care of (*shall attend to the matter myself; attend to the older people*). **5** *tr.* (usu. in *passive*) follow as a result from (*the error was attended by serious consequences*). ▫▫ **attender** *n.* [ME f. OF *atendre* f. L *attendere* (as AD-, *tendere tent-* stretch)]
■ **1a, 2a** be present (at), go (to), appear (at), put in an appearance (at), turn up (at), sit in (on), assist (at); be at; be there. **1 b** go to, be at, take, be enrolled *or* registered at, be a member of, haunt, frequent, *US* audit. **2 b** see WAIT *v.* 6b. **3 a** escort, accompany, serve, conduct, convoy, squire, follow, usher, wait (up)on; chaperon. **4** (*attend to*) **a** pay attention to, heed, listen to, take notice *or* account of, mind, concentrate on. **b** take care of, deal with, handle, look after, see to, reckon with, occupy oneself with, devote oneself to; turn *or* come to; tend, watch over, wait on *or* upon, care for, minister to, look out for. **5** accompany, be associated with, go along *or* together with, come with; result in *or* from, give rise to, lead to; bring on *or* about, produce, create, generate. ▫▫ **attender** member, frequenter, participant, attendee; see also ATTENDANT *n.*

attendance /əténdənss/ *n.* **1** the act of attending or being present. **2** the number of people present (*a high attendance*). ▫ **attendance allowance** (in the UK) a State benefit paid to disabled people in need of constant care at home. **attendance centre** *Brit.* a place where young offenders report by order of a court as a minor penalty. **in attendance** on hand, available for service. [ME f. OF *atendance* (as ATTEND, -ANCE)]
■ **1** presence, appearance, being. **2** turnout, gate, audience; gathering, crowd, assembly, assemblage, *Austral. sl.* muster. ▫ **in attendance** on hand, available, serving.

attendant /əténdənt/ *n.* & *adj.* ● *n.* a person employed to wait on others or provide a service (*cloakroom attendant; museum attendant*). ● *adj.* **1** accompanying (*attendant circumstances*). **2** waiting on; serving (*ladies attendant on the queen*). [ME f. OF (as ATTEND, -ANT)]
■ *n.* escort, servant, menial, helper, steward, stewardess, valet, usher, usherette, chaperon; aide, subordinate, underling, boy, page, assistant, henchman, second; waiter, waitress, *garçon*, butler, *Mil.* batman, batwoman, *esp. Brit.* commissionaire, scout, *archaic* pursuivant, servitor, *derog.* lackey, flunkey, *hist.* squire, varlet. ● *adj.* **1** accompanying, following; resultant, related, consequent, concomitant, dependent, accessory, associated. **2** serving, waiting on, ministering to.

attendee /áttendée/ *n.* a person who attends (a meeting etc.).
■ see *attender* (ATTEND).

attention /aténsh'n/ *n.* & *int.* ● *n.* **1** the act or faculty of applying one's mind (*give me your attention; attract his attention*). **2 a** consideration (*give attention to the problem*). **b** care (*give special attention to your handwriting*). **c** notice, publicity (*only needs a bit of attention; labelled an attention seeker*). **3** (in *pl.*) **a** ceremonious politeness (*he paid his attentions to her*). **b** wooing, courting (*she was the subject of his attentions*). **4** *Mil.* an erect attitude of readiness (*stand at attention*). ● *int.* (in full **stand to attention!**) an order to assume an attitude of attention. [ME f. L *attentio* (as ATTEND, -ION)]
■ *n.* **1** awareness, consciousness, attentiveness. **2 a** heed, regard, notice, concentration. **b** see CARE *n.* 3. **c** notice, publicity, distinction, acclaim, prominence, notoriety; limelight. **3** (*attentions*) **a** see RESPECT *n.* 1. **b** suit, courtship.

attentive /əténtiv/ *adj.* **1** concentrating; paying attention. **2** assiduously polite. **3** heedful. ▫▫ **attentively** *adv.* **attentiveness** *n.* [ME f. F *attentif -ive* f. *attente*, OF *atente*, fem. past part. of *atendre* ATTEND]
■ **1** observant, awake, alert, on the qui vive, aware, intent, watchful, assiduous, *colloq.* on the ball. **2** polite, courteous, courtly, gallant, gracious, accommodating, considerate, thoughtful, solicitous, civil, respectful, deferential. **3** see MINDFUL. ▫▫ **attentively** intently, closely, carefully, observantly, watchfully, vigilantly, alertly, heedfully, mindfully, assiduously, concentratedly; politely, courteously, graciously, considerately, solicitously, civilly. **attentiveness**

attention, awareness, consciousness, concentration; see also RESPECT *n.* 1.

attenuate *v.* & *adj.* ● *v.tr.* /ətényoo-ayt/ **1** make thin. **2** reduce in force, value, or virulence. **3** *Electr.* reduce the amplitude of (a signal or current). ● *adj.* /əténγooət/ **1** slender. **2** tapering gradually. **3** rarefied. ▫▫ **attenuated** *adj.* **attenuation** /-áysh'n/ *n.* **attenuator** *n.* [L *attenuare* (as AD-, *tenuis* thin)]
■ *adj.* attenuated; slender, tapering; rarefied.
▫▫ **attenuated** see NARROW *adj.* 1a, THIN *adj.* 2.

attest /ətést/ *v.* **1** *tr.* certify the validity of. **2** *tr.* enrol (a recruit) for military service. **3** *intr.* (foll. by *to*) bear witness to. **4** *intr.* enrol oneself for military service. ▫▫ **attestable** *adj.* **attestor** *n.* [F *attester* f. L *attestari* (as AD-, *testis* witness)]
■ **1, 3** confirm, verify, substantiate, vouch for, validate, assert, asseverate, affirm, vow, declare, *Law* depose, *formal* aver; (*attest to*) bear witness to, bear out, swear to, testify to, certify. **2, 4** see ENROL 1, 2.

attestation /áttestáysh'n/ *n.* **1** the act of attesting. **2** a testimony. [F *attestation* or LL *attestatio* (as ATTEST, -ATION)]

Attic /áttik/ *adj.* & *n.* ● *adj.* of ancient Athens or Attica, or the form of Greek spoken there. ● *n.* the form of Greek used by the ancient Athenians. ▫ **Attic salt** (or **wit**) refined wit. [L *Atticus* f. Gk *Attikos*]

attic /áttik/ *n.* **1** the uppermost storey in a house, usu. under the roof. **2** a room in the attic area. [F *attique*, as ATTIC: orig. (Archit.) a small order above a taller one]

atticism /áttisiz'm/ *n.* **1** extreme elegance of speech. **2** an instance of this. [Gk *Attikismos* (as ATTIC, -ISM)]

attire /ətír/ *v.* & *n. formal* ● *v.tr.* dress, esp. in fine clothes or formal wear. ● *n.* clothes, esp. fine or formal. [ME f. OF *atir(i)er* equip f. *à tire* in order, of unkn. orig.]
■ *v.* see DRESS *v.* 1a. ● *n.* see CLOTHES.

attitude /áttityōōd/ *n.* **1 a** a settled opinion or way of thinking. **b** behaviour reflecting this (*I don't like his attitude*). **2 a** a bodily posture. **b** a pose adopted in a painting or a play, esp. for dramatic effect (*strike an attitude*). **3** the position of an aircraft, spacecraft, etc., in relation to specified directions. ▫ **attitude of mind** a settled way of thinking. ▫▫ **attitudinal** /áttityōōdin'l/ *adj.* [F f. It. *attitudine* fitness, posture, f. LL *aptitudo -dinis* f. *aptus* fit]
■ **1** position, opinion, feeling, view, point of view, viewpoint, outlook, approach, leaning, thought, inclination, bent, tendency, orientation; disposition, demeanour. **2** pose, posture, position, stance, aspect; form, shape. ▫▫ **attitudinal** postural, positional, aspectual.

attitudinize /áttityōōdinīz/ *v.intr.* (also **-ise**) **1** practise or adopt attitudes, esp. for effect. **2** speak, write, or behave affectedly. [It. *attitudine* f. LL (as ATTITUDE) + -IZE]
■ **2** see POSE[1] *v.* 3.

attn. *abbr.* **1** attention. **2** for the attention of.

atto- /áttō/ *comb. form Math.* denoting a factor of 10^{-18} (*attometre*). [Da. or Norw. *atten* eighteen + -O-]

attorney /ətúrni/ *n.* (*pl.* **-eys**) **1** a person, esp. a lawyer, appointed to act for another in business or legal matters. **2** *US* a qualified lawyer, esp. one representing a client in a lawcourt. ▫ **Attorney-General** the chief legal officer in England, the US, and other countries. **District Attorney** see DISTRICT. **power of attorney** the authority to act for another person in legal or financial matters. ▫▫ **attorneyship** *n.* [ME f. OF *atorné* past part. of *atorner* assign f. *à* to + *torner* turn]
■ see LAWYER.

attract /ətrákt/ *v.tr.* **1** (also *absol.*) draw or bring to oneself or itself (*attracts many admirers*; *attracts attention*). **2** be attractive to; fascinate. **3** (of a magnet, gravity, etc.) exert a pull on (an object). ▫▫ **attractable** *adj.* **attractor** *n.* [L *attrahere* (as AD-, *trahere tract-* draw)]
■ **1** draw, catch, capture, bring in *or* out *or* forth, *colloq.* pull. **2** entice, lure, allure, appeal to, charm, captivate, fascinate, *colloq.* turn on. ▫▫ **attractor** drawer, *colloq.* puller; charmer.

attractant /əträktənt/ *n.* & *adj.* ● *n.* a substance which attracts (esp. insects). ● *adj.* attracting.

attraction /ətráksh'n/ *n.* **1 a** the act or power of attracting (*the attraction of foreign travel*). **b** a person or thing that attracts by arousing interest (*the fair is a big attraction*). **2** *Physics* the force by which bodies attract or approach each other (opp. REPULSION). **3** *Gram.* the influence exerted by one word on another which causes it to change to an incorrect form, e.g. *the wages of sin is death.* [F *attraction* or L *attractio* (as ATTRACT, -ION)]
■ **1 a** draw, appeal, lure, magnetism, (personal) charm, attractiveness, seductiveness, allure, fascination, captivation, pull, winsomeness. **b** draw, lure, enticement, pull, inducement, allurement, *sl.* come-on; show, entertainment, presentation, performance, crowd-puller, crowd-pleaser. **2** magnetism, polarity; gravitation.

attractive /ətráktiv/ *adj.* **1** attracting or capable of attracting; interesting (*an attractive proposition*). **2** aesthetically pleasing or appealing. ▫▫ **attractively** *adv.* **attractiveness** *n.* [F *attractif -ive* f. LL *attractivus* (as ATTRACT, -IVE)]
■ **1** captivating, appealing, luring, catching, taking, inviting, seductive, engaging, enchanting, interesting, pleasing, pleasant, winning, winsome, alluring. **2** good-looking, pretty, handsome, fetching, comely, beautiful, *Sc.* & *N.Engl.* bonny; aesthetic. ▫▫ **attractiveness** see ATTRACTION 1a, BEAUTY 1.

attribute *v.* & *n.* ● *v.tr.* /ətríbyōōt/ (usu. foll. by *to*) **1** regard as belonging or appropriate (*a poem attributed to Shakespeare*). **2** ascribe; regard as the effect of a stated cause (*the delays were attributed to the heavy traffic*). ● *n.* /átribyōōt/ **1 a** a quality ascribed to a person or thing. **b** a characteristic quality. **2** a material object recognized as appropriate to a person, office, or status (*a large car is an attribute of seniority*). **3** *Gram.* an attributive adjective or noun. ▫▫ **attributable** /ətríbyootəb'l/ *adj.* **attribution** /átribyōōsh'n/ *n.* [ME f. L *attribuere attribut-* (as AD-, *tribuere* assign): (n.) f. OF *attribut* or L *attributum*]
■ *v.* ascribe, impute, assign, put down, trace, charge, credit. ● *n.* **1** quality, character, characteristic, property, feature, trait, virtue. **2** see INDICATION 1b. ▫▫ **attributable** assignable, ascribable, imputable; traceable, chargeable; connectable. **attribution** assignment, ascription, imputation, credit, tracing; connection, association, linkage.

attributive /ətríbyootiv/ *adj. Gram.* (of an adjective or noun) preceding the word described and expressing an attribute, as *old* in *the old dog* (but not in *the dog is old*) and *expiry* in *expiry date* (opp. PREDICATIVE). ▫▫ **attributively** *adv.* [F *attributif -ive* (as ATTRIBUTE, -IVE)]

attrit /ətrít/ *v.tr. US colloq.* wear (an enemy or opponent) down by attrition. [back-form. f. ATTRITION]

attrition /ətrísh'n/ *n.* **1 a** the act or process of gradually wearing out, esp. by friction. **b** abrasion. **2** *Theol.* sorrow for sin, falling short of contrition. ▫ **war of attrition** a war in which one side wins by gradually wearing the other down with repeated attacks etc. ▫▫ **attritional** *adj.* [ME f. LL *attritio* f. *atterere attrit-* rub]
■ **1** see EROSION.

attune /ətyōōn/ *v.tr.* **1** (usu. foll. by *to*) adjust (a person or thing) to a situation. **2** bring (an orchestra, instrument, etc.) into musical accord. [AT- + TUNE]
■ **1** (*attune to*) see ADAPT 1a. **2** see TUNE *v.* 1

Atty. *abbr.* Attorney.

atypical /áytíppik'l/ *adj.* not typical; not conforming to a type. ▫▫ **atypically** *adv.*
■ see PECULIAR *adj.* 1.

AU *abbr.* **1** (also **au.**) astronomical unit. **2** ångström unit.

Au *symb. Chem.* the element gold. [L *aurum*]

aubade /ōbaád/ *n.* a poem or piece of music appropriate to the dawn or early morning. [F f. Sp. *albada* f. *alba* dawn]

auberge /ōbáirzh/ *n.* an inn. [F]

aubergine /ōbərzheen/ *n.* **1** a tropical plant, *Solanum melongena*, having erect or spreading branches bearing white or purple egg-shaped fruit. **2** this fruit eaten as a vegetable. Also called EGGPLANT. **3** the dark purple colour of this fruit. [F f. Cat. *albergínia* f. Arab. *al-bādinjān* f. Pers. *bādingān* f. Skr. *vātiṃgaṇa*]

aubrietia /awbréeshə/ *n.* (also **aubretia**) any dwarf perennial rock-plant of the genus *Aubrietia*, having purple or pink flowers in spring. [mod.L f. Claude *Aubriet*, Fr. botanist d. 1743]

auburn /áwbərn/ *adj.* reddish brown (usu. of a person's hair). [ME, orig. yellowish white, f. OF *auborne, alborne*, f. L *alburnus* whitish f. *albus* white]

AUC *abbr.* (of a date) from the foundation of the city (of Rome). [L *ab urbe condita*]

au courant /ō koorón/ *predic.adj.* (usu. foll. by *with, of*) knowing what is going on; well-informed. [F, = in the (regular) course]

auction /áwksh'n/ *n.* & *v.* ● *n.* **1** a sale of goods, usu. in public, in which articles are sold to the highest bidder. **2** the sequence of bids made at auction bridge. ● *v.tr.* sell by auction. □ **auction bridge** a form of bridge in which players bid for the right to name trumps. **Dutch auction** a sale, usu. public, of goods in which the price is reduced by the auctioneer until a buyer is found. [L *auctio* increase, auction f. *augēre auct-* increase]

auctioneer /áwkshənéer/ *n.* a person who conducts auctions professionally, by calling for bids and declaring goods sold. □□ **auctioneering** *n.*

audacious /awdáyshəss/ *adj.* **1** daring, bold. **2** impudent. □□ **audaciously** *adv.* **audaciousness** *n.* **audacity** /awdássiti/ *n.* [L *audax -acis* bold f. *audēre* dare]

■ **1** daring, bold, confident, intrepid, brave, courageous, adventurous, fearless, unafraid, venturesome, mettlesome, *archaic or joc.* doughty, *colloq.* gutsy; reckless, rash, foolhardy, daredevil, devil-may-care. **2** presumptuous, shameless, bold, impudent, defiant, impertinent, insolent, brazen, unabashed, rude, disrespectful, cheeky, forward. □□ **audaciousness, audacity** see GUT *n.* 3, GALL[1] 1.

audible /áwdib'l/ *adj.* capable of being heard. □□ **audibility** /-bílliti/ *n.* **audibleness** *n.* **audibly** *adv.* [LL *audibilis* f. *audire* hear]

audience /áwdiənss/ *n.* **1 a** the assembled listeners or spectators at an event, esp. a stage performance, concert, etc. **b** the people addressed by a film, book, play, etc. **2** a formal interview with a person in authority. **3** *archaic* a hearing (*give audience to my plea*). [ME f. OF f. L *audientia* f. *audire* hear]

■ **1 a** see ATTENDANCE 2. **2** see INTERVIEW *n.* 3.

audile /áwdīl/ *adj.* of or referring to the sense of hearing. [irreg. f. L *audire* hear, after *tactile*]

audio /áwdiō/ *n.* (usu. *attrib.*) sound or the reproduction of sound. □ **audio frequency** a frequency capable of being perceived by the human ear. **audio typist** a person who types direct from a recording. [AUDIO-]

audio- /áwdiō/ *comb. form* hearing or sound. [L *audire* hear + -O-]

audiology /áwdiólləji/ *n.* the science of hearing. □□ **audiologist** *n.*

audiometer /áwdiómmitər/ *n.* an instrument for testing hearing.

audiophile /áwdiōfīl/ *n.* a hi-fi enthusiast.

audiotape /áwdiōtayp/ *n.* & *v.* ● *n.* **1 a** magnetic tape on which sound can be recorded. **b** a length of this. **2** a sound recording on tape. ● *v.tr.* record (sound, speech, etc.) on tape.

audiovisual /áwdiōvizhyooəl/ *adj.* (esp. of teaching methods) using both sight and sound.

audit /áwdit/ *n.* & *v.* ● *n.* an official examination of accounts. ● *v.tr.* (**audited, auditing**) **1** conduct an audit of. **2** *US* attend (a class) informally, without working for credits. [ME f. L *auditus* hearing f. *audire audit-* hear]

■ *v.* **1** see MONITOR *v.* **2** see ATTEND 1b.

audition /awdísh'n/ *n.* & *v.* ● *n.* **1** an interview for a role as a singer, actor, dancer, etc., consisting of a practical demonstration of suitability. **2** the power of hearing or listening. ● *v.* **1** *tr.* interview (a candidate at an audition). **2** *intr.* be interviewed at an audition. [F *audition* or L *auditio* f. *audire audit-* hear]

auditive /áwditiv/ *adj.* concerned with hearing. [F *auditif -ive* (as AUDITION, -IVE)]

■ auditory, aural, auricular.

auditor /áwditər/ *n.* **1** a person who audits accounts. **2** a listener. □□ **auditorial** /-tóriəl/ *adj.* [ME f. AF *auditour* f. L *auditor -oris* (as AUDITIVE, -OR[1])]

auditorium /áwditóriəm/ *n.* (*pl.* **auditoriums** or **auditoria** /-riə/) the part of a theatre etc. in which the audience sits. [L neut. of *auditorius* (adj.): see AUDITORY, -ORIUM]

auditory /áwditəri/ *adj.* **1** concerned with hearing. **2** received by the ear. [L *auditorius* (as AUDITOR, -ORY[2])]

■ **1** auditive, aural, auricular. **2** aural.

AUEW *abbr.* (in the UK) Amalgamated Union of Engineering Workers.

au fait /ō fáy/ *predic.adj.* (usu. foll. by *with*) having current knowledge; conversant (*fully* au fait *with the arrangements*). □ **put** (or **make**) ***au fait* with** instruct in. [F]

■ see AWARE 2.

au fond /ō fón/ *adv.* basically; at bottom. [F]

■ see *in essence* (ESSENCE).

Aug. *abbr.* August.

Augean /awjéeən/ *adj.* filthy; extremely dirty. [L *Augeas* f. Gk *Augeias* (in Gk mythology, the owner of stables cleaned by Hercules by diverting a river through them)]

■ see DIRTY *adj.* 1.

auger /áwgər/ *n.* **1** a tool resembling a large corkscrew, for boring holes in wood. **2** a similar larger tool for boring holes in the ground. [OE *nafogār* f. *nafu* NAVE[2], + *gār* pierce: for loss of *n* cf. ADDER]

aught[1] /awt/ *n.* (also **ought**) *archaic* (usu. implying *neg.*) anything at all. [OE *āwiht* f. Gmc]

aught[2] var. of OUGHT[2].

augite /áwjīt/ *n. Mineral.* a complex calcium magnesium aluminous silicate occurring in many igneous rocks. [L *augites* f. Gk *augitēs* f. *augē* lustre]

augment *v.* & *n.* ● *v.tr.* & *intr.* /awgmént/ make or become greater; increase. ● *n.* /áwgment/ *Gram.* a vowel prefixed to the past tenses in the older Indo-European languages. □ **augmented interval** *Mus.* a perfect or major interval that is increased by a semitone. □□ **augmenter** *n.* [ME f. OF *augment* (n.), F *augmenter* (v.), or LL *augmentum, augmentare* f. L *augēre* increase]

■ *v.* see INCREASE *v.* 1.

augmentation /áwgmentáysh'n/ *n.* **1** enlargement; growth; increase. **2** *Mus.* the lengthening of the time-values of notes in melodic parts. [ME f. F f. LL *augmentatio -onis* f. *augmentare* (as AUGMENT)]

■ **1** see INCREASE *n.* 1, 2.

augmentative /awgméntətiv/ *adj.* **1** having the property of increasing. **2** *Gram.* (of an affix or derived word) reinforcing the idea of the original word. [F *augmentatif -ive* or med.L *augmentativus* (as AUGMENT)]

au gratin /ō gratán/ *adj. Cookery* cooked with a crisp brown crust usu. of breadcrumbs or melted cheese. [F f. *gratter*, = by grating, f. GRATE[1]]

augur /áwgər/ *v.* & *n.* ● *v.* **1** *intr.* **a** (of an event, circumstance, etc.) suggest a specified outcome (usu. *augur well* or *ill*). **b** portend, bode (*all augured well for our success*). **2** *tr.* **a** foresee, predict. **b** portend. ● *n.* a Roman religious official who observed natural signs, esp. the behaviour of birds, interpreting these as an indication of divine approval or disapproval of a proposed action. □□ **augural** *adj.* [L]

■ *v.* **1 b** see PROMISE *v.* 2a. **2 a** see FORESEE. **b** see FORESHADOW. ● *n.* see SEER[1].

augury /áwgyəri/ *n.* (*pl.* **-ies**) **1** an omen; a portent. **2** the work of an augur; the interpretation of omens. [ME f. OF *augurie* or L *augurium* f. AUGUR]

■ **1** see OMEN *n.* **2** see PROPHECY 2.

August /áwgəst/ *n.* the eighth month of the year. [OE f. L *Augustus* Caesar, the first Roman emperor]

august /awgúst/ *adj.* inspiring reverence and admiration; venerable, impressive. □□ **augustly** *adv.* **augustness** *n.* [F *auguste* or L *augustus* consecrated, venerable]
■ see VENERABLE.

Augustan /awgústən/ *adj.* & *n.* ● *adj.* **1** connected with, occurring during, or influenced by the reign of the Roman emperor Augustus, esp. as an outstanding period of Latin literature. **2** (of a nation's literature) refined and classical in style (in England of the literature of the 17th–18th c.). ● *n.* a writer of the Augustan age of any literature. [L *Augustanus* f. *Augustus*]

Augustine /awgústeen/ *n.* an Augustinian friar. [ME f. OF *augustin* f. L *Augustinus*: see AUGUSTINIAN]

Augustinian /áwgəstínniən/ *adj.* & *n.* ● *adj.* **1** of or relating to St Augustine, a Doctor of the Church (d. 430), or his doctrines. **2** belonging to a religious order observing a rule derived from St Augustine's writings. ● *n.* **1** an adherent of the doctrines of St Augustine. **2** one of the order of Augustinian friars. [L *Augustinus* Augustine]

auk /awk/ *n.* any sea diving-bird of the family Alcidae, with heavy body, short wings, and black and white plumage, e.g. the guillemot, puffin, and razorbill. □ **great auk** an extinct flightless auk, *Alca impennis.* **little auk** a small Arctic auk, *Plautus alle.* [ON *álka*]

auld /awld/ *adj. Sc.* old. [OE *ald*, Anglian form of OLD]
■ see OLD 1, 5.

auld lang syne /áwld lang sín/ *n.* times long past. [Sc., = old long since: also as the title and refrain of a song]

aumbry /áwmbri/ *n.* (also **ambry** /ámbri/) (*pl.* **-ies**) **1** a small recess in the wall of a church. **2** *hist.* a small cupboard. [ME f. OF *almarie, armarie* f. L *armarium* closet, chest f. *arma* utensils]

au naturel /ō natyərél/ *predic.adj.* & *adv. Cookery* uncooked; (cooked) in the most natural or simplest way. [F, = in the natural state]

aunt /aant/ *n.* **1** the sister of one's father or mother. **2** an uncle's wife. **3** *colloq.* an unrelated woman friend of a child or children. □ **Aunt Sally 1** a game in which players throw sticks or balls at a wooden dummy. **2** the object of an unreasonable attack. **my** (or **my sainted** etc.) **aunt** *sl.* an exclamation of surprise, disbelief, etc. [ME f. AF *aunte*, OF *ante*, f. L *amita*]
■ □ **Aunt Sally 2** see BUTT[2].

auntie /áanti/ *n.* (also **aunty**) (*pl.* **-ies**) *colloq.* **1** = AUNT. **2** (**Auntie**) an institution considered to be conservative or cautious, esp. the BBC.

au pair /ō páir/ *n.* a young foreign person, esp. a woman, helping with housework etc. in exchange for room, board, and pocket money, esp. as a means of learning a language. [F]

aura /áwrə/ *n.* (*pl.* **aurae** /-ree/ or **auras**) **1** the distinctive atmosphere diffused by or attending a person, place, etc. **2** (in mystic or spiritualistic use) a supposed subtle emanation, visible as a sphere of white or coloured light, surrounding the body of a living creature. **3** a subtle emanation or aroma from flowers etc. **4** *Med.* premonitory symptom(s) in epilepsy etc. [ME f. L f. Gk, = breeze, breath]
■ **1** air, atmosphere, feeling, ambience, spirit, sense, mood, character, quality. **3** odour, aroma, emanation, fragrance, scent, perfume; see also HINT *n.* 3.

aural[1] /áwrəl/ *adj.* of or relating to or received by the ear. □□ **aurally** *adv.* [L *auris* ear]
■ auditive, auditory, auricular.

aural[2] /áwrəl/ *adj.* of, relating to, or resembling an aura; atmospheric. [as AURA]
■ auric, atmospheric.

aureate /áwriət/ *adj.* **1** golden, gold-coloured. **2** resplendent. **3** (of a language) highly ornamented. [ME f. LL *aureatus* f. L *aureus* golden f. *aurum* gold]

aureole /áwriōl/ *n.* (also **aureola** /awreéələ/) **1** a halo or circle of light, esp. round the head or body of a portrayed religious figure. **2** a corona round the sun or moon. [ME f. L *aureola (corona)*, = golden (crown), fem. of *aureolus* f. *aureus* f. *aurum* gold: *aureole* f. OF f. L *aureola*]

aureomycin /áwriōmísin/ *n.* an antibiotic used esp. in lung diseases. [L *aureus* golden + Gk *mukēs* fungus + -IN]

au revoir /ō rəvwáar/ *int.* & *n.* goodbye (until we meet again). [F]

auric[1] /áwrik/ *adj.* of or relating to trivalent gold. [L *aurum* gold]

auric[2] /áwrik/ *adj.* = AURAL[2].

auricle /áwrik'l/ *n. Anat.* **1 a** a small muscular pouch on the surface of each atrium of the heart. **b** the atrium itself. **2** the external ear of animals. Also called PINNA. **3** an appendage shaped like the ear. [AURICULA]

auricula /awríkyoolə/ *n.* a primula, *Primula auricula*, with leaves shaped like bears' ears. [L, dimin. of *auris* ear]

auricular /awríkyoolər/ *adj.* **1** of or relating to the ear or hearing. **2** of or relating to the auricle of the heart. **3** shaped like an auricle. □□ **auricularly** *adv.* [LL *auricularis* (as AURICULA)]

auriculate /awríkyoolət/ *adj.* having one or more auricles or ear-shaped appendages. [L]
■ auditive, auditory, aural.

auriferous /awríffərəss/ *adj.* naturally bearing gold. [L *aurifer* f. *aurum* gold]

Aurignacian /áwrignáysh'n/ *n.* & *adj.* ● *n.* a flint culture of the palaeolithic period in Europe following the Mousterian and preceding the Solutrean. ● *adj.* of this culture. [F *Aurignacien* f. *Aurignac* in SW France, where remains of it were found]

aurochs /áwroks, ówroks/ *n.* (*pl.* same) an extinct wild ox, *Bos primigenius*, ancestor of domestic cattle and formerly native to many parts of the world. Also called URUS. [G f. OHG *ūrohso* f. *ūr-* urus + *ohso* ox]

aurora /awrórə/ *n.* (*pl.* **auroras** or **aurorae** /-ree/) **1** a luminous electrical atmospheric phenomenon, usu. of streamers of light in the sky above the northern or southern magnetic pole. **2** *poet.* the dawn. □ **aurora australis** /awstráyliss/ a southern occurrence of aurora. **aurora borealis** /bórriáyliss/ a northern occurrence of aurora. □□ **auroral** *adj.* [L, = dawn, goddess of dawn]

auscultation /áwskəltáysh'n/ *n.* the act of listening, esp. to sounds from the heart, lungs, etc., as a part of medical diagnosis. □□ **auscultatory** /-kúltətəri/ *adj.* [L *auscultatio* f. *auscultare* listen to]

auspice /áwspiss/ *n.* **1** (in *pl.*) patronage (esp. *under the auspices of*). **2** a forecast. [orig. 'observation of bird-flight in divination': F *auspice* or L *auspicium* f. *auspex* observer of birds f. *avis* bird]
■ **1** (*auspices*) aegis, sponsorship, authority, protection, support, backing, supervision, guidance, patronage, sanction, approval, control, influence. **2** see FORECAST *n.*

auspicious /awspíshəss/ *adj.* **1** of good omen; favourable. **2** prosperous. □□ **auspiciously** *adv.* **auspiciousness** *n.* [AUSPICE + -OUS]
■ **1** see PROPITIOUS 1.

Aussie /ózzi/ *n.* & *adj.* (also **Ossie, Ozzie**) *colloq.* ● *n.* **1** an Australian. **2** Australia. ● *adj.* Australian. [abbr.]

austere /osteér/ *adj.* (**austerer, austerest**) **1** severely simple. **2** morally strict. **3** harsh, stern. □□ **austerely** *adv.* [ME f. OF f. L *austerus* f. Gk *austēros* severe]
■ **1** see SIMPLE *adj.* 2. **2** see STRICT 2a. **3** see STERN[1].

austerity /ostérriti/ *n.* (*pl.* **-ies**) **1** sternness; moral severity. **2** severe simplicity, e.g. of nationwide economies. **3** (esp. in *pl.*) an austere practice (*the austerities of a monk's life*).
■ **1** see *severity* (SEVERE). **3** rigours, asceticism; see also HARDSHIP.

Austin /óstin/ *n.* = AUGUSTINIAN. [contr. of AUGUSTINE]

austral /áwstrəl, óstrəl/ *adj.* **1** southern. **2** (**Austral**) of Australia or Australasia (*Austral English*). [ME f. L *australis* f. *Auster* south wind]

Australasian /óstrəláyzh'n, -sh'n/ *adj.* of or relating to Australasia, a region consisting of Australia and islands of the SW Pacific. [*Australasia* f. F *Australasie*, formed as *Australia* + *Asia*]

Australian /ostráyliən/ *n.* & *adj.* ● *n.* **1** a native or national of Australia. **2** a person of Australian descent. ● *adj.* of or relating to Australia. □ **Australian bear** a koala bear. **Australian National Football** = *Australian Rules*. **Australian Rules** a form of football played with a Rugby ball by teams of 18. **Australian terrier** a wire-haired Australian breed of terrier. □□ **Australianism** *n.* **Australianize** *v.* [F *australien* f. L (as AUSTRAL)]

Australiana /ostráyliaánə/ *n. pl.* objects relating to or characteristic of Australia.

Australoid /óstrəloyd/ *adj.* of the ethnological type of the Australian Aborigines.

Australopithecus /óstrəlōpíthikəss/ *n.* any extinct bipedal primate of the genus *Australopithecus* having apelike and human characteristics, or its fossilized remains. □□ **australopithecine** /-píthiseen/ *n.* & *adj.* [mod.L f. L *australis* southern + Gk *pithēkos* ape]

Austro- /óstrō/ *comb. form* Austrian; Austrian and (*Austro-Hungarian*).

AUT *abbr.* (in the UK) Association of University Teachers.

autarchy /áwtaarki/ *n.* (*pl.* **-ies**) **1** absolute sovereignty. **2** despotism. **3** an autarchic country or society. □□ **autarchic** /awtaárkik/ *adj.* **autarchical** /awtaárkik'l/ *adj.* [mod.L *autarchia* (as AUTO-, Gk *-arkhia* f. *arkhō* rule)]
■ **1** see SUPREMACY 2. **2** see DESPOTISM.

autarky /áwtaarki/ *n.* (*pl.* **-ies**) **1** self-sufficiency, esp. as an economic system. **2** a state etc. run according to such a system. □□ **autarkic** /awtaárkik/ *adj.* **autarkical** /awtaárkik'l/ *adj.* **autarkist** *n.* [Gk *autarkeia* (as AUTO-, *arkeō* suffice)]

authentic /awthéntik/ *adj.* **1 a** of undisputed origin; genuine. **b** reliable or trustworthy. **2** *Mus.* (of a mode) containing notes between the final and an octave higher (cf. PLAGAL). □□ **authentically** *adv.* **authenticity** /áwthentíssiti/ *n.* [ME f. OF *autentique* f. LL *authenticus* f. Gk *authentikos* principal, genuine]
■ **1** genuine, real, actual, bona fide, sterling, factual, accurate, true, exact, legitimate, valid, *echt*, *colloq.* honest-to-goodness, kosher, *Austral.* & *NZ colloq.* (fair) dinkum; authoritative, reliable, incontrovertible, veritable, trustworthy, dependable, faithful, undisputed, indubitable. □□ **authentically** genuinely, bona fide; reliably, authoritatively, faithfully. **authenticity** reality, realness, fact, truth, genuineness, accuracy, legitimacy, validity; reliability, trustworthiness, dependability, authoritativeness, incontrovertibility.

authenticate /awthéntikayt/ *v.tr.* **1** establish the truth or genuineness of. **2** validate. □□ **authentication** /-káysh'n/ *n.* **authenticator** *n.* [med.L *authenticare* f. LL *authenticus*: see AUTHENTIC]
■ verify, validate, certify, endorse, vouch for, confirm; clinch, seal; corroborate, substantiate, prove, sustain, make good, justify, support. □□ **authentication** verification, validation, certification, confirmation; corroboration; see also PROOF *n.* 3.

author /áwthər/ *n.* & *v.* ● *n.* (*fem.* **authoress** /áwthriss, áwthəréss/) **1** a writer, esp. of books. **2** the originator of an event, a condition, etc. (*the author of all my woes*). ● *v.tr. disp.* be the author of (a book, the universe, a child, etc.). □□ **authorial** /awthóriəl/ *adj.* [ME f. AF *autour*, OF *autor* f. L *auctor* f. *augēre auct-* increase, originate, promote]
■ *n.* **1** writer, man *or* woman of letters, penman, littérateur, wordsmith, *often derog.* scribbler; novelist, playwright, dramatist, essayist, poet; journalist, columnist. **2** creator, originator, inventor, father, founder, framer, initiator, maker, producer, begetter, prime mover, instigator, architect, designer, engineer; cause. ● *v.* see CREATE 1, WRITE 7.

authoritarian /awthórritáiriən/ *adj.* & *n.* ● *adj.* **1** favouring, encouraging, or enforcing strict obedience to authority, as opposed to individual freedom. **2** tyrannical or domineering. ● *n.* a person favouring absolute obedience to a constituted authority. □□ **authoritarianism** *n.*
■ *adj.* dictatorial, imperious, totalitarian, autocratic, tyrannical, despotic, autarchic(al), arbitrary, absolute, dogmatic, domineering, high-handed, overweening, strict, rigid, inflexible, severe, tough, unyielding. ● *n.* disciplinarian, absolutist. □□ **authoritarianism** strictness, inflexibility, rigidity, severity; see also TYRANNY.

authoritative /awthórritətiv/ *adj.* **1** being recognized as true or dependable. **2** (of a person, behaviour, etc.) commanding or self-confident. **3** official; supported by authority (*an authoritative document*). **4** having or claiming influence through recognized knowledge or expertise. □□ **authoritatively** *adv.* **authoritativeness** *n.*
■ **1** dependable, reliable, trustworthy, authentic, definitive, valid, sound, veritable, verifiable, accurate, factual, faithful, true, truthful. **2** see DOMINANT *adj.*, *self-assured* (SELF-ASSURANCE). **3** official, approved, valid, authentic, documented, certified, validated, legitimate, lawful, accredited, sanctioned, recognized, accepted. **4** influential, scholarly, learned, knowledgeable, well-informed, *colloq.* in the know. □□ **authoritatively** officially, learnedly, knowledgeably; reliably, dependably, definitively, soundly, faithfully, truthfully; self-confidently, confidently, self-assuredly, with certainty *or* conviction, convincingly. **authoritativeness** authority, knowledgeability, scholarliness, learnedness; reliability, dependability, soundness, faithfulness, truthfulness; legitimacy; see also CONFIDENCE 2b.

authority /awthórriti/ *n.* (*pl.* **-ies**) **1 a** the power or right to enforce obedience. **b** (often foll. by *for*, or *to* + infin.) delegated power. **2** (esp. in *pl.*) a person or body having authority, esp. political or administrative. **3 a** an influence exerted on opinion because of recognized knowledge or expertise. **b** such an influence expressed in a book, quotation, etc. (*an authority on vintage cars*). **c** a person whose opinion is accepted, esp. an expert in a subject. **4** the weight of evidence. [ME f. OF *autorité* f. L *auctoritas* f. *auctor*: see AUTHOR]
■ **1 a** power, jurisdiction, dominion, right, control, prerogative. **b** authorization, licence; see also PERMISSION. **2** (*authorities*) government, establishment, officials, officialdom, powers that be. **3 a** see INFLUENCE *n.* **c** expert, specialist, scholar, sage, judge, arbiter, connoisseur, *US colloq.* maven. **4** word, testimony, evidence, attestation, averment, asseveration, *colloq.* say-so.

authorize /áwthərīz/ *v.tr.* (also **-ise**) **1** sanction. **2** (foll. by *to* + infin.) **a** give authority. **b** commission (a person or body) (*authorized to trade*). □ **Authorized Version** an English translation of the Bible made in 1611 and traditionally used in Anglican worship. □□ **authorization** /-záysh'n/ *n.* [ME f. OF *autoriser* f. med.L *auctorizare* f. *auctor*: see AUTHOR]
■ **1** sanction, approve, countenance, consent *or* subscribe to, permit, allow, license, endorse, give the go-ahead to, *colloq.* OK, give the green light to; legalize, legitimatize, legitimize. **2 a** permit, give leave *or* permission, allow, license, entitle, empower. **b** commission, license. □□ **authorization** see LICENCE, PERMISSION.

authorship /áwthərship/ *n.* **1** the origin of a book or other written work (*of unknown authorship*). **2** the occupation of writing.

autism /áwtiz'm/ *n. Psychol.* a mental condition, usu. present from childhood, characterized by complete self-absorption and a reduced ability to respond to or communicate with the outside world. □□ **autistic** /awtístik/ *adj.* [mod.L *autismus* (as AUTO-, -ISM)]

auto /áwtō/ *n.* (*pl.* **-os**) *US colloq.* a motor car. [abbr. of AUTOMOBILE]

auto- /áwtō/ *comb. form* (usu. **aut-** before a vowel) **1** self (*autism*). **2** one's own (*autobiography*). **3** by oneself or spontaneous (*auto-suggestion*). **4** by itself or automatic (*automobile*). [from or after Gk *auto-* f. *autos* self]

autobahn /áwtōbaan/ *n.* (*pl.* ***autobahns*** or ***autobahnen*** /-nən/) a German, Austrian, or Swiss motorway. [G f. *Auto* motor car + *Bahn* path, road]

autobiography /áwtōbīógrəfi/ *n.* (*pl.* **-ies**) **1** a personal account of one's own life, esp. for publication. **2** this as a process or literary form. □□ **autobiographer** *n.* **autobiographic** /-bīəgráffik/ *adj.* **autobiographical** /-bīəgráffik'l/ *adj.*

autocade /áwtōkayd/ *n. US* a motorcade. ¶ *Motorcade* is more usual. [AUTOMOBILE + CAVALCADE]

autocar /áwtōkaar/ *n. archaic* a motor vehicle.

autocephalous /áwtōséffələss/ *adj.* **1** (esp. of an Eastern church) appointing its own head. **2** (of a bishop, church, etc.) independent. [Gk *autokephalos* (as AUTO-, *kephalē* head)]

autochthon /awtókthən/ *n.* (*pl.* **autochthons** or **autochthones** /-thəneez/) (in *pl.*) the original or earliest known inhabitants of a country; aboriginals. □□ **autochthonal** *adj.* **autochthonic** /-thónnik/ *adj.* **autochthonous** *adj.* [Gk, = sprung from the earth (as AUTO-, *khthōn*, *-onos* earth)]
■ see ABORIGINAL *n.* 1.

autoclave /áwtəklayv/ *n.* **1** a strong vessel used for chemical reactions at high pressures and temperatures. **2** a sterilizer using high-pressure steam. [AUTO- + L *clavus* nail or *clavis* key]

autocracy /awtókrəsi/ *n.* (*pl.* **-ies**) **1** absolute government by one person. **2** the power exercised by such a person. **3** an autocratic country or society. [Gk *autokrateia* (as AUTOCRAT)]
■ **1** see TYRANNY. **3** tyranny, dictatorship.

autocrat /áwtəkrat/ *n.* **1** an absolute ruler. **2** a dictatorial person. □□ **autocratic** /-kráttik/ *adj.* **autocratically** /-kráttikəli/ *adv.* [F *autocrate* f. Gk *autokratēs* (as AUTO-, *kratos* power)]
■ **1** see DICTATOR 1, 2. **2** see DICTATOR 3.

autocross /áwtōkross/ *n.* motor-racing across country or on unmade roads. [AUTOMOBILE + CROSS- 1]

Autocue /áwtōkyōō/ *n. propr.* a device, unseen by the audience, displaying a television script to a speaker or performer as an aid to memory (cf. TELEPROMPTER).

auto-da-fé /áwtōdaafáy/ *n.* (*pl.* ***autos-da-fé***) /áwtōz-/ **1** a sentence of punishment by the Spanish Inquisition. **2** the execution of such a sentence, esp. the burning of a heretic. [Port., = act of the faith]

autodidact /áwtōdīdakt/ *n.* a self-taught person. □□ **autodidactic** /-dáktik/ *adj.* [AUTO- + *didact* as DIDACTIC]

auto-erotism /áwtō-érrətiz'm/ *n.* (also **auto-eroticism** /-iróttisiz'm/) *Psychol.* sexual excitement generated by stimulating one's own body; masturbation. □□ **auto-erotic** /-iróttik/ *adj.*

autofocus /áwtōfōkəss/ *n.* a device for focusing a camera etc. automatically.

autogamy /awtóggəmi/ *n. Bot.* self-fertilization in plants. □□ **autogamous** *adj.* [AUTO- + Gk *-gamia* f. *gamos* marriage]

autogenous /awtójinəss/ *adj.* self-produced. □ **autogenous welding** a process of joining metal by melting the edges together, without adding material.

autogiro /áwtōjīrō/ *n.* (also **autogyro**) (*pl.* **-os**) an early form of helicopter with freely rotating horizontal vanes and a propeller. [Sp. (as AUTO-, *giro* gyration)]

autograft /áwtəgraaft/ *n. Surgery* a graft of tissue from one point to another of the same person's body.

autograph /áwtəgraaf/ *n.* & *v.* ● *n.* **1 a** a signature, esp. that of a celebrity. **b** handwriting. **2** a manuscript in an author's own handwriting. **3** a document signed by its author. ● *v.tr.* **1** sign (a photograph, autograph album, etc.). **2** write (a letter etc.) by hand. [F *autographe* or LL *autographum* f. Gk *autographon* neut. of *autographos* (as AUTO-, -GRAPH)]
■ *n.* **2** holograph. ● *v.* **1** see SIGN *v.* 1.

autography /awtógrəfi/ *n.* **1** writing done with one's own hand. **2** the facsimile reproduction of writing or illustration. □□ **autographic** /-təgráffik/ *adj.*

autogyro var. of AUTOGIRO.

autoharp /áwtōhaarp/ *n.* a kind of zither with a mechanical device to allow the playing of chords.

autoimmune /áwtō-imyōōn/ *adj. Med.* (of a disease) caused by antibodies produced against substances naturally present in the body. □□ **autoimmunity** *n.*

autointoxication /áwtō-intóksikáysh'n/ *n. Med.* poisoning by a toxin formed within the body itself.

autolysis /awtóllisiss/ *n.* the destruction of cells by their own enzymes. □□ **autolytic** /áwtəlíttik/ *adj.* [G *Autolyse* (as AUTO-, -LYSIS)]

automat /áwtəmat/ *n. US* **1** a slot-machine that dispenses goods. **2** a cafeteria containing slot-machines dispensing food and drink. [G f. F *automate*, formed as AUTOMATION]

automate /áwtəmayt/ *v.tr.* convert to or operate by automation (*the ticket office has been automated*). [back-form. f. AUTOMATION]
■ automatize.

automatic /áwtəmáttik/ *adj.* & *n.* ● *adj.* **1** (of a machine, device, etc., or its function) working by itself, without direct human intervention. **2 a** done spontaneously, without conscious thought or intention (*an automatic reaction*). **b** necessary and inevitable (*an automatic penalty*). **3** *Psychol.* performed unconsciously or subconsciously. **4** (of a firearm) that continues firing until the ammunition is exhausted or the pressure on the trigger is released. **5** (of a motor vehicle or its transmission) using gears that change automatically according to speed and acceleration. ● *n.* **1** an automatic device, esp. a gun or transmission. **2** *colloq.* a vehicle with automatic transmission. □ **automatic pilot** a device for keeping an aircraft on a set course. □□ **automatically** *adv.* **automaticity** /áwtəmətíssiti/ *n.* [formed as AUTOMATON + -IC]
■ *adj.* **1** self-acting, self-governing, self-regulating, self-executing, mechanical, robotic, automated. **2 a** mechanical, involuntary, instinctive, instinctual, natural, spontaneous, impulsive, immediate, conditioned, unconscious, subconscious, intuitive, reflex, knee-jerk, gut, robot-like, robotic, unbidden. **b** unavoidable, inevitable, inescapable, ineluctable; mandatory, compulsory; assured, definite. **3** see sense 2a above. ● *n.* **1** (*spec.*) *Mil.* machine-gun, MG, tommy-gun, pom-pom, Bren, Gatling (gun), Lewis gun, Sten gun, *US sl.* chopper. □ **automatic pilot** autopilot, *Brit. sl.* George. □□ **automatically** mechanically, by itself *or* oneself, on its *or* one's own; involuntarily, instinctively, instinctually, intuitively, spontaneously, impulsively, immediately, unconsciously, unthinkingly; see also NECESSARILY.

automation /áwtəmáysh'n/ *n.* **1** the use of automatic equipment to save mental and manual labour. **2** the automatic control of the manufacture of a product through its successive stages. [irreg. f. AUTOMATIC + -ATION]

automatism /awtómmətiz'm/ *n.* **1** *Psychol.* the performance of actions unconsciously or subconsciously; such action. **2** involuntary action. **3** unthinking routine. [F *automatisme* f. *automate* AUTOMATON]

automatize /awtómmətīz/ *v.tr.* (also **-ise**) **1** make (a process etc.) automatic. **2** subject (a business, enterprise, etc.) to automation. □□ **automatization** /-záysh'n/ *n.* [AUTOMATIC + -IZE]
■ automate.

automaton /awtómmət'n/ *n.* (*pl.* **automata** /-tə/ or **automatons**) **1** a piece of mechanism with concealed motive power. **2** a person who behaves mechanically, like an automaton. [L f. Gk, neut. of *automatos* acting of itself: see AUTO-]
■ **1** see ROBOT 1, 2. **2** see ROBOT 3.

automobile /áwtəməbeel/ *n. US* a motor car. [F (as AUTO-, MOBILE)]
■ see CAR 1.
automotive /áwtəmṓtiv/ *adj.* concerned with motor vehicles.
autonomic /áwtənómmik/ *adj.* esp. *Physiol.* functioning involuntarily. □ **autonomic nervous system** the part of the nervous system responsible for control of the bodily functions not consciously directed, e.g. heartbeat. [AUTONOMY + -IC]
autonomous /awtónnəməss/ *adj.* **1** having self-government. **2** acting independently or having the freedom to do so. □□ **autonomously** *adv.* [Gk *autonomos* (as AUTONOMY)]
■ **1** see INDEPENDENT *adj.* 1b.
autonomy /awtónnəmi/ *n.* (*pl.* **-ies**) **1** the right of self-government. **2** personal freedom. **3** freedom of the will. **4** a self-governing community. □□ **autonomist** *n.* [Gk *autonomia* f. *autos* self + *nomos* law]
■ **1** see SELF-GOVERNMENT 1. **2** see FREEDOM 1, 2. **3** freedom, independence, self-determination.
autopilot /áwtōpīlət/ *n.* an automatic pilot. [abbr.]
autopista /ówtōpeéstə/ *n.* a Spanish motorway. [Sp. (as AUTOMOBILE, *pista* track)]
autopsy /áwtopsi, awtópsi/ *n.* (*pl.* **-ies**) **1** a post-mortem examination. **2** any critical analysis. **3** a personal inspection. [F *autopsie* or mod.L *autopsia* f. Gk f. *autoptēs* eye-witness]
■ **1** post-mortem, necropsy. **2** *colloq.* post-mortem; see also ANALYSIS 1.
autoradiograph /áwtəráydiəgraaf/ *n.* a photograph of an object, produced by radiation from radioactive material in the object. □□ **autoradiographic** /áwtəráydiəgráffik/ *adj.* **autoradiography** /áwtəráydiógrəfi/ *n.*
autoroute /áwtōroōt/ *n.* a French motorway. [F (as AUTOMOBILE, ROUTE)]
autostrada /ówtōstraadə/ *n.* (*pl.* ***autostradas*** or ***autostrade*** /-de/) an Italian motorway. [It. (as AUTOMOBILE, *strada* road)]
auto-suggestion /áwtōsəjéss-chən/ *n.* a hypnotic or subconscious suggestion made by a person to himself or herself and affecting behaviour.
autotelic /áwtətéllik/ *adj.* having or being a purpose in itself. [AUTO- + Gk *telos* end]
autotomy /awtóttəmi/ *n. Zool.* the casting off of a part of the body when threatened, e.g. the tail of a lizard.
autotoxin /áwtətóksin/ *n.* a poisonous substance originating within an organism. □□ **autotoxic** *adj.*
autotrophic /áwtətróffik/ *adj. Biol.* able to form complex nutritional organic substances from simple inorganic substances such as carbon dioxide (cf. HETEROTROPHIC). [AUTO- + Gk *trophos* feeder]
autotype /áwtətīp/ *n.* **1** a facsimile. **2 a** a photographic printing process for monochrome reproduction. **b** a print made by this process.
autoxidation /awtóksidáysh'n/ *n. Chem.* oxidation by exposure to air at room temperature.
autumn /áwtəm/ *n.* **1** the third season of the year, when crops and fruits are gathered, and leaves fall, in the N. hemisphere from September to November and in the S. hemisphere from March to May. **2** *Astron.* the period from the autumnal equinox to the winter solstice. **3** a time of maturity or incipient decay. □ **autumn crocus** any plant of the genus *Colchicum*, esp. meadow saffron, of the lily family and unrelated to the true crocus. [ME f. OF *autompne* f. L *autumnus*]
■ **1** *US* fall.
autumnal /awtúmn'l/ *adj.* **1** of, characteristic of, or appropriate to autumn (*autumnal colours*). **2** occurring in autumn (*autumnal equinox*). **3** maturing or blooming in autumn. **4** past the prime of life. [L *autumnalis* (as AUTUMN, -AL)]
auxanometer /áwksənómmitər/ *n.* an instrument for measuring the linear growth of plants. [Gk *auxanō* increase + -METER]
auxiliary /awgzílyəri/ *adj.* & *n.* ● *adj.* **1** (of a person or thing) that gives help. **2** (of services or equipment) subsidiary, additional. ● *n.* (*pl.* **-ies**) **1** an auxiliary person or thing. **2** (in *pl.*) *Mil.* auxiliary troops. **3** *Gram.* an auxiliary verb. □ **auxiliary troops** *Mil.* foreign or allied troops in a belligerent nation's service. **auxiliary verb** *Gram.* one used in forming tenses, moods, and voices of other verbs. [L *auxiliarius* f. *auxilium* help]
■ *adj.* supportive, support; additional, accessory, supplementary, supplemental, subsidiary, ancillary, secondary, extra, reserve. ● *n.* **1** help, assistance, aid, support, accessory; helper, assistant, aide, supporter, helpmate, man Friday, girl Friday; subordinate, deputy.
auxin /áwksin/ *n.* a plant hormone that regulates growth. [G f. Gk *auxō* increase + -IN]
AV *abbr.* **1** audiovisual (teaching aids etc.). **2** Authorized Version (of the Bible).
avadavat var. of AMADAVAT.
avail /əváyl/ *v.* & *n.* ● *v.* **1** *tr.* help, benefit. **2** *refl.* (foll. by *of*) profit by; take advantage of. **3** *intr.* **a** provide help. **b** be of use, value, or profit. ● *n.* (usu. in *neg.* or *interrog.* phrases) use, profit (*to no avail*; *without avail*; *of what avail?*). [ME f. obs. *vail* (v.) f. OF *valoir* be worth f. L *valēre*]
■ *v.* **2** (*avail oneself of*) see PROFIT *v.* 2. ● *n.* see PROFIT *n.* 1.
available /əváyləb'l/ *adj.* (often foll. by *to*, *for*) **1** capable of being used; at one's disposal. **2** within one's reach. **3** (of a person) **a** free. **b** able to be contacted. □□ **availability** /-bílliti/ *n.* **availableness** *n.* **availably** *adv.* [ME f. AVAIL + -ABLE]
■ **1** at one's disposal, free, unoccupied, unengaged, not busy; on the market, in stock, on sale. **2** at *or* to hand, close at hand, accessible, handy, present, ready, (readily) obtainable, nearby, close by, within (easy) reach, on hand, at one's elbow, *colloq.* get-at-able, on tap. **3** free, unoccupied, at liberty, not busy, on hand, in attendance; contactable, accessible.
avalanche /ávvəlaansh/ *n.* & *v.* ● *n.* **1** a mass of snow and ice, tumbling rapidly down a mountain. **2** a sudden appearance or arrival of anything in large quantities (*faced with an avalanche of work*). ● *v.* **1** *intr.* descend like an avalanche. **2** *tr.* carry down like an avalanche. [F, alt. of dial. *lavanche* after *avaler* descend]
avant-garde /ávvoN-gaárd/ *n.* & *adj.* ● *n.* pioneers or innovators esp. in art and literature. ● *adj.* (of ideas etc.) new, progressive. □□ **avant-gardism** *n.* **avant-gardist** *n.* [F, = vanguard]
■ *n.* vanguard, innovators, pioneers, trend-setters. ● *adj.* innovative, advanced, progressive, experimental, original, new, trend-setting, pioneering; unconventional, eccentric, far-out, unusual, unorthodox, offbeat, *colloq.* way-out; revolutionary, extreme, extremist.
□□ **avant-gardist** innovator, pioneer, trend-setter, experimenter; eccentric; extremist, revolutionary.
avarice /ávvəriss/ *n.* extreme greed for money or gain; cupidity. □□ **avaricious** /-ríshəss/ *adj.* **avariciously** /-ríshəsli/ *adv.* **avariciousness** /-ríshəsniss/ *n.* [ME f. OF f. L *avaritia* f. *avarus* greedy]
■ avariciousness, greed, greediness, acquisitiveness, cupidity, covetousness, graspingness, rapacity, selfishness, itching palm. □□ **avaricious** greedy, acquisitive, grasping, covetous, mercenary, selfish, rapacious. **avariciously** greedily, covetously, acquisitively, graspingly. **avariciousness** see AVARICE above.
avast /əvaást/ *int. Naut.* stop, cease. [Du. *houd vast* hold fast]
avatar /ávvətaar/ *n.* **1** (in Hindu mythology) the descent of a deity or released soul to earth in bodily form. **2** incarnation; manifestation. **3** a manifestation or phase. [Skr. *avatāra* descent f. *áva* down + *tṛ-* pass over]
avaunt /əváwnt/ *int. archaic* begone. [ME f. AF f. OF *avant* ult. f. L *ab* from + *ante* before]
Ave. *abbr.* Avenue.
ave /aávay, aávi/ *int.* & *n.* ● *int.* **1** welcome. **2** farewell. ● *n.* **1** (in full **Ave Maria**) a prayer to the Virgin Mary, the

opening line from Luke 1:28. Also called *Hail Mary*. **2** a shout of welcome or farewell. [ME f. L, 2nd sing. imper. of *avēre* fare well]

avenge /əvénj/ *v.tr.* **1** inflict retribution on behalf of (a person, a violated right, etc.). **2** take vengeance for (an injury). □ **be avenged** avenge oneself. □□ **avenger** *n.* [ME f. OF *avengier* f. *à* to + *vengier* f. L *vindicare* vindicate]
■ **2** see REVENGE *v.* 2.

avens /ávv'nz/ *n.* any of various plants of the genus *Geum*. □ **mountain avens** a related plant (*Dryas octopetala*). [ME f. OF *avence* (med.L *avencia*), of unkn. orig.]

aventurine /əvéntyooreen/ *n. Mineral.* **1** brownish glass or mineral containing sparkling gold-coloured particles usu. of copper or gold. **2** a variety of spangled quartz resembling this. [F f. It. *avventurino* f. *avventura* chance (because of its accidental discovery)]

avenue /ávvənyoo/ *n.* **1 a** a broad road or street, often with trees at regular intervals along its sides. **b** a tree-lined approach to a country house. **2** a way of approaching or dealing with something (*explored every avenue to find an answer*). [F, fem. past part. of *avenir* f. L *advenire* come to]
■ **1 a** see ROAD[1] 1. **2** see ROUTE *n.*

aver /əvér/ *v.tr.* (**averred, averring**) *formal* assert, affirm. [ME f. OF *averer* (as AD-, L *verus* true)]
■ see DECLARE 3.

average /ávvərij/ *n.*, *adj.*, & *v.* ● *n.* **1 a** the usual amount, extent, or rate. **b** the ordinary standard. **2** an amount obtained by dividing the total of given amounts by the number of amounts in the set. **3** *Law* the distribution of loss resulting from damage to a ship or cargo. ● *adj.* **1 a** usual, typical. **b** mediocre, undistinguished. **2** estimated or calculated by average. ● *v.tr.* **1** amount on average to (*the sale of the product averaged one hundred a day*). **2** do on average (*averages six hours' work a day*). **3 a** estimate the average of. **b** estimate the general standard of. □ **average adjustment** *Law* the apportionment of average. **average out** result in an average. **average out at** result in an average of. **batting average 1** *Cricket* a batsman's runs scored per completed innings. **2** *Baseball* a batter's safe hits per time at bat. **bowling average** *Cricket* a bowler's conceded runs per wicket taken. **law of averages** the principle that if one of two extremes occurs the other will also tend to so as to maintain the normal average. **on** (or **on an**) **average** as an average rate or estimate. □□ **averagely** *adv.* [F *avarie* damage to ship or cargo (see sense 3), f. It. *avaria* f. Arab. *'awārīya* damaged goods f. *'awār* damage at sea, loss: *-age* after *damage*]
■ *n.* **1** standard, usual, mean, norm, (happy) medium. ● *adj.* **1 a** normal, common, usual, customary, general, typical, ordinary, regular, standard. **b** mediocre, middling, run-of-the-mill, commonplace, undistinguished, unexceptional, indifferent, so so, *colloq.* no great shakes. **2** mean. □ **on average** in the main, generally, in general, normally, usually, ordinarily, typically, commonly, customarily, as a rule, for the most part. □□ **averagely** see QUITE 2.

averment /əvérmənt/ *n.* a positive statement; an affirmation, esp. *Law* one with an offer of proof. [ME f. AF, OF *aver(r)ement* (as AVER, -MENT)]
■ see PROFESSION 3.

averse /əvérss/ *predic.adj.* (usu. foll. by *to*; also foll. by *from*) opposed, disinclined (*was not averse to helping me*). ¶ Construction with *to* is now more common. [L *aversus* (as AVERT)]
■ disinclined, unwilling, reluctant, resistant, loath, opposed, antipathetic, ill-disposed, indisposed, hostile, antagonistic; anti, against.

aversion /əvérsh'n/ *n.* **1** (usu. foll. by *to, from, for*) a dislike or unwillingness (*has an aversion to hard work*). **2** an object of dislike (*my pet aversion*). □ **aversion therapy** therapy designed to make a subject averse to an existing habit. [F *aversion* or L *aversio* (as AVERT, -ION)]
■ **1** dislike, abhorrence, repugnance, antipathy, antagonism, animosity, hostility, loathing, hatred, odium, horror; disinclination, unwillingness, resistance, reluctance, distaste. **2** dislike, bugbear, *bête noire*, *colloq.* hate, peeve.

avert /əvért/ *v.tr.* (often foll. by *from*) **1** turn away (one's eyes or thoughts). **2** prevent or ward off (an undesirable occurrence). □□ **avertable** *adj.* **avertible** *adj.* [ME f. L *avertere* (as AB-, *vertere vers-* turn): partly f. OF *avertir* f. Rmc]
■ **1** see DEFLECT. **2** see PREVENT 1.

Avesta /əvéstə/ *n.* (usu. prec. by *the*) the sacred writings of Zoroastrianism (cf. ZEND). [Pers.]

Avestan /əvéstən/ *adj.* & *n.* ● *adj.* of or relating to the Avesta. ● *n.* the ancient Iranian language of the Avesta.

avian /áyviən/ *adj.* of or relating to birds. [L *avis* bird]
■ ornithological.

aviary /áyviəri/ *n.* (*pl.* **-ies**) a large enclosure or building for keeping birds. [L *aviarium* (as AVIAN, -ARY[1])]

aviate /áyviayt/ *v.* **1** *intr.* fly in an aeroplane. **2** *tr.* pilot (an aeroplane). [back-form. f. AVIATION]

aviation /áyviáysh'n/ *n.* **1** the skill or practice of operating aircraft. **2** aircraft manufacture. [F f. L *avis* bird]

aviator /áyviaytər/ *n.* (*fem.* **aviatrix** /áyviətriks/) an airman or airwoman. [F *aviateur* f. L *avis* bird]

aviculture /áyvikulchər/ *n.* the rearing and keeping of birds. □□ **aviculturist** /-kúlchərist/ *n.* [L *avis* bird, after AGRICULTURE]

avid /ávvid/ *adj.* (usu. foll. by *of, for*) eager, greedy. □□ **avidity** /əvídditi/ *n.* **avidly** *adv.* [F *avide* or L *avidus* f. *avēre* crave]
■ see EAGER.

avifauna /áyvifawnə/ *n.* birds of a region or country collectively. [L *avis* bird + FAUNA]

avionics /áyvióniks/ *n.pl.* (treated as *sing.*) electronics as applied to aviation.

avitaminosis /ayvíttəminōsiss/ *n. Med.* a condition resulting from a deficiency of one or more vitamins.

avizandum /ávvizándəm/ *n. Sc. Law* a period of time for further consideration of a judgement. [med.L, gerund of *avizare* consider (as ADVISE)]

avocado /ávvəkaádō/ *n.* (*pl.* **-os**) **1** (in full **avocado pear**) a pear-shaped fruit with rough leathery skin, a smooth oily edible flesh, and a large stone. **2** the tropical evergreen tree, *Persea americana*, native to Central America, bearing this fruit. Also called *alligator pear*. **3** the light green colour of the flesh of this fruit. [Sp., = advocate (substituted for Aztec *ahuacatl*)]

avocation /ávvəkáysh'n/ *n.* **1** a minor occupation. **2** *colloq.* a vocation or calling. [L *avocatio* f. *avocare* call away]
■ calling, vocation; see also INTEREST *n.* 2.

avocet /ávvəset/ *n.* any wading bird of the genus *Recurvirostra* with long legs and a long slender upward-curved bill and usu. black and white plumage. [F *avocette* f. It. *avosetta*]

Avogadro's constant /ávvəgaádrōz/ *n.* (also **Avogadro's number**) *Physics* the number of atoms or molecules in one mole of a substance. [A. *Avogadro*, It. physicist d. 1856]

Avogadro's law /ávvəgaádrōz/ *n. Physics* the law that equal volumes of all gases at the same temperature and pressure contain the same number of molecules.

avoid /əvóyd/ *v.tr.* **1** refrain or keep away from (a thing, person, or action). **2** escape; evade. **3** *Law* **a** nullify (a decree or contract). **b** quash (a sentence). □□ **avoidable** *adj.* **avoidably** *adv.* **avoidance** *n.* **avoider** *n.* [AF *avoider*, OF *evuider* clear out, get quit of, f. *vuide* empty, VOID]
■ **1** shun, keep *or* stay (away) from, keep off, leave alone, keep *or* steer clear of, keep at arm's length, fight shy of, give a wide berth to, refrain from, abstain from, miss, *literary* eschew. **2** escape, evade, get away from *or* without, miss; dodge, circumvent, sidestep, elude, skirt (round), keep *or* steer clear of, fight shy of; ward *or* fend

or stave off, keep away. □□ **avoidable** escapable, evadable. **avoidance** see EVASION 1.

avoirdupois /ávvərdəpóyz/ *n.* (in full **avoirdupois weight**) **1** a system of weights based on a pound of 16 ounces or 7,000 grains. **2** weight, heaviness. [ME f. OF *aveir de peis* goods of weight f. *aveir* f. L *habēre* have + *peis* (see POISE[1])]

avouch /əvówch/ *v.tr.* & *intr. archaic* or *rhet.* guarantee, affirm, confess. □□ **avouchment** *n.* [ME f. OF *avochier* f. L *advocare* (as AD-, *vocare* call)]
■ see DECLARE 3.

avow /əvów/ *v.tr.* **1** admit, confess. **2 a** *refl.* admit that one is (*avowed himself the author*). **b** (as **avowed** *adj.*) admitted (*the avowed author*). □□ **avowal** *n.* **avowedly** /əvówidli/ *adv.* [ME f. OF *avouer* acknowledge f. L *advocare* (as AD-, *vocare* call)]
■ **1** see CONFESS 1a.

avulsion /əvúlsh'n/ *n.* **1** a tearing away. **2** *Law* a sudden removal of land by a flood etc. to another person's estate. [F *avulsion* or L *avulsio* f. *avellere avuls-* pluck away]

avuncular /əvúngkyoolər/ *adj.* like or of an uncle; kind and friendly, esp. towards a younger person. [L *avunculus* maternal uncle, dimin. of *avus* grandfather]

AWACS /áywaks/ *n.* a long-range radar system for detecting enemy aircraft. [abbr. of *a*irborne *w*arning *a*nd *c*ontrol *s*ystem]

await /əwáyt/ *v.tr.* **1** wait for. **2** (of an event or thing) be in store for (*a surprise awaits you*). [ME f. AF *awaitier*, OF *aguaitier* (as AD-, *waitier* WAIT)]

awake /əwáyk/ *v.* & *adj.* ● *v.* (*past* **awoke** /əwṓk/; *past part.* **awoken** /əwṓkən/) **1** *intr.* **a** cease to sleep. **b** become active. **2** *intr.* (foll. by *to*) become aware of. **3** *tr.* rouse, esp. from sleep. ● *predic.adj.* **1 a** not asleep. **b** vigilant. **2** (foll. by *to*) aware of. [OE *āwæcnan*, *āwacian* (as A-[2], WAKE[1])]
■ *v.* **1 a** wake (up), awaken, get up, rouse *or* bestir oneself, come to, *colloq.* surface. **b** see STIR[1] *v.* 2c. **2** (*awake to*) awaken to, wake up to, realize, understand, become aware *or* conscious of, become sensitive *or* alive to, become informed *or* knowledgeable about, *colloq.* get wise to, get on to, *sl.* drop to. **3** awaken, animate, arouse, rouse, stimulate, revive, incite, excite, activate, alert; stir up, fan, kindle, ignite, fire. ● *predic.adj.* **1 a** up (and about), aroused, roused, astir, wide awake, open-eyed, conscious. **b** vigilant, alert, on the alert, on the qui vive, watchful, on one's guard *or* toes, on the spot, attentive, aware, conscious, alive; heedful. **2** see AWARE 1.

awaken /əwáykən/ *v.tr.* & *intr.* **1** = AWAKE *v.* **2** *tr.* (often foll. by *to*) make aware. [OE *onwæcnan* etc. (as A-[2], WAKEN)]
■ **1** see AWAKE *v.* **2** arouse, rouse, alert; (*awaken to*) make aware *or* conscious *or* apprised of, arouse *or* alert to, inform *or* apprise *or* advise of.

award /əwáwrd/ *v.* & *n.* ● *v.tr.* **1** give or order to be given as a payment, compensation, or prize (*awarded him a knighthood*; *was awarded damages*). **2** grant, assign. ● *n.* **1 a** a payment, compensation, or prize awarded. **b** the act or process of awarding. **2** a judicial decision. □□ **awarder** *n.* [ME f. AF *awarder*, ult. f. Gmc: see WARD]
■ *v.* grant, give (out), donate; confer on, bestow on, present to, furnish with, endow with; assign, apportion, accord. ● *n.* **1 a** a prize, trophy, reward, honour(s); payment, subsidy, grant, donation, gift, compensation, damages, subvention. **b** grant, bestowal, presentation, endowment, *esp. US* conferral. **2** see DECISION 2, 3.

aware /əwáir/ *predic.adj.* **1** (often foll. by *of*, or *that* + clause) conscious; not ignorant; having knowledge. **2** well-informed. ¶ Also found in *attrib.* use in sense 2, as in *a very aware person*; this is *disp.* □□ **awareness** *n.* [OE *gewær*]
■ **1** awake, alert, on the qui vive, *colloq.* switched-on, *poet.* ware; (*aware of*) conscious *or* cognizant *or* sensible of, sensitive *or* awake *or* alert to, informed *or* apprised *or* seized of, *colloq.* wise to. **2** well-informed, knowledgeable, knowing, posted, in the know, enlightened, *au fait*, *au courant*, *colloq.* switched-on, *sl.* hip. □□ **awareness** see SENSITIVITY, UNDERSTANDING *n.* 1, 5.

awash /əwósh/ *predic.adj.* **1** level with the surface of water, so that it just washes over. **2** carried or washed by the waves; flooded or as if flooded.

away /əwáy/ *adv.*, *adj.*, & *n.* ● *adv.* **1** to or at a distance from the place, person, or thing in question (*go away*; *give away*; *look away*; *they are away*; *5 miles away*). **2** towards or into non-existence (*sounds die away*; *explain it away*; *idled their time away*). **3** constantly, persistently, continuously (*work away*; *laugh away*). **4** without delay (*ask away*). ● *adj. Sport* played on an opponent's ground etc. (*away match*; *away win*). ● *n. Sport* an away match or win. □ **away with** (as *imper.*) take away; let us be rid of. [OE *onweg*, *aweg* on one's way f. A[2] + WAY]
■ □ **away with** down with.

awe /aw/ *n.* & *v.* ● *n.* reverential fear or wonder (*stand in awe of*). ● *v.tr.* inspire with awe. □ **awe-inspiring** causing awe or wonder; amazing, magnificent. □□ **awe-inspiringly** *adv.* [ME *age* f. ON *agi* f. Gmc]
■ *n.* see WONDER *n.* 1. □□ **awe-inspiring** see AWESOME 1.

aweary /əwéeri/ *predic.adj. poet.* (often foll. by *of*) weary. [aphetic *a* + WEARY]

aweigh /əwáy/ *predic.adj. Naut.* (of an anchor) clear of the sea or river bed; hanging. [A[2] + WEIGH[1]]

awesome /áwsəm/ *adj.* **1** inspiring awe. **2** *sl.* excellent, superb. □□ **awesomely** *adv.* **awesomeness** *n.* [AWE + -SOME[1]]
■ **1** awe-inspiring, imposing, overwhelming, formidable, daunting, dreadful, fearsome, fearful, frightening, horrifying, terrifying, terrible; breathtaking, amazing, wonderful, marvellous, moving, stirring, affecting, *poet.* awful, wondrous; unbelievable, incredible; alarming, shocking, stupefying, astounding, astonishing, *colloq.* stunning. **2** see GREAT *adj.* 10.

awestricken /áwstrikkən/ *adj.* (also **awestruck** /-struk/) struck or affected by awe.

awful /áwfŏŏl/ *adj.* **1** *colloq.* **a** unpleasant or horrible (*awful weather*). **b** poor in quality; very bad (*has awful writing*). **c** (*attrib.*) excessive; remarkably large (*an awful lot of money*). **2** *poet.* inspiring awe. □□ **awfulness** *n.* [AWE + -FUL]
■ **1 a, b** unpleasant, horrible, atrocious, horrendous, disagreeable, nasty, abhorrent, repellent, gruesome, desperate, detestable, woeful, unspeakable, grotesque, execrable, *colloq.* terrible, horrid, ghastly, hideous, dreadful, abominable, lousy, shocking, frightful, wicked, accursed, infernal, *Brit. colloq.* chronic, *sl.* rotten, gross; bad, inferior, base. **c** see EXCESSIVE, LARGE *adj.* 1, 2. **2** see AWESOME 1.

awfully /áwfəli, -fli/ *adv.* **1** *colloq.* in an unpleasant, bad, or horrible way (*he played awfully*). **2** *colloq.* very (*she's awfully pleased*; *thanks awfully*). **3** *poet.* reverently.
■ **1** terribly, woefully, atrociously, shockingly, poorly, ineptly, *colloq.* lousily, dreadfully, abominably, abysmally; see also BADLY 1. **2** very, extremely, really, greatly, remarkably, exceedingly, excessively, fearfully, inordinately, incomparably, *colloq.* terribly, dreadfully, beastly, *Sc.* & *US colloq.* real; very much, a lot, *Brit. colloq.* ever so (much).

awhile /əwī́l/ *adv.* for a short time. [OE *āne hwīle* a while]

awkward /áwkwərd/ *adj.* **1** ill-adapted for use; causing difficulty in use. **2** clumsy or bungling. **3 a** embarrassed (*felt awkward about it*). **b** embarrassing (*an awkward situation*). **4** difficult to deal with (*an awkward customer*). □ **the awkward age** adolescence. □□ **awkwardly** *adv.* **awkwardness** *n.* [obs. *awk* backhanded, untoward (ME f. ON *afugr* turned the wrong way) + -WARD]
■ **1** unwieldy, cumbersome, cumbrous; unfriendly, ill-adapted; tricky. **2** clumsy, ungainly, left-handed, blundering, lumbersome, bungling, maladroit, uncoordinated, ungraceful, graceless, ungainly, inelegant, gawky, wooden, artless, blockish, cloddish, lumpish, inexpert, gauche, unhandy, inept, oafish, unskilled, unskilful, all thumbs, *colloq.* cack-handed, ham-fisted, ham-handed. **3 a** embarrassed, shamefaced, uncomfortable, ill at ease, uneasy, out of place,

discomfited, disconcerted, self-conscious. **b** embarrassing, uncomfortable, humiliating. **4** difficult, touchy, sensitive, embarrassing, delicate, unpleasant, uncomfortable, ticklish, tricky, trying, troublesome, problematic, problematical, scabrous, knotty, *colloq.* sticky. □ **the awkward age** adolescence, puberty, (the) teenage years.

awl /awl/ *n.* a small pointed tool used for piercing holes, esp. in leather. [OE *æl*]

awn /awn/ *n.* a stiff bristle growing from the grain-sheath of grasses, or terminating a leaf etc. □□ **awned** *adj.* [ME f. ON *ögn*]

awning /áwning/ *n.* a sheet of canvas or similar material stretched on a frame and used to shade a shop window, doorway, ship's deck, or other area from the sun or rain. [17th c. (Naut.): orig. uncert.]
■ see SHADE *n.* 7, 8.

awoke *past* of AWAKE.

awoken *past part.* of AWAKE.

AWOL /áywol/ *abbr. colloq.* absent without leave.

awry /ərī/ *adv.* & *adj.* ● *adv.* **1** crookedly or askew. **2** improperly or amiss. ● *predic.adj.* crooked; deviant or unsound (*his theory is awry*). □ **go awry** go or do wrong. [ME f. A[2] + WRY]
■ *adv.* **1** see ASKEW *adv.* **2** see AMISS *adv.* ● *adj.* see CROOKED 1, WRONG *adj.* 4.

axe /aks/ *n.* & *v.* (*US* **ax**) ● *n.* **1** a chopping-tool, usu. of iron with a steel edge and wooden handle. **2** the drastic cutting or elimination of expenditure, staff, etc. ● *v.tr.* (**axing**) **1** cut (esp. costs or services) drastically. **2** remove or dismiss. □ **axe-breaker** a hard-wooded Australian tree. **an axe to grind** private ends to serve. [OE *æx* f. Gmc]

axel /áks'l/ *n.* a jumping movement in skating, similar to a loop (see LOOP *n.* 7) but from one foot to the other. [*Axel* R. Paulsen, Norw. skater d. 1938]

axes *pl.* of AXIS[1].

axial /áksiəl/ *adj.* **1** forming or belonging to an axis. **2** round an axis (*axial rotation; axial symmetry*). □□ **axiality** /-siálliti/ *n.* **axially** *adv.*

axil /áksil/ *n.* the upper angle between a leaf and the stem it springs from, or between a branch and the trunk. [L *axilla*: see AXILLA]

axilla /aksíllə/ *n.* (*pl.* **axillae** /-lee/) **1** *Anat.* the armpit. **2** an axil. [L, = armpit, dimin. of *ala* wing]

axillary /aksílləri/ *adj.* **1** *Anat.* of or relating to the armpit. **2** *Bot.* in or growing from the axil.

axiom /áksiəm/ *n.* **1** an established or widely accepted principle. **2** esp. *Geom.* a self-evident truth. [F *axiome* or L *axioma* f. Gk *axiōma axiōmat-* f. *axios* worthy]
■ **1** see PRINCIPLE 1.

axiomatic /áksiəmáttik/ *adj.* **1** self-evident. **2** relating to or containing axioms. □□ **axiomatically** *adv.* [Gk *axiōmatikos* (as AXIOM)]
■ **1** see SELF-EVIDENT. **2** see PROVERBIAL 2.

axis[1] /áksiss/ *n.* (*pl.* **axes** /-seez/) **1 a** an imaginary line about which a body rotates or about which a plane figure is conceived as generating a solid. **b** a line which divides a regular figure symmetrically. **2** *Math.* a fixed reference line for the measurement of coordinates etc. **3** *Bot.* the central column of an inflorescence or other growth. **4** *Anat.* the second cervical vertebra. **5** *Physiol.* the central part of an organ or organism. **6 a** an agreement or alliance between two or more countries forming a centre for an eventual larger grouping of nations sharing an ideal or objective. **b** (**the Axis**) the alliance of Germany and Italy formed before and during the war of 1939–45, later extended to include Japan and other countries; these countries as a group. [L, = axle, pivot]

axis[2] /áksiss/ *n.* a white spotted deer, *Cervus axis*, of S. Asia. Also called CHITAL. [L]

axle /áks'l/ *n.* a rod or spindle (either fixed or rotating) on which a wheel or group of wheels is fixed. [orig. *axle-tree* f. ME *axel-tre* f. ON *öxull-tré*]

Axminster /áksminstər/ *n.* (in full **Axminster carpet**) a kind of machine-woven patterned carpet with a cut pile. [*Axminster* in S. England]

axolotl /áksəlott'l/ *n.* an aquatic newtlike salamander, *Ambystoma mexicanum*, from Mexico, which in natural conditions retains its larval form for life but is able to breed. [Nahuatl f. *atl* water + *xolotl* servant]

axon /ákson/ *n. Anat.* & *Zool.* a long threadlike part of a nerve cell, conducting impulses from the cell body. [mod.L f. Gk *axōn* axis]

ay var. of AYE[1].

ayah /íə/ *n.* a native nurse or maidservant, esp. in India and other former British territories abroad. [Anglo-Ind. f. Port. *aia* nurse]

ayatollah /íətóllə/ *n.* a Shiite religious leader in Iran. [Pers. f. Arab., = token of God]

aye[1] /ī/ *adv.* & *n.* (also **ay**) ● *adv.* **1** *archaic* or *dial.* yes. **2** (in voting) I assent. **3** (as **aye aye**) *Naut.* a response accepting an order. ● *n.* an affirmative answer or assent, esp. in voting. □ **the ayes have it** the affirmative votes are in the majority. [16th c.: prob. f. first pers. personal pron. expressing assent]
■ yes, *archaic* yea.

aye[2] /ay/ *adv. archaic* ever, always. □ **for aye** for ever. [ME f. ON *ei*, *ey* f. Gmc]
■ see ALWAYS 1. □ **for aye** see ALWAYS 4.

aye-aye /í-ī/ *n.* an arboreal nocturnal lemur, *Daubentonia madagascariensis*, native to Madagascar. [F f. Malagasy *aiay*]

Aylesbury /áylzbəri/ *n.* (*pl.* **Aylesburys**) **1** a bird of a breed of large white domestic ducks. **2** this breed. [*Aylesbury* in S. England]

Ayrshire /áirshər/ *n.* **1** an animal of a mainly white breed of dairy cattle. **2** this breed. [name of a former Scottish county]

AZ *abbr. US* Arizona (in official postal use).

azalea /əzáyliə/ *n.* any of various flowering deciduous shrubs of the genus *Rhododendron*, with large pink, purple, white, or yellow flowers. [mod.L f. Gk, fem. of *azaleos* dry (from the dry soil in which it was believed to flourish)]

azeotrope /əzéeətrōp/ *n. Chem.* a mixture of liquids in which the boiling-point remains constant during distillation, at a given pressure, without change in composition. □□ **azeotropic** /əzéeətróppik/ *adj.* [A-[1] + Gk *zeō* boil + *tropos* turning]

azide /áyzīd/ *n. Chem.* any compound containing the radical N_3-.

Azilian /əzílliən/ *n.* & *adj. Archaeol.* ● *n.* the transitional culture between the palaeolithic and neolithic ages in Europe. ● *adj.* of or relating to this culture. [Mas d'*Azil* in the French Pyrenees, where remains of it were found]

azimuth /ázziməth/ *n.* **1** the angular distance from a north or south point of the horizon to the intersection with the horizon of a vertical circle passing through a given celestial body. **2** the horizontal angle or direction of a compass bearing. □□ **azimuthal** /-myōōthəl/ *adj.* [ME f. OF *azimut* f. Arab. *as-sumūt* f. *al* the + *sumūt* pl. of *samt* way, direction]

azine /áyzeen/ *n. Chem.* any organic compound with two or more nitrogen atoms in a six-atom ring. [AZO- + -INE[4]]

azo- /ázzō, áy-/ *prefix Chem.* containing two adjacent nitrogen atoms between carbon atoms. [F *azote* nitrogen f. Gk *azōos* without life]

azoic /əzō-ik/ *adj.* **1** having no trace of life. **2** *Geol.* (of an age etc.) having left no organic remains. [Gk *azōos* without life]

AZT /áyzedtée/ *n.* a drug intended for use against the Aids virus. [chem. name *azidothymidine*]

Aztec /áztek/ *n.* & *adj.* ● *n.* **1** a member of the native people dominant in Mexico before the Spanish conquest of the 16th century. **2** the language of the Aztecs. ● *adj.* of the Aztecs or their language (see also NAHUATL). [F *Aztèque* or Sp. *Azteca* f. Nahuatl *aztecatl* men of the north]

azuki var. of ADZUKI.

azure /ázhər, ázyər, áy-/ *n.* & *adj.* ● *n.* **1 a** a deep sky-blue colour. **b** *Heraldry* blue. **2** *poet.* the clear sky. ● *adj.* **1 a** of the colour azure. **b** *Heraldry* blue. **2** serene, untroubled. [ME f. OF *asur*, *azur*, f. med.L *azzurum*, *azolum* f. Arab. *al* the + *lāzaward* f. Pers. *lāžward* lapis lazuli]
■ *adj.* **1 a** see BLUE[1] *adj.* 1. **2** see SERENE *adj.*

azygous /ázzigəss/ *adj.* & *n.* *Anat.* ● *adj.* (of any organic structure) single, not existing in pairs. ● *n.* an organic structure occurring singly. [Gk *azugos* unyoked f. *a-* not + *zugon* yoke]

Bb

B[1] /bee/ *n.* (also **b**) (*pl.* **Bs** or **B's**) **1** the second letter of the alphabet. **2** *Mus.* the seventh note of the diatonic scale of C major. **3** the second hypothetical person or example. **4** the second highest class or category (of roads, academic marks, etc.). **5** *Algebra* (usu. **b**) the second known quantity. **6** a human blood type of the ABO system. □ **B film** a supporting film in a cinema programme.

B[2] *symb.* **1** *Chem.* the element boron. **2** *Physics* magnetic flux density.

B[3] *abbr.* (also **B.**) **1** Bachelor. **2** bel(s). **3** bishop. **4** black (pencil-lead). **5** Blessed.

b *symb. Physics* barn.

b. *abbr.* **1** born. **2** *Cricket* **a** bowled by. **b** bye. **3** billion.

BA *abbr.* **1** Bachelor of Arts. **2** British Academy. **3** British Airways. **4** British Association.

Ba *symb. Chem.* the element barium.

BAA *abbr.* British Airports Authority.

baa /baa/ *v.* & *n.* ● *v.intr.* (**baas, baaed** or **baa'd**) (esp. of a sheep) bleat. ● *n.* (*pl.* **baas**) the cry of a sheep or lamb. [imit.]

baas /baass/ *n. S.Afr.* boss, master (often as a form of address). [Du.: cf. BOSS[1]]

baasskap /ba̋askaap/ *n. S.Afr.* domination, esp. of non-Whites by Whites. [Afrik. f. *baas* master + *-skap* condition]

baba /ba̋abaa/ *n.* (in full **rum baba**) a small rich sponge cake, usu. soaked in rum-flavoured syrup. [F f. Pol.]

babacoote /ba̋abəko͞ot/ *n.* = INDRI. [Malagasy *babakoto*]

Babbitt[1] /bábbit/ *n.* **1** (in full **Babbitt metal**) any of a group of soft alloys of tin, antimony, copper, and usu. lead, used for lining bearings etc., to diminish friction. **2** (**babbitt**) a bearing-lining made of this. [I. *Babbitt*, Amer. inventor d. 1862]

Babbitt[2] /bábbit/ *n.* a materialistic, complacent businessman. □□ **Babbittry** *n.* [George *Babbitt*, a character in the novel *Babbitt* (1922) by S. Lewis]
■ see PHILISTINE 2.

babble /bább'l/ *v.* & *n.* ● *v.* **1** *intr.* **a** talk in an inarticulate or incoherent manner. **b** chatter excessively or irrelevantly. **c** (of a stream etc.) murmur, trickle. **2** *tr.* repeat foolishly; divulge through chatter. ● *n.* **1 a** incoherent speech. **b** foolish, idle, or childish talk. **2** the murmur of voices, water, etc. **3** *Telephony* background disturbance caused by interference from conversations on other lines. □□ **babblement** *n.* [ME f. MLG *babbelen*, or imit.]
■ *v.* **1 a, b** burble, gabble, gurgle, jabber, gibber, blab, blabber; prattle, twaddle, chatter, prate, blather, tattle, tittle-tattle, gossip, clack, *colloq.* gab, natter, witter, *colloq. or dial.* yammer, yatter (on), *esp. Austral. colloq.* mag, *Brit. colloq.* rabbit (on), *sl. derog.* yack. **c** murmur, trickle, whisper, gurgle, purl, burble, bubble. **2** divulge, tell, disclose, broadcast, repeat, reveal, blurt (out), burst out with, give away, blab, let out, *colloq.* let on. ● *n.* **1 a** gibberish, gibber, jabber, gabble. **b** twaddle, prattle, chatter, burble, prate, blather, tattle, tittle-tattle, gossip, *bavardage*, *colloq.* chit-chat, gab, natter, *colloq. or dial.* yatter, *sl. derog.* yack; nonsense, drivel, rubbish; baby-talk. **2** murmur, gurgle, whisper, purl, *literary* susurration; buzz.

babbler /bábblər/ *n.* **1** a chatterer. **2** a person who reveals secrets. **3** any of a large group of passerine birds with loud chattering voices.

babe /bayb/ *n.* **1** *literary* a baby. **2** an innocent or helpless person (*babes and sucklings*; *babes in the wood*). **3** *US sl.* a young woman (often as a form of address). [ME: imit. of child's *ba*, *ba*]
■ **1** see BABY *n.* 1.

babel /báyb'l/ *n.* **1** a confused noise, esp. of voices. **2** a noisy assembly. **3** a scene of confusion. □ **Tower of Babel** a visionary or unrealistic plan. [ME f. Heb. *Bāḇel* Babylon f. Akkad. *bab ili* gate of god (with ref. to the biblical account of the tower that was built to reach heaven but ended in chaos when Jehovah confused the builders' speech: see Gen. 11)]
■ **1** see DIN *n.*

Babis /bábbiss/ *n.* a member of a Persian eclectic sect founded in 1844 whose doctrine includes Muslim, Christian, Jewish, and Zoroastrian elements. □□ **Babism** *n.* [Pers. *Bab*-ed-Din, gate (= intermediary) of the Faith]

baboon /bəbo͞on/ *n.* **1** any of various large Old World monkeys of the genus *Papio*, having a long doglike snout, large teeth, and naked callosities on the buttocks. **2** an ugly or uncouth person. [ME f. OF *babuin* or med.L *babewynus*, of unkn. orig.]

babu /ba̋abo͞o/ *n.* (also **baboo**) *Ind.* **1** a title of respect, esp. to Hindus. **2** *derog.* formerly, an English-writing Indian clerk. [Hindi *bābū*]

babushka /bəbo͞oshkə/ *n.* a headscarf tied under the chin. [Russ., = grandmother]

baby /báybi/ *n.* & *v.* ● *n.* (*pl.* **-ies**) **1** a very young child or infant, esp. one not yet able to walk. **2** an unduly childish person (*is a baby about injections*). **3** the youngest member of a family, team, etc. **4** (often *attrib.*) **a** a young or newly born animal. **b** a thing that is small of its kind (*baby car*; *baby rose*). **5** *sl.* a young woman; a sweetheart (often as a form of address). **6** *sl.* a person or thing regarded with affection or familiarity. **7** one's own responsibility, invention, concern, achievement, etc., regarded in a personal way. ● *v.tr.* (**-ies, -ied**) **1** treat like a baby. **2** pamper. □ **baby boom** *colloq.* a temporary marked increase in the birthrate. **baby boomer** a person born during a baby boom, esp. after the war of 1939–45. **baby-bouncer** *Brit.* a frame supported by elastic or springs, into which a child is harnessed to exercise its limbs. **Baby Buggy** (*pl.* **-ies**) *Brit. propr.* a kind of child's collapsible pushchair. **baby carriage** *US* a pram. **baby grand** the smallest size of grand piano. **baby-snatcher** *colloq.* **1** a person who kidnaps babies. **2** = *cradle-snatcher*. **baby-talk** childish talk used by or to young children. **baby-walker** a wheeled frame in which a baby learns to walk. **carry** (or **hold**) **the baby** bear unwelcome responsibility. **throw away the baby with the bath-water** reject the essential with the inessential. □□ **babyhood** *n.* [ME, formed as BABE, -Y[2]]
■ *n.* **1** infant, neonate, child, toddler, tot, *Sc.* & *N.Engl.* bairn, *colloq.* new arrival, *literary* babe (in arms), *sl.* sprog. **3** youngest, smallest, littlest. **5** see DARLING *n.* 1. ● *v.* cosset, coddle, pamper, mollycoddle, indulge, spoil,

pet, dandle. □ **baby-talk** see BABBLE *n.* 1b. □□ **babyhood** infancy, early childhood, early *or* initial stage(s) *or* days.

Babygro /báybigrō/ *n.* (*pl.* **-os**) *propr.* a kind of all-in-one stretch garment for babies. [BABY + GROW]

babyish /báybi-ish/ *adj.* **1** childish, simple. **2** immature. □□ **babyishly** *adv.* **babyishness** *n.*

■ **2** see CHILDISH 2.

Babylonian /bábbilṓniən/ *n.* & *adj.* ● *n.* an inhabitant of Babylon, an ancient city and kingdom in Mesopotamia. ● *adj.* of or relating to Babylon. [L *Babylonius* f. Gk *Babulonios* f. *Babulon* f. Heb. *Bābel*]

babysit /báybisit/ *v.intr.* (**-sitting**; *past* and *past part.* **-sat**) look after a child or children while the parents are out. □□ **babysitter** *n.*

■ see MIND *v.* 3. □□ **babysitter** see MINDER 1.

Bacardi /bəkaárdi/ *n.* (*pl.* **Bacardis**) *propr.* a West Indian rum produced orig. in Cuba. [name of the company producing it]

baccalaureate /bákkəláwriət/ *n.* **1** the university degree of bachelor. **2** an examination intended to qualify successful candidates for higher education. [F *baccalauréat* or med.L *baccalaureatus* f. *baccalaureus* bachelor]

baccarat /bákkəraa/ *n.* a gambling card-game played by punters in turn against the banker. [F]

baccate /bákkayt/ *adj. Bot.* **1** bearing berries. **2** of or like a berry. [L *baccatus* berried f. *bacca* berry]

bacchanal /bákkən'l/ *n.* & *adj.* ● *n.* **1** a wild and drunken revelry. **2** a drunken reveller. **3** a priest, worshipper, or follower of Bacchus. ● *adj.* **1** of or like Bacchus, the Greek or Roman god of wine, or his rites. **2** riotous, roistering. [L *bacchanalis* f. *Bacchus* god of wine f. Gk *Bakkhos*]

■ *n.* **1** see REVEL *n.*

Bacchanalia /bákkənáyliə/ *n.pl.* **1** the Roman festival of Bacchus. **2** (**bacchanalia**) a drunken revelry. □□ **Bacchanalian** *adj.* & *n.* [L, neut. pl. of *bacchanalis*: see BACCHANAL]

■ **2** see ORGY 1.

bacchant /bákkənt/ *n.* & *adj.* ● *n.* (*pl.* **bacchants** or **bacchantes** /bəkánteez/; *fem.* **bacchante** /bəkánti/) **1** a priest, worshipper, or follower of Bacchus. **2** a drunken reveller. ● *adj.* **1** of or like Bacchus or his rites. **2** riotous, roistering. □□ **bacchantic** /bəkántik/ *adj.* [F *bacchante* f. L *bacchari* celebrate Bacchanal rites]

Bacchic /bákkik/ *adj.* = BACCHANAL *adj.* [L *bacchicus* f. Gk *bakkhikos* of Bacchus]

baccy /bákki/ *n.* (*pl.* **-ies**) *Brit. colloq.* tobacco. [abbr.]

bachelor /báchələr/ *n.* **1** an unmarried man. **2** a man or woman who has taken the degree of Bachelor of Arts or Science etc. **3** *hist.* a young knight serving under another's banner. □ **bachelor girl** an independent unmarried young woman. **bachelor's buttons** any of various button-like flowers, esp. the double buttercup. □□ **bachelorhood** *n.* **bachelorship** *n.* [ME & OF *bacheler* aspirant to knighthood, of uncert. orig.]

■ **2** graduate. □ **bachelor girl** see MISS[2].

bacillary /bəsílləri/ *adj.* relating to or caused by bacilli.

bacilliform /bəsílliform/ *adj.* rod-shaped.

bacillus /bəsílləs/ *n.* (*pl.* **bacilli** /-lī/) **1** any rod-shaped bacterium. **2** (usu. in *pl.*) any pathogenic bacterium. [LL, dimin. of L *baculus* stick]

back /bak/ *n.*, *adv.*, *v.*, & *adj.* ● *n.* **1 a** the rear surface of the human body from the shoulders to the hips. **b** the corresponding upper surface of an animal's body. **c** the spine (*fell and broke his back*). **d** the keel of a ship. **2 a** any surface regarded as corresponding to the human back, e.g. of the head or hand, or of a chair. **b** the part of a garment that covers the back. **3 a** the less active or visible or important part of something functional, e.g. of a knife or a piece of paper (*write it on the back*). **b** the side or part normally away from the spectator or the direction of motion or attention, e.g. of a car, house, or room (*stood at the back*). **4 a** a defensive player in field games. **b** this position. **5** (**the Backs**) the grounds of Cambridge colleges which back on to the River Cam. ● *adv.* **1** to the rear; away from what is considered to be the front (*go back a bit*; *ran off without looking back*). **2 a** in or into an earlier or normal position or condition (*came back late*; *went back home*; *ran back to the car*; *put it back on the shelf*). **b** in return (*pay back*). **3** in or into the past (*back in June*; *three years back*). **4** at a distance (*stand back from the road*). **5** in check (*hold him back*). **6** (foll. by *of*) *US* behind (*was back of the house*). ● *v.* **1** *tr.* **a** help with moral or financial support. **b** bet on the success of (a horse etc.). **2** *tr.* & *intr.* move, or cause (a vehicle etc.) to move, backwards. **3** *tr.* **a** put or serve as a back, background, or support to. **b** *Mus.* accompany. **4** *tr.* lie at the back of (*a beach backed by steep cliffs*). **5** *intr.* (of the wind) move round in an anticlockwise direction. ● *adj.* **1** situated behind, esp. as remote or subsidiary (*backstreet*; *back teeth*; *back entrance*). **2** of or relating to the past; not current (*back pay*; *back issue*). **3** reversed (*back flow*). □ **at a person's back** in pursuit or support. **at the back of one's mind** remembered but not consciously thought of. **back and forth** to and fro. **back bench** a back-bencher's seat in the House of Commons. **back-bencher** a member of Parliament not holding a senior office. **back-boiler** *Brit.* a boiler behind and integral with a domestic fire. **back-breaking** (esp. of manual work) extremely hard. **back country** esp. *Austral.* & *NZ* an area away from settled districts. **back-crawl** = BACKSTROKE. **back-cross** *Biol.* **1** cross a hybrid with one of its parents. **2** an instance or the product of this. **back door** a secret or ingenious means of gaining an objective. **back-door** *adj.* (of an activity) clandestine, underhand (*back-door deal*). **back down** withdraw one's claim or point of view etc.; concede defeat in an argument etc. **back-down** *n.* an instance of backing down. **back-fill** refill an excavated hole with the material dug out of it. **back-formation 1** the formation of a word from its seeming derivative (e.g. *laze* from *lazy*). **2** a word formed in this way. **back number 1** an issue of a periodical earlier than the current one. **2** *sl.* an out-of-date person or thing. **the back of beyond** a very remote or inaccessible place. **back off 1** draw back, retreat. **2** abandon one's intention, stand, etc. **back on to** have its back adjacent to (*the house backs on to a field*). **back out** (often foll. by *of*) withdraw from a commitment. **back passage** *colloq.* the rectum. **back-pedal** (**-pedalled, -pedalling**; *US* **-pedaled, -pedaling**) **1** pedal backwards on a bicycle etc. **2** reverse one's previous action or opinion. **back-projection** the projection of a picture from behind a translucent screen for viewing or filming. **back room** (often (with hyphen) *attrib.*) a place where secret work is done. **back-scattering** the scattering of radiation in a reverse direction. **back seat** an inferior position or status. **back-seat driver** a person who is eager to advise without responsibility (orig. of a passenger in a car etc.). **back slang** slang using words spelt backwards (e.g. *yob*). **back-stop** = LONGSTOP. **back talk** *US* = BACKCHAT. **back to back** with backs adjacent and opposite each other (*we stood back to back*). **back-to-back** *adj.* esp. *Brit.* (of houses) with a party wall at the rear. **back to front 1** with the back at the front and the front at the back. **2** in disorder. **back-to-nature** (usu. *attrib.*) applied to a movement or enthusiast for the reversion to a simpler way of life. **back up 1** give (esp. moral) support to. **2** *Computing* make a spare copy of (data, a disk, etc.). **3** (of running water) accumulate behind an obstruction. **4** reverse (a vehicle) into a desired position. **5** *US* form a queue of vehicles etc., esp. in congested traffic. **back water** reverse a boat's forward motion using oars. **get** (or **put**) **a person's back up** annoy or anger a person. **get off a person's back** stop troubling a person. **go back on** fail to honour (a promise or commitment). **know like the back of one's hand** be entirely familiar with. **on one's back** injured or ill in bed. **on the back burner** see BURNER. **put one's back into** approach (a task etc.) with vigour. **see the back of** see SEE[1]. **turn one's back on 1** abandon. **2** disregard, ignore. **with one's back to** (or **up against**) **the wall** in a desperate situation; hard-pressed. □□ **backer** *n.* (in sense 1 of *v.*). **backless** *adj.* [OE *bæc* f. Gmc]

■ *n.* **1, 2** rear; spine. **3 a** reverse, rear, other *or* opposite side, wrong side, verso, underside, *colloq.* flip side. **b** rear, far side *or* corner. **4** defender, full-back, half-back, *Football* sweeper, stopper, *Rugby Football* three-quarter (back), *colloq.* half. ● *adv.* **1** to *or* toward(s) the rear, rearward(s), backward(s), behind; away, off. **2 a** again, re-. **b** in return *or* repayment *or* requital *or* retaliation; again. **3** in the past, ago, in time(s) past, earlier, before. **4** away, at a distance, at arm's length; aside, to one side. **5** in check, under control. **6** (*back of*) behind, on *or* round the other side of, at the rear of. ● *v.* **1 a** back up, support, stand behind, encourage, help, second, side with, aid, abet, assist; uphold, endorse, promote; sponsor, subsidize, fund, underwrite, finance, *US colloq.* bankroll, stake. **b** invest in, wager *or* bet on, lay *or* stake *or* place a bet on. **2** back up, reverse, go *or* move in reverse, go *or* move backwards. **3 b** accompany, provide the backing *or* harmony *or* accompaniment for. ● *adj.* **1** rear, side; service, servants'. **2** in arrears, overdue, past due, late; behindhand; old, past, out-of-date, out-dated. **3** reversed, backward. □ **at a person's back** behind, following, pursuing, in (hot) pursuit, chasing, *US* in back of; supporting, seconding. **back and forth** see AROUND *adv.* 2. **back-breaking** see *exhausting* (EXHAUST). **back country** bush, backwater, interior, wilds, back of beyond, backwoods, hinterland, *esp. Austral.* outback, backblocks, *S.Afr.* backveld, platteland, *colloq.* middle of nowhere, sticks, *Austral.* & *NZ sl.* woop woop, *US sl.* boondocks. **back-door** covert, clandestine, secret, hidden, backstage, secretive, private, hugger-mugger; underhand, furtive, shady, sneaky, deceitful, conspiratorial, cloak-and-dagger, dishonest, under-the-counter. **back down** see *give in*, WITHDRAW 2. **back-down** see SURRENDER *n.* **back number 2** see FOGY. **the back of beyond** see *back country* above. **back off 1** see RETREAT *v.* 1a. **2** see *give in.* **back out** see RENEGE 1a. **back passage** rectum, anus. **back-pedal** back up, backtrack, go backwards, *Naut.* make sternway. **back seat** (*take a back seat*) play second fiddle. **back-stop** longstop, last resort, *pis aller*, sheet anchor, last port of call. **back talk** see *impudence* (IMPUDENT). **back to front 1** inside out, wrong way round, wrong side out. **2** see DISORDERLY 1. **back up 1** see BACK *v.* 1a above. **4** see BACK *v.* 2 above. **get a person's back up** get on a person's nerves, *colloq.* get in a person's hair, *Brit. colloq.* get on a person's wick, *sl.* get up a person's nose; see also ANNOY 1. **go back on** renege on, back out of, back down from *or* on, backtrack on, retract, take back, default on, fail to honour, break, repudiate, forsake; *colloq.* chicken out of. **know like the back of one's hand** know backwards *or* inside out. **on one's back** see ILL *adj.* 1. **put one's back into** put (some *or* a lot of) elbow grease into, put effort into, throw oneself into. **turn one's back on 1** abandon, forsake, reject, repudiate, cast off, disown, deny. **2** disregard, overlook; see also IGNORE 2. **with one's back to** (or **up against**) **the wall** hard-pressed, struggling (against odds), without hope, with little *or* no hope, helpless, in dire straits, in (serious) trouble. □□ **backer** investor, benefactor, benefactress, underwriter, patron, advocate, promoter, sponsor, *sl.* angel; better, punter; see also SUPPORTER.

backache /bákkayk/ *n.* a (usu. prolonged) pain in one's back.

backbite /bákbīt/ *v.tr.* slander; speak badly of. □□ **backbiter** *n.*

■ see DISPARAGE 1.

backblocks /bákbloks/ *n.pl. Austral.* & *NZ* land in the remote and sparsely inhabited interior. □□ **backblocker** *n.*

■ see *back country.*

backboard /bákbord/ *n.* **1** a board worn to support or straighten the back. **2** a board placed at or forming the back of anything.

backbone /bákbōn/ *n.* **1** the spine. **2** the main support of a structure. **3** firmness of character. **4** *US* the spine of a book.

■ **1** spine, spinal column, vertebrae. **2** mainstay, chief *or* main support, buttress, pillar. **3** resoluteness, sturdiness, firmness, determination, strength (of character), mettle, purposefulness, resolution, perseverance, tenacity, tenaciousness, courage, fortitude, resolve, will, will-power, stability, stamina, staying power, *colloq.* guts, grit.

backchat /bákchat/ *n. Brit. colloq.* the practice of replying rudely or impudently.

■ see *impudence* (IMPUDENT).

backcloth /bák-kloth/ *n. Brit. Theatr.* a painted cloth at the back of the stage as a main part of the scenery.

■ see BACKDROP.

backcomb /bák-kōm/ *v.tr.* comb (the hair) towards the scalp to make it look thicker.

backdate /bákdáyt/ *v.tr.* **1** put an earlier date to (an agreement etc.) than the actual one. **2** make retrospectively valid.

backdrop /bákdrop/ *n.* = BACKCLOTH.

backfire *v.* & *n.* ● *v.intr.* /bákfír/ **1** undergo a mistimed explosion in the cylinder or exhaust of an internal-combustion engine. **2** (of a plan etc.) rebound adversely on the originator; have the opposite effect to what was intended. ● *n.* /bákfīr/ an instance of backfiring.

■ *v.* **2** see BOOMERANG *v.* ● *n.* see REPORT *n.* 6.

backgammon /bákgámmən/ *n.* **1** a game for two played on a board with pieces moved according to throws of the dice. **2** the most complete form of win in this. [BACK + GAMMON²]

background /bákgrownd/ *n.* **1** part of a scene, picture, or description, that serves as a setting to the chief figures or objects and foreground. **2** an inconspicuous or obscure position (*kept in the background*). **3** a person's education, knowledge, or social circumstances. **4** explanatory or contributory information or circumstances. **5** *Physics* low-intensity ambient radiation from radioisotopes present in the natural environment. **6** *Electronics* unwanted signals, such as noise in the reception or recording of sound. □ **background music** music intended as an unobtrusive accompaniment to some activity, or to provide atmosphere in a film etc.

■ **1** backing, surroundings, surround; field, distance, horizon, obscurity. **2** (*in the background*) inconspicuous, unnoticed, unobtrusive, behind the scenes, out of the limelight *or* spotlight, unseen, out of *or* away from the public eye, backstage; see also *hidden* (HIDE). **3** history, experience, qualifications, credentials, grounding, training, knowledge; circumstances, breeding, upbringing, past, life, story, family; curriculum vitae, c.v. □ **background music** incidental music, *usu. derog.* muzak, wallpaper music.

backhand /bák-hand/ *n. Tennis* etc. **1** a stroke played with the back of the hand turned towards the opponent. **2** (*attrib.*) of or made with a backhand (*backhand volley*).

■ **1** backhander. **2** (*attrib.*) backhanded.

backhanded /bák-hándid/ *adj.* **1** (of a blow etc.) delivered with the back of the hand, or in a direction opposite to the usual one. **2** indirect; ambiguous (*a backhanded compliment*). **3** = BACKHAND *attrib.*

backhander /bák-hándər/ *n.* **1 a** a backhand stroke. **b** a backhanded blow. **2** *colloq.* an indirect attack. **3** *Brit. sl.* a bribe.

backing /bákking/ *n.* **1 a** support. **b** a body of supporters. **c** material used to form a back or support. **2** musical accompaniment, esp. to a singer.

■ **1 a** support, help, aid, assistance, succour, backup, reinforcement; approval, endorsement, patronage, sponsorship, promotion, financing; grant, contribution, subsidy, investment, money, funds, funding. **b** backers, supporters, helpers, campaigners, patrons, sponsors, benefactors, investors, financiers. **c** lining, interlining, underlay, reinforcement, support, mount, mounting, background, setting, coating. **2** accompaniment, harmony.

backlash /báklash/ *n.* **1** an excessive or marked adverse reaction. **2 a** a sudden recoil or reaction between parts of a mechanism. **b** excessive play between such parts.
■ **1** reaction, retaliation, retort, reprisal, repercussion, counteraction, rebound, *sl.* comeback; revenge, retribution. **2** recoil, counteraction, rebound, backfire, boomerang, *colloq.* kickback.

backlist /báklist/ *n.* a publisher's list of books published before the current season and still in print.

backlit /báklit/ *adj.* (esp. in photography) illuminated from behind.

backlog /báklog/ *n.* **1** arrears of uncompleted work etc. **2** a reserve; reserves (*a backlog of goodwill*).

backmarker /bákmaarkər/ *n. Brit.* a competitor who has the least favourable handicap in a race etc.

backmost /bákmōst/ *adj.* furthest back.

backpack /bákpak/ *n.* & *v.* ● *n.* a rucksack. ● *v.intr.* travel or hike with a backpack. □□ **backpacker** *n.*
■ *n.* see PACK[1] *n.* 1.

backrest /bákrest/ *n.* a support for the back.

backscratcher /bákskrachər/ *n.* **1** a rod terminating in a clawed hand for scratching one's own back. **2** a person who performs mutual services with another for gain.

backsheesh var. of BAKSHEESH.

backside /báksīd/ *n. colloq.* the buttocks.
■ see BUTTOCK.

backsight /báksīt/ *n.* **1** the sight of a rifle etc. that is nearer the stock. **2** *Surveying* a sight or reading taken backwards or towards the point of starting.

backslapping /bákslapping/ *adj.* vigorously hearty.

backslash /bákslash/ *n.* a backward-sloping diagonal line; a reverse solidus (\).

backslide /bákslīd/ *v.intr.* (*past* **-slid**; *past part.* **-slid** or **-slidden**) relapse into bad ways or error. □□ **backslider** *n.*
■ see RELAPSE *v.*

backspace /bákspayss/ *v.intr.* move a typewriter carriage etc. back one or more spaces.

backspin /bákspin/ *n.* a backward spin imparted to a ball causing it to fly off at an angle on hitting a surface.

backstage /bákstáyj/ *adv.* & *adj.* ● *adv.* **1** *Theatr.* out of view of the audience, esp. in the wings or dressing-rooms. **2** not known to the public. ● *adj.* that is backstage; concealed.
■ *adv.* see *in the background* (BACKGROUND 2). ● *adj.* see *back-door.*

backstairs /bákstairz/ *n.pl.* **1** stairs at the back or side of a building. **2** (also **backstair**) (*attrib.*) denoting underhand or clandestine activity.
■ **2** (*attrib.*) see STEALTHY.

backstay /bákstay/ *n.* a rope etc. leading downwards and aft from the top of a mast.
■ see STAY[2] *n.*

backstitch /bákstich/ *n.* & *v.* ● *n.* sewing with overlapping stitches. ● *v.tr.* & *intr.* sew using backstitch.

backstreet /bákstreet/ *n.* **1** a street in a quiet part of a town, away from the main streets. **2** (*attrib.*) denoting illicit or illegal activity (*a backstreet abortion*).

backstroke /bákstrōk/ *n.* a swimming stroke performed on the back with the arms lifted alternately out of the water in a backward circular motion and the legs extended in a kicking action.
■ back-crawl.

backtrack /báktrak/ *v.intr.* **1** retrace one's steps. **2** reverse one's previous action or opinion.
■ **1** see REVERSE 3.

backup /bákkup/ *n.* **1** moral or technical support (*called for extra backup*). **2** a reserve. **3** *Computing* (often *attrib.*) **a** the procedure for making security copies of data (*backup facilities*). **b** the copy itself (*made a backup*). **4** *US* a queue of vehicles etc., esp. in congested traffic. □ **backup light** *US* a reversing light.
■ **1** see SUPPORT *n.* 1. **2** see RESERVE 6.

backveld /bákvelt/ *n. S.Afr.* remote country districts, esp. those strongly conservative. □□ **backvelder** *n.*
■ see *back country*.

backward /bákwərd/ *adv.* & *adj.* ● *adv.* = BACKWARDS. ¶ *Backwards* is now more common, esp. in literal senses. ● *adj.* **1** directed to the rear or starting-point (*a backward look*). **2** reversed. **3 a** mentally retarded or slow. **b** slow to progress; late. **4** reluctant, shy, unassertive. □□ **backwardness** *n.* [earlier *abackward*, assoc. with BACK]
■ *adv.* see BACKWARDS 2. ● *adj.* **1** rearward, to the rear, behind; to the past. **2** reversed, reverse, contrariwise, in the opposite way *or* direction; retrograde, retrogressive, regressive. **3 a** (mentally) retarded, *US* retardate; slow, dull, stupid, slow-witted, simple, simple-minded, soft-headed, feeble-minded, thick-witted, *colloq.* dim, dim-witted, *esp. Brit. colloq.* gormless, *US colloq.* dumb. **b** slow, late, behindhand, retarded. **4** bashful, shy, reticent, diffident, retiring, unassertive, coy, timid, unwilling, loath, chary, reluctant, averse.

backwardation /bákwərdáysh'n/ *n.* esp. *Brit. Stock Exch.* the percentage paid by a person selling stock for the right of delaying the delivery of it (cf. CONTANGO).

backwards /bákwərdz/ *adv.* **1** away from one's front (*lean backwards; look backwards*). **2 a** with the back foremost (*walk backwards*). **b** in reverse of the usual way (*count backwards; spell backwards*). **3 a** into a worse state (*new policies are taking us backwards*). **b** into the past (*looked backwards over the years*). **c** (of a thing's motion) back towards the starting-point (*rolled backwards*). □ **backwards and forwards** in both directions alternately; to and fro. **bend** (or **fall** or **lean**) **over backwards** (often foll. by *to* + infin.) *colloq.* make every effort, esp. to be fair or helpful. **know backwards** be entirely familiar with.
■ **1** see BACK *adv.* 1. **2** rearward(s), in reverse, regressively, retrogressively, backward; in the wrong direction *or* way; withershins, against the sun, anticlockwise, *US* counter-clockwise; back to front. **3 a** (*go backwards*) see DETERIORATE. **b** into the past, into an earlier time, back. **c** back. □ **backwards and forwards** back and forth, to and fro, up and down; see also AROUND *adv.* 2. **bend over backwards** do one's utmost *or* best, make every effort. **know backwards** know inside out, know like the back of one's hand.

backwash /bákwosh/ *n.* **1 a** receding waves created by the motion of a ship etc. **b** a backward current of air created by a moving aircraft. **2** repercussions.
■ **1** see WAKE[2] 1. **2** see UPSHOT.

backwater /bákwawtər/ *n.* **1** a place or condition remote from the centre of activity or thought. **2** stagnant water fed from a stream.

backwoods /bákwŏŏdz/ *n.pl.* **1** remote uncleared forest land. **2** any remote or sparsely inhabited region.
■ **2** see STICK[1] 11.

backwoodsman /bákwŏŏdzmən/ *n.* (*pl.* **-men**) **1** an inhabitant of backwoods. **2** an uncouth person.
■ **1** see BOOR 3.

backyard /bakyaárd/ *n.* a yard at the back of a house etc. □ **in one's own backyard** *colloq.* near at hand.

baclava var. of BAKLAVA.

bacon /báykən/ *n.* cured meat from the back or sides of a pig. □ **bring home the bacon** *colloq.* **1** succeed in one's undertaking. **2** supply material provision or support. [ME f. OF f. Frank. *bako* = OHG *bahho* ham, flitch]

Baconian /baykṓniən/ *adj.* & *n.* ● *adj.* of or relating to the English philosopher Sir Francis Bacon (d. 1626), or to his inductive method of reasoning and philosophy. ● *n.* **1** a supporter of the view that Bacon was the author of Shakespeare's plays. **2** a follower of Bacon.

bacteria *pl.* of BACTERIUM.

bactericide /baktéérisīd/ *n.* a substance capable of destroying bacteria. ▫▫ **bactericidal** /-sīd'l/ *adj.*

bacteriology /bákteeriólləji/ *n.* the study of bacteria. ▫▫ **bacteriological** /-riəlójik'l/ *adj.* **bacteriologically** /-riəlójikəli/ *adv.* **bacteriologist** *n.*

bacteriolysis /bakteeriólississ/ *n.* the rupture of bacterial cells.

bacteriolytic /bakteeriəlíttik/ *adj.* capable of lysing bacteria.

bacteriophage /bakteeriōfayj, -faazh/ *n.* a virus parasitic on a bacterium, by infecting it and reproducing inside it. [BACTERIUM + Gk *phagein* eat]

bacteriostasis /bakteeriōstáysiss/ *n.* the inhibition of the growth of bacteria without destroying them. ▫▫ **bacteriostatic** /-státtik/ *adj.*

bacterium /bakteeriəm/ *n.* (*pl.* **bacteria** /-riə/) a member of a large group of unicellular micro-organisms lacking organelles and an organized nucleus, some of which can cause disease. ▫▫ **bacterial** *adj.* [mod.L f. Gk *baktērion* dimin. of *baktron* stick]

■ see MICROBE.

Bactrian /báktriən/ *adj.* of or relating to Bactria in central Asia. ▫ **Bactrian camel** a camel, *Camelus bactrianus*, native to central Asia, with two humps. [L *Bactrianus* f. Gk *Baktrianos*]

bad /bad/ *adj.*, *n.*, & *adv.* ● *adj.* (**worse** /wurss/; **worst**) /wurst/ **1** inferior, inadequate, defective (*bad work*; *a bad driver*; *bad light*). **2 a** unpleasant, unwelcome (*bad weather*; *bad news*). **b** unsatisfactory, unfortunate (*a bad business*). **3** harmful (*is bad for you*). **4 a** (of food) decayed, putrid. **b** polluted (*bad air*). **5** *colloq.* ill, injured (*am feeling bad today*; *a bad leg*). **6** *colloq.* regretful, guilty, ashamed (*feels bad about it*). **7** (of an unwelcome thing) serious, severe (*a bad headache*; *a bad mistake*). **8 a** morally wicked or offensive (*a bad man*; *bad language*). **b** naughty; badly behaved (*a bad child*). **9** worthless; not valid (*a bad cheque*). **10** (**badder**, **baddest**) esp. *US sl.* good, excellent. ● *n.* **1 a** ill fortune (*take the bad with the good*). **b** ruin; a degenerate condition (*go to the bad*). **2** the debit side of an account (*£500 to the bad*). **3** (as *pl.*; prec. by *the*) bad or wicked people. ● *adv. US colloq.* badly (*took it bad*). ▫ **bad blood** ill feeling. **bad books** see BOOK. **bad breath** unpleasant-smelling breath. **bad debt** a debt that is not recoverable. **bad egg** see EGG[1]. **bad faith** see FAITH. **bad form** see FORM. **a bad job** *colloq.* an unfortunate state of affairs. **bad-mannered** having bad manners; rude. **bad mouth** *US* malicious gossip or criticism. **bad-mouth** *v.tr. US* subject to malicious gossip or criticism. **bad news** *colloq.* an unpleasant or troublesome person or thing. **from bad to worse** into an even worse state. **in a bad way** ill; in trouble (*looked in a bad way*). **not** (or **not so**) **bad** *colloq.* fairly good. **too bad** *colloq.* (of circumstances etc.) regrettable but now beyond retrieval. ▫▫ **baddish** *adj.* **badness** *n.* [ME, perh. f. OE *bæddel* hermaphrodite, womanish man: for loss of *l* cf. MUCH, WENCH]

■ *adj.* **1** poor, inferior, defective, worthless, substandard, shoddy, second-rate, second-class, not up to par *or* scratch *or* standard, low-quality, unsatisfactory, disappointing, inadequate, indifferent, insufficient, wretched, *colloq.* not up to snuff, lousy, crummy, *sl.* rotten, naff, *Brit. sl.* grotty, *US sl.* bum; see also AWFUL 1a, b. **2 a** unpleasant, unwelcome, unwanted, offensive, disagreeable, inclement, unfavourable, adverse, undesirable, *colloq.* lousy, *sl.* rotten; see also AWFUL 1a, b. **b** unsatisfactory; unfavourable, unlucky, untoward, unpropitious, unfortunate, inauspicious, inopportune; troubled, sad, wretched, unhappy, grim, distressing, lamentable, regrettable, discouraging, unpleasant. **3** injurious, dangerous, harmful, hurtful, detrimental, pernicious, deleterious, ruinous, inimical; unhealthful, unhealthy, noxious, mephitic, poisonous, baleful, destructive, evil, malignant, pestilent, *archaic* miasmic, miasmatic, *literary* nocuous, noisome. **4 a** off, spoilt, mouldy, stale, rotten, decayed, putrefied, putrid, addled, contaminated, tainted. **b** corrupt, polluted, vitiated, debased, base, vile, foul, rotten. **5** injured, wounded, diseased, lame, game, *Brit. sl.* gammy; see also ILL *adj.* 1. **6** sorry, regretful, apologetic, guilty, ashamed, conscience-stricken, remorseful, contrite; rueful, sad, unhappy, depressed, upset, distressed, dejected, downhearted, disconsolate, melancholy, inconsolable. **7** distressing, severe, grave, serious, critical, terrible, awful, dreadful, dire, dangerous. **8 a** evil, ill, immoral, wicked, vicious, vile, sinful, depraved, awful, villainous, corrupt, amoral, criminal, wrong, unspeakable; see also OFFENSIVE *adj.* 1. **b** naughty, ill-behaved, badly behaved, disobedient, unruly, wild, mischievous, rebellious, recalcitrant, *Brit.* unbiddable. **9** see INVALID[2]. **10** see EXCELLENT. ● *adv.* see BADLY. ▫ **bad blood** see *ill will*. **bad-mouth** see RUBBISH *v.* **in a bad way** see ILL *adj.* 1, *in trouble* 1 (TROUBLE). **not bad** see OK[1] *adj.* **too bad** see REGRETTABLE. ▫▫ **badness** see EVIL *n.* 2, *misbehaviour* (MISBEHAVE).

baddy /báddi/ *n.* (*pl.* **-ies**) *colloq.* a villain or criminal, esp. in a story, film, etc.

bade see BID.

badge /baj/ *n.* **1** a distinctive emblem worn as a mark of office, membership, achievement, licensed employment, etc. **2** any feature or sign which reveals a characteristic condition or quality. [ME: orig. unkn.]

■ **1** see EMBLEM 1, 3.

badger /bájər/ *n.* & *v.* ● *n.* **1** an omnivorous grey-coated nocturnal mammal of the family Mustelidae with a white stripe flanked by black stripes on its head, which lives in sets. **2** a fishing-fly, brush, etc., made of its hair. ● *v.tr.* pester, harass, tease. [16th c.: perh. f. BADGE, with ref. to its white forehead mark]

■ *v.* see HARASS 1.

badinage /báddinaázh/ *n.* humorous or playful ridicule. [F f. *badiner* to joke]

■ see CHAFF *n.* 3.

badlands /bádlandz/ *n.* extensive uncultivable eroded tracts in arid areas. [transl. F *mauvaises terres*]

badly /bádli/ *adv.* (**worse** /wurss/; **worst** /wurst/) **1** in a bad manner (*works badly*). **2** *colloq.* very much (*wants it badly*). **3** severely (*was badly defeated*).

■ **1** poorly, defectively, incorrectly, shoddily, deficiently, faultily, inaccurately, erroneously, unacceptably, insufficiently, inadequately, unfavourably, unsatisfactorily, unsuccessfully, carelessly, ineptly, inartistically, amateurishly, abysmally, *colloq.* awfully, lousily, crummily, terribly; unkindly, cruelly, wickedly, harshly, severely, damagingly, critically, wretchedly, dreadfully, improperly, immorally, viciously, mischievously, naughtily, shamefully, villainously; atrociously, horribly, unspeakably, *US colloq.* bad. **2** very much, greatly, seriously, *US colloq.* bad. **3** severely, gravely, critically, grievously, seriously, dangerously.

badminton /bádmintən/ *n.* **1** a game with rackets in which a shuttlecock is played back and forth across a net. **2** a summer drink of claret, soda, and sugar. [*Badminton* in S. England]

bad-tempered /bádtémpərd/ *adj.* having a bad temper; irritable; easily annoyed. ▫▫ **bad-temperedly** *adv.*

■ see IRRITABLE 1.

Baedeker /báydikər/ *n.* any of various travel guidebooks published by the firm founded by the German Karl *Baedeker* (d. 1859).

baffle /báff'l/ *v.* & *n.* ● *v.tr.* **1** confuse or perplex (a person, one's faculties, etc.). **2 a** frustrate or hinder (plans etc.). **b** restrain or regulate the progress of (fluids, sounds, etc.). ● *n.* (also **baffle-plate**) a device used to restrain the flow of fluid, gas, etc., through an opening, often found in microphones etc. to regulate the emission of sound. ▫ **baffle-board** a device to prevent sound from spreading in different directions, esp. round a loudspeaker cone. ▫▫ **bafflement** *n.* **baffling** *adj.* **bafflingly** *adv.* [perh. rel. to F *bafouer* ridicule, OF *beffer* mock]

■ *v.* **1** see PERPLEX 1. **2** see FRUSTRATE *v.* 2.

baffler /báflər/ *n.* = BAFFLE *n.*

BAFTA /báftə/ *abbr.* British Association of Film and Television Arts.

bag /bag/ *n.* & *v.* ● *n.* **1** a receptacle of flexible material with an opening at the top. **2 a** (usu. in *pl.*) a piece of luggage (*put the bags in the boot*). **b** a woman's handbag. **3** (in *pl.*; usu. foll. by *of*) *colloq.* a large amount; plenty (*bags of time*). **4** (in *pl.*) *Brit. colloq.* trousers. **5** *sl. derog.* a woman, esp. regarded as unattractive or unpleasant. **6** an animal's sac containing poison, honey, etc. **7** an amount of game shot by a sportsman. **8** (usu. in *pl.*) baggy folds of skin under the eyes. **9** *sl.* a person's particular interest or preoccupation, esp. in a distinctive style or category of music (*his bag is Indian music*). ● *v.* (**bagged, bagging**) **1** *tr.* put in a bag. **2** *tr. colloq.* **a** secure; get hold of (*bagged the best seat*). **b** *colloq.* steal. **c** shoot (game). **d** (often in phr. **bags I**) *Brit. colloq.* claim on grounds of being the first to do so (*bagged first go*; *bags I go first*). **3 a** *intr.* hang loosely; bulge; swell. **b** *tr.* cause to do this. **4** *tr. Austral. sl.* criticize, disparage. □ **bag and baggage** with all one's belongings. **bag lady** *US* a homeless woman who carries her possessions around in shopping bags. **bag** (or **whole bag**) **of tricks** *colloq.* everything; the whole lot. **in the bag** *colloq.* achieved; as good as secured. □□ **bagful** *n.* (*pl.* **-fuls**). [ME, perh. f. ON *baggi*]

■ *n.* **1** sack, shopping bag, string bag, plastic bag, *Austral.* port, *Brit.* carrier bag, carrier, *dial.* poke, *usu. hist.* reticule. **2 a** valise, satchel, grip, suitcase, case, overnight bag, vanity case, carry-on luggage *or* bag, Gladstone bag, carpet-bag, portmanteau; briefcase, attaché case, dispatch-box, dispatch-case, *Austral.* port, *US sl.* keister; (*bags*) baggage, luggage, gear, belongings. **b** handbag, evening bag, clutch bag, shoulder-bag, wallet, *US* pocketbook, purse. **3** (*bags*) see LOT *n.* 1. **4** (*bags*) see TROUSERS. **5** crone, (old) hag, ogress, gorgon, dragon, witch, harridan, *archaic* beldam, *colloq.* battleaxe, *sl.* (old) cow, old bag, *sl. derog.* dog. **9** occupation, hobby, avocation, business, vocation, speciality, field, *métier*, department, concern, affair, passion, *esp. US* specialty, *colloq.* lookout, thing, cup of tea. ● *v.* **2 a** see SECURE *v.* 3. **b** see STEAL *v.* 1. **c** kill, shoot, flight, gun down, pick off, *colloq.* blast, *sl.* plug; catch, trap, ensnare, snare, entrap, capture, land. **d** claim, lay claim to. **3** see SWELL *v.* 3. **4** see CRITICIZE 1. □ **whole bag of tricks** see EVERYTHING 1.

bagarre /baagaar/ *n.* a scuffle or brawl. [F]

bagasse /bəgáss/ *n.* the dry pulpy residue left after the extraction of juice from sugar cane, usable as fuel or to make paper etc. [F f. Sp. *bagazo*]

bagatelle /bággətél/ *n.* **1** a game in which small balls are struck into numbered holes on a board, with pins as obstructions. **2** a mere trifle; a negligible amount. **3** *Mus.* a short piece of music, esp. for the piano. [F f. It. *bagatella* dimin., perh. f. *baga* BAGGAGE]

■ **2** see TRIFLE *n.* 1.

bagel /báyg'l/ *n.* (also **beigel**) *US* a hard bread roll in the shape of a ring. [Yiddish *beygel*]

baggage /bággij/ *n.* **1** everyday belongings packed up in suitcases etc. for travelling; luggage. **2** the portable equipment of an army. **3** *joc.* or *derog.* a girl or woman. □ **baggage check** *US* a luggage ticket. [ME f. OF *bagage* f. *baguer* tie up or *bagues* bundles: perh. rel. to BAG]

■ **1** see LUGGAGE. **3** see WOMAN 1.

baggy /bággi/ *adj.* (**baggier, baggiest**) **1** hanging in loose folds. **2** puffed out. □□ **baggily** *adv.* **bagginess** *n.*

■ **1** see LOOSE *adj.* 3–5.

bagman /bágmən/ *n.* (*pl.* **-men**) **1** *Brit. sl.* a travelling salesman. **2** *Austral.* a tramp. **3** *US sl.* an agent who collects or distributes money for illicit purposes.

bagnio /baányō/ *n.* (*pl.* **-os**) **1** a brothel. **2** an Oriental prison. [It. *bagno* f. L *balneum* bath]

■ **1** see BROTHEL.

bagpipe /bágpīp/ *n.* (usu. in *pl.*) a musical instrument consisting of a windbag connected to two kinds of reeded pipes: drone pipes which produce single sustained notes and a fingered melody pipe or 'chanter'. □□ **bagpiper** *n.*

baguette /bagét/ *n.* **1** a long narrow French loaf. **2** a gem cut in a long rectangular shape. **3** *Archit.* a small moulding, semicircular in section. [F f. It. *bacchetto* dimin. of *bacchio* f. L *baculum* staff]

bah /baa/ *int.* an expression of contempt or disbelief. [prob. F]

Baha'i /bəhaa-i/ *n.* (*pl.* **Baha'is**) a member of a monotheistic religion founded in 1863 as a branch of Babism (see BABIS), emphasizing religious unity and world peace. □□ **Baha'ism** *n.* [Pers. *bahá* splendour]

Bahamian /bəháymiən/ *n.* & *adj.* ● *n.* **1** a native or national of the Bahamas in the W. Indies. **2** a person of Bahamian descent. ● *adj.* of or relating to the Bahamas.

Bahasa Indonesia /baahaassə indəneeziə/ *n.* the official language of Indonesia. [Indonesian *bahasa* language f. Skr. *bhāṣā* f. *bhāṣate* he speaks: see INDONESIAN]

bail[1] /bayl/ *n.* & *v.* ● *n.* **1** money etc. required as security against the temporary release of a prisoner pending trial. **2** a person or persons giving such security. ● *v.tr.* (usu. foll. by *out*) **1** release or secure the release of (a prisoner) on payment of bail. **2** (also **bale** by assoc. with *bale out* 1: see BALE[1]) release from a difficulty; come to the rescue of. □ **forfeit** (*colloq.* **jump**) **bail** fail to appear for trial after being released on bail. **go** (or **stand**) **bail** (often foll. by *for*) act as surety (for an accused person). □□ **bailable** *adj.* [ME f. OF *bail* custody, *bailler* take charge of, f. L *bajulare* bear a burden]

■ *n.* **1** see PAWN[2] *n.* ● *v.* (*bail out*) see SAVE *v.* 1.

bail[2] /bayl/ *n.* & *v.* ● *n.* **1** *Cricket* either of the two crosspieces bridging the stumps. **2** the bar on a typewriter holding the paper against the platen. **3** a bar separating horses in an open stable. **4** *Austral.* & *NZ* a framework for securing the head of a cow during milking. ● *v. Austral.* & *NZ* (usu. foll. by *up*) **1** *tr.* secure (a cow) during milking. **2 a** *tr.* make (a person) hold up his or her arms to be robbed. **b** *intr.* surrender by throwing up one's arms. **c** *tr.* buttonhole (a person). [ME f. OF *bail(e)*, perh. f. *bailler* enclose]

bail[3] /bayl/ *v.tr.* (also **bale**) **1** (usu. foll. by *out*) scoop water out of (a boat etc.). **2** scoop (water etc.) out. □ **bail out** var. of *bale out* 1 (see BALE[1]). □□ **bailer** *n.* [obs. *bail* (n.) bucket f. F *baille* ult. f. L *bajulus* carrier]

■ (*bail out*) scoop out, spoon out.

bailee /baylée/ *n. Law* a person or party to whom goods are committed for a purpose, e.g. custody or repair, without transfer of ownership. [BAIL[1] + -EE]

bailey /báyli/ *n.* (*pl.* **-eys**) **1** the outer wall of a castle. **2** a court enclosed by it. [ME, var. of BAIL[2]]

Bailey bridge /báyli/ *n.* a temporary bridge of lattice steel designed for rapid assembly from prefabricated standard parts, used esp. in military operations. [Sir D. *Bailey* (d. 1985), its designer]

bailie /báyli/ *n.* esp. *hist.* a municipal officer and magistrate in Scotland. [ME, f. OF *bailli(s)* BAILIFF]

bailiff /báylif/ *n.* **1** a sheriff's officer who executes writs and processes and carries out distraints and arrests. **2** *Brit.* the agent or steward of a landlord. **3** *US* an official in a court of law who keeps order, looks after prisoners, etc. **4** *Brit.* (*hist.* except in formal titles) the sovereign's representative in a district, esp. the chief officer of a hundred. **5** the first civil officer in the Channel Islands. [ME f. OF *baillif* ult. f. L *bajulus* carrier, manager]

bailiwick /báyliwik/ *n.* **1** *Law* the district or jurisdiction of a bailie or bailiff. **2** *joc.* a person's sphere of operations or particular area of interest. [BAILIE + WICK[2]]

■ **1** see JURISDICTION 2. **2** see AREA 4.

bailment /báylmənt/ *n.* the act of delivering goods etc. for a (usu. specified) purpose.

bailor /báylər/ *n. Law* a person or party that entrusts goods to a bailee. [BAIL[1] + -OR]

bailsman /báylzmən/ *n.* (*pl.* **-men**) a person who stands bail for another. [BAIL[1] + MAN]

bain-marie /báɴmareé/ *n.* (*pl.* **bains-marie** *pronunc.* same) a cooking utensil consisting of a vessel of hot water in which a receptacle containing a sauce etc. can be slowly and gently heated; a double boiler. [F, transl. med.L *balneum Mariae* bath of Maria (an alleged Jewish alchemist)]

Bairam /bīrám, bīram/ *n.* either of two annual Muslim festivals. □ **Greater Bairam** at the end of the Islamic year. **Lesser Bairam** at the end of Ramadan. [Turk. & Pers.]

bairn /bairn/ *n. Sc. & N.Engl.* a child. [OE *bearn*]

bait[1] /bayt/ *n.* & *v.* ● *n.* **1** food used to entice a prey, esp. a fish or an animal. **2** an allurement; something intended to tempt or entice. **3** *archaic* a halt on a journey for refreshment or a rest. **4** = BATE. ● *v.* **1** *tr.* **a** harass or annoy (a person). **b** torment (a chained animal). **2** *tr.* put bait on (a hook, trap, etc.) to entice a prey. **3** *archaic* **a** *tr.* give food to (horses on a journey). **b** *intr.* stop on a journey to take food or a rest. [ME f. ON *beita* hunt or chase]
■ *n.* **1, 2** see *enticement* (ENTICE). ● *v.* **1 a** see HARASS 1. **b** see TANTALIZE.

bait[2] var. of BATE.

baize /bayz/ *n.* a coarse usu. green woollen material resembling felt used as a covering or lining, esp. on the tops of billiard- and card-tables. [F *baies* (pl.) fem. of *bai* chestnut-coloured (BAY[4]), treated as sing.: cf. BODICE]

bajra /baájrə/ *n. Ind.* pearl millet or similar grain. [Hindi]

bake /bayk/ *v.* & *n.* ● *v.* **1 a** *tr.* cook (food) by dry heat in an oven or on a hot surface, without direct exposure to a flame. **b** *intr.* undergo the process of being baked. **2** *intr. colloq.* **a** (usu. as **be baking**) (of weather etc.) be very hot. **b** (of a person) become hot. **3 a** *tr.* harden (clay etc.) by heat. **b** *intr.* (of clay etc.) be hardened by heat. **4 a** *tr.* (of the sun) affect by its heat, e.g. ripen (fruit). **b** *intr.* (e.g. of fruit) be affected by the sun's heat. ● *n.* **1** the act or an instance of baking. **2** a batch of baking. **3** *US* a social gathering at which baked food is eaten. □ **baked Alaska** see ALASKA. **baked beans** baked haricot beans, usu. tinned in tomato sauce. **baking-powder** a mixture of sodium bicarbonate, cream of tartar, etc., used instead of yeast in baking. **baking-soda** sodium bicarbonate. [OE *bacan*]
■ *v.* **2 a** (**be baking**) see BOIL[1] *v.* 3c.

bakehouse /báyk-howss/ *n.* = BAKERY.

Bakelite /báykəlīt/ *n. propr.* any of various thermosetting resins or plastics made from formaldehyde and phenol and used for cables, buttons, plates, etc. [G *Bakelit* f. L.H. *Baekeland* its Belgian-born inventor d. 1944]

Baker /báykər/ *n.* □ **Baker day** *colloq.* a day set aside for in-service training of teachers in England and Wales. [*Kenneth Baker*, the name of the Education Secretary responsible for introducing them]

baker /báykər/ *n.* a person who bakes and sells bread, cakes, etc., esp. professionally. □ **baker's dozen** thirteen (so called from the former bakers' custom of adding an extra loaf to a dozen sold; the exact reason for this is unclear). [OE *bæcere*]

bakery /báykəri/ *n.* (*pl.* **-ies**) a place where bread and cakes are made or sold.

Bakewell tart /báykwel/ *n.* a baked open pie consisting of a pastry case lined with jam and filled with a rich almond paste. [*Bakewell* in Derbyshire]

baklava /báklәvә, -vaá/ *n.* (also **baclava**) a rich sweetmeat of flaky pastry, honey, and nuts. [Turk.]

baksheesh /báksheésh/ *n.* (also **backsheesh**) (in some oriental countries) a small sum of money given as a gratuity or as alms. [ult. f. Pers. *bakšīš* f. *bakšīdan* give]
■ see TIP[3] *n.* 1.

Balaclava /bálləklaávə/ *n.* (in full **Balaclava helmet**) a tight woollen garment covering the whole head and neck except for parts of the face, worn orig. by soldiers on active service in the Crimean War. [*Balaclava* in the Crimea, the site of a battle in 1854]

balalaika /bálləlīkə/ *n.* a guitar-like musical instrument having a triangular body and 2–4 strings, popular in Russia and other Slav countries. [Russ.]

balance /bállənss/ *n.* & *v.* ● *n.* **1** an apparatus for weighing, esp. one with a central pivot, beam, and two scales. **2 a** a counteracting weight or force. **b** (in full **balance-wheel**) the regulating device in a clock etc. **3 a** an even distribution of weight or amount. **b** stability of body or mind (*regained his balance*). **4** a preponderating weight or amount (*the balance of opinion*). **5 a** an agreement between or the difference between credits and debits in an account. **b** the difference between an amount due and an amount paid (*will pay the balance next week*). **c** an amount left over; the rest. **6 a** *Art* harmony of design and proportion. **b** *Mus.* the relative volume of various sources of sound (*bad balance between violins and trumpets*). **c** proportion. **7** (**the Balance**) the zodiacal sign or constellation Libra. ● *v.* **1** *tr.* (foll. by *with*, *against*) offset or compare (one thing) with another (*must balance the advantages with the disadvantages*). **2** *tr.* counteract, equal, or neutralize the weight or importance of. **3 a** *tr.* bring into or keep in equilibrium (*balanced a book on her head*). **b** *intr.* be in equilibrium (*balanced on one leg*). **4** *tr.* (usu. as **balanced** *adj.*) establish equal or appropriate proportions of elements in (*a balanced diet*; *balanced opinion*). **5** *tr.* weigh (arguments etc.) against each other. **6 a** *tr.* compare and esp. equalize debits and credits of (an account). **b** *intr.* (of an account) have credits and debits equal. □ **balance of payments** the difference in value between payments into and out of a country. **balance of power 1** a situation in which the chief States of the world have roughly equal power. **2** the power held by a small group when larger groups are of equal strength. **balance of trade** the difference in value between imports and exports. **balance sheet** a statement giving the balance of an account. **in the balance** uncertain; at a critical stage. **on balance** all things considered. **strike a balance** choose a moderate course or compromise. □□ **balanceable** *adj.* **balancer** *n.* [ME f. OF, ult. f. LL (*libra*) *bilanx bilancis* two-scaled (balance)]
■ *n.* **1** (weighing) scale(s), pair of scales, steelyard, spring balance, trebuchet, weigher. **3 a** even spread *or* cover, evenness, symmetry, equality, harmony. **b** equilibrium, equilibration, stability, steadiness, footing; poise, control, composure, self-possession. **4** weight, preponderance; control, command, authority. **5 a** bank balance. **b, c** difference, remainder, residue, rest; extra, excess, surplus. **6** see PROPORTION *n.* 2. ● *v.* **1** weigh, estimate, consider, assess, measure, compare, evaluate, offset, counterbalance; compensate, make up; (*balance with* or *against*) put *or* place *or* set against. **2** counteract, neutralize, cancel (out), offset; match (up with), equal, counterbalance, countervail, compensate (for), counterpoise, equipoise. **3 a** equilibrate, steady, poise. **b** be steadied *or* steady *or* poised, poise; stabilize, level (up *or* out), even out *or* up. **4** proportion, equilibrate, moderate, regulate, stablilize, equalize; (**balanced**) well-balanced; delicately balanced. **5** weigh up, compare, set side by side, contrast, measure. □ **in the balance** see UNCERTAIN 1. **on balance** see *on the whole* (WHOLE). **strike a balance** find a happy medium, strike *or* take a middle course, compromise. □□ **balancer** harmonizer, steadier.

balander /bəlándər/ *n.* (also **balanda**) *Austral.* (Aboriginal English) a white man. [Maccasarese corruption of *Hollander*]

balata /bállətə/ *n.* **1** any of several latex-yielding trees of Central America, esp. *Manilkara bidentata*. **2** the dried sap of this used as a substitute for gutta-percha. [ult. f. Carib]

Balbriggan /balbríggən/ *n.* a knitted cotton fabric used for underwear etc. [*Balbriggan* in Ireland, where it was orig. made]

balcony /bálkəni/ *n.* (*pl.* **-ies**) **1** a usu. balustraded platform on the outside of a building, with access from an upper-floor window or door. **2 a** the tier of seats in a theatre above the dress circle. **b** the upstairs seats in a cinema etc. **c** *US* the dress circle in a theatre. □□ **balconied** *adj.* [It. *balcone*]

bald /bawld/ *adj.* **1** (of a person) with the scalp wholly or partly lacking hair. **2** (of an animal, plant, etc.) not covered by the usual hair, feathers, leaves, etc. **3** *colloq.* with the surface worn away (*a bald tyre*). **4 a** blunt, unelaborated (*a bald statement*). **b** undisguised (*the bald effrontery*). **5** meagre or dull (*a bald style*). **6** marked with white, esp. on the face (*a bald horse*). □ **bald eagle** a white-headed eagle (*Haliaeetus leucocephalus*), used as the emblem of the United States. □□ **balding** *adj.* (in senses 1–3). **baldish** *adj.* **baldly** *adv.* (in sense 4). **baldness** *n.* [ME *ballede*, orig. 'having a white blaze', prob. f. an OE root *ball-* 'white patch']
■ **1, 2** see *hairless* (HAIR). **4 b** see OUTRIGHT *adj.* 1.

baldachin /báwldəkin/ *n.* (also **baldaquin**) **1** a ceremonial canopy over an altar, throne, etc. **2** a rich brocade. [It. *baldacchino* f. *Baldacco* Baghdad, its place of origin]

balderdash /báwldərdash/ *n.* senseless talk or writing; nonsense. [earlier = 'mixture of drinks': orig. unkn.]
■ see NONSENSE.

baldhead /báwldhed/ *n.* a person with a bald head.

baldmoney /báwldmunni/ *n.* (*pl.* **-eys**) an aromatic white-flowered umbelliferous mountain plant *Meum athamanticum*. [ME in sense 'gentian': orig. unkn.]

baldric /báwldrik/ *n. hist.* a belt for a sword, bugle, etc., hung from the shoulder across the body to the opposite hip. [ME *baudry* f. OF *baudrei*: cf. MHG *balderich*, of unkn. orig.]

baldy /báwldi/ *n.* & *adj.* (also **bally**) *Austral. colloq.* ● *n.* **1** a Hereford. **2** a white-faced beast. ● *adj.* **1** Hereford (cattle). **2** (of cattle) with a white marking on the face. [Brit. dial.]

bale[1] /bayl/ *n.* & *v.* ● *n.* **1** a bundle of merchandise or hay etc. tightly wrapped and bound with cords or hoops. **2** the quantity in a bale as a measure, esp. *US* 500 lb. of cotton. ● *v.tr.* make up into bales. □ **bale** (or **bail**) **out 1** (of an airman) make an emergency parachute descent from an aircraft (cf. BAIL[3]). **2** = BAIL[1] *v.* 2. [ME prob. f. MDu., ult. identical with BALL[1]]
■ *n.* **1** see BUNDLE *n.* 1.

bale[2] /bayl/ *n. archaic* or *poet.* evil, destruction, woe, pain, misery. [OE *b(e)alu*]

bale[3] var. of BAIL[3].

baleen /bəleén/ *n.* whalebone. □ **baleen whale** any of various whales of the suborder Mysticeti, having plates of baleen fringed with bristles for straining plankton from the water. [ME f. OF *baleine* f. L *balaena* whale]

baleful /báylfŏŏl/ *adj.* **1** (esp. of a manner, look, etc.) gloomy, menacing. **2** harmful, malignant, destructive. □□ **balefully** *adv.* **balefulness** *n.* [BALE[2] + -FUL]
■ **2** see HARMFUL.

baler /báylər/ *n.* a machine for making bales of hay, straw, metal, etc.

Balinese /baàlineéz/ *n.* & *adj.* ● *n.* (*pl.* same) **1** a native of Bali, an island in Indonesia. **2** the language of Bali. ● *adj.* of or relating to Bali or its people or language.

balk var. of BAULK.

Balkan /báwlkən/ *adj.* & *n.* ● *adj.* **1** of or relating to the region of SE Europe bounded by the Adriatic, the Aegean, and the Black Sea. **2** of or relating to its peoples or countries. ● *n.* (**the Balkans**) the Balkan countries. [Turk.]

balky var. of BAULKY.

ball[1] /bawl/ *n.* & *v.* ● *n.* **1** a solid or hollow sphere, esp. for use in a game. **2 a** a ball-shaped object; material forming the shape of a ball (*ball of snow*; *ball of wool*; *rolled himself into a ball*). **b** a rounded part of the body (*ball of the foot*). **3** a solid non-explosive missile for a cannon etc. **4** a single delivery of a ball in cricket, baseball, etc., or passing of a ball in football. **5** (in *pl.*) *coarse sl.* **a** the testicles. **b** (usu. as an exclam. of contempt) nonsense, rubbish. **c** = *balls-up*. **d** courage, 'guts'. ¶ Sense 5 is usually considered a taboo use. ● *v.* **1** *tr.* squeeze or wind into a ball. **2** *intr.* form or gather into a ball or balls. □ **ball-and-socket joint** *Anat.* a joint in which a rounded end lies in a concave cup or socket, allowing freedom of movement. **ball-bearing 1** a bearing in which the two halves are separated by a ring of small metal balls which reduce friction. **2** one of these balls. **ball game 1 a** any game played with a ball. **b** *US* a game of baseball. **2** esp. *US colloq.* a particular affair or concern (*a whole new ball game*). **the ball is in your** etc. **court** you etc. must be next to act. **ball lightning** a rare globular form of lightning. **ball-point** (**pen**) a pen with a tiny ball as its writing point. **balls** (or **ball**) **up** *coarse sl.* bungle; make a mess of. **balls-up** *n. coarse sl.* a mess; a confused or bungled situation. **have the ball at one's feet** have one's best opportunity. **keep the ball rolling** maintain the momentum of an activity. **on the ball** *colloq.* alert. **play ball** *colloq.* cooperate. **start** etc. **the ball rolling** set an activity in motion; make a start. [ME f. ON *böllr* f. Gmc]
■ *n.* **1, 2a** see ORB *n.* **3** see SHOT[1] 3. □ **ball game 2** see SITUATION 2. **ball-point** (**pen**) see PEN[1] *n.* **on the ball** see ALERT *adj.* 1. **play ball** cooperate, agree, work together, work hand in glove, play along.

ball[2] /bawl/ *n.* **1** a formal social gathering for dancing. **2** *sl.* an enjoyable time (esp. *have a ball*). [F *bal* f. LL *ballare* to dance]
■ **1** see DANCE *n.*

ballad /bállad/ *n.* **1** a poem or song narrating a popular story. **2** a slow sentimental or romantic song. □ **ballad metre** = *common metre*. [ME f. OF *balade* f. Prov. *balada* dancing-song f. *balar* to dance]
■ see LAY[3].

ballade /balaàd/ *n.* **1** a poem of one or more triplets of stanzas with a repeated refrain and an envoy. **2** *Mus.* a short lyrical piece, esp. for piano. [earlier spelling and pronunc. of BALLAD]
■ **1** see LAY[3].

balladeer /bálladeér/ *n.* a singer or composer of ballads.
■ see *singer* (SING).

balladry /bálladri/ *n.* ballad poetry.

ballast /bállast/ *n.* & *v.* ● *n.* **1** any heavy material placed in a ship or the car of a balloon etc. to secure stability. **2** coarse stone etc. used to form the bed of a railway track or road. **3** *Electr.* any device used to stabilize the current in a circuit. **4** anything that affords stability or permanence. ● *v.tr.* **1** provide with ballast. **2** afford stability or weight to. [16th c.: f. LG or Scand., of uncert. orig.]

ballboy /báwlboy/ *n.* (*fem.* **ballgirl** /-gurl/) (in lawn tennis) a boy or girl who retrieves balls that go out of play during a game.

ballcock /báwlkok/ *n.* a floating ball on a hinged arm, whose movement up and down controls the water level in a cistern.

ballerina /bállareéna/ *n.* a female ballet-dancer. [It., fem. of *ballerino* dancing-master f. *ballare* dance f. LL: see BALL[2]]

ballet /bállay/ *n.* **1 a** a dramatic or representational style of dancing and mime, using set steps and techniques and usu. (esp. in classical ballet) accompanied by music. **b** a particular piece or performance of ballet. **c** the music for this. **2** a company performing ballet. □ **ballet-dancer** a dancer who specializes in ballet. □□ **balletic** /bəléttik/ *adj.* [F f. It. *balletto* dimin. of *ballo* BALL[2]]

balletomane /bállitōmayn/ *n.* a devotee of ballet. □□ **balletomania** /-máynia/ *n.*

ballista /bəlistə/ *n.* (*pl.* **ballistae** /-stee/) a catapult used in ancient warfare for hurling large stones etc. [L f. Gk *ballō* throw]

ballistic /bəlistik/ *adj.* **1** of or relating to projectiles. **2** moving under the force of gravity only. □ **ballistic missile** a missile which is initially powered and guided but falls under gravity on its target. □□ **ballistically** *adv.* [BALLISTA + -IC]
■ □ **ballistic missile** see MISSILE.

ballistics /bəlistiks/ *n.pl.* (usu. treated as *sing.*) the science of projectiles and firearms.

ballocks var. of BOLLOCKS.

ballon d'essai /balóɴ desáy/ *n.* (*pl.* ***ballons d'essai*** *pronunc.* same) an experiment to see how a new policy etc. will be received. [F, = trial balloon]

balloon /bəlóon/ *n.* & *v.* ● *n.* **1** a small inflatable rubber pouch with a neck, used as a child's toy or as decoration. **2** a large usu. round bag inflatable with hot air or gas to make it rise in the air, often carrying a basket for passengers. **3** *colloq.* a balloon shape enclosing the words or thoughts of characters in a comic strip or cartoon. **4** a large globular drinking glass, usu. for brandy. ● *v.* **1** *intr.* & *tr.* swell out or cause to swell out like a balloon. **2** *intr.* travel by balloon. **3** *tr. Brit.* hit or kick (a ball etc.) high in the air. □ **when the balloon goes up** *colloq.* when the action or trouble starts. □□ **balloonist** *n.* [F *ballon* or It. *ballone* large ball]

■ *v.* **1** see SWELL *v.* 3.

ballot /bállət/ *n.* & *v.* ● *n.* **1** a process of voting, in writing and usu. secret. **2** the total of votes recorded in a ballot. **3** the drawing of lots. **4** a paper or ticket etc. used in voting. ● *v.* (**balloted, balloting**) **1** *intr.* (usu. foll. by *for*) **a** hold a ballot; give a vote. **b** draw lots for precedence etc. **2** *tr.* take a ballot of (*the union balloted its members*). □ **ballot-box** a sealed box into which voters put completed ballot-papers. **ballot-paper** a slip of paper used to register a vote. [It. *ballotta* dimin. of *balla* BALL[1]]

■ *n.* **1** see VOTE *n.* 1. ● *v.* **1 a** see VOTE *v.* 1.

ballpark /báwlpaark/ *n. US* **1** a baseball ground. **2** (*attrib.*) *colloq.* approximate, rough (*a ballpark figure*). □ **in the ballpark of** *colloq.* approximately, in the region of. **in the right ballpark** *colloq.* close to one's objective; approximately correct.

■ **2** see APPROXIMATE *adj.*

ballroom /báwlroom, -room/ *n.* a large room or hall for dancing. □ **ballroom dancing** formal social dancing as a recreation.

bally[1] /bálli/ *adj.* & *adv. Brit. sl.* a mild form of *bloody* (see BLOODY *adj.* 3) (*took the bally lot*). [alt. of BLOODY]

bally[2] var. of BALDY.

ballyhoo /bállihóo/ *n.* **1** a loud noise or fuss; a confused state or commotion. **2** extravagant or sensational publicity. [19th or 20th c., orig. US (in sense 2): orig. unkn.]

■ **1** see NOISE *n.* **2** see FANFARE 2.

ballyrag /bállirag/ *v.tr.* (also **bullyrag** /bóol-/) (**-ragged, -ragging**) *sl.* play tricks on; scold, harass. [18th c.: orig. unkn.]

balm /baam/ *n.* **1** an aromatic ointment for anointing, soothing, or healing. **2** a fragrant and medicinal exudation from certain trees and plants. **3** a healing or soothing influence or consolation. **4** an Asian and N. African tree yielding balm. **5** any aromatic herb, esp. one of the genus *Melissa*. **6** a pleasant perfume or fragrance. □ **balm of Gilead** (cf. Jer. 8:22) **1 a** a fragrant resin formerly much used as an unguent. **b** a plant of the genus *Commiphora* yielding such resin. **2** the balsam fir or poplar. [ME f. OF *ba(s)me* f. L *balsamum* BALSAM]

■ **1** see OINTMENT.

balmoral /balmórrəl/ *n.* **1** a type of brimless boat-shaped cocked hat with a cockade or ribbons attached, usu. worn by certain Scottish regiments. **2** a heavy leather walking-boot with laces up the front. [*Balmoral* Castle in Scotland]

balmy /baámi/ *adj.* (**balmier, balmiest**) **1** mild and fragrant; soothing. **2** yielding balm. **3** *sl.* = BARMY. □□ **balmily** *adv.* **balminess** *n.*

■ **1** see MILD 3.

balneology /bálniólləji/ *n.* the scientific study of bathing and medicinal springs. □□ **balneological** /-niəlójik'l/ *adj.* **balneologist** *n.* [L *balneum* bath + -LOGY]

baloney var. of BOLONEY.

BALPA *abbr.* British Air Line Pilots' Association.

balsa /bólsə, báwl-/ *n.* **1** (in full **balsa-wood**) a type of tough lightweight wood used for making models etc. **2** the tropical American tree, *Ochroma lagopus*, from which it comes. [Sp., = raft]

balsam /bólsəm, báwl-/ *n.* **1** any of several aromatic resinous exudations, such as balm, obtained from various trees and shrubs and used as a base for certain fragrances and medical preparations. **2** an ointment, esp. one composed of a substance dissolved in oil or turpentine. **3** any of various trees or shrubs which yield balsam. **4** any of several flowering plants of the genus *Impatiens*. **5** a healing or soothing agency. □ **balsam apple** any of various gourdlike plants of the genus *Momordica*, having warted orange-yellow fruits. **balsam fir** a N. American tree (*Abies balsamea*) which yields balsam. **balsam poplar** any of various N. American poplars, esp. *Populus balsamifera*, yielding balsam. □□ **balsamic** /-sámmik/ *adj.* [OE f. L *balsamum*]

■ □□ **balsamic** see *soothing* (SOOTHE).

Baltic /báwltik, ból-/ *n.* & *adj.* ● *n.* **1** (**the Baltic**) **a** an almost land-locked sea of NE Europe. **b** the States bordering this sea. **2** an Indo-European branch of languages comprising Old Prussian, Lithuanian, and Latvian. ● *adj.* of or relating to the Baltic or the branch of languages called *Baltic*. [med.L *Balticus* f. LL *Balthae* dwellers near the Baltic Sea]

baluster /bálləstər/ *n.* each of a series of often ornamental short posts or pillars supporting a rail or coping etc. ¶ Often confused with *banister*. [F *balustre* f. It. *balaustro* f. L f. Gk *balaustion* wild-pomegranate flower]

■ see RAIL[1] *n.* 1.

balustrade /bálləstráyd/ *n.* a railing supported by balusters, esp. forming an ornamental parapet to a balcony, bridge, or terrace. [F (as BALUSTER)]

■ see RAIL[1] *n.* 1.

bama /bámmə, pámmə/ *n.* (also **pama**) *Austral.* an Aboriginal person, esp. one from northern Queensland. [f. many north Qld. languages *bama* person or man]

bambino /bambeénō/ *n.* (*pl.* ***bambini*** /-ni/) *colloq.* a young (esp. Italian) child. [It., dimin. of *bambo* silly]

bamboo /bambóo/ *n.* **1** a mainly tropical giant woody grass of the subfamily Bambusidae. **2** its hollow jointed stem, used as a stick or to make furniture etc. [Du. *bamboes* f. Port. *mambu* f. Malay]

bamboozle /bambóoz'l/ *v.tr. colloq.* cheat, hoax, mystify. □□ **bamboozlement** *n.* **bamboozler** *n.* [*c.*1700: prob. of cant orig.]

■ see CHEAT *v.* 1.

ban /ban/ *v.* & *n.* ● *v.tr.* (**banned, banning**) forbid, prohibit (an action etc.), esp. formally; refuse admittance to (a person). ● *n.* **1** a formal or authoritative prohibition (*a ban on smoking*). **2** a tacit prohibition by public opinion. **3** a sentence of outlawry. **4** *archaic* a curse or execration. [OE *bannan* summon f. Gmc]

■ *v.* prohibit, forbid, outlaw, interdict, stop, prevent, bar, disallow; debar, proscribe, banish, exile. ● *n.* **1, 2** prohibition, taboo, proscription, interdiction, interdict; embargo, boycott. **4** see CURSE *n.* 1.

banal /bənaál/ *adj.* trite, feeble, commonplace. □□ **banality** /-nálliti/ *n.* (*pl.* **-ies**). **banally** *adv.* [orig. in sense 'compulsory', hence 'common to all', f. F f. *ban* (as BAN)]

■ trite, hackneyed, stereotyped, clichéd, stereotypical, commonplace, stock, common, everyday, ordinary, pedestrian, humdrum, tired, well-worn, feeble, threadbare, unoriginal, unimaginative, uninspired, bourgeois, platitudinous; petty, jejune, *vieux jeu*, *archaic* trivial, *colloq.* corny, old hat. □□ **banality** triteness, pedestrianism, tiredness, feebleness, unimaginativeness, triviality, corniness; see also CLICHÉ. **banally** tritely, stereotypically, unimaginatively, unoriginally, *colloq.* cornily.

banana /bənaánə/ *n.* **1** a long curved fruit with soft pulpy flesh and yellow skin when ripe, growing in clusters. **2** (in full **banana-tree**) the tropical and subtropical treelike plant, *Musa sapientum*, bearing this. □ **banana republic** *derog.* a small State, esp. in Central America, dependent on the influx of foreign capital. **banana skin 1** the skin of a banana. **2** a cause of upset or humiliation; a blunder. **banana split** a sweet dish made with split bananas, ice-cream, sauce, etc. **go bananas** *sl.* become crazy or angry. [Port. or Sp., f. a name in Guinea]

banausic /bənáwsik/ *adj. derog.* **1 a** uncultivated. **b** materialistic. **2** suitable only for artisans. [Gk *banausikos* for artisans]

Banbury cake /bánbəri/ *n.* a flat pastry with a spicy currant filling. [*Banbury* in S. England, where it was orig. made]

banc /bangk/ *n.* □ **in banc** *Law* sitting as a full court. [AF (= bench) f. med.L (as BANK²)]

band¹ /band/ *n.* & *v.* ● *n.* **1** a flat, thin strip or loop of material (e.g. paper, metal, or cloth) put round something esp. to hold it together or decorate it (*headband*). **2 a** a strip of material forming part of a garment (*hatband*; *waistband*). **b** a stripe of a different colour or material on an object. **3 a** a range of frequencies or wavelengths in a spectrum (esp. of radio frequencies). **b** a range of values within a series. **4** *Mech.* a belt connecting wheels or pulleys. **5** (in *pl.*) a collar having two hanging strips, worn by some lawyers, ministers, and academics in formal dress. **6** *archaic* a thing that restrains, binds, connects, or unites; a bond. ● *v.tr.* **1** put a band on. **2 a** mark with stripes. **b** (as **banded** *adj.*) *Bot.* & *Zool.* marked with coloured bands or stripes. □ **band-saw** a mechanical saw with a blade formed by an endless toothed band. [ME f. OF *bande*, *bende* (sense 6 f. ON *band*) f. Gmc]

■ *n.* **1** strip, ribbon, headband, belt, bandeau, fillet, tie, string, *literary* cincture. **2 b** strip, stripe, line, streak, bar, border, edging, edge, frame, fringe, *Heraldry* bordure, orle. **3 a** frequency, wavelength. ● *v.* **1** tie (up), keep, bind, fasten, secure; encircle, belt, *literary* gird. **2 a** line, stripe, border, streak, striate; edge, frame, fringe.

band² /band/ *n.* & *v.* ● *n.* **1** an organized group of people having a common object, esp. of a criminal nature (*band of cutthroats*). **2 a** a group of musicians, esp. playing wind instruments (*brass band*; *military band*). **b** a group of musicians playing jazz, pop, or dance music. **c** *colloq.* an orchestra. **3** *US* a herd or flock. ● *v.tr.* & *intr.* form into a group for a purpose (*band together for mutual protection*). □ **Band of Hope** an association promoting total abstinence from alcohol. [ME f. OF *bande*, *bander*, med.L *banda*, prob. of Gmc orig.]

■ *n.* **1** company, troop, platoon, corps, group, body, gang, horde, party, pack, *colloq.* bunch, crew, mob. **2** group, ensemble, combination, orchestra, *sl.* combo. ● *v.* (*band together*) unite, confederate, ally, gather *or* join *or* league together, team *or* join up, affiliate, merge, federate.

bandage /bándij/ *n.* & *v.* ● *n.* **1** a strip of material for binding up a wound etc. **2** a piece of material used as a blindfold. ● *v.tr.* bind (a wound etc.) with a bandage. [F f. *bande* (as BAND¹)]

■ *v.* see BIND *v.* 10a.

bandanna /bandánnə/ *n.* a large coloured handkerchief or neckerchief, usu. of silk or cotton, and often having white spots. [prob. Port. f. Hindi]

b. & b. *abbr.* bed and breakfast.

■ see HOTEL 1.

bandbox /bándboks/ *n.* a usu. circular cardboard box for carrying hats. □ **out of a bandbox** extremely neat. [BAND¹ + BOX¹]

bandeau /bándō/ *n.* (*pl.* **bandeaux** /-dōz/) a narrow band worn round the head. [F]

■ see BAND¹ *n.* 1.

banderilla /bándərílyə/ *n.* a decorated dart thrust into a bull's neck or shoulders during a bullfight. [Sp.]

banderole /bándərōl/ *n.* (also **banderol**) **1 a** a long narrow flag with a cleft end, flown at a masthead. **b** an ornamental streamer on a knight's lance. **2 a** a ribbon-like scroll. **b** a stone band resembling a banderole, bearing an inscription. [F *banderole* f. It. *banderuola* dimin. of *bandiera* BANNER]

■ **1** see STREAMER.

bandicoot /bándikoot/ *n.* **1** any of the insect- and plant-eating marsupials of the family *Peramelidae*. **2** (in full **bandicoot rat**) *Ind.* a destructive rat, *Bandicota benegalensis*. [Telugu *pandikokku* pig-rat]

bandit /bándit/ *n.* (*pl.* **bandits** or **banditti** /-ditti/) **1** a robber or murderer, esp. a member of a gang; a gangster. **2** an outlaw. □□ **banditry** *n.* [It. *bandito* (pl. *-iti*), past part. of *bandire* ban, = med.L *bannire* proclaim: see BANISH]

■ see OUTLAW *n.*

bandmaster /bándmaastər/ *n.* the conductor of a (esp. military or brass) band. [BAND² + MASTER]

bandolier /bándəléer/ *n.* (also **bandoleer**) a shoulder belt with loops or pockets for cartridges. [Du. *bandelier* or F *bandoulière*, prob. formed as BANDEROLE]

bandsman /bándzmən/ *n.* (*pl.* **-men**) a player in a (esp. military or brass) band.

bandstand /bándstand/ *n.* a covered outdoor platform for a band to play on, usu. in a park.

bandwagon /bándwaggən/ *n.* *US* a wagon used for carrying a band in a parade etc. □ **climb** (or **jump**) **on the bandwagon** join a party, cause, or group that seems likely to succeed.

bandwidth /bándwitth, -width/ *n.* the range of frequencies within a given band (see BAND¹ *n.* 3a).

bandy¹ /bándi/ *adj.* (**bandier, bandiest**) **1** (of the legs) curved so as to be wide apart at the knees. **2** (also **bandy-legged**) (of a person) having bandy legs. [perh. f. obs. *bandy* curved stick]

bandy² /bándi/ *v.tr.* (**-ies, -ied**) **1** (often foll. by *about*) **a** pass (a story, rumour, etc.) to and fro. **b** throw or pass (a ball etc.) to and fro. **2** (often foll. by *about*) discuss disparagingly (*bandied her name about*). **3** (often foll. by *with*) exchange (blows, insults, etc.) (*don't bandy words with me*). [perh. f. F *bander* take sides f. *bande* BAND²]

bane /bayn/ *n.* **1** the cause of ruin or trouble; the curse (esp. *the bane of one's life*). **2** *poet.* ruin; woe. **3** *archaic* (except in *comb.*) poison (*ratsbane*). □□ **baneful** *adj.* **banefully** *adv.* [OE *bana* f. Gmc]

■ **1** see CURSE *n.* 4. **2** see RUIN *n.* 1–3a. **3** see POISON *n.* 1.

baneberry /báynbəri/ *n.* (*pl.* **-ies**) **1** a plant of the genus *Actaea*. **2** the bitter poisonous berry of this plant.

bang /bang/ *n.*, *v.*, & *adv.* ● *n.* **1 a** a loud short sound. **b** an explosion. **c** the report of a gun. **2 a** a sharp blow. **b** the sound of this. **3** esp. *US* a fringe of hair cut straight across the forehead. **4** *coarse sl.* **a** an act of sexual intercourse. **b** a partner in sexual intercourse. **5** *sl.* a drug injection (cf. BHANG). **6** *US sl.* a thrill (*got a bang from going fast*). ● *v.* **1** *tr.* & *intr.* strike or shut noisily (*banged the door shut*; *banged on the table*). **2** *tr.* & *intr.* make or cause to make the sound of a blow or an explosion. **3** *tr.* esp. *US* cut (hair) in a bang. **4** *coarse sl.* **a** *intr.* have sexual intercourse. **b** *tr.* have sexual intercourse with. ● *adv.* **1** with a bang or sudden impact. **2** *colloq.* exactly (*bang in the middle*). □ **bang off** *Brit. sl.* immediately. **bang on** *Brit. colloq.* exactly right. **bang up** *Brit. sl.* lock up, imprison. **bang-up** *US sl.* first-class, excellent (esp. *bang-up job*). **go bang 1** (of a door etc.) shut noisily. **2** explode. **3** *colloq.* be suddenly destroyed (*bang went their chances*). **go with a bang** go successfully. [16th c.: perh. f. Scand.]

■ *n.* **1** see EXPLOSION 2. **2a** see HIT *n.* 1a. ● *v.* **1** see HIT *v.* 1a, BEAT *v.* 2a. **2** see BOOM¹ *v.* □ **bang on** see RIGHT *adj.* 2.

banger /bángər/ *n. Brit.* **1** *sl.* a sausage. **2** *sl.* an old car, esp. a noisy one. **3** a loud firework.

bangle /bángg'l/ *n.* a rigid ornamental band worn round the arm or occas. the ankle. [Hindi *bangri* glass bracelet]

bangtail /bángtayl/ *n.* & *v.* ● *n.* a horse, esp. with its tail cut straight across. ● *v.tr. Austral.* cut the tails of (horses or cattle) as an aid to counting or identification. □ **bangtail muster** *Austral.* the counting of cattle involving cutting across the tufts at the tail-ends as each is counted.

banian var. of BANYAN.

banish /bánnish/ *v.tr.* **1** formally expel (a person), esp. from a country. **2** dismiss from one's presence or mind. □□ **banishment** *n.* [ME f. OE *banir* ult. f. Gmc]

■ **1** exile, expatriate, deport, extradite, transport, eject, oust, proscribe, expel, drive out *or* away, dismiss, outlaw, ban, ostracize, rusticate, relegate, *Eccl.* excommunicate.

2 drive out *or* away, expel, cast out, dismiss, push out, reject. □□ **banishment** see EXILE *n.* 1.

banister /bánnistər/ *n.* (also **bannister**) **1** (in *pl.*) the uprights and handrail at the side of a staircase. **2** (usu. in *pl.*) an upright supporting a handrail. ¶ Often confused with *baluster*. [earlier *barrister*, corrupt. of BALUSTER]
■ **1** (*banisters*) see RAIL[1] 1.

banjo /bánjō/ *n.* (*pl.* **-os** or **-oes**) a stringed musical instrument with a neck and head like a guitar and an open-backed body consisting of parchment stretched over a metal hoop. □□ **banjoist** *n.* [US southern corrupt. of earlier *bandore* ult. f. Gk *pandoura* three-stringed lute]

bank[1] /bangk/ *n.* & *v.* ● *n.* **1 a** the sloping edge of land by a river. **b** the area of ground alongside a river (*had a picnic on the bank*). **2** a raised shelf of ground; a slope. **3** an elevation in the sea or a river bed. **4** the artificial slope of a road etc., enabling vehicles to maintain speed round a curve. **5** a mass of cloud, fog, snow, etc. **6** the edge of a hollow place (e.g. the top of a mine-shaft). ● *v.* **1** *tr.* & *intr.* (often foll. by *up*) heap or rise into banks. **2** *tr.* heap up (a fire) tightly so that it burns slowly. **3 a** *intr.* (of a vehicle or aircraft or its occupant) travel with one side higher than the other in rounding a curve. **b** *tr.* cause (a vehicle or aircraft) to do this. **4** *tr.* contain or confine within a bank or banks. **5** *tr.* build (a road etc.) higher at the outer edge of a bend to enable fast cornering. [ME f. Gmc f. ON *banki* (unrecorded: cf. OIcel. *bakki*): rel. to BENCH]
■ *n.* **1a, 2, 4** see SLOPE *n.* 1–3. **3** see SHALLOW *n.* ● *v.* **1** see HEAP *v.* 1.

bank[2] /bangk/ *n.* & *v.* ● *n.* **1 a** a financial establishment which uses money deposited by customers for investment, pays it out when required, makes loans at interest, exchanges currency, etc. **b** a building in which this business takes place. **2** = *piggy bank*. **3 a** the money or tokens held by the banker in some gambling games. **b** the banker in such games. **4** a place for storing anything for future use (*blood bank*; *data bank*). ● *v.* **1** *tr.* deposit (money or valuables) in a bank. **2** *intr.* engage in business as a banker. **3** *intr.* (often foll. by *at*, *with*) keep money (at a bank). **4** *intr.* act as banker in some gambling games. □ **bank balance** the amount of money held in a bank account at a given moment. **bank-bill 1** *Brit.* a bill drawn by one bank on another. **2** *US* = BANKNOTE. **bank-book** = PASSBOOK. **bank card** = *cheque card*. **bank holiday** a day on which banks are officially closed, (in the UK) usu. kept as a public holiday. **bank manager** a person in charge of a local branch of a bank. **the Bank of England** the central bank of England and Wales, issuing banknotes and having the Government as its main customer. **bank on** rely on (*I'm banking on your help*). **bank statement** a printed statement of transactions and balance issued periodically to the holder of a bank account. [F *banque* or It. *banca* f. med.L *banca*, *bancus*, f. Gmc: rel. to BANK[1]]
■ *n.* **4** see STOREHOUSE. ● *v.* **1** see DEPOSIT *v.* 2. □ **bank on** see RELY.

bank[3] /bangk/ *n.* **1** a row of similar objects, esp. of keys, lights, or switches. **2** a tier of oars. [ME f. OF *banc* f. Gmc: rel. to BANK[1], BENCH]

bankable /bángkəb'l/ *adj.* **1** acceptable at a bank. **2** reliable (*a bankable reputation*). **3** certain to bring profit; good for the box office (*Hollywood's most bankable stars*).

banker[1] /bángkər/ *n.* **1** a person who manages or owns a bank or group of banks. **2 a** a keeper of the bank or dealer in some gambling games. **b** a card-game involving gambling. **3** *Brit.* a result forecast identically (while other forecasts differ) in several football-pool entries on one coupon. □ **banker's card** = *cheque card*. **banker's order** an instruction to a bank to pay money or deliver property, signed by the owner or the owner's agent. [F *banquier* f. *banque* BANK[2]]

banker[2] /bángkər/ *n.* **1 a** a fishing boat off Newfoundland. **b** a Newfoundland fisherman. **2** *Austral. colloq.* a river flooded to the top of its banks. [BANK[1] + -ER[1]]

banking /bángking/ *n.* the business transactions of a bank.

banknote /bángk-nōt/ *n.* a banker's promissory note, esp. from a central bank, payable to the bearer on demand, and serving as money.

bankroll /bángkrōl/ *n.* & *v.* *US* ● *n.* **1** a roll of banknotes. **2** funds. ● *v.tr. colloq.* support financially.

bankrupt /bángkrupt/ *adj.*, *n.*, & *v.* ● *adj.* **1 a** insolvent; declared in law unable to pay debts. **b** undergoing the legal process resulting from this. **2** (often foll. by *of*) exhausted or drained (of some quality etc.); deficient, lacking. ● *n.* **1 a** an insolvent person whose estate is administered and disposed of for the benefit of the creditors. **b** an insolvent debtor. **2** a person exhausted of or deficient in a certain attribute (*a moral bankrupt*). ● *v.tr.* make bankrupt. □□ **bankruptcy** /-ruptsi/ *n.* (*pl.* **-ies**). [16th c.: f. It *banca rotta* broken bench (as BANK[2], L *rumpere rupt-* break), assim. to L]
■ *adj.* **1** see INSOLVENT *adj.* ● *n.* **1** see PAUPER. ● *v.* see RUIN *v.* 1a.

banksia /bángksiə/ *n.* any evergreen flowering shrub of the genus *Banksia*, native to Australia. □ **banksia rose** a Chinese climbing rose with small flowers. [Sir J. *Banks*, Engl. naturalist d. 1820]

banner /bánnər/ *n.* **1 a** a large rectangular sign bearing a slogan or design and usu. carried on two side-poles or a crossbar in a demonstration or procession. **b** a long strip of cloth etc. hung across a street or along the front of a building etc. and bearing a slogan. **2** a flag on a pole used as the standard of a king, knight, etc., esp. in battle. **3** (*attrib.*) *US* excellent, outstanding (*a banner year in sales*). □ **banner headline** a large newspaper headline, esp. one across the top of the front page. **join** (or **follow**) **the banner of** adhere to the cause of. **under the banner of** associated with the cause of, esp. by the use of the same slogans as, adherence to the same principles as, etc. □□ **bannered** *adj.* [ME f. AF *banere*, OF *baniere* f. Rmc ult. f. Gmc]
■ **1, 2** standard, flag, pennant, ensign, burgee, gonfalon, pennon, streamer, colour, banderole, *Eccl.* vexillium, *Naut.* jack, house-flag. **3** (*attrib.*) outstanding, celebrated, exceptional, momentous, memorable, notable, important, noteworthy, distinguished; see also EXCELLENT. □ **under the banner of** in association with, using the slogan(s) *or* rallying cry *or* motto *or* catchword(s) of.

banneret /bánnərit/ *n. hist.* **1** a knight who commanded his own troops in battle under his own banner. **2** a knighthood given on the battlefield for courage. [ME & OF *baneret* f. *baniere* BANNER + *-et* as -ATE[1]]

bannister var. of BANISTER.

bannock /bánnək/ *n.* *Sc.* & *N.Engl.* a round flat loaf, usu. unleavened. [OE *bannuc*, perh. f. Celt.]

banns /banz/ *n.pl.* a notice read out on three successive Sundays in a parish church, announcing an intended marriage and giving the opportunity for objections. □ **forbid the banns** raise an objection to an intended marriage, esp. in church following the reading of the banns. [pl. of BAN]

banquet /bángkwit/ *n.* & *v.* ● *n.* **1** an elaborate usu. extensive feast. **2** a dinner for many people followed by speeches in favour of a cause or in celebration of an event. ● *v.* (**banqueted, banqueting**) **1** *intr.* hold a banquet; feast. **2** *tr.* entertain with a banquet. □□ **banqueter** *n.* [F, dimin. of *banc* bench, BANK[2]]
■ *n.* feast, dinner, sumptuous meal, ceremonial dinner, lavish dinner, function, *formal* sumptuous repast. ● *v.* feast, indulge, wine and dine, carouse; regale. □□ **banqueter** diner, feaster.

banquette /bangkét/ *n.* **1** an upholstered bench along a wall, esp. in a restaurant or bar. **2** a raised step behind a rampart. [F f. It. *banchetta* dimin. of *banca* bench, BANK[2]]

banshee /bánsheé/ *n.* *Ir.* & *Sc.* a female spirit whose wailing warns of a death in a house. [Ir. *bean sídhe* f. OIr. *ben síde* woman of the fairies]

bantam /bántəm/ *n.* **1** any of several small breeds of domestic fowl, of which the cock is very aggressive. **2** a small but aggressive person. [app. f. *Banten* in Java, although the fowl is not native there]

bantamweight /bántəmwayt/ *n.* **1** a weight in certain sports intermediate between flyweight and featherweight, in the amateur boxing scale 51–4 kg but differing for professional boxers, wrestlers, and weightlifters. **2** a sportsman of this weight.

banter /bántər/ *n.* & *v.* ● *n.* good-humoured teasing. ● *v.* **1** *tr.* ridicule in a good-humoured way. **2** *intr.* talk humorously or teasingly. □□ **banterer** *n.* [17th c.: orig. unkn.]

■ *n.* raillery, *badinage*, persiflage, pleasantries, jesting, jests, joking, repartee; teasing, chaff, *colloq.* kidding, ribbing, *Austral.* & *NZ sl.* borak. ● *v.* **1** tease, kid, joke, poke fun at, jolly, chaff, ridicule, *colloq.* have on, rib, *sl.* josh, take the mickey out of, *US sl.* razz. **2** kid, joke (around), jest, fool (about *or* around).

Bantu /bantóo/ *n.* & *adj.* ● *n.* (*pl.* same or **Bantus**) **1** often *offens.* **a** a large group of Negroid peoples of central and southern Africa. **b** a member of any of these peoples. **2** the group of languages spoken by them. ● *adj.* of or relating to these peoples or languages. [Bantu, = people]

Bantustan /bántoostaán/ *n.* *S.Afr. hist.* often *offens.* any of several partially self-governing areas formerly reserved for Black South Africans (see also HOMELAND). [BANTU + *-stan* as in *Hindustan*]

banyan /bányən/ *n.* (also **banian**) **1** an Indian fig tree, *Ficus benghalensis*, the branches of which hang down and root themselves. **2** a Hindu trader. **3** a loose flannel jacket, shirt, or gown worn in India. [Port. *banian* f. Gujarati *vāṇiyo* man of trading caste, f. Skr.: applied orig. to one such tree under which banyans had built a pagoda]

banzai /baanzī́/ *int.* **1** a Japanese battle cry. **2** a form of greeting used to the Japanese emperor. [Jap., = ten thousand years (of life to you)]

baobab /báyōbab/ *n.* an African tree, *Adansonia digitata*, with an enormously thick trunk and large fruit containing edible pulp. [L (1592), prob. f. an Afr. lang.]

BAOR *abbr.* British Army of the Rhine.

bap /bap/ *n. Brit.* a soft flattish bread roll. [16th c.: orig. unkn.]

■ see ROLL *n.* 6a.

baptism /báptiz'm/ *n.* **1 a** the religious rite, symbolizing admission to the Christian Church, of sprinkling the forehead with water, or (usu. only with adults) by immersion, generally accompanied by name-giving. **b** the act of baptizing or being baptized. **2** an initiation, e.g. into battle. **3** the naming of ships, church bells, etc. □ **baptism of fire 1** initiation into battle. **2** a painful new undertaking or experience. □□ **baptismal** /-tízm'l/ *adj.* [ME f. OF *ba(p)te(s)me* f. eccl.L *baptismus* f. eccl.Gk *baptismos* f. *baptizō* BAPTIZE]

baptist /báptist/ *n.* **1** a person who baptizes, esp. John the Baptist. **2** (**Baptist**) a Christian advocating baptism by total immersion, esp. of adults, as a symbol of membership of and initiation into the Church. [ME f. OF *baptiste* f. eccl.L *baptista* f. eccl.Gk *baptistēs* f. *baptizō* BAPTIZE]

baptistery /báptistəri/ *n.* (also **baptistry** /-tri/) (*pl.* **-ies**) **1 a** the part of a church used for baptism. **b** *hist.* a building next to a church, used for baptism. **2** (in a Baptist chapel) a sunken receptacle used for total immersion. [ME f. OF *baptisterie* f. eccl.L *baptisterium* f. eccl.Gk *baptistērion* bathing-place f. *baptizō* BAPTIZE]

baptize /báptī́z/ *v.tr.* (also **-ise**) **1** (also *absol.*) administer baptism to. **2** give a name or nickname to; christen. [ME f. OF *baptiser* f. eccl.L *baptizare* f. Gk *baptizō* immerse, baptize]

■ **1** christen. **2** see CALL *v.* 7.

bar[1] /baar/ *n.*, *v.*, & *prep.* ● *n.* **1** a long rod or piece of rigid wood, metal, etc., esp. used as an obstruction, confinement, fastening, weapon, etc. **2 a** something resembling a bar in being (thought of as) straight, narrow, and rigid (*bar of soap*; *bar of chocolate*). **b** a band of colour or light, esp. on a flat surface. **c** the heating element of an electric fire. **d** = CROSSBAR. **e** *Brit.* a metal strip below the clasp of a medal, awarded as an extra distinction. **f** a sandbank or shoal at the mouth of a harbour or an estuary. **g** *Brit.* a rail marking the end of each chamber in the Houses of Parliament. **h** *Heraldry* a narrow horizontal stripe across a shield. **3 a** a barrier of any shape. **b** a restriction (*colour bar*; *a bar to promotion*). **4 a** a counter in a public house, restaurant, or café across which alcohol or refreshments are served. **b** a room in a public house in which customers may sit and drink. **c** *US* a public house. **d** a small shop or stall serving refreshments (*snack bar*). **e** a specialized department in a large store (*heel bar*). **5 a** an enclosure in which a prisoner stands in a lawcourt. **b** a public standard of acceptability, before which a person is said to be tried (*bar of conscience*). **c** a plea arresting an action or claim in a law case. **d** a particular court of law. **6** *Mus.* **a** any of the sections of usu. equal time-value into which a musical composition is divided by vertical lines across the staff. **b** = *bar-line*. **7** (**the Bar**) *Law* **a** barristers collectively. **b** the profession of barrister. ● *v.tr.* (**barred, barring**) **1 a** fasten (a door, window, etc.) with a bar or bars. **b** (usu. foll. by *in*, *out*) shut or keep in or out (*barred him in*). **2** obstruct, prevent (*bar his progress*). **3 a** (usu. foll. by *from*) prohibit, exclude (*bar them from attending*). **b** exclude from consideration (cf. BARRING). **4** mark with stripes. **5** *Law* prevent or delay (an action) by objection. ● *prep.* **1** except (*all were there bar a few*). **2** *Racing* except (the horses indicated: used in stating the odds, indicating the number of horses excluded) (*33–1 bar three*). □ **bar billiards** a form of billiards in which balls are knocked into holes in the table. **bar chart** a chart using bars to represent quantity. **bar-code** a machine-readable code in the form of a pattern of stripes printed on and identifying a commodity, used esp. for stock-control. **bar-line** *Mus.* a vertical line used to mark divisions between bars. **bar none** with no exceptions. **bar person** a barmaid or barman. **bar sinister** = *bend sinister* (see BEND[2]). **bar tracery** tracery with strips of stone across an aperture. **be called to the Bar** *Brit.* be admitted as a barrister. **be called within the Bar** *Brit.* be appointed a Queen's Counsel. **behind bars** in prison. **the outer Bar** barristers who are not Queen's Counsels. [ME f. OF *barre*, *barrer*, f. Rmc]

■ *n.* **1** rod, shaft, pole, stick, stake, beam, railing, rail. **2 a** see BLOCK *n.* 1. **b** strip, stripe, band, belt, streak, line. **f** sand bar, shallow, shoal, bank, sandbank. **3** barrier, obstacle, obstruction, barricade, hindrance, block, deterrent, impediment, restriction, control, check, restraint, constraint; ban, embargo, boycott. **4 a** counter. **b, c** bar-room, saloon, public house, café, lounge (bar), cocktail lounge, wine bar, taproom, inn, *Austral.* & *NZ* hotel, *Brit.* beerhouse, *archaic or literary* hostelry, *literary* tavern, *Brit. colloq.* local, pub, boozer, *hist.* alehouse. **d** counter, kiosk, stall, booth, shop. **5 d** tribunal, court (of justice), courtroom, lawcourt, court of law, bench. ● *v.* **1 a** fasten, close up, secure, make fast, shut up, barricade, lock, lock up, padlock. **b** (*bar in*) see *keep in* 2; (*bar out*) see *shut out* 1. **2** block, obstruct, stop, hinder, prevent, impede, hamper, inhibit, frustrate, check, retard, baulk, *archaic or literary* stay. **3** keep (out), shut out, exclude, forbid, prohibit, outlaw, disallow, prevent; ban. **4** stripe, band, line. ● *prep.* **1** except (for), excepting, excluding, barring, outside (*disp.* of), but (for), apart from, other than, *US* aside from, *archaic or poet.* save (for). □ **behind bars** in prison *or* jail, *colloq.* doing time, *esp. US colloq.* in hock, *sl.* inside, in clink *or* jug *or* stir, in the can *or* cooler *or* nick *or* slammer, *Brit. sl.* in the choky, doing bird *or* porridge, banged up, *US sl.* in hoosegow, in the slam.

bar[2] /baar/ *n.* esp. *Meteorol.* a unit of pressure, 10^5 newton per square metre, approx. one atmosphere. [Gk *baros* weight]

barathea /bárrəthéeə/ *n.* a fine woollen cloth, sometimes mixed with silk or cotton, used esp. for coats, suits, etc. [19th c.: orig. unkn.]

barb /baarb/ *n.* & *v.* ● *n.* **1** a secondary backward-facing projection from an arrow, fish-hook, etc., angled to make extraction difficult. **2** a deliberately hurtful remark. **3** a beardlike filament at the mouth of some fish, e.g. barbel and catfish. **4** any one of the fine hairlike filaments growing from the shaft of a feather, forming the vane. ● *v.tr.* **1** provide (an arrow, a fish-hook, etc.) with a barb or barbs. **2** (as **barbed** *adj.*) (of a remark etc.) deliberately hurtful. □ **barbed wire** wire bearing sharp pointed spikes close together and used in fencing, or in warfare as an obstruction. [ME f. OF *barbe* f. L *barba* beard]
■ *n.* **1** see SPINE 2. **2** see WISECRACK *n.* ● *v.* **2** (**barbed**) see TART[3] 2.

Barbadian /baarbáydiən/ *n.* & *adj.* ● *n.* **1** a native or national of Barbados in the W. Indies. **2** a person of Barbadian descent. ● *adj.* of or relating to Barbados or its people.

barbarian /baarbáiriən/ *n.* & *adj.* ● *n.* **1** an uncultured or brutish person; a lout. **2** a member of a primitive community or tribe. ● *adj.* **1** rough and uncultured. **2** uncivilized. [orig. of any foreigner with a different language or customs: F *barbarien* f. *barbare* (as BARBAROUS)]
■ *n.* **1** boor, lowbrow, lout, oaf, clod, lubber, churl, philistine, ignoramus, yahoo; hooligan, vandal, ruffian, tough, hoodlum, *Austral.* larrikin, *Brit.* skinhead, *colloq.* hobbledehoy, *derog.* peasant, *sl.* trog, *dial. sl.* roughie, *Brit sl.* yob, yobbo, skin, bovver boy, *esp. US sl.* lug. **2** savage, brute, native. ● *adj.* uncivilized, uncultivated, uncultured, philistine, savage; barbarous, barbaric, coarse, vulgar, uncouth, rude; boorish, loutish, oafish, crude, rough, insensitive, churlish, uncivil.

barbaric /baarbárrik/ *adj.* **1** brutal; cruel (*flogging is a barbaric punishment*). **2** rough and uncultured; unrestrained. **3** of or like barbarians and their art or taste; primitive. □□ **barbarically** *adv.* [ME f. OF *barbarique* or L *barbaricus* f. Gk *barbarikos* f. *barbaros* foreign]
■ **1** see BRUTAL. **2, 3** see SAVAGE *adj.* 2.

barbarism /ba͞arbəriz'm/ *n.* **1 a** the absence of culture and civilized standards; ignorance and rudeness. **b** an example of this. **2** a word or expression not considered correct; a solecism. **3** anything considered to be in bad taste. [F *barbarisme* f. L *barbarismus* f. Gk *barbarismos* f. *barbarizō* speak like a foreigner f. *barbaros* foreign]
■ **1 b** see OUTRAGE *n.* 1, INSULT *n.* **2** see SOLECISM.

barbarity /baarbárriti/ *n.* (*pl.* **-ies**) **1** savage cruelty. **2** an example of this.
■ **1** cruelty, inhumanity, ruthlessness, savagery, brutishness, barbarousness, heartlessness, viciousness, cold-bloodedness, bloodthirstiness. **2** atrocity, outrage, villainy.

barbarize /ba͞arbərīz/ *v.tr.* & *intr.* (also **-ise**) make or become barbarous. □□ **barbarization** /-záysh'n/ *n.*

barbarous /ba͞arbərəss/ *adj.* **1** uncivilized. **2** cruel. **3** coarse and unrefined. □□ **barbarously** *adv.* **barbarousness** *n.* [orig. of any foreign language or people: f. L f. Gk *barbaros* foreign]
■ **1** see UNCIVILIZED 1. **2** see CRUEL *adj.* **3** see UNGRACEFUL.

Barbary ape /ba͞arbəri/ *n.* a macaque, *Macaca sylvana*, of N. Africa and Gibraltar. [*Barbary*, an old name of the western part of N. Africa, ult. f. Arab. *barbar* BERBER]

barbecue /ba͞arbikyoo/ *n.* & *v.* ● *n.* **1 a** a meal cooked on an open fire out of doors, esp. meat grilled on a metal appliance. **b** a party at which such a meal is cooked and eaten. **2 a** the metal appliance used for the preparation of a barbecue. **b** a fireplace, usu. of brick, containing such an appliance. ● *v.tr.* (**barbecues, barbecued, barbecuing**) cook (esp. meat) on a barbecue. □ **barbecue sauce** a highly seasoned sauce, usu. containing chillies, in which meat etc. may be cooked. [Sp. *barbacoa* f. Haitian *barbacòa* wooden frame on posts]

barbel /ba͞arb'l/ *n.* **1** any large European freshwater fish of the genus *Barbus*, with fleshy filaments hanging from its mouth. **2** such a filament growing from the mouth of any fish. [ME f. OF f. LL *barbellus* dimin. of *barbus* barbel f. *barba* beard]

barbell /ba͞arbel/ *n.* an iron bar with a series of graded discs at each end, used for weightlifting exercises. [BAR[1] + BELL[1]]

barber /ba͞arbər/ *n.* & *v.* ● *n.* a person who cuts men's hair and shaves or trims beards as an occupation; a men's hairdresser. ● *v.tr.* **1** cut the hair, shave or trim the beard of. **2** cut or trim closely (*barbered the grass*). □ **barber-shop** (or **barber-shop quartet**) *US colloq.* a popular style of close harmony singing for four male voices. **barber's pole** a spirally painted striped red and white pole hung outside barbers' shops as a business sign. [ME & AF f. OF *barbeor* f. med.L *barbator -oris* f. *barba* beard]
■ *v.* see TRIM *v.* 1b.

barberry /ba͞arbəri/ *n.* (*pl.* **-ies**) **1** any shrub of the genus *Berberis*, with spiny shoots, yellow flowers, and ovoid red berries, often grown as hedges. **2** its berry. [ME f. OF *berberis*, of unkn. orig.: assim. to BERRY]

barbet /ba͞arbit/ *n.* any small brightly coloured tropical bird of the family Capitonidae, with bristles at the base of its beak. [F f. *barbe* beard]

barbette /baarbét/ *n.* a platform in a fort or ship from which guns can be fired over a parapet etc. without an embrasure. [F, dimin. of *barbe* beard]

barbican /ba͞arbikən/ *n.* the outer defence of a city, castle, etc., esp. a double tower above a gate or drawbridge. [ME f. OF *barbacane*, of unkn. orig.]

barbie /ba͞arbi/ *n. Austral. colloq.* a barbecue. [abbr.]

barbitone /ba͞arbitōn/ *n.* (*US* **barbital** /ba͞arbit'l/) a sedative drug. [as BARBITURIC ACID + -ONE, *-al* as in *veronal*]

barbiturate /baarbítyoorət, -rayt/ *n.* any derivative of barbituric acid used in the preparation of sedative and sleep-inducing drugs. [BARBITURIC + -ATE[1]]
■ see SEDATIVE *n.*

barbituric acid /ba͞arbityo͞orik/ *n. Chem.* an organic acid from which various sedatives and sleep-inducing drugs are derived. [F *barbiturique* f. G *Barbitursäure* (*Säure* acid) f. the name *Barbara*]

barbola /baarbṓlə/ *n.* (in full **barbola work**) **1** the craft of making small models of fruit, flowers, etc. from a plastic paste. **2** articles, e.g. mirrors, decorated with such models. [arbitr. f. *barbotine* clay slip for ornamenting pottery]

barbule /ba͞arbyool/ *n.* a minute filament projecting from the barb of a feather. [L *barbula*, dimin. of *barba* beard]

barbwire /ba͞arbwīr/ *n. US* = *barbed wire* (see BARB).

barcarole /ba͞arkərōl/ *n.* (also **barcarolle** /-ról/) **1** a song sung by Venetian gondoliers. **2** music in imitation of this. [F *barcarolle* f. Venetian It. *barcarola* boatman's song f. *barca* boat]

Barcoo /baarko͞o/ *adj. Austral.* of or relating to a remote area of the country. □ **Barcoo rot** scurvy. **Barcoo sickness** illness marked by attacks of vomiting. **Barcoo sore** an ulcer characteristic of Barcoo rot. [river in W. Qld.]

bard[1] /baard/ *n.* **1 a** *hist.* a Celtic minstrel. **b** the winner of a prize for Welsh verse at an Eisteddfod. **2** *poet.* a poet, esp. one treating heroic themes. □ **the Bard** (or **the Bard of Avon**) Shakespeare. □□ **bardic** *adj.* [Gael. & Ir. *bárd*, Welsh *bardd*, f. OCelt.]
■ **1 a** see MINSTREL.

bard[2] /baard/ *n.* & *v.* ● *n.* a rasher of fat bacon placed on meat or game before roasting. ● *v.tr.* cover (meat etc.) with bards. [F *barde*, orig. = horse's breastplate, ult. f. Arab.]

bardy /ba͞ardi/ *n.* (*pl.* **-ies**) *Austral.* an edible wood-boring grub. [Aboriginal]

bare /bair/ *adj.* & *v.* ● *adj.* **1** (esp. of part of the body) unclothed or uncovered (*with bare head*). **2** without appropriate covering or contents: **a** (of a tree) leafless. **b** unfurnished; empty (*bare rooms*; *the cupboard was bare*). **c** (of a floor) uncarpeted. **3 a** undisguised (*the bare truth*). **b** unadorned (*bare facts*). **4** (*attrib.*) **a** scanty (*a bare majority*). **b** mere (*bare necessities*). ● *v.tr.* **1** uncover, unsheathe (*bared his teeth*). **2** reveal (*bared his soul*). □ **bare contract** *Law* a contract lacking a consideration and therefore void unless under seal. **bare of** without. **with one's bare hands**

without using tools or weapons. □□ **bareness** *n.* [OE *bær*, *barian* f. Gmc]
■ *adj.* **1** unclothed, naked, nude, stark naked, unclad, exposed, uncovered, undressed, in a state of nature, in the raw, *colloq.* in the altogether, in the buff, *joc.* in one's birthday suit, *sl.* sky-clad, *Austral. sl.* bollocky, *Brit. sl.* starkers. **2 a** denuded, stripped, leafless, defoliated, shorn, barren. **b** unfurnished, undecorated, vacant, stripped; empty, uninhabited, unoccupied, deserted. **3** unconcealed, undisguised, open, revealed, literal, bald, manifest, out-and-out, overt, uncovered, straightforward, direct, unvarnished, unembellished, unadulterated, cold, hard, plain, unadorned, basic, simple. **4** plain, mere, simple, minimal, essential, absolute, basic; meagre, scant, scanty. ● *v.* **1** expose, lay bare, uncover, unsheathe, reveal; unveil, strip, divest, denude; defoliate. **2** disclose, reveal, lay bare, uncover, divulge, unfold, unveil, tell, expose, betray, unmask, bring to light, show. □ **bare of** without, minus, less. □□ **bareness** nakedness, nudity; see also *emptiness* (EMPTY), SIMPLICITY.

bareback /báirbak/ *adj.* & *adv.* on an unsaddled horse, donkey, etc.

barefaced /báirfáyst/ *adj.* undisguised; impudent (*barefaced cheek*). □□ **barefacedly** /-fáysidli/ *adv.* **barefacedness** *n.*
■ unconcealed, open, undisguised, blatant, manifest, unmitigated, outright, downright, arrant, out-and-out, sheer, unalloyed, undiluted; audacious, impudent, shameless, insolent, impertinent, immodest, bold, unabashed, forward, brazen, brassy, saucy, cocky, pert, unblushing, *archaic* malapert. □□ **barefacedness** see *impudence* (IMPUDENT).

barefoot /báirfŏŏt/ *adj.* & *adv.* (also **barefooted** /-fŏŏtid/) with nothing on the feet. □ **barefoot doctor** a paramedical worker with basic medical training, esp. in China.

barège /bəráyzh/ *n.* a silky gauze made from wool or other material. [F f. *Barèges* in SW France, where it was orig. made]

bareheaded /báirhéddid/ *adj.* & *adv.* without a covering for the head.

barely /báirli/ *adv.* **1** only just; scarcely (*barely escaped*). **2** scantily (*barely furnished*). **3** *archaic* openly, explicitly.
■ **1** scarcely, only, just, not quite, hardly, only just, no more than. **2** scantily, sparsely, sparely, austerely, simply, plainly.

barf /baarf/ *v.* & *n. sl.* ● *v.intr.* vomit or retch. ● *n.* an attack of vomiting. [20th c.: orig. unkn.]
■ *v.* see VOMIT *v.* 1.

barfly /baárflī/ *n.* (*pl.* **-flies**) *colloq.* a person who frequents bars.

bargain /baárgin/ *n.* & *v.* ● *n.* **1 a** an agreement on the terms of a transaction or sale. **b** this seen from the buyer's viewpoint (*a bad bargain*). **2** something acquired or offered cheaply. ● *v.intr.* (often foll. by *with, for*) discuss the terms of a transaction (*expected him to bargain, but he paid up*; *bargained with her*; *bargained for the table*). □ **bargain away** part with for something worthless (*had bargained away the estate*). **bargain basement** the basement of a shop where bargains are displayed. **bargain for** (or *colloq.* **on**) (usu. with *neg.* actual or implied) be prepared for; expect (*didn't bargain for bad weather*; *more than I bargained for*). **bargain on** rely on. **drive a hard bargain** pursue one's own profit in a transaction keenly. **into** (*US* **in**) **the bargain** moreover; in addition to what was expected. **make** (or **strike**) **a bargain** agree a transaction. □□ **bargainer** *n.* [ME f. OF *bargaine, bargaignier*, prob. f. Gmc]
■ *n.* **1** agreement, contract, understanding, arrangement, covenant, pact, compact, settlement, transaction, deal. **2** good deal, best buy, square deal, *Brit.* snip, *colloq.* give-away, steal. ● *v.* negotiate, trade, haggle, barter, chaffer, huckster, *esp. US* dicker. □ **bargain for** expect, be prepared for, count on *or* upon, reckon on *or* upon, envisage, envision, foresee, take into account, allow for, *disp.* anticipate. **bargain on** see *count on*. **into the bargain** see MOREOVER. **make a bargain** agree terms.

barge /baarj/ *n.* & *v.* ● *n.* **1** a long flat-bottomed boat for carrying freight on canals, rivers, etc. **2** a long ornamental boat used for pleasure or ceremony. **3** a boat used by the chief officers of a man-of-war. ● *v.intr.* **1** (often foll. by *around*) lurch or rush clumsily about. **2** (foll. by *in, into*) **a** intrude or interrupt rudely or awkwardly (*barged in while we were kissing*). **b** collide with (*barged into her*). [ME f. OF perh. f. med.L *barica* f. Gk *baris* Egyptian boat]
■ *v.* **2 a** see INTRUDE 1.

bargeboard /baárjbord/ *n.* a board (often ornamental) fixed to the gable-end of a roof to hide the ends of the roof timbers. [perh. f. med.L *bargus* gallows]

bargee /baarjeé/ *n. Brit.* a person in charge of or working on a barge.

bargepole /baárjpōl/ *n.* a long pole used for punting barges etc. and for fending off obstacles. □ **would not touch with a bargepole** refuse to be associated or concerned with (a person or thing).

barilla /bərillə/ *n.* **1** any plant of the genus *Salsola* found chiefly in Spain and Sicily. **2** an impure alkali made by burning either this or kelp. [Sp.]

barite /báirīt/ *n. US* = BARYTES.

baritone /bárritōn/ *n.* & *adj.* ● *n.* **1 a** the second-lowest adult male singing voice. **b** a singer with this voice. **c** a part written for it. **2 a** an instrument that is second-lowest in pitch in its family. **b** its player. ● *adj.* of the second-lowest range. [It. *baritono* f. Gk *barutonos* f. *barus* heavy + *tonos* TONE]

barium /báiriəm/ *n. Chem.* a white reactive soft metallic element of the alkaline earth group. ¶ Symb.: **Ba.** □ **barium meal** a mixture of barium sulphate and water, which is opaque to X-rays, and is given to patients requiring radiological examination of the stomach and intestines. [BARYTA + -IUM]

bark[1] /baark/ *n.* & *v.* ● *n.* **1** the sharp explosive cry of a dog, fox, etc. **2** a sound resembling this cry. ● *v.* **1** *intr.* (of a dog, fox, etc.) give a bark. **2** *tr.* & *intr.* speak or utter sharply or brusquely. **3** *intr.* cough fiercely. **4** *tr. US* sell or advertise publicly by calling out. □ **one's bark is worse than one's bite** one is not as ferocious as one appears. **bark up the wrong tree** be on the wrong track; make an effort in the wrong direction. [OE *beorcan*]
■ *n.* **1** see YAP *n.* 1. **2** see WHOOP *n.* ● *v.* **1, 2** see YAP *v.* 1.

bark[2] /baark/ *n.* & *v.* ● *n.* **1** the tough protective outer sheath of the trunks, branches, and twigs of trees or woody shrubs. **2** this material used for tanning leather or dyeing material. ● *v.tr.* **1** graze or scrape (one's shin etc.). **2** strip bark from (a tree etc.). **3** tan or dye (leather etc.) using the tannins found in bark. [ME f. OIcel. *börkr bark-*: perh. rel. to BIRCH]
■ *v.* **1** see SCRAPE *v.* 3b.

bark[3] /baark/ *n. poet.* a ship or boat. [= BARQUE]
■ see VESSEL 2.

barkeeper /baárkeepər/ *n.* (also **barkeep**) *US* a person serving drinks in a bar.

barkentine esp. *US* var. of BARQUENTINE.

barker /baárkər/ *n.* a tout at an auction, sideshow, etc., who calls out for custom to passers-by. [BARK[1] + -ER[1]]

barley /baárli/ *n.* **1** any of various hardy awned cereals of the genus *Hordeum* widely used as food and in malt liquors and spirits such as whisky. **2** the grain produced from this (cf. *pearl barley*). □ **barley sugar** an amber-coloured sweet made of boiled sugar, traditionally shaped as a twisted stick. **barley water** a drink made from water and a boiled barley mixture. [OE *bærlic* (adj.) f. *bære, bere* barley]

barleycorn /baárlikorn/ *n.* **1** the grain of barley. **2** a former unit of measure (about a third of an inch) based on the length of a grain of barley.

barleymow /baárlimō/ *n. Brit.* a stack of barley.

barm /baarm/ *n.* **1** the froth on fermenting malt liquor. **2** *archaic* or *dial.* yeast or leaven. [OE *beorma*]

barmaid /baármayd/ *n.* a woman serving behind the bar of a public house, hotel, etc.

barman /baármən/ *n.* (*pl.* **-men**) a man serving behind the bar of a public house, hotel, etc.

barmbrack /baármbrak/ *n.* (also **barnbrack** /baárn-/) *Ir.* soft spicy bread with currants etc. [Ir. *bairigen breac* speckled cake]

Barmecide /baármisīd/ *adj.* & *n.* ● *adj.* illusory, imaginary; such as to disappoint. ● *n.* a giver of benefits that are illusory or disappointing. [the name of a wealthy man in the *Arabian Nights' Entertainments* who gave a beggar a feast consisting of ornate but empty dishes]

bar mitzvah /baa mítsvə/ *n.* **1** the religious initiation ceremony of a Jewish boy who has reached the age of 13. **2** the boy undergoing this ceremony. [Heb., = 'son of the commandment']

barmy /baármi/ *adj.* (**barmier, barmiest**) esp. *Brit. sl.* crazy, stupid. □□ **barmily** *adv.* **barminess** *n.* [earlier = frothy, f. BARM]
■ see CRAZY 1.

barn[1] /baarn/ *n.* **1** a large farm building for storing grain etc. **2** *derog.* a large plain or unattractive building. **3** *US* a large shed for storing road or railway vehicles. □ **barn dance 1** an informal social gathering for country dancing, orig. in a barn. **2** a dance for a number of couples forming a line or circle, with couples moving along it in turn. **barn-owl** a kind of owl, *Tyto alba*, frequenting barns. [OE *bern, beren* f. *bere* barley + *ern, ærn* house]
■ **1** see STALL[1] *n.* 2.

barn[2] /baarn/ *n. Physics* a unit of area, 10^{-28} square metres, used esp. in particle physics. ¶ Symb.: **b**. [perh. f. phrase 'as big as a barn']

barnacle /baárnək'l/ *n.* **1** any of various species of small marine crustaceans of the class Cirripedia which in adult form cling to rocks, ships' bottoms, etc. **2** a tenacious attendant or follower who cannot easily be shaken off. □ **barnacle goose** an Arctic goose, *Branta leucopsis*, which visits Britain in winter. □□ **barnacled** *adj.* [ME *bernak* (= med.L *bernaca*), of unkn. orig.]

barnbrack var. of BARMBRACK.

barney /baárni/ *n.* (*pl.* **-eys**) *Brit. colloq.* a noisy quarrel. [perh. dial.]
■ see QUARREL[1] *n.* 1.

barnstorm /baárnstorm/ *v.intr.* **1** tour rural districts giving theatrical performances (formerly often in barns). **2** *US* make a rapid tour holding political meetings. **3** *US Aeron.* give informal flying exhibitions; do stunt flying. □□ **barnstormer** *n.*

barnyard /baárnyaard/ *n.* the area around a barn; a farmyard.

barograph /bárrəgraaf/ *n.* a barometer equipped to record its readings. [Gk *baros* weight + -GRAPH]

barometer /bərómmitər/ *n.* **1** an instrument measuring atmospheric pressure, esp. in forecasting the weather and determining altitude. **2** anything which reflects changes in circumstances, opinions, etc. □□ **barometric** /bárrōmétrik/ *adj.* **barometrical** /bárrōmétrik'l/ *adj.* **barometry** *n.*

baron /bárrən/ *n.* **1 a** a member of the lowest order of the British nobility. **b** a similar member of a foreign nobility. **2** an important businessman or other powerful or influential person (*sugar baron*; *newspaper baron*). **3** *hist.* a person who held lands or property from the sovereign or a powerful overlord. □ **baron of beef** an undivided double sirloin. [ME f. AF *barun*, OF *baron* f. med.L *baro, -onis* man, of unkn. orig.]

baronage /bárrənij/ *n.* **1** barons or nobles collectively. **2** an annotated list of barons or peers. [ME f. OF *barnage* (as BARON)]

baroness /bárrəniss/ *n.* **1** a woman holding the rank of baron either as a life peerage or as a hereditary rank. **2** the wife or widow of a baron. [ME f. OF *baronesse* (as BARON)]

baronet /bárrənit/ *n.* a member of the lowest hereditary titled British order. [ME f. AL *baronettus* (as BARON)]

baronetage /bárrənitij/ *n.* **1** baronets collectively. **2** an annotated list of baronets.

baronetcy /bárrənitsi/ *n.* (*pl.* **-ies**) the domain, rank, or tenure of a baronet.

baronial /bərṓniəl/ *adj.* of, relating to, or befitting barons.

barony /bárrəni/ *n.* (*pl.* **-ies**) **1** the domain, rank, or tenure of a baron. **2** (in Ireland) a division of a county. **3** (in Scotland) a large manor or estate. [ME f. OF *baronie* (as BARON)]

baroque /bərók/ *adj.* & *n.* ● *adj.* **1** highly ornate and extravagant in style, esp. of European art, architecture, and music of the 17th and 18th c. **2** of or relating to this period. ● *n.* **1** the baroque style. **2** baroque art collectively. [F (orig. = 'irregular pearl') f. Port. *barroco*, of unkn. orig.]
■ *adj.* **1** see ORNATE.

barouche /bəroósh/ *n.* a horse-drawn carriage with four wheels and a collapsible hood over the rear half, used esp. in the 19th c. [G (dial.) *Barutsche* f. It. *baroccio* ult. f. L *birotus* two-wheeled]

barque /baark/ *n.* **1** a sailing-ship with the rear mast fore-and-aft-rigged and the remaining (usu. two) masts square-rigged. **2** *poet.* any boat. [ME f. F prob. f. Prov. *barca* f. L *barca* ship's boat]
■ see VESSEL 2.

barquentine /baárkənteen/ *n.* (also **barkentine, barquantine**) a sailing ship with the foremast square-rigged and the remaining (usu. two) masts fore-and-aft-rigged. [BARQUE after *brigantine*]

barrack[1] /bárrək/ *n.* & *v.* ● *n.* (usu. in *pl.*, often treated as *sing.*) **1** a building or building complex used to house soldiers. **2** any building used to accommodate large numbers of people. **3** a large building of a bleak or plain appearance. ● *v.tr.* place (soldiers etc.) in barracks. □ **barrack-room lawyer** *Brit.* a pompously argumentative person. **barrack-square** a drill-ground near a barracks. [F *baraque* f. It. *baracca* or Sp. *barraca* soldier's tent, of unkn. orig.]

barrack[2] /bárrək/ *v. Brit.* **1** *tr.* shout or jeer at (players in a game, a performer, speaker, etc.). **2** *intr.* (of spectators at games etc.) shout or jeer. [app. f. BORAK]
■ see JEER *v.* 1.

barracouta /bárrəkóótə/ *n.* (*pl.* same or **barracoutas**) **1** a long slender fish, *Thyrsites atun*, usu. found in southern oceans. **2** *NZ* a small narrow loaf of bread. [var. of BARRACUDA]

barracuda /bárrəkóódə/ *n.* (*pl.* same or **barracudas**) a large and voracious tropical marine fish of the family Sphyraenidae. [Amer. Sp. *barracuda*]

barrage /bárraazh/ *n.* **1** a concentrated artillery bombardment over a wide area. **2** a rapid succession of questions or criticisms. **3** an artificial barrier, esp. in a river. **4** a heat or deciding event in fencing, show jumping, etc. □ **barrage balloon** a large anchored balloon, often with netting suspended from it, used (usu. as one of a series) as a defence against low-flying aircraft. [F f. *barrer* (as BAR[1])]
■ **1** see VOLLEY *n.* 1. **2** see STREAM *n.* 2.

barramundi /bárrəmúndi/ *n.* (*pl.* same or **barramundis**) any of various Australian freshwater fishes, esp. *Lates calcarifer*, used as food. [Aboriginal]

barrator /bárrətər/ *n.* **1** a malicious person causing discord. **2** *hist.* a vexatious litigant. [ME f. AF *baratour*, OF *barateor* trickster, f. *barat* deceit]

barratry /bárrətri/ *n.* **1** fraud or gross negligence of a ship's master or crew at the expense of its owners or users. **2** *hist.* vexatious litigation or incitement to it. **3** *hist.* trade in the sale of Church or State appointments. □□ **barratrous** *adj.* [ME f. OF *baraterie* (as BARRATOR)]

barre /baar/ *n.* a horizontal bar at waist level used in dance exercises. [F]

barré /bárray/ *n. Mus.* a method of playing a chord on the guitar etc. with a finger laid across the strings at a particular fret, raising their pitch. [F, past part. of *barrer* bar]

barrel /bárrəl/ *n.* & *v.* ● *n.* **1** a cylindrical container usu. bulging out in the middle, traditionally made of wooden

staves with metal hoops round them. **2** the contents of this. **3** a measure of capacity, usu. varying from 30 to 40 gallons. **4** a cylindrical tube forming part of an object such as a gun or a pen. **5** the belly and loins of a four-legged animal, e.g. a horse. ● *v.* (**barrelled, barrelling**; *US* **barreled, barreling**) **1** *tr.* put into a barrel or barrels. **2** *intr. US sl.* drive fast. □ **barrel-chested** having a large rounded chest. **barrel-organ** a mechanical musical instrument in which a rotating pin-studded cylinder acts on a series of pipe-valves, strings, or metal tongues. **barrel roll** an aerobatic manoeuvre in which an aircraft follows a single turn of a spiral while rolling once about its longitudinal axis. **barrel vault** *Archit.* a vault forming a half cylinder. **over a barrel** *colloq.* in a helpless position; at a person's mercy. [ME f. OF *baril* perh. f. Rmc.: rel to BAR[1]]
■ *n.* **1, 2** see KEG.

barren /bárrən/ *adj.* & *n.* ● *adj.* (**barrener, barrenest**) **1 a** unable to bear young. **b** unable to produce fruit or vegetation. **c** devoid of vegetation or other signs of life. **2** meagre, unprofitable. **3** dull, unstimulating. **4** (foll. by *of*) lacking in (*barren of wit*). ● *n.* a barren tract or tracts of land esp. (in *pl.*) in N. America. □□ **barrenly** *adv.* **barrenness** *n.* [ME f. AF *barai(g)ne*, OF *barhaine* etc., of unkn. orig.]
■ *adj.* **1 a** sterile, childless, infertile. **b** unproductive, sterile, infertile, fruitless, unfruitful. **c** bare, dry, bleak, desolate, deserted, uninhabited, empty, unpeopled, trackless, waste, austere. **2** unprofitable, unrewarding, poor, meagre, profitless, deficient. **3** see DREARY. ● *n.* (*barrens*) see WILD *n.* □□ **barrenness** sterility, childlessness, infertility, fruitlessness, unfruitfulness; unprofitability, poverty; bareness, desolation, waste, emptiness, tracklessness, bleakness, austerity; dullness, tedium, dreariness, drabness, tediousness, changelessness.

barrette /barét/ *n.* a woman's bar-shaped clip or ornament for the hair. [F, dimin. of *barre* BAR[1]]

barricade /bárrikáyd/ *n.* & *v.* ● *n.* a barrier, esp. one improvised across a street etc. ● *v.tr.* block or defend with a barricade. [F f. *barrique* cask f. Sp. *barrica*, rel. to BARREL]
■ *n.* see BAR[1] *n.* 3. ● *v.* see BAR[1] *v.* 1a.

barrier /bárriər/ *n.* **1** a fence or other obstacle that bars advance or access. **2** an obstacle or circumstance that keeps people or things apart, or prevents communication (*class barriers; a language barrier*). **3** anything that prevents progress or success. **4** a gate at a car park, railway station, etc., that controls access. **5** *colloq.* = *sound barrier*. □ **barrier cream** a cream used to protect the skin from damage or infection. **barrier reef** a coral reef separated from the shore by a broad deep channel. [ME f. AF *barrere*, OF *barriere*]
■ **1** bar, fence, railing, wall, barrage, barricade. **2, 3** obstacle, bar, obstruction, block, impediment, hindrance, encumbrance. **4** gate, toll.

barring /baáring/ *prep.* except, not including. [BAR[1] + -ING[2]]
■ excluding, exclusive of, bar, omitting, not including, leaving out, excepting, except (for), save for, besides, but, *US* aside from.

barrio /baáriō/ *n.* (*pl.* **-os**) (in the US) the Spanish-speaking quarter of a town or city. [Sp., = district of a town]

barrister /bárristər/ *n.* (in full **barrister-at-law**) **1** *Brit.* a person called to the bar and entitled to practise as an advocate in the higher courts. **2** *US* a lawyer. [16th c.: f. BAR[1], perh. after *minister*]
■ see LAWYER.

barrow[1] /bárrō/ *n.* **1** *Brit.* a two-wheeled handcart used esp. by street vendors. **2** = WHEELBARROW. **3** a metal frame with two wheels used for transporting luggage etc. □ **barrow boy** *Brit.* a boy who sells wares from a barrow. [OE *bearwe* f. Gmc]
■ **1, 3** see CART *n.* 2.

barrow[2] /bárrō/ *n. Archaeol.* an ancient grave-mound or tumulus. [OE *beorg* f. Gmc]
■ see MOUND[1] *n.* 1, 2.

Bart. /baart/ *abbr.* Baronet.

bartender /baártendər/ *n.* a person serving behind the bar of a public house.

barter /baártər/ *v.* & *n.* ● *v.* **1** *tr.* exchange (goods or services) without using money. **2** *intr.* make such an exchange. ● *n.* trade by exchange of goods. □□ **barterer** *n.* [prob. OF *barater*: see BARRATOR]
■ *v.* see EXCHANGE *v.* ● *n.* see EXCHANGE *n.* 1.

bartizan /baártiz'n, -tizán/ *n. Archit.* a battlemented parapet or an overhanging corner turret at the top of a castle or church tower. □□ **bartizaned** *adj.* [var. of *bertisene*, erron. spelling of *bratticing*: see BRATTICE]

baryon /bárrion/ *n. Physics* an elementary particle that is of equal mass to or greater mass than a proton (i.e. is a nucleon or a hyperon). □□ **baryonic** /-ónnik/ *adj.* [Gk *barus* heavy + -ON]

barysphere /bárrisfeer/ *n.* the dense interior of the earth, including the mantle and core, enclosed by the lithosphere. [Gk *barus* heavy + *sphaira* sphere]

baryta /bərī́tə/ *n.* barium oxide or hydroxide. □□ **barytic** /-ríttik/ *adj.* [BARYTES, after *soda* etc.]

barytes /bərī́teez/ *n.* a mineral form of barium sulphate. [Gk *barus* heavy, partly assim. to mineral names in *-ites*]

basal /báys'l/ *adj.* **1** of, at, or forming a base. **2** fundamental. □ **basal metabolism** the chemical processes occurring in an organism at complete rest. [BASE[1] + -AL]

basalt /bássawlt/ *n.* **1** a dark basic volcanic rock whose strata sometimes form columns. **2** a kind of black stoneware resembling basalt. □□ **basaltic** /bəsáwltik/ *adj.* [L *basaltes* var. of *basanites* f. Gk f. *basanos* touchstone]

bascule bridge /báskyōōl/ *n.* a type of drawbridge which is raised and lowered using counterweights. [F, earlier *bacule* see-saw f. *battre* bump + *cul* buttocks]

base[1] /bayss/ *n.* & *v.* ● *n.* **1 a** a part that supports from beneath or serves as a foundation for an object or structure. **b** a notional structure or entity on which something draws or depends (*power base*). **2** a principle or starting-point; a basis. **3** esp. *Mil.* a place from which an operation or activity is directed. **4 a** a main or important ingredient of a mixture. **b** a substance, e.g. water, in combination with which pigment forms paint etc. **5** a substance used as a foundation for make-up. **6** *Chem.* a substance capable of combining with an acid to form a salt and water and usu. producing hydroxide ions when dissolved in water. **7** *Math.* a number in terms of which other numbers or logarithms are expressed (see RADIX). **8** *Archit.* the part of a column between the shaft and pedestal or pavement. **9** *Geom.* a line or surface on which a figure is regarded as standing. **10** *Surveying* a known line used as a geometrical base for trigonometry. **11** *Electronics* the middle part of a transistor separating the emitter from the collector. **12** *Linguistics* a root or stem as the origin of a word or a derivative. **13** *Baseball* etc. one of the four stations that must be reached in turn when scoring a run. **14** *Bot. & Zool.* the end at which an organ is attached to the trunk. **15** *Heraldry* the lowest part of a shield. ● *v.tr.* **1** (usu. foll. by *on, upon*) found or establish (*a theory based on speculation; his opinion was soundly based*). **2** (foll. by *at, in*, etc.) station (*troops were based in Malta*). □ **base hospital** esp. *Austral.* a hospital in a rural area, or (in warfare) removed from the field of action. **base pairing** *Biochem.* complementary binding by means of hydrogen bonds of a purine to a pyrimidine base in opposite strands of nucleic acids. **base rate** *Brit.* the interest rate set by the Bank of England, used as the basis for other banks' rates. **base unit** a unit that is defined arbitrarily and not by combinations of other units. [F *base* or L *basis* stepping f. Gk]
■ *n.* **1 a** bottom, foot, support, stand, pedestal. **b** centre, hub, focus, nucleus, focal point. **2** basis, starting-point, point of departure, groundwork, background, (fundamental *or* underlying) principle, foundation, underpinning, infrastructure. **3** home, station, camp, starting-point, point of departure, post, centre,

headquarters, (G)HQ. **12** root, stem, theme, radical, core. ● *v.* **1** establish, found, secure, build, ground, anchor, fix, hinge, form, bottom; derive, draw. **2** establish, post, station, position, place, quarter.

base[2] /bayss/ *adj.* **1** lacking moral worth; cowardly, despicable. **2** menial. **3** not pure; alloyed (*base coin*). **4** (of a metal) low in value (opp. NOBLE, PRECIOUS). **5** cheap, shoddy. **6** mean, degraded. ▫▫ **basely** *adv.* **baseness** *n.* [ME in sense 'of small height', f. F *bas* f. med.L *bassus* short (in L as a cognomen)]

■ **1** low, undignified, cowardly, mean, despicable, abject, contemptible, dastardly, evil, sordid, ignoble, dishonourable, disreputable, degenerate, vile, scurrilous, wicked, iniquitous, corrupt, depraved, shameful, currish, loathsome, scurvy, insufferable, villainous, verminous, sordid, offensive, lewd, lascivious, obscene, profane, rude, ribald, unseemly, vulgar, coarse, dirty, indecent, evil-minded, filthy, pornographic, *poet. or archaic* caitiff, whoreson, *literary* recreant. **2** degrading, menial, inferior, mean, unworthy, lowly, low, grovelling, servile, slavish, subservient, *colloq.* infra dig. **3** see IMPURE 1. **5** mean, poor, common, low-quality, low-grade, second-rate, shoddy, shabby, cheap, tawdry, fake, pinchbeck, inferior, counterfeit, fraudulent, debased, forged, spurious, worthless, bad, *US colloq.* two-bit. **6** mean, degraded, poor, downtrodden, abject, miserable, wretched, undignified.

baseball /báysbawl/ *n.* **1** a game played esp. in the US with teams of nine, a bat and ball, and a circuit of four bases which the batsman must complete. **2** the ball used in this game.

baseboard /báysbord/ *n. US* a skirting-board.

baseless /báysliss/ *adj.* unfounded, groundless. ▫▫ **baselessly** *adv.* **baselessness** *n.*

■ see UNFOUNDED.

baseline /báyslīn/ *n.* **1** a line used as a base or starting-point. **2** (in lawn tennis) the line marking each end of a court.

baseload /báyslōd/ *n. Electr.* the permanent load on power supplies etc.

baseman /báysmən/ *n.* (*pl.* **-men**) *Baseball* a fielder stationed near a base.

basement /báysmənt/ *n.* the lowest floor of a building, usu. at least partly below ground level. [prob. Du., perh. f. It. *basamento* column-base]

■ see CELLAR *n.*

bases *pl.* of BASE[1], BASIS.

bash /bash/ *v.* & *n.* ● *v.* **1** *tr.* **a** strike bluntly or heavily. **b** (often foll. by *up*) *colloq.* attack violently. **c** (often foll. by *down, in,* etc.) damage or break by striking forcibly. **2** *intr.* (foll. by *into*) collide with. ● *n.* **1** a heavy blow. **2** *sl.* an attempt (*had a bash at painting*). **3** *sl.* a party or social event. [imit., perh. f. *bang, smash, dash,* etc.]

■ *v.* **1 a, b** see STRIKE *v.* 1. ● *n.* **3** see PARTY[1] *n.* 1.

bashful /báshfo͝ol/ *adj.* **1** shy, diffident, self-conscious. **2** sheepish. ▫▫ **bashfully** *adv.* **bashfulness** *n.* [obs. *bash* (v.), = ABASH]

■ shy, retiring, embarrassed, meek, abashed, shamefaced, sheepish, timid, timorous, diffident, coy, demure, self-effacing, reserved, restrained; ill at ease, uneasy, uncomfortable, nervous, self-conscious, awkward.

BASIC /báysik/ *n.* a computer programming language using familiar English words, designed for beginners and widely used on microcomputers. [*B*eginner's *A*ll-purpose *S*ymbolic *I*nstruction *C*ode]

basic /báysik/ *adj.* & *n.* ● *adj.* **1** forming or serving as a base. **2** fundamental. **3 a** simplest or lowest in level (*basic pay*; *basic requirements*). **b** vulgar (*basic humour*). **4** *Chem.* having the properties of or containing a base. **5** *Geol.* (of volcanic rocks etc.) having less than 50 per cent silica. **6** *Metallurgy* of or produced in a furnace etc. which is made of a basic material. ● *n.* (usu. in *pl.*) the fundamental facts or principles. ▫ **basic dye** a dye consisting of salts of organic bases. **Basic English** a simplified form of English limited to 850 selected words intended for international communication. **basic industry** an industry of fundamental economic importance. **basic slag** fertilizer containing phosphates formed as a by-product during steel manufacture. **basic wage** *Austral.* & *NZ* the minimum living wage, fixed by industrial tribunal. ▫▫ **basically** *adv.* [BASE[1] + -IC]

■ *adj.* **2** fundamental, essential, key, underlying, prime, primary, root, principal, central, focal, vital. **3 a** elementary, elemental, primary, simple. **b** see VULGAR 1. ● *n.* (*basics*) see ELEMENT 6. ▫▫ **basically** see *in essence* (ESSENCE).

basicity /baysíssiti/ *n. Chem.* the number of protons with which a base will combine.

basidium /bəsíddiəm/ *n.* (*pl.* **basidia** /-diə/) a microscopic spore-bearing structure produced by certain fungi. [mod.L f. Gk *basidion* dimin. of BASIS]

basil /bázz'l/ *n.* an aromatic herb of the genus *Ocimum*, esp. *O. basilicum* (in full **sweet basil**), whose leaves are used as a flavouring in savoury dishes. [ME f. OF *basile* f. med.L *basilicus* f. Gk *basilikos* royal]

basilar /bázzilər/ *adj.* of or at the base (esp. of the skull). [mod.L *basilaris* (as BASIS)]

basilica /bəzíllikə/ *n.* **1** an ancient Roman public hall with an apse and colonnades, used as a lawcourt and place of assembly. **2** a similar building used as a Christian church. **3** a church having special privileges from the Pope. ▫▫ **basilican** *adj.* [L f. Gk *basilikē* (*oikia, stoa*) royal (house, portico) f. *basileus* king]

basilisk /bázzilisk/ *n.* **1** a mythical reptile with a lethal breath and look. **2** any small American lizard of the genus *Basiliscus*, with a crest from its back to its tail. **3** *Heraldry* a cockatrice. [ME f. L *basiliscus* f. Gk *basiliskos* kinglet, serpent]

basin /báys'n/ *n.* **1** a wide shallow open container, esp. a fixed one for holding water. **2** a hollow rounded depression. **3** any sheltered area of water where boats can moor safely. **4** a round valley. **5** an area drained by rivers and tributaries. **6** *Geol.* **a** a rock formation where the strata dip towards the centre. **b** an accumulation of rock strata formed in this dip as a result of subsidence and sedimentation. ▫▫ **basinful** *n.* (*pl.* **-fuls**). [ME f. OF *bacin* f. med.L *ba(s)cinus*, perh. f. Gaulish]

■ **2** see HOLLOW *n.* 1. **4** see HOLLOW *n.* 2.

basipetal /baysíppit'l/ *adj. Bot.* (of each new part produced) developing nearer the base than the previous one did. ▫▫ **basipetally** *adv.* [BASIS + L *petere* seek]

basis /báysiss/ *n.* (*pl.* **bases** /-seez/) **1** the foundation or support of something, esp. an idea or argument. **2** the main or determining principle or ingredient (*on a purely friendly basis*). **3** the starting-point for a discussion etc. [L f. Gk, = BASE[1]]

■ **1, 2** foundation, base, support, footing, grounding, (fundamental *or* underlying) principle, main ingredient *or* constituent, underpinning, infrastructure; essence, bottom, heart, centre, focus; grounds, background, reason, explanation, justification, motive. **3** starting-point, base, point of departure, beginning.

bask /baask/ *v.intr.* **1** sit or lie back lazily in warmth and light (*basking in the sun*). **2** (foll. by *in*) derive great pleasure (from) (*basking in glory*). ▫ **basking shark** a very large shark, *Cetorhinus maximus*, which often lies near the surface. [ME, app. f. ON: rel. to BATHE]

■ **1** see SUN *v.* 1, 3. **2** see REVEL *v.* 2.

basket /baáskit/ *n.* **1** a container made of interwoven cane etc. **2** a container resembling this. **3** the amount held by a basket. **4** the goal in basketball, or a goal scored. **5** *Econ.* a group or range (of currencies). **6** *euphem. colloq.* bastard. ▫ **basket weave** a weave resembling that of a basket. ▫▫ **basketful** *n.* (*pl.* **-fuls**). [AF & OF *basket*, AL *baskettum*, of unkn. orig.]

basketball /baáskitbawl/ *n.* **1** a game between two teams of five or six, in which goals are scored by making the ball drop through hooped nets fixed high up at each end of the court. **2** the ball used in this game.

basketry /baáskitri/ *n.* **1** the art of making baskets. **2** baskets collectively.

basketwork /baáskitwurk/ *n.* **1** material woven in the style of a basket. **2** the art of making this.

basmati /bazmaáti/ *n.* (in full **basmati rice**) a superior kind of Indian rice. [Hindi, = fragrant]

Basque /bask, baask/ *n.* & *adj.* ● *n.* **1** a member of a people of the Western Pyrenees. **2** the language of this people. ● *adj.* of or relating to the Basques or their language. [F f. L *Vasco -onis*]

basque /bask/ *n.* a close-fitting bodice extending from the shoulders to the waist and often with a short continuation below waist level. [BASQUE]

bas-relief /básrileéf/ *n.* sculpture or carving in which the figures project slightly from the background. [earlier *basse relieve* f. It. *basso rilievo* low relief: later altered to F form]

bass[1] /bayss/ *n.* & *adj.* ● *n.* **1 a** the lowest adult male singing voice. **b** a singer with this voice. **c** a part written for it. **2** the lowest part in harmonized music. **3 a** an instrument that is the lowest in pitch in its family. **b** its player. **4** *colloq.* **a** a bass guitar or double-bass. **b** its player. **5** the low-frequency output of a radio, record-player, etc., corresponding to the bass in music. ● *adj.* **1** lowest in musical pitch. **2** deep-sounding. □ **bass clef** a clef placing F below middle C on the second highest line of the staff. **bass viol 1 a** a viola da gamba. **b** its player. **2** *US* a double-bass. □□ **bassist** *n.* (in sense 4b). [alt. of BASE[2] after It. *basso*]

bass[2] /bass/ *n.* (*pl.* same or **basses**) **1** the common perch. **2 a** a marine fish of the family Serranidae, with spiny fins. **b** a similar N. American marine fish, *Morone saxatilis*. **3** any of various American freshwater fish, esp. *Micropterus salmoides*. [earlier *barse* f. OE *bærs*]

bass[3] /bass/ *n.* = BAST. [alt. f. BAST]

basset /bássit/ *n.* (in full **basset-hound**) **1** a sturdy hunting-dog of a breed with a long body, short legs, and big ears. **2** this breed. [F, dimin. of *bas basse* low: see BASE[2]]

basset-horn /bássit-horn/ *n.* an alto clarinet in F, with a dark tone. [G, transl. of F *cor de bassette* f. It. *corno di bassetto* f. *corno* horn + *bassetto* dimin. of *basso* BASE[2]]

bassinet /bássinét/ *n.* a child's wicker cradle, usu. with a hood. [F, dimin. of *bassin* BASIN]

basso /bássō/ *n.* (*pl.* **-os** or **bassi** /-si/) a singer with a bass voice. □ **basso profondo** a bass singer with an exceptionally low range. [It., = BASS[1]; *profondo* deep]

bassoon /bəsoōn/ *n.* **1 a** a bass instrument of the oboe family, with a double reed. **b** its player. **2** an organ stop with the quality of a bassoon. □□ **bassoonist** *n.* (in sense 1b). [F *basson* f. *bas* BASS[1]]

basso-relievo /bássō-rileévō/ *n.* (also **basso-rilievo** /bássō-rilyáyvō/) (*pl.* **-os**) = BAS-RELIEF. [It. *basso-rilievo* = BAS-RELIEF]

basso-rilievo var. of BASSO-RELIEVO.

basswood /báswŏŏd/ *n.* **1** the American lime, *Tilia americana*. **2** the wood of this tree. [BASS[3] + WOOD]

bast /bast/ *n.* the inner bark of lime, or other flexible fibrous bark, used as fibre in matting etc. [OE *bæst* f. Gmc]

bastard /baástərd/ *n.* & *adj.* ● *n.* **1** a person born of parents not married to each other. **2** *sl.* **a** an unpleasant or despicable person. **b** a person of a specified kind (*poor bastard*; *rotten bastard*; *lucky bastard*). **3** *sl.* a difficult or awkward thing, undertaking, etc. ● *adj.* **1** born of parents not married to each other; illegitimate. **2** (of things): **a** unauthorized, counterfeit. **b** hybrid. □□ **bastardy** *n.* (in sense 1 of *n.*). [ME f. OF f. med.L *bastardus*, perh. f. *bastum* pack-saddle]
■ *n.* **2 a** son of a bitch, *Brit. sl.* toerag, *US sl.* bummer; person, chap, fellow, man, boy, lad, child, *colloq.* guy, devil, beggar, *sl.* geezer, *Brit. sl.* bloke; *sl.* jerk; fool, idiot, *Brit. sl.* git. ● *adj.* **1** see ILLEGITIMATE *adj.* 1.

bastardize /baástərdīz/ *v.tr.* (also **-ise**) **1** declare (a person) illegitimate. **2** corrupt, debase. □□ **bastardization** /-záysh'n/ *n.*
■ **2** see ADULTERATE *v.*

baste[1] /bayst/ *v.tr.* moisten (meat) with gravy or melted fat during cooking. [16th c.: orig. unkn.]

baste[2] /bayst/ *v.tr.* stitch loosely together in preparation for sewing; tack. [ME f. OF *bastir* sew lightly, ult. f. Gmc]
■ see TACK[1] *v.* 2.

baste[3] /bayst/ *v.tr.* beat soundly; thrash. [perh. figurative use of BASTE[1]]
■ see CLUB *v.* 1.

bastille /basteél/ *n. hist.* a fortress or prison. [ME f. OF *bastille* f. Prov. *bastir* build: orig. of the fortress and prison in Paris, destroyed in 1789]

bastinado /bástináydō/ *n.* & *v.* ● *n.* punishment by beating with a stick on the soles of the feet. ● *v.tr.* (**-oes, -oed**) punish (a person) in this way. [Sp. *bastonada* f. *baston* BATON]

bastion /bástiən/ *n.* **1** a projecting part of a fortification built at an angle of, or against the line of, a wall. **2** a thing regarded as protecting (*bastion of freedom*). **3** a natural rock formation resembling a bastion. [F f. It. *bastione* f. *bastire* build]
■ **1, 2** see STRONGHOLD 1, 3.

basuco /bəzoōkō/ *n.* a cheap impure form of cocaine smoked for its stimulating effect. [Colombian Sp.]

bat[1] /bat/ *n.* & *v.* ● *n.* **1** an implement with a handle, usu. of wood and with a flat or curved surface, used for hitting balls in games. **2** a turn at using this. **3** a batsman, esp. in cricket, usu. described in some way (*an excellent bat*). **4** (usu. in *pl.*) an object like a table-tennis bat used to guide aircraft when taxiing. ● *v.* (**batted, batting**) **1** *tr.* hit with or as with a bat. **2** *intr.* take a turn at batting. □ **bat around 1** *sl.* potter aimlessly. **2** *US* discuss (an idea or proposal). **off one's own bat** unprompted, unaided. **right off the bat** *US* immediately. [ME f. OE *batt* club, perh. partly f. OF *batte* club f. *battre* strike]
■ *v.* **1** see HIT *v.* 1a. □ **right off the bat** see *rapidly* (RAPID).

bat[2] /bat/ *n.* any mouselike nocturnal mammal of the order Chiroptera, capable of flight by means of membranous wings extending from its forelimbs. □ **have bats in the belfry** be eccentric or crazy. **like a bat out of hell** very fast. [16th c., alt. of ME *bakke* f. Scand.]

bat[3] /bat/ *v.tr.* (**batted, batting**) wink (one's eyelid) (now usu. in phr.). □ **not** (or **never**) **bat an eyelid** *colloq.* show no reaction or emotion. [var. of obs. *bate* flutter]

batch /bach/ *n.* & *v.* ● *n.* **1** a number of things or persons forming a group or dealt with together. **2** an instalment (*have sent off the latest batch*). **3** the loaves produced at one baking. **4** (*attrib.*) using or dealt with in batches, not as a continuous flow (*batch production*). **5** *Computing* a group of records processed as a single unit. ● *v.tr.* arrange or deal with in batches. [ME f. OE *bæcce* f. *bacan* BAKE]
■ *n.* **1, 2** set, group, number, quantity, assortment, lot, bunch, pack, bundle, collection, assemblage; consignment, instalment. ● *v.* group, sort, bunch, pack, bundle, collect, assemble.

bate /bayt/ *n.* (also **bait**) *Brit. sl.* a rage; a cross mood (*is in an awful bate*). [BAIT[1] = state of baited person]

bateau /báttō/ *n.* (*pl.* **bateaux** /-tōz/) a light river-boat, esp. of the flat-bottomed kind used in Canada. [F, = boat]

bated /báytid/ *adj.* □ **with bated breath** very anxiously. [past part. of obs. *bate* (v.) restrain, f. ABATE]
■ □ **with bated breath** see EXPECTANT *adj.* 1.

bateleur /báttəlőr/ *n.* a short-tailed African eagle, *Terathopius ecaudatus*. [F, = juggler]

bath /baath/ *n.* & *v.* ● *n.* (*pl.* **baths** /baathz/) **1 a** (in full **bath-tub**) a container for liquid, usu. water, used for immersing and washing the body. **b** this with its contents (*your bath is ready*). **2** the act or process of immersing the body for washing or therapy (*have a bath*; *take a bath*). **3 a** a vessel containing liquid in which something is immersed, e.g. a film for developing, for controlling temperature, etc. **b** this with its contents. **4** (usu. in *pl.*) a building with baths or a swimming pool, usu. open to the public. ● *v. Brit.* **1** *tr.* wash (esp. a person) in a bath. **2** *intr.* take a bath. □ **bath cube** a cube of compacted bath salts. **bath salts** soluble salts used for softening or scenting bath-water. [OE *bæth* f. Gmc]

■ *n.* **2** see WASH *n.* 1. ● *v.* see WASH *v.* 1, 3.

Bath bun /baath/ *n. Brit.* a yeast bun with currants, topped with granules of sugar. [*Bath* in S. England, named from its hot springs]

Bath chair /baath/ *n.* a wheelchair for invalids.

Bath chap see CHAP[3].

bathe /bay*th*/ *v.* & *n.* ● *v.* **1** *intr.* immerse oneself in water, esp. to swim or esp. *US* wash oneself. **2** *tr.* immerse in or wash or treat with liquid esp. for cleansing or medicinal purposes. **3** *tr.* (of sunlight etc.) envelop. ● *n. Brit.* an immersion in liquid, esp. to swim. □ **bathing-costume** (or **-suit**) a garment worn for swimming. [OE *bathian* f. Gmc]

■ *v.* **1** see CLEAN *v.* 4. **2** see DIP *v.* 1. **3** see SUFFUSE. ● *n.* see DIP *n.* 3.

bather /báy*th*ər/ *n.* **1** a person who bathes. **2** (in *pl.*) *Austral.* a bathing-suit.

bathhouse /baáth-howss/ *n.* a building with baths for public use.

batholith /báthəlith/ *n.* a dome of igneous rock extending inwards to an unknown depth. [G f. Gk *bathos* depth + -LITH]

Bath Oliver /baáth óllivər/ *n. Brit. propr.* a kind of savoury biscuit. [Dr W. *Oliver* of *Bath* d. 1764, who invented it]

bathometer /bəthómmitər/ *n.* an instrument used to measure the depth of water. [Gk *bathos* depth + -METER]

bathos /báythoss/ *n.* an unintentional lapse in mood from the sublime to the absurd or trivial; a commonplace or ridiculous feature offsetting an otherwise sublime situation; an anticlimax. □□ **bathetic** /bəthéttik/ *adj.* **bathotic** /bəthóttik/ *adj.* [Gk, = depth]

bathrobe /baáthrōb/ *n. US* a loose coat usu. of towelling worn before and after taking a bath.

■ see WRAPPER 4 .

bathroom /baáthrōōm, -rŏŏm/ *n.* **1** a room containing a bath and usu. other washing facilities. **2** esp. *US* a room containing a lavatory.

■ **2** see LAVATORY.

bathyscaphe /báthiskaf/ *n.* a manned vessel for deep-sea diving. [Gk *bathus* deep + *skaphos* ship]

bathysphere /báthisfeer/ *n.* a spherical vessel for deep-sea observation. [Gk *bathus* deep + SPHERE]

batik /bəteék, báttik/ *n.* a method (orig. used in Java) of producing coloured designs on textiles by applying wax to the parts to be left uncoloured; a piece of cloth treated in this way. [Jav., = painted]

batiste /bateést/ *n.* & *adj.* ● *n.* a fine linen or cotton cloth. ● *adj.* made of batiste. [F (earlier *batiche*), perh. rel. to *battre* BATTER[1]]

batman /bátmən/ *n.* (*pl.* **-men**) *Mil.* an attendant serving an officer. [OF *bat, bast* f. med.L *bastum* pack-saddle + MAN]

baton /bátt'n/ *n.* **1** a thin stick used by a conductor to direct an orchestra, choir, etc. **2** *Athletics* a short stick or tube carried and passed on by the runners in a relay race. **3** a long stick carried and twirled by a drum major. **4** a staff of office or authority, esp. a Field Marshal's. **5** a policeman's truncheon. **6** *Heraldry* a narrow truncated bend. **7** *Horol.* a short bar replacing some figures on dials. □ **baton round** a rubber or plastic bullet. [F *bâton, baston* ult. f. LL *bastum* stick]

■ **1–5** see STAFF[1] *n.* 1a, b.

batrachian /bətráykiən/ *n.* & *adj.* ● *n.* any of the amphibians that discard gills and tails, esp. the frog and toad. ● *adj.* of or relating to the batrachians. [Gk *batrakhos* frog]

bats /bats/ *predic.adj. sl.* crazy. [f. phr. (*have*) *bats in the belfry*: see BAT[2]]

■ see CRAZY 1.

batsman /bátsmən/ *n.* (*pl.* **-men**) **1** a person who bats or is batting, esp. in cricket. **2** a signaller using bats to guide aircraft on the ground. □□ **batsmanship** *n.* (in sense 1).

battalion /bətálliən/ *n.* **1** a large body of men ready for battle, esp. an infantry unit forming part of a brigade. **2** a large group of people pursuing a common aim or sharing a major undertaking. [F *battaillon* f. It. *battaglione* f. *battaglia* BATTLE]

■ **1** see CORPS.

battels /bátt'lz/ *n.pl. Brit.* an Oxford college account for expenses, esp. for board and the supply of provisions. [perh. f. obs. *battle* (v.) fatten f. obs. *battle* (adj.) nutritious: cf. BATTEN[2]]

batten[1] /bátt'n/ *n.* & *v.* ● *n.* **1** a long flat strip of squared timber or metal, esp. used to hold something in place or as a fastening against a wall etc. **2** a strip of wood used for clamping the boards of a door etc. **3** *Naut.* a strip of wood or metal for securing a tarpaulin over a ship's hatchway. ● *v.tr.* strengthen or fasten with battens. □ **batten down the hatches 1** *Naut.* secure a ship's tarpaulins. **2** prepare for a difficulty or crisis. [OF *batant* part. of *batre* beat f. L *battuere*]

batten[2] /bátt'n/ *v.intr.* (foll. by *on*) thrive or prosper at another's expense. [ON *batna* get better f. *bati* advantage]

Battenberg /bátt'nberg/ *n.* a kind of oblong cake, usu. of two colours of sponge and covered with marzipan. [*Battenberg* in Germany]

batter[1] /báttər/ *v.* **1 a** *tr.* strike repeatedly with hard blows, esp. so as to cause visible damage. **b** *intr.* (often foll. by *against*, *at*, etc.) strike repeated blows; pound heavily and insistently (*batter at the door*). **2** *tr.* (often in *passive*) **a** handle roughly, esp. over a long period. **b** censure or criticize severely. □ **battered baby** an infant that has suffered repeated violence from adults, esp. its parents. **battered wife** a wife subjected to repeated violence by her husband. **battering-ram** *hist.* a heavy beam, orig. with an end in the form of a carved ram's head, used in breaching fortifications. □□ **batterer** *n.* **battering** *n.* [ME f. AF *baterer* f. OF *batre* beat f. L *battuere*]

■ **1 a** beat, beat up, knock about, hit, strike, clout, belabour, pound, buffet, pummel, pelt, bash, bang, thrash, *sl.* wallop, clobber, *archaic or literary* smite; bombard. **b** pound, beat, strike, bang, thrash. **2 a** maltreat, mistreat, ill-treat, abuse, mishandle, harm; maul, bruise, mangle. **b** attack, blast, flay, cut up, roast, *colloq.* pan, lambaste, rubbish, *Brit. colloq.* slate, *sl.* knock, clobber, slam, take to the cleaners; censure, criticize, damn, condemn, reprobate. □□ **batterer** maltreater, abuser, (child) molester.

batter[2] /báttər/ *n.* **1** a fluid mixture of flour, egg, and milk or water, used in cooking, esp. for pancakes and for coating food before frying. **2** *Printing* an area of damaged type. [ME f. AF *batour* f. OF *bateüre* f. *batre*: see BATTER[1]]

batter[3] /báttər/ *n. Sport* a player batting, esp. in baseball.

batter[4] /báttər/ *n.* & *v.* ● *n.* **1** a wall etc. with a sloping face. **2** a receding slope. ● *v.intr.* have a receding slope. [ME: orig. unkn.]

battered /báttərd/ *adj.* (esp. of fish) coated in batter and deep-fried.

battery /báttəri/ *n.* (*pl.* **-ies**) **1** a usu. portable container of a cell or cells carrying an electric charge, as a source of current. **2** (often *attrib.*) esp. *Brit.* a series of cages for the intensive breeding and rearing of poultry or cattle. **3** a set of similar units of equipment, esp. connected. **4** a series of tests, esp. psychological. **5 a** a fortified emplacement for heavy guns. **b** an artillery unit of guns, men, and vehicles. **6** *Law* an act inflicting unlawful personal violence on another (see ASSAULT). **7** *Baseball* the pitcher and the catcher. [F *batterie* f. *batre, battre* strike f. L *battuere*]

batting /bátting/ *n.* **1** the action of hitting with a bat. **2** cotton wadding prepared in sheets for use in quilts etc. □

batting order the order in which people act or take their turn, esp. of batsmen in cricket.

battle /bátt'l/ *n.* & *v.* ● *n.* **1** a prolonged fight between large organized armed forces. **2** a contest; a prolonged or difficult struggle (*life is a constant battle; a battle of wits*). ● *v.* **1** *intr.* struggle; fight persistently (*battled against the elements; battled for women's rights*). **2** *tr.* fight (one's way etc.). **3** *tr. US* engage in battle with. □ **battle-cruiser** *hist.* a heavy-gunned ship faster and more lightly armoured than a battleship. **battle-cry** a cry or slogan of participants in a battle or contest. **battle fatigue** = *combat fatigue*. **battle royal 1** a battle in which several combatants or all available forces engage; a free fight. **2** a heated argument. **half the battle** the key to the success of an undertaking. □□ **battler** *n.* [ME f. OF *bataille* ult. f. LL *battualia* gladiatorial exercises f. L *battuere* beat]
■ *n.* **1** fight, conflict, combat, war, action, encounter, clash, engagement, struggle, Donnybrook, fray. **2** contest, competition, match, tournament, game, encounter; struggle, fight, war, conflict, crusade, campaign; brawl, fracas, mêlée; duel, hand-to-hand encounter, *Law* affray; argument, dispute, altercation, quarrel. ● *v.* **1** fight, struggle, combat, wage war, war, wrestle, crusade, campaign, lobby; (*battle with* or *against*) oppose, stand against, engage with, grapple with, strive *or* contend with *or* against, take up arms against. **3** see FIGHT *v.* 1a. □ **battle-cry** see SLOGAN. **battle royal 1** see BRAWL *n.* **2** see ROW[3] *n.* 2. □□ **battler** fighter, soldier, pugilist, warrior, militant, combatant, campaigner.

battleaxe /bátt'laks/ *n.* **1** a large axe used in ancient warfare. **2** *colloq.* a formidable or domineering older woman. □ **battleaxe block** *Austral.* a battleaxe-shaped block of land, one lacking a frontage and accessible through a lane.
■ **2** see WITCH *n.* 2.

battledore /bátt'ldor/ *n. hist.* **1 a** (in full **battledore and shuttlecock**) a game played with a shuttlecock and rackets. **b** the racket used in this. **2** a kind of wooden utensil like a paddle, formerly used in washing, baking, etc. [15th c., perh. f. Prov. *batedor* beater f. *batre* beat]

battledress /bátt'ldress/ *n.* the everyday uniform of a soldier.

battlefield /bátt'lfeeld/ *n.* (also **battleground** /-grownd/) the piece of ground on which a battle is or was fought.

battlement /bátt'lmənt/ *n.* (usu. in *pl.*) **1** a parapet with recesses along the top of a wall, as part of a fortification. **2** a section of roof enclosed by this (*walking on the battlements*). □□ **battlemented** *adj.* [OF *bataillier* furnish with ramparts + -MENT]

battleship /bátt'lship/ *n.* a warship with the heaviest armour and the largest guns.

battue /batyoō, -toō/ *n.* **1 a** the driving of game towards hunters by beaters. **b** a shooting-party arranged in this way. **2** wholesale slaughter. [F, fem. past part. of *battre* beat f. L *battuere*]

batty /bátti/ *adj.* (**battier, battiest**) *sl.* crazy. □□ **battily** *adv.* **battiness** *n.* [BAT[2] + -Y[1]]
■ see CRAZY 1.

batwing /bátwing/ *adj.* (esp. of a sleeve or a flame) shaped like the wing of a bat.

batwoman /bátwoŏmmən/ *n.* (*pl.* **-women**) a female attendant serving an officer in the women's services. [as BATMAN + WOMAN]

bauble /báwb'l/ *n.* **1** a showy trinket or toy of little value. **2** a baton formerly used as an emblem by jesters. [ME f. OF *ba(u)bel* child's toy, of unkn. orig.]
■ **1** gewgaw, trinket, *bijou*, ornament, trifle, gimcrack, kickshaw, bagatelle, knick-knack, falderal, frippery, toy, plaything.

baud /bōd, bawd/ *n.* (*pl.* same or **bauds**) *Computing* etc. **1** a unit used to express the speed of electronic code signals, corresponding to one information unit per second. **2** (loosely) a unit of data-transmission speed of one bit per second. [J. M. E. *Baudot*, Fr. engineer d. 1903]

Bauhaus /bówhowss/ *n.* **1** a German school of architectural design (1919–33). **2** its principles, based on functionalism and development of existing skills. [G f. *Bau* building + *Haus* house]

baulk /bawlk, bawk/ *v.* & *n.* (also **balk**) ● *v.* **1** *intr.* **a** refuse to go on. **b** (often foll. by *at*) hesitate. **2** *tr.* **a** thwart, hinder. **b** disappoint. **3** *tr.* **a** miss, let slip (a chance etc.). **b** ignore, shirk. ● *n.* **1** a hindrance; a stumbling-block. **2 a** a roughly-squared timber beam. **b** a tie-beam of a house. **3** *Billiards* etc. the area on a billiard-table from which a player begins a game. **4** *Baseball* an illegal action made by a pitcher. **5** a ridge left unploughed between furrows. □□ **baulker** *n.* [OE *balc* f. ON *bálkr* f. Gmc]
■ *v.* **1** see RECOIL *v.* 1, 2. **2a** see HINDER[1]. ● *n.* **1** see *prevention* (PREVENT). **2** see BEAM *n.* 1.

baulky /báwlki, báwki/ *adj.* (also **balky**) (**-ier, -iest**) reluctant, perverse. □□ **baulkiness** *n.* [BAULK + -Y[1]]

bauxite /báwksīt/ *n.* a claylike mineral containing varying proportions of alumina, the chief source of aluminium. □□ **bauxitic** /-síttik/ *adj.* [F f. *Les Baux* near Arles in S. France + -ITE[1]]

bavardage /bávaardaázh/ *n.* idle gossip, chit-chat. [Fr., f. *bavarder* to chatter]

bawd /bawd/ *n.* a woman who runs a brothel. [ME *bawdstrot* f. OF *baudetrot*, *baudestroyt* procuress]
■ see PROCURER.

bawdy /báwdi/ *adj.* & *n.* ● *adj.* (**bawdier, bawdiest**) (esp. humorously) indecent; raunchy. ● *n.* bawdy talk or writing. □ **bawdy-house** a brothel. □□ **bawdily** *adv.* **bawdiness** *n.* [BAWD + -Y[1]]
■ *adj.* lewd, obscene, taboo, vulgar, dirty, smutty, saucy, randy, filthy, coarse, earthy, gross, scatological, rude, lascivious, lubricious, salacious, indelicate, indecent, indecorous, broad, crude, ribald, risqué, suggestive, Rabelaisian, uninhibited, unrestrained, *Gk Hist.* ithyphallic. ● *n.* scatology, obscenity, smut, filth, pornography, ribaldry, *colloq.* porn. □ **bawdy-house** see BROTHEL. □□ **bawdily** lewdly, obscenely, rudely, dirtily, filthily, smuttily, saucily, coarsely, grossly, lasciviously, salaciously, indelicately, crudely, indecorously, suggestively. **bawdiness** see RIBALDRY.

bawl /bawl/ *v.* **1** *tr.* speak or call out noisily. **2** *intr.* weep loudly. □ **bawl out** *colloq.* reprimand angrily. □□ **bawler** *n.* [imit.: cf. med.L *baulare* bark, Icel. *baula* (Sw. *böla*) to low]
■ **1** shout, bellow, vociferate, roar, yell, cry, trumpet, thunder, *US colloq.* holler. **2** cry, wail, weep, howl, keen, sob, squall, blubber, whimper, *Sc.* greet, *colloq. or dial.* yammer, *sl.* blub. □ **bawl out** see REPRIMAND *v.* □□ **bawler** shouter, bellower, roarer; weeper, cry-baby, sobber, howler, wailer, blubberer, *colloq. or dial.* yammerer.

bay[1] /bay/ *n.* **1** a broad inlet of the sea where the land curves inwards. **2** a recess in a mountain range. □ **Bay State** *US* Massachusetts. [ME f. OF *baie* f. OSp. *bahia*]
■ **1** see GULF *n.* 1.

bay[2] /bay/ *n.* **1** (in full **bay laurel**) a laurel, *Laurus nobilis*, having deep green leaves and purple berries. Also called SWEET BAY. **2** (in *pl.*) a wreath made of bay-leaves, for a victor or poet. □ **bay-leaf** the aromatic (usu. dried) leaf of the bay-tree, used in cooking. **bay rum** a perfume, esp. for the hair, distilled orig. from bayberry leaves in rum. [OF *baie* f. L *baca* berry]
■ **2** (*bays*) see TROPHY 1.

bay[3] /bay/ *n.* **1** a space created by a window-line projecting outwards from a wall. **2** a recess; a section of wall between buttresses or columns, esp. in the nave of a church etc. **3** a compartment (*bomb bay*). **4** an area specially allocated or marked off (*sick bay; loading bay*). **5** *Brit.* the terminus of a branch line at a railway station also having through lines, usu. at the side of an outer platform. □ **bay window** a window built into a bay. [ME f. OF *baie* f. *ba(y)er* gape f. med.L *batare*]
■ **1, 2** see RECESS *n.* 1.

bay[4] /bay/ *adj.* & *n.* ● *adj.* (esp. of a horse) dark reddish-brown. ● *n.* a bay horse with a black mane and tail. [OF *bai* f. L *badius*]

bay[5] /bay/ *v.* & *n.* ● *v.* **1** *intr.* (esp. of a large dog) bark or howl loudly and plaintively. **2** *tr.* bay at. ● *n.* the sound of baying, esp. in chorus from hounds in close pursuit. □ **at bay 1** cornered, apparently unable to escape. **2** in a desperate situation. **bring to bay** gain on in pursuit; trap. **hold** (or **keep**) **at bay** hold off (a pursuer). **stand at bay** turn to face one's pursuers. [ME f. OF *bai, baiier* bark f. It. *baiare*, of imit. orig.]
■ *v.* **1** see HOWL *v.* 1.

bayberry /báybəri/ *n.* (*pl.* **-ies**) any of various N. American plants of the genus *Myrica*, having aromatic leaves and bearing berries covered in a wax coating. [BAY[2] + BERRY]

bayonet /báyənét/ *n.* & *v.* ● *n.* **1** a stabbing blade attachable to the muzzle of a rifle. **2** an electrical or other fitting engaged by being pushed into a socket and twisted. ● *v.tr.* (**bayoneted, bayoneting**) stab with a bayonet. [F *baïonnette*, perh. f. *Bayonne* in SW France, where they were first made]

bayou /bī́-ōō/ *n.* a marshy offshoot of a river etc. in the southern US. [Amer. F: cf. Choctau *bayuk*]

bazaar /bəzaár/ *n.* **1** a market in an oriental country. **2** a fund-raising sale of goods, esp. for charity. **3** a large shop selling fancy goods etc. [Pers. *bāzār*, prob. through Turk. and It.]
■ **1, 3** see MARKET *n.* 2. **2** see FAIR[2] 2.

bazoo /bəzóō/ *n. sl.* the mouth. [19th c.: orig. unkn.]

bazooka /bəzóōkə/ *n.* **1** a tubular short-range rocket-launcher used against tanks. **2** a crude trombone-like musical instrument. [app. f. *bazoo* mouth, of unkn. orig.]

BB *abbr.* double-black (pencil-lead).

BBC *abbr.* British Broadcasting Corporation. □ **BBC English** English as supposedly pronounced by BBC announcers.

bbl. *abbr.* barrels (esp. of oil).

BC *abbr.* **1** (of a date) before Christ. **2** British Columbia.

BCD /beéseedeé/ *n. Computing* a code representing decimal numbers as a string of binary digits. [abbr. for *binary coded decimal*]

BCE *abbr.* before the Common Era.

BCG *abbr.* Bacillus Calmette-Guérin, an anti-tuberculosis vaccine.

BD *abbr.* Bachelor of Divinity.

Bde *abbr.* Brigade.

bdellium /délliəm/ *n.* **1** any of various trees, esp. of the genus *Commiphora*, yielding resin. **2** this fragrant resin used in perfumes. [L f. Gk *bdellion* f. Heb. *bᵉdhōlaḥ*]

Bdr. *abbr.* (before a name) Bombardier.

BDS *abbr.* Bachelor of Dental Surgery.

BE *abbr.* **1** Bachelor of Education. **2** Bachelor of Engineering. **3** bill of exchange.

Be *symb. Chem.* the element beryllium.

be /bee, bi/ *v.* & *v.aux.* (*sing. present* **am** /am, əm/; **are** /aar, ər/; **is** /iz/; *pl. present* **are**; *1st and 3rd sing. past* **was** /woz, wəz/; *2nd sing. past and pl. past* **were** /wer, wər/; *present subj.* **be**; *past subj.* **were**; *pres. part.* **being**; *past part.* **been** /been, bin/) ● *v.intr.* **1** (often prec. by *there*) exist, live (*I think, therefore I am*; *there is a house on the corner*; *there is no God*). **2 a** occur; take place (*dinner is at eight*). **b** occupy a position in space (*he is in the garden*; *she is from abroad*; *have you been to Paris?*). **3** remain, continue (*let it be*). **4** linking subject and predicate, expressing: **a** identity (*she is the person*; *today is Thursday*). **b** condition (*he is ill today*). **c** state or quality (*he is very kind*; *they are my friends*). **d** opinion (*I am against hanging*). **e** total (*two and two are four*). **f** cost or significance (*it is £5 to enter*; *it is nothing to me*). ● *v.aux.* **1** with a past participle to form the passive mood (*it was done*; *it is said*; *we shall be helped*). **2** with a present participle to form continuous tenses (*we are coming*; *it is being cleaned*). **3** with an infinitive to express duty or commitment, intention, possibility, destiny, or hypothesis (*I am to tell you*; *we are to wait here*; *he is to come at four*; *it was not to be found*; *they were never to meet again*; *if I were to die*). **4** *archaic* with the past participle of intransitive verbs to form perfect tenses (*the sun is set*; *Babylon is fallen*). □ **be about** occupy oneself with (*is about his business*). **be-all and end-all** *colloq.* (often foll. by *of*) the whole being or essence. **be at** occupy oneself with (*what is he at?*; *mice have been at the food*). **been** (or **been and gone**) **and** *sl.* an expression of protest or surprise (*he's been and taken my car!*). **be off** *colloq.* go away; leave. **be that as it may** see MAY. **-to-be** of the future (in *comb.*: *bride-to-be*). [OE *beo(m)*, *(e)am*, *is*, *(e)aron*; past f. OE *wǣs* f. *wesan* to be; there are numerous Gmc cognates]
■ *v.* **1** see EXIST 1, 2a. □ **be-all and end-all** see TOTALITY.

be- /bi/ *prefix* forming verbs: **1** (from transitive verbs) **a** all over; all round (*beset*; *besmear*). **b** thoroughly, excessively (*begrudge*; *belabour*). **2** (from intransitive verbs) expressing transitive action (*bemoan*; *bestride*). **3** (from adjectives and nouns) expressing transitive action (*befool*; *befoul*). **4** (from nouns) **a** affect with (*befog*). **b** treat as (*befriend*). **c** (forming adjectives in *-ed*) having; covered with (*bejewelled*; *bespectacled*). [OE *be-*, weak form of *bī* BY as in *bygone*, *byword*, etc.]

BEA *abbr.* British Epilepsy Association.

beach /beech/ *n.* & *v.* ● *n.* a pebbly or sandy shore esp. of the sea between high- and low-water marks. ● *v.tr.* run or haul up (a boat etc.) on to a beach. □ **beach-ball** a large inflated ball for games on the beach. **beach buggy** a low wide-wheeled motor vehicle for recreational driving on sand. **beach plum 1** a maritime N. American shrub, *Prunus maritima*. **2** its edible fruit. [16th c.: orig. unkn.]
■ *n.* shore, lakeshore, bank, seashore, seaside, plage, lido, coast, margin, littoral, *rhet. or poet.* strand. ● *v.* ground, run aground, strand; land.

beachcomber /beéchkōmər/ *n.* **1** a vagrant who lives by searching beaches for articles of value. **2** a long wave rolling in from the sea.
■ **1** see TRAMP *n.* 1.

beachhead /beéch-hed/ *n. Mil.* a fortified position established on a beach by landing forces. [after *bridgehead*]

Beach-la-mar /beéchləmaár/ *n. Brit.* an English-based Creole language spoken in the W. Pacific. [corrupt. f. Port. *bicho do mar* BÊCHE-DE-MER]

beacon /beékən/ *n.* **1 a** a fire or light set up in a high or prominent position as a warning etc. **b** *Brit.* (now often in place-names) a hill suitable for this. **2** a visible warning or guiding point or device (e.g. a lighthouse, navigation buoy, etc.). **3** a radio transmitter whose signal helps fix the position of a ship or aircraft. **4** *Brit.* = BELISHA BEACON. [OE *bēacn* f. WG]
■ **1a, 2** fire, light, bonfire, flare, signal fire, Very light, rocket; signal, sign, guide, guiding light; lighthouse, pharos.

bead /beed/ *n.* & *v.* ● *n.* **1 a** a small usu. rounded and perforated piece of glass, stone, etc., for threading with others to make jewellery, or sewing on to fabric, etc. **b** (in *pl.*) a string of beads; a rosary. **2** a drop of liquid; a bubble. **3** a small knob in the foresight of a gun. **4** the inner edge of a pneumatic tyre that grips the rim of the wheel. **5** *Archit.* **a** a moulding like a series of beads. **b** a narrow moulding with a semicircular cross-section. ● *v.* **1** *tr.* furnish or decorate with beads. **2** *tr.* string together. **3** *intr.* form or grow into beads. □ **draw a bead on** take aim at. **tell one's beads** use the beads of a rosary etc. in counting prayers. □□ **beaded** *adj.* [orig. = 'prayer' (for which the earliest use of beads arose): OE *gebed* f. Gmc, rel. to BID]
■ *n.* **1a** see ROUND *n.* 1. **2** see DROP *n.* 1. **5** see BORDER *n.* 3.

beading /beéding/ *n.* **1** decoration in the form of or resembling a row of beads, esp. lacelike looped edging. **2** *Archit.* a bead moulding. **3** the bead of a tyre.

beadle /beéd'l/ *n.* **1** *Brit.* a ceremonial officer of a church, college, etc. **2** *Sc.* a church officer attending on the minister. **3** *Brit. hist.* a minor parish officer dealing with petty offenders etc. □□ **beadleship** *n.* [ME f. OF *bedel* ult. f. Gmc]

beadsman /beédzmən/ *n.* (*pl.* **-men**) *hist.* **1** a pensioner provided for by a benefactor in return for prayers. **2** an inmate of an almshouse.

beady /beédi/ *adj.* (**beadier, beadiest**) **1** (of the eyes) small, round, and bright. **2** covered with beads or drops. □ **beady-eyed** with beady eyes. □□ **beadily** *adv.* **beadiness** *n.*

beagle /beég'l/ *n.* & *v.* ● *n.* **1 a** a small hound of a breed with a short coat, used for hunting hares. **b** this breed. **2** *hist.* an informer or spy; a constable. ● *v.intr.* (often as **beagling** *n.*) hunt with beagles. □□ **beagler** *n.* [ME f. OF *beegueule* noisy person, prob. f. *beer* open wide + *gueule* throat]

beak[1] /beek/ *n.* **1 a** a bird's horny projecting jaws; a bill. **b** the similar projecting jaw of other animals, e.g. a turtle. **2** *sl.* a hooked nose. **3** *Naut. hist.* the projection at the prow of a warship. **4** a spout. □□ **beaked** *adj.* **beaky** *adj.* [ME f. OF *bec* f. L *beccus*, of Celt. orig.]

■ **1** see BILL[2] *n.* 1, 2.

beak[2] /beek/ *n.* *Brit. sl.* **1** a magistrate. **2** a schoolmaster. [19th c.: prob. f. thieves' cant]

■ **1** see JUDGE *n.* 1.

beaker /beékər/ *n.* **1** a tall drinking-vessel, usu. of plastic and tumbler-shaped. **2** a lipped cylindrical glass vessel for scientific experiments. **3** *archaic* or *literary* a large drinking-vessel with a wide mouth. □ **Beaker Folk** *Archaeol.* a people thought to have come to Britain from Central Europe in the early Bronze Age, named after beaker-shaped pottery found in their graves. [ME f. ON *bikarr*, perh. f. Gk *bikos* drinking-bowl]

■ **1, 3** see GLASS *n.* 2a.

beam /beem/ *n.* & *v.* ● *n.* **1** a long sturdy piece of squared timber or metal spanning an opening or room, usu. to support the structure above. **2 a** a ray or shaft of light. **b** a directional flow of particles or radiation. **3** a bright look or smile. **4 a** a series of radio or radar signals as a guide to a ship or aircraft. **b** the course indicated by this (*off beam*). **5** the crossbar of a balance. **6 a** a ship's breadth at its widest point. **b** the width of a person's hips (esp. *broad in the beam*). **7** (in *pl.*) the horizontal cross-timbers of a ship supporting the deck and joining the sides. **8** the side of a ship (*land on the port beam*). **9** the chief timber of a plough. **10** the cylinder in a loom on which the warp or cloth is wound. **11** the main stem of a stag's antlers. **12** the lever in an engine connecting the piston-rod and crank. **13** the shank of an anchor. ● *v.* **1** *tr.* emit or direct (light, radio waves, etc.). **2** *intr.* **a** shine. **b** look or smile radiantly. □ **beam-compass** (or **-compasses**) compasses with a beam connecting sliding sockets, used for large circles. **a beam in one's eye** a fault that is greater in oneself than in the person one is finding fault with (see Matt. 7:3). **off** (*or* **off the**) **beam** *colloq.* mistaken. **on the beam** *colloq.* on the right track. **on the beam-ends** (of a ship) on its side; almost capsizing. **on one's beam-ends** near the end of one's resources. [OE *bēam* tree f. WG]

■ *n.* **1** timber, baulk, pile, purlin, collar-beam, tie-beam, crosspiece, summer, summer-tree, hammerbeam, scantling, girder, rafter, cantilever; bar, brace, plank, board, stud, trestle, *Archit.* breastsummer. **2 a** ray, gleam, shaft. ● *v.* **1** emit, radiate, shed, give off *or* out, send out; direct, shine, train, aim, focus. **2 a** radiate, shine (out *or* forth), pour out *or* forth, emanate, gleam, glow, blaze. **b** smile, grin. □ **off** (*or* **off the**) **beam** see WRONG *adj.* 1. **on the beam** on the right track, along the right lines, close, *colloq.* warm. **on one's beam-ends** see BROKE.

beamer /beémər/ *n.* *Cricket colloq.* a ball bowled at a batsman's head.

beamy /beémi/ *adj.* (of a ship) broad-beamed.

■ broad-beamed, broad, wide, broad in the beam.

bean /been/ *n.* & *v.* ● *n.* **1 a** any kind of leguminous plant with edible usu. kidney-shaped seeds in long pods. **b** one of these seeds. **2** a similar seed of coffee and other plants. **3** *US sl.* the head, esp. as a source of common sense. **4** (in *pl.*; with *neg.*) *US sl.* anything at all (*doesn't know beans about it*). ● *v.tr.* *US sl.* hit on the head. □ **bean curd** jelly or paste made from beans, used esp. in Asian cookery. **bean sprout** a sprout of a bean seed, esp. of the mung bean, used as food. **full of beans** *colloq.* lively; in high spirits. **not a bean** *Brit. sl.* no money. **old bean** *Brit. sl.* a friendly form of address, usu. to a man. [OE *bēan* f. Gmc]

■ *n.* **3** see HEAD *n.* 1.

beanbag /beénbag/ *n.* **1** a small bag filled with dried beans and used esp. in children's games. **2** a large cushion filled usu. with polystyrene beads and used as a seat.

beanery /beénəri/ *n.* (*pl.* **-ies**) *US sl.* a cheap restaurant.

beanfeast /beénfeest/ *n.* **1** *Brit. colloq.* a celebration; a merry time. **2** an employer's annual dinner given to employees. [BEAN + FEAST, beans and bacon being regarded as an indispensable dish]

■ see PARTY *n.* 1.

beanie /beéni/ *n.* a small close-fitting hat worn on the back of the head. [perh. f. BEAN 'head' + -IE]

beano /beénō/ *n.* (*pl.* **-os**) *Brit. sl.* a celebration; a party. [abbr. of BEANFEAST]

■ see PARTY *n.* 1.

beanpole /beénpōl/ *n.* **1** a stick for supporting bean plants. **2** *colloq.* a tall thin person.

beanstalk /beénstawk/ *n.* the stem of a bean plant.

bear[1] /bair/ *v.* (*past* **bore** /bor/; *past part.* **borne, born** /born/) ¶ In the passive *born* is used with reference to birth (e.g. *was born in July*), except for *borne by* foll. by the name of the mother (e.g. *was borne by Sarah*). **1** *tr.* carry, bring, or take (esp. visibly) (*bear gifts*). **2** *tr.* show; be marked by; have as an attribute or characteristic (*bear marks of violence; bears no relation to the case; bore no name*). **3** *tr.* **a** produce, yield (fruit etc.). **b** give birth to (*has borne a son; was born last week*). **4** *tr.* **a** sustain (a weight, responsibility, cost, etc.). **b** stand, endure (an ordeal, difficulty, etc.). **5** *tr.* (usu. with *neg.* or *interrog.*) **a** tolerate; put up with (*can't bear him; how can you bear it?*). **b** admit of; be fit for (*does not bear thinking about*). **6** *tr.* carry in thought or memory (*bear a grudge*). **7** *intr.* veer in a given direction (*bear left*). **8** *tr.* bring or provide (something needed) (*bear him company*). **9** *refl.* behave (in a certain way). □ **bear arms 1** carry weapons; serve as a soldier. **2** wear or display heraldic devices. **bear away** (or **off**) win (a prize etc.). **bear down** exert downward pressure. **bear down on** approach rapidly or purposefully. **bear fruit** have results. **bear a hand** help. **bear hard on** oppress. **bear in mind** take into account having remembered. **bear on** (or **upon**) be relevant to. **bear out** support or confirm (an account or the person giving it). **bear repeating** be worth repetition. **bear up 1** raise one's spirits; not despair. **2** (often foll. by *against*, *under*) endure, survive. **bear with** treat forbearingly; tolerate patiently. **bear witness** testify. [OE *beran* f. Gmc]

■ **1** carry, transport, convey, move, take, deliver, bring, *colloq.* schlep, *esp. US colloq.* tote, *sl.* cart. **2** have, carry, show, hold, exhibit, display, be marked by. **3** produce, yield, develop, breed, generate; give birth to, spawn, bring forth, have, *archaic* engender; (*be born*) come into the world, *colloq.* arrive. **4** carry, support, sustain, shoulder, take, uphold; endure, stand, withstand, hold *or* stand up under, hold out against, weather, suffer, cope with, undergo, go through with, experience. **5 a** stand, put up with, abide, tolerate, endure, submit (oneself) to, reconcile oneself to, *literary* brook. **b** merit, admit of, be worthy of, warrant, be fit for, deserve, rate; invite. **6** carry, harbour, keep, hold, retain, maintain, foster, have; entertain. **7** turn, veer, swing, shift, wheel, incline. **9** (*bear oneself*) see ACT *v.* 1, 2. □ **bear away** see WIN *v.* 1. **bear down on** travel headlong towards, head towards, approach, home in on. **bear a hand** see HELP *v.* 1. **bear hard on** see OPPRESS 1, 2. **bear in mind** remember, keep in mind, do not forget *or* overlook, recollect, recall, be aware *or* cognizant *or* mindful of; see also CONSIDER 4.

bear on (or **upon**) relate to, have relevance to, be relevant to, pertain to, be *or* have to do with, touch on *or* upon, affect, concern, have a bearing on *or* upon, appertain to. **bear out** confirm, support, corroborate, substantiate, uphold, back up, authenticate, verify, bear witness to. **bear up 1** cheer up, be encouraged, raise *or* lift one's spirits, buoy oneself up, uplift *or* hearten *or* comfort oneself. **2** endure, survive, hold out *or* up, stand up, withstand. **bear with** put up with, be patient *or* tolerant with, tolerate, make allowance(s) *or* concessions for, excuse. **bear witness** see TESTIFY 1.

bear[2] /bair/ *n.* & *v.* ● *n.* **1** any large heavy mammal of the family Ursidae, having thick fur and walking on its soles. **2** a rough, unmannerly, or uncouth person. **3** *Stock Exch.* a person who sells shares hoping to buy them back later at a lower price. **4** = TEDDY. **5** (**the Bear**) *colloq.* Russia. ● *v. Stock Exch.* **1** *intr.* speculate for a fall in price. **2** *tr.* produce a fall in the price of (stocks etc.). □ **bear-baiting** *hist.* an entertainment involving setting dogs to attack a captive bear. **bear-hug** a tight embrace. **bear market** *Stock Exch.* a market with falling prices. **bear's breech** a kind of acanthus, *Acanthus mollis.* **bear's ear** auricula. **bear's foot** a hellebore, *Helleborus fetidus.* **the Great Bear, the Little Bear** two constellations near the North Pole. **like a bear with a sore head** *Brit. colloq.* very irritable. [OE *bera* f. WG]

bearable /báirəb'l/ *adj.* that may be endured or tolerated. □□ **bearability** /-bílliti/ *n.* **bearableness** *n.* **bearably** *adv.*

■ tolerable, supportable, endurable, acceptable, manageable, sufferable. □□ **bearability, bearableness** see *acceptability* (ACCEPTABLE). **bearably** see *acceptably* (ACCEPTABLE)

beard /beerd/ *n.* & *v.* ● *n.* **1** hair growing on the chin and lower cheeks of the face. **2** a similar tuft or part on an animal (esp. a goat). **3** the awn of a grass, sheath of barley, etc. ● *v.tr.* oppose openly; defy. □□ **bearded** *adj.* **beardless** *adj.* [OE f. WG]

■ □□ **bearded** see HAIRY 1.

beardie /béerdi/ *n. Brit. colloq.* a bearded man.

■ *sl.* beaver.

bearer /báirər/ *n.* **1** a person or thing that bears, carries, or brings. **2** a carrier of equipment on an expedition etc. **3** a person who presents a cheque or other order to pay money. **4** (*attrib.*) payable to the possessor (*bearer stock*). **5** *hist.* (in India etc.) a personal servant.

beargarden /báirgaard'n/ *n.* a rowdy or noisy scene.

bearing /báiring/ *n.* **1** a person's bodily attitude or outward behaviour. **2** (foll. by *on, upon*) relation or relevance to (*his comments have no bearing on the subject*). **3** endurability (*beyond bearing*). **4** a part of a machine that supports a rotating or other moving part. **5** direction or position relative to a fixed point, measured esp. in degrees. **6** (in *pl.*) **a** one's position relative to one's surroundings. **b** awareness of this; a sense of one's orientation (*get one's bearings*; *lose one's bearings*). **7** *Heraldry* a device or charge. **8** = *ball-bearing* (see BALL[1]). □ **bearing-rein** a fixed rein from bit to saddle that forces a horse to arch its neck.

■ **1** carriage, deportment, manner, behaviour, conduct, aspect, demeanour, posture, stance, air, attitude, presence, *literary* mien. **2** relation, reference, relationship, correlation, pertinence, relevance, connection, relevancy, applicability, application, germaneness, significance. **3** endurance, endurability, tolerance, tolerability, acceptance, acceptability, sufferance, manageability. **5** see POSITION *n.* 1. **6** (*bearings*) (sense of) direction, orientation, (relative) position.

bearish /báirish/ *adj.* **1** like a bear, esp. in temper. **2** *Stock Exch.* causing or associated with a fall in prices.

■ **1** see *short-tempered.*

Béarnaise sauce /báyaarnáyz/ *n.* a rich sauce thickened with egg yolks and flavoured with tarragon. [F, fem. of *béarnais* of *Béarn* in SW France]

bearskin /báirskin/ *n.* **1 a** the skin of a bear. **b** a wrap etc. made of this. **2** a tall furry hat worn ceremonially by some regiments.

beast /beest/ *n.* **1** an animal other than a human being, esp. a wild quadruped. **2 a** a brutal person. **b** *colloq.* an objectionable or unpleasant person or thing (*he's a beast for not inviting her*; *a beast of a problem*). **3** (prec. by *the*) a human being's brutish or uncivilized characteristics (*saw the beast in him*). □ **beast of burden** an animal, e.g. an ox, used for carrying loads. **beast of prey** see PREY. [ME f. OF *beste* f. Rmc *besta* f. L *bestia*]

■ **1** animal, creature, living thing; being. **2 a** brute, savage, animal, monster, fiend, ogre, barbarian, demon. **b** see STINKER.

beastie /béesti/ *n. Sc.* or *joc.* a small animal.

beastly /béestli/ *adj.* & *adv.* ● *adj.* (**beastlier, beastliest**) **1** *colloq.* objectionable, unpleasant. **2** like a beast; brutal. ● *adv. colloq.* very, extremely. □□ **beastliness** *n.*

■ *adj.* **1** objectionable, horrible, awful, unpleasant, atrocious, disagreeable, intolerable, offensive, hateful, execrable, vile, nasty, unspeakable, woeful, *colloq.* terrible, horrid, hideous, dreadful, abominable, lousy, shocking, frightful, ghastly, wicked, accursed, infernal, foul, *sl.* rotten. **2** uncivilized, uncultivated, uncivil, rude, crude, uncouth, insensitive, vulgar, boorish, unrefined, coarse; cruel, inhuman, savage, barbaric, barbarous, bestial, brutal. ● *adv.* see AWFULLY 2. □□ **beastliness** see *brutality* (BRUTAL).

beat /beet/ *v., n.,* & *adj.* ● *v.* (*past* **beat**; *past part.* **beaten** /béet'n/) **1** *tr.* **a** strike (a person or animal) persistently or repeatedly, esp. to harm or punish. **b** strike (a thing) repeatedly, e.g. to remove dust from (a carpet etc.), to sound (a drum etc.). **2** *intr.* (foll. by *against, at, on,* etc.) **a** pound or knock repeatedly (*waves beat against the shore*; *beat at the door*). **b** = *beat down* 3. **3** *tr.* **a** overcome; surpass; win a victory over. **b** complete an activity before (another person etc.). **c** be too hard for; perplex. **4** *tr.* (often foll. by *up*) stir (eggs etc.) vigorously into a frothy mixture. **5** *tr.* (often foll. by *out*) fashion or shape (metal etc.) by blows. **6** *intr.* (of the heart, a drum, etc.) pulsate rhythmically. **7** *tr.* (often foll. by *out*) **a** indicate (a tempo or rhythm) by gestures, tapping, etc. **b** sound (a signal etc.) by striking a drum or other means (*beat a tattoo*). **8 a** *intr.* (of a bird's wings) move up and down. **b** *tr.* cause (wings) to move in this way. **9** *tr.* make (a path etc.) by trampling. **10** *tr.* strike (bushes etc.) to rouse game. **11** *intr. Naut.* sail in the direction from which the wind is blowing. ● *n.* **1 a** a main accent or rhythmic unit in music or verse (*three beats to the bar*; *missed a beat and came in early*). **b** the indication of rhythm by a conductor's movements (*watch the beat*). **c** the tempo or rhythm of a piece of music as indicated by the repeated fall of the main beat. **d** (in popular music) a strong rhythm. **e** (*attrib.*) characterized by a strong rhythm (*beat music*). **2 a** a stroke or blow (e.g. on a drum). **b** a measured sequence of strokes (*the beat of the waves on the rocks*). **c** a throbbing movement or sound (*the beat of his heart*). **3 a** a route or area allocated to a police officer etc. **b** a person's habitual round. **4** *Physics* a pulsation due to the combination of two sounds or electric currents of similar but not equivalent frequencies. **5** *colloq.* = BEATNIK. ● *adj.* **1** (*predic.*) *sl.* exhausted, tired out. **2** (*attrib.*) of the beat generation or its philosophy. □ **beat about** (often foll. by *for*) search (for an excuse etc.). **beat about the bush** discuss a matter without coming to the point. **beat the bounds** *Brit.* mark parish boundaries by striking certain points with rods. **beat one's breast** strike one's chest in anguish or sorrow. **beat the clock** complete a task within a stated time. **beat down 1 a** bargain with (a seller) to lower the price. **b** cause a seller to lower (the price). **2** strike (a resisting object) until it falls (*beat the door down*). **3** (of the sun, rain, etc.) radiate heat or fall continuously and vigorously. **beat the drum for** publicize, promote. **beaten at the post** defeated at the last moment. **beat generation** the members of a movement of young people esp. in the 1950s who rejected conventional society in their dress, habits, and beliefs. **beat in** crush. **beat it** *sl.* go away. **beat off** drive back (an attack etc.). **beat a retreat** withdraw; abandon an undertaking. **beat time** indicate or follow a musical tempo with a baton or other means. **beat a person to it** arrive or achieve something before another person. **beat up** give a beating to, esp. with punches and kicks. **beat-up** *adj. colloq.* dilapidated; in a state of disrepair. **it beats me** I do not understand (it). □□ **beatable** *adj.* [OE *bēatan* f. Gmc]

■ *v.* **1** strike, pound, bash, batter, baste, pummel, pommel, belabour, pelt, clout, thrash, trounce, give a person a thrashing *or* beating, drub, thump, cane, scourge, whip, flail, strap, bludgeon, club, cudgel, leather, flog, lash, welt, *Austral.* give a person bondi, *archaic or literary* smite, *colloq.* manhandle, whack, thwack, give a person a good hiding *or* licking, lambaste, *esp. US colloq.* whale, *sl.* clobber, whop, wallop, belt, duff up, paste, tan a person's hide, fill in, give a person a going-over, *Austral. sl.* quilt. **2 a** pound, knock, dash, strike, hit, rap, bang, hammer; (*beat against*) break against. **3 a** defeat, worst, win (out) over, trounce, rout, break, outdo, subdue, overcome, overwhelm, surpass, outstrip, conquer, crush, master, get the better *or* best of, thrash, *US* scalp, *archaic* confound, *colloq.* lick, best, slaughter, pull the plug on, knock *or* take the stuffing out of, take apart, *US colloq.* cream, *literary* vanquish, *sl.* crucify, clobber, snooker, whip, whop, *US sl.* skunk, shellac. **b** pre-empt. **c** see PERPLEX 1. **4** mix, whip (up), stir (up), blend (together). **5** hammer (out), forge, shape, form, fashion, make, mould, work. **6** throb, pulsate, pulse, palpitate, pound, thump, hammer. **8** flap, flutter. **9** tread, wear, trample. **11** *Naut.* tack. ● *n.* **1 a** accent, stress; throb, pulsation. **c** rhythm, tempo, measure, cadence, time, timing, pulse. **2 a** stroke, blow, rap. **b** rhythm, cadence. **c** throb, thump, pulse, pulsation, palpitation, throbbing. **3** course, round, tour, route, circuit, run, path; area, zone, territory, *Law* bailiwick. ● *adj.* **1** exhausted, spent, beaten, drained, worn out, played out, weary, bone-tired, dog-tired, tired out, fatigued, ragged, shattered, *Brit.* whacked, *colloq.* all in, done in, dead beat, shot, fagged (out), frazzled, *US colloq.* pooped, tuckered (out), *Austral.* & *NZ sl.* stonkered, *Brit. sl.* knackered, cooked. □ **beat about** see SEARCH *v.* 4. **beat about the bush** see PUSSYFOOT 2. **beat one's breast** see GRIEVE[1] 2. **beat down 1** knock *or* bring down. **2** knock *or* batter *or* pound *or* bash down. **3** blaze, shine, burn. **beat the drum for** see PROMOTE 3. **beat it** go away, depart, leave, abscond, run off *or* away, take oneself off, *US* hit the road, *colloq.* push off, be off, clear off *or* out, scram, *sl.* buzz off, shove off, kiss off, get lost, naff off, take a running jump, slope off, *Brit. sl.* hop it, *US sl.* go on the lam, skiddoo. **beat off** drive off *or* away *or* back, rout, put to rout, repel, fight off, ward off, *Mil.* repulse. **beat a retreat** see WITHDRAW 5. **beat-up** see DILAPIDATED. **it beats me** see *ask me another*.

beaten /beét'n/ *adj.* **1** outwitted; defeated. **2** exhausted; dejected. **3** (of gold or any other metal) shaped by a hammer. **4** (of a path etc.) well-trodden, much-used. □ **off the beaten track 1** in or into an isolated place. **2** unusual. [past part. of BEAT]

beater /beétər/ *n.* **1** a person employed to rouse game for shooting. **2** an implement used for beating (esp. a carpet or eggs). **3** a person who beats metal.

■ **2** see WHISK *n.* 2.

beatific /beéətiffik/ *adj.* **1** *colloq.* blissful (*a beatific smile*). **2 a** of or relating to blessedness. **b** making blessed. □□ **beatifically** *adv.* [F *béatifique* or L *beatificus* f. *beatus* blessed]

■ **1** see ECSTATIC 3. **2** see SAINTLY.

beatification /bee-áttifikáysh'n/ *n.* **1** *RC Ch.* the act of formally declaring a dead person 'blessed', often a step towards canonization. **2** making or being blessed. [F *béatification* or eccl.L *beatificatio* (as BEATIFY)]

beatify /bee-áttifī/ *v.tr.* (**-ies, -ied**) **1** *RC Ch.* announce the beatification of. **2** make happy. [F *béatifier* or eccl.L *beatificare* f. L *beatus* blessed]

■ **1** see SANCTIFY 1.

beating /beéting/ *n.* **1** a physical punishment or assault. **2** a defeat. □ **take some** (or **a lot of**) **beating** be difficult to surpass.

beatitude /bee-áttityōōd/ *n.* **1** blessedness. **2** (in *pl.*) the declarations of blessedness in Matt. 5:3-11. **3** a title given to patriarchs in the Orthodox Church. [F *béatitude* or L *beatitudo* f. *beatus* blessed]

beatnik /beétnik/ *n.* a member of the beat generation (see BEAT). [BEAT + *-nik* after *sputnik*, perh. infl. by US use of Yiddish *-nik* agent-suffix]

beau /bō/ *n.* (*pl.* **beaux** or **beaus** /bōz, bō/) **1** esp. *US* an admirer; a boyfriend. **2** a fop; a dandy. [F, = handsome, f. L *bellus*]

■ **1** see ADMIRER 1. **2** see DANDY *n.* 1.

Beaufort scale /bṓfərt/ *n.* a scale of wind speed ranging from 0 (calm) to 12 (hurricane). [Sir F. *Beaufort*, Engl. admiral d. 1857]

beau geste /bō zhést/ *n.* (*pl.* ***beaux gestes*** *pronunc.* same) a generous or gracious act. [F, = splendid gesture]

■ see FAVOUR *n.* 1.

beau idéal /bṓ eedayál/ *n.* (*pl.* ***beaux idéals*** /bṓz eedayál/) the highest type of excellence or beauty. [F *beau idéal* = ideal beauty: see BEAU, IDEAL]

■ see PARAGON.

Beaujolais /bṓzhəlay/ *n.* a red or white burgundy wine from the Beaujolais district of France. □ **Beaujolais nouveau** Beaujolais wine sold in the first year of a vintage.

beau monde /bō mónd/ *n.* fashionable society. [F]

■ see SOCIETY 5a.

beaut /byōōt/ *n.* & *adj. Austral.* & *NZ sl.* ● *n.* an excellent or beautiful person or thing. ● *adj.* excellent; beautiful. [abbr. of BEAUTY]

beauteous /byṓōtiəss/ *adj. poet.* beautiful. [ME f. BEAUTY + -OUS, after *bounteous*, *plenteous*]

■ see FAIR[1] *adj.* 6.

beautician /byootísh'n/ *n.* **1** a person who gives beauty treatment. **2** a person who runs or owns a beauty salon.

beautiful /byṓōtifŏŏl/ *adj.* **1** delighting the aesthetic senses (*a beautiful voice*). **2** pleasant, enjoyable (*had a beautiful time*). **3** excellent (*a beautiful specimen*). □□ **beautifully** *adv.*

■ **1** attractive, charming, comely, lovely, good-looking, fair, pretty, alluring, appealing, exquisite, handsome, radiant, gorgeous, divine, aesthetic, *Sc.* & *N.Engl.* bonny, *colloq.* smashing, *literary* pulchritudinous, *poet.* beauteous, *Austral.* & *NZ sl.* beaut; scenic, picturesque. **2** see PLEASANT. **3** excellent, first-rate, unequalled, fine, skilful, admirable, ideal, superb, spectacular, splendid, beyond comparison, first-class, marvellous, remarkable, superlative, wonderful, rip-roaring, incomparable, superior, sovereign, exquisite, *US* elegant, *colloq.* smashing, swinging, magnificent, tremendous, grand, terrific, out of sight, out of this world, way-out, A1, divine, capital, *US colloq.* swell, *literary* beyond compare, *sl.* wicked, cracking, *archaic sl.* spiffing, *Austral. sl.* bonzer, *Austral.* & *NZ sl.* beaut, *sl. esp. Brit.* wizard, *Brit. archaic sl.* topping, *sl. esp. US* cool, *US sl.* bang-up, copacetic. □□ **beautifully** attractively, exquisitely, gorgeously, charmingly, prettily, alluringly, handsomely, radiantly, divinely, appealingly, fashionably, delightfully, elegantly, chicly; scenically, picturesquely; splendidly, admirably, superbly, excellently, wonderfully, marvellously, remarkably, superlatively, *Sc.* & *N.Engl.* bonnily, *US* elegantly, *colloq.* smashingly, brilliantly, fantastically, magnificently, tremendously, capitally.

beautify /byṓōtifī/ *v.tr.* (**-ies, -ied**) make beautiful; adorn. □□ **beautification** /-fikáysh'n/ *n.* **beautifier** /-fīər/ *n.*

■ adorn, embellish, decorate, ornament, elaborate, garnish,

deck (out), bedeck, smarten (up), *colloq.* titivate.
□□ **beautification** see *embellishment* (EMBELLISH). **beautifier** embellisher, decorator, elaborator.

beauty /byóoti/ *n.* (*pl.* **-ies**) **1 a** a combination of qualities such as shape, colour, etc., that pleases the aesthetic senses, esp. the sight. **b** a combination of qualities that pleases the intellect or moral sense (*the beauty of the argument*). **2** *colloq.* **a** an excellent specimen (*what a beauty!*). **b** an attractive feature; an advantage (*that's the beauty of it!*). **3** a beautiful woman. □ **beauty is only skin-deep** a pleasing appearance is not a guide to character. **beauty parlour** (or **salon**) an establishment in which massage, manicure, hairdressing, make-up, etc., are offered to women. **beauty queen** the woman judged most beautiful in a competition. **beauty sleep** sleep before midnight, supposed to be health-giving. **beauty spot 1** a place known for its beauty. **2** a small natural or artificial mark such as a mole on the face, considered to enhance another feature. **beauty treatment** cosmetic treatment received in a beauty parlour. [ME f. AF *beuté*, OF *bealté*, *beauté*, ult. f. L (as BEAU)]
■ **1** loveliness, attractiveness, handsomeness, comeliness, fairness, prettiness, gorgeousness, charm(s), *Sc. & N.Engl.* bonniness, *literary* pulchritude; picturesqueness, aestheticism, elegance, exquisiteness, grandeur, fineness, splendour, radiance, splendidness, gracefulness, delicacy, glory, glamour. **2 a** perfect specimen, jewel, pearl, gem, dream, winner, *crème de la crème*, treasure, prize, *chef-d'œuvre*, masterpiece, *colloq.* stunner, smasher, knockout, *Austral. colloq.* trimmer, *sl.* corker, gasser, *Austral. & NZ sl.* beaut. **b** attraction, appeal, charm, allure, draw, lure, seductiveness, pull; strength, advantage, asset, benefit, boon, selling-point, plus, added extra. **3** belle, vision, beauty queen, English rose, picture, good-looker, peach, *archaic* fair, *colloq.* pippin, looker, bit of crackling, knockout, smasher, dreamboat, a fair treat, stunner, *poet.* Venus, *sl.* bombshell, bit of all right, dish, *Austral. & NZ sl.* beaut, *Brit. sl.* cracker, *US sl.* fox. □ **beauty is only skin-deep** all that glitters is not gold.

beaux *pl.* of BEAU.

beaux arts /bōz aár/ *n.pl.* **1** fine arts. **2** (*attrib.*) relating to the rules and conventions of the École des Beaux-Arts in Paris (later called Académie des Beaux Arts). [F *beaux-arts*]

beaver[1] /beévər/ *n.* & *v.* ● *n.* (*pl.* same or **beavers**) **1 a** any large amphibious broad-tailed rodent of the genus *Castor*, native to N. America, Europe, and Asia, and able to cut down trees and build dams. **b** its soft light-brown fur. **c** a hat of this. **2** (in full **beaver cloth**) a heavy woollen cloth like beaver fur. **3** (**Beaver**) a boy aged six or seven who is an affiliate member of the Scout Association. ● *v.intr. colloq.* (usu. foll. by *away*) work hard. □ **beaver lamb** lamb's wool made to look like beaver fur. **eager beaver** *colloq.* an over-zealous person. [OE *be(o)for* f. Gmc]
■ *v.* (*beaver away*) see *peg away*. □ **eager beaver** fanatic, zealot, workaholic, *colloq.* buff, freak, maniac, *sl.* fiend, nut.

beaver[2] /beévər/ *n. hist.* the lower face-guard of a helmet. [OF *baviere* bib f. *baver* slaver f. *beve* saliva f. Rmc]

beaver[3] /beévər/ *n. sl.* a bearded man. [20th c.: orig. uncert.]

Beaverboard /beévərbord/ *n. propr.* a kind of fibreboard. [BEAVER[1] + BOARD]

bebop /beébop/ *n.* a type of jazz originating in the 1940s and characterized by complex harmony and rhythms. □□ **bebopper** *n.* [imit. of the typical rhythm]

becalm /bikaám/ *v.tr.* (usu. in *passive*) deprive (a ship) of wind.

became *past* of BECOME.

because /bikóz/ *conj.* for the reason that; since. □ **because of** on account of; by reason of. [ME f. BY *prep.* + CAUSE, after OF *par cause de* by reason of]
■ for, since, as, inasmuch as, seeing that, owing *or* due to the fact that.

béchamel /béshəmel/ *n.* a kind of thick white sauce. [invented by the Marquis de *Béchamel*, Fr. courtier d. 1703]

bêche-de-mer /béshdəmáir/ *n.* (*pl.* same or ***bêches-de-mer*** *pronunc.* same) **1** a kind of sea cucumber eaten in China usu. in long dried strips. **2** = BEACH-LA-MAR. [F, alt. of *biche de mer* f. Port. *bicho do mar* sea-worm]

beck[1] /bek/ *n. N.Engl.* a brook; a mountain stream. [ME f. ON *bekkr* f. Gmc]
■ see BROOK[1].

beck[2] /bek/ *n. poet.* a gesture requesting attention, e.g. a nod, wave, etc. □ **at a person's beck and call** having constantly to obey a person's orders. [*beck* (v.) f. BECKON]
■ □ **at a person's beck and call** see UNDER *prep.* 3a.

becket /békkit/ *n. Naut.* a contrivance such as a hook, bracket, or rope-loop, for securing loose ropes, tackle, or spars. [18th c.: orig. unkn.]

beckon /békkən/ *v.* **1** *tr.* attract the attention of; summon by gesture. **2** *intr.* (usu. foll. by *to*) make a signal to attract a person's attention; summon a person by doing this. [OE *bīecnan*, *bēcnan* ult. f. WG *baukna* BEACON]
■ **1** summon, call, *archaic or literary* bid. **2** signal, gesture, motion, sign, gesticulate.

becloud /biklówd/ *v.tr.* **1** obscure (*becloud the argument*). **2** cover with clouds.
■ see OBSCURE *v.* 1, 2.

become /bikúm/ *v.* (*past* **became** /bikáym/; *past part.* **become**) **1** *intr.* (foll. by compl.) begin to be; come to be, turn into (*became president*; *will become famous*; *tadpoles become frogs*). **2** *tr.* **a** look well on; suit (*blue becomes him*). **b** befit (*it ill becomes you to complain*). **3** *intr.* (as **becoming** *adj.*) **a** flattering the appearance. **b** suitable; decorous. □ **become of** happen to (*what will become of me?*). □□ **becomingly** *adj.* **becomingness** *n.* [OE *becuman* f. Gmc: cf. BE-, COME]
■ **1** be; turn, grow, get, fall; turn *or* change *or* transform *or* metamorphose into, grow *or* develop *or* evolve into, mature *or* ripen into. **2** look good *or* well on, suit; fit, befit, be proper *or* appropriate *or* suitable, *formal* behove. **3** (**becoming**) **a** flattering, seemly; attractive, fetching, chic, stylish, fashionable, tasteful. **b** appropriate, apt, fitting, fit, befitting, proper, suitable, well-suited, *archaic* meet; see also DECOROUS. □ **become of** come of, happen to, *archaic* hap to, *poet.* befall, betide. □□ **becomingly** flatteringly, attractively, fetchingly, stylishly, tastefully. **becomingness** see PROPRIETY 1.

becquerel /békkərel/ *n. Physics* the SI unit of radioactivity, corresponding to one disintegration per second. [A. H. *Becquerel*, Fr. physicist d. 1908]

B.Ed. *abbr.* Bachelor of Education.

bed /bed/ *n.* & *v.* ● *n.* **1 a** a piece of furniture used for sleeping on, usu. a framework with a mattress and coverings. **b** such a mattress, with or without coverings. **2** any place used by a person or animal for sleep or rest; a litter. **3 a** a garden plot, esp. one used for planting flowers. **b** a place where other things may be grown (*osier bed*). **4** the use of a bed: **a** *colloq.* for sexual intercourse (*only thinks of bed*). **b** for rest (*needs his bed*). **5** something flat, forming a support or base as in: **a** the bottom of the sea or a river. **b** the foundations of a road or railway. **c** the slates etc. on a billiard-table. **6** a stratum, such as a layer of oysters etc. ● *v.* (**bedded, bedding**) **1** *tr.* & *intr.* (usu. foll. by *down*) put or go to bed. **2** *tr. colloq.* have sexual intercourse with. **3** *tr.* (usu. foll. by *out*) plant in a garden bed. **4** *tr.* cover up or fix firmly in something. **5 a** *tr.* arrange as a layer. **b** *intr.* be or form a layer. □ **bed and board 1** lodging and food. **2** marital relations. **bed and breakfast 1** one night's lodging and breakfast in a hotel etc. **2** an establishment that provides this. **bed of roses** a life of ease. **brought to bed** (often foll. by *of*) delivered of a child. **get out of bed on the wrong side** be bad-tempered all day long. **go to bed 1** retire for the night. **2** have sexual intercourse. **3** (of a

newspaper) go to press. **keep one's bed** stay in bed because of illness. **make the bed** tidy and arrange the bed for use. **make one's bed and lie in it** accept the consequences of one's acts. **put to bed 1** cause to go to bed. **2** make (a newspaper) ready for press. **take to one's bed** stay in bed because of illness. [OE *bed(d)*, *beddian* f. Gmc]
■ *n.* **3 a** see BORDER *n.* 4. **5 a** see BOTTOM *n.* 4. **6** see SEAM *n.* 4. ● *v.* **2** see LAY[1] *v.* 16. **3** see PLANT *v.* 1.

bedabble /bidább'l/ *v.tr.* stain or splash with dirty liquid, blood, etc.
■ see DABBLE 3.

bedad /bidád/ *int. Ir.* by God! [corrupt.: cf. GAD[2]]

bedaub /bidáwb/ *v.tr.* smear or daub with paint etc.; decorate gaudily.
■ see SMEAR *v.* 1.

bedazzle /bidázz'l/ *v.tr.* **1** dazzle. **2** confuse (a person). □□ **bedazzlement** *n.*
■ see DAZE *v.*

bedbug /bédbug/ *n.* either of two flat, wingless, evil-smelling insects of the genus *Cimex* infesting beds and unclean houses and sucking blood.

bedchamber /bédchaymbər/ *n.* **1** *archaic* a bedroom. **2** (**Bedchamber**) part of the title of some of the sovereign's attendants (*Lady of the Bedchamber*).

bedclothes /bédklōthz/ *n.pl.* coverings for a bed, such as sheets, blankets, etc.
■ see COVER *n.* 1f.

beddable /béddəb'l/ *adj. colloq.* sexually attractive. [BED + -ABLE]

bedder /béddər/ *n.* **1** a plant suitable for a garden bed. **2** *Brit. colloq.* a college bedmaker.

bedding /bédding/ *n.* **1** a mattress and bedclothes. **2** litter for cattle, horses, etc. **3** a bottom layer. **4** *Geol.* the stratification of rocks, esp. when clearly visible. □ **bedding plant** a plant suitable for a garden bed.
■ **1** see COVER *n.* 1f.

bedeck /bidék/ *v.tr.* adorn.
■ see DECORATE 1, 3.

bedeguar /béddigaar/ *n.* a mosslike growth on rose-bushes produced by a gall wasp. [F *bédegar* f. Pers. *bād-āwar* wind-brought]

bedel /béed'l, bidél/ *n.* (also **bedell**) *Brit.* a university official with chiefly processional duties. [= BEADLE]

bedevil /bidévv'l/ *v.tr.* (**bedevilled, bedevilling**; *US* **bedeviled, bedeviling**) **1** plague; afflict. **2** confound; confuse. **3** possess as if with a devil; bewitch. **4** treat with diabolical violence or abuse. □□ **bedevilment** *n.*
■ **1** see PESTER. **3** see OBSESS.

bedew /bidyóō/ *v.tr.* **1** cover or sprinkle with dew or drops of water. **2** *poet.* sprinkle with tears.
■ **1** see DAMPEN 1.

bedfellow /bédfellō/ *n.* **1** a person who shares a bed. **2** an associate.

Bedford cord /bédfərd/ *n.* a tough woven fabric having prominent ridges, similar to corduroy. [*Bedford* in S. England]

bedight /bidī́t/ *adj. archaic* arrayed; adorned. [ME past part. of *bedight* (v.) (as BE-, DIGHT)]

bedim /bidím/ *v.tr.* (**bedimmed, bedimming**) *poet.* make (the eyes, mind, etc.) dim.
■ see OBSCURE *v.* 1, 2.

bedizen /bidī́z'n, -dízz'n/ *v.tr. poet.* deck out gaudily. [BE- + obs. *dizen* deck out]

bedjacket /bédjakkit/ *n.* a jacket worn when sitting up in bed.

bedlam /bédləm/ *n.* **1** a scene of uproar and confusion (*the traffic was bedlam*). **2** *archaic* a madhouse; an asylum. [hospital of St Mary of *Bethlehem* in London]
■ **1** pandemonium, uproar, chaos, hubbub, commotion, confusion, tumult, turmoil, furore, pie, *colloq.* madhouse, *sl.* snafu. **2** (mental) asylum, (mental) institution, mental home *or* hospital, *archaic or colloq.* madhouse, *hist.* lunatic asylum, *sl.* loony-bin, nut-house, funny-farm, *esp. US sl.* booby-hatch.

bedlinen /bédlinnin/ *n.* sheets and pillowcases.

Bedlington terrier /bédlingtən/ *n.* **1** a terrier of a breed with narrow head, long legs, and curly grey hair. **2** this breed. [*Bedlington* in Northumberland]

bedmaker /bédmaykər/ *n. Brit.* a person employed to clean and tidy students' rooms in a college.

Bedouin /béddoo-in/ *n.* & *adj.* (also **Beduin**) (*pl.* same) ● *n.* **1** a nomadic Arab of the desert. **2** a wanderer; a nomad. ● *adj.* **1** of or relating to the Bedouin. **2** wandering; nomadic. [ME f. OF *beduin* ult. f. Arab. *badwiyyīn* (oblique case) dwellers in the desert f. *badw* desert]

bedpan /bédpan/ *n.* a receptacle used by a bedridden patient for urine and faeces.

bedplate /bédplayt/ *n.* a metal plate forming the base of a machine.

bedpost /bédpōst/ *n.* any of the four upright supports of a bedstead. □ **between you and me and the bedpost** *colloq.* in strict confidence.

bedraggle /bidrágg'l/ *v.tr.* **1** (often as **bedraggled** *adj.*) wet (a dress etc.) by trailing it, or so that it hangs limp. **2** (as **bedraggled** *adj.*) untidy; dishevelled. [BE- + DRAGGLE]
■ (**bedraggled**) **1** wet, sloppy, soaking (wet), sopping (wet), wringing wet, soaked, drenched. **2** untidy, dishevelled, scruffy, messy, unkempt, rumpled, disorderly, ragged, raggedy, ungroomed; soiled, dirty, muddy, muddied.

bedrest /bédrest/ *n.* confinement of an invalid to bed.

bedridden /bédridd'n/ *adj.* **1** confined to bed by infirmity. **2** decrepit. [OE *bedreda* f. *ridan* ride]

bedrock /bédrok/ *n.* **1** solid rock underlying alluvial deposits etc. **2** the underlying principles or facts of a theory, character, etc.

bedroll /bédrōl/ *n.* esp. *US* portable bedding rolled into a bundle, esp. a sleeping-bag.

bedroom /bédrōōm, -rŏŏm/ *n.* **1** a room for sleeping in. **2** (*attrib.*) of or referring to sexual relations (*bedroom comedy*).
■ **1** see CHAMBER 3. **2** (*attrib.*) see SEXY 1.

Beds. *abbr.* Bedfordshire.

bedside /bédsīd/ *n.* **1** the space beside esp. a patient's bed. **2** (*attrib.*) of or relating to the side of a bed (*bedside lamp*). □ **bedside manner** (of a doctor) an approach or attitude to a patient.

bedsitter /bédsíttər/ *n.* (also **bedsit**) *colloq.* = BEDSITTING ROOM. [contr.]

bedsitting room /bédsítting/ *n. Brit.* a one-roomed unit of accommodation usu. consisting of combined bedroom and sitting-room with cooking facilities.

bedsock /bédsok/ *n.* each of a pair of thick socks worn in bed.

bedsore /bédsor/ *n.* a sore developed by an invalid because of pressure caused by lying in bed.

bedspread /bédspred/ *n.* an often decorative cloth used to cover a bed when not in use.
■ see SPREAD *n.* 10.

bedstead /bédsted/ *n.* the framework of a bed.

bedstraw /bédstraw/ *n.* **1** any herbaceous plant of the genus *Galium*, once used as straw for bedding. **2** (in full **Our Lady's bedstraw**) a bedstraw, *G. verum*, with yellow flowers.

bedtable /bédtayb'l/ *n.* a portable table or tray with legs used by a person sitting up in bed.

bedtime /bédtīm/ *n.* **1** the usual time for going to bed. **2** (*attrib.*) of or relating to bedtime (*bedtime drink*).

Beduin var. of BEDOUIN.

bedwetting /bédwetting/ *n.* involuntary urination during the night.

bee /bee/ *n.* **1** any four-winged insect of the superfamily Apoidea which collects nectar and pollen, produces wax and honey, and lives in large communities. **2** any insect of a similar type. **3** (usu. **busy bee**) a busy person. **4** esp. *US* a meeting for communal work or amusement. □ **bee-bread** honey or pollen used as food by bees. **bee dance** a dance performed by worker bees to inform the colony of the location of food. **bee-eater** any bright-plumaged insect-eating bird of the family Meropidae with a long slender curved bill. **a bee in one's bonnet** an obsession. **bee-keeper** a keeper of bees. **bee-keeping** the occupation of keeping bees. **bee-master** a bee-keeper. **bee orchid** a kind of European orchid, *Ophrys apifera*, with bee-shaped flowers. **the bee's knees** *sl.* something outstandingly good (*thinks he's the bee's knees*). [OE *bēo* f. Gmc]

Beeb /beeb/ *n.* (prec. by *the*) *Brit. colloq.* the BBC. [abbr.]

beech /beech/ *n.* **1** any large forest tree of the genus *Fagus*, having smooth grey bark and glossy leaves. **2** (also **beechwood**) its wood. **3** *Austral.* any of various similar trees in Australia. □ **beech-fern** a fern, *Thelypteris phagopteris*, found in damp woods. **beech-marten** a white-breasted marten, *Martes foina*, of S. Europe and Asia. □□ **beechy** *adj.* [OE *bēce* f. Gmc]

beechmast /béechmaast/ *n.* (*pl.* same) the small rough-skinned fruit of the beech tree. [BEECH + MAST²]

beef /beef/ *n.* & *v.* ● *n.* **1** the flesh of the ox, bull, or esp. the cow, for eating. **2** *colloq.* well-developed male muscle. **3** (*pl.* **beeves** /beevz/ or *US* **beefs**) a cow, bull, or ox fattened for beef; its carcass. **4** (*pl.* **beefs**) *sl.* a complaint; a protest. ● *v.intr. sl.* complain. □ **beef tea** stewed extract of beef, given to invalids. **beef up** *sl.* strengthen, reinforce, augment. **beef-wood 1** any of various Australian and W. Indian hardwood trees. **2** the close-grained red timber of these. [ME f. AF, OF *boef* f. L *bos bovis* ox]
▪ *n.* **4** see PROTEST *n.* 1. ● *v.* see COMPLAIN 1.

beefburger /béefburgər/ *n.* = HAMBURGER.

beefcake /béefkayk/ *n.* esp. *US sl.* well-developed male muscles, esp. when displayed for admiration.

beefeater /béefeetər/ *n.* a warder in the Tower of London; a Yeoman of the Guard. [f. obs. sense 'well-fed menial']

beefsteak /béefstáyk/ *n.* a thick slice of lean beef, esp. from the rump, usu. for grilling or frying. □ **beefsteak fungus** a red edible fungus, *Fistulina hepatica*, resembling beef.

beefy /béefi/ *adj.* (**beefier, beefiest**) **1** like beef. **2** solid; muscular. □□ **beefily** *adv.* **beefiness** *n.*
▪ **2** see BRAWNY.

beehive /béehīv/ *n.* **1** an artificial habitation for bees. **2** a busy place. **3** anything resembling a wicker beehive in being domed.

beeline /béelīn/ *n.* a straight line between two places. □ **make a beeline for** hurry directly to.

Beelzebub /bee-élzibub/ *n.* the Devil. [OE f. L f. Gk *beelzeboub* & Heb. *ba'al zᵉbûḇ* lord of the flies, name of a Philistine god]
▪ see DEVIL *n.* 1, 2.

been *past part.* of BE.

beep /beep/ *n.* & *v.* ● *n.* **1** the sound of a motor-car horn. **2** any similar high-pitched noise. ● *v.intr.* emit a beep. □□ **beeper** *n.* [imit.]

beer /beer/ *n.* **1 a** an alcoholic drink made from yeast-fermented malt etc., flavoured with hops. **b** a glass of this, esp. a pint or half-pint. **2** any of several other fermented drinks, e.g. ginger beer. □ **beer and skittles** amusement (*life is not all beer and skittles*). **beer-cellar 1** an underground room for storing beer. **2** a basement or cellar for selling or drinking beer. **beer-engine** *Brit.* a machine that draws up beer from a barrel in a cellar. **beer garden** a garden where beer is sold and drunk. **beer hall** a large room where beer is sold and drunk. **beer-mat** a small table-mat for a beer-glass. **beer pump** *US* = *beer-engine*. **beer-up** *Austral. colloq.* a beer-drinking party or session. [OE *bēor* f. LL *biber* drink f. L *bibere*]
▪ **1 a** ale, lager, stout; *Austral.* & *NZ colloq.* hop, *Austral. joc.* sherbet. □ **beer-up** see BENDER.

beerhouse /béerhowss/ *n. Brit.* a public house licensed to sell beer but not spirits.

beery /béeri/ *adj.* (**beerier, beeriest**) **1** showing the influence of drink in one's appearance or behaviour. **2** smelling or tasting of beer. □□ **beerily** *adv.* **beeriness** *n.*

beestings /béestingz/ *n.pl.* (also treated as *sing.*) the first milk (esp. of a cow) after giving birth. [OE *bēsting* (implied by *bēost*), of unkn. orig.]

beeswax /béezwaks/ *n.* & *v.* ● *n.* **1** the wax secreted by bees to make honeycombs. **2** this wax refined and used to polish wood. ● *v.tr.* polish (furniture etc.) with beeswax.

beeswing /béezwing/ *n.* a filmy second crust on old port.

beet /beet/ *n.* any plant of the genus *Beta* with an edible root (see BEETROOT, *sugar beet*). [OE *bēte* f. L *beta*, perh. of Celt. orig.]

beetle¹ /béet'l/ *n.* & *v.* ● *n.* **1** any insect of the order Coleoptera, with modified front wings forming hard protective cases closing over the back wings. **2** *colloq.* any similar, usu. black, insect. **3** *sl.* a type of compact rounded Volkswagen saloon car. **4** a dice game in which a beetle is drawn or assembled. ● *v.intr. colloq.* (foll. by *about*, *away*, *etc.*) *Brit.* hurry, scurry. □ **beetle-crusher** *Brit. colloq.* a large boot or foot. [OE *bitula* biter f. *bītan* BITE]
▪ **1, 2** see BUG *n.* 1.

beetle² /béet'l/ *n.* & *v.* ● *n.* **1** a tool with a heavy head and a handle, used for ramming, crushing, driving wedges, etc. **2** a machine used for heightening the lustre of cloth by pressure from rollers. ● *v.tr.* **1** ram, crush, drive, etc., with a beetle. **2** finish (cloth) with a beetle. [OE *bētel* f. Gmc]

beetle³ /béet'l/ *adj.* & *v.* ● *adj.* (esp. of the eyebrows) projecting, shaggy, scowling. ● *v.intr.* (usu. as **beetling** *adj.*) (of brows, cliffs, etc.) projecting; overhanging threateningly. □ **beetle-browed** with shaggy, projecting, or scowling eyebrows. [ME: orig. unkn.]
▪ *v.* see PROJECT *v.* 2.

beetroot /béetrōōt/ *n.* esp. *Brit.* **1** a beet, *Beta vulgaris*, with an edible spherical dark red root. **2** this root used as a vegetable.

beeves *pl.* of BEEF.

BEF *abbr. hist.* British Expeditionary Force.

befall /bifáwl/ *v.* (*past* **befell** /bifél/; *past part.* **befallen** /bifáwlən/) *poet.* **1** *intr.* happen (*so it befell*). **2** *tr.* happen to (a person etc.) (*what has befallen her?*). [OE *befeallan* (as BE-, *feallan* FALL)]
▪ **1** see HAPPEN *v.* 1. **2** see HAPPEN *v.* 3.

befit /bifít/ *v.tr.* (**befitted, befitting**) **1** be fitted or appropriate for; suit. **2** be incumbent on. □□ **befitting** *adj.* **befittingly** *adv.*
▪ be appropriate *or* suitable *or* fitting *or* apt for, suit; be required of, be incumbent on, be proper to *or* for, *formal* behove. □□ **befitting** fitting, becoming, due, suitable, appropriate, apt, apropos, proper, seemly, correct, right, *archaic* meet. **befittingly** see *appropriately* (APPROPRIATE).

befog /bifóg/ *v.tr.* (**befogged, befogging**) **1** confuse; obscure. **2** envelop in fog.

befool /bifōōl/ *v.tr.* make a fool of; delude.

before /bifór/ *conj.*, *prep.*, & *adv.* ● *conj.* **1** earlier than the time when (*crawled before he walked*). **2** rather than that (*would starve before he stole*). ● *prep.* **1 a** in front of (*before her in the queue*). **b** ahead of (*crossed the line before him*). **c** under the impulse of (*recoil before the attack*). **d** awaiting (*the future before them*). **2** earlier than; preceding (*Lent comes before Easter*). **3** rather than (*death before dishonour*). **4 a** in the presence of (*appear before the judge*). **b** for the attention of (*a plan put before the committee*). ● *adv.* **1 a** earlier than the time in question; already (*heard it before*). **b** in the past (*happened long before*). **2** ahead (*go before*). **3** on the front (*hit before and behind*). □ **Before Christ** (of a date) reckoned backwards from the birth of Christ. **before God** a solemn oath meaning 'as God sees me'. **before time** see TIME. [OE *beforan* f. Gmc]
▪ *conj.* **1** previous to *or* preceding the time when, earlier than. ● *prep.* **1 a, b** ahead of, in advance of, in front of, forward of. **d** awaiting, waiting for, ahead of. **2** earlier

than, at an earlier time than; preceding, previous to, anterior to, prior to, ahead of; on the eve of; ante-, pre-. **3** in preference to, rather than, sooner than, more willingly than; instead of, in place of, in lieu of. ● *adv.* **1 a** previously, earlier, already, beforehand. **b** formerly, in the past, in time(s) past, ago, back; once. **2** (up) ahead, in advance, in (the) front, in the forefront, first, in the lead *or* vanguard, *colloq.* up front.

beforehand /bifórhand/ *adv.* in anticipation; in advance; in readiness (*had prepared the meal beforehand*). □ **be beforehand with** anticipate; forestall. [ME f. BEFORE + HAND: cf. AF *avant main*]
■ see *in advance* (ADVANCE).

befoul /bifówl/ *v.tr. poet.* **1** make foul or dirty. **2** degrade; defile (*befouled her name*).
■ **1** see DIRTY *v.* **2** see DESECRATE.

befriend /bifrénd/ *v.tr.* act as a friend to; help.
■ see *fall in with* 1.

befuddle /bifúdd'l/ *v.tr.* **1** make drunk. **2** confuse. □□ **befuddlement** *n.*
■ **1** see INTOXICATE 1. **2** see CONFUSE 1a.

beg /beg/ *v.* (**begged, begging**) **1 a** *intr.* (usu. foll. by *for*) ask for (esp. food, money, etc.) (*begged for alms*). **b** *tr.* ask for (food, money, etc.) as a gift. **c** *intr.* live by begging. **2** *tr.* & *intr.* (usu. foll. by *for*, or *to* + infin.) ask earnestly or humbly (*begged for forgiveness*; *begged to be allowed out*; *please, I beg of you*; *beg your indulgence for a time*). **3** *tr.* ask formally for (*beg leave*). **4** *intr.* (of a dog etc.) sit up with the front paws raised expectantly. **5** *tr.* take or ask leave (to do something) (*I beg to differ*; *beg to enclose*). □ **beg one's bread** live by begging. **begging bowl 1** a bowl etc. held out for food or alms. **2** an earnest appeal for help. **beg off 1** decline to take part in or attend. **2** get (a person) excused a penalty etc. **beg pardon** see PARDON. **beg the question 1** assume the truth of an argument or proposition to be proved, without arguing it. **2** *disp.* pose the question. **3** *colloq.* evade a difficulty. **go begging** (or **a-begging**) (of a chance or a thing) not be taken; be unwanted. [ME prob. f. OE *bedecian* f. Gmc: rel. to BID]
■ **1 a** (*beg for*) see ASK 4. **b, c** beg one's bread, solicit, sponge, cadge, *colloq.* scrounge, *US colloq.* panhandle, mooch, *US sl.* bum, freeload. **2** entreat, beseech, plead (with), ask for, request, call on *or* upon, crave, implore, press, importune, appeal to, invoke, supplicate, pray, petition. **3** see ASK 4. □ **beg off 1** abstain from, decline to, *US* take a rain check on, *colloq.* cry off. **go begging** be unwanted, be available, be there for the taking *or* asking.

begad /bigád/ *int. archaic colloq.* by God! [corrupt.: cf. GAD[2]]

began *past* of BEGIN.

begat *archaic past* of BEGET.

beget /bigét/ *v.tr.* (**begetting**; *past* **begot** /bigót/; *archaic* **begat** /bigát/; *past part.* **begotten** /bigótt'n/) *literary* **1** (usu. of a father, sometimes of a father and mother) procreate. **2** give rise to; cause (*beget strife*). □□ **begetter** *n.* [OE *begietan*, formed as BE- + GET = procreate]
■ **1** see FATHER *v.* 1. **2** see CREATE 1.

beggar /béggər/ *n.* & *v.* ● *n.* **1** a person who begs, esp. one who lives by begging. **2** a poor person. **3** *colloq.* a person; a fellow (*poor beggar*). ● *v.tr.* **1** reduce to poverty. **2** outshine. **3** exhaust the resources of (*beggar description*). □ **beggar-my-neighbour 1** a card-game in which a player seeks to capture an opponent's cards. **2** (*attrib.*) (esp. of national policy) self-aggrandizing at the expense of competitors. **beggars cannot** (or **must not**) **be choosers** those without other resources must take what is offered. [ME f. BEG + -AR[3]]
■ *n.* **1, 2** mendicant, sponger, tramp, vagrant, pauper, down-and-out, cadger, *colloq.* scrounger, have-not, *US* panhandler, hobo, *esp. US sl.* schnorrer, freeloader, bum; supplicant, suppliant. **3** fellow, man, person, *Sc.* carl, *colloq.* chap, guy, devil, lad, scout, *Brit. colloq.* johnny, *sl.* joker, *sl. often derog.* gink, *Brit. sl.* bloke, old cock, josser, *Brit. sl. archaic* cove, *US sl.* dude. ● *v.* **2** see OUTDO. **3** see EXCEED.

beggarly /béggərli/ *adj.* **1** poverty-stricken; needy. **2** intellectually poor. **3** mean; sordid. **4** ungenerous. □□ **beggarliness** *n.*
■ **1** see PENURIOUS 1. **3** see PITIFUL 2. **4** see PALTRY.

beggary /béggəri/ *n.* extreme poverty.
■ see POVERTY 1.

begin /bigín/ *v.* (**beginning**; *past* **began** /bigán/; *past part.* **begun** /bigún/) **1** *tr.* perform the first part of; start (*begin work*; *begin crying*; *begin to understand*). **2** *intr.* come into being; arise: **a** in time (*war began in 1939*). **b** in space (*Wales begins beyond the river*). **3** *tr.* (usu. foll. by *to* + infin.) start at a certain time (*then began to feel ill*). **4** *intr.* be begun (*the meeting will begin at 7*). **5** *intr.* **a** start speaking (*'No,' he began*). **b** take the first step; be the first to do something (*who wants to begin?*). **6** *intr. colloq.* (usu. with *neg.*) show any attempt or likelihood (*can't begin to compete*). □ **begin at** start from. **begin on** (or **upon**) set to work at. **begin school** attend school for the first time. **begin with** take (a subject, task, etc.) first or as a starting-point. **to begin with** in the first place; as the first thing. [OE *beginnan* f. Gmc]
■ **1** start (out *or* off *or* in *or* on), initiate, enter on *or* upon, set out *or* about, set out on *or* upon, *formal* commence; inaugurate, get going, get off the ground, put into operation *or* motion. **2, 4** arise, start, originate, come into being, emerge, open, get under way, be inaugurated *or* initiated, get going, get off the ground, be put into operation *or* motion, *colloq.* kick off, *formal* commence. **5 b** take the first step, be first, set the ball rolling, *colloq.* get cracking, take the first crack *or* shot at. □ **to begin with** see *originally* (ORIGINAL).

beginner /bigínnər/ *n.* a person just beginning to learn a skill etc. □ **beginner's luck** good luck supposed to attend a beginner at games etc.

beginning /bigínning/ *n.* **1** the time or place at which anything begins. **2** a source or origin. **3** the first part. □ **the beginning of the end** the first clear sign of a final result.
■ **1, 2** start, outset, onset, inception, dawn, dawning, birth, genesis, origin, creation, day one, *formal* commencement, *rhet.* birth; origination, source, well-spring. **3** opening, start, inception, *formal* commencement; first part.

begone /bigón/ *int. poet.* go away at once!
■ see SHOO *int.*

begonia /bigṓnyə/ *n.* any plant of the genus *Begonia* with brightly coloured sepals and no petals, and often having brilliant glossy foliage. [M. *Bégon*, Fr. patron of science d. 1710]

begorra /bigórrə/ *int. Ir.* by God! [corrupt.]

begot *past* of BEGET.

begotten *past part.* of BEGET.

begrime /bigrī́m/ *v.tr.* make grimy.
■ see DIRTY *v.*

begrudge /bigrúj/ *v.tr.* **1** resent; be dissatisfied at. **2** envy (a person) the possession of. **3** be reluctant or unwilling to give (a thing to a person). □□ **begrudgingly** *adv.*
■ **1, 2** resent, feel envious *or* jealous about, feel embittered *or* bitter about, have hard feelings about, be disgruntled *or* dissatisfied at; envy, grudge. **3** grudge, give (be)grudgingly *or* unwillingly *or* reluctantly, deny, refuse. □□ **begrudgingly** unwillingly, grudgingly, under protest, reluctantly, without good grace; jealously, enviously.

beguile /bigī́l/ *v.tr.* **1** charm; amuse. **2** divert attention pleasantly from (toil etc.). **3** (often foll. by *of*, *out of*, or *into* + verbal noun) delude; cheat (*beguiled him into paying*). □□ **beguilement** *n.* **beguiler** *n.* **beguiling** *adj.* **beguilingly** *adv.* [BE- + obs. *guile* to deceive]
■ **1** charm, divert, amuse, distract, fascinate, allure, seduce; captivate, enchant, enthral, entrance, enrapture, engross, engage, occupy, absorb. **3** delude, deceive, cheat, swindle, dupe, gull, fool, mislead, entrap, hoodwink, seduce, jockey, take in, *Brit.* have, *archaic* chicane, *colloq.* pull a fast one on, bamboozle, *Brit. colloq.* twist, *literary*

cozen, *sl.* con, bilk, chisel, cross, gyp, stitch up, *US sl.* snow, bunco; (*beguile out of*) defraud of, deprive of. □□ **beguilement** see AMUSEMENT 2, TRICKERY. **beguiler** see *charmer* (CHARM), *swindler* (SWINDLE). **beguiling** see *enchanting* (ENCHANT). **beguilingly** charmingly, enchantingly, seductively, enticingly, winsomely, winningly, alluringly, engagingly.

beguine /bigeén/ *n.* **1** a popular dance of W. Indian origin. **2** its rhythm. [Amer. F f. F *béguin* infatuation]

begum /báygəm/ *n.* in the Indian subcontinent: **1** a Muslim lady of high rank. **2** (**Begum**) the title of a married Muslim woman, equivalent to Mrs. [Urdu *begam* f. E.Turk. *bīgam* princess, fem. of *big* prince: cf. BEY]

begun *past part.* of BEGIN.

behalf /biha'af/ *n.* □ **on** (*US* **in**) **behalf of** (or **on a person's behalf**) **1** in the interests of (a person, principle, etc.). **2** as representative of (*acting on behalf of my client*). [mixture of earlier phrases *on his halve* and *bihalve him*, both = on his side: see BY, HALF]

■ in the interest of, for the benefit *or* advantage of, for, as a representative of, in place of, instead of, in the name of, on the part of.

behave /biháyv/ *v.* **1** *intr.* **a** act or react (in a specified way) (*behaved well*). **b** (esp. to or of a child) conduct oneself properly. **c** (of a machine etc.) work well (or in a specified way) (*the computer is not behaving today*). **2** *refl.* (esp. of or to a child) show good manners (*behaved herself*). □ **behave towards** treat (in a specified way). **ill-behaved** having bad manners or conduct. **well-behaved** having good manners or conduct. [BE- + HAVE]

■ **1 a** act, react, function, operate, perform, work, do, conduct *or* deport *or* bear *or* demean *or* acquit oneself, *colloq.* play, *literary* comport oneself. **b** act obediently, act properly, be good, *sl.* keep one's nose clean. **c** work, operate, function. **2** see BEHAVE 1b above. □ **ill-behaved** see NAUGHTY 1, IMPOLITE. **well-behaved** good, orderly, well-mannered, obedient, well-bred, polite, proper, correct, decorous, seemly, civil, respectful, courteous, mannerly, *colloq.* house-broken, *Brit. colloq.* house-trained, *joc.* couth.

behaviour /biháyvyər/ *n.* (*US* **behavior**) **1 a** the way one conducts oneself; manners. **b** the treatment of others; moral conduct. **2** the way in which a ship, machine, chemical substance, etc., acts or works. **3** *Psychol.* the response (of a person, animal, etc.) to a stimulus. □ **behaviour therapy** the treatment of neurotic symptoms by training the patient's reactions (see BEHAVIOURISM). **be on one's good** (or **best**) **behaviour** behave well when being observed. [BEHAVE after *demeanour* and obs. *haviour* f. *have*]

■ **1 a** conduct, demeanour, deportment, bearing, manners, action(s), *literary* comportment. **2** operation, action, performance, working, functioning.

behavioural /biháyvyərəl/ *adj.* (*US* **behavioral**) of or relating to behaviour. □ **behavioural science** the scientific study of human behaviour (see BEHAVIOURISM). □□ **behaviouralist** *n.*

behaviourism /biháyvyəriz'm/ *n.* (*US* **behaviorism**) *Psychol.* **1** the theory that human behaviour is determined by conditioning rather than by thoughts or feelings, and that psychological disorders are best treated by altering behaviour patterns. **2** such study and treatment in practice. □□ **behaviourist** *n.* **behaviouristic** /-rístik/ *adj.*

behead /bihéd/ *v.tr.* **1** cut off the head of (a person), esp. as a form of execution. **2** kill by beheading. [OE *behēafdian* (as BE-, *hēafod* HEAD)]

■ decapitate, guillotine, *formal* decollate.

beheld *past* and *past part.* of BEHOLD.

behemoth /biheémoth/ *n.* an enormous creature or thing. [ME f. Heb. *bᵉhēmôṯ* intensive pl. of *bᵉhēmāh* beast, perh. f. Egyptian *p-ehe-mau* water-ox]

■ see JUMBO *n.*

behest /bihést/ *n. literary* a command; an entreaty (*went at his behest*). [OE *behǣs* f. Gmc]

■ see COMMAND *n.* 1.

behind /bihínd/ *prep.*, *adv.*, & *n.* ● *prep.* **1 a** in, towards, or to the rear of. **b** on the further side of (*behind the bush*). **c** hidden by (*something behind that remark*). **2 a** in the past in relation to (*trouble is behind me now*). **b** late in relation to (*behind schedule*). **3** inferior to; weaker than (*rather behind the others in his maths*). **4 a** in support of (*she's right behind us*). **b** responsible for; giving rise to (*the man behind the project*; *the reasons behind his resignation*). **5** in the tracks of; following. ● *adv.* **1 a** in or to or towards the rear; further back (*the street behind*; *glance behind*). **b** on the further side (*a high wall with a field behind*). **2** remaining after departure (*leave behind*; *stay behind*). **3** (usu. foll. by *with*) **a** in arrears (*behind with the rent*). **b** late in accomplishing a task etc. (*working too slowly and getting behind*). **4** in a weak position; backward (*behind in Latin*). **5** following (*his dog running behind*). ● *n.* **1** *colloq.* the buttocks. **2** (in Australian Rules) a kick etc. scoring one point. □ **behind a person's back** without a person's knowledge. **behind the scenes** see SCENE. **behind time** late. **behind the times** antiquated. **come from behind** win after lagging. **fall** (or **lag**) **behind** see FALL. **put behind one 1** refuse to consider. **2** get over (an unhappy experience etc.). [OE *behindan*, *bihindan* f. *bi* BY + *hindan* from behind, *hinder* below]

■ *prep.* **1 a, b** round the back of, in *or* at *or* to the rear of, on *or* to the other side of. **c** hidden *or* concealed by. **3** below, inferior to, weaker *or* worse *or* lower than. **4 a** in support of; at a person's back, supporting, seconding; see also *in favour* (FAVOUR). **b** responsible for; for, explaining. **5** see *at a person's back* (BACK). ● *adv.* **1 a** see BACK *adv.* 1. **b** see BACK *adv.* 6. **3** in arrear(s), late, overdue, behindhand, belated, *US* delinquent. ● *n.* **1** see BUTTOCK. □ **behind a person's back** surreptitiously, secretly, in secret, covertly, clandestinely, privately, furtively, sneakily, slyly, on the sly, *colloq.* on the q.t.; underhandedly, treacherously, traitorously, perfidiously, deceitfully, insidiously. **behind time** see LATE *adj.* 1. **behind the times** antiquated, old-fashioned, outdated, out of date, dated, outmoded, *passé*, obsolete, outworn, antique, rusty, mouldy, *colloq.* fossilized, old hat, medieval, prehistoric, antediluvian. **put behind one 2** see *get over* 1.

behindhand /bihíndhand/ *adv.* & *predic.adj.* **1** (usu. foll. by *with*, *in*) late (in discharging a duty, paying a debt, etc.). **2** out of date; behind time. [BEHIND + HAND: cf. BEFOREHAND]

■ see LATE *adj.* 1.

behold /bihṓld/ *v.tr.* (*past* & *past part.* **beheld** /bihéld/) *literary* (esp. in *imper.*) see, observe. □□ **beholder** *n.* [OE *bihaldan* (as BE-, *haldan* hold)]

■ see, look at *or* upon, observe, regard, set *or* lay eyes on, gaze at *or* upon, watch, notice, note, spy, perceive, view, *colloq.* clap eyes on, *literary* descry, espy. □□ **beholder** see OBSERVER.

beholden /bihṓldən/ *predic.adj.* (usu. foll. by *to*) under obligation. [past part. (obs. except in this use) of BEHOLD, = bound]

■ obliged, obligated, indebted, bound, grateful, in debt, under (an) obligation.

behoof /bihōōf/ *n. archaic* (prec. by *to*, *for*, *on*; foll. by *of*) benefit; advantage. [OE *behōf*]

■ see PROFIT *n.*1.

behove /bihṓv/ *v.tr.* (*US* **behoove** /-hōōv/) *formal* (prec. by *it* as subject; foll. by *to* + infin.) **1** be incumbent on. **2** (usu. with *neg.*) befit (*ill behoves him to protest*). [OE *behōfian* f. *behōf*: see BEHOOF]

■ be required of, be incumbent on, be proper to *or* for, be fitting of *or* for, befit; be appropriate *or* suitable *or* apt for, suit; be advisable for, be worthwhile for, be expeditious for *or* of, be advantageous to *or* for, be useful to *or* for, be beneficial to *or* for.

beige /bayzh/ *n.* & *adj.* ● *n.* a pale sandy fawn colour. ● *adj.* of this colour. [F: orig. unkn.]

■ *adj.* see NEUTRAL *adj.* 3, 5.

beigel var. of BAGEL.

being /beé-ing/ *n.* **1** existence. **2** the nature or essence (of a person etc.) (*his whole being revolted*). **3** a human being. **4** anything that exists or is imagined. □ **in being** existing.
■ **1** see EXISTENCE 1. **2** see ESSENCE 1. **3** see PERSON. **4** see ENTITY 1.

bejabers /bijáybərz/ *int.* (also **bejabbers** /-jábbərz/) *Ir.* by Jesus! [corrupt.]

bejewelled /bijóoəld/ *adj.* (*US* **bejeweled**) adorned with jewels.

bel /bel/ *n.* a unit used in the comparison of power levels in electrical communication or intensities of sound, corresponding to an intensity ratio of 10 to 1 (cf. DECIBEL). [A. G. *Bell*, inventor of telephone d. 1922]

belabour /biláybər/ *v.tr.* (*US* **belabor**) **1 a** thrash; beat. **b** attack verbally. **2** argue or elaborate (a subject) in excessive detail. [BE- + LABOUR = exert one's strength]
■ **1 a** see BEAT *v.* 1. **b** see BERATE. **2** dissect, scrutinize, go over *or* through again, look at again; elaborate (on), enlarge *or* expand *or* expatiate on.

belated /biláytid/ *adj.* **1** coming late or too late. **2** overtaken by darkness. □□ **belatedly** *adv.* **belatedness** *n.* [past part. of obs. *belate* delay (as BE-, LATE)]
■ **1** late; behind time, behindhand, out of date, overdue, behind; delayed, detained. □□ **belatedly** see LATE *adv.* 1. **belatedness** lateness, tardiness.

belay /biláy/ *v.* & *n.* ● *v.* **1** *tr.* fix (a running rope) round a cleat, pin, rock, etc., to secure it. **2** *tr.* & *intr.* (usu. in *imper.*) *Naut. sl.* stop; enough! (esp. *belay there!*). ● *n.* **1** an act of belaying. **2** a spike of rock etc. used for belaying. □ **belaying-pin** a fixed wooden or iron pin used for fastening a rope round. [Du. *beleggen*]

bel canto /bel kántō/ *n.* **1** a lyrical style of operatic singing using a full rich broad tone and smooth phrasing. **2** (*attrib.*) (of a type of aria or voice) characterized by this type of singing. [It., = fine song]

belch /belch/ *v.* & *n.* ● *v.* **1** *intr.* emit wind noisily from the stomach through the mouth. **2** *tr.* **a** (of a chimney, volcano, gun, etc.) send (smoke etc.) out or up. **b** utter forcibly. ● *n.* an act of belching. [OE *belcettan*]

beldam /béldəm/ *n.* (also **beldame**) *archaic* **1** an old woman; a hag. **2** a virago. [ME & OF *bel* beautiful + DAM[2], DAME]
■ see HAG[1].

beleaguer /bileégər/ *v.tr.* **1** besiege. **2** vex; harass. [Du. *belegeren* camp round (as BE-, *leger* a camp)]
■ **1** see BESIEGE 1. **2** see MOLEST 1.

belemnite /bélləmnīt/ *n.* any extinct cephalopod of the order Belemnoidea, having a bullet-shaped internal shell often found in fossilized form. [mod.L *belemnites* f. Gk *belemnon* dart + -ITE[1]]

bel esprit /bél espreé/ *n.* (*pl.* ***beaux esprits*** /bṓz espreé/) a witty person. [F, lit. fine mind]

belfry /bélfri/ *n.* (*pl.* **-ies**) **1** a bell tower or steeple housing bells, esp. forming part of a church. **2** a space for hanging bells in a church tower. □ **bats in the belfry** see BAT[2]. [ME f. OF *berfrei* f. Frank.: altered by assoc. with *bell*]
■ **1** see TOWER *n.* 1.

Belgian /béljən/ *n.* & *adj.* ● *n.* **1** a native or national of Belgium in W. Europe. **2** a person of Belgian descent. ● *adj.* of or relating to Belgium. □ **Belgian hare** a dark-red long-eared breed of domestic rabbit.

Belgic /béljik/ *adj.* **1** of the ancient Belgae of N. Gaul. **2** of the Low Countries. [L *Belgicus* f. *Belgae*]

Belial /beéliəl/ *n.* the Devil. [Heb. *b*[e]*liyya'al* worthless]
■ see DEVIL *n.* 1, 2.

belie /bilī́/ *v.tr.* (**belying**) **1** give a false notion of; fail to corroborate (*its appearance belies its age*). **2 a** fail to fulfil (a promise etc.). **b** fail to justify (a hope etc.). [OE *belēogan* (as BE-, *lēogan* LIE[2])]
■ **1** see MISREPRESENT.

belief /bileéf/ *n.* **1 a** a person's religion; religious conviction (*has no belief*). **b** a firm opinion (*my belief is that he did it*). **c** an acceptance (of a thing, fact, statement, etc.) (*belief in the afterlife*). **2** (usu. foll. by *in*) trust or confidence. □ **beyond belief** incredible. **to the best of my belief** in my genuine opinion. [ME f. OE *gelēafa* (as BELIEVE)]
■ **1** religion, faith, conviction, creed, doctrine, dogma, principle(s), axiom, maxim, opinion, judgement, persuasion, tenet, view, idea, sentiment, intuition; acceptance, credence; assent. **2** trust, confidence, faith, conviction, certitude, certainty, sureness; reliance, security, assurance. □ **beyond belief** see INCREDIBLE 1. **to the best of my belief** as far as I know *or* can see *or* can tell, a priori.

believe /bileév/ *v.* **1** *tr.* accept as true or as conveying the truth (*I believe it; don't believe him; believes what he is told*). **2** *tr.* think, suppose (*I believe it's raining; Mr Smith, I believe?*). **3** *intr.* (foll. by *in*) **a** have faith in the existence of (*believes in God*). **b** have confidence in (a remedy, a person, etc.) (*believes in alternative medicine*). **c** have trust in the advisability of (*believes in telling the truth*). **4** *intr.* have (esp. religious) faith. □ **believe one's ears** (or **eyes**) accept that what one apparently hears or sees etc. is true. **believe it or not** *colloq.* it is true though surprising. **make believe** (often foll. by *that* + clause, or *to* + infin.) pretend (*let's make believe that we're young again*). **would you believe it?** *colloq.* = *believe it or not.* □□ **believable** *adj.* **believability** /-leévəbílliti/ *n.* [OE *belȳfan, belēfan*, with change of prefix f. *gelēfan* f. Gmc: rel. to LIEF]
■ **1** accept, put faith *or* credence in *or* into, find credible *or* believable, be convinced *or* assured of, take (it) as given *or* read. **2** think, suppose, assume, hold, maintain, feel, take it, allow, fancy, imagine. **3** (*believe in*) trust to *or* in, rely upon *or* on, have faith *or* confidence in, put one's trust in, be convinced *or* assured of, swear by, credit. **4** have faith; have found faith, have seen the light. □ **make believe** pretend, suppose, imagine, fancy, conjecture, assume, make out; play-act. □□ **believable** see PLAUSIBLE 1. **believability** credibility, feasibility, likelihood, conceivability, plausibility, tenability, dependability, reliability, trustworthiness, cogency.

believer /bileévər/ *n.* **1** an adherent of a specified religion. **2** a person who believes, esp. in the efficacy of something (*a great believer in exercise*).

Belisha beacon /bəleéshə/ *n. Brit.* a flashing orange ball mounted on a striped post, marking some pedestrian crossings. [L. Hore-*Belisha* d. 1957, Minister of Transport 1934]

belittle /bilítt'l/ *v.tr.* **1** depreciate. **2** make small; dwarf. □□ **belittlement** *n.* **belittler** *n.* **belittlingly** *adv.*
■ disparage, decry, cry down, detract from, depreciate, trivialize, deprecate, degrade, denigrate, downgrade, discredit, criticize, pooh-pooh, put down, run down, undervalue, underestimate, underrate, slight, *colloq.* play down, *esp. US colloq.* trash, *formal* derogate, *Austral.* & *NZ sl.* sling off at; minimize, diminish, reduce, lessen. □□ **belittlement** disparagement, deprecation, depreciation, denigration, derogation; diminution. **belittler** decrier, deprecator, denigrator. **belittlingly** deprecatingly, disparagingly, depreciatingly, slightingly.

bell[1] /bel/ *n.* & *v.* ● *n.* **1** a hollow usu. metal object in the shape of a deep upturned cup usu. widening at the lip, made to sound a clear musical note when struck (either externally or by means of a clapper inside). **2 a** a sound or stroke of a bell, esp. as a signal. **b** (prec. by a numeral) *Naut.* the time as indicated every half-hour of a watch by the striking of the ship's bell one to eight times. **3** anything that sounds like or functions as a bell, esp. an electronic device that rings etc. as a signal. **4 a** any bell-shaped object or part, e.g. of a musical instrument. **b** the corolla of a flower when bell-shaped. **5** (in *pl.*) *Mus.* a set of cylindrical metal tubes of different lengths, suspended in a frame and played by being struck with a hammer. ● *v.tr.* **1** provide with a bell or bells; attach a bell to. **2** (foll. by *out*) form into the shape of the lip of a bell. □ **bell-bottom 1** a marked flare below the knee (of a trouser-leg). **2** (in *pl.*) trousers with bell-bottoms. **bell-bottomed** having bell-bottoms. **bell-buoy** a buoy equipped with a warning bell rung by the motion of the sea. **bell-founder** a person who casts large bells in a foundry. **bell-glass** a bell-shaped glass cover for plants. **bell-jar** a bell-shaped glass cover or container for use in a laboratory. **bell-metal** an alloy of copper and tin for making bells (the tin content being greater than in bronze). **bell-pull** a cord or handle which rings a bell when pulled. **bell-push** a button that operates an electric bell when pushed. **bell-ringer** a person who rings church bells or handbells. **bell-ringing** this as an activity. **bells and whistles** *colloq.* attractive but unnecessary additional features, esp. in computing. **bell-tent** a cone-shaped tent supported by a central pole. **bell-wether 1** the leading sheep of a flock, with a bell on its neck. **2** a ringleader. **clear** (or **sound**) **as a bell** perfectly clear or sound. **give a person a bell** *colloq.* telephone a person. **ring a bell** *colloq.* revive a distant recollection; sound familiar. [OE *belle*: perh. rel. to BELL[2]]

■ *n.* **2 a** see ALARM *n.* 2a.

bell[2] /bel/ *n.* & *v.* ● *n.* the cry of a stag or buck at rutting-time. ● *v.intr.* make this cry. [OE *bellan* bark, bellow]

belladonna /béllədónnə/ *n.* **1** *Bot.* a poisonous plant, *Atropa belladonna*, with purple flowers and purple-black berries. Also called *deadly nightshade*. **2** *Med.* a drug prepared from this. □ **belladonna lily** a S. African amaryllis with white or pink flowers, *Amaryllis belladonna*. [mod.L f. It., = fair lady, perh. from its use as a cosmetic]

bellbird /bélburd/ *n.* any of various birds with a bell-like song, esp. any Central or S. American bird of the genus *Procnias*, a New Zealand honey-eater, *Anthornis melanura*, and an Australian bird, *Oreoica gutturalis*.

bellboy /bélboy/ *n.* esp. *US* a page in a hotel or club.

■ see PAGE[2] *n.*

belle /bel/ *n.* **1** a beautiful woman. **2** a woman recognized as the most beautiful (*the belle of the ball*). [F f. L *bella* fem. of *bellus* beautiful]

■ see BEAUTY 3.

belle époque /bél epók/ *n.* the period of settled and comfortable life preceding the war of 1914–18. [F, = fine period]

belle laide /bel láyd/ *n.* (*pl.* ***belles laides*** *pronunc.* same) a fascinatingly ugly woman. [F f. *belle* beautiful + *laide* ugly]

■ *jolie laide.*

belles-lettres /bel-létrə/ *n.pl.* (also treated as *sing.*) writings or studies of a literary nature, esp. essays and criticisms. □□ **belletrism** /bel-létriz'm/ *n.* **belletrist** /bel-létrist/ *n.* **belletristic** /bél-letrístik/ *adj.* [F, = fine letters]

■ see WRITING 3.

bellflower /bélflowr/ *n.* = CAMPANULA.

bellicose /béllikōz/ *adj.* eager to fight; warlike. □□ **bellicosity** /-kóssiti/ *n.* [ME f. L *bellicosus* f. *bellum* war]

■ see WARLIKE 1.

belligerence /bilíjərənss/ *n.* (also **belligerency** /-rənsi/) **1** aggressive or warlike behaviour. **2** the status of a belligerent.

■ **1** see AGGRESSION 1.

belligerent /bilíjərənt/ *adj.* & *n.* ● *adj.* **1** engaged in war or conflict. **2** given to constant fighting; pugnacious. ● *n.* a nation or person engaged in war or conflict. □□ **belligerently** *adv.* [L *belligerare* wage war f. *bellum* war + *gerere* wage]

■ *adj.* **1** warring, militant, warmongering, hawkish, jingoistic, bellicose, martial. **2** quarrelsome, pugnacious, contentious, disputatious, truculent, aggressive, hostile, combative, antagonistic, bellicose, argumentative, cantankerous, contrary; *US sl.* feisty. ● *n.* warring party, fighter, antagonist, adversary, contender, contestant; opposition, other side; quarreller, squabbler; aggressor.

bellman /bélmən/ *n.* (*pl.* **-men**) *hist.* a town crier.

bellow /béllō/ *v.* & *n.* ● *v.* **1** *intr.* **a** emit a deep loud roar. **b** cry or shout with pain. **2** *tr.* utter loudly and usu. angrily. ● *n.* a bellowing sound. [ME: perh. rel. to BELL[2]]

■ *v.* roar, yell, shout, cry, blare, trumpet, thunder, howl, bawl, halloo, holla, vociferate, sing out, *US colloq.* holler. ● *n.* roar, yell, shout, cry, call, blare, holla, howl, *US colloq.* holler.

bellows /béllōz/ *n.pl.* (also treated as *sing.*) **1** a device with an air bag that emits a stream of air when squeezed, esp.: **a** (in full **pair of bellows**) a kind with two handles used for blowing air on to a fire. **b** a kind used in a harmonium or small organ. **2** an expandable component, e.g. joining the lens to the body of a camera. [ME prob. f. OE *belga* pl. of *belig* belly]

belly /bélli/ *n.* & *v.* ● *n.* (*pl.* **-ies**) **1** the part of the human body below the chest, containing the stomach and bowels. **2** the stomach, esp. representing the body's need for food. **3** the front of the body from the waist to the groin. **4** the underside of a four-legged animal. **5 a** a cavity or bulging part of anything. **b** the surface of an instrument of the violin family, across which the strings are placed. ● *v.tr.* & *intr.* (**-ies, -ied**) (often foll. by *out*) swell or cause to swell; bulge. □ **belly button** *colloq.* the navel. **belly-dance** an oriental dance performed by a woman, involving voluptuous movements of the belly. **belly-dancer** a woman who performs belly-dances, esp. professionally. **belly-dancing** the performance of belly-dances. **belly-landing** a crash-landing of an aircraft on the underside of the fuselage, without lowering the undercarriage. **belly-laugh** a loud unrestrained laugh. **go belly up** *US colloq.* fail financially. [OE *belig* (orig. = bag) f. Gmc]

■ *n.* **1–3** see STOMACH *n.* 2a. ● *v.* see SWELL *v.* 3. □ **belly button** see NAVEL 1. **go belly up** see FAIL *v.* 7.

bellyache /bélliayk/ *n.* & *v.* ● *n.* *colloq.* a stomach pain. ● *v.intr.* *sl.* complain noisily or persistently. □□ **bellyacher** *n.*

■ *n.* see GRIPE *n.* 1. ● *v.* see GRIPE *v.*

bellyband /bélliband/ *n.* a band placed round a horse's belly, holding the shafts of a cart etc.

bellyflop /bélliflop/ *n.* & *v.* *colloq.* ● *n.* a dive into water in which the body lands with the belly flat on the water. ● *v.intr.* (**-flopped, -flopping**) perform this dive.

bellyful /béllifōōl/ *n.* (*pl.* **-fuls**) **1** enough to eat. **2** *colloq.* enough or more than enough of anything (esp. unwelcome).

belong /bilóng/ *v.intr.* **1** (foll. by *to*) **a** be the property of. **b** be rightly assigned to as a duty, right, part, member, characteristic, etc. **c** be a member of (a club, family, group, etc.). **2** have the right personal or social qualities to be a member of a particular group (*he's nice but just doesn't belong*). **3** (foll. by *in, under*) **a** be rightly placed or classified. **b** fit a particular environment. □□ **belongingness** *n.* [ME f. intensive BE- + *longen* belong f. OE *langian* (*gelang* at hand)]

■ **1** (*belong to*) **a** be owned by, be the property *or* possession of. **b** be assigned *or* allocated to. **c** be a member of, be affiliated *or* associated *or* connected with, be attached *or* bound to, be a part of. **2** fit, be suited, have a (proper) place, be suitable, be clubbable, be one of us, have the right stuff.

belonging /bilónging/ *n.* **1** (in *pl.*) one's movable possessions or luggage. **2** membership, relationship; esp. a person's membership of, and acceptance by, a group or society.

■ **1** (*belongings*) (personal) property, effects, possessions, goods, chattels, goods and chattels, *colloq.* gear, stuff, things; baggage, luggage, cases. **2** association, connection, alliance, relationship, affinity, relation; membership, acceptance.

Belorussian /béllōrúsh'n/ *n.* & *adj.* (also **Byelorussian** /byéllō-/) ● *n.* **1** a native of Belorussia, now officially the Republic of Belarus. **2** the East Slavonic language of Belorussia. ● *adj.* of or relating to Belorussia or its people or language. [Russ. *Belorussiya* f. *belyi* white + *Russiya* Russia]

beloved /bilúvvid, *predic.* also -lúvd/ *adj.* & *n.* ● *adj.* much loved. ● *n.* a much loved person. [obs. *belove* (v.)]

■ *adj.* loved, cherished, adored, dear, dearest, darling, precious, treasured; admired, worshipped, revered, esteemed, idolized, respected, valued, prized. ● *n.*

sweetheart, darling, dearest, love, sweet, true-love, *colloq.* honey, girl, young lady *or* man, *sl.* baby, *Brit. sl.* dona; lover, boyfriend, girlfriend, inamorata, inamorato, gallant, lady, queen, *archaic* paramour, leman, *colloq.* flame, *Sc.* & *N.Engl.* hinny, jo.

below /bilṓ/ *prep.* & *adv.* ● *prep.* **1** lower in position (vertically, down a slope or stream, etc.) than. **2** beneath the surface of; at or to a greater depth than (*head below water; below 500 feet*). **3** lower or less than in amount or degree (*below freezing-point*). **4** lower in rank, position, or importance than. **5** unworthy of. ● *adv.* **1** at or to a lower point or level. **2 a** downstairs (*lives below*). **b** downstream. **3** (of a text reference) further forward on a page or in a book (*as noted below*). **4** on the lower side (*looks similar above and below*). **5** *rhet.* on earth; in hell. **6** below zero; esp. below freezing-point. □ **below stairs** in the basement of a house esp. as the part occupied by servants. [BE- + LOW[1]]

■ *prep.* **1, 2** under, underneath, (submerged) beneath. **3** less *or* lower *or* cheaper than; under. **4** inferior *or* secondary *or* subordinate to, lower than, under, beneath. **5** beneath, unworthy of, unbefitting (of). ● *adv.* **1** lower down, further *or* farther down, beneath. **2 a** beneath, underneath; downstairs, below stairs, in the basement, *Naut.* below deck(s). **3** further on *or* down, *infra.* **4** on the other *or* lower side, on the back; behind. **5** on earth, here (below), in this world, beneath *or* under the sun, in this sublunary world; see also HELL 1.

Bel Paese /bél paa-áyzay/ *n. propr.* a rich white mild creamy cheese of a kind orig. made in Italy. [It., = fair country]

belt /belt/ *n.* & *v.* ● *n.* **1** a strip of leather or other material worn round the waist or across the chest, esp. to retain or support clothes or to carry weapons or as a safety-belt. **2** a belt worn as a sign of rank or achievement. **3 a** a circular band of material used as a driving medium in machinery. **b** a conveyor belt. **c** a flexible strip carrying machine-gun cartridges. **4** a strip of colour or texture etc. differing from that on each side. **5** a distinct region or extent (*cotton belt; commuter belt; a belt of rain*). **6** *sl.* a heavy blow. ● *v.* **1** *tr.* put a belt round. **2** *tr.* (often foll. by *on*) fasten with a belt. **3** *tr.* **a** beat with a belt. **b** *sl.* hit hard. **4** *intr. sl.* rush, hurry (usu. with compl.: *belted along; belted home*). □ **below the belt** unfair or unfairly; disregarding the rules. **belt and braces** (of a policy etc.) of twofold security. **belt out** *sl.* sing or utter loudly and forcibly. **belt up** *Brit.* **1** *sl.* be quiet. **2** *colloq.* put on a seat belt. **tighten one's belt** live more frugally. **under one's belt 1** (of food) eaten. **2** securely acquired (*has a degree under her belt*). □□ **belter** *n.* (esp. in sense of *belt out*). [OE f. Gmc f. L *balteus*]

■ *n.* **1** sash, girdle, cord, *archaic* zone, *literary* cincture. **4** see BAND[2] *n.* 2b. **5** zone, band, sector, strip, area, region, district, quarter, swath, tract, stretch, sphere. **6** see BLOW[2] 1. ● *v.* **3** see BEAT *v.* 1. **4** see HURRY *v.* 1. □ **below the belt** unfair, unjust, unsporting, unsportsmanlike, underhand(ed), improper, dirty, unscrupulous, unprincipled, wrong; unfairly, unjustly, unsportingly, underhandedly, improperly, dirtily, unscrupulously. **belt out** sing *or* perform stridently *or* loudly; put over *or* across loudly. **belt up 1** see *wrap up* 1. **tighten one's belt** see ECONOMIZE 1.

Beltane /béltayn/ *n.* an ancient Celtic festival celebrated on May Day. [Gael. *bealltainn*]

beltman /béltman/ *n.* (*pl.* **-men**) *Austral.* a member of a life-saving team of surfers.

beluga /bəlṓōgə/ *n.* **1 a** a large kind of sturgeon, *Huso huso.* **b** caviare obtained from it. **2** a white whale. [Russ. *beluga* f. *belyi* white]

belvedere /bélvideer/ *n.* a summer-house or open-sided gallery usu. at rooftop level. [It. f. *bel* beautiful + *vedere* see]

belying *pres. part.* of BELIE.

BEM *abbr.* British Empire Medal.

bemire /bimī́r/ *v.tr.* **1** cover or stain with mud. **2** (in *passive*) be stuck in mud. [BE- + MIRE]

bemoan /bimṓn/ *v.tr.* **1** express regret or sorrow over; lament. **2** complain about. [BE- + MOAN]

■ **1** bewail, mourn (for *or* over), grieve *or* weep *or* sorrow *or* moan for *or* over; see also LAMENT. **2** moan *or* grumble *or* complain about, *colloq.* gripe *or* grouse *or* whinge about, bitch about, *sl.* beef about.

bemuse /bimyṓōz/ *v.tr.* stupefy or bewilder (a person). □□ **bemusedly** /-zidli/ *adv.* **bemusement** *n.* [BE- + MUSE[2]]

■ confuse, mystify, perplex, bewilder, puzzle, baffle, muddle, mix up, addle, befuddle, confound, bedazzle, bedevil, maze, *archaic* wilder, *colloq.* tie in knots, flummox, *US joc.* discombobulate; stupefy, benumb, numb, dizzy, paralyse.

ben[1] /ben/ *n. Sc.* a high mountain or mountain peak, esp. in names (*Ben Nevis*). [Gael. *beann*]

■ see MOUNTAIN 1.

ben[2] /ben/ *n. Sc.* an inner room, esp. of a two-roomed cottage. [ellipt. use of *ben* (adv.), = within (OE *binnan*)]

bench /bench/ *n.* & *v.* ● *n.* **1** a long seat of wood or stone for seating several people. **2** a working-table, e.g. for a carpenter, mechanic, or scientist. **3** (prec. by *the*) **a** the office of judge or magistrate. **b** a judge's seat in a lawcourt. **c** a lawcourt. **d** judges and magistrates collectively. **4** (often in *pl.*) *Sport* an area to the side of a pitch, with seating where coaches and players not taking part can watch the game. **5** *Brit. Parl.* a seat appropriated as specified (*front bench*). **6** a level ledge in masonry or an earthwork, on a hill-slope, etc. ● *v.tr.* **1** exhibit (a dog) at a show. **2** *Sport US* withdraw (a player) from the pitch to the benches. □ **bench test** esp. *Computing n.* a test made by benchmarking. ● *v.tr.* run a series of tests on (a computer etc.) before its use. **King's** (or **Queen's**) **Bench** (in the UK) a division of the High Court of Justice. **on the bench** appointed a judge or magistrate. [OE *benc* f. Gmc]

■ *n.* **1** see SEAT *n.* 1.

bencher /bénchər/ *n. Brit.* **1** *Law* a senior member of any of the Inns of Court. **2** (in *comb.*) *Parl.* an occupant of a specified bench (*backbencher*).

■ **1** see LAWYER.

benchmark /bénchmaark/ *n.* & *v.* ● *n.* **1** a surveyor's mark cut in a wall, pillar, building, etc., used as a reference point in measuring altitudes. **2** a standard or point of reference. **3** a means of testing a computer, usu. by a set of programs run on a series of different machines. ● *v.tr.* evaluate (a computer) by a benchmark. □ **benchmark test** a test using a benchmark.

■ *n.* **2** see STANDARD *n.* 1, 8.

bend[1] /bend/ *v.* & *n.* ● *v.* (*past* **bent**; *past part.* **bent** exc. in *bended knee*) **1 a** *tr.* force or adapt (something straight) into a curve or angle. **b** *intr.* (of an object) be altered in this way. **2** *intr.* move or stretch in a curved course (*the road bends to the left*). **3** *intr.* & *tr.* (often foll. by *down, over,* etc.) incline or cause to incline from the vertical (*bent down to pick it up*). **4** *tr.* interpret or modify (a rule) to suit oneself. **5** *tr.* & *refl.* (foll. by *to, on*) direct or devote (oneself or one's attention, energies, etc.). **6** *tr.* turn (one's steps or eyes) in a new direction. **7** *tr.* (in *passive*; foll. by *on*) have firmly decided; be determined (*was bent on selling; on pleasure bent*). **8 a** *intr.* stoop or submit (*bent before his master*). **b** *tr.* force to submit. **9** *tr. Naut.* attach (a sail or cable) with a knot. ● *n.* **1** a curve in a road or other course. **2** a departure from a straight course. **3** a bent part of anything. **4** (in *pl.*; prec. by *the*) *colloq.* sickness due to too rapid decompression underwater. □ **bend over backwards** see BACKWARDS. **round the bend** *colloq.* crazy, insane. □□ **bendable** *adj.* [OE *bendan* f. Gmc]

■ *v.* **1** arch, bow, curve, crook. **2** incline, turn, curve, wind, deflect, veer, swing, bear. **3** see STOOP *v.* 1. **4** change, modify, adapt, revise, adjust, interpret; see also TWIST *v.* 5. **5, 6** incline, channel, focus, direct, steer, set, fix, turn, train. **7** (*be bent on*) see BENT[1] *adj.* 4. **8 a** bow, curtsy, make *or* drop a curtsy; kowtow, salaam; kneel, genuflect; submit, yield, give way *or* in, be pliant *or* subservient *or* tractable. ● *n.* **1, 3** curve, turn, turning, corner; angle, crook, hook, bow, curvature, flexure. □ **round the bend** see CRAZY 1. □□ **bendable** see PLASTIC *adj.* 1a.

bend[2] /bend/ *n.* **1** *Naut.* any of various knots for tying ropes (*fisherman's bend*). **2** *Heraldry* **a** a diagonal stripe from top right to bottom left of a shield. **b** (**bend sinister**) a diagonal stripe from top left to bottom right, as a sign of bastardy. [OE *bend* band, bond f. Gmc]

bender /béndər/ *n. sl.* a wild drinking spree. [BEND[1] + -ER[1]]
■ drinking-bout, drinking-spree, revel, carousal, carouse, bacchanal, *Sc.* skite, *archaic* wassail, *colloq.* bust, *Austral. colloq.* beer-up, *Brit. colloq.* pub-crawl, *sl.* binge, booze-up, jag, drunk, *Brit. sl.* blind.

bendy /béndi/ *adj.* (**bendier, bendiest**) *colloq.* capable of bending; soft and flexible. □□ **bendiness** *n.*
■ see PLIABLE 1.

beneath /binéeth/ *prep.* & *adv.* ● *prep.* **1** not worthy of; too demeaning for (*it was beneath him to reply*). **2** below, under. ● *adv.* below, under, underneath. □ **beneath contempt** see CONTEMPT. [OE *binithan, bineothan* f. *bi* BY + *nithan* etc. below f. Gmc]
■ *prep.* **1** below, unworthy of, unbefitting of, undeserving of, too demeaning for, lower than. **2** under, underneath, below, behind. ● *adv.* low *or* lower down, below, under, underneath; underground.

benedicite /bénnidísiti/ *n.* a blessing, esp. a grace said at table in religious communities. [ME f. L, = bless ye: see BENEDICTION]

Benedictine /bénnidíktin, (in sense 2) -teen/ *n.* & *adj.* ● *n.* **1** a monk or nun of an order following the rule of St Benedict established *c.*540. **2** *propr.* a liqueur based on brandy, orig. made by Benedictines in France. ● *adj.* of St Benedict or the Benedictines. [F *bénédictine* or mod.L *benedictinus* f. *Benedictus* Benedict]

benediction /bénnidíksh'n/ *n.* **1** the utterance of a blessing, esp. at the end of a religious service or as a special Roman Catholic service. **2** the state of being blessed. [ME f. OF f. L *benedictio -onis* f. *benedicere -dict-* bless]
■ **1** see BLESSING 1.

benedictory /bénnidíktəri/ *adj.* of or expressing benediction. [L *benedictorius* (as BENEDICTION)]

Benedictus /bénnidíktəss/ *n.* **1** the section of the Roman Catholic Mass beginning *Benedictus qui venit in nomine Domini* (Blessed is he who comes in the name of the Lord). **2** a canticle beginning *Benedictus Dominus Deus* (Blessed be the Lord God) from Luke 1:68–79. [L, = blessed: see BENEDICTION]

benefaction /bénnifáksh'n/ *n.* **1** a donation or gift. **2** an act of giving or doing good. [LL *benefactio* (as BENEFIT)]
■ **1** see GIFT *n.* 1.

benefactor /bénnifaktər/ *n.* (*fem.* **benefactress** /-triss/) a person who gives support (esp. financial) to a person or cause. [ME f. LL (as BENEFIT)]
■ patron, supporter, sponsor, donor, philanthropist; backer, investor, underwriter, *sl.* angel.

benefice /bénnifiss/ *n.* **1** a living from a church office. **2** the property attached to a church office, esp. that bestowed on a rector or vicar. □□ **beneficed** *adj.* [ME f. OF f. L *beneficium* favour f. *bene* well + *facere* do]

beneficent /binéffis'nt/ *adj.* doing good; generous, actively kind. □□ **beneficence** *n.* **beneficently** *adv.* [L *beneficent-* (as BENEFICE)]
■ see GENEROUS 2. □□ **beneficence** see KINDNESS 1.

beneficial /bénnifísh'l/ *adj.* **1** advantageous; having benefits. **2** *Law* relating to the use or benefit of property; having rights to this use or benefit. □□ **beneficially** *adv.* [ME f. F *bénéficial* or LL *beneficialis* (as BENEFICE)]
■ **1** advantageous, serviceable, useful, profitable, valuable, helpful, supportive, favourable, constructive, worthwhile, good, gainful, propitious, efficacious, effective; healthful, healthy, salutary, salubrious.

beneficiary /bénnifíshəri/ *n.* (*pl.* **-ies**) **1** a person who receives benefits, esp. under a person's will. **2** a holder of a church living. [L *beneficiarius* (as BENEFICE)]
■ **1** see HEIR.

benefit /bénnifit/ *n.* & *v.* ● *n.* **1** a favourable or helpful factor or circumstance; advantage, profit. **2** (often in *pl.*) payment made under insurance, social security, welfare, etc. (*sickness benefit*). **3** a public performance or game of which the proceeds go to a particular player or company or charitable cause. ● *v.* (**benefited, benefiting**; *US* **benefitted, benefitting**) **1** *tr.* do good to; bring advantage to. **2** *intr.* (often foll. by *from, by*) receive an advantage or gain. □ **benefit of clergy 1** *hist.* exemption of the English tonsured clergy and nuns from the jurisdiction of the ordinary civil courts. **2** ecclesiastical sanction or approval (*marriage without benefit of clergy*). **the benefit of the doubt** a concession that a person is innocent, correct, etc., although doubt exists. **benefit society** a society for mutual insurance against illness or the effects of old age. [ME f. AF *benfet*, OF *bienfet*, f. L *benefactum* f. *bene facere* do well]
■ *n.* **1** advantage, profit, good, gain, aid, help, service; strength, attraction, asset, added extra, boon, plus, appeal, pull, beauty, selling-point; sake. **2** payment, payout; sick pay; *Brit. colloq.* dole; (*benefits*) perquisites, emoluments, allowance(s), extras, fringe benefits, *colloq.* perks. **3** charity event. ● *v.* **1** do good to; improve, aid, help, better, promote, further, advance, forward, advantage. **2** profit, gain.

Benelux /bénniluks/ *n.* Belgium, the Netherlands, and Luxembourg in association as a regional economic group. [*Be*lgium + *Ne*therlands + *Lux*embourg]

benevolent /binévvələnt/ *adj.* **1** wishing to do good; actively friendly and helpful. **2** charitable (*benevolent fund; benevolent society*). □□ **benevolence** *n.* **benevolently** *adv.* [ME f. OF *benivolent* f. L *bene volens -entis* well wishing f. *velle* wish]
■ **1** well-disposed, gracious, good, kind, kindly, friendly, cordial, genial, congenial, humane, helpful, humanitarian, altruistic, philanthropic, well-wishing, thoughtful, considerate, sympathetic, caring, kind-hearted, warm-hearted, compassionate, benign, benignant; liberal, generous, magnanimous, open-handed. **2** charitable, good, philanthropic, eleemosynary. □□ **benevolence** charity, kindness, kindliness, kind-heartedness, warm-heartedness, friendliness, humanity, humanitarianism, compassion, beneficence, charitableness, goodness, altruism, good will, unselfishness, philanthropy, generosity, magnanimity, open-handedness, helpfulness, thoughtfulness, considerateness.

B.Eng. *abbr.* Bachelor of Engineering.

Bengali /benggáwli/ *n.* & *adj.* ● *n.* **1** a native of Bengal, a former Indian province now consisting of Bangladesh and the Indian State of W. Bengal. **2** the language of this people. ● *adj.* of or relating to Bengal or its people or language.

Bengal light /benggáwl/ *n.* a kind of firework giving off a blue flame, used for signals.

benighted /binítid/ *adj.* **1** intellectually or morally ignorant. **2** overtaken by darkness. □□ **benightedness** *n.* [obs. *benight* (v.)]
■ **1** unenlightened, naïve, uninformed, ignorant, in the dark, unknowing, unaware, unversed, uneducated, uninformed, *literary* nescient.

benign /binín/ *adj.* **1** gentle, mild, kindly. **2** fortunate, salutary. **3** (of the climate, soil, etc.) mild, favourable. **4** *Med.* (of a disease, tumour, etc.) not malignant. □□ **benignly** *adv.* [ME f. OF *benigne* f. L *benignus* f. *bene* well + *-genus* born]
■ **1** kindly, gracious, good, kind, kind-hearted, benevolent, benignant, warm, mild, warm-hearted, cordial, genial, congenial, tender, gentle, tender-hearted, compassionate, sympathetic, caring, soft-hearted. **2** salutary, congenial, propitious, beneficial, helpful, wholesome, healthful, healthy; fortunate, advantageous, favourable, auspicious, benignant. **3** mild, temperate, moderate, clement, gentle, mellow, kind, salubrious, favourable, advantageous,

promising. **4** non-fatal, non-malignant, non-virulent, curable, harmless, benignant.

benignant /binígnənt/ *adj.* **1** kindly, esp. to inferiors. **2** salutary, beneficial. **3** *Med.* = BENIGN 4. ▫▫ **benignancy** *n.* **benignantly** *adv.* [f. BENIGN or L *benignus*, after *malignant*]
■ **1** see BENEVOLENT 1, BENIGN 1. **2** see BENIGN 2. **3** see BENIGN 4.

benignity /binígniti/ *n.* (*pl.* **-ies**) **1** kindliness. **2** an act of kindness. [ME f. OF *benignité* or L *benignitas* (as BENIGN)]
■ **1** see KINDNESS 1.

benison /bénniz'n/ *n. archaic* a blessing. [ME f. OF *beneiçun* f. L *benedictio -onis*]

bent[1] /bent/ *past* and *past part.* of BEND[1] *v.* ● *adj.* **1** curved or having an angle. **2** *sl.* dishonest, illicit. **3** *sl.* **a** sexually deviant. **b** strange, weird, warped. **4** (foll. by *on*) determined to do or have. ● *n.* **1** an inclination or bias. **2** (foll. by *for*) a talent for something specified (*a bent for mimicry*).
■ *adj.* **1** curved, deflected, bowed, crooked, distorted, contorted, twisted, warped, gnarled. **2** illegal, illicit, criminal, unlawful; dishonest, untrustworthy, deceitful, corrupt, unprincipled, unscrupulous, sharp, *colloq.* crooked. **3 a** deviant, warped, perverted, degenerate, perverse, abnormal, unnatural, depraved, twisted, *colloq.* kinky. **b** strange, weird, peculiar, wry, awry, warped, corrupt, corrupted. **4** (*bent on*) determined about *or* to, intent on, set on, resolved about *or* to, resolute about, decided on *or* to, fixed on. ● *n.* **1** inclination, direction, disposition, predisposition, tendency, bias, leaning, proclivity, propensity, partiality, prejudice. **2** ability, aptitude, talent, gift, skill, faculty, facility, flair, feel, knack, genius.

bent[2] /bent/ *n.* **1 a** any stiff grass of the genus *Agrostis*. **b** any of various grasslike reeds, rushes, or sedges. **2** a stiff stalk of a grass usu. with a flexible base. **3** *archaic* or *dial.* a heath or unenclosed pasture. [ME repr. OE *beonet-* (in place-names), f. Gmc]

Benthamism /bénthəmiz'm/ *n.* the utilitarian philosophy of Jeremy Bentham, Engl. philosopher d. 1832. ▫▫ **Benthamite** *n.* & *adj.*

benthos /bénthoss/ *n.* the flora and fauna found at the bottom of a sea or lake. ▫▫ **benthic** *adj.* [Gk, = depth of the sea]

bentonite /béntənīt/ *n.* a kind of absorbent clay used esp. as a filler. [Fort *Benton* in Montana, US]

ben trovato /bén trōvaàtō/ *adj.* **1** well invented. **2** characteristic if not true. [It., = well found]

bentwood /béntwŏŏd/ *n.* wood that is artificially shaped for use in making furniture.

benumb /binúm/ *v.tr.* **1** make numb; deaden. **2** paralyse (the mind or feelings). [orig. = deprived, as past part. of ME *benimen* f. OE *beniman* (as BE-, *niman* take)]
■ see DEADEN 2.

Benzedrine /bénzidreen/ *n. propr.* amphetamine. [BENZOIC + EPHEDRINE]

benzene /bénzeen/ *n.* a colourless carcinogenic volatile liquid found in coal tar, petroleum, etc., and used as a solvent and in the manufacture of plastics etc. ¶ Chem. formula: C_6H_6. ▫ **benzene ring** the hexagonal unsaturated ring of six carbon atoms in the benzene molecule. ▫▫ **benzenoid** *adj.* [BENZOIC + -ENE]

benzine /bénzeen/ *n.* (also **benzin** /-zin/) a mixture of liquid hydrocarbons obtained from petroleum. [BENZOIN + -INE[4]]

benzoic /benzṓ-ik/ *adj.* containing or derived from benzoin or benzoic acid. ▫ **benzoic acid** a white crystalline substance used as a food preservative. ¶ Chem. formula: $C_7H_6O_2$. [BENZOIN + -IC]

benzoin /bénzō-in/ *n.* **1** a fragrant gum resin obtained from various E. Asian trees of the genus *Styrax*, and used in the manufacture of perfumes and incense. **2** the white crystalline constituent of this. Also called *gum benjamin*. [earlier *benjoin* ult. f. Arab. *lubān jāwī* incense of Java]

benzol /bénzol/ *n.* (also **benzole** /-zōl/) benzene, esp. unrefined and used as a fuel.

benzoyl /bénzō-il/ *n.* (usu. *attrib.*) *Chem.* the radical C_6H_5CO.

benzyl /bénzīl, -zil/ *n.* (usu. *attrib.*) *Chem.* the radical $C_6H_5CH_2$.

bequeath /bikwee̲th̲/ *v.tr.* **1** leave (a personal estate) to a person by a will. **2** hand down to posterity. ▫▫ **bequeathal** *n.* **bequeather** *n.* [OE *becwethan* (as BE-, *cwethan* say: cf. QUOTH)]
■ leave, make over, will, pass on, hand down *or* on, transmit, *Law* devise.

bequest /bikwést/ *n.* **1** the act or an instance of bequeathing. **2** a thing bequeathed. [ME f. BE- + obs. *quiste* f. OE *-cwiss*, *cwide* saying]
■ **2** legacy, inheritance, heritage, patrimony, *Law* hereditament; heirloom.

berate /biráyt/ *v.tr.* scold, rebuke. [BE- + RATE[2]]
■ scold, reprimand, rebuke, rate, upbraid, chastise, reprove, reproach, reprehend, revile, abuse, rail at, excoriate, castigate, keelhaul, belabour, harangue, rap a person's knuckles, slap a person's wrist, take to task, *archaic* lesson, *archaic or literary* chide, *colloq.* dress down, tell off, lay into, *literary* objurgate, *sl.* ballyrag, *Austral.* & *NZ sl.* go off at.

Berber /bérbər/ *n.* & *adj.* ● *n.* **1** a member of the indigenous mainly Muslim Caucasian peoples of N. Africa. **2** the language of these peoples. ● *adj.* of the Berbers or their language. [Arab. *barbar*]

berberis /bérbəriss/ *n.* = BARBERRY. [med.L & OF, of unkn. orig.]

berceuse /bairsṓz/ *n.* (*pl.* ***berceuses*** *pronunc.* same) **1** a lullaby. **2** an instrumental piece in the style of a lullaby. [F]

bereave /birééev/ *v.tr.* (esp. as **bereaved** *adj.*) (foll. by *of*) deprive of a relation, friend, etc., esp. by death. ▫▫ **bereavement** *n.* [OE *berēafian* (as BE-, REAVE)]
■ deprive, strip, rob, dispossess; widow. ▫▫ **bereavement** see LOSS 1, MOURNING 1.

bereft /biréft/ *adj.* (foll. by *of*) deprived (esp. of a non-material asset) (*bereft of hope*). [past part. of BEREAVE]

beret /bérray/ *n.* a round flattish cap of felt or cloth. [F *béret* Basque cap f. Prov. *berret*]

berg[1] /berg/ *n.* = ICEBERG. [abbr.]

berg[2] /berg/ *n. S.Afr.* a mountain or hill. ▫ **berg wind** a hot dry northerly wind blowing from the interior to coastal districts. [Afrik. f. Du.]

bergamot[1] /bérgəmot/ *n.* **1** an aromatic herb, esp. *Mentha citrata*. **2** an oily perfume extracted from the rind of the fruit of the citrus tree *Citrus bergamia*, a dwarf variety of the Seville orange tree. **3** the tree itself. [*Bergamo* in N. Italy]

bergamot[2] /bérgəmot/ *n.* a variety of fine pear. [F *bergamotte* f. It. *bergamotta* f. Turk. *begarmūdi* prince's pear f. *beg* prince + *armudi* pear]

bergschrund /báirkshrŏŏnt/ *n.* a crevasse or gap at the head of a glacier or névé. [G]

beriberi /bérribérri/ *n.* a disease causing inflammation of the nerves due to a deficiency of vitamin B_1. [Sinh., f. *beri* weakness]

berk /berk/ *n.* (also **burk**) *Brit. sl.* a fool; a stupid person. ¶ Usu. not considered *offens.* despite the etymology. [abbr. of *Berkeley* or *Berkshire Hunt*, rhyming sl. for *cunt*]

berkelium /berkeéliəm, bérkliəm/ *n. Chem.* a transuranic radioactive metallic element produced by bombardment of americium. ¶ Symb.: **Bk**. [mod.L f. *Berkeley* in California (where first made) + -IUM]

Berks. /baarks/ *abbr.* Berkshire.

Berliner /berlínnər/ *n.* **1** a native or citizen of Berlin in Germany. **2** a lightly fried yeast bun with jam filling and vanilla icing. [G]

berm /berm/ *n.* **1** a narrow path or grass strip beside a road, canal, etc. **2** a narrow ledge, esp. in a fortification between a ditch and the base of a parapet. [F *berme* f. Du. *berm*]

Bermuda shorts /bərmyŏŏdə/ *n.pl.* (also **Bermudas**) close-fitting shorts reaching the knees. [*Bermuda* in the W. Atlantic]

Bermuda triangle /bərmyŏŏdə/ *n.* an area of the western Atlantic where ships and aircraft are reported to have disappeared without trace.

berry /bérri/ *n.* & *v.* ● *n.* (*pl.* **-ies**) **1** any small roundish juicy fruit without a stone. **2** *Bot.* a fruit with its seeds enclosed in a pulp (e.g. a banana, tomato, etc.). **3** any of various kernels or seeds (e.g. coffee bean etc.). **4** a fish egg or roe of a lobster etc. ● *v.intr.* (**-ies, -ied**) **1** (usu. as **berrying** *n.*) go gathering berries. **2** form a berry; bear berries. □□ **berried** *adj.* (also in *comb.*). [OE *berie* f. Gmc]

berserk /bərsérk, -zérk/ *adj.* & *n.* ● *adj.* (esp. in **go berserk**) wild, frenzied; in a violent rage. ● *n.* (also **berserker** /-kər/) an ancient Norse warrior who fought with a wild frenzy. [Icel. *berserkr* (n.) prob. f. *bern-* BEAR² + *serkr* coat]
■ *adj.* mad, violent, wild, crazy, deranged, crazed, frenzied, maniacal, manic, insane, hysterical, frantic, raving, out of control, out of one's mind, *sl.* loopy, loony, bonkers, out of one's skull; fuming, irate, enraged, incensed, furious, angry.

berth /berth/ *n.* & *v.* ● *n.* **1** a fixed bunk on a ship, train, etc., for sleeping in. **2** a ship's place at a wharf. **3** room for a ship to swing at anchor. **4** adequate sea room. **5** *colloq.* a situation or appointment. **6** the proper place for anything. ● *v.* **1** *tr.* moor (a ship) in its berth. **2** *tr.* provide a sleeping place for. **3** *intr.* (of a ship) come to its mooring-place. □ **give a wide berth to** stay away from. [prob. f. naut. use of BEAR¹ + -TH²]
■ *n.* **1** see CABIN *n.* 2. **5** see APPOINTMENT 2a. ● *v.* **1, 3** see MOOR².

bertha /bérthə/ *n.* **1** a deep falling collar often of lace. **2** a small cape on a dress. [F *berthe* f. *Berthe* Bertha (the name)]

beryl /bérril/ *n.* **1** a kind of transparent precious stone, esp. pale green, blue, or yellow, and consisting of beryllium aluminium silicate in a hexagonal form. **2** a mineral species which includes this, emerald, and aquamarine. [ME f. OF f. L *beryllus* f. Gk *bērullos*]

beryllium /bərilliəm/ *n. Chem.* a hard white metallic element used in the manufacture of light corrosion-resistant alloys. ¶ Symb.: **Be**. [BERYL + -IUM]

beseech /biseéch/ *v.tr.* (*past* and *past part.* **besought** /-sáwt/ or **beseeched**) **1** (foll. by *for*, or *to* + infin.) entreat. **2** ask earnestly for. □□ **beseeching** *adj.* [ME f. BE- + *secan* SEEK]
■ supplicate, entreat, implore, plead (with), beg, importune, appeal to *or* for, pray, petition.

beset /bisét/ *v.tr.* (**besetting**; *past* and *past part.* **beset**) **1** attack or harass persistently (*beset by worries*). **2** surround or hem in (a person etc.). **3** *archaic* cover round with (*beset with pearls*). □ **besetting sin** the sin that especially or most frequently tempts one. □□ **besetment** *n.* [OE *besettan* f. Gmc]
■ **1** assail, attack, harass, beleaguer, besiege, bedevil, harry, hector, bother, nag, afflict, trouble, distress, oppress, torment, hound, badger, *colloq.* plague, crowd in. **2** encompass, surround, besiege, hem in, encircle.

beside /bisíd/ *prep.* **1** at the side of; near. **2** compared with. **3** irrelevant to (*beside the point*). □ **beside oneself** overcome with worry, anger, etc. [OE *be sīdan* (as BY, SIDE)]
■ **1** alongside, near, next to, with, close to, hard by, by. **3** irrelevant to, away from, wide of, apart from, unconnected with, off. □ **beside oneself** out of one's mind *or* wits, at the end of one's tether, overwrought, agitated, distracted, distraught, upset, crazy, mad; excited, worked up, wound up, *colloq.* in a tizzy, in a flap *or* fluster, all of a dither, in a state, *sl.* doing one's head *or* nut.

besides /bisídz/ *prep.* & *adv.* ● *prep.* in addition to; apart from. ● *adv.* also; as well; moreover.
■ *prep.* over and above, above and beyond, in addition to, additionally to, as well as; barring, bar, excepting, except (for), excluding, exclusive of, not counting *or* including, leaving out, beyond, apart from, other than, but for, *US* aside from, *archaic or poet.* save for. ● *adv.* in addition, additionally, also; further, furthermore, moreover, as well, too, more than that; to boot, on top of everything else, into the bargain.

besiege /biseéj/ *v.tr.* **1** lay siege to. **2** crowd round oppressively. **3** harass with requests. □□ **besieger** *n.* [ME f. *assiege* by substitution of BE-, f. OF *asegier* f. Rmc]
■ **1** lay siege to, beleaguer, invest. **2** blockade, block (off *or* up), hem in, cut off; surround, crowd round, encircle. **3** beleaguer, harass, bedevil, beset, assail, pressurize, press, hound, badger, *colloq.* plague; overwhelm, inundate.

besmear /bismeér/ *v.tr.* **1** smear with greasy or sticky stuff. **2** sully (a reputation etc.). [OE *bismierwan* (as BE-, SMEAR)]

besmirch /bismúrch/ *v.tr.* **1** soil, discolour. **2** dishonour; sully the reputation or name of. [BE- + SMIRCH]
■ **1** see DIRTY *v.* **2** see SULLY.

besom /beéz'm/ *n.* **1** a broom made of twigs tied round a stick. **2** esp. *N.Engl. derog.* or *joc.* a woman. [OE *besema*]
■ **1** see BRUSH *n.* 1.

besotted /bisóttid/ *adj.* **1** infatuated. **2** foolish, confused. **3** intoxicated, stupefied. [*besot* (v.) (as BE-, SOT)]
■ **1** see INFATUATED. **3** see DRUNK *adj.* 1.

besought *past* and *past part.* of BESEECH.

bespangle /bispángg'l/ *v.tr.* adorn with spangles.

bespatter /bispáttər/ *v.tr.* **1** spatter (an object) all over. **2** spatter (liquid etc.) about. **3** overwhelm with abuse etc.
■ **1, 2** see SPATTER *v.* 1.

bespeak /bispeék/ *v.tr.* (*past* **bespoke** /-spṓk/; *past part.* **bespoken** /-spṓkən/ or as *adj.* **bespoke**) **1** engage in advance. **2** order (goods). **3** suggest; be evidence of (*his gift bespeaks a kind heart*). **4** *literary* speak to. [OE *bisprecan* (as BE-, SPEAK)]
■ **1** see ENGAGE 5. **3** see INDICATE 2.

bespectacled /bispéktək'ld/ *adj.* wearing spectacles.

bespoke *past* and *past part.* of BESPEAK. ● *adj.* **1** (of goods, esp. clothing) made to order. **2** (of a tradesman) making goods to order.
■ **1** see *tailor-made* 1.

bespoken *past part.* of BESPEAK.

besprinkle /bispríngk'l/ *v.tr.* sprinkle or strew all over with liquid etc. [ME f. BE- + *sprengen* in the same sense]
■ see SPATTER *v.* 1a.

Bessemer converter /béssimər/ *n.* a special furnace used to purify pig-iron using the Bessemer process. [Sir H. *Bessemer*, Engl. engineer d. 1898]

Bessemer process /béssimər/ *n.* a process once widely used, in which air is blown through molten pig-iron to remove carbon, silicon, and other impurities in order to render it suitable for making steel.

best /best/ *adj.*, *adv.*, *n.*, & *v.* ● *adj.* (*superl.* of GOOD) of the most excellent or outstanding or desirable kind (*my best work*; *the best solution*; *the best thing to do would be to confess*). ● *adv.* (*superl.* of WELL¹). **1** in the best manner (*does it best*). **2** to the greatest degree (*like it best*). **3** most usefully (*is best ignored*). ● *n.* **1** that which is best (*the best is yet to come*). **2** the chief merit or advantage; the best aspect or side; a person's best performance, achievement, etc. (*brings out the best in him*; *gave their best to the task*). **3** (foll. by *of*) a winning majority of (a certain number of games etc. played) (*the best of five*). **4** = Sunday best. ● *v.tr. colloq.* defeat, outwit, outbid, etc. □ **all the best** an expression used to wish a person good fortune. **as best one can** (or **may**) as effectively as possible under the circumstances. **at best** on the most optimistic view. **at one's best** in peak condition etc. **at the best of times** even in the most favourable circumstances. **be for** (or **all for**) **the best** be desirable in the end. **best end of neck** the rib end of a neck of lamb etc. for cooking. **best man** the bridegroom's chief attendant at a wedding. **the best part of** most of. **best seller 1** a book or other item that has sold in large numbers. **2** the author of such a book. **do one's best** do all one can. **get**

the best of defeat, outwit. **give a person the best** admit the superiority of that person. **had best** would find it wisest to. **make the best of** derive what limited advantage one can from (something unsatisfactory or unwelcome); put up with. **to the best of one's ability, knowledge,** etc. as far as one can do, know, etc. **with the best of them** as well as anyone. [OE *betest* (adj.), *bet(o)st* (adv.), f. Gmc]

■ *adj.* top, superlative, unexcelled, unrivalled, finest, pre-eminent, first, superb, unsurpassed, peerless, superior, excellent, paramount, first-rate, foremost, choicest, *colloq.* A1; first-class, upper-class, *colloq.* upper-crust. ● *adv.* **2** most, to the greatest extent *or* degree. **3** better. ● *n.* **1, 2** finest, first, prime, cream, pearl, winner, choice, flower, *crème de la crème*; utmost, *sl.* the most. **3** majority. **4** finery, best clothes, best bib and tucker, *colloq.* glad rags, *joc.* Sunday best. ● *v.* win (out) over, conquer, beat, surpass, get the better of, subdue, defeat, worst, trounce, rout, crush, master, outdo, overwhelm, overcome, outwit, *literary* vanquish; outbid; see also BEAT *v.* 3a. □ **all the best** see REGARD *n.* 5. **at best** see *ideally* (IDEAL). **at one's best** on *or* in top form, in the best of health, in good *or* great shape, *colloq.* in tiptop condition. **the best part of** most of, the majority of, the better part of, the greater part of. **get the best of** see BEAT *v.* 3a. **had best** had better, ought to, must, should. **make the best of** see *put up with*.

bestial /béstiəl/ *adj.* **1** brutish, cruel, savage. **2** sexually depraved; lustful. **3** of or like a beast. □□ **bestialize** *v.tr.* (also **-ise**). **bestially** *adv.* [ME f. OF f. LL *bestialis* f. *bestia* beast]

■ **1** see SAVAGE *adj.* 1, 2. **2** see LIBERTINE *adj.* 1.

bestiality /béstiálliti/ *n.* (*pl.* **-ies**) **1** bestial behaviour or an instance of this. **2** sexual intercourse between a person and an animal. [F *bestialité* (as BESTIAL)]

bestiary /béstiəri/ *n.* (*pl.* **-ies**) a moralizing medieval treatise on real and imaginary beasts. [med.L *bestiarium* f. L *bestia* beast]

bestir /bistúr/ *v.refl.* (**bestirred, bestirring**) exert or rouse (oneself).

■ see ROUSE 2a.

bestow /bistṓ/ *v.tr.* **1** (foll. by *on, upon*) confer (a gift, right, etc.). **2** deposit. □□ **bestowal** *n.* [ME f. BE- + OE *stow* a place]

■ **1** confer, give, award, present, donate, grant, cede, afford. □□ **bestowal** see AWARD *n.* 1b.

bestrew /bistrṓo/ *v.tr.* (*past part.* **bestrewed** or **bestrewn** /-strṓon/) **1** (foll. by *with*) cover or partly cover (a surface). **2** scatter (things) about. **3** lie scattered over. [OE *bestrēowian* (as BE-, STREW)]

■ **1, 2** see STREW.

bestride /bistrī́d/ *v.tr.* (*past* **bestrode** /-strṓd/; *past part.* **bestridden** /-stridd'n/) **1** sit astride on. **2** stand astride over. [OE *bestrīdan*]

bet /bet/ *v.* & *n.* ● *v.* (**betting**; *past* and *past part.* **bet** or **betted**) **1** *intr.* (foll. by *on* or *against* with ref. to the outcome) risk a sum of money etc. against another's on the basis of the outcome of an unpredictable event (esp. the result of a race, game, etc., or the outcome in a game of chance). **2** *tr.* risk (an amount) on such an outcome or result (*bet £10 on a horse*). **3** *tr.* risk a sum of money against (a person). **4** *tr. colloq.* feel sure (*bet they've forgotten it*). ● *n.* **1** the act of betting (*make a bet*). **2** the money etc. staked (*put a bet on*). **3** *colloq.* an opinion, esp. a quickly formed or spontaneous one (*my bet is that he won't come*). **4** *colloq.* a choice or course of action (*she's our best bet*). □ **you bet** *colloq.* you may be sure. [16th c.: perh. a shortened form of ABET]

■ *v.* **1, 2** wager, stake, gamble, risk, hazard, play, lay (down), put, chance, venture, try one's luck, *Brit. colloq.* punt. ● *n.* **1, 2** wager, stake, risk, venture, *Brit. colloq.* punt, *Brit. sl.* flutter. **4** see OPTION 1. □ **you bet** see ABSOLUTELY 6.

beta /béetə/ *n.* **1** the second letter of the Greek alphabet (*Β, β*). **2** a second-class mark given for a piece of work or in an examination. **3** *Astron.* the second brightest star in a constellation. **4** the second member of a series. □ **beta-blocker** *Pharm.* a drug that prevents the stimulation of increased cardiac action, used to treat angina and reduce high blood pressure. **beta particle** (or **ray**) a fast-moving electron emitted by radioactive decay of substances (orig. regarded as rays). [ME f. L f. Gk]

betake /bitáyk/ *v.refl.* (*past* **betook** /bitŏŏk/; *past part.* **betaken** /bitáykən/) (foll. by *to*) go to (a place or person).

betatron /béetətron/ *n. Physics* an apparatus for accelerating electrons in a circular path by magnetic induction. [BETA + -TRON]

betel /béet'l/ *n.* the leaf of the Asian evergreen climbing plant *Piper betle*, chewed in the East with parings of the areca nut. □ **betel-nut** the areca nut. [Port. f. Malayalam *veṭṭila*]

bête noire /bayt nwaár/ *n.* (*pl.* ***bêtes noires*** *pronunc.* same) a person or thing one particularly dislikes or fears. [F, = black beast]

■ see AVERSION 2.

bethink /bithingk/ *v.refl.* (*past* and *past part.* **bethought** /-tháwt/) (foll. by *of, how,* or *that* + clause) *formal* **1** reflect; stop to think. **2** be reminded by reflection. [OE *bithencan* f. Gmc (as BE-, THINK)]

betide /bitī́d/ *v. poet.* (only in infin. and 3rd sing. subj.) **1** *tr.* happen to (*woe betide him*). **2** *intr.* happen (*whate'er may betide*). [ME f. obs. *tide* befall f. OE *tīdan*]

■ **1** see HAPPEN *v.* 3. **2** see HAPPEN *v.* 1.

betimes /bitī́mz/ *adv. literary* early; in good time. [ME f. obs. *betime* (as BY, TIME)]

■ see EARLY *adj.* & *adv.* 1.

bêtise /baytéez/ *n.* **1** a foolish or ill-timed remark or action. **2** a piece of folly. [F]

betoken /bitṓkən/ *v.tr.* **1** be a sign of; indicate. **2** augur. [OE (as BE-, *tācnian* signify: see TOKEN)]

■ **1** see INDICATE 2. **2** see BODE.

betony /béttəni/ *n.* **1** a purple-flowered plant, *Stachys officinalis*. **2** any of various similar plants. [ME f. OF *betoine* f. L *betonica*]

betook *past* of BETAKE.

betray /bitráy/ *v.tr.* **1** place (a person, one's country, etc.) in the hands or power of an enemy. **2** be disloyal to (another person, a person's trust, etc.). **3** reveal involuntarily or treacherously; be evidence of (*his shaking hand betrayed his fear*). **4** lead astray or into error. □□ **betrayal** *n.* **betrayer** *n.* [ME f. obs. *tray*, ult. f. L *tradere* hand over]

■ **2** be *or* prove false *or* disloyal to, sell out, break faith with, let down, fail, inform on, stab in the back, double-cross, give away, *colloq.* sell down the river, rat on, *sl.* stitch up, *Brit. sl.* shop, grass (on). **3** reveal, disclose, divulge, display, show, demonstrate, make known, expose, lay bare, evidence. **4** lead astray, mislead, misguide, deceive, take in, dupe, beguile, fool, hoodwink. □□ **betrayal** treachery, treason, disloyalty, perfidy, traitorousness, faithlessness, bad faith, breach of faith, stab in the back, sell-out; revelation, exposure, disclosure, divulgence, *colloq.* give-away.

betroth /bitrṓth/ *v.tr.* (usu. as **betrothed** *adj.*) bind with a promise to marry. □□ **betrothal** *n.* [ME f. BE- + *trouthe, treuthe* TRUTH, later assim. to TROTH]

■ (**betrothed**) see ENGAGED 1. □□ **betrothal** see MATCH[1] *n.* 3.

better[1] /béttər/ *adj., adv., n.,* & *v.* ● *adj.* (*compar.* of GOOD). **1** of a more excellent or outstanding or desirable kind (*a better product; it would be better to go home*). **2** partly or fully recovered from illness (*feeling better*). ● *adv.* (*compar.* of WELL[1]). **1** in a better manner (*she sings better*). **2** to a greater degree (*like it better*). **3** more usefully or advantageously (*is better forgotten*). ● *n.* **1** that which is better (*the better of the two; had the better of me*). **2** (usu. in *pl.*; prec. by *my* etc.) one's superior in ability or rank (*take notice of your betters*). ● *v.* **1** *tr.* improve on; surpass (*I can better his offer*). **2** *tr.* make better; improve. **3** *refl.* improve one's position etc. **4**

intr. become better; improve. □ **better feelings** one's conscience. **better half** *colloq.* one's wife or husband. **better off** in a better (esp. financial) position. **the better part of** most of. **for better or for worse** on terms accepting all results; whatever the outcome. **get the better of** defeat, outwit; win an advantage over. **go one better 1** outbid etc. by one. **2** (*go one better than*) outdo another person. **had better** would find it wiser to. [OE *betera* f. Gmc]

■ *adj.* **1** superior; preferable. **2** healthier, haler, heartier, less ill *or esp. US* sick, improved; cured, recovered. ● *adv.* **3** best. ● *n.* **1** advantage, mastery, superiority, control; the edge. **2** (*betters*) superiors, masters, elders. ● *v.* **1** surpass, excel, outdo, outstrip, beat, improve on, outmatch, exceed, eclipse, *colloq.* lick, best. **2** improve, advance, raise, elevate, upgrade, enhance, lift, extend, increase, *formal* ameliorate, *literary* meliorate. **3** improve, advance, promote. **4** see IMPROVE 1a. □ **better feelings** see CONSCIENCE. **better half** see PARTNER *n.* 4. **better off** improved; wealthier, richer. **the better part of** the best part of, most of, the greater part of, the majority of. **get the better of** see DEFEAT *v.* 1. **go one better 2** see OUTDO. **had better** had best, ought to, should, must.

better[2] /béttər/ *n.* (also **bettor**) a person who bets.
■ gambler, speculator, gamester, punter.

betterment /béttərmənt/ *n.* **1** making better; improvement. **2** *Econ.* enhanced value (of real property) arising from local improvements.

betting /bétting/ *n.* **1** gambling by risking money on an unpredictable outcome. **2** the odds offered in this. □ **betting-shop** *Brit.* a bookmaker's shop or office. **what's the betting?** *colloq.* it is likely or to be expected (*what's the betting he'll be late?*).

bettor var. of BETTER[2].

between /bitweén/ *prep.* & *adv.* ● *prep.* **1 a** at or to a point in the area or interval bounded by two or more other points in space, time, etc. (*broke down between London and Dover*; *we must meet between now and Friday*). **b** along the extent of such an area or interval (*there are five shops between here and the main road*; *works best between five and six*; *the numbers between 10 and 20*). **2** separating, physically or conceptually (*the distance between here and Leeds*; *the difference between right and wrong*). **3 a** by combining the resources of (*great potential between them*; *between us we could afford it*). **b** shared by; as the joint resources of (*£5 between them*). **c** by joint or reciprocal action (*an agreement between us*; *sorted it out between themselves*). ¶ Use in sense 3 with reference to more than two people or things is established and acceptable (e.g. *relations between Britain, France, and Germany*). **4** to and from (*runs between London and Sheffield*). **5** taking one and rejecting the other of (*decide between eating here and going out*). ● *adv.* (also **in between**) at a point or in the area bounded by two or more other points in space, time, sequence, etc. (*not fat or thin but in between*). □ **between ourselves** (or **you and me**) in confidence. **between times** (or **whiles**) in the intervals between other actions; occasionally. [OE *betwēonum* f. Gmc (as BY, TWO)]

betwixt /bitwíkst/ *prep.* & *adv. archaic* between. □ **betwixt and between** *colloq.* neither one thing nor the other. [ME f. OE *betwēox* f. Gmc: cf. AGAINST]

BeV *abbr.* a billion ($=10^9$) electron-volts. Also called GEV.

bevatron /bévvətron/ *n.* a synchrotron used to accelerate protons to energies in the billion electronvolt range. [BEV + -TRON]

bevel /bévv'l/ *n.* & *v.* ● *n.* **1** a slope from the horizontal or vertical in carpentry and stonework; a sloping surface or edge. **2** (in full **bevel square**) a tool for marking angles in carpentry and stonework. ● *v.* (**bevelled, bevelling**; *US* **beveled, beveling**) **1** *tr.* reduce (a square edge) to a sloping edge. **2** *intr.* slope at an angle; slant. □ **bevel gear** a gear working another gear at an angle to it by means of bevel wheels. **bevel wheel** a toothed wheel whose working face is oblique to the axis. [OF *bevel* (unrecorded) f. *baïf* f. *baer* gape]
■ *n.* **1** see SLOPE 1–3. ● *v.* see SLANT 1, 2.

beverage /bévvərij/ *n. formal* a drink (*hot beverage*; *alcoholic beverage*). [ME f. OF *be(u)vrage*, ult. f. L *bibere* drink]
■ see DRINK *n.* 1a.

bevvy /bévvi/ *n.* (also **bevy**) *sl.* (a) drink, esp. (of) beer or other alcoholic liquor. [shortened f. BEVERAGE]

bevy /bévvi/ *n.* (*pl.* **-ies**) **1** a flock of quails or larks. **2** a company or group (orig. of women). [15th c.: orig. unkn.]
■ **1** see FLIGHT[1] *n.* 3a. **2** see GROUP *n.* 1.

bewail /biwáyl/ *v.tr.* **1** greatly regret or lament. **2** wail over; mourn for. □□ **bewailer** *n.*
■ lament (for *or* over), regret, mourn (for *or* over), bemoan, rue; grieve for *or* over, sorrow for *or* over, moan over, weep *or* cry *or* keen *or* wail over, beat one's breast over, *archaic or poet.* plain for.

beware /biwáir/ *v.* (only in *imper.* or *infin.*) **1** *intr.* (often foll. by *of*, or *that*, *lest*, etc. + clause) be cautious, take heed (*beware of the dog*; *told us to beware*; *beware that you don't fall*). **2** *tr.* be cautious of (*beware the Ides of March*). [BE + WARE[3]]
■ take heed, be careful, be wary, be cautious, be on one's guard, exercise caution, watch out, look out, take care; (*beware of*) mind, watch for, heed.

bewilder /biwíldər/ *v.tr.* utterly perplex or confuse. □□ **bewilderedly** *adv.* **bewildering** *adj.* **bewilderingly** *adv.* **bewilderment** *n.* [BE- + obs. *wilder* lose one's way]
■ confuse, confound, perplex, puzzle, mystify, befuddle, nonplus, baffle, bemuse, maze, bedazzle, bedevil, distract, *US* gravel, *archaic* wilder, *colloq.* flummox. □□ **bewildering** see *perplexing* (PERPLEX).

bewitch /biwích/ *v.tr.* **1** enchant; greatly delight. **2** cast a spell on. □□ **bewitching** *adj.* **bewitchingly** *adv.* [ME f. BE- + OE *wiccian* enchant f. *wicca* WITCH]
■ **1** enchant, entrance, spellbind, charm, fascinate, beguile, captivate, enrapture, enthral, seduce, *archaic* witch, *poet.* glamour; delight, thrill, excite. **2** cast a spell on *or* over, charm, bedevil, voodoo, *Austral.* point the bone at, *US* hex, *esp. US* hoodoo, *archaic* witch; *colloq.* jinx.

bey /bay/ *n. hist.* (in the Ottoman Empire) the title of a governor of a province. [Turk.]

beyond /biyónd/ *prep.*, *adv.*, & *n.* ● *prep.* **1** at or to the further side of (*beyond the river*). **2** outside the scope, range, or understanding of (*beyond repair*; *beyond a joke*; *it is beyond me*). **3** more than. ● *adv.* **1** at or to the further side. **2** further on. ● *n.* (prec. by *the*) the unknown after death. □ **the back of beyond** see BACK. **beyond words** inexpressible. [OE *beg(e)ondan* (as BY, YON, YONDER)]
■ *prep.* **1** see OVER *prep.* 3, 4. **2** see ABOVE *prep.* 4b. **3** see OVER *prep.* 10. ● *adv.* **1** see OVER *adv.* 4. □ **beyond words** see INEXPRESSIBLE.

bezant /bézz'nt, bizánt/ *n.* **1** *hist.* a gold or silver coin orig. minted at Byzantium. **2** *Heraldry* a gold roundel. [ME f. OF *besanz -ant* f. L *Byzantius* Byzantine]

bezel /bézz'l/ *n.* **1** the sloped edge of a chisel. **2** the oblique faces of a cut gem. **3 a** a groove holding a watch-glass or gem. **b** a rim holding a glass etc. cover. [OF *besel* (unrecorded: cf. F *béseau*, *bizeau*) of unkn. orig.]

bezique /bizeék/ *n.* **1** a card-game for two with a double pack of 64 cards, including the ace to seven only in each suit. **2** a combination of the queen of spades and the jack of diamonds in this game. [F *bésigue*, perh. f. Pers. *bāzīgar* juggler]

bezoar /beézor, bézzō-aar/ *n.* a small stone which may form in the stomachs of certain animals, esp. ruminants, and which was once used as an antidote for various ills. [ult. f. Pers. *pādzahr* antidote, Arab. *bāzahr*]

b.f. *abbr.* **1** *Brit. colloq.* bloody fool. **2** brought forward. **3** *Printing* bold face.

bhang /bang/ *n.* the leaves and flower-tops of Indian hemp used as a narcotic. [Port. *bangue*, Pers. *bang*, & Urdu etc. *bhāng* f. Skr. *bhangā*]

bhangra /baánggrə/ *n.* a kind of pop music that combines Punjabi folk traditions with Western popular music. [Punjabi *bhāngrā*, a traditional folk-dance]

bharal /búrrəl/ *n.* (also **burhel**) a Himalayan wild sheep, *Pseudois nayaur*, with blue-black coat and horns curved rearward. [Hindi]

b.h.p. *abbr.* brake horsepower.

Bi *symb. Chem.* the element bismuth.

bi- /bī/ *comb. form* (often **bin-** before a vowel) forming nouns and adjectives meaning: **1** having two; a thing having two (*bilateral*; *binaural*; *biplane*). **2 a** occurring twice in every one or once in every two (*bi-weekly*). **b** lasting for two (*biennial*). **3** doubly; in two ways (*biconcave*). **4** *Chem.* a substance having a double proportion of the acid etc. indicated by the simple word (*bicarbonate*). **5** *Bot.* & *Zool.* (of division and subdivision) twice over (*bipinnate*). [L]

biannual /bīányooəl/ *adj.* occurring, appearing, etc., twice a year (cf. BIENNIAL). ▫▫ **biannually** *adv.*

bias /bīəss/ *n.* & *v.* ● *n.* **1** (often foll. by *towards*, *against*) a predisposition or prejudice. **2** *Statistics* a systematic distortion of a statistical result due to a factor not allowed for in its derivation. **3** an edge cut obliquely across the weave of a fabric. **4** *Sport* **a** the irregular shape given to a bowl. **b** the oblique course this causes it to run. **5** *Electr.* a steady voltage, magnetic field, etc., applied to an electronic system or device. ● *v.tr.* (**biased, biasing; biassed, biassing**) **1** (esp. as **biased** *adj.*) influence (usu. unfairly); prejudice. **2** give a bias to. ▫ **bias binding** a strip of fabric cut obliquely and used to bind edges. **on the bias** obliquely, diagonally. [F *biais*, of unkn. orig.]

■ *n.* **1** prejudice, predisposition, partiality, inclination, leaning, bent, disposition, propensity, tendency, predilection, proclivity. **2** skew, skewness, distortion. **3** angle, slant, diagonal. ● *v.* **1** affect unduly *or* unfairly, prejudice, colour, taint, predispose, influence, sway, incline; skew; (**biased**) prejudiced, partial; warped, distorted, one-sided, subjective, jaundiced; skewed.

biathlon /bīáthlən/ *n. Sport* an athletic contest in skiing and shooting. ▫▫ **biathlete** *n.* [BI-, after PENTATHLON]

biaxial /bīáksiəl/ *adj.* (esp. of crystals) having two axes along which polarized light travels with equal velocity.

bib[1] /bib/ *n.* **1** a piece of cloth or plastic fastened round a child's neck to keep the clothes clean while eating. **2** the top front part of an apron, dungarees, etc. **3** the edible marine fish *Trisopterus luscus* of the cod family. Also called POUT[2]. ▫ **best bib and tucker** best clothes. **stick** (or **poke** etc.) **one's bib in** *Austral. sl.* interfere. [perh. f. BIB[2]]

■ ▫ **stick** (or **poke**) **one's bib in** see INTERFERE 2.

bib[2] /bib/ *v.intr.* (**bibbed, bibbing**) *archaic* drink much or often. ▫▫ **bibber** *n.* [ME, perh. f. L *bibere* drink]

■ ▫▫ **bibber** see DRUNK *n.* 1.

bib-cock /bíbkok/ *n.* a tap with a bent nozzle fixed at the end of a pipe. [perh. f. BIB[1] + COCK[1]]

bibelot /beéblō/ *n.* a small curio or artistic trinket. [F]

Bible /bīb'l/ *n.* **1 a** the Christian scriptures consisting of the Old and New Testaments. **b** the Jewish scriptures. **c** (**bible**) any copy of these (*three bibles on the table*). **d** a particular edition of the Bible (*New English Bible*). **2** *colloq.* any authoritative book (*Wisden is his Bible*). **3** the scriptures of any non-Christian religion. ▫ **Bible-basher** (or **-thumper** etc.) *sl.* a person given to Bible-bashing. **Bible-bashing** (or **-thumping** etc.) *sl.* aggressive fundamentalist preaching. **Bible belt** esp. *US* the reputedly puritanical area of the southern and central US. **Bible oath** a solemn oath taken on the Bible. [ME f. OF f. eccl.L *biblia* f. Gk *biblia* books (pl. of *biblion*), orig. dimin. of *biblos*, *bublos* papyrus]

■ **1, 3** see SCRIPTURE.

biblical /bíblik'l/ *adj.* **1** of, concerning, or contained in the Bible. **2** resembling the language of the Authorized Version of the Bible. ▫▫ **biblically** *adv.*

biblio- /bíbliō/ *comb. form* denoting a book or books. [Gk f. *biblion* book]

bibliography /bíbliógrəfi/ *n.* (*pl.* **-ies**) **1 a** a list of the books referred to in a scholarly work, usu. printed as an appendix. **b** a list of the books of a specific author or publisher, or on a specific subject, etc. **2 a** the history or description of books, including authors, editions, etc. **b** any book containing such information. ▫▫ **bibliographer** *n.* **bibliographic** /-liəgráffik/ *adj.* **bibliographical** /-liəgráffik'l/ *adj.* **bibliographically** /-liəgráffikəli/ *adv.* **bibliographize** *v.tr.* (also **-ise**). [F *bibliographie* f. mod.L *bibliographia* f. Gk (as BIBLE, -GRAPHY)]

bibliomancy /bíbliōmansi/ *n.* foretelling the future by the analysis of a randomly chosen passage from a book, esp. the Bible.

bibliomania /bíbliōmáyniə/ *n.* an extreme enthusiasm for collecting and possessing books. ▫▫ **bibliomaniac** /-niak/ *n.* & *adj.*

bibliophile /bíbliōfīl/ *n.* (also **bibliophil** /-fil/) a person who collects or is fond of books. ▫▫ **bibliophilic** /-fíllik/ *adj.* **bibliophily** /-lióffili/ *n.* [F *bibliophile* (as BIBLIO-, -PHILE)]

■ see BOOKWORM.

bibliopole /bíbliōpōl/ *n.* a seller of (esp. rare) books. ▫▫ **bibliopoly** /-lióppəli/ *n.* [L *bibliopola* f. Gk *bibliopōlēs* f. *biblion* book + *pōlēs* seller]

bibulous /bíbyooləss/ *adj.* given to drinking alcoholic liquor. ▫▫ **bibulously** *adv.* **bibulousness** *n.* [L *bibulus* freely drinking f. *bibere* drink]

■ ▫▫ **bibulousness** see *drunkenness* (DRUNKEN).

bicameral /bīkámmərəl/ *adj.* (of a parliament or legislative body) having two chambers. ▫▫ **bicameralism** *n.* [BI- + L *camera* chamber]

bicarb /bīkaarb/ *n. colloq.* = BICARBONATE 2. [abbr.]

bicarbonate /bīkaárbənit/ *n.* **1** *Chem.* any acid salt of carbonic acid. **2** (in full **bicarbonate of soda**) sodium bicarbonate used as an antacid or in baking powder.

bice /bīss/ *n.* **1** any of various pigments made from blue or green basic copper carbonate. **2** any similar pigment made from smalt. **3** a shade of blue or green given by these. ▫ **blue bice** a shade of blue between ultramarine and azure derived from smalt. **green bice** a yellowish green colour derived by adding yellow orpiment to smalt. [orig. = brownish grey, f. OF *bis* dark grey, of unkn. orig.]

bicentenary /bīsenteénəri/ *n.* & *adj.* ● *n.* (*pl.* **-ies**) **1** a two-hundredth anniversary. **2** a celebration of this. ● *adj.* of or concerning a bicentenary.

bicentennial /bīsenténniəl/ *n.* & *adj.* esp. *US* ● *n.* a bicentenary. ● *adj.* **1** lasting two hundred years or occurring every two hundred years. **2** of or concerning a bicentenary.

bicephalous /bīséffələss/ *adj.* having two heads.

biceps /bīseps/ *n.* a muscle having two heads or attachments, esp. the one which bends the elbow. [L, = two-headed, formed as BI- + *-ceps* f. *caput* head]

bicker /bíkkər/ *v.intr.* **1** quarrel pettily; wrangle. **2** *poet.* **a** (of a stream, rain, etc.) patter (over stones etc.). **b** (of a flame, light, etc.) flash, flicker. ▫▫ **bickerer** *n.* [ME *biker*, *beker*, of unkn. orig.]

■ **1** squabble, quarrel, dispute, wrangle, argue, disagree, tiff, *colloq.* row, *US colloq.* spat, *joc.* argy-bargy. **2 a** see PATTER[1] *v.* 1. **b** see FLASH *v.* 1, 3.

bickie /bíkki/ *n.* (also **bikkie**) *colloq.* a biscuit. ▫ **big bickies** *Austral. colloq.* a large sum of money. [abbr.]

■ ▫ **big bickies** see PILE[1] *n.* 3b.

bicolour /bīkúllər/ *adj.* & *n.* ● *adj.* having two colours. ● *n.* a bicolour blossom or animal.

biconcave /bīkónkayv/ *adj.* (esp. of a lens) concave on both sides.

biconvex /bīkónveks/ *adj.* (esp. of a lens) convex on both sides.

bicultural /bīkúlchərəl/ *adj.* having or combining two cultures.

bicuspid /bīkúspid/ *adj.* & *n.* ● *adj.* having two cusps or points. ● *n.* **1** the premolar tooth in humans. **2** a tooth with two cusps. ▫▫ **bicuspidate** *adj.* [BI- + L *cuspis -idis* sharp point]

bicycle /bī́sik'l/ *n.* & *v.* ● *n.* a vehicle of two wheels held in a frame one behind the other, propelled by pedals and steered with handlebars attached to the front wheel. ● *v.intr.* ride a bicycle. □ **bicycle-chain** a chain transmitting power from the bicycle pedals to the wheels. **bicycle-clip** either of two metal clips used to confine a cyclist's trousers at the ankle. **bicycle-pump** a portable pump for inflating bicycle tyres. □□ **bicycler** *n.* **bicyclist** /-klist/ *n.* [F f. BI- + Gk *kuklos* wheel]

■ *n.* see CYCLE *n.* 4.

bid /bid/ *v.* & *n.* ● *v.* (**bidding**; *past* **bid**, *archaic* **bade** /bayd, bad/; *past part.* **bid**, *archaic* **bidden** /bídd'n/) **1** *tr.* & *intr.* (*past* and *past part.* **bid**) (often foll. by *for*, *against*) **a** (esp. at an auction) offer (a certain price) (*did not bid for the vase*; *bid against the dealer*; *bid £20*). **b** offer to do work etc. for a stated price. **2** *tr. archaic* or *literary* **a** command; order (*bid the soldiers shoot*). **b** invite (*bade her start*). **3** *tr. archaic* or *literary* **a** utter (greeting or farewell) to (*I bade him welcome*). **b** proclaim (defiance etc.). **4** (*past* and *past part.* **bid**) *Cards* **a** *intr.* state before play how many tricks one intends to make. **b** *tr.* state (one's intended number of tricks). ● *n.* **1 a** (esp. at an auction) an offer (of a price) (*a bid of £5*). **b** an offer (to do work, supply goods, etc.) at a stated price; a tender. **2** *Cards* a statement of the number of tricks a player proposes to make. **3** *colloq.* an attempt; an effort (*a bid for power*). □ **bid fair to** seem likely to. **make a bid for** try to gain (*made a bid for freedom*). □□ **bidder** *n.* [OE *biddan* ask f. Gmc, & OE *bēodan* offer, command]

■ *v.* **1** (*tr.*) offer, make an offer of, tender, proffer, put up, put forward; (*bid for*) make an offer for, tender for. **2 a** command *or* order *or* direct *or* tell *or* enjoin to. **b** invite *or* summon *or* ask *or* request *or* entreat *or* beg to. ● *n.* **1** offer, tender, *literary* proffer. **3** see ATTEMPT *n.* □ **bid fair to** see LIKELY *adj.* 2.

biddable /bíddəb'l/ *adj.* **1** obedient. **2** *Cards* (of a hand or suit) suitable for being bid. □□ **biddability** /-bílliti/ *n.*

■ **1** see TRACTABLE 1.

bidden *archaic past part.* of BID.

bidding /bídding/ *n.* **1** the offers at an auction. **2** *Cards* the act of making a bid or bids. **3** a command, request, or invitation. □ **bidding-prayer** one inviting the congregation to join in.

■ **3** invitation, summons, call, *colloq.* invite; command, order, dictate, direction, instruction, demand, requisition, *archaic* hest, *formal* pleasure, *literary* behest; request, entreaty, solicitation, plea, petition, supplication, appeal, obsecration.

biddy /bíddi/ *n.* (*pl.* **-ies**) *sl. derog.* a woman (esp. *old biddy*). [pet-form of the name *Bridget*]

bide /bīd/ *v.intr. archaic* or *dial.* remain; stay. □ **bide one's time** await one's best opportunity. [OE *bīdan* f. Gmc]

■ see STAY[1] *v.* 1. □ **bide one's time** see WAIT *v.* 1a.

bidet /béeday/ *n.* a low oval basin used esp. for washing the genital area. [F, = pony]

Biedermeier /béedərmīər/ *attrib.adj.* **1** (of styles, furnishings, etc.) characteristic of the period 1815–48 in Germany. **2** *derog.* conventional; bourgeois. [*Biedermaier* a fictitious German poet (1854)]

biennial /bīénniəl/ *adj.* & *n.* ● *adj.* **1** lasting two years. **2** recurring every two years (cf. BIANNUAL). ● *n.* **1** *Bot.* a plant that takes two years to grow from seed to fruition and die (cf. ANNUAL, PERENNIAL). **2** an event celebrated or taking place every two years. □□ **biennially** *adv.* [L *biennis* (as BI-, *annus* year)]

biennium /bīénniəm/ *n.* (*pl.* **bienniums** or **biennia** /-niə/) a period of two years. [L (as BIENNIAL)]

bier /beer/ *n.* a movable frame on which a coffin or a corpse is placed, or taken to a grave. [OE *bēr* f. Gmc]

biff /bif/ *n.* & *v. sl.* ● *n.* a sharp blow. ● *v.tr.* strike (a person). [imit.]

■ *n.* see PUNCH[1] *n.* 1. ● *v.* see PUNCH[1] *v.* 1.

biffin /bíffin/ *n. Brit.* a deep-red cooking-apple. [= *beefing* f. BEEF + -ING[1], with ref. to the colour]

bifid /bī́fid/ *adj.* divided by a deep cleft into two parts. [L *bifidus* (as BI-, *fidus* f. stem of *findere* cleave)]

bifocal /bīfṓk'l/ *adj.* & *n.* ● *adj.* having two focuses, esp. of a lens with a part for distant vision and a part for near vision. ● *n.* (in *pl.*) bifocal spectacles.

■ *n.* (*bifocals*) see GLASS *n.* 3a.

bifurcate /bī́fərkayt/ *v.* & *adj.* ● *v.tr.* & *intr.* divide into two branches; fork. ● *adj.* forked; branched. [med.L *bifurcare* f. L *bifurcus* two-forked (as BI-, *furca* fork)]

■ *v.* see BRANCH *v.* 2.

bifurcation /bī́fərkáysh'n/ *n.* **1 a** a division into two branches. **b** either or both of such branches. **2** the point of such a division.

big /big/ *adj.* & *adv.* ● *adj.* (**bigger**, **biggest**) **1 a** of considerable size, amount, intensity, etc. (*a big mistake*; *a big helping*). **b** of a large or the largest size (*big toe*; *big drum*). **c** (of a letter) capital, upper-case. **2 a** important; significant; outstanding (*the big race*; *my big chance*). **b** *colloq.* (of a person) famous, important, esp. in a named field. **3 a** grown up (*a big boy now*). **b** elder (*big sister*). **4** *colloq.* **a** boastful (*big words*). **b** often *iron.* generous (*big of him*). **c** ambitious (*big ideas*). **5** (usu. foll. by *with*) advanced in pregnancy; fecund (*big with child*; *big with consequences*). ● *adv. colloq.* in a big manner, esp.: **1** effectively (*went over big*). **2** boastfully (*talk big*). **3** ambitiously (*think big*). □ **Big Apple** *US sl.* New York City. **big band** a large jazz or pop orchestra. **big bang** *Stock Exch.* (in the UK) the introduction in 1986 of important changes in the regulations and procedures for trading, esp. the widening of membership, the relaxation of rules for brokers, and the introduction of computerized communications. **big bang theory** the theory that the universe began with the explosion of dense matter. **Big Ben** the great clock tower of the Houses of Parliament and its bell. **Big Board** *US colloq.* the New York Stock Exchange. **Big Brother** an all-powerful supposedly benevolent dictator (as in Orwell's *1984*). **big bud** a plant disease caused by the gall-mite. **big bug** *sl.* = BIGWIG. **big business** large-scale financial dealings, esp. when sinister or exploitative. **Big Chief** (or **Daddy**) *sl.* = BIGWIG. **big deal!** *sl. iron.* I am not impressed. **big dipper 1** a fairground switchback. **2** *US* = *the Great Bear* (see BEAR[2]). **big end** (in a motor vehicle) the end of the connecting-rod that encircles the crankpin. **big game** large animals hunted for sport. **big gun** *sl.* = BIGWIG. **big-head** *colloq.* a conceited person. **big-headed** *colloq.* conceited. **big-headedness** *colloq.* conceitedness. **big-hearted** generous. **big house 1** the principal house in a village etc. **2** *sl.* a prison. **big idea** often *iron.* the important intention or scheme. **big money** large amounts; high profit; high pay. **big mouth** *colloq.* loquacity; talkativeness. **big-mouth** *colloq.* a boastful or talkative person; a gossip-monger. **big name** a famous person. **big noise** (or **pot** or **shot**) *colloq.* = BIGWIG. **big smoke** *Brit. sl.* **1** London. **2** any large town. **big stick** a display of force. **Big Three** (or **Four** etc.) the predominant few. **the big time** *sl.* success in a profession, esp. show business. **big-timer** *sl.* a person who achieves success. **big top** the main tent in a circus. **big tree** *US* a giant evergreen conifer, *Sequoiadendron giganteum*, usu. with a trunk of large girth. **big wheel 1** a Ferris wheel. **2** *US sl.* = BIGWIG. **come** (or **go**) **over big** make a great effect. **in a big way 1** on a large scale. **2** *colloq.* with great enthusiasm, display, etc. **talk big** boast. **think big** be ambitious. **too big for one's boots** (or **breeches**) *sl.* conceited. □□ **biggish** *adj.* **bigness** *n.* [ME: orig. unkn.]

■ *adj.* **1 a** large, great, grand, huge, enormous, immense, gigantic, giant, monstrous, tremendous, colossal, gargantuan, elephantine, mammoth, king-size, hefty, *colloq.* jumbo, hulking, *Brit. colloq.* socking *or* whacking great, *sl.* humongous, *Brit. sl.* ginormous. **c** capital, large, upper case, majuscule. **2** important, significant, outstanding, weighty, consequential, major, momentous, critical, *disp.* vital, *colloq. disp.* crucial; prominent, leading, foremost, noted, noteworthy, notable, renowned, well-known, illustrious, distinguished, esteemed, mighty, powerful, popular, famous, successful. **3 a** grown, mature, grown-up. **b** elder, older. **4 b** generous, magnanimous, charitable, unselfish, good, high-minded. **c** ambitious, grandiose, showy, overambitious, inflated, overblown, puffed up, exaggerated; above one's station. ● *adv.* **1** successfully, well, effectively, outstandingly, like a charm *or* dream, perfectly, wonderfully, like clockwork, without a hitch, *Brit. colloq.* like a bomb. **2** pompously, boastfully, conceitedly, arrogantly, pretentiously. **3** ambitiously, determinedly, enterprisingly, enthusiastically. □ **big deal** *colloq.* so what?, so?, I couldn't (*US* could) care less. **big-headed** see CONCEITED. **big-headedness** see VANITY 1. **big-hearted** see GENEROUS 1. **big house 2** see PRISON *n.* 1. **the big time** success, good fortune, the jackpot, the top. **big-timer** see SOMEBODY *n.* **in a big way 1** on a large *or* grand scale. **2** extravagantly, showily, ostentatiously, grandly, pretentiously, lavishly, unstintingly; wholeheartedly, enthusiastically, zealously, energetically; to the fullest extent, to the utmost. **talk big** see BOAST *v.* 1. **too big for one's boots** see CONCEITED.

bigamy /bíggəmi/ *n.* (*pl.* **-ies**) the crime of marrying when one is lawfully married to another person. □□ **bigamist** *n.* **bigamous** *adj.* [ME f. OF *bigamie* f. *bigame* bigamous f. LL *bigamus* (as BI-, Gk *gamos* marriage)]

bighorn /bíg-horn/ *n.* an American sheep, *Ovis canadensis*, esp. native to the Rocky Mountains.

bight /bīt/ *n.* **1** a curve or recess in a coastline, river, etc. **2** a loop of rope. [OE *byht*, MLG *bucht* f. Gmc: see BOW[2]]
■ **1** see GULF *n.* 1.

bigot /bíggət/ *n.* an obstinate and intolerant believer in a religion, political theory, etc. □□ **bigotry** *n.* [16th c. f. F: orig. unkn.]
■ dogmatist, partisan, sectionalist, intransigent, *S.Afr. verkrampte.* □□ **bigotry** prejudice, intolerance, narrow-mindedness, partiality, partisanship, dogmatism; discrimination.

bigoted /bíggətid/ *adj.* unreasonably prejudiced and intolerant.
■ intolerant, narrow-minded, uncompromising, inflexible, rigid, set, dogmatic, opinionated; prejudiced, biased, jaundiced, one-sided, partial, *S.Afr. verkrampte*; distorted, warped, twisted.

bigwig /bígwig/ *n. colloq.* an important person.
■ kingpin, king, queen, nabob, chief, VIP, *Austral.* joss, *colloq.* boss, big shot, big noise, *Brit. colloq.* brass hat, *esp. US colloq.* hotshot, *sl.* big bug, (big) cheese, big gun, Big Chief *or* Daddy, *Brit. sl.* nob, *US sl.* big wheel, honcho.

bijou /beézhōō/ *n.* & *adj.* ● *n.* (*pl.* ***bijoux*** *pronunc.* same) a jewel; a trinket. ● *attrib.adj.* (**bijou**) small and elegant. [F]
■ *n.* see JEWEL *n.* 1a.

bijouterie /beezhōōtəri/ *n.* jewellery; trinkets. [F (as BIJOU, -ERY)]
■ see JEWELLERY.

bike /bīk/ *n.* & *v.* ● *n.* **1** *colloq.* a bicycle or motor cycle. **2** *Austral. sl.* a promiscuous woman (*the town bike*). ● *v.intr.* ride a bicycle or motor cycle. [abbr.]
■ *n.* **1** see CYCLE *n.* 4. **2** see TART[2] *n.*

biker /bīkər/ *n.* a cyclist, esp. a motor cyclist.

bikie /bīki/ *n. Austral. colloq.* a member of a gang of motor cyclists.

bikini /bikéeni/ *n.* a two-piece swimsuit for women. □ **bikini briefs** women's scanty briefs. [*Bikini*, an atoll in the Marshall Islands in the Pacific where an atomic bomb was exploded in 1946, from the supposed 'explosive' effect]

bikkie var. of BICKIE.

bilabial /bīláybiəl/ *adj. Phonet.* (of a sound etc.) made with closed or nearly closed lips.

bilateral /bīláttərəl/ *adj.* **1** of, on, or with two sides. **2** affecting or between two parties, countries, etc. (*bilateral negotiations*). □ **bilateral symmetry** symmetry about a plane. □□ **bilaterally** *adv.*

bilberry /bílbəri/ *n.* (*pl.* **-ies**) **1** a hardy dwarf shrub, *Vaccinium myrtillus*, of N. Europe, growing on heaths and mountains, and having red drooping flowers and dark-blue berries. **2** the small blue edible berry of this species. **3** any of various shrubs of the genus *Vaccinium* having dark-blue berries. [orig. uncert.: cf. Da. *böllebær*]

bilbo /bílbō/ *n.* (*pl.* **-os** or **-oes**) *hist.* a sword noted for the temper and elasticity of its blade. [*Bilboa* = Bilbao in Spain]

bilboes /bílbōz/ *n.pl. hist.* an iron bar with sliding shackles for a prisoner's ankles. [16th c.: orig. unkn.]
■ see SHACKLE 2.

Bildungsroman /bíldōōngzrōmaan/ *n.* a novel dealing with one person's early life and development. [G]

bile /bīl/ *n.* **1** a bitter greenish-brown alkaline fluid which aids digestion and is secreted by the liver and stored in the gall-bladder. **2** bad temper; peevish anger. □ **bile-duct** the duct which conveys bile from the liver and the gall-bladder to the duodenum. [F f. L *bilis*]
■ **2** see GALL[1] 2, 3.

bilge /bilj/ *n.* & *v.* ● *n.* **1 a** the almost flat part of a ship's bottom, inside or out. **b** (in full **bilge-water**) filthy water that collects inside the bilge. **2** *sl.* nonsense; rot (*don't talk bilge*). ● *v.* **1** *tr.* stave in the bilge of (a ship). **2** *intr.* spring a leak in the bilge. **3** *intr.* swell out; bulge. □ **bilge-keel** a plate or timber fastened under the bilge to prevent rolling. [prob. var. of BULGE]
■ *n.* **1 b** see MUCK *n.* 1, 2. **2** see NONSENSE.

bilharzia /bilhaártsiə/ *n.* **1** a tropical flatworm of the genus *Schistosoma* (formerly *Bilharzia*) which is parasitic in blood vessels in the human pelvic region. Also called SCHISTOSOME. **2** the chronic tropical disease produced by its presence. Also called BILHARZIASIS, SCHISTOSOMIASIS. [mod.L f. T. *Bilharz*, Ger. physician d. 1862]

bilharziasis /bílhaartsīəsiss/ *n.* the disease of bilharzia. Also called SCHISTOSOMIASIS.

biliary /bílliəri/ *adj.* of the bile. [F *biliaire*: see BILE, -ARY[2]]

bilingual /bīlínggwəl/ *adj.* & *n.* ● *adj.* **1** able to speak two languages, esp. fluently. **2** spoken or written in two languages. ● *n.* a bilingual person. □□ **bilingualism** *n.* [L *bilinguis* (as BI-, *lingua* tongue)]

bilious /bílyəss/ *adj.* **1** affected by a disorder of the bile. **2** bad-tempered. □□ **biliously** *adv.* **biliousness** *n.* [L *biliosus* f. *bilis* bile]
■ **2** ill-tempered, bad-tempered, ill-natured, ill-humoured, peevish, irritable, crotchety, splenetic, testy, cross, petulant, irascible, tetchy, crabbed, crabby, choleric, angry, *esp. US* cranky, *literary* wrathful.

bilirubin /bíllirōōbin/ *n.* the orange-yellow pigment occurring in bile. [G f. L *bilis* BILE + *ruber* red]

bilk /bilk/ *v.tr. sl.* **1** cheat. **2** give the slip to. **3** avoid paying (a creditor or debt). □□ **bilker** *n.* [orig. uncert., perh. = BAULK: earliest use (17th c.) in cribbage, = spoil one's opponent's score]
■ **1** see CHEAT *v.* 1a.

bill[1] /bil/ *n.* & *v.* ● *n.* **1 a** a printed or written statement of charges for goods supplied or services rendered. **b** the amount owed (*ran up a bill of £300*). **2** a draft of a proposed law. **3 a** a poster; a placard. **b** = HANDBILL. **4 a** a printed list, esp. a theatre programme. **b** the entertainment itself (*top of the bill*). **5** *US* a banknote (*ten dollar bill*). ● *v.tr.* **1** put in the programme; announce. **2** (foll. by *as*) advertise. **3** send a note of charges to (*billed him for the books*). □ **bill of exchange** *Econ.* a written order to pay a sum of money on a given date to the drawer or to a named payee. **bill of fare 1** a menu. **2** a programme (for a theatrical event). **bill of health 1** *Naut.* a certificate regarding infectious disease on a ship or in a port at the time of sailing. **2** (**clean bill of health**) **a** such a certificate stating that there is no disease. **b** a declaration that a person or thing examined has been found to be free of illness or in good condition. **bill of indictment** *hist.* or *US* a written accusation as presented to a grand jury. **bill of lading** *Naut.* **1** a shipmaster's detailed list of the ship's cargo. **2** *US* = WAYBILL. **Bill of**

Rights 1 *Law* the English constitutional settlement of 1689. **2** *Law* (in the US) the constitutional amendments of 1791. **3** a statement of the rights of a class of people. **bill of sale** *Econ.* a certificate of transfer of personal property, esp. as a security against debt. □□ **billable** *adj.* [ME f. AF *bille*, AL *billa*, prob. alt. of med.L *bulla* seal, sealed documents, BULL[2]]

■ *n.* **1** statement, invoice, account, tally, reckoning, tabulation, *US* (restaurant) check, *US colloq.* tab. **3 a** see POSTER 1. **b** handbill, *US* flyer, dodger. **4 a** playbill, programme, bill of fare. **5** note, banknote; (*bills*) paper money, *esp. US colloq.* folding money, *sl.* green, *Brit. sl.* wad, *US sl.* kale. ● *v.* **1, 2** see ANNOUNCE 1, PROMOTE 3. **3** invoice, charge, debit. □ **bill of fare 1** menu; wine list. **2** see BILL[1] *n.* 4 above.

bill[2] /bil/ *n.* & *v.* ● *n.* **1** the beak of a bird, esp. when it is slender, flattened, or weak, or belongs to a web-footed bird or a bird of the pigeon family. **2** the muzzle of a platypus. **3** a narrow promontory. **4** the point of an anchor-fluke. ● *v.intr.* (of doves etc.) stroke a bill with a bill. □ **bill and coo** exchange caresses. □□ **billed** *adj.* (usu. in *comb.*). [OE *bile*, of unkn. orig.]

■ **1, 2** beak, *Sc.* & *N.Engl.* neb; jaws. **3** promontory, headland, bluff, cape, foreland, head, ness, point, tongue, *Sc.* mull. □ **bill and coo** see CUDDLE *v.* 2.

bill[3] /bil/ *n.* **1** *hist.* a weapon like a halberd with a hook instead of a blade. **2** = BILLHOOK. [OE *bil*, ult. f. Gmc]

billabong /bílləbong/ *n. Austral.* a branch of a river forming a backwater or a stagnant pool. [Aboriginal *Billibang* Bell River f. *billa* water]

billboard /bílbord/ *n.* esp. *US* a large outdoor board for advertisements etc.

billet[1] /bíllit/ *n.* & *v.* ● *n.* **1 a** a place where troops etc. are lodged, usu. with civilians. **b** a written order requiring a householder to lodge the bearer, usu. a soldier. **2** *colloq.* a situation; a job. ● *v.tr.* (**billeted, billeting**) **1** (usu. foll. by *on, in, at*) quarter (soldiers etc.). **2** (of a householder) provide (a soldier etc.) with board and lodging. □□ **billetee** /-teé/ *n.* **billeter** *n.* [ME f. AF *billette*, AL *billetta*, dimin. of *billa* BILL[1]]

■ *n.* **1 a** see QUARTER *n.* 9b. **2** see POSITION *n.* 8. ● *v.* **1** see QUARTER *v.* **2** see ACCOMMODATE 1.

billet[2] /bíllit/ *n.* **1** a thick piece of firewood. **2** a small metal bar. **3** *Archit.* each of a series of short rolls inserted at intervals in Norman decorative mouldings. [ME f. F *billette* small log, ult. prob. of Celtic orig.]

billet-doux /billidoó/ *n.* (*pl.* **billets-doux** /-doóz/) often *joc.* a love-letter. [F, = sweet note]

■ see NOTE *n.* 3.

billfold /bílfōld/ *n. US* a wallet for keeping banknotes.

■ see WALLET.

billhead /bílhed/ *n.* a printed account form.

billhook /bílhook/ *n.* a sickle-shaped tool with a sharp inner edge, used for pruning, lopping, etc.

billiards /bílyərdz/ *n.* **1** a game played on an oblong cloth-covered table, with three balls struck with cues into pockets round the edge of the table. **2** (**billiard**) (in *comb.*) used in billiards (*billiard-ball*; *billiard-table*). [orig. pl., f. F *billard* billiards, cue, dimin. of *bille* log: see BILLET[2]]

billion /bílyən/ *n.* & *adj.* ● *n.* (*pl.* same or (in sense 3) **billions**) (in *sing.* prec. by *a* or *one*) **1** a thousand million (1,000,000,000 or 10^9). **2** (now less often, esp. *Brit.*) a million million (1,000,000,000,000 or 10^{12}). **3** (in *pl.*) *colloq.* a very large number (*billions of years*). ● *adj.* that amount to a billion. □□ **billionth** *adj.* & *n.* [F (as BI-, MILLION)]

■ *n.* **3** (*billions*) see LOT *n.* 1.

billionaire /bílyənáir/ *n.* a person possessing over a billion pounds, dollars, etc. [after MILLIONAIRE]

■ see TYCOON.

billon /bíllən/ *n.* an alloy of gold or silver with a predominating admixture of a base metal. [F f. *bille* BILLET[2]]

billow /bíllō/ *n.* & *v.* ● *n.* **1** a wave. **2** a soft upward-curving flow. **3** any large soft mass. ● *v.intr.* move or build up in billows. □□ **billowy** *adj.* [ON *bylgja* f. Gmc]

■ *n.* **1** see WAVE *n.* 1, 2. ● *v.* see WAVE *v.* 2.

billposter /bílpōstər/ *n.* (also **billsticker** /-stikkər/) a person who pastes up advertisements on hoardings. □□ **billposting** *n.*

billy[1] /bílli/ *n.* (*pl.* **-ies**) (in full **billycan**) orig. *Austral.* a tin or enamel cooking-pot with a lid and wire handle, for use out of doors. [perh. f. Aboriginal *billa* water]

billy[2] /bílli/ *n.* (*pl.* **-ies**) **1** = BILLY-GOAT. **2** a bludgeon.

billycan /bíllikan/ *n.* = BILLY[1].

billycart /bíllikaart/ *n. Austral.* **1** a small handcart. **2** a go-kart.

■ **1** see CART *n.* 1.

billy-goat /bílligōt/ *n.* a male goat. [*Billy*, pet-form of the name *William*]

billy-oh /bílliō/ *n.* □ **like billy-oh** *sl.* very much, hard, strongly, etc. (*raining like billy-oh*). [19th c.: orig. unkn.]

bilobate /bīlṓbət/ *adj.* (also **bilobed** /-lōbd/) having or consisting of two lobes.

biltong /bíltong/ *n. S.Afr.* boneless meat salted and dried in strips. [Afrik., of uncert. orig.]

BIM *abbr.* British Institute of Management.

bimanal /bímmən'l/ *adj.* (also **bimanous** /-nəss/) having two hands. [BI- + L *manus* hand]

bimbo /bímbō/ *n.* (*pl.* **-os** or **-oes**) *sl.* usu. *derog.* **1** a person. **2** a woman, esp. a young empty-headed one. [It., = little child]

■ **2** see MISS[2].

bimetallic /bīmitállik/ *adj.* **1** made of two metals. **2** of or relating to bimetallism. □ **bimetallic strip** a sensitive element in some thermostats made of two bands of different metals that expand at different rates when heated, causing the strip to bend. [F *bimétallique* (as BI-, METALLIC)]

bimetallism /bīméttəliz'm/ *n.* a system of allowing the unrestricted currency of two metals (e.g. gold and silver) at a fixed ratio to each other, as coined money. □□ **bimetallist** *n.*

bimillenary /bīmilénnəri/ *adj.* & *n.* ● *adj.* of or relating to a two-thousandth anniversary. ● *n.* (*pl.* **-ies**) a bimillenary year or festival.

bimonthly /bīmúnthli/ *adj.*, *adv.*, & *n.* ● *adj.* occurring twice a month or every two months. ● *adv.* twice a month or every two months. ● *n.* (*pl.* **-ies**) a periodical produced bimonthly. ¶ Often avoided, because of the ambiguity of meaning, in favour of *two-monthly* and *twice-monthly*.

bin /bin/ *n.* & *v.* ● *n.* a large receptacle for storage or for depositing rubbish. ● *v.tr. colloq.* (**binned, binning**) store or put in a bin. □ **bin end** one of the last bottles from a bin of wine, usu. sold at a reduced price. **bin-liner** a bag (usu. of plastic) for lining a rubbish bin. [OE *bin(n)*, *binne*]

bin- /bin, bīn/ *prefix* var. of BI- before a vowel.

binary /bīnəri/ *adj.* & *n.* ● *adj.* **1 a** dual. **b** of or involving pairs. **2** of the arithmetical system using 2 as a base. ● *n.* (*pl.* **-ies**) **1** something having two parts. **2** a binary number. **3** a binary star. □ **binary code** *Computing* a coding system using the binary digits 0 and 1 to represent a letter, digit, or other character in a computer (see BCD). **binary compound** *Chem.* a compound having two elements or radicals. **binary fission** the division of a cell or organism into two parts. **binary number** (or **digit**) one of two digits (usu. 0 or 1) in a binary system of notation. **binary star** a system of two stars orbiting each other. **binary system** a system in which information can be expressed by combinations of the digits 0 and 1 (corresponding to 'off' and 'on' in computing). **binary tree** a data structure in which a record is branched to the left when greater and to the right when less than the previous record. [LL *binarius* f. *bini* two together]

binate /bīnayt/ *adj. Bot.* **1** growing in pairs. **2** composed of two equal parts. [mod.L *binatus* f. L *bini* two together]

binaural /bīnáwrəl/ *adj.* **1** of or used with both ears. **2** (of sound) recorded using two microphones and usu. transmitted separately to the two ears.

bind /bīnd/ *v.* & *n.* ● *v.* (*past* and *past part.* **bound** /bownd/) (see also BOUNDEN). **1** *tr.* (often foll. by *to, on, together*) tie or fasten tightly. **2** *tr.* **a** restrain; put in bonds. **b** (as **-bound** *adj.*) constricted, obstructed (*snowbound*). **3** *tr.* esp. *Cookery* cause (ingredients) to cohere using another ingredient. **4** *tr.* fasten or hold together as a single mass. **5** *tr.* compel; impose an obligation or duty on. **6** *tr.* **a** edge (fabric etc.) with braid etc. **b** fix together and fasten (the pages of a book) in a cover. **7** *tr.* constipate. **8** *tr.* ratify (a bargain, agreement, etc.). **9** *tr.* (in *passive*) be required by an obligation or duty (*am bound to answer*). **10** *tr.* (often foll. by *up*) **a** put a bandage or other covering round. **b** fix together with something put round (*bound her hair*). **11** *tr.* indenture as an apprentice. **12** *intr.* (of snow etc.) cohere, stick. **13** *intr.* be prevented from moving freely. **14** *intr. sl.* complain. ● *n.* **1** *colloq.* **a** a nuisance; a restriction. **b** esp. *US* a tight or difficult situation. **2** = BINE. □ **be bound up with** be closely associated with. **bind over** *Law* order (a person) to do something, esp. keep the peace. **bind up** bandage. **I'll be bound** a statement of assurance, or guaranteeing the truth of something. [OE *bindan*]
■ *v.* **1** tie (up), fasten, make fast, secure, attach, join; cement, stick, fuse. **2 a** see TIE *v.* 1a, 3. **3** mix, blend, combine. **5** constrain, restrain, confine, restrict; commit, hold, oblige, obligate, pledge; compel, force, require, impel, drive; burden. **6 a** edge, border, band, frame, fringe. **9** see sense 5 above. **10 a** bind up, swathe, bandage, swaddle, wrap, cover. **b** see TIE *v.* 1a; encircle, wreathe, surround, encompass, ring, circle, hem in, enclose, *literary* gird. **11** apprentice, indenture, *archaic* prentice. **14** see COMPLAIN 1. ● *n.* **1 a** nuisance, annoyance, irritant, bother, bore, pest, trial, irritation, vexation, *colloq.* pain (in the neck), *joc.* menace, *US sl.* bummer, *esp. US sl.* pain in the butt; restriction, restraint, difficulty, problem, snag, hindrance, obstacle. **b** predicament, tight corner *or* place *or* spot, (difficult) situation, *colloq.* pickle, fix, jam, *disp.* dilemma; (*in a bind*) in a cleft stick.

binder /bīndər/ *n.* **1** a cover for sheets of paper, for a book, etc. **2** a substance that acts cohesively. **3** a reaping-machine that binds grain into sheaves. **4** a bookbinder.

bindery /bīndəri/ *n.* (*pl.* **-ies**) a workshop or factory for binding books.

bindi-eye /bíndi-ī/ *n. Austral.* a small perennial Australian herb, *Calotis cuneifolia*, which has a burlike fruit. [20th c.: orig. unkn.]

binding /bīnding/ *n.* & *adj.* ● *n.* something that binds, esp. the covers, glue, etc., of a book. ● *adj.* (often foll. by *on*) obligatory.
■ *n.* see COVER *n.* 1b. ● *adj.* see INCUMBENT *adj.* 1.

bindweed /bīndweed/ *n.* **1** convolvulus. **2** any of various species of climbing plants such as honeysuckle.

bine /bīn/ *n.* **1** the twisting stem of a climbing plant, esp. the hop. **2** a flexible shoot. [orig. a dial. form of BIND]

Binet-Simon test /beénaysémon/ *adj.* (also **Binet test**) *Psychol.* a test used to measure intelligence, esp. of children. [A. *Binet* d. 1911 and T. *Simon* d. 1961, Fr. psychologists]

binge /binj/ *n.* & *v. sl.* ● *n.* a spree; a period of uncontrolled eating, drinking, etc. ● *v.intr.* go on a spree; indulge in uncontrolled eating, drinking, etc. [prob. orig. dial., = soak]
■ *n.* see SPREE *n.* 2. ● *v.* see DRINK *v.* 2.

bingle /bingg'l/ *n. Austral. colloq.* a collision. [Brit. dial. *bing* thump, blow]
■ see COLLISION 1.

bingo /binggō/ *n.* & *int.* ● *n.* a game for any number of players, each having a card of squares with numbers, which are marked off as numbers are randomly drawn by a caller. ● *int.* expressing sudden surprise, satisfaction, etc., as in winning at bingo. [prob. imit.: cf. dial. *bing* 'with a bang']

bingy /binji/ *n.* (also **bingie**) *Austral. colloq.* the stomach, the belly. [Dharuk *bindhi* belly]
■ see STOMACH *n.* 2.

binman /binman/ *n.* (*pl.* **-men**) *colloq.* a dustman.

binnacle /binnək'l/ *n.* a built-in housing for a ship's compass. [earlier *bittacle*, ult. f. L *habitaculum* habitation f. *habitare* inhabit]

binocular /bīnókyoolər/ *adj.* adapted for or using both eyes. [BIN- + L *oculus* eye]

binoculars /binókyoolərz/ *n.pl.* an optical instrument with a lens for each eye, for viewing distant objects.

binomial /bīnṓmiəl/ *n.* & *adj.* ● *n.* **1** an algebraic expression of the sum or the difference of two terms. **2** a two-part name, esp. in taxonomy. ● *adj.* consisting of two terms. □ **binomial classification** a system of classification using two terms, the first one indicating the genus and the second the species. **binomial distribution** a frequency distribution of the possible number of successful outcomes in a given number of trials in each of which there is the same probability of success. **binomial theorem** a formula for finding any power of a binomial without multiplying at length. □□ **binomially** *adv.* [F *binôme* or mod.L *binomium* (as BI-, Gk *nomos* part, portion)]

binominal /bīnṓmin'l/ *adj.* = BINOMIAL. [L *binominis* (as BI-, *nomen -inis* name)]

bint /bint/ *n. sl.* usu. *offens.* a girl or woman. [Arab., = daughter, girl]

binturong /bíntyoorong/ *n.* a civet, *Arctictis binturong*, of S. Asia, with a shaggy black coat and a prehensile tail. [Malay]

bio / bīō/ *n.* & *adj.* ● *n.* **1** biology. **2** (*pl.* **bios**) biography. ● *adj.* biological. [abbr.]

bio- /bīō/ *comb. form* **1** life (*biography*). **2** biological (*biomathematics*). **3** of living beings (*biophysics*). [Gk *bios* (course of) human life]

biochemistry /bīōkémmistri/ *n.* the study of the chemical and physico-chemical processes of living organisms. □□ **biochemical** *adj.* **biochemist** *n.*

biocoenosis /bīōseenṓsiss/ *n.* (*US* **biocenosis**) (*pl.* **-noses** /-seez/) **1** an association of different organisms forming a community. **2** the relationship existing between such organisms. □□ **biocoenology** /-nólləji/ *n.* **biocoenotic** /-nóttik/ *adj.* [mod.L f. BIO- + Gk *koinōsis* sharing f. *koinos* common]

biodegradable /bīōdigráydəb'l/ *adj.* capable of being decomposed by bacteria or other living organisms. □□ **biodegradability** /-bílliti/ *n.* **biodegradation** /bīōdégrədáysh'n/ *n.*

bioengineering /bīō-énjineéring/ *n.* **1** the application of engineering techniques to biological processes. **2** the use of artificial tissues, organs, or organ components to replace damaged or absent parts of the body, e.g. artificial limbs, heart pacemakers, etc. □□ **bioengineer** *n.* & *v.*

bioethics /bīō-éthiks/ *n.pl.* (treated as *sing.*) the ethics of medical and biological research. □□ **bioethicist** *n.*

biofeedback /bīōfeédbak/ *n.* the technique of using the feedback of a normally automatic bodily response to a stimulus, in order to acquire voluntary control of that response.

bioflavonoid /bīōfláyvənoyd/ *n.* = CITRIN. [BIO- + *flavonoid* f. FLAVINE + -OID]

biogenesis /bīōjénnisiss/ *n.* **1** the synthesis of substances by living organisms. **2** the hypothesis that a living organism arises only from another similar living organism. □□ **biogenetic** /-jinéttik/ *adj.*

biogenic /bīōjénnik/ *adj.* produced by living organisms.

biogeography /bīōjiógrəfi/ *n.* the scientific study of the geographical distribution of plants and animals. □□ **biogeographical** /-jiəgráffik'l/ *adj.*

biography /bīógrəfi/ *n.* (*pl.* **-ies**) **1 a** a written account of a person's life, usu. by another. **b** such writing as a branch of literature. **2** the course of a living (usu. human) being's life. □□ **biographer** *n.* **biographic** /bīəgráffik/ *adj.* **biographical** /bīəgráffik'l/ *adj.* [F *biographie* or mod.L *biographia* f. med.Gk]

■ **1a** see LIFE 10.

biological /bīəlójik'l/ *adj.* of or relating to biology or living organisms. □ **biological clock** an innate mechanism controlling the rhythmic physiological activities of an organism. **biological control** the control of a pest by the introduction of a natural enemy. **biological warfare** warfare involving the use of toxins or micro-organisms. □□ **biologically** *adv.*

biology /bīólləji/ *n.* **1** the study of living organisms. **2** the plants and animals of a particular area. □□ **biologist** *n.* [F *biologie* f. G *Biologie* (as BIO-, -LOGY)]

bioluminescence /bīōlōōminéss'nss/ *n.* the emission of light by living organisms such as the firefly and glow-worm. □□ **bioluminescent** *adj.*

biomass /bīōmass/ *n.* the total quantity or weight of organisms in a given area or volume. [BIO- + MASS[1]]

biomathematics /bīōmáthimáttiks/ *n.* the science of the application of mathematics to biology.

biome /bīōm/ *n.* **1** a large naturally occurring community of flora and fauna adapted to the particular conditions in which they occur, e.g. tundra. **2** the geographical region containing such a community. [BIO- + -OME]

biomechanics /bīōmikánniks/ *n.* the study of the mechanical laws relating to the movement or structure of living organisms.

biometry /bīómmitri/ *n.* (also **biometrics** /bīōmétriks/) the application of statistical analysis to biological data. □□ **biometric** /bīōmétrik/ *adj.* **biometrical** /bīōmétrik'l/ *adj.* **biometrician** /bīōmitrísh'n/ *n.*

biomorph /bīōmorf/ *n.* a decorative form based on a living organism. □□ **biomorphic** /-mórfik/ *adj.* [BIO- + Gk *morphē* form]

bionic /bīónnik/ *adj.* **1** having artificial body parts or the superhuman powers resulting from these. **2** relating to bionics. □□ **bionically** *adv.* [BIO- after ELECTRONIC]

bionics /bīónniks/ *n.pl.* (treated as *sing.*) the study of mechanical systems that function like living organisms or parts of living organisms.

bionomics /bīənómmiks/ *n.pl.* (treated as *sing.*) the study of the mode of life of organisms in their natural habitat and their adaptations to their surroundings. □□ **bionomic** *adj.* [BIO- after ECONOMICS]

biophysics /bīōfizziks/ *n.pl.* (treated as *sing.*) the science of the application of the laws of physics to biological phenomena. □□ **biophysical** *adj.* **biophysicist** *n.*

biopsy /bīopsi/ *n.* (*pl.* **-ies**) the examination of tissue removed from a living body to discover the presence, cause, or extent of a disease. [F *biopsie* f. Gk *bios* life + *opsis* sight, after *necropsy*]

biorhythm /bīōrithəm/ *n.* **1** any of the recurring cycles of biological processes thought to affect a person's emotional, intellectual, and physical activity. **2** any periodic change in the behaviour or physiology of an organism. □□ **biorhythmic** /-ríthmik/ *adj.* **biorhythmically** /-ríthmikəli/ *adv.*

bioscope /bīəskōp/ *n. S.Afr. sl.* a cinema.

biosphere /bīōsfeer/ *n.* the regions of the earth's crust and atmosphere occupied by living organisms. [G *Biosphäre* (as BIO-, SPHERE)]

biosynthesis /bīōsínthisiss/ *n.* the production of organic molecules by living organisms. □□ **biosynthetic** /-théttik/ *adj.*

biota /bīōtə/ *n.* the animal and plant life of a region. [mod.L: cf. Gk *biotē* life]

biotechnology /bīōteknólləji/ *n.* the exploitation of biological processes for industrial and other purposes, esp. genetic manipulation of micro-organisms (for the production of antibiotics, hormones, etc.).

biotic /bīóttik/ *adj.* **1** relating to life or to living things. **2** of biological origin. [F *biotique* or LL *bioticus* f. Gk *biōtikos* f. *bios* life]

biotin /bīətin/ *n.* a vitamin of the B complex, found in egg yolk, liver, and yeast, and involved in the metabolism of carbohydrates, fats, and proteins. [G f. Gk *bios* life + -IN]

biotite /bīətīt/ *n. Mineral.* a black, dark brown, or green micaceous mineral occurring as a constituent of metamorphic and igneous rocks. [J. B. *Biot*, Fr. physicist d. 1862]

bipartisan /bīpaartizán, bīpaártiz'n/ *adj.* of or involving two (esp. political) parties. □□ **bipartisanship** *n.*

bipartite /bīpaártīt/ *adj.* **1** consisting of two parts. **2** shared by or involving two parties. **3** *Law* (of a contract, treaty, etc.) drawn up in two corresponding parts or between two parties. [L *bipartitus* f. *bipartire* (as BI-, *partire* PART)]

biped /bīped/ *n.* & *adj.* ● *n.* a two-footed animal. ● *adj.* two-footed. □□ **bipedal** *adj.* [L *bipes -edis* (as BI-, *pes pedis* foot)]

bipinnate /bīpínnayt/ *adj.* (of a pinnate leaf) having leaflets that are further subdivided in a pinnate arrangement.

biplane /bīplayn/ *n.* an early type of aeroplane having two sets of wings, one above the other.

bipolar /bīpōlər/ *adj.* having two poles or extremities. □□ **bipolarity** /-lárriti/ *n.*

birch /burch/ *n.* & *v.* ● *n.* **1** any tree of the genus *Betula*, having thin peeling bark, bearing catkins, and found predominantly in northern temperate regions. **2** (in full **birchwood**) the hard fine-grained pale wood of these trees. **3** *NZ* any of various similar trees. **4** (in full **birch-rod**) a bundle of birch twigs used for flogging. ● *v.tr.* beat with a birch (in sense 4). □ **birch-bark 1** the bark of *Betula papyrifera* used to make canoes. **2** *US* such a canoe. □□ **birchen** *adj.* [OE *bi(e)rce* f. Gmc]

■ *n.* **4** see ROD 3a. ● *v.* see SWITCH *v.* 6a.

bird /burd/ *n.* **1** a feathered vertebrate with a beak, two wings, and two feet, egg-laying and usu. able to fly. **2** a game-bird. **3** *Brit. sl.* a young woman. **4** *colloq.* a person (*a wily old bird*). **5** *sl.* **a** a prison. **b** *rhyming sl.* a prison sentence (short for *birdlime* = time). □ **bird-bath** a basin in a garden etc. with water for birds to bathe in. **bird-call 1** a bird's natural call. **2** an instrument imitating this. **bird cherry** a wild cherry *Prunus padus*. **bird-fancier** a person who knows about, collects, breeds, or deals in, birds. **a bird in the hand** something secured or certain. **the bird is** (or **has**) **flown** the prisoner, quarry, etc., has escaped. **bird-** (or **birds'-**) **nesting** hunting for birds' nests, usu. to get eggs. **bird of paradise** any bird of the family Paradiseidae found chiefly in New Guinea, the males having very beautiful brilliantly coloured plumage. **bird of passage 1** a migrant. **2** any transient visitor. **bird of prey** see PREY. **bird sanctuary** an area where birds are protected and encouraged to breed. **the birds and the bees** *euphem.* sexual activity and reproduction. **bird's-eye** ● *n.* **1** any of several plants having small bright round flowers, such as the germander speedwell. **2** a pattern with many small spots. ● *adj.* of or having small bright round flowers (*bird's-eye primrose*). **bird's-eye view** a general view from above. **bird's-foot** (*pl.* **bird's-foots**) any plant like the foot of a bird, esp. of the genus *Lotus*, having claw-shaped pods. **bird's nest soup** soup made (esp. in Chinese cookery) from the dried gelatinous coating of the nests of swifts and other birds. **birds of a feather** people of like character. **bird-strike** a collision between a bird and an aircraft. **bird table** a raised platform on which food for birds is placed. **bird-watcher** a person who observes birds in their natural surroundings. **bird-watching** this occupation. **for** (or **strictly for**) **the birds** *colloq.* trivial, uninteresting. **get the bird** *sl.* **1** be dismissed. **2** be hissed at or booed. **like a bird** without difficulty or hesitation. **a little bird** an unnamed informant. [OE *brid*, of unkn. orig.]

■ **3** see WOMAN 1. □ **bird of passage 1** see MIGRANT *n.*

birdbrain /búrdbrayn/ *n. colloq.* a stupid or flighty person. □□ **birdbrained** *adj.*

■ see HALFWIT. □□ **birdbrained** see FRIVOLOUS 2.

birdcage /búrdkayj/ *n.* **1** a cage for birds usu. made of wire or cane. **2** an object of a similar design.

birder /búrdər/ *n. US* a bird-watcher. ▫▫ **birding** *n.*

birdie /búrdi/ *n.* & *v.* ● *n.* **1** *colloq.* a little bird. **2** *Golf* a score of one stroke less than par at any hole. ● *v.tr.* (**birdies, birdied, birdying**) *Golf* play (a hole) in a birdie.

birdlime /búrdlīm/ *n.* sticky material painted on to twigs to trap small birds.

birdseed /búrdseed/ *n.* a blend of seed for feeding birds, esp. ones which are caged.

birdsong /búrdsong/ *n.* the musical cry of a bird or birds.

birefringent /bīrifrínjənt/ *adj. Physics* having two different refractive indices. ▫▫ **birefringence** *n.*

bireme /bīreem/ *n. hist.* an ancient Greek warship, with two files of oarsmen on each side. [L *biremis* (as BI-, *remus* oar)]

biretta /birέttə/ *n.* a square usu. black cap with three flat projections on top, worn by (esp. Roman Catholic) clergymen. [It. *berretta* or Sp. *birreta* f. LL *birrus* cape]

biriani /birriaáni/ *n.* (also **biryani**) an orig. Indian dish made with highly seasoned rice, and meat or fish etc. [Urdu]

Biro /bīrō/ *n.* (*pl.* **-os**) *Brit. propr.* a kind of ball-point pen. [L. *Biró*, Hung. inventor d. 1985]

■ see PEN[1] *n.*

birth /burth/ *n.* & *v.* ● *n.* **1** the emergence of a (usu. fully developed) infant or other young from the body of its mother. **2** *rhet.* the beginning or coming into existence of something (*the birth of civilization*; *the birth of socialism*). **3 a** origin, descent, ancestry (*of noble birth*). **b** high or noble birth; inherited position. ● *v.tr. US colloq.* **1** to give birth to. **2** to assist (a woman) to give birth. ▫ **birth certificate** an official document identifying a person by name, place, date of birth, and parentage. **birth control** the control of the number of children one conceives, esp. by contraception. **birth pill** the contraceptive pill. **birth rate** the number of live births per thousand of population per year. **give birth** bear a child etc. **give birth to 1** produce (young) from the womb. **2** cause to begin, found. [ME f. ON *byrth* f. Gmc: see BEAR[1], -TH[2]]

■ *n.* **1** childbirth, delivery, nativity, *formal* parturition. **2** origin, creation, emergence, genesis, beginning, start, origination, dawn, dawning. **3** origin, extraction, parentage, line, lineage, ancestry, descent, family, blood. ● *v.* **1** give birth to, have, deliver, bear, bring forth *or* into the world, mother, *derog.* whelp. ▫ **birth control** family planning, contraception. **give birth to 1** see BIRTH *v.* above. **2** see FOUND[2] 1.

birthday /búrthday/ *n.* **1** the day on which a person etc. was born. **2** the anniversary of this. ▫ **birthday honours** *Brit.* titles etc. given on a sovereign's official birthday. **in one's birthday suit** *joc.* naked.

■ ▫ **in one's birthday suit** see NAKED 1.

birthmark /búrthmaark/ *n.* an unusual brown or red mark on one's body at or from birth.

birthplace /búrthplayss/ *n.* the place where a person was born.

birthright /búrthrīt/ *n.* a right of possession or privilege one has from birth, esp. as the eldest son.

■ see INHERITANCE 1.

birthstone /búrthstōn/ *n.* a gemstone popularly associated with the month of one's birth.

biryani var. of BIRIANI.

biscuit /bískit/ *n.* & *adj.* ● *n.* **1** *Brit.* a small unleavened cake, usu. flat and crisp and often sweet. **2** fired unglazed pottery. **3** a light brown colour. ● *adj.* biscuit-coloured. [ME f. OF *bescoit* etc. ult. f. L *bis* twice + *coctus* past part. of *coquere* cook]

bise /beez/ *n.* a keen dry northerly wind in Switzerland, S. France, etc. [ME f. OF]

bisect /bīsékt/ *v.tr.* divide into two (strictly, equal) parts. ▫▫ **bisection** *n.* **bisector** *n.* [BI- + L *secare sect-* cut]

■ see CLEAVE[1] 1a.

bisexual /bīséksyooəl, -sékshooəl/ *adj.* & *n.* ● *adj.* **1** sexually attracted by persons of both sexes. **2** *Biol.* having characteristics of both sexes. **3** of or concerning both sexes. ● *n.* a bisexual person. ▫▫ **bisexuality** /-séksyoo-álliti, sékshoo-álliti/ *n.*

■ *adj.* **2** hermaphrodite, hermaphroditical, hermaphroditic, androgynous, *Zool.* monoecious. ● *n.* androgyne, hermaphrodite.

bish /bish/ *n. sl.* a mistake. [20th c.: orig. uncert.]

bishop /bíshəp/ *n.* **1** a senior member of the Christian clergy usu. in charge of a diocese, and empowered to confer holy orders. **2** a chess piece with the top sometimes shaped like a mitre. **3** mulled and spiced wine. [OE *biscop*, ult. f. Gk *episkopos* overseer (as EPI-, *-skopos* -looking)]

bishopric /bíshəprik/ *n.* **1** the office of a bishop. **2** a diocese. [OE *bisceoprīce* (as BISHOP, *rīce* realm)]

bismuth /bízməth/ *n. Chem.* **1** a brittle reddish-white metallic element, occurring naturally and used in alloys. ¶ Symb.: **Bi**. **2** any compound of this element used medicinally. [mod.L *bisemutum*, Latinization of G *Wismut*, of unkn. orig.]

bison /bīs'n/ *n.* (*pl.* same) either of two wild hump-backed shaggy-haired oxen of the genus *Bison*, native to N. America (*B. bison*) or Europe (*B. bonasus*). [ME f. L f. Gmc]

bisque[1] /bisk/ *n.* a rich shellfish soup, made esp. from lobster. [F]

bisque[2] /bisk/ *n. Tennis, Croquet,* & *Golf* an advantage of scoring one free point, or taking an extra turn or stroke. [F]

bisque[3] /bisk/ *n.* = BISCUIT 2.

bistable /bīstáyb'l/ *adj.* (of an electrical circuit etc.) having two stable states.

bister var. of BISTRE.

bistort /bístort/ *n.* a herb, *Polygonum bistorta*, with a twisted root and a cylindrical spike of flesh-coloured flowers. [F *bistorte* or med.L *bistorta* f. *bis* twice + *torta* fem. past part. of *torquēre* twist]

bistoury /bístəri/ *n.* (*pl.* **-ies**) a surgical scalpel. [F *bistouri*, *bistorie*, orig. = dagger, of unkn. orig.]

bistre /bístər/ *n.* & *adj.* (*US* **bister**) ● *n.* **1** a brownish pigment made from the soot of burnt wood. **2** the brownish colour of this. ● *adj.* of this colour. [F, of unkn. orig.]

bistro /beéstrō/ *n.* (*pl.* **-os**) a small restaurant. [F]

■ see CAFÉ 1.

bisulphate /bīsúlfayt/ *n.* (*US* **bisulfate**) *Chem.* a salt or ester of sulphuric acid.

bit[1] /bit/ *n.* **1** a small piece or quantity (*a bit of cheese*; *give me another bit*; *that bit is too small*). **2** (prec. by *a*) **a** a fair amount (*sold quite a bit*; *needed a bit of persuading*). **b** *colloq.* somewhat (*am a bit tired*). **c** (foll. by *of*) *colloq.* rather (*a bit of an idiot*). **d** (foll. by *of*) *colloq.* only a little; a mere (*a bit of a boy*). **3** a short time or distance (*wait a bit*; *move up a bit*). **4** *US sl.* a unit of 12 $^1/_2$ cents (used only in even multiples). ▫ **bit by bit** gradually. **bit of all right** *sl.* a pleasing person or thing, esp. a woman. **bit of fluff** (or **skirt** or **stuff**) see FLUFF, SKIRT, STUFF. **bit on the side** *sl.* an extramarital sexual relationship. **bit part** a minor part in a play or a film. **bits and pieces** (or **bobs**) an assortment of small items. **do one's bit** *colloq.* make a useful contribution to an effort or cause. **every bit as** see EVERY. **not a bit** (or **not a bit of it**) not at all. **to bits** into pieces. [OE *bita* f. Gmc, rel. to BITE]

■ **1** piece, segment, share, portion, part, fraction; morsel, scrap, fragment, shred, sliver, particle, grain, crumb, drop, sippet, snippet, mite, pinch, spot, *colloq.* smidgen; jot, tittle, whit, rap, iota, speck, atom, *US* & *Austral. colloq.* skerrick; touch, trifle, scintilla, trace, hint, suggestion, suspicion, *US colloq.* tad. **2 b, c** see RATHER 4. **d** slip. **3** moment, minute, second, little while, flash, two shakes (of a lamb's *or* dog's tail), *colloq.* mo, sec; (*in a bit*) very soon, very quickly, in a wink, *colloq.* before you can say knife *or* Jack Robinson, *joc.* in less than no time; little, inch. ▫ **bit by bit** see *gradually* (GRADUAL). **bit of all right** see BEAUTY 3. **bit on the side** see AFFAIR 3. **bits and pieces** odds and ends, oddments, bits. **not a bit** see *by no means* (MEANS). **to bits** see APART 2.

bit[2] *past* of BITE.

bit[3] /bit/ *n.* & *v.* ● *n.* **1** a metal mouthpiece on a bridle, used to control a horse. **2** a (usu. metal) tool or piece for boring or drilling. **3** the cutting or gripping part of a plane, pincers, etc. **4** the part of a key that engages with the lock-lever. **5** the copper head of a soldering-iron. ● *v.tr.* **1** put a bit into the mouth of (a horse). **2** restrain. □ **take the bit between one's teeth 1** take decisive personal action. **2** escape from control. [OE *bite* f. Gmc, rel. to BITE]

bit[4] /bit/ *n. Computing* a unit of information expressed as a choice between two possibilities; a 0 or 1 in binary notation. [BINARY + DIGIT]

bitch /bich/ *n.* & *v.* ● *n.* **1** a female dog or other canine animal. **2** *sl. offens.* a malicious or spiteful woman. **3** *sl.* a very unpleasant or difficult thing or situation. ● *v. colloq.* **1** *intr.* (often foll. by *about*) **a** speak scathingly. **b** complain. **2** *tr.* be spiteful or unfair to. **3** *tr.* spoil, botch. [OE *bicce*]

■ *n.* **2** shrew, hag, termagant, ogress, witch, harridan, virago, harpy, fury, *archaic* scold, beldam, *sl.* cow, (old) bag. **3** *Austral.* & *NZ* cow, *colloq.* beast, pig, swine, pain, *sl.* bastard, stinker, *US sl.* bummer. ● *v.* **1 a** (*bitch about*) criticize, censure, find fault with, malign, come down on, have a go at, lay into, carp at, *colloq.* slag (off), put down, knock, jump on, *Austral. sl.* bag, *US sl.* diss; gossip about. **b** complain, object, protest, grumble, whine, bleat, carp, *colloq.* gripe, grouse, whine, moan, *sl.* beef, bellyache, bind. **2** see ATTACK *v.* 3. **3** bungle, botch, ruin, spoil.

bitchy /bíchi/ *adj.* (**bitchier**, **bitchiest**) *sl.* spiteful; bad-tempered. □□ **bitchily** *adv.* **bitchiness** *n.*

■ see VICIOUS 1. □□ **bitchiness** see SPITE *n.* 1.

bite /bīt/ *v.* & *n.* ● *v.* (*past* **bit** /bit/; *past part.* **bitten** /bítt'n/) **1** *tr.* cut or puncture using the teeth. **2** *tr.* (foll. by *off*, *away*, etc.) detach with the teeth. **3** *tr.* (of an insect, snake, etc.) wound with a sting, fangs, etc. **4** *intr.* (of a wheel, screw, etc.) grip, penetrate. **5** *intr.* accept bait or an inducement. **6** *intr.* have a (desired) adverse effect. **7** *tr.* (in *passive*) **a** take in; swindle. **b** (foll. by *by*, *with*, etc.) be infected by (enthusiasm etc.). **8** *tr.* (as **bitten** *adj.*) cause a glowing or smarting pain to (*frostbitten*). **9** *intr.* (foll. by *at*) snap at. ● *n.* **1** an act of biting. **2** a wound or sore made by biting. **3 a** a mouthful of food. **b** a snack or light meal. **4** the taking of bait by a fish. **5** pungency (esp. of flavour). **6** incisiveness, sharpness. **7** = OCCLUSION 3. □ **bite back** restrain (one's speech etc.) by or as if by biting the lips. **bite** (or **bite on**) **the bullet** *sl.* behave bravely or stoically. **bite the dust** *sl.* **1** die. **2** fail; break down. **bite the hand that feeds one** hurt or offend a benefactor. **bite a person's head off** *colloq.* respond fiercely or angrily. **bite one's lip** see LIP. **bite off more than one can chew** take on a commitment one cannot fulfil. **once bitten twice shy** an unpleasant experience induces caution. **put the bite on** *US sl.* borrow or extort money from. **what's biting you?** *sl.* what is worrying you? □□ **biter** *n.* [OE *bītan* f. Gmc]

■ *v.* **1, 2** nip, chew, gnaw, nibble; savage. **3** sting. **7 a** see SWINDLE *v.* 1. ● *n.* **1** nibble, chew. **2** sting. **3 a** mouthful; taste; morsel, bit, piece. **b** snack, meal, lunch, *Austral.* & *NZ* crib, *Ind.* tiffin, *US sl.* nosh. **5** see SPICE *n.* 3a. **6** see EDGE *n.* 7a. □ **bite back** hold back, keep back, suppress, restrain, check, control. **bite the bullet** brave it, bear up, steel oneself, face up to it, grit one's teeth, grin and bear it, screw *or* pluck up one's courage. **bite the dust 1** see DIE[1] 1. **2** see *pack up*. **what's biting you?** what's bugging you?, what's up (with you)?, who rattled your cage?, what's eating you?

biting /bīting/ *adj.* **1** stinging; intensely cold (*a biting wind*). **2** sharp; effective (*biting wit*; *biting sarcasm*). □□ **bitingly** *adv.*

■ **1** cold, wintry, freezing, icy, raw, chilling, *colloq.* arctic, perishing, polar, *literary* chill; severe, harsh, cutting, piercing, stinging, penetrating, keen, sharp, bitter, *archaic* shrewd. **2** cutting, piercing, keen, sharp, effective, trenchant, incisive, mordant, rapier-like, penetrating, pungent; acid, acerbic, bitter, caustic, searing, astringent.

bitten *past part.* of BITE.

bitter /bíttər/ *adj.* & *n.* ● *adj.* **1** having a sharp pungent taste; not sweet. **2 a** caused by or showing mental pain or resentment (*bitter memories*; *bitter rejoinder*). **b** painful or difficult to accept (*bitter disappointment*). **3 a** harsh; virulent (*bitter animosity*). **b** piercingly cold. ● *n.* **1** *Brit.* beer strongly flavoured with hops and having a bitter taste. **2** (in *pl.*) liquor with a bitter flavour (esp. of wormwood) used as an additive in cocktails. □ **bitter-apple** = COLOCYNTH. **bitter orange** = SEVILLE ORANGE. **bitter pill** something unpleasant that has to be accepted. **bitter-sweet** *adj.* **1** sweet with a bitter after-taste. **2** arousing pleasure tinged with pain or sorrow. ● *n.* **1 a** sweetness with a bitter after-taste. **b** pleasure tinged with pain or sorrow. **2** = *woody nightshade* (see NIGHTSHADE). **to the bitter end** to the very end in spite of difficulties. □□ **bitterly** *adv.* **bitterness** *n.* [OE *biter* prob. f. Gmc: *to the bitter end* may be assoc. with a Naut. word *bitter* = 'last part of a cable': see BITTS]

■ *adj.* **1** harsh, acerbic, acrid, sharp. **2 a** disturbing, dispiriting, distressing, disquieting, upsetting, grievous, cruel, distressful, painful, agonizing, severe, harrowing, excruciating, heart-breaking, heart-rending, hurtful; aggrieved, pained, wronged, resentful, embittered, rancorous, sour. **b** painful, unwelcome, unpalatable, disagreeable, unappetizing, distasteful, unsavoury, unpleasant, hard (to swallow), hurtful. **3 a** stinging, cutting, biting, acerbic, caustic, searing, harsh, vicious, acrimonious, virulent, venomous, vindictive, malicious, spiteful, malevolent, cruel, unkind, unpleasant, nasty. **b** see BITING 1. □□ **bitterness** harshness, acerbity, spleen, gall, gall and wormwood, causticity, asperity; viciousness, virulence, venomousness, animosity, acrimony, acrimoniousness, vindictiveness, maliciousness, spitefulness, cruelty, unkindness, nastiness; hatred, resentment, hostility, antagonism, venom, rancour, hate, malice.

bitterling /bíttərling/ *n.* a small brightly coloured freshwater fish, *Rhodeus amarus*, from Central Europe. [BITTER + -LING[1]]

bittern /bíttərn/ *n.* **1** any of a group of wading birds of the heron family, esp. of the genus *Botaurus* with a distinctive booming call. **2** *Chem.* the liquid remaining after the crystallization of common salt from sea water. [ME f. OF *butor* ult. f. L *butio* bittern + *taurus* bull; *-n* perh. f. assoc. with HERON]

bitts /bits/ *n.pl. Naut.* a pair of posts on the deck of a ship, for fastening cables etc. [ME prob. f. LG: cf. LG & Du. *beting*]

bitty /bítti/ *adj.* (**bittier**, **bittiest**) made up of unrelated bits; scrappy. □□ **bittily** *adv.* **bittiness** *n.*

bitumen /bítyoomin/ *n.* **1** any of various tarlike mixtures of hydrocarbons derived from petroleum naturally or by distillation and used for road surfacing and roofing. **2** *Austral. colloq.* a tarred road. [L *bitumen -minis*]

■ **1** see PITCH[2] *n.*

bituminize /bityoōminīz/ *v.tr.* (also **-ise**) convert into, impregnate with, or cover with bitumen. □□ **bituminization** /-záysh'n/ *n.*

bituminous /bityoōminəss/ *adj.* of, relating to, or containing bitumen. □ **bituminous coal** a form of coal burning with a smoky flame.

bitzer /bítsər/ *n.* (also **bitser**) *Austral. colloq.* **1** a contraption made from previously unrelated parts. **2** a mongrel dog. [prob. abbr. of *bits and pieces*]

bivalent /bīváylənt/ *adj.* & *n.* ● *adj.* **1** *Chem.* having a valency of two. **2** *Biol.* (of homologous chromosomes) associated in pairs. ● *n. Biol.* any pair of homologous chromosomes. □□ **bivalency** *n.* [BI- + *valent-* pres. part. stem formed as VALENCE[1]]

bivalve /bīvalv/ *n.* & *adj.* ● *n.* any of a group of aquatic molluscs of the class Bivalvia, with laterally compressed bodies enclosed within two hinged shells, e.g. oysters, mussels, etc. • *adj.* **1** with a hinged double shell. **2** *Biol.* having two valves, e.g. of a pea-pod.

bivouac /bívvoo-ak/ *n.* & *v.* • *n.* a temporary open encampment without tents, esp. of soldiers. • *v.intr.* (**bivouacked, bivouacking**) camp in a bivouac, esp. overnight. [F, prob. f. Swiss G *Beiwacht* additional guard at night]
▪ *n.* see CAMP[1] *n.* 2. • *v.* see CAMP[1] *v.*

biweekly /bīwéékli/ *adv.*, *adj.*, & *n.* • *adv.* **1** every two weeks. **2** twice a week. • *adj.* produced or occurring biweekly. • *n.* (*pl.* **-ies**) a biweekly periodical. ¶ See the note at *bimonthly*.

biyearly /bīyéérli/ *adv.* & *adj.* • *adv.* **1** every two years. **2** twice a year. • *adj.* produced or occurring biyearly. ¶ See the note at *bimonthly*.

biz /biz/ *n. colloq.* business. [abbr.]

bizarre /bizaár/ *adj.* strange in appearance or effect; eccentric; grotesque. ▫▫ **bizarrely** *adv.* **bizarreness** *n.* [F, = handsome, brave, f. Sp. & Port. *bizarro* f. Basque *bizarra* beard]
▪ eccentric, unusual, strange, weird, odd, peculiar, queer, different, curious, offbeat, fantastic, unconventional, idiosyncratic, outlandish, *outré*, fantastic, incongruous, deviant, kinky, extravagant, whimsical; grotesque, freakish, irregular.

bizarrerie /bizaárəri/ *n.* a bizarre quality; bizarreness. [F]

Bk *symb. Chem.* the element berkelium.

bk. *abbr.* book.

BL *abbr.* **1** *Sc.* & *Ir.* Bachelor of Law. **2** British Library. **3** *hist.* British Leyland. **4** bill of lading.

bl. *abbr.* **1** barrel. **2** black.

blab /blab/ *v.* & *n.* • *v.* (**blabbed, blabbing**) **1** *intr.* **a** talk foolishly or indiscreetly. **b** reveal secrets. **2** *tr.* reveal (a secret etc.) by indiscreet talk. • *n.* a person who blabs. [ME prob. f. Gmc]
▪ *v.* **1** gossip, prattle, chatter, (tittle-)tattle, blather, blether; see also BABBLE *v.* 1a, b. **2** broadcast, betray, reveal, disclose, divulge, expose; see also BABBLE *v.* 2. • *n.* see BLABBER *n.*

blabber /blábbər/ *n.* & *v.* • *n.* (also **blabbermouth** /blábbərmowth/) a person who blabs. • *v.intr.* (often foll. by *on*) talk foolishly or inconsequentially, esp. at length.
▪ *n.* tell-tale, babbler, chatterer, gossip, chatterbox, gossip-monger, blatherskite, blab, *US* tattle-tale, *archaic* rattle, *colloq.* big-mouth, *esp. Austral. colloq.* mag. • *v.* see BABBLE *v.* 1a, b.

black /blak/ *adj.*, *n.*, & *v.* • *adj.* **1** very dark, having no colour from the absorption of all or nearly all incident light (like coal or soot). **2** completely dark from the absence of a source of light (*black night*). **3** (**Black**) **a** of the human group having dark-coloured skin, esp. of African or Aboriginal descent. **b** of or relating to Black people (*Black rights*). **4** (of the sky, a cloud, etc.) dusky; heavily overcast. **5** angry, threatening (*a black look*). **6** implying disgrace or condemnation (*in his black books*). **7** wicked, sinister, deadly (*black-hearted*). **8** gloomy, depressed, sullen (*a black mood*). **9** portending trouble or difficulty (*things looked black*). **10** (of hands, clothes, etc.) dirty, soiled. **11** (of humour or its representation) with sinister or macabre, as well as comic, import (*black comedy*). **12** (of tea or coffee) without milk. **13** *Brit.* **a** (of industrial labour or its products) boycotted, esp. by a trade union, in an industrial dispute. **b** (of a person) doing work or handling goods that have been boycotted. **14** dark in colour as distinguished from a lighter variety (*black bear*; *black pine*). • *n.* **1** a black colour or pigment. **2** black clothes or material (*dressed in black*). **3 a** (in a game or sport) a black piece, ball, etc. **b** the player using such pieces. **4** the credit side of an account (*in the black*). **5** (**Black**) a member of a dark-skinned race, esp. a Negro or Aboriginal. • *v.tr.* **1** make black (*blacked his face*). **2** polish with blacking. **3** *Brit.* declare (goods etc.) 'black'. ▫ **beyond the black stump** *Austral. colloq.* in the remote outback. **Black Africa** the area of Africa, generally south of the Sahara, where Blacks predominate. **black and blue** discoloured by bruises. **Black and Tans** an armed force recruited to fight Sinn Fein in Ireland in 1921, wearing a mixture of military and constabulary uniforms. **black and white 1** recorded in writing or print (*down in black and white*). **2** (of film etc.) not in colour. **3** consisting of extremes only, oversimplified (*interpreted the problem in black and white terms*). **the black art** = *black magic*. **black beetle** the common cockroach, *Blatta orientalis*. **black belt 1** a black belt worn by an expert in judo, karate, etc. **2** a person qualified to wear this. **black body** *Physics* a hypothetical perfect absorber and radiator of energy, with no reflecting power. **black box 1** a flight-recorder in an aircraft. **2** any complex piece of equipment, usu. a unit in an electronic system, with contents which are mysterious to the user. **black bread** a coarse dark-coloured type of rye bread. **black bryony** a rooted climber, *Tamus communis*, with clusters of red berries. **Black Country** (usu. prec. by *the*) a district of the Midlands with heavy industry. **black damp** = *choke-damp*. **Black Death** (usu. prec. by *the*) a widespread epidemic of bubonic plague in Europe in the 14th c. **black diamond** (in *pl.*) coal. **black disc** a long-playing gramophone record, as distinct from a compact disc. **black earth** = CHERNOZEM. **black economy** unofficial economic activity. **Black English** the form of English spoken by many Blacks, esp. as an urban dialect of the US. **black eye** bruised skin around the eye resulting from a blow. **black-eyed** (or **black-eye**) **bean** a variety of bean, *Vigna sinensis*, with seeds often dried and stored prior to eating (so called from its black hilum). **black-eyed Susan** any of several flowers, esp. of the genus *Rudbeckia*, with yellow-coloured petals and a dark centre. **black-face 1** a variety of sheep with a black face. **2** the make-up used by a non-Black performer playing a Black role. **black flag** see FLAG[1]. **black forest gateau** a chocolate sponge with layers of morello cherries or cherry jam and whipped cream and topped with chocolate icing, orig. from S. Germany. **Black Friar** a Dominican friar. **black frost** see FROST. **black game** (or **grouse**) a European grouse, *Lyrurus tetrix*. **black hole 1** a region of space possessing a strong gravitational field from which matter and radiation cannot escape: also called COLLAPSAR. **2** a place of confinement for punishment, esp. in the armed services. **black ice** thin hard transparent ice, esp. on a road surface. **black in the face** livid with strangulation, exertion, or passion. **black leopard** = PANTHER. **black letter** an old heavy style of type. **black light** *Physics* the invisible ultraviolet or infrared radiations of the electromagnetic spectrum. **black magic** magic involving supposed invocation of evil spirits. **Black Maria** *sl.* a police vehicle for transporting prisoners. **black mark** a mark of discredit. **black market** an illicit traffic in officially controlled or scarce commodities. **black marketeer** a person who engages in a black market. **Black Mass** a travesty of the Roman Catholic Mass in worship of Satan. **Black Monk** a Benedictine monk. **Black Muslim** *US* a member of an exclusively Black Islamic sect proposing a separate Black community. **Black Nationalism** advocacy of the national civil rights of US (and occas. other) Blacks. **black nightshade** see NIGHTSHADE. **black out 1 a** effect a blackout on. **b** undergo a blackout. **2** obscure windows etc. or extinguish all lights for protection esp. against an air attack. **Black Panther** *US* one of a group of extremist fighters for Blacks' rights. **black pepper** pepper made by grinding the whole dried berry, including the husk, of the pepper plant. **Black Power** a movement in support of rights and political power for Blacks. **black pudding** a black sausage containing pork, dried pig's blood, suet, etc. **Black Rod** *Brit.* the principal usher of the Lord Chamberlain's department, House of Lords, etc. **black sheep** *colloq.* an unsatisfactory member of a family, group, etc.; a scoundrel. **black spot** a place of danger or difficulty, esp. on a road (*an accident black spot*). **black stump** *Austral. colloq.* a mythical marker of distance in the outback. **black swan 1** something extremely rare. **2** an Australian swan, *Cygnus atratus*, with black plumage. **black tea** tea that is fully fermented before drying. **black tie 1** a black bow-tie worn with a dinner jacket. **2** *colloq.* formal evening dress. **black tracker** *Austral.* an Aboriginal employed to help find persons lost or hiding in the bush. **black velvet** a drink of stout and champagne. **Black Watch** (usu. prec. by *the*) the Royal Highland Regiment (so called from its dark tartan uniform). **black-water fever** a complication of malaria, in which blood cells are rapidly destroyed, resulting in dark urine. **black widow** a venomous spider, *Latrodectus mactans*, of which the female devours the male. □□ **blackish** *adj.* **blackly** *adv.* **blackness** *n.* [OE *blæc*]

■ *adj.* **1** jet, jet-black, coal-black, inky, sooty, swarthy, raven, ebony, *archaic* swart, *literary* ebon. **2** dark, pitch-black, jet-black, coal-black, *literary* Stygian; starless, moonless. **3** non-White, Coloured, dark-skinned, Negroid, *often offens.* Negro; African, African-American, Afro-American, Afro-Caribbean; Aboriginal; Melanesian. **4** dark, sombre, overcast, dusky, murky, gloomy, menacing, glowering, louring, threatening, funereal. **5** angry, furious, frowning, bad-tempered, sulky, resentful, clouded, threatening, glowering, *literary* wrathful. **7** bad, foul, iniquitous, wicked, evil, diabolical, infernal, hellish, atrocious, awful, malicious, abominable, outrageous, vicious, villainous, flagitious, vile, disgraceful, unscrupulous, unconscionable, unprincipled, blackguardly, knavish, perfidious, insidious, nefarious, dastardly, treacherous, unspeakable, disgraceful, shameful, scurvy, criminal, felonious. **8** see GLOOMY 2. **9** malignant, baleful, baneful, deadly, deathly, sinister, grim, dismal, hateful, disastrous. **10** dirty, soiled, sullied, filthy, grubby, unclean, dingy. ● *v.* **1** blacken. **2** polish. **3** boycott, embargo, blacklist, ban, interdict. □ **black and blue** bruised (all over), contused, a mass of bruises. **black and white** (*in black and white*) **1** written, printed, in writing *or* print, in written *or* printed form, typewritten, typeset, on paper. **2** in monochrome, not in colour. **3** oversimplified, simplistic. **black eye** *colloq.* shiner, *sl.* mouse. **black magic** see MAGIC *n.* 1. **black out 1b** see FAINT *v.* 1. **2** see SHADE *v.* 1–3. **black sheep** scoundrel, wastrel, slacker, good-for-nothing, ne'er-do-well; odd man out, pariah, outcast, *persona non grata*.

blackamoor /blákkəmoor, -mor/ *n. archaic* a dark-skinned person, esp. a Negro. [BLACK + MOOR[2]]

blackball /blákbawl/ *v.tr.* reject (a candidate) in a ballot (orig. by voting with a black ball).

blackberry /blákbəri/ *n.* & *v.* ● *n.* (*pl.* **-ies**) **1** a climbing thorny rosaceous shrub, *Rubus fruticosus*, bearing white or pink flowers. Also called BRAMBLE. **2** a black fleshy edible fruit of this plant. ● *v.intr.* (**-ies, -ied**) gather blackberries.

blackbird /blákburd/ *n.* **1** a common thrush, *Turdus merula*, of which the male is black with an orange beak. **2** *US* any of various birds, esp. a grackle, with black plumage. **3** *hist.* a kidnapped Negro or Polynesian on a slave-ship.

blackboard /blákbord/ *n.* a board with a smooth usu. dark surface for writing on with chalk.

blackboy /blákboy/ *n.* any tree of the genus *Xanthorrhea*, native to Australia, with a thick dark trunk and a head of grasslike leaves. Also called *grass tree*.

blackbuck /blákbuk/ *n.* a small Indian gazelle, *Antilope cervicapra*, with a black back and white underbelly. Also called SASIN.

blackcap /blák-kap/ *n.* a small warbler, *Sylvia atricapilla*, the male of which has a black-topped head.

blackcock /blák-kok/ *n.* the male of the black grouse (cf. *grey-hen*).

blackcurrant /blák-kúrrənt/ *n.* **1** a widely cultivated shrub, *Ribes nigrum*, bearing flowers in racemes. **2** the small dark edible berry of this plant.

blacken /blákkən/ *v.* **1** *tr.* & *intr.* make or become black or dark. **2** *tr.* speak evil of, defame (*blacken someone's character*).

■ **1** black, darken, smudge, begrime. **2** slander, libel, asperse, cast aspersions on, traduce, smear, sully, soil, besmirch, taint, tarnish, defame, revile, malign, vilify, discredit, denigrate, defile, drag through the mire, heap dirt on.

blackfellow /blákfellō/ *n. hist.* an Australian Aboriginal.

blackfish /blákfish/ *n.* **1** any of several species of dark-coloured fish. **2** a salmon at spawning.

blackfly /blákflī/ *n.* (*pl.* **-flies**) any of various thrips or aphids, esp. *Aphis fabae*, infesting plants.

blackguard /blággaard, -gərd/ *n.* & *v.* ● *n.* a villain; a scoundrel; an unscrupulous, unprincipled person. ● *v.tr.* abuse scurrilously. □□ **blackguardly** *adj.* [BLACK + GUARD: orig. applied collectively to menials etc.]

■ *n.* see SCOUNDREL.

blackhead /blák-hed/ *n.* a black-topped pimple on the skin.

■ see PIMPLE.

blacking /blákking/ *n.* any black paste or polish, esp. for shoes.

blackjack[1] /blákjak/ *n.* **1** the card-game pontoon. **2** *US* a flexible leaded bludgeon. [BLACK + JACK[1]]

■ **2** see CLUB *n.* 1.

blackjack[2] /blákjak/ *n.* a pirates' black flag. [BLACK + JACK[1]]

blackjack[3] /blákjak/ *n.* a tarred-leather vessel for alcoholic liquor. [BLACK + JACK[2]]

blacklead /blákled/ *n.* & *v.* ● *n.* graphite. ● *v.tr.* polish with graphite.

blackleg /blákleg/ *n.* & *v.* ● *n.* (often *attrib.*) *Brit. derog.* a person who fails or declines to take part in industrial action. ● *v.intr.* (**-legged, -legging**) act as a blackleg.

■ *n.* strikebreaker, *colloq. derog.* scab.

blacklist /bláklist/ *n.* & *v.* ● *n.* a list of persons under suspicion, in disfavour, etc. ● *v.tr.* put the name of (a person) on a blacklist.

■ *n.* see BOYCOTT *n.* ● *v.* see BOYCOTT *v.*

blackmail /blákmayl/ *n.* & *v.* ● *n.* **1 a** an extortion of payment in return for not disclosing discreditable information, a secret, etc. **b** any payment extorted in this way. **2** the use of threats or moral pressure. ● *v.tr.* **1** extort or try to extort money etc. from (a person) by blackmail. **2** threaten, coerce. □□ **blackmailer** *n.* [BLACK + obs. *mail* rent, OE *māl* f. ON *mál* agreement]

■ *n.* **1** bribe, protection money, hush money, protection, ransom, tribute. **2** extortion, bribery, exaction, milking. ● *v.* **1** see *shake down* 4. **2** threaten, force, coerce, compel, make, *colloq.* put the thumbscrews on.

blackout /blákkowt/ *n.* **1** a temporary or complete loss of vision, consciousness, or memory. **2** a loss of power, radio reception, etc. **3** a compulsory period of darkness as a precaution against air raids. **4** a temporary suppression of the release of information, esp. from police or government sources. **5** a sudden darkening of a theatre stage.

■ **1** see FAINT *n.*

blackshirt /blákshurt/ *n.* a member of a Fascist organization. [f. the colour of the It. Fascist uniform]

blacksmith /bláksmith/ *n.* a smith who works in iron.

blackthorn /blákthorn/ *n.* **1** a thorny rosaceous shrub, *Prunus spinosa*, bearing white-petalled flowers before small blue-black fruits. Also called SLOE. **2** a cudgel or walking-stick made from its wood. □ **blackthorn winter** the time when the plant flowers, usu. marked by cold NE winds.

blacktop /bláktop/ *n. US* a type of road-surfacing material.

bladder /bládər/ *n.* **1 a** any of various membranous sacs in some animals, containing urine (**urinary bladder**), bile (**gall-bladder**), or air (**swim-bladder**). **b** this or part of it or a similar object prepared for various uses. **2** an inflated pericarp or vesicle in various plants. **3** anything inflated and hollow. [OE *blǣdre* f. Gmc]

bladderwort /bládərwurt/ *n.* any insect-consuming aquatic plant of the genus *Utricularia*, with leaves having small bladders for trapping insects.

bladderwrack /bládərak/ *n.* a common brown seaweed, *Fucus vesiculosus*, with fronds containing air bladders which give buoyancy to the plant.

blade /blayd/ *n.* **1 a** the flat part of a knife, chisel, etc., that forms the cutting edge. **b** = *razor-blade*. **2** the flattened functional part of an oar, spade, propeller, bat, skate, etc. **3 a** the flat, narrow, usu. pointed leaf of grass and cereals. **b**

the whole of such plants before the ear is formed (*in the blade*). **c** *Bot.* the broad thin part of a leaf apart from the petiole. **4** (in full **blade-bone**) a flat bone, e.g. in the shoulder. **5** *Archaeol.* a long narrow flake (see FLAKE[1] 3). **6** *poet.* a sword. **7** *colloq.* (usu. *archaic*) a carefree young fellow. ▫▫ **bladed** *adj.* (also in *comb.*). [OE *blæd* f. Gmc]
■ **1 a** knife, cutting edge, cutter. **3** leaf, leaflet, frond, shoot. **6** sword, rapier, sabre, dagger, stiletto, cutlass, bayonet, knife, penknife, jackknife, *hist.* skean, *literary* poniard, *poet.* brand. **7** playboy, ladies' man, man about town, fop, dandy, beau, gallant, lady-killer, rake, *colloq.* swell.

blaeberry /bláybəri/ *n.* (*pl.* **-ies**) *Brit.* = BILBERRY. [ME f. *blae* (Sc. and N.Engl. dial. f. ME *blo* f. ON *blár* f. Gmc: see BLUE[1]) + BERRY]

blag /blag/ *n.* & *v. sl.* ● *n.* robbery, esp. with violence; theft. ● *v.tr.* & *intr.* (**blagged, blagging**) rob (esp. with violence); steal. ▫▫ **blagger** *n.* [19th c.: orig. unkn.]

blague /blaag/ *n.* humbug, claptrap. [F]

blagueur /blaagőr/ *n.* a pretentious talker. [F]

blah /blaa/ *n.* (also **blah-blah**) *colloq.* pretentious nonsense. [imit.]

blain /blayn/ *n.* an inflamed swelling or sore on the skin. [OE *blegen* f. WG]

blakey /bláyki/ *n.* (also **Blakey**) (*pl.* **-eys**) a metal cap on the heel or toe of a shoe or boot. [*Blakey*, name of the manufacturer]

blame /blaym/ *v.* & *n.* ● *v.tr.* **1** assign fault or responsibility to. **2** (foll. by *on*) assign the responsibility for (an error or wrong) to a person etc. (*blamed his death on a poor diet*). ● *n.* **1** responsibility for a bad result; culpability (*shared the blame equally*; *put the blame on the bad weather*). **2** the act of blaming or attributing responsibility; censure (*she got all the blame*). ▫ **be to blame** (often foll. by *for*) be responsible; deserve censure (*she is not to blame for the accident*). **have only oneself to blame** be solely responsible (for something one suffers). **I don't blame you** etc. I think your etc. action was justifiable. ▫▫ **blameable** *adj.* [ME f. OF *bla(s)mer* (v.), *blame* (n.) f. pop.L *blastemare* f. eccl.L *blasphemare* reproach f. Gk *blasphēmeō* blaspheme]
■ *v.* **1** find fault with, hold responsible, censure, criticize, fault; accuse, charge, indict, condemn, point (the finger) at, rebuke, reprimand, reproach, scold, reprehend, reprove, denounce, incriminate. **2** fix (the) responsibility upon *or* on, put *or* place *or* lay (the) blame on, lay at the door of. ● *n.* **1** culpability, responsibility; guilt. **2** censure, criticism, reproof, rebuke, recrimination, disapproval, disapprobation, reproach, condemnation, reprehension, *literary* objurgation, *sl.* rap.

blameful /bláymfŏŏl/ *adj.* deserving blame; guilty. ▫▫ **blamefully** *adv.*

blameless /bláymliss/ *adj.* innocent; free from blame. ▫▫ **blamelessly** *adv.* **blamelessness** *n.*
■ faultless, guiltless, innocent, irreproachable, unimpeachable, virtuous, not guilty, in the clear, spotless, unblemished, above suspicion, above reproach, *sl.* clean.

blameworthy /bláymwurthi/ *adj.* deserving blame. ▫▫ **blameworthiness** *n.*
■ see GUILTY 1, 4.

blanch /blaanch/ *v.* **1** *tr.* make white or pale by extracting colour. **2** *intr.* & *tr.* grow or make pale from shock, fear, etc. **3** *tr. Cookery* **a** peel (almonds etc.) by scalding. **b** immerse (vegetables or meat) briefly in boiling water. **4** *tr.* whiten (a plant) by depriving it of light. ▫ **blanch over** give a deceptively good impression of (a fault etc.) by misrepresentation. [ME f. OF *blanchir* f. *blanc* white, BLANK]
■ **1** see BLEACH *v.* **2** see PALE[1] *v.* 1.

blancmange /bləmónj/ *n.* a sweet opaque gelatinous dessert made with flavoured cornflour and milk. [ME f. OF *blancmanger* f. *blanc* white, BLANK + *manger* eat f. L *manducare* MANDUCATE]

blanco /blángkō/ *n.* & *v. Mil.* ● *n.* **1** a white substance for whitening belts etc. **2** a similar coloured substance. ● *v.tr.* (**-oes, -oed**) treat with blanco. [F *blanc* white, BLANK]

bland /bland/ *adj.* **1 a** mild, not irritating. **b** tasteless, unstimulating, insipid. **2** gentle in manner; suave. ▫▫ **blandly** *adv.* **blandness** *n.* [L *blandus* soft, smooth]
■ **1 a** gentle, soothing, smooth, mild. **b** insipid, boring, dull, unstimulating, uninteresting, uninspiring, uninspired, unexciting, characterless, vapid, neutral, prosaic, tasteless, flavourless, watery, flat, tame, wishy-washy. **2** gentle; suave, urbane, cool, unruffled, calm, composed, unemotional, nonchalant, insouciant.

blandish /blándish/ *v.tr.* flatter; coax, cajole. [ME f. OF *blandir* (-ISH[2]) f. L *blandiri* f. *blandus* soft, smooth]
■ see ENTICE.

blandishment /blándishmənt/ *n.* (usu. in *pl.*) flattery; cajolery.
■ see *cajolery* (CAJOLE).

blank /blangk/ *adj.*, *n.*, & *v.* ● *adj.* **1 a** (of paper) not written or printed on. **b** (of a document) with spaces left for a signature or details. **2 a** not filled; empty (*a blank space*). **b** unrelieved; plain, undecorated (*a blank wall*). **3 a** having or showing no interest or expression (*a blank face*). **b** void of incident or result. **c** puzzled, nonplussed. **d** having (temporarily) no knowledge or understanding (*my mind went blank*). **4** (with neg. import) complete, downright (*a blank refusal*; *blank despair*). **5** *euphem.* used in place of an adjective regarded as coarse or abusive. ● *n.* **1 a** a space left to be filled in a document. **b** a document having blank spaces to be filled. **2** (in full **blank cartridge**) a cartridge containing gunpowder but no bullet, used for training etc. **3** an empty space or period of time. **4 a** a coin-disc before stamping. **b** a metal or wooden block before final shaping. **5 a** a dash written instead of a word or letter, esp. instead of an obscenity. **b** *euphem.* used in place of a noun regarded as coarse. **6** a domino with one or both halves blank. **7** a lottery ticket that gains no prize. **8** the white centre of the target in archery etc. ● *v.tr.* **1** (usu. foll. by *off*, *out*) screen, obscure (*clouds blanked out the sun*). **2** (usu. foll. by *out*) cut (a metal blank). **3** *US* defeat without allowing to score. ▫ **blank cheque 1** a cheque with the amount left for the payee to fill in. **2** *colloq.* unlimited freedom of action (cf. CARTE BLANCHE). **blank test** *Chem.* a scientific test done without a specimen, to verify the absence of the effects of reagents etc. **blank verse** unrhymed verse, esp. iambic pentameters. **draw a blank** elicit no response; fail. ▫▫ **blankly** *adv.* **blankness** *n.* [ME f. OF *blanc* white, ult. f. Gmc]
■ *adj.* **1 a** unused, plain, virgin, clean, clear, unfilled. **2 a** empty, plain, bare, vacant, unfilled. **b** unornamented, unadorned, undecorated, unrelieved, void. **3 a** passive, impassive, expressionless, emotionless, vacuous, mindless, unexpressive. **c** disconcerted, discomfited, nonplussed, confused, helpless, resourceless, perplexed, dazed, puzzled, bewildered. **4** unrelieved, stark, sheer, utter, pure, unmixed, complete, downright, absolute, unqualified. ● *n.* **1 a** space; line, box. **3** nothing, zero, nil, *esp. US sl.* zilch; void, emptiness, nothingness, vacuum.

blanket /blángkit/ *n.*, *adj.*, & *v.* ● *n.* **1** a large piece of woollen or other material used esp. as a bed-covering or to wrap up a person or an animal for warmth. **2** (usu. foll. by *of*) a thick mass or layer that covers something (*blanket of fog*; *blanket of silence*). **3** *Printing* a rubber surface transferring an impression from a plate to paper etc. in offset printing. ● *adj.* covering all cases or classes; inclusive (*blanket condemnation*; *blanket agreement*). ● *v.tr.* (**blanketed, blanketing**) **1** cover with or as if with a blanket (*snow blanketed the land*). **2** stifle; keep quiet (*blanketed all discussion*). **3** *Naut.* take wind from the sails of (another craft) by passing to windward. ▫ **blanket bath** a body wash given to a bedridden patient. **blanket stitch** a stitch used to neaten the edges of a blanket or other material. **born on the wrong side of the blanket** illegitimate. **electric blanket** an electrically wired blanket used for heating a bed. **wet**

blanket *colloq.* a gloomy person preventing the enjoyment of others. [ME f. OF *blancquet, blanchet* f. *blanc* white, BLANK]
■ *n.* **1** see COVER *n.* 1f. **2** see MANTLE *n.* 2. ● *adj.* see INCLUSIVE 3. ● *v.* **1** see COVER *v.* 2. **2** see SMOTHER *v.* 1.

blankety /blángkəti/ *adj.* & *n.* (also **blanky** /blángki/) *Brit. colloq.* = BLANK *adj.*& *n.* 5.

blanky var. of BLANKETY.

blanquette /blonkét/ *n. Cookery* a dish consisting of white meat, e.g. veal, in a white sauce. [F (as BLANKET)]

blare /blair/ *v.* & *n.* ● *v.* **1** *tr.* & *intr.* sound or utter loudly. **2** *intr.* make the sound of a trumpet. ● *n.* a loud sound resembling that of a trumpet. [ME f. MDu. *blaren, bleren*, imit.]
■ *v.* blast, bellow, trumpet, ring, boom, thunder, roar, bray; resound, echo, reverberate, resonate. ● *n.* blast, bellow, ring, roar, boom, noise, sound, clamour.

blarney /blaárni/ *n.* & *v.* ● *n.* **1** cajoling talk; flattery. **2** nonsense. ● *v.* (**-eys, -eyed**) **1** *tr.* flatter (a person) with blarney. **2** *intr.* talk flatteringly. [*Blarney*, an Irish castle near Cork with a stone said to confer a cajoling tongue on whoever kisses it]
■ *n.* **2** see FLANNEL *n.*

blasé /blaázay/ *adj.* **1** unimpressed or indifferent because of over-familiarity. **2** tired of pleasure; surfeited. [F]
■ **1** indifferent, cool, superior, supercilious, sophisticated, unmoved, unimpressed, nonchalant, emotionless, phlegmatic, apathetic, carefree, light-hearted, insouciant; cavalier. **2** bored, jaded, weary, jaundiced; surfeited.

blaspheme /blasfeém/ *v.* **1** *intr.* talk profanely, making use of religious names, etc. **2** *tr.* talk profanely about; revile. □□ **blasphemer** *n.* [ME f. OF *blasfemer* f. eccl.L *blasphemare* f. Gk *blasphēmeō*: cf. BLAME]
■ **1** curse, swear, execrate, damn. **2** abuse, malign, calumniate, defame, disparage, revile, put down, decry, deprecate, depreciate, belittle.

blasphemy /blásfəmi/ *n.* (*pl.* **-ies**) **1** profane talk. **2** an instance of this. □□ **blasphemous** *adj.* **blasphemously** *adv.* [ME f. OF *blasfemie* f. eccl.L f. Gk *blasphēmia* slander, blasphemy]
■ see PROFANITY 2. □□ **blasphemous** profane, impious, irreverent, disrespectful, sacrilegious, irreligious, sinful, wicked, evil, iniquitous.

blast /blaast/ *n., v.,* & *int.* ● *n.* **1** a strong gust of wind. **2 a** a destructive wave of highly compressed air spreading outwards from an explosion. **b** such an explosion. **3** the single loud note of a wind instrument, car horn, whistle, etc. **4** *colloq.* a severe reprimand. **5** a strong current of air used in smelting etc. **6** *sl.* a party; a good time. ● *v.* **1** *tr.* blow up (rocks etc.) with explosives. **2** *tr.* **a** wither, shrivel, or blight (a plant, animal, limb, etc.) (*blasted oak*). **b** destroy, ruin (*blasted her hopes*). **c** strike with divine anger; curse. **3** *intr.* & *tr.* make or cause to make a loud or explosive noise (*blasted away on his trumpet*). **4** *tr. colloq.* reprimand severely. **5** *colloq.* **a** *tr.* shoot; shoot at. **b** *intr.* shoot. ● *int.* expressing annoyance. □ **at full blast** *colloq.* working at maximum speed etc. **blast-furnace** a smelting furnace into which compressed hot air is driven. **blast-hole** a hole containing an explosive charge for blasting. **blast off** (of a rocket etc.) take off from a launching site. **blast-off** *n.* **1** the launching of a rocket etc. **2** the initial thrust for this. [OE *blǣst* f. Gmc]
■ *n.* **1** blow, gust, wind, gale. **2** explosion, burst, eruption, discharge; detonation. **3** blare, sound, noise, racket, din, bellow, roar; boom, report. ● *v.* **1** blow up, explode, dynamite, demolish, destroy, ruin, waste, lay waste, shatter, devastate. **2 b** see DESTROY 2. **c** curse, damn. **4** defame, discredit, denounce, impugn, put down, criticize, attack, *colloq.* lambaste, pan, knock, slate. **5 a** fire at, shoot (at), bombard, shell. **b** open fire, fire, shoot. □ **at full blast** fully, at full tilt, at *or* to the maximum, completely, thoroughly, entirely, maximally, *US sl.* to the max.

-blast /blaast/ *comb. form Biol.* **1** an embryonic cell (*erythroblast*) (cf. -CYTE). **2** a germ layer of an embryo (*epiblast*). [Gk *blastos* sprout]

blasted /blaástid/ *adj.* & *adv.* ● *attrib.adj.* damned; annoying (*that blasted dog!*). ● *adv. colloq.* damned; extremely (*it's blasted cold*).

blaster /blaástər/ *n.* **1** in senses of BLAST *v.* **2** *Golf* a heavy lofted club for playing from a bunker.

blastula /blástyoolə/ *n.* (*pl.* **blastulae** /-lee/ or *US* **blastulas**) *Biol.* an animal embryo at an early stage of development when it is a hollow ball of cells. [mod.L f. Gk *blastos* sprout]

blatant /bláyt'nt/ *adj.* **1** flagrant, unashamed (*blatant attempt to steal*). **2** offensively noisy or obtrusive. □□ **blatancy** *n.* **blatantly** *adv.* [a word used by Spenser (1596), perh. after Sc. *blatand* = bleating]
■ **1** obvious, flagrant, palpable, obtrusive, arrant, shameless, unashamed, brazen, overt, glaring. **2** noisy, clamorous, loud, bellowing, strident, vociferous, rowdy, boisterous, obstreperous, uproarious; obtrusive.

blather /bláthər/ *n.* & *v.* (also **blether** /bléthər/) ● *n.* foolish chatter. ● *v.intr.* chatter foolishly. [ME *blather*, Sc. *blether*, f. ON *blathra* talk nonsense f. *blathr* nonsense]
■ *n.* see WAFFLE[1] *n.* ● *v.* see WAFFLE[1] *v.*

blatherskite /bláthərskīt/ (also **bletherskate** /bléthərskayt/) *n.* **1** a person who blathers. **2** = BLATHER *n.* [BLATHER + *skite*, corrupt. of derog. use of SKATE[2]]
■ **1** see BLABBER *n.*

blaze[1] /blayz/ *n.* & *v.* ● *n.* **1** a bright flame or fire. **2 a** a bright glaring light (*the sun set in a blaze of orange*). **b** a full light (*a blaze of publicity*). **3** a violent outburst (of passion etc.) (*a blaze of patriotic fervour*). **4 a** a glow of colour (*roses were a blaze of scarlet*). **b** a bright display (*a blaze of glory*). ● *v.intr.* **1** burn with a bright flame. **2** be brilliantly lighted. **3** be consumed with anger, excitement, etc. **4 a** show bright colours (*blazing with jewels*). **b** emit light (*stars blazing*). □ **blaze away** (often foll. by *at*) **1** fire continuously with rifles etc. **2** work enthusiastically. **blaze up 1** burst into flame. **2** burst out in anger. **like blazes** *sl.* **1** with great energy. **2** very fast. **what the blazes!** *sl.* what the hell! □□ **blazingly** *adv.* [OE *blæse* torch, f. Gmc: ult. rel. to BLAZE[2]]
■ *n.* **1** flame, fire, holocaust, inferno, conflagration. **2, 4** brightness, brilliance, brilliancy, glow. **3** outburst, eruption, flare-up, explosion, outbreak. ● *v.* **1** burn, flare (up), flame. **2, 4** glow, glare, dazzle, sparkle, shine, gleam, coruscate, twinkle, shimmer, glitter; see also FLASH *v.* 1, 3; 2. □ **blaze away 1** fire, shoot, open fire, blast; (*blaze away at*) bombard, shell.

blaze[2] /blayz/ *n.* & *v.* ● *n.* **1** a white mark on an animal's face. **2** a mark made on a tree by slashing the bark esp. to mark a route. ● *v.tr.* mark (a tree or a path) by chipping bark. □ **blaze a trail 1** mark out a path or route. **2** be the first to do, invent, or study something; pioneer. [17th c.: ult. rel. to BLAZE[1]]

blaze[3] /blayz/ *v.tr.* proclaim as with a trumpet. □ **blaze abroad** spread (news) about. [ME f. LG or Du. *blāzen* blow, f. Gmc *blǣsan*]

blazer /bláyzər/ *n.* **1** a coloured, often striped, summer jacket worn by schoolchildren, sportsmen, etc., esp. as part of a uniform. **2** a man's plain jacket, often dark blue, not worn with matching trousers. [BLAZE[1] + -ER[1]]

blazon /bláyz'n/ *v.* & *n.* ● *v.tr.* **1** proclaim (esp. *blazon abroad*). **2** *Heraldry* **a** describe or paint (arms). **b** inscribe or paint (an object) with arms, names, etc. ● *n.* **1** *Heraldry* **a** a shield, coat of arms, bearings, or a banner. **b** a correct description of these. **2** a record or description, esp. of virtues etc. □□ **blazoner** *n.* **blazonment** *n.* [ME f. OF *blason* shield, of unkn. orig.; verb also f. BLAZE[3]]

blazonry /bláyzənri/ *n. Heraldry* **1 a** the art of describing or painting heraldic devices or armorial bearings. **b** such devices or bearings. **2** brightly coloured display.

bleach /bleech/ *v.* & *n.* ● *v.tr.* & *intr.* whiten by exposure to sunlight or by a chemical process. ● *n.* **1** a bleaching substance. **2** the process of bleaching. □ **bleaching-powder** calcium hypochlorite used esp. to remove colour from materials. [OE *blǣcan* f. Gmc]

■ *v.* whiten, lighten, fade, blanch. ● *n.* **1** whitener, chlorine.

bleacher /bléechər/ *n.* **1 a** a person who bleaches (esp. textiles). **b** a vessel or chemical used in bleaching. **2** (usu. in *pl.*) esp. *US* a bench-seat at a sports ground, esp. one in an outdoor uncovered stand usu. arranged in tiers and very cheap.

bleak[1] /bleek/ *adj.* **1** bare, exposed; windswept. **2** unpromising; dreary (*bleak prospects*). □□ **bleakly** *adv.* **bleakness** *n.* [16th c.: rel. to obs. adjs. *bleach, blake* (f. ON *bleikr*) pale, ult. f. Gmc: cf. BLEACH]

■ **1** austere, inhospitable, grim, harsh, barren, bare, exposed, windswept, desolate. **2** cheerless, dreary, unpromising, disheartening, forebidding, inauspicious, unpropitious, depressing, dismal, gloomy, sombre, melancholy, sad, unhappy, mournful.

bleak[2] /bleek/ *n.* any of various species of small river-fish, esp. *Alburnus alburnus.* [ME prob. f. ON *bleikja*, OHG *bleicha* f. Gmc]

blear /bleer/ *adj.* & *v. archaic* ● *adj.* **1** (of the eyes or the mind) dim, dull, filmy. **2** indistinct. ● *v.tr.* make dim or obscure; blur. [ME, of uncert. orig.]

bleary /bléeri/ *adj.* (**blearier, bleariest**) **1** (of the eyes or mind) dim; blurred. **2** indistinct. □ **bleary-eyed** having dim sight or wits. □□ **blearily** *adv.* **bleariness** *n.*

■ **1** see FILMY 2. **2** see INDISTINCT 2.

bleat /bleet/ *v.* & *n.* ● *v.* **1** *intr.* (of a sheep, goat, or calf) make a weak, wavering cry. **2** *intr.* & *tr.* (often foll. by *out*) speak or say feebly, foolishly, or plaintively. ● *n.* **1** the sound made by a sheep, goat, etc. **2** a weak, plaintive, or foolish cry. □□ **bleater** *n.* **bleatingly** *adv.* [OE *blǣtan* (imit.)]

bleb /bleb/ *n.* **1** esp. *Med.* a small blister on the skin. **2** a small bubble in glass or on water. [var. of BLOB]

bleed /bleed/ *v.* & *n.* ● *v.* (*past* and *past part.* **bled** /bled/) **1** *intr.* emit blood. **2** *tr.* draw blood from surgically. **3 a** *tr.* extort money from. **b** *intr.* part with money lavishly; suffer extortion. **4** *intr.* (often foll. by *for*) suffer wounds or violent death (*bled for the Revolution*). **5** *intr.* **a** (of a plant) emit sap. **b** (of dye) come out in water. **6** *tr.* **a** allow (fluid or gas) to escape from a closed system through a valve etc. **b** treat (such a system) in this way. **7** *Printing* **a** *intr.* (of a printed area) be cut into when pages are trimmed. **b** *tr.* cut into the printed area of when trimming. **c** *tr.* extend (an illustration) to the cut edge of a page. ● *n.* an act of bleeding (cf. NOSEBLEED). □ **one's heart bleeds** usu. *iron.* one is very sorrowful. [OE *blēdan* f. Gmc]

■ **3 a** see FLEECE *v.* 1.

bleeder /bléedər/ *n.* **1** *coarse sl.* a person (esp. as a term of contempt or disrespect) (*you bleeder; lucky bleeder*). **2** *colloq.* a haemophiliac.

bleeding /bléeding/ *adj.* & *adv. Brit. coarse sl.* expressing annoyance or antipathy (*a bleeding nuisance*). □ **bleeding heart 1** *colloq.* a dangerously soft-hearted person. **2** any of various plants, esp. *Dicentra spectabilis* having heart-shaped crimson flowers hanging from an arched stem.

bleep /bleep/ *n.* & *v.* ● *n.* an intermittent high-pitched sound made electronically. ● *v.intr.* & *tr.* **1** make or cause to make such a sound, esp. as a signal. **2** alert or summon by a bleep or bleeps. [imit.]

bleeper /bléepər/ *n.* a small portable electronic device which emits a bleep when the wearer is contacted.

blemish /blémmish/ *n.* & *v.* ● *n.* a physical or moral defect; a stain; a flaw (*not a blemish on his character*). ● *v.tr.* spoil the beauty or perfection of; stain (*spots blemished her complexion*). [ME f. OF *ble(s)mir* (-ISH[2]) make pale, prob. of Gmc orig.]

■ *n.* disfigurement, scar, mark, impairment, stain, smear, blot; defect, flaw, error, fault, imperfection, erratum. ● *v.* deface, mar, scar, impair, disfigure, tarnish, stain, spoil, flaw, harm, damage, scar, injure, bruise, besmirch, *poet.* sully.

blench /blench/ *v.intr.* flinch; quail. [ME f. OE *blencan*, ult. f. Gmc]

■ see FLINCH[1] *v.*

blend /blend/ *v.* & *n.* ● *v.* **1** *tr.* **a** mix (esp. sorts of tea, spirits, tobacco, etc.) together to produce a desired flavour etc. **b** produce by this method (*blended whisky*). **2** *intr.* form a harmonious compound; become one. **3 a** *tr.* & *intr.* (often foll. by *with*) mingle or be mingled (*truth blended with lies; blends well with the locals*). **b** *tr.* (often foll. by *in, with*) mix thoroughly. **4** *intr.* (esp. of colours): **a** pass imperceptibly into each other. **b** go well together; harmonize. ● *n.* **1 a** a mixture, esp. of various sorts of tea, spirits, tobacco, fibre, etc. **b** a combination (of different abstract or personal qualities). **2** a portmanteau word. [ME prob. f. ON *blanda* mix]

■ *v.* **1 a** mix, mingle, combine, meld, intermingle, *literary* commingle. **2** join, amalgamate, merge, integrate, fuse, unite. **4 a** shade, grade, gradate, graduate, merge, coalesce, fuse, unite. ● *n.* **1 a** amalgamation, mixture, mix, combination. **b** fusion, composite, amalgam, compound, combination.

blende /blend/ *n.* any naturally occurring metal sulphide, esp. zinc blende. [G f. *blenden* deceive, so called because while often resembling galena it yielded no lead]

blender /bléndər/ *n.* **1** a mixing machine used in food preparation for liquidizing, chopping, or puréeing. **2 a** a thing that blends. **b** a person who blends.

Blenheim /blénnim/ *n.* **1** a small spaniel of a red and white breed. **2** this breed. [the Duke of Marlborough's seat at Woodstock in S. England, named after his victory at Blenheim in Bavaria (1704)]

Blenheim Orange /blénnim/ *n.* a golden-coloured apple which ripens late in the season.

blenny /blénni/ *n.* (*pl.* **-ies**) any of a family of small spiny-finned marine fish, esp. of the genus *Blennius*, having scaleless skins. [L *blennius* f. Gk *blennos* mucus, with reference to its mucous coating]

blent /blent/ *poet. past* and *past part.* of BLEND.

blepharitis /bléffərítiss/ *n.* inflammation of the eyelids. [Gk *blepharon* eyelid + -ITIS]

blesbok /blésbok/ *n.* (also **blesbuck** /-buk/) a subspecies of bontebok, native to southern Africa, having small lyre-shaped horns. [Afrik. f. *bles* BLAZE[2], (from the white mark on its forehead) + *bok* goat]

bless /bless/ *v.tr.* (*past* and *past part.* **blessed**, *poet.* **blest** /blest/) **1** (of a priest etc.) pronounce words, esp. in a religious rite, asking for divine favour; ask God to look favourably on (*bless this house*). **2 a** consecrate (esp. bread and wine). **b** sanctify by the sign of the cross. **3** call (God) holy; adore. **4** attribute one's good fortune to (an auspicious time, one's fate, etc.); thank (*bless the day I met her; bless my stars*). **5** (usu. in *passive*; often foll. by *with*) make happy or successful (*blessed with children; they were truly blessed*). **6** *euphem.* curse; damn (*bless the boy!*). □ (**God**) **bless me** (or **my soul**) an exclamation of surprise, pleasure, indignation, etc. (**God**) **bless you! 1** an exclamation of endearment, gratitude, etc. **2** an exclamation made to a person who has just sneezed. **I'm** (or **well, I'm**) **blessed** (or **blest**) an exclamation of surprise etc. **not have a penny to bless oneself with** be impoverished. [OE *blēdsian, blēdsian, blētsian*, f. *blōd* blood (hence mark with blood, consecrate): meaning infl. by its use at the conversion of the English to translate L *benedicare* praise]

■ **2** consecrate, hallow, sanctify, dedicate. **3** extol, glorify, praise, revere, adore, exalt, honour, venerate, *archaic* magnify. **4** thank, pay homage to, pay respect to. **5** make happy *or* fortunate, endow, favour, furnish, provide, supply, grace. **6** curse, damn, confound.

blessed /bléssid, blest/ *adj.* (also *poet.* **blest**) **1 a** consecrated (*Blessed Sacrament*). **b** revered. **2** /blest/ (usu. foll. by *with*) often *iron.* fortunate (in the possession of) (*blessed with good* *health*; *blessed with children*). **3** *euphem.* cursed; damned (*blessed nuisance!*). **4 a** in paradise. **b** *RC Ch.* a title given to a dead person as an acknowledgement of his or her holy life; beatified. **5** bringing happiness; blissful (*blessed ignorance*). □□ **blessedly** *adv.*

■ **2** see FORTUNATE 1.

blessedness /bléssidniss/ *n.* **1** happiness. **2** the enjoyment of divine favour. □ **single blessedness** *joc.* the state of being unmarried (perversion of Shakesp. *Midsummer Night's Dream* I. i. 78).

■ **1** see BLISS 1.

blessing /bléssing/ *n.* **1** the act of declaring, seeking, or bestowing (esp. divine) favour (*sought God's blessing*; *mother gave them her blessing*). **2** grace said before or after a meal. **3** a gift of God, nature, etc.; a thing one is glad of (*what a blessing he brought it!*). □ **blessing in disguise** an apparent misfortune that eventually has good results.

■ **1** benediction, prayer, consecration, sanction, approbation, endorsement, imprimatur, favour; see also APPROVAL. **3** boon, favour, advantage, good fortune, godsend, luck, profit, gain, help, asset, gift, bounty.

blest /blest/ *poet.* var. of BLESSED.

blether var. of BLATHER.

bletherskate var. of BLATHERSKITE.

blew *past* of BLOW[1], BLOW[3].

blewits /bloo-its/ *n.* any fungus of the genus *Tricholoma*, with edible lilac-stemmed mushrooms. [prob. f BLUE[1]]

blight /blīt/ *n.* & *v.* ● *n.* **1** any plant disease caused by mildews, rusts, smuts, fungi, or insects. **2** any insect or parasite causing such a disease. **3** any obscure force which is harmful or destructive. **4** an unsightly or neglected urban area. ● *v.tr.* **1** affect with blight. **2** harm, destroy. **3** spoil. [17th c.: orig. unkn.]

■ *n.* **1** disease, plague, infestation. **3** affliction, disease, plague, pestilence, misfortune, curse, trouble, calamity, bane, *archaic or literary* woe, scourge. **4** eyesore, wasteland, blot, taint, stain. ● *v.* **1** afflict, infest, plague, scourge. **2** wither, blast, wreck, ruin, destroy, harm, spoil. **3** mar, taint, deface, mutilate, damage, disfigure, blot.

blighter /blītər/ *n. Brit. colloq.* a person (esp. as a term of contempt or disparagement). [BLIGHT + -ER[1]]

■ person, chap, fellow, man, boy, lad, *colloq.* guy, devil, beggar, *sl.* geezer, bastard, son of a bitch, *Brit. sl.* bloke; *sl.* jerk; fool, idiot, *Brit. sl.* git.

Blighty /blīti/ *n.* (*pl.* **-ies**) *sl.* (used by soldiers, esp. during the war of 1914–18) England; home. [Anglo-Ind. corrupt. of Hind. *bilāyatī*, *wilāyatī* foreign, European]

blimey /blīmi/ *int.* (also **cor blimey** /kor/) *Brit. sl.* an expression of surprise, contempt, etc. [corrupt. of (*God*) *blind me!*]

blimp /blimp/ *n.* **1** (also **(Colonel) Blimp**) a proponent of reactionary establishment opinions. **2 a** a small non-rigid airship. **b** a barrage balloon. **3** a soundproof cover for a cine-camera. □□ **blimpery** *n.* **blimpish** *adj.* [20th. c., of uncert. orig.: in sense 1, a pompous, obese, elderly character invented by cartoonist David Low (d. 1963), and used in anti-German or anti-Government drawings before and during the war of 1939-45]

■ □□ **blimpish** see REACTIONARY *adj.*

blind /blīnd/ *adj.*, *v.*, *n.*, & *adv.* ● *adj.* **1** lacking the power of sight. **2 a** without foresight, discernment, intellectual perception, or adequate information (*blind effort*). **b** (often foll. by *to*) unwilling or unable to appreciate (a factor, circumstance, etc.) (*blind to argument*). **3** not governed by purpose or reason (*blind forces*). **4** reckless (*blind hitting*). **5 a** concealed (*blind ditch*). **b** (of a door, window, etc.) walled up. **c** closed at one end. **6** *Aeron.* (of flying) without direct observation, using instruments only. **7** *Cookery* (of a flan case, pie base, etc.) baked without a filling. **8** *sl.* drunk. ● *v.* **1** *tr.* deprive of sight, permanently or temporarily (*blinded by tears*). **2** *tr.* (often foll. by *to*) rob of judgement; deceive (*blinded them to the danger*). **3** *intr. sl.* go very fast and dangerously, esp. in a motor vehicle. ● *n.* **1 a** a screen for a window, esp. on a roller, or with slats (*roller blind*; *Venetian blind*). **b** an awning over a shop window. **2 a** something designed or used to hide the truth; a pretext. **b** a legitimate business concealing a criminal enterprise (*he's a spy, and his job is just a blind*). **3** any obstruction to sight or light. **4** *Brit. sl.* a heavy drinking-bout. **5** *Cards* a stake put up by a poker player before the cards dealt are seen. **6** *US* = HIDE[1] *n.* ● *adv.* blindly (*fly blind*; *bake it blind*). □ **blind alley 1** a cul-de-sac. **2** a course of action leading nowhere. **blind as a bat** completely blind. **blind coal** coal burning without a flame. **blind corner** a corner round which a motorist etc. cannot see. **blind date 1** a social engagement between a man and a woman who have not previously met. **2** either of the couple on a blind date. **blind drunk** extremely drunk. **blind gut** the caecum. **blind man's buff** a game in which a blindfold player tries to catch others while being pushed about by them. **blind side** a direction in which one cannot see the approach of danger etc. **blind spot 1** *Anat.* the point of entry of the optic nerve on the retina, insensitive to light. **2** an area in which a person lacks understanding or impartiality. **3** a point of unusually weak radio reception. **blind stamping** (or **tooling**) embossing a book cover without the use of colour or gold leaf. **blind-stitch** *n.* sewing visible on one side only. ● *v.tr.* & *intr.* sew with this stitch. **blind to** incapable of appreciating. **blind with science** overawe with a display of (often spurious) knowledge. **go it blind** act recklessly or without proper consideration. **not a blind bit of** (or **not a blind**) *sl.* not the slightest; not a single (*took not a blind bit of notice*; *not a blind word out of him*). **turn a** (or **one's**) **blind eye to** pretend not to notice. □□ **blindly** *adv.* **blindness** *n.* [OE f. Gmc]

■ *adj.* **1** sightless, eyeless, visionless, unseeing, unsighted, purblind; partially sighted, visually handicapped; *Austral.* boko. **2 a** imperceptive, slow, myopic, heedless, inconsiderate, thoughtless, insensitive, thick, dense, obtuse, stupid, weak-minded, dull-witted, slow-witted, dim-witted, *esp. Brit. colloq.* gormless. **b** (*blind to*) unaware *or* unconscious of, impervious *or* insensible to, unaffected *or* untouched *or* unmoved by, heedless of, oblivious to *or* of. **3** indiscriminate, undiscriminating, unreasoning, mindless, senseless, irrational. **4** wild, reckless, rash, impetuous, unthinking. ● *v.* **1** put *or* poke a person's eyes out, cause a person's eyes to fog *or* mist over, dazzle, blindfold; see also DAZZLE *v.* 1. **2** deceive, blindfold, blinker; hoodwink, fool, *colloq.* bamboozle. ● *n.* **1** shade, curtain, screen, cover, shutter(s), covering, *esp. US* window shade; awning. **2** pretence, pretext, front, cover, smokescreen, stratagem, subterfuge, ruse, trick, deception, dodge; *US sl.* scam. □ **turn a blind eye to** see IGNORE 2. □□ **blindly** recklessly, heedlessly, deludedly, indiscriminately, rashly, impetuously, irrationally, thoughtlessly, mindlessly, senselessly, unthinkingly.

blinder /blīndər/ *n. colloq.* **1** an excellent piece of play in a game. **2** (in *pl.*) *US* blinkers.

blindfold /blīndfōld/ *v.*, *n.*, *adj.*, & *adv.* ● *v.tr.* **1** deprive (a person) of sight by covering the eyes, esp. with a tied cloth. **2** deprive of understanding; hoodwink. ● *n.* **1** a bandage or cloth used to blindfold. **2** any obstruction to understanding. ● *adj.* & *adv.* **1** with eyes bandaged. **2** without care or circumspection (*went into it blindfold*). **3** *Chess* without sight of board and men. [replacing (by assoc. with FOLD[1]) ME *blindfellen*, past part. *blindfelled* (FELL[1]) strike blind]

■ *v.* **1** see BLIND *v.* 1. **2** see BLIND *v.* 2.

blinding /blīnding/ *n.* **1** the process of covering a newly made road etc. with grit to fill cracks. **2** such grit.

blindworm /blīndwurm/ *n.* = SLOW-WORM.

blink /blingk/ *v.* & *n.* ● *v.* **1** *intr.* shut and open the eyes quickly and usu. involuntarily. **2** *intr.* (often foll. by *at*) look with eyes opening and shutting. **3** *tr.* **a** (often foll. by *back*) prevent (tears) by blinking. **b** (often foll. by *away*, *from*) clear (dust etc.) from the eyes by blinking. **4** *tr.* &

(foll. by *at*) *intr.* shirk consideration of; ignore; condone. **5** *intr.* **a** shine with an unsteady or intermittent light. **b** cast a momentary gleam. **6** *tr.* blink with (eyes). ● *n.* **1** an act of blinking. **2** a momentary gleam or glimpse. **3** = ICEBLINK. □ **on the blink** *sl.* out of order, esp. intermittently. [partly var. of *blenk* = BLENCH, partly f. MDu. *blinken* shine]
■ *v.* **1** wink, flicker, flutter, nictitate, bat one's eyelid. **2** squint, screw up one's eyes; be shocked, be surprised, be startled, flinch, wince, shrink, quail, blench, recoil, start, move. **4** (*blink at*) wink at, ignore, overlook, disregard; condone, turn a blind eye to. **5** twinkle, flicker, gleam, glimmer, shimmer, flash, sparkle, scintillate, coruscate. ● *n.* **1** wink, flicker, flutter, waver. **2** flash, sparkle, twinkle, shimmer, flicker, gleam, glimmer. □ **on the blink** out of order, broken, in disrepair, not working *or* operating, not operational, down, *esp. US sl.* out of whack, *US sl.* on the fritz.

blinker /blíngkər/ *n.* & *v.* ● *n.* **1** (usu. in *pl.*) either of a pair of screens attached to a horse's bridle to prevent it from seeing sideways. **2** a device that blinks, esp. a vehicle's indicator. ● *v.tr.* **1** obscure with blinkers. **2** (as **blinkered** *adj.*) having narrow and prejudiced views.
■ *v.* **2** (**blinkered**) see NEAR-SIGHTED.

blinking /blíngking/ *adj.* & *adv. Brit. sl.* an intensive, esp. expressing disapproval (*a blinking idiot*; *a blinking awful time*). [BLINK + -ING[2] (euphem. for BLOODY)]

blip /blip/ *n.* & *v.* ● *n.* **1** a quick popping sound, as of dripping water or an electronic device. **2** a small image of an object on a radar screen. **3** a minor deviation or error. ● *v.* (**blipped, blipping**) **1** *intr.* make a blip. **2** *tr.* strike briskly. [imit.]
■ *n.* **3** see MISTAKE *n.*

bliss /bliss/ *n.* **1 a** perfect joy or happiness. **b** enjoyment; gladness. **2 a** being in heaven. **b** a state of blessedness. [OE *blīths, bliss* f. Gmc *blīthsjō* f. *blīthiz* BLITHE: sense infl. by BLESS]
■ **1** happiness, gladness, joy, blessedness, delight, felicity, glee, enjoyment, pleasure, joyousness, cheer, exhilaration, gaiety, blissfulness, rapture, ecstasy, *poet.* blitheness. **2** paradise, nirvana; see also HEAVEN 2.

blissful /blísfo͝ol/ *adj.* perfectly happy; joyful. □ **blissful ignorance** fortunate unawareness of something unpleasant. □□ **blissfully** *adv.* **blissfulness** *n.*
■ see ELATE *v.*

blister /blístər/ *n.* & *v.* ● *n.* **1** a small bubble on the skin filled with serum and caused by friction, burning, etc. **2** a similar swelling on any other surface. **3** *Med.* anything applied to raise a blister. **4** *sl.* an annoying person. ● *v.* **1** *tr.* raise a blister on. **2** *intr.* come up in a blister or blisters. **3** *tr.* attack sharply (*blistered them with his criticisms*). **4** (as **blistering** *adj.*) causing blisters; severe; hot. □ **blister copper** copper which is almost pure. **blister gas** a poison gas causing blisters on the skin. **blister pack** a bubble pack. □□ **blistery** *adj.* [ME perh. f. OF *blestre, blo(u)stre* swelling, pimple]
■ *n.* **1, 2** see LUMP[1] *n.* 3. ● *v.* **4** see SEVERE 3, 4, HOT *adj.* 1.

blithe /blīth/ *adj.* **1** *poet.* gay, joyous. **2** careless, casual (*with blithe indifference*). □□ **blithely** *adv.* **blitheness** *n.* **blithesome** /blīthsəm/ *adj.* [OE *blīthe* f. Gmc]
■ **1** blithesome, blissful, happy, cheerful, joyous, merry, light-hearted, well-pleased, delighted, gay, joyful, elated, jubilant. **2** happy-go-lucky, insouciant, heedless, carefree, unconcerned, blasé, casual, detached, indifferent, uncaring, careless, blithesome.

blithering /blíthəring/ *adj. colloq.* **1** senselessly talkative. **2 a** (*attrib.*) utter; hopeless (*blithering idiot*). **b** contemptible. [*blither*, var. of BLATHER + -ING[2]]

B.Litt. *abbr.* Bachelor of Letters. [L *Baccalaureus Litterarum*]

blitz /blits/ *n.* & *v. colloq.* ● *n.* **1 a** an intensive or sudden (esp. aerial) attack. **b** an energetic intensive attack, usu. on a specific task (*must have a blitz on this room*). **2** (**the Blitz**) the German air raids on London in 1940. ● *v.tr.* attack, damage, or destroy by a blitz. [abbr. of BLITZKRIEG]
■ *n.* **1 a** see RAID *n.* 1. ● *v.* see SHELL *v.* 2.

blitzkrieg /blítskreeg/ *n.* an intense military campaign intended to bring about a swift victory. [G, = lightning war]
■ see PUSH *n.* 4.

blizzard /blízzərd/ *n.* a severe snowstorm with high winds. [US 'violent blow' (1829), 'snowstorm' (1859), perh. imit.]
■ see STORM *n.* 1.

bloat /blōt/ *v.* **1** *tr.* & *intr.* inflate, swell (*wind bloated the sheets*; *bloated with gas*). **2** *tr.* (as **bloated** *adj.*) **a** swollen, puffed. **b** puffed up with pride or excessive wealth (*bloated plutocrat*). **3** *tr.* cure (a herring) by salting and smoking lightly. [obs. *bloat* swollen, soft and wet, perh. f. ON *blautr* soaked, flabby]
■ **1** see SWELL *v.* 3. **2** (**bloated**) **a** swollen, distended, full, puffy, bulging, puffed up, tumescent. **b** puffed up, overgrown, inflated, pompous, conceited, big-headed, self-important, arrogant.

bloater /blṓtər/ *n.* a herring cured by bloating.

blob /blob/ *n.* **1** a small roundish mass; a drop of matter. **2** a drop of liquid. **3** a spot of colour. **4** *Cricket sl.* a score of 0. [imit.: cf. BLEB]
■ **1** gobbet, globule, drop, droplet, bit, lump, dab, glob, *archaic* gout, *colloq.* smidgen, *Brit. sl.* gob. **2** drop, droplet, raindrop, bead, drip, spot, *archaic* gout.

bloc /blok/ *n.* a combination of parties, governments, groups, etc. sharing a common purpose. □ **bloc vote** = *block vote*. [F, = block]
■ see COMBINATION 3.

block /blok/ *n.*, *v.*, & *adj.* ● *n.* **1** a solid hewn or unhewn piece of hard material, esp. of rock, stone, or wood (*block of ice*). **2** a flat-topped block used as a base for chopping, beheading, standing something on, hammering on, or for mounting a horse from. **3 a** a large building, esp. when subdivided (*block of flats*). **b** a compact mass of buildings bounded by (usu. four) streets. **4** an obstruction; anything preventing progress or normal working (*a block in the pipe*). **5** a chock for stopping the motion of a wheel etc. **6** a pulley or system of pulleys mounted in a case. **7** (in *pl.*) any of a set of solid cubes etc., used as a child's toy. **8** *Printing* a piece of wood or metal engraved for printing on paper or fabric. **9** a head-shaped mould used for shaping hats or wigs. **10** *sl.* the head (*knock his block off*). **11** *US* **a** the area between streets in a town or suburb. **b** the length of such an area, esp. as a measure of distance (*lives three blocks away*). **12** a stolid, unimaginative, or hard-hearted person. **13** a large quantity or allocation of things treated as a unit, esp. shares, seats in a theatre, etc. **14** a set of sheets of paper used for writing, or esp. drawing, glued along one edge. **15** *Cricket* a spot on which a batsman blocks the ball before the wicket, and rests the bat before playing. **16** *Athletics* = *starting-block*. **17** *Amer. Football* a blocking action. **18** *Austral.* **a** a tract of land offered to an individual settler by a government. **b** a large area of land. ● *v.tr.* **1 a** (often foll. by *up*) obstruct (a passage etc.) (*the road was blocked*; *you are blocking my view*). **b** put obstacles in the way of (progress etc.). **2** restrict the use or conversion of (currency or any other asset). **3** use a block for making (a hat, wig, etc.). **4** emboss or impress a design on (a book cover). **5** *Cricket* stop (a ball) with a bat defensively. **6** *Amer. Football* intercept (an opponent) with one's body. ● *attrib.adj.* treating (many similar things) as one unit (*block booking*). □ **block and tackle** a system of pulleys and ropes, esp. for lifting. **block capitals** (or **letters**) letters printed without serifs, or written with each letter separate and in capitals. **block diagram** a diagram showing the general arrangement of parts of an apparatus. **block in 1** sketch roughly; plan. **2** confine. **block mountain** *Geol.* a mountain formed by natural faults. **block out 1 a** shut out (light, noise, etc.). **b** exclude from memory, as being too painful. **2** sketch roughly; plan. **block-ship** *Naut.* a ship used to block a channel. **block system** a system by which no railway train may enter a section that is not clear. **block tin** refined tin cast in ingots. **block up 1** confine; shut (a person etc.) in. **2** infill (a window, doorway, etc.) with bricks etc. **block vote** a vote proportional in power to the number of people a delegate represents. **mental** (or **psychological**) **block** a particular mental inability due to subconscious emotional factors. **on the block** *US* being auctioned. **put the blocks on** prevent from proceeding. □□ **blocker** *n.* [ME f. OF *bloc, bloquer* f. MDu. *blok*, of unkn. orig.]

■ *n.* **1** piece, chunk, hunk, lump, slab; stump; brick, cube. **2** plinth. **3 a** tenement, apartment house. **4** bar, obstacle, obstruction, hindrance, stumbling-block, deterrent, impediment, barrier, blockage. **7** (*blocks*) *Brit.* bricks. **10** head, *archaic joc.* costard, *archaic sl.* crumpet, *colloq.* noddle, *sl.* loaf, nut, dome, noodle, noggin, *Brit. sl.* bonce, chump, *US sl.* bean. ● *v.* **1 a** obstruct, clog, close off, barricade; bar, shut off; stuff (up), congest, bung up. **b** hinder, hamper, balk, impede, prevent, thwart. □ **block out 1 a** shut out, mask, screen, blank (out), erase, eliminate, exclude, blot out. **b** deny, repress, suppress. **2** rough out, design, outline, sketch, lay out, plan. **block up 1** lock up, imprison, confine, shut in. **2** stuff (up), congest, clog, bung up; infill, fill in, close up, brick up.

blockade /blokáyd/ *n.* & *v.* ● *n.* **1** the surrounding or blocking of a place, esp. a port, by an enemy to prevent entry and exit of supplies etc. **2** anything that prevents access or progress. **3** *US* an obstruction by snow etc. ● *v. tr.* **1** subject to a blockade. **2** obstruct (a passage, a view, etc.). □ **blockade-runner 1** a vessel which runs or attempts to run into a blockaded port. **2** the owner, master, or one of the crew of such a vessel. **run a blockade** enter or leave a blockaded port by evading the blockading force. □□ **blockader** *n.* [BLOCK + -ADE[1], prob. after *ambuscade*]

blockage /blókkij/ *n.* **1** an obstruction. **2** a blocked state.

■ **1** see JAM[1] *n.* 4.

blockboard /blókbord/ *n.* a plywood board with a core of wooden strips.

blockbuster /blókbustər/ *n. sl.* **1** something of great power or size, esp. an epic film or a book. **2** a huge bomb capable of destroying a whole block of buildings.

blockhead /blók-hed/ *n.* a stupid person. □□ **blockheaded** *adj.*

■ see CLOD 2. □□ **blockheaded** see FOOLISH.

blockhouse /blók-howss/ *n.* **1** a reinforced concrete shelter used as an observation point etc. **2** *hist.* a one-storeyed timber building with loopholes, used as a fort. **3** a house made of squared logs.

blockish /blókkish/ *adj.* **1** resembling a block. **2** excessively dull; stupid, obtuse. **3** clumsy, rude, roughly hewn. □□ **blockishly** *adv.* **blockishness** *n.*

■ **2** see SLOW *adj.* 5.

bloke /blōk/ *n. Brit. sl.* a man, a fellow. [Shelta]

■ see MAN *n.* 1.

blond /blond/ *adj.* & *n.* ● *adj.* **1** (of hair) light-coloured; fair. **2** (of the complexion, esp. as an indication of race) light-coloured. ● *n.* a person, esp. a man, with fair hair and skin. □□ **blondish** *adj.* **blondness** *n.* [ME f. F f. med.L *blondus, blundus* yellow, perh. of Gmc orig.]

■ *adj.* **1** see FAIR[1] *adj.* 2.

blonde /blond/ *adj.* & *n.* ● *adj.* (of a woman or a woman's hair) blond. ● *n.* a blond-haired woman. [F fem. of *blond*; see BLOND]

■ *adj.* see FAIR[1] *adj.* 2.

blood /blud/ *n.* & *v.* ● *n.* **1** a liquid, usually red and circulating in the arteries and veins of vertebrates, that carries oxygen to and carbon dioxide from the tissues of the body. **2** a corresponding fluid in invertebrates. **3** bloodshed, esp. killing. **4** passion, temperament. **5** race, descent, parentage (*of the same blood*). **6** a relationship; relations (*own flesh and blood; blood is thicker than water*). **7** a dandy; a man of fashion. ● *v.tr.* **1** give (a hound) a first taste of blood. **2** initiate (a person) by experience. □ **bad blood** ill feeling. **blood-and-thunder** (*attrib.*) *colloq.* sensational, melodramatic. **blood bank** a place where supplies of blood or plasma for transfusion are stored. **blood bath** a massacre. **blood-brother** a brother by birth or by the ceremonial mingling of blood. **blood count 1** the counting of the number of corpuscles in a specific amount of blood. **2** the number itself. **blood-curdling** horrifying. **blood donor** a person who gives blood for transfusion. **blood feud** a feud between families involving killing or injury. **blood group** any one of the various types of human blood determining compatibility in transfusion. **blood-heat** the normal body temperature of a healthy human being, about 37 °C or 98.4 °F. **blood horse** a thoroughbred. **one's blood is up** one is in a fighting mood. **blood-letting 1** the surgical removal of some of a patient's blood. **2** *joc.* bloodshed. **blood-lust** the desire for shedding blood. **blood-money 1** money paid to the next of kin of a person who has been killed. **2** money paid to a hired murderer. **3** money paid for information about a murder or murderer. **blood orange** an orange with red or red-streaked pulp. **blood-poisoning** a diseased state caused by the presence of micro-organisms in the blood. **blood pressure** the pressure of the blood in the circulatory system, often measured for diagnosis since it is closely related to the force and rate of the heartbeat and the diameter and elasticity of the arterial walls. **blood-red** red as blood. **blood relation** (or **relative**) a relative by blood, not by marriage. **blood royal** the royal family. **blood serum** see SERUM. **blood sport** sport involving the wounding or killing of animals, esp. hunting. **blood sugar** the amount of glucose in the blood. **blood test** a scientific examination of blood, esp. for diagnosis. **blood transfusion** the injection of a volume of blood, previously taken from a healthy person, into a patient. **blood-vessel** a vein, artery, or capillary carrying blood. **blood-wort** any of various plants having red roots or leaves, esp. the red-veined dock. **first blood 1** the first shedding of blood, esp. in boxing. **2** the first point gained in a contest etc. **in one's blood** inherent in one's character. **make a person's blood boil** infuriate. **make a person's blood run cold** horrify. **new** (or **fresh**) **blood** new members admitted to a group, esp. as an invigorating force. **of the blood** royal. **out for a person's blood** set on getting revenge. **taste blood** be stimulated by an early success. **young blood 1** a younger member or members of a group. **2** a rake or fashionable young man. [OE *blōd* f. Gmc]

■ *n.* **3** see GORE[1]. **5** see RACE[2] 7. **6** see *one's own flesh and blood* (FLESH). **7** see DANDY *n.* □ **blood-and-thunder** see *melodramatic* (MELODRAMA). **blood bath** see MASSACRE *n.* 1. **blood-curdling** see HORRIBLE 1. **blood-letting 2** see BLOODSHED. **blood-vessel** vein, *Anat.* venule.

blooded /blúddid/ *adj.* **1** (of horses etc.) of good pedigree. **2** (in *comb.*) having blood or a disposition of a specified kind (*cold-blooded; red-blooded*).

bloodhound /blúdhownd/ *n.* **1** a large hound of a breed used in tracking and having a very keen sense of smell. **2** this breed.

bloodless /blúdliss/ *adj.* **1** without blood. **2** unemotional; cold. **3** pale. **4** without bloodshed (*a bloodless coup*). **5** feeble; lifeless. □□ **bloodlessly** *adv.* **bloodlessness** *n.*

■ **3** see PALE[1] *adj.* 1, 4.

bloodline /blúdlīn/ *n.* a line of descent; pedigree, descent.

bloodshed /blúdshed/ *n.* **1** the spilling of blood. **2** slaughter.

■ **2** slaughter, carnage, butchery, killing, murder, *joc.* blood-letting; violence; genocide.

bloodshot /blúdshot/ *adj.* (of an eyeball) inflamed, tinged with blood.

bloodstain /blúdstayn/ *n.* a discoloration caused by blood.

bloodstained /blúdstaynd/ *adj.* **1** stained with blood. **2** guilty of bloodshed.

bloodstock /blúdstok/ *n.* thoroughbred horses.

bloodstone /blúdstōn/ *n.* a type of green chalcedony spotted or streaked with red, often used as a gemstone.

bloodstream /blúdstreem/ *n.* blood in circulation.

bloodsucker /blúdsukkər/ *n.* **1** an animal or insect that sucks blood, esp. a leech. **2** an extortioner. **3** a person who lives off others; a parasite. □□ **bloodsucking** *adj.*

■ **2, 3** leech, extortionist, extortioner, blackmailer; parasite, barnacle, sponge(r), scrounger, *esp. US colloq.* moocher, *US sl.* freeloader.

bloodthirsty /blúdthursti/ *adj.* (**bloodthirstier, bloodthirstiest**) eager for bloodshed. □□ **bloodthirstily** *adv.* **bloodthirstiness** *n.*

■ murderous, slaughterous, homicidal, savage, feral, cruel, ruthless, pitiless, vicious, brutal, sadistic, ferocious, fierce, sanguinary, *poet. or rhet.* fell.

bloodworm /blúdwurm/ *n.* **1** any of a variety of bright-red midge-larvae. **2** a small tubifex worm used as food for aquarium fish.

bloody /blúddi/ *adj., adv., & v.* ● *adj.* (**bloodier, bloodiest**) **1 a** of or like blood. **b** running or smeared with blood (*bloody bandage*). **2 a** involving, loving, or resulting from bloodshed (*bloody battle*). **b** sanguinary; cruel (*bloody butcher*). **3** *coarse sl.* expressing annoyance or antipathy, or as an intensive (*a bloody shame; a bloody sight better; not a bloody chocolate left*). **4** red. ● *adv. coarse sl.* as an intensive (*a bloody good job; I'll bloody thump him*). ● *v.tr.* (**-ies, -ied**) make bloody; stain with blood. □ **bloody hand** *Heraldry* the armorial device of a baronet. **Bloody Mary** a drink composed of vodka and tomato juice. **bloody-minded** *colloq.* deliberately uncooperative. **bloody-mindedly** *colloq.* in a perverse or uncooperative manner. **bloody-mindedness** *colloq.* perversity, contrariness. □□ **bloodily** *adv.* **bloodiness** *n.* [OE *blōdig* (as BLOOD, -Y[1])]

■ *adj.* **2 a** see GORY. **b** see MURDEROUS 1. □ **bloody-minded** see DIFFICULT 2. **bloody-mindedness** see *obstinacy* (OBSTINATE).

bloom[1] /bloom/ *n. & v.* ● *n.* **1 a** a flower, esp. one cultivated for its beauty. **b** the state of flowering (*in bloom*). **2** a state of perfection or loveliness; the prime (*in full bloom*). **3 a** (of the complexion) a flush; a glow. **b** a delicate powdery surface deposit on plums, grapes, leaves, etc., indicating freshness. **c** a cloudiness on a shiny surface. ● *v.* **1** *intr.* bear flowers; be in flower. **2** *intr.* **a** come into, or remain in, full beauty. **b** flourish; be in a healthy, vigorous state. **3** *tr. Photog.* coat (a lens) so as to reduce reflection from its surface. □ **take the bloom off** make stale. **water-bloom** scum formed by algae on the surface of standing water. [ME f. ON *blóm, blómi* etc. f. Gmc: cf. BLOSSOM]

■ *n.* **1 a** see FLOWER *n.* **3 a** see FLUSH[1] *n.* 1. ● *v.* **1** see FLOWER *v.* 1. **2 b** see THRIVE 3.

bloom[2] /bloom/ *n. & v.* ● *n.* a mass of puddled iron hammered or squeezed into a thick bar. ● *v.tr.* make into bloom. [OE *blōma*]

bloomer[1] /bloomər/ *n. sl.* a blunder. [= BLOOMING *error*]

■ see ERROR 1.

bloomer[2] /bloomər/ *n. Brit.* an oblong loaf with a rounded diagonally slashed top. [20th c.: orig. uncert.]

bloomer[3] /bloomər/ *n.* a plant that blooms (in a specified way) (*early autumn bloomer*).

bloomers /bloomərz/ *n.pl.* **1** women's loose-fitting almost knee-length knickers. **2** *colloq.* any women's knickers. **3** *hist.* women's loose-fitting trousers, gathered at the knee or (orig.) the ankle. [Mrs A. *Bloomer*, Amer. social reformer d. 1894, who advocated a similar costume]

■ **1, 2** see PANTS 1. **3** see TROUSERS 1.

bloomery /bloomәri/ *n.* (*pl.* **-ies**) a factory that makes puddled iron into blooms.

blooming /blooming/ *adj. & adv.* ● *adj.* **1** flourishing; healthy. **2** *Brit. sl.* an intensive (*a blooming miracle*). ● *adv. Brit. sl.* an intensive (*was blooming difficult*). [BLOOM[1] + -ING[2]: euphem. for BLOODY]

■ *adj.* **1** see SOUND[2] *adj.* 1. **2** see FLAMING 3b.

Bloomsbury /bloomzbəri, -bri/ *n. & adj.* ● *n.* (in full **Bloomsbury Group**) a group of writers, artists, and philosophers living in or associated with Bloomsbury in London in the early 20th c. ● *adj.* **1** associated with or similar to the Bloomsbury Group. **2** intellectual; highbrow.

blooper /bloopər/ *n.* esp. *US colloq.* an embarrassing error. [imit. *bloop* + -ER[1]]

■ see MISTAKE *n.*

blossom /blóssəm/ *n. & v.* ● *n.* **1** a flower or a mass of flowers, esp. of a fruit-tree. **2** the stage or time of flowering (*the cherry tree in blossom*). **3** a promising stage (*the blossom of youth*). ● *v.intr.* **1** open into flower. **2** reach a promising stage; mature, thrive. □□ **blossomy** *adj.* [OE *blōstm(a)* prob. formed as BLOOM[1]]

■ *n.* **1** see FLOWER *n.* ● *v.* **1** see FLOWER *v.* 1.

blot /blot/ *n. & v.* ● *n.* **1** a spot or stain of ink etc. **2** a moral defect in an otherwise good character; a disgraceful act or quality. **3** any disfigurement or blemish. ● *v.* (**blotted, blotting**) **1 a** *tr.* spot or stain with ink; smudge. **b** *intr.* (of a pen, ink, etc.) make blots. **2** *tr.* **a** use blotting-paper or other absorbent material to absorb excess ink. **b** (of blotting-paper etc.) soak up (esp. ink). **3** *tr.* disgrace (*blotted his reputation*). □ **blot one's copybook** damage one's reputation. **blot on the escutcheon** a disgrace to the family name. **blot out 1 a** obliterate (writing). **b** obscure (a view, sound, etc.). **2** obliterate (from the memory) as too painful. **3** destroy. **blotting-paper** unglazed absorbent paper used for soaking up excess ink. [ME prob. f. Scand.: cf. Icel. *blettr* spot, stain]

■ *n.* **1** stain, spot, mark, smudge, blotch, discoloration, *colloq.* splodge, splotch. **2, 3** blemish, smear, smirch, scar, taint, flaw, fault, imperfection, black mark, failing, weakness. ● *v.* **1 a** stain, spot, spatter, smudge, mark, blur. **3** spoil, discredit, dishonour, disgrace, shame. □ **blot one's copybook** err, destroy *or* ruin *or* mar *or* spoil one's reputation, commit an indiscretion, transgress, sin, disgrace oneself, discredit oneself, shame oneself. **blot out 1a, 2** obscure, conceal, cover (up), hide, eclipse, dim, cloud, block out; obliterate, erase, efface, annihilate, delete, rub *or* wipe out, block out, expunge, eradicate, eliminate.

blotch /bloch/ *n. & v.* ● *n.* **1** a discoloured or inflamed patch on the skin. **2** an irregular patch of ink or colour. ● *v.tr.* cover with blotches. □□ **blotchy** *adj.* (**blotchier, blotchiest**). [17th c.: f. obs. *plotch* and BLOT]

■ *n.* see SPOT *n.* 1a, b. ● *v.* see STAIN *v.* 1.

blotter /blóttər/ *n.* **1** a sheet or sheets of blotting-paper, usu. inserted into a frame. **2** *US* a temporary recording-book, esp. a police charge-sheet.

blotto /blóttō/ *adj. sl.* very drunk, esp. unconscious from drinking. [20th c.: perh. f. BLOT]

■ see DRUNK *adj.* 1.

blouse /blowz/ *n. & v.* ● *n.* **1 a** a woman's loose, usu. lightweight, upper garment, usu. buttoned and collared. **b** the upper part of a soldier's or airman's battledress. **2** a workman's or peasant's loose linen or cotton garment, usu. belted at the waist. ● *v.tr.* make (a bodice etc.) loose like a blouse. [F, of unkn. orig.]

blouson /bloozon/ *n.* a short blouse-shaped jacket. [F]

blow[1] /blō/ *v. & n.* ● *v.* (*past* **blew** /bloo/; *past part.* **blown** /blōn/) **1 a** *intr.* (of the wind or air, or impersonally) move along; act as an air-current (*it was blowing hard*). **b** *intr.* be driven by an air-current (*waste paper blew along the gutter*). **c** *tr.* drive with an air-current (*blew the door open*). **2 a** *tr.* send out (esp. air) by breathing (*blew cigarette smoke; blew a bubble*). **b** *intr.* send a directed air-current from the mouth. **3** *tr. & intr.* sound or be sounded by blowing (*the whistle blew; they blew the trumpets*). **4** *tr.* **a** direct an air-current at (*blew the embers*). **b** (foll. by *off, away,* etc.) clear of by means of an air-current (*blew the dust off*). **5** *tr.* (*past part.* **blowed**) *sl.* (esp. in *imper.*) curse, confound (*blow it!; I'll be blowed!; let's take a taxi and blow the expense*). **6** *tr.* **a** clear (the nose) of mucus by blowing. **b** remove contents from (an egg) by blowing through it. **7 a** *intr.* puff, pant. **b** *tr.* (esp. in *passive*) exhaust of breath. **8** *sl.* **a** *tr.* depart suddenly from (*blew the town yesterday*). **b** *intr.* depart suddenly. **9** *tr.* shatter or send flying by an explosion (*the bomb blew the tiles off the roof; blew them to smithereens*). **10** *tr.* make or shape (glass or a bubble) by blowing air in. **11** *tr. & intr.* melt or cause to melt from overloading (*the fuse has blown*). **12** *intr.* (of a whale) eject air and water through a blow-hole.

13 *tr.* break into (a safe etc.) with explosives. **14** *tr. sl.* **a** squander, spend recklessly (*blew £20 on a meal*). **b** spoil, bungle (an opportunity etc.) (*he's blown his chances of winning*). **c** reveal (a secret etc.). **15** *intr.* (of a food-tin etc.) swell and eventually burst from internal gas pressure. **16** *tr.* work the bellows of (an organ). **17** *tr.* (of flies) deposit eggs in. **18** *intr. US* & *Austral. colloq.* boast. ● *n.* **1 a** an act of blowing (e.g. one's nose, a wind instrument). **b** *colloq.* a turn or spell of playing jazz (on any instrument); a musical session. **2 a** a gust of wind or air. **b** exposure to fresh air. **3** = *fly-blow* (see FLY[2]). **4** *US* a boaster. □ **be blowed if one will** *sl.* be unwilling to. **blow-ball** the globular seed-head of a dandelion etc. **blow-dry** arrange (the hair) while drying it with a hand-held drier. **blow-drier** (or **-dryer**) a drier used for this. **blow the gaff** reveal a secret inadvertently. **blow-hole 1** the nostril of a whale, on the top of its head. **2** a hole (esp. in ice) for breathing or fishing through. **3** a vent for air, smoke, etc., in a tunnel etc. **blow hot and cold** *colloq.* vacillate. **blow in 1** break inwards by an explosion. **2** *colloq.* arrive unexpectedly. **blow-job** *coarse sl.* fellatio; cunnilingus. **blow a kiss** kiss one's hand and wave it to a distant person. **blow a person's mind** *sl.* cause a person to have drug-induced hallucinations or a similar experience. **blow off 1** escape or allow (steam etc.) to escape forcibly. **2** *sl.* break wind noisily. **blow on** (or **upon**) make stale; discredit. **blow out 1 a** extinguish by blowing. **b** send outwards by an explosion. **2** (of a tyre) burst. **3** (of a fuse etc.) melt. **blow-out** *n. colloq.* **1** a burst tyre. **2** a melted fuse. **3** a huge meal. **blow over** (of trouble etc.) fade away without serious consequences. **blow one's own trumpet** praise oneself. **blow one's top** (*US* **stack**) *colloq.* explode in rage. **blow up 1 a** shatter or destroy by an explosion. **b** explode, erupt. **2** *colloq.* rebuke strongly. **3** inflate (a tyre etc.). **4** *colloq.* **a** enlarge (a photograph). **b** exaggerate. **5** *colloq.* come to notice; arise. **6** *colloq.* lose one's temper. **blow-up** *n.* **1** *colloq.* an enlargement (of a photograph etc.). **2** an explosion. **blow the whistle on** see WHISTLE. [OE *blāwan* f. Gmc]

■ *v.* **1 a, b** waft, puff, whistle, whine, blast. **2** breathe, puff, exhale; expel. **7a** see PUFF *v.* 4. **8 b** see ESCAPE *v.* 1. **9** blast, shatter. **11** short-circuit, burn out. **14 a** spend, lavish, squander, waste, throw away, *sl.* blue. **b** bungle, botch, mess up, make a mess of, muff, spoil, wreck, mismanage, *Brit. colloq.* muck up, fluff, *sl.* louse up, goof (up), screw up. **c** see REVEAL 2. ● *n.* **1 a** exhalation, breath, expiration. **2 a** breeze, gust, wind, blast, puff, gale, storm, tempest, whirlwind, tornado, cyclone, hurricane, typhoon. □ **blow hot and cold** vacillate, be inconsistent, be fickle, shilly-shally. **blow out 1 a** extinguish, snuff (out), smother, put out. **b** explode, burst, blast. **3** short-circuit, burn out. **blow one's top** (or *US* **stack**) become angry, become furious *or* infuriated, rage, rant, lose one's temper, *sl.* blow *or* lose one's cool, get hot under the collar. **blow up 1 a** puncture, rupture, shatter, *colloq.* bust; dynamite, destroy, blast. **b** fly apart, go off, explode, burst; erupt. **3** inflate, dilate, pump up, puff up. **4 a** enlarge, magnify. **b** amplify, expand, exaggerate, inflate, overstate. **6** become furious *or* angry *or* enraged, flare up, lose one's temper, *colloq.* lose one's cool, blow one's top, *US colloq.* blow one's stack, *Austral.* & *NZ colloq.* go crook, *sl.* blow a gasket, flip one's lid.

blow[2] /blō/ *n.* **1** a hard stroke with a hand or weapon. **2** a sudden shock or misfortune. □ **at one blow** by a single stroke; in one operation. **blow-by-blow** (of a description etc.) giving all the details in sequence. **come to blows** end up fighting. **strike a blow for** (or **against**) help (or oppose). [15th c.: orig. unkn.]

■ **1** cuff, rap, smack, stroke, punch, clout, hit, knock, thump, *colloq.* whack, thwack, *esp. US colloq.* bust, *sl.* wallop, belt. **2** shock, surprise, bombshell, jolt, bolt from the blue, revelation, set-back, disappointment, frustration, let-down.

blow[3] /blō/ *v.* & *n. archaic* ● *v.intr.* (*past* **blew** /bloo͞/; *past part.* **blown** /blōn/) burst into or be in flower. ● *n.* blossoming, bloom (*in full blow*). [OE *blōwan* f. Gmc]

blower /blṓər/ *n.* **1** in senses of BLOW[1] *v.* **2** a device for creating a current of air. **3** *colloq.* a telephone.

■ **3** see TELEPHONE *n.*

blowfish /blṓfish/ *n.* any of several kinds of fish able to inflate their bodies when frightened etc.

blowfly /blṓflī/ *n.* (*pl.* **-flies**) a meat-fly, a bluebottle.

blowgun /blṓgun/ *n. US* = BLOWPIPE.

blowhard /blṓhaard/ *n.* & *adj. colloq.* ● *n.* a boastful person. ● *adj.* boastful; blustering.

■ *n.* see *show-off* (SHOW).

blowlamp /blṓlamp/ *n.* a portable device with a very hot flame used for burning off paint, soldering, etc.

blown *past part.* of BLOW[1], BLOW[3].

blowpipe /blṓpīp/ *n.* **1** a tube used esp. by primitive peoples for propelling arrows or darts by blowing. **2** a tube used to intensify the heat of a flame by blowing air or other gas through it at high pressure. **3** a tube used in glass-blowing.

blowtorch /blṓtorch/ *n. US* = BLOWLAMP.

blowy /blṓ-i/ *adj.* (**blowier**, **blowiest**) windy, windswept. □□ **blowiness** *n.*

■ see WINDY 1.

blowzy /bló̈wzi/ *adj.* (**blowzier**, **blowziest**) **1** coarse-looking; red-faced. **2** dishevelled, slovenly. □□ **blowzily** *adv.* **blowziness** *n.* [obs. *blowze* beggar's wench, of unkn. orig.]

■ **2** see UNKEMPT.

blub /blub/ *v.intr.* (**blubbed**, **blubbing**) *sl.* sob. [abbr. of BLUBBER[1]]

■ see WEEP *v.* 1, 2.

blubber[1] /blúbbər/ *n.* & *v.* ● *n.* **1** whale fat. **2** a spell of weeping. ● *v.* **1** *intr.* sob loudly. **2** *tr.* sob out (words). □□ **blubberer** *n.* **blubberingly** *adv.* **blubbery** *adj.* [ME perh. imit. (obs. meanings 'foaming, bubble')]

■ *v.* see SOB *v.*

blubber[2] /blúbbər/ *adj.* (of the lips) swollen, protruding. [earlier *blabber*, *blobber*, imit.]

bluchers /bloo͝kərz/ *n.pl. hist.* strong leather half-boots or high shoes. [G. L. von *Blücher*, Prussian general d. 1819]

bludge /bluj/ *v.* & *n. Austral.* & *NZ sl.* ● *v.intr.* avoid work. ● *n.* an easy job or assignment. □ **bludge on** impose on. [back-form. f. BLUDGER]

■ *v.* see TRUANT *v.* ● *n.* see BREEZE[1] *n.* 5.

bludgeon /blújən/ *n.* & *v.* ● *n.* a club with a heavy end. ● *v.tr.* **1** beat with a bludgeon. **2** coerce. [18th c.: orig. unkn.]

■ *n.* see CLUB *n.* 1. ● *v.* **1** see BEAT *v.* 1.

bludger /blújər/ *n. Austral.* & *NZ sl.* **1** a hanger-on. **2** a loafer. [orig. E sl., = pimp, f. obs. *bludgeoner* f. BLUDGEON]

blue[1] /bloo͞/ *adj.*, *n.*, & *v.* ● *adj.* **1** having a colour like that of a clear sky. **2** sad, depressed; (of a state of affairs) gloomy, dismal (*feel blue*; *blue times*). **3** indecent, pornographic (*a blue film*). **4** with bluish skin through cold, fear, anger, etc. **5** *Brit.* politically conservative. **6** having blue as a distinguishing colour (*blue jay*). ● *n.* **1** a blue colour or pigment. **2** blue clothes or material (*dressed in blue*). **3** *Brit.* **a** a person who has represented a university in a sport, esp. Oxford or Cambridge. **b** this distinction. **4** *Brit.* a supporter of the Conservative party. **5** any of various small blue-coloured butterflies of the family Lycaenidae. **6** blue powder used to whiten laundry. **7** *Austral. sl.* **a** an argument or row. **b** (as a nickname) a red-headed person. **8** a blue ball, piece, etc. in a game or sport. **9** (prec. by *the*) the clear sky. ● *v.tr.* (**blues**, **blued**, **bluing** or **blueing**) **1** make blue. **2** treat with laundering blue. □ **blue baby** a baby with a blue complexion from lack of oxygen in the blood due to a congenital defect of the heart or great vessels. **blue bag** a lawyer's brief-bag. **blue blood** noble birth. **blue-blooded** of noble birth. **Blue Book** a report issued by Parliament or the Privy Council. **blue cheese** cheese produced with veins of blue mould, e.g. Stilton and Danish Blue. **blue-chip** (*attrib.*) of shares of reliable investment, though less secure than gilt-edged stock. **blue-collar** (*attrib.*) of manual or unskilled work. **blue dahlia** something rare or impossible. **blue ensign** see ENSIGN. **blue-eyed boy** esp. *Brit. colloq.* usu. *derog.* a favoured person; a favourite. **blue funk** *sl.* a state of great terror or panic. **blue-green alga** = CYANOBACTERIUM. **blue ground** = KIMBERLITE. **blue in the face** in a state of extreme anger or exasperation. **blue metal** broken blue stone used for road-making. **blue mould** a bluish fungus growing on food and other organic matter. **blue-pencil** (**-pencilled, -pencilling;** *US* **-penciled, -penciling**) censor or make cuts in (a manuscript, film, etc.). **Blue Peter** a blue flag with a white square raised on board a ship leaving port. **blue ribbon 1** a high honour. **2** *Brit.* the ribbon of the Order of the Garter. **blue rinse** a preparation for tinting grey hair. **blue roan** see ROAN[1]. **blue rock** = *rock-dove* (see ROCK[1]). **blue stone** (or **vitriol**) copper sulphate crystals. **blue tit** a common tit, *Parus caeruleus*, with a distinct blue crest on a black and white head. **blue water** open sea. **blue whale** a rorqual, *Balaenoptera musculus*, the largest known living mammal. **once in a blue moon** very rarely. **out of the blue** unexpectedly. ▫▫ **blueness** *n.* [ME f. OF *bleu* f. Gmc]

■ *adj.* **1** azure, sapphire, aquamarine, turquoise, ultramarine, lapis lazuli, navy, indigo, cyan, hyacinth, lavender, cobalt, saxe, teal, Wedgewood. **2** depressed, low-spirited, dispirited, sad, dismal, gloomy, unhappy, glum, downcast, crestfallen, chap-fallen, dejected, melancholy, despondent, downhearted, morose, *colloq.* down in the mouth. **3** obscene, vulgar, indecent, pornographic, dirty, filthy, lewd, smutty, risqué, bawdy, sexy, X(-rated), 18, *euphem.* adult; indelicate, suggestive, erotic, coarse, offensive, improper, *US* off colour. **5** conservative, right-wing, rightist, Tory, reactionary.

blue[2] /bloo/ *v.tr.* (**blues, blued, bluing** or **blueing**) *sl.* squander (money). [perh. var. of BLOW[1]]

■ see BLOW[1] *v.* 14a.

Bluebeard /bloobeerd/ *n.* **1** a man who murders his wives. **2** a person with a horrible secret. [a character in a fairy-tale told orig. in F (*Barbe-Bleue*) by Perrault]

bluebell /loobel/ *n.* **1** a liliaceous plant, *Hyacinthoides nonscripta*, with clusters of bell-shaped blue flowers on a stem arising from a rhizome. Also called *wild hyacinth, wood hyacinth* (see HYACINTH). **2** *Sc.* a plant, *Campanula rotundifolia*, with solitary bell-shaped blue flowers on long stalks. Also called HAREBELL. **3** any of several plants with blue bell-shaped flowers.

blueberry /bloobəri/ *n.* (*pl.* **-ies**) **1** any of several plants of the genus *Vaccinium*, cultivated for their edible fruit. **2** the small blue-black fruit of these plants.

bluebird /blooburd/ *n.* any of various N. American songbirds of the thrush family, esp. of the genus *Sialia*, with distinctive blue plumage usu. on the back or head.

bluebottle /eloobott'l/ *n.* **1** a large buzzing fly, *Calliphora vomitoria*, with a metallic-blue body. Also called BLOWFLY. **2** *Austral.* a Portuguese man-of-war. **3** a dark blue cornflower. **4** *Brit. colloq.* a policeman.

bluefish /bloofish/ *n.* a voracious marine fish, *Pomatomus saltatrix*, inhabiting tropical waters and popular as a game-fish.

bluegrass /bloograass/ *n. US* **1** any of several bluish-green grasses, esp. of Kentucky. **2** a kind of instrumental country-and-western music characterized by virtuosic playing of banjos, guitars, etc.

bluegum /bloogum/ *n.* any tree of the genus *Eucalyptus*, esp. *E. regnans* with blue-green aromatic leaves.

bluejacket /bloojakkit/ *n.* a seaman in the Navy.

■ see SAILOR.

Bluemantle /bloomant'l/ *n.* one of four pursuivants of the English College of Arms.

blueprint /blooprint/ *n.* & *v.* ● *n.* **1** a photographic print of the final stage of engineering or other plans in white on a blue background. **2** a detailed plan, esp. in the early stages of a project or idea. ● *v.tr.* *US* work out (a programme, plan, etc.).

■ *n.* see PLAN *n.* 4.

blues /blooz/ *n.pl.* **1** (prec. by *the*) a bout of depression (*had a fit of the blues*). **2 a** (prec. by *the*; often treated as *sing.*) melancholic music of Black American folk origin, often in a twelve-bar sequence (*always singing the blues*). **b** (*pl.* same) (as *sing.*) a piece of such music (*the band played a blues*). ▫▫ **bluesy** *adj.* (in sense 2).

bluestocking /bloostokking/ *n.* usu. *derog.* an intellectual or literary woman. [from the (less formal) blue stockings worn by one man at a literary society meeting *c.*1750]

■ see ACADEMIC *n.*

bluet /bloo-it/ *n. US* a blue-flowered plant of the genus *Houstonia*.

bluey /bloo-i/ *n.* (*pl.* **-eys**) *Austral. colloq.* **1** a bundle carried by a bushman. **2** = BLUE[1] *n.* 7b.

bluff[1] /bluf/ *v.* & *n.* ● *v.* **1** *intr.* make a pretence of strength or confidence to gain an advantage. **2** *tr.* mislead by bluffing. ● *n.* an act of bluffing; a show of confidence or assertiveness intended to deceive. ▫ **call a person's bluff** challenge a person thought to be bluffing. ▫▫ **bluffer** *n.* [19th c. (orig. in poker) f. Du. *bluffen* brag]

■ *v.* **1** pretend, fake, feign, bluster, boast, brag. **2** deceive, hoodwink, dupe, mislead, delude, trick, fool, cheat, pull the wool over a person's eyes, *colloq.* bamboozle, *literary* cozen. ● *n.* bombast, bravado, sham, boasting, bragging, bluster, show, puffery; deception, rodomontade; *sl.* hot air.

bluff[2] /bluf/ *adj.* & *n.* ● *adj.* **1** (of a cliff, or a ship's bows) having a vertical or steep broad front. **2** (of a person or manner) blunt, frank, hearty. ● *n.* a steep cliff or headland. ▫▫ **bluffly** *adv.* (in sense 2 of *adj.*). **bluffness** *n.* (in sense 2 of *adj.*). [17th-c. Naut. word: orig. unkn.]

■ *adj.* **1** steep, abrupt, sheer, perpendicular, acclivitous, precipitous. **2** blustering, gruff, rough, abrupt, blunt, curt, short, crude, frank, open, hearty, straightforward, plain, plain-spoken, outspoken; affable, approachable, good-natured, friendly. ● *n.* cliff, precipice, scarp, *Geol.* escarpment; headland, promontory, *US* palisades.

bluish /bloo-ish/ *adj.* somewhat blue.

blunder /blúndər/ *n.* & *v.* ● *n.* a clumsy or foolish mistake, esp. an important one. ● *v.* **1** *intr.* make a blunder; act clumsily or ineptly. **2** *tr.* deal incompetently with; mismanage. **3** *intr.* move about blindly or clumsily; stumble. ▫▫ **blunderer** *n.* **blunderingly** *adv.* [ME prob. f. Scand.: cf. MSw *blundra* shut the eyes]

■ *n.* mistake, error, gaffe, *faux pas*, impropriety, slip, accident, bungle, solecism, *US* bull, *colloq.* (bad) break, slip-up, howler, fluff, *esp. US colloq.* blooper, *sl.* bloomer, clanger, fluff, goof, boner, screw-up, *US sl.* clinker. ● *v.* **1** make a mess *or* mistake *or* gaffe *or faux pas*, *sl.* fluff. **2** botch, bungle, make a mess of, mess up, muff, mismanage, *Brit. colloq.* muck up, fluff, *sl.* louse up, goof (up), screw up. **3** stumble, flounder, grope about, stagger, lurch.

blunderbuss /blúndərbuss/ *n. hist.* a short large-bored gun firing balls or slugs. [alt. of Du. *donderbus* thunder gun, assoc. with BLUNDER]

blunge /blunj/ *v.tr.* (in ceramics etc.) mix (clay etc.) with water. ▫▫ **blunger** *n.* [after *plunge, blend*]

blunt /blunt/ *adj.* & *v.* ● *adj.* **1** (of a knife, pencil, etc.) lacking in sharpness; having a worn-down point or edge. **2** (of a person or manner) direct, uncompromising, outspoken. ● *v.tr.* make blunt or less sharp. ▫▫ **bluntly** *adv.* (in sense 2 of *adj.*). **bluntness** *n.* [ME perh. f. Scand.: cf. ON *blunda* shut the eyes]

■ *adj.* **1** dull, blunted, obtuse, unpointed, worn (down). **2** abrupt, curt, rough-spoken, plain-spoken, short, direct, candid, frank, unceremonious, undiplomatic, inconsiderate, thoughtless, brusque, outspoken, bluff, brash, indelicate, rude, uncivil, ungracious, discourteous, impolite; straightforward, straight, uncomplicated, uncompromising. ● *v.* dull, take the edge off, soften, mitigate, mollify, soothe.

blur /blur/ *v.* & *n.* ● *v.* (**blurred, blurring**) **1** *tr.* & *intr.* make or become unclear or less distinct. **2** *tr.* smear; partially efface. **3** *tr.* make (one's memory, perception, etc.) dim or less clear. ● *n.* something that appears or sounds indistinct or unclear. □□ **blurry** *adj.* (**blurrier, blurriest**). [16th c.: perh. rel. to BLEAR]
■ *v.* **1** obscure, hide, conceal, veil, mask; muddle, jumble, mix up, confuse, muffle, muddy. **2** smudge; smear. **3** dim, befog, obscure, cloud, becloud, *poet.* bedim. ● *n.* indistinctness, dimness, haziness, cloudiness, fogginess; cloud, mist, veil, smudge, fog, haze.

blurb /blurb/ *n.* a (usu. eulogistic) description of a book, esp. printed on its jacket, as promotion by its publishers. [coined by G. Burgess, Amer. humorist d. 1951]
■ see LITERATURE 5.

blurt /blurt/ *v.tr.* (usu. foll. by *out*) utter abruptly, thoughtlessly, or tactlessly. [prob. imit.]
■ (*blurt out*) burst out with, utter, tattle; reveal, disclose, give away, divulge, blab.

blush /blush/ *v.* & *n.* ● *v.intr.* **1 a** develop a pink tinge in the face from embarrassment or shame. **b** (of the face) redden in this way. **2** feel embarrassed or ashamed. **3** be or become red or pink. ● *n.* **1** the act of blushing. **2** a pink tinge. □ **at first blush** on the first glimpse or impression. **spare a person's blushes** refrain from causing embarrassment esp. by praise. [ME f. OE *blyscan*]
■ *v.* **1, 3** redden, flush, colour, be *or* become red-faced, burn. **2** be *or* feel shamefaced, be red-faced *or* sheepish *or* mortified.

blusher /blúshər/ *n.* a cosmetic used to give a warmth of colour to the face.

bluster /blústər/ *v.* & *n.* ● *v.intr.* **1** behave pompously and boisterously; utter empty threats. **2** (of the wind etc.) blow fiercely. ● *n.* **1** noisily self-assertive talk. **2** empty threats. □□ **blusterer** *n.* **blustery** *adj.* [16th c.: ult. imit.]
■ *v.* **1** swagger, strut, boast, brag, blow one's own trumpet, show off, *colloq.* talk big. **2** storm, rage. ● *n.* **1** swagger, rhetoric, bombast, puffery, bravado, grandiloquence, rodomontade, *sl.* hot air.

BM *abbr.* **1** British Museum. **2** Bachelor of Medicine.

BMA *abbr.* British Medical Association.

B.Mus. *abbr.* Bachelor of Music.

BMX /beé-eméks/ *n.* **1** organized bicycle-racing on a dirt-track, esp. for youngsters. **2** a kind of bicycle used for this. **3** (*attrib.*) of or related to such racing or the equipment used (*BMX gloves*). [abbr. of *bicycle moto-cross*]

Bn. *abbr.* Battalion.

bn. *abbr.* billion.

BO *abbr. colloq.* body odour.

bo[1] /bō/ *int.* = BOO. [imit.]

bo[2] /bō/ *n. US colloq.* (as a form of address) pal; old chap. [19th c.: perh. f. BOY]

boa /bṓə/ *n.* **1** any large non-poisonous snake from tropical America esp. of the genus *Boa*, which kills its prey by crushing and suffocating it in its coils. **2** any snake which is similar in appearance, such as Old World pythons. **3** a long thin stole made of feathers or fur. □ **boa constrictor** a large snake, *Boa constrictor*, native to tropical America and the West Indies, which crushes its prey. [L]
■ **3** see STOLE[1].

boar /bor/ *n.* **1** (in full **wild boar**) the tusked wild pig, *Sus scrofa*, from which domestic pigs are descended. **2** an uncastrated male pig. **3** its flesh. **4** a male guinea-pig etc. [OE *bār* f. WG]

board /bord/ *n.* & *v.* ● *n.* **1 a** a flat thin piece of sawn timber, usu. long and narrow. **b** a piece of material resembling this, made from compressed fibres. **c** a thin slab of wood or a similar substance, often with a covering, used for any of various purposes (*chessboard*; *ironing-board*; *notice-board*). **d** thick stiff card used in bookbinding. **2** the provision of regular meals, usu. with accommodation, for payment. **3** *archaic* a table spread for a meal. **4** the directors of a company; any other specially constituted administrative body, e.g. a committee or group of councillors, examiners, etc. **5** (in *pl.*) the stage of a theatre (cf. *tread the boards*). **6** *Naut.* the side of a ship. ● *v.* **1** *tr.* **a** go on board (a ship, train, aircraft, etc.). **b** force one's way on board (a ship etc.) in attack. **2 a** *intr.* receive regular meals, or (esp. of a schoolchild) meals and lodging, for payment. **b** *tr.* (often foll. by *out*) arrange accommodation away from home for (esp. a child). **c** *tr.* provide (a lodger etc.) with regular meals. **3** *tr.* (usu. foll. by *up*) cover with boards; seal or close. □ **board-game** a game played on a board. **board of trade** *US* a chamber of commerce. **go by the board** be neglected, omitted, or discarded. **on board** on or on to a ship, aircraft, oil rig, etc. **take on board** consider (a new idea etc.). [OE *bord* f. Gmc]
■ *n.* **1 a** plank, timber. **2** food, meals, provisions. **4** council, committee, directors, directorship, management, cabinet, panel, trustees, advisers, delegates. ● *v.* **1 a** go aboard; enter. **2 a** eat, take meals. **b** accommodate, put up, lodge, house, quarter, *Mil.* billet. **3** see SEAL *v.* 1. □ **go by the board** see STOP *v.* 2. **on board** aboard, on; on to. **take on board** see CONSIDER 4.

boarder /bórdər/ *n.* **1** a person who boards (see BOARD *v.* 2a), esp. a pupil at a boarding-school. **2** a person who boards a ship, esp. an enemy.

boarding-house /bórding-howss/ *n.* an unlicensed establishment providing board and lodging, esp. to holiday-makers.

boarding-school /bórdingskōōl/ *n.* a school where pupils are resident in term-time.

boardroom /bórdrōōm, -rŏŏm/ *n.* a room in which a board of directors etc. meets regularly.

boardsailing /bórdsayling/ *n.* = WINDSURFING. □□ **boardsailor** *n.* (also **boardsailer**).

boardwalk /bórdwawk/ *n. US* **1** a wooden walkway across sand, marsh, etc. **2** a promenade along a beach.
■ see WALK *n.* 3a.

boart var. of BORT.

boast /bōst/ *v.* & *n.* ● *v.* **1** *intr.* declare one's achievements, possessions, or abilities with indulgent pride and satisfaction. **2** *tr.* own or have as something praiseworthy etc. (*the hotel boasts magnificent views*). ● *n.* **1** an act of boasting. **2** something one is proud of. □□ **boaster** *n.* **boastingly** *adv.* [ME f. AF *bost*, of unkn. orig.]
■ *v.* **1** brag, blow one's (own) trumpet, rodomontade, talk tall, vapour, *colloq.* talk big, show off, bounce, *Austral.* & *NZ colloq.* skite, *Austral.* & *US colloq.* blow, *literary* vaunt. **2** see PROVIDE 1. ● *n.* **1** brag, buck, fanfaronade, rodomontade, braggadocio, *literary* vaunt, *sl.* hot air. □□ **boaster** see BRAGGART *n.*

boastful /bṓstfŏŏl/ *adj.* **1** given to boasting. **2** characterized by boasting (*boastful talk*). □□ **boastfully** *adv.* **boastfulness** *n.*
■ braggart, magniloquent, grandiloquent, ostentatious, puffed up, swanky, rodomontade, bragging, egotistical, vain, pompous, conceited, *colloq.* loud-mouthed, blowhard, *literary* vainglorious.

boat /bōt/ *n.* & *v.* ● *n.* **1** a small vessel propelled on water by an engine, oars, or sails. **2** (in general use) a ship of any size. **3** an elongated boat-shaped jug used for holding sauce etc. ● *v.intr.* travel or go in a boat, esp. for pleasure. □ **boat-hook** a long pole with a hook and a spike at one end, for moving boats. **boat-house** a shed at the edge of a river, lake, etc., for housing boats. **boat people** refugees who have left a country by sea. **boat race** a race between rowing crews, esp. (**Boat Race**) the one between Oxford and Cambridge. **boat-train** a train scheduled to meet or go on a boat. **in the same boat** sharing the same adverse circumstances. **push the boat out** *colloq.* celebrate lavishly. □□ **boatful** *n.* (*pl.* **-fuls**). [OE *bāt* f. Gmc]
■ *n.* **1** vessel, craft, skiff, motor boat, speedboat, powerboat, launch, yacht, sailing-boat, yawl, *Brit.* rowing-boat, *US* row-boat, sailboat, *colloq.* ship. ● *v.* sail, go boating, cruise. □ **push the boat out** see REVEL *v.* 1.

boatel var. of BOTEL.

boater /bṓtər/ *n.* a flat-topped hardened straw hat with a brim.

boating /bṓting/ *n.* rowing or sailing in boats as a sport or form of recreation.

boatload /bṓtlōd/ *n.* **1** enough to fill a boat. **2** *colloq.* a large number of people.

boatman /bṓtmən/ *n.* (*pl.* **-men**) a person who hires out boats or provides transport by boat.

boatswain /bṓs'n/ *n.* (also **bo'sun, bosun, bo's'n**) a ship's officer in charge of equipment and the crew. □ **boatswain's chair** a seat suspended from ropes for work on the side of a ship or building. [OE *bātswegen* (as BOAT, SWAIN)]

bob[1] /bob/ *v.* & *n.* ● *v.intr.* (**bobbed, bobbing**) **1** move quickly up and down; dance. **2** (usu. foll. by *back, up*) **a** bounce buoyantly. **b** emerge suddenly; become active or conspicuous again after a defeat etc. **3** curtsy. **4** (foll. by *for*) try to catch with the mouth alone (fruit etc. floating or hanging). ● *n.* **1** a jerking or bouncing movement, esp. upward. **2** a curtsy. **3** one of several kinds of change in long peals in bell-ringing. [14th c.: prob. imit.]
■ *v.* **1** see WAG[1] *v.*

bob[2] /bob/ *n.* & *v.* ● *n.* **1** a short hairstyle for women and children. **2** a weight on a pendulum, plumb-line, or kite-tail. **3** = BOB-SLEIGH. **4** a horse's docked tail. **5** a short line at or towards the end of a stanza. **6** a knot of hair; a tassel-shaped curl. ● *v.* (**bobbed, bobbing**) **1** *tr.* cut (a woman's or child's hair) so that it hangs clear of the shoulders. **2** *intr.* ride on a bob-sleigh. [ME: orig. unkn.]
■ *v.* **1** see TRIM *v.* 1b.

bob[3] /bob/ *n.* (*pl.* same) *Brit. sl.* a former shilling (now = 5 decimal pence). [19th c.: orig. unkn.]

bob[4] /bob/ *n.* □ **bob's your uncle** *Brit. sl.* an expression of completion or satisfaction. [pet-form of the name *Robert*]

bobbin /bóbbin/ *n.* **1 a** a cylinder or cone holding thread, yarn, wire, etc., used esp. in weaving and machine sewing. **b** a spool or reel. **2** a small bar and string for raising a door-latch. □ **bobbin-lace** lace made by hand with thread wound on bobbins. [F *bobine*]

bobbinet /bóbbinet/ *n.* machine-made cotton net (imitating lace made with bobbins on a pillow). [BOBBIN + NET[1]]

bobble /bóbb'l/ *n.* a small woolly or tufted ball as a decoration or trimming. [dimin. of BOB[2]]

bobby[1] /bóbbi/ *n.* (*pl.* **-ies**) *Brit. colloq.* a policeman. [Sir *Robert* Peel, Engl. statesman d. 1850, founder of the metropolitan police force]
■ see *police officer.*

bobby[2] /bóbbi/ *n.* (*pl.* **-ies**) (in full **bobby calf**) *Austral.* & *NZ* an unweaned calf slaughtered for veal. [Eng. dial.]

bobby-dazzler /bóbbidazlər/ *n. colloq.* a remarkable or excellent person or thing. [dial., rel. to DAZZLE]

bobby-pin /bóbbipin/ *n. US, Austral.,* & *NZ* a flat hairpin. [BOB[2] + -Y[2]]

bobby socks /bóbbi soks/ *n.pl.* esp. *US* short socks reaching just above the ankle.

bobcat /bóbkat/ *n.* a small N. American lynx, *Felix rufus*, with a spotted reddish-brown coat and a short tail. [BOB[2] + CAT]

bobolink /bóbbəlingk/ *n.* a N. American oriole, *Dolichonyx oryzivorus*. [orig. *Bob (o') Lincoln*: imit. of its call]

bob-sled /bóbsled/ *n. US* = BOB-SLEIGH.

bob-sleigh /bóbslay/ *n.* & *v.* ● *n.* a mechanically-steered and -braked sledge used for racing down a steep ice-covered run. ● *v.intr.* race in a bob-sleigh. [BOB[2] + SLEIGH]

bobstay /bóbstay/ *n.* the chain or rope holding down a ship's bowsprit. [prob. BOB[1] + STAY[2]]

bobtail /bóbtayl/ *n.* a docked tail; a horse or a dog with a bobtail. [BOB[2] + TAIL[1]]

bocage /bəkaázh/ *n.* the representation of silvan scenery in ceramics. [F f. OF *boscage*: see BOSCAGE]

Boche /bosh/ *n.* & *adj. sl. derog.* ● *n.* **1** a German, esp. a soldier. **2** (prec. by *the*) Germans, esp. German soldiers, collectively. ● *adj.* German. [F sl., orig. = rascal: applied to Germans in the war of 1914–18]

bock /bok/ *n.* a strong dark German beer. [F f. G abbr. of *Eimbockbier* f. *Einbeck* in Hanover]

BOD *abbr.* biochemical oxygen demand.

bod /bod/ *n. Brit. colloq.* a person. [abbr. of BODY]
■ see FELLOW 1.

bode /bōd/ *v.* **1** *tr.* portend, foreshow. **2** *tr.* foresee, foretell (evil). □ **bode well** (or **ill**) show good (or bad) signs for the future. □□ **boding** *n.* [OE *bodian* f. *boda* messenger]
■ portend, promise, augur, betoken, omen, forebode, presage, foreshadow, foreshow, foretell; foresee.

bodega /bōdeegə/ *n.* a cellar or shop selling wine and food, esp. in a Spanish-speaking country. [Sp. f. L *apotheca* f. Gk *apothēkē* storehouse]

bodge var. of BOTCH.

bodgie /bóji/ *n. Austral. colloq.* **1** a male youth of the 1950s, as distinguished by dress etc., analogous to the Brit. TEDDY BOY. **2** something flawed or worthless. [f. Brit. dial. *bodge* work clumsily]
■ **2** botch, mess, hash.

Bodhisattva /bṓdisátvə/ *n.* in Mahayana Buddhism, one who is able to reach nirvana but delays doing so through compassion for suffering beings. [Skr., = one whose essence is perfect knowledge]

bodice /bóddiss/ *n.* **1** the part of a woman's dress (excluding sleeves) which is above the waist. **2** a woman's undergarment, like a vest, for the same part of the body. [orig. *pair of bodies* = stays, corsets]

bodiless /bóddiliss/ *adj.* **1** lacking a body. **2** incorporeal, insubstantial.
■ **2** see INSUBSTANTIAL 2.

bodily /bóddili/ *adj.* & *adv.* ● *adj.* of or concerning the body. ● *adv.* **1** with the whole bulk; as a whole (*threw them bodily*). **2** in the body; as a person.
■ *adj.* physical, corporal.

bodkin /bódkin/ *n.* **1** a blunt thick needle with a large eye used esp. for drawing tape etc. through a hem. **2** a long pin for fastening hair. **3** a small pointed instrument for piercing cloth, removing a piece of type for correction, etc. [ME perh. f. Celt.]
■ **3** see PUNCH[2].

body /bóddi/ *n.* & *v.* ● *n.* (*pl.* **-ies**) **1** the physical structure, including the bones, flesh, and organs, of a person or an animal, whether dead or alive. **2** the trunk apart from the head and the limbs. **3 a** the main or central part of a thing (*body of the car*; *body of the attack*). **b** the bulk or majority; the aggregate (*body of opinion*). **4 a** a group of persons regarded collectively, esp. as having a corporate function (*governing body*). **b** (usu. foll. by *of*) a collection (*body of facts*). **5** a quantity (*body of water*). **6** a piece of matter (*heavenly body*). **7** *colloq.* a person. **8** a full or substantial quality of flavour, tone, etc., e.g. in wine, musical sounds, etc. ● *v.tr.* (**-ies, -ied**) (usu. foll. by *forth*) give body or substance to. □ **body-blow** a severe set-back. **body-building** the practice of strengthening the body, esp. shaping and enlarging the muscles, by exercise. **body-colour** an opaque pigment. **body language** the process of communicating through conscious or unconscious gestures and poses. **body-line bowling** *Cricket* persistent fast bowling on the leg side threatening the batsman's body. **body odour** the smell of the human body, esp. when unpleasant. **body politic** the nation or State as a corporate body. **body scanner** a scanning X-ray machine for taking tomograms of the whole body. **body shop** a workshop where repairs to the bodywork of vehicles are carried out. **body stocking** a woman's undergarment, usually made of knitted nylon, which covers the torso. **body warmer** a sleeveless quilted or padded jacket worn as an outdoor garment. **in a body** all together. **keep body and soul together** keep alive, esp. barely. **over my dead body** *colloq.* entirely without my assent. □□ **-bodied** *adj.* (in *comb.*) (*able-bodied*). [OE *bodig*, of unkn. orig.]
■ *n.* **1** (*dead body*) corpse, remains, carcass, *esp. Med.*

cadaver, *archaic* corse, *sl.* stiff. **2** trunk, torso, carcass. **3 a** main part *or* portion, hull, fuselage, bodywork, chassis; substance, essentials, essence, heart, centre, core. **b** majority, bulk, main part *or* portion, better *or* best part, most, mass(es), greater number; aggregate, whole, sum, (grand *or* sum) total, totality. **4 a** association, league, band, organization, corps, union, confederation, federation, confederacy, fraternity, society; committee, council; group, assemblage, assembly, congress, company. **b** see COLLECTION 2. **5** see AMOUNT *n.* 1. **7** see SOUL 4. **8** richness, substance, firmness, consistency, fullness, solidity, thickness, density, viscosity. ● *v.* (*body forth*) embody. □ **body-blow** see *set-back* 1 (SET[1]). **in a body** all together, together, as a group, as one. **keep body and soul together** see SURVIVE 1.

body-check /bóddichek/ *n.* & *v. Sport* ● *n.* a deliberate obstruction of one player by another. ● *v.tr.* obstruct in this way.

bodyguard /bóddigaard/ *n.* a person or group of persons escorting and protecting another person (esp. a dignitary).
■ see ESCORT *n.* 1.

bodysuit /bóddisoot, -syoot/ *n.* a close-fitting one-piece stretch garment for women, used mainly for sport.

bodywork /bóddiwurk/ *n.* the outer shell of a vehicle.

Boer /bōər, boor/ *n.* & *adj.* ● *n.* a South African of Dutch descent. ● *adj.* of or relating to the Boers. [Du.: see BOOR]

boffin /bóffin/ *n.* esp. *Brit. colloq.* a person engaged in scientific (esp. military) research. [20th c.: orig. unkn.]

Bofors gun /bṓfərz/ *n.* a type of light anti-aircraft gun. [*Bofors* in Sweden]

bog /bog/ *n.* & *v.* ● *n.* **1 a** wet spongy ground. **b** a stretch of such ground. **2** *Brit. sl.* a lavatory. ● *v.tr.* (**bogged, bogging**) (foll. by *down*; usu. in *passive*) impede (*was bogged down by difficulties*). □ **bog-bean** = BUCKBEAN. **bog myrtle** a deciduous shrub, *Myrica gale*, which grows in damp open places and has short upright catkins and aromatic grey-green leaves: also called *sweet-gale* (see GALE[2]). **bog oak** an ancient oak which has been preserved in a black state in peat. **bog spavin** see SPAVIN. **bog-trotter** *sl. derog.* an Irishman. □□ **boggy** *adj.* (**boggier, boggiest**). **bogginess** *n.* [Ir. or Gael. *bogach* f. *bog* soft]
■ *n.* **1** swamp, fen, marsh, quagmire, mire, slough, ooze, sink, *US* moor, *literary* morass. **2** see TOILET 1. ● *v.* (*bog down*) impede, slow (down), hamper, encumber, stay, inhibit, interfere with; set back, hold back *or* up, delay. □ **bog-trotter** Irishman, *colloq. often offens.* Paddy, *sl. offens.* mick.

bogan /bṓgən/ *n. Austral. sl.* a gormless person. [20th c.: orig. uncert.]
■ see TWIT[1].

bogey[1] /bṓgi/ *n.* & *v. Golf* ● *n.* (*pl.* **-eys**) **1** a score of one stroke more than par at any hole. **2** (formerly) a score that a good player should do a hole or course in; par. ● *v.tr.* (**-eys, -eyed**) play (a hole) in one stroke more than par. [perh. f. *Bogey* as an imaginary player]

bogey[2] /bṓgi/ *n.* (also **bogy**) (*pl.* **-eys** or **-ies**) **1** an evil or mischievous spirit; a devil. **2** an awkward thing or circumstance. **3** *sl.* a piece of dried nasal mucus. [19th c., orig. as a proper name: cf. BOGLE]
■ **1** see DEVIL *n.* 1, 2. **2** see JINX *n.*

bogey[3] /bṓgi/ *n.* & *v.* (also **bogie**) *Austral.* ● *n.* a swim or bathe; a bath. ● *v.intr.* swim, bathe. [Dharuk *bugi* to bathe or dive]

bogeyman /bṓgiman/ *n.* (also **bogyman**) (*pl.* **-men**) a person (real or imaginary) causing fear or difficulty.
■ see MONSTER 1.

boggle /bógg'l/ *v.intr. colloq.* **1** be startled or baffled (esp. *the mind boggles*). **2** (usu. foll. by *about, at*) hesitate, demur. [prob. f. dial. *boggle* BOGEY[2]]
■ **2** see HESITATE 2.

bogie /bṓgi/ *n.* esp. *Brit.* **1** a wheeled undercarriage pivoted below the end of a rail vehicle. **2** a small truck used for carrying coal, rubble, etc. [19th-c. north. dial. word: orig. unkn.]

bogle /bṓg'l/ *n.* **1** = BOGEY[2]. **2** a phantom. **3** a scarecrow. [orig. Sc. (16th c.), prob. rel. to BOGEY[2]]

bogus /bṓgəss/ *adj.* sham, fictitious, spurious. □□ **bogusly** *adv.* **bogusness** *n.* [19th-c. US word: orig. unkn.]
■ counterfeit, spurious, fake, false, fraudulent, sham, imitation, fictitious, *colloq.* phoney.

bogy var. of BOGEY[2].

bogyman var. of BOGEYMAN.

bohea /bōhée/ *n.* a black China tea, the last crop of the season and usu. regarded as of low quality. [*Bu-i* (Wuyi) Hills in China]

Bohemian /bōhéemiən/ *n.* & *adj.* ● *n.* **1** a native of Bohemia, a former kingdom in central Europe corresponding to part of the modern Czech Republic; Czech. **2** (also **bohemian**) a socially unconventional person, esp. an artist or writer. ● *adj.* **1** of, relating to, or characteristic of Bohemia or its people. **2** socially unconventional. □□ **bohemianism** *n.* (in sense 2). [*Bohemia* + -AN: sense 2 f. F *bohémien* gypsy]
■ *n.* **2** eccentric, nonconformist, dissident, individualist, avant-gardist; *colloq.* hippie. ● *adj.* **2** alternative, radical, experimental, avant-garde; nonconformist, unconventional, unorthodox, casual, free and easy; *colloq.* arty.

boil[1] /boyl/ *v.* & *n.* ● *v.* **1** *intr.* **a** (of a liquid) start to bubble up and turn into vapour; reach a temperature at which this happens. **b** (of a vessel) contain boiling liquid (*the kettle is boiling*). **2 a** *tr.* bring (a liquid or vessel) to a temperature at which it boils. **b** *tr.* cook (food) by boiling. **c** *intr.* (of food) be cooked by boiling. **d** *tr.* subject to the heat of boiling water, e.g. to clean. **3** *intr.* **a** (of the sea etc.) undulate or seethe like boiling water. **b** (of a person or feelings) be greatly agitated, esp. by anger. **c** *colloq.* (of a person or the weather) be very hot. ● *n.* the act or process of boiling; boiling-point (*on the boil; bring to the boil*). □ **boil down 1** reduce volume by boiling. **2** reduce to essentials. **3** (foll. by *to*) amount to; signify basically. **boiled shirt** a dress shirt with a starched front. **boiled sweet** *Brit.* a sweet made of boiled sugar. **boil over 1** spill over in boiling. **2** lose one's temper; become over-excited. **make one's blood boil** see BLOOD. [ME f. AF *boiller*, OF *boillir*, f. L *bullire* to bubble f. *bulla* bubble]
■ *v.* **1 a** bubble, seethe, simmer; evaporate. **2 b, c** simmer, stew, steam. **3 a** undulate, seethe, foam, fret; ferment, sputter, splutter. **b** seethe, fume, foam at the mouth, rage, storm, rant and rave, bristle, smoulder, chafe, *colloq.* sizzle, *US sl.* burn up. **c** swelter, roast, *esp. US* broil, *colloq.* bake, sizzle, fry, scorch. □ **boil down 2** see TELESCOPE *v.* 3. **3** (*boil down to*) amount to, come down to, mean, signify. **boil over 2** see EXPLODE 2.

boil[2] /boyl/ *n.* an inflamed pus-filled swelling caused by infection of a hair follicle etc. [OE *bȳl(e)* f. WG]
■ abscess, carbuncle, pustule, lump, pimple, spot, *Med.* furuncle.

boiler /bóylər/ *n.* **1** a fuel-burning apparatus for heating a hot-water supply. **2** a tank for heating water, esp. for turning it to steam under pressure. **3** a metal tub for boiling laundry etc. **4** a fowl, vegetable, etc., suitable for cooking only by boiling. □ **boiler-room** a room with a boiler and other heating equipment, esp. in the basement of a large building. **boiler suit** a one-piece suit worn as overalls for heavy manual work.

boiling /bóyling/ *adj.* (also **boiling hot**) *colloq.* very hot.
■ see HOT *adj.* 1.

boiling-point /bóyling-poynt/ *n.* **1** the temperature at which a liquid starts to boil. **2** high excitement (*feelings reached boiling-point*).

boisterous /bóystərəss/ *adj.* **1** (of a person) rough; noisily exuberant. **2** (of the sea, weather, etc.) stormy, rough. □□ **boisterously** *adv.* **boisterousness** *n.* [var. of ME *boist(u)ous*, of unkn. orig.]
■ **1** rowdy, rough, noisy, clangorous, uproarious,

rip-roaring, tumultuous, roistering, lively, exuberant, clamorous, unruly, stormy, wild, riotous, undisciplined, uncontrolled, irrepressible, knockabout, *Sc.* randy, *colloq.* rumbustious, raunchy, *US colloq.* rambunctious. **2** rough, tempestuous, stormy, turbulent, blustery, wild, raging, roaring, howling.

boko /bṓkō/ *n.* & *adj. Austral.* ● *n.* an animal or person who is blind in one eye. ● *adj.* blind. [perh. f. an Aboriginal language]
■ *adj.* see BLIND *adj.* 1.

bolas /bṓləss/ *n.* (as *sing.* or *pl.*) (esp. in S. America) a missile consisting of a number of balls connected by strong cord, which when thrown entangles the limbs of the quarry. [Sp. & Port., pl. of *bola* ball]

bold /bōld/ *adj.* **1** confidently assertive; adventurous, courageous. **2** forthright, impudent. **3** vivid, distinct, well-marked (*bold colours*; *a bold imagination*). **4** *Printing* (in full **bold-face** or **-faced**) printed in a thick black typeface. □ **as bold as brass** excessively bold or self-assured. **make** (or **be**) **so bold as to** presume to; venture to. □□ **boldly** *adv.* **boldness** *n.* [OE *bald* dangerous f. Gmc]
■ **1** courageous, brave, gallant, adventurous, plucky, spirited, confident, stout-hearted, assertive, lion-hearted, daring, enterprising, audacious, fearless, unafraid, intrepid, resolute, dauntless, undaunted, valiant, stout, staunch, valorous, stalwart, venturesome, heroic, *colloq.* gutsy, *US sl.* feisty; reckless, foolhardy, incautious, daredevil, rash, *literary* temerarious. **2** audacious, forthright, self-assertive, outspoken, presumptuous, familiar, forward, aggressive, brazen, brash, impudent, impertinent, insolent, immodest, shameless, barefaced, *colloq.* fresh, pushy. **3** pronounced, prominent, well-marked, strong, vivid, distinct, striking, loud, noisy, vigorous, clear, conspicuous, glaring, outstanding. □ **make so bold as to** see PRESUME 2. □□ **boldly** see *adventurously* (ADVENTUROUS), *assertively* (ASSERTIVE).

bole[1] /bōl/ *n.* the stem or trunk of a tree. [ME f. ON *bolr*, perh. rel. to BALK[1]]
■ see TRUNK 1.

bole[2] /bōl/ *n.* fine compact earthy clay. [LL BOLUS]

bolero /bōláirō/ *n.* (*pl.* **-os**) **1 a** a Spanish dance in simple triple time. **b** music for or in the time of a bolero. **2** /also bóllərō/ a woman's short open jacket. [Sp.]

boll /bōl/ *n.* a rounded capsule containing seeds, esp. flax or cotton. □ **boll-weevil** a small American or Mexican weevil, *Anthonomus grandis*, whose larvae destroy cotton bolls. [ME f. MDu. *bolle*: see BOWL[1]]

bollard /bóllaard/ *n.* **1** *Brit.* a short metal, concrete, or plastic post in the road, esp. as part of a traffic island. **2** a short post on a quay or ship for securing a rope. [ME perh. f. ON *bolr* BOLE[1] + -ARD]

bollocking /bólləking/ *n. coarse sl.* a severe reprimand.

bollocks /bólləks/ *n.* (also **ballocks**) *coarse sl.* ¶ Usually considered a taboo word. **1** the testicles. **2** (usu. as an exclam. of contempt) nonsense, rubbish. [OE *beallucc*, rel. to BALL[1]]
■ **2** see DRIVEL *n.*

bollocky /bólləki/ *adj. Austral. sl.* naked.
■ see BARE *adj.* 1.

bologna /bəlṓnyə, bəlṓni/ *n. US* = BOLOGNA SAUSAGE.

Bologna sausage /bəlṓnyə, bəlṓni/ *n. US* a large smoked sausage made of bacon, veal, pork-suet, and other meats, and sold ready for eating. [*Bologna* in Italy]

bolometer /bəlómmitər/ *n.* a sensitive electrical instrument for measuring radiant energy. □□ **bolometry** *n.* **bolometric** /bṓləmétrik/ *adj.* [Gk *bolē* ray + -METER]

boloney /bəlṓni/ *n.* (also **baloney**) (*pl.* **-eys**) *sl.* **1** humbug, nonsense. **2** = BOLOGNA SAUSAGE. [20th c.: alt. of BOLOGNA]
■ **1** see NONSENSE.

Bolshevik /bólshəvik/ *n.* & *adj.* ● *n.* **1** *hist.* a member of the radical faction of the Russian Social Democratic party, which became the Communist party in 1918. **2** a Russian communist. **3** (in general use) any revolutionary socialist. ● *adj.* **1** of, relating to, or characteristic of the Bolsheviks. **2** communist. □□ **Bolshevism** *n.* **Bolshevist** *n.* [Russ., = a member of the majority, from the fact that this faction formed the majority group of the Russian Social Democratic party in 1903, f. *bol'she* greater]
■ *n.* **3** see *left-winger*. □□ **Bolshevist** see *left-winger*.

Bolshie /bólshi/ *adj.* & *n.* (also **Bolshy**) *sl.* ● *adj.* (usu. **bolshie**) **1** uncooperative, rebellious, awkward; bad-tempered. **2** left-wing, socialist. ● *n.* (*pl.* **-ies**) a Bolshevik. □□ **bolshiness** *n.* (in sense 1 of *adj.*). [abbr.]
■ *adj.* **1** see DIFFICULT 2. ● *n.* see *left-winger*.

bolster[1] /bṓlstər/ *n.* & *v.* ● *n.* **1** a long thick pillow. **2** a pad or support, esp. in a machine. **3** *Building* a short timber cap over a post to increase the bearing of the beams it supports. ● *v.tr.* (usu. foll. by *up*) **1** encourage, reinforce (*bolstered our morale*). **2** support with a bolster; prop up. □□ **bolsterer** *n.* [OE f. Gmc]
■ *v.* support, prop up, shore up, buttress, hold up, uphold, back (up), reinforce, strengthen; aid, help, assist, encourage, further, advance, *colloq.* boost.

bolster[2] /bṓlstər/ *n.* a chisel for cutting bricks. [20th c.: orig. uncert.]

bolt[1] /bōlt/ *n.*, *v.*, & *adv.* ● *n.* **1** a sliding bar and socket used to fasten or lock a door, gate, etc. **2** a large usu. metal pin with a head, usu. riveted or used with a nut, to hold things together. **3** a discharge of lightning. **4** an act of bolting (cf. sense 4 of *v.*); a sudden escape or dash for freedom. **5** *hist.* an arrow for shooting from a crossbow. **6** a roll of fabric (orig. as a measure). ● *v.* **1** *tr.* fasten or lock with a bolt. **2** *tr.* (foll. by *in*, *out*) keep (a person etc.) from leaving or entering by bolting a door. **3** *tr.* fasten together with bolts. **4** *intr.* **a** dash suddenly away, esp. to escape. **b** (of a horse) suddenly gallop out of control. **5** *tr.* gulp down (food) unchewed; eat hurriedly. **6** *intr.* (of a plant) run to seed. ● *adv.* (usu. in **bolt upright**) rigidly, stiffly. □ **a bolt from the blue** a complete surprise. **bolt-hole 1** a means of escape. **2** a secret refuge. **shoot one's bolt** do all that is in one's power. □□ **bolter** *n.* (in sense 4 of *v.*). [OE *bolt* arrow]
■ *n.* **1** pin, bar, rod, catch, latch. **3** lightning flash, thunderbolt, streak (of lightning), shaft, fulmination, *archaic* levin. **4** see DASH *n.* 1. **5** arrow, dart, projectile, missile, shaft, *hist.* quarrel. **6** roll, length. ● *v.* **1** fasten, lock, latch, secure. **2** (*bolt in*) see LOCK *v.* 2; (*bolt out*) see *lock out*. **3** fix, attach, fasten, connect. **4 a** dart off, race off, shoot off, run (away *or* off), rush (off *or* away), dash (off *or* away), take off, take to one's heels, vanish, do a disappearing act, flee, decamp, abscond, escape, take flight, do a moonlight flit, *colloq.* skedaddle, scram, make oneself scarce, *Brit. colloq.* flit, *US colloq.* hightail (it), *sl.* take a powder, cut and run, *Austral.* & *NZ sl.* shoot through, *Brit. sl.* scarper, do a bunk. **b** break away, go out of control. **5** gulp (down), swallow whole, ingurgitate; gobble, guzzle, wolf down, stuff down, *colloq.* gollop, pig (down), scoff. ● *adv.* (**bolt upright**) erect, straight; rigidly, stiffly, woodenly, fixedly. □ **bolt from the blue** surprise, shock, bombshell, blow, jolt, revelation. **bolt-hole 2** see REFUGE 1, 2. **shoot one's bolt** exhaust *or* use up one's resources, run out of steam *or US* gas, *esp. US* burn oneself out.

bolt[2] /bōlt/ *v.tr.* (also **boult**) sift (flour etc.). □□ **bolter** *n.* [ME f. OF *bulter*, *buleter*, of unkn. orig.]

bolus /bṓləss/ *n.* (*pl.* **boluses**) **1** a soft ball, esp. of chewed food. **2** a large pill. [LL f. Gk *bōlos* clod]
■ **2** see PILL 1a.

bomb /bom/ *n.* & *v.* ● *n.* **1 a** a container with explosive, incendiary material, smoke, or gas etc., designed to explode on impact or by means of a time-mechanism or remote-control device. **b** an ordinary object fitted with an explosive device (*letter-bomb*). **2** (prec. by *the*) the atomic or hydrogen bomb considered as a weapon with supreme destructive power. **3** *Brit. sl.* a large sum of money (*cost a bomb*). **4** a mass of solidified lava thrown from a volcano. **5** *US colloq.* a bad failure (esp. a theatrical one). **6** *sl.* a drugged cigarette. **7** *Med.* = *radium bomb*. ● *v.* **1** *tr.* attack with bombs; drop bombs on. **2** *tr.* (foll. by *out*) drive (a person etc.) out of a building or refuge by using bombs. **3** *intr.* throw or drop bombs. **4** *intr.* esp. *US sl.* fail badly. **5** *intr. colloq.* (usu. foll. by *along*, *off*) move or go very quickly. **6** *tr. US sl.* criticize fiercely. □ **bomb-bay** a compartment in an aircraft used to hold bombs. **bomb-disposal** the defusing or removal and detonation of an unexploded bomb. **bomb-sight** a device in an aircraft for aiming bombs. **bomb-site** an area where buildings have been destroyed by bombs. **go down a bomb** *colloq.*, often *iron.* be very well received. **like a bomb** *Brit. colloq.* **1** often *iron.* very successfully. **2** very fast. [F *bombe* f. It. *bomba* f. L *bombus* f. Gk *bombos* hum]

■ *n.* **1** bombshell, shell, explosive, maroon, device, *US* torpedo. **3** (*make a bomb*) make a killing *or* a pretty penny *or* big money *or* a mint *or* a fortune, *colloq.* make a packet *or* a pile, *sl.* make a bundle, *US sl.* make big bucks; (*cost a bomb*) cost an arm and a leg, *colloq.* cost the earth *or* a packet. **5** see FLOP *n.* ● *v.* **1** bombard, shell, blow up, drop bombs on. **4** see FAIL *v.* 1, 2a. **5** see RUSH[1] *v.* 1. **6** see SLAM *v.* 5. □ **like a bomb 1** see WELL *adv.* 9. **2** see *rapidly* (RAPID).

bombard /bombaárd/ *v.tr.* **1** attack with a number of heavy guns or bombs. **2** (often foll. by *with*) subject to persistent questioning, abuse, etc. **3** *Physics* direct a stream of high-speed particles at (a substance). □□ **bombardment** *n.* [F *bombarder* f. *bombarde* f. med.L *bombarda* a stone-throwing engine: see BOMB]

■ **1, 2** bomb, shell, gun; hail, pelt, shower, pepper, volley, assail, attack, assault, set upon; see also BESIEGE 3. □□ **bombardment** see ATTACK *n.* 1.

bombardier /bómbərdeér/ *n.* **1** *Brit.* a non-commissioned officer in the artillery. **2** *US* a member of a bomber crew responsible for sighting and releasing bombs. [F (as BOMBARD)]

bombardon /bombaárd'n, bómbərd'n/ *n. Mus.* **1** a type of valved bass tuba. **2** an organ stop imitating this. [It. *bombardone* f. *bombardo* bassoon]

bombasine var. of BOMBAZINE.

bombast /bómbast/ *n.* pompous or extravagant language. □□ **bombastic** /-bástik/ *adj.* **bombastically** /-bástikəli/ *adv.* [earlier *bombace* cotton wool f. F f. med.L *bombax -acis* alt. f. *bombyx*; see BOMBAZINE]

■ pretentious language, fustian, pomposity, turgidity, bluster, show, wind, bluff, grandiloquence, magniloquence, bravado, boast, buck, braggadocio, rodomontade, fanfaronade, flatulence, *sl.* hot air; burlesque, rhetoric. □□ **bombastic** high-flown, extravagant, rhetorical, pompous, pretentious, highfalutin, high-sounding, grandiose, grandiloquent, magniloquent, euphuistic, flowery, inflated, fustian, flatulent, turgid, tumid, mouthy.

Bombay duck /bómbay dúk/ *n.* a dried fish, esp. bummalo, usu. eaten with curried dishes. [corrupt. of *bombil*: see BUMMALO]

bombazine /bómbəzeén/ (also **bombasine**) *n.* a twilled dress-material of worsted with or without an admixture of silk or cotton, esp., when black, formerly used for mourning. [F *bombasin* f. med.L *bombacinum* f. LL *bombycinus* silken f. *bombyx -ycis* silk or silkworm f. Gk *bombux*]

bombe /bonb/ *n. Cookery* a dome-shaped dish or confection, freq. frozen. [F, = BOMB]

bomber /bómmər/ *n.* **1** an aircraft equipped to carry and drop bombs. **2** a person using bombs, esp. illegally. □ **bomber jacket** a short leather or cloth jacket tightly gathered at the waist and cuffs.

bombora /bombórə/ *n. Austral.* a dangerous sea area where waves break over a submerged reef. [Aboriginal]

bombproof /bómpro͞of/ *adj.* strong enough to resist the effects of blast from a bomb.

bombshell /bómshel/ *n.* **1** an overwhelming surprise or disappointment. **2** an artillery bomb. **3** *sl.* a very attractive woman (*blonde bombshell*).

■ **1** surprise, shock, bomb, blow, jolt, revelation, bolt from *or* out of the blue. **3** see BEAUTY 3.

bona fide /bṓnə fídi/ *adj.* & *adv.* ● *adj.* genuine; sincere. ● *adv.* genuinely; sincerely. [L, ablat. sing. of BONA FIDES]

■ *adj.* genuine, authentic, attested, real, veritable, undisputed, legitimate, true, valid; reliable, trustworthy, dependable, solid, indubitable, sincere, honest. ● *adv.* see *authentically* (AUTHENTIC).

bona fides /bṓnə fídeez/ *n.* **1** *esp. Law.* an honest intention; sincerity. **2** (as *pl.*) *colloq.* documentary evidence of acceptability (*his bona fides are in order*). [L, = good faith]

bonanza /bənánzə/ *n.* & *adj.* ● *n.* **1** a source of wealth or prosperity. **2** a large output (esp. of a mine). **3 a** prosperity; good luck. **b** a run of good luck. ● *adj.* greatly prospering or productive. [orig. US f. Sp., = fair weather, f. L *bonus* good]

■ *n.* **3** see WINDFALL.

bona vacantia /bṓnə vəkántiə/ *n. Law* goods without an apparent owner. [L, = ownerless goods]

bon-bon /bónbon/ *n.* a piece of confectionery; a sweet. [F f. *bon* good f. L *bonus*]

■ see SWEET *n.* 1.

bonce /bonss/ *n. Brit.* **1** *sl.* the head. **2** a large playing-marble. [19th c.: orig. unkn.]

bond /bond/ *n.* & *v.* ● *n.* **1 a** a thing that ties another down or together. **b** (usu. in *pl.*) a thing restraining bodily freedom (*broke his bonds*). **2** (often in *pl.*) **a** a uniting force (*sisterly bond*). **b** a restraint; a responsibility (*bonds of duty*). **3** a binding engagement; an agreement (*his word is his bond*). **4** *Commerce* a certificate issued by a government or a public company promising to repay borrowed money at a fixed rate of interest at a specified time; a debenture. **5** adhesiveness. **6** *Law* a deed by which a person is bound to make payment to another. **7** *Chem.* linkage between atoms in a molecule or a solid. **8** *Building* the laying of bricks in one of various patterns in a wall in order to ensure strength (*English bond*; *Flemish bond*). ● *v.* **1** *tr.* **a** lay (bricks) overlapping. **b** bind together (resin with fibres, etc.). **2** *intr.* adhere; hold together. **3** *tr.* connect with a bond. **4** *tr.* place (goods) in bond. **5** *intr.* become emotionally attached. □ **bond paper** high-quality writing-paper. **bond-washing** dividend-stripping. **in bond** (of goods) stored in a bonded warehouse until the importer pays the duty owing (see BONDED). [ME var. of BAND[1]]

■ *n.* **1 a** cement, adhesive; glue, mortar; fastening. **b** (*bonds*) tie(s), shackles, chains, fetters, manacles, handcuffs, trammels, thongs, cord(s), rope(s); restraint(s), constraint(s), check(s), control(s), rein(s). **2 a** connection, tie, attachment, link, linkage, union, relationship, alliance. **b** responsibility, charge, duty, trust, obligation, commitment, burden; see also sense 1b above. **3** covenant, pact, contract, agreement, engagement, compact, treaty, arrangement, settlement, *colloq.* deal; word (of honour), assurance, guarantee, warrant, pledge, vow, oath, promise. ● *v.* **2, 3** adhere, hold together; cement, bind, glue, weld, connect, splice, stick, cohere, attach, put together, solder, marry, join, fuse, combine.

bondage /bóndij/ *n.* **1** serfdom; slavery. **2** subjection to constraint, influence, obligation, etc. **3** sado-masochistic practices, including the use of physical restraints or mental enslavement. [ME f. AL *bondagium*: infl. by BOND]

■ **1** slavery, servitude, serfdom, subjection, enslavement, enthralment, *hist.* vassalage, villeinage, peonage, *literary* thraldom, thrall. **2** subjection, subjugation, oppression, repression, suppression; confinement, yoke, restraint, constraint; bonds, fetters, chains, shackles; imprisonment, captivity, *archaic* durance.

bonded /bóndid/ *adj.* **1** (of goods) placed in bond. **2** (of material) reinforced by or cemented to another. **3** (of a debt) secured by bonds. □ **bonded warehouse** a Customs-controlled warehouse for the retention of imported goods until the duty owed is paid.

bondi /bóndī/ *n. Austral.* a heavy club with a knob on the end. □ **give a person bondi** attack savagely. [Wiradhuri *bundi*]
■ □ **give a person bondi** see BEAT *v.* 1.

bondsman /bóndzmən/ *n.* (*pl.* **-men**) **1** a slave. **2** a person in thrall to another. [var. of *bondman* (f. archaic *bond* in serfdom or slavery) as though f. *bond's* genitive of BOND[1]]

bone /bōn/ *n.* & *v.* ● *n.* **1** any of the pieces of hard tissue making up the skeleton in vertebrates. **2** (in *pl.*) **a** the skeleton, esp. as remains after death. **b** the body, esp. as a seat of intuitive feeling (*felt it in my bones*). **3 a** the material of which bones consist. **b** a similar substance such as ivory, dentine, or whalebone. **4** a thing made of bone. **5** (in *pl.*) the essential part of a thing (*the bare bones*). **6** (in *pl.*) **a** dice. **b** castanets. **7** a strip of stiffening in a corset etc. ● *v.* **1** *tr.* take out the bones from (meat or fish). **2** *tr.* stiffen (a garment) with bone etc. **3** *tr. Brit. sl.* steal. □ **bone china** fine china made of clay mixed with the ash from bones. **bone-dry** quite dry. **bone idle** (or **lazy**) utterly idle or lazy. **bone-meal** crushed or ground bones used esp. as a fertilizer. **bone of contention** a source or ground of dispute. **bone-setter** a person who sets broken or dislocated bones, esp. without being a qualified surgeon. **bone spavin** see SPAVIN. **bone up** (often foll. by *on*) *colloq.* study (a subject) intensively. **close to** (or **near**) **the bone 1** tactless to the point of offensiveness. **2** destitute; hard up. **have a bone to pick** (usu. foll. by *with*) have a cause for dispute (with another person). **make no bones about 1** admit or allow without fuss. **2** not hesitate or scruple. **point the bone** (usu. foll. by *at*) *Austral.* **1** wish bad luck on. **2** cast a spell on in order to kill. **to the bone 1** to the bare minimum. **2** penetratingly. **work one's fingers to the bone** work very hard, esp. thanklessly. □□ **boneless** *adj.* [OE *bān* f. Gmc]
■ □ **bone up** see STUDY *v.* 1.

bonefish /bṓnfish/ *n. US* any of several species of large game-fish, esp. *Albula vulpes*, having many small bones.

bonehead /bṓnhed/ *n. sl.* a stupid person. □□ **boneheaded** *adj.*
■ see DOLT. □□ **boneheaded** see STUPID *adj.* 1, 5.

boner /bṓnər/ *n. sl.* a stupid mistake. [BONE + -ER[1]]
■ see BLUNDER *n.*

boneshaker /bṓnshaykər/ *n.* **1** a decrepit or uncomfortable old vehicle. **2** an old type of bicycle with solid tyres.

bonfire /bónfīr/ *n.* a large open-air fire for burning rubbish, as part of a celebration, or as a signal. □ **Bonfire Night** *Brit.* 5 Nov., on which fireworks are displayed and an effigy of Guy Fawkes burnt (see GUY[1]). **make a bonfire of** destroy by burning. [earlier *bonefire* f. BONE (bones being the chief material formerly used) + FIRE]

bongo[1] /bónggō/ *n.* (*pl.* **-os** or **-oes**) either of a pair of small long-bodied drums usu. held between the knees and played with the fingers. [Amer. Sp. *bongó*]

bongo[2] /bónggō/ *n.* (*pl.* same or **-os**) a rare antelope, *Tragelaphus euryceros*, native to the forests of central Africa, having spiralled horns and a chestnut-red coat with narrow white vertical stripes. [cf. Bangi *mbangani*, Lingala *mongu*]

bonhomie /bónnomeé/ *n.* geniality; good-natured friendliness. [F f. *bonhomme* good fellow]

bonhomous /bónnəməss/ *adj.* full of *bonhomie*.

bonito /bəneétō/ *n.* (*pl.* **-os**) any of several tunny-like fish which are striped like mackerel and are common in tropical seas. [Sp.]

bonk /bongk/ *v.* & *n.* ● *v.* **1** *tr.* hit resoundingly. **2** *intr.* bang; bump. **3** *coarse sl.* **a** *intr.* have sexual intercourse. **b** *tr.* have sexual intercourse with. ● *n.* an instance of bonking (*a bonk on the head*). □□ **bonker** *n.* [imit.: cf. BANG, BUMP[1], CONK[2]]
■ *v.* **1** see BUMP *v.* 1, 2. ● *n.* see BUMP *n.* 1.

bonkers /bóngkərz/ *adj. sl.* crazy. [20th c.: orig. unkn.]
■ see CRAZY 1.

bon mot /boɴ mṓ/ *n.* (*pl.* ***bons mots*** *pronunc.* same or /-mṓz/) a witty saying. [F]
■ see WITTICISM.

bonne bouche /bon bo͞osh/ *n.* (*pl.* ***bonne bouches*** or ***bonnes bouches*** *pronunc.* same) a titbit, esp. to end a meal with. [F f. *bonne* fem. good + *bouche* mouth]
■ see TITBIT.

bonnet /bónnit/ *n.* **1 a** a woman's or child's hat tied under the chin and usu. with a brim framing the face. **b** a soft round brimless hat like a beret worn by men and boys in Scotland (cf. TAM-O'-SHANTER). **c** *colloq.* any hat. **2** *Brit.* a hinged cover over the engine of a motor vehicle. **3** the ceremonial feathered head-dress of an American Indian. **4** the cowl of a chimney etc. **5** a protective cap in various machines. **6** *Naut.* additional canvas laced to the foot of a sail. □ **bonnet monkey** an Indian macaque, *Macaca radiata*, with a bonnet-like tuft of hair. □□ **bonneted** *adj.* [ME f. OF *bonet* short for *chapel de bonet* cap of some kind of material (med.L *bonetus*)]

bonnethead /bónnit-hed/ *n.* = SHOVELHEAD.

bonny /bónni/ *adj.* (**bonnier, bonniest**) esp. *Sc.* & *N.Engl.* **1 a** physically attractive. **b** healthy-looking. **2** good, fine, pleasant. □□ **bonnily** *adv.* **bonniness** *n.* [16th c.: perh. f. F *bon* good]
■ **1 a** pretty, comely, good-looking, fair, attractive, lovely, beautiful; see also FINE *adj.* 4. **2** see FINE[1] *adj.* 2, 6, PLEASANT.

bonsai /bónsī/ *n.* (*pl.* same) **1** the art of cultivating ornamental artificially dwarfed varieties of trees and shrubs. **2** a tree or shrub grown by this method. [Jap.]

bonspiel /bónspeel/ *n.* esp. *Sc.* a curling-match (usu. between two clubs). [16th c.: perh. f. LG]

bontebok /bóntibuk/ *n.* (also **bontbok** /bóntbuk/) (*pl.* same or **-boks**) a large chestnut antelope, *Damaliscus dorcas*, native to southern Africa, having a white tail and a white patch on its head and rump. [Afrik. f. *bont* spotted + *bok* BUCK[1]]

bonus /bṓnəss/ *n.* **1** an unsought or unexpected extra benefit. **2 a** a usu. seasonal gratuity to employees beyond their normal pay. **b** an extra dividend or issue paid to the shareholders of a company. **c** a distribution of profits to holders of an insurance policy. [L *bonus*, *bonum* good (thing)]
■ **1** see BENEFIT *n.* 1. **2** reward, hand-out, perquisite, extra, gratuity, allowance, tip, remuneration, compensation, appanage, largesse, *Brit. colloq.* perk.

bon vivant /bóɴ veevóɴ/ *n.* (*pl.* ***bon vivants*** or ***bons vivants*** *pronunc.* same) a person indulging in good living; a gourmand. [F, lit. good liver f. *vivre* to live]
■ see GOURMET.

bon viveur /bóɴ veevṓr/ *n.* (*pl.* ***bon viveurs*** or ***bons viveurs*** *pronunc.* same) = BON VIVANT. [pseudo-F]
■ see GOURMET.

bon voyage /bóɴ vwaayaázh/ *int.* & *n.* an expression of good wishes to a departing traveller. [F]

bony /bṓni/ *adj.* (**bonier, boniest**) **1** (of a person) thin with prominent bones. **2** having many bones. **3** of or like bone. **4** (of a fish) having bones rather than cartilage. □□ **boniness** *n.*
■ **1** see THIN *adj.* 4.

bonze /bonz/ *n.* a Japanese or Chinese Buddhist priest. [F *bonze* or Port. *bonzo* perh. f. Jap. *bonzō* f. Chin. *fanseng* religious person, or f. Jap. *bō-zi* f. Chin. *fasi* teacher of the law]

bonzer /bónzər/ *adj. Austral. sl.* excellent, first-rate. [perh. f. BONANZA]
■ see EXCELLENT.

boo /boo/ *int., n.,* & *v.* ● *int.* **1** an expression of disapproval or contempt. **2** a sound, made esp. to a child, intended to surprise. ● *n.* an utterance of *boo*, esp. as an expression of disapproval or contempt made to a performer etc. ● *v.* (**boos, booed**) **1** *intr.* utter a boo or boos. **2** *tr.* jeer at (a performer etc.) by booing. □ **can't** (or **wouldn't**) **say boo to a goose** is very shy or timid. [imit.]
■ *v.* see JEER *v.* 1.

boob[1] /bōōb/ *n.* & *v. sl.* ● *n.* **1** *Brit.* an embarrassing mistake. **2** a simpleton. ● *v.intr. Brit.* make an embarrassing mistake. [abbr. of BOOBY]
■ *n.* **1** see MISTAKE *n.* ● *v.* see ERR 1.

boob[2] /bōōb/ *n. sl.* a woman's breast. □ **boob tube** *sl.* **1** a woman's low-cut close-fitting usu. strapless top. **2** (usu. prec. by *the*) *US* television; one's television set. [earlier *bubby*, *booby*, of uncert. orig.]
■ see BREAST *n.* 1a. □ **boob tube 2** see TELEVISION 2, 3.

booboo /bōōbōō/ *n. sl.* a mistake. [BOOB[1]]
■ see MISTAKE *n.*

boobook /bōōbōōk/ *n. Austral.* a brown spotted owl, *Ninox novae-seelandiae*, native to Australia and New Zealand. [imit. of its call]

booby /bōōbi/ *n.* (*pl.* **-ies**) **1** a stupid or childish person. **2** a small gannet of the genus *Sula*. □ **booby-hatch** esp. *US sl.* a mental hospital. **booby prize** a prize given to the least successful competitor in any contest. **booby trap 1** a trap intended as a practical joke, e.g. an object placed on top of a door ajar. **2** *Mil.* an apparently harmless explosive device intended to kill or injure anyone touching it. **booby-trap** *v.tr.* place a booby trap or traps in or on. [prob. f. Sp. *bobo* (in both senses) f. L *balbus* stammering]
■ **1** see SILLY *n.* □ **booby-hatch** see BEDLAM 2. **booby trap 1** see TRAP[1] *n.* 3.

boodle /bōōd'l/ *n. sl.* money, esp. when gained or used dishonestly, e.g. as a bribe. [Du. *boedel* possessions]
■ see MONEY 1.

boofhead /bōōfhed/ *n. Austral. sl.* a fool. [prob. f. *bufflehead* fool]
■ see TWIT[1].

boogie /bōōgi/ *v.* & *n.* ● *v.intr.* (**boogies, boogied, boogying**) *sl.* dance enthusiastically to pop music. ● *n.* **1** = BOOGIE-WOOGIE. **2** *sl.* a dance to pop music. [BOOGIE-WOOGIE]

boogie-woogie /bōōgiwōōgi/ *n.* a style of playing blues or jazz on the piano, marked by a persistent bass rhythm. [20th c.: orig. unkn.]

book /bōōk/ *n.* & *v.* ● *n.* **1 a** a written or printed work consisting of pages glued or sewn together along one side and bound in covers. **b** a literary composition intended for publication (*is working on her book*). **2** a bound set of blank sheets for writing or keeping records in. **3** a set of tickets, stamps, matches, cheques, samples of cloth, etc., bound up together. **4** (in *pl.*) a set of records or accounts. **5** a main division of a literary work, or of the Bible (*the Book of Deuteronomy*). **6** (in full **book of words**) **a** a libretto, script of a play, etc. **b** a set of rules or regulations. **7** *colloq.* a magazine. **8** a telephone directory (*his number's in the book*). **9** a record of bets made and money paid out at a race meeting by a bookmaker. **10** a set of six tricks collected together in a card-game. **11** an imaginary record or list (*the book of life*). ● *v.* **1** *tr.* **a** engage (a seat etc.) in advance; make a reservation of. **b** engage (a guest, supporter, etc.) for some occasion. **2** *tr.* **a** take the personal details of (an offender or rule-breaker). **b** enter in a book or list. **3** *tr.* issue a railway etc. ticket to. **4** *intr.* make a reservation (*no need to book*). □ **book club** a society which sells its members selected books on special terms. **book-end** a usu. ornamental prop used to keep a row of books upright. **book in** esp. *Brit.* register one's arrival at a hotel etc. **book learning** mere theory. **book-plate** a decorative label stuck in the front of a book bearing the owner's name. **book-rest** an adjustable support for an open book on a table. **book token** *Brit.* a voucher which can be exchanged for books to a specified value. **book up 1** buy tickets in advance for a theatre, concert, holiday, etc. **2** (as **booked up**) with all places reserved. **book value** the value of a commodity as entered in a firm's books (opp. *market value*). **bring to book** call to account. **closed** (or **sealed**) **book** a subject of which one is ignorant. **go by the book** proceed according to the rules. **the good Book** the Bible. **in a person's bad** (or **good**) **books** in disfavour (or favour) with a person. **in my book** in my opinion. **make a book** take bets and pay out winnings at a race meeting. **not in the book** disallowed. **on the books** contained in a list of members etc. **suits my book** is convenient to me. **take a leaf out of a person's book** imitate a person. **throw the book at** *colloq.* charge or punish to the utmost. [OE *bōc*, *bōcian*, f. Gmc, usu. taken to be rel. to BEECH (the bark of which was used for writing on)]
■ *n.* **1** volume, tome, work, publication; paperback, hardback; composition, creation, writing. **4** (*books*) records, accounts, documents. **6 a** libretto, words, lyrics, script, play; continuity. **b** rules, laws, regulations; *colloq.* Bible. **7** see MAGAZINE 1. ● *v.* **1** engage, reserve, earmark, save, set *or* put aside, take, ticket; order. **2 b** register, enrol, list, log, record, post. **4** book up. □ **book in** register, check in, sign in, log in. **book up 2** (**booked up**) full up, all taken, fully booked. **bring to book** see *take to task* (TASK). **go by the book** follow the rules *or* regulations, abide by the law *or* rules *or* regulations, stick to the rules. **not in the book** see UNLAWFUL. **suits my book** suits me (fine), is fine *or* all right *or* okay by me. **take a leaf out of a person's book** see IMITATE 1. **throw the book at** see ACCUSE 2, PUNISH 1.

bookbinder /bōōkbīndər/ *n.* a person who binds books professionally. □□ **bookbinding** *n.*

bookcase /bōōk-kayss/ *n.* a set of shelves for books in the form of a cabinet.

bookie /bōōkki/ *n. colloq.* = BOOKMAKER.

booking /bōōkking/ *n.* the act or an instance of booking or reserving a seat, a room in a hotel, etc.; a reservation (see BOOK *v.* 1). □ **booking-clerk** an official selling tickets at a railway station. **booking-hall** (or **-office**) *Brit.* a room or area at a railway station in which tickets are sold.
■ reservation, order, arrangement.

bookish /bōōkkish/ *adj.* **1** studious; fond of reading. **2** acquiring knowledge from books rather than practical experience. **3** (of a word, language, etc.) literary; not colloquial. □□ **bookishly** *adv.* **bookishness** *n.*
■ **1** see STUDIOUS 1.

bookkeeper /bōōk-keepər/ *n.* a person who keeps accounts for a trader, a public office, etc. □□ **bookkeeping** *n.*
■ clerk, accountant, cashier, *Brit.* chartered accountant, *Can.* & *Sc.* CA, *US* CPA, certified public accountant.

bookland /bōōkland/ *n. hist.* an area of common land granted by charter to a private owner.

booklet /bōōklit/ *n.* a small book consisting of a few sheets usu. with paper covers.

bookmaker /bōōkmaykər/ *n.* a person who takes bets, esp. on horse-races, calculates odds, and pays out winnings. □□ **bookmaking** *n.*
■ *Brit.* turf accountant, *colloq.* bookie.

bookman /bōōkmən/ *n.* (*pl.* **-men**) a literary man, esp. a reviewer.

bookmark /bōōkmaark/ *n.* (also **bookmarker**) a strip of leather, card, etc., used to mark one's place in a book.

bookmobile /bōōkməbeel/ *n. US* a mobile library. [after AUTOMOBILE]

bookseller /bōōksellər/ *n.* a dealer in books.

bookshop /bōōkshop/ *n.* a shop where books are sold.

bookstall /bōōkstawl/ *n.* a stand for selling books, newspapers, etc., esp. out of doors or at a station.

bookstore /bōōkstor/ *n. US* = BOOKSHOP.

booksy /bōōksi/ *adj. colloq.* having literary or bookish pretensions.

bookwork /bōōkwurk/ *n.* the study of books (as opposed to practical work).
■ see STUDY *n.* 1, 2.

bookworm /bōōkwurm/ *n.* **1** *colloq.* a person devoted to reading. **2** the larva of a moth or beetle which feeds on the paper and glue used in books.
■ **1** bibliophile, book-lover, inveterate *or* ardent reader.

Boolean /bōōliən/ *adj.* denoting a system of algebraic notation to represent logical propositions. □ **Boolean logic** the use of the logical operators 'and', 'or', and 'not' in retrieving information from a computer database. [G. *Boole*, Engl. mathematician d. 1864]

boom[1] /bo͞om/ *n.* & *v.* ● *n.* a deep resonant sound. ● *v.intr.* make or speak with a boom. [imit.]

▪ *n.* rumble, roar, blare, report, peal, blast. ● *v.* sound, resound, resonate, rumble, thunder, roar, bellow; blast, bang.

boom[2] /bo͞om/ *n.* & *v.* ● *n.* a period of prosperity or sudden activity in commerce. ● *v.intr.* (esp. of commercial ventures) be suddenly prosperous or successful. □ **boom town** a town undergoing sudden growth due to a boom. □□ **boomlet** *n.* [19th-c. US word, perhaps f. BOOM[1] (cf. *make things hum*)]

▪ *n.* growth, increase, development, *archaic* flourish, *colloq.* bulge; prosperity, profitability. ● *v.* prosper, thrive, flourish, bloom, blossom, succeed, progress, make progress, grow, increase, be on the upgrade, *Brit. colloq.* be on the up and up, *literary* burgeon.

boom[3] /bo͞om/ *n.* **1** *Naut.* a pivoted spar to which the foot of a sail is attached, allowing the angle of the sail to be changed. **2** a long pole over a film or television set, carrying microphones and other equipment. **3** a floating barrier across the mouth of a harbour or river. [Du., = BEAM *n.*]

boomer /bo͞omər/ *n.* **1** a large male kangaroo. **2** a N. American mountain beaver, *Aplodontia rufa.* **3** a large wave.

boomerang /bo͞omərang/ *n.* & *v.* ● *n.* **1** a curved flat hardwood missile used by Australian Aboriginals to kill prey, and often of a kind able to return in flight to the thrower. **2** a plan or scheme that recoils on its originator. ● *v.intr.* **1** act as a boomerang. **2** (of a plan or action) backfire. [Aboriginal name, perh. modified]

▪ *v.* **2** rebound, recoil, backfire, redound; miscarry, go wrong, fail.

boomslang /bo͞omslang/ *n.* a large venomous tree-snake, *Dispholidus typus*, native to southern Africa. [Afrik. f. *boom* tree + *slang* snake]

boon[1] /bo͞on/ *n.* **1** an advantage; a blessing. **2** *archaic* **a** a thing asked for; a request. **b** a gift; a favour. [ME, orig. = prayer, f. ON *bón* f. Gmc]

▪ **1** blessing, godsend, stroke of good fortune, piece *or* bit of luck, benefit, advantage, asset, plus, added extra, *colloq.* break, *Austral. colloq.* purple patch, *Austral.* & *NZ sl.* spin. **2 a** see REQUEST *n.* 1, 2. **b** gift, award, reward, gratuity, present, offering, donation; service, favour, kindness, courtesy, good deed, *beau geste.*

boon[2] /bo͞on/ *adj.* close, intimate, favourite (usu. *boon companion*). [ME (orig. = jolly, congenial) f. OF *bon* f. L *bonus* good]

boondock /bo͞ondok/ *n.* (usu. in *pl.*) *US sl.* rough or isolated country. [Tagalog *bundok* mountain]

boong /bo͞ong/ *n. Austral. sl. offens.* an Aborigine. [orig. uncert.]

boonies /bo͞oneez/ *n.pl.* (prec. by *the*) *US sl.* = BOONDOCK.

boor /boor/ *n.* **1** a rude, ill-mannered person. **2** a clumsy person. **3** a rustic, a yokel. □□ **boorish** *adj.* **boorishly** *adv.* **boorishness** *n.* [LG *būr* or Du. *boer* farmer: cf. BOWER[3]]

▪ **1** barbarian, yahoo, lout, brute, churl, hoodlum, philistine, *Austral.* larrikin, *colloq.* slob, pig, hobbledehoy, *derog.* peasant, *sl.* trog, *Austral. sl.* ocker, *Brit. sl.* yob, yobbo. **2** oaf, lubber, clown, *colloq.* galoot, hobbledehoy, *US colloq.* lummox, *sl.* goop, clod. **3** rustic, peasant, yokel, (country) bumpkin, provincial, backwoodsman, kern, *archaic* churl, villain, *esp. US colloq.* hick, *US colloq.* hayseed, hill-billy, *hist.* hind. □□ **boorish** rustic, barbarian, rude, crude, ill-mannered, uncultured, coarse, uncivilized, uncouth, churlish, uncivil, loutish, vulgar, ill-bred, *colloq.* slobbish; oafish, clownish, lubberly, gawky, clumsy, *sl.* cloddish.

boost /bo͞ost/ *v.* & *n. colloq.* ● *v.tr.* **1 a** promote or increase the reputation of (a person, scheme, commodity, etc.) by praise or advertising; push; increase or assist (*boosted his spirits; boost sales*). **b** push from below; assist (*boosted me up the tree*). **2 a** raise the voltage in (an electric circuit etc.). **b** amplify (a radio signal). ● *n.* **1** an act, process, or result of boosting; a push (*asked for a boost up the hill*). **2 a** an advertisement campaign. **b** the resulting advance in value, reputation, etc. [19th-c. US word: orig. unkn.]

▪ *v.* **1 a** encourage, promote, help, kick-start, aid, support, assist, strengthen, bolster, build up, improve, enhance, exalt; increase, raise, swell, extend, lift, *sl.* crank up; inspire, push. **b** lift, shove *or* push (up *or* upward(s)), give a person a leg up; raise; help, assist. **2 b** see AMPLIFY 1. ● *n.* **1** lift, shove, push, leg up, kick-start; raise; help, hand, encouragement, support, furtherance, tonic; increase, rise, jump, leap, revival, (up)surge, *esp. US* raise, hike.

booster /bo͞ostər/ *n.* **1** a device for increasing electrical power or voltage. **2** an auxiliary engine or rocket used to give initial acceleration. **3** *Med.* a dose of an immunizing agent increasing or renewing the effect of an earlier one. **4** *colloq.* a person who boosts by helping or encouraging.

▪ **4** see FAN[2].

boot[1] /bo͞ot/ *n.* & *v.* ● *n.* **1** an outer covering for the foot, esp. of leather, reaching above the ankle, often to the knee. **2** *Brit.* the luggage compartment of a motor car, usu. at the rear. **3** *colloq.* a firm kick. **4** (prec. by *the*) *colloq.* dismissal, esp. from employment (*gave them the boot*). **5** a covering to protect the lower part of a horse's leg. **6** *hist.* an instrument of torture encasing and crushing the foot. ● *v.tr.* **1** kick, esp. hard. **2** (often foll. by *out*) dismiss (a person) forcefully. **3** (usu. foll. by *up*) put (a computer) in a state of readiness (cf. BOOTSTRAP 2). □ **the boot is on the other foot** (or **leg**) the truth or responsibility is the other way round. **die with one's boots on** (of a soldier etc.) die fighting. **put the boot in 1** kick brutally. **2** act decisively against a person. **you bet your boots** *sl.* it is quite certain. □□ **booted** *adj.* [ME f. ON *bóti* or f. OF *bote*, of unkn. orig.]

▪ *n.* **2** luggage compartment, *US* trunk. **3** see KICK[1] *n.* 1. **4** see SACK[1] *n.* 2. ● *v.* **1** see KICK[1] *v.* 1. **2** (*boot out*) eject, expel, throw *or* cast *or* turn out, push *or* drive *or* force *or* fling out, *colloq.* kick out, *Brit. colloq.* turf out, *sl.* bounce; see also DISMISS 2. □ **you bet your boots** see *of course* (COURSE).

boot[2] /bo͞ot/ *n.* □ **to boot** as well; to the good; in addition. [orig. = 'advantage': OE *bōt* f. Gmc]

▪ □ **to boot** in addition, into the bargain, besides, moreover, as well, also, too, additionally, for good measure, on top of everything else, as a bonus, *archaic* withal.

bootblack /bo͞otblak/ *n. US* a person who polishes boots and shoes.

bootee /bo͞otee/ *n.* **1** a soft shoe, esp. a woollen one, worn by a baby. **2** a woman's short boot.

booth /bo͞oth, bo͞oth/ *n.* **1** a small temporary roofed structure of canvas, wood, etc., used esp. as a market stall, for puppet shows, etc. **2** an enclosure or compartment for various purposes, e.g. telephoning or voting. **3** a set of a table and benches in a restaurant or bar. [ME f. Scand.]

▪ **1** stall, stand, table. **2** compartment, cubicle, box, kiosk, alcove, carrel, enclosure.

bootjack /bo͞otjak/ *n.* a device for holding a boot by the heel to ease withdrawal of the leg.

bootlace /bo͞otlayss/ *n.* a cord or leather thong for lacing boots.

▪ see LACE *n.* 2.

bootleg /bo͞otleg/ *adj.* & *v.* ● *adj.* (esp. of liquor) smuggled; illicitly sold. ● *v.tr.* (**-legged, -legging**) make, distribute, or smuggle (illicit goods, esp. alcohol). □□ **bootlegger** *n.* [f. the smugglers' practice of concealing bottles in their boots]

▪ *v.* see RUN *v.* 24.

bootless /bo͞otliss/ *adj. archaic* unavailing, useless. [OE *bōtlēas* (as BOOT[2], LESS)]

▪ pointless, unavailing, vain, purposeless, hopeless, useless, futile, worthless, unproductive, non-productive, ineffective, ineffectual, inefficacious, fruitless, idle, unprofitable, profitless, unremunerative, unrewarding, wasteful, time-wasting, Sisyphean.

bootlicker /bóotlikkər/ *n. colloq.* a person who behaves obsequiously or servilely; a toady. □□ **bootlick** *v.intr.* **bootlicking** *n.* & *adj.*
■ see *flatterer* (FLATTER).

boots /bōōts/ *n. Brit.* a hotel employee who cleans boots and shoes, carries luggage, etc.

bootstrap /bóotstrap/ *n.* **1** a loop at the back of a boot used to pull it on. **2** *Computing* a technique of loading a program into a computer by means of a few initial instructions which enable the introduction of the rest of the program from an input device. □ **pull oneself up by one's bootstraps** better oneself by one's own efforts.

booty /bóoti/ *n.* **1** plunder gained esp. in war or by piracy. **2** *colloq.* something gained or won. [ME f. MLG *būte*, *buite* exchange, of uncert. orig.]
■ **1** plunder, gain, spoil(s), contraband, takings, loot, *sl.* swag, boodle, (hot) goods. **2** gain, pickings, takings, winnings, *esp. US* take; prize, haul.

booze /bōōz/ *n.* & *v. colloq.* ● *n.* **1** alcoholic drink. **2** the drinking of this (*on the booze*). ● *v.intr.* drink alcoholic liquor, esp. excessively or habitually. □ **booze-up** *sl.* a drinking-bout. [earlier *bouse*, *bowse*, f. MDu. *būsen* drink to excess]
■ *n.* **1** drink, (hard) liquor, spirit(s), alcohol, *Ir.* poteen, *colloq.* fire-water, mother's ruin, plonk, *US colloq.* hooch, *sl.* gut-rot, rot-gut, bevvy, gargle, hard stuff, *Brit. sl.* wallop, *esp. US sl.* lush, *US sl.* red-eye, juice. **2** (*on the booze*) on the drink, *sl.* on a bender *or* a binge *or* the hard stuff, on the bottle. ● *v.* drink, tipple, imbibe, fuddle, sot, carouse, *archaic or literary* tope, *esp. N.Engl. colloq.* sup, *sl.* hit the bottle, *Brit. sl.* knock it back, *esp. US sl.* lush. □ **booze-up** see BENDER.

boozer /bóozər/ *n. colloq.* **1** a person who drinks alcohol, esp. to excess. **2** *Brit.* a public house.
■ **1** see DRUNK *n.* 1. **2** see PUB 1.

boozy /bóozi/ *adj.* (**boozier**, **booziest**) *colloq.* intoxicated; addicted to drink. □□ **boozily** *adv.* **booziness** *n.*
■ see DRUNK *adj.* 1.

bop[1] /bop/ *n.* & *v. colloq.* ● *n.* **1** = BEBOP. **2 a** a spell of dancing, esp. to pop music. **b** an organized social occasion for this. ● *v.intr.* (**bopped**, **bopping**) dance, esp. to pop music. □□ **bopper** *n.* [abbr. of BEBOP]
■ *n.* **2** see DANCE *n.* ● *v.* dance, *sl.* hoof it.

bop[2] /bop/ *v.* & *n. colloq.* ● *v.tr.* (**bopped**, **bopping**) hit, punch lightly. ● *n.* a light blow or hit. [imit.]

bo-peep /bōpéep/ *n.* a game of hiding and suddenly reappearing, played with a young child. [BO[1] + PEEP[1]]

bora[1] /bórə/ *n.* a strong cold dry NE wind blowing in the upper Adriatic. [It. dial. f. L *boreas* north wind: see BOREAL]

bora[2] /bórə/ *n. Austral.* an Aboriginal rite in which boys are initiated into manhood. [Aboriginal]

boracic /bərássik/ *adj.* of borax; containing boron. □ **boracic acid** = *boric acid.* [med.L *borax -acis*]

borage /bórrij/ *n.* any plant of the genus *Borago*, esp. *Borago officinalis* with bright blue flowers and leaves used as flavouring. [OF *bourrache* f. med.L *borrago* f. Arab. *'abu 'āraḳ* father of sweat (from its use as a diaphoretic)]

borak /bórak/ *n. Austral.* & *NZ sl.* banter, ridicule, nonsense. □ **poke borak at** make fun of. [Aboriginal Austral.]

borane /bórayn/ *n. Chem.* any hydride of boron.

borate /bórayt/ *n.* a salt or ester of boric acid.

borax /bóraks/ *n.* **1** the mineral salt sodium borate, occurring in alkaline deposits as an efflorescence or as crystals. **2** the purified form of this salt, used in making glass and china, and as an antiseptic. [ME f. OF *boras* f. med.L *borax* f. Arab. *būraḳ* f. Pers. *būrah*]

borazon /bórəzon/ *n.* a hard form of boron nitride, resistant to oxidation. [BORON + AZO- nitrogen + *-on*]

borborygmus /bórbərígməss/ *n.* (*pl.* **borborygmi** /-mī/) a rumbling of gas in the intestines. □□ **borborygmic** *adj.* [mod.L f. Gk]
■ see WIND[1] *n.* 4.

Bordeaux /bordṓ/ *n.* (*pl.* same /-dṓz/) any of various red, white, or rosé wines from the district of Bordeaux in SW France. □ **Bordeaux mixture** a fungicide for vines, fruit-trees, etc., composed of equal quantities of copper sulphate and calcium oxide in water.

bordello /bordéllō/ *n.* (*pl.* **-os**) esp. *US* a brothel. [ME (f. It. *bordello*) f. OF *bordel* small farm, dimin. of *borde* ult. f. Frank.: see BOARD]
■ see BROTHEL.

border /bórdər/ *n.* & *v.* ● *n.* **1** the edge or boundary of anything, or the part near it. **2 a** the line separating two political or geographical areas, esp. countries. **b** the district on each side of this. **c** (**the Border**) a particular boundary and its adjoining districts, esp. between Scotland and England (usu. **the Borders**), or N. Ireland and the Irish Republic. **3** a distinct edging round anything, esp. for strength or decoration. **4** a long narrow bed of flowers or shrubs in a garden (*herbaceous border*). ● *v.* **1** *tr.* be a border to. **2** *tr.* provide with a border. **3** *intr.* (usu. foll. by *on*, *upon*) **a** adjoin; come close to being. **b** approximate, resemble. □ **Border collie** a common working sheepdog of the North Country. **Border terrier 1** a small terrier of a breed with rough hair. **2** this breed. [ME f. OF *bordure*: cf. BOARD]
■ *n.* **1** boundary, edge, fringe, verge, rim; periphery, outskirts, margin, extremity. **2 a** boundary, frontier, borderline, divide, dividing line. **b** hinterland(s). **3** edge, margin, hem, band, binding, trimming, trim, edging, fringe, *archaic* purfle, purfling; frame, frieze, mount, moulding. **4** bed, flower-bed, herbaceous border. ● *v.* **1, 2** edge, trim, bind, fringe, purfle; ring. **3 a** (*border on*) lie alongside, adjoin, line, abut (on *or* upon), butt on to, verge upon *or* on, touch, be adjacent to, flank, join on to; approach (closely), near, come close to. **b** (*border on*) approximate (to), resemble (closely), seem *or* be similar to, be like, verge upon *or* on.

borderer /bórdərər/ *n.* a person who lives near a border, esp. that between Scotland and England.

borderland /bórdərland/ *n.* **1** the district near a border. **2** an intermediate condition between two extremes. **3** an area for debate.

borderline /bórdərlīn/ *n.* & *adj.* ● *n.* **1** the line dividing two (often extreme) conditions. **2** a line marking a boundary. ● *adj.* **1** on the borderline. **2** verging on an extreme condition; only just acceptable.
■ *n.* see LINE[1] *n.* 8a. ● *adj.* **2** see MARGINAL 2b.

bordure /bórdyoor/ *n. Heraldry* a border round the edge of a shield. [ME form of BORDER]

bore[1] /bor/ *v.* & *n.* ● *v.* **1** *tr.* make a hole in, esp. with a revolving tool. **2** *tr.* hollow out (a tube etc.). **3** *tr.* **a** make (a hole) by boring or excavation. **b** make (one's way) through a crowd etc. **4** *intr.* (of an athlete, racehorse, etc.) push another competitor out of the way. **5** *intr.* drill a well (for oil etc.). ● *n.* **1** the hollow of a firearm barrel or of a cylinder in an internal-combustion engine. **2** the diameter of this; the calibre. **3** = BOREHOLE. [OE *borian* f. Gmc]
■ *v.* **1–3a** pierce, drill, perforate, penetrate, puncture, punch; tunnel, excavate, sink, dig (out), gouge (out), ream, burrow out; hollow *or* scoop out. **3 b** (*bore one's way*) barge, make *or* thread *or* pick one's way, plough, push one's way. **5** drill, excavate, dig. ● *n.* **2** see CALIBRE 1.

bore[2] /bor/ *n.* & *v.* ● *n.* a tiresome or dull person or thing. ● *v.tr.* weary by tedious talk or dullness. □ **bore a person to tears** weary (a person) in the extreme. [18th c.: orig. unkn.]
■ *n.* see NUISANCE. ● *v.* weary, wear out, tire, exhaust, jade, stultify; make a person yawn, make a person fed up, *Brit. sl.* cheese a person off.

bore[3] /bor/ *n.* a high tidal wave rushing up a narrow estuary. Also called EAGRE. [ME, perh. f. ON *bára* wave]

bore[4] *past* of BEAR[1].

boreal /bóriəl/ *adj.* **1** of the North or northern regions. **2** of the north wind. [ME f. F *boréal* or LL *borealis* f. L *Boreas* f. Gk *Boreas* god of the north wind]

boredom /bórdəm/ *n.* the state of being bored; ennui.
■ dullness, dreariness, ennui, tedium, monotony.

borehole /bórhōl/ *n.* **1** a deep narrow hole, esp. one made in the earth to find water, oil, etc. **2** *Austral.* a water-hole for cattle.
■ **1** see WELL² *n.* 1.

borer /bórər/ *n.* **1** any of several worms, molluscs, insects, or insect larvae which bore into wood, other plant material, and rock. **2** a tool for boring.

boric /bórik/ *adj.* of or containing boron. □ **boric acid** an acid derived from borax, used as a mild antiseptic and in the manufacture of heat-resistant glass and enamels.

boring /bóring/ *adj.* that makes one bored; uninteresting, tedious, dull. □□ **boringly** *adv.* **boringness** *n.*
■ dull, monotonous, tedious, humdrum, routine, mundane, tiresome, dreary, flat, dead, uninteresting, unexciting, uninspiring; wearisome, soporific.

born /born/ *adj.* **1** existing as a result of birth. **2 a** being such or likely to become such by natural ability or quality (*a born leader*). **b** (usu. foll. by *to* + infin.) having a specified destiny or prospect (*born lucky*; *born to be king*; *born to lead men*). **3** (in *comb.*) of a certain status by birth (*French-born*; *well-born*). □ **born-again** (*attrib.*) converted (esp. to fundamentalist Christianity). **born and bred** by birth and upbringing. **in all one's born days** *colloq.* in one's life so far. **not born yesterday** *colloq.* not stupid; shrewd. [past part. of BEAR¹]

borne /born/ **1** *past part.* of BEAR¹. **2** (in *comb.*) carried or transported by (*airborne*).

borné /bórnay/ *adj.* **1** narrow-minded; of limited ideas. **2** having limitations. [F]

Bornholm's disease /bórnhōmz/ *n.* a viral infection with fever and pain in the muscles of the ribs. [*Bornholm* in Denmark]

boro- /bórō/ *comb. form* indicating salts containing boron.

boron /bóron/ *n. Chem.* a non-metallic yellow crystalline or brown amorphous element extracted from borax and boracic acid and mainly used for hardening steel. ¶ Symb.: **B.** [BORAX + *-on* f. *carbon* (which it resembles in some respects)]

boronia /bərṓniə/ *n. Austral.* any sweet-scented shrub of the genus *Boronia.* [F. *Borone*, It. botanist d. 1794]

borosilicate /bórōsíllikayt/ *n.* any of many substances containing boron, silicon, and oxygen generally used in glazes and enamels and in the production of glass.

borough /búrrə/ *n.* **1** *Brit.* **a** a town represented in the House of Commons. **b** a town or district granted the status of a borough. **2** *Brit. hist.* a town with a municipal corporation and privileges conferred by a royal charter. **3** *US* a municipal corporation in certain States. **4** *US* each of five divisions of New York City. **5** *US* (in Alaska) a county. [OE *burg*, *burh* f. Gmc: cf. BURGH]
■ **1, 2** see TOWN 1.

borrow /bórrō/ *v.* **1 a** *tr.* acquire temporarily with the promise or intention of returning. **b** *intr.* obtain money in this way. **2** *tr.* use (an idea, invention, etc.) originated by another; plagiarize. **3** *intr. Golf* **a** play the ball uphill so that it rolls back towards the hole. **b** allow for the wind or a slope. □ **borrowed time** an unexpected extension esp. of life. □□ **borrower** *n.* **borrowing** *n.* [OE *borgian* give a pledge]
■ **1** be lent *or* loaned; cadge, sponge, *US* hire, *sl.* touch a person for, *US sl.* bum. **2** see TAKE *v.* 14a.

borsch var. of BORTSCH.

Borstal /bórst'l/ *n. Brit. hist.* an institution for reforming and training young offenders. ¶ Now replaced by *detention centre* and *youth custody centre*. [*Borstal* in S. England, where the first of these was established]
■ youth custody centre, detention centre, reform school, *hist.* approved school, *US* & *hist.* reformatory.

bort /bort/ *n.* (also **boart**) **1** an inferior or malformed diamond, used for cutting. **2** fragments of diamonds produced in cutting. [Du. *boort*]

bortsch /borch/ *n.* (also **borsch** /borsh/) a highly seasoned Russian or Polish soup with various ingredients including beetroot and cabbage and served with sour cream. [Russ. *borshch*]

borzoi /bórzoy/ *n.* **1** a large Russian wolfhound of a breed with a narrow head and silky, usu. white, coat. **2** this breed. [Russ. f. *borzyi* swift]

boscage /bóskij/ *n.* (also **boskage**) **1** masses of trees or shrubs. **2** wooded scenery. [ME f. OF *boscage* f. Gmc: cf. BUSH¹]
■ see BRUSH *n.* 6.

bosh /bosh/ *n.* & *int. sl.* nonsense; foolish talk. [Turk. *boş* empty]
■ see NONSENSE.

bosky /bóski/ *adj.* (**boskier, boskiest**) *literary* wooded, bushy. [ME *bosk* thicket]
■ see WOODED.

bo's'n var. of BOATSWAIN.

bosom /bŏŏzz'm/ *n.* & *adj.* ● *n.* **1 a** a person's breast or chest, esp. a woman's. **b** *colloq.* each of a woman's breasts. **c** the enclosure formed by a person's breast and arms. **2** the seat of the emotions; an emotional centre, esp. as the source of an enfolding relationship (*in the bosom of one's family*). **3** the part of a woman's dress covering the breast. ● *adj.* (esp. in **bosom friend**) close, intimate. [OE *bōsm* f. Gmc]
■ *n.* **1** breast, chest, bust; (*bosoms*) *sl.* boobs, *Austral. sl.* norks, *Brit. sl.* bristols, charlies. **2** soul, heart (of hearts), blood; midst, interior, core, centre. ● *adj.* close, intimate, dear, beloved, cherished, boon, special, confidential; (**bosom friend**) best friend, intimate, second self, crony; see also FRIEND *n.* 1.

bosomy /bŏŏzzəmi/ *adj.* (of a woman) having large breasts.
■ busty, buxom, *colloq.* chesty, well-endowed.

boson /bṓzon/ *n. Physics* any of several elementary particles obeying the relations stated by Bose and Einstein, with a zero or integral spin, e.g. photons (cf. FERMION). [S. N. *Bose*, Ind. physicist d. 1974]

boss¹ /boss/ *n.* & *v. colloq.* ● *n.* **1** a person in charge; an employer, manager, or overseer. **2** *US* a person who controls or dominates a political organization. ● *v.tr.* **1** (usu. foll. by *about*, *around*) treat domineeringly; give constant peremptory orders to. **2** be the master or manager of. [orig. US: f. Du. *baas* master]
■ *n.* **1** chief, supervisor, head, administrator, manager, foreman, superintendent, overseer, employer, leader, director, managing director, MD, supremo, kingpin, *Austral.* & *NZ* trump, *esp. Ir.* himself, *US* president, *colloq.* super, *Brit. colloq.* gaffer, *sl.* governor, gov., big cheese, Big Chief *or* Daddy, *US sl.* honcho, Mr Big, prex. ● *v.* **1** push *or* shove around *or* about, dominate, order about *or* around, lord it over, dictate to. **2** supervise, head, manage, run, oversee, watch *or* preside over, overlook, direct, control, superintend, command, have charge of, be in charge of, govern.

boss² /boss/ *n.* **1** a round knob, stud, or other protuberance, esp. on the centre of a shield or in ornamental work. **2** *Archit.* a piece of ornamental carving etc. covering the point where the ribs in a vault or ceiling cross. **3** *Geol.* a large mass of igneous rock. **4** *Mech.* an enlarged part of a shaft. [ME f. OF *boce* f. Rmc]

bossa nova /bóssə nṓvə/ *n.* **1** a dance like the samba, originating in Brazil. **2** a piece of music for this or in its rhythm. [Port., = new flair]

boss-eyed /bóssīd/ *adj. Brit. colloq.* **1** having only one good eye; cross-eyed. **2** crooked; out of true. [dial. *boss* miss, bungle]

boss-shot /bóss-shot/ *n. Brit. dial.* & *sl.* **1** a bad shot or aim. **2** an unsuccessful attempt. [as BOSS-EYED]

bossy /bóssi/ *adj.* (**bossier**, **bossiest**) *colloq.* domineering; tending to boss. □ **bossy-boots** *colloq.* a domineering person. □□ **bossily** *adv.* **bossiness** *n.*
■ overbearing, domineering, high-handed, dictatorial, authoritarian, tyrannical, despotic, imperious, lordly, *colloq.* pushy.

bosun (also **bo'sun**) var. of BOATSWAIN.

bot /bot/ *n.* (also **bott**) any of various parasitic larvae of flies of the family Oestridae, infesting horses, sheep, etc. □ **bot-fly** (*pl.* **-flies**) any dipterous fly of the genus *Oestrus*, with stout hairy bodies. [prob. of LG orig.]

bot. *abbr.* **1** bottle. **2** botanic; botanical; botany. **3** bought.

botanize /bóttənīz/ *v.intr.* (also **-ise**) study plants, esp. in their habitat.

Botany /bóttəni/ *n.* (in full **Botany wool**) merino wool, esp. from Australia. [*Botany Bay*, New S. Wales, named from the variety of its flora]

botany /bóttəni/ *n.* **1** the study of the physiology, structure, genetics, ecology, distribution, classification, and economic importance of plants. **2** the plant life of a particular area or time. □□ **botanic** /bətánnik/ *adj.* **botanical** /bətánnik'l/ *adj.* **botanically** /bətánnikəli/ *adv.* **botanist** *n.* [*botanic* f. F *botanique* or LL *botanicus* f. Gk *botanikos* f. *botanē* plant]

botch /boch/ *v.* & *n.* (also **bodge**) ● *v.tr.* **1** bungle; do badly. **2** patch or repair clumsily. ● *n.* bungled or spoilt work (*made a botch of it*). □□ **botcher** *n.* [ME: orig. unkn.]
■ *v.* **1** bungle, mismanage, spoil, mess up, muff, make a mess of, *colloq.* make a pig's ear of, make a hash of, *Brit. colloq.* muck up, fluff, *sl.* screw up, louse up, blow, goof (up), *Brit. sl.* cock up. **2** patch up; (*botch it up*) paper over the cracks, stick it back together. ● *n.* mess, hash, *Austral. colloq.* bodgie.

botel /bōtél/ *n.* (also **boatel**) a waterside hotel with facilities for mooring boats. [blend of BOAT and HOTEL]

both /bōth/ *adj.*, *pron.*, & *adv.* ● *adj.* & *pron.* the two, not only one (*both boys; both the boys; both of the boys; the boys are both here*). ¶ Widely used with *of*, esp. when followed by a pronoun (e.g. *both of us*) or a noun implying separate rather than collective consideration, e.g. *both of the boys* suggests *each boy* rather than the two together. ● *adv.* with equal truth in two cases (*both the boy and his sister are here; are both here and hungry*). □ **both ways** = *each way*. **have it both ways** alternate between two incompatible points of view to suit the needs of the moment. [ME f. ON *báthir*]

bother /bóthər/ *v.*, *n.*, & *int.* ● *v.* **1** *tr.* **a** give trouble to; worry, disturb. **b** *refl.* (often foll. by *about*) be anxious or concerned. **2** *intr.* **a** (often foll. by *about*, or *to* + infin.) worry or trouble oneself (*don't bother about that; didn't bother to tell me*). **b** (foll. by *with*) be concerned. ● *n.* **1 a** a person or thing that bothers or causes worry. **b** a minor nuisance. **2** trouble, worry, fuss; a state of worry. ● *int.* esp. *Brit.* expressing annoyance or impatience. □ **cannot be bothered** will not make the effort needed. [Ir. *bodhraim* deafen]
■ *v.* **1 a** annoy, pester, keep on at, irritate, trouble, hector, harass, hound, dog, nag, badger, plague, *colloq.* hassle, get at; inconvenience; perturb, disturb, worry, upset, unsettle, make uneasy, disquiet, disconcert, concern, aggravate, distress, discomfit, *archaic* ail, *sl.* bug. **b** see sense 2 below. **2** worry, trouble (oneself), be anxious, fret, concern oneself, upset oneself, lose sleep, burden oneself, get worked up *or* upset, *colloq.* get het up; fuss, make a fuss; be concerned *or* interested. ● *n.* **1** nuisance, pest, annoyance, inconvenience, vexation, irritation, bore, burden, *colloq.* bind, headache, hassle, drag, pain, pain in the neck, thorn in the side *or* flesh, *Brit. colloq.* fag, *esp. US sl.* pain in the butt, *US sl.* bummer. **2** trouble, worry, inconvenience, discomfort, *colloq.* hassle; disturbance, ado, commotion, fuss, disorder; dither, flutter, *colloq.* tizzy, pet, stew, lather, sweat. ● *int.* blast, damn, hang it all, *colloq.* dash (it), dash it all, hell, *euphem.* sugar, *sl.* blow (it), rats, *Brit. sl.* flaming heck, *esp. US sl.* doggone it. □ **cannot be bothered** cannot be fussed *or Brit. colloq.* fagged.

botheration /bóthəráysh'n/ *n.* & *int. colloq.* = BOTHER *n.*, *int.*

bothersome /bóthərsəm/ *adj.* causing bother; troublesome.
■ see TROUBLESOME 2.

bothy /bóthi/ *n.* (also **bothie**) (*pl.* **-ies**) *Sc.* a small hut or cottage, esp. one for housing labourers. [18th c.: orig. unkn.: perh. rel. to BOOTH]
■ see CABIN *n.* 1.

bo-tree /bṓtree/ *n.* the Indian fig-tree, *Ficus religiosa*, regarded as sacred by Buddhists. Also called PIPAL or PEEPUL. [repr. Sinh. *bogaha* tree of knowledge (Buddha's enlightenment having occurred beneath such a tree)]

bott var. of BOT.

bottle /bótt'l/ *n.* & *v.* ● *n.* **1** a container, usu. of glass or plastic and with a narrow neck, for storing liquid. **2** the amount that will fill a bottle. **3** a baby's feeding-bottle. **4** = *hot-water bottle*. **5** a metal cylinder for liquefied gas. **6** *Brit. sl.* courage, confidence. ● *v.tr.* **1** put into bottles or jars. **2** preserve (fruit etc.) in jars. **3** (foll. by *up*) **a** conceal or restrain for a time (esp. a feeling). **b** keep (an enemy force etc.) contained or entrapped. **4** (as **bottled** *adj.*) *sl.* drunk. □ **bottle bank** a place where used bottles may be deposited for recycling. **bottle-brush 1** a cylindrical brush for cleaning inside bottles. **2** any of various plants with a flower of this shape. **bottle-green** a dark shade of green. **bottle party** a party to which guests bring bottles of drink. **bottle tree** any of various Australian trees of the genus *Brachychiton* with a swollen bottle-shaped trunk. **hit the bottle** *sl.* drink heavily. **on the bottle** *sl.* drinking (alcoholic drink) heavily. □□ **bottleful** *n.* (*pl.* **-fuls**). [ME f. OF *botele*, *botaille* f. med.L *butticula* dimin. of LL *buttis* BUTT[4]]
■ *n.* **1** flask, container; decanter. **6** courage, nerve, confidence, daring, manliness, manfulness, backbone, mettle, pluck, *colloq.* guts, spunk, grit, gumption, *US colloq.* sand, *US sl.* moxie. ● *v.* **3** (*bottle up*) **a** contain, restrain, hold back, control, suppress, repress, hold *or* keep in check, stifle; conceal, hide, cover (up), mask, bury. **b** entrap, trap, contain, confine, hem in, box *or* shut in *or* up, coop (up); surround. **4** (**bottled**) see DRUNK *adj.* 1. □ **hit the bottle** see BOOZE *v.* **on the bottle** see BOOZE *n.* 2.

bottle-feed /bótt'lfeed/ *v.tr.* (*past* and *past part.* **-fed**) feed (a baby) with milk by means of a bottle.

bottleneck /bótt'lnek/ *n.* **1** a point at which the flow of traffic, production, etc., is constricted. **2** a narrow place causing constriction.

bottlenose /bótt'lnōz/ *n.* (also **bottlenosed**) a swollen nose. □ **bottlenose dolphin** a dolphin, *Tursiops truncatus*, with a bottle-shaped snout.

bottler /bótlər/ *n.* **1** a person who bottles drinks etc. **2** *Austral.* & *NZ sl.* an excellent person or thing.
■ **2** see KILLER 2a.

bottom /bóttəm/ *n.*, *adj.*, & *v.* ● *n.* **1 a** the lowest point or part (*bottom of the stairs*). **b** the part on which a thing rests (*bottom of a saucepan*). **c** the underneath part (*scraped the bottom of the car*). **d** the furthest or inmost part (*bottom of the garden*). **2** *colloq.* **a** the buttocks. **b** the seat of a chair etc. **3 a** the less honourable, important, or successful end of a table, a class, etc. (*at the bottom of the list of requirements*). **b** a person occupying this place (*he's always bottom of the class*). **4** the ground under the water of a lake, a river, etc. (*swam until he touched the bottom*). **5** the basis; the origin (*he's at the bottom of it*). **6** the essential character; reality. **7** *Naut.* **a** the keel or hull of a ship. **b** a ship, esp. as a cargo-carrier. **8** staying power; endurance. ● *adj.* **1** lowest (*bottom button*). **2** last (*got the bottom score*). ● *v.* **1** *tr.* put a bottom to (a chair, saucepan, etc.). **2** *intr.* (of a ship) reach or touch the bottom. **3** *tr.* find the extent or real nature of; work out. **4** *tr.* (usu. foll. by *on*) base (an argument etc.) (*reasoning bottomed on logic*). **5** *tr.* touch the bottom or lowest point of. □ **at bottom** basically, essentially. **be at the bottom of** have caused. **bet one's bottom dollar** *sl.*

stake all. **bottom dog** = UNDERDOG. **bottom drawer** *Brit.* linen etc. stored by a woman in preparation for her marriage. **bottom falls out** collapse occurs. **bottom gear** see GEAR. **bottom line** *colloq.* the underlying or ultimate truth; the ultimate, esp. financial, criterion. **bottom out** reach the lowest level. **bottoms up!** a call to drain one's glass. **bottom up** upside-down. **get to the bottom of** fully investigate and explain. **knock the bottom out of** prove (a thing) worthless. □□ **bottommost** /bóttəm-mōst/ *adj.* [OE *botm* f. Gmc]

■ *n.* **1 a, b** base, foot, foundation. **c** underneath, underside. **d** (far) end, foot. **2 a** seat, buttocks, rump, posterior, hindquarters, hams, *Anat.* nates, gluteus maximus, *archaic* breech, *colloq.* backside, behind, rear, sit-upon, *colloq. euphem. derrière*, *joc.* fundament, *sl.* prat, cheeks, *Brit. sl.* bum, *esp. US sl.* butt, *US sl.* keister, fanny, can. **4** bed, floor, ground, depths, *sl.* Davy Jones's (locker). **5** root, basis, base, foundation, source, origin, cause, heart, seat, centre, nub, hub, crux. ● *v.* **2** sink, ground, run aground. **4** see BASE[1] *v.* 1. □ **at bottom** basically, fundamentally, in the final *or* last analysis, really, in reality, truly, in fact, actually, essentially, in essence, *au fond*, *literary* in truth. **be at the bottom of** be behind, be responsible for, have caused, be involved with, be implicated in. **bottom drawer** *US* hope chest. **bottoms up!** (to) your (very good) health, here's to —, *skol*, *prosit*, *colloq.* here's mud in your eye, *Brit. colloq.* cheers, *sl.* down the hatch. **bottom up** bottom side up, upside-down, wrong side up, the other way about *or* round, inverted.

bottomless /bóttəmliss/ *adj.* **1** without a bottom. **2** (of a supply etc.) inexhaustible.

■ **1** unfathomed, unfathomable, abyssal, unplumbable, unsounded. **2** inexhaustible, unlimited, boundless, limitless, illimitable; interminable, never-ending, endless, unending, undying, everlasting, inestimable, measureless, immeasurable, infinite.

bottomry /bóttəmri/ *n.* & *v. Naut.* ● *n.* a system of using a ship as security against a loan to finance a voyage, the lender losing his or her money if the ship sinks. ● *v.tr.* (**-ies, -ied**) pledge (a ship) in this way. [BOTTOM = ship + -RY, after Du. *bodemerij*]

botulism /bótyooliz'm/ *n.* poisoning caused by a toxin produced by the bacillus *Clostridium botulinum* growing in poorly preserved food. [G *Botulismus* f. L *botulus* sausage]

bouclé /bŏŏklay/ *n.* **1** a looped or curled yarn (esp. wool). **2** a fabric, esp. knitted, made of this. [F, = buckled, curled]

boudoir /bŏŏdwaar/ *n.* a woman's small private room or bedroom. [F, lit. sulking-place f. *bouder* sulk]

bouffant /bŏŏfoN/ *adj.* (of a dress, hair, etc.) puffed out. [F]

bougainvillaea /bŏŏgənvílliə/ *n.* any tropical widely cultivated plant of the genus *Bougainvillaea*, with large coloured bracts (usu. purple, red, or white) almost concealing the inconspicuous flowers. [L. A. de *Bougainville*, Fr. navigator d. 1811]

bough /bow/ *n.* a branch of a tree, esp. a main one. [OE *bōg*, *bōh* f. Gmc]

■ see BRANCH *n.* 1.

bought *past* and *past part.* of BUY.

boughten /báwt'n/ *adj. US* or *dial.* bought at a shop, not home-made. [var. of past part. of BUY]

bougie /bŏŏzhee/ *n.* **1** *Med.* a thin flexible surgical instrument for exploring, dilating, etc. the passages of the body. **2** a wax candle. [F f. Arab. *Bujiya* Algerian town with a wax trade]

bouillabaisse /bŏŏyəbéss/ *n. Cookery* a rich, spicy fish-stew, orig. from Provence. [F]

bouilli /bŏŏyée/ *n. Cookery* stewed or boiled meat. [F, = boiled]

bouillon /bŏŏyóN, bŏŏyon/ *n.* thin soup; broth. [F f. *bouillir* to boil]

■ see BROTH.

boulder /bṓldər/ *n.* a large stone worn smooth by erosion. □ **boulder-clay** *Geol.* a mixture of boulders etc. formed by deposition from massive bodies of melting ice, to give distinctive glacial formations. [short for *boulderstone*, ME f. Scand.]

■ see ROCK[1] 4.

boule[1] /bōōl/ *n.* (also **boules** *pronunc.* same) a French form of bowls, played on rough ground with usu. metal balls. [F, = BOWL[2]]

boule[2] /bŏŏli/ *n.* a legislative body of an ancient Greek city or of modern Greece. [Gk *boulē* senate]

boule[3] var. of BUHL.

boules var. of BOULE[1].

boulevard /bŏŏləvaard, bŏŏlvaar/ *n.* **1** a broad tree-lined avenue. **2** esp. *US* a broad main road. [F f. G *Bollwerk* BULWARK, orig. of a promenade on a demolished fortification]

■ see STREET 1.

boulle var. of BUHL.

boult var. of BOLT[2].

bounce /bownss/ *v.* & *n.* ● *v.* **1 a** *intr.* (of a ball etc.) rebound. **b** *tr.* cause to rebound. **c** *tr.* & *intr.* bounce repeatedly. **2** *intr. sl.* (of a cheque) be returned by a bank when there are insufficient funds to meet it. **3** *intr.* **a** (foll. by *about*, *up*) (of a person, dog, etc.) jump or spring energetically. **b** (foll. by *in*, *out*, etc.) rush noisily, angrily, enthusiastically, etc. (*bounced into the room*; *bounced out in a temper*). **4** *tr. colloq.* (usu. foll. by *into* + verbal noun) hustle, persuade (*bounced him into signing*). **5** *intr. colloq.* talk boastfully. **6** *tr. sl.* eject forcibly (from a dancehall, club, etc.). ● *n.* **1 a** a rebound. **b** the power of rebounding (*this ball has a good bounce*). **2** *colloq.* **a** swagger, self-confidence (*has a lot of bounce*). **b** liveliness. **c** resilience. **3** *sl.* (often prec. by *the*) dismissal or ejection. □ **bounce back** regain one's good health, spirits, prosperity, etc. [ME *bunsen* beat, thump, (perh. imit.), or f. LG *bunsen*, Du. *bons* thump]

■ *v.* **1** bound, rebound, ricochet, glance, *Billiards* cannon, *US Billiards* carom; (*bounce back*) recoil, spring *or* jump back, resile. **3** see SPRING *v.* 1. **4** see HUSTLE *v.* 2. **5** see BOAST *v.* 1. **6** see *throw out* 3. ● *n.* **1** bound, leap, hop; recoil, ricochet, rebound. **2 a** see SELF-ASSURANCE. **b** vitality, energy, verve, zest, vivacity, vivaciousness, liveliness, animation, dynamism, vigour, life, spirit, *colloq.* pep, zip, go, get-up-and-go. **3** see EXPULSION.

bouncer /bównsər/ *n.* **1** *sl.* a person employed to eject troublemakers from a dancehall, club, etc. **2** *Cricket* = BUMPER.

bouncing /bównsing/ *adj.* **1** (esp. of a baby) big and healthy. **2** boisterous.

bouncy /bównsi/ *adj.* (**bouncier, bounciest**) **1** (of a ball etc.) that bounces well. **2** cheerful and lively. **3** resilient, springy (*a bouncy sofa*). □□ **bouncily** *adv.* **bounciness** *n.*

■ **1** see ELASTIC *adj.* 1, 2. **2** see LIVELY 1. □□ **bounciness** see SPRING *n.* 3.

bound[1] /bownd/ *v.* & *n.* ● *v.intr.* **1 a** spring, leap (*bounded out of bed*). **b** walk or run with leaping strides. **2** (of a ball etc.) recoil from a wall or the ground; bounce. ● *n.* **1** a springy movement upwards or outwards; a leap. **2** a bounce. □ **by leaps and bounds** see LEAP. [F *bond*, *bondir* (orig. of sound) f. LL *bombitare* f. L *bombus* hum]

■ *v.* **1** leap, jump, hop, spring, vault, bounce; gambol, caper, romp, frolic, skip, prance, *colloq.* galumph, *sl.* cavort. **2** see BOUNCE *v.* 1. ● *n.* **1** leap, jump, vault, spring, hop.

bound[2] /bownd/ *n.* & *v.* ● *n.* (usu. in *pl.*) **1** a limitation; a restriction (*beyond the bounds of possibility*). **2** a border of a territory; a boundary. ● *v.tr.* **1** (esp. in *passive*; foll. by *by*) set bounds to; limit (*views bounded by prejudice*). **2** be the boundary of. □ **out of bounds 1** outside the part of a school etc. in which one is allowed to be. **2** beyond what is acceptable; forbidden. [ME f. AF *bounde*, OF *bonde* etc., f. med.L *bodina*, earlier *butina*, of unkn. orig.]

■ *n.* **1** (*bounds*) limit(s), extent, confines, margin(s), pale, compass, parameter; limitation, restriction, constraint. **2** (*bounds*) boundary, boundary line, border(s), margins, circuit, pale, edge, line, mete, rim. ● *v.* limit, restrict, confine, enclose, surround, delimit, define, circumscribe, control, restrain, constrain, hem in, *archaic* compass. □ **out of bounds 1** off limits. **2** forbidden, prohibited, proscribed, *verboten*, taboo; inadmissible, unacceptable, beyond the pale, out of order, below the belt, *colloq.* not on.

bound[3] /bownd/ *adj.* **1** (usu. foll. by *for*) ready to start or having started (*bound for stardom*). **2** (in *comb.*) moving in a specified direction (*northbound*; *outward bound*). [ME f. ON *búinn* past part. of *búa* get ready: *-d* euphonic, or partly after BIND[1]]

■ **1** destined, headed, directed, *en route*, on the way.

bound[4] /bownd/ *past* and *past part.* of BIND. □ **bound to** certain to (*he's bound to come*).

■ □ **bound to** certain to, sure to.

boundary /bówndəri, -dri/ *n.* (*pl.* **-ies**) **1** a real or notional line marking the limits of an area, territory, etc.; the limit itself or the area near it (*the fence is the boundary*; *boundary between liberty and licence*). **2** *Cricket* a hit crossing the limits of the field, scoring 4 or 6 runs. □ **boundary layer** the fluid immediately surrounding an object that is immersed and moving. **boundary rider** *Austral.* & *NZ* a person employed to ride round the fences etc. of a cattle or sheep station and keep them in good order. **boundary umpire** (in Australian Rules) an umpire on the sidelines who signals when the ball is out. [dial. *bounder* f. BOUND[2] + -ER[1] perh. after *limitary*]

■ **1** border, frontier, boundary line, line, borderline, dividing line; parameter, limit, extent, compass; division; edge, bound(s), confines, perimeter, fringe, margin.

bounden /bówndən/ *adj. archaic* obligatory. □ **bounden duty** solemn responsibility. [archaic past part. of BIND]

bounder /bówndər/ *n. colloq.* or *joc.* a cad; an ill-bred person.

■ see RASCAL.

boundless /bówndliss/ *adj.* unlimited; immense (*boundless enthusiasm*). □□ **boundlessly** *adv.* **boundlessness** *n.*

■ limitless, unbounded, unlimited, illimitable, endless, unending, never-ending, infinite, immeasurable, incalculable, measureless, untold, unrestricted, unchecked, inexhaustible, bottomless, unstoppable, unbridled, uncontrolled; vast, immense, enormous, tremendous, great.

bounteous /bówntiəss/ *adj. poet.* **1** generous, liberal. **2** freely given (*bounteous affection*). □□ **bounteously** *adv.* **bounteousness** *n.* [ME f. OF *bontif* f. *bonté* BOUNTY after *plenteous*]

■ generous, beneficent, munificent, liberal, ungrudging, big-hearted, open-handed, charitable, eleemosynary, magnanimous, bountiful; free, unsparing, unstinting.

bountiful /bówntifōōl/ *adj.* **1** = BOUNTEOUS. **2** ample. □ **Lady Bountiful** a charitable but patronizing lady of a neighbourhood (after a character in Farquhar's *Beaux' Stratagem*, 1707). □□ **bountifully** *adv.* [BOUNTY + -FUL]

■ **2** ample, abundant, plentiful, copious, generous, substantial, lavish, princely, profuse, prodigal, opulent, *poet.* bounteous, plenteous.

bounty /bównti/ *n.* (*pl.* **-ies**) **1** liberality; generosity. **2** a gift or reward, made usu. by the State, esp.: **a** a sum paid for a valiant act. **b** a sum paid to encourage a trading enterprise etc. **c** a sum paid to army or navy recruits on enlistment. □ **bounty-hunter** a person who pursues a criminal or seeks an achievement for the sake of the reward. **King's** (or **Queen's**) **bounty** *hist.* a grant made to a mother of triplets. [ME f. OF *bonté* f. L *bonitas -tatis* f. *bonus* good]

■ **1** generosity, liberality, munificence, prodigality, charitableness, philanthropy, charity, unselfishness, beneficence, largesse, goodness, *poet.* bounteousness. **2** gift, present, reward, gratuity, prize, premium, tribute, honour, award, favour, return, recompense; largesse.

bouquet /bookáy, bō-/ *n.* **1** a bunch of flowers, esp. for carrying at a wedding or other ceremony. **2** the scent of wine etc. **3** a favourable comment; a compliment. □ **bouquet garni** /gaárni/ *Cookery* a bunch of herbs used for flavouring stews etc. [F f. dial. var. of OF *bos*, *bois* wood]

■ **1** nosegay, posy, bunch, arrangement, spray. **2** aroma, scent, odour, fragrance, perfume, smell, redolence. **3** compliment(s), honour, tribute, homage, commendation, eulogy, plaudit, encomium, accolade, paean; praise.

Bourbon /bóorb'n, -BON/ *n.* **1** a chocolate-flavoured biscuit with chocolate-cream filling. **2** *US* a reactionary. [the Bourbon family, whose descendants founded dynasties in France and Spain]

bourbon /búrb'n, bóor-/ *n. US* whisky distilled from maize and rye. [*Bourbon* County, Kentucky, where it was first made]

■ see WHISKY.

bourdon /bóord'n/ *n. Mus.* **1** a low-pitched stop in an organ or harmonium. **2** the lowest bell in a peal of bells. **3** the drone pipe of a bagpipe. [F, = bagpipe-drone, f. Rmc, imit.]

bourgeois /bóorzhwaa/ *adj.* & *n.* often *derog.* ● *adj.* **1 a** conventionally middle-class. **b** humdrum, unimaginative. **c** selfishly materialistic. **2** upholding the interests of the capitalist class; non-communist. ● *n.* a bourgeois person. [F: see BURGESS]

■ *adj.* **1 a** middle-class, conventional, conservative, conformist; propertied, capitalist; see also NARROW-MINDED, PHILISTINE *adj.* **b** see BANAL. **c** materialistic, capitalistic, greedy, selfish, acquisitive, *archaic or joc.* esurient, *colloq.* money-grubbing, *colloq. usu. derog.* yuppie. **2** capitalistic, capitalist; non-communist. ● *n.* capitalist, materialist, professional, *colloq. usu. derog.* yuppie.

bourgeoisie /bóorzhwaazée/ *n.* **1** the capitalist class. **2** the middle class. [F]

bourn[1] /born, boorn/ *n.* a small stream. [ME: S. Engl. var. of BURN[2]]

bourn[2] /born, boorn/ *n.* (also **bourne**) *archaic* **1** a goal; a destination. **2** a limit. [F *borne* f. OF *bodne* BOUND[2]]

■ **2** see EDGE *n.* 1.

bourrée /bóorray/ *n.* **1** a lively French dance like a gavotte. **2** the music for this dance. [F]

bourse /boorss/ *n.* **1** (**Bourse**) the Paris equivalent of the Stock Exchange. **2** a money-market. [F, = purse, f. med.L *bursa*: cf. PURSE[1]]

■ see EXCHANGE *n.* 4.

boustrophedon /bówstrəfeéd'n, bōō-/ *adj.* & *adv.* (of written words) from right to left and from left to right in alternate lines. [Gk (adv.) = as an ox turns in ploughing f. *bous* ox + *-strophos* turning]

bout /bowt/ *n.* (often foll. by *of*) **1 a** a limited period (of intensive work or exercise). **b** a drinking session. **c** a period (of illness) (*a bout of flu*). **2 a** a wrestling- or boxing-match. **b** a trial of strength. [16th c.: app. the same as obs. *bought* bending]

■ **1 a, c** spell, period, session, stint, term, stretch; round; attack, fit, outburst, burst. **b** see BENDER. **2 a** fight, contest, match, boxing-match, wrestling-match, prizefight, meet, fist fight, spar, mill, fall, encounter, engagement, *colloq.* set-to.

boutique /bōōteék/ *n.* a small shop or department of a store, selling (esp. fashionable) clothes or accessories. [F, = small shop, f. L (as BODEGA)]

■ shop, *esp. US* store.

boutonnière /bōōtoniáir/ *n.* a spray of flowers worn in a buttonhole. [F]

■ buttonhole, corsage.

bouzouki /boozōōki/ *n.* a Greek form of mandolin. [mod. Gk]

bovate /bṓvayt/ *n. hist.* a measure of land, as much as one ox could plough in a year, varying from 10 to 18 acres. [med.L *bovata* f. L *bos bovis* ox]

bovine /bṓvīn/ *adj.* **1** of or relating to cattle. **2** stupid, dull. ▫▫ **bovinely** *adv.* [LL *bovinus* f. L *bos bovis* ox]
▪ **2** see DULL *adj.* 1.

Bovril /bóvril/ *n. propr.* a concentrated essence of beef diluted with hot water to make a drink. [L *bos bovis* ox, cow]

bovver /bóvvər/ *n. Brit. sl.* deliberate troublemaking. ▫ **bovver boot** a heavy laced boot worn typically by skinheads. **bovver boy** a violent hooligan. [cockney pronunc. of BOTHER]
▪ see *rowdyism* (ROWDY). ▫ **bovver boy** see ROWDY *n.*

bow[1] /bō/ *n.* & *v.* ● *n.* **1 a** a slip-knot with a double loop. **b** a ribbon, shoelace, etc., tied with this. **c** a decoration (on clothing, or painted etc.) in the form of a bow. **2** a device for shooting arrows with a taut string joining the ends of a curved piece of wood etc. **3 a** a rod with horsehair stretched along its length, used for playing the violin, cello, etc. **b** a single stroke of a bow over strings. **4 a** a shallow curve or bend. **b** a rainbow. **5** = *saddle-bow*. **6** a metal ring forming the handle of scissors, a key, etc. **7** *US* the side-piece of a spectacle-frame. **8** *Archery* = BOWMAN[1]. ● *v.tr.* (also *absol.*) use a bow on (a violin etc.) (*he bowed vigorously*). ▫ **bow-compass** (or **-compasses**) compasses with jointed legs. **bow-legged** having bandy legs. **bow-legs** bandy legs. **bow-saw** *Carpentry* a narrow saw stretched like a bowstring on a light frame. **bow-tie** a necktie in the form of a bow (sense 1). **bow-window** a curved bay window. **two strings to one's bow** a twofold resource. [OE *boga* f. Gmc: cf. BOW[2]]

bow[2] /bow/ *v.* & *n.* ● *v.* **1** *intr.* incline the head or trunk, esp. in greeting or assent or acknowledgement of applause. **2** *intr.* submit (*bowed to the inevitable*). **3** *tr.* cause to incline or submit (*bowed his head; bowed his will to hers*). **4** *tr.* express (thanks, assent, etc.) by bowing (*bowed agreement to the plan*). **5** *tr.* (foll. by *in*, *out*) usher or escort obsequiously (*bowed us out of the restaurant*). ● *n.* an inclining of the head or body in greeting, assent, or in the acknowledgement of applause, etc. ▫ **bow and scrape** be obsequious; fawn. **bow down 1** bend or kneel in submission or reverence (*bowed down before the king*). **2** (usu. in *passive*) make stoop; crush (*was bowed down by care*). **bowing acquaintance** a person one acknowledges but does not know well enough to speak to. **bow out 1** make one's exit (esp. formally). **2** retreat, withdraw; retire gracefully. **make one's bow** make a formal exit or entrance. **take a bow** acknowledge applause. [OE *būgan*, f. Gmc: cf. BOW[1]]
▪ *v.* **1** nod; curtsy, salaam, genuflect, prostrate oneself, make (an) obeisance, *archaic* show reverence, *hist.* kowtow. **2** defer, yield, submit, give in, give way, bow down, capitulate, surrender, succumb; (*bow to*) see OBEY. **3** bend, incline, lower, drop; make submit *or* surrender *or* yield. **5** usher, conduct, escort, guide, show (the way). ● *n.* nod; salaam, genuflection, prostration, obeisance, *archaic* reverence, *hist.* kowtow. ▫ **bow and scrape** fawn, kowtow, kiss a person's feet, grovel, prostrate oneself, demean *or* lower oneself, toady, lick a person's boots, cringe, dance to a person's tune, truckle, *colloq.* crawl, creep, bootlick. **bow down 1** bend, kneel, salaam, prostate oneself, make obeisance, *hist.* kowtow. **2** weigh down, crush, overload, load (down), wear *or* press down; overburden, burden, oppress, overwhelm. **bowing acquaintance** nodding acquaintance. **bow out 1** make one's exit, take one's leave. **2** see WITHDRAW 5.

bow[3] /bow/ *n. Naut.* **1** (often in *pl.*) the fore-end of a boat or a ship. **2** = BOWMAN[2]. ▫ **bow wave** a wave set up at the bows of a moving ship or in front of a body moving in air. **on the bow** within 45° of the point directly ahead. **shot across the bows** a warning. [LG *boog*, Du. *boeg*, ship's bow, orig. shoulder: see BOUGH]

bowdlerize /bówdlərīz/ *v.tr.* (also **-ise**) expurgate (a book etc.). ▫▫ **bowdlerism** *n.* **bowdlerization** /-záysh'n/ *n.* [T. *Bowdler* (d. 1825), expurgator of Shakesp.]
▪ see EDIT *v.* 5a.

bowel /bówəl/ *n.* **1** the part of the alimentary canal below the stomach; the intestine. **2** (in *pl.*) the depths, the innermost parts (*the bowels of the earth*). ▫ **bowel movement 1** discharge from the bowels; defecation. **2** the faeces discharged from the body. [ME f. OF *buel* f. L *botellus* little sausage]
▪ **1** intestine, gut, guts; (*bowels*) viscera, vitals, belly, *colloq.* innards. **2** (*bowels*) interior, inside(s), depths, innermost reaches, heart, centre, core. ▫ **bowel movement 1** defecation, movement, motion, evacuation, *sl.* pooh. **2** faeces, excrement, excreta, motion(s), stool(s), *sl.* pooh.

bower[1] /bowr/ *n.* & *v.* ● *n.* **1 a** a secluded place, esp. in a garden, enclosed by foliage; an arbour. **b** a summer-house. **2** *poet.* an inner room; a boudoir. ● *v.tr. poet.* embower. ▫▫ **bowery** *adj.* [OE *būr* f. Gmc]

bower[2] /bowr/ *n.* (in full **bower-anchor**) either of two anchors carried at a ship's bow. ▫ **best bower** the starboard bower. **bower-cable** the cable attached to a bower-anchor. **small bower** the port bower. [BOW[3] + -ER[1]]

bower[3] /bowr/ *n.* either of two cards at euchre and similar games. ▫ **left bower** the jack of the same colour as the right bower. **right bower** the jack of trumps. [G *Bauer* peasant, jack at cards, rel. to Du. *boer*: see BOOR]

bowerbird /bówrburd/ *n.* **1** any of various birds of the Ptilonorhyncidae family, native to Australia and New Guinea, the males of which construct elaborate bowers of feathers, grasses, shells, etc. during courtship. **2** a person who collects bric-à-brac.

bowery /bówri/ *n.* (also **Bowery**) (*pl.* **-ies**) *US* a district known as a resort of drunks and down-and-outs. [orig. the Bowery, a street in New York City, f. Du. *bouwerij* farm]

bowfin /bṓfin/ *n.* a voracious American freshwater fish, *Amia calva*. [BOW[1] + FIN]

bowhead /bṓhed/ *n.* an Arctic whale, *Balaena mysticetus*.

bowie /bṓ-i/ *n.* (in full **bowie knife**) a long knife with a blade double-edged at the point, used as a weapon by American pioneers. [J. *Bowie*, Amer. soldier d. 1836]

bowl[1] /bōl/ *n.* **1 a** a usu. round deep basin used for food or liquid. **b** the quantity (of soup etc.) a bowl holds. **c** the contents of a bowl. **2 a** any deep-sided container shaped like a bowl (*lavatory bowl*). **b** the bowl-shaped part of a tobacco-pipe, spoon, balance, etc. **3** esp. *US* a bowl-shaped region or building, esp. an amphitheatre (*Hollywood Bowl*). ▫▫ **bowlful** *n.* (*pl.* **-fuls**). [OE *bolle*, *bolla*, f. Gmc]
▪ **1 a** dish, plate; basin, pan.

bowl[2] /bōl/ *n.* & *v.* ● *n.* **1 a** a wooden or hard rubber ball, slightly asymmetrical so that it runs on a curved course, used in the game of bowls. **b** a wooden ball or disc used in playing skittles. **c** a large ball with indents for gripping, used in tenpin bowling. **2** (in *pl.*; usu. treated as *sing.*) **a** a game played with bowls (sense 1a) on grass. **b** tenpin bowling. **c** skittles. **3** a spell or turn of bowling in cricket. ● *v.* **1 a** *tr.* roll (a ball, a hoop, etc.) along the ground. **b** *intr.* play bowls or skittles. **2** *tr.* (also *absol.*) *Cricket* etc. **a** deliver (a ball, an over, etc.) (*bowled six overs; bowled well*). **b** (often foll. by *out*) dismiss (a batsman) by knocking down the wicket with a ball (*soon bowled him out*). **c** (often foll. by *down*) knock (a wicket) over. **3** *intr.* (often foll. by *along*) go along rapidly by revolving, esp. on wheels (*the cart bowled along the road*). ▫ **bowl out** *Cricket* dismiss (a batsman or a side). **bowl over 1** knock down. **2** *colloq.* **a** impress greatly. **b** overwhelm (*bowled over by her energy*). [ME & F *boule* f. L *bulla* bubble]
▪ *v.* **3** move, trundle, wheel, roll, spin, whirl; hurtle. ▫ **bowl over 1** knock down *or* over, bring down, fell, floor, cut *or* strike down, flatten. **2** see OVERWHELM 3.

bowler[1] /bṓlər/ *n.* **1** *Cricket* etc. a member of the fielding side who bowls or is bowling. **2** a player at bowls.

bowler[2] /bṓlər/ *n.* (in full **bowler hat**) a man's hard felt hat with a round dome-shaped crown. □ **bowler-hat** (**-hatted, -hatting**) *sl.* retire (a person) from the army etc. (*he's been bowler-hatted*). [*Bowler*, a hatter, who designed it in 1850]

bowline /bṓlin/ *n. Naut.* **1** a rope attaching the weather side of a square sail to the bow. **2** a simple knot for forming a non-slipping loop at the end of a rope. [ME f. MLG *bōlīne* (as BOW[3], LINE[1])]

bowling /bṓling/ *n.* the game of bowls as a sport or recreation. □ **bowling-alley 1** a long enclosure for skittles or tenpin bowling. **2** a building containing these. **bowling-crease** *Cricket* the line from behind which a bowler delivers the ball. **bowling-green** a lawn used for playing bowls.

bowman[1] /bṓmən/ *n.* (*pl.* **-men**) an archer.

bowman[2] /bówmən/ *n.* (*pl.* **-men**) the rower nearest the bow of esp. a racing boat.

bowser /bówzər/ *n.* **1** a tanker used for fuelling aircraft etc. **2** *Austral.* & *NZ* a petrol pump. [trade name, orig. propr.]

bowshot /bṓshot/ *n.* the distance to which a bow can send an arrow.

bowsprit /bṓsprit/ *n. Naut.* a spar running out from a ship's bow to which the forestays are fastened. [ME f. Gmc (as BOW[3], SPRIT)]

Bow Street runner /bō/ *n.* (also **Bow Street officer**) *hist.* a London policeman. [*Bow Street* in London, containing the chief metropolitan police-court]

■ see *police officer*.

bowstring /bṓstring/ *n.* & *v.* ● *n.* the string of an archer's bow. ● *v.tr.* strangle with a bowstring (a former Turkish method of execution).

■ see CHOKE *v.* 1.

bow-wow /bów-wów/ *int.* & *n.* ● *int.* an imitation of a dog's bark. ● *n.* **1** *colloq.* a dog. **2** a dog's bark. [imit.]

bowyang /bṓ-yang/ *n. Austral.* & *NZ* either of a pair of bands or straps worn round the trouser-legs below the knee. [dial. *bowy-yangs* etc.]

bowyer /bṓ-yər/ *n.* a maker or seller of archers' bows.

box[1] /boks/ *n.* & *v.* ● *n.* **1** a container, usu. with flat sides and of firm material such as wood or card, esp. for holding solids. **2 a** the amount that will fill a box. **b** *Brit.* a gift of a kind formerly given to tradesmen etc. at Christmas. **3** a separate compartment for any of various purposes, e.g. for a small group in a theatre, for witnesses in a lawcourt, for horses in a stable or vehicle. **4** an enclosure or receptacle for a special purpose (often in *comb.*: *money box*; *telephone box*). **5** a facility at a newspaper office for receiving replies to an advertisement. **6** (prec. by *the*) *colloq.* television; one's television set (*what's on the box?*). **7** an enclosed area or space. **8** a space or area of print on a page, enclosed by a border. **9** *Brit.* a small country house for use when shooting, fishing, or for other sporting activity. **10** a protective casing for a piece of mechanism. **11** a light shield for protecting the genitals in sport, esp. in cricket. **12** (prec. by *the*) *Football colloq.* the penalty area. **13** *Baseball* the area occupied by the batter or the pitcher. **14** a coachman's seat. ● *v.tr.* **1** put in or provide with a box. **2** (foll. by *in*, *up*) confine; restrain from movement. **3** (foll. by *up*) *Austral.* & *NZ* mix up (different flocks of sheep). □ **box camera** a simple box-shaped hand camera. **box the compass** *Naut.* recite the points of the compass in the correct order. **box girder** a hollow girder square in cross-section. **box junction** *Brit.* a road area at a junction marked with a yellow grid, which a vehicle should enter only if its exit from it is clear. **box kite** a kite in the form of a long box open at each end. **box number** a number by which replies are made to a private advertisement in a newspaper. **box office 1** an office for booking seats and buying tickets at a theatre, cinema, etc. **2** the commercial aspect of the arts and entertainment (often *attrib.*: *a box-office failure*). **box pleat** a pleat consisting of two parallel creases forming a raised band. **box spanner** a spanner with a box-shaped end fitting over the head of a nut. **box spring** each of a set of vertical springs housed in a frame, e.g. in a mattress. □□ **boxful** *n.* (*pl.* **-fuls**). **boxlike** *adj.* [OE f. LL *buxis* f. L PYXIS]

■ *n.* **1, 2a** case, receptacle, crate, carton, container, casket, coffer, caddy, chest. **2 b** tip, bonus, gratuity. **3** compartment, stall, booth, cubicle, enclosure. **6** televison, TV, *Brit. colloq.* goggle-box, telly, *US colloq.* tube, *US sl.* boob tube. **7** see ENCLOSURE 2. ● *v.* **1** crate, encase, package, pack, containerize, case, wrap up. **2** (*box in* or *up*) trap, confine, hem *or* block in, shut up *or* in, coop up, bound, enclose, surround.

box[2] /boks/ *v.* & *n.* ● *v.* **1 a** *tr.* fight (an opponent) at boxing. **b** *intr.* practise boxing. **2** slap (esp. a person's ears). ● *n.* a slap with the hand, esp. on the ears. □ **box clever** *colloq.* act in a clever or effective way. [ME: orig. unkn.]

■ *v.* **1 a** fight (with), come to blows with, spar with, *sl.* mill. **b** fight, engage in fisticuffs, spar, battle. **2** strike, slap, smack, rap, punch, hit, clout, thump, cuff, *US* slug, *colloq.* sock, whack, thwack *sl.* mill, belt, clobber, wallop, whop. ● *n.* blow, slap, smack, rap, punch, hit, strike, clout, thump, cuff, buffet, *US* slug, *colloq.* sock, whack, thwack, *sl.* belt, clobber, whop, wallop.

box[3] /boks/ *n.* **1** any small evergreen tree or shrub of the genus *Buxus*, esp. *B. sempervirens*, a slow-growing tree with glossy dark green leaves which is often used in hedging. **2** its wood, used for carving, turning, engraving, etc. **3** any of various trees in Australasia which have similar wood or foliage, esp. those of several species of *Eucalyptus*. □ **box elder** the American ash-leaved maple, *Acer negundo*. [OE f. L *buxus*, Gk *puxos*]

Box and Cox /bóks ənd kóks/ *n.* & *v.* ● *n.* (often *attrib.*) two persons sharing accommodation etc., and using it at different times. ● *v.intr.* share accommodation, duties, etc. by a strictly timed arrangement. [the names of characters in a play (1847) by J. M. Morton]

boxcar /bókskaar/ *n. US* an enclosed railway goods wagon, usu. with sliding doors on the sides.

Boxer /bóksər/ *n. hist.* a member of a fiercely nationalistic Chinese secret society that flourished in the 19th c. [transl. of Chin. *i ho chuan*, lit. 'righteous harmony fists']

boxer /bóksər/ *n.* **1** a person who practises boxing, esp. for sport. **2 a** a medium-size dog of a breed with a smooth brown coat and puglike face. **b** this breed. □ **boxer shorts** men's underpants similar to shorts worn in boxing, with a shallow curved slit at each side.

■ **1** see PUGILIST. □ **boxer shorts** see PANTS 1.

boxing /bóksing/ *n.* the practice of fighting with the fists, esp. in padded gloves as a sport. □ **boxing glove** each of a pair of heavily padded gloves used in boxing. **boxing weight** each of a series of fixed weight-ranges at which boxers are matched.

■ see *pugilism* (PUGILIST).

Boxing Day /bóksing/ *n.* the first weekday after Christmas. [from the custom of giving tradesmen gifts or money: see BOX[1] *n.* 2b]

boxroom /bóksrōōm, -rŏŏm/ *n. Brit.* a room or large cupboard for storing boxes, cases, etc.

boxwood /bókswŏŏd/ *n.* **1** the wood of the box used esp. by engravers for the fineness of its grain and for its hardness. **2** = BOX[3] 1.

boxy /bóksi/ *adj.* (**boxier, boxiest**) reminiscent of a box; (of a room or space) very cramped.

boy /boy/ *n.* & *int.* ● *n.* **1** a male child or youth. **2** a young man, esp. regarded as not yet mature. **3** a male servant, attendant, etc. **4** (**the boys**) *colloq.* a group of men mixing socially. ● *int.* expressing pleasure, surprise, etc. □ **boy scout** = SCOUT[1] 4. **boys in blue** *Brit.* policemen. □□ **boyhood** *n.* **boyish** *adj.* **boyishly** *adv.* **boyishness** *n.* [ME = servant, perh. ult. f. L *boia* fetter]

■ *n.* **1, 2** lad, youth, young man, stripling, youngster, schoolboy, juvenile, minor, *Austral.* & *dial.* tacker, *colloq.* kid, laddie, (little) shaver, fellow, chap, *US colloq.* bub, *Welsh* & *Ir. colloq.* boyo, *usu. derog.* brat, *esp. joc.* little man. **3** servant, house-servant, attendant, *hist.* varlet;

lackey, slave; waiter, *garçon*. ● *int.* wow, (my) god, Lord, golly, goodness, gosh, whew, ooh, *archaic* marry, *Brit. sl.* coo, cor, *US sl.* jeepers. □ **boys in blue** see POLICE *n.*
□□ **boyish** young, youthful, adolescent, childlike; childish, puerile, juvenile, immature, infantile, *US* sophomoric.

boyar /bō-yaár/ *n. hist.* a member of the old aristocracy in Russia. [Russ. *boyarin* grandee]

boycott /bóykot/ *v.* & *n.* ● *v.tr.* **1** combine in refusing social or commercial relations with (a person, group, country, etc.) usu. as punishment or coercion. **2** refuse to handle (goods) to this end. ● *n.* such a refusal. [Capt. C. C. *Boycott*, Irish land-agent d. 1897, so treated from 1880]
■ *v.* blacklist, embargo, ostracize; avoid, refuse, shun, reject, pass over *or* by, *Brit.* black, *literary* eschew. ● *n.* embargo, blacklist, ban; interdiction, prohibition.

boyfriend /bóyfrend/ *n.* a person's regular male companion or lover.
■ see SWEETHEART 1.

Boyle's law /boylz/ *n.* the law that the pressure of a given mass of gas is inversely proportional to its volume at a constant temperature. [Robert *Boyle*, Irish scientist d. 1691]

boyo /bóyō/ *n.* (*pl.* **-os**) *Welsh* & *Ir. colloq.* boy, fellow (esp. as a form of address).
■ see BOY *n.* 1, 2.

boysenberry /bóyz'nbəri/ *n.* (*pl.* **-ies**) **1** a hybrid of several species of bramble. **2** the large red edible fruit of this plant. [R. *Boysen*, 20th-c. Amer. horticulturalist]

BP *abbr.* **1** boiling-point. **2** blood pressure. **3** before the present (era). **4** British Petroleum. **5** British Pharmacopoeia.

Bp. *abbr.* Bishop.

BPC *abbr.* British Pharmaceutical Codex.

B.Phil. *abbr.* Bachelor of Philosophy.

Bq *abbr.* becquerel.

BR *abbr.* British Rail.

Br *symb. Chem.* the element bromine.

Br. *abbr.* **1** British. **2** Brother.

bra /braa/ *n.* (*pl.* **bras**) *colloq.* = BRASSIÈRE. [abbr.]

brace /brayss/ *n.* & *v.* ● *n.* **1 a** a device that clamps or fastens tightly. **b** a strengthening piece of iron or timber in building. **2** (in *pl.*) *Brit.* straps supporting trousers from the shoulders. **3** a wire device for straightening the teeth. **4** (*pl.* same) a pair (esp. of game). **5** a rope attached to the yard of a ship for trimming the sail. **6 a** a connecting mark { or } used in printing. **b** *Mus.* a similar mark connecting staves to be performed at the same time. ● *v.tr.* **1** fasten tightly, give firmness to. **2** make steady by supporting. **3** (esp. as **bracing** *adj.*) invigorate, refresh. **4** (often *refl.*) prepare for a difficulty, shock, etc. □ **brace and bit** a revolving tool with a D-shaped central handle for boring. □□ **bracingly** *adv.* **bracingness** *n.* [ME f. OF *brace* two arms, *bracier* embrace, f. L *bra(c)chia* arms]
■ *n.* **1 a** clasp, clamp, vice, fastener, staple, clip, holdfast, catch, coupler, coupling. **b** bracket, stiffener, reinforcement, reinforcer, support, buttress, prop, stay, strut, truss. **2** (*braces*) *US* suspenders, *dial.* & *US* galluses. **4** pair, couple, set, team (of two). ● *v.* **1** see SECURE *v.* 2. **2** steady, stabilize, reinforce, support, secure, strengthen, prop *or* shore *or* hold up, bolster, buttress, strut. **3** (**bracing**) invigorating, tonic, stimulating, refreshing, exhilarating, fortifying, strengthening, restorative, vitalizing; brisk, fresh. **4** (*brace oneself*) steady *or* gird *or* prepare oneself, gird one's loins, *colloq.* gear oneself up; get *or* make ready, prepare, hold on, hold tight, *colloq.* get fired *or* geared up, hang on. □ **brace and bit** see DRILL[1] *n.* 1.

bracelet /bráyslit/ *n.* **1** an ornamental band, hoop, or chain worn on the wrist or arm. **2** *sl.* a handcuff. [ME f. OF, dimin. of *bracel* f. L *bracchiale* f. *bra(c)chium* arm]

bracer /bráysər/ *n. colloq.* a tonic.
■ see TONIC *n.*

brachial /bráykiəl/ *adj.* **1** of or relating to the arm (*brachial artery*). **2** like an arm. [L *brachialis* f. *bra(c)chium* arm]

brachiate /bráykiayt/ *v.* & *adj.* ● *v.intr.* (of certain apes and monkeys) move by using the arms to swing from branch to branch. ● *adj. Biol.* **1** having arms. **2** having paired branches on alternate sides. □□ **brachiation** /-áysh'n/ *n.* **brachiator** *n.* [L *bra(c)chium* arm]

brachiopod /bráykiəpod, brák-/ *n.* any marine invertebrate of the phylum Brachiopoda (esp. a fossil one) having a two-valved chalky shell and a ciliated feeding arm. [mod.L f. Gk *brakhiōn* arm + *pous podos* foot]

brachiosaurus /bráykiəsáwrəss, brák-/ *n.* any huge plant-eating dinosaur of the genus *Brachiosaurus* with forelegs longer than its hind legs. [mod.L f. Gk *brakhiōn* arm + *sauros* lizard]

brachistochrone /brakístəkrōn/ *n.* a curve between two points along which a body can move in a shorter time than for any other curve. [Gk *brakhistos* shortest + *khronos* time]

brachy- /brákki/ *comb. form* short. [Gk *brakhus* short]

brachycephalic /brákkisifállik/ *adj.* having a broad short head. □□ **brachycephalous** /brákkiséffələss/ *adj.* [BRACHY- + Gk *kephalē* head]

brachylogy /brəkílləji/ *n.* (*pl.* **-ies**) **1** over-conciseness of expression. **2** an instance of this.

brack /brak/ *n. Ir.* cake or bread containing dried fruit etc. [abbr. of BARMBRACK]

bracken /brákkən/ *n.* **1** any large coarse fern, esp. *Pteridium aquilinum*, abundant on heaths and moorlands, and in woods. **2** a mass of such ferns. Also called BRAKE[5]. [north. ME f. ON]

bracket /brákkit/ *n.* & *v.* ● *n.* **1** a right-angled or other support attached to and projecting from a vertical surface. **2** a shelf fixed with such a support to a wall. **3** each of a pair of marks () [] {} used to enclose words or figures. **4** a group classified as containing similar elements or falling between given limits (*income bracket*). **5** *Mil.* the distance between two artillery shots fired either side of the target to establish range. ● *v.tr.* (**bracketed, bracketing**) **1 a** couple (names etc.) with a bracket. **b** imply a connection or equality between. **2 a** enclose in brackets as parenthetic or spurious. **b** *Math.* enclose in brackets as having specific relations to what precedes or follows. **3** *Mil.* establish the range of (a target) by firing two preliminary shots one short of and the other beyond it. [F *braguette* or Sp. *bragueta* codpiece, dimin. of F *brague* f. Prov. *braga* f. L *braca*, pl. *bracae* breeches]
■ *n.* **1** support, console, cantilever, gusset, *Archit.* corbel. **2** shelf. **3** parenthesis, brace. **4** category, class, set, group, grouping, classification, division, level, stratum; range, span; order, grade, rank. ● *v.* **1** couple, join, link, connect, put together, place side by side, ally, attach, unite, combine; classify, rank, group, class, order, bunch together; associate, affiliate, relate.

brackish /brákkish/ *adj.* (of water etc.) slightly salty. □□ **brackishness** *n.* [obs. *brack* (adj.) f. MLG, MDu. *brac*]
■ see SALT *adj.*

bract /brakt/ *n.* a modified and often brightly coloured leaf, with a flower or an inflorescence in its axil. □□ **bracteal** *adj.* **bracteate** /-ti-it/ *adj.* [L *bractea* thin plate, gold-leaf]

brad /brad/ *n.* a thin flat nail with a head in the form of slight enlargement at the top. [var. of ME *brod* goad, pointed instrument, f. ON *broddr* spike]

bradawl /bráddawl/ *n.* a small tool with a pointed end for boring holes by hand. [BRAD + AWL]

bradycardia /bráddikaárdiə/ *n. Med.* abnormally slow heart-action. [Gk *bradus* slow + *kardia* heart]

brae /bray/ *n. Sc.* a steep bank or hillside. [ME f. ON *brá* eyelash]
■ see HILL *n.* 1.

brag /brag/ *v.* & *n.* ● *v.* (**bragged, bragging**) **1** *intr.* talk boastfully. **2** *tr.* boast about. ● *n.* **1** a card-game like poker. **2** a boastful statement; boastful talk. □□ **bragger** *n.* **braggingly** *adv.* [ME, orig. adj., = spirited, boastful: orig. unkn.]

■ *v.* **1** boast, crow, swagger, rodomontade, blow one's (own) trumpet, talk tall, *colloq.* show off, bounce, gas, talk big, *Austral.* & *NZ colloq.* skite, *Austral.* & *US colloq.* blow, *literary* vaunt. **2** boast of, trumpet, *literary* vaunt. ● *n.* **2** see BOAST *n.* □□ **bragger** see BRAGGART *n.*

braggadocio /bråggədṓchiō, -dṓshiō/ *n.* empty boasting; a boastful manner of speech and behaviour. [*Braggadochio*, a braggart in Spenser's *Faerie Queene*, f. BRAG or BRAGGART + It. augment. suffix *-occio*]

■ see BRAVADO.

braggart /bråggərt/ *n.* & *adj.* ● *n.* a person given to bragging. ● *adj.* boastful. [F *bragard* f. *braguer* BRAG]

■ *n.* boaster, bragger, peacock, gascon, *archaic* scaramouch, *colloq.* show-off, big-mouth, loud-mouth, blowhard, *Austral. sl.* lair, *US sl.* flannel-mouth. ● *adj.* see BOASTFUL.

Brahma /bra'amə/ *n.* **1** the Hindu Creator. **2** the supreme divine reality in Hindu belief. [Skr., = creator]

Brahman /bra'amən/ *n.* (also **brahman**) (*pl.* **-mans**) **1** a member of the highest Hindu caste, whose members are traditionally eligible for the priesthood. **2** = BRAHMA 2. □□ **Brahmanic** /-mánnik/ *adj.* **Brahmanical** /-mánnik'l/ *adj.* **Brahmanism** *n.* [Skr. *brāhmaṇas* f. *brahmaṇ* priest]

brahmaputra /bra'aməpṓōtrə/ *n.* (also **brahma**) **1** any bird of a large Asian breed of domestic fowl. **2** this breed. [river *Brahmaputra* in India, from where it was brought]

Brahmin /bra'amin/ *n.* **1** = BRAHMAN. **2** *US* a socially or intellectually superior person. [var. of BRAHMAN]

braid /brayd/ *n.* & *v.* ● *n.* **1** a woven band of silk or thread used for edging or trimming. **2** a length of entwined hair. ● *v.tr.* **1** plait or intertwine (hair or thread). **2** trim or decorate with braid. □□ **braider** *n.* [OE *bregdan* f. Gmc]

■ *n.* **1** trimming, trim, fillet, ribbon, twine, soutache, edging, piping, lace, lacing, rickrack, *passementerie*, thread, ruche, welt, *archaic* purfle; band. **2** plait. ● *v.* **1** plait, intertwine, interlace, weave, twist, twine, interweave. **2** trim, edge, pipe, lace, fringe; see also DECORATE 1, 3.

braiding /bráyding/ *n.* **1** various types of braid collectively. **2** braided work.

Braille /brayl/ *n.* & *v.* ● *n.* a system of writing and printing for the blind, in which characters are represented by patterns of raised dots. ● *v.tr.* print or transcribe in Braille. [L. *Braille*, Fr. teacher d. 1852, its inventor]

brain /brayn/ *n.* & *v.* ● *n.* **1** an organ of soft nervous tissue contained in the skull of vertebrates, functioning as the coordinating centre of sensation, and of intellectual and nervous activity. **2** (in *pl.*) the substance of the brain, esp. as food. **3 a** a person's intellectual capacity (*has a poor brain*). **b** (often in *pl.*) intelligence; high intellectual capacity (*has a brain*; *has brains*). **c** *colloq.* a clever person. **4** (in *pl.*; prec. by *the*) *colloq.* **a** the cleverest person in a group. **b** a person who originates a complex plan or idea (*the brains behind the robbery*). **5** an electronic device with functions comparable to those of a brain. ● *v.tr.* **1** dash out the brains of. **2** strike hard on the head. □ **brain-dead** suffering from brain death. **brain death** irreversible brain damage causing the end of independent respiration, regarded as indicative of death. **brain drain** *colloq.* the loss of skilled personnel by emigration. **brain fever** inflammation of the brain. **brain-pan** *colloq.* the skull. **brain stem** the central trunk of the brain, upon which the cerebrum and cerebellum are set, and which continues downwards to form the spinal cord. **brains** (*US* **brain**) **trust** a group of experts who give impromptu answers to questions, usu. publicly. **brain-teaser** (or **-twister**) *colloq.* a puzzle or problem. **brain trust** *US* a group of expert advisers. **on the brain** *colloq.* obsessively in one's thoughts. [OE *brægen* f. WG]

■ *n.* **3a, b** intelligence, intellect, brainpower, understanding, cleverness, brightness, smartness, sense, thought, imagination, capacity, perspicacity, perspicaciousness, perceptiveness, perception, percipience, braininess, *Philos.* nous; head, mind, *archaic* headpiece, *colloq.* grey matter, *sl.* loaf; wisdom, sagacity, wit(s), discernment, acumen; knowledge, cognition. **3c, 4** (*brains*) genius, mastermind, intellectual, thinker, maestro, authority, *colloq.* whiz-kid, highbrow, *esp. Brit. colloq.* boffin; leader, planner. ● *v.* **1** see MURDER *v.* 1. **2** head-butt, clout, cuff, *colloq.* sock, whack, thwack, *sl.* clobber, whop, wallop. □ **brain-teaser** see PUZZLE *n.* 2.

brainchild /bráynchīld/ *n.* (*pl.* **-children**) *colloq.* an idea, plan, or invention regarded as the result of a person's mental effort.

brainless /bráynliss/ *adj.* stupid, foolish.

■ see STUPID *adj.* 1, 5.

brainpower /bráynpowr/ *n.* mental ability or intelligence.

■ see INTELLIGENCE 1b.

brainstorm /bráynstorm/ *n.* **1** a violent or excited outburst often as a result of a sudden mental disturbance. **2** *colloq.* mental confusion. **3** *US* a brainwave. **4** a concerted intellectual treatment of a problem by discussing spontaneous ideas about it. □□ **brainstorming** *n.* (in sense 4).

■ **3** see THOUGHT[1] 4.

brainwash /bráynwosh/ *v.tr.* subject (a person) to a prolonged process by which ideas other than and at variance with those already held are implanted in the mind. □□ **brainwashing** *n.*

■ see INDOCTRINATE.

brainwave /bráynwayv/ *n.* **1** (usu. in *pl.*) an electrical impulse in the brain. **2** *colloq.* a sudden bright idea.

■ **2** see INSPIRATION 2.

brainy /bráyni/ *adj.* (**brainier**, **brainiest**) intellectually clever or active. □□ **brainily** *adv.* **braininess** *n.*

■ see INTELLECTUAL *adj.* 2.

braise /brayz/ *v.tr.* fry lightly and then stew slowly with a little liquid in a closed container. [F *braiser* f. *braise* live coals]

brake[1] /brayk/ *n.* & *v.* ● *n.* **1** (often in *pl.*) a device for checking the motion of a mechanism, esp. a wheel or vehicle, or for keeping it at rest. **2** anything that has the effect of hindering or impeding (*shortage of money was a brake on their enthusiasm*). ● *v.* **1** *intr.* apply a brake. **2** *tr.* retard or stop with a brake. □ **brake block** a block used to hold a brake shoe. **brake drum** a cylinder attached to a wheel on which the brake shoe presses to brake. **brake fluid** fluid used in a hydraulic brake system. **brake horsepower** the power of an engine reckoned in terms of the force needed to brake it. **brake lining** a strip of fabric which increases the friction of the brake shoe. **brake shoe** a long curved block which presses on the brake drum to brake. **brake van** *Brit.* a railway coach or vehicle from which the train's brakes can be controlled. □□ **brakeless** *adj.* [prob. obs. *brake* in sense 'machine-handle, bridle']

■ *n.* **2** curb, check, restraint, restriction, constraint, control, rein. ● *v.* **1** put on *or* apply the brakes. **2** slow, slow up *or* down, pull up, reduce the speed of, decelerate, slacken, hold up; stop, halt, bring to a stop *or* halt.

brake[2] /brayk/ *n.* a large estate car. [var. of BREAK[2]]

brake[3] /brayk/ *n.* & *v.* ● *n.* **1** a toothed instrument used for crushing flax and hemp. **2** (in full **brake harrow**) a heavy kind of harrow for breaking up large lumps of earth. ● *v.tr.* crush (flax or hemp) by beating it. [ME, rel. to BREAK[1]]

brake[4] /brayk/ *n.* **1** a thicket. **2** brushwood. [ME f. OF *bracu*, MLG *brake* branch, stump]

brake[5] /brayk/ *n.* bracken. [ME, perh. shortened f. BRACKEN, *-en* being taken as a pl. ending]

brake[6] *archaic past* of BREAK[1].

brakeman /bráykmən/ *n.* (*pl.* **-men**) **1** *US* an official on a train, responsible for maintenance on a journey. **2** a person in charge of brakes. [BRAKE[1] + MAN]

brakesman /bráyksmən/ *n.* (*pl.* **-men**) *Brit.* = BRAKEMAN 2.

bramble /brámb'l/ *n.* **1** any of various thorny shrubs bearing fleshy red or black berries, esp. the blackberry bush, *Rubus fructicosus*. **2** the edible berry of these shrubs. **3** any of

various other rosaceous shrubs with similar foliage, esp. the dog rose (*Rosa canina*). □□ **brambly** *adj.* [OE *brǣmbel* (earlier *brǣmel*): see BROOM]
■ □□ **brambly** see THORNY 1.

brambling /brámbling/ *n.* the speckled finch, *Fringilla montifringilla*, native to northern Eurasia, the male having a distinctive red breast. [G *Brämling* f. WG (cf. BRAMBLE)]

Bramley /brámli/ *n.* (*pl.* **-eys**) (in full **Bramley's seedling**) a large green variety of cooking apple. [M. *Bramley*, Engl. butcher in whose garden it may have first grown *c.*1850]

bran /bran/ *n.* grain husks separated from the flour. □ **bran-tub** *Brit.* a lucky dip with prizes concealed in bran. [ME f. OF. of unkn. orig.]

branch /braanch/ *n.* & *v.* ● *n.* **1** a limb extending from a tree or bough. **2** a lateral extension or subdivision, esp. of a river, road, or railway. **3** a conceptual extension or subdivision, as of a family, knowledge, etc. **4** a local division or office etc. of a large business, as of a bank, library, etc. ● *v.intr.* (often foll. by *off*) **1** diverge from the main part. **2** divide into branches. **3** (of a tree) bear or send out branches. □ **branch out** extend one's field of interest. □□ **branched** *adj.* **branchlet** *n.* **branchlike** *adj.* **branchy** *adj.* [ME f. OF *branche* f. LL *branca* paw]
■ *n.* **1** offshoot, arm; limb, bough. **2, 3** extension, offshoot; wing, side; department, section, subsection, division, subdivision, ramification, part, area, sphere, field. **4** office, bureau; affiliate, subsidiary. ● *v.* **1** (*branch off*) diverge, deviate, turn off *or* away, separate, depart, divaricate. **2** divide, subdivide, fork, separate, split, ramify, break up. □ **branch out** diversify, spread *or* stretch one's wings.

branchia /brángkiə/ *n.pl.* (also **branchiae** /-ki-ee/) gills. □□ **branchial** *adj.* **branchiate** /-kiayt/ *adj.* [L *branchia*, pl. *-ae*, f. Gk *bragkhia* pl.]

brand /brand/ *n.* & *v.* ● *n.* **1 a** a particular make of goods. **b** an identifying trade mark, label, etc. **2** (usu. foll. by *of*) a special or characteristic kind (*brand of humour*). **3** an identifying mark burned on livestock or (formerly) prisoners etc. with a hot iron. **4** an iron used for this. **5** a piece of burning, smouldering, or charred wood. **6** a stigma; a mark of disgrace. **7** *poet.* **a** a torch. **b** a sword. **8** a kind of blight, leaving leaves with a burnt appearance. ● *v.tr.* **1** mark with a hot iron. **2** stigmatize; mark with disgrace (*they branded him a liar; was branded for life*). **3** impress unforgettably on one's mind. **4** assign a trademark or label to. □ **brand-new** completely or obviously new. □□ **brander** *n.* [OE f. Gmc]
■ *n.* **1 a** kind, make, type, sort, variety. **b** brand name, trade *or* proprietary name, trade mark, label, mark, marque, name brand, *Brit. archaic* chop. **2** see TYPE *n.* 1. **6** see STIGMA 1. **7 a** see TORCH *n.* **b** see BLADE 6. ● *v.* **2** discredit, disgrace, dishonour, besmirch, smear, tarnish, taint, blacken; accuse of being, stigmatize as, pronounce; label, characterize as, mark (down) as. **3** see IMPRESS[1] *v.* 3, 4. **4** mark, stamp, identify, tag, label; register (as a trade mark). □ **brand-new** new, unused, fresh, firsthand, mint, virgin; latest, today's, up to date, up to the minute, just out, hot, hot off the press, red-hot.

brandish /brándish/ *v.tr.* wave or flourish as a threat or in display. □□ **brandisher** *n.* [OF *brandir* ult. f. Gmc, rel. to BRAND]
■ see FLOURISH *v.* 4.

brandling /brándling/ *n.* a red earthworm, *Eisenia foetida*, with rings of a brighter colour, which is often found in manure and used as bait. [BRAND + -LING[1]]

brandy /brándi/ *n.* (*pl.* **-ies**) a strong alcoholic spirit distilled from wine or fermented fruit juice. □ **brandy-ball** *Brit.* a kind of brandy-flavoured sweet. **brandy butter** a rich sweet hard sauce made with brandy, butter, and sugar. **brandy-snap** a crisp rolled gingerbread wafer usu. filled with cream. [earlier *brand(e)wine* f. Du. *brandewijn* burnt (distilled) wine]

brank-ursine /brangkúrsīn/ *n.* the plant *Acanthus mollis* or *A. spinosus*, with three-lobed flowers and spiny leaves, used as a motif for the Corinthian capital. Also called *bear's breech* (see BEAR[2]). [F *branche ursine*, med.L *branca ursina* bear's claw: see BRANCH, URSINE]

brant *US* var. of BRENT.

brash[1] /brash/ *adj.* **1** vulgarly or ostentatiously self-assertive. **2** hasty, rash. **3** impudent. □□ **brashly** *adv.* **brashness** *n.* [orig. dial., perh. f. RASH[1]]
■ **1** see BOLD 2. **2** hasty, rash, abrupt, impetuous, precipitate, impulsive, unpremeditated, unplanned, unreflective, unreasoned, headlong, reckless. **3** impudent, rude, impertinent, disrespectful, insolent, cheeky, uncivil, discourteous, impolite, forward, self-assertive, audacious, presumptuous, pushing, loud, brassy, brazen, bold, cocksure, cocky, tactless, undiplomatic, *colloq.* fresh, pushy.

brash[2] /brash/ *n.* **1** loose broken rock or ice. **2** clippings from hedges, shrubs, etc. [18th c.: orig. unkn.]

brash[3] /brash/ *n.* an eruption of fluid from the stomach. [16th c., perh. imit.]

brass /braass/ *n.* & *adj.* ● *n.* **1** a yellow alloy of copper and zinc. **2 a** an ornament or other decorated piece of brass. **b** brass objects collectively. **3** *Mus.* brass wind instruments (including trumpet, horn, trombone) forming a band or a section of an orchestra. **4** *Brit. sl.* money. **5** (in full **horse-brass**) a round flat brass ornament for the harness of a draught-horse. **6** (in full **top brass**) *colloq.* persons in authority or of high (esp. military) rank. **7** an inscribed or engraved memorial tablet of brass. **8** *colloq.* effrontery (*then had the brass to demand money*). **9** a brass block or die used for making a design on a book binding. ● *adj.* made of brass. □ **brass band** a group of musicians playing brass instruments, sometimes also with percussion. **brassed off** *sl.* fed up. **brass hat** *Brit. colloq.* an officer of high rank, usu. one with gold braid on the cap. **brass monkey** *coarse sl.* used in various phrases to indicate extreme cold. **brass neck** *Brit. colloq.* cheek, effrontery; = BRASS 8 above. **brass-rubbing 1** the rubbing of heelball etc. over paper laid on an engraved brass to take an impression of its design. **2** the impression obtained by this. **brass tacks** *sl.* actual details; real business (*get down to brass tacks*). **not have a brass farthing** *colloq.* have no money or assets at all. [OE *bræs*, of unkn. orig.]
■ *n.* **4** see MONEY 1. **6** see MANAGEMENT 2b, c. **8** effrontery, nerve, cheek, audacity, presumption, brazenness, brashness, barefacedness, shamelessness, cockiness, temerity, impudence, insolence, rudeness, *colloq.* nerve, sauce, *Brit. colloq.* brass neck, *sl.* gall, chutzpah. □ **brassed off** see *discontented* (DISCONTENT *v.*). **brass hat** see BIGWIG. **brass tacks** see DETAIL *n.* 1. **not have a brass farthing** not have a shot in one's locker, *colloq.* be broke *or* penniless, not have a cent, *Austral.* & *NZ sl.* not have a brass razoo, *Brit. sl.* not have a bean; see also BROKE.

brassard /brássaard/ *n.* a band worn on the sleeve, esp. with a uniform. [F *bras* arm + -ARD]

brasserie /brássəri/ *n.* a restaurant, orig. one serving beer with food. [F, = brewery]
■ see CAFÉ 1.

brassica /brássikə/ *n.* any cruciferous plant of the genus *Brassica*, having tap roots and erect branched stems, including cabbage, swede, Brussels sprout, mustard, rape, cauliflower, kohlrabi, calabrese, kale, and turnip. [L, = cabbage]

brassie /brássi/ *n.* (also **brassy**) (*pl.* **-ies**) a wooden-headed golf club with a brass sole.

brassière /brázziər, -siair/ *n.* an undergarment worn by women to support the breasts. [F, = child's vest]

brassy[1] /braássi/ *adj.* (**brassier**, **brassiest**) **1** impudent. **2** pretentious, showy. **3** loud and blaring. **4** of or like brass. □□ **brassily** *adv.* **brassiness** *n.*
■ **1** impudent, forward, self-assertive, insolent, saucy, brash, rude, cheeky, brazen, bold, pert, shameless, barefaced, cocky, cocksure, loud, coarse, *colloq.* fresh, pushy. **2** pretentious, showy, ostentatious, flashy, florid, flamboyant. **3** harsh, blaring, loud, strident, tinny,

grating, jarring, dissonant, discordant, unharmonious, coarse, raucous, shrill.

brassy[2] var. of BRASSIE.

brat /brat/ *n.* usu. *derog.* a child, esp. an ill-behaved one. □ **brat pack** a rowdy or ostentatious group of young celebrities, esp. film stars. □□ **bratty** *adj.* [perh. abbr. of Sc. *bratchart* hound, or f. *brat* rough garment]

■ see IMP *n.* 1.

brattice /bráttiss/ *n.* a wooden partition or shaft-lining in a coalmine. [ME ult. f. OE *brittisc* BRITISH]

bratwurst /brátvoorst, -vurst/ *n.* a type of small German pork sausage. [G f. *braten* fry, roast + *Wurst* sausage]

bravado /brəvaádō/ *n.* a bold manner or a show of boldness intended to impress. [Sp. *bravata* f. *bravo*: cf. BRAVE, -ADO]

■ boldness, bluster, boasting, bluff, braggadocio, swagger, boastfulness, self-assurance, rodomontade, *Austral.* & *NZ colloq.* skite, *Brit. sl.* side; machismo.

brave /brayv/ *adj.*, *n.*, & *v.* ● *adj.* **1** able or ready to face and endure danger or pain. **2** *formal* splendid, spectacular (*make a brave show*). ● *n.* an American Indian warrior. ● *v.tr.* defy; encounter bravely. □ **brave it out** behave defiantly under suspicion or blame; see a thing through to the end. □□ **bravely** *adv.* **braveness** *n.* [ME f. F, ult. f. L *barbarus* BARBAROUS]

■ *adj.* **1** fearless, intrepid, bold, courageous, daring, gallant, stout, stout-hearted, lion-hearted, valiant, valorous, stalwart, plucky, staunch, undaunted, dauntless, unafraid, mettlesome, indomitable, heroic, *archaic or joc.* doughty, *colloq.* gutsy. **2** fine, handsome, grand, splendid, showy, dramatic, colourful, spectacular, awe-inspiring, *Sc.* braw. ● *v.* brazen out, weather, face (up to), confront, encounter, meet head on, come *or* go up against, withstand, put up with; challenge, defy, stand up to, dare; (*brave it*) see *bite the bullet*. □ **brave it out** brave it, weather the storm, brazen it out, sit *or* stick it out, stay till the bitter end.

bravery /bráyvəri/ *n.* **1** brave conduct. **2** a brave nature. [F *braverie* or It. *braveria* (as BRAVE)]

■ daring, courage, valour, heroism, gallantry, fortitude, fearlessness, intrepidity, intrepidness, determination, staunchness, firmness, resoluteness, resolution, indomitability, stalwartness, stout-heartedness, manliness, manhood; pluck, nerve, mettle, *colloq.* grit, guts.

bravo[1] /braavṓ/ *int.* & *n.* ● *int.* expressing approval of a performer etc. ● *n.* (*pl.* **-os**) a cry of bravo. [F f. It.]

bravo[2] /braávō/ *n.* (*pl.* **-oes** or **-os**) a hired ruffian or killer. [It.: see BRAVE]

bravura /brəvoórə, -vyoórə/ *n.* (often *attrib.*) **1** a brilliant or ambitious action or display. **2 a** a style of (esp. vocal) music requiring exceptional ability. **b** a passage of this kind. **3** bravado. [It.]

■ **1** see VIRTUOSO 1b.

braw /braw/ *adj. Sc.* fine, good. [var. of *brawf* BRAVE]

brawl /brawl/ *n.* & *v.* ● *n.* a noisy quarrel or fight. ● *v.intr.* **1** quarrel noisily or roughly. **2** (of a stream) run noisily. □□ **brawler** *n.* [ME f. OProv., rel. to BRAY[1]]

■ *n.* fight, fist-fight, mêlée, scrimmage, scuffle, battle, battle royal, Donnybrook, fray, *bagarre*, free-for-all, maul, *esp. US* ruckus, *colloq.* scrap, rumpus, shindy, ruction, set-to, dust-up, ding-dong, *Brit. colloq.* punch-up, *US colloq.* spat, *sl.* shemozzle, rough-house, *Sc. sl.* rammy; riot, unrest, disturbance, commotion, uproar, fracas, rout; wrangle, dispute, quarrel, squabble, *colloq.* row. ● *v.* **1** fight, scuffle, wrangle, clash, quarrel, squabble, dispute, *colloq.* scrap, row, *Austral. sl.* go the knuckle; riot.

brawn /brawn/ *n.* **1** muscular strength. **2** muscle; lean flesh. **3** *Brit.* a jellied preparation of the chopped meat from a boiled pig's head. [ME f. AF *braun*, OF *braon* f. Gmc]

■ **1** muscle(s), strength, robustness, brawniness, might, power, toughness, huskiness, *archaic* puissance. **2** muscle, sinew, flesh.

brawny /bráwni/ *adj.* (**brawnier**, **brawniest**) muscular, strong. □□ **brawniness** *n.*

■ muscular, well-muscled, muscly, strong, tough, robust, mighty, powerful, burly, sturdy, strapping, beefy, hefty, bulky, husky. □□ **brawniness** see BRAWN 1.

bray[1] /bray/ *n.* & *v.* ● *n.* **1** the cry of a donkey. **2** a sound like this cry, e.g. that of a harshly-played brass instrument, a laugh, etc. ● *v.* **1** *intr.* make a braying sound. **2** *tr.* utter harshly. [ME f. OF *braire*, perh. ult. f. Celt.]

■ *v.* see BLARE *v.*

bray[2] /bray/ *v.tr. archaic* pound or crush to small pieces, esp. with a pestle and mortar. [ME f. AF *braier*, OF *breier* f. Gmc]

braze[1] /brayz/ *v.* & *n.* ● *v.tr.* solder with an alloy of brass and zinc at a high temperature. ● *n.* **1** a brazed joint. **2** the alloy used for brazing. [F *braser* solder f. *braise* live coals]

■ *v.* see WELD[1] *v.* 1a, b.

braze[2] /brayz/ *v.tr.* **1 a** make of brass. **b** cover or ornament with brass. **2** make hard like brass. [OE *bræsen* f. *bræs* BRASS]

brazen /bráyz'n/ *adj.* & *v.* ● *adj.* **1** (also **brazen-faced**) flagrant and shameless; insolent. **2** made of brass. **3** of or like brass, esp. in colour or sound. ● *v.tr.* (foll. by *out*) face or undergo defiantly. □ **brazen it out** be defiantly unrepentant under censure. □□ **brazenly** *adv.* **brazenness** /bráyz'n-niss/ *n.* [OE *bræsen* f. *bræs* brass]

■ *adj.* **1** brassy, shameless, barefaced, unashamed, shameless, unabashed, audacious, flagrant, blatant, outright, out-and-out; outspoken, forward, bold, brash, immodest, presumptuous, candid, open; rude, impertinent, insolent, impudent, cheeky, saucy, cocksure, cocky, *colloq.* fresh, pushy, *US colloq.* sassy. ● *v.* (*brazen out*) see BRAVE *v.* □ **brazen it out** see *brave it out*. □□ **brazenness** see BRASS *n.* 8.

brazier[1] /bráyziər, -zhər/ *n.* a portable heater consisting of a pan or stand for holding lighted coals. [F *brasier* f. *braise* hot coals]

brazier[2] /bráyziər, -zhər/ *n.* a worker in brass. □□ **braziery** *n.* [ME prob. f. BRASS + -IER, after *glass*, *glazier*]

Brazil /brəzíl/ *n.* **1 a** a lofty tree, *Bertholletia excelsa*, forming large forests in S. America. **b** (in full **Brazil nut**) a large three-sided nut with an edible kernel from this tree. **2** (in full **Brazil-wood**) a hard red wood from any tropical tree of the genus *Caesalpina*, that yields dyes. [the name of a S.Amer. country, named from *Brazil-wood*, ult. f. med.L *brasilium*]

BRCS *abbr.* British Red Cross Society.

breach /breech/ *n.* & *v.* ● *n.* **1** (often foll. by *of*) the breaking of or failure to observe a law, contract, etc. **2 a** a breaking of relations; an estrangement. **b** a quarrel. **3 a** a broken state. **b** a gap, esp. one made by artillery in fortifications. ● *v.tr.* **1** break through; make a gap in. **2** break (a law, contract, etc.). □ **breach of the peace** an infringement or violation of the public peace by any disturbance or riot etc. **breach of promise** the breaking of a promise, esp. a promise to marry. **stand in the breach** bear the brunt of an attack. **step into the breach** give help in a crisis, esp. by replacing someone who has dropped out. [ME f. OF *breche*, ult. f. Gmc]

■ *n.* **1** break, violation, non-observance, infringement, contravention, *Law* infraction, *archaic* delict; betrayal. **2 a** break, rift, gulf, split, break-up, separation, rupture, severance, schism, split, alienation, estrangement, *colloq.* bust-up. **b** see QUARREL *n.* 1. **3 b** gap, fissure, crack, hole, opening, aperture. ● *v.* **1** rupture, burst, break through, force oneself *or* itself through; split, fracture, break, *colloq.* bust. **2** see BREAK[1] *v.* 3.

bread /bred/ *n.* & *v.* ● *n.* **1** baked dough made of flour usu. leavened with yeast and moistened, eaten as a staple food. **2 a** necessary food. **b** (also **daily bread**) one's livelihood. **3** *sl.* money. ● *v.tr.* coat with breadcrumbs for cooking. □ **bread and butter 1** bread spread with butter. **2 a** one's livelihood. **b** routine work to ensure an income. **bread-and-butter letter** a letter of thanks for hospitality.

bread and circuses the public provision of subsistence and entertainment. **bread and wine** the Eucharist. **bread basket 1** a basket for bread or rolls. **2** *sl.* the stomach. **bread bin** a container for keeping bread in. **bread sauce** a white sauce thickened with breadcrumbs. **cast one's bread upon the waters** do good without expecting gratitude or reward. **know which side one's bread is buttered** know where one's advantage lies. **take the bread out of a person's mouth** take away a person's living, esp. by competition etc. [OE *brēad* f. Gmc]

■ *n.* **2 a** see FOOD 1a. **3** see MONEY 1, 2. □ **bread basket 2** see STOMACH *n.* 2.

breadboard /brédbord/ *n.* **1** a board for cutting bread on. **2** a board for making an experimental model of an electric circuit.

breadcrumb /brédkrum/ *n.* **1** a small fragment of bread. **2** (in *pl.*) bread crumbled for use in cooking.

breadfruit /brédfroot/ *n.* **1** a tropical evergreen tree, *Artocarpus altilis*, bearing edible usu. seedless fruit. **2** the fruit of this tree which when roasted becomes soft like new bread.

breadline /brédlīn/ *n.* **1** subsistence level (esp. *on the breadline*). **2** *US* a queue of people waiting to receive free food.

breadth /bredth/ *n.* **1** the distance or measurement from side to side of a thing; broadness. **2** a piece (of cloth etc.) of standard or full breadth. **3** extent, distance, room. **4** (usu. foll. by *of*) capacity to respect other opinions; freedom from prejudice or intolerance (esp. *breadth of mind* or *view*). **5** *Art* unity of the whole, achieved by the disregard of unnecessary details. □□ **breadthways** *adv.* **breadthwise** *adv.* [obs. *brede*, OE *brǣdu*, f. Gmc, rel. to BROAD]

■ **1** width, wideness, broadness, span, spread, thickness, *Naut.* beam. **3** extent, magnitude, degree, amount, area, expanse, depth, range, scope, room, leeway; distance, stretch, measurement. **4** liberality, largeness, catholicity, latitude, width, broadness, wideness.

breadwinner /brédwinnər/ *n.* a person who earns the money to support a family.

break[1] /brayk/ *v.* & *n.* ● *v.* (*past* **broke** /brōk/ or *archaic* **brake** /brayk/; *past part.* **broken** /brōkən/ or *archaic* **broke**) **1** *tr.* & *intr.* **a** separate into pieces under a blow or strain; shatter. **b** make or become inoperative, esp. from damage (*the toaster has broken*). **c** break a bone in or dislocate (part of the body). **d** break the skin of (the head or crown). **2 a** *tr.* cause or effect an interruption in (*broke our journey*; *the spell was broken*; *broke the silence*). **b** *intr.* have an interval between spells of work (*let's break now*; *we broke for tea*). **3** *tr.* fail to observe or keep (a law, promise, etc.). **4 a** *tr.* & *intr.* make or become subdued or weakened; yield or cause to yield (*broke his spirit*; *he broke under the strain*). **b** *tr.* weaken the effect of (a fall, blow, etc.). **c** *tr.* = *break in* 3c. **d** *tr.* defeat, destroy (*broke the enemy's power*). **e** *tr.* defeat the object of (a strike, e.g. by engaging other personnel). **5** *tr.* surpass (a record). **6** *intr.* (foll. by *with*) **a** quarrel or cease association with (another person etc.). **b** repudiate, depart from (a tradition, practice, etc.) **7** *tr.* **a** be no longer subject to (a habit). **b** (foll. by *of*) cause (a person) to be free of a habit (*broke them of their addiction*). **8** *tr.* & *intr.* reveal or be revealed; (cause to) become known (*broke the news*; *the story broke on Friday*). **9** *intr.* **a** (of the weather) change suddenly, esp. after a fine spell. **b** (of waves) curl over and dissolve into foam. **c** (of the day) dawn. **d** (of clouds) move apart; show a gap. **e** (of a storm) begin violently. **10** *tr. Electr.* disconnect (a circuit). **11** *intr.* **a** (of the voice) change with emotion. **b** (of a boy's voice) change in register etc. at puberty. **12** *tr.* **a** (often foll. by *up*) divide (a set etc.) into parts, e.g. by selling to different buyers. **b** change (a banknote etc.) for coins. **13** *tr.* ruin (an individual or institution) financially (see also BROKE *adj.*). **14** *tr.* penetrate (e.g. a safe) by force. **15** *tr.* decipher (a code). **16** *tr.* make (a way, path, etc.) by separating obstacles. **17** *intr.* burst forth (*the sun broke through the clouds*). **18** *Mil.* **a** *intr.* (of troops) disperse in confusion. **b** *tr.* make a rupture in (ranks). **19 a** *intr.* (usu. foll. by *free*, *loose*, *out*, etc.) escape from constraint by a sudden effort. **b** *tr.* escape or emerge from (prison, bounds, cover, etc.). **20** *tr. Tennis* etc. win a game against (an opponent's service). **21** *intr. Boxing* etc. (of two fighters, usu. at the referee's command) come out of a clinch. **22** *tr. Mil.* demote (an officer). **23** *intr.* esp. *Stock Exch.* (of prices) fall sharply. **24** *intr. Cricket* (of a bowled ball) change direction on bouncing. **25** *intr. Billiards* etc. disperse the balls at the beginning of a game. **26** *tr.* unfurl (a flag etc.). **27** *tr. Phonet.* subject (a vowel) to fracture. **28** *tr.* fail to rejoin (one's ship) after absence on leave. **29** *tr.* disprove (an alibi). ● *n.* **1 a** an act or instance of breaking. **b** a point where something is broken; a gap. **2** an interval, an interruption; a pause in work; a holiday. **3** a sudden dash (esp. to escape). **4** *colloq.* **a** a piece of good luck; a fair chance. **b** (also **bad break**) an unfortunate remark or action, a blunder. **c** *US* (in *pl.*, prec. by *the*) fate. **5** *Cricket* a change in direction of a bowled ball on bouncing. **6** *Billiards* etc. **a** a series of points scored during one turn. **b** the opening shot that disperses the balls. **7** *Mus.* (in jazz) a short unaccompanied passage for a soloist, usu. improvised. **8** *Electr.* a discontinuity in a circuit. □ **bad break** *colloq.* **1** a piece of bad luck. **2** a mistake or blunder. **break away** make or become free or separate (see also BREAKAWAY). **break the back of 1** do the hardest or greatest part of; crack (a problem etc.). **2** overburden (a person) physically or mentally; crush, defeat. **break bulk** see BULK. **break crop** a crop grown to avoid the continual growing of cereals. **break-dancing** an energetic style of street-dancing, developed by US Blacks. **break down 1 a** fail in mechanical action; cease to function. **b** (of human relationships etc.) fail, collapse. **c** (of health) fail, deteriorate; (of a person) fail in (esp. mental) health. **d** be overcome by emotion; collapse in tears. **2 a** demolish, destroy. **b** suppress (resistance). **c** force (a person) to yield under pressure. **3** analyse into components (see also BREAKDOWN). **break even** emerge from a transaction etc. with neither profit nor loss. **break a person's heart** see HEART. **break the ice 1** begin to overcome formality or shyness, esp. between strangers. **2** make a start. **break in 1** enter premises by force, esp. with criminal intent. **2** interrupt. **3 a** accustom to a habit etc. **b** wear etc. until comfortable. **c** tame or discipline (an animal); accustom (a horse) to saddle and bridle etc. **4** *Austral.* & *NZ* bring (virgin land) into cultivation. **break-in** *n.* an illegal forced entry into premises, esp. with criminal intent. **breaking and entering** (formerly) the illegal entering of a building with intent to commit a felony. **breaking-point** the point of greatest strain, at which a thing breaks or a person gives way. **break in on** disturb; interrupt. **break into 1** enter forcibly or violently. **2 a** suddenly begin, burst forth with (a song, laughter, etc.). **b** suddenly change one's pace for (a faster one) (*broke into a gallop*). **3** interrupt. **break-line** *Printing* the last line of a paragraph (usu. not of full length). **break new ground** innovate; start on something new. **break of day** dawn. **break off 1** detach by breaking. **2** bring to an end. **3** cease talking etc. **break open** open forcibly. **break out 1** escape by force, esp. from prison. **2** begin suddenly; burst forth (*then violence broke out*). **3** (foll. by *in*) become covered in (a rash etc.). **4** exclaim. **5** release (a run-up flag). **6** *US* **a** open up (a receptacle) and remove its contents. **b** remove (articles) from a place of storage. **break-out** *n.* a forcible escape. **break point 1** a place or time at which an interruption or change is made. **2** *Computing* (usu. **breakpoint**) a place in a computer program where the sequence of instructions is interrupted, esp. by another program. **3 a** (in lawn tennis) a point which would win the game for the player(s) receiving service. **b** the situation at which the receiver(s) may break service by winning such a point. **4** = *breaking-point*. **break step** get out of step. **break up 1** break into small pieces. **2** disperse; disband. **3** end the school term. **4 a** terminate a relationship; disband. **b** cause to do this. **5** (of the weather) change suddenly (esp. after a fine spell). **6** esp. *US* **a** upset or be upset. **b** excite or be excited. **c** convulse or be convulsed (see also BREAKUP). **break wind** release gas from

the anus. **break one's word** see WORD. [OE *brecan* f. Gmc]
■ *v.* **1 a** break apart *or* up, fracture, rupture, break into bits, fall to bits *or* apart *or* in two, come apart, shatter, shiver, crack, snap, splinter, fragment, comminute, split, burst, explode, collapse, *colloq.* bust, *literary* break *or* fall asunder. **b** (*tr.*) stop, *colloq.* bust; (*intr.*) break down, stop working *or* functioning, go wrong, give out, die, *archaic or colloq.* give up the ghost, *colloq.* conk out, pack up *or* in, crock up, go phut, *sl.* bite the dust. **2 a** break off, discontinue, suspend, interrupt, hold up, delay, disrupt, punctuate; sever, cut off *or* short. **b** have *or* take a break, stop, pause. **3** violate, transgress, disobey, overstep, go counter to *or* against, contravene, defy, infringe, breach, fail to observe, go beyond, ignore, disregard, flout, fly in the face of. **4 a** weary, exhaust, subdue, sap, drain, wear out, weaken, enfeeble, debilitate, cripple, demoralize, undermine, crush, quash, overcome, defeat, cow; see also YIELD *v.* 3a. **b** lessen, soften, mitigate, cushion, pad, allay, alleviate, take the edge off. **d** demolish, smash, destroy, crush, ruin, defeat, quell, overcome, put down, quash, foil, frustrate, *literary* vanquish. **5** see EXCEED 1, 3. **6** (*break with*) **a** see LEAVE *v.* 1b, 3, 4, QUARREL *v.* 2. **b** renounce, repudiate, disavow, dispense with, depart from. **7 a** give up, put an end to, relinquish, *sl.* kick. **8** reveal, announce, disclose, divulge, let *or* put out, release, tell, make public *or* known, spread about, bruit about *or* abroad. **9 a** change, fail; shift, switch, vary. **c** dawn, begin, start. **d** break up, move apart, part, spread out *or* apart, divide, disperse, scatter, dissipate. **e** break forth *or* out, burst forth, erupt. **11 a** see QUAVER *v.* **13** ruin, bankrupt, reduce to penury *or* destitution, put out of business, put into receivership. **14** break *or* force open, get *or* break into. **15** decipher, decode, decrypt. **17** burst forth, emerge, come out, appear. **19 a** see ESCAPE *v.* 1. **22** demote, downgrade, degrade, reduce to the ranks, relegate, *esp. US colloq.* bust. **23** see FALL *v.* 1. **29** see DISPROVE. ● *n.* **1 a** fracture, split, separation, rupture, cut-off, severance, burst, breach, rift, schism, *Prosody* caesura, *archaic* discerption. **b** gap, opening, hole, space, aperture, breach, chink, crack, slit. **2** interruption, interval, discontinuity, discontinuation, disruption, hesitation, delay, lapse, lull, wait, suspension, hiatus, gap, lacuna, *colloq.* let-up; stop, pause, cease, cessation, *literary* surcease; rest, respite, rest period, time off *or US* out, holiday, leave (of absence), *US* vacation; coffee-break, tea break, intermission, interlude, entr'acte, *Sport* half-time, *US* recess, *colloq.* breather, *Austral.* & *NZ colloq.* smoko. **3** see DASH *n.* 1, ESCAPE *n.* 1. **4 a** chance, stroke of luck, opportunity, opening, foot in the door. **b** see BLUNDER *n.* 2. □ **bad break 1** see MISFORTUNE 2. **2** see BLUNDER *n.* **break away** leave, depart, separate (oneself *or* itself); branch off, diverge, turn away, separate off; split. **break the back of 1** overcome, master, get the better of, *colloq.* crack. **2** overburden, overload; weaken, enfeeble, cripple, disable, put out of action; overcome, crush, smash, ruin, destroy, defeat, quell, put down, quash, *literary* vanquish. **break down 1 a** see BREAK[1] *v.* 1b above. **b** see FAIL 1, 2a. **c** see DETERIORATE, *go to pieces* (PIECE). **d** be overcome; burst *or* dissolve into tears. **2 a** see DESTROY 1. **b** see SUPPRESS 1. **3** separate, dissect, anatomize, take apart *or* to pieces, break up, reduce; analyse, examine, sort, classify, codify, organize. **break the ice 2** see *break new ground* below. **break in 1** force one's way in, *sl.* crack a crib. **2** see INTERRUPT 1. **3 a** train, educate, prepare; accustom, condition, habituate. **b** wear in. **c** break, tame, discipline, train, condition, domesticate. **break in on** see INTERRUPT 1. **break into 1** force one's way into, burst into, irrupt into. **2 a** burst *or* erupt *or* explode into, burst forth with. **3** see INTERRUPT 1. **break new ground** be innovative, innovate, take the initiative *or* lead, take the first steps, make the first move, make a start, make great strides, break the ice, blaze a trail, start the ball rolling, *colloq.* take the plunge. **break of day** see DAWN *n.* 1. **break off 1** see SNAP *v.* 1. **2** see STOP *v.* 1a, b. **3** discontinue; come to a stop, stop, cease, end, halt. **break out 1** see ESCAPE *v.* 1. **2** burst forth *or* out, erupt, come forth, flare up. **3** (*break out in*) come out in. **4** see EXCLAIM 1. **break-out** see ESCAPE *n.* 1. **break up 1** see BREAK[1] *v.* 1a above, DISINTEGRATE. **2** see DISPERSE 2. **4 a** see SPLIT *v.* 3a. **6 a** see UPSET *v.* 2. **b** see EXCITE 1. **break wind** *Brit. colloq.* let off, *sl.* blow off.

break[2] /brayk/ *n.* **1** a carriage-frame without a body, for breaking in young horses. **2** = BRAKE[2]. [perh. = *brake* framework: 17th c., of unkn. orig.]

breakable /bráykəb'l/ *adj.* & *n.* ● *adj.* that may or is apt to be broken easily. ● *n.* (esp. in *pl.*) a breakable thing.
■ *adj.* see FRAGILE 1.

breakage /bráykij/ *n.* **1 a** a broken thing. **b** damage caused by breaking. **2** an act or instance of breaking.
■ **2** see FRACTURE *n.* 1.

breakaway /bráykəway/ *n.* **1** the act or an instance of breaking away or seceding. **2** (*attrib.*) that breaks away or has broken away; separate. **3** *Austral.* a stampede, esp. at the sight or smell of water. **4** a false start in a race. **5** *Rugby Football* an outside second-row forward.

breakdown /bráykdown/ *n.* **1 a** a mechanical failure. **b** a loss of (esp. mental) health and strength. **2 a** a collapse or disintegration (*breakdown of communication*). **b** physical or chemical decomposition. **3** a detailed analysis (of statistics, chemical components, etc.).
■ **1 a** collapse, failure, failing, *Computing* crash. **b** (mental) collapse, nervous breakdown, trauma, *colloq.* crack-up. **2 a** collapse, disintegration, failure, downfall, decline, deterioration, degeneration. **b** decomposition, dissolution, corruption, degeneration. **3** analysis, review, run-down; itemization, classification, listing, dissection, distillation, fractionation; examination, investigation.

breaker /bráykər/ *n.* **1** a person or thing that breaks something, esp. disused machinery. **2** a person who breaks in a horse. **3** a heavy wave that breaks.
■ **3** see WAVE *n.* 1, 2.

breakfast /brékfəst/ *n.* & *v.* ● *n.* the first meal of the day. ● *v.intr.* have breakfast. □□ **breakfaster** *n.* [BREAK[1] interrupt + FAST[2]]
■ *n.* see MEAL[1].

breakneck /bráyk-nek/ *adj.* (of speed) dangerously fast.
■ reckless, dangerous, daredevil, careless; excessive, headlong, rash; (*at breakneck speed*) at full speed *or* gallop, headlong, flat out, (at) full tilt, *ventre à terre*, all out, hell for leather, *colloq.* lickety-split.

breakthrough /bráykthroo/ *n.* **1** a major advance or discovery. **2** an act of breaking through an obstacle etc.

breakup /bráykup/ *n.* **1** disintegration, collapse. **2** dispersal.
■ **1** see DISSOLUTION 1. **2** see DISSOLUTION 3.

breakwater /bráykwawtər/ *n.* a barrier built out into the sea to break the force of waves.

bream[1] /breem/ *n.* (*pl.* same) **1** a yellowish arch-backed freshwater fish, *Abramis brama.* **2** (in full **sea bream**) a similarly shaped marine fish of the family Sparidae. [ME f. OF *bre(s)me* f. WG]

bream[2] /breem/ *v.tr. Naut. hist.* clean (a ship's bottom) by burning and scraping. [prob. f. LG: rel. to BROOM]

breast /brest/ *n.* & *v.* ● *n.* **1 a** either of two milk-secreting organs on the upper front of a woman's body. **b** the corresponding usu. rudimentary part of a man's body. **2 a** the upper front part of a human body; the chest. **b** the corresponding part of an animal. **3** the part of a garment that covers the breast. **4** the breast as a source of nourishment or emotion. ● *v.tr.* **1** face, meet in full opposition (*breast the wind*). **2** contend with, face (*prepared to breast the difficulties of the journey*). **3** reach the top of (a hill). □ **breast-feed** (*past* and *past part.* **-fed**) feed (a baby) from the breast. **breast-high** as high as the breast; submerged to the breast. **breast-pin** a brooch etc. worn on the breast. **breast-stroke** a stroke made while swimming on the breast by extending arms forward and sweeping them back in unison. **breast the tape** see TAPE. **make a clean breast**

of confess fully. ▫▫ **breasted** *adj.* (also in *comb.*). **breastless** *adj.* [OE *brēost* f. Gmc]

■ *n.* **1 a** teat, mamma, mammary gland; (*breasts*) *colloq.* bosoms, *sl.* boobs, *Austral. sl.* norks, *Brit. sl.* bristols, charlies. **2** chest, bust, front. **4** soul, core, heart (of hearts); see also BOSOM 2. ● *v.* **1, 2** see FACE *v.* 3a. ▫ **make a clean breast of** see CONFESS 1a.

breastbone /bréstbōn/ *n.* a thin flat vertical bone and cartilage in the chest connecting the ribs.

breastplate /bréstplayt/ *n.* a piece of armour covering the breast.

breastsummer /bréssəmər/ *n. Archit.* a beam across a broad opening, sustaining a superstructure. [BREAST + SUMMER²]

breastwork /bréstwurk/ *n.* a low temporary defence or parapet.

■ see RAMPART.

breath /breth/ *n.* **1 a** the air taken into or expelled from the lungs. **b** one respiration of air. **c** an exhalation of air that can be seen, smelt, or heard (*breath steamed in the cold air*; *bad breath*). **2 a** a slight movement of air; a breeze. **b** a whiff of perfume etc. **3** a whisper, a murmur (esp. of a scandalous nature). **4** the power of breathing; life (*is there breath in him?*). ▫ **below** (or **under**) **one's breath** in a whisper. **breath of fresh air 1** a small amount of or a brief time in the fresh air. **2** a refreshing change. **breath of life** a necessity. **breath test** *Brit.* a test of a person's alcohol consumption, using a breathalyser. **catch one's breath 1** cease breathing momentarily in surprise, suspense, etc. **2** rest after exercise to restore normal breathing. **draw breath** breathe; live. **hold one's breath 1** cease breathing temporarily. **2** *colloq.* wait in eager anticipation. **in the same breath** (esp. of saying two contradictory things) within a short time. **out of breath** gasping for air, esp. after exercise. **take breath** pause for rest. **take a person's breath away** astound; surprise; awe; delight. **waste one's breath** talk or give advice without effect. [OE *brǣth* f. Gmc]

■ **1** see EXHALATION 1. **2 a** gust, breeze, puff, stirring, stir, draught, waft, wind, air, *literary* zephyr. **b** smell, whiff, aroma, sniff, scent, waft, wind. **3** murmur, whisper, suggestion, hint, suspicion, indication, intimation, undercurrent, undertone; touch, dash, drop, trace, tinge, soupçon. **4** life. ▫ **breath of fresh air 2** see TONIC *n.*; (*like a breath of fresh air*) see REFRESHING. **breath of life** see NECESSITY 1a. **draw breath** see LIVE *v.* 4, 6. **in the same breath** see *at once* 2 (ONCE). **out of breath** see BREATHLESS 1. **take breath** see REST¹ *v.* 1. **take a person's breath away** astound, astonish, surprise, dazzle, startle, shock, stagger, stun, take aback, *colloq.* knock sideways, floor, knock for six, *sl.* knock out; awe, amaze, overawe; delight, excite, thrill.

Breathalyser /bréthəlīzər/ *n.* (also **Breathalyzer**) *Brit. propr.* an instrument for measuring the amount of alcohol in the breath (and hence in the blood) of a driver. ▫▫ **breathalyse** *v.tr.* (also **-lyze**). [BREATH + ANALYSE + -ER¹]

breathe /breeth/ *v.* **1** *intr.* take air into and expel it from the lungs. **2** *intr.* be or seem alive (*is she breathing?*). **3** *tr.* **a** utter; say (esp. quietly) (*breathed her forgiveness*). **b** express; display (*breathed defiance*). **4** *intr.* take breath, pause. **5** *tr.* send out or take in (as if) with breathed air (*breathed enthusiasm into them*; *breathed whisky*). **6** *intr.* (of wine, fabric, etc.) be exposed to fresh air. **7** *intr.* **a** sound, speak (esp. quietly). **b** (of wind) blow softly. **8** *tr.* allow (a horse etc.) to breathe; give rest after exertion. ▫ **breathe again** (or **freely**) recover from a shock, fear, etc., and be at ease. **breathe down a person's neck** follow or check up on a person, esp. menacingly. **breathe new life into** revitalize, refresh. **breathe one's last** die. **breathe upon** tarnish, taint. **not breathe a word** keep silent. **not breathe a word of** keep quite secret. [ME f. BREATH]

■ **1** inhale and exhale, respire, draw breath. **2** live, be alive *or* living, exist, draw breath, *joc.* be in the land of the living. **3 a** whisper, murmur, mutter, say under one's breath, hint (at), suggest; tell, speak, say, utter. **4** see REST¹ *v.* 1. **5** exhale, breathe out, expel, puff, blow, send out, emit, give forth, pour out *or* forth, spew forth. ▫ **breathe new life into** see REFRESH 1. **breathe one's last** see *pass away* 1. **breathe upon** see TAINT *v.* 1. **not breathe a word** see *play one's cards close to one's chest* (CHEST), *dummy up*.

breather /bréethər/ *n.* **1** *colloq.* **a** a brief pause for rest. **b** a short spell of exercise. **2** a safety-vent in the crankcase of a motor vehicle etc.

■ **1 a** see BREAK¹ *n.* 2.

breathing /bréething/ *n.* **1** the process of taking air into and expelling it from the lungs. **2** *Phonet.* a sign in Greek indicating that an initial vowel or rho is aspirated (**rough breathing**) or not aspirated (**smooth breathing**). ▫ **breathing-space** time to breathe; a pause.

■ ▫ **breathing-space** see PAUSE *n.*

breathless /bréthliss/ *adj.* **1** panting, out of breath. **2** (as if) holding the breath because of excitement, suspense, etc. (*a state of breathless expectancy*). **3** unstirred by wind; still. ▫▫ **breathlessly** *adv.* **breathlessness** *n.*

■ **1** panting, short *or* out of breath, winded, short-winded, gasping (for air *or* breath), puffed (out), puffy; exhausted, spent, worn out, tired out. **2** eager, agog, feverish, excited, keen, expectant, impatient, anxious, frenzied, restive; with bated breath, speechless, surprised, amazed, astonished, astounded, awestruck, thunderstruck, staggered, *poet.* athirst. **3** see STILL *adj.* 1

breathtaking /bréthtayking/ *adj.* astounding; awe-inspiring. ▫▫ **breathtakingly** *adv.*

■ see TERRIFIC 1b.

breathy /bréthi/ *adj.* (**breathier, breathiest**) (of a singing-voice etc.) containing the sound of breathing. ▫▫ **breathily** *adv.* **breathiness** *n.*

breccia /bréchiə/ *n.* & *v.* ● *n.* a rock of angular stones etc. cemented by finer material. ● *v.tr.* form into breccia. ▫▫ **brecciate** *v.tr.* **brecciation** /-chiáysh'n/ *n.* [It., = gravel, f. Gmc, rel. to BREAK¹]

bred /bred/ *past* and *past part.* of BREED.

breech /breech/ *n.* & *v.* ● *n.* **1 a** the part of a cannon behind the bore. **b** the back part of a rifle or gun barrel. **2** *archaic* the buttocks. ● *v.tr. archaic* put (a boy) into breeches after being in petticoats since birth. ▫ **breech birth** (or **delivery**) the delivery of a baby with the buttocks or feet foremost. **breech-block** a metal block which closes the breech aperture in a gun. **breech-loader** a gun loaded at the breech, not through the muzzle. **breech-loading** (of a gun) loaded at the breech, not through the muzzle. [OE *brōc*, pl. *brēc* (treated as sing. in ME), f. Gmc]

■ *n.* **2** see BOTTOM *n.* 2a.

breeches /bríchiz/ *n.pl.* (also **pair of breeches** *sing.*) **1** short trousers, esp. fastened below the knee, now used esp. for riding or in court costume. **2** *colloq.* any trousers, knickerbockers, or underpants. ▫ **Breeches Bible** the Geneva Bible of 1560 with *breeches* for *aprons* in Gen. 3:7. **breeches buoy** a lifebuoy suspended from a rope which has canvas breeches for the user's legs. [pl. of BREECH]

breed /breed/ *v.* & *n.* ● *v.* (*past* and *past part.* **bred** /bred/) **1** *tr.* & *intr.* bear, generate (offspring); reproduce. **2** *tr.* & *intr.* propagate or cause to propagate; raise (livestock). **3** *tr.* **a** yield, produce; result in (*war breeds famine*). **b** spread (*discontent bred by rumour*). **4** *intr.* arise; spread (*disease breeds in the Tropics*). **5** *tr.* bring up; train (*bred to the law*; *Hollywood breeds stars*). **6** *tr. Physics* create (fissile material) by nuclear reaction. ● *n.* **1** a stock of animals or plants within a species, having a similar appearance, and usu. developed by deliberate selection. **2** a race; a lineage. **3** a sort, a kind. ▫ **bred and born** = *born and bred.* **bred in the bone** hereditary. **breeder reactor** a nuclear reactor that can create more fissile material than it consumes. **breed in** mate with or marry near relations. ▫▫ **breeder** *n.* [OE *brēdan*: rel. to BROOD]

■ *v.* **1** produce, generate, bring forth, give birth to, create, spawn, hatch, bear, develop, *archaic* engender, get, *literary* beget; see also REPRODUCE 3. **2** raise, rear, cultivate, propagate, farm; mate, couple, pair (up). **3 a** yield, produce, make, generate, create, bring forth *or* out *or* about, give rise to, spark *or* trigger (off), set off; result in, lead to, cause, bring, *literary* beget. **b** see SPREAD *v.* 3. **4** arise, originate, appear, begin, start (off *or* up), spring up; develop, grow, increase, multiply, spread, proliferate, *literary* burgeon. **5** see *bring up* 1, TRAIN *v.* 1a. ● *n.* **1** stock, strain. **2** race, lineage, stock, family, tribe, strain, blood, extraction, ancestry, descent, parentage, birth. **3** kind, sort, type, form, variety, species, class, group, category, brand, make, stamp, stripe, manner, description, *disp.* ilk. □ **bred in the bone** see HEREDITARY 1.

breeding /bréeding/ *n.* **1** the process of developing or propagating (animals, plants, etc.). **2** generation; childbearing. **3** the result of training or education; behaviour. **4** good manners (as produced by an aristocratic heredity) (*has no breeding*).
■ **1** rearing, bringing-up, raising, cultivation, development, propagation. **2** generation, (re)production, creation, making, bearing, childbearing. **3** see UPBRINGING. **4** (good) upbringing, (good) manners, civility, politeness, *politesse*, gentility, (good) behaviour; decorum, etiquette, social code *or* graces, propriety; refinement, class, sophistication, discernment, taste, urbanity, urbaneness, *savoir faire*.

breeks /breeks/ *n.pl. Sc.* var. of BREECHES.

breeze[1] /breez/ *n.* & *v.* ● *n.* **1** a gentle wind. **2** *Meteorol.* a wind of 4–31 m.p.h. and between force 2 and force 6 on the Beaufort scale. **3** a wind blowing from land at night or sea during the day. **4** esp. *Brit. colloq.* a quarrel or display of temper. **5** esp. *US colloq.* an easy task. ● *v.intr.* (foll. by *in*, *out*, *along*, etc.) *colloq.* come or go in a casual or lighthearted manner. [prob. f. OSp. & Port. *briza* NE wind]
■ *n.* **1** breath, puff, stir, waft, wind, draught, gust, air, *Naut.* cat's-paw, *literary* zephyr. **4** see QUARREL *n.* 1, TANTRUM. **5** easy *or* simple job *or* task, child's play, nothing, five-finger exercise, *Bridge* pianola, *colloq.* cinch, cakewalk, gift, cushy number, sitter, steal, piece of cake, picnic, kids' stuff, *Brit. colloq.* doddle, *sl.* snip, *Austral sl.* snack, *Austral.* & *NZ sl.* bludge, *US sl.* snap, duck soup. ● *v.* drift, waft, float; saunter, cruise, roam, wander.

breeze[2] /breez/ *n.* small cinders. □ **breeze-block** any lightweight building block, esp. one made from breeze mixed with sand and cement. [F *braise* live coals]

breeze[3] /breez/ *n.* a gadfly or cleg. [OE *briosa*, of unkn. orig.]

breezy /bréezi/ *adj.* (**breezier**, **breeziest**) **1 a** windswept. **b** pleasantly windy. **2** *colloq.* lively; jovial. **3** *colloq.* careless (*with breezy indifference*). □□ **breezily** *adv.* **breeziness** *n.*
■ **1** airy, fresh, windy, blowy, brisk, gusty, draughty; windswept. **2** carefree, light-hearted, free and easy, sunny, easy, easygoing, jovial, cheerful, jaunty, perky, cheery, lively, bright, spirited, buoyant, animated, energetic, *poet.* blithesome. **3** casual, careless, heedless, thoughtless, offhand.

bremsstrahlung /brémz-shtraaloong/ *n. Physics* the electromagnetic radiation produced by the acceleration or esp. the deceleration of a charged particle after passing through the electric and magnetic fields of a nucleus. [G, = braking radiation]

Bren /bren/ *n.* (in full **Bren gun**) a lightweight quick-firing machine-gun. [*Br*no in the Czech Republic (where orig. made) + *En*field in England (where later made)]

brent /brent/ *n.* (*US* **brant**) (in full **brent-goose**) a small migratory goose, *Branta bernicla*. [16th c.: orig. unkn.]

brethren see BROTHER.

Breton /brétt'n, brətóɴ/ *n.* & *adj.* ● *n.* **1** a native of Brittany. **2** the Celtic language of Brittany. ● *adj.* of or relating to Brittany or its people or language. [OF, = BRITON]

bretzel var. of PRETZEL.

breve /breev/ *n.* **1** *Mus.* a note, now rarely used, having the time value of two semibreves. **2** a written or printed mark (˘) indicating a short or unstressed vowel. **3** *hist.* an authoritative letter from a sovereign or pope. [ME var. of BRIEF]

brevet /brévvit/ *n.* & *v.* ● *n.* (often *attrib.*) a document conferring a privilege from a sovereign or government, esp. a rank in the army, without the appropriate pay (*was promoted by brevet; brevet major*). ● *v.tr.* (**breveted**, **breveting** or **brevetted**, **brevetting**) confer brevet rank on. [ME f. OF dimin. of *bref* BRIEF]

breviary /bréeviəri/ *n.* (*pl.* **-ies**) *RC Ch.* a book containing the service for each day, to be recited by those in orders. [L *breviarium* summary f. *breviare* abridge: see ABBREVIATE]

brevity /brévviti/ *n.* **1** economy of expression; conciseness. **2** shortness (of time etc.) (*the brevity of happiness*). [AF *breveté*, OF *brieveté* f. *bref* BRIEF]
■ conciseness, concision, terseness, succinctness, pithiness, compactness, laconicism, laconism, economy; shortness, briefness.

brew /broo/ *v.* & *n.* ● *v.* **1** *tr.* **a** make (beer etc.) by infusion, boiling, and fermentation. **b** make (tea etc.) by infusion or (punch etc.) by mixture. **2** *intr.* undergo either of these processes (*the tea is brewing*). **3** *intr.* (of trouble, a storm, etc.) gather force; threaten (*mischief was brewing*). **4** *tr.* bring about; set in train; concoct (*brewed their fiendish scheme*). ● *n.* **1** an amount (of beer etc.) brewed at one time (*this year's brew*). **2** what is brewed (esp. with regard to its quality) (*a good strong brew*). **3** the action or process of brewing. □ **brew up 1** make tea. **2** = BREW *v.* 2 above. **3** = BREW *v.* 4 above. **brew-up** *n.* an instance of making tea. □□ **brewer** *n.* [OE *brēowan* f. Gmc]
■ *v.* **1, 2** ferment, cook, boil; infuse. **3** gather force, impend, approach, brew up, be (close) at hand *or* near *or* imminent *or* forthcoming *or* in the wind *or* in prospect *or* in store *or* in the offing *or* on the horizon, hatch, develop, take shape, begin, form, *esp. US* be upcoming, *colloq.* cook; threaten, loom, menace. **4** brew up, concoct, devise, plan, plot, contrive, conceive, prepare, develop, formulate, *colloq.* cook up; bring about, cause, produce, hatch; set in train *or* motion, set going, institute, launch. ● *n.* **2** see POTION.

brewery /bróoəri/ *n.* (*pl.* **-ies**) a place where beer etc. is brewed commercially.

briar[1] var. of BRIER[1].

briar[2] var. of BRIER[2].

bribe /brīb/ *v.* & *n.* ● *v.tr.* (often foll. by *to* + infin.) persuade (a person etc.) to act improperly in one's favour by a gift of money, services, etc. (*bribed the guard to release the suspect*). ● *n.* money or services offered in the process of bribing. □□ **bribable** *adj.* **briber** *n.* **bribery** *n.* [ME f. OF *briber*, *brimber* beg, of unkn. orig.]
■ *v.* pay *or* buy off, buy (over), oil a person's hand *or* palm, *colloq.* fix, grease the palm of, square; corrupt, suborn. ● *n.* inducement, pay-off, *colloq.* kickback, graft, sweetener, *esp. US* payola, plugola, *sl.* drop, dropsy, *Austral. sl.* sling, *Brit. sl.* backhander. □□ **bribery** extortion, blackmail, subornation, corruption, *colloq.* graft.

bric-à-brac /bríkkəbrak/ *n.* (also **bric-a-brac**, **bricabrac**) miscellaneous, often old, ornaments, trinkets, furniture, etc., of no great value. [F f. obs. *à bric et à brac* at random]
■ curiosities, knick-knacks, bits and pieces *or* bobs, sundries, collectibles, trinkets, gewgaws, gimcracks, falderals, kickshaws, *bijoux*, bibelots, curios, *objets d'art*; rummage, lumber, junk, *Brit.* jumble.

brick /brik/ *n.*, *v.*, & *adj.* ● *n.* **1 a** a small, usu. rectangular, block of fired or sun-dried clay, used in building. **b** the material used to make these. **c** a similar block of concrete etc. **2** *Brit.* a child's toy building-block. **3** a brick-shaped solid object (*a brick of ice-cream*). **4** *sl.* a generous or loyal person. ● *v.tr.* (foll. by *in*, *up*) close or block with brickwork. ● *adj.* **1** built of brick (*brick wall*). **2** of a dull red colour. □ **bang** (or **knock** or **run**) **one's head against a brick wall** attempt the impossible. **brick-field** a place at which bricks are made. **brick-red** the colour of bricks. **like a load** (or **ton**) **of bricks** *colloq.* with crushing weight, force, or authority. **see through a brick wall** have miraculous insight. ▫▫ **bricky** *adj.* [ME f. MLG, MDu. *bri(c)ke*, of unkn. orig.]

▪ *n.* **2** (*bricks*) blocks. **3** block, cube, chunk, hunk, slab, lump, square. **4** the salt of the earth, good chap, *colloq.* good sort, topper, trump. ● *v.* see WALL *v.* 2a.

brickbat /brikbat/ *n.* **1** a piece of brick, esp. when used as a missile. **2** an uncomplimentary remark.

▪ **1** see MISSILE. **2** see TAUNT *n.*

brickfielder /brikfeeldər/ *n. Austral.* a hot, dry north wind.

brickie /brikki/ *n. sl.* a bricklayer.

bricklayer /briklayər/ *n.* a worker who builds with bricks. ▫▫ **bricklaying** *n.*

brickwork /brikwurk/ *n.* **1** building in brick. **2** a wall, building, etc. made of brick.

brickyard /brikyaard/ *n.* a place where bricks are made.

bridal /brīd'l/ *adj.* of or concerning a bride or a wedding. ▫▫ **bridally** *adv.* [orig. as noun, = wedding-feast, f. OE *brȳd-ealu* f. *brȳd* BRIDE + *ealu* ale-drinking]

▪ nuptial, wedding, marriage, *literary* hymeneal.

bride /brīd/ *n.* a woman on her wedding day and for some time before and after it. ▫ **bride-cake** a wedding cake. **bride-price** money or goods given to a bride's family esp. in primitive societies. [OE *brȳd* f. Gmc]

▪ see WIFE.

bridegroom /brīdgroom, -groom/ *n.* a man on his wedding day and for some time before and after it. [OE *brȳdguma* (as BRIDE, *guma* man, assim. to GROOM)]

▪ see HUSBAND.

bridesmaid /brīdzmayd/ *n.* a girl or unmarried woman attending a bride on her wedding day. [earlier *bridemaid*, f. BRIDE + MAID]

bridewell /brīdwəl, -wel/ *n. archaic* a prison; a reformatory. [St *Bride's Well* in London, near which such a building stood]

▪ see PRISON *n.* 1.

bridge[1] /brij/ *n.* & *v.* ● *n.* **1 a** a structure carrying a road, path, railway, etc., across a stream, ravine, road, railway, etc. **b** anything providing a connection between different things (*English is a bridge between nations*). **2** the superstructure on a ship from which the captain and officers direct operations. **3** the upper bony part of the nose. **4** *Mus.* an upright piece of wood on a violin etc. over which the strings are stretched. **5** = BRIDGEWORK. **6** *Billiards* etc. **a** a long stick with a structure at the end which is used to support a cue for a difficult shot. **b** a support for a cue formed by a raised hand. **7** = *land-bridge*. ● *v.tr.* **1 a** be a bridge over (*a fallen tree bridges the stream*). **b** make a bridge over; span. **2** span as if with a bridge (*bridged their differences with understanding*). ▫ **bridge of asses** = *pons asinorum*. **bridge of boats** a bridge formed by mooring boats together abreast across a river etc. **bridge passage** *Mus.* a transitional piece between main themes. **bridging loan** a loan from a bank etc. to cover the short interval between buying a house etc. and selling another. **cross a** (or **that**) **bridge when one comes to it** deal with a problem when and if it arises. ▫▫ **bridgeable** *adj.* [OE *brycg* f. Gmc]

▪ *n.* **1 a** viaduct. **b** link, connection, tie, bond. ● *v.* **1** span, cross (over), go *or* pass *or* stretch *or* extend *or* reach over, traverse, go across. **2** overcome, reconcile.

bridge[2] /brij/ *n.* a card-game derived from whist, in which one player's cards are exposed and are played by his or her partner (cf. *auction bridge*, *contract bridge*). ▫ **bridge roll** a small soft bread roll. [19th c.: orig. unkn.]

bridgehead /brijhed/ *n. Mil.* a fortified position held on the enemy's side of a river or other obstacle.

bridgework /brijwurk/ *n. Dentistry* a dental structure used to cover a gap, joined to and supported by the teeth on either side.

bridle /brīd'l/ *n.* & *v.* ● *n.* **1 a** the headgear used to control a horse, consisting of buckled leather straps, a metal bit, and reins. **b** a restraining device or influence (*put a bridle on your tongue*). **2** *Naut.* a mooring-cable. **3** *Physiol.* a ligament checking the motion of a part. ● *v.* **1** *tr.* put a bridle on (a horse etc.). **2** *tr.* bring under control; curb. **3** *intr.* (often foll. by *at* or *up at*) express offence, resentment, etc., esp. by throwing up the head and drawing in the chin. ▫ **bridle-path** (or **-road** or **-way**) a rough path or road fit only for riders or walkers, not vehicles. [OE *brīdel*]

▪ *n.* **1 b** restraint, curb, check, control, brake, rein; command. ● *v.* **2** curb, check, restrain, hold in (check), control, subdue; command, master, hold sway over, govern. **3** (*bridle (up) at*) bristle at, draw oneself up at, be *or* become indignant at *or* with, take offence *or* umbrage *or* affront at, be affronted *or* offended by.

bridoon /bridoon/ *n.* the snaffle and rein of a military bridle. [F *bridon* f. *bride* bridle]

Brie /bree/ *n.* a kind of soft cheese. [*Brie* in N. France]

brief /breef/ *adj.*, *n.*, & *v.* ● *adj.* **1** of short duration; fleeting. **2** concise in expression. **3** abrupt, brusque (*was rather brief with me*). **4** scanty; lacking in substance (*wearing a brief skirt*). ● *n.* **1** (in *pl.*) **a** women's brief pants. **b** men's brief underpants. **2** *Law* **a** a summary of the facts and legal points of a case drawn up for counsel. **b** a piece of work for a barrister. **3** instructions given for a task, operation, etc. (orig. a bombing plan given to an aircrew). **4** *RC Ch.* a letter from the Pope to a person or community on a matter of discipline. **5** *US* a short account or summary; a synopsis. ● *v.tr.* **1** *Brit. Law* instruct (a barrister) by brief. **2** instruct (an employee, a participant, etc.) in preparation for a task; inform or instruct thoroughly in advance (*briefed him for the interview*) (cf. DEBRIEF). ▫ **be brief** use few words. **hold a brief for 1** argue in favour of. **2** be retained as counsel for. **in brief** in short. **watching brief 1** a brief held by a barrister following a case for a client not directly involved. **2** a state of interest maintained in a proceeding not directly or immediately concerning one. ▫▫ **briefly** *adv.* **briefness** *n.* [ME f. AF *bref*, OF *brief*, f. L *brevis* short]

▪ *adj.* **1** short, momentary, short-lived; flying, brisk, hasty, speedy, swift; transitory, fleeting, transient, evanescent, passing. **2** short, concise, thumbnail, succinct, compact, to the point, laconic, terse, summary, compendious. **3** curt, abrupt, terse, short, blunt, brusque, direct, unceremonious. **4** see SCANTY. ● *n.* **1** (*briefs*) pants, knickers, bikini briefs, G-string; underpants, boxer shorts, *US* shorts, *propr.* Y-fronts. **3** instructions, guideline(s), directive(s), orders, directions. **5** summary, outline, digest, précis, résumé, *aperçu*, abstract, abridgement, synopsis. ● *v.* **2** coach, instruct, train, drill, prime, prepare, make *or* get ready; advise, inform, apprise, acquaint, put in the picture, *colloq.* fill in, put a person wise. ▫ **hold a brief for 1** see ADVOCATE *v.* **in brief** in short, briefly, concisely, in sum, in summary, to sum up, succinctly, in a word, to cut a long story short, in a nutshell. ▫▫ **briefly** momentarily, for a few moments *or* seconds *or* minutes, fleetingly, hurriedly, hastily, quickly; see also *in brief* (BRIEF) above.

briefcase /breefkayss/ *n.* a flat rectangular case for carrying documents etc.

▪ see BAG *n.* 2a.

briefing /breefing/ *n.* **1** a meeting for giving information or instructions. **2** the information or instructions given; a brief. **3** the action of informing or instructing.

▪ see ORIENTATION 3.

briefless /breefliss/ *adj. Law* (of a barrister) having no clients.

brier[1] /brīər/ *n.* (also **briar**) any prickly bush esp. of a wild rose. ▫ **brier-rose** dog-rose. **sweet-brier** a wild rose, *Rosa eglanteria*, with small fragrant leaves and flowers. ▫▫ **briery** *adj.* [OE *brǣr*, *brēr*, of unkn. orig.]

brier[2] /brīər/ *n.* (also **briar**) **1** a white heath, *Erica arborea*, native to S. Europe. **2** a tobacco pipe made from its root. [19th-c. *bruyer* f. F *bruyère* heath]

■ **2** see PIPE *n.* 2a.

Brig. *abbr.* Brigadier.

brig[1] /brig/ *n.* **1** a two-masted square-rigged ship, with an additional lower fore-and-aft sail on the gaff and a boom to the mainmast. **2** *US* a prison, esp. on a warship. [abbr. of BRIGANTINE]
■ **2** see PRISON *n.* 1.

brig[2] /brig/ *n. Sc.* & *N.Engl.* var. of BRIDGE[1].

brigade /brigáyd/ *n.* & *v.* ● *n.* **1** *Mil.* **a** a subdivision of an army. **b** a British infantry unit consisting usu. of 3 battalions and forming part of a division. **c** a corresponding armoured unit. **2** an organized or uniformed band of workers (*fire brigade*). **3** *colloq.* any group of people with a characteristic in common (*the couldn't-care-less brigade*). ● *v.tr.* form into a brigade. [F f. It. *brigata* company f. *brigare* be busy with f. *briga* strife]
■ *n.* **1 a** see CORPS.

brigadier /bríggədeer/ *n. Mil.* **1** an officer commanding a brigade. **2 a** a staff officer of similar standing, above a colonel and below a major-general. **b** the titular rank granted to such an officer. □ **brigadier general** *US* an officer ranking next above colonel. [F (as BRIGADE, -IER)]

brigalow /bríggəlō/ *n. Austral.* any of various acacia trees, esp. *Acacia harpophylla.* [Aboriginal]

brigand /bríggənd/ *n.* a member of a robber band living by pillage and ransom, usu. in wild terrain. □□ **brigandage** *n.* **brigandish** *adj.* **brigandism** *n.* **brigandry** *n.* [ME f. OF f. It. *brigante* f. *brigare*: see BRIGADE]
■ see ROBBER.

brigantine /bríggənteen/ *n.* a two-masted sailing-ship with a square-rigged foremast and a fore-and-aft rigged mainmast. [OF *brigandine* or It. *brigantino* f. *brigante* BRIGAND]

bright /brīt/ *adj.* & *adv.* ● *adj.* **1** emitting or reflecting much light; shining. **2** (of colour) intense, vivid. **3** clever, talented, quick-witted (*a bright idea*; *a bright child*). **4 a** (of a person) cheerful, vivacious. **b** (of prospects, the future, etc.) promising, hopeful. ● *adv.* esp. *poet.* brightly (*the moon shone bright*). □ **bright and early** very early in the morning. **bright-eyed and bushy-tailed** *colloq.* alert and sprightly. **the bright lights** the glamour and excitement of the city. **look on the bright side** be optimistic. □□ **brightish** *adj.* **brightly** *adv.* **brightness** *n.* [OE *beorht*, (adv.) *beorhte*, f. Gmc]
■ *adj.* **1** light, shining, gleaming, radiant, brilliant, luminous, resplendent, glittering, sparkling, *formal* splendent, *literary* refulgent, effulgent, *poet. or rhet.* fulgent; alight, aglow, beaming, dazzling, glowing, lambent, incandescent, ablaze; shiny, polished, lustrous, glossy, sheeny. **2** brilliant, vivid, intense, bold, strong, striking, loud, fluorescent, *prop.* Day-Glo. **3** intelligent, clever, quick, quick-witted, brilliant, keen, sharp-witted, sharp, brainy, astute, receptive, alert, smart, *colloq.* on the ball; precocious; talented, gifted. **4 a** cheerful, gay, happy, cheery, exuberant, bubbly, lively, active, dynamic, animated, vivacious, spirited, vibrant, perky, perk, energetic, enthusiastic, eager. **b** hopeful, optimistic, favourable, propitious, auspicious, promising, rosy. ● *adv.* brightly, radiantly, brilliantly, luminously, resplendently, *literary* refulgently, effulgently, lambently. □ **bright and early** see EARLY *adj.* & *adv.* 1. **bright-eyed and bushy-tailed** see ALERT *adj.* 2, PERKY 2. □□ **brightly** see BRIGHT *adv.* above.

brighten /brī́t'n/ *v.tr.* & *intr.* (often foll. by *up*) **1** make or become brighter. **2** make or become more cheerful or hopeful.
■ **1** see LIGHTEN[2]. **2** enliven, lighten, cheer (up), liven up, perk *or* lift up, hearten.

Bright's disease /brīts/ *n.* inflammation of the kidney from any of various causes; nephritis. [R. *Bright*, Engl. physician d. 1858]

brill[1] /bril/ *n.* a European flat-fish, *Scophthalmus rhombus*, resembling a turbot. [15th c.: orig. unkn.]

brill[2] /bril/ *adj. colloq.* = BRILLIANT *adj.* 4. [abbr.]

brilliance /brílliənss/ *n.* (also **brilliancy** /-ənsi/) **1** great brightness; sparkling or radiant quality. **2** outstanding talent or intelligence.
■ **1** brightness, radiance, lustrousness, lustre, luminosity, resplendence, refulgence, lambency, incandesence, splendour, magnificence, pomp, glory, sparkle, dazzle, glitter, *literary* effulgence. **2** intelligence, cleverness, brightness, wit, intellect, keenness, sharpness, smartness, acuteness, quickness, genius, excellence, talent, flair, ability, aptitude; precocity.

brilliancy var. of BRILLIANCE.

brilliant /brílliənt/ *adj.* & *n.* ● *adj.* **1** very bright; sparkling. **2** outstandingly talented or intelligent. **3** showy; outwardly impressive. **4** *colloq.* excellent, superb. ● *n.* a diamond of the finest cut with many facets. □□ **brilliantly** *adv.* [F *brillant* part. of *briller* shine f. It. *brillare*, of unkn. orig.]
■ *adj.* **1** bright, shining, lustrous, radiant, resplendent, dazzling, luminous; incandescent, glittering, sparkling, gleaming, scintillating, coruscating, twinkling, *formal* splendent, *literary* effulgent, refulgent, *poet. or rhet.* fulgent. **2** intelligent, clever, gifted, bright, smart, quick-witted, sharp-witted; outstanding, exceptional, excellent, superior, superlative; talented, expert, masterful, masterly, accomplished, ingenious, imaginative, creative, enlightened; resourceful, discerning, able, competent. **3** showy, glittering, dazzling, sparkling, scintillating, gaudy, garish, impressive, pyrotechnic. **4** excellent, splendid, superb, distinguished, striking, glorious, remarkable, marvellous, admirable, exceptional, outstanding, superlative, first-rate, first-class, matchless, peerless, sovereign; great, fine, *colloq.* A1, brill, fab, smashing, super, fabulous, magnificent, magic, dreamy, tremendous, grand, terrific, out of sight, out of this world, way-out, capital, *Brit. colloq.* top-hole, *sl.* wicked, cracking, *Austral. sl.* bonzer, *esp. Brit. sl.* wizard, *Brit. archaic sl.* topping, spiffing, *esp. US sl.* cool, *US sl.* bang-up, copacetic.

brilliantine /brílliənteen/ *n.* **1** an oily liquid dressing for making the hair glossy. **2** *US* a lustrous dress fabric. [F *brillantine* (as BRILLIANT)]

brim /brim/ *n.* & *v.* ● *n.* **1** the edge or lip of a cup or other vessel, or of a hollow. **2** the projecting edge of a hat. ● *v.tr.* & *intr.* (**brimmed**, **brimming**) fill or be full to the brim. □ **brim over** overflow. □□ **brimless** *adj.* **brimmed** *adj.* (usu. in *comb.*). [ME *brimme*, of unkn. orig.]
■ *n.* **1** edge, margin, lip, rim, side; brink. ● *v.* be full *or* filled. □ **brim over** overflow, spill *or* slosh over, bubble over.

brim-full /brimfŏŏl/ *adj.* (also **brimful**) (often foll. by *of*) filled to the brim.
■ see FULL[1] *adj.* 1.

brimstone /brímstōn/ *n.* **1** *archaic* the element sulphur. **2** a butterfly, *Gonepteryx rhamni*, or moth, *Opisthograptis luteolata*, having yellow wings. [ME prob. f. OE *bryne* burning + STONE]

brindled /brínd'ld/ *adj.* (also **brindle**) brownish or tawny with streaks of other colour (esp. of domestic animals). [earlier *brinded*, *brended* f. *brend*, perh. of Scand. orig.]
■ see *speckled* (SPECKLE *v.*).

brine /brīn/ *n.* & *v.* ● *n.* **1** water saturated or strongly impregnated with salt. **2** sea water. ● *v.tr.* soak in or saturate with brine. [OE *brīne*, of unkn. orig.]

bring /bring/ *v.tr.* (*past* and *past part.* **brought** /brawt/) **1 a** come conveying esp. by carrying or leading. **b** come with. **2** cause to come or be present (*what brings you here?*). **3** cause or result in (*war brings misery*). **4** be sold for; produce as income. **5 a** prefer (a charge). **b** initiate (legal action). **6** cause to become or to reach a particular state (*brings me alive*; *brought them to their senses*; *cannot bring myself to agree*). **7** adduce (evidence, an argument, etc.). □ **bring about 1** cause to happen. **2** turn (a ship) around. **bring-and-buy sale** *Brit.* a kind of charity sale at which participants bring items for sale and buy what is brought by others. **bring back** call to mind. **bring down 1** cause to fall. **2** lower (a price). **3** *sl.* make unhappy or less happy. **4** *colloq.* damage the reputation of; demean. **bring forth 1** give birth to. **2** produce, emit, cause. **bring forward 1** move to an earlier date or time. **2** transfer from the previous page or account. **3** draw attention to; adduce. **bring home to** cause to realize fully (*brought home to me that I was wrong*). **bring the house down** receive rapturous applause. **bring in 1** introduce (legislation, a custom, fashion, topic, etc.). **2** yield as income or profit. **bring into play** cause to operate; activate. **bring low** overcome. **bring off** achieve successfully. **bring on 1** cause to happen or appear. **2** accelerate the progress of. **bring out 1** emphasize; make evident. **2** publish. **bring over** convert to one's own side. **bring round 1** restore to consciousness. **2** persuade. **bring through** aid (a person) through adversity, esp. illness. **bring to 1** restore to consciousness (*brought him to*). **2** check the motion of. **bring to bear** (usu. foll. by *on*) direct and concentrate (forces). **bring to mind** recall; cause one to remember. **bring to pass** cause to happen. **bring under** subdue. **bring up 1** rear (a child). **2** vomit, regurgitate. **3** call attention to; broach. **4** (*absol.*) stop suddenly. **bring upon oneself** be responsible for (something one suffers). ▫▫ **bringer** *n.* [OE *bringan* f. Gmc]

▪ **1 a** bring along, carry, bear, transport, fetch, take (along), convey, *esp. US colloq.* tote. **b** bring along, escort, invite, accompany, take (along); see, usher, show, conduct, lead. **2** lead, draw, direct, attract, lure, allure, entice. **3** result in, lead to, bring on, bring about, occasion, give rise to, be the source *or* cause of, create, cause, spark *or* trigger (off), set off, produce, *archaic* engender; contribute to. **4** see *bring in* 2 below. **5 a** see PREFER 2. **b** see INITIATE *v.* 1. **7** see QUOTE *v.* 1. ▫ **bring about 1** occasion, cause, give rise to, bring (on), spark *or* trigger (off), set off, induce; accomplish, effect, effectuate, achieve, engineer, produce. **bring down 1** overthrow, depose, oust, unseat, dethrone, overturn; see also TOPPLE 1b. **2** decrease, reduce, lower, drop, mark down, diminish, cut, cut back *or* down (on), slash, *colloq.* knock down. **3** see DEPRESS 2. **4** see MORTIFY 1. **bring forth 1** bear, give birth to, bring into the world, spawn, procreate, have, deliver, *archaic* engender, *literary* beget; yield, produce, generate, put out *or* forth. **2** produce, set forth, bring out *or* in *or* up, introduce, present, put out, submit, offer, advance; see also CAUSE *v.* 1, EMIT 1. **bring forward 1** advance. **3** see *bring up* 3 below. **bring home to** make a person realize *or* be aware, impress upon, drive home to, make clear to, stress *or* emphasize to. **bring in 1** see INTRODUCE 3, 7. **2** earn, reap, make, pocket, return, net, yield, produce; fetch, sell for, get, bring, pick up. **bring into play** see ACTIVATE 1, USE *v.* 1a. **bring low** see PROSTRATE *v.* 3. **bring off** succeed (in), achieve, accomplish, do, carry out *or* off, perform, pull off; *US* put over. **bring on 1** produce, introduce, bring in *or* out; see also *bring about* 1 above. **2** see HASTEN 2. **bring out 1** emphasize, focus on, make noticeable *or* conspicuous *or* evident, display, feature, illuminate, reveal, show up, throw up. **2** publish, issue, release, put *or* turn out, come out with, make known *or* public, produce, launch; put on, stage. **bring round 1** revive, resuscitate, bring to; restore. **2** persuade, win over, sway, convince, convert. **bring to 1** see *bring round* 1 above. **bring to bear** see EXERT 1. **bring to mind** see RECALL *v.* 2. **bring up 1** rear, raise, care for, look after, nurture, breed, mother, parent; educate, teach, train, tutor. **2** vomit, throw up, regurgitate, disgorge, spew up, *colloq.* fetch up, *Brit. colloq.* sick up, *sl.* puke (up). **3** introduce, broach, bring in, raise, call attention to, mention, touch on, talk about, voice, discuss, suggest, allude to, moot, set forth. **bring upon oneself** be responsible *or* to blame for, ask for, invite, attract, provoke, court; bring about one's ears; be at fault for.

brinjal /brínjəl/ *n.* (in India and Africa) an aubergine. [ult. Port. *berinjela* formed as AUBERGINE]

brink /bringk/ *n.* **1** the extreme edge of land before a precipice, river, etc., esp. when a sudden drop follows. **2** the furthest point before something dangerous or exciting is discovered. ▫ **on the brink of** about to experience or suffer; in imminent danger of. [ME f. ON: orig. unkn.]

▪ **1** edge, brim, rim, margin, lip, border. ▫ **on the brink of** on the threshold *or* point *or* verge of, within an ace of, close *or* near to, approaching; about to, at *or* on the point of.

brinkmanship /bríngkmənship/ *n.* the art or policy of pursuing a dangerous course to the brink of catastrophe before desisting.

briny /bríni/ *adj.* & *n.* ● *adj.* (**brinier, briniest**) of brine or the sea; salty. ● *n.* (prec. by *the*) *Brit. sl.* the sea. ▫▫ **brininess** *n.*

▪ *adj.* see SALT *adj.* ● *n.* see SEA 1.

brio /brée-ō/ *n.* dash, vigour, vivacity. [It.]

▪ see VERVE.

brioche /brée-osh/ *n.* a small rounded sweet roll made with a light yeast dough. [F]

briquette /brikét/ *n.* (also **briquet**) a block of compressed coal dust used as fuel. [F *briquette*, dimin. of *brique* brick]

brisk /brisk/ *adj.* & *v.* ● *adj.* **1** quick, lively, keen (*a brisk pace*; *brisk trade*). **2** enlivening, fresh, keen (*a brisk wind*). **3** curt, peremptory (*a brisk manner*). ● *v.tr.* & *intr.* (often foll. by *up*) make or grow brisk. ▫▫ **brisken** *v.tr.* & *intr.* **briskly** *adv.* **briskness** *n.* [prob. F *brusque* BRUSQUE]

▪ *adj.* **1** active, lively, busy, vigorous, bustling, vibrant; quick, fast, prompt, rapid, smart, snappy, speedy, swift, keen, expeditious; animated, sprightly, spry, energetic, spirited, jaunty. **2** breezy, strong, steady, fresh, refreshing, bracing, invigorating, stimulating, enlivening, vitalizing, energizing; crisp, biting, keen, sharp, chilly, cool, cold, *colloq.* nippy, *literary* chill. ▫▫ **briskly** see FAST[1] *adv.* 1.

brisket /brískit/ *n.* an animal's breast, esp. as a joint of meat. [AF f. OF *bruschet*, perh. f. ON]

brisling /brízling, brís-/ *n.* a small herring or sprat. [Norw. & Da., = sprat]

bristle /bríss'l/ *n.* & *v.* ● *n.* **1** a short stiff hair, esp. one of those on an animal's back. **2** this, or a man-made substitute, used in clumps to make a brush. ● *v.* **1 a** *intr.* (of the hair) stand upright, esp. in anger or pride. **b** *tr.* make (the hair) do this. **2** *intr.* show irritation or defensiveness. **3** *intr.* (usu. foll. by *with*) be covered or abundant (in). [ME *bristel*, *brestel* f. OE *byrst*]

▪ *n.* **1** hair, whisker(s); *Bot.* & *Zool.* seta. ● *v.* **1** rise, stand up. **2** draw oneself up, take offence *or* umbrage (at); seethe, foam at the mouth, be angry *or* infuriated *or* furious *or* maddened, get *or* have one's hackles up, boil, flare up, rage, storm, see red, bridle. **3** teem, crawl, swarm, throng, be thick *or* crowded *or* packed *or* jammed, be infested, be alive, abound, be abundant *or* rich *or* covered.

bristletail /bríss'ltayl/ *n.* = SILVERFISH.

bristly /brísli/ *adj.* (**bristlier, bristliest**) full of bristles; rough, prickly.

▪ see PRICKLY 1.

Bristol board /bríst'l/ *n.* a kind of fine smooth pasteboard for drawing on. [*Bristol* in S. England]

Bristol fashion /bríst'l/ *n.* (functioning as *predic.adj.*) (in full **shipshape and Bristol fashion**) orig. *Naut.* with all in good order.

▪ see SHIPSHAPE.

bristols /bríst'lz/ *n.pl. Brit. sl.* a woman's breasts. [rhyming sl. f. *Bristol cities* = *titties*]

▪ see BOSOM *n.* 1.

Brit /brit/ *n. colloq.* a British person. [abbr.]

Brit. *abbr.* **1** British. **2** Britain.

Britannia /britányə/ *n.* the personification of Britain, esp. as a helmeted woman with shield and trident. ▫ **Britannia metal** a silvery alloy of tin, antimony, and copper. [L f. Gk *Brettania* f. *Brettanoi* Britons]

Britannic /británnik/ *adj.* (esp. in **His** (**or Her**) **Britannic Majesty**) of Britain. [L *Britannicus* (as BRITANNIA)]

Briticism /bríttisiz'm/ *n.* (also **Britishism** /-tishiz'm/) an idiom used in Britain but not in other English-speaking countries. [BRITISH, after GALLICISM]

British /bríttish/ *adj.* & *n.* ● *adj.* **1** of or relating to Great Britain or the United Kingdom, or to its people or language. **2** of the British Commonwealth or (formerly) the British Empire (*British subject*). ● *n.* **1** (prec. by *the*; treated as *pl.*) the British people. **2** *US* = *British English.* □ **British English** English as used in Great Britain, as distinct from that used elsewhere. **British Legion** = *Royal British Legion.* **British summer time** = *summer time* (see SUMMER[1]). **British thermal unit** see THERMAL. □□ **Britishness** *n.* [OE *Brettisc* etc. f. *Bret* f. L *Britto* or OCelt.]

Britisher /bríttishər/ *n.* a British subject, esp. of British descent. ¶ Not used in British English.

Britishism var. of BRITICISM.

Briton /brítt'n/ *n.* **1** one of the people of S. Britain before the Roman conquest. **2** a native or inhabitant of Great Britain or (formerly) of the British Empire. [ME & OF *Breton* f. L *Britto -onis* f. OCelt.]

brittle /brítt'l/ *adj.* & *n.* ● *adj.* **1** hard and fragile; apt to break. **2** frail, weak; unstable. ● *n.* a brittle sweet made from nuts and set melted sugar. □ **brittle-bone disease** = OSTEOPOROSIS. **brittle-star** an echinoderm of the class Ophiuroidea, with long brittle arms radiating from a small central body. □□ **brittlely** *adv.* **brittleness** *n.* **brittly** *adv.* [ME ult. f. a Gmc root rel. to OE *brēotan* break up]

■ *adj.* **1** fragile, frangible, breakable, delicate; friable. **2** frail, weak, delicate, sensitive, insecure, unstable.

bro. *abbr.* brother.

broach /brōch/ *v.* & *n.* ● *v.tr.* **1** raise (a subject) for discussion. **2** pierce (a cask) to draw liquor. **3** open and start using contents of (a box, bale, bottle, etc.). **4** begin drawing (liquor). ● *n.* **1** a bit for boring. **2** a roasting-spit. □ **broach spire** an octagonal church spire rising from a square tower without a parapet. [ME f. OF *broche* (n.), *brocher* (v.) ult. f. L *brocc(h)us* projecting]

■ *v.* **1** introduce, raise, open (up), venture, put *or* bring forward, suggest, mention, moot, voice, hint at, touch on *or* upon, bring up *or* in, talk about, advance.

broad /brawd/ *adj.* & *n.* ● *adj.* **1** large in extent from one side to the other; wide. **2** (following a measurement) in breadth (*2 metres broad*). **3** spacious or extensive (*broad acres*; *a broad plain*). **4** full and clear (*broad daylight*). **5** explicit, unmistakable (*broad hint*). **6** general; not taking account of detail (*broad intentions*; *a broad inquiry*; *in the broadest sense of the word*). **7** chief or principal (*the broad facts*). **8** tolerant, liberal (*take a broad view*). **9** somewhat coarse (*broad humour*). **10** (of speech) markedly regional (*broad Scots*). ● *n.* **1** the broad part of something (*broad of the back*). **2** *US sl.* a young woman. **3** (**the Broads**) large areas of fresh water in E. Anglia, formed where rivers widen. □ **broad arrow** see ARROW. **broad bean 1** a kind of bean, *Vicia faba*, with pods containing large edible flat seeds. **2** one of these seeds. **Broad Church** a group within the Anglican Church favouring a liberal interpretation of doctrine. **broad gauge** a railway track with a gauge wider than the standard one. **broad-leaved** (of a tree) deciduous and hard-timbered. **broad pennant** a short swallow-tailed pennant distinguishing the commodore's ship in a squadron. **broad spectrum** (of a medicinal substance) effective against a large variety of micro-organisms. □□ **broadness** *n.* **broadways** *adv.* **broadwise** *adv.* [OE *brād* f. Gmc]

■ *adj.* **2** in breadth, in width, wide. **3** wide, expansive, wide-ranging, large, extensive, spacious, sweeping, sizeable, spread out, far-reaching, ample. **4** clear, bright, plain, open, full, complete, undiminished, pure, total. **5** plain, clear, obvious, unmistakable, explicit, direct, unconcealed, undisguised, unsubtle, overt, bald, bald-faced, self-evident. **6** general, generalized, basic, overall, sweeping, rough, approximate; imprecise, unspecific, non-specific, unfocused. **7** see MAIN[1] *adj.* 1. **8** liberal, tolerant, catholic, ecumenical, latitudinarian, open-minded, broad-minded, unprejudiced, undogmatic, enlightened. **9** dirty, blue, coarse, rude, indecent, vulgar, improper, indelicate, gross, obscene, lewd, lascivious, filthy, pornographic; inelegant, unrefined, unladylike, ungentlemanly. ● *n.* **2** woman, girl, *sl.* chick, doll, Judy, petticoat, *Austral.* & *NZ sl.* brush, sheila, *Brit. sl.* bird, *US sl.* dame, cookie, babe, frail, *sl. offens.* (bit of) skirt, *derog. sl.* piece (of baggage).

broadcast /bráwdkaast/ *v.*, *n.*, *adj.*, & *adv.* ● *v.* (*past* **broadcast** or **broadcasted**; *past part.* **broadcast**) **1** *tr.* **a** transmit (programmes or information) by radio or television. **b** disseminate (information) widely. **2** *intr.* undertake or take part in a radio or television transmission. **3** *tr.* scatter (seed etc.) over a large area, esp. by hand. ● *n.* a radio or television programme or transmission. ● *adj.* **1** transmitted by radio or television. **2 a** scattered widely. **b** (of information etc.) widely disseminated. ● *adv.* over a large area. □□ **broadcaster** *n.* **broadcasting** *n.* [BROAD + CAST *past part.*]

■ *v.* **1 a** air, transmit, relay; radio; screen, televise, telecast. **b** announce, advertise, circulate, publish, proclaim, pronounce; put *or* give out, report; disseminate. **3** sow, scatter, strew, seed, litter, sprinkle, disperse, disseminate. ● *n.* programme, show; transmission, telecast. □□ **broadcaster** see ANNOUNCER.

broadcloth /bráwdkloth/ *n.* a fine cloth of wool, cotton, or silk. [orig. with ref. to width and quality]

broaden /bráwd'n/ *v.tr.* & *intr.* make or become broader.

■ see WIDEN.

broadloom /bráwdloom/ *adj.* (esp. of carpet) woven in broad widths.

broadly /bráwdli/ *adv.* in a broad manner; widely (*grinned broadly*). □ **broadly speaking** disregarding minor exceptions.

■ □ **broadly speaking** see GENERALLY 2.

broad-minded /bráwdmíndid/ *adj.* tolerant or liberal in one's views. □□ **broad-mindedly** *adv.* **broad-mindedness** *n.*

■ see LIBERAL *adj.* 3.

broadsheet /bráwdsheet/ *n.* **1** a large sheet of paper printed on one side only, esp. with information. **2** a newspaper with a large format.

■ **2** see JOURNAL 1.

broadside /bráwdsīd/ *n.* **1** the firing of all guns from one side of a ship. **2** a vigorous verbal onslaught. **3** the side of a ship above the water between the bow and quarter. □ **broadside on** sideways on.

broadsword /bráwdsord/ *n.* a sword with a broad blade, for cutting rather than thrusting.

broadtail /bráwdtayl/ *n.* **1** the karacul sheep. **2** the fleece or wool from its lamb.

broadway /bráwdway/ *n.* a large open or main road.

brocade /brəkáyd, brō-/ *n.* & *v.* ● *n.* a rich fabric with a silky finish woven with a raised pattern, and often with gold or silver thread. ● *v.tr.* weave with this design. [Sp. & Port. *brocado* f. It. *broccato* f. *brocco* twisted thread]

broccoli /brókkəli/ *n.* **1** a variety of cabbage, similar to the cauliflower, with a loose cluster of greenish flower buds. **2** the flower-stalk and head used as a vegetable. [It., pl. of *broccolo* dimin. of *brocco* sprout]

broch /brok, brokh/ *n.* (in Scotland) a prehistoric circular stone tower. [ON *borg* castle]

brochette /broshét/ *n.* a skewer on which chunks of meat are cooked, esp. over an open fire. [F, dimin. of *broche* BROACH]

brochure /brṓshər, brōshyóor/ *n.* a pamphlet or leaflet, esp. one giving descriptive information. [F, lit. 'stitching', f. *brocher* stitch]

■ pamphlet, leaflet, booklet, insert, catalogue, folder.

brock /brok/ *n.* (esp. in rural use) a badger. [OE *broc(c)* f. OBrit. *brokkos*]

brocket /brókkit/ *n.* any small deer of the genus *Mazama*, native to Central and S. America, having short straight antlers. [ME f. AF *broque* (= *broche* BROACH)]

broderie anglaise /brṓdəri ONGGLÁYZ/ *n.* open embroidery on white linen or cambric, esp. in floral patterns. [F, = English embroidery]

brogue[1] /brōg/ *n.* **1** a strong outdoor shoe with ornamental perforated bands. **2** a rough shoe of untanned leather. [Gael. & Ir. *brōg* f. ON *brók*]

brogue[2] /brōg/ *n.* a marked accent, esp. Irish. [18th c.: orig. unkn.: perh. allusively f. BROGUE[1]]
▪ see DIALECT 1.

broil[1] /broyl/ *v.* esp. *US* **1** *tr.* cook (meat) on a rack or a gridiron. **2** *tr.* & *intr.* make or become very hot, esp. from the sun. [ME f. OF *bruler* burn f. Rmc]
▪ **1** grill, barbecue, griddle, frizzle; cook. **2** swelter, roast, *colloq.* bake, sizzle, boil, fry, scorch.

broil[2] /broyl/ *n.* a row; a tumult. [obs. *broil* to muddle: cf. EMBROIL]

broiler /bróylər/ *n.* **1** a young chicken raised for broiling or roasting. **2** a gridiron etc. for broiling. **3** *colloq.* a very hot day. □ **broiler house** a building for rearing broiler chickens in close confinement.

broke /brōk/ *past* of BREAK[1]. ● *predic.adj. colloq.* having no money; financially ruined. □ **go for broke** *sl.* risk everything in a strenuous effort. [(adj.) archaic past part. of BREAK[1]]
▪ penniless, indigent, down and out, poverty-stricken, penurious, impoverished, insolvent, destitute, poor, needy, bankrupt, ruined, on one's beam-ends, close to the bone, hard up, *Austral.* unfinancial, *colloq.* on one's uppers, strapped (for cash), flat broke, up against it, on the skids, *Brit. sl.* skint, stony-broke; (*be broke*) not have a penny to one's name, not have a shot in one's locker, *US* not have a red cent, *colloq.* not have a brass farthing, not have a cent, *Austral.* & *NZ sl.* not have a (brass) razoo, *Brit. sl.* not have a bean. □ **go for broke** throw caution to the wind, take one's life in one's hands, give one's all, *colloq.* go for it, go all out, *Austral. sl.* go for the doctor.

broken /brṓkən/ *past part.* of BREAK[1]. ● *adj.* **1** that has been broken; out of order. **2** (of a person) reduced to despair; beaten. **3** (of a language or of speech) spoken falteringly and with many mistakes, as by a foreigner (*broken English*). **4** disturbed, interrupted (*broken time*). **5** uneven (*broken ground*). **6** (of an animal) trained to obey; tamed. **7** trangressed, not observed (*broken rules*). □ **broken chord** *Mus.* a chord in which the notes are played successively. **broken-down 1** worn out by age, use, or ill-treatment. **2** out of order. **broken-hearted** overwhelmed with sorrow or grief. **broken-heartedness** grief. **broken home** a family in which the parents are divorced or separated. **broken reed** a person who has become unreliable or ineffective. **broken wind** heaves (see HEAVE *n.* 3). **broken-winded** (of a horse) disabled by ruptured air-cells in the lungs. □□ **brokenly** *adv.* **brokenness** *n.*
▪ **1** fragmented, shattered, shivered, splintered, ruptured, cracked, fractured, split, smashed; broken-down, out of order *or* commission, not working *or* functioning, in (a state of) disrepair, in pieces, inoperative, faulty, malfunctioning, out of kilter, failed, *colloq.* bust, busted, *sl.* on the blink, kaput, dud, *Brit. sl.* duff, *US sl.* on the fritz, out of whack. **2** enfeebled, weakened, crushed, defeated, beaten, ruined; dispirited, dejected, discouraged, demoralized, subdued, debilitated, *colloq.* licked. **3** shaky, unsteady, faltering, wobbly, hesitant, halting, stumbling; poor, faulty. **4** interrupted, disturbed, discontinuous, disjointed, disconnected, fragmented, fragmentary, intermittent, erratic, sporadic. **5** see BUMPY 1. **6** tamed, trained, disciplined, obedient, docile, domesticated, subdued; house-broken, house-trained; conditioned. **7** violated, transgressed, disobeyed, contravened, defied, flouted, disregarded, ignored, infringed. □ **broken-down 1** worn out, worn, decrepit, ageing, effete, raddled, toil-worn, time-worn, *Brit. sl.* clapped out; delapidated, ramshackle, tumbledown, crumbling, run-down, down at heel; see also BEAT *adj.*, BROKEN 2 above. **2** see BROKEN 1 above. **broken-hearted** heartbroken, depressed, downhearted, dejected, devastated, crushed, desolate, overwhelmed, heartsick, downcast, cast down, upset, forlorn, sorrowful, disconsolate, inconsolable, grief-stricken, miserable, wretched, melancholy, heavy-hearted, sad, doleful, woeful, woebegone, gloomy, morose, glum, cheerless, down, *archaic* stricken, *literary or joc.* dolorous. **broken-heartedness** see GRIEF 1.

broker /brṓkər/ *n.* **1** an agent who buys and sells for others; a middleman. **2** a member of the Stock Exchange dealing in stocks and shares. ¶ In the UK from Oct. 1986 officially called **broker-dealer** and entitled to act as agent and principal in share dealings. **3** *Brit.* an official appointed to sell or appraise distrained goods. [ME f. AF *brocour*, of unkn. orig.]
▪ **1** agent, dealer, merchant, trader, factor, wholesaler, middleman, intermediary, mediator, go-between, contact, negotiator, *Brit.* stockjobber, scrivener, *US* jobber. **2** broker-dealer, stockbroker, *derog.* jobber, *US derog.* stockjobber.

brokerage /brṓkərij/ *n.* a broker's fee or commission.

broking /brṓking/ *n.* the trade or business of a broker.

brolga /brólgə/ *n. Austral.* a large Australian crane, *Grus rubicunda*, with a booming call. [Aboriginal]

brolly /brólli/ *n.* (*pl.* **-ies**) *Brit.* **1** *colloq.* an umbrella. **2** *sl.* a parachute. [abbr.]
▪ **1** see UMBRELLA 1.

bromate /brṓmayt/ *n. Chem.* a salt or ester of bromic acid.

brome /brōm/ *n.* any oatlike grass of the genus *Bromus*, having slender stems with flowering spikes. [mod.L *Bromus* f. Gk *bromos* oat]

bromelia /brōmeéliə/ *n.* (also **bromeliad** /-liəd/) any plant of the family Bromeliaceae (esp. of the genus *Bromelia*), native to the New World, having short stems with rosettes of stiff usu. spiny leaves, e.g. pineapple. [O. *Bromel*, Sw. botanist d. 1705]

bromic /brṓmik/ *adj. Chem.* of or containing bromine. □ **bromic acid** a strong acid used as an oxidizing agent.

bromide /brṓmīd/ *n.* **1** *Chem.* any binary compound of bromine. **2** *Pharm.* a preparation of usu. potassium bromide, used as a sedative. **3** a trite remark. □ **bromide paper** a photographic printing paper coated with silver bromide emulsion.
▪ **2** see TRANQUILLIZER. **3** see TRUISM.

bromine /brṓmeen/ *n. Chem.* a dark fuming liquid element with a choking irritating smell, extracted from bittern and used in the manufacture of chemicals for photography and medicine. ¶ Symb.: **Br.** □□ **bromism** *n.* [F *brome* f. Gk *brōmos* stink]

bromo- /brṓmō/ *comb. form Chem.* bromine.

bronc /brongk/ *n. US colloq.* = BRONCO. [abbr.]

bronchi *pl.* of BRONCHUS.

bronchial /bróngkiəl/ *adj.* of or relating to the bronchi or bronchioles. □ **bronchial tree** the branching system of bronchi and bronchioles conducting air from the windpipe to the lungs.

bronchiole /bróngkiōl/ *n.* any of the minute divisions of a bronchus. □□ **bronchiolar** /-ṓlər/ *adj.*

bronchitis /brongkítiss/ *n.* inflammation of the mucous membrane in the bronchial tubes. □□ **bronchitic** /-kíttik/ *adj.* & *n.*

broncho- /bróngkō/ *comb. form* bronchi.

bronchocele /bróngkəseel/ *n.* a goitre.

bronchopneumonia /bróngkōnyoomṓniə/ *n.* inflammation of the lungs, arising in the bronchi or bronchioles.

bronchoscope /bróngkəskōp/ *n.* a usu. fibre-optic instrument for inspecting the bronchi. □□ **bronchoscopy** /-kóskəpi/ *n.*

bronchus /bróngkəss/ *n.* (*pl.* **bronchi** /-kī/) any of the major air passages of the lungs, esp. either of the two main divisions of the windpipe. [LL f. Gk *brogkhos* windpipe]

bronco /bróngkō/ *n.* (*pl.* **-os**) a wild or half-tamed horse of the western US. □ **bronco-buster** *US sl.* a person who breaks in horses. [Sp., = rough]

brontosaurus /bróntəsáwrəss/ *n.* (also **brontosaur** /bróntəsawr/) a large plant-eating dinosaur of the genus *Brontosaurus*, with a long whiplike tail and trunk-like legs. [Gk *brontē* thunder + *sauros* lizard]

bronze /bronz/ *n.*, *adj.*, & *v.* ● *n.* **1** any alloy of copper and tin. **2** its brownish colour. **3** a thing made of bronze, esp. as a work of art. ● *adj.* made of or coloured like bronze. ● *v.* **1** *tr.* give a bronzelike surface to. **2** *tr.* & *intr.* make or become brown; tan. □ **Bronze Age** *Archaeol.* the period preceding the Iron Age, when weapons and tools were usu. made of bronze. **bronze medal** a medal usu. awarded to a competitor who comes third (esp. in sport). □□ **bronzy** *adj.* [F f. It. *bronzo*, prob. f. Pers. *birinj* copper]
■ *n.* **3** see SCULPTURE. ● *v.* **2** see SUN *v.*

brooch /brōch/ *n.* an ornament fastened to clothing with a hinged pin. [ME *broche* = BROACH *n.*]
■ clasp, pin, badge; fastening, clip.

brood /brōōd/ *n.* & *v.* ● *n.* **1** the young of an animal (esp. a bird) produced at one hatching or birth. **2** *colloq.* the children in a family. **3** a group of related things. **4** bee or wasp larvae. **5** (*attrib.*) kept for breeding (*brood-mare*). ● *v.* **1** *intr.* (often foll. by *on*, *over*, etc.) worry or ponder (esp. resentfully). **2 a** *intr.* sit as a hen on eggs to hatch them. **b** *tr.* sit on (eggs) to hatch them. **3** *intr.* (usu. foll. by *over*) (of silence, a storm, etc.) hang or hover closely. □□ **broodingly** *adv.* [OE *brōd* f. Gmc]
■ *n.* **1** young, offspring, litter, progeny, issue, progeniture, *archaic* seed, *derog.* spawn. **2** children, family, *colloq.* kids, *derog.* spawn, *sl.* sprogs. **3** see SET² *n.* 1, 2, 7. ● *v.* **1** ponder, deliberate, reflect, meditate, ruminate, *literary* muse; mope, sulk, be sullen *or* moody *or* resentful, harbour a grudge, get *or* be worked up, eat one's heart out, fret, worry; (*brood over*) mull over. **2 b** incubate, hatch, sit on, cover. **3** see LOOM *v.* 2.

brooder /brōōdər/ *n.* **1** a heated house for chicks, piglets, etc. **2** a person who broods.

broody /brōōdi/ *adj.* (**broodier**, **broodiest**) **1** (of a hen) wanting to brood. **2** sullenly thoughtful or depressed. **3** *colloq.* (of a woman) wanting to have a baby. □□ **broodily** *adv.* **broodiness** *n.*
■ **2** see MOODY *adj.*

brook¹ /brŏŏk/ *n.* a small stream. □□ **brooklet** /brŏŏklit/ *n.* [OE *brōc*, of unkn. orig.]
■ stream, rivulet, brooklet, streamlet, runlet, runnel, rill, bourn, *Brit.* gill, *N.Engl.* beck, *Sc.* burn, *US* run, *US*, *Austral.* & *NZ* creek.

brook² /brŏŏk/ *v.tr.* (usu. with *neg.*) *literary* tolerate, allow. [OE *brūcan* f. Gmc]
■ endure, tolerate, stand, abide, put up with, support, bear, stomach; see also ALLOW 1.

brooklime /brŏŏklīm/ *n.* a kind of speedwell, *Veronica beccabunga*, growing in wet areas.

brookweed /brŏŏkweed/ *n.* a small herb, *Samolus valerandi*, having slender stems with tiny white flowers and growing in wet places.

broom /brōōm/ *n.* **1** a long-handled brush of bristles, twigs, etc. for sweeping (orig. one made of twigs of broom). **2** any of various shrubs, esp. *Cytisus scoparius* bearing bright yellow flowers. □ **new broom** a newly appointed person eager to make changes. [OE *brōm*]
■ **1** brush, besom.

broomrape /brōōmrayp/ *n.* any parasitic plant of the genus *Orobanche*, with tubular flowers on a leafless brown stem, and living on the roots of broom and similar plants. [BROOM + L *rapum* tuber]

broomstick /brōōmstik/ *n.* the handle of a broom, esp. as allegedly ridden on through the air by witches.

Bros. *abbr.* Brothers (esp. in the name of a firm).

brose /brōz/ *n.* esp. *Sc. Cookery* a dish of oatmeal with boiling water or milk poured on it. [Sc. form of *brewis* broth: ME f. OF *bro(u)ez*, ult. f. Gmc]

broth /broth/ *n.* **1** *Cookery* **a** a thin soup of meat or fish stock. **b** unclarified meat or fish stock. **2** *Biol.* meat stock as a nutrient medium for bacteria. [OE f. Gmc: rel. to BREW]
■ **1** stock, consommé, decoction, liquor; soup, bouillon, potage, *pot-au-feu*, *Brit.* skilly, *US* chowder, *archaic* pottage.

brothel /bróthəl/ *n.* a house etc. where prostitution takes place. [orig. *brothel-house* f. ME *brothel* worthless man, prostitute, f. OE *brēothan* go to ruin]
■ whore-house, bawdy-house, bagnio, *Law* disorderly house, *esp. US* bordello, *US* house, sporting house, *archaic* house of ill fame *or* ill repute, stews, *euphem.* massage parlour, *sl.* crib, drum, *Brit. sl.* kip, kip-house, kip-shop, knocking-shop.

brother /brú<u>th</u>ər/ *n.* **1** a man or boy in relation to other sons and daughters of his parents. **2 a** (often as a form of address) a close male friend or associate. **b** a male fellow member of a trade union etc. **3** (*pl.* also **brethren** /bré<u>th</u>rin/) **a** a member of a male religious order, esp. a monk. **b** a fellow member of the Christian Church, a religion, or (formerly) a guild etc. **4** a fellow human being. □ **brother german** see GERMAN. **brother-in-law** (*pl.* **brothers-in-law**) **1** the brother of one's wife or husband. **2** the husband of one's sister. **3** the husband of one's sister-in-law. **brother uterine** see UTERINE 2. □□ **brotherless** *adj.* **brotherly** *adj.* & *adv.* **brotherliness** *n.* [OE *brōthor* f. Gmc]
■ **1** sibling; cousin, relation, relative, kin, kinsman. **2**, **4** fellow, fellow-man, fellow-citizen, fellow-countryman, fellow-creature; associate, colleague, confrère, comrade, comrade-in-arms, fellow-worker, co-worker, companion; mate, friend, *colloq.* pal, chum, *Austral.* & *NZ colloq.* cobber, *esp. US colloq.* buddy, *US colloq.* homeboy, *amigo*. **3 a** see MONK. □□ **brotherly** fraternal, neighbourly, comradely, loyal, devoted, kind, affectionate, cordial, friendly, amicable, amiable, congenial, convivial, loving, matey, *colloq.* chummy, pally.

brotherhood /brú<u>th</u>ərhŏŏd/ *n.* **1 a** the relationship between brothers. **b** brotherly friendliness; companionship. **2 a** an association, society, or community of people linked by a common interest, religion, trade, etc. **b** its members collectively. **3** *US* a trade union. **4** community of feeling between all human beings. [ME alt. f. *brotherrede* f. OE *brōthor-rǣden* (cf. KINDRED) after words in -HOOD, -HEAD]
■ **1 b** brotherliness, fellowship, companionship, alliance, friendship, comradeship, camaraderie, kinship, amity. **2** fraternity, confraternity, guild, society, association, order, league, union, organization, syndicate, club, clan, community, circle, set, clique. **3** trade(s) union, union, *US* labour union. **4** harmony, love, affinity, sympathy, togetherness, communality, accord, unity.

brougham /brōōəm, brōōm/ *n. hist.* **1** a horse-drawn closed carriage with a driver perched outside in front. **2** a motor car with an open driver's seat. [Lord *Brougham*, d. 1868]

brought *past* and *past part.* of BRING.

brouhaha /brōōhaahaa/ *n.* commotion, sensation; hubbub, uproar. [F]
■ see UPROAR.

brow /brow/ *n.* **1** the forehead. **2** (usu. in *pl.*) an eyebrow. **3** the summit of a hill or pass. **4** the edge of a cliff etc. **5** *colloq.* intellectual level. □□ **browed** *adj.* [OE *brū* f. Gmc]

browbeat /brówbeet/ *v.tr.* (*past* **-beat**; *past part.* **-beaten**) intimidate with stern looks and words. □□ **browbeater** *n.*
■ bully, persecute, torment, intimidate, threaten, badger, cow, frighten, tyrannize, terrorize, hector, harass, hound, dog, plague, keep after, nag, *colloq.* hassle.

brown /brown/ *adj.*, *n.*, & *v.* ● *adj.* **1** having the colour produced by mixing red, yellow, and black, as of dark wood or rich soil. **2** dark-skinned or suntanned. **3** (of bread) made from a dark flour as wholemeal or wheatmeal. **4** (of species or varieties) distinguished by brown coloration. ● *n.* **1** a brown colour or pigment. **2** brown clothes or material (*dressed in brown*). **3** (in a game or sport) a brown ball, piece, etc. **4** (prec. by *the*) *Brit.* a brown mass of flying game-birds. ● *v.tr.* & *intr.* make or become brown by cooking, sunburn, etc. □ **brown ale** a dark, mild, bottled beer. **brown bear** a large N. American brown bear, *Ursus arctos*. **brown coal** = LIGNITE. **browned off** *Brit. sl.* fed up, disheartened. **brown fat** a dark-coloured adipose tissue with a rich supply of blood vessels. **brown holland** see HOLLAND. **brown-nose** *US coarse sl.* toady; be servile. **brown-noser** *US coarse sl.* a toady, a yes-man. **brown owl 1** any of various owls, esp. the tawny owl. **2** (**Brown Owl**) an adult leader of a Brownie Guides pack. **brown rice** unpolished rice with only the husk of the grain removed. **Brown-shirt** a Nazi; a member of a fascist organization. **brown sugar** unrefined or partially refined sugar. **in a brown study** see STUDY. □□ **brownish** *adj.* **brownness** *n.* **browny** *adj.* [OE *brūn* f. Gmc]
■ *adj.* **2** see DARK *adj.* 3. ● *v.* see SUN *v.*

Brownian movement /brównian/ *n.* (also **Brownian motion**) *Physics* the erratic random movement of microscopic particles in a liquid, gas, etc., as a result of continuous bombardment from molecules of the surrounding medium. [R. *Brown*, Sc. botanist d. 1858]

Brownie /brówni/ *n.* **1** (in full **Brownie Guide**) a member of the junior branch of the Guides. **2** (**brownie**) *Cookery* **a** a small square of rich, usu. chocolate, cake with nuts. **b** *Austral.* & *NZ* a sweet currant-bread. **3** (**brownie**) a benevolent elf said to haunt houses and do household work secretly. □ **Brownie point** *colloq.* a notional credit for something done to please or win favour.

browning /brówning/ *n. Brit. Cookery* browned flour or any other additive to colour gravy.

brownstone /brównstōn/ *n. US* **1** a kind of reddish-brown sandstone used for building. **2** a building faced with this.

browse /browz/ *v.* & *n.* ● *v.* **1** *intr.* & *tr.* read or survey desultorily. **2** *intr.* (often foll. by *on*) feed (on leaves, twigs, or scanty vegetation). **3** *tr.* crop and eat. ● *n.* **1** twigs, young shoots, etc., as fodder for cattle. **2** an act of browsing. □□ **browser** *n.* [(n.) f. earlier *brouse* f. OF *brost* young shoot, prob. f. Gmc; (v.) f. F *broster*]
■ *v.* **1** (*tr.*) look over *or* through, skim (through), scan, run one's eye over, thumb *or* flip *or* flick *or* leaf through, dip into. **2, 3** graze, pasture; feed. ● *n.* **2** look, scan, skim, glance, *Brit. colloq.* shufti, *Brit. sl.* dekko, *rhyming sl.* butcher's.

BRS *abbr.* British Road Services.

brucellosis /brōōssəlṓsiss/ *n.* a disease caused by bacteria of the genus *Brucella*, affecting esp. cattle and causing undulant fever in humans. [*Brucella* f. Sir D. *Bruce*, Sc. physician d. 1931 + -OSIS]

brucite /brōōssīt/ *n.* a mineral form of magnesium hydroxide. [A. *Bruce*, US mineralogist d. 1818]

Bruin /brōō-in/ *n.* a personal name used for a bear. [ME f. Du., = BROWN: used as a name in *Reynard the Fox*]

bruise /brōōz/ *n.* & *v.* ● *n.* **1** an injury appearing as an area of discoloured skin on a human or animal body, caused by a blow or impact. **2** a similar area of damage on a fruit etc. ● *v.* **1** *tr.* **a** inflict a bruise on. **b** hurt mentally. **2** *intr.* be susceptible to bruising. **3** *tr.* crush or pound. [ME f. OE *brȳsan* crush, reinforced by AF *bruser*, OF *bruisier* break]
■ *n.* injury, hurt, contusion, bump, welt, weal; blotch, blemish, mark, spot, discoloration. ● *v.* **1** contuse, hurt, harm, wound, damage; see also INJURE 1, 2. **3** see POUND[2] *v.* 1.

bruiser /brōōzər/ *n. colloq.* **1** a large tough-looking person. **2** a professional boxer.
■ **1** tough, ruffian, bodyguard, thug, hoodlum, bouncer, gangster, hooligan, bully-boy, enforcer, *Austral.* larrikin, *colloq.* tough guy, toughie, roughneck, *sl.* minder, trog, *dial. sl.* roughie, *Brit. sl.* yob, yobbo, bovver boy, *US sl.* hood, lug, plug-ugly. **2** prizefighter, boxer, fighter, pugilist, welter, *US* slugger, *sl.* pug.

bruit /brōōt/ *v.* & *n.* ● *v.tr.* (often foll. by *abroad*, *about*) spread (a report or rumour). ● *n. archaic* a report or rumour. [F, = noise f. *bruire* roar]
■ *v.* see RUMOUR *v.*

Brum /brum/ *n. colloq.* Birmingham (in England). [abbr. of BRUMMAGEM]

brumby /brúmbi/ *n.* (*pl.* **-ies**) *Austral.* a wild or unbroken horse. [19th c.: orig. unkn.]

brume /brōōm/ *n. literary* mist, fog. [F f. L *bruma* winter]

Brummagem /brúmməjəm/ *adj.* **1** cheap and showy (*Brummagem goods*). **2** counterfeit. [dial. form of *Birmingham*, England, with ref. to counterfeit coins and plated goods once made there]
■ **1** see GARISH 2.

Brummie /brúmmi/ *n.* & *adj.* (also **Brummy**) *colloq.* ● *n.* (*pl.* **-ies**) a native of Birmingham. ● *adj.* of or characteristic of a Brummie (*a Brummie accent*). [BRUM]

brunch /brunch/ *n.* & *v.* ● *n.* a late-morning meal eaten as the first meal of the day. ● *v.intr.* eat brunch. [BR(EAKFAST) + (L)UNCH]

brunette /brōōnét/ *n.* & *adj.* ● *n.* a woman with dark brown hair. ● *adj.* (of a woman) having dark brown hair. [F, fem. of *brunet*, dimin. of *brun* BROWN]
■ *adj.* see DARK *adj.* 3.

brunt /brunt/ *n.* the chief or initial impact of an attack, task, etc. (esp. *bear the brunt of*). [ME: orig. unkn.]
■ (full) force, burden, onus, weight, impact, thrust; effect, repercussion(s), consequence(s), responsibility.

brush /brush/ *n.* & *v.* ● *n.* **1** an implement with bristles, hair, wire, etc. varying in firmness set into a block or projecting from the end of a handle, for any of various purposes, esp. cleaning or scrubbing, painting, arranging the hair, etc. **2** the application of a brush; brushing. **3 a** (usu. foll. by *with*) a short esp. unpleasant encounter (*a brush with the law*). **b** a skirmish. **4 a** the bushy tail of a fox. **b** a brushlike tuft. **5** *Electr.* **a** a piece of carbon or metal serving as an electrical contact esp. with a moving part. **b** (in full **brush discharge**) a brushlike discharge of sparks. **6** esp. *US* & *Austral.* **a** undergrowth, thicket; small trees and shrubs. **b** *US* such wood cut in faggots. **c** land covered with brush. **d** *Austral.* dense forest. **7** *Austral.* & *NZ sl.* a girl or young woman. ● *v.* **1** *tr.* **a** sweep or scrub or put in order with a brush. **b** treat (a surface) with a brush so as to change its nature or appearance. **2** *tr.* **a** remove (dust etc.) with a brush. **b** apply (a liquid preparation) to a surface with a brush. **3** *tr.* & *intr.* graze or touch in passing. **4** *intr.* perform a brushing action or motion. □ **brush aside** dismiss or dispose of (a person, idea, etc.) curtly or lightly. **brushed aluminium** aluminium with a lustreless surface. **brushed fabric** fabric brushed so as to raise the nap. **brush off** rebuff; dismiss abruptly. **brush-off** *n.* a rebuff; an abrupt dismissal. **brush over** paint lightly. **brush turkey** *Austral.* a large mound-building bird, *Alectura lathami*. **brush up 1** clean up or smarten. **2** revive one's former knowledge of (a subject). **brush-up** *n.* the process of cleaning up. □□ **brushlike** *adj.* **brushy** *adj.* [ME f. OF *brosse*]
■ *n.* **1** broom, besom. **2** groom; sweep. **3** encounter, altercation, exchange, incident, to-do, clash, collision, wrangle, tussle, run-in, confrontation, quarrel, disagreement, dispute, engagement, *colloq.* set-to, *joc.* argy-bargy, *Brit. sl.* (spot of) bovver; see also SKIRMISH *n.* 1. **6** brushwood, shrubs, branches, scrub, bracken, brambles, boscage, coppice; thicket, undergrowth, underwood, brake, cover, thickset, copsewood, *Brit.* spinney, *US* underbrush, chaparral. **7** see BROAD *n.* ● *v.* **1, 4** sweep, dust, scrub, clean, wipe; groom, curry. **3** graze, touch, rub *or* press against. □ **brush aside** disregard, discount, discard, dismiss, put *or* push aside,

dispose of, shrug off, reject, laugh away *or* off, pooh-pooh; make light of, write off, gloss over, blink at, ridicule, play down, belittle, minimize, trivialize, de-emphasize, underrate, underestimate, undervalue. **brush off** give a person the brush-off, dismiss, ignore, spurn, snub, rebuff, turn one's back on, send off *or* away *or* packing, show a person the door, tell a person where to go *or* get off, cut, give a person the cold shoulder, *colloq.* give a person his *or* her walking papers *or* marching orders, give a person the boot, *sl.* tell a person to get lost. **brush-off** see REBUFF *n.* **brush up 1** see CLEAN *v.* 1, SPRUCE. **2** (*brush up on*) polish up, review, restudy, go over, study, *archaic* con (over), *colloq.* bone up (on), *Brit. colloq.* swot up (on), *sl.* get clued up on, *Brit. sl.* gen up on.

brushless /brúshliss/ *adj.* not requiring the use of a brush.

brushwood /brúshwŏŏd/ *n.* **1** cut or broken twigs etc. **2** undergrowth; a thicket.
■ see BRUSH *n.* 6.

brushwork /brúshwurk/ *n.* **1** manipulation of the brush in painting. **2** a painter's style in this.

brusque /brŏŏsk, brōōsk, brusk/ *adj.* abrupt or offhand in manner or speech. □□ **brusquely** *adv.* **brusqueness** *n.* **brusquerie** /brŏŏskəree/ *n.* [F f. It. *brusco* sour]
■ blunt, gruff, abrupt, short, curt, sharp, terse, brash, bluff, rough, indelicate, tactless, undiplomatic, overbearing; offhand(ed), unceremonious, cursory, careless, rude, impolite, uncivil, discourteous, ungracious, ill-mannered, unmannerly.

Brussels carpet /brúss'lz/ *n.* a carpet with a wool pile and a stout linen back. [*Brussels* in Belgium]

Brussels lace /brúss'lz/ *n.* an elaborate needlepoint or pillow lace.

Brussels sprout /brúss'lz/ *n.* **1** a variety of cabbage with small compact cabbage-like buds borne close together along a tall single stem. **2** any of these buds used as a vegetable.

brut /brōōt/ *adj.* (of wine) unsweetened. [F]

brutal /brōōt'l/ *adj.* **1** savagely or coarsely cruel. **2** harsh, merciless. □□ **brutality** /-tálliti/ *n.* (*pl.* **-ies**). **brutally** *adv.* [F *brutal* or med.L *brutalis* f. *brutus* BRUTE]
■ inhuman, savage, cruel, pitiless, merciless, unmerciful, harsh, severe, Draconian, barbaric, barbarous, beastly, bestial, sadistic; inhumane, heartless, callous, hard-hearted, fierce, stony-hearted, insensitive, unfeeling, cold-blooded, unsympathetic, remorseless, ruthless, ferocious, deadly, *poet. or rhet.* fell; oppressive, tyrannical, repressive, tyrannous, despotic, unjust. □□ **brutality** bestiality, cruelty, savagery, barbarousness, barbarity, inhumanity, beastliness, monstrousness, horribleness, fiendishness, wildness; vulgarity, crudeness, coarseness, boorishness, grossness, insensitivity.

brutalism /brōōtəliz'm/ *n.* **1** brutality. **2** a heavy plain style of architecture etc.

brutalize /brōōtəlīz/ *v.tr.* (also **-ise**) **1** make brutal. **2** treat brutally. □□ **brutalization** /-záysh'n/ *n.*
■ **2** see MISTREAT.

brute /brōōt/ *n.* & *adj.* ● *n.* **1 a** a brutal or violent person or animal. **b** *colloq.* an unpleasant person. **2** an animal as opposed to a human being. ● *adj.* **1** not possessing the capacity to reason. **2 a** animal-like, cruel. **b** stupid, sensual. **3** unthinking, merely material (*brute force*; *brute matter*). □□ **brutehood** *n.* **brutish** *adj.* **brutishly** *adv.* **brutishness** *n.* [F f. L *brutus* stupid]
■ *n.* **1 a** see BEAST 2a. **b** see STINKER. **2** animal, creature, beast. ● *adj.* **2 a** see CRUEL *adj.* **b** see CARNAL 1, SIMPLE 5. **3** brutish, unfeeling, unthinking, senseless, blind, unintelligent, insensate, thoughtless, mindless, unreasoning, irrational, instinctive, unconscious, physical, material, bodily. □□ **brutish** see BRUTE *adj.* above.

bruxism /brúksiz'm/ *n.* the involuntary or habitual grinding or clenching of the teeth. [Gk *brukhein* gnash the teeth]

bryology /brīólləji/ *n.* the study of bryophytes. □□ **bryological** /brīəlójik'l/ *adj.* **bryologist** *n.* [Gk *bruon* moss]

bryony /brīəni/ *n.* (*pl.* **-ies**) any climbing plant of the genus *Bryonia*, esp. *B. dioica* bearing greenish-white flowers and red berries. □ **black bryony** a similar unrelated plant, *Tamus communis*, bearing poisonous berries. [L *bryonia* f. Gk *bruōnia*]

bryophyte /brīəfīt/ *n.* any plant of the phylum Bryophyta, including mosses and liverworts. □□ **bryophytic** /-fittik/ *adj.* [mod.L *Bryophyta* f. Gk *bruon* moss + *phuton* plant]

bryozoan /brīəzōən/ *n.* & *adj.* ● *n.* any aquatic invertebrate animal of the phylum Bryozoa, forming colonies attached to rocks, seaweeds, etc. Also called POLYZOAN. ● *adj.* of or relating to the phylum Bryozoa. □□ **bryozoology** /-zō-ólləji/ *n.* [Gk *bruon* moss + *zōia* animals]

Brythonic /brithónnik/ *n.* & *adj.* ● *n.* the language of the Celts of southern Britain and Brittany. ● *adj.* of or relating to this people or their language. [W *Brython* Britons f. OCelt.]

BS *abbr.* **1** *US* Bachelor of Science. **2** Bachelor of Surgery. **3** Blessed Sacrament. **4** British Standard(s).

B.Sc. *abbr.* Bachelor of Science.

BSE *abbr.* bovine spongiform encephalopathy, a usu. fatal disease of cattle involving the central nervous system and causing extreme agitation.

BSI *abbr.* British Standards Institution.

B-side /beéssīd/ *n.* the side of a gramophone record regarded as less important.

BST *abbr.* **1** British Summer Time. **2** British Standard Time (in use 1968–71). **3** bovine somatotrophin, a growth hormone found naturally in cows and introduced into cattle-feed to boost milk production.

BT *abbr.* British Telecom.

Bt. *abbr.* Baronet.

B.th.u. *abbr.* (also **B.t.u.**, **BTU**, **B.Th.U.**) British thermal unit(s).

bu. *abbr.* bushel(s).

bub /bub/ *n.* *US colloq.* a boy or a man, often used as a form of address. [earlier *bubby*, perh. a childish form of BROTHER or f. G *Bube* boy]

bubal /byōōb'l/ *n.* = HARTEBEEST. [L *bubalus* f. Gk *boubalos* oxlike antelope]

bubble /búbb'l/ *n.* & *v.* ● *n.* **1 a** a thin sphere of liquid enclosing air etc. **b** an air-filled cavity in a liquid or a solidified liquid such as glass or amber. **c** (in *pl.*) froth, foam. **2** the sound or appearance of boiling. **3** a transparent domed cavity. **4** a visionary or unrealistic project or enterprise (*the South Sea Bubble*). ● *v.intr.* **1** rise in or send up bubbles. **2** make the sound of boiling. □ **bubble and squeak** *Brit.* cooked cabbage fried with cooked potatoes or meat. **bubble bath 1** a preparation for adding to bath water to make it foam. **2** a bath with this added. **bubble car** *Brit.* a small motor car with a transparent dome. **bubble chamber** *Physics* an apparatus designed to make the tracks of ionizing particles visible as a row of bubbles in a liquid. **bubble gum** chewing-gum that can be blown into bubbles. **bubble memory** *Computing* a type of memory which stores data as a pattern of magnetized regions in a thin layer of magnetic material. **bubble over** (often foll. by *with*) be exuberant with laughter, excitement, anger, etc. **bubble pack** a small package enclosing goods in a transparent material on a backing. [ME: prob. imit.]
■ *n.* **1 a, b** blister, air pocket, globule, droplet. **c** (*bubbles*) froth, foam, suds, lather, spume, *Technical* barm; effervescence, carbonation, fizz. **4** pipedream, fantasy, illusion, day-dream, castle in the air *or* Spain, pie in the sky, hare-brained scheme. ● *v.* foam, froth, boil, seethe, fizz, simmer. □ **bubble over** see GUSH *v.* 2.

bubbly /búbli/ *adj.* & *n.* ● *adj.* (**bubblier**, **bubbliest**) **1** having or resembling bubbles. **2** exuberant. ● *n.* *colloq.* champagne. □ **bubbly-jock** *Sc.* a turkeycock.
■ *adj.* **1** effervescent, foamy, frothy, spumy, sudsy, lathery,

fizzy, sparkling, sparkly. **2** effervescent, exuberant, merry, gay, buoyant, ebullient, bouncy, animated, vivacious, dynamic, vibrant, radiant, sunny, bright, cheerful, cheery, perky, perk, lively, spirited, energetic, excited. ● *n.* champagne, sparkling wine, (Asti) spumante, *colloq.* fizz, *sl.* champers.

bubo /byóōbō/ *n.* (*pl.* **-oes**) a swollen inflamed lymph node in the armpit or groin. [med.L *bubo -onis* swelling f. Gk *boubōn* groin]

bubonic /byoobónnik/ *adj.* relating to or characterized by buboes. □ **bubonic plague** a contagious bacterial disease characterized by fever, delirium, and the formation of buboes.

buccal /búkk'l/ *adj.* **1** of or relating to the cheek. **2** of or in the mouth. [L *bucca* cheek]

buccaneer /búkkənéer/ *n.* & *v.* ● *n.* **1** a pirate, orig. off the Spanish-American coasts. **2** an unscrupulous adventurer. ● *v.intr.* be a buccaneer. □□ **buccaneering** *n.* & *adj.* **buccaneerish** *adj.* [F *boucanier* f. *boucaner* cure meat on a barbecue f. *boucan* f. Tupi *mukem*]
■ *n.* **1** see PIRATE *n.* 1a.

buccinator /búksinaytər/ *n.* a flat thin cheek muscle. [L f. *buccinare* blow a trumpet (*buccina*)]

buck[1] /buk/ *n.* & *v.* ● *n.* **1** the male of various animals, esp. the deer, hare, or rabbit. **2** *archaic* a fashionable young man. **3** (*attrib.*) **a** *sl.* male (*buck antelope*). **b** *US Mil.* of the lowest rank (*buck private*). ● *v.* **1** *intr.* (of a horse) jump upwards with back arched and feet drawn together. **2** *tr.* **a** (usu. foll. by *off*) throw (a rider or burden) in this way. **b** *US* oppose, resist. **3** *tr.* & *intr.* (usu. foll. by *up*) *colloq.* **a** make or become more cheerful. **b** hurry. **4** *tr.* (as **bucked** *adj.*) *colloq.* encouraged, elated. □ **buck fever** *US* nervousness when called on to act. **buck-horn** horn of buck as a material for knife-handles etc. **buck-hound** a small kind of staghound. **buck rarebit** Welsh rarebit with a poached egg on top. **buck-tooth** an upper tooth that projects. □□ **bucker** *n.* [OE *buc* male deer, *bucca* male goat, f. ON]
■ *v.* **3 a** see CHEER *v.* 3.

buck[2] /buk/ *n. US* etc. *sl.* a dollar. □ **big bucks** a great deal of money. **a fast buck** easy money. [19th c.: orig. unkn.]

buck[3] /buk/ *n. sl.* an article placed as a reminder before a player whose turn it is to deal at poker. □ **pass the buck** *colloq.* shift responsibility (to another). [19th c.: orig. unkn.]

buck[4] /buk/ *n.* **1** *US* a saw-horse. **2** a vaulting-horse. [Du. (*zaag*)*boc*]

buck[5] /buk/ *n.* the body of a cart. [perh. f. obs. *bouk* belly, f. OE *būc* f. Gmc]

buck[6] /buk/ *n.* conversation; boastful talk. [Hindi *buk buk*]

buckbean /búkbeen/ *n.* a bog plant, *Menyanthes trifoliata*, with white or pinkish hairy flowers. Also called *bog-bean*.

buckboard /búkbord/ *n. US* a horse-drawn vehicle with the body formed by a plank fixed to the axles. [BUCK[5] + BOARD]

bucket /búkkit/ *n.* & *v.* ● *n.* **1 a** a roughly cylindrical open container, esp. of metal, with a handle, used for carrying, drawing, or holding water etc. **b** the amount contained in this (*need three buckets to fill the bath*). **2** (in *pl.*) large quantities of liquid, esp. rain or tears (*wept buckets*). **3** a compartment on the outer edge of a water wheel. **4** the scoop of a dredger or a grain-elevator. ● *v.* (**bucketed, bucketing**) **1** *intr.* & *tr.* (often foll. by *along*) *Brit.* move or drive jerkily or bumpily. **2** *intr.* (often foll. by *down*) (of liquid, esp. rain) pour heavily. □ **bucket seat** a seat with a rounded back to fit one person, esp. in a car. **bucket-shop** **1** an office for gambling in stocks, speculating on markets, etc. **2** *colloq.* a travel agency specializing in cheap air tickets. □□ **bucketful** *n.* (*pl.* **-fuls**). [ME & AF *buket*, *buquet*, perh. f. OE *būc* pitcher]
■ *n.* **1** pail, scuttle. ● *v.* **1** see BUMP *v.* 4. **2** see POUR 3.

buckeye /búkkī/ *n.* **a** any shrub of the genus *Aesculus*, with large sticky buds and showy red or white flowers. **b** the shiny brown fruit of this plant.

buckle /búkk'l/ *n.* & *v.* ● *n.* **1** a flat often rectangular frame with a hinged pin, used for joining the ends of a belt, strap, etc. **2** a similarly shaped ornament, esp. on a shoe. ● *v.* **1** *tr.* (often foll. by *up*, *on*, etc.) fasten with a buckle. **2** *tr.* & *intr.* (often foll. by *up*) give way or cause to give way under longitudinal pressure; crumple up. □ **buckle down** make a determined effort. **buckle to** (or **down to**) prepare for, set about (work etc.). **buckle to** get to work, make a vigorous start. [ME f. OF *boucle* f. L *buccula* cheek-strap of a helmet f. *bucca* cheek: sense 2 of *v.* f. F *boucler* bulge]
■ *n.* **1** clasp, fastener, clip, fastening, hook, catch. **2** brooch, pin, badge. ● *v.* **1** clasp, fasten, bracket, strap, lash, clip, pin, hook. **2** collapse, cave in, give way, crumple (up), knuckle under, fall *or* come apart, bend, warp, distort, twist, bulge. □ **buckle down** see *put one's shoulder to the wheel* (SHOULDER). **buckle to** (or **down to**) get down to, work at, knuckle down to, set to work on, set to, set out on, get going on, launch into, get cracking on, concentrate on, focus on, apply oneself to, *sl.* get stuck into, *Austral.* & *NZ sl.* hoe into.

buckler /búklər/ *n.* **1** *hist.* a small round shield held by a handle. **2** *Bot.* any of several ferns of the genus *Dryopteris*, having buckler-shaped indusia. Also called *shield-fern*. [ME f. OF *bocler* lit. 'having a boss' f. *boucle* BOSS[2]]

Buckley's /búkliz/ *n.* (in full **Buckley's chance**) *Austral.* & *NZ colloq.* little or no chance. [19th c.: orig. uncert.]

buckling /búkling/ *n.* a smoked herring. [G *Bückling* bloater]

bucko /búkkō/ *n.* & *adj. Naut. sl.* ● *n.* (*pl.* **-oes**) a swaggering or domineering fellow. ● *adj.* blustering, swaggering, bullying. [BUCK[1] + -O]

buckram /búkrəm/ *n.* & *adj.* ● *n.* **1** a coarse linen or other cloth stiffened with gum or paste, and used as interfacing or in bookbinding. **2** *archaic* stiffness in manner. ● *adj.* *archaic* starchy; formal. □ **men in buckram** non-existent persons, figments (Shakesp. *1 Henry IV* II. iv. 210–50). [ME f. AF *bukeram*, OF *boquerant*, perh. f. *Bokhara* in central Asia]

Bucks. /buks/ *abbr.* Buckinghamshire.

Buck's Fizz /buks/ *n.* a cocktail of champagne or sparkling white wine and orange juice. [*Buck's* Club in London + FIZZ]

buckshee /búkshée/ *adj.* & *adv. Brit. sl.* free of charge. [corrupt. of BAKSHEESH]
■ see FREE *adj.* 7.

buckshot /búkshot/ *n.* coarse lead shot.
■ see SHOT[1] 3.

buckskin /búkskin/ *n.* **1 a** the skin of a buck. **b** leather made from a buck's skin. **2** a thick smooth cotton or woollen cloth.

buckthorn /búkthorn/ *n.* any thorny shrub of the genus *Rhamnus*, esp. *R. cathartica* with berries formerly used as a cathartic.

buckwheat /búkweet/ *n.* any cereal plant of the genus *Fagopyrum*, esp. *F. esculentum* with seeds used for fodder and for flour to make bread and pancakes. [MDu. *boecweite* beech wheat, its grains being shaped like beechmast]

bucolic /byookóllik/ *adj.* & *n.* ● *adj.* of or concerning shepherds, the pastoral life, etc.; rural. ● *n.* **1** (usu. in *pl.*) a pastoral poem or poetry. **2** a peasant. □□ **bucolically** *adv.* [L *bucolicus* f. Gk *boukolikos* f. *boukolos* herdsman f. *bous* ox]
■ *adj.* see PASTORAL *adj.* 1. ● *n.* **2** see PEASANT.

bud[1] /bud/ *n.* & *v.* ● *n.* **1 a** an immature knoblike shoot from which a stem, leaf, or flower develops. **b** a flower or leaf that is not fully open. **2** *Biol.* an asexual outgrowth from a parent organism that separates to form a new individual. **3** anything still undeveloped. ● *v.* (**budded, budding**) **1** *intr. Bot.* & *Zool.* form a bud. **2** *intr.* begin to grow or develop (*a budding cricketer*). **3** *tr. Hort.* graft a bud (of a plant) on to another plant. □ **in bud** having newly formed buds. [ME: orig. unkn.]
■ *n.* **1** see SHOOT. ● *v.* **1** see SPROUT *v.* 2.

bud[2] /bud/ *n. US colloq.* (as a form of address) = BUDDY. [abbr.]

Buddha /bŏŏddə/ *n.* **1** a title given to successive teachers of Buddhism, esp. to its founder, Gautama. **2** a statue or picture of the Buddha. [Skr., = enlightened, past part. of *budh* know]

Buddhism /bŏŏddiz'm/ *n.* a widespread Asian religion or philosophy, founded by Gautama Buddha in India in the 5th c. BC, which teaches that elimination of the self and earthly desires is the highest goal (cf. NIRVANA). □□ **Buddhist** *n.* & *adj.* **Buddhistic** /-dístik/ *adj.* **Buddhistical** /-dístik'l/ *adj.*

buddleia /búdliə/ *n.* any shrub of the genus *Buddleia*, with fragrant lilac, yellow, or white flowers attractive to butterflies. [A. *Buddle*, Engl. botanist d. 1715]

buddy /búddi/ *n.* & *v.* esp. *US colloq.* ● *n.* (*pl.* **-ies**) (often as a form of address) a close friend or mate. ● *v.intr.* (**-ies, -ied**) (often foll. by *up*) become friendly. [perh. corrupt. of *brother*, or var. of BUTTY[1]]
■ *n.* see MATE[1] *n.* 1.

budge /buj/ *v.* (usu. with *neg.*) **1** *intr.* **a** make the slightest movement. **b** change one's opinion (*he's stubborn, he won't budge*). **2** *tr.* cause or compel to budge (*nothing will budge him*). □ **budge up** (or **over**) make room for another person by moving. [F *bouger* stir ult. f. L *bullire* boil]
■ **1a, 2** see SHIFT *v.* 1.

budgerigar /bújərigaar/ *n.* a small green parrot, *Melopsittacus undulatus*, native to Australia, and bred in coloured varieties which are often kept as cage-birds. [Aboriginal, = good cockatoo]

budget /bújit/ *n.* & *v.* ● *n.* **1** the amount of money needed or available (for a specific item etc.) (*a budget of £200*; *mustn't exceed the budget*). **2 a** (**the Budget**) *Brit.* the usu. annual estimate of national revenue and expenditure. **b** an estimate or plan of expenditure in relation to income. **c** a private person's or family's similar estimate. **3** (*attrib.*) inexpensive. **4** *archaic* a quantity of material etc., esp. written or printed. ● *v.tr.* & *intr.* (**budgeted, budgeting**) (often foll. by *for*) allow or arrange for in a budget (*have budgeted for a new car*; *can budget £60*). □ **budget account** (or **plan**) a bank account, or account with a store, into which one makes regular, usu. monthly, payments to cover bills. **on a budget** avoiding expense; cheap. □□ **budgetary** *adj.* [ME = pouch, f. OF *bougette* dimin. of *bouge* leather bag f. L *bulga* (f. Gaulish) knapsack: cf. BULGE]
■ *n.* **3** (*attrib.*) see CHEAP *adj.* 1, 2. ● *v.* see RATION 1.
□□ **budgetary** see ECONOMIC 1.

budgie /búji/ *n. colloq.* = BUDGERIGAR. [abbr.]

buff /buf/ *adj.*, *n.*, & *v.* ● *adj.* of a yellowish beige colour (*buff envelope*). ● *n.* **1** a yellowish beige colour. **2** *colloq.* an enthusiast, esp. for a particular hobby (*railway buff*). **3** *colloq.* the human skin unclothed. **4 a** a velvety dull-yellow ox-leather. **b** (*attrib.*) (of a garment etc.) made of this (*buff gloves*). **5** (**the Buffs**) the former East Kent Regiment (from the colour of its uniform facings). ● *v.tr.* **1** polish (metal, fingernails, etc.). **2** make (leather) velvety like buff, by removing the surface. □ **buff-stick** a stick covered with buff and used for polishing. **in the buff** *colloq.* naked. [orig. sense 'buffalo', prob. f. F *buffle*; sense 2 of *n.* orig. f. buff uniforms formerly worn by New York volunteer firemen, applied to enthusiastic fire-watchers]
■ *n.* **2** see ENTHUSIAST. ● *v.* **1** see POLISH *v.* 1. □ **in the buff** see NAKED 1.

buffalo /búffəlō/ *n.* & *v.* ● *n.* (*pl.* same or **-oes**) **1** either of two species of ox, *Synceros caffer*, native to Africa, or *Bubalus arnee*, native to Asia with heavy backswept horns. **2** a N. American bison, *Bison bison*. ● *v.tr.* (**-oes, -oed**) *US sl.* overawe, outwit. □ **buffalo grass 1** a grass, *Buchloe dactyloides*, of the N. American plains. **2** a grass, *Stenotaphrum secundatum*, of Australia and New Zealand. [prob. f. Port. *bufalo* f. LL *bufalus* f. L *bubalus* f. Gk *boubalos* antelope, wild ox]
■ *v.* see OVERAWE, SWINDLE *v.*

buffer[1] /búffər/ *n.* & *v.* ● *n.* **1 a** a device that protects against or reduces the effect of an impact. **b** *Brit.* such a device (usu. one of a pair) on the front and rear of a railway vehicle or at the end of a track. **2** *Biochem.* a substance that maintains the hydrogen ion concentration of a solution when an acid or alkali is added. **3** *Computing* a temporary memory area or queue for data to aid its transfer between devices or programs operating at different speeds etc. ● *v.tr.* **1** act as a buffer to. **2** *Biochem.* treat with a buffer. □ **buffer State** a small State situated between two larger ones potentially hostile to one another and regarded as reducing the likelihood of open hostilities. **buffer stock** a reserve of commodity to offset price fluctuations. [prob. f. obs. *buff* (v.), imit. of the sound of a soft body struck]
■ *n.* **1** see PROTECTION 1b, c. ● *v.* **1** see CUSHION *v.* 3.

buffer[2] /búffər/ *n. Brit. sl.* a silly or incompetent old man (esp. *old buffer*). [18th c.: prob. formed as BUFFER[1] or with the sense 'stutterer']

buffet[1] /bŏŏffay, búffay/ *n.* **1** a room or counter where light meals or snacks may be bought (*station buffet*). **2** a meal consisting of several dishes set out from which guests serve themselves (*buffet lunch*). **3** /also búffit/ a sideboard or recessed cupboard for china etc. □ **buffet car** *Brit.* a railway coach serving light meals or snacks. [F f. OF *bufet* stool, of unkn. orig.]

buffet[2] /búffit/ *v.* & *n.* ● *v.* (**buffeted, buffeting**) **1** *tr.* **a** strike or knock repeatedly (*wind buffeted the trees*). **b** strike, esp. repeatedly, with the hand or fist. **2** *tr.* (of fate etc.) treat badly; plague (*cheerful though buffeted by misfortune*). **3 a** *intr.* struggle; fight one's way (through difficulties etc.). **b** *tr.* contend with (waves etc.). ● *n.* **1** a blow, esp. of the hand or fist. **2** a shock. [ME f. OF dimin. of *bufe* blow]
■ *v.* **1** see STRIKE *v.* 1. ● *n.* **1** see BUMP *n.* 1.

buffeting /búffiting/ *n.* **1** a beating; repeated blows. **2** *Aeron.* an irregular oscillation, caused by air eddies, of any part of an aircraft.

bufflehead /búff'lhed/ *n.* a duck, *Bucephala albeola*, native to N. America, with a head that appears over-large. [obs. *buffle* buffalo + HEAD]

buffo /bŏŏffō/ *n.* & *adj.* ● *n.* (*pl.* **-os**) a comic actor, esp. in Italian opera. ● *adj.* comic, burlesque. [It.]

buffoon /bəfŏŏn/ *n.* **1** a jester; a mocker. **2** a stupid person. □□ **buffoonery** *n.* **buffoonish** *adj.* [F *bouffon* f. It. *buffone* f. med.L *buffo* clown f. Rmc]
■ **1** see FOOL[1] *n.* 2. see FOOL[1] *n.* 1.

bug /bug/ *n.* & *v.* ● *n.* **1 a** any of various hemipterous insects with oval flattened bodies and mouthparts modified for piercing and sucking. **b** *US* any small insect. **2** *sl.* a micro-organism, esp. a bacterium, or a disease caused by it. **3** a concealed microphone. **4** *sl.* an error in a computer program or system etc. **5** *sl.* **a** an obsession, enthusiasm, etc. **b** an enthusiast. ● *v.* (**bugged, bugging**) **1** *tr.* conceal a microphone in (esp. a building or room). **2** *tr. sl.* annoy, bother. **3** *intr.* (often foll. by *out*) *US sl.* leave quickly. □ **bug-eyed** with bulging eyes. [17th c.: orig. unkn.]
■ *n.* **1** insect, beetle, fly, midge, *Sc. or joc.* beastie, *US* no-see-em, *Brit. colloq.* creepy-crawly. **2** microbe, micro-organism, germ, virus, bacterium; disease, affliction, illness, sickness, ailment, disorder, malady, infection, complaint. **3** microphone, transmitter. **4** fault, error, mistake, failing, shortcoming, irregularity, flaw, *colloq.* glitch. **5 a** obsession, enthusiasm, craze, fad, mania, rage, passion, *colloq.* thing, *sl.* bag; hobby, interest, pastime. **b** enthusiast, faddist, fan, fanatic, hobbyist, *colloq.* buff. ● *v.* **1** tap, wire-tap. **2** see ANNOY 1, BOTHER *v.* 1a. **3** see BOLT[1] *v.* 4a.

bugaboo /búggəbōō/ *n.* a bogey (see BOGEY[2]) or bugbear. [prob. of dial. orig.: cf. Welsh *bwcibo* the Devil, *bwci* hobgoblin]
■ see AVERSION 2.

bugbear /búgbair/ *n.* **1** a cause of annoyance or anger; a *bête noire*. **2** an object of baseless fear. **3** *archaic* a sort of hobgoblin or any being invoked to intimidate children. [obs. *bug* + BEAR[2]]
■ **1** see AVERSION 2. **3** see DEVIL *n.* 1, 2.

bugger /búggər/ *n.*, *v.*, & *int. coarse sl.* (except in sense 2 of *n.* and 3 of *v.*) ¶ Usually considered a taboo word. ● *n.* **1 a**

an unpleasant or awkward person or thing (*the bugger won't fit*). **b** a person of a specified kind (*he's a miserable bugger; you clever bugger!*). **2** a person who commits buggery. ● *v.tr.* **1** as an exclamation of annoyance (*bugger the thing!*). **2** (often foll. by *up*) *Brit.* **a** ruin; spoil (*really buggered it up; no good, it's buggered*). **b** exhaust, tire out. **3** commit buggery with. ● *int.* expressing annoyance. □ **bugger about** (or **around**) **1** (often foll. by *with*) fool about. **2** mislead; persecute; make things awkward for. **bugger-all** nothing. **bugger off** (often in *imper.*) go away. [ME f. MDu. f. OF *bougre*, orig. 'heretic' f. med.L *Bulgarus* Bulgarian (member of the Greek Church)]

buggery /búggəri/ *n.* **1** anal intercourse. **2** = BESTIALITY 2. [ME f. MDu. *buggerie* f. OF *bougerie*: see BUGGER]

buggy[1] /búggi/ *n.* (*pl.* **-ies**) **1** a light, horse-drawn, esp. two-wheeled, vehicle for one or two people. **2** a small, sturdy, esp. open, motor vehicle (*beach buggy; dune buggy*). **3** *US* a pram. [18th c.: orig. unkn.]

■ **2** see CAR 1.

buggy[2] /búggi/ *adj.* (**buggier, buggiest**) infested with bugs.

bugle[1] /byóóg'l/ *n.* & *v.* ● *n.* (also **bugle-horn**) a brass instrument like a small trumpet, used esp. by huntsmen and for military signals. ● *v.* **1** *intr.* sound a bugle. **2** *tr.* sound (a note, a call, etc.) on a bugle. □□ **bugler** /byóóglə/ *n.* **buglet** /byóóglit/ *n.* [ME, orig. = 'buffalo', f. OF f. L *buculus* dimin. of *bos* ox]

bugle[2] /byóóg'l/ *n.* a blue-flowered mat-forming plant, *Ajuga reptans.* [ME f. LL *bugula*]

bugle[3] /byóóg'l/ *n.* a tube-shaped bead sewn on a dress etc. for ornament. [16th c.: orig. unkn.]

bugloss /byóógloss/ *n.* **1** any of various bristly plants related to borage, esp. of the genus *Anchusa* with bright blue tubular flowers. **2** = *viper's bugloss* (see VIPER). [F *buglosse* or L *buglossus* f. Gk *bouglōssos* ox-tongued]

buhl /bōōl/ *n.* (also **boule, boulle**) **1** pieces of brass, tortoiseshell, etc., cut to make a pattern and used as decorative inlays esp. on furniture. **2** work inlaid with buhl. **3** (*attrib.*) inlaid with buhl. [(*buhl* Germanized) f. A. C. *Boule*, Fr. wood-carver d. 1732]

build /bild/ *v.* & *n.* ● *v.tr.* (*past* and *past. part.* **built** /bilt/) **1 a** construct (a house, vehicle, fire, road, model, etc.) by putting parts or material together. **b** commission, finance, and oversee the building of (*the council has built two new schools*). **2 a** (often foll. by *up*) establish, develop, make, or accumulate gradually (*built the business up from nothing*). **b** (often foll. by *on*) base (hopes, theories, etc.) (*ideas built on a false foundation*). **3** (as **built** *adj.*) having a specified build (*sturdily built; brick-built*). ● *n.* **1** the proportions of esp. the human body (*a slim build*). **2** a style of construction; a make (*build of his suit was pre-war*). □ **build in** incorporate as part of a structure. **build in** (or **round** or **up**) surround with houses etc.; block up. **build on** add (an extension etc.). **build up 1** increase in size or strength. **2** praise; boost. **3** gradually become established. **build-up** *n.* **1** a favourable description in advance; publicity. **2** a gradual approach to a climax or maximum (*the build-up was slow but sure*). **built-in 1** forming an integral part of a structure. **2** forming an integral part of a person's character (*built-in integrity*). **built on sand** unstable. **built-up 1** (of a locality) densely covered by houses etc. **2** increased in height etc. by the addition of parts. **3** composed of separately prepared parts. [OE *byldan* f. *bold* dwelling f. Gmc: cf. BOWER[1], BOOTH]

■ *v.* **1** construct, erect, raise, set up, assemble, put together, fabricate, shape, make, produce. **2** build up, develop, expand, extend, cultivate, increase, intensify, enlarge, strengthen; establish, base, found, secure, create, set up, constitute. **3** (**built**) made, constructed. ● *n.* **1** physique, figure, body, shape, form, frame, make-up, proportions, size. **2** see MOULD[1] *n.* 3. □ **build in** incorporate, include. **build on** add (on), annex, append, attach, tag on, tack on, *colloq.* stick on *or* up, *Brit. sl.* bung on. **build up 1** see BUILD *v.* 2 above. **2** see BOOST *v.* 1a. **build-up 2** see INCREASE *n.* 1, 2. **built-in 1, 2** see INHERENT. **built on sand** see UNSOUND 2. **built-up 1** populous, (heavily) populated.

builder /bíldər/ *n.* **1** a contractor for building houses etc.; a master builder. **2** a person engaged as a bricklayer etc. on a building site.

building /bílding/ *n.* **1** a permanent fixed structure forming an enclosure and providing protection from the elements etc. (e.g. a house, school, factory, or stable). **2** the constructing of such structures. □ **building line** a limit or boundary between a house and a street beyond which the owner may not build. **building site** an area before or during the construction of a house etc. **building society** *Brit.* a public finance company which accepts investments at interest and lends capital for mortgages on houses etc.

■ edifice, structure; construction, erection, fabrication, manufacture, production, assemblage, assembly. □ **building site** construction site, hard hat area.

built *past* and *past part.* of BUILD.

bulb /bulb/ *n.* **1 a** an underground fleshy-leaved storage organ of some plants (e.g. lily, onion) sending roots downwards and leaves upwards. **b** a plant grown from this, e.g. a daffodil. **2** = *light-bulb* (see LIGHT[1]). **3** any object or part shaped like a bulb. [L *bulbus* f. Gk *bolbos* onion]

■ **1 a** see SEED *n.* 1a.

bulbous /búlbəss/ *adj.* **1** shaped like a bulb; fat or bulging. **2** having a bulb or bulbs. **3** (of a plant) growing from a bulb.

■ **1** see PROTUBERANT.

bulbul /bóólbóól/ *n.* **1** any songbird of the family Pycnonotidae, of dull plumage with contrasting bright patches. **2** a singer or poet. [Pers. f. Arab., of imit. orig.]

Bulgar /búlgaar/ *n.* **1** a member of a tribe who settled in what is now Bulgaria in the 7th c. **2** a Bulgarian. [med.L *Bulgarus* f. OBulg. *Blŭgarinŭ*]

bulgar var. of BULGUR.

Bulgarian /bulgáiriən/ *n.* & *adj.* ● *n.* **1 a** a native or national of Bulgaria. **b** a person of Bulgarian descent. **2** the language of Bulgaria. ● *adj.* of or relating to Bulgaria or its people or language. [med.L *Bulgaria* f. *Bulgarus*: see BULGAR]

bulge /bulj/ *n.* & *v.* ● *n.* **1 a** a convex part of an otherwise flat or flatter surface. **b** an irregular swelling; a lump. **2** *colloq.* a temporary increase in quantity or number (*baby bulge*). **3** *Naut.* the bilge of a ship. **4** *Mil.* a salient. ● *v.* **1** *intr.* swell outwards. **2** *intr.* be full or replete. **3** *tr.* swell (a bag, cheeks, etc.) by stuffing. □ **have** (or **get**) **the bulge on** *sl.* have or get an advantage over. □□ **bulgingly** *adv.* **bulgy** *adj.* [ME f. OF *boulge, bouge* f. L *bulga*: see BUDGET]

■ *n.* **1** lump, hump, protuberance, bump, swelling, projection, protrusion, excrescence, knob, knop, tumescence, *Anat.* node. **2** see BOOM[2] *n.* ● *v.* **1** protrude, stick out, swell (out); bag, sag, belly out, knob out, project, flare out, stand out, *Naut.* bilge. **2** (*bulging*) see REPLETE 1. **3** see SWELL *v.* 3. □ **have** (or **get**) **the bulge on** have an advantage over, have the edge on *or* over, have something on *or* over, have (a certain amount) to the good over, *colloq.* have the drop *or* jump on, *sl.* have the goods on.

bulgur /búlgər/ *n.* (also **bulgar, bulghur**) a cereal food of whole wheat partially boiled then dried, eaten esp. in Turkey. [Turk.]

bulimarexia /byoolímmərékslə/ *n.* esp. *US* = BULIMIA 2. □□ **bulimarexic** *adj.* & *n.* [BULIMIA + ANOREXIA]

bulimia /byoolímmiə/ *n. Med.* **1** insatiable overeating. **2** (in full **bulimia nervosa**) an emotional disorder in which bouts of extreme overeating are followed by depression and self-induced vomiting, purging, or fasting. □□ **bulimic** *adj.* & *n.* [mod.L f. Gk *boulimia* f. *bous* ox + *limos* hunger]

bulk /bulk/ *n.* & *v.* ● *n.* **1 a** size; magnitude (esp. large). **b** a large mass. **c** a large quantity. **2** a large shape, body, or person (*jacket barely covered his bulk*). **3** (usu. prec. by *the*; treated as *pl.*) the greater part or number (*the bulk of the applicants are women*). **4** roughage. **5** *Naut.* cargo, esp. unpackaged. ● *v.* **1** *intr.* seem in respect of size or importance (*bulks large in his reckoning*). **2** *tr.* (often foll. by *out*) make (a book, a textile yarn, etc.) seem thicker by suitable treatment (*bulked it with irrelevant stories*). **3** *tr.* combine (consignments etc.). □ **break bulk** begin unloading (cargo). **bulk-buy** buy in bulk; engage in bulk-buying. **bulk-buying 1** buying in large amounts at a discount. **2** the purchase by one buyer of all or most of a producer's output. **in bulk 1** in large quantities. **2** (of a cargo) loose, not packaged. [sense 'cargo' f. OIcel. *búlki*; sense 'mass' etc. perh. alt. f. obs. *bouk* (cf. BUCK[3])]

■ *n.* **1 a** volume, magnitude, mass, size, weight, quantity, amount, extent; largeness, hugeness, immensity, vastness, enormousness, massiveness; fatness, obesity. **3** see MAJORITY 1. **4** fibre, roughage. **5** see CARGO 1a, 2a. ● *v.* **1** see LOOM[2] *v.* 1. **2** see PAD *v.* 2. □ **bulk-buying 1** wholesale buying. **in bulk 1** wholesale, *en bloc*, by the gross.

bulkhead /búlk-hed/ *n.* an upright partition separating the compartments in a ship, aircraft, vehicle, etc. [*bulk* stall f. ON *bálkr* + HEAD]

■ see WALL *n.* 2.

bulky /búlki/ *adj.* (**bulkier**, **bulkiest**) **1** taking up much space, large. **2** awkwardly large, unwieldy. □□ **bulkily** *adv.* **bulkiness** *n.*

■ large, voluminous, unwieldy, awkward, ungainly, cumbersome, weighty, *colloq.* hulking; heavy, chunky, large, big, fat, hefty, brawny, husky, burly, beefy, mighty, stout, obese, overweight, corpulent, *colloq.* poddy.

bull[1] /bo͝ol/ *n.*, *adj.*, & *v.* ● *n.* **1 a** an uncastrated male bovine animal. **b** a male of the whale, elephant, and other large animals. **2** (**the Bull**) the zodiacal sign or constellation Taurus. **3** *Brit.* the bull's-eye of a target. **4** *Stock Exch.* a person who buys shares hoping to sell them at a higher price later (cf. BEAR[2]). ● *adj.* like that of a bull (*bull neck*). ● *v.* **1** *tr.* & *intr.* act or treat violently. **2** *Stock Exch.* **a** *intr.* speculate for a rise. **b** *tr.* raise price of (stocks, etc.). □ **bull ant** *Austral.* = *bulldog ant*. **bull at a gate** a hasty or rash person. **bull-fiddle** *US colloq.* a double-bass. **bull-horn** a megaphone. **bull in a china shop** a reckless or clumsy person. **bull market** a market with shares rising in price. **bull-nose** (or **-nosed**) with rounded end. **bull session** *US* an informal group discussion. **bull's-eye 1** the centre of a target; a shot that hits this. **2** a large hard peppermint-flavoured sweet. **3** a hemisphere or thick disc of glass in a ship's deck or side to admit light. **4** a small circular window. **5 a** a hemispherical lens. **b** a lantern fitted with this. **6** a boss of glass at the centre of a blown glass sheet. **bull-terrier 1** a short-haired dog of a breed that is a cross between a bulldog and a terrier. **2** this breed. **take the bull by the horns** face danger or challenge boldly. □□ **bullish** *adj.* [ME f. ON *boli* = MLG, MDu *bulle*]

■ □ **bull session** see DISCUSSION 1. **bull's-eye 1** see MIDDLE *n.* 1. **3, 4** see PANE.

bull[2] /bo͝ol/ *n.* a papal edict. [ME f. OF *bulle* f. L *bulla* rounded object, in med.L 'seal']

bull[3] /bo͝ol/ *n.* **1** (also **Irish bull**) an expression containing a contradiction in terms or implying ludicrous inconsistency. **2** *sl.* **a** unnecessary routine tasks or discipline. **b** nonsense. **c** trivial or insincere talk or writing. **d** *US* a bad blunder (cf. BULLSHIT). [17th c.: orig. unkn.]

■ **2 b** see NONSENSE.

bullace /bo͝oliss/ *n.* a thorny shrub, *Prunus insititia*, bearing globular yellow or purple-black fruits, of which the damson is the cultivated form. [ME f. OF *buloce*, *beloce*]

bulldog /bo͝oldog/ *n.* **1 a** a dog of a sturdy powerful breed with a large head and smooth hair. **b** this breed. **2** a tenacious and courageous person. □ **bulldog ant** *Austral.* a large ant with a powerful sting. **bulldog clip** a strong sprung clip for papers.

bulldoze /bo͝oldōz/ *v.tr.* **1** clear with a bulldozer. **2** *colloq.* **a** intimidate. **b** make (one's way) forcibly.

■ **1** see LEVEL *v.* 2. **2** see FORCE[1] *v.* 1.

bulldozer /bo͝oldōzər/ *n.* **1** a powerful tractor with a broad curved vertical blade at the front for clearing ground. **2** a forceful and domineering person. [*bulldose* (or *-doze*) *US* = intimidate, f. BULL[1]: second element uncert.]

bullet /bo͝ollit/ *n.* a small round or cylindrical missile with a pointed end, fired from a rifle, revolver, etc. □ **bullet-headed** having a round head. [F *boulet*, *boulette* dimin. of *boule* ball f. L *bulla* bubble]

■ see PROJECTILE *n.*

bulletin /bo͝ollitin/ *n.* **1** a short official statement of news. **2** a regular list of information etc. issued by an organization or society. □ **bulletin-board** *US* a notice-board. [F f. It. *bullettino* dimin. of *bulletta* passport, dimin. of *bulla* seal, BULL[2]]

■ **1** report, account, flash, news item, newsflash, update, announcement, communiqué, dispatch, statement, *US* advisory; see also WORD *n.* 7. **2** newsletter, news-sheet, pamphlet, leaflet, message, notice, communication.

bulletproof /bo͝ollitproof/ *adj.* & *v.* ● *adj.* (of a material) designed to resist the penetration of bullets. ● *v.tr.* make bulletproof.

bullfight /bo͝olfīt/ *n.* a sport of baiting and (usu.) killing bulls as a public spectacle, esp. in Spain. □□ **bullfighter** *n.* **bullfighting** *n.*

bullfinch /bo͝olfinch/ *n.* a finch, *Pyrrhula pyrrhula*, with a short stout beak and bright plumage.

bullfrog /bo͝olfrog/ *n.* a large frog, *Rana catesbiana*, native to N. America, with a deep croak.

bullhead /bo͝olhed/ *n.* any of various marine fishes with large flattened heads.

bull-headed /bo͝olhéddid/ *adj.* obstinate; impetuous; blundering. □□ **bull-headedly** *adv.* **bull-headedness** *n.*

■ see STUBBORN.

bullion /bo͝ollian/ *n.* a metal (esp. gold or silver) in bulk before coining, or valued by weight. [AF = mint, var. of OF *bouillon* ult. f. L *bullire* boil]

bullish /bo͝ollish/ *adj.* **1** like a bull, esp. in temper. **2** *Stock Exch.* causing or associated with a rise in prices.

■ **2** see *optimistic* (OPTIMISM).

bullock /bo͝ollək/ *n.* & *v.* ● *n.* a castrated bull. ● *v.intr.* (often foll. by *at*) *Austral. colloq.* work very hard. [OE *bulluc*, dimin. of BULL[1]]

■ *v.* see SLAVE *v.* 1.

bullocky /bo͝olləki/ *n. Austral.* & *NZ colloq.* a bullock-driver.

bullring /bo͝olring/ *n.* an arena for bullfights.

bullshit /bo͝olshit/ *n.* & *v. coarse sl.* ● *n.* **1** (often as *int.*) nonsense, rubbish. **2** trivial or insincere talk or writing. ● *v.intr.* (**-shitted**, **-shitting**) talk nonsense; bluff. □□ **bullshitter** *n.* [BULL[3] + SHIT]

■ *n.* **1** see RUBBISH 3. **2** see TALK *n.* 4c. ● *v.* see BLUFF[1] *v.* 1.

bulltrout /bo͝oltrowt/ *n. Brit.* a salmon trout.

bully[1] /bo͝olli/ *n.* & *v.* ● *n.* (*pl.* **-ies**) a person who uses strength or power to coerce others by fear. ● *v.tr.* (**-ies**, **-ied**) **1** persecute or oppress by force or threats. **2** (foll. by *into* + verbal noun) pressure or coerce (a person) to do something (*bullied him into agreeing*). □ **bully-boy** a hired ruffian. [orig. as a term of endearment, prob. f. MDu. *boele* lover]

■ *n.* hooligan, bully-boy, rowdy, thug, ruffian, rough, *colloq.* roughneck, bruiser, tough guy, *Brit. sl.* bovver boy, *US sl.* hood; persecutor, oppressor, intimidator, tyrant, hector, swashbuckler. ● *v.* **1** persecute, victimize, intimidate, tyrannize, torment, browbeat, terrorize, oppress, hector, menace, harass, pick on, push around, *colloq.* heavy, bulldoze. **2** see RAILROAD *v.* □ **bully-boy** see BULLY[1] *n.* above.

bully[2] /bo͝olli/ *adj.* & *int. colloq.* ● *adj.* very good; first-rate. ● *int.* (foll. by *for*) expressing admiration or approval, or *iron.* (*bully for them!*). [perh. f BULLY[1]]

■ *adj.* see *first-rate*. ● *int.* (*bully for you!*) bravo, great, fantastic, fabulous, marvellous, spectacular, good on *or* for you, *US* dandy; (*iron.*) big deal, so (what)?, what of it?

bully[3] /bŏŏlli/ *n.* & *v.* (in full **bully off**) ● *n.* (*pl.* **-ies**) the start of play in hockey in which two opponents strike each other's sticks three times and then go for the ball. ● *v.intr.* (**-ies, -ied**) start play in this way. [19th c.: perh. f. *bully* scrum in Eton football, of unkn. orig.]

bully[4] /bŏŏlli/ *n.* (in full **bully beef**) corned beef. [F *bouilli* boiled beef f. *bouillir* BOIL[1]]

bullyrag var. of BALLYRAG.

bully tree /bŏŏlli/ *n.* = BALATA. [corrupt.]

bulrush /bŏŏlrush/ *n.* **1** = *reed-mace* (see REED[1]). **2** a rushlike water-plant, *Scirpus lacustris*, used for weaving. **3** *Bibl.* a papyrus plant. [perh. f. BULL[1] = large, coarse, as in *bullfrog*, *bulltrout*, etc.]

bulwark /bŏŏlwərk/ *n.* & *v.* ● *n.* **1** a defensive wall, esp. of earth; a rampart; a mole or breakwater. **2** a person, principle, etc., that acts as a defence. **3** (usu. in *pl.*) a ship's side above deck. ● *v.tr.* serve as a bulwark to; defend, protect. [ME f. MLG, MDu. *bolwerk*: see BOLE[1], WORK]
■ *n.* **1** see RAMPART *n.* 1a. **2** defence, safeguard, protection, shield, shelter, cover, guard, security, provision, buffer, barrier, fortification. ● *v.* defend, protect, shelter.

bum[1] /bum/ *n. Brit. sl.* the buttocks. □ **bum-bag** *Brit. colloq.* a small pouch for money and other valuables, on a belt worn round the waist or hips. **bum-bailiff** *hist.* a bailiff empowered to collect debts or arrest debtors for non-payment. **bum-boat** any small boat plying with provisions etc. for ships. **bum-sucker** *sl.* a toady. **bum-sucking** *sl.* toadying. [ME *bom*, of unkn. orig.]
■ buttocks, seat, posterior, rump, hindquarters, hams, *Anat.* nates, gluteus maximus, *colloq.* backside, behind, bottom, rear, sit-upon, *colloq. euphem. derrière*, *joc.* fundament, *sl.* prat, cheeks, *esp. US sl.* butt, *US sl.* fanny, can, keister.

bum[2] /bum/ *n.*, *v.*, & *adj. US sl.* ● *n.* a habitual loafer or tramp; a lazy dissolute person. ● *v.* (**bummed, bumming**) **1** *intr.* (often foll. by *about*, *around*) loaf or wander around; be a bum. **2** *tr.* get by begging; cadge. ● *attrib.adj.* **1** of poor quality; bad, worthless. **2** false, fabricated. □ **bum rap** imprisonment on a false charge. **bum's rush** forcible ejection. **bum steer** false information. **on the bum** vagrant, begging. [prob. abbr. or back-form. f. BUMMER]
■ *n.* tramp, beggar, down-and-out, vagrant, loafer, drifter, traveller, vagabond, derelict, pauper, grubber, gypsy, *Austral.* bagman, *Sc.* & *Ir.* tinker, *US* hobo, (shopping-)bag lady, *colloq.* panhandler, have-not; sponge, sponger, cadger, scrounger, scrounge, slob, *esp. US colloq.* moocher, *US sl.* freeloader, lug. ● *v.* **1** see LOAF[2] *v.* 1. **2** borrow, beg, sponge, cadge, solicit, *colloq.* scrounge, *US colloq.* panhandle, mooch; (*bum off*) *sl.* touch, put the touch on, *US sl.* freeload. ● *attrib.adj.* **1** see BAD *adj.* 1. **2** improper, unjustified, false, trumped up, untrue, fabricated, made-up, bogus. □ **bum's rush** see EXPULSION. **bum steer** bad *or* poor tip, bad *or* false information, *Brit. sl.* bad *or* duff gen. **on the bum** begging, *colloq.* on the scrounge; see also MIGRANT *adj.*

bumble /búmb'l/ *v.intr.* **1** (foll. by *on*) speak in a rambling incoherent way. **2** (often as **bumbling** *adj.*) move or act ineptly; blunder. **3** make a buzz or hum. □□ **bumbler** *n.* [BOOM[1] + -LE[4]: partly f. *bumble* = blunderer]
■ **2** (**bumbling**) see INEPT 1.

bumble-bee /búmb'lbee/ *n.* any large loud humming bee of the genus *Bombus*. [as BUMBLE]

bumf /bumf/ *n.* (also **bumph**) *Brit. colloq.* **1** usu. *derog.* papers, documents. **2** lavatory paper. [abbr. of *bum-fodder*]

bummalo /búmməlō/ *n.* (*pl.* same) a small fish, *Harpodon nehereus*, of S. Asian coasts, dried and used as food (see BOMBAY DUCK). [perh. f. Marathi *bombīl(a)*]

bummer /búmmər/ *n. US sl.* **1** an idler; a loafer. **2** an unpleasant occurrence. [19th c.: perh. f. G *Bummler*]

bump /bump/ *n.*, *v.*, & *adv.* ● *n.* **1** a dull-sounding blow or collision. **2** a swelling or dent caused by this. **3** an uneven patch on a road, field, etc. **4** *Phrenol.* any of various prominences on the skull thought to indicate different mental faculties. **5** (in narrow-river races where boats make a spaced start one behind another) the point at which a boat begins to overtake (and usu. touches) the boat ahead, thereby defeating it. **6** *Aeron.* **a** an irregularity in an aircraft's motion. **b** a rising air current causing this. ● *v.* **1 a** *tr.* hit or come against with a bump. **b** *intr.* (of two objects) collide. **2** *intr.* (foll. by *against*, *into*) hit with a bump; collide with. **3** *tr.* (often foll. by *against*, *on*) hurt or damage by striking (*bumped my head on the ceiling*; *bumped the car while parking*). **4** *intr.* (usu. foll. by *along*) move or travel with much jolting (*we bumped along the road*). **5** *tr.* (in a boat-race) gain a bump against. **6** *tr. US* displace, esp. by seniority. ● *adv.* with a bump; suddenly; violently. □ **bump into** *colloq.* meet by chance. **bump off** *sl.* murder. **bump up** *colloq.* increase (prices etc.). [16th c., imit.: perh. f. Scand.]
■ *n.* **1** blow, collision, thud, thump, hit, knock, buffet, clunk, jerk, jolt, plump, *colloq.* whack, *sl.* wallop. **2** lump, protuberance, welt, swelling, tumescence, knob, bulge, protrusion, excrescence, irregularity; dent, indentation, depression, impression, mark, nick. ● *v.* **1, 2** knock (against), strike, hit, bang, bash, dash, smack, slam, collide (with), run into, drive into, ram, smash, crash, *sl.* wallop. **3** hurt, injure, bruise, hit; scrape, damage. **4** lurch, jerk, jolt, jostle, jog, bounce, jump, *Brit.* bucket. **6** see SUPPLANT. ● *adv.* crash, *colloq.* smack, plump; suddenly, all of a sudden; violently, hard. □ **bump into** meet, encounter, run into *or* across, come across, stumble over *or* upon *or* across, chance upon, fall in with, rencounter. **bump off** see MURDER *v.* 1. **bump up** see INCREASE *v.* 1.

bumper /búmpər/ *n.* **1** a horizontal bar or strip fixed across the front or back of a motor vehicle to reduce damage in a collision or as a trim. **2** (usu. *attrib.*) an unusually large or fine example (*a bumper crop*). **3** *Cricket* a ball rising high after pitching. **4** a brim-full glass of wine etc. □ **bumper car** = DODGEM.
■ **2** (*attrib.*) see PLENTIFUL.

bumph var. of BUMF.

bumpkin /búmpkin/ *n.* a rustic or socially inept person. [perh. Du. *boomken* little tree or MDu. *bommekijn* little barrel]
■ see RUSTIC *n.*

bumptious /búmpshəss/ *adj.* offensively self-assertive or conceited. □□ **bumptiously** *adv.* **bumptiousness** *n.* [BUMP, after FRACTIOUS]
■ see PUSHY.

bumpy /búmpi/ *adj.* (**bumpier, bumpiest**) **1** having many bumps (*a bumpy road*). **2** affected by bumps (*a bumpy ride*). □□ **bumpily** *adv.* **bumpiness** *n.*
■ **1** lumpy, rough, uneven, irregular, broken, knobby, knobbly, pitted; potholed, rutted, rocky. **2** rough, bouncy, jarring, jerky, jolty.

bun /bun/ *n.* **1** a small usu. sweetened bread roll or cake, often with dried fruit. **2** *Sc.* a rich fruit cake or currant bread. **3** hair worn in the shape of a bun. □ **bun fight** *Brit. sl.* a tea party. **have a bun in the oven** *sl.* be pregnant. **hot cross bun** a bun marked with a cross, traditionally eaten on Good Friday. [ME: orig. unkn.]
■ **1, 2** see CAKE *n.* 1.

buna /byŏŏnə, bŏŏnə/ *n.* a synthetic rubber made by polymerization of butadiene. [G (as BUTADIENE, *natrium* sodium)]

bunch /bunch/ *n.* & *v.* ● *n.* **1** a cluster of things growing or fastened together (*bunch of grapes*; *bunch of keys*). **2** a collection; a set or lot (*best of the bunch*). **3** *colloq.* a group; a gang. ● *v.* **1** *tr.* make into a bunch or bunches; gather into close folds. **2** *intr.* form into a group or crowd. □ **bunch grass** a N. American grass that grows in clumps. **bunch of**

fives *sl.* a fist; hence also, a punch. ▫▫ **bunchy** *adj.* [ME: orig. unkn.]

■ *n.* **1** bundle, cluster, batch, clump; bouquet, nosegay, posy, spray. **2** collection, group, lot, set, clutch, batch, number. **3** group, body, band, gathering, company, cluster, assemblage, assembly, assortment, mass, crowd, huddle, knot; gang, pack, party, *colloq.* crew. ● *v.* sort, class, classify, categorize, organize, arrange, group, bracket, order; gather, collect, band, crowd, group, cluster, assemble, mass, huddle, knot, congregate, accumulate. ▫ **bunch of fives** see PUNCH *n.* 1.

bunco /bo͝ongkō/ *n.* & *v. US sl.* ● *n.* (*pl.* **-os**) a swindle, esp. by card-sharping or a confidence trick. ● *v.tr.* (**-oes, -oed**) swindle, cheat. [perh. f. Sp. *banca* a card-game]

■ *n.* see SWINDLE *n.* 1, 3. ● *v.* see SWINDLE *v.*

buncombe var. of BUNKUM.

Bundesrat /bo͝ondəsraat/ *n.* the Upper House of Parliament in Germany or in Austria. [G f. *Bund* federation + *Rat* council]

Bundestag /bo͝ondəstaag/ *n.* the Lower House of Parliament in Germany. [G f. *Bund* federation + *tagen* confer]

bundle /búnd'l/ *n.* & *v.* ● *n.* **1** a collection of things tied or fastened together. **2** a set of nerve fibres etc. banded together. **3** *sl.* a large amount of money. ● *v.* **1** *tr.* (usu. foll. by *up*) tie in or make into a bundle (*bundled up my squash kit*). **2** *tr.* (usu. foll. by *into*) throw or push, esp. quickly or confusedly (*bundled the papers into the drawer*). **3** *tr.* (usu. foll. by *out*, *off*, *away*, etc.) send (esp. a person) away hurriedly or unceremoniously (*bundled them off the premises*). **4** *intr.* sleep clothed with another person, esp. a fiancé(e), as a local custom. ▫ **be a bundle of nerves** (or **prejudices** etc.) be extremely nervous (or prejudiced etc.). **bundle up** dress warmly or cumbersomely. **go a bundle on** *sl.* be very fond of. ▫▫ **bundler** *n.* [ME, perh. f. OE *byndelle* a binding, but also f. LG, Du *bundel*]

■ *n.* **1** bunch, collection, assemblage, cluster, group, package, parcel, packet, pack, *Austral.* shiralee, *Austral. sl.* Matilda; bale, sheaf. **3** (*make a bundle*) see BOMB *n.* 3. ● *v.* **1** tie up; collect, gather (together), pack (up), package. **2** throw, push, thrust, stuff, cram, squeeze, ram, *colloq.* shove. **3** (*bundle off*) dispatch, pack off, hustle *or* hurry off *or* away, send away *or* off, dismiss, drive off, order off *or* out *or* away. ▫ **be a bundle of nerves** see WORRY *v.* 1. **go a bundle on** see LOVE *v.* 2–4.

bung[1] /bung/ *n.* & *v.* ● *n.* a stopper for closing a hole in a container, esp. a cask. ● *v.tr.* **1** stop with a bung. **2** *Brit. sl.* throw, toss. ▫ **bunged up** closed, blocked. **bung-hole** a hole for filling or emptying a cask etc. [MDu. *bonghe*]

■ *n.* see STOPPER *n.* ● *v.* **1** see PLUG *v.* 1. **2** see THROW *v.* 1, 2.

bung[2] /bung/ *adj. Austral.* & *NZ sl.* dead; ruined, useless. ▫ **go bung 1** die. **2** fail; go bankrupt. [Aboriginal]

■ see DEAD *adj.* 1. ▫ **go bung 1** see DIE[1] 1.

bungalow /búnggəlō/ *n.* a one-storeyed house. [Gujarati *bangalo* f. Hind. *baṅglā* belonging to Bengal]

■ see CABIN *n.* 1.

bungee /búnji/ *n.* (in full **bungee cord, rope**) elasticated cord or rope used for securing baggage and in bungee jumping. ▫ **bungee jumping** the sport of jumping from a height while secured by a bungee from the ankles or a harness. [20th c.: orig. unkn.]

bungle /búngg'l/ *v.* & *n.* ● *v.* **1** *tr.* blunder over, mismanage, or fail at (a task). **2** *intr.* work badly or clumsily. ● *n.* a bungled attempt; bungled work. ▫▫ **bungler** *n.* [imit.: cf. BUMBLE]

■ *v.* **1** see BOTCH *v.* 1. **2** bumble, fumble, make a blunder *or faux pas*, blunder, *colloq.* slip up, drop a brick, *US colloq.* flub, *sl.* screw *or* louse up, mess up, goof, make a mess, drop a clanger, *Brit. sl.* boob. ● *n.* see MISTAKE *n.*

bunion /búnyən/ *n.* a swelling on the foot, esp. at the first joint of the big toe. [OF *buignon* f. *buigne* bump on the head]

bunk[1] /bungk/ *n.* a sleeping-berth, esp. a shelflike bed against a wall, e.g. in a ship. ▫ **bunk-bed** each of two or more beds one above the other, forming a unit. **bunk-house** a house where workers etc. are lodged. [18th c.: orig. unkn.]

bunk[2] /bungk/ *n.* ▫ **do a bunk** *Brit. sl.* leave or abscond hurriedly. [19th c.: orig. unkn.]

bunk[3] /bungk/ *n. sl.* nonsense, humbug. [abbr. of BUNKUM]

■ see NONSENSE.

bunker /búngkər/ *n.* & *v.* ● *n.* **1** a large container or compartment for storing fuel. **2** a reinforced underground shelter, esp. for use in wartime. **3** a hollow filled with sand, used as an obstacle in a golf-course. ● *v.tr.* **1** fill the fuel bunkers of (a ship etc.). **2** (usu. in *passive*) **a** trap in a bunker (in sense 3). **b** bring into difficulties. [19th c.: orig. unkn.]

bunkum /búngkəm/ *n.* (also **buncombe**) nonsense; humbug. [orig. *buncombe* f. *Buncombe* County in N. Carolina, mentioned in a nonsense speech by its Congressman, *c.*1820]

■ see NONSENSE.

bunny /búnni/ *n.* (*pl.* **-ies**) **1** a child's name for a rabbit. **2** *Austral. sl.* a victim or dupe. **3** (in full **bunny girl**) a club hostess, waitress, etc., wearing a skimpy costume with ears and a tail suggestive of a rabbit. [dial. *bun* rabbit]

Bunsen burner /búns'n/ *n.* a small adjustable gas burner used in scientific work as a source of great heat. [R. W. *Bunsen*, Ger. chemist d. 1899]

bunt[1] /bunt/ *n.* the baggy centre of a fishing-net, sail, etc. [16th c.: orig. unkn.]

bunt[2] /bunt/ *n.* a disease of wheat caused by the fungus *Tilletia caries*. [18th c.: orig. unkn.]

bunt[3] /bunt/ *v.* & *n.* ● *v.* **1** *tr.* & *intr.* push with the head or horns; butt. **2** *tr. US Baseball* stop (a ball) with the bat without swinging. ● *n.* an act of bunting. [19th c.: cf. BUTT[1]]

buntal /búnt'l/ *n.* the straw from a talipot palm. [Tagalog]

bunting[1] /búnting/ *n.* any of numerous seed-eating birds of the family Emberizidae, related to the finches and sparrows. [ME: orig. unkn.]

bunting[2] /búnting/ *n.* **1** flags and other decorations. **2** a loosely-woven fabric used for these. [18th c.: orig. unkn.]

buntline /búntlīn/ *n.* a line for confining the bunt (see BUNT[1]) when furling a sail.

bunya /búnyə/ *n.* (also **bunya bunya**) *Austral.* a tall coniferous tree, *Araucaria bidwillii*, bearing large nutritious cones. [Aboriginal]

bunyip /búnyip/ *n. Austral.* **1** a fabulous monster inhabiting swamps and lagoons. **2** an impostor. [Aboriginal]

■ **2** see IMPOSTOR 1.

buoy /boy/ *n.* & *v.* ● *n.* **1** an anchored float serving as a navigation mark or to show reefs etc. **2** a lifebuoy. ● *v.tr.* **1** (usu. foll. by *up*) **a** keep afloat. **b** sustain the courage or spirits of (a person etc.); uplift, encourage. **2** (often foll. by *out*) mark with a buoy or buoys. [ME prob. f. MDu. *bo(e)ye*, ult. f. L *boia* collar f. Gk *boeiai* ox-hides]

■ *n.* **1** (navigational *or* channel) marker, float, beacon, dan, dolphin, drogue. **2** lifebuoy, lifebelt. ● *v.* **1** keep afloat, keep a person's head above water; uplift, lift (up), raise, keep up, elevate, support, sustain, hearten, cheer (up), comfort, enliven, gladden.

buoyancy /bóyənsi/ *n.* **1** the capacity to be or remain buoyant. **2** resilience; recuperative power. **3** cheerfulness.

buoyant /bóyənt/ *adj.* **1 a** able or apt to keep afloat or rise to the top of a liquid or gas. **b** (of a liquid or gas) able to keep something afloat. **2** light-hearted, resilient. ▫▫ **buoyantly** *adv.* [F *buoyant* or Sp. *boyante* part. of *boyar* float f. *boya* BUOY]

■ **1 a** afloat, floating, floatable. **2** light, lively, vivacious, bubbly, bright, cheerful, happy, carefree, animated, jaunty, bouncy, cheery, sunny, ebullient, light-hearted, easy-going, *colloq.* peppy; resilient, robust, tough, strong, *poet.* blithe.

bur /bur/ *n.* (also **burr**) **1 a** a prickly clinging seed-case or flower-head. **b** any plant producing these. **2** a person hard to shake off. **3** = BURR *n.* 2. ▫ **bur oak** a N. American oak,

Quercus macrocarpa with large fringed acorn-cups. [ME: cf. Da. *burre* bur, burdock, Sw. *kard-borre* burdock]

burble /búrb'l/ *v.* & *n.* • *v.intr.* **1** speak ramblingly; make a murmuring noise. **2** *Aeron.* (of an air-flow) break up into turbulence. • *n.* **1** a murmuring noise. **2** rambling speech. ▫▫ **burbler** *n.* [19th c.: imit.]
■ *v.* **1** see BABBLE *v.* 1a, b. • *n.* **1** see GURGLE *n.* **2** see BABBLE *n.* 1b.

burbot /búrbət/ *n.* an eel-like flat-headed bearded freshwater fish, *Lota lota.* [ME: cf. OF *barbote*]

burden /búrd'n/ *n.* & *v.* • *n.* **1** a load, esp. a heavy one. **2** an oppressive duty, obligation, expense, emotion, etc. **3** the bearing of loads (*beast of burden*). **4** (also *archaic* **burthen** /búrthən/) a ship's carrying-capacity, tonnage. **5 a** the refrain or chorus of a song. **b** the chief theme or gist of a speech, book, poem, etc. • *v.tr.* load with a burden; encumber, oppress. ▫ **burden of proof** the obligation to prove one's case. ▫▫ **burdensome** *adj.* **burdensomeness** *n.* [OE *byrthen*: rel. to BIRTH]
■ *n.* **1, 2** load, weight, onus; strain, stress, pressure, trouble, trial, tribulation, hardship, imposition, trouble, responsibility, anxiety, worry, charge, millstone, cross, albatross, encumbrance; brunt, force, impact; see also BOTHER *n.* 1. **5 a** refrain, chorus, reprise. **b** see THEME 1. • *v.* load (down), weigh down, saddle, encumber, bow *or* press *or* wear down, crush, overload, lumber; tax, oppress, trouble, pressure, overwhelm. ▫▫ **burdensome** onerous, cumbersome, oppressive, weighty, troublesome, wearisome, exhausting, bothersome, distressing, worrying, worrisome, vexatious, irksome, trying; arduous, difficult, exacting, hard, heavy, punishing, toilsome, gruelling, back-breaking.

burdock /búrdok/ *n.* any plant of the genus *Arctium*, with prickly flowers and docklike leaves. [BUR + DOCK³]

bureau /byóorō/ *n.* (*pl.* **bureaux** or **bureaus** /-rōz/) **1 a** *Brit.* a writing-desk with drawers and usu. an angled top opening downwards to form a writing surface. **b** *US* a chest of drawers. **2 a** an office or department for transacting specific business. **b** a government department. [F, = desk, orig. its baize covering, f. OF *burel* f. *bure, buire* dark brown ult. f. Gk *purros* red]
■ **1** writing-desk, desk, escritoire, *Brit.* Davenport; chest of drawers, chest, commode, *US* dresser, highboy, tallboy. **2** office, agency, department, division, section, subdivision, subsection, desk; ministry.

bureaucracy /byoorókrəsi/ *n.* (*pl.* **-ies**) **1 a** government by central administration. **b** a State or organization so governed. **2** the officials of such a government, esp. regarded as oppressive and inflexible. **3** conduct typical of such officials. [F *bureaucratie*: see BUREAU]
■ **2, 3** officialdom, officialism, red tape, rigmarole, formalities, punctiliousness, punctilio.

bureaucrat /byóorəkrat/ *n.* **1** an official in a bureaucracy. **2** an inflexible or insensitive administrator. ▫▫ **bureaucratic** /-krátik/ *adj.* **bureaucratically** /-krátikəli/ *adv.* [F *bureaucrate* (as BUREAUCRACY)]
■ **1** see FUNCTIONARY.

bureaucratize /byoorókrətīz/ *v.tr.* (also **-ise**) govern by or transform into a bureaucratic system. ▫▫ **bureaucratization** /-záysh'n/ *n.*

burette /byoorét/ *n.* (*US* **buret**) a graduated glass tube with an end-tap for measuring small volumes of liquid in chemical analysis. [F]

burg /burg/ *n. US colloq.* a town or city. [see BOROUGH]
■ see CITY 1a.

burgage /búrgij/ *n. hist.* (in England and Scotland) tenure of land in a town on a yearly rent. [ME f. med.L *burgagium* f. *burgus* BOROUGH]

burgee /burjée/ *n.* a triangular or swallow-tailed flag bearing the colours or emblem of a sailing-club. [18th c.: perh. = (ship)owner, ult. F *bourgeois*: see BURGESS]
■ see PENNANT.

burgeon /búrjən/ *v.* & *n. literary* • *v.intr.* **1** begin to grow rapidly; flourish. **2** put forth young shoots; bud. • *n.* a bud or young shoot. [ME f. OF *bor-*, *burjon* ult. f. LL *burra* wool]
■ *v.* **1** see FLOURISH *v.* 1a, d. **2** see SHOOT *v.* 5.

burger /búrgər/ *n.* **1** *colloq.* a hamburger. **2** (in *comb.*) a certain kind of hamburger or variation of it (*beefburger*; *nutburger*). [abbr.]

burgess /búrjiss/ *n.* **1** *Brit.* an inhabitant of a town or borough, esp. of one with full municipal rights. **2** *Brit. hist.* a Member of Parliament for a borough, corporate town, or university. **3** *US* a borough magistrate or governor. [ME f. OF *burgeis* ult. f. LL *burgus* BOROUGH]
■ **1** see CITIZEN 2a.

burgh /búrrə/ *n. hist.* a Scottish borough or chartered town. ¶ This status was abolished in 1975. ▫▫ **burghal** /búrg'l/ *adj.* [Sc. form of BOROUGH]
■ see TOWN 1.

burgher /búrgər/ *n.* **1** a citizen or freeman, esp. of a Continental town. **2** *S.Afr. hist.* a citizen of a Boer republic. **3** a descendant of a Dutch or Portuguese colonist in Sri Lanka. [G *Burger* or Du. *burger* f. *Burg, burg* BOROUGH]

burglar /búrglər/ *n.* a person who commits burglary. ▫▫ **burglarious** /-gláiriəss/ *adj.* [legal AF *burgler*, rel. to OF *burgier* pillage]
■ housebreaker, thief, robber, cat burglar, night-hawk, picaroon, *archaic* lurcher, *rhyming sl.* tea-leaf, *sl.* cracksman, drummer, *US sl.* yegg.

burglarize /búrglərīz/ *v.tr.* & *intr.* (also **-ise**) *US* = BURGLE.

burglary /búrgləri/ *n.* (*pl.* **-ies**) **1** entry into a building illegally with intent to commit theft, do bodily harm, or do damage. **2** an instance of this. ¶ Before 1968 in English law a crime under statute and in common law; after 1968 a statutory crime only (cf. HOUSEBREAKING). [legal AF *burglarie*: see BURGLAR]

burgle /búrg'l/ *v.* **1** *tr.* commit burglary on (a building or person). **2** *intr.* commit burglary. [back-form. f BURGLAR]
■ see ROB 1.

burgomaster /búrgəmaastər/ *n.* the mayor of a Dutch or Flemish town. [Du. *burgemeester* f. *burg* BOROUGH: assim. to MASTER]

burgrave /búrgrayv/ *n. hist.* the ruler of a town or castle. [G *Burggraf* f. *Burg* BOROUGH + *Graf* COUNT²]

burgundy /búrgəndi/ *n.* (*pl.* **-ies**) **1 a** the wine (usu. red) of Burgundy in E. France. **b** a similar wine from another place. **2** the red colour of Burgundy wine.

burhel var. of BHARAL.

burial /bérriəl/ *n.* **1 a** the burying of a dead body. **b** a funeral. **2** *Archaeol.* a grave or its remains. ▫ **burial-ground** a cemetery. [ME, erron. formed as sing. of OE *byrgels* f. Gmc: rel. to BURY]
■ **1** interment, entombment, *literary* sepulture; funeral, obsequies. **2** grave, tomb, burial vault *or* chamber *or* mound, sepulchre, tumulus, *Archaeol.* barrow.
▫ **burial-ground** see GRAVEYARD.

burin /byóorin/ *n.* **1** a steel tool for engraving on copper or wood. **2** *Archaeol.* a flint tool with a chisel point. [F]

burk var. of BERK.

burka /búrkə/ *n.* a long enveloping garment worn in public by Muslim women. [Hind. f. Arab. *burḳa'*]

Burkitt's lymphoma /búrkits/ *n. Med.* a malignant tumour of the lymphatic system, esp. affecting children of Central Africa. [D. P. *Burkitt*, Brit. surgeon b. 1911]

burl /burl/ *n.* **1** a knot or lump in wool or cloth. **2** *US* a flattened knotty growth on a tree. [ME f. OF *bourle* tuft of wool, dimin. of *bourre* coarse wool f. LL *burra* wool]

burlap /búrlap/ *n.* **1** coarse canvas esp. of jute used for sacking etc. **2** a similar lighter material for use in dressmaking or furnishing. [17th c.: orig. unkn.]

burlesque /burlésk/ *n.*, *adj.*, & *v.* • *n.* **1 a** a comic imitation, esp. in parody of a dramatic or literary work. **b** a performance or work of this kind. **c** bombast, mock-seriousness. **2** *US* a variety show, often including striptease. • *adj.* of or in the nature of burlesque. • *v.tr.* (**burlesques, burlesqued,**

burlesquing) make or give a burlesque of. ▫▫ **burlesquer** *n.* [F f. It. *burlesco* f. *burla* mockery]

■ *n.* **1** imitation, caricature, satirization, mimicry, lampoonery, ridicule, derision, *colloq.* spoofery; lampoon, parody, satire, mockery, travesty, *colloq.* spoof, take-off, *Brit. colloq.* send-up; see also BOMBAST. **2** variety show, *Brit.* music-hall, *esp. US* vaudeville; striptease, strip show, *colloq.* girlie show. ● *adj.* satirical, derisive, mocking, sardonic, ironic, ironical, mock-heroic, mock-serious, mock-pathetic. ● *v.* satirize, lampoon, parody, caricature, imitate, travesty, ridicule, mock, mimic, *colloq.* spoof, take off, *Brit. colloq.* send up.

burly /búrli/ *adj.* (**burlier**, **burliest**) of stout sturdy build; big and strong. ▫▫ **burliness** *n.* [ME *borli* prob. f. an OE form = 'fit for the bower' (BOWER[1])]

■ stout, sturdy, corpulent, large, big, hefty, stocky, thickset, brawny, chunky, heavy, beefy, muscular, muscly, strong, strapping, rugged, tough, husky.

Burman /búrmən/ *adj.* & *n.* (*pl.* **Burmans**) = BURMESE.

Burmese /búrmeéz/ *n.* & *adj.* ● *n.* (*pl.* same) **1 a** a native or national of Burma (now Myanmar) in SE Asia. **b** a person of Burmese descent. **2** a member of the largest ethnic group of Burma. **3** the language of this group. ● *adj.* of or relating to Burma or its people or language.

burn[1] /burn/ *v.* & *n.* ● *v.* (*past* and *past part.* **burnt** or **burned**) **1** *tr.* & *intr.* be or cause to be consumed or destroyed by fire. **2** *intr.* **a** blaze or glow with fire. **b** be in the state characteristic of fire. **3** *tr.* & *intr.* be or cause to be injured or damaged by fire or great heat or by radiation. **4** *tr.* & *intr.* use or be used as a source of heat, light, or other energy. **5** *tr.* & *intr.* char or scorch in cooking (*burned the vegetables*; *the vegetables are burning*). **6** *tr.* produce (a hole, a mark, etc.) by fire or heat. **7** *tr.* **a** subject (clay, chalk, etc.) to heat for a purpose. **b** harden (bricks) by fire. **c** make (lime or charcoal) by heat. **8** *tr.* colour, tan, or parch with heat or light (*we were burnt brown by the sun*). **9** *tr.* & *intr.* put or be put to death by fire. **10** *tr.* **a** cauterize, brand. **b** (foll. by *in*) imprint by burning. **11** *tr.* & *intr.* make or be hot, give or feel a sensation or pain of or like heat. **12 a** *tr.* & *intr.* (often foll. by *with*) make or be passionate; feel or cause to feel great emotion (*burn with shame*). **b** *intr.* (usu. foll. by *to* + infin.) desire passionately, long. **13** *intr. sl.* drive fast. **14** *tr. US sl.* anger, infuriate. **15** *intr.* (foll. by *into*) (of acid etc.) gradually penetrate (into) causing disintegration. ● *n.* **1** a mark or injury caused by burning. **2** the ignition of a rocket engine in flight, giving extra thrust. **3** *US*, *Austral.*, & *NZ* a forest area cleared by burning. **4** *sl.* a cigarette. **5** *sl.* a car race. ▫ **burn one's boats** (or **bridges**) commit oneself irrevocably. **burn the candle at both ends** exhaust one's strength or resources by undertaking too much. **burn down 1 a** destroy (a building) by burning. **b** (of a building) be destroyed by fire. **2** burn less vigorously as fuel fails. **burn one's fingers** suffer for meddling or rashness. **burn a hole in one's pocket** (of money) be quickly spent. **burning-glass** a lens for concentrating the sun's rays on an object to burn it. **burn low** (of fire) be nearly out. **burn the midnight oil** read or work late into the night. **burn out 1** be reduced to nothing by burning. **2** fail or cause to fail by burning. **3** (usu. *refl.*) esp. *US* suffer physical or emotional exhaustion. **4** consume the contents of by burning. **5** make (a person) homeless by burning his or her house. **burn-out** *n. US* **1** physical or emotional exhaustion, esp. caused by stress. **2** depression, disillusionment. **burnt ochre** (or **sienna** or **umber**) a pigment darkened by burning. **burnt offering 1** an offering burnt on an altar as a sacrifice. **2** *joc.* overcooked food. **burnt-out** physically or emotionally exhausted. **burn up 1** get rid of by fire. **2** begin to blaze. **3** *US sl.* be or make furious. **have money to burn** have more money than one needs. [OE *birnan*, *bærnan* f. Gmc]

■ *v.* **1** ignite, set on fire, set alight, set fire to, burn up, fire, light, kindle, incinerate, *US sl.* torch. **2** blaze, flame, flare (up), glow, smoulder, be on fire *or* ablaze *or* in flames, burn up. **5** overcook, blacken, char, singe, scorch. **8** tan, colour, suntan; bake, parch, scorch, char, wither, dry out *or* up, *archaic* sear. **11** see BROIL[1] 2. **12 a** see FLUSH[1] *v.* 1a, PULSATE, SMART *v.* **b** desire, yearn, wish, long, itch. **13** see RACE *v.* 6a. **14** see INFURIATE *v.* ● *n.* **1** scorch, scar, brand. **4** see CIGARETTE 1. ▫ **burn the candle at both ends** see *overdo it*. **burn the midnight oil** see STUDY *v.* 2. **burn out 3** see EXHAUST *v.* 2. **burn-out 1** see EXHAUSTION 2. **2** see DEPRESSION 1b. **burnt-out** see *spent* (SPEND 3). **burn up 2** see BURN[1] *v.* 1, 2 above. **3** see MADDEN.

burn[2] /burn/ *n. Sc.* a small stream. [OE *burna* etc. f. Gmc]

■ see STREAM *n.* 1.

burner /búrnər/ *n.* the part of a gas cooker, lamp, etc. that emits and shapes the flame. ▫ **on the back** (or **front**) **burner** *colloq.* receiving little (or much) attention.

burnet /búrnit/ *n.* **1** any rosaceous plant of the genus *Sanguisorba*, with pink or red flowers. **2** any of several diurnal moths of the family Zygaenidae, with crimson spots on greenish-black wings. [obs. *burnet* (adj.) dark brown f. OF *burnete*]

burning /búrning/ *adj.* **1** ardent, intense (*burning desire*). **2** hotly discussed, exciting (*burning question*). **3** flagrant (*burning shame*). **4** that burns; on fire; very hot. ▫ **burning bush 1** any of various shrubs with red fruits or red autumn leaves (with ref. to Exod. 3:2). **2** fraxinella. ▫▫ **burningly** *adv.*

■ **1** vehement, ardent, excited, passionate, impassioned, fervent, fervid, avid, intense, fiery, fierce, strong, violent, raging, towering, enthusiastic, *literary* perfervid. **2** see *thrilling* (THRILL). **3** see FLAGRANT. **4** flaming, blazing, fiery; ablaze, aflame, afire, on fire; see also HOT *adj.* 1.

burnish /búrnish/ *v.tr.* polish by rubbing. ▫▫ **burnisher** *n.* [ME f. OF *burnir* = *brunir* f. *brun* BROWN]

■ see POLISH *v.* 1.

burnous /burnóoss/ *n.* an Arab or Moorish hooded cloak. [F f. Arab. *burnus* f. Gk *birros* cloak]

burnt see BURN[1].

burp /burp/ *v.* & *n. colloq.* ● *v.* **1** *intr.* belch. **2** *tr.* make (a baby) belch, usu. by patting its back. ● *n.* a belch. ▫ **burp gun** *US sl.* an automatic pistol. [imit.]

burr /bur/ *n.* & *v.* ● *n.* **1 a** a whirring sound. **b** a rough sounding of the letter *r*. **2** (also **bur**) **a** a rough edge left on cut or punched metal or paper. **b** a surgeon's or dentist's small drill. **3 a** a siliceous rock used for millstones. **b** a whetstone. **4** = BUR 1, 2. **5** the coronet of a deer's antler. ● *v.* **1** *tr.* pronounce with a burr. **2** *intr.* speak indistinctly. **3** *intr.* make a whirring sound. [var. of BUR]

burrawang /búrrəwang/ *n. Austral.* **1** any palmlike tree of the genus *Macrozamia*. **2** the nut produced by this tree. [Mount *Budawang* in New South Wales]

burrito /bəreétō/ *n.* (*pl.* **-os**) *US* a tortilla rolled round a savoury filling. [Amer. Sp., dimin. of *burro* BURRO]

burro /búrrō/ *n.* (*pl.* **-os**) *US* a small donkey used as a pack-animal. [Sp.]

burrow /búrrō/ *n.* & *v.* ● *n.* a hole or tunnel dug by a small animal, esp. a rabbit, as a dwelling. ● *v.* **1** *intr.* make or live in a burrow. **2** *tr.* make (a hole etc.) by digging. **3** *intr.* hide oneself. **4** *intr.* (foll. by *into*) investigate, search. ▫▫ **burrower** *n.* [ME, app. var. of BOROUGH]

■ *n.* excavation, hole, warren, tunnel; den, set, lair. ● *v.* **1, 2** dig, tunnel, bore, root (around *or* about), *poet.* delve; excavate. **3** see HIDE[1] *v.* 2. **4** (*burrow into*) see INVESTIGATE.

bursa /búrsə/ *n.* (*pl.* **bursae** /-see/ or **bursas**) *Anat.* a fluid-filled sac or saclike cavity to lessen friction. ▫▫ **bursal** *adj.* [med.L = bag: cf. PURSE]

bursar /búrsər/ *n.* **1** a treasurer, esp. the person in charge of the funds and other property of a college. **2** the holder of a bursary. ▫▫ **bursarship** *n.* [F *boursier* or (in sense 1) med.L *bursarius* f. *bursa* bag]

■ ▫▫ **bursarship** see SCHOLARSHIP 2.

bursary /búrsəri/ *n.* (*pl.* **-ies**) **1** a grant, esp. a scholarship. **2** the post or room of a bursar. ▫▫ **bursarial** /-sáiriəl/ *adj.* [med.L *bursaria* (as BURSAR)]

■ **1** see SCHOLARSHIP 2.

bursitis /bursítiss/ *n.* inflammation of a bursa.

burst /burst/ *v.* & *n.* ● *v.* (*past* and *past part.* **burst**) **1 a** *intr.* break suddenly and violently apart by expansion of contents or internal pressure. **b** *tr.* cause to do this. **c** *tr.* send (a container etc.) violently apart. **2 a** *tr.* open forcibly. **b** *intr.* come open or be opened forcibly. **3 a** *intr.* (usu. foll. by *in, out*) make one's way suddenly, dramatically, or by force. **b** *tr.* break away from or through (*the river burst its banks*). **4** *tr.* & *intr.* fill or be full to overflowing. **5** *intr.* appear or come suddenly (*burst into flame; burst upon the view; sun burst out*). **6** *intr.* (foll. by *into*) suddenly begin to shed or utter (esp. *burst into tears* or *laughter* or *song*). **7** *intr.* be as if about to burst because of effort, excitement, etc. **8** *tr.* suffer bursting of (*burst a blood-vessel*). **9** *tr.* separate (continuous stationery) into single sheets. ● *n.* **1** the act of or an instance of bursting; a split. **2** a sudden issuing forth (*burst of flame*). **3** a sudden outbreak (*burst of applause*). **4 a** a short sudden effort; a spurt. **b** a gallop. **5** an explosion. □ **burst out 1** suddenly begin (*burst out laughing*). **2** exclaim. [OE *berstan* f. Gmc]

■ *v.* **1** break (apart), rupture, split, shatter, come apart, explode, blow up, *colloq.* bust, *literary* break asunder; puncture, pop. **2** break *or* force open. **3 a** force *or* break *or* push *or* drive *or* thrust one's way. **5** break (out *or* forth), erupt; (*burst out*) emerge, come out *or* forth, appear, show *or* manifest (oneself *or* itself), be revealed. **6** (*burst into*) burst out in, break into, burst forth with, erupt *or* collapse *or* dissolve into. **7** (*bursting*) see TENSE *adj.* 1. ● *n.* **1** see SPLIT *n.* 2. **3** see OUTBURST. **4** see SPURT *n.* 2. **5** see BLAST *n.* 2. □ **burst out 1** break out, erupt *or* explode into. **2** see BLURT, EXCLAIM 1.

burstproof /búrstproof/ *adj.* (of a door lock) able to withstand a violent impact.

burthen *archaic* var. of BURDEN *n.* 4.

burton[1] /búrt'n/ *n.* □ **go for a burton** *Brit. sl.* be lost or destroyed or killed. [20th c.: perh. *Burton* ale f. *Burton-on-Trent* in England]

burton[2] /búrt'n/ *n.* a light two-block tackle for hoisting. [ME *Breton tackles*: see BRETON]

bury /bérri/ *v.tr.* (**-ies, -ied**) **1** place (a dead body) in the earth, in a tomb, or in the sea. **2** lose by death (*has buried three husbands*). **3 a** put under ground (*bury alive*). **b** hide (treasure, a bone, etc.) in the earth. **c** cover up; submerge. **4 a** put out of sight (*buried his face in his hands*). **b** consign to obscurity (*the idea was buried after brief discussion*). **c** put away; forget. **5** involve deeply (*buried himself in his work; was buried in a book*). □ **bury the hatchet** cease to quarrel. **burying-beetle** a sexton beetle. **burying-ground** (or **-place**) a cemetery. [OE *byrgan* f. WG: cf. BURIAL]

■ **1** inter, lay to rest, *literary* inhume. **3 b, c** conceal, hide, secrete, cache, keep secret, *colloq.* stash (away); cover (up), submerge, obscure, cloak, veil, shroud, screen, wrap, enclose, envelop. **4 b, c** see ABANDON *v.* 2a, DISREGARD *v.* 1. **5** see IMMERSE 2. □ **bury the hatchet** see *make up* 4. **burying-ground** see GRAVEYARD.

bus /buss/ *n.* & *v.* ● *n.* (*pl.* **buses** or *US* **busses**) **1** a large passenger vehicle, esp. one serving the public on a fixed route. **2** *colloq.* a motor car, aeroplane, etc. **3** *Computing* a defined set of conductors carrying data and control signals within a computer. ● *v.* (**buses** or **busses, bussed, bussing**) **1** *intr.* go by bus. **2** *tr. US* transport by bus, esp. to promote racial integration. □ **bus lane** a part of a road's length marked off mainly for use by buses. **bus shelter** a shelter from rain etc. beside a bus stop. **bus station** a centre, esp. in a town, where (esp. long-distance) buses depart and arrive. **bus-stop 1** a regular stopping-place of a bus. **2** a sign marking this. [abbr. of OMNIBUS]

■ *n.* **1** see COACH *n.* 1. □ **bus station** see STATION *n.* 1.

busbar /búsbaar/ *n. Electr.* a system of conductors in a generating or receiving station on which power is concentrated for distribution.

busby /búzbi/ *n.* (*pl.* **-ies**) (not in official use) a tall fur hat worn by hussars etc. [18th c.: orig. unkn.]

bush[1] /boosh/ *n.* **1** a shrub or clump of shrubs with stems of moderate length. **2** a thing resembling this, esp. a clump of hair or fur. **3** (esp. in Australia and Africa) a wild uncultivated district; woodland or forest. **4** *hist.* a bunch of ivy as a vintner's sign. □ **bush-baby** (*pl.* **-ies**) a small African tree-climbing lemur; a galago. **bush basil** a culinary herb, *Ocimum minimum*. **bush jacket** a light cotton jacket with a belt. **bush lawyer 1** *Austral.* & *NZ* a person claiming legal knowledge without qualifications for it. **2** *NZ* a bramble. **bush-ranger** *hist.* an Australian outlaw living in the bush. **bush sickness** a disease of animals due to a lack of cobalt in the soil. **bush telegraph** rapid spreading of information, a rumour, etc. **go bush** *Austral.* leave one's usual surroundings; run wild. [ME f. OE & ON, ult. f. Gmc]

■ **3** see STICK[1] *n.* 11. □ **bush-ranger** see THIEF.

bush[2] /boosh/ *n.* & *v.* ● *n.* **1** a metal lining for a round hole enclosing a revolving shaft etc. **2** a sleeve providing electrical insulation. ● *v.tr.* provide with a bush. [MDu. *busse* BOX[1]]

bushbuck /booshbuk/ *n.* a small antelope, *Tragelaphus scriptus*, of southern Africa, having a chestnut coat with white stripes. [BUSH[1] + BUCK[1], after Du. *boschbok* f. *bosch* bush]

bushed /boosht/ *adj. colloq.* **1** *Austral.* & *NZ* **a** lost in the bush. **b** bewildered. **2** *US* tired out.

■ **2** see TIRED 1.

bushel /boosh'l/ *n.* a measure of capacity for corn, fruit, liquids, etc. (*Brit.* 8 gallons, or 36.4 litres; *US* 64 US pints). □□ **bushelful** *n.* (*pl.* **-fuls**). [ME f. OF *buissiel* etc., perh. of Gaulish orig.]

bushfire /booshfīr/ *n.* a fire in a forest or in scrub often spreading widely.

bushido /boosheédō/ *n.* the code of honour and morals evolved by the Japanese samurai. [Jap., = military knight's way]

bushing /booshing/ *n.* = BUSH[2] *n.*

bushman /booshmən/ *n.* (*pl.* **-men**) **1** a person who lives or travels in the Australian bush. **2** (**Bushman**) **a** a member of an aboriginal people in S. Africa. **b** the language of this people. [BUSH[1] + MAN: sense 2 after Du. *boschjesman* f. *bosch* bush]

bushmaster /booshmaastər/ *n.* a venomous viper, *Lachesis muta*, of Central and S. America. [perh. f. Du. *boschmeester*]

bushveld /booshfelt/ *n.* open country consisting largely of bush. [BUSH[1] + VELD, after Afrik. *bosveld*]

bushwhack /booshwak/ *v.* **1** *intr. US, Austral.*, & *NZ* **a** clear woods and bush country. **b** live or travel in bush country. **2** *tr. US* ambush.

■ **2** see AMBUSH *v.*

bushwhacker /booshwakkər/ *n.* **1** *US, Austral.*, & *NZ* **a** a person who clears woods and bush country. **b** a person who lives or travels in bush country. **2** *US* a guerrilla fighter (orig. in the American Civil war).

bushy[1] /booshi/ *adj.* (**bushier, bushiest**) **1** growing thickly like a bush. **2** having many bushes. **3** covered with bush. □□ **bushily** *adv.* **bushiness** *n.*

■ **1** see THICK *adj.* 3c.

bushy[2] /booshi/ *n.* (*pl.* **-ies**) *Austral.* & *NZ colloq.* a person who lives in the bush (as distinct from in a town).

busily /bizzili/ *adv.* in a busy manner.

business /bízniss/ *n.* **1** one's regular occupation, profession, or trade. **2** a thing that is one's concern. **3 a** a task or duty. **b** a reason for coming (*what is your business?*). **4** serious work or activity (*get down to business*). **5** *derog.* **a** an affair, a matter (*sick of the whole business*). **b** a structure (*a lath-and-plaster business*). **6** a thing or series of things needing to be dealt with (*the business of the day*). **7** trade, relations; dealings, esp. of a commercial nature (*good stroke of business*). **8** a commercial house or firm. **9** *Theatr.* action on stage. **10** a difficult matter (*what a business it is!; made a great business of it*). □ **business card** a card printed with one's name and professional details. **the business end** *colloq.* the functional part of a tool or device. **business**

park an area designed to accommodate businesses and light industry. **business person** a businessman or businesswoman. **business studies** training in economics, management, etc. **has no business to** has no right to. **in business 1** trading or dealing. **2** able to begin operations. **in the business of 1** engaged in. **2** intending to (*we are not in the business of surrendering*). **like nobody's business** *colloq.* extraordinarily. **make it one's business to** undertake to. **mind one's own business** not meddle. **on business** with a definite purpose, esp. one relating to one's regular occupation. **send a person about his or her business** dismiss a person; send a person away. [OE *bisignis* (as BUSY, -NESS)]

▪ **1** occupation, calling, vocation, trade, profession, career, *métier*, (line of) work, field, job, employment. **2** concern, affair, interest, responsibility, province, area, job. **3** duty, function, task, job, responsibility, role, charge, obligation. **4** work, serious business, *sl.* brass tacks, nitty-gritty. **5 a** affair, matter, topic, subject, question, problem, situation, thing; see also PALAVER *n.* 4. **6** concern(s), agenda, matter(s) (in hand), job, assignment, charge, task, subject, question, problem, issue, proceeding(s), point, affair. **7** dealing(s), relations, transaction(s), truck, exchange; trade, commerce, industry, traffic; custom. **8** concern, establishment, operation, practice, organization, company, firm, house, enterprise, *colloq.* outfit; corporation, partnership, proprietorship. **10** see PALAVER *n.* 4. □ **has no business to** see LICENCE *n.* 2. **like nobody's business** see *amazingly* (AMAZE). **make it one's business to** see UNDERTAKE 2. **mind one's own business** stop butting in *or* prying *or* interfering, stick to one's last, keep off *or* out, *colloq.* keep one's paws off, stop poking *or* sticking one's nose in. **send a person about his or her business** see DISMISS 2.

businesslike /bíznislīk/ *adj.* efficient, systematic, practical.
▪ see SYSTEMATIC 1.

businessman /bíznismən/ *n.* (*pl.* **-men**; *fem.* **businesswoman**, *pl.* **-women**) a man or woman engaged in trade or commerce, esp. at a senior level (see also *business person*).
▪ see TRADER.

busk /busk/ *v.intr.* perform (esp. music) for voluntary donations, usu. in the street or in subways. □□ **busker** *n.* **busking** *n.* [*busk* peddle etc. (perh. f. obs. F *busquer* seek)]

buskin /búskin/ *n.* **1** either of a pair of thick-soled laced boots worn by an ancient Athenian tragic actor to gain height. **2** (usu. prec. by *the*) tragic drama; its style or spirit. **3** *hist.* either of a pair of calf- or knee-high boots of cloth or leather worn in the Middle Ages. □□ **buskined** *adj.* [prob. f. OF *bouzequin*, var. of *bro(u)sequin*, of unkn. orig.]

busman /búsmən/ *n.* (*pl.* **-men**) the driver of a bus. □ **busman's holiday** leisure time spent in an activity similar to one's regular work.

buss /buss/ *n.* & *v. archaic* or *US colloq.* ● *n.* a kiss. ● *v.tr.* kiss. [earlier *bass* (n. & v.): cf. F *baiser* f. L *basiare*]
▪ *n.* see KISS *n.* ● *v.* see KISS *v.* 1, 2.

bust[1] /bust/ *n.* **1 a** the human chest, esp. that of a woman; the bosom. **b** the circumference of the body at bust level (*a 36-inch bust*). **2** a sculpture of a person's head, shoulders, and chest. [F *buste* f. It. *busto*, of unkn. orig.]
▪ **1** see BOSOM *n.* 1. **2** see STATUE.

bust[2] /bust/ *v.*, *n.*, & *adj. colloq.* ● *v.* (*past* and *past part.* **busted** or **bust**) **1** *tr.* & *intr.* burst, break. **2** *tr.* esp. *US* reduce (a soldier etc.) to a lower rank; dismiss. **3** *tr.* esp. *US* **a** raid, search. **b** arrest. ● *n.* **1** a sudden failure; a bankruptcy. **2** esp. *US* **a** a police raid. **b** an arrest. **3** a drinking-bout. **4** esp. *US* a punch; a hit. **5** a worthless thing. **6** a bad hand at cards. ● *adj.* (also **busted**) **1** broken, burst, collapsed. **2** bankrupt. □ **bust a gut** make every possible effort. **bust up 1** bring or come to collapse; explode. **2** (of esp. a married couple) separate. **bust-up** *n.* **1** a quarrel. **2** a collapse; an explosion. **go bust** become bankrupt; fail. [orig. a (dial.) pronunc. of BURST]
▪ *v.* **1** see BREAK[1] 1b. **2** see DOWNGRADE *v.* 1. **3 a** see RAID *v.* 2. **b** see ARREST *v.* 1a. ● *n.* **2** raid, search; see also ARREST *n.* 1. **3** see ORGY 1. **4** see HIT *n.* 1a. ● *adj.* **1** see DUD *adj.* 1. **2** see INSOLVENT *adj.* □ **bust a gut** see *strain every nerve*.

bustard /bústərd/ *n.* any large terrestrial bird of the family Otididae, with long neck, long legs, and stout tapering body. [ME f. OF *bistarde* f. L *avis tarda* slow bird (? = slow on the ground; but possibly a perversion of a foreign word)]

bustee /bústee/ *n. Ind.* a shanty town; a slum. [Hind. *bastī* dwelling]

buster /bústər/ *n.* **1** esp. *US sl.* mate; fellow (used esp. as a disrespectful form of address). **2** a violent gale.

bustier /bústiay/ *n.* a strapless close-fitting bodice, usu. boned. [F]

bustle[1] /búss'l/ *v.* & *n.* ● *v.* **1** *intr.* (often foll. by *about*) **a** work etc. showily, energetically, and officiously. **b** hasten (*bustled about the kitchen banging saucepans*). **2** *tr.* make (a person) hurry or work hard (*bustled him into his overcoat*). **3** *intr.* (as **bustling** *adj.*) *colloq.* full of activity. ● *n.* excited activity; a fuss. □□ **bustler** *n.* [perh. f. *buskle* frequent. of *busk* prepare]
▪ *v.* **1** see RUSH[1] *v.* 1. **3** (**bustling**) see ACTIVE *adj.* 1a. ● *n.* rush, hustle (and bustle), hurry; haste.

bustle[2] /búss'l/ *n. hist.* a pad or frame worn under a skirt and puffing it out behind. [18th c.: orig. unkn.]

busty /bústi/ *adj.* (**bustier, bustiest**) (of a woman) having a prominent bust. □□ **bustiness** *n.*
▪ see BUXOM.

busy /bízzi/ *adj.*, *v.*, & *n.* ● *adj.* (**busier, busiest**) **1** (often foll. by *in*, *with*, *at*, or pres. part.) occupied or engaged in work etc. with the attention concentrated (*busy at their needlework*; *he was busy packing*). **2** full of activity or detail; fussy (*a busy evening*; *a picture busy with detail*). **3** employed continuously; unresting (*busy as a bee*). **4** meddlesome; prying. **5** esp. *US* (of a telephone line) engaged. ● *v.tr.* (**-ies, -ied**) (often *refl.*) keep busy; occupy (*the work busied him for many hours*; *busied herself with the accounts*). ● *n.* (*pl.* **-ies**) *sl.* a detective; a policeman. □ **busy Lizzie** a house-plant, *Impatiens Walleriana*, with usu. toothed leaves and pendulous flowers. □□ **busily** /bízzili/ *adv.* **busyness** /bízziniss/ *n.* (cf. BUSINESS). [OE *bisig*]
▪ *adj.* **1** occupied, engaged, tied up, wrapped up. **2** hectic, frantic, active, full, brisk, eventful; fancy, fussy, ornate, elaborate, detailed, complicated, complex, (over-)decorated, intricate, baroque, rococo. **3** working, industrious, active, tireless, hard-working; bustling, hectic, unresting, frantic, lively, hustling, energetic. **4** see NOSY *adj.* ● *v.* occupy, involve, employ, divert, absorb, engross, preoccupy, hold a person's attention. ● *n.* see DETECTIVE *n.*, *police officer*.

busybody /bízziboddi/ *n.* (*pl.* **-ies**) **1** a meddlesome person. **2** a mischief-maker.
▪ **1** snoop(er), gossip, meddler, *colloq.* kibitzer, *esp. Brit. colloq.* Nosy Parker, *Austral.* & *NZ sl.* stickybeak. **2** see TROUBLEMAKER.

but[1] /but, bət/ *conj.*, *prep.*, *adv.*, *pron.*, *n.*, & *v.* ● *conj.* **1 a** nevertheless, however (*tried hard but did not succeed*; *I am old, but I am not weak*). **b** on the other hand; on the contrary (*I am old but you are young*). **2** (prec. by *can* etc.; in *neg.* or *interrog.*) except, other than, otherwise than (*cannot choose but do it*; *what could we do but run?*). **3** without the result that (*it never rains but it pours*). **4** prefixing an interruption to the speaker's train of thought (*the weather is ideal - but is that a cloud on the horizon?*). ● *prep.* except; apart from; other than (*everyone went but me*; *nothing but trouble*). ● *adv.* **1** only; no more than; only just (*we can but try*; *is but a child*; *had but arrived*; *did it but once*). **2** introducing emphatic repetition; definitely (*wanted to see nobody, but nobody*). **3** *Austral.*, *NZ*, & *Sc.* though, however (*didn't like it, but*). ● *rel.pron.* who not; that not (*there is not a man but feels pity*). ● *n.* an objection (*ifs and buts*). ● *v.tr.* (in phr. **but me no buts**) do not raise objections. □ **but for** without the help or hindrance etc. of (*but for you I'd be rich by now*). **but one** (or **two** etc.) excluding one (or two etc.) from the number (*next door but one*; *last but one*). **but that** (prec. by *neg.*) that (*I don't deny but that it's true*). **but that** (or *colloq.* **what**) other than that; except that (*who knows but that it is true?*). **but then** (or **yet**) however, on the other hand (*I won, but then the others were beginners*). [OE *be-ūtan*, *būtan*, *būta* outside, without]

■ *conj.* **1 a** see NEVERTHELESS. **b** however, on the other hand, on the contrary, contrariwise. ● *prep.* see EXCEPT *prep.* ● *adv.* **3** see HOWEVER 2.

but[2] /but/ *n. Sc.* □ **but and ben** the outer and inner rooms of a two-roomed house (see BEN[2]). [BUT[1] = outside]

butadiene /byōōtədī́-een/ *n. Chem.* a colourless gaseous hydrocarbon used in the manufacture of synthetic rubbers. ¶ Chem. formula: C_4H_6. [BUTANE + DI-[2] + -ENE: cf. BUNA]

butane /byōōtayn/ *n. Chem.* a gaseous hydrocarbon of the alkane series used in liquefied form as fuel. ¶ Chem. formula: C_4H_{10}. [BUTYL + -ANE[2]]

butch /bŏŏch/ *adj.* & *n. sl.* ● *adj.* masculine; tough-looking. ● *n.* **1** (often *attrib.*) **a** a mannish woman. **b** a mannish lesbian. **2** a tough, usu. muscular, youth or man. [perh. abbr. of BUTCHER]

butcher /bŏŏchər/ *n.* & *v.* ● *n.* **1 a** a person whose trade is dealing in meat. **b** a person who slaughters animals for food. **2** a person who kills or has people killed indiscriminately or brutally. ● *v.tr.* **1** slaughter or cut up (an animal) for food. **2** kill (people) wantonly or cruelly. **3** ruin (esp. a job or a musical composition) through incompetence. □ **the butcher, the baker, the candlestick-maker** people of all kinds or trades. **butcher-bird** a shrike of the genus *Lanius*, native to Australia and New Guinea, with a long hook-tipped bill for catching prey. **butcher's** *rhyming sl.* a look (short for *butcher's hook*). **butcher's-broom** a low spiny-leaved evergreen shrub, *Ruscus aculeatus*. **butcher's meat** slaughtered fresh meat excluding game, poultry, and bacon. □□ **butcherly** *adj.* [ME f. OF *bo(u)chier* f. *boc* BUCK[1]]

■ *n.* **2** murderer, slaughterer, killer, ripper, cutthroat, executioner, annihilator. ● *v.* **2** slaughter, massacre, murder, exterminate, annihilate, kill, liquidate, mow down, cut down, wipe out; cut *or* hack *or* hew to pieces, mutilate, dismember, cut up, disembowel. **3** see RUIN *v.* 1b. □ **butcher's** see LOOK *n.* 1.

butchery /bŏŏchəri/ *n.* (*pl.* **-ies**) **1** needless or cruel slaughter (of people). **2** the butcher's trade. **3** a slaughterhouse. [ME f. OF *boucherie* (as BUTCHER)]

■ **1** see SLAUGHTER *n.* 2. **2** slaughter, butchering.

butle var. of BUTTLE.

butler /bútlər/ *n.* the principal manservant of a household, usu. in charge of the wine cellar, pantry, etc. [ME f. AF *buteler*, OF *bouteillier*: see BOTTLE]

butt[1] /but/ *v.* & *n.* ● *v.* **1** *tr.* & *intr.* push with the head or horns. **2 a** *intr.* (usu. foll. by *against*, *upon*) come with one end flat against, meet end to end with, abut. **b** *tr.* (usu. foll. by *against*) place (timber etc.) with the end flat against a wall etc. ● *n.* **1** a push with the head. **2** a join of two edges. □ **butt in** interrupt, meddle. [ME f. AF *buter*, OF *boter* f. Gmc: infl. by BUTT[2] and ABUT]

■ *v.* **1** ram, head-butt, prod, poke, jab, charge. **2 a** (*butt on to*) join, meet, abut (on *or* against), come up against, border (on *or* upon), touch, adjoin. ● *n.* **1** head-butt, poke, jab, prod, dig, stab, jog, nudge, push. □ **butt in** interfere, intrude, intervene, meddle, put *or* stick one's oar in, trespass on a person's preserves, *colloq.* poke one's nose in, kibitz; interrupt, cut in, break in, burst out, *colloq.* chip in.

butt[2] /but/ *n.* **1** (often foll. by *of*) an object (of ridicule etc.) (*the butt of his jokes*; *made him their butt*). **2 a** a mound behind a target. **b** (in *pl.*) a shooting-range. **c** a target. **3** a grouse-shooter's stand screened by low turf or a stone wall. [ME f. OF *but* goal, of unkn. orig.]

■ **1** target, end, object; prey, victim, quarry, scapegoat, dupe, gull, pigeon, cat's-paw, Aunt Sally, *sl.* sucker, fall guy, *US sl.* patsy.

butt[3] /but/ *n.* **1** (also **butt-end**) the thicker end, esp. of a tool or a weapon (*gun butt*). **2 a** the stub of a cigar or a cigarette. **b** (also **butt-end**) a remnant (*the butt of the evening*). **3** esp. *US sl.* the buttocks. **4** (also **butt-end**) the square end of a plank meeting a similar end. **5** the trunk of a tree, esp. the part just above the ground. □ **butt weld** a weld in which the pieces are joined end to end. [Du. *bot* stumpy]

butt[4] /but/ *n.* a cask, esp. as a measure of wine or ale. [AL *butta*, *bota*, AF *but*, f. OF *bo(u)t* f. LL *buttis*]

butt[5] /but/ *n.* a flat-fish (e.g. a sole, plaice, or turbot). [MLG, MDu. *but* flat-fish]

butte /byōōt/ *n. US* a high isolated steep-sided hill. [F, = mound]

butter /búttər/ *n.* & *v.* ● *n.* **1 a** a pale yellow edible fatty substance made by churning cream and used as a spread or in cooking. **b** a substance of a similar consistency or appearance (*peanut butter*). **2** excessive flattery. ● *v.tr.* spread, cook, or serve with butter (*butter the bread*; *buttered carrots*). □ **butter-and-eggs** any of several plants having two shades of yellow in the flower, e.g. toadflax. **butter-bean 1** the flat, dried, white lima bean. **2** a yellow-podded bean. **butter-cream** (or **-icing**) a mixture of butter, icing sugar, etc. used as a filling or a topping for a cake. **butter-fingers** *colloq.* a clumsy person prone to drop things. **butter-knife** a blunt knife used for cutting butter at table. **butter muslin** a thin, loosely-woven cloth with a fine mesh, orig. for wrapping butter. **butter-nut 1** a N. American tree, *Juglans cinerea*. **2** the oily nut of this tree. **butter up** *colloq.* flatter excessively. **look as if butter wouldn't melt in one's mouth** seem demure or innocent, probably deceptively. [OE *butere* f. L *butyrum* f. Gk *bouturon*]

butterball /búttərbawl/ *n.* **1** a piece of butter shaped into a ball. **2** *US* = BUFFLEHEAD (because it is very fat in autumn). **3** *US sl.* a fat person.

butterbur /búttərbur/ *n.* any of several plants of the genus *Petasites* with large soft leaves, formerly used to wrap butter.

buttercup /búttərkup/ *n.* any common yellow-flowered plant of the genus *Ranunculus*.

butterfat /búttərfat/ *n.* the essential fats of pure butter.

butterfish /búttərfish/ *n.* = GUNNEL[1].

butterfly /búttərflī/ *n.* (*pl.* **-flies**) **1** any diurnal insect of the order Lepidoptera, with knobbed antennae, a long thin body, and four usu. brightly coloured wings erect when at rest. **2** a showy or frivolous person. **3** (in *pl.*) *colloq.* a nervous sensation felt in the stomach. □ **butterfly net** a fine net on a ring attached to a pole, used for catching butterflies. **butterfly nut** a kind of wing-nut. **butterfly stroke** a stroke in swimming, with both arms raised and lifted forwards together. **butterfly valve** a valve with hinged semicircular plates. [OE *buttor-flēoge* (as BUTTER, FLY[2])]

buttermilk /búttərmilk/ *n.* a slightly acid liquid left after churning butter.

butterscotch /búttərskoch/ *n.* a brittle sweet made from butter, brown sugar, etc. [SCOTCH]

butterwort /búttərwurt/ *n.* any bog plant of the genus *Pinguicula*, esp. *P. vulgaris* with violet-like flowers and fleshy leaves that secrete a fluid to trap small insects for nutrient.

buttery[1] /búttəri/ *n.* (*pl.* **-ies**) a room, esp. in a college, where provisions are kept and supplied to students etc. [ME f. AF *boterie* butt-store (as BUTT[4])]

buttery[2] /búttəri/ *adj.* like, containing, or spread with butter. □□ **butteriness** *n.*

buttle /bútt'l/ *v.intr.* (also **butle**) *joc.* work as a butler. [back-form. f. BUTLER]

buttock /búttək/ *n.* (usu. in *pl.*) **1** each of two fleshy protuberances on the lower rear part of the human body. **2** the corresponding part of an animal. [*butt* ridge + -OCK]
■ (*buttocks*) seat, posterior, rump, hindquarters, hams, *Anat.* nates, gluteus maximus, *colloq.* backside, behind, bottom, rear, sit-upon, *colloq. euphem. derrière, joc.* fundament, *sl.* prat, cheeks, *Brit. sl.* bum, *esp. US sl.* butt, *US sl.* fanny, can, keister.

button /bútt'n/ *n.* & *v.* ● *n.* **1** a small disc or knob sewn on to a garment, either to fasten it by being pushed through a buttonhole, or as an ornament or badge. **2** a knob on a piece of esp. electronic equipment which is pressed to operate it. **3 a** a small round object (*chocolate buttons*). **b** (*attrib.*) anything resembling a button (*button nose*). **4 a** a bud. **b** a button mushroom. **5** *Fencing* a terminal knob on a foil making it harmless. ● *v.* **1** *tr.* & *intr.* = *button up* 1. **2** *tr.* supply with buttons. □ **buttonball tree** (or **button wood**) *US* a plane-tree, *Platanus occidentalis.* **button chrysanthemum** a variety of chrysanthemum with small spherical flowers. **buttoned up** *colloq.* **1** formal and inhibited in manner. **2** silent. **button one's lip** esp. *US sl.* remain silent. **button mushroom** a young unopened mushroom. **button-through** (of a dress) fastened with buttons from neck to hem like a coat. **button up 1** fasten with buttons. **2** *colloq.* complete (a task etc.) satisfactorily. **3** *colloq.* become silent. **not worth a button** worthless. **on the button** esp. *US sl.* precisely. □□ **buttoned** *adj.* **buttonless** *adj.* **buttony** *adj.* [ME f. OF *bouton*, ult. f. Gmc]

buttonhole /bútt'nhōl/ *n.* & *v.* ● *n.* **1** a slit made in a garment to receive a button for fastening. **2** a flower or spray worn in a lapel buttonhole. ● *v.tr.* **1** *colloq.* accost and detain (a reluctant listener). **2** make buttonholes in. □ **buttonhole stitch** a looped stitch used for making buttonholes.
■ *n.* **2** corsage, boutonnière. ● *v.* **1** corner, detain, hold up, accost, importune, waylay, *Austral.* & *NZ* bail (up).

buttonhook /bútt'nhŏŏk/ *n.* a hook formerly used esp. for pulling the buttons on tight boots into place for fastening.

buttons /bútt'nz/ *n. colloq.* a liveried page-boy. [from the rows of buttons on his jacket]
■ see PAGE[2] *n.* 1, 2.

buttress /bútriss/ *n.* & *v.* ● *n.* **1 a** a projecting support of stone or brick etc. built against a wall. **b** a source of help or encouragement (*she was a buttress to him in his trouble*). **2** a projecting portion of a hill or mountain. ● *v.tr.* (often foll. by *up*) **1** support with a buttress. **2** support by argument etc. (*claim buttressed by facts*). [ME f. OF (*ars*) *bouterez* thrusting (arch) f. *bouteret* f. *bouter* BUTT[1]]
■ *n.* **1** support, prop, stay, reinforcement, reinforcer, strengthener, bolster, brace, bracket. ● *v.* sustain, support, bolster, strengthen, reinforce, fortify, prop (up), hold up, brace, shore up, *archaic* stay; back up, provide backing for, consolidate, firm up, secure; aid, help, assist, encourage, further, advance, *colloq.* boost.

butty[1] /búttі/ *n.* (*pl.* **-ies**) **1** *colloq.* or *dial.* a mate; a companion. **2** *hist.* a middleman negotiating between a mine-owner and the miners. **3** a barge or other craft towed by another. □ **butty-gang** a gang of men contracted to work on a large job and sharing the profits equally. [19th c.: perh. f. BOOTY in phr. *play booty* join in sharing plunder]

butty[2] /bútti/ *n.* (*pl.* **-ies**) *N.Engl.* **1** a sandwich (*bacon butty*). **2** a slice of bread and butter. [BUTTER + -Y[2]]

butyl /byŏŏtīl/ *n. Chem.* the univalent alkyl radical C_4H_9. □ **butyl rubber** a synthetic rubber used in the manufacture of tyre inner tubes. [BUTYRIC (ACID) + -YL]

butyric acid /byootírrik/ *n. Chem.* either of two colourless syrupy liquid organic acids found in rancid butter or arnica oil. □□ **butyrate** /byŏŏtirayt/ *n.* [L *butyrum* BUTTER + -IC]

buxom /búksəm/ *adj.* (esp. of a woman) plump and healthy-looking; large and shapely; busty. □□ **buxomly** *adv.* **buxomness** *n.* [earlier sense *pliant*: ME f. stem of OE *būgan* BOW[2] + -SOME[1]]
■ hearty, healthy, vigorous, solid, sizeable, large, plump, stout, substantial, lusty, voluptuous, attractive, comely, shapely, hefty; busty, bosomy, *colloq.* curvaceous, well-endowed, chesty.

buy /bī/ *v.* & *n.* ● *v.* (**buys, buying**; *past* and *past part.* **bought** /bawt/) **1** *tr.* **a** obtain in exchange for money etc. **b** (usu. in *neg.*) serve to obtain (*money can't buy happiness*). **2** *tr.* **a** procure (the loyalty etc.) of a person by bribery, promises, etc. **b** win over (a person) in this way. **3** *tr.* get by sacrifice, great effort, etc. (*dearly bought*; *bought with our sweat*). **4** *tr. sl.* accept, believe in, approve of (*it's a good scheme, I'll buy it*; *he bought it, he's so gullible*). **5** *absol.* be a buyer for a store etc. (*buys for Selfridges*; *are you buying or selling?*). ● *n. colloq.* a purchase (*that sofa was a good buy*). □ **best buy** the purchase giving the best value in proportion to its price; a bargain. **buy in 1** buy a stock of. **2** withdraw (an item) at auction because of failure to reach the reserve price. **buy into** obtain a share in (an enterprise) by payment. **buy it** (usu. in *past*) *sl.* be killed. **buy off** get rid of (a claim, a claimant, a blackmailer) by payment. **buy oneself out** obtain one's release (esp. from the armed services) by payment. **buy out** pay (a person) to give up an ownership, interest, etc. **buy-out** *n.* the purchase of a controlling share in a company etc. **buy over** bribe. **buy time** delay an event, conclusion, etc., temporarily. **buy up 1** buy as much as possible of. **2** absorb (another firm etc.) by purchase. [OE *bycgan* f. Gmc]
■ *v.* **1** purchase; acquire, obtain, get, procure, gain, come by, secure, get *or* lay one's hands on, get hold of, pick up. **2 b** bribe, pay off, buy off *or* over, *colloq.* fix, grease the palm of, square; suborn, corrupt. **4** accept, allow, take, believe (in), find credible *or* believable, be convinced *or* assured of, take as given *or* read, trust, swallow, go for. **5** see TRADE *v.* 1. ● *n.* purchase, acquisition, deal. □ **best buy** bargain, good deal *or* buy, square deal, *Brit.* snip, *colloq.* steal, give-away. **buy it** be *or* get killed, *sl.* bite the dust, *Brit. sl.* snuff it; see also DIE[1] *v.* 1. **buy off** see BUY *v.* 2b above. **buy over** see BUY *v.* 2b above. **buy time** see STALL[2] *v.* 1.

buyer /bīər/ *n.* **1** a person employed to select and purchase stock for a large store etc. **2** a purchaser, a customer. □ **buyer's** (or **buyers'**) **market** an economic position in which goods are plentiful and cheap and buyers have the advantage.
■ **2** customer, consumer, client, purchaser, patron, *colloq.* punter, regular; (*buyers*) see CLIENTELE.

buzz /buz/ *n.* & *v.* ● *n.* **1** the hum of a bee etc. **2** the sound of a buzzer. **3 a** a confused low sound as of people talking; a murmur. **b** a stir; hurried activity (*a buzz of excitement*). **c** *colloq.* a rumour. **4** *sl.* a telephone call. **5** *sl.* a thrill; a euphoric sensation. ● *v.* **1** *intr.* make a humming sound. **2 a** *tr.* & *intr.* signal or signal to with a buzzer. **b** *tr. sl.* telephone. **3** *intr.* **a** (often foll. by *about*) move or hover busily. **b** (of a place) have an air of excitement or purposeful activity. **4** *tr. colloq.* throw hard. **5** *tr. Aeron. colloq.* fly fast and very close to (another aircraft, the ground, etc.). □ **buzz off** *sl.* go or hurry away. **buzz-saw** *US* a circular saw. **buzz-word** *sl.* **1** a fashionable piece of esp. technical or computer jargon. **2** a catchword; a slogan. [imit.]
■ *n.* **1** hum, drone. **3 a** murmur, undercurrent, undertone, background noise, mumble, murmuring, drone, hum, burble, whispering, *literary* susurration, susurrus. **b** see STIR *n.* 2. **c** rumour, a piece of gossip *or* hearsay, *on dit*; see also WORD *n.* 7. **4** telephone call, phone call, call, *colloq.* ring, *Brit. colloq.* tinkle. **5** thrill, feeling of excitement, sensation, stimulation, *colloq.* kick, *sl.* high, bang, *US sl.* hit. ● *v.* **1** hum, murmur, drone. **2 a** summon, signal, buzz *or* ring for. **b** telephone, call (up), *Brit.* ring (up), *colloq.* phone, give a person a bell *or* ring, *Brit. colloq.* give a person a tinkle. **3 a** bustle, fuss (about), rush about *or* around; flutter, hover, fly. **b** be alive, bristle, swarm, hum. **4** see THROW *v.* 1, 2. **5** fly close to, fly down on, zoom on to. □ **buzz off** see *beat it.* **buzz-word 2** see SLOGAN.

buzzard /búzzərd/ *n.* **1** any of a group of predatory birds of the hawk family, esp. of the genus *Butea*, with broad wings well adapted for soaring flight. **2** *US* a turkey buzzard. [ME f. OF *busard*, *buson* f. L *buteo -onis* falcon]

buzzer /búzzər/ *n.* **1** an electrical device, similar to a bell, that makes a buzzing noise. **2** a whistle or hooter.

BVM *abbr.* Blessed Virgin Mary.

bwana /bwaanə/ *n. Afr.* master, sir. [Swahili]

BWI *abbr. hist.* British West Indies.

BWR *abbr.* boiling-water (nuclear) reactor.

by /bī/ *prep., adv., & n.* ● *prep.* **1** near, beside, in the region of (*stand by the door*; *sit by me*; *path by the river*). **2** through the agency, means, instrumentality, or causation of (*by proxy*; *bought by a millionaire*; *a poem by Donne*; *went by bus*; *succeeded by persisting*; *divide four by two*). **3** not later than; as soon as (*by next week*; *by now*; *by the time he arrives*). **4 a** past, beyond (*drove by the church*; *came by us*). **b** passing through; via (*went by Paris*). **5** in the circumstances of (*by day*; *by daylight*). **6** to the extent of (*missed by a foot*; *better by far*). **7** according to; using as a standard or unit (*judge by appearances*; *paid by the hour*). **8** with the succession of (*worse by the minute*; *day by day*; *one by one*). **9** concerning; in respect of (*did our duty by them*; *Smith by name*; *all right by me*). **10** used in mild oaths (orig. = as surely as one believes in) (*by God*; *by gum*; *swear by all that is sacred*). **11** placed between specified lengths in two directions (*three feet by two*). **12** avoiding, ignoring (*pass by him*; *passed us by*). **13** inclining to (*north by north-west*). ● *adv.* **1** near (*sat by, watching*; *lives close by*). **2** aside; in reserve (*put £5 by*). **3** past (*they marched by*). ● *n.* = BYE. □ **by and by** before long; eventually. **by and large** on the whole, everything considered. **by the by** (or **bye**) incidentally, parenthetically. **by oneself 1 a** unaided. **b** without prompting. **2** alone; without company. [OE *bī*, *bi*, *be* f. Gmc]

■ *prep.* **1** near, beside, next to, close to, alongside, with, hard by, *archaic or dial.* nigh. **2** by means of, through. **3** before, not later than, sooner than, as soon as. **4 b** via, by way of, through. **5** during, at. **7** see ACCORDING 1b. **9** see CONCERNING. ● *adv.* **1** near, nearby, at hand, close, about, around, *archaic or dial.* nigh. **2** away, aside, in reserve, on one side. □ **by and by** see PRESENTLY 1. **by and large** see *on the whole* (WHOLE). **by the by** see INCIDENTALLY 1. **by oneself 1** see ALONE 1b. **2** see ALONE 1a.

by- /bī/ *prefix* (also **bye-**) subordinate, incidental, secondary (*by-effect*; *by-road*).

by-blow /bíblō/ *n.* **1** a side-blow not at the main target. **2** an illegitimate child.

bye[1] /bī/ *n.* **1** *Cricket* a run scored from a ball that passes the batsman without being hit. **2** the status of an unpaired competitor in a sport, who proceeds to the next round as if having won. **3** *Golf* one or more holes remaining unplayed after the match has been decided. □ **by the bye** = *by the by*. **leg-bye** *Cricket* a run scored from a ball that touches the batsman. [BY as noun]

bye[2] /bī/ *int. colloq.* = GOODBYE. [abbr.]

bye- *prefix* var. of BY-.

bye-bye[1] /bíbí, bəbí/ *int. colloq.* = GOODBYE. [childish corrupt.]

bye-bye[2] /bíbī/ *n.* (also **bye-byes** /-bīz/) (a child's word for) sleep. [ME, f. the sound used in lullabies]

by-election /bí-ilekshʼn/ *n.* the election of an MP in a single constituency to fill a vacancy arising during a government's term of office.

Byelorussian var. of BELORUSSIAN.

by-form /bíform/ *n.* a collateral form of a word etc.

bygone /bígon/ *adj.* & *n.* ● *adj.* past, antiquated (*bygone years*). ● *n.* (in *pl.*) past offences (*let bygones be bygones*).

■ *adj.* past, former, antiquated, ancient, *archaic* olden, *colloq.* antediluvian, medieval; of old, *literary* of yore. ● *n.* (*bygones*) past indiscretions *or* offences; (*let bygones be bygones*) let sleeping dogs lie, bury the hatchet, bury *or* forget one's differences, call a truce.

by-law /bílaw/ *n.* (also **bye-law**) **1** *Brit.* a regulation made by a local authority or corporation. **2** a rule made by a company or society for its members. [ME prob. f. obs. *byrlaw* local custom (ON *býjar* genitive sing. of *býr* town, but assoc. with BY)]

byline /bílīn/ *n.* **1** a line in a newspaper etc. naming the writer of an article. **2** a secondary line of work. **3** a goal-line or touch-line.

byname /bínaym/ *n.* a sobriquet; a nickname.

bypass /bípaass/ *n.* & *v.* ● *n.* **1** a road passing round a town or its centre to provide an alternative route for through traffic. **2 a** a secondary channel or pipe etc. to allow a flow when the main one is closed or blocked. **b** an alternative passage for the circulation of blood during a surgical operation on the heart. ● *v.tr.* **1** avoid; go round. **2** provide with a bypass.

■ *n.* **1** ring road, orbital road *or* route; detour, alternative way *or* route, diversion. ● *v.* **1** avoid, evade, circumvent, sidestep, skirt, go *or* get round, steer *or* keep clear of, keep away from, fight shy of, detour; pass over, skip, skip *or* jump over, leave out; ignore, gloss over, overlook, brush over.

bypath /bípaath/ *n.* **1** a secluded path. **2** a minor or obscure branch of a subject.

byplay /bíplay/ *n.* a secondary action or sequence of events, esp. in a play.

by-product /bíprodukt/ *n.***1** an incidental product of the manufacture of something else. **2** a secondary result.

■ see DERIVATIVE *n.* 1.

byre /bīr/ *n.* a cowshed. [OE *bȳre*: perh. rel. to BOWER[1]]

byroad /bí-rōd/ *n.* a minor road.

Byronic /bīrónnik/ *adj.* **1** characteristic of Lord Byron, English poet d. 1824, or his romantic poetry. **2** (of a man) handsomely dark, mysterious, or moody.

byssinosis /bíssinṓsiss/ *n. Med.* a lung disease caused by prolonged inhalation of textile fibre dust. [mod.L f. Gk *bussinos* made of byssus + -OSIS]

byssus /bíssəss/ *n. hist.* (*pl.* **byssuses** or **byssi** /-sī/) **1** *hist.* a fine textile fibre and fabric of flax. **2** a tuft of tough silky filaments by which some molluscs adhere to rocks etc. [ME f. L f. Gk *bussos*]

bystander /bístandər/ *n.* a person who stands by but does not take part; a mere spectator.

■ spectator, onlooker, looker-on, observer, witness, passer-by, eyewitness.

byte /bīt/ *n. Computing* a group of eight binary digits, often used to represent one character. [20th c.: perh. based on BIT[4] and BITE]

byway /bíway/ *n.* **1** a byroad or bypath. **2** a minor activity.

■ **1** byroad, bypath, minor road, lane, track, side-street.

byword /bíwurd/ *n.* **1** a person or thing cited as a notable example (*is a byword for luxury*). **2** a familiar saying; a proverb.

■ **2** proverb, proverbial saying, maxim, adage, motto, slogan, apophthegm, aphorism, catchword, catch-phrase.

Byzantine /bizántīn, bī-, bízzənteen, -tīn/ *adj.* & *n.* ● *adj.* **1** of Byzantium or the E. Roman Empire. **2** (of a political situation etc.): **a** extremely complicated. **b** inflexible. **c** carried on by underhand methods. **3** *Archit.* & *Painting* of a highly decorated style developed in the Eastern Empire. ● *n.* a citizen of Byzantium or the E. Roman Empire. □□ **Byzantinism** *n.* **Byzantinist** *n.* [F *byzantin* or L *Byzantinus* f. *Byzantium*, later Constantinople and now Istanbul]

Cc

C[1] /see/ *n.* (also **c**) (*pl.* **Cs** or **C's**) **1** the third letter of the alphabet. **2** *Mus.* the first note of the diatonic scale of C major (the major scale having no sharps or flats). **3** the third hypothetical person or example. **4** the third highest class or category (of academic marks etc.). **5** *Algebra* (usu. **c**) the third known quantity. **6** (as a Roman numeral) 100. **7** (**c**) the speed of light in a vacuum. **8** (also ©) copyright.

C[2] *symb. Chem.* the element carbon.

C[3] *abbr.* (also **C.**) **1** Cape. **2** Conservative. **3** Command Paper (second series, 1870–99). **4** Celsius, Centigrade. **5** coulomb(s), capacitance.

c. *abbr.* **1** century; centuries. **2** chapter. **3** cent(s). **4** cold. **5** cubic. **6** colt. **7** *Cricket* caught by. **8** centi-.

c. *abbr. circa*, about.

c/- *abbr. Austral.* & *NZ* care of.

CA *abbr.* **1** *US* California (in official postal use). **2** *Sc.* & *Can.* chartered accountant.
■ **2** see BOOKKEEPER.

Ca *symb. Chem.* the element calcium.

ca. *abbr. circa*, about.

CAA *abbr.* (in the UK) Civil Aviation Authority.

Caaba var. of KAABA.

CAB *abbr.* **1** Citizens' Advice Bureau. **2** *US* Civil Aeronautics Board.

cab /kab/ *n.* **1** a taxi. **2** the driver's compartment in a lorry, train, or crane. **3** *hist.* a hackney carriage. [abbr. of CABRIOLET]
■ **1** taxi, hackney carriage, *Brit.* minicab, *US* hack.

cabal /kəbál/ *n.* & *v.* ● *n.* **1** a secret intrigue. **2** a political clique or faction. **3** *hist.* a committee of five ministers under Charles II, whose surnames happened to begin with C, A, B, A, and L. ● *v.intr.* (**caballed, caballing**) (often foll. by *together*, *against*) plot, intrigue. [F *cabale* f. med.L *cabala*, CABBALA]
■ *n.* **1** intrigue, plot, conspiracy, scheme, machination. **2** junta, clique, faction, set, sect, coterie, body, band, camarilla, league, pressure group, *Brit.* ginger group; ring, gang, mafia; unit, party, caucus, club. ● *v.* intrigue, plot, conspire, connive, machinate, scheme, collude.

cabala var. of CABBALA.

caballero /kábbəlyáirō/ *n.* (*pl.* **-os**) a Spanish gentleman. [Sp.: see CAVALIER]

cabana /kəbaánə/ *n. US* a hut or shelter at a beach or swimming-pool. [Sp. *cabaña* f. LL (as CABIN)]

cabaret /kábbəray/ *n.* **1** an entertainment in a nightclub or restaurant while guests eat or drink at tables. **2** such a nightclub etc. [F, = wooden structure, tavern]
■ **1** floor show, show, entertainment, performance, amusement. **2** nightclub, club, nightspot, *sl.* drum.

cabbage /kábbij/ *n.* **1 a** any of several cultivated varieties of *Brassica oleracea*, with thick green or purple leaves forming a round heart or head. **b** this head usu. eaten as a vegetable. **2** *colloq. derog.* a person who is inactive or lacks interest. □ **cabbage palm** a palm tree, *Cordyline australis*, with edible cabbage-like terminal buds. **cabbage rose** a double rose with a large round compact flower. **cabbage tree** = *cabbage palm*. **cabbage white** a butterfly, *Pieris brassicae*, whose caterpillars feed on cabbage leaves. □□ **cabbagy** *adj.* [earlier *cabache*, *-oche* f. OF (Picard) *caboche* head, OF *caboce*, of unkn. orig.]
■ **2** deadhead, *colloq.* vegetable.

cabbala /kəbaálə, kábbələ/ *n.* (also **cabala, kabbala**) **1** the Jewish mystical tradition. **2** mystic interpretation; any esoteric doctrine or occult lore. □□ **cabbalism** *n.* **cabbalist** *n.* **cabbalistic** /-lístik/ *adj.* [med.L f. Rabbinical Heb. *ḳabbālâ* tradition]
■ **2** see *the occult* (OCCULT). □□ **cabbalistic** see OCCULT *adj.* 2.

cabby /kábbi/ *n.* (also **cabbie**) (*pl.* **-ies**) *colloq.* a taxi-driver. [CAB + -Y[2]]

caber /káybər/ *n.* a roughly trimmed tree-trunk used in the Scottish Highland sport of tossing the caber. [Gael. *cabar* pole]

cabin /kábbin/ *n.* & *v.* ● *n.* **1** a small shelter or house, esp. of wood. **2** a room or compartment in an aircraft or ship for passengers or crew. **3** a driver's cab. ● *v.tr.* (**cabined, cabining**) confine in a small place, cramp. □ **cabin-boy** a boy who waits on a ship's officers or passengers. **cabin class** the intermediate class of accommodation in a ship. **cabin crew** the crew members on an aeroplane attending to passengers and cargo. **cabin cruiser** a large motor boat with living accommodation. [ME f. OF *cabane* f. Prov. *cabana* f. LL *capanna*, *cavanna*]
■ *n.* **1** hut, shack, cottage, crib, shanty, shelter, *Sc.* bothy, *poet.* cot; bungalow, lodge, chalet, *Austral. colloq.* weekender. **2** compartment, berth, room. ● *v.* see IMPRISON 2.

cabinet /kábbinit/ *n.* **1 a** a cupboard or case with drawers, shelves, etc., for storing or displaying articles. **b** a piece of furniture housing a radio or television set etc. **2** (**Cabinet**) the committee of senior ministers responsible for controlling government policy. **3** *archaic* a small private room. □ **cabinet-maker** a skilled joiner. **Cabinet Minister** *Brit.* a member of the Cabinet. **cabinet photograph** one of about 6 by 4 inches. **cabinet pudding** a steamed pudding with dried fruit. [CABIN + -ET[1], infl. by F *cabinet*]
■ **1 a** cupboard, bureau, commode, chiffonier, chest (of drawers), tallboy, *US* highboy, lowboy. **2** council, ministry, committee, board, advisers, senate. **3** closet, cell, cubby, den, antechamber, ante-room, boudoir, *Brit.* snug, *poet. or archaic* chamber.

cable /káyb'l/ *n.* & *v.* ● *n.* **1** a thick rope of wire or hemp. **2** an encased group of insulated wires for transmitting electricity or electrical signals. **3** a cablegram. **4 a** *Naut.* the chain of an anchor. **b** a measure of 200 yards. **5** (in full **cable stitch**) a knitted stitch resembling twisted rope. **6** *Archit.* a rope-shaped ornament. ● *v.* **1 a** *tr.* transmit (a message) by cablegram. **b** *tr.* inform (a person) by cablegram. **c** *intr.* send a cablegram. **2** *tr.* furnish or fasten with a cable or cables. **3** *Archit. tr.* furnish with cables. □ **cable-car 1** a small cabin (often one of a series) suspended on an endless cable and drawn up and down a mountainside etc. by an engine at one end. **2** a carriage drawn along a cable railway. **cable-laid** (of rope) having three triple strands. **cable railway** a railway along which carriages are drawn by an endless cable. **cable television** a broadcasting system with

signals transmitted by cable to subscribers' sets. [ME f. OF *chable*, ult. f. LL *capulum* halter f. Arab. *ḥabl*]
▪ *n.* **1** wire, line, rope, lead, chain, strand, twine, guy, *Naut.* hawser, stay. **2** lead, cord, wire, *Brit.* flex. **3** telegram, cablegram, radiogram, *esp. US colloq.* wire. ● *v.* **1** telegraph, radio, *esp. US colloq.* wire; see also TRANSMIT 1a.

cablegram /káyb'lgram/ *n.* a telegraph message sent by undersea cable etc.
▪ see TELEGRAM.

cableway /káyb'lway/ *n.* a transporting system with a usu. elevated cable.

cabman /kábmən/ *n.* (*pl.* **-men**) the driver of a cab.

cabochon /kábbəshon/ *n.* a gem polished but not faceted. □ ***en cabochon*** (of a gem) treated in this way. [F dimin. of *caboche*: see CABBAGE]

caboodle /kəbo͞od'l/ *n.* □ **the whole** (**kit and**) **caboodle** *sl.* the whole lot (of persons or things). [19th c. US: perh. f. phr. *kit and boodle*]

caboose /kəbo͞oss/ *n.* **1** a kitchen on a ship's deck. **2** *US* a guard's van; a car on a freight train for workmen etc. [Du. *cabūse*, of unkn. orig.]
▪ **1** see KITCHEN.

cabotage /kábbətaazh, -tij/ *n.* **1** *Naut.* coastal navigation and trade. **2** esp. *Aeron.* the reservation to a country of (esp. air) traffic operation within its territory. [F f. *caboter* to coast, perh. f. Sp. *cabo* CAPE[2]]

cabotin /kaabətán/ *n.* (*fem.* ***cabotine*** /-téen/) a second-rate actor; a strolling player. [F, = strolling player, perh. formed as CABOTAGE, from the resemblance to vessels travelling from port to port]

cabriole /kábriōl/ *n.* a kind of curved leg characteristic of Queen Anne and Chippendale furniture. [F f. *cabrioler*, *caprioler* f. It. *capriolare* to leap in the air; from the resemblance to a leaping animal's foreleg: see CAPRIOLE]

cabriolet /kábriōláy/ *n.* **1** a light two-wheeled carriage with a hood, drawn by one horse. **2** a motor car with a folding top. [F f. *cabriole* goat's leap (cf. CAPRIOLE), applied to its motion]

ca'canny /kaakánni/ *n.* **1** the practice of 'going slow' at work; a trade union policy of limiting output. **2** extreme caution. [Sc., = proceed warily: see CALL *v.* 16, CANNY]

cacao /kəkaá-ō, -káyō/ *n.* (*pl.* **-os**) **1** a seed pod from which cocoa and chocolate are made. **2** a small widely cultivated evergreen tree, *Theobroma cacao*, bearing these. [Sp. f. Nahuatl *cacauatl* (*uatl* tree)]

cachalot /káshəlot, -lōt/ *n.* a sperm whale. [F f. Sp. & Port. *cachalote*, of unkn. orig.]

cache /kash/ *n.* & *v.* ● *n.* **1** a hiding-place for treasure, provisions, ammunition, etc. **2** what is hidden in a cache. ● *v.tr.* put in a cache. [F f. *cacher* to hide]
▪ *n.* **1** hiding-place, hole, vault, repository, *colloq.* hidey-hole, stash. **2** store, hoard, supply, reserve, stock, fund, nest egg, stockpile, *Law* (treasure) trove, *colloq.* stash. ● *v.* hide, store, conceal, hoard, put *or* stow away, squirrel away, secrete, bury, *colloq.* stash (away).

cachectic /kəkéktik/ *adj.* relating to or having the symptoms of cachexia.

cachet /káshay/ *n.* **1** a distinguishing mark or seal. **2** prestige. **3** *Med.* a flat capsule enclosing a dose of unpleasant-tasting medicine. [F f. *cacher* press ult. f. L *coactare* constrain]
▪ **1** stamp, seal, sign, hallmark, (distinguishing) mark, identification (mark), tag. **2** distinction, importance, prestige, status, stature, reputation, renown, prominence, pre-eminence, superiority, merit, value, dignity, style.

cachexia /kəkéksiə/ *n.* (also **cachexy** /-kéksi/) a condition of weakness of body or mind associated with chronic disease. [F *cachexie* or LL *cachexia* f. Gk *kakhexia* f. *kakos* bad + *hexis* habit]

cachinnate /kákkinayt/ *v.intr. literary* laugh loudly. □□ **cachinnation** /-náysh'n/ *n.* **cachinnatory** /-náytəri/ *adj.* [L *cachinnare cachinnat-*]

cacholong /káshəlong/ *n.* a kind of opal. [F f. Mongolian *kashchilon* beautiful stone]

cachou /káshoo/ *n.* **1** a lozenge to sweeten the breath. **2** var. of CATECHU. [F f. Port. *cachu* f. Malay *kāchu*: cf. CATECHU]

cachucha /kəcho͞ochə/ *n.* a Spanish solo dance. [Sp.]

cacique /kəséek/ *n.* **1** a W. Indian or American Indian native chief. **2** a political boss in Spain or Latin America. [Sp., of Carib orig.]

cack-handed /kák-hándid/ *adj. colloq.* **1** awkward, clumsy. **2** left-handed. □□ **cack-handedly** *adv.* **cack-handedness** *n.* [dial. *cack* excrement]
▪ **1** see AWKWARD 2. **2** see LEFT-HANDED 1.

cackle /kákk'l/ *n.* & *v.* ● *n.* **1** a clucking sound as of a hen or a goose. **2** a loud silly laugh. **3** noisy inconsequential talk. ● *v.* **1** *intr.* emit a cackle. **2** *intr.* talk noisily and inconsequentially. **3** *tr.* utter or express with a cackle. □ **cut the cackle** *colloq.* stop talking aimlessly and come to the point. [ME prob. f. MLG, MDu. *kākelen* (imit.)]
▪ *n.* **2** see LAUGH *n.* 1. **3** see PRATTLE *n.* ● *v.* **1, 3** see SQUAWK *v.* **2** see JABBER *v.*1.

cacodemon /kákkədéemən/ *n.* (also **cacodaemon**) **1** an evil spirit. **2** a malignant person. [Gk *kakodaimōn* f. *kakos* bad + *daimōn* spirit]
▪ **1** see DEMON[1] 1a.

cacodyl /kákkədīl/ *n.* a malodorous, toxic, spontaneously flammable liquid, tetramethyldiarsine. □□ **cacodylic** /-dílik/ *adj.* [Gk *kakōdēs* stinking f. *kakos* bad]

cacoethes /kákkō-éetheez/ *n.* an urge to do something inadvisable. [L f. Gk *kakoēthes* neut. adj. f. *kakos* bad + *ēthos* disposition]
▪ see MANIA 2.

cacography /kəkógrəfi/ *n.* **1** bad handwriting. **2** bad spelling. □□ **cacographer** *n.* **cacographic** /kákkəgráffik/ *adj.* **cacographical** /kákkəgráffik'l/ *adj.* [Gk *kakos* bad, after *orthography*]

cacology /kəkólləji/ *n.* **1** bad choice of words. **2** bad pronunciation. [LL *cacologia* f. Gk *kakologia* vituperation f. *kakos* bad]

cacomistle /kákkəmis'l/ *n.* any racoon-like animal of several species of the genus *Bassariscus*, native to Central America, having a dark-ringed tail. [Amer. Sp. *cacomixtle* f. Nahuatl *tlacomiztli*]

cacophony /kəkóffəni/ *n.* (*pl.* **-ies**) **1** a harsh discordant mixture of sound. **2** dissonance; discord. □□ **cacophonous** *adj.* [F *cacophonie* f. Gk *kakophōnia* f. *kakophōnos* f. *kakos* bad + *phōnē* sound]
▪ □□ **cacophonous** see DISCORDANT 2.

cactus /káktəss/ *n.* (*pl.* **cacti** /-tī/or **cactuses**) any succulent plant of the family Cactaceae, with a thick fleshy stem, usu. spines but no leaves, and brilliantly coloured flowers. □ **cactus dahlia** any kind of dahlia with quilled petals resembling a cactus flower. □□ **cactaceous** /-táyshəss/ *adj.* [L f. Gk *kaktos* cardoon]

cacuminal /kakyo͞omin'l/ *adj. Phonet.* pronounced with the tongue-tip curled up towards the hard palate. [L *cacuminare* make pointed f. *cacumen -minis* tree-top]

CAD *abbr.* computer-aided design.

cad /kad/ *n.* a person (esp. a man) who behaves dishonourably. □□ **caddish** *adj.* **caddishly** *adv.* **caddishness** *n.* [abbr. of CADDIE in sense 'odd-job man']
▪ see ROGUE *n.* 1.

cadastral /kədástrəl/ *adj.* of or showing the extent, value, and ownership, of land for taxation. [F f. *cadastre* register of property f. Prov. *cadastro* f. It. *catast(r)o*, earlier *catastico* f. late Gk *katastikhon* list, register f. *kata stikhon* line by line]

cadaver /kədáyvər, -daávər/ *n.* esp. *Med.* a corpse. □□ **cadaveric** /-dávvərik/ *adj.* [ME f. L f. *cadere* fall]
▪ corpse, (dead) body, remains, *archaic* corse, *sl.* stiff.

cadaverous /kədávvərəss/ *adj.* **1** corpselike. **2** deathly pale. [L *cadaverosus* (as CADAVER)]

caddie /káddi/ *n.* & *v.* (also **caddy**) ● *n.* (*pl.* **-ies**) a person who assists a golfer during a match, by carrying clubs etc.

• *v.intr.* (**caddies, caddied, caddying**) act as caddie. □ **caddie car** (or **cart**) a light two-wheeled trolley for transporting golf clubs during a game. [orig. Sc. f. F CADET]

caddis-fly /káddisflī/ *n.* (*pl.* **-flies**) any small hairy-winged nocturnal insect of the order Trichoptera, living near water. [17th c.: orig. unkn.]

caddish see CAD.

caddis-worm /káddiswurm/ *n.* (also **caddis**) a larva of the caddis-fly, living in water and making protective cylindrical cases of sticks, leaves, etc., and used as fishing-bait. [as CADDIS-FLY]

caddy[1] /káddi/ *n.* (*pl.* **-ies**) a small container, esp. a box for holding tea. [earlier *catty* weight of $1^1/_3$ lb., f. Malay *kātī*]
▪ see BOX[1] *n.* 1.

caddy[2] var. of CADDIE.

cadence /káyd'nss/ *n.* **1** a fall in pitch of the voice, esp. at the end of a phrase or sentence. **2** intonation, tonal inflection. **3** *Mus.* the close of a musical phrase. **4** rhythm; the measure or beat of sound or movement. □□ **cadenced** *adj.* [ME f. OF f. It. *cadenza*, ult. f. L *cadere* fall]
▪ **2** see INTONATION 1. **4** measure, beat, rhythm, tempo, accent, pulse, metre; lilt, swing.

cadential /kədénsh'l/ *adj.* of a cadence or cadenza.

cadenza /kədénzə/ *n. Mus.* a virtuosic passage for a solo instrument or voice, usu. near the close of a movement of a concerto, sometimes improvised. [It.: see CADENCE]
▪ improvisation, bravura.

cadet /kədét/ *n.* **1** a young trainee in the armed services or police force. **2** *NZ* an apprentice in sheep-farming. **3** a younger son. □□ **cadetship** *n.* [F f. Gascon dial. *capdet*, ult. f. L *caput* head]

cadge /kaj/ *v.* **1** *tr.* get or seek by begging. **2** *intr.* beg. □□ **cadger** *n.* [19th c., earlier = ? bind, carry: orig. unkn.]
▪ see BEG 1b, c.

cadi /kaádi, káydi/ *n.* (also **kadi**) (*pl.* **-is**) a judge in a Muslim country. [Arab. *ḳāḍī* f. *ḳaḍā* to judge]

Cadmean /kadmeéən/ *adj.* = PYRRHIC[1]. [L *Cadmeus* f. Gk *Kadmeios* f. *Kadmos* Cadmus: see CADMIUM]

cadmium /kádmiəm/ *n.* a soft bluish-white metallic element occurring naturally with zinc ores, and used in the manufacture of solders and in electroplating. ¶ Symb.: **Cd.** □ **cadmium cell** *Electr.* a standard primary cell. **cadmium yellow** an intense yellow pigment containing cadmium sulphide and used in paints etc. [obs. *cadmia* calamine f. L *cadmia* f. Gk *kadm(e)ia* (*gē*) Cadmean (earth), f. *Cadmus* legendary founder of Thebes: see -IUM]

cadre /kaádər, kaádrə/ *n.* **1** a basic unit, esp. of servicemen, forming a nucleus for expansion when necessary. **2** /also káydər/ **a** a group of activists in a communist or any revolutionary party. **b** a member of such a group. [F f. It. *quadro* f. L *quadrus* square]
▪ **1** see CORPS. **2 a** see FACTION[1] 1.

caduceus /kədyoóssiəss/ *n.* (*pl.* **caducei** /-si-ī/) an Ancient Greek or Roman herald's wand, esp. as carried by the messenger-god Hermes or Mercury. [L f. Doric Gk *karuk(e)ion* f. *kērux* herald]
▪ see STAFF[1] *n.* 1a, b.

caducous /kədyoókəss/ *adj. Biol.* (of organs and parts) easily detached or shed at an early stage. □□ **caducity** /-dyoóssiti/ *n.* [L *caducus* falling f. *cadere* fall]

caecilian /seesílliən/ *n.* (also **coecilian**) any burrowing wormlike amphibian of the order Gymnophiona, having poorly developed eyes and no limbs. [L *caecilia* kind of lizard]

caecitis /sikítiss/ *n.* (*US* **cecitis**) inflammation of the caecum.

caecum /seékəm/ *n.* (*US* **cecum**) (*pl.* **-ca** /-kə/) a blind-ended pouch at the junction of the small and large intestines. □□ **caecal** *adj.* [L for *intestinum caecum* f. *caecus* blind, transl. of Gk *tuphlon enteron*]

Caenozoic var. of CENOZOIC.

Caerns. *abbr.* Caernarvonshire (a former county in Wales).

Caerphilly /kairfílli, kər-/ *n.* a kind of mild white cheese orig. made in Caerphilly in Wales.

Caesar /seézər/ *n.* **1** the title of the Roman emperors, esp. from Augustus to Hadrian. **2** an autocrat. **3** *Med. sl.* a Caesarean section; a case of this. □ **Caesar's wife** a person required to be above suspicion. [L, family name of Gaius Julius *Caesar*, Roman statesman d. 44 BC]

Caesarean /sizáiriən/ *adj.* & *n.* (also **Caesarian,** *US* **Ces-**) • *adj.* **1** of Caesar or the Caesars. **2** (of a birth) effected by Caesarean section. • *n.* a Caesarean section. □ **Caesarean section** an operation for delivering a child by cutting through the wall of the abdomen (Julius Caesar supposedly having been born this way). [L *Caesarianus*]

caesious /seéziəss/ *adj. Bot.* bluish or lavender. [L *caesius*]

caesium /seéziəm/ *n.* (*US* **cesium**) a soft silver-white element of the alkali metal group, occurring naturally in a number of minerals, and used in photoelectric cells. ¶ Symb.: **Cs.** □ **caesium clock** an atomic clock that uses caesium. [as CAESIOUS (from its spectrum lines)]

caesura /sizyoórə/ *n.* (*pl.* **caesuras**) *Prosody* **1** (in Greek and Latin verse) a break between words within a metrical foot. **2** (in modern verse) a pause near the middle of a line. □□ **caesural** *adj.* [L f. *caedere caes-* cut]
▪ see PAUSE *n.*

CAF *abbr. US* cost and freight.

cafard /kaafaár/ *n.* melancholia. [F, = cockroach, hypocrite]

café /káffay, káffi/ *n.* (also **cafe** /also *joc.* kaf, kayf/) **1** a small coffee-house or teashop; a simple restaurant. **2** *US* a bar. □ ***café au lait*** /ō láy/ **1** coffee with milk. **2** the colour of this. ***café noir*** /nwaar/ black coffee. **café society** the regular patrons of fashionable restaurants and nightclubs. [F, = coffee, coffee-house]
▪ **1** coffee-house, coffee bar, coffee-shop, bistro, snack bar, brasserie; tearoom, lunch-room, restaurant, eating-house, canteen, cafeteria, *esp. Brit.* teashop, *Brit.* pull-in, *US* diner, *US colloq.* eatery, *Brit. sl.* caff. **2** see BAR[1] *n.* 4b, c.

cafeteria /káffiteériə/ *n.* a restaurant in which customers collect their meals on trays at a counter and usu. pay before sitting down to eat. [Amer. Sp. *cafetería* coffee-shop]

caff /kaf/ *n. Brit. sl.* = CAFÉ. [abbr.]

caffeine /káffeen/ *n.* an alkaloid drug with stimulant action found in tea leaves and coffee beans. [F *caféine* f. *café* coffee]

caftan /káftan/ *n.* (also **kaftan**) **1** a long usu. belted tunic worn by men in countries of the Near East. **2 a** a woman's long loose dress. **b** a loose shirt or top. [Turk. *ḳafṭān*, partly through F *cafetan*]
▪ see SHIFT *n.* 4a.

cage /kayj/ *n.* & *v.* • *n.* **1** a structure of bars or wires, esp. for confining animals or birds. **2** any similar open framework, esp. an enclosed platform or lift in a mine or the compartment for passengers in a lift. **3** *colloq.* a camp for prisoners of war. • *v.tr.* place or keep in a cage. □ **cage-bird** a bird of the kind customarily kept in a cage. [ME f. OF f. L *cavea*]
▪ *n.* **1** crate, enclosure, pen, pound, coop, hutch. • *v.* cage up *or* in, confine, enclose, pen, impound, shut up *or* in, coop (up), lock up *or* in, fence in, close in, imprison; hem in.

cagey /káyji/ *adj.* (also **cagy**) (**cagier, cagiest**) *colloq.* cautious and uncommunicative; wary. □□ **cagily** *adv.* **caginess** *n.* (also **cageyness**). [20th-c. US: orig. unkn.]
▪ see WARY.

cagoule /kəgoól/ *n.* a hooded thin windproof garment worn in mountaineering etc. [F]

cahoots /kəhoóts/ *n.pl.* □ **in cahoots** (often foll. by *with*) *sl.* in collusion. [19th c.: orig. uncert.]
▪ □ **in cahoots** see *in league* (LEAGUE[1]).

CAI *abbr.* computer-assisted (or -aided) instruction.

caiman var. of CAYMAN.

Cain /kayn/ *n.* □ **raise Cain** *colloq.* make a disturbance; create trouble. [*Cain*, eldest son of Adam (Gen. 4)]

Cainozoic var. of CENOZOIC.

caique /kī-éek/ *n.* **1** a light rowing-boat on the Bosporus. **2** a Levantine sailing-ship. [F f. It. *caicco* f. Turk. *kayik*]

cairn /kairn/ *n.* **1** a mound of rough stones as a monument or landmark. **2** (in full **cairn terrier**) **a** a small terrier of a breed with short legs, a longish body, and a shaggy coat (perhaps so called from its being used to hunt among cairns). **b** this breed. [Gael. *carn*]
■ **1** see LANDMARK 1.

cairngorm /káirngorm/ *n.* a yellow or wine-coloured semi-precious form of quartz. [found on *Cairngorm*, a mountain in Scotland f. Gael. *carn gorm* blue cairn]

caisson /káys'n, kəsóon/ *n.* **1** a watertight chamber in which underwater construction work can be done. **2** a floating vessel used as a floodgate in docks. **3** an ammunition chest or wagon. □ **caisson disease** = *decompression sickness.* [F (f. It. *cassone*) assim. to *caisse* CASE[2]]

caitiff /káytif/ *n.* & *adj. poet.* or *archaic* ● *n.* a base or despicable person; a coward. ● *adj.* base, despicable, cowardly. [ME f. OF *caitif*, *chaitif* ult. f. L *captivus* CAPTIVE]
■ *n.* see WRETCH 2. ● *adj.* see BASE[2] 1.

cajole /kəjṓl/ *v.tr.* (often foll. by *into*, *out of*) persuade by flattery, deceit, etc. □□ **cajolement** *n.* **cajoler** *n.* **cajolery** *n.* [F *cajoler*]
■ wheedle, coax, beguile, seduce, inveigle, persuade, entice, bring round, *colloq.* soft-soap, jolly (along), cosy (along), butter (up), sweet-talk, smooth-talk; (*cajole into*) talk into; (*cajole out of*) talk out of. □□ **cajolery** wheedling, coaxing, blandishment, beguilement, persuasion, seduction, palaver, inveiglement, blarney, *colloq.* soft soap, buttering-up, sweet talk.

cake /kayk/ *n.* & *v.* ● *n.* **1 a** a mixture of flour, butter, eggs, sugar, etc., baked in the oven. **b** a quantity of this baked in a flat round or ornamental shape and often iced and decorated. **2 a** other food in a flat round shape (*fish cake*). **b** = *cattle-cake.* **3** a flattish compact mass (*a cake of soap*). **4** *Sc.* & *N.Engl.* thin oaten bread. ● *v.* **1** *tr.* & *intr.* form into a compact mass. **2** *tr.* (usu. foll. by *with*) cover (with a hard or sticky mass) (*boots caked with mud*). □ **cakes and ale** merrymaking. **have one's cake and eat it** *colloq.* enjoy both of two mutually exclusive alternatives. **like hot cakes** rapidly or successfully. **a piece of cake** *colloq.* something easily achieved. **a slice of the cake** participation in benefits. [ME f. ON *kaka*]
■ *n.* **1** pastry, bun, gateau. **2 a** burger, pat, *US* patty. **3** piece, chunk, bar, block, cube, lump, loaf, slab, hunk. ● *v.* **1** harden, solidify, thicken, congeal, dry, coagulate, set. **2** encrust, coat, cover, layer. □ **cakes and ale** see *revelry* (REVEL). **have one's cake and eat it** get the best of both worlds. **like hot cakes** see *quickly* (QUICK). **piece of cake** see BREEZE[1] *n.* 5. **slice of the cake** see SHARE[1] *n.*

cakewalk /káykwawk/ *n.* **1** a dance developed from an American Black contest in graceful walking with a cake as a prize. **2** *colloq.* an easy task. **3** a form of fairground entertainment consisting of a promenade moved by machinery.

CAL *abbr.* computer-assisted learning.

Cal *abbr.* large calorie(s).

Cal. *abbr.* California.

cal *abbr.* small calorie(s).

Calabar bean /kálləbaar/ *n.* a poisonous seed of the tropical African climbing plant *Physostigma venosum*, yielding a medicinal extract. [*Calabar* in Nigeria]

calabash /kálləbash/ *n.* **1 a** an evergreen tree, *Crescentia cujete*, native to tropical America, bearing fruit in the form of large gourds. **b** a gourd from this tree. **2** the shell of this or a similar gourd used as a vessel for water, to make a tobacco pipe, etc. [F *calebasse* f. Sp. *calabaza* perh. f. Pers. *karbuz* melon]

calaboose /kálləbóoss/ *n. US* a prison. [Black F *calabouse* f. Sp. *calabozo* dungeon]
■ see PRISON *n.* 1.

calabrese /kálləbréez, kálləbráysay/ *n.* a large succulent variety of sprouting broccoli. [It., = Calabrian]

calamanco /kálləmángkō/ *n.* (*pl.* **-oes**) *hist.* a glossy woollen cloth chequered on one side. [16th c.: orig. unkn.]

calamander /kálləmandər/ *n.* a fine-grained red-brown ebony streaked with black, from the Asian tree *Diospyros qualsita*, used in furniture. [19th c.: orig. unkn.: perh. conn. with Sinh. word for the tree *kalu-madīriya*]

calamary /kálləməri/ *n.* (*pl.* **-ies**) any cephalopod mollusc with a long tapering penlike horny internal shell, esp. a squid of the genus *Loligo*. [med.L *calamarium* pen-case f. L *calamus* pen]

calamine /kálləmīn/ *n.* **1** a pink powder consisting of zinc carbonate and ferric oxide used as a lotion or ointment. **2** a zinc mineral usu. zinc carbonate. [ME f. F f. med.L *calamina* alt. f. L *cadmia*: see CADMIUM]

calamint /kálləmint/ *n.* any aromatic herb or shrub of the genus *Calamintha*, esp. *C. officinalis* with purple or lilac flowers. [ME f. OF *calament* f. med.L *calamentum* f. LL *calaminthe* f. Gk *kalaminthē*]

calamity /kəlámmiti/ *n.* (*pl.* **-ies**) **1** a disaster, a great misfortune. **2 a** adversity. **b** deep distress. □ **Calamity Jane** a prophet of disaster. □□ **calamitous** *adj.* **calamitously** *adv.* [ME f. F *calamité* f. L *calamitas -tatis*]
■ **1** disaster, catastrophe, cataclysm, devastation, tragedy, blight, crisis, misfortune, reverse, accident, misadventure, mischance, mishap. **2** distress, affliction, trouble, tragedy, misfortune, adversity, hardship, misery, grief, suffering, unhappiness, ruin, ruination, desolation, despair, wretchedness, gloom, *archaic or literary* woe. □□ **calamitous** disastrous, cataclysmic, catastrophic, distressful, dire, tragic, troublesome, woeful, sad, grievous, destructive, ruinous, unfortunate, awful, dreadful, terrible, devastating, desperate, pernicious.

calando /kalándō/ *adv. Mus.* gradually decreasing in speed and volume. [It., = slackening]

calash /kəlásh/ *n. hist.* **1 a** a light low-wheeled carriage with a removable folding hood. **b** the folding hood itself. **2** *Can.* a two-wheeled horse-drawn vehicle. **3** a woman's hooped silk hood. [F *calèche* f. G *Kalesche* f. Pol. *kolaska* or Czech *kolesa*]

calc- /kalk/ *comb. form* lime or calcium. [G *Kalk* f. L CALX]

calcaneus /kalkáyniəss/ *n.* (also **calcaneum** /-niəm/) (*pl.* **calcanei** /-ni-ī/ or **calcanea** /-niə/) the bone forming the heel. [L]

calcareous /kalkáiriəss/ *adj.* (also **calcarious**) of or containing calcium carbonate; chalky. [L *calcarius* (as CALX)]

calceolaria /kálsiəláiriə/ *n. Bot.* any plant of the genus *Calceolaria*, native to S. America, with slipper-shaped flowers. [mod.L f. L *calceolus* dimin. of *calceus* shoe + *-aria* fem. = -ARY[1]]

calceolate /kálsiəlayt/ *adj. Bot.* slipper-shaped.

calces *pl.* of CALX.

calciferol /kalsíffərol/ *n.* one of the D vitamins, routinely added to dairy products, essential for the deposition of calcium in bones. Also called ERGOCALCIFEROL, *vitamin* D_2. [CALCIFEROUS + -OL[1]]

calciferous /kalsíffərəss/ *adj.* yielding calcium salts, esp. calcium carbonate. [L CALX lime + -FEROUS]

calcify /kálsifī/ *v.tr.* & *intr.* (**-ies, -ied**) **1** harden or become hardened by deposition of calcium salts; petrify. **2** convert or be converted to calcium carbonate. □□ **calcific** /-síffik/ *adj.* **calcification** /-fikáysh'n/ *n.*

calcine /kálsin, -sīn/ *v.* **1** *tr.* **a** reduce, oxidize, or desiccate by strong heat. **b** burn to ashes; consume by fire; roast. **c** reduce to calcium oxide by roasting or burning. **2** *tr.* consume or purify as if by fire. **3** *intr.* undergo any of these. □□ **calcination** /-náysh'n/ *n.* [ME f. OF *calciner* or med.L *calcinare* f. LL *calcina* lime f. L CALX]

calcite /kálsīt/ *n.* natural crystalline calcium carbonate. [G *Calcit* f. L CALX lime]

calcium /kálsiəm/ *n.* a soft grey metallic element of the alkaline earth group occurring naturally in limestone, marble, chalk, etc., that is important in industry and essential for normal growth in living organisms. ¶ Symb.: **Ca.** □ **calcium carbide** a greyish solid used in the production of acetylene. **calcium carbonate** a white insoluble solid occurring naturally as chalk, limestone, marble, and calcite, and used in the manufacture of lime and cement. **calcium hydroxide** a white crystalline powder used in the manufacture of plaster and cement; slaked lime. **calcium oxide** a white crystalline solid from which many calcium compounds are manufactured: also called QUICKLIME, CALX. **calcium phosphate** the main constituent of animal bones and used as bone ash fertilizer. **calcium sulphate** a white crystalline solid occurring as anhydrite and gypsum. [L CALX lime + -IUM]

calcrete /kálkreet/ *n. Geol.* a conglomerate formed by the cementation of sand and gravel with calcium carbonate. [L *calc* lime + con*crete*]

calcspar /kálkspaar/ *n.* = CALCITE. [CALC- + SPAR³]

calculable /kálkyooləb'l/ *adj.* able to be calculated or estimated. □□ **calculability** /-bílliti/ *n.* **calculably** *adv.*

calculate /kálkyoolayt/ *v.* **1** *tr.* ascertain or determine beforehand, esp. by mathematics or by reckoning. **2** *tr.* plan deliberately. **3** *intr.* (foll. by *on, upon*) rely on; make an essential part of one's reckoning (*calculated on a quick response*). **4** *tr. US colloq.* suppose, believe. □□ **calculative** /-lətiv/ *adj.* [LL *calculare* (as CALCULUS)]
■ **1** compute, work out, determine, ascertain, reckon, assess, evaluate, figure (out), measure, estimate, gauge, calibrate. **3** (*calculate on* or *upon*) see RECKON 6, RELY.

calculated /kálkyoolaytid/ *adj.* **1** (of an action) done with awareness of the likely consequences. **2** (foll. by *to* + infin.) designed or suitable; intended. □□ **calculatedly** *adv.*
■ **2** arranged, intended, designed, planned, prepared, adjusted, adapted, fit, fitted, suited, suitable; deliberate, purposeful, purposive, intentional, premeditated; studied, well-thought-out, conscious.

calculating /kálkyoolayting/ *adj.* (of a person) shrewd, scheming. □□ **calculatingly** *adv.*
■ shrewd, conniving, crafty, sly, wily, scheming, designing, machiavellian, manipulative, canny, cunning, artful, astute.

calculation /kálkyooláysh'n/ *n.* **1** the act or process of calculating. **2** a result got by calculating. **3** a reckoning or forecast. [ME f. OF f. LL *calculatio* (as CALCULATE)]
■ **1** computation, reckoning, estimation, determining, measurement. **2** answer, product, result, figure, count, tally, estimate, amount. **3** estimate, forecast, projection, expectation, prediction.

calculator /kálkyoolaytər/ *n.* **1** a device (esp. a small electronic one) used for making mathematical calculations. **2** a person or thing that calculates. **3** a set of tables used in calculation. [ME f. L (as CALCULATE)]
■ **1** computer, adding machine; abacus.

calculus /kálkyooləss/ *n.* (*pl.* **calculuses** or **calculi** /-lī/) **1** *Math.* **a** a particular method of calculation or reasoning (*calculus of probabilities*). **b** the infinitesimal calculuses of integration or differentiation (see *integral calculus, differential calculus*). **2** *Med.* a stone or concretion of minerals formed within the body. □□ **calculous** *adj.* (in sense 2). [L, = small stone used in reckoning on an abacus]

caldera /kaaldáirə/ *n.* a large volcanic depression. [Sp. f. LL *caldaria* boiling-pot]

caldron var. of CAULDRON.

Caledonian /kállidṓniən/ *adj.* & *n.* ● *adj.* **1** of or relating to Scotland. **2** *Geol.* of a mountain-forming period in Europe in the Palaeozoic era. ● *n.* a Scotsman. [L *Caledonia* northern Britain]

calefacient /kállifáysh'nt/ *n.* & *adj. Med.* ● *n.* a substance producing or causing a sensation of warmth. ● *adj.* of this substance. [L *calefacere* f. *calēre* be warm + *facere* make]

calendar /kállindər/ *n.* & *v.* ● *n.* **1** a system by which the beginning, length, and subdivisions of the year are fixed. **2** a chart or series of pages showing the days, weeks, and months of a particular year, or giving special seasonal information. **3** a timetable or programme of appointments, special events, etc. ● *v.tr.* register or enter in a calendar or timetable etc. □ **calendar month** (or **year**) see MONTH, YEAR. □□ **calendric** /-léndrik/ *adj.* **calendrical** /-léndrik'l/ *adj.* [ME f. AF *calender*, OF *calendier* f. L *calendarium* account-book (as CALENDS)]
■ *n.* **2** almanac, chronicle, annal(s), yearbook; appointment book, journal, diary, *US law* docket. **3** schedule, timetable, programme, register, diary, listing.

calender /kállindər/ *n.* & *v.* ● *n.* a machine in which cloth, paper, etc., is pressed by rollers to glaze or smooth it. ● *v.tr.* press in a calender. [F *calendre(r)*, of unkn. orig.]
■ *n.* see ROLLER 1a. ● *v.* see SMOOTH *v.* 1.

calends /kállendz/ *n.pl.* (also **kalends**) the first of the month in the ancient Roman calendar. [ME f. OF *calendes* f. L *kalendae*]

calendula /kəléndyoolə/ *n.* any plant of the genus *Calendula*, with large yellow or orange flowers, e.g. marigold. [mod.L dimin. of *calendae* (as CALENDS), perh. = little clock]

calenture /kállenchər/ *n. hist.* a tropical delirium of sailors, who think the sea is green fields. [F f. Sp. *calentura* fever f. *calentar* be hot ult. f. L *calēre* be warm]

calf¹ /kaaf/ *n.* (*pl.* **calves** /kaavz/) **1** a young bovine animal, used esp. of domestic cattle. **2** the young of other animals, e.g. elephant, deer, and whale. **3** *Naut.* a floating piece of ice detached from an iceberg. □ **calf-love** romantic attachment or affection between adolescents. **in** (or **with**) **calf** (of a cow) pregnant. □□ **calfhood** *n.* **calfish** *adj.* **calflike** *adj.* [OE *cælf* f. WG]

calf² /kaaf/ *n.* (*pl.* **calves** /kaavz/) the fleshy hind part of the human leg below the knee. □□ **-calved** /kaavd/ *adj.* (in *comb.*). [ME f. ON *kálfi*, of unkn. orig.]

calfskin /ka̋afskin/ *n.* calf-leather, esp. in bookbinding and shoemaking.

calibrate /kállibrayt/ *v.tr.* **1** mark (a gauge) with a standard scale of readings. **2** correlate the readings of (an instrument) with a standard. **3** determine the calibre of (a gun). **4** determine the correct capacity or value of. □□ **calibration** /-bráysh'n/ *n.* **calibrator** *n.* [CALIBRE + -ATE³]
■ **1, 2** adjust, tune (up), regulate, attune, align, set; graduate, mark, scale, grade; standardize. **4** see CALCULATE 1.

calibre /kállibər/ *n.* (*US* **caliber**) **1 a** the internal diameter of a gun or tube. **b** the diameter of a bullet or shell. **2** strength or quality of character; ability, importance (*we need someone of your calibre*). □□ **calibred** *adj.* (also in *comb.*). [F *calibre* or It. *calibro*, f. Arab. *ḳālib* mould]
■ **1** diameter, size, bore, gauge, width, breadth. **2** merit, ability, talent, capability, competence, proficiency, capacity, quality, strength, stature, importance.

caliche /kəle̋echi/ *n.* **1** a mineral deposit of gravel, sand, and nitrates, esp. Chile saltpetre, found in dry areas of America. **2** = CALCRETE. [Amer. Sp.]

calico /kállikō/ *n.* & *adj.* ● *n.* (*pl.* **-oes** or *US* **-os**) **1** a cotton cloth, esp. plain white or unbleached. **2** *US* a printed cotton fabric. ● *adj.* **1** made of calico. **2** *US* multicoloured, piebald. [earlier *calicut* f. *Calicut* in India]

Calif. *abbr.* California.

californium /kállifórniəm/ *n. Chem.* a transuranic radioactive metallic element produced artificially from curium. ¶ Symb.: **Cf.** [*California* (where it was first made) + -IUM]

caliper var. of CALLIPER.

caliph /káylif, kál-/ *n.* esp. *hist.* the chief Muslim civil and religious ruler, regarded as the successor of Muhammad. □□ **caliphate** *n.* [ME f. OF *caliphe* f. Arab. *Ḳalīfa* successor]

calisthenics var. of CALLISTHENICS.

calk *US* var. of CAULK.

call /kawl/ *v.* & *n.* ● *v.* **1** *intr.* **a** (often foll. by *out*) cry, shout; speak loudly. **b** (of a bird or animal) emit its characteristic note or cry. **2** *tr.* communicate or converse with by telephone or radio. **3** *tr.* **a** bring to one's presence by calling; summon (*will you call the children?*). **b** arrange for (a person or thing) to come or be present (*called a taxi*). **4** *intr.* (often foll. by *at, in, on*) pay a brief visit (*called at the house*; *called in to see you*; *come and call on me*). **5** *tr.* **a** order to take place; fix a time for (*called a meeting*). **b** direct to happen; announce (*call a halt*). **6** **a** *intr.* require one's attention or consideration (*duty calls*). **b** *tr.* urge, invite, nominate (*call to the bar*). **7** *tr.* name; describe as (*call her Della*). **8** *tr.* consider; regard or estimate as (*I call that silly*). **9** *tr.* rouse from sleep (*call me at 8*). **10** *intr.* guess the outcome of tossing a coin etc. **11** *intr.* (foll. by *for*) order, require, demand (*called for silence*). **12** *tr.* (foll. by *over*) read out (a list of names to determine those present). **13** *intr.* (foll. by *on, upon*) invoke; appeal to; request or require (*called on us to be quiet*). **14** *tr. Cricket* (of an umpire) disallow a ball from (a bowler). **15** *tr. Cards* specify (a suit or contract) in bidding. **16** *tr. Sc.* drive (an animal, vehicle, etc.). ● *n.* **1** a shout or cry; an act of calling. **2** **a** the characteristic cry of a bird or animal. **b** an imitation of this. **c** an instrument for imitating it. **3** a brief visit (*paid them a call*). **4** **a** an act of telephoning. **b** a telephone conversation. **5** **a** an invitation or summons to appear or be present. **b** an appeal or invitation (from a specific source or discerned by a person's conscience etc.) to follow a certain profession, set of principles, etc. **6** (foll. by *for*, or *to* + infin.) a duty, need, or occasion (*no call to be rude*; *no call for violence*). **7** (foll. by *for, on*) a demand (*not much call for it these days*; *a call on one's time*). **8** a signal on a bugle etc.; a signalling-whistle. **9** *Stock Exch.* an option of buying stock at a fixed price at a given date. **10** *Cards* **a** a player's right or turn to make a bid. **b** a bid made. □ **at call** = *on call*. **call away** divert, distract. **call-box** a public telephone box or kiosk. **call-boy** a theatre attendant who summons actors when needed on stage. **call down** **1** invoke. **2** reprimand. **call forth** elicit. **call-girl** a prostitute who accepts appointments by telephone. **call in** *tr.* **1** withdraw from circulation. **2** seek the advice or services of. **calling-card** *US* = *visiting-card*. **call in** (or **into**) **question** dispute; doubt the validity of. **call into play** give scope for; make use of. **call a person names** abuse a person verbally. **call off** **1** cancel (an arrangement etc.). **2** order (an attacker or pursuer) to desist. **call of nature** a need to urinate or defecate. **call out** **1** summon (troops etc.) to action. **2** order (workers) to strike. **call-over** **1** a roll-call. **2** reading aloud of a list of betting prices. **call the shots** (or **tune**) be in control; take the initiative. **call-sign** (or **-signal**) a broadcast signal identifying the radio transmitter used. **call to account** see ACCOUNT. **call to mind** recollect; cause one to remember. **call to order** **1** request to be orderly. **2** declare (a meeting) open. **call up** **1** reach by telephone. **2** imagine, recollect. **3** summon, esp. to serve in the army. **call-up** *n.* the act or process of calling up (sense 3). **on call** **1** (of a doctor etc.) available if required but not formally on duty. **2** (of money lent) repayable on demand. **within call** near enough to be summoned by calling. [OE *ceallian* f. ON *kalla*]

■ *v.* **1** **a** shout, cry (out), hail, yell, roar, bellow, call out, bawl, howl, *US colloq.* holler. **2** call up, telephone, dial, *Brit.* ring (up), *colloq.* buzz, phone, give a person a bell *or* ring, *Brit. colloq.* give a person a tinkle; radio. **3** **a** summon, collect, muster, rally, assemble, convene, *formal* convoke; page, send for *or* after. **4** call in *or* by, visit, attend, pay a visit, look in, stop in *or* by, pop in *or* by, come by, *colloq.* drop in *or* by. **5** **a** see ARRANGE 2, 3. **b** see ORDER *v.* 1, 2, 5, 6. **6** **a** beckon, summon. **7** name, designate, denominate, term, style, nickname, label, title, tag, identify, dub, christen, baptize, *archaic* entitle; (*be called*) answer to the name of. **8** see CONSIDER 6. **9** awake, awaken, wake up, rouse, get up, *Brit.* knock up. **11** (*call for*) see DEMAND *v.* 1. **13** (*call on*) invoke, appeal to, request, entreat, ask. **16** drive, herd, shepherd, *US* ride, herd on. ● *n.* **1** shout, cry, yell, hail, whoop, *US colloq.* holler. **2** song, cry. **3** visit. **4** telephone call, phone call, *colloq.* ring, bell, *Brit. colloq.* tinkle, *sl.* buzz. **5** summons, bidding, notice, notification, order, demand, command, dictate, instruction, requisition, *archaic* hest, *literary* behest; invitation; request, appeal, entreaty, plea, petition; subpoena; vocation, calling. **6** reason, justification, case, pretext, ground(s), cause, motive, need, occasion, right, excuse; requirement; duty, responsibility. **7** see DEMAND *n.* 2. □ **call away** see DISTRACT 1. **call down** **1** invoke, summon (up), call forth, conjure up, muster. **2** see BERATE. **call forth** summon (up), invoke, draw on *or* upon, evoke, conjure up, muster, call down; elicit, bring *or* draw forth, bring *or* draw out, attract; excite, inspire, incite, occasion, bring about. **call-girl** see PROSTITUTE *n.* 1a. **call in** (or **into**) **question** see CHALLENGE *v.* 2. **call into play** see USE *v.* 1a. **call a person names** see ABUSE *v.* 2. **call off** **1** cancel; see also POSTPONE. **call the shots** (or **tune**) be in charge *or* command *or* control, rule the roost, be in the driver's seat, be in the saddle, be at the wheel, pull the strings, take the initiative, run *or* direct *or* manage *or* administer *or* control things, *colloq.* run the show. **call to mind** see RECALL *v.* 2, REMIND *v.* 1. **call up** **1** see CALL *v.* 2 above. **2** see IMAGINE 1, *call forth* above. **3** summon, enlist, recruit, conscript, *US* draft. **call-up** enlistment, conscription, recruitment, *US* induction, draft, *Brit. hist.* national service, *US hist.* selective service. **on call** **1** ready, on duty, standing by, on stand-by, awaiting orders. **within call** within earshot *or* hearing *or* (easy) reach; nearby, close by, close at hand, in the vicinity, about, around.

calla /kállə/ *n.* **1** (in full **calla lily**) = *arum lily*. **2** an aquatic plant, *Calla palustris*. [mod.L]

caller /káwlər/ *n.* **1** a person who calls, esp. one who pays a visit or makes a telephone call. **2** *Austral.* a racing commentator.

■ **1** see VISITOR.

calligraphy /kəlígrəfi/ *n.* **1** handwriting, esp. when fine or pleasing. **2** the art of handwriting. □□ **calligrapher** *n.* **calligraphic** /kálligráffik/ *adj.* **calligraphist** *n.* [Gk *kalligraphia* f. *kallos* beauty]

■ see WRITING 2.

calling /káwling/ *n.* **1** a profession or occupation. **2** an inwardly felt call or summons; a vocation.

■ **1** profession, occupation, business, trade, employment, work, line, job, *métier*, pursuit, career, craft, area, province, (area of) expertise, speciality, *colloq.* racket. **2** vocation, mission, purpose, call, summons.

calliope /kəlíəpi/ *n. US* a keyboard instrument resembling an organ, with a set of steam whistles producing musical notes. [Gk *Kalliopē* muse of epic poetry (lit. 'beautiful-voiced')]

■ steam organ.

calliper /kállipər/ *n.* & *v.* (also **caliper**) ● *n.* **1** (in *pl.*) (also **calliper compasses**) compasses with bowed legs for measuring the diameter of convex bodies, or with out-turned points for measuring internal dimensions. **2** (in full **calliper splint**) a metal splint to support the leg. ● *v.tr.* measure with callipers. [app. var. of CALIBRE]

callisthenics /kálliss-thénniks/ *n.pl.* (also **calisthenics**) gymnastic exercises to achieve bodily fitness and grace of movement. □□ **callisthenic** *adj.* [Gk *kallos* beauty + *sthenos* strength]

■ see EXERCISE *n.* 3.

callop /kálləp/ *n. Austral.* a gold-coloured freshwater fish, *Plectroplites ambiguus*, used as food. Also called *golden perch*. [Aboriginal]

callosity /kəlóssiti/ *n.* (*pl.* **-ies**) a hard thick area of skin usu. occurring in parts of the body subject to pressure or friction. [F *callosité* or L *callositas* (as CALLOUS)]

callous /kálləss/ *adj.* & *n.* ● *adj.* **1** unfeeling, insensitive. **2** (of skin) hardened or hard. ● *n.* = CALLUS 1. □□ **callously** *adv.* (in sense 1 of *adj.*). **callousness** *n.* [ME f. L *callosus* (as CALLUS) or F *calleux*]

■ *adj.* **1** thick-skinned, unfeeling, uncaring, insensitive, hard, hard-hearted, cold, cold-hearted, stony-hearted, heartless, cruel, ruthless, indifferent, unsympathetic, *colloq.* hard-nosed, hardbitten. **2** hard, hardened, tough, leathery.

callow /kállō/ *adj.* inexperienced, immature. □□ **callowly** *adv.* **callowness** *n.* [OE *calu*]
■ inexperienced, immature, juvenile, young, naïve, green, fresh, new, tender, guileless, unsophisticated, innocent, raw, unfledged, untried, (still) wet behind the ears.

calluna /kəlōōnə/ *n.* any common heather of the genus *Calluna*, native to Europe and N. Africa. [mod.L f. Gk *kallunō* beautify f. *kallos* beauty]

callus /kálləs/ *n.* **1** a hard thick area of skin or tissue. **2** a hard tissue formed round bone ends after a fracture. **3** *Bot.* a new protective tissue formed over a wound. [L]

calm /kaam/ *adj.*, *n.*, & *v.* ● *adj.* **1** tranquil, quiet, windless (*a calm sea; a calm night*). **2** (of a person or disposition) settled; not agitated (*remained calm throughout the ordeal*). **3** self-assured, confident (*his calm assumption that we would wait*). ● *n.* **1** a state of being calm; stillness, serenity. **2** a period without wind or storm. ● *v.tr.* & *intr.* (often foll. by *down*) make or become calm. □□ **calmly** *adv.* **calmness** *n.* [ME ult. f. LL *cauma* f. Gk *kauma* heat]
■ *adj.* **1** quiet, still, tranquil, serene, peaceful, balmy, halcyon, undisturbed, windless, placid, pacific; motionless, smooth, even. **2** composed, cool, controlled, cool-headed, level-headed, self-controlled, impassive, dispassionate, unimpassioned, unmoved, nonchalant, unexcited, unexcitable, unruffled, unbothered, unhurried, settled, equable, collected, serene, quiet, tranquil, sedate, stoical, *colloq.* laid-back, together. **3** see CONFIDENT *adj.* 1. ● *n.* **1** calmness, quiet, tranquillity, quietness, serenity, peacefulness, composure, placidity, placidness, sang-froid, coolness, self-control, equanimity, self-possession; stillness, motionlessness. **2** hush, peace; see also LULL *n.* ● *v.* quiet, still, soothe, hush, lull, pacify, quell; mollify, appease, placate, *Austral.* square off, *Brit.* quieten (down); relax, take it easy, cool off *or* down, wind down, *colloq.* unwind; subside, abate, moderate, let up, ease up, die down, slacken (off), diminish, lessen.

calmative /kálmətiv, ka'am-/ *adj.* & *n. Med.* ● *adj.* tending to calm or sedate. ● *n.* a calmative drug etc.
■ *adj.* see SEDATIVE *adj.* ● *n.* see SEDATIVE *n.*

calomel /káləmel/ *n.* a compound of mercury, esp. when used medicinally as a cathartic. [mod.L perh. f. Gk *kalos* beautiful + *melas* black]

Calor gas /kállər/ *n. propr.* liquefied butane gas stored under pressure in containers for domestic use and used as a substitute for mains gas. [L *calor* heat]

caloric /kállərik/ *adj.* & *n.* ● *adj.* of heat or calories. ● *n. hist.* a supposed material form or cause of heat. [F *calorique* f. L *calor* heat]

calorie /kálləri/ *n.* (also **calory**) (*pl.* **-ies**) a unit of quantity of heat: **1** (in full **small calorie**) the amount needed to raise the temperature of 1 gram of water through 1 °C. ¶ Abbr.: **cal. 2** (in full **large calorie**) the amount needed to raise the temperature of 1 kilogram of water through 1 °C, often used to measure the energy value of foods. ¶ Abbr.: **Cal.** [F, arbitr. f. L *calor* heat + *-ie*]

calorific /kállərífik/ *adj.* producing heat. □ **calorific value** the amount of heat produced by a specified quantity of fuel, food, etc. □□ **calorifically** *adv.* [L *calorificus* f. *calor* heat]

calorimeter /kállərímmitər/ *n.* any of various instruments for measuring quantity of heat, esp. to find calorific values. □□ **calorimetric** /-métrik/ *adj.* **calorimetry** *n.* [L *calor* heat + -METER]

calory var. of CALORIE.

calque /kalk/ *n. Philol.* = *loan-translation.* [F, = copy, tracing f. *calquer* trace ult. f. L *calcare* tread]

caltrop /káltrəp/ *n.* (also **caltrap**) **1** *hist.* a four-spiked iron ball thrown on the ground to impede cavalry horses. **2** *Heraldry* a representation of this. **3** any creeping plant of the genus *Tribulus*, with woody carpels usu. having hard spines. [(sense 3) OE *calcatrippe* f. med.L *calcatrippa*: (senses 1–2) ME f. OF *chauchetrape* f. *chauchier* tread, *trappe* trap: ult. the same word]

calumet /kályoomet/ *n.* a N. American Indian peace-pipe. [F, ult. f. L *calamus* reed]

calumniate /kəlúmniayt/ *v.tr.* slander. □□ **calumniation** /-áysh'n/ *n.* **calumniator** *n.* **calumniatory** *adj.* [L *calumniari*]
■ see SLANDER *v.*

calumny /kálləmni/ *n.* & *v.* ● *n.* (*pl.* **-ies**) **1** slander; malicious representation. **2** an instance of this. ● *v.tr.* (**-ies, -ied**) slander. □□ **calumnious** *adj.* [L *calumnia*]
■ *n.* see SLANDER *n.* ● *v.* see SLANDER *v.* □□ **calumnious** see *slanderous* (SLANDER).

calvados /kálvədoss/ *n.* an apple brandy. [*Calvados* in France]

Calvary /kálvəri/ *n.* the place where Christ was crucified. [ME f. LL *calvaria* skull, transl. Gk *golgotha*, Aram. *gûlgûltâ* (Matt. 27:33)]

calve /kaav/ *v.* **1 a** *intr.* give birth to a calf. **b** *tr.* (esp. in *passive*) give birth to (a calf). **2** *tr.* (also *absol.*) (of an iceberg) break off or shed (a mass of ice). [OE *calfian*]

calves *pl.* of CALF[1], CALF[2].

Calvinism /kálviniz'm/ *n.* the theology of the French theologian J. Calvin (d. 1564) or his followers, in which predestination and justification by faith are important elements. □□ **Calvinist** *n.* **Calvinistic** /-nístik/ *adj.* **Calvinistical** /-nístik'l/ *adj.* [F *calvinisme* or mod.L *calvinismus*]

calx /kalks/ *n.* (*pl.* **calces** /kálseez/) **1** a powdery metallic oxide formed when an ore or mineral has been heated. **2** calcium oxide. [L *calx calcis* lime prob. f. Gk *khalix* pebble, limestone]

calypso /kəlípsō/ *n.* (*pl.* **-os**) a W. Indian song in African rhythm, usu. improvised on a topical theme. [20th c.: orig. unkn.]

calyx /káyliks, kál-/ *n.* (also **calix**) (*pl.* **calyces** /-liseez/ or **calyxes**) **1** *Bot.* the sepals collectively, forming the protective layer of a flower in bud. **2** *Biol.* any cuplike cavity or structure. [L f. Gk *kalux* case of bud, husk: cf. *kaluptō* hide]

cam /kam/ *n.* a projection on a rotating part in machinery, shaped to impart reciprocal or variable motion to the part in contact with it. [Du. *kam* comb: cf. Du. *kamrad* cog-wheel]

camaraderie /kámmərа́adəri/ *n.* mutual trust and sociability among friends. [F]
■ see COMPANIONSHIP.

camarilla /kámmərílla/ *n.* a cabal or clique. [Sp., dimin. of *camara* chamber]
■ see FACTION[1] 1.

Camb. *abbr.* Cambridge.

camber /kámbər/ *n.* & *v.* ● *n.* **1** the slightly convex or arched shape of the surface of a road, ship's deck, aircraft wing, etc. **2** the slight sideways inclination of the front wheel of a motor vehicle. ● *v.* **1** *intr.* (of a surface) have a camber. **2** *tr.* give a camber to; build with a camber. [F *cambre* arched f. L *camurus* curved inwards]
■ *n.* **1** see SLANT *n.* 1.

Camberwell Beauty /kámbərwel/ *n.* a deep purple butterfly, *Nymphalis antiopa*, with yellow-bordered wings. [*Camberwell* in London]

cambium /kámbiəm/ *n.* (*pl.* **cambia** /-biə/ or **cambiums**) *Bot.* a cellular plant tissue responsible for the increase in girth of stems and roots. □□ **cambial** *adj.* [med.L, = change, exchange]

Cambodian /kambṓdiən/ *n.* & *adj.* ● *n.* **1 a** a native or national of Cambodia (Kampuchea) in SE Asia. **b** a person of Cambodian descent. **2** the language of Cambodia. ● *adj.* of or relating to Cambodia or its people or language. Also called KAMPUCHEAN.

Cambrian /kámbriən/ *adj.* & *n.* ● *adj.* **1** Welsh. **2** *Geol.* of or relating to the first period in the Palaeozoic era, marked by the occurrence of many forms of invertebrate life (including trilobites and brachiopods). ¶ Cf. Appendix VII. ● *n.* this period or system. [L *Cambria* var. of *Cumbria* f. Welsh *Cymry* Welshman or *Cymru* Wales]

cambric /kámbrik/ *n.* a fine white linen or cotton fabric. [*Kamerijk*, Flem. form of *Cambrai* in N. France, where it was orig. made]

Cambridge blue /káymbrij/ *n.* & *adj.* a pale blue. [*Cambridge* in S. England]

Cambs. *abbr.* Cambridgeshire.

camcorder /kámkordər/ *n.* a combined video camera and sound recorder. [*camera* + *recorder*]

came *past* of COME.

camel /kámm'l/ *n.* **1** either of two kinds of large cud-chewing mammals having slender cushion-footed legs and one hump (**Arabian camel**, *Camelus dromedarius*) or two humps (**Bactrian camel**, *Camelus bactrianus*). **2** a fawn colour. **3** an apparatus for providing additional buoyancy to ships etc. □ **camel** (or **camel's**) **-hair 1** the hair of a camel. **2 a** a fine soft hair used in artists' brushes. **b** a fabric made of this. [OE f. L *camelus* f. Gk *kamēlos*, of Semitic orig.]

cameleer /kámməleér/ *n.* a camel-driver.

camellia /kəmeéliə/ *n.* any evergreen shrub of the genus *Camellia*, native to E. Asia, with shiny leaves and showy flowers. [J. *Camellus* or *Kamel*, 17th-c. Jesuit botanist]

camelopard /kámmələpaard, kəmél-/ *n. archaic* a giraffe. [L *camelopardus* f. Gk *kamēlopardalis* (as CAMEL, PARD)]

camelry /kámməlri/ *n.* (*pl.* **-ies**) troops mounted on camels.

Camembert /kámməmbair/ *n.* a kind of soft creamy cheese, usu. with a strong flavour. [*Camembert* in N. France, where it was orig. made]

cameo /kámmiō/ *n.* (*pl.* **-os**) **1 a** a small piece of onyx or other hard stone carved in relief with a background of a different colour. **b** a similar relief design using other materials. **2 a** a short descriptive literary sketch or acted scene. **b** a small character part in a play or film, usu. brief and played by a distinguished actor. [ME f. OF *camahieu* and med.L *cammaeus*]

camera /kámrə, kámmərə/ *n.* **1** an apparatus for taking photographs, consisting of a lightproof box to hold light-sensitive film, a lens, and a shutter mechanism, either for still photographs or for motion-picture film. **2** *Telev.* a piece of equipment which forms an optical image and converts it into electrical impulses for transmission or storage. □ **camera obscura** /obskyoórə/ an internally darkened box with an aperture for projecting the image of an external object on a screen inside it. **camera-ready** *Printing* (of copy) in a form suitable for immediate photographic reproduction. **in camera 1** *Law* in a judge's private room. **2** privately; not in public. **on camera** (esp. of an actor or actress) being filmed or televised at a particular moment. [orig. = chamber f. L *camera* f. Gk *kamara* vault etc.]

■ □ **in camera** see *in private* (PRIVATE).

cameraman /kámrəmən/ *n.* (*pl.* **-men**) a person who operates a camera professionally, esp. in film-making or television.

■ see *photographer* (PHOTOGRAPH).

camiknickers /kámminikkərz/ *n.pl. Brit.* a one-piece close-fitting undergarment formerly worn by women. [CAMISOLE + KNICKERS]

camisole /kámmisōl/ *n.* an under-bodice, usu. embroidered. [F f. It. *camiciola* or Sp. *camisola*: see CHEMISE]

camomile /kámməmīl/ *n.* (also **chamomile**) any aromatic plant of the genus *Anthemis* or *Matricaria*, with daisy-like flowers. □ **camomile tea** an infusion of its dried flowers used as a tonic. [ME f. OF *camomille* f. LL *camomilla* or *chamomilla* f. Gk *khamaimēlon* earth-apple (from the apple-smell of its flowers)]

camouflage /kámməflaazh/ *n.* & *v.* ● *n.* **1 a** the disguising of military vehicles, aircraft, ships, artillery, and installations by painting them or covering them to make them blend with their surroundings. **b** such a disguise. **2** the natural colouring of an animal which enables it to blend in with its surroundings. **3** a misleading or evasive precaution or expedient. ● *v.tr.* hide or disguise by means of camouflage. [F f. *camoufler* disguise f. It. *camuffare* disguise, deceive]

■ *n.* **1** disguise, concealment. **2** *Zool.* cryptic colouring *or* coloration. **3** smokescreen, cover-up, cover, guise, cloak, mask, screen, blind, (false) front, show, façade. ● *v.* disguise, cloak, mask, cover (up), hide, obscure, conceal, screen, veil, shroud, dress up; bury, dissemble, dissimulate, misrepresent, falsify.

camp[1] /kamp/ *n.* & *v.* ● *n.* **1 a** a place where troops are lodged or trained. **b** the military life (*court and camp*). **2** temporary overnight lodging in tents etc. in the open. **3 a** temporary accommodation of various kinds, usu. consisting of huts or tents, for detainees, homeless persons, and other emergency use. **b** a complex of buildings for holiday accommodation, usu. with extensive recreational facilities. **4** an ancient fortified site or its remains. **5** the adherents of a particular party or doctrine regarded collectively (*the Labour camp was jubilant*). **6** *S.Afr.* a portion of veld fenced off for pasture on farms. **7** *Austral.* & *NZ* an assembly place of sheep or cattle. ● *v.intr.* **1** set up or spend time in a camp (in senses 1 and 2 of *n.*). **2** (often foll. by *out*) lodge in temporary quarters or in the open. **3** *Austral.* & *NZ* (of sheep or cattle) flock together esp. for rest. □ **camp-bed** a folding portable bed of a kind used in camping. **camp-fire** an open-air fire in a camp etc. **camp-follower 1** a civilian worker in a military camp. **2** a disciple or adherent. **camp-site** a place for camping. □□ **camping** *n.* [F f. It. *campo* f. L *campus* level ground]

■ *n.* **1 a** base, station, barrack(s), cantonment, encampment. **2** bivouac, *esp. S.Afr.* laager. **4** fortification, rampart(s), defence(s), earthwork(s). **5** faction, wing, front, set, coterie, clique, side, group, party, body, band, lobby. ● *v.* **1** encamp, pitch camp, tent, lodge, bivouac. **2** (*camp out*) tent, bivouac, stay (over), *sl.* crash. □ **camp-bed** *US* cot. **camp-follower 2** follower, disciple; see also DEVOTEE. **camp-site** camping site.

camp[2] /kamp/ *adj.*, *n.*, & *v. colloq.* ● *adj.* **1** affected, effeminate. **2** homosexual. **3** done in an exaggerated way for effect. ● *n.* a camp manner or style. ● *v.intr.* & *tr.* behave or do in a camp way. □ **camp it up** overact; behave affectedly. □□ **campy** *adj.* (**campier**, **campiest**). **campily** *adv.* **campiness** *n.* [20th c.: orig. uncert.]

■ *adj.* **1** affected, effeminate, mincing, niminy-piminy, minikin, chichi, *colloq.* campy. **3** *outré*, outrageous, outlandish, exaggerated, affected, extravagant, artificial, theatrical, mannered, flamboyant, showy, ostentatious, flashy. ● *v.* exaggerate, overact, go too far, overdo it, go overboard, overshoot the mark, *colloq.* camp it up; show off, strut, flaunt, flounce, prance, posture, *sl.* ham. □ **camp it up** see CAMP[2] *v.* above.

campaign /kampáyn/ *n.* & *v.* ● *n.* **1** an organized course of action for a particular purpose, esp. to arouse public interest (e.g. before a political election). **2 a** a series of military operations in a definite area or to achieve a particular objective. **b** military service in the field (*on campaign*). ● *v.intr.* conduct or take part in a campaign. □□ **campaigner** *n.* [F *campagne* open country f. It. *campagna* f. LL *campania*]

■ *n.* **1** drive, offensive, push, effort, crusade; move, strategy, scheme, movement, plan. **2** operation(s), manoeuvre(s), movement, crusade, action, offensive; battle, conflict, engagement. ● *v.* run, electioneer, canvass, compete, vie, contend, *Brit.* stand, *US* stump; agitate, push, press, fight, work; (*campaign for*) promote, support, back, advocate, champion, speak up for *or* on behalf of.

campanile /kámpəneéli/ *n.* a bell-tower (usu. free-standing), esp. in Italy. [It. f. *campana* bell]

■ see TOWER *n.* 1.

campanology /kámpənólləji/ *n.* **1** the study of bells. **2** the art or practice of bell-ringing. □□ **campanologer** *n.* **campanological** /-nəlójik'l/ *adj.* **campanologist** *n.* [mod.L *campanologia* f. LL *campana* bell]

campanula /kampányoolə/ *n.* any plant of the genus *Campanula*, with bell-shaped usu. blue, purple, or white flowers. Also called BELLFLOWER. [mod.L dimin. of L *campana* bell]

campanulate /kampányoolət/ *adj. Bot.* & *Zool.* bell-shaped.

Campeachy wood /kampeéchi/ *n.* = LOGWOOD. [*Campeche* in Mexico, from where it was first exported]

camper /kámpər/ *n.* **1** a person who camps out or lives temporarily in a tent, hut, etc., esp. on holiday. **2** a large motor vehicle with accommodation for camping out.

camphor /kámfər/ *n.* a white translucent crystalline volatile substance with aromatic smell and bitter taste, used to make celluloid and in medicine. □□ **camphoric** /-fórrik/ *adj.* [ME f. OF *camphore* or med.L *camphora* f. Arab. *kāfūr* f. Skr. *karpūram*]

camphorate /kámfərayt/ *v.tr.* impregnate or treat with camphor.

campion /kámpiən/ *n.* **1** any plant of the genus *Silene*, with usu. pink or white notched flowers. **2** any of several similar cultivated plants of the genus *Lychnis*. [perh. f. obs. *campion* f. OF, = CHAMPION: transl. of Gk *lukhnis stephanōmatikē* a plant used for (champions') garlands]

campus /kámpəss/ *n.* (*pl.* **campuses**) **1** the grounds of a university or college. **2** esp. *US* a university, esp. as a teaching institution. [L, = field]

CAMRA /kámrə/ *abbr.* Campaign for Real Ale.

camshaft /kámshaaft/ *n.* a shaft with one or more cams attached to it.

camwood /kámwŏŏd/ *n.* a hard red wood from a tree *Pterocarpus soyauxii*, native to W. Africa. [perh. f. Temne]

Can. *abbr.* Canada; Canadian.

can[1] /kan, kən/ *v.aux.* (*3rd sing. present* **can**; *past* **could** /kŏŏd/) (foll. by infin. without *to*, or *absol.*; present and past only in use) **1 a** be able to; know how to (*I can run fast; can he?; can you speak German?*). **b** be potentially capable of (*you can do it if you try*). **2** be permitted to (*can we go to the party?*). [OE *cunnan* know]

can[2] /kan/ *n.* & *v.* ● *n.* **1** a metal vessel for liquid. **2** a tin container in which food or drink is hermetically sealed to enable storage over long periods. **3** (prec. by *the*) *sl.* **a** prison (*sent to the can*). **b** *US* lavatory. **4** *US sl.* the buttocks. ● *v.tr.* (**canned, canning**) **1** put or preserve in a can. **2** record on film or tape for future use. □ **can of worms** *colloq.* a complicated problem. **can-opener** a device for opening cans (in sense 2 of *n.*). **in the can** *colloq.* completed, ready (orig. of filmed or recorded material). □□ **canner** *n.* [OE *canne*]

■ *n.* **1, 2** see RECEPTACLE. **3 a** see PRISON *n.* 1. **b** see LAVATORY. ● *v.* **1** see PRESERVE *v.* 4a. □ **can of worms** see PROBLEM 1, 2.

Canaan /káynən/ *n.* **1** a promised land (orig. that west of the River Jordan, the Promised Land of the Israelites). **2** heaven. [eccl.L f. eccl.Gk *Khanaan* f. Heb. *kᵉna'an*]

Canada balsam /kánnədə/ *n. Biol.* a yellow resin obtained from the balsam fir and used for mounting preparations on microscope slides (its refractive index being similar to that of glass).

Canada goose /kánnədə/ *n.* a wild goose, *Branta canadensis*, of N. America, with a brownish-grey body and white cheeks and breast.

canaille /kənaá-i/ *n.* the rabble; the populace. [F f. It. *canaglia* pack of dogs f. *cane* dog]

■ see RABBLE[1] 3.

canal /kənál/ *n.* **1** an artificial waterway for inland navigation or irrigation. **2** any of various tubular ducts in a plant or animal, for carrying food, liquid, or air. **3** *Astron.* any of a network of apparent linear markings on the planet Mars, which are observed from earth but not at close range. □ **canal boat** a long narrow boat for use on canals. **canal ray** a beam of positive ions moving through a bored hole in the cathode of a high-vacuum tube. [ME f. OF (earlier *chanel*) f. L *canalis* or It. *canale*]

■ **1** see CHANNEL[1] *n.* 5a, 6. **2** see VESSEL 3.

canalize /kánnəlīz/ *v.tr.* (also **-ise**) **1** make a canal through. **2** convert (a river) into a canal. **3** provide with canals. **4** give the desired direction or purpose to. □□ **canalization** /-záysh'n/ *n.* [F *canaliser*: see CANAL]

canapé /kánnəpi/ *n.* **1** a small piece of bread or pastry with a savoury on top, often served as an hors-d'œuvre. **2** a sofa. [F]

canard /kənaárd, kánnaard/ *n.* **1** an unfounded rumour or story. **2** an extra surface attached to an aeroplane forward of the main lifting surface, for extra stability or control. [F, = duck]

Canarese var. of KANARESE.

canary /kənáiri/ *n.* (*pl.* **-ies**) **1** any of various small finches of the genus *Serinus*, esp. *S. canaria*, a songbird native to the Canary Islands, with mainly yellow plumage. **2** *hist.* a sweet wine from the Canary Islands. □ **canary-coloured** coloured canary yellow. **canary creeper** a climbing plant, *Tropaeolium peregrinum*, with flowers of bright yellow deeply toothed petals which give the appearance of a small bird in flight. **canary grass** a Mediterranean plant *Phalaris canariensis*, grown as a crop plant for bird seed. **canary yellow** bright yellow. [*Canary* Islands f. F *Canarie* f. Sp. & L *Canaria* f. *canis* dog, one of the islands being noted in Roman times for large dogs]

canasta /kənástə/ *n.* **1** a card-game using two packs and resembling rummy, the aim being to collect sets (or melds) of cards. **2** a set of seven cards in this game. [Sp., = basket]

canaster /kənástər/ *n.* tobacco made from coarsely broken dried leaves. [orig. the container: Sp. *canastro* ult. f. Gk *kanastron*]

cancan /kánkan/ *n.* a lively stage-dance with high kicking, performed by women in long skirts and petticoats. [F]

cancel /káns'l/ *v.* & *n.* ● *v.* (**cancelled, cancelling**; *US* **canceled, canceling**) **1** *tr.* **a** withdraw or revoke (a previous arrangement). **b** discontinue (an arrangement in progress). **2** *tr.* obliterate or delete (writing etc.). **3** *tr.* mark or pierce (a ticket, stamp, etc.) to invalidate it. **4** *tr.* annul; make void; abolish. **5** (often foll. by *out*) **a** *tr.* (of one factor or circumstance) neutralize or counterbalance (another). **b** *intr.* (of two factors or circumstances) neutralize each other. **6** *tr. Math.* strike out (an equal factor) on each side of an equation or from the numerator and denominator of a fraction. ● *n.* **1** a countermand. **2** the cancellation of a postage stamp. **3** *Printing* a new page or section inserted in a book to replace the original text, usu. to correct an error. **4** *Mus. US* a natural-sign. □□ **canceller** *n.* [ME f. F *canceller* f. L *cancellare* f. *cancelli* crossbars, lattice]

■ *v.* **1 a** revoke, call off, retract, withdraw, rescind, countermand, do away with, dispense with, *colloq.* scrub, *sl.* nix. **b** see STOP *v.* 1c. **2** delete, obliterate, cross *or* strike *or* blot *or* scratch out, rub out, erase, *Printing* dele; expunge, efface, eradicate; eliminate, do away with, get rid of, dispense with, take away, omit. **3** stamp, clip; postmark. **4** void, annul, declare null and void, invalidate, nullify, quash, recall, set aside, wipe off, wash out, write off, remit, dissolve, repeal, abolish, undo, unmake, *Law* defeat, repeal, reverse, vacate, discharge. **5** neutralize, nullify, counterbalance, countervail, counter, compensate (for), make up for, offset, counteract.

cancellate /kánsilət/ *adj.* (also **cancellated** /-laytid/) *Biol.* marked with crossing lines. [L *cancelli* lattice]

cancellation /kánsəláysh'n/ *n.* **1** the act or an instance of cancelling or being cancelled. **2** something that has been cancelled, esp. a booking or reservation. [L *cancellatio* (as CANCEL)]

■ **1** annulment, nullification, abrogation, invalidation, rescission, rescindment, reversal, recall, repeal, abandonment, withdrawal, revocation; deletion, elimination; discontinuance, termination, stoppage, cessation.

cancellous /kánsiləss/ *adj.* (of a bone) with pores. [L *cancelli* lattice]

cancer /kánsər/ *n.* **1 a** any malignant growth or tumour from an abnormal and uncontrolled division of body cells. **b** a disease caused by this. **2** an evil influence or corruption spreading uncontrollably. **3** (**Cancer**) **a** a constellation, traditionally regarded as contained in the figure of a crab. **b** the fourth sign of the zodiac (the Crab). **c** a person born when the sun is in this sign. □ **cancer stick** *sl.* a cigarette. **Tropic of Cancer** see TROPIC. □□ **Cancerian** /-seériən/ *n.* & *adj.* (in sense 3). **cancerous** *adj.* [ME f. L, = crab, cancer, after Gk *karkinos*]

■ **1** see TUMOUR. **2** see POISON *n.* 2.

cancroid /kángkroyd/ *adj.* & *n.* ● *adj.* **1** crablike. **2** resembling cancer. ● *n.* a disease resembling cancer.

candela /kandeélə, -dáylə/ *n.* the SI unit of luminous intensity. ¶ Abbr.: **cd.** [L, = candle]

candelabrum /kándilaábrəm/ *n.* (also **candelabra** /-brə/) (*pl.* **candelabra,** *US* **candelabrums, candelabras**) a large branched candlestick or lamp-holder. □ **candelabrum tree** a tropical E. African tree, *Euphorbia candelabrum*, with foliage shaped like a candelabrum. [L f. *candela* CANDLE]

candescent /kandéss'nt/ *adj.* glowing with or as with white heat. □□ **candescence** *n.* [L *candēre* be white]

candid /kándid/ *adj.* **1** frank; not hiding one's thoughts. **2** (of a photograph) taken informally, usu. without the subject's knowledge. □ **candid camera** a small camera for taking candid photographs. □□ **candidly** *adv.* **candidness** *n.* [F *candide* or L *candidus* white]

■ **1** frank, open, plain, sincere, ingenuous, straight, straightforward, truthful, forthright, direct, unequivocal, plain-spoken, round, blunt, outspoken, honest, artless, guileless, above-board, undeceitful, undeceiving, *colloq.* upfront, on the level. **2** unposed, informal, impromptu, extemporaneous, extemporary, unofficial, natural, spontaneous.

candida /kándidə/ *n.* any yeastlike parasitic fungus of the genus *Candida*, esp. *C. albicans* causing thrush. [mod.L fem. of L *candidus*: see CANDID]

candidate /kándidət, -dayt/ *n.* **1** a person who seeks or is nominated for an office, award, etc. **2** a person or thing likely to gain some distinction or position. **3** a person entered for an examination. □□ **candidacy** *n.* **candidature** *n. Brit.* [F *candidat* or L *candidatus* white-robed (Roman candidates wearing white)]

■ **1, 3** runner, nominee; aspirant, seeker, pretender; applicant, entrant, interviewee, examinee. **2** prospect, possibility.

candle /kánd'l/ *n.* & *v.* ● *n.* **1** a cylinder or block of wax or tallow with a central wick, for giving light when burning. **2** = CANDLEPOWER. ● *v.tr.* test (an egg) for freshness by holding it to the light. □ **cannot hold a candle to** cannot be compared with; is much inferior to. **not worth the candle** not justifying the cost or trouble. □□ **candler** *n.* [OE *candel* f. L *candela* f. *candēre* shine]

■ *n.* **1** see LIGHT[1] *n.* 4a.

candlelight /kánd'l-līt/ *n.* **1** light provided by candles. **2** dusk. □□ **candlelit** *adj.*

■ **1** see LIGHT[1] *n.* 2.

Candlemas /kánd'lməss, -mass/ *n.* a feast with blessing of candles (2 Feb.), commemorating the Purification of the Virgin Mary and the presentation of Christ in the Temple. [OE *Candelmæsse* (as CANDLE, MASS[2])]

candlepower /kánd'lpowr/ *n.* a unit of luminous intensity.

candlestick /kánd'lstik/ *n.* a holder for one or more candles.

candlewick /kánd'lwik/ *n.* **1** a thick soft cotton yarn. **2** material made from this, usu. with a tufted pattern.

candour /kándər/ *n.* (*US* **candor**) candid behaviour or action; frankness. [F *candeur* or L *candor* whiteness]

■ candidness, openness, frankness, straightness, straightforwardness, ingenuousness, simplicity, naïvety, outspokenness, unreservedness, forthrightness, honesty, truthfulness, sincerity, directness, bluntness, unequivocalness.

C. & W. *abbr.* country-and-western.

candy /kándi/ *n.* & *v.* ● *n.* (*pl.* **-ies**) **1** (in full **sugar-candy**) sugar crystallized by repeated boiling and slow evaporation. **2** *US* sweets; a sweet. ● *v.tr.* (**-ies, -ied**) (usu. as **candied** *adj.*) preserve by coating and impregnating with a sugar syrup (*candied fruit*). [F *sucre candi* candied sugar f. Arab. *ḳand* sugar]

■ *n.* **2** sweet(s), bon-bon(s), sweetmeat(s), confectionery. ● *v.* (**candied**) sugar-coated, preserved, crystallized.

candyfloss /kándifloss/ *n. Brit.* a fluffy mass of spun sugar wrapped round a stick.

candystripe /kándistrīp/ *n.* a pattern consisting of alternate stripes of white and a colour (usu. pink). □□ **candystriped** *adj.*

candytuft /kándituft/ *n.* any of various plants of the genus *Iberis*, native to W. Europe, with white, pink, or purple flowers in tufts. [obs. *Candy* (*Candia* Crete) + TUFT]

cane /kayn/ *n.* & *v.* ● *n.* **1 a** the hollow jointed stem of giant reeds or grasses (*bamboo cane*). **b** the solid stem of slender palms (*malacca cane*). **2** = *sugar cane*. **3** a raspberry-cane. **4** material of cane used for wickerwork etc. **5 a** a cane used as a walking-stick or a support for a plant or an instrument of punishment. **b** any slender walking-stick. ● *v.tr.* **1** beat with a cane. **2** weave cane into (a chair etc.). □ **cane-brake** *US* a tract of land overgrown with canes. **cane chair** a chair with a seat made of woven cane strips. **cane-sugar** sugar obtained from sugar-cane. **cane-trash** see TRASH. □□ **caner** *n.* (in sense 2 of *v.*). **caning** *n.* [ME f. OF f. L *canna* f. Gk *kanna*]

■ *n.* **1** see STEM[1] 2. **5** see STICK[1] 1b. ● *v.* **1** see BEAT *v.* 1.

canine /káynīn, kán-/ *adj.* & *n.* ● *adj.* **1** of a dog or dogs. **2** of or belonging to the family Canidae, including dogs, wolves, foxes, etc. ● *n.* **1** a dog. **2** (in full **canine tooth**) a pointed tooth between the incisors and premolars. [ME f. *canin -ine* or f. L *caninus* f. *canis* dog]

canister /kánnistər/ *n.* **1** a small container, usu. of metal and cylindrical, for storing tea etc. **2 a** a cylinder of shot, tear-gas, etc., that explodes on impact. **b** such cylinders collectively. [L *canistrum* f. Gk f. *kanna* CANE]

canker /kángkər/ *n.* & *v.* ● *n.* **1 a** a destructive fungus disease of trees and plants. **b** an open wound in the stem of a tree or plant. **2** *Zool.* an ulcerous ear disease of animals esp. cats and dogs. **3** *Med.* an ulceration esp. of the lips. **4** a corrupting influence. ● *v.tr.* **1** consume with canker. **2** corrupt. **3** (as **cankered** *adj.*) soured, malignant, crabbed. □ **canker-worm** any caterpillar of various wingless moths which consume the buds and leaves of shade and fruit trees in N. America. □□ **cankerous** *adj.* [OE *cancer* & ONF *cancre*, OF *chancre* f. L *cancer* crab]

■ *n.* **2, 3** see ULCER 1. **4** see POISON *n.* 2. ● *v.* **3** (**cankered**) see MALIGNANT 2.

canna /kánnə/ *n.* any tropical plant of the genus *Canna* with bright flowers and ornamental leaves. [L: see CANE]

cannabis /kánnəbiss/ *n.* **1** any hemp plant of the genus *Cannabis*, esp. Indian hemp. **2** a preparation of parts of this used as an intoxicant or hallucinogen. □ **cannabis resin** a sticky product, esp. from the flowering tops of the female cannabis plant. [L f. Gk]

canned /kand/ *adj.* **1** pre-recorded (*canned laughter*; *canned music*). **2** supplied in a can (*canned beer*). **3** *sl.* drunk.

cannel /kánn'l/ *n.* (in full **cannel coal**) a bituminous coal burning with a bright flame. [16th c.: orig. N.Engl.]

cannelloni /kánnəlṓni/ *n.pl.* tubes or rolls of pasta stuffed with meat or a vegetable mixture. [It. f. *cannello* stalk]

cannelure /kánnəlyoor/ *n.* the groove round a bullet etc. [F f. *canneler* f. *canne* reed, CANE]

cannery /kánnəri/ *n.* (*pl.* **-ies**) a factory where food is canned.

cannibal /kánnib'l/ *n.* & *adj.* ● *n.* **1** a person who eats human flesh. **2** an animal that feeds on flesh of its own species. ● *adj.* of or like a cannibal. □□ **cannibalism** *n.* **cannibalistic** /-bəlístik/ *adj.* **cannibalistically** /-bəl ístikəli/ *adv.* [orig. pl. *Canibales* f. Sp.: var. of *Caribes* name of a W.Ind. nation]

cannibalize /kánnibəlīz/ *v.tr.* (also **-ise**) use (a machine etc.) as a source of spare parts for others. □□ **cannibalization** /-záysh'n/ *n.*

cannikin /kánnikin/ *n.* a small can. [Du. *kanneken* (as CAN², -KIN)]

cannon /kánnən/ *n.* & *v.* ● *n.* **1** *hist.* (*pl.* same) a large heavy gun installed on a carriage or mounting. **2** an automatic aircraft gun firing shells. **3** *Billiards* the hitting of two balls successively by the cue-ball. **4** *Mech.* a hollow cylinder moving independently on a shaft. **5** (in full **cannon-bit**) a smooth round bit for a horse. ● *v.intr.* **1** (usu. foll. by *against*, *into*) collide heavily or obliquely. **2** *Billiards* make a cannon shot. □ **cannon-ball** *hist.* a large usu. metal ball fired by a cannon. **cannon-bone** the tube-shaped bone between the hock and fetlock of a horse. **cannon-fodder** soldiers regarded merely as material to be expended in war. [F *canon* f. It. *cannone* large tube f. *canna* CANE: in Billiards sense f. older CAROM]
■ □ **cannon-ball** see SHOT¹ 3.

cannonade /kánnənáyd/ *n.* & *v.* ● *n.* a period of continuous heavy gunfire. ● *v.tr.* bombard with a cannonade. [F f. It. *cannonata*]
■ *n.* see VOLLEY *n.* 1. ● *v.* see SHELL *v.* 2.

cannot /kánnot, kanót/ *v.aux.* can not.

cannula /kányoolə/ *n.* (*pl.* **cannulae** /-lee/ or **cannulas**) *Surgery* a small tube for inserting into the body to allow fluid to enter or escape. [L, dimin. of *canna* cane]

cannulate /kányoolayt/ *v.tr.* *Surgery* introduce a cannula into.

canny /kánni/ *adj.* (**cannier**, **canniest**) **1 a** shrewd, worldly-wise. **b** thrifty. **c** circumspect. **2** sly, drily humorous. **3** *Sc.* & *N.Engl.* pleasant, agreeable. □□ **cannily** *adv.* **canniness** *n.* [CAN¹ (in sense 'know') + -Y¹]
■ **1 a** see SHREWD. **b** see THRIFTY 1.

canoe /kənóó/ *n.* & *v.* ● *n.* a small narrow boat with pointed ends usu. propelled by paddling. ● *v.intr.* (**canoes, canoed, canoeing**) travel in a canoe. □□ **canoeist** *n.* [Sp. and Haitian *canoa*]

canon /kánnən/ *n.* **1 a** a general law, rule, principle, or criterion. **b** a church decree or law. **2** (*fem.* **canoness**) **a** a member of a cathedral chapter. **b** a member of certain RC orders. **3 a** a collection or list of sacred books etc. accepted as genuine. **b** the recognized genuine works of a particular author; a list of these. **4** the part of the Roman Catholic Mass containing the words of consecration. **5** *Mus.* a piece with different parts taking up the same theme successively, either at the same or at a different pitch. □ **canon law** ecclesiastical law. **canon regular** (or **regular canon**) see REGULAR *adj.* 9b. [OE f. L f. Gk *kanōn*, in ME also f. AF & OF *canun*, *-on*; in sense 2 ME f. OF *canonie* f. eccl.L *canonicus*: cf. CANONICAL]
■ **1** see LAW 1a. **2** see CLERGYMAN.

cañon var. of CANYON.

canonic /kənónnik/ *adj.* = CANONICAL *adj.* [OE f. OF *canonique* or L *canonicus* f. Gk *kanonikos* (as CANON)]

canonical /kənónnik'l/ *adj.* & *n.* ● *adj.* **1 a** according to or ordered by canon law. **b** included in the canon of Scripture. **2** authoritative, standard, accepted. **3** of a cathedral chapter or a member of it. **4** *Mus.* in canon form. ● *n.* (in *pl.*) the canonical dress of the clergy. □ **canonical hours** *Eccl.* the times fixed for a formal set of prayers or for the celebration of marriage. □□ **canonically** *adv.* [med.L *canonicalis* (as CANONIC)]

canonicate /kənónnikət/ *n.* = CANONRY.

canonicity /kánnənissiti/ *n.* the status of being canonical. [L *canonicus* canonical]

canonist /kánnənist/ *n.* an expert in canon law. [ME f. F *canoniste* or f. med.L *canonista*: see CANON]

canonize /kánnənīz/ *v.tr.* (also **-ise**) **1 a** declare officially to be a saint, usu. with a ceremony. **b** regard as a saint. **2** admit to the canon of Scripture. **3** sanction by Church authority. □□ **canonization** /-záysh'n/ *n.* [ME f. med.L *canonizare*: see CANON]
■ **2, 3** see SANCTIFY 3.

canonry /kánnənri/ *n.* (*pl.* **-ies**) the office or benefice of a canon.

canoodle /kənóód'l/ *v.intr.* *colloq.* kiss and cuddle amorously. [19th-c. US: orig. unkn.]
■ see KISS *v.* 3.

Canopic /kənópik/ *adj.* □ **Canopic jar** (or **vase**) an urn used for holding the entrails of an embalmed body in an ancient Egyptian burial. [L *Canopicus* f. *Canopus* in ancient Egypt]

canopy /kánnəpi/ *n.* & *v.* ● *n.* (*pl.* **-ies**) **1 a** a covering hung or held up over a throne, bed, person, etc. **b** the sky. **c** an overhanging shelter. **2** *Archit.* a rooflike projection over a niche etc. **3** the uppermost layers of foliage etc. in a forest. **4 a** the expanding part of a parachute. **b** the cover of an aircraft's cockpit. ● *v.tr.* (**-ies, -ied**) supply or be a canopy to. [ME f. med.L *canopeum* f. L *conopeum* f. Gk *kōnōpeion* couch with mosquito-curtains f. *kōnōps* gnat]
■ **1** see MANTLE *n.* 2.

canorous /kənórəss/ *adj.* melodious, resonant. [L *canorus* f. *canere* sing]

canst /kanst/ *archaic 2nd person sing.* of CAN¹.

Cant. *abbr.* Canticles (Old Testament).

cant¹ /kant/ *n.* & *v.* ● *n.* **1** insincere pious or moral talk. **2** ephemeral or fashionable catchwords. **3** language peculiar to a class, profession, sect, etc.; jargon. ● *v.intr.* use cant. □ **canting arms** *Heraldry* arms containing an allusion to the name of the bearer. [earlier of musical sound, of intonation, and of beggars' whining; perh. from the singing of religious mendicants: prob. f. L *canere* sing]
■ *n.* **1** hypocrisy, insincerity, sham, pretence, humbug, sanctimony, sanctimoniousness, piety, lip-service, pretension. **3** jargon, language, argot, vernacular, idiom, slang, dialect, patois, *colloq.* lingo.

cant² /kant/ *n.* & *v.* ● *n.* **1 a** a slanting surface, e.g. of a bank. **b** a bevel of a crystal etc. **2** an oblique push or movement that upsets or partly upsets something. **3** a tilted or sloping position. ● *v.* **1** *tr.* push or pitch out of level; tilt. **2** *intr.* take or lie in a slanting position. **3** *tr.* impart a bevel to. **4** *intr.* *Naut.* swing round. □ **cant-dog** (or **-hook**) an iron hook at the end of a long handle, used for rolling logs. [ME f. MLG *kant*, *kante*, MDu. *cant*, point, side, edge, ult. f. L *cant(h)us* iron tire]

can't /kaant/ *contr.* can not.

Cantab. /kántab/ *abbr.* of Cambridge University. [L *Cantabrigiensis*]

cantabile /kantaábili/ *adv.*, *adj.*, & *n.* *Mus.* ● *adv.* & *adj.* in a smooth singing style. ● *n.* a cantabile passage or movement. [It., = singable]

Cantabrigian /kántəbríjiən/ *adj.* & *n.* ● *adj.* of Cambridge or Cambridge University. ● *n.* **1** a member of Cambridge University. **2** a native of Cambridge. [L *Cantabrigia* Cambridge]

cantal /kánt'l/ *n.* a type of hard strong French cheese. [name of a department of Auvergne, France]

cantaloup /kántəloop/ *n.* (also **cantaloupe**) a small round ribbed variety of melon with orange flesh. [F *cantaloup* f. *Cantaluppi* near Rome, where it was first grown in Europe]

cantankerous /kantángkərəss/ *adj.* bad-tempered, quarrelsome. □□ **cantankerously** *adv.* **cantankerousness** *n.* [perh. f. Ir. *cant* outbidding + *rancorous*]
■ ill-natured, quarrelsome, cross, grumpy, choleric, cross-grained, crabby, curmudgeonly, crusty, surly, irascible, snappish, bad-tempered, moody, ill-tempered, bearish, bilious, splenetic, peevish, testy, irritable, crotchety, touchy, disagreeable, tetchy, contrary, *Sc.*

thrawn, *esp. US* cranky, *colloq.* grouchy, *literary* atrabilious, *Austral. & NZ sl.* lemony.

cantata /kantaátə/ *n. Mus.* a short narrative or descriptive composition with vocal solos and usu. chorus and orchestral accompaniment. [It. *cantata (aria)* sung (air) f. *cantare* sing]

canteen /kanteén/ *n.* **1 a** a restaurant for employees in an office or factory etc. **b** a shop selling provisions or liquor in a barracks or camp. **2** a case or box of cutlery. **3** a soldier's or camper's water-flask or set of eating or drinking utensils. [F *cantine* f. It. *cantina* cellar]
▪ **1** see CAFÉ 1. **2** see SET² 4, 5.

canter /kántər/ *n. & v.* ● *n.* a gentle gallop. ● *v.* **1** *intr.* (of a horse or its rider) go at a canter. **2** *tr.* make (a horse) canter. ▫ **in a canter** easily (*win in a canter*). [short for *Canterbury pace*, from the supposed easy pace of medieval pilgrims to Canterbury]

canterbury /kántərbəri/ *n.* (*pl.* **-ies**) a piece of furniture with partitions for holding music etc. [*Canterbury* in Kent]

Canterbury bell /kántərbəri/ *n.* a cultivated campanula with large flowers. [after the bells of Canterbury pilgrims' horses: see CANTER]

cantharides /kanthárrideez/ *n.pl.* a preparation made from dried bodies of a beetle *Lytta vesicatoria*, causing blistering of the skin and formerly used in medicine and as an aphrodisiac. Also called *Spanish fly*. [L f. Gk *kantharis* Spanish fly]

canthus /kánthəss/ *n.* (*pl.* **canthi** /-thī/) the outer or inner corner of the eye, where the upper and lower lids meet. [L f. Gk *kanthos*]

canticle /kántik'l/ *n.* **1** a song or chant with a Biblical text. **2** (also **Canticle of Canticles**) the Song of Solomon. [ME f. OF *canticle* (var. of *cantique*) or L *canticulum* dimin. of *canticum* f. *canere* sing]
▪ **1** see CHANT *n.*

cantilena /kántileénə/ *n. Mus.* a simple or sustained melody. [It.]

cantilever /kántileevər/ *n. & v.* ● *n.* **1** a long bracket or beam etc. projecting from a wall to support a balcony etc. **2** a beam or girder fixed at only one end. ● *v.intr.* **1** project as a cantilever. **2** be supported by cantilevers. ▫ **cantilever bridge** a bridge made of cantilevers projecting from the piers and connected by girders. [17th c.: orig. unkn.]

cantillate /kántilayt/ *v.tr. & intr.* chant or recite with musical tones. ▫▫ **cantillation** /-láysh'n/ *n.* [L *cantillare* sing low: see CHANT]

cantina /kanteénə/ *n.* a bar-room or wine-shop. [Sp. & It.]

canto /kántō/ *n.* (*pl.* **-os**) a division of a long poem. [It., = song, f. L *cantus*]
▪ see PASSAGE¹ 6.

canton *n. & v.* ● *n.* **1** /kánton/ **a** a subdivision of a country. **b** a State of the Swiss confederation. **2** /kántən/ *Heraldry* a square division, less than a quarter, in the upper (usu. dexter) corner of a shield. ● *v.tr.* **1** /kantoōn/ put (troops) into quarters. **2** /kantón/ divide into cantons. ▫▫ **cantonal** /kántən'l, kantónn'l/ *adj.* [OF, = corner (see CANT²): (v.) also partly f. F *cantonner*]

Cantonese /kántəneéz/ *adj. & n.* ● *adj.* of Canton or the Cantonese dialect of Chinese. ● *n.* (*pl.* same) **1** a native of Canton. **2** the dialect of Chinese spoken in SE China and Hong Kong. [*Canton* in China]

cantonment /kantoōnmənt/ *n.* **1** a lodging assigned to troops. **2** a permanent military station in India. [F *cantonnement*: see CANTON]
▪ **1** see QUARTER *n.* 9b.

cantor /kántor/ *n.* **1** the leader of the singing in church; a precentor. **2** the precentor in a synagogue. [L, = singer f. *canere* sing]
▪ see VOCALIST.

cantorial /kantóriəl/ *adj.* **1** of or relating to the cantor. **2** of the north side of the choir in a church (cf. DECANAL).

cantoris /kantóriss/ *adj. Mus.* to be sung by the cantorial side of the choir in antiphonal singing (cf. DECANI). [L, genit. of CANTOR precentor]

cantrail /kántrayl/ *n. Brit.* a timber etc. support for the roof of a railway carriage. [CANT² + RAIL]

cantrip /kántrip/ *n. Sc.* **1** a witch's trick. **2** a piece of mischief; a playful act. [18th c.: orig. unkn.]
▪ see TRICK *n.* 5.

Canuck /kənúk/ *n. & adj. US sl.* usu. *derog.* ● *n.* **1** a Canadian, esp. a French Canadian. **2** a Canadian horse or pony. ● *adj.* Canadian, esp. French Canadian. [app. f. *Canada*]

canvas /kánvəss/ *n. & v.* ● *n.* **1 a** a strong coarse kind of cloth made from hemp or flax or other coarse yarn and used for sails and tents etc. and as a surface for oil-painting. **b** a piece of this. **2** a painting on canvas, esp. in oils. **3** an open kind of canvas used as a basis for tapestry and embroidery. **4** *sl.* the floor of a boxing or wrestling ring. **5** a racing-boat's covered end. ● *v.tr.* (**canvassed, canvassing;** *US* **canvased, canvasing**) cover with canvas. ▫ **by a canvas** (in boat-racing) by a small margin (*win by a canvas*). **canvas-back** a wild duck *Aythya valisineria*, of N. America, with back feathers the colour of unbleached canvas. **under canvas 1** in a tent or tents. **2** with sails spread. [ME & ONF *canevas*, ult. f. L *cannabis* hemp]

canvass /kánvəss/ *v. & n.* ● *v.* **1 a** *intr.* solicit votes. **b** *tr.* solicit votes from (electors in a constituency). **2** *tr.* **a** ascertain opinions of. **b** seek custom from. **c** discuss thoroughly. **3** *tr. Brit.* propose (an idea or plan etc.). **4** *intr. US* check the validity of votes. ● *n.* the process of or an instance of canvassing, esp. of electors. ▫▫ **canvasser** *n.* [orig. = toss in a sheet, agitate, f. CANVAS]
▪ *v.* **1 a** electioneer, campaign, *Brit.* stand, *US* stump. **b** solicit. **2 a** survey, poll, study, examine, investigate, interview, question, sound (out). **3** see PROPOSE 1. **4** see CHECK¹ *v.* 1. ● *n.* solicitation, campaign; survey, study, investigation, poll, examination, analysis.

canyon /kányən/ *n.* (also **cañon**) a deep gorge, often with a stream or river. [Sp. *cañón* tube, ult. f. L *canna* CANE]
▪ gorge, ravine, gully, pass, defile, *Brit.* gill, *US* coulée, gulch, pass, arroyo.

canzonetta /kánzənéttə/ *n.* (also **canzonet** /-nét/) **1** a short light song. **2** a kind of madrigal. [It., dimin. of *canzone* song f. L *cantio -onis* f. *canere* sing]

caoutchouc /kówchoōk/ *n.* raw rubber. [F f. Carib *cahuchu*]

CAP *abbr.* Common Agricultural Policy (of the EEC).

cap /kap/ *n. & v.* ● *n.* **1 a** a soft brimless head-covering, usu. with a peak. **b** a head-covering worn in a particular profession (*nurse's cap*). **c** esp. *Brit.* a cap awarded as a sign of membership of a sports team. **d** an academic mortarboard or soft hat. **e** a special hat as part of Highland costume. **2 a** a cover like a cap in shape or position (*kneecap; toecap*). **b** a device to seal a bottle or protect the point of a pen, lens of a camera, etc. **3 a** = *Dutch cap*. **b** = *percussion cap*. **4** = CROWN *n.* 9b. ● *v.tr.* (**capped, capping**) **1 a** put a cap on. **b** cover the top or end of. **c** set a limit to (*rate-capping*). **2 a** esp. *Brit.* award a sports cap to. **b** *Sc. & NZ* confer a university degree on. **3 a** lie on top of; form the cap of. **b** surpass, excel. **c** improve on (a story, quotation, etc.) esp. by producing a better or more apposite one. ▫ **cap in hand** humbly. **cap of maintenance** a cap or hat worn as a symbol of official dignity or carried before the sovereign etc. **cap rock** a hard rock or stratum overlying a deposit of oil, gas, coal, etc. **cap sleeve** a sleeve extending only a short distance from the shoulder. **if the cap fits** (said of a generalized comment) it seems to be true (of a particular person). **set one's cap at** try to attract as a suitor. ▫▫ **capful** *n.* (*pl.* **-fuls**). **capping** *n.* [OE *cæppe* f. LL *cappa*, perh. f. L *caput* head]
▪ *n.* **1 a** hat, head-covering. **d** mortarboard, square, trencher, trencher cap. **2 b** lid, top, cover, covering.
● *v.* **1 a, b** cover, protect, shelter, shield, screen, sheathe. **c** curb, check, restrain; see also CONTROL *v.* 3. **3 a** see COVER *v.* 2a. **b, c** surpass, exceed, break, top, improve on,

improve on, outdo, outmatch, outshine, eclipse, outstrip, better, beat, excel, *colloq.* lick, best. □ **cap in hand** humbly, meekly, servilely, submissively, subserviently, docilely, respectfully. **set one's cap at** see COURT *v.* 1b.

cap. *abbr.* **1** capital. **2** capital letter. **3** chapter. [L *capitulum* or *caput*]

capability /káypəbílliti/ *n.* (*pl.* **-ies**) **1** (often foll. by *of*, *for*, *to*) ability, power; the condition of being capable. **2** an undeveloped or unused faculty.
■ ability, power, capacity, means, faculty, talent, gift, touch, proficiency, aptitude, facility, adeptness, skill, competence, prowess, calibre, *colloq.* wherewithal; potential, promise.

capable /káypəb'l/ *adj.* **1** competent, able, gifted. **2** (foll. by *of*) **a** having the ability or fitness or necessary quality for. **b** susceptible or admitting of (explanation or improvement etc.). □□ **capably** *adv.* [F f. LL *capabilis* f. L *capere* hold]
■ **1** able, competent, efficient, proficient, qualified, experienced, talented, gifted, skilled, skilful, expert, masterly, masterful, accomplished, apt, adept, clever, effective, effectual. **2 a** (*capable of*) disposed to, inclined to, predisposed to; up to; (*be capable of*) have the potential to, have it in one to, *colloq.* have what it takes to.

capacious /kəpáyshəss/ *adj.* roomy; able to hold much. □□ **capaciously** *adv.* **capaciousness** *n.* [L *capax -acis* f. *capere* hold]
■ see ROOMY.

capacitance /kəpássit'nss/ *n. Electr.* **1** the ability of a system to store an electric charge. **2** the ratio of the change in an electric charge in a system to the corresponding change in its electric potential. ¶ Symb.: **C**. [CAPACITY + -ANCE]

capacitate /kəpássitayt/ *v.tr.* **1** (usu. foll. by *for*, or *to* + infin.) render capable. **2** make legally competent.
■ see ENABLE 1.

capacitor /kəpássitər/ *n. Electr.* a device of one or more pairs of conductors separated by insulators used to store an electric charge.

capacity /kəpássiti/ *n.* (*pl.* **-ies**) **1 a** the power of containing, receiving, experiencing, or producing (*capacity for heat, pain*, etc.). **b** the maximum amount that can be contained or produced etc. **c** the volume, e.g. of the cylinders in an internal-combustion engine. **d** (*attrib.*) fully occupying the available space, resources, etc. (*a capacity audience*). **2 a** mental power. **b** a faculty or talent. **3** a position or function (*in a civil capacity*; *in my capacity as a critic*). **4** legal competence. **5** *Electr.* capacitance. □ **measure of capacity** a measure used for vessels and liquids or grains etc. **to capacity** fully; using all resources (*working to capacity*). □□ **capacitative** /-tətiv/ *adj.* (also **capacitive**) (in sense 5). [ME f. F f. L *capacitas -tatis* (as CAPACIOUS)]
■ **1 a** see POTENTIAL *n.* 1. **b** volume, content, size, dimensions, measurements, proportions, magnitude; range, scope, extent, reach, limit; room, space. **2 a** potential, ability, power, capability, competence, intelligence, brainpower, cleverness, brightness, wit, brain(s), acumen, understanding, sense, judgement, perspicacity, perspicaciousness, perceptiveness, imagination, perception, discernment, mother wit, intellect, genius, talent, flair, instinct. **b** genius, skill, gift, faculty, talent, flair, knack, instinct, power. **3** position, function, condition, character, place, post, role, job, office, duty, responsibility. **4** *Law* competency, qualification. □ **to capacity** see *completely* (COMPLETE).

caparison /kəpárris'n/ *n.* & *v.* ● *n.* **1** (usu. in *pl.*) a horse's trappings. **2** equipment, finery. ● *v.tr.* put caparisons on; adorn richly. [obs. F *caparasson* f. Sp. *caparazón* saddle-cloth f. *capa* CAPE[1]]
■ *n.* see TRAPPINGS. ● *v.* see DECORATE 1, 3.

cape[1] /kayp/ *n.* **1** a sleeveless cloak. **2** a short sleeveless cloak as a fixed or detachable part of a longer cloak or coat. [F f. Prov. *capa* f. LL *cappa* CAP]
■ **1** cloak; mantle, shawl, stole, wrap, *hist.* mantelet.

cape[2] /kayp/ *n.* **1** a headland or promontory. **2** (**the Cape**) **a** the Cape of Good Hope. **b** the S. African province containing it. □ **Cape Coloured** *adj. S.Afr.* of the Coloured (see COLOURED 2) population of Cape Province. ● *n.* a member of this population. **Cape doctor** *S.Afr. colloq.* a strong SE wind. **Cape Dutch** *archaic* Afrikaans. **Cape gooseberry 1** an edible soft roundish yellow berry enclosed in a lantern-like husk. **2** the plant, *Physalis peruviana*, bearing these. [ME f. OF *cap* f. Prov. *cap* ult. f. L *caput* head]
■ **1** headland, promontory, neck, point, tip, ness, bluff, bill, foreland, head, point, tongue, *Sc.* mull.

capelin /káplin/ *n.* (also **caplin**) a small smeltlike fish, *Mallotus villosus*, of the N. Atlantic, used as food and as bait for catching cod etc. [F f. Prov. *capelan*: see CHAPLAIN]

caper[1] /káypər/ *v.* & *n.* ● *v.intr.* jump or run about playfully. ● *n.* **1** a playful jump or leap. **2 a** a fantastic proceeding; a prank. **b** *sl.* any activity or occupation. □ **cut a caper** (or **capers**) act friskily. □□ **caperer** *n.* [abbr. of CAPRIOLE]
■ *v.* skip, hop, frolic, leap, jump, frisk, romp, bound, spring, gambol, prance, *colloq.* galumph, *sl.* cavort; curvet. ● *n.* **1** skip, leap, jump, spring, frolic, hop, gambol, frisk, bound, curvet, gambade. **2 a** escapade, stunt, trick, prank, gambade, high jinks, antic, nonsense, *colloq.* shenanigans, lark, *US colloq.* dido. **b** affair, matter, thing, *colloq.* palaver, *Brit. colloq.* lark, *derog.* business, *Brit. sl.* carry-on.

caper[2] /káypər/ *n.* **1** a bramble-like S. European shrub, *Capparis spinosa*. **2** (in *pl.*) its flower buds cooked and pickled for use as flavouring esp. for a savoury sauce. [ME *capres* & F *câpres* f. L *capparis* f. Gk *kapparis*, treated as pl.: cf. CHERRY, PEA]

capercaillie /káppərkáyli/ *n.* (also **capercailzie** /-káylzi/) a large European grouse, *Tetrao urogallus*. [Gael. *capull coille* horse of the wood]

capeskin /káypskin/ *n.* a soft leather made from S. African sheepskin.

capias /káppiass, káyp-/ *n. Law* a writ ordering the arrest of the person named. [L, = you are to seize, f. *capere* take]

capillarity /káppilárriti/ *n.* a phenomenon at liquid boundaries resulting in the rise or depression of liquids in narrow tubes. Also called *capillary action*. [F *capillarité* (as CAPILLARY)]

capillary /kəpílləri/ *adj.* & *n.* ● *adj.* **1** of or like a hair. **2** (of a tube) of hairlike internal diameter. **3** of one of the delicate ramified blood vessels intervening between arteries and veins. ● *n.* (*pl.* **-ies**) **1** a capillary tube. **2** a capillary blood vessel. □ **capillary action** = CAPILLARITY. [L *capillaris* f. *capillus* hair]

capital[1] /káppit'l/ *n.*, *adj.*, & *int.* ● *n.* **1** the most important town or city of a country or region, usu. its seat of government and administrative centre. **2 a** the money or other assets with which a company starts in business. **b** accumulated wealth, esp. as used in further production. **c** money invested or lent at interest. **3** capitalists generally. **4** a capital letter. ● *adj.* **1 a** principal; most important; leading. **b** *colloq.* excellent, first-rate. **2 a** involving or punishable by death (*capital punishment*; *a capital offence*). **b** (of an error etc.) vitally harmful; fatal. **3** (of letters of the alphabet) large in size and of the form used to begin sentences and names etc. ● *int.* expressing approval or satisfaction. □ **capital gain** a profit from the sale of investments or property. **capital goods** goods, esp. machinery, plant, etc., used or to be used in producing commodities (opp. *consumer goods*). **capital levy 1** the appropriation by the State of a fixed proportion of the wealth in the country. **2** a wealth tax. **capital sum** a lump sum of money, esp. payable to an insured person. **capital territory** a territory containing the capital city of a country. **capital transfer tax** *hist.* (in the UK) a tax levied on the transfer of capital by gift or bequest etc. ¶ Replaced in 1986 by *inheritance tax*. **make capital out of** use to one's advantage. **with a capital —** emphatically such (*art with a*

capital A). ▫▫ **capitally** *adv.* [ME f. OF f. L *capitalis* f. *caput -itis* head]
■ *n.* **2** money, assets, funds, stocks, finance(s), riches, cash, *colloq.* wherewithal, shekels, *derog. or joc.* pelf, *sl.* readies, dosh, dough, scratch, *Brit. sl.* lolly; wealth, means, property, resources, savings, principal. **4** capital letter, upper case letter, initial. ● *adj.* **1 a** chief, main, major, important, cardinal, central, principal, prime, primary, paramount, pre-eminent, foremost, leading. **b** see BRILLIANT 4. **2 b** see GRAVE² *adj.* 2. **3** upper case, initial, large, big. ▫ **make capital out of** see PROFIT *v.* 2.

capital² /káppit'l/ *n. Archit.* the head or cornice of a pillar or column. [ME f. OF *capitel* f. LL *capitellum* dimin. of L *caput* head]
■ head, top, crown, cap, cornice.

capitalism /káppitəliz'm/ *n.* **1 a** an economic system in which the production and distribution of goods depend on invested private capital and profit-making. **b** the possession of capital or wealth. **2** *Polit.* the dominance of private owners of capital and production for profit.

capitalist /káppitəlist/ *n.* & *adj.* ● *n.* **1** a person using or possessing capital; a rich person. **2** an advocate of capitalism. ● *adj.* of or favouring capitalism. ▫▫ **capitalistic** /-lístik/ *adj.* **capitalistically** /-lístikəli/ *adv.*

capitalize /káppitəlīz/ *v.* (also **-ise**) **1** *tr.* **a** convert into or provide with capital. **b** calculate or realize the present value of an income. **c** reckon (the value of an asset) by setting future benefits against the cost of maintenance. **2** *tr.* **a** write (a letter of the alphabet) as a capital. **b** begin (a word) with a capital letter. **3** *intr.* (foll. by *on*) use to one's advantage; profit from. ▫▫ **capitalization** /-záysh'n/ *n.* [F *capitaliser* (as CAPITAL¹)]

capitation /káppitáysh'n/ *n.* **1** a tax or fee at a set rate per person. **2** the levying of such a tax or fee. ▫ **capitation grant** a grant of a sum calculated from the number of people to be catered for, esp. in education. [F *capitation* or LL *capitatio* poll-tax f. *caput* head]

capitular /kəpítyoolər/ *adj.* **1** of or relating to a cathedral chapter. **2** *Anat.* of or relating to a terminal protuberance of a bone. [LL *capitularis* f. L *capitulum* CHAPTER]

capitulary /kəpítyooləri/ *n.* (*pl.* **-ies**) a collection of ordinances, esp. of the Frankish kings. [LL *capitularius* (as CAPITULAR)]

capitulate /kəpítyoolayt/ *v.intr.* surrender, esp. on stated conditions. ▫▫ **capitulator** *n.* **capitulatory** /-lətəri/ *adj.* [med.L *capitulare* draw up under headings f. L *caput* head]
■ surrender, yield, give up *or* in *or* way, bow (down), submit, succumb, throw in the towel.

capitulation /kəpítyooláysh'n/ *n.* **1** the act of capitulating; surrender. **2** a statement of the main divisions of a subject. **3** an agreement or set of conditions.

capitulum /kəpítyooləm/ *n.* (*pl.* **capitula** /-lə/) *Bot.* an inflorescence with flowers clustered together like a head, as in the daisy family. [L, dimin. of *caput* head]

caplin var. of CAPELIN.

cap'n /kápp'n/ *n. sl.* captain. [contr.]

capo /káppō/ *n.* (in full **capo tasto** /tástō/) (*pl.* **capos** or **capo tastos**) *Mus.* a device secured across the neck of a fretted instrument to raise equally the tuning of all strings by the required amount. [It. *capo tasto* head stop]

capon /káyp'n/ *n.* a domestic cock castrated and fattened for eating. ▫▫ **caponize** *v.tr.* (also **-ise**). [OE f. AF *capun*, OF *capon*, ult. f. L *capo -onis*]
■ ▫▫ **caponize** see NEUTER *v.*

caponier /káppənéer/ *n.* a covered passage across a ditch round a fort. [Sp. *caponera*, lit. 'capon-pen']

capot /kəpót/ *n.* & *v.* ● *n.* (in piquet) the winning of all the tricks by one player. ● *v.tr.* (**capotted, capotting**) score a capot against (an opponent). [F]

capote /kəpṓt/ *n. hist.* a long cloak with a hood, formerly worn by soldiers and travellers etc. [F, dimin. of *cape* CAPE¹]

cappuccino /káppoochéenō/ *n.* (*pl.* **-os**) coffee with milk made frothy with pressurized steam. [It., = CAPUCHIN]

capriccio /kəpríchiō/ *n.* (*pl.* **-os**) **1** a lively and usu. short musical composition. **2** a painting etc. representing a fantasy or a mixture of real and imaginary features. [It., = sudden start, orig. 'horror']

capriccioso /kəpríchiṓsō/ *adv.*, *adj.*, & *n. Mus.* ● *adv.* & *adj.* in a free and impulsive style. ● *n.* (*pl.* **-os**) a capriccioso passage or movement. [It., = capricious]

caprice /kəpréess/ *n.* **1 a** an unaccountable or whimsical change of mind or conduct. **b** a tendency to this. **2** a work of lively fancy in painting, drawing, or music; a capriccio. [F f. It. CAPRICCIO]
■ **1** see FANCY *n.* 2.

capricious /kəpríshəss/ *adj.* **1** guided by or given to caprice. **2** irregular, unpredictable. ▫▫ **capriciously** *adv.* **capriciousness** *n.* [F *capricieux* f. It. CAPRICCIOSO]
■ erratic, kittle(-cattle), unsteady, variable, fitful, unstable, wayward, unpredictable, undependable, inconsistent, irregular, changeable, unreliable, inconstant; giddy, mercurial, volatile, temperamental, wanton, fickle, impulsive, quirky, whimsical, flighty, fanciful.

Capricorn /káprikorn/ *n.* (also **Capricornus** /-kórnəss/) **1** a constellation, traditionally regarded as contained in the figure of a goat's horns. **2 a** the tenth sign of the zodiac (the Goat). **b** a person born when the sun is in this sign. ▫▫ **Capricornian** *n.* & *adj.* [ME f. OF *capricorne* f. L *capricornus* f. *caper -pri* goat + *cornu* horn]

caprine /káprīn/ *adj.* of or like a goat. [ME f. L *caprinus* f. *caper -pri* goat]

capriole /kápriōl/ *n.* & *v.* ● *n.* **1** a leap or caper. **2** a trained horse's high leap and kick without advancing. ● *v.* **1** *intr.* (of a horse or its rider) perform a capriole. **2** *tr.* make (a horse) capriole. [F f. It. *capriola* leap, ult. f. *caper -pri* goat]
■ *v.* **1** see PRANCE *v.*

Capris /kəpréez/ *n.pl.* (also **Capri pants**) women's close-fitting tapered trousers. [*Capri*, an island in the bay of Naples]

caps. *abbr.* capital letters.

Capsian /kápsiən/ *adj.* & *n.* ● *adj.* of or relating to a palaeolithic culture of N. Africa and S. Europe. ● *n.* this culture. [L *Capsa* = Gafsa in Tunisia]

capsicum /kápsikəm/ *n.* **1** any plant of the genus *Capsicum*, having edible capsular fruits containing many seeds, esp. *C. annuum* yielding several varieties of pepper. **2** the fruit of any of these plants, which vary in size, colour, and pungency. [mod.L, perh. f. L *capsa* box]

capsid¹ /kápsid/ *n.* any bug of the family Capsidae, esp. one that feeds on plants. [mod.L *Capsus* a genus of them]

capsid² /kápsid/ *n.* the protein coat or shell of a virus. [F *capside* f. L *capsa* box]

capsize /kapsīz/ *v.* **1** *tr.* upset or overturn (a boat). **2** *intr.* be capsized. ▫▫ **capsizal** *n.* [*cap-* as in Prov. *capvirar*, F *chavirer*: *-size* unexpl.]
■ keel, overturn, turn upside down, turn over, invert, tip over; upset; turn turtle.

capstan /kápstən/ *n.* **1** a thick revolving cylinder with a vertical axis, for winding an anchor cable or a halyard etc. **2** a revolving spindle on a tape recorder, that guides the tape past the head. ▫ **capstan lathe** a lathe with a revolving tool-holder. [Prov. *cabestan*, ult. f. L *capistrum* halter f. *capere* seize]

capstone /kápstōn/ *n.* coping; a coping-stone.

capsule /kápsyōōl/ *n.* **1** a small soluble case of gelatine enclosing a dose of medicine and swallowed with it. **2** a detachable compartment of a spacecraft or nose-cone of a rocket. **3** an enclosing membrane in the body. **4 a** a dry fruit that releases its seeds when ripe. **b** the spore-producing part of mosses and liverworts. **5** *Biol.* an enveloping layer surrounding certain bacteria. **6** (*attrib.*) concise; highly condensed (*a capsule history of jazz*). ▫▫ **capsular** *adj.* **capsulate** *adj.* [F f. L *capsula* f. *capsa* CASE²]
■ **1** see PILL 1a.

capsulize /kápsyoolīz/ *v.tr.* (also **-ise**) put (information etc.) in compact form.

Capt. *abbr.* Captain.

captain /káptin/ *n.* & *v.* ● *n.* **1 a** a chief or leader. **b** the leader of a team, esp. in sports. **c** a powerful or influential person (*captain of industry*). **2 a** the person in command of a merchant or passenger ship. **b** the pilot of a civil aircraft. **3** (as a title **Captain**) **a** an army or *US* Air Force officer next above lieutenant. **b** a Navy officer in command of a warship; one ranking below commodore or rear admiral and above commander. **c** *US* a police officer in charge of a precinct, ranking below Chief Officer. **4 a** a foreman. **b** a head boy or girl in a school. **c** *US* a supervisor of waiters or bellboys. **5 a** a great soldier or strategist. **b** an experienced commander. ● *v.tr.* be captain of; lead. □ **captain-general** an honorary officer, esp. of artillery. **Captain of the Fleet** *Brit.* a Navy staff officer in charge of maintenance. □□ **captaincy** *n.* (*pl.* **-ies**). **captainship** *n.* [ME & OF *capitain* f. LL *capitaneus* chief f. L *caput capit-* head]
■ *n.* **1, 4, 5** see CHIEF *n.* **2** see SKIPPER[1] *n.* ● *v.* see LEAD[1] *v.* 6, 7a.

caption /kápsh'n/ *n.* & *v.* ● *n.* **1** a title or brief explanation appended to an illustration, cartoon, etc. **2** wording appearing on a cinema or television screen as part of a film or broadcast. **3** the heading of a chapter or article etc. **4** *Law* a certificate attached to or written on a document. ● *v.tr.* provide with a caption. [ME f. L *captio* f. *capere capt-* take]
■ *n.* **1, 3** see TITLE *n.* 2. **2** see TITLE *n.* 4.

captious /kápshəss/ *adj.* given to finding fault or raising petty objections. □□ **captiously** *adv.* **captiousness** *n.* [ME f. OF *captieux* or L *captiosus* (as CAPTION)]
■ see OVERCRITICAL.

captivate /káptivayt/ *v.tr.* **1** overwhelm with charm or affection. **2** fascinate. □□ **captivating** *adj.* **captivatingly** *adv.* **captivation** /-váysh'n/ *n.* [LL *captivare* take captive (as CAPTIVE)]
■ beguile, charm, delight, enamour, enchant, bewitch, enrapture, dazzle, infatuate, transport, attract, allure, seduce, win (over), take *or* draw in, regale, take by storm; intrigue, fascinate, enthral, hypnotize, entrance.

captive /káptiv/ *n.* & *adj.* ● *n.* a person or animal that has been taken prisoner or confined. ● *adj.* **1 a** taken prisoner. **b** kept in confinement or under restraint. **2 a** unable to escape. **b** in a position of having to comply (*captive audience*; *captive market*). **3** of or like a prisoner (*captive state*). □ **captive balloon** a balloon held by a rope from the ground. [ME f. L *captivus* f. *capere capt-* take]
■ *n.* prisoner, hostage, detainee, internee; capture, catch; slave, bondsman. ● *adj.* **1** imprisoned, incarcerated, confined, caged, locked up, chained, shackled, fettered, under lock and key, behind bars; under restraint.

captivity /kaptívviti/ *n.* (*pl.* **-ies**) **1 a** the condition or circumstances of being a captive. **b** a period of captivity. **2** (**the Captivity**) the captivity of the Jews in Babylon in the 6th c. BC.
■ **1** confinement, imprisonment, internment, detention, custody, incarceration, restraint, duress, *archaic* durance; bondage, slavery, enslavement, enthralment, servitude, *literary* thraldom.

captor /káptər, -tor/ *n.* a person who captures (a person, place, etc.). [L (as CAPTIVE)]

capture /kápchər/ *v.* & *n.* ● *v.tr.* **1 a** take prisoner; seize as a prize. **b** obtain by force or trickery. **2** portray in permanent form (*could not capture the likeness*). **3** *Physics* absorb (a subatomic particle). **4** (in board games) make a move that secures the removal of (an opposing piece) from the board. **5** (of a stream) divert the upper course of (another stream) by encroaching on its basin. **6** cause (data) to be stored in a computer. ● *n.* **1** the act of capturing. **2 a** thing or person captured. □□ **capturer** *n.* [F f. L *captura* f. *capere capt-* take]
■ *v.* **1** seize, take, take captive *or* prisoner, catch, lay *or* take hold of, grab, ensnare, entrap, snare, hook, apprehend, arrest, collar, *sl.* pinch, nab, *Brit. sl.* nick; kidnap, take as hostage; carry off *or* away, secure, snap up, snatch, take possession of, take over, get, net, conquer, take away, make off with, *US* snag, *colloq.* bag, land. **2** see CHARACTERIZE 1, 2. ● *n.* **1** seizure, taking, arrest, apprehension, *sl.* pinch; kidnap. **2** see CAPTIVE *n.*, CATCH *n.* 2b.

Capuchin /kápyoochin/ *n.* **1** a Franciscan friar of the new rule of 1529. **2** a cloak and hood formerly worn by women. **3** (**capuchin**) **a** any monkey of the genus *Cebus* of S. America, with cowl-like head hair. **b** a variety of pigeon with head and neck feathers resembling a cowl. [F f. It. *cappuccino* f. *cappuccio* cowl f. *cappa* CAPE[1]]

capybara /káppibaárə/ *n.* a very large semi-aquatic rodent, *Hydrochoerus hydrochaeris*, native to S. America. [Tupi]

car /kaar/ *n.* **1** (in full **motor car**) a road vehicle with an enclosed passenger compartment, powered by an internal-combustion engine. **2** (in *comb.*) **a** a wheeled vehicle, esp. of a specified kind (*tramcar*). **b** a railway carriage of a specified type (*dining-car*). **3** *US* any railway carriage or van. **4** the passenger compartment of a lift, cableway, balloon, etc. **5** *poet.* a wheeled vehicle; a chariot. □ **car bomb** a terrorist bomb concealed in or under a parked car. **car-boot sale** an outdoor sale at which participants sell unwanted possessions from the boots of their cars. **car coat** a short coat designed esp. for car drivers. **car park** an area for parking cars. **car phone** a radio-telephone for use in a motor vehicle. □□ **carful** *n.* (*pl.* **-fuls**). [ME f. AF & ONF *carre* ult. f. L *carrum*, *carrus*, of OCelt. orig.]
■ **1** (motor) vehicle, motor car, passenger car, *Brit.* motor, *US* automobile, *archaic* horseless carriage, *colloq.* machine, buggy, bus, wagon, *US colloq.* auto, *sl.* wheels, drag. **2, 3** (railway) carriage, van, wagon. □ **car-boot sale** see *jumble sale*.

carabineer /kárrəbineér/ *n.* (also **carabinier**) *hist.* **1** a soldier whose principal weapon is a carbine. **2** (**the Carabineers**) the Royal Scots Dragoon Guards. [F *carabinier* f. *carabine* CARBINE]

carabiniere /kárrəbinyáiri/ *n.* (*pl.* ***carabinieri*** /*pronunc.* same/) an Italian gendarme. [It.]

caracal /kárrəkal/ *n.* a lynx, *Felis caracal*, native to N. Africa and SW Asia. [F or Sp. f. Turk. *karakulak* f. *kara* black + *kulak* ear]

caracole /kárrəkōl/ *n.* & *v.* ● *n.* a horse's half-turn to the right or left. ● *v.* **1** *intr.* (of a horse or its rider) perform a caracole. **2** *tr.* make (a horse) caracole. [F]

caracul var. of KARAKUL.

carafe /kəráf, -raáf/ *n.* a glass container for water or wine, esp. at a table or bedside. [F f. It. *caraffa*, ult. f. Arab. *ġarrāfa* drinking vessel]
■ see JUG *n.* 1, 2.

carambola /kárrəmbṓlə/ *n.* **1** a small tree, *Averrhoa carambola*, native to SE Asia, bearing golden-yellow ribbed fruit. **2** this fruit. Also called *star fruit*. [Port., prob. of Indian or E. Indian orig.]

caramel /kárrəmel/ *n.* **1 a** sugar or syrup heated until it turns brown, then used as a flavouring or to colour spirits etc. **b** a kind of soft toffee made with sugar, butter, etc., melted and further heated. **2** the light-brown colour of caramel. [F f. Sp. *caramelo*]

caramelize /kárrəməlīz/ *v.* (also **-ise**) **1 a** *tr.* convert (sugar or syrup) into caramel. **b** *intr.* (of sugar or syrup) be converted into caramel. **2** *tr.* coat or cook (food) with caramelized sugar or syrup. □□ **caramelization** /-záysh'n/ *n.*

carapace /kárrəpayss/ *n.* the hard upper shell of a tortoise or a crustacean. [F f. Sp. *carapacho*]

carat /kárrət/ *n.* **1** a unit of weight for precious stones, now equivalent to 200 milligrams. **2** (*US* **karat**) a measure of purity of gold, pure gold being 24 carats. [F f. It. *carato* f. Arab. *ḳīrāṭ* weight of four grains, f. Gk *keration* fruit of the carob (dimin. of *keras* horn)]

caravan /kárrəvan/ *n.* & *v.* ● *n.* **1 a** *Brit.* a vehicle equipped for living in and usu. towed by a motor vehicle or a horse. **b** *US* a covered motor vehicle equipped for living in. **2** a company of merchants or pilgrims etc. travelling together,

esp. across a desert in Asia or N. Africa. **3** a covered cart or carriage. ● *v.intr.* (**caravanned, caravanning**) travel or live in a caravan. □ **caravan site** (or **park**) a place where caravans are parked as dwellings, often with special amenities. □□ **caravanner** *n.* [F *caravane* f. Pers. *kārwān*]
■ *n.* **1 a** mobile home, *Brit.* van, *US* trailer. **b** motor caravan, caravanette, *propr.* Dormobile.

caravanette /kárrəvanét/ *n.* a motor vehicle with a caravan-like rear compartment for eating, sleeping, etc.

caravanserai /kárrəvánsəri, -rī/ *n.* an Eastern inn with a central court where caravans (see CARAVAN 2) may rest. [Pers. *kārwānsarāy* f. *sarāy* palace]

caravel /kárrəvel/ *n.* (also **carvel** /kaárv'l/) *hist.* a small light fast ship, chiefly Spanish and Portuguese of the 15th–17th c. [F *caravelle* f. Port. *caravela* f. Gk *karabos* horned beetle, light ship]

caraway /kárrəway/ *n.* an umbelliferous plant, *Carum carvi*, bearing clusters of tiny white flowers. □ **caraway seed** its fruit used as flavouring and as a source of oil. [prob. OSp. *alcarahueya* f. Arab. *alkarāwiyā*, perh. f. Gk *karon, kareon* cumin]

carb /kaarb/ *n. colloq.* a carburettor. [abbr.]

carbamate /kaárbəmayt/ *n. Chem.* a salt or ester of an amide of carbonic acid. [CARBONIC + AMIDE]

carbide /kaárbīd/ *n. Chem.* **1** a binary compound of carbon. **2** = *calcium carbide.*

carbie /kaárbi/ *n.* (also **carby**) *Austral. colloq.* a carburettor. [abbr.]

carbine /kaárbīn/ *n.* a short firearm, usu. a rifle, orig. for cavalry use. [F *carabine* (this form also earlier in Engl.), weapon of the *carabin* mounted musketeer]

carbo- /kaárbō/ *comb. form* carbon (*carbohydrate; carbolic; carboxyl*).

carbohydrate /kaárbəhī́drayt/ *n. Biochem.* any of a large group of energy-producing organic compounds containing carbon, hydrogen, and oxygen, e.g. starch, glucose, and other sugars.

carbolic /kaarbóllik/ *n.* (in full **carbolic acid**) phenol, esp. when used as a disinfectant. □ **carbolic soap** soap containing this. [CARBO- + -OL[1] + -IC]

carbon /kaárb'n/ *n.* **1** a non-metallic element occurring naturally as diamond, graphite, and charcoal, and in all organic compounds. ¶ Symb.: **C**. **2 a** = *carbon copy*. **b** = *carbon paper*. **3** a rod of carbon in an arc lamp. □ **carbon black** a fine carbon powder made by burning hydrocarbons in insufficient air. **carbon copy 1** a copy made with carbon paper. **2** a person or thing identical or similar to another (*is a carbon copy of his father*). **carbon cycle** *Biol.* the cycle in which carbon compounds are interconverted, usu. by living organisms. **carbon dating** the determination of the age of an organic object from the ratio of isotopes which changes as carbon-14 decays. **carbon dioxide** a colourless odourless gas occurring naturally in the atmosphere and formed by respiration. ¶ Chem. formula: CO_2. **carbon disulphide** a colourless liquid used as a solvent. ¶ Chem. formula: CS_2. **carbon fibre** a thin strong crystalline filament of carbon used as strengthening material in resins, ceramics, etc. **carbon-14** a long-lived radioactive carbon isotope of mass 14, used in radiocarbon dating, and as a tracer in biochemistry. **carbon monoxide** a colourless odourless toxic gas formed by the incomplete burning of carbon. ¶ Chem. formula: CO. **carbon paper** a thin carbon-coated paper used for making (esp. typed) copies. **carbon steel** a steel with properties dependent on the percentage of carbon present. **carbon tax** a tax on the carbon emissions that result from burning fossil fuels (e.g. in motor vehicles) because of their contribution to the greenhouse effect. **carbon tetrachloride** a colourless volatile liquid used as a solvent. ¶ Chem. formula: CCl_4. **carbon-12** a carbon isotope of mass 12, used in calculations of atomic mass units. [F *carbone* f. L *carbo -onis* charcoal]
■ □ **carbon copy 1** see DUPLICATE *n.*

carbonaceous /kaárbənáyshəss/ *adj.* **1** consisting of or containing carbon. **2** of or like coal or charcoal.

carbonade /kaárbənáyd/ *n.* a rich beef stew made with onions and beer. [F]

carbonado /kaárbənáydō/ *n.* (*pl.* **-os**) a dark opaque or impure kind of diamond used as an abrasive, for drills etc. [Port.]

carbonate /kaárbənayt/ *n.* & *v.* ● *n. Chem.* a salt of carbonic acid. ● *v.tr.* **1** impregnate with carbon dioxide; aerate. **2** convert into a carbonate. □□ **carbonation** /-náysh'n/ *n.* [F *carbonat* f. mod.L *carbonatum* (as CARBON)]

carbonic /kaarbónnik/ *adj. Chem.* containing carbon. □ **carbonic acid** a very weak acid formed from carbon dioxide dissolved in water. **carbonic acid gas** *archaic* carbon dioxide.

carboniferous /kaárbəníffərəss/ *adj.* & *n.* ● *adj.* **1** producing coal. **2** (**Carboniferous**) *Geol.* of or relating to the fifth period in the Palaeozoic era, with evidence of the first reptiles and extensive coal-forming swamp forests. ¶ Cf. Appendix VII. ● *n.* (**Carboniferous**) *Geol.* this period or system.

carbonize /kaárbənīz/ *v.tr.* (also **-ise**) **1** convert into carbon by heating. **2** reduce to charcoal or coke. **3** coat with carbon. □□ **carbonization** /-záysh'n/ *n.*

carbonyl /kaárbənīl/ *n.* (used *attrib.*) *Chem.* the divalent radical CO.

carborundum /kaábərúndəm/ *n.* a compound of carbon and silicon used esp. as an abrasive. [CARBON + CORUNDUM]

carboxyl /kaarbóksil/ *n. Chem.* the univalent acid radical (-COOH), present in most organic acids. □□ **carboxylic** *adj.* [CARBON + OXYGEN + -YL]

carboy /kaárboy/ *n.* a large globular glass bottle usu. protected by a frame, for containing liquids. [Pers. *ḳarāba* large glass flagon]

carbuncle /kaárbungk'l/ *n.* **1** a severe abscess in the skin. **2** a bright red gem. □□ **carbuncular** /-búngkyoolər/ *adj.* [ME f. OF *charbucle* etc. f. L *carbunculus* small coal f. *carbo* coal]
■ **1** see BOIL[2].

carburation /kaárbyooráysh'n/ *n.* the process of charging air with a spray of liquid hydrocarbon fuel, esp. in an internal-combustion engine. [as CARBURET]

carburet /kaárbyoorét/ *v.tr.* (**carburetted, carburetting**; *US* **carbureted, carbureting**) combine (a gas etc.) with carbon. [earlier *carbure* f. F f. L *carbo* (as CARBON)]

carburettor /kaárbyoorétтər, kaárbər-/ *n.* (also **carburetter**, *US* **carburetor** /kaárbyooraytər/) an apparatus for carburation of petrol and air in an internal-combustion engine. [as CARBURET + -OR[1]]

carby var. of CARBIE.

carcajou /kaárkəjōō, -kazhōō/ *n. US* = WOLVERINE. [F, app. of Amer. Ind. orig.]

carcass /kaárkəss/ *n.* (also **carcase**) **1** the dead body of an animal, esp. a trunk for cutting up as meat. **2** the bones of a cooked bird. **3** *derog.* the human body, living or dead. **4** the skeleton, framework of a building, ship, etc. **5** worthless remains. □ **carcass meat** raw meat, not preserved. [ME f. AF *carcois* (OF *charcois*) & f. F *carcasse*: ult. orig. unkn.]
■ **1** see BODY *n.* 1.

carcinogen /kaarsínnəjən/ *n.* any substance that produces cancer. [as CARCINOMA + -GEN]

carcinogenesis /kaársinəjénnisiss/ *n.* the production of cancer.

carcinogenic /kaársinəjénnik/ *adj.* producing cancer. □□ **carcinogenicity** /-níssiti/ *n.*

carcinoma /kaársinṓmə/ *n.* (*pl.* **carcinomata** /-mətə/ or **carcinomas**) a cancer, esp. one arising in epithelial tissue. □□ **carcinomatous** *adj.* [L f. Gk *karkinōma* f. *karkinos* crab]
■ see TUMOUR.

Card. *abbr.* Cardinal.

card[1] /kaard/ *n.* & *v.* ● *n.* **1** thick stiff paper or thin pasteboard. **2 a** a flat piece of this, esp. for writing or printing on. **b** = POSTCARD. **c** a card used to send greetings, issue an invitation, etc. (*birthday card*). **d** = *visiting-card*. **e** = *business card*. **f** a ticket of admission or membership. **3 a**

= PLAYING-CARD. **b** a similar card in a set designed for particular games, e.g. happy families. **c** (in *pl.*) card-playing; a card-game. **4** (in *pl.*) *colloq.* an employee's documents, esp. for tax and national insurance, held by the employer. **5 a** a programme of events at a race-meeting etc. **b** *Cricket* a score-card. **c** a list of holes on a golf course, on which a player's scores are entered. **6** *colloq.* a person, esp. an odd or amusing one (*what a card!*; *a knowing card*). **7** a plan or expedient (*sure card*). **8** a printed or written notice, set of rules, etc., for display. **9** a small rectangular piece of plastic issued by a bank, building society, etc., with personal (often machine-readable) data on it, chiefly to obtain cash or credit (*cheque card*; *credit card*; *do you have a card?*). ● *v.tr.* **1** fix to a card. **2** write on a card, esp. for indexing. □ **ask for** (or **get**) **one's cards** ask (or be told) to leave one's employment. **card-carrying** being a registered member of an organization, esp. a political party or trade union. **card-game** a game in which playing-cards are used. **card index** an index in which each item is entered on a separate card. **card-index** *v.tr.* make a card index of. **card-playing** the playing of card-games. **card-sharp** (or **-sharper**) a swindler at card-games. **card-table** a table for card-playing, esp. a folding one. **card up one's sleeve** a plan in reserve. **card vote** a block vote, esp. in trade-union meetings. **on** (*US* **in**) **the cards** possible or likely. **put** (or **lay**) **one's cards on the table** reveal one's resources, intentions, etc. [ME f. OF *carte* f. L *charta* f. Gk *khartēs* papyrus-leaf]

■ *n.* **4** (*cards*) documents, papers, records, credentials. **6** character, eccentric, original, *Austral.* hard doer, *Austral.* & *NZ* hard case; joker, prankster, practical joker, wag, wit, humorist, comedian, comedienne, *archaic* droll, *colloq.* scream, laugh, *Austral.* & *NZ sl.* dag. □ **get one's cards** get one's notice, *colloq.* get the boot *or* sack, get one's walking papers *or* marching orders, *Brit. sl.* get the chop. **on** (*US* **in**) **the cards** likely, probable, possible, expected, in the offing, on the horizon, in view *or* prospect *or* store, to come, *disp.* liable. **put** (or **lay**) **one's cards on the table** act openly, play fair, reveal all, be open *or* honest *or* straight, show one's cards *or* hand, *colloq.* come clean.

card[2] /kaard/ *n.* & *v.* ● *n.* a toothed instrument, wire brush, etc., for raising a nap on cloth or for disentangling fibres before spinning. ● *v.tr.* brush, comb, cleanse, or scratch with a card. □ **carding-wool** short-stapled wool. □□ **carder** *n.* [ME f. OF *carde* f. Prov. *carda* f. *cardar* tease, comb, ult. f. L *carere* card]

cardamom /kaárdəməm/ *n.* (also **cardamum**) **1** an aromatic SE Asian plant, *Elettaria cardamomum*. **2** the seed-capsules of this used as a spice. [L *cardamomum* or F *cardamome* f. Gk *kardamōmon* f. *kardamon* cress + *amōmon* a spice plant]

cardan joint /kaárd'n/ *n. Engin.* a universal joint. [G. *Cardano*, It. mathematician d. 1576]

cardan shaft /kaárd'n/ *n. Engin.* a shaft with a universal joint at one or both ends.

cardboard /kaárdbord/ *n.* & *adj.* ● *n.* pasteboard or stiff paper, esp. for making cards or boxes. ● *adj.* **1** made of cardboard. **2** flimsy, insubstantial. □ **cardboard city** a place where homeless people gather at night using cardboard boxes etc. for shelter.

cardiac /kaárdiak/ *adj.* & *n.* ● *adj.* **1** of or relating to the heart. **2** of or relating to the part of the stomach nearest the oesophagus. ● *n.* a person with heart disease. [F *cardiaque* or L *cardiacus* f. Gk *kardiakos* f. *kardia* heart]

■ *adj.* cardio-.

cardie var. of CARDY.

cardigan /kaárdigən/ *n.* a knitted jacket fastening down the front, usu. with long sleeves. [named after the 7th Earl of *Cardigan* d. 1868]

cardinal /kaárdin'l/ *n.* & *adj.* ● *n.* **1** (as a title **Cardinal**) a leading dignitary of the RC Church, one of the college electing the Pope. **2** any small American songbird of the genus *Richmondena*, the males of which have scarlet plumage. **3** *hist.* a woman's cloak, orig. of scarlet cloth with a hood. ● *adj.* **1** chief, fundamental; on which something hinges. **2** of deep scarlet (like a cardinal's cassock). □ **cardinal-flower** the scarlet lobelia. **cardinal humour** see HUMOUR. **cardinal numbers** those denoting quantity (one, two, three, etc.), as opposed to ordinal numbers (first, second, third, etc.). **cardinal points** the four main points of the compass (N., S., E., W.). **cardinal virtues** the chief moral attributes: justice, prudence, temperance, and fortitude. □□ **cardinalate** /-nəlayt/ *n.* (in sense 1 of *n.*). **cardinally** *adv.* **cardinalship** *n.* (in sense 1 of *n.*). [ME f. OF f. L *cardinalis* f. *cardo -inis* hinge: in Eng. first applied to the four virtues on which conduct 'hinges']

■ *adj.* **1** important, chief, major, key, special, main, central, principal, prime, primary, essential, necessary, fundamental; supreme, paramount, highest, first, foremost, leading, pre-eminent. **2** scarlet, cinnabar, vermilion, *poet.* vermeil.

cardio- /kaárdiō/ *comb. form* heart (*cardiogram*; *cardiology*). [Gk *kardia* heart]

cardiogram /kaárdiōgram/ *n.* a record of muscle activity within the heart, made by a cardiograph.

cardiograph /kaárdiōgraaf/ *n.* an instrument for recording heart muscle activity. □□ **cardiographer** /-diógrəfər/ *n.* **cardiography** /-diógrəfi/ *n.*

cardiology /kaárdióllәji/ *n.* the branch of medicine concerned with diseases and abnormalities of the heart. □□ **cardiologist** *n.*

cardiovascular /kaárdiōváskyoolər/ *adj.* of or relating to the heart and blood vessels.

cardoon /kaardóon/ *n.* a thistle-like plant, *Cynara cardunculus*, allied to the globe artichoke, with leaves used as a vegetable. [F *cardon* ult. f. L *cardu(u)s* thistle]

cardphone /kaárdfōn/ *n.* a public telephone operated by the insertion of a prepaid plastic machine-readable card instead of money.

cardy /kaárdi/ *n.* (also **cardie**) (*pl.* **-ies**) *colloq.* a cardigan. [abbr.]

care /kair/ *n.* & *v.* ● *n.* **1** worry, anxiety. **2** an occasion for this. **3** serious attention; heed, caution, pains (*assembled with care*; *handle with care*). **4 a** protection, charge. **b** *Brit.* = *child care*. **5** a thing to be done or seen to. ● *v.intr.* **1** (usu. foll. by *about*, *for*, *whether*) feel concern or interest. **2** (usu. foll. by *for*, *about*, and with neg. expressed or implied) feel liking, affection, regard, or deference (*don't care for jazz*). **3** (foll. by *to* + infin.) wish or be willing (*should not care to be seen with him*; *would you care to try them?*). □ **care for** provide for; look after. **care-label** a label attached to clothing, with instructions for washing etc. **care of** at the address of (*sent it care of his sister*). **for all one cares** *colloq.* denoting uninterest or unconcern (*for all I care they can leave tomorrow*; *I could be dying for all you care*). **have a care** take care; be careful. **I** (etc.) **couldn't** (*US* **could**) **care less** *colloq.* an expression of complete indifference. **in care** *Brit.* (of a child) taken into the care of a local authority. **take care 1** be careful. **2** (foll. by *to* + infin.) not fail or neglect. **take care of 1** look after; keep safe. **2** deal with. **3** dispose of. [OE *caru*, *carian*, f. Gmc]

■ *n.* **1, 2** anxiety, worry, trouble, anguish, uneasiness, disquiet, distress, grief, sorrow, sadness, suffering, misery, tribulation, *archaic or literary* woe, *literary* dolour; see also BURDEN *n.* 1, 2. **3** heedfulness, attention, thought, consideration, deliberation, awareness, pains, heed, carefulness, meticulousness, punctiliousness; caution, cautiousness, vigilance, mindfulness, circumspection, watchfulness. **4 a** responsibility, charge, protection, guardianship, custody, custodianship, keeping, safe keeping, trust; control, direction, supervision, management, authority. **5** see RESPONSIBILITY 2. ● *v.* **1** be concerned *or* bothered, trouble oneself, feel interest, worry, fret, trouble, mind. **2** see LIKE[2] *v.* 1. **3** see WISH *v.* 1. □ **care for** look after, tend, attend (to), watch over, mind, protect, take care of, provide for, nurse, minister to, wait on; be responsible for. **have a care** see BEWARE. **take care 1** see BEWARE. **take care of 1** look after, attend to, be responsible for, take charge of, take responsibility for, be careful of; tend, nurse, minister to, care for; watch over, mind; keep safe, safeguard, protect, conserve. **2** see DEAL[1] *v.* 1a. **3** see *dispose of* (DISPOSE) 1a, c.

careen /kəre͞en/ *v.* **1** *tr.* turn (a ship) on one side for cleaning, caulking, or repair. **2 a** *intr.* tilt; lean over. **b** *tr.* cause to do this. **3** *intr. US* swerve about; career. ¶ Sense 3 is infl. by *career* (v.). ▫▫ **careenage** *n.* [earlier as noun, = careened position of ship, f. F *carène* f. It. *carena* f. L *carina* keel]
■ **2** see TILT *v.* 1. **3** career, sway, veer, swerve, lurch, reel, totter, swing.

career /kəre͞er/ *n.* & *v.* ● *n.* **1 a** one's advancement through life, esp. in a profession. **b** the progress through history of a group or institution. **2** a profession or occupation, esp. as offering advancement. **3** (*attrib.*) **a** pursuing or wishing to pursue a career (*career woman*). **b** working permanently in a specified profession (*career diplomat*). **4** swift course; impetus (*in full career*). ● *v.intr.* **1** move or swerve about wildly. **2** go swiftly. [F *carrière* f. It. *carriera* ult. f. L *carrus* CAR]
■ *n.* **1 a** life's work *or* journey. **b** see PROGRESS *n.* 2. **2** occupation, profession, job, trade, craft, *métier*, (line of) work, business, livelihood, calling, vocation, pursuit. **4** see PROGRESS *n.* 1, IMPETUS 1. ● *v.* **1** see SWERVE *v.* **2** speed, race, rush, dash, dart, zip, sprint, fly, whirl, roar, zoom, hurtle, bolt, shoot, *colloq.* tear, *US colloq.* hightail.

careerist /kəre͞erist/ *n.* a person predominantly concerned with personal advancement.

carefree /káirfree/ *adj.* free from anxiety or responsibility; light-hearted. ▫▫ **carefreeness** *n.*
■ nonchalant, easy, easygoing, insouciant, light-hearted, blithe, debonair, happy-go-lucky, gay, breezy, airy, unworried, careless, trouble-free, worry-free, relaxed, contented, happy.

careful /káirfo͝ol/ *adj.* **1** painstaking, thorough. **2** cautious. **3** done with care and attention. **4** (usu. foll. by *that* + clause, or *to* + infin.) taking care; not neglecting. **5** (foll. by *for*, *of*) concerned for; taking care of. ▫▫ **carefully** *adv.* **carefulness** *n.* [OE *carful* (as CARE, -FUL)]
■ **1, 3** meticulous, painstaking, attentive, punctilious, (well-)organized, systematic, precise, accurate, fastidious, thorough, scrupulous, nice, conscientious, assiduous, diligent, particular, finicky, finical, fussy, *colloq.* pernickety; sedulous, deliberate, measured, judicious, studious, ceremonious. **2** cautious, wary, circumspect, guarded, chary, prudent, watchful, aware, alert, vigilant, sharp-eyed, on one's guard *or* toes; suspicious, distrustful, *sl.* leery. **4** (*be careful*) see BEWARE. **5** (*be careful of*) see *take care of* 1 (CARE).

careless /káirliss/ *adj.* **1** not taking care or paying attention. **2** unthinking, insensitive. **3** done without care; inaccurate. **4** light-hearted. **5** (foll. by *of*) not concerned about; taking no heed of. **6** effortless; casual. ▫▫ **carelessly** *adv.* **carelessness** *n.* [OE *carlēas* (as CARE, -LESS)]
■ **1** inattentive, negligent, thoughtless, foolhardy, absent-minded, neglectful, remiss, slapdash, devil-may-care, irresponsible, lackadaisical, perfunctory, *US* derelict; unobservant, unthinking, unmindful, incautious, unwary, reckless, rash. **2** unconcerned, unthinking, insensitive, thoughtless, casual, blithe, indifferent, inconsiderate, uncaring. **3** casual, cursory; inaccurate, imprecise, inexact, incorrect, wrong, error-ridden, erroneous, sloppy. **4** see CAREFREE. **5** see *heedless* (HEED). **6** unstudied, ingenuous, artless, casual, nonchalant; effortless.

carer /káirər/ *n.* a person who cares for a sick or elderly person.

caress /kəréss/ *v.* & *n.* ● *v.tr.* **1** touch or stroke gently or lovingly; kiss. **2** treat fondly or kindly. ● *n.* a loving or gentle touch or kiss. [F *caresse* (n.), *caresser* (v.), f. It. *carezza* ult. f. L *carus* dear]
■ *v.* **1** touch, stroke, pet, fondle, pat, cuddle, embrace, hug, nuzzle; kiss, *colloq.* neck. ● *n.* touch, stroke, pat; cuddle, embrace, hug; kiss.

caret /kárrət/ *n.* a mark (‸, ⁁) indicating a proposed insertion in printing or writing. [L, = is lacking]

caretaker /káirtaykər/ *n.* **1** a person employed to look after something, esp. a house in the owner's absence, or *Brit.* a public building. **2** (*attrib.*) exercising temporary authority (*caretaker government*).
■ **1** see PORTER[2].

careworn /káirworn/ *adj.* showing the effects of prolonged worry.
■ see HAGGARD *adj.*

carfare /kaarfair/ *n. US* a passenger's fare to travel by public transport.

cargo /kaargō/ *n.* (*pl.* **-oes** or **-os**) **1 a** goods carried on a ship or aircraft. **b** a load of such goods. **2** *US* **a** goods carried in a motor vehicle. **b** a load of such goods. ▫ **cargo cult** (orig. in the Pacific Islands) a belief in the forthcoming arrival of ancestral spirits bringing cargoes of food and other goods. [Sp. (as CHARGE)]
■ **1a, 2a** freight, goods, merchandise, freightage, *Naut.* bulk. **1b, 2b** shipment, consignment, shipload, truckload, wagon-load, load, trainload.

carhop /kaarhop/ *n. US colloq.* a waiter at a drive-in restaurant.

cariama var. of SERIEMA.

Carib /kárrib/ *n.* & *adj.* ● *n.* **1** an aboriginal inhabitant of the southern W. Indies or the adjacent coasts. **2** the language of this people. ● *adj.* of or relating to this people. [Sp. *Caribe* f. Haitian]

Caribbean /kárribe͞eən, kəríbbiən/ *n.* & *adj.* ● *n.* the part of the Atlantic between the southern W. Indies and Central America. ● *adj.* **1** of or relating to this region. **2** of the Caribs or their language or culture.

caribou /kárribo͞o/ *n.* (*pl.* same) a N. American reindeer. [Can. F, prob. f. Amer. Ind.]

caricature /kárrikətyoor/ *n.* & *v.* ● *n.* **1** a grotesque usu. comic representation of a person by exaggeration of characteristic traits, in a picture, writing, or mime. **2** a ridiculously poor or absurd imitation or version. ● *v.tr.* make or give a caricature of. ▫▫ **caricatural** *adj.* **caricaturist** *n.* [F f. It. *caricatura* f. *caricare* load, exaggerate: see CHARGE]
■ *n.* **1** cartoon, parody, satire, satirization, burlesque, lampoon, pasquinade, *colloq.* take-off, spoof, *Brit. colloq.* send-up. **2** see JOKE *n.* 2. ● *v.* parody, satirize, lampoon, burlesque, guy; ridicule, mock, distort, *colloq.* take off, *Brit. colloq.* send up.

caries /káireez, -ri-eez/ *n.* (*pl.* same) decay and crumbling of a tooth or bone. [L]

carillon /kərílyən, kárrilyən/ *n.* **1** a set of bells sounded either from a keyboard or mechanically. **2** a tune played on bells. **3** an organ-stop imitating a peal of bells. [F f. OF *quarregnon* peal of four bells, alt. of Rmc *quaternio* f. L *quattuor* four]
■ **1** see PEAL[1] *n.*

carina /kəre͞enə/ *n. Biol.* a keel-shaped structure, esp. the ridge of a bird's breastbone. ▫▫ **carinal** *adj.* [L, = keel]

carinate /kárrinayt/ *adj.* (of a bird) having a keeled breastbone (opp. RATITE). [L *carinatus* keeled f. *carina* keel]

caring /káiring/ *adj.* **1** compassionate. **2** involving the care of the sick, elderly, or disabled.
■ **1** see SYMPATHETIC *adj.* 1.

carioca /kárriṓkə/ *n.* **1 a** a Brazilian dance like the samba. **b** the music for this. **2** a native of Rio de Janeiro. [Port.]

cariogenic /káiriōjénnik/ *adj.* causing caries.

carious /káiriəss/ *adj.* (of bones or teeth) decayed. [L *cariosus*]
■ see MOULDY 1.

carking /kaarking/ *adj. archaic* burdensome (*carking care*). [part. of obs. *cark* (v.) f. ONF *carkier* f. Rmc, rel. to CHARGE]

carl /kaarl/ *n. Sc.* a man; a fellow. [OE f. ON *karl*, rel. to CHURL]

carline /kaárlin/ *n.* any plant of the genus *Carlina*, esp. the thistle-like *C. vulgaris*. [F f. med.L *carlina* perh. for *cardina* (L *carduus* thistle), assoc. with *Carolus Magnus* Charlemagne]

carload /kaárlōd/ *n.* **1** a quantity that can be carried in a car. **2** *US* the minimum quantity of goods for which a lower rate is charged for transport.

Carlovingian var. of CAROLINGIAN.

carman /kaárman/ *n. US* **1** the driver of a van. **2** a carrier.

Carmelite /kaármilīt/ *n.* & *adj.* ● *n.* **1** a friar of the Order of Our Lady of Mount Carmel, following a rule of extreme asceticism. **2** a nun of a similar order. ● *adj.* of or relating to the Carmelites. [F *Carmelite* or med.L *carmelita* f. Mt. *Carmel* in Palestine, where the order was founded in the 12th c.]

carminative /kaárminətiv/ *adj.* & *n.* ● *adj.* relieving flatulence. ● *n.* a carminative drug. [F *carminatif -ive* or med.L *carminare* heal (by incantation): see CHARM]

carmine /kaármīn/ *adj.* & *n.* ● *adj.* of a vivid crimson colour. ● *n.* **1** this colour. **2** a vivid crimson pigment made from cochineal. [F *carmin* or med.L *carminium* perh. f. *carmesinum* crimson + *minium* cinnabar]

carnage /kaárnij/ *n.* great slaughter, esp. of human beings in battle. [F f. It. *carnaggio* f. med.L *carnaticum* f. L *caro carnis* flesh]
■ bloodshed, slaughter, butchery, massacre, killing, mass murder, genocide, holocaust, blood bath, *joc.* blood-letting.

carnal /kaárn'l/ *adj.* **1** of the body or flesh; worldly. **2** sensual, sexual. □ **carnal knowledge** *Law* sexual intercourse. □□ **carnality** /-nálliti/ *n.* **carnalize** *v.tr.* (also **-ise**). **carnally** *adv.* [ME f. LL *carnalis* f. *caro carnis* flesh]
■ **1** bodily, physical, corporeal, fleshly, animal, brute; worldly, earthly, material, non-spiritual. **2** sensual, sexual, fleshly, erotic, voluptuous, libidinous, lustful, lecherous, lascivious, licentious, lewd, prurient, *formal* concupiscent. □ **carnal knowledge** see *sexual intercourse*.

carnassial /kaarnássiəl/ *adj.* & *n.* ● *adj.* (of a carnivore's upper premolar and lower molar teeth) adapted for shearing flesh. ● *n.* such a tooth. Also called SECTORIAL. [F *carnassier* carnivorous]

carnation[1] /kaarnáysh'n/ *n.* **1** any of several cultivated varieties of clove-scented pink, with variously coloured showy flowers (see also CLOVE[1] 2). **2** this flower. [orig. uncert.: in early use varying with *coronation*]

carnation[2] /kaarnáysh'n/ *n.* & *adj.* ● *n.* a rosy pink colour. ● *adj.* of this colour. [F f. It. *carnagione* ult. f. L *caro carnis* flesh]

carnauba/kaarnówbə, -náwbə, -nṓbə/ *n.* **1** a fan palm, *Copernicia cerifera*, native to NE Brazil. **2** (in full **carnauba wax**) the yellowish leaf-wax of this tree used as a polish etc. [Port.]

carnelian var. of CORNELIAN.

carnet /kaárnay/ *n.* **1** a customs permit to take a motor vehicle across a frontier for a limited period. **2** a permit allowing use of a camp-site. [F, = notebook]

carnival /kaárniv'l/ *n.* **1 a** the festivities usual during the period before Lent in Roman Catholic countries. **b** any festivities, esp. those occurring at a regular date. **2** merrymaking, revelry. **3** *US* a travelling funfair or circus. [It. *carne-*, *carnovale* f. med.L *carnelevarium* etc. Shrovetide f. L *caro carnis* flesh + *levare* put away]
■ **1b, 2** see JAMBOREE.

carnivore /kaárnivor/ *n.* **1 a** any mammal of the order Carnivora, with powerful jaws and teeth adapted for stabbing, tearing, and eating flesh, including cats, dogs, and bears. **b** any other flesh-eating mammal. **2** any flesh-eating plant.

carnivorous /kaarnívvərəss/ *adj.* **1** (of an animal) feeding on flesh. **2** (of a plant) digesting trapped insects or other animal substances. **3** of or relating to the order Carnivora. □□ **carnivorously** *adv.* **carnivorousness** *n.* [L *carnivorus* f. *caro carnis* flesh + -VOROUS]

carob /kárrəb/ *n.* **1** (in full **carob-tree**) an evergreen tree, *Ceratonia siliqua*, native to the Mediterranean, bearing edible pods. **2** its bean-shaped edible seed pod sometimes used as a substitute for chocolate. [obs. F *carobe* f. med.L *carrubia*, *-um* f. Arab. *ḵarrūba*]

carol /kárrəl/ *n.* & *v.* ● *n.* a joyous song, esp. a Christmas hymn. ● *v.* (**carolled, carolling**; *US* **caroled, caroling**) **1** *intr.* sing carols, esp. outdoors at Christmas. **2** *tr.* & *intr.* sing joyfully. □□ **caroler** *n.* (also **caroller**). [ME f. OF *carole*, *caroler*, of unkn. orig.]
■ *n.* see SONG. ● *v.* see SING *v.* 1, 2.

Caroline /kárrəlīn/ *adj.* **1** (also **Carolean** /-leéən/) of the time of Charles I or II of England. **2** = CAROLINGIAN *adj.* 2. [L *Carolus* Charles]

Carolingian /kárrəlínjiən/ *adj.* & *n.* (also **Carlovingian** /kaárləvínjiən/) ● *adj.* **1** of or relating to the second Frankish dynasty, founded by Charlemagne (d. 814). **2** of a style of script developed in France at the time of Charlemagne. ● *n.* **1** a member of the Carolingian dynasty. **2** the Carolingian style of script. [F *carlovingien* f. *Karl* Charles after *mérovingien* (see MEROVINGIAN): re-formed after L *Carolus*]

carom /kárrəm/ *n.* & *v. US Billiards* ● *n.* a cannon. ● *v.intr.* **1** make a carom. **2** (usu. foll. by *off*) strike and rebound. [abbr. of *carambole* f. Sp. *carambola*]
■ *v.* see BOUNCE *v.* 1.

carotene /kárrəteen/ *n.* any of several orange-coloured plant pigments found in carrots, tomatoes, etc., acting as a source of vitamin A. [G *Carotin* f. L *carota* CARROT]

carotenoid /kəróttinoyd/ *n.* any of a group of yellow, orange, or brown pigments giving characteristic colour to plant organs, e.g. ripe tomatoes, carrots, autumn leaves, etc.

carotid /kəróttid/ *n.* & *adj.* ● *n.* each of the two main arteries carrying blood to the head and neck. ● *adj.* of or relating to either of these arteries. [F *carotide* or mod.L *carotides* f. Gk *karōtides* (pl.) f. *karoō* stupefy (compression of these arteries being thought to cause stupor)]

carouse /kərówz/ *v.* & *n.* ● *v.intr.* **1** have a noisy or lively drinking-party. **2** drink heavily. ● *n.* a noisy or lively drinking-party. □□ **carousal** *n.* **carouser** *n.* [orig. as adv. = right out, in phr. *drink carouse* f. G *gar aus trinken*]
■ *v.* **1** make merry, revel, party, *archaic* wassail, *colloq.* go on a pub-crawl, make whoopee, paint the town red. **2** see BOOZE *v.* ● *n.* revel, party, carousal, bacchanal, orgy, *Austral.* corroboree, *Sc.* skite, *archaic* wassail, *colloq.* (drinking) spree, rave, rave-up, shindig, pub-crawl, *Brit. colloq.* knees-up, *sl.* jag, bender, drunk, binge, booze-up.

carousel /kárrəsél, -zél/ *n.* (*US* **carrousel**) **1** *US* a merry-go-round or roundabout. **2** a rotating delivery or conveyor system, esp. for passengers' luggage at an airport. **3** *hist.* a kind of equestrian tournament. [F *carrousel* f. It. *carosello*]
■ **1** see ROUNDABOUT *n.* 2.

carp[1] /kaarp/ *n.* (*pl.* same) any freshwater fish of the family Cyprinidae, esp. *Cyprinus carpio*, often bred for use as food. [ME f. OF *carpe* f. Prov. or f. LL *carpa*]

carp[2] /kaarp/ *v.intr.* (usu. foll. by *at*) find fault; complain pettily. □□ **carper** *n.* [obs. ME senses 'talk, say, sing' f. ON *karpa* to brag: mod. sense (16th c.) from or infl. by L *carpere* pluck at, slander]
■ find fault, cavil, complain, grumble, niggle, *colloq.* gripe, whinge; (*carp at*) criticize, fault, pick at *or* on, nag (at), peck at, put down, pick holes in, *colloq.* check, *sl.* knock.

carpal /kaárp'l/ *adj.* & *n.* ● *adj.* of or relating to the bones in the wrist. ● *n.* any of the bones forming the wrist. [CARPUS + -AL]

carpel /kaárp'l/ *n. Bot.* the female reproductive organ of a flower, consisting of a stigma, style, and ovary. □□ **carpellary** *adj.* [F *carpelle* or mod.L *carpellum* f. Gk *karpos* fruit]

carpenter /kaárpintər/ *n.* & *v.* • *n.* a person skilled in woodwork, esp. of a structural kind (cf. JOINER). • *v.* **1** *intr.* do carpentry. **2** *tr.* make by means of carpentry. **3** *tr.* (often foll. by *together*) construct; fit together. □ **carpenter ant** any large ant of the genus *Camponotus*, boring into wood to nest. **carpenter bee** any of various solitary bees, which bore into wood. [ME & AF; OF *carpentier* f. LL *carpentarius* f. *carpentum* wagon f. Gaulish]

carpentry /kaárpintri/ *n.* **1** the work or occupation of a carpenter. **2** timber-work constructed by a carpenter. [ME f. OF *carpenterie* f. L *carpentaria*: see CARPENTER]

carpet /kaárpit/ *n.* & *v.* • *n.* **1 a** thick fabric for covering a floor or stairs. **b** a piece of this fabric. **2** an expanse or layer resembling a carpet in being smooth, soft, bright, or thick (*carpet of snow*). • *v.tr.* (**carpeted, carpeting**) **1** cover with or as with a carpet. **2** *colloq.* reprimand, reprove. □ **carpet-bag** a travelling-bag of a kind orig. made of carpet-like material. **carpet-bagger 1** esp. *US* a political candidate in an area where the candidate has no local connections (orig. a northerner in the southern US after the Civil War). **2** an unscrupulous opportunist. **carpet bombing** intensive bombing. **carpet slipper** a kind of slipper with the upper made orig. of carpet-like material. **carpet-sweeper** a household implement with a revolving brush or brushes for sweeping carpets. **on the carpet 1** *colloq.* being reprimanded. **2** under consideration. **sweep under the carpet** conceal (a problem or difficulty) in the hope that it will be forgotten. [ME f. OF *carpite* or med.L *carpita*, f. obs. It. *carpita* woollen counterpane, ult. f. L *carpere* pluck, pull to pieces]

▪ *v.* **2** see REPRIMAND *v.* □ **carpet-bag** see BAG *n.* 2a.

carpeting /kaárpiting/ *n.* **1** material for carpets. **2** carpets collectively.

carpology /kaarpólləji/ *n.* the study of the structure of fruit and seeds. [Gk *karpos* fruit]

carport /kaárport/ *n.* a shelter with a roof and open sides for a car, usu. beside a house.

carpus /kaárpəss/ *n.* (*pl.* **carpi** /-pī/) the small bones between the forelimb and metacarpus in terrestrial vertebrates, forming the wrist in humans. [mod.L f. Gk *karpos* wrist]

carrack /kárrək/ *n. hist.* a large armed merchant-ship. [ME f. F *caraque* f. Sp. *carraca* f. Arab. *ḳarāḳir*]

carrageen /kárrəgeen/ *n.* (also **carragheen**) an edible red seaweed, *Chondrus crispus*, of the N. hemisphere. Also called *Irish moss*. [orig. uncert.: perh. f. Ir. *cosáinín carraige* carrageen, lit. 'little stem of the rock']

carrel /kárrəl/ *n.* **1** a small cubicle for a reader in a library. **2** *hist.* a small enclosure or study in a cloister. [OF *carole*, med.L *carola*, of unkn. orig.]

carriage /kárrij/ *n.* **1** *Brit.* a railway passenger vehicle. **2** a wheeled passenger vehicle, esp. one with four wheels and pulled by horses. **3 a** the conveying of goods. **b** the cost of this (*carriage paid*). **4** the part of a machine (e.g. a typewriter) that carries other parts into the required position. **5** a gun-carriage. **6** a manner of carrying oneself; one's bearing or deportment. □ **carriage and pair** a carriage with two horses pulling it. **carriage clock** a portable clock in a rectangular case with a handle on top. **carriage-dog** a dalmatian. [ME f. ONF *cariage* f. *carier* CARRY]

▪ **1** (railway) coach, *US* car. **3 a** freight, freightage, transportation, transport, haulage, movement, conveyance, shipping, shipment, transit. **b** cartage, postage, haulage, freightage. **6** bearing, air, deportment, demeanour, attitude, posture, stance, presence, *literary* comportment.

carriageway /kárrijway/ *n. Brit.* the part of a road intended for vehicles.

carrick bend /kárrik/ *n. Naut.* a kind of knot used to join ropes. [BEND[2]: *carrick* perh. f. CARRACK]

carrier /kárriər/ *n.* **1** a person or thing that carries. **2** a person or company undertaking to convey goods or passengers for payment. **3** = *carrier bag*. **4** a part of a bicycle etc. for carrying luggage or a passenger. **5** a person or animal that may transmit a disease or a hereditary characteristic without suffering from or displaying it. **6** = *aircraft-carrier*. **7** a substance used to support or convey a pigment, a catalyst, radioactive material, etc. **8** *Physics* a mobile electron or hole that carries a charge in a semiconductor. □ **carrier bag** *Brit.* a disposable plastic or paper bag with handles. **carrier pigeon** a pigeon trained to carry messages tied to its neck or leg. **carrier wave** a high-frequency electromagnetic wave modulated in amplitude or frequency to convey a signal.

▪ **1, 2** bearer, porter, conveyor, transporter, carter, shipper, *US* carman; hauler, *Brit.* haulier. **3** see BAG *n.* 1. **5** transmitter, *Immunology* vector. □ **carrier bag** see BAG *n.* 1.

carriole /kárriōl/ *n.* **1** a small open carriage for one. **2** a covered light cart. **3** a Canadian sledge. [F f. It. *carriuola*, dimin. of *carro* CAR]

carrion /kárriən/ *n.* & *adj.* • *n.* **1** dead putrefying flesh. **2** something vile or filthy. • *adj.* rotten, loathsome. □ **carrion crow** a black crow, *Corvus corone*, native to Europe, feeding mainly on carrion. **carrion flower** = STAPELIA. [ME f. AF & ONF *caroine*, *-oigne*, OF *charoigne* ult. f. L *caro* flesh]

carrot /kárrət/ *n.* **1 a** an umbelliferous plant, *Daucus carota*, with a tapering orange-coloured root. **b** this root as a vegetable. **2** a means of enticement or persuasion. **3** (in *pl.*) *sl.* a red-haired person. □□ **carroty** *adj.* [F *carotte* f. L *carota* f. Gk *karōton*]

▪ **2** see INCENTIVE *n.* 1.

carrousel *US* var. of CAROUSEL.

carry /kárri/ *v.* & *n.* • *v.* (**-ies, -ied**) **1** *tr.* support or hold up, esp. while moving. **2** *tr.* convey with one from one place to another. **3** *tr.* have on one's person (*carry a watch*). **4** *tr.* conduct or transmit (*pipe carries water*; *wire carries electric current*). **5** *tr.* take (a process etc.) to a specified point (*carry into effect*; *carry a joke too far*). **6** *tr.* (foll. by *to*) continue or prolong (*carry modesty to excess*). **7** *tr.* involve, imply; have as a feature or consequence (*carries a two-year guarantee*; *principles carry consequences*). **8** *tr.* (in reckoning) transfer (a figure) to a column of higher value. **9** *tr.* hold in a specified way (*carry oneself erect*). **10** *tr.* **a** (of a newspaper or magazine) publish; include in its contents, esp. regularly. **b** (of a radio or television station) broadcast, esp. regularly. **11** *tr.* (of a retailing outlet) keep a regular stock of (particular goods for sale) (*have stopped carrying that brand*). **12** *intr.* **a** (of sound, esp. a voice) be audible at a distance. **b** (of a missile) travel, penetrate. **13** *tr.* (of a gun etc.) propel to a specified distance. **14** *tr.* **a** win victory or acceptance for (a proposal etc.). **b** win acceptance from (*carried the audience with them*). **c** win, capture (a prize, a fortress, etc.). **d** *US* gain (a State or district) in an election. **e** *Golf* cause the ball to pass beyond (a bunker etc.). **15** *tr.* **a** endure the weight of; support (*columns carry the dome*). **b** be the chief cause of the effectiveness of; be the driving force in (*you carry the sales department*). **16** *tr.* be pregnant with (*is carrying twins*). **17** *tr.* **a** (of a motive, money, etc.) cause or enable (a person) to go to a specified place. **b** (of a journey) bring (a person) to a specified point. • *n.* (*pl.* **-ies**) **1** an act of carrying. **2** *Golf* the distance a ball travels before reaching the ground. **3** a portage between rivers etc. **4** the range of a gun etc. □ **carry-all 1** a light carriage (cf. CARRIOLE). **2** *US* a car with seats placed sideways. **3** *US* a large bag or case. **carry all before one** succeed; overcome all opposition. **carry away 1** remove. **2** inspire; affect emotionally or spiritually. **3** deprive of self-control (*got carried away*). **4** *Naut.* **a** lose (a mast etc.) by breakage. **b** break off or away. **carry back** take (a person) back in thought to a past time. **carry one's bat** *Cricket* be not out at the end of a side's completed innings. **carry the can** *colloq.* bear the responsibility or blame. **carry conviction** be convincing. **carry-cot** a portable cot for a baby. **carry the day** be victorious or successful. **carry forward** transfer to a new page or account. **carrying-on** (or **carryings-on**) = *carry-on*. **carrying-trade** the conveying of goods from one country to another by water or air as a business. **carry it off** (or

carry it off well) do well under difficulties. **carry off 1** take away, esp. by force. **2** win (a prize). **3** (esp. of a disease) kill. **4** render acceptable or passable. **carry on 1** continue (*carry on eating*; *carry on, don't mind me*). **2** engage in (a conversation or a business). **3** *colloq.* behave strangely or excitedly. **4** (often foll. by *with*) *colloq.* flirt or have a love affair. **5** advance (a process) by a stage. **carry-on** *n. Brit. sl.* **1** a state of excitement or fuss. **2** a questionable piece of behaviour. **3** a flirtation or love affair. **carry out** put (ideas, instructions, etc.) into practice. **carry-out** *attrib.adj.* & *n.* esp. *Sc.* & *US* = *take-away*. **carry over 1** = *carry forward*. **2** postpone (work etc.). **3** *Stock Exch.* keep over to the next settling-day. **carry-over** *n.* **1** something carried over. **2** *Stock Exch.* postponement to the next settling-day. **carry through 1** complete successfully. **2** bring safely out of difficulties. **carry weight** be influential or important. **carry with one** bear in mind. [ME f. AF & ONF *carier* (as CAR)]

■ *v.* **1, 2** transport, convey, bear, deliver, bring, haul, lug, cart, ship, move, *colloq.* schlep, hump, *esp. US colloq.* tote; drive, take; hold. **4** conduct, transmit, convey, take, transport, transfer, bear. **7** see INCLUDE 1. **9** bear, deport, hold (up), maintain, keep. **10** publish, put out; broadcast, air, screen; disseminate, communicate, present, announce, offer, give, release. **11** stock, keep, have in stock, sell, offer, trade in, deal in, take, have. **14 c** win, take, sweep, carry off *or* away, capture, gain, secure, pick up, *colloq.* walk away *or* off with. **15** see SUPPORT *v.* 1, 2. **16** be pregnant with, be expecting, *literary or Zool.* be gravid with. □ **carry-all 3** see CASE[2] *n.* 4. **carry away 1** see REMOVE *v.* 2a. **2** see INSPIRE 1, 2. **carry back** take back, remind. **carry the can** take *or* shoulder the blame. **carry conviction** be convincing, hold up, stand up, carry weight, bear scrutiny, hold water. **carry the day** see TRIUMPH *v.* 1. **carry off 1** abscond with, take (away), make away *or* off with, run off with, spirit off *or* away, whisk away *or* off, cart off, drag away, kidnap, abduct. **2** win, gain, capture, secure, pick up, take, *colloq.* walk away *or* off with. **3** kill (off), be *or* cause the death of, cause to die, put out of one's misery, *colloq.* finish off. **4** accomplish, achieve, perform, effect, effectuate, do, execute, succeed in *or* with, handle, manage, work, bring off, carry out *or* through, pull off. **carry on 1** continue, go on, keep on; keep (on) going, last, remain; persist, persevere, push *or* press on. **2** engage in, be involved *or* busy *or* absorbed in, occupy oneself with; follow, pursue, prosecute; manage, conduct, operate, run, administer, proceed with, transact. **4** have a fling *or* affair, flirt. **carry-on 1** see PALAVER *n.* 1. **3** see AFFAIR 3. **carry out** perform, carry on *or* through, continue, implement, administer, transact, put into practice, see through, execute, discharge, prosecute, effect, complete, accomplish, conclude. **carry over 2** see POSTPONE. **carry through 1** see ACCOMPLISH, *carry out* above.

carse /kaarss/ *n. Sc.* fertile lowland beside a river. [ME, perh. f. *carrs* swamps]

carsick /kaársik/ *adj.* affected with nausea caused by the motion of a car. □□ **carsickness** *n.*

cart /kaart/ *n.* & *v.* ● *n.* **1** a strong vehicle with two or four wheels for carrying loads, usu. drawn by a horse. **2** a light vehicle for pulling by hand. **3** a light vehicle with two wheels for driving in, drawn by a single horse. ● *v.tr.* **1** convey in or as in a cart. **2** *sl.* carry (esp. a cumbersome thing) with difficulty or over a long distance (*carted it all the way home*). □ **cart-horse** a thickset horse suitable for heavy work. **cart-load 1** an amount filling a cart. **2** a large quantity of anything. **cart off** remove, esp. by force. **cart-track** (or **-road**) a track or road too rough for ordinary vehicles. **cart-wright** a maker of carts. **in the cart** *sl.* in trouble or difficulty. **put the cart before the horse 1** reverse the proper order or procedure. **2** take an effect for a cause. □□ **carter** *n.* **cartful** *n.* (*pl.* **-fuls**). [ME f. ON *kartr* cart & OE *cræt*, prob. infl. by AF & ONF *carete* dimin. of *carre* CAR]

■ *n.* **1** dray, trailer, wagon, *hist.* tumbrel. **2** handcart, pushcart, trolley, *Austral.* billycart, *Austral.* & *NZ* dray, *Brit.* barrow. **3** carriole, float. ● *v.* **2** carry, lug, drag, haul, transport, *colloq.* schlep, hump, *esp. US colloq.* tote. □ **cart-load 2** see LOT *n.* 1. **cart off** see *carry off* 1. **in the cart** see *in trouble* (TROUBLE) 1.

cartage /kaártij/ *n.* the price paid for carting.

carte var. of QUART 4.

carte blanche /kaart blónsh/ *n.* full discretionary power given to a person. [F, = blank paper]

■ licence, free rein, permission, sanction, warrant, freedom, free hand, liberty, power, authority, discretion, *colloq.* blank cheque.

cartel /kaartél/ *n.* **1** an informal association of manufacturers or suppliers to maintain prices at a high level, and control production, marketing arrangements, etc. **2** a political combination between parties. □□ **cartelize** /kaártəlīz/ *v.tr.* & *intr.* (also **-ise**). [G *Kartell* f. F *cartel* f. It. *cartello* dimin. of *carta* CARD[1]]

■ **1** see SYNDICATE *n.*

Cartesian /kaartéeziən, -zh'n/ *adj.* & *n.* ● *adj.* of or relating to R. Descartes, 17th-c. French philosopher and mathematician. ● *n.* a follower of Descartes. □ **Cartesian coordinates** a system for locating a point by reference to its distance from two or three axes intersecting at right angles. □□ **Cartesianism** *n.* [mod.L *Cartesianus* f. *Cartesius*, name of *Descartes*]

Carthusian /kaarthyóoziən/ *n.* & *adj.* ● *n.* a monk of a contemplative order founded by St Bruno in 1084. ● *adj.* of or relating to this order. [med.L *Carthusianus* f. L *Cart(h)usia* Chartreuse, near Grenoble]

cartilage /kaártilij/ *n.* gristle, a firm flexible connective tissue forming the infant skeleton, which is mainly replaced by bone in adulthood. □□ **cartilaginoid** /-lájinoyd/ *adj.* **cartilaginous** /-lájinəss/ *adj.* [F f. L *cartilago -ginis*]

■ □□ **cartilaginoid, cartilaginous** see TOUGH *adj.* 1.

cartogram /kaártəgram/ *n.* a map with diagrammatic statistical information. [F *cartogramme* f. *carte* map, card]

cartography /kaartógrəfi/ *n.* the science or practice of map-drawing. □□ **cartographer** *n.* **cartographic** /-təgráffik/ *adj.* **cartographical** /-təgráffik'l/ *adj.* [F *cartographie* f. *carte* map, card]

cartomancy /kaártəmansi/ *n.* fortune-telling by interpreting a random selection of playing-cards. [F *cartomancie* f. *carte* CARD[1]]

carton /kaárt'n/ *n.* a light box or container, esp. one made of cardboard. [F (as CARTOON)]

■ see BOX[1] *n.* 1, 2a.

cartoon /kaartóon/ *n.* & *v.* ● *n.* **1** a humorous drawing in a newspaper, magazine, etc., esp. as a topical comment. **2** a sequence of drawings, often with speech indicated, telling a story (*strip cartoon*). **3** a filmed sequence of drawings using the technique of animation. **4** a full-size drawing on stout paper as an artist's preliminary design for a painting, tapestry, mosaic, etc. ● *v.* **1** *tr.* draw a cartoon of. **2** *intr.* draw cartoons. □□ **cartoonist** *n.* [It. *cartone* f. *carta* CARD[1]]

cartouche /kaartóosh/ *n.* **1 a** *Archit.* a scroll-like ornament, e.g. the volute of an Ionic capital. **b** a tablet imitating, or a drawing of, a scroll with rolled-up ends, used ornamentally or bearing an inscription. **c** an ornate frame. **2** *Archaeol.* an oval ring enclosing Egyptian hieroglyphs, usu. representing the name and title of a king. [F, = cartridge, f. It. *cartoccio* f. *carta* CARD[1]]

■ **2** see SIGN *n.* 2.

cartridge /kaártrij/ *n.* **1** a case containing a charge of propelling explosive for firearms or blasting, with a bullet or shot if for small arms. **2** a spool of film, magnetic tape, etc., in a sealed container ready for insertion. **3** a component carrying the stylus on the pick-up head of a record-player. **4** an ink-container for insertion in a pen. □ **cartridge-belt** a belt with pockets or loops for cartridges (in sense 1). **cartridge paper** thick rough paper used for cartridges,

for drawing, and for strong envelopes. [corrupt. of CARTOUCHE (but recorded earlier)]
■ **1** see SHELL *n.* 2.

cartwheel /kaártweel/ *n.* **1** the (usu. spoked) wheel of a cart. **2** a circular sideways handspring with the arms and legs extended.

caruncle /kárrəngk'l, kərúngk'l/ *n.* **1** *Zool.* a fleshy excrescence, e.g. a turkeycock's wattles or the red prominence at the inner angle of the eye. **2** *Bot.* an outgrowth from a seed near the micropyle. □□ **caruncular** /kərúngkyoolər/ *adj.* [obs. F f. L *caruncula* f. *caro carnis* flesh]

carve /kaarv/ *v.* **1** *tr.* produce or shape (a statue, representation in relief, etc.) by cutting into a hard material (*carved a figure out of rock; carved it in wood*). **2** *tr.* **a** cut patterns, designs, letters, etc. in (hard material). **b** (foll. by *into*) form a pattern, design, etc., from (*carved it into a bust*). **c** (foll. by *with*) cover or decorate (material) with figures or designs cut in it. **3** *tr.* (*absol.*) cut (meat etc.) into slices for eating. □ **carve out 1** take from a larger whole. **2** establish (a career etc.) purposefully (*carved out a name for themselves*). **carve up** divide into several pieces; subdivide (territory etc.). **carve-up** *n. sl.* a sharing-out, esp. of spoils. **carving knife** a knife with a long blade, for carving meat. [OE *ceorfan* cut f. WG]
■ **1, 2** hew, cut, sculpt, sculpture, shape, chisel, model, fashion, whittle, chip; engrave, incise, inscribe, *archaic* grave; chase, enchase. **3** slice, cut. □ **carve out 2** see ESTABLISH 1, FORGE[1] 3. **carve up** divide (up), cut (up), subdivide, partition, split (up); share (out), apportion, parcel out, allot.

carvel /kaárv'l/ *n.* var. of CARAVEL. □ **carvel-built** (of a boat) made with planks flush, not overlapping (cf. CLINKER-BUILT). [as CARAVEL]

carven /kaárv'n/ *archaic past part.* of CARVE.

Carver /kaárvər/ *n. US* a chair with arms, a rush seat, and a back having horizontal and vertical spindles. [J. *Carver*, first governor of Plymouth Colony, d. 1621, for whom a prototype was allegedly made]

carver /kaárvər/ *n.* **1** a person who carves. **2 a** a carving knife. **b** (in *pl.*) a knife and fork for carving. **3** *Brit.* the principal chair, with arms, in a set of dining-chairs, intended for the person who carves. ¶ To be distinguished (in sense 3) from *Carver*.

carvery /kaárvəri/ *n.* (*pl.* **-ies**) a buffet or restaurant with joints of meat displayed, and carved as required, in front of customers.

carving /kaárving/ *n.* a carved object, esp. as a work of art.

caryatid /kárriáttid/ *n.* (*pl.* **caryatides** /-deez/ or **caryatids**) *Archit.* a pillar in the form of a draped female figure, supporting an entablature. [F *caryatide* f. It. *cariatide* or L f. Gk *karuatis -idos* priestess at Caryae (*Karuai*) in Laconia]
■ see STATUE.

caryopsis /kárriópsiss/ *n.* (*pl.* **caryopses** /-seez/) *Bot.* a dry one-seeded indehiscent fruit, as in wheat and maize. [mod.L f. Gk *karuon* nut + *opsis* appearance]

Casanova /kássənṓvə/ *n.* a man notorious for seducing women. [G. J. *Casanova* de Seingalt, It. adventurer d. 1798]
■ see *philanderer* (PHILANDER).

casbah var. of KASBAH.

cascade /kaskáyd/ *n.* & *v.* ● *n.* **1** a small waterfall, esp. forming one in a series or part of a large broken waterfall. **2** a succession of electrical devices or stages in a process. **3** a quantity of material etc. draped in descending folds. **4** a process of disseminating information from senior to junior levels in an organization. ● *v.intr.* fall in or like a cascade. [F f. It. *cascata* f. *cascare* to fall ult. f. L *casus*: see CASE[1]]
■ *n.* **1** see WATERFALL. ● *v.* see STREAM *v.* 1.

cascara /kaskaárə/ *n.* (in full **cascara sagrada** /səgraádə/) the bark of a Californian buckthorn, *Rhamnus purshiana*, used as a purgative. [Sp., = sacred bark]

case[1] /kayss/ *n.* **1** an instance of something occurring. **2** a state of affairs, hypothetical or actual. **3 a** an instance of a person receiving professional guidance, e.g. from a doctor or social worker. **b** this person or the circumstances involved. **4** a matter under official investigation, esp. by the police. **5** *Law* **a** a cause or suit for trial. **b** a statement of the facts in a cause *sub judice*, drawn up for a higher court's consideration (*judge states a case*). **c** a cause that has been decided and may be cited (*leading case*). **6 a** the sum of the arguments on one side, esp. in a lawsuit (*that is our case*). **b** a set of arguments, esp. in relation to persuasiveness (*have a good case; have a weak case*). **c** a valid set of arguments (*have no case*). **7** *Gram.* **a** the relation of a word to other words in a sentence. **b** a form of a noun, adjective, or pronoun expressing this. **8** *colloq.* a comical person. **9** the position or circumstances in which one is. □ **as the case may be** according to the situation. **case history** information about a person for use in professional treatment, e.g. by a doctor. **case-law** the law as established by the outcome of former cases (cf. *common law, statute law*). **case-load** the cases with which a doctor etc. is concerned at one time. **case-study 1** an attempt to understand a person, institution, etc., from collected information. **2** a record of such an attempt. **3** the use of a particular instance as an exemplar of general principles. **in any case** whatever the truth is; whatever may happen. **in case 1** in the event that; if. **2** lest; in provision against a stated or implied possibility (*take an umbrella in case it rains; took it in case*). **in case of** in the event of. **in the case of** as regards. **in no case** under no circumstances. **in that case** if that is true; should that happen. **is** (or **is not**) **the case** is (or is not) so. [ME f. OF *cas* f. L *casus* fall f. *cadere cas-* to fall]
■ **1** instance, example, specimen, illustration. **2, 9** happening, occasion, event, occurrence, (set of) circumstance(s), state (of affairs), situation, eventuality, contingency, position. **3 b** patient, client; subject. **5 a** action, suit, lawsuit, dispute; cause. **6 a, b** see ARGUMENT 2. □ **in any case** in any event, come what may, at all events, at any rate, anyhow, anyway, regardless, just the same, for all that; always. **in case 1** if, in the event that, if it happens *or* proves *or* turns out that. **2** lest, for fear that. **in the case of** as regards, regarding, in the matter of, with respect *or* regard to, re. **in no case** see NEVER 1b, 2. **is** (or **is not**) **the case** is (not) so, is (not) the fact *or* actuality *or* truth *or* reality, is (not) what really happened *or* happens *or* took place *or* takes place.

case[2] /kayss/ *n.* & *v.* ● *n.* **1** a container or covering serving to enclose or contain. **2** a container with its contents. **3** the outer protective covering of a watch, book, seed-vessel, sausage, etc. **4** an item of luggage, esp. a suitcase. **5** *Printing* a partitioned receptacle for type. **6** a glass box for showing specimens, curiosities, etc. ● *v.tr.* **1** enclose in a case. **2** (foll. by *with*) surround. **3** *sl.* reconnoitre (a house etc.) esp. with a view to robbery. □ **case-bound** (of a book) in a hard cover. **case-harden 1** harden the surface of, esp. give a steel surface to (iron) by carbonizing. **2** make callous. **case-knife** a knife carried in a sheath. **case-shot 1** bullets in an iron case fired from a cannon. **2** shrapnel. **lower case** small letters. **upper case** capitals. [ME f. OF *casse, chasse*, f. L *capsa* f. *capere* hold]
■ *n.* **1, 3** box, container, carton, crate, chest, holder, receptacle, casket, caddy; shell, husk, skin, *US* shuck; covering, cover, casing, housing, outside, envelope, wrapper, protection, shield. **4** piece of luggage *or* baggage, bag, trunk, suitcase, hold-all, grip, valise, *Austral.* port, *US* carry-all, *US sl.* keister. ● *v.* **1** encase, box, crate, pack, package, containerize, contain; house, cover, wrap, envelop, enclose. **3** see RECONNOITRE *v.* □ **upper case** capital letter(s), capital(s), majuscule (letters *or* characters).

casebook /káysbŏŏk/ *n.* a book containing a record of legal or medical cases.

casein /káysi-in, kayseen/ *n.* the main protein in milk, esp. in coagulated form as in cheese. [L *caseus* cheese]

caseinogen /kaysínnəjən/ *n.* the soluble form of casein as it occurs in milk.

casemate /káysmayt/ *n.* **1** a chamber in the thickness of the wall of a fortress, with embrasures. **2** an armoured enclosure for guns on a warship. [F *casemate* & It. *casamatta* or Sp. *-mata*, f. *camata*, perh. f. Gk *khasma -atos* gap]

casement /káysmənt/ *n.* **1** a window or part of a window hinged vertically to open like a door. **2** *poet.* a window. [ME f. AL *cassimentum* f. *cassa* CASE[2]]

casework /káyswurk/ *n.* social work concerned with individuals, esp. involving understanding of the client's family and background. □□ **caseworker** *n.*

cash[1] /kash/ *n.* & *v.* ● *n.* **1** money in coins or notes, as distinct from cheques or orders. **2** (also **cash down**) money paid as full payment at the time of purchase, as distinct from credit. **3** *colloq.* wealth. ● *v.tr.* give or obtain cash for (a note, cheque, etc.). □ **cash and carry 1** a system of wholesaling in which goods are paid for in cash and taken away by the purchaser. **2** a store where this system operates. **cash-book** a book in which receipts and payments of cash are recorded. **cash crop** a crop produced for sale, not for use as food etc. **cash desk** a counter or compartment in a shop where goods are paid for. **cash dispenser** an automatic machine from which customers of a bank etc. may withdraw cash, esp. by using a cashcard. **cash flow** the movement of money into and out of a business, as a measure of profitability, or as affecting liquidity. **cash in 1** obtain cash for. **2** *colloq.* (usu. foll. by *on*) profit (from); take advantage (of). **3** pay into a bank etc. **4** (in full **cash in one's chips** or **checks**) *colloq.* die. **cash on delivery** a system of paying the carrier for goods when they are delivered. **cash register** a machine in a shop etc. with a drawer for money, recording the amount of each sale, totalling receipts, etc. **cash up** *Brit.* count and check cash takings at the end of a day's trading. □□ **cashable** *adj.* **cashless** *adj.* [obs. F *casse* box or It. *cassa* f. L *capsa* CASE[2]]

■ *n.* **1** money, currency, funds, bills, notes, banknotes, change, hard cash, specie, coin of the realm, purse, *colloq.* shekels, *derog. or joc.* pelf, *sl.* moolah, dough, bread, loot, spondulicks, ready, readies, dosh, scratch, splosh, stuff, doubloons, green(s), *Brit. sl.* lolly, brass, tin, *US sl.* jack, kale, rock. **3** see WEALTH 1. ● *v.* cash in, redeem, exchange; realize. □ **cash in 1** see CASH *v.* 1 above. **2** see PROFIT *v.* 2. **3** see DEPOSIT *v.* 2. **4** see DIE[1] 1. **cash register** register, till, money box, cash box.

cash[2] /kash/ *n.* (*pl.* same) *hist.* any of various small coins of China or the E. Indies. [ult. f. Port. *ca(i)xa* f. Tamil *kāsu* f. Skr. *karsha*]

cashcard /káshkaard/ *n.* a plastic card (see CARD[1] *n.* 9) which enables the holder to draw money from a cash dispenser.

cashew /káshoo, kashóo/ *n.* **1** a bushy evergreen tree, *Anacardium occidentale*, native to Central and S. America, bearing kidney-shaped nuts attached to fleshy fruits. **2** (in full **cashew nut**) the edible nut of this tree. □ **cashew apple** the edible fleshy fruit of this tree. [Port. f. Tupi *(a)caju*]

cashier[1] /kasheér/ *n.* a person dealing with cash transactions in a shop, bank, etc. [Du. *cassier* or F *caissier* (as CASH[1])]

■ see BOOKKEEPER.

cashier[2] /kasheér/ *v.tr.* dismiss from service, esp. from the armed forces with disgrace. [Flem. *kasseren* disband, revoke, f. F *casser* f. L *quassare* QUASH]

■ see DISMISS 2.

cashmere /káshmeer/ *n.* **1** a fine soft wool, esp. that of a Kashmir goat. **2** a material made from this. [*Kashmir* in Asia]

cashpoint /káshpoynt/ *n.* = *cash dispenser*.

casing /káysing/ *n.* **1** a protective or enclosing cover or shell. **2** the material for this.

■ **1** see HOUSING[1] 3.

casino /kəseénō/ *n.* (*pl.* **-os**) a public room or building for gambling. [It., dimin. of *casa* house f. L *casa* cottage]

cask /kaask/ *n.* **1** a large barrel-like container made of wood, metal, or plastic, esp. one for alcoholic liquor. **2** its contents. **3** its capacity. [F *casque* or Sp. *casco* helmet]

■ see KEG.

casket /kaáskit/ *n.* **1** a small often ornamental box or chest for jewels, letters, etc. **2 a** a small wooden box for cremated ashes. **b** *US* a coffin, esp. a rectangular one. [perh. f. AF form of OF *cassette* f. It. *cassetta* dimin. of *cassa* f. L *capsa* CASE[2]]

■ **1** chest, box, container, case, coffer, receptacle.

casque /kask/ *n.* **1** *hist.* or *poet.* a helmet. **2** *Zool.* a helmet-like structure, e.g. the process on the bill of the cassowary. [F f. Sp. *casco*]

Cassandra /kəsándrə/ *n.* a prophet of disaster, esp. one who is disregarded. [L f. Gk *Kassandra*, daughter of Priam King of Troy: she was condemned by Apollo to prophesy correctly but not be believed]

■ see KILLJOY.

cassata /kəsaátə/ *n.* a type of ice-cream containing candied or dried fruit and nuts. [It.]

cassation /kəsáysh'n/ *n.* *Mus.* an informal instrumental composition of the 18th c., similar to a divertimento and orig. often for outdoor performance. [It. *cassazione*]

cassava /kəsaávə/ *n.* **1 a** any plant of the genus *Manihot*, esp. the cultivated varieties *M. esculenta* (**bitter cassava**) and *M. dulcis* (**sweet cassava**), having starchy tuberous roots. **b** the roots themselves. **2** a starch or flour obtained from these roots. Also called TAPIOCA, MANIOC. [earlier *cas(s)avi* etc., f. Taino *casavi*, infl. by F *cassave*]

casserole /kássərōl/ *n.* & *v.* ● *n.* **1** a covered dish, usu. of earthenware or glass, in which food is cooked, esp. slowly in the oven. **2** food cooked in a casserole. ● *v.tr.* cook in a casserole. [F f. *cassole* dimin. of *casse* f. Prov. *casa* f. LL *cattia* ladle, pan f. Gk *kuathion* dimin. of *kuathos* cup]

■ *n.* **1** see PAN[1] *n.* 1. **2** see STEW[1] *n.* 1. ● *v.* see STEW[1] *v.* 1.

cassette /kasét, kə-/ *n.* a sealed case containing a length of tape, ribbon, etc., ready for insertion in a machine, esp.: **1** a length of magnetic tape wound on to spools, ready for insertion in a tape recorder. **2** a length of photographic film, ready for insertion in a camera. [F, dimin. of *casse* CASE[2]]

■ **1** see TAPE *n.* 4.

cassia /kássiə, káshə/ *n.* **1** any tree of the genus *Cassia*, bearing leaves from which senna is extracted. **2** the cinnamon-like bark of this tree used as a spice. [L f. Gk *kasia* f. Heb. *ḳᵉṣîʿāh* bark like cinnamon]

cassis /kaseéss/ *n.* a syrupy usu. alcoholic blackcurrant flavouring for drinks etc. [F, = blackcurrant]

cassiterite /kəsíttərīt/ *n.* a naturally occurring ore of tin dioxide, from which tin is extracted. Also called TINSTONE. [Gk *kassiteros* tin]

cassock /kássək/ *n.* a long close-fitting usu. black or red garment worn by clergy, members of choirs, etc. □□ **cassocked** *adj.* [F *casaque* long coat f. It. *casacca* horseman's coat, prob. f. Turkic: cf. COSSACK]

cassoulet /kássoolay/ *n.* a ragout of meat and beans. [F, dimin. of dial. *cassolo* stew-pan]

cassowary /kássəwairi/ *n.* (*pl.* **-ies**) any large flightless Australasian bird of the genus *Casuarius*, with heavy body, stout legs, a wattled neck, and a bony crest on its forehead. [Malay *kasuārī*, *kasavārī*]

cast /kaast/ *v.* & *n.* ● *v.* (*past* and *past part.* **cast**) **1** *tr.* throw, esp. deliberately or forcefully. **2** *tr.* (often foll. by *on*, *over*) **a** direct or cause to fall (one's eyes, a glance, light, a shadow, a spell, etc.). **b** express (doubts, aspersions, etc.). **3** *tr.* throw out (a fishing-line) into the water. **4** *tr.* let down (an anchor or sounding-lead). **5** *tr.* **a** throw off, get rid of. **b** shed (skin etc.) esp. in the process of growth. **c** (of a horse) lose (a shoe). **6** *tr.* record, register, or give (a vote). **7** *tr.* **a** shape (molten metal or plastic material) in a mould. **b** make (a product) in this way. **8** *tr.* *Printing* make (type). **9** *tr.* **a** (usu. foll. by *as*) assign (an actor) to play a particular character. **b** allocate roles in (a play, film, etc.). **10** *tr.* (foll. by *in*, *into*) arrange or formulate (facts etc.) in a specified form. **11** *tr.* & *intr.* reckon, add up, calculate (accounts or figures). **12** *tr.* calculate and record details of (a horoscope).

● *n.* **1 a** the throwing of a missile etc. **b** the distance reached by this. **2** a throw or a number thrown at dice. **3** a throw of a net, sounding-lead, or fishing-line. **4** *Fishing* **a** that which is cast, esp. the gut with hook and fly. **b** a place for casting (*a good cast*). **5 a** an object of metal, clay, etc., made in a mould. **b** a moulded mass of solidified material, esp. plaster protecting a broken limb. **6** the actors taking part in a play, film, etc. **7** form, type, or quality (*cast of features*; *cast of mind*). **8** a tinge or shade of colour. **9 a** (in full **cast in the eye**) a slight squint. **b** a twist or inclination. **10 a** a mass of earth excreted by a worm. **b** a mass of indigestible food thrown up by a hawk, owl, etc. **11** the form into which any work is thrown or arranged. **12 a** a wide area covered by a dog or pack to find a trail. **b** *Austral.* & *NZ* a wide sweep made by a sheepdog in mustering sheep. □ **cast about** (or **around** or **round**) make an extensive search (actually or mentally) (*cast about for a solution*). **cast adrift** leave to drift. **cast ashore** (of waves etc.) throw to the shore. **cast aside** give up using; abandon. **cast away 1** reject. **2** (in *passive*) be shipwrecked (cf. CASTAWAY). **cast one's bread upon the waters** see BREAD. **cast down** depress, deject (cf. DOWNCAST). **casting vote** a deciding vote usu. given by the chairperson when the votes on two sides are equal. ¶ From an obsolete sense of *cast* = turn the scale. **cast iron** a hard alloy of iron, carbon, and silicon cast in a mould. **cast-iron** *adj.* **1** made of cast iron. **2** hard, unchallengeable, unchangeable. **cast loose** detach; detach oneself. **cast lots** see LOT. **cast-net** a net thrown out and immediately drawn in. **cast off 1** abandon. **2** *Knitting* take the stitches off the needle by looping each over the next to finish the edge. **3** *Naut.* **a** set a ship free from a quay etc. **b** loosen and throw off (rope etc.). **4** *Printing* estimate the space that will be taken in print by manuscript copy. **cast-off** *adj.* abandoned, discarded. ● *n.* a cast-off thing, esp. a garment. **cast on** *Knitting* make the first row of loops on the needle. **cast out** expel. **cast up 1** (of the sea) deposit on the shore. **2** add up (figures etc.). [ME f. ON *kasta*]

■ *v.* **1** throw, toss, pitch, fling, let fly, sling, hurl, bowl, launch, discharge, dash, send, shoot, shy, *colloq.* chuck. **2 a** see DIRECT *v.* 4, SHED² 5. **5 a** see *throw off*. **b** see SHED² 1. **7** shape, mould, form, fashion. **9 a** give *or* assign the part; appoint, designate, name, nominate, choose, pick, select. **10** see FORMULATE 1. **11** see CALCULATE 1. ● *n.* **1 a** throw, toss, pitch, shy, lob, hurl, *colloq.* chuck. **5 a** model, casting, mould, plaster cast. **6** actors and actresses, players, performers, troupe, company, act. **7** form, shape, mould, cut, figure; stamp, type, quality, character, nature, kind, sort, brand, style, genre, class, variety, strain, fibre; turn, inclination, bent. **8** tinge, tint, shade, tone, colouring, colour; hint, touch, suggestion. **9 b** twist, turn, inclination, bend, kink, tilt, bias, irregularity, warp. **11** organization, structure, pattern, formation, formulation, arrangement, grouping, form, layout, make-up, composition, array, categorization, systematization, classification. □ **cast about** (*cast about for*) search for, look (around) for, seek. **cast aside** reject, discard, cast *or* throw away, cast *or* throw out, dispense with, get rid of, dispose of, abandon; see also REJECT *v.* 1. **cast away 1** see REJECT *v.* 3 **2** (*be cast away*) be marooned *or* shipwrecked. **cast down** see DEPRESS 2. **cast-iron 2** see SOLID *adj.* 4, 6a. **cast loose** see DETACH 1. **cast off 1** see ABANDON *v.* 2a. **cast-off** (*adj.*) see ABANDONED 1a; (*n.*) see REJECT *n.* **cast out** expel, drive *or* force *or* throw *or* fling *or* push *or* turn out, kick *or* boot out, evict, eject, oust, exile, banish, remove, *colloq.* chuck out, *Brit. colloq.* turf out, *sl.* bounce. **cast up 1** throw *or* bring up, deposit. **2** see ADD 2.

castanet /kástənét/ *n.* (usu. in *pl.*) a small concave piece of hardwood, ivory, etc., in pairs held in the hands and clicked together by the fingers as a rhythmic accompaniment, esp. by Spanish dancers. [Sp. *castañeta* dimin. of *castaña* f. L *castanea* chestnut]

castaway /kaástəway/ *n.* & *adj.* ● *n.* a shipwrecked person. ● *adj.* **1** shipwrecked. **2** cast aside; rejected.

■ *adj.* **1** shipwrecked, marooned, stranded. **2** see ABANDONED 1a.

caste /kaast/ *n.* **1** any of the Hindu hereditary classes, distinguished by relative degrees of purity or pollution, whose members are socially equal with one another and often follow the same occupations. **2** a more or less exclusive social class. **3** a system of such classes. **4** the position it confers. **5** *Zool.* a form of social insect having a particular function. □ **caste mark** a symbol on the forehead denoting a person's caste. **lose caste** descend in the social order. [Sp. and Port. *casta* lineage, race, breed, fem. of *casto* pure, CHASTE]

■ **1, 2** (social) class, order, level, stratum, rank, station, *archaic or literary* estate. **4** standing, position, status, rank.

casteism /kaástiz'm/ *n.* often *derog.* the caste system.

castellan /kástələn/ *n. hist.* the governor of a castle. [ME f. ONF *castelain* f. med.L *castellanus*: see CASTLE]

castellated /kástəlaytid/ *adj.* **1** having battlements. **2** castle-like. □□ **castellation** /-láysh'n/ *n.* [med.L *castellatus*: see CASTLE]

caster /kaástər/ *n.* **1** var. of CASTOR¹. **2** a person who casts. **3** a machine for casting type.

castigate /kástigayt/ *v.tr.* rebuke or punish severely. □□ **castigation** /-gáysh'n/ *n.* **castigator** *n.* **castigatory** *adj.* [L *castigare* reprove f. *castus* pure]

■ chastise, rebuke, scold, reprimand, berate, upbraid, reproach, call down, drop on, pull up, read the Riot Act to, lecture, tear into, keelhaul, haul *or* call over the coals, rap on *or* over the knuckles, give a rating to, give a piece of one's mind to, strafe, criticize, *archaic or literary* chide, *colloq.* tell off, dress down, tick off, bawl out, blast, dust down, carpet, put *or* call on to the carpet, give a person an earful, give a person a dressing-down *or* talking-to *or* telling-off *or* wigging, give a person what for, row, slap (down), *Brit. colloq.* slate, *US colloq.* chew out, *Austral.* & *NZ sl.* go off at, give a person a serve; punish, discipline, chasten, correct, penalize.

Castile soap /kastéel/ *n.* a fine hard white or mottled soap made with olive oil and soda. [as CASTILIAN]

Castilian /kəstílliən/ *n.* & *adj.* ● *n.* **1** a native of Castile in Spain. **2** the language of Castile, standard spoken and literary Spanish. ● *adj.* of or relating to Castile.

casting /kaásting/ *n.* an object made by casting, esp. of molten metal.

■ see STATUE.

castle /kaás'l/ *n.* & *v.* ● *n.* **1 a** a large fortified building or group of buildings; a stronghold. **b** a formerly fortified mansion. **2** *Chess* = ROOK². ● *v. Chess* **1** *intr.* make a special move (once only in a game on each side) in which the king is moved two squares along the back rank and the nearer rook is moved to the square passed over by the king. **2** *tr.* move (the king) by castling. □ **castles in the air** (or **in Spain**) a visionary unattainable scheme; a day-dream. □□ **castled** *adj.* [AF & ONF *castel*, *chastel* f. L *castellum* dimin. of *castrum* fort]

■ *n.* **1 a** fortress, stronghold, citadel, fastness, tower. **b** mansion, palace, manor-house, manor, hall, château, *Brit.* stately home. □ **castles in the air** (or **in Spain**) see *day-dream n.*

castor¹ /kaástər/ *n.* (also **caster**) **1** a small swivelled wheel (often one of a set) fixed to a leg (or the underside) of a piece of furniture. **2** a small container with holes in the top for sprinkling the contents. □ **castor action** swivelling of vehicle wheels to ensure stability. **castor sugar** finely granulated white sugar. [orig. a var. of CASTER (in the general sense)]

castor² /kaástər/ *n.* an oily substance secreted by beavers and used in medicine and perfumes. [F or L f. Gk *kastōr* beaver]

castor oil /kaástər/ *n.* **1** an oil from the seeds of a plant, *Ricinus communis*, used as a purgative and lubricant. **2** (in full **castor oil plant**) this plant. □ **castor oil bean** (or

castor bean) a seed of the castor oil plant. [18th c.: orig. uncert.: perh. so called as having succeeded CASTOR[2] in the medical sense]

castrate /kastráyt/ *v.tr.* **1** remove the testicles of; geld. **2** deprive of vigour. □□ **castration** *n.* **castrator** *n.* [L *castrare*]
■ **1** see NEUTER *v.*

castrato /kastraátō/ *n.* (*pl.* **castrati** /-ti/) *hist.* a male singer castrated in boyhood so as to retain a soprano or alto voice. [It., past part. of *castrare*: see CASTRATE]

casual /kázhooəl, kázyoo-/ *adj.* & *n.* ● *adj.* **1** accidental; due to chance. **2** not regular or permanent; temporary, occasional (*casual work; a casual affair*). **3 a** unconcerned, uninterested (*was very casual about it*). **b** made or done without great care or thought (*a casual remark*). **c** acting carelessly or unmethodically. **4** (of clothes) informal. ● *n.* **1** a casual worker. **2** (usu. in *pl.*) casual clothes or shoes. □□ **casually** *adv.* **casualness** *n.* [ME f. OF *casuel* & L *casualis* f. *casus* CASE[1]]
■ *adj.* **1** accidental, chance, coincidental, adventitious, aleatoric, aleatory, random, incidental, spontaneous, fortuitous, unexpected, impromptu, unforeseen, unpremeditated, unplanned, unlooked-for, unforeseeable, unpredictable, serendipitous, haphazard. **2** occasional, temporary, part-time, impermanent, makeshift, stopgap, irregular, intermittent; superficial, passing, transient, fleeting. **3 a** indifferent, nonchalant, offhand, lax, insouciant, apathetic, cool, unconcerned, unbothered, uninterested, dispassionate, blasé, blithe, relaxed, lackadaisical, indiscriminate, *colloq.* laid-back. **b** thoughtless, unthinking, offhand, extempore, careless, cursory, passing, stray, ill-considered, ill-judged, inadvertent, unguarded, unpremeditated, hasty, *colloq.* off the cuff. **c** unmethodical, unsystematic, unsystematized, disorderly, disordered, disorganized, unorganized, haphazard, sporadic, erratic, chaotic, confused, careless, hit-or-miss, *colloq.* slap-happy. **4** see INFORMAL. ● *n.* **1** freelance, freelancer; temporary, *colloq.* temp.

casualty /kázhooəlti, kázyoo-/ *n.* (*pl.* **-ies**) **1** a person killed or injured in a war or accident. **2** a thing lost or destroyed. **3** = *casualty department*. **4** an accident, mishap, or disaster. □ **casualty department** (or **ward**) the part of a hospital where casualties are treated. [ME f. med.L *casualitas* (as CASUAL), after ROYALTY etc.]
■ **1** victim, fatality, death; (*casualties*) wounded, injured, dead, *Mil.* missing in action, losses. **4** disaster, catastrophe, calamity, tragedy; accident, mischance, misfortune, misadventure, mishap.

casuarina /kássyooreénə/ *n.* any tree of the genus *Casuarina*, native to Australia and SE Asia, having tiny scale leaves on slender jointed branches, resembling gigantic horsetails. [mod.L *casuarius* cassowary (from the resemblance between branches and feathers)]

casuist /kázhoo-ist, kázyoo-/ *n.* **1** a person, esp. a theologian, who resolves problems of conscience, duty, etc., often with clever but false reasoning. **2** a sophist or quibbler. □□ **casuistic** /-ístik/ *adj.* **casuistical** /-ístik'l/ *adj.* **casuistically** /-ístikəli/ *adv.* **casuistry** *n.* [F *casuiste* f. Sp. *casuista* f. L *casus* CASE[1]]
■ □□ **casuistic, casuistical** see SPECIOUS.

casus belli /kaázəss bélli, káysəss/ *n.* an act or situation provoking or justifying war. [L]

CAT *abbr.* **1** computer-assisted (or -aided) testing. **2** *Med.* computerized axial tomography.

cat /kat/ *n.* & *v.* ● *n.* **1** a small soft-furred four-legged domesticated animal, *Felis catus*. **2 a** any wild animal of the genus *Felis*, e.g. a lion, tiger, or leopard. **b** = *wild cat*. **3** a catlike animal of any other species (*civet cat*). **4** *colloq.* a malicious or spiteful woman. **5** *sl.* a jazz enthusiast. **6** *Naut.* = CATHEAD. **7** = *cat-o'-nine-tails*. **8** a short tapered stick in the game of tipcat. ● *v.tr.* (also *absol.*) (**catted, catting**) *Naut.* raise (an anchor) from the surface of the water to the cathead. □ **cat-and-dog** (of a relationship etc.) full of quarrels. **cat burglar** a burglar who enters by climbing to an upper storey. **cat flap** (or **door**) a small swinging flap in an outer door, for a cat to pass in and out. **cat-ice** thin ice unsupported by water. **cat-o'-nine-tails** *hist.* a rope whip with nine knotted lashes for flogging sailors, soldiers, or criminals. **cat's cradle** a child's game in which a loop of string is held between the fingers and patterns are formed. **Cat's-eye** *Brit. propr.* one of a series of reflector studs set into a road. **cat's-eye** a precious stone of Sri Lanka and Malabar. **cat's-foot** any small plant of the genus *Antennaria*, having soft woolly leaves and growing on the surface of the ground. **cat's-paw 1** a person used as a tool by another. **2** a slight breeze rippling the surface of the water. **cat's-tail** = *reed-mace* (see REED[1]). **cat's whiskers** (or **pyjamas**) *sl.* an excellent person or thing. **let the cat out of the bag** reveal a secret, esp. involuntarily. **like a cat on hot bricks** (or **on a hot tin roof**) very agitated or agitatedly. **put** (or **set**) **the cat among the pigeons** cause trouble. **rain cats and dogs** *colloq.* rain very hard. [OE *catt(e)* f. LL *cattus*]
■ □ **cat-o'-nine-tails** see WHIP *n.* **cat's-paw 1** see BUTT[2].

cata- /káttə/ *prefix* (usu. **cat-** before a vowel or *h*) **1** down, downwards (*catadromous*). **2** wrongly, badly (*catachresis*). [Gk *kata* down]

catabolism /kətábbəliz'm/ *n.* (also **katabolism**) *Biochem.* the breakdown of complex molecules in living organisms to form simpler ones with the release of energy; destructive metabolism (opp. ANABOLISM). □□ **catabolic** /káttəbóllik/ *adj.* [Gk *katabolē* descent f. *kata* down + *bolē* f. *ballō* throw]

catachresis /káttəkreéssiss/ *n.* (*pl.* **catachreses** /-seez/) an incorrect use of words. □□ **catachrestic** /-kreéstik, -kréstik/ *adj.* [L f. Gk *katakhrēsis* f. *khraomai* use]
■ see MISUSE *n.*

cataclasis /káttəkláysiss/ *n.* (*pl.* **cataclases** /-seez/) *Geol.* the natural process of fracture, shearing, or breaking up of rocks. □□ **cataclastic** /-klástik/ *adj.* [mod.L f. Gk *kataklasis* breaking down]

cataclasm /káttəklaz'm/ *n.* a violent break; a disruption. [Gk *kataklasma* (as CATA-, *klaō* to break)]

cataclysm /káttəkliz'm/ *n.* **1 a** a violent, esp. social or political, upheaval or disaster. **b** a great change. **2** a great flood or deluge. □□ **cataclysmal** /-klízm'l/ *adj.* **cataclysmic** /-klízmik/ *adj.* **cataclysmically** /-klízmikəli/ *adv.* [F *cataclysme* f. L *cataclysmus* f. Gk *kataklusmos* f. *klusmos* flood f. *kluzō* wash]
■ **1** see DISASTER 1.

catacomb /káttəkoōm, -kōm/ *n.* (often in *pl.*) **1** an underground cemetery, esp. a Roman subterranean gallery with recesses for tombs. **2** a similar underground construction; a cellar. [F *catacombes* f. LL *catacumbas* (name given in the 5th c. to the cemetery of St Sebastian near Rome), of unkn. orig.]
■ **1** see CRYPT.

catadromous /kətádrəməss/ *adj.* (of a fish, e.g. the eel) that swims down rivers to the sea to spawn (cf. ANADROMOUS). [Gk *katadromos* f. *kata* down + *dromos* running]

catafalque /káttəfalk/ *n.* a decorated wooden framework for supporting the coffin of a distinguished person during a funeral or while lying in state. [F f. It. *catafalco*, of unkn. orig.: cf. SCAFFOLD]

Catalan /káttəlan/ *n.* & *adj.* ● *n.* **1** a native of Catalonia in Spain. **2** the language of Catalonia. ● *adj.* of or relating to Catalonia or its people or language. [F f. Sp.]

catalase /káttəlayz/ *n.* *Biochem.* an enzyme that catalyses the reduction of hydrogen peroxide. [CATALYSIS]

catalepsy /káttəlepsi/ *n.* a state of trance or seizure with loss of sensation and consciousness accompanied by rigidity of the body. □□ **cataleptic** /-léptik/ *adj.* & *n.* [F *catalepsie* or LL *catalepsia* f. Gk *katalēpsis* (as CATA-, *lēpsis* seizure)]

catalogue /káttəlog/ *n.* & *v.* (*US* **catalog**) ● *n.* **1** a complete list of items (e.g. articles for sale, books held by a library), usu. in alphabetical or other systematic order and often with a description of each. **2** an extensive list (*a catalogue of crimes*). **3** *US* a university course-list etc. ● *v.tr.* (**catalogues, catalogued, cataloguing;** *US* **catalogs, cataloged, cataloging**) **1** make a catalogue of. **2** enter in a catalogue. ◻◻ **cataloguer** *n.* (*US* **cataloger**). [F f. LL *catalogus* f. Gk. *katalogos* f. *katalegō* enrol (as CATA-, *legō* choose)]

■ *n.* see LIST¹ *n.* ● *v.* see LIST¹ *v.*

catalogue raisonné /káttəlog ráyzonáy/ *n.* a descriptive catalogue with explanations or comments. [F, = explained catalogue]

■ see LIST¹ *n.* 1.

catalpa /kətálpə/ *n.* any tree of the genus *Catalpa*, with heart-shaped leaves, trumpet-shaped flowers, and long pods. [Amer. Ind. (Creek)]

catalyse /káttəlīz/ *v.tr.* (*US* **catalyze**) *Chem.* produce (a reaction) by catalysis. [as CATALYSIS after *analyse*]

catalysis /kətállisiss/ *n.* (*pl.* **catalyses** /-seez/) *Chem.* & *Biochem.* the acceleration of a chemical or biochemical reaction by a catalyst. [Gk *katalusis* dissolution (as CATA-, *luō* set free)]

catalyst /káttəlist/ *n.* **1** *Chem.* a substance that, without itself undergoing any permanent chemical change, increases the rate of a reaction. **2** a person or thing that precipitates a change. [as CATALYSIS after *analyst*]

catalytic /káttəlíttik/ *adj. Chem.* relating to or involving catalysis. ◻ **catalytic converter** a device incorporated in the exhaust system of a motor vehicle, with a catalyst for converting pollutant gases into harmless products. **catalytic cracker** a device for cracking (see CRACK *v.* 9) petroleum oils by catalysis.

catalyze *US* var. of CATALYSE.

catamaran /káttəmərán/ *n.* **1** a boat with twin hulls in parallel. **2** a raft of yoked logs or boats. **3** *colloq.* a quarrelsome woman. [Tamil *kaṭṭumaram* tied wood]

catamite /káttəmīt/ *n.* **1** a boy kept for homosexual practices. **2** the passive partner in sodomy. [L *catamitus* through Etruscan f. Gk *Ganumēdēs* Ganymede, cupbearer of Zeus]

■ see PROSTITUTE *n.* 1b.

catamountain /káttəmowntin/ *n.* **1** a lynx, leopard, puma, or other tiger-cat. **2** a wild quarrelsome person. [ME f. *cat of the mountain*]

catananche /káttənángki/ *n.* any composite plant of the genus *Catananche*, with blue or yellow flowers. [mod.L f. L *catanancē* plant used in love-potions f. Gk *katanagkē* (as CATA-, *anagkē* compulsion)]

cataplexy /káttəpleksi/ *n.* sudden temporary paralysis due to fright etc. ◻◻ **cataplectic** /-pléktik/ *adj.* [Gk *kataplēxis* stupefaction]

catapult /káttəpult/ *n.* & *v.* ● *n.* **1** a forked stick etc. with elastic for shooting stones. **2** *hist.* a military machine worked by a lever and ropes for hurling large stones etc. **3** a mechanical device for launching a glider, an aircraft from the deck of a ship, etc. ● *v.* **1** *tr.* **a** hurl from or launch with a catapult. **b** fling forcibly. **2** *intr.* leap or be hurled forcibly. [F *catapulte* or L *catapulta* f. Gk *katapeltēs* (as CATA-, *pallō* hurl)]

■ *n.* **1** see SLING¹ *n.* 3. ● *v.* **1** see LAUNCH¹ *v.* 2.

cataract /káttərakt/ *n.* **1 a** a large waterfall or cascade. **b** a downpour; a rush of water. **2** *Med.* a condition in which the eye-lens becomes progressively opaque resulting in blurred vision. [L *cataracta* f. Gk *katarrhaktēs* down-rushing; in med. sense prob. f. obs. sense 'portcullis']

■ **1 a** see WATERFALL. **b** see STREAM *n.* 2.

catarrh /kətaár/ *n.* **1** inflammation of the mucous membrane of the nose, air passages, etc. **2** a watery discharge in the nose or throat due to this. ◻◻ **catarrhal** *adj.* [F *catarrhe* f. LL *catarrhus* f. Gk *katarrhous* f. *katarrheō* flow down]

catarrhine /káttərīn/ *adj.* & *n. Zool.* ● *adj.* (of primates) having nostrils close together, and directed downwards, e.g. a baboon, chimpanzee, or human. ● *n.* such an animal (cf. PLATYRRHINE). [CATA- + *rhis rhinos* nose]

catastrophe /kətástrəfi/ *n.* **1** a great and usu. sudden disaster. **2** the denouement of a drama. **3** a disastrous end; ruin. **4** an event producing a subversion of the order of things. ◻◻ **catastrophic** /káttəstróffik/ *adj.* **catastrophically** /káttəstróffikəli/ *adv.* [L *catastropha* f. Gk *katastrophē* (as CATA-, *strophē* turning f. *strephō* turn)]

■ **1** disaster, calamity, cataclysm, casualty, misfortune, tragedy, reverse, affliction, visitation; fiasco. **3** ruin, disaster, destruction, devastation, downfall, havoc, collapse, disintegration, ruination, failure, débâcle; the abyss.

catastrophism /kətástrəfiz'm/ *n. Geol.* the theory that changes in the earth's crust have occurred in sudden violent and unusual events. ◻◻ **catastrophist** *n.*

catatonia /káttətṓniə/ *n.* **1** schizophrenia with intervals of catalepsy and sometimes violence. **2** catalepsy. ◻◻ **catatonic** /-tónnik/ *adj.* & *n.* [G *Katatonie* (as CATA-, TONE)]

catawba /kətáwbə/ *n.* **1** a US variety of grape. **2** a white wine made from it. [River *Catawba* in S. Carolina]

catboat /kátbōt/ *n.* a sailing-boat with a single mast placed well forward and carrying only one sail. [perh. f. *cat* a former type of coaler in NE England, + BOAT]

catcall /kátkawl/ *n.* & *v.* ● *n.* a shrill whistle of disapproval made at meetings etc. ● *v.* **1** *intr.* make a catcall. **2** *tr.* make a catcall at.

■ *n.* see JEER *n.* ● *v.* **1** see JEER *v.* 1. **2** see JEER *v.* 2.

catch /kach/ *v.* & *n.* ● *v.* (*past* and *past part.* **caught** /kawt/) **1** *tr.* **a** lay hold of so as to restrain or prevent from escaping; capture in a trap, in one's hands, etc. **b** (also **catch hold of**) get into one's hands so as to retain, operate, etc. (*caught hold of the handle*). **2** *tr.* detect or surprise (a person, esp. in a wrongful or embarrassing act) (*caught me in the act*; *caught him smoking*). **3** *tr.* **a** intercept and hold (a moving thing) in the hands etc. (*failed to catch the ball*; *a bowl to catch the drips*). **b** *Cricket* dismiss (a batsman) by catching the ball before it reaches the ground. **4** *tr.* **a** contract (a disease) by infection or contagion. **b** acquire (a quality or feeling) from another's example (*caught her enthusiasm*). **5** *tr.* **a** reach in time and board (a train, bus, etc.). **b** be in time to see etc. (a person or thing about to leave or finish) (*if you hurry you'll catch them*; *caught the end of the performance*). **6** *tr.* **a** apprehend with the senses or the mind (esp. a thing occurring quickly or briefly) (*didn't catch what he said*). **b** (of an artist etc.) reproduce faithfully. **7 a** *intr.* become fixed or entangled; be checked (*the bolt began to catch*). **b** *tr.* cause to do this (*caught her tights on a nail*). **c** *tr.* (often foll. by *on*) hit, deal a blow to (*caught him on the nose*; *caught his elbow on the table*). **8** *tr.* draw the attention of; captivate (*caught his eye*; *caught her fancy*). **9** *intr.* begin to burn. **10** *tr.* (often foll. by *up*) reach or overtake (a person etc. ahead). **11** *tr.* check suddenly (*caught his breath*). **12** *tr.* (foll. by *at*) grasp or try to grasp. ● *n.* **1 a** an act of catching. **b** *Cricket* a chance or act of catching the ball. **2 a** an amount of a thing caught, esp. of fish. **b** a thing or person caught or worth catching, esp. in marriage. **3 a** a question, trick, etc., intended to deceive, incriminate, etc. **b** an unexpected or hidden difficulty or disadvantage. **4** a device for fastening a door or window etc. **5** *Mus.* a round, esp. with words arranged to produce a humorous effect. ◻ **catch-all** (often *attrib.*) a thing designed to be all-inclusive. **catch-as-catch-can** a style of wrestling with few holds barred. **catch at a straw** see STRAW. **catch crop** a crop grown between two staple crops (in position or time). **catch one's death** see DEATH. **catch fire** see FIRE. **catch it** *sl.* be punished or in trouble. **catch me!** etc. (often foll. by *pres. part.*) *colloq.* you may be sure I etc. shall not. **catch on** *colloq.* **1** (of a practice, fashion, etc.) become popular. **2** (of a person) understand what is meant. **catch out 1** detect in a mistake etc. **2** take unawares; cause to be bewildered or confused. **3** = sense 3b of *v.* **catch-phrase** a phrase in frequent use. **catch the sun 1** be in a sunny position. **2** become sunburnt. **catch up 1 a** (often foll. by *with*) reach a person etc. ahead (*he caught up in the end*; *he caught us up*; *he caught up with us*). **b** (often foll. by *with*, *on*) make up arrears (of work etc.) (*must catch up with my correspondence*). **2** snatch or pick up hurriedly. **3** (often in *passive*) **a** involve; entangle (*caught up in suspicious dealings*). **b** fasten up (*hair caught up in a ribbon*). □□ **catchable** *adj.* [ME f. AF & ONF *cachier*, OF *chacier*, ult. f. L *captare* try to catch]

■ *v.* **1 a** capture, seize, apprehend, take *or* get (hold of), grab, take captive, arrest, take prisoner, collar, *sl.* nab, pinch, *Austral. sl.* snavel, *Brit. sl.* nick; trap, ensnare, entrap, snare, net, bag, hook, land. **b** grab (hold of), grip, grasp, seize, clasp, clutch, take *or* lay *or* get hold of, fasten on *or* upon. **2** surprise, discover, find, detect, uncover, take unawares. **3 a** intercept, field, stop; grab, seize, snatch, take possession of. **4 a** contract, get, develop, be seized by, be taken hold of by *or* with, come down with, pick up, acquire, be afflicted by *or* with, suffer from, *Brit.* go down with, *archaic* be stricken by *or* with. **5 a** make; take, get, get on (to), board, *colloq.* hop. **6 a** understand, comprehend, ascertain, grasp, apprehend, follow, take in, hear, gather, fathom, perceive, discern, *colloq.* get, catch on to, get the drift of, cotton on to, twig. **7 a** tangle, be enmeshed, stick, lodge, become entangled *or* stuck *or* trapped *or* fixed *or* hooked *or* wedged. **b** snag, wedge, fix, entangle, hook; tear, rip. **c** see BOX[2] *v.* 2. **8** attract, draw, capture; appeal to, engage, captivate, bewitch. **9** ignite, light, flare up. **10** reach, draw level *or* even with, get to, come to, make it to, catch up (with); overtake, pass, go past, overhaul. **11** restrain, control, stop, check, curb. ● *n.* **2 a** take, bag, haul, yield, harvest. **b** find; conquest. **3 a** trick, trap, wile, dodge, *colloq.* ploy, *sl.* con. **b** disadvantage, hitch, snag, problem, drawback, difficulty, twist, rub, fly in the ointment, complication, small print, stumbling block, joker (in the pack). **4** clasp, bolt, hook, pin, clip, buckle, fastening, fastener. □ **catch-all** (*attrib.*) see INCLUSIVE 3. **catch it** be in trouble *or* deep water, *colloq.* get it in the neck, get a dressing-down *or* telling-off, get a piece of a person's mind. **catch on 1** take hold, become popular *or* fashionable. **2** understand, comprehend, see daylight, *colloq.* get it, cotton on, get the drift, twig. **catch out 1, 2** catch in the act *or* red-handed; take unawares, catch napping, catch off guard, take aback, surprise, *colloq.* catch flat-footed. **catch up 1 a** see CATCH *v.* 10 above. **b** clear the backlog (of); make up time. **3 a** absorb, involve, enthral, immerse, engross, preoccupy, wrap up; engage, occupy; mix up, bind up, entangle, embroil, implicate, draw in, enmesh, ensnare.

catcher /káchər/ *n.* **1** a person or thing that catches. **2** *Baseball* a fielder who stands behind the batter.

catchfly /káchflī/ *n.* (*pl.* **-ies**) any plant of the genus *Silene* or *Lychnis* with a sticky stem.

catching /káching/ *adj.* **1 a** (of a disease) infectious. **b** (of a practice, habit, etc.) likely to be imitated. **2** attractive; captivating.

■ **1 a** contagious, infectious, transmissible, transmittable, communicable. **2** attractive, captivating, fascinating, enchanting, bewitching, entrancing, engaging, winning, enticing, alluring, fetching, winsome.

catchline /káchlīn/ *n.* *Printing* a short line of type esp. at the head of copy or as a running headline.

catchment /káchmənt/ *n.* the collection of rainfall. □ **catchment area 1** the area from which rainfall flows into a river etc. **2** the area served by a school, hospital, etc.

catchpenny /káchpenni/ *adj.* intended merely to sell quickly; superficially attractive.

catch-22 /káchtwentitóō/ *n.* (often *attrib.*) *colloq.* a dilemma or circumstance from which there is no escape because of mutually conflicting or dependent conditions. [title of a novel by J. Heller (1961) featuring a dilemma of this kind]

■ see DILEMMA 1.

catchup var. of KETCHUP.

catchweight /káchwayt/ *adj.* & *n.* ● *adj.* unrestricted as regards weight. ● *n.* unrestricted weight, as a weight category in sports.

catchword /káchwurd/ *n.* **1** a word or phrase in common (often temporary) use; a topical slogan. **2** a word so placed as to draw attention. **3** *Theatr.* an actor's cue. **4** *Printing* the first word of a page given at the foot of the previous one.

■ **1, 2** see SLOGAN.

catchy /káchi/ *adj.* (**catchier**, **catchiest**) **1** (of a tune) easy to remember; attractive. **2** that snares or entraps; deceptive. **3** (of the wind etc.) fitful, spasmodic. □□ **catchily** *adv.* **catchiness** *n.* [CATCH + -Y[1]]

■ **1** see MEMORABLE.

cate /kayt/ *n.* *archaic* (usu. in *pl.*) choice food, delicacies. [obs. *acate* purchase f. AF *acat*, OF *achat* f. *acater*, *achater* buy: see CATER]

catechetical /káttikéttik'l/ *adj.* (also **catechetic**) **1** of or by oral teaching. **2** according to the catechism of a Church. **3** consisting of or proceeding by question and answer. □□ **catechetically** *adv.* **catechetics** *n.* [eccl.Gk *katēkhētikos* f. *katēkhētēs* oral teacher: see CATECHIZE]

catechism /káttikiz'm/ *n.* **1 a** a summary of the principles of a religion in the form of questions and answers. **b** a book containing this. **2** a series of questions put to anyone. □□ **catechismal** /-kízm'l/ *adj.* [eccl.L *catechismus* (as CATECHIZE)]

■ **2** see EXAMINATION 5.

catechist /káttikist/ *n.* a religious teacher, esp. one using a catechism.

catechize /káttikīz/ *v.tr.* (also **-ise**) **1** instruct by means of question and answer, esp. from a catechism. **2** put questions to; examine. □□ **catechizer** *n.* [LL *catechizare* f. eccl.Gk *katēkhizō* f. *katēkheō* make hear (as CATA-, *ēkheō* sound)]

■ **2** see EXAMINE 5.

catechu /káttichoo/ *n.* (also **cachou** /káshoo/) gambier or similar vegetable extract, containing tannin. [mod.L f. Malay *kachu*]

catechumen /káttikyóomən/ *n.* a Christian convert under instruction before baptism. [ME f. OF *catechumene* or eccl.L *catechumenus* f. Gk *katēkheō*: see CATECHIZE]

■ see INITIATE *n.*

categorical /káttigórrik'l/ *adj.* (also **categoric**) unconditional, absolute; explicit, direct (*a categorical refusal*). □ **categorical imperative** *Ethics* an unconditional moral obligation derived from pure reason; the bidding of conscience as ultimate moral law. □□ **categorically** *adv.* [F *catégorique* or LL *categoricus* f. Gk *katēgorikos*: see CATEGORY]

■ direct, explicit, express, unconditional, firm, positive, absolute, unmitigated, unqualified, definitive, unequivocal, unambiguous, specific, unreserved, unrestricted, outright, downright, flat, point-blank, emphatic, apodictic.

categorize /káttigərīz/ *v.tr.* (also **-ise**) place in a category or categories. □□ **categorization** /-záysh'n/ *n.*

■ compartmentalize, classify, class, sort, organize, group, assort, rank, order, section, departmentalize, compartmentalize, file, label, arrange.

category /káttigəri, -gri/ *n.* (*pl.* **-ies**) **1** a class or division. **2** *Philos.* **a** one of a possibly exhaustive set of classes among which all things might be distributed. **b** one of the a priori conceptions applied by the mind to sense-impressions. **c** any relatively fundamental philosophical concept. □□ **categorial** /-góriəl/ *adj.* [F *catégorie* or LL *categoria* f. Gk *katēgoria* statement f. *katēgoros* accuser]

■ **1** class, type, sort, kind, variety, species, form, order, breed, nature, manner, description; division, section, sector, league, bracket, genre, set, group, area, sphere, realm, domain, grouping, grade, department, head, heading.

catena /kateénə/ *n.* (*pl.* **catenae** /-nee/ or **catenas**) **1** a connected series of patristic comments on Scripture. **2** a series or chain. [L, = chain: orig. *catena patrum* chain of the Fathers (of the Church)]

catenary /kəteénəri/ *n.* & *adj.* ● *n.* (*pl.* **-ies**) a curve formed by a uniform chain hanging freely from two points not in the same vertical line. ● *adj.* of or resembling such a curve. □ **catenary bridge** a suspension bridge hung from such chains. [L *catenarius* f. *catena* chain]

catenate /káttinayt/ *v.tr.* connect like links of a chain. □□ **catenation** /-náysh'n/ *n.* [L *catenare catenat-* (as CATENARY)]

cater /káytər/ *v.intr.* **1** (often foll. by *for*) provide food. **2** (foll. by *for, to*) provide what is desired or needed by. **3** (foll. by *to*) pander to (esp. low tastes). [obs. noun *cater* (now *caterer*), f. *acater* f. AF *acatour* buyer f. *acater* buy f. Rmc]

■ **1** (*cater for*) provision, victual, provide. **2** (*cater for* or *to*) provide (services) for, accommodate, be host to, host, entertain, receive, deal with, handle, see to; care for, look after, minister to; make allowances for, take into consideration *or* account, consider, bear in mind, have regard for. **3** (*cater to*) indulge, pander to, minister to, humour, serve.

cateran /káttərən/ *n. Sc.* a Highland irregular fighting man; a marauder. [ME f. med.L *cateranus* & Gael. *ceathairne* peasantry]

cater-cornered /káttərkórnərd/ *adj.* & *adv.* (also **cater-corner, catty-cornered** /kátti-/) *US* ● *adj.* placed or situated diagonally. ● *adv.* diagonally. [dial. adv. *cater* diagonally (cf. obs. *cater* the four on dice f. F *quatre* f. L *quattuor* four)]

caterer /káytərər/ *n.* a person who supplies food for social events, esp. professionally.

catering /káytəring/ *n.* the profession or work of a caterer.

caterpillar /káttərpillər/ *n.* **1 a** the larva of a butterfly or moth. **b** (in general use) any similar larva of various insects. **2** (**Caterpillar**) **a** (in full **Caterpillar track** or **tread**) *propr.* a steel band passing round the wheels of a tractor etc. for travel on rough ground. **b** a vehicle with these tracks, e.g. a tractor or tank. [perh. AF var. of OF *chatepelose* lit. hairy cat, infl. by obs. *piller* ravager]

caterwaul /káttərwawl/ *v.* & *n.* ● *v.intr.* make the shrill howl of a cat. ● *n.* a caterwauling noise. [ME f. CAT + *-waul* etc. imit.]

■ *v.* see SCREAM *v.* 1, 2. ● *n.* see SCREAM *n.* 1.

catfish /kátfish/ *n.* any of various esp. freshwater fish, usu. having whisker-like barbels round the mouth.

catgut /kátgut/ *n.* a material used for the strings of musical instruments and surgical sutures, made of the twisted intestines of the sheep, horse, or ass (but not the cat).

Cath. *abbr.* **1** Cathedral. **2** Catholic.

Cathar /káthər/ *n.* (*pl.* **Cathars** or **Cathari** /-ri/) a member of a medieval sect which sought to achieve great spiritual purity. □□ **Catharism** *n.* **Catharist** *n.* [med.L *Cathari* (pl.) f. Gk *katharoi* pure]

catharsis /kəthaársiss/ *n.* (*pl.* **catharses** /-seez/) **1** an emotional release in drama or art. **2** *Psychol.* the process of freeing repressed emotion by association with the cause, and elimination by abreaction. **3** *Med.* purgation. [mod.L f. Gk *katharsis* f. *kathairō* cleanse: sense 1 f. Aristotle's *Poetics*]

cathartic /kəthaártik/ *adj.* & *n.* ● *adj.* **1** effecting catharsis. **2** purgative. ● *n.* a cathartic drug. □□ **cathartically** *adv.* [LL *catharticus* f. Gk *kathartikos* (as CATHARSIS)]

■ *adj.* see PURGATIVE *adj.* 1, 2. ● *n.* see PURGATIVE *n.* 2.

Cathay /katháy/ *n. archaic* or *poet.* the country China. [med.L *Cataya*]

cathead /kát-hed/ *n. Naut.* a horizontal beam from each side of a ship's bow for raising and carrying the anchor.

cathectic see CATHEXIS.

cathedral /kəthe͞edrəl/ *n.* the principal church of a diocese, containing the bishop's throne. □ **cathedral city** a city in which there is a cathedral. [ME (as adj.) f. OF *cathedral* or f. LL *cathedralis* f. L f. Gk *kathedra* seat]

Catherine wheel /káthrin/ *n.* **1** a firework in the form of a flat coil which spins when fixed and lit. **2** a circular window with radial divisions. [mod.L *Catharina* f. Gk *Aikaterina* name of a saint martyred on a spiked wheel]

catheter /káthitər/ *n. Med.* a tube for insertion into a body cavity for introducing or removing fluid. [LL f. Gk *kathetēr* f. *kathiēmi* send down]

catheterize /káthitərīz/ *v.tr.* (also **-ise**) *Med.* insert a catheter into.

cathetometer /káthitómmitər/ *n.* a telescope mounted on a graduated scale along which it can slide, used for accurate measurement of small vertical distances. [L *cathetus* f. Gk *kathetos* perpendicular line (as CATHETER + -METER)]

cathexis /kəthéksiss/ *n.* (*pl.* **cathexes** /-seez/) *Psychol.* concentration of mental energy in one channel. □□ **cathectic** *adj.* [Gk *kathexis* retention]

cathode /káthōd/ *n.* (also **kathode**) *Electr.* **1** the negative electrode in an electrolytic cell or electronic valve or tube. **2** the positive terminal of a primary cell such as a battery (opp. ANODE). □ **cathode ray** a beam of electrons emitted from the cathode of a high-vacuum tube. **cathode-ray tube** a high-vacuum tube in which cathode rays produce a luminous image on a fluorescent screen. ¶ Abbr.: **CRT**. □□ **cathodal** *adj.* **cathodic** /kəthóddik/ *adj.* [Gk *kathodos* descent f. *kata* down + *hodos* way]

catholic /káthəlik, káthlik/ *adj.* & *n.* ● *adj.* **1** of interest or use to all; universal. **2** all-embracing; of wide sympathies or interests (*has catholic tastes*). **3** (**Catholic**) **a** of the Roman Catholic religion. **b** including all Christians. **c** including all of the Western Church. ● *n.* (**Catholic**) a Roman Catholic. □□ **catholically** *adv.* **Catholicism** /kəthóllisiz'm/ *n.* **catholicity** /káthəlíssiti/ *n.* **catholicly** *adv.* [ME f. OF *catholique* or LL *catholicus* f. Gk *katholikos* universal f. *kata* in respect of + *holos* whole]

■ *adj.* **1** universal, general, widespread. **2** inclusive, all-inclusive, broad, wide, wide-ranging, comprehensive, widespread, all-embracing, extensive, eclectic, liberal, tolerant, open-minded, broad-minded, unprejudiced, unbigoted, latitudinarian, enlightened. **3 b** ecumenical, Christian.

catholicize /kəthóllisīz/ *v.tr.* & *intr.* (also **-ise**) **1** make or become catholic. **2** (**Catholicize**) make or become a Roman Catholic.

cation /káttīən/ *n.* a positively charged ion; an ion that is attracted to the cathode in electrolysis (opp. ANION). [CATA- + ION]

cationic /káttīónnik/ *adj.* **1** of a cation or cations. **2** having an active cation.

catkin /kátkin/ *n.* a spike of usu. downy or silky male or female flowers hanging from a willow, hazel, etc. [obs. Du. *katteken* kitten]

catlick /kátlik/ *n. colloq.* a perfunctory wash.

catlike /kátlīk/ *adj.* **1** like a cat. **2** stealthy.

catmint /kátmint/ *n.* a white-flowered plant, *Nepeta cataria*, having a pungent smell attractive to cats. Also called CATNIP.

catnap /kátnap/ *n.* & *v.* ● *n.* a short sleep. ● *v.intr.* (**-napped, -napping**) have a catnap.

■ *n.* see DOZE *n.* ● *v.* see DOZE *v.*

catnip /kátnip/ *n.* = CATMINT. [CAT + dial. *nip* catmint, var. of dial. *nep*]

catoptric /kətóptrik/ *adj.* of or relating to a mirror, a reflector, or reflection. □□ **catoptrics** *n.* [Gk *katoptrikos* f. *katoptron* mirror]

catsuit /kátso͞ot, -syo͞ot/ *n.* a close-fitting garment with trouser legs, covering the body from neck to feet.

catsup /kátsəp/ esp. *US* var. of KETCHUP.

cattery /káttəri/ *n.* (*pl.* **-ies**) a place where cats are boarded or bred.

cattish /káttish/ *adj.* = CATTY. □□ **cattishly** *adv.* **cattishness** *n.*

cattle /kátt'l/ *n.pl.* **1** bison, buffalo, yaks, or domesticated bovine animals, esp. of the genus *Bos*. **2** *archaic* livestock. □ **cattle-cake** *Brit.* a concentrated food for cattle, in cake form. **cattle-dog** *Austral.* & *NZ* a dog trained to work with cattle. **cattle-duff** *Austral.* to steal cattle. **cattle-duffer** *Austral.* a cattle thief. **cattle-grid** *Brit.* a grid covering a ditch, allowing vehicles to pass over but not cattle, sheep, etc.

cattle-guard *US* = *cattle-grid*. **cattle-plague** rinderpest. **cattle-stop** *NZ* = *cattle-grid*. [ME & AF *catel* f. OF *chatel* CHATTEL]
■ **1, 2** cows, bulls, bullocks, steers, oxen; stock, livestock.

cattleman /kátt'lmən/ *n.* (*pl.* **-men**) *US* a person who tends or rears cattle.

cattleya /kátliə/ *n.* any epiphytic orchid of the genus *Cattleya*, with handsome violet, pink, or yellow flowers. [mod.L f. W. *Cattley*, Engl. patron of botany d. 1832]

catty /kátti/ *adj.* (**cattier**, **cattiest**) **1** sly, spiteful; deliberately hurtful in speech. **2** catlike. □□ **cattily** *adv.* **cattiness** *n.*

catty-cornered var. of CATER-CORNERED.

catwalk /kátwawk/ *n.* **1** a narrow footway along a bridge, above a theatre stage, etc. **2** a narrow platform or gangway used in fashion shows etc.

Caucasian /kawkáyzh'n, -káyziən/ *adj.* & *n.* ● *adj.* **1** of or relating to the White or light-skinned division of mankind. **2** of or relating to the Caucasus. ● *n.* a Caucasian person. [*Caucasus*, mountains between the Black and Caspian Seas, the supposed place of origin of this people]
■ *adj.* **1** see WHITE *adj.* 4.

Caucasoid /káwkəsoyd/ *adj.* of or relating to the Caucasian division of mankind.
■ see WHITE *adj.* 4.

caucus /káwkəss/ *n.* **1** *US* **a** a meeting of the members of a political party, esp. in the Senate etc., to decide policy. **b** a bloc of such members. **c** this system as a political force. **2** often *derog.* (esp. in the UK) **a** a usu. secret meeting of a group within a larger organization or party. **b** such a group. [18th-c. US, perh. f. Algonquian *cau'-cau-as'u* adviser]
■ **1a, 2a** see MEETING 2, 5. **1b, 2b** see PARTY[1] *n.* 3.

caudal /káwd'l/ *adj.* **1** of or like a tail. **2** of the posterior part of the body. □□ **caudally** *adv.* [mod.L *caudalis* f. L *cauda* tail]

caudate /káwdayt/ *adj.* having a tail. [see CAUDAL]

caudillo /kowdéelyō/ *n.* (*pl.* **-os**) (in Spanish-speaking countries) a military or political leader. [Sp. f. LL *capitellum* dimin. of *caput* head]

caught *past* and *past part.* of CATCH.

caul /kawl/ *n.* **1 a** the inner membrane enclosing a foetus. **b** part of this occasionally found on a child's head at birth, thought to bring good luck. **2** *hist.* **a** a woman's close-fitting indoor head-dress. **b** the plain back part of a woman's indoor head-dress. **3** the omentum. [ME perh. f. OF *cale* small cap]

cauldron /káwldrən/ *n.* (also **caldron**) a large deep bowl-shaped vessel for boiling over an open fire; an ornamental vessel resembling this. [ME f. AF & ONF *caudron*, ult. f. L *caldarium* hot bath f. *calidus* hot]
■ see POT[1] *n.* 1.

cauliflower /kólliflowr/ *n.* **1** a variety of cabbage with a large immature flower-head of small usu. creamy-white flower-buds. **2** the flower-head eaten as a vegetable. □ **cauliflower cheese** a savoury dish of cauliflower in a cheese sauce. **cauliflower ear** an ear thickened by repeated blows, esp. in boxing. [earlier *cole-florie* etc. f. obs. F *chou fleuri* flowered cabbage, assim. to COLE and FLOWER]

caulk /kawk/ *v.tr.* (*US* **calk**) **1** stop up (the seams of a boat etc.) with oakum etc. and waterproofing material, or by driving plate-junctions together. **2** make (esp. a boat) watertight by this method. □□ **caulker** *n.* [OF dial. *cauquer* tread, press with force, f. L *calcare* tread f. *calx* heel]
■ **1** see STOP *v.* 7.

causal /káwz'l/ *adj.* **1** of, forming, or expressing a cause or causes. **2** relating to, or of the nature of, cause and effect. □□ **causally** *adv.* [LL *causalis*: see CAUSE]

causality /kawzálliti/ *n.* **1** the relation of cause and effect. **2** the principle that everything has a cause.

causation /kawzáysh'n/ *n.* **1** the act of causing or producing an effect. **2** = CAUSALITY. [F *causation* or L *causatio* pretext etc., in med.L the action of causing, f. *causare* CAUSE]

causative /káwzətiv/ *adj.* **1** acting as cause. **2** (foll. by *of*) producing; having as effect. **3** *Gram.* expressing cause. □□ **causatively** *adv.* [ME f. OF *causatif* or f. LL *causativus*: see CAUSATION]

cause /kawz/ *n.* & *v.* ● *n.* **1 a** that which produces an effect, or gives rise to an action, phenomenon, or condition. **b** a person or thing that occasions something. **c** a reason or motive; a ground that may be held to justify something (*no cause for complaint*). **2** a reason adjudged adequate (*show cause*). **3** a principle, belief, or purpose which is advocated or supported (*faithful to the cause*). **4 a** a matter to be settled at law. **b** an individual's case offered at law (*plead a cause*). **5** the side taken by any party in a dispute. ● *v.tr.* **1** be the cause of, produce, make happen (*caused a commotion*). **2** (foll. by *to* + infin.) induce (*caused me to smile*; *caused it to be done*). □ **in the cause of** to maintain, defend, or support (*in the cause of justice*). **make common cause with** join the side of. □□ **causable** *adj.* **causeless** *adj.* **causer** *n.* [ME f. OF f. L *causa*]
■ *n.* **1 a** origin, derivation, basis, source, root, rise, genesis, agent, reason, occasion, prime mover, well-spring. **b** source, originator, creator, producer, agent, agency, initiator, instigator. **c** reason, ground(s), motive, justification, basis, call, occasion; right, excuse, pretext, case. **3** see PRINCIPLE 1. **4 b** see CASE[1] 5a. **5** see SIDE *n.* 5b. ● *v.* **1** effect, bring (on *or* about *or* forth), give rise to, result in, produce, create, precipitate, occasion, lead to, spark (off), trigger *or* set off, excite, set in motion, touch off, induce, generate, breed, provoke, promote, engender. **2** induce, compel, motivate, prompt, stimulate, encourage; (*cause to*) make. □ **make common cause with** join forces with.

'cause /koz/ *conj.* & *adv. colloq.* = BECAUSE. [abbr.]

cause célèbre /káwz selébrə/ *n.* (*pl.* **causes célèbres** /*pronunc.* same/) a lawsuit that attracts much attention. [F]

causerie /kṓzəri/ *n.* (*pl.* **causeries** /*pronunc.* same/) an informal article or talk, esp. on a literary subject. [F f. *causer* talk]

causeway /káwzway/ *n.* **1** a raised road or track across low or wet ground or a stretch of water. **2** a raised path by a road. [earlier *cauce*, *cauceway* f. ONF *caucié* ult. f. L CALX lime, limestone]

causey /káwzi/ *n. archaic* or *dial.* = CAUSEWAY.

caustic /káwstik/ *adj.* & *n.* ● *adj.* **1** that burns or corrodes organic tissue. **2** sarcastic, biting. **3** *Chem.* strongly alkaline. **4** *Physics* formed by the intersection of reflected or refracted parallel rays from a curved surface. ● *n.* **1** a caustic substance. **2** *Physics* a caustic surface or curve. □ **caustic potash** potassium hydroxide. **caustic soda** sodium hydroxide. □□ **caustically** *adv.* **causticity** /-tíssiti/ *n.* [L *causticus* f. Gk *kaustikos* f. *kaustos* burnt f. *kaiō* burn]
■ *adj.* **1** burning, corrosive, destructive, mordant. **2** sarcastic, biting, acrimonious, sharp, bitter, mordant, sardonic, cutting, trenchant, critical, scathing, acidic, astringent, stinging, acerbic, searing, harsh, pungent, virulent.

cauterize /káwtərīz/ *v.tr.* (also **-ise**) *Med.* burn or coagulate (tissue) with a heated instrument or caustic substance, esp. to stop bleeding. □□ **cauterization** /-záysh'n/ *n.* [F *cautériser* f. LL *cauterizare* f. Gk *kautēriazō* f. *kautērion* branding-iron f. *kaiō* burn]

cautery /káwtəri/ *n.* (*pl.* **-ies**) *Med.* **1** an instrument or caustic for cauterizing. **2** the operation of cauterizing. [L *cauterium* f. Gk *kautērion*: see CAUTERIZE]

caution /káwsh'n/ *n.* & *v.* ● *n.* **1** attention to safety; prudence, carefulness. **2 a** esp. *Brit.* a warning, esp. a formal one in law. **b** a formal warning and reprimand. **3** *colloq.* an amusing or surprising person or thing. ● *v.tr.* **1** (often foll. by *against*, or *to* + infin.) warn or admonish. **2** esp. *Brit.* issue a caution to. □ **caution money** *Brit.* a sum deposited as security for good conduct. [ME f. OF f. L *cautio -onis* f. *cavēre caut-* take heed]
■ *n.* **1** wariness, prudence, care, cautiousness, carefulness,

vigilance, forethought, heed, heedfulness, watchfulness, alertness, circumspection, discretion, consideration. **2** warning, admonition, admonishment, caveat, injunction, *literary* monition; see also REPRIMAND *n.* **3** *Austral.* doer, *Austral.* & *NZ* hard case, *colloq.* hoot, scream, riot, laugh, card, giggle, *sl.* gas, yell. ● *v.* **1** see WARN.

cautionary /káwshənəri, -shənri/ *adj.* that gives or serves as a warning (*a cautionary tale*).

cautious /káwshəss/ *adj.* careful, prudent; attentive to safety. □□ **cautiously** *adv.* **cautiousness** *n.* [ME f. OF f. L: see CAUTION]
■ wary, heedful, careful, prudent, circumspect, watchful, vigilant, alert, discreet, guarded, measured, *sl.* leery.

cavalcade /kávvəlkáyd/ *n.* a procession or formal company of riders, motor vehicles, etc. [F f. It. *cavalcata* f. *cavalcare* ride ult. f. L *caballus* pack-horse]
■ see PROCESSION 1.

cavalier /kávvəleér/ *n.* & *adj.* ● *n.* **1** *hist.* (**Cavalier**) a supporter of Charles I in the Civil War. **2** a courtly gentleman, esp. as a lady's escort. **3** *archaic* a horseman. ● *adj.* offhand, supercilious, blasé. □□ **cavalierly** *adv.* [F f. It. *cavaliere*: see CHEVALIER]
■ *adj.* see OFFHAND *adj.*

cavalry /kávvəlri/ *n.* (*pl.* **-ies**) (usu. treated as *pl.*) soldiers on horseback or in armoured vehicles. □ **cavalry twill** a strong fabric in a double twill. [F *cavallerie* f. It. *cavalleria* f. *cavallo* horse f. L *caballus*]

cavalryman /kávvəlrimən/ *n.* (*pl.* **-men**) a soldier of a cavalry regiment.

cavatina /kávvəteénə/ *n.* **1** a short simple song. **2** a similar piece of instrumental music, usu. slow and emotional. [It.]

cave[1] /kayv/ *n.* & *v.* ● *n.* **1** a large hollow in the side of a cliff, hill, etc., or underground. **2** *Brit. hist.* a dissident political group. ● *v.intr.* explore caves, esp. interconnecting or underground. □ **cave-bear** an extinct kind of large bear, whose bones have been found in caves. **cave-dweller** = CAVEMAN. **cave in 1 a** (of a wall, earth over a hollow, etc.) subside, collapse. **b** cause (a wall, earth, etc.) to do this. **2** yield or submit under pressure; give up. **cave-in** *n.* a collapse, submission, etc. □□ **cavelike** *adj.* **caver** *n.* [ME f. OF f. L *cava* f. *cavus* hollow: *cave in* prob. f. E. Anglian dial. *calve in*]
■ *n.* **1** cavern, grotto, hollow, hole, cavity; den, lair. □ **cave in 1 a** collapse, give (way), subside, buckle, fall in *or* inwards, crumple, crumble. **b** knock *or* break down, pull down, tear down, push down, collapse. **2** yield, submit, give way *or* in *or* up, surrender, knuckle under, capitulate. **cave-in** see BREAKDOWN 2a, SUBMISSION 1a.

cave[2] /káyvi/ *int. Brit. school sl.* look out! (as a warning cry). □ **keep cave** act as lookout. [L, = beware]

caveat /kávviat/ *n.* **1** a warning or proviso. **2** *Law* a process in court to suspend proceedings. [L, = let a person beware]
■ **1** see QUALIFICATION 3a, WARNING 1.

caveat emptor /kávviat émptor/ *n.* the principle that the buyer alone is responsible if dissatisfied. [L, = let the buyer beware]

caveman /káyvman/ *n.* (*pl.* **-men**) **1** a prehistoric man living in a cave. **2** a primitive or crude man.

cavern /kávvərn/ *n.* **1** a cave, esp. a large or dark one. **2** a dark cavelike place, e.g. a room. □□ **cavernous** *adj.* **cavernously** *adv.* [ME f. OF *caverne* or f. L *caverna* f. *cavus* hollow]

caviare /kávviaar/ *n.* (*US* **caviar**) the pickled roe of sturgeon or other large fish, eaten as a delicacy. [early forms repr. It. *caviale*, Fr. *caviar*, prob. f. med.Gk *khaviari*]

cavil /kávvil/ *v.* & *n.* ● *v.intr.* (**cavilled, cavilling**; *US* **caviled, caviling**) (usu. foll. by *at*, *about*) make petty objections; carp. ● *n.* a trivial objection. □□ **caviller** *n.* [F *caviller* f. L *cavillari* f. *cavilla* mockery]
■ *v.* carp, quibble, split hairs, complain, find fault, object, demur, niggle, pick holes, *colloq.* nit-pick, gripe, whinge. ● *n.* quibble, complaint, criticism, niggle, *colloq.* whinge, gripe.

caving /káyving/ *n.* exploring caves as a sport or pastime.
■ speleology, *Brit.* potholing, *US* spelunking.

cavitation /kávvitáysh'n/ *n.* **1** the formation of a cavity in a structure. **2** the formation of bubbles, or of a vacuum, in a liquid.

cavity /kávviti/ *n.* (*pl.* **-ies**) **1** a hollow within a solid body. **2** a decayed part of a tooth. □ **cavity wall** a wall formed from two skins of brick or blockwork with a space between. [F *cavité* or LL *cavitas* f. L *cavus* hollow]
■ **1** pit, hole, hollow, gap, space, opening, crater, pan.

cavort /kəvórt/ *v.intr. sl.* caper excitedly; gambol, prance. [US, perh. f. CURVET]
■ prance, caper, frisk, bound, gambol, frolic, romp, skip, leap, jump, bound, spring, dance, trip, sport, *colloq.* galumph; curvet.

cavy /káyvi/ *n.* (*pl.* **-ies**) any small rodent of the family Caviidae, native to S. America and having a sturdy body and vestigial tail, including guinea pigs. [mod.L *cavia* f. Galibi *cabiai*]

caw /kaw/ *n.* & *v.* ● *n.* the harsh cry of a rook, crow, etc. ● *v.intr.* utter this cry. [imit.]

cay /kay/ *n.* a low insular bank or reef of coral, sand, etc. (cf. KEY[2]). [Sp. *cayo* shoal, reef f. F *quai*: see QUAY]
■ see ISLAND 1.

cayenne /kayén/ *n.* (in full **cayenne pepper**) a pungent red powder obtained from various plants of the genus *Capsicum* and used for seasoning. [Tupi *kyynha* assim. to *Cayenne* capital of French Guiana]

cayman /káymən/ *n.* (also **caiman**) any of various S. American alligator-like reptilians, esp. of the genus *Caiman*. [Sp. & Port. *caiman*, f. Carib *acayuman*]

CB *abbr.* **1** citizens' band. **2** (in the UK) Companion of the Order of the Bath.

Cb *symb. US Chem.* the element columbium.

CBC *abbr.* Canadian Broadcasting Corporation.

CBE *abbr.* Commander of the Order of the British Empire.

CBI *abbr.* (in the UK) Confederation of British Industry.

CBS *abbr.* (in the US) Columbia Broadcasting System.

CC *abbr.* **1** *Brit.* **a** City Council. **b** County Council. **c** County Councillor. **2** Cricket Club. **3** Companion of the Order of Canada.

cc *abbr.* (also **c.c.**) **1** cubic centimetre(s). **2** carbon copy.

CD *abbr.* **1** compact disc. **2** Civil Defence. **3** *Corps Diplomatique.*

Cd *symb. Chem.* the element cadmium.

Cd. *abbr.* Command Paper (1900–18).

cd *abbr.* candela.

Cdr. *abbr. Mil.* Commander.

Cdre. *abbr.* Commodore.

CD-ROM /seédee-róm/ *abbr.* compact disc read-only memory (for retrieval of text or data on a VDU screen).

CDT *abbr.* (in the US) Central Daylight Time.

CD-video /seédeevíddiō/ *n.* a system of simultaneously reproducing high-quality sound and video pictures from a compact disc.

CE *abbr.* **1** Church of England. **2** civil engineer. **3** Common Era.

Ce *symb. Chem.* the element cerium.

ceanothus /seéənṓthəss/ *n.* any shrub of the genus *Ceanothus*, with small blue or white flowers. [mod.L f. Gk *keanōthos* kind of thistle]

cease /seess/ *v.* & *n.* ● *v.tr.* & *intr.* stop; bring or come to an end (*ceased breathing*). ● *n.* (in **without cease**) unendingly. □ **cease fire** *Mil.* stop firing. **cease-fire** *n.* **1** the order to do this. **2** a period of truce; a suspension of hostilities. [ME f. OF *cesser*, L *cessare* frequent. of *cedere cess-* yield]

■ *v.* stop, end, finish, terminate, halt, discontinue, break *or* leave off (from), refrain (from), *Austral.* give away, *literary* desist (from); abandon, cut off, bring to a close *or* an end *or* a halt, suspend, drop, sever; die away, come to a close *or* an end, grind to a halt, expire, die a natural death. ● *n.* (**without cease**) ceaselessly, endlessly, unendingly, incessantly, interminably, continuously, continually, constantly, ad infinitum, infinitely, perpetually, for ever, eternally, everlastingly, non-stop, unremittingly, without respite, *colloq.* without (a) let-up. □ **cease-fire 2** see TRUCE.

ceaseless /seésliss/ *adj.* without end; not ceasing. □□ **ceaselessly** *adv.*

cecitis *US* var. of CAECITIS.

cecum *US* var. of CAECUM.

cedar /seédər/ *n.* **1** any spreading evergreen conifer of the genus *Cedrus*, bearing tufts of small needles and cones of papery scales. **2** any of various similar conifers yielding timber. **3** (in full **cedar wood**) the fragrant durable wood of any cedar tree. □□ **cedarn** *adj. poet.* [ME f. OF *cedre* f. L *cedrus* f. Gk *kedros*]

cede /seed/ *v.tr.* give up one's rights to or possession of. [F *céder* or L *cedere* yield]

■ yield, give up, grant, surrender, deliver up, turn *or* make *or* hand over, *archaic* render; relinquish, forgo, abandon, renounce, abdicate, forfeit, resign, *colloq.* pass up.

cedilla /sidíllə/ *n.* **1** a mark written under the letter *c*, esp. in French, to show that it is sibilant (as in *façade*). **2** a similar mark under *s* in Turkish and other oriental languages. [Sp. *cedilla* dimin. of *zeda* f. Gk *zēta* letter Z]

Ceefax /seéfaks/ *n. Brit. propr.* a teletext service provided by the BBC.

ceilidh /káyli/ *n.* orig. *Ir.* & *Sc.* an informal gathering for conversation, music, dancing, songs, and stories. [Gael.]

ceiling /seéling/ *n.* **1 a** the upper interior surface of a room or other similar compartment. **b** the material forming this. **2** an upper limit on prices, wages, performance, etc. **3** *Aeron.* the maximum altitude a given aircraft can reach. **4** *Naut.* the inside planking of a ship's bottom and sides. [ME *celynge*, *siling*, perh. ult. f. L *caelum* heaven or *celare* hide]

celadon /séllədon/ *n.* & *adj.* ● *n.* **1** a willow-green colour. **2** a grey-green glaze used on some pottery. **3** Chinese pottery glazed in this way. ● *adj.* of a grey-green colour. [F, f. the name of a character in d'Urfé's *L'Astrée* (1607–27)]

celandine /sélləndīn/ *n.* either of two yellow-flowered plants, the greater celandine, *Chelidonium majus*, and the lesser celandine, *Ranunculus ficaria*. [ME and OF *celidoine* ult. f. Gk *khelidōn* swallow: the flowering of the plant was associated with the arrival of swallows]

-cele /seel/ *comb. form* (also **-coele**) *Med.* swelling, hernia (*gastrocele*). [Gk *kēlē* tumour]

celeb /siléb/ *n. colloq.* a celebrity, a star.

celebrant /séllibrənt/ *n.* a person who performs a rite, esp. a priest at the Eucharist. [F *célébrant* or L *celebrare celebrant-*: see CELEBRATE]

■ officiant, officiator, celebrator; priest.

celebrate /séllibrayt/ *v.* **1** *tr.* mark (a festival or special event) with festivities etc. **2** *tr.* perform publicly and duly (a religious ceremony etc.). **3 a** *tr.* officiate at (the Eucharist). **b** *intr.* officiate, esp. at the Eucharist. **4** *intr.* engage in festivities, usu. after a special event etc. **5** *tr.* (esp. as **celebrated** *adj.*) honour publicly, make widely known. □□ **celebration** /-bráysh'n/ *n.* **celebrator** *n.* **celebratory** *adj.* [L *celebrare* f. *celeber -bris* frequented, honoured]

■ **1** mark, memorialize, commemorate, solemnize, honour; hold, keep, observe, recognize. **2** perform, solemnize, ritualize, officiate at; sanctify, hallow, consecrate, dedicate. **4** have a party, have a good time, revel, rejoice, make merry, *archaic* wassail, *colloq.* party, paint the town red, whoop it up, make whoopee. **5** extol, praise, exalt, glorify, laud, eulogize, honour, immortalize, lionize; publicize, advertise, broadcast; (**celebrated**) acclaimed; famous, renowned, well-known, famed, legendary, great, memorable, prominent, noted, notable, eminent, noteworthy, distinguished, illustrious; notorious. □□ **celebration** commemoration, memorialization, observance, solemnization, sanctification, ritualization, dedication, consecration; performance, officiation; party, function, festival, fête, gala, revel; festivities, revelry, merrymaking, merriment.

celebrity /silébriti/ *n.* (*pl.* **-ies**) **1** a well-known person. **2** fame. [F *célébrité* or L *celebritas* f. *celeber*: see CELEBRATE]

■ **1** notable, dignitary, star, luminary, personage, name, personality, superstar, somebody, success story. **2** renown, fame, repute, reputation, prominence, eminence, distinction, prestige, famousness, popularity, notability, acclaim, glory; notoriety.

celeriac /silérriak/ *n.* a variety of celery with a swollen turnip-like stem-base used as a vegetable. [CELERY: *-ac* is unexplained]

celerity /silérriti/ *n. archaic* or *literary* swiftness (esp. of a living creature). [ME f. F *célérité* f. L *celeritas -tatis* f. *celer* swift]

■ see SPEED *n.* 1.

celery /séllәri/ *n.* an umbelliferous plant, *Apium graveolens*, with closely packed succulent leaf-stalks used as a vegetable. □ **celery pine** an Australasian tree, *Phyllocladus trichomanoides*, with branchlets like celery leaves. [F *céleri* f. It. dial. *selleri* f. L *selinum* f. Gk *selinon* parsley]

celesta /siléstə/ *n. Mus.* a small keyboard instrument resembling a glockenspiel, with hammers striking steel plates suspended over wooden resonators, giving an ethereal bell-like sound. [pseudo-L f. F *céleste*: see CELESTE]

celeste /silést/ *n. Mus.* **1** an organ and harmonium stop with a soft tremulous tone. **2** = CELESTA. [F *céleste* heavenly f. L *caelestis* f. *caelum* heaven]

celestial /siléstiəl/ *adj.* **1** heavenly; divinely good or beautiful; sublime. **2 a** of the sky; of the part of the sky commonly observed in astronomy etc. **b** of heavenly bodies. □ **celestial equator** the great circle of the sky in the plane perpendicular to the earth's axis. **celestial horizon** see HORIZON 1c. **celestial navigation** navigation by the stars etc. □□ **celestially** *adv.* [ME f. OF f. med.L *caelestialis* f. L *caelestis*: see CELESTE]

■ **1** heavenly, divine, spiritual, godly, godlike, holy, paradisiacal, paradisal, sublime, empyrean, empyreal, Elysian, ethereal, immortal, supernatural, unearthly; perfect, ideal, exquisite, blissful, idyllic. **2 a** astronomical. **b** astral, stellar, solar, planetary, nebular, *attrib.* star.

celiac *US* var. of COELIAC.

celibate /séllibət/ *adj.* & *n.* ● *adj.* **1** committed to abstention from sexual relations and from marriage, esp. for religious reasons. **2** abstaining from sexual relations. ● *n.* a celibate person. □□ **celibacy** *n.* [F *célibat* or L *caelibatus* unmarried state f. *caelebs -ibis* unmarried]

■ *adj.* **1** abstinent, abstemious, continent, ascetic, temperate, self-restrained, self-disciplined; unmarried, single, unwed. **2** virgin, virginal, pure, chaste, unsullied, undefiled, virtuous, immaculate. □□ **celibacy** abstemiousness, self-denial, continence, (self-)restraint, abstinence, temperance, asceticism; chastity, virginity, purity, virtue, maidenhead, maidenhood.

cell /sel/ *n.* **1** a small room, esp. in a prison or monastery. **2** a small compartment, e.g. in a honeycomb. **3** a small group as a nucleus of political activity, esp. of a subversive kind. **4** *hist.* a small monastery or nunnery dependent on a larger one. **5** *Biol.* **a** the structural and functional usu. microscopic unit of an organism, consisting of cytoplasm and a nucleus enclosed in a membrane. **b** an enclosed cavity in an organism etc. **6** *Electr.* a vessel for containing electrodes within an electrolyte

for current-generation or electrolysis. □□ **celled** *adj.* (also in *comb.*). [ME f. OF *celle* or f. L *cella* storeroom etc.]
■ **1** room, closet, cubby(-hole), den, cubicle, stall, apartment, *archaic* cabinet, *poet. or archaic* chamber. **2** see COMPARTMENT *n.* 1. **3** set, circle, ring, gang, band, team, confederacy, federation, clique, coterie, fraternity, brotherhood, secret society.

cellar /séllər/ *n.* & *v.* ● *n.* **1** a room below ground level in a house, used for storage, esp. of wine or coal. **2** a stock of wine in a cellar (*has a good cellar*). ● *v.tr.* store or put in a cellar. [ME f. AF *celer*, OF *celier* f. LL *cellarium* storehouse]
■ *n.* **1** basement, vault. ● *v.* see STORE *v.* 1.

cellarage /séllərij/ *n.* **1** cellar accommodation. **2** the charge for the use of a cellar or storehouse.

cellarer /séllərər/ *n.* a monastic officer in charge of wine.

cellaret /séllərét/ *n.* a case or sideboard for holding wine bottles in a dining-room.

cello /chéllō/ *n.* (*pl.* **-os**) a bass instrument of the violin family, held upright on the floor between the legs of the seated player. □□ **cellist** *n.* [abbr. of VIOLONCELLO]

Cellophane /sélləfayn/ *n. propr.* a thin transparent wrapping material made from viscose. [CELLULOSE + *-phane* (cf. DIAPHANOUS)]

cellphone /sélfōn/ *n.* a small portable radio-telephone having access to a cellular radio system.

cellular /sélyoolər/ *adj.* **1** of or having small compartments or cavities. **2** of open texture; porous. **3** *Physiol.* of or consisting of cells. □ **cellular blanket** a blanket of open texture. **cellular plant** a plant with no distinct stem, leaves, etc. **cellular radio** a system of mobile radio-telephone transmission with an area divided into 'cells' each served by its own small transmitter. □□ **cellularity** /-lárriti/ *n.* **cellulate** *adj.* **cellulation** /-láysh'n/ *n.* **cellulous** *adj.* [F *cellulaire* f. mod.L *cellularis*: see CELLULE]

cellule /sélyōōl/ *n. Biol.* a small cell or cavity. [F *cellule* or L *cellula* dimin. of *cella* CELL]

cellulite /sélyoolīt/ *n.* a lumpy form of fat, esp. on the hips and thighs of women, causing puckering of the skin. [F (as CELLULE)]

cellulitis /sélyoolī́tiss/ *n.* inflammation of cellular tissue.

celluloid /sélyooloyd/ *n.* **1** a transparent flammable plastic made from camphor and cellulose nitrate. **2** cinema film. [irreg. f. CELLULOSE]

cellulose /sélyoolōz, -lōss/ *n.* **1** *Biochem.* a carbohydrate forming the main constituent of plant-cell walls, used in the production of textile fibres. **2** (in general use) a paint or lacquer consisting of esp. cellulose acetate or nitrate in solution. □□ **cellulosic** /-lṓsik/ *adj.* [F (as CELLULE)]

celom *US* var. of COELOM.

Celsius /sélsiəss/ *adj.* of or denoting a temperature on the Celsius scale. □ **Celsius scale** a scale of temperature on which water freezes at 0° and boils at 100° under standard conditions. [A. *Celsius*, Sw. astronomer d. 1744]

Celt /kelt, selt/ *n.* (also **Kelt**) a member of a group of W. European peoples, including the pre-Roman inhabitants of Britain and Gaul and their descendants, esp. in Ireland, Wales, Scotland, Cornwall, Brittany, and the Isle of Man. [L *Celtae* (pl.) f. Gk *Keltoi*]

celt /kelt/ *n. Archaeol.* a stone or metal prehistoric implement with a chisel edge. [med.L *celtes* chisel]

Celtic /kéltik, séltik/ *adj.* & *n.* ● *adj.* of or relating to the Celts. ● *n.* a group of languages spoken by Celtic peoples, including Gaelic, Welsh, Cornish, and Breton. □ **Celtic cross** a Latin cross with a circle round the centre. □□ **Celticism** /-tisiz'm/ *n.* [L *celticus* (as CELT) or F *celtique*]

cembalo /chémbəlō/ *n.* (*pl.* **-os**) a harpsichord. [abbr. of CLAVICEMBALO]

cement /simént/ *n.* & *v.* ● *n.* **1** a powdery substance made by calcining lime and clay, mixed with water to form mortar or used in concrete (see also *Portland cement*). **2** any similar substance that hardens and fastens on setting. **3** a uniting factor or principle. **4** a substance for filling cavities in teeth. **5** (also **cementum**) *Anat.* a thin layer of bony material that fixes teeth to the jaw. ● *v.tr.* **1 a** unite with or as with cement. **b** establish or strengthen (a friendship etc.). **2** apply cement to. **3** line or cover with cement. □ **cement-mixer** a machine (usu. with a revolving drum) for mixing cement with water. □□ **cementer** *n.* [ME f. OF *ciment* f. L *caementum* quarry stone f. *caedere* hew]
■ *n.* **2** mortar, bond, glue, gum, paste, solder, adhesive. ● *v.* **1 a** stick, glue, paste, solder, weld, braze, bond; join, bind, combine, unite, fuse. **b** see REINFORCE.

cementation /seémentáysh'n/ *n.* **1** the act or process of cementing or being cemented. **2** the heating of iron with charcoal powder to form steel.

cemetery /sémmitəri, -tri/ *n.* (*pl.* **-ies**) a burial ground, esp. one not in a churchyard. [LL *coemeterium* f. Gk *koimētērion* dormitory f. *koimaō* put to sleep]
■ see GRAVEYARD.

C.Eng. *abbr. Brit.* chartered engineer.

cenobite *US* var. of COENOBITE.

cenotaph /sénnətaaf/ *n.* a tomblike monument, esp. a war memorial, to a person whose body is elsewhere. [F *cénotaphe* f. LL *cenotaphium* f. Gk *kenos* empty + *taphos* tomb]
■ see MONUMENT 1–3.

Cenozoic /seénəzṓ-ik/ (also **Cainozoic** /kī́nə-/, **Caenozoic** /seénə-/) *adj.* & *n. Geol.* ● *adj.* of or relating to the most recent era of geological time, marked by the evolution and development of mammals, birds, and flowers. ¶ Cf. Appendix VII. ● *n.* this era (cf. MESOZOIC, PALAEOZOIC). [Gk *kainos* new + *zōion* animal]

censer /sénsər/ *n.* a vessel in which incense is burnt, esp. during a religious procession or ceremony. [ME f. AF *censer*, OF *censier* aphetic of *encensier* f. *encens* INCENSE[1]]

censor /sénsər/ *n.* & *v.* ● *n.* **1** an official authorized to examine printed matter, films, news, etc., before public release, and to suppress any parts on the grounds of obscenity, a threat to security, etc. **2** *Rom.Hist.* either of two annual magistrates responsible for holding censuses and empowered to supervise public morals. **3** *Psychol.* an impulse which is said to prevent certain ideas and memories from emerging into consciousness. ● *v.tr.* **1** act as a censor of. **2** make deletions or changes in. ¶ As a verb, often confused with *censure.* □□ **censorial** /-sóriəl/ *adj.* **censorship** *n.* [L f. *censēre* assess: in sense 3 mistransl. of G *Zensur* censorship]
■ *v.* see EDIT *v.* 5b.

censorious /sensóriəss/ *adj.* severely critical; fault-finding; quick or eager to criticize. □□ **censoriously** *adv.* **censoriousness** *n.* [L *censorius*: see CENSOR]
■ see CRITICAL 1.

censure /sénsyər/ *v.* & *n.* ● *v.tr.* criticize harshly; reprove. ¶ Often confused with *censor.* ● *n.* harsh criticism; expression of disapproval. □□ **censurable** *adj.* [ME f. OF f. L *censura* f. *censēre* assess]
■ *v.* see CRITICIZE 1. ● *n.* see CRITICISM 1a.

census /sénsəss/ *n.* (*pl.* **censuses**) the official count of a population or of a class of things, often with various statistics noted. [L f. *censēre* assess]
■ see POLL[1] *n.* 2.

cent /sent/ *n.* **1 a** a monetary unit valued at one-hundredth of a dollar or other metric unit. **b** a coin of this value. **2** *colloq.* a very small sum of money. **3** see PER CENT. [F *cent* or It. *cento* or L *centum* hundred]

cent. *abbr.* century.

centaur /séntawr/ *n.* a creature in Greek mythology with the head, arms, and torso of a man and the body and legs of a horse. [ME f. L *centaurus* f. Gk *kentauros*, of unkn. orig.]

centaury /séntawri/ *n.* (*pl.* **-ies**) any plant of the genus *Centaurium*, esp. *C. erythraea*, formerly used in medicine. [LL *centaurea* ult. f. Gk *kentauros* CENTAUR: from the legend that it was discovered by the centaur Chiron]

centavo /sentaávō/ *n.* a small coin of Spain, Portugal, and some Latin American countries, worth one-hundredth of the standard unit. [Sp. f. L *centum* hundred]

centenarian /séntináiriən/ *n.* & *adj.* ● *n.* a person a hundred or more years old. ● *adj.* a hundred or more years old.

centenary /sentéenəri/ *n.* & *adj.* ● *n.* (*pl.* **-ies**) **1** a hundredth anniversary. **2** a celebration of this. ● *adj.* **1** of or relating to a centenary. **2** occurring every hundred years. [L *centenarius* f. *centeni* a hundred each f. *centum* a hundred]

centennial /senténniəl/ *adj.* & *n.* ● *adj.* **1** lasting for a hundred years. **2** occurring every hundred years. ● *n. US* = CENTENARY *n.* [L *centum* a hundred, after BIENNIAL]

center *US* var. of CENTRE.

centerboard *US* var. of CENTREBOARD.

centerfold *US* var. of CENTREFOLD.

centering *US* var. of CENTRING.

centesimal /sentéssim'l/ *adj.* reckoning or reckoned by hundredths. □□ **centesimally** *adv.* [L *centesimus* hundredth f. *centum* hundred]

centi- /sénti/ *comb. form* **1** one-hundredth, esp. of a unit in the metric system (*centigram*; *centilitre*). **2** hundred. ¶ Abbr.: **c.** [L *centum* hundred]

centigrade /séntigrayd/ *adj.* **1** = CELSIUS. **2** having a scale of a hundred degrees. ¶ In sense 1 *Celsius* is usually preferred in technical use. [F f. L *centum* hundred + *gradus* step]

centigram /séntigram/ *n.* (also **centigramme**) a metric unit of mass, equal to one-hundredth of a gram.

centilitre /séntileetər/ *n.* (*US* **centiliter**) a metric unit of capacity, equal to one-hundredth of a litre.

centime /sóNteem/ *n.* **1** a monetary unit valued at one-hundredth of a franc. **2** a coin of this value. [F f. L *centum* a hundred]

centimetre /séntimeetər/ *n.* (*US* **centimeter**) a metric unit of length, equal to one-hundredth of a metre. □ **centimetre-gram-second system** the system using these as basic units of length, mass, and time. ¶ Abbr.: **cgs system**.

centipede /séntipeed/ *n.* any arthropod of the class Chilopoda, with a wormlike body of many segments each with a pair of legs. [F *centipède* or L *centipeda* f. *centum* hundred + *pes pedis* foot]

cento /séntō/ *n.* (*pl.* **-os**) a composition made up of quotations from other authors. [L, = patchwork garment]

central /séntrəl/ *adj.* **1** of, at, or forming the centre. **2** from the centre. **3** chief, essential, most important. □ **Central America** the isthmus joining North and South America. **central bank** a national bank issuing currency etc. **central heating** a method of warming a building by pipes, radiators, etc., fed from a central source of heat. **central nervous system** *Anat.* the complex of nerve tissues that controls the activities of the body, in vertebrates the brain and spinal cord. **central processor** (or **processing unit**) the principal operating part of a computer. □□ **centrality** /-trálliti/ *n.* **centrally** *adv.* [F *central* or L *centralis* f. *centrum* CENTRE]
■ **1** middle, centre, medial, median, mid, *Anat.* mesial; inner, inside. **3** chief, main, principal, major, key, leading, dominant, prime, primary, pre-eminent; important, significant; essential, vital, crucial, critical, fundamental, cardinal, pivotal, capital, basic.

centralism /séntrəliz'm/ *n.* a system that centralizes (esp. an administration) (see also *democratic centralism*). □□ **centralist** *n.*

centralize /séntrəlīz/ *v.* (also **-ise**) **1** *tr.* & *intr.* bring or come to a centre. **2** *tr.* **a** concentrate (administration) at a single centre. **b** subject (a State) to this system. □□ **centralization** /-záysh'n/ *n.*
■ **1** see CONCENTRATE *v.* 2, CONVERGE.

centre /séntər/ *n.* & *v.* (*US* **center**) ● *n.* **1** the middle point, esp. of a line, circle, or sphere, equidistant from the ends or from any point on the circumference or surface. **2** a pivot or axis of rotation. **3 a** a place or group of buildings forming a central point in a district, city, etc., or a main area for an activity (*shopping centre*; *town centre*). **b** (with preceding word) a piece or set of equipment for a number of connected functions (*music centre*). **4** a point of concentration or dispersion; a nucleus or source. **5** a political party or group holding moderate opinions. **6** the filling in a chocolate etc. **7** *Sport* **a** the middle player in a line or group in some field games. **b** a kick or hit from the side to the centre of the pitch. **8** (in a lathe etc.) a conical adjustable support for the workpiece. **9** (*attrib.*) of or at the centre. ● *v.* **1** *intr.* (foll. by *in*, *on*; *disp.* foll. by *round*) have as its main centre. **2** *tr.* place in the centre. **3** *tr.* mark with a centre. **4** *tr.* (foll. by *in* etc.) concentrate. **5** *tr. Sport* kick or hit (the ball) from the side to the centre of the pitch. □ **centre-bit** a boring tool with a centre point and side cutters. **centre forward** *Sport* the middle player or position in a forward line. **centre half** *Sport* the middle player or position in a half-back line. **centre of attention 1** a person or thing that draws general attention. **2** *Physics* the point to which bodies tend by gravity. **centre of gravity** (or **mass**) the point at which the weight of a body may be considered to act. **centre-piece 1** an ornament for the middle of a table. **2** a principal item. **centre spread** the two facing middle pages of a newspaper etc. □□ **centred** *adj.* (often in *comb.*). **centremost** *adj.* **centric** *adj.* **centrical** *adj.* **centricity** /-trissiti/ *n.* [ME f. OF *centre* or L *centrum* f. Gk *kentron* sharp point]
■ *n.* **1** middle; mid-point, halfway point *or* line; bull's-eye. **2** pivot, axis, fulcrum, nave, hub. **3 a** focal point, hub, focus. **4** nucleus, source, nub, core, heart, kernel, navel, bosom; midst, interior, bowels. **6** filling, inside, middle. **9** (*attrib.*) see CENTRAL 1. ● *v.* **1** (*centre on* or *in*) cluster *or* collect *or* congregate around, converge on. **4** focus, concentrate, direct, train, turn.

centreboard /séntərbord/ *n.* (*US* **centerboard**) a board for lowering through a boat's keel to prevent leeway.

centrefold /séntərfōld/ *n.* (*US* **centerfold**) a printed and usu. illustrated sheet folded to form the centre spread of a magazine etc.

centreing var. of CENTRING.

-centric /séntrik/ *comb. form* forming adjectives with the sense 'having a (specified) centre' (*anthropocentric*; *eccentric*). [after *concentric* etc. f. Gk *kentrikos*: see CENTRE]

centrifugal /séntrifyóog'l, sentrifyoog'l/ *adj.* moving or tending to move from a centre (cf. CENTRIPETAL). □ **centrifugal force** an apparent force that acts outwards on a body moving about a centre. □□ **centrifugally** *adv.* [mod.L *centrifugus* f. L *centrum* centre + *fugere* flee]

centrifuge /séntrifyooj/ *n.* & *v.* ● *n.* a machine with a rapidly rotating device designed to separate liquids from solids or other liquids (e.g. cream from milk). ● *v.tr.* **1** subject to the action of a centrifuge. **2** separate by centrifuge. □□ **centrifugation** /-fyoogáysh'n/ *n.*

centring /séntring/ (also **centreing** /séntəring/, *US* **centering** /séntəring/) *n.* a temporary frame used to support an arch, dome, etc., while under construction.

centriole /séntriōl/ *n. Biol.* a minute organelle usu. within a centrosome involved esp. in the development of spindles in cell division. [med.L *centriolum* dimin. of *centrum* centre]

centripetal /sentríppit'l/ *adj.* moving or tending to move towards a centre (cf. CENTRIFUGAL). □ **centripetal force** the force acting on a body causing it to move about a centre. □□ **centripetally** *adv.* [mod.L *centripetus* f. L *centrum* centre + *petere* seek]

centrist /séntrist/ *n. Polit.* often *derog.* a person who holds moderate views. □□ **centrism** *n.*
■ see MODERATE *n.*

centromere /séntrəmeer/ *n. Biol.* the point on a chromosome to which the spindle is attached during cell division. [L *centrum* centre + Gk *meros* part]

centrosome /séntrəsōm/ *n. Biol.* a distinct part of the cytoplasm in a cell, usu. near the nucleus, that contains the centriole. [G *Centrosoma* f. L *centrum* centre + Gk *sōma* body]

centuple /séntyoop'l/ *n.*, *adj.*, & *v.* ● *n.* a hundredfold amount. ● *adj.* increased a hundredfold. ● *v.tr.* multiply by a hundred; increase a hundredfold. [F *centuple* or eccl.L *centuplus*, *centuplex* f. L *centum* hundred]

centurion /sentyŏŏriən/ *n.* the commander of a century in the ancient Roman army. [ME f. L *centurio -onis* (as CENTURY)]

century /sénchəri, séntyoori/ *n.* (*pl.* **-ies**) **1 a** a period of one hundred years. **b** any of the centuries reckoned from the birth of Christ (*twentieth century* = 1901–2000; *fifth century* BC = 500–401 BC). ¶ In modern use often reckoned as (e.g.) 1900–1999. **2 a** a score etc. of a hundred in a sporting event, esp. a hundred runs by one batsman in cricket. **b** a group of a hundred things. **3 a** a company in the ancient Roman army, orig. of 100 men. **b** an ancient Roman political division for voting. □ **century plant** a plant, *Agave americana*, flowering once in many years and yielding sap from which tequila is distilled: also called *American aloe* (see ALOE). [L *centuria* f. *centum* hundred]

cep /sep/ *n.* an edible mushroom, *Boletus edulis*, with a stout stalk and brown smooth cap. [F *cèpe* f. Gascon *cep* f. L *cippus* stake]

cephalic /sifállik, ke-/ *adj.* of or in the head. □ **cephalic index** *Anthropol.* a number expressing the ratio of a head's greatest breadth and length. [F *céphalique* f. L *cephalicus* f. Gk *kephalikos* f. *kephalē* head]

-cephalic /sifállik/ *comb. form* = -CEPHALOUS.

cephalopod /séffəlәpod/ *n.* any mollusc of the class Cephalopoda, having a distinct tentacled head, e.g. octopus, squid, and cuttlefish. [Gk *kephalē* head + *pous podos* foot]

cephalothorax /séffəlōthóraks/ *n.* (*pl.* **-thoraces** /-thórəseez/ or **-thoraxes**) *Anat.* the fused head and thorax of a spider, crab, or other arthropod.

-cephalous /séffələss/ *comb. form* -headed (*brachycephalous; dolichocephalic*). [Gk *kephalē* head]

cepheid /seéfi-id, séf-/ *n.* (in full **cepheid variable**) *Astron.* any of a class of variable stars with a regular cycle of brightness that can be used to measure distances. [L *Cepheus* f. Gk *Kēpheus*, a mythical king whose name was given to a constellation]

ceramic /sirámmik, ki-/ *adj.* & *n.* ● *adj.* **1** made of (esp.) clay and permanently hardened by heat (*a ceramic bowl*). **2** of or relating to ceramics (*the ceramic arts*). ● *n.* **1** a ceramic article or product. **2** a substance, esp. clay, used to make ceramic articles. [Gk *keramikos* f. *keramos* pottery]

ceramics /sirámmiks, ki-/ *n.pl.* **1** ceramic products collectively (*exhibition of ceramics*). **2** (usu. treated as *sing.*) the art of making ceramic articles.

■ **1** see POTTERY.

ceramist /sérrəmist/ *n.* a person who makes ceramics.

cerastes /sirásteez/ *n.* any viper of the genus *Cerastes*, esp. *C. cerastes* having a sharp upright spike over each eye and moving forward in a lateral motion. [L f. Gk *kerastēs* f. *keras* horn]

cerastium /sirástiəm/ *n.* any plant of the genus *Cerastium*, with white flowers and often horn-shaped capsules. [mod.L f. Gk *kerastes* horned f. *keras* horn]

cere /seer/ *n.* a waxy fleshy covering at the base of the upper beak in some birds. [L *cera* wax]

cereal /seériəl/ *n.* & *adj* ● *n.* **1** (usu. in *pl.*) **a** any kind of grain used for food. **b** any grass producing this, e.g. wheat, maize, rye, etc. **2** a breakfast food made from a cereal and requiring no cooking. ● *adj.* of edible grain or products of it. [L *cerealis* f. *Ceres* goddess of agriculture]

■ *n.* **1 a** see GRAIN *n.* 2.

cerebellum /sérribélləm/ *n.* (*pl.* **cerebellums** or **cerebella** /-lə/) the part of the brain at the back of the skull in vertebrates, which coordinates and regulates muscular activity. □□ **cerebellar** *adj.* [L dimin. of CEREBRUM]

cerebral /sérribrəl/ *adj.* **1** of the brain. **2** intellectual rather than emotional. **3** = CACUMINAL. □ **cerebral hemisphere** each of the two halves of the vertebrate cerebrum. **cerebral palsy** *Med.* spastic paralysis from brain damage before or at birth, with jerky or uncontrolled movements. □□ **cerebrally** *adv.* [L *cerebrum* brain]

■ **2** see INTELLECTUAL *adj.* 1.

cerebration /sérribráysh'n/ *n.* working of the brain. □ **unconscious cerebration** action of the brain with results reached without conscious thought. □□ **cerebrate** /sérribrayt/ *v.intr.*

■ see THOUGHT[1] 1, 3a.

cerebro- /sérribrō/ *comb. form* brain (*cerebrospinal*).

cerebrospinal /sérribrōspīn'l/ *adj.* of the brain and spine.

cerebrovascular /sérribrōváskyoolər/ *adj.* of the brain and its blood vessels.

cerebrum /sérribrəm/ *n.* (*pl.* **cerebra** /-brə/) the principal part of the brain in vertebrates, located in the front area of the skull, which integrates complex sensory and neural functions. [L, = brain]

cerecloth /seérkloth/ *n. hist.* waxed cloth used as a waterproof covering or (esp.) as a shroud. [earlier *cered cloth* f. *cere* to wax f. L *cerare* f. *cera* wax]

■ see SHROUD *n.* 1.

cerement /seérmənt/ *n.* (usu. in *pl.*) *literary* grave-clothes; cerecloth. [first used by Shakesp. in *Hamlet* (1602): app. f. CERECLOTH]

■ see SHROUD *n.* 1.

ceremonial /sérrimṓniəl/ *adj.* & *n.* ● *adj.* **1** with or concerning ritual or ceremony. **2** formal (*a ceremonial bow*). ● *n.* **1** a system of rites etc. to be used esp. at a formal or religious occasion. **2** the formalities or behaviour proper to any occasion (*with all due ceremonial*). **3** *RC Ch.* a book containing an order of ritual. □□ **ceremonialism** *n.* **ceremonialist** *n.* **ceremonially** *adv.* [LL *caerimonialis* (as CEREMONY)]

■ *adj.* **1** ritual, celebratory, commemorative, state. **2** formal, solemn, stately, official, dignified, ceremonious, ritual, ritualistic, august, grand. ● *n.* **1** rite, ritual, service. **2** formality, ceremony, observance, form.

ceremonious /sérrimṓniəss/ *adj.* **1** excessively polite; punctilious. **2** having or showing a fondness for ritualistic observance or formality. □□ **ceremoniously** *adv.* **ceremoniousness** *n.* [F *cérémonieux* or LL *caerimoniosus* (as CEREMONY)]

■ **1** punctilious, nice, courtly, over-nice, exact, precise, correct, proper, prim, scrupulous, formal, stuffy, stiff, starchy, conventional, meticulous, careful. **2** ceremonial, formal, dignified, solemn, ritual, ritualistic, stately, official.

ceremony /sérriməni/ *n.* (*pl.* **-ies**) **1** a formal religious or public occasion, esp. celebrating a particular event or anniversary. **2** formalities, esp. of an empty or ritualistic kind (*ceremony of exchanging compliments*). **3** excessively polite behaviour (*bowed low with great ceremony*). □ **Master of Ceremonies 1** (also **MC**) a person introducing speakers at a banquet, or entertainers in a variety show. **2** a person in charge of ceremonies at a state or public occasion. **stand on ceremony** insist on the observance of formalities. **without ceremony** informally. [ME f. OF *ceremonie* or L *caerimonia* religious worship]

■ **1** rite(s), solemnity, service, ceremonial, ritual; function, celebration, pageant; formality, observance. **2** formalities, formality, pageantry, pomp, convention(s), niceties, proprieties, social graces *or* conventions, convenances, form, protocol; rigmarole. **3** punctiliousness, courtesy, etiquette, decorum, politeness, *politesse*, civility. □ **without ceremony** informally, casually, familiarly; unceremoniously.

Cerenkov radiation /chiréngkof/ *n.* (also **Cherenkov**) the electromagnetic radiation emitted by particles moving in a medium at speeds faster than that of light in the same medium. [P. A. *Cherenkov*, Russian physicist b. 1904]

ceresin /sérrisin/ *n.* a hard whitish wax used with or instead of beeswax. [mod.L *ceres* f. L *cera* wax + -IN]

cerise /səreéz, -reéss/ *adj.* & *n.* ● *adj.* of a light clear red. ● *n.* this colour. [F, = CHERRY]

■ *adj.* see ROSY 1.

cerium /seériəm/ *n. Chem.* a silvery metallic element of the lanthanide series occurring naturally in various minerals and used in the manufacture of lighter flints. ¶ Symb.: **Ce.** [named after the asteroid *Ceres*, discovered (1801) about the same time as this]

cermet /sérmet/ *n.* a heat-resistant material made of ceramic and sintered metal. [*cer*amic + *met*al]

CERN /sern/ *abbr.* European Organization for Nuclear Research. [F *Conseil Européen pour la Recherche Nucléaire*, its former title]

cero- /seérō/ *comb. form* wax (cf. CEROGRAPHY, CEROPLASTIC). [L *cera* or Gk *kēros* wax]

cerography /seerógrəfi/ *n.* the technique of engraving or designing on or with wax.

ceroplastic /seéröplástik/ *adj.* **1** modelled in wax. **2** of or concerning wax-modelling.

cert /sert/ *n. sl.* (esp. **dead cert**) **1** an event or result regarded as certain to happen. **2** a horse strongly tipped to win. [abbr. of CERTAIN, CERTAINTY]

cert. /sert/ *abbr.* **1** a certificate. **2** certified.

certain /sért'n, -tin/ *adj.* & *pron.* ● *adj.* **1 a** (often foll. by *of*, or *that* + clause) confident, convinced (*certain that I put it here*). **b** (often foll. by *that* + clause) indisputable; known for sure (*it is certain that he is guilty*). **2** (often foll. by *to* + infin.) **a** that may be relied on to happen (*it is certain to rain*). **b** destined (*certain to become a star*). **3** definite, unfailing, reliable (*a certain indication of the coming storm; his touch is certain*). **4** (of a person, place, etc.) that might be specified, but is not (*a certain lady; of a certain age*). **5** some though not much (*a certain reluctance*). **6** (of a person, place, etc.) existing, though probably unknown to the reader or hearer (*a certain John Smith*). ● *pron.* (as *pl.*) some but not all (*certain of them were wounded*). □ **for certain** without doubt. **make certain** = *make sure* (see SURE). [ME f. OF ult. f. L *certus* settled]

■ *adj.* **1 a** confident, convinced, sure, positive, satisfied, assured, persuaded. **b** sure, definite, indubitable, indisputable, undisputed, undoubted, clear, unequivocal, incontestable, undeniable, incontrovertible, irrefutable, unquestionable, unarguable; inevitable, inescapable, ineluctable, inexorable, unavoidable. **2 a** bound, sure. **b** destined, predestined, fated. **3** definite, firm, sure, decided, settled, stable, invariable, established, standard, constant, unchanging, steady, unfluctuating, non-fluctuating, final; unerring, dependable, unfailing, infallible, reliable, assured, guaranteed, necessary. **4** unnamed, unspecified, non-specified, undefined; particular. **5** some, a few; a bit of, a little. **6** see ONE *adj.* 3a. ● *pron.* some, a number. □ **for certain** see *for a certainty* (CERTAINTY).

certainly /sért'nli, -tinli/ *adv.* **1** undoubtedly, definitely. **2** confidently. **3** (in affirmative answer to a question or command) yes; by all means.

■ **1** see *undoubtedly* (UNDOUBTED). **3** see ABSOLUTELY 6.

certainty /sért'nti, -tinti/ *n.* (*pl.* **-ies**) **1 a** an undoubted fact. **b** a certain prospect (*his return is a certainty*). **2** (often foll. by *of*, or *that* + clause) an absolute conviction (*has a certainty of his own worth*). **3** (often foll. by *to* + infin.) a thing or person that may be relied on (*a certainty to win the Derby*). □ **for a certainty** beyond the possibility of doubt. [ME f. AF *certainté*, OF *-eté* (as CERTAIN)]

■ **1 a** fact, actuality, reality, truth, *archaic* surety. **b** sure thing, moral certainty, *colloq.* cinch, *sl.* (dead) cert. **2** assurance, self-assurance, assuredness, definiteness, confidence, conviction, faith, authoritativeness, positiveness, certitude, sureness, fixedness. □ **for a certainty** for certain, assuredly, definitely, certainly, surely, positively; undoubtedly, indubitably, without (a) doubt, beyond *or* without a shadow of a doubt, undeniably, unquestionably, absolutely, *colloq.* for sure.

Cert. Ed. *abbr.* (in the UK) Certificate in Education.

certifiable /sértifīəb'l/ *adj.* **1** able or needing to be certified. **2** *colloq.* insane.

■ **2** see INSANE 1.

certificate *n.* & *v.* ● *n.* /sərtíffikət/ a formal document attesting a fact, esp. birth, marriage, or death, a medical condition, a level of achievement, a fulfilment of requirements, ownership of shares, etc. ● *v.tr.* /sərtíffikayt/ (esp. as **certificated** *adj.*) provide with or license or attest by a certificate. □ **Certificate of Secondary Education** *hist.* **1** an examination set for secondary-school pupils in England and Wales. **2** the certificate gained by passing it. ¶ Replaced in 1988 by the *General Certificate of Secondary Education.* □□ **certification** /sértifikáysh'n/ *n.* [F *certificat* or med.L *certificatum* f. *certificare*: see CERTIFY]

■ *n.* see DOCUMENT *n.*

certify /sértifī/ *v.tr.* (**-ies, -ied**) **1** make a formal statement of; attest; attest to (*certified that he had witnessed the crime*). **2** declare by certificate (that a person is qualified or competent) (*certified as a trained bookkeeper*). **3** officially declare insane (*he should be certified*). □ **certified cheque** a cheque the validity of which is guaranteed by a bank. **certified mail** *US* = *recorded delivery* (see RECORD). **certified milk** milk guaranteed free from the tuberculosis bacillus. **certified public accountant** *US* a member of an officially accredited professional body of accountants. [ME f. OF *certifier* f. med.L *certificare* f. L *certus* certain]

■ **1** confirm, attest (to), verify, vouch for, testify (to), bear witness to, affirm, declare, asseverate, corroborate, substantiate, endorse, guarantee, warrant, *formal* aver; swear.

certiorari /sértioráirī/ *n. Law* a writ from a higher court requesting the records of a case tried in a lower court. [LL passive of *certiorare* inform f. *certior* compar. of *certus* certain]

certitude /sértityōōd/ *n.* a feeling of absolute certainty or conviction. [ME f. LL *certitudo* f. *certus* certain]

■ see CONVICTION 2a.

cerulean /sərōōliən/ *adj.* & *n. literary* ● *adj.* deep blue like a clear sky. ● *n.* this colour. [L *caeruleus* sky-blue *f. caelum* sky]

cerumen /sərōōmen/ *n.* the yellow waxy substance in the outer ear. □□ **ceruminous** *adj.* [mod.L f. L *cera* wax]

ceruse /seérōōss, sirōōss/ *n.* white lead. [ME f. OF f. L *cerussa*, perh. f. Gk *kēros* wax]

cervelat /sérvəlaa, -lat/ *n.* a kind of smoked pork sausage. [obs. F f. It. *cervellata*]

cervical /servīk'l, sérvik'l/ *adj. Anat.* **1** of or relating to the neck (*cervical vertebrae*). **2** of or relating to the cervix. □ **cervical screening** examination of a large number of apparently healthy women for cervical cancer. **cervical smear** a specimen of cellular material from the neck of the womb for detection of cancer. [F *cervical* or mod.L *cervicalis* f. L *cervix -icis* neck]

cervine /sérvīn/ *adj.* of or like a deer. [L *cervinus* f. *cervus* deer]

cervix /sérviks/ *n.* (*pl.* **cervices** /-viseez/) *Anat.* **1** the neck. **2** any necklike structure, esp. the neck of the womb. [L]

Cesarean (also **Cesarian**) *US* var. of CAESAREAN.

cesarevitch /sizárrivich/ *n.* (also **cesarewitch** /-wich/) **1** *hist.* the eldest son of the emperor of Russia (cf. TSAREVICH). **2** (**Cesarewitch**) a horse-race run annually at Newmarket. [Russ. *tsesarevich*]

cesium *US* var. of CAESIUM.

cess[1] /sess/ *n.* (also **sess**) *Sc., Ir.,* & *Ind.* etc. a tax, a levy. [properly *sess* for obs. *assess* n.: see ASSESS]

■ see TAX *n.* 1.

cess[2] /sess/ *n. Ir.* □ **bad cess to** may evil befall (*bad cess to their clan*). [perh. f. CESS[1]]

cessation /sesáysh'n/ *n.* **1** a ceasing (*cessation of the truce*). **2** a pause (*resumed fighting after the cessation*). [ME f. L *cessatio* f. *cessare* CEASE]

■ **1** see END *n.* 3a, b. **2** see REST[1] *n.* 3.

cesser /séssər/ *n. Law* a coming to an end; a cessation (of a term, a liability, etc.). [AF & OF, = CEASE]

cession /sésh'n/ *n.* **1** (often foll. by *of*) the ceding or giving up (of rights, property, and esp. of territory by a State). **2** the territory etc. so ceded. [ME f. OF *cession* or L *cessio* f. *cedere cess-* go away]

■ **1** see SURRENDER *n.*

cessionary /séshənəri/ *n.* (*pl.* **-ies**) *Law* = ASSIGN *n.*

cesspit /séspit/ *n.* **1** a pit for the disposal of refuse. **2** = CESSPOOL. [*cess* in CESSPOOL + PIT[1]]

cesspool /séspo͞ol/ *n.* **1** an underground container for the temporary storage of liquid waste or sewage. **2** a centre of corruption, depravity, etc. [perh. alt., after POOL[1], f. earlier *cesperalle*, f. *suspiral* vent, water-pipe, f. OF *souspirail* air-hole f. L *suspirare* breathe up, sigh (as SUB-, *spirare* breathe)]

cestode /séstōd/ *n.* (also **cestoid** /séstoyd/) any flatworm of the class Cestoda, including tapeworms. [L *cestus* f. Gk *kestos* girdle]

CET *abbr.* Central European Time.

cetacean /sitáysh'n/ *n.* & *adj.* ● *n.* any marine mammal of the order Cetacea with streamlined hairless body and dorsal blowhole for breathing, including whales, dolphins, and porpoises. ● *adj.* of cetaceans. □□ **cetaceous** *adj.* [mod.L *Cetacea* f. L *cetus* f. Gk *kētos* whale]

cetane /séetayn/ *n. Chem.* a colourless liquid hydrocarbon of the alkane series used in standardizing ratings of diesel fuel. □ **cetane number** a measure of the ignition properties of diesel fuel. [f. SPERMACETI after *methane* etc.]

ceteris paribus /séttəriss párriboōss/ *adv.* other things being equal. [L]

Ceylon moss /silón/ *n.* a red seaweed, *Gracilaria lichenoides*, from E. India. [*Ceylon*, now Sri Lanka]

CF *abbr. Brit.* Chaplain to the Forces.

Cf *symb. Chem.* the element californium.

cf. *abbr.* compare. [L *confer* imper. of *conferre* compare]

c.f. *abbr.* carried forward.

CFC *abbr. Chem.* chloro-fluorocarbon, any of various usu. gaseous compounds of carbon, hydrogen, chlorine, and fluorine, used in refrigerants, aerosol propellants, etc., and thought to be harmful to the ozone layer in the earth's atmosphere.

CFE *abbr.* College of Further Education.

cg *abbr.* centigram(s).

CGS *abbr.* Chief of General Staff.

cgs *abbr.* centimetre-gram-second.

CH *abbr.* (in the UK) Companion of Honour.

ch. *abbr.* **1** church. **2** chapter. **3** chestnut.

cha var. of CHAR[3].

Chablis /shábli/ *n.* (*pl.* same /-liz/) a dry white burgundy wine. [*Chablis* in E. France]

cha-cha /cha'achaa/ (also **cha-cha-cha** /cha'achaachaa'/) *n.* & *v.* ● *n.* **1** a ballroom dance with a Latin-American rhythm. **2** music for or in the rhythm of a cha-cha. ● *v.intr.* (**cha-chas, cha-chaed** /-chaad/ or **cha-cha'd, cha-chaing** /-chaa-ing/) dance the cha-cha. [Amer. Sp.]

chaconne /shəkón/ *n. Mus.* **1 a** a musical form consisting of variations on a ground bass. **b** a musical composition in this style. **2** *hist.* a dance performed to this music. [F f. Sp. *chacona*]

chador /chúddər/ *n.* (also **chadar, chuddar**) a large piece of cloth worn in some countries by Muslim women, wrapped around the body to leave only the face exposed. [Pers. *chador*, Hindi *chador*]

chaetognath /kéetəgnath/ *n.* any dart-shaped worm of the phylum Chaetognatha, usu. living among marine plankton, and having a head with external thorny teeth. [mod.L *Chaetognatha* f. Gk *khaitē* long hair + *gnathos* jaw]

chafe /chayf/ *v.* & *n.* ● *v.* **1** *tr.* & *intr.* make or become sore or damaged by rubbing. **2** *tr.* rub (esp. the skin to restore warmth or sensation). **3** *tr.* & *intr.* make or become annoyed; fret (*was chafed by the delay*). ● *n.* **1 a** an act of chafing. **b** a sore resulting from this. **2** a state of annoyance. [ME f. OF *chaufer* ult. f. L *calefacere* f. *calēre* be hot + *facere* make]

■ *v.* **1** rub, abrade, fret, gall, irritate, make sore. **3** fume, rage, seethe, fizz, fret, foam at the mouth, storm, rant and rave, smoulder, *US sl.* burn up; see also IRRITATE 2. ● *n.* **1 b** sore, abrasion, bruise, soreness, irritation. **2** see RAGE *n.* 2.

chafer /cháyfər/ *n.* any of various large slow-moving beetles of the family Scarabeidae, esp. the cockchafer. [OE *ceafor, cefer* f. Gmc]

chaff /chaaf/ *n.* & *v.* ● *n.* **1** the husks of corn or other seed separated by winnowing or threshing. **2** chopped hay and straw used as fodder. **3** light-hearted joking; banter. **4** worthless things; rubbish. **5** strips of metal foil released in the atmosphere to obstruct radar detection. ● *v.tr.* **1** tease; banter. **2** chop (straw etc.). □ **chaff-cutter** a machine for chopping fodder. **separate the wheat from the chaff** distinguish good from bad. □□ **chaffy** *adj.* [OE *ceaf, cæf* prob. f. Gmc: sense 3 of *n.* & 1 of *v.* perh. f. CHAFE]

■ *n.* **3** banter, raillery, ridicule, *badinage*, joking, teasing, jest, persiflage, *colloq.* ribbing, *Austral.* & *NZ* chiack(ing), *Austral.* & *NZ sl.* borak. **4** see RUBBISH *n.* 1, 2. ● *v.* **1** banter, poke fun (at), gibe (at), jeer (at), *sl.* take the mickey (out of); tease, jolly, kid, twit, pull a person's leg, mock, ridicule, *Austral.* & *NZ* chiack, *colloq.* have on, rib, rag, *sl.* josh, *Austral.* & *NZ sl.* poke borak at.

chaffer /cháffər/ *v.* & *n.* ● *v.intr.* haggle; bargain. ● *n.* bargaining; haggling. □□ **chafferer** *n.* [ME f. OE *ceapfaru* f. *ceap* bargain + *faru* journey]

■ *v.* see HAGGLE *v.* ● *n.* see DISPUTE *n.* 1, 2.

chaffinch /cháffinch/ *n. Brit.* a common European finch, *Fringilla coelebs*, the male of which has a blue-grey head with pinkish cheeks. [OE *ceaffinc*: see CHAFF, FINCH]

chafing-dish /cháyfing/ *n.* **1** a cooking pot with an outer pan of hot water, used for keeping food warm. **2** a dish with a spirit-lamp etc. for cooking at table. [obs. sense of CHAFE =warm]

Chagas' disease /cha'agəss/ (also **Chagas's disease**) *n.* a kind of sleeping sickness caused by a protozoan transmitted by blood-sucking bugs. [C. *Chagas*, Braz. physician d. 1934]

chagrin /shágrin, shəgréen/ *n.* & *v.* ● *n.* acute vexation or mortification. ● *v.tr.* affect with chagrin. [F *chagrin(er)*, of uncert. orig.]

■ *n.* see *embarrassment* (EMBARRASS). ● *v.* see MORTIFY *v.* 1.

chain /chayn/ *n.* & *v.* ● *n.* **1 a** a connected flexible series of esp. metal links as decoration or for a practical purpose. **b** something resembling this (*formed a human chain*). **2** (in *pl.*) **a** fetters used to confine prisoners. **b** any restraining force. **3** a sequence, series, or set (*chain of events*; *mountain chain*). **4** a group of associated hotels, shops, newspapers, etc. **5** a badge of office in the form of a chain worn round the neck (*mayoral chain*). **6 a** a jointed measuring-line consisting of linked metal rods. **b** its length (66 ft.). **7** *Chem.* a group of (esp. carbon) atoms bonded in sequence in a molecule. **8** a figure in a quadrille or similar dance. **9** (in *pl.*) *Naut.* channels (see CHANNEL[2]). **10** (also **chain-shot**) *hist.* two cannon-balls or half balls joined by a chain and used in sea battles for bringing down a mast etc. ● *v.tr.* **1** (often foll. by *up*) secure or confine with a chain. **2** confine or restrict (a person) (*is chained to the office*). □ **chain-armour** armour made of interlaced rings. **chain bridge** a suspension bridge on chains. **chain drive** a system of transmission by endless chains. **chain-gang** a team of convicts chained together and forced to work in the open air. **chain-gear** a gear transmitting motion by means of an endless chain. **chain-letter** one of a sequence of letters the recipient of which is requested to send copies to a specific number of other people. **chain-link** made of wire in a diamond-shaped mesh (*chain-link fencing*). **chain-mail** = *chain-armour*. **chain reaction 1** *Physics* a self-sustaining nuclear reaction, esp. one in which a neutron from a fission reaction initiates a series of these reactions. **2** *Chem.* a self-sustaining molecular reaction in which intermediate products initiate further reactions. **3** a series of events, each caused by the previous one. **chain-saw** a motor-driven saw with teeth on an endless chain. **chain-smoker** a person who smokes continually, esp. one who lights a cigarette etc. from the stub of the last one smoked. **chain-stitch** an ornamental embroidery or crochet stitch resembling chains. **chain store** one of a series of shops owned by one firm and selling the same sort of goods. **chain-wale** = CHANNEL[2]. **chain-wheel** a wheel transmitting power by a chain fitted to its edges. [ME f. OF *cha(e)ine* f. L *catena*]

■ *n.* **2** (*chains*) **a** see BOND *n.* 1b. **b** restriction(s), restraint, constraint(s), checks, trammels, control, confinement. **3** string, series, set, stream, combination; sequence, succession, procession, concatenation, train, course; range, line, row. ● *v.* **1** shackle, secure, fasten, bind (up), fetter, tie up, manacle, trammel; leash, tether, lash, hitch; confine, restrain. **2** restrict, tie, limit.

chair /chair/ *n.* & *v.* ● *n.* **1** a separate seat for one person, of various forms, usu. having a back and four legs. **2 a** a professorship (*offered the chair in physics*). **b** a seat of authority, esp. on a board of directors. **c** a mayoralty. **3 a** a chairperson. **b** the seat or office of a chairperson (*will you take the chair?; I'm in the chair*). **4** *US* = *electric chair*. **5** an iron or steel socket holding a railway rail in place. **6** *hist.* = *sedan chair*. ● *v.tr.* **1** act as chairperson of or preside over (a meeting). **2** *Brit.* carry (a person) aloft in a chair or in a sitting position, in triumph. **3** install in a chair, esp. as a position of authority. □ **chair-bed** a chair that unfolds into a bed. **chair-borne** *colloq.* (of an administrator) not active. **chair-car** a railway carriage with chairs instead of long seats; a parlour car. **chair-lift** a series of chairs on an endless cable for carrying passengers up and down a mountain etc. **take a chair** sit down. [ME f. AF *chaere*, OF *chaiere* f. L *cathedra* f. Gk *kathedra*: see CATHEDRAL]

■ *n.* **2 a, b** professorship; seat, position, place; directorship. **3 a** chairperson, chairman, chairwoman, chairlady, presiding officer, leader, moderator. ● *v.* **1** preside over, head (up), lead, moderate, run, direct, manage, oversee. □ **chair-borne** see INACTIVE 1, 2. **take a chair** see SIT *v.* 1.

chairlady /cháirlaydi/ *n.* (*pl.* **-ies**) = CHAIRWOMAN.

chairman /cháirmən/ *n.* (*pl.* **-men**; *fem.* **chairwoman**, *pl.* **-women**) **1** a person chosen to preside over a meeting. **2** the permanent president of a committee, a board of directors, a firm, etc. **3** the master of ceremonies at an entertainment etc. **4** *hist.* either of two sedan-bearers. □□ **chairmanship** *n.*

■ **1, 2** see HEAD *n.* 6a.

chairperson /cháirpers'n/ *n.* a chairman or chairwoman (used as a neutral alternative).

■ see HEAD *n.* 6a.

chaise /shayz/ *n.* **1** esp. *hist.* a horse-drawn carriage for one or two persons, esp. one with an open top and two wheels. **2** = *post-chaise* (see POST[2]). [F var. of *chaire*, formed as CHAIR]

chaise longue /sháyz lóngg/ *n.* a sofa with only one arm rest. [F, lit. long chair]

■ see COUCH[1] *n.*

chalaza /kəláyzə/ *n.* (*pl.* **chalazae** /-zee/) each of two twisted membranous strips joining the yolk to the ends of an egg. [mod.L f. Gk, = hailstone]

chalcedony /kalséddəni/ *n.* a type of quartz occurring in several different forms, e.g. onyx, agate, tiger's eye, etc. □□ **chalcedonic** /kálsidónnik/ *adj.* [ME f. L *c(h)alcedonius* f. Gk *khalkēdōn*]

chalcolithic /kálkəlíthik/ *adj.* *Archaeol.* of a prehistoric period in which both stone and bronze implements were used. [Gk *khalkos* copper + *lithos* stone]

chalcopyrite /kálkəpīrīt/ *n.* a yellow mineral of copper-iron sulphide, which is the principal ore of copper. [Gk *khalkos* copper + PYRITE]

Chaldean /kaldeéən/ *n.* & *adj.* ● *n.* **1 a** a native of ancient Chaldea or Babylonia. **b** the language of the Chaldeans. **2** an astrologer. **3** a member of the Uniat (formerly Nestorian) sect in Iran etc. ● *adj.* **1** of or relating to ancient Chaldea or its people or language. **2** of or relating to astrology. **3** of or relating to the Uniat sect. [L *Chaldaeus* f. Gk *Khaldaios* f. Assyr. *Kaldu*]

Chaldee /kaldeé/ *n.* **1** the language of the Chaldeans. **2** a native of ancient Chaldea. **3** the Aramaic language as used in Old Testament books. [ME, repr. L *Chaldaei* (pl.) (as CHALDEAN)]

chalet /shállay/ *n.* **1** a small suburban house or bungalow, esp. with an overhanging roof. **2** a small, usu. wooden, hut or house on a beach or in a holiday camp. **3** a Swiss cowherd's hut, or wooden cottage, with overhanging eaves. [Swiss F]

■ **1** see COTTAGE. **2, 3** see CABIN *n.* 1.

chalice /chálliss/ *n.* **1** *literary* a goblet. **2** a wine-cup used in the Communion service. [ME f. OF f. L *calix -icis* cup]

chalk /chawk/ *n.* & *v.* ● *n.* **1** a white soft earthy limestone (calcium carbonate) formed from the skeletal remains of sea creatures. **2 a** a similar substance (calcium sulphate), sometimes coloured, used for writing or drawing. **b** a piece of this (*a box of chalks*). **3** a series of strata consisting mainly of chalk. **4** = *French chalk*. ● *v.tr.* **1** rub, mark, draw, or write with chalk. **2** (foll. by *up*) **a** write or record with chalk. **b** register (a success etc.). **c** charge (to an account). □ **as different as chalk and** (or **from**) **cheese** fundamentally different. **by a long chalk** *Brit.* by far (from the use of chalk to mark the score in games). **chalk and talk** traditional teaching (employing blackboard, chalk, and interlocution). **chalk out** sketch or plan a thing to be accomplished. **chalk-pit** a quarry in which chalk is dug. **chalk-stone** a concretion of urates like chalk in tissues and joints esp. of hands and feet. **chalk-stripe** a pattern of thin white stripes on a dark background. **chalk-striped** having chalk-stripes. [OE *cealc* ult. f. WG f. L CALX]

chalkboard /cháwkbord/ *n.* *US* = BLACKBOARD.

chalkie /cháwki/ *n.* *Austral. colloq.* a schoolteacher.

■ see TEACHER.

chalky /cháwki/ *adj.* (**chalkier**, **chalkiest**) **1 a** abounding in chalk. **b** white as chalk. **2** like or containing chalk stones. □□ **chalkiness** *n.*

■ **1 b** see WHITE *adj.* 1.

challenge /chállinj/ *n.* & *v.* ● *n.* **1 a** a summons to take part in a contest or a trial of strength etc., esp. to a duel. **b** a summons to prove or justify something. **2** a demanding or difficult task (*rose to the challenge of the new job*). **3** an act of disputing or denying a statement, claim, etc. **4** *Law* an objection made to a jury member. **5** a call to respond, esp. a sentry's call for a password etc. **6** an invitation to a sporting contest, esp. one issued to a reigning champion. **7** *Med.* a test of immunity after immunization treatment. ● *v.tr.* **1** (often foll. by *to* + infin.) **a** invite to take part in a contest, game, debate, duel, etc. **b** invite to prove or justify something. **2** dispute, deny (*I challenge that remark*). **3 a** stretch, stimulate (*challenges him to produce his best*). **b** (as **challenging** *adj.*) demanding; stimulatingly difficult. **4** (of a sentry) call to respond. **5** claim (attention, etc.). **6** *Law* object to (a jury member, evidence, etc.). **7** *Med.* test by a challenge. □□ **challengeable** /-jəb'l/ *adj.* **challenger** *n.* [ME f. OF *c(h)alenge*, *c(h)alenger* f. L *calumnia calumniari* calumny]

■ *n.* **1** defiance, gage, gauntlet, invitation, dare, summons; provocation; ultimatum; (*take up a challenge*) throw one's hat in the ring, take up the glove, enter the lists. **2** demand(s), needs, requirement(s); test, trial, examination; difficulties, problems. **3** question, impeachment, dispute, doubt, refutation, contradiction, objection, protest, opposition, remonstration. ● *v.* **1 a** invite, dare, summon, call out, provoke, *archaic* defy; take on; (*challenge a person*) throw down the glove *or* gauntlet, enter the lists. **b** defy. **2** question, dispute, object to, take exception to, cast doubt upon, query, contest, contend, doubt, call into doubt, call in *or* into question, impugn, impeach; deny, disagree with, *disp.* refute; oppose. **3 a** stretch, test; stimulate, drive. **b** (**challenging**) demanding, formidable, difficult, exacting, hard; stimulating. **5** see CLAIM *v.* 1a.

challis /shálliss, shálli/ *n.* a lightweight soft clothing fabric. [perh. f. a surname]

chalybeate /kəlíbbiət/ *adj.* (of mineral water etc.) impregnated with iron salts. [mod.L *chalybeatus* f. L *chalybs* f. Gk *khalups -ubos* steel]

chamaephyte /kámmifīt/ *n.* a plant whose buds are on or near the ground. [Gk *khamai* on the ground + -PHYTE]

chamber /cháymbər/ *n.* **1 a** a hall used by a legislative or judicial body. **b** the body that meets in it. **c** any of the houses of a parliament (*Chamber of Deputies*; *second chamber*). **2** (in *pl.*) *Brit. Law* **a** rooms used by a barrister or group of barristers, esp. in the Inns of Court. **b** a judge's room used for hearing cases not needing to be taken in court. **3** *poet.* or *archaic* a room, esp. a bedroom. **4** *Mus.* (*attrib.*) of or for a small group of instruments (*chamber orchestra*; *chamber music*). **5** an enclosed space in machinery etc. (esp. the part of a gun-bore that contains the charge). **6 a** a cavity in a plant or in the body of an animal. **b** a compartment in a structure. **7** = *chamber-pot*. □ **Chamber of Commerce** an association to promote local commercial interests. **chamber-pot** a receptacle for urine etc., used in a bedroom. [ME f. OF *chambre* f. L CAMERA]

■ **1 a** hall, meeting-hall, assembly room. **b, c** assembly, body, legislature, judicature, judiciary, diet, *Brit.* convocation, *US* caucus; house, congress, senate. **3** room, apartment; bedroom, bedchamber; (*chambers*) (living) quarters, rooms. **5** enclosure, magazine, *Mech.* manifold. **6 a** *Anat.* antrum, vestibule. **b** compartment, cell, cavity, space, hole, hollow, niche, nook, recess, alcove. □ **chamber-pot** chamber, commode, *colloq.* potty, *Brit. colloq.* po, *Brit. sl.* jerry.

chambered /cháymbərd/ *adj.* (of a tomb) containing a burial chamber.

chamberlain /cháymbərlin/ *n.* **1** an officer managing the household of a sovereign or a great noble. **2** the treasurer of a corporation etc. □ **Lord Chamberlain (of the Household)** the official in charge of the Royal Household, formerly the licenser of plays. **Lord Great Chamberlain of England** the hereditary holder of a ceremonial office. □□ **chamberlainship** *n.* [ME f. OF *chamberlain* etc. f. Frank. f. L *camera* CAMERA]

chambermaid /cháymbərmayd/ *n.* **1** a housemaid at a hotel etc. **2** *US* a housemaid.

■ see MAID 1.

Chambertin /shóɴbərtaɴ/ *n.* a high-quality dry red burgundy wine. [*Gevrey Chambertin* region in E. France]

chambray /shámbray/ *n.* a linen-finished gingham cloth with a white weft and a coloured warp. [irreg. f. *Cambrai*: see CAMBRIC]

chambré /shóɴbray/ *adj.* (of red wine) brought to room temperature. [F, past part. of *chambrer* f. *chambre* room: see CHAMBER]

chameleon /kəmeeliən/ *n.* **1** any of a family of small lizards having grasping tails, long tongues, protruding eyes, and the power of changing colour. **2** a variable or inconstant person. □□ **chameleonic** /-liónnik/ *adj.* [ME f. L f. Gk *khamaileōn* f. *khamai* on the ground + *leōn* lion]

■ □□ **chameleonic** see VARIABLE 2.

chamfer /chámfər/ *v.* & *n.* ● *v.tr.* bevel symmetrically (a right-angled edge or corner). ● *n.* a bevelled surface at an edge or corner. [back-form. f. *chamfering* f. F *chamfrain* f. *chant* edge (CANT[2]) + *fraint* broken f. OF *fraindre* break f. L *frangere*]

chamois *n.* (*pl.* same) **1** /shámwaa/ (*pl.* /-waaz/) an agile goat antelope, *Rupicapra rupicapra*, native to the mountains of Europe and Asia. **2** /shámmi, shámwaa/ (in full **chamois leather**) **a** soft pliable leather from sheep, goats, deer, etc. **b** a piece of this for polishing etc. [F: cf. Gallo-Roman *camox*]

chamomile var. of CAMOMILE.

champ[1] /champ/ *v.* & *n.* ● *v.* **1** *tr.* & *intr.* munch or chew noisily. **2** *tr.* (of a horse etc.) work (the bit) noisily between the teeth. **3** *intr.* fret with impatience (*is champing to be away*). ● *n.* a chewing noise or motion. □ **champ at the bit** be restlessly impatient. [prob. imit.]

■ *v.* **1** see MUNCH.

champ[2] /champ/ *n. sl.* a champion. [abbr.]

■ see WINNER 1.

champagne /shampáyn/ *n.* **1 a** a white sparkling wine from Champagne. **b** (loosely) a similar wine from elsewhere. ¶ Use in sense b is strictly incorrect. **2** a pale cream or straw colour. [*Champagne*, former province in E. France]

■ **1** see FIZZ *n.* 2.

champaign /shampáyn/ *n. literary* **1** open country. **2** an expanse of open country. [ME f. OF *champagne* f. LL *campania*: cf. CAMPAIGN]

champers /shámpərz/ *n. sl.* champagne.

■ see FIZZ *n.* 2.

champerty /chámpərti/ *n.* (*pl.* **-ies**) *Law* an illegal agreement in which a person not naturally interested in a lawsuit finances it with a view to sharing the disputed property. □□ **champertous** *adj.* [ME f. AF *champartie* f. OF *champart* feudal lord's share of produce, f. L *campus* field + *pars part*]

champion /chámpiən/ *n.*, *v.*, *adj.*, & *adv.* ● *n.* **1** (often *attrib.*) a person (esp. in a sport or game), an animal, plant, etc., that has defeated or surpassed all rivals in a competition etc. **2 a** a person who fights or argues for a cause or on behalf of another person. **b** *hist.* a knight etc. who fought in single combat on behalf of a king etc. ● *v.tr.* support the cause of, defend, argue in favour of. ● *adj. colloq.* or *dial.* first-class, splendid. ● *adv. colloq.* or *dial.* splendidly, well. □ **Champion of England** (or **King's** or **Queen's Champion**) a hereditary official at coronations. [ME f. OF f. med.L *campio -onis* fighter f. L *campus* field]

■ *n.* **1** victor, winner, conqueror, title-holder, prizewinner, victor ludorum, gold-medallist, *sl.* champ; (*attrib.*) prize, winning, prizewinning, victorious. **2 a** defender, guardian, protector, hero, saviour, knight in shining armour, supporter, backer, advocate, proponent, upholder, apologist, patron, *disp.* protagonist; fighter, campaigner, lobbyist. **b** fighter, combatant, hero, warrior, campaigner. ● *v.* defend, protect, guard; support, back, stand up for, speak *or* plead *or* argue in favour of, hold a brief for, fight for, lobby for *or* on behalf of, maintain, sustain, uphold; espouse, forward, promote, advocate, urge. ● *adj.* see FIRST-RATE. ● *adv.* see WELL[1] *adv.* 9.

championship /chámpiənship/ *n.* **1** (often in *pl.*) a contest for the position of champion in a sport etc. **2** the position of champion over all rivals. **3** the advocacy or defence (of a cause etc.).

■ **1** see CONTEST *n.* 1. **2** see TITLE *n.* 6. **3** see FURTHERANCE.

champlevé /shóɴləváy/ *n.* & *adj.* ● *n.* a type of enamel-work in which hollows made in a metal surface are filled with coloured enamels. ● *adj.* of or relating to *champlevé* (cf. CLOISONNÉ). [F, = raised field]

chance /chaanss/ *n.*, *adj.*, & *v.* ● *n.* **1 a** a possibility (*just a chance we will catch the train*). **b** (often in *pl.*) probability (*the chances are against it*). **2** a risk (*have to take a chance*). **3 a** an undesigned occurrence (*just a chance that they met*). **b** the absence of design or discoverable cause (*here merely because of chance*). **4** an opportunity (*didn't have a chance to speak to him*). **5** the way things happen; fortune; luck (*we'll just leave it to chance*). **6** (often **Chance**) the course of events regarded as a power; fate (*blind Chance rules the universe*). **7** *Cricket* an opportunity for dismissing a batsman. ● *adj.* fortuitous, accidental (*a chance meeting*). ● *v.* **1** *tr. colloq.* risk (*we'll chance it and go*). **2** *intr.* (often foll. by *that* + clause, or *to* + infin.) happen without intention (*it chanced that I found it*; *I chanced to find it*). □ **by any chance** as it happens; perhaps. **by chance** without design; unintentionally. **chance one's arm** make an attempt though unlikely to succeed. **chance on** (or **upon**) happen to find, meet, etc. **game of chance** a game decided by luck, not skill. **the off chance** the slight possibility. **on the chance** (often foll. by *of*, or *that* + clause) in view of the possibility. **stand a chance** have a prospect of success etc. **take a chance** (or **chances**) behave riskily; risk failure.

take a (or **one's**) **chance on** (or **with**) consent to take the consequences of; trust to luck. [ME f. AF *ch(e)aunce*, OF *chëance chëoir* fall ult. f. L *cadere*]

■ *n.* **1** conceivability, possibility; eventuality; (*chances*) likelihood, odds, probability, prospect(s). **2** risk, gamble, venture. **3** accident, coincidence, fluke, fortuity, *US* happenstance. **4** opportunity, time, turn, occasion, moment; window, opening, start, hearing, say, *colloq.* break, show; see also SHOT[1] 5b. **5, 6** fortune, luck, fate, destiny, fortuity, fortuitousness, kismet. ● *adj.* fortuitous, casual, accidental, coincidental, adventitious, aleatoric, aleatory, incidental, arbitrary; unintentional, inadvertent, unplanned, unpremeditated; unexpected, unforeseen, unlooked-for. ● *v.* **1** risk, hazard, venture. **2** happen, occur, come to pass, take place, come about, *poet.* betide, befall. □ **by any chance** see POSSIBLY 2. **by chance** accidentally, coincidentally, fortuitously, adventitiously, incidentally, unexpectedly, unintentionally, inadvertently. **take a chance on** see TRUST *v.* 1.

chancel /chaáns'l/ *n.* the part of a church near the altar, reserved for the clergy, the choir, etc., usu. enclosed by a screen or separated from the nave by steps. [ME f. OF f. L *cancelli* lattice]

chancellery /chaánsələri/ *n.* (*pl.* **-ies**) **1 a** the position, office, staff, department, etc., of a chancellor. **b** the official residence of a chancellor. **2** *US* an office attached to an embassy or consulate. [ME f. OF *chancellerie* (as CHANCELLOR)]

chancellor /chaánsələr/ *n.* **1** a State or legal official of various kinds. **2** the head of the government in some European countries, e.g. Germany. **3** the non-resident honorary head of a university. **4** a bishop's law officer. **5** *US* the president of a chancery court. □ **Chancellor of the Duchy of Lancaster** a member of the government legally representing the Queen as Duke of Lancaster, often a Cabinet Minister employed on non-departmental work. **Chancellor of the Exchequer** the finance minister of the United Kingdom. **Chancellor of the Garter** etc. a government officer who seals commissions etc. **Lord** (or **Lord High**) **Chancellor** an officer presiding in the House of Lords, the Chancery Division, or the Court of Appeal. □□ **chancellorship** *n.* [OE f. AF *c(h)anceler*, OF *-ier* f. LL *cancellarius* porter, secretary, f. *cancelli* lattice]

■ **2** see PREMIER *n.* **3** see PRINCIPAL *n.* 2.

chance-medley /chaánsmédli/ *n.* (*pl.* **-eys**) **1** *Law* a fight, esp. homicidal, beginning unintentionally. **2** inadvertency. [AF *chance medlee* (see MEDDLE) mixed chance]

chancery /chaánsəri/ *n.* (*pl.* **-ies**) **1** *Law* (**Chancery**) the Lord Chancellor's court, a division of the High Court of Justice. **2** *hist.* the records office of an order of knighthood. **3** *hist.* the court of a bishop's chancellor. **4** an office attached to an embassy or consulate. **5** a public record office. **6** *US* a court of equity. □ **in chancery** *sl.* (of a boxer or wrestler) with the head held under the opponent's arm and being pummelled. [ME, contracted f. CHANCELLERY]

chancre /shángkər/ *n.* a painless ulcer developing in venereal disease etc. [F f. L CANCER]

■ see ULCER 1.

chancroid /shángkroyd/ *n.* ulceration of lymph nodes in the groin, from venereal disease.

chancy /chaánsi/ *adj.* (**chancier**, **chanciest**) subject to chance; uncertain; risky. □□ **chancily** *adv.* **chanciness** *n.*

■ see RISKY.

chandelier /shándiléer/ *n.* an ornamental branched hanging support for several candles or electric light bulbs. [F (*chandelle* f. as CANDLE)]

chandler /chaándlər/ *n.* a dealer in candles, oil, soap, paint, groceries, etc. □ **corn chandler** a dealer in corn. **ship** (or **ship's**) **chandler** a dealer in cordage, canvas, etc. [ME f. AF *chaundeler*, OF *chandelier* (as CANDLE)]

chandlery /chaándləri/ *n.* the goods sold by a chandler.

change /chaynj/ *n.* & *v.* ● *n.* **1 a** the act or an instance of making or becoming different. **b** an alteration or modification (*the change in her expression*). **2 a** money given in exchange for money in larger units or a different currency. **b** money returned as the balance of that given in payment. **c** = *small change*. **3** a new experience; variety (*fancied a change*; *for a change*). **4 a** the substitution of one thing for another; an exchange (*change of scene*). **b** a set of clothes etc. put on in place of another. **5** (in full **change of life**) *colloq.* the menopause. **6** (usu. in *pl.*) the different orders in which a peal of bells can be rung. **7** (**Change**) (also **'Change**) *hist.* a place where merchants etc. met to do business. **8** (of the moon) arrival at a fresh phase, esp. at the new moon. ● *v.* **1** *tr.* & *intr.* undergo, show, or subject to change; make or become different (*the wig changed his appearance*; *changed from an introvert into an extrovert*). **2** *tr.* **a** take or use another instead of; go from one to another (*change one's socks*; *changed his doctor*; *changed trains*). **b** (usu. foll. by *for*) give up or get rid of in exchange (*changed the car for a van*). **3** *tr.* **a** give or get change in smaller denominations for (*can you change a ten-pound note?*). **b** (foll. by *for*) exchange (a sum of money) for (*changed his dollars for pounds*). **4** *tr.* & *intr.* put fresh clothes or coverings on (*changed the baby as he was wet*; *changed into something loose*). **5** *tr.* (often foll. by *with*) give and receive, exchange (*changed places with him*; *we changed places*). **6** *intr.* change trains etc. (*changed at Crewe*). **7** *intr.* (of the moon) arrive at a fresh phase, esp. become new. □ **change colour** blanch or flush. **change down** engage a lower gear in a vehicle. **change gear** engage a different gear in a vehicle. **change hands 1** pass to a different owner. **2** substitute one hand for another. **change one's mind** adopt a different opinion or plan. **change of air** a different climate; variety. **change of heart** a conversion to a different view. **change over** change from one system or situation to another. **change-over** *n.* such a change. **change step** begin to keep step with the opposite leg when marching etc. **change the subject** begin talking of something different, esp. to avoid embarrassment. **change one's tune 1** voice a different opinion from that expressed previously. **2** change one's style of language or manner, esp. from an insolent to a respectful tone. **change up** engage a higher gear in a vehicle. **get no change out of** *sl.* **1** fail to get information from. **2** fail to get the better of (in business etc.). **ring the changes** (**on**) vary the ways of expressing, arranging, or doing something. □□ **changeful** *adj.* **changer** *n.* [ME f. AF *chaunge*, OF *change*, *changer* f. LL *cambiare*, L *cambire* barter, prob. of Celt. orig.]

■ *n.* **1** alteration, transformation, mutation, shift, fluctuation, swing, modulation, metamorphosis, revolution, conversion; modification, adjustment, amendment; transition, flux, movement, motion, upheaval. **2 c** small change, coin(s), coppers, silver, cash, specie. **3** variation, difference, variety, novelty. **4** substitution, switch, interchange, replacement, exchange, change-over, *US* trade. ● *v.* **1** modify, alter, modulate, sway, transmute, transfigure, convert, adapt, change over, ring the changes; mutate, transform, metamorphose, *joc.* transmogrify; fluctuate, shift, vary; influence, affect, have an impact on; distort, warp, deform, disfigure; (*change to* or *into*) turn into, become; make into. **2, 5** exchange, interchange, switch, swap, trade; replace, substitute. □ **change colour** see FLUSH[1] *v.* 1a, PALE[1] *v.* 1. **change one's mind** think twice *or* again, have a change of heart, change one's position *or* plan(s); (*change one's mind about*) think better of. **change of air** see VARIETY 1. **change over** change, convert, switch, shift. **change-over** change, conversion, switch, shift, revolution; transition, move.

changeable /cháynjəb'l/ *adj.* **1** irregular, inconstant. **2** that can change or be changed. □□ **changeability** /-bílliti/ *n.* **changeableness** *n.* **changeably** *adv.* [ME f. OF, formed as CHANGE]

■ **1** variable, protean, inconstant, unstable, unsettled, shifting, fluctuating, uncertain, irregular, erratic, inconsistent, uneven, unsteady, unpredictable, *Chem.*

labile, *archaic* versatile, *literary* mutable; capricious, erratic, fickle, flighty, fitful, unreliable, undependable, mercurial, volatile. **2** alterable, modifiable, transformable, convertible, variable, adaptable, flexible.

changeless /cháynjliss/ *adj.* unchanging. ▫▫ **changelessly** *adv.* **changelessness** *n.*

▪ unchanging, unvaried, constant, unvarying, invariable, steadfast, firm, unwavering, fixed, stable, static, unchangeable, immutable, unalterable; see also ABIDING.

changeling /cháynjling/ *n.* a child believed to be substituted for another by stealth, esp. an elf-child left by fairies.

channel[1] /chánn'l/ *n.* & *v.* ● *n.* **1 a** a length of water wider than a strait, joining two larger areas, esp. seas. **b** (**the Channel**) the English Channel between Britain and France. **2** a medium of communication; an agency for conveying information (*through the usual channels*). **3** *Broadcasting* **a** a band of frequencies used in radio and television transmission, esp. as used by a particular station. **b** a service or station using this. **4** the course in which anything moves; a direction. **5 a** a natural or artificial hollow bed of water. **b** the navigable part of a waterway. **6** a tubular passage for liquid. **7** *Electronics* a lengthwise strip on recording tape etc. **8** a groove or a flute, esp. in a column. ● *v.tr.* (**channelled, channelling**; *US* **channeled, channeling**) **1** guide, direct (*channelled them through customs*). **2** form channels in; groove. [ME f. OF *chanel* f. L *canalis* CANAL]

▪ *n.* **2** avenue, path, course, passage, route, artery, conduit; means, agency, vehicle, method, device, way, approach. **5a, 6** watercourse, canal, waterway, stream, ditch, drain, duct, aqueduct, sluice, conduit, flume, chute, race, pipe, trench, trough, gutter, moat. **8** furrow, groove, slot, chase, gouge, *Anat.* sulcus, *Anat.* & *Bot.* vallecula, *Archit.* flute, glyph. ● *v.* **1** direct, convey, pass, guide, lead, conduct, channelize; focus, train, turn, concentrate, centre, bend; divert, sublimate.

channel[2] /chánn'l/ *n. Naut.* any of the broad thick planks projecting horizontally from a ship's side abreast of the masts, used to widen the basis for the shrouds. [for *chain-wale*: cf. *gunnel* for *gunwale*]

channelize /chánnəlīz/ *v.tr.* (also **-ise**) convey in, or as if in, a channel; guide.

chanson de geste /shonsón də zhést/ *n.* (*pl.* ***chansons*** /*pronunc.* same/) any of a group of medieval French epic poems. [F, = song of heroic deeds]

chant /chaant/ *n.* & *v.* ● *n.* **1 a** a spoken singsong phrase, esp. one performed in unison by a crowd etc. **b** a repetitious singsong way of speaking. **2** *Mus.* **a** a short musical passage in two or more phrases used for singing unmetrical words, e.g. psalms, canticles. **b** the psalm or canticle so sung. **c** a song, esp. monotonous or repetitive. **3** a musical recitation, esp. of poetry. ● *v.tr.* & *intr.* **1** talk or repeat monotonously (*a crowd chanting slogans*). **2** sing or intone (a psalm etc.). [ME (orig. as verb) f. OF *chanter* sing f. L *cantare* frequent. of *canere cant-* sing]

▪ *n.* **2 b** song, psalm, canticle, plainsong, plainchant, mantra. ● *v.* **1** singsong, recite, repeat; shout (out), cry out, yell (out), *sl.* belt out. **2** sing, intone, cantillate.

chanter /chaántər/ *n. Mus.* the melody-pipe, with finger-holes, of a bagpipe.

chanterelle /chántərél/ *n.* an edible fungus, *Cantharellus cibarius*, with a yellow funnel-shaped cap and smelling of apricots. [F f. mod.L *cantharellus* dimin. of *cantharus* f. Gk *kantharos* a kind of drinking vessel]

chanteuse /shaantǒz/ *n.* a female singer of popular songs. [F]

▪ see *singer* (SING).

chanticleer /chántikleér, chaán-, shán-, shaán-/ *n. literary* a name given to a domestic cock, esp. in fairy tales etc. [ME f. OF *chantecler* (as CHANT, CLEAR), a name in *Reynard the Fox*]

Chantilly /shantílli, shóNteeyeé/ *n.* **1** a delicate kind of bobbin-lace. **2** sweetened or flavoured whipped cream. [*Chantilly* near Paris]

chantry /chaántri/ *n.* (*pl.* **-ies**) **1** an endowment for a priest or priests to celebrate masses for the founder's soul. **2** the priests, chapel, altar, etc., endowed. [ME f. AF *chaunterie*, OF *chanterie* f. *chanter* CHANT]

chanty var. of SHANTY[2].

Chanukkah var. of HANUKKAH.

chaology /kayólləji/ *n. Math.* = *chaos theory*.

chaos /káyoss/ *n.* **1 a** utter confusion. **b** *Math.* the unpredictable and apparently random behaviour of a deterministic system that is extremely sensitive to infinitesimal changes in initial parameters. **2** the formless matter supposed to have existed before the creation of the universe. ▫ **chaos theory** *Math.* the study of the apparently random behaviour of deterministic systems. ▫▫ **chaotic** /kayóttik/ *adj.* **chaotically** /kayóttikəli/ *adv.* [F or L f. Gk *khaos*: *-otic* after *erotic* etc.]

▪ **1 a** pandemonium, bedlam, havoc, mayhem, babel, turmoil, disarray, tumult, uproar, maelstrom, pie, tailspin, pell-mell, topsy-turvy, higgledy-piggledy, hugger-mugger, *sl.* snafu; disorder, confusion, disorganization. **2** formlessness; the abyss. ▫▫ **chaotic** formless, shapeless, incoherent, disordered, disorderly, disorganized, unorganized, unsystematic, unsystematized, unmethodical, haphazard, irregular, helter-skelter, confused, topsy-turvy, all over the place, at sixes and sevens, jumbled, turbulent, tumultuous, higgledy-piggledy, hugger-mugger, *colloq.* shambolic, all over the shop, *sl.* snafu.

chap[1] /chap/ *v.* & *n.* ● *v.* (**chapped, chapping**) **1** *intr.* (esp. of the skin; also of dry ground etc.) crack in fissures, esp. because of exposure and dryness. **2** *tr.* (of the wind, cold, etc.) cause to chap. ● *n.* (usu. in *pl.*) **1** a crack in the skin. **2** an open seam. [ME, perh. rel. to MLG, MDu. *kappen* chop off]

chap[2] /chap/ *n. colloq.* a man; a boy; a fellow. [abbr. of CHAPMAN]

▪ fellow, lad, man, boy, customer, *Sc.* carl, *colloq.* guy, chappie, *Brit. colloq.* blighter, johnny, *sl.* geezer, *Brit. sl.* bloke, josser, *Brit. sl. archaic* cove, *US sl.* dude, *sl. often derog.* gink.

chap[3] /chap/ *n.* the lower jaw or half of the cheek, esp. of a pig as food. ▫ **chap-fallen** dispirited, dejected (with the lower jaw hanging). [16th c.: var. of CHOP[2], of unkn. orig.]

chap. *abbr.* chapter.

chaparejos /sháppəráyōss, cháp-/ *n.pl. US* a cowboy's leather protection for the front of the legs. [Mex. Sp.]

chaparral /chápparál, sháp-/ *n. US* dense tangled brushwood; undergrowth. ▫ **chaparral cock** = ROADRUNNER. [Sp. f. *chaparra* evergreen oak]

chapatti /chəpaáti, -pátti/ *n.* (also **chapati, chupatty**) (*pl.* **-is** or **chupatties**) *Ind.* a flat thin cake of unleavened wholemeal bread. [Hindi *capātī*]

chap-book /chápbŏŏk/ *n. hist.* a small pamphlet containing tales, ballads, tracts, etc., hawked by chapmen. [19th c.: see CHAPMAN]

chape /chayp/ *n.* **1** the metal cap of a scabbard-point. **2** the back-piece of a buckle attaching it to a strap etc. **3** a sliding loop on a belt or strap. [ME f. OF, = cope, hood, formed as CAP]

chapeau-bras /sháppōbraá/ *n.* (*pl.* ***chapeaux-bras*** /*pronunc.* same/) a three-cornered flat silk hat often carried under the arm. [F f. *chapeau* hat + *bras* arm]

chapel /chápp'l/ *n.* **1 a** a place for private Christian worship in a large church or esp. a cathedral, with its own altar and dedication (*Lady chapel*). **b** a place of Christian worship attached to a private house or institution. **2** *Brit.* **a** a place of worship for nonconformist bodies. **b** (*predic.*) an attender at or believer in nonconformist worship (*they are strictly chapel*). **c** a chapel service. **d** attendance at a chapel. **3** an Anglican church subordinate to a parish church. **4** *Printing* **a** the members or branch of a printers' trade union at a specific place of work. **b** a meeting of them. ▫ **chapel of ease** an Anglican chapel for the convenience of remote parishioners. **chapel of rest** an undertaker's mortuary. **chapel royal** a chapel in a royal palace. **father of chapel** (or **the chapel**) the shop steward of a printers' chapel. [ME f. OF *chapele* f. med.L *cappella* dimin. of *cappa* cloak: the first chapel was a sanctuary in which St Martin's sacred cloak (*cappella*) was preserved]

■ **1** see SANCTUARY 1. **2 a** see TEMPLE[1].

chapelry /cháppəlri/ *n.* (*pl.* **-ies**) a district served by an Anglican chapel.

chaperon /sháppərōn/ *n.* & *v.* (also **chaperone**) ● *n.* **1** a person, esp. an older woman, who ensures propriety by accompanying a young unmarried woman on social occasions. **2** a person who takes charge of esp. young people in public. ● *v.tr.* act as a chaperon to. □□ **chaperonage** /sháppərənij/ *n.* [F, = hood, chaperon, dimin. of *chape* cope, formed as CAP]

■ *n.* see ESCORT *n.* 1. ● *v.* see ACCOMPANY 1.

chaplain /cháplin/ *n.* a member of the clergy attached to a private chapel, institution, ship, regiment, etc. □□ **chaplaincy** *n.* (*pl.* **-ies**). [ME f. AF & OF *c(h)apelain* f. med.L *cappellanus*, orig. custodian of the cloak of St Martin: see CHAPEL]

■ see CLERGYMAN.

chaplet /cháplit/ *n.* **1** a garland or circlet for the head. **2** a string of 55 beads (one-third of the rosary number) for counting prayers, or as a necklace. **3** a bead-moulding. □□ **chapleted** *adj.* [ME f. OF *chapelet*, ult. f. LL *cappa* CAP]

■ **1** see GARLAND *n.* 1. **2** see STRING *n.* 6.

chapman /chápmən/ *n.* (*pl.* **-men**) *hist.* a pedlar. [OE *cēapman* f. *cēap* barter]

■ see PEDLAR.

chappal /chápp'l/ *n.* an Indian sandal, usu. of leather. [Hindi]

chappie /cháppi/ *n. colloq.* = CHAP[2].

chappy /cháppi/ *adj.* full of chaps; chapped (*chappy knuckles*).

chaps /chaps, shaps/ *n.* = CHAPAREJOS. [abbr.]

chapstick /chápstik/ *n.* *US* a cylinder of a cosmetic substance used to prevent chapping of the lips.

chapter /cháptər/ *n.* **1** a main division of a book. **2** a period of time (in a person's life, a nation's history, etc.). **3** a series or sequence (*a chapter of misfortunes*). **4 a** the canons of a cathedral or other religious community or knightly order. **b** a meeting of these. **5** an Act of Parliament numbered as part of a session's proceedings. **6** *US* a local branch of a society. □ **chapter and verse** an exact reference or authority. **chapter house 1** a building used for the meetings of a chapter. **2** *US* the place where a college fraternity or sorority meets. [ME f. OF *chapitre* f. L *capitulum* dimin. of *caput -itis* head]

■ **1** see EPISODE 2. **2** see ERA. **6** see LODGE *n.* 5, 6.

char[1] /chaar/ *v.tr.* & *intr.* (**charred**, **charring**) **1** make or become black by burning; scorch. **2** burn or be burnt to charcoal. [app. back-form. f. CHARCOAL]

■ **1** see SCORCH *v.* 1, 2.

char[2] /chaar/ *n.* & *v.* *Brit. colloq.* ● *n.* = CHARWOMAN. ● *v.intr.* (**charred**, **charring**) work as a charwoman. [earlier *chare* f. OE *cerr* a turn, *cierran* to turn]

char[3] /chaar/ *n.* (also **cha** /chaar/) *Brit. sl.* tea. [Chin. *cha*]

char[4] /chaar/ *n.* (also **charr**) (*pl.* same) any small troutlike fish of the genus *Salvelinus*. [17th c.: orig. unkn.]

charabanc /shárrəbang/ *n. Brit. hist.* an early form of motor coach. [F *char à bancs* seated carriage]

character /kárriktər/ *n.* & *v.* ● *n.* **1** the collective qualities or characteristics, esp. mental and moral, that distinguish a person or thing. **2 a** moral strength (*has a weak character*). **b** reputation, esp. good reputation. **3 a** a person in a novel, play, etc. **b** a part played by an actor; a role. **4** *colloq.* a person, esp. an eccentric or outstanding individual (*he's a real character*). **5 a** a printed or written letter, symbol, or distinctive mark (*Chinese characters*). **b** *Computing* any of a group of symbols representing a letter etc. **6** a written description of a person's qualities; a testimonial. **7** a characteristic (esp. of a biological species). ● *v.tr. archaic* inscribe; describe. □ **character actor** an actor who specializes in playing eccentric or unusual persons. **character assassination** a malicious attempt to harm or destroy a person's good reputation. **in** (or **out of**) **character** consistent (or inconsistent) with a person's character. □□ **characterful** *adj.* **characterfully** *adv.* **characterless** *adj.* [ME f. OF *caractere* f. L *character* f. Gk *kharaktēr* stamp, impress]

■ *n.* **1** personality, nature, temperament, disposition, temper, make-up, complexion, spirit; qualities, features, properties, attributes, traits; aroma, feel, feeling, atmosphere, aura, quality, air, tone, flavour, tenor; sort, kind, type, description. **2 a** morality, (moral) fibre, honesty, integrity, uprightness, decency, principle, respectability, rectitude, honour, courage, goodness, nobility. **b** see REPUTATION 2. **3 b** role, part, personality; (*characters*) dramatis personae. **4** eccentric, original, individual, individualist, *colloq.* card, *Brit. sl.* oner. **5** mark, symbol, monogram, sign; letter, number, figure, type, sort, rune, hieroglyphic, hieroglyph. **6** see TESTIMONIAL 1. **7** see CHARACTERISTIC *n.* ● *v.* see DESCRIBE 1a. □ **in** (or **out of**) **character** (*in character*) in keeping, typical, normal, expected, characteristic; fitting, proper, suitable; (*out of character*) untypical, atypical, uncharacteristic, abnormal, unexpected, unfitting, unbecoming.

characteristic /kárriktərístik/ *adj.* & *n.* ● *adj.* typical, distinctive (*with characteristic expertise*). ● *n.* **1** a characteristic feature or quality. **2** *Math.* the whole number or integral part of a logarithm. □ **characteristic curve** a graph showing the relationship between two variable but interdependent quantities. **characteristic radiation** radiation the wavelengths of which are peculiar to the element which emits them. □□ **characteristically** *adv.* [F *caractéristique* or med.L *characterizare* f. Gk *kharaktērizō*]

■ *adj.* typical, representative; emblematic, symbolic, distinctive, symptomatic; in character. ● *n.* **1** mark, trait, attribute, feature, quality, property, character, aspect, peculiarity, idiosyncrasy; hallmark, indication, sign, symbol, emblem, symptom.

characterize /kárriktərīz/ *v.tr.* (also **-ise**) **1 a** describe the character of. **b** (foll. by *as*) describe as. **2** be characteristic of. **3** impart character to. □□ **characterization** /-záysh'n/ *n.* [F *caractériser* or med.L *characterizare* f. Gk *kharaktērizō*]

■ **1, 2** describe, define, categorize; delineate, portray, depict, represent, paint, identify, mark. **3** see TYPIFY.

charade /shəraád/ *n.* **1 a** (usu. in *pl.*, treated as *sing.*) a game of guessing a word from a written or acted clue given for each syllable and for the whole. **b** one such clue. **2** an absurd pretence. [F f. mod.Prov. *charrado* conversation f. *charra* chatter]

■ **2** travesty, absurdity, mockery, farce, parody, nonsense.

charas /chaárəss/ *n.* a narcotic resin from the flower-heads of hemp; cannabis resin. [Hindi]

charcoal /chaárkōl/ *n.* **1 a** an amorphous form of carbon consisting of a porous black residue from partially burnt wood, bones, etc. **b** (usu. in *pl.*) a piece of this used for drawing. **2** a drawing in charcoal. **3** (in full **charcoal grey**) a dark grey colour. □ **charcoal biscuit** a biscuit containing wood-charcoal to aid digestion. [ME COAL = charcoal: first element perh. *chare* turn (cf. CHAR[1], CHAR[2])]

chard /chaard/ *n.* a kind of beet, *Beta vulgaris*, with edible broad white leaf-stalks and green blades. Also called *seakale beet*. [F *carde*, and *chardon* thistle: cf. CARDOON]

Chardonnay /shaárdonay/ *n.* **1** a variety of white grape used for making champagne and other wines. **2** the vine on which this grape grows. **3** a wine made from Chardonnay grapes. [F]

charge /chaarj/ *v.* & *n.* ● *v.* **1** *tr.* **a** ask (an amount) as a price (*charges £5 a ticket*). **b** ask (a person) for an amount as a price (*you forgot to charge me*). **2** *tr.* **a** (foll. by *to*, *up to*) debit the cost of to (a person or account) (*charge it to my account*; *charge it up to me*). **b** debit (a person or an account) (*bought a new car and charged the company*). **3** *tr.* **a** (often foll. by *with*) accuse (of an offence) (*charged him with theft*). **b** (foll. by *that* + clause) make an accusation that. **4** *tr.* (foll. by *to* + infin.) instruct or urge. **5** (foll. by *with*) **a** *tr.* entrust with. **b** *refl.* undertake. **6 a** *intr.* make a rushing attack; rush headlong. **b** *tr.* make a rushing attack on; throw oneself against. **7** *tr.* (often foll. by *up*) **a** give an electric charge to (a body). **b** store energy in (a battery). **8** *tr.* (often foll. by *with*) load or fill (a vessel, gun, etc.) to the full or proper extent. **9** *tr.* (usu. as **charged** *adj.*) **a** (foll. by *with*) saturated with (*air charged with vapour*). **b** (usu. foll. by *with*) pervaded (with strong feelings etc.) (*atmosphere charged with emotion; a charged atmosphere*). • *n.* **1 a** a price asked for goods or services. **b** a financial liability or commitment. **2** an accusation, esp. against a prisoner brought to trial. **3 a** a task, duty, or commission. **b** care, custody, responsible possession. **c** a person or thing entrusted; a minister's congregation. **4 a** an impetuous rush or attack, esp. in a battle. **b** the signal for this. **5** the appropriate amount of material to be put into a receptacle, mechanism, etc. at one time, esp. of explosive for a gun. **6 a** a property of matter that is a consequence of the interaction between its constituent particles and exists in a positive or negative form, causing electrical phenomena. **b** the quantity of this carried by a body. **c** energy stored chemically for conversion into electricity. **d** the process of charging a battery. **7** an exhortation; directions, orders. **8** a burden or load. **9** *Heraldry* a device; a bearing. □ **charge account** *US* a credit account at a shop etc. **charge card** a credit card for which the account must be paid in full when a statement is issued. **charge-hand** *Brit.* a worker, ranking below a foreman, in charge of others on a particular job. **charge-nurse** *Brit.* a nurse in charge of a ward etc. **charge-sheet** *Brit.* a record of cases and charges made at a police station. **free of charge** gratis. **give a person in charge** hand a person over to the police. **in charge** having command. **lay to a person's charge** accuse a person of. **put a person on a charge** charge a person with a specified offence. **return to the charge** begin again, esp. in argument. **take charge** (often foll. by *of*) assume control or direction. □□ **chargeable** *adj.* [ME f. OF *charger* f. LL *car(ri)care* load f. L *carrus* CAR]

■ *v.* **1 a** ask, demand, claim, require, expect. **b** bill, invoice. **2 a** (*charge to*) put on a person's account, put down *or* write to a person's account, chalk up to, *Brit.* put on the slate of. **3** accuse, indict, impeach, arraign, incriminate, inculpate; allege; assert, claim, hold, asseverate, maintain, contend. **4** instruct, command, order, direct, tell, enjoin, exhort, urge, press, push, beg, call on, *archaic or literary* bid. **5 a** entrust, trust. **b** (*charge oneself with*) see UNDERTAKE 1. **6 a** bear down; see also RUSH[1] *v.* 1. **b** rush at, attack, assault, storm, assail, set upon, come at, descend upon. **9** fill, imbue, load, instil, saturate, steep, suffuse, infuse, surcharge, impregnate, permeate. • *n.* **1 a** price, fee, cost, payment, rate, tariff, fare, toll, *sl.* damage. **b** debt, debit, expense, assessment, liability. **2** accusation, imputation, indictment, allegation, complaint, *Law* information, *Brit. Law* plaint. **3 a** see OBLIGATION 2. **b** care, custody, protection, safe keeping, keeping, trust, guardianship, wardship, custodianship; supervision, jurisdiction, control, guidance, leadership, direction. **c** concern, responsibility; protégé; flock, congregation. **4 a** attack, onset, assault, sally, sortie, going forth, raid, foray. **7** order(s), mandate, injunction, precept, command, dictate, direction, instruction, demand, exhortation. **8** see LOAD *n.* 1. □ **free of charge** see FREE *adj.* 7. **in charge** (*be in charge*) see *call the shots, have the initiative* (INITIATIVE). **take charge** see HEAD *v.* 2.

chargé d'affaires /shaárzhay dafáir/ *n.* (also **chargé**) (*pl.* **chargés** /*pronunc.* same/) **1** an ambassador's deputy. **2** an envoy to a minor country. [F, = in charge (of affairs)]

■ see MINISTER *n.* 1, 3.

charger[1] /chaárjər/ *n.* **1 a** a cavalry horse. **b** *poet.* any horse. **2** an apparatus for charging a battery. **3** a person or thing that charges.

■ **1** see MOUNT[1] *n.* 3.

charger[2] /chaárjər/ *n. archaic* a large flat dish. [ME f. AF *chargeour*]

■ see PLATE *n.* 1a.

chariot /chárriət/ *n.* & *v.* • *n.* **1** *hist.* **a** a two-wheeled vehicle drawn by horses, used in ancient warfare and racing. **b** a four-wheeled carriage with back seats only. **2** *poet.* a stately or triumphal vehicle. • *v.tr. literary* convey in or as in a chariot. [ME f. OF, augment. of *char* CAR]

charioteer /chárriəteér/ *n.* a chariot-driver.

charisma /kərízmə/ *n.* (*pl.* **charismata** /-mətə/) **1 a** the ability to inspire followers with devotion and enthusiasm. **b** an attractive aura; great charm. **2** a divinely conferred power or talent. [eccl.L f. Gk *kharisma* f. *kharis* favour, grace]

■ **1** see APPEAL *n.* 4.

charismatic /kárrizmáttik/ *adj.* **1** having charisma; inspiring enthusiasm. **2** (of Christian worship) characterized by spontaneity, ecstatic utterances, etc. □ **charismatic movement** a neo-pentecostal movement affecting Roman Catholic, Anglican, and other Christian Churches. □□ **charismatically** *adv.*

■ **1** see MAGNETIC.

charitable /chárritəb'l/ *adj.* **1** generous in giving to those in need. **2** of, relating to, or connected with a charity or charities. **3** apt to judge favourably of persons, acts, and motives. □□ **charitableness** *n.* **charitably** *adv.* [ME f. OF f. *charité* CHARITY]

■ **1** generous, liberal, bountiful, munificent, beneficent, unselfish, open-handed, magnanimous, philanthropic, public-spirited, well-meaning, good, eleemosynary, *poet.* bounteous; free, unsparing, unstinting, ungrudging. **3** sympathetic, magnaminous, well-disposed, lenient, tolerant, forgiving, indulgent, understanding, compassionate, humane, considerate, non-judgemental, uncritical.

charity /chárriti/ *n.* (*pl.* **-ies**) **1 a** giving voluntarily to those in need; alms-giving. **b** the help, esp. money, so given. **2** an institution or organization for helping those in need. **3 a** kindness, benevolence. **b** tolerance in judging others. **c** love of one's fellow men. □ **Charity Commission** (in the UK) a board established to control charitable trusts. [OE f. OF *charité* f. L *caritas -tatis* f. *carus* dear]

■ **1 b** help, aid, support, assistance; relief, benefit, Welfare, *Brit. colloq.* dole; donation, contribution, largesse, *hist.* alms. **3 a** generosity, benevolence, kindness, charitableness, kind-heartedness, munificence, liberality, open-handedness, magnanimity, beneficence, largesse, bounty, philanthropy, unselfishness, altruism, humanity, humanitarianism, good will. **b** leniency, tolerance, big-heartedness, magnanimity, indulgence, considerateness, consideration, compassion, understanding, sympathy.

charivari /shaárivaári/ *n.* (also **shivaree** /shívvəreé/) **1** a serenade of banging saucepans etc. to a newly-married couple. **2** a medley of sounds; a hubbub. [F, = serenade with pans, trays, etc., to an unpopular person]

■ **2** see NOISE *n.* 1, 2.

charlady /chaárlaydi/ *n.* (*pl.* **-ies**) = CHARWOMAN.

charlatan /shaárlət'n/ *n.* a person falsely claiming a special knowledge or skill. □□ **charlatanism** *n.* **charlatanry** *n.* [F f. It. *ciarlatano* f. *ciarlare* babble]

■ see FRAUD 3.

Charles' Law /chaárlz/ (also **Charles's Law** /chaárlziz/) *n. Chem.* the law stating that the volume of an ideal gas at constant pressure is directly proportional to the absolute temperature. [J. A. C. *Charles*, Fr. scientist d. 1823]

Charles's Wain /chaárlziz wáyn/ *n.* the constellation Ursa Major or its seven bright stars. Also called PLOUGH. [OE *Carles wægn* the wain of Carl (Charles the Great, Charlemagne), perh. by assoc. of the star Arcturus with legends of King Arthur and Charlemagne]

charleston /chaárlstən/ *n.* & *v.* (also **Charleston**) ● *n.* a lively American dance of the 1920s with side-kicks from the knee. ● *v.intr.* dance the charleston. [*Charleston* in S. Carolina, US]

charley horse /chaárli/ *n. US sl.* stiffness or cramp in an arm or leg. [19th c.: orig. uncert.]

charlie /chaárli/ *n. Brit. sl.* **1** a fool. **2** (in *pl.*) a woman's breasts. [dimin. of the name *Charles*]
■ **2** (*charlies*) see BREAST *n.* 1a.

charlock /chaárlok/ *n.* a wild mustard, *Sinapis arvensis*, with yellow flowers. Also called *field mustard*. [OE *cerlic*, of unkn. orig.]

charlotte /shaárlot/ *n.* a pudding made of stewed fruit with a casing or layers or covering of bread, sponge cake, biscuits, or breadcrumbs (*apple charlotte*). □ **charlotte russe** /rōōss/ custard etc. enclosed in sponge cake or a casing of sponge fingers. [F]

charm /chaarm/ *n.* & *v.* ● *n.* **1 a** the power or quality of giving delight or arousing admiration. **b** fascination, attractiveness. **c** (usu. in *pl.*) an attractive or enticing quality. **2** a trinket on a bracelet etc. **3 a** an object, act, or word(s) supposedly having occult or magic power; a spell. **b** a thing worn to avert evil etc.; an amulet. **4** *Physics* a property of matter manifested by some elementary particles. ● *v.tr.* **1** delight, captivate (*charmed by the performance*). **2** influence or protect as if by magic (*leads a charmed life*). **3 a** gain by charm (*charmed agreement out of him*). **b** influence by charm (*charmed her into consenting*). **4** cast a spell on, bewitch. □ **charm-bracelet** a bracelet hung with small trinkets. **like a charm** perfectly, wonderfully. □□ **charmer** *n.* [ME f. OF *charme*, *charmer* f. L *carmen* song]
■ *n.* **1 a, b** attractiveness, appeal, fascination, attraction, allure, magnetism, draw, pull, desirability, winsomeness, seductiveness. **3 a** spell, incantation, conjuration. **b** amulet, talisman, good-luck piece, periapt, phylactery, ju-ju, churinga; horseshoe, toadstone, rabbit's foot. ● *v.* **1** see CAPTIVATE, DELIGHT *v.* 1. **3 b** influence, seduce, coax, disarm, wheedle, hypnotize, mesmerize; see also BEGUILE 3. **4** put *or* cast a spell on, bewitch, bedevil, voodoo, possess, *Austral.* point the bone at, *esp. US* hoodoo, *US* hex, *archaic* witch. □ **like a charm** successfully, perfectly, wonderfully, marvellously, especially well; like a dream, like clockwork, without a hitch *or* hiccup. □□ **charmer** enchanter, enchantress, sorcerer, sorceress, magician; vamp, siren, temptress, seductress; seducer, Romeo, Don Juan, Lothario, Casanova, lady-killer, ladies' man; smooth talker, beguiler, flatterer, wheedler, *colloq.* smoothie.

charmeuse /shaarmőz/ *n.* a soft smooth silky dress-fabric. [F, fem. of *charmeur* (as CHARM)]

charming /chaárming/ *adj.* **1** delightful, attractive, pleasing. **2** (often as *int.*) *iron.* expressing displeasure or disapproval. □□ **charmingly** *adv.*
■ **1** see DELIGHTFUL.

charmless /chaármliss/ *adj.* lacking charm; unattractive. □□ **charmlessly** *adv.* **charmlessness** *n.*

charnel-house /chaárn'lhowss/ *n.* a house or vault in which dead bodies or bones are piled. [ME & OF *charnel* burying-place f. med.L *carnale* f. LL *carnalis* CARNAL]

Charollais /shárrəlay/ *n.* (also **Charolais**) (*pl.* same) **1** an animal of a breed of large white beef-cattle. **2** this breed. [Monts du *Charollais* in E. France]

charpoy /chaárpoy/ *n. Ind.* a light bedstead. [Hind. *chārpāī*]

charr var. of CHAR[4].

chart /chaart/ *n.* & *v.* ● *n.* **1** a geographical map or plan, esp. for navigation by sea or air. **2** a sheet of information in the form of a table, graph, or diagram. **3** (usu. in *pl.*) *colloq.* a listing of the currently most popular gramophone records. ● *v.tr.* make a chart of, map. [F *charte* f. L *charta* CARD[1]]
■ *n.* **1** plan, map. **2** map, table, tabulation, graph, diagram. ● *v.* plot, map (out), chart out, draw, mark (out); delineate, sketch (out), trace, rough out, outline, frame, draft, particularize, spell out.

chartbuster /chaártbustər/ *n. colloq.* a best-selling popular song, record, etc.

charter /chaártər/ *n.* & *v.* ● *n.* **1 a** a written grant of rights, by the sovereign or legislature, esp. the creation of a borough, company, university, etc. **b** a written constitution or description of an organization's functions etc. **2** a contract to hire an aircraft, ship, etc., for a special purpose. **3** = CHARTER-PARTY. ● *v.tr.* **1** grant a charter to. **2** hire (an aircraft, ship, etc.). □ **chartered accountant, engineer, librarian, surveyor**, etc. *Brit.* a member of a professional body that has a royal charter. **chartered libertine** a person allowed to do as he or she pleases. **charter flight** a flight by a chartered aircraft. **charter-member** an original member of a society, corporation, etc. **Great Charter** = MAGNA CARTA. □□ **charterer** *n.* [ME f. OF *chartre* f. L *chartula* dimin. of *charta* CARD[1]]
■ *n.* **1 a** document, contract, compact, agreement, covenant, accord, bill of rights; permit, permission, licence, grant, franchise, diploma, patent. **b** constitution, rules, code, law. **2** lease, contract. ● *v.* **1** license, authorize, commission, franchise, approve, certify, qualify, sanction. **2** let, lease, rent, hire, engage, contract, reserve, engage, secure.

charter-party /chaártərpaárti/ *n.* (*pl.* **-ies**) a deed between a ship-owner and a merchant for the hire of a ship and the delivery of cargo. [F *charte partie* f. med.L *charta partita* divided charter, indenture]

Chartism /chaártiz'm/ *n. hist.* the principles of the UK Parliamentary reform movement of 1837–48. □□ **Chartist** *n.* [L *charta* charter + -ISM: name taken from the manifesto 'People's Charter']

chartreuse /shaartrőz/ *n.* **1** a pale green or yellow liqueur of brandy and aromatic herbs etc. **2** the pale yellow or pale green colour of this. **3** a dish of fruit enclosed in jelly etc. [La Grande *Chartreuse* (Carthusian monastery near Grenoble)]

charwoman /chaárwōōmmən/ *n.* (*pl.* **-women**) a woman employed as a cleaner in houses or offices.
■ see SERVANT 1.

chary /cháiri/ *adj.* (**charier, chariest**) **1** cautious, wary (*chary of employing such people*). **2** sparing; ungenerous (*chary of giving praise*). **3** shy. □□ **charily** *adv.* **chariness** *n.* [OE *cearig*]
■ **1** see WARY. **3** see SHY *adj.* 2.

Charybdis see SCYLLA AND CHARYBDIS.

Chas. *abbr.* Charles.

chase[1] /chayss/ *v.* & *n.* ● *v.* **1** *tr.* pursue in order to catch. **2** *tr.* (foll. by *from*, *out of*, *to*, etc.) drive. **3** *intr.* **a** (foll. by *after*) hurry in pursuit of (a person). **b** (foll. by *round* etc.) *colloq.* act or move about hurriedly. **4** *tr.* (usu. foll. by *up*) *colloq.* pursue (overdue work, payment, etc. or the person responsible for it). **5** *tr. colloq.* **a** try to attain. **b** court persistently and openly. ● *n.* **1** pursuit. **2** unenclosed hunting-land. **3** (prec. by *the*) hunting, esp. as a sport. **4** an animal etc. that is pursued. **5** = STEEPLECHASE. □ **go and chase oneself** (usu. in *imper.*) *colloq.* depart. [ME f. OF *chace chacier*, ult. f. L *capere* take]
■ *v.* **1, 4** chase after, run after, follow, pursue, track, hunt, go (out) after, take off after, trail, *colloq.* tail. **2** drive, hound; expel, throw *or* cast out; (*chase away* or *off*, etc.) rout, put to rout, put to flight, *colloq.* send packing. **3 a** (*chase after*) see CHASE[1] *v.* 1, 4 above. **b** see RUSH[1] *v.* 1. **5 a** see PURSUE 1, 5. **b** see COURT *v.* 1b. ● *n.* **1** search, hunt, tracking, stalking; pursuance. □ **go and chase oneself** see DEPART 1.

chase[2] /chayss/ *v.tr.* emboss or engrave (metal). [app. f. earlier *enchase* f. F *enchâsser* (as EN-[1], CASE[2])]

chase[3] /chayss/ *n. Printing* a metal frame holding composed type. [F *châsse* f. L *capsa* CASE[2]]

chase[4] /chayss/ *n.* **1** the part of a gun enclosing the bore. **2** a trench or groove cut to receive a pipe etc. [F *chas* enclosed space f. Prov. *ca(u)s* f. med.L *capsum* thorax]

chaser /cháysər/ *n.* **1** a person or thing that chases. **2** a horse for steeplechasing. **3** *colloq.* a drink taken after another of a different kind, e.g. beer after spirits. **4** *US colloq.* an amorous pursuer of women.

chasm /kázz'm/ *n.* **1** a deep fissure or opening in the earth, rock, etc. **2** a wide difference of feeling, interests, etc.; a gulf. **3** *archaic* a hiatus. □□ **chasmic** *adj.* [L *chasma* f. Gk *khasma* gaping hollow]
■ **1** see GORGE *n.* 1. **3** see SPLIT *n.* 2.

chasse /shaass/ *n.* a liqueur taken after coffee etc. [F f. *chasser* CHASE[1]]

chassé /shássay/ *n.* & *v.* ● *n.* a gliding step in dancing. ● *v.intr.* (***chasséd***; ***chasséing***) make this step. [F, = chasing]

chassis /shássi/ *n.* (*pl.* same /-siz/) **1** the base-frame of a motor vehicle, carriage, etc. **2** a frame to carry radio etc. components. [F *châssis* ult. f. L *capsa* CASE[2]]
■ see FRAME *n.* 2.

chaste /chayst/ *adj.* **1** abstaining from extramarital, or from all, sexual intercourse. **2** (of behaviour, speech, etc.) pure, virtuous, decent. **3** (of artistic etc. style) simple, unadorned. □ **chaste-tree** an ornamental shrub, *Vitex agnus-castus*, with blue or white flowers. □□ **chastely** *adv.* **chasteness** *n.* [ME f. OF f. L *castus*]
■ **1** pure, virginal, virgin, vestal, immaculate, celibate, abstinent, continent, virtuous, undefiled, stainless, unstained, unsullied, unblemished, *archaic or poet.* maiden, maidenly. **2** pure, innocent, platonic, uncorrupted, sinless, blameless, immaculate, spotless, stainless, unstained, unsullied, unblemished, untarnished, untainted, undefiled, virtuous, decent, clean, flawless, faultless, irreproachable, pristine, good, wholesome, moral, honest, *colloq.* white. **3** simple, unadorned, undecorated, unembellished, subdued, restrained, austere, severe, pure, clean.

chasten /cháys'n/ *v.tr.* **1** (esp. as **chastening, chastened** *adjs.*) subdue, restrain (*a chastening experience*; *chastened by his failure*). **2** discipline, punish. **3** moderate. □□ **chastener** *n.* [obs. *chaste* (v.) f. OF *chastier* f. L *castigare* CASTIGATE]
■ **1** subdue, humble, bring *or* pull down, take down a peg, shame, mortify; curb, restrain, control, check, repress, suppress. **2** discipline, correct, chastise, punish, penalize; see also CASTIGATE. **3** temper, tame, quieten *or* tone down, mellow, soften; see also MODERATE *v.* 1.

chastise /chastī́z/ *v.tr.* **1** rebuke or reprimand severely. **2** punish, esp. by beating. □□ **chastisement** *n.* **chastiser** *n.* [ME, app. irreg. formed f. obs. verbs *chaste*, *chasty*: see CHASTEN]
■ **1** see REBUKE *v.* **2** punish, beat, thrash, belabour, spank, whip, flog, scourge, birch, cane, flail, strap, give a person a thrashing *or* beating, *colloq.* give a person a good hiding *or* licking, *sl.* tan a person's hide; discipline, chasten, castigate, correct.

chastity /chástiti/ *n.* **1** being chaste. **2** sexual abstinence; virginity. **3** simplicity of style or taste. □ **chastity belt** *hist.* a garment designed to prevent a woman from having sexual intercourse. [ME f. OF *chasteté* f. L *castitas -tatis* f. *castus* CHASTE]
■ **1, 2** purity, continence, virginity, maidenhood, maidenhead, virtue, honour, celibacy, abstinence, abstention, abstemiousness, restraint, self-restraint, forbearance. **3** see SIMPLICITY.

chasuble /cházyoob'l/ *n.* a loose sleeveless usu. ornate outer vestment worn by a priest celebrating Mass or the Eucharist. [ME f. OF *chesible*, later *-uble*, ult. f. L *casula* hooded cloak, little cottage, dimin. of *casa* cottage]

chat[1] /chat/ *v.* & *n.* ● *v.intr.* (**chatted, chatting**) talk in a light familiar way. ● *n.* **1** informal conversation or talk. **2** an instance of this. □ **chat show** *Brit.* a television or radio programme in which celebrities are interviewed informally. **chat up** *Brit. colloq.* chat to, esp. flirtatiously or with an ulterior motive. [ME: shortening of CHATTER]
■ *v.* converse, gossip, talk, chatter, palaver, confabulate, *US* visit, *colloq.* natter, chit-chat, jaw, *colloq. or dial.* yatter, *sl.* chew the fat *or* rag, rap. ● *n.* **1** small talk, gossip, palaver, *bavardage*, *colloq.* chit-chat, gab, *colloq. or dial.* yatter. **2** conversation, colloquy, talk, gossip, confabulation, froth, *US* bull session, visit, *colloq.* confab, natter, *sl.* chin-wag, rap. □ **chat up** flirt *or* dally with, make advances to, make overtures to, seduce, proposition; work on, ingratiate oneself with, court, pay court to, *US* shine up to, *colloq.* butter up, suck up to, soft-soap, sweet-talk.

chat[2] /chat/ *n.* any of various small birds with harsh calls, esp. a stonechat or whinchat or any of certain American or Australian warblers. [prob. imit.]

château /shátt ō/ *n.* (*pl.* **châteaux** /-tōz/) a large French country house or castle, often giving its name to wine made in its neighbourhood. [F f. OF *chastel* CASTLE]
■ see CASTLE *n.* 1b.

chateaubriand /sháttōbreé-ON/ *n.* a thick fillet of beef steak. [Vicomte de *Chateaubriand* (d. 1848), Fr. writer and statesman]

chatelaine /sháttəlayn/ *n.* **1** the mistress of a large house. **2** *hist.* a set of short chains attached to a woman's belt, for carrying keys etc. [F *châtelaine*, fem. of *-ain* lord of a castle, f. med.L *castellanus* CASTELLAN]

chattel /chátt'l/ *n.* (usu. in *pl.*) a moveable possession; any possession or piece of property other than real estate or a freehold. □ **chattel mortgage** *US* the conveyance of chattels by mortgage as security for a debt. **goods and chattels** personal possessions. [ME f. OF *chatel*: see CATTLE]
■ (*chattels*) see EFFECT *n.* 4.

chatter /cháttər/ *v.* & *n.* ● *v.intr.* **1** talk quickly, incessantly, trivially, or indiscreetly. **2** (of a bird) emit short quick notes. **3** (of the teeth) click repeatedly together (usu. from cold). **4** (of a tool) clatter from vibration. ● *n.* **1** chattering talk or sounds. **2** the vibration of a tool. □□ **chatterer** *n.* **chattery** *adj.* [ME: imit.]
■ *v.* **1** prattle, gabble, jabber, prate, twaddle, blather, tattle, tittle-tattle, patter, gibber, clack, blab, blabber, drivel on, run *or* go on, talk the hind leg off a donkey, *Brit.* talk nineteen to the dozen, *colloq.* gab, jaw, natter, witter, yap, *colloq. or dial.* yatter, yammer, *esp. Austral. colloq.* mag, *esp. Brit. colloq.* waffle, *Brit. colloq.* rabbit on, *sl. derog.* yack. **3** clatter, rattle, shake, shiver, vibrate, jiggle. ● *n.* **1** prattle, prate, prating, patter, gossip, palaver, chattering, babble, twaddle, blather, tattle, rattle, tittle-tattle, *bavardage*, *colloq.* chit-chat, gab, natter, *colloq. or dial.* yatter, *sl.* gas, *sl. derog.* yack.

chatterbox /cháttərboks/ *n.* a talkative person.
■ blabber, babbler, natterer, chatterer, prater, gossip, blatherskite, *colloq.* blab, big-mouth.

chatty /chátti/ *adj.* (**chattier, chattiest**) **1** fond of chatting; talkative. **2** resembling chat; informal and lively (*a chatty letter*). □□ **chattily** *adv.* **chattiness** *n.*
■ **1** see TALKATIVE.

Chaucerian /chawseériən/ *adj.* & *n.* ● *adj.* of or relating to the English poet Chaucer (d. 1400) or his style. ● *n.* a student of Chaucer.

chaud-froid /shōfrwaá/ *n.* a dish of cold cooked meat or fish in jelly or sauce. [F f. *chaud* hot + *froid* cold]

chauffeur /shṓfər, -fṓr/ *n.* & *v.* ● *n.* (*fem.* **chauffeuse** /-fṓz/) a person employed to drive a private or hired motor car. ● *v.tr.* drive (a car or a person) as a chauffeur. [F, = stoker]

chaulmoogra /chawlmoógrə/ *n.* any tree of the genus *Hydnocarpus*, esp. *H. wightiana*, with seeds yielding an oil formerly used in the treatment of leprosy. [Bengali]

chautauqua /chawtáwkwə, shaw-/ *n.* *US* a summer school or similar educational course. [*Chautauqua* in New York State]

chauvinism /shṓviniz'm/ *n.* **1** exaggerated or aggressive patriotism. **2** excessive or prejudiced support or loyalty for one's cause or group or sex (*male chauvinism*). [*Chauvin*, a

Napoleonic veteran in the Cogniards' *Cocarde Tricolore* (1831)]
■ **1** see *jingoism* (JINGO).

chauvinist /shṓvinist/ *n.* **1** a person exhibiting chauvinism. **2** (in full **male chauvinist**) a man showing excessive loyalty to men and prejudice against women. □□ **chauvinistic** /-nístik/ *adj.* **chauvinistically** /-nístikəli/ *adv.*

Ch.B. *abbr.* Bachelor of Surgery. [L *Chirurgiae Baccalaureus*]

cheap /cheep/ *adj.* & *adv.* ● *adj.* **1** low in price; worth more than its cost (*a cheap holiday*; *cheap labour*). **2** charging low prices; offering good value (*a cheap restaurant*). **3** of poor quality; inferior (*cheap housing*). **4 a** costing little effort or acquired by discreditable means and hence of little worth (*cheap popularity*; *a cheap joke*). **b** contemptible; despicable (*a cheap criminal*). ● *adv.* cheaply (*got it cheap*). □ **cheap and nasty** of low cost and bad quality. **dirt cheap** very cheap. **feel cheap** feel ashamed or contemptible. **on the cheap** cheaply. □□ **cheapish** *adj.* **cheaply** *adv.* **cheapness** *n.* [obs. phr. *good cheap* f. *cheap* a bargain f. OE *cēap* barter, ult. f. L *caupo* innkeeper]
■ *adj.* **1, 2** inexpensive, low-priced, low-cost, cut-price, cut-rate, reasonable, budget, *sl.* cheapo. **3** shoddy, shabby, tawdry, tatty, seedy, base, pinchbeck, cheapjack; inferior, low-grade, poor, second-rate, trashy, worthless, chintzy, *Brit.* tinpot, *Brit. colloq.* twopenny, twopenny-halfpenny, *US colloq.* two-bit, tacky, *sl.* cheesy, tinhorn. **4** see LOW[1] *adj.* 11. ● *adv.* inexpensively, cheaply, on the cheap, *colloq.* for a song, for peanuts. □ **on the cheap** see CHEAP *adv.* above.

cheapen /cheép'n/ *v.tr.* & *intr.* make or become cheap or cheaper; depreciate, degrade.
■ see DEPRECIATE 1.

cheapjack /cheépjak/ *n.* & *adj.* ● *n.* a seller of inferior goods at low prices. ● *adj.* inferior, shoddy. [CHEAP + JACK[1]]
■ *n.* see PEDLAR. ● *adj.* see SHODDY *adj.* 1.

cheapo /cheépō/ *attrib.adj.* *sl.* cheap.

cheapskate /cheépskayt/ *n.* esp. *US colloq.* a mean or contemptible person.
■ see MISER.

cheat /cheet/ *v.* & *n.* ● *v.* **1** *tr.* **a** (often foll. by *into*, *out of*) deceive or trick (*cheated into parting with his savings*). **b** (foll. by *of*) deprive of (*cheated of a chance to reply*). **2** *intr.* gain unfair advantage by deception or breaking rules, esp. in a game or examination. **3** *tr.* avoid (something undesirable) by luck or skill (*cheated the bad weather*). **4** *tr.* *archaic* divert attention from, beguile (time, tedium, etc.). ● *n.* **1** a person who cheats. **2** a trick, fraud, or deception. **3** an act of cheating. □ **cheat on** *colloq.* be sexually unfaithful to. □□ **cheatingly** *adv.* [ME *chete* f. *achete*, var. of ESCHEAT]
■ *v.* **1 a** swindle, deceive, trick, fleece, defraud, euchre, hoodwink, take in, beguile, dupe, rook, flimflam, *archaic* chicane, *colloq.* finagle, diddle, rip off, bamboozle, two-time, take for a ride, do down, *literary* cozen, *sl.* con, fiddle, bilk, chisel, cross, double-cross, clip, *US sl.* bunco. **b** (*cheat of*) deny, refuse, deprive of, strip *or* divest of, rob of, do out of. **2** move the goalposts, break the rules. ● *n.* **1** cheater, swindler, deceiver, impostor, faker, trickster, confidence man, charlatan, mountebank, rogue, card-sharp(er), sharper, flimflammer, *US* four-flusher, *colloq.* shark, sharp, two-timer, *Brit. colloq.* twister, *sl.* fiddler, con man, bilker, chiseller, *Austral. sl.* shicer, spieler, magsman. **2** see TRICK *n.* 1. □ **cheat on** be unfaithful to, *colloq.* two-time.

cheater /cheétər/ *n.* **1** a person who cheats. **2** (in *pl.*) *US sl.* spectacles.

check[1] /chek/ *v.*, *n.*, & *int.* ● *v.* **1** *tr.* (also *absol.*) **a** examine the accuracy, quality, or condition of. **b** (often foll. by *that* + clause) make sure; verify; establish to one's satisfaction (*checked that the doors were locked*; *checked the train times*). **2** *tr.* **a** stop or slow the motion of; curb, restrain (*progress was checked by bad weather*). **b** *colloq.* find fault with; rebuke. **3** *tr.* *Chess* move a piece into a position that directly threatens (the opposing king). **4** *intr.* *US* agree or correspond when compared. **5** *tr.* *US* mark with a tick etc. **6** *tr.* *US* deposit (luggage etc.) for storage or dispatch. **7** *intr.* (of hounds) pause to ensure or regain scent. ● *n.* **1** a means or act of testing or ensuring accuracy, quality, satisfactory condition, etc. **2 a** a stopping or slowing of motion; a restraint on action. **b** a rebuff or rebuke. **c** a person or thing that restrains. **3** *Chess* (also as *int.*) **a** the exposure of a king to direct attack from an opposing piece. **b** an announcement of this by the attacking player. **4** *US* a bill in a restaurant. **5** esp. *US* a token of identification for left luggage etc. **6** *US Cards* a counter used in various games. **7** a temporary loss of the scent in hunting. **8** a crack or flaw in timber. **9** *US* = TICK[1] *n.* 3. ● *int.* *US* expressing assent or agreement. □ **check in 1** arrive or register at a hotel, airport, etc. **2** record the arrival of. **check-in** *n.* the act or place of checking in. **check into** register one's arrival at (a hotel etc.). **check-list** a list for reference and verification. **check-nut** = *lock-nut*. **check off** mark on a list etc. as having been examined or dealt with. **check on** examine carefully or in detail; ascertain the truth about; keep a watch on (a person, work done, etc.). **check out 1** (often foll. by *of*) leave a hotel etc. with due formalities. **2** *colloq.* investigate; examine for authenticity or suitability. **check over** examine for errors; verify. **check-rein** a rein attaching one horse's rein to another's bit, or preventing a horse from lowering its head. **check through** inspect or examine exhaustively; verify successive items of. **check up** ascertain, verify, make sure. **check-up** *n.* a thorough (esp. medical) examination. **check up on** = *check on*. **check-valve** a valve allowing flow in one direction only. **in check** under control, restrained. □□ **checkable** *adj.* [ME f. OF *eschequier* play chess, give check to, and OF *eschec*, ult. f. Pers. *šāh* king]
■ *v.* **1** authenticate, verify, confirm, substantiate, validate, corroborate, look into, check over *or* through, check up on, test out, *colloq.* check out; examine, investigate, inspect, scrutinize, make sure of, look at *or* over, pass one's eye over, keep an eye on, monitor, check on, keep track of, oversee, watch; make sure *or* certain, check up, ascertain. **2 a** stop, arrest, halt, hold up, stall; limit, interfere with, stunt; retard, slow, brake, stanch, stem, curb, *archaic or literary* stay; obstruct, block, hinder, hamper, impede, inhibit, thwart, dampen, frustrate; restrain, control, repress, contain, restrict, bridle, rein in, govern, hold in *or* down. **b** see REBUKE *v.* **4** correspond, coincide, agree, tally, accord, concur, match, conform, fit, mesh, chime, *US colloq.* jibe; compare. **5** check off, tick (off), mark. **6** see LEAVE[1] *v.* 10a. ● *n.* **1** control, test, verification, substantiation, authentication, confirmation, validation, corroboration; investigation, examination, inspection, enquiry, look. **2 a** stop, arrest, halt, cessation, discontinuation, discontinuance, *literary* surcease; break, pause, hesitation, interruption, suspension, delay. **b** see REBUKE *n.* **c** restraint, curb, restriction, bridle, control, constraint, hindrance, brake, deterrent, obstruction, impediment, damper, limitation, stint, inhibitor. **4** bill, *US colloq.* tab. **5** token, receipt, counterfoil, stub; voucher, chit, certificate. **6** chip, counter, token. □ **check in 1** register, sign in, enrol; see also ARRIVE 1. **check off** tick (off), mark, check. **check on** see CHECK[1] *v.* 1 above. **check out 1** depart, leave; go. **2** investigate, research, explore, enquire into, look into *or* at *or* over, scrutinize, examine, inspect, probe, sound out, survey, check (up) on, follow up, check, check into, check over, *colloq.* vet, size up; see also CHECK[1] *v.* 1 above. **check over** see CHECK[1] *v.* 1 above. **check through** see CHECK[1] *v.* 1 above. **check up** see CHECK[1] *v.* 1 above. **check-up** examination, *colloq.* going-over.**check up on** see CHECK[1] *v.* 1 above. **in check** under control *or* restraint, back, down; restrained.

check[2] /chek/ *n.* **1** a pattern of small squares. **2** fabric having this pattern. [ME, prob. f. CHEQUER]

check[3] *US* var. of CHEQUE.

checked /chekt/ *adj.* having a check pattern.

checker[1] /chékkər/ *n.* **1** a person or thing that verifies or examines, esp. in a factory etc. **2** *US* a cashier in a supermarket etc.

checker[2] /chékkər/ *n.* **1** var. of CHEQUER. **2** *US* **a** (in *pl.*, usu. treated as *sing.*) the game of draughts. **b** = CHECKERMAN.

checkerberry /chékkərbəri/ *n.* (*pl.* **-ies**) **1** a wintergreen, *Gaultheria procumbens.* **2** the fruit of this plant. [*checkers* berries of service-tree]

checkerboard /chékkərbord/ *n. US* = DRAUGHTBOARD.

checkerman /chékkərman/ *n.* (*pl.* **-men**) each of the 'men' in a game of draughts.

checking account /chékking/ *n. US* a current account at a bank. [CHECK[3]]

checkmate /chékmayt/ *n.* & *v.* ● *n.* **1** (also as *int.*) *Chess* **a** check from which a king cannot escape. **b** an announcement of this. **2** a final defeat or deadlock. ● *v.tr.* **1** *Chess* put into checkmate. **2** defeat; frustrate. [ME f. OF *eschec mat* f. Pers. *šāh māt* the king is dead]

checkout /chékkowt/ *n.* **1** an act of checking out. **2** a point at which goods are paid for in a supermarket etc.

checkpoint /chékpoynt/ *n.* a place, esp. a barrier or manned entrance, where documents, vehicles, etc., are inspected.

checkroom /chékroom, -rōōm/ *n. US* **1** a cloakroom in a hotel or theatre. **2** an office for left luggage etc.

Cheddar /chéddər/ *n.* a kind of firm smooth cheese orig. made in Cheddar in S. England.

cheek /cheek/ *n.* & *v.* ● *n.* **1 a** the side of the face below the eye. **b** the side-wall of the mouth. **2 a** impertinent speech. **b** impertinence; cool confidence (*had the cheek to ask for more*). **3** *sl.* either buttock. **4 a** either of the side-posts of a door etc. **b** either of the jaws of a vice. **c** either of the side-pieces of various parts of machines arranged in lateral pairs. ● *v.tr.* speak impertinently to. □ **cheek-bone** the bone below the eye. **cheek by jowl** close together; intimate. **turn the other cheek** accept attack etc. meekly; refuse to retaliate. [OE *cē(a)ce, cēoce*]
■ **2** see *impertinence* (IMPERTINENT). □ **cheek by jowl** see *side by side*.

cheeky /cheéki/ *adj.* (**cheekier, cheekiest**) impertinent, impudent. □□ **cheekily** *adv.* **cheekiness** *n.*
■ impudent, impertinent, insolent, audacious, disrespectful, rude, uncivil, forward, brazen, pert, saucy, cocky, cocksure, *US* nervy, *colloq.* fresh, lippy, *esp. US colloq.* sassy.

cheep /cheep/ *n.* & *v.* ● *n.* the weak shrill cry of a young bird. ● *v.intr.* make such a cry. [imit.: cf. PEEP[2]]
■ *n.* see PEEP[2] *n.* 1. ● *v.* see PEEP[2] *v.*

cheer /cheer/ *n.* & *v.* ● *n.* **1** a shout of encouragement or applause. **2** mood, disposition (*full of good cheer*). **3** cheerfulness, joy. **4** (in *pl.*; as *int.*) *Brit. colloq.* **a** expressing good wishes on parting. **b** expressing good wishes before drinking. **c** expressing gratitude. ● *v.* **1** *tr.* **a** applaud with shouts. **b** (usu. foll. by *on*) urge or encourage with shouts. **2** *intr.* shout for joy. **3** *tr.* gladden; comfort. □ **cheer-leader** a person who leads cheers of applause etc. **cheer up** make or become less depressed. **three cheers** three successive hurrahs for a person or thing honoured. [ME f. AF *chere* face etc., OF *chiere* f. LL *cara* face f. Gk *kara* head]
■ *n.* **1** shout, cry, whoop, hurrah, hooray. **2** temper, spirit(s), humour, feelings, sentiments, temperament, nature, disposition, frame of mind, mood. **3** cheerfulness, gladness, mirth, joy, gaiety, happiness, buoyancy, light-heartedness, merrymaking, *poet.* blitheness. **4** (*cheers!*) **a** see GOODBYE *int.* **b** see *bottoms up!* (BOTTOM). **c** thank you, thanks, much obliged, *Brit. colloq.* ta. ● *v.* **1 a** applaud, clap, *colloq.* give a person a (big) hand, hail. **b** (*cheer on*) urge (on), encourage, egg on, spur on, goad on; halloo. **2** shout, hurrah, clap; see also APPLAUD 1. **3** gladden, comfort, enliven, cheer up, hearten, console, buoy up, brighten, uplift, encourage, lift up, raise a person's spirits, relieve, *colloq.* buck up. □ **cheer up** brighten, perk up, liven up, *colloq.* buck up; see also CHEER *v.* 3 above.

cheerful /cheérfōōl/ *adj.* **1** in good spirits, noticeably happy (*a cheerful disposition*). **2** bright, pleasant (*a cheerful room*). **3** willing, not reluctant. □□ **cheerfully** *adv.* **cheerfulness** *n.*
■ **1** happy, cheery, jolly, merry, gay, light-hearted, breezy, optimistic, positive, sunny, upbeat, bubbly, joyous, glad, joyful, exuberant, *poet.* gladsome, blithesome, blithe. **2** cheering, bright, enlivening, genial, cheery, gay; pleasant, charming, agreeable, attractive.

cheerio /chírrió/ *int. Brit. colloq.* expressing good wishes on parting or before drinking.
■ see GOODBYE *int.*, *bottoms up!* (BOTTOM).

cheerless /cheérliss/ *adj.* gloomy, dreary, miserable. □□ **cheerlessly** *adv.* **cheerlessness** *n.*
■ see GLOOMY 2, 3.

cheerly /cheérli/ *adv.* & *adj.* ● *adv.* esp. *Naut.* heartily, with a will. ● *adj. archaic* cheerful.

cheery /cheéri/ *adj.* (**cheerier, cheeriest**) lively; in good spirits; genial, cheering. □□ **cheerily** *adv.* **cheeriness** *n.*
■ see GENIAL[1] 1.

cheese[1] /cheez/ *n.* **1 a** a food made from the pressed curds of milk. **b** a complete cake of this with rind. **2** a conserve having the consistency of soft cheese (*lemon cheese*). **3** a round flat object, e.g. the heavy flat wooden disc used in skittles. □ **cheese-cutter 1** a knife with a broad curved blade. **2** a device for cutting cheese by pulling a wire through it. **cheese-fly** (*pl.* **-flies**) a small black fly, *Piophila casei*, breeding in cheese. **cheese-head** the squat cylindrical head of a screw etc. **cheese-mite** any mite of the genus *Tyroglyphus* feeding on cheese. **cheese-paring** *adj.* stingy. ● *n.* stinginess. **cheese plant** = *Swiss cheese plant.* **cheese-skipper** = *cheese-fly.* **cheese straw** a thin cheese-flavoured strip of pastry. **hard cheese** *sl.* bad luck. [OE *cēse* etc. ult. f. L *caseus*]
■ □ **cheese-paring** see MISERLY.

cheese[2] /cheez/ *v.tr. Brit. sl.* (as **cheesed** *adj.*) (often foll. by *off*) bored, fed up. □ **cheese it** stop it, leave off. [19th c.: orig. unkn.]
■ (**cheesed**) see DISGRUNTLED.

cheese[3] /cheez/ *n.* (also **big cheese**) *sl.* an important person. [perh. f. Hind. *chīz* thing]

cheeseboard /cheézbord/ *n.* **1** a board from which cheese is served. **2** a selection of cheeses.

cheeseburger /cheézburgər/ *n.* a hamburger with cheese in or on it.

cheesecake /cheézkayk/ *n.* **1** a tart filled with sweetened curds etc. **2** *sl.* the portrayal of women in a sexually attractive manner.

cheesecloth /cheézkloth/ *n.* thin loosely woven cloth, used orig. for wrapping cheese.

cheesemonger /cheézmunggər/ *n.* a dealer in cheese, butter, etc.

cheesewood /cheézwōōd/ *n.* **1** an Australian tree of the genus *Pittosporum.* **2** its hard yellowish wood.

cheesy /cheézi/ *adj.* (**cheesier, cheesiest**) **1** like cheese in taste, smell, appearance, etc. **2** *sl.* inferior; cheap and nasty. □□ **cheesiness** *n.*
■ **2** see INFERIOR *adj.* 2.

cheetah /cheétə/ *n.* a swift-running feline, *Acinonyx jubatus*, with a leopard-like spotted coat. [Hindi *cītā*, perh. f. Skr. *citraka* speckled]

chef /shef/ *n.* a (usu. male) cook, esp. the chief cook in a restaurant etc. [F, = head]

chef-d'œuvre /shaydővrə/ *n.* (*pl.* ***chefs-d'œuvre*** /*pronunc.* same/) a masterpiece. [F]
■ see MASTERPIECE.

cheiro- *comb. form* var. of CHIRO-.

chela[1] /keélə/ *n.* (*pl.* **chelae** /-lee/) a prehensile claw of crabs, lobsters, scorpions, etc. [mod.L f. L *chele*, or Gk *khēlē* claw]

chela[2] /cháylə/ *n.* **1** (in esoteric Buddhism) a novice qualifying for initiation. **2** a disciple; a pupil. [Hindi, = servant]

chelate /kéelayt/ *n.*, *adj.*, & *v.* ● *n. Chem.* a usu. organometallic compound containing a bonded ring of atoms including a metal atom. ● *adj.* **1** *Chem.* of a chelate. **2** *Zool.* & *Anat.* of or having chelae. ● *v.intr. Chem.* form a chelate. □□ **chelation** /-láysh'n/ *n.*

Chellean /shélliən/ *adj. Archaeol.* = ABBEVILLIAN. [F *chelléen* f. *Chelles* near Paris]

chelonian /kilṓniən/ *n.* & *adj.* ● *n.* any reptile of the order Chelonia, including turtles, terrapins, and tortoises, having a shell of bony plates covered with horny scales. ● *adj.* of or relating to this order. [mod.L *Chelonia* f. Gk *khelōnē* tortoise]

Chelsea bun /chélsi/ *n.* a kind of currant bun in the form of a flat spiral. [*Chelsea* in London]

Chelsea pensioner /chélsi/ *n.* an inmate of the Chelsea Royal Hospital for old or disabled soldiers.

Chelsea ware /chélsi/ *n.* any of various soft-paste porcelains made at Chelsea in the 18th c.

chemi- *comb. form* var. of CHEMO-.

chemical /kémmik'l/ *adj.* & *n.* ● *adj.* of, made by, or employing chemistry or chemicals. ● *n.* a substance obtained or used in chemistry. □ **chemical bond** the force holding atoms together in a molecule or crystal. **chemical engineer** one engaged in chemical engineering, esp. professionally. **chemical engineering** the design, manufacture, and operation of industrial chemical plants. **chemical reaction** a process that involves change in the structure of atoms, molecules, or ions. **chemical warfare** warfare using poison gas and other chemicals. **fine chemicals** chemicals of high purity usu. used in small amounts. **heavy chemicals** bulk chemicals used in industry and agriculture. □□ **chemically** *adv.* [*chemic* alchemic f. F *chimique* or mod.L *chimicus*, *chymicus*, f. med.L *alchymicus*: see ALCHEMY]

chemico- /kémmikō/ *comb. form* chemical; chemical and (*chemico-physical*).

chemiluminescence /kémmiloōminéss'nss, -lyoōmin éss'nss/ *n.* the emission of light during a chemical reaction. □□ **chemiluminescent** *adj.* [G *Chemilumineszenz* (as CHEMI-, LUMINESCENCE)]

chemin de fer /shəmán də fáir/ *n.* a form of baccarat. [F, = railway, lit. road of iron]

chemise /shəméez/ *n. hist.* a woman's loose-fitting undergarment or dress hanging straight from the shoulders. [ME f. OF f. LL *camisia* shirt]

■ see SHIFT *n.* 4.

chemisorption /kémmisórpsh'n/ *n.* adsorption by chemical bonding. [CHEMI- + ADSORPTION (see ADSORB)]

chemist /kémmist/ *n.* **1** *Brit.* **a** a dealer in medicinal drugs, usu. also selling other medical goods and toiletries. **b** an authorized dispenser of medicines. **2** a person practising or trained in chemistry. [earlier *chymist* f. F *chimiste* f. mod.L *chimista* f. *alchimista* ALCHEMIST (see ALCHEMY)]

■ **1b** see PHARMACIST.

chemistry /kémmistri/ *n.* (*pl.* **-ies**) **1** the study of the elements and the compounds they form and the reactions they undergo. **2** any complex (esp. emotional) change or process (*the chemistry of fear*). **3** *colloq.* a person's personality or temperament.

chemo- /kéemō/ *comb. form* (also **chemi-** /kémmi/) chemical.

chemosynthesis /kéeməsínthisiss/ *n.* the synthesis of organic compounds by energy derived from chemical reactions.

chemotherapy /kéeməthérrəpi/ *n.* the treatment of disease, esp. cancer, by use of chemical substances. □□ **chemotherapist** *n.*

chemurgy /kémmurji/ *n. US* the chemical and industrial use of organic raw materials. □□ **chemurgic** /-úrjik/ *adj.* [CHEMO-, after *metallurgy*]

chenille /shənéel/ *n.* **1** a tufty velvety cord or yarn, used in trimming furniture etc. **2** fabric made from this. [F, = hairy caterpillar f. L *canicula* dimin. of *canis* dog]

cheongsam /chiongsám/ *n.* a Chinese woman's garment with a high neck and slit skirt. [Chin.]

cheque /chek/ *n.* (*US* **check**) **1** a written order to a bank to pay the stated sum from the drawer's account. **2** the printed form on which such an order is written. **3** *Austral.* the total sum received by a rural worker at the end of a seasonal contract. □ **cheque-book** a book of forms for writing cheques. **cheque-book journalism** the payment of large sums for exclusive rights to material for (esp. personal) newspaper stories. **cheque card** a card issued by a bank to guarantee the honouring of cheques up to a stated amount. [special use of CHECK¹ to mean 'device for checking the amount of an item']

■ **1, 2** see DRAFT *n.* 2a.

chequer /chékkər/ *n.* & *v.* (also **checker**) ● *n.* **1** (often in *pl.*) a pattern of squares often alternately coloured. **2** (in *pl.*) (usu. as **checkers**) *US* the game of draughts. ● *v.tr.* **1** mark with chequers. **2** variegate; break the uniformity of. **3** (as **chequered** *adj.*) with varied fortunes (*a chequered career*). □ **chequer-board** **1** a chessboard. **2** a pattern resembling it. [ME f. EXCHEQUER]

■ *v.* **3** (**chequered**) variable, varied, varying, mixed, changeable, unsettled, up and down, diversified, heterogeneous; uncertain.

Cherenkov radiation /chiréngkof/ var. of CERENKOV RADIATION.

cherish /chérrish/ *v.tr.* **1** protect or tend (a child, plant, etc.) lovingly. **2** hold dear, cling to (hopes, feelings, etc.). [ME f. OF *cherir* f. *cher* f. L *carus* dear]

■ **1** foster, tend, cultivate, protect, preserve, sustain, nurture, nourish, nurse, cosset. **2** treasure, hold *or* keep dear, prize, cling to, hold to.

chernozem /chérnōzem/ *n.* a fertile black soil rich in humus, found in temperate regions, esp. S. Russia. Also called *black earth*. [Russ. f. *chernyĭ* black + *zemlya* earth]

Cherokee /chérrəki/ *n.* & *adj.* ● *n.* **1 a** an American Indian tribe formerly inhabiting much of the southern US. **b** a member of this tribe. **2** the language of this tribe. ● *adj.* of or relating to the Cherokees or their language. □ **Cherokee rose** a fragrant white rose, *Rosa laevigata*, of the southern US. [Cherokee *Tsálăgĭ*]

cheroot /shəroōt/ *n.* a cigar with both ends open. [F *cheroute* f. Tamil *shuruṭṭu* roll]

cherry /chérri/ *n.* & *adj.* ● *n.* (*pl.* **-ies**) **1 a** a small soft round stone-fruit. **b** any of several trees of the genus *Prunus* bearing this or grown for its ornamental flowers. **2** (in full **cherry wood**) the wood of a cherry. **3** *US sl.* **a** virginity. **b** a virgin. ● *adj.* of a light red colour. □ **cherry brandy** a dark-red liqueur of brandy in which cherries have been steeped. **cherry-laurel** *Brit.* a small evergreen tree, *Prunus laurocerasus*, with white flowers and cherry-like fruits. **cherry-picker** *colloq.* a crane for raising and lowering people. **cherry-pie** **1** a pie made with cherries. **2** a garden heliotrope. **cherry plum** **1** a tree, *Prunus cerasifera*, native to SW Asia, with solitary white flowers and red fruits. **2** the fruit of this tree. **cherry tomato** a miniature tomato with a strong flavour. [ME f. ONF *cherise* (taken as pl.: cf. PEA) f. med.L *ceresia* perh. f. L f. Gk *kerasos*]

■ *adj.* see ROSY 1.

chersonese /kérsəneess/ *n.* a peninsula, esp. the Thracian peninsula west of the Hellespont. [L *chersonesus* f. Gk *khersonēsos* f. *khersos* dry + *nēsos* island]

chert /chert/ *n.* a flintlike form of quartz composed of chalcedony. □□ **cherty** *adj.* [17th c.: orig. unkn.]

cherub /chérrəb/ *n.* **1** (*pl.* **cherubim** /-bim/) an angelic being of the second order of the celestial hierarchy. **2 a** a representation of a winged child or the head of a winged child. **b** a beautiful or innocent child. □□ **cherubic** /chiroōbik/ *adj.* **cherubically** /chiroōbikəli/ *adv.* [ME f. OE *cherubin* and f. Heb. *kᵉrūḇ*, pl. *kᵉrūḇîm*]

chervil /chérvil/ *n.* an umbelliferous plant, *Anthriscus cerefolium*, with small white flowers, used as a herb for flavouring soup, salads, etc. [OE *cerfille* f. L *chaerephylla* f. Gk *khairephullon*]

Ches. *abbr.* Cheshire.

Cheshire /chéshər/ *n.* a kind of firm crumbly cheese, orig. made in Cheshire. □ **like a Cheshire cat** with a broad fixed grin. [*Cheshire*, a county in England]

chess /chess/ *n.* a game for two with 16 men each, played on a chessboard. [ME f. OF *esches* pl. of *eschec* CHECK[1]]

chessboard /chésbord/ *n.* a chequered board of 64 squares on which chess and draughts are played.

chessman /chésman/ *n.* (*pl.* **-men**) any of the 32 pieces and pawns with which chess is played.

chest /chest/ *n.* **1** a large strong box, esp. for storage or transport e.g. of blankets, tea, etc. **2 a** the part of a human or animal body enclosed by the ribs. **b** the front surface of the body from neck to waist. **3** a small cabinet for medicines etc. **4 a** the treasury or financial resources of an institution. **b** the money available from it. □ **chest of drawers** a piece of furniture consisting of a set of drawers in a frame. **chest-voice** the lowest register of the voice in singing or speaking. **get a thing off one's chest** *colloq.* disclose a fact, secret, etc., to relieve one's anxiety about it. **play** (**one's cards, a thing**, etc.) **close to one's chest** *colloq.* be cautious or secretive about. □□ **-chested** *adj.* (in *comb.*). [OE *cest*, *cyst* f. Gmc f. L f. Gk *kistē*]

■ **1** box, coffer, trunk, strongbox, crate, caddy, case, receptacle, container. **2** breast, front; *Anat.* & *Zool.* thorax. **4** coffers, treasury, exchequer; funds, resources, cache. □ **chest of drawers** chest, commode, *US* dresser, bureau, highboy, tallboy, lowboy. **get a thing off one's chest** get a load *or* weight off one's mind, unburden oneself of a thing, say one's piece about a thing, say what is on one's mind. **play one's cards** (or **a thing** etc.) **close to one's chest** give nothing away, not give the game away, keep quiet, say nothing; play it cool *or* safe, keep one's powder dry; be unforthcoming *or* tight-lipped.

chesterfield /chéstərfeeld/ *n.* **1** a sofa with arms and back of the same height and curved outwards at the top. **2** a man's plain overcoat usu. with a velvet collar. [19th-c. Earl of *Chesterfield*]

chestnut /chésnut/ *n.* & *adj.* ● *n.* **1 a** a glossy hard brown edible nut. **b** the tree *Castanea sativa*, bearing flowers in catkins and nuts enclosed in a spiny fruit. Also called *Spanish chestnut* or *sweet chestnut*. **2** any other tree of the genus *Castanea*. **3** = *horse chestnut*. **4** (in full **chestnut-wood**) the heavy wood of any chestnut tree. **5** a horse of a reddish-brown or yellowish-brown colour. **6** *colloq.* a stale joke or anecdote. **7** a small hard patch on a horse's leg. **8** a reddish-brown colour. ● *adj.* of the colour chestnut. □ **liver chestnut** a dark kind of chestnut horse. [obs. *chesten* f. OF *chastaine* f. L *castanea* f. Gk *kastanea*]

■ *n.* **6** see JOKE *n.* 1.

chesty /chésti/ *adj.* (**chestier, chestiest**) **1** *Brit. colloq.* inclined to or symptomatic of chest disease. **2** *colloq.* having a large chest or prominent breasts. **3** *US sl.* arrogant. □□ **chestily** *adv.* **chestiness** *n.*

■ **2** see BUXOM.

chetnik /chétnik/ *n. hist.* a member of a guerrilla force in the Balkans, esp. during the wars of 1914–18 and 1939–45. [Serbian *četnik* f. *četa* band, troop]

cheval-glass /shəválglaass/ *n.* a tall mirror swung on an upright frame. [F *cheval* horse, frame]

chevalier /shévvəleér/ *n.* **1 a** a member of certain orders of knighthood, and of modern French orders, as the Legion of Honour. **b** *archaic* or *hist.* a knight. **2** *hist.* the title of the Old and Young Pretenders. **3** a chivalrous man; a cavalier. [ME f. AF *chevaler*, OF *chevalier* f. med.L *caballarius* f. L *caballus* horse]

chevet /shəváy/ *n.* the apsidal end of a church, sometimes with an attached group of apses. [F, = pillow, f. L *capitium* f. *caput* head]

Cheviot /chévviət, chéev-/ *n.* **1 a** a large sheep of a breed with short thick wool. **b** this breed. **2** (**cheviot**) the wool or cloth obtained from this breed. [*Cheviot* Hills in N. England and Scotland]

chèvre /shévrə/ *n.* a variety of goat's-milk cheese. [F, = goat, she-goat]

chevron /shévrən/ *n.* **1** a badge in a V shape on the sleeve of a uniform indicating rank or length of service. **2** *Heraldry* & *Archit.* a bent bar of an inverted V shape. **3** any V-shaped line or stripe. [ME f. OF ult. f. L *caper* goat: cf. L *capreoli* pair of rafters]

chevrotain /shévrətayn/ (also **chevrotin** /-tin/) *n.* any small deerlike animal of the family Tragulidae, native to Africa and SE Asia, having small tusks. Also called *mouse deer*. [F, dimin. of OF *chevrot* dimin. of *chèvre* goat]

chevy var. of CHIVVY.

chew /choo/ *v.* & *n.* ● *v.tr.* (also *absol.*) work (food etc.) between the teeth; crush or indent with the teeth. ● *n.* **1** an act of chewing. **2** something for chewing, esp. a chewy sweet. □ **chew the cud** reflect, ruminate. **chew the fat** (or **rag**) *sl.* **1** chat. **2** grumble. **chewing-gum** flavoured gum, esp. chicle, for chewing. **chew on 1** work continuously between the teeth (*chewed on a piece of string*). **2** think about; meditate on. **chew out** *US colloq.* reprimand. **chew over 1** discuss, talk over. **2** think about; meditate on. □□ **chewable** *adj.* **chewer** *n.* [OE *cēowan*]

■ *v.* **1** masticate, munch, grind, champ, *literary* manducate; bite, gnaw. □ **chew the cud** see MEDITATE 1. **chew the fat** (or **rag**) **1** see CHAT[1] *v.* **2** see COMPLAIN 1. **chew on 2** think about *or* on *or* over, reflect on, consider, review, ponder, ruminate on, meditate on *or* over, mull over, deliberate on *or* over, give thought to. **chew out** see REPRIMAND *v.* **chew over 1** see DISCUSS 1. **2** see *chew on* above.

chewy /chóo-i/ *adj.* (**chewier, chewiest**) **1** needing much chewing. **2** suitable for chewing. □□ **chewiness** *n.*

■ **1** see TOUGH *adj.* 1.

Cheyenne /shīán/ *n.* & *adj.* ● *n.* **1 a** an American Indian tribe formerly living between the Missouri and Arkansas rivers. **b** a member of this tribe. **2** the language of this tribe. ● *adj.* of or relating to the Cheyennes or their language. [Canadian F f. Dakota *Sahiyena*]

Cheyne-Stokes respiration /cháynstóks/ *adj. Med.* (of a breathing cycle) with a gradual decrease of movement to a complete stop, followed by a gradual increase. [J. *Cheyne*, Sc. physician d. 1836, and W. *Stokes*, Ir. physician d. 1878]

chez /shay/ *prep.* at the house or home of. [F f. OF *chiese* f. L *casa* cottage]

chi /kī/ *n.* the twenty-second letter of the Greek alphabet (*X*, *χ*). □ **chi-rho** a monogram of chi and rho as the first two letters of Greek *Khristos* Christ. **chi-square test** a method of comparing observed and theoretical values in statistics. [ME f. Gk *khi*]

chiack /chīak/ *v.* & *n.* (also **chyack**) *Austral.* & *NZ* ● *v.tr.* jeer, taunt. ● *n.* jeering, banter. □□ **chiacking** *n.* [19th c.: orig. unkn.]

Chianti /kiánti/ *n.* (*pl.* **Chiantis**) a dry red Italian wine. [*Chianti*, an area in Tuscany, Italy]

chiaroscuro /kiaárəskóorō/ *n.* **1** the treatment of light and shade in drawing and painting. **2** the use of contrast in literature etc. **3** (*attrib.*) half-revealed. [It. f. *chiaro* CLEAR + *oscuro* dark, OBSCURE]

chiasma /kīázmə/ *n.* (*pl.* **chiasmata** /-mətə/) *Biol.* the point at which paired chromosomes remain in contact after crossing over during meiosis. [mod.L f. Gk *chiasma* a cross-shaped mark]

chiasmus /kīázməss/ *n.* inversion in the second of two parallel phrases of the order followed in the first (e.g. *to stop too fearful and too faint to go*). □□ **chiastic** *adj.* [mod.L f. Gk *khiasmos* crosswise arrangement f. *khiazō* mark with letter CHI]

chibouk /chibóok/ *n.* (also **chibouque**) a long Turkish tobacco-pipe. [Turk. *çubuk* tube]

■ see PIPE *n.* 2a.

chic /sheek/ *adj.* & *n.* ● *adj.* (**chic-er, chic-est**) stylish, elegant (in dress or appearance). ● *n.* stylishness, elegance. □□ **chicly** *adv.* [F]

■ *adj*. stylish, fashionable, à la mode, modish, in fashion *or* vogue, smart, snappy, tasteful, elegant, sophisticated, glamorous, becoming, in, swish, swell, *colloq. often derog.* trendy; exclusive. ● *n*. good taste, tastefulness, elegance, stylishness, style, fashion, modishness. □□ **chicly** see *beautifully* (BEAUTIFUL).

chicane /shikáyn/ *n*. & *v*. ● *n*. **1** chicanery. **2** an artificial barrier or obstacle on a motor racecourse. **3** *Bridge* a hand without trumps, or without cards of one suit. ● *v*. *archaic* **1** *intr*. use chicanery. **2** *tr*. (usu. foll. by *into*, *out of*, etc.) cheat (a person). [F *chicane(r)* quibble]
■ *n*. **1** see CHICANERY 2. ● *v*. see CHEAT *v*. 1a.

chicanery /shikáynəri/ *n*. (*pl*. **-ies**) **1** clever but misleading talk; a false argument. **2** trickery, deception. [F *chicanerie* (as CHICANE)]
■ **1** sophistry, equivocation, humbug, flimflam; . **2** trickery, deception, chicane, deceit, sharp practice, cheating, deviousness, duplicity, pettifoggery, double-dealing, legerdemain, artifice, skulduggery, underhandedness, cunning, artfulness, dissimulation, foul play, *Brit. colloq.* jiggery-pokery, *sl.* funny business.

chicano /chikaánō/ *n*. (*pl*. **-os**) *US* an American of Mexican origin. [Sp. *mejicano* Mexican]

chichi /shéeshee/ *adj*. & *n*. ● *adj*. **1** (of a thing) frilly, showy. **2** (of a person or behaviour) fussy, affected. ● *n*. **1** over-refinement, pretentiousness, fussiness. **2** a frilly, showy, or pretentious object. [F]
■ *adj*. **1** see SWANKY 1. **2** see AFFECTED 3.

chick[1] /chik/ *n*. **1** a young bird, esp. one newly hatched. **2** *sl*. **a** a young woman. **b** a child. [ME: shortening of CHICKEN]
■ **2 a** see GIRL 2.

chick[2] /chik/ *n*. *Ind*. a screen for a doorway etc., made from split bamboo and twine. [Hindi *chik*]

chickadee /chíkkədee/ *n*. *US* any of various small birds of the tit family, esp. *Parus atricapillus* with a distinctive dark-crowned head. [imit.]

chicken /chíkkin/ *n*., *adj*., & *v*. ● *n*. (*pl*. same or **chickens**) **1** a young bird of a domestic fowl. **2 a** a domestic fowl prepared as food. **b** its flesh. **3** a youthful person (usu.with *neg*.: *is no chicken*). **4** *colloq*. a children's pastime testing courage, usu. recklessly. ● *adj*. *colloq*. cowardly. ● *v.intr*. (foll. by *out*) *colloq*. withdraw from or fail in some activity through fear or lack of nerve. □ **chicken-and-egg problem** (or **dilemma** etc.) the unresolved question as to which of two things caused the other. **chicken brick** an earthenware container in two halves for roasting a chicken in its own juices. **chicken cholera** see CHOLERA. **chicken-feed 1** food for poultry. **2** *colloq*. an unimportant amount, esp. of money. **chicken-hearted** (or **-livered**) easily frightened; lacking nerve or courage. **chicken-wire** a light wire netting with a hexagonal mesh. [OE *cīcen*, *cȳcen* f. Gmc]
■ *adj*. see TIMID. □ **chicken-feed 2** see PITTANCE. **chicken-hearted** (or **-livered**) see COWARDLY *adj*.

chickenpox /chíkkinpoks/ *n*. an infectious disease, esp. of children, with a rash of small blisters. Also called VARICELLA.

chick-pea /chíkpee/ *n*. **1** a leguminous plant, *Cicer arietinum*, with short swollen pods containing yellow beaked seeds. **2** this seed used as a vegetable. [orig. *ciche pease* f. L *cicer*: see PEASE]

chickweed /chíkweed/ *n*. any of numerous small plants, esp. *Stellaria media*, a garden weed with slender stems and tiny white flowers.

chicle /chíkk'l, chéeklee/ *n*. the milky juice of the sapodilla tree, used in the manufacture of chewing-gum. [Amer. Sp. f. Nahuatl *tzietli*]

chicory /chíkkəri/ *n*. (*pl*. **-ies**) **1** a blue-flowered plant, *Cichorium intybus*, cultivated for its salad leaves and its root. **2** its root, roasted and ground for use with or instead of coffee. **3** *US* = ENDIVE. [ME f. obs. F *cicorée* endive f. med.L *cic(h)orea* f. L *cichorium* f. Gk *kikhorion* SUCCORY]

chide /chīd/ *v.tr*. & *intr*. (*past* **chided** or **chid** /chid/; *past part*. **chided** or **chidden** /chídd'n/) *archaic* or *literary* scold, rebuke. □□ **chider** *n*. **chidingly** *adv*. [OE *cīdan*, of unkn. orig.]
■ see SCOLD *v*.

chief /cheef/ *n*. & *adj*. ● *n*. **1 a** a leader or ruler. **b** the head of a tribe, clan, etc. **2** the head of a department; the highest official. **3** *Heraldry* the upper third of a shield. ● *adj*. (usu. *attrib*.) **1** first in position, importance, influence, etc. (*chief engineer*). **2** prominent, leading. □ **Chief of Staff** the senior staff officer of a service or command. **-in-Chief** supreme (*Commander-in-Chief*). □□ **chiefdom** *n*. [ME f. OF *ch(i)ef* ult. f. L *caput* head]
■ *n*. **1, 2** head, leader, principal, employer, manager, managing director, MD, superior, director, supervisor, superintendent, manager, overseer, captain, master, kingpin, king, ruler, supremo, ringleader, *Ir*. himself, *colloq*. boss, super, top dog, *Brit. colloq*. brass hat, gaffer, *US colloq*. man, *sl*. big cheese, big bug, big gun, Big Chief *or* Daddy, governor, *Brit. sl*. guv, *US sl*. (head *or* chief) honcho, Mr Big; chieftain, headman. ● *adj*. **1** head, superior, supreme, foremost, premier, first, greatest, leading, *US* ranking. **2** principal, leading, prominent, most important, outstanding, key, paramount, dominant, overriding, predominant, primary, prime, main, major. □ **-in-Chief** see SUPREME *adj*. 1.

chiefly /chéefli/ *adv*. above all; mainly but not exclusively.
■ mainly, in particular, especially, primarily, particularly, above all, most of all, pre-eminently, principally, primarily, mostly, for the most part, predominantly, largely, by and large, on the whole, in the main.

chieftain /chéeftən/ *n*. (*fem*. **chieftainess** /-təniss/) the leader of a tribe, clan, etc. □□ **chieftaincy** /-tənsi/ *n*. (*pl*. **-ies**). **chieftainship** *n*. [ME f. OF *chevetaine* f. LL *capitaneus* CAPTAIN: assim. to CHIEF]
■ see LEADER 1.

chiffchaff /chífchaf/ *n*. a small European bird, *Phylloscopus collybita*, of the warbler family. [imit.]

chiffon /shíffon/ *n*. & *adj*. ● *n*. a light diaphanous fabric of silk, nylon, etc. ● *adj*. **1** made of chiffon. **2** (of a pie-filling, dessert, etc.) light-textured. [F f. *chiffe* rag]

chiffonier /shíffənéer/ *n*. a movable low cupboard with a sideboard top. [F *chiffonnier*, *-ière* rag-picker, chest of drawers for odds and ends]

chigger /chíggər/ *n*. **1** = CHIGOE. **2** any harvest mite of the genus *Leptotrombidium* with parasitic larvae. [var. of CHIGOE]

chignon /shéenyon/ *n*. a coil or mass of hair at the back of a woman's head. [F, orig. = nape of the neck]

chigoe /chíggō/ *n*. a tropical flea, *Tunga penetrans*, the females of which burrow beneath the skin causing painful sores. Also called CHIGGER. [Carib]

chihuahua /chiwaáwə/ *n*. **1** a very small dog of a smooth-haired large-eyed breed originating in Mexico. **2** this breed. [*Chihuahua* State and city in Mexico]

chilblain /chílblayn/ *n*. a painful itching swelling of the skin usu. on a hand, foot, etc., caused by exposure to cold and by poor circulation. □□ **chilblained** *adj*. [CHILL + BLAIN]

child /chīld/ *n*. (*pl*. **children** /chíldrən/) **1 a** a young human being below the age of puberty. **b** an unborn or newborn human being. **2** one's son or daughter (at any age). **3** (foll. by *of*) a descendant, follower, adherent, or product of (*children of Israel*; *child of God*; *child of nature*). **4** a childish person. □ **child abuse** maltreatment of a child, esp. by physical violence or sexual interference. **child benefit** (in the UK) regular payment by the State to the parents of a child up to a certain age. **child care** the care of children, esp. by a local authority. **child-minder** a person who looks after children for payment. **child's play** an easy task. □□ **childless** *adj*. **childlessness** *n*. [OE *cild*]
■ **1 a** toddler, youngster, little one, juvenile, minor, chit, whippersnapper, adolescent, teenager, teen, *Ir*. spalpeen, *Sc*. & *N.Engl*. bairn, *colloq*. kid, *Austral. colloq*. ankle-biter, *Brit. colloq*. nipper, young 'un; boy, young

man *or* gentleman, lad, youth, stripling, *colloq.* laddie, (little) shaver; girl, young woman *or* lady, *Sc.* & *N.Engl. or poet.* lass, *colloq.* lassie. **b** neonate, infant, baby, tot, *colloq.* new arrival, *literary* babe (in arms), *sl.* sprog. **2** descendant, son, daughter; (*children*) offspring, family, progeny, *Law* issue, *colloq.* brood, *derog.* spawn. **3** descendant; adherent, follower, disciple, votary, devotee, student; product, consequence, issue, result. □ **child-minder** baby-sitter, nanny, au pair, minder. **child's play** see BREEZE[1] *n.* 5.

childbed /chīldbed/ *n. archaic* = CHILDBIRTH.

childbirth /chīldburth/ *n.* the act of giving birth to a child.
■ see LABOUR *n.* 3.

Childe /chīld/ *n. archaic* a youth of noble birth (*Childe Harold*). [var. of CHILD]

Childermas /childərmass/ *n. archaic* the feast of the Holy Innocents, 28 Dec. [OE *cildramæsse* f. *cildra* genit. pl. of *cild* CHILD + *mæsse* MASS[2]]

childhood /chīldhŏŏd/ *n.* the state or period of being a child. □ **second childhood** a person's dotage. [OE *cildhād*]
■ boyhood, girlhood, youth, prepubescence, puberty, minority, adolescence, teens; infancy, babyhood, juvenescence.

childish /chīldish/ *adj.* **1** of, like, or proper to a child. **2** immature, silly. □□ **childishly** *adv.* **childishness** *n.*
■ **1** childlike, boyish, girlish, youthful. **2** juvenile, puerile, adolescent, infantile, babyish; immature, inexperienced, naïve, silly, *US* sophomoric.

childlike /chīldlīk/ *adj.* having the good qualities of a child as innocence, frankness, etc.
■ youthful, young, innocent, trustful, ingenuous, unsophisticated, naïve, trusting, credulous, open, undissembling, unassuming, guileless, artless, undeceitful, truthful, simple, natural, unaffected.

childproof /chīldprōōf/ *adj.* that cannot be damaged or operated by a child.

children *pl.* of CHILD.

Chilean /chílliən/ *n.* & *adj.* ● *n.* **1** a native or national of Chile in S. America. **2** a person of Chilean descent. ● *adj.* of or relating to Chile.

Chile pine /chílli/ *n.* a monkey-puzzle tree.

Chile saltpetre /chílli/ *n.* (also **Chile nitre**) naturally occurring sodium nitrate.

chili var. of CHILLI.

chiliad /kílliad/ *n.* **1** a thousand. **2** a thousand years. [LL *chilias chiliad-* f. Gk *khilias -ados*]

chiliasm /kílliaz'm/ *n.* the doctrine of or belief in Christ's prophesied reign of 1000 years on earth (see MILLENNIUM). [Gk *khiliasmos*: see CHILIAD]

chiliast /kílliast/ *n.* a believer in chiliasm. □□ **chiliastic** /-ástik/ *adj.* [LL *chiliastes*: see CHILIAD, CHILIASM]
■ millenarian, millennialist.

chill /chil/ *n.*, *v.*, & *adj.* ● *n.* **1 a** an unpleasant cold sensation; lowered body temperature. **b** a feverish cold (*catch a chill*). **2** unpleasant coldness (of air, water, etc.). **3 a** a depressing influence (*cast a chill over*). **b** a feeling of fear or dread accompanied by coldness. **4** coldness of manner. ● *v.* **1** *tr.* & *intr.* make or become cold. **2** *tr.* depress, dispirit. **3** *tr.* cool (food or drink); preserve by cooling. **4** *tr.* harden (molten metal) by contact with cold material. ● *adj. literary* chilly. □ **take the chill off** warm slightly. □□ **chiller** *n.* **chillingly** *adv.* **chillness** *n.* **chillsome** *adj. literary*. [OE *cele, ciele*, etc.: in mod. use the verb is the oldest (ME), and is of obscure orig.]
■ *n.* **1 b** cold, sniffle(s), influenza, ague, *Med.* coryza, *archaic or colloq.* grippe, *colloq.* flu. **2** coldness, cold, nip, chilliness, chillness, coolness; sharpness, keenness, rawness. **3 a** pall, black *or* dark cloud, dampener. **4** chillness, chilliness, coolness, iciness, frostiness, frigidity, aloofness, stiffness; unfriendliness; hostility. ● *v.* **1** cool, refrigerate, freeze, ice; numb. **2** see DEPRESS 2. **3** cool, refrigerate, freeze, ice. ● *adj.* see CHILLY.

chilli /chílli/ *n.* (*pl.* **-ies**) (also *US* **chili**) a small hot-tasting dried red pod of a capsicum, *Capsicum frutescens*, used as seasoning and in curry powder, cayenne pepper, etc. □ **chilli con carne** /kon kaárni/ a stew of chilli-flavoured minced beef and beans. **chilli sauce** a hot sauce made with tomatoes, chillies, and spices. [Sp. *chile, chili*, f. Aztec *chilli*]

chilly /chílli/ *adj.* (**chillier, chilliest**) **1** (of the weather or an object) somewhat cold. **2** (of a person or animal) feeling somewhat cold; sensitive to the cold. **3** unfriendly; unemotional. □□ **chilliness** *n.*
■ **1** cool, coldish, cold, frosty, icy, wintry, crisp, *colloq.* nippy, *dial. literary* chill, chillsome. **3** unemotional, emotionless, unfeeling, passionless, lukewarm, unresponsive, unforthcoming, unreceptive, frosty, stiff, crisp, cool, cold, icy, cold-blooded, stony, flinty, steely, unfriendly, unwelcoming, *literary* chill; distant, aloof, remote, formal; hostile.

Chiltern Hundreds /chíltərn/ *n.pl.* a Crown manor, whose administration is a nominal office for which an MP applies as a way of resigning from the House of Commons. [*Chiltern* Hills in S. England]

chimaera var. of CHIMERA.

chime[1] /chīm/ *n.* & *v.* ● *n.* **1 a** a set of attuned bells. **b** the series of sounds given by this. **c** (usu. in *pl.*) a set of attuned bells as a door bell. **2** agreement, correspondence, harmony. ● *v.* **1 a** *intr.* (of bells) ring. **b** *tr.* sound (a bell or chime) by striking. **2** *tr.* show (the hour) by chiming. **3** *intr.* (usu. foll. by *together, with*) be in agreement, harmonize. □ **chime in 1** interject a remark. **2** join in harmoniously. **3** (foll. by *with*) agree with. □□ **chimer** *n.* [ME, prob. f. *chym(b)e* bell f. OE *cimbal* f. L *cymbalum* f. Gk *kumbalon* CYMBAL]
■ *n.* **1 a** carillon, ring, peal. **b** ringing, ring, peal, chiming, tolling, tintinnabulation, clanging, ding-dong; tinkle, jingle, jangle. **2** see HARMONY 3. ● *v.* **1** ring, toll, sound, clang, strike; see also PEAL[1] *v.* **2** sound, mark, denote, indicate, announce. **3** see ACCORD *v.* 1. □ **chime in 1** interrupt, intercede, interfere, interpose, interject, break in, cut in, butt in, pipe up, *colloq.* chip in. **2** join in, come in. **3** see ACCORD *v.* 1.

chime[2] /chīm/ *n.* (also **chimb**) the projecting rim at the end of a cask. [ME: cf. MDu., MLG *kimme*]

chimera /kīmeérə, ki-/ (also **chimaera**) *n.* **1** (in Greek mythology) a fire-breathing female monster with a lion's head, a goat's body, and a serpent's tail. **2** a fantastic or grotesque product of the imagination; a bogey. **3** any fabulous beast with parts taken from various animals. **4** *Biol.* **a** an organism containing genetically different tissues, formed by grafting, mutation, etc. **b** a nucleic acid formed by laboratory manipulation. **5** any cartilaginous fish of the family Chimaeridae, usu. having a long tapering caudal fin. □□ **chimeric** /-mérrik/ *adj.* **chimerical** /-mérrik'l/ *adj.* **chimerically** /-mérrikəli/ *adv.* [L f. Gk *khimaira* she-goat, chimera]
■ **2** see PHANTOM *n.* 2. □□ **chimerical** see IMAGINARY.

chimney /chímni/ *n.* (*pl.* **-eys**) **1** a vertical channel conducting smoke or combustion gases etc. up and away from a fire, furnace, engine, etc. **2** the part of this which projects above a roof. **3** a glass tube protecting the flame of a lamp. **4** a narrow vertical crack in a rock-face, often used by mountaineers to ascend. □ **chimney-breast** a projecting interior wall surrounding a chimney. **chimney-piece** an ornamental structure around an open fireplace; a mantelpiece. **chimney-pot** an earthenware or metal pipe at the top of a chimney, narrowing the aperture and increasing the up draught. **chimney-stack 1** a number of chimneys grouped in one structure. **2** = sense 2. **chimney-sweep** a person whose job is removing soot from inside chimneys. [ME f. OF *cheminée* f. LL *caminata* having a fire-place, f. L *caminus* f. Gk *kaminos* oven]
■ **1** see STACK *n.* 4.

chimp /chimp/ *n. colloq.* = CHIMPANZEE. [abbr.]

chimpanzee /chímpənzeé/ *n.* a small African anthropoid ape, *Pan troglodytes*. [F *chimpanzé* f. Kongo]

chin /chin/ *n.* the front of the lower jaw. □ **chin-strap** a strap for fastening a hat etc. under the chin. **chin up** *colloq.* cheer up. **chin-wag** *sl. n.* a talk or chat. ● *v.intr.* (**-wagged, -wagging**) have a gossip. **keep one's chin up** *colloq.* remain cheerful, esp. in adversity. **take on the chin 1** suffer a severe blow from (a misfortune etc.). **2** endure courageously. □□ **-chinned** *adj.* (in *comb.*). [OE *cin(n)* f. Gmc]
■ □ **chin-wag** (*v.*) see TALK *v.* 1, 3a. (*n.*) see CHAT[1] *n.* 2.

china /chī́nə/ *n.* & *adj.* ● *n.* **1** a kind of fine white or translucent ceramic ware, porcelain, etc. **2** things made from ceramic, esp. household tableware. **3** *rhyming sl.* one's 'mate', i.e. husband or wife (short for *china plate*). ● *adj.* made of china. □ **china clay** kaolin. **China tea** smoke-cured tea from a small-leaved tea plant grown in China. [orig. *China ware* (from China in Asia): name f. Pers. *chīnī*]
■ **1, 2** see POTTERY. **3** see MATE[1] *n.* 3b.

Chinagraph /chī́nəgraaf/ *n. propr.* a waxy coloured pencil used to write on china, glass, etc.

Chinaman /chī́nəmən/ *n.* (*pl.* **-men**) **1** *archaic* or *derog.* (now usu. *offens.*) a native of China. **2** *Cricket* a ball bowled by a left-handed bowler that spins from off to leg.

Chinatown /chī́nətown/ *n.* a district of any non-Chinese town, esp. a city or seaport, in which the population is predominantly Chinese.

chinch /chinch/ *n.* (in full **chinch-bug**) *US* **1** a small insect, *Blissus leucopterus*, that destroys the shoots of grasses and grains. **2** a bedbug. [Sp. *chinche* f. L *cimex -icis*]

chincherinchee /chínchərincheé/ *n.* a white-flowered bulbous plant, *Ornithogalum thyrsoides*, native to S. Africa. [imit. of the squeaky rubbing of its stalks]

chinchilla /chinchíllə/ *n.* **1 a** any small rodent of the genus *Chinchilla*, native to S. America, having soft silver-grey fur and a bushy tail. **b** its highly valued fur. **2** a breed of cat or rabbit. [Sp. prob. f. S. Amer. native name]

chin-chin /chínchín/ *int. Brit. colloq.* a toast; a greeting or farewell. [Chin. *qingqing* (pr. ch-)]

Chindit /chíndit/ *n. hist.* a member of the Allied forces behind the Japanese lines in Burma (now Myanmar) in 1943–5. [Burm. *chinthé*, a mythical creature]

chine[1] /chīn/ *n.* & *v.* ● *n.* **1 a** a backbone, esp. of an animal. **b** a joint of meat containing all or part of this. **2** a ridge or arête. ● *v.tr.* cut (meat) across or along the backbone. [ME f. OF *eschine* f. L *spina* SPINE]

chine[2] /chīn/ *n.* a deep narrow ravine in the Isle of Wight or Dorset. [OE *cinu* chink etc. f. Gmc]

chine[3] /chīn/ *n.* the join between the side and the bottom of a ship etc. [var. of CHIME[2]]

Chinese /chīnéez/ *adj.* & *n.* ● *adj.* **a** of or relating to China. **b** of Chinese descent. ● *n.* **1** the Chinese language. **2** (*pl.* same) **a** a native or national of China. **b** a person of Chinese descent. □ **Chinese cabbage** = *Chinese leaf*. **Chinese gooseberry** = *kiwi fruit*. **Chinese lantern 1** a collapsible paper lantern. **2** a solanaceous plant, *Physalis alkekengi*, bearing white flowers and globular orange fruits enclosed in an orange-red papery calyx. **Chinese leaf** a lettuce-like cabbage, *Brassica chinensis*. **Chinese puzzle** a very intricate puzzle or problem. **Chinese water chestnut** see *water chestnut* 2. **Chinese white** zinc oxide as a white pigment.

Chink /chingk/ *n. sl. offens.* a Chinese. □□ **Chinky** *adj.* [abbr.]

chink[1] /chingk/ *n.* **1** an unintended crack that admits light or allows an attack; a flaw. **2** a narrow opening; a slit. [16th c.: rel. to CHINE[2]]
■ **1** fissure, breach, split, rift, crack, crevice, gap, opening, cleft, cranny; see also FLAW[1] *n.* 1. **2** slit, aperture, gap, opening.

chink[2] /chingk/ *v.* & *n.* ● *v.* **1** *intr.* make a slight ringing sound, as of glasses or coins striking together. **2** *tr.* cause to make this sound. ● *n.* this sound. [imit.]

chinless /chínliss/ *adj. colloq.* weak or feeble in character. □ **chinless wonder** *Brit.* an ineffectual esp. upper class person.

chino /cheénō/ *n. US* (*pl.* **-os**) **1** a cotton twill fabric, usu. khaki-coloured. **2** (in *pl.*) a garment, esp. trousers, made from this. [Amer. Sp., = toasted]

Chino- /chī́nō/ *comb. form* = SINO-.

chinoiserie /sheenwaázəri/ *n.* **1** the imitation of Chinese motifs and techniques in painting and in decorating furniture. **2** an object or objects in this style. [F]

chinook /shənoŏk, chə-, -noŏk/ *n.* **1** a warm dry wind which blows east of the Rocky Mountains. **2** a warm wet southerly wind west of the Rocky Mountains. □ **chinook salmon** a large salmon, *Oncorhynchus tshawytscha*, of the N. Pacific. [Amer. Ind. name of a tribe]

chintz /chints/ *n.* & *adj.* ● *n.* a printed multicoloured cotton fabric with a glazed finish. ● *adj.* made from or upholstered with this fabric. [earlier *chints* (pl.) f. Hindi *chīṇt* f. Skr. *citra* variegated]

chintzy /chíntsi/ *adj.* (**chintzier, chintziest**) **1** like chintz. **2** gaudy, cheap. **3** characteristic of the décor associated with chintz soft furnishings. □□ **chintzily** *adv.* **chintziness** *n.*
■ **2** see GAUDY[1].

chionodoxa /kīənədóksə/ *n.* any liliaceous plant of the genus *Chionodoxa*, having early-blooming blue flowers. Also called *glory-of-the-snow*. [mod.L f. Gk *khiōn* snow + *doxa* glory]

chip /chip/ *n.* & *v.* ● *n.* **1** a small piece removed by or in the course of chopping, cutting, or breaking, esp. from hard material such as wood or stone. **2** the place where such a chip has been made. **3 a** (usu. in *pl.*) a strip of potato, deep fried. **b** (in *pl.*) *US* potato crisps. **4** a counter used in some gambling games to represent money. **5** *Electronics* = MICROCHIP. **6 a** a thin strip of wood, straw, etc., used for weaving hats, baskets, etc. **b** a basket made from these. **7** *Football* etc. & *Golf* a short shot, kick, or pass with the ball describing an arc. ● *v.* (**chipped, chipping**) **1** *tr.* (often foll. by *off*, *away*) cut or break (a piece) from a hard material. **2** *intr.* (foll. by *at*, *away at*) cut pieces off (a hard material) to alter its shape, break it up, etc. **3** *intr.* (of stone, china, etc.) be susceptible to being chipped; be apt to break at the edge (*will chip easily*). **4** *tr.* (also *absol.*) *Football* etc. & *Golf* strike or kick (the ball) with a chip (cf. sense 7 of *n.*). **5** *tr.* (usu. as **chipped** *adj.*) cut (potatoes) into chips. □ **chip heater** *Austral.* & *NZ* a domestic water-heater that burns wood chips. **chip in** *colloq.* **1** interrupt or contribute abruptly to a conversation (*chipped in with a reminiscence*). **2** contribute (money or resources). **a chip off the old block** a child who resembles a parent, esp. in character. **a chip on one's shoulder** *colloq.* a disposition or inclination to feel resentful or aggrieved. **chip shot** = sense 7 of *n.* **have had one's chips** *Brit. colloq.* be unable to avoid defeat, punishment, etc. **in the chips** *sl.* moneyed, affluent. **when the chips are down** *colloq.* when it comes to the point. [ME f. OE *cipp*, *cyp* beam]
■ *n.* **1** fragment, piece, shard, sherd, splinter, flake, sliver. **2** nick. **3 a** (*chips*) potato chips, chipped potatoes, French fried potatoes, *US* French fries. **4** counter, marker, token, *US Cards* check. ● *v.* **1** cut, break, snap. **2** chisel, whittle; (*chip away at*) hew. □ **chip in 1** interrupt, break in, intrude, interfere, intercede, interpose, cut in, butt in, chime in. **2** contribute, help out, *colloq.* shell out, *Brit. colloq.* stump up, *sl.* fork out *or* up.

chipboard /chípbord/ *n.* a rigid sheet or panel made from compressed wood chips and resin.

chipmunk /chípmungk/ *n.* any ground squirrel of the genus *Tamias* or *Eutamias*, having alternate light and dark stripes running down the body. [Algonquian]

chipolata /chíppəlaátə/ *n. Brit.* a small thin sausage. [F f. It. *cipollata* a dish of onions f. *cipolla* onion]

Chippendale /chíppəndayl/ *adj.* **1** (of furniture) designed or made by the English cabinet-maker Thomas Chippendale (d. 1779). **2** in the ornately elegant style of Chippendale's furniture.

chipper /chíppər/ *adj.* esp. *US colloq.* **1** cheerful. **2** smartly dressed. [perh. f. N.Engl. dial. *kipper* lively]
■ **1** see SPRIGHTLY.

chippie var. of CHIPPY.

chipping /chípping/ *n.* **1** a small fragment of stone, wood, etc. **2** (in *pl.*) these used as a surface for roads, roofs, etc.

chippy /chíppi/ *n.* (also **chippie**) (*pl.* **-ies**) *Brit. colloq.* **1** a fish-and-chip shop. **2** a carpenter.

Chips /chips/ *n. Naut. sl.* a ship's carpenter.

chiral /kīrəl/ *adj. Chem.* (of a crystal etc.) not superposable on its mirror image. □□ **chirality** /-rálliti/ *n.* [Gk *kheir* hand]

chiro- /kīrō/ (also **cheiro-**) *comb. form* of the hand. [Gk *kheir* hand]

chirography /kīrógrəfi/ *n.* handwriting, calligraphy.
■ see WRITING 2.

chiromancy /kīrōmansi/ *n.* palmistry.

chiropody /kiróppədi/ *n.* the treatment of the feet and their ailments. □□ **chiropodist** *n.* [CHIRO- + Gk *pous podos* foot]

chiropractic /kīrōpráktik/ *n.* the diagnosis and manipulative treatment of mechanical disorders of the joints, esp. of the spinal column. □□ **chiropractor** *n.* [CHIRO- + Gk *praktikos*: see PRACTICAL]

chiropteran /kīróptərən/ *n.* any member of the order Chiroptera, with membraned limbs serving as wings including bats and flying foxes. □□ **chiropterous** *adj.* [CHIRO- + Gk *pteron* wing]

chirp /churp/ *v.* & *n.* ● *v.* **1** *intr.* (usu. of small birds, grasshoppers, etc.) utter a short sharp high-pitched note. **2** *tr.* & *intr.* (esp. of a child) speak or utter in a lively or jolly way. ● *n.* a chirping sound. □□ **chirper** *n.* [ME, earlier *chirk*, *chirt*: imit.]
■ *v.* **1** tweet, sing, twitter, chirrup, warble, trill, cheep, chirr, pipe. ● *n.* tweet, peep, twitter, chirrup, warble, trill, cheep, chirr.

chirpy /chúrpi/ *adj. colloq.* (**chirpier**, **chirpiest**) cheerful, lively. □□ **chirpily** *adv.* **chirpiness** *n.*
■ see LIVELY 1.

chirr /chur/ *v.* & *n.* (also **churr**) ● *v.intr.* (esp. of insects) make a prolonged low trilling sound. ● *n.* this sound. [imit.]
■ *v.* see CHIRP *v.* ● *n.* see CHIRP *n.*

chirrup /chírrəp/ *v.* & *n.* ● *v.intr.* (**chirruped**, **chirruping**) (esp. of small birds) chirp, esp. repeatedly; twitter. ● *n.* a chirruping sound. □□ **chirrupy** *adj.* [trilled form of CHIRP]
■ *v.* see CHIRP *v.* ● *n.* see CHIRP *n.*

chisel /chízz'l/ *n.* & *v.* ● *n.* a hand tool with a squared bevelled blade for shaping wood, stone, or metal. ● *v.* **1** *tr.* (**chiselled**, **chiselling**; *US* **chiseled**, **chiseling**) cut or shape with a chisel. **2** *tr.* (as **chiselled** *adj.*) (of facial features) clear-cut, fine. **3** *tr.* & *intr. sl.* cheat, swindle. □□ **chiseller** *n.* [ME f. ONF ult. f. LL *cisorium* f. L *caedere caes-* cut]
■ *v.* **1** carve, cut, sculpt, sculpture, shape, fashion, model; incise, engrave, inscribe, *archaic* grave; gouge, groove, dig, hollow out. **2** (**chiselled**) fine, distinct, distinctive, crisp, well-defined, clear-cut, marked, honed. **3** see CHEAT *v.* 1a.

chit[1] /chit/ *n.* **1** *derog.* or *joc.* a young, small, or frail girl or woman (esp. *a chit of a girl*). **2** a young child. [ME, = whelp, cub, kitten, perh. = dial. *chit* sprout]
■ **1** see LASS.

chit[2] /chit/ *n.* **1** a note of requisition; a note of a sum owed, esp. for food or drink. **2** esp. *Brit.* a note or memorandum. [earlier *chitty*: Anglo-Ind. f. Hindi *ciṭṭhī* pass f. Skr. *citra* mark]
■ **2** see MEMORANDUM.

chital /cheet'l/ *n.* = AXIS[2]. [Hindi *cītal*]

chit-chat /chítchat/ *n.* & *v. colloq.* ● *n.* light conversation; gossip. ● *v.intr.* (**-chatted**, **-chatting**) talk informally; gossip. [redupl. of CHAT[1]]
■ *n.* see GOSSIP *n.* 1. ● *v.* see CHAT[1] *v.*

chitin /kītin/ *n. Chem.* a polysaccharide forming the major constituent in the exoskeleton of arthropods and in the cell walls of fungi. □□ **chitinous** *adj.* [F *chitine* irreg. f. Gk *khitōn*: see CHITON]

chiton /kīt'n/ *n.* **1** a long woollen tunic worn by ancient Greeks. **2** any marine mollusc of the class Amphineura, having a shell of overlapping plates. [Gk *khitōn* tunic]

chitterling /chíttərling/ *n.* (usu. in *pl.*) the smaller intestines of pigs etc., esp. as cooked for food. [ME: orig. uncert.]

chivalrous /shívvəlrəss/ *adj.* **1** (usu. of a male) gallant, honourable, courteous. **2** involving or showing chivalry. □□ **chivalrously** *adv.* [ME f. OF *chevalerous*: see CHEVALIER]
■ honourable, courtly, gracious, courteous, gallant, heroic, noble, chivalric, gentlemanly, decent, dignified, well-bred, well-mannered, *poet.* knightly.

chivalry /shívvəlri/ *n.* **1** the medieval knightly system with its religious, moral, and social code. **2** the combination of qualities expected of an ideal knight, esp. courage, honour, courtesy, justice, and readiness to help the weak. **3** a man's courteous behaviour, esp. towards women. **4** *archaic* knights, noblemen, and horsemen collectively. □□ **chivalric** *adj.* [ME f. OF *chevalerie* etc. f. med.L *caballerius* for LL *caballarius* horseman: see CAVALIER]
■ **2** honour, courtliness, gallantry, nobility, knightliness, knight-errantry, graciousness, gentlemanliness, decency, dignity, virtuousness; bravery, courage. **3** see COURTESY.

chive /chīv/ *n.* a small alliaceous plant, *Allium schoenoprasum*, having purple-pink flowers and dense tufts of long tubular leaves which are used as a herb. [ME f. OF *cive* f. L *cepa* onion]

chivvy /chívvi/ *v.tr.* (**-ies**, **-ied**) (also **chivy**, **chevy** /chévvi/) harass, nag; pursue. [*chevy* (n. & v.), prob. f. the ballad of *Chevy Chase*, a place on the Scottish border]
■ see HARASS 1.

chlamydia /kləmíddiə/ *n.* (*pl.* **chlamydiae** /-di-ee/) any parasitic bacterium of the genus *Chlamydia*, some of which cause diseases such as trachoma, psittacosis, and non-specific urethritis. [mod.L f. Gk *khlamus -udos* cloak]

chlamydomonas /klámmidəmōnəss/ *n.* any unicellular green freshwater alga of the genus *Chlamydomonas*. [mod.L (as CHLAMYDIA)]

chlor- var. of CHLORO-.

chloral /klórəl/ *n.* **1** a colourless liquid aldehyde used in making DDT. **2** (in full **chloral hydrate**) *Pharm.* a colourless crystalline solid made from chloral and used as a sedative. [F f. *chlore* chlorine + *alcool* alcohol]

chloramphenicol /klóramfénnikol/ *n. Pharm.* an antibiotic prepared from *Streptomyces venezuelae* or produced synthetically and used esp. against typhoid fever. [CHLORO- + AMIDE + PHENO- + NITRO- + GLYCOL]

chlorate /klórayt/ *n. Chem.* any salt of chloric acid.

chlorella /klorélla/ *n.* any non-motile unicellular green alga of the genus *Chlorella*. [mod.L, dimin. of Gk *khlōros* green]

chloric acid /klórik/ *n. Chem.* a colourless liquid acid with strong oxidizing properties. [CHLORO- + -IC]

chloride /klórīd/ *n. Chem.* **1** any compound of chlorine with another element or group. **2** any bleaching agent containing chloride. [CHLORO- + -IDE]

chlorinate /klórinayt/ *v.tr.* **1** impregnate or treat with chlorine. **2** *Chem.* cause to react or combine with chlorine. □□ **chlorinator** *n.*

chlorination /klórináysh'n/ *n.* **1** the treatment of water with chlorine to disinfect it. **2** *Chem.* a reaction in which chlorine is introduced into a compound.

chlorine /klóreen/ *n. Chem.* a poisonous greenish-yellow gaseous element of the halogen group occurring naturally in salt, sea-water, rock-salt, etc., and used for purifying water, bleaching, and the manufacture of many organic chemicals. ¶ Symb.: **Cl**. [Gk *khlōros* green + -INE[4]]

chlorite /klórīt/ *n. Chem.* any salt of chlorous acid. □□ **chloritic** /-ríttik/ *adj.*

chloro- /klórō, klórro/ *comb. form* (also **chlor-** esp. before a vowel) **1** *Bot.* & *Mineral.* green. **2** *Chem.* chlorine. [Gk *khlōros* green: in sense 2 f. CHLORINE]

chloro-fluorocarbon see CFC.

chloroform /klórrəform, klórə-/ *n.* & *v.* ● *n.* a colourless volatile sweet-smelling liquid used as a solvent and formerly used as a general anaesthetic. ¶ Chem. formula: $CHCl_3$. ● *v.tr.* render (a person) unconscious with this. [F *chloroforme* formed as CHLORO- + *formyle*: see FORMIC (ACID)]

Chloromycetin /klórōmīseétin/ *n. propr.* = CHLORAMPHENICOL. [CHLORO- + Gk *mukēs -ētos* fungus]

chlorophyll /klórrəfil/ *n.* the green pigment found in most plants, responsible for light absorption to provide energy for photosynthesis. □□ **chlorophyllous** /-fílləss/ *adj.* [F *chlorophylle* f. Gk *phullon* leaf: see CHLORO-]

chloroplast /klórōplast/ *n.* a plastid containing chlorophyll, found in plant cells undergoing photosynthesis. [G: (as CHLORO-, PLASTID)]

chlorosis /klərṓsiss, klor-/ *n.* **1** *hist.* a severe form of anaemia from iron deficiency esp. in young women, causing a greenish complexion (cf. GREENSICK). **2** *Bot.* a reduction or loss of the normal green coloration of plants. □□ **chlorotic** *adj.* [CHLORO- + -OSIS]

chlorous acid /klórəss/ *n. Chem.* a pale yellow liquid acid with oxidizing properties. ¶ Chem. formula: $HClO_2$. [CHLORO- + -OUS]

chlorpromazine /klorprómməzeen/ *n. Pharm.* a drug used as a sedative and to control nausea and vomiting. [F (as CHLORO-, PROMETHAZINE)]

Ch.M. *abbr.* Master of Surgery. [L *Chirurgiae Magister*]

choc /chok/ *n.* & *adj. colloq.* chocolate. □ **choc-ice** a bar of ice-cream covered with a thin coating of chocolate. [abbr.]

chocho /chṓchō/ *n.* (*pl.* **-os**) *W.Ind.* = CHOKO.

chock /chok/ *n.*, *v.*, & *adv.* ● *n.* a block or wedge of wood to check motion, esp. of a cask or a wheel. ● *v.tr.* **1** fit or make fast with chocks. **2** (usu. foll. by *up*) *Brit.* cram full. ● *adv.* as closely or tightly as possible. [prob. f. OF *çouche*, *çoche*, of unkn. orig.]

■ *n.* see WEDGE[1] *n.* 1.

chock-a-block /chókkəblók/ *adj.* & *adv.* crammed close together; crammed full (*a street chock-a-block with cars*). [orig. Naut., with ref. to tackle with the two blocks run close together]

■ see FULL[1] *adj.* 1.

chocker /chókkər/ *adj. Brit. sl.* fed up, disgusted. [CHOCK-A-BLOCK]

chock-full /chókfŏŏl/ *adj.* & *adv.* = CHOCK-A-BLOCK (*chock-full of rubbish*). [CHOCK + FULL[1]: ME *chokkefulle* (rel. to CHOKE[1]) is doubtful]

chocolate /chókkələt, chóklət/ *n.* & *adj.* ● *n.* **1 a** a food preparation in the form of a paste or solid block made from roasted and ground cacao seeds, usually sweetened. **b** a sweet made of or coated with this. **c** a drink made with chocolate. **2** a deep brown colour. ● *adj.* **1** made from or of chocolate. **2** chocolate-coloured. □ **chocolate-box 1** a decorated box filled with chocolates. **2** (*attrib.*) stereotypically pretty or romantic. □□ **chocolatey** *adj.* (also **chocolaty**). [F *chocolat* or Sp. *chocolate* f. Aztec *chocolatl*]

Choctaw /chóktaw/ *n.* (*pl.* same or **Choctaws**) **1 a** a member of a N. American people orig. from Alabama. **b** the language of this people. **2** (in skating) a step from one edge of a skate to the other edge of the other skate in the opposite direction. [native name]

choice /choyss/ *n.* & *adj.* ● *n.* **1 a** the act or an instance of choosing. **b** a thing or person chosen (*not a good choice*). **2** a range from which to choose. **3** (usu. foll. by *of*) the élite, the best. **4** the power or opportunity to choose (*what choice have I?*). ● *adj.* of superior quality; carefully chosen. □□ **choicely** *adv.* **choiceness** *n.* [ME f. OF *chois* f. *choisir* CHOOSE]

■ *n.* **1** selection, election, preference, pick. **2** see SELECTION 3. **3** finest, pick, élite, flower, best, select, cream, *crème de la crème*. **4** option, discretion; possibility, opportunity, alternative. ● *adj.* special, fine, good, superior, prime, high-quality, excellent, outstanding, pre-eminent, best, prize, first-rate, first-class, exceptional, splendid, preferred, *colloq.* plum, plummy; dainty; selected, select, elect, hand-picked, well-chosen, fit, appropriate, fitting, apposite, apt.

choir /kwīr/ *n.* **1** a regular group of singers, esp. taking part in church services. **2** the part of a cathedral or large church between the altar and the nave, used by the choir and clergy. **3** a company of singers, birds, angels etc. (*a heavenly choir*). **4** *Mus.* a group of instruments of one family playing together. □ **choir organ** the softest of three parts making up a large organ having its row of keys the lowest of the three. **choir-stall** = STALL[1] *n.* 3a. [ME f. OF *quer* f. L *chorus*: see CHORUS]

■ **1, 4** see ENSEMBLE 3.

choirboy /kwīrboy/ *n.* a boy who sings in a church or cathedral choir.

■ see *singer* (SING).

choke[1] /chōk/ *v.* & *n.* ● *v.* **1** *tr.* hinder or impede the breathing of (a person or animal) esp. by constricting the windpipe or (of gas, smoke, etc.) by being unbreathable. **2** *intr.* suffer a hindrance or stoppage of breath. **3** *tr.* & *intr.* make or become speechless from emotion. **4** *tr.* retard the growth of or kill (esp. plants) by the deprivation of light, air, nourishment, etc. **5** *tr.* (often foll. by *back*) suppress (feelings) with difficulty. **6** *tr.* block or clog (a passage, tube, etc.). **7** *tr.* (as **choked** *adj.*) *colloq.* disgusted, disappointed. **8** *tr.* enrich the fuel mixture in (an internal-combustion engine) by reducing the intake of air. ● *n.* **1** the valve in the carburettor of an internal-combustion engine that controls the intake of air, esp. to enrich the fuel mixture. **2** *Electr.* an inductance coil used to smooth the variations of an alternating current or to alter its phase. □ **choke-chain** a chain looped round a dog's neck to exert control by pressure on its windpipe when the dog pulls. **choke-cherry** (*pl.* **-cherries**) an astringent N. American cherry, *Prunus virginiana*. **choke-damp** carbon dioxide in mines, wells, etc. **choke down** swallow with difficulty. **choke up** block (a channel etc.). [ME f. OE *ācēocian* f. *cēoce*, *cēce* CHEEK]

■ *v.* **1** suffocate, asphyxiate, smother, stifle, strangle, throttle, garrotte. **2** gag, retch. **5** (*choke back*) hold *or* keep back, hold in (check), suppress, repress, stifle, swallow (back), restrain, withhold. **6** choke up, stop *or* clog *or* bung *or* block (up), fill (up), obstruct, congest, dam (up), constrict, stuff *or* silt (up), foul (up). **7** (**choked**) see *disappointed* (DISAPPOINT). □ **choke up** see CHOKE *v.* 6 above.

choke[2] /chōk/ *n.* the centre part of an artichoke. [prob. confusion of the ending of *artichoke* with CHOKE[1]]

chokeberry /chṓkbəri/ *n.* (*pl.* **-ies**) *Bot.* **1** any rosaceous shrub of the genus *Aronia*. **2** its scarlet berry-like fruit.

choker /chṓkər/ *n.* **1** a close-fitting necklace or ornamental neckband. **2** a clerical or other high collar.

■ **1** see STRING *n.* 6.

choko /chṓkō/ *n.* (*pl.* **-os**) *Austral.* & *NZ* a succulent green pear-shaped vegetable like a cucumber in flavour. [Braz. Ind. *chocho*]

choky[1] /chṓki/ *n.* (also **chokey**) (*pl.* **-ies** or **-eys**) *Brit. sl.* prison. [orig. Anglo-Ind., f. Hindi *caukī* shed]

■ see PRISON *n.* 1.

choky[2] /chṓki/ *adj.* (**chokier**, **chokiest**) tending to choke or to cause choking.

cholangiography /kóllanjiógrəfi/ *n. Med.* X-ray examination of the bile ducts, used to find the site and nature of any obstruction. [CHOLE- + Gk *aggeion* vessel + -GRAPHY]

chole- /kólli/ *comb. form* (also **chol-** esp. before a vowel) *Med.* & *Chem.* bile. [Gk *kholē* gall, bile]

cholecalciferol /kóllikalsíffərol/ *n.* one of the D vitamins, produced by the action of sunlight on a cholesterol derivative widely distributed in the skin, a deficiency of which results in rickets in children and osteomalacia in adults. Also called *vitamin* D_3. [CHOLE- + CALCIFEROL]

cholecystography /kóllisistógrəfi/ *n. Med.* X-ray examination of the gall-bladder, esp. used to detect the presence of any gallstones. [CHOLE- + CYSTO- + -GRAPHY]

choler /kóllər/ *n.* **1** *hist.* one of the four humours, bile. **2** *poet.* or *archaic* anger, irascibility. [ME f. OF *colere* bile,

anger f. L *cholera* f. Gk *kholera* diarrhoea, in LL = bile, anger, f. Gk *kholē* bile]
▪ **2** see ANGER *n.*

cholera /kóllərə/ *n. Med.* an infectious and often fatal disease of the small intestine caused by the bacterium *Vibrio cholerae*, resulting in severe vomiting and diarrhoea. ▫ **chicken** (or **fowl**) **cholera** an infectious disease of fowls. ▫▫ **choleraic** /-ráyik/ *adj.* [ME f. L f. Gk *kholera*: see CHOLER]

choleric /kóllərik/ *adj.* irascible, angry. ▫▫ **cholerically** *adv.* [ME f. OF *cholerique* f. L *cholericus* f. Gk *kholerikos*: see CHOLER]
▪ see CANTANKEROUS.

cholesterol /kəléstərol/ *n. Biochem.* a sterol found in most body tissues, including the blood, where high concentrations promote arteriosclerosis. [*cholesterin* f. Gk *kholē* bile + *stereos* stiff]

choli /chṓli/ *n.* (*pl.* **cholis**) a type of short-sleeved bodice worn by Indian women. [Hindi *colī*]

choliamb /kṓliamb/ *n. Prosody* = SCAZON. ▫▫ **choliambic** /-ámbik/ *adj.* [LL *choliambus* f. Gk *khōliambos* f. *khōlos* lame: see IAMBUS]

choline /kṓleen, -lin/ *n. Biochem.* a basic nitrogenous organic compound occurring widely in living matter. [G *Cholin* f. Gk *kholē* bile]

chomp /chomp/ *v.tr.* = CHAMP[1]. [imit.]

chondrite /kóndrīt/ *n.* a stony meteorite containing small mineral granules. [G *Chondrit* f. Gk *khondros* granule]

chondrocranium /kóndrōkráyniəm/ *n. Anat.* the embryonic skull composed of cartilage and later replaced by bone. [Gk *khondros* grain, cartilage]

choo-choo /chóochoo/ *n. colloq.* (esp. as a child's word) a railway train or locomotive, esp. a steam engine. [imit.]
▪ see TRAIN *n.* 1.

chook /chook/ *n.* (also **chookie**) *Austral.* & *NZ colloq.* **1** a chicken or fowl. **2** *sl.* an older woman. [E dial. *chuck* chicken]

choose /chooz/ *v.* (*past* **chose** /chōz/; *past part.* **chosen** /chṓz'n/) **1** *tr.* select out of a greater number. **2** *intr.* (usu. foll. by *between, from*) take or select one or another. **3** *tr.* (usu. foll. by *to* + infin.) decide, be determined (*chose to stay behind*). **4** *tr.* (foll. by complement) select as (*was chosen king*). **5** *tr. Theol.* (esp. as **chosen** *adj.*) destine to be saved (*God's chosen people*). ▫ **cannot choose but** *archaic* must. **nothing** (or **little**) **to choose between them** they are equivalent. ▫▫ **chooser** *n.* [OE *cēosan* f. Gmc]
▪ **1** select, elect, pick (out), opt for, go for, settle *or* decide *or* fix *or* fasten upon *or* on, single out, pitch on *or* upon. **3** determine, opt, elect, resolve, make up one's mind, undertake; see also DECIDE 1. **5** elect, save. ▫ **cannot choose but** have to, be obliged *or* obligated to, be required to, can only, can but, cannot but; can't help.

choosy /choozi/ *adj.* (**choosier**, **choosiest**) *colloq.* fastidious. ▫▫ **choosily** *adv.* **choosiness** *n.*
▪ discriminating, discerning, fastidious, finicky, finical, particular, over-particular, fussy, demanding, exacting, difficult, hard to please, *colloq.* picky, pernickety.

chop[1] /chop/ *v.* & *n.* ● *v.tr.* (**chopped**, **chopping**) **1** (usu. foll. by *off, down*, etc.) cut or fell by a blow, usu. with an axe. **2** (often foll. by *up*) cut (esp. meat or vegetables) into small pieces. **3** strike (esp. a ball) with a short heavy edgewise blow. **4** *Brit. colloq.* dispense with; shorten or curtail. ● *n.* **1** a cutting blow, esp. with an axe. **2** a thick slice of meat (esp. pork or lamb) usu. including a rib. **3** a short heavy edgewise stroke or blow in tennis, cricket, boxing, etc. **4** the broken motion of water, usu. owing to the action of the wind against the tide. **5** (prec. by *the*) *Brit. sl.* **a** dismissal from employment. **b** the action of killing or being killed. ▫ **chop logic** argue pedantically. [ME, var. of CHAP[1]]
▪ *v.* **1** cut, hack, hew, lop, crop, slice; fell; (*chop off*) sever. **2** (*chop up*) cut up, mince, dice; hash (up). **4** see ABOLISH, CURTAIL 1. ● *n.* **1** cut, blow, stroke; swing, *colloq.* swipe. **5 a** (*the chop*) see SACK[1] *n.* 2. ▫ **chop logic** see QUIBBLE *v.*

chop[2] /chop/ *n.* (usu. in *pl.*) the jaw of an animal etc. [16th-c. var. (occurring earlier) of CHAP[3], of unkn. orig.]

chop[3] /chop/ *v.intr.* (**chopped**, **chopping**) ▫ **chop and change** vacillate; change direction frequently. [ME, perh. rel. to *chap* f. OE *cēapian* (as CHEAP)]

chop[4] /chop/ *n. Brit. archaic* a trade mark; a brand of goods. ▫ **not much chop** esp. *Austral.* & *NZ* no good. [orig. in India & China, f. Hindi *chāp* stamp]

chop-chop /chópchóp/ *adv.* & *int.* (pidgin English) quickly, quick. [f. Chin. dial. *k'wâi-k'wâi*]
▪ see *at the double* (DOUBLE).

chopper /chóppər/ *n.* **1 a** *Brit.* a short axe with a large blade. **b** a butcher's cleaver. **2** *colloq.* a helicopter. **3** a device for regularly interrupting an electric current or light-beam. **4** *colloq.* a type of bicycle or motor cycle with high handlebars. **5** (in *pl.*) *Brit. sl.* teeth. **6** *US sl.* a machine-gun.

choppy /chóppi/ *adj.* (**choppier**, **choppiest**) (of the sea, the weather, etc.) fairly rough. ▫▫ **choppily** *adv.* **choppiness** *n.* [CHOP[1] + -Y[1]]
▪ see ROUGH *adj.* 5.

chopstick /chópstik/ *n.* each of a pair of small thin sticks of wood or ivory etc., held both in one hand as eating utensils by the Chinese, Japanese, etc. [pidgin Engl. f. *chop* = quick + STICK[1] equivalent of Cantonese *k'wâi-tsze* nimble ones]

chopsuey /chopsóo-i/ *n.* (*pl.* **-eys**) a Chinese-style dish of meat stewed and fried with bean sprouts, bamboo shoots, onions, and served with rice. [Cantonese *shap sui* mixed bits]

choral /kórəl/ *adj.* of, for, or sung by a choir or chorus. ▫ **choral society** a group which meets regularly to sing choral music. ▫▫ **chorally** *adv.* [med.L *choralis* f. L *chorus*: see CHORUS]

chorale /koraál/ *n.* (also **choral**) **1** a stately and simple hymn tune; a harmonized version of this. **2** esp. *US* a choir or choral society. [G *Choral(gesang)* f. med.L *cantus choralis*]

chord[1] /kord/ *n. Mus.* a group of (usu. three or more) notes sounded together, as a basis of harmony. ▫▫ **chordal** *adj.* [orig. *cord* f. ACCORD: later confused with CHORD[2]]

chord[2] /kord/ *n.* **1** *Math.* & *Aeron.* etc. a straight line joining the ends of an arc, the wings of an aeroplane, etc. **2** *Anat.* = CORD. **3** *poet.* the string of a harp etc. **4** *Engin.* one of the two principal members, usu. horizontal, of a truss. ▫ **strike a chord 1** recall something to a person's memory. **2** elicit sympathy. **touch the right chord** appeal skilfully to the emotions. ▫▫ **chordal** *adj.* [16th-c. refashioning of CORD after L *chorda*]

chordate /kórdayt/ *n.* & *adj.* ● *n.* any animal of the phylum Chordata, possessing a notochord at some stage during its development. ● *adj.* of or relating to the chordates. [mod.L *chordata* f. L *chorda* CHORD[2] after *Vertebrata* etc.]

chore /chor/ *n.* a tedious or routine task, esp. domestic. [orig. dial. & US form of CHAR[2]]
▪ see TASK *n.*

chorea /koreéə/ *n. Med.* a disorder characterized by jerky involuntary movements affecting esp. the shoulders, hips, and face. ▫ **Huntington's chorea** chorea accompanied by a progressive dementia. **Sydenham's chorea** chorea esp. in children as one of the manifestations of rheumatic fever: also called ST VITUS'S DANCE. [L f. Gk *khoreia* (as CHORUS)]

choreograph /kórriəgraaf/ *v.tr.* compose the choreography for (a ballet etc.). ▫▫ **choreographer** /-ríógrəfər/ *n.* [back-form. f. CHOREOGRAPHY]

choreography /kórriógrəfi/ *n.* **1** the design or arrangement of a ballet or other staged dance. **2** the sequence of steps and movements in dance. **3** the written notation for this. ▫▫ **choreographic** /-riəgráffik/ *adj.* **choreographically** /-riəgráffikəli/ *adv.* [Gk *khoreia* dance + -GRAPHY]

choreology /kórriólləji/ *n.* the study and description of the movements of dancing. ▫▫ **choreologist** *n.*

choriambus /kórriámbəss/ *n.* (*pl.* **choriambi** /-bī/) *Prosody* a metrical foot consisting of two short (unstressed) syllables between two long (stressed) ones. ▫▫ **choriambic** *adj.* [LL Gk *khoriambos* f. *khoreios* of the dance + IAMBUS]

choric /kórik/ *adj.* of, like, or for a chorus in drama or recitation. [LL *choricus* f. Gk *khorikos* (as CHORUS)]

chorine /kóreen/ *adj. US* a chorus girl. [CHORUS + -INE[3]]

chorion /kóriən/ *n.* the outermost membrane surrounding an embryo of a reptile, bird, or mammal. ▫▫ **chorionic** /-riónnik/ *adj.* [Gk *khorion*]

chorister /kórristər/ *n.* **1** a member of a choir, esp. a choirboy. **2** *US* the leader of a church choir. [ME, ult. f. OF *cueriste* f. *quer* CHOIR]
▪ see *singer* (SING).

chorography /kərógrəfi/ *n.* the systematic description of regions or districts. ▫▫ **chorographer** *n.* **chorographic** /kórrəgráffik/ *adj.* [F *chorographie* or L f. Gk *khōrographia* f. *khōra* region]

choroid /kóroyd/ *adj.* & *n.* ● *adj.* like a chorion in shape or vascularity. ● *n.* (in full **choroid coat** or **membrane**) a layer of the eyeball between the retina and the sclera. [Gk *khoroeidēs* for *khorioeidēs*: see CHORION]

chorology /kərólləji/ *n.* the study of the geographical distribution of animals and plants. ▫▫ **chorological** /kórrəlójik'l/ *adj.* **chorologist** *n.* [Gk *khōra* region + -LOGY]

chortle /chórt'l/ *v.* & *n.* ● *v.intr. colloq.* chuckle gleefully. ● *n.* a gleeful chuckle. [portmanteau word coined by Lewis Carroll, prob. f. CHUCKLE + SNORT]
▪ *v.* see CHUCKLE *v.* ● *n.* see CHUCKLE *n.*

chorus /kórəss/ *n.* & *v.* ● *n.* (*pl.* **choruses**) **1** a group (esp. a large one) of singers; a choir. **2** a piece of music composed for a choir. **3** the refrain or the main part of a popular song, in which a chorus participates. **4** any simultaneous utterance by many persons etc. (*a chorus of disapproval followed*). **5** a group of singers and dancers performing in concert in a musical comedy, opera, etc. **6** *Gk Antiq.* **a** in Greek tragedy, a group of performers who comment together in voice and movement on the main action. **b** an utterance of the chorus. **7** esp. in Elizabethan drama, a character who speaks the prologue and other linking parts of the play. **8** the part spoken by this character. ● *v.tr.* & *intr.* (of a group) speak or utter simultaneously. ▫ **chorus girl** a young woman who sings or dances in the chorus of a musical comedy etc. **in chorus** (uttered) together; in unison. [L f. Gk *khoros*]
▪ *n.* **1** see ENSEMBLE 3. **3** see REFRAIN[2].

chose *past* of CHOOSE.

chosen *past part.* of CHOOSE.

chough /chuf/ *n.* any corvine bird of the genus *Pyrrhocorax*, with a glossy blue-black plumage and red legs. [ME, prob. orig. imit.]

choux pastry /shōō/ *n.* very light pastry enriched with eggs. [F, pl. of *chou* cabbage, rosette]

chow /chow/ *n.* **1** *sl.* food. **2** *offens.* a Chinese. **3 a** a dog of a Chinese breed with long hair and bluish-black tongue. **b** this breed. [shortened f. CHOW-CHOW]
▪ **1** see FOOD 1.

chow-chow /chówchow/ *n.* **1** = CHOW. **2** a Chinese preserve of ginger, orange-peel, etc., in syrup. **3** a mixed vegetable pickle. [pidgin Engl.]

chowder /chówdər/ *n. US* a soup or stew usu. of fresh fish, clams, or corn with bacon, onions, etc. [perh. F *chaudière* pot: see CAULDRON]

chow mein /chów máyn/ *n.* a Chinese-style dish of fried noodles with shredded meat or shrimps etc. and vegetables. [Chin. *chao mian* fried flour]

Chr. *abbr.* Chronicles (Old Testament).

chrestomathy /krestómməthi/ *n.* (*pl.* **-ies**) a selection of passages used esp. to help in learning a language. [F *chrestomathie* or Gk *khrēstomatheia* f. *khrēstos* useful + *-matheia* learning]

chrism /krízz'm/ *n.* a consecrated oil or unguent used esp. for anointing in Catholic and Greek Orthodox rites. [OE *crisma* f. eccl.L f. Gk *khrisma* anointing]

chrisom /krízz'm/ *n.* **1** = CHRISM. **2** (in full **chrisom-cloth**) *hist.* a white robe put on a child at baptism, and used as its shroud if it died within the month. [ME, as pop. pronunc. of CHRISM]

Christ /krīst/ *n.* & *int.* ● *n.* **1** the title, also now treated as a name, given to Jesus of Nazareth, believed by Christians to have fulfilled the Old Testament prophecies of a coming Messiah. **2** the Messiah as prophesied in the Old Testament. **3** an image or picture of Jesus. ● *int. sl.* expressing surprise, anger, etc. ▫▫ **Christhood** *n.* **Christlike** *adj.* **Christly** *adj.* [OE *Crīst* f. L *Christus* f. Gk *khristos* anointed one f. *khriō* anoint: transl. of Heb. *māšîaḥ* MESSIAH]
▪ *n.* **1, 2** see LORD *n.* 4.

Christadelphian /krístədélfiən/ *n.* & *adj.* ● *n.* a member of a Christian sect rejecting the doctrine of the Trinity and expecting a second coming of Christ on earth. ● *adj.* of or adhering to this sect and its beliefs. [CHRIST + Gk *adelphos* brother]

christen /kríss'n/ *v.tr.* **1** give a Christian name to at baptism as a sign of admission to a Christian Church. **2** give a name to anything, esp. formally or with a ceremony. **3** *colloq.* use for the first time. ▫▫ **christener** *n.* **christening** *n.* [OE *crīstnian* make Christian]
▪ **1** baptize. **2** see CALL *v.* 7.

Christendom /kríss'ndəm/ *n.* Christians worldwide, regarded as a collective body. [OE *cristendōm* f. *cristen* CHRISTIAN + -DOM]

Christian /krístiən, kríss-chən/ *adj.* & *n.* ● *adj.* **1** of Christ's teaching or religion. **2** believing in or following the religion of Jesus Christ. **3** showing the qualities associated with Christ's teaching. **4** *colloq.* (of a person) kind, fair, decent. ● *n.* **1 a** a person who has received Christian baptism. **b** an adherent of Christ's teaching. **2** a person exhibiting Christian qualities. ▫ **Christian era** the era reckoned from the traditional date of Christ's birth. **Christian name** a forename, esp. as given at baptism. **Christian Science** a Christian sect believing in the power of healing by prayer alone. **Christian Scientist** an adherent of Christian Science. ▫▫ **Christianize** *v.tr.* & *intr.* (also **-ise**). **Christianization** /krístiənīzáysh'n/ *n.* **Christianly** *adv.* [*Christianus* f. *Christus* CHRIST]

Christianity /krístiánniti/ *n.* **1** the Christian religion; its beliefs and practices. **2** being a Christian; Christian quality or character. **3** = CHRISTENDOM. [ME *cristianite* f. OF *crestienté* f. *crestien* CHRISTIAN]

Christie /krísti/ *n.* (also **Christy**) (*pl.* **-ies**) *Skiing* a sudden turn in which the skis are kept parallel, used for changing direction fast or stopping short. [abbr. of *Christiania* (now Oslo) in Norway]

Christingle /krístingg'l/ *n.* a lighted candle symbolizing Christ as the light of the world, held by children esp. at Advent services. [perh. f. G *Christkindl* dimin. of *Christkind* Christ child]

Christmas /krísməss/ *n.* & *int.* ● *n.* (*pl.* **Christmases**) **1** (also **Christmas Day**) the annual festival of Christ's birth, celebrated on 25 Dec. **2** the season in which this occurs; the time immediately before and after 25 Dec. ● *int. sl.* expressing surprise, dismay, etc. ▫ **Christmas-box** a present or gratuity given at Christmas esp. to tradesmen and employees. **Christmas cake** *Brit.* a rich fruit cake usu. covered with marzipan and icing and eaten at Christmas. **Christmas card** a card sent with greetings at Christmas. **Christmas Eve** the day or the evening before Christmas Day. **Christmas pudding** *Brit.* a rich boiled pudding eaten at Christmas, made with flour, suet, dried fruit, etc. **Christmas rose** a white-flowered winter-blooming evergreen, *Helleborus niger*. **Christmas tree** an evergreen (usu. spruce) or artificial tree set up with decorations at Christmas. ▫▫ **Christmassy** *adj.* [OE *Crīstes mæsse* (MASS[2])]

Christo- /krístō/ *comb. form* Christ.

Christology /kristólləji/ *n.* the branch of theology relating to Christ.

Christy var. of CHRISTIE. [abbr.]

chroma /krṓmə/ *n.* purity or intensity of colour. [Gk *khrōma* colour]

chromate /krṓmayt/ *n. Chem.* a salt or ester of chromic acid.

chromatic /krəmáttik/ *adj.* **1** of or produced by colour; in (esp. bright) colours. **2** *Mus.* **a** of or having notes not belonging to a diatonic scale. **b** (of a scale) ascending or descending by semitones. □ **chromatic aberration** *Optics* the failure of different wavelengths of electromagnetic radiation to come to the same focus after refraction. **chromatic semitone** *Mus.* an interval between a note and its flat or sharp. □□ **chromatically** *adv.* **chromaticism** /-tisiz'm/ *n.* [F *chromatique* or L *chromaticus* f. Gk *khrōmatikos* f. *khrōma -atos* colour

chromaticity /krṓmətíssiti/ *n.* the quality of colour regarded independently of brightness.

chromatid /krṓmətid/ *n.* either of two threadlike strands into which a chromosome divides longitudinally during cell division. [Gk *khrōma -atos* colour + -ID²]

chromatin /krṓmətin/ *n.* the material in a cell nucleus that stains with basic dyes and consists of protein, RNA, and DNA, of which eukaryotic chromosomes are composed. [G: see CHROMATID]

chromato- /krṓmətō/ *comb. form* (also **chromo-** /krṓmō/) colour (*chromatopsia*). [Gk *khrōma -atos* colour]

chromatography /krṓmətógrəfi/ *n. Chem.* the separation of the components of a mixture by slow passage through or over a material which adsorbs them differently. □□ **chromatograph** /-máttəgraaf/ *n.* **chromatographic** /-mətōgráffik/ *adj.* [G *Chromatographie* (as CHROMATO-, -GRAPHY)]

chromatopsia /krṓmətópsiə/ *n. Med.* abnormally coloured vision. [CHROMATO- + Gk *-opsia* seeing]

chrome /krōm/ *n.* **1** chromium, esp. as plating. **2** (in full **chrome yellow**) a yellow pigment obtained from lead chromate. □ **chrome leather** leather tanned with chromium salts. **chrome-nickel** (of stainless steel) containing chromium and nickel. **chrome steel** a hard fine-grained steel containing much chromium and used for tools etc. [F, = chromium, f. Gk *khrōma* colour]

chromic /krṓmik/ *adj. Chem.* of or containing trivalent chromium. □ **chromic acid** an acid that exists only in solution or in the form of chromate salts.

chromite /krṓmīt/ *n.* **1** *Mineral.* a black mineral of chromium and iron oxides, which is the principal ore of chromium. **2** *Chem.* a salt of bivalent chromium.

chromium /krṓmiəm/ *n. Chem.* a hard white metallic transition element, occurring naturally as chromite and used as a shiny decorative electroplated coating. ¶ Symb.: **Cr.** □ **chromium steel** = *chrome steel.* [mod.L f. F CHROME]

chromium-plate /krṓmiəmpláyt/ *n.* & *v.* ● *n.* an electrolytically deposited protective coating of chromium. ● *v.tr.* **1** coat with this. **2** (as **chromium-plated** *adj.*) pretentiously decorative.

chromo /krṓmō/ *n.* (*pl.* **-os**) *Austral. sl.* a prostitute. [abbr. of CHROMOLITHOGRAPH, with ref. to her make-up]
■ see PROSTITUTE *n.* 1a.

chromo-¹ /krṓmō/ *comb. form Chem.* chromium.

chromo-² *comb. form* var. of CHROMATO-.

chromolithograph /krṓmōlíthəgraaf/ *n.* & *v.* ● *n.* a coloured picture printed by lithography. ● *v.tr.* print or produce by this process. □□ **chromolithographer** /-lithógrəfər/ *n.* **chromolithographic** /-lithəgráffik/ *adj.* **chromolithography** /-lithógrəfi/ *n.*

chromosome /krṓməsōm/ *n. Biochem.* one of the threadlike structures, usu. found in the cell nucleus, that carry the genetic information in the form of genes. □ **chromosome map** a plan showing the relative positions of genes along the length of a chromosome. □□ **chromosomal** *adj.* [G *Chromosom* (as CHROMO-², -SOME³)]

chromosphere /krṓməsfeer/ *n.* a gaseous layer of the sun's atmosphere between the photosphere and the corona. □□ **chromospheric** /-sférrik/ *adj.* [CHROMO-² + SPHERE]

Chron. *abbr.* Chronicles (Old Testament).

chronic /krónnik/ *adj.* **1** persisting for a long time (usu. of an illness or a personal or social problem). **2** having a chronic complaint. **3** *colloq. disp.* habitual, inveterate (*a chronic liar*). **4** *Brit. colloq.* very bad; intense, severe. □□ **chronically** *adv.* **chronicity** /kronníssiti/ *n.* [F *chronique* f. L *chronicus* (in LL of disease) f. Gk *khronikos* f. *khronos* time]
■ **1** long-lasting, long-standing, lingering, inveterate, persistent, continuing, lasting, long-lived, long-established, deep-rooted, perennial, nagging. **3** inveterate, habitual, persistent, dyed in the wool, confirmed, hardened, incorrigible, out and out, unalterable, intractable, obdurate. **4** see AWFUL 1a, b, INTENSE 1, 3.

chronicle /krónnik'l/ *n.* & *v.* ● *n.* **1** a register of events in order of their occurrence. **2** a narrative, a full account. **3** (**Chronicles**) the name of two of the historical books of the Old Testament or Hebrew bible. ● *v.tr.* record (events) in the order of their occurrence. □□ **chronicler** *n.* [ME f. AF *cronicle* ult. f. L *chronica* f. Gk *khronika* annals: see CHRONIC]
■ *n.* **1, 2** record, history, report, register, annals, chronology, diary, journal, account, narrative, description, commentary. ● *v.* record, register, list, enter, document, put *or* set down, write down, enrol; tell, describe, recount, narrate, report, relate, retail.

chrono- /krṓnō/ *comb. form* time. [Gk *khronos* time]

chronograph /krónnəgraaf, krṓnə-, -graf/ *n.* **1** an instrument for recording time with extreme accuracy. **2** a stopwatch. □□ **chronographic** /-gráffik/ *adj.*

chronological /krónnəlójik'l/ *adj.* **1** (of a number of events) arranged or regarded in the order of their occurrence. **2** of or relating to chronology. □□ **chronologically** *adv.*

chronology /krənólləji/ *n.* (*pl.* **-ies**) **1** the study of historical records to establish the dates of past events. **2 a** the arrangement of events, dates, etc. in the order of their occurrence. **b** a table or document displaying this. □□ **chronologist** *n.* **chronologize** *v.tr.* (also **-ise**). [mod.L *chronologia* (as CHRONO-, -LOGY)]
■ **2 a** see SEQUENCE *n.* **b** account, record, calendar, almanac, journal, log, register, document, list.

chronometer /krənómmitər/ *n.* a time-measuring instrument, esp. one keeping accurate time at all temperatures and used in navigation.
■ see WATCH *n.* 1.

chronometry /krənómmitri/ *n.* the science of accurate time-measurement. □□ **chronometric** /krónnəmétrik/ *adj.* **chronometrical** /krónnəmétrik'l/ *adj.* **chronometrically** /krónnəmétrikəli/ *adv.*

chrysalis /kríssəliss/ *n.* (*pl.* **chrysalises** or **chrysalides** /krisállideez/) **1 a** a quiescent pupa of a butterfly or moth. **b** the hard outer case enclosing it. **2** a preparatory or transitional state. [L f. Gk *khrusallis -idos* f. *khrusos* gold]

chrysanth /krisánth/ *n. colloq.* any of the autumn-blooming cultivated varieties of chrysanthemum. [abbr.]

chrysanthemum /krisánthəməm/ *n.* any composite plant of the genus *Chrysanthemum*, having brightly coloured flowers. [L f. Gk *khrusanthemon* f. *khrusos* gold + *anthemon* flower]

chryselephantine /krísselifántīn/ *adj.* (of ancient Greek sculpture) overlaid with gold and ivory. [Gk *khruselephantinos* f. *khrusos* gold + *elephas* ivory]

chrysoberyl /kríssəbérril/ *n.* a yellowish-green gem consisting of a beryllium salt. [L *chrysoberyllus* f. Gk *khrusos* gold + *bērullos* beryl]

chrysolite /kríssəlīt/ *n.* a precious stone, a yellowish-green or brownish variety of olivine. [ME f. OF *crisolite* f. med.L *crisolitus* f. L *chrysolithus* f. Gk *khrusolithos* f. *khrusos* gold + *lithos* stone]

chrysoprase /kríssəprayz/ *n.* **1** an apple-green variety of chalcedony containing nickel and used as a gem. **2** (in the New Testament) prob. a golden-green variety of beryl. [ME f. OF *crisopace* f. L *chrysopassus* var. of L *chrysoprasus* f. Gk *khrusoprasos* f. *khrusos* gold + *prason* leek]

chthonic /kthónnik, thón-/ (also **chthonian** /kthṓniən, thṓ-/) *adj.* of, relating to, or inhabiting the underworld. [Gk *khthōn* earth]

chub /chub/ *n.* a thick-bodied coarse-fleshed river fish, *Leuciscus cephalus*. [15th c.: orig. unkn.]

chubby /chúbbi/ *adj.* (**chubbier**, **chubbiest**) plump and rounded (esp. of a person or a part of the body). □□ **chubbily** *adv.* **chubbiness** *n.* [CHUB]
■ podgy, stumpy, stubby, chunky, tubby, plump, dumpy, rotund, *colloq.* pudgy; thickset, heavy-set, heavy, overweight, fat.

chuck[1] /chuk/ *v.* & *n.* ● *v.tr.* **1** *colloq.* fling or throw carelessly or with indifference. **2** *colloq.* (often foll. by *in, up*) give up; reject, abandon; jilt (*chucked in my job*; *chucked her boyfriend*). **3** touch playfully, esp. under the chin. ● *n.* a playful touch under the chin. □ **the chuck** *sl.* dismissal (*he got the chuck*). **chucker-out** *colloq.* a person employed to expel troublesome people from a gathering etc. **chuck it** *sl.* stop, desist. **chuck off** *Austral.* & *NZ sl.* sneer, scoff. **chuck out** *colloq.* **1** expel (a person) from a gathering etc. **2** get rid of, discard. [16th c., perh. f. F *chuquer, choquer* to knock]
■ *v.* **1** see THROW *v.* 1, 2. **2** see DROP *v.* 4. □ **chuck out 1** see *cast out*. **2** see *throw away* 1.

chuck[2] /chuk/ *n.* & *v.* ● *n.* **1** a cut of beef between the neck and the ribs. **2** a device for holding a workpiece in a lathe or a tool in a drill. ● *v.tr.* fix (wood, a tool, etc.) to a chuck. [var. of CHOCK]

chuck[3] /chuk/ *n.* *US colloq.* food. □ **chuck-wagon 1** a provision-cart on a ranch etc. **2** a roadside eating-place. [19th c.: perh. f. CHUCK[2]]

chuckle /chúkk'l/ *v.* & *n.* ● *v.intr.* laugh quietly or inwardly. ● *n.* a quiet or suppressed laugh. □□ **chuckler** *n.* [*chuck* cluck]
■ *v.* laugh, chortle, giggle, titter, tee-hee, snigger, snicker. ● *n.* titter, tee-hee, laugh, chortle, giggle, snigger, snicker.

chucklehead /chúkk'lhed/ *n.* *colloq.* a stupid person. □□ **chuckleheaded** *adj.* [*chuckle* clumsy, prob. rel. to CHUCK[2]]
■ see FOOL[1] *n.* 1.

chuddar var. of CHADOR.

chuff /chuf/ *v.intr.* (of a steam engine etc.) work with a regular sharp puffing sound. [imit.]

chuffed /chuft/ *adj.* *Brit. sl.* delighted. [dial. *chuff* pleased]
■ see GLAD[1] 1.

chug /chug/ *v.* & *n.* ● *v.intr.* (**chugged**, **chugging**) **1** emit a regular muffled explosive sound, as of an engine running slowly. **2** move with this sound. ● *n.* a chugging sound. [imit.]

chukar /chukaár/ *n.* a red-legged partridge, *Alectoris chukar*, native to India. [Hindi *cakor*]

chukker /chúkkər/ *n.* (also **chukka**) each of the periods of play into which a game of polo is divided. □ **chukka boot** an ankle-high leather boot as worn for polo. [Hindi *cakkar* f. Skr. *cakra* wheel]

chum[1] /chum/ *n.* & *v.* ● *n.* *colloq.* (esp. among schoolchildren) a close friend. ● *v.intr.* (often foll. by *with*) share rooms. □ **chum up** (often foll. by *with*) become a close friend (of). □□ **chummy** *adj.* (**chummier**, **chummiest**). **chummily** *adv.* **chumminess** *n.* [17th c.: prob. short for *chamber-fellow*]
■ *n.* friend, comrade, mate, playmate, (boon) companion, crony, confidant(e), intimate, second self, familiar, *colloq.* pal, sidekick, *Austral.* & *NZ colloq.* cobber, *Brit. colloq.* oppo, *esp. US colloq.* buddy, amigo, *sl.* mucker; fellow, colleague. □ **chum up** (*chum up with*) ally (oneself) with, be friendly with, go with, associate with, team up with, *colloq.* pal up with. □□ **chummy** friendly, intimate, close, attached, matey, on good terms, *colloq.* pally, thick, *US colloq.* solid.

chum[2] /chum/ *n.* & *v.* *US* ● *n.* **1** refuse from fish. **2** chopped fish used as bait. ● *v.* **1** *intr.* fish using chum. **2** *tr.* bait (a fishing place) using chum. [19th c.: orig. unkn.]

chump /chump/ *n.* **1** *colloq.* a foolish person. **2** *Brit.* the thick end, esp. of a loin of lamb or mutton (*chump chop*). **3** a short thick block of wood. **4** *Brit. sl.* the head. □ **off one's chump** *Brit. sl.* crazy. [18th c.: blend of CHUNK and LUMP[1]]
■ **1** see FOOL[1] *n.* 1. **4** see BLOCK *n.* 10.

chunder /chúndər/ *v.intr.* & *n.* *Austral. sl.* vomit. [20th c.: orig. unkn.]
■ *v.* see VOMIT *v.* 1. ● *n.* see VOMIT *n.*

chunk /chungk/ *n.* **1** a thick solid slice or piece of something firm or hard. **2** a substantial amount or piece. [prob. var. of CHUCK[2]]
■ see PIECE *n.* 1a.

chunky /chúngki/ *adj.* (**chunkier**, **chunkiest**) **1** containing or consisting of chunks. **2** short and thick; small and sturdy. **3** (of clothes) made of a thick material. □□ **chunkiness** *n.*
■ **1** see LUMPY 1. **2** see STOCKY. **3** see BULKY.

Chunnel /chúnn'l/ *n.* *colloq.* a tunnel under the English Channel linking England and France. [portmanteau word f. *Channel tunnel*]

chunter /chúntər/ *v.intr.* *Brit. colloq.* mutter, grumble. [prob. imit.]
■ see MUTTER *v.* 2.

chupatty var. of CHAPATTI.

church /church/ *n.* & *v.* ● *n.* **1** a building for public (usu. Christian) worship. **2** a meeting for public worship in such a building (*go to church*; *met after church*). **3** (**Church**) the body of all Christians. **4** (**Church**) the clergy or clerical profession (*went into the Church*). **5** (**Church**) an organized Christian group or society of any time, country, or distinct principles of worship (*the primitive Church*; *Church of Scotland*; *High Church*). **6** (**Church**) institutionalized religion as a political or social force (*Church and State*). ● *v.tr.* bring (esp. a woman after childbirth) to church for a service of thanksgiving. □ **Church Army** an organization of the Church of England concerned with social welfare. **Church Commissioners** a body managing the finances of the Church of England. **Church of England** the English Church, recognized by the State and having the sovereign as its head. **church school** a school founded by or associated with the Church of England. [OE *cirice, circe*, etc. f. med. Gk *kurikon* f. Gk *kuriakon* (*dōma*) Lord's (house) f. *kurios* Lord: cf. KIRK]
■ *n.* **1** see TEMPLE[1]. **4** see MINISTRY 2, 3. **5** see DENOMINATION 1.

churchgoer /chúrchgōər/ *n.* a person who goes to church, esp. regularly. □□ **churchgoing** *n.* & *adj.*

churchman /chúrchmən/ *n.* (*pl.* **-men**) **1** a member of the clergy or of a church. **2** a supporter of the church.
■ **1** see CLERGYMAN.

churchwarden /chúrchwáwrd'n/ *n.* **1** either of two elected lay representatives of a parish, assisting with routine administration. **2** a long-stemmed clay pipe.

churchwoman /chúrchwoomman/ *n.* (*pl.* **-women**) **1** a woman member of the clergy or of a church. **2** a woman supporter of the Church.

churchy /chúrchi/ *adj.* **1** obtrusively or intolerantly devoted to the Church or opposed to religious dissent. **2** like a church. □□ **churchiness** *n.*

churchyard /chúrchyaard/ *n.* the enclosed ground around a church, esp. as used for burials.
■ see GRAVEYARD.

churinga /churínggə/ *n.* (*pl.* same or **churingas**) a sacred object, esp. an amulet, among the Australian Aboriginals. [Aboriginal]

churl /churl/ *n.* **1** an ill-bred person. **2** *archaic* a peasant; a person of low birth. **3** *archaic* a surly or mean person. [OE *ceorl* f. a WG root, = man]
■ **1** see SLOB. **2** see PEASANT.

churlish /chúrlish/ *adj.* surly; mean. □□ **churlishly** *adv.* **churlishness** *n.* [OE *cierlisc, ceorlisc* f. *ceorl* CHURL]
■ see MEAN[2] 5.

churn /churn/ *n.* & *v.* ● *n.* **1** *Brit.* a large milk-can. **2** a machine for making butter by agitating milk or cream. ● *v.*

1 *tr.* agitate (milk or cream) in a churn. **2** *tr.* produce (butter) in this way. **3** *tr.* (usu. foll. by *up*) cause distress to; upset, agitate. **4** *intr.* (of a liquid) seethe, foam violently (*the churning sea*). **5** *tr.* agitate or move (liquid) vigorously, causing it to foam. □ **churn out** produce routinely or mechanically, esp. in large quantities. [OE *cyrin* f. Gmc]
■ *n.* **2** see AGITATOR 2. ● *v.* **1** see STIR[1] *v.* 1. **3** see DISTURB 1. **4** see SWIRL *v.* □ **churn out** see *run off* 2.

churr var. of CHIRR.

chute[1] /shoot/ *n.* **1** a sloping channel or slide, with or without water, for conveying things to a lower level. **2** a slide into a swimming-pool. **3** *US* a cataract or cascade of water; a steep descent in a river-bed producing a swift current. [F *chute* fall (of water etc.), f. OF *cheoite* fem. past part. of *cheoir* fall f. L *cadere*; in some senses = SHOOT]
■ **1** slide, shaft, channel, ramp, runway, trough, conduit, race. **2** slide, flume. **3** waterfall, rapid.

chute[2] /shoot/ *n. colloq.* parachute. □□ **chutist** *n.* [abbr.]

chutney /chútni/ *n.* (*pl.* **-eys**) a pungent orig. Indian condiment made of fruits or vegetables, vinegar, spices, sugar, etc. [Hindi *caṭnī*]

chutzpah /khootspə/ *n. sl.* shameless audacity; cheek. [Yiddish]
■ see NERVE *n.* 2b.

chyack var. of CHIACK.

chyle /kīl/ *n.* a milky fluid consisting of lymph and absorbed food materials from the intestine after digestion. □□ **chylous** *adj.* [LL *chylus* f. Gk *khulos* juice]

chyme /kīm/ *n.* the acidic semisolid and partly digested food produced by the action of gastric secretion. □□ **chymous** *adj.* [LL *chymus* f. Gk *khumos* juice]

chypre /sheeprə/ *n.* a heavy perfume made from sandalwood. [F, = Cyprus, perh. where it was first made]

CI *abbr.* **1** Channel Islands. **2** *hist.* Order of the Crown of India.

Ci *abbr.* curie.

CIA *abbr.* Central Intelligence Agency (US).

ciao /chow/ *int. colloq.* **1** goodbye. **2** hello. [It.]
■ **1** see GOODBYE *int.* **2** see HELLO *int.*

ciborium /sibóriəm/ *n.* (*pl.* **ciboria** /-riə/) **1** a vessel with an arched cover used to hold the Eucharist. **2** *Archit.* **a** a canopy. **b** a shrine with a canopy. [med.L f. Gk *kibōrion* seed-vessel of the water-lily, a cup made from it]

cicada /sikaadə, -káydə/ *n.* (also **cicala** /sikaalə/) any transparent-winged large insect of the family Cicadidae, the males of which make a loud rhythmic chirping sound. [L *cicada*, It. f. L *cicala*, It. *cigala*]

cicatrice /síkkətriss/ *n.* (also **cicatrix** /-triks/) (*pl.* **cicatrices** /-trīseez/) **1** any mark left by a healed wound; a scar. **2** *Bot.* **a** a mark on a stem etc. left when a leaf or other part becomes detached. **b** a scar on the bark of a tree. □□ **cicatricial** /-trísh'l/ *adj.* [ME f. OF *cicatrice* or L *cicatrix -icis*]

cicatrize /síkkətrīz/ *v.* (also **-ise**) **1** *tr.* heal (a wound) by scar formation. **2** *intr.* (of a wound) heal by scar formation. □□ **cicatrization** /-záysh'n/ *n.* [F *cicatriser*: see CICATRICE]

cicely /síssəli/ *n.* (*pl.* **-ies**) any of various umbelliferous plants, esp. sweet cicely (see SWEET). [app. f. L *seselis* f. Gk, assim. to the woman's Christian name]

cicerone /chíchərōni, síssə-/ *n.* (*pl.* **ciceroni** /*pronunc.* same/) a guide who gives information about antiquities, places of interest, etc. to sightseers. [It.: see CICERONIAN]
■ see GUIDE *n.* 1–3.

Ciceronian /síssərōniən/ *adj.* (of language) eloquent, classical, or rhythmical, in the style of Cicero. [L *Ciceronianus* f. *Cicero -onis* Roman statesman and orator d. 43 BC]

cichlid /síklid/ *n.* any tropical freshwater fish of the family Cichlidae, esp. the kinds kept in aquariums. [mod.L *Cichlidae* f. Gk *kikhlē* a kind of fish]

CID *abbr.* (in the UK) Criminal Investigation Department.

-cide /sīd/ *suffix* forming nouns meaning: **1** a person or substance that kills (*regicide*; *insecticide*). **2** the killing of (*infanticide*; *suicide*). [F f. L *-cida* (sense 1), *-cidium* (sense 2), *caedere* kill]

cider /sīdər/ *n.* (also **cyder**) **1** *Brit.* an alcoholic drink made from fermented apple-juice. **2** *US* an unfermented drink made from apple-juice. □ **cider-press** a press for crushing apples to make cider. [ME f. OF *sidre*, ult. f. Heb. *šēkār* strong drink]

ci-devant /seedəvón/ *adj.* & *adv.* that has been (with person's earlier name or status); former or formerly. [F, = heretofore]
■ *adj.* see FORMER[1] 2. ● *adv.* see FORMERLY.

CIE *abbr. hist.* Companion (of the Order) of the Indian Empire.

c.i.f. *abbr.* cost, insurance, freight (as being included in a price).

cig /sig/ *n. colloq.* cigarette, cigar. [abbr.]
■ see CIGARETTE.

cigala /sigaalə/ *n.* = CICADA. [F *cigale*, It. & Prov. *cigala* f. L *cicada*]

cigar /sigaar/ *n.* a cylinder of tobacco rolled in tobacco leaves for smoking. [F *cigare* or Sp. *cigarro*]

cigarette /síggərét/ *n.* (*US* also **cigaret**) **1** a thin cylinder of finely-cut tobacco rolled in paper for smoking. **2** a similar cylinder containing a narcotic or medicated substance. □ **cigarette card** a small picture card of a kind formerly included in a packet of cigarettes. **cigarette-end** the unsmoked remainder of a cigarette. [F, dimin. of *cigare* CIGAR]
■ **1** *colloq.* cig, ciggy, smoke, *sl.* fag, burn, coffin-nail, cancer stick, *Brit. sl.* gasper, snout. **2** *sl.* joint, reefer, spliff, *US sl.* bomb.

cigarillo /síggərílló/ *n.* (*pl.* **-os**) a small cigar. [Sp., dimin. of *cigarro* CIGAR]

ciggy /síggi/ *n.* (*pl.* **-ies**) *colloq.* cigarette. [abbr.]
■ see CIGARETTE.

CIGS *abbr. hist.* Chief of the Imperial General Staff.

cilice /sílliss/ *n.* **1** haircloth. **2** a garment of this. [F f. L *cilicium* f. Gk *kilikion* f. *Kilikia* Cilicia in Asia Minor]

cilium /sílliəm/ *n.* (*pl.* **cilia** /-liə/) **1** a short minute hairlike vibrating structure on the surface of some cells, causing currents in the surrounding fluid. **2** an eyelash. □□ **ciliary** *adj.* **ciliate** /-liayt, -liət/ *adj.* **ciliated** *adj.* **ciliation** /-liáysh'n/ *n.* [L, = eyelash]

cill var. of SILL.

cimbalom /símbələm/ *n.* a dulcimer. [Magyar f. It. *cembalo*]

C.-in-C. *abbr.* Commander-in-Chief.

cinch /sinch/ *n.* & *v.* ● *n.* **1** *colloq.* **a** a sure thing; a certainty. **b** an easy task. **2** a firm hold. **3** esp. *US* a girth for a saddle or pack. ● *v.tr.* **1** **a** tighten as with a cinch (*cinched at the waist with a belt*). **b** secure a grip on. **2** *sl.* make certain of. **3** esp. *US* put a cinch (sense 3) on. [Sp. *cincha*]
■ *n.* **1** **a** see CERTAINTY 1b. **b** see PUSHOVER 1. **3** see GIRTH *n.* 2.

cinchona /singkónə/ *n.* **1** **a** any evergreen tree or shrub of the genus *Cinchona*, native to S. America, with fragrant flowers and yielding cinchona bark. **b** the bark of this tree, containing quinine. **2** any drug from this bark formerly used as a tonic and to stimulate the appetite. □□ **cinchonic** /-kónnik/ *adj.* **cinchonine** /síngkəneen/ *n.* [mod.L f. Countess of Chinchón d. 1641, introducer of drug into Spain]

cincture /síngkchər/ *n.* **1** *literary* a girdle, belt, or border. **2** *Archit.* a ring at either end of a column-shaft. [L *cinctura* f. *cingere cinct-* gird]
■ **1** see BELT *n.* 1.

cinder /síndər/ *n.* **a** the residue of coal or wood etc. that has stopped giving off flames but still has combustible matter in it. **b** slag. **c** (in *pl.*) ashes. □ **burnt to a cinder** made useless by burning. □□ **cindery** *adj.* [OE *sinder*, assim. to the unconnected F *cendre* and L *cinis* ashes]

Cinderella /síndərélla/ *n.* **1** a person or thing of unrecognized or disregarded merit or beauty. **2** a neglected or despised member of a group. [the name of a girl in a fairy-tale]

cine- /sínni/ *comb. form* cinematographic (*cine-camera*; *cine-photography*). [abbr.]

cineaste /sínniast/ *n.* (also **cineast**) a cinema enthusiast. [F *cinéaste* (as CINE-): cf. ENTHUSIAST]

cinema /sínnimaa, -mə/ *n.* **1** *Brit.* a theatre where motion-picture films (see FILM *n.* 3) are shown. **2 a** films collectively. **b** the production of films as an art or industry; cinematography. □ **cinema organ** *Mus.* a kind of organ with extra stops and special effects. [F *cinéma*: see CINEMATOGRAPH]
■ **1** (film) theatre, cinematheque, flea-pit, *Brit. archaic* picture-palace, picture-theatre, *esp. US colloq.* movie-house, *S.Afr. sl.* bioscope. **2 a** see PICTURE *n.* 3.

cinematheque /sínnimətek/ *n.* **1** a film library or archive. **2** a small cinema. [F]

cinematic /sínnimáttik/ *adj.* **1** having the qualities characteristic of the cinema. **2** of or relating to the cinema. □□ **cinematically** *adv.*

cinematograph /sínnimáttəgraaf/ (also **kinematograph** /kín-/) *n.* an apparatus for showing motion-picture films. [F *cinématographe* f. Gk *kinēma -atos* movement f. *kineō* move]

cinematography /sínnimətógrəfi/ *n.* the art of making motion-picture films. □□ **cinematographer** *n.* **cinematographic** /-máttəgráffik/ *adj.* **cinematographically** /-máttəgráffikəli/ *adv.*
■ □□ **cinematographer** see *photographer* (PHOTOGRAPH).

cinéma-vérité /sínnemaá vérritáy/ *n. Cinematog.* **1** the art or process of making realistic (esp. documentary) films which avoid artificiality and artistic effect. **2** such films collectively. [F, = cinema truth]

cineraria /sínnəráiriə/ *n.* any of several varieties of the composite plant, *Cineraria cruentus*, having bright flowers and ash-coloured down on its leaves. [mod.L, fem. of L *cinerarius* of ashes f. *cinis -eris* ashes, from the ash-coloured down on the leaves]

cinerarium /sínnəráiriəm/ *n.* (*pl.* **cinerariums**) a place where a cinerary urn is deposited. [LL, neut. of *cinerarius*: see CINERARIA]

cinerary /sínnərəri/ *adj.* of ashes. □ **cinerary urn** an urn for holding the ashes after cremation. [L *cinerarius*: see CINERARIA]

cinereous /sineériəss/ *adj.* (esp. of a bird or plumage) ash-grey. [L *cinereus* f. *cinis -eris* ashes]

ciné-vérité /sínnevérritáy/ *n. Cinematog.* = CINÉMA-VÉRITÉ.

Cingalese /sínggəléez/ *adj.* & *n.* (*pl.* same) *archaic* Sinhalese. [F *cing(h)alais*: see SINHALESE]

cingulum /síngyooləm/ *n.* (*pl.* **cingula** /-lə/) *Anat.* a girdle, belt, or analogous structure, esp. a ridge surrounding the base of the crown of a tooth. [L, = belt]
■ see RING[1] *n.* 2.

cinnabar /sínnəbaar/ *n.* **1** a bright red mineral form of mercuric sulphide from which mercury is obtained. **2** vermilion. **3** a moth (*Callimorpha jacobaeae*) with reddish marked wings. [ME f. L *cinnabaris* f. Gk *kinnabari*, of oriental orig.]

cinnamon /sínnəmən/ *n.* **1** an aromatic spice from the peeled, dried, and rolled bark of a SE Asian tree. **2** any tree of the genus *Cinnamomum*, esp. *C. zeylanicum* yielding the spice. **3** yellowish-brown. [ME f. OF *cinnamome* f. L *cinnamomum* f. Gk *kinnamōmon*, and L *cinnamon* f. Gk *kinnamon*, f. Semitic (cf. Heb. *ḳinnāmôn*)]

cinque /singk/ *n.* (also **cinq**) the five on dice. [ME f. OF *cinc, cink*, f. L *quinque* five]

cinquecento /chíngkwichéntō/ *n.* the style of Italian art and literature of the 16th c., with a reversion to classical forms. □□ **cinquecentist** *n.* [It., = 500, used with ref. to the years 1500-99]

cinquefoil /síngkfoyl/ *n.* **1** any plant of the genus *Potentilla*, with compound leaves of five leaflets. **2** *Archit.* a five-cusped ornament in a circle or arch. [ME f. L *quinquefolium* f. *quinque* five + *folium* leaf]

Cinque Ports /síngk pórts/ *n.pl.* a group of ports (orig. five only) on the SE coast of England with ancient privileges. [ME f. OF *cink porz*, L *quinque portus* five ports]

cion *US* var. of SCION 1.

cipher /sífər/ *n.* & *v.* (also **cypher**) ● *n.* **1 a** a secret or disguised way of writing. **b** a thing written in this way. **c** the key to it. **2** the arithmetical symbol (0) denoting no amount but used to occupy a vacant place in decimal etc. numeration (as in 12.05). **3** a person or thing of no importance. **4** the interlaced initials of a person or company etc.; a monogram. **5** any Arabic numeral. **6** continuous sounding of an organ-pipe, caused by a mechanical defect. ● *v.* **1** *tr.* put into secret writing, encipher. **2 a** *tr.* (usu. foll. by *out*) work out by arithmetic, calculate. **b** *intr. archaic* do arithmetic. [ME, f. OF *cif(f)re*, ult. f. Arab *ṣifr* ZERO]
■ *n.* **1 a** see CODE *n.* 2. **2** see ZERO *n.* 1. **3** see NOBODY *n.* **4** see SIGN *n.* 2. **5** see FIGURE *n.* 6a.

cipolin /síppəlin/ *n.* an Italian white-and-green marble. [F *cipolin* or It. *cipollino* f. *cipolla* onion]

circa /súrkə/ *prep.* (preceding a date) about. [L]
■ see AROUND *prep.* 4b.

circadian /surkáydiən/ *adj. Physiol.* occurring or recurring about once per day. [irreg. f. L *circa* about + *dies* day]
■ see DAILY *adj.* 1.

Circe /súrsi/ *n.* a dangerously attractive enchantress. [L f. Gk *Kirkē*, an enchantress in Gk mythol.]

circinate /súrsinayt/ *adj. Bot.* & *Zool.* rolled up with the apex in the centre, e.g. of young fronds of ferns. [L *circinatus* past part. of *circinare* make round f. *circinus* pair of compasses]

circle /súrk'l/ *n.* & *v.* ● *n.* **1 a** a round plane figure whose circumference is everywhere equidistant from its centre. **b** the line enclosing a circle. **2** a roundish enclosure or structure. **3** a ring. **4** a curved upper tier of seats in a theatre etc. (*dress circle*). **5** a circular route. **6** *Archaeol.* a group of (usu. large embedded) stones arranged in a circle. **7** *Hockey* = *striking-circle*. **8** persons grouped round a centre of interest. **9** a set or class or restricted group (*literary circles*; *not done in the best circles*). **10** a period or cycle (*the circle of the year*). **11** (in full **vicious circle**) **a** an unbroken sequence of reciprocal cause and effect. **b** an action and reaction that intensify each other (cf. *virtuous circle*). **c** the fallacy of proving a proposition from another which depends on the first for its own proof. ● *v.* **1** *intr.* (often foll. by *round, about*) move in a circle. **2** *tr.* **a** revolve round. **b** form a circle round. □ **circle back** move in a wide loop towards the starting-point. **come full circle** return to the starting-point. **go round in circles** make no progress despite effort. **great** (or **small**) **circle** a circle on the surface of a sphere whose plane passes (or does not pass) through the sphere's centre. **run round in circles** *colloq.* be fussily busy with little result. □□ **circler** *n.* [ME f. OF *cercle* f. L *circulus* dimin. of *circus* ring]
■ *n.* **1** disc, round. **3** ring, hoop, band, loop, coil; *esp. Math.* & *Biol.* annulus. **9** set, coterie, clique, class, sphere, division, group, camp, faction, *Austral. sl.* push; society, company, crowd. **10** see CYCLE *n.* 1a. ● *v.* **1** see REVOLVE 1, 2. **2** go (a)round, tour, circumnavigate, *formal* circumambulate; encircle, surround, enclose, circumscribe, ring, hoop, girth, clasp, enlace, environ, orb, fillet, wreathe, fringe, *literary* gird; shut in, hem in. □ **go round in circles** get nowhere, take two steps forward and one step back. **run round in circles** see FUSS *v.* 1c.

circlet /súrklit/ *n.* **1** a small circle. **2** a circular band, esp. of gold or jewelled etc., as an ornament.
■ see RING[1] *n.* 2.

circs /surks/ *n.pl. colloq.* circumstances. [abbr.]

circuit /súrkit/ *n.* **1 a** a line or course enclosing an area; the distance round; the circumference. **b** the area enclosed. **2** *Electr.* **a** the path of a current. **b** the apparatus through which a current passes. **3 a** the journey of a judge in a particular district to hold courts. **b** this district. **c** the lawyers following a circuit. **4** a chain of theatres or cinemas etc. under a single management. **5** *Brit.* a motor-racing track. **6 a** a sequence of sporting events (*the US tennis circuit*). **b** a sequence of athletic exercises. **7** a roundabout journey. **8 a** a group of local Methodist churches forming a minor administrative unit. **b** the journey of an itinerant minister within this. □ **circuit-breaker** an automatic device for stopping the flow of current in an electrical circuit. [ME f. OF, f. L *circuitus* f. CIRCUM- + *ire it-* go]

■ **1 a** round, tour, ambit, circle, orbit, course, lap, revolution; compass, circumference, perimeter, periphery, girth, border, boundary, edge, limit, ambit, margin, outline, confine(s), bound, pale. **3, 8b** see ROUND *n.* 3. **6 a** sequence, series. **b** see SEQUENCE *n.* **7** see JOURNEY *n.*

circuitous /surkyóō-itəss/ *adj.* **1** indirect (and usu. long). **2** going a long way round. □□ **circuitously** *adv.* **circuitousness** *n.* [med.L *circuitosus* f. *circuitus* CIRCUIT]

■ see INDIRECT 1, 2.

circuitry /súrkitri/ *n.* (*pl.* **-ies**) **1** a system of electric circuits. **2** the equipment forming this.

circular /súrkyoolər/ *adj.* & *n.* ● *adj.* **1 a** having the form of a circle. **b** moving or taking place along a circle; indirect, circuitous (*circular tour*). **2** *Logic* (of reasoning) depending on a vicious circle. **3** (of a letter or advertisement etc.) printed for distribution to a large number of people. ● *n.* a circular letter, leaflet, etc. □ **circular saw** a power saw with a rapidly rotating toothed disc. □□ **circularity** /-lárriti/ *n.* **circularly** *adv.* [ME f. AF *circuler*, OF *circulier*, *cerclier* f. LL *circularis* f. L *circulus* CIRCLE]

■ *adj.* **1 a** round, disc-shaped, disc-like, discoid; ring-shaped, ring-like, annular. **b** roundabout, indirect, circuitous, tortuous, twisting, twisted, anfractuous; periphrastic, circumlocutory; devious. **2** illogical, inconsistent, redundant, fallacious, irrational, sophistic, sophistical.

circularize /súrkyoolərīz/ *v.tr.* (also **-ise**) **1** distribute circulars to. **2** *US* seek opinions of (people) by means of a questionnaire. □□ **circularization** /-záysh'n/ *n.*

circulate /súrkyoolayt/ *v.* **1** *intr.* go round from one place or person etc. to the next and so on; be in circulation. **2** *tr.* **a** cause to go round; put into circulation. **b** give currency to (a report etc.). **c** circularize. **3** *intr.* be actively sociable at a party, gathering, etc. □ **circulating library** a small library with books lent to a group of subscribers in turn. **circulating medium** notes or gold etc. used in exchange. □□ **circulative** *adj.* **circulator** *n.* [L *circulare circulat-* f. *circulus* CIRCLE]

■ **1** move *or* go about *or* round *or* around, orbit, flow, course, run, circle. **2 a, b** spread, distribute, disseminate, issue, publish, air, announce, proclaim, make known, noise abroad, bruit about, report, broadcast, reveal, divulge, advertise, publicize, promulgate, put about, bring *or* put out, pass out *or* round *or* around. **3** go round *or* around, mix, mingle, move around, socialize, fraternize.

circulation /súrkyooláysh'n/ *n.* **1 a** movement to and fro, or from and back to a starting point, esp. of a fluid in a confined area or circuit. **b** the movement of blood from and to the heart. **c** a similar movement of sap etc. **2 a** the transmission or distribution (of news or information or books etc.). **b** the number of copies sold, esp. of journals and newspapers. **3 a** currency, coin, etc. **b** the movement or exchange of this in a country etc. □ **in** (or **out of**) **circulation** participating (or not participating) in activities etc. [F *circulation* or L *circulatio* f. *circulare* CIRCULATE]

■ **1** circuit, course, orbit, flow, motion. **2 a** spreading, dissemination, transmission, passage, distribution, diffusion, publication, advertisement, announcement, issuance, pronouncement, proclamation, promulgation, broadcast, broadcasting. **3 a** currency, coin, specie; change, cash, silver.

circulatory /súrkyooláytəri, -lətəri/ *adj.* of or relating to the circulation of blood or sap.

circum- /súrkəm/ *comb. form* round, about, around, used: **1** adverbially (*circumambient*; *circumfuse*). **2** prepositionally (*circumlunar*; *circumocular*). [from or after L *circum* prep. = round, about]

circumambient /súrkəmámbiənt/ *adj.* (esp. of air or another fluid) surrounding. □□ **circumambience** *n.* **circumambiency** *n.*

■ see *surrounding* (SURROUND).

circumambulate /súrkəmámbyoolayt/ *v.tr.* & *intr. formal* walk round or about. □□ **circumambulation** /-láysh'n/ *n.* **circumambulatory** *adj.* [CIRCUM- + *ambulate* f. L *ambulare* walk]

circumcircle /súrkəmsurk'l/ *n. Geom.* a circle touching all the vertices of a triangle or polygon.

circumcise /súrkəmsīz/ *v.tr.* **1** cut off the foreskin, as a Jewish or Muslim rite or a surgical operation. **2** cut off the clitoris (and sometimes the labia), usu. as a religious rite. **3** *Bibl.* purify (the heart etc.). [ME f. OF f. L *circumcidere circumcis-* (as CIRCUM-, *caedere* cut)]

circumcision /súrkəmsízh'n/ *n.* **1** the act or rite of circumcising or being circumcised. **2** (**Circumcision**) *Eccl.* the feast of the Circumcision of Christ, 1 Jan. [ME f. OF *circoncision* f. LL *circumcisio -onis* (as CIRCUMCISE)]

circumference /sərkúmfərənss/ *n.* **1** the enclosing boundary, esp. of a circle or other figure enclosed by a curve. **2** the distance round. □□ **circumferential** /súrkəmfərénsh'l/ *adj.* **circumferentially** /súrkəmfərénshəli/ *adv.* [ME f. OF *circonference* f. L *circumferentia* (as CIRCUM-, *ferre* bear)]

■ **1** see PERIMETER.

circumflex /súrkəmfleks/ *n.* & *adj.* ● *n.* (in full **circumflex accent**) a mark (ˆ) placed over a vowel in some languages to indicate a contraction, length, or a special quality. ● *adj. Anat.* curved, bending round something else (*circumflex nerve*). [L *circumflexus* (as CIRCUM-, *flectere flex-* bend), transl. of Gk *perispōmenos* drawn around]

circumfluent /sərkúmflooənt/ *adj.* flowing round, surrounding. □□ **circumfluence** *n.* [L *circumfluere* (as CIRCUM-, *fluere* flow)]

circumfuse /súrkəmfyóōz/ *v.tr.* pour round or about. [CIRCUM- + L *fundere fus-* pour]

circumjacent /súrkəmjáys'nt/ *adj.* situated around. [L *circumjacēre* (as CIRCUM-, *jacēo* lie)]

■ see *surrounding* (SURROUND).

circumlocution /súrkəmləkyóōsh'n/ *n.* **1 a** a roundabout expression. **b** evasive talk. **2** the use of many words where fewer would do; verbosity. □□ **circumlocutional** *adj.* **circumlocutionary** *adj.* **circumlocutionist** *n.* **circumlocutory** /-lókyootəri/ *adj.* [ME f. F *circumlocution* or L *circumlocutio* (as CIRCUM-, LOCUTION), transl. of Gk PERIPHRASIS]

■ **1 a** periphrasis. **b** see EVASION 2. **2** see TAUTOLOGY 1.

circumlunar /súrkəmlóōnər/ *adj.* moving or situated around the moon.

circumnavigate /súrkəmnávvigayt/ *v.tr.* sail round (esp. the world). □□ **circumnavigation** /-gáysh'n/ *n.* **circumnavigator** *n.* [L *circumnavigare* (as CIRCUM-, NAVIGATE)]

■ see CIRCLE *v.* 2.

circumpolar /súrkəmpṓlər/ *adj.* **1** *Geog.* around or near one of the earth's poles. **2** *Astron.* (of a star or motion etc.) above the horizon at all times in a given latitude.

circumscribe /súrkəmskrīb/ *v.tr.* **1** (of a line etc.) enclose or outline. **2** lay down the limits of; confine, restrict. **3** *Geom.* draw (a figure) round another, touching it at points but not cutting it (cf. INSCRIBE). □□ **circumscribable** /-skrībəb'l/ *adj.* **circumscriber** *n.* **circumscription** /-skrípsh'n/ *n.* [L *circumscribere* (as CIRCUM-, *scribere script-* write)]

■ **1** see DEFINE 4. **2** see RESTRICT.

circumsolar /súrkəmsṓlər/ *adj.* moving or situated around or near the sun.

circumspect /súrkəmspekt/ *adj.* wary, cautious; taking everything into account. □□ **circumspection** /-spéksh'n/ *n.* **circumspectly** *adv.* [ME f. L *circumspicere circumspect-* (as CIRCUM-, *specere spect-* look)]

■ see CAUTIOUS.

circumstance /súrkəmstənss/ *n.* **1 a** a fact, occurrence, or condition, esp. (in *pl.*) the time, place, manner, cause, occasion etc., or surroundings of an act or event. **b** (in *pl.*) the external conditions that affect or might affect an action. **2** (often foll. by *that* + clause) an incident, occurrence, or fact, as needing consideration (*the circumstance that he left early*). **3** (in *pl.*) one's state of financial or material welfare (*in reduced circumstances*). **4** ceremony, fuss (*pomp and circumstance*). **5** full detail in a narrative (*told it with much circumstance*). □ **in** (or **under**) **the** (or **these**) **circumstances** the state of affairs being what it is. **in** (or **under**) **no circumstances** not at all; never. □□ **circumstanced** *adj.* [ME f. OF *circonstance* or L *circumstantia* (as CIRCUM-, *stantia* f. *sto* stand)]

■ **1** situation, condition(s), state (of affairs), *colloq.* circs; fact; event, incident, episode, occurrence, affair, happening, occasion. **2** see INCIDENT *n.* 1a. **3** (*circumstances*) status, station, resources, income, finances. **4** see CEREMONY 2, 3. **5** see *elaboration* (ELABORATE). □ **in** (or **under**) **no circumstances** see NEVER 1b, 2.

circumstantial /súrkəmstánsh'l/ *adj.* **1** given in full detail (*a circumstantial account*). **2** (of evidence, a legal case, etc.) tending to establish a conclusion by inference from known facts hard to explain otherwise. **3 a** depending on circumstances. **b** adventitious, incidental. □□ **circumstantiality** /-shiálliti/ *n.* **circumstantially** *adv.* [L *circumstantia*: see CIRCUMSTANCE]

■ **1** detailed, particular, precise, explicit, specific. **2** indirect, presumptive, deduced, presumed, presumable, implicative, implied, inferred, inferential. **3 b** accidental, incidental, indirect, unimportant, adventitious, provisional, secondary, unessential, non-essential, fortuitous, chance, extraneous.

circumterrestrial /súrkəmtəréstriəl/ *adj.* moving or situated around the earth.

circumvallate /súrkəmvállayt/ *v.tr.* surround with or as with a rampart. [L *circumvallare circumvallat-* (as CIRCUM-, *vallare* f. *vallum* rampart)]

circumvent /súrkəmvént/ *v.tr.* **1 a** evade (a difficulty); find a way round. **b** baffle, outwit. **2** entrap (an enemy) by surrounding. □□ **circumvention** *n.* [L *circumvenire circumvent-* (as CIRCUM-, *venire* come)]

■ **1 a** see EVADE 1, 2. **b** see FOIL[1] *v.*

circumvolution /súrkəmvəlyóosh'n/ *n.* **1** rotation. **2** the winding of one thing round another. **3** a sinuous movement. [ME f. L *circumvolvere circumvolut-* (as CIRCUM-, *volvere* roll)]

circus /súrkəss/ *n.* (*pl.* **circuses**) **1** a travelling show of performing animals, acrobats, clowns, etc. **2** *colloq.* **a** a scene of lively action; a disturbance. **b** a group of people in a common activity, esp. sport. **3** *Brit.* an open space in a town, where several streets converge (*Piccadilly Circus*). **4** a circular hollow surrounded by hills. **5** *Rom. Antiq.* **a** a rounded or oval arena with tiers of seats, for equestrian and other sports and games. **b** a performance given there (*bread and circuses*). [L, = ring]

■ **5 a** see RING[1] *n.* 6a.

ciré /séeray/ *n.* & *adj.* ● *n.* a fabric with a smooth shiny surface obtained esp. by waxing and heating. ● *adj.* having such a surface. [F, = waxed]

cire perdue /séer perdyóo/ *n.* a method of bronze-casting using a clay core and a wax coating placed in a mould: the wax is melted in the mould and bronze poured into the space left, producing a hollow bronze figure when the core is discarded. [F, = lost wax]

cirque /surk/ *n.* **1** *Geol.* a deep bowl-shaped hollow at the head of a valley or on a mountainside. **2** *poet.* **a** a ring. **b** an amphitheatre or arena. [F f. L CIRCUS]

cirrhosis /sirósiss/ *n.* a chronic disease of the liver marked by the degeneration of cells and the thickening of surrounding tissues, as a result of alcoholism, hepatitis, etc. □□ **cirrhotic** /siróttik/ *adj.* [mod.L f. Gk *kirrhos* tawny]

cirriped /sírriped/ *n.* (also **cirripede** /sírripeed/) any marine crustacean of the class Cirripedia, having a valved shell and usu. sessile when adult, e.g. a barnacle. [mod.L *Cirripedia* f. L *cirrus* curl (from the form of the legs) + *pes pedis* foot]

cirro- /sírrō/ *comb. form* cirrus (cloud).

cirrus /sírrəss/ *n.* (*pl.* **cirri** /-rī/) **1** *Meteorol.* a form of white wispy cloud, esp. at high altitude. **2** *Bot.* a tendril. **3** *Zool.* a long slender appendage or filament. □□ **cirrose** *adj.* **cirrous** *adj.* [L, = curl]

cis- /siss/ *prefix* (opp. TRANS- or ULTRA-). **1** on this side of; on the side nearer to the speaker or writer (*cisatlantic*). **2** *Rom. Antiq.* on the Roman side of (*cisalpine*). **3** (of time) closer to the present (*cis-Elizabethan*). **4** *Chem.* (of an isomer) having two atoms or groups on the same side of a given plane in the molecule. [L *cis* on this side of]

cisalpine /sisálpīn/ *adj.* on the southern side of the Alps.

cisatlantic /síssətlántik/ *adj.* on this side of the Atlantic.

cisco /sískō/ *n.* (*pl.* **-oes**) any of various freshwater whitefish of the genus *Coregonus*, native to N. America. [19th c.: orig. unkn.]

cislunar /sislóonər/ *adj.* between the earth and the moon.

cispontine /sispóntīn/ *adj.* on the north side of the Thames in London. [CIS- (orig. the better-known side) + L *pons pont-* bridge]

cissy var. of SISSY.

cist[1] /sist, kist/ *n.* (also **kist** /kist/) *Archaeol.* a coffin or burial-chamber made from stone or a hollowed tree. [Welsh, = CHEST]

cist[2] /sist/ *n.* *Gk Antiq.* a box used for sacred utensils. [L *cista* f. Gk *kistē* box]

Cistercian /sistérsh'n/ *n.* & *adj.* ● *n.* a monk or nun of an order founded in 1098 as a stricter branch of the Benedictines. ● *adj.* of the Cistercians. [F *cistercien* f. L *Cistercium* Cîteaux near Dijon in France, where the order was founded]

cistern /sístərn/ *n.* **1** a tank for storing water, esp. one in a roof-space supplying taps or as part of a flushing lavatory. **2** an underground reservoir for rainwater. [ME f. OF *cisterne* f. L *cisterna* (as CIST[2])]

cistus /sístəss/ *n.* any shrub of the genus *Cistus*, with large white or red flowers. Also called *rock rose*. [mod.L f. Gk *kistos*]

citadel /síttəd'l, -del/ *n.* **1** a fortress, usu. on high ground protecting or dominating a city. **2** a meeting-hall of the Salvation Army. [F *citadelle* or It. *citadella*, ult. f. L *civitas -tatis* city]

■ **1** see STRONGHOLD 1.

citation /sītáysh'n/ *n.* **1** the citing of a book or other source; a passage cited. **2** a mention in an official dispatch. **3** a note accompanying an award, describing the reasons for it.

■ **1** see QUOTATION 2. **2** see MENTION *n.* 1.

cite /sīt/ *v.tr.* **1** adduce as an instance. **2** quote (a passage, book, or author) in support of an argument etc. **3** mention in an official dispatch. **4** summon to appear in a lawcourt. □□ **citable** *adj.* [ME f. F f. L *citare* f. *ciēre* set moving]

■ **1, 2** see QUOTE *v.* 1. **3** see MENTION *v.* 1, 2. **4** subpoena.

citified /síttifīd/ *adj.* (also **cityfied**) usu. *derog.* city-like or urban in appearance or behaviour.

citizen /síttiz'n/ *n.* **1** a member of a State or Commonwealth, either native or naturalized (*British citizen*). **2** (usu. foll. by *of*) **a** an inhabitant of a city. **b** a freeman of a city. **3** *US* a civilian. □ **citizen of the world** a person who is at home anywhere; a cosmopolitan. **Citizens' Advice Bureau** (in the UK) an office at which the public can receive free advice and information on civil matters. **citizen's arrest** an arrest by an ordinary person without a warrant, allowable in certain cases. **citizen's band** a system of local intercommunication by individuals on special radio frequencies. □□ **citizenhood** *n.* **citizenry** *n.* **citizenship** *n.* [ME f. AF *citesein*, OF *citeain* ult. f. L *civitas -tatis* city: cf. DENIZEN]

■ **1** voter; native, resident, inhabitant, dweller, *poet.* denizen; subject. **2 a** city-dweller, town-dweller, townsman, townswoman, *Brit.* burgess.

citole /sitōl/ *n.* a small cittern. [ME f. OF: rel. to CITTERN with dimin. suffix]

citric /sítrik/ *adj.* derived from citrus fruit. □ **citric acid** a sharp-tasting water-soluble organic acid found in the juice of lemons and other sour fruits. □□ **citrate** *n.* [F *citrique* f. L *citrus* citron]

citrin /sítrin/ *n.* a group of substances occurring mainly in citrus fruits and blackcurrants, and formerly thought to be a vitamin. Also called BIOFLAVONOID.

citrine /sítrin/ *adj.* & *n.* ● *adj.* lemon-coloured. ● *n.* a transparent yellow variety of quartz. Also called *false topaz.* [ME f. OF *citrin* (as CITRUS)]

citron /sítrən/ *n.* **1** a shrubby tree, *Citrus medica*, bearing large lemon-like fruits with thick fragrant peel. **2** this fruit. [F f. L CITRUS, after *limon* lemon]

citronella /sítrənéllə/ *n.* **1** any fragrant grass of the genus *Cymbopogon*, native to S. Asia. **2** the scented oil from these, used in insect repellent, and perfume and soap manufacture. [mod.L, formed as CITRON + dimin. suffix]

citrus /sítrəss/ *n.* **1** any tree of the genus *Citrus*, including citron, lemon, lime, orange, and grapefruit. **2** (in full **citrus fruit**) a fruit from such a tree. □□ **citrous** *adj.* [L, = citron-tree or thuja]

cittern /síttərn/ *n. hist.* a wire-stringed lutelike instrument usu. played with a plectrum. [L *cithara*, Gk *kithara* a kind of harp, assim. to GITTERN]

city /sítti/ *n.* (*pl.* **-ies**) **1 a** a large town. **b** *Brit.* (strictly) a town created a city by charter and containing a cathedral. **c** *US* a municipal corporation occupying a definite area. **2** (**the City**) **a** the part of London governed by the Lord Mayor and the Corporation. **b** the business part of this. **c** commercial circles; high finance. **3** (*attrib.*) of a city or the City. □ **City Company** a corporation descended from an ancient trade-guild. **city desk** a department of a newspaper dealing with business news or *US* with local news. **City editor 1** the editor dealing with financial news in a newspaper or magazine. **2** (**city editor**) *US* the editor dealing with local news. **city father** (usu. in *pl.*) a person concerned with or experienced in the administration of a city. **city hall** *US* municipal offices or officers. **city manager** *US* an official directing the administration of a city. **city page** *Brit.* the part of a newspaper or magazine dealing with the financial and business news. **city slicker** usu. *derog.* **1** a smart and sophisticated city-dweller. **2** a plausible rogue as found in cities. **city-state** esp. *hist.* a city that with its surrounding territory forms an independent state. □□ **cityward** *adj.* & *adv.* **citywards** *adv.* [ME f. OF *cité* f. L *civitas -tatis* f. *civis* citizen]

■ **1 a** metropolis, municipality, borough, town; conurbation, megalopolis, urban area, *US colloq.* burg. **3** (*attrib.*) metropolitan, urban, municipal, civic. □ **city slicker 1** *US colloq.* slicker, *derog.* townee. **2** *US colloq.* slicker.

cityfied var. of CITIFIED.

cityscape /síttiskayp/ *n.* **1** a view of a city (actual or depicted). **2** city scenery.

■ see VIEW *n.* 2a, b.

civet /sívvit/ *n.* **1** (in full **civet-cat**) any catlike animal of the mongoose family, esp. *Civettictis civetta* of Central Africa, having well developed anal scent glands. **2** a strong musky perfume obtained from the secretions of these scent glands. [F *civette* f. It. *zibetto* f. med.L *zibethum* f. Arab. *azzabād* f. *al* the + *zabād* this perfume]

civic /sívvik/ *adj.* **1** of a city; municipal. **2** of or proper to citizens (*civic virtues*). **3** of citizenship, civil. □ **civic centre** *Brit.* the area where municipal offices and other public buildings are situated; the buildings themselves. □□ **civically** *adv.* [F *civique* or L *civicus* f. *civis* citizen]

■ **1** see MUNICIPAL. **2** see PUBLIC *adj.* 1.

civics /sívviks/ *n.pl.* (usu. treated as *sing.*) the study of the rights and duties of citizenship.

civil /sívv'l, -vil/ *adj.* **1** of or belonging to citizens. **2** of ordinary citizens and their concerns, as distinct from military or naval or ecclesiastical matters. **3** polite, obliging, not rude. **4** *Law* relating to civil law (see below), not criminal or political matters (*civil court*; *civil lawyer*). **5** (of the length of a day, year, etc.) fixed by custom or law, not natural or astronomical. **6** occurring within a community or among fellow citizens; internal (*civil unrest*). □ **civil aviation** non-military, esp. commercial aviation. **civil commotion** a riot or similar disturbance. **civil defence** the organization and training of civilians for the protection of lives and property during and after attacks in wartime. **civil disobedience** the refusal to comply with certain laws or to pay taxes etc. as a peaceful form of political protest. **civil engineer** an engineer who designs or maintains roads, bridges, dams, etc. **civil engineering** this work. **civil law 1** law concerning private rights (opp. *criminal law*). **2** *hist.* Roman or non-ecclesiastical law. **civil libertarian** an advocate of increased civil liberty. **civil liberty** (often in *pl.*) freedom of action and speech subject to the law. **civil list** (in the UK) an annual allowance voted by Parliament for the royal family's household expenses. **civil marriage** a marriage solemnized as a civil contract without religious ceremony. **civil rights** the rights of citizens to political and social freedom and equality. **civil servant** a member of the civil service. **civil service** the permanent professional branches of State administration, excluding military and judicial branches and elected politicians. **civil state** being single or married or divorced etc. **civil war** a war between citizens of the same country. **civil year** see YEAR 2. □□ **civilly** *adv.* [ME f. OF f. L *civilis* f. *civis* citizen]

■ **2** civilian, non-military; lay, laic, laical, non-clerical, secular. **3** polite, courteous, respectful, well-mannered, proper, civilized, cordial, genial, formal, courtly, gallant, chivalrous, urbane, polished, refined, gracious, obliging, *Brit.* decent. **6** internal, domestic; public. □ **civil servant** civil-service employee *or* worker, public servant, (government *or* state) official, office-holder, government worker.

civilian /sivíllian/ *n.* & *adj.* ● *n.* a person not in the armed services or the police force. ● *adj.* of or for civilians.

civilianize /sivílliənīz/ *v.tr.* (also **-ise**) make civilian in character or function. □□ **civilianization** /-záysh'n/ *n.*

civility /sivílliti/ *n.* (*pl.* **-ies**) **1** politeness. **2** an act of politeness. [ME f. OF *civilité* f. L *civilitas -tatis* (as CIVIL)]

■ **1** courtesy, politeness, respect, comity, urbanity, amiability, consideration, courteousness, cordiality, propriety, tact, diplomacy, *politesse*, protocol. **2** courtesy, politeness.

civilization /sívvilīzáysh'n, sívvili-/ *n.* (also **-isation**) **1** an advanced stage or system of social development. **2** those peoples of the world regarded as having this. **3** a people or nation (esp. of the past) regarded as an element of social evolution (*ancient civilizations*; *the Inca civilization*). **4** making or becoming civilized.

■ **1** culture, refinement, cultivation, enlightenment, edification, sophistication, polish. **3** see PEOPLE *n.* 1a, NATION.

civilize /sívvilīz/ *v.tr.* (also **-ise**) **1** bring out of a barbarous or primitive stage of society. **2** enlighten; refine and educate. □□ **civilizable** *adj.* **civilizer** *n.* [F *civiliser* (as CIVIL)]

■ **2** enlighten, refine, polish, edify, educate, acculturate, broaden, elevate.

civvies /sívviz/ *n.pl. sl.* civilian clothes. [abbr.]

Civvy Street /sívvi/ *n. sl.* civilian life. [abbr.]

CJ *abbr.* Chief Justice.

Cl *symb. Chem.* the element chlorine.

cl *abbr.* **1** centilitre(s). **2** class.

clack /klak/ *v.* & *n.* ● *v.intr.* **1** make a sharp sound as of boards struck together. **2** chatter, esp. loudly. ● *n.* **1** a clacking sound. **2** clacking talk. □□ **clacker** *n.* [ME, = to chatter, prob. f. ON *klaka*, of imit. orig.]

■ *v.* **2** see CHATTER *v.* 1. ● *n.* **2** see PRATTLE *n.*

clad[1] /klad/ *adj.* **1** clothed. **2** provided with cladding. [past part. of CLOTHE]

clad[2] /klad/ *v.tr.* (**cladding**; *past* and *past part.* **cladded** or **clad**) provide with cladding. [app. f. CLAD[1]]

cladding /kládding/ *n.* a covering or coating on a structure or material etc.
■ see FACING 1a.

clade /klayd/ *n. Biol.* a group of organisms evolved from a common ancestor. [Gk *klados* branch]

cladistics /klədístiks/ *n.pl.* (usu. treated as *sing.*) *Biol.* a method of classification of animals and plants on the basis of shared characteristics, which are assumed to indicate common ancestry. □□ **cladism** /kláddiz'm/ *n.* [as CLADE + -IST + -ICS]

cladode /kláydōd/ *n.* a flattened leaflike stem. [Gk *kladōdēs* many-shooted f. *klados* shoot]

claim /klaym/ *v.* & *n.* ● *v.tr.* **1 a** (often foll. by *that* + clause) demand as one's due or property. **b** (usu. *absol.*) submit a request for payment under an insurance policy. **2 a** represent oneself as having or achieving (*claim victory*; *claim accuracy*). **b** (foll. by *to* + infin.) profess (*claimed to be the owner*). **c** assert, contend (*claim that one knows*). **3** have as an achievement or a consequence (*could then claim five wins*; *the fire claimed many victims*). **4** (of a thing) deserve (one's attention etc.). ● *n.* **1 a** a demand or request for something considered one's due (*lay claim to*; *put in a claim*). **b** an application for compensation under the terms of an insurance policy. **2** (foll. by *to*, *on*) a right or title to a thing (*his only claim to fame*; *have many claims on my time*). **3** a contention or assertion. **4** a thing claimed. **5** a statement of the novel features in a patent. **6** *Mining* a piece of land allotted or taken. □ **no claim** (or **claims**) **bonus** a reduction of an insurance premium after an agreed period without a claim under the terms of the policy. □□ **claimable** *adj.* **claimer** *n.* [ME f. OF *claime* f. *clamer* call out f. L *clamare*]
■ *v.* **1 a** demand, seek, ask *or* call (for), exact, insist on *or* upon. **2** profess, declare, assert, allege, state, put *or* set forth, affirm, contend, maintain. **4** see DESERVE 1. ● *n.* **1** demand, request, requisition, petition, application. **2** (*claim to*) right to, title to; (*claim on*) call on, demand on. **3** see ASSERTION 1, 2.

claimant /kláymənt/ *n.* a person making a claim, esp. in a lawsuit or for a State benefit.

clairaudience /klairórdiənss/ *n.* the supposed faculty of perceiving, as if by hearing, what is inaudible. □□ **clairaudient** *adj.* & *n.* [F *clair* CLEAR, + AUDIENCE, after CLAIRVOYANCE]

clairvoyance /klairvóyənss/ *n.* **1** the supposed faculty of perceiving things or events in the future or beyond normal sensory contact. **2** exceptional insight. [F *clairvoyance* f. *clair* CLEAR + *voir voy-* see]

clairvoyant /klairvóyənt/ *n.* & *adj.* ● *n.* (*fem.* **clairvoyante**) a person having clairvoyance. ● *adj.* having clairvoyance. □□ **clairvoyantly** *adv.*
■ *n.* see PSYCHIC *n.* ● *adj.* see PSYCHIC *adj.* 1a.

clam /klam/ *n.* & *v.* ● *n.* **1** any bivalve mollusc, esp. the edible N. American hard or round clam (*Mercenaria mercenaria*) or the soft or long clam (*Mya arenaria*). **2** *colloq.* a shy or withdrawn person. ● *v.intr.* (**clammed**, **clamming**) **1** dig for clams. **2** (foll. by *up*) *colloq.* refuse to talk. [16th c.: app. f. *clam* a clamp]

clamant /kláymənt/ *adj. literary* noisy; insistent, urgent. □□ **clamantly** *adv.* [L *clamare clamant-* cry out]

clamber /klámbər/ *v.* & *n.* ● *v.intr.* climb with hands and feet, esp. with difficulty or laboriously. ● *n.* a difficult climb. [ME, prob. f. *clamb*, obs. past tense of CLIMB]
■ *v.* see SCRAMBLE *v.* 1.

clammy /klámmi/ *adj.* (**clammier**, **clammiest**) **1** unpleasantly damp and sticky or slimy. **2** (of weather) cold and damp. □□ **clammily** *adv.* **clamminess** *n.* [ME f. *clam* to daub]
■ **1** moist, damp, sticky, gummy, pasty, viscous, slimy. **2** moist, damp, wet.

clamour /klámmər/ *n.* & *v.* (*US* **clamor**) ● *n.* **1** loud or vehement shouting or noise. **2** a protest or complaint; an appeal or demand. ● *v.* **1** *intr.* make a clamour. **2** *tr.* utter with a clamour. □□ **clamorous** *adj.* **clamorously** *adv.* **clamorousness** *n.* [ME f. OF f. L *clamor -oris* f. *clamare* cry out]
■ *n.* **1** see NOISE *n.* 1, 2. **2** see OUTCRY.

clamp[1] /klamp/ *n.* & *v.* ● *n.* **1** a device, esp. a brace or band of iron etc., for strengthening other materials or holding things together. **2** a device for immobilizing an illegally parked car. ● *v.tr.* **1** strengthen or fasten with a clamp. **2** place or hold firmly. **3** immobilize (an illegally parked car) by fixing a clamp to one of its wheels. □ **clamp down 1** (often foll. by *on*) be rigid in enforcing a rule etc. **2** (foll. by *on*) try to suppress. **clamp-down** *n.* severe restriction or suppression. [ME prob. f. MDu., MLG *klamp(e)*]
■ *n.* **1** clasp, vice, brace, clip, fastener. ● *v.* **1** fasten (together), clip (together), bracket, make fast, clasp. **2** grip, grasp, clutch, clasp, hold. □ **clamp down 2** see SUPPRESS 1. **clamp-down** see *suppression* (SUPPRESS).

clamp[2] /klamp/ *n.* **1** a heap of potatoes or other root vegetables stored under straw or earth. **2** a pile of bricks for burning. **3** a pile of turf or peat or garden rubbish etc. [16th c.: prob. f. Du. *klamp* heap (in sense 2 related to CLUMP)]

clan /klan/ *n.* **1** a group of people with a common ancestor, esp. in the Scottish Highlands. **2** a large family as a social group. **3** a group with a strong common interest. **4 a** a genus, species, or class. **b** a family or group of animals, e.g. elephants. [ME f. Gael. *clann* f. L *planta* sprout]
■ **1** tribe, family, sib, dynasty, line, house. **3** fraternity, brotherhood, party, set, clique, coterie, circle, crowd, group, fellowship, society, faction; band, ring, gang. **4 a** genus, species, class; see also KIND[1] 2.

clandestine /klandéstin/ *adj.* surreptitious, secret. □□ **clandestinely** *adv.* **clandestinity** /-tínniti/ *n.* [F *clandestin* or L *clandestinus* f. *clam* secretly]
■ see SECRET *adj.* 3.

clang /klang/ *n.* & *v.* ● *n.* a loud resonant metallic sound as of a bell or hammer etc. ● *v.* **1** *intr.* make a clang. **2** *tr.* cause to clang. [imit.: infl. by L *clangere* resound]
■ *n.* see CLASH *n.* 1a. ● *v.* see CLASH *v.* 1.

clanger /klángər/ *n. sl.* a mistake or blunder. □ **drop a clanger** commit a conspicuous indiscretion.
■ see MISTAKE *n.*

clangour /klánggər/ *n.* (*US* **clangor**) **1** a prolonged or repeated clanging noise. **2** an uproar or commotion. □□ **clangorous** *adj.* **clangorously** *adv.* [L *clangor* noise of trumpets etc.]
■ see NOISE *n.* 1, 2.

clank /klangk/ *n.* & *v.* ● *n.* a sound as of heavy pieces of metal meeting or a chain rattling. ● *v.* **1** *intr.* make a clanking sound. **2** *tr.* cause to clank. □□ **clankingly** *adv.* [imit.: cf. CLANG, CLINK[1], Du. *klank*]
■ *n.* see JANGLE *n.* ● *v.* see JANGLE *v.* 1.

clannish /klánnish/ *adj.* usu. *derog.* **1** (of a family or group) tending to hold together. **2** of or like a clan. □□ **clannishly** *adv.* **clannishness** *n.*
■ **1** see EXCLUSIVE *adj.* 3, 4. **2** see SECTARIAN *adj.* 1.

clanship /klánship/ *n.* **1** a patriarchal system of clans. **2** loyalty to one's clan.

clansman /klánzmən/ *n.* (*pl.* **-men**; *fem.* **clanswoman**, *pl.* **-women**) a member or fellow-member of a clan.

clap[1] /klap/ *v.* & *n.* ● *v.* (**clapped**, **clapping**) **1 a** *intr.* strike the palms of one's hands together as a signal or repeatedly as applause. **b** *tr.* strike (the hands) together in this way. **2** *tr.* **a** applaud or show one's approval of (esp. a person) in this way. **b** slap with the palm of the hand as a sign of approval or encouragement. **3** *tr.* (of a bird) flap (its wings) audibly. **4** *tr.* put or place quickly or with determination (*clapped him in prison*; *clap a tax on whisky*). ● *n.* **1** the act of clapping, esp. as applause. **2** an explosive sound, esp. of thunder. **3** a slap, a pat. □ **clap eyes on** *colloq.* see. **clap on the back** = *slap on the back*. **clapped out** *Brit. sl.* worn out (esp. of machinery etc.); exhausted. [OE *clappian* throb, beat, of imit. orig.]
■ *v.* **1 a** applaud, cheer. **2 a** applaud, cheer, give a person a

round of applause, *colloq.* give a person a (big) hand. **b** slap, strike, pat. **3** beat, flutter, flap, thrash. **4** put, place, slap, fling, toss, cast, *colloq.* stick; impose, lay, apply. ● *n.* **2** crack, slap, report, crash, bang, snap. **3** see SLAP *n.*, PAT[1] *n.* 1, 2.

clap[2] /klap/ *n. coarse sl.* venereal disease, esp. gonorrhoea. [OF *clapoir* venereal bubo]

clapboard /klápbord, klábbərd/ *n. US* = WEATHERBOARD. [Anglicized f. LG *klappholt* cask-stave]

clapper /kláppər/ *n.* the tongue or striker of a bell. □ **like the clappers** *Brit. sl.* very fast or hard.
■ tongue, striker. □ **like the clappers** see FAST[1] *adv.* 1.

clapperboard /kláppərbord/ *n. Cinematog.* a device of hinged boards struck together to synchronize the starting of picture and sound machinery in filming.

claptrap /kláptrap/ *n.* **1** insincere or pretentious talk, nonsense. **2** language used or feelings expressed only to gain applause. [CLAP[1] + TRAP[1]]
■ **1** see NONSENSE 1. **2** see MOUTH *n.* 4.

claque /klak, klaak/ *n.* a group of people hired to applaud in a theatre etc. [F f. *claquer* to clap]
■ see CROWD *n.* 3.

claqueur /klakṓr, klaa-/ *n.* a member of a claque. [F (as CLAQUE)]

clarabella /klárrəbéllə, klaár-/ *n.* an organ-stop of flute quality. [fem. forms of L *clarus* clear and *bellus* pretty]

clarence /klárrənss/ *n. hist.* a four-wheeled closed carriage with seats for four inside and two on the box. [Duke of *Clarence*, afterwards William IV]

Clarenceux /klárrənsyoo/ *n. Heraldry* (in the UK) the title given to the second King of Arms, with jurisdiction south of the Trent (cf. NORROY, *King of Arms*). [ME f. AF f. Duke of *Clarence* f. *Clare* in Suffolk]

claret /klárrət/ *n.* & *adj.* ● *n.* **1** red wine, esp. from Bordeaux. **2** a deep purplish-red. **3** *archaic sl.* blood. ● *adj.* claret-coloured. [ME f. OF (*vin*) *claret* f. med.L *claratum* (*vinum*) f. L *clarus* clear]

clarify /klárrifī/ *v.* (**-ies, -ied**) **1** *tr.* & *intr.* make or become clearer. **2** *tr.* **a** free (liquid, butter, etc.) from impurities. **b** make transparent. **c** purify. □□ **clarification** /-fikáysh'n/ *n.* **clarificatory** /-fikáytəri/ *n.* **clarifier** *n.* [ME f. OF *clarifier* f. L *clarus* clear]
■ **1** elucidate, make clear, simplify, make plain, clear up, explain, shed *or* throw light (up)on, illuminate, explicate. **2 a** clear, purify, clean. **c** see PURIFY.

clarinet /klárrinét/ *n.* **1 a** a woodwind instrument with a single-reed mouthpiece, a cylindrical tube with a flared end, holes, and keys. **b** its player. **2** an organ-stop with a quality resembling a clarinet. □□ **clarinettist** *n.* (*US* **clarinetist**). [F *clarinette*, dimin. of *clarine* a kind of bell]

clarion /klárriən/ *n.* & *adj.* ● *n.* **1** a clear rousing sound. **2** *hist.* a shrill narrow-tubed war trumpet. **3** an organ-stop with the quality of a clarion. ● *adj.* clear and loud. [ME f. med.L *clario -onis* f. L *clarus* clear]
■ *adj.* see CLEAR *adj.* 6a.

clarity /klárriti/ *n.* the state or quality of being clear, esp. of sound or expression. [ME f. L *claritas* f. *clarus* clear]
■ clearness, lucidity, limpidity, pellucidity, definition, definiteness, distinctness; comprehensibility, intelligibility.

clarkia /klaárkiə/ *n.* any plant of the genus *Clarkia*, with showy white, pink, or purple flowers. [mod.L f. W. *Clark*, US explorer d. 1838]

clary /kláiri/ *n.* (*pl.* **-ies**) any of various aromatic herbs of the genus *Salvia*. [ME f. obs. F *clarie* repr. med.L *sclarea*]

clash /klash/ *n.* & *v.* ● *n.* **1 a** a loud jarring sound as of metal objects being struck together. **b** a collision, esp. with force. **2 a** a conflict or disagreement. **b** a discord of colours etc. ● *v.* **1 a** *intr.* make a clashing sound. **b** *tr.* cause to clash. **2** *intr.* collide; coincide awkwardly. **3** *intr.* (often foll. by *with*) **a** come into conflict or be at variance. **b** (of colours) be discordant. □□ **clasher** *n.* [imit.: cf. *clack*, *clang*, *crack*, *crash*]
■ *n.* **1 a** crash, clang, clank, clangour. **b** collision, smash. **2 a** (hostile) encounter, conflict, engagement, fight, battle, disagreement, difference, argument, dispute, altercation, quarrel, squabble. ● *v.* **1** crash, clang, clank, smash, bang, boom. **3 a** come into conflict, disagree, differ, argue, dispute, quarrel, squabble, feud, wrangle, cross swords. **b** disharmonize, jar, be at odds *or* out of keeping; (*clash with*) *colloq.* swear at.

clasp /klaasp/ *n.* & *v.* ● *n.* **1 a** a device with interlocking parts for fastening. **b** a buckle or brooch. **c** a metal fastening on a book-cover. **2 a** an embrace; a person's reach. **b** a grasp or handshake. **3** a bar of silver on a medal-ribbon with the name of the battle etc. at which the wearer was present. ● *v.* **1** *tr.* fasten with or as with a clasp. **2** *tr.* **a** grasp, hold closely. **b** embrace, encircle. **3** *intr.* fasten a clasp. □ **clasp hands** shake hands with fervour or affection. **clasp one's hands** interlace one's fingers. **clasp-knife** a folding knife, usu. with a catch holding the blade when open. □□ **clasper** *n.* [ME: orig. unkn.]
■ *n.* **1** fastener, fastening, hook, catch, clip, pin, brooch, buckle. **2** embrace, hug, hold, grasp, grip; handshake; reach. ● *v.* **1** fasten, secure, close, hold, hook, clip, pin, clamp. **2** hold, embrace, take hold of, hug, enclose, encircle, envelop; grab, grasp, seize, clutch, grip.

clasper /klaáspər/ *n.* (in *pl.*) the appendages of some male fish and insects used to hold the female in copulation.

class /klaass/ *n.* & *v.* ● *n.* **1** any set of persons or things grouped together, or graded or differentiated from others esp. by quality (*first class*; *economy class*). **2 a** a division or order of society (*upper class*; *professional classes*). **b** a caste system, a system of social classes. **c** (**the classes**) *archaic* the rich or educated. **3** *colloq.* distinction or high quality in appearance, behaviour, etc.; stylishness. **4 a** a group of students or pupils taught together. **b** the occasion when they meet. **c** their course of instruction. **5** *US* all the college or school students of the same standing or graduating in a given year (*the class of 1990*). **6** (in conscripted armies) all the recruits of a given year (*the 1950 class*). **7** *Brit.* a division of candidates according to merit in an examination. **8** *Biol.* a grouping of organisms, the next major rank below a division or phylum. ● *v.tr.* assign to a class or category. □ **class-conscious** aware of and reacting to social divisions or one's place in a system of social class. **class-consciousness** this awareness. **class-list** *Brit.* a list of candidates in an examination with the class achieved by each. **class war** conflict between social classes. **in a class of** (or **on**) **its** (or **one's**) **own** unequalled. **no class** *colloq.* a lack of quality or distinction. [L *classis* assembly]
■ *n.* **1** category, division, classification, group, genre, league, realm, domain; kind, sort, type. **2 a** rank, grade, level, order, stratum; caste, lineage, birth, pedigree, stock, extraction, descent. **b** caste system, social ladder, hierarchy; caste, *often derog.* casteism. **3** excellence, merit, refinement, elegance, stylishness, prestige, importance, taste, discernment, distinction, bearing, presence, *savoir faire*, *savoir vivre*, breeding. **4a, c** form; year, *US* grade. **6** recruits, conscripts. ● *v.* classify, group, arrange, assort, type, categorize, rank, grade, rate, order. □ **in a class of** (or **on**) **its** (or **one's**) **own** see UNPARALLELED.

classic /klássik/ *adj.* & *n.* ● *adj.* **1 a** of the first class; of acknowledged excellence. **b** remarkably typical; outstandingly important (*a classic case*). **c** having enduring worth; timeless. **2 a** of ancient Greek and Latin literature, art, or culture. **b** (of style in art, music, etc.) simple, harmonious, well-proportioned; in accordance with established forms (cf. ROMANTIC). **3** having literary or historic associations (*classic ground*). **4** (of clothes) made in a simple elegant style not much affected by changes in fashion. ● *n.* **1** a classic writer, artist, work, or example. **2 a** an ancient Greek or Latin writer. **b** (in *pl.*) the study of ancient Greek and Latin literature and history. **c** *archaic* a scholar of ancient Greek and Latin. **3** a follower of classic models (cf. ROMANTIC). **4** a garment in classic style. **5** (in *pl.*) *Brit.* the classic races. □ **classic races** *Brit.* the five main flat races, namely the Two Thousand and the One Thousand Guineas, the Derby, the Oaks, and the St Leger. [F *classique* or L *classicus* f. *classis* class]

■ *adj.* **1 a** outstanding, first-rate, superior, excellent, noteworthy, notable, exemplary. **b** typical, standard, leading, outstanding, prototypic(al), definitive, model, ideal, archetypal, paradigmatic; see also IMPORTANT 1, 2. **c** legendary, immortal, enduring, deathless, ageless, timeless, undying, venerable, time-honoured, vintage. **2b, 4** see SIMPLE *adj.* 2. ● *n.* **1** paragon, epitome, outstanding example, exemplar, model, paradigm, prototype; masterpiece, master-work.

classical /klássik'l/ *adj.* **1 a** of ancient Greek or Latin literature or art. **b** (of language) having the form used by the ancient standard authors (*classical Latin*; *classical Hebrew*). **c** based on the study of ancient Greek and Latin (*a classical education*). **d** learned in classical studies. **2 a** (of music) serious or conventional; following traditional principles and intended to be of permanent rather than ephemeral value (cf. POPULAR, LIGHT). **b** of the period from *c.*1750–1800 (cf. ROMANTIC). **3 a** in or following the restrained style of classical antiquity (cf. ROMANTIC). **b** (of a form or period of art etc.) representing an exemplary standard; having a long-established worth. **4** *Physics* relating to the concepts which preceded relativity and quantum theory. □□ **classicalism** *n.* **classicalist** *n.* **classicality** /-kálliti/ *n.* **classically** *adv.* [L *classicus* (as CLASSIC)]

■ **1 a** Greek, Latin, Roman. **3 b** standard, model, exemplary, traditional, established, influential, authoritative, serious, weighty.

classicism /klássisiz'm/ *n.* **1** the following of a classic style. **2 a** classical scholarship. **b** the advocacy of a classical education. **3** an ancient Greek or Latin idiom. □□ **classicist** *n.*

classicize /klássisīz/ *v.* (also **-ise**) **1** *tr.* make classic. **2** *intr.* imitate a classical style.

classified /klássifīd/ *adj.* **1** arranged in classes or categories. **2** (of information etc.) designated as officially secret. **3** *Brit.* (of a road) assigned to a category according to its importance. **4** *Brit.* (of newspaper advertisements) arranged in columns according to various categories.

■ **2** see CONFIDENTIAL 1.

classify /klássifī/ *v.tr.* (**-ies, -ied**) **1 a** arrange in classes or categories. **b** assign (a thing) to a class or category. **2** designate as officially secret or not for general disclosure. □□ **classifiable** *adj.* **classification** /-fikáysh'n/ *n.* **classificatory** /-fikáytəri/ *adj.* **classifier** *n.* [back-form. f. *classification* f. F (as CLASS)]

■ **1** see ORGANIZE 1.

classless /klaásliss/ *adj.* making or showing no distinction of classes (*classless society*; *classless accent*). □□ **classlessness** *n.*

■ see DEMOCRATIC 2.

classmate /klaásmayt/ *n.* a fellow-member of a class, esp. at school.

classroom /klaásrōōm, -rōōm/ *n.* a room in which a class of students is taught, esp. in a school.

classy /klaássi/ *adj.* (**classier, classiest**) *colloq.* superior, stylish. □□ **classily** *adv.* **classiness** *n.*

■ see STYLISH 1.

clastic /klástik/ *adj. Geol.* composed of broken pieces of older rocks. □ **clastic rocks** conglomerates, sandstones, etc. [F *clastique* f. Gk *klastos* broken in pieces]

clathrate /kláthrayt/ *n. Chem.* a solid in which one component is enclosed in the structure of another. [L *clathratus* f. *clathri* lattice-bars f. Gk *klēthra*]

clatter /kláttər/ *n.* & *v.* ● *n.* **1** a rattling sound as of many hard objects struck together. **2** noisy talk. ● *v.* **1** *intr.* **a** make a clatter. **b** fall or move etc. with a clatter. **2** *tr.* cause (plates etc.) to clatter. [OE, of imit. orig.]

■ *n.* **1** see RATTLE *n.* 1. ● *v.* see RATTLE *v.* 1a.

claudication /kláwdikáysh'n/ *n. Med.* a cramping pain, esp. in the leg, caused by arterial obstruction; limping. [L *claudicare* limp f. *claudus* lame]

■ see LIMP[1] *n.*

clause /klawz/ *n.* **1** *Gram.* a distinct part of a sentence, including a subject and predicate. **2** a single statement in a treaty, law, bill, or contract. □□ **clausal** *adj.* [ME f. OF f. L *clausula* conclusion f. *claudere claus-* shut]

■ **1** see PHRASE *n.* 1. **2** see *stipulation* (STIPULATE[1]).

claustral /kláwstrəl/ *adj.* **1** of or associated with the cloister; monastic. **2** narrow-minded. [ME f. LL *claustralis* f. *claustrum* CLOISTER]

claustrophobia /kláwstrəfṓbiə/ *n.* an abnormal fear of confined places. □□ **claustrophobe** /kláwstrəfōb/ *n.* [mod.L f. L *claustrum*: see CLOISTER]

claustrophobic /kláwstrəfṓbik/ *adj.* **1** suffering from claustrophobia. **2** inducing claustrophobia. □□ **claustrophobically** *adv.*

clavate /kláyvayt/ *adj. Bot.* club-shaped. [mod.L *clavatus* f. L *clava* club]

clave[1] /klayv, klaav/ *n. Mus.* a hardwood stick used in pairs to make a hollow sound when struck together. [Amer. Sp. f. Sp., = keystone, f. L *clavis* key]

clave[2] *past* of CLEAVE[2].

clavicembalo /klávvichémbəlō/ *n.* (*pl.* **-os**) a harpsichord. [It.]

clavichord /klávvikord/ *n.* a small keyboard instrument with a very soft tone. [ME f. med.L *clavichordium* f. L *clavis* key, *chorda* string: see CHORD[2]]

clavicle /klávvik'l/ *n.* the collar-bone. □□ **clavicular** /kləvíkyoolər/ *adj.* [L *clavicula* dimin. of *clavis* key (from its shape)]

clavier /kləvéer, klávviər/ *n. Mus.* **1** any keyboard instrument. **2** its keyboard. [F *clavier* or G *Klavier* f. med.L *claviarius*, orig. = key-bearer, f. L *clavis* key]

claviform /klávviform/ *adj.* club-shaped. [L *clava* club]

claw /klaw/ *n.* & *v.* ● *n.* **1 a** a pointed horny nail on an animal's or bird's foot. **b** a foot armed with claws. **2** the pincers of a shellfish. **3** a device for grappling, holding, etc. ● *v.* **1 a** *tr.* & *intr.* scratch, maul, or pull (a person or thing) with claws. **b** *intr.* (often foll. by *at*) grasp, clutch, or scrabble at as with claws. **2** *tr.* & *intr. Sc.* scratch gently. **3** *intr. Naut.* beat to windward. □ **claw back 1** regain laboriously or gradually. **2** recover (money paid out) from another source (e.g. taxation). **claw-back** *n.* **1** the act of clawing back. **2** money recovered in this way. **claw-hammer** a hammer with one side of the head forked for extracting nails. □□ **clawed** *adj.* (also in *comb.*). **clawer** *n.* **clawless** *adj.* [OE *clawu*, *clawian*]

■ *n.* **1** talon, nail. **3** vice. ● *v.* **1 a** scratch, tear, scrape, rake, slash. **b** grapple, grab, grasp, clutch, scrabble. □ **claw back 2** see RECOVER *v.* 1.

clay /klay/ *n.* **1** a stiff sticky earth, used for making bricks, pottery, ceramics, etc. **2** *poet.* the substance of the human body. **3** (in full **clay pipe**) a tobacco-pipe made of clay. □ **clay-pan** *Austral.* a natural hollow in clay soil, retaining water after rain. **clay pigeon** a breakable disc thrown up from a trap as a target for shooting. □□ **clayey** *adj.* **clayish** *adj.* **claylike** *adj.* [OE *clǣg* f. WG]

■ **1** see EARTH *n.* 2b.

claymore /kláymor/ *n.* **1** *hist.* **a** a Scottish two-edged broadsword. **b** a broadsword, often with a single edge, having a hilt with a basketwork design. **2** *US* a type of anti-personnel mine. [Gael. *claidheamh mór* great sword]

-cle /k'l/ *suffix* forming (orig. diminutive) nouns (*article*; *particle*). [as -CULE]

clean /kleen/ *adj.*, *adv.*, *v.*, & *n.* ● *adj.* **1** (often foll. by *of*) free from dirt or contaminating matter, unsoiled. **2** clear; unused or unpolluted; preserving what is regarded as the original state (*clean air*; *clean page*). **3** free from obscenity or indecency. **4 a** attentive to personal hygiene and cleanliness. **b** (of children and animals) toilet-trained or house-trained. **5** complete, clear-cut, unobstructed, even. **6 a** (of a ship, aircraft, or car) streamlined, smooth. **b** well-formed, slender and shapely (*clean-limbed*; *the car has clean lines*). **7** adroit, skilful (*clean fielding*). **8** (of a nuclear weapon) producing relatively little fallout. **9 a** free from ceremonial defilement or from disease. **b** (of food) not prohibited. **10 a** free from any record of a crime, offence, etc. (*a clean driving-licence*). **b** *sl.* not carrying a weapon or incriminating material; free from suspicion. **11** (of a taste, smell, etc.) sharp, fresh, distinctive. **12** (of timber) free from knots. ● *adv.* **1** completely, outright, simply (*clean bowled*; *cut clean through*; *clean forgot*). **2** in a clean manner. ● *v.* **1** *tr.* (also foll. by *of*) & *intr.* make or become clean. **2** *tr.* eat all the food on (one's plate). **3** *tr. Cookery* remove the innards of (fish or fowl). **4** *intr.* make oneself clean. ● *n.* the act or process of cleaning or being cleaned (*give it a clean*). □ **clean bill of health** see BILL[1]. **clean break** a quick and final separation. **clean-cut** sharply outlined. **clean down** clean by brushing or wiping. **clean hands** freedom from guilt. **clean-living** of upright character. **clean out 1** clean or clear thoroughly. **2** *sl.* empty or deprive (esp. of money). **clean-shaven** without beard, whiskers, moustache. **clean sheet** (or **slate**) freedom from commitments or imputations; the removal of these from one's record. **clean up 1 a** clear (a mess) away. **b** (also *absol.*) put (things) tidy. **c** make (oneself) clean. **2** restore order or morality to. **3** *sl.* **a** acquire as gain or profit. **b** make a gain or profit. **clean-up** *n.* an act of cleaning up. **come clean** *colloq.* own up; confess everything. **make a clean breast of** see BREAST. **make a clean job of** *colloq.* do thoroughly. **make a clean sweep of** see SWEEP. □□ **cleanable** *adj.* **cleanish** *adj.* **cleanness** *n.* [OE *clǣne* (adj. & adv.), *clēne* (adv.), f. WG]

■ *adj.* **1** pure, undefiled, unsullied, unmixed, unadulterated, uncontaminated, unpolluted, uninfected, unsoiled, untainted, unstained, unspoiled, unspoilt, sanitary, disinfected; antiseptic, decontaminated, purified, sterile; cleanly, (freshly) laundered, washed, scrubbed, *usu. formal* cleansed; spotless, immaculate, clear. **2, 3** see PURE 3, 4. **4 a** hygienic, cleanly. **5** complete, clean-cut, neat, simple, definite, clear-cut, unobstructed, uncomplicated, smooth, even, straight, trim, tidy. **6 a** see STREAMLINE *v.* 3a. **b** see SLENDER 1, SHAPELY. **7** see SKILFUL. **9 a** undefiled, uninfected, uncontaminated. **b** halal, kosher. **10 a** innocent, inoffensive, respectable; *Brit.* not endorsed; see also BLAMELESS. **b** unarmed, weaponless. ● *adv.* **1** completely, outright, entirely, thoroughly, fully, totally, wholly, altogether, quite, utterly, simply, absolutely. ● *v.* **1** wash, sponge, mop, scrub, scour, sweep, brush, wipe, clean down *or* out, dust, vacuum, launder, hoover, *esp. Brit.* wash up, *usu. formal* cleanse, *literary* lave; tidy, neaten, do up, straighten up *or* out. **4** wash, (have *or* take a) shower, have *or* take a bath, clean oneself up, *Brit.* bath, *esp. US* bathe, wash up. □ **clean-cut** see CLEAR *adj.* 6c. **clean down** see CLEAN *v.* 1 above. **clean-living** see UPRIGHT *adj.* 3. **clean hands** a clear conscience. **clean out 2** see DEFRAUD. **clean up 1 a, b** see *clear up* 1. **c** clean, wash, (have *or* take a) shower, have *or* take a bath, *Brit.* bath, *esp. US* bathe, wash up. **clean-up** clean; see also PROFIT *n.* 2. **come clean** confess, acknowledge *or* admit guilt, make a clean breast of it, own up, *sl.* sing.

cleaner /kléenər/ *n.* **1** a person employed to clean the interior of a building. **2** (usu. in *pl.*) a commercial establishment for cleaning clothes. **3** a device or substance for cleaning. □ **take to the cleaners** *sl.* **1** defraud or rob (a person) of all his or her money. **2** criticize severely.

■ **1** see SERVANT 1. **3** see DETERGENT *n.*

cleanly[1] /kléenli/ *adv.* **1** in a clean way. **2** efficiently; without difficulty. [OE *clǣnlīce*: see CLEAN, -LY[2]]

■ **1** clean. **2** see EASILY 1.

cleanly[2] /klénli/ *adj.* (**cleanlier**, **cleanliest**) habitually clean; with clean habits. □□ **cleanlily** *adv.* **cleanliness** *n.* [OE *clǣnlic*: see CLEAN, -LY[1]]

■ □□ **cleanliness** see PURITY 1.

cleanse /klenz/ *v.tr.* **1** usu. *formal.* make clean. **2** (often foll. by *of*) purify from sin or guilt. **3** *archaic* cure (a leper etc.). □ **cleansing cream** cream for removing unwanted matter from the face, hands, etc. **cleansing department** *Brit.* a local service of refuse collection etc. □□ **cleanser** *n.* [OE *clǣnsian* (see CLEAN)]

■ **1** wash, scour, scrub; see also CLEAN *v.* 1. **2** purify, depurate, purge.

cleanskin /kléenskin/ *n. Austral.* **1** an unbranded animal. **2** *sl.* a person free from blame, without a police record, etc.

clear /kleer/ *adj.*, *adv.*, & *v.* ● *adj.* **1** free from dirt or contamination. **2** (of weather, the sky, etc.) not dull or cloudy. **3 a** transparent. **b** lustrous, shining; free from obscurity. **c** (of the complexion) fresh and unblemished. **4** (of soup) not containing solid ingredients. **5** (of a fire) burning with little smoke. **6 a** distinct, easily perceived by the senses. **b** unambiguous, easily understood (*make a thing clear*; *make oneself clear*). **c** manifest; not confused or doubtful (*clear evidence*). **7** that discerns or is able to discern readily and accurately (*clear thinking*; *clear-sighted*). **8** (usu. foll. by *about*, *on*, or *that* + clause) confident, convinced, certain. **9** (of a conscience) free from guilt. **10** (of a road etc.) unobstructed, open. **11 a** net, without deduction (*a clear £1000*). **b** complete (*three clear days*). **12** (often foll. by *of*) free, unhampered; unencumbered by debt, commitments, etc. **13** (foll. by *of*) not obstructed by. ● *adv.* **1** clearly (*speak loud and clear*). **2** completely (*he got clear away*). **3** apart, out of contact (*keep clear*; *stand clear of the doors*). **4** (foll. by *to*) *US* all the way. ● *v.* **1** *tr.* & *intr.* make or become clear. **2 a** *tr.* (often foll. by *of*) free from prohibition or obstruction. **b** *tr.* & *intr.* make or become empty or unobstructed. **c** *tr.* free (land) for cultivation or building by cutting down trees etc. **d** *tr.* cause people to leave (a room etc.). **3** *tr.* (often foll. by *of*) show or declare (a person) to be innocent (*cleared them of complicity*). **4** *tr.* approve (a person) for special duty, access to information, etc. **5** *tr.* pass over or by safely or without touching, esp. by jumping. **6** *tr.* make (an amount of money) as a net gain or to balance expenses. **7** *tr.* pass (a cheque) through a clearing-house. **8** *tr.* pass through (a customs office etc.). **9** *tr.* remove (an obstruction, an unwanted object, etc.) (*clear them out of the way*). **10** *tr.* (also *absol.*) *Football* send (the ball) out of one's defensive zone. **11** *intr.* (often foll. by *away*, *up*) (of physical phenomena) disappear, gradually diminish (*mist cleared by lunchtime*; *my cold has cleared up*). **12** *tr.* (often foll. by *off*) discharge (a debt). □ **clear the air 1** make the air less sultry. **2** disperse an atmosphere of suspicion, tension, etc. **clear away 1** remove completely. **2** remove the remains of a meal from the table. **clear-cut** sharply defined. **clear the decks** prepare for action, esp. fighting. **clear off 1** get rid of. **2** *colloq.* go away. **clear out 1** empty. **2** remove. **3** *colloq.* go away. **clear one's throat** cough slightly to make one's voice clear. **clear up 1** tidy up. **2** solve (a mystery etc.); remove (a difficulty etc.). **3** (of weather) become fine. **clear the way 1** remove obstacles. **2** stand aside. **clear a thing with** get approval or authorization for a thing from (a person). **in clear** not in cipher or code. **in the clear** free from suspicion or difficulty. **out of a clear sky** as a complete surprise. □□ **clearable** *adj.* **clearer** *n.* **clearly** *adv.* **clearness** *n.* [ME f. OF *cler* f. L *clarus*]

■ *adj.* **1** see CLEAN *adj.* 1. **2** unclouded, cloudless, sunny, fair, sunlit, fine. **3 a** transparent, limpid, crystalline; translucent, uncloudy, unclouded, pellucid. **b** bright, lustrous, shining, shiny, sparkling. **c** bright, fresh, unblemished, unscarred. **6 a** distinct, sharp, well-defined, definite, vivid; legible, readable; pure, unwavering, clarion. **b** understandable, intelligible, perspicuous, lucid, comprehensible, apprehensible, discernible, plain, obvious, patent, unambiguous, unequivocal, explicit, definite, unmistakable, indisputable, undisputed, unquestionable, incontrovertible. **c** manifest, distinct, evident, unclouded, unconfused, explicit, plain, definite, clear-cut, palpable. **7** acute, sensitive, perspicacious, discerning, keen; see also PERCEPTIVE. **8** certain, sure, convinced, confident, positive, determined, definite, assured. **9** pure, guiltless, blameless, faultless; not guilty; see also INNOCENT *adj.* 2. **10** open, unencumbered, free, unblocked, unobstructed, unimpeded, direct. **11 a** unencumbered, free, net. **b** complete, entire, whole; uninterrupted. **12** see UNIMPEDED. **13** disengaged, disentangled, unentangled, free, freed, rid, quit, loose, released. ● *adv.* **1** distinctly, clearly, audibly. **2** completely, utterly, entirely, clean(ly), wholly, totally. **3** see APART 3a. ● *v.* **1** (*tr.*) clarify, clean, purify, purge, *usu. formal* cleanse. **2 b** open (up), free; unblock, unclog, unstop. **d** vacate, evacuate. **3** exonerate, absolve, acquit; excuse, forgive. **5** leap *or* jump over, vault, hurdle. **9** remove, eliminate, take (away); clear away, cut away *or* down, dislodge. **11** see DISAPPEAR 1, DIMINISH 1. **12** settle, discharge, pay, square. □ **clear away 1** see REMOVE *v.* 2a. **clear-cut** see CLEAR *adj.* 6c above. **clear off 1** see *get rid of* (RID). **2** see LEAVE[1] *v.* 1b, 3, 4. **clear out 1** see EMPTY *v.* 1. **2** see REMOVE *v.* 2a. **3** see *go away* (GO[1]). **clear up 1** tidy (up), neaten (up), put *or* set in order, clear. **2** explain, elucidate, explicate, clarify, make plain *or* clear, disambiguate; settle, remove, eliminate. **3** become fair *or* fine *or* cloudless *or* sunny. **in the clear** innocent, not guilty; exonerated, forgiven, absolved; unburdened, disburdened, unencumbered, free. **out of a clear sky** see *suddenly* (SUDDEN). □□ **clearly** distinctly, audibly, understandably, clear; evidently, plainly, apparently, manifestly, obviously, certainly, definitely, positively, unequivocally, unquestionably, incontestably, without doubt, undoubtedly, indubitably, demonstrably.

clearance /kléeranss/ *n.* **1** the removal of obstructions etc., esp. removal of buildings, persons, etc., so as to clear land. **2** clear space allowed for the passing of two objects or two parts in machinery etc. **3** special authorization or permission (esp. for an aircraft to take off or land, or for access to information etc.). **4 a** the clearing of a person, ship, etc., by customs. **b** a certificate showing this. **5** the clearing of cheques. **6** *Football* a kick sending the ball out of a defensive zone. **7** making clear. □ **clearance order** an order for the demolition of buildings. **clearance sale** *Brit.* a sale to get rid of superfluous stock.
■ **2** margin, leeway, space, gap, hole, interval, separation, room, allowance. **3** approval, endorsement, authorization, licence, leave, permission, consent.

clearcole /kléerkōl/ *n.* & *v.* ● *n.* a mixture of size and whiting or white lead, used as a primer for distemper. ● *v.tr.* paint with clearcole. [F *claire colle* clear glue]

clearing /kléering/ *n.* **1** in senses of CLEAR *v.* **2** an area in a forest cleared for cultivation. □ **clearing bank** *Brit.* a bank which is a member of a clearing-house. **clearing-house 1** a bankers' establishment where cheques and bills from member banks are exchanged, so that only the balances need be paid in cash. **2** an agency for collecting and distributing information etc.
■ **2** see FIELD *n.* 1.

clearstory *US* var. of CLERESTORY.

clearway /kléerway/ *n.* *Brit.* a main road (other than a motorway) on which vehicles are not normally permitted to stop.

cleat /kleet/ *n.* **1** a piece of metal, wood, etc., bolted on for fastening ropes to, or to strengthen woodwork etc. **2** a projecting piece on a spar, gangway, boot, etc., to give footing or prevent a rope from slipping. **3** a wedge. [OE: cf. CLOT]

cleavage /kléevij/ *n.* **1** the hollow between a woman's breasts, esp. as exposed by a low-cut garment. **2** a division or splitting. **3** the splitting of rocks, crystals, etc., in a preferred direction.
■ **2, 3** see SPLIT *n.* 2.

cleave[1] /kleev/ *v.* (*past* **clove** /klōv/ or **cleft** /kleft/ or **cleaved**; *past part.* **cloven** /klṓv'n/ or **cleft** or **cleaved**) *literary* **1 a** *tr.* chop or break apart, split, esp. along the grain or the line of cleavage. **b** *intr.* come apart in this way. **2** *tr.* make one's way through (air or water). □□ **cleavable** *adj.* [OE *clēofan* f. Gmc]
■ **1 a** split, divide, cut, cut *or* chop *or* hew in two, bisect, halve, separate, slit, *archaic or poet.* rive, *literary* cut *or* chop *or* hew asunder. **b** see *come apart*.

cleave[2] /kleev/ *v.intr.* (*past* **cleaved** or **clave** /klayv/) (foll. by *to*) *literary* stick fast; adhere. [OE *cleofian, clifian* f. WG: cf. CLAY]

cleaver /kléevar/ *n.* **1** a tool for cleaving, esp. a heavy chopping tool used by butchers. **2** a person who cleaves.

cleavers /kléevarz/ *n.* (also **clivers** /klívvarz/) (treated as *sing.* or *pl.*) a plant, *Galium aparine*, having hooked bristles on its stem that catch on clothes etc. Also called GOOSEGRASS. [OE *clife*, formed as CLEAVE[2]]

clef /klef/ *n.* *Mus.* any of several symbols placed at the beginning of a staff, indicating the pitch of the notes written on it. [F f. L *clavis* key]

cleft[1] /kleft/ *adj.* split, partly divided. □ **cleft lip, palate** a congenital split in the lip or the roof of the mouth. **in a cleft stick** in a difficult position, esp. one allowing neither retreat nor advance. [past part. of CLEAVE[1]]
■ □ **in a cleft stick** see QUANDARY 2.

cleft[2] /kleft/ *n.* a split or fissure; a space or division made by cleaving. [OE (rel. to CLEAVE[1]): assim. to CLEFT[1]]
■ see SPLIT *n.* 2.

cleg /kleg/ *n.* *Brit.* a horsefly. [ON *kleggi*]

cleistogamic /klīstagámmik/ *adj.* *Bot.* (of a flower) permanently closed and self-fertilizing. [Gk *kleistos* closed + *gamos* marriage]

clematis /klémmatiss, klamáytiss/ *n.* any erect or climbing plant of the genus *Clematis*, bearing white, pink, or purple flowers and feathery seeds, e.g. old man's beard. [L f. Gk *klēmatis* f. *klēma* vine branch]

clement /klémmant/ *adj.* **1** mild (*clement weather*). **2** merciful. □□ **clemency** *n.* [ME f. L *clemens -entis*]
■ **1** see MILD 3. **2** see MERCIFUL.

clementine /klémmanteen, -tīn/ *n.* a small citrus fruit, thought to be a hybrid between a tangerine and sweet orange. [F *clémentine*]

clench /klench/ *v.* & *n.* ● *v.tr.* **1** close (the teeth or fingers) tightly. **2** grasp firmly. **3** = CLINCH *v.* 4. ● *n.* **1** a clenching action. **2** a clenched state. [OE f. Gmc: cf. CLING]

clepsydra /klépsidra/ *n.* an ancient time-measuring device worked by a flow of water. [L f. Gk *klepsudra* f. *kleptō* steal + *hudōr* water]
■ water-clock.

clerestory /kléerstari, -stori/ *n.* (*US* **clearstory**) (*pl.* **-ies**) **1** an upper row of windows in a cathedral or large church, above the level of the aisle roofs. **2** *US* a raised section of the roof of a railway carriage, with windows or ventilators. [ME f. CLEAR + STOREY]

clergy /klérji/ *n.* (*pl.* **-ies**) (usu. treated as *pl.*) **1** (usu. prec. by *the*) the body of all persons ordained for religious duties in the Christian churches. **2** a number of such persons (*ten clergy were present*). [ME, partly f. OF *clergé* f. eccl.L *clericatus*, partly f. OF *clergie* f. *clerc* CLERK]
■ **1** see MINISTRY 2, 3.

clergyman /klérjiman/ *n.* (*pl.* **-men**) a member of the clergy, esp. of the Church of England.
■ ecclesiastic, churchman, cleric, divine, man of the cloth, man of God, holy man, priest, minister, chaplain, father, pastor, parson, rector, vicar, dean, bishop, canon, presbyter, deacon, *archaic* clerk, *colloq.* reverend, *formal* clerk in holy orders, *sl.* sky pilot, *orig. Naut. sl.* holy Joe.

cleric /klérrik/ *n.* a member of the clergy. [(orig. adj.) f. eccl.L f. Gk *klērikos* f. *klēros* lot, heritage, as in Acts 1:17]
■ see CLERGYMAN.

clerical /klérrik'l/ *adj.* **1** of the clergy or clergymen. **2** of or done by a clerk or clerks. □ **clerical collar** a stiff upright white collar fastening at the back, as worn by the clergy in some Churches. **clerical error** an error made in copying or writing out. □□ **clericalism** *n.* **clericalist** *n.* **clerically** *adv.* [eccl.L *clericalis* (as CLERIC)]

■ **1** ecclesiastical, churchly, pastoral, sacerdotal, priestly, hieratic, ministerial, episcopal. **2** white-collar, office, secretarial, stenographic.

clerihew /klérrihyōō/ *n.* a short comic or nonsensical verse, usu. in two rhyming couplets with lines of unequal length and referring to a famous person. [E. *Clerihew* Bentley, Engl. writer d. 1956, its inventor]

clerk /klaark/ *n.* & *v.* ● *n.* **1** a person employed in an office, bank, shop, etc., to keep records, accounts, etc. **2** a secretary, agent, or record-keeper of a local council (*town clerk*), court, etc. **3** a lay officer of a church (*parish clerk*), college chapel, etc. **4** a senior official in Parliament. **5** *US* an assistant in a shop or hotel. **6** *archaic* a clergyman. ● *v.intr.* work as a clerk. □ **clerk in holy orders** *formal* a clergyman. **clerk of the course** the judges' secretary etc. in horse or motor racing. **clerk of the works** (or **of works**) an overseer of building works etc. □□ **clerkdom** *n.* **clerkess** *n. Sc.* **clerkish** *adj.* **clerkly** *adj.* **clerkship** *n.* [OE *cleric*, *clerc*, & OF *clerc*, f. eccl.L *clericus* CLERIC]

■ *n.* **1** see BOOKKEEPER. **2** see SCRIBE *n.* 1. **5** see SALESPERSON. **6** see CLERGYMAN.

clever /klévvər/ *adj.* (**cleverer**, **cleverest**) **1 a** skilful, talented; quick to understand and learn. **b** showing good sense or wisdom, wise. **2** adroit, dextrous. **3** (of the doer or the thing done) ingenious, cunning. □ **clever Dick** (or **clogs** etc.) *colloq.* a person who is or purports to be smart or knowing. **not too clever** *Austral. colloq.* unwell, indisposed. □□ **cleverly** *adv.* **cleverness** *n.* [ME, = adroit: perh. rel. to CLEAVE[2], with sense 'apt to seize']

■ **1 a** skilled, talented, skilful, gifted, quick-witted, intelligent, brainy, smart, perceptive, discerning, sharp, sharp-witted, adept, able. **b** sensible, wise, sage. **2** deft, adroit, nimble-fingered, handy, agile, skilful, skilled; see also DEXTEROUS. **3** ingenious, original, resourceful, , inventive, creative, imaginative; shrewd, cunning, guileful, canny, artful, crafty, sly, wily, foxy. □ **clever Dick** (or **clogs** etc.) see BRAIN *n.* 3c, 4.

clevis /klévviss/ *n.* **1** a U-shaped piece of metal at the end of a beam for attaching tackle etc. **2** a connection in which a bolt holds one part that fits between the forked ends of another. [16th c.: rel. to CLEAVE[1]]

clew /klōō/ *n.* & *v.* ● *n.* **1** *Naut.* **a** a lower or after corner of a sail. **b** a set of small cords suspending a hammock. **2** *archaic* **a** a ball of thread or yarn, esp. with reference to the legend of Theseus and the labyrinth. **b** = CLUE. ● *v.tr. Naut.* **1** (foll. by *up*) draw the lower ends of (a sail) to the upper yard or the mast ready for furling. **2** (foll. by *down*) let down (a sail) by the clews in unfurling. [OE *cliwen*, *cleowen*]

clianthus /kliánthəss/ *n.* any leguminous plant of the genus *Clianthus*, native to Australia and New Zealand, bearing drooping clusters of red pealike flowers. [mod.L, app. f. Gk *klei-*, *kleos* glory + *anthos* flower]

cliché /kléeshay/ *n.* **1** a hackneyed phrase or opinion. **2** *Brit.* a metal casting of a stereotype or electrotype. [F f. *clicher* to stereotype]

■ **1** stereotype, bromide, trite saying, old saw *or* maxim, truism, platitude, commonplace, banality.

clichéd /kléeshayd/ *adj.* (also **cliché'd**) hackneyed; full of clichés.

click /klik/ *n.* & *v.* ● *n.* **1** a slight sharp sound as of a switch being operated. **2** a sharp non-vocal suction, used as a speech-sound in some languages. **3** a catch in machinery acting with a slight sharp sound. **4** (of a horse) an action causing a hind foot to touch the shoe of a fore foot. ● *v.* **1 a** *intr.* make a click. **b** *tr.* cause (one's tongue, heels, etc.) to click. **2** *intr. colloq.* **a** become clear or understandable (often prec. by *it* as subject: *when I saw them it all clicked*). **b** be successful, secure one's object. **c** (foll. by *with*) become friendly, esp. with a person of the opposite sex. **d** come to an agreement. □ **click beetle** any of a family of beetles (Elateridae) that make a click in recovering from being overturned. □□ **clicker** *n.* [imit.: cf. Du. *klikken*, F *cliquer*]

■ *n.* **1** see SNAP *n.* 1. ● *v.* **1 a** see SNAP *v.* 2, 3. **2 b** see ACHIEVE 3.

client /klīənt/ *n.* **1** a person using the services of a lawyer, architect, social worker, or other professional person. **2** a customer. **3** *Rom.Hist.* a plebeian under the protection of a patrician. **4** *archaic* a dependant or hanger-on. □□ **clientship** *n.* [ME f. L *cliens -entis* f. *cluere* hear, obey]

■ **1** patron; patient. **2** customer, shopper; patron. **4** see *hanger-on* (HANGER[1]).

clientele /klée-ontél/ *n.* **1** clients collectively. **2** customers, esp. of a shop. **3** the patrons of a theatre etc. [L *clientela* clientship & F *clientèle*]

■ **1** clients, patrons, customers. **2** clients, patrons, customers; custom, business, trade, patronage, following. **3** patrons; public, audience.

cliff /klif/ *n.* a steep rock-face, esp. at the edge of the sea. □ **cliff-hanger** a story etc. with a strong element of suspense; a suspenseful ending to an episode of a serial. **cliff-hanging** full of suspense. □□ **clifflike** *adj.* **cliffy** *adj.* [OE *clif* f. Gmc]

■ precipice, bluff, escarpment, scarp, rock-face, scar, *Geog.* cuesta, *Brit.* crag.

climacteric /klīmáktərik, klīmaktérrik/ *n.* & *adj.* ● *n.* **1** *Med.* the period of life when fertility and sexual activity are in decline. **2** a supposed critical period in life (esp. occurring at intervals of seven years). ● *adj.* **1** *Med.* occurring at the climacteric. **2** constituting a crisis; critical. [F *climatérique* or L *climactericus* f. Gk *klimaktērikos* f. *klimaktēr* critical period f. *klimax -akos* ladder]

■ **1** menopause, male menopause.

climactic /klīmáktik/ *adj.* of or forming a climax. □□ **climactically** *adv.* [CLIMAX + -IC, perh. after SYNTACTIC or CLIMACTERIC]

climate /klīmit/ *n.* **1** the prevailing weather conditions of an area. **2** a region with particular weather conditions. **3** the prevailing trend of opinion or public feeling. □□ **climatic** /-máttik/ *adj.* **climatical** /-máttik'l/ *adj.* **climatically** /-máttikəli/ *adv.* [ME f. OF *climat* or LL *clima climat-* f. Gk *klima* f. *klinō* slope]

■ **1** weather, *literary* clime. **3** consensus; atmosphere, ambience, air; feeling, mood, aura, milieu, feel.

climatology /klīmətólləji/ *n.* the scientific study of climate. □□ **climatological** /-təlójik'l/ *adj.* **climatologist** *n.*

climax /klīmaks/ *n.* & *v.* ● *n.* **1** the event or point of greatest intensity or interest; a culmination or apex. **2** a sexual orgasm. **3** *Rhet.* **a** a series arranged in order of increasing importance etc. **b** the last term in such a series. **4** *Ecol.* a state of equilibrium reached by a plant community. ● *v.tr.* & *intr. colloq.* bring or come to a climax. [LL f. Gk *klimax -akos* ladder, climax]

■ *n.* **1** culmination, height, acme, apex, summit, zenith, apogee, peak, high point, maximum, supreme moment. ● *v.* (*intr.*) culminate, peak, come to a head.

climb /klīm/ *v.* & *n.* ● *v.* **1** *tr.* & *intr.* (often foll. by *up*) ascend, mount, go or come up, esp. by using one's hands. **2** *intr.* (of a plant) grow up a wall, tree, trellis, etc. by clinging with tendrils or by twining. **3** *intr.* make progress from one's own efforts, esp. in social rank, intellectual or moral strength, etc. **4** *intr.* (of an aircraft, the sun, etc.) go upwards. **5** *intr.* slope upwards. ● *n.* **1** an ascent by climbing. **2 a** a place, esp. a hill, climbed or to be climbed. **b** a recognized route up a mountain etc. □ **climb down 1** descend with the help of one's hands. **2** withdraw from a stance taken up in argument, negotiation, etc. **climb-down** *n.* such a withdrawal. **climbing-frame** a structure of joined bars etc. for children to climb on. **climbing-iron** a set of spikes attachable to a boot for climbing trees or ice slopes. □□ **climbable** *adj.* [OE *climban* f. WG, rel. to CLEAVE[2]]

■ *v.* **1** mount, ascend, go up, scale, shin (up), clamber up, *US colloq.* shinny (up). **2** creep, trail, twine; grow. **3** see PROGRESS *v.* 1. **4** rise, ascend, go up, *esp. archaic* & *poet.* arise. □ **climb down 1** descend, go *or* come down, move down, get down. **2** retreat, withdraw, back away *or* off, give up, back-pedal; (*climb down from*) abandon, renounce. **climb-down** withdrawal, pull-back, retraction.

climber /klímər/ *n.* **1** a mountaineer. **2** a climbing plant. **3** a person with strong social etc. aspirations.

clime /klīm/ *n. literary* **1** a region. **2** a climate. [LL *clima*: see CLIMATE]
■ **2** see CLIMATE 1.

clinch /klinch/ *v.* & *n.* ● *v.* **1** *tr.* confirm or settle (an argument, bargain, etc.) conclusively. **2** *intr. Boxing* & *Wrestling* (of participants) become too closely engaged. **3** *intr. colloq.* embrace. **4** *tr.* secure (a nail or rivet) by driving the point sideways when through. **5** *tr. Naut.* fasten (a rope) with a particular half hitch. ● *n.* **1 a** a clinching action. **b** a clinched state. **2** *colloq.* an (esp. amorous) embrace. **3** *Boxing* & *Wrestling* an action or state in which participants become too closely engaged. [16th-c. var. of CLENCH]
■ *v.* **1** secure, settle, confirm, determine, conclude, dispose of, complete, wind up, finalize, *colloq.* sew up. **3** see EMBRACE *v.* 1. ● *n.* **2** hug, clasp, embrace, cuddle, squeeze.

clincher /klínchər/ *n. colloq.* a remark or argument that settles a matter conclusively.
■ finishing touch *or* stroke, punch-line, *coup de grâce*, final *or* crowning blow, *sl.* pay-off.

clincher-built var. of CLINKER-BUILT.

cline /klīn/ *n. Biol.* the graded sequence of differences within a species etc. □□ **clinal** *adj.* [Gk *klinō* to slope]

cling /kling/ *v.* & *n.* ● *v.intr.* (*past* and *past part.* **clung** /klung/) **1** (foll. by *to*) adhere, stick, or hold on (by means of stickiness, suction, grasping, or embracing). **2** (foll. by *to*) remain persistently or stubbornly faithful (to a friend, habit, idea, etc.). **3** maintain one's grasp; keep hold; resist separation. ● *n.* = CLINGSTONE. □ **cling film** a very thin clinging transparent plastic film, used as a covering esp. for food. **cling together** remain in one body or in contact. □□ **clinger** *n.* **clingingly** *adv.* [OE *clingan* f. Gmc: cf. CLENCH]
■ *v.* **1** adhere; see also STICK[2] 4. **2** (*cling to*) favour, be *or* remain devoted *or* attached to, embrace, hang on to, retain, keep, cherish. □ **cling together** stick *or* stay together, embrace, hug, clasp one another, clutch one another, hold (fast) to one another, grasp one another, *literary* cleave to one another.

clingstone /klingstōn/ *n.* a variety of peach or nectarine in which the flesh adheres to the stone (cf. FREESTONE 2).

clingy /klíngi/ *adj.* (**clingier, clingiest**) liable to cling. □□ **clinginess** *n.*

clinic /klínnik/ *n.* **1** *Brit.* a private or specialized hospital. **2** a place or occasion for giving specialist medical treatment or advice (*eye clinic*; *fertility clinic*). **3** a gathering at a hospital bedside for the teaching of medicine or surgery. **4** *US* a conference or short course on a particular subject (*golf clinic*). □□ **clinician** /klinísh'n/ *n.* [F *clinique* f. Gk *klinikē* (*tekhnē*) clinical, lit. bedside (art)]
■ **1** see INFIRMARY 1.

clinical /klínnik'l/ *adj.* **1** *Med.* **a** of or for the treatment of patients. **b** taught or learnt at the hospital bedside. **2** dispassionate, coldly detached. □ **clinical death** death judged by observation of a person's condition. **clinical medicine** medicine dealing with the observation and treatment of patients. **clinical thermometer** a thermometer with a small range, for taking a person's temperature. □□ **clinically** *adv.* [L *clinicus* f. Gk *klinikos* f. *klinē* bed]
■ **2** see COLD *adj.* 4.

clink[1] /klingk/ *n.* & *v.* ● *n.* a sharp ringing sound. ● *v.* **1** *intr.* make a clink. **2** *tr.* cause (glasses etc.) to clink. [ME, prob. f. MDu. *klinken*; cf. CLANG, CLANK]
■ *n.* see JINGLE *n.* 1. ● *v.* see JINGLE *v.*

clink[2] /klingk/ *n.* (often prec. by *in*) *sl.* prison. [16th c.: orig. unkn.]
■ see PRISON *n.* 1.

clinker[1] /klíngkər/ *n.* **1** a mass of slag or lava. **2** a stony residue from burnt coal. [earlier *clincard* etc. f. obs. Du. *klinkaerd* f. *klinken* CLINK[1]]

clinker[2] /klíngkər/ *n.* **1** *Brit. sl.* something excellent or outstanding. **2** *US sl.* a mistake or blunder. [CLINK[1] + -ER[1]]
■ **2** see BLUNDER *n.*

clinker-built /klíngkərbilt/ *adj.* (also **clincher-built** /klínchərbilt/) (of a boat) having external planks overlapping downwards and secured with clinched copper nails. [*clink* N.Engl. var. of CLINCH + -ER[1]]

clinkstone /klíngkstōn/ *n.* a kind of feldspar that rings like iron when struck.

clinometer /klīnómmitər/ *n. Surveying* an instrument for measuring slopes. [Gk *klinō* to slope + -METER]

cliometrics /klīəmétriks/ *n.pl.* (usu. treated as *sing.*) a method of historical research making much use of statistical information and methods. [*Clio*, Muse of history + METRIC + -ICS]

clip[1] /klip/ *n.* & *v.* ● *n.* **1** a device for holding things together or for attachment to an object as a marker, esp. a paper-clip or a device worked by a spring. **2** a piece of jewellery fastened by a clip. **3** a set of attached cartridges for a firearm. ● *v.tr.* (**clipped, clipping**) **1** fix with a clip. **2** grip tightly. **3** surround closely. □ **clip-on** attached by a clip. [OE *clyppan* embrace f. WG]
■ *n.* **1** clasp, fastener. ● *v.* **1** clasp, fasten, fix, attach, hold; staple. **2** grip, grasp, clutch, clasp, hold. **3** see CIRCLE *v.* 2.

clip[2] /klip/ *v.* & *n.* ● *v.tr.* (**clipped, clipping**) **1** cut with shears or scissors, esp. cut short or trim (hair, wool, etc.). **2** trim or remove the hair or wool of (a person or animal). **3** *colloq.* hit smartly. **4 a** curtail, diminish, cut short. **b** omit (a letter etc.) from a word; omit letters or syllables of (words pronounced). **5** *Brit.* remove a small piece of (a ticket) to show that it has been used. **6** cut (an extract) from a newspaper etc. **7** *sl.* swindle, rob. **8** pare the edge of (a coin). ● *n.* **1** an act of clipping, esp. shearing or hair-cutting. **2** *colloq.* a smart blow, esp. with the hand. **3** a short sequence from a motion picture. **4** the quantity of wool clipped from a sheep, flock, etc. **5** *colloq.* speed, esp. rapid. □ **clip-joint** *sl.* a club etc. charging exorbitant prices. **clip a person's wings** prevent a person from pursuing ambitions or acting effectively. □□ **clippable** *adj.* [ME f. ON *klippa*, prob. imit.]
■ *v.* **1** trim (off), lop (off), cut (off), cut short, crop, chop, snip. **2** shear, fleece. **3** strike, hit, punch, smack, box, cuff, clout, *colloq.* sock, thwack, whack; *sl.* wallop. **4** shorten, reduce, abbreviate, diminish, curtail, cut (short), truncate. **7** cheat, overcharge, *sl.* rook, bilk; see also SWINDLE *v.* ● *n.* **1** cut, trim, hair-cutting, shearing. **2** blow, cuff, punch, hit, strike, smack, box, clout, *colloq.* whack, sock, *sl.* wallop, *Brit. sl.* clock. **3** segment, section, part, portion, extract, cutting, excerpt, bit, snippet, scrap, fragment. **5** pace, rate, speed. □ **clip a person's wings** see THWART *v.*

clipboard /klípbord/ *n.* a small board with a spring clip for holding papers etc. and providing support for writing.

clip-clop /klípklóp/ *n.* & *v.* ● *n.* a sound such as the beat of a horse's hooves. ● *v.intr.* (**-clopped, -clopping**) make such a sound. [imit.]

clipper /klíppər/ *n.* **1** (usu. in *pl.*) any of various instruments for clipping hair, fingernails, hedges, etc. **2** a fast sailing-ship, esp. one with raking bows and masts. **3** a fast horse.

clippie /klíppi/ *n. Brit. colloq.* a bus conductress.

clipping /klípping/ *n.* a piece clipped or cut from something, esp. from a newspaper.
■ see EXTRACT *n.* 1.

clique /kleek/ *n.* a small exclusive group of people. □□ **cliquey** *adj.* (**cliquier, cliquiest**). **cliquish** *adj.* **cliquishness** *n.* **cliquism** *n.* [F f. *cliquer* CLICK]
■ set, coterie, crowd, circle, group, *Austral.* push.

C.Lit. *abbr. Brit.* Companion of Literature.

clitic /klíttik/ *n.* (often *attrib.*) an enclitic or proclitic. ▫▫ **cliticization** /-tikīzáysh'n/ *n.*

clitoris /klíttəriss, klī́-/ *n.* a small erectile part of the female genitals at the upper end of the vulva. ▫▫ **clitoral** *adj.* [mod.L f. Gk *kleitoris*]

clivers var. of CLEAVERS.

Cllr. *abbr. Brit.* Councillor.

cloaca /klō-áykə/ *n.* (*pl.* **cloacae** /-áysee/) **1** the genital and excretory cavity at the end of the intestinal canal in birds, reptiles, etc. **2** a sewer. ▫▫ **cloacal** *adj.* [L, = sewer]
■ **2** see DRAIN *n.* 1a.

cloak /klōk/ *n.* & *v.* ● *n.* **1** an outdoor over-garment, usu. sleeveless, hanging loosely from the shoulders. **2** a covering (*cloak of snow*). **3** (in *pl.*) = CLOAKROOM. ● *v.tr.* **1** cover with a cloak. **2** conceal, disguise. ▫ **cloak-and-dagger** involving intrigue and espionage. **under the cloak of** using as a pretext. [ME f. OF *cloke*, dial. var. of *cloche* bell, cloak (from its bell shape) f. med.L *clocca* bell: see CLOCK[1]]
■ *n.* **1** mantle, cape, robe, wrap, poncho, overcoat. **2** mantle, covering, cover, screen, shroud, veil. ● *v.* **1** see DRESS *v.* 1. **2** conceal, hide, mask, screen, veil, shroud, cover up; disguise.

cloakroom /klṓkrōōm, -rŏŏm/ *n.* **1** a room where outdoor clothes or luggage may be left by visitors, clients, etc. **2** *Brit. euphem.* a lavatory.

clobber[1] /klóbbər/ *n. Brit. sl.* clothing or personal belongings. [19th c.: orig. unkn.]
■ see CLOTHES.

clobber[2] /klóbbər/ *v.tr. sl.* **1** hit repeatedly; beat up. **2** defeat. **3** criticize severely. [20th c.: orig. unkn.]
■ **1** see HIT *v.* 1a. **2** see SLAUGHTER *v.* 3.

cloche /klosh, klōsh/ *n.* **1** a small translucent cover for protecting or forcing outdoor plants. **2** (in full **cloche hat**) a woman's close-fitting bell-shaped hat. [F, = bell, f. med.L *clocca*: see CLOCK[1]]

clock[1] /klok/ *n.* & *v.* ● *n.* **1** an instrument for measuring time, driven mechanically or electrically and indicating hours, minutes, etc., by hands on a dial or by displayed figures. **2 a** any measuring device resembling a clock. **b** *colloq.* a speedometer, taximeter, or stopwatch. **3** time taken as an element in competitive sports etc. (*ran against the clock*). **4** *Brit. sl.* a person's face. **5** a downy seed-head, esp. that of a dandelion. ● *v.tr.* **1** *colloq.* **a** (often foll. by *up*) attain or register (a stated time, distance, or speed, esp. in a race). **b** time (a race) with a stopwatch. **2** *Brit. sl.* hit, esp. on the head. ▫ **clock golf** a game in which a golf ball is putted into a hole from successive points in a circle. **clock in** (or **on**) register one's arrival at work, esp. by means of an automatic recording clock. **clock off** (or **out**) register one's departure similarly. **clock radio** a combined radio and alarm clock. **round the clock** all day and (usu.) night. **watch the clock** = CLOCK-WATCH. [ME f. MDu., MLG *klocke* f. med.L *clocca* bell, perh. f. Celt.]
■ *n.* **1** see WATCH *n.* 1. **4** see MUG[1] *n.* 2. ▫ **clock in** see REPORT *v.* 4. **clock off** see *knock off* 2a.

clock[2] /klok/ *n.* an ornamental pattern on the side of a stocking or sock near the ankle. [16th c.: orig. unkn.]

clock-watch /klókwoch/ *v.intr.* work over-anxiously to time, esp. so as not to exceed minimum working hours. ▫▫ **clock-watcher** *n.* **clock-watching** *n.*

clockwise /klókwīz/ *adj.* & *adv.* in a curve corresponding in direction to the movement of the hands of a clock.

clockwork /klókwurk/ *n.* **1** a mechanism like that of a mechanical clock, with a spring and gears. **2** (*attrib.*) **a** driven by clockwork. **b** regular, mechanical. ▫ **like clockwork** smoothly, regularly, automatically.
■ **1** see WORK *n.* 8.

clod /klod/ *n.* **1** a lump of earth, clay, etc. **2** *sl.* a silly or foolish person. **3** meat cut from the neck of an ox. ▫▫ **cloddy** *adj.* [ME: var. of CLOT]
■ **1** lump, mass, wad, hunk, chunk, piece. **2** idiot, fool, dolt, blockhead, simpleton, nincompoop, dunce, oaf, ass, clown, ninny, bumpkin, clodhopper, *colloq.* imbecile, *Brit. colloq.* clot, *sl.* jerk, dope, clodpoll, *Austral. sl.* hoon.

cloddish /klóddish/ *adj.* loutish, foolish, clumsy. ▫▫ **cloddishly** *adv.* **cloddishness** *n.*

clodhopper /klódhoppər/ *n.* **1** (usu. in *pl.*) *colloq.* a large heavy shoe. **2** = CLOD 2.

clodhopping /klódhopping/ *adj.* = CLODDISH.

clodpoll /klódpol/ *n. sl.* = CLOD 2.

clog /klog/ *n.* & *v.* ● *n.* **1** a shoe with a thick wooden sole. **2** *archaic* an encumbrance or impediment. **3** a block of wood to impede an animal's movement. ● *v.* (**clogged, clogging**) **1** (often foll. by *up*) **a** *tr.* obstruct, esp. by accumulation of glutinous matter. **b** *intr.* become obstructed. **2** *tr.* impede, hamper. **3** *tr.* & *intr.* (often foll. by *up*) fill with glutinous or choking matter. ▫ **clog-dance** a dance performed in clogs. [ME: orig. unkn.]
■ *n.* **2** see IMPEDIMENT. ● *v.* **1** obstruct, choke (up), block, congest, jam. **2** see IMPEDE.

cloggy /klóggi/ *adj.* (**cloggier, cloggiest**) **1** lumpy, knotty. **2** sticky.

cloisonné /klwaázonay/ *n.* & *adj.* ● *n.* **1** an enamel finish produced by forming areas of different colours separated by strips of wire placed edgeways on a metal backing. **2** this process. ● *adj.* (of enamel) made by this process. [F f. *cloison* compartment]

cloister /klóystər/ *n.* & *v.* ● *n.* **1** a covered walk, often with a wall on one side and a colonnade open to a quadrangle on the other, esp. in a convent, monastery, college, or cathedral. **2** monastic life or seclusion. **3** a convent or monastery. ● *v.tr.* seclude or shut up usu. in a convent or monastery. ▫▫ **cloistral** *adj.* [ME f. OF *cloistre* f. L *claustrum, clostrum* lock, enclosed place f. *claudere claus-* CLOSE[2]]
■ *n.* **3** see MONASTERY. ● *v.* see ISOLATE 1.

cloistered /klóystərd/ *adj.* **1** secluded, sheltered. **2** monastic.
■ **1** see SECLUDE 2.

clomp var. of CLUMP *v.* 2.

clone /klōn/ *n.* & *v.* ● *n.* **1 a** a group of organisms produced asexually from one stock or ancestor. **b** one such organism. **2** a person or thing regarded as identical with another. ● *v.tr.* propagate as a clone. ▫▫ **clonal** *adj.* [Gk *klōn* twig, slip]
■ *n.* **1b, 2** see DUPLICATE *n.* 1. ● *v.* see IMITATE 3.

clonk /klongk/ *n.* & *v.* ● *n.* an abrupt heavy sound of impact. ● *v.* **1** *intr.* make such a sound. **2** *tr. colloq.* hit. [imit.]
■ *n.* see THUD *n.* ● *v.* **1** see THUD *v.* **2** see HIT *v.* 1a.

clonus /klṓnəss/ *n. Physiol.* a spasm with alternate muscular contractions and relaxations. ▫▫ **clonic** *adj.* [Gk *klonos* turmoil]

clop /klop/ *n.* & *v.* ● *n.* the sound made by a horse's hooves. ● *v.intr.* (**clopped, clopping**) make this sound. [imit.]

cloqué /klṓkay/ *n.* a fabric with an irregularly raised surface. [F, = blistered]

close[1] /klōss/ *adj.*, *adv.*, & *n.* ● *adj.* **1** (often foll. by *to*) situated at only a short distance or interval. **2 a** having a strong or immediate relation or connection (*close friend; close relative*). **b** in intimate friendship or association (*were very close*). **c** corresponding almost exactly (*close resemblance*). **d** fitting tightly (*close cap*). **e** (of hair etc.) short, near the surface. **3** in or almost in contact (*close combat; close proximity*). **4** dense, compact, with no or only slight intervals (*close texture; close writing; close formation; close thicket*). **5** in which competitors are almost equal (*close contest; close election*). **6** leaving no gaps or weaknesses, rigorous (*close reasoning*). **7** concentrated, searching (*close examination; close attention*). **8** (of air etc.) stuffy or humid. **9 a** closed, shut. **b** shut up, under secure confinement. **10** limited or restricted to certain persons etc. (*close corporation; close scholarship*). **11 a** hidden, secret, covered. **b** secretive. **12** (of a danger etc.) directly threatening, narrowly avoided (*that was close*). **13** niggardly. **14** (of a vowel) pronounced with a relatively narrow opening of the mouth. **15** narrow, confined, contracted. **16** under prohibition. ● *adv.* **1** (often foll. by *by, on, to, upon*) at only a short distance or interval (*they live close by; close to the church*). **2** closely, in a close manner (*shut close*). ● *n.* **1** an enclosed space. **2** *Brit.* a street closed at one end. **3** *Brit.* the precinct of a cathedral. **4** *Brit.* a school playing-field or playground. **5** *Sc.* an entry from the street to a common stairway or to a court at the back. □ **at close quarters** very close together. **close-fisted** niggardly. **close-fitting** (of a garment) fitting close to the body. **close-grained** without gaps between fibres etc. **close harmony** harmony in which the notes of the chord are close together. **close-hauled** (of a ship) with the sails hauled aft to sail close to the wind. **close-knit** tightly bound or interlocked; closely united in friendship. **close-mouthed** reticent. **close score** *Mus.* a score with more than one part on the same staff. **close season** *Brit.* the season when something, esp. the killing of game etc., is illegal. **close-set** separated only by a small interval or intervals. **close shave** *colloq.* a narrow escape. **close to the wind** see SAIL. **close-up 1** a photograph etc. taken at close range and showing the subject on a large scale. **2** an intimate description. **go close** (of a racehorse) win or almost win. □□ **closely** *adv.* **closeness** *n.* **closish** *adj.* [ME f. OF *clos* f. L *clausum* enclosure & *clausus* past part. of *claudere* shut]

■ *adj.* **1** adjacent, near. **2 a, b** intimate, devoted, familiar, inseparable, close-knit, solid, fast; attached, friendly, *colloq.* thick, thick as thieves, pally. **d** see TIGHT *adj.* 1, 2a. **4** dense, compact, tight, cramped, compressed. **5** nearly equal *or* even, neck and neck, tight. **6** see METICULOUS. **7** careful, assiduous, precise, detailed, concentrated, strict, rigorous, minute, searching, attentive, alert, intent, intense, thorough, painstaking. **8** stuffy, humid, musty, stale, fusty, oppressive, airless, unventilated, stifling, suffocating. **9 b** shut up, secure, fast. **11 a** private, secret, guarded, closely guarded, confidential; secluded, concealed, shut up *or* away, hidden, covered, *archaic* privy. **b** secretive, reticent, taciturn, reserved, close-mouthed, tight-lipped, silent. **13** stingy, mean, miserly, niggardly, tight-fisted, close-fisted, parsimonious, penurious, penny-pinching, cheese-paring, Scrooge-like, skinflinty, near, *Brit. colloq.* mingy. **15** see NARROW *adj.* 1b. ● *adv.* **1** near, in the neighbourhood (of), not far (from *or* off), adjacent (to); alongside; at hand, nearby, close by; (*close to* or *on*) nearly, almost, practically, approximately, approaching, *archaic or dial.* nigh unto *or* on. **2** see *tightly* (TIGHT). □ **at close quarters** close, near, cheek by jowl. **close-fisted** see CLOSE *adj.* 13 above. **close-fitting** tight-fitting, tight, skin-tight, snug. **close-knit** see CLOSE *adj.* 2a, b above. **close-mouthed** see *reticent* (RETICENCE).

close[2] /klōz/ *v.* & *n.* ● *v.* **1 a** *tr.* shut (a lid, box, door, room, house, etc.). **b** *intr.* become shut (*the door closed slowly*). **c** *tr.* block up. **2 a** *tr.* & *intr.* bring or come to an end. **b** *intr.* finish speaking (*closed with an expression of thanks*). **c** *tr.* settle (a bargain etc.). **3 a** *intr.* end the day's business. **b** *tr.* end the day's business at (a shop, office, etc.). **4** *tr.* & *intr.* bring or come closer or into contact (*close ranks*). **5** *tr.* make (an electric circuit etc.) continuous. **6** *intr.* (foll. by *with*) express agreement (with an offer, terms, or the person offering them). **7** *intr.* (often foll. by *with*) come within striking distance; grapple. **8** *intr.* (foll. by *on*) (of a hand, box, etc.) grasp or entrap. ● *n.* **1** a conclusion, an end. **2** *Mus.* a cadence. □ **close down 1** (of a shop, factory, etc.) discontinue business, esp. permanently. **2** *Brit.* (of a broadcasting station) end transmission esp. until the next day. **close one's eyes 1** (foll. by *to*) pay no attention. **2** die. **close in 1** enclose. **2** come nearer. **3** (of days) get successively shorter with the approach of the winter solstice. **close off** prevent access to by blocking or sealing the entrance. **close out** *US* discontinue, terminate, dispose of (a business). **close up 1** (often foll. by *to*) move closer. **2** shut, esp. temporarily. **3** block up. **4** (of an aperture) grow smaller. **5** coalesce. **closing-time** the time at which a public house, shop, etc., ends business. □□ **closable** *adj.* **closer** *n.* [ME f. OF *clos-* stem of *clore* f. L *claudere* shut]

■ *v.* **1 a** shut, close up, seal; close off, lock, padlock, secure, fasten. **b** shut, be shut. **2 a** conclude, end, finish, bring to a close *or* an end, terminate, climax; complete, wind up; come to a close *or* an end. **b** end, conclude, terminate, finish. **c** conclude, sign, seal, make, settle, clinch, agree, arrange, work out, establish. **3 a** shut, put up the shutters. **b** shut. ● *n.* **1** end, termination, conclusion, finish, completion; culmination. □ **close down 1** shut down, go out of business, shut up shop, cease operations, close (up), wind up, put up the shutters. **close one's eyes 1** (*close one's eyes to*) ignore, overlook, disregard. **close in 1** see ENCLOSE 1, 6. **2** see APPROACH *v.* 1, 2. **close off** seal, make inaccessible, shut (off), obstruct, block. **close out** see TERMINATE. **close up 1** see APPROACH *v.* 1, 2. **2** close, shut (up), lock up. **3** see CLOG *v.* **5** see COMBINE *v.* 3.

closed /klōzd/ *adj.* **1** not giving access; shut. **2** (of a shop etc.) having ceased business temporarily. **3** (of a society, system, etc.) self-contained; not communicating with others. **4** (of a sport etc.) restricted to specified competitors etc. □ **closed book** see BOOK. **closed-circuit** (of television) transmitted by wires to a restricted set of receivers. **closed-end** having a predetermined extent (cf. *open-ended*). **closed season** *US* = *close season* (see CLOSE[1]). **closed shop 1** a place of work etc. where all employees must belong to an agreed trade union. **2** this system. **closed syllable** a syllable ending in a consonant.

■ **3** self-contained, withdrawn, uncommunicative, aloof, distant.

closet /klózzit/ *n.* & *v.* ● *n.* **1** a small or private room. **2** a cupboard or recess. **3** = *water-closet*. **4** (*attrib.*) secret, covert (*closet homosexual*). ● *v.tr.* (**closeted, closeting**) shut away, esp. in private conference or study. □ **Clerk of the Closet** (in the UK) the sovereign's principal chaplain. **closet play** a play to be read rather than acted. **come out of the closet** stop hiding something about oneself, esp. one's homosexuality. [ME f. OF, dimin. of *clos*: see CLOSE[1]]

■ *n.* **1** see CABINET 3. **2** see WARDROBE 1. **4** see STEALTHY. □ **come out of the closet** come out.

closure /klṓzhər/ *n.* & *v.* ● *n.* **1** the act or process of closing. **2** a closed condition. **3** something that closes or seals, e.g. a cap or tie. **4** a procedure for ending a debate and taking a vote, esp. in Parliament. ● *v.tr.* apply the closure to (a motion, speakers, etc.). [ME f. OF f. LL *clausura* f. *claudere claus-* CLOSE[2]]

■ *n.* **1** *Parl.* guillotine, *US* cloture. ● *v. Parl.* guillotine, *US* cloture.

clot /klot/ *n.* & *v.* ● *n.* **1 a** a thick mass of coagulated liquid, esp. of blood exposed to air. **b** a mass of material stuck together. **2** *Brit. colloq.* a silly or foolish person. ● *v.tr.* & *intr.* (**clotted, clotting**) form into clots. □ **clotted cream** esp. *Brit.* thick cream obtained by slow scalding. [OE *clot(t)* f. WG: cf. CLEAT]

■ *n.* **1** see LUMP[1] *n.* 1, 2. **2** see DOLT. ● *v.* see COAGULATE.

cloth /kloth/ *n.* (*pl.* **cloths** /kloths, klothz/) **1** woven or felted material. **2** a piece of this. **3** a piece of cloth for a particular purpose; a tablecloth, dishcloth, etc. **4** woollen woven fabric as used for clothes. **5 a** profession or status, esp. of the clergy, as shown by clothes (*respect due to his cloth*). **b** (prec. by *the*) the clergy. □ **cloth-cap** relating to or associated with the working class. **cloth-eared** *colloq.* somewhat deaf. **cloth of gold** (or **silver**) tissue of gold (or silver) threads interwoven with silk or wool. [OE *clāth*, of unkn. orig.]

■ **1** fabric, material, textile. **5 b** (*the cloth*) the clergy, the (religious) ministry, the priesthood.

clothe /klōth/ *v.tr.* (*past* and *past part.* **clothed** or *formal* **clad**) **1** put clothes on; provide with clothes. **2** cover as with clothes or a cloth. **3** (foll. by *with*) endue (with qualities etc.). [OE: rel. to CLOTH]

■ **1** dress, garb, outfit, fit out *or* up, accoutre, kit out *or* up, *archaic* apparel, *formal* attire. **2** cover, garb, robe, sheathe, *formal* attire. **3** endow, endue, invest, caparison, provide, supply, furnish.

clothes /klōthz/ *n.pl.* **1** garments worn to cover the body and limbs. **2** bedclothes. □ **clothes-horse 1** a frame for airing washed clothes. **2** *colloq.* an affectedly fashionable person. **clothes-line** a rope or wire etc. on which washed clothes are hung to dry. **clothes-moth** any moth of the family Tineidae, with a larva destructive to wool, fur, etc. **clothes-peg** *Brit.* a clip or forked device for securing clothes to a clothes-line. **clothes-pin** *US* a clothes-peg. [OE *clāthas* pl. of *clāth* CLOTH]

■ **1** clothing, wear, dress, garments, wardrobe, vestment(s), *archaic* raiment, *colloq.* togs, gear, *formal* attire, apparel, *sl.* duds, *Austral. sl.* mocker, *Brit. sl.* clobber, (set of) threads.

clothier /klṓthiər/ *n.* a seller of men's clothes. [ME *clother* f. CLOTH]

■ see TAILOR *n.*

clothing /klṓthing/ *n.* clothes collectively.

cloture /klṓchər, klṓtyoor/ *n.* & *v.* *US* ● *n.* the closure of a debate. ● *v.tr.* closure. [F *clôture* f. OF CLOSURE]

clou /kloo/ *n.* **1** the point of greatest interest; the chief attraction. **2** the central idea. [F, = nail]

cloud /klowd/ *n.* & *v.* ● *n.* **1** a visible mass of condensed watery vapour floating in the atmosphere high above the general level of the ground. **2** a mass of smoke or dust. **3** (foll. by *of*) a great number of insects, birds, etc., moving together. **4 a** a state of gloom, trouble, or suspicion. **b** a frowning or depressed look (*a cloud on his brow*). **5** a local dimness or a vague patch of colour in or on a liquid or a transparent body. **6** an unsubstantial or fleeting thing. **7** obscurity. ● *v.* **1** *tr.* cover or darken with clouds or gloom or trouble. **2** *intr.* (often foll. by *over, up*) become overcast or gloomy. **3** *tr.* make unclear. **4** *tr.* variegate with vague patches of colour. □ **cloud-castle** a daydream. **cloud chamber** a device containing vapour for tracking the paths of charged particles, X-rays, and gamma rays. **clouded leopard** a mottled arboreal S. Asian feline, *Neofelis nebulosa*. **cloud-hopping** movement of an aircraft from cloud to cloud esp. for concealment. **cloud-land** a Utopia or fairyland. **in the clouds 1** unreal, imaginary, mystical. **2** (of a person) abstracted, inattentive. **on cloud nine** (or **seven**) *colloq.* extremely happy. **under a cloud** out of favour, discredited, under suspicion. **with one's head in the clouds** day-dreaming, unrealistic. □□ **cloudless** *adj.* **cloudlessly** *adv.* **cloudlet** *n.* [OE *clūd* mass of rock or earth, prob. rel. to CLOD]

■ *n.* **1, 2** see VAPOUR *n.* 1. **3** see SWARM[1] *n.* 1–3. ● *v.* **1** see SHADE *v.* 1, 2. **2** see FOG *v.* 1a, 2. **3** see MUDDY *v.* □ **cloud-land** see UTOPIA. **in the clouds** see ABSENT-MINDED. **on cloud nine** see HAPPY 1. □□ **cloudless** see CLEAR *adj.* 2.

cloudberry /klówdbəri/ *n.* (*pl.* **-ies**) a small mountain bramble, *Rubus chamaemorus*, with a white flower and an orange-coloured fruit.

cloudburst /klówdburst/ *n.* a sudden violent rainstorm.

■ see STORM *n.* 1.

cloud-cuckoo-land /klowdkóókkooland/ *n.* a fanciful or ideal place. [transl. of Gk *Nephelokokkugia* f. *nephelē* cloud + *kokkux* cuckoo (in Aristophanes' *Birds*)]

■ see UTOPIA.

cloudscape /klówdskayp/ *n.* **1** a picturesque grouping of clouds. **2** a picture or view of clouds. [CLOUD *n.*, after *landscape*]

cloudy /klówdi/ *adj.* (**cloudier, cloudiest**) **1 a** (of the sky) covered with clouds, overcast. **b** (of weather) characterized by clouds. **2** not transparent; unclear. □□ **cloudily** *adv.* **cloudiness** *n.*

■ **1** see DULL *adj.* 3. **2** see OPAQUE *adj.* 1, 2.

clough /kluf/ *n. dial.* a steep valley usu. with a torrent bed; a ravine. [OE *clōh* f. Gmc]

■ see RAVINE.

clout /klowt/ *n.* & *v.* ● *n.* **1** a heavy blow. **2** *colloq.* influence, power of effective action esp. in politics or business. **3** *dial.* a piece of cloth or clothing (*cast not a clout*). **4** *Archery hist.* a piece of canvas on a frame, used as a mark. **5** a nail with a large flat head. **6** a patch. ● *v.tr.* **1** hit hard. **2** mend with a patch. [OE *clūt*, rel. to CLEAT, CLOT]

■ *n.* **1** see BLOW[2] 1. **2** see INFLUENCE *n.* ● *v.* **1** see HIT *v.* 1a.

clove[1] /klōv/ *n.* **1 a** a dried flower-bud of a tropical plant, *Eugenia aromatica*, used as a pungent aromatic spice. **b** this plant. **2** (in full **clove gillyflower** or **clove pink**) a clove-scented pink, *Dianthus caryophyllus*, the original of the carnation and other double pinks. [ME f. OF *clou* (*de girofle*) nail (of gillyflower), from its shape, GILLYFLOWER being orig. the name of the spice; later applied to the similarly scented pink]

clove[2] /klōv/ *n.* any of the small bulbs making up a compound bulb of garlic, shallot, etc. [OE *clufu*, rel. to CLEAVE[1]]

clove[3] *past* of CLEAVE[1].

clove hitch /klōv/ *n.* a knot by which a rope is secured by passing it twice round a spar or rope that it crosses at right angles. [old past part. of CLEAVE[1], as showing parallel separate lines]

cloven /klṓv'n/ *adj.* split, partly divided. □ **cloven hoof** (or **foot**) the divided hoof of ruminant quadrupeds (e.g. oxen, sheep, goats); also ascribed to the god Pan, and so to the Devil. **show the cloven hoof** reveal one's evil nature. □□ **cloven-footed** /-fóottid/ *adj.* **cloven-hoofed** /-hóoft/ *adj.* [past part. of CLEAVE[1]]

clover /klṓvər/ *n.* any leguminous fodder plant of the genus *Trifolium*, having dense flower heads and leaves each consisting of usu. three leaflets. □ **clover leaf** a junction of roads intersecting at different levels with connecting sections forming the pattern of a four-leaved clover. **in clover** in ease and luxury. [OE *clāfre* f. Gmc]

■ □ **in clover** see OPULENT 1.

clown /klown/ *n.* & *v.* ● *n.* **1** a comic entertainer, esp. in a pantomime or circus, usu. with traditional costume and make-up. **2** a silly, foolish, or playful person. **3** *archaic* a rustic. ● *v.* **1** *intr.* (often foll. by *about, around*) behave like a clown; act foolishly or playfully. **2** *tr.* perform (a part, an action, etc.) like a clown. □□ **clownery** *n.* **clownish** *adj.* **clownishly** *adv.* **clownishness** *n.* [16th c.: perh. of LG orig.]

■ *n.* **1** jester, fool, zany, comic, comedian, comedienne, funny man *or* woman, merry andrew. **2** buffoon, clod, clodhopper, fool, *US colloq.* lummox, *sl.* jerk. **3** boor, rustic, yahoo, oaf, lout, bumpkin, provincial, peasant, yokel, *esp. US colloq.* hick, *US colloq. often derog.* hill-billy. ● *v.* **1** (*clown around* or *about*) fool (around *or* about), play *or* act the fool, horse around *or* about, mess around *or* about, engage in high jinks, *US* cut up, *US colloq.* cut (up) didoes.

cloy /kloy/ *v.tr.* (usu. foll. by *with*) satiate or sicken with an excess of sweetness, richness, etc. □□ **cloyingly** *adv.* [ME f. obs. *acloy* f. AF *acloyer*, OF *encloyer* f. Rmc: cf. ENCLAVE]

■ see SATE 2.

cloze /klōz/ *n.* the exercise of supplying a word that has been omitted from a passage as a test of readability or comprehension (usu. *attrib.*: *cloze test*). [CLOSURE]

club /klub/ *n.* & *v.* ● *n.* **1** a heavy stick with a thick end, used as a weapon etc. **2** a stick used in a game, esp. a stick with a head used in golf. **3 a** a playing-card of a suit denoted by a black trefoil. **b** (in *pl.*) this suit. **4** an association of persons united by a common interest, usu. meeting periodically for a shared activity (*tennis club*; *yacht club*). **5 a** an organization or premises offering members social amenities, meals and temporary residence, etc. **b** a nightclub. **6** an organization offering subscribers certain benefits (*book club*). **7** a group of persons, nations, etc., having something in common. **8** = CLUBHOUSE. **9** a structure or organ, esp. in a plant, with a knob at the end. ● *v.* (**clubbed, clubbing**) **1** *tr.* beat with or as with a club. **2** *intr.* (foll. by *together, with*) combine for joint action, esp. making up a sum of money for a purpose. **3** *tr.* contribute (money etc.) to a common stock. □ **club-class** a class of fare on aircraft etc. designed for the business traveller. **club-foot** a congenitally deformed foot. **club-footed** having a club-foot. **club-man** (*pl.* **-men**) a member of one or more clubs (in sense 5 of *n.*). **club-root** a disease of cabbages etc. with swelling at the base of the stem. **club sandwich** *US* a sandwich with two layers of filling between three slices of toast or bread. **in the club** *Brit. sl.* pregnant. **on the club** *colloq.* receiving relief from the funds of a benefit society. □□ **clubber** *n.* [ME f. ON *klubba* assim. form of *klumba* club, rel. to CLUMP]

■ *n.* **1** cudgel, bat, bludgeon, billy, truncheon, lathi, *Austral.* & *NZ* waddy, *US* blackjack, *Brit. colloq.* cosh, *hist.* mace, *US sl.* sap. **4** association, society, organization, fraternity, sorority, fellowship, brotherhood, sisterhood, federation, union, guild, lodge. **5 b** nightclub, cabaret, *colloq.* nightspot. **7** alliance, league, order, consortium, company, federation. ● *v.* **1** beat, cudgel, bludgeon, bat, belabour, baste, thrash, trounce, *colloq.* lambaste. **2** (*club together*) band *or* join *or* league (together), team (up), join forces, combine, associate, confederate, cooperate. **3** pool.

clubbable /klúbbəb'l/ *adj.* sociable; fit for membership of a club. □□ **clubbability** /-bílliti/ *n.* **clubbableness** *n.*

clubby /klúbbi/ *adj.* (**clubbier, clubbiest**) esp. *US* sociable; friendly.

■ see FRIENDLY *adj.* 2.

clubhouse /klúbhowss/ *n.* the premises used by a club.

clubland /klúbland/ *n. Brit.* an area where many clubs are, esp. St James's in London.

clubmoss /klúbmoss/ *n.* any pteridophyte of the family Lycopodiaceae, bearing upright spikes of spore-cases.

cluck /kluk/ *n.* & *v.* ● *n.* **1** a guttural cry like that of a hen. **2** *sl.* a silly or foolish person (*dumb cluck*). ● *v.intr.* emit a cluck or clucks. [imit.]

clucky /klúkki/ *adj.* (of a hen) sitting on eggs.

clue /kloo/ *n.* & *v.* ● *n.* **1** a fact or idea that serves as a guide, or suggests a line of inquiry, in a problem or investigation. **2** a piece of evidence etc. in the detection of a crime. **3** a verbal formula serving as a hint as to what is to be inserted in a crossword. **4 a** the thread of a story. **b** a train of thought. ● *v.tr.* (**clues, clued, cluing** or **clueing**) provide a clue to. □ **clue in** (or **up**) *sl.* inform. **not have a clue** *colloq.* be ignorant or incompetent. [var. of CLEW]

■ *n.* **1, 2** hint, indication, pointer, lead, trace, intimation, suggestion; inkling, idea; key, answer, indicator. **4 a** see THREAD *n.* 3. □ **clue in** see INFORM 1. **not have a clue** see IGNORANT 1a, INCOMPETENT *adj.*

clueless /kloóliss/ *adj. colloq.* ignorant, stupid. □□ **cluelessly** *adv.* **cluelessness** *n.*

clump /klump/ *n.* & *v.* ● *n.* **1** (foll. by *of*) a cluster of plants, esp. trees or shrubs. **2** an agglutinated mass of blood-cells etc. **3** a thick extra sole on a boot or shoe. ● *v.* **1 a** *intr.* form a clump. **b** *tr.* heap or plant together. **2** *intr.* (also **clomp** /klomp/) walk with heavy tread. **3** *tr. colloq.* hit. □□ **clumpy** *adj.* (**clumpier, clumpiest**). [MLG *klumpe*, MDu. *klompe*: see CLUB]

■ *n.* **1** bunch, cluster; thicket. **2** lump, mass, clot, clod, glob, *Brit. sl.* gob. ● *v.* **1 b** lump, mass, clot, heap, collect, gather, bunch, pile. **3** see HIT *v.* 1a.

clumsy /klúmzi/ *adj.* (**clumsier, clumsiest**) **1** awkward in movement or shape; ungainly. **2** difficult to handle or use. **3** tactless. □□ **clumsily** *adv.* **clumsiness** *n.* [obs. *clumse* be numb with cold (prob. f. Scand.)]

■ **1** awkward, ungainly, ungraceful, gawky, maladroit, unhandy, unskilful, inept, bungling, bumbling, cloddish, uncoordinated, lubberly, oafish, gauche, *colloq.* butter-fingered, ham-fisted, ham-handed, cack-handed. **2** see UNWIELDY. **3** see TACTLESS.

clung *past* and *past part.* of CLING.

clunk /klungk/ *n.* & *v.* ● *n.* a dull sound as of thick pieces of metal meeting. ● *v.intr.* make such a sound. [imit.]

■ *n.* see THUD *n.* ● *v.* see THUD *v.*

cluster /klústər/ *n.* & *v.* ● *n.* **1** a close group or bunch of similar things growing together. **2** a close group or swarm of people, animals, faint stars, gems, etc. **3** a group of successive consonants or vowels. ● *v.* **1** *tr.* bring into a cluster or clusters. **2** *intr.* be or come into a cluster or clusters. **3** *intr.* (foll. by *round, around*) gather, congregate. □ **cluster bomb** an anti-personnel bomb spraying pellets on impact. **cluster pine** a Mediterranean pine *Pinus pinaster* with clustered cones: also called PINASTER. [OE *clyster*: cf. CLOT]

■ *n.* **1, 2** collection, bunch, clutch, tuft, bundle, knot; group, swarm, body, band, company, gathering, crowd, assembly, congregation, throng, flock, assemblage. ● *v.* **2, 3** collect, gather, bunch, group, band, congregate, assemble, accumulate, mass, aggregate; crowd, throng.

clustered /klústərd/ *adj.* **1** growing in or brought into a cluster. **2** *Archit.* (of pillars, columns, or shafts) several close together, or disposed round or half detached from a pier.

clutch[1] /kluch/ *v.* & *n.* ● *v.* **1** *tr.* seize eagerly; grasp tightly. **2** *intr.* (foll. by *at*) snatch suddenly. ● *n.* **1 a** a tight grasp. **b** (foll. by *at*) grasping. **2** (in *pl.*) grasping hands, esp. as representing a cruel or relentless grasp or control. **3 a** (in a motor vehicle) a device for connecting and disconnecting the engine to the transmission. **b** the pedal operating this. **c** an arrangement for connecting or disconnecting working parts of a machine. □ **clutch bag** a slim flat handbag without handles. [ME *clucche*, *clicche* f. OE *clyccan* crook, clench, f. Gmc]

■ *v.* **1** seize, snatch, grab, grasp, take *or* lay hold of; hold, grip. **2** snatch, grab, grasp, pluck. ● *n.* **1 a** grasp, hold, grip, clasp, embrace, lock. **2** (*clutches*) grasp, hold, *literary* thraldom; embrace; domination, dominance, influence, control, power, possession.

clutch[2] /kluch/ *n.* **1** a set of eggs for hatching. **2** a brood of chickens. [18th c.: prob. S.Engl. var. of *cletch* f. *cleck* to hatch f. ON *klekja*, assoc. with CLUTCH[1]]

clutter /klúttər/ *n.* & *v.* ● *n.* **1** a crowded and untidy collection of things. **2** an untidy state. ● *v.tr.* (often foll. by *up, with*) crowd untidily, fill with clutter. [partly var. of *clotter* coagulate, partly assoc. with CLUSTER, CLATTER]

■ *n.* **1** mess, litter, jumble, mishmash, olla podrida, olio, confusion, hash, gallimaufry, hotchpotch, muddle, farrago, medley. **2** confusion, tangle; see also CHAOS 1a. ● *v.* mess up, litter, strew.

Clydesdale /klídzdayl/ *n.* **1 a** a horse of a heavy powerful breed, used as draught-horses. **b** this breed. **2** a kind of small terrier. [orig. bred near the river *Clyde* in Scotland: see DALE]

clypeus /klíppiəss/ *n.* (*pl.* **clypei** /-pi-ī/) the hard protective area of an insect's head. □□ **clypeal** *adj.* **clypeate** *adj.* [L, = round shield]

clyster /klístər/ *n.* & *v. archaic* ● *n.* an enema. ● *v.tr.* treat with an enema. [ME f. OF *clystere* or f. L f. Gk *klustēr* syringe f. *kluzō* wash out]

CM *abbr.* Member of the Order of Canada.

Cm *symb. Chem.* the element curium.

Cm. *abbr. Brit.* Command Paper (1986–).

cm *abbr.* centimetre(s).

Cmd. *abbr. Brit.* Command Paper (1918–56).

Cmdr. *abbr.* Commander.

Cmdre. *abbr.* Commodore.

CMG *abbr.* (in the UK) Companion (of the Order) of St Michael and St George.

Cmnd. *abbr. Brit.* Command Paper (1956–86).

CNAA *abbr.* Council for National Academic Awards.

CND *abbr.* (in the UK) Campaign for Nuclear Disarmament.

cnr. *abbr.* corner.

CO *abbr.* **1** Commanding Officer. **2** conscientious objector. **3** *US* Colorado (in official postal use).

Co *symb. Chem.* the element cobalt.

Co. *abbr.* **1** company. **2** county. □ **and Co.** /kō/ *colloq.* and the rest of them; and similar things.

co- /kō/ *prefix* **1** added to: **a** nouns, with the sense 'joint, mutual, common' (*co-author*; *coequality*). **b** adjectives and adverbs, with the sense 'jointly, mutually' (*co-belligerent*; *coequal*; *coequally*). **c** verbs, with the sense 'together with another or others' (*cooperate*; *co-author*). **2** *Math.* **a** of the complement of an angle (*cosine*). **b** the complement of (*co-latitude*; *coset*). [orig. a form of COM-]

c/o *abbr.* care of.

coach /kōch/ *n.* & *v.* ● *n.* **1** a single-decker bus, usu. comfortably equipped for longer journeys. **2** a railway carriage. **3** a horse-drawn carriage, usu. closed, esp. a State carriage or a stagecoach. **4 a** an instructor or trainer in sport. **b** a private tutor. **5** *US* economy-class seating in an aircraft. **6** *Austral.* a docile cow or bullock used as a decoy to attract wild cattle. ● *v.* **1** *tr.* **a** train or teach (a pupil, sports team, etc.) as a coach. **b** give hints to; prime with facts. **2** *intr.* travel by stagecoach (*in the old coaching days*). □ **coach-built** (of motor-car bodies) individually built by craftsmen. **coach-house** an outhouse for carriages. **coach station** a stopping-place for a number of coaches, usu. with buildings and amenities. [F *coche* f. Magyar *kocsi* (adj.) f. *Kocs* in Hungary]
■ *n.* **1** bus, motor coach, *formal* omnibus, *Brit. hist.* charabanc. **4** tutor, trainer, instructor, crammer; see also TEACHER. ● *v.* **1** tutor, train, instruct, guide, direct, drill, prepare, prompt, school, exercise, cram.

coachload /kṓchlōd/ *n.* a number of people, esp. holiday-makers, taken by coach.

coachman /kṓchmən/ *n.* (*pl.* **-men**) the driver of a horse-drawn carriage.

coachwood /kṓchwŏŏd/ *n.* *Austral.* any tree esp. *Ceratopetalum apetalum* with close-grained wood suitable for cabinet-making.

coachwork /kṓchwurk/ *n.* the bodywork of a road or rail vehicle.

coadjutor /kō-ájootər/ *n.* an assistant, esp. an assistant bishop. [ME f. OF *coadjuteur* f. LL *coadjutor* (as CO-, *adjutor* f. *adjuvare -jut-* help)]
■ see AIDE.

coagulant /kō-ágyoolənt/ *n.* a substance that produces coagulation.

coagulate /kō-ágyoolayt/ *v.tr.* & *intr.* **1** change from a fluid to a solid or semisolid state. **2** clot, curdle. **3** set, solidify. □□ **coagulable** *adj.* **coagulative** /-lətiv/ *adj.* **coagulator** *n.* [ME f. L *coagulare* f. *coagulum* rennet]
■ congeal, gel, clot, curdle, *colloq.* jell; set, solidify.

coagulation /kō-agyooláysh'n/ *n.* the process by which a liquid changes to a semisolid mass. [as COAGULATE]

coagulum /kō-ágyooləm/ *n.* (*pl.* **coagula** /-lə/) a mass of coagulated matter. [L: see COAGULATE]

coal /kōl/ *n.* & *v.* ● *n.* **1 a** a hard black or blackish rock, mainly carbonized plant matter, found in underground seams and used as a fuel and in the manufacture of gas, tar, etc. **b** *Brit.* a piece of this for burning. **2** a red-hot piece of coal, wood, etc. in a fire. ● *v.* **1** *intr.* take in a supply of coal. **2** *tr.* put coal into (an engine, fire, etc.). □ **coal-bed** a stratum of coal. **coal-black** completely black. **coal-fired** heated or driven by coal. **coal gas** mixed gases extracted from coal and used for lighting and heating. **coal-hole** *Brit.* a compartment or small cellar for storing coal. **coal measures** a series of rocks formed by seams of coal with intervening strata. **coal oil** *US* petroleum or paraffin. **coal-sack 1** a sack for carrying coal. **2** a black patch in the Milky Way, esp. the one near the Southern Cross. **coal-scuttle** a container for coal to supply a domestic fire. **coal-seam** a stratum of coal suitable for mining. **coals to Newcastle** something brought or sent to a place where it is already plentiful. **coal tar** a thick black oily liquid distilled from coal and used as a source of benzene. **coal-tit** (or **cole-tit**) a small greyish bird, *Parus ater*, with a black head: also called COALMOUSE. **haul** (or **call**) **over the coals** reprimand. □□ **coaly** *adj.* [OE *col* f. Gmc]

coaler /kṓlər/ *n.* a ship etc. transporting coal.

coalesce /kṓəléss/ *v.intr.* **1** come together and form one whole. **2** combine in a coalition. □□ **coalescence** *n.* **coalescent** *adj.* [L *coalescere* (as CO-, *alescere alit-* grow f. *alere* nourish)]
■ see MERGE.

coalface /kṓlfayss/ *n.* an exposed surface of coal in a mine.

coalfield /kṓlfeeld/ *n.* an extensive area with strata containing coal.

coalfish /kṓlfish/ *n.* = SAITHE.

coalition /kṓəlísh'n/ *n.* **1** *Polit.* a temporary alliance for combined action, esp. of distinct parties forming a government, or of States. **2** fusion into one whole. □□ **coalitionist** *n.* [med.L *coalitio* (as COALESCE)]
■ **1** see ALLIANCE 1.

coalman /kṓlmən/ *n.* (*pl.* **-men**) a man who carries or delivers coal.

coalmine /kṓlmīn/ *n.* a mine in which coal is dug. □□ **coalminer** *n.*

coalmouse /kṓlmowss/ *n.* (also **colemouse**) (*pl.* **-mice**) = *coal-tit*. [OE *colmāse* f. *col* COAL + *māse* as TITMOUSE]

coaming /kṓming/ *n.* a raised border round the hatches etc. of a ship to keep out water. [17th c.: orig. unkn.]

coarse /korss/ *adj.* **1 a** rough or loose in texture or grain; made of large particles. **b** (of a person's features) rough or large. **2** lacking refinement or delicacy; crude, obscene (*coarse humour*). **3** rude, uncivil. **4** inferior, common. □ **coarse fish** *Brit.* any freshwater fish other than salmon and trout. □□ **coarsely** *adv.* **coarseness** *n.* **coarsish** *adj.* [ME: orig. unkn.]
■ **1 a** rough, uneven, scratchy, prickly, bristly; crude, rough-hewn, unfinished, unrefined. **b** rough, thickset, rough-hewn, heavy, large, crude. **2** boorish, loutish, crude, unpolished, rough, uncouth, unrefined; rude, indecent, improper, indelicate, obscene, lewd, vulgar, gross, smutty, dirty, filthy, foul, offensive, lascivious, ribald, bawdy; foul-mouthed. **3** ill-mannered, impolite, uncivil; see also RUDE 1. **4** inferior, common, low-quality, second-rate, shoddy, tawdry, trashy.

coarsen /kórs'n/ *v.tr.* & *intr.* make or become coarse.

coast /kōst/ *n.* & *v.* ● *n.* **1 a** the border of the land near the sea; the seashore. **b** (**the Coast**) *US* the Pacific coast of the US. **2 a** a run, usu. downhill, on a bicycle without pedalling or in a motor vehicle without using the engine. **b** *US* a toboggan slide or slope. ● *v.intr.* **1** ride or move, usu. downhill, without use of power, free-wheel. **2** make progress without much effort. **3** *US* slide down a hill on a toboggan. **4 a** sail along the coast. **b** trade between ports on the same coast. □ **the coast is clear** there is no danger of being observed or caught. **coast-to-coast** across an island or continent. □□ **coastal** *adj.* [ME f. OF *coste*, *costeier* f. L *costa* rib, flank, side]
■ *n.* **1 a** seaside, seashore, shore, beach, littoral, coastline, seaboard, *rhet. or poet.* strand. ● *v.* **1** glide, skim, slide, sail; free-wheel. **2** free-wheel.

coaster /kṓstər/ *n.* **1** a ship that travels along the coast from port to port. **2** a small tray or mat for a bottle or glass. **3** *US* **a** a sledge for coasting. **b** a roller-coaster.

coastguard /kṓstgaard/ *n.* **1** an organization keeping watch on the coasts and on local shipping to save life, prevent smuggling, etc. **2** a member of this.

coastline /kṓstlīn/ *n.* the line of the seashore, esp. with regard to its shape (*a rugged coastline*).

coastwise /kṓstwīz/ *adj.* & *adv.* along, following, or connected with the coast.

coat /kōt/ *n.* & *v.* ● *n.* **1** an outer garment with sleeves and often extending below the hips; an overcoat or jacket. **2 a** an animal's fur, hair, etc. **b** *Physiol.* a structure, esp. a membrane, enclosing or lining an organ. **c** a skin, rind, or husk. **d** a layer of a bulb etc. **3 a** a layer or covering. **b** a covering of paint etc. laid on a surface at one time. ● *v.tr.* **1** (usu. foll. by *with*, *in*) **a** apply a coat of paint etc. to; provide with a layer or covering. **b** (as **coated** *adj.*) covered with. **2** (of paint etc.) form a covering to. □ **coat armour** coats of arms. **coat dress** a woman's tailored dress resembling a coat. **coat-hanger** see HANGER[1]. **coat of arms** the heraldic bearings or shield of a person, family, or corporation. **coat of mail** a jacket of mail armour (see MAIL[2]). **on a person's coat-tails** undeservedly benefiting from another's success. □□ **coated** *adj.* (also in *comb.*). [ME f. OF *cote* f. Rmc f. Frank., of unkn. orig.]

■ *n.* **1** overcoat, topcoat, greatcoat, coatee; jacket, anorak, parka. **2 c** see SKIN *n.* 4. **3** coating, layer, covering, film. ● *v.* **1 a** cover, paint, spread. **b** (**coated**) see SPREAD *v.* 4a.

coatee /kōtée/ *n.* **1** a woman's or infant's short coat. **2** *archaic* a close-fitting short coat.

coati /kō-aáti/ *n.* (*pl.* **coatis**) any racoon-like flesh-eating mammal of the genus *Nasua*, with a long flexible snout and a long usu. ringed tail. [Tupi f. *cua* belt + *tim* nose]

coatimundi /kō-aatimúndi/ *n.* (*pl.* **coatimundis**) = COATI. [as COATI + Tupi *mondi* solitary]

coating /kōting/ *n.* **1** a thin layer or covering of paint etc. **2** material for making coats.

co-author /kō-áwthər/ *n.* & *v.* ● *n.* a joint author. ● *v.tr.* be a joint author of.

coax /kōks/ *v.tr.* **1** (usu. foll. by *into*, or *to* + infin.) persuade (a person) gradually or by flattery. **2** (foll. by *out of*) obtain (a thing from a person) by coaxing. **3** manipulate (a thing) carefully or slowly. □□ **coaxer** *n.* **coaxingly** *adv.* [16th c.: f. 'make a *cokes* of' f. obs. *cokes* simpleton, of unkn. orig.]

■ **1, 2** persuade, wheedle, cajole, beguile, charm, inveigle, manipulate, *colloq.* jolly.

coaxial /kō-áksiəl/ *adj.* **1** having a common axis. **2** *Electr.* (of a cable or line) transmitting by means of two concentric conductors separated by an insulator. □□ **coaxially** *adv.*

cob[1] /kob/ *n.* **1** a roundish lump of coal etc. **2** *Brit.* a domed loaf of bread. **3** *Brit.* = *corn-cob* (see CORN[1]). **4** (in full **cob-nut**) a large hazelnut. **5** a sturdy riding- or driving-horse with short legs. **6** a male swan. [ME: orig. unkn.]

cob[2] /kob/ *n.* a material for walls, made from compressed earth, clay, or chalk reinforced with straw. [17th c.: orig. unkn.]

cobalt /kōbawlt, -bolt/ *n. Chem.* a silvery-white magnetic metallic element occurring naturally as a mineral in combination with sulphur and arsenic, and used in many alloys. ¶ Symb.: **Co.** □ **cobalt blue 1** a pigment containing a cobalt salt. **2** the deep-blue colour of this. □□ **cobaltic** /kəbáwltik/ *adj.* **cobaltous** /kəbáwltəss/ *adj.* [G *Kobalt* etc., prob. = KOBOLD in mines]

cobber /kóbbər/ *n. Austral.* & *NZ colloq.* a companion or friend. [19th c.: perh. rel. to E dial. *cob* take a liking to]

■ see FRIEND *n.* 1.

cobble[1] /kóbb'l/ *n.* & *v.* ● *n.* **1** (in full **cobblestone**) a small rounded stone of a size used for paving. **2** (in *pl.*) *Brit.* coal in lumps of this size. ● *v.tr.* pave with cobbles. [ME *cobel(-ston)*, f. COB[1]]

cobble[2] /kóbb'l/ *v.tr.* **1** mend or patch up (esp. shoes). **2** (often foll. by *together*) join or assemble roughly. [back-form. f. COBBLER]

cobbler /kóblər/ *n.* **1** a person who mends shoes, esp. professionally. **2** an iced drink of wine etc., sugar, and lemon (*sherry cobbler*). **3 a** a fruit pie topped with scones. **b** esp. *US* a fruit pie with a rich thick crust. **4** (in *pl.*) *Brit. sl.* nonsense. **5** *Austral.* & *NZ sl.* the last sheep to be shorn. □ **cobbler's wax** a resinous substance used for waxing thread. [ME, of unkn. orig.: sense 4 f. rhyming sl. *cobbler's awls* = *balls*: sense 5 with pun on LAST[3]]

■ **4** (*cobblers*) see NONSENSE.

co-belligerent /kōbilíjərənt/ *n.* & *adj.* ● *n.* any of two or more nations engaged in war as allies. ● *adj.* of or as a co-belligerent. □□ **co-belligerence** *n.* **co-belligerency** *n.*

coble /kōb'l/ *n.* a flat-bottomed fishing-boat in Scotland and NE England. [OE, perh. f. Celt.]

COBOL /kōbol/ *n. Computing* a programming language designed for use in commerce. [*co*mmon *b*usiness *o*riented *l*anguage]

cobra /kōbrə, kóbrə/ *n.* any venomous snake of the genus *Naja*, native to Africa and Asia, with a neck dilated like a hood when excited. [Port. f. L *colubra* snake]

cobweb /kóbweb/ *n.* **1 a** a fine network of threads spun by a spider from a liquid secreted by it, used to trap insects etc. **b** the thread of this. **2** anything compared with a cobweb, esp. in flimsiness of texture. **3** a trap or insidious entanglement. **4** (in *pl.*) a state of languishing; fustiness. □□ **cobwebbed** *adj.* **cobwebby** *adj.* [ME *cop(pe)web* f. obs. *coppe* spider]

coca /kōkə/ *n.* **1** a S. American shrub, *Erythroxylum coca*. **2** its dried leaves, chewed as a stimulant. [Sp. f. Quechua *cuca*]

Coca-Cola /kōkəkōlə/ *n. propr.* an aerated non-alcoholic drink sometimes flavoured with cola seeds.

cocaine /kəkáyn, kō-/ *n.* a drug derived from coca or prepared synthetically, used as a local anaesthetic and as a stimulant. [COCA + -INE[4]]

coccidiosis /kóksidiōsiss/ *n.* a disease of birds and mammals caused by any of various parasitic protozoa, esp. of the genus *Eimeria*, affecting the intestine. [*coccidium* (mod.L f. Gk *kokkis* dimin. of *kokkos* berry) + -OSIS]

coccus /kókkəss/ *n.* (*pl.* **cocci** /-ki/) any spherical or roughly spherical bacterium. □□ **coccal** *adj.* **coccoid** *adj.* [mod.L f. Gk *kokkos* berry]

coccyx /kóksiks/ *n.* (*pl.* **coccyges** /-sijeez/ or **coccyxes**) the small triangular bone at the base of the spinal column in humans and some apes. □□ **coccygeal** /koksíjiəl/ *adj.* [L f. Gk *kokkux -ugos* cuckoo (from being shaped like its bill)]

cochin /kōchin/ *n.* (in full **cochin-china**) **1** a fowl of an Asian breed with feathery legs. **2** this breed. [*Cochin China* in Vietnam]

cochineal /kóchineél/ *n.* **1** a scarlet dye used esp. for colouring food. **2** the dried bodies of the female of the Mexican insect, *Dactylopius coccus*, yielding this. [F *cochenille* or Sp. *cochinilla* f. L *coccinus* scarlet f. Gk *kokkos* berry]

cochlea /kókliə/ *n.* (*pl.* **cochleae** /-li-ee/) the spiral cavity of the internal ear. □□ **cochlear** *adj.* [L, = snail-shell, f. Gk *kokhlias*]

■ □□ **cochlear** see SPIRAL *adj.*

cock[1] /kok/ *n.* & *v.* ● *n.* **1 a** a male bird, esp. of a domestic fowl. **b** a male lobster, crab, or salmon. **c** = WOODCOCK. **2** *Brit. sl.* (usu. **old cock** as a form of address) a friend; a fellow. **3** *coarse sl.* the penis. **4** *Brit. sl.* nonsense. ¶ In senses 3, 4 usually considered a taboo word. **5 a** a firing lever in a gun which can be raised to be released by the trigger. **b** the cocked position of this (*at full cock*). **6** a tap or valve controlling flow. ● *v.tr.* **1** raise or make upright or erect. **2** turn or move (the eye or ear) attentively or knowingly. **3** set aslant, or turn up the brim of (a hat). **4** raise the cock of (a gun). □ **at half cock** only partly ready. **cock-a-doodle-doo** a cock's crow. **cock-and-bull story** an absurd or incredible account. **cock crow** dawn. **cocked hat** a brimless triangular hat pointed at the front, back, and top. **cock-fight** a fight between cocks as sport. **cock-fighting** this sport. **cock-of-the-rock** a S. American bird, *Rupicola rupicola*, having a crest and bright orange plumage. **cock-of-the-walk** a dominant or arrogant person. **cock-of-the-wood 1** a capercaillie. **2** *US* a red-crested woodpecker. **cock-shy 1 a** a target for throwing at with sticks, stones, etc. **b** a throw at this. **2** an object of ridicule or criticism. **cock a snook** see SNOOK[1]. **cock sparrow 1** a male sparrow. **2** a lively quarrelsome person. **cock up** *Brit. sl.* bungle; make a mess of. **cock-up** *n. Brit. sl.* a muddle or mistake. **knock into a cocked hat** defeat utterly. [OE *cocc* and OF *coq* prob. f. med.L *coccus*]

■ *n.* **6** see TAP[1] *n.* 1. □ **cock-and-bull story** see YARN *n.* 2. **cock crow** see DAWN *n.* 1. **cock up** see BOTCH *v.* 1. **cock-up** see MUDDLE *n.*

cock[2] /kok/ *n.* & *v.* ● *n.* a small pile of hay, straw, etc. with vertical sides and a rounded top. ● *v.tr.* pile into cocks. [ME, perh. of Scand. orig.]

■ *n.* see STACK *n.* 2.

cockade /kokáyd/ *n.* a rosette etc. worn in a hat as a badge of office or party, or as part of a livery. □□ **cockaded** *adj.* [F *cocarde* orig. in *bonnet à la coquarde*, f. fem. of obs. *coquard* saucy f. *coq* COCK[1]]

cock-a-hoop /kókkəhóop/ *adj.* & *adv.* ● *adj.* exultant; crowing boastfully. ● *adv.* exultantly. [16th c.: orig. in phr. *set cock a hoop* denoting some action preliminary to hard drinking]
■ *adj.* see *exultant* (EXULT).

cock-a-leekie /kókkəleéki/ *n.* (also **cocky-leeky** /kókki-/) a soup traditionally made in Scotland with boiling fowl and leeks. [COCK[1] + LEEK]

cockalorum /kókkəlórəm/ *n. colloq.* a self-important little man. [18th c.: arbitr. f. COCK[1]]

cockatiel /kókkəteél/ *n.* (also **cockateel**) *Austral.* a small delicately coloured crested parrot, *Nymphicus hollandicus.* [Du. *kaketielje*]

cockatoo /kókkətóo/ *n.* **1** any of several parrots of the family Cacatuinae, having powerful beaks and erectile crests. **2** *Austral.* & *NZ colloq.* a small farmer. [Du. *kaketoe* f. Malay *kakatua*, assim. to COCK[1]]

cockatrice /kókkətriss, -trīss/ *n.* **1** = BASILISK 1. **2** *Heraldry* a fabulous animal, a cock with a serpent's tail. [ME f. OF *cocatris* f. L *calcare* tread, track, rendering Gk *ikhneumōn* tracker: see ICHNEUMON]

cockboat /kókbōt/ *n.* a small ship's-boat. [obs. *cock* small boat (f. OF *coque*) + BOAT]

cockchafer /kókchayfər/ *n.* a large nocturnal beetle, *Melolontha melolontha*, which feeds on leaves and whose larva feeds on roots of crops etc. Also called *May-bug*. [perh. f. COCK[1] as expressing size or vigour + CHAFER]

cocker /kókkər/ *n.* (in full **cocker spaniel**) **1** a small spaniel of a breed with a silky coat. **2** this breed. [as COCK[1], from use in hunting woodcocks etc.]

cockerel /kókrəl/ *n.* a young cock. [ME: dimin. of COCK[1]]

cock-eyed /kókkīd/ *adj. colloq.* **1** crooked, askew, not level. **2** (of a scheme etc.) absurd, not practical. **3** drunk. **4** squinting. [19th c.: app. f. COCK[1] + EYE]
■ **1** see LOPSIDED. **2** see STUPID *adj.* 2. **3** see DRUNK *adj.* 1.

cockle[1] /kókk'l/ *n.* **1 a** any edible mollusc of the genus *Cardium*, having a chubby ribbed bivalve shell. **b** its shell. **2** (in full **cockle-shell**) a small shallow boat. □ **warm the cockles of one's heart** make one contented; be satisfying. [ME f. OF *coquille* shell ult. f. Gk *kogkhulion* f. *kogkhē* CONCH]

cockle[2] /kókk'l/ *n.* **1** any of various plants, esp. the pink-flowered corn-cockle, *Agrostemma githago*, growing among corn, esp. wheat. **2** a disease of wheat that turns the grains black. [OE *coccul*, perh. ult. f. LL COCCUS]

cockle[3] /kókk'l/ *v.* & *n.* ● *v.* **1** *intr.* pucker, wrinkle. **2** *tr.* cause to cockle. ● *n.* a pucker or wrinkle in paper, glass, etc. [F *coquiller* blister (bread in cooking) f. *coquille*: see COCKLE[1]]

cockney /kókni/ *n.* & *adj.* ● *n.* (*pl.* **-eys**) **1 a** a native of East London, esp. one born within hearing of Bow Bells. **b** the dialect or accent typical of this area. **2** *Austral.* a young snapper fish, *Chrysophrys auratus.* ● *adj.* of or characteristic of cockneys or their dialect or accent. □□ **cockneyism** *n.* [ME *cokeney* cock's egg, later derog. for 'townsman']

cockpit /kókpit/ *n.* **1 a** a compartment for the pilot (or the pilot and crew) of an aircraft or spacecraft. **b** a similar compartment for the driver in a racing car. **c** a space for the helmsman in some small yachts. **2** an arena of war or other conflict. **3** a place where cock-fights are held. [orig. in sense 3, f. COCK[1] + PIT[1]]

cockroach /kókrōch/ *n.* any of various flat brown insects, esp. *Blatta orientalis*, infesting kitchens, bathrooms, etc. [Sp. *cucaracha*, assim. to COCK[1], ROACH[1]]

cockscomb /kókskōm/ *n.* **1** the crest or comb of a cock. **2** a garden plant *Celosia cristata*, with a terminal plume of tiny white or red flowers.

cocksfoot /kóksfoot/ *n.* any pasture grass of the genus *Dactylis*, with broad leaves and green or purplish spikes.

cocksure /kókshoór, -shór/ *adj.* **1** presumptuously or arrogantly confident. **2** (foll. by *of*, *about*) absolutely sure. □□ **cocksurely** *adv.* **cocksureness** *n.* [*cock* = God + SURE]
■ **1** see CONFIDENT 1.

cocktail /kóktayl/ *n.* **1** a usu. alcoholic drink made by mixing various spirits, fruit juices, etc. **2** a dish of mixed ingredients (*fruit cocktail*; *shellfish cocktail*). **3** any hybrid mixture. □ **cocktail dress** a usu. short evening dress suitable for wearing at a drinks party. **cocktail stick** a small pointed stick for serving an olive, cherry, small sausage, etc. [orig. unkn.: cf. earlier sense 'docked horse' f. COCK[1]: the connection is unclear]

cocky[1] /kókki/ *adj.* (**cockier**, **cockiest**) **1** conceited, arrogant. **2** saucy, impudent. □□ **cockily** *adv.* **cockiness** *n.* [COCK[1] + -Y[1]]
■ **1** overconfident, arrogant, haughty, conceited, self-important, egotistical, proud, vain, prideful, cocksure. **2** saucy, cheeky, brash; see also IMPUDENT 1, 2.

cocky[2] /kókki/ *n.* (*pl.* **-ies**) *Austral.* & *NZ colloq.* = COCKATOO 2. [abbr.]

cocky-leeky var. of COCK-A-LEEKIE.

coco /kōkō/ *n.* (also **cocoa**) (*pl.* **cocos** or **cocoas**) a tall tropical palm tree, *Cocos nucifera*, bearing coconuts. [Port. & Sp. *coco* grimace: the base of the shell resembles a face]

cocoa /kōkō/ *n.* **1** a powder made from crushed cacao seeds, often with other ingredients. **2** a drink made from this. □ **cocoa bean** a cacao seed. **cocoa butter** a fatty substance obtained from cocoa beans and used for confectionery, cosmetics, etc. [alt. of CACAO]

coco-de-mer /kōkōdəmáir/ *n.* a tall palm-tree, *Lodoicea maldivica*, of the Seychelles. [F]

coconut /kōkənut/ *n.* (also **cocoanut**) **1 a** a large ovate brown seed of the coco, with a hard shell and edible white fleshy lining enclosing a milky juice. **b** = COCO. **c** the edible white fleshy lining of a coconut. **2** *sl.* the human head. □ **coconut butter** a solid oil obtained from the lining of the coconut, and used in soap, candles, ointment, etc. **coconut ice** a sweet of sugar and desiccated coconut. **coconut matting** a matting made of fibre from coconut husks. **coconut shy** a fairground sideshow where balls are thrown to dislodge coconuts. **double coconut** a very large nut of the coco-de-mer. [COCO + NUT]
■ **2** see HEAD *n.* 1.

cocoon /kəkóon/ *n.* & *v.* ● *n.* **1 a** a silky case spun by many insect larvae for protection as pupae. **b** a similar structure made by other animals. **2** a protective covering, esp. to prevent corrosion of metal equipment. ● *v.* **1** *tr.* & *intr.* wrap in or form a cocoon. **2** *tr.* spray with a protective coating. [F *cocon* f. mod. Prov. *coucoun* dimin. of *coca* shell]

cocotte /kəkót/ *n.* **1 a** a small fireproof dish for cooking and serving an individual portion of food. **b** a deep cooking pot with a tight-fitting lid and handles. **2** *archaic* a fashionable prostitute. [F]
■ **2** see PROSTITUTE *n.* 1a.

COD *abbr.* **1 a** cash on delivery. **b** *US* collect on delivery. **2** Concise Oxford Dictionary.

cod[1] /kod/ *n.* (*pl.* same) any large marine fish of the family Gadidae, used as food, esp. *Gadus morhua.* □ **cod-liver oil** an oil pressed from the fresh liver of cod, which is rich in vitamins D and A. [ME: orig. unkn.]

cod[2] /kod/ *n.* & *v. Brit. sl.* ● *n.* **1** a parody. **2** a hoax. **3** (*attrib.*) = MOCK *adj.* ● *v.* (**codded**, **codding**) **1 a** *intr.* perform a hoax. **b** *tr.* play a trick on; fool. **2** *tr.* parody. [19th c.: orig. unkn.]
■ *n.* **2** see HOAX *n.* ● *v.* **1 b** see FOOL[1] *v.* 1, 3.

cod[3] /kod/ *n. sl.* nonsense. [abbr. of CODSWALLOP]

coda /kōdə/ *n.* **1** *Mus.* the concluding passage of a piece or movement, usu. forming an addition to the basic structure. **2** *Ballet* the concluding section of a dance. **3** a concluding event or series of events. [It. f. L *cauda* tail]

coddle /kódd'l/ *v.tr.* **1 a** treat as an invalid; protect attentively. **b** (foll. by *up*) strengthen by feeding. **2** cook (an egg) in water below boiling point. □□ **coddler** *n.* [prob. dial. var. of *caudle* invalids' gruel]
■ **1 a** pamper, baby, cosset, mollycoddle, indulge, humour, spoil.

code /kōd/ *n.* & *v.* ● *n.* **1** a system of words, letters, figures, or symbols, used to represent others for secrecy or brevity. **2** a system of prearranged signals, esp. used to ensure secrecy in transmitting messages. **3** *Computing* a piece of program text. **4 a** a systematic collection of statutes, a body of laws so arranged as to avoid inconsistency and overlapping. **b** a set of rules on any subject. **5 a** the prevailing morality of a society or class (*code of honour*). **b** a person's standard of moral behaviour. ● *v.tr.* put (a message, program, etc.) into code. □ **code-book** a list of symbols etc. used in a code. **code-name** (or **-number**) a word or symbol (or number) used for secrecy or convenience instead of the usual name. □□ **coder** *n.* [ME f. OF f. L CODEX]
■ *n.* **2** cipher. **4** law(s), regulation(s), rule(s), constitution. **5** system, practice(s), convention(s), standard(s), criteria, principle(s), rule(s), maxim(s), custom(s), pattern(s), structure, tradition(s), protocol. ● *v.* encode, encipher, encrypt.

codeine /kṓdeen/ *n.* an alkaloid derived from morphine and used to relieve pain. [Gk *kōdeia* poppy-head + -INE[4]]

codependency /kṓdipéndənsi/ *n.* addiction to a supportive role in a relationship. □□ **codependent** *adj.* & *n.* [CO- + DEPENDENCY]

co-determination /kṓditérmináysh'n/ *n.* cooperation between management and workers in decision-taking. [CO- + DETERMINATION, after G *Mitbestimmung*]

codex /kṓdeks/ *n.* (*pl.* **codices** /kṓdiseez, kód-/) **1** an ancient manuscript text in book form. **2** a collection of pharmaceutical descriptions of drugs etc. [L, = block of wood, tablet, book]

codfish /kódfish/ *n.* = COD[1].

codger /kójər/ *n.* (usu. in **old codger**) *colloq.* a person, esp. an old or strange one. [perh. var. of *cadger*: see CADGE]

codices *pl.* of CODEX.

codicil /kṓdisil, kód-/ *n.* an addition explaining, modifying, or revoking a will or part of one. □□ **codicillary** /kóddisílləri/ *adj.* [L *codicillus*, dimin. of CODEX]
■ see SUPPLEMENT *n.* 1, 2.

codicology /kṓdikólləji/ *n.* the study of manuscripts. □□ **codicological** /-kəlójik'l/ *adj.* **codicologically** /-kəlójikəli/ *adv.* [F *codicologie* f. L *codex codicis*: see CODEX]

codify /kṓdifī, kód-/ *v.tr.* (**-ies**, **-ied**) arrange (laws etc.) systematically into a code. □□ **codification** /-fikáysh'n/ *n.* **codifier** *n.*
■ see ORGANIZE 1.

codling[1] /kódling/ *n.* (also **codlin**) **1** any of several varieties of cooking-apple, having a long tapering shape. **2** a small moth, *Carpocapsa pomonella*, the larva of which feeds on apples. □ **codlings-and-cream** the great willow-herb, *Epilobium angustifolium*. [ME f. AF *quer de lion* lion-heart]

codling[2] /kódling/ *n.* a small codfish.

codomain /kṓdōmayn/ *n. Math.* a set that includes all the possible expressions of a given function. [CO- 2 + DOMAIN]

codon /kṓdon/ *n. Biochem.* a sequence of three nucleotides, forming a unit of genetic code in a DNA or RNA molecule. [CODE + -ON]

codpiece /kódpeess/ *n. hist.* an appendage like a small bag or flap at the front of a man's breeches. [ME, f. *cod* scrotum + PIECE]

co-driver /kṓdrīvər/ *n.* a person who shares the driving of a vehicle with another, esp. in a race, rally, etc.

codswallop /kódzwolləp/ *n. Brit. sl.* nonsense. [20th c.: orig. unkn.]
■ see RUBBISH *n.* 3.

coecilian var. of CAECILIAN.

coed *n.* & *adj. colloq.* ● *n.* /kó-ed/ **1** a coeducational system or institution. **2** esp. *US* a female student at a coeducational institution. ● *adj.* /kṓ-éd/ coeducational. [abbr.]
■ *n.* **2** see MISS[2].

coeducation /kó-edyookáysh'n/ *n.* the education of pupils of both sexes together. □□ **coeducational** *adj.*

coefficient /kṓ-ifish'nt/ *n.* **1** *Math.* a quantity placed before and multiplying an algebraic expression (e.g. *4* in $4x^y$). **2** *Physics* a multiplier or factor that measures some property (*coefficient of expansion*). [mod.L *coefficiens* (as CO-, EFFICIENT)]

coelacanth /seéləkanth/ *n.* a large bony marine fish, *Latimeria chalumnae*, formerly thought to be extinct, having a trilobed tail-fin and fleshy pectoral fins. [mod.L *Coelacanthus* f. Gk *koilos* hollow + *akantha* spine]

-coele *comb. form* var. of -CELE.

coelenterate /seeléntərayt/ *n.* any marine animal of the phylum Coelenterata with a simple tube-shaped or cup-shaped body, e.g. jellyfish, corals, and sea anemones. [mod.L *Coelenterata* f. Gk *koilos* hollow + *enteron* intestine]

coeliac /seéliak/ *adj.* (*US* **celiac**) of or affecting the belly. □ **coeliac disease** a digestive disease of the small intestine brought on by contact with dietary gluten. [L *coeliacus* f. Gk *koiliakos* f. *koilia* belly]

coelom /seéləm, -lōm/ *n.* (*US* **celom**) (*pl.* **-oms** or **-omata** /-lṓmətə/) *Zool.* the principal body cavity in animals, between the intestinal canal and the body wall. □□ **coelomate** *adj.* & *n.* [Gk *koilōma* cavity]

coelostat /seéləstat/ *n. Astron.* an instrument with a rotating mirror that continuously reflects the light from the same area of sky allowing the path of a celestial body to be monitored. [L *caelum* sky + -STAT]

coenobite /seénəbīt/ *n.* (*US* **cenobite**) a member of a monastic community. □□ **coenobitic** /-bíttik/ *adj.* **coenobitical** /-bíttik'l/ *adj.* [OF *cenobite* or eccl.L *coenobita* f. LL *coenobium* f. Gk *koinobion* convent f. *koinos* common + *bios* life]
■ see MONK.

coenzyme /kó-enzīm/ *n. Biochem.* a non-proteinaceous compound that assists in the action of an enzyme.

coequal /kō-eékwəl/ *adj.* & *n. archaic* or *literary* ● *adj.* equal with one another. ● *n.* an equal. □□ **coequality** /kṓ-ikwólliti/ *n.* **coequally** *adv.* [ME f. L or eccl.L *coaequalis* (as CO-, EQUAL)]

coerce /kō-érss/ *v.tr.* (often foll. by *into*) persuade or restrain (an unwilling person) by force (*coerced you into signing*). □□ **coercible** *adj.* [ME f. L *coercēre* restrain (as CO-, *arcēre* restrain)]
■ see FORCE[1] *v.* 1.

coercion /kō-érsh'n/ *n.* **1** the act or process of coercing. **2** government by force. □□ **coercive** *adj.* **coercively** *adv.* **coerciveness** *n.* [OF *cohercion*, *-tion* f. L *coer(c)tio*, *coercitio -onis* (as COERCE)]
■ **1** see FORCE[1] *n.* 2.

coeval *adj.* & *n.* ● *adj.* /kṓ-eév'l/ **1** having the same age or date of origin. **2** living or existing at the same epoch. **3** having the same duration. ● *n.* /kō-eév'l/ a coeval person, a contemporary. □□ **coevality** /kṓ-eeválliti/ *n.* **coevally** *adv.* [LL *coaevus* (as CO-, L *aevum* age)]
■ *adj.* **1, 2** see CONTEMPORARY *adj.* 1.

coexist /kṓ-igzíst/ *v.intr.* (often foll. by *with*) **1** exist together (in time or place). **2** (esp. of nations) exist in mutual tolerance though professing different ideologies etc. □□ **coexistence** *n.* **coexistent** *adj.* [LL *coexistere* (as CO-, EXIST)]
■ □□ **coexistent** see CONTEMPORARY *adj.* 1.

coextensive /kṓ-iksténsiv/ *adj.* extending over the same space or time.
■ see IDENTICAL 1.

C. of E. *abbr.* Church of England.

coffee /kóffi/ *n.* **1 a** a drink made from the roasted and ground beanlike seeds of a tropical shrub. **b** a cup of this. **2 a** any shrub of the genus *Coffea*, yielding berries containing one or more seeds. **b** these seeds raw, or roasted and ground. **3** a pale brown colour, of coffee mixed with milk. □ **coffee bar** a bar or café serving coffee and light refreshments from a counter. **coffee bean** the beanlike seeds of the coffee shrub. **coffee-cup** a small cup for serving coffee. **coffee-essence** a concentrated extract of coffee usu. containing chicory. **coffee-house** a place serving coffee and other refreshments. **coffee-mill** a small machine for grinding roasted coffee beans. **coffee-morning** a morning gathering at which coffee is served, often in aid of charity. **coffee nibs** coffee beans removed from their shells. **coffee-shop** a small informal restaurant, esp. in a hotel or department store. **coffee-table** a small low table. **coffee-table book** a large lavishly illustrated book. [ult. f. Turk. *kahveh* f. Arab. *ḳahwa*, the drink]

■ □ **coffee-shop** see CAFÉ 1.

coffer /kóffər/ *n.* **1** a box, esp. a large strongbox for valuables. **2** (in *pl.*) a treasury or store of funds. **3** a sunken panel in a ceiling etc. □ **coffer-dam** a watertight enclosure pumped dry to permit work below the waterline on building bridges etc., or for repairing a ship. □□ **coffered** *adj.* [ME f. OF *coffre* f. L *cophinus* f. Gk *kophinos* basket]

■ **1** see SAFE *n.* 1. **2** (*coffers*) see TREASURY 1.

coffin /kóffin/ *n.* & *v.* ● *n.* **1** a long narrow usu. wooden box in which a corpse is buried or cremated. **2** the part of a horse's hoof below the coronet. ● *v.tr.* (**coffined, coffining**) put in a coffin. □ **coffin-bone** a bone in a horse's hoof. **coffin corner** *US Football* the corner between the goal-line and sideline. **coffin-joint** the joint at the top of a horse's hoof. **coffin-nail** *sl.* a cigarette. [ME f. OF *cof(f)in* little basket etc. f. L *cophinus*: see COFFER]

■ *n.* **1** *US* casket; sarcophagus. □ **coffin-nail** see CIGARETTE.

coffle /kóff'l/ *n.* a line of animals, slaves, etc., fastened together. [Arab. *ḳāfila* caravan]

cog /kog/ *n.* **1** each of a series of projections on the edge of a wheel or bar transferring motion by engaging with another series. **2** an unimportant member of an organization etc. □ **cog-wheel** a wheel with cogs. □□ **cogged** *adj.* [ME: prob. of Scand. orig.]

■ **1** tooth, gear-tooth, sprocket. **2** underling, pawn, subordinate, nonentity, zero, cipher, nothing, nobody.

cogent /kṓjənt/ *adj.* (of arguments, reasons, etc.) convincing, compelling. □□ **cogency** *n.* **cogently** *adv.* [L *cogere* compel (as CO-, *agere act-* drive)]

■ see PERSUASIVE. □□ **cogency** see FORCE[1] *n.* 4.

cogitable /kójitəb'l/ *adj.* able to be grasped by the mind; conceivable. [L *cogitabilis* (as COGITATE)]

cogitate /kójitayt/ *v.tr.* & *intr.* ponder, meditate. □□ **cogitation** /-táysh'n/ *n.* **cogitative** /-tətiv/ *adj.* **cogitator** *n.* [L *cogitare* think (as CO-, AGITATE)]

■ see PONDER. □□ **cogitative** see THOUGHTFUL 1.

cogito /kṓgitō/ *n. Philos.* the principle establishing the existence of a being from the fact of its thinking or awareness. [L, = I think, in Fr. philosopher Descartes's formula (1641) *cogito, ergo sum* I think, therefore I exist]

cognac /kónyak/ *n.* a high-quality brandy, properly that distilled in Cognac in W. France.

cognate /kógnayt/ *adj.* & *n.* ● *adj.* **1** related to or descended from a common ancestor (cf. AGNATE). **2** *Philol.* (of a word) having the same linguistic family or derivation (as another); representing the same original word or root (e.g. English *father*, German *Vater*, Latin *pater*). ● *n.* **1** a relative. **2** a cognate word. □ **cognate object** *Gram.* an object that is related in origin and sense to the verb governing it (as in *live a good life*). □□ **cognately** *adv.* **cognateness** *n.* [L *cognatus* (as CO-, *natus* born)]

■ *adj.* **1** see LIKE[1] *adj.* 1a.

cognition /kognísh'n/ *n.* **1** *Philos.* knowing, perceiving, or conceiving as an act or faculty distinct from emotion and volition. **2** a result of this; a perception, sensation, notion, or intuition. □□ **cognitional** *adj.* **cognitive** /kógnitiv/ *adj.* [L *cognitio* (as CO-, *gnoscere gnit-* apprehend)]

■ **1** see KNOWLEDGE 1a.

cognizable /kógnizəb'l, kón-/ *adj.* (also **-isable**) **1** perceptible, recognizable; clearly identifiable. **2** within the jurisdiction of a court. □□ **cognizably** *adv.* [COGNIZANCE + -ABLE]

■ **1** see SENSIBLE 2.

cognizance /kógniz'nss, kón-/ *n.* (also **cognisance**) **1** knowledge or awareness; perception, notice. **2** the sphere of one's observation or concern. **3** *Law* the right of a court to deal with a matter. **4** *Heraldry* a distinctive device or mark. □ **have cognizance of** know, esp. officially. **take cognizance of** attend to; take account of. [ME f. OF *conoisance* ult. f. L *cognoscent-* f. *cognitio*: see COGNITION]

■ **1** knowledge, awareness, perception, notice, consciousness, mindfulness. **2** sphere, scope, province, domain. **3** see JURISDICTION 2. **4** see DEVICE 3.

cognizant /kógniz'nt, kón-/ *adj.* (also **cognisant**) (foll. by *of*) having knowledge or being aware of.

■ see AWARE 1.

cognomen /kognṓmen/ *n.* **1** a nickname. **2** an ancient Roman's personal name or epithet, as in Marcus Tullius *Cicero*, Publius Cornelius Scipio *Africanus*. [L]

cognoscente /kónyəshénti/ *n.* (*pl.* ***cognoscenti*** /*pronunc.* same/) (usu. in *pl.*) a connoisseur. [*obs.* It.]

cohabit /kōhábbit/ *v.intr.* (**cohabited, cohabiting**) live together, esp. as husband and wife without being married to one another. □□ **cohabitant** *n.* **cohabitation** /-táysh'n/ *n.* **cohabitee** /-teé/ *n.* **cohabiter** *n.* [L *cohabitare* (as CO-, *habitare* dwell)]

cohere /kōheér/ *v.intr.* **1** (of parts or a whole) stick together, remain united. **2** (of reasoning etc.) be logical or consistent. [L *cohaerēre cohaes-* (as CO-, *haerēre* stick)]

■ **1** see STICK[2] *v.* 4. **2** hold, hang together, be logical.

coherent /kōheérənt/ *adj.* **1** (of a person) able to speak intelligibly and articulately. **2** (of speech, an argument, etc.) logical and consistent; easily followed. **3** cohering; sticking together. **4** *Physics* (of waves) having a constant phase relationship. □□ **coherence** *n.* **coherency** *n.* **coherently** *adv.* [L *cohaerēre cohaerent-* (as COHERE)]

■ **1, 2** consistent, orderly, organized, well-organized, logical, rational, reasonable, sensible, well-ordered; understandable, comprehensible, intelligible, articulate, lucid, clear. □□ **coherence** see UNITY 1.

cohesion /kōheézh'n/ *n.* **1 a** the act or condition of sticking together. **b** a tendency to cohere. **2** *Chem.* the force with which molecules cohere. □□ **cohesive** /-heéssiv/ *adj.* **cohesively** /-heéssivli/ *adv.* **cohesiveness** /-heéssivniss/ *n.* [L *cohaes-* (see COHERE) after *adhesion*]

coho /kṓhō/ *n.* (also **cohoe**) (*pl.* **-os** or **-oes**) a silver salmon, *Oncorhynchus kisutch*, of the N. Pacific. [19th c.: orig. unkn.]

cohort /kṓhort/ *n.* **1** an ancient Roman military unit, equal to one-tenth of a legion. **2** a band of warriors. **3 a** persons banded or grouped together, esp. in a common cause. **b** a group of persons with a common statistical characteristic. **4** *US* a companion or colleague. [ME f. F *cohorte* or L *cohors cohort-* enclosure, company]

■ **2** troop, squad, squadron, platoon, brigade, unit, cadre, wing, detachment, contingent. **3 a** company, band, group, faction, set, body, corps. **4** companion, confederate, accomplice, associate, fellow, comrade, friend, confrère.

COHSE /kṓzi/ *abbr.* (in the UK) Confederation of Health Service Employees.

COI *abbr.* (in the UK) Central Office of Information.

coif /koyf/ *n. hist.* **1** a close-fitting cap, esp. as worn by nuns under a veil. **2** a protective metal skullcap worn under armour. [ME f. OF *coife* f. LL *cofia* helmet]

coiffeur /kwaafṓr/ *n.* (*fem.* ***coiffeuse*** /-fṓz/) a hairdresser. [F]

coiffure /kwaafyoór/ *n.* the way hair is arranged; a hairstyle. [F]

coign /koyn/ *n.* □ **coign of vantage** a favourable position for observation or action. [earlier spelling of COIN in the sense 'cornerstone']

coil[1] /koyl/ *n.* & *v.* ● *n.* **1** anything arranged in a joined sequence of concentric circles. **2** a length of rope, a spring, etc., arranged in this way. **3** a single turn of something coiled, e.g. a snake. **4** a lock of hair twisted and coiled. **5** an intra-uterine contraceptive device in the form of a coil. **6** *Electr.* a device consisting of a coiled wire for converting low voltage to high voltage, esp. for transmission to the sparking plugs of an internal-combustion engine. **7** a piece of wire, piping, etc., wound in circles or spirals. **8** a roll of postage stamps. ● *v.* **1** *tr.* arrange in a series of concentric loops or rings. **2** *tr.* & *intr.* twist or be twisted into a circular or spiral shape. **3** *intr.* move sinuously. [OF *coillir* f. L *colligere* COLLECT[1]]

■ *n.* **1–3** circle, loop, twist, turn, *Naut.* fake; winding, whorl, spiral, helix. ● *v.* **1, 2** wind, twist, snake, wrap, spiral, *Naut.* fake, *literary* enwrap. **3** see WIND[2] *v.* 1.

coil[2] /koyl/ *n.* □ **this mortal coil** the difficulties of earthly life (with ref. to Shakesp. *Hamlet* III. i. 67). [16th c.: orig. unkn.]

coin /koyn/ *n.* & *v.* ● *n.* **1** a piece of flat usu. round metal stamped and issued by authority as money. **2** (*collect.*) metal money. ● *v.tr.* **1** make (coins) by stamping. **2** make (metal) into coins. **3** invent or devise (esp. a new word or phrase). □ **coin-box 1** a telephone operated by inserting coins. **2** the receptacle for these. **coin money** make much money quickly. **coin-op** a launderette etc. with automatic machines operated by inserting coins. **to coin a phrase** *iron.* introducing a banal remark or cliché. [ME f. OF, = stamping-die, f. L *cuneus* wedge]

■ *n.* **2** specie; change, cash, silver. ● *v.* **1** mint, stamp. **3** invent, devise, make up, create, conceive, originate, start, fabricate, concoct, think *or* dream up. □ **coin money** earn *or* make money, become wealthy, enrich oneself, *colloq.* rake it in.

coinage /kóynij/ *n.* **1** the act or process of coining. **2 a** coins collectively. **b** a system or type of coins in use (*decimal coinage*; *bronze coinage*). **3** an invention, esp. of a new word or phrase. [ME f. OF *coigniage*]

■ **3** see NEOLOGISM.

coincide /kō-insíd/ *v.intr.* **1** occur at or during the same time. **2** occupy the same portion of space. **3** (often foll. by *with*) be in agreement; have the same view. [med.L *coincidere* (as CO-, INCIDENT)]

■ **1, 2** fall *or* come *or* go together, co-occur, synchronize. **3** agree, (be in) accord, *US colloq.* jibe; correspond, match, tally.

coincidence /kō-ínsid'nss/ *n.* **1 a** occurring or being together. **b** an instance of this. **2** a remarkable concurrence of events or circumstances without apparent causal connection. **3** *Physics* the presence of ionizing particles etc. in two or more detectors simultaneously, or of two or more signals simultaneously in a circuit. [med.L *coincidentia* (as COINCIDE)]

■ **1** co-occurrence, simultaneity, correspondence, concurrence, contemporaneity, synchronism, synchrony, coextension, coevality, coinstantaneity, concomitance, congruence. **2** chance occurrence, fluke, chance, accident, luck, fortuity, *US* happenstance.

coincident /kō-ínsid'nt/ *adj.* **1** occurring together in space or time. **2** (foll. by *with*) in agreement; harmonious. □□ **coincidently** *adv.*

coincidental /kō-ínsidént'l/ *adj.* **1** in the nature of or resulting from a coincidence. **2** happening or existing at the same time. □□ **coincidentally** *adv.*

■ **1** chance, fortuitous, accidental, unexpected, unpredicted, unpredictable, unforeseen. **2** see SIMULTANEOUS.

coiner /kóynər/ *n.* **1** a person who coins money, esp. *Brit.* the maker of counterfeit coin. **2** a person who invents or devises something (esp. a new word or phrase).

Cointreau /kwáantrō/ *n. propr.* a colourless orange-flavoured liqueur. [F]

coir /kóyər/ *n.* fibre from the outer husk of the coconut, used for ropes, matting, etc. [Malayalam *kāyar* cord f. *kāyaru* be twisted]

coition /kō-ísh'n/ *n. Med.* = COITUS. [L *coitio* f. *coire coit-* go together]

coitus /kō-itəss/ *n. Med.* sexual intercourse. □ **coitus interruptus** /intərúptəss/ sexual intercourse in which the penis is withdrawn before ejaculation. □□ **coital** *adj.* [L (as COITION)]

■ see *sexual intercourse.*

Coke /kōk/ *n. propr.* Coca-Cola. [abbr.]

coke[1] /kōk/ *n.* & *v.* ● *n.* **1** a solid substance left after the gases have been extracted from coal. **2** a residue left after the incomplete combustion of petrol etc. ● *v.tr.* convert (coal) into coke. [prob. f. N.Engl. dial. *colk* core, of unkn. orig.]

coke[2] /kōk/ *n. sl.* cocaine. [abbr.]

Col. *abbr.* **1** Colonel. **2** Colossians (New Testament).

col /kol/ *n.* **1** a depression in the summit-line of a chain of mountains, generally affording a pass from one slope to another. **2** *Meteorol.* a low-pressure region between anticyclones. [F, = neck, f. L *collum*]

■ **1** see PASS[2]. **2** depression, low-pressure area, cyclone.

col. *abbr.* column.

col- /kol/ *prefix* assim. form of COM- before *l*.

cola /kṓlə/ *n.* (also **kola**) **1** any small tree of the genus *Cola*, native to W. Africa, bearing seeds containing caffeine. **2** a carbonated drink usu. flavoured with these seeds. □ **cola nut** a seed of the tree. [W.Afr.]

■ **2** see POP[1] *n.* 2.

colander /kúlləndər/ *n.* a perforated vessel used to strain off liquid in cookery. [ME, ult. f. L *colare* strain]

■ see SCREEN *n.* 11.

co-latitude /kōláttityōōd/ *n. Astron.* the complement of the latitude, the difference between it and 90°.

colchicine /kólchiseen, kólki-/ *n.* a yellow alkaloid obtained from colchicum, used in the treatment of gout.

colchicum /kólchikəm, kólki-/ *n.* **1** any liliaceous plant of the genus *Colchicum*, esp. meadow saffron. **2** its dried corm or seed. Also called *autumn crocus.* [L f. Gk *kolkhikon* of Kolkhis, a region east of the Black Sea]

cold /kōld/ *adj.*, *n.*, & *adv.* ● *adj.* **1** of or at a low or relatively low temperature, esp. when compared with the human body. **2** not heated; cooled after being heated. **3** (of a person) feeling cold. **4** lacking ardour, friendliness, or affection; undemonstrative, apathetic. **5** depressing, dispiriting, uninteresting (*cold facts*). **6 a** dead. **b** *colloq.* unconscious. **7** *colloq.* at one's mercy (*had me cold*). **8** sexually frigid. **9** (of soil) slow to absorb heat. **10** (of a scent in hunting) having become weak. **11** (in children's games) far from finding or guessing what is sought. **12** without preparation or rehearsal. ● *n.* **1 a** the prevalence of a low temperature, esp. in the atmosphere. **b** cold weather; a cold environment (*went out into the cold*). **2** an infection in which the mucous membrane of the nose and throat becomes inflamed, causing running at the nose, sneezing, sore throat, etc. ● *adv.* esp. *US* completely, entirely (*was stopped cold mid-sentence*). □ **catch a cold 1** become infected with a cold. **2** encounter trouble or difficulties. **cold call** sell goods or services by making unsolicited calls on prospective customers by telephone or in person. **cold cathode** a cathode that emits electrons without being heated. **cold chisel** a chisel suitable for cutting metal. **cold comfort** poor or inadequate consolation. **cold cream** ointment for cleansing and softening the skin. **cold cuts** slices of cold cooked meats. **cold feet** *colloq.* loss of nerve or confidence. **cold frame** an unheated frame with a glass top for growing small plants. **cold front** the forward edge of an advancing mass of cold air. **cold fusion** nuclear fusion at room temperature esp. as a possible energy source. **cold shoulder** a show of intentional unfriendliness. **cold-shoulder** *v.tr.* be deliberately unfriendly to. **cold sore** inflammation and blisters in and around the mouth, caused by a virus infection. **cold storage 1** storage in a refrigerator or other cold place for preservation. **2** a state in which something (esp. an idea) is put aside temporarily. **cold sweat** a state of sweating induced by fear or illness. **cold table** a selection of dishes of cold food. **cold turkey** *US sl.* **1** a series of blunt statements or behaviour. **2** abrupt withdrawal from addictive drugs; the symptoms of this. **cold war** a state of hostility between nations without actual fighting. **cold wave 1** a temporary spell of cold weather over a wide area.

2 a kind of permanent wave for the hair using chemicals and without heat. **in cold blood** without feeling or passion; deliberately, ruthlessly. **out in the cold** ignored, neglected. **throw** (or **pour**) **cold water on** be discouraging or depreciatory about. ▫▫ **coldish** *adj.* **coldly** *adv.* **coldness** *n.* [OE *cald* f. Gmc, rel. to L *gelu* frost]

▪ *adj.* **1** chilly, frosty, icy, freezing, frigid, ice-cold, stone-cold, bitter, raw, keen, biting, gelid, wintry, glacial, polar, hyperborean, Siberian, *colloq.* nippy, arctic, *literary* chill. **2** chilled, cooled; unheated. **3** freezing, frozen, stone-cold. **4** indifferent, apathetic, chilly, cool, icy, dispassionate, unsympathetic, aloof, unresponsive, clinical, spiritless, frigid, unfriendly, uncordial, lukewarm; cold-blooded, insensitive, uncaring, unemotional, undemonstrative, reserved, unmoved, callous, remote, distant, standoffish, unapproachable, stony-hearted, emotionless, unfeeling, cold-hearted. **5** depressing, cheerless, gloomy, dispiriting, deadening, disheartening, bleak, dismal, discouraging; uninteresting. **6 a** see DEAD *adj.* 1. **b** see DEAD *adj.* 4. **7** at one's mercy, vulnerable, *colloq.* over a barrel. **8** see FRIGID 2. **10** weak, faint, stale, old, dead. **11** off the track, far away, distant, remote. **12** see UNPREPARED. ● *n.* **1** coldness, frigidity, iciness. **2** common cold, sniffle(s), *Med.* coryza, , *sl.* bug. ● *adv.* completely, thoroughly, entirely, absolutely, unhesitatingly, promptly, immediately, unreservedly, abruptly. ▫ **cold-shoulder** rebuff, snub, ostracize, put down, reject, exclude, shun, cut (dead), give the cold shoulder to, send to Coventry, *US colloq.* freeze out.

cold-blooded /kōldblúddid/ *adj.* **1** having a body temperature varying with that of the environment (e.g. of fish); poikilothermic. **2 a** callous; deliberately cruel. **b** without excitement or sensibility, dispassionate. ▫▫ **cold-bloodedly** *adv.* **cold-bloodedness** *n.*

▪ **2 a** callous, cruel, brutal, savage, inhuman, barbarous, vicious, barbaric, merciless, pitiless, ruthless; thick-skinned, insensitive, heartless, uncaring, stony, steely, stony-hearted, cold-hearted, unsympathetic. **b** indifferent, unresponsive, dispassionate, unemotional, cool, unimpassioned.

cold-hearted /kōldhaártid/ *adj.* lacking affection or warmth; unfriendly. ▫▫ **cold-heartedly** *adv.* **cold-heartedness** *n.*

▪ unfriendly, insensitive, unsympathetic, indifferent, unfeeling, uncaring, callous, thick-skinned, cold, cool, frigid, cold-blooded, hard-hearted, heartless, unkind, thoughtless, unthoughtful, uncharitable, ruthless, pitiless, unmerciful, cruel, merciless.

cold-short /kōldshort/ *adj.* (of a metal) brittle in its cold state. [Sw. *kallskör* f. *kall* cold + *skör* brittle: assim. to SHORT]

cole /kōl/ *n.* (usu. in *comb.*) **1** cabbage. **2** = RAPE[2]. [ME f. ON *kál* f. L *caulis* stem, cabbage]

colemouse var. of COALMOUSE.

coleopteron /kólliópteron/ *n.* any insect of the order Coleoptera, with front wings modified into sheaths to protect the hinder wings, e.g. a beetle or weevil. ▫▫ **coleopterist** *n.* **coleopterous** *adj.* [mod.L *Coleoptera* f. Gk *koleopteros* f. *koleon* sheath + *pteron* wing]

coleoptile /kólliópt̄il/ *n. Bot.* a sheath protecting a young shoot tip in grasses. [Gk *koleon* sheath + *ptilon* feather]

coleseed /kōlseed/ *n.* = COLE 2.

coleslaw /kōlslaw/ *n.* a dressed salad of sliced raw cabbage, carrot, onion, etc. [Du. *koolsla*: see COLE, SLAW]

cole-tit var. of *coal-tit*.

coleus /kōliəss/ *n.* any plant of the genus *Coleus*, having variegated coloured leaves. [mod.L f. Gk *koleon* sheath]

coley /kōli/ *n.* (*pl.* **-eys**) *Brit.* any of various fish used as food, esp. the saithe or rock-salmon. [perh. f. *coal-fish*]

colic /kóllik/ *n.* a severe spasmodic abdominal pain. ▫▫ **colicky** *adj.* [ME f. F *colique* f. LL *colicus*: see COLON[2]]

▪ see GRIPE *n.* 1.

coliseum /kólliseéəm/ *n. US* = COLOSSEUM.

colitis /kəl̄ītiss/ *n.* inflammation of the lining of the colon.

Coll. *abbr.* College.

collaborate /kəlábbərayt/ *v.intr.* (often foll. by *with*) **1** work jointly, esp. in a literary or artistic production. **2** cooperate traitorously with an enemy. ▫▫ **collaboration** /-ráysh'n/ *n.* **collaborationist** /-ráyshənist/ *n.* & *adj.* **collaborative** /-rətiv/ *adj.* **collaborator** *n.* [L *collaborare collaborat-* (as COM-, *laborare* work)]

▪ **1** cooperate, join (forces), work together, team up.

collage /kóllaazh, kəlaázh/ *n.* **1** a form of art in which various materials (e.g. photographs, pieces of paper, matchsticks) are arranged and glued to a backing. **2** a work of art done in this way. **3** a collection of unrelated things. ▫▫ **collagist** *n.* [F, = gluing]

collagen /kólləjən/ *n.* a protein found in animal connective tissue, yielding gelatin on boiling. [F *collagène* f. Gk *kolla* glue + *-gène* = -GEN]

collapsar /kolápsaar/ *n. Astron.* = *black hole* 1.

collapse /kəláps/ *n.* & *v.* ● *n.* **1** the tumbling down or falling in of a structure; folding up; giving way. **2** a sudden failure of a plan, undertaking, etc. **3** a physical or mental breakdown. ● *v.* **1 a** *intr.* undergo or experience a collapse. **b** *tr.* cause to collapse. **2** *intr. colloq.* lie or sit down and relax, esp. after prolonged effort (*collapsed into a chair*). **3 a** *intr.* (of furniture etc.) be foldable into a small space. **b** *tr.* fold (furniture) in this way. ▫▫ **collapsible** *adj.* **collapsibility** /-sibílliti/ *n.* [L *collapsus* past part. of *collabi* (as COM-, *labi* slip)]

▪ *n.* **1** cave-in, breakdown, disintegration, subsidence; see also RUIN *n.* 2a. **2** failure, downfall, ruin; disintegration, dissolution, bankruptcy. **3** (mental *or* nervous) breakdown, prostration, *colloq.* crack-up. ● *v.* **1 a** fall (down *or* in *or* apart), crumple, cave in, deflate, crumble, tumble down, break down; fail, (come to an) end, fall through, peter out, disintegrate, dissolve, fall flat, founder, break up *or* down, disappear, evaporate, go up in smoke, go bankrupt, go under, go to the wall; pass out, faint, drop, keel over, *literary* swoon; have a (mental *or* nervous) breakdown, go to pieces, *colloq.* crack up.

collar /kóllər/ *n.* & *v.* ● *n.* **1** the part of a shirt, dress, coat, etc., that goes round the neck, either upright or turned over. **2** a band of linen, lace, etc., completing the upper part of a costume. **3** a band of leather or other material put round an animal's (esp. a dog's) neck. **4** a restraining or connecting band, ring, or pipe in machinery. **5** a coloured marking resembling a collar round the neck of a bird or animal. **6** *Brit.* a piece of meat rolled up and tied. ● *v.tr.* **1** seize (a person) by the collar or neck. **2** capture, apprehend. **3** *colloq.* accost. **4** *sl.* take, esp. illicitly. ▫ **collar-beam** a horizontal beam connecting two rafters and forming with them an A-shaped roof-truss. **collar-bone** either of two bones joining the breastbone and the shoulder-blades. **collared dove** a dove, *Streptopelia decaoto*, having distinct neck-markings. ▫▫ **collared** *adj.* (also in *comb.*). **collarless** *adj.* [ME f. AF *coler*, OF *colier*, f. L *collare* f. *collum* neck]

▪ *v.* **2** see CAPTURE *v.* 1.

collate /kəláyt/ *v.tr.* **1** analyse and compare (texts, statements, etc.) to identify points of agreement and difference. **2** *Bibliog.* verify the order of (sheets) by their signatures. **3** assemble (information) from different sources. **4** (often foll. by *to*) *Eccl.* appoint (a clergyman) to a benefice. ▫▫ **collator** *n.* [L *collat-* past part. stem of *conferre* compare]

▪ **1** see SEPARATE *v.* 6a. **3** see COMPILE 1.

collateral /kəláttərəl/ *n.* & *adj.* ● *n.* **1** security pledged as a guarantee for repayment of a loan. **2** a person having the same descent as another but by a different line. ● *adj.* **1** descended from the same stock but by a different line. **2** side by side; parallel. **3 a** additional but subordinate. **b** contributory. **c** connected but aside from the main subject, course, etc. ▫▫ **collaterality** /-rálliti/ *n.* **collaterally** *adv.* [ME f. med.L *collateralis* (as COM-, LATERAL)]

▪ *n.* **1** see SECURITY 4. ● *adj.* **3** see EXTRA *adj.*

collation /kəláysh'n/ *n.* **1** the act or an instance of collating. **2** *RC Ch.* a light meal allowed during a fast. **3** a light informal meal. [ME f. OF f. L *collatio -onis* (see COLLATE):

sense 2 f. Cassian's *Collationes Patrum* (= *Lives of the Fathers*) read by Benedictines and followed by a light meal]
▪ **2, 3** see MEAL[1].

colleague /kólleeg/ *n.* a fellow official or worker, esp. in a profession or business. [F *collègue* f. L *collega* (as COM-, *legare* depute)]
▪ team-mate, fellow-worker, co-worker; associate, comrade, ally, confrère.

collect[1] /kəlékt/ *v.*, *adj.*, & *adv.* ● *v.* **1** *tr.* & *intr.* bring or come together; assemble, accumulate. **2** *tr.* systematically seek and acquire (books, stamps, etc.), esp. as a continuing hobby. **3 a** *tr.* obtain (taxes, contributions, etc.) from a number of people. **b** *intr. colloq.* receive money. **4** *tr.* call for; fetch (*went to collect the laundry*). **5 a** *refl.* regain control of oneself esp. after a shock. **b** *tr.* concentrate (one's energies, thoughts, etc.). **c** *tr.* (as **collected** *adj.*) calm and cool; not perturbed or distracted. **6** *tr.* infer, gather, conclude. ● *adj.* & *adv. US* to be paid for by the receiver (of a telephone call, parcel, etc.). □□ **collectable** *adj.* **collectedly** *adv.* [F *collecter* or med.L *collectare* f. L *collectus* past part. of *colligere* (as COM-, *legere* pick)]
▪ *v.* **1** gather (together), get *or* bring *or* come together, amass, accumulate, assemble, compile, pile up, heap up, *US* rack up; convene, congregate, converge, rally, meet. **3 b** see RECEIVE 1, 2. **4** see FETCH[1] *v.* 1. **5 a** see COMPOSE 4a. **b** summon (up), concentrate, draw (up), muster, gather (up). **c** (**collected**) calm, serene, controlled, cool, sedate, composed, nonchalant, poised, unruffled, unperturbed, undistracted, at ease, comfortable, tranquil, unexcited; imperturbable; confident.

collect[2] /kóllekt, -ikt/ *n.* a short prayer of the Anglican and Roman Catholic Church, esp. one assigned to a particular day or season. [ME f. OF *collecte* f. L *collecta* fem. past part. of *colligere*: see COLLECT[1]]

collectible /kəléktib'l/ *adj.* & *n.* ● *adj.* worth collecting. ● *n.* an item sought by collectors.

collection /kəléksh'n/ *n.* **1** the act or process of collecting or being collected. **2** a group of things collected together (e.g. works of art, literary items, or specimens), esp. systematically. **3** (foll. by *of*) an accumulation; a mass or pile (*a collection of dust*). **4 a** the collecting of money, esp. in church or for a charitable cause. **b** the amount collected. **5** the regular removal of mail, esp. from a postbox, for dispatch. **6** (in *pl.*) *Brit.* college examinations held at the end of a term, esp. at Oxford University. [ME f. OF f. L *collectio -onis* (as COLLECT[1])]
▪ **1** accumulation, amassment, aggregation. **2** accumulation, hoard, store, assemblage; anthology. **3** see MASS[1] *n.* 1, 2. **4a** *Brit. colloq.* whip-round.

collective /kəléktiv/ *adj.* & *n.* ● *adj.* **1** formed by or constituting a collection. **2** taken as a whole; aggregate (*our collective opinion*). **3** of or from several or many individuals; common. ● *n.* **1 a** = *collective farm.* **b** any cooperative enterprise. **c** its members. **2** = *collective noun.* □ **collective bargaining** negotiation of wages etc. by an organized body of employees. **collective farm** a jointly-operated esp. State-owned amalgamation of several smallholdings. **collective noun** *Gram.* a noun that is grammatically singular and denotes a collection or number of individuals (e.g. *assembly*, *family*, *troop*). **collective ownership** ownership of land, means of production, etc., by all for the benefit of all. **collective unconscious** *Psychol.* (in Jungian theory) the part of the unconscious mind derived from ancestral memory and experience common to all mankind, as distinct from the personal unconscious. □□ **collectively** *adv.* **collectiveness** *n.* **collectivity** /kóllektívviti/ *n.* [F *collectif* or L *collectivus* (as COLLECT[1])]
▪ *adj.* **2** see JOINT *adj.* **3** see COMMON *adj.* 2.

collectivism /kəléktiviz'm/ *n.* the theory and practice of the collective ownership of land and the means of production. □□ **collectivist** *n.* **collectivistic** /-vístik/ *adj.*

collectivize /kəléktivīz/ *v.tr.* (also **-ise**) organize on the basis of collective ownership. □□ **collectivization** /-záysh'n/ *n.*

collector /kəléktər/ *n.* **1** a person who collects, esp. things of interest as a hobby. **2** a person who collects money etc. due (*tax-collector*; *ticket-collector*). **3** *Electronics* the region in a transistor that absorbs carriers of a charge. □ **collector's item** (or **piece**) a valuable object, esp. one of interest to collectors. [ME f. AF *collectour* f. med.L *collector* (as COLLECT[1])]
▪ **1** gatherer, accumulator, hoarder.

colleen /koléen/ *n. Ir.* a girl. [Ir. *cailín*, dimin. of *caile* country-woman]
▪ see GIRL 1.

college /kóllij/ *n.* **1** an establishment for further or higher education, sometimes part of a university. **2** an establishment for specialized professional education (*business college*; *college of music*; *naval college*). **3** the buildings or premises of a college (*lived in college*). **4** the students and teachers in a college. **5** *Brit.* a public school. **6** an organized body of persons with shared functions and privileges (*College of Physicians*). □ **College of Arms** (in the UK) a corporation recording lineage and granting arms. **college of education** *Brit.* a training college for schoolteachers. **college pudding** *Brit.* a small baked or steamed suet pudding with dried fruit. □□ **collegial** /kəléejəl/ *adj.* [ME f. OF *college* or L *collegium* f. *collega* (*as* COLLEAGUE)]
▪ **1–5** see INSTITUTE *n.* 1.

collegian /kəléejən/ *n.* a member of a college. [med.L *collegianus* (as COLLEGE)]

collegiate /kəléejət/ *adj.* constituted as or belonging to a college; corporate. □ **collegiate church 1** a church endowed for a chapter of canons but without a bishop's see. **2** *US* & *Sc.* a church or group of churches established under a joint pastorate. □□ **collegiately** *adv.* [LL *collegiatus* (as COLLEGE)]

collenchyma /koléngkimə/ *n. Bot.* a tissue of cells with thick cellulose cell walls, strengthening young stems etc. [Gk *kolla* glue + *egkhuma* infusion]

Colles' fracture /kólliss/ *n.* a fracture of the lower end of the radius with a backward displacement of the hand. [A. *Colles*, Ir. surgeon d. 1843]

collet /kóllit/ *n.* **1** a flange or socket for setting a gem in jewellery. **2** *Engin.* a segmented band or sleeve put round a shaft or spindle and tightened to grip it. **3** *Horol.* a small collar to which the inner end of a balance spring is attached. [F, dimin. of COL]

collide /kəlīd/ *v.intr.* (often foll. by *with*) **1** come into abrupt or violent impact. **2** be in conflict. [L *collidere collis-* (*as* COM-, *laedere* strike, damage)]
▪ **1** crash, strike *or* dash together; (*collide with*) crash into, smash into, run into, bump into, smack into. **2** see CONFLICT *v* 1.

collie /kólli/ *n.* **1** a sheepdog orig. of a Scottish breed, with a long pointed nose and usu. dense long hair. **2** this breed. [perh. f. *coll* COAL (as being orig. black)]

collier /kólliər/ *n.* **1** a coalminer. **2 a** a coal-ship. **b** a member of its crew. [ME, f. COAL + -IER]

colliery /kólliəri/ *n.* (*pl.* **-ies**) a coalmine and its associated buildings.
▪ see MINE[2] *n.* 1.

colligate /kólligayt/ *v.tr.* bring into connection (esp. isolated facts by a generalization). □□ **colligation** /-gáysh'n/ *n.* [L *colligare colligat-* (as COM-, *ligare* bind)]

collimate /kóllimayt/ *v.tr.* **1** adjust the line of sight of (a telescope etc.). **2** make (telescopes or rays) accurately parallel. □□ **collimation** /-máysh'n/ *n.* [L *collimare*, erron. for *collineare* align (as COM-, *linea* line)]

collimator /kóllimaytər/ *n.* **1** a device for producing a parallel beam of rays or radiation. **2** a small fixed telescope used for adjusting the line of sight of an astronomical telescope, etc.

collinear /kəlínniər/ *adj. Geom.* (of points) lying in the same straight line. □□ **collinearity** /-niárriti/ *n.* **collinearly** *adv.*

Collins /kóllinz/ *n.* an iced drink made of gin or whisky etc. with soda, lemon or lime juice, and sugar. [20th c.: orig. unkn.]

collision /kəlízh'n/ *n.* **1** a violent impact of a moving body, esp. a vehicle or ship, with another or with a fixed object. **2** the clashing of opposed interests or considerations. **3** *Physics* the action of particles striking or coming together. □ **collision course** a course or action that is bound to cause a collision or conflict. □□ **collisional** *adj.* [ME f. LL *collisio* (as COLLIDE)]
▪ **1** smash, crash, *colloq.* smash-up, pile-up, crack-up, *Austral. colloq.* bingle, *Brit. sl.* prang. **2** clash, conflict, difference; see also STRUGGLE *n.* 2.

collocate /kólləkayt/ *v.tr.* **1** place together or side by side. **2** arrange; set in a particular place. **3** (often foll. by *with*) *Linguistics* juxtapose (a word etc.) with another. □□ **collocation** /-káysh'n/ *n.* [L *collocare collocat-* (as COM-, *locare* to place)]
▪ □□ **collocation** see PHRASE *n.* 1.

collocutor /kólləkyootər, kəlókyootər/ *n.* a person who takes part in a conversation. [LL f. *colloqui* (as COM-, *loqui locut-* talk)]

collodion /kəlṓdiən/ *n.* a syrupy solution of cellulose nitrate in a mixture of alcohol and ether, used in photography and surgery. [Gk *kollōdēs* gluelike f. *kolla* glue]

collogue /kəlṓg/ *v.intr.* (**collogues, collogued, colloguing**) (foll. by *with*) talk confidentially. [prob. alt. of obs. *colleague* conspire, by assoc. with L *colloqui* converse]

colloid /kólloyd/ *n.* **1** *Chem.* **a** a substance consisting of ultramicroscopic particles. **b** a mixture of such a substance uniformly dispersed through a second substance esp. to form a viscous solution. **2** *Med.* a substance of a homogeneous gelatinous consistency. □□ **colloidal** /-lóyd'l/ *adj.* [Gk *kolla* glue + -OID]

collop /kólləp/ *n.* a slice, esp. of meat or bacon; an escalope. [ME, = fried bacon and eggs, of Scand. orig.]
▪ see SLICE *n.* 1.

colloquial /kəlṓkwiəl/ *adj.* belonging to or proper to ordinary or familiar conversation, not formal or literary. □□ **colloquially** *adv.* [L *colloquium* COLLOQUY]
▪ see VERNACULAR *adj.*

colloquialism /kəlṓkwiəliz'm/ *n.* **1** a colloquial word or phrase. **2** the use of colloquialisms.

colloquium /kəlṓkwiəm/ *n.* (*pl.* **colloquiums** or **colloquia** /-kwiə/) an academic conference or seminar. [L: see COLLOQUY]
▪ see CONFERENCE 2.

colloquy /kólləkwi/ *n.* (*pl.* **-quies**) **1** the act of conversing. **2** a conversation. **3** *Eccl.* a gathering for discussion of theological questions. [L *colloquium* (as COM-, *loqui* speak)]
▪ **1, 2** see CONVERSATION. **3** see CONFERENCE 1.

collotype /kóllətīp/ *n.* *Printing* **1** a thin sheet of gelatin exposed to light, treated with reagents, and used to make high quality prints by lithography. **2** a print made by this process. [Gk *kolla* glue + TYPE]

collude /kəlṓōd, -lyṓōd/ *v.intr.* come to an understanding or conspire together, esp. for a fraudulent purpose. □□ **colluder** *n.* [L *colludere collus-* (as COM-, *ludere lus-* play)]
▪ see PLOT *v.* 2.

collusion /kəlṓōzh'n, -lyṓōzh'n/ *n.* **1** a secret understanding, esp. for a fraudulent purpose. **2** *Law* such an understanding between ostensible opponents in a lawsuit. □□ **collusive** *adj.* **collusively** *adv.* [ME f. OF *collusion* or L *collusio* (as COLLUDE)]
▪ **1** see INTRIGUE *n.* 1.

collyrium /kəlírriəm/ *n.* (*pl.* **collyria** /-riə/) a medicated eye-lotion. [L f. Gk *kollurion* poultice f. *kollura* coarse bread-roll]
▪ see WASH *n.* 7, 10.

collywobbles /kólliwobb'lz/ *n.pl. colloq.* **1** a rumbling or pain in the stomach. **2** a feeling of strong apprehension. [fanciful, f. COLIC + WOBBLE]

Colo. *abbr.* Colorado.

colobus /kólləbəss/ *n.* any leaf-eating monkey of the genus *Colobus*, native to Africa, having shortened thumbs. [mod.L f. Gk *kolobos* docked]

colocynth /kólləsinth/ *n.* (also **coloquintida** /kólləkwíntidə/) **1 a** a plant of the gourd family, *Citrullus colocynthis*, bearing a pulpy fruit. **b** this fruit. **2** a bitter purgative drug obtained from the fruit. [L *colocynthis* f. Gk *kolokunthis*]

cologne /kəlṓn/ *n.* (in full **cologne water**) eau-de-Cologne or a similar scented toilet water. [abbr.]

colon[1] /kṓlən, -lon/ *n.* a punctuation mark (:), used esp. to introduce a quotation or a list of items or to separate clauses when the second expands or illustrates the first; also between numbers in a statement of proportion (as in 10:1) and in Biblical references (as in Exodus 3:2). [L f. Gk *kōlon* limb, clause]

colon[2] /kṓlən, -lon/ *n.* *Anat.* the lower and greater part of the large intestine, from the caecum to the rectum. □□ **colonic** /kəlónnik/ *adj.* [ME, ult. f. Gk *kolon*]

colonel /kṓn'l/ *n.* **1** an army officer in command of a regiment, immediately below a brigadier in rank. **2** *US* an officer of corresponding rank in the Air Force. **3** = *lieutenant-colonel.* □ **Colonel Blimp** see BLIMP *n.* 1. □□ **colonelcy** *n.* (*pl.* **-ies**). [obs. F *coronel* f. It. *colonnello* f. *colonna* COLUMN]

colonial /kəlṓniəl/ *adj.* & *n.* ● *adj.* **1** of, relating to, or characteristic of a colony or colonies, esp. of a British Crown Colony. **2** (esp. of architecture or furniture) built or designed in, or in a style characteristic of, the period of the British colonies in America before independence. ● *n.* **1** a native or inhabitant of a colony. **2** a house built in colonial style. □ **colonial goose** *Austral.* & *NZ* a boned and stuffed roast leg of mutton. □□ **colonially** *adv.*

colonialism /kəlṓniəliz'm/ *n.* **1** a policy of acquiring or maintaining colonies. **2** *derog.* this policy regarded as the esp. economic exploitation of weak or backward peoples by a larger power. □□ **colonialist** *n.*
▪ **2** neocolonialism, *usu. derog.* imperialism.

colonist /kóllənist/ *n.* a settler in or inhabitant of a colony.
▪ see SETTLER.

colonize /kóllənīz/ *v.* (also **-ise**) **1** *tr.* **a** establish a colony or colonies in (a country or area). **b** settle as colonists. **2** *intr.* establish or join a colony. **3** *tr. US Polit.* plant voters in (a district) for party purposes. **4** *tr. Biol.* (of plants and animals) become established (in an area). □□ **colonization** /-záysh'n/ *n.* **colonizer** *n.*
▪ **1, 2** see SETTLE[1] 12.

colonnade /kóllənáyd/ *n.* a row of columns, esp. supporting an entablature or roof. □□ **colonnaded** *adj.* [F f. *colonne* COLUMN]
▪ see PORTICO.

colony /kólləni/ *n.* (*pl.* **-ies**) **1 a** a group of settlers in a new country (whether or not already inhabited) fully or partly subject to the mother country. **b** the settlement or its territory. **2 a** people of one nationality or race or occupation in a city, esp. if living more or less in isolation or in a special quarter. **b** a separate or segregated group (*nudist colony*). **3** *Biol.* a collection of animals, plants, etc., connected, in contact, or living close together. [ME f. L *colonia* f. *colonus* farmer f. *colere* cultivate]
▪ **1** see SETTLEMENT 2.

colophon /kólləfon, -f'n/ *n.* **1** a publisher's device or imprint, esp. on the title-page. **2** a tailpiece in a manuscript or book, often ornamental, giving the writer's or printer's name, the date, etc. [LL f. Gk *kolophōn* summit, finishing touch]
▪ **1** see STAMP *n.* 2, 4.

colophony /kəlóffəni/ *n.* = ROSIN. [L *colophonia* (resin) from Colophon in Asia Minor]

coloquintida var. of COLOCYNTH.

color etc. *US* var. of COLOUR etc.

Colorado beetle /kóllərâadō/ *n.* a yellow and black striped beetle, *Leptinotarsa decemlineata*, the larva of which is highly destructive to the potato plant. [*Colorado* in the US]

coloration /kúlləráysh'n/ *n.* (also **colouration**) **1** colouring; a scheme or method of applying colour. **2** the natural (esp.

variegated) colour of living things or animals. [F *coloration* or LL *coloratio* f. *colorare* COLOUR]

coloratura /kòllərətóórə/ *n.* **1** elaborate ornamentation of a vocal melody. **2** a singer (esp. a soprano) skilled in coloratura singing. [It. f. L *colorare* COLOUR]

colorific /kólləríffik, kúl-/ *adj.* **1** producing colour. **2** highly coloured. [F *colorifique* or mod.L *colorificus* (as COLOUR)]

colorimeter /kóllərímmitər, kúl-/ *n.* an instrument for measuring the intensity of colour. □□ **colorimetric** /-métrik/ *adj.* **colorimetry** *n.* [L *color* COLOUR + -METER]

colossal /kəlóss'l/ *adj.* **1** of immense size; huge, gigantic. **2** *colloq.* remarkable, splendid. **3** *Archit.* (of an order) having more than one storey of columns. **4** *Sculpture* (of a statue) about twice life size. □□ **colossally** *adv.* [F f. *colosse* COLOSSUS]

■ **1** huge, vast, enormous, gigantic, giant, mammoth, massive, gargantuan, immense, monumental, titanic, elephantine, *colloq.* jumbo; Herculean. **2** spectacular, remarkable, splendid, stupendous, wonderful, awe-inspiring, staggering, extraordinary, incredible, overwhelming, unbelievable, *colloq.* fantastic.

colosseum /kólləseéəm/ *n.* a large stadium or amphitheatre. [med.L, neut. of *colosseus* gigantic (as COLOSSUS)]

colossus /kəlóssəss/ *n.* (*pl.* **colossi** /-sī/ or **colossuses**) **1** a statue much bigger than life size. **2** a gigantic person, animal, building, etc. **3** an imperial power personified. [L f. Gk *kolossos*]

■ **1** see STATUE. **2** see GIANT *n.* 1.

colostomy /kəlóstəmi/ *n.* (*pl.* **-ies**) *Surgery* an operation on the colon to make an opening in the abdominal wall to provide an artificial anus. [as COLON[2] + Gk *stoma* mouth]

colostrum /kəlóstrəm/ *n.* the first secretion from the mammary glands occurring after giving birth. [L]

colotomy /kəlóttəmi/ *n.* (*pl.* **-ies**) *Surgery* an incision in the colon. [as COLON[2] + -TOMY]

colour /kúllər/ *n.* & *v.* ● *n.* (*US* **color**) **1 a** the sensation produced on the eye by rays of light when resolved as by a prism, selective reflection, etc., into different wavelengths. **b** perception of colour; a system of colours. **2** one, or any mixture, of the constituents into which light can be separated as in a spectrum or rainbow, sometimes including (loosely) black and white. **3** a colouring substance, esp. paint. **4** the use of all colours, not only black and white, as in photography and television. **5 a** pigmentation of the skin, esp. when dark. **b** this as a ground for prejudice or discrimination. **6** ruddiness of complexion (*a healthy colour*). **7** (in *pl.*) appearance or aspect (*see things in their true colours*). **8** (in *pl.*) **a** *Brit.* a coloured ribbon or uniform etc. worn to signify membership of a school, club, team, etc. **b** the flag of a regiment or ship. **c** a national flag. **9** quality, mood, or variety in music, literature, speech, etc.; distinctive character or timbre. **10** a show of reason; a pretext (*lend colour to*; *under colour of*). ● *v.* **1** *tr.* apply colour to, esp. by painting or dyeing or with coloured pens or pencils. **2** *tr.* influence (*an attitude coloured by experience*). **3** *tr.* **a** misrepresent, exaggerate, esp. with spurious detail (*a highly coloured account*). **b** disguise. **4** *intr.* take on colour; blush. □ **colour bar** the denial of services and facilities to non-White people. **colour-blind** unable to distinguish certain colours. **colour-blindness** the condition of being colour-blind. **colour code** use of colours as a standard means of identification. **colour-code** *v.tr.* identify by means of a colour code. **colour-fast** dyed in colours that will not fade or be washed out. **colour-fastness** the condition of being colour-fast. **colour scheme** an arrangement or planned combination of colours esp. in interior design. **colour-sergeant** the senior sergeant of an infantry company. **colour supplement** *Brit.* a magazine with coloured illustrations, issued as a supplement to a newspaper. **colour wash** coloured distemper. **colour-wash** *v.tr.* paint with coloured distemper. **Queen's** (or **King's** or **regimental**) **colour** a flag carried by a regiment. **show one's true colours** reveal one's true character or intentions. **under false colours** falsely, deceitfully. **with flying colours** see FLYING. [ME f. OF *color*, *colorer* f. L *color*, *colorare*]

■ *n.* **2** hue, tint, shade, tone, tinge, tincture. **3** pigmentation, pigment, dye, paint. **5 a** coloration, colouring. **6** bloom, flush, blush, redness, ruddiness, rosiness, glow. **7** (*colours*) appearance, aspect, identity, light. **8** (*colours*) **a** badge, emblem, insignia, symbol(s). **b** flag, ensign, standard, pennant, banner. **9** see CHARACTER *n.* 1. ● *v.* **1** tint, dye, stain, paint, tincture, tinge; pigment. **2** affect, bias; see also INFLUENCE *v.* **3 a** misrepresent, exaggerate, distort, falsify, taint, warp, twist, skew, slant, pervert. **b** mask, disguise, conceal. **4** blush, redden, flush, become red-faced.

colourable /kúllərəb'l/ *adj.* (*US* **colorable**) **1** specious, plausible. **2** counterfeit. □□ **colourably** *adv.*

colourant /kúllərənt/ *n.* (*US* **colorant**) a colouring substance.

■ see TINT *n.* 3.

colouration var. of COLORATION.

coloured /kúllərd/ *adj.* & *n.* (*US* **colored**) ● *adj.* **1** having colour(s). **2** (**Coloured**) **a** wholly or partly of non-White descent. **b** *S.Afr.* of mixed White and non-White descent. **c** of or relating to Coloured people (*a Coloured audience*). ● *n.* (**Coloured**) **1** a Coloured person. **2** *S.Afr.* a person of mixed descent speaking Afrikaans or English as the mother tongue.

■ **2** see BLACK *adj.* 3.

colourful /kúllərfōōl/ *adj.* (*US* **colorful**) **1** having much or varied colour; bright. **2** full of interest; vivid, lively. □□ **colourfully** *adv.* **colourfulness** *n.*

■ **1** see VIVID 1. **2** see DRAMATIC 4.

colouring /kúlləring/ *n.* (*US* **coloring**) **1** the process of or skill in using colour(s). **2** the style in which a thing is coloured, or in which an artist uses colour. **3** facial complexion.

colourist /kúllərist/ *n.* (*US* **colorist**) a person who uses colour, esp. in art.

colourless /kúllərliss/ *adj.* (*US* **colorless**) **1** without colour. **2** lacking character or interest. **3** dull or pale in hue. **4** neutral, impartial, indifferent. □□ **colourlessly** *adv.*

■ **1, 3** pale, pallid, blanched, white; wan, washed out, ashen, sallow, waxen, sickly; dull. **2** dull, drab, uninteresting, vacuous, vapid, lifeless, boring, tedious, spiritless, dry, dry as dust, dreary, characterless, insipid, bland, lacklustre, uninspiring, uninspired. **4** see INDIFFERENT 4.

coloury /kúlləri/ *adj.* *US* (**colory**) having a distinctive colour, esp. as indicating good quality.

colposcopy /kolpóskəpi/ *n.* examination of the vagina and the neck of the womb. □□ **colposcope** *n.* [Gk *kolpos* womb + -SCOPY]

colt /kōlt/ *n.* **1** a young uncastrated male horse, usu. less than four years old. **2** *Sport* a young or inexperienced player; a member of a junior team. □□ **colthood** *n.* **coltish** *adj.* **coltishly** *adv.* **coltishness** *n.* [OE, = young ass or camel]

colter *US* var. of COULTER.

coltsfoot /kóltsfōōt/ *n.* (*pl.* **coltsfoots**) a wild composite plant, *Tussilago farfara*, with large leaves and yellow flowers.

colubrine /kólyoobrīn/ *adj.* **1** snakelike. **2** of the subfamily Colubrinae of non-poisonous snakes. [L *colubrinus* f. *coluber* snake]

Columbine /kólləmbīn/ *n.* the partner of Harlequin in pantomime. [F *Colombine* f. It. *Colombina* f. *colombino* dovelike]

columbine /kólləmbīn/ *n.* any plant of the genus *Aquilegia*, esp. *A. vulgaris*, having purple-blue flowers. Also called AQUILEGIA. [ME f. OF *colombine* f. med.L *colombina herba* dovelike plant f. L *columba* dove (from the supposed resemblance of the flower to a cluster of 5 doves)]

columbite /kəlúmbīt/ *n.* *US Chem.* an ore of iron and niobium found in America. [*Columbia*, a poetic name for America, + -ITE[1]]

columbium /kəlúmbiəm/ *n.* *US Chem.* = NIOBIUM.

column /kólləm/ *n.* **1** *Archit.* an upright cylindrical pillar often slightly tapering and usu. supporting an entablature or arch, or standing alone as a monument. **2** a structure or part shaped like a column. **3** a vertical cylindrical mass of liquid or vapour. **4 a** a vertical division of a page, chart, etc., containing a sequence of figures or words. **b** the figures or words themselves. **5** a part of a newspaper regularly devoted to a particular subject (*gossip column*). **6 a** *Mil.* an arrangement of troops in successive lines, with a narrow front. **b** *Naut.* a similar arrangement of ships. □ **column-inch** a quantity of print (esp. newsprint) occupying a one-inch length of a column. **dodge the column** *colloq.* shirk one's duty; avoid work. □□ **columnar** /kəlúmnər/ *adj.* **columned** *adj.* [ME f. OF *columpne* & L *columna* pillar]
■ **1–3** see PILLAR 1. **5** see EDITORIAL.

columnist /kólləmnist, -mist/ *n.* a journalist contributing regularly to a newspaper.
■ see JOURNALIST.

colure /kəloȯr/ *n. Astron.* either of two great circles intersecting at right angles at the celestial poles and passing through the ecliptic at either the equinoxes or the solstices. [ME f. LL *colurus* f. Gk *kolouros* truncated]

colza /kólzə/ *n.* = RAPE[2]. [F *kolza(t)* f. LG *kōlsāt* (as COLE, SEED)]

COM *abbr.* computer output on microfilm or microfiche.

com- /kom, kəm, kum/ *prefix* (also **co-**, **col-**, **con-**, **cor-**) with, together, jointly, altogether. ¶ *com-* is used before *b*, *m*, *p*, and occas. before vowels and *f*; *co-* esp. before vowels, *h*, and *gn*; *col-* before *l*, *cor-* before *r*, and *con-* before other consonants. [L *com-*, *cum* with]

coma[1] /kṓmə/ *n.* (*pl.* **comas**) a prolonged deep unconsciousness, caused esp. by severe injury or excessive use of drugs. [med.L f. Gk *kōma* deep sleep]
■ see STUPOR.

coma[2] /kṓmə/ *n.* (*pl.* **comae** /-mee/) **1** *Astron.* a cloud of gas and dust surrounding the nucleus of a comet. **2** *Bot.* a tuft of silky hairs at the end of some seeds. [L f. Gk *komē* hair of head]

comatose /kṓmətōz/ *adj.* **1** in a coma. **2** drowsy, sleepy, lethargic.
■ **1** see UNCONSCIOUS *adj.* **2** see *lethargic* (LETHARGY).

comb /kōm/ *n.* & *v.* ● *n.* **1** a toothed strip of rigid material for tidying and arranging the hair, or for keeping it in place. **2** a part of a machine having a similar design or purpose. **3 a** the red fleshy crest of a fowl, esp. a cock. **b** an analogous growth in other birds. **4** a honeycomb. ● *v.tr.* **1** arrange or tidy (the hair) by drawing a comb through. **2** curry (a horse). **3** dress (wool or flax) with a comb. **4** search (a place) thoroughly. □ **comb out 1** tidy and arrange (hair) with a comb. **2** remove with a comb. **3** search or attack systematically. **4** search out and get rid of (anything unwanted). □□ **combed** *adj.* [OE *camb* f. Gmc]
■ *v.* **4** see SEARCH *v.* 1, 3.

combat /kómbat, kúm-/ *n.* & *v.* ● *n.* **1** a fight, an armed encounter or conflict; fighting, battle. **2** a struggle, contest, or dispute. ● *v.* (**combated**, **combating**) **1** *intr.* engage in combat. **2** *tr.* engage in combat with. **3** *tr.* oppose; strive against. □ **combat fatigue** a mental disorder caused by stress in wartime combat. **single combat** a duel. [F *combat* f. *combattre* f. LL (as COM-, L *batuere* fight)]
■ *n.* **1** fight, encounter, engagement, duel, conflict, skirmish; action, fighting, battle. **2** struggle, contest, strife, controversy, dispute, quarrel, disagreement, altercation, confrontation. ● *v.* **1** fight, (do) battle, engage, war, clash, contend, duel, wrestle, come to blows, spar, grapple, *hist.* joust. **3** fight, struggle *or* strive against, oppose, defy, withstand; challenge, enter the lists against. □ **combat fatigue** shell-shock.

combatant /kómbət'nt, kúm-/ *n.* & *adj.* ● *n.* a person engaged in fighting. ● *adj.* **1** fighting. **2** for fighting.
■ *n.* see CHAMPION *n.* 2b. ● *adj.* **1** see MILITANT *adj.* 2.

combative /kómbətiv, kúm-/ *adj.* ready or eager to fight; pugnacious. □□ **combatively** *adv.* **combativeness** *n.*
■ see PUGNACIOUS.

combe var. of COOMB.

comber[1] /kṓmər/ *n.* **1** a person or thing that combs, esp. a machine for combing cotton or wool very fine. **2** a long curling wave; a breaker.
■ **2** see WAVE *n.* 1, 2.

comber[2] /kṓmər/ *n. Brit.* a fish of the perch family, *Serranus cabrilla*. [18th c.: orig. unkn.]

combination /kómbináysh'n/ *n.* **1** the act or an instance of combining; the process of being combined. **2** a combined state (*in combination with*). **3** a combined set of things or people. **4** a sequence of numbers or letters used to open a combination lock. **5** *Brit.* a motor cycle with side-car attached. **6** (in *pl.*) *Brit.* a single undergarment for the body and legs. **7** a group of things chosen from a larger number without regard to their arrangement. **8 a** united action. **b** *Chess* a coordinated and effective sequence of moves. **9** *Chem.* a union of substances in a compound with new properties. □ **combination lock** a lock that can be opened only by a specific sequence of movements. □□ **combinative** /kómbinətiv/ *adj.* **combinational** *adj.* **combinatory** /kómbinətəri/ *adj.* [obs. F *combination* or LL *combinatio* (as COMBINE)]
■ **1** union, conjunction, mixture, mix, grouping, amalgamation, compound; blend. **2** conjunction, tandem; see also ASSOCIATION 2. **3** set, array; association, alliance, coalition, union, federation, confederation, combine, syndicate, consortium, trust, bloc, cartel, party, society, organization, league; see also MIXTURE 2.

combinatorial /kómbinətóriəl/ *adj. Math.* relating to combinations of items.

combine *v.* & *n.* ● *v.* /kəmbī́n/ **1** *tr.* & *intr.* join together; unite for a common purpose. **2** *tr.* possess (qualities usually distinct) together (*combines charm and authority*). **3 a** *intr.* coalesce in one substance. **b** *tr.* cause to do this. **c** *intr.* form a chemical compound. **4** *intr.* cooperate. **5** /kómbīn/ *tr.* harvest (crops etc.) by means of a combine harvester. ● *n.* /kómbīn/ a combination of esp. commercial interests to control prices etc. □ **combine harvester** a mobile machine that reaps and threshes in one operation. **combining form** *Gram.* a linguistic element used in combination with another element to form a word (e.g. *Anglo-* = English, *bio-* = life, *-graphy* writing). ¶ In this dictionary, *combining form* is used of an element that contributes to the particular sense of words (as with both elements of *biography*), as distinct from a prefix or suffix that adjusts the sense of or determines the function of words (as with *un-*, *-able*, and *-ation*). □□ **combinable** *adj.* [ME f. OF *combiner* or LL *combinare* (as COM-, L *bini* two)]
■ *v.* **1** unite, unify, join, connect, relate, link, conjoin, integrate, merge, pool; band, ally, join forces. **2** see FUSE[1] *v.* **3** come together; blend, fuse, synthesize, bind, bond, unite, coalesce, join, mingle, amalgamate, mix, merge, integrate, meld, bind, bond, *literary* commingle; compound, bring *or* put together, conflate. **4** see COOPERATE.

combing /kṓming/ *n.* (in *pl.*) hairs combed off. □ **combing wool** long-stapled wool, suitable for combing and making into worsted.

combo /kómbō/ *n.* (*pl.* **-os**) *sl.* a small jazz or dance band. [abbr. of COMBINATION + -O]
■ see BAND[2] *n.* 2.

combs /komz/ *n.pl. colloq.* combinations (see COMBINATION 6).

combust /kəmbúst/ *v.tr.* subject to combustion. [obs. *combust* (adj.) f. L *combustus* past part. (as COMBUSTION)]

combustible /kəmbústib'l/ *adj.* & *n.* ● *adj.* **1** capable of or used for burning. **2** excitable; easily irritated. ● *n.* a combustible substance. □□ **combustibility** /-bílliti/ *n.* [F *combustible* or med.L *combustibilis* (as COMBUSTION)]
■ *adj.* **1** see INFLAMMABLE *adj.* 1. **2** see INFLAMMABLE *adj.* 2.

combustion /kəmbúss-chən/ *n.* **1** burning; consumption by fire. **2** *Chem.* the development of light and heat from the chemical combination of a substance with oxygen. □□ **combustive** *adj.* [ME f. F *combustion* or LL *combustio* f. L *comburere combust-* burn up]

come /kum/ *v.* & *n.* ● *v.intr.* (*past* **came** /kaym/; *past part.* **come**) **1** move, be brought towards, or reach a place thought of as near or familiar to the speaker or hearer (*come and see me*; *shall we come to your house?*; *the books have come*). **2** reach or be brought to a specified situation or result (*you'll come to no harm*; *have come to believe it*; *has come to be used wrongly*; *came into prominence*). **3** reach or extend to a specified point (*the road comes within a mile of us*). **4** traverse or accomplish (with compl.: *have come a long way*). **5** occur, happen; become present instead of future (*how did you come to break your leg?*). **6** take or occupy a specified position in space or time (*it comes on the third page*; *Nero came after Claudius*; *it does not come within the scope of the inquiry*). **7** become perceptible or known (*the church came into sight*; *the news comes as a surprise*; *it will come to me*). **8** be available (*the dress comes in three sizes*; *this model comes with optional features*). **9** become (with compl.: *the handle has come loose*). **10** (foll. by *of*) **a** be descended from (*comes of a rich family*). **b** be the result of (*that comes of complaining*). **11** *colloq.* play the part of; behave like (with compl.: *don't come the bully with me*). **12** *sl.* have a sexual orgasm. **13** (in *subj.*) *colloq.* when a specified time is reached (*come next month*). **14** (as *int.*) expressing caution or reserve (*come, it cannot be that bad*). ● *n. sl.* semen ejaculated at a sexual orgasm. □ **as . . . as they come** typically or supremely so (*is as tough as they come*). **come about 1** happen; take place. **2** *Naut.* tack. **come across 1** be effective or understood. **2** (foll. by *with*) *sl.* hand over what is wanted. **3** meet or find by chance (*came across an old jacket*). **come again** *colloq.* **1** make a further effort. **2** (as *imper.*) what did you say? **come along 1** make progress; move forward. **2** (as *imper.*) hurry up. **come and go 1** pass to and fro; be transitory. **2** pay brief visits. **come apart** fall or break into pieces, disintegrate. **come at 1** reach, discover; get access to. **2** attack (*came at me with a knife*). **come-at-able** /kumáttəb'l/ *adj.* reachable, accessible. **come away 1** become detached or broken off (*came away in my hands*). **2** (foll. by *with*) be left with a feeling, impression, etc. (*came away with many misgivings*). **come back 1** return. **2** recur to one's memory. **3** become fashionable or popular again. **4** *US* reply, retort. **come before** be dealt with by (a judge etc.). **come between 1** interfere with the relationship of. **2** separate; prevent contact between. **come by 1** pass; go past. **2** call on a visit (*why not come by tomorrow?*). **3** acquire, obtain; attain (*came by a new bicycle*). **come clean** see CLEAN. **come down 1** come to a place or position regarded as lower. **2** lose position or wealth (*has come down in the world*). **3** be handed down by tradition or inheritance. **4** be reduced; show a downward trend (*prices are coming down*). **5** (foll. by *against*, *in favour of*) reach a decision or recommendation (*the report came down against change*). **6** (foll. by *to*) signify or betoken basically; be dependent on (a factor) (*it comes down to who is willing to go*). **7** (foll. by *on*) criticize harshly; rebuke, punish. **8** (foll. by *with*) begin to suffer from (a disease). **come for 1** come to collect or receive. **2** attack (*came for me with a hammer*). **come forward 1** advance. **2** offer oneself for a task, post, etc. **come-hither** *attrib.adj. colloq.* (of a look or manner) enticing, flirtatious. **come in 1** enter a house or room. **2 a** take a specified position in a race etc. (*came in third*). **b** *colloq.* win. **3** become fashionable or seasonable. **4 a** have a useful role or function. **b** (with compl.) prove to be (*came in very handy*). **c** have a part to play (*where do I come in?*). **5** be received (*more news has just come in*). **6** begin speaking, esp. in radio transmission. **7** be elected; come to power. **8** *Cricket* begin an innings. **9** (foll. by *for*) receive; be the object of (usu. something unwelcome) (*came in for much criticism*). **10** (foll. by *on*) join (an enterprise etc.). **11** (of a tide) turn to high tide. **12** (of a train, ship, or aircraft) approach its destination. **come into 1** see senses 2, 7 of *v.* **2** receive, esp. as heir. **come near** see NEAR. **come of age** see AGE. **come off 1** *colloq.* (of an action) succeed; be accomplished. **2** (with compl.) fare; turn out (*came off badly*; *came off the winner*). **3** *coarse sl.* have a sexual orgasm. **4** be detached or detachable (from). **5** fall (from). **6** be reduced or subtracted from (*£5 came off the price*). **come off it** (as *imper.*) *colloq.* an expression of disbelief or refusal to accept another's opinion, behaviour, etc. **come on 1** continue to come. **2** advance, esp. to attack. **3** make progress; thrive (*is really coming on*). **4** (foll. by *to* + infin.) begin (*it came on to rain*). **5** appear on the stage, field of play, etc. **6** be heard or seen on television, on the telephone, etc. **7** arise to be discussed. **8** (as *imper.*) expressing encouragement. **9** = *come upon*. **come-on** *n. sl.* a lure or enticement. **come out 1 a** emerge; become known (*it came out that he had left*). **b** end, turn out. **2** appear or be published (*comes out every Saturday*). **3 a** declare oneself; make a decision (*came out in favour of joining*). **b** openly declare that one is a homosexual. **4** *Brit.* go on strike. **5 a** be satisfactorily visible in a photograph etc., or present in a specified way (*the dog didn't come out*; *he came out badly*). **b** (of a photograph) be produced satisfactorily or in a specified way (*only three have come out*; *they all came out well*). **6** attain a specified result in an examination etc. **7** (of a stain etc.) be removed. **8** make one's début on stage or in society. **9** (foll. by *in*) be covered with (*came out in spots*). **10** (of a problem) be solved. **11** (foll. by *with*) declare openly; disclose. **come over 1** come from some distance or nearer to the speaker (*came over from Paris*; *come over here a moment*). **2** change sides or one's opinion. **3 a** (of a feeling etc.) overtake or affect (a person). **b** *colloq.* feel suddenly (*came over faint*). **4** appear or sound in a specified way (*you came over very well*; *the ideas came over clearly*). **5** affect or influence (*I don't know what came over me*). **come round 1** pay an informal visit. **2** recover consciousness. **3** be converted to another person's opinion. **4** (of a date or regular occurrence) recur; be imminent again. **come through 1** be successful; survive. **2** be received by telephone. **3** survive or overcome (a difficulty) (*came through the ordeal*). **come to 1** recover consciousness. **2** *Naut.* bring a vessel to a stop. **3** reach in total; amount to. **4** *refl.* **a** recover consciousness. **b** stop being foolish. **5** have as a destiny; reach (*what is the world coming to?*). **6** be a question of (*when it comes to wine, he is an expert*). **come to hand** become available; be recovered. **come to light** see LIGHT[1]. **come to nothing** have no useful result in the end; fail. **come to pass** happen, occur. **come to rest** cease moving. **come to one's senses** see SENSE. **come to that** *colloq.* in fact; if that is the case. **come under 1** be classified as or among. **2** be subject to (influence or authority). **come up 1** come to a place or position regarded as higher. **2** attain wealth or position (*come up in the world*). **3** (of an issue, problem, etc.) arise; present itself; be mentioned or discussed. **4** (often foll. by *to*) **a** approach a person, esp. to talk. **b** approach or draw near to a specified time, event, etc. (*is coming up to eight o'clock*). **5** (foll. by *to*) match (a standard etc.). **6** (foll. by *with*) produce (an idea etc.), esp. in response to a challenge. **7** (of a plant etc.) spring up out of the ground. **8** become brighter (e.g. with polishing); shine more brightly. **come up against** be faced with or opposed by. **come upon 1** meet or find by chance. **2** attack by surprise. **come what may** no matter what happens. **have it coming to one** *colloq.* be about to get one's deserts. **how come?** *colloq.* how did that happen? **if it comes to that** in that case. **to come** future; in the future (*the year to come*; *many problems were still to come*). [OE *cuman* f. Gmc]

■ *v.* **1** approach, advance, (draw) near, move closer, *archaic or dial.* draw nigh; arrive, appear, make *or* put in an appearance, turn *or* show up, *colloq.* blow in. **3** extend, reach, stretch *or* spread (out), range, go. **5** see CHANCE *v.* 2. **9** see BECOME 1. **10 a** see SPRING *v.* 3. **b** see SPRING *v.* 4. **11** see ACT *v.* 5a. **12** climax. □ **come about 1** occur, happen, take place, *disp.* transpire, *poet.* befall. **2** *Naut.* tack, go about. **come across 1** be communicated *or* understandable, penetrate, sink in. **2** see DELIVER 5. **3** find, discover, encounter, run across *or* into, happen *or* chance upon, hit *or* light upon, stumble (up)on. **come**

again 1 see PERSEVERE. **come along 1** do, progress, move along, *literary* fare; see also *get on* 1. **2** see HURRY *v.* 1. **come apart** disintegrate, crumble, fall apart *or* to pieces, separate, break (apart *or* up). **come at 1** see REACH *v.* 4. **2** attack, assault, charge, rush (at), fly at, descend (up)on, make for, *colloq.* go for. **come-at-able** see ACCESSIBLE 1. **come away 1** see DETACH 1, BREAK[1] *v.* 1a. **2** go, go away *or* off, leave, depart. **come back 1** see RETURN *v.* 1. **4** reply, answer, respond, retort, rejoin, return. **come between 1** see INTERFERE 2. **2** see SEPARATE *v.* 1. **come by 1** pass (by), go past, move *or* proceed past. **2** see CALL *v.* 4. **3** acquire, obtain, get, procure; secure, find, take *or* get possession of, get *or* lay hold of, get *or* lay *or* put (one's) hands on; win, earn, attain. **come down 1** see DESCEND 1. **4** see FALL *v.* 8. **5** resolve, rule; see also DECIDE 1. **6** see DEPEND 1. **7** (*come down on*) punish, pounce on *or* upon, rebuke, criticize, revile, reprimand, bear down on. **8** (*come down with*) succumb to, contract, catch, be afflicted with, get, *archaic* be stricken with. **come for 2** see ATTACK *v.* 1. **come forward 1** see ADVANCE *v.* 1, 2. **come-hither** see *flirtatious* (FLIRT). **come in 1** enter, go in *or* into. **2 a** finish, end up, come, arrive. **b** win, succeeed, *colloq.* finish (in the money). **4 b** be, prove (to be), turn out (to be). **9** see INCUR. **12** arrive. **come into 2** see RECEIVE 1, 2. **come off 1** succeed; occur, happen, be accomplished, come to pass, take place. **2** turn out, emerge, result as, end up; see also FARE *v.* 1. **4** see DETACH 1. **5** see FALL *v.* 1a. **come off it** see *go on!* **come on 3** see ADVANCE *v.* 1, 2, BOOM[2] *v.* **4** start, begin. **5** see ENTER 1c. **6** appear. **7** see ARISE 3. **come-on** lure, attraction, enticement, inducement, temptation, bait. **come out 1 a** be revealed, become public *or* known *or* common knowledge, get about *or* around, get *or* leak out, emerge. **b** end, conclude, terminate, finish, turn out. **2** appear, be published *or* issued *or* produced *or* distributed, be shown, be in print, première. **3 a** see DECIDE 1. **b** come out of the closet. **4** strike, go on strike. **7** go, vanish, disappear. **11** see DISCLOSE 1. **come over 1** see JOURNEY *v.*, COME *v.* 1 above. **2** change over, change, convert, switch, shift. **3 a** see OVERTAKE 2, AFFECT[1] 2. **4** go over, come across, be received; sound, appear; be communicated. **come round 1** see VISIT *v.* 1. **2** see *come to* 1 below. **3** see *change one's mind*. **4** see RECUR. **come through 1** succeed, be successful, not fail *or* disappoint; survive, get well *or* better. **3** recover from, recuperate from. **come to 1** regain *or* recover consciousness, awake(n), revive, wake up, come round. **3** amount to, add up to, total, aggregate, (be) equal (to), mount up to, tot up to, make. **4 a** see *come to* 1 above. **5** see BECOME 1. **6** regard, concern, relate to, be a question of, involve, be relevant to, be involved. **come to hand** see APPEAR 2. **come to nothing** see FAIL *v.* 1, 2a. **come to pass** see HAPPEN *v.* 1. **come to rest** see STOP *v.* 3. **come to that** see *in fact* 1 (FACT). **come under 2** see SUBJECT *adj.* 1. **come up 1** rise, *esp. archaic & poet.* arise. **2** see PROSPER. **3** arise, surface, present itself, be brought up, be broached, crop up. **4** see APPROACH *v.* 1, 2. **6** see *think up*. **7** appear, sprout, spring up, shoot up, grow. **come up against** face, experience, meet (with), contend with, be faced with, come into contact with, wrestle with. **come upon 1** see STUMBLE *v.* 4. **how come?** why? **if it comes to that** in that case. **to come** see FORTHCOMING 1.

comeback /kúmbak/ *n.* **1** a return to a previous (esp. successful) state. **2** *sl.* a retaliation or retort. **3** *Austral.* a sheep bred from crossbred and purebred parents for both wool and meat.
■ **1** see REVIVAL 1, 3. **2** see RETORT *n.* 1, 3.

Comecon /kómmikon/ *n.* an economic association of East European countries. [abbr. of *Council for Mutual Economic Assistance*]

comedian /kəméédiən/ *n.* **1** a humorous entertainer on stage, television, etc. **2** an actor in comedy. [F *comédien* f. *comédie* COMEDY]
■ **1** comic, comedienne, humorist, wit, wag, funny man *or* woman, jokesmith.

comedienne /kəméédi-én/ *n.* a female comedian. [F fem. (as COMEDIAN)]

comedist /kómmidist/ *n.* a writer of comedies.

comedo /kómmidō/ *n.* (*pl.* **comedones** /-dṓneez/) *Med.* a blackhead. [L, = glutton f. *comedere* eat up]
■ see SPOT *n.* 1c.

comedown /kúmdown/ *n.* **1** a loss of status; decline or degradation. **2** a disappointment.

comedy /kómmidi/ *n.* (*pl.* **-ies**) **1 a** a play, film, etc., of an amusing or satirical character, usu. with a happy ending. **b** the dramatic genre consisting of works of this kind (*she excels in comedy*) (cf. TRAGEDY). **2** an amusing or farcical incident or series of incidents in everyday life. **3** humour, esp. in a work of art etc. □ **comedy of manners** see MANNER. □□ **comedic** /kəméédik/ *adj.* [ME f. OF *comedie* f. L *comoedia* f. Gk *kōmōidia f. kōmōidos* comic poet f. *kōmos* revel]
■ **3** see HUMOUR *n.* 1.

comely /kúmli/ *adj.* (**comelier, comeliest**) (usu. of a woman) pleasant to look at. □□ **comeliness** /kúmliniss/ *n.* [ME *cumelich, cumli* prob. f. *becumelich* f. BECOME]
■ good-looking, pretty, lovely, fair, beautiful, handsome, attractive, appealing, wholesome, winsome, *Sc. & N.Engl.* bonny.

comer /kúmmər/ *n.* **1** a person who comes, esp. as an applicant, participant, etc. (*offered the job to the first comer*). **2** *colloq.* a person likely to be a success. □ **all comers** any applicants (with reference to a position, or esp. a challenge to a champion, that is unrestricted in entry).

comestible /kəméstib'l/ *n.* (usu. in *pl.*) *formal* or *joc.* food. [ME f. F f. med.L *comestibilis* f. L *comedere comest-* eat up]
■ see FOOD 1.

comet /kómmit/ *n.* a hazy object usu. with a nucleus of ice and dust surrounded by gas and with a tail pointing away from the sun, moving about the sun in an eccentric orbit. □□ **cometary** *adj.* [ME f. OF *comete* f. L *cometa* f. Gk *komētes* long-haired (star)]
■ see STAR *n.* 1.

comeuppance /kumúppənss/ *n. colloq.* one's deserved fate or punishment (*got his comeuppance*). [COME + UP + -ANCE]
■ see DESERT[3] 1b.

comfit /kúmfit/ *n. archaic* a sweet consisting of a nut, seed, etc., coated in sugar. [ME f. OF *confit* f. L *confectum* past part. of *conficere* prepare: see CONFECTION]
■ see SWEET *n.* 1.

comfort /kúmfərt/ *n.* & *v.* ● *n.* **1** consolation; relief in affliction. **2 a** a state of physical well-being; being comfortable (*live in comfort*). **b** (usu. in *pl.*) things that make life easy or pleasant (*has all the comforts*). **3** a cause of satisfaction (*a comfort to me that you are here*). **4** a person who consoles or helps one (*he's a comfort to her in her old age*). **5** *US* a warm quilt. ● *v.tr.* **1** soothe in grief; console. **2** make comfortable (*comforted by the warmth of the fire*). □ **comfort station** *US euphem.* a public lavatory. [ME f. OF *confort(er)* f. LL *confortare* strengthen (as COM-, L *fortis* strong)]
■ *n.* **1** consolation, solace, relief, cheer, help, support. **2 a** ease, luxury, security, abundance, plenty, opulence. **3** pleasure, delight, joy, treat, blessing. **4** see HELP *n.* 2. ● *v.* **1** console, solace, soothe, assuage, reassure, relieve, hearten, cheer, gladden.

comfortable /kúmftəb'l, -fərtəb'l/ *adj.* & *n.* ● *adj.* **1 a** such as to avoid hardship or trouble and give comfort or ease (*a comfortable pair of shoes*). **b** (of a person) relaxing to be with, congenial. **2** free from discomfort; at ease (*I'm quite comfortable thank you*). **3** *colloq.* having an adequate standard of living; free from financial worry. **4 a** having an easy conscience (*did not feel comfortable about refusing him*). **b** *colloq.* complacent, placidly self-satisfied. **5** with a wide margin (*a comfortable win*). ● *n. US* a warm quilt. □□ **comfortableness** *n.* **comfortably** *adv.* [ME f. AF *confortable* (as COMFORT)]

■ *adj.* **1** congenial, amiable, pleasant, agreeable, relaxing; see also SNUG *adj.* 1a, b. **2** at ease, easy; relaxed, untroubled, undisturbed. **3** see *well off* 1 (WELL[1]). **4 a** see RIGHT *adj.* 1. **b** self-satisfied, complacent, smug. **5** easy, secure; see also *assured* (ASSURE 5a).

comforter /kúmfərtər/ *n.* **1** a person who comforts. **2** a baby's dummy. **3** *archaic* a woollen scarf. **4** *US* a warm quilt. [ME f. AF *confortour*, OF *-ëor* (as COMFORT)]
■ **4** see COVER *n.* 1f.

comfortless /kúmfərtliss/ *adj.* **1** dreary, cheerless. **2** without comfort.

comfrey /kúmfri/ *n.* (*pl.* **-eys**) any of various plants of the genus *Symphytum*, esp. *S. officinale* having large hairy leaves and clusters of usu. white or purple bell-shaped flowers. [ME f. AF *cumfrie*, ult. f. L *conferva* (as COM-, *fervēre* boil)]

comfy /kúmfi/ *adj.* (**comfier, comfiest**) *colloq.* comfortable. □□ **comfily** *adv.* **comfiness** *n.* [abbr.]

comic /kómmik/ *adj.* & *n.* ● *adj.* **1** (often *attrib.*) of, or in the style of, comedy (*a comic actor*; *comic opera*). **2** causing or meant to cause laughter; funny (*comic to see his struggles*). ● *n.* **1** a professional comedian. **2 a** a children's periodical, mainly in the form of comic strips. **b** a similar publication intended for adults. □ **comic opera 1** an opera with much spoken dialogue, usu. with humorous treatment. **2** this genre of opera. **comic strip** a horizontal series of drawings in a comic, newspaper, etc., telling a story. [L *comicus* f. Gk *kōmikos* f. *kōmos* revel]
■ *adj.* **2** funny, amusing, droll, comical, comedic, humorous, hilarious, side-splitting, mirthful, jocose, jocular, witty, waggish. ● *n.* **1** see COMEDIAN. □ **comic opera** opera buffa.

comical /kómmik'l/ *adj.* funny; causing laughter. □□ **comicality** /-kálliti/ *n.* **comically** *adv.* [COMIC]

coming /kúmming/ *adj.* & *n.* ● *attrib.adj.* **1** approaching, next (*in the coming week*; *this coming Sunday*). **2** of potential importance (*a coming man*). ● *n.* arrival; approach.

Comintern /kómmintern/ *n.* the Third International (see INTERNATIONAL *n.* 2), a communist organization (1919-43). [Russ. *Komintern* f. Russ. forms of *communist, international*]

comitadji /kómmitáji/ *n.* (also **komitadji, komitaji**) a member of an irregular band of soldiers in the Balkans. [Turk. *komitacı*, lit. 'member of a (revolutionary) committee']

comity /kómmiti/ *n.* (*pl.* **-ies**) **1** courtesy, civility; considerate behaviour towards others. **2 a** an association of nations etc. for mutual benefit. **b** (in full **comity of nations**) the mutual recognition by nations of the laws and customs of others. [L *comitas* f. *comis* courteous]
■ **1** see CIVILITY 1.

comma /kómmə/ *n.* **1** a punctuation mark (,) indicating a pause between parts of a sentence, or dividing items in a list, string of figures, etc. **2** *Mus.* a definite minute interval or difference of pitch. □ **comma bacillus** a comma-shaped bacillus causing cholera. [L f. Gk *komma* clause]

command /kəmaánd/ *v.* & *n.* ● *v.tr.* **1** (also *absol.*; often foll. by *to* + infin., or *that* + clause) give formal order or instructions to (*commands us to obey*; *commands that it be done*). **2** (also *absol.*) have authority or control over. **3 a** (often *refl.*) restrain, master. **b** gain the use of; have at one's disposal or within reach (skill, resources, etc.) (*commands an extensive knowledge of history*; *commands a salary of £40,000*). **4** deserve and get (sympathy, respect, etc.). **5** *Mil.* dominate (a strategic position) from a superior height; look down over. ● *n.* **1** an authoritative order; an instruction. **2** mastery, control, possession (*a good command of languages*; *has command of the resources*). **3** the exercise or tenure of authority, esp. naval or military (*has command of this ship*). **4** *Mil.* **a** a body of troops etc. (*Bomber Command*). **b** a district under a commander (*Western Command*). **5** *Computing* **a** an instruction causing a computer to perform one of its basic functions. **b** a signal initiating such an operation. □ **at command** ready to be used at will. **at** (or **by**) **a person's command** in pursuance of a person's bidding. **command module** the control compartment in a spacecraft. **Command Paper** (in the UK) a paper laid before Parliament by command of the Crown. **command performance** (in the UK) a theatrical or film performance given by royal command. **command post** the headquarters of a military unit. **in command of** commanding; having under control. **under command of** commanded by. **word of command 1** *Mil.* an order for a movement in a drill etc. **2** a prearranged spoken signal for the start of an operation. [ME f. AF *comaunder*, OF *comander* f. LL *commandare* COMMEND]
■ *v.* **1** order, direct, enjoin, charge, request, require, demand, instruct, *archaic or literary* bid; say, prescribe, decree. **2, 5** control, dominate, wield authority *or* influence over, hold sway over; lead, rule, govern, have under one's thumb; head (up); look down on *or* over. **3 b** have, enjoy, possess; muster, draw (up)on, summon. **4** attract, earn; exact, compel, demand. ● *n.* **1** order, direction, instruction, mandate, charge, bidding, *literary* behest. **2** mastery, control, (thorough) grasp *or* knowledge, possession. **3** control, authority, power, sovereignty, dominion, regulation, direction, management, government, supervision, oversight, leadership, charge, sway, stewardship, jurisdiction. □ **at command** see *at will* 1 (WILL[2]). **in command of** (*be in command*) see *call the shots*.

commandant /kómməndánt, -daánt/ *n.* a commanding officer, esp. of a particular force, military academy, etc. □ **Commandant-in-Chief** the supreme commandant. □□ **commandantship** *n.* [F *commandant*, or It. or Sp. *commandante* (as COMMAND)]
■ see LEADER 1.

commandeer /kómməndéer/ *v.tr.* **1** seize (men or goods) for military purposes. **2** take possession of without authority. [S.Afr. Du. *kommanderen* f. F *commander* COMMAND]
■ see SEIZE 2.

commander /kəmaándər/ *n.* **1** a person who commands, esp.: **a** a naval officer next in rank below captain. **b** = *wing commander*. **2** an officer in charge of a London police district. **3** (in full **knight commander**) a member of a higher class in some orders of knighthood. **4** a large wooden mallet. □ **commander-in-chief** the supreme commander, esp. of a nation's forces. **Commander of the Faithful** a title of a Caliph. □□ **commandership** *n.* [ME f. OF *comandere*, *-eör* f. Rmc (as COMMAND)]
■ **1, 2** see MASTER *n.* 1.

commanding /kəmaánding/ *adj.* **1** dignified, exalted, impressive. **2** (of a hill or other high point) giving a wide view. **3** (of an advantage, a position, etc.) controlling; superior (*has a commanding lead*). □□ **commandingly** *adv.*
■ **1** see MAGNIFICENT 1. **2** see *panoramic* (PANORAMA). **3** see DOMINANT *adj.*

commandment /kəmaándmənt/ *n.* a divine command. □ **the Ten Commandments** the divine rules of conduct given by God to Moses on Mount Sinai, according to Exod. 20:1–17. [ME f. OF *comandement* (as COMMAND)]
■ see ORDER *n.* 2.

commando /kəmaándō/ *n.* (*pl.* **-os**) *Mil.* **1 a** a unit of British amphibious shock troops. **b** a member of such a unit. **c** a similar unit or member of such a unit elsewhere. **2 a** a party of men called out for military service. **b** a body of troops. **3** (*attrib.*) of or concerning a commando (*a commando operation*). [Port. f. *commandar* COMMAND]

comme ci, comme ça /komsée komsaá/ *adv.* & *adj.* so so; middling or middlingly. [F, = like this, like that]
■ see *so so adj.* (SO[1]).

commedia dell'arte /komáydiə delaártay/ *n.* an improvised kind of popular comedy in Italian theatres in the 16th–18th c., based on stock characters. [It., = comedy of art]

comme il faut /kóm eel fṓ/ *adj.* & *adv.* ● *predic.adj.* (esp. of behaviour, etiquette, etc.) proper, correct. ● *adv.* properly, correctly. [F, = as is necessary]
■ *adj.* see PROPER *adj.* 2.

commemorate /kəmémmərayt/ *v.tr.* **1** celebrate in speech or writing. **2 a** preserve in memory by some celebration. **b** (of a stone, plaque, etc.) be a memorial of. □□ **commemorative** /-rətiv/ *adj.* **commemorator** *n.* [L *commemorare* (as COM-, *memorare* relate f. *memor* mindful)]
■ **1** see CELEBRATE 1. **2** memorialize, remember, celebrate, observe; reverence, revere, honour, venerate, pay tribute *or* homage to, salute, solemnize, sanctify, hallow; immortalize.

commemoration /kəmémməráysh'n/ *n.* **1** an act of commemorating. **2** a service or part of a service in memory of a person, an event, etc. [ME f. F *commemoration* or L *commemoratio* (as COMMEMORATE)]

commence /kəménss/ *v.tr.* & *intr. formal* begin. [ME f. OF *com(m)encier* f. Rmc (as COM-, L *initiare* INITIATE)]
■ begin, enter upon, start, open, initiate, launch, inaugurate, embark on *or* upon.

commencement /kəménsmənt/ *n. formal* **1** a beginning. **2** esp. *US* a ceremony of degree conferment. [ME f. OF (as COMMENCE)]

commend /kəménd/ *v.tr.* **1** (often foll. by *to*) entrust, commit (*commends his soul to God*). **2** praise (*commends her singing voice*). **3** recommend (*method commends itself*). □ **commend me to** *archaic* remember me kindly to. **highly commended** (of a competitor etc.) just missing the top places. [ME f. L *commendare* (as COM-, *mendare* = *mandare* entrust: see MANDATE)]
■ **1** see TRUST *v.* 4. **2** see PRAISE *v.* 1. **3** see RECOMMEND 1b, SUGGEST 1.

commendable /kəméndəb'l/ *adj.* praiseworthy. □□ **commendably** *adv.* [ME f. OF f. L *commendabilis* (as COMMEND)]
■ see PRAISEWORTHY.

commendation /kómmendáysh'n/ *n.* **1** an act of commending or recommending (esp. a person to another's favour). **2** praise. [ME f. OF f. L *commendatio* (as COMMEND)]
■ **1** see *recommendation* (RECOMMEND). **2** see PRAISE *n.*

commendatory /kəméndətəri/ *adj.* commending, recommending. [LL *commendatorius* (as COMMEND)]
■ see COMPLIMENTARY 1.

commensal /kəméns'l/ *adj.* & *n.* ● *adj.* **1** *Biol.* of, relating to, or exhibiting commensalism. **2** (of a person) eating at the same table as another. ● *n.* **1** *Biol.* a commensal organism. **2** one who eats at the same table as another. □□ **commensality** /kómmənsálliti/ *n.* [ME f. F *commensal* or med.L *commensalis* (in sense 2) (as COM-, *mensa* table)]

commensalism /kəménsəliz'm/ *n. Biol.* an association between two organisms in which one benefits and the other derives no benefit or harm.

commensurable /kəménshərəb'l, -syoorəb'l/ *adj.* **1** (often foll. by *with*, *to*) measurable by the same standard. **2** (foll. by *to*) proportionate to. **3** *Math.* (of numbers) in a ratio equal to the ratio of integers. □□ **commensurability** /-bílliti/ *n.* **commensurably** *adv.* [LL *commensurabilis* (as COM-, MEASURE)]

commensurate /kəménshərət, -syoorət/ *adj.* **1** (usu. foll. by *with*) having the same size, duration, etc.; coextensive. **2** (often foll. by *to*, *with*) proportionate. □□ **commensurately** *adv.* [LL *commensuratus* (as COM-, MEASURE)]
■ **1** see EQUAL *adj.* 1, 3, 4. **2** see PROPORTIONAL *adj.*

comment /kómment/ *n.* & *v.* ● *n.* **1 a** a remark, esp. critical; an opinion (*passed a comment on her hat*). **b** commenting; criticism (*his behaviour aroused much comment*; *an hour of news and comment*). **2 a** an explanatory note (e.g. on a written text). **b** written criticism or explanation (e.g. of a text). **3** (of a play, book, etc.) a critical illustration; a parable (*his art is a comment on society*). ● *v.intr.* **1** (often foll. by *on*, *upon*, or *that* + clause) make (esp. critical) remarks (*commented on her choice of friends*). **2** (often foll. by *on*, *upon*) write explanatory notes. □ **no comment** *colloq.* I decline to answer your question. □□ **commenter** *n.* [ME f. L *commentum* contrivance (in LL also = interpretation), neut. past part. of *comminisci* devise, or F *commenter* (v.)]
■ *n.* **1** opinion, remark, view, observation, reaction; animadversion, criticism. **2 a** remark, reference, note, annotation, exposition, explanation, elucidation, clarification, footnote. **3** statement, judgment; see also CRITICISM 2. ● *v.* **1** remark, observe, opine, say; (*comment on* or *about*) discuss, talk about, remark on. **2** (*comment on* or *upon*) annotate.

commentary /kómməntəri, -tri/ *n.* (*pl.* **-ies**) **1** a set of explanatory or critical notes on a text etc. **2** a descriptive spoken account (esp. on radio or television) of an event or a performance as it happens. [L *commentarius*, *-ium* adj. used as noun (as COMMENT)]
■ **1** see EXPLANATION 1. **2** see DESCRIPTION 1b.

commentate /kómməntayt/ *v.intr. disp.* act as a commentator. [back-form. f. COMMENTATOR]

commentator /kómməntaytər/ *n.* **1** a person who provides a commentary on an event etc. **2** the writer of a commentary. **3** a person who writes or speaks on current events. [L f. *commentari* frequent. of *comminisci* devise]
■ **1, 3** see JOURNALIST.

commerce /kómmerss/ *n.* **1** financial transactions, esp. the buying and selling of merchandise, on a large scale. **2** social intercourse (*the daily commerce of gossip and opinion*). **3** *archaic* sexual intercourse. [F *commerce* or L *commercium* (as COM-, *mercium* f. *merx mercis* merchandise)]
■ **1** business, marketing; see also TRADE *n.* 1a, b. **2** see INTERCOURSE. **3** see *sexual intercourse*.

commercial /kəmérsh'l/ *adj.* & *n.* ● *adj.* **1** of, engaged in, or concerned with, commerce. **2** having profit as a primary aim rather than artistic etc. value; philistine. **3** (of chemicals) supplied in bulk more or less unpurified. ● *n.* **1** a television or radio advertisement. **2** *archaic* a commercial traveller. □ **commercial art** art used in advertising, selling, etc. **commercial broadcasting** television or radio broadcasting in which programmes are financed by advertisements. **commercial traveller** a firm's travelling salesman or saleswoman who visits shops to get orders. **commercial vehicle** a vehicle used for carrying goods or fare-paying passengers. □□ **commercialism** *n.* **commerciality** /-shiálliti/ *n.* **commercially** *adv.*
■ *adj.* **1** see ECONOMIC 1. **2** see PHILISTINE *adj.* ● *n.* **1** see ADVERTISEMENT 1. □ **commercial traveller** see REPRESENTATIVE *n.* 2b.

commercialize /kəmérshəlīz/ *v.tr.* (also **-ise**) **1** exploit or spoil for the purpose of gaining profit. **2** make commercial. □□ **commercialization** /-záysh'n/ *n.*

commère /kómmair/ *n. Brit.* a female compère. [F, fem. of COMPÈRE]

Commie /kómmi/ *n. sl. derog.* a Communist. [abbr.]

commination /kómmináysh'n/ *n.* **1** the threatening of divine vengeance. **2 a** the recital of divine threats against sinners in the Anglican Liturgy for Ash Wednesday. **b** the service that includes this. [ME f. L *comminatio* f. *comminari* threaten]
■ **1** see THREAT 1a.

comminatory /kómminətəri/ *adj.* threatening, denunciatory. [med.L *comminatorius* (as COMMINATION)]
■ see *threatening* (THREATEN).

commingle /kəmíngg'l/ *v.tr.* & *intr. literary* mingle together.

comminute /kómminyoot/ *v.tr.* **1** reduce to small fragments. **2** divide (property) into small portions. □ **comminuted fracture** a fracture producing multiple bone splinters. □□ **comminution** /-nyoosh'n/ *n.* [L *comminuere comminut-* (as COM-, *minuere* lessen)]
■ **1** see PULVERIZE 1, 2.

commis /kómmi, kómmiss/ *n.* (*pl.* **commis** /kómmi, kómmiz/) a junior waiter or chef. [orig. = deputy, clerk, f. F, past part. of *commettre* entrust (as COMMIT)]

commiserate /kəmízzərayt/ *v.* **1** *intr.* (usu. foll. by *with*) express or feel pity. **2** *tr. archaic* express or feel pity for (*commiserate you on your loss*). □□ **commiseration** /-ráysh'n/ *n.* **commiserative** /-rətiv/ *adj.* **commiserator**

n. [L *commiserari* (as COM-, *miserari* pity f. *miser* wretched)]
■ see SYMPATHIZE 1.

commissar /kómmisaar/ *n. hist.* **1** an official of the former Soviet Communist Party responsible for political education and organization. **2** the head of a government department in the former USSR before 1946. [Russ. *komissar* f. F *commissaire* (as COMMISSARY)]

commissariat /kómmisáiriət, -sárriat/ *n.* **1** esp. *Mil.* **a** a department for the supply of food etc. **b** the food supplied. **2** *hist.* a government department of the former USSR before 1946. [F *commissariat* & med.L *commissariatus* (as COMMISSARY)]

commissary /kómmisəri, kəmíss-/ *n.* (*pl.* **-ies**) **1** a deputy or delegate. **2** a representative or deputy of a bishop. **3** *Mil.* an officer responsible for the supply of food etc. to soldiers. **4** *US* **a** a restaurant in a film studio etc. **b** the food supplied. **5** *US Mil.* a store for the supply of food etc. to soldiers. □□ **commissarial** /-sáiriəl/ *adj.* **commissaryship** *n.* [ME f. med.L *commissarius* person in charge (as COMMIT)]

commission /kəmísh'n/ *n.* & *v.* ● *n.* **1 a** the authority to perform a task or certain duties. **b** a person or group entrusted esp. by a government with such authority (*set up a commission to look into it*). **c** an instruction, command, or duty given to such a group or person (*their commission was to simplify the procedure*; *my commission was to find him*). **2** an order for something, esp. a work of art, to be produced specially. **3** *Mil.* **a** a warrant conferring the rank of officer in the army, navy, or air force. **b** the rank so conferred. **4 a** the authority to act as agent for a company etc. in trade. **b** a percentage paid to the agent from the profits of goods etc. sold, or business obtained (*his wages are low, but he gets 20 per cent commission*). **c** the pay of a commissioned agent. **5** the act of committing (a crime, sin, etc.). **6** the office or department of a commissioner. ● *v.tr.* **1** authorize or empower by a commission. **2 a** give (an artist etc.) a commission for a piece of work. **b** order (a work) to be written (*commissioned a new concerto*). **3** *Naut.* **a** give (an officer) the command of a ship. **b** prepare (a ship) for active service. **4** bring (a machine, equipment, etc.) into operation. □ **commission-agent** a bookmaker. **commission of the peace 1** Justices of the Peace. **2** the authority given to them. **in commission** (of a warship etc.) manned, armed, and ready for service. **out of commission** (esp. of a ship) not in service, not in working order. **Royal Commission 1** a commission of inquiry appointed by the Crown at the instance of the Government. **2** a committee so appointed. [ME f. OF f. L *commissio -onis* (as COMMIT)]
■ *n.* **1 b** see COMMITTEE. **2** see ORDER *n.* 6. **4 b** see CUT *n.* 9. **6** see OFFICE 2, 3, 7. ● *v.* **1** see AUTHORIZE 2. **2** see ORDER *v.* 3. □ **out of commission** see *out of order* 1 (ORDER).

commissionaire /kəmíshənáir/ *n.* esp. *Brit.* a uniformed door-attendant at a theatre, cinema, etc. [F (as COMMISSIONER)]

commissioner /kəmíshənər/ *n.* **1** a person appointed by a commission to perform a specific task, e.g. the head of the London police, a delegate to the General Assembly of the Church of Scotland, etc. **2** a person appointed as a member of a government commission (*Charity Commissioner*; *Civil Service Commissioner*). **3** a representative of the supreme authority in a district, department, etc. □ **Commissioner for Oaths** a solicitor authorized to administer an oath to a person making an affidavit. **Lord** (or **Lord High**) **Commissioner** the representative of the Crown at the General Assembly of the Church of Scotland. [ME f. med.L *commissionarius* (as COMMISSION)]
■ see OFFICER *n.* 1, 3, 4.

commissure /kómmisyoor/ *n.* **1** a junction, joint, or seam. **2** *Anat.* **a** the joint between two bones. **b** a band of nerve tissue connecting the hemispheres of the brain, the two sides of the spinal cord, etc. **c** the line where the upper and lower lips, or eyelids, meet. **3** *Bot.* any of several joints etc. between different parts of a plant. □□ **commissural** /-syoórəl/ *adj.* [ME f. L *commissura* junction (as COMMIT)]

commit /kəmít/ *v.tr.* (**committed, committing**) **1** (usu. foll. by *to*) entrust or consign for: **a** safe keeping (*I commit him to your care*). **b** treatment, usu. destruction (*committed the book to the flames*). **c** official custody as a criminal or as insane (*you could be committed for such behaviour*). **2** perpetrate, do (esp. a crime, sin, or blunder). **3** pledge, involve, or bind (esp. oneself) to a certain course or policy (*does not like committing herself*; *committed by the vow he had made*). **4** (as **committed** *adj.*) (often foll. by *to*) **a** morally dedicated or politically aligned (*a committed Christian*; *committed to the cause*; *a committed socialist*). **b** obliged (to take certain action) (*felt committed to staying there*). **5** *Polit.* refer (a bill etc.) to a committee. □ **commit to memory** memorize. **commit to prison** consign officially to custody, esp. on remand. □□ **committable** *adj.* **committer** *n.* [ME f. L *committere* join, entrust (as COM-, *mittere miss-* send)]
■ **1 a** entrust, consign, transfer, assign, delegate, hand over, deliver, give; allot, pledge, allocate. **c** sentence, confine, shut up, intern, put away, imprison, commit to prison, incarcerate, *Brit.* send down, *US* send up. **2** do, perform, carry out; see also PERPETRATE. **3** (*commit oneself*) pledge, promise, covenant, agree, assure, swear, give one's word, vow, engage, undertake, guarantee, bind oneself. **4 a** (**committed**) see DEVOTED. **5** see REFER 3. □ **commit to prison** see COMMIT 1c above.

commitment /kəmítmənt/ *n.* **1** an engagement or (esp. financial) obligation that restricts freedom of action. **2** the process or an instance of committing oneself; a pledge or undertaking. **3** dedication, application.
■ **1** see BOND *n.* 2b. **2** see UNDERTAKING 2. **3** see APPLICATION 4.

committal /kəmítt'l/ *n.* **1** the act of committing a person to an institution, esp. prison or a mental hospital. **2** the burial of a dead body.

committee /kəmítti/ *n.* **1 a** a body of persons appointed for a specific function by, and usu. out of, a larger body. **b** such a body appointed by Parliament etc. to consider the details of proposed legislation. **c** (**Committee**) *Brit.* the whole House of Commons when sitting as a committee. **2** /kómmitée/ *Law* a person entrusted with the charge of another person or another person's property. □ **committee-man** (*pl.* **-men**; *fem.* **committee-woman**, *pl.* **-women**) a member of a committee, esp. a habitual member of committees. **committee stage** *Brit.* the third of five stages of a bill's progress through Parliament when it may be considered in detail and amendments made. **select committee** a small parliamentary committee appointed for a special purpose. **standing committee** a committee that is permanent during the existence of the appointing body. [COMMIT + -EE]
■ **1** council, board, cabinet, panel, body, commission, working party.

commix /kəmíks/ *v.tr.* & *intr. archaic* or *poet.* mix. □□ **commixture** *n.* [ME: back-form. f. *commixt* past part. f. L *commixtus* (as COM-, MIXED)]

Commo /kómmō/ *n.* (*pl.* **-os**) chiefly *Austral.* & *NZ sl.* a Communist. [abbr.]

commode /kəmṓd/ *n.* **1** a chest of drawers. **2** (also **night-commode**) **a** a bedside table with a cupboard containing a chamber-pot. **b** a chamber-pot concealed in a chair with a hinged cover. **3** = CHIFFONIER. [F, adj. (as noun) f. L *commodus* convenient (as COM-, *modus* measure)]
■ **1** see CHEST OF DRAWERS. **2** see CHAMBER-POT.

commodious /kəmṓdiəss/ *adj.* **1** roomy and comfortable. **2** *archaic* convenient. □□ **commodiously** *adv.* **commodiousness** *n.* [F *commodieux* or f. med.L *commodiosus* f. L *commodus* (as COMMODE)]
■ **1** see ROOMY. **2** see CONVENIENT 1.

commodity /kəmódditi/ *n.* (*pl.* **-ies**) **1** *Commerce* an article or raw material that can be bought and sold, esp. a product as opposed to a service. **2** a useful thing. [ME f. OF *commodité* or f. L *commoditas* (as COMMODE)]
■ **1** see PRODUCT 1. **2** see THING 2, 3.

commodore /kómmədor/ *n.* **1** a naval officer above a captain and below a rear-admiral. **2** the commander of a squadron or other division of a fleet. **3** the president of a yacht-club. **4** the senior captain of a shipping line. □ **Commodore-in-Chief** the supreme officer in the air force. [prob. f. Du. *komandeur* f. F *commandeur* COMMANDER]

common /kómmən/ *adj.* & *n.* ● *adj.* (**commoner, commonest**) **1 a** occurring often (*a common mistake*). **b** occurring too frequently, overused, trite. **c** ordinary; of ordinary qualities; without special rank or position (*no common mind*; *common soldier*; *the common people*). **2 a** shared by, coming from, or done by, more than one (*common knowledge*; *by common consent*; *our common benefit*). **b** belonging to, open to, or affecting, the whole community or the public (*common land*). **3** *derog.* low-class; vulgar; inferior (*a common little man*). **4** of the most familiar type (*common cold*; *common nightshade*). **5** *Math.* belonging to two or more quantities (*common denominator*; *common factor*). **6** *Gram.* (of gender) referring to individuals of either sex (e.g. *teacher*). **7** *Prosody* (of a syllable) that may be either short or long. **8** *Mus.* having two or four beats, esp. four crotchets, in a bar. **9** *Law* (of a crime) of lesser importance (cf. GRAND, PETTY). ● *n.* **1** a piece of open public land, esp. in a village or town. **2** *sl.* = *common sense* (*use your common*). **3** *Eccl.* a service used for each of a group of occasions. **4** (in full **right of common**) *Law* a person's right over another's land, e.g. for pasturage. □ **common carrier** a person or firm undertaking to transport any goods or person in a specified category. **common chord** *Mus.* any note with its major or minor third and perfect fifth. **common crier** see CRIER. **common denominator** see DENOMINATOR. **Common Era** the Christian era. **common ground** a point or argument accepted by both sides in a dispute. **common jury** a jury with members of no particular social standing (cf. *special jury*). **common law** law derived from custom and judicial precedent rather than statutes (cf. *case-law* (see CASE[1]), *statute law*). **common-law husband** (or **wife**) a partner in a marriage recognized by common law, esp. after a period of cohabitation. **Common Market** the European Economic Community. **common metre** a hymn stanza of four lines with 8, 6, 8, and 6 syllables. **common noun** (or **name**) *Gram.* a name denoting a class of objects or a concept as opposed to a particular individual (e.g. *boy*, *chocolate*, *beauty*). **common or garden** *colloq.* ordinary. **Common Prayer** the Church of England liturgy orig. set forth in the *Book of Common Prayer* of Edward VI (1549). **common-room 1** a room in some colleges, schools, etc., which members may use for relaxation or work. **2** the members who use this. **common salt** see SALT. **common seal** the official seal of a corporate body. **common sense** sound practical sense, esp. in everyday matters. **Common Serjeant** see SERJEANT. **common soldier** see SOLDIER. **common stock** *US* = *ordinary shares*. **common weal** public welfare. **common year** see YEAR 2. **in common 1** in joint use; shared. **2** of joint interest (*have little in common*). **in common with** in the same way as. **least** (or **lowest**) **common denominator, multiple** see DENOMINATOR, MULTIPLE. **out of the common** unusual. □□ **commonly** *adv.* **commonness** *n.* [ME f. OF *comun* f. L *communis*]

■ *adj.* **1 a** frequent, usual, familiar, customary, prevalent. **b** trite, stale, hackneyed, worn out, banal, tired, overused, clichéd, stereotypic(al). **c** ordinary, everyday, commonplace, prosaic, run-of-the-mill, general, normal, standard, conventional, regular, routine, stock, average, mediocre, middling, plain, simple, workaday, undistinguished, unexceptional, *colloq.* common or garden. **2** public, general, community, communal, collective, non-private; well-known; universal, joint, shared, *colloq. disp.* mutual. **3** low-class, inferior, low-grade, mean, cheap, vulgar, base, ordinary, plain, simple, plebeian, bourgeois, proletarian, vulgar, unrefined. **4** familiar, commonplace, plain, simple, *colloq.* common or garden; see also FAMILIAR 1. □ **common or garden** see ORDINARY *adj.* **common sense** see GUMPTION 2. **in common with** (just) like, in the same way as. **out of the common** see UNUSUAL 2.

commonable /kómmənəb'l/ *adj.* **1** (of an animal) that may be pastured on common land. **2** (of land) that may be held in common. [obs. *common* to exercise right of common + -ABLE]

commonage /kómmənij/ *n.* **1** = *right of common* (see COMMON *n.* 4). **2 a** land held in common. **b** the state of being held in common. **3** the common people; commonalty.

commonality /kómmənálliti/ *n.* (*pl.* **-ies**) **1** the sharing of an attribute. **2** a common occurrence. **3** = COMMONALTY. [var. of COMMONALTY]

commonalty /kómmənəlti/ *n.* (*pl.* **-ies**) **1** the common people. **2** the general body (esp. of mankind). **3** a corporate body. [ME f. OF *comunalté* f. med.L *communalitas -tatis* (as COMMON)]

■ **1** see PEOPLE *n.* 2.

commoner /kómmənər/ *n.* **1** one of the common people, as opposed to the aristocracy. **2** a person who has the right of common. **3** a student at a British university who does not have a scholarship. [ME f. med.L *communarius* f. *communa* (as COMMUNE[1])]

■ **1** see PLEBEIAN *n.*

commonplace /kómmənplayss/ *adj.* & *n.* ● *adj.* lacking originality; trite. ● *n.* **1 a** an everyday saying; a platitude (*uttered a commonplace about the weather*). **b** an ordinary topic of conversation. **2** anything usual or trite. **3** a notable passage in a book etc. copied into a commonplace-book. □ **commonplace-book** a book into which notable extracts from other works are copied for personal use. □□ **commonplaceness** *n.* [transl. of L *locus communis* = Gk *koinos topos* general theme]

■ *adj.* see BANAL. ● *n.* **1 a** see TRUISM.

commons /kómmənz/ *n.pl.* **1** (**the Commons**) = *House of Commons*. **2 a** the common people. **b** (prec. by *the*) the common people regarded as a part of a political, esp. British, system. **3** provisions shared in common; daily fare. □ **short commons** insufficient food. [ME pl. of COMMON]

commonsensical /kómmənsénsik'l/ *adj.* possessing or marked by common sense. [*common sense* (see COMMON)]

■ see SENSIBLE 1, 3.

commonweal /kómmənweel/ *n. archaic* **1** = *common weal*. **2** = COMMONWEALTH.

commonwealth /kómmənwelth/ *n.* **1 a** an independent State or community, esp. a democratic republic. **b** such a community or organization of shared interests in a non-political field (*the commonwealth of learning*). **2** (**the Commonwealth**) **a** (in full **the British Commonwealth of Nations**) an international association consisting of the UK together with States that were previously part of the British Empire. **b** the republican period of government in Britain 1649–60. **c** *US* a part of the title of Puerto Rico and some of the States of the US. **d** the title of the federated Australian States. □ **Commonwealth Day** a day each year commemorating the British Commonwealth (formerly called *Empire Day*). [COMMON + WEALTH]

commotion /kəmṓsh'n/ *n.* **1 a** a confused and noisy disturbance or outburst. **b** loud and confusing noise. **2** a civil insurrection. [ME f. OF *commotion* or L *commotio* (as COM-, MOTION)]

■ **1** see NOISE 1, 2. **2** see DISORDER *n.* 2.

communal /kómyoon'l/ *adj.* **1** relating to or benefiting a community; for common use (*communal baths*). **2** of a commune, esp. the Paris Commune. □□ **communality** /-nálliti/ *n.* **communally** *adv.* [F f. LL *communalis* (as COMMUNE[1])]

■ **1** see COMMON *adj.* 2.

communalism /kómyoonəliz'm/ *n.* **1** a principle of political organization based on federated communes. **2** the principle of communal ownership etc. □□ **communalist** *n.* **communalistic** /-lístik/ *adj.*

communalize /kómyoonəlīz/ *v.tr.* (also **-ise**) make communal. □□ **communalization** /-záysh'n/ *n.*

communard /kómyoonaard/ *n.* **1** a member of a commune. **2** (also **Communard**) *hist.* a supporter of the Paris Commune. [F (as COMMUNE¹)]

commune¹ /kómyoon/ *n.* **1 a** a group of people, not necessarily related, sharing living accommodation, goods, etc., esp. as a political act. **b** a communal settlement esp. for the pursuit of shared interests. **2 a** the smallest French territorial division for administrative purposes. **b** a similar division elsewhere. **3** (**the Commune**) the communalistic government in Paris in 1871. [F f. med.L *communia* neut. pl. of L *communis* common]

commune² /kəmyóon/ *v.intr.* **1** (usu. foll. by *with*) **a** speak confidentially and intimately (*communed together about their loss; communed with his heart*). **b** feel in close touch (with nature etc.) (*communed with the hills*). **2** *US* receive Holy Communion. [ME f. OF *comuner* share f. *comun* COMMON]
■ **2** communicate.

communicable /kəmyóonikəb'l/ *adj.* **1** (esp. of a disease) able to be passed on. **2** *archaic* communicative. □□ **communicability** /-bílliti/ *n.* **communicably** *adv.* [ME f. OF *communicable* or LL *communicabilis* (as COMMUNICATE)]
■ **1** see INFECTIOUS 2, 3.

communicant /kəmyóonikənt/ *n.* **1** a person who receives Holy Communion, esp. regularly. **2** a person who imparts information. [L *communicare communicant-* (as COMMON)]

communicate /kəmyóonikayt/ *v.* **1** *tr.* **a** transmit or pass on by speaking or writing (*communicated his ideas*). **b** transmit (heat, motion, etc.). **c** pass on (an infectious illness). **d** impart (feelings etc.) non-verbally (*communicated his affection*). **2** *intr.* (often foll. by *with*) be in communication; succeed in conveying information, evoking understanding etc. (*he communicates well*). **3** *intr.* (often foll. by *with*) share a feeling or understanding; relate socially. **4** *intr.* (often foll. by *with*) (of a room etc.) have a common door (*my room communicates with yours*). **5 a** *tr.* administer Holy Communion to. **b** *intr.* receive Holy Communion. □□ **communicator** *n.* **communicatory** *adj.* [L *communicare communicat-* (as COMMON)]
■ **1 a** make known, impart, confer, transmit, transfer, hand on *or* down, share, pass on *or* along, get *or* put across, make understandable, send on, spread; tell, divulge, disclose, reveal, announce, promulgate, proffer, tender, offer, convey, present. **2** be in communication, converse, talk, correspond, associate, be in contact *or* touch; get through, make oneself understood. **3** be of one mind, be in tune, relate, be in rapport, be *en rapport*, *colloq.* be on the same wavelength.

communication /kəmyóonikáysh'n/ *n.* **1 a** the act of imparting, esp. news. **b** an instance of this. **c** the information etc. communicated. **2** a means of connecting different places, such as a door, passage, road, or railway. **3** social intercourse (*it was difficult to maintain communication in the uproar*). **4** (in *pl.*) the science and practice of transmitting information esp. by electronic or mechanical means. **5** (in *pl.*) *Mil.* the means of transport between a base and the front. **6** a paper read to a learned society. □ **communication cord** *Brit.* a cord or chain in a railway carriage that may be pulled to stop the train in an emergency. **communication** (or **communications**) **satellite** an artificial satellite used to relay telephone circuits or broadcast programmes. **communication theory** the study of the principles and methods by which information is conveyed.
■ **1** see INFORMATION 1, 3. **4** (*communications*) see TRANSMISSION 1.

communicative /kəmyóonikətiv/ *adj.* **1** open, talkative, informative. **2** ready to communicate. □□ **communicatively** *adv.* [LL *communicativus* (as COMMUNICATE)]
■ **1** see TALKATIVE. **2** see RESPONSIVE.

communion /kəmyóoniən/ *n.* **1** a sharing, esp. of thoughts etc.; fellowship (*their minds were in communion*). **2** participation; a sharing in common (*communion of interests*). **3** (**Communion, Holy Communion**) **a** the Eucharist. **b** participation in the Communion service. **c** (*attrib.*) of or used in the Communion service (*Communion-table; Communion-cloth; Communion-rail*). **4** fellowship, esp. between branches of the Catholic Church. **5** a body or group within the Christian faith (*the Methodist communion*). □ **communion of saints** fellowship between Christians living and dead. [ME f. OF *communion* or L *communio* f. *communis* common]

communiqué /kəmyóonikay/ *n.* an official communication, esp. a news report. [F, = communicated]
■ see BULLETIN 1.

communism /kómyooniz'm/ *n.* **1** a political theory derived from Marx, advocating class war and leading to a society in which all property is publicly owned and each person is paid and works according to his or her needs and abilities. **2** (usu. **Communism**) **a** the communistic form of society established in the former USSR and elsewhere. **b** any movement or political doctrine advocating communism. **3** = COMMUNALISM. [F *communisme* f. *commun* COMMON]

communist /kómyoonist/ *n.* & *adj.* ● *n.* **1** a person advocating or practising communism. **2** (**Communist**) a member of a Communist Party. ● *adj.* of or relating to communism (*a communist play*). □□ **communistic** /-nístik/ *adj.* [COMMUNISM]
■ *n.* **1** see *left winger* (LEFT¹). ● *adj.* see LEFT¹ *adj.* 3.

communitarian /kəmyóonitáiriən/ *n.* & *adj.* ● *n.* a member of a communistic community. ● *adj.* of or relating to such a community. [COMMUNITY + -ARIAN after *unitarian* etc.]

community /kəmyóoniti/ *n.* (*pl.* **-ies**) **1 a** all the people living in a specific locality. **b** a specific locality, including its inhabitants. **2** a body of people having a religion, a profession, etc., in common (*the immigrant community*). **3** fellowship of interests etc.; similarity (*community of intellect*). **4** a monastic, socialistic, etc. body practising common ownership. **5** joint ownership or liability (*community of goods*). **6** (prec. by *the*) the public. **7** a body of nations unified by common interests. **8** *Ecol.* a group of animals or plants living or growing together in the same area. □ **community centre** a place providing social etc. facilities for a neighbourhood. **community charge** *hist.* (in the UK) a local tax on every adult in a community. **community chest** *US* a fund for charity and welfare work in a community. **community home** *Brit.* a centre for housing young offenders and other juveniles in need of custodial care. **community service order** an order for a convicted offender to perform a period of unpaid work in the community. **community singing** singing by a large crowd or group, esp. of old popular songs or hymns. **community spirit** a feeling of belonging to a community, expressed in mutual support etc. [ME f. OF *comuneté* f. L *communitas -tatis* (as COMMON)]
■ **1 b** see DISTRICT *n.* **2** see BROTHERHOOD 2. **6** see PUBLIC *n.* 1. □ **community home** see REFORM SCHOOL.

communize /kómyoonīz/ *v.tr.* (also **-ise**) **1** make (land etc.) common property. **2** make (a person etc.) communistic. □□ **communization** /-záysh'n/ *n.* [L *communis* COMMON]

commutable /kəmyóotəb'l/ *adj.* **1** convertible into money; exchangeable. **2** *Law* (of a punishment) able to be commuted. **3** within commuting distance. □□ **commutability** /-bílliti/ *n.* [L *commutabilis* (as COMMUTE)]

commutate /kómyootayt/ *v.tr. Electr.* **1** regulate the direction of (an alternating current), esp. to make it a direct current. **2** reverse the direction (of an electric current). [L *commutare commutat-* (as COMMUTE)]

commutation /kómyootáysh'n/ *n.* **1** the act or process of commuting or being commuted (in legal and exchange senses). **2** *Electr.* the act or process of commutating or being commutated. **3** *Math.* the reversal of the order of two quantities. □ **commutation ticket** *US* a season ticket. [F *commutation* or L *commutatio* (as COMMUTE)]

commutative /kəmyóotətiv/ *adj.* **1** relating to or involving substitution. **2** *Math.* unchanged in result by the interchange of the order of quantities. [F *commutatif* or med.L *commutativus* (as COMMUTE)]

commutator /kómyootaytər/ *n.* **1** *Electr.* a device for reversing electric current. **2** an attachment connected with the armature of a dynamo which directs and makes continuous the current produced.

commute /kəmyóot/ *v.* **1** *intr.* travel to and from one's daily work, usu. in a city, esp. by car or train. **2** *tr. Law* (usu. foll. by *to*) change (a judicial sentence etc.) to another less severe. **3** *tr.* (often foll. by *into, for*) **a** change (one kind of payment) for another. **b** make a payment etc. to change (an obligation etc.) for another. **4** *tr.* **a** exchange; interchange (two things). **b** change (to another thing). **5** *tr. Electr.* commutate. **6** *intr. Math.* have a commutative relation. **7** *intr. US* buy and use a season ticket. [L *commutare commutat-* (as COM-, *mutare* change)]
■ **1** see TRAVEL *v.* 1. **2** see REPRIEVE *v.* **3, 4** see TRANSPOSE.

commuter /kəmyóotər/ *n.* a person who travels some distance to work, esp. in a city, usu. by car or train.

comose /kómōss/ *adj. Bot.* (of seeds etc.) having hairs, downy. [L *comosus* (as COMA²)]
■ see HAIRY 1.

comp /komp/ *n.* & *v. colloq.* ● *n.* **1** a competition. **2** *Printing* a compositor. **3** *Mus.* an accompaniment. ● *v.* **1** *Mus.* **a** *tr.* accompany. **b** *intr.* play an accompaniment. **2** *Printing* **a** *intr.* work as a compositor. **b** *tr.* work as a compositor on. [abbr.]

compact¹ *adj., v.,* & *n.* ● *adj.* /kəmpákt/ **1** closely or neatly packed together. **2** (of a piece of equipment, a room, etc.) well-fitted and practical though small. **3** (of style etc.) condensed; brief. **4** (esp. of the human body) small but well-proportioned. **5** (foll. by *of*) composed or made up of. ● *v.tr.* /kəmpákt/ **1** join or press firmly together. **2** condense. **3** (usu. foll. by *of*) compose; make up. ● *n.* /kómpakt/ **1** a small, flat, usu. decorated, case for face-powder, a mirror, etc. **2** an object formed by compacting powder. **3** *US* a medium-sized motor car. □ **compact disc** /kómpakt/ a disc on which information or sound is recorded digitally and reproduced by reflection of laser light. □□ **compaction** *n.* **compactly** *adv.* **compactness** *n.* **compactor** *n.* [ME f. L *compingere compact-* (as COM-, *pangere* fasten)]
■ *adj.* **1** packed, compacted, closely-knit, condensed, consolidated, compressed; dense, solid, firm, tight, thick. **3** condensed, terse, laconic, close, pithy, succinct, concise, brief, compendious, epigrammatic, aphoristic. ● *v.* **1, 2** compress, condense, squash (together), squeeze *or* push *or* press together.

compact² /kómpakt/ *n.* an agreement or contract between two or more parties. [L *compactum* f. *compacisci compact-* (as COM-, *pacisci* covenant): cf. PACT]

compages /kəmpáyjeez/ *n.* (*pl.* same) **1** a framework; a complex structure. **2** something resembling a compages in complexity etc. [L *compages* (as COM-, *pages* f. *pangere* fasten)]

companion¹ /kəmpányən/ *n.* & *v.* ● *n.* **1 a** (often foll. by *in, of*) a person who accompanies, associates with, or shares with, another (*a companion in adversity; they were close companions*). **b** a person, esp. an unmarried or widowed woman, employed to live with and assist another. **2** a handbook or reference book on a particular subject (*A Companion to North Wales*). **3** a thing that matches another (*the companion of this book-end is over there*). **4** (**Companion**) a member of the lowest grade of some orders of knighthood (*Companion of the Bath*). **5** *Astron.* a star etc. that accompanies another. **6** equipment or a piece of equipment that combines several uses. ● *v.* **1** *tr.* accompany. **2** *intr. literary* (often foll. by *with*) be a companion. □ **companion in arms** a fellow-soldier. **Companion of Honour** (in the UK) a member of an order founded in 1917. **Companion of Literature** (in the UK) a member of an order founded in 1961. **companion-set** a set of fireside implements on a stand. [ME f. OF *compaignon* ult. f. L *panis* bread]
■ *n.* **1 a** fellow, associate, comrade, colleague, confrère, brother, mate, *colloq.* pal, chum, *esp. US colloq.* buddy. **2** vade-mecum, manual, handbook, guide, reference book, *formal* enchiridion. **3** complement, counterpart, match, fellow. ● *v.* see ACCOMPANY 1.

companion² /kəmpányən/ *n. Naut.* **1** a raised frame on a quarterdeck used for lighting the cabins etc. below. **2** = *companion-way*. □ **companion-hatch** a wooden covering over a companion-way. **companion hatchway** an opening in a deck leading to a cabin. **companion ladder** a ladder from a deck to a cabin. **companion-way** a staircase to a cabin. [obs. Du. *kompanje* quarterdeck f. OF *compagne* f. It. (*camera della*) *compagna* pantry, prob. ult. rel. to COMPANION¹]

companionable /kəmpányənəb'l/ *adj.* agreeable as a companion; sociable. □□ **companionableness** *n.* **companionably** *adv.*
■ see SOCIABLE *adj.*

companionate /kəmpányənit/ *adj.* **1** well-suited; (of clothes) matching. **2** of or like a companion.

companionship /kəmpányənship/ *n.* good fellowship; friendship.
■ fellowship, friendship, camaraderie, comradeship, company, society, amity, fraternity, *Austral.* mateship.

company /kúmpəni/ *n.* & *v.* ● *n.* (*pl.* **-ies**) **1 a** a number of people assembled; a crowd; an audience (*addressed the company*). **b** guests or a guest (*am expecting company*). **2** a state of being a companion or fellow; companionship, esp. of a specific kind (*enjoys low company; do not care for his company*). **3 a** a commercial business. **b** (usu. **Co.**) the partner or partners not named in the title of a firm (*Smith and Co.*). **4** a troupe of actors or entertainers. **5** *Mil.* a subdivision of an infantry battalion usu. commanded by a major or a captain. **6** a group of Guides. ● *v.* (**-ies, -ied**) **1** *tr. archaic* accompany. **2** *intr. literary* (often foll. by *with*) be a companion. □ **company officer** a captain or a lower commissioned officer. **company sergeant-major** see SERGEANT. **err** (or **be**) **in good company** discover that one's companions, or better people, have done the same as oneself. **good** (or **bad**) **company 1** a pleasant (or dull) companion. **2** a suitable (or unsuitable) associate or group of friends. **in company** not alone. **in company with** together with. **keep company** (often foll. by *with*) associate habitually. **keep** (*archaic* **bear**) **a person company** accompany a person; be sociable. **part company** (often foll. by *with*) cease to associate. **ship's company** the entire crew. [ME f. AF *compainie*, OF *compai(g)nie* f. Rmc (as COMPANION¹)]
■ *n.* **1 a** assemblage, party, audience, band, group, circle, assembly, gathering, convention, body, crowd, throng; troop, followers, following, retinue, entourage, suite, train. **b** guest(s), visitor(s), caller(s). **2** companionship, society, fellowship; attendance, presence. **3 a** firm, business, house, concern, institution, establishment, enterprise; partnership, corporation. **4** troupe, cast, ensemble, players, actors and actresses, performers. ● *v.* see ACCOMPANY 1.

comparable /kómpərəb'l, *disp.* kəmpárrəb'l/ *adj.* **1** (often foll. by *with*) able to be compared. **2** (often foll. by *to*) fit to be compared; worth comparing. ¶ Use with *to* and *with* corresponds to the senses at *compare*; *to* is more common. □□ **comparability** /-bílliti/ *n.* **comparableness** *n.* **comparably** *adv.* [ME f. OF f. L *comparabilis* (as COMPARE)]

comparative /kəmpárrətiv/ *adj.* & *n.* ● *adj.* **1** perceptible by comparison; relative (*in comparative comfort*). **2** estimated by comparison (*the comparative merits of the two ideas*). **3** of or involving comparison (esp. of sciences etc.). **4** *Gram.* (of an adjective or adverb) expressing a higher degree of a quality, but not the highest possible (e.g. *braver, more fiercely*) (cf. POSITIVE, SUPERLATIVE). ● *n. Gram.* **1** the comparative expression or form of an adjective or adverb. **2** a word in the comparative. □□ **comparatively** *adv.* [ME f. L *comparativus* (as COMPARE)]

comparator /kəmpárrətər/ *n. Engin.* a device for comparing a product, an output, etc., with a standard, esp. an electronic circuit comparing two signals.

compare /kəmpáir/ *v.* & *n.* ● *v.* **1** *tr.* (usu. foll. by *to*) express similarities in; liken (*compared the landscape to a* *painting*). **2** *tr.* (often foll. by *to, with*) estimate the similarity or dissimilarity of; assess the relation between (*compared radio with television; that lacks quality compared to this*). ¶ In current use *to* and *with* are generally interchangeable, but *with* often implies a greater element of formal analysis, as in *compared my account with yours*. **3** *intr.* (often foll. by *with*) bear comparison (*compares favourably with the rest*). **4** *intr.* (often foll. by *with*) be equal or equivalent to. **5** *tr. Gram.* form the comparative and superlative degrees of (an adjective or an adverb). ● *n. literary* comparison (*beyond compare; without compare; has no compare*). □ **compare notes** exchange ideas or opinions. [ME f. OF *comparer* f. L *comparare* (as COM-, *parare* f. *par* equal)]

■ *v.* **1** liken, associate, make (an) analogy of *or* between, analogize. **2** contrast, weigh up, juxtapose, set side by side, relate, correlate. **3, 4** (*compare with*) resemble, be *or* look like, be on a par with, be in the same class with, correspond, match, parallel, approach, approximate (to), bear *or* merit comparison with; rival, compete with *or* against, be a match for. ● *n.* see COMPARISON 3, MATCH[1] *n.* 2a, b.

comparison /kəmpárris'n/ *n.* **1** the act or an instance of comparing. **2** a simile or semantic illustration. **3** capacity for being likened; similarity (*there's no comparison*). **4** (in full **degrees of comparison**) *Gram.* the positive, comparative, and superlative forms of adjectives and adverbs. □ **bear** (or **stand**) **comparison** (often foll. by *with*) be able to be compared favourably. **beyond comparison 1** totally different in quality. **2** greatly superior; excellent. **in comparison with** compared to. [ME f. OF *comparesoun* f. L *comparatio -onis* (as COMPARE)]

■ **1** contrasting, contrast, juxtaposing, juxtaposition, balance, weighing up, likening. **3** match, similarity, resemblance, likeness, comparability, relation, relationship, commensurability, kinship, point of agreement *or* correspondence, *literary* compare. □ **bear** (or **stand**) **comparison** see COMPARE *v.* 3, 4. **beyond comparison 1** see *poles apart* (POLE[2]). **2** see *peerless* (PEER[2]). **in comparison with** compared to *or* with, beside, in contrast with, against, over against.

compartment /kəmpaártmənt/ *n.* & *v.* ● *n.* **1** a space within a larger space, separated from the rest by partitions, e.g. in a railway carriage, wallet, desk, etc. **2** *Naut.* a watertight division of a ship. **3** an area of activity etc. kept apart from others in a person's mind. ● *v.tr.* put into compartments. □□ **compartmentation** /-táysh'n/ *n.* [F *compartiment* f. It. *compartimento* f. LL *compartiri* (as COM-, *partiri* share)]

■ *n.* **1** division, section, partition, part, space, chamber, bay, alcove, cell, pigeon-hole, locker, cubby-hole, cubby, niche, cubicle, slot. **3** see AREA 4. ● *v.* compartmentalize, separate; see also DIVIDE *v.* 1, 3a.

compartmental /kómpaartmént'l/ *adj.* consisting of or relating to compartments or a compartment. □□ **compartmentally** *adv.*

compartmentalize /kómpaartméntəlīz/ *v.tr.* (also **-ise**) divide into compartments or categories. □□ **compartmentalization** /-záysh'n/ *n.*

■ see DIVIDE *v.* 1, 3a.

compass /kúmpəss/ *n.* & *v.* ● *n.* **1** (in full **magnetic compass**) an instrument showing the direction of magnetic north and bearings from it. **2** (usu. in *pl.*) an instrument for taking measurements and describing circles, with two arms connected at one end by a movable joint. **3** a circumference or boundary. **4** area, extent; scope (e.g. of knowledge or experience) (*beyond my compass*). **5** the range of tones of a voice or a musical instrument. ● *v.tr. literary* **1** hem in. **2** grasp mentally. **3** contrive, accomplish. **4** go round. □ **compass card** a circular rotating card showing the 32 principal bearings, forming the indicator of a magnetic compass. **compass rose** a circle of the principal directions marked on a chart. **compass-saw** a saw with a narrow blade, for cutting curves. **compass window** a bay window with a semi-circular curve. □□ **compassable** *adj.* [ME f. OF *compas* ult. f. L *passus* PACE[1]]

■ *n.* **3** see BOUNDARY. **4** see SCOPE[1].

compassion /kəmpásh'n/ *n.* pity inclining one to help or be merciful. □ **compassion fatigue** indifference to human suffering, esp. as a result of overexposure to charitable appeals. [ME f. OF f. eccl.L *compassio -onis* f. *compati* (as COM-, *pati pass-* suffer)]

■ see PITY *n.* 1.

compassionate /kəmpáshənət/ *adj.* sympathetic, pitying. □ **compassionate leave** *Brit.* leave granted on grounds of bereavement etc. □□ **compassionately** *adv.* [obs. F *compassioné* f. *compassioner* feel pity (as COMPASSION)]

■ see SYMPATHETIC *adj.* 1.

compatible /kəmpáttəb'l/ *adj.* **1** (often foll. by *with*) **a** able to coexist; well-suited; mutually tolerant (*a compatible couple*). **b** consistent (*their views are not compatible with their actions*). **2** (of equipment, machinery, etc.) capable of being used in combination. □□ **compatibility** /-bílliti/ *n.* **compatibly** *adv.* [F f. med.L *compatibilis* (as COMPASSION)]

■ **1 a** well-matched, well-suited. **b** see CONSISTENT 1.

compatriot /kəmpátriət/ *n.* a fellow-countryman. □□ **compatriotic** /-rióttik/ *adj.* [F *compatriote* f. LL *compatriota* (as COM-, *patriota* PATRIOT)]

compeer /kómpeer, -péer/ *n.* **1** an equal, a peer. **2** a comrade. [ME f. OF *comper* (as COM-, PEER[2])]

■ **1** see PEER[2] *n.* 2. **2** see FRIEND *n.* 1.

compel /kəmpél/ *v.tr.* (**compelled, compelling**) **1** (usu. foll. by *to* + infin.) force, constrain (*compelled them to admit it*). **2** bring about (an action) by force (*compel submission*). **3** (as **compelling** *adj.*) rousing strong interest, attention, conviction, or admiration. **4** *archaic* drive forcibly. □□ **compellable** *adj.* **compellingly** *adv.* [ME f. L *compellere compuls-* (as COM-, *pellere* drive)]

■ **1, 2, 4** see FORCE[1] *v.* 1. **3** (**compelling**) see INTERESTING.

compendious /kəmpéndiəss/ *adj.* (esp. of a book etc.) comprehensive but fairly brief. □□ **compendiously** *adv.* **compendiousness** *n.* [ME f. OF *compendieux* f. L *compendiosus* brief (as COMPENDIUM)]

■ see CONCISE.

compendium /kəmpéndiəm/ *n.* (*pl.* **compendiums** or **compendia** /-diə/) **1** esp. *Brit.* a usu. one-volume handbook or encyclopedia. **2 a** a summary or abstract of a larger work. **b** an abridgement. **3 a** a collection of games in a box. **b** any collection or mixture. **4** a package of writing paper, envelopes, etc. [L, = what is weighed together, f. *compendere* (as COM-, *pendere* weigh)]

■ **2 a** see SUMMARY *n.* **b** see ABRIDGEMENT 1a.

compensate /kómpensayt/ *v.* **1** *tr.* (often foll. by *for*) recompense (a person) (*compensated him for his loss*). **2** *intr.* (usu. foll. by *for* a thing, *to* a person) make amends (*compensated for the insult; will compensate to her in full*). **3** *tr.* counterbalance. **4** *tr. Mech.* provide (a pendulum etc.) with extra or less weight etc. to neutralize the effects of temperature etc. **5** *intr. Psychol.* offset a disability or frustration by development in another direction. □□ **compensative** /-pénsətiv, -saytiv/ *adj.* **compensator** *n.* **compensatory** /-pénsətəri, -sáytəri/ *adj.* [L *compensare* (as COM-, *pensare* frequent. of *pendere pens-* weigh)]

■ **1** recompense, make restitution *or* reparation to, repay, indemnify, repay, reimburse, requite. **2** atone, make amends; (*compensate for*) expiate, offset, make up for, make good, make restitution *or* reparation for, redress. **3** counterbalance, balance, counterpoise, equalize, neutralize, even (up), offset. □□ **compensative, compensatory** restitutive, restitutory, expiatory, reparative, reparatory, compensational, *formal* piacular.

compensation /kómpensáysh'n/ *n.* **1 a** the act of compensating. **b** the process of being compensated. **2** something, esp. money, given as a recompense. **3** *Psychol.* **a** an act of compensating. **b** the result of compensating. **4** *US* a salary or wages. □ **compensation pendulum** *Physics* a pendulum designed to neutralize the effects of temperature variation. □□ **compensational** *adj.* [ME f. OF f. L *compensatio* (as COMPENSATE)]

■ **1, 2** see RESTITUTION 2. **4** see SALARY *n.*

compère /kómpair/ *n.* & *v. Brit.* ● *n.* a person who introduces and links the artistes in a variety show etc.; a master of ceremonies. ● *v.* **1** *tr.* act as a compère to. **2** *intr.* act as compère. [F, = godfather f. Rmc (as COM-, L *pater* father)]
■ *n.* see HOST² *n.* 5. ● *v.* see PRESENT² *v.* 3b.

compete /kəmpeét/ *v.intr.* **1** (often foll. by *with*, *against* a person, *for* a thing) strive for superiority or supremacy (*competed with his brother; compete against the Russians; compete for the victory*). **2** (often foll. by *in*) take part (in a contest etc.) (*competed in the hurdles*). [L *competere competit-*, in late sense 'strive after or contend for (something)' (as COM-, *petere* seek)]
■ **1** contend, vie, struggle, strive; fight, battle, fence, *hist.* joust.

competence /kómpit'nss/ *n.* (also **competency** /kómpitənsi/) **1** (often foll. by *for*, or *to* + infin.) ability; the state of being competent. **2** an income large enough to live on, usu. unearned. **3** *Law* the legal capacity (of a court, a magistrate, etc.) to deal with a matter.
■ **1** see *proficiency* (PROFICIENT).

competent /kómpit'nt/ *adj.* **1 a** (usu. foll. by *to* + infin. or *for*) properly qualified or skilled (*not competent to drive*); adequately capable, satisfactory. **b** effective (*a competent batsman*). **2** *Law* (of a judge, court, or witness) legally qualified or qualifying. □□ **competently** *adv.* [ME f. OF *competent* or L *competent-* (as COMPETE)]
■ **1 a** qualified, skilled, fit, capable; adequate, suitable, sufficient, satisfactory, acceptable, all right, *colloq.* OK. **b** see PROFICIENT *adj.*

competition /kómpətish'n/ *n.* **1** (often foll. by *for*) competing, esp. in an examination, in trade, etc. **2** an event or contest in which people compete. **3 a** the people competing against a person. **b** the opposition they represent. [LL *competitio* rivalry (as COMPETITIVE)]
■ **1** contention, striving, struggle; see also RIVALRY. **2** contest, match, meet, game, tournament, event, championship. **3** see COMPETITOR.

competitive /kəmpéttitiv/ *adj.* **1** involving, offered for, or by competition (*competitive contest*). **2** (of prices etc.) low enough to compare well with those of rival traders. **3** (of a person) having a strong urge to win; keen to compete. □□ **competitively** *adv.* **competitiveness** *n.* [*competit-*, past part. stem of L *competere* COMPETE]

competitor /kəmpéttitər/ *n.* a person who competes; a rival, esp. in business or commerce. [F *compétiteur* or L *competitor* (as COMPETE)]
■ rival, opponent, adversary, antagonist; contestant, contender; (*competitors*) competition, opposition.

compilation /kómpiláysh'n/ *n.* **1 a** the act of compiling. **b** the process of being compiled. **2** something compiled, esp. a book etc. composed of separate articles, stories, etc. [ME f. OF f. L *compilatio -onis* (as COMPILE)]

compile /kəmpíl/ *v.tr.* **1 a** collect (material) into a list, volume, etc. **b** make up (a volume etc.) from such material. **2** accumulate (a large number of) (*compiled a score of 160*). **3** *Computing* produce (a machine-coded form of a high-level program). [ME f. OF *compiler* or its apparent source, L *compilare* plunder, plagiarize]
■ **1** collect, put together, gather, accumulate, assemble, amass, collate, organize, order, systematize; anthologize, compose. **2** see AMASS.

compiler /kəmpílər/ *n.* **1** *Computing* a program for translating a high-level programming language into machine code. **2** a person who compiles.
■ **2** see EDITOR 3.

complacency /kəmpláysənsi/ *n.* (also **complacence**) **1** smug self-satisfaction. **2** tranquil pleasure. [med.L *complacentia* f. L *complacēre* (as COM-, *placēre* please)]

complacent /kəmpláys'nt/ *adj.* **1** smugly self-satisfied. **2** calmly content. ¶ Often confused with *complaisant*. □□ **complacently** *adv.* [L *complacēre*: see COMPLACENCY]
■ **1** see SMUG.

complain /kəmpláyn/ *v.intr.* **1** (often foll. by *about*, *at*, or *that* + clause) express dissatisfaction (*complained at the state of the room; is always complaining*). **2** (foll. by *of*) **a** announce that one is suffering from (an ailment) (*complained of a headache*). **b** state a grievance concerning (*complained of the delay*). **3** make a mournful sound; groan, creak under a strain. □□ **complainer** *n.* **complainingly** *adv.* [ME f. OF *complaindre* (stem *complaign-*) f. med.L *complangere* bewail (as COM-, *plangere planct-* lament)]
■ **1, 2b** grumble, moan, groan, wail, carp, whimper, cry, squawk, kick, *colloq.* gripe, grouch, grouse, whinge, bitch, *sl.* beef, chew the fat *or* rag. **3** see GROAN *v.* 1.

complainant /kəmpláynənt/ *n. Law* a plaintiff in certain lawsuits.

complaint /kəmpláynt/ *n.* **1** an act of complaining. **2** a grievance. **3** an ailment or illness. **4** *US Law* the plaintiff's case in a civil action. [ME f. OF *complainte* f. *complaint* past part. of *complaindre*: see COMPLAIN]
■ **1** moan (and groan). **2** grumble, grievance, squawk, *colloq.* gripe, grouse, *sl.* beef(s) . **3** see AILMENT.

complaisant /kəmpláyz'nt/ *adj.* **1** politely deferential. **2** willing to please; acquiescent. ¶ Often confused with *complacent*. □□ **complaisance** *n.* [F f. *complaire* (stem *complais-*) acquiesce to please, f. L *complacēre*: see COMPLACENCY]
■ **1** see PASSIVE 2. **2** see ACCOMMODATING.

compleat *archaic* var. of COMPLETE.

complement *n.* & *v.* ● *n.* /kómplimənt/ **1 a** something that completes. **b** one of a pair, or one of two things that go together. **2** (often **full complement**) the full number needed to man a ship, fill a conveyance, etc. **3** *Gram.* a word or phrase added to a verb to complete the predicate of a sentence. **4** *Biochem.* a group of proteins in the blood capable of lysing bacteria etc. **5** *Math.* any element not belonging to a specified set or class. **6** *Geom.* the amount by which an angle is less than 90° (cf. SUPPLEMENT). ● *v.tr.* /kómpliment/ **1** complete. **2** form a complement to (*the scarf complements her dress*). □□ **complemental** /-mént'l/ *adj.* [ME f. L *complementum* (as COMPLETE)]
■ *n.* **1 a** completion, finishing touch, consummation. **b** companion, twin, fellow. **2** crew, team, company, band, outfit; quota, allowance, quorum. ● *v.* **1** complete, perfect, round out *or* off, set off, top off. **2** supplement, add to; see also ENHANCE.

complementarity /kómplimentárriti/ *n.* (*pl.* **-ies**) **1** a complementary relationship or situation. **2** *Physics* the concept that a single model may not be adequate to explain atomic systems in different experimental conditions.

complementary /kómpliméntəri, -tri/ *adj.* **1** completing; forming a complement. **2** (of two or more things) complementing each other. □ **complementary angle** either of two angles making up 90°. **complementary colour** a colour that combined with a given colour makes white or black. **complementary medicine** alternative medicine. □□ **complementarily** *adv.* **complementariness** *n.*
■ **1** see COORDINATE *adj.* 1. **2** see HARMONIOUS 2.

complete /kəmpleét/ *adj.* & *v.* ● *adj.* **1** having all its parts; entire (*the set is complete*). **2** finished (*my task is complete*). **3** of the maximum extent or degree (*a complete surprise; a complete stranger*). **4** (also **compleat** after Walton's *Compleat Angler*) *joc.* accomplished (*the complete horseman*). ● *v.tr.* **1** finish. **2 a** make whole or perfect. **b** make up the amount of (*completes the quota*). **3** fill in the answers to (a questionnaire etc.). **4** (usu. *absol.*) *Law* conclude a sale of property. □ **complete with** having (as an important accessory) (*comes complete with instructions*). □□ **completely** *adv.* **completeness** *n.* **completion** /-pleésh'n/ *n.* [ME f. OF *complet* or L *completus* past part. of *complēre* fill up]
■ *adj.* **1** entire, whole, intact, uncut, unbroken, undivided, unabridged, full, undiminished, unabated, unreduced. **2** finished, ended, concluded, over, done, accomplished, terminated; settled, executed, performed. **3** entire, total, thorough, absolute, utter, unqualified, unmixed,

unalloyed, pure, unmitigated, rank, *colloq.* blithering. **4** accomplished, perfect, consummate, exemplary, ideal, model, superior, superlative, superb, faultless, flawless. ● *v.* **1** conclude, finish (off), end, bring to an end, wrap up; accomplish, achieve, do; finalize. **2** round out, round off, perfect; crown, culminate; see also *make up* 2. **3** fill in *or* up *or US* out, answer, make out. ▫▫ **completely** entirely, fully, quite, wholly, totally, altogether, *in toto*, thoroughly, perfectly, exactly, precisely, from the word go, in full; lock, stock, and barrel; hook, line, and sinker; with all one's heart, root and branch, unqualifiedly, unconditionally, utterly, absolutely, unreservedly, clearly, expressly, explicitly, unambiguously, unequivocally, truly, categorically, flatly. **completion** conclusion, end, close, termination, culmination, finish; fulfilment, realization, accomplishment; finalization, wind-up, finishing-off, completing.

complex /kómpleks/ *n.* & *adj.* ● *n.* **1** a building, a series of rooms, a network, etc. made up of related parts (*the arts complex*). **2** *Psychol.* a related group of usu. repressed feelings or thoughts which cause abnormal behaviour or mental states (see *inferiority complex* (see OEDIPUS COMPLEX)). **3** (in general use) a preoccupation or obsession (*has a complex about punctuality*). **4** *Chem.* a compound in which molecules or ions form coordinate bonds to a metal atom or ion. ● *adj.* **1** consisting of related parts; composite. **2** complicated (*a complex problem*). **3** *Math.* containing real and imaginary parts (cf. IMAGINARY). ▫ **complex sentence** a sentence containing a subordinate clause or clauses. ▫▫ **complexity** /kəmpléksiti/ *n.* (*pl.* **-ies**). **complexly** *adv.* [F *complexe* or L *complexus* past part. of *complectere* embrace, assoc. with *complexus* plaited]
■ *n.* **3** see OBSESSION. ● *adj.* **2** see COMPLICATE 2. ▫▫ **complexity** complication, convolution; intricacy, involvement, complicatedness; inscrutability.

complexion /kəmpléksh'n/ *n.* **1** the natural colour, texture, and appearance, of the skin, esp. of the face. **2** an aspect; a character (*puts a different complexion on the matter*). ▫▫ **complexioned** *adj.* (also in *comb.*) [ME f. OF f. L *complexio -onis* (as COMPLEX): orig. = combination of supposed qualities determining the nature of a body]
■ **2** see CHARACTER *n.* 1.

complexionless /kəmplékshənliss/ *adj.* pale-skinned.

compliance /kəmplī́ənss/ *n.* **1** the act or an instance of complying; obedience to a request, command, etc. **2** *Mech.* **a** the capacity to yield under an applied force. **b** the degree of such yielding. **3** unworthy acquiescence. ▫ **in compliance with** according to (a wish, command, etc.).
■ **1** see OBEDIENCE.

compliant /kəmplī́ənt/ *adj.* disposed to comply; yielding, obedient. ▫▫ **compliantly** *adv.*
■ see OBEDIENT.

complicate /kómplikayt/ *v.tr.* & *intr.* **1** (often foll. by *with*) make or become difficult, confused, intricate, or complex. **2** (as **complicated** *adj.*) complex; intricate. ▫▫ **complicatedly** *adv.* **complicatedness** *n.* [L *complicare complicat-* (as COM-, *plicare* fold)]
■ **1** make complicated *or* complex, make involved *or* intricate, make a mess *or* muddle of; tangle, entangle, mix up, confuse, confound, muddle. **2** (**complicated**) involved, intricate, complex, elaborate; ornate, Byzantine, tangled, knotty, confused, labyrinthine.

complication /kómplikáysh'n/ *n.* **1 a** an involved or confused condition or state. **b** a complicating circumstance; a difficulty. **2** *Med.* a secondary disease or condition aggravating a previous one. [F *complication* or LL *complicatio* (as COMPLICATE)]
■ **1 a** complexity, involvement, intricacy, convolution; see also SUBTLETY 1. **b** difficulty, problem, predicament, obstacle, obstruction, snag, drawback, *disp.* dilemma.

complicity /kəmplíssiti/ *n.* partnership in a crime or wrongdoing. [*complice* (see ACCOMPLICE) + -ITY]

compliment *n.* & *v.* ● *n.* /kómplimənt/ **1 a** a spoken or written expression of praise. **b** an act or circumstance implying praise (*their success was a compliment to their efforts*). **2** (in *pl.*) **a** formal greetings, esp. as a written accompaniment to a gift etc. (*with the compliments of the management*). **b** praise (*my compliments to the cook*). ● *v.tr.* /kómpliment/ **1** (often foll. by *on*) congratulate; praise (*complimented him on his roses*). **2** (often foll. by *with*) present as a mark of courtesy (*complimented her with his attention*). ▫ **compliments of the season** greetings appropriate to the time of year, esp. Christmas. **compliments slip** a printed slip of paper sent with a gift etc., esp. from a business firm. **pay a compliment to** praise. **return the compliment 1** give a compliment in return for another. **2** retaliate or recompense in kind. [F *complimenter* f. It. *complimento* ult. f. L (as COMPLEMENT)]
■ *n.* **1** commendation, bouquet, tribute, honour. **2** (*compliments*) **a** respects, regards, good *or* best wishes, felicitations, salutations, greetings. ● *v.* **1, 2** congratulate, praise, felicitate, pay homage *or* tribute to, commend, slap on the back, laud, honour; flatter. ▫ **pay a compliment to** see PRAISE *v.* 1. **return the compliment 2** see RETALIATE 1.

complimentary /kómpliméntəri, -tri/ *adj.* **1** expressing a compliment; praising. **2** (of a ticket for a play etc.) given free of charge, esp. as a mark of favour. ▫▫ **complimentarily** *adv.*
■ **1** laudatory, laudative, congratulatory, commendatory, approving, encomiastic, panegyrical, eulogistic, flattering. **2** gratis, on the house; see also FREE *adj.* 7.

compline /kómplin, -plīn/ *n. Eccl.* **1** the last of the canonical hours of prayer. **2** the service taking place during this. [ME f. OF *complie*, fem. past part. of obs. *complir* complete, ult. f. L *complēre* fill up]

comply /kəmplī́/ *v.intr.* (**-ies, -ied**) (often foll. by *with*) act in accordance (with a wish, command, etc.) (*complied with her expectation; had no choice but to comply*). [It. *complire* f. Cat. *complir*, Sp. *cumplir* f. L *complēre* fill up]
■ agree, obey, conform, consent, acquiesce, concur, submit, yield, accede.

compo /kómpō/ *n.* & *adj.* ● *n.* (*pl.* **-os**) a composition of plaster etc., e.g. stucco. ● *adj.* = COMPOSITE. ▫ **compo rations** a large pack of food designed to last for several days. [abbr.]

component /kəmpṓnənt/ *n.* & *adj.* ● *n.* **1** a part of a larger whole, esp. part of a motor vehicle. **2** *Math.* one of two or more vectors equivalent to a given vector. ● *adj.* being part of a larger whole (*assembled the component parts*). ▫▫ **componential** /kómpənénsh'l/ *adj.* [L *componere component-* (as COM-, *ponere* put)]
■ *n.* **1** see PART *n.* 3.

comport /kəmpórt/ *v.refl. literary* conduct oneself; behave. ▫ **comport with** suit, befit. ▫▫ **comportment** *n.* [L *comportare* (as COM-, *portare* carry)]
■ see BEHAVE 1a. ▫▫ **comportment** see BEHAVIOUR 1a.

compos var. of COMPOS MENTIS.

compose /kəmpṓz/ *v.* **1 a** *tr.* construct or create (a work of art, esp. literature or music). **b** *intr.* compose music (*gave up composing in 1917*). **2** *tr.* constitute; make up (*six tribes which composed the German nation*). ¶ Preferred to *comprise* in this sense. **3** *tr.* put together to form a whole, esp. artistically; order; arrange (*composed the group for the photographer*). **4** *tr.* **a** (often *refl.*) calm; settle (*compose your expression; composed himself to wait*). **b** (as **composed** *adj.*) calm, settled. **5** *tr.* settle (a dispute etc.). **6** *tr. Printing* **a** set up (type) to form words and blocks of words. **b** set up (a manuscript etc.) in type. ▫ **composed of** made up of, consisting of (*a flock composed of sheep and goats*). ▫▫ **composedly** /-zidli/ *adv.* [F *composer*, f. L *componere* (as COM-, *ponere* put)]
■ **1 a** write, create, imagine, think up, originate, frame, formulate, make (up), devise, construct, *disp.* author; set to music, arrange. **2** constitute, form, make (up), be the constituents *or* ingredients *or* components *or* elements of. **3** see ARRANGE 1. **4 a** settle; (*compose oneself*) calm (down), quiet *or Brit.* quieten (down), pacify, control

oneself, get control of *or* over oneself. **b** (**composed**) see *collected* (COLLECT[1] *v.* 5c). **5** see SETTLE[1] 5–7, 8b. □ **composed of** consisting of *or* in, comprising, formed *or* made (up) of, constituted of.

composer /kəmpṓzər/ *n.* a person who composes (esp. music).

composite /kómpəzit, -zīt/ *adj.*, *n.*, & *v.* ● *adj.* **1** made up of various parts; blended. **2** (esp. of a synthetic building material) made up of recognizable constituents. **3** *Archit.* of the fifth classical order of architecture, consisting of elements of the Ionic and Corinthian orders. **4** *Bot.* of the plant family Compositae. ● *n.* **1** a thing made up of several parts or elements. **2** a synthetic building material. **3** *Bot.* any plant of the family Compositae, having a head of many small flowers forming one bloom, e.g. the daisy or the dandelion. **4** *Polit.* a resolution composed of two or more related resolutions. ● *v.tr. Polit.* amalgamate (two or more similar resolutions). □□ **compositely** *adv.* **compositeness** *n.* [F f. L *compositus* past part. of *componere* (as COM-, *ponere posit-* put)]
■ *adj.* **1** compound, multiform, multifaceted. ● *n.* **1** see COMPOUND[1] *n.* 1.

composition /kómpəzísh'n/ *n.* **1 a** the act of putting together; formation or construction. **b** something so composed; a mixture. **c** the constitution of such a mixture; the nature of its ingredients (*the composition is two parts oil to one part vinegar*). **2 a** a literary or musical work. **b** the act or art of producing such a work. **c** an essay, esp. written by a schoolchild. **d** an artistic arrangement (of parts of a picture, subjects for a photograph, etc.). **3** mental constitution; character (*jealousy is not in his composition*). **4** (often *attrib.*) a compound artificial substance, esp. one serving the purpose of a natural one. **5** *Printing* the setting-up of type. **6** *Gram.* the formation of words into a compound word. **7** *Law* **a** a compromise, esp. a legal agreement to pay a sum in lieu of a larger sum, or other obligation (*made a composition with his creditors*). **b** a sum paid in this way. **8** *Math.* the combination of functions in a series. □□ **compositional** *adj.* **compositionally** *adv.* [ME f. OF, f. L *compositio -onis* (as COMPOSITE)]
■ **1a, c, 2d** formation, construction, combination, make-up, structure, form, assembly, set-up, organization, layout, arrangement, configuration, shaping; balance, harmony, proportion, placement, placing. **1 b** combination, aggregate, mixture, compound, mix, formulation, composite, amalgam, alloy, *mélange*, medley. **2 a** see WORK *n.* 5. **b** creation, production, making, generation; writing; see also FORMATION 1, 2. **c** essay, article, paper, story. **3** see CHARACTER *n.* 1.

compositor /kəmpózzitər/ *n. Printing* a person who sets up type for printing. [ME f. AF *compositour* f. L *compositor* (as COMPOSITE)]
■ typesetter.

compos mentis /kómposs méntiss/ *adj.* (also ***compos***) having control of one's mind; sane. [L]
■ see SANE 1.

compossible /kəmpóssib'l/ *adj. formal* (often foll. by *with*) able to coexist. [OF f. med.L *compossibilis* (as COM-, POSSIBLE)]

compost /kómpost/ *n.* & *v.* ● *n.* **1 a** mixed manure, esp. of organic origin. **b** a loam soil or other medium with added compost, used for growing plants. **2** a mixture of ingredients (*a rich compost of lies and innuendo*). ● *v.tr.* **1** treat (soil) with compost. **2** make (manure, vegetable matter, etc.) into compost. □ **compost heap** (or **pile**) a layered structure of garden refuse, soil, etc., which decays to become compost. [ME f. OF *composte* f. L *compos(i)tum* (as COMPOSITE)]
■ *v.* **1** see FERTILIZE 1.

composure /kəmpṓzhər/ *n.* a tranquil manner; calmness. [COMPOSE + -URE]
■ see CALM *n.* 1.

compote /kómpōt, -pot/ *n.* fruit preserved or cooked in syrup. [F f. OF *composte* (as COMPOSITE)]

compound[1] *n.*, *adj.*, & *v.* ● *n.* /kómpownd/ **1** a mixture of two or more things, qualities, etc. **2** (also **compound word**) a word made up of two or more existing words. **3** *Chem.* a substance formed from two or more elements chemically united in fixed proportions. ● *adj.* /kómpownd/ **1 a** made up of several ingredients. **b** consisting of several parts. **2** combined; collective. **3** *Zool.* consisting of individual organisms. **4** *Biol.* consisting of several or many parts. ● *v.* /kəmpównd/ **1** *tr.* mix or combine (ingredients, ideas, motives, etc.) (*grief compounded with fear*). **2** *tr.* increase or complicate (difficulties etc.) (*anxiety compounded by discomfort*). **3** *tr.* make up or concoct (a composite whole). **4** *tr.* (also *absol.*) settle (a debt, dispute, etc.) by concession or special arrangement. **5** *tr. Law* **a** condone (a liability or offence) in exchange for money etc. **b** forbear from prosecuting (a felony) from private motives. **6** *intr.* (usu. foll. by *with*, *for*) *Law* come to terms with a person, for forgoing a claim etc. for an offence. **7** *tr.* combine (words or elements) into a word. □ **compound eye** an eye consisting of numerous visual units, as found in insects and crustaceans. **compound fracture** a fracture complicated by a skin wound. **compound interest** interest payable on capital and its accumulated interest (cf. *simple interest*). **compound interval** *Mus.* an interval exceeding one octave. **compound leaf** a leaf consisting of several or many leaflets. **compound sentence** a sentence with more than one subject or predicate. **compound time** *Mus.* music having more than one group of simple-time units in each bar. □□ **compoundable** /kəmpówndəb'l/ *adj.* [ME *compoun(e)* f. OF *compondre* f. L *componere* (as COM-, *ponere* put: *-d* as in *expound*)]
■ *n.* **1** composite, blend, synthesis, combination, consolidation, mixture, amalgam, alloy, mix. ● *adj.* **1** composite, multiform, multifaceted. **2** combined; collective; see also JOINT *adj.* ● *v.* **1, 7** put together, mix, blend, merge, unite, fuse; see also COMBINE *v.* 3. **2** aggravate, intensify, exacerbate, heighten, augment, add to, worsen, increase, enhance, multiply, complicate. **3** concoct, compose, formulate; see also MAKE *v.* 1.

compound[2] /kómpownd/ *n.* **1** a large open enclosure for housing workers etc., esp. miners in S. Africa. **2** an enclosure, esp. in India, China, etc., in which a factory or a house stands (cf. KAMPONG). **3** a large enclosed space in a prison or prison camp. **4** = POUND[3]. [Port. *campon* or Du. *kampong* f. Malay]

comprador /kómprədór/ *n.* (also **compradore**) **1** *hist.* a Chinese business agent of a foreign company. **2** an agent of a foreign power. [Port. *comprador* buyer f. LL *comparator* f. L *comparare* purchase]

comprehend /kómprihénd/ *v.tr.* **1** grasp mentally; understand (a person or a thing). **2** include; take in. [ME f. OF *comprehender* or L *comprehendere comprehens-* (as COM-, *prehendere* grasp)]
■ **1** understand, see, grasp, conceive, take in, apprehend, realize, fathom, perceive, discern, appreciate; see also DIGEST *v.* 2. **2** include, take in, comprise, assimilate, absorb.

comprehensible /kómprihénsib'l/ *adj.* **1** that can be understood; intelligible. **2** that can be included or contained. □□ **comprehensibility** /-bílliti/ *n.* **comprehensibly** *adv.* [F *compréhensible* or L *comprehensibilis* (as COMPREHEND)]
■ **1** see INTELLIGIBLE.

comprehension /kómprihénsh'n/ *n.* **1 a** the act or capability of understanding, esp. writing or speech. **b** an extract from a text set as an examination, with questions designed to test understanding of it. **2** inclusion. **3** *Eccl. hist.* the inclusion of Nonconformists in the Anglican Church. [F *compréhension* or L *comprehensio* (as COMPREHENSIBLE)]
■ **1 a** see UNDERSTANDING *n.* 1.

comprehensive /kómprihénsiv/ *adj.* & *n.* ● *adj.* **1** complete; including all or nearly all elements, aspects, etc. (*a comprehensive grasp of the subject*). **2** of or relating to understanding (*the comprehensive faculty*). **3** (of motor-vehicle insurance) providing complete protection. ● *n.* (in full

comprehensive school) *Brit.* a secondary school catering for children of all abilities from a given area. □□ **comprehensively** *adv.* **comprehensiveness** *n.* [F *compréhensif -ive* or LL *comprehensivus* (as COMPREHENSIBLE)]
■ *adj.* **1** (all-)inclusive, (all-)encompassing, thorough, extensive, full, exhaustive, complete, sweeping, all-embracing, wide, broad, encyclopedic. **2** cognitive; see also MENTAL *adj.* 1, 2.

compress *v.* & *n.* ● *v.tr.* /kəmpréss/ **1** squeeze together. **2** bring into a smaller space or shorter extent. ● *n.* /kómpress/ a pad of lint etc. pressed on to part of the body to relieve inflammation, stop bleeding, etc. □ **compressed air** air at more than atmospheric pressure. □□ **compressible** /kəmpréssib'l/ *adj.* **compressibility** /kəmpréssibílliti/ *n.* **compressive** /kəmpréssiv/ *adj.* [ME f. OF *compresser* or LL *compressare* frequent. of L *comprimere compress-* (as COM-, *premere* press)]
■ *v.* **1** see SQUEEZE *v.* 1. **2** see CONTRACT *v.* 1.

compression /kəmprésh'n/ *n.* **1** the act of compressing or being compressed. **2** the reduction in volume (causing an increase in pressure) of the fuel mixture in an internal-combustion engine before ignition. [F f. L *compressio* (as COMPRESS)]
■ **1** see PRESSURE *n.* 1a, b.

compressor /kəmpréssər/ *n.* an instrument or device for compressing, esp. a machine used for increasing the pressure of air or other gases.

comprise /kəmpríz/ *v.tr.* **1** include; comprehend. **2** consist of, be composed of (*the book comprises 350 pages*). **3** *disp.* make up, compose (*the essays comprise his total work*). □□ **comprisable** *adj.* [ME f. F, fem. past part. of *comprendre* COMPREHEND]
■ **1** see INCLUDE 1.

compromise /kómprəmīz/ *n.* & *v.* ● *n.* **1** the settlement of a dispute by mutual concession (*reached a compromise by bargaining*). **2** (often foll. by *between*) an intermediate state between conflicting opinions, actions, etc., reached by mutual concession or modification (*a compromise between ideals and material necessity*). ● *v.* **1 a** *intr.* settle a dispute by mutual concession (*compromised over the terms*). **b** *tr. archaic* settle (a dispute) by mutual concession. **2** *tr.* bring into disrepute or danger esp. by indiscretion or folly. □□ **compromiser** *n.* **compromisingly** *adv.* [ME f. OF *compromis* f. LL *compromissum* neut. past part. of *compromittere* (as COM-, *promittere* PROMISE)]
■ *n.* see ACCOMMODATION 2b. ● *v.* **1** see *come to terms* (TERM).

compte rendu /kónt rondyōō/ *n.* (*pl.* ***comptes rendus*** /*pronunc.* same/) a report; a review; a statement. [F]

Comptometer /komptómmitər/ *n. propr.* an early type of calculating-machine. [app. f. F *compte* COUNT[1] + -METER]

comptroller /kəntrṓlər/ *n.* a controller (used in the title of some financial officers) (*Comptroller and Auditor General*). [var. of CONTROLLER, by erron. assoc. with COUNT[1], L *computus*]

compulsion /kəmpúlsh'n/ *n.* **1** a constraint; an obligation. **2** *Psychol.* an irresistible urge to a form of behaviour, esp. against one's conscious wishes. □ **under compulsion** because one is compelled. [ME f. F f. LL *compulsio -onis* (as COMPEL)]
■ **1** see OBLIGATION 1, 3. **2** see URGE *n.* 1.

compulsive /kəmpúlsiv/ *adj.* **1** compelling. **2** resulting or acting from, or as if from, compulsion (*a compulsive gambler*). **3** *Psychol.* resulting or acting from compulsion against one's conscious wishes. **4** irresistible (*compulsive viewing*). □□ **compulsively** *adv.* **compulsiveness** *n.* [med.L *compulsivus* (as COMPEL)]
■ **1** compelling, coercive, urgent, overwhelming; compulsory, obligatory, required; see also FORCEFUL 2. **2** obsessive, unshakeable; see also INCORRIGIBLE 2. **4** irresistible, compelling, gripping; see also FORCEFUL 2.

compulsory /kəmpúlsəri/ *adj.* **1** required by law or a rule (*it is compulsory to keep dogs on leads*). **2** essential; necessary. □ **compulsory purchase** the enforced purchase of land or property by a local authority etc., for public use. □□ **compulsorily** *adv.* **compulsoriness** *n.* [med.L *compulsorius* (as COMPEL)]
■ **1** see MANDATORY *adj.* **2** see NECESSARY *adj.* 1.

compunction /kəmpúngksh'n/ *n.* (usu. with *neg.*) **1** the pricking of the conscience. **2** a slight regret; a scruple (*without compunction*; *have no compunction in refusing him*). □□ **compunctious** /-shəss/ *adj.* **compunctiously** /-shəsli/ *adv.* [ME f. OF *componction* f. eccl.L *compunctio -onis* f. L *compungere compunct-* (as COM-, *pungere* prick)]
■ **1** remorse, contrition, regret, uneasiness of mind, pang *or* pricking of conscience, self-reproach. **2** regret, second thought(s), misgiving, qualm; see also SCRUPLE *n.*

compurgation /kómpurgáysh'n/ *n. Law hist.* an acquittal from a charge or accusation obtained by the oaths of witnesses. □□ **compurgatory** /kəmpúrgətəri/ *adj.* [med.L *compurgatio* f. L *compurgare* (as COM-, *purgare* purify)]

compurgator /kómpurgaytər/ *n. Law hist.* a witness who swore to the innocence or good character of an accused person.

compute /kəmpyōōt/ *v.* **1** *tr.* (often foll. by *that* + clause) reckon or calculate (a number, an amount, etc.). **2** *intr.* make a reckoning, esp. using a computer. □□ **computability** /-pyōōtəbílliti/ *n.* **computable** /-pyōōtəb'l/ *adj.* **computation** /kómpyootáysh'n/ *n.* **computational** /kómpyootáyshən'l/ *adj.* [F *computer* or L *computare* (as COM-, *putare* reckon)]
■ **1** calculate, reckon, figure (out), work out, determine, ascertain, estimate. □□ **computation** see CALCULATION 1.

computer /kəmpyōōtər/ *n.* **1** a usu. electronic device for storing and processing data (usu. in binary form), according to instructions given to it in a variable program. **2** a person who computes or makes calculations. □ **computer-literate** able to use computers; familiar with the operation of computers. **computer science** the study of the principles and use of computers. **computer virus** a hidden code within a computer program intended to corrupt a system or destroy data stored in it.

computerize /kəmpyōōtərīz/ *v.tr.* (also **-ise**) **1** equip with a computer; install a computer in. **2** store, perform, or produce by computer. □□ **computerization** /-záysh'n/ *n.*

comrade /kómrayd, -rid/ *n.* **1** (also **comrade-in-arms**) **a** (usu. of males) a workmate, friend, or companion. **b** fellow soldier etc. **2** *Polit.* a fellow socialist or communist (often as a form of address). □□ **comradely** *adj.* **comradeship** *n.* [earlier *cama- camerade* f. F *camerade*, *camarade* (orig. fem.) f. Sp. *camarada* room-mate (as CHAMBER)]
■ **1 a** colleague, associate, friend, companion, crony, mate, confrère, *colloq.* pal, chum, *Austral.* & *NZ colloq.* cobber, *esp. US colloq.* buddy. **2** brother, sister, tovarish.

Comsat /kómsat/ *n. propr.* a communication satellite. [abbr.]

con[1] /kon/ *n.* & *v. sl.* ● *n.* a confidence trick. ● *v.tr.* (**conned, conning**) swindle; deceive (*conned him into thinking he had won*). □ **con man** = *confidence man*. [abbr.]
■ *n.* see SWINDLE *n.* 1, 3. ● *v.* see SWINDLE *v.*

con[2] /kon/ *n.*, *prep.*, & *adv.* ● *n.* (usu. in *pl.*) a reason against. ● *prep.* & *adv.* against (cf. PRO[2]). [L *contra* against]

con[3] /kon/ *n. sl.* a convict. [abbr.]
■ see CONVICT *n.*

con[4] /kon/ *v.tr.* (*US* **conn**) (**conned, conning**) *Naut.* direct the steering of (a ship). [app. weakened form of obs. *cond*, *condie*, f. F *conduire* f. L *conducere* CONDUCT]
■ see NAVIGATE 1, 5.

con[5] /kon/ *v.tr.* (**conned, conning**) *archaic* (often foll. by *over*) study, learn by heart (*conned his part well*). [ME *cunn-*, *con*, forms of CAN[1]]
■ see STUDY *v.* 2.

con- /kon, kən/ *prefix* assim. form of COM- before *c*, *d*, *f*, *g*, *j*, *n*, *q*, *s*, *t*, *v*, and sometimes before vowels.

conacre /kónnaykər/ *n. Ir.* the letting by a tenant of small portions of land prepared for crops or grazing. [CORN[1] + ACRE]

con amore /kón amóri/ *adv.* **1** with devotion or zeal. **2** (**con amore**) *Mus.* tenderly. [It., = with love]

conation /kənáysh'n/ *n. Philos.* & *Psychol.* **1** the desire to perform an action. **2** voluntary action; volition. □□ **conative** /kónnətiv, kṓ-/ *adj.* [L *conatio* f. *conari* try]

con brio /kón brée-ō/ *adv. Mus.* with vigour. [It.]

concatenate /kənkáttinayt/ *v.* & *adj.* ● *v.tr.* link together (a chain of events, things, etc.). ● *adj.* joined; linked. □□ **concatenation** /-náysh'n/ *n.* [LL *concatenare* (as COM-, *catenare* f. *catena* chain)]
■ *v.* see LINK[1] *v.* 1. □□ **concatenation** see CHAIN *n.* 3.

concave /kónkayv/ *adj.* having an outline or surface curved like the interior of a circle or sphere (cf. CONVEX). □□ **concavely** *adv.* **concavity** /-kávviti/ *n.* [L *concavus* (as COM-, *cavus* hollow), or through F *concave*]
■ see HOLLOW *adj.* 1b.

conceal /kənséel/ *v.tr.* **1** (often foll. by *from*) keep secret (*concealed her motive from him*). **2** not allow to be seen; hide (*concealed the letter in her pocket*). □□ **concealer** *n.* **concealment** *n.* [ME f. OF *conceler* f. L *concelare* (as COM-, *celare* hide)]
■ **1** keep secret *or* hidden, keep quiet about, disguise; see also HIDE[1] *v.* 3. **2** hide, secrete, bury, squirrel away, cover (up), disguise, camouflage.

concede /kənséed/ *v.tr.* **1 a** (often foll. by *that* + clause) admit (a defeat etc.) to be true (*conceded that his work was inadequate*). **b** admit defeat in. **2** (often foll. by *to*) grant, yield, or surrender (a right, a privilege, points or a start in a game, etc.). **3** *Sport* allow an opponent to score (a goal) or to win (a match), etc. □□ **conceder** *n.* [F *concéder* or L *concedere concess-* (as COM-, *cedere* yield)]
■ **1 a** admit, allow, grant, acknowledge, confess, own (up to), accept. **b** see *give up* 1. **2** grant, yield, surrender, cede, give up, submit, resign, relinquish, abandon, waive.

conceit /kənséet/ *n.* **1** personal vanity; pride. **2** *literary* **a** a far-fetched comparison, esp. as a stylistic affectation; a convoluted or unlikely metaphor. **b** a fanciful notion. [ME f. CONCEIVE after *deceit*, *deceive*, etc.]
■ **1** vanity, pride, egotism, self-admiration, self-love, narcissism, arrogance, *literary* vainglory. **2 a** elaborate figure (of speech), trope, affectation; mixed metaphor. **b** see FANCY *n.* 2.

conceited /kənséetid/ *adj.* vain, proud. □□ **conceitedly** *adv.* **conceitedness** *n.*
■ vain, egotistical, self-centred, egocentric, self-admiring, narcissistic, prideful, proud, arrogant, self-important, self-satisfied, smug, complacent, snobbish, *colloq.* stuck-up, snotty, *literary* vainglorious, *esp. Brit. sl.* toffee-nosed.

conceivable /kənséevəb'l/ *adj.* capable of being grasped or imagined; understandable. □□ **conceivability** /-bílliti/ *n.* **conceivably** *adv.*
■ see PLAUSIBLE 1.

conceive /kənséev/ *v.* **1** *intr.* become pregnant. **2** *tr.* become pregnant with (a child). **3** *tr.* (often foll. by *that* + clause) **a** imagine, fancy, think (*can't conceive that he could be guilty*). **b** (usu. in *passive*) formulate, express (a belief, a plan, etc.). □ **conceive of** form in the mind; imagine. [ME f. OF *conceiv-* stressed stem of *concevoir* f. L *concipere concept-* (as COM-, *capere* take)]
■ **3 a** conceive of, think (up), imagine, fancy, speculate (on), perceive, see, understand, realize, comprehend, envision, envisage, conjure up, dream up, hypothesize, postulate, posit, suggest, suppose. **b** see EXPRESS[1] 1, 2. □ **conceive of** see CONCEIVE 3a above.

concelebrate /kənsélllibrayt/ *v.intr. RC Ch.* **1** (of two or more priests) celebrate the mass together. **2** (esp. of a newly ordained priest) celebrate the mass with the ordaining bishop. □□ **concelebrant** /-brənt/ *n.* **concelebration** /-bráysh'n/ *n.* [L *concelebrare* (as COM-, *celebrare* CELEBRATE)]

concentrate /kónsəntrayt/ *v.* & *n.* ● *v.* **1** *intr.* (often foll. by *on*, *upon*) focus all one's attention or mental ability. **2** *tr.* bring together (troops, power, attention, etc.) to one point; focus. **3** *tr.* increase the strength of (a liquid etc.) by removing water or any other diluting agent. **4** *tr.* (as **concentrated** *adj.*) (of hate etc.) intense, strong. ● *n.* **1** a concentrated substance. **2** a concentrated form of esp. food. □□ **concentratedly** *adv.* **concentrative** *adj.* **concentrator** *n.* [after *concentre* f. F *concentrer* (as CON- + CENTRE)]
■ *v.* **1** focus; think, focus one's thoughts *or* attention, apply oneself. **2** focus, direct, centre, concentre, centralize, consolidate; gather, collect, congregate, draw *or* bring together, crowd, cluster, group. **3** condense, reduce, distil, intensify, refine, strengthen. **4** (**concentrated**) see INTENSE 1, 3. ● *n.* **1** see ESSENCE 2a.

concentration /kónsəntráysh'n/ *n.* **1 a** the act or power of concentrating (*needs to develop concentration*). **b** an instance of this (*interrupted my concentration*). **2** something concentrated (*a concentration of resources*). **3** something brought together; a gathering. **4** the weight of substance in a given weight or volume of material. □ **concentration camp** a camp for the detention of political prisoners, internees, etc., esp. in Nazi Germany.
■ **1** see THOUGHT[1] 3a. **2** see POCKET *n.* 4.

concentre /kənséntər/ *v.tr.* & *intr.* (*US* **concenter**) bring or come to a common centre. [F *concentrer*: see CONCENTRATE]

concentric /kənséntrik/ *adj.* (often foll. by *with*) (esp. of circles) having a common centre (cf. ECCENTRIC). □□ **concentrically** *adv.* **concentricity** /kónsentríssiti/ *n.* [ME f. OF *concentrique* or med.L *concentricus* (as COM-, *centricus* as CENTRE)]

concept /kónsept/ *n.* **1** a general notion; an abstract idea (*the concept of evolution*). **2** *colloq.* an idea or invention to help sell or publicize a commodity (*a new concept in swimwear*). **3** *Philos.* an idea or mental picture of a group or class of objects formed by combining all their aspects. [LL *conceptus* f. *concept-*: see CONCEIVE]
■ **1, 2** see IDEA 1, 2a, b.

conception /kənsépsh'n/ *n.* **1 a** the act or an instance of conceiving; the process of being conceived. **b** the faculty of conceiving in the mind, apprehension, imagination. **2** an idea or plan, esp. as being new or daring (*the whole conception showed originality*). □ **no conception of** an inability to imagine. □□ **conceptional** *adj.* [ME f. OF f. L *conceptio -onis* (as CONCEPT)]
■ **1** birth, beginning, genesis, inception, emergence, start, inauguration, initiation, launch, origin, origination, formation, formulation, introduction, *formal* commencement; understanding, apprehension, knowledge, appreciation, imagination, comprehension. **2** design, scheme, proposal, outline; see also IDEA 1, 2a, b, PLAN *n.* 1a.

conceptive /kənséptiv/ *adj.* **1** conceiving mentally. **2** of conception. [L *conceptivus* (as CONCEPTION)]

conceptual /kənséptyooəl/ *adj.* of mental conceptions or concepts. □□ **conceptually** *adv.* [med.L *conceptualis* (*conceptus* as CONCEPT)]
■ see ABSTRACT *adj.* 1a.

conceptualism /kənséptyooəliz'm/ *n. Philos.* the theory that universals exist, but only as concepts in the mind. □□ **conceptualist** *n.*

conceptualize /kənséptyooəlīz/ *v.tr.* (also **-ise**) form a concept or idea of. □□ **conceptualization** /-záysh'n/ *n.*
■ see IMAGINE 1.

concern /kənsérn/ *v.* & *n.* ● *v.tr.* **1 a** be relevant or important to (*this concerns you*). **b** relate to; be about. **2** (usu. *refl.*; often foll. by *with*, *in*, *about*, or *to* + infin.) interest or involve oneself (*don't concern yourself with my problems*). **3** worry, cause anxiety to (*it concerns me that he is always late*). ● *n.* **1 a** anxiety, worry (*felt a deep concern*). **b** solicitous regard; care, consideration. **2 a** a matter of interest or importance to one (*no concern of mine*). **b** (usu. in *pl.*) affairs, private business (*meddling in my concerns*). **3** a business, a firm (*quite a prosperous concern*). **4** *colloq.* a complicated or awkward thing (*have lost the whole concern*).

□ **have a concern in** have an interest or share in. **have no concern with** have nothing to do with. **to whom it may concern** to those who have a proper interest in the matter (as an address to the reader of a testimonial, reference, etc.). [F *concerner* or LL *concernere* (as COM-, *cernere* sift, discern)]

■ *v.* **1 a** be relevant to, affect, have (a) bearing *or* (an) influence on, involve, touch; interest, be of importance *or* interest to. **b** refer *or* relate to, have relation *or* reference to, be about, pertain *or* appertain to, be pertinent *or* relevant to, regard, apply to, be connected *or* involved with, bear on, be germane to, involve, touch (on). **2** see BOTHER *v.* 2. **3** worry, trouble, disturb, bother, perturb, unsettle, upset, distress. ● *n.* **1 a** anxiety, worry, solicitude, apprehension, distress, apprehensiveness, uneasiness, disquiet, disquietude. **b** interest, regard, consideration, care, thought, awareness, attention. **2 a** business, affair, problem, matter, issue; responsibility, duty, charge, task, *colloq.* thing, *sl.* bag. **b** affairs, matters, business, concerns, things. **3** business, firm, company, house, establishment, enterprise, organization.

concerned /kənsérnd/ *adj.* **1** involved, interested (*the people concerned*; *concerned with proving his innocence*). **2** (often foll. by *that*, *about*, *at*, *for*, or *to* + infin.) troubled, anxious (*concerned about him*; *concerned to hear that*). □ **as** (or **so**) **far as I am concerned** as regards my interests. **be concerned** (often foll. by *in*) take part. **I am not concerned** it is not my business. □□ **concernedly** /-sérnidli/ *adv.* **concernedness** /-sérnidniss/ *n.*

■ **1** involved, responsible, interested. **2** troubled, vexed, anxious, worried, distressed, uneasy, perturbed, bothered, upset, disturbed. □ **as** (or **so**) **far as I am concerned** as for me, for myself. **be concerned** see *take part* (PART).

concerning /kənsérning/ *prep.* about, regarding.

■ about, regarding, relative *or* relating to, referring to, with *or* in reference to, as regards, in *or* with regard to, with an eye to, with respect to, respecting, apropos (of), as to *or* for, in the matter of, on the subject of, *archaic or Sc. or US* anent, *colloq.* re.

concernment /kənsérnmənt/ *n. formal* **1** an affair or business. **2** importance. **3** (often foll. by *with*) a state of being concerned; anxiety.

concert *n.* & *v.* ● *n.* /kónsərt/ **1** a musical performance of usu. several separate compositions. **2** agreement, accordance, harmony. **3** a combination of voices or sounds. ● *v.tr.* /kənsért/ arrange (by mutual agreement or coordination). □ **concert-goer** a person who often goes to concerts. **concert grand** the largest size of grand piano, used for concerts. **concert-master** esp. *US* the leading first-violin player in some orchestras. **concert overture** *Mus.* a piece like an overture but intended for independent performance. **concert performance** *Mus.* a performance (of an opera etc.) without scenery, costumes, or action. **concert pitch 1** *Mus.* the pitch internationally agreed in 1960 whereby the A above middle C = 440 Hz. **2** a state of unusual readiness, efficiency, and keenness (for action etc.). **in concert 1** (often foll. by *with*) acting jointly and accordantly. **2** (*predic.*) (of a musician) in a performance. [F *concert* (n.), *concerter* (v.) f. It. *concertare* harmonize]

■ *n.* **1** see PERFORMANCE 2. **2** see ACCORD *n.* 1. □ **concert-master** see LEADER 2.

concerted /kənsértid/ *adj.* **1** combined together; jointly arranged or planned (*a concerted effort*). **2** *Mus.* arranged in parts for voices or instruments.

■ **1** see UNITED 2a.

concertina /kónsərteénə/ *n.* & *v.* ● *n.* a musical instrument held in the hands and stretched and squeezed like bellows, having reeds and a set of buttons at each end to control the valves. ● *v.tr.* & *intr.* (**concertinas**, **concertinaed** /-nəd/ or **concertina'd**, **concertinaing**) compress or collapse in folds like those of a concertina (*the car concertinaed into the bridge*). [CONCERT + -INA]

■ *v.* crush, squash, telescope.

concertino /kónchərteénō/ *n.* (*pl.* **-os**) *Mus.* **1** a simple or short concerto. **2** a solo instrument or solo instruments playing in a concerto. [It., dimin. of CONCERTO]

concerto /kəncháirtō, -chértō/ *n.* (*pl.* **-os** or **concerti** /-ti/) *Mus.* a composition for a solo instrument or instruments accompanied by an orchestra. □ **concerto grosso** /gróssō, grṓ-/ (*pl.* **concerti grossi** /-si/ or **concerto grossos**) a composition for a group of solo instruments accompanied by an orchestra. [It. (see CONCERT): *grosso* big]

concession /kənsésh'n/ *n.* **1 a** the act or an instance of conceding (*made the concession that we were right*). **b** a thing conceded. **2** a reduction in price for a certain category of person. **3 a** the right to use land or other property, granted esp. by a government or local authority, esp. for a specific use. **b** the right, given by a company, to sell goods, esp. in a particular territory. **c** the land or property used or given. □□ **concessionary** *adj.* (also **concessional**). [F *concession* f. L *concessio* (as CONCEDE)]

■ **1** see ADMISSION 1. **3 a, b** see PRIVILEGE *n.* 1a.

concessionaire /kənséshənáir/ *n.* (also **concessionnaire**) the holder of a concession or grant, esp. for the use of land or trading rights. [F *concessionnaire* (as CONCESSION)]

concessive /kənséssiv/ *adj.* **1** of or tending to concession. **2** *Gram.* **a** (of a preposition or conjunction) introducing a phrase or clause which might be expected to preclude the action of the main clause, but does not (e.g. *in spite of*, *although*). **b** (of a phrase or clause) introduced by a concessive preposition or conjunction. [LL *concessivus* (as CONCEDE)]

conch /kongk, konch/ *n.* (*pl.* **conchs** /kongks/ or **conches** /kónchiz/) **1 a** a thick heavy spiral shell, occasionally bearing long projections, of various marine gastropod molluscs of the family Strombidae. **b** any of these gastropods. **2** *Archit.* the domed roof of a semicircular apse. **3** = CONCHA. [L *concha* shell f. Gk *kogkhē*]

concha /kóngkə/ *n.* (*pl.* **conchae** /-kee/) *Anat.* any part resembling a shell, esp. the depression in the external ear leading to its central cavity. [L: see CONCH]

conchie /kónchi/ *n.* (also **conchy**) (*pl.* **-ies**) *sl. derog.* a conscientious objector. [abbr.]

conchoidal /kongkóyd'l/ *adj. Mineral.* (of a solid fracture etc.) resembling the surface of a bivalve shell.

conchology /kongkólləji/ *n. Zool.* the scientific study of shells. □□ **conchological** /-kəlójik'l/ *adj.* **conchologist** *n.* [Gk *kogkhē* shell + -LOGY]

conchy var. of CONCHIE.

concierge /kónsiáirzh, kón-/ *n.* (esp. in France) a door-keeper or porter of a block of flats etc. [F, prob. ult. f. L *conservus* fellow slave]

■ see PORTER[2].

conciliar /kənsílliər/ *adj.* of or concerning a council, esp. an ecclesiastical council. [med.L *consiliarius* counsellor]

conciliate /kənsílliayt/ *v.tr.* **1** make calm and amenable; pacify. **2** gain (esteem or goodwill). **3** *archaic* reconcile, make compatible. □□ **conciliative** /-sílliətiv/ *adj.* **conciliator** *n.* **conciliatory** /-sílliətəri, -tri/ *adj.* **conciliatoriness** /-sílliətəriniss, -triniss/ *n.* [L *conciliare* combine, gain (*concilium* COUNCIL)]

■ **1** see DISARM 6. □□ **conciliator** see *mediator* (MEDIATE).

conciliation /kənsílliáysh'n/ *n.* the use of conciliating measures; reconcilement. [L *conciliatio* (as CONCILIATE)]

■ see *reconciliation* (RECONCILE).

concinnity /kənsínniti/ *n.* elegance or neatness of literary style. □□ **concinnous** *adj.* [L *concinnitas* f. *concinnus* well-adjusted]

concise /kənsíss/ *adj.* (of speech, writing, style, or a person) brief but comprehensive in expression. □□ **concisely** *adv.* **conciseness** *n.* [F *concis* or L *concisus* past part. of *concidere* (as COM-, *caedere* cut)]

■ brief, terse, laconic, compact, direct, succinct, epigrammatic, cogent, pithy, compendious, summary, trenchant, compressed, condensed, short; shortened, abridged, curtailed, abbreviated.

concision /kənsízh'n/ *n.* (esp. of literary style) conciseness. [ME f. L *concisio* (as CONCISE)]
■ see BREVITY.

conclave /kónklayv/ *n.* **1** a private meeting. **2** *RC Ch.* **a** the assembly of cardinals for the election of a pope. **b** the meeting-place for a conclave. [ME f. OF f. L *conclave* lockable room (as COM-, *clavis* key)]
■ **1** see MEETING 2, 5.

conclude /kənklóod/ *v.* **1** *tr.* & *intr.* bring or come to an end. **2** *tr.* (often foll. by *from*, or *that* + clause) infer (from given premisses) (*what did you conclude?*; *concluded from the evidence that he had been mistaken*). **3** *tr.* settle, arrange (a treaty etc.). **4** *intr.* (usu. foll. by *to* + infin.) esp. *US* decide. [ME f. L *concludere* (as COM-, *claudere* shut)]
■ **1** see END *v.* 1. **2** see INFER 1. **3, 4** see SETTLE[1] 5–7, 8b.

conclusion /kənklóozh'n/ *n.* **1** a final result; a termination. **2** a judgement reached by reasoning. **3** the summing-up of an argument, article, book, etc. **4** a settling; an arrangement (*the conclusion of peace*). **5** *Logic* a proposition that is reached from given premisses; the third and last part of a syllogism. □ **in conclusion** lastly, to conclude. **try conclusions with** engage in a trial of skill etc. with. [ME f. OF *conclusion* or L *conclusio* (as CONCLUDE)]
■ **1** see RESULT *n.* 1. **2** see THINKING *n.* 1.

conclusive /kənklóossiv/ *adj.* decisive, convincing. □□ **conclusively** *adv.* **conclusiveness** *n.* [LL *conclusivus* (as CONCLUSION)]
■ see UNQUESTIONABLE.

concoct /kənkókt/ *v.tr.* **1** make by mixing ingredients (*concocted a stew*). **2** invent (a story, a lie, etc.). □□ **concocter** *n.* **concoction** /-kóksh'n/ *n.* **concoctor** *n.* [L *concoquere concoct-* (as COM-, *coquere* cook)]
■ **2** see INVENT 1.

concomitance /kənkómmit'nss/ *n.* (also **concomitancy**) **1** coexistence. **2** *Theol.* the doctrine of the coexistence of the body and blood of Christ both in the bread and in the wine of the Eucharist. [med.L *concomitantia* (as CONCOMITANT)]
■ **1** see COINCIDENCE 1.

concomitant /kənkómmit'nt/ *adj.* & *n.* ● *adj.* going together; associated (*concomitant circumstances*). ● *n.* an accompanying thing. □□ **concomitantly** *adv.* [LL *concomitari* (as COM-, *comitari* f. L *comes -mitis* companion)]
■ *adj.* see ATTENDANT *adj.* 1.

concord /kónkord/ *n.* **1** agreement or harmony between people or things. **2** a treaty. **3** *Mus.* a chord that is pleasing or satisfactory in itself. **4** *Gram.* agreement between words in gender, number, etc. [ME f. OF *concorde* f. L *concordia* f. *concors* of one mind (as COM-, *cors* f. *cor cordis* heart)]
■ **1** see AGREEMENT 1, 2. **2** see PACT.

concordance /kənkórd'nss/ *n.* **1** agreement. **2** a book containing an alphabetical list of the important words used in a book or by an author, usu. with citations of the passages concerned. [ME f. OF f. med.L *concordantia* (as CONCORDANT)]
■ **1** see AGREEMENT 1, 2. **2** see INDEX *n.* 1.

concordant /kənkórd'nt/ *adj.* **1** (often foll. by *with*) agreeing, harmonious. **2** *Mus.* in harmony. □□ **concordantly** *adv.* [ME f. OF f. L *concordare* f. *concors* (as CONCORD)]
■ **1** see HARMONIOUS 2.

concordat /kənkórdat/ *n.* an agreement, esp. between the Roman Catholic Church and a State. [F *concordat* or L *concordatum* neut. past part. of *concordare* (as CONCORDANCE)]
■ see AGREEMENT 3.

concourse /kónkorss/ *n.* **1** a crowd. **2** a coming together; a gathering (*a concourse of ideas*). **3** an open central area in a large public building, a railway station, etc. [ME f. OF *concours* f. L *concursus* (as CONCUR)]

concrescence /kənkréss'nss/ *n.* *Biol.* coalescence; growing together. □□ **concrescent** *adj.* [CON-, after *excrescence* etc.]

concrete /kónkreet/ *adj.*, *n.*, & *v.* ● *adj.* **1 a** existing in a material form; real. **b** specific, definite (*concrete evidence*; *a concrete proposal*). **2** *Gram.* (of a noun) denoting a material object as opposed to an abstract quality, state, or action. ● *n.* (often *attrib.*) a composition of gravel, sand, cement, and water, used for building. ● *v.* **1** *tr.* **a** cover with concrete. **b** embed in concrete. **2 a** *tr.* & *intr.* form into a mass; solidify. **b** *tr.* make concrete instead of abstract. □ **concrete-mixer** a machine, usu. with a revolving drum, used for mixing concrete. **concrete music** music constructed by mixing recorded sounds. **concrete poetry** poetry using unusual typographical layout to enhance the effect on the page. **in the concrete** in reality or in practice. □□ **concretely** *adv.* **concreteness** *n.* [F *concret* or L *concretus* past part. of *concrescere* (as COM-, *crescere cret-* GROW)]
■ *adj.* **1** real, actual, literal, realistic, authentic, valid, genuine, bona fide, reliable; specific, particular, definite, definitive, clear-cut, material, physical, tangible, substantial. ● *v.* **2 a** see SOLIDIFY. **b** see EMBODY 1, 3. □ **in the concrete** see *in practice* 1 (PRACTICE).

concretion /kənkréesh'n/ *n.* **1 a** a hard solid concreted mass. **b** the forming of this by coalescence. **2** *Med.* a stony mass formed within the body. **3** *Geol.* a small round mass of rock particles embedded in limestone or clay. □□ **concretionary** *adj.* [F f. L *concretio* (as CONCRETE)]
■ **1 a** see MASS *n.* 1, 2.

concretize /kónkritīz/ *v.tr.* (also **-ise**) make concrete instead of abstract. □□ **concretization** /-záysh'n/ *n.*
■ see EMBODY 1, 3.

concubinage /kənkyóobinij/ *n.* **1** the cohabitation of a man and woman not married to each other. **2** the state of being or having a concubine. [ME f. F (as CONCUBINE)]

concubine /kónkyoobīn/ *n.* **1** a woman who lives with a man as his wife. **2** (among polygamous peoples) a secondary wife. □□ **concubinary** /kənkyóobinəri/ *adj.* [ME f. OF f. L *concubina* (as COM-, *cubina* f. *cubare* lie)]
■ see WOMAN 3.

concupiscence /kənkyóopis'nss/ *n.* *formal* sexual desire. □□ **concupiscent** *adj.* [ME f. OF f. LL *concupiscentia* f. L *concupiscere* begin to desire (as COM-, inceptive f. *cupere* desire)]
■ see DESIRE *n.* 2.

concur /kənkúr/ *v.intr.* (**concurred**, **concurring**) **1** happen together; coincide. **2** (often foll. by *with*) **a** agree in opinion. **b** express agreement. **3** combine together for a cause; act in combination. [L *concurrere* (as COM-, *currere* run)]
■ **1** see AGREE 3a. **2** see AGREE 1.

concurrent /kənkúrrənt/ *adj.* **1** (often foll. by *with*) **a** existing or in operation at the same time (*served two concurrent sentences*). **b** existing or acting together. **2** *Geom.* (of three or more lines) meeting at or tending towards one point. **3** agreeing, harmonious. □□ **concurrence** *n.* **concurrently** *adv.*
■ **1** see SIMULTANEOUS.

concuss /kənkúss/ *v.tr.* **1** subject to concussion. **2** shake violently. **3** *archaic* intimidate. [L *concutere concuss-* (as COM-, *cutere* = *quatere* shake)]

concussion /kənkúsh'n/ *n.* **1** *Med.* temporary unconsciousness or incapacity due to injury to the head. **2** violent shaking; shock. [L *concussio* (as CONCUSS)]

condemn /kəndém/ *v.tr.* **1** express utter disapproval of; censure (*was condemned for his irresponsible behaviour*). **2 a** find guilty; convict. **b** (usu. foll. by *to*) sentence to (a punishment, esp. death). **c** bring about the conviction of (*his looks condemn him*). **3** pronounce (a building etc.) unfit for use or habitation. **4** (usu. foll. by *to*) doom or assign (to something unwelcome or painful) (*condemned to spending hours at the kitchen sink*). **5 a** declare (smuggled goods, property, etc.) to be forfeited. **b** pronounce incurable. □ **condemned cell** a cell for a prisoner condemned to death. □□ **condemnable** /-démnəb'l/ *adj.* **condemnation** /kóndemnáysh'n/ *n.* **condemnatory** /-démnətəri/ *adj.* [ME f. OF *condem(p)ner* f. L *condemnare* (as COM-, *damnare* DAMN)]

■ **1** censure, blame, criticize, remonstrate with *or* against, denounce, disparage, reproach, rebuke, reprove, scold, reprimand, upbraid. **2 a** convict, find guilty. **b** sentence. **4** doom, damn, destine, fate, ordain, foreordain; consign, assign.

condensate /kəndénsayt, kóndən-/ *n.* a substance produced by condensation.

condensation /kóndensáysh'n/ *n.* **1** the act of condensing. **2** any condensed material (esp. water on a cold surface). **3** an abridgement. **4** *Chem.* the combination of molecules with the elimination of water or other small molecules. □ **condensation trail** = *vapour trail.* [LL *condensatio* (as CONDENSE)]

■ **3** see ABRIDGEMENT 1a.

condense /kəndénss/ *v.* **1** *tr.* make denser or more concentrated. **2** *tr.* express in fewer words; make concise. **3** *tr.* & *intr.* reduce or be reduced from a gas or solid to a liquid. □ **condensed milk** milk thickened by evaporation and sweetened. □□ **condensable** *adj.* [F *condenser* or L *condensare* (as COM-, *densus* thick)]

■ **1, 3** see CONCENTRATE *v.* 3. **2** see ABRIDGE 1.

condenser /kəndénsər/ *n.* **1** an apparatus or vessel for condensing vapour. **2** *Electr.* = CAPACITOR. **3** a lens or system of lenses for concentrating light. **4** a person or thing that condenses.

condescend /kóndisénd/ *v.intr.* **1** (usu. foll. by *to* + infin.) be gracious enough (to do a thing) esp. while showing one's sense of dignity or superiority (*condescended to attend the meeting*). **2** (foll. by *to*) behave as if one is on equal terms with (an inferior), usu. while maintaining an attitude of superiority. **3** (as **condescending** *adj.*) patronizing; kind to inferiors. □□ **condescendingly** *adv.* [ME f. OF *condescendre* f. eccl.L *condescendere* (as COM-, DESCEND)]

■ **1** stoop, deign, vouchsafe, lower *or* humble *or* demean oneself, come down off one's high horse. **3** (**condescending**) patronizing, belittling, disdainful, contemptuous, pompous, overbearing, high-handed, imperious, snobbish, haughty, supercilious, *colloq.* snooty, snotty, *Brit. sl.* toffee-nosed.

condescension /kóndisénsh'n/ *n.* **1** a patronizing manner. **2** affability towards inferiors. [obs. F f. eccl.L *condescensio* (as CONDESCEND)]

condign /kəndín/ *adj.* (of a punishment etc.) severe and well-deserved. □□ **condignly** *adv.* [ME f. OF *condigne* f. L *condignus* (as COM-, *dignus* worthy)]

■ see JUST *adj.* 2.

condiment /kóndimənt/ *n.* a seasoning or relish for food. [ME f. L *condimentum* f. *condire* pickle]

■ see SPICE *n.* 1.

condition /kəndísh'n/ *n.* & *v.* ● *n.* **1** a stipulation; something upon the fulfilment of which something else depends. **2 a** the state of being or fitness of a person or thing (*arrived in bad condition; not in a condition to be used*). **b** an ailment or abnormality (*a heart condition*). **3** (in *pl.*) circumstances, esp. those affecting the functioning or existence of something (*working conditions are good*). **4** *archaic* social rank (*all sorts and conditions of men*). **5** *Gram.* a clause expressing a condition. **6** *US* a subject in which a student must pass an examination within a stated time to maintain a provisionally granted status. ● *v.tr.* **1 a** bring into a good or desired state or condition. **b** make fit (esp. dogs or horses). **2** teach or accustom to adopt certain habits etc. (*conditioned by society*). **3** govern, determine (*his behaviour was conditioned by his drunkenness*). **4 a** impose conditions on. **b** be essential to (*the two things condition each other*). **5** test the condition of (textiles etc.). **6** *US* subject (a student) to re-examination. □ **conditioned reflex** a reflex response to a non-natural stimulus, established by training. **in** (or **out of**) **condition** in good (or bad) condition. **in no condition to** certainly not fit to. **on condition that** with the stipulation that. [ME f. OF *condicion* (n.), *condicionner* (v.) or med.L *condicionare* f. L *condicio -onis* f. *condicere* (as COM-, *dicere* say)]

■ *n.* **1** stipulation, proviso, demand, requirement, term, qualification, contingency, requisite, prerequisite. **2 a** state, circumstance, shape; working order; fitness, form, fettle, health. **3** (*conditions*) circumstances; environment, surroundings. **4** see RANK[1] *n.* 1a. ● *v.* **1 a** ready, get *or* make ready, prepare, equip, outfit, fit (out *or* up), adapt, modify. **2** train, educate, teach; brainwash; influence, mould; accustom, inure, adapt, acclimatize, *US* acclimate; (*conditioned to*) used to. **3** see DETERMINE 3. **4 b** demand, cry out for, necessitate, need, want, call for, require. □ **in condition** fit, in good shape. **out of condition** unfit, out of shape. **on condition that** see PROVIDED *conj.*

conditional /kəndíshən'l/ *adj.* & *n.* ● *adj.* **1** (often foll. by *on*) dependent; not absolute; containing a condition or stipulation (*a conditional offer*). **2** *Gram.* (of a clause, mood, etc.) expressing a condition. ● *n. Gram.* **1** a conditional clause etc. **2** the conditional mood. □ **conditional discharge** *Law* an order made by a criminal court whereby an offender will not be sentenced for an offence unless a further offence is committed within a stated period. □□ **conditionality** /-nálliti/ *n.* **conditionally** *adv.* [ME f. OF *condicionel* or f. LL *conditionalis* (as CONDITION)]

■ *adj.* **1** see PROVISIONAL *adj.*

conditioner /kəndíshənər/ *n.* an agent that brings something into good condition, esp. a substance applied to the hair.

condo /kóndō/ *n.* (*pl.* **-os**) *US colloq.* a condominium. [abbr.]

condolatory /kəndṓlətəri/ *adj.* expressing condolence. [CONDOLE, after *consolatory* etc.]

condole /kəndṓl/ *v.intr.* (foll. by *with*) express sympathy with a person over a loss, grief, etc. ¶ Often confused with *console*. [LL *condolēre* (as COM-, *dolēre* suffer)]

■ see SYMPATHIZE 1.

condolence /kəndṓlənss/ *n.* (often in *pl.*) an expression of sympathy (*sent my condolences*).

■ see PITY *n.* 1.

condom /kóndom/ *n.* a rubber sheath worn on the penis during sexual intercourse as a contraceptive or to prevent infection. [18th c.: orig. unkn.]

condominium /kóndəmínniəm/ *n.* **1** the joint control of a State's affairs by other States. **2** *US* a building containing flats which are individually owned. [mod.L (as COM-, *dominium* DOMINION)]

condone /kəndṓn/ *v.tr.* **1** forgive or overlook (an offence or wrongdoing). **2** approve or sanction, usu. reluctantly. **3** (of an action) atone for (an offence); make up for. □□ **condonation** /kóndənáysh'n/ *n.* **condoner** *n.* [L *condonare* (as COM-, *donare* give)]

condor /kóndor/ *n.* **1** (in full **Andean condor**) a large vulture, *Vultur gryphus*, of S. America, having black plumage with a white neck ruff and a fleshy wattle on the forehead. **2** (in full **California condor**) a small vulture, *Gymnogyps californianus*, of California. [Sp. f. Quechua *cuntur*]

condottiere /kóndotiyáiri/ *n.* (*pl.* ***condottieri*** /*pronunc.* same/) *hist.* a leader or a member of a troop of mercenaries in Italy etc. [It. f. *condotto* troop under contract (*condotta*) (as CONDUCT)]

conduce /kəndyóoss/ *v.intr.* (foll. by *to*) (usu. of an event or attribute) lead or contribute to (a result). [L *conducere conduct-* (as COM-, *ducere duct-* lead)]

conducive /kəndyóossiv/ *adj.* (often foll. by *to*) contributing or helping (towards something) (*not a conducive atmosphere for negotiation; good health is conducive to happiness*).

■ see INSTRUMENTAL *adj.*

conduct *n.* & *v.* ● *n.* /kóndukt/ **1** behaviour (esp. in its moral aspect). **2** the action or manner of directing or managing (business, war, etc.). **3** *Art* mode of treatment, execution. **4** leading, guidance. ● *v.* /kəndúkt/ **1** *tr.* lead or guide (a person or persons). **2** *tr.* direct or manage (business etc.). **3** *tr.* (also *absol.*) be the conductor of (an orchestra, choir, etc.). **4** *tr.* transmit (heat, electricity, etc.) by conduction; serve as a channel for. **5** *refl.* behave (*conducted himself appropriately*). □ **conducted tour** a tour led by a guide on a fixed itinerary. **conduct sheet** a record of a person's offences and punishments. □□ **conductible** /kəndúktib'l/ *adj.* **conductibility** /kəndúktibílliti/ *n.* [ME f. L *conductus* (as COM-, *ducere duct-* lead): (v.) f. OF *conduite* past part. of *conduire*]

■ *n.* **1** behaviour, actions, demeanour, manners, deportment, attitude, *literary* comportment. **2, 4** guidance, direction, management, supervision, leadership, administration, government, running, handling, control, command, regulation, operation. ● *v.* **1** guide, escort, show, usher; see also LEAD[1] *v.* 1. **2** direct, supervise, manage, carry on, run, control, administer, regulate, operate. **4** channel, carry, transmit, convey; direct. **5** (*conduct oneself*) act, demean oneself, deport oneself, acquit oneself, *literary* comport oneself; see also BEHAVE 1a.

conductance /kəndúkt'nss/ *n. Physics* the power of a specified material to conduct electricity.

conduction /kəndúksh'n/ *n.* **1 a** the transmission of heat through a substance from a region of higher temperature to a region of lower temperature. **b** the transmission of electricity through a substance by the application of an electric field. **2** the transmission of impulses along nerves. **3** the conducting of liquid through a pipe etc. [F *conduction* or L *conductio* (as CONDUCT)]

conductive /kəndúktiv/ *adj.* having the property of conducting (esp. heat, electricity, etc.). □ **conductive education** a system of education for children and adults with motor disorders. □□ **conductively** *adv.*

conductivity /kónduktívviti/ *n.* the conducting power of a specified material.

conductor /kəndúktər/ *n.* **1** a person who directs the performance of an orchestra or choir etc. **2** (*fem.* **conductress** /-triss/) **a** a person who collects fares in a bus etc. **b** *US* an official in charge of a train. **3** *Physics* **a** a thing that conducts or transmits heat or electricity, esp. regarded in terms of its capacity to do this (*a poor conductor*). **b** = *lightning-conductor*. **4** a guide or leader. **5** a manager or director. □ **conductor rail** a rail transmitting current to an electric train etc. □□ **conductorship** *n.* [ME f. F *conducteur* f. L *conductor* (as CONDUCT)]

■ **1** maestro, *esp. US* director, *US* leader. **2 b** *Brit.* guard. **4** see GUIDE *n.* 1–3. **5** see LEADER 1.

conductus /kəndúktəss/ *n.* (*pl.* **conducti** /-tī/) a musical composition of the 12th–13th c., with Latin text. [med.L: see CONDUIT]

conduit /kóndit, -dyoo-it/ *n.* **1** a channel or pipe for conveying liquids. **2 a** a tube or trough for protecting insulated electric wires. **b** a length or stretch of this. [ME f. OF *conduit* f. med.L *conductus* CONDUCT *n.*]

■ **1** see CHANNEL[1] *n.* 5a, 6.

condyle /kóndil/ *n. Anat.* a rounded process at the end of some bones, forming an articulation with another bone. □□ **condylar** *adj.* **condyloid** *adj.* [F f. L *condylus* f. Gk *kondulos* knuckle]

cone /kōn/ *n.* & *v.* ● *n.* **1** a solid figure with a circular (or other curved) plane base, tapering to a point. **2** a thing of a similar shape, solid or hollow, e.g. as used to mark off areas of roads. **3** the dry fruit of a conifer. **4** an ice-cream cornet. **5** any of the minute cone-shaped structures in the retina. **6** a conical mountain esp. of volcanic origin. **7** (in full **cone-shell**) any marine gastropod mollusc of the family Conidae. **8** *Pottery* a ceramic pyramid, melting at a known temperature, used to indicate the temperature of a kiln. ● *v.tr.* **1** shape like a cone. **2** (foll. by *off*) *Brit.* mark off (a road etc.) with cones. [F *cône* f. L *conus* f. Gk *kōnos*]

coney var. of CONY.

confab /kónfab/ *n.* & *v. colloq.* ● *n.* = CONFABULATION (see CONFABULATE). ● *v.intr.* (**confabbed, confabbing**) = CONFABULATE. [abbr.]

confabulate /kənfábyoolayt/ *v.intr.* **1** converse, chat. **2** *Psychol.* fabricate imaginary experiences as compensation for the loss of memory. □□ **confabulation** /-láysh'n/ *n.* **confabulatory** *adj.* [L *confabulari* (as COM-, *fabulari* f. *fabula* tale)]

■ **1** see CHAT[1] *v.* □□ **confabulation** see CHAT[1] *n.* 2.

confect /kənfékt/ *v.tr. literary* make by putting together ingredients. [L *conficere confect-* put together (as COM-, *facere* make)]

confection /kənféksh'n/ *n.* **1** a dish or delicacy made with sweet ingredients. **2** mixing, compounding. **3** a fashionable or elaborate article of women's dress. □□ **confectionary** *adj.* (in sense 1). [ME f. OF f. L *confectio -onis* (as CONFECT)]

■ **1** see SWEET *n.* 1.

confectioner /kənfékshənər/ *n.* a maker or retailer of confectionery.

confectionery /kənfékshənəri, -shənri/ *n.* sweets and other confections.

■ see CANDY *n.*

confederacy /kənféddərəsi/ *n.* (*pl.* **-ies**) **1** a league or alliance, esp. of confederate States. **2** a league for an unlawful or evil purpose; a conspiracy. **3** the condition or fact of being confederate; alliance; conspiracy. [ME, AF, OF *confederacie* (as CONFEDERATE)]

■ **1, 2** see LEAGUE[1] *n.* 1, 3.

confederate *adj.*, *n.*, & *v.* ● *adj.* /kənféddərət/ esp. *Polit.* allied; joined by an agreement or treaty. ● *n.* /kənféddərət/ **1** an ally, esp. (in a bad sense) an accomplice. **2** (**Confederate**) a supporter of the Confederate States. ● *v.* /kənféddərayt/ (often foll. by *with*) **1** *tr.* bring (a person, State, or oneself) into alliance. **2** *intr.* come into alliance. □ **Confederate States** States which seceded from the US in 1860–1. [LL *confoederatus* (as COM-, FEDERATE)]

■ *n.* **1** see ACCOMPLICE. ● *v.* see ASSOCIATE *v.* 1.

confederation /kənféddəráysh'n/ *n.* **1** a union or alliance of States etc. **2** the act or an instance of confederating; the state of being confederated. [F *confédération* (as CONFEDERATE)]

■ **1** see ALLIANCE 1.

confer /kənfér/ *v.* (**conferred, conferring**) **1** *tr.* (often foll. by *on*, *upon*) grant or bestow (a title, degree, favour, etc.). **2** *intr.* (often foll. by *with*) converse, consult. □□ **conferrable** *adj.* [L *conferre* (as COM-, *ferre* bring)]

■ **1** give, grant, present, award, bestow. **2** converse, consult, talk, take counsel, communicate, parley, negotiate, have a (little) talk, (have a) chat, confabulate.

conferee /kónfəreé/ *n.* **1** a person on whom something is conferred. **2** a participant in a conference.

conference /kónfərənss/ *n.* **1** consultation, discussion. **2** a meeting for discussion, esp. a regular one held by an association or organization. **3** an annual assembly of the Methodist Church. **4** an association in commerce, sport, etc. **5** the linking of several telephones, computer terminals, etc., so that each user may communicate with the others simultaneously. □ **in conference** engaged in discussion. □□ **conferential** /kónfərénsh'l/ *adj.* [F *conférence* or med.L *conferentia* (as CONFER)]

■ **1** consultation, talk, colloquy, *US* bull session; see also DISCUSSION 1. **2** meeting, convention, symposium, congress, seminar, forum, colloquium. **4** see ASSOCIATION 1.

conferment /kənférmənt/ *n.* **1** the conferring of a degree, honour, etc. **2** an instance of this.

conferral /kənférəl/ *n.* esp. *US* = CONFERMENT.

confess /kənféss/ *v.* **1 a** *tr.* (also *absol.*) acknowledge or admit (a fault, wrongdoing, etc.). **b** *intr.* (foll. by *to*) admit to (*confessed to having lied*). **2** *tr.* admit reluctantly (*confessed it would be difficult*). **3 a** *tr.* (also *absol.*) declare (one's sins) to a priest. **b** *tr.* (of a priest) hear the confession of. **c** *refl.* declare one's sins to a priest. [ME f. OF *confesser* f. Rmc f. L *confessus* past part. of *confitēri* (as COM-, *fatēri* declare, avow)]

■ **1 a** acknowledge, admit, own (up to), declare, confirm, concede, affirm, testify, avow, make a clean breast of; disclose, reveal, divulge, *formal* aver. **b** see *come clean* (CLEAN).

confessant /kənféss'nt/ *n.* a person who confesses to a priest.

confessedly /kənféssidli/ *adv.* by one's own or general admission.

confession /kənfésh'n/ *n.* **1 a** confessing or acknowledgement of a fault, wrongdoing, a sin to a priest, etc. **b** an instance of this. **c** a thing confessed. **2** (in full **confession of faith**) **a** a declaration of one's religious beliefs. **b** a statement of one's principles. ▫▫ **confessionary** *adj.* [ME f. OF f. L *confessio -onis* (as CONFESS)]
■ **1** see ADMISSION 1. **2** see PROFESSION 3.

confessional /kənféshən'l/ *n.* & *adj.* ● *n.* an enclosed stall in a church in which a priest hears confessions. ● *adj.* **1** of or relating to confession. **2** denominational. [F f. It. *confessionale* f. med.L, neut. of *confessionalis* (as CONFESSION)]

confessor /kənféssər/ *n.* **1** a person who makes a confession. **2** /also kón-/ a priest who hears confessions and gives spiritual counsel. **3** a person who avows a religion in the face of its suppression, but does not suffer martyrdom. [ME f. AF *confessur*, OF *-our*, f. eccl.L *confessor* (as CONFESS)]
■ **2** see PRIEST.

confetti /kənfétti/ *n.* small bits of coloured paper thrown by wedding guests at the bride and groom. [It., = sweetmeats f. L (as COMFIT)]

confidant /kónfidánt/ *n.* (*fem.* **confidante** /*pronunc.* same/) a person trusted with knowledge of one's private affairs. [18th-c. for earlier CONFIDENT *n.*, prob. to represent the pronunc. of F *confidente* (as CONFIDE)]
■ see INTIMATE[1] *n.*

confide /kənfíd/ *v.* **1** *tr.* (usu. foll. by *to*) tell (a secret etc.) in confidence. **2** *tr.* (foll. by *to*) entrust (an object of care, a task, etc.) to. **3** *intr.* (foll. by *in*) **a** have trust or confidence in. **b** talk confidentially to. ▫▫ **confidingly** *adv.* [L *confidere* (as COM-, *fidere* trust)]
■ **1** see IMPART 1. **2** see TRUST *v.* 4. **3 a** see TRUST *v.* 1.

confidence /kónfid'nss/ *n.* **1** firm trust (*have confidence in his ability*). **2 a** a feeling of reliance or certainty. **b** a sense of self-reliance; boldness. **3 a** something told confidentially. **b** the telling of private matters with mutual trust. ▫ **confidence man** a man who robs by means of a confidence trick. **confidence trick** (*US* **game**) a swindle in which the victim is persuaded to trust the swindler in some way. **in confidence** as a secret. **in a person's confidence** trusted with a person's secrets. **take into one's confidence** confide in. [ME f. L *confidentia* (as CONFIDE)]
■ **1** trust, faith, belief. **2 a** reliance; conviction, certitude; see also CERTAINTY 2. **b** assurance, self-confidence, boldness, courage, nerve, self-assurance, self-reliance, poise, aplomb, coolness. **3 a** secret, private *or* confidential matter *or* affair. ▫ **confidence man** see FRAUD 3. **confidence trick** (*US* **game**) see SWINDLE *n.* 1, 3. **in confidence** in secrecy, secretly, in privacy, privately, confidentially, intimately, on the quiet, *colloq.* on the q.t.

confident /kónfid'nt/ *adj.* & *n.* ● *adj.* **1** feeling or showing confidence; self-assured, bold (*spoke with a confident air*). **2** (often foll. by *of*, or *that* + clause) assured, trusting (*confident of your support*; *confident that he will come*). ● *n.* *archaic* = CONFIDANT. ▫▫ **confidently** *adv.* [F f. It. *confidente* (as CONFIDE)]
■ *adj.* **1** self-confident, self-assured, self-possessed, reliant, self-reliant, dauntless, bold, cool, cocksure, fearless, courageous. **2** secure, sure, certain, assured, positive, convinced, trusting, satisfied.

confidential /kónfidénsh'l/ *adj.* **1** spoken or written in confidence. **2** entrusted with secrets (*a confidential secretary*). **3** confiding. ▫▫ **confidentiality** /-shiálliti/ *n.* **confidentially** *adv.*
■ **1** private, secret, classified, top secret, *colloq.* hush-hush. **3** see also INTIMATE[1] *adj.* 1.

configuration /kənfigyooráysh'n, -gəráysh'n/ *n.* **1 a** an arrangement of parts or elements in a particular form or figure. **b** the form, shape, or figure resulting from such an arrangement. **2** *Astron.* & *Astrol.* the relative position of planets etc. **3** *Psychol.* = GESTALT. **4** *Physics* the distribution of electrons among the energy levels of an atom, or of nucleons among the energy levels of a nucleus, as specified by quantum numbers. **5** *Chem.* the fixed three-dimensional relationship of the atoms in a molecule. **6** *Computing* **a** the interrelating or interconnecting of a computer system or elements of it so that it will accommodate a particular specification. **b** an instance of this. ▫▫ **configurational** *adj.* **configure** *v.tr.* (in senses 1, 2, 6). [LL *configuratio* f. L *configurare* (as COM-, *figurare* fashion)]
■ **1** see FORM *n.* 1a.

confine *v.* & *n.* ● *v.tr.* /kənfín/ (often foll. by *in*, *to*, *within*) **1** keep or restrict (within certain limits etc.). **2** hold captive; imprison. ● *n.* /kónfīn/ (usu. in *pl.*) a limit or boundary (*within the confines of the town*). ▫ **be confined** be in childbirth. [(v.) f. F *confiner*, (n.) ME f. F *confins* (pl.), f. L *confinia* (as COM-, *finia* neut. pl. f. *finis* end, limit)]
■ *v.* **1** see RESTRICT. **2** see IMPRISON 2. ● *n.* see BOUND[2] *n.* 1.

confinement /kənfínmənt/ *n.* **1** the act or an instance of confining; the state of being confined. **2** the time of a woman's giving birth.
■ **1** see CAPTIVITY. **2** see LABOUR *n.* 3.

confirm /kənfúrm/ *v.tr.* **1** provide support for the truth or correctness of; make definitely valid (*confirmed my suspicions*; *confirmed his arrival time*). **2** ratify (a treaty, possession, title, etc.); make formally valid. **3** (foll. by *in*) encourage (a person) in (an opinion etc.). **4** establish more firmly (power, possession, etc.). **5** administer the religious rite of confirmation to. ▫▫ **confirmative** *adj.* **confirmatory** *adj.* [ME f. OF *confermer* f. L *confirmare* (as COM-, FIRM[1])]
■ **1, 2** strengthen, encourage, fortify, support, reinforce, uphold, back up, corroborate, substantiate, buttress, prove; ratify, sanction, authorize, endorse, sustain, approve, validate, verify, recognize; authenticate, accredit. **3** see SUPPORT *v.* 4, 6. **4** establish, settle, affirm, ensure, clinch, substantiate, guarantee, bind, seal.

confirmand /kónfərmand/ *n.* *Eccl.* a person who is to be or has just been confirmed.

confirmation /kónfərmáysh'n/ *n.* **1 a** the act or an instance of confirming; the state of being confirmed. **b** an instance of this. **2 a** a religious rite confirming a baptized person, esp. at the age of discretion, as a member of the Christian Church. **b** a ceremony of confirming persons of about this age in the Jewish faith. [ME f. OF f. L *confirmatio -onis* (as CONFIRM)]
■ **1** see ENDORSEMENT 1.

confirmed /kənfúrmd/ *adj.* firmly settled in some habit or condition (*confirmed in his ways*; *a confirmed bachelor*).
■ see HABITUAL 3.

confiscate /kónfiskayt/ *v.tr.* **1** take or seize by authority. **2** appropriate to the public treasury (by way of a penalty). ▫▫ **confiscable** /kənfískəb'l/ *adj.* **confiscation** /-skáysh'n/ *n.* **confiscator** *n.* **confiscatory** /kənfískətəri/ *adj.* [L *confiscare* (as COM-, *fiscare* f. *fiscus* treasury)]
■ **1, 2** appropriate, seize, impound, expropriate, take (away), commandeer, *Law* sequester, sequestrate.

conflagration /kónfləgráysh'n/ *n.* a great and destructive fire. [L *conflagratio* f. *conflagrare* (as COM-, *flagrare* blaze)]
■ fire, holocaust, inferno.

conflate /kənfláyt/ *v.tr.* blend or fuse together (esp. two variant texts into one). ▫▫ **conflation** /-fláysh'n/ *n.* [L *conflare* (as COM-, *flare* blow)]

conflict *n.* & *v.* ● *n.* /kónflikt/ **1 a** a state of opposition or hostilities. **b** a fight or struggle. **2** (often foll. by *of*) **a** the clashing of opposed principles etc. **b** an instance of this. **3** *Psychol.* **a** the opposition of incompatible wishes or needs in a person. **b** an instance of this. **c** the distress resulting from this. ● *v.intr.* /kənflíkt/ **1** clash; be incompatible. **2** (often foll. by *with*) struggle or contend. **3** (as **conflicting** *adj.*) contradictory. ▫ **in conflict** conflicting. ▫▫ **confliction** /kənflíksh'n/ *n.* **conflictual** /kənflíkchooəl/ *adj.* [ME f. L *confligere conflict-* (as COM-, *figere* strike)]
■ *n.* **1 a** battle, combat, war; dispute, controversy,

contention, disagreement. **b** fight, engagement, struggle, fray, fracas, affray, Donnybrook; dispute, argument, wrangle, altercation, feud, quarrel, squabble, tiff, *colloq.* row, *US colloq.* spat, set-to. **2** antagonism, opposition, disagreement, variance, discord; clash, dispute; see also *disagreement* (DISAGREE). ● *v.* **1** clash, disagree, differ, be incompatible *or* at odds *or* at variance, be in opposition. **2** see STRUGGLE *v.* 3. **3** (**conflicting**) see CONTRADICTORY. □ **in conflict** see CONTRADICTORY.

confluence /kónflooənss/ *n.* **1** a place where two rivers meet. **2 a** a coming together. **b** a crowd of people. [L *confluere* (as COM-, *fluere* flow)]
■ **1, 2a** see MEETING 1.

confluent /kónflooənt/ *adj.* & *n.* ● *adj.* flowing together, uniting. ● *n.* a stream joining another.

conflux /kónfluks/ *n.* = CONFLUENCE. [LL *confluxus* (as CONFLUENCE)]

conform /kənfórm/ *v.* **1** *intr.* comply with rules or general custom. **2** *intr.* & *tr.* (often foll. by *to*) be or make accordant or suitable. **3** *tr.* (often foll. by *to*) form according to a pattern; make similar. **4** *intr.* (foll. by *to, with*) comply with; be in accordance with. □□ **conformer** *n.* [ME f. OF *conformer* f. L *conformare* (as COM-, FORM)]
■ **1** fit (in), harmonize. **2** accord, agree, concur, coincide, correspond, harmonize, square, tally, fit in, be consistent, be in accord *or* in accordance; match, fit. **4** (*conform to* or *with*) comply with, follow, observe, obey, respect, abide by, adapt *or* adjust to.

conformable /kənfórməb'l/ *adj.* **1** (often foll. by *to*) similar. **2** (often foll. by *with*) consistent. **3** (often foll. by *to*) adapted. **4** tractable, submissive. **5** *Geol.* (of strata in contact) lying in the same direction. □□ **conformability** /-bíliti/ *n.* **conformably** *adv.* [med.L *conformabilis* (as CONFORM)]
■ **4** see OBEDIENT.

conformal /kənfórm'l/ *adj.* (of a map) showing any small area in its correct shape. □□ **conformally** *adv.* [LL *conformalis* (as CONFORM)]

conformance /kənfórmənss/ *n.* (often foll. by *to, with*) = CONFORMITY 1, 2.

conformation /kónformáysh'n/ *n.* **1** the way in which a thing is formed; shape, structure. **2** (often foll. by *to*) adjustment in form or character; adaptation. **3** *Chem.* any spatial arrangement of atoms in a molecule from the rotation of part of the molecule about a single bond. [L *conformatio* (as CONFORM)]
■ **1** see FORM *n.* 1a. **2** see ACCOMMODATION 2a.

conformist /kənfórmist/ *n.* & *adj.* ● *n.* **1** a person who conforms to an established practice; a conventional person. **2** *Brit.* a person who conforms to the practices of the Church of England. ● *adj.* (of a person) conforming to established practices; conventional. □□ **conformism** *n.*
■ *n.* **1** see SQUARE *n.* 6. ● *adj.* see CONSERVATIVE *adj.* 1a.

conformity /kənfórmiti/ *n.* **1** (often foll. by *to, with*) action or behaviour in accordance with established practice; compliance. **2** (often foll. by *to, with*) correspondence in form or manner; likeness, agreement. **3** *Brit.* compliance with the practices of the Church of England. [ME f. OF *conformité* or LL *conformitas* (as CONFORM)]
■ **1** see OBEDIENCE. **2** see ACCORD *n.* 1.

confound /kənfównd/ *v.* & *int.* ● *v.tr.* **1** throw into perplexity or confusion. **2** mix up; confuse (in one's mind). **3** *archaic* defeat, overthrow. ● *int.* expressing annoyance (*confound you!*). [ME f. AF *conf(o)undre*, OF *confondre* f. L *confundere* mix up (as COM-, *fundere fus-* pour)]
■ **1** see PERPLEX 1. **2** see CONFUSE 2.

confounded /kənfówndid/ *adj. colloq.* damned (*a confounded nuisance!*). □□ **confoundedly** *adv.*

confraternity /kónfrətérniti/ *n.* (*pl.* **-ies**) a brotherhood, esp. religious or charitable. [ME f. OF *confraternité* f. med.L *confraternitas* (as COM-, FRATERNITY)]

confrère /kónfrair/ *n.* a fellow member of a profession, scientific body, etc. [ME f. OF f. med.L *confrater* (as COM-, *frater* brother)]
■ see COLLEAGUE.

confront /kənfrúnt/ *v.tr.* **1 a** face in hostility or defiance. **b** face up to and deal with (a problem, difficulty, etc.). **2** (of a difficulty etc.) present itself to (*countless obstacles confronted us*). **3** (foll. by *with*) **a** bring (a person) face to face with (a circumstance), esp. by way of accusation (*confronted them with the evidence*). **b** set (a thing) face to face with (another) for comparison. **4** meet or stand facing. □□ **confrontation** /kónfruntáysh'n/ *n.* **confrontational** /kónfruntáyshən'l/ *adj.* [F *confronter* f. med.L *confrontare* (as COM-, *frontare* f. *frons frontis* face)]
■ **1** see FACE *v.* 3a, b.

Confucian /kənfyóosh'n/ *adj.* & *n.* ● *adj.* of or relating to Confucius, Chinese philosopher d. 479 BC, or his philosophy. ● *n.* a follower of Confucius. □□ **Confucianism** *n.* **Confucianist** *n.* [*Confucius*, Latinization of *Kongfuze* Kong the master]

confusable /kənfyóozəb'l/ *adj.* that is able or liable to be confused. □□ **confusability** /-bíliti/ *n.*

confuse /kənfyóoz/ *v.tr.* **1 a** disconcert, perplex, bewilder. **b** embarrass. **2** mix up in the mind; mistake (one for another). **3** make indistinct (*that point confuses the issue*). **4** (as **confused** *adj.*) **a** mentally decrepit. **b** puzzled, perplexed. **5** (often as **confused** *adj.*) make muddled or disorganized, throw into disorder (*a confused jumble of clothes*). □□ **confusedly** /kənfyóozidli/ *adv.* **confusing** *adj.* **confusingly** *adv.* [19th-c. back-form. f. *confused* (14th c.) f. OF *confus* f. L *confusus*: see CONFOUND]
■ **1 a** disconcert, perplex, puzzle, bewilder, mystify, baffle, bemuse, befuddle, discomfit, confound, fluster, upset, disorient, *colloq.* flummox, rattle, throw, *US joc.* discombobulate. **b** abash, shame, embarrass. **2** confuse, muddle (up), mistake, get the wrong way round. **3** disorder, confound, throw into disarray, muddle, mix up, snarl (up), ensnarl, tangle (up), entangle; blur. **4** (**confused**) **a** muddle-headed, decrepit; see also SENILE *adj.* **b** bewildered, perplexed, puzzled, nonplussed, baffled, befuddled, bemused, mixed up, dazed, flustered, *colloq.* flummoxed, stumped, *Austral.* & *NZ colloq.* bushed. **5** (**confused**) mixed up, jumbled, disordered, disorganized, disorderly, muddled, messy, topsy-turvy, chaotic, higgledy-piggledy, *colloq.* shambolic.

confusion /kənfyóozh'n/ *n.* **1 a** the act of confusing (*the confusion of fact and fiction*). **b** an instance of this; a misunderstanding (*confusions arise from a lack of communication*). **2 a** the result of confusing; a confused state; embarrassment, disorder (*thrown into confusion by his words; trampled in the confusion of battle*). **b** (foll. by *of*) a disorderly jumble (*a confusion of ideas*). **3 a** a civil commotion (*confusion broke out at the announcement*). **b** an instance of this. [ME f. OF *confusion* or L *confusio* (as CONFUSE)]
■ **1 a** confounding, muddling, jumbling, blurring. **b** misconception, mix-up; see also MISUNDERSTANDING 1. **2 a** disorder, disarray, disarrangement, chaos, tumult, commotion, turmoil, pandemonium, bedlam; embarrassment, discomfiture, mortification, abashment, chagrin. **b** mix-up, mess, jumble, muddle, *colloq.* shambles; assortment, mixture, pot-pourri, gallimaufry, hotchpotch. **3** see UPROAR.

confute /kənfyóot/ *v.tr.* **1** prove (a person) to be in error. **2** prove (an argument) to be false. □□ **confutation** /kónfyootáysh'n/ *n.* [L *confutare* restrain]
■ see DISPROVE.

conga /kónggə/ *n.* & *v.* ● *n.* **1** a Latin-American dance of African origin, usu. with several persons in a single line, one behind the other. **2** (also **conga drum**) a tall, narrow, low-toned drum beaten with the hands. ● *v.intr.* (**congas, congaed** /-gəd/ or **conga'd, congaing** /-gəing/) perform the conga. [Amer. Sp. f. Sp. *conga* (fem.) of the Congo]

congé /kónzhay/ *n.* an unceremonious dismissal; leave-taking. [F: earlier *congee*, ME f. OF *congié* f. L *commeatus*

leave of absence f. *commeare* go and come (as COM-, *meare* go): now usu. treated as mod. F]
▪ see *dismissal* (DISMISS).

congeal /kənjéel/ *v.tr.* & *intr.* **1** make or become semi-solid by cooling. **2** (of blood etc.) coagulate. □□ **congealable** *adj.* **congealment** *n.* [ME f. OF *congeler* f. L *congelare* (as COM-, *gelare* f. *gelu* frost)]
▪ see COAGULATE.

congelation /kónjiláysh'n/ *n.* **1** the process of congealing. **2** a congealed state. **3** a congealed substance. [ME f. OF *congelation* or L *congelatio* (as CONGEAL)]

congener /kənjéenər/ *n.* a thing or person of the same kind or category as another, esp. animals or plants of a specified genus (*the goldfinch is a congener of the canary*). [L (as CON-, GENUS)]

congeneric /kónjinérrik/ *adj.* **1** of the same genus, kind, or race. **2** allied in nature or origin; akin. □□ **congenerous** /kənjénnərəss/ *adj.*

congenial /kənjéeniəl/ *adj.* **1** (often foll. by *with*, *to*) (of a person, character, etc.) pleasant because akin to oneself in temperament or interests. **2** (often foll. by *to*) suited or agreeable. □□ **congeniality** /-niálliti/ *n.* **congenially** *adv.* [CON- + GENIAL[1]]
▪ **1** see LIKEABLE.

congenital /kənjénnit'l/ *adj.* **1** (esp. of a disease, defect, etc.) existing from birth. **2** that is (or as if) such from birth (*a congenital liar*). □□ **congenitally** *adv.* [L *congenitus* (as COM-, *genitus* past part. of *gigno* beget)]
▪ **1** see INBORN. **2** see INHERENT 1.

conger /kónggər/ *n.* (in full **conger eel**) any large marine eel of the family Congridae. [ME f. OF *congre* f. L *conger*, *congrus*, f. Gk *goggros*]

congeries /kənjéereez, -jérri-eez/ *n.* (*pl.* same) a disorderly collection; a mass or heap. [L, formed as CONGEST]
▪ see HEAP *n.* 1.

congest /kənjést/ *v.tr.* (esp. as **congested** *adj.*) affect with congestion; obstruct, block (*congested streets*; *congested lungs*). □□ **congestive** *adj.* [L *congerere congest-* (as COM-, *gerere* bring)]
▪ see BLOCK *v.* 1a; (**congested**) snarled up, obstructed, (over)crowded; blocked (up), stuffed (up).

congestion /kənjéss-chən/ *n.* abnormal accumulation, crowding, or obstruction, esp. of traffic etc. or of blood or mucus in a part of the body. [F f. L *congestio -onis* (as CONGEST)]

conglomerate *adj.*, *n.*, & *v.* • *adj.* /kənglómmərət/ **1** gathered into a rounded mass. **2** *Geol.* (of rock) made up of small stones held together (cf. AGGLOMERATE). • *n.* /kənglómmərət/ **1** a number of things or parts forming a heterogeneous mass. **2** a group or corporation formed by the merging of separate and diverse firms. **3** *Geol.* conglomerate rock. • *v.tr.* & *intr.* /kənglómmərayt/ collect into a coherent mass. □□ **conglomeration** /-ráysh'n/ *n.* [L *conglomeratus* past part. of *conglomerare* (as COM-, *glomerare* f. *glomus -eris* ball)]
▪ *n.* **2** see ORGANIZATION 2.

Congolese /kónggəléez/ *adj.* & *n.* • *adj.* of or relating to the Republic of the Congo in Central Africa, or the region surrounding the Congo river. • *n.* a native of either of these regions. [F *congolais*]

congou /kónggoō, -gō/ *n.* a variety of black China tea. [Chin. dial. *kung hu tē* tea laboured for]

congrats /kəngráts/ *n.pl.* & *int. colloq.* congratulations. [abbr.]

congratulate /kəngrátyoolayt/ *v.tr.* & *refl.* (often foll. by *on*, *upon*) **1** *tr.* express pleasure at the happiness or good fortune or excellence of (a person) (*congratulated them on their success*). **2** *refl.* think oneself fortunate or clever. □□ **congratulant** *adj.* & *n.* **congratulator** *n.* **congratulatory** /-lətəri/ *adj.* [L *congratulari* (as COM-, *gratulari* show joy f. *gratus* pleasing)]
▪ **1** see COMPLIMENT *v.* **2** pat oneself on the back.

congratulation /kəngrátyooláysh'n/ *n.* **1** congratulating. **2** (also as *int.*; usu. in *pl.*) an expression of this (*congratulations on winning!*). [L *congratulatio* (as CONGRATULATE)]
▪ **2** (*congratulations*) felicitations, well done, good for *or* on you, *colloq.* nice going, good show; many happy returns.

congregant /kónggrigənt/ *n.* a member of a congregation (esp. Jewish). [L *congregare* (as CONGREGATE)]

congregate /kónggrigayt/ *v.intr.* & *tr.* collect or gather into a crowd or mass. [ME f. L *congregare* (as COM-, *gregare* f. *grex gregis* flock)]
▪ see GATHER *v.* 1.

congregation /kónggrigáysh'n/ *n.* **1** the process of congregating; collection into a crowd or mass. **2** a crowd or mass gathered together. **3 a** a body assembled for religious worship. **b** a body of persons regularly attending a particular church etc. **c** *RC Ch.* a body of persons obeying a common religious rule. **d** *RC Ch.* any of several permanent committees of the Roman Catholic College of Cardinals. **4** (**Congregation**) *Brit.* (in some universities) a general assembly of resident senior members. [ME f. OF *congregation* or L *congregatio* (as CONGREGATE)]
▪ **2, 3a, 4** see ASSEMBLY 1, 2a.

congregational /kónggrigáyshən'l/ *adj.* **1** of a congregation. **2** (**Congregational**) of or adhering to Congregationalism.

Congregationalism /kónggrigáyshənəliz'm/ *n.* a system of ecclesiastical organization whereby individual churches are largely self-governing. □□ **Congregationalist** *n.* **Congregationalize** *v.tr.* (also **-ise**).

congress /kónggress/ *n.* **1** a formal meeting of delegates for discussion. **2** (**Congress**) a national legislative body, esp. that of the US. **3** a society or organization. **4** coming together, meeting. □□ **congressional** /kəngréshən'l/ *adj.* [L *congressus* f. *congredi* (as COM-, *gradi* walk)]
▪ **1** see CONFERENCE 2. **2** see PARLIAMENT 2.

congressman /kónggresmən/ *n.* (*pl.* **-men**; *fem.* **congresswoman**, *pl.* **-women**) a member of the US Congress.
▪ see REPRESENTATIVE *n.* 4.

congruence /kónggrooənss/ *n.* (also **congruency** /-ənsi/) **1** agreement, consistency. **2** *Geom.* the state of being congruent. [ME f. L *congruentia* (as CONGRUENT)]
▪ **1** see ACCORD *n.* 2. **2** see COINCIDENCE 1.

congruent /kónggrooənt/ *adj.* **1** (often foll. by *with*) suitable, agreeing. **2** *Geom.* (of figures) coinciding exactly when superimposed. □□ **congruently** *adv.* [ME f. L *congruere* agree]
▪ **2** see PARALLEL *adj.* 2.

congruous /kónggrooəss/ *adj.* (often foll. by *with*) suitable, agreeing; fitting. □□ **congruity** /-grŏŏ-iti/ *n.* **congruously** *adv.* [L *congruus* (as CONGRUENT)]
▪ □□ **congruity** see HARMONY 3.

conic /kónnik/ *adj.* & *n.* • *adj.* of a cone. • *n.* **1** a conic section. **2** (in *pl.*) the study of conic sections. □ **conic section** a figure formed by the intersection of a cone and a plane. [mod.L *conicus* f. Gk *kōnikos* (as CONE)]

conical /kónnik'l/ *adj.* cone-shaped. □□ **conically** *adv.*

conidium /kəníddiəm/ *n.* (*pl.* **conidia** /-diə/) a spore produced asexually by various fungi. [mod.L dimin. f. Gk *konis* dust]

conifer /kónnifər, kṓn-/ *n.* any evergreen tree of a group usu. bearing cones, including pines, yews, cedars, and redwoods. □□ **coniferous** /kəníffərəss/ *adj.* [L (as CONE, -FEROUS)]

coniform /kṓniform/ *adj.* cone-shaped. [L *conus* cone + -FORM]

coniine /kṓni-een/ *n.* a poisonous alkaloid found in hemlock, that paralyses the nerves. [L *conium* f. Gk *kōneion* hemlock]

conjectural /kənjékchərəl/ *adj.* based on, involving, or given to conjecture. □□ **conjecturally** *adv.* [F f. L *conjecturalis* (as CONJECTURE)]
▪ see SPECULATIVE 1.

conjecture /kənjékchər/ *n.* & *v.* • *n.* **1 a** the formation of an opinion on incomplete information; guessing. **b** an opinion or conclusion reached in this way. **2 a** (in textual criticism) the guessing of a reading not in the text. **b** a proposed reading. • *v.* **1** *tr.* & *intr.* guess. **2** *tr.* (in textual

criticism) propose (a reading). ▫▫ **conjecturable** *adj.* [ME f. OF *conjecture* or L *conjectura* f. *conjicere* (as COM-, *jacere* throw)]
■ *n.* **1** see GUESS *n.* ● *v.* **1** see GUESS *v.*2.

conjoin /kənjóyn/ *v.tr.* & *intr.* join, combine. [ME f. OF *conjoign-* pres. stem of *conjoindre* f. L *conjungere* (as COM-, *jungere junct-* join)]
■ see COMBINE *v.* 1.

conjoint /kənjóynt/ *adj.* associated, conjoined. ▫▫ **conjointly** *adv.* [ME f. OF, past part. (as CONJOIN)]

conjugal /kónjoog'l/ *adj.* of marriage or the relation between husband and wife. ▫ **conjugal rights** those rights (esp. to sexual relations) regarded as exercisable in law by each partner in a marriage. ▫▫ **conjugality** /-gálliti/ *n.* **conjugally** *adv.* [L *conjugalis* f. *conjux* consort (as COM-, *-jux -jugis* f. root of *jungere* join)]
■ see *matrimonial* (MATRIMONY).

conjugate *v.*, *adj.*, & *n.* ● *v.* /kónjoogayt/ **1** *tr. Gram.* give the different forms of (a verb). **2** *intr.* **a** unite sexually. **b** (of gametes) become fused. **3** *intr. Chem.* (of protein) combine with non-protein. ● *adj.* /kónjoogət/ **1** joined together, esp. as a pair. **2** *Gram.* derived from the same root. **3** *Biol.* fused. **4** *Chem.* (of an acid or base) related by loss or gain of an electron. **5** *Math.* joined in a reciprocal relation, esp. having the same real parts, and equal magnitudes but opposite signs of imaginary parts. ● *n.* /kónjoogət/ a conjugate word or thing. ▫▫ **conjugately** /kónjoogətli/ *adv.* [L *conjugare* yoke together (as COM-, *jugare* f. *jugum* yoke)]

conjugation /kónjoogáysh'n/ *n.* **1** *Gram.* a system of verbal inflection. **2 a** the act or an instance of conjugating. **b** an instance of this. **3** *Biol.* the fusion of two gametes in reproduction. ▫▫ **conjugational** *adj.* [L *conjugatio* (as CONJUGATE)]

conjunct /kənjúngkt/ *adj.* joined together; combined; associated. [ME f. L *conjunctus* (as CONJOIN)]

conjunction /kənjúngksh'n/ *n.* **1 a** the action of joining; the condition of being joined. **b** an instance of this. **2** *Gram.* a word used to connect clauses or sentences or words in the same clause (e.g. *and*, *but*, *if*). **3 a** a combination (of events or circumstances). **b** a number of associated persons or things. **4** *Astron.* & *Astrol.* the alignment of two bodies in the solar system so that they have the same longitude as seen from the earth. ▫ **in conjunction with** together with. ▫▫ **conjunctional** *adj.* [ME f. OF *conjonction* f. L *conjunctio -onis* (as CONJUNCT)]
■ **1** see JUNCTION 2, 3. **3 a** see COMBINATION 3.

conjunctiva /kónjungktī́və, kənjúngktivə/ *n.* (*pl.* **conjunctivas**) *Anat.* the mucous membrane that covers the front of the eye and lines the inside of the eyelids. ▫▫ **conjunctival** *adj.* [med.L (*membrana*) *conjunctiva* (as CONJUNCTIVE)]

conjunctive /kənjúngktiv/ *adj.* & *n.* ● *adj.* **1** serving to join; connective. **2** *Gram.* of the nature of a conjunction. ● *n. Gram.* a conjunctive word. ▫▫ **conjunctively** *adv.* [LL *conjunctivus* (as CONJOIN)]

conjunctivitis /kənjúngktivī́tiss/ *n.* inflammation of the conjunctiva.

conjuncture /kənjúngkchər/ *n.* a combination of events; a state of affairs. [obs. F f. It. *congiuntura* (as CONJOIN)]

conjuration /kónjooráysh'n/ *n.* an incantation; a magic spell. [ME f. OF f. L *conjuratio -onis* (as CONJURE)]
■ see MUMBO-JUMBO 1.

conjure /kúnjər/ *v.* **1** *intr.* perform tricks which are seemingly magical, esp. by rapid movements of the hands. **2** *tr.* (usu. foll. by *out of*, *away*, *to*, etc.) cause to appear or disappear as if by magic (*conjured a rabbit out of a hat*; *conjured them to a desert island*; *his pain was conjured away*). **3** *tr.* call upon (a spirit) to appear. **4** *intr.* perform marvels. **5** *tr.* /kənjóor/ (often foll. by *to* + infin.) appeal solemnly to (a person). ▫ **conjure up 1** bring into existence or cause to appear as if by magic. **2** cause to appear to the eye or mind; evoke. [ME f. OF *conjurer* plot, exorcise f. L *conjurare* band together by oath (as COM-, *jurare* swear)]
■ ▫ **conjure up 2** see EVOKE 2.

conjuror /kúnjərər/ *n.* (also **conjurer**) a performer of conjuring tricks. [CONJURE + -ER[1] & AF *conjurour* (OF *-eor*) f. med.L *conjurator* (as CONJURE)]
■ magician, illusionist, *formal* prestidigitator.

conk[1] /kongk/ *v.intr.* (usu. foll. by *out*) *colloq.* **1** (of a machine etc.) break down. **2** (of a person) become exhausted and give up; faint; die. [20th c.: orig. unkn.]
■ **1** see BREAK[1] *v.* 1b. **2** see DIE[1] 1.

conk[2] /kongk/ *n.* & *v. sl.* ● *n.* **1 a** the nose. **b** the head. **2 a** a punch on the nose or head. **b** a blow. ● *v.tr.* punch on the nose; hit on the head etc. [19th c.: perh. = CONCH]
■ *n.* **1 b** see HEAD *n.* 1. **2** see HIT *n.* 1a. ● *v.* see HIT *v.* 1a.

conker /kóngkər/ *n.* **1** the hard fruit of a horse chestnut. **2** (in *pl.*) *Brit.* a children's game played with conkers on strings, one hit against another to try to break it. [dial. *conker* snail-shell (orig. used in the game), assoc. with CONQUER]

con moto /kón mṓtō/ *adv. Mus.* with movement. [It., = with movement]

Conn. *abbr.* Connecticut.

conn *US* var. of CON[4].

connate /kónnayt/ *adj.* **1** existing in a person or thing from birth; innate. **2** formed at the same time. **3** allied, congenial. **4** *Bot.* (of organs) congenitally united so as to form one part. **5** *Geol.* (of water) trapped in sedimentary rock during its deposition. [LL *connatus* past part. of *connasci* (as COM-, *nasci* be born)]
■ **1** see INBORN.

connatural /kənáchərəl/ *adj.* **1** (often foll. by *to*) innate; belonging naturally. **2** of like nature. ▫▫ **connaturally** *adv.* [LL *connaturalis* (as COM-, NATURAL)]

connect /kənékt/ *v.* **1 a** *tr.* (often foll. by *to*, *with*) join (one thing with another) (*connected the hose to the tap*). **b** *tr.* join (two things) (*a track connected the two villages*). **c** *intr.* be joined or joinable (*the two parts do not connect*). **2** *tr.* (often foll. by *with*) associate mentally or practically (*did not connect the two ideas*; *never connected her with the theatre*). **3** *intr.* (foll. by *with*) (of a train etc.) be synchronized at its destination with another train etc., so that passengers can transfer (*the train connects with the boat*). **4** *tr.* put into communication by telephone. **5 a** *tr.* (usu. in *passive*; foll. by *with*) unite or associate with others in relationships etc. (*am connected with the royal family*). **b** *intr.* form a logical sequence; be meaningful. **6** *intr. colloq.* hit or strike effectively. ▫ **connecting-rod** the rod between the piston and the crankpin etc. in an internal-combustion engine or between the wheels of a locomotive. ▫▫ **connectable** *adj.* **connector** *n.* [L *connectere connex-* (as COM-, *nectere* bind)]
■ **1 a, b** join *or* link *or* tie (together); fasten, bind, attach, couple, put together, secure, fit together, fix, affix, stick together; pin, hook, staple, tack, glue, cement, fuse, seal, strap, bolt, lash. **c** join, fit together. **2, 5a** associate, affiliate, link, relate, league, tie (in), make a connection between. **5 b** follow, make sense; see also *add up* 3.

connected /kənéktid/ *adj.* **1** joined in sequence. **2** (of ideas etc.) coherent. **3** related or associated. ▫ **well-connected** associated, esp. by birth, with persons of good social position. ▫▫ **connectedly** *adv.* **connectedness** *n.*

connection /kənéksh'n/ *n.* (also *Brit.* **connexion**) **1 a** the act of connecting; the state of being connected. **b** an instance of this. **2** the point at which two things are connected (*broke at the connection*). **3 a** a thing or person that connects; a link, a relationship or association (*a radio formed the only connection with the outside world*; *cannot see the connection between the two ideas*). **b** a telephone link (*got a bad connection*). **4** arrangement or opportunity for catching a connecting train etc.; the train etc. itself (*missed the connection*). **5** *Electr.* **a** the linking up of an electric current by contact. **b** a device for effecting this. **6** (often in *pl.*) a relative or associate, esp. one with influence (*has connections in the Home Office*; *heard it through a business connection*). **7** a relation of ideas; a context (*in this connection I have to* *disagree*). **8** *sl.* a supplier of narcotics. **9** a religious body, esp. Methodist. □ **in connection with** with reference to. **in this** (or **that**) **connection** with reference to this (or that). □□ **connectional** *adj.* [L *connexio* (as CONNECT): spelling *-ct-* after CONNECT]

■ **1** linking, linkage, union, join, bond, link; tie, relationship, association, relevance, appropriateness. **2** see JOINT *n.* 1. **3 a** see LINK[1] *n.* 2a, b. **6** (*connections*) contacts, friends (at court); influence, pull, *colloq.* clout, *US sl.* drag; relatives, relations, family, kin, kith and kin. **7** see CONTEXT.

connective /kənéktiv/ *adj.* & *n.* ● *adj.* serving or tending to connect. ● *n.* something that connects. □ **connective tissue** *Anat.* a fibrous tissue that supports, binds, or separates more specialized tissue.

conning tower /kónning/ *n.* **1** the superstructure of a submarine from which steering, firing, etc., are directed on or near the surface, and which contains the periscope. **2** the armoured pilot-house of a warship. [CON[4] + -ING[1]]

connivance /kənī́v'nss/ *n.* **1** (often foll. by *at, in*) conniving (*connivance in the crime*). **2** tacit permission (*done with his connivance*). [F *connivence* or L *conniventia* (as CONNIVE)]

■ **1** see CONSPIRACY 2.

connive /kənī́v/ *v.intr.* **1** (foll. by *at*) disregard or tacitly consent to (a wrongdoing). **2** (usu. foll. by *with*) conspire. □□ **conniver** *n.* [F *conniver* or L *connivēre* shut the eyes (to)]

■ **1** see ABET. **2** see SCHEME *v.* 1.

connoisseur /kónnəsőr/ *n.* (often foll. by *of, in*) an expert judge in matters of taste (*a connoisseur of fine wine*). □□ **connoisseurship** *n.* [F, obs. spelling of *connaisseur* f. pres. stem of *connaître* know + *-eur* -OR[1]: cf. *reconnoitre*]

■ see EXPERT *n.*

connotation /kónnətáysh'n/ *n.* **1** that which is implied by a word etc. in addition to its literal or primary meaning (*a letter with sinister connotations*). **2** the act of connoting or implying.

■ see IMPLICATION.

connote /kənṓt/ *v.tr.* **1** (of a word etc.) imply in addition to the literal or primary meaning. **2** (of a fact) imply as a consequence or condition. **3** mean, signify. □□ **connotative** /kónnətaytiv, kənṓtətiv/ *adj.* [med.L *connotare* mark in addition (as COM-, *notare* f. *nota* mark)]

■ **1, 2** see IMPLY 3. **3** see MEAN[1] 4, 6.

connubial /kənyṓobiəl/ *adj.* of or relating to marriage or the relationship of husband and wife. □□ **connubiality** /-biálliti/ *n.* **connubially** *adv.* [L *connubialis* f. *connubium* (*nubium* f. *nubere* marry)]

■ see *matrimonial* (MATRIMONY).

conoid /kṓnoyd/ *adj.* & *n.* ● *adj.* (also **conoidal** /-nóyd'l/) cone-shaped. ● *n.* a cone-shaped object.

conquer /kóngkər/ *v.tr.* **1 a** overcome and control (an enemy or territory) by military force. **b** *absol.* be victorious. **2** overcome (a habit, emotion, disability, etc.) by effort (*conquered his fear*). **3** climb (a mountain) successfully. □□ **conquerable** *adj.* [ME f. OF *conquerre* f. Rmc f. L *conquirere* (as COM-, *quaerere* seek, get)]

■ **1 a** overcome, beat, defeat, subdue, crush, subjugate, *literary* vanquish; capture, seize, win, gain, acquire, obtain; occupy, annex. **2** overcome, triumph *or* prevail over, beat, surmount, master, win out (over); *sl.* kick.

conqueror /kóngkərər/ *n.* **1** a person who conquers. **2** *Brit.* = CONKER. [ME f. AF *conquerour* (OF *-eor*) f. *conquerre* (as CONQUER)]

■ **1** see VICTOR.

conquest /kóngkwest/ *n.* **1** the act or an instance of conquering; the state of being conquered. **2 a** conquered territory. **b** something won. **3** a person whose affection or favour has been won. **4** (**the Conquest** or **Norman Conquest**) the conquest of England by William of Normandy in 1066. □ **make a conquest of** win the affections of. [ME f. OF *conquest(e)* f. Rmc (as CONQUER)]

■ **1** subjugation, domination, subjection; (*conquest of*) mastery *or* control of, triumph over; see also DEFEAT *n.* **2 b** see TROPHY 1. □ **make a conquest of** see CAPTIVATE.

conquistador /konkwístədor/ *n.* (*pl.* **conquistadores** /-dórez/ or **conquistadors**) a conqueror, esp. one of the Spanish conquerors of Mexico and Peru in the 16th c. [Sp.]

con-rod /kónrod/ *n. colloq.* connecting-rod. [abbr.]

Cons. *abbr.* Conservative.

consanguineous /kónsanggwínniəss/ *adj.* descended from the same ancestor; akin. □□ **consanguinity** *n.* [L *consanguineus* (as COM-, *sanguis -inis* blood)]

■ see KIN *adj.*

conscience /kónsh'nss/ *n.* **1** a moral sense of right and wrong esp. as felt by a person and affecting behaviour (*my conscience won't allow me to do that*). **2** an inner feeling as to the goodness or otherwise of one's behaviour (*my conscience is clear*; *has a guilty conscience*). □ **case of conscience** a matter in which one's conscience has to decide a conflict of principles. **conscience clause** a clause in a law, ensuring respect for the consciences of those affected. **conscience money** a sum paid to relieve one's conscience, esp. about a payment previously evaded. **conscience-stricken** (or **-struck**) made uneasy by a bad conscience. **for conscience** (or **conscience's**) **sake** to satisfy one's conscience. **freedom of conscience** a system allowing all citizens a free choice of religion. **in all conscience** *colloq.* by any reasonable standard; by all that is fair. **on one's conscience** causing one feelings of guilt. **prisoner of conscience** a person imprisoned by a State for holding political or religious views it does not tolerate. □□ **conscienceless** *adj.* [ME f. OF f. L *conscientia* f. *conscire* be privy to (as COM-, *scire* know)]

■ **1, 2** morality, morals, judgement, fairness, sense of right and wrong, ethics, honour, standards, principles, scruples. □ **conscience-stricken** (or **-struck**) see BAD *adj.* 6. **in all conscience** in all fairness, reasonably.

conscientious /kónshi-énshəss/ *adj.* (of a person or conduct) governed by a sense of duty; diligent and scrupulous. □ **conscientious objector** a person who for reasons of conscience objects to conforming to a requirement, esp. that of military service. □□ **conscientiously** *adv.* **conscientiousness** *n.* [F *consciencieux* f. med.L *conscientiosus* (as CONSCIENCE)]

■ principled, fair, moral, ethical, strict, righteous, right-minded, upstanding, upright, honourable, just, responsible, high-minded, incorruptible; careful, exacting, scrupulous, meticulous, punctilious, painstaking, diligent, particular, rigorous, thorough; prudent, sensible, attentive, serious.

conscious /kónshəss/ *adj.* & *n.* ● *adj.* **1** awake and aware of one's surroundings and identity. **2** (usu. foll. by *of*, or *that* + clause) aware, knowing (*conscious of his inferiority*). **3** (of actions, emotions, etc.) realized or recognized by the doer; intentional (*made a conscious effort not to laugh*). **4** (in *comb.*) aware of; concerned with (*appearance-conscious*). ● *n.* (prec. by *the*) the conscious mind. □□ **consciously** *adv.* [L *conscius* knowing with others or in oneself f. *conscire* (as COM-, *scire* know)]

■ *adj.* **1** aware, alert; see also AWAKE *adj.* 1b. **2** see AWARE 1. **3** deliberate, intentional, purposive, purposeful, wilful, studied.

consciousness /kónshəsniss/ *n.* **1** the state of being conscious (*lost consciousness during the fight*). **2 a** awareness, perception (*had no consciousness of being ridiculed*). **b** (in *comb.*) awareness of (*class-consciousness*). **3** the totality of a person's thoughts and feelings, or of a class of these (*moral consciousness*). □ **consciousness-raising** the activity of increasing esp. social or political sensitivity or awareness.

■ **2** see PERCEPTION. **3** see SPIRIT *n.* 1.

conscribe /kənskrī́b/ *v.tr.* = CONSCRIPT *v.* [L *conscribere* (as CONSCRIPTION)]

conscript *v.* & *n.* ● *v.tr.* /kənskrípt/ enlist by conscription. ● *n.* /kónskript/ a person enlisted by conscription. [(v.)

back-form. f. CONSCRIPTION: (n.) f. F *conscrit* f. L *conscriptus* (as CONSCRIPTION)]
■ *v.* see ENLIST 1. ● *n.* see RECRUIT *n.* 1, 2.

conscription /kənskrípsh'n/ *n.* compulsory enlistment for State service, esp. military service. [F f. LL *conscriptio* levying of troops f. L *conscribere conscript-* enrol (as COM-, *scribere* write)]
■ impressment, call-up, *Brit. hist.* national service, *US* draft, *US hist.* selective service.

consecrate /kónsikrayt/ *v.tr.* **1** make or declare sacred; dedicate formally to a religious or divine purpose. **2** (in Christian belief) make (bread and wine) into the body and blood of Christ. **3** (foll. by *to*) devote (one's life etc.) to (a purpose). **4** ordain (esp. a bishop) to a sacred office. □□ **consecration** /-kráysh'n/ *n.* **consecrator** *n.* **consecratory** *adj.* [ME f. L *consecrare* (as COM-, *secrare* = *sacrare* dedicate f. *sacer* sacred)]
■ **1** see SANCTIFY 1. **3** see DEVOTE.

consecution /kónsikyoósh'n/ *n.* **1** logical sequence (in argument or reasoning). **2** sequence, succession (of events etc.). [L *consecutio* f. *consequi consecut-* overtake (as COM-, *sequi* pursue)]

consecutive /kənsékyootiv/ *adj.* **1 a** following continuously. **b** in unbroken or logical order. **2** *Gram.* expressing consequence. □ **consecutive intervals** *Mus.* intervals of the same kind (esp. fifths or octaves), occurring in succession between two voices or parts in harmony. □□ **consecutively** *adv.* **consecutiveness** *n.* [F *consécutif -ive* f. med.L *consecutivus* (as CONSECUTION)]
■ **1** see SUCCESSIVE.

consensual /kənsénsyooəl, -sénshooəl/ *adj.* of or by consent or consensus. □□ **consensually** *adv.* [L *consensus* (see CONSENSUS) + -AL]

consensus /kənsénsəss/ *n.* (often foll. by *of*) **1 a** general agreement (of opinion, testimony, etc.). **b** an instance of this. **2** (*attrib.*) majority view, collective opinion (*consensus politics*). [L, = agreement (as CONSENT)]
■ **1** see AGREEMENT 1, 2.

consent /kənsént/ *v.* & *n.* ● *v.intr.* (often foll. by *to*) express willingness, give permission, agree. ● *n.* voluntary agreement, permission, compliance. □ **age of consent** the age at which consent to sexual intercourse is valid in law. **consenting adult** an adult who consents to something, esp. a homosexual act. [ME f. OF *consentir* f. L *consentire* (as COM-, *sentire sens-* feel)]
■ *v.* agree, comply, concur, accede, acquiesce, concede, yield, submit, cede, conform, give in; (*consent to*) permit, allow, agree to, give in to, approve, authorize. ● *n.* approval, assent, permission, sanction, authorization, imprimatur, seal of approval, go-ahead, *colloq.* OK, okay; agreement, acceptance, acquiescence, compliance, approval, concurrence.

consentient /kənsénsh'nt/ *adj.* **1** agreeing, united in opinion. **2** concurrent. **3** (often foll. by *to*) consenting. [L *consentient-* (as CONSENT)]

consequence /kónsikwənss/ *n.* **1** the result or effect of an action or condition. **2 a** importance (*it is of no consequence*). **b** social distinction (*persons of consequence*). **3** (in *pl.*) a game in which a narrative is made up by the players, each ignorant of what has already been contributed. □ **in consequence** as a result. **take the consequences** accept the results of one's choice or action. [ME f. OF f. L *consequentia* (as CONSEQUENT)]
■ **1** see RESULT *n.* 1. **2** see IMPORTANCE 2, 3.
□ **in consequence** see ACCORDINGLY 2.

consequent /kónsikwənt/ *adj.* & *n.* ● *adj.* **1** (often foll. by *on*, *upon*) following as a result or consequence. **2** logically consistent. ● *n.* **1** a thing that follows another. **2** *Logic* the second part of a conditional proposition, dependent on the antecedent. [ME f. OF f. L *consequi* (as CONSECUTION)]
■ *adj.* **1** see ATTENDANT *adj.* 1. **2** see NATURAL *adj.* 8.

consequential /kónsikwénsh'l/ *adj.* **1** following as a result or consequence. **2** resulting indirectly (*consequential damage*). **3** (of a person) self-important. □□ **consequentiality** /-shiálliti/ *n.* **consequentially** *adv.* [L *consequentia*]

consequently /kónsikwentli/ *adv.* & *conj.* as a result; therefore.
■ so, therefore, as a result *or* consequence, in consequence, accordingly, *ergo*, hence, *formal* thus.

conservancy /kənsérvənsi/ *n.* (*pl.* **-ies**) **1** *Brit.* a commission etc. controlling a port, river, etc. (*Thames Conservancy*). **2** a body concerned with the preservation of natural resources (*Nature Conservancy*). **3** conservation; official preservation (of forests etc.). [18th-c. alt. of obs. *conservacy* f. AF *conservacie* f. AL *conservatia* f. L *conservatio* (as CONSERVE)]

conservation /kónsərváysh'n/ *n.* preservation, esp. of the natural environment. □ **conservation area** an area containing a noteworthy environment and specially protected by law against undesirable changes. **conservation of energy** (or **mass** or **momentum** etc.) *Physics* the principle that the total quantity of energy etc. of any system not subject to external action remains constant. □□ **conservational** *adj.* [ME f. OF *conservation* or L *conservatio* (as CONSERVE)]
■ preservation, protection, safe keeping, maintenance, upkeep, management, safeguarding; husbandry, environmentalism, greenness.

conservationist /kónsərváyshənist/ *n.* a supporter or advocate of environmental conservation.
■ environmentalist, ecologist, preservationist; see also NATURALIST.

conservative /kənsérvətiv/ *adj.* & *n.* ● *adj.* **1 a** averse to rapid change. **b** (of views, taste, etc.) moderate, avoiding extremes (*conservative in his dress*). **2** (of an estimate etc.) purposely low; moderate, cautious. **3** (**Conservative**) of or characteristic of Conservatives or the Conservative Party. **4** tending to conserve. ● *n.* **1** a conservative person. **2** (**Conservative**) a supporter or member of the Conservative Party. □ **Conservative Judaism** Judaism allowing only minor changes in traditional ritual etc. **Conservative Party 1** a British political party promoting free enterprise and private ownership. **2** a similar party elsewhere. **conservative surgery** surgery that seeks to preserve tissues as far as possible. □□ **conservatism** *n.* **conservatively** *adv.* **conservativeness** *n.* [ME f. LL *conservativus* (as CONSERVE)]
■ *adj.* **1 a** unprogressive, orthodox, traditional, conformist, hidebound, conventional, fundamentalist, true-blue, dyed in the wool, inveterate. **b** cautious, careful, prudent, moderate, traditional, temperate, middle-of-the-road, sober, stable. **2** low, moderate; cautious, tentative, hesitant. **3** Tory. ● *n.* **1** reactionary, fundamentalist; moderate, middle-of-the-roader. **2** Tory.

conservatoire /kənsérvətwaar/ *n.* a (usu. European) school of music or other arts. [F f. It. *conservatorio* (as CONSERVATORY)]
■ *Austral.* conservatorium, *US* conservatory.

conservator /kónsərvaytər, kənsérvətər/ *n.* a person who preserves something; an official custodian (of a museum etc.). [ME f. AF *conservatour*, OF *-ateur* f. L *conservator -oris* (as CONSERVE)]

conservatorium /kənsérvətóriəm/ *n.* *Austral.* = CONSERVATOIRE.

conservatory /kənsérvətəri, -tri/ *n.* (*pl.* **-ies**) **1** a greenhouse for tender plants, esp. one attached to and communicating with a house. **2** esp. *US* = CONSERVATOIRE. [LL *conservatorium* (as CONSERVE): sense 2 through It. *conservatorio*]
■ **1** see HOTHOUSE *n.* 1.

conserve /kənsérv/ *v.* & *n.* ● *v.tr.* **1** store up; keep from harm or damage, esp. for later use. **2** *Physics* maintain a quantity of (heat etc.). **3** preserve (food, esp. fruit), usu. with sugar. ● *n.* /also kónserv/ **1** fruit etc. preserved in sugar. **2** fresh fruit jam. [ME f. OF *conserver* f. L *conservare* (as COM-, *servare* keep)]
■ *v.* **1** keep, preserve, hold on to, store up, save, spare, reserve; maintain, keep up, take care of. **3** see PRESERVE *v.* 4a. ● *n.* **2** see PRESERVE *n.* 1.

consider /kənsíddər/ *v.tr.* (often *absol.*) **1** contemplate mentally, esp. in order to reach a conclusion. **2** examine the merits of (a course of action, a candidate, claim, etc.). **3** give attention to. **4** reckon with; take into account. **5** (foll. by *that* + clause) have the opinion. **6** (foll. by compl.) believe; regard as (*consider it to be genuine*; *consider it settled*). **7** (as **considered** *adj.*) formed after careful thought (*a considered opinion*). □ **all things considered** taking everything into account. [ME f. OF *considerer* f. L *considerare* examine]

■ **1** think about *or* over, deliberate (over *or* about), contemplate, ponder, mull over, cogitate on, meditate (on *or* upon *or* over *or* about), reflect (on *or* upon *or* about), ruminate (on *or* over *or* about), chew over, study, examine. **2** see DELIBERATE *v.* 2. **3** see HEED *v.* **4** heed, mark, take into account *or* consideration, reckon with, bear in mind, think of *or* about, note, observe, make allowance for; respect, have regard for. **5** see RECKON 4a. **6** regard, look upon; judge, take to be, think, believe, gauge, rate, estimate, reckon, *formal* deem.

considerable /kənsíddərəb'l/ *adj.* **1** enough in amount or extent to need consideration. **2** much; a lot of (*considerable pain*). **3** notable, important. □□ **considerably** *adv.*

■ **1, 2** sizeable, substantial, large, big, great, no little, appreciable, respectable, noticeable, largish, biggish, goodly, decent, fair, *colloq.* tidy; much, a lot of. **3** important, worthy, of consequence, of distinction, distinguished, illustrious, noteworthy, notable, remarkable, estimable, influential, respectable.

considerate /kənsíddərət/ *adj.* **1** thoughtful towards other people; careful not to cause hurt or inconvenience. **2** *archaic* careful. □□ **considerately** *adv.*

■ **1** thoughtful, kind, kindly, kind-hearted, good-hearted, helpful, friendly, neighbourly, gracious, obliging, accommodating, charitable, generous, unselfish; sympathetic, compassionate, sensitive, attentive, solicitous, *Psychol.* empathetic, empathic.

consideration /kənsíddəráysh'n/ *n.* **1** the act of considering; careful thought. **2** thoughtfulness for others; being considerate. **3** a fact or a thing taken into account in deciding or judging something. **4** compensation; a payment or reward. **5** *Law* (in a contractual agreement) anything given or promised or forborne by one party in exchange for the promise or undertaking of another. **6** *archaic* importance or consequence. □ **in consideration of** in return for; on account of. **take into consideration** include as a factor, reason, etc.; make allowance for. **under consideration** being considered. [ME f. OF f. L *consideratio -onis* (as CONSIDER)]

■ **1** thought, deliberation, reflection, contemplation, rumination, cogitation; study, examination. **2** thoughtfulness, regard, concern, attentiveness, solicitude, compassion, kindness, kindliness, kind-heartedness, considerateness, respect, care, concern, *Psychol.* empathy. **3** see POINT *n.* 11. **4** reward, compensation, remuneration, fee, payment, recompense, emolument, tip, gratuity, *pourboire*, baksheesh, honorarium. **6** see IMPORTANCE 2.

considering /kənsíddəring/ *prep.* **1** in view of; taking into consideration (*considering their youth*; *considering that it was snowing*). **2** (without compl.) *colloq.* all in all; taking everything into account (*not so bad, considering*).

■ **1** in view of, in (the) light of, bearing in mind, making allowance for, taking into consideration *or* account, looking at, inasmuch as, insomuch as. **2** all things *or* everything considered; see also *on the whole* (WHOLE).

consign /kənsín/ *v.tr.* (often foll. by *to*) **1** hand over; deliver to a person's possession or trust. **2** assign; commit decisively or permanently (*consigned it to the dustbin*; *consigned to years of misery*). **3** transmit or send (goods), usu. by a public carrier. □□ **consignee** /kónsīneé/ *n.* **consignor** *n.* [ME f. F *consigner* or L *consignare* mark with a seal (as COM-, SIGN)]

■ **1** see ENTRUST 1. **2** dispatch, dismiss, relegate; see also DOWNGRADE *v.* 1. **3** see SEND 1a.

consignment /kənsínmənt/ *n.* **1** the act or an instance of consigning; the process of being consigned. **2** a batch of goods consigned.

■ **2** see CARGO 1b, 2b.

consist /kənsíst/ *v.intr.* **1** (foll. by *of*) be composed; have specified ingredients or elements. **2** (foll. by *in*, *of*) have its essential features as specified (*its beauty consists in the use of colour*). **3** (usu. foll. by *with*) harmonize; be consistent. [L *consistere* exist (as COM-, *sistere* stop)]

■ **1** (*consist of*) contain, comprise, be composed of, include, have in it.

consistency /kənsístənsi/ *n.* (also **consistence**) (*pl.* **-ies** or **-es**) **1** the degree of density, firmness, or viscosity, esp. of thick liquids. **2** the state of being consistent; conformity with other or earlier attitudes, practice, etc. **3** the state or quality of holding or sticking together and retaining shape. [F *consistence* or LL *consistentia* (as CONSIST)]

■ **1** texture, viscosity, density, firmness, compactness. **2** see UNIFORMITY.

consistent /kənsístənt/ *adj.* (usu. foll. by *with*) **1** compatible or in harmony; not contradictory. **2** (of a person) constant to the same principles of thought or action. □□ **consistently** *adv.* [L *consistere* (as CONSIST)]

■ **1** in agreement, in harmony, in keeping, harmonious, in concordance, in conformance *or* conformity, accordant, compatible, in accord *or* accordance, consonant, consequent. **2** dependable, regular, constant, predictable, undeviating, steady, steadfast, unchanging, unswerving. □□ **consistently** steadily, constantly, regularly, often, frequently; reliably, dependably, uniformly, unswervingly, devotedly, firmly, resolutely, faithfully, unfailingly, undeviatingly.

consistory /kənsístəri/ *n.* (*pl.* **-ies**) **1** *RC Ch.* the council of cardinals (with or without the pope). **2** (in full **consistory court**) (in the Church of England) a court presided over by a bishop, for the administration of ecclesiastical law in a diocese. **3** (in other Churches) a local administrative body. □□ **consistorial** /kónsistóriəl/ *adj.* [ME f. AF *consistorie*, OF *-oire* f. LL *consistorium* (as CONSIST)]

consociation /kənsṓshiáysh'n, kənsṓsi-/ *n.* **1** close association, esp. of Churches or religious communities. **2** *Ecol.* a closely-related sub-group of plants having one dominant species. [L *consociatio, -onis* f. *consociare* (as COM-, *socius* fellow)]

■ **1** see SOCIETY 8.

consolation /kónsəláysh'n/ *n.* **1** the act or an instance of consoling; the state of being consoled. **2** a consoling thing, person, or circumstance. □ **consolation prize** a prize given to a competitor who just fails to win a main prize. □□ **consolatory** /kənsóllətəri, -tri/ *adj.* [ME f. OF, f. L *consolatio -onis* (as CONSOLE[1])]

■ see COMFORT *n.* 1.

console[1] /kənsṓl/ *v.tr.* comfort, esp. in grief or disappointment. ¶ Often confused with *condole*. □□ **consolable** *adj.* **consoler** *n.* **consolingly** *adv.* [F *consoler* f. L *consolari*]

■ comfort, soothe, calm, assuage, solace, cheer (up), reassure, relieve, hearten, cheer, gladden.

console[2] /kónsōl/ *n.* **1** a panel or unit accommodating a set of switches, controls, etc. **2** a cabinet for television or radio equipment etc. **3** *Mus.* a cabinet with the keyboards, stops, pedals, etc., of an organ. **4** an ornamented bracket supporting a shelf etc. □ **console table** a table supported by a bracket against a wall. [F, perh. f. *consolider* (as CONSOLIDATE)]

consolidate /kənsóllidayt/ *v.* **1** *tr.* & *intr.* make or become strong or solid. **2** *tr.* reinforce or strengthen (one's position, power, etc.). **3** *tr.* combine (territories, companies, debts, etc.) into one whole. □ **consolidated fund** (or **annuities**) *Brit.* a Bank of England fund into which tax revenue is paid and from which payments not dependent on annual votes in Parliament are made. □□ **consolidation** /-dáysh'n/ *n.*

consolidator *n.* **consolidatory** *adj.* [L *consolidare* (as COM-, *solidare* f. *solidus* solid)]
■ **1, 2** see STRENGTHEN. **3** see AMALGAMATE.

consols /kónsolz/ *n.pl.* British government securities without redemption date and with fixed annual interest. [abbr. of *consolidated annuities*]

consommé /kənsómmay/ *n.* a clear soup made with meat stock. [F, past part. of *consommer* f. L *consummare* (as CONSUMMATE)]
■ see BROTH.

consonance /kónsənənss/ *n.* **1** agreement, harmony. **2** *Prosody* a recurrence of similar-sounding consonants. **3** *Mus.* a harmonious combination of notes; a harmonious interval. [ME f. OF *consonance* or L *consonantia* (as CONSONANT)]
■ **1** see HARMONY 3.

consonant /kónsənənt/ *n.* & *adj.* ● *n.* **1** a speech sound in which the breath is at least partly obstructed, and which to form a syllable must be combined with a vowel. **2** a letter or letters representing this. ● *adj.* (foll. by *with, to*) **1** consistent; in agreement or harmony. **2** similar in sound. **3** *Mus.* making a concord. □□ **consonantal** /-nánt'l/ *adj.* **consonantly** *adv.* [ME f. F f. L *consonare* (as COM-, *sonare* sound f. *sonus*)]
■ *adj.* **1** see CONSISTENT 1.

con sordino /kón sordéenō/ *adv. Mus.* with the use of a mute. [It.]

consort[1] *n.* & *v.* ● *n.* /kónsort/ **1** a wife or husband, esp. of royalty (*prince consort*). **2** a ship sailing with another. ● *v.* /kənsórt/ **1** *intr.* (usu. foll. by *with, together*) **a** keep company; associate. **b** harmonize. **2** *tr.* class or bring together. [ME f. F f. L *consors* sharer, comrade (as COM-, *sors sortis* lot, destiny)]
■ *n.* **1** see MATE[1] *n.* 3b. ● *v.* **1 a** see ASSOCIATE *v.* 5.

consort[2] /kónsort/ *n. Mus.* a group of players or instruments, esp. playing early music (*recorder consort*). [earlier form of CONCERT]

consortium /kənsórtiəm/ *n.* (*pl.* **consortia** /-tiə/ or **consortiums**) **1** an association, esp. of several business companies. **2** *Law* the right of association with a husband or wife (*loss of consortium*). [L, = partnership (as CONSORT[1])]
■ **1** see ASSOCIATION 1.

conspecific /kónspisíffik/ *adj. Biol.* of the same species.

conspectus /kənspéktəss/ *n.* **1** a general or comprehensive survey. **2** a summary or synopsis. [L f. *conspicere conspect-* (as COM-, *spicere* look at)]
■ **2** see SYNOPSIS 1, 2.

conspicuous /kənspíkyooəss/ *adj.* **1** clearly visible; striking to the eye; attracting notice. **2** remarkable of its kind (*conspicuous extravagance*). □□ **conspicuously** *adv.* **conspicuousness** *n.* [L *conspicuus* (as CONSPECTUS)]
■ **1** obvious, unmistakable, prominent, outstanding, noticeable, impressive, vivid, obtrusive; striking, loud, blatant; evident, apparent, clear-cut, unquestionable, incontestable, incontrovertible. **2** notable, noteworthy, exceptional, outstanding, eminent, unusual, marked, extraordinary, remarkable, distinguished, impressive, awesome, awe-inspiring, glorious.

conspiracy /kənspírrəsi/ *n.* (*pl.* **-ies**) **1** a secret plan to commit a crime or do harm, often for political ends; a plot. **2** the act of conspiring. □ **conspiracy of silence** an agreement to say nothing. [ME f. AF *conspiracie*, alt. form of OF *conspiration* f. L *conspiratio -onis* (as CONSPIRE)]
■ **1** plot, scheme, stratagem, cabal, intrigue, machination. **2** collusion, connivance, intrigue, foul play, dirty work *or* tricks.

conspirator /kənspírrətər/ *n.* a person who takes part in a conspiracy. □□ **conspiratorial** /-tóriəl/ *adj.* **conspiratorially** /-tóriəli/ *adv.* [ME f. AF *conspiratour*, OF *-teur* (as CONSPIRE)]
■ see ACCOMPLICE.

conspire /kənspír/ *v.intr.* **1** combine secretly to plan and prepare an unlawful or harmful act. **2** (often foll. by *against*, or *to* + infin.) (of events or circumstances) seem to be working together, esp. disadvantageously. [ME f. OF *conspirer* f. L *conspirare* agree, plot (as COM-, *spirare* breathe)]
■ **1** see PLOT *v.* 2.

constable /kúnstəb'l/ *n.* **1** *Brit.* **a** a policeman or policewoman. **b** (also **police constable**) a police officer of the lowest rank. **2** the governor of a royal castle. **3** *hist.* the principal officer in a royal household. □ **Chief Constable** the head of the police force of a county or other region. [ME f. OF *conestable* f. LL *comes stabuli* count of the stable]
■ **1 a** policeman, policewoman, (police) officer, PC, WPC, *US* lawman, *colloq.* flattie, *Brit. colloq.* bobby, bluebottle, *sl.* cop, flatfoot, fuzz, busy, finger, jack, *Austral. sl.* walloper, John Hop, *Brit. sl.* copper, rozzer, *Brit. archaic sl. or dial.* peeler, *sl. derog.* pig. **b** *US* patrolman.

constabulary /kənstábyooləri/ *n.* & *adj.* ● *n.* (*pl.* **-ies**) an organized body of police; a police force. ● *attrib.adj.* of or concerning the police force. [med.L *constabularius* (as CONSTABLE)]
■ *n.* see POLICE *n.*

constancy /kónstənsi/ *n.* **1** the quality of being unchanging and dependable; faithfulness. **2** firmness, endurance. [L *constantia* (as CONSTANT)]
■ **1** see LOYALTY. **2** see DETERMINATION 1.

constant /kónstənt/ *adj.* & *n.* ● *adj.* **1** continuous (*needs constant attention*). **2** occurring frequently (*receive constant complaints*). **3** (often foll. by *to*) unchanging, faithful, dependable. ● *n.* **1** anything that does not vary. **2** *Math.* a component of a relationship between variables that does not change its value. **3** *Physics* **a** a number expressing a relation, property, etc., and remaining the same in all circumstances. **b** such a number that remains the same for a substance in the same conditions. □□ **constantly** *adv.* [ME f. OF f. L *constare* (as COM-, *stare* stand)]
■ *adj.* **1** continuous, continual; incessant, unceasing, ceaseless, perpetual, persistent, uninterrupted, steady, regular, invariable, unremitting, unvarying, relentless, unrelenting, unending, endless, never-ending, non-stop, perennial, eternal, everlasting, *rhet.* sempiternal. **2** frequent, numerous; see also MANY *adj.* **3** unchanging, invariable, unvarying, fixed, uniform, unalterable, inalterable, immutable, changeless; resolute, immovable, steadfast, firm, dependable, unshakeable, determined, unswerving, undeviating, persevering, unwearying, unwearied, untiring, indefatigable, tireless, unflagging, unwavering, unfailing, unfaltering, persistent; loyal, true, tried and true, devoted, staunch, faithful, *archaic* trusty.

constantan /kónstəntan/ *n.* an alloy of copper and nickel used in electrical equipment. [CONSTANT + -AN]

constellate /kónstəlayt/ *v.tr.* **1** form into (or as if into) a constellation. **2** adorn as with stars.

constellation /kónstəláysh'n/ *n.* **1** a group of fixed stars whose outline is traditionally regarded as forming a particular figure. **2** a group of associated persons, ideas, etc. [ME f. OF f. LL *constellatio -onis* (as COM-, *stella* star)]

consternate /kónstərnayt/ *v.tr.* (usu. in *passive*) dismay; fill with anxiety. [L *consternare* (as COM-, *sternere* throw down)]

consternation /kónstərnáysh'n/ *n.* anxiety or dismay causing mental confusion. [F *consternation* or L *consternatio* (as CONSTERNATE)]
■ see DISMAY *n.* 1.

constipate /kónstipayt/ *v.tr.* (esp. as **constipated** *adj.*) affect with constipation. [L *constipare* (as COM-, *stipare* press)]

constipation /kónstipáysh'n/ *n.* **1** a condition with hardened faeces and difficulty in emptying the bowels. **2** a restricted state. [ME f. OF *constipation* or LL *constipatio* (as CONSTIPATE)]

constituency /kənstítyooənsi/ *n.* (*pl.* **-ies**) **1** a body of voters in a specified area who elect a representative member to a legislative body. **2** the area represented in this way. **3** a body of customers, supporters, etc.

constituent /kənstítyooənt/ *adj.* & *n.* ● *adj.* **1** composing or helping to make up a whole. **2** able to make or change a (political etc.) constitution (*constituent assembly*). **3** appointing or electing. ● *n.* **1** a member of a constituency (esp. political). **2** a component part. **3** *Law* a person who appoints another as agent. [L *constituent-* partly through F *-ant* (as CONSTITUTE)]
■ *n.* **2** see INGREDIENT.

constitute /kónstityoot/ *v.tr.* **1** be the components or essence of; make up, form. **2 a** be equivalent or tantamount to (*this constitutes an official warning*). **b** formally establish (*does not constitute a precedent*). **3** give legal or constitutional form to; establish by law. □□ **constitutor** *n.* [L *constituere* (as COM-, *statuere* set up)]
■ **1** see FORM *v.* 3. **2 a** see MAKE *v.* 5. **b** see ESTABLISH 1.

constitution /kónstityóosh'n/ *n.* **1** the act or method of constituting; the composition (of something). **2 a** the body of fundamental principles or established precedents according to which a State or other organization is acknowledged to be governed. **b** a (usu. written) record of this. **3** a person's physical state as regards vitality, health, strength, etc. **4** a person's mental or psychological make-up. **5** *hist.* a decree or ordinance. [ME f. OF *constitution* or L *constitutio* (as CONSTITUTE)]
■ **1** see STRUCTURE *n.* 2. **2, 5** see LAW 1a, b. **3** see HEALTH 2. **4** see MAKE-UP 5.

constitutional /kónstityóoshən'l/ *adj.* & *n.* ● *adj.* **1** of, consistent with, authorized by, or limited by a political constitution (*a constitutional monarchy*). **2** inherent in, stemming from, or affecting the physical or mental constitution. ● *n.* a walk taken regularly to maintain or restore good health. □□ **constitutionality** /-nálliti/ *n.* **constitutionalize** *v.tr.* (also **-ise**). **constitutionally** *adv.*
■ *adj.* **1** see LEGITIMATE *adj.* 1, 2. **2** see INHERENT 1. ● *n.* see WALK *n.* 2b.

constitutionalism /kónstityóoshənəliz'm/ *n.* **1** a constitutional system of government. **2** the adherence to or advocacy of such a system. □□ **constitutionalist** *n.*

constitutive /kónstityootiv/ *adj.* **1** able to form or appoint. **2** component. **3** essential. □□ **constitutively** *adv.* [LL *constitutivus* (as CONSTITUTE)]

constrain /kənstráyn/ *v.tr.* **1** compel; urge irresistibly or by necessity. **2 a** confine forcibly; imprison. **b** restrict severely as regards action, behaviour, etc. **3** bring about by compulsion. **4** (as **constrained** *adj.*) forced, embarrassed (*a constrained voice*; *a constrained manner*). □□ **constrainedly** /-nidli/ *adv.* [ME f. OF *constraindre* f. L *constringere* (as COM-, *stringere strict-* tie)]
■ **1, 3** see FORCE[1] *v.* 1. **2** see BOUND[2] *v.* **4** (**constrained**) see STRAINED 1.

constraint /kənstráynt/ *n.* **1** the act or result of constraining or being constrained; restriction of liberty. **2** something that constrains; a limitation on motion or action. **3** the restraint of natural feelings or their expression; a constrained manner. [ME f. OF *constreinte*, fem. past part. (as CONSTRAIN)]

constrict /kənstríkt/ *v.tr.* **1** make narrow or tight; compress. **2** *Biol.* cause (organic tissue) to contract. □□ **constriction** *n.* **constrictive** *adj.* [L (as CONSTRAIN)]
■ **1** see CONTRACT *v.* 1.

constrictor /kənstríktər/ *n.* **1** any snake (esp. a boa) that kills by coiling round its prey and compressing it. **2** *Anat.* any muscle that compresses or contracts an organ or part of the body. [mod.L (as CONSTRICT)]

construct *v.* & *n.* ● *v.tr.* /kənstrúkt/ **1** make by fitting parts together; build, form (something physical or abstract). **2** *Geom.* draw or delineate, esp. accurately to given conditions (*construct a triangle*). ● *n.* /kónstrukt/ **1** a thing constructed, esp. by the mind. **2** *Linguistics* a group of words forming a phrase. □□ **constructor** *n.* [L *construere construct-* (as COM-, *struere* pile, build)]
■ *v.* **1** build, erect, make, put together, frame, set up, put up, assemble; fabricate, devise, create, forge, invent, formulate, compose, form, shape, fashion. ● *n.* **1** see INVENTION 1.

construction /kənstrúksh'n/ *n.* **1** the act or a mode of constructing. **2** a thing constructed. **3** an interpretation or explanation (*they put a generous construction on his act*). **4** *Gram.* an arrangement of words according to syntactical rules. □□ **constructional** *adj.* **constructionally** *adv.* [ME f. OF f. L *constructio -onis* (as CONSTRUCT)]
■ **1, 2** see STRUCTURE *n.* 1a, b, 2. **3** see RENDITION 1.

constructionism /kənstrúkshəniz'm/ *n.* = CONSTRUCTIVISM.

constructive /kənstrúktiv/ *adj.* **1 a** of construction; tending to construct. **b** tending to form a basis for ideas (*constructive criticism*). **2** helpful, positive (*a constructive approach*). **3** derived by inference; not expressed (*constructive permission*). **4** belonging to the structure of a building. □□ **constructively** *adv.* **constructiveness** *n.* [LL *constructivus* (as CONSTRUCT)]
■ **2** helpful, useful, practicable, practical, productive, beneficial, positive. **3** virtual, inferential, implicit, inferred, derived, deduced. **4** structural.

constructivism /kənstrúktiviz'm/ *n.* *Art* a Russian movement in which assorted (usu. mechanical or industrial) objects are combined into non-representational and mobile structural forms. □□ **constructivist** *n.* [Russ. *konstruktivizm* (as CONSTRUCT)]

construe /kənstróo/ *v.tr.* (**construes, construed, construing**) **1** interpret (words or actions) (*their decision can be construed in many ways*). **2** (often foll. by *with*) combine (words) grammatically (*'rely' is construed with 'on'*). **3** analyse the syntax of (a sentence). **4** translate word for word. □□ **construable** *adj.* **construal** *n.* [ME f. L *construere* CONSTRUCT]
■ **1** see INTERPRET 4.

consubstantial /kónsəbstánsh'l/ *adj.* *Theol.* of the same substance (esp. of the three persons of the Trinity). □□ **consubstantiality** /-shiálliti/ *n.* [ME f. eccl.L *consubstantialis*, transl. Gk *homoousios* (as COM-, SUBSTANTIAL)]

consubstantiation /kónsəbstánshiáysh'n/ *n.* *Theol.* the real substantial presence of the body and blood of Christ together with the bread and wine in the Eucharist. [mod.L *consubstantiatio*, after *transubstantiatio* TRANSUBSTANTIATION]

consuetude /kónswityood/ *n.* a custom, esp. one having legal force in Scotland. □□ **consuetudinary** /kónswityóodinəri/ *adj.* [ME f. OF *consuetude* or L *consuetudo -dinis* f. *consuetus* accustomed]

consul /kóns'l/ *n.* **1** an official appointed by a State to live in a foreign city and protect the State's citizens and interests there. **2** *hist.* either of two annually elected chief magistrates in ancient Rome. **3** any of the three chief magistrates of the French republic (1799–1804). □□ **consular** /kónsyoolər/ *adj.* **consulship** *n.* [ME f. L, rel. to *consulere* take counsel]
■ **1** see MINISTER *n.* 1, 3.

consulate /kónsyoolət/ *n.* **1** the building officially used by a consul. **2** the office, position, or period of office of consul. **3** *hist.* government by consuls. **4** *hist.* the period of office of a consul. **5** *hist.* (**Consulate**) the government of France by three consuls (1799–1804). [ME f. L *consulatus* (as CONSUL)]

consult /kənsúlt/ *v.* **1** *tr.* seek information or advice from (a person, book, watch, etc.). **2** *intr.* (often foll. by *with*) refer to a person for advice, an opinion, etc. **3** *tr.* seek permission or approval from (a person) for a proposed action. **4** *tr.* take into account; consider (feelings, interests, etc.). □□ **consultative** /-tətiv/ *adj.* [F *consulter* f. L *consultare* frequent. of *consulere consult-* take counsel]
■ **1, 2** refer to, look in *or* at; confer (with), discuss (with), deliberate (with), talk over (with), inquire *or* enquire (of), seek advice (from), ask (of), question, take counsel (with). **4** see CONSIDER 4.

consultancy /kənsúltənsi/ *n.* (*pl.* **-ies**) the professional practice or position of a consultant.

consultant /kənsúlt'nt/ *n.* **1** a person providing professional advice etc., esp. for a fee. **2** a senior specialist in a branch of medicine responsible for patients in a hospital. [prob. F (as CONSULT)]
■ **1** expert, counsellor; see also ADVISER. **2** specialist, expert.

consultation /kónsəltáysh'n/ *n.* **1** a meeting arranged to consult (esp. with a consultant). **2** the act or an instance of consulting. **3** a conference. [ME f. OF *consultation* or L *consultatio* (as CONSULTANT)]

■ **1, 2** see TALK *n.* 1. **3** see CONFERENCE 1.

consulting /kənsúlting/ *attrib.adj.* giving professional advice to others working in the same field or subject (*consulting physician*).

consumable /kənsyóōməb'l/ *adj.* & *n.* ● *adj.* that can be consumed; intended for consumption. ● *n.* (usu. in *pl.*) a commodity that is eventually used up, worn out, or eaten.

consume /kənsyóōm/ *v.tr.* **1** eat or drink. **2** completely destroy; reduce to nothing or to tiny particles (*fire consumed the building*). **3** (often as **consumed** *adj.*) possess or entirely take up (foll. by *with*: *consumed with rage*). **4** use up (time, energy, etc.). ▫▫ **consumingly** *adv.* [ME f. L *consumere* (as COM-, *sumere sumpt-* take up): partly through F *consumer*]

■ **1** devour, eat (up), gulp (down), swallow, put away, gobble (up); drink (up); digest. **2** destroy, ruin, (lay) waste, demolish, devastate, wreck, ravage, gut, raze, *US sl.* total. **3** overcome, overwhelm, possess, eat up, devour; (**consumed**) preoccupied, obsessed, absorbed. **4** use up, exhaust, occupy, absorb, deplete, drain, expend; waste, squander, fritter away, dissipate, lose, throw away, lavish, *sl.* blow.

consumer /kənsyóōmər/ *n.* **1** a person who consumes, esp. one who uses a product. **2** a purchaser of goods or services. ▫ **consumer durable** a household product with a relatively long useful life (e.g. a radio or washing-machine). **consumer goods** goods put to use by consumers, not used in producing other goods (opp. *capital goods* (see CAPITAL[1])). **consumer research** investigation of purchasers' needs and opinions. **consumer society** a society in which the marketing of goods and services is an important social and economic activity.

■ **1** see USER 1. **2** see BUYER.

consumerism /kənsyóōməriz'm/ *n.* the protection or promotion of consumers' interests in relation to the producer. ▫▫ **consumerist** *adj.* & *n.*

consummate *v.* & *adj.* ● *v.tr.* /kónsəmayt/ **1** complete; make perfect. **2** complete (a marriage) by sexual intercourse. ● *adj.* /kənsúmmit, kónsəmit/ complete, perfect; fully skilled (*a consummate general*). ▫▫ **consummately** *adv.* **consummative** *adj.* **consummator** /kónsəmaytər/ *n.* [L *consummare* (as COM-, *summare* complete f. *summus* utmost)]

■ *v.* **1** see FINISH *v.* 1a. ● *adj.* see COMPLETE *adj.* 4.

consummation /kónsəmáysh'n/ *n.* **1** completion, esp. of a marriage by sexual intercourse. **2** a desired end or goal; perfection. [ME f. OF *consommation* or L *consummatio* (as CONSUMMATE)]

■ **1** completion, accomplishment, fulfilment, finish, end, realization, attainment, achievement, success. **2** acme, perfection, peak, culmination, finishing touch, conclusion, grand finale, climax.

consumption /kənsúmpsh'n/ *n.* **1** the act or an instance of consuming; the process of being consumed. **2** any disease causing wasting of tissues, esp. pulmonary tuberculosis. **3** an amount consumed. **4** the purchase and use of goods etc. [ME f. OF *consomption* f. L *consumptio* (as CONSUME)]

■ **1, 4** see USE *n.* 1.

consumptive /kənsúmptiv/ *adj.* & *n.* ● *adj.* **1** of or tending to consumption. **2** tending to or affected with pulmonary tuberculosis. ● *n.* a consumptive patient. ▫▫ **consumptively** *adv.* [med.L *consumptivus* (as CONSUMPTION)]

■ *adj.* **2** tuberculate, tuberculous, tubercular, phthisic(al); see also EMACIATE. ● *n.* tubercular.

cont. *abbr.* **1** contents. **2** continued.

contact *n.* & *v.* ● *n.* /kóntakt/ **1** the state or condition of touching, meeting, or communicating. **2** a person who is or may be communicated with for information, supplies, assistance, etc. **3** *Electr.* **a** a connection for the passage of a current. **b** a device for providing this. **4** a person likely to carry a contagious disease through being associated with an infected person. **5** (usu. in *pl.*) *colloq.* a contact lens. ● *v.tr.* /kóntakt, kəntákt/ **1** get into communication with (a person). **2** begin correspondence or personal dealings with. ▫ **contact lens** a small lens placed directly on the eyeball to correct the vision. **contact print** a photographic print made by placing a negative directly on sensitized paper etc. and illuminating it. **contact sport** a sport in which participants necessarily come into bodily contact with one another. ▫▫ **contactable** *adj.* [L *contactus* f. *contingere* (as COM-, *tangere* touch)]

■ *n.* **1** conjunction, connection, touch, communication, meeting, association. **2** acquaintance, friend; see also CONNECTION 6. ● *v.* **1, 2** get in touch with, communicate with, reach, get hold of, speak to *or* with, write to.

contagion /kəntáyjən/ *n.* **1 a** the communication of disease from one person to another by bodily contact. **b** a contagious disease. **2** a contagious or harmful influence. **3** moral corruption, esp. when tending to be widespread. [ME f. L *contagio* (as COM-, *tangere* touch)]

■ **1 b** see DISEASE 3. **2, 3** see POISON *n.* 2.

contagious /kəntáyjəss/ *adj.* **1 a** (of a person) likely to transmit disease by contact. **b** (of a disease) transmitted in this way. **2** (of emotions, reactions, etc.) likely to affect others (*contagious enthusiasm*). ▫ **contagious abortion** brucellosis of cattle. ▫▫ **contagiously** *adv.* **contagiousness** *n.* [ME f. LL *contagiosus* (as CONTAGION)]

■ **1b, 2** see INFECTIOUS 2, 3.

contain /kəntáyn/ *v.tr.* **1** hold or be capable of holding within itself; include, comprise. **2** (of measures) consist of or be equal to (*a gallon contains eight pints*). **3** prevent (an enemy, difficulty, etc.) from moving or extending. **4** control or restrain (oneself, one's feelings, etc.). **5** (of a number) be divisible by (a factor) without a remainder. ▫▫ **containable** *adj.* [ME f. OF *contenir* f. L *continēre content-* (as COM-, *tenēre* hold)]

■ **1** hold, have in it, comprise, lodge; bear, carry; see also INCLUDE 1. **2** consist of, equal; hold. **3, 4** restrain, control, restrict, confine, repress, hold back *or* in, curb, bridle, keep under control, suppress, check, stifle.

container /kəntáynər/ *n.* **1** a vessel, box, etc., for holding particular things. **2** a large boxlike receptacle of standard design for the transport of goods, esp. one readily transferable from one form of transport to another (also *attrib.*: *container ship*).

■ see RECEPTACLE.

containerize /kəntáynərīz/ *v.tr.* (also **-ise**) **1** pack in or transport by container. **2** adapt to transport by container. ▫▫ **containerization** /-záysh'n/ *n.*

■ **1** see PACKAGE *v.*

containment /kəntáynmənt/ *n.* the action or policy of preventing the expansion of a hostile country or influence.

contaminate /kəntámminayt/ *v.tr.* **1** pollute, esp. with radioactivity. **2** infect; corrupt. ▫▫ **contaminant** *n.* **contamination** /-náysh'n/ *n.* **contaminator** *n.* [L *contaminare* (as COM-, *tamen-* rel. to *tangere* touch)]

■ **1** defile, pollute, dirty, poison, foul, spoil, grime, *poet.* befoul, sully; debase, adulterate, vitiate. **2** stain, corrupt, soil, taint, infect.

contango /kəntánggō/ *n.* (*pl.* **-os**) *Brit. Stock Exch.* **1** the postponement of the transfer of stock from one account day to the next. **2** a percentage paid by the buyer for such a postponement. ▫ **contango day** the eighth day before settling day. [19th c.: prob. an arbitrary formation]

conte /KONT/ *n.* **1** a short story (as a form of literary composition). **2** a medieval narrative tale. [F]

contemn /kəntém/ *v.tr. literary* despise; treat with disregard. ▫▫ **contemner** /-témmər, -témnər/ *n.* [ME f. OF *contemner* or L *contemnere* (as COM-, *temnere tempt-* despise)]

■ see DESPISE.

contemplate /kóntəmplayt/ *v.* **1** *tr.* survey with the eyes or in the mind. **2** *tr.* regard (an event) as possible. **3** *tr.* intend; have as one's purpose (*we contemplate leaving tomorrow*). **4**

intr. meditate. □□ **contemplation** /-pláysh'n/ *n.* **contemplator** *n.* [L *contemplari* (as COM-, *templum* place for observations)]

■ **1** look at *or* (up)on, gaze at *or* (up)on, view, survey, observe, regard, eye, scan, *literary* behold; ruminate on *or* over, ponder on *or* over, deliberate over, meditate *or* reflect on, think about *or* over, mull over, cogitate over, turn over in one's mind, brood on *or* over, chew on *or* over, consider, *literary* muse on *or* over. **2** see ENVISAGE 2. **3** plan, think of *or* about, consider, entertain the idea *or* notion of; see also INTEND 1, 2. **4** see MEDITATE 1.

contemplative /kəntémplətiv/ *adj.* & *n.* ● *adj.* of or given to (esp. religious) contemplation; meditative. ● *n.* a person whose life is devoted to religious contemplation. □□ **contemplatively** *adv.* [ME f. OF *contemplatif -ive*, or L *contemplativus* (as CONTEMPLATE)]

■ *adj.* see MEDITATIVE.

contemporaneous /kəntémpəráyniəss/ *adj.* (usu. foll. by *with*) **1** existing or occurring at the same time. **2** of the same period. □□ **contemporaneity** /-née-iti/ *n.* **contemporaneously** *adv.* **contemporaneousness** *n.* [L *contemporaneus* (as COM-, *temporaneus* f. *tempus -oris* time)]

■ see SIMULTANEOUS. □□ **contemporaneity** see COINCIDENCE 1.

contemporary /kəntémpərəri/ *adj.* & *n.* ● *adj.* **1** living or occurring at the same time. **2** approximately equal in age. **3** following modern ideas or fashion in style or design. ● *n.* (*pl.* **-ies**) **1** a person or thing living or existing at the same time as another. **2** a person of roughly the same age as another. □□ **contemporarily** *adv.* **contemporariness** *n.* **contemporarize** *v.tr.* (also **-ise**). [med.L *contemporarius* (as CONTEMPORANEOUS)]

■ *adj.* **1** contemporaneous, coeval, coexistent, concurrent, synchronous, synchronic. **3** modern, current, present-day, new, up to date, stylish, fashionable, modish, à la mode, latest, in, novel, *colloq.* with it, *colloq. often derog.* trendy, *derog.* newfangled. ● *n.* **1** peer, compeer, coeval.

contempt /kəntémpt/ *n.* **1** a feeling that a person or a thing is beneath consideration or worthless, or deserving scorn or extreme reproach. **2** the condition of being held in contempt. **3** (in full **contempt of court**) disobedience to or disrespect for a court of law and its officers. □ **beneath contempt** utterly despicable. **hold in contempt** despise. [ME f. L *contemptus* (as CONTEMN)]

■ **1** scorn, disdain, disgust; loathing, abhorrence, hatred, odium, hate. **2** contumely. □ **beneath contempt** see DESPICABLE.

contemptible /kəntémptib'l/ *adj.* deserving contempt; despicable. □□ **contemptibility** *n.* **contemptibly** *adv.* [ME f. OF or LL *contemptibilis* (as CONTEMN)]

■ despicable, unworthy, shabby, shameful, scurvy, cheap, low, mean, base, measly, fiddling, frippery, misbegotten, miserable, wretched, paltry, petty, pitiable, pitiful, *US* picayune, *colloq.* nasty, blithering, pipsqueak, snotty, *Brit. colloq.* pathetic, *sl.* putrid; loathsome, detestable; currish, vile, ignominious.

contemptuous /kəntémptyooəss/ *adj.* (often foll. by *of*) showing contempt, scornful; insolent. □□ **contemptuously** *adv.* [med.L *contemptuosus* f. L *contemptus* (as CONTEMPT)]

■ scornful, disdainful, sneering, derisive, insulting, contumelious, insolent.

contend /kənténd/ *v.* **1** *intr.* (usu. foll. by *with*) strive, fight. **2** *intr.* compete (*contending emotions*). **3** *tr.* (usu. foll. by *that* + clause) assert, maintain. □□ **contender** *n.* [OF *contendre* or L *contendere* (as COM-, *tendere tent-* stretch, strive)]

■ **1, 2** see STRIVE 2. **3** see MAINTAIN 3.

content[1] /kəntént/ *adj.*, *v.*, & *n.* ● *predic.adj.* **1** satisfied; adequately happy; in agreement. **2** (foll. by *to* + infin.) willing. ● *v.tr.* make content; satisfy. ● *n.* a contented state; satisfaction. □ **to one's heart's content** to the full extent of one's desires. [ME f. OF f. L *contentus* satisfied, past part. of *continēre* (as CONTAIN)]

■ *adj.* **1** pleased, satisfied, happy, delighted, contented, gratified, glad, cheerful; comfortable, fulfilled; in agreement. **2** see WILLING *adj.* ● *v.* satisfy, please, gratify, soothe, cheer, gladden, delight. ● *n.* pleasure, satisfaction, gratification, happiness, contentment, contentedness, felicity, delight.

content[2] /kóntent/ *n.* **1** (usu. in *pl.*) what is contained in something, esp. in a vessel, book, or house. **2** the amount of a constituent contained (*low sodium content*). **3** the substance or material dealt with (in a speech, work of art, etc.) as distinct from its form or style; significance. **4** the capacity or volume of a thing. [ME f. med.L *contentum* (as CONTAIN)]

■ **1** (*contents*) components, constituents; load. **3** substance, subject-matter, material, theme, topic, thesis, text; see also SIGNIFICANCE 2. **4** capacity, volume, size.

contented /kənténtid/ *adj.* (often foll. by *with*, or *to* + infin.) **1** happy, satisfied. **2** (foll. by *with*) willing to be content (*was contented with the outcome*). □□ **contentedly** *adv.* **contentedness** *n.*

contention /kənténsh'n/ *n.* **1** a dispute or argument; rivalry. **2** a point contended for in an argument (*it is my contention that you are wrong*). □ **in contention** competing, esp. with a good chance of success. [ME f. OF *contention* or L *contentio* (as CONTEND)]

■ **1** see RIVALRY. **2** see ARGUMENT 2.

contentious /kənténshəss/ *adj.* **1** argumentative, quarrelsome. **2** likely to cause an argument; disputed, controversial. □□ **contentiously** *adv.* **contentiousness** *n.* [ME f. OF *contentieux* f. L *contentiosus* (as CONTENTION)]

■ **1** see ARGUMENTATIVE. **2** see CONTROVERSIAL 1.

contentment /kənténtmənt/ *n.* a satisfied state; tranquil happiness.

■ ease, comfort, tranquillity, serenity, peace, peacefulness; see also JOY *n.* 1.

conterminous /kontérminəss/ *adj.* (often foll. by *with*) **1** having a common boundary. **2** coextensive, coterminous. □□ **conterminously** *adv.* [L *conterminus* (as COM-, *terminus* boundary)]

contessa /kontéssə/ *n.* an Italian countess. [It. f. LL *comitissa*: see COUNTESS]

contest *n.* & *v.* ● *n.* /kóntest/ **1** a process of contending; a competition. **2** a dispute; a controversy. ● *v.tr.* /kəntést/ **1** challenge or dispute (a decision etc.). **2** debate (a point, statement, etc.). **3** contend or compete for (a prize, parliamentary seat, etc.); compete in (an election). □□ **contestable** /kəntéstəb'l/ *adj.* **contester** /kəntéstər/ *n.* [L *contestari* (as COM-, *testis* witness)]

■ *n.* **1** competition, match, tournament, championship, meet, game. **2** controversy, dispute, debate, altercation, argument, *archaic* velitation; conflict, struggle, fight, battle, war; strife, contention. ● *v.* **1** argue against, dispute, challenge, (call into) question, oppose, counter, object to, *Law* litigate, *disp.* refute. **2** debate. **3** contend for, compete in *or* for.

contestant /kəntéstənt/ *n.* a person who takes part in a contest or competition.

■ contender, competitor, entrant, player, participant; opponent, rival, adversary.

contestation /kóntestáysh'n/ *n.* **1** a disputation. **2** an assertion contended for. [L *contestatio* partly through F (as CONTEST)]

context /kóntekst/ *n.* **1** the parts of something written or spoken that immediately precede and follow a word or passage and clarify its meaning. **2** the circumstances relevant to something under consideration (*must be seen in context*). □ **out of context** without the surrounding words or circumstances and so not fully understandable. □□ **contextual** /kəntékstyooəl/ *adj.* **contextualize** /kəntékstyooəlīz/ *v.tr.* (also **-ise**). **contextualization** /kəntékstyooəlīzáysh'n/ *n.* **contextually** /kəntékstyooəli/ *adv.* [ME f. L *contextus* (as COM-, *texere text-* weave)]

■ structure, framework, environment, situation, circumstance(s); surround, surroundings, frame (of reference), setting, background, connection.

contiguity /kóntigyóō-iti/ *n.* **1** being contiguous; proximity; contact. **2** *Psychol.* the proximity of ideas or impressions in place or time, as a principle of association.
■ **1** see PROXIMITY.

contiguous /kəntígyooəss/ *adj.* (usu. foll. by *with, to*) touching, esp. along a line; in contact. ◻◻ **contiguously** *adv.* [L *contiguus* (as COM-, *tangere* touch)]
■ see NEAR *adj.* 1.

continent[1] /kóntinənt/ *n.* **1** any of the main continuous expanses of land (Europe, Asia, Africa, N. and S. America, Australia, Antarctica). **2** (**the Continent**) *Brit.* the mainland of Europe as distinct from the British Isles. **3** continuous land; a mainland. [L *terra continens* (see CONTAIN) continuous land]

continent[2] /kóntinənt/ *adj.* **1** able to control movements of the bowels and bladder. **2** exercising self-restraint, esp. sexually. ◻◻ **continence** *n.* **continently** *adv.* [ME f. L (as CONTAIN)]
■ **2** see TEMPERATE 4. ◻◻ **continence** see *celibacy* (CELIBATE).

continental /kóntinént'l/ *adj.* & *n.* ● *adj.* **1** of or characteristic of a continent. **2** (**Continental**) *Brit.* of, relating to, or characteristic of mainland Europe. ● *n.* an inhabitant of mainland Europe. ◻ **continental breakfast** a light breakfast of coffee, rolls, etc. **continental climate** a climate having wide variations of temperature. **continental drift** *Geol.* the hypothesis that the continents are moving slowly over the surface of the earth on a deep-lying plastic substratum. **continental quilt** *Brit.* a duvet. **continental shelf** an area of relatively shallow seabed between the shore of a continent and the deeper ocean. ◻◻ **continentally** *adv.*

contingency /kəntínjənsi/ *n.* (*pl.* **-ies**) **1** a future event or circumstance regarded as likely to occur, or as influencing present action. **2** something dependent on another uncertain event or occurrence. **3** uncertainty of occurrence. **4 a** one thing incident to another. **b** an incidental expense etc. ◻ **contingency fund** a fund to cover incidental or unforeseen expenses. [earlier *contingence* f. LL *contingentia* (as CONTINGENT)]
■ **1** see EVENTUALITY. **2** see CONDITION *n.* 1.

contingent /kəntínjənt/ *adj.* & *n.* ● *adj.* **1** (usu. foll. by *on, upon*) conditional, dependent (on an uncertain event or circumstance). **2** associated. **3** (usu. foll. by *to*) incidental. **4 a** that may or may not occur. **b** fortuitous; occurring by chance. **5** true only under existing or specified conditions. ● *n.* a body (esp. of troops, ships, etc.) forming part of a larger group. ◻◻ **contingently** *adv.* [L *contingere* (as COM-, *tangere* touch)]
■ *adj.* **1** see PROVISIONAL. ● *n.* see COHORT 2.

continual /kəntínyooəl/ *adj.* constantly or frequently recurring; always happening. ◻◻ **continually** *adv.* [ME f. OF *continuel* f. *continuer* (as CONTINUE)]
■ constant, incessant, perpetual, non-stop, persistent, uninterrupted, regular, steady, unbroken, unceasing, ceaseless, eternal, unremitting, interminable, endless, unending, continuous.

continuance /kəntínyooənss/ *n.* **1** a state of continuing in existence or operation. **2** the duration of an event or action. **3** *US Law* an adjournment. [ME f. OF (as CONTINUE)]

continuant /kəntínyooənt/ *n.* & *adj.* *Phonet.* ● *n.* a speech sound in which the vocal tract is only partly closed, allowing the breath to pass through and the sound to be prolonged (as with *f, r, s, v*). ● *adj.* of or relating to such a sound. [F *continuant* and L *continuare* (as CONTINUE)]

continuation /kəntínyoo-áysh'n/ *n.* **1** the act or an instance of continuing; the process of being continued. **2** a part that continues something else. **3** *Brit. Stock Exch.* the carrying over of an account to the next settling day. ◻ **continuation day** *Stock Exch.* = *contango day*. [ME f. OF f. L *continuatio -onis* (as CONTINUE)]
■ **1** see MAINTENANCE 1. **2** see SUPPLEMENT *n.* 1.

continuative /kəntínyooətiv/ *adj.* tending or serving to continue. [LL *continuativus* (as CONTINUATION)]

continue /kəntínyōō/ *v.* (**continues, continued, continuing**) **1** *tr.* (often foll. by verbal noun, or *to* + infin.) persist in, maintain, not stop (an action etc.). **2 a** *tr.* (also *absol.*) resume or prolong (a narrative, journey, etc.). **b** *intr.* recommence after a pause (*the concert will continue shortly*). **3** *tr.* be a sequel to. **4** *intr.* **a** remain in existence or unchanged. **b** (with compl.) remain in a specified state (*the weather continued fine*). **5** *tr. US Law* adjourn (proceedings). ◻◻ **continuable** *adj.* **continuer** *n.* [ME f. OF *continuer* f. L *continuare* make or be CONTINUOUS]
■ **1** carry on (with), proceed with, keep (up *or* on *or* at), go on (with), pursue, persist (in *or* with), persevere in; maintain, prolong, sustain. **2** resume, pick up, take up, carry on (with); prolong. **4 a** endure, last, go on, persist, be prolonged, remain, extend.

continuity /kóntinyóō-iti/ *n.* (*pl.* **-ies**) **1 a** the state of being continuous. **b** an unbroken succession. **c** a logical sequence. **2** the detailed and self-consistent scenario of a film or broadcast. **3** the linking of broadcast items. ◻ **continuity girl** (or **man**) the person responsible for agreement of detail between different sessions of filming. [F *continuité* f. L *continuitas -tatis* (as CONTINUOUS)]
■ **1** see UNITY 2.

continuo /kəntínyoo-ō/ *n.* (*pl.* **-os**) *Mus.* an accompaniment providing a bass line and harmonies which are indicated by figures, usu. played on a keyboard instrument. [*basso continuo* (It., = continuous bass)]

continuous /kəntínyooəss/ *adj.* **1** unbroken, uninterrupted, connected throughout in space or time. **2** *Gram.* = PROGRESSIVE. ◻ **continuous assessment** the evaluation of a pupil's progress throughout a course of study, as well as or instead of by examination. **continuous creation** the creation of the universe or the matter in it regarded as a continuous process. **continuous stationery** a continuous ream of paper, usu. perforated to form single sheets. ◻◻ **continuously** *adv.* **continuousness** *n.* [L *continuus* uninterrupted f. *continēre* (as COM-, *tenēre* hold)]
■ **1** connected, unbroken, uninterrupted; incessant, persistent, perpetual, non-stop, unceasing, ceaseless, constant, unremitting, interminable, endless, unending, continual.

continuum /kəntínyooəm/ *n.* (*pl.* **continua** /-yooə/) anything seen as having a continuous, not discrete, structure (*space-time continuum*). [L, neut. of *continuus*: see CONTINUOUS]

contort /kəntórt/ *v.tr.* twist or force out of normal shape. [L *contorquēre contort-* (as COM-, *torquēre* twist)]
■ see TWIST *v.* 1a, b.

contortion /kəntórsh'n/ *n.* **1** the act or process of twisting. **2** a twisted state, esp. of the face or body. [L *contortio* (as CONTORT)]
■ see WARP *n.*

contortionist /kəntórshənist/ *n.* an entertainer who adopts contorted postures.

contour /kóntoor/ *n.* & *v.* ● *n.* **1** an outline, esp. representing or bounding the shape or form of something. **2** the outline of a natural feature, e.g. a coast or mountain mass. **3** a line separating differently coloured parts of a design. ● *v.tr.* **1** mark with contour lines. **2** carry (a road or railway) round the side of a hill. ◻ **contour line** a line on a map joining points of equal altitude. **contour map** a map marked with contour lines. **contour ploughing** ploughing along lines of constant altitude to minimize soil erosion. [F f. It. *contorno* f. *contornare* draw in outline (as COM-, *tornare* turn)]
■ *n.* **1, 2** see OUTLINE *n.* 4. ● *v.* **1** see LINE[1] *v.* 1.

contra /kóntrə/ *n.* (*pl.* **contras**) a member of a counter-revolutionary guerrilla force in Nicaragua. [abbr. of Sp. *contrarevolucionario* counter-revolutionary]

contra- /kóntrə/ *comb. form* **1** against, opposite (*contradict*). **2** *Mus.* (of instruments, organ-stops, etc.) pitched an octave below (*contra-bassoon*). [L *contra* against]

contraband /kóntrəband/ *n.* & *adj.* ● *n.* **1** goods that have been smuggled, or imported or exported illegally. **2**

prohibited trade; smuggling. **3** (in full **contraband of war**) goods forbidden to be supplied by neutrals to belligerents. ● *adj.* **1** forbidden to be imported or exported (at all or without payment of duty). **2** concerning traffic in contraband (*contraband trade*). ◻◻ **contrabandist** *n.* [Sp. *contrabanda* f. It. (as CONTRA-, *bando* proclamation)]

contrabass /kóntrəbayss/ *n. Mus.* = *double-bass*. [It. (*basso* BASS[1])]

contraception /kóntrəsépsh'n/ *n.* the intentional prevention of pregnancy; the use of contraceptives. [CONTRA- + CONCEPTION]
■ birth control.

contraceptive /kóntrəséptiv/ *adj.* & *n.* ● *adj.* preventing pregnancy. ● *n.* a contraceptive device or drug.

contract *n.* & *v.* ● *n.* /kóntrakt/ **1** a written or spoken agreement between two or more parties, intended to be enforceable by law. **2** a document recording this. **3** marriage regarded as a binding commitment. **4** *Bridge* etc. an undertaking to win the number of tricks bid. ● *v.* /kəntrákt/ **1** *tr.* & *intr.* make or become smaller. **2 a** *intr.* (usu. foll. by *with*) make a contract. **b** *intr.* (usu. foll. by *for*, or *to* + infin.) enter formally into a business or legal arrangement. **c** *tr.* (often foll. by *out*) arrange (work) to be done by contract. **3** *tr.* catch or develop (a disease). **4** *tr.* form or develop (a friendship, habit, etc.). **5** *tr.* enter into (marriage). **6** *tr.* incur (a debt etc.). **7** *tr.* shorten (a word) by combination or elision. **8** *tr.* draw (one's muscles, brow, etc.) together. ◻ **contract bridge** the most common form of bridge, in which only tricks bid and won count towards the game. **contract in** (or **out**) (also *refl.*) *Brit.* choose to be involved in (or withdraw or remain out of) a scheme or commitment. ◻◻ **contractive** *adj.* [earlier as adj., = contracted: OF, f. L *contractus* (as COM-, *trahere tract-* draw)]
■ *n.* **1** agreement, understanding, deal, bargain, arrangement, pact, compact. **2** agreement, *Law* memorandum. ● *v.* **1** diminish, reduce, shrink, draw together, narrow, constrict, compress, condense. **2 b** engage, agree, promise, covenant, undertake. **3** catch, acquire, get, come down with, develop, become infected with, *Brit.* go down with. **4** form, forge; see also DEVELOP 1. **8** wrinkle, knit, crease, corrugate, pucker.

contractable /kəntráktəb'l/ *adj.* (of a disease) that can be contracted.

contractible /kəntráktib'l/ *adj.* that can be shrunk or drawn together.

contractile /kəntráktīl/ *adj.* capable of or producing contraction. ◻◻ **contractility** /kóntraktílliti/ *n.*
■ see ELASTIC *adj.* 1, 2.

contraction /kəntráksh'n/ *n.* **1** the act of contracting. **2** *Med.* (usu. in *pl.*) shortening of the uterine muscles during childbirth. **3** shrinking, diminution. **4 a** a shortening of a word by combination or elision. **b** a contracted word or group of words. [F f. L *contractio -onis* (as CONTRACT)]
■ **2** see LABOUR *n.* 3. **4** see ABBREVIATION.

contractor /kəntráktər/ *n.* a person who undertakes a contract, esp. to provide materials, conduct building operations, etc. [LL (as CONTRACT)]

contractual /kəntráktyooəl/ *adj.* of or in the nature of a contract. ◻◻ **contractually** *adv.*

contradict /kóntrədíkt/ *v.tr.* **1** deny or express the opposite of (a statement). **2** deny or express the opposite of a statement made by (a person). **3** be in opposition to or in conflict with (*new evidence contradicted our theory*). ◻◻ **contradictor** *n.* [L *contradicere contradict-* (as CONTRA-, *dicere* say)]
■ **1** counter, dispute, controvert, rebut, deny, reject, *disp.* refute. **2** rebut, argue against, oppose, *archaic or literary* gainsay.

contradiction /kóntrədíksh'n/ *n.* **1 a** statement of the opposite; denial. **b** an instance of this. **2** inconsistency. ◻ **contradiction in terms** a self-contradictory statement or group of words. [ME f. OF f. L *contradictio -onis* (as CONTRADICT)]

contradictory /kóntrədíktəri/ *adj.* **1** expressing a denial or opposite statement. **2** (of statements etc.) mutually opposed or inconsistent. **3** (of a person) inclined to contradict. **4** *Logic* (of two propositions) so related that one and only one must be true. ◻◻ **contradictorily** *adv.* **contradictoriness** *n.* [ME f. LL *contradictorius* (as CONTRADICT)]
■ **2** inconsistent, opposed, conflicting, incompatible, discrepant.

contradistinction /kóntrədistíngksh'n/ *n.* a distinction made by contrasting.

contradistinguish /kóntrədistínggwish/ *v.tr.* (usu. foll. by *from*) distinguish two things by contrasting them.
■ see DIFFERENTIATE 2.

contraflow /kóntrəflō/ *n. Brit.* a flow (esp. of road traffic) alongside, and in a direction opposite to, an established or usual flow, esp. as a temporary or emergency arrangement.

contrail /kóntrayl/ *n.* a condensation trail, esp. from an aircraft. [abbr.]

contraindicate /kóntrəíndikayt/ *v.tr. Med.* act as an indication against (the use of a particular substance or treatment). ◻◻ **contraindication** /-káysh'n/ *n.*

contralto /kəntráltō/ *n.* (*pl.* **-os**) **1 a** the lowest female singing-voice. **b** a singer with this voice. **2** a part written for contralto. [It. (as CONTRA-, ALTO)]

contraposition /kóntrəpəzísh'n/ *n.* **1** opposition or contrast. **2** *Logic* conversion of a proposition from *all A is B* to *all not-B is not-A*. ◻◻ **contrapositive** /-pózzitiv/ *adj.* & *n.* [LL *contrapositio* (as CONTRA-, *ponere posit-* place)]

contraption /kəntrápsh'n/ *n.* often *derog.* or *joc.* a machine or device, esp. a strange or cumbersome one. [19th c.: perh. f. CONTRIVE, INVENTION: assoc. with TRAP[1]]
■ machine, contrivance, device, gadget, implement, mechanism, apparatus, doodah, toy, Heath Robinson device, *Brit.* gubbins, *colloq.* widget, *US colloq.* hickey, *sl.* gismo, jigger.

contrapuntal /kóntrəpúnt'l/ *adj. Mus.* of or in counterpoint. ◻◻ **contrapuntally** *adv.* **contrapuntist** *n.* [It. *contrappunto* counterpoint]

contrariety /kóntrərī́-iti/ *n.* **1** opposition in nature, quality, or action. **2** disagreement, inconsistency. [ME f. OF *contrarieté* f. LL *contrarietas -tatis* (as CONTRARY)]
■ **2** see DISCREPANCY.

contrariwise /kəntráiriwīz/ *adv.* **1** on the other hand. **2** in the opposite way. **3** perversely. [ME f. CONTRARY + -WISE]
■ **2** see VICE VERSA.

contrary /kóntrəri/ *adj.*, *n.*, & *adv.* ● *adj.* **1** (usu. foll. by *to*) opposed in nature or tendency. **2** /kəntráiri/ *colloq.* perverse, self-willed. **3** (of a wind) unfavourable, impeding. **4** mutually opposed. **5** opposite in position or direction. ● *n.* (*pl.* **-ies**) (prec. by *the*) the opposite. ● *adv.* (foll. by *to*) in opposition or contrast (*contrary to expectations it rained*). ◻ **on the contrary** intensifying a denial of what has just been implied or stated. **to the contrary** to the opposite effect (*can find no indication to the contrary*). ◻◻ **contrarily** /kóntrərili/ (/kəntráirili/ in sense 2 of *adj.*) *adv.* **contrariness** /kóntrəriniss/ (/kəntráiriniss/ in sense 2 of *adj.*) *n.* [ME f. AF *contrarie*, OF *contraire*, f. L *contrarius* f. *contra* against]
■ *adj.* **1** antipathetic; opposite, opposing, opposed, different, contradictory, conflicting, antagonistic. **2** antagonistic, perverse, contrarious, hostile, unfriendly, inimical, cross-grained, intractable, awkward, difficult, refractory, stubborn, contumacious, self-willed, argumentative, unaccommodating, uncooperative, antipathetic, *archaic* froward. **3** adverse, unfavourable, impeding. ● *n.* opposite, reverse, converse, antithesis.

contrast *n.* & *v.* ● *n.* /kóntraast/ **1 a** a juxtaposition or comparison showing striking differences. **b** a difference so revealed. **2** (often foll. by *to*) a thing or person having qualities noticeably different from another. **3 a** the degree of difference between tones in a television picture or a photograph. **b** the change of apparent brightness or colour of an object caused by the juxtaposition of other objects.

● *v.* /kəntraást/ (often foll. by *with*) **1** *tr.* distinguish or set together so as to reveal a contrast. **2** *intr.* have or show a contrast. ▫▫ **contrastingly** /kəntraástingli/ *adv.* **contrastive** /kəntraástiv/ *adj.* [F *contraste*, *contraster*, f. It. *contrasto* f. med.L *contrastare* (as CONTRA-, *stare* stand)]

■ *n.* **1** comparison, juxtaposition; difference, distinction, disparity, dissimilarity. ● *v.* **1** juxtapose, oppose, compare, distinguish, differentiate, discriminate, set *or* place against *or* together. **2** conflict, differ, diverge.

contrasty /kóntraasti/ *adj.* (of photographic negatives or prints or of a television picture) showing a high degree of contrast.

contra-suggestible /kóntrəsəjéstib'l/ *adj. Psychol.* tending to respond to a suggestion by believing or doing the contrary.

contrate wheel /kóntrayt/ *n.* = *crown wheel*. [med.L & Rmc *contrata*: see COUNTRY]

contravene /kóntrəvéen/ *v.tr.* **1** infringe (a law or code of conduct). **2** (of things) conflict with. ▫▫ **contravener** *n.* [LL *contravenire* (as CONTRA-, *venire vent-* come)]

■ **1** see INFRINGE 1.

contravention /kóntrəvénsh'n/ *n.* **1** infringement. **2** an instance of this. ▫ **in contravention of** infringing, violating (a law etc.). [F f. med.L *contraventio* (as CONTRAVENE)]

contretemps /káwntrətoN/ *n.* **1** an awkward or unfortunate occurrence. **2** an unexpected mishap. [F]

■ see MISFORTUNE 2.

contribute /kəntríbyōōt, *disp.* kóntribyōōt/ *v.* (often foll. by *to*) **1** *tr.* give (money, an idea, help, etc.) towards a common purpose (*contributed £5 to the fund*). **2** *intr.* help to bring about a result etc. (*contributed to their downfall*). **3** *tr.* (also *absol.*) supply (an article etc.) for publication with others in a journal etc. ▫▫ **contributive** /kəntríbyootiv/ *adj.* [L *contribuere contribut-* (as COM-, *tribuere* bestow)]

■ **1** give, donate, bestow, grant, present, provide, supply. **2** (*contribute to*) add to, promote, advance, help, aid, support, forward, have a hand in, play a part *or* role in.

contribution /kóntribyōōsh'n/ *n.* **1** the act of contributing. **2** something contributed, esp. money. **3** an article etc. contributed to a publication. [ME f. OF *contribution* or LL *contributio* (as CONTRIBUTE)]

■ **1** see DONATION 1. **2** see DONATION 2.

contributor /kəntríbyootər/ *n.* a person who contributes (esp. an article or literary work).

contributory /kəntríbyootəri, -tri/ *adj.* & *n.* ● *adj.* **1** that contributes. **2** operated by means of contributions (*contributory pension scheme*). ● *n. Brit. Law* a person liable to contribute towards the payment of a wound-up company's debts. ▫ **contributory negligence** *Law* negligence on the part of the injured party through failure to take precautions against an accident. [med.L *contributorius* (as CONTRIBUTE)]

■ *adj.* **1** see INSTRUMENTAL *adj.*

contrite /kóntrīt, kəntrīt/ *adj.* **1** completely penitent. **2** feeling remorse or penitence; affected by guilt. **3** (of an action) showing a contrite spirit. ▫▫ **contritely** *adv.* **contriteness** *n.* [ME f. OF *contrit* f. L *contritus* bruised (as COM-, *terere trit-* rub)]

■ **1, 2** see REMORSEFUL.

contrition /kəntrísh'n/ *n.* the state of being contrite; thorough penitence. [ME f. OF f. LL *contritio -onis* (as CONTRITE)]

■ see *penitence* (PENITENT).

contrivance /kəntrív'nss/ *n.* **1** something contrived, esp. a mechanical device or a plan. **2** an act of contriving, esp. deceitfully. **3** inventive capacity.

■ **1** see DEVICE 1a. **2** see SUBTERFUGE 1.

contrive /kəntrív/ *v.tr.* **1** devise; plan or make resourcefully or with skill. **2** (often foll. by *to* + infin.) manage (*contrived to make matters worse*). ▫▫ **contrivable** *adj.* **contriver** *n.* [ME f. OF *controver* find, imagine f. med.L *contropare* compare]

■ **1** see DEVISE *v.* 1. **2** see MANAGE *v.* 2, 3, 5a.

contrived /kəntrívd/ *adj.* planned so carefully as to seem unnatural; artificial, forced (*the plot seemed contrived*).

■ see ARTIFICIAL 3.

control /kəntrṓl/ *n.* & *v.* ● *n.* **1** the power of directing, command (*under the control of*). **2** the power of restraining, esp. self-restraint. **3** a means of restraint; a check. **4** (usu. in *pl.*) a means of regulating prices etc. **5** (usu. in *pl.*) switches and other devices by which a machine, esp. an aircraft or vehicle, is controlled (also *attrib.*: *control panel*; *control room*). **6 a** a place where something is controlled or verified. **b** a person or group that controls something. **7** a standard of comparison for checking the results of a survey or experiment. ● *v.tr.* (**controlled, controlling**) **1** have control or command of; dominate. **2** exert control over; regulate. **3** hold in check; restrain (*told him to control himself*). **4** serve as control to. **5** check, verify. ▫ **controlling interest** a means of determining the policy of a business etc., esp. by ownership of a majority of the stock. **control rod** a rod of neutron-absorbing material used to vary the output power of a nuclear reactor. **control tower** a tall building at an airport etc. from which air traffic is controlled. **in control** (often foll. by *of*) directing an activity. **out of control** no longer subject to containment, restraint, or guidance. **under control** being controlled; in order. ▫▫ **controllable** *adj.* **controllability** /-trṓləbilliti/ *n.* **controllably** *adv.* [ME f. AF *contreroller* keep a copy of a roll of accounts, f. med.L *contrarotulare* (as CONTRA-, *rotulus* ROLL *n.*): (n.) perh. f. F *contrôle*]

■ *n.* **1** command, direction, power, authority, leadership, management, guidance, supervision, oversight, charge; sway, rule, jurisdiction. **2** restraint, self-restraint, mastery, command, dominance, domination. **3** check, curb. **5** knob, button, dial, handle, lever, switch; device, mechanism. ● *v.* **1, 2** command, dominate, direct, steer, pilot, hold sway over, rule, exercise power *or* authority over, govern, manage, lead, conduct, be in control of, guide, oversee, supervise, regulate. **3** check, hold back *or* in check, restrain, curb, repress, contain, manage; suppress, put down, master, subdue.

controller /kəntrṓlər/ *n.* **1** a person or thing that controls. **2** a person in charge of expenditure, esp. a steward or comptroller. ▫▫ **controllership** *n.* [ME *counterroller* f. AF *contrerollour* (as CONTROL)]

controversial /kóntrəvérsh'l/ *adj.* **1** causing or subject to controversy. **2** of controversy. **3** given to controversy. ▫▫ **controversialism** *n.* **controversialist** *n.* **controversially** *adv.* [LL *controversialis* (as CONTROVERSY)]

■ **1** debatable, contentious, disputable, questionable, litigious, moot, doubtful, unsettled. **2** polemic(al). **3** disputatious, argumentative, provocative, litigious, factious.

controversy /kóntrəversi, *disp.* kəntróvvərsi/ *n.* (*pl.* **-ies**) a prolonged argument or dispute, esp. when conducted publicly. [ME f. L *controversia* (as CONTROVERT)]

■ dispute, debate, contention, disagreement, argument, wrangling, confrontation, questioning; quarrel.

controvert /kóntrəvert, -vért/ *v.tr.* **1** dispute, deny. **2** argue about; discuss. ▫▫ **controvertible** *adj.* [orig. past part.; f. F *controvers(e)* f. L *controversus* (as CONTRA-, *vertere vers-* turn)]

■ **1** see DENY 1.

contumacious /kóntyoomáyshəss/ *adj.* insubordinate; stubbornly or wilfully disobedient, esp. to a court order. ▫▫ **contumaciously** *adv.* [L *contumax*, perh. rel. to *tumēre* swell]

■ see INSUBORDINATE.

contumacy /kóntyoomәsi/ *n.* stubborn refusal to obey or comply. [L *contumacia* f. *contumax*: see CONTUMACIOUS]

■ see REBELLION.

contumelious /kóntyoomeéliəss/ *adj.* reproachful, insulting, or insolent. ▫▫ **contumeliously** *adv.* [ME f. OF *contumelieus* f. L *contumeliosus* (as CONTUMELY)]

■ see INSOLENT.

contumely /kóntyoomli/ *n.* **1** insolent or reproachful language or treatment. **2** disgrace. [ME f. OF *contumelie* f. L *contumelia* (as COM-, *tumēre* swell)]
■ **1** see DERISION. **2** see DISGRACE *n.*

contuse /kəntyóoz/ *v.tr.* injure without breaking the skin; bruise. □□ **contusion** *n.* [L *contundere contus-* (as COM-, *tundere* thump)]
■ see BRUISE *v.* 1. □□ **contusion** see BRUISE *n.*

conundrum /kənúndrəm/ *n.* **1** a riddle, esp. one with a pun in its answer. **2** a hard or puzzling question. [16th c.: orig. unkn.]
■ **1** see RIDDLE[1] *n.*

conurbation /kónnurbáysh'n/ *n.* an extended urban area, esp. one consisting of several towns and merging suburbs. [CON- + L *urbs urbis* city + -ATION]
■ see CITY 1a.

conure /kónyoor/ *n.* any medium-sized parrot of the genus *Pyrrhura*, with mainly green plumage and a long gradated tail. [mod.L *conurus* f. Gk *kōnos* cone + *oura* tail]

convalesce /kónvəléss/ *v.intr.* recover one's health after illness or medical treatment. [ME f. L *convalescere* (as COM-, *valēre* be well)]
■ recover, improve, get better, recuperate.

convalescent /kónvəléss'nt/ *adj.* & *n.* ● *adj.* **1** recovering from an illness. **2** of or for persons in convalescence. ● *n.* a convalescent person. □□ **convalescence** *n.*
■ *adj.* **1** see *on the mend* (MEND). ● *n.* see INVALID[1] *n.* 1.

convection /kənvéksh'n/ *n.* **1** transference of heat in a gas or liquid by upward movement of the heated and less dense medium. **2** *Meteorol.* the transfer of heat by the upward flow of hot air or downward flow of cold air. □ **convection current** circulation that results from convection. □□ **convectional** *adj.* **convective** *adj.* [LL *convectio* f. L *convehere convect-* (as COM-, *vehere vect-* carry)]

convector /kənvéktər/ *n.* a heating appliance that circulates warm air by convection.

convenance /kónvənonss/ *n.* (usu. in *pl.*) conventional propriety. [F f. *convenir* be fitting (as CONVENE)]

convene /kənvéen/ *v.* **1** *tr.* summon or arrange (a meeting etc.). **2** *intr.* assemble. **3** *tr.* summon (a person) before a tribunal. □□ **convenable** *adj.* **convener** *n.* **convenor** *n.* [ME f. L *convenire convent-* assemble, agree, fit (as COM-, *venire* come)]
■ **1** see SUMMON 3. **2** see ASSEMBLE 1.

convenience /kənvéeniənss/ *n.* & *v.* ● *n.* **1** the quality of being convenient; suitability. **2** freedom from difficulty or trouble; material advantage (*for convenience*). **3** an advantage (*a great convenience*). **4** a useful thing, esp. an installation or piece of equipment. **5** *Brit.* a lavatory, esp. a public one. ● *v.tr.* afford convenience to; suit, accommodate. □ **at one's convenience** at a time or place that suits one. **at one's earliest convenience** as soon as one can. **convenience food** food, esp. complete meals, sold in convenient form and requiring very little preparation. **convenience store** *US* a large shop with extended opening hours. **make a convenience of** take advantage of (a person) insensitively. [ME f. L *convenientia* (as CONVENE)]
■ *v.* **2** see ADVANTAGE *n.* 1, 3. **5** see TOILET 1. □ **at one's convenience** see *at leisure* 2 (LEISURE).

convenient /kənvéeniənt/ *adj.* **1** (often foll. by *for, to*) **a** serving one's comfort or interests; easily accessible. **b** suitable. **c** free of trouble or difficulty. **2** available or occurring at a suitable time or place (*will try to find a convenient moment*). **3** well situated for some purpose (*convenient for the shops*). □□ **conveniently** *adv.* [ME (as CONVENE)]
■ **1** suitable, useful, helpful, handy, serviceable, expedient, advantageous, *archaic* commodious; trouble-free; see also CONVENIENT 3 below. **2** opportune, well-timed. **3** accessible, well placed *or* situated, nearby, within (easy) reach, at one's fingertips, close at hand, handy, available, (at the) ready.

convent /kónv'nt, -vent/ *n.* **1** a religious community, esp. of nuns, under vows. **2** the premises occupied by this. **3** (in full **convent school**) a school attached to and run by a convent. [ME f. AF *covent*, OF *convent* f. L *conventus* assembly (as CONVENE)]

conventicle /kənvéntik'l/ *n.* esp. *hist.* **1** a secret or unlawful religious meeting, esp. of dissenters. **2** a building used for this. [ME f. L *conventiculum* (place of) assembly, dimin. of *conventus* (as CONVENE)]

convention /kənvénsh'n/ *n.* **1 a** general agreement, esp. agreement on social behaviour etc. by implicit consent of the majority. **b** a custom or customary practice, esp. an artificial or formal one. **2 a** a formal assembly or conference for a common purpose. **b** *US* an assembly of the delegates of a political party to select candidates for office. **c** *hist.* a meeting of Parliament without a summons from the sovereign. **3 a** a formal agreement. **b** an agreement between States, esp. one less formal than a treaty. **4** *Cards* an accepted method of play (in leading, bidding, etc.) used to convey information to a partner. **5** the act of convening. [ME f. OF f. L *conventio -onis* (as CONVENE)]
■ **1 b** practice, custom, tradition, usage, formality, rule. **2 a** assembly, meeting, gathering, congregation, congress, conference, symposium, council, conclave, diet, synod, seminar.

conventional /kənvénshən'l/ *adj.* **1** depending on or according with convention. **2** (of a person) attentive to social conventions. **3** usual; of agreed significance. **4** not spontaneous or sincere or original. **5** (of weapons or power) non-nuclear. **6** *Art* following tradition rather than nature. □□ **conventionalism** *n.* **conventionalist** *n.* **conventionality** /-nálliti/ *n.* **conventionalize** *v.tr.* (also **-ise**). **conventionally** *adv.* [F *conventionnel* or LL *conventionalis* (as CONVENTION)]
■ **1** traditional, orthodox, established, accustomed, received, agreed. **2** formal, conservative, conformist, petty-bourgeois, old-fashioned, respectable, ordinary, stodgy, stuffy, *colloq.* straight, *US colloq.* uptight, *derog.* Biedermeier, *sl.* square. **3** usual, normal, regular, standard, customary, habitual, ordinary, everyday, common, commonplace. **4** insincere, unoriginal, unspontaneous, formal, formulaic, formulistic, stock, hackneyed, *colloq.* old hat. **6** classical, traditional.

conventioneer /kənvénshənéer/ *n.* *US* a person attending a convention.

conventual /kənvéntyooəl/ *adj.* & *n.* ● *adj.* **1** of or belonging to a convent. **2** of the less strict branch of the Franciscans, living in large convents. ● *n.* **1** a member or inmate of a convent. **2** a conventual Franciscan. [ME f. med.L *conventualis* (as CONVENT)]

converge /kənvérj/ *v.intr.* **1** come together as if to meet or join. **2** (of lines) tend to meet at a point. **3** (foll. by *on, upon*) approach from different directions. **4** *Math.* (of a series) approximate in the sum of its terms towards a definite limit. [LL *convergere* (as COM-, *vergere* incline)]
■ **1** come *or* go together, meet, join, unite, merge, coincide.

convergent /kənvérjənt/ *adj.* **1** converging. **2** *Biol.* (of unrelated organisms) having the tendency to become similar while adapting to the same environment. **3** *Psychol.* (of thought) tending to reach only the most rational result. □□ **convergence** *n.* **convergency** *n.*

conversant /kənvérs'nt, kónvərs'nt/ *adj.* (foll. by *with*) well experienced or acquainted with a subject, person, etc. □□ **conversance** *n.* **conversancy** *n.* [ME f. OF, pres. part. of *converser* CONVERSE[1]]
■ see FAMILIAR *adj.* 2.

conversation /kónvərsáysh'n/ *n.* **1** the informal exchange of ideas by spoken words. **2** an instance of this. □ **conversation piece 1** a small genre painting of a group of figures. **2** a thing that serves as a topic of conversation because of its unusualness etc. **conversation stopper** *colloq.* an unexpected remark, esp. one that cannot readily be answered. [ME f. OF f. L *conversatio -onis* (as CONVERSE[1])]

■ discussion, gossip, chattering, chatter, *archaic* converse, *colloq.* crack, nattering, chit-chat, *literary* discourse; talk, chat, dialogue, colloquy, parley, *US* bull session, *sl.* chin-wag.

conversational /kónvərsáyshən'l/ *adj.* **1** of or in conversation. **2** fond of or good at conversation. **3** colloquial. □□ **conversationally** *adv.*

conversationalist /kónvərsáyshənəlist/ *n.* one who is good at or fond of conversing.
■ talker, chatterer, deipnosophist.

conversazione /kónvərsátsióni/ *n.* (*pl.* **conversaziones** or **conversazioni** /*pronunc.* same/) a social gathering held by a learned or art society. [It. f. L (as CONVERSATION)]

converse[1] *v.* & *n.* ● *v.intr.* /kənvérss/ (often foll. by *with*) engage in conversation (*conversed with him about various subjects*). ● *n.* /kónverss/ *archaic* conversation. □□ **converser** /kənvérsər/ *n.* [ME f. OF *converser* f. L *conversari* keep company (with), frequent. of *convertere* (CONVERT)]
■ *v.* discuss, talk, speak, chat, parley, discourse, gossip, chatter, *colloq.* natter, chit-chat, *Austral.* & *NZ colloq.* yabber, *sl.* chin-wag.

converse[2] /kónverss/ *adj.* & *n.* ● *adj.* opposite, contrary, reversed. ● *n.* **1** something that is opposite or contrary. **2** a statement formed from another statement by the transposition of certain words, e.g. *some philosophers are men* from *some men are philosophers*. **3** *Math.* a theorem whose hypothesis and conclusion are the conclusion and hypothesis of another. □□ **conversely** /kónversli, kənvérsli/ *adv.* [L *conversus*, past part. of *convertere* (CONVERT)]

conversion /kənvérsh'n/ *n.* **1** the act or an instance of converting or the process of being converted, esp. in belief or religion. **2 a** an adaptation of a building for new purposes. **b** a converted building. **3** transposition, inversion. **4** *Theol.* the turning of sinners to God. **5** the transformation of fertile into fissile material in a nuclear reactor. **6** *Rugby Football* the scoring of points by a successful kick at goal after scoring a try. **7** *Psychol.* the change of an unconscious conflict into a physical disorder or disease. [ME f. OF f. L *conversio -onis* (as CONVERT)]
■ **2 a** see *alteration* (ALTER). **3** see TRANSFORMATION.

convert *v.* & *n.* ● *v.* /kənvért/ **1** *tr.* (usu. foll. by *into*) change in form, character, or function. **2** *tr.* cause (a person) to change beliefs, opinion, party, etc. **3** *tr.* change (money, stocks, units in which a quantity is expressed, etc.) into others of a different kind. **4** *tr.* make structural alterations in (a building) to serve a new purpose. **5** *tr.* (also *absol.*) **a** *Rugby Football* score extra points from (a try) by a successful kick at goal. **b** *Amer. Football* complete (a touchdown) by kicking a goal or crossing the goal-line. **6** *intr.* be converted or convertible (*the sofa converts into a bed*). **7** *tr. Logic* interchange the terms of (a proposition). ● *n.* /kónvert/ (often foll. by *to*) a person who has been converted to a different belief, opinion, etc. □ **convert to one's own use** wrongfully make use of (another's property). [ME f. OF *convertir* ult. f. L *convertere convers-* turn about (as COM-, *vertere* turn)]
■ *v.* **1, 4** change, modify, alter, transform, transmute, mutate, transfigure, remodel, remake, metamorphose, *joc.* transmogrify. **2** proselytize, *US* proselyte. **6** change, turn; metamorphose. ● *n.* proselyte, neophyte.

converter /kənvértər/ *n.* (also **convertor**) **1** a person or thing that converts. **2** *Electr.* **a** an electrical apparatus for the interconversion of alternating current and direct current. **b** *Electronics* an apparatus for converting a signal from one frequency to another. **3** a reaction vessel used in making steel. □ **converter reactor** a nuclear reactor that converts fertile material into fissile material.

convertible /kənvértib'l/ *adj.* & *n.* ● *adj.* **1** that may be converted. **2** (of currency etc.) that may be converted into other forms, esp. into gold or US dollars. **3** (of a car) having a folding or detachable roof. **4** (of terms) synonymous. ● *n.* a car with a folding or detachable roof. □□ **convertibility** /-bílliti/ *n.* **convertibly** *adv.* [OF f. L *convertibilis* (as CONVERT)]
■ *adj.* **1** see CHANGEABLE 2. **2** see LIQUID *adj.* 5.

convex /kónveks/ *adj.* having an outline or surface curved like the exterior of a circle or sphere (cf. CONCAVE). □□ **convexity** /-véksiti/ *n.* **convexly** *adv.* [L *convexus* vaulted, arched]

convey /kənváy/ *v.tr.* **1** transport or carry (goods, passengers, etc.). **2** communicate (an idea, meaning, etc.). **3** *Law* transfer the title to (property). **4** transmit (sound, smell, etc.). □□ **conveyable** *adj.* [ME f. OF *conveier* f. med.L *conviare* (as COM-, L *via* way)]
■ **1** see TRANSPORT *v.* 1. **2** see COMMUNICATE 1a. **4** see TRANSMIT 1a.

conveyance /kənváyənss/ *n.* **1 a** the act or process of carrying. **b** the communication (of ideas etc.). **c** transmission. **2** a means of transport; a vehicle. **3** *Law* **a** the transfer of property from one owner to another. **b** a document effecting this. □□ **conveyancer** *n.* (in sense 3). **conveyancing** *n.* (in sense 3).
■ **1** see TRANSMISSION 1. **2** vehicle.

conveyor /kənváyər/ *n.* (also **conveyer**) a person or thing that conveys. □ **conveyor belt** an endless moving belt for conveying articles or materials, esp. in a factory.
■ see CARRIER 1, 2.

convict *v.* & *n.* ● *v.tr.* /kənvíkt/ **1** (often foll. by *of*) prove to be guilty (of a crime etc.). **2** declare guilty by the verdict of a jury or the decision of a judge. ● *n.* /kónvikt/ **1** a person found guilty of a criminal offence. **2** a person serving a prison sentence, esp. (*hist.*) in a penal colony. [ME f. L *convincere convict-* (as COM-, *vincere* conquer): noun f. obs. *convict* convicted]
■ *v.* **1** find *or* prove guilty. ● *n.* **2** prisoner, captive, jailbird, *sl.* con, (old) lag, *US sl.* yardbird.

conviction /kənvíksh'n/ *n.* **1 a** the act or process of proving or finding guilty. **b** an instance of this (*has two previous convictions*). **2 a** the action or resulting state of being convinced. **b** a firm belief or opinion. **c** an act of convincing. [L *convictio* (as CONVICT)]
■ **2 a** certainty, sureness, positiveness, confidence, assurance, certitude. **b** (firm) belief, opinion, view, persuasion, position.

convince /kənvínss/ *v.tr.* **1** (often foll. by *of*, or *that* + clause) persuade (a person) to believe or realize. **2** (as **convinced** *adj.*) firmly persuaded (*a convinced pacifist*). □□ **convincer** *n.* **convincible** *adj.* [L (as CONVICT)]
■ **1** win over, persuade, bring (a)round, sway.
2 (**convinced**) see CERTAIN *adj.* 1a.

convincing /kənvínsing/ *adj.* **1** able to or such as to convince. **2** leaving no margin of doubt, substantial (*a convincing victory*). □□ **convincingly** *adv.*

convivial /kənvívviəl/ *adj.* **1** fond of good company; sociable and lively. **2** festive (*a convivial atmosphere*). □□ **conviviality** /-viálliti/ *n.* **convivially** *adv.* [L *convivialis* f. *convivium* feast (as COM-, *vivere* live)]
■ **1** see SOCIABLE.

convocation /kónvəkáysh'n/ *n.* **1** the act of calling together. **2** a large formal gathering of people, esp.: **a** *Brit.* a provincial synod of the Anglican clergy of Canterbury or York. **b** *Brit.* a legislative or deliberative assembly of a university. □□ **convocational** *adj.* [ME f. L *convocatio* (as CONVOKE)]
■ **2** see ASSEMBLY 1, 2a.

convoke /kənvṓk/ *v.tr. formal* call (people) together to a meeting etc.; summon to assemble. [L *convocare convocat-* (as COM-, *vocare* call)]
■ see SUMMON 3.

convoluted /kónvəlōōtid/ *adj.* **1** coiled, twisted. **2** complex, intricate. □□ **convolutedly** *adv.* [past part. of *convolute* f. L *convolutus* (as COM-, *volvere volut-* roll)]
■ **1** see TORTUOUS 1. **2** see INTRICATE.

convolution /kónvəlōōsh'n/ *n.* **1** coiling, twisting. **2** a coil or twist. **3** complexity. **4** a sinuous fold in the surface of the brain. □□ **convolutional** *adj.* [med.L *convolutio* (as CONVOLUTED)]

■ **2** see TWIST *n.* 4. **3** see *complexity* (COMPLEX).

convolve /kənvólv/ *v.tr.* & *intr.* (esp. as **convolved** *adj.*) roll together; coil up. [L *convolvere* (as CONVOLUTED)]

convolvulus /kənvólvyooləss/ *n.* any twining plant of the genus *Convolvulus*, with trumpet-shaped flowers, e.g. bindweed. [L]

convoy /kónvoy/ *n.* & *v.* ● *n.* **1** a group of ships travelling together or under escort. **2** a supply of provisions etc. under escort. **3** a group of vehicles travelling on land together or under escort. **4** the act of travelling or moving in a group or under escort. ● *v.tr.* **1** (of a warship) escort (a merchant or passenger vessel). **2** escort, esp. with armed force. [OF *convoyer* var. of *conveier* CONVEY]

■ *n.* **1** see FLEET[1]. ● *v.* see ESCORT *v.*

convulsant /kənvúls'nt/ *adj.* & *n. Pharm.* ● *adj.* producing convulsions. ● *n.* a drug that may produce convulsions. [F f. *convulser* (as CONVULSE)]

convulse /kənvúlss/ *v.tr.* **1** (usu. in *passive*) affect with convulsions. **2** cause to laugh uncontrollably. **3** shake violently; agitate, disturb. [L *convellere convuls-* (as COM-, *vellere* pull)]

convulsion /kənvúlsh'n/ *n.* **1** (usu. in *pl.*) violent irregular motion of a limb or limbs or the body caused by involuntary contraction of muscles, esp. as a disorder of infants. **2** a violent natural disturbance, esp. an earthquake. **3** violent social or political agitation. **4** (in *pl.*) uncontrollable laughter. □□ **convulsionary** *adj.* [F *convulsion* or L *convulsio* (as CONVULSE)]

■ **1** see FIT[2] 1. **3** see AGITATION 1.

convulsive /kənvúlsiv/ *adj.* **1** characterized by or affected with convulsions. **2** producing convulsions. □□ **convulsively** *adv.*

■ **1** see SPASMODIC 1.

cony /kóni/ *n.* (also **coney**) (*pl.* **-ies** or **-eys**) **1 a** a rabbit. **b** its fur. **2** *Bibl.* a hyrax. [ME *cunin(g)* f. AF *coning*, OF *conin*, f. L *cuniculus*]

coo /koo/ *n.*, *v.*, & *int.* ● *n.* a soft murmuring sound like that of a dove or pigeon. ● *v.* (**coos, cooed**) **1** *intr.* make the sound of a coo. **2** *intr.* & *tr.* talk or say in a soft or amorous voice. ● *int. Brit. sl.* expressing surprise or incredulity. □□ **cooingly** *adv.* [imit.]

cooee /kóo-ee/ *n.*, *int.*, & *v. colloq.* ● *n.* & *int.* a sound used to attract attention, esp. at a distance. ● *v.intr.* (**cooees, cooeed, cooeeing**) make this sound. □ **within cooee** (or **a cooee**) **of** *Austral.* & *NZ colloq.* very near to. [imit. of a signal used by Australian Aboriginals and copied by settlers]

cook /kook/ *v.* & *n.* ● *v.* **1** *tr.* prepare (food) by heating it. **2** *intr.* (of food) undergo cooking. **3** *tr. colloq.* falsify (accounts etc.); alter to produce a desired result. **4** *tr. sl.* ruin, spoil. **5** *tr.* (esp. as **cooked** *adj.*) *Brit. sl.* fatigue, exhaust. **6** *tr.* & *intr. US colloq.* do or proceed successfully. **7** *intr.* (as **be cooking**) *colloq.* be happening or about to happen (*went to find out what was cooking*). ● *n.* a person who cooks, esp. professionally or in a specified way (*a good cook*). □ **cook-chill 1** the process of cooking and refrigerating food ready for reheating at a later time. **2** (*attrib.*) (of food) prepared in this way. **cook a person's goose** ruin a person's chances. **cook up** *colloq.* invent or concoct (a story, excuse, etc.). □□ **cookable** *adj.* & *n.* [OE *cōc* f. pop.L *cocus* for L *coquus*]

■ **1** see PREPARE 2. **3** see FALSIFY 1. □ **cook up** see INVENT 2.

cookbook /kookbook/ *n. US* a cookery book.

cooker /kookkər/ *n.* **1 a** a container or device for cooking food. **b** *Brit.* an appliance powered by gas, electricity, etc., for cooking food. **2** *Brit.* a fruit etc. (esp. an apple) that is more suitable for cooking than for eating raw.

■ **1** stove, cooking-stove, *US* range, *propr.* Aga.

cookery /kookkəri/ *n.* (*pl.* **-ies**) **1** the art or practice of cooking. **2** *US* a place or establishment for cooking. □ **cookery book** *Brit.* a book containing recipes and other information about cooking.

cookhouse /kook-howss/ *n.* **1** a camp kitchen. **2** an outdoor kitchen in warm countries. **3** a ship's galley.

■ see KITCHEN.

cookie /kookki/ *n.* **1** *US* a small sweet biscuit. **2** *US sl.* a person. **3** *Sc.* a plain bun. □ **the way the cookie crumbles** *US colloq.* how things turn out; the unalterable state of affairs. [Du. *koekje* dimin. of *koek* cake]

cooking /kookking/ *n.* **1** the art or process by which food is cooked. **2** (*attrib.*) suitable for or used in cooking (*cooking apple; cooking utensils*).

cookout /kookkowt/ *n. US* a gathering with an open-air cooked meal; a barbecue.

■ see PICNIC *n.* 2.

cookshop /kookshop/ *n. NZ* the kitchen of a sheep-station.

cookware /kookwair/ *n.* utensils for cooking, esp. dishes, pans, etc.

cool /kool/ *adj.*, *n.*, & *v.* ● *adj.* **1** of or at a fairly low temperature, fairly cold (*a cool day; a cool bath*). **2** suggesting or achieving coolness (*cool colours; cool clothes*). **3 a** (of a person) calm, unexcited. **b** (of an act) done without emotion. **4** lacking zeal or enthusiasm. **5** unfriendly; lacking cordiality (*got a cool reception*). **6** (of jazz playing) restrained, relaxed. **7** calmly audacious (*a cool customer*). **8** (prec. by *a*) *colloq.* at least; not less than (*cost me a cool thousand*). **9** *sl.* esp. *US* excellent, marvellous; suave, stylish. ● *n.* **1** coolness. **2** cool air; a cool place. **3** *sl.* calmness, composure (*keep one's cool; lose one's cool*). ● *v.* (often foll. by *down, off*) **1** *tr.* & *intr.* make or become cool. **2** *intr.* (of anger, emotions, etc.) lessen, become calmer. □ **cool-bag** (or **-box**) an insulated container for keeping food cool. **cool-headed** not easily excited. **cool one's heels** see HEEL[1]. **cooling-off period** an interval to allow for a change of mind before commitment to action. **cooling tower** a tall structure for cooling hot water before reuse, esp. in industry. **cool it** *sl.* relax, calm down. □□ **coolish** *adj.* **coolly** /kool-li/ *adv.* **coolness** *n.* [OE *cōl*, *cōlian*, f. Gmc: cf. COLD]

■ *adj.* **1** chilly, cold, fresh, *literary* chill; chilled; unheated. **3 a** calm, serene, collected, level-headed, quiet, unexcited, unemotional, undisturbed, unexcitable, unruffled, cool-headed, relaxed, controlled, under control, self-possessed, self-controlled, unperturbed, phlegmatic, composed, imperturbable, *colloq.* unflappable. **b** dispassionate, cold, cold-blooded, emotionless, deliberate, cold-hearted, calculated, wilful, premeditated, purposeful, purposive. **4** unenthusiastic, uninvolved, uninterested, unconcerned, apathetic. **5** unfriendly, lukewarm, unsympathetic, uncordial, unsociable, unapproachable, standoffish, forbidding, unwelcoming, cold, cold-hearted, cold-blooded; distant, remote, aloof, detached, removed. **7** bold, audacious, brazen, overconfident, presumptuous, shameless, unabashed, impertinent, impudent, insolent. **9** see SUPERB, WORLDLY 2. ● *n.* **1** coolness, chill, chilliness. **3** calmness, control, self-control, composure, sang-froid, aplomb, poise, sedateness. ● *v.* **1** (*tr.*) chill, refrigerate, ice. **2** diminish, reduce, lessen, abate, moderate. □ **cool-headed** see CALM *adj.* 2, COOL *adj.* 3a above. **cool it** see RELAX 4.

coolabah /kooləbaa/ *n.* (also **coolibah** /-libaa/) *Austral.* any of various gum-trees, esp. *Eucalyptus microtheca.* [Aboriginal]

coolant /koolənt/ *n.* **1** a cooling agent, esp. fluid, to remove heat from an engine, nuclear reactor, etc. **2** a fluid used to lessen the friction of a cutting tool. [COOL + -ANT after *lubricant*]

cooler /koolər/ *n.* **1** a vessel in which a thing is cooled. **2** *US* a refrigerator. **3** a long drink, esp. a spritzer. **4** *sl.* prison or a prison cell.

■ **4** see PRISON *n.* 1.

Coolgardie safe /koolgaárdi/ *n. Austral.* a food safe cooled by strips of wetted fabric. [*Coolgardie*, a town in Western Australia]

coolibah var. of COOLABAH.

coolie /kóoli/ *n.* (also **cooly**) (*pl.* **-ies**) an unskilled native labourer in Eastern countries. □ **coolie hat** a broad conical hat as worn by coolies. [perh. f. *Kulī*, an aboriginal tribe of Gujarat, India]

coomb /kōom/ *n.* (also **combe**) *Brit.* **1** a valley or hollow on the side of a hill. **2** a short valley running up from the coast. [OE *cumb*: cf. CWM]
■ see VALLEY.

coon /kōon/ *n.* **1** *US* a racoon. **2** *sl. offens.* a Black. [abbr.]

coon-can /kóonkan/ *n.* a simple card-game like rummy (orig. Mexican). [Sp. *con quién* with whom?]

coonskin /kóonskin/ *n.* **1** the skin of a racoon. **2** a cap etc. made of this.

coop /kōop/ *n.* & *v.* ● *n.* **1** a cage placed over sitting or fattening fowls. **2** a fowl-run. **3** a small place of confinement, esp. a prison. **4** *Brit.* a basket used in catching fish. ● *v.tr.* **1** put or keep (a fowl) in a coop. **2** (often foll. by *up*, *in*) confine (a person) in a small space. [ME *cupe* basket f. MDu., MLG *kūpe*, ult. f. L *cupa* cask]
■ *n.* **1, 2** see CAGE *n.* **3** see JAIL *n.* 1. ● *v.* see *shut up* 2.

co-op /kó-op/ *n. colloq.* **1** *Brit.* a cooperative society or shop. **2** a cooperative business or enterprise. [abbr.]
■ **1** see STORE *n.* 3b.

cooper /kóopər/ *n.* & *v.* ● *n.* a maker or repairer of casks, barrels, etc. ● *v.tr.* make or repair (a cask). [ME f. MDu., MLG *kūper* f. *kūpe* COOP]

cooperage /kóopərij/ *n.* **1** the work or establishment of a cooper. **2** money payable for a cooper's work.

cooperate /kō-óppərayt/ *v.intr.* (also **co-operate**) **1** (often foll. by *with*) work or act together; assist. **2** (of things) concur in producing an effect. □□ **cooperant** *adj.* **cooperator** *n.* [eccl.L *cooperari* (as CO-, *operari* f. *opus operis* work)]
■ **1** collaborate, work together, join, unite, interact, team up, join forces, act jointly *or* in concert, coordinate (one's efforts); participate, contribute, lend a hand, help, assist.

cooperation /kō-óppəráysh'n/ *n.* (also **co-operation**) **1** working together to the same end; assistance. **2** *Econ.* the formation and operation of cooperatives. [ME f. L *cooperatio* (as COOPERATE): partly through F *coopération*]
■ **1** collaboration, teamwork, interaction, coordination; support, help, aid, assistance, patronage, backing, advocacy, favour, helping hand, friendship, blessing, sponsorship, auspices, backup.

cooperative /kō-óppərətiv/ *adj.* & *n.* (also **co-operative**) ● *adj.* **1** of or affording cooperation. **2** willing to cooperate. **3** *Econ.* (of a farm, shop, or other business, or a society owning such businesses) owned and run jointly by its members, with profits shared among them. ● *n.* a cooperative farm or society or business. □□ **cooperatively** *adv.* **cooperativeness** *n.* [LL *cooperativus* (as COOPERATE)]

co-opt /kō-ópt/ *v.tr.* appoint to membership of a body by invitation of the existing members. □□ **co-optation** /-táysh'n/ *n.* **co-option** *n.* **co-optive** *adj.* [L *cooptare* (as CO-, *optare* choose)]

coordinate *v.*, *adj.*, & *n.* (also **co-ordinate**) ● *v.* /kō-órdinayt/ **1** *tr.* bring (various parts, movements, etc.) into a proper or required relation to ensure harmony or effective operation etc. **2** *intr.* work or act together effectively. **3** *tr.* make coordinate; organize, classify. ● *adj.* /kō-órdinət/ **1** equal in rank or importance. **2** in which the parts are coordinated; involving coordination. **3** *Gram.* (of parts of a compound sentence) equal in status (cf. SUBORDINATE). **4** *Chem.* denoting a type of covalent bond in which one atom provides both the shared electrons. ● *n.* /kō-órdinət/ **1** *Math.* each of a system of magnitudes used to fix the position of a point, line, or plane. **2** a person or thing equal in rank or importance. **3** (in *pl.*) matching items of clothing. □□ **coordinately** /-nətli/ *adv.* **coordination** /-náysh'n/ *n.* **coordinative** /-naytiv/ *adj.* **coordinator** /-naytər/ *n.* [CO- + L *ordinare ordinat-* f. *ordo -inis* order]
■ *v.* **1** harmonize, correlate, synchronize, integrate; see also UNIFY. **2** pull together, work together; see also COOPERATE. **3** organize, classify, order, arrange, systemize, systematize, codify, categorize, group, match (up), rate, rank, grade. ● *adj.* **1** equivalent, parallel, corresponding, complementary, equal, *archaic* correspondent. **2** coordinating, coordinative, coordinated. □□ **coordination** see HARMONY 3, COOPERATION, ORGANIZATION 1.

coot /kōot/ *n.* **1** any black aquatic bird of the genus *Fulica*, esp. *F. atra* with the upper mandible extended backwards to form a white plate on the forehead. **2** *colloq.* a stupid person. [ME, prob. f. LG]

cootie /kóoti/ *n. sl.* a body louse. [perh. f. Malay *kutu* a biting parasite]

cop[1] /kop/ *n.* & *v. sl.* ● *n.* **1** a policeman. **2** *Brit.* a capture or arrest (*it's a fair cop*). ● *v.tr.* (**copped**, **copping**) **1** catch or arrest (an offender). **2** receive, suffer. **3** take, seize. □ **cop it 1** get into trouble; be punished. **2** be killed. **cop out 1** withdraw; give up an attempt. **2** go back on a promise. **3** escape. **cop-out** *n.* **1** a cowardly or feeble evasion. **2** an escape; a way of escape. **cop-shop** a police station. **not much** (or **no**) **cop** *Brit.* of little or no value or use. [perh. f. obs. *cap* arrest f. OF *caper* seize f. L *capere*: (n.) cf. COPPER[2]]
■ *n.* **1** see *police officer*. **2** see ARREST *n.* 1. ● *v.* **1** see ARREST *v.* 1a.

cop[2] /kop/ *n.* (in spinning) a conical ball of thread wound on a spindle. [OE *cop* summit]

copacetic /kṓpəséttik, -seétik/ *adj. US sl.* excellent; in good order. [20th c.: orig. unkn.]
■ see FABULOUS 2.

copaiba /kəpíbə/ *n.* an aromatic oil or resin from any plant of the genus *Copaifera*, used in medicine and perfumery. [Sp. & Port. f. Guarani *cupauba*]

copal /kṓp'l/ *n.* a resin from any of various tropical trees, used for varnish. [Sp. f. Aztec *copalli* incense]

copartner /kōpaártnər/ *n.* a partner or associate, esp. when sharing equally. □□ **copartnership** *n.*

cope[1] /kōp/ *v.intr.* **1** (foll. by *with*) deal effectively or contend successfully with a person or task. **2** manage successfully; deal with a situation or problem (*found they could no longer cope*). [ME f. OF *coper*, *colper* f. *cop*, *colp* blow f. med.L *colpus* f. L *colaphus* f. Gk *kolaphos* blow with the fist]
■ **1** (*cope with*) withstand, contend with, handle, dispose of; see also DEAL[1] *v.* 1a. **2** manage, get along *or* by, make do, survive, subsist, come *or* pull through, scrape by *or* along, muddle through, *colloq.* make out.

cope[2] /kōp/ *n.* & *v.* ● *n.* **1** *Eccl.* a long cloaklike vestment worn by a priest or bishop in ceremonies and processions. **2** esp. *poet.* a covering compared with a cope. ● *v.tr.* cover with a cope or coping. [ME ult. f. LL *cappa* CAP, CAPE[1]]

copeck /kṓpek, kóppek/ *n.* (also **kopeck, kopek**) a Russian coin and monetary unit worth one-hundredth of a rouble. [Russ. *kopeĭka* dimin. of *kop'ë* lance (from the figure of Ivan IV bearing a lance instead of a sword in 1535)]

copepod /kṓpipod/ *n.* any small aquatic crustacean of the class Copepoda, many of which form the minute components of plankton. [Gk *kōpē* oar-handle + *pous podos* foot]

coper /kṓpər/ *n.* a horse-dealer. [obs. *cope* buy, f. MDu., MLG *kōpen*, G *kaufen*: rel. to CHEAP]

Copernican system /kəpérnikən/ *n.* (also **Copernican theory**) *Astron.* the theory that the planets (including the earth) move round the sun (cf. *Ptolemaic system*). [*Copernicus* latinized f. M. *Kopernik*, Polish astronomer d. 1543]

copestone /kṓpstōn/ *n.* **1** = *coping-stone*. **2** a finishing touch. [COPE[2] + STONE]

copiable /kóppiəb'l/ *adj.* that can or may be copied.

copier /kóppiər/ *n.* a machine or person that copies (esp. documents).
■ see SCRIBE *n.* 1.

copilot /kṓpīlət/ *n.* a second pilot in an aircraft.

coping /kṓping/ *n.* the top (usu. sloping) course of masonry in a wall or parapet. □ **coping-stone** a stone used in a coping.

coping saw /kṓping/ *n.* a D-shaped saw for cutting curves in wood. [*cope* cut wood f. OF *coper*: see COPE[1]]

copious /kṓpiəss/ *adj.* **1** abundant, plentiful. **2** producing much. **3** providing much information. **4** profuse in speech. ▫▫ **copiously** *adv.* **copiousness** *n.* [ME f. OF *copieux* or f. L *copiosus* f. *copia* plenty]
■ **1** see ABUNDANT 1. **2** see PROFUSE 2.

copita /kəpeétə/ *n.* **1** a tulip-shaped sherry-glass. **2** a glass of sherry. [Sp., dimin. of *copa* cup]

coplanar /kōpláynər/ *adj. Geom.* in the same plane. ▫▫ **coplanarity** /-plənárriti/ *n.*

copolymer /kōpóllimər/ *n. Chem.* a polymer with units of more than one kind. ▫▫ **copolymerize** *v.tr.* & *intr.* (also **-ise**).

copper[1] /kóppər/ *n.*, *adj.*, & *v.* ● *n.* **1** *Chem.* a malleable red-brown metallic element of the transition series occurring naturally esp. in cuprous oxide and malachite, and used esp. for electrical cables and apparatus. ¶ Symb.: **Cu**. **2** a bronze coin. **3** a large metal vessel for boiling esp. laundry. **4** any of various butterflies with copper-coloured wings. ● *adj.* made of or coloured like copper. ● *v.tr.* cover (a ship's bottom, a pan, etc.) with copper. ▫ **copper beech** a variety of beech with copper-coloured leaves. **copper belt** a copper-mining area of Central Africa. **copper-bit** a soldering tool pointed with copper. **copper-bottomed 1** having a bottom sheathed with copper (esp. of a ship or pan). **2** genuine or reliable (esp. financially). **copper pyrites** a double sulphide of copper and iron: also called CHALCOPYRITE. **copper sulphate** a blue crystalline solid used in electroplating, textile dyeing, etc. **copper vitriol** copper sulphate. [OE *copor*, *coper*, ult. f. L *cyprium aes* Cyprus metal]

copper[2] /kóppər/ *n. Brit. sl.* a policeman. [COP[1] + ER[1]]
■ see *police officer*.

copperas /kóppərəss/ *n.* green iron-sulphate crystals. [ME *coperose* f. OF *couperose* f. med.L *cup(e)rosa*: perh. orig. *aqua cuprosa* copper water]

copperhead /kóppərhed/ *n.* **1** a venomous viper, *Agkistrodon contortrix*, native to N. America. **2** a venomous cobra, *Denisonia superba*, native to Australia.

copperplate /kóppərplayt/ *n.* & *adj.* ● *n.* **1 a** a polished copper plate for engraving or etching. **b** a print made from this. **2** an ornate style of handwriting resembling that orig. used in engravings. ● *adj.* of or in copperplate writing.

coppersmith /kóppərsmith/ *n.* a person who works in copper.

coppery /kóppəri/ *adj.* of or like copper, esp. in colour.

coppice /kóppiss/ *n.* & *v.* ● *n.* an area of undergrowth and small trees, grown for periodic cutting. ● *v.tr.* cut back (young trees) periodically to stimulate growth of shoots. ▫▫ **coppiced** *adj.* [OF *copeïz* ult. f. med.L *colpus* blow: see COPE[1]]
■ *n.* grove, wood, stand, thicket, brake, *Brit.* spinney.

copra /kóprə/ *n.* the dried kernels of the coconut. [Port. f. Malayalam *koppara* coconut]

co-precipitation /kṓprisíppitáysh'n/ *n. Chem.* the simultaneous precipitation of more than one compound from a solution.

copro- /kóprō/ *comb. form* dung, faeces. [Gk *kopros* dung]

co-production /kṓprədúksh'n/ *n.* a production of a play, broadcast, etc., jointly by more than one company.

coprolite /kóprəlīt/ *n. Archaeol.* fossil dung or a piece of it.

coprophagous /kopróffəgəss/ *adj. Zool.* dung-eating. [COPRO-]

coprophilia /kóprəfilliə/ *n.* an abnormal interest in faeces and defecation.

coprosma /kəprózmə/ *n.* any small evergreen plant of the genus *Coprosma*, native to Australasia. [mod.L f. Gk *kopros* dung + *osmē* smell]

copse /kops/ *n.* **1** = COPPICE. **2** (in general use) a small wood. ▫▫ **copsy** *adj.* [shortened f. COPPICE]

copsewood /kópswŏŏd/ *n.* undergrowth.

Copt /kopt/ *n.* **1** a native Egyptian in the Hellenistic and Roman periods. **2** a native Christian of the independent Egyptian Church. [F *Copte* or mod.L *Coptus* f. Arab. *al-ḳibṭ*, *al-ḳubṭ* Copts f. Coptic *Gyptios* f. Gk *Aiguptios* Egyptian]

Coptic /kóptik/ *n.* & *adj.* ● *n.* the language of the Copts, now used only in the Coptic Church. ● *adj.* of or relating to the Copts.

copula /kópyoolə/ *n.* (*pl.* **copulas**) *Logic* & *Gram.* a connecting word, esp. a part of the verb *be* connecting a subject and predicate. ▫▫ **copular** *adj.* [L (as CO-, *apere* fasten)]

copulate /kópyoolayt/ *v.intr.* (often foll. by *with*) have sexual intercourse. ▫▫ **copulatory** *adj.* [L *copulare* fasten together (as COPULA)]
■ see MATE[1] *v.* 1b.

copulation /kópyooláysh'n/ *n.* **1** sexual union. **2** a grammatical or logical connection. [ME f. OF f. L *copulatio* (as COPULATE)]
■ **1** see SEX *n.* 5.

copulative /kópyoolətiv/ *adj.* **1** serving to connect. **2** *Gram.* **a** (of a word) that connects words or clauses linked in sense (cf. DISJUNCTIVE). **b** connecting a subject and predicate. **3** relating to sexual union. ▫▫ **copulatively** *adv.* [ME f. OF *copulatif -ive* or LL *copulativus* (as COPULATE)]

copy /kóppi/ *n.* & *v.* ● *n.* (*pl.* **-ies**) **1** a thing made to imitate or be identical to another. **2** a single specimen of a publication or issue (*ordered twenty copies*). **3 a** matter to be printed. **b** material for a newspaper or magazine article (*scandals make good copy*). **c** the text of an advertisement. **4 a** a model to be copied. **b** a page written after a model (of penmanship). ● *v.* (**-ies**, **-ied**) **1** *tr.* **a** make a copy of. **b** (often foll. by *out*) transcribe. **2** *intr.* make a copy, esp. clandestinely. **3** *tr.* (foll. by *to*) send a copy of (a letter) to a third party. **4** *tr.* do the same as; imitate. ▫ **copy-edit** edit (copy) for printing. **copy editor** a person who edits copy for printing. **copy-typist** a person who makes typewritten transcripts of documents. [ME f. OF *copie*, *copier*, ult. f. L *copia* abundance (in med.L = transcript)]
■ *n.* **1** reproduction, replica, facsimile, likeness, imitation, duplication, duplicate, transcript, replication; carbon (copy), photocopy, print. **2** example, sample, specimen; number, issue. **3** text, writing, material. ● *v.* **1** reproduce, duplicate, replicate, transcribe; see also IMITATE 3. **4** mimic, impersonate, emulate, ape, echo; see also IMITATE 1, 2. ▫ **copy-edit** copyread, *Brit.* sub-edit. **copy editor** copyreader, *Brit.* sub-editor.

copybook /kóppibŏŏk/ *n.* **1** a book containing models of handwriting for learners to imitate. **2** (*attrib.*) **a** tritely conventional. **b** accurate, exemplary.

copycat /kóppikat/ *n. colloq.* (esp. as a child's word) a person who copies another, esp. slavishly.
■ see MIMIC *n.*

copydesk /kóppidesk/ *n.* the desk at which copy is edited for printing.

copyhold /kóppihōld/ *n. Brit. hist.* **1** tenure of land based on manorial records. **2** land held in this way. ▫▫ **copyholder** *n.*

copyist /kóppi-ist/ *n.* **1** a person who makes (esp. written) copies. **2** an imitator. [earlier *copist* f. F *copiste* or med.L *copista* (as COPY)]
■ **1** see SCRIBE *n.* 1.

copyreader /kóppireedər/ *n.* a person who reads and edits copy for a newspaper or book. ▫▫ **copyread** *v.tr.*

copyright /kóppirīt/ *n.*, *adj.*, & *v.* ● *n.* the exclusive legal right granted for a specified period to an author, designer, etc., or another appointed person, to print, publish, perform, film, or record original literary, artistic, or musical material. ● *adj.* (of such material) protected by copyright. ● *v.tr.* secure copyright for (material). ▫ **copyright library** *Brit.* a library entitled to a free copy of each book published in the UK.

copywriter /kóppirītər/ *n.* a person who writes or prepares copy (esp. of advertising material) for publication. ▫▫ **copywriting** *n.*

coq au vin /kók ō váN/ *n.* a casserole of chicken pieces cooked in wine. [F]

coquetry /kókkitri, kṓk-/ *n.* (*pl.* **-ies**) **1** coquettish behaviour. **2** a coquettish act. **3** trifling with serious matters. [F *coquetterie* f. *coqueter* (as COQUETTE)]

coquette /kokét, kəkét/ *n.* **1** a woman who flirts. **2** any crested humming-bird of the genus *Lophornis.* □□ **coquettish** *adj.* **coquettishly** *adv.* **coquettishness** *n.* [F, fem. of *coquet* wanton, dimin. of *coq* cock]
■ **1** see FLIRT *n.* 1.

coquina /kəkeénə/ *n. US* a soft limestone of broken shells, used in road-making. [Sp., = cockle]

coquito /kəkeétō/ *n.* (*pl.* **-os**) a palm-tree, *Jubaea chilensis*, native to Chile, yielding honey from its sap, and fibre. [Sp., dimin. of *coco* coconut]

Cor. *abbr.* **1** Corinthians (New Testament). **2** *US* corner.

cor /kor/ *int. Brit. sl.* expressing surprise, alarm, exasperation, etc. □ **cor blimey** see BLIMEY. [corrupt. of *God*]

cor- /kər/ *prefix* assim. form of COM- before *r*.

coracle /kórrək'l/ *n. Brit.* a small boat of wickerwork covered with watertight material, used on Welsh and Irish lakes and rivers. [Welsh *corwgl* (*corwg* = Ir. *currach* boat: cf. CURRACH)]

coracoid /kórrəkoyd/ *n.* (in full **coracoid process**) a short projection from the shoulder-blade in vertebrates. [mod.L *coracoides* f. Gk *korakoeidēs* raven-like f. *korax -akos* raven]

coral /kórrəl/ *n.* & *adj.* ● *n.* **1 a** a hard red, pink, or white calcareous substance secreted by various marine polyps for support and habitation. **b** any of these usu. colonial organisms. **2** the unimpregnated roe of a lobster or scallop. ● *adj.* **1** like coral, esp. in colour. **2** made of coral. □ **coral island** (or **reef**) one formed by the growth of coral. **coral rag** limestone containing beds of petrified corals. **coral-snake** any of various brightly-coloured poisonous snakes, esp. *Micrurus nigrocinctus*, native to Central America. [ME f. OF f. L *corallum* f. Gk *korallion*, prob. of Semitic orig.]

coralline /kórrəlīn/ *n.* & *adj.* ● *n.* **1** any seaweed of the genus *Corallina* having a calcareous jointed stem. **2** (in general use) the name of various plantlike compound organisms. ● *adj.* **1** coral-red. **2** of or like coral. [F *corallin* & It. *corallina* f. LL *corallinus* (as CORAL)]

corallite /kórrəlīt/ *n.* **1** the coral skeleton of a marine polyp. **2** fossil coral. [L *corallum* CORAL]

coralloid /kórrəloyd/ *adj.* & *n.* ● *adj.* like or akin to coral. ● *n.* a coralloid organism.

coram populo /kórəm pópyoolō/ *adv.* in public. [L, = in the presence of the people]

cor anglais /kór ónglay, ONGláy/ *n.* (*pl.* **cors anglais** /*pronunc.* same/) *Mus.* **1** an alto woodwind instrument of the oboe family. **2** its player. **3** an organ stop with the quality of a cor anglais. [F, = English horn]
■ English horn.

corbel /kórb'l/ *n.* & *v. Archit.* ● *n.* **1** a projection of stone, timber, etc., jutting out from a wall to support a weight. **2** a short timber laid longitudinally under a beam to help support it. ● *v.tr.* & *intr.* (**corbelled, corbelling**; *US* **corbeled, corbeling**) (foll. by *out, off*) support or project on corbels. □ **corbel-table** a projecting course resting on corbels. [ME f. OF, dimin. of *corp*: see CORBIE]
■ *n.* **1** see BRACKET *n.* 1.

corbie /kórbi/ *n. Sc.* **1** a raven. **2** a carrion crow. □ **corbie-steps** the steplike projections on the sloping sides of a gable. [ME f. OF *corb, corp* f. L *corvus* crow]

cord /kord/ *n.* & *v.* ● *n.* **1 a** long thin flexible material made from several twisted strands. **b** a piece of this. **2** *Anat.* a structure in the body resembling a cord (*spinal cord*). **3 a** ribbed fabric, esp. corduroy. **b** (in *pl.*) corduroy trousers. **c** a cordlike rib on fabric. **4** an electric flex. **5** a measure of cut wood (usu. 128 cu.ft., 3.6 cubic metres). **6** a moral or emotional tie (*cords of affection*; *fourfold cord of evidence*). ● *v.tr.* **1** fasten or bind with cord. **2** (as **corded** *adj.*) **a** (of cloth) ribbed. **b** provided with cords. **c** (of muscles) standing out like taut cords. □□ **cordlike** *adj.* [ME f. OF *corde* f. L *chorda* f. Gk *khordē* gut, string of musical instrument]
■ *n.* **1** line, twine, rope, *Brit.* flex; see also STRING *n.* 1, 2.

cordage /kórdij/ *n.* cords or ropes, esp. in the rigging of a ship. [ME f. F (as CORD)]

cordate /kórdayt/ *adj.* heart-shaped. [mod.L *cordatus* f. L *cor cordis* heart]

cordelier /kórdileér/ *n.* a Franciscan friar of the strict rule (wearing a knotted cord round the waist). [ME f. OF f. *cordele* dimin. of *corde* CORD]

cordial /kórdiəl/ *adj.* & *n.* ● *adj.* **1** heartfelt, sincere. **2** warm, friendly. ● *n.* **1** a fruit-flavoured drink. **2** a comforting or pleasant-tasting medicine. □□ **cordiality** /-diálliti/ *n.* **cordially** *adv.* [ME f. med.L *cordialis* f. L *cor cordis* heart]
■ *adj.* **1** see SINCERE. **2** friendly, warm, affable, amiable, kindly, genial, gracious, welcoming, open-armed, pleasant, good-natured, nice, courteous, polite.

cordillera /kórdilyáirə/ *n.* a system or group of usu. parallel mountain ranges together with intervening plateaux etc., esp. of the Andes and in Central America and Mexico. [Sp. f. *cordilla* dimin. of *cuerda* CORD]

cordite /kórdīt/ *n.* a smokeless explosive made from cellulose nitrate and nitroglycerine. [CORD (from its appearance) + -ITE[1]]

cordless /kórdliss/ *adj.* (of an electrical appliance, telephone, etc.) working from an internal source of energy etc. (esp. a battery) and without a connection to a mains supply or central unit.

cordon /kórd'n/ *n.* & *v.* ● *n.* **1** a line or circle of police, soldiers, guards, etc., esp. preventing access to or from an area. **2 a** an ornamental cord or braid. **b** the ribbon of a knightly order. **3** a fruit-tree trained to grow as a single stem. **4** *Archit.* a string-course. ● *v.tr.* (often foll. by *off*) enclose or separate with a cordon of police etc. [It. *cordone* augmentative of *corda* CORD, & F *cordon* (as CORD)]
■ *n.* **2a** see BRAID *n.* 1. ● *v.* see *lay siege to* (SIEGE).

cordon bleu /kórdon blṓ/ *adj.* & *n. Cookery* ● *adj.* of the highest class. ● *n.* a cook of this class. [F, = blue ribbon]

cordon sanitaire /kórdon sánnitáir/ *n.* **1** a guarded line between infected and uninfected districts. **2** any measure designed to prevent communication or the spread of undesirable influences.

cordovan /kórdəv'n/ *n.* a kind of soft leather. [Sp. *cordovan* of Cordova (Córdoba) where it was orig. made]

corduroy /kórdəroy, -dyooroy/ *n.* **1** a thick cotton fabric with velvety ribs. **2** (in *pl.*) corduroy trousers. □ **corduroy road** a road made of tree-trunks laid across a swamp. [18th c.: prob. f. CORD ribbed fabric + obs. *duroy* coarse woollen fabric]

cordwainer /kórdwaynər/ *n. Brit. archaic* a shoemaker (usu. in names of guilds etc.). [obs. *cordwain* CORDOVAN]

cordwood /kórdwŏŏd/ *n.* wood that is or can easily be measured in cords.

CORE *abbr. US* Congress of Racial Equality.

core /kor/ *n.* & *v.* ● *n.* **1** the horny central part of various fruits, containing the seeds. **2 a** the central or most important part of anything (also *attrib.*: *core curriculum*). **b** the central part, of different character from the surroundings. **3** the central region of the earth. **4** the central part of a nuclear reactor, containing the fissile material. **5** a magnetic structural unit in a computer, storing one bit of data (see BIT[4]). **6** the inner strand of an electric cable, rope, etc. **7** a piece of soft iron forming the centre of an electromagnet or an induction coil. **8** an internal mould filling a space to be left hollow in a casting. **9** the central part cut out (esp. of rock etc. in boring). **10** *Archaeol.* a piece of flint from which flakes or blades have been removed. ● *v.tr.* remove the core from. □ **core memory** *Computing* the memory of a computer consisting of many cores. **core time** (in a flexitime system) the central part of the working day, when all employees must be present. □□ **corer** *n.* [ME: orig. unkn.]

■ *n.* **1** centre, heart, middle, inside(s), kernel, stone, pip(s). **2 a** essence, marrow, heart, pith, quintessence, substance, crux, nub; basics, fundamentals, *sl.* nitty-gritty. ● *v.* seed, stone, pip, *US* pit.

corelation var. of CORRELATION.

co-religionist /kō-rilíjənist/ *n.* (*US* **coreligionist**) an adherent of the same religion.

corella /kərélla/ *n. Austral.* either of two small white cockatoos, *Cacatua tenuirostris* or *C. sanguinea.* [app. Latinized f. Aboriginal *ca-rall*]

coreopsis /kórriópsiss/ *n.* any composite plant of the genus *Coreopsis*, having rayed usu. yellow flowers. [mod.L f. Gk *koris* bug + *opsis* appearance, with ref. to the shape of the seed]

co-respondent /kō-rispóndənt/ *n.* (*US* **corespondent**) a person cited in a divorce case as having committed adultery with the respondent.

corf /korf/ *n.* (*pl.* **corves** /korvz/) *Brit.* **1** a basket in which fish are kept alive in the water. **2** a small wagon, formerly a large basket, used in mining. [MDu., MLG *korf*, OHG *chorp*, *korb* f. L *corbis* basket]

corgi /kórgi/ *n.* (*pl.* **corgis**) (in full **Welsh corgi**) **1** a dog of a short-legged breed with foxlike head. **2** this breed. [Welsh f. *cor* dwarf + *ci* dog]

coriaceous /kórriáyshəss/ *adj.* like leather; leathery. [LL *coriaceus* f. *corium* leather]

coriander /kórriándər/ *n.* **1** a plant, *Coriandrum sativum*, with leaves used for flavouring and small round aromatic fruits. **2** (also **coriander seed**) the dried fruit used for flavouring curries etc. [ME f. OF *coriandre* f. L *coriandrum* f. Gk *koriannon*]

Corinthian /kərínthiən/ *adj.* & *n.* ● *adj.* **1** of ancient Corinth in southern Greece. **2** *Archit.* of an order characterized by ornate decoration and flared capitals with rows of acanthus leaves, used esp. by the Romans. **3** *archaic* profligate. ● *n.* a native of Corinth. [L *Corinthius* f. Gk *Korinthios* + -AN]

Coriolis effect /kórriṓliss/ *n.* a hypothetical force used to explain rotating systems, such that the movement of air or water over the surface of the rotating earth is directed clockwise in the northern hemisphere and anticlockwise in the southern hemisphere. [G. G. *Coriolis*, Fr. scientist d. 1843]

corium /kóriəm/ *n. Anat.* the dermis. [L, = skin]

cork /kork/ *n.* & *v.* ● *n.* **1** the buoyant light-brown bark of the cork-oak. **2** a bottle-stopper of cork or other material. **3** a float of cork used in fishing etc. **4** *Bot.* a protective layer of dead cells immediately below the bark of woody plants. **5** (*attrib.*) made of cork. ● *v.tr.* (often foll. by *up*) **1** stop or confine. **2** restrain (feelings etc.). **3** blacken with burnt cork. □ **cork-oak** a S. European oak, *Quercus suber*. **cork-tipped** *Brit.* (of a cigarette) having a filter of corklike material. □□ **corklike** *adj.* [ME f. Du. & LG *kork* f. Sp. *alcorque* cork sole, perh. f. Arab.]

■ *n.* **2** see STOPPER *n.* ● *v.* **1** see PLUG *v.* 1.

corkage /kórkij/ *n.* a charge made by a restaurant or hotel for serving wine etc. when brought in by customers.

corked /korkt/ *adj.* **1** stopped with a cork. **2** (of wine) spoilt by a decayed cork. **3** blackened with burnt cork.

corker /kórkər/ *n. sl.* an excellent or astonishing person or thing.

corking /kórking/ *adj. sl.* strikingly large or splendid.

corkscrew /kórkskroo/ *n.* & *v.* ● *n.* **1** a spirally twisted steel device for extracting corks from bottles. **2** (often *attrib.*) a thing with a spiral shape. ● *v.tr.* & *intr.* move spirally; twist.

■ *n.* **2** see SPIRAL *n.*

corkwood /kórkwood/ *n.* **1** any shrub of the genus *Duboisia*, yielding a light porous wood. **2** this wood.

corky /kórki/ *adj.* (**corkier, corkiest**) **1** corklike. **2** (of wine) corked.

corm /korm/ *n. Bot.* an underground swollen stem base of some plants, e.g. crocus. [mod.L *cormus* f. Gk *kormos* trunk with boughs lopped off]

cormorant /kórmərənt/ *n.* any diving sea bird of the family Phalacrocoracidae, esp. *Phalacrocorax carbo* having lustrous black plumage. [ME f. OF *cormaran* f. med.L *corvus marinus* sea-raven: for ending *-ant* cf. *peasant*, *tyrant*]

corn[1] /korn/ *n.* & *v.* ● *n.* **1 a** any cereal before or after harvesting, esp. the chief crop of a region: wheat, oats, or (in the US and Australia) maize. **b** a grain or seed of a cereal plant. **2** *colloq.* something corny or trite. ● *v.tr.* (as **corned** *adj.*) sprinkled or preserved with salt or brine (*corned beef*). □ **corn-cob** the cylindrical centre of the maize ear to which rows of grains are attached. **corn-cob pipe** a tobacco-pipe made from a corn-cob. **corn-cockle** see COCKLE[2]. **corn dolly** a symbolic or decorative figure made of plaited straw. **corn exchange** a place for trade in corn. **corn-factor** *Brit.* a dealer in corn. **corn marigold** a daisy-like yellow-flowered plant, *Chrysanthemum segetum*, growing amongst corn. **corn on the cob** maize cooked and eaten from the corn-cob. **corn-salad** = *lamb's lettuce* (see LAMB). **corn-spurry** see SPURRY. **corn-whiskey** *US* whisky distilled from maize. [OE f. Gmc: rel. to L *granum* grain]

■ *n.* **1** see GRAIN *n.* 2. **2** see *sentimentality* (SENTIMENTAL). ● *v.* (**corned**) see SALT *adj.*

corn[2] /korn/ *n.* a small area of horny usu. tender skin esp. on the toes, extending into subcutaneous tissue. [ME f. AF f. L *cornu* horn]

■ see LUMP[1] *n.* 3.

cornbrash /kórnbrash/ *n. Geol. Brit.* an earthy limestone layer of the Jurassic period. [CORN[1] + BRASH[2]]

corncrake /kórnkrayk/ *n.* a rail, *Crex crex*, inhabiting grassland and nesting on the ground.

cornea /kórniə/ *n.* the transparent circular part of the front of the eyeball. □□ **corneal** *adj.* [med.L *cornea tela* horny tissue, f. L *corneus* horny f. *cornu* horn]

cornel /kórn'l/ *n.* any plant of the genus *Cornus*, esp. a dwarf kind, *C. suecica*. [ME f. L *cornus*]

cornelian /kornéeliən/ *n.* (also **carnelian** /kaar-/) **1** a dull red or reddish-white variety of chalcedony. **2** this colour. [ME f. OF *corneline*; *car-* after L *caro carnis* flesh]

corneous /kórniəss/ *adj.* hornlike, horny. [L *corneus* f. *cornu* horn]

corner /kórnər/ *n.* & *v.* ● *n.* **1** a place where converging sides or edges meet. **2** a projecting angle, esp. where two streets meet. **3** the internal space or recess formed by the meeting of two sides, esp. of a room. **4** a difficult position, esp. one from which there is no escape (*driven into a corner*). **5** a secluded or remote place. **6** a region or quarter, esp. a remote one (*from the four corners of the earth*). **7** the action or result of buying or controlling the whole available stock of a commodity, thereby dominating the market. **8** *Boxing* & *Wrestling* **a** an angle of the ring, esp. one where a contestant rests between rounds. **b** a contestant's supporters offering assistance at the corner between rounds. **9** *Football* & *Hockey* a free kick or hit from a corner of the pitch after the ball has been kicked over the goal-line by a defending player. **10** a triangular cut of gammon or ham. ● *v.* **1** *tr.* force (a person or animal) into a difficult or inescapable position. **2** *tr.* **a** establish a corner in (a commodity). **b** dominate (dealers or the market) in this way. **3** *intr.* (esp. of or in a vehicle) go round a corner. □ **corner shop** a small local shop, esp. at a street corner. **just round** (or **around**) **the corner** *colloq.* very near, imminent. [ME f. AF ult. f. L *cornu* horn]

■ *n.* **1, 2** see ANGLE[1] *n.* 2. **3** see NOOK. **4** see HOLE *n.* 5. **6** see PART *n.* 11. ● *v.* **1** see TRAP[1] *v.* 1, 2. **2** see MONOPOLIZE. **3** see TURN *v.* 3b.

cornerstone /kórnərstōn/ *n.* **1 a** a stone in a projecting angle of a wall. **b** a foundation-stone. **2** an indispensable part or basis of something.

■ **2** see KEYSTONE.

cornerwise /kórnərwīz/ *adv.* diagonally.

cornet[1] /kórnit/ *n.* **1** *Mus.* **a** a brass instrument resembling a trumpet but shorter and wider. **b** its player. **c** an organ stop with the quality of a cornet. **d** a cornetto. **2** *Brit.* a conical wafer for holding ice-cream. ▫▫ **cornetist** /kornéttist, kórnitist/ *n.* **cornettist** /kornéttist/ *n.* [ME f. OF ult. f. L *cornu* horn]

cornet[2] /kórnit/ *n. Brit. hist.* the fifth commissioned officer in a cavalry troop, who carried the colours. ▫▫ **cornetcy** *n.* (*pl.* **-ies**). [earlier sense 'pennon, standard' f. F *cornette* dimin. of *corne* ult. f. L *cornua* horns]

cornett /kórnit/ *n. Mus.* = CORNETTO. [var. of CORNET[1]]

cornetto /kornéttō/ *n.* (*pl.* **cornetti** /-ti/) *Mus.* an old woodwind instrument like a flageolet. [It., dimin. of *corno* horn (as CORNET[1])]

cornfield /kórnfeeld/ *n.* a field in which corn is being grown.

cornflake /kórnflayk/ *n.* **1** (in *pl.*) a breakfast cereal of toasted flakes made from maize flour. **2** a flake of this cereal.

cornflour /kórnflowr/ *n.* **1** a fine-ground maize flour. Also called CORNSTARCH. **2** a flour of rice or other grain.

cornflower /kórnflowr/ *n.* any plant of the genus *Centaurea* growing among corn, esp. *C. cyanus*, with deep-blue flowers.

cornice /kórniss/ *n.* **1** *Archit.* **a** an ornamental moulding round the wall of a room just below the ceiling. **b** a horizontal moulded projection crowning a building or structure, esp. the uppermost member of the entablature of an order, surmounting the frieze. **2** *Mountaineering* an overhanging mass of hardened snow at the edge of a precipice. ▫▫ **corniced** *adj.* [F *corniche* etc. f. It. *cornice*, perh. f. L *cornix -icis* crow]

corniche /kórnish, kornéesh/ *n.* (in full **corniche road**) **1** a road cut into the edge of a cliff etc. **2** a coastal road with wide views. [F: see CORNICE]

Cornish /kórnish/ *adj.* & *n.* ● *adj.* of or relating to Cornwall in SW England. ● *n.* the ancient Celtic language of Cornwall. ▫ **Cornish cream** clotted cream. **Cornish pasty** seasoned meat and vegetables baked in a pastry envelope.

cornstarch /kórnstaarch/ *n.* = CORNFLOUR.

cornstone /kórnstōn/ *n. Brit. Geol.* a mottled red and green limestone usu. formed under arid conditions, esp. in the Devonian period.

cornucopia /kórnyookṓpiə/ *n.* **1 a** a symbol of plenty consisting of a goat's horn overflowing with flowers, fruit, and corn. **b** an ornamental vessel shaped like this. **2** an abundant supply. ▫▫ **cornucopian** *adj.* [LL f. L *cornu copiae* horn of plenty]

■ **2** see ABUNDANCE 1.

corny /kórni/ *adj.* (**cornier**, **corniest**) **1** *colloq.* **a** trite. **b** feebly humorous. **c** sentimental. **d** old-fashioned; out of date. **2** of or abounding in corn. ▫▫ **cornily** *adv.* **corniness** *n.* [CORN[1] + -Y[1]: sense 1 f. sense 'rustic']

■ **1 a** see BANAL. **c** see SENTIMENTAL. **d** see *out of date* (DATE).

corolla /kəróllə/ *n. Bot.* a whorl or whorls of petals forming the inner envelope of a flower. [L, dimin. of *corona* crown]

corollary /kəróllәri/ *n.* & *adj.* ● *n.* (*pl.* **-ies**) **1 a** a proposition that follows from (and is often appended to) one already proved. **b** an immediate deduction. **2** (often foll. by *of*) a natural consequence or result. ● *adj.* **1** supplementary, associated. **2** (often foll. by *to*) forming a corollary. [ME f. L *corollarium* money paid for a garland, gratuity: neut. adj. f. COROLLA]

corona[1] /kərṓnə/ *n.* (*pl.* **coronae** /-nee/) **1 a** a small circle of light round the sun or moon. **b** the rarefied gaseous envelope of the sun, seen as an irregularly shaped area of light around the moon's disc during a total solar eclipse. **2** a circular chandelier hung from a roof. **3** *Anat.* a crown or crownlike structure. **4** *Bot.* a crownlike outgrowth from the inner side of a corolla. **5** *Archit.* a broad vertical face of a cornice, usu. of considerable projection. **6** *Electr.* the glow around a conductor at high potential. [L, = crown]

■ **1** see HALO *n.* 1, 3.

corona[2] /kərṓnə/ *n.* a long cigar with straight sides. [Sp. *La Corona* the crown]

coronach /kórrənək, -nəkh/ *n. Sc.* & *Ir.* a funeral-song or dirge. [Ir. *coranach*, Gael. *corranach* f. *comh-* together + *rànach* outcry]

■ see LAMENT *n.* 2.

coronagraph /kərṓnəgraaf/ *n.* an instrument for observing the sun's corona, esp. other than during a solar eclipse.

coronal[1] /kərṓn'l, kórrən'l/ *adj.* **1** *Astron.* & *Bot.* of a corona. **2** *Anat.* of the crown of the head. ▫ **coronal bone** the frontal bone of the skull. **coronal plane** an imaginary plane dividing the body into dorsal and ventral parts. **coronal suture** a transverse suture of the skull separating the frontal bone from the parietal bones. [F *coronal* or L *coronalis* (as CORONA[1])]

coronal[2] /kórrən'l/ *n.* **1** a circlet (esp. of gold or gems) for the head. **2** a wreath or garland. [ME, app. f. AF f. *corone* CROWN]

coronary /kórrənəri/ *adj.* & *n.* ● *adj. Anat.* resembling or encircling like a crown. ● *n.* (*pl.* **-ies**) **1** = *coronary thrombosis*. **2** a heart attack. ▫ **coronary artery** an artery supplying blood to the heart. **coronary thrombosis** *Med.* a blockage of the blood flow caused by a blood clot in a coronary artery. [L *coronarius* f. *corona* crown]

coronation /kórrənáysh'n/ *n.* the ceremony of crowning a sovereign or a sovereign's consort. [ME f. OF f. med.L *coronatio -onis* f. *coronare* to crown f. CORONA[1]]

■ see *inauguration* (INAUGURATE).

coroner /kórrənər/ *n.* **1** an officer of a county, district, or municipality, holding inquests on deaths thought to be violent or accidental, and inquiries in cases of treasure trove. **2** *hist.* an officer charged with maintaining the rights of the private property of the Crown. ▫▫ **coronership** *n.* [ME f. AF *cor(o)uner* f. *coro(u)ne* CROWN]

coronet /kórrənit, -net/ *n.* **1** a small crown (esp. as worn, or used as a heraldic device, by a peer or peeress). **2** a circlet of precious materials, esp. as a woman's head-dress or part of one. **3** a garland for the head. **4** the lowest part of a horse's pastern. **5** a ring of bone at the base of a deer's antler. ▫▫ **coroneted** *adj.* [OF *coronet(t)e* dimin. of *corone* CROWN]

■ **1, 2** see CROWN *n.* 1.

corozo /kərṓzō/ *n.* (*pl.* **-os**) *Bot.* any of various palm-trees native to S. America. ▫ **corozo-nut** a seed of one species of palm, *Phytelephas macrocarpa*, which when hardened forms vegetable ivory: also called *ivory-nut*. [Sp.]

Corp. *abbr.* **1** Corporal. **2** *US* Corporation.

corpora *pl.* of CORPUS.

corporal[1] /kórprəl/ *n.* **1** a non-commissioned army or air-force officer ranking next below sergeant. **2** (in full **ship's corporal**) *Brit.* an officer under the master-at-arms, attending to police matters. **3** *US* a freshwater fallfish, *Semotilis corporalis*. [obs. F, var. of *caporal* f. It. *caporale* prob. f. L *corporalis* (as CORPORAL[2]), confused with It. *capo* head]

corporal[2] /kórpərəl/ *adj.* of or relating to the human body (cf. CORPOREAL). ▫ **corporal punishment** punishment inflicted on the body, esp. by beating. ▫▫ **corporally** *adv.* [ME f. OF f. L *corporalis* f. *corpus -oris* body]

■ bodily, physical.

corporal[3] /kórpərəl/ *n.* a cloth on which the vessels containing the consecrated elements are placed during the celebration of the Eucharist. [OE f. OF *corporal* or med.L *corporale pallium* body cloth (as CORPORAL[2])]

corporality /kórpərálliti/ *n.* (*pl.* **-ies**) **1** material existence. **2** a body. [ME f. LL *corporalitas* (as CORPORAL[2])]

corporate /kórpərət/ *adj.* **1** forming a corporation (*corporate body; body corporate*). **2** forming one body of many individuals. **3** of or belonging to a corporation or group (*corporate responsibility*). **4** corporative. ▫ **corporate raider** *US* a person who mounts an unwelcome takeover bid by buying up a company's shares on the stock market. ▫▫ **corporately** *adv.* **corporatism** *n.* [L *corporare corporat-* form into a body (*corpus -oris*)]

corporation /kórpəráysh'n/ *n.* **1** a group of people authorized to act as an individual and recognized in law as a single entity, esp. in business. **2** the municipal authorities of a borough, town, or city. **3** *joc.* a protruding stomach. [LL *corporatio* (as CORPORATE)]
■ **1** see COMPANY *n.* 3a. **3** see PAUNCH *n.*

corporative /kórpərətiv/ *adj.* **1** of a corporation. **2** governed by or organized in corporations, esp. of employers and employed. □□ **corporativism** *n.*

corporeal /korpóriəl/ *adj.* **1** bodily, physical, material, esp. as distinct from spiritual (cf. CORPORAL²). **2** *Law* consisting of material objects. □□ **corporeality** /-riálliti/ *n.* **corporeally** *adv.* [LL *corporealis* f. L *corporeus* f. *corpus -oris* body]
■ **1** see PHYSICAL *adj.* 2.

corporeity /kórpərée-iti/ *n.* **1** the quality of being or having a material body. **2** bodily substance. [F *corporéité* or med.L *corporeitas* f. L *corporeus* (as CORPOREAL)]

corposant /kórpəzant/ *n.* a luminous electrical discharge sometimes seen on a ship or aircraft during a storm. [OSp., Port., It. *corpo santo* holy body]

corps /kor/ *n.* (*pl.* **corps** /korz/) **1** *Mil.* **a** a body of troops with special duties (*intelligence corps*; *Royal Army Medical Corps*). **b** a main subdivision of an army in the field, consisting of two or more divisions. **2** a body of people engaged in a special activity (*diplomatic corps*; *press corps*). [F (as CORPSE)]
■ **1 a** troop(s), cadre, unit, detachment, cohort, division, battalion, brigade, platoon, squad, squadron.

corps de ballet /kór də bállay/ *n.* the company of ensemble dancers in a ballet. [F]

corps d'élite /kór dayleét/ *n.* a select group. [F]

corps diplomatique /kór díplәmateék/ *n.* a diplomatic corps. [F]

corpse /korps/ *n.* a dead (usu. human) body. □ **corpse-candle 1** a lambent flame seen in a churchyard or over a grave, regarded as an omen of death. **2** a lighted candle placed beside a corpse before burial. [ME *corps*, var. spelling of *cors* (CORSE), f. OF *cors* f. L *corpus* body]
■ body, remains, cadaver, *archaic* corse, *sl.* stiff; carcass.

corpulent /kórpyoolənt/ *adj.* bulky in body, fat. □□ **corpulence** *n.* **corpulency** *n.* [ME f. L *corpulentus* f. *corpus* body]
■ see FAT *adj.* 1. □□ **corpulence** see FAT *n.* 3.

corpus /kórpəss/ *n.* (*pl.* **corpora** /kórpərə/ or **corpuses**) **1** a body or collection of writings, texts, spoken material, etc. **2** *Anat.* a structure of a special character in the animal body. [ME f. L, = body]

Corpus Christi /kórpəss krísti/ *n.* a feast commemorating the Eucharist, observed on the Thursday after Trinity Sunday. [ME f. L, = Body of Christ]

corpuscle /kórpus'l/ *n.* a minute body or cell in an organism, esp. (in *pl.*) the red or white cells in the blood of vertebrates. □□ **corpuscular** /korpúskyoolər/ *adj.* [L *corpusculum* (as CORPUS)]

corpus delicti /kórpəss dilíktī/ *n.* *Law* the facts and circumstances constituting a breach of a law. [L, = body of offence]

corpus luteum /kórpəss lóotiəm/ *n.* *Anat.* a body developed in the ovary after discharge of the ovum, remaining in existence only if pregnancy has begun. [mod.L f. CORPUS + *luteus*, *-um* yellow]

corral /koraál/ *n.* & *v.* ● *n.* **1** *US* a pen for cattle, horses, etc. **2** an enclosure for capturing wild animals. **3** esp. *US hist.* a defensive enclosure of wagons in an encampment. ● *v.tr.* (**corralled**, **corralling**) **1** put or keep in a corral. **2** form (wagons) into a corral. **3** *US colloq.* acquire. [Sp. & OPort. (as KRAAL)]
■ *n.* **1, 2** see PEN² *n.* 1. ● *v.* **1** see PEN² *v.* 2.

corrasion /kəráyzh'n/ *n.* *Geol.* erosion of the earth's surface by rock material being carried over it by water, ice, etc. [L *corradere corras-* scrape together (as COM-, *radere* scrape)]

correct /kərékt/ *adj.* & *v.* ● *adj.* **1** true, right, accurate. **2** (of conduct, manners, etc.) proper, right. **3** in accordance with good standards of taste etc. ● *v.tr.* **1** set right; amend (an error, omission, etc., or the person responsible for it). **2** mark the errors in (written or printed work etc.). **3** substitute the right thing for (the wrong one). **4 a** admonish or rebuke (a person). **b** punish (a person or fault). **5** counteract (a harmful quality). **6** adjust (an instrument etc.) to function accurately or accord with a standard. □□ **correctly** *adv.* **correctness** *n.* [ME (adj. through F) f. L *corrigere correct-* (as COM-, *regere* guide)]
■ *adj.* **1** accurate, right, precise, exact, factual, valid, true, proper, suitable, appropriate. **2, 3** proper, decorous, decent, appropriate, (socially) acceptable, suitable, fit, right, *comme il faut*, meet, fitting, befitting, apt; faultless, perfect, unimpeachable; in order, *de rigueur*, *colloq.* done; conventional, set, established, standard, normal, orthodox, approved, usual, natural, customary, traditional. ● *v.* **1** right, set *or* put right, amend, redress, rectify, remedy, repair, fix, cure. **2** mark, grade; revise, edit. **4 a** scold, admonish, rebuke, reprimand, berate, reprove, castigate, chastise, *archaic or literary* chide; censure, blame. **b** chastise, chasten, discipline, castigate; see also PUNISH 1. **5** reverse, offset, counteract, counterbalance, neutralize, nullify, make up for, annul, cancel. **6** see ADJUST 1.

correction /kəréksh'n/ *n.* **1 a** the act or process of correcting. **b** an instance of this. **2** a thing substituted for what is wrong. **3** *archaic* punishment (*house of correction*). □□ **correctional** *adj.* [ME f. OF f. L *correctio -onis* (as CORRECT)]
■ **1** emendation, rectification, redress, reparation, amendment; improvement. **3** castigation, chastisement; see also PUNISHMENT 1, 2.

correctitude /kəréktityood/ *n.* correctness, esp. conscious correctness of conduct. [19th c., f. CORRECT + RECTITUDE]

corrective /kəréktiv/ *adj.* & *n.* ● *adj.* serving or tending to correct or counteract something undesired or harmful. ● *n.* a corrective measure or thing. □□ **correctively** *adv.* [F *correctif -ive* or LL *correctivus* (as CORRECT)]
■ *adj.* see THERAPEUTIC 1. ● *n.* see ANTIDOTE 2.

corrector /kəréktər/ *n.* a person who corrects or points out faults. [ME f. AF *correctour* f. L *corrector* (as CORRECT)]

correlate /kórrəlayt/ *v.* & *n.* ● *v.* **1** *intr.* (foll. by *with*, *to*) have a mutual relation. **2** *tr.* (usu. foll. by *with*) bring into a mutual relation. ● *n.* each of two related or complementary things (esp. so related that one implies the other). [back-form. f. CORRELATION, CORRELATIVE]
■ *v.* see RELATE 3.

correlation /kórrəláysh'n/ *n.* (also **corelation** /kṓ-ri-/) **1** a mutual relation between two or more things. **2 a** interdependence of variable quantities. **b** a quantity measuring the extent of this. **3** the act of correlating. □□ **correlational** *adj.* [med.L *correlatio* (as CORRELATIVE)]
■ **1, 3** see PARALLEL *n.* 2.

correlative /korélləttiv, kə-/ *adj.* & *n.* ● *adj.* **1** (often foll. by *with*, *to*) having a mutual relation. **2** *Gram.* (of words) corresponding to each other and regularly used together (as *neither* and *nor*). ● *n.* a correlative word or thing. □□ **correlatively** *adv.* **correlativity** /-tívviti/ *n.* [med.L *correlativus* (as COM-, RELATIVE)]
■ *adj.* **1** see RECIPROCAL *adj.* 4.

correspond /kórrispónd/ *v.intr.* **1 a** (usu. foll. by *to*) be analogous or similar. **b** (usu. foll. by *to*) agree in amount, position, etc. **c** (usu. foll. by *with*, *to*) be in harmony or agreement. **2** (usu. foll. by *with*) communicate by interchange of letters. □ **corresponding member** an honorary member of a learned society etc. with no voice in the society's affairs. □□ **correspondingly** *adv.* [F *correspondre* f. med.L *correspondere* (as COM-, RESPOND)]
■ **1** be alike *or* similar *or* analogous; agree, conform, tally, comply, accord, harmonize, be congruous, coincide; (*correspond to*) match. **2** write (letters), communicate, exchange letters.

correspondence /kórrispóndənss/ *n.* **1** (usu. foll. by *with, to, between*) agreement, similarity, or harmony. **2 a** communication by letters. **b** letters sent or received. □ **correspondence college** (or **school**) a college conducting correspondence courses. **correspondence column** the part of a newspaper etc. that contains letters from readers. **correspondence course** a course of study conducted by post. [ME f. OF f. med.L *correspondentia* (as CORRESPOND)]
■ **1** see ACCORD *n.* 1. **2** see LETTER *n.* 2a.

correspondent /kórrispóndənt/ *n.* & *adj.* ● *n.* **1** a person who writes letters to a person or a newspaper, esp. regularly. **2** a person employed to contribute material for publication in a periodical or for broadcasting (*our chess correspondent; the BBC's Moscow correspondent*). **3** a person or firm having regular business relations with another, esp. in another country. ● *adj.* (often foll. by *to, with*) *archaic* corresponding. □□ **correspondently** *adv.* [ME f. OF *correspondant* or med.L (as CORRESPOND)]
■ *n.* **2** journalist, reporter, newspaperman, pressman, newsman, newsperson, *colloq.* stringer.

corrida /koreédə/ *n.* **1** a bullfight. **2** bullfighting. [Sp. *corrida de toros* running of bulls]

corridor /kórridor/ *n.* **1** a passage from which doors lead into rooms (orig. an outside passage connecting parts of a building, now usu. a main passage in a large building). **2** a passage in a railway carriage from which doors lead into compartments. **3** a strip of the territory of one State passing through that of another, esp. securing access to the sea. **4** a route to which aircraft are restricted, esp. over a foreign country. □ **corridors of power** places where covert influence is said to be exerted in government. [F f. It. *corridore* corridor for *corridojo* running-place f. *correre* run, by confusion with *corridore* runner]
■ **1** hallway, passage, passageway, *US* hall.

corrie /kórri/ *n. Sc.* a circular hollow on a mountainside; a cirque. [Gael. *coire* cauldron]
■ see VALLEY.

corrigendum /kórrigéndəm, -jéndəm/ *n.* (*pl.* **corrigenda** /-də/) a thing to be corrected, esp. an error in a printed book. [L, neut. gerundive of *corrigere*: see CORRECT]

corrigible /kórrijib'l/ *adj.* **1** capable of being corrected. **2** (of a person) submissive; open to correction. □□ **corrigibly** *adv.* [ME f. F f. med.L *corrigibilis* (as CORRECT)]

corroborate /kəróbbərayt/ *v.tr.* confirm or give support to (a statement or belief, or the person holding it), esp. in relation to witnesses in a law court. □□ **corroboration** /-ráysh'n/ *n.* **corroborative** /-rətiv/ *adj.* **corroborator** *n.* **corroboratory** /-rətəri/ *adj.* [L *corroborare* strengthen (as COM-, *roborare* f. *robur -oris* strength)]
■ see SUBSTANTIATE.

corroboree /kəróbbəri/ *n.* **1** a festive or warlike dance-drama with song of Australian Aboriginals. **2** a noisy party. [Aboriginal dial.]

corrode /kərṓd/ *v.* **1 a** *tr.* wear away, esp. by chemical action. **b** *intr.* be worn away; decay. **2** *tr.* destroy gradually (*optimism corroded by recent misfortunes*). □□ **corrodible** *adj.* [ME f. L *corrodere corros-* (as COM-, *rodere* gnaw)]
■ **1** see WEAR[1] *v.* 5.

corrosion /kərṓzh'n/ *n.* **1** the process of corroding, esp. of a rusting metal. **2 a** damage caused by corroding. **b** a corroded area.

corrosive /kərṓsiv/ *adj.* & *n.* ● *adj.* tending to corrode or consume. ● *n.* a corrosive substance. □ **corrosive sublimate** mercuric chloride, a strong acid poison, used as a fungicide, antiseptic, etc. □□ **corrosively** *adv.* **corrosiveness** *n.* [ME f. OF *corosif -ive* (as CORRODE)]
■ *adj.* see CAUSTIC *adj.* 1, INCISIVE 3.

corrugate /kórroogayt/ *v.* **1** *tr.* (esp. as **corrugated** *adj.*) form into alternate ridges and grooves, esp. to strengthen (*corrugated iron; corrugated paper*). **2** *tr.* & *intr.* contract into wrinkles or folds. □□ **corrugation** /-gáysh'n/ *n.* [L *corrugare* (as COM-, *rugare* f. *ruga* wrinkle)]
■ see WRINKLE *v.* 1.

corrugator /kórroogaytər/ *n. Anat.* either of two muscles that contract the brow in frowning. [mod.L (as CORRUGATE)]

corrupt /kərúpt/ *adj.* & *v.* ● *adj.* **1** morally depraved; wicked. **2** influenced by or using bribery or fraudulent activity. **3** (of a text, language, etc.) harmed (esp. made suspect or unreliable) by errors or alterations. **4** rotten. ● *v.* **1** *tr.* & *intr.* make or become corrupt or depraved. **2** *tr.* affect or harm by errors or alterations. **3** *tr.* infect, taint. □ **corrupt practices** fraudulent activity, esp. at elections. □□ **corrupter** *n.* **corruptible** *adj.* **corruptibility** /-rúptibílliti/ *n.* **corruptive** *adj.* **corruptly** *adv.* **corruptness** *n.* [ME f. OF *corrupt* or L *corruptus* past part. of *corrumpere corrupt-* (as COM-, *rumpere* break)]
■ *adj.* **1** debased, depraved, perverted, evil, wicked, degraded, corrupted; see also DEGENERATE *adj.* **2** dishonest, untrustworthy, dishonourable, underhand(ed), venal, *colloq.* crooked, *sl.* bent. **3** harmed, debased, corrupted; unreliable. ● *v.* **1** debase, pervert, subvert, degrade, deprave, warp; bribe, suborn, buy (off). **3** infect, contaminate, pollute, taint, defile, spoil, poison, adulterate.

corruption /kərúpsh'n/ *n.* **1** moral deterioration, esp. widespread. **2** use of corrupt practices, esp. bribery or fraud. **3 a** irregular alteration (of a text, language, etc.) from its original state. **b** an irregularly altered form of a word. **4** decomposition, esp. of a corpse or other organic matter. [ME f. OF *corruption* or L *corruptio* (as CORRUPT)]
■ **1** see SIN[1] *n.* 1. **2** see GRAFT[2] *n.* 1. **3** see MISUSE *n.* **4** see ROT *n.* 1.

corsac /kórsak/ *n.* (also **corsak**) a fox, *Vulpes corsac*, of Central Asia. [Turki]

corsage /korsaázh/ *n.* **1** a small bouquet worn by a woman. **2** the bodice of a woman's dress. [ME f. OF f. *cors* body: see CORPSE]
■ **1** buttonhole, boutonnière.

corsair /kórsair/ *n.* **1** a pirate ship. **2** a pirate. **3** *hist.* a privateer, esp. of the Barbary Coast. [F *corsaire* f. med.L *cursarius* f. *cursus* inroad f. *currere* run]
■ **2, 3** see PIRATE *n.* 1a.

corsak var. of CORSAC.

corse /korss/ *n. archaic* a corpse. [var. of CORPSE]

corselet var. of CORSLET, CORSELETTE.

corselette /kórslit, kórsəlét/ *n.* (also **corselet**) a woman's foundation garment combining corset and brassière.

corset /kórsit/ *n.* & *v.* ● *n.* **1** a closely-fitting undergarment worn by women to support the abdomen. **2** a similar garment worn by men and women because of injury, weakness, or deformity. ● *v.tr.* (**corseted, corseting**) **1** provide with a corset. **2** control closely. □□ **corseted** *adj.* **corsetry** *n.* [ME f. OF, dimin. of *cors* body: see CORPSE]

corsetière /kórsityáir/ *n.* a woman who makes or fits corsets. [F, fem. of *corsetier* (as CORSET, -IER)]

Corsican /kórsikən/ *adj.* & *n.* ● *adj.* of or relating to Corsica, an island in the Mediterranean under French rule. ● *n.* **1** a native of Corsica. **2** the Italian dialect of Corsica.

corslet /kórslit/ *n.* (also **corselet**) **1** a garment (usu. tight-fitting) covering the trunk but not the limbs. **2** *hist.* a piece of armour covering the trunk. [OF *corselet*, dimin. formed as CORSET]

cortège /kortáyzh/ *n.* **1** a procession, esp. for a funeral. **2** a train of attendants. [F]
■ **1** see PROCESSION 1. **2** see TRAIN *n.* 4.

Cortes /kórtess, -tez/ *n.* the legislative assembly of Spain and formerly of Portugal. [Sp. & Port., pl. of *corte* COURT]

cortex /kórteks/ *n.* (*pl.* **cortices** /-tiseez/) **1** *Anat.* the outer part of an organ, esp. of the brain (**cerebral cortex**) or kidneys (**renal cortex**). **2** *Bot.* **a** an outer layer of tissue immediately below the epidermis. **b** bark. □□ **cortical** /-tik'l/ *adj.* [L *cortex, -icis* bark]

Corti /kórti/ *n.* □ **organ of Corti** *Anat.* a structure in the inner ear of mammals, responsible for converting sound signals into nerve impulses. [A. *Corti*, It. anatomist d. 1876]

corticate /kórtikayt/ *adj.* (also **corticated**) **1** having bark or rind. **2** barklike. [L *corticatus* (as CORTEX)]

corticotrophic hormone /kórtikōtróffik/ *adj.* (also **corticotropic**) = ADRENOCORTICOTROPHIC HORMONE.

corticotrophin /kórtikōtrṓfin/ *n.* (also **corticotropin**) = ADRENOCORTICOTROPHIN.

cortisone /kórtizōn/ *n. Biochem.* a steroid hormone produced by the adrenal cortex or synthetically, used medicinally esp. against inflammation and allergy. [Chem. name 17-hydroxy-11-dehydro*corti*co*s*ter*one*]

corundum /kərúndəm/ *n. Mineral.* extremely hard crystallized alumina, used esp. as an abrasive, and varieties of which, e.g. ruby and sapphire, are used for gemstones. [Tamil *kurundam* f. Skr. *kuruvinda* ruby]

coruscate /kórrəskayt/ *v.intr.* **1** give off flashing light; sparkle. **2** be showy or brilliant. □□ **coruscation** /-skáysh'n/ *n.* [L *coruscare* glitter]
■ **1** see SPARKLE *v.* 1a.

corvée /korváy/ *n.* **1** *hist.* a day's work of unpaid labour due to a lord from a vassal. **2** labour exacted in lieu of paying taxes. **3** an onerous task. [ME f. OF ult. f. L *corrogare* ask for, collect (as COM-, *rogare* ask)]

corves *pl.* of CORF.

corvette /korvét/ *n. Naut.* **1** a small naval escort-vessel. **2** *hist.* a flush-decked warship with one tier of guns. [F f. MDu. *korf* kind of ship + dimin. -ETTE]

corvine /kórvīn/ *adj.* of or akin to the raven or crow. [L *corvinus* f. *corvus* raven]

corybantic /kórribántik/ *adj.* wild, frenzied. [*Corybantes* priests of Cybele performing wild dances (L f. Gk *Korubantes*)]

corymb /kórrimb/ *n. Bot.* a flat-topped cluster of flowers with the flower-stalks proportionally longer lower down the stem. □□ **corymbose** *adj.* [F *corymbe* or L *corymbus* f. Gk *korumbos* cluster]

coryphée /kórrifay/ *n.* a leading dancer in a *corps de ballet*. [F f. Gk *koruphaios* leader of a chorus f. *koruphē* head]

coryza /kərīzə/ *n.* **1** a catarrhal inflammation of the mucous membrane in the nose; a cold in the head. **2** any disease with this as a symptom. [L f. Gk *koruza* running at the nose]
■ see COLD *n.* 2.

cos[1] /koss/ *n.* a variety of lettuce with crisp narrow leaves forming a long upright head. [L f. Gk *Kōs*, island in the Aegean, where it originated]
■ *US* romaine.

cos[2] /koss, koz/ *abbr.* cosine.

cos[3] /koz/ *conj.* & *adv.* (also **'cos**) *colloq.* because. [abbr.]

Cosa Nostra /kṓzə nóstrə/ *n.* a US criminal organization resembling and related to the Mafia. [It., = our affair]
■ see UNDERWORLD 1.

cosec /kṓsek/ *abbr.* cosecant.

cosecant /kōséekənt/ *n. Math.* the ratio of the hypotenuse (in a right-angled triangle) to the side opposite an acute angle; the reciprocal of sine. [mod.L *cosecans* and F *cosécant* (as CO-, SECANT)]

coseismal /kōsīzm'l/ *adj.* & *n.* ● *adj.* of or relating to points of simultaneous arrival of an earthquake wave. ● *n.* a straight line or a curve connecting these points. [CO- + SEISMAL (see SEISMIC)]

coset /kṓset/ *n. Math.* a set composed of all the products obtained by multiplying on the right or on the left each element of a subgroup in turn by one particular element of the group containing the subgroup. [CO- + SET[2]]

cosh[1] /kosh/ *n.* & *v. Brit. colloq.* ● *n.* a heavy blunt weapon. ● *v.tr.* hit with a cosh. [19th c.: orig. unkn.]
■ *n.* see CLUB *n.* 1.

cosh[2] /kosh, kosáych/ *abbr. Math.* hyperbolic cosine.

co-signatory /kṓsígnətəri, -tri/ *n.* & *adj.* (*US* **cosignatory**) ● *n.* (*pl.* **-ies**) a person or State signing (a treaty etc.) jointly with others. ● *adj.* signing jointly.

cosine /kṓsīn/ *n. Math.* the ratio of the side adjacent to an acute angle (in a right-angled triangle) to the hypotenuse. [mod.L *cosinus* (as CO-, SINE)]

cosmea /kózmiə/ *n.* = COSMOS[2]. [mod.L, formed as COSMOS[2]]

cosmetic /kozméttik/ *adj.* & *n.* ● *adj.* **1** intended to adorn or beautify the body, esp. the face. **2** intended to improve only appearances; superficially improving or beneficial (*a cosmetic change*). **3** (of surgery or a prosthetic device) imitating, restoring, or enhancing the normal appearance. ● *n.* a cosmetic preparation, esp. for the face. □□ **cosmetically** *adv.* [F *cosmétique* f. Gk *kosmētikos* f. *kosmeō* adorn f. *kosmos* order, adornment]
■ *adj.* **2** see SUPERFICIAL 3.

cosmic /kózmik/ *adj.* **1** of the universe or cosmos, esp. as distinct from the earth. **2** of or for space travel. □ **cosmic dust** small particles of matter distributed throughout space. **cosmic rays** (or **radiation**) radiations from space etc. that reach the earth from all directions, usu. with high energy and penetrative power. □□ **cosmical** *adj.* **cosmically** *adv.*
■ **1** see UNIVERSAL *adj.*

cosmogony /kozmóggəni/ *n.* (*pl.* **-ies**) **1** the origin of the universe. **2** a theory about this. □□ **cosmogonic** /-məgónnik/ *adj.* **cosmogonical** /-məgónnik'l/ *adj.* **cosmogonist** *n.* [Gk *kosmogonia* f. *kosmos* world + *-gonia* -begetting]

cosmography /kozmógrəfi/ *n.* (*pl.* **-ies**) a description or mapping of general features of the universe. □□ **cosmographer** *n.* **cosmographic** /-məgráffik/ *adj.* **cosmographical** /-məgráffik'l/ *adj.* [ME f. F *cosmographie* or f. LL f. Gk *kosmographia* (as COSMOS[1], -GRAPHY)]

cosmology /kozmólləji/ *n.* the science or theory of the universe. □□ **cosmological** /-məlójik'l/ *adj.* **cosmologist** *n.* [F *cosmologie* or mod.L *cosmologia* (as COSMOS[1], -LOGY)]

cosmonaut /kózmənawt/ *n.* a Russian astronaut. [Russ. *kosmonavt*, as COSMOS[1], after *astronaut*]

cosmopolis /kozmóppəliss/ *n.* a cosmopolitan city. [Gk *kosmos* world + *polis* city]

cosmopolitan /kózməpóllit'n/ *adj.* & *n.* ● *adj.* **1 a** of or from or knowing many parts of the world. **b** consisting of people from many or all parts. **2** free from national limitations or prejudices. **3** *Ecol.* (of a plant, animal, etc.) widely distributed. ● *n.* **1** a cosmopolitan person. **2** *Ecol.* a widely distributed animal or plant. □□ **cosmopolitanism** *n.* **cosmopolitanize** *v.tr.* & *intr.* (also **-ise**). [COSMOPOLITE + -AN]
■ **1** see INTERNATIONAL *adj.* **2** see WORLDLY 2.

cosmopolite /kozmóppəlīt/ *n.* & *adj.* ● *n.* **1** a cosmopolitan person. **2** *Ecol.* = COSMOPOLITAN *n.* 2. ● *adj.* free from national attachments or prejudices. [F f. Gk *kosmopolitēs* f. *kosmos* world + *politēs* citizen]

cosmos[1] /kózmoss/ *n.* **1** the universe, esp. as a well-ordered whole. **2 a** an ordered system of ideas etc. **b** a sum total of experience. [Gk *kosmos*]
■ **1** see UNIVERSE 1a.

cosmos[2] /kózmoss/ *n.* any composite plant of the genus *Cosmos*, bearing single dahlia-like blossoms of various colours. [mod.L f. Gk *kosmos* in sense 'ornament']

COSPAR *abbr.* Committee on Space Research.

Cossack /kóssak/ *n.* & *adj.* ● *n.* **1** a member of a people of southern Imperial Russia, orig. famous for their military skill. **2** a member of a Cossack military unit. ● *adj.* of, relating to, or characteristic of the Cossacks. [F *cosaque* f. Russ. *kazak* f. Turki *quzzāq* nomad, adventurer]

cosset /kóssit/ *v.tr.* (**cosseted, cosseting**) pamper. [dial. *cosset* = pet lamb, prob. f. AF *coscet*, *cozet* f. OE *cotsǣta* cottager (as COT[2], SIT)]
■ see PAMPER.

cossie /kózzi/ *n.* (also **cozzie**) chiefly *Austral. sl.* a swimming costume. [abbr.]

cost /kost/ *v.* & *n.* ● *v.* (*past* and *past part.* **cost**) **1** *tr.* be obtainable for (a sum of money); have as a price (*what does it cost?; it cost me £50*). **2** *tr.* involve as a loss or sacrifice (*it cost them much effort; it cost him his life*). **3** *tr.* (*past* and *past part.* **costed**) fix or estimate the cost or price of. **4** *colloq.* **a**

tr. be costly to (*it'll cost you*). **b** *intr.* be costly. ● *n.* **1** what a thing costs; the price paid or to be paid. **2** a loss or sacrifice; an expenditure of time, effort, etc. **3** (in *pl.*) legal expenses, esp. those allowed in favour of the winning party or against the losing party in a suit. □ **at all costs** (or **at any cost**) no matter what the cost or risk may be. **at cost** at the initial cost; at cost price. **at the cost of** at the expense of losing or sacrificing. **cost accountant** an accountant who records costs and (esp. overhead) expenses in a business concern. **cost-benefit** assessing the relation between the cost of an operation and the value of the resulting benefits (*cost-benefit analysis*). **cost** (or **costing**) **clerk** a clerk who records costs and expenses in a business concern. **cost a person dear** (or **dearly**) involve a person in a high cost or a heavy penalty. **cost-effective** effective or productive in relation to its cost. **cost of living** the level of prices esp. of the basic necessities of life. **cost-plus** calculated as the basic cost plus a profit factor. **cost price** the price paid for a thing by one who later sells it. **cost push** *Econ.* factors other than demand that cause inflation. **to a person's cost** at a person's expense; with loss or disadvantage to a person. [ME f. OF *coster, couster, coust* ult. f. L *constare* stand firm, stand at a price (as COM-, *stare* stand)]

■ *v.* **1** sell for, get, fetch, bring in; *colloq.* set a person back. **2** see INVOLVE 2. ● *n.* **1** price, payment, charge, expense, expenditure, rate, tariff; outlay. **2** see LOSS 1. □ **at all costs** see *by all means* 3 (MEANS).

costal /kóst'l/ *adj.* of the ribs. [F f. mod.L *costalis* f. L *costa* rib]

co-star /kṓstaar/ *n.* & *v.* ● *n.* a cinema or stage star appearing with another or others of equal importance. ● *v.* (**-starred, -starring**) **1** *intr.* take part as a co-star. **2** *tr.* (of a production) include as a co-star.

costard /kóstərd/ *n. Brit.* **1** a large ribbed variety of apple. **2** *archaic joc.* the head. [ME f. AF f. *coste* rib f. L *costa*]

costate /kóstayt/ *adj.* ribbed; having ribs or ridges. [L *costatus* f. *costa* rib]

coster /kóstər/ *n. Brit.* = COSTERMONGER. [abbr.]

costermonger /kóstərmunggər/ *n. Brit.* a person who sells fruit, vegetables, etc., in the street from a barrow. [COSTARD + MONGER]

costive /kóstiv/ *adj.* **1** constipated. **2** niggardly. □□ **costively** *adv.* **costiveness** *n.* [ME f. OF *costivé* f. L *constipatus*: see CONSTIPATE]

costly /kóstli/ *adj.* (**costlier, costliest**) **1** costing much; expensive. **2** of great value. □□ **costliness** *n.*

■ **1** see EXPENSIVE 1. **2** see PRECIOUS *adj.* 1.

costmary /kóstmairi/ *n.* (*pl.* **-ies**) an aromatic composite plant, *Balsamita major*, formerly used in medicine and for flavouring ale. [OE *cost* f. L *costum* f. Gk *kostos* f. Arab. *ḳusṭ* an aromatic plant + (*St*) *Mary* (with whom it was associated in medieval times)]

costume /kóstyoom/ *n.* & *v.* ● *n.* **1** a style or fashion of dress, esp. that of a particular place, time, or class. **2** a set of clothes. **3** clothing for a particular activity (*swimming-costume*). **4** an actor's clothes for a part. **5** a woman's matching jacket and skirt. ● *v.tr.* provide with a costume. □ **costume jewellery** artificial jewellery worn to adorn clothes. **costume play** (or **piece** or **drama**) a play or television drama in which the actors wear historical costume. [F f. It. f. L *consuetudo* CUSTOM]

■ *n.* **1, 2** dress, clothing, clothes, garb, garments, outfit, vestment, livery, uniform, kit, *archaic* raiment, *colloq.* togs, *formal* attire, apparel, *sl.* threads. **5** suit. ● *v.* see DRESS *v.* 1a.

costumier /kostyóomiər/ *n.* (also **costumer** /-mər/) a person who makes or deals in costumes, esp. for theatrical use. [F *costumier* (as COSTUME)]

■ see TAILOR *n.*

cosy /kṓzi/ *adj.*, *n.*, & *v.* (*US* **cozy**) ● *adj.* (**cosier, cosiest**) **1** comfortable and warm; snug. **2** *derog.* complacent; self-serving. **3** warm and friendly. ● *n.* (*pl.* **-ies**) **1** a cover to keep something hot, esp. a teapot or a boiled egg. **2** a canopied corner seat for two. ● *v.tr.* (**-ies, -ied**) (often foll. by *along*) *colloq.* reassure, esp. deceptively. □ **cosy up to** *US colloq.* **1** ingratiate oneself with. **2** snuggle up to. □□ **cosily** *adv.* **cosiness** *n.* [18th c. f. Sc., of unkn. orig.]

■ *adj.* **1** comfortable, snug, warm, restful, secure, relaxing, *colloq.* comfy. **2** complacent, self-serving; see also SMUG. **3** see WARM *adj.* 3a. □ **cosy up to 1** see INGRATIATE.

cot[1] /kot/ *n.* **1** *Brit.* a small bed with high sides, esp. for a baby or very young child. **2** a hospital bed. **3** *US* a small folding bed. **4** *Ind.* a light bedstead. **5** *Naut.* a kind of swinging bed hung from deck beams, formerly used by officers. □ **cot-case** a person too ill to leave his or her bed. **cot-death** the unexplained death of a baby while sleeping. [Anglo-Ind., f. Hindi *khāṭ* bedstead, hammock]

■ **1** bed, crib, cradle. **3** camp-bed. **4** *Ind.* charpoy.

cot[2] /kot/ *n.* & *v.* ● *n.* **1** a small shelter; a cote (*bell-cot*; *sheep-cot*). **2** *poet.* a cottage. ● *v.tr.* (**cotted, cotting**) put (sheep) in a cot. [OE f. Gmc, rel. to COTE]

cot[3] /kot/ *abbr. Math.* cotangent.

cotangent /kōtánjənt/ *n. Math.* the ratio of the side adjacent to an acute angle (in a right-angled triangle) to the opposite side.

cote /kōt/ *n.* a shelter, esp. for animals or birds; a shed or stall (*sheep-cote*). [OE f. Gmc, rel. to COT[2]]

■ see STALL[1] *n.* 2.

coterie /kṓtəri/ *n.* **1** an exclusive group of people sharing interests. **2** a select circle in society. [F, orig. = association of tenants, ult. f. MLG *kote* COTE]

■ see GROUP *n.* 3.

coterminous /kōtérminəss/ *adj.* (often foll. by *with*) having the same boundaries or extent (in space, time, or meaning). [CO- + TERMINUS + -OUS]

■ coextensive, conterminous.

coth /koth/ *abbr. Math.* hyperbolic cotangent.

co-tidal line /kōtíd'l/ *n.* a line on a map connecting points at which tidal levels (as high tide or low tide) occur simultaneously.

cotillion /kətílyən/ *n.* **1** any of various French dances with elaborate steps, figures, and ceremonial. **2** *US* **a** a ballroom dance resembling a quadrille. **b** a formal ball. [F *cotillon* petticoat, dimin. of *cotte* f. OF *cote* COAT]

cotoneaster /kətṓniástər/ *n.* any rosaceous shrub of the genus *Cotoneaster*, bearing usu. bright red berries. [mod.L f. L *cotoneum* QUINCE + -ASTER]

cotta /kóttə/ *n. Eccl.* a short surplice. [It., formed as COAT]

cottage /kóttij/ *n.* **1** a small simple house, esp. in the country. **2** a dwelling forming part of a farm establishment, used by a worker. □ **cottage cheese** soft white cheese made from curds of skimmed milk without pressing. **cottage hospital** *Brit.* a small hospital not having resident medical staff. **cottage industry** a business activity partly or wholly carried on at home. **cottage loaf** a loaf formed of two round masses, the smaller on top of the larger. **cottage pie** *Brit.* a dish of minced meat topped with browned mashed potato. □□ **cottagey** *adj.* [ME f. AF, formed as COT[2], COTE]

■ **1** hut, cabin, bungalow, lodge, chalet, shanty, *Sc.* bothy, *poet.* cot.

cottager /kóttijər/ *n.* a person who lives in a cottage.

cottar /kóttər/ *n.* (also **cotter**) **1** *Sc.* & *hist.* a farm-labourer or tenant occupying a cottage in return for labour as required. **2** *Ir. hist.* = COTTIER. [COT[2] + -ER[1] (Sc. *-ar*)]

cotter /kóttər/ *n.* **1** a bolt or wedge for securing parts of machinery etc. **2** (in full **cotter pin**) a split pin that opens after passing through a hole. [17th c. (rel. to earlier *cotterel*): orig. unkn.]

cottier /kóttiər/ *n. Brit.* **1** a cottager. **2** *hist.* an Irish peasant under cottier tenure. □ **cottier tenure** *hist.* the letting of land in small portions at a rent fixed by competition. [ME f. OF *cotier* f. med.L *cotarius*: see COTERIE]

cotton /kótt'n/ *n.* & *v.* ● *n.* **1** a soft white fibrous substance covering the seeds of certain plants. **2 a** (in full **cotton plant**) such a plant, esp. any of the genus *Gossypium*. **b** cotton plants cultivated as a crop for the fibre or the seeds.

3 thread or cloth made from the fibre. **4** (*attrib.*) made of cotton. ● *v.intr.* (foll. by *to*) be attracted by (a person). □ **cotton-cake** compressed cotton seed used as food for cattle. **cotton candy** *US* candyfloss. **cotton-gin** a machine for separating cotton from its seeds. **cotton-grass** any grasslike plant of the genus *Eriophorum*, with long white silky hairs. **cotton on** (often foll. by *to*) *colloq.* begin to understand. **cotton-picking** *US sl.* unpleasant, wretched. **cotton waste** refuse yarn used to clean machinery etc. **cotton wool 1** esp. *Brit.* fluffy wadding of a kind orig. made from raw cotton. **2** *US* raw cotton. □□ **cottony** *adj.* [ME f. OF *coton* f. Arab. *ḳuṭn*]

■ □ **cotton on** see REALIZE 2.

cottontail /kótt'ntayl/ *n.* any rabbit of the genus *Sylvilagus*, native to America, having a mainly white fluffy tail.

cottonwood /kótt'nwŏŏd/ *n.* **1** any of several poplars, native to N. America, having seeds covered in white cottony hairs. **2** any of several trees native to Australia, esp. a downy-leaved tree, *Bedfordia arborescens*.

cotyledon /kóttiléed'n/ *n.* **1** an embryonic leaf in seed-bearing plants. **2** any succulent plant of the genus *Umbilicus*, e.g. pennywort. □□ **cotyledonary** *adj.* **cotyledonous** *adj.* [L, = pennywort, f. Gk *kotulēdōn* cup-shaped cavity f. *kotulē* cup]

coucal /kōōkal/ *n.* any ground-nesting bird of the genus *Centropus*, related to the cuckoos. [F, perh. f. *coucou* cuckoo + *alouette* lark]

couch[1] /kowch/ *n.* & *v.* ● *n.* **1** an upholstered piece of furniture for several people; a sofa. **2** a long padded seat with a headrest at one end, esp. one on which a psychiatrist's or doctor's patient reclines during examination. ● *v.* **1** *tr.* (foll. by *in*) express in words of a specified kind (*couched in simple language*). **2** *tr.* lay on or as on a couch. **3** *intr.* **a** (of an animal) lie, esp. in its lair. **b** lie in ambush. **4** *tr.* lower (a spear etc.) to the position for attack. **5** *tr. Med.* treat (a cataract) by displacing the lens of the eye. □ **couch potato** *US sl.* a person who likes lazing at home. [ME f. OF *couche*, *coucher* f. L *collocare* (as COM-, *locare* place)]

■ *n.* **1** sofa, settee, divan, love-seat, studio couch, settle, *chaise longue*; tête-à-tête, canapé, chesterfield, squab, *US* Davenport. ● *v.* **1** phrase, embed, frame, formulate, style; see also EXPRESS[1] 1, 2. □ **couch potato** see LOAFER.

couch[2] /kōōch, kowch/ *n.* (in full **couch grass**) any of several grasses of the genus *Agropyron*, esp. *A. repens*, having long creeping roots. [var. of QUITCH]

couchant /kówchənt/ *adj.* (placed after noun) *Heraldry* (of an animal) lying with the body resting on the legs and the head raised. [F, pres. part. of *coucher*: see COUCH[1]]

couchette /kōōshét/ *n.* **1** a railway carriage with seats convertible into sleeping-berths. **2** a berth in this. [F, = little bed, dimin. of *couche* COUCH[1]]

coudé /kōōdáy/ *adj.* & *n.* ● *adj.* of or relating to a telescope in which rays are bent to a focus off the axis. ● *n.* such a telescope. [F, past part. of *couder* bend at right angles f. *coude* elbow formed as CUBIT]

Couéism /kōō-ayiz'm/ *n.* a system of usu. optimistic auto-suggestion as psychotherapy. [E. *Coué*, Fr. psychologist d. 1926]

cougar /kōōgər/ *n. US* a puma. [F, repr. Guarani *guaçu ara*]

cough /kof/ *v.* & *n.* ● *v.intr.* **1** expel air from the lungs with a sudden sharp sound produced by abrupt opening of the glottis, to remove an obstruction or congestion. **2** (of an engine, gun, etc.) make a similar sound. **3** *sl.* confess. ● *n.* **1** an act of coughing. **2** a condition of the respiratory organs causing coughing. **3** a tendency to cough. □ **cough drop** (or **sweet**) a medicated lozenge to relieve a cough. **cough mixture** a liquid medicine to relieve a cough. **cough out 1** eject by coughing. **2** say with a cough. **cough up 1** = *cough out*. **2** *sl.* bring out or give (money or information) reluctantly. □□ **cougher** *n.* [ME *coghe*, *cowhe*, rel. to MDu. *kuchen*, MHG *kūchen*, of imit. orig.]

■ □ **cough up 2** see PAY[1] *v.* 2.

could *past* of CAN[1].

couldn't /kŏŏdd'nt/ *contr.* could not.

coulée /kōōlay, kōōli/ *n. Geol.* **1** a solidified lava-flow. **2** *US* a deep ravine. [F, fem. past part. of *couler* flow, f. L *colare* strain, filter]

■ **2** see CANYON.

coulisse /kōōléess/ *n.* **1** (usu. in *pl.*) *Theatr.* a piece of side scenery or a space between two of these; the wings. **2** a place of informal discussion or negotiation. [F f. *coulis* sliding: see PORTCULLIS]

couloir /kōōlwaar/ *n.* a steep narrow gully on a mountainside. [F f. *couler* glide: see COULÉE]

■ see PASS[2].

coulomb /kōōlom/ *n. Electr.* the SI unit of electric charge, equal to the quantity of electricity conveyed in one second by a current of one ampere. ¶ Symb.: **C**. [C. A. de *Coulomb*, Fr. physicist d. 1806]

coulometry /kōōlómmitri/ *n. Chem.* a method of chemical analysis by measurement of the number of coulombs used in electrolysis. □□ **coulometric** /kōōləmétrik/ *adj.*

coulter /kōltər/ *n.* (*US* **colter**) a vertical cutting blade fixed in front of a ploughshare. [OE f. L *culter*]

coumarin /kōōmərin/ *n.* an aromatic substance found in many plants and formerly used for flavouring food. [F *coumarine* f. Tupi *cumarú* tonka bean]

coumarone /kōōmərōn/ *n.* an organic liquid obtained from coal tar by synthesis and used in paints and varnishes. □ **coumarone resin** a thermoplastic resin formed by polymerization of coumarone. [COUMARIN + -ONE]

council /kówns'l/ *n.* **1 a** an advisory, deliberative, or administrative body of people formally constituted and meeting regularly. **b** a meeting of such a body. **2 a** the elected local administrative body of a parish, district, town, city, or administrative county and its paid officers and workforce. **b** (*attrib.*) (esp. of housing) provided by a local council (*council flat*; *council estate*). **3** a body of persons chosen as advisers (*Privy Council*). **4** an ecclesiastical assembly (*ecumenical council*). □ **council-chamber** a room in which a council meets. **council-house** a building in which a council meets. **council of war 1** an assembly of officers called in a special emergency. **2** any meeting held to plan a response to an emergency. **the Queen** (or **King**) **in Council** the Privy Council as issuing Orders in Council or receiving petitions etc. [ME f. AF *cuncile* f. L *concilium* convocation, assembly f. *calare* summon: cf. COUNSEL]

■ **1 a** board, ministry, directors, cabinet, panel, committee, body, directorate, *hist.* Directory. **b** assembly, meeting, conclave, conference, convention, congress, congregation, gathering, convocation.

councillor /kównsələr/ *n.* an elected member of a council, esp. a local one. □□ **councillorship** *n.* [ME, alt. of COUNSELLOR: assim. to COUNCIL]

councilman /kówns'lmən/ *n.* (*pl.* **-men**; *fem.* **councilwoman**, *pl.* **-women**) esp. *US* a member of a council; a councillor.

counsel /kówns'l/ *n.* & *v.* ● *n.* **1** advice, esp. formally given. **2** consultation, esp. to seek or give advice. **3** (*pl.* same) a barrister or other legal adviser; a body of these advising in a case. **4** a plan of action. ● *v.tr.* (**counselled**, **counselling**; *US* **counseled**, **counseling**) **1** (often foll. by *to* + infin.) advise (a person). **2 a** give advice to (a person) on social or personal problems, esp. professionally. **b** assist or guide (a person) in resolving personal difficulties. **3** (often foll. by *that*) recommend (a course of action). □ **counsel of despair** action to be taken when all else fails. **counsel of perfection 1** advice that is ideal but not feasible. **2** advice guiding towards moral perfection. **keep one's own counsel** not confide in others. **Queen's** (or **King's**) **Counsel** *Brit.* a counsel to the Crown, taking precedence over other barristers. **take counsel** (usu. foll. by *with*) consult. [ME f. OF

c(o)unseil, conseiller f. L *consilium* consultation, advice]
■ *n.* **1** advice, judgement, direction, opinion, guidance, instruction, recommendation, exhortation. **2** consultation, deliberation; see also DISCUSSION 1. **3** adviser, guide, counsellor; lawyer, *Brit.* barrister, *Ir.* counsellor-at-law, *US* attorney, counselor-at-law. ● *v.* **1** direct, instruct; see also ADVISE 1, 2. **3** recommend, urge, exhort, advocate; see also SUGGEST 1. □ **take counsel** see CONSULT 1, 2.

counselling /kównsəling/ *n.* (*US* **counseling**) **1** the act or process of giving counsel. **2** the process of assisting and guiding clients, esp. by a trained person on a professional basis, to resolve esp. personal, social, or psychological problems and difficulties (cf. COUNSEL *v.* 2b).

counsellor /kównsələr/ *n.* (*US* **counselor**) **1** a person who gives counsel; an adviser. **2** a person trained to give guidance on personal, social, or psychological problems (*marriage guidance counsellor*). **3** a senior officer in the diplomatic service. **4 a** (also **counselor-at-law**) *US* a barrister. **b** (also **counsellor-at-law**) *Ir.* an advising barrister. □ **Counsellor of State** *Brit.* a temporary regent during a sovereign's absence. [ME f. OF *conseiller* (f. L *consiliarius*), *conseillour, -eur* (f. L *consiliator*): see COUNSEL]
■ **4** adviser, counsel, lawyer, barrister, *Sc.* advocate, *US* attorney.

count[1] /kownt/ *v.* & *n.* ● *v.* **1** *tr.* determine the total number or amount of, esp. by assigning successive numbers (*count the stations*). **2** *intr.* repeat numbers in ascending order; conduct a reckoning. **3 a** *tr.* (often foll. by *in*) include in one's reckoning or plan (*you can count me in; fifteen people, counting the guide*). **b** *intr.* be included in a reckoning or plan. **4** *tr.* consider (a thing or a person) to be (lucky etc.) (*count no man happy until he is dead*). **5** *intr.* (often foll. by *for*) have value; matter (*his opinion counts for a great deal*). ● *n.* **1 a** the act of counting; a reckoning (*after a count of fifty*). **b** the sum total of a reckoning (*blood count; pollen count*). **2** *Law* each charge in an indictment (*guilty on ten counts*). **3** a count of up to ten seconds by a referee when a boxer is knocked down. **4** *Polit.* the act of counting the votes after a general or local election. **5** one of several points under discussion. **6** the measure of the fineness of a yarn expressed as the weight of a given length or the length of a given weight. **7** *Physics* the number of ionizing particles detected by a counter. □ **count against** be reckoned to the disadvantage of. **count one's blessings** be grateful for what one has. **count one's chickens** be over-optimistic or hasty in anticipating good fortune. **count the cost** consider the risks before taking action; calculate the damage resulting from an action. **count the days** (or **hours** etc.) be impatient. **count down** recite numbers backwards to zero, esp. as part of a rocket-launching procedure. **counting-house** a place where accounts are kept. **count noun** a countable noun (see COUNTABLE 2). **count on** (or **upon**) depend on, rely on; expect confidently. **count out 1** count while taking from a stock. **2** complete a count of ten seconds over (a fallen boxer etc.), indicating defeat. **3** (in children's games) select (a player) for dismissal or a special role by use of a counting rhyme etc. **4** *colloq.* exclude from a plan or reckoning (*I'm too tired, count me out*). **5** *Brit. Polit.* procure the adjournment of (the House of Commons) when fewer than 40 members are present. **count up** find the sum of. **keep count** take note of how many there have been etc. **lose count** fail to take note of the number etc. **not counting** excluding from the reckoning. **out for the count 1** *Boxing* defeated by being unable to rise within ten seconds. **2 a** defeated or demoralized. **b** sound asleep. **take the count** *Boxing* be defeated. [ME f. OF *co(u)nter, co(u)nte* f. LL *computus, computare* COMPUTE]
■ *v.* **1** count up *or* off, enumerate, number, calculate, add up, total, reckon, compute, tally, figure (out), quantify. **3 a** include, consider. **4** see CONSIDER 6. **5** see MATTER *v.* □ **count on** (or **upon**) rely on *or* upon, depend on *or* upon, be sure of, trust, bank on, be confident of, *colloq.* reckon on, *US* figure on *or* upon. **count out 4** see EXCLUDE 3. **count up** see COUNT[1] *v.* 1 above. **out for the count 2 a** defeated, demoralized; see also *dejected* (DEJECT). **b** sound asleep, sleeping like a baby; see also *dead to the world.*

count[2] /kownt/ *n.* a foreign noble corresponding to an earl. □ **Count Palatine** *hist.* a high official of the Holy Roman Empire with royal authority within his domain. □□ **countship** *n.* [OF *conte* f. L *comes comitis* companion]

countable /kówntəb'l/ *adj.* **1** that can be counted. **2** *Gram.* (of a noun) that can form a plural or be used with the indefinite article (e.g. *book, kindness*).

countdown /kówntdown/ *n.* **1 a** the act of counting down, esp. at the launching of a rocket etc. **b** the procedures carried out during this time. **2** the final moments before any significant event.

countenance /kówntinənss/ *n.* & *v.* ● *n.* **1 a** the face. **b** the facial expression. **2** composure. **3** moral support. ● *v.tr.* **1** give approval to (an act etc.) (*cannot countenance this breach of the rules*). **2** (often foll. by *in*) encourage (a person or a practice). □ **change countenance** alter one's expression as an effect of emotion. **keep one's countenance** maintain composure, esp. by refraining from laughter. **keep a person in countenance** support or encourage a person. **lose countenance** become embarrassed. **out of countenance** disconcerted. [ME f. AF *c(o)untenance*, OF *contenance* bearing f. *contenir*: see CONTAIN]
■ *n.* **1 a** see FACE *n.* 1. **b** see EXPRESSION 4. ● *v.* **1** see APPROVE. **2** see SUPPORT *v.* 11.

counter[1] /kówntər/ *n.* **1 a** a long flat-topped fitment in a shop, bank, etc., across which business is conducted with customers. **b** a similar structure used for serving food etc. in a cafeteria or bar. **2 a** a small disc used for keeping the score etc. esp. in table-games. **b** a token representing a coin. **c** something used in bargaining; a pawn (*a counter in the struggle for power*). **3** an apparatus used for counting. **4** *Physics* an apparatus used for counting individual ionizing particles etc. **5** a person or thing that counts. □ **over the counter** by ordinary retail purchase. **under the counter** (esp. of the sale of scarce goods) surreptitiously, esp. illegally. [AF *count(e)our*, OF *conteo(i)r*, f. med.L *computatorium* (as COMPUTE)]
■ **1** table, bar; desk. **2 a, b** token, disc, chip, piece, marker. □ **under the counter** see *on the sly* (SLY), *illegally* (ILLEGAL).

counter[2] /kówntər/ *v.*, *adv.*, *adj.*, & *n.* ● *v.* **1** *tr.* **a** oppose, contradict (*countered our proposal with their own*). **b** meet by a countermove. **2** *intr.* **a** make a countermove. **b** make an opposing statement (*'I shall!' he countered*). **3** *intr. Boxing* give a return blow while parrying. ● *adv.* **1** in the opposite direction (*ran counter to the fox*). **2** contrary (*his action was counter to my wishes*). ● *adj.* **1** opposed; opposite. **2** duplicate; serving as a check. ● *n.* **1** a parry; a countermove. **2** something opposite or opposed. □ **act** (or **go**) **counter to** disobey (instructions etc.). **go** (or **hunt** or **run**) **counter** run or ride against the direction taken by a quarry. **run counter to** act contrary to. [ME f. OF *countre* f. L *contra* against: see COUNTER-]

counter[3] /kówntər/ *n.* **1** the part of a horse's breast between the shoulders and under the neck. **2** the curved part of the stern of a ship. **3** *Printing* a part of a printing-type etc. that is completely enclosed by an outline (e.g. the loop of P). [17th c.: orig. unkn.]

counter[4] /kówntər/ *n.* the back part of a shoe or a boot round the heel. [abbr. of *counterfort* buttress]

counter- /kówntər/ *comb. form* denoting: **1** retaliation, opposition, or rivalry (*counter-threat; counter-cheers*). **2** opposite direction (*counter-current*). **3** correspondence, duplication, or substitution (*counterpart; countersign*). [from or after AF *countre-*, OF *contre* f. L *contra* against]

counteract /kówntərákt/ *v.tr.* **1** hinder or oppose by contrary action. **2** neutralize. □□ **counteraction** *n.* **counteractive** *adj.*
■ **1** see HINDER[1], OPPOSE 1–3. **2** counterbalance, neutralize, correct, annul, nullify, cancel, mitigate.

counter-attack *n.* & *v.* ● *n.* /kówntərətak/ an attack in reply to an attack by an enemy or opponent. ● *v.tr.* & *intr.* /kówntərəták/ attack in reply.

■ *v.* see OPPOSE 1–3.

counter-attraction /kówntəratráksh'n/ *n.* **1** a rival attraction. **2** the attraction of a contrary tendency.

counterbalance *n.* & *v.* ● *n.* /kówntərballənss/ **1** a weight balancing another. **2** an argument, force, etc., balancing another. ● *v.tr.* /kówntərbálləns/act as a counterbalance to.
■ *n.* **2** see OFFSET *n.* ● *v.* see BALANCE *v.* 1, 2.

counterblast /kówntərblaast/ *n.* (often foll. by *to*) an energetic or violent verbal or written reply to an argument etc.

counterchange /kówntərcháynj/ *v.* **1** *tr.* change (places or parts); interchange. **2** *tr. literary* chequer, esp. with contrasting colours etc. **3** *intr.* change places or parts. [F *contrechanger* (as COUNTER-, CHANGE)]

countercharge *n.* & *v.* ● *n.* /kówntərchaarj/ a charge or accusation in return for one received. ● *v.tr.* /kówntərcháarj/ make a countercharge against.
■ *n.* see *recrimination* (RECRIMINATE).

countercheck *n.* & *v.* ● *n.* /kówntərchek/ **1 a** a restraint that opposes something. **b** a restraint that operates against another. **2** a second check, esp. for security or accuracy. **3** *archaic* a retort. ● *v.tr.* /kówntərchék/ make a countercheck on.

counter-claim *n.* & *v.* ● *n.* /kówntərklaym/ **1** a claim made against another claim. **2** *Law* a claim made by a defendant in a suit against the plaintiff. ● *v.tr.* & *intr.* /kówntərkláym/ make a counter-claim (for).

counter-clockwise /kówntərklókwīz/ *adv.* & *adj. US* = ANTICLOCKWISE.

counter-culture /kówntərkulchər/ *n.* a way of life etc. opposed to that usually considered normal.

counter-espionage /kówntəréspiənaazh, -nij/ *n.* action taken to frustrate enemy spying.

counterfeit /kówntərfit, -feet/ *adj.*, *n.*, & *v.* ● *adj.* **1** (of a coin, writing, etc.) made in imitation; not genuine; forged. **2** (of a claimant etc.) pretended. ● *n.* a forgery; an imitation. ● *v.tr.* **1 a** imitate fraudulently (a coin, handwriting, etc.); forge. **b** make an imitation of. **2** simulate (feelings etc.) (*counterfeited interest*). **3** resemble closely. □□ **counterfeiter** *n.* [ME f. OF *countrefet*, *-fait*, past part. of *contrefaire* f. Rmc]
■ *adj.* **1** forged, fake, fraudulent, imitation, bogus, spurious, sham, *colloq.* phoney. **2** make-believe, sham, pretended, feigned, insincere, fake, faked, false, artificial, meretricious, pseudo, factitious, fictitious, synthetic, unreal, simulated, *colloq.* pretend. ● *n.* fake, imitation, forgery, reproduction, *colloq.* phoney. ● *v.* **1** forge, falsify; copy, reproduce, imitate. **2** feign, pretend, simulate, put on, fake, make a pretence of, dissemble, sham, affect. □ **counterfeiter** forger, *Brit.* coiner.

counterfoil /kówntərfoyl/ *n.* the part of a cheque, receipt, etc., retained by the payer and containing details of the transaction.
■ see STUB *n.* 2.

counter-intelligence /kówntərintéllijənss/ *n.* = COUNTER-ESPIONAGE.

counterirritant /kówntərírrit'nt/ *n.* **1** *Med.* something used to produce surface irritation of the skin, thereby counteracting more painful symptoms. **2** anything resembling a counterirritant in its effects. □□ **counterirritation** /-táysh'n/ *n.*

countermand *v.* & *n.* ● *v.tr.* /kówntərmaánd/ **1** *Mil.* **a** revoke (an order or command). **b** recall (forces etc.) by a contrary order. **2** cancel an order for (goods etc.). ● *n.* /kówntərmaand/ an order revoking a previous one. [ME f. OF *contremander* f. med.L *contramandare* (as CONTRA-, *mandare* order)]
■ *v.* **1a, 2** see CANCEL *v.* 1a.

countermarch *v.* & *n.* ● *v.intr.* & *tr.* /kówntərmaárch/esp. *Mil.* march or cause to march in the opposite direction, e.g. with the front marchers turning and marching back through the ranks. ● *n.* /kówntərmaarch/ an act of countermarching.

countermeasure /kówntərmezhər/ *n.* an action taken to counteract a danger, threat, etc.
■ see PREVENTIVE *n.*

countermine *n.* & *v.* ● *n.* /kówntərmīn/ **1** *Mil.* **a** a mine dug to intercept another dug by an enemy. **b** a submarine mine sunk to explode an enemy's mines. **2** a counterplot. ● *v.tr.* /kówntərmīn/ make a countermine against.

countermove *n.* & *v.* ● *n.* /kówntərmoov/ a move or action in opposition to another. ● *v.intr.* /kówntərmóov/ make a countermove. □□ **countermovement** *n.*

counter-offensive /kówntərəfénsiv/ *n.* **1** *Mil.* an attack made from a defensive position in order to effect an escape. **2** any attack made from a defensive position.

counterpane /kówntərpayn/ *n.* a bedspread. [alt. (with assim. to *pane* in obs. sense 'cloth') f. obs. *counterpoint* f. OF *contrepointe* alt. f. *cou(l)tepointe* f. med.L *culcita puncta* quilted mattress]

counterpart /kówntərpaart/ *n.* **1 a** a person or thing extremely like another. **b** a person or thing forming a natural complement or equivalent to another. **2** *Law* one of two copies of a legal document. □ **counterpart funds** *US* funds etc. in a local currency equivalent to goods etc. received from abroad.
■ **1** see MATCH[1] *n.* 2c.

counterplot *n.* & *v.* ● *n.* /kówntərplot/ a plot intended to defeat another plot. ● *v.* /kówntərplót/ (**-plotted, -plotting**) **1** *intr.* make a counterplot. **2** *tr.* make a counterplot against.

counterpoint /kówntərpoynt/ *n.* & *v.* ● *n.* **1** *Mus.* **a** the art or technique of setting, writing, or playing a melody or melodies in conjunction with another, according to fixed rules. **b** a melody played in conjunction with another. **2** a contrasting argument, plot, idea, or literary theme, etc., used to set off the main element. ● *v.tr.* **1** *Mus.* add counterpoint to. **2** set (an argument, plot, etc.) in contrast to (a main element). □ **strict counterpoint** an academic exercise in writing counterpoint, not necessarily intended as a composition. [OF *contrepoint* f. med.L *contrapunctum* pricked or marked opposite, i.e. to the original melody (as CONTRA-, *pungere punct-* prick)]
■ *n.* **1** polyphony.

counterpoise *n.* & *v.* ● *n.* /kówntərpoyz/ **1** a force etc. equivalent to another on the opposite side. **2** a state of equilibrium. **3** a counterbalancing weight. ● *v.tr.* /kówntərpóyz/ **1** counterbalance. **2** compensate. **3** bring into or keep in equilibrium. [ME f. OF *contrepeis*, *-pois*, *contrepeser* (as COUNTER-, *peis*, *pois* f. L *pensum* weight: cf. POISE[1])]
■ *v.* **1** see BALANCE *v.* 2.

counter-productive /kówntərprədúktiv/ *adj.* having the opposite of the desired effect.
■ see PREJUDICIAL.

counter-reformation /kówntəréffərmáysh'n/ *n.* **1** (**Counter-Reformation**) *hist.* the reform of the Church of Rome in the 16th and 17th centuries which took place in response to the Protestant Reformation. **2** a reformation running counter to another.

counter-revolution /kówntərévvəlóosh'n/ *n.* a revolution opposing a former one or reversing its results. □□ **counter-revolutionary** *adj.* & *n.* (*pl.* **-ies**).

counterscarp /kówntərskaarp/ *n. Mil.* the outer wall or slope of a ditch in a fortification. [F *contrescarpe* f. It. *contrascarpa* (as CONTRA-, SCARP)]

countershaft /kówntərshaaft/ *n.* **1** an intermediate shaft driven by a main shaft and transmitting motion to a particular machine etc. **2** *US* = LAYSHAFT.

countersign *v.* & *n.* ● *v.tr.* /kówntərsīn/ **1** add a signature to (a document already signed by another). **2** ratify. ● *n.* /kówntərsīn/ **1** a watchword or password spoken to a person on guard. **2** a mark used for identification etc. □□ **counter-signature** /-sígnəchər/ *n.* [F *contresigner* (v.), *contresigne* (n.) f. It. *contrasegno* (as COUNTER-, SIGN)]
■ *v.* **1** see SIGN *v.* 1. **2** see ENDORSE 2. ● *n.* **1** see PASSWORD.

countersink /kówntərsingk/ *v.tr.* (*past* and *past part.* **-sunk**) **1** enlarge and bevel (the rim of a hole) so that a screw or bolt can be inserted flush with the surface. **2** sink (a screw etc.) in such a hole.

counterstroke /kówntərstrōk/ *n.* a blow given in return for another.

counter-tenor /kówntərtennər/ *n. Mus.* **1 a** a male alto singing-voice. **b** a singer with this voice. **2** a part written for counter-tenor. [ME f. F *contre-teneur* f. obs. It. *contratenore* (as CONTRA-, TENOR)]

countervail /kówntərváyl/ *v.* **1** *tr.* counterbalance. **2** *tr.* & *intr.* (often foll. by *against*) oppose forcefully and usu. successfully. □ **countervailing duty** a tax put on imports to offset a subsidy in the exporting country or a tax on similar goods not from abroad. [ME f. AF *contrevaloir* f. L *contra valēre* be of worth against]
■ **1** see BALANCE *v.* 2. **2** see RESIST *v.* 1, 2.

countervalue /kówntərvalyōō/ *n.* an equivalent value, esp. in military strategy.

counterweight /kówntərwayt/ *n.* a counterbalancing weight.

countess /kówntiss/ *n.* **1** the wife or widow of a count or an earl. **2** a woman holding the rank of count or earl. [ME f. OF *contesse*, *cuntesse*, f. LL *comitissa* fem. of *comes* COUNT²]
■ see PEER² *n.* 1.

countless /kówntliss/ *adj.* too many to be counted.

countrified /kúntrifīd/ *adj.* (also **countryfied**) often *derog.* rural or rustic, esp. of manners, appearance, etc. [past part. of *countrify* f. COUNTRY]
■ see RUSTIC *adj.* 2.

country /kúntri/ *n.* (*pl.* **-ies**) **1 a** the territory of a nation with its own government; a State. **b** a territory possessing its own language, people, culture, etc. **2** (often *attrib.*) rural districts as opposed to towns or the capital (*a cottage in the country*; *a country town*). **3** the land of a person's birth or citizenship; a fatherland. **4 a** a territory, esp. an area of interest or knowledge. **b** a region associated with a particular person, esp. a writer (*Hardy country*). **5** *Brit.* a national population, esp. as voters (*the country won't stand for it*). □ **across country** not keeping to roads. **country-and-western** rural or cowboy songs originating in the US, and usu. accompanied by a guitar etc. **country club** a sporting and social club in a rural setting. **country cousin** often *derog.* a person with a countrified appearance or manners. **country dance** a traditional sort of dance, esp. English, with couples facing each other in long lines. **country gentleman** a gentleman with landed property. **country house** a usu. large house in the country, often the seat of a country gentleman. **country music** = *country-and-western*. **country party** a political party supporting agricultural interests. **country seat** a large country house belonging to an aristocratic family. **country-wide** extending throughout a nation. **go** (or **appeal**) **to the country** *Brit.* test public opinion by dissolving Parliament and holding a general election. **in the country** *Cricket sl.* far from the wickets; in the deep field. **line of country** a subject about which a person is knowledgeable. **unknown country** an unfamiliar place or topic. [ME f. OF *cuntree*, f. med.L *contrata* (*terra*) (land) lying opposite (CONTRA)]
■ **1** nation, state, power; territory, *formal esp. Law* realm. **2** countryside, rural area, provinces, hinterlands, *esp. Austral.* outback, *literary* champaign, *sl.* sticks. **3** (native) land, homeland, fatherland, motherland, mother country. **4 a** see TERRITORY 1, 7, SPHERE *n.* 4a. **b** territory, land, terrain. **5** see POPULATION 1a. □ **country cousin** see RUSTIC *n.*

countryfied var. of COUNTRIFIED.

countryman /kúntrimən/ *n.* (*pl.* **-men**; *fem.* **countrywoman**, *pl.* **-women**) **1** a person living in a rural area. **2 a** (also **fellow-countryman**) a person of one's own country or district. **b** (often in *comb.*) a person from a specified country or district (*north-countryman*).
■ **1** see RUSTIC *n.*

countryside /kúntrisīd/ *n.* **1 a** a rural area. **b** rural areas in general. **2** the inhabitants of a rural area.
■ **1** see COUNTRY 2.

county /kównti/ *n.* & *adj.* ● *n.* (*pl.* **-ies**) **1 a** any of the territorial divisions of some countries, forming the chief unit of local administration. **b** *US* a political and administrative division of a State. **2** the people of a county, esp. the leading families. ● *adj.* having the social status or characteristics of county families. □ **county borough** *hist.* a large borough ranking as a county for administrative purposes. **county corporate** *hist.* a city or town ranking as an administrative county. **county council** the elected governing body of an administrative county. **county court** a judicial court for civil cases (in the US for civil and criminal cases). **county cricket** cricket matches between teams representing counties. **county family** an aristocratic family with an ancestral seat in a county. **County Palatine** the territory of a Count or Earl Palatine. **county town** (*US* **seat**) the administrative capital of a county. [ME f. AF *counté*, OF *conté*, *cunté*, f. L *comitatus* (as COUNT²)]
■ *adj.* see GENTEEL 2.

coup /kōō/ *n.* (*pl.* **coups** /kōōz/) **1** a notable or successful stroke or move. **2** = COUP D'ÉTAT. **3** *Billiards* a direct pocketing of the ball. [F f. med.L *colpus* blow: see COPE¹]
■ **1** see TRIUMPH *n.* 1b.

coup de grâce /kōō də graàss/ *n.* a finishing stroke, esp. to kill a wounded animal or person. [F, lit. stroke of grace]
■ see KILL¹ *n.* 1.

coup de main /kōō də máN/ *n.* a sudden vigorous attack. [F, lit. stroke of the hand]

coup d'état /kōō daytaà/ *n.* a violent or illegal seizure of power. [F, lit. stroke of the State]
■ see REVOLT *n.*

coup d'œil /kōō dő-i/ *n.* **1** a comprehensive glance. **2** a general view. [F, lit. stroke of the eye]
■ **1** see GLANCE¹ *n.* 1.

coupe /kōōp/ *n.* **1** a shallow glass or dish used for serving fruit, ice-cream, etc. **2** fruit, ice-cream, etc. served in this. [F, = goblet]

coupé /kōōpay/ *n.* (*US* **coupe** /kōōp/) **1** a car with a hard roof, esp. one with two seats and a sloping rear. **2** *hist.* a four-wheeled enclosed carriage for two passengers and a driver. [F, past part. of *couper* cut (formed as COUP)]

couple /kúpp'l/ *n.* & *v.* ● *n.* **1** (usu. foll. by *of*; often as *sing.*) **a** two (*a couple of girls*). **b** about two (*a couple of hours*). **2** (often as *sing.*) **a** a married or engaged pair. **b** a pair of partners in a dance, a game, etc. **c** a pair of rafters. **3** (*pl.* **couple**) a pair of hunting dogs (*six couple of hounds*). **4** (in *pl.*) a pair of joined collars used for holding hounds together. **5** *Mech.* a pair of equal and parallel forces acting in opposite directions, and tending to cause rotation about an axis perpendicular to the plane containing them. ● *v.* **1** *tr.* fasten or link together; connect (esp. railway carriages). **2** *tr.* (often foll. by *together*, *with*) associate in thought or speech (*papers coupled their names*; *couple our congratulations with our best wishes*). **3** *intr.* copulate. **4** *tr. Physics* connect (oscillators) with a coupling. [ME f. OF *cople*, *cuple*, *copler*, *cupler* f. L *copulare*, L COPULA]
■ *n.* **1 a** two; pair, brace, yoke. **b** (*a couple of*) a few, a handful (of), two or three; see also SEVERAL *adj.* **2** pair, duo, twosome. ● *v.* **1** join, connect, link, fasten, yoke, lock, combine, unite. **2** see ASSOCIATE *v.* 1. **3** see *make love* (LOVE).

coupler /kúplər/ *n.* **1** *Mus.* **a** a device in an organ for connecting two manuals, or a manual with pedals, so that they both sound when only one is played. **b** (also **octave coupler**) a similar device for connecting notes with their octaves above or below. **2** anything that connects two things, esp. a transformer used for connecting electric circuits.
■ **2** see TERMINAL *n.* 4.

couplet /kúplit/ *n. Prosody* two successive lines of verse, usu. rhyming and of the same length. [F dimin. of *couple*, formed as COUPLE]

coupling /kúpling/ *n.* **1 a** a link connecting railway carriages etc. **b** a device for connecting parts of machinery. **2** *Physics* a connection between two systems, causing one to oscillate when the other does so. **3** *Mus.* **a** the arrangement of items on a gramophone record. **b** each such item. **4** (an act of) sexual intercourse.
■ **1** see JUNCTION 3. **4** see SEX *n.* 5.

coupon /kóopon/ *n.* **1** a form etc. in a newspaper, magazine, etc., which may be filled in and sent as an application for a purchase, information, etc. **2** *Brit.* an entry form for a football pool or other competition. **3** a voucher given with a retail purchase, a certain number of which entitle the holder to a discount etc. **4 a** a detachable ticket entitling the holder to a ration of food, clothes, etc., esp. in wartime. **b** a similar ticket entitling the holder to payment, goods, services, etc. [F, = piece cut off f. *couper* cut: see COUPÉ]

courage /kúrrij/ *n.* the ability to disregard fear; bravery. □ **courage of one's convictions** the courage to act on one's beliefs. **lose courage** become less brave. **pluck up** (or **take**) **courage** muster one's courage. **take one's courage in both hands** nerve oneself to a venture. [ME f. OF *corage*, f. L *cor* heart]
■ courageousness, bravery, valour, boldness, intrepidity, gallantry, dauntlessness, daring, fearlessness, heroism, nerve, pluck, *colloq.* grit, guts, spunk, *US colloq.* sand, *Brit. sl.* bottle, *US sl.* moxie.

courageous /kəráyjəss/ *adj.* brave, fearless. □□ **courageously** *adv.* **courageousness** *n.* [ME f. AF *corageous*, OF *corageus* (as COURAGE)]
■ brave, valiant, valorous, bold, intrepid, unafraid, gallant, dauntless, undaunted, daring, fearless, heroic, plucky, audacious, stalwart, *archaic or joc.* doughty, *colloq.* spunky, gutsy.

courante /koorónt/ *n.* **1** *hist.* a running or gliding dance. **2** *Mus.* the music used for this, esp. as a movement of a suite. [F, fem. pres. part. (as noun) of *courir* run f. L *currere*]

courgette /koorzhét/ *n.* a small green variety of vegetable marrow. Also called ZUCCHINI. [F, dimin. of *courge* gourd]

courier /kóorriər/ *n.* **1** a person employed, usu. by a travel company, to guide and assist a group of tourists. **2** a special messenger. [ME f. obs. F, f. It. *corriere*, & f. OF *coreor*, both f. L *currere* run]
■ **2** see MESSENGER.

course /korss/ *n.* & *v.* ● *n.* **1** a continuous onward movement or progression. **2 a** a line along which a person or thing moves; a direction taken (*has changed course*; *the course of the winding river*). **b** a correct or intended direction or line of movement. **c** the direction taken by a ship or aircraft. **3 a** the ground on which a race (or other sport involving extensive linear movement) takes place. **b** a series of fences, hurdles, or other obstacles to be crossed in a race etc. **4 a** a series of lectures, lessons, etc., in a particular subject. **b** a book for such a course (*A Modern French Course*). **5** any of the successive parts of a meal. **6** *Med.* a sequence of medical treatment etc. (*prescribed a course of antibiotics*). **7** a line of conduct (*disappointed by the course he took*). **8** *Archit.* a continuous horizontal layer of brick, stone, etc., in a building. **9** a channel in which water flows. **10** the pursuit of game (esp. hares) with hounds, esp. greyhounds, by sight rather than scent. **11** *Naut.* a sail on a square-rigged ship (*fore course*; *main course*). ● *v.* **1** *intr.* (esp. of liquid) run, esp. fast (*blood coursed through his veins*). **2** *tr.* (also *absol.*) **a** use (hounds) to hunt. **b** pursue (hares etc.) in hunting. □ **the course of nature** ordinary events or procedure. **in course of** in the process of. **in the course of** during. **in the course of time** as time goes by; eventually. **a matter of course** the natural or expected thing. **of course** naturally; as is or was to be expected; admittedly. **on** (or **off**) **course** following (or deviating from) the desired direction or goal. **run** (or **take**) **its course** (esp. of an illness) complete its natural development. □□ **courser** *n.* (in sense 2 of *v.*). [ME f. OF *cours* f. L *cursus* f. *currere curs-* run]
■ *n.* **2** path, way, orbit, route, run, track, ambit, line, circuit, passage; direction, tack. **4 a** class, seminar. **9** see CHANNEL[1] *n.* 5a, 6. ● *v.* **1** see RUN *v.* 11a, 13. □ **in the course of time** see *eventually* (EVENTUAL). **of course** naturally, certainly, positively, obviously, definitely, assuredly, by all means; undoubtedly, indubitably, without (a) doubt, no doubt, absolutely, that goes without saying, *colloq.* (for) sure, you bet, *sl.* you bet your boots *or* bottom dollar; admittedly, needless to say, it goes without saying (that), to be sure.

courser[1] /kórsər/ *n. poet.* a swift horse. [ME f. OF *corsier* f. Rmc]

courser[2] /kórsər/ *n.* any fast-running plover-like bird of the genus *Cursorius*, native to Africa and Asia, having long legs and a slender bill. [LL *cursorius* adapted for running]

court /kort/ *n.* & *v.* ● *n.* **1** (in full **court of law**) **a** an assembly of judges or other persons acting as a tribunal in civil and criminal cases. **b** = COURTROOM. **2 a** an enclosed quadrangular area for games, which may be open or covered (*tennis-court*; *squash-court*). **b** an area marked out for lawn tennis etc. (*hit the ball out of court*). **3 a** a small enclosed street in a town, having a yard surrounded by houses, and adjoining a larger street. **b** *Brit.* = COURTYARD. **c** (**Court**) the name of a large house, block of flats, street, etc. (*Grosvenor Court*). **d** (at Cambridge University) a college quadrangle. **e** a subdivision of a building, usu. a large hall extending to the ceiling with galleries and staircases. **4 a** the establishment, retinue, and courtiers of a sovereign. **b** a sovereign and his or her councillors, constituting a ruling power. **c** a sovereign's residence. **d** an assembly held by a sovereign; a State reception. **5** attention paid to a person whose favour, love, or interest is sought (*paid court to her*). **6 a** the qualified members of a company or a corporation. **b** (in some Friendly Societies) a local branch. **c** a meeting of a court. ● *v.tr.* **1 a** try to win the affection or favour of (a person). **b** pay amorous attention to (*courting couples*). **2** seek to win (applause, fame, etc.). **3** invite (misfortune) by one's actions (*you are courting disaster*). □ **court-card** a playing-card that is a king, queen, or jack (orig. *coat-card*). **court circular** *Brit.* a daily report of royal court affairs, published in some newspapers. **court dress** formal dress worn at a royal court. **court-house 1** a building in which a judicial court is held. **2** *US* a building containing the administrative offices of a county. **Court leet** see LEET[1]. **Court of Appeal** a court of law hearing appeals against judgements in the Crown Court, High Court, County Court, etc. **Court of Protection** *Brit.* the department of the Supreme Court attending to the affairs of the mentally unfit. **court of record** a court whose proceedings are recorded and available as evidence of fact. **Court of St James's** the British sovereign's court. **Court of Session** the supreme civil court in Scotland. **court of summary jurisdiction** a court having the authority to use summary proceedings and arrive at a judgement or conviction. **court order** a direction issued by a court or a judge, usu. requiring a person to do or not do something. **court plaster** *hist.* sticking-plaster for cuts etc. (formerly used by ladies at court for face-patches). **court roll** *hist.* a manorial-court register of holdings. **court shoe** a woman's light, usu. high-heeled, shoe with a low-cut upper. **court tennis** *US* real tennis. **go to court** take legal action. **in court** appearing as a party or an advocate in a court of law. **out of court 1** (of a plaintiff) not entitled to be heard. **2** (of a settlement) arranged before a hearing or judgement can take place. **3** not worthy of consideration (*that suggestion is out of court*). [ME f. AF *curt*, OF *cort*, ult. f. L *cohors*, *-hortis* yard, retinue: (v.) after OIt. *corteare*, OF *courtoyer*]
■ *n.* **1 a** see TRIBUNAL 2. **4 a** see TRAIN *n.* 4. ● *v.* **1 a** see CULTIVATE 3b. **b** woo, pay suit *or* court to, seek the hand of, press one's suit with, set one's cap at, go after, chase, pursue, *archaic* make love to, *Austral. sl.* track with.

court bouillon /kóor bóo-yóN/ *n.* stock usu. made from wine, vegetables, etc., often used in fish dishes. [F f. *court* short + BOUILLON]

courteous /kúrtiəss/ *adj.* polite, kind, or considerate in manner; well-mannered. □□ **courteously** *adv.* **courteousness** *n.* [ME f. OF *corteis*, *curteis* f. Rmc (as COURT): assim. to words in -OUS]
■ polite, well-mannered, well-behaved, chivalrous, gentlemanly, ladylike, well-bred, polished, urbane, civilized, respectful, civil, courtly, proper, decorous, tactful, considerate, diplomatic, *joc.* couth.

courtesan /kórtizán/ *n. literary* **1** a prostitute, esp. one with wealthy or upper-class clients. **2** the mistress of a wealthy man. [F *courtisane* f. It. *cortigiana*, fem. of *cortigiano* courtier f. *corte* COURT]
■ **1** see PROSTITUTE *n.* 1a.

courtesy /kúrtisi/ *n.* (*pl.* **-ies**) **1** courteous behaviour; good manners. **2** a courteous act. **3** *archaic* = CURTSY. □ **by courtesy** by favour, not by right. **by courtesy of** with the formal permission of (a person etc.). **courtesy light** a light in a car that is switched on by opening a door. **courtesy title** a title held by courtesy, usu. having no legal validity, e.g. a title given to the heir of a duke etc. [ME f. OF *curtesie*, *co(u)rtesie* f. *curteis* etc. COURTEOUS]
■ **1** politeness, courtliness, *politesse*, chivalry, courteousness, respect, respectfulness, good manners, formality, civility.

courtier /kórtiər/ *n.* a person who attends or frequents a sovereign's court. [ME f. AF *courte(i)our*, f. OF f. *cortoyer* be present at court]

courtly /kórtli/ *adj.* (**courtlier**, **courtliest**) **1** polished or refined in manners. **2** obsequious. **3** punctilious. □ **courtly love** the conventional medieval tradition of knightly love for a lady, and the etiquette used in its (esp. literary) expression. □□ **courtliness** *n.* [COURT]
■ **1, 3** see *polished* (POLISH *v.* 2). **2** see SMOOTH *adj.* 9.

court martial /kórt maársh'l/ *n.* & *v.* ● *n.* (*pl.* **courts martial**) a judicial court for trying members of the armed services. ● *v.tr.* (**court-martial**) (**-martialled**, **-martialling**; *US* **-martialed**, **-martialing**) try by a court martial.

courtroom /kórtroom, -room/ *n.* the place or room in which a court of law meets.
■ see BAR[1] *n.* 5d.

courtship /kórtship/ *n.* **1 a** a courting with a view to marriage. **b** the courting behaviour of male animals, birds, etc. **c** a period of courting. **2** an attempt, often protracted, to gain advantage by flattery, attention, etc.

courtyard /kórtyaard/ *n.* an area enclosed by walls or buildings, often opening off a street.
■ see AREA 5.

couscous /kóoskooss/ *n.* a N. African dish of wheat grain or coarse flour steamed over broth, often with meat or fruit added. [F f. Arab. *kuskus* f. *kaskasa* to pound]

cousin /kúzz'n/ *n.* **1** (also **first cousin**, **cousin-german**) the child of one's uncle or aunt. **2** (usu. in *pl.*) applied to the people of kindred races or nations (*our American cousins*). **3** *hist.* a title formerly used by a sovereign in addressing another sovereign or a noble of his or her own country. □ **second cousin** a child of one's parent's first cousin. □□ **cousinhood** *n.* **cousinly** *adj.* **cousinship** *n.* [ME f. OF *cosin*, *cusin*, f. L *consobrinus* mother's sister's child]

couth /kooth/ *adj. joc.* cultured; well-mannered. [back-form. as antonym of UNCOUTH]

couture /kootyóor/ *n.* the design and manufacture of fashionable clothes; = HAUTE COUTURE. [F, = sewing, dressmaking]

couturier /kootyóoriay/ *n.* (*fem.* **couturière** /-riáir/) a fashion designer or dressmaker. [F]
■ see DRESSMAKER.

couvade /koovaád/ *n.* a custom by which a father appears to undergo labour and childbirth when his child is being born. [F f. *couver* hatch f. L *cubare* lie down]

couvert /koováir/ *n.* = COVER *n.* 6. [F]

couverture /kóovərtyoor/ *n.* chocolate for covering sweets, cakes, etc. [F, = covering]

covalency /kōváylənsi/ *n. Chem.* **1** the linking of atoms by a covalent bond. **2** the number of pairs of electrons an atom can share with another.

covalent /kōváylənt/ *adj. Chem.* of, relating to, or characterized by covalency. □ **covalent bond** *Chem.* a bond formed by sharing of electrons usu. in pairs by two atoms in a molecule. □□ **covalence** *n.* **covalently** *adv.* [CO- + *valent*, after *trivalent* etc.]

cove[1] /kōv/ *n.* & *v.* ● *n.* **1** a small, esp. sheltered, bay or creek. **2** a sheltered recess. **3** *Archit.* a concave arch or arched moulding, esp. one formed at the junction of a wall with a ceiling. ● *v.tr. Archit.* **1** provide (a room, ceiling, etc.) with a cove. **2** slope (the sides of a fireplace) inwards. [OE *cofa* chamber f. Gmc]
■ *n.* **1** see CREEK 1.

cove[2] /kōv/ *n. Brit. sl. archaic* a fellow; a chap. [16th-c. cant: orig. unkn.]
■ see CHAP[2].

coven /kúvv'n/ *n.* an assembly of witches. [var. of *covent*; see CONVENT]

covenant /kúvvənənt/ *n.* & *v.* ● *n.* **1** an agreement; a contract. **2** *Law* **a** a contract drawn up under a seal, esp. undertaking to make regular payments to a charity. **b** a clause of a covenant. **3** (**Covenant**) *Bibl.* the agreement between God and the Israelites (see *Ark of the Covenant*). ● *v.tr.* & *intr.* agree, esp. by legal covenant. □ **land of the Covenant** Canaan. □□ **covenantal** /-nánt'l/ *adj.* **covenantor** *n.* [ME f. OF, pres. part. of *co(n)venir*, formed as CONVENE]
■ *n.* **1, 2** see AGREEMENT 3. ● *v.* see UNDERTAKE 2.

covenanted /kúvvənəntid/ *adj.* bound by a covenant.

covenanter /kúvvənəntər/ *n.* **1** a person who covenants. **2** (**Covenanter**) *hist.* an adherent of the National Covenant of the Solemn League and Covenant in 17th-c. Scotland, in support of Presbyterianism.

Coventry /kóvvəntri/ *n.* □ **send a person to Coventry** refuse to associate with or speak to a person. [*Coventry* in W. Midlands]

cover /kúvvər/ *v.* & *n.* ● *v.tr.* **1 a** (often foll. by *with*) protect or conceal by means of a cloth, lid, etc. **b** prevent the perception or discovery of, conceal (*to cover my embarrassment*). **2 a** extend over; occupy the whole surface of (*covered in dirt*; *covered with writing*). **b** (often foll. by *with*) strew thickly or thoroughly (*covered the floor with straw*). **c** lie over; be a covering to (*the blanket scarcely covered him*). **3 a** protect; clothe. **b** (as **covered** *adj.*) wearing a hat; having a roof. **4** include; comprise; deal with (*the talk covered recent discoveries*). **5** travel (a specified distance) (*covered sixty miles*). **6** *Journalism* **a** report (events, a meeting, etc.). **b** investigate as a reporter. **7** be enough to defray (expenses, a bill, etc.) (*£20 should cover it*). **8 a** *refl.* take precautionary measures so as to protect oneself (*had covered myself by saying I might be late*). **b** (*absol.*; foll. by *for*) deputize or stand in for (a colleague etc.) (*will you cover for me?*). **9** *Mil.* **a** aim a gun etc. at. **b** (of a fortress, guns, etc.) command (a territory). **c** stand behind (a person in the front rank). **d** protect (an exposed person etc.) by being able to return fire. **10 a** esp. *Cricket* stand behind (another player) to stop any missed balls. **b** (in team games) mark (a corresponding player of the other side). **11** (also *absol.*) (in some card-games) play a card higher than (one already played to the same trick). **12** (of a stallion, a bull, etc.) copulate with. ● *n.* **1** something that covers or protects, esp.: **a** a lid. **b** the binding of a book. **c** either board of this. **d** an envelope or the wrapper of a parcel (*under separate cover*). **e** the outer case of a pneumatic tyre. **f** (in *pl.*) bedclothes. **2** a hiding-place; a shelter. **3** woods or undergrowth sheltering game or covering the ground (see COVERT). **4 a** a pretence; a screen (*under cover of humility*). **b** a spy's pretended identity or activity, intended as concealment. **c** *Mil.* a supporting force protecting an advance party from attack. **5 a** funds, esp. obtained by insurance, to meet a liability or secure against a contingent loss. **b** the state of being protected (*third-party cover*). **6** a place setting at table, esp. in a restaurant. **7** *Cricket* = *cover-point*. □ **break cover** (of an animal, esp. game, or a hunted person) leave a place of shelter, esp. vegetation. **cover charge** an extra charge levied per head in a restaurant, nightclub, etc. **cover crop** a crop grown for the protection and enrichment of the soil. **cover-drive** *Cricket* a drive past cover-point. **cover girl** a female model whose picture appears on magazine covers etc. **cover in** provide with a roof etc. **covering letter** (or **note**) an explanatory letter sent with an enclosure. **cover note** *Brit.* a temporary certificate of current insurance. **cover-point** *Cricket* **1** a fielding position on the off side and half way to the boundary. **2** a fielder at this position. **cover story** a news story in a magazine, that is illustrated or advertised on the front cover. **cover one's tracks** conceal evidence of what one has done. **cover up 1** completely cover or conceal. **2** conceal (circumstances etc., esp. illicitly) (also *absol.*: *refused to cover up for them*). **cover-up** *n.* an act of concealing circumstances, esp. illicitly. **from cover to cover** from beginning to end of a book etc. **take cover** use a natural or prepared shelter against an attack. □□ **coverable** *adj.* **coverer** *n.* [ME f. OF *covrir, cuvrir* f. L *cooperire* (as CO-, *operire opert-* cover)]

■ *v.* **1 a** conceal, hide, bury, mask, shroud, obscure; enclose, envelop, wrap, swaddle. **b** see HIDE[1] *v.* 3. **2 a** overlie, spread *or* extend over, overspread, lie on, coat, blanket. **b** see STREW. **3 a** protect, shelter, shield, screen; dress (up), clothe, garb, robe, sheathe, *formal* attire. **4** include, comprehend, take in, deal with, comprise, contain, embody, incorporate, account for, take into account. **5** traverse, complete, pass *or* travel over, travel, cross. **7** pay *or* compensate for, defray, be enough *or* sufficient for; counter, offset, counterbalance, make up for. **8 b** deputize, act, take over responsibility, stand *or* sit in, substitute, take over, run things, hold the fort. **9 b** guard, defend, command. ● *n.* **1 a** lid, top, cap, covering. **b** binding, boards, wrapper, dust-jacket, jacket. **f** (*covers*) blankets, bedclothes, bedding, covering(s), (bed) linen, quilt, eiderdown, duvet, *US* comfort(er). **2** shelter, hiding-place, hide-out, retreat, refuge, *colloq.* hidey-hole; *Brit.* hide, *US* blind; protection, concealment. **4 a** cloak, screen, disguise, pretence, front, camouflage, smokescreen, cover-up, mask, covering. □ **cover up 1** see CONCEAL 2. **2** see HIDE[1] *v.* 3. **cover-up** see PRETENCE 2b.

coverage /kúvvərij/ *n.* **1** an area or an amount covered. **2** *Journalism* the amount of press etc. publicity received by a particular story, person, etc. **3** a risk covered by an insurance policy. **4** an area reached by a particular broadcasting station or advertising medium.

coverall /kúvvərawl/ *n.* & *adj.* esp. *US* ● *n.* **1** something that covers entirely. **2** (usu. in *pl.*) a full-length protective outer garment often zipped up the front. ● *attrib.adj.* covering entirely (*a coverall term*).

covering /kúvvəring/ *n.* something that covers, esp. a bedspread, blanket, etc., or clothing.

coverlet /kúvvərlit/ *n.* a bedspread. [ME f. AF *covrelet, -lit* f. OF *covrir* cover + *lit* bed]

■ see SPREAD *n.* 10.

covert /kúvvərt/ *adj.* & *n.* ● *adj.* secret or disguised (*a covert glance*; *covert operations*). ● *n.* **1** a shelter, esp. a thicket hiding game. **2** a feather covering the base of a bird's flight-feather. □ **covert coat** a short, light, overcoat worn for shooting, riding, etc. □□ **covertly** *adv.* **covertness** *n.* [ME f. OF *covert* past part. of *covrir* COVER]

■ *adj.* see SECRET *adj.* 4. ● *n.* **1** see THICKET.

coverture /kúvvərtyoor, -vərchər/ *n.* **1** covering; shelter. **2** *Law hist.* the position of a married woman, considered to be under her husband's protection. [ME f. OF (as COVERT)]

covet /kúvvit/ *v.tr.* (**coveted, coveting**) desire greatly (esp. something belonging to another person) (*coveted her friend's earrings*). □□ **covetable** *adj.* [ME f. OF *cu-, coveitier* f. Rmc]

■ see DESIRE *v.* 1.

covetous /kúvvitəss/ *adj.* (usu. foll. by *of*) **1** greatly desirous (esp. of another person's property). **2** grasping, avaricious. □□ **covetously** *adv.* **covetousness** *n.* [ME f. OF *coveitous* f. Gallo-Roman]

■ **1** see HUNGRY 3a. **2** see *avaricious* (AVARICE).

covey /kúvvi/ *n.* (*pl.* **-eys**) **1** a brood of partridges. **2** a small party or group of people or things. [ME f. OF *covee* f. Rmc f. L *cubare* lie]

■ **1** see FLIGHT[1] *n.* 3a. **2** see GROUP *n.* 1.

covin /kúvvin/ *n.* **1** *Law* a conspiracy to commit a crime etc. against a third party. **2** *archaic* fraud, deception. [ME f. OF *covin(e)* f. med.L *convenium -ia* f. *convenire*: see CONVENE]

coving *n.* = COVE[1] *n.* 3.

cow[1] /kow/ *n.* **1** a fully grown female of any bovine animal, esp. of the genus *Bos*, used as a source of milk and beef. **2** the female of other large animals, esp. the elephant, whale, and seal. **3** *sl. derog.* **a** a woman esp. a coarse or unpleasant one. **b** *Austral.* & *NZ* an unpleasant person, thing, situation, etc. □ **cow-fish 1** any of several small plant-eating mammals, e.g. the manatee. **2** a marine fish, *Lactoria diaphana*, covered in hard bony plates and having hornlike spines over the eyes and on other parts of the body. **cow-heel** the foot of a cow or an ox stewed to a jelly. **cow-lick** a projecting lock of hair. **cow-parsley** a hedgerow plant *Anthriscus sylvestris*, having lacelike umbels of flowers: also called *Queen Anne's lace*. **cow-pat** a flat round piece of cow-dung. **cow-tree** a tree, *Brosimum galactodendron*, native to S. America, yielding a milklike juice which is used as a substitute for cow's milk. **cow-wheat** any plant of the genus *Melampyrum*, esp. *M. pratense* growing on heathland. **till the cows come home** *colloq.* an indefinitely long time. [OE *cū* f. Gmc, rel. to L *bos*, Gk *bous*]

■ **3 a** see BAG *n.* 5. □ **till the cows come home** see EVER 1.

cow[2] /kow/ *v.tr.* (usu. in *passive*) intimidate or dispirit (*cowed by ill-treatment*). [prob. f. ON *kúga* oppress]

■ see INTIMIDATE.

cowage /kówij/ *n.* (also **cowhage**) a climbing plant, *Mucuna pruritum*, having hairy pods which cause stinging and itching. [Hindi *kawānch*]

coward /kówərd/ *n.* & *adj.* ● *n.* a person who is easily frightened or intimidated by danger or pain. ● *adj. poet.* easily frightened. [ME f. OF *cuard, couard* ult. f. L *cauda* tail]

■ *n.* poltroon, craven, baby, mouse, milksop, *archaic* scaramouch, *colloq.* sissy, yellow-belly, *Austral. colloq.* gutless wonder, *Austral. sl.* dingo.

cowardice /kówərdiss/ *n.* a lack of bravery. [ME f. OF *couardise* (as COWARD)]

■ cowardliness, chicken-heartedness, faint-heartedness, timidity, timorousness, pusillanimity.

cowardly /kówərdli/ *adj.* & *adv.* ● *adj.* **1** of or like a coward; lacking courage. **2** (of an action) done against one who cannot retaliate. ● *adv. archaic* like a coward; with cowardice. □□ **cowardliness** *n.*

■ *adj.* **1** timid, faint-hearted, timorous, chicken-hearted, chicken-livered, lily-livered, craven, fearful, frightened, afraid, scared, dastardly, pusillanimous, *colloq.* yellow, yellow-bellied, chicken.

cowbane /kówbayn/ *n.* = *water hemlock*.

cowbell /kówbel/ *n.* **1** a bell worn round a cow's neck for easy location of the animal. **2** a similar bell used as a percussion instrument.

cowberry /kówbəri/ *n.* (*pl.* **-ies**) **1** an evergreen shrub, *Vaccinium vitis-idaea*, bearing dark-red berries. **2** the berry of this plant.

cowboy /kówboy/ *n.* **1** (*fem.* **cowgirl**) a person who herds and tends cattle, esp. in the western US. **2** this as a conventional figure in American folklore, esp. in films. **3** *colloq.* an unscrupulous or reckless person in business, esp. an unqualified one.

cowcatcher /kówkachər/ *n. US* a peaked metal frame at the front of a locomotive for pushing aside obstacles on the line.

cower /kowr/ *v.intr.* **1** crouch or shrink back, esp. in fear; cringe. **2** stand or squat in a bent position. [ME f. MLG *kūren* lie in wait, of unkn. orig.]

■ **1** see CRINGE *v.* 1.

cowhage var. of COWAGE.

cowherd /kówherd/ *n.* a person who tends cattle.

cowhide /kówhīd/ *n.* **1 a** a cow's hide. **b** leather made from this. **2** a leather whip made from cowhide.

cowhouse /kówhowss/ *n.* a shed or shelter for cows.

cowl /kowl/ *n.* **1 a** the hood of a monk's habit. **b** a loose hood. **c** a monk's hooded habit. **2** the hood-shaped covering of a chimney or ventilating shaft. **3** the removable cover of a vehicle or aircraft engine. ▫▫ **cowled** *adj.* (in sense 1). [OE *cugele*, *cūle* f. eccl.L *cuculla* f. L *cucullus* hood of a cloak]

cowling /kówling/ *n.* = COWL 3.

cowman /kówmən/ *n.* (*pl.* **-men**) **1** = COWHERD. **2** *US* a cattle-owner.

co-worker /kṓ-wúrkər/ *n.* a person who works in collaboration with another.

■ see COLLEAGUE.

cowpoke /kówpōk/ *n. US* = COWBOY 1.

cowpox /kówpoks/ *n.* a disease of cows, of which the virus was formerly used in vaccination against smallpox.

cowpuncher /kówpunchər/ *n. US* = COWBOY 1.

cowrie /kówri/ *n.* (also **cowry**) (*pl.* **-ies**) **1** any gastropod mollusc of the family Cypraeidae, having a smooth glossy and usu. brightly-coloured shell. **2** its shell, esp. used as money in parts of Africa and S. Asia. [Urdu & Hindi *kaurī*]

cowshed /kówshed/ *n.* **1** a shed for cattle that are not at pasture. **2** a milking-shed.

■ see STALL[1] *n.* 2.

cowslip /kówslip/ *n.* **1** a primula, *Primula veris*, with fragrant yellow flowers and growing in pastures. **2** *US* a marsh marigold. [OE *cūslyppe* f. *cū* COW[1] + *slyppe* slimy substance, i.e. cow-dung]

Cox /koks/ *n.* (in full **Cox's orange pippin**) a variety of eating-apple with a red-tinged green skin. [R. *Cox*, amateur Eng. fruit grower d. 1825]

cox /koks/ *n.* & *v.* ● *n.* a coxswain, esp. of a racing-boat. ● *v.* **1** *intr.* act as a cox (*coxed for Cambridge*). **2** *tr.* act as cox for (*coxed the winning boat*). [abbr.]

coxa /kóksə/ *n.* (*pl.* **coxae** /-see/) **1** *Anat.* the hip-bone or hip-joint. **2** *Zool.* the first segment of an insect's leg. ▫▫ **coxal** *adj.* [L]

coxcomb /kókskōm/ *n.* an ostentatiously conceited man; a dandy. ▫▫ **coxcombry** /-kəmri/ *n.* (*pl.* **-ies**). [= *cock's comb* (see COCK[1]), orig. (a cap worn by) a jester]

■ see DANDY *n.*

coxswain /kóks'n/ *n.* & *v.* ● *n.* **1** a person who steers, esp. in a rowing-boat. **2** the senior petty officer in a small ship. ● *v.* **1** *intr.* act as a coxswain. **2** *tr.* act as a coxswain of. ▫▫ **coxswainship** *n.* [ME f. *cock* (see COCKBOAT) + SWAIN: cf. BOATSWAIN]

Coy. *abbr.* esp. *Mil.* Company.

coy /koy/ *adj.* (**coyer, coyest**) **1** archly or affectedly shy. **2** irritatingly reticent (*always coy about her age*). **3** (esp. of a girl) modest or shy. ▫▫ **coyly** *adv.* **coyness** *n.* [ME f. OF *coi*, *quei* f. L *quietus* QUIET]

■ **2** reticent, reluctant, evasive. **3** shy, modest, diffident, demure, timid, bashful, self-conscious, sheepish, timorous, unassuming, unpretentious, reserved, self-effacing, retiring.

coyote /koyṓti, kóyōt/ *n.* (*pl.* same or **coyotes**) a wolflike wild dog, *Canis latrans*, native to N. America. [Mex. Sp. f. Aztec *coyotl*]

coypu /kóypōō/ *n.* (*pl.* **coypus**) an aquatic beaver-like rodent, *Myocastor coypus*, native to S. America and kept in captivity for its fur. [Araucan]

coz /kuz/ *n. archaic* cousin. [abbr.]

cozen /kúzz'n/ *v. literary* **1** *tr.* (often foll. by *of*, *out of*) cheat, defraud. **2** *tr.* (often foll. by *into*) beguile; persuade. **3** *intr.* act deceitfully. ▫▫ **cozenage** *n.* [16th-c. cant, perh. rel. to COUSIN]

■ see CHEAT *v.* 1a.

cozy *US* var. of COSY.

cozzie var. of COSSIE.

CP *abbr.* **1** Cape Province. **2** Communist Party. **3** *Austral.* Country Party.

cp. *abbr.* compare.

c.p. *abbr.* candlepower.

CPA *abbr. US* certified public accountant.

Cpl. *abbr.* Corporal.

CPO *abbr.* Chief Petty Officer.

CPR *abbr.* Canadian Pacific Railway.

CPRE *abbr.* Council for the Protection of Rural England.

cps *abbr.* (also **c.p.s.**) **1** *Computing* characters per second. **2** cycles per second.

CPSA *abbr.* (in the UK) Civil and Public Services Association.

CPU *abbr. Computing* central processing unit.

CR *abbr.* Community of the Resurrection.

Cr *symb. Chem.* the element chromium.

Cr. *abbr.* **1** Councillor. **2** creditor.

crab[1] /krab/ *n.* **1 a** any of numerous ten-footed crustaceans having the first pair of legs modified as pincers. **b** the flesh of a crab, esp. *Cancer pagurus*, as food. **2** (**the Crab**) the zodiacal sign or constellation Cancer. **3** (in full **crab-louse**) (often in *pl.*) a parasitic louse, *Phthirus pubis*, infesting hairy parts of the body and causing extreme irritation. **4** a machine for hoisting heavy weights. ▫ **catch a crab** *Rowing* effect a faulty stroke in which the oar is jammed under water or misses the water altogether. **crab-grass** *US* a creeping grass infesting lawns. **crab-pot** a wicker trap for crabs. ▫▫ **crablike** *adj.* [OE *crabba*, rel. to ON *krafla* scratch]

crab[2] /krab/ *n.* **1** (in full **crab-apple**) a small sour apple-like fruit. **2** (in full **crab tree** or **crab-apple tree**) any of several trees bearing this fruit. **3** a sour person. [ME, perh. alt. (after CRAB[1] or CRABBED) of earlier *scrab*, prob. of Scand. orig.]

crab[3] /krab/ *v.* (**crabbed, crabbing**) *colloq.* **1** *tr.* & *intr.* criticize adversely or captiously; grumble. **2** *tr.* act so as to spoil (*the mistake crabbed his chances*). [orig. of hawks fighting, f. MLG *krabben*]

crabbed /krábbid/ *adj.* **1** irritable or morose. **2** (of handwriting) ill-formed and hard to decipher. **3** perverse or cross-grained. **4** difficult to understand. ▫▫ **crabbedly** *adv.* **crabbedness** *n.* [ME f. CRAB[1], assoc. with CRAB[2]]

■ **1** see IRRITABLE 1.

crabby /krábbi/ *adj.* (**crabbier, crabbiest**) = CRABBED 1, 3. ▫▫ **crabbily** *adv.* **crabbiness** *n.*

crabwise /krábwīz/ *adv.* & *attrib.adj.* (of movement) sideways or backwards like a crab.

■ see SIDEWAYS *adv.*

crack /krak/ *n.*, *v.*, & *adj.* ● *n.* **1 a** a sudden sharp or explosive noise (*the crack of a whip*; *a rifle crack*). **b** (in a voice) a sudden harshness or change in pitch. **2** a sharp blow (*a crack on the head*). **3 a** a narrow opening formed by a break (*entered through a crack in the wall*). **b** a partial fracture, with the parts still joined (*the teacup has a crack in it*). **c** a chink (*looked through the crack formed by the door*; *a crack of light*). **4** *colloq.* a mischievous or malicious remark or aside (*a nasty crack about my age*). **5** *colloq.* an attempt (*I'll have a crack at it*). **6** the exact moment (*at the crack of noon*; *the crack of dawn*). **7** *colloq.* a first-rate player, horse, etc. **8** *dial. colloq.* conversation; good company; fun (*only went there for the crack*). **9** *sl.* a potent hard crystalline form of cocaine broken into small pieces and inhaled or smoked for its stimulating effect. ● *v.* **1** *tr.* & *intr.* break without a complete separation of the parts (*cracked the window*; *the* *cup cracked on hitting the floor*). **2** *intr.* & *tr.* make or cause to make a sudden sharp or explosive sound. **3** *intr.* & *tr.* break or cause to break with a sudden sharp sound. **4** *intr.* & *tr.* give way or cause to give way (under torture etc.); yield. **5** *intr.* (of the voice, esp. of an adolescent boy or a person under strain) become dissonant; break. **6** *tr. colloq.* find a solution to (a problem, code, etc.). **7** *tr.* say (a joke etc.) in a jocular way. **8** *tr. colloq.* hit sharply or hard (*cracked her head on the ceiling*). **9** *tr. Chem.* decompose (heavy oils) by heat and pressure with or without a catalyst to produce lighter hydrocarbons (such as petrol). **10** *tr.* break (wheat) into coarse pieces. ● *attrib.adj. colloq.* excellent; first-rate (*a crack regiment*; *a crack shot*). □ **crack a bottle** open a bottle, esp. of wine, and drink it. **crack-brained** *colloq.* crazy. **crack a crib** *sl.* break into a house. **crack-down** *colloq.* severe measures (esp. against law-breakers etc.). **crack down on** *colloq.* take severe measures against. **crack-jaw** *colloq.* ● *adj.* (of a word) difficult to pronounce. ● *n.* such a word. **crack of doom** a thunder-peal announcing the Day of Judgement. **crack on** *colloq.* (often foll. by *with*) proceed briskly or vigorously. **crack up** *colloq.* **1** collapse under strain. **2** laugh. **3** repute (*not all it's cracked up to be*). **crack-up** *n. colloq.* **1** a mental breakdown. **2** a car crash. **crack-willow** a species of willow, *Salix fragilis*, with brittle branches. **fair crack of the whip** *colloq.* a fair chance to participate etc. **get cracking** *colloq.* begin promptly and vigorously. **have a crack at** *colloq.* attempt. [OE *cracian* resound]

■ *n.* **1 a** snap, report, bang, clap, shot, slap. **2** see KNOCK *n.* 3. **3** break, fracture, crevice, rift, rupture, breach, slit, gap, cleft, check; split, fissure, flaw; chink; (*cracks*) craquelure. **4** see GIBE *n.* **5** see ATTEMPT *n.* **6** moment, instant, time, second. **8** see CONVERSATION. ● *v.* **1** break, fracture, rupture; fissure, split; craze. **2** snap. **4** see *give way* 1 (WAY). **6** see SOLVE. **8** see HIT *v.* 1a.
□ **crack-brained** see CRAZY 1. **crack-down** see *suppression* (SUPPRESS). **crack up 1** see COLLAPSE *v.* **2** see LAUGH *v.* 1. **3** (*cracked up*) reputed, supposed, suggested, rumoured, reported, intimated, whispered, said. **crack-up 1** see BREAKDOWN 1b. **2** see COLLISION 1. **get cracking** see *get a move on* 2 (MOVE). **have a crack at** see TRY *v.* 1, 2.

cracked /krakt/ *adj.* **1** having cracks. **2** (*predic.*) *sl.* crazy. □ **cracked wheat** wheat that has been crushed into small pieces.
■ **1** see BROKEN 1. **2** see CRAZY 1.

cracker /krákkər/ *n.* **1** a paper cylinder both ends of which are pulled at Christmas etc. making a sharp noise and releasing a small toy etc. **2** a firework exploding with a sharp noise. **3** (usu. in *pl.*) an instrument for cracking (*nutcrackers*). **4** a thin dry biscuit often eaten with cheese. **5** *Brit. sl.* a notable or attractive person. **6** *US* a biscuit. **7** *US offens.* = *poor White*. □ **cracker-barrel** *US* (of philosophy etc.) homespun; unsophisticated.

crackerjack /krákkərjak/ *adj.* & *n. US sl.* ● *adj.* exceptionally fine or expert. ● *n.* an exceptionally fine thing or person.
■ *adj.* see EXPERT *adj.* 1. ● *n.* see MASTER *n.* 5.

crackers /krákkərz/ *predic.adj. Brit. sl.* crazy.
■ see CRAZY 1.

cracking /krákking/ *adj.* & *adv. sl.* ● *adj.* **1** outstanding; very good (*a cracking performance*). **2** (*attrib.*) fast and exciting (*a cracking speed*). ● *adv.* outstandingly (*a cracking good time*).
■ **1** see BRILLIANT 4. **2** see SMART *adj.* 5.

crackle /krákk'l/ *v.* & *n.* ● *v.intr.* make a repeated slight cracking sound (*radio crackled*; *fire was crackling*). ● *n.* **1** such a sound. **2 a** paintwork, china, or glass decorated with a pattern of minute surface cracks. **b** the smooth surface of such paintwork etc. □□ **crackly** *adj.* [CRACK + -LE[4]]
■ *n.* **1** see RATTLE *n.* 1.

crackling /krákling/ *n.* **1** the crisp skin of roast pork. **2** *joc.* or *offens.* attractive women regarded collectively as objects of sexual desire. □ **bit of crackling** *colloq.* an attractive woman.

cracknel /kráknəl/ *n.* a light crisp biscuit. [ME f. F *craquelin* f. MDu. *krākelinc* f. *krāken* CRACK]

crackpot /krákpot/ *n.* & *adj. sl.* ● *n.* an eccentric or impractical person. ● *adj.* mad, unworkable (*a crackpot scheme*).
■ *n.* see WEIRDO. ● *adj.* see IMPRACTICAL 1.

cracksman /kráksmən/ *n.* (*pl.* **-men**) *sl.* a burglar, esp. a safe-breaker.
■ see BURGLAR.

cracky /krákki/ *adj.* covered with cracks. □□ **crackiness** *n.*

-cracy /krəsi/ *comb. form* denoting a particular form of government, rule, or influence (*aristocracy*; *bureaucracy*). [from or after F *-cratie* f. med.L *-cratia* f. Gk *-kratia* f. *kratos* strength, power]

cradle /kráyd'l/ *n.* & *v.* ● *n.* **1 a** a child's bed or cot, esp. one mounted on rockers. **b** a place in which a thing begins, esp. a civilization etc., or is nurtured in its infancy (*cradle of choral singing*; *cradle of democracy*). **2** a framework resembling a cradle, esp.: **a** that on which a ship, a boat, etc., rests during construction or repairs. **b** that on which a worker is suspended to work on a ceiling, a ship, the vertical side of a building, etc. **c** the part of a telephone on which the receiver rests when not in use. ● *v.tr.* **1** contain or shelter as if in a cradle (*cradled his head in her arms*). **2** place in a cradle. □ **cradle-snatcher** *sl.* a person amorously attached to a much younger person. **cradle-song** a lullaby. **from the cradle** from infancy. **from the cradle to the grave** from infancy till death (esp. of State welfare). [OE *cradol*, perh. rel. to OHG *kratto* basket]
■ *n.* **1 a** cot, bed, crib. **b** see ORIGIN 1. ● *v.* **1** see HOLD[1] *v.* 1a, c.

cradling /kráydling/ *n. Archit.* a wooden or iron framework, esp. one used as a structural support in a ceiling.

craft /kraaft/ *n.* & *v.* ● *n.* **1** skill, esp. in practical arts. **2 a** (esp. in *comb.*) a trade or an art (*statecraft*; *handicraft*; *priestcraft*; *the craft of pottery*). **b** the members of a craft. **3** (*pl.* **craft**) **a** a boat or vessel. **b** an aircraft or spacecraft. **4** cunning or deceit. **5** (**the Craft**) the brotherhood of Freemasons. ● *v.tr.* make in a skilful way (*crafted a poem*; *a well-crafted piece of work*). □ **craft-brother** a fellow worker in the same trade. **craft-guild** *hist.* a guild of workers of the same trade. [OE *cræft*]
■ *n.* **1** skill, ability, artisanship, craftsmanship, workmanship, ingenuity, skilfulness, art, talent, dexterity, cleverness, mastery, expertness, expertise, flair, genius, technique, know-how. **2 a** trade, art, occupation, calling, vocation, *métier*, profession. **3** vessel, ship, boat; aircraft, *esp. Brit.* aeroplane, *US* airplane, *colloq.* plane; spaceship, spacecraft, rocket. **4** deceit, guile, cunning, art, fraud, trickery, wiliness, foxiness, artfulness, craftiness, duplicity. ● *v.* make, fashion, fabricate.

craftsman /kraáftsmən/ *n.* (*pl.* **-men**; *fem.* **craftswoman**, *pl.* **-women**) **1** a skilled and usu. time-served worker. **2** a person who practises a handicraft. **3** a private soldier in the Royal Electrical and Mechanical Engineers. □□ **craftsmanship** *n.* [ME, orig. *craft's man*]
■ **1** see TRADESMAN. □□ **craftsmanship** see WORKMANSHIP.

crafty /kraáfti/ *adj.* (**craftier**, **craftiest**) cunning, artful, wily. □□ **craftily** *adv.* **craftiness** *n.* [OE *cræftig*]
■ artful, cunning, clever, shrewd, foxy, canny, wily, sly, scheming, calculating, designing, plotting, tricky, sneaky, deceitful, dodgy, guileful, insidious, double-dealing, two-faced, duplicitous, treacherous, *colloq.* shifty.

crag[1] /krag/ *n. Brit.* a steep or rugged rock. [ME, of Celt. orig.]
■ cliff, bluff, tor, rock, scarp, precipice, *Geol.* escarpment; (*crags*) *US* palisades.

crag[2] /krag/ *n. Geol.* rock consisting of a shelly sand. [18th c.: perh. f. CRAG[1]]

craggy /krággi/ *adj.* (**craggier, craggiest**) **1** (esp. of a person's face) rugged; rough-textured. **2** (of a landscape) having crags. □□ **craggily** *adv.* **cragginess** *n.*

cragsman /krágzmən/ *n.* (*pl.* **-men**) a skilled climber of crags.

crake /krayk/ *n.* **1** any rail (see RAIL³), esp. a corncrake. **2** the cry of a corncrake. [ME f. ON *kráka* (imit.): cf. CROAK]

cram /kram/ *v.* (**crammed, cramming**) **1** *tr.* **a** fill to bursting; stuff (*the room was crammed*). **b** (foll. by *in, into*) force (a thing) into (*cram the sandwiches into the bag*). **2** *tr.* & *intr.* prepare for an examination by intensive study. **3** *tr.* (often foll. by *with*) feed (poultry etc.) to excess. **4** *tr.* & *intr. colloq.* eat greedily. □ **cram-full** as full as possible. **cram in** push in to bursting point (*crammed in another five minutes' work*). [OE *crammian* f. Gmc]
■ **1** pack, stuff, overstuff, overcrowd, jam, fill (to bursting); force, shove. **2** study, burn the midnight oil, grind (away), *Brit. colloq.* swot, *literary* lucubrate.
□ **cram-full** see *jam-packed*.

crambo /krámbō/ *n.* a game in which a player gives a word or verse-line to which each of the others must find a rhyme. [earlier *crambe*, app. allusive f. L *crambe repetita* cabbage served up again]

crammer /krámmər/ *n.* a person or institution that crams pupils for examinations.

cramp /kramp/ *n.* & *v.* ● *n.* **1 a** a painful involuntary contraction of a muscle or muscles from the cold, exertion, etc. **b** = *writer's cramp* (see WRITER). **2** (also **cramp-iron**) a metal bar with bent ends for holding masonry etc. together. **3** a portable tool for holding two planks etc. together; a clamp. **4** a restraint. ● *v.tr.* **1** affect with cramp. **2** confine narrowly. **3** restrict (energies etc.). **4** (as **cramped** *adj.*) **a** (of handwriting) small and difficult to read. **b** (of a room etc.) uncomfortably crowded, lacking space. **5** fasten with a cramp. □ **cramp a person's style** prevent a person from acting freely or naturally. **cramp up** confine narrowly. [ME f. OF *crampe* f. MDu., MLG *krampe*, OHG *krampfo* f. adj. meaning 'bent': cf. CRIMP]
■ *n.* **1 a** see GRIPE *n.* 1. **4** see RESTRAINT 2. ● *v.* **2** see BOX¹ *v.* 2. **3** see INHIBIT 1. **4 b** (**cramped**) tight, crowded, incommodious, uncomfortable, close.

crámpon /krámpən/ *n.* (*US* **crampoon** /-po͞on/) (usu. in *pl.*) **1** an iron plate with spikes fixed to a boot for walking on ice, climbing, etc. **2** a metal hook for lifting timber, rock, etc.; a grappling-iron. [ME f. F (as CRAMP)]

cran /kran/ *n. Sc.* a measure for fresh herrings (37½ gallons). [= Gael. *crann*, of uncert. orig.]

cranage /kráynij/ *n.* **1** the use of a crane or cranes. **2** the money paid for this.

cranberry /kránbəri/ *n.* (*pl.* **-ies**) **1** any evergreen shrub of the genus *Vaccinium*, esp. *V. macrocarpon* of America and *V. oxycoccos* of Europe, yielding small red acid berries. **2** a berry from this used for a sauce and in cooking. Also called *fen-berry*. [17th c.: named by Amer. colonists f. G *Kranbeere*, LG *kranebere* crane-berry]

crane /krayn/ *n.* & *v.* ● *n.* **1** a machine for moving heavy objects, usu. by suspending them from a projecting arm or beam. **2** any tall wading bird of the family Gruidae, with long legs, long neck, and straight bill. **3** a moving platform supporting a television camera or cine-camera. ● *v.tr.* **1** (also *absol.*) stretch out (one's neck) in order to see something. **2** *tr.* move (an object) by a crane. □ **crane-fly** (*pl.* **-flies**) any fly of the family Tipulidae, having two wings and long legs: also called *daddy-long-legs*. [OE *cran*, rel. to L *grus*, Gk *geranos*]
■ *n.* **1** see HOIST *n.* ● *v.* **1** see STRAIN¹ *v.* 1.

cranesbill /kráynzbil/ *n.* any of various plants of the genus *Geranium*, having beaked fruits.

cranial /kráyniəl/ *adj.* of or relating to the skull. □ **cranial index** the ratio of the width and length of a skull. [CRANIUM + -AL]

craniate /kráyniət/ *adj.* & *n.* ● *adj.* having a skull. ● *n.* a craniate animal. [mod.L *craniatus* f. CRANIUM]

cranio- /kráyniō/ *comb. form* cranium.

craniology /kráyniólləji/ *n.* the scientific study of the shape and size of the human skull. □□ **craniological** /-niəlójik'l/ *adj.* **craniologist** *n.*

craniometry /kráyniómmitri/ *n.* the scientific measurement of skulls. □□ **craniometric** /-niəmétrik/ *adj.*

craniotomy /kráynióttəmi/ *n.* (*pl.* **-ies**) **1** surgical removal of a portion of the skull. **2** surgical perforation of the skull of a dead foetus to ease delivery.

cranium /kráyniəm/ *n.* (*pl.* **craniums** or **crania** /-niə/) **1** the skull. **2** the part of the skeleton that encloses the brain. [ME f. med.L f. Gk *kranion* skull]
■ see HEAD *n.* 1.

crank¹ /krangk/ *n.* & *v.* ● *n.* **1** part of an axle or shaft bent at right angles for interconverting reciprocal and circular motion. **2** an elbow-shaped connection in bell-hanging. ● *v.tr.* **1** cause to move by means of a crank. **2 a** bend into a crank-shape. **b** furnish or fasten with a crank. □ **crank up 1** start (a car engine) by turning a crank. **2** *sl.* increase (speed etc.) by intensive effort. [OE *cranc*, app. f. *crincan*, rel. to *cringan* fall in battle, orig. 'curl up']

crank² /krangk/ *n.* **1 a** an eccentric person, esp. one obsessed by a particular theory (*health-food crank*). **b** *US* a bad-tempered person. **2** *literary* a fanciful turn of speech (*quips and cranks*). [back-form. f. CRANKY]
■ **1 a** eccentric, character, oddity, *sl.* nut, nutcase, *Brit. sl.* nutter; monomaniac, zealot, fanatic, freak.

crank³ /krangk/ *adj. Naut.* liable to capsize. [perh. f. *crank* weak, shaky, or CRANK¹]

crankcase /krángk-kayss/ *n.* a case enclosing a crankshaft.

crankpin /krángkpin/ *n.* a pin by which a connecting-rod is attached to a crank.

crankshaft /krángkshaaft/ *n.* a shaft driven by a crank (see CRANK¹ *n.* 1).

cranky /krángki/ *adj.* (**crankier, crankiest**) **1** *colloq.* eccentric, esp. obsessed with a particular theory (*cranky ideas about women*). **2** working badly; shaky. **3** esp. *US* ill-tempered or crotchety. □□ **crankily** *adv.* **crankiness** *n.* [perh. f. obs. *crank* rogue feigning sickness]
■ **1** eccentric, odd, weird, strange, queer, peculiar, quirky, obsessed, obsessive, capricious, whimsical. **2** see SHAKY. **3** ill-tempered, crotchety, testy, grouchy, crabby, short-tempered, surly, irascible, waspish, churlish, gruff, curmudgeonly, cantankerous, choleric, bilious, snappish, petulant, peevish, contentious, querulous, irritable, splenetic. □□ **crankily** see BADLY 1. **crankiness** see *eccentricity* (ECCENTRIC), *ill humour*.

crannog /krànnəg/ *n.* an ancient lake-dwelling in Scotland or Ireland. [Ir. f. *crann* tree, beam]

cranny /kránni/ *n.* (*pl.* **-ies**) a chink, a crevice, a crack. □□ **crannied** /-nid/ *adj.* [ME f. OF *crané* past part. of *craner* f. *cran* f. pop.L *crena* notch]
■ chink, crevice, crack, fissure, fracture, break, furrow, split, cleft.

crap¹ /krap/ *n.* & *v. coarse sl.* ● *n.* **1** (often as *int.*) nonsense, rubbish (*he talks crap*). **2** faeces. ● *v.intr.* (**crapped, crapping**) defecate. ¶ Usually considered a taboo word. □ **crap out** *US* **1** be unsuccessful. **2** withdraw from a game etc. [earlier senses 'chaff, refuse from fat-boiling': ME f. Du. *krappe*]
■ *n.* **1** see NONSENSE.

crap² /krap/ *n. US* a losing throw of 2, 3, or 12 in craps. □ **crap game** a game of craps. [formed as CRAPS]

crape /krayp/ *n.* **1** crêpe, usu. of black silk or imitation silk, formerly used for mourning clothes. **2** a band of this formerly worn round a person's hat etc. as a sign of mourning. □ **crape fern** a NZ fern, *Leptopteris superba*, with tall dark-green fronds. **crape hair** artificial hair used in stage make-up. □□ **crapy** *adj.* [earlier *crispe*, *crespe* f. F *crespe* CRÊPE]

crappy /kráppi/ *adj.* (**crappier, crappiest**) *coarse sl.* **1** rubbishy, cheap. **2** disgusting.
■ **1** see SHODDY *adj.* 1.

craps /kraps/ *n.pl. US* a gambling game played with dice. □ **shoot craps** play craps. [19th c.: perh. f. *crab* lowest throw at dice]

crapulent /krápyoolənt/ *adj.* **1** given to indulging in alcohol. **2** resulting from drunkenness. **3 a** drunk. **b** suffering from the effects of drunkenness. □□ **crapulence** *n.* **crapulous** *adj.* [LL *crapulentus* very drunk f. L *crapula* inebriation f. Gk *kraipalē* drunken headache]
■ **1** see EPICUREAN *adj.* **3** see DRUNK *adj.* 1.

craquelure /krákkəlyoor/ *n.* a network of fine cracks in a painting or its varnish. [F]

crash[1] /krash/ *v., n., & adv.* ● *v.* **1** *intr. & tr.* make or cause to make a loud smashing noise (*the cymbals crashed; crashed the plates together*). **2** *tr. & intr.* throw, drive, move, or fall with a loud smashing noise. **3** *intr. & tr.* **a** collide or cause (a vehicle) to collide violently with another vehicle, obstacle, etc.; overturn at high speed. **b** fall or cause (an aircraft) to fall violently on to the land or the sea (*crashed the plane; the airman crashed into the sea*). **4** *intr.* (usu. foll. by *into*) collide violently (*crashed into the window*). **5** *intr.* undergo financial ruin. **6** *tr. colloq.* enter without permission (*crashed the cocktail party*). **7** *intr. colloq.* be heavily defeated (*crashed to a 4–0 defeat*). **8** *intr. Computing* (of a machine or system) fail suddenly. **9** *tr. colloq.* pass (a red traffic-light etc.). **10** *intr.* (often foll. by *out*) *sl.* sleep for a night, esp. in an improvised setting. ● *n.* **1 a** a loud and sudden smashing noise (*a thunder crash; the crash of crockery*). **b** a breakage (esp. of crockery, glass, etc.). **2 a** a violent collision, esp. of one vehicle with another or with an object. **b** the violent fall of an aircraft on to the land or sea. **3** ruin, esp. financial. **4** *Computing* a sudden failure which puts a system out of action. **5** (*attrib.*) done rapidly or urgently (*a crash course in first aid*). ● *adv.* with a crash (*the window went crash*). □ **crash barrier** a barrier intended to prevent a car from leaving the road etc. **crash-dive** ● *v.* **1** *intr.* **a** (of a submarine or its pilot) dive hastily and steeply in an emergency. **b** (of an aircraft or airman) dive and crash. **2** *tr.* cause to crash-dive. ● *n.* such a dive. **crash-halt** a sudden stop by a vehicle. **crash-helmet** a helmet worn esp. by a motorcyclist to protect the head in a crash. **crash-land 1** *intr.* (of an aircraft or airman) land hurriedly with a crash, usu. without lowering the undercarriage. **2** *tr.* cause (an aircraft) to crash-land. **crash landing** a hurried landing with a crash. **crash pad** *sl.* a place to sleep, esp. in an emergency. **crash-stop** = *crash-halt*. **crash-tackle** *Football* a vigorous tackle. [ME: imit.]
■ *v.* **1** bang, boom, smash, clash, clang, clank. **3 a** smash (into); collide, bang together; (*crash into*) drive *or* run into. **4** see COLLIDE 1. **5** see FAIL *v.* 7b. **6** gatecrash, invade, intrude *or* break into. ● *n.* **1 a** bang, smash, clash, explosion, blast, clangour; see also BOOM[1] *n.* **2 a** see COLLISION 1. **3** ruin, disaster, collapse, failure.

crash[2] /krash/ *n.* a coarse plain linen, cotton, etc., fabric. [Russ. *krashenina* coloured linen]

crashing /kráshing/ *adj. colloq.* overwhelming (*a crashing bore*).

crasis /kráysiss/ *n.* (*pl.* **crases** /-seez/) the contraction of two adjacent vowels in ancient Greek into one long vowel or diphthong. [Gk *krasis* mixture]

crass /krass/ *adj.* **1** grossly stupid (*a crass idea*). **2** gross (*crass stupidity*). **3** *literary* thick or gross. □□ **crassitude** *n.* **crassly** *adv.* **crassness** *n.* [L *crassus* solid, thick]
■ see GROSS *adj.* 2.

-crat /krat/ *comb. form* a member or supporter of a particular form of government or rule (*autocrat; democrat*). [from or after F *-crate*: see -CRACY]

cratch /krach/ *n.* a rack used for holding food for farm animals out of doors. [ME f. OF *creche* f. Gmc: rel. to CRIB]

crate /krayt/ *n. & v.* ● *n.* **1** a large wickerwork basket or slatted wooden case etc. for packing esp. fragile goods for transportation. **2** *sl.* an old aeroplane or other vehicle. ● *v.tr.* pack in a crate. □□ **crateful** *n.* (*pl.* **-fuls**). [ME, perh. f. Du. *krat* basket etc.]
■ *n.* **1** see BOX[1] *n.* 1, 2a. ● *v.* see BOX[1] *v.* 1.

crater /kráytər/ *n. & v.* ● *n.* **1** the mouth of a volcano. **2** a bowl-shaped cavity, esp. that made by the explosion of a shell or bomb. **3** *Astron.* a hollow with a raised rim on the surface of a planet or moon, caused by the impact of a meteorite. **4** *Antiq.* a large ancient Greek bowl, used for mixing wine. ● *v.tr.* form a crater in. □□ **craterous** *adj.* [L f. Gk *kratēr* mixing-bowl: see CRASIS]
■ **1–3** see HOLLOW *n.* 1.

-cratic /kráttik/ *comb. form* (also **-cratical**) denoting a particular kind of government or rule (*autocratic; democratic*). □□ **-cratically** *comb. form* (*adv.*) [from or after F *-cratique*: see -CRACY]

cravat /krəvát/ *n.* **1** a scarf worn by men inside an open-necked shirt. **2** *hist.* a necktie. □□ **cravatted** *adj.* [F *cravate* f. G *Krawat, Kroat* f. Serbo-Croatian *Hrvat* Croat]
■ see TIE *n.* 2.

crave /krayv/ *v.* **1** *tr.* **a** long for (*craved affection*). **b** beg for (*craves a blessing*). **2** *intr.* (foll. by *for*) long for; beg for (*craved for comfort*). □□ **craver** *n.* [OE *crafian*, rel. to ON *krefja*]
■ **1a, 2** see LONG[2]. **1 b** see BEG 2.

craven /kráyv'n/ *adj. & n.* ● *adj.* (of a person, behaviour, etc.) cowardly; abject. ● *n.* a cowardly person. □□ **cravenly** *adv.* **cravenness** *n.* [ME *cravand* etc. perh. f. OF *cravanté* defeated, past part. of *cravanter* ult. f. L *crepare* burst; assim. to -EN[3]]
■ *adj.* see COWARDLY *adj.* ● *n.* see COWARD *n.*

craving /kráyving/ *n.* (usu. foll. by *for*) a strong desire or longing.
■ see LONGING *n.*

craw /kraw/ *n. Zool.* the crop of a bird or insect. □ **stick in one's craw** be unacceptable. [ME, rel. to MDu. *crāghe*, MLG *krage*, MHG *krage* neck, throat]

crawfish /kráwfish/ *n. & v.* ● *n.* (*pl.* same) a large marine spiny lobster. ● *v.intr. US* retreat; back out. [var. of CRAYFISH]

crawl /krawl/ *v. & n.* ● *v.intr.* **1** move slowly, esp. on hands and knees. **2** (of an insect, snake, etc.) move slowly with the body close to the ground etc. **3** walk or move slowly (*the train crawled into the station*). **4** (often foll. by *to*) *colloq.* behave obsequiously or ingratiatingly in the hope of advantage. **5** (often foll. by *with*) be covered or filled with crawling or moving things, or with people etc. compared to this. **6** (esp. of the skin) feel a creepy sensation. **7** swim with a crawl stroke. ● *n.* **1** an act of crawling. **2** a slow rate of movement. **3** a high-speed swimming stroke with alternate overarm movements and rapid straight-legged kicks. **4 a** (usu. in *comb.*) *colloq.* a leisurely journey between places of interest (*church-crawl*). **b** = *pub-crawl*. □□ **crawlingly** *adv.* **crawly** *adj.* (in senses 5, 6 of *v.*). [ME: orig. unkn.: cf. Sw. *kravla*, Da. *kravle*]
■ *v.* **2** creep, worm, wriggle, squirm, slither, *colloq.* wiggle. **3** inch, creep; see also EDGE *v.* 1. **4** grovel, toady, fawn, cower, *colloq.* creep, suck up; (*crawl to*) *archaic* lackey; see also CRINGE *v.* 2. **5** (*crawl with*) see TEEM[1] 2.

crawler /kráwlər/ *n.* **1** *sl.* a person who behaves obsequiously in the hope of advantage. **2** anything that crawls, esp. an insect. **3** a tractor moving on an endless chain. **4** (usu. in *pl.*) esp. *US* a baby's overall for crawling in; rompers.

cray /kray/ *n. Austral. & NZ* = CRAYFISH.

crayfish /kráyfish/ *n.* (*pl.* same) **1** a small lobster-like freshwater crustacean. **2** a crawfish. [ME f. OF *crevice, crevis*, ult. f. OHG *krebiz* CRAB[1]: assim. to FISH[1]]

crayon /kráyən, -on/ *n. & v.* ● *n.* **1** a stick or pencil of coloured chalk, wax, etc. used for drawing. **2** a drawing made with this. ● *v.tr.* draw with crayons. [F f. *craie* f. L *creta* chalk]

craze /krayz/ *v. & n.* ● *v.* **1** *tr.* (usu. as **crazed** *adj.*) make insane (*crazed with grief*). **2 a** *tr.* produce fine surface cracks on (pottery glaze etc.). **b** *intr.* develop such cracks. ● *n.* **1 a** a usu. temporary enthusiasm (*a craze for hula hoops*). **b** the object of this. **2** an insane fancy or condition. [ME, orig. = break, shatter, perh. f. ON]

■ *v.* **1** (**crazed**) see MAD *adj.* 1. ● *n.* **1 a** fashion, trend, enthusiasm, mania, obsession. **b** rage, fad, thing; last word, *dernier cri.*

crazy /kráyzi/ *adj.* (**crazier, craziest**) **1** *colloq.* (of a person, an action, etc.) insane or mad; foolish. **2** *colloq.* (usu. foll. by *about*) extremely enthusiastic. **3** *sl.* **a** exciting, unrestrained. **b** excellent. **4** (*attrib.*) (of paving, a quilt, etc.) made of irregular pieces fitted together. **5** *archaic* (of a ship, building, etc.) unsound, shaky. □ **crazy bone** *US* the funny bone. **like crazy** *colloq.* = *like mad* (see MAD). □□ **crazily** *adv.* **craziness** *n.*

■ **1** mad, insane, demented, deranged, unbalanced, unhinged, lunatic, *non compos mentis, non compos*, certifiable, touched, out of one's mind *or* head, crazed, *colloq.* mental, dotty, crack-brained, out to lunch, round the bend, *sl.* bananas, off one's head *or* rocker *or* trolley, cuckoo, cracked, dippy, daffy, nuts, bonkers, batty, bats, loony, screwy, gaga, goofy, nutty (as a fruit cake), loco, up the creek, *sl.* balmy, *Brit. sl.* barmy, crackers, potty, round the twist, off one's chump, *esp. US sl.* flaky; silly, absurd, foolish, nonsensical, inane, ridiculous, preposterous, laughable, risible, ludicrous, asinine, stupid, imbecile, *colloq.* imbecilic, idiotic, moronic, cretinous, *esp. Brit. colloq.* daft, *sl.* crackpot, *US sl.* screwball; impractical, impracticable, unworkable, unsound, pointless, imprudent, rash, reckless, hare-brained, ill-considered; (*be crazy*) have a screw loose, be as mad as a hatter *or* March hare, have bats in the belfry; (*go crazy*) *sl.* go ape. **2** enthusiastic, avid, zealous, keen, excited; infatuated, obsessed, wild, mad, *colloq.* dotty, mental, *sl.* nuts, nutty. **3 a** see WILD *adj.* 4. **b** see EXCELLENT. □□ **crazily** see MADLY 1.

creak /kreek/ *n.* & *v.* ● *n.* a harsh scraping or squeaking sound. ● *v.intr.* **1** make a creak. **2 a** move with a creaking noise. **b** move stiffly and awkwardly. **c** show weakness or frailty under strain. □□ **creakingly** *adv.* [ME, imit.: cf. CRAKE, CROAK]

creaky /kreéki/ *adj.* (**creakier, creakiest**) **1** liable to creak. **2 a** stiff or frail (*creaky joints*). **b** (of a practice, institution, etc.) decrepit, dilapidated, outmoded. □□ **creakily** *adv.* **creakiness** *n.*

■ **2 b** see DECREPIT 2.

cream /kreem/ *n.*, *v.*, & *adj.* ● *n.* **1 a** the fatty content of milk which gathers at the top and can be made into butter by churning. **b** this eaten (often whipped) with a dessert, as a cake-filling, etc. (*strawberries and cream; cream gateau*). **2** the part of a liquid that gathers at the top. **3** (usu. prec. by *the*) the best or choicest part of something, esp.: **a** the point of an anecdote. **b** an élite group of people (*the cream of the nation*). **4** a creamlike preparation, esp. a cosmetic (*hand cream*). **5** a very pale yellow or off-white colour. **6 a** a dish or sweet like or made with cream. **b** a soup or sauce containing milk or cream. **c** a full-bodied mellow sweet sherry. **d** a biscuit with a creamy sandwich filling. **e** a chocolate-covered usu. fruit-flavoured fondant. ● *v.* **1** *tr.* (usu. foll. by *off*) **a** take the cream from (milk). **b** take the best or a specified part from (*creamed off the brightest pupils*). **2** *tr.* work (butter etc.) to a creamy consistency. **3** *tr.* treat (the skin etc.) with cosmetic cream. **4** *tr.* add cream to (coffee etc.). **5** *intr.* (of milk or any other liquid) form a cream or scum. **6** *tr. US colloq.* defeat (esp. in a sporting contest). ● *adj.* pale yellow; off-white. □ **cream bun** (or **cake**) a bun or cake filled or topped with cream. **cream cheese** a soft rich cheese made from unskimmed milk and cream. **cream-coloured** pale yellowish white. **cream cracker** *Brit.* a crisp dry unsweetened biscuit usu. eaten with cheese. **cream-laid** (or **-wove**) laid (or wove) cream-coloured paper. **cream of tartar** purified and crystallized potassium hydrogen tartrate, used in medicine, baking powder, etc. **cream puff 1** a cake made of puff pastry filled with cream. **2** *colloq.* an ineffectual or effeminate person. **cream soda** a carbonated vanilla-flavoured soft drink. **cream tea** afternoon tea with scones, jam, and cream. [ME f. OF *cre(s)me* f. LL *cramum* (perh. f. Gaulish) & eccl.L *chrisma* CHRISM]

■ *n.* **3** see BEST *n.* 1, 2. **4** see LOTION. ● *v.* **1** (*cream off*) skim off. **2** see PRESS^1 *v.* 2b. **6** see BEAT *v.* 3a. □ **cream puff 2** see DRIP *n.* 2.

creamer /kreémər/ *n.* **1** a flat dish used for skimming the cream off milk. **2** a machine used for separating cream from milk. **3** *US* a jug for cream.

creamery /kreéməri/ *n.* (*pl.* **-ies**) **1** a factory producing butter and cheese. **2** a shop where milk, cream, etc., are sold; a dairy. [CREAM, after F *crémerie*]

creamy /kreémi/ *adj.* (**creamier, creamiest**) **1** like cream in consistency or colour. **2** rich in cream. □□ **creamily** *adv.* **creaminess** *n.*

■ **1** see WHITE *adj.* 1. **2** see RICH 6.

crease^1 /kreess/ *n.* & *v.* ● *n.* **1 a** a line in paper etc. caused by folding. **b** a fold or wrinkle. **2** *Cricket* a line marking the position of the bowler or batsman (see POPPING-CREASE, *bowling-crease*). **3** an area near the goal in ice hockey or lacrosse into which the puck or the ball must precede the players. ● *v.* **1** *tr.* make creases in (material). **2** *intr.* become creased (*linen creases badly*). **3** *tr.* & *intr. sl.* (often foll. by *up*) make or become incapable through laughter. **4** *tr.* esp. *US sl.* **a** tire out. **b** stun or kill. [earlier *creast* = CREST ridge in material]

■ *n.* **1** see FOLD^1 *n.* ● *v.* **1** see FOLD^1 *v.* 1.

crease^2 var. of KRIS.

create /kree-áyt/ *v.* **1** *tr.* **a** (of natural or historical forces) bring into existence; cause (*poverty creates resentment*). **b** (of a person or persons) make or cause (*create a diversion; create a good impression*). **2** *tr.* originate (*an actor creates a part*). **3** *tr.* invest (a person) with a rank (*created him a lord*). **4** *intr. Brit. sl.* make a fuss; grumble. □□ **creatable** *adj.* [ME f. L *creare*]

■ **1** make, cause, produce, form, bring into being, originate, conceive, generate, invent, imagine, think up, frame, forge, fashion, fabricate, manufacture, develop, design, contrive, devise, produce, dream up, initiate; engender, give rise to, spawn, *literary* beget. **4** grumble, fuss, make a fuss, kick up a fuss; see also MOAN *v.* 2.

creatine /kreéətin/ *n.* a product of protein metabolism found in the muscles of vertebrates. [Gk *kreas* meat + -INE^4]

creation /kree-áysh'n/ *n.* **1 a** the act of creating. **b** an instance of this. **2 a** (usu. **the Creation**) the creating of the universe regarded as an act of God. **b** (usu. **Creation**) everything so created; the universe. **3** a product of human intelligence, esp. of imaginative thought or artistic ability. **4 a** the act of investing with a title or rank. **b** an instance of this. [ME f. OF f. L *creatio -onis* (as CREATE)]

■ **1 a** generation, making; beginning, origin, start, inception, genesis, *rhet.* birth; see also FORMATION 1, 2. **2 b** the world, the universe, the cosmos. **3** see INVENTION 1, 2.

creationism /kree-áyshəniz'm/ *n. Theol.* a theory attributing all matter, biological species, etc., to separate acts of creation, rather than to evolution. □□ **creationist** *n.*

creative /kree-áytiv/ *adj.* **1** inventive and imaginative. **2** creating or able to create. □□ **creatively** *adv.* **creativeness** *n.* **creativity** /-tívviti/ *n.*

■ **1** imaginative, inventive, originative, artistic, original, ingenious, resourceful. **2** see PRODUCTIVE 2b.

creator /kree-áytər/ *n.* **1** a person who creates. **2** (as **the Creator**) God. [ME f. OF *creat(o)ur* f. L *creator -oris* (as CREATE)]

■ **1** originator, author, initiator, founder, father, inventor, architect, designer, framer, maker, prime mover. **2** (**the Creator**) God, the Supreme Being, the Deity.

creature /kreéchər/ *n.* **1 a** an animal, as distinct from a human being. **b** any living being (*we are all God's creatures*). **2** a person of a specified kind (*poor creature*). **3** a person owing status to and obsequiously subservient to another. **4** anything created; a creation. □ **creature comforts** material comforts such as good food, warmth, etc. **creature of habit** a person set in an unvarying routine. □□ **creaturely** *adj.* [ME f. OF f. LL *creatura* (as CREATE)]

■ **1** animal, beast; being, organism, entity, living thing. **2** see PERSON. □ **creature comforts** luxuries, material comforts, *colloq.* mod cons.

crèche /kresh, kraysh/ *n.* **1** a day nursery for babies and young children. **2** *US* a representation of a Nativity scene. [F (as CRATCH)]

credal see CREED.

credence /kreéd'nss/ *n.* **1** belief. **2** (in full **credence table**) a small side-table, shelf, or niche which holds the elements of the Eucharist before they are consecrated. □ **give credence to** believe. **letter of credence** a letter of introduction, esp. of an ambassador. [ME f. OF f. med.L *credentia* f. *credere* believe]

■ **1** see BELIEF 1.

credential /kridénsh'l/ *n.* (usu. in *pl.*) **1** evidence of a person's achievements or trustworthiness, usu. in the form of certificates, references, etc. **2** a letter or letters of introduction. [med.L *credentialis* (as CREDENCE)]

■ **1** see WARRANT *n.* 2.

credenza /kridénzə/ *n.* a sideboard or cupboard. [It. f. med.L (as CREDENCE)]

credibility /kréddibílliti/ *n.* **1** the condition of being credible or believable. **2** reputation, status. □ **credibility gap** an apparent difference between what is said and what is true.

credible /kréddib'l/ *adj.* **1** (of a person or statement) believable or worthy of belief. **2** (of a threat etc.) convincing. □□ **credibly** *adv.* [ME f. L *credibilis* f. *credere* believe]

■ see PLAUSIBLE 1.

credit /kréddit/ *n.* & *v.* ● *n.* **1** (usu. of a person) a source of honour, pride, etc. (*is a credit to the school*). **2** the acknowledgement of merit (*must give him credit for consistency*). **3** a good reputation (*his credit stands high*). **4 a** belief or trust (*I place credit in that*). **b** something believable or trustworthy (*that statement has credit*). **5 a** a person's financial standing; the sum of money at a person's disposal in a bank etc. **b** the power to obtain goods etc. before payment (based on the trust that payment will be made). **6** (usu. in *pl.*) an acknowledgement of a contributor's services to a film, television programme, etc. **7** a grade above a pass in an examination. **8** a reputation for solvency and honesty in business. **9 a** (in bookkeeping) the acknowledgement of being paid by an entry on the credit side of an account. **b** the sum entered. **c** the credit side of an account. **10** *US* a certificate indicating that a student has completed a course. ● *v.tr.* (**credited, crediting**) **1** believe (*cannot credit it*). **2** (usu. foll. by *to, with*) **a** enter on the credit side of an account (*credited £20 to him*; *credited him with £20*). **b** ascribe a good quality or achievement to (*the goal was credited to Barnes*; *he was credited with the improved sales*). □ **credit account** *Brit.* an account with a shop etc. for obtaining goods or services before payment. **credit card** a card from a bank etc. authorizing the obtaining of goods on credit. **credit note** a note given by a shop etc. in return for goods returned, stating the value of goods owed to the customer. **credit rating** an estimate of a person's suitability to receive commercial credit. **credit sale** the sale of goods on credit. **credit title** a person's name appearing at the beginning or end of a film or broadcast etc. as an acknowledgement. **credit transfer** a transfer from one person's bank account to another's. **credit a person with** ascribe (a good quality) to a person. **do credit to** (or **do a person credit**) enhance the reputation of. **get credit for** be given credit for. **give a person credit for 1** enter (a sum) to a person's credit. **2** ascribe (a good quality) to a person. **give credit to** believe. **letter of credit** a letter from a banker authorizing a person to draw money up to a specified amount, usu. from another bank. **on credit** with an arrangement to pay later. **to one's credit** in one's praise, commendation, or defence (*to his credit, he refused the offer*). [F *crédit* f. It. *credito* or L *creditum* f. *credere credit-* believe, trust]

■ *n.* **2** praise, commendation, tribute, recognition, acknowledgement, acclaim. **3** honour, esteem, merit, reputation, standing, stature, position, status, name, repute. **4 a** belief, faith, trust, credence; confidence. **b** believability, credibility, conceivability, plausibility; reliability, trustworthiness, honesty, probity, dependability. **6** (*credits*) end credits, acknowledgements, titles, credit titles. ● *v.* **1** give credit to, believe, trust, accept, put *or* place one's faith *or* confidence in, have faith *or* confidence in, rely on, depend on *or* upon. **2 b** accredit, ascribe, attribute, assign. □ **give credit to** see CREDIT *v.* 1 above.

creditable /krédditəb'l/ *adj.* (often foll. by *to*) bringing credit or honour. □□ **creditability** /-bílliti/ *n.* **creditably** *adv.*

■ see MERITORIOUS.

creditor /krédditər/ *n.* **1** a person to whom a debt is owing. **2** a person or company that gives credit for money or goods (cf. DEBTOR). [ME f. AF *creditour* (OF *-eur*) f. L *creditor* *-oris* (as CREDIT)]

creditworthy /krédditwurthi/ *adj.* considered suitable to receive commercial credit. □□ **creditworthiness** *n.*

■ see SOLVENT *adj.*

credo /kráydō, kreé-/ *n.* (*pl.* **-os**) **1** (**Credo**) a statement of belief; a creed, esp. the Apostles' or Nicene creed beginning in Latin with *credo*. **2** a musical setting of the Nicene Creed. [ME f. L, = I believe]

■ **1** see CREED.

credulous /krédyooləss/ *adj.* **1** too ready to believe; gullible. **2** (of behaviour) showing such gullibility. □□ **credulity** /kridyoóliti/ *n.* **credulously** *adv.* **credulousness** *n.* [L *credulus* f. *credere* believe]

■ see GULLIBLE.

Cree /kree/ *n.* & *adj.* ● *n.* (*pl.* same or **Crees**) **1 a** an American Indian people of N. America. **b** a member of this people. **2** the language of this people. ● *adj.* of or relating to the Crees or their language. [Canadian F *Cris* (earlier *Cristinaux*) f. Algonquian]

creed /kreed/ *n.* **1** a set of principles or opinions, esp. as a philosophy of life (*his creed is moderation in everything*). **2 a** (often **the Creed**) = *Apostles' Creed* (see APOSTLE). **b** a brief formal summary of Christian doctrine (cf. NICENE CREED, *Athanasian Creed*). **c** the Creed as part of the Mass. □□ **credal** /kreéd'l/ *adj.* **creedal** *adj.* [OE *crēda* f. L CREDO]

■ **1** dogma, doctrine, Credo, teaching, principles, belief, set of beliefs, philosophy, maxim.

creek /kreek/ *n.* **1** *Brit.* **a** a small bay or harbour on a sea-coast. **b** a narrow inlet on a sea-coast or in a river-bank. **2** *US, Austral.,* & *NZ* a stream or brook. □ **up shit creek** *coarse sl.* = *up the creek* 1. **up the creek** *sl.* **1** in difficulties or trouble. **2** crazy. [ME *crike* f. ON *kriki* nook (or partly f. OF *crique* f. ON), & ME *crēke* f. MDu. *krēke* (or f. *crike* by lengthening): ult. orig. unkn.]

■ **1** inlet, bay, cove, harbour. **2** stream, streamlet, brook, rivulet, rill, runnel, *Sc.* burn, *US* run. □ **up the creek** **1** see *in trouble* 1 (TROUBLE). **2** see CRAZY 1.

creel /kreel/ *n.* **1** a large wicker basket for fish. **2** an angler's fishing-basket. [ME, orig. Sc.: ult. orig. unkn.]

creep /kreep/ *v.* & *n.* ● *v.intr.* (*past* and *past part.* **crept** /krept/) **1** move with the body prone and close to the ground; crawl. **2** (often foll. by *in, out, up,* etc.) come, go, or move slowly and stealthily or timidly (*crept out without being seen*). **3** enter slowly (into a person's affections, life, awareness, etc.) (*a feeling crept over her*; *crept into her heart*). **4** *colloq.* act abjectly or obsequiously in the hope of advancement. **5** (of a plant) grow along the ground or up a wall by means of tendrils etc. **6** (as **creeping** *adj.*) developing slowly and steadily (*creeping inflation*). **7** (of the flesh) feel as if insects etc. were creeping over it, as a result of fear, horror, etc. **8** (of metals etc.) undergo creep. ● *n.* **1 a** the act of creeping. **b** an instance of this. **2** (in *pl.*; prec. by *the*) *colloq.* a nervous feeling of revulsion or fear (*gives*

me the creeps). **3** *sl.* an unpleasant person. **4** the gradual downward movement of disintegrated rock due to gravitational forces etc. **5** (of metals etc.) a gradual change of shape under stress. **6** a low arch under a railway embankment, road, etc. □ **creeping barrage** a barrage moving ahead of advancing troops. **creeping Jenny** any of various creeping plants, esp. moneywort. **creeping Jesus** *sl.* an abject or hypocritical person. **creep up on** approach (a person) stealthily or unnoticed. [OE *crēopan* f. Gmc]
■ *v.* **1** crawl, slither, inch, squirm, wriggle, *colloq.* wiggle; (*creep by*) drag. **2** steal, sneak; slink, skulk, tiptoe, pussyfoot, sidle. **3** make its way. **4** see CRAWL *v.* 4. ● *n.* **2** (*the creeps*) see JITTER *n.* **3** see WRETCH 2. □ **creeping Jesus** see WRETCH 2, HYPOCRITE.

creeper /kréepər/ *n.* **1** *Bot.* any climbing or creeping plant. **2** any bird that climbs, esp. a treecreeper. **3** *sl.* a soft-soled shoe.
■ **1** see RUNNER 2b.

creepy /kréepi/ *adj.* (**creepier, creepiest**) **1** *colloq.* having or producing a creeping of the flesh (*I feel creepy*; *a creepy film*). **2** given to creeping. □□ **creepily** *adv.* **creepiness** *n.* [CREEP]
■ **1** see SCARY.

creepy-crawly /kréepikráwli/ *n.* & *adj. Brit. colloq.* ● *n.* (*pl.* **-ies**) an insect, worm, etc. ● *adj.* creeping and crawling.
■ *n.* see BUG *n.* 1.

creese var. of KRIS.

cremate /krimáyt/ *v.tr.* consume (a corpse etc.) by fire. □□ **cremation** /-máysh'n/ *n.* **cremator** *n.* [L *cremare* burn]
■ □□ **cremation** see FUNERAL *n.*

crematorium /krémmətóriəm/ *n.* (*pl.* **crematoria** or **crematoriums**) a place for cremating corpses in a furnace. [mod.L (as CREMATE, -ORY)]

crematory /krémmətəri/ *adj.* & *n.* ● *adj.* of or relating to cremation. ● *n.* (*pl.* **-ies**) *US* = CREMATORIUM.

crème /krem/ *n.* **1** = CREAM *n.* 6a. **2** a name for various creamy liqueurs (*crème de cassis*). □ ***crème brûlée*** /brooláy/ a pudding of cream or custard topped with caramelized sugar. ***crème caramel*** a custard coated with caramel. ***crème de la crème*** /də laa krém/ the best part; the élite. ***crème de menthe*** /də mónth/ a peppermint-flavoured liqueur. [F, = cream]
■ □ **crème de la crème** see BEST *n.* 1, 2.

crenate /kréenayt/ *adj. Bot.* & *Zool.* having a notched edge or rounded teeth. □□ **crenated** *adj.* **crenation** /-náysh'n/ *n.* **crenature** /krénnətyoor, krée-/ *n.* [mod.L *crenatus* f. pop.L *crena* notch]
■ see *notched* (NOTCH).

crenel /krénn'l/ *n.* (also **crenelle** /krinél/) an indentation or gap in the parapet of a tower, castle, etc., orig. for shooting through etc. [ME f. OF *crenel*, ult. f. pop.L *crena* notch]

crenellate /krénnəlayt/ *v.tr.* provide (a tower etc.) with battlements or loopholes. □□ **crenellation** /-láysh'n/ *n.* [F *créneler* (as CRENEL)]

Creole /krée-ōl/ *n.* & *adj.* ● *n.* **1 a** a descendant of European (esp. Spanish) settlers in the W. Indies or Central or S. America. **b** a White descendant of French settlers in the southern US. **c** a person of mixed European and Black descent. **2** a mother tongue formed from the contact of a European language (esp. English, French, or Portuguese) with another (esp. African) language. ● *adj.* **1** of or relating to a Creole or Creoles. **2** (usu. **creole**) of Creole origin or production (*creole cooking*). [F *créole*, *criole* f. Sp. *criollo*, prob. f. Port. *crioulo* home-born slave f. *criar* breed f. L *creare* CREATE]

creolize /kréeəlīz/ *v.tr.* (also **-ise**) form a Creole from (another language). □□ **creolization** /-záysh'n/ *n.*

creosote /kréeəsōt/ *n.* & *v.* ● *n.* **1** (in full **creosote oil**) a dark-brown oil distilled from coal tar, used as a wood-preservative. **2** a colourless oily fluid distilled from wood tar, used as an antiseptic. ● *v.tr.* treat with creosote. [G *Kreosote* f. Gk *kreas* flesh + *sōtēr* preserver, with ref. to its antiseptic properties]

crêpe /krayp/ *n.* **1** a fine often gauzelike fabric with a wrinkled surface. **2** a thin pancake, usu. with a savoury or sweet filling. **3** (also **crêpe rubber**) a very hard-wearing wrinkled sheet rubber used for the soles of shoes etc. □ **crêpe de Chine** /də shéen/ a fine silk crêpe. **crêpe paper** thin crinkled paper. **crêpe Suzette** /soozét/ a small dessert pancake flamed in alcohol at the table. □□ **crêpey** *adj.* **crêpy** *adj.* [F f. OF *crespe* curled f. L *crispus*]

crepitate /kréppitayt/ *v.intr.* **1** make a crackling sound. **2** *Zool.* (of a beetle) eject pungent fluid with a sharp report. □□ **crepitant** *adj.* [L *crepitare* frequent. of *crepare* creak]

crepitation /kréppitáysh'n/ *n.* **1** *Med.* = CREPITUS. **2** the action or sound of crackling or rattling.

crepitus /kréppitəss/ *n. Med.* **1** a grating noise from the ends of a fractured bone rubbing together. **2** a similar sound heard from the chest in pneumonia etc. [L f. *crepare* rattle]

crept *past* and *past part.* of CREEP.

crepuscular /kripúskyoolər/ *adj.* **1 a** of twilight. **b** dim. **2** *Zool.* appearing or active in twilight. [L *crepusculum* twilight]
■ **1 a** see TWILIGHT 6. **b** see DIM *adj.* 1a.

Cres. *abbr.* Crescent.

cresc. *abbr.* (also **cres.**) *Mus.* = CRESCENDO.

crescendo /krishéndō/ *n.*, *adv.*, *adj.*, & *v.* ● *n.* (*pl.* **-os**) **1** *Mus.* a passage gradually increasing in loudness. **2 a** progress towards a climax (*a crescendo of emotions*). **b** *disp.* a climax (*reached a crescendo then died away*). ● *adv.* & *adj.* with a gradual increase in loudness. ● *v.intr.* (**-oes, -oed**) increase gradually in loudness or intensity. [It., part. of *crescere* grow (as CRESCENT)]
■ *n.* **2** see HEAD *n.* 21.

crescent /krézz'nt, kréss-/ *n.* & *adj.* ● *n.* **1** the curved sickle shape of the waxing or waning moon. **2** anything of this shape, esp. *Brit.* a street forming an arc. **3 a** the crescent-shaped emblem of Islam or Turkey. **b** (**the Crescent**) the world or power of Islam. ● *adj.* **1** *poet.* increasing. **2** crescent-shaped. □□ **crescentic** /kriséntik/ *adj.* [ME f. AF *cressaunt*, OF *creissant*, f. L *crescere* grow]
■ *n.* **2** arc, lunette, *Geom.* lune, *Math.* meniscus. ● *adj.* **1** increasing, growing. **2** crescentic, *Math.* meniscoid.

cresol /kréessol/ *n.* any of three isomeric phenols present in creosote and used as disinfectants. □□ **cresyl** /kréessil/ *adj.* [CREOSOTE + -OL[2]]

cress /kress/ *n.* any of various cruciferous plants usu. with pungent edible leaves, e.g. watercress. [OE *cresse* f. WG]

cresset /kréssit/ *n. hist.* a metal container filled with fuel, lighted and usu. mounted on a pole for illumination. [ME f. OF *cresset*, *craisset*, f. *craisse* = *graisse* GREASE]

crest /krest/ *n.* & *v.* ● *n.* **1 a** a comb or tuft of feathers, fur, etc. on a bird's or animal's head. **b** something resembling this, esp. a plume of feathers on a helmet. **c** a helmet; the top of a helmet. **2** the top of something, esp. of a mountain, wave, roof, etc. **3** *Heraldry* **a** a device above the shield and helmet of a coat of arms. **b** such a device reproduced on writing paper or on a seal, signifying a family. **4 a** a line along the top of the neck of some animals. **b** the hair growing from this; a mane. **5** *Anat.* a ridge along the surface of a bone. ● *v.* **1** *tr.* reach the crest of (a hill, wave, etc.). **2** *tr.* **a** provide with a crest. **b** serve as a crest to. **3** *intr.* (of a wave) form into a crest. □ **on the crest of a wave** at the most favourable moment in one's progress. □□ **crested** *adj.* (also in *comb.*). **crestless** *adj.* [ME f. OF *creste* f. L *crista* tuft]
■ *n.* **2** top, summit, pinnacle, peak, head, ridge. **3** seal, device, figure, badge, emblem, insignia, symbol, design. ● *v.* **2 a** top, crown, surmount, cap. **3** level out *or* off.

crestfallen /kréstfawlən/ *adj.* **1** dejected, dispirited. **2** with a fallen or drooping crest.
■ **1** see *dejected* (DEJECT).

cretaceous /kritáyshəss/ *adj.* & *n.* ● *adj.* **1** of the nature of chalk. **2** (**Cretaceous**) *Geol.* of or relating to the last period of the Mesozoic era, with evidence of the first flowering plants, the extinction of dinosaurs, and extensive deposits of chalk. ¶ Cf. Appendix VII. ● *n. Geol.* this era or system. [L *cretaceus* f. *creta* chalk]

Cretan /kreét'n/ *n.* & *adj.* ● *n.* a native of Crete, an island SE of the Greek mainland. ● *adj.* of or relating to Crete or the Cretans. [L *Cretanus* f. *Creta* f. Gk *Krētē* Crete]

cretic /kreétik/ *n. Prosody* a foot containing one short or unstressed syllable between two long or stressed ones. [L *Creticus* f. Gk *Krētikos* (as CRETAN)]

cretin /kréttin/ *n.* **1** a person who is deformed and mentally retarded as the result of a thyroid deficiency. **2** *colloq.* a stupid person. ▫▫ **cretinism** *n.* **cretinize** *v.tr.* (also **-ise**). **cretinous** *adj.* [F *crétin* f. Swiss F. *creitin, crestin* f. L *Christianus* CHRISTIAN]
▪ ▫▫ **cretinism** see *stupidity* (STUPID).

cretonne /kretón, krétton/ *n.* (often *attrib.*) a heavy cotton fabric with a usu. floral pattern printed on one or both sides, used for upholstery. [F f. *Creton* in Normandy]

crevasse /krəváss/ *n.* **1** a deep open crack, esp. in a glacier. **2** *US* a breach in a river levee. [F f. OF *crevace*: see CREVICE]
▪ gorge, chasm, abyss, ravine, fissure, crack, furrow.

crevice /krévviss/ *n.* a narrow opening or fissure, esp. in a rock or building etc. [ME f. OF *crevace* f. *crever* burst f. L *crepare*]
▪ crack, fissure, chink, cleft, cranny, groove, furrow, break, split, rift.

crew[1] /kro͞o/ *n.* & *v.* ● *n.* (often treated as *pl.*) **1 a** a body of people manning a ship, aircraft, train, etc. **b** such a body as distinguished from the captain or officers. **c** a body of people working together; a team. **2** *colloq.* a company of people; a gang (*a motley crew*). ● *v.* **1** *tr.* supply or act as a crew or member of a crew for. **2** *intr.* act as a crew or member of a crew. ▫ **crew cut** an orig. man's haircut which is short all over the head. **crew neck** a close-fitting round neckline, esp. on a sweater. [ME f. OF *creüe* increase, fem. past part. of *croistre* grow f. L *crescere*]
▪ *n.* group, company, band, troupe, party, gang, team, corps, body.

crew[2] *past* of CROW[2].

crewel /kro͞oəl/ *n.* a thin worsted yarn used for tapestry and embroidery. ▫ **crewel-work** a design worked in crewel on linen or cloth. [ME *crule* etc., of unkn. orig.]

crewman /kro͞omən/ *n.* (*pl.* **-men**) a member of a crew.

crib /krib/ *n.* & *v.* ● *n.* **1 a** a child's bed with barred or latticed sides; a cot. **b** a model of the Nativity of Christ, with a manger as a bed. **2** a barred container or rack for animal fodder. **3** *colloq.* **a** a translation of a text for the (esp. surreptitious) use of students. **b** plagiarized work etc. **4** a small house or cottage. **5** a framework lining the shaft of a mine. **6** *colloq.* **a** cribbage. **b** a set of cards given to the dealer at cribbage by all the players. **7** heavy crossed timbers used in foundations in loose soil etc. **8** *sl.* a brothel. **9** *Austral.* & *NZ* a light meal; food. ● *v.tr.* (also *absol.*) (**cribbed, cribbing**) **1** *colloq.* copy (another person's work) unfairly or without acknowledgement. **2** confine in a small space. **3** *colloq.* pilfer, steal. **4** *colloq.* grumble. ▫ **crib-biting** a horse's habit of biting the manger while noisily breathing in and swallowing. ▫▫ **cribber** *n.* [OE *crib(b)*]
▪ *n.* **1 a** cot, cradle, bed. **b** *US* crèche. **3 a** translation, gloss, interpretation, *US sl.* trot. **4** see CABIN *n.* 1. **7** cribwork. **8** see BROTHEL. **9** see BITE *n.* 3b. ● *v.* **1** copy, plagiarize. **2** see RESTRICT. **3** see STEAL *v.* 1. **4** see MOAN *v.* 2.

cribbage /kríbbij/ *n.* a card game for two, three, or four players, in which the dealer may score from the cards in the crib (see CRIB *n.* 6b). ▫ **cribbage-board** a board with pegs and holes used for scoring at cribbage. [17th c.: orig. unkn.]

cribo /kríbbō, krībō/ *n.* (*pl.* **-os**) a large harmless snake, *Drymarchon corais*, of tropical America. Also called *gopher snake* (see GOPHER[1]). [19th c.: orig. unkn.]

cribriform /kríbriform/ *adj. Anat.* & *Bot.* having numerous small holes. [L *cribrum* sieve + -FORM]

cribwork /kríbwurk/ *n.* = CRIB *n.* 7.

crick /krik/ *n.* & *v.* ● *n.* a sudden painful stiffness in the neck or the back etc. ● *v.tr.* produce a crick in (the neck etc.). [ME: orig. unkn.]

cricket[1] /kríkkit/ *n.* & *v.* ● *n.* a game played on a grass pitch with two teams of 11 players taking turns to bowl at a wicket defended by a batting player of the other team. ● *v.intr.* (**cricketed, cricketing**) play cricket. ▫ **cricket-bag** a long bag used for carrying a cricketer's bat etc. **not cricket** *Brit. colloq.* underhand or unfair behaviour. ▫▫ **cricketer** *n.* [16th c.: orig. uncert.]

cricket[2] /kríkkit/ *n.* any of various grasshopper-like insects of the order Orthoptera, the males of which produce a characteristic chirping sound. [ME f. OF *criquet* f. *criquer* creak etc. (imit.)]

cricoid /krīkoyd/ *adj.* & *n.* ● *adj.* ring-shaped. ● *n.* (in full **cricoid cartilage**) *Anat.* the ring-shaped cartilage of the larynx. [mod.L *cricoides* f. Gk *krikoeidēs* f. *krikos* ring]

cri de cœur /kreé də kőr/ *n.* (*pl.* ***cris de cœur*** /*pronunc.* same/) a passionate appeal, complaint, or protest. [F, = cry from the heart]

cried *past* and *past part.* of CRY.

crier /krīər/ *n.* (also **cryer**) **1** a person who cries. **2** an officer who makes public announcements in a court of justice. ▫ **town** (or **common**) **crier** *hist.* an officer employed by a town council etc. to make public announcements in the streets or market-place. [ME f. AF *criour*, OF *criere* f. *crier* CRY]

crikey /krīki/ *int. Brit. sl.* an expression of astonishment. [euphem. for CHRIST]

crim /krim/ *n.* & *adj. Austral. sl.* = CRIMINAL. [abbr.]

crime /krīm/ *n.* & *v.* ● *n.* **1 a** an offence punishable by law. **b** illegal acts as a whole (*resorted to crime*). **2** an evil act (*a crime against humanity*). **3** *colloq.* a shameful act (*a crime to tease them*). **4** a soldier's offence against military regulations. ● *v.tr. Mil.* etc. charge with or convict of an offence. ▫ **crime-sheet** *Mil.* a record of a defendant's offences. **crime wave** a sudden increase in crime. **crime-writer** a writer of detective fiction or thrillers. [ME f. OF f. L *crimen -minis* judgement, offence]
▪ *n.* **1 a** offence, violation, misdeed, wrong, misdemeanour; felony. **b** lawlessness. **2** see EVIL *n.* 1.

crime passionnel /kreém pásyonél/ *n.* (*pl.* ***crimes passionnels*** /*pronunc.* same/) a crime, esp. murder, committed in a fit of sexual jealousy. [F, = crime of passion]

criminal /krímmin'l/ *n.* & *adj.* ● *n.* a person who has committed a crime or crimes. ● *adj.* **1** of, involving, or concerning crime (*criminal records*). **2** having committed (and usu. been convicted of) a crime. **3** *Law* relating to or expert in criminal law rather than civil or political matters (*criminal code; criminal lawyer*). **4** *colloq.* scandalous, deplorable. ▫ **criminal law** law concerned with punishment of offenders (opp. *civil law*). **criminal libel** see LIBEL. ▫▫ **criminality** /-nálliti/ *n.* **criminally** *adv.* [ME f. LL *criminalis* (as CRIME)]
▪ *n.* felon, lawbreaker, outlaw, culprit, offender, malefactor, wrongdoer, racketeer, *colloq.* crook, *Brit. colloq.* villain, *Austral. sl.* crim; villain, miscreant, scoundrel, knave, blackguard; *colloq.* roughneck, bad guy, black hat, bad hat, baddy; see also THUG. ● *adj.* **2** illegal, unlawful, illicit, lawless, dishonest, *colloq.* crooked. **4** scandalous, deplorable, disgraceful, reprehensible, *colloq.* awful; wicked, evil, bad, wrong, corrupt, vile, immoral, amoral, sinful, villainous, iniquitous, flagitious.

criminalistic /krímminəlístik/ *adj.* relating to criminals or their habits.

criminalistics /krímminəlístiks/ *n.pl.* esp. *US* forensic science.

criminology /krímminólləji/ *n.* the scientific study of crime. ▫▫ **criminological** /-nəlójik'l/ *adj.* **criminologist** *n.* [L *crimen -minis* CRIME + -OLOGY]

crimp /krimp/ *v.* & *n.* ● *v.tr.* **1** compress into small folds or ridges; frill. **2** make narrow wrinkles or flutings in; corrugate.

3 make waves in (the hair) with a hot iron. ● *n.* a crimped thing or form. □ **put a crimp in** *US sl.* thwart; interfere with. □□ **crimper** *n.* **crimpy** *adj.* **crimpily** *adv.* **crimpiness** *n.* [ME, prob. ult. f. OHG *krimphan*]
■ *v.* **1, 2** see WRINKLE *v.* 1. ● *n.* see FOLD[1] *n.*

Crimplene /krímpleen/ *n. propr.* a synthetic crease-resistant fibre and fabric.

crimson /krímz'n/ *adj.*, *n.*, & *v.* ● *adj.* of a rich deep red inclining to purple. ● *n.* this colour. ● *v.tr.* & *intr.* make or become crimson. [ME *cremesin, crimesin*, ult. f. Arab. *ḳirmizī* KERMES]
■ *adj.* see RED *adj.* 1. ● *v.* see FLUSH[1] *v.* 1a.

cringe /krinj/ *v.* & *n.* ● *v.intr.* **1** shrink back in fear or apprehension; cower. **2** (often foll. by *to*) behave obsequiously. ● *n.* the act or an instance of cringing. □□ **cringer** *n.* [ME *crenge, crenche*, OE *cringan, crincan*: see CRANK[1]]
■ *v.* **1** cower, wince, flinch, quail, recoil, blench, tremble, quiver, shrink back, *colloq.* quake *or* shake in one's boots *or* shoes. **2** defer, kowtow, grovel, fawn, *Austral.* & *NZ* smoodge, *colloq.* bootlick, crawl, suck up; (*cringe to*) *archaic* lackey. ● *n.* embarrassment.

cringle /kríngg'l/ *n. Naut.* an eye of rope containing a thimble for another rope to pass through. [LG *kringel* dimin. of *kring* ring f. root of CRANK[1]]

crinkle /kríngk'l/ *n.* & *v.* ● *n.* a wrinkle or crease in paper, cloth, etc. ● *v.* **1** *intr.* form crinkles. **2** *tr.* form crinkles in. □ **crinkle-cut** (of vegetables) cut with wavy edges. □□ **crinkly** *adj.* [ME f. OE *crincan*: see CRANK[1]]
■ *n.* see WRINKLE *n.* 1, 2. ● *v.* see WRINKLE *v.* 2.

crinoid /krínnoyd/ *n.* & *adj.* ● *n.* any echinoderm of the class Crinoidea, usu. sedentary with feathery arms, e.g. sea lilies and feather stars. ● *adj.* lily-shaped. □□ **crinoidal** /-nóyd'l/ *adj.* [Gk *krinoeidēs* f. *krinon* lily]

crinoline /krínnəlin/ *n.* **1** a stiffened or hooped petticoat formerly worn to make a long skirt stand out. **2** a stiff fabric of horsehair etc. used for linings, hats, etc. [F f. L *crinis* hair + *linum* thread]

cripple /krípp'l/ *n.* & *v.* ● *n.* a person who is permanently lame. ● *v.tr.* **1** make a cripple of; lame. **2** disable, impair. **3** weaken or damage (an institution, enterprise, etc.) seriously (*crippled by the loss of funding*). □□ **crippledom** *n.* **cripplehood** *n.* **crippler** *n.* [OE *crypel*, rel. to CREEP]
■ *n.* invalid, paralytic, paraplegic. ● *v.* disable, lame; incapacitate, handicap, maim; impair, damage, weaken, debilitate, emasculate.

cris var. of KRIS.

crisis /krī́siss/ *n.* (*pl.* **crises** /-seez/) **1 a** a decisive moment. **b** a time of danger or great difficulty. **2** the turning-point, esp. of a disease. [L f. Gk *krisis* decision f. *krinō* decide]
■ **1 b** disaster, emergency, calamity, catastrophe, danger. **2** turning-point, critical time *or* moment.

crisp /krisp/ *adj.*, *n.*, & *v.* ● *adj.* **1** hard but brittle. **2 a** (of air) bracing. **b** (of a style or manner) lively, brisk and decisive. **c** (of features etc.) neat and clear-cut. **d** (of paper) stiff and crackling. **e** (of hair) closely curling. ● *n.* **1** (in full **potato crisp**) *Brit.* a thin fried slice of potato sold in packets etc. and eaten as a snack or appetizer. **2** a thing overdone in roasting etc. (*burnt to a crisp*). ● *v.tr.* & *intr.* **1** make or become crisp. **2** curl in short stiff folds or waves. □□ **crisply** *adv.* **crispness** *n.* [OE f. L *crispus* curled]
■ *adj.* **1** brittle, crunchy, friable, breakable, crumbly, frangible. **2 a** see *bracing* (BRACE *v.* 3). **b** see LIVELY 1, 2, EMPHATIC. **c** see *chiselled* (CHISEL *v.* 2). **e** curly, crispy, crinkly, frizzy, frizzled.

crispate /kríspayt/ *adj.* **1** crisped. **2** *Bot.* & *Zool.* having a wavy margin. [L *crispare* curl]

crispbread /kríspbred/ *n.* **1** a thin crisp biscuit of crushed rye etc. **2** these collectively (*a packet of crispbread*).

crisper /kríspər/ *n.* a compartment in a refrigerator for storing fruit and vegetables.

crispy /kríspi/ *adj.* (**crispier**, **crispiest**) **1** crisp, brittle. **2** curly. **3** brisk. □□ **crispiness** *n.*

criss-cross /krískróss/ *n.*, *adj.*, *adv.*, & *v.* ● *n.* **1** a pattern of crossing lines. **2** the crossing of lines or currents etc. ● *adj.* crossing; in cross lines (*criss-cross marking*). ● *adv.* crosswise; at cross purposes. ● *v.* **1** *intr.* **a** intersect repeatedly. **b** move crosswise. **2** *tr.* mark or make with a criss-cross pattern. [15th c., f. *Christ's cross*: later treated as redupl. of CROSS]
■ *n.* **1** see NETWORK *n.* 2. ● *v.* **1** see TRAVERSE *v.* 1.

crista /krístə/ *n.* (*pl.* **cristae** /-tee/) **1** *Anat.* & *Zool.* a ridge or crest. **2** *Anat.* an infold of the inner membrane of a mitochondrion. □□ **cristate** *adj.* [L]

cristobalite /kristṓbəlīt/ *n. Mineral.* a principal form of silica, occurring as opal. [G *Cristobalit* f. Cerro San *Cristóbal* in Mexico]

crit /krit/ *n. colloq.* **1** = CRITICISM 2. **2** = CRITIQUE. **3** *Physics* critical mass. [abbr.]

criterion /krīteériən/ *n.* (*pl.* **criteria** /-riə/) a principle or standard that a thing is judged by. □□ **criterial** *adj.* [Gk *kritērion* means of judging (cf. CRITIC)]
■ see STANDARD *n.* 1, 8.

critic /kríttik/ *n.* **1** a person who censures. **2** a person who reviews or judges the merits of literary, artistic, or musical works etc., esp. regularly or professionally. **3** a person engaged in textual criticism. [L *criticus* f. Gk *kritikos* f. *kritēs* judge f. *krinō* judge, decide]
■ **1** see ASSAILANT. **2** see JUDGE *n.* 3b.

critical /kríttik'l/ *adj.* **1 a** making or involving adverse or censorious comments or judgements. **b** expressing or involving criticism. **2** skilful at or engaged in criticism. **3** providing textual criticism (*a critical edition of Milton*). **4 a** of or at a crisis; involving risk or suspense (*in a critical condition*; *a critical operation*). **b** decisive, crucial (*of critical importance*; *at the critical moment*). **5 a** *Math.* & *Physics* marking transition from one state etc. to another (*critical angle*). **b** *Physics* (of a nuclear reactor) maintaining a self-sustaining chain reaction. □ **critical apparatus** = APPARATUS 4. **critical mass** *Physics* the amount of fissile material needed to maintain a nuclear chain reaction. **critical path** the sequence of stages determining the minimum time needed for an operation. **critical temperature** *Chem.* the temperature above which a gas cannot be liquefied. □□ **criticality** /-kálliti/ *n.* (in sense 5). **critically** *adv.* **criticalness** *n.* [L *criticus*: see CRITIC]
■ **1** censorious, disparaging, depreciatory, deprecatory, deprecative, deprecating, judgemental; adverse. **4 a** risky, uncertain, perilous, dangerous, touch-and-go, ticklish, sensitive, touchy, *archaic or joc.* parlous; grave, severe, serious. **b** crucial, important, essential, basic, key, decisive, pivotal, vital, momentous, climacteric.

criticaster /kríttikástər/ *n.* a minor or inferior critic.

criticism /kríttisiz'm/ *n.* **1 a** finding fault; censure. **b** a statement or remark expressing this. **2 a** the work of a critic. **b** an article, essay, etc., expressing or containing an analytical evaluation of something. □ **the higher criticism** criticism dealing with the origin and character etc. of texts, esp. of Biblical writings. **the lower criticism** textual criticism of the Bible. [CRITIC or L *criticus* + -ISM]
■ **1 a** censure, fault-finding, disapproval, condemnation, disparagement. **2 a** judgement, evaluation, appraisal, analysis, assessment, estimation, valuation. **b** critique, review, commentary.

criticize /kríttisīz/ *v.tr.* (also **-ise**) (also *absol.*) **1** find fault with; censure. **2** discuss critically. □□ **criticizable** *adj.* **criticizer** *n.*
■ **1** censure, find fault (with), carp (at), cavil (at), condemn, attack, cut up, denounce, impugn, *colloq.* pan, lambaste, put down, *Brit. colloq.* slate, *sl.* knock, *Austral. sl.* bag. **2** judge, evaluate, assess, appraise; discuss, analyse, critique.

critique /kriteék/ *n.* & *v.* ● *n.* a critical essay or analysis; an instance or the process of formal criticism. ● *v.tr.* (**critiques**, **critiqued**, **critiquing**) discuss critically. [F f. Gk *kritikē tekhnē* critical art]

■ *n.* see ANALYSIS 1. ● *v.* see ANALYSE 3.

critter /krĭttər/ *n.* **1** *dial.* or *joc.* a creature. **2** *derog.* a person. [var. of CREATURE]

croak /krōk/ *n.* & *v.* ● *n.* **1** a deep hoarse sound as of a frog or a raven. **2** a sound resembling this. ● *v.* **1 a** *intr.* utter a croak. **b** *tr.* utter with a croak or in a dismal manner. **2** *sl.* **a** *intr.* die. **b** *tr.* kill. [ME: imit.]

■ *v.* **1** see RASP *v.* 2. **2 a** see DIE[1] 1.

croaker /krṓkər/ *n.* **1** an animal that croaks. **2** a prophet of evil.

croaky /krṓki/ *adj.* (**croakier**, **croakiest**) (of a voice) croaking; hoarse. □□ **croakily** *adv.* **croakiness** *n.*

Croat /krṓ-at/ *n.* & *adj.* ● *n.* **1 a** a native of Croatia in the former Yugoslavia. **b** a person of Croatian descent. **2** the Slavonic dialect of the Croats (cf. SERBO-CROAT). ● *adj.* of or relating to the Croats or their dialect. [mod.L *Croatae* f. Serbo-Croatian *Hrvat*]

Croatian /krō-áysh'n/ *n.* & *adj.* = CROAT.

croc /krok/ *n.* *colloq.* a crocodile. [abbr.]

croceate /krṓsiayt/ *adj.* saffron-coloured. [L *croceus* f. CROCUS]

crochet /krṓshay, -shi/ *n.* & *v.* ● *n.* **1** a handicraft in which yarn is made up into a patterned fabric by means of a hooked needle. **2** work made in this way. ● *v.* (**crocheted** /-shayd/; **crocheting** /-shaying/) **1** *tr.* make by crocheting. **2** *intr.* do crochet. □□ **crocheter** /krṓshayər/ *n.* [F, dimin. of *croc* hook]

crocidolite /krōsíddəlīt/ *n.* a fibrous blue or green silicate of iron and sodium; blue asbestos. [Gk *krokis -idos* nap of cloth]

crock[1] /krok/ *n.* & *v.* *colloq.* ● *n.* **1** an inefficient, broken-down, or worn-out person. **2** a worn-out vehicle, ship, etc. ● *v.* **1** *intr.* (foll. by *up*) break down, collapse. **2** *tr.* (often foll. by *up*) disable, cause to collapse. [orig. Sc., perh. f. Flem.]

■ *v.* **1** see BREAK[1] *v.* 1b.

crock[2] /krok/ *n.* **1** an earthenware pot or jar. **2** a broken piece of earthenware. [OE *croc(ca)*]

■ **1** see JAR[1] 1.

crockery /krókkəri/ *n.* earthenware or china dishes, plates, etc. [obs. *crocker* potter: see CROCK[2]]

■ see POTTERY.

crocket /krókkit/ *n.* *Archit.* a small carved ornament (usu. a bud or curled leaf) on the inclined side of a pinnacle etc. [ME f. var. of OF *crochet*: see CROCHET]

crocodile /krókkədīl/ *n.* **1 a** any large tropical amphibious reptile of the order Crocodilia, with thick scaly skin, long tail, and long jaws. **b** leather from its skin, used to make bags, shoes, etc. **2** *Brit.* *colloq.* a line of schoolchildren etc. walking in pairs. □ **crocodile clip** a clip with teeth for gripping. **crocodile tears** insincere grief (from the belief that crocodiles wept while devouring or alluring their prey). □□ **crocodilian** /-dílliən/ *adj.* [ME f. OF *cocodrille* f. med.L *cocodrillus* f. L *crocodilus* f. Gk *krokodilos* f. *krokē* pebble + *drilos* worm]

■ **2** see LINE[1] *n.* 9a.

crocus /krṓkəss/ *n.* (*pl.* **crocuses**) any dwarf plant of the genus *Crocus*, growing from a corm and having brilliant usu. yellow or purple flowers. [ME, = saffron, f. L f. Gk *krokos* crocus, of Semitic orig.]

Croesus /kréessəss/ *n.* a person of great wealth. [name of a king of Lydia (6th c. BC)]

croft /kroft/ *n.* & *v.* *Brit.* ● *n.* **1** an enclosed piece of (usu. arable) land. **2** a small rented farm in Scotland or N. England. ● *v.intr.* farm a croft; live as a crofter. [OE: orig. unkn.]

■ *n.* **2** see FARM *n.*

crofter /króftər/ *n.* *Brit.* a person who rents a smallholding, esp. a joint tenant of a divided farm in parts of Scotland.

croissant /krwússon/ *n.* a crescent-shaped roll made of rich yeast pastry. [F, formed as CRESCENT]

Cro-Magnon /krōmənyóɴ, -mágnən/ *adj.* *Anthropol.* of a tall broad-faced European race of late palaeolithic times. [name of a hill in the Dordogne, France, where remains were found in 1868]

cromlech /krómlekh/ *n.* **1** a dolmen; a megalithic tomb. **2** a circle of upright prehistoric stones. [Welsh f. *crom* fem. of *crwm* bent + *llech* flat stone]

crone /krōn/ *n.* **1** a withered old woman. **2** an old ewe. [ME, ult. f. ONF *carogne* CARRION]

■ **1** see HAG[1] 1.

cronk /krongk/ *adj.* *Austral.* *colloq.* **1** unsound; liable to collapse. **2 a** fraudulent. **b** (of a horse) dishonestly run, unfit. [19th c.: cf. CRANK[3]]

■ **1** see DODGY 1. **2 a** see FRAUDULENT 2.

crony /krṓni/ *n.* (*pl.* **-ies**) a close friend or companion. [17th-c. *chrony*, university sl. f. Gk *khronios* long-standing f. *khronos* time]

■ see FRIEND *n.* 1.

crook /krŏŏk/ *n.*, *v.*, & *adj.* ● *n.* **1** the hooked staff of a shepherd or bishop. **2 a** a bend, curve, or hook. **b** anything hooked or curved. **3** *colloq.* **a** a rogue; a swindler. **b** a professional criminal. ● *v.tr.* & *intr.* bend, curve. ● *adj.* **1** crooked. **2** *Austral.* & *NZ colloq.* **a** unsatisfactory, out of order; (of a person) unwell, injured. **b** unpleasant. **c** dishonest, unscrupulous. **d** bad-tempered, irritable, angry. □ **crook-back** a hunchback. **crook-backed** hunchbacked. **go crook** (usu. foll. by *at*, *on*) *Austral.* & *NZ colloq.* lose one's temper; become angry. □□ **crookery** *n.* [ME f. ON *krókr* hook]

■ *n.* **1** see STAFF[1] *n.* 1a, b. **2** see BEND[1] *n.* **3** see CRIMINAL *n.* ● *v.* see BEND[1] *v.* 1. ● *adj.* **2 a** see SICK[1] *adj.* 2. **d** see ANGRY 1.

crooked /krŏŏkid/ *adj.* (**crookeder**, **crookedest**) **1 a** not straight or level; bent, curved, twisted. **b** deformed, bent with age. **2** *colloq.* not straightforward; dishonest. **3** /krŏŏkt/ *Austral.* & *NZ sl.* = CROOK *adj.* 2. **4** (foll. by *on*) *Austral.* *sl.* hostile to. □□ **crookedly** *adv.* **crookedness** *n.* [ME f. CROOK, prob. after ON *krókóttr*]

■ **1** bent, bowed, curved, askew, awry, deformed, distorted, contorted, lopsided, twisted, misshapen, disfigured, warped, gnarled, *Brit.* *colloq.* boss-eyed. **2** criminal, dishonest, *sl.* bent; illegal, unlawful, illicit, wrong; perverse. **4** see HOSTILE 2.

croon /kroon/ *v.* & *n.* ● *v.tr.* & *intr.* hum or sing in a low subdued voice, esp. in a sentimental manner. ● *n.* such singing. □□ **crooner** *n.* [ME (orig. Sc. & N.Engl.) f. MDu. & MLG *krōnen* groan, lament]

■ *v.* see SING *v.* 1, 2.

crop /krop/ *n.* & *v.* ● *n.* **1 a** the produce of cultivated plants, esp. cereals. **b** the season's total yield of this (*a good crop*). **2** a group or an amount produced or appearing at one time (*this year's crop of students*). **3** (in full **hunting crop**) the stock or handle of a whip. **4 a** a style of hair cut very short. **b** the cropping of hair. **5** *Zool.* **a** the pouch in a bird's gullet where food is prepared for digestion. **b** a similar organ in other animals. **6** the entire tanned hide of an animal. **7** a piece cut off or out of something. ● *v.* (**cropped**, **cropping**) **1** *tr.* **a** cut off. **b** (of animals) bite off (the tops of plants). **2** *tr.* cut (hair, cloth, edges of a book, etc.) short. **3** *tr.* gather or reap (produce). **4** *tr.* (foll. by *with*) sow or plant (land) with a crop. **5** *intr.* (of land) bear a crop. □ **crop circle** a circular depression in a standing crop, often only visible from the air. **crop-dusting** the sprinkling of powdered insecticide or fertilizer on crops, esp. from the air. **crop-eared** having the ears (esp. of animals) or hair cut short. **crop-full** having a full crop or stomach. **crop out** *Geol.* appear at the surface. **crop-over** a W. Indian celebration marking the end of the sugar-cane harvest. **crop up 1** (of a subject, circumstance, etc.) appear or come to one's notice unexpectedly. **2** *Geol.* appear at the surface. [OE *crop(p)*]

■ *n.* **1** see HARVEST *n.* 2. **3** see WHIP *n.* ● *v.* **1, 2** see CUT *v.* 3a. □ **crop up 1** see ARISE 3.

cropper /króppər/ *n.* a crop-producing plant of specified quality (*a good cropper*; *a heavy cropper*). □ **come a cropper** *sl.* **1** fall heavily. **2** fail badly.

croquet /krṓkay, -ki/ *n.* & *v.* ● *n.* **1** a game played on a lawn, with wooden balls which are driven through a series of hoops with mallets. **2** the act of croqueting a ball. ● *v.tr.* (**croqueted** /-kayd/; **croqueting** /-kaying/) drive away (one's opponent's ball in croquet) by placing one's own against it and striking one's own. [perh. dial. form of F CROCHET hook]

croquette /krəkét/ *n.* a fried breaded roll or ball of mashed potato or minced meat etc. [F f. *croquer* crunch]

crore /kror/ *n. Ind.* **1** ten million. **2** one hundred lakhs (of rupees, units of measurement, persons, etc.). [Hindi *k(a)rōr*, ult. f. Skr. *koṭi* apex]

crosier /krṓziər, -zhər/ *n.* (also **crozier**) **1** a hooked staff carried by a bishop as a symbol of pastoral office. **2** a crook. [orig. = bearer of a crook, f. OF *crocier* & OF *croisier* f. *crois* CROSS]

cross /kross/ *n.*, *v.*, & *adj.* ● *n.* **1** an upright post with a transverse bar, as used in antiquity for crucifixion. **2 a** (**the Cross**) in Christianity, the cross on which Christ was crucified. **b** a representation of this as an emblem of Christianity. **c** = *sign of the cross*. **3** a staff surmounted by a cross and borne before an archbishop or in a religious procession. **4 a** a thing or mark shaped like a cross, esp. a figure made by two short intersecting lines (+ or x). **b** a monument in the form of a cross, esp. one in the centre of a town or on a tomb. **5** a cross-shaped decoration indicating rank in some orders of knighthood or awarded for personal valour. **6 a** an intermixture of animal breeds or plant varieties. **b** an animal or plant resulting from this. **7** (foll. by *between*) a mixture or compromise of two things. **8 a** a crosswise movement, e.g. of an actor on stage. **b** *Football* etc. a pass of the ball across the direction of play. **c** *Boxing* a blow with a crosswise movement of the fist. **9** a trial or affliction; something to be endured (*bear one's crosses*). ● *v.* **1** *tr.* (often foll. by *over*; also *absol.*) go across or to the other side of (a road, river, sea, etc.). **2 a** *intr.* intersect or be across one another (*the roads cross near the bridge*). **b** *tr.* cause to do this; place crosswise (*cross one's legs*). **3** *tr.* **a** draw a line or lines across. **b** *Brit.* mark (a cheque) with two parallel lines, and often an annotation, to indicate that it must be paid into a named bank account. **4** *tr.* (foll. by *off*, *out*, *through*) cancel or obliterate or remove from a list with lines drawn across. **5** *tr.* (often *refl.*) make the sign of the cross on or over. **6** *intr.* **a** pass in opposite or different directions. **b** (of letters between two correspondents) each be dispatched before receipt of the other. **c** (of telephone lines) become wrongly interconnected so that intrusive calls can be heard. **7** *tr.* **a** cause to interbreed. **b** cross-fertilize (plants). **8** *tr.* thwart or frustrate (*crossed in love*). **9** *tr. sl.* cheat. ● *adj.* **1** (often foll. by *with*) peevish, angry. **2** (usu. *attrib.*) transverse; reaching from side to side. **3** (usu. *attrib.*) intersecting. **4** (usu. *attrib.*) contrary, opposed, reciprocal. □ **as cross as two sticks** extremely angry or peevish. **at cross purposes** misunderstanding or conflicting with one another. **cross one's fingers** (or **keep one's fingers crossed**) **1** put one finger across another as a sign of hoping for good luck. **2** trust in good luck. **cross the floor** join the opposing side in a debating-assembly. **cross one's heart** make a solemn pledge, esp. by crossing one's front. **cross one's mind** (of a thought etc.) occur to one, esp. transiently. **cross a person's palm** (usu. foll. by *with*) pay a person for a favour. **cross the path of 1** meet with (a person). **2** thwart. **cross swords** (often foll. by *with*) encounter in opposition; have an argument or dispute. **cross wires** (or **get one's wires crossed**) **1** become wrongly connected by telephone. **2** have a misunderstanding. **on the cross 1** diagonally. **2** *sl.* fraudulently, dishonestly. □□ **crossly** *adv.* **crossness** *n.* [OE *cros* f. ON *kross* f. OIr. *cros* f. L *crux cruc-*]

■ *n.* **1, 2b** crucifix, rood. **6 b** hybrid, cross-breed, mongrel. **7** mixture, blend, combination. **9** see TRIAL 3. ● *v.* **1** cross over, go across, pass over, span, traverse. **2 a** intersect; meet, join. **4** (*cross off* or *out*) obliterate, strike out, erase, cancel, rub out, delete, wipe out. **7** interbreed, cross-breed, cross-fertilize, cross-pollinate. **8** see FRUSTRATE *v.* 2. ● *adj.* **1** irritated, annoyed, piqued, in a huff *or* mood, *colloq.* shirty; peevish, irritable, testy, snappish, irascible, crotchety, choleric, splenetic, grouchy, huffish, huffy, pettish, grumpy, touchy, moody, fractious, vexed, curmudgeonly, petulant, waspish, querulous, cantankerous, crusty, short-tempered, *esp. US* cranky, *colloq.* on a short fuse. □ **as cross as two sticks** see FURIOUS 1, 2. **cross one's fingers 2** hope *or* pray for the best, touch wood, keep one's fingers crossed, *US* knock (on) wood. **cross one's heart** see SWEAR *v.* 1a, 2. **cross one's mind** see OCCUR 2. **cross the path of 1** see MEET[1] *v.* 1. **cross swords** see CLASH *v.* 3a.

cross- /kross/ *comb. form* **1** denoting movement or position across something (*cross-channel*; *cross-country*). **2** denoting interaction (*cross-breed*; *cross-cultural*; *cross-fertilize*). **3 a** passing from side to side; transverse (*crossbar*; *cross-current*). **b** having a transverse part (*crossbow*). **4** describing the form or figure of a cross (*cross-keys*; *crossroads*).

crossbar /krósbaar/ *n.* a horizontal bar, esp. held on a pivot or between two upright bars etc., e.g. of a bicycle or of a football goal.

cross-bedding /krósbedding/ *n. Geol.* lines of stratification crossing the main rock strata. Also called *false bedding*.

cross-bench /krósbench/ *n. Brit.* a seat in Parliament (now only the House of Lords) occupied by a member not taking the whip from a political party. □□ **cross-bencher** *n.*

crossbill /krósbil/ *n.* any stout finch of the genus *Loxia*, having a bill with crossed mandibles for opening pine cones.

crossbones /krósbōnz/ *n.* a representation of two crossed thigh-bones (see SKULL).

crossbow /krósbō/ *n.* esp. *hist.* a bow fixed across a wooden stock, with a groove for an arrow and a mechanism for drawing and releasing the string. □□ **crossbowman** *n.* (*pl.* **-men**).

cross-breed *n.* & *v.* ● *n.* /krósbreed/ **1** a breed of animals or plants produced by crossing. **2** an individual animal or plant of a cross-breed. ● *v.tr.* /krósbreéd/ (*past* and *past part.* **-bred**) produce by crossing.

■ *n.* see HYBRID *n.* 1.

cross-check *v.* & *n.* ● *v.tr.* /króss-chék/ check by a second or alternative method, or by several methods. ● *n.* /króss-chek/ an instance of cross-checking.

cross-country /króskúntri/ *adj.* & *adv.* **1** across fields or open country. **2** not keeping to main or direct roads.

cross-cut *adj.* & *n.* ● *adj.* /króskút/ cut across the main grain or axis. ● *n.* /króskut/ a diagonal cut, path, etc. □ **cross-cut saw** a saw for cutting across the grain of wood.

cross-dating /krósdáyting/ *n. Archaeol.* dating by correlation with another site or level.

crosse /kross/ *n.* a stick with a triangular net at the end for conveying the ball in lacrosse. [F f. OF *croce*, *croc* hook]

cross-examine /króssigzámmin/ *v.tr.* examine (esp. a witness in a lawcourt) to check or extend testimony already given. □□ **cross-examination** /-náysh'n/ *n.* **cross-examiner** *n.*

cross-eyed /króssīd/ *adj.* (as a disorder) having one or both eyes turned permanently inwards towards the nose.

cross-fade /krósfáyd/ *v.intr. Radio* etc. fade in one sound as another is faded out.

cross-fertilize /krósfértilīz/ *v.tr.* (also **-ise**) **1** fertilize (an animal or plant) from one of a different species. **2** help by the interchange of ideas etc. □□ **cross-fertilization** /-záysh'n/ *n.*

crossfire /krósfīr/ *n.* **1** firing in two crossing directions simultaneously. **2 a** attack or criticism from several sources at once. **b** a lively or combative exchange of views etc.

cross-grain /krósgrayn/ *n.* a grain in timber, running across the regular grain.

cross-grained /krósgráynd/ *adj.* **1** (of timber) having a cross-grain. **2** perverse, intractable.

■ **2** see PERVERSE 2.

cross-hair /króss-hair/ *n.* a fine wire at the focus of an optical instrument for use in measurement.

cross-hatch /króss-hách/ *v.tr.* shade with intersecting sets of parallel lines.

cross-head /króss-hed/ *n.* **1** a bar between the piston-rod and connecting-rod in a steam engine. **2** = CROSS-HEADING.

cross-heading /króss-hedding/ *n.* a heading to a paragraph printed across a column in the body of an article in a newspaper etc.

crossing /króssing/ *n.* **1** a place where things (esp. roads) cross. **2** a place at which one may cross a street etc. (*pedestrian crossing*). **3** a journey across water (*had a smooth crossing*). **4** the intersection of a church nave and transepts. **5** *Biol.* mating. □ **crossing over** *Biol.* an exchange of genes between homologous chromosomes (cf. RECOMBINATION).
■ **1** see JUNCTION 2. **3** see PASSAGE[1] 1, 4.

cross-legged /krósslégd, -léggid/ *adj.* with one leg crossed over the other.

cross-link /króslingk/ *n.* (also **cross-linkage**) *Chem.* a bond between chains of atoms in a polymer etc.

crossmatch /krósmách/ *v.tr. Med.* test the compatibility of (a donor's and a recipient's blood). □□ **crossmatching** *n.*

crossover /króssōvər/ *n.* & *adj.* ● *n.* a point or place of crossing from one side to the other. ● *adj.* having a crossover.

crosspatch /króspach/ *n. colloq.* a bad-tempered person. [CROSS *adj.* 1 + obs. *patch* fool, clown]

crosspiece /króspeess/ *n.* a transverse beam or other component of a structure etc.

cross-ply /krósplī́/ *adj.* (of a tyre) having fabric layers with cords lying crosswise.

cross-pollinate /króspóllinayt/ *v.tr.* pollinate (a plant) from another. □□ **cross-pollination** /-náysh'n/ *n.*

cross-question /króskwéss-chən/ *v.tr.* = CROSS-EXAMINE.

cross-refer /krósrifér/ *v.intr.* (**-referred, -referring**) refer from one part of a book, article, etc., to another.

cross-reference /krósréfərənss/ *n.* & *v.* ● *n.* a reference from one part of a book, article, etc., to another. ● *v.tr.* provide with cross-references.

crossroad /krósrōd/ *n.* **1** (usu. in *pl.*) an intersection of two or more roads. **2** *US* a road that crosses a main road or joins two main roads. □ **at the crossroads** at a critical point in one's life.

cross-ruff /krósrúf/ *n.* & *v. Bridge* etc. ● *n.* the alternate trumping of partners' leads. ● *v.intr.* play in this way.

cross-section /króss-séksh'n/ *n.* **1 a** a cutting of a solid at right angles to an axis. **b** a plane surface produced in this way. **c** a representation of this. **2** a representative sample, esp. of people. **3** *Physics* a quantity expressing the probability of interaction between particles. □□ **cross-sectional** *adj.*
■ **2** see SAMPLE *n.* 1.

cross-stitch /króss-stich/ *n.* **1** a stitch formed of two stitches crossing each other. **2** needlework done using this stitch.

crosstalk /króss-tawk/ *n.* **1** unwanted transfer of signals between communication channels. **2** *Brit.* witty talk; repartee.

cross-trees /króss-treez/ *n.pl. Naut.* a pair of horizontal timbers at the top of a lower mast, supporting the topmast.

cross-voting /krósvōting/ *n.* voting for a party not one's own, or for more than one party.

crosswalk /króswawk/ *n. US* a pedestrian crossing.

crossways /krósswayz/ *adv.* = CROSSWISE.

crosswind /króswind/ *n.* a wind blowing across one's direction of travel.

crosswise /króswīz/ *adj.* & *adv.* **1** in the form of a cross; intersecting. **2** transverse or transversely.

crossword /króswurd/ *n.* (also **crossword puzzle**) a puzzle of a grid of squares and blanks into which words crossing vertically and horizontally have to be filled from clues.

crotch /kroch/ *n.* a place where something forks, esp. the legs of the human body or a garment (cf. CRUTCH). [perh. = ME & OF *croc(he)* hook, formed as CROOK]

crotchet /króchit/ *n.* **1** *Mus.* a note having the time value of a quarter of a semibreve and usu. representing one beat, drawn as a large dot with a stem. Also called *quarter note.* **2** a whimsical fancy. **3** a hook. [ME f. OF *crochet* dimin. of *croc* hook (see CROTCH)]
■ **2** see FANCY *n.* 2.

crotchety /króchiti/ *adj.* peevish, irritable. □□ **crotchetiness** *n.* [CROTCHET + -Y[1]]
■ see CROSS *adj.* 1, IRRITABLE 1.

croton /krṓt'n/ *n.* **1** any small tree or shrub of the genus *Croton*, producing a capsule-like fruit. **2** any small tree or shrub of the genus *Codiaeum*, esp. *C. variegatum*, with coloured ornamental leaves. □ **croton oil** a powerful purgative obtained from the fruit of *Croton tiglium.* [mod.L f. Gk *krotōn* sheep-tick, croton (from the shape of its seeds)]

crouch /krowch/ *v.* & *n.* ● *v.intr.* lower the body with the limbs close to the chest, esp. for concealment, or (of an animal) before pouncing; be in this position. ● *n.* an act of crouching; a crouching position. [ME, perh. f. OF *crochir* be bent f. *croc* hook: cf. CROOK]
■ *v.* bend (down), squat (down); scrunch down, stoop.
● *n.* squat, bend; see also STOOP[1] *n.* 1.

croup[1] /kro͞op/ *n.* an inflammation of the larynx and trachea in children, with a hard cough and difficulty in breathing. □□ **croupy** *adj.* [*croup* to croak (imit.)]

croup[2] /kro͞op/ *n.* the rump or hindquarters esp. of a horse. [ME f. OF *croupe*, rel. to CROP]
■ see TAIL[1] *n.* 1.

croupier /kro͞opiər, -iay/ *n.* **1** the person in charge of a gaming-table, raking in and paying out money etc. **2** the assistant chairperson at a public dinner, seated at the foot of the table. [F, orig. = rider on the croup: see CROUP[2]]

croûton /kro͞oton/ *n.* a small piece of fried or toasted bread served with soup or used as a garnish. [F f. *croûte* CRUST]

crow[1] /krō/ *n.* **1** any large black bird of the genus *Corvus*, having a powerful black beak. **2** any similar bird of the family Corvidae, e.g. the raven, rook, and jackdaw. **3** *sl. derog.* a woman, esp. an old or ugly one. □ **as the crow flies** in a straight line. **crow-bill** forceps for extracting bullets etc. **crow's-foot** (*pl.* **-feet**) **1** (usu. in *pl.*) a wrinkle at the outer corner of a person's eye. **2** *Mil.* a caltrop. **crow's-nest** a barrel or platform fixed at the masthead of a sailing vessel as a shelter for a lookout man. **crow steps** corbie-steps. **crow-toe** *archaic* or *dial.* any of various flowers, esp. the bluebell or buttercup. **eat crow** *US* submit to humiliation. [OE *crāwe* ult. f. WG]
■ □ **as the crow flies** see STRAIGHT *adv.* 1. **crow's-foot 1** see WRINKLE *n.* 1.

crow[2] /krō/ *v.* & *n.* ● *v.intr.* **1** (*past* **crowed** or **crew** /kro͞o/) (of a cock) utter its characteristic loud cry. **2** (of a baby) utter happy cries. **3** (usu. foll. by *over*) express unrestrained gleeful satisfaction. ● *n.* **1** the cry of a cock. **2** a happy cry of a baby. [OE *crāwan*, of imit. orig.]
■ *v.* **3** see GLOAT *v.*

crowbar /krṓbaar/ *n.* an iron bar with a flattened end, used as a lever.

crowberry /krṓbəri/ *n.* (*pl.* **-ies**) **1 a** a heathlike evergreen shrub *Empetrum nigrum*, bearing black berries. **b** the flavourless edible berry of this plant. **2** *US* a cranberry.

crowd /krowd/ *n.* & *v.* ● *n.* **1** a large number of people gathered together, usu. without orderly arrangement. **2** a mass of spectators; an audience. **3** *colloq.* a particular company or set of people (*met the crowd from the sales department*). **4** (prec. by *the*) the mass or multitude of people (*go along with the crowd*). **5** a large number (of things). **6** actors representing a crowd. ● *v.* **1 a** *intr.* come together in a crowd. **b** *tr.* cause to do this. **c** *intr.* force one's way. **2** *tr.* **a** (foll. by *into*) force or compress into a confined space. **b** (often foll. by *with*; usu. in *passive*) fill or make abundant with (*was crowded with tourists*). **3** *tr.* **a** (of a number of people) come aggressively close to. **b** *colloq.* harass or pressure (a person). □ **crowd out** exclude by crowding. □□ **crowdedness** *n.* [OE *crūdan* press, drive]

■ *n.* **1** throng, multitude, horde, host, swarm, mass, press, flood, mob, flock, pack. **3** company, set, circle, lot, gang, bunch, group, coterie, clique, claque, faction. **5** see MASS[1] *n.* 3. ● *v.* **1 a** throng, swarm, herd, pour, pile, press, cluster, gather, get together, flood, flock, assemble, congregate, collect. **2 a** compress, squeeze, pack, jam, stuff, cram, push, press, drive, shove, thrust, force, load. **b** see *packed out* (PACK[1]). **3 b** see HARASS 1.

crowfoot /krṓfŏŏt/ *n.* any of various aquatic plants of the genus *Ranunculus*, with white buttercup-like flowers held above the water.

crown /krown/ *n.* & *v.* ● *n.* **1** a monarch's ornamental and usu. jewelled head-dress. **2** (**the Crown**) **a** the monarch, esp. as head of State. **b** the power or authority residing in the monarchy. **3 a** a wreath of leaves or flowers etc. worn on the head, esp. as an emblem of victory. **b** an award or distinction gained by a victory or achievement, esp. in sport. **4** a crown-shaped thing, esp. a device or ornament. **5** the top part of a thing, esp. of the head or a hat. **6 a** the highest or central part of an arched or curved thing (*crown of the road*). **b** a thing that completes or forms the summit. **7** the part of a plant just above and below the ground. **8** the upper part of a cut gem above the girdle. **9 a** the part of a tooth projecting from the gum. **b** an artificial replacement or covering for this. **10 a** a former British coin equal to five shillings (25p). **b** any of several foreign coins with a name meaning 'crown', esp. the krona or krone. **11** a former size of paper, 504 x 384 mm. ● *v.tr.* **1** put a crown on (a person or a person's head). **2** invest (a person) with a royal crown or authority. **3** be a crown to; encircle or rest on the top of. **4 a** (often as **crowning** *adj.*) be or cause to be the consummation, reward, or finishing touch to (*the crowning glory*). **b** bring (efforts) to a happy issue. **5** fit a crown to (a tooth). **6** *sl.* hit on the head. □ **crown cap** a cork-lined metal cap for a bottle. **Crown Colony** a British colony controlled by the Crown. **Crown Court** a court of criminal jurisdiction in England and Wales. **Crown Derby** a soft-paste porcelain made at Derby and often marked with a crown above the letter 'D'. **crown glass** glass made without lead or iron and orig. in a circular sheet; used formerly in windows, now as optical glass of low refractive index. **crown green** a kind of bowling-green rising towards the middle. **crown imperial** a tall fritillary, *Fritillaria imperialis*, with a flower-cluster at the top of the stalk. **crown jewels** the regalia and other jewellery worn by the sovereign on certain State occasions. **Crown Office** (in the UK) an office of the Supreme Court transacting common-law business of Chancery. **crown of thorns** any starfish of the genus *Acanthaster* feeding on coral. **Crown prince** a male heir to a sovereign throne. **Crown princess** **1** the wife of a Crown prince. **2** a female heir to a sovereign throne. **crown roast** a roast of rib-pieces of pork or lamb arranged like a crown. **crown saw** a cylinder with a toothed edge for making a circular hole. **crown wheel** a wheel with teeth set at right angles to its plane, esp. in the gears of motor vehicles. [ME f. AF *corune*, OF *corone* f. L *corona*]

■ *n.* **1** coronet, diadem, circlet, tiara. **2 a** monarch, ruler, sovereign, potentate; king, queen; His *or* Her Majesty, His *or* Her Highness. **b** monarchy, government, *formal esp. Law* realm. ● *v.* **2** enthrone. **3** see ENCIRCLE 1, TOP[1] *v.* 1. **4** cap, top, surmount, culminate, climax, consummate, fulfil, reward. **6** see BRAIN *v.* 2.

crozier var. of CROSIER.

CRT *abbr.* cathode-ray tube.

cru /kroo/ *n.* **1** a French vineyard or wine-producing region. **2** the grade of wine produced from it. [F f. *crû* grown]

cruces *pl.* of CRUX.

crucial /kroosh'l/ *adj.* **1** decisive, critical. **2** *colloq. disp.* very important. **3** *sl.* excellent. □□ **cruciality** /-shiálliti/ *n.* (*pl.* **-ies**). **crucially** *adv.* [F f. L *crux crucis* cross]

■ **1** critical, decisive, pivotal, vital, momentous, essential, major; key. **3** see EXCELLENT.

crucian /kroosh'n/ *n.* a yellow cyprinoid fish, *Carassius carassius*, allied to the goldfish. [LG *karusse* etc.]

cruciate /krooshiayt/ *adj. Zool.* cross-shaped. [mod.L *cruciatus* f. L (as CRUCIBLE)]

crucible /kroossib'l/ *n.* **1** a melting-pot for metals etc. **2** a severe test or trial. [ME f. med.L *crucibulum* night-lamp, crucible, f. L *crux crucis* cross]

crucifer /kroossifər/ *n.* a cruciferous plant.

cruciferous /kroosíffərəss/ *adj. Bot.* of the family Cruciferae, having flowers with four petals arranged in a cross. [LL *crucifer* (as CRUCIAL, -FEROUS)]

crucifix /kroossifiks/ *n.* a model or image of a cross with a figure of Christ on it. [ME f. OF f. eccl.L *crucifixus* f. L *cruci fixus* fixed to a cross]

■ cross, rood.

crucifixion /kroossifiksh'n/ *n.* **1 a** crucifying or being crucified. **b** an instance of this. **2** (**Crucifixion**) **a** the crucifixion of Christ. **b** a representation of this. [eccl.L *crucifixio* (as CRUCIFIX)]

cruciform /kroossiform/ *adj.* cross-shaped (esp. of a church with transepts). [L *crux crucis* cross + -FORM]

crucify /kroossifī/ *v.tr.* (**-ies, -ied**) **1** put to death by fastening to a cross. **2 a** cause extreme pain to. **b** persecute, torment. **c** *sl.* defeat thoroughly in an argument, match, etc. □□ **crucifier** *n.* [ME f. OF *crucifier* f. LL *crucifigere* (as CRUCIFIX)]

■ **2** see TORMENT *v.* 1.

cruck /kruk/ *n. Brit. hist.* either of a pair of curved timbers extending to the ground in the framework of a type of medieval house-roof. [var. of CROOK]

crud /krud/ *n. sl.* **1 a** a deposit of unwanted impurities, grease, etc. **b** a corrosive deposit in a nuclear reactor. **2** an unpleasant person. **3** nonsense. □□ **cruddy** *adj.* (**cruddier, cruddiest**). [var. of CURD]

■ **1** see FILTH 1. □□ **cruddy** see FILTHY *adj.* 1.

crude /krood/ *adj.* & *n.* ● *adj.* **1 a** in the natural or raw state; not refined. **b** rough, unpolished; lacking finish. **2 a** (of an action or statement or manners) rude, blunt. **b** offensive, indecent (*a crude gesture*). **3 a** *Statistics* (of figures) not adjusted or corrected. **b** rough (*a crude estimate*). ● *n.* natural mineral oil. □□ **crudely** *adv.* **crudeness** *n.* **crudity** *n.* [ME f. L *crudus* raw, rough]

■ *adj.* **1 a** unrefined, raw, natural, original, unprocessed. **b** rough, unpolished, unfinished, rudimentary, immature, undeveloped, primitive, unrefined. **2 a** blunt, rough, coarse, rude, brusque, unsophisticated, indelicate, unrefined, uncouth, crass, gross, rustic, uncivil, impolite. **b** obscene, rude, indecent, offensive, vulgar, tasteless. **3** see ROUGH *adj.* 11a.

crudités /krooditáy/ *n.pl.* an hors-d'œuvre of mixed raw vegetables often served with a sauce into which they are dipped. [F]

cruel /krooəl/ *adj.* & *v.* ● *adj.* (**crueller, cruellest** or **crueler, cruelest**) **1** indifferent to or gratified by another's suffering. **2** causing pain or suffering, esp. deliberately. ● *v.tr.* (**cruelled, cruelling**) *Austral. sl.* thwart, spoil. □□ **cruelly** *adv.* **cruelness** *n.* [ME f. OF f. L *crudelis*, rel. to *crudus* (as CRUDE)]

■ *adj.* merciless, pitiless, hard-hearted, harsh, stony-hearted, heartless, unsparing, callous, sadistic, beastly, cold-blooded, ruthless, vicious, unkind, hard; ferocious, inhuman, barbaric, barbarous, brutal, brute, savage, fiendish. ● *v.* see THWART *v.*

cruelty /krooəlti/ *n.* (*pl.* **-ies**) **1** a cruel act or attitude; indifference to another's suffering. **2** a succession of cruel acts; a continued cruel attitude (*suffered much cruelty*). **3** *Law* physical or mental harm inflicted (whether or not intentional), esp. as a ground for divorce. □ **cruelty-free** (of cosmetics etc.) produced without involving any cruelty to animals in the development or manufacturing process. [OF *crualté* ult. f. L *crudelitas*]

cruet /kroo-it/ *n.* **1** a small container for salt, pepper, oil, or vinegar for use at table. **2** (in full **cruet-stand**) a stand holding cruets. **3** *Eccl.* a small container for the wine and the water in the celebration of the Eucharist. [ME through AF f. OF *crue* pot f. OS *krūka*: rel. to CROCK[2]]

cruise /krooz/ *v.* & *n.* ● *v.* **1** *intr.* make a journey by sea calling at a series of ports usu. according to a predetermined plan, esp. for pleasure. **2** *intr.* sail about without a precise destination. **3** *intr.* **a** (of a motor vehicle or aircraft) travel at a moderate or economical speed. **b** (of a vehicle or its driver) travel at random, esp. slowly. **4** *intr.* achieve an objective, win a race etc., with ease. **5** *intr.* & *tr. sl.* walk or drive about (the streets etc.) in search of a sexual (esp. homosexual) partner. ● *n.* a cruising voyage, esp. as a holiday. □ **cruise missile** one able to fly at a low altitude and guide itself by reference to the features of the region it traverses. **cruising speed** a comfortable and economical speed for a motor vehicle, below its maximum speed. [prob. f. Du. *kruisen* f. *kruis* CROSS]
■ *v.* **1** sail, coast, travel, journey, voyage. ● *n.* sail, voyage, journey, boat trip.

cruiser /kroozər/ *n.* **1** a warship of high speed and medium armament. **2** = *cabin cruiser*. **3** *US* a police patrol car. [Du. *kruiser* (as CRUISE)]

cruiserweight /kroozərwayt/ *n.* esp. *Brit.* = *light heavyweight* (see HEAVYWEIGHT).

cruller /krúllər/ *n.* *US* a small cake made of a rich dough twisted or curled and fried in fat. [prob. f. Du. *krullen* curl]

crumb /krum/ *n.* & *v.* ● *n.* **1 a** a small fragment, esp. of bread. **b** a small particle (*a crumb of comfort*). **2** the soft inner part of a loaf of bread. **3** *sl.* an objectionable person. ● *v.tr.* **1** cover with breadcrumbs. **2** break into crumbs. [OE *cruma*]
■ *n.* **1** fragment, morsel, bite, scrap, particle, shred, snippet, sliver, bit, speck, *colloq.* atom. **3** see WRETCH 2.

crumble /krúmb'l/ *v.* & *n.* ● *v.* **1** *tr.* & *intr.* break or fall into crumbs or fragments. **2** *intr.* (of power, a reputation, etc.) gradually disintegrate. ● *n.* **1** *Brit.* a mixture of flour and fat, rubbed to the texture of breadcrumbs and cooked as a topping for fruit etc. (*apple crumble*; *vegetable crumble*). **2** a crumbly or crumbled substance. [ME f. OE, formed as CRUMB]
■ *v.* **1** disintegrate, fragment, break apart, break up, shiver, come to pieces. **2** see COLLAPSE *v.*

crumbly /krúmbli/ *adj.* (**crumblier**, **crumbliest**) consisting of, or apt to fall into, crumbs or fragments. □□ **crumbliness** *n.*

crumbs /krumz/ *int. Brit. sl.* expressing dismay or surprise. [euphem. for *Christ*]

crumby /krúmmi/ *adj.* (**crumbier**, **crumbiest**) **1** like or covered in crumbs. **2** = CRUMMY.

crumhorn var. of KRUMMHORN.

crummy /krúmmi/ *adj.* (**crummier**, **crummiest**) *colloq.* dirty, squalid; inferior, worthless. □□ **crummily** *adv.* **crumminess** *n.* [var. of CRUMBY]
■ see INFERIOR *adj.* 2.

crump /krump/ *n.* & *v.* *Mil. sl.* ● *n.* the sound of a bursting bomb or shell. ● *v.intr.* make this sound. [imit.]

crumpet /krúmpit/ *n.* **1** a soft flat cake of a yeast mixture cooked on a griddle and eaten toasted and buttered. **2** *Brit. joc.* or *offens.* **a** a sexually attractive person, esp. a woman. **b** women regarded collectively, esp. as objects of sexual desire. **3** *archaic sl.* the head. [17th c.: orig. uncert.]
■ **2 a** see GIRL 2. **3** see HEAD *n.* 1.

crumple /krúmp'l/ *v.* & *n.* ● *v.* **1** *tr.* & *intr.* (often foll. by *up*) **a** crush or become crushed into creases. **b** ruffle, wrinkle. **2** *intr.* (often foll. by *up*) collapse, give way. ● *n.* a crease or wrinkle. □ **crumple zone** a part of a motor vehicle, esp. the extreme front and rear, designed to crumple easily in a crash and absorb impact. □□ **crumply** *adj.* [obs. *crump* (v. & adj.) (make or become) curved]
■ *v.* **1** wrinkle, crease, rumple, ruffle, crinkle, crush, mangle. **2** see COLLAPSE *v.* ● *n.* see WRINKLE *n.* 1, 2.

crunch /krunch/ *v.* & *n.* ● *v.* **1** *tr.* **a** crush noisily with the teeth. **b** grind (gravel, dry snow, etc.) under foot, wheels, etc. **2** *intr.* (often foll. by *up*, *through*) make a crunching sound in walking, moving, etc. ● *n.* **1** crunching; a crunching sound. **2** *colloq.* a decisive event or moment. [earlier *cra(u)nch*, assim. to *munch*]
■ *v.* **1 a** chew, bite, crush, grind, munch, champ, chomp, scrunch. ● *n.* **2** moment of truth, decision time, crisis, critical moment, showdown, crux, juncture.

crunchy /krúnchi/ *adj.* (**crunchier**, **crunchiest**) that can be or has been crunched or crushed into small pieces; hard and crispy. □□ **crunchily** *adv.* **crunchiness** *n.*
■ see CRISP *adj.* 1.

crupper /krúppər/ *n.* **1** a strap buckled to the back of a saddle and looped under the horse's tail to hold the harness back. **2** the hindquarters of a horse. [ME f. OF *cropiere* (cf. CROUP[2])]

crural /kroorəl/ *adj. Anat.* of the leg. [F *crural* or L *cruralis* f. *crus cruris* leg]

crusade /kroosáyd/ *n.* & *v.* ● *n.* **1 a** any of several medieval military expeditions made by Europeans to recover the Holy Land from the Muslims. **b** a war instigated by the Church for alleged religious ends. **2** a vigorous campaign in favour of a cause. ● *v.intr.* engage in a crusade. □□ **crusader** *n.* [earlier *croisade* (F f. *croix* cross) or *crusado* (Sp. f. *cruz* cross)]
■ *n.* **1 b** campaign, expedition, holy war; jihad. **2** see CAMPAIGN *n.* 1. ● *v.* campaign, war, battle; lobby, fight.

cruse /krooz/ *n. archaic* an earthenware pot or jar. [OE *crūse*, of unkn. orig.]

crush /krush/ *v.* & *n.* ● *v.tr.* **1** compress with force or violence, so as to break, bruise, etc. **2** reduce to powder by pressure. **3** crease or crumple by rough handling. **4** defeat or subdue completely (*crushed by my reply*). ● *n.* **1** an act of crushing. **2** a crowded mass of people. **3** a drink made from the juice of crushed fruit. **4** *colloq.* **a** (usu. foll. by *on*) a (usu. passing) infatuation. **b** the object of an infatuation (*who's the latest crush?*). □ **crush bar** a place in a theatre for audiences to buy drinks in the intervals. **crush barrier** a barrier, esp. a temporary one, for restraining a crowd. □□ **crushable** *adj.* **crusher** *n.* **crushingly** *adv.* [ME f. AF *crussir*, *corussier*, OF *croissir*, *cruissir*, gnash (teeth), crack, f. Rmc]
■ *v.* **1** break, smash, crunch, shiver, splinter; squash, pulp, mash, mangle, squeeze, compress, press. **2** pulverize, pound; see also GRIND *v.* 1a. **3** crumple, wrinkle, crease, crinkle, rumple. **4** overcome, defeat, conquer, beat, thrash, *literary* vanquish; subdue, put down, quash, quell, overwhelm, squelch, suppress, repress; mortify, depress, devastate. ● *n.* **2** press, crowd, squeeze, jam, squash. **4 a** (*have a crush on*) see LOVE *v.* 1. **b** see PASSION 3b.

crust /krust/ *n.* & *v.* ● *n.* **1 a** the hard outer part of a loaf of bread. **b** a piece of this with some soft bread attached. **c** a hard dry scrap of bread. **d** esp. *Austral. sl.* a livelihood (*what do you do for a crust?*). **2** the pastry covering of a pie. **3** a hard casing of a softer thing, e.g. a harder layer over soft snow. **4** *Geol.* the outer portion of the earth. **5 a** a coating or deposit on the surface of anything. **b** a hard dry formation on the skin, a scab. **6** a deposit of tartar formed in bottles of old wine. **7 a** *sl.* impudence (*you have a crust!*). **b** a superficial hardness of manner. ● *v.tr.* & *intr.* **1** cover or become covered with a crust. **2** form into a crust. □□ **crustal** *adj.* (in sense 4 of *n.*). [ME f. OF *crouste* f. L *crusta* rind, shell]
■ *n.* **1** see HEEL[1] *n.* 5. **3–5** see SKIN *n.* 4. **7 a** see GALL[1] 1.

crustacean /krustáysh'n/ *n.* & *adj.* ● *n.* any arthropod of the class Crustacea, having a hard shell and usu. aquatic, e.g. the crab, lobster, and shrimp. ● *adj.* of or relating to crustaceans. □□ **crustaceology** /-shióllәji/ *n.* **crustaceous** /-shәss/ *adj.* [mod.L *crustaceus* f. *crusta*: see CRUST]

crusted /krústid/ *adj.* **1 a** having a crust. **b** (of wine) having deposited a crust. **2** antiquated, venerable (*crusted prejudice*).

crusty /krústi/ *adj.* (**crustier**, **crustiest**) **1** having a crisp crust (*a crusty loaf*). **2** irritable, curt. **3** hard, crustlike. □□ **crustily** *adv.* **crustiness** *n.*
■ **2** see IRRITABLE 1.

crutch /kruch/ *n.* **1** a support for a lame person, usu. with a crosspiece at the top fitting under the armpit (*pair of crutches*). **2** any support or prop. **3** the crotch of the human body or garment. [OE *cryc(c)* f. Gmc]

crux /kruks/ *n.* (*pl.* **cruxes** or **cruces** /kroōsseez/) **1** the decisive point at issue. **2** a difficult matter; a puzzle. [L, = cross]

▪ **1** see NUB 1.

cruzado /kroozaádō/ *n.* (*pl.* **-os**) the chief monetary unit of Brazil from 1986. [Port. *cruzado, crusado,* = marked with the cross]

cruzeiro /kroozáirō/ *n.* (*pl.* **-os**) the former monetary unit of Brazil; from 1986 one-thousandth of a cruzado. [Port., = large cross]

cry /krī/ *v.* & *n.* ● *v.* (**cries, cried**) **1** *intr.* (often foll. by *out*) make a loud or shrill sound, esp. to express pain, grief, etc., or to appeal for help. **2 a** *intr.* shed tears; weep. **b** *tr.* shed (tears). **3** *tr.* (often foll. by *out*) say or exclaim loudly or excitedly. **4** *intr.* (of an animal, esp. a bird) make a loud call. **5** *tr.* (of a hawker etc.) proclaim (wares etc.) in the street. ● *n.* (*pl.* **cries**) **1** a loud inarticulate utterance of grief, pain, fear, joy, etc. **2** a loud excited utterance of words. **3** an urgent appeal or entreaty. **4** a spell of weeping. **5 a** public demand; a strong movement of opinion. **b** a watchword or rallying call. **6** the natural utterance of an animal, esp. of hounds on the scent. **7** the street-call of a hawker etc. □ **cry-baby** a person, esp. a child, who sheds tears frequently. **cry down** disparage, belittle. **cry one's eyes** (or **heart**) **out** weep bitterly. **cry for the moon** ask for what is unattainable. **cry from the heart** a passionate appeal or protest. **cry off** *colloq.* withdraw from a promise or undertaking. **cry out for** demand as a self-evident requirement or solution. **cry over spilt milk** see MILK. **cry stinking fish** disparage one's own efforts, products, etc. **cry up** praise, extol. **cry wolf** see WOLF. **a far cry 1** a long way. **2** a very different thing. **for crying out loud** *colloq.* an exclamation of surprise or annoyance. **in full cry** (of hounds) in keen pursuit. [ME f. OF *crier, cri* f. L *quiritare* wail]

▪ *v.* **1** see SHOUT *v.* **2 a** weep, sob, wail, keen, bawl, shed tears, whimper, snivel, mewl, *colloq.* turn on the waterworks, *Brit. colloq.* grizzle, *literary* pule. ● *n.* **1, 2** scream, shriek, wail, howl, yowl, screech, yelp, whoop, yell, shout. **3** see APPEAL *n.* 1. **5 b** war cry, battle-cry, rallying cry; slogan, watchword. **6** call, sound, note. □ **cry down** see DISPARAGE 1. **cry off** see WITHDRAW 5. **cry out for** demand, need, call *or* ask for, beg *or* plead for. **cry stinking fish** do *or* put oneself down, belittle oneself. **cry up** see PRAISE *v.* 1. **a far cry 1** a long way, quite a distance, remote, distant, far-away, far-off. **2** (*a far cry from*) not (at all), not quite *or* exactly, very different from, anything but.

cryer var. of CRIER.

crying /krī́-ing/ *attrib.adj.* (of an injustice or other evil) flagrant, demanding redress (*a crying need; a crying shame*).

cryo- /krī́ō/ *comb. form* (extreme) cold. [Gk *kruos* frost]

cryobiology /krī́ōbīóllәji/ *n.* the biology of organisms below their normal temperatures. □□ **cryobiological** /-bīәlójik'l/ *adj.* **cryobiologist** *n.*

cryogen /krī́ōjәn/ *n.* a freezing-mixture; a substance used to produce very low temperatures.

cryogenics /krī́ōjénniks/ *n.* the branch of physics dealing with the production and effects of very low temperatures. □□ **cryogenic** *adj.*

cryolite /krī́ōlīt/ *n. Mineral.* a lustrous mineral of sodium-aluminium fluoride, used in the manufacture of aluminium.

cryopump /krī́ōpump/ *n.* a vacuum pump using liquefied gases.

cryostat /krī́ōstat/ *n.* an apparatus for maintaining a very low temperature.

cryosurgery /krī́ōsúrjәri/ *n.* surgery using the local application of intense cold for anaesthesia or therapy.

crypt /kript/ *n.* an underground room or vault, esp. one beneath a church, used usu. as a burial-place. [ME f. L *crypta* f. Gk *kruptē* f. *kruptos* hidden]

▪ tomb, vault, mausoleum, sepulchre, grave, catacomb; cellar, basement.

cryptanalysis /kríptәnállisiss/ *n.* the art or process of deciphering cryptograms by analysis. □□ **cryptanalyst** /-ánnәlist/ *n.* **cryptanalytic** /-anәlíttik/ *adj.* **cryptanalytical** /-anәlíttik'l/ *adj.* [CRYPTO- + ANALYSIS]

cryptic /kríptik/ *adj.* **1 a** obscure in meaning. **b** (of a crossword clue etc.) indirect; indicating the solution in a way that is not obvious. **c** secret, mysterious, enigmatic. **2** *Zool.* (of coloration etc.) serving for concealment. □□ **cryptically** *adv.* [LL *crypticus* f. Gk *kruptikos* (as CRYPTO-)]

▪ **1 a** obscure, unclear, nebulous, vague, inscrutable, recondite, puzzling. **c** secret, occult, mystical, hidden, esoteric, mystic, cabbalistic; mysterious, arcane, enigmatic.

crypto /kríptō/ *n.* (*pl.* **-os**) *colloq.* a person having a secret allegiance to a political creed etc., esp. communism. [as CRYPTO-]

crypto- /kríptō/ *comb. form* concealed, secret (*crypto-communist*). [Gk *kruptos* hidden]

cryptocrystalline /kríptōkrístәlīn/ *adj.* having a crystalline structure visible only when magnified.

cryptogam /kríptәgam/ *n.* a plant that has no true flowers or seeds, e.g. ferns, mosses, algae, and fungi. □□ **cryptogamic** /-gámmik/ *adj.* **cryptogamous** /-tóggәmәss/ *adj.* [F *cryptogame* f. mod.L *cryptogamae* (*plantae*) formed as CRYPTO- + Gk *gamos* marriage]

cryptogram /kríptәgram/ *n.* a text written in cipher.

cryptography /kriptógrәfi/ *n.* the art of writing or solving ciphers. □□ **cryptographer** *n.* **cryptographic** /-tәgráffik/ *adj.* **cryptographically** /-tәgráffikәli/ *adv.*

▪ □□ **cryptographic** see SECRET *adj.* 1.

cryptomeria /kríptәmeériә/ *n.* a tall evergreen tree, *Cryptomeria japonica*, native to China and Japan, with long curved spirally arranged leaves and short cones. Also called *Japanese cedar.* [CRYPTO- + Gk *meros* part (because the seeds are enclosed by scales)]

crystal /kríst'l/ *n.* & *adj.* ● *n.* **1 a** a clear transparent mineral, esp. rock crystal. **b** a piece of this. **2** (in full **crystal glass**) **a** highly transparent glass; flint glass. **b** articles made of this. **3** the glass over a watch-face. **4** *Electronics* a crystalline piece of semiconductor. **5** *Chem.* **a** an aggregation of molecules with a definite internal structure and the external form of a solid enclosed by symmetrically arranged plane faces. **b** a solid whose constituent particles are symmetrically arranged. ● *adj.* (usu. *attrib.*) made of, like, or clear as crystal. □ **crystal ball** a glass globe used in crystal-gazing. **crystal class** *Crystallog.* any of 32 categories of crystals classified according to their symmetry. **crystal clear** unclouded, transparent. **crystal-gazing** the process of concentrating one's gaze on a crystal ball supposedly in order to obtain a picture of future events etc. **crystal lattice** *Crystallog.* the regular repeating pattern of atoms, ions, or molecules in a crystalline substance. **crystal set** a simple early form of radio receiving apparatus with a crystal touching a metal wire as the rectifier. **crystal system** *Crystallog.* any of seven possible unique combinations of unit cells, crystal lattices, and symmetry elements of a crystal class. [OE f. OF *cristal* f. L *crystallum* f. Gk *krustallos* ice, crystal]

▪ *n.* **1 b** see GRAIN *n.* 3. □ **crystal clear** see PLAIN[1] *adj.* 1, 2. **crystal-gazing** see PROPHECY 2.

crystalline /krístәlīn/ *adj.* **1** of, like, or clear as crystal. **2** *Chem.* & *Mineral.* having the structure and form of a crystal. □ **crystalline lens** a transparent lens enclosed in a membranous capsule behind the iris of the eye. □□ **crystallinity** /-línniti/ *n.* [ME f. OF *cristallin* f. L *crystallinus* f. Gk *krustallinos* (as CRYSTAL)]

▪ **1** see CLEAR *adj.* 3a.

crystallite /krístәlīt/ *n.* **1** a small crystal. **2** an individual perfect crystal or grain in a metal etc. **3** *Bot.* a region of cellulose etc. with a crystal-like structure.

crystallize /krístəlīz/ *v.* (also **-ise**) **1** *tr.* & *intr.* form or cause to form crystals. **2** (often foll. by *out*) **a** *intr.* (of ideas or plans) become definite. **b** *tr.* make definite. **3** *tr.* & *intr.* coat or impregnate or become coated or impregnated with sugar (*crystallized fruit*). ▫▫ **crystallizable** *adj.* **crystallization** /-záysh'n/ *n.*
■ **2** see FORM *v.* 2. ▫▫ **crystallization** see FORMATION 1, 2.

crystallography /krístəlógrəfi/ *n.* the science of crystal form and structure. ▫▫ **crystallographer** *n.* **crystallographic** /-ləgráffik/ *adj.*

crystalloid /krístəloyd/ *adj.* & *n.* ● *adj.* **1** crystal-like. **2** having a crystalline structure. ● *n.* a substance that in solution is able to pass through a semipermeable membrane (cf. COLLOID).

CS *abbr.* **1** Civil Service. **2** chartered surveyor. **3** Court of Session.

Cs *symb. Chem.* the element caesium.

c/s *abbr.* cycles per second.

csardas /chaárdaash/ *n.* (also **czardas**) (*pl.* same) a Hungarian dance with a slow start and a quick wild finish. [Magyar *csárdás* f. *csárda* inn]

CSC *abbr.* **1** Civil Service Commission. **2** Conspicuous Service Cross.

CSE *abbr. hist.* (in the UK) Certificate of Secondary Education. ¶ Replaced in 1988 by GCSE.

CS gas /seé-éss/ *n.* a gas causing tears and choking, used to control riots etc. [B. B. *C*orson & R. W. *S*toughton, Amer. chemists]

CSI *abbr.* Companion of the Order of the Star of India.

CSIRO *abbr.* Commonwealth Scientific and Industrial Research Organization.

CSM *abbr.* (in the UK) Company Sergeant-Major.

CST *abbr.* (in the US) Central Standard Time.

CSU *abbr.* (in the UK) Civil Service Union.

CT *abbr. US* Connecticut (in official postal use).

ct. *abbr.* **1** carat. **2** cent.

CTC *abbr.* **1** (in the UK) Cyclists' Touring Club. **2** (in the UK) City Technology College.

ctenoid /teénoyd, tén-/ *adj. Zool.* (of fish scales) characterized by tiny toothlike processes (cf. PLACOID). [Gk *kteis ktenos* comb]

ctenophore /teénəfor, tén-/ *n.* any marine animal of the phylum Ctenophora, having a jellyfish-like body bearing rows of cilia, e.g. sea gooseberries. [mod.L *ctenophorus* (as CTENOID)]

CU *abbr.* Cambridge University.

Cu *symb. Chem.* the element copper.

cu. *abbr.* cubic.

cub /kub/ *n.* & *v.* ● *n.* **1** the young of a fox, bear, lion, etc. **2** an ill-mannered young man. **3** (**Cub**) (in full **Cub Scout**) a member of the junior branch of the Scout Association. **4** (in full **cub reporter**) *colloq.* a young or inexperienced newspaper reporter. **5** *US* an apprentice. ● *v.tr.* (**cubbed, cubbing**) (also *absol.*) give birth to (cubs). ▫▫ **cubhood** *n.* [16th c.: orig. unkn.]
■ **2** see PUP *n.* 3.

Cuban /kyoōb'n/ *adj.* & *n.* ● *adj.* of or relating to Cuba, an island republic in the Caribbean, or its people. ● *n.* a native or national of Cuba. ▫ **Cuban heel** a moderately high straight heel of a man's or woman's shoe.

cubby /kúbbi/ *n.* (*pl.* **-ies**) (in full **cubby-hole**) **1** a very small room. **2** a snug or confined space. [dial. *cub* stall, pen, of LG orig.]
■ **2** see SANCTUM 2, COMPARTMENT *n.* 1.

cube /kyoōb/ *n.* & *v.* ● *n.* **1** a solid contained by six equal squares. **2** a cube-shaped block. **3** *Math.* the product of a number multiplied by its square. ● *v.tr.* **1** find the cube of (a number). **2** cut (food for cooking etc.) into small cubes. ▫ **cube root** the number which produces a given number when cubed. ▫▫ **cuber** *n.* [F *cube* or L *cubus* f. Gk *kubos*]
■ *n.* **2** see BLOCK *n.* 1. ● *v.* **2** see *cut up* 1.

cubeb /kyoōbeb/ *n.* **1** a climbing plant, *Piper cubeba*, bearing pungent berries. **2** this berry crushed for use in medicated cigarettes. [ME f. OF *cubebe*, *quibibe* ult. f. Arab. *kobāba*, *kubāba*]

cubic /kyoōbik/ *adj.* **1** cube-shaped. **2** of three dimensions. **3** involving the cube (and no higher power) of a number (*cubic equation*). **4** *Crystallog.* having three equal axes at right angles. ▫ **cubic content** the volume of a solid expressed in cubic metres. **cubic metre** etc. the volume of a cube whose edge is one metre etc. [F *cubique* or L *cubicus* f. Gk *kubikos* (as CUBE)]
■ **2** solid, three-dimensional.

cubical /kyoōbik'l/ *adj.* cube-shaped. ▫▫ **cubically** *adv.*

cubicle /kyoōbik'l/ *n.* **1** a small partitioned space, screened for privacy. **2** a small separate sleeping-compartment. [L *cubiculum* f. *cubare* lie down]
■ **1** see BOOTH 2.

cubiform /kyoōbiform/ *adj.* cube-shaped.

cubism /kyoōbiz'm/ *n.* a style and movement in art, esp. painting, in which objects are represented as an assemblage of geometrical forms. ▫▫ **cubist** *n.* & *adj.* [F *cubisme* (as CUBE)]

cubit /kyoōbit/ *n.* an ancient measure of length, approximately equal to the length of a forearm. [ME f. L *cubitum* elbow, cubit]

cubital /kyoōbit'l/ *adj.* **1** *Anat.* of the forearm. **2** *Zool.* of the corresponding part in animals. [ME f. L *cubitalis* (as CUBIT)]

cuboid /kyoōboyd/ *adj.* & *n.* ● *adj.* cube-shaped; like a cube. ● *n.* **1** *Geom.* a rectangular parallelepiped. **2** (in full **cuboid bone**) *Anat.* the outer bone of the tarsus. ▫▫ **cuboidal** /-bóyd'l/ *adj.* [mod.L *cuboides* f. Gk *kuboeidēs* (as CUBE)]

cucking-stool /kúkkingstōol/ *n. hist.* a chair on which disorderly women were ducked as a punishment. [ME f. obs. *cuck* defecate]

cuckold /kúkkōld/ *n.* & *v.* ● *n.* the husband of an adulteress. ● *v.tr.* make a cuckold of. ▫▫ **cuckoldry** *n.* [ME *cukeweld*, *cokewold*, f. OF *cucu* cuckoo]

cuckoo /kóokkōo/ *n.* & *adj.* ● *n.* any bird of the family Cuculidae, esp. *Cuculus canorus*, having a characteristic cry, and depositing its eggs in the nests of small birds. ● *predic.adj. sl.* crazy, foolish. ▫ **cuckoo clock** a clock that strikes the hour with a sound like a cuckoo's call, usu. with the emergence on each note of a mechanical cuckoo. **cuckoo flower 1** a meadow plant, *Cardamine pratensis*, with pale lilac flowers. **2** = *ragged robin*. **cuckoo in the nest** an unwelcome intruder. **cuckoo-pint** a wild arum, *Arum maculatum*, with arrow-shaped leaves and scarlet berries: also called *lords and ladies* (see LORD). **cuckoo-spit** froth exuded by larvae of insects of the family Cercopidae on leaves, stems, etc. [ME f. OF *cucu*, imit.]
■ *adj.* see CRAZY 1.

cucumber /kyoōkumbər/ *n.* **1** a long green fleshy fruit, used in salads. **2** the climbing plant, *Cucumis sativus*, yielding this fruit. [ME f. OF *co(u)combre* f. L *cucumer*]

cucurbit /kyookúrbit/ *n.* = GOURD. ▫▫ **cucurbitaceous** /-táyshəss/ *adj.* [L *cucurbita*]

cud /kud/ *n.* half-digested food returned from the first stomach of ruminants to the mouth for further chewing. [OE *cwidu*, *cudu* what is chewed, corresp. to OHG *kuti*, *quiti* glue]

cuddle /kúdd'l/ *v.* & *n.* ● *v.* **1** *tr.* hug, embrace, fondle. **2** *intr.* nestle together, lie close and snug; kiss and fondle amorously. ● *n.* a prolonged and fond hug. ▫▫ **cuddlesome** *adj.* [16th c.: perh. f. dial. *couth* snug]
■ *v.* **1** see CARESS *v.* **2** nestle together, embrace, snuggle up, bill and coo; pet, *Austral.* & *NZ* smoodge, *archaic* make love, *colloq.* neck, smooch, *Brit. sl.* snog. ● *n.* see CARESS *n.*

cuddly /kúdli/ *adj.* (**cuddlier, cuddliest**) tempting to cuddle; given to cuddling.

cuddy /kúddi/ *n.* (*pl.* **-ies**) *Sc.* **1** a donkey. **2** a stupid person. [perh. a pet-form of the name *Cuthbert*]

cudgel /kújəl/ *n.* & *v.* ● *n.* a short thick stick used as a weapon. ● *v.tr.* (**cudgelled, cudgelling**; *US* **cudgeled,**

cudgeling) beat with a cudgel. □ **cudgel one's brains** think hard about a problem. **take up the cudgels** (often foll. by *for*) make a vigorous defence. [OE *cycgel*, of unkn. orig.]
■ *n.* see CLUB *n.* 1. ● *v.* see CLUB *v.* 1. □ **cudgel one's brains** see WONDER *v.* 3.

cudweed /kúdweed/ *n.* any wild composite plant of the genus *Gnaphalium*, with scales and round flower-heads, formerly given to cattle that had lost their cud.

cue[1] /kyōō/ *n.* & *v.* ● *n.* **1 a** the last words of an actor's speech serving as a signal to another actor to enter or speak. **b** a similar signal to a singer or player etc. **2 a** a stimulus to perception etc. **b** a signal for action. **c** a hint on how to behave in particular circumstances. **3** a facility for or an instance of cueing audio equipment (see sense 2 of *v.*). ● *v.tr.* (**cues, cued, cueing** or **cuing**) **1** give a cue to. **2** put (a piece of audio equipment, esp. a record-player or tape recorder) in readiness to play a particular part of the recorded material. □ **cue-bid** *Bridge* an artificial bid to show a particular card etc. in the bidder's hand. **cue in 1** insert a cue for. **2** give information to. **on cue** at the correct moment. **take one's cue from** follow the example or advice of. [16th c.: orig. unkn.]
■ *n.* **1, 2** prompt, hint, reminder, signal, sign. ● *v.* **1** signal, prompt, remind. □ **take one's cue from** see FOLLOW 5.

cue[2] /kyōō/ *n.* & *v.* *Billiards* etc. ● *n.* a long straight tapering rod for striking the ball. ● *v.* (**cues, cued, cueing** or **cuing**) **1** *tr.* strike (a ball) with a cue. **2** *intr.* use a cue. □ **cue-ball** the ball that is to be struck with the cue. □□ **cueist** *n.* [var. of QUEUE]

cuesta /kwéstə/ *n. Geog.* a gentle slope, esp. one ending in a steep drop. [Sp., = slope, f. L *costa*: see COAST]
■ see CLIFF.

cuff[1] /kuf/ *n.* **1 a** the end part of a sleeve. **b** a separate band of linen worn round the wrist so as to appear under the sleeve. **c** the part of a glove covering the wrist. **2** *US* a trouser turn-up. **3** (in *pl.*) *colloq.* handcuffs. □ **cuff-link** a device of two joined studs etc. to fasten the sides of a cuff together. **off the cuff** *colloq.* without preparation, extempore. □□ **cuffed** *adj.* (also in *comb.*). [ME: orig. unkn.]
■ □ **off the cuff** see EXTEMPORANEOUS.

cuff[2] /kuf/ *v.* & *n.* ● *v.tr.* strike with an open hand. ● *n.* such a blow. [16th c.: perh. imit.]
■ *v.* see HIT *v.* 1a. ● *n.* see BLOW[2] 1.

Cufic var. of KUFIC.

cui bono? /kweé bónnō, bṓ-/ who stands, or stood, to gain? (with the implication that this person is responsible). [L, = to whom (is it) a benefit?]

cuirass /kwiráss/ *n.* **1** *hist.* a piece of armour consisting of breastplate and back-plate fastened together. **2** a device for artificial respiration. [ME f. OF *cuirace*, ult. f. LL *coriaceus* f. *corium* leather]

cuirassier /kwirrəseér/ *n. hist.* a cavalry soldier wearing a cuirass. [F (as CUIRASS)]

cuish var. of CUISSE.

cuisine /kwizeén/ *n.* a style or method of cooking, esp. of a particular country or establishment. [F f. L *coquina* f. *coquere* to cook]

cuisse /kwiss/ *n.* (also **cuish** /kwish/) (usu. in *pl.*) *hist.* thigh armour. [ME, f. OF *cuisseaux* pl. of *cuissel* f. LL *coxale* f. *coxa* hip]

cul-de-sac /kúldəsak, kŏŏl-/ *n.* (*pl.* **culs-de-sac** /*pronunc.* same/) **1** a street or passage closed at one end. **2** a route or course leading nowhere; a position from which one cannot escape. **3** *Anat.* = DIVERTICULUM. [F, = sack-bottom]

-cule /kyōōl/ *suffix* forming (orig. diminutive) nouns (*molecule*). [F *-cule* or L *-culus*]

culinary /kúllinəri/ *adj.* of or for cooking or the kitchen. □□ **culinarily** *adv.* [L *culinarius* f. *culina* kitchen]

cull /kul/ *v.* & *n.* ● *v.tr.* **1** select, choose, or gather from a large quantity or amount (*knowledge culled from books*). **2** pick or gather (flowers, fruit, etc.). **3** select (animals) according to quality, esp. poor surplus specimens for killing. ● *n.* **1** an act of culling. **2** an animal or animals culled. □□ **culler** *n.* [ME f. OF *coillier* etc. ult. f. L *colligere* COLLECT[1]]
■ *v.* see PICK[1] *v.* 1.

cullet /kúllit/ *n.* recycled waste or broken glass used in glass-making. [var. of COLLET]

culm[1] /kulm/ *n.* **1** coal-dust, esp. of anthracite. **2** *Geol.* strata under coal measures, esp. in SW England. [ME, prob. rel. to COAL]

culm[2] /kulm/ *n. Bot.* the stem of a plant, esp. of grasses. □□ **culmiferous** /-míffərəss/ *adj.* [L *culmus* stalk]

culminant /kúlminənt/ *adj.* **1** at or forming the top. **2** *Astron.* on the meridian. [as CULMINATE + -ANT]

culminate /kúlminayt/ *v.* **1** *intr.* (usu. foll. by *in*) reach its highest or final point (*the antagonism culminated in war*). **2** *tr.* bring to its highest or final point. **3** *intr. Astron.* be on the meridian. □□ **culmination** /-náysh'n/ *n.* [LL *culminare culminat-* f. *culmen* summit]
■ **1, 2** see FINISH *v.* 2a.

culottes /kyoolóts/ *n.pl.* women's (usu. short) trousers cut to resemble a skirt. [F, = knee-breeches]

culpable /kúlpəb'l/ *adj.* deserving blame. □□ **culpability** /-bílliti/ *n.* **culpably** *adv.* [ME f. OF *coupable* f. L *culpabilis* f. *culpare* f. *culpa* blame]
■ see GUILTY 1, 4.

culprit /kúlprit/ *n.* a person accused of or guilty of an offence. [17th c.: orig. in the formula *Culprit, how will you be tried?*, said by the Clerk of the Crown to a prisoner pleading Not Guilty: perh. abbr. of AF *Culpable: prest d'averrer* etc. (You are) guilty: (I am) ready to prove etc.]
■ offender, criminal, malefactor, wrongdoer.

cult /kult/ *n.* **1** a system of religious worship esp. as expressed in ritual. **2 a** devotion or homage to a person or thing (*the cult of aestheticism*). **b** a popular fashion esp. followed by a specific section of society. **3** (*attrib.*) denoting a person or thing popularized in this way (*cult film; cult figure*). □□ **cultic** *adj.* **cultism** *n.* **cultist** *n.* [F *culte* or L *cultus* worship f. *colere cult-* inhabit, till, worship]
■ □□ **cultist** see SECTARIAN *n.* 1.

cultivar /kúltivaar/ *n. Bot.* a plant variety produced by cultivation. [CULTIVATE + VARIETY]

cultivate /kúltivayt/ *v.tr.* **1 a** prepare and use (soil etc.) for crops or gardening. **b** break up (the ground) with a cultivator. **2 a** raise or produce (crops). **b** culture (bacteria etc.). **3 a** (often as **cultivated** *adj.*) apply oneself to improving or developing (the mind, manners, etc.). **b** pay attention to or nurture (a person or a person's friendship); ingratiate oneself with (a person). □□ **cultivable** *adj.* **cultivatable** *adj.* **cultivation** /-váysh'n/ *n.* [med.L *cultivare* f. *cultiva* (*terra*) arable (land) (as CULT)]
■ **1 a** till, plough, farm, work. **2 a** grow, raise, tend, produce. **3 a** (**cultivated**) sophisticated, cultured, educated, refined, elegant, *soigné*, civilized, polished, aristocratic, urbane, suave, cosmopolitan. **b** develop, nurture, work on, pay attention to, promote, further, encourage, foster, advance; woo, court, make advances to; ingratiate oneself with, pay court to, curry favour with, *US* shine up to, *sl.* suck up to, butter up. □□ **cultivation** see CULTURE *n.* 1b, *farming* (FARM).

cultivator /kúltivaytər/ *n.* **1** a mechanical implement for breaking up the ground and uprooting weeds. **2** a person or thing that cultivates.

cultural /kúlchərəl/ *adj.* of or relating to the cultivation of the mind or manners, esp. through artistic or intellectual activity. □□ **culturally** *adv.*

culture /kúlchər/ *n.* & *v.* ● *n.* **1 a** the arts and other manifestations of human intellectual achievement regarded collectively (*a city lacking in culture*). **b** a refined understanding of this; intellectual development (*a person of culture*). **2** the customs, civilization, and achievements of a particular time or people (*studied Chinese culture*). **3** improvement by mental or physical training. **4 a** the cultivation of plants; the rearing of bees, silkworms, etc. **b** the cultivation of the soil. **5** a quantity of micro-organisms and the nutrient material supporting their growth. ● *v.tr.*

maintain (bacteria etc.) in conditions suitable for growth. □ **culture shock** the feeling of disorientation experienced by a person suddenly subjected to an unfamiliar culture or way of life. **culture vulture** *colloq.* a person eager to acquire culture. **the two cultures** the arts and science. [ME f. F *culture* or L *cultura* (as CULT): (v.) f. obs. F *culturer* or med.L *culturare*]

■ *n.* **1 b** cultivation, refinement, sophistication, urbanity, suavity, elegance, (good) breeding, background, erudition, education, enlightenment, learning, taste, discrimination, *savoir faire*, *savoir vivre*, discernment. **2** civilization, mores, customs, lifestyle, way of life, (sense of) values. **4** see BREEDING 1, *farming* (FARM).

cultured /kúlchərd/ *adj.* having refined taste and manners and a good education. □ **cultured pearl** a pearl formed by an oyster after the insertion of a foreign body into its shell.

cultus /kúltəss/ *n.* a system of religious worship; a cult. [L: see CULT]

culverin /kúlvərin/ *n. hist.* **1** a long cannon. **2** a small firearm. [ME f. OF *coulevrine* f. *couleuvre* snake ult. f. L *colubra*]

culvert /kúlvərt/ *n.* **1** an underground channel carrying water across a road etc. **2** a channel for an electric cable. [18th c.: orig. unkn.]

■ **1** see DRAIN *n.* 1a.

cum /kum/ *prep.* (usu. in *comb.*) with, combined with, also used as (*a bedroom-cum-study*). [L]

cumber /kúmbər/ *v.* & *n.* ● *v.tr. literary* hamper, hinder, inconvenience. ● *n.* a hindrance, obstruction, or burden. [ME, prob. f. ENCUMBER]

■ *v.* see OVERLOAD *v.*

cumbersome /kúmbərsəm/ *adj.* inconvenient in size, weight, or shape; unwieldy. □□ **cumbersomely** *adv.* **cumbersomeness** *n.* [ME f. CUMBER + -SOME[1]]

■ see UNWIELDY.

Cumbrian /kúmbriən/ *adj.* & *n.* ● *adj.* **1** of Cumberland. **2 a** of the ancient British kingdom of Cumbria. **b** of the modern county of Cumbria. ● *n.* a native of Cumberland or of ancient or modern Cumbria. [med.L *Cumbria* f. Welsh *Cymry* Welshmen + -AN]

cumbrous /kúmbrəss/ *adj.* = CUMBERSOME. □□ **cumbrously** *adv.* **cumbrousness** *n.* [CUMBER + -OUS]

cum grano salis /kúm graánō saáliss/ *adv.* with a grain of salt (see *take with a pinch of salt* (see SALT)). [L]

cumin /kúmmin/ *n.* (also **cummin**) **1** an umbelliferous plant, *Cuminum cyminum*, bearing aromatic seeds. **2** these seeds used as flavouring, esp. ground and used in curry powder. [ME f. OF *cumin*, *comin* f. L *cuminum* f. Gk *kuminon*, prob. of Semitic orig.]

cummerbund /kúmmərbund/ *n.* a waist sash. [Hind. & Pers. *kamar-band* loin-band]

cummin var. of CUMIN.

cumquat var. of KUMQUAT.

cumulate *v.* & *adj.* ● *v.tr.* & *intr.* /kyoōmyoolayt/ accumulate, amass; combine. ● *adj.* /kyoōmyoolət/ heaped up, massed. □□ **cumulation** /-láysh'n/ *n.* [L *cumulare* f. *cumulus* heap]

■ *v.* see ACCUMULATE 1.

cumulative /kyoōmyoolətiv/ *adj.* **1 a** increasing or increased in amount, force, etc., by successive additions (*cumulative evidence*). **b** formed by successive additions (*learning is a cumulative process*). **2** *Stock Exch.* (of shares) entitling holders to arrears of interest before any other distribution is made. □ **cumulative error** an error that increases with the size of the sample revealing it. **cumulative voting** a system in which each voter has as many votes as there are candidates and may give all to one candidate. □□ **cumulatively** *adv.* **cumulativeness** *n.*

cumulo- /kyoōmyoolō/ *comb. form* cumulus (cloud).

cumulus /kyoōmyooləss/ *n.* (*pl.* **cumuli** /-lī/) a cloud formation consisting of rounded masses heaped on each other above a horizontal base. □□ **cumulous** *adj.* [L, = heap]

cuneate /kyoōniət/ *adj.* wedge-shaped. [L *cuneus* wedge]

cuneiform /kyoōniform/ *adj.* & *n.* ● *adj.* **1** wedge-shaped. **2** of, relating to, or using the wedge-shaped writing impressed usu. in clay in ancient Babylonian etc. inscriptions. ● *n.* cuneiform writing. [F *cunéiforme* or mod.L *cuneiformis* f. L *cuneus* wedge]

cunjevoi /kúnjivoy/ *n. Austral.* **1** the green arum or spoon lily *Alocasia macrorrhiza*. **2** a sea squirt. [Aboriginal]

cunnilingus /kúnnilínggəss/ *n.* (also **cunnilinctus** /-língktəss/) oral stimulation of the female genitals. [L f. *cunnus* vulva + *lingere* lick]

cunning /kúnning/ *adj.* & *n.* ● *adj.* (**cunninger**, **cunningest**) **1 a** skilled in ingenuity or deceit. **b** selfishly clever or crafty. **2** ingenious (*a cunning device*). **3** *US* attractive, quaint. ● *n.* **1** craftiness; skill in deceit. **2** skill, ingenuity. □□ **cunningly** *adv.* **cunningness** *n.* [ME f. ON *kunnandi* knowing f. *kunna* know: cf. CAN[1]]

■ *adj.* **1** see CRAFTY. **2** see INGENIOUS. ● *n.* **1** see CRAFT *n.* 4. **2** see INGENUITY.

cunt /kunt/ *n. coarse sl.* **1** the female genitals. **2** *offens.* an unpleasant or stupid person. ¶ A highly taboo word. [ME f. Gmc]

CUP *abbr.* Cambridge University Press.

cup /kup/ *n.* & *v.* ● *n.* **1** a small bowl-shaped container, usu. with a handle for drinking from. **2 a** its contents (*a cup of tea*). **b** = CUPFUL. **3** a cup-shaped thing, esp. the calyx of a flower or the socket of a bone. **4** flavoured wine, cider, etc., usu. chilled. **5** an ornamental cup-shaped trophy as a prize for victory or prowess, esp. in a sports contest. **6** one's fate or fortune (*a bitter cup*). **7** either of the two cup-shaped parts of a brassière. **8** the chalice used or the wine taken at the Eucharist. **9** *Golf* the hole on a putting-green or the metal container in it. ● *v.tr.* (**cupped**, **cupping**) **1** form (esp. one's hands) into the shape of a cup. **2** take or hold as in a cup. **3** *hist.* bleed (a person) by using a glass in which a partial vacuum is formed by heating. □ **cup-cake** a small cake baked in a cup-shaped foil or paper container and often iced. **Cup Final** a final match in a competition for a cup. **cup lichen** a lichen, *Cladonia pyxidata*, with cup-shaped processes arising from the thallus. **one's cup of tea** *colloq.* what interests or suits one. **cup-tie** a match in a competition for a cup. **in one's cups** while drunk; drunk. [OE *cuppe* f. med.L *cuppa* cup, prob. differentiated from L *cupa* tub]

■ *n.* **1** see MUG[1] *n.* 1. **5** see TROPHY 1. □ **in one's cups** see DRUNK *adj.* 1.

cupbearer /kúpbairər/ *n.* a person who serves wine, esp. an officer of a royal or noble household.

■ see WAITER.

cupboard /kúbbərd/ *n.* a recess or piece of furniture with a door and (usu.) shelves, in which things are stored. □ **cupboard love** a display of affection meant to secure some gain. [ME f. CUP + BOARD]

■ see CABINET 1a.

cupel /kyoōp'l/ *n.* & *v.* ● *n.* a small flat porous vessel used in assaying gold or silver in the presence of lead. ● *v.tr.* (**cupelled**, **cupelling**; *US* **cupeled**, **cupeling**) assay or refine in a cupel. □□ **cupellation** /-pəláysh'n/ *n.* [F *coupelle* f. LL *cupella* dimin. of *cupa*: see CUP]

cupful /kúpfōōl/ *n.* (*pl.* **-fuls**) **1** the amount held by a cup, esp. *US* a half-pint or 8-ounce measure in cookery. **2** a cup full of a substance (*drank a cupful of water*). ¶ A *cupful* is a measure, and so *three cupfuls* is a quantity regarded in terms of a cup; *three cups full* denotes the actual cups, as in *three cups full of water*. Sense 2 is an intermediate use.

Cupid /kyoōpid/ *n.* **1** (in Roman mythology) the Roman god of love represented as a naked winged boy with a bow and arrows. **2** (also **cupid**) a representation of Cupid. □ **Cupid's bow** the upper lip etc. shaped like the double-curved bow carried by Cupid. [ME f. L *Cupido* f. *cupere* desire]

cupidity /kyoopídditi/ *n.* greed for gain; avarice. [ME f. OF *cupidité* or L *cupiditas* f. *cupidus* desirous]

■ see AVARICE.

cupola /kyóopələ/ *n.* **1 a** a rounded dome forming a roof or ceiling. **b** a small rounded dome adorning a roof. **2 a** revolving dome protecting mounted guns on a warship or in a fort. **3** (in full **cupola-furnace**) a furnace for melting metals. ▫▫ **cupolaed** /-ləd/ *adj.* [It. f. LL *cupula* dimin. of *cupa* cask]

cuppa /kúppə/ *n.* (also **cupper** /kúppə/) *Brit. colloq.* **1** a cup of. **2** a cup of tea. [corruption]

cuprammonium /kyóoprəmṓniəm/ *n.* a complex ion of divalent copper and ammonia, solutions of which dissolve cellulose. [LL *cuprum* + AMMONIUM]

cupreous /kyóopriəss/ *adj.* of or like copper. [LL *cupreus* f. *cuprum* copper]

cupric /kyóoprik/ *adj.* of copper, esp. divalent copper. ▫▫ **cupriferous** /-príffərəss/ *adj.* [LL *cuprum* copper]

cupro- /kyóoprō/ *comb. form* copper (*cupro-nickel*).

cupro-nickel /kyóoprōníkk'l/ *n.* an alloy of copper and nickel, esp. in the proportions 3:1 as used in 'silver' coins.

cuprous /kyóoprəss/ *adj.* of copper, esp. monovalent copper. [LL *cuprum* copper]

cupule /kyóopyool/ *n. Bot.* & *Zool.* a cup-shaped organ, receptacle, etc. [LL *cupula* CUPOLA]

cur /kur/ *n.* **1** a worthless or snappy dog. **2** *colloq.* a contemptible person. [ME, prob. orig. in *cur-dog*, perh. f. ON *kurr* grumbling]

■ **1** see MONGREL *n.* **2** see WRETCH 2.

curable /kyóorəb'l/ *adj.* that can be cured. ▫▫ **curability** /-bílliti/ *n.* [CURE]

■ see BENIGN 4.

curaçao /kyóorəsō/ *n.* (also **curaçoa** /-sṓə/) (*pl.* **-os** or **curaçoas**) a liqueur of spirits flavoured with the peel of bitter oranges. [F *Curaçao*, name of the Caribbean island producing these oranges]

curacy /kyóorəsi/ *n.* (*pl.* **-ies**) a curate's office or the tenure of it.

curare /kyooraári/ *n.* a resinous bitter substance prepared from S. American plants of the genera *Strychnos* and *Chondodendron*, paralysing the motor nerves, used by American Indians to poison arrows and blowpipe darts, and formerly used as a muscle relaxant in surgery. [Carib]

curassow /kyóorəsō/ *n.* any game bird of the family Cracidae, found in Central and S. America. [Anglicized f. CURAÇAO]

curate /kyóorət/ *n.* **1** a member of the clergy engaged as assistant to a parish priest. **2** *archaic* an ecclesiastical pastor. ▫ **curate-in-charge** a curate appointed to take charge of a parish in place of a priest. **curate's egg** a thing that is partly good and partly bad. [ME f. med.L *curatus* f. L *cura* CURE]

■ see MINISTER *n.* 2.

curative /kyóorətiv/ *adj.* & *n.* ● *adj.* tending or able to cure (esp. disease). ● *n.* a curative medicine or agent. [F *curatif -ive* f. med.L *curativus* f. L *curare* CURE]

■ *adj.* see THERAPEUTIC 1.

curator /kyooráytər/ *n.* a keeper or custodian of a museum or other collection. ▫▫ **curatorial** /kyóorətóriəl/ *adj.* **curatorship** *n.* [ME f. AF *curatour* (OF *-eur*) or L *curator* (as CURATIVE)]

curb /kurb/ *n.* & *v.* ● *n.* **1** a check or restraint. **2** a strap etc. fastened to the bit and passing under a horse's lower jaw, used as a check. **3** an enclosing border or edging such as the frame round the top of a well or a fender round a hearth. **4** = KERB. ● *v.tr.* **1** restrain. **2** put a curb on (a horse). ▫ **curb roof** a roof of which each face has two slopes, the lower one steeper. [ME f. OF *courber* f. L *curvare* bend, CURVE]

■ *n.* **1** restraint, control; see also CHECK[1] *n.* 2c. ● *v.* **1** check, bridle, control, contain, repress, subdue, suppress; see also RESTRAIN 1.

curcuma /kúrkyoomə/ *n.* **1** the spice turmeric. **2** any tuberous plant of the genus *Curcuma*, yielding this and other commercial substances. [med.L or mod.L f. Arab. *kurkum* saffron f. Skr. *kuṅkuma*]

curd /kurd/ *n.* **1** (often in *pl.*) a coagulated substance formed by the action of acids on milk, which may be made into cheese or eaten as food. **2** a fatty substance found between flakes of boiled salmon flesh. **3** the edible head of a cauliflower. ▫ **curds and whey** the result of acidulating milk. **curd soap** a white soap made of tallow and soda. ▫▫ **curdy** *adj.* [ME: orig. unkn.]

curdle /kúrd'l/ *v.tr.* & *intr.* make into or become curds, (of milk) turn sour; congeal. ▫ **make one's blood curdle** fill one with horror. ▫▫ **curdler** *n.* [frequent. form of CURD (as verb)]

■ see TURN *v.* 10, COAGULATE.

cure /kyoor/ *v.* & *n.* ● *v.* **1** *tr.* (often foll. by *of*) restore (a person or animal) to health (*was cured of pleurisy*). **2** *tr.* eliminate (a disease, evil, etc.). **3** *tr.* preserve (meat, fruit, tobacco, or skins) by salting, drying, etc. **4** *tr.* **a** vulcanize (rubber). **b** harden (concrete or plastic). **5** *intr.* effect a cure. **6** *intr.* undergo a process of curing. ● *n.* **1** restoration to health. **2** a thing that effects a cure. **3** a course of medical or healing treatment. **4 a** the office or function of a curate. **b** a parish or other sphere of spiritual ministration. **5 a** the process of curing rubber or plastic. **b** (with qualifying adj.) the degree of this. ▫ **cure-all** a panacea; a universal remedy. ▫▫ **curer** *n.* [ME f. OF *curer* f. L *curare* take care of f. *cura* care]

■ *v.* **1** heal, restore to health, make better. **2** see ELIMINATE 1a. **3** preserve; smoke, pickle, dry, salt, corn, marinate. ● *n.* **1** restoration, healing. **2, 3** course of treatment, therapy, remedy, medication, medicament, medicine, drug, prescription; cure-all. ▫ **cure-all** heal-all, panacea, universal remedy.

curé /kyóoray/ *n.* a parish priest in France etc. [F f. med.L *curatus*: see CURATE]

■ see MINISTER *n.* 2.

curettage /kyooréttij, -ritaázh/ *n.* the use of or an operation involving the use of a curette. [F (as CURETTE)]

curette /kyoorét/ *n.* & *v.* ● *n.* a surgeon's small scraping-instrument. ● *v.tr.* & *intr.* clean or scrape with a curette. [F, f. *curer* cleanse (as CURE)]

curfew /kúrfyoo/ *n.* **1 a** a regulation restricting or forbidding the public circulation of people, esp. requiring people to remain indoors between specified hours, usu. at night. **b** the hour designated as the beginning of such a restriction. **c** a daily signal indicating this. **2** *hist.* **a** a medieval regulation requiring people to extinguish fires at a fixed hour in the evening. **b** the hour for this. **c** the bell announcing it. **3** the ringing of a bell at a fixed evening hour. [ME f. AF *coeverfu*, OF *cuevrefeu* f. the stem of *couvrir* COVER + *feu* fire]

Curia /kyóoriə/ *n.* (also **curia**) the papal court; the government departments of the Vatican. ▫▫ **Curial** *adj.* [L: orig. a division of an ancient Roman tribe, the senate house at Rome, a feudal court of justice]

curie /kyóori/ *n.* **1** a unit of radioactivity, corresponding to 3.7×10^{10} disintegrations per second. ¶ Abbr.: **Ci**. **2** a quantity of radioactive substance having this activity. [P. *Curie*, Fr. scientist d. 1906]

curio /kyóoriō/ *n.* (*pl.* **-os**) a rare or unusual object or person. [19th-c. abbr. of CURIOSITY]

■ see RARITY 2.

curiosa /kyóoriṓsə/ *n.pl.* **1** curiosities. **2** erotic or pornographic books. [neut. pl. of L *curiosus*: see CURIOUS]

curiosity /kyóoriósiti/ *n.* (*pl.* **-ies**) **1** an eager desire to know; inquisitiveness. **2** strangeness. **3** a strange, rare, or interesting object. [ME f. OF *curiouseté* f. L *curiositas -tatis* (as CURIOUS)]

■ **1** inquisitiveness, interest, *colloq.* nosiness. **2** strangeness, peculiarity, unusualness, uncommonness, weirdness; see also ODDITY 3. **3** curio, oddity, rarity, conversation piece, *objet d'art*; knick-knack, bauble, trinket, gewgaw, bibelot.

curious /kyóoriəss/ *adj.* **1** eager to learn; inquisitive. **2** strange, surprising, odd. **3** *euphem.* (of books etc.) erotic, pornographic. ▫▫ **curiously** *adv.* **curiousness** *n.* [ME f. OF *curios* f. L *curiosus* careful f. *cura* care]

■ **1** inquisitive, interested, inquiring, prying, investigative, *colloq.* nosy, snoopy. **2** odd, peculiar, eccentric, strange, *outré*, queer, unusual, outrageous, offbeat, weird, bizarre, unconventional, freakish, exotic, surprising, singular, out of the ordinary, extraordinary, erratic, quaint, outlandish, aberrant, abnormal, irregular, deviant, *colloq.* kinky. **3** see EROTIC.

curium /kyóoriəm/ *n.* an artificially made transuranic radioactive metallic element, first produced by bombarding plutonium with helium ions. ¶ Symb.: **Cm**. [M. *Curie* d. 1934 and P. *Curie* d. 1906, Fr. scientists]

curl /kurl/ *v.* & *n.* ● *v.* **1** *tr.* & *intr.* (often foll. by *up*) bend or coil into a spiral; form or cause to form curls. **2** *intr.* move in a spiral form (*smoke curling upwards*). **3 a** *intr.* (of the upper lip) be raised slightly on one side as an expression of contempt or disapproval. **b** *tr.* cause (the lip) to do this. **4** *intr.* play curling. ● *n.* **1** a lock of curled hair. **2** anything spiral or curved inwards. **3 a** a curling movement or act. **b** the state of being curled. **4** a disease of plants in which the leaves are curled up. □ **curl up 1** lie or sit with the knees drawn up. **2** *colloq.* writhe with embarrassment, horror, or amusement. **make a person's hair curl** *colloq.* shock or horrify a person. **out of curl** lacking energy. [ME; earliest form *crolled, crulled* f. obs. adj. *crolle, crulle* curly f. MDu. *krul*]

■ *v.* **1, 2** se WIND[2] *v.* 4. ● *n.* **1** see LOCK[2] 1a. **2** see SPIRAL *n.* □ **curl up 1** see NESTLE. **2** cringe, shrink; collapse into giggles *or* hysterics, *sl.* crease up.

curler /kúrlər/ *n.* **1** a pin or roller etc. for curling the hair. **2** a player in the game of curling.

curlew /kúrlyoo/ *n.* any wading bird of the genus *Numenius*, esp. *N. arquatus*, possessing a usu. long slender downcurved bill. [ME f. OF *courlieu, courlis* orig. imit., but assim. to *courliu* courier f. *courre* run + *lieu* place]

curlicue /kúrlikyoo/ *n.* a decorative curl or twist. [CURLY + CUE[2] (= pigtail) or Q[1]]

■ see KINK *n.* 1.

curling /kúrling/ *n.* **1** in senses of CURL *v.* **2** a game played on ice, esp. in Scotland, in which large round flat stones are slid across the surface towards a mark. □ **curling-tongs** (or **-iron** or **-pins**) a heated device for twisting the hair into curls.

curly /kúrli/ *adj.* (**curlier, curliest**) **1** having or arranged in curls. **2** moving in curves. □ **curly kale** see KALE. □□ **curliness** *n.*

■ **1** see KINKY 3.

curmudgeon /kərmújən/ *n.* a bad-tempered person. □□ **curmudgeonly** *adj.* [16th c.: orig. unkn.]

■ □□ **curmudgeonly** see IRRITABLE 1.

currach /kúrrə/ *n.* (also **curragh**) *Ir.* a coracle. [Ir.: cf. CORACLE]

currajong var. of KURRAJONG.

currant /kúrrənt/ *n.* **1** a dried fruit of a small seedless variety of grape grown in the Levant and much used in cookery. **2 a** any of various shrubs of the genus *Ribes* producing red, white, or black berries. **b** a berry of these shrubs. □ **flowering currant** an ornamental species of currant native to N. America. [ME *raysons of coraunce* f. AF, = grapes of Corinth (the orig. source)]

currawong /kúrrəwong/ *n. Austral.* any crowlike songbird of the genus *Strepera*, possessing a resonant call. [Aboriginal]

currency /kúrrənsi/ *n.* (*pl.* **-ies**) **1 a** the money in general use in a country. **b** any other commodity used as a medium of exchange. **2** the condition of being current; prevalence (e.g. of words or ideas). **3** the time during which something is current.

■ **1** see MONEY 1.

current /kúrrənt/ *adj.* & *n.* ● *adj.* **1** belonging to the present time; happening now (*current events; the current week*). **2** (of money, opinion, a rumour, a word, etc.) in general circulation or use. ● *n.* **1** a body of water, air, etc., moving in a definite direction, esp. through a stiller surrounding body. **2 a** an ordered movement of electrically charged particles. **b** a quantity representing the intensity of such movement. **3** (usu. foll. by *of*) a general tendency or course (of events, opinions, etc.). □ **current account** a bank account from which money may be drawn without notice. **pass current** be generally accepted as true or genuine. □□ **currentness** *n.* [ME f. OF *corant* f. L *currere* run]

■ *adj.* **1** contemporary, ongoing, present, contemporaneous, latest, up to date. **2** prevalent, prevailing, common, popular, accepted, known, widespread, reported, in circulation, going round *or* around, bruited about, widely known, in the air, present-day. ● *n.* **1** stream, flow, undercurrent, tide. **3** course, progress, tendency, tenor, drift, trend, inclination, stream, direction, tide, mainstream.

currently /kúrrəntli/ *adv.* at the present time; now.

curricle /kúrrik'l/ *n. hist.* a light open two-wheeled carriage drawn by two horses abreast. [L *curriculum*: see CURRICULUM]

curriculum /kəríkyooləm/ *n.* (*pl.* **curricula** /-lə/) **1** the subjects that are studied or prescribed for study in a school (*not part of the school curriculum*). **2** any programme of activities. □□ **curricular** *adj.* [L, = course, race-chariot, f. *currere* run]

■ see PROGRAMME *n.* 4.

curriculum vitae /kəríkyooləm véetī/ *n.* (*pl.* **curricula vitae** or **vitarum**) a brief account of one's education, qualifications, and previous occupations. [L, = course of life]

■ see RÉSUMÉ 2.

currier /kúrriər/ *n.* a person who dresses and colours tanned leather. [ME f. OF *corier*, f. L *coriarius* f. *corium* leather]

currish /kúrrish/ *adj.* **1** like a cur; snappish. **2** ignoble. □□ **currishly** *adv.* **currishness** *n.*

■ see CONTEMPTIBLE.

curry[1] /kúrri/ *n.* & *v.* ● *n.* (*pl.* **-ies**) a dish of meat, vegetables, etc., cooked in a sauce of hot-tasting spices, usu. served with rice. ● *v.tr.* (**-ies, -ied**) prepare or flavour with a sauce of hot-tasting spices (*curried eggs*). □ **curry-powder** a preparation of turmeric and other spices for making curry. [Tamil]

curry[2] /kúrri/ *v.tr.* (**-ies, -ied**) **1** groom (a horse) with a curry-comb. **2** treat (tanned leather) to improve its properties. **3** thrash. □ **curry-comb** a hand-held metal serrated device for grooming horses. **curry favour** ingratiate oneself. [ME f. OF *correier* ult. f. Gmc]

■ **1** see GROOM *v.* 1. □ **curry favour** see INGRATIATE.

curse /kurss/ *n.* & *v.* ● *n.* **1** a solemn utterance intended to invoke a supernatural power to inflict destruction or punishment on a person or thing. **2** the evil supposedly resulting from a curse. **3** a violent exclamation of anger; a profane oath. **4** a thing that causes evil or harm. **5** (prec. by *the*) *colloq.* menstruation. **6** a sentence of excommunication. ● *v.* **1** *tr.* **a** utter a curse against. **b** (in *imper.*) may God curse. **2** *tr.* (usu. in *passive*; foll. by *with*) afflict with (*cursed with blindness*). **3** *intr.* utter expletive curses; swear. **4** *tr.* excommunicate. □□ **curser** *n.* [OE *curs, cursian*, of unkn. orig.]

■ *n.* **1** malediction, imprecation, denunciation, execration, anathema, *archaic* ban. **2** *archaic or joc.* plague. **3** profanity, oath, expletive, blasphemy, obscenity, dirty word, swear-word, damn, curse-word, *colloq.* cuss, *US colloq.* cuss-word. **4** evil, bane, misfortune, affliction, torment, scourge, blight, cross to bear. ● *v.* **1 a** damn, execrate, denounce, anathematize, *colloq.* cuss; swear at, blaspheme at. **b** damn, confound, *colloq.* drat, *euphem.* bless, *sl.* blow. **2** afflict with, burden, saddle, weigh down, handicap. **3** swear, *sl. euphem.* eff.

cursed /kúrsid, kurst/ *adj.* damnable, abominable. □□ **cursedly** *adv.* **cursedness** *n.*

■ see DAMNABLE.

cursillo /koorsíllō/ *n.* (*pl.* **-os**) *RC Ch.* a short informal spiritual retreat by a group of devotees esp. in Latin America. [Sp., = little course]

cursive /kúrsiv/ *adj.* & *n.* ● *adj.* (of writing) done with joined characters. ● *n.* cursive writing (cf. PRINT *v.* 4, UNCIAL). □□ **cursively** *adv.* [med.L (*scriptura*) *cursiva* f. L *currere curs-* run]

cursor /kúrsər/ *n.* **1** *Math.* etc. a transparent slide engraved with a hairline and forming part of a slide-rule. **2** *Computing* a movable indicator on a VDU screen identifying a particular position in the display, esp. the position that the program will operate on with the next keystroke. [L, = runner (as CURSIVE)]

cursorial /kursóriəl/ *adj. Anat.* having limbs adapted for running. [as CURSOR + -IAL]

cursory /kúrsəri/ *adj.* hasty, hurried (*a cursory glance*). □□ **cursorily** *adv.* **cursoriness** *n.* [L *cursorius* of a runner (as CURSOR)]
■ superficial, hasty, hurried, passing, quick, slapdash, perfunctory, rapid, summary.

curst *archaic* var. of CURSED.

curt /kurt/ *adj.* noticeably or rudely brief. □□ **curtly** *adv.* **curtness** *n.* [L *curtus* cut short, abridged]
■ abrupt, short, terse, brief, laconic, concise; blunt, gruff, harsh, brusque, unceremonious, snappish, crusty, rude.

curtail /kurtáyl/ *v.tr.* **1** cut short; reduce; terminate esp. prematurely (*curtailed his visit to America*). **2** (foll. by *of*) *archaic* deprive of. □□ **curtailment** *n.* [obs. *curtal* horse with docked tail f. F *courtault* f. *court* short f. L *curtus*: assim. to *tail*]
■ **1** shorten, abbreviate, cut short, abridge; diminish, reduce, cut, cut back, cut down, *Brit. colloq.* chop; terminate. **2** see DIVEST 2.

curtain /kúrt'n/ *n.* & *v.* ● *n.* **1** a piece of cloth etc. hung up as a screen, usu. moveable sideways or upwards, esp. at a window or between the stage and auditorium of a theatre. **2** *Theatr.* **a** the rise or fall of the stage curtain at the beginning or end of an act or scene. **b** = *curtain-call*. **3** a partition or cover. **4** (in *pl.*) *sl.* the end. ● *v.tr.* **1** furnish or cover with a curtain or curtains. **2** (foll. by *off*) shut off with a curtain or curtains. □ **curtain-call** *Theatr.* an audience's summons to actor(s) to take a bow after the fall of the curtain. **curtain-fire** *Mil.* a concentration of rapid and continuous fire. **curtain lecture** a wife's private reproof to her husband, orig. behind bed-curtains. **curtain-raiser 1** *Theatr.* a piece prefaced to the main performance. **2** a preliminary event. **curtain-wall 1** *Fortification* the plain wall of a fortified place, connecting two towers etc. **2** *Archit.* a piece of plain wall not supporting a roof. [ME f. OF *cortine* f. LL *cortina* transl. Gk *aulaia* f. *aulē* court]

curtana /kurtáynə, -taánə/ *n. Brit.* an unpointed sword borne before English sovereigns at their coronation, as an emblem of mercy. [ME f. AL *curtana* (*spatha* sword) f. AF *curtain*, OF *cortain* name of Roland's similar sword f. *cort* short (as CURT)]

curtilage /kúrtilij/ *n.* an area attached to a dwelling-house and forming one enclosure with it. [ME f. AF *curtilage*, OF *co(u)rtillage* f. *co(u)rtil* small court f. *cort* COURT]

curtsy /kúrtsi/ *n.* & *v.* (also **curtsey**) ● *n.* (*pl.* **-ies** or **-eys**) a woman's or girl's formal greeting or salutation made by bending the knees and lowering the body. ● *v.intr.* (**-ies, -ied** or **-eys, -eyed**) make a curtsy. [var. of COURTESY]

curule /kyóoroōl/ *adj. Rom.Hist.* designating or relating to the authority exercised by the senior Roman magistrates, chiefly the consul and praetor, who were entitled to use the *sella curulis* ('curule seat' or seat of office). [L *curulis* f. *currus* chariot (in which the chief magistrate was conveyed to the seat of office)]

curvaceous /kurváyshəss/ *adj. colloq.* (esp. of a woman) having a shapely curved figure.
■ see SHAPELY.

curvature /kúrvəchər/ *n.* **1** the act or state of curving. **2** a curved form. **3** *Geom.* **a** the deviation of a curve from a straight line, or of a curved surface from a plane. **b** the quantity expressing this. [OF f. L *curvatura* (as CURVE)]
■ **1, 2** see BEND[1] *n.*

curve /kurv/ *n.* & *v.* ● *n.* **1** a line or surface having along its length a regular deviation from being straight or flat, as exemplified by the surface of a sphere or lens. **2** a curved form or thing. **3** a curved line on a graph. **4** *Baseball* a ball caused to deviate by the pitcher's spin. ● *v.tr.* & *intr.* bend or shape so as to form a curve. □□ **curved** *adj.* [orig. as adj. (in *curve line*) f. L *curvus* bent: (v.) f. L *curvare*]
■ *n.* **1–3** see BEND[1] *n.* ● *v.* see BEND[1] *v.* 1.

curvet /kurvét/ *n.* & *v.* ● *n.* a horse's leap with the forelegs raised together and the hind legs raised with a spring before the forelegs reach the ground. ● *v.intr.* (**curvetted, curvetting** or **curveted, curveting**) (of a horse or rider) make a curvet. [It. *corvetta* dimin. of *corva* CURVE]
■ *n.* see CAPER[1] *n.* 1. ● *v.* see LEAP *v.* 1.

curvi- /kúrvi/ *comb. form* curved. [L *curvus* curved]

curvifoliate /kúrvifṓliət/ *adj. Bot.* with the leaves bent back.

curviform /kúrviform/ *adj.* having a curved shape.

curvilinear /kúrvilínniər/ *adj.* contained by or consisting of curved lines. □□ **curvilinearly** *adv.* [CURVI- after *rectilinear*]
■ see ROUND *adj.* 1.

curvirostral /kúrviróstrəl/ *adj.* with a curved beak.

curvy /kúrvi/ *adj.* (**curvier, curviest**) **1** having many curves. **2** (of a woman's figure) shapely. □□ **curviness** *n.*
■ **1** see SERPENTINE *adj.* 2. **2** *colloq.* curvaceous; see also SHAPELY.

cuscus[1] /kúskəss/ *n.* the aromatic fibrous root of an Indian grass, *Vetiveria zizanoides*, used for making fans etc. [Pers. *ḵašḵaš*]

cuscus[2] /kúskəss/ *n.* any of several nocturnal, usu. arboreal, marsupial mammals of the genus *Phalanger*, native to New Guinea and N. Australia. [native name]

cusec /kyóossek/ *n.* a unit of flow (esp. of water) equal to one cubic foot per second. [abbr.]

cush /kōōsh/ *n.* esp. *Billiards colloq.* a cushion. [abbr.]

cushat /kúshət/ *n. Sc.* a woodpigeon. [OE *cūscute*, of unkn. orig.]

cush-cush /kōōshkōōsh/ *n.* a yam, *Dioscorea trifida*, native to S. America. [native name]

cushion /kōōsh'n/ *n.* & *v.* ● *n.* **1** a bag of cloth etc. stuffed with a mass of soft material, used as a soft support for sitting or leaning on etc. **2** a means of protection against shock. **3** the elastic lining of the sides of a billiard-table, from which the ball rebounds. **4** a body of air supporting a hovercraft etc. **5** the frog of a horse's hoof. ● *v.tr.* **1** provide or protect with a cushion or cushions. **2** provide with a defence; protect. **3** mitigate the adverse effects of (*cushioned the blow*). **4** quietly suppress. **5** place or bounce (the ball) against the cushion in billiards. □□ **cushiony** *adj.* [ME f. OF *co(i)ssin*, *cu(i)ssin* f. Gallo-Roman f. L *culcita* mattress, cushion]
■ *n.* **1** pillow, bolster, pad. **2** see DEFENCE 2a, b. ● *v.* **2** see PROTECT. **3** soften, absorb, buffer, damp, lessen. **4** see SUPPRESS 2.

Cushitic /kooshíttik/ *n.* & *adj.* ● *n.* a group of E. African languages of the Hamitic type. ● *adj.* of this group. [*Cush* an ancient country in the Nile valley + -ITE[1] + -IC]

cushy /kōōshi/ *adj.* (**cushier, cushiest**) *colloq.* **1** (of a job etc.) easy and pleasant. **2** *US* (of a seat, surroundings, etc.) soft, comfortable. □□ **cushiness** *n.* [Anglo-Ind. f. Hind. *ḵhūsh* pleasant]
■ **1** see EASY *adj.* 1.

cusp /kusp/ *n.* **1** an apex or peak. **2** the horn of a crescent moon etc. **3** *Astrol.* the initial point of a house. **4** *Archit.* a projecting point between small arcs in Gothic tracery. **5** *Geom.* the point at which two arcs meet from the same direction terminating with a common tangent. **6** *Bot.* a pointed end, esp. of a leaf. **7** a cone-shaped prominence on the surface of a tooth esp. a molar or premolar. **8** a pocket or fold in a valve of the heart. □□ **cuspate** /kúspayt/ *adj.* **cusped** *adj.* **cuspidal** *adj.* [L *cuspis*, *-idis* point, apex]

■ **1** see ANGLE[1] *n.* 2.

cuspidor /kúspidor/ *n. US* a spittoon. [Port., = spitter f. *cuspir* spit f. L *conspuere*]

cuss /kuss/ *n.* & *v. colloq.* ● *n.* **1** a curse. **2** usu. *derog.* a person; a creature. ● *v.tr.* & *intr.* curse. □ **cuss-word** *US* a swear-word. [var. of CURSE]

■ *n.* **1** see CURSE *n.* 1. ● *v.* see CURSE *v.* 1a. □ **cuss-word** see CURSE *n.* 3.

cussed /kússid/ *adj. colloq.* awkward and stubborn. □□ **cussedly** *adv.* **cussedness** *n.* [var. of CURSED]

custard /kústərd/ *n.* **1** a dish made with milk and eggs, usu. sweetened. **2** a sweet sauce made with milk and flavoured cornflour. □ **custard-apple** a W. Indian fruit, *Annona reticulata*, with a custard-like pulp. **custard-pie 1** a pie containing custard, commonly thrown in slapstick comedy. **2** (*attrib.*) denoting slapstick comedy. **custard powder** a preparation of cornflour etc. for making custard. [ME, earlier *crusta(r)de* f. AF f. OF *crouste* CRUST]

custodian /kustṓdiən/ *n.* a guardian or keeper, esp. of a public building etc. □□ **custodianship** *n.* [CUSTODY + -AN, after *guardian*]

■ see GUARD *n.* 2. □□ **custodianship** see CARE *n.* 4a.

custody /kústədi/ *n.* **1** guardianship; protective care. **2** imprisonment. □ **take into custody** arrest. □□ **custodial** /kustṓdiəl/ *adj.* [L *custodia* f. *custos -odis* guardian]

■ **1** care, custodianship, safe keeping, protection, charge, guardianship, keeping. **2** imprisonment, detention, incarceration, confinement. □ **take into custody** see ARREST *v.* 1a.

custom /kústəm/ *n.* **1 a** the usual way of behaving or acting (*a slave to custom*). **b** a particular established way of behaving (*our customs seem strange to foreigners*). **2** *Law* established usage having the force of law. **3** business patronage; regular dealings or customers (*lost a lot of custom*). **4** (in *pl.*; also treated as *sing.*) **a** a duty levied on certain imported and exported goods. **b** the official department that administers this. **c** the area at a port, frontier, etc., where customs officials deal with incoming goods, baggage, etc. □ **custom-built** (or **-made** etc.) made to a customer's order. **custom-house** the office at a port or frontier etc. at which customs duties are levied. **customs union** a group of States with an agreed common tariff, and usu. free trade with each other. [ME and OF *custume* ult. f. L *consuetudo -dinis*: see CONSUETUDE]

■ **1 a** practice, habit, usage, fashion, tradition, routine, convention, form, formality; *formal or joc.* wont. **b** (*customs*) ways, way of life, traditions, conventions, mores. **3** patronage, support, business, trade. **4** (*customs*) **a** toll, duty, impost, tax, excise, levy, dues, tariff. □ **custom-built** (or **-made** etc.) built specially *or* especially *or* expressly *or* exclusively *or* particularly *or* to order, customized.

customary /kústəməri/ *adj.* & *n.* ● *adj.* **1** usual; in accordance with custom. **2** *Law* in accordance with custom. ● *n.* (*pl.* **-ies**) *Law* a book etc. listing the customs and established practices of a community. □□ **customarily** *adv.* **customariness** *n.* [med.L *custumarius* f. *custuma* f. AF *custume* (as CUSTOM)]

■ *adj.* **1** usual, normal, conventional, routine, everyday, common, commonplace, ordinary, traditional; accustomed, habitual, regular, wonted.

customer /kústəmər/ *n.* **1** a person who buys goods or services from a shop or business. **2** a person one has to deal with (*an awkward customer*). [ME f. AF *custumer* (as CUSTOMARY), or f. CUSTOM + -ER[1]]

■ **1** client, patron, buyer, purchaser; consumer. **2** fellow, character, person, soul, individual, being, *colloq.* chap.

customize /kústəmīz/ *v.tr.* (also **-ise**) make to order or modify according to individual requirements.

cut /kut/ *v.* & *n.* ● *v.* (**cutting**; *past* and *past part.* **cut**) **1** *tr.* (also *absol.*) penetrate or wound with a sharp-edged instrument (*cut his finger*; *the knife won't cut*). **2** *tr.* & *intr.* (often foll. by *into*) divide or be divided with a knife etc. (*cut the bread*; *cut the cloth into metre lengths*). **3** *tr.* **a** trim or reduce the length of (hair, a hedge, etc.) by cutting. **b** detach all or the significant part of (flowers, corn, etc.) by cutting. **c** reduce the length of (a book, film, etc.). **4** *tr.* (foll. by *loose*, *open*, etc.) make loose, open, etc. by cutting. **5** *tr.* (esp. as **cutting** *adj.*) cause sharp physical or mental pain to (*a cutting remark*; *a cutting wind*; *was cut to the quick*). **6** *tr.* (often foll. by *down*) **a** reduce (wages, prices, time, etc.). **b** reduce or cease (services etc.). **7** *tr.* **a** shape or fashion (a coat, gem, key, record, etc.) by cutting. **b** make (a path, tunnel, etc.) by removing material. **8** *tr.* perform, execute, make (*cut a caper*; *cut a sorry figure*; *cut a deal*). **9** *tr.* (also *absol.*) cross, intersect (*the line cuts the circle at two points*; *the two lines cut*). **10** *intr.* (foll. by *across*, *through*, etc.) pass or traverse, esp. in a hurry or as a shorter way (*cut across the grass*). **11** *tr.* **a** ignore or refuse to recognize (a person). **b** renounce (a connection). **12** *tr.* esp. *US* deliberately fail to attend (a class etc.). **13** *Cards* **a** *tr.* divide (a pack) into two parts. **b** *intr.* select a dealer etc. by dividing the pack. **14** *Cinematog.* **a** *tr.* edit (a film or tape). **b** *intr.* (often in *imper.*) stop filming or recording. **c** *intr.* (foll. by *to*) go quickly to (another shot). **15** *tr.* switch off (an engine etc.). **16** *tr.* **a** hit (a ball) with a chopping motion. **b** *Golf* slice (the ball). **17** *tr. US* dilute, adulterate. **18** *tr.* (as **cut** *adj.*) *Brit. sl.* drunk. **19** *intr. Cricket* (of the ball) turn sharply on pitching. **20** *intr. sl.* run. **21** *tr.* castrate. ● *n.* **1** an act of cutting. **2** a division or wound made by cutting. **3** a stroke with a knife, sword, whip, etc. **4 a** a reduction (in prices, wages, etc.). **b** a cessation (of a power supply etc.). **5** an excision of part of a play, film, book, etc. **6** a wounding remark or act. **7** the way or style in which a garment, the hair, etc., is cut. **8** a piece of meat etc. cut from a carcass. **9** *colloq.* commission; a share of profits. **10** *Tennis* & *Cricket* etc. a stroke made by cutting. **11** ignoring of or refusal to recognize a person. **12 a** an engraved block for printing. **b** a woodcut or other print. **13** a railway cutting. **14** a new channel made for a river. □ **a cut above** *colloq.* noticeably superior to. **be cut out** (foll. by *for*, or *to* + infin.) be suited (*was not cut out to be a teacher*). **cut across 1** transcend or take no account of (normal limitations etc.) (*their concern cuts across normal rivalries*). **2** see sense 10 of *v.* **cut-and-come-again** *n.* a green vegetable etc. that can be frequently cut or picked. ● *adj.* inexhaustible. **cut and dried 1** completely decided; prearranged; inflexible. **2** (of opinions etc.) ready-made, lacking freshness. **cut and run** *sl.* run away. **cut and thrust 1** a lively interchange of argument etc. **2** the use of both the edge and the point of a sword. **cut back 1** reduce (expenditure etc.). **2** prune (a tree etc.). **3** *Cinematog.* repeat part of a previous scene for dramatic effect. **cut-back** *n.* an instance or the act of cutting back, esp. a reduction in expenditure. **cut both ways 1** serve both sides of an argument etc. **2** (of an action) have both good and bad effects. **cut one's coat according to one's cloth 1** adapt expenditure to resources. **2** limit ambition to what is feasible. **cut a corner** go across and not round it. **cut corners** do a task etc. perfunctorily or incompletely, esp. to save time. **cut a dash** see DASH. **cut dead** completely refuse to recognize (a person). **cut down 1 a** bring or throw down by cutting. **b** kill by means of a sword or disease. **2** see sense 6 of *v.* **3** reduce the length of (*cut down the trousers to make shorts*). **4** (often foll. by *on*) reduce one's consumption (*tried to cut down on beer*). **cut a person down to size** *colloq.* ruthlessly expose the limitations of a person's importance, ability, etc. **cut one's eye-teeth** attain worldly wisdom. **cut glass** glass with patterns and designs cut on it. **cut in 1** interrupt. **2** pull in too closely in front of another vehicle (esp. having overtaken it). **3** give a share of profits etc. to (a person). **4** connect (a source of electricity). **5** join in a card-game by taking the place of a player who cuts out. **6** interrupt a dancing couple to take over from one partner. **cut into 1** make a cut in (*they cut into the cake*). **2** interfere with and reduce (*travelling cuts into my free time*). **cut it fine** see FINE[1]. **cut it out** (usu. in *imper.*) *sl.* stop doing that (esp. quarrelling). **cut the knot** solve a problem in an irregular but efficient way. **cut-line 1** a caption to an illustration. **2** the line in squash above which a served ball must strike the wall. **cut loose 1**

begin to act freely. **2** see sense 4 of *v.* **cut one's losses** (or **a loss**) abandon an unprofitable enterprise before losses become too great. **cut the mustard** *US sl.* reach the required standard. **cut no ice** *sl.* **1** have no influence or importance. **2** achieve little or nothing. **cut off 1** remove (an appendage) by cutting. **2 a** (often in *passive*) bring to an abrupt end or (esp. early) death. **b** intercept, interrupt; prevent from continuing (*cut off supplies*; *cut off the gas*). **c** disconnect (a person engaged in a telephone conversation) (*was suddenly cut off*). **3 a** prevent from travelling or venturing out (*was cut off by the snow*). **b** (as **cut off** *adj.*) isolated, remote (*felt cut off in the country*). **4 a** disinherit (*was cut off without a penny*). **b** sever a relationship (*was cut off from the children*). **cut-off** *n.* **1** the point at which something is cut off. **2** a device for stopping a flow. **3** *US* a short cut. **cut out 1** remove from the inside by cutting. **2** make by cutting from a larger whole. **3** omit; leave out. **4** *colloq.* stop doing or using (something) (*managed to cut out chocolate*; *let's cut out the arguing*). **5** cease or cause to cease functioning (*the engine cut out*). **6** outdo or supplant (a rival). **7** *US* detach (an animal) from the herd. **8** *Cards* be excluded from a card-game as a result of cutting the pack. **9** *colloq.* prepare, plan (*has his work cut out*). **cut-out 1** a figure cut out of paper etc. **2** a device for automatic disconnection, the release of exhaust gases, etc. **cut-out box** *US* = *fuse-box* (see FUSE[1]). **cut-price** (or **-rate**) selling or sold at a reduced price. **cut short 1** interrupt; terminate prematurely (*cut short his visit*). **2** make shorter or more concise. **cut one's teeth on** acquire initial practice or experience from (something). **cut a tooth** have it appear through the gum. **cut up 1** cut into pieces. **2** destroy utterly. **3** (usu. in *passive*) distress greatly (*was very cut up about it*). **4** criticize severely. **5** *US* behave in a comical or unruly manner. **cut up rough** *Brit. sl.* show anger or resentment. **cut up well** *sl.* bequeath a large fortune. **have one's work cut out** see WORK. [ME *cutte*, *kitte*, *kette*, perh. f. OE *cyttan* (unrecorded)]

■ *v.* **1** gash, slash; see also SLIT *v.* **2** slice, carve. **3 a** trim, snip, lop, clip, crop, shorten, shear, chop off; mow; dock. **c** abbreviate, shorten, crop, condense, abridge, edit, cut back, reduce, cut down, curtail. **5** cut up, hurt, wound, pain, upset, grieve, distress, slight, insult, offend, affront; (**cutting**) sarcastic, sardonic, bitter, scornful, sneering, acid, scathing, acerb, acerbic, wounding, stern, harsh, caustic, mordant, acrimonious, contemptuous; malicious, invidious, vicious, venomous; severe, biting, cold, icy, frigid, freezing, raw, piercing, penetrating, *literary* chill. **6** reduce, cut back (on), cut down (on), slash, diminish, decrease, retrench (on), curtail; discount, mark down; lessen, lower. **7 a** see SHAPE *v.* 1. **b** dig, burrow, gouge (out), scoop (out), hollow out; tunnel. **8** make, present, exhibit, display; perform, execute, do; conclude, settle, agree. **9** cross (over), intersect, meet; see also JOIN *v.* 8. **10** pass, go, make one's way; take a short cut. **11 a** see IGNORE 1. **12** avoid, fail to attend, *colloq.* skip, *literary* eschew. **15** turn *or* switch off. **17** dilute, thin, water (down), weaken; degrade, adulterate. **18** (**cut** *adj.*) see DRUNK *adj.* 1. **20** see RUN *v.* 1, 3. ● *n.* **2** gash, slash, incision, nick, wound. **3** stroke, *colloq.* swipe. **4 a** reduction, cut-back, curtailment, decrease. **b** failure, breakdown; blackout. **5** deletion, excision, omission. **6** affront, insult, offence, slight, snub, dig, slap in the face, *US colloq.* jibe. **7** see STYLE *n.* 1, 6. **9** share, portion, percentage, dividend, commission. **12** engraving, plate, artwork, picture, illustration, plate, drawing, woodcut, linocut, print, half-tone. □ **a cut above** better than, superior to, *colloq.* streets ahead of. **be cut out** be suited *or* fit(ted) *or* equipped. **cut across 1** see TRANSCEND. **2** see CUT *v.* 10 above. **cut and dried 1** clear-cut, settled, arranged, decided; predetermined, prearranged, inflexible. **2** ready-made, automatic; stale, unoriginal, trite, hackneyed, old; dull, boring, manufactured, unchanging, unchanged. **cut and run** see RUN *v.* 2. **cut back 1** see CUT *v.* 6 above. **2** see PRUNE[2] 1. **cut-back** see DECREASE *n.* **cut dead** cut, snub, slight, spurn, shun, ignore, give the cold shoulder. **cut down 1 a** fell, chop *or* hew down. **b** kill, cut off; murder, assassinate; see also KILL[1] *v.* 1a. **2** see CUT *v.* 6 above. **cut in 1** interrupt, butt in. **cut it out** see *pack it in* (PACK[1]). **cut the mustard** see *make it* 2. **cut off 1** chop *or* lop *or* hack off, *literary* cleave; see also SEVER 1. **2 a** see *cut down* 1b above. **b** intercept, interrupt, discontinue, cease; end, stop, terminate, break off. **3 b** (*adj.*) see ISOLATED 1. **4 a** disinherit, disown, reject. **b** separate, sever, split, estrange. **cut out 1** extract, excise, remove, take out. **3** leave out, delete, remove, excise, strike *or* cross out, edit out, omit, cut, kill, *Printing* dele. **4, 5** stop, cease, quit, *literary* desist (from). **6** see OUTDO. **9** plan, prepare, ready, organize; destine. **cut-price** (or **-rate**) marked down, bargain-priced, reduced (in price), on offer. **cut short 1** see INTERRUPT 1, 3. **2** abbreviate, shorten, crop, condense, abridge, edit, trim, cut, cut back *or* down, reduce; curtail. **cut up 1** chop (up), dice, cube, mince, cut, divide (up), carve (up). **2** see DEVASTATE 1. **3** see DISTRESS *v.* **4** see CRITICIZE 1. **5** misbehave. **cut up rough** get angry, lose one's temper; see also EXPLODE 2.

cutaneous /kyootáyniəss/ *adj.* of the skin. [mod.L *cutaneus* f. L *cutis* skin]

cutaway /kúttəway/ *adj.* **1** (of a diagram etc.) with some parts left out to reveal the interior. **2** (of a coat) with the front below the waist cut away.

cutch var. of COUCH[2].

cute /kyōōt/ *adj. colloq.* **1** esp. *US* **a** attractive, quaint. **b** affectedly attractive. **2** clever, ingenious. □□ **cutely** *adv.* **cuteness** *n.* [shortening of ACUTE]

■ **1 a** pretty, attractive, adorable, dainty, lovely, beautiful; quaint, *US* cunning. **2** clever, shrewd, ingenious, adroit, crafty, cunning.

cuticle /kyōōtik'l/ *n.* **1 a** the dead skin at the base of a fingernail or toenail. **b** the epidermis or other superficial skin. **2** *Bot.* a thin surface film on plants. □□ **cuticular** /-tíkyoolər/ *adj.* [L *cuticula*, dimin. of *cutis* skin]

cutie /kyōōti/ *n. sl.* an attractive young woman.

cutis /kyōōtiss/ *n. Anat.* the true skin or dermis, underlying the epidermis. [L, = skin]

cutlass /kútləss/ *n.* a short sword with a slightly curved blade, esp. of the type formerly used by sailors. [F *coutelas* ult. f. L *cultellus*: see CUTLER]

■ see KNIFE *n.* 1b.

cutler /kútlər/ *n.* a person who makes or deals in knives and similar utensils. [ME f. AF *cotillere*, OF *coutelier* f. *coutel* f. L *cultellus* dimin. of *culter* COULTER]

cutlery /kútləri/ *n.* knives, forks, and spoons for use at table. [OF & F *coutel(l)erie* (as CUTLER)]

■ *US* flatware.

cutlet /kútlit/ *n.* **1** a neck-chop of mutton or lamb. **2** a small piece of veal etc. for frying. **3** a flat cake of minced meat or nuts and breadcrumbs etc. [F *côtelette*, OF *costelet* dimin. of *coste* rib f. L *costa*]

cutpurse /kútpurss/ *n. archaic* a pickpocket; a thief.

■ see THIEF.

cutter /kúttər/ *n.* **1** a tailor etc. who takes measurements and cuts cloth. **2** *Naut.* **a** a small fast sailing-ship. **b** a small boat carried by a large ship. **3** *Cricket* a ball turning sharply on pitching. **4** *US* a light horse-drawn sleigh.

cutthroat /kút-thrōt/ *n.* & *adj.* ● *n.* **1** a murderer. **2** (in full **cutthroat razor**) a razor having a long blade set in a handle and usu. folding like a penknife. **3** a species of trout, *Salmo clarki*, with a red mark under the jaw. ● *adj.* **1** (of competition) ruthless and intense. **2** (of a person) murderous. **3** (of a card-game) three-handed.

■ *n.* **1** murderer, pirate, killer, gunman, assassin, *colloq.* hatchet man, *sl.* hit man, *esp. US sl.* gunslinger, *US sl.* gunsel. ● *adj.* **1** intense, merciless, ruthless, unmerciful, unprincipled, relentless, pitiless, brutal, cold-blooded, cold-hearted. **2** murderous, homicidal, lethal, deadly, barbaric, fierce, cruel, barbarous, savage, inhuman, brutal, violent, ferocious, bloodthirsty, sanguinary, bloody, feral, vicious.

cutting /kútting/ *n.* & *adj.* ● *n.* **1** a piece cut from a newspaper etc. **2** a piece cut from a plant for propagation. **3** an excavated channel through high ground for a railway or road. ● *adj.* see CUT *v.* 5. □□ **cuttingly** *adv.*
■ *n.* **1, 2** scion, slip; clipping.

cuttle /kútt'l/ *n.* = CUTTLEFISH. □ **cuttle-bone** the internal shell of the cuttlefish crushed and used for polishing teeth etc. or as a supplement to the diet of a cage-bird. [OE *cudele*, ME *codel*, rel. to *cod* bag, with ref. to its ink-bag]

cuttlefish /kútt'lfish/ *n.* any marine cephalopod mollusc of the genera *Sepia* and *Sepiola*, having ten arms and ejecting a black fluid when threatened or pursued.

cutty /kútti/ *adj.* & *n.* *Sc.* & *N.Engl.* ● *adj.* cut short; abnormally short. ● *n.* (*pl.* **-ies**) a short tobacco pipe. □ **cutty-stool** *hist.* a stool of repentance.

cutwater /kútwawtər/ *n.* **1** the forward edge of a ship's prow. **2** a wedge-shaped projection from a pier or bridge.

cutworm /kútwurm/ *n.* any of various caterpillars that eat through the stems of young plants level with the ground.

cuvée /kyoováy/ *n.* a blend or batch of wine. [F, = vatful f. *cuve* cask f. L *cupa*]

cuvette /kyoovét/ *n.* a shallow vessel for liquid. [F, dimin. of *cuve* cask f. L *cupa*]

c.v. *abbr.* curriculum vitae.

CVO *abbr.* Commander of the Royal Victorian Order.

CVS *abbr.* chorionic villus sample, a test on a pregnant woman to detect any chromosomal abnormalities in the foetus.

Cwlth. *abbr.* Commonwealth.

cwm /koom/ *n.* **1** (in Wales) = COOMB. **2** *Geog.* a cirque. [Welsh]

c.w.o. *abbr.* cash with order.

cwt. *abbr.* hundredweight.

-cy /si/ *suffix* (see also -ACY, -ANCY, -CRACY, -ENCY, -MANCY). **1** denoting state or condition (*bankruptcy*; *idiocy*). **2** denoting rank or status (*captaincy*). [from or after L *-cia*, *-tia*, Gk *-k(e)ia*, *-t(e)ia*]

cyan /sían/ *adj.* & *n.* ● *adj.* of a greenish-blue. ● *n.* a greenish-blue colour. [Gk *kuan(e)os* dark blue]

cyanamide /síánnəmīd/ *n.* *Chem.* a colourless crystalline amide of cyanogen; any salt of this, esp. the calcium one which is used as a fertilizer. ¶ Chem. formula: CH_2N_2. [CYANOGEN + AMIDE]

cyanic acid /síánnik/ *n.* an unstable colourless pungent acid gas. ¶ Chem. formula: HCNO. [CYANOGEN]

cyanide /síənīd/ *n.* any of the highly poisonous salts or esters of hydrocyanic acid, esp. the potassium salt used in the extraction of gold and silver. [CYANOGEN + -IDE]

cyanobacterium /síənōbakteériəm/ *n.* any prokaryotic organism of the division Cyanobacteria, found in many environments and capable of photosynthesizing. Also called *blue-green alga* (see BLUE[1]). [CYANOGEN + BACTERIUM]

cyanocobalamin /síənōkəbálləmin/ *n.* a vitamin of the B complex, found in foods of animal origin such as liver, fish, and eggs, a deficiency of which can cause pernicious anaemia. Also called *vitamin* B_{12}. [CYANOGEN + *cobalamin* f. COBALT + VITAMIN]

cyanogen /síánnəjən/ *n.* *Chem.* a colourless highly poisonous gas intermediate in the preparation of many fertilizers. ¶ Chem. formula: C_2N_2. [F *cyanogène* f. Gk *kuanos* dark-blue mineral, as being a constituent of Prussian blue]

cyanosis /síənōsiss/ *n.* *Med.* a bluish discoloration of the skin due to the presence of oxygen-deficient blood. □□ **cyanotic** /-nóttik/ *adj.* [mod.L f. Gk *kuanōsis* blueness (as CYANOGEN)]

cybernation /síbərnáysh'n/ *n.* control by machines. □□ **cybernate** *v.tr.* [f. CYBERNETICS + -ATION]

cybernetics /síbərnéttiks/ *n.pl.* (usu. treated as *sing.*) the science of communications and automatic control systems in both machines and living things. □□ **cybernetic** *adj.* **cybernetician** /-tísh'n/ *n.* **cyberneticist** /-tisist/ *n.* [Gk *kubernētēs* steersman]

cycad /síkad/ *n.* *Bot.* any of the palmlike plants of the order Cycadales (including fossil forms) inhabiting tropical and subtropical regions and often growing to a great height. [mod.L *cycas*, *cycad-* f. supposed Gk *kukas*, scribal error for *koikas*, pl. of *koix* Egyptian palm]

Cycladic /sikláddik, si-/ *adj.* of the Cyclades, a group of islands east of the Greek mainland, esp. of the Bronze Age civilization that flourished there. [*Cyclades*, L f. Gk *Kuklades* f. *kuklos* circle (of islands)]

cyclamate /síkləmayt, sík-/ *n.* any of various salts or esters of sulphamic acid formerly used as artificial sweetening agents. [Chem. name *cyclohexylsulphamate*]

cyclamen /sikləmən/ *n.* **1** any plant of the genus *Cyclamen*, originating in Europe, having pink, red, or white flowers with reflexed petals, often grown in pots. **2** the shade of colour of the red or pink cyclamen flower. [med.L f. Gk *kuklaminos*, perh. f. *kuklos* circle, with ref. to its bulbous roots]

cycle /sík'l/ *n.* & *v.* ● *n.* **1 a** a recurrent round or period (of events, phenomena, etc.). **b** the time needed for one such round or period. **2 a** *Physics* etc. a recurrent series of operations or states. **b** *Electr.* = HERTZ. **3** a series of songs, poems, etc., usu. on a single theme. **4** a bicycle, tricycle, or similar machine. ● *v.intr.* **1** ride a bicycle etc. **2** move in cycles. □ **cycle-track** (or **-way**) a path or road for bicycles. [ME f. OF, or f. LL *cyclus* f. Gk *kuklos* circle]
■ *n.* **1 a** round, rotation, circle, course; series, sequence, run, succession, pattern. **4** bicycle, pedal cycle, *colloq.* bike, *Brit. colloq.* push-bike; tricycle. ● *v.* **2** recur, return, rotate, circle.

cyclic /síklik/ *adj.* **1 a** recurring in cycles. **b** belonging to a chronological cycle. **2** *Chem.* with constituent atoms forming a ring. **3** of a cycle of songs etc. **4** *Bot.* (of a flower) with its parts arranged in whorls. **5** *Math.* of a circle or cycle. [F *cyclique* or L *cyclicus* f. Gk *kuklikos* (as CYCLE)]
■ **1** see PERIODIC.

cyclical /síklik'l, sík-/ *adj.* = CYCLIC 1. □□ **cyclically** *adv.*

cyclist /síklist/ *n.* a rider of a bicycle.

cyclo- /síklō/ *comb. form* circle, cycle, or cyclic (*cyclometer*; *cyclorama*). [Gk *kuklos* circle]

cycloalkane /síklō-álkayn/ *n.* *Chem.* a saturated cyclic hydrocarbon.

cyclo-cross /síklōkross/ *n.* cross-country racing on bicycles.

cyclograph /síkləgraaf/ *n.* an instrument for tracing circular arcs.

cyclohexane /síklōhéksayn/ *n.* *Chem.* a colourless liquid cycloalkane used as a solvent and paint remover. ¶ Chem. formula: C_6H_{12}.

cycloid /síkloyd/ *n.* *Math.* a curve traced by a point on a circle when the circle is rolled along a straight line. □□ **cycloidal** /-klóyd'l/ *adj.* [Gk *kukloeidēs* (as CYCLE, -OID)]

cyclometer /síklómmitər/ *n.* **1** an instrument for measuring circular arcs. **2** an instrument for measuring the distance traversed by a bicycle etc.

cyclone /síklōn/ *n.* **1** a system of winds rotating inwards to an area of low barometric pressure; a depression. **2** a violent hurricane of limited diameter. □□ **cyclonic** /-klónnik/ *adj.* **cyclonically** /-klónnikəli/ *adv.* [prob. repr. Gk *kuklōma* wheel, coil of a snake]
■ **1** see DEPRESSION 3. **2** see HURRICANE 1, 2.

cycloparaffin /síklōpárrəfin/ *n.* *Chem.* = CYCLOALKANE.

Cyclopean /síkləpeéən, -klōpiən/ *adj.* (also **Cyclopian**) **1** (of ancient masonry) made with massive irregular blocks. **2** of or resembling a Cyclops.

cyclopedia /síkləpeédiə/ *n.* (also **cyclopaedia**) an encyclopedia. □□ **cyclopedic** *adj.* [shortening of ENCYCLOPEDIA]

cyclopropane /síklōprōpayn/ *n.* *Chem.* a colourless gaseous cycloalkane used as a general anaesthetic. ¶ Chem. formula: C_3H_6.

Cyclops /síklops/ *n.* **1** (*pl.* **Cyclops** or **Cyclopses** or **Cyclopes** /síklōpeez/) (in Greek mythology) a member of a race of one-eyed giants. **2** (**cyclops**) (*pl.* **cyclops** or **cyclopes**) *Zool.* a crustacean of the genus *Cyclops*, with a single central eye. [L f. Gk *Kuklōps* f. *kuklos* circle + *ōps* eye]

cyclorama /sī́klō-raamə/ *n.* a circular panorama, curved wall, or cloth at the rear of a stage, esp. one used to represent the sky. □□ **cycloramic** /-rámmik/ *adj.*

cyclostome /sī́kləstōm/ *n.* any fishlike jawless vertebrate of the subclass Cyclostomata, having a large sucking mouth, e.g. a lamprey. □□ **cyclostomate** /-klóstəmət/ *adj.* [CYCLO- + Gk *stoma* mouth]

cyclostyle /sī́kləstīl/ *n.* & *v.* ● *n.* an apparatus for printing copies of writing from a stencil. ● *v.tr.* print or reproduce with this.

cyclothymia /sī́klōthī́miə/ *n. Psychol.* a disorder characterized by the occurrence of marked swings of mood from cheerfulness to misery. □□ **cyclothymic** *adj.* [CYCLO- + Gk *thumos* temper]

cyclotron /sī́klətron/ *n. Physics* an apparatus in which charged atomic and subatomic particles are accelerated by an alternating electric field while following an outward spiral or circular path in a magnetic field.

cyder var. of CIDER.

cygnet /sígnit/ *n.* a young swan. [ME f. AF *cignet* dimin. of OF *cigne* swan f. med.L *cycnus* f. Gk *kuknos*]

cylinder /síllindər/ *n.* **1 a** a uniform solid or hollow body with straight sides and a circular section. **b** a thing of this shape, e.g. a container for liquefied gas. **2** a cylinder-shaped part of various machines, esp. a piston-chamber in an engine. **3** *Printing* a metal roller. □ **cylinder saw** = *crown saw*. **cylinder seal** *Antiq.* a small barrel-shaped object of stone or baked clay bearing a cuneiform inscription, esp. for use as a seal. □□ **cylindrical** /-líndrik'l/ *adj.* **cylindrically** /-líndrikəli/ *adv.* [L *cylindrus* f. Gk *kulindros* f. *kulindō* roll]
■ **1** see ROLL *n.* 5a. **3** see ROLLER 1a.

cyma /sī́mə/ *n.* **1** *Archit.* an ogee moulding of a cornice. **2** = CYME. [mod.L f. Gk *kuma* wave, wavy moulding]

cymbal /símb'l/ *n.* a musical instrument consisting of a concave brass or bronze plate, struck with another or with a stick etc. to make a ringing sound. □□ **cymbalist** *n.* [ME f. L *cymbalum* f. Gk *kumbalon* f. *kumbē* cup]

cymbidium /simbíddiəm/ *n.* any tropical orchid of the genus *Cymbidium*, with a recess in the flower-lip. [mod.L f. Gk *kumbē* cup]

cymbiform /símbiform/ *adj. Anat.* & *Bot.* boat-shaped. [L *cymba* f. Gk *kumbē* boat + -FORM]

cyme /sīm/ *n. Bot.* an inflorescence in which the primary axis bears a single terminal flower that develops first, the system being continued by the axes of secondary and higher orders each with a flower (cf. RACEME). □□ **cymose** *adj.* [F, var. of *cime* summit, ult. f. Gk *kuma* wave]

Cymric /kímrik/ *adj.* Welsh. [Welsh *Cymru* Wales]

cynic /sínnik/ *n.* & *adj.* ● *n.* **1** a person who has little faith in human sincerity and goodness. **2** (**Cynic**) one of a school of ancient Greek philosophers founded by Antisthenes, marked by ostentatious contempt for ease and pleasure. ● *adj.* **1** (**Cynic**) of the Cynics. **2** = CYNICAL. □□ **cynicism** /-nisiz'm/ *n.* [L *cynicus* f. Gk *kunikos* f. *kuōn kunos* dog, nickname for a Cynic]
■ *n.* **1** see SCEPTIC *n.* 1.

cynical /sínnik'l/ *adj.* **1** of or characteristic of a cynic; incredulous of human goodness. **2** (of behaviour etc.) disregarding normal standards. **3** sneering, mocking. □□ **cynically** *adv.*
■ **1** see SCEPTICAL. **3** see SARDONIC 1.

cynocephalus /sī́nōséffələss/ *n.* **1** a fabled dog-headed man. **2** any flying lemur of the genus *Cynocephalus*, native to SE Asia. [Gk *kunokephalos* f. *kuōn kunos* dog + *kephalē* head]

cynosure /sī́nəzyoor, sín-/ *n.* **1** a centre of attraction or admiration. **2** a guiding star. [F *cynosure* or L *cynosura* f. Gk *kunosoura* dog's tail, Ursa Minor f. *kuōn kunos* dog + *oura* tail]
■ **1** see FOCUS *n.* 3.

cypher var. of CIPHER.

cy pres /seé práy/ *adv.* & *adj. Law* as near as possible to the testator's or donor's intentions when these cannot be precisely followed. [AF, = *si près* so near]

cypress /sī́prəss/ *n.* **1** any coniferous tree of the genus *Cupressus* or *Chamaecyparis*, with hard wood and dark foliage. **2** this, or branches from it, as a symbol of mourning. [ME f. OF *cipres* f. LL *cypressus* f. Gk *kuparissos*]

Cyprian /sípriən/ *n.* & *adj.* = CYPRIOT. [L *Cyprius* of Cyprus]

cyprinoid /síprinoyd/ *adj.* & *n.* ● *adj.* of or like a carp. ● *n.* a carp or related fish. [L *cyprinus* f. Gk *kuprinos* carp]

Cypriot /sípriət/ *n.* & *adj.* (also **Cypriote** /-ōt/) ● *n.* a native or national of Cyprus. ● *adj.* of Cyprus. [Gk *Kupriōtes* f. *Kupros* Cyprus in E. Mediterranean]

cypripedium /sípripeédiəm/ *n.* any orchid of the genus *Cypripedium*, esp. the lady's slipper. [mod.L f. Gk *Kupris* Aphrodite + *pedilon* slipper]

cypsela /sípsilə/ *n.* (*pl.* **cypselae** /-lee/) *Bot.* a dry single-seeded fruit formed from a double ovary of which only one develops into a seed, characteristic of the daisy family Compositae. [mod.L f. Gk *kupselē* hollow vessel]

Cyrillic /siríllik/ *adj.* & *n.* ● *adj.* denoting the alphabet used by the Slavonic peoples of the Orthodox Church; now used esp. for Russian and Bulgarian. ● *n.* this alphabet. [St *Cyril* d. 869, its reputed inventor]

cyst /sist/ *n.* **1** *Med.* a sac containing morbid matter, a parasitic larva, etc. **2** *Biol.* **a** a hollow organ, bladder, etc., in an animal or plant, containing a liquid secretion. **b** a cell or cavity enclosing reproductive bodies, an embryo, parasite, micro-organism, etc. [LL *cystis* f. Gk *kustis* bladder]
■ **1** see LUMP[1] *n.* 3.

cysteine /sísti-een, -ti-in/ *n. Biochem.* a sulphur-containing amino acid, essential in the human diet and a constituent of many enzymes. [CYSTINE + *-eine* (var. of -INE[4])]

cystic /sístik/ *adj.* **1** of the urinary bladder. **2** of the gall-bladder. **3** of the nature of a cyst. □ **cystic fibrosis** *Med.* a hereditary disease affecting the exocrine glands and usu. resulting in respiratory infections. [F *cystique* or mod.L *cysticus* (as CYST)]

cystitis /sistī́tiss/ *n.* an inflammation of the urinary bladder, often caused by infection, and usu. accompanied by frequent painful urination.

cysto- /sístō/ *comb. form* the urinary bladder (*cystoscope*; *cystotomy*). [Gk *kustē*, *kustis* bladder]

cystoscope /sístəskōp/ *n.* an instrument inserted in the urethra for examining the urinary bladder. □□ **cystoscopic** /-skóppik/ *adj.* **cystoscopy** /sistóskəpi/ *n.*

cystotomy /sistóttəmi/ *n.* (*pl.* **-ies**) a surgical incision into the urinary bladder.

-cyte /sīt/ *comb. form Biol.* a mature cell (*leucocyte*) (cf. -BLAST). [Gk *kutos* vessel]

cytidine /sī́tideen/ *n.* a nucleoside obtained from RNA by hydrolysis. [G *Cytidin* (as -CYTE)]

cyto- /sī́tō/ *comb. form Biol.* cells or a cell. [as -CYTE]

cytochrome /sī́tōkrōm/ *n. Biochem.* a compound consisting of a protein linked to a haem, which is involved in electron transfer reactions.

cytogenetics /sī́tōjinéttiks/ *n.* the study of inheritance in relation to the structure and function of cells. □□ **cytogenetic** *adj.* **cytogenetical** *adj.* **cytogenetically** *adv.* **cytogeneticist** /-tisist/ *n.*

cytology /sītólləji/ *n.* the study of cells. □□ **cytological** /sī́təlójik'l/ *adj.* **cytologically** /sī́təlójikəli/ *adv.* **cytologist** *n.*

cytoplasm /sī́tōplaz'm/ *n.* the protoplasmic content of a cell apart from its nucleus. □□ **cytoplasmic** /-plázmik/ *adj.*

cytosine /sī́tōseen/ *n.* one of the principal component bases of the nucleotides and the nucleic acids DNA and RNA, derived from pyrimidine.

cytotoxic /sī́tōtóksik/ *adj.* toxic to cells.

czar etc. var. of TSAR etc.

czardas var. of CSARDAS.

Czech /chek/ *n.* & *adj.* ● *n.* **1** a native or national of the Czech Republic, Bohemia, or (*hist.*) Czechoslovakia. **2** the West Slavonic language of the Czech people. ● *adj.* of or relating to the Czechs or their language. [Pol. spelling of Bohemian *Čech*]

Czechoslovak /chékkəslṓvak/ *n.* & *adj.* (also **Czechoslovakian** /-sləvákkiən/) ● *n.* a native or national of Czechoslovakia, a former State in central Europe including Bohemia, Moravia, and Slovakia. ● *adj.* of or relating to Czechoslovaks or the former State of Czechoslovakia. [CZECH + SLOVAK]

Dd

D[1] /dee/ *n.* (also **d**) (*pl.* **Ds** or **D's**) **1** the fourth letter of the alphabet. **2** *Mus.* the second note of the diatonic scale of C major. **3** (as a Roman numeral) 500. **4** = DEE. **5** the fourth highest class or category (of academic marks etc.).

D[2] *symb. Chem.* the element deuterium.

D[3] *abbr.* (also **D.**) **1** *US* Democrat. **2** dimension (*3-D*).

d. *abbr.* **1** died. **2** departs. **3** delete. **4** daughter. **5** *Brit.* (pre-decimal) penny. **6** depth. **7** deci-. [sense 5 f. L *denarius* silver coin]

'd *v. colloq.* (usu. after pronouns) had, would (*I'd; he'd*). [abbr.]

DA *abbr.* **1** *US* District Attorney. **2** *sl.* = *duck's arse* (see DUCK[1]).

D/A *abbr. Computing* digital to analogue.

da *abbr.* deca-.

dab[1] /dab/ *v.* & *n.* ● *v.* (**dabbed, dabbing**) **1** *tr.* press (a surface) briefly with a cloth, sponge, etc., without rubbing, esp. in cleaning or to apply a substance. **2** *tr.* press (a sponge etc.) lightly on a surface. **3** *tr.* (foll. by *on*) apply (a substance) by dabbing a surface. **4** *intr.* (usu. foll. by *at*) aim a feeble blow; tap. **5** *tr.* strike lightly; tap. ● *n.* **1** a brief application of a cloth, sponge, etc., to a surface without rubbing. **2** a small amount of something applied in this way (*a dab of paint*). **3** a light blow or tap. **4** (in *pl.*) *Brit. sl.* fingerprints. □□ **dabber** *n.* [ME, imit.]

■ *v.* **3** daub, touch; see also APPLY 4a. **5** see TAP[2] *v.* 1, 2. ● *n.* **1** daub, application, touch, administration, rubbing in, putting on. **2** touch, drop, trace, bit, mite, hint, suggestion, pinch, dash, spot, tinge, *colloq.* smidgen. **3** poke, pat, tap, touch; see also TAP[2] *n.*

dab[2] /dab/ *n.* any flat-fish of the genus *Limanda*. [15th c.: orig. unkn.]

dab[3] /dab/ *adj.* esp. *Brit. colloq.* □ **dab hand** (usu. foll. by *at*) a person especially skilled (in) (*a dab hand at cooking*). [17th c.: orig. unkn.]

■ □ **dab hand** past master, expert, master, adept, authority, wizard, ace.

dabble /dább'l/ *v.* **1** *intr.* (usu. foll. by *in, at*) take a casual or superficial interest or part (in a subject or activity). **2** *intr.* move the feet, hands, etc. about in (usu. a small amount of) liquid. **3** *tr.* wet partly or intermittently; moisten, stain, splash. □□ **dabbler** *n.* [16th c.: f. Du. *dabbelen* or DAB[1]]

■ **1** tinker, trifle, potter, dally; experiment. **3** moisten, dampen; splash, spatter, sprinkle, bespatter, besprinkle, bedabble, stain. □□ **dabbler** see DILETTANTE *n.*

dabchick /dábchik/ *n.* = *little grebe* (see GREBE). [16th c., in earlier forms *dap-, dop-*: perh. rel. to OE *dūfedoppa*, DEEP, DIP]

da capo /daá kaápō/ *adv. Mus.* repeat from the beginning. [It.]

dace /dayss/ *n.* (*pl.* same) any small freshwater fish, esp. of the genus *Leuciscus*, related to the carp. [OF *dars*: see DART]

dacha /dáchə/ *n.* a country house or cottage in Russia. [Russ., = gift]

dachshund /dáks-hŏŏnd/ *n.* **1** a dog of a short-legged long-bodied breed. **2** this breed. [G, = badger-dog]

dacoit /dəkóyt/ *n.* (in India or Burma) a member of a band of armed robbers. [Hindi *ḍakait* f. *ḍākā* gang-robbery]

dactyl /dáktil/ *n.* a metrical foot (¯ ˘ ˘) consisting of one long (or stressed) syllable followed by two short (or unstressed). [ME f. L *dactylus* f. Gk *daktulos* finger, the three bones corresponding to the three syllables]

dactylic /daktíllik/ *adj.* & *n.* ● *adj.* of or using dactyls. ● *n.* (usu. in *pl.*) dactylic verse. [L *dactylicus* f. Gk *daktulikos* (as DACTYL)]

dad /dad/ *n. colloq.* father. [perh. imit. of a child's *da, da* (cf. DADDY)]

■ see FATHER *n.* 1a.

Dada /daádaa/ *n.* an early 20th-c. international movement in art, literature, music, and film, repudiating and mocking artistic and social conventions. □□ **Dadaism** /-dəiz'm/ *n.* **Dadaist** /-dəist/ *n.* & *adj.* **Dadaistic** /-dəístik/ *adj.* [F (the title of an early 20th-c. review) f. *dada* hobby-horse]

daddy /dáddi/ *n.* (*pl.* **-ies**) *colloq.* **1** father. **2** (usu. foll. by *of*) the oldest or supreme example (*had a daddy of a headache*). □ **daddy-long-legs 1** a crane-fly. **2** *US* a harvestman. [DAD + -Y[3]]

■ **1** see FATHER *n.* 1a.

dado /dáydō/ *n.* (*pl.* **-os**) **1** the lower part of the wall of a room when visually distinct from the upper part. **2** the plinth of a column. **3** the cube of a pedestal between the base and the cornice. [It., = DIE[2]]

daemon var. of DEMON[1] 5.

daemonic var. of DEMONIC.

daff /daf/ *n. colloq.* = DAFFODIL. [abbr.]

daffodil /dáffədil/ *n.* **1 a** a bulbous plant, *Narcissus pseudonarcissus*, with a yellow trumpet-shaped crown. **b** any of various other large-flowered plants of the genus *Narcissus*. **c** a flower of any of these plants. **2** a pale-yellow colour. [earlier *affodill*, as ASPHODEL]

daffy /dáffi/ *adj.* (**daffier, daffiest**) *sl.* = DAFT. □□ **daffily** *adv.* **daffiness** *n.* [*daff* simpleton + -Y[2]]

daft /daaft/ *adj.* esp. *Brit. colloq.* **1** silly, foolish, crazy. **2** (foll. by *about*) fond of; infatuated with. □□ **daftly** *adv.* **daftness** *n.* [ME *daffte* = OE *gedæfte* mild, meek, f. Gmc]

■ **1** foolish, silly, giddy, senseless, absurd, ridiculous, stupid, nonsensical, fatuous, imbecile, imbecilic, idiotic, cretinous, boneheaded, fat-headed, dim-witted, witless, asinine, weak-minded, simple-minded, brainless, feeble-minded, feather-brained, hare-brained, slow-witted, addle-brained, *colloq.* dumb, dopey, moronic, cock-eyed, halfwitted, *esp. Brit. colloq.* gormless, *esp. US colloq.* dumb, *sl.* daffy, *Austral. sl.* dilly; see also CRAZY 1. **2** (*daft about*) fond of, mad about, infatuated with, besotted by *or* with, *colloq.* nuts about, sweet on, crazy about.

dag[1] /dag/ *n.* & *v. Austral.* & *NZ* ● *n.* (usu. in *pl.*) a lock of wool clotted with dung on the hinder parts of a sheep. ● *v.tr.* (**dagged, dagging**) remove dags from (a sheep). □ **rattle one's dags** *sl.* hurry up. □□ **dagger** *n.* [orig. Engl. dial.]

■ □ **rattle one's dags** see HURRY *v.* 1.

dag[2] /dag/ *n. Austral.* & *NZ sl.* an eccentric or noteworthy person; a character (*he's a bit of a dag*). [orig. Engl. dial., = a dare, challenge]

■ see ECCENTRIC *n.*

dagga /dággə/ *n. S.Afr.* **1** hemp used as a narcotic. **2** any plant of the genus *Leontis* used similarly. [Afrik. f. Hottentot *dachab*]

dagger /dággər/ *n.* **1** a short stabbing-weapon with a pointed and edged blade. **2** *Printing* = OBELUS. □ **at daggers drawn** in bitter enmity. **look daggers at** glare angrily or venomously at. [ME, perh. f. obs. *dag* pierce, infl. by OF *dague* long dagger]
■ **1** knife, short sword, stiletto, dirk, kris, *hist.* skean, *literary* poniard, *poet.* blade. □ **look daggers at** see GLARE[1] *v.* 1.

dago /dáygō/ *n.* (*pl.* **-os**) *sl. offens.* a foreigner, esp. a Spaniard, Portuguese, or Italian. [Sp. *Diego* = James]

daguerreotype /dəgérrōtīp/ *n.* **1** a photograph taken by an early photographic process employing an iodine-sensitized silvered plate and mercury vapour. **2** this process. [L. *Daguerre*, Fr. inventor d. 1851]

dah /daa/ *n.* esp. *US Telegraphy* (in the Morse system) = DASH (cf. DIT). [imit.]

dahlia /dáyliə/ *n.* any composite garden plant of the genus *Dahlia*, of Mexican origin, cultivated for its many-coloured single or double flowers. [A. *Dahl*, Sw. botanist d. 1789]

Dáil /doyl/ *n.* (in full **Dáil Éireann** /áirən/) the lower house of parliament in the Republic of Ireland. [Ir., = assembly (of Ireland)]

daily /dáyli/ *adj.*, *adv.*, & *n.* ● *adj.* **1** done, produced, or occurring every day or every weekday. **2** constant, regular. ● *adv.* **1** every day; from day to day. **2** constantly. ● *n.* (*pl.* **-ies**) *colloq.* **1** a daily newspaper. **2** *Brit.* a charwoman or domestic help working daily. □ **daily bread** necessary food; a livelihood. **daily dozen** *Brit. colloq.* regular exercises, esp. on rising. [ME f. DAY + -LY[1], -LY[2]]
■ *adj.* **1** diurnal, everyday, quotidian, *Physiol.* circadian. **2** constant, continual, everyday, routine, regular, common, commonplace. ● *adv.* **1** every day, day after day. **2** constantly, always, habitually, routinely, regularly, continually, continuously. ● *n.* **2** see DOMESTIC *n.* □ **daily bread** see SUSTENANCE 2.

daimon /dīmōn/ *n.* = DEMON[1] 5. □□ **daimonic** /-mónnik/ *adj.* [Gk, = deity]

dainty /dáynti/ *adj.* & *n.* ● *adj.* (**daintier**, **daintiest**) **1** delicately pretty. **2** delicate of build or in movement. **3** (of food) choice. **4** fastidious; having delicate taste and sensibility. ● *n.* (*pl.* **-ies**) a choice morsel; a delicacy. □□ **daintily** *adv.* **daintiness** *n.* [AF *dainté*, OF *daintié*, *deintié* f. L *dignitas -tatis* f. *dignus* worthy]
■ *adj.* **1, 2** delicate, graceful, fine, elegant, exquisite, neat. **3** delicious, tasty, appetizing, palatable, toothsome, *literary* delectable; see also CHOICE *adj.* **4** fastidious, sensitive, squeamish, finicky, finical, over-nice, overrefined, genteel, mincing. ● *n.* delicacy, sweetmeat, treat, titbit, *bonne bouche*, morsel.

daiquiri /dákkəri, dī-/ *n.* (*pl.* **daiquiris**) a cocktail of rum, lime-juice, etc. [*Daiquiri* in Cuba]

dairy /dáiri/ *n.* (*pl.* **-ies**) **1** a building or room for the storage, processing, and distribution of milk and its products. **2** a shop where milk and milk products are sold. **3** (*attrib.*) **a** of, containing, or concerning milk and its products (and sometimes eggs). **b** used for dairy products (*dairy cow*). [ME *deierie* f. *deie* maidservant f. OE *dǣge* kneader of dough]

dairying /dáiri-ing/ *n.* the business of producing, storing, and distributing milk and its products.

dairymaid /dáirimayd/ *n.* a woman employed in a dairy.

dairyman /dáirimən/ *n.* (*pl.* **-men**) **1** a man dealing in dairy products. **2** a man employed in a dairy.

dais /dáyiss/ *n.* a low platform, usu. at the upper end of a hall and used to support a table, lectern, etc. [ME f. OF *deis* f. L *discus* disc, dish, in med.L = table]

daisy /dáyzi/ *n.* (*pl.* **-ies**) **1 a** a small composite plant, *Bellis perennis*, bearing flowers each with a yellow disc and white rays. **b** any other plant with daisy-like flowers, esp. the larger ox-eye daisy, the Michaelmas daisy, or the Shasta daisy. **2** *sl.* a first-rate specimen of anything. □ **daisy-chain** a string of daisies threaded together. **daisy-cutter** *Cricket* a ball bowled so as to roll along the ground. **daisy wheel** *Computing* a disc of spokes extending radially from a central hub, each terminating in a printing character, used as a printer in word processors and typewriters. **pushing up the daisies** *sl.* dead and buried. [OE *dæges ēage* day's eye, the flower opening in the morning]

Dak. *abbr.* Dakota.

dal var. of DHAL.

Dalai lama /dállī laámə/ *n.* the spiritual head of Tibetan Buddhism, formerly also the chief ruler of Tibet (see LAMA). [Mongolian *dalai* ocean; see LAMA]

dale /dayl/ *n.* a valley, esp. in N. England. [OE *dæl* f. Gmc]
■ see VALLEY *n.*

dalesman /dáylzmən/ *n.* (*pl.* **-men**) an inhabitant of the dales in Northern England.

dalliance /dálliənss/ *n.* **1** a leisurely or frivolous passing of time. **2** the act or an instance of light-hearted flirting. [DALLY + -ANCE]
■ **1** see SPORT *n.* 3. **2** see ROMANCE *n.* 2c.

dally /dálli/ *v.intr.* (**-ies**, **-ied**) **1** delay; waste time, esp. frivolously. **2** (often foll. by *with*) play about; flirt, treat frivolously (*dallied with her affections*). □ **dally away** waste or fritter (one's time, life, etc.). [ME f. OF *dalier* chat]
■ **1** see DELAY *v.* 3. **2** see FLIRT *v.* 1.

Dalmatian /dalmáysh'n/ *n.* **1** a dog of a large white short-haired breed with dark spots. **2** this breed. [*Dalmatia* in Croatia]

dalmatic /dalmáttik/ *n.* a wide-sleeved long loose vestment open at the sides, worn by deacons and bishops, and by a monarch at his or her coronation. [ME f. OF *dalmatique* or LL *dalmatica* (*vestis* robe) of Dalmatia]

dal segno /dal sáynyō/ *adv. Mus.* repeat from the point marked by a sign. [It., = from the sign]

daltonism /dáwltəniz'm/ *n.* colour-blindness, esp. a congenital inability to distinguish between red and green. [F *daltonisme* f. J. *Dalton*, Engl. chemist d. 1844, who suffered from it]

dam[1] /dam/ *n.* & *v.* ● *n.* **1** a barrier constructed to hold back water and raise its level, forming a reservoir or preventing flooding. **2** a barrier constructed in a stream by a beaver. **3** anything functioning as a dam does. **4** a causeway. ● *v.tr.* (**dammed**, **damming**) **1** furnish or confine with a dam. **2** (often foll. by *up*) block up; hold back; obstruct. [ME f. MLG, MDu.]
■ *v.* see PLUG *v.* 1.

dam[2] /dam/ *n.* the female parent of an animal, esp. a four-footed one. [ME: var. of DAME]

damage /dámmij/ *n.* & *v.* ● *n.* **1** harm or injury impairing the value or usefulness of something, or the health or normal function of a person. **2** (in *pl.*) *Law* a sum of money claimed or awarded in compensation for a loss or an injury. **3** the loss of what is desirable. **4** (prec. by *the*) *sl.* cost (*what's the damage?*). ● *v.tr.* **1** inflict damage on. **2** (esp. as **damaging** *adj.*) detract from the reputation of (*a most damaging admission*). □□ **damagingly** *adv.* [ME f. OF *damage* (n.), *damagier* (v.), f. *dam(me)* loss f. L *damnum* loss, damage]
■ *n.* **1** harm, injury, hurt, impairment, mutilation, destruction, devastation. **2** (*damages*) compensation, reparation, indemnity. **4** expense, price, cost; bill. ● *v.* **1** harm, hurt, injure, impair, mar, deface. **2** spoil, impair; see also DETRACT.

damascene /dámməseén/ *v.*, *n.*, & *adj.* ● *v.tr.* decorate (metal, esp. iron or steel) by etching or inlaying esp. with gold or silver, or with a watered pattern produced in welding. ● *n.* a design or article produced in this way. ● *adj.* of, relating to, or produced by this process. [*Damascene* of Damascus, f. L *Damascenus* f. Gk *Damaskēnos*]

damask /dámməsk/ *n.*, *adj.*, & *v.* ● *n.* **1 a** a figured woven fabric (esp. silk or linen) with a pattern visible on both sides. **b** twilled table linen with woven designs shown by the reflection of light. **2** a tablecloth made of this material. **3** *hist.* steel with a watered pattern produced in welding. ● *adj.* **1** made of or resembling damask. **2** coloured like a damask rose, velvety pink or vivid red. ● *v.tr.* **1** weave with figured designs. **2** = DAMASCENE *v.* **3** ornament. □ **damask rose** an old sweet-scented variety of rose, with very soft velvety petals, used to make attar. [ME, ult. f. L *Damascus*]

dame /daym/ *n.* **1** (**Dame**) **a** (in the UK) the title given to a woman with the rank of Knight Commander or holder of the Grand Cross in the Orders of Chivalry. **b** a woman holding this title. **2** *Brit.* a comic middle-aged woman in modern pantomime, usu. played by a man. **3** *archaic* a mature woman. **4** *US sl.* a woman. □ **dame-school** *hist.* a primary school kept by an elderly woman. [ME f. OF f. L *domina* mistress]
■ **4** see WOMAN 1.

damfool /dámfōōl/ *adj. colloq.* foolish, stupid. [DAMN + FOOL[1]]

dammar /dámmər/ *n.* **1** any E. Asian tree, esp. one of the genus *Agathis* or *Shorea*, yielding a resin used in varnish-making. **2** this resin. [Malay *damar*]

dammit /dámmit/ *int.* damn it.

damn /dam/ *v., n., adj., & adv.* ● *v.tr.* **1** (often *absol.* or as *int.* of anger or annoyance, = *may God damn*) curse (a person or thing). **2** doom to hell; cause the damnation of. **3** condemn, censure (*a review damning the performance*). **4 a** (often as **damning** *adj.*) (of a circumstance, piece of evidence, etc.) show or prove to be guilty; bring condemnation upon (*evidence against them was damning*). **b** be the ruin of. ● *n.* **1** an uttered curse. **2** *sl.* a negligible amount (*not worth a damn*). ● *adj.* & *adv. colloq.* = DAMNED. □ **damn all** *sl.* nothing at all. **damn well** *colloq.* (as an emphatic) simply (*damn well do as I say*). **damn with faint praise** commend so unenthusiastically as to imply disapproval. **I'm** (or **I'll be**) **damned if** *colloq.* I certainly do not, will not, etc. **not give a damn** see GIVE. **well I'm** (or **I'll be**) **damned** *colloq.* exclamation of surprise, dismay, etc. □□ **damningly** *adv.* [ME f. OF *damner* f. L *damnare* inflict loss on f. *damnum* loss]
■ *v.* **1** see CURSE *v.* 1. **2** doom, condemn, sentence. **3** condemn, criticize, find fault with, censure, berate, castigate, upbraid, attack, blast, reprimand, reprove, remonstrate, denounce. **4 b** see RUIN *v.* 1a. ● *n.* **1** see CURSE *n.* 1. **2** jot, tittle, *colloq.* brass farthing, *sl.* hoot, two hoots (in hell). □ **damn all** see NOTHING *n.* 1, 2. **damn well** well enough, *colloq.* jolly well. **well I'm** (or **I'll be**) **damned** well I never, *colloq.* you don't say, *sl.* well I'll be blowed.

damnable /dámnəb'l/ *adj.* hateful, annoying. □□ **damnably** *adv.* [ME f. OF *damnable* (as DAMN)]
■ hateful, terrible, horrible, horrid, atrocious, abominable, dreadful, hideous, execrable, accursed, cursed, detestable, abhorrent, despicable, loathsome, wicked, sinful, offensive, heinous, pernicious, infernal, malicious, malevolent, outrageous, foul, rotten, base, vile, odious, *colloq.* awful, damned; see also IRKSOME.

damnation /damnáysh'n/ *n.* & *int.* ● *n.* condemnation to eternal punishment, esp. in hell. ● *int.* expressing anger or annoyance. [ME f. OF *damnation* (as DAMN)]
■ *n.* see PERDITION.

damnatory /dámnətəri, -tri/ *adj.* conveying or causing censure or damnation. [L *damnatorius* (as DAMN)]

damned /damd/ *adj.* & *adv. colloq.* ● *adj.* damnable, infernal, unwelcome. ● *adv.* extremely (*damned hot*; *damned lovely*). □ **damned well** (as an emphatic) simply (*you've damned well got to*). **do one's damnedest** do one's utmost.
■ *adj.* see INFERNAL 1, FLAMING 3b. ● *adv.* see *extremely* (EXTREME).

damnify /dámnifī/ *v.tr.* (**-ies, -ied**) *Law* cause injury to. □□ **damnification** /-fikáysh'n/ *n.* [OF *damnifier* etc. f. LL *damnificare* injure (as DAMN)]

damp /damp/ *adj., n., & v.* ● *adj.* slightly wet; moist. ● *n.* **1** diffused moisture in the air, on a surface, or in a solid, esp. as a cause of inconvenience or danger. **2** dejection; discouragement. **3** = FIREDAMP. ● *v.tr.* **1** make damp; moisten. **2** (often foll. by *down*) **a** take the force or vigour out of (*damp one's enthusiasm*). **b** make flaccid or spiritless. **c** make (a fire) burn less strongly by reducing the flow of air to it. **3** reduce or stop the vibration of (esp. the strings of a musical instrument). **4** quieten. □ **damp** (or **damp-proof**) **course** a layer of waterproof material in the wall of a building near the ground, to prevent rising damp. **damp off** (of a plant) die from a fungus attack in damp conditions. **damp squib** an unsuccessful attempt to impress etc. □□ **damply** *adv.* **dampness** *n.* [ME f. MLG, = vapour etc., OHG *dampf* steam f. WG]
■ *adj.* moist, wettish; humid, dank, steamy, clammy, muggy. ● *n.* **1** moistness, moisture, dampness, clamminess, humidity, wetness. **2** see DEPRESSION 1b. ● *v.* **1** see DAMPEN 1. **2 a, b** see DAMPEN 2. **4** see QUIETEN. □ **damp squib** see FLOP *n.* □□ **dampness** see DAMP *n.* 1 above.

dampen /dámpən/ *v.* **1** *v.tr.* & *intr.* make or become damp. **2** *tr.* make less forceful or vigorous; stifle, choke. □□ **dampener** *n.*
■ **1** damp, moisten, bedew; see also WET *v.* **2** stifle, deaden, choke, damp, damp down, check, chill, cool, restrain, retard, lessen, diminish, reduce, suppress, abate, moderate, allay, subdue, temper, dull, discourage.

damper /dámpər/ *n.* **1** a person or thing that discourages, or tempers enthusiasm. **2** a device that reduces shock or noise. **3** a metal plate in a flue to control the draught, and so the rate of combustion. **4** *Mus.* a pad silencing a piano string except when removed by means of a pedal or by the note's being struck. **5** esp. *Austral.* & *NZ* unleavened bread or cake of flour and water baked in wood ashes. □ **put a damper on** take the vigour or enjoyment out of.
■ **1** see SPOILSPORT.

damsel /dámz'l/ *n. archaic* or *literary* a young unmarried woman. [ME f. OF *dam(e)isele* ult. f. L *domina* mistress]
■ see MAID 2.

damselfish /dámz'lfish/ *n.* a small brightly-coloured fish, *Chromis chromis*, found in or near coral reefs.

damselfly /dámz'lflī/ *n.* (*pl.* **-flies**) any of various insects of the order Odonata, like a dragonfly but with its wings folded over the body when resting.

damson /dámz'n/ *n.* & *adj.* ● *n.* **1** (in full **damson plum**) **a** a small dark-purple plumlike fruit. **b** the small deciduous tree, *Prunus institia*, bearing this. **2** a dark-purple colour. ● *adj.* damson-coloured. □ **damson cheese** a solid preserve of damsons and sugar. [ME *damacene, -scene, -sene* f. L *damascenum* (*prunum* plum) of *Damascus*: see DAMASCENE]

Dan. *abbr.* Daniel (Old Testament).

dan[1] /dan/ *n.* **1** any of twelve degrees of advanced proficiency in judo. **2** a person who has achieved any of these. [Jap.]

dan[2] /dan/ *n.* (in full **dan buoy**) a small buoy used as a marker in deep-sea fishing, or to mark the limits of an area cleared by minesweepers. [17th c.: orig. unkn.]

dance /daanss/ *v.* & *n.* ● *v.* **1** *intr.* move about rhythmically alone or with a partner or in a set, usu. in fixed steps or sequences to music, for pleasure or as entertainment. **2** *intr.* move in a lively way; skip or jump about. **3** *tr.* **a** perform (a specified dance or form of dancing). **b** perform (a specified role) in a ballet etc. **4** *intr.* move up and down (on water, in the field of vision, etc.). **5** *tr.* move (esp. a child) up and down; dandle. ● *n.* **1 a** a piece of dancing; a sequence of steps in dancing. **b** a special form of this. **2** a single round or turn of a dance. **3** a social gathering for dancing, a ball. **4** a piece of music for dancing to or in a dance rhythm. **5** a dancing or lively motion. □ **dance attendance on** follow or wait on (a person) obsequiously. **dance of death** a medieval dance in which a personified Death is represented as leading all to the grave. **dance to a person's tune** accede obsequiously to a person's demands and wishes. **lead a person a dance** (or **merry dance**) *Brit.* cause a person much trouble in following a course one has instigated. □□ **danceable** *adj.* [ME f. OF *dance, danse* (n.), *dancer, danser* (v.), f. Rmc, of unkn. orig.]
■ *v.* **1** *colloq.* bop, *sl.* hoof it. **2** gambol, caper, skip, leap, romp, jump about, frolic, *sl.* cavort. **4** see WAG[1] *v.* ● *n.* **3** ball, social, dancing party, tea dance, *thé dansant*, *US*

promenade, *colloq.* hop, bop, rave(-up), *US colloq.* prom.

dancehall /daánss-hawl/ *n.* a public hall for dancing.

dancer /daánsər/ *n.* **1** a person who performs a dance. **2** a person whose profession is dancing.

d. and c. *n.* dilatation (of the cervix) and curettage (of the uterus), performed after a miscarriage or for the removal of cysts, tumours, etc.

dandelion /dándilīən/ *n.* a composite plant, *Taraxacum officinale*, with jagged leaves and a large bright-yellow flower on a hollow stalk, followed by a globular head of seeds with downy tufts. □ **dandelion clock** the downy seed-head of a dandelion. **dandelion coffee** dried and powdered dandelion roots; a drink made from this. [F *dent-de-lion* transl. med.L *dens leonis* lion's tooth]

dander /dándər/ *n. colloq.* temper, anger, indignation. □ **get one's dander up** lose one's temper; become angry. [19th c.: orig. uncert.]

dandify /dándifī/ *v.tr.* (**-ies, -ied**) cause to resemble a dandy.

dandle /dánd'l/ *v.tr.* **1** dance (a child) on one's knees or in one's arms. **2** pamper, pet. [16th c.: orig. unkn.]
■ **2** see BABY *v.*

dandruff /dándruf/ *n.* **1** dead skin in small scales among the hair. **2** the condition of having this. [16th c.: *-ruff* perh. rel. to ME *rove* scurfiness f. ON *hrufa* or MLG, MDu. *rōve*]

dandy /dándi/ *n.* & *adj.* ● *n.* (*pl.* **-ies**) **1** a man unduly devoted to style, smartness, and fashion in dress and appearance. **2** *colloq.* an excellent thing. ● *adj.* (**dandier, dandiest**) esp. *US colloq.* very good of its kind; splendid, first-rate. □ **dandy-brush** a brush for grooming a horse. **dandy roll** (or **roller**) a device for solidifying, and impressing a watermark in, paper during manufacture. □□ **dandyish** *adj.* **dandyism** *n.* [18th c.: perh. orig. = *Andrew*, in *Jack-a-dandy*]
■ *n.* **1** fop, coxcomb, *petit-maître*, beau, blood, *archaic* gallant, *colloq.* swell, clothes-horse, *Brit. sl.* toff, *US sl.* dude. ● *adj.* see SPLENDID 3.

Dane /dayn/ *n.* **1** a native or national of Denmark. **2** *hist.* a Viking invader of England in the 9th–11th c. □ **Great Dane 1** a dog of a very large short-haired breed. **2** this breed. [ME f. ON *Danir* (pl.), LL *Dani*]

Danegeld /dáyngeld/ *n. hist.* **1** (in pre-Conquest England) an annual tax to raise funds for protection against Danish invaders. **2** appeasement by bribery. [OE (as DANE + ON *gjald* payment)]

Danelaw /dáynlaw/ *n. hist.* the part of N. & E. England occupied or administered by Danes in the 9th–11th c. [OE *Dena lagu* Danes' law]

danger /dáynjər/ *n.* **1** liability or exposure to harm. **2** a thing that causes or is likely to cause harm. **3** the status of a railway signal directing a halt or caution. □ **danger list** a list of those dangerously ill, esp. in a hospital. **danger money** extra payment for dangerous work. **in danger of** likely to incur or to suffer from. [earlier sense 'jurisdiction, power': ME f. OF *dangier* ult. f. L *dominus* lord]
■ **1, 2** peril, risk, threat, jeopardy, endangerment, hazard; (*in danger*) in jeopardy, at risk, under threat. □ **in danger of** likely to, liable to.

dangerous /dáynjərəss/ *adj.* involving or causing danger. □□ **dangerously** *adv.* **dangerousness** *n.* [ME f. AF *dangerous*, *daungerous*, OF *dangereus* (as DANGER)]
■ risky, perilous, treacherous, hazardous, unsafe, precarious, chancy; threatening, menacing, harmful. □□ **dangerously** perilously, hazardously, unsafely, precariously, recklessly; ominously, alarmingly.

dangle /dángg'l/ *v.* **1** *intr.* be loosely suspended, so as to be able to sway to and fro. **2** *tr.* hold or carry loosely suspended. **3** *tr.* hold out (a hope, temptation, etc.) enticingly. □□ **dangler** *n.* [16th c. (imit.): cf. Sw. *dangla*, Da. *dangle*]
■ **1** hang down, droop, swing, *archaic poet.* depend; see also HANG *v.* 10. **3** hold out, flaunt, brandish, wave, flourish.

Daniell cell /dányəl/ *n. Physics* & *Chem.* a primary voltaic cell with a copper anode and a zinc-amalgam cathode giving a standard electromotive force when either copper sulphate or sulphuric acid is used as the electrolyte. [John *Daniell*, Brit. chemist d. 1845, its inventor]

Danish /dáynish/ *adj.* & *n.* ● *adj.* of or relating to Denmark or the Danes. ● *n.* **1** the Danish language. **2** (prec. by *the*; treated as *pl.*) the Danish people. □ **Danish blue** a soft salty white cheese with blue veins. **Danish pastry** a cake of sweetened yeast pastry topped with icing, fruit, nuts, etc. [ME f. AF *danes*, OF *daneis* f. med.L *Danensis* (as DANE)]

dank /dangk/ *adj.* disagreeably damp and cold. □□ **dankly** *adv.* **dankness** *n.* [ME prob. f. Scand.: cf. Sw. *dank* marshy spot]
■ see DAMP *adj.*

danse macabre /dónss məkaábrə/ *n.* = *dance of death*. [F (as DANCE, MACABRE)]

danseur /donsőr/ *n.* (*fem.* ***danseuse*** /-sőz/) a ballet-dancer. [F, = dancer]

Dantean /dántiən, dantéeən/ *adj.* & *n.* ● *adj.* **1** of Dante. **2** in the style of or reminiscent of Dante's writings. ● *n.* a student or imitator of Dante. □□ **Dantesque** /-tésk/ *adj.* [*Dante* Alighieri, It. poet d. 1321]

danthonia /danthṓniə/ *n. Austral.* & *NZ* any tufted pasture grass of the genus *Danthonia*. [mod.L f. E. *Danthoine* 19th-c. Fr. botanist]

dap /dap/ *v.* (**dapped, dapping**) **1** *intr.* fish by letting the bait bob on the water. **2** *tr.* & *intr.* dip lightly. **3** *tr.* & *intr.* bounce on the ground. [cf. DAB[1]]

daphne /dáfni/ *n.* any flowering shrub of the genus *Daphne*, e.g. the spurge laurel or mezereon. [ME, = laurel, f. Gk *daphnē*]

daphnia /dáfniə/ *n.* any freshwater branchiopod crustacean of the genus *Daphnia*, enclosed in a transparent carapace and with long antennae and prominent eyes. Also called *freshwater flea*. [mod.L f. *Daphne* name of a nymph in Gk mythol., f. DAPHNE]

dapper /dáppər/ *adj.* **1** neat and precise, esp. in dress or movement. **2** sprightly. □□ **dapperly** *adv.* **dapperness** *n.* [ME f. MLG, MDu. *dapper* strong, stout]
■ **1** neat, spruce, smart, trim, well-dressed, well turned out, stylish, fashionable, elegant, chic, dressy, dressed up to the nines, dressed to kill, swanky, *colloq.* nifty, swell, classy, sharp, ritzy, *esp. US colloq.* swank, *sl.* snazzy, *esp. US sl.* spiffy. **2** see SPRIGHTLY.

dapple /dápp'l/ *v.* & *n.* ● *v.* **1** *tr.* mark with spots or rounded patches of colour or shade. **2** *intr.* become marked in this way. ● *n.* **1** a dappled effect. **2** a dappled animal, esp. a horse. □ **dapple grey 1** (of an animal's coat) grey or white with darker spots. **2** a horse of this colour. [ME *dappled*, *dappeld*, (adj.), of unkn. orig.]
■ *v.* **1** spot, dot, mottle, speckle, stipple. ● *n.* **2** piebald, skewbald, dapple grey, *US* pinto. □ **dapple grey 1** spotted, mottled, speckled, flecked, dappled, brindled; pied, piebald, skewbald, *US* pinto. **2** see DAPPLE *n.* 2 above.

darbies /daárbiz/ *n.pl. Brit. sl.* handcuffs. [allusive use of *Father Darby's bands*, some rigid form of agreement for debtors (16th c.)]

Darby and Joan /daárbi ənd jṓn/ *n.* a devoted old married couple. □ **Darby and Joan club** *Brit.* a club for people over 60. [18th c.: perh. f. a poem of 1735 in the *Gentleman's Magazine*]

dare /dair/ *v.* & *n.* ● *v.tr.* (*3rd sing. present* usu. **dare** before an expressed or implied infinitive without *to*) **1** (foll. by infin. with or without *to*) venture (to); have the courage or impudence (to) (*dare he do it?*; *if they dare to come*; *how dare you?*; *I dare not speak*; *I do not dare to jump*). **2** (usu. foll. by *to* + infin.) defy or challenge (a person) (*I dare you to own up*). **3** *literary* attempt; take the risk of (*dare all things*; *dared their anger*). ● *n.* **1** an act of daring. **2** a challenge, esp. to prove courage. □ **I dare say 1** (often foll. by *that* + clause) it is probable. **2** probably; I grant that much (*I dare say, but*

you are still wrong). ▫▫ **darer** *n*. [OE *durran* with Gmc cognates: cf. Skr. *dhṛsh*, Gk *tharseō* be bold]
▪ *v*. **1** venture, risk, hazard, make bold, be so bold as. **2** challenge, defy. **3** see ATTEMPT *v*. ● *n*. **2** challenge, provocation, taunt.

daredevil /dáirdevv'l/ *n*. & *adj*. ● *n*. a recklessly daring person. ● *adj*. recklessly daring. ▫▫ **daredevilry** *n*. **daredeviltry** *n*.
▪ *n*. adventurer, adventuress, swashbuckler, hero, heroine, soldier of fortune, *Austral. colloq*. Ned Kelly. ● *adj*. reckless, rash, death-defying, impulsive, daring, impetuous, incautious, wild, foolhardy, madcap, devil-may-care; audacious, bold, brave, fearless, gallant, courageous, intrepid.

darg /daarg/ *n*. *Sc*., *N.Engl*., & *Austral*. **1** a day's work. **2** a definite amount of work; a task. [ME f. *daywerk* or *daywark* day-work]

daring /dáiring/ *n*. & *adj*. ● *n*. adventurous courage. ● *adj*. adventurous, bold; prepared to take risks. ▫▫ **daringly** *adv*.
▪ *n*. courage, boldness, bravery, valour, intrepidity, fearlessness, pluck, spirit, mettle, nerve, adventurousness, *colloq*. guts, grit, spunk, *literary joc*. derring-do, *Brit. sl*. bottle. ● *adj*. bold, adventurous, audacious, courageous, brave, valorous, intrepid, fearless, unafraid, plucky, mettlesome, venturesome, *archaic or joc*. doughty, *colloq*. gutsy, *US* nervy; rash, reckless.

dariole /dárriōl/ *n*. a savoury or sweet dish cooked and served in a small mould usu. shaped like a flowerpot. [ME f. OF]

Darjeeling /daarjéeling/ *n*. a high-quality tea from Darjeeling in NE India.

dark /daark/ *adj*. & *n*. ● *adj*. **1** with little or no light. **2** of a deep or sombre colour. **3** (of a person) with deep brown or black hair, complexion, or skin. **4** gloomy, depressing, dismal (*dark thoughts*). **5** evil, sinister (*dark deeds*). **6** sullen, angry (*a dark mood*). **7** remote, secret, mysterious, little-known (*the dark and distant past*; *keep it dark*). **8** ignorant, unenlightened. ● *n*. **1** absence of light. **2** nightfall (*don't go out after dark*). **3** a lack of knowledge. **4** a dark area or colour, esp. in painting (*the skilled use of lights and darks*). ▫ **the Dark Ages** (or **Age**) **1** the period of European history preceding the Middle Ages, esp. the 5th–10th c. **2** any period of supposed unenlightenment. **the Dark Continent** a name for Africa, esp. when little known to Europeans. **dark glasses** spectacles with dark-tinted lenses. **dark horse** a little-known person who is unexpectedly successful or prominent. **dark star** an invisible star known to exist from reception of physical data other than light. **in the dark** lacking information. ▫▫ **darkish** *adj*. **darkly** *adv*. **darkness** *n*. **darksome** *poet*. *adj*. [OE *deorc* prob. f. Gmc]
▪ *adj*. **1** unlit, unlighted, unilluminated, ill-lit, sunless, *poet*. darkling; dim, murky, gloomy, dusky, shady, shadowy, *formal* subfusc, *literary* tenebrous; black, pitch-dark, pitch-black, jet-black, *literary* Stygian. **2** deep; inky, sooty; dreary, dull, drab, sombre. **3** brunette; black, swarthy, dark-hued, brown, *archaic* swart; (sun)tanned. **4** gloomy, depressing, dismal, bleak, cheerless, mournful, pessimistic, sombre, doleful, joyless, grim, sad, melancholy, sorrowful. **5** evil, wicked, vile, base, foul, iniquitous, nefarious, black-hearted, villainous, sinister, satanic, devilish, hellish. **6** see SULLEN *adj*. 1. **7** mysterious, deep, remote, hidden, concealed, secret, incomprehensible, impenetrable, unfathomable, abstruse, little-known, recondite, arcane, obscure, occult, mystic, mystical, cryptic, enigmatic, puzzling. **8** unenlightened, benighted; see also IGNORANT 1a. ● *n*. **1** darkness, blackness, gloominess, murk, murkiness; see also GLOOM *n*. 1. **2** night, night-time, nightfall; dusk, twilight, sunset, sundown, evening, *archaic or poet*. eventide, *poet*. gloaming, vesper. **3** darkness, obscurity; see also IGNORANCE. ▫ **in the dark** see IGNORANT 1a. ▫▫ **darkness** see DARK *n*. 1 above.

darken /daárkən/ *v*. **1** *tr*. make dark or darker. **2** *intr*. become dark or darker. ▫ **never darken a person's door** keep away permanently. ▫▫ **darkener** *n*.
▪ **1** see SHADE *v*. 3. **2** see DIM *v*. 1.

darkie var. of DARKY.

darkling /daárkling/ *adj*. & *adv*. *poet*. in the dark; in the night.
▪ *adj*. see *sunless* (SUN).

darkroom /daárkrōōm, -rōōm/ *n*. a room for photographic work, with normal light excluded.

darky /daárki/ *n*. (also **darkie**) (*pl*. **-ies**) *sl*. *offens*. a Black person.

darling /daárling/ *n*. & *adj*. ● *n*. **1** a beloved or lovable person or thing. **2** a favourite. **3** *colloq*. a pretty or endearing person or thing. ● *adj*. **1** beloved, lovable. **2** favourite. **3** *colloq*. charming or pretty. [OE *dēorling* (as DEAR, -LING[1])]
▪ *n*. **1** sweetheart, beloved, love, dear, dearest, true-love, *archaic* leman. **2** pet, favourite, apple of one's eye, *colloq*. golden boy *or* girl, *Brit. colloq*. blue-eyed boy. ● *adj*. **1** beloved, loved, cherished, adored, dear, precious, treasured. **2** see FAVOURITE *adj*. **3** pleasing, fetching, attractive, adorable, enchanting, lovely, alluring, engaging, bewitching, charming.

darn[1] /daarn/ *v*. & *n*. ● *v.tr*. **1** mend (esp. knitted material, or a hole in it) by interweaving yarn across the hole with a needle. **2** embroider with a large running stitch. ● *n*. a darned area in material. ▫ **darning needle 1** a long needle with a large eye, used in darning. **2** *US* a dragonfly. [16th c.: perh. f. obs. *dern* hide]
▪ *v*. **1** see PATCH *v*. 1, 2.

darn[2] /daarn/ *v.tr*., *int*., *adj*., & *adv*. (*US* **durn** /durn/) *colloq*. = DAMN (in imprecatory senses). [corrupt. of DAMN]

darned /daarnd/ *adj*. & *adv*. (*US* **durned** /durnd/) *colloq*. = DAMNED.
▪ see *extremely* (EXTREME).

darnel /daárn'l/ *n*. any of several grasses of the genus *Lolium*, growing as weeds among cereal crops. [ME: cf. Walloon *darnelle*]

darner /daárnər/ *n*. a person or thing that darns, esp. a darning needle.

darning /daárning/ *n*. **1** the action of a person who darns. **2** things to be darned.

dart /daart/ *n*. & *v*. ● *n*. **1** a small pointed missile used as a weapon or in a game. **2** (in *pl*.; usu. treated as *sing*.) an indoor game in which light feathered darts are thrown at a circular target to score points. **3** a sudden rapid movement. **4** *Zool*. a dartlike structure, such as an insect's sting or the calcareous projections of a snail (used during copulation). **5** a tapering tuck stitched in a garment. ● *v*. **1** *intr*. (often foll. by *out*, *in*, *past*, etc.) move or go suddenly or rapidly (*darted into the shop*). **2** *tr*. throw (a missile). **3** *tr*. direct suddenly (a glance etc.). [ME f. OF *darz*, *dars*, f. Frank.]
▪ *n*. **1** see BOLT[1] *n*. 5. **3** see DASH *n*. 1. ● *v*. **1** see DASH *v*. 1.

dartboard /daártbord/ *n*. a circular board marked with numbered segments, used as a target in darts.

darter /daártər/ *n*. **1** any large water-bird of the genus *Anhinga*, having a narrow head and long thin neck. **2** any of various small quick-moving freshwater fish of the family Percidae, native to N. America.

Dartmoor pony /daártmoor, -mor/ *n*. **1** a small pony of a shaggy-coated breed. **2** this breed. [*Dartmoor* in SW England]

Darwinian /daarwinniən/ *adj*. & *n*. ● *adj*. of or relating to Darwin's theory of the evolution of species by the action of natural selection. ● *n*. an adherent of this theory. ▫▫ **Darwinism** /daárwiniz'm/ *n*. **Darwinist** /daárwinist/ *n*. [C. *Darwin*, Engl. naturalist d. 1882]

dash /dash/ *v*. & *n*. ● *v*. **1** *intr*. rush hastily or forcefully (*dashed up the stairs*). **2** *tr*. strike or fling with great force, esp. so as to shatter (*dashed it to the ground*; *the cup was dashed from my hand*). **3** *tr*. frustrate, daunt, dispirit (*dashed their hopes*). **4** *tr*. *colloq*. (esp. **dash it** or **dash it all**) = DAMN *v*. 1. ● *n*. **1** a rush or onset; a sudden advance (*made* *a dash for shelter*). **2** a horizontal stroke in writing or printing to mark a pause or break in sense or to represent omitted letters or words. **3** impetuous vigour or the capacity for this. **4** showy appearance or behaviour. **5** *US* a sprinting-race. **6** the longer signal of the two used in Morse code (cf. DOT[1] *n.* 3). **7** a slight admixture, esp. of a liquid. **8** = DASHBOARD. □ **cut a dash** make a brilliant show. **dash down** (or **off**) write or finish hurriedly. [ME, prob. imit.]

■ *v.* **1** rush, run, dart, spring, bolt, bound, race, sprint; hasten, fly, hurry, speed. **2** strike; hurl, toss, throw, fling, cast, pitch, *colloq.* chuck. **3** frustrate, daunt, dispirit, destroy, ruin, spoil, *colloq.* put paid to. ● *n.* **1** dart, bolt, rush, run; spurt, bound, sprint. **3** vigour, energy, vivacity, impetuosity; *élan*, flair, liveliness, style, panache, spirit, brio, verve, zest; ardour, fervour. **4** see OSTENTATION. **7** bit, pinch, soupçon, hint, suggestion, touch, trace, sprinkling, tinge, taste, drop, splash, piece, *colloq.* smidgen, *US colloq.* tad. □ **dash down** (or **off**) scribble, rush off.

dashboard /dáshbord/ *n.* **1** the surface below the windscreen of a motor vehicle or aircraft, containing instruments and controls. **2** *hist.* a board of wood or leather in front of a carriage, to keep out mud.

dashiki /daáshiki/ *n.* a loose brightly-coloured shirt worn by American Blacks. [W. Afr.]

dashing /dáshing/ *adj.* **1** spirited, lively. **2** stylish. □□ **dashingly** *adv.* **dashingness** *n.*

■ **1** spirited, impetuous, energetic, vigorous, dynamic, animated, bouncy, *colloq.* peppy; see also LIVELY 1. **2** fashionable, stylish, chic, à la mode, modish, smart, elegant, dapper, *colloq.* swish.

dashpot /dáshpot/ *n.* a device for damping shock or vibration.

dassie /dássi, daássi/ *n. S.Afr.* **1** the Cape hyrax *Procavia capensis*. Also called *rock-rabbit* (see ROCK[1]). **2** a small coastal fish *Diplodus sargus* with rows of black stripes. [Afrik. f. Du. *dasje* dimin. of *das* badger]

dastardly /dástərdli/ *adj.* cowardly, despicable. □□ **dastardliness** *n.* [*dastard* base coward, prob. f. *dazed* past part. + -ARD, or obs. *dasart* dullard, DOTARD]

■ see COWARDLY.

dasyure /dássiyoor/ *n.* any small flesh-eating marsupial of the genus *Dasyurus*. [F f. mod.L *dasyurus* f. Gk *dasus* rough + *oura* tail]

DAT *abbr.* digital audio tape.

data /dáytə/ *n.pl.* (also treated as *sing.*, as in *that is all the data we have*, although the singular form is strictly *datum*) **1** known facts or things used as a basis for inference or reckoning. **2** quantities or characters operated on by a computer etc. □ **data bank 1** a store or source of data. **2** = DATABASE. **data capture** the action or process of entering data into a computer. **data processing** a series of operations on data, esp. by a computer, to retrieve or classify etc. information. **data processor** a machine, esp. a computer, that carries out data processing. **data protection** legal control over access to data stored in computers. [pl. of DATUM]

■ **1** facts, information, statistics, figures, details, observations, material(s), evidence; text.

database /dáytəbayss/ *n.* a structured set of data held in a computer, esp. one that is accessible in various ways.

datable /dáytəb'l/ *adj.* (often foll. by *to*) capable of being dated (to a particular time).

date[1] /dayt/ *n.* & *v.* ● *n.* **1** a day of the month, esp. specified by a number. **2** a particular day or year, esp. when a given event occurred. **3** a statement (usu. giving the day, month, and year) in a document or inscription etc., of the time of composition or publication. **4** the period to which a work of art etc. belongs. **5** the time when an event happens or is to happen. **6** *colloq.* **a** an engagement or appointment, esp. with a person of the opposite sex. **b** *US* a person with whom one has a social engagement. ● *v.* **1** *tr.* mark with a date. **2** *tr.* **a** assign a date to (an object, event, etc.). **b** (foll. by *to*) assign to a particular time, period, etc. **3** *intr.* (often foll. by *from*, *back to*, etc.) have its origins at a particular time. **4** *intr.* be recognizable as from a past or particular period; become evidently out of date (*a design that does not date*). **5** *tr.* indicate or expose as being out of date (*that hat really dates you*). **6** *colloq.* **a** *tr.* make an arrangement with (a person) to meet socially. **b** *intr.* meet socially by agreement (*they are now dating regularly*). □ **date-line 1** the line from north to south partly along the meridian 180° from Greenwich, to the east of which the date is a day earlier than it is to the west. **2** a line at the head of a dispatch or special article in a newspaper showing the date and place of writing. **date-stamp** *n.* **1** an adjustable rubber stamp etc. used to record a date. **2** the impression made by this. ● *v.tr.* mark with a date-stamp. **out of date** (*attrib.* **out-of-date**) old-fashioned, obsolete. **to date** until now. **up to date** (*attrib.* **up-to-date**) meeting or according to the latest requirements, knowledge, or fashion; modern. [ME f. OF f. med.L *data*, fem. past part. of *dare* give: from the L formula used in dating letters, *data* (*epistola*) (letter) given or delivered (at a particular time or place)]

■ *n.* **4** time, year, season, period, day, age, era, epoch, stage, phase. **5** fixture, time. **6 a** appointment, meeting, engagement, rendezvous, assignation, *archaic* tryst. **b** escort, companion, friend; boyfriend, girlfriend, sweetheart, *colloq.* girl. ● *v.* **3** (*date from* or *back to*) belong to, come from. **4** show one's *or* its age; go out of fashion. **6** escort; have a relationship (with), *colloq.* go steady (with); be together; see also *go out* 4 (GO[1]). □ **out of date** outdated, old-fashioned, behind the times, old, ancient, archaic, antiquated, dated, *passé*, outmoded, outworn, obsolete, fossil, obsolescent, anachronistic, anachronic, behindhand, *colloq.* old hat, fossilized, antediluvian, medieval, prehistoric, corny. **up to date** modern, latest, current, contemporary, à la mode, fashionable, *colloq.* *often derog.* trendy.

date[2] /dayt/ *n.* **1** a dark oval single-stoned fruit. **2** (in full **date-palm**) the tall tree *Phoenix dactylifera*, native to W. Asia and N. Africa, bearing this fruit. [ME f. OF f. L *dactylus* f. Gk *daktulos* finger, from the shape of its leaf]

dateless /dáytliss/ *adj.* **1** having no date. **2** of immemorial age. **3** not likely to become out of date.

dative /dáytiv/ *n.* & *adj. Gram.* ● *n.* the case of nouns and pronouns (and words in grammatical agreement with them) indicating an indirect object or recipient. ● *adj.* of or in the dative. □□ **datival** /dətī́v'l/ *adj.* **datively** /dətī́vəli/ *adv.* [ME f. L (*casus*) *dativus* f. *dare dat-* give]

datum /dáytəm, daátəm/ *n.* (*pl.* **data**: see DATA as main entry). **1** a piece of information. **2** a thing known or granted; an assumption or premiss from which inferences may be drawn (see *sense-datum*). **3** a fixed starting-point of a scale etc. (*datum-line*). [L, = thing given, neut. past part. of *dare* give]

datura /dətyoórə/ *n.* any poisonous plant of the genus *Datura*, e.g. the thorn apple. [mod.L f. Hindi *dhatura*]

daub /dawb/ *v.* & *n.* ● *v.tr.* **1** spread (paint, plaster, or some other thick substance) crudely or roughly on a surface. **2** coat or smear (a surface) with paint etc. **3 a** (also *absol.*) paint crudely or unskilfully. **b** lay (colours) on crudely and clumsily. ● *n.* **1** paint or other substance daubed on a surface. **2** plaster, clay, etc., for coating a surface, esp. mixed with straw and applied to laths or wattles to form a wall. **3** a crude painting. [ME f. OF *dauber* f. L *dealbare* whitewash f. *albus* white]

■ *v.* see SMEAR *v.* 1.

daube /dōb/ *n.* a stew of braised meat (usu. beef) with wine etc. [F]

dauber /dáwbər/ *n.* a person or implement that daubs, esp. in painting. □ **get one's dauber down** *US sl.* become dispirited or depressed.

daughter /dáwtər/ *n.* **1** a girl or woman in relation to either or both of her parents. **2** a female descendant. **3** (foll. by *of*) a female member of a family, nation, etc. **4** (foll. by *of*) a woman who is regarded as the spiritual descendant of, or as

spiritually attached to, a person or thing. **5** a product or attribute personified as a daughter in relation to its source (*Fortune and its daughter Confidence*). **6** *Physics* a nuclide formed by the radioactive decay of another. **7** *Biol.* a cell etc. formed by the division etc. of another. □ **daughter-in-law** (*pl.* **daughters-in-law**) the wife of one's son. □□ **daughterhood** *n.* **daughterly** *adj.* [OE *dohtor* f. Gmc]
■ **1** see CHILD 2.

daunt /dawnt/ *v.tr.* discourage, intimidate. □□ **daunting** *adj.* **dauntingly** *adv.* [ME f. AF *daunter*, OF *danter*, *donter* f. L *domitare* frequent. of *domare* tame]
■ intimidate, discourage, put off, dishearten, dispirit, unnerve, shake, upset, disconcert, discomfit, awe, overawe, appal, alarm, threaten, frighten, terrify, scare.

dauntless /dáwntliss/ *adj.* intrepid, persevering. □□ **dauntlessly** *adv.* **dauntlessness** *n.*
■ fearless, undaunted, unafraid, unflinching, stalwart, brave, courageous, bold, audacious, intrepid, valorous, daring, gallant, heroic, venturesome, plucky, stout-hearted, valiant, persevering.

dauphin /dáwfin, dṓfaN/ *n. hist.* the eldest son of the King of France. [ME f. F, ult. f. L *delphinus* DOLPHIN, as a family name]

Davenport /dávv'nport/ *n.* **1** *Brit.* an ornamental writing-desk with drawers and a sloping surface for writing. **2** *US* a large heavily upholstered sofa. [19th c.: from the name *Davenport*]

davit /dávvit, dáyvit/ *n.* a small crane on board a ship, esp. one of a pair for suspending or lowering a lifeboat. [AF & OF *daviot* dimin. of *Davi* David]

Davy /dáyvi/ *n.* (*pl.* **-ies**) (in full **Davy lamp**) a miner's safety lamp with the flame enclosed by wire gauze to prevent an explosion of gas. [Sir H. *Davy*, Engl. chemist d. 1829, who invented it]

Davy Jones /dáyvi jṓnz/ *n. sl.* **1** (in full **Davy Jones's locker**) the bottom of the sea, esp. regarded as the grave of those drowned at sea. **2** the evil spirit of the sea. [18th c.: orig. unkn.]

daw /daw/ *n.* = JACKDAW. [ME: cf. OHG *tāha*]

dawdle /dáwd'l/ *v.* & *n.* ● *v.* **1** *intr.* **a** walk slowly and idly. **b** delay; waste time. **2** *tr.* (foll. by *away*) waste (time). ● *n.* an act or instance of dawdling. □□ **dawdler** *n.* [perh. rel. to dial. *daddle*, *doddle* idle, dally]
■ *v.* **1** linger, loiter, straggle, delay, procrastinate, dally, lounge, laze, idle, lag, lie about, waste time, *colloq.* dilly-dally, shilly-shally.

dawn /dawn/ *n.* & *v.* ● *n.* **1** the first light of day; daybreak. **2** the beginning or incipient appearance of something. ● *v.intr.* **1** (of a day) begin; grow light. **2** begin to appear or develop. **3** (often foll. by *on*, *upon*) begin to become evident or understood (by a person). □ **dawn chorus** the singing of many birds at the break of day. [orig. as verb: back-form. f. *dawning*, ME f. earlier *dawing* after Scand. (as DAY)]
■ *n.* **1** daybreak, sunrise, break of day, crack of dawn, first light, dawning, cock crow, *esp. US* sun-up, *poet.* aurora. **2** dawning, beginning, start, awakening, inception, genesis, onset, origin, appearance, arrival, advent, emergence, inauguration, rise, *formal* commencement, *rhet.* birth. ● *v.* **1** break; brighten, lighten. **2** begin, originate, arise, appear, emerge, start, arrive, develop, unfold, *formal* commence. **3** (*dawn on* or *upon*) occur to, come to a person's mind, become apparent *or* evident to.

dawning /dáwning/ *n.* **1** daybreak. **2** the first beginning of something.
■ **1** see DAWN *n.* 1. **2** see DAWN *n.* 2.

day /day/ *n.* **1** the time between sunrise and sunset. **2 a** a period of 24 hours as a unit of time, esp. from midnight to midnight, corresponding to a complete revolution of the earth on its axis. **b** a corresponding period on other planets (*Martian day*). **3** daylight (*clear as day*). **4** the time in a day during which work is normally done (*an eight-hour day*). **5 a** (also *pl.*) a period of the past or present (*the modern day*; *the old days*). **b** (prec. by *the*) the present time (*the issues of the day*). **6** the lifetime of a person or thing, esp. regarded as useful or productive (*have had my day*; *in my day things were different*). **7** a point of time (*will do it one day*). **8 a** the date of a specific festival. **b** a day associated with a particular event or purpose (*graduation day*; *payday*; *Christmas day*). **9** a particular date; a date agreed on. **10** a day's endeavour, or the period of an endeavour, esp. as bringing success (*win the day*). □ **all in a** (or **the**) **day's work** part of normal routine. **at the end of the day** in the final reckoning, when all is said and done. **call it a day** end a period of activity, esp. resting content that enough has been done. **day after day** without respite. **day and night** all the time. **day-boy** (or **-girl**) *Brit.* a boy or girl who goes daily from home to school, esp. a school that also has boarders. **day by day** gradually. **day care** the supervision of young children during the working day. **day centre** a place providing care for the elderly or handicapped during the day. **day-dream** *n.* a pleasant fantasy or reverie. ● *v.intr.* indulge in this. **day-dreamer** a person who indulges in day-dreams. **day in, day out** routinely, constantly. **day labourer** an unskilled labourer hired by the day. **day lily** any plant of the genus *Hemerocallis*, whose flowers last only a day. **day nursery** a nursery where children are looked after during the working day. **day off** a day's holiday from work. **Day of Judgement** = *Judgement Day*. **day of reckoning** see RECKONING. **day of rest** the Sabbath. **day out** a trip or excursion for a day. **day-owl** any owl hunting by day esp. the short-eared owl. **day release** *Brit.* a system of allowing employees days off work for education. **day return** a fare or ticket at a reduced rate for a journey out and back in one day. **day-room** a room, esp. a communal room in an institution, used during the day. **day-school** a school for pupils living at home. **day-to-day** mundane, routine. **day-trip** a trip or excursion completed in one day. **day-tripper** *Brit.* a person who goes on a day-trip. **from day one** *colloq.* originally. **not one's day** a day of successive misfortunes for a person. **on one's day** at one's peak of capability. **one of these days** before very long. **one of those days** a day when things go badly. **some day** at some point in the future. **that will be the day** *colloq.* that will never happen. **this day and age** the present time or period. □□ **dayless** *adj.* [OE *dæg* f. Gmc]
■ **3** daytime, daylight, broad daylight, light of day. **5 a** age, period, era, epoch; date. **b** see PRESENT[1] *n.*, NOW *adv.* 1, 4. **6** time, lifetime; hour, prime, heyday. □ **at the end of the day** see *ultimately* (ULTIMATE). **day after day** see *all the time* 2 (TIME). **day and night** see *all the time* 2 (TIME). **day by day** see *gradually* (GRADUAL). **day-dream** (*n.*) reverie, fantasy, fancy, dream, musing, castle(s) in the air *or* in Spain, pipedream. (*v.*) fantasize, dream; (*day-dream about*) imagine, fancy, envisage, envision. **day-dreamer** see DREAMER. **day in, day out** see *all the time* 2 (TIME). **day out** day-trip, outing, trip, jaunt, excursion. **day-to-day** see ROUTINE *adj.* 1. **from day one** see *originally* (ORIGINAL). **one of these days** see SOON 1. **this day and age** see PRESENT[1] *n.*, NOW *adv.* 1, 4.

Dayak var. of DYAK.

daybook /dáybŏŏk/ *n.* an account-book in which a day's transactions are entered, for later transfer to a ledger.
■ journal, ledger.

daybreak /dáybrayk/ *n.* the first appearance of light in the morning.
■ see DAWN *n.* 1.

Day-Glo /dáyglō/ *n.* & *adj.* ● *n. propr.* a make of fluorescent paint or other colouring. ● *adj.* coloured with or like this. [DAY + GLOW]

daylight /dáylīt/ *n.* **1** the light of day. **2** dawn (*before daylight*). **3 a** openness, publicity. **b** open knowledge. **4** a visible gap or interval, e.g. between boats in a race. **5** (usu. in *pl.*) *sl.* one's life or consciousness (orig. the internal organs) esp. as representing vulnerability to fear, attack, etc. (*scared the daylights out of me*; *beat the living daylights out of them*). □ **daylight robbery** *colloq.* a blatantly excessive

charge. **daylight saving** the achieving of longer evening daylight, esp. in summer, by setting the time an hour ahead of the standard time. **see daylight** begin to understand what was previously obscure.
■ **1** sunlight, sun, sunshine, light. **2** see DAWN *n*. 1.
□ **see daylight** see *catch on* 2.

daylong /dáylong/ *adj*. lasting for a day.

dayside /dáysīd/ *n*. **1** *US* staff, esp. of a newspaper, who work during the day. **2** *Astron*. the side of a planet that faces the sun.

daytime /dáytīm/ *n*. the part of the day when there is natural light.
■ see DAY 3.

daywork /dáywurk/ *n*. work paid for according to the time taken.

daze /dayz/ *v*. & *n*. ● *v.tr*. stupefy, bewilder. ● *n*. a state of confusion or bewilderment (*in a daze*). □□ **dazedly** /-zidli/ *adv*. [ME *dased* past part., f. ON *dasathr* weary]
■ *v*. stun, stupefy, blind, dazzle, bedazzle; shock, stagger, startle, take aback, astonish, astound, amaze, surprise, overcome, overpower, dumbfound, benumb, paralyse, *colloq*. bowl over, floor, flabbergast, knock sideways, knock for six, *sl*. knock out; befuddle, confuse, bemuse, bewilder, puzzle, mystify, baffle, perplex, nonplus. ● *n*. (*in a daze*) stupefied, in a trance, bewildered, confused, bemused, baffled, puzzled, mystified; perplexed, disoriented, dizzy, dazzled, bedazzled, overcome, overpowered, nonplussed, befuddled, flustered; startled, surprised, shocked, stunned, astonished, astounded, amazed, staggered, *colloq*. flabbergasted, bowled over, floored.

dazzle /dázz'l/ *v*. & *n*. ● *v*. **1** *tr*. blind temporarily or confuse the sight of by an excess of light. **2** *tr*. impress or overpower (a person) with knowledge, ability, or any brilliant display or prospect. **3** *intr*. *archaic* (of eyes) be dazzled. ● *n*. bright confusing light. □□ **dazzlement** *n*. **dazzler** *n*. **dazzling** *adj*. **dazzlingly** *adv*. [ME, f. DAZE + -LE[4]]
■ *v*. **1** blind, stun, stupefy, bedazzle, overpower. **2** impress, bewitch, enchant, charm, beguile, intrigue, captivate, fascinate, spellbind, entrance, hypnotize, mesmerize; overpower. □□ **dazzling** bright, brilliant, resplendent, radiant, splendid, magnificent, glorious, sparkling, scintillating, *colloq*. *or joc*. splendiferous; overwhelming, overpowering, stupefying, dizzying, *colloq*. stunning, mind-boggling; gorgeous.

dB *abbr*. decibel(s).

DBE *abbr*. (in the UK) Dame Commander of the Order of the British Empire.

DBS *abbr*. **1** direct-broadcast satellite. **2** direct broadcasting by satellite.

DC *abbr*. **1** (also **d.c.**) direct current. **2** District of Columbia. **3** da capo. **4** District Commissioner.

DCB *abbr*. (in the UK) Dame Commander of the Order of the Bath.

DCL *abbr*. Doctor of Civil Law.

DCM *abbr*. (in the UK) Distinguished Conduct Medal.

DCMG *abbr*. (in the UK) Dame Commander of the Order of St Michael and St George.

DCVO *abbr*. (in the UK) Dame Commander of the Royal Victorian Order.

DD *abbr*. Doctor of Divinity.

D-Day /déeday/ *n*. **1** the day (6 June 1944) on which British and American forces invaded N. France. **2** the day on which an important operation is to begin or a change to take effect. [*D* for *day* + DAY]

DDT *abbr*. dichlorodiphenyltrichloroethane, a colourless chlorinated hydrocarbon used as an insecticide.

DE *abbr*. *US* Delaware (in official postal use).

de- /di, dee/ *prefix* **1** forming verbs and their derivatives: **a** down, away (*descend*; *deduct*). **b** completely (*declare*; *denude*; *deride*). **2** added to verbs and their derivatives to form verbs and nouns implying removal or reversal (*decentralize*; *de-ice*; *demoralization*). [from or after L *de* (adv. & prep.) = off, from: sense 2 through OF *des-* f. L *dis-*]

deacon /déekən/ *n*. & *v*. ● *n*. **1** (in Episcopal churches) a minister of the third order, below bishop and priest. **2** (in Nonconformist churches) a lay officer attending to a congregation's secular affairs. **3** (in the early Church) an appointed minister of charity. ● *v.tr*. appoint or ordain as a deacon. □□ **deaconate** *n*. **deaconship** *n*. [OE *diacon* f. eccl.L *diaconus* f. Gk *diakonos* servant]

deaconess /déekənéss, déekəniss/ *n*. a woman in the early Church and in some modern Churches with functions analogous to a deacon's. [DEACON, after LL *diaconissa*]

deactivate /dee-áktivayt/ *v.tr*. make inactive or less reactive. □□ **deactivation** /-váysh'n/ *n*. **deactivator** *n*.
■ see STOP *v*. 1a.

dead /ded/ *adj*., *adv*., & *n*. ● *adj*. **1** no longer alive. **2** *colloq*. extremely tired or unwell. **3** benumbed; affected by loss of sensation (*my fingers are dead*). **4** (foll. by *to*) unappreciative or unconscious of; insensitive to. **5** no longer effective or in use; obsolete, extinct. **6** (of a match, of coal, etc.) no longer burning; extinguished. **7** inanimate. **8 a** lacking force or vigour; dull, lustreless, muffled. **b** (of sound) not resonant. **c** (of sparkling wine etc.) no longer effervescent. **9 a** quiet; lacking activity (*the dead season*). **b** motionless, idle. **10 a** (of a microphone, telephone, etc.) not transmitting any sound, esp. because of a fault. **b** (of a circuit, conductor, etc.) carrying or transmitting no current; not connected to a source of electricity (*a dead battery*). **11** (of the ball in a game) out of play. **12** abrupt, complete, exact, unqualified, unrelieved (*come to a dead stop*; *a dead faint*; *a dead calm*; *in dead silence*; *a dead certainty*). **13** without spiritual life. ● *adv*. **1** absolutely, exactly, completely (*dead on target*; *dead level*; *dead tired*). **2** *colloq*. very, extremely (*dead good*; *dead easy*). ● *n*. (prec. by *the*) **1** (treated as *pl*.) those who have died. **2** a time of silence or inactivity (*the dead of night*). □ **dead-and-alive** *Brit*. (of a place, person, activity, etc.) dull, monotonous; lacking interest. **dead as the dodo** see DODO. **dead as a doornail** see DOORNAIL. **dead bat** *Cricket* a bat held loosely so that it imparts no motion to the ball when struck. **dead beat 1** *colloq*. exhausted. **2** *Physics* (of an instrument) without recoil. **dead-beat** *n*. **1** *colloq*. a penniless person. **2** *US sl*. a person constantly in debt. **dead centre 1** the exact centre. **2** the position of a crank etc. in line with the connecting-rod and not exerting torque. **dead cert** see CERT. **dead duck** *sl*. an unsuccessful or useless person or thing. **dead end 1** a closed end of a road, passage, etc. **2** (often (with hyphen) *attrib*.) a situation offering no prospects of progress or advancement. **dead-eye** *Naut*. a round flat three-holed block for extending shrouds. **dead from the neck up** *colloq*. stupid. **dead hand** an oppressive persisting influence, esp. posthumous control. **dead heat 1** a race in which two or more competitors finish exactly level. **2** the result of such a race. **dead-heat** *v.intr*. run a dead heat. **dead language** a language no longer commonly spoken, e.g. Latin. **dead letter** a law or practice no longer observed or recognized. **dead lift** the exertion of one's utmost strength to lift something. **dead loss 1** *colloq*. a useless person or thing. **2** a complete loss. **dead man's fingers 1** a kind of orchis, *Orchis mascula*. **2** any soft coral of the genus *Alcyonium*, with spongy lobes. **3** the finger-like divisions of a lobster's or crab's gills. **dead man's handle** (or **pedal** etc.) a controlling-device on an electric train, allowing power to be connected only as long as the operator presses on it. **dead march** a funeral march. **dead men** *colloq*. bottles after the contents have been drunk. **dead-nettle** any plant of the genus *Lamium*, having nettle-like leaves but without stinging hairs. **dead-on** exactly right. **dead reckoning** *Naut*. calculation of a ship's position from the log, compass, etc., when observations are impossible. **dead ringer** see RINGER. **dead shot** one who is extremely accurate. **dead time** *Physics* the period after the recording of a pulse etc. when the detector is unable to record another. **dead to the world** *colloq*. fast asleep; unconscious. **dead weight** (or **dead-weight**) **1 a** an inert mass. **b** a heavy weight or burden. **2** a debt not covered by assets. **3** the total weight carried on a ship. **dead wood** *colloq.* one or more useless people or things. **make a dead set at** see SET[2]. **wouldn't be seen dead in** (or **with** etc.) *colloq.* shall have nothing to do with; shall refuse to wear etc. ▫▫ **deadness** *n.* [OE *dēad* f. Gmc, rel. to DIE[1]]

■ *adj.* **1** defunct, extinct, gone, departed, late, lifeless, no more, *formal* deceased, *Brit. sl.* gone for a burton. **2** tired (out), exhausted, worn out, fatigued, spent, in a state of collapse, beaten, *colloq.* all in, done in, dead beat, *US colloq.* bushed, pooped, fagged (out), *sl.* beat, *Brit. sl.* knackered, cooked. **3** insensate, insensible, numb, paralysed, benumbed, unfeeling, deadened, senseless, sensationless; without feeling. **4** insensible, unconscious, out; insensitive, indifferent, unconcerned, uninterested; hardened, impervious, inured. **5** extinct, obsolete, perished, past, outmoded, disused, expired. **6** out, smothered, extinguished. **7** lifeless, inert, inorganic; see also INANIMATE 1, 2. **8 a** dull, lustreless, flat, neutral, vapid, empty, bland, colourless, grey, beige, dun; boring, tedious, tiresome, monotonous, prosaic, uninteresting, run-of-the-mill, ordinary, commonplace, dry, insipid, two-dimensional, lifeless, stiff, rigid. **b** dull, muffled, deadened, anechoic, unresounding, non-resonant. **9 a** see INACTIVE 1, 2. **b** stagnant, motionless, still, standing, static, inert, unmoving, inactive, idle, quiet, calm. **12** complete, entire, total, full, absolute, downright, thorough, through and through, utter, all-out, out-and-out, unqualified, unrelieved, unbroken, categorical, outright; profound, deep; sudden, abrupt; exact, precise. ● *adv.* **1** completely, entirely, absolutely, totally, utterly, categorically, thoroughly, unconditionally, unqualifiedly; abruptly, suddenly; directly, exactly, precisely. **2** see VERY *adv.* ● *n.* **2** depth(s), extreme, midst, middle. ▫ **dead-and-alive** see MONOTONOUS. **dead beat 1** see DEAD *adj.* 2 above. **dead duck** see DISASTER 2b. **dead from the neck up** see STUPID *adj.* 1, 5. **dead heat** tie, stalemate, draw, deadlock. **dead loss 1** see DISASTER 2b. **dead-on** see RIGHT *adj.* 2. **dead to the world** (fast) asleep, unconscious, out, out for the count, *colloq.* (out) cold. **dead weight 1 b** see ENCUMBRANCE 1.

deadbolt /dédbōlt/ *n.* esp. *US* a bolt engaged by turning a knob or key, rather than by spring action.

deaden /dédd'n/ *v.* **1** *tr.* & *intr.* deprive of or lose vitality, force, brightness, sound, feeling, etc. **2** *tr.* (foll. by *to*) make insensitive. ▫▫ **deadener** *n.*

■ **1** weaken, tire (out), weary, lessen, diminish, reduce, decrease; drain, tax, exhaust, sap, debilitate, enfeeble, fatigue, wear out, dull, subdue, devitalize, take it out of, strain, break, crush, depress, dispirit, *Brit. sl.* knacker; moderate, soothe, mitigate, assuage, alleviate, cushion, soften, blunt, dull, dampen; grow tired, languish, falter, fail, dwindle, fade, deteriorate, waste away, degenerate, decline, abate, peter out, die, taper (off), ease (up), subside, slump, fall off, wane, ebb, sink, lag, *colloq.* let up. **2** numb, benumb, paralyse, anaesthetize, desensitize, dull.

deadeye /déddī/ *n.* **1** *Naut.* a circular wooden block with a groove round the circumference to take a lanyard, used singly or in pairs to tighten a shroud. **2** *US colloq.* an expert marksman.

deadfall /dédfawl/ *n. US* a trap in which a raised weight is made to fall on and kill esp. large game.

deadhead /dédhed/ *n.* & *v.* ● *n.* **1** a faded flower-head. **2** a passenger or member of an audience who has made use of a free ticket. **3** a useless or unenterprising person. ● *v.* **1** *tr.* remove deadheads from (a plant). **2** *intr. US* (of a driver etc.) complete a journey with an empty train, bus, etc.

deadlight /dédlīt/ *n. Naut.* **1** a shutter inside a porthole. **2** *US* a skylight that cannot be opened.

deadline /dédlīn/ *n.* **1** a time-limit for the completion of an activity etc. **2** *hist.* a line beyond which prisoners were not allowed to go.

deadlock /dédlok/ *n.* & *v.* ● *n.* **1** a situation, esp. one involving opposing parties, in which no progress can be made. **2** a type of lock requiring a key to open or close it. ● *v.tr.* & *intr.* bring or come to a standstill.

■ *n.* **1** standstill, impasse, stalemate, draw, *US* stand-off. ● *v.* bring *or* come to a standstill *or* impasse, stall, stop, halt.

deadly /dédli/ *adj.* & *adv.* ● *adj.* (**deadlier, deadliest**) **1 a** causing or able to cause fatal injury or serious damage. **b** poisonous (*deadly snake*). **2** intense, extreme (*deadly dullness*). **3** (of an aim etc.) extremely accurate or effective. **4** deathlike (*deadly pale*; *deadly faintness*; *deadly gloom*). **5** *colloq.* dreary, dull. **6** implacable. ● *adv.* **1** like death; as if dead (*deadly faint*). **2** extremely, intensely (*deadly serious*). ▫ **deadly nightshade** = BELLADONNA. **deadly sin** a sin regarded as leading to damnation, esp. pride, covetousness, lust, gluttony, envy, anger, and sloth. ▫▫ **deadliness** *n.* [OE *dēadlic*, *dēadlīce* (as DEAD, -LY[1])]

■ *adj.* **1** lethal, fatal; dangerous, poisonous, toxic; baleful, harmful, noxious, *literary* nocuous. **2** see INTENSE 1, 3. **3** exact, precise, accurate, true, unerring, unfailing. **4** deathly, deathlike; pale, pallid, ghostly, cadaverous, ghastly, wan, livid, ashen. **5** boring, excruciating, dull, tiresome, tedious, dreary, humdrum, lacklustre, wearying, wearisome. **6** see MORTAL *adj.* 5. ● *adv.* **2** see *extremely* (EXTREME).

deadpan /dédpán/ *adj.* & *adv.* with a face or manner totally lacking expression or emotion.

■ *adj.* see WOODEN 3a.

deadstock /dédstok/ *n.* slaughtered farm stock, esp. diseased animals.

de-aerate /dee-áirayt/ *v.tr.* remove air from. ▫▫ **de-aeration** /-ráysh'n/ *n.*

deaf /def/ *adj.* **1** wholly or partly without hearing (*deaf in one ear*). **2** (foll. by *to*) refusing to listen or comply. **3** insensitive to harmony, rhythm, etc. (*tone-deaf*). ▫ **deaf-aid** *Brit.* a hearing-aid. **deaf-and-dumb alphabet** (or **language** etc.) = *sign language* ¶ *Sign language* is preferred in official use. **deaf as a post** completely deaf. **deaf mute** a deaf and dumb person. **fall on deaf ears** be ignored. **turn a deaf ear** (usu. foll. by *to*) be unresponsive. ▫▫ **deafly** *adv.* **deafness** *n.* [OE *dēaf* f. Gmc]

■ **1** hard of hearing, stone-deaf. **2** unheedful, heedless, insensible, insensitive, impervious, indifferent, oblivious, unresponsive, unmoved, unconcerned, unyielding. ▫ **fall on deaf ears** fall on stony ground. **turn a deaf ear** see IGNORE 2.

deafen /déff'n/ *v.tr.* **1** (often as **deafening** *adj.*) overpower with sound. **2** deprive of hearing by noise, esp. temporarily. ▫▫ **deafeningly** *adv.*

deal[1] /deel/ *v.* & *n.* ● *v.* (*past* and *past part.* **dealt** /delt/) **1** *intr.* **a** (foll. by *with*) take measures concerning (a problem, person, etc.), esp. in order to put something right. **b** (foll. by *with*) do business with; associate with. **c** (foll. by *with*) discuss or treat (a subject). **d** (often foll. by *by*) behave in a specified way towards a person (*dealt honourably by them*). **2** *intr.* (foll. by *in*) to sell or be concerned with commercially (*deals in insurance*). **3** *tr.* (often foll. by *out, round*) distribute or apportion to several people etc. **4** *tr.* (also *absol.*) distribute (cards) to players for a game or round. **5** *tr.* cause to be received; administer (*deal a heavy blow*). **6** *tr.* assign as a share or deserts to a person (*Providence dealt them much happiness*). **7** *tr.* (foll. by *in*) *colloq.* include (a person) in an activity (*you can deal me in*). ● *n.* **1** (usu. **a good** or **great deal**) *colloq.* **a** a large amount (*a good deal of trouble*). **b** to a considerable extent (*is a great deal better*). **2** *colloq.* a business arrangement; a transaction. **3** a specified form of treatment given or received (*gave them a rough deal*; *got a fair deal*). **4 a** the distribution of cards by dealing. **b** a player's turn to do this (*it's my deal*). **c** the round of play following this. **d** a set of hands dealt to players. ▫ **it's a deal** *colloq.* expressing assent to an agreement. [OE *dǣl*, *dǣlan*, f. Gmc]

■ *v.* **1 a** (*deal with*) treat, handle, take care of, attend to, see to, reckon with, grapple with, act on. **b** see ASSOCIATE *v.* 5. **c** (*deal with*) see TREAT *v.* 4. **d** behave, act, conduct oneself, deport oneself, *literary* comport oneself. **2** (*deal in*) buy and sell, handle, stock, do business in, trade in, traffic in. **3, 4** distribute, dole out, give *or* hand out, parcel out, allot, apportion, *literary* mete out; administer, dispense. **6** see ASSIGN *v.* 1a. ● *n.* **1** (**a good** or **great deal**) see LOT *n.* 1. **2** transaction, arrangement, negotiation, agreement, contract, bargain, understanding. **3** see TREATMENT 1.

deal[2] /deel/ *n.* **1** fir or pine timber, esp. sawn into boards of a standard size. **2 a** a board of this timber. **b** such boards collectively. [ME f. MLG, MDu. *dele* plank f. Gmc]

dealer /deélər/ *n.* **1** a person or business dealing in (esp. retail) goods (*contact your dealer*; *car-dealer*; *a dealer in tobacco*). **2** the player dealing at cards. **3** a jobber on the Stock Exchange. ¶ In the UK from Oct. 1986 the name has been merged with **broker** (see BROKER 2, JOBBER 1). □□ **dealership** *n.* (in sense 1).

■ **1, 3** trader, businessman, businesswoman, merchant, tradesman, retailer, shopkeeper, vendor, merchandiser, *US* storekeeper; wholesaler, distributor, supplier, *Brit.* stockist, *US* jobber; broker, agent, salesman; trafficker.

dealings /deélingz/ *n.pl.* contacts or transactions, esp. in business. □ **have dealings with** associate with.

■ business, commerce, exchange, trade, traffic, transactions, negotiations; relations, relationships, affairs, contacts. □ **have dealings with** see ASSOCIATE *v.* 5.

dealt *past* and *past part.* of DEAL[1].

dean[1] /deen/ *n.* **1 a** the head of the chapter of a cathedral or collegiate church. **b** (usu. **rural dean**) *Brit.* a member of the clergy exercising supervision over a group of parochial clergy within a division of an archdeaconry. **2 a** a college or university official, esp. one of several fellows of a college, with disciplinary and advisory functions. **b** the head of a university faculty or department or of a medical school. **3** = DOYEN. □ **Dean of Faculty** the president of the Faculty of Advocates in Scotland. [ME f. AF *deen*, OF *deien*, f. LL *decanus* f. *decem* ten; orig. = chief of a group of ten]

dean[2] var. of DENE[1].

deanery /deénəri/ *n.* (*pl.* **-ies**) **1** a dean's house or office. **2** *Brit.* the group of parishes presided over by a rural dean.

dear /deer/ *adj.*, *n.*, *adv.*, & *int.* ● *adj.* **1 a** beloved or much esteemed. **b** as a merely polite or ironic form (*my dear man*). **2** used as a formula of address, esp. at the beginning of letters (*Dear Sir*). **3** (often foll. by *to*) precious; much cherished. **4** (usu. in *superl.*) earnest, deeply felt (*my dearest wish*). **5 a** high-priced relative to its value. **b** having high prices. **c** (of money) available as a loan only at a high rate of interest. ● *n.* (esp. as a form of address) dear person. ● *adv.* at a high price or great cost (*buy cheap and sell dear*; *will pay dear*). ● *int.* expressing surprise, dismay, pity, etc. (*dear me!*; *oh dear!*; *dear, dear!*). □ **Dear John** *colloq.* a letter terminating a personal relationship. **for dear life** see LIFE. □□ **dearly** *adv.* (esp. in sense 3 of *adj.*). **dearness** *n.* [OE *dēore* f. Gmc]

■ *adj.* **1 a** beloved, loved, adored, darling, favoured, esteemed, admired, venerated, honoured. **3** precious, cherished, prized, valued, treasured. **4** see EARNEST *adj.* **5 a** expensive, costly, high-priced, highly priced, exorbitant, *colloq.* pricey, steep. ● *n.* dearest, darling, sweetheart, beloved, love, true-love, sweet, precious, pet, *Ir.* acushla, *esp. US* honey, *colloq.* sweetie, sweetie-pie, treasure, *sl.* baby. ● *adv.* dearly; at great cost *or* expense, at a high *or* excessive price; (*cost dear*) cost an arm and a leg, cost a pretty penny, *colloq.* cost the earth *or* a packet, *Brit. sl.* cost a bomb. □□ **dearly** greatly, very much, indeed, sincerely; affectionately, fondly, lovingly, tenderly; expensively, dear, at great cost *or* expense, at a high *or* excessive price, punitively.

dearie /deéri/ *n.* (esp. as a form of address) usu. *joc.* or *iron.* my dear. □ **dearie me!** *int.* expressing surprise, dismay, etc.

dearth /derth/ *n.* scarcity or lack, esp. of food. [ME, formed as DEAR]

■ scarcity, want, need, lack, deficiency, sparseness, sparsity, scantiness, insufficiency, inadequacy, shortage, paucity, exiguity, poverty, exiguousness; absence.

deasil /déss'l/ *adv. Sc.* in the direction of the sun's apparent course (considered as lucky); clockwise. [Gael. *deiseil*]

death /deth/ *n.* **1** the final cessation of vital functions in an organism; the ending of life. **2** the event that terminates life. **3 a** the fact or process of being killed or killing (*stone to death*; *fight to the death*). **b** the fact or state of being dead (*eyes closed in death*; *their deaths caused rioting*). **4 a** the destruction or permanent cessation of something (*was the death of our hopes*). **b** *colloq.* something terrible or appalling. **5** (usu. **Death**) a personification of death, esp. as a destructive power, usu. represented by a skeleton. **6** a lack of religious faith or spiritual life. □ **as sure as death** quite certain. **at death's door** close to death. **be in at the death 1** be present when an animal is killed, esp. in hunting. **2** witness the (esp. sudden) ending of an enterprise etc. **be the death of 1** cause the death of. **2** be very harmful to. **catch one's death** *colloq.* catch a serious chill etc. **death adder** any of various venomous snakes of the genus *Acanthopis* esp. *A. antarcticus* of Australia. **death cap** a poisonous toadstool, *Amanita phalloides*. **death cell** a prison cell for a person condemned to death. **death certificate** an official statement of the cause and date and place of a person's death. **death duty** *Brit. hist.* a tax levied on property after the owner's death. ¶ Replaced in 1975 by *capital transfer tax* and in 1986 by *inheritance tax*. **death grant** *Brit.* a State grant towards funeral expenses. **death-knell 1** the tolling of a bell to mark a person's death. **2** an event that heralds the end or destruction of something. **death-mask** a cast taken of a dead person's face. **death penalty** punishment by being put to death. **death rate** the number of deaths per thousand of population per year. **death-rattle** a gurgling sound sometimes heard in a dying person's throat. **death-roll 1** those killed in an accident, battle, etc. **2** a list of these. **death row** *US* a prison block or section for prisoners sentenced to death. **death's head** a human skull as an emblem of mortality. **death's head moth** a large dark hawk moth, *Acherontia atropos*, with skull-like markings on the back of the thorax. **death squad** an armed paramilitary group formed to kill political enemies etc. **death tax** *US* a tax on property payable on the owner's death. **death-toll** the number of people killed in an accident, battle, etc. **death-trap** *colloq.* a dangerous or unhealthy building, vehicle, etc. **death-warrant 1** an order for the execution of a condemned person. **2** anything that causes the end of an established practice etc. **death-watch** (in full **death-watch beetle**) a small beetle (*Xestobium rufovillosum*) which makes a sound like a watch ticking, once supposed to portend death, and whose larva bores in old wood. **death-wish** *Psychol.* a desire (usu. unconscious) for the death of oneself or another. **do to death 1** kill. **2** overdo. **fate worse than death** *colloq.* a disastrous misfortune or experience. **like death warmed up** *sl.* very tired or ill. **put to death** kill or cause to be killed. **to death** to the utmost, extremely (*bored to death*; *worked to death*). □□ **deathless** *adj.* **deathlessness** *n.* **deathlike** *adj.* [OE *dēath* f. Gmc: rel. to DIE[1]]

■ **1** demise, dying, end, exit, quietus, expiry, expiration, *euphem.* passing (away), *formal esp. Law* decease. **4 a** end, termination, cessation, expiration, expiry, finish; extinction, destruction, extermination, annihilation, eradication, obliteration, extirpation, liquidation; ruin, downfall, undoing. □ **as sure as death** see CERTAIN *adj.* 1a. **catch one's death** catch a cold *or* chill, get pneumonia. **do to death 1** see KILL[1] *v.* 1. **2** see OVERDO 1. **put to death** see KILL[1] *v.* 1. **to death** see *extremely* (EXTREME). □□ **deathless** eternal, everlasting, immortal, undying, imperishable, permanent, unending, timeless, never-ending.

deathbed /déthbed/ *n.* a bed as the place where a person is dying or has died.

deathblow /déthblō/ *n.* **1** a blow or other action that causes death. **2** an event or circumstance that abruptly ends an activity, enterprise, etc.

▪ see KILL[1] *n.* 1.

deathly /déthli/ *adj.* & *adv.* ● *adj.* (**deathlier, deathliest**) suggestive of death (*deathly silence*). ● *adv.* in a deathly way (*deathly pale*).

▪ *adj.* see DEADLY *adj.* 4.

deb /deb/ *n. colloq.* a débutante. [abbr.]

débâcle /daybaák'l/ *n.* (*US* **debacle**) **1 a** an utter defeat or failure. **b** a sudden collapse or downfall. **2** a confused rush or rout; a stampede. **3 a** a break-up of ice in a river, with resultant flooding. **b** a sudden rush of water carrying along blocks of stone and other debris. [F f. *débâcler* unbar]

▪ **1** see RUIN *n.* 2a. **3** see FLOOD *n.* 1.

debag /deebág/ *v.tr.* (**debagged, debagging**) *Brit. sl.* remove the trousers of (a person), esp. as a joke.

debar /dibaár, dee-/ *v.tr.* (**debarred, debarring**) (foll. by *from*) exclude from admission or from a right; prohibit from an action (*was debarred from entering*). ▫▫ **debarment** *n.* [ME f. F *débarrer*, OF *desbarrer* (as DE-, BAR[1])]

▪ see BAN *v.*

debark[1] /deebaárk, di-/ *v.tr.* & *intr.* land from a ship. ▫▫ **debarkation** /-káysh'n/ *n.* [F *débarquer* (as DE-, BARK[3])]

▪ see LAND *v.* 1, 3.

debark[2] /deébaárk/ *v.tr.* remove the bark from (a tree).

debase /dibáyss/ *v.tr.* **1** lower in quality, value, or character. **2** depreciate (coin) by alloying etc. ▫▫ **debasement** *n.* **debaser** *n.* [DE- + obs. *base* for ABASE]

▪ **1** lower, degrade, devalue, depreciate, depress, demote, deprecate, belittle, diminish, reduce, disparage.

debatable /dibáytəb'l/ *adj.* **1** questionable; subject to dispute. **2** capable of being debated. ▫▫ **debatably** *adv.* [OF *debatable* or AL *debatabilis* (as DEBATE)]

▪ **1** controversial, arguable, questionable, doubtful, dubious, problematic, problematical, disputable, open *or* subject to dispute *or* doubt *or* question, in dispute *or* doubt *or* question, moot, polemic, polemical; unsure, uncertain, unsettled, undecided.

debate /dibáyt/ *v.* & *n.* ● *v.* **1** *tr.* (also *absol.*) discuss or dispute about (an issue, proposal, etc.) esp. formally in a legislative assembly, public meeting, etc. **2 a** *tr.* consider, ponder (a matter). **b** *intr.* consider different sides of a question. ● *n.* **1** a formal discussion on a particular matter, esp. in a legislative assembly etc. **2** debating, discussion (*open to debate*). ▫ **debating point** an inessential matter used to gain advantage in a debate. ▫▫ **debater** *n.* [ME f. OF *debatre*, *debat* f. Rmc (as DE-, BATTLE)]

▪ *v.* **1** argue *or* wrangle *or* dispute about, contest; discuss, moot, question. **2 a** deliberate, consider, reflect on, mull over, ponder (over), weigh up, ruminate (over), meditate (on *or* over), think over *or* about, think through. ● *n.* **1** discussion, argument, dispute, altercation, polemic. **2** discussion, argumentation, argument, dispute, contention.

debauch /dibáwch/ *v.* & *n.* ● *v.tr.* **1** corrupt morally. **2** make intemperate or sensually indulgent. **3** deprave or debase (taste or judgement). **4** (as **debauched** *adj.*) dissolute. **5** seduce (a woman). ● *n.* **1** a bout of sensual indulgence. **2** debauchery. ▫▫ **debaucher** *n.* [F *débauche(r)*, OF *desbaucher*, of unkn. orig.]

▪ *v.* **1** see DEMORALIZE 2. **4** (**debauched**) see DISSOLUTE. **5** see SEDUCE 1. ● *n.* **1** see ORGY 1.

debauchee /díbbawcheé, déb-/ *n.* a person addicted to excessive sensual indulgence. [F *débauché* past part.: see DEBAUCH]

▪ see *sensualist* (SENSUAL).

debauchery /dibáwchəri/ *n.* excessive sensual indulgence.

▪ see DISSIPATION 1.

debenture /dibénchər/ *n.* **1** *Brit.* an acknowledgement of indebtedness, esp. a bond of a company or corporation acknowledging a debt and providing for payment of interest at fixed intervals. **2** *US* (in full **debenture bond**) a fixed-interest bond of a company or corporation, backed by general credit rather than specified assets. ▫ **debenture stock** *Brit.* stock comprising debentures, with only the interest secured. [ME f. L *debentur* are owing f. *debēre* owe: assim. to -URE]

debilitate /dibíllitayt/ *v.tr.* enfeeble, enervate. ▫▫ **debilitatingly** *adv.* **debilitation** /-táysh'n/ *n.* **debilitative** /-tətiv/ *adj.* [L *debilitare* (as DEBILITY)]

▪ see ENERVATE *v.*

debility /dibílliti/ *n.* feebleness, esp. of health. [ME f. OF *debilité* f. L *debilitas -tatis* f. *debilis* weak]

▪ see *infirmity* (INFIRM).

debit /débbit/ *n.* & *v.* ● *n.* **1** an entry in an account recording a sum owed. **2** the sum recorded. **3** the total of such sums. **4** the debit side of an account. ● *v.tr.* (**debited, debiting**) **1** (foll. by *against*, *to*) enter (an amount) on the debit side of an account (*debited £500 against me*). **2** (foll. by *with*) enter (a person) on the debit side of an account (*debited me with £500*). [F *débit* f. L *debitum* DEBT]

▪ *n.* see CHARGE *n.* 1b. ● *v.* bill, charge, invoice.

debonair /débbənáir/ *adj.* **1** carefree, cheerful, self-assured. **2** having pleasant manners. ▫▫ **debonairly** *adv.* [ME f. OF *debonaire* = *de bon aire* of good disposition]

▪ **1** carefree, insouciant, gay, nonchalant, light-hearted, dashing, charming, cheerful, buoyant, jaunty, sprightly; smooth, unruffled; see also *self-assured* (SELF-ASSURANCE). **2** suave, elegant, urbane, refined, genteel, well-bred, courteous, civil, mannerly, gracious, polite, affable, obliging, pleasant.

debouch /dibówch, -bo͝osh/ *v.intr.* **1** (of troops or a stream) issue from a ravine, wood, etc., into open ground. **2** (often foll. by *into*) (of a river, road, etc.) merge into a larger body or area. ▫▫ **debouchment** *n.* [F *déboucher* (as DE-, *bouche* mouth)]

debrief /deebreéf/ *v.tr. colloq.* interrogate (a person, e.g. a diplomat or pilot) about a completed mission or undertaking. ▫▫ **debriefing** *n.*

debris /débree, dáy-/ *n.* **1** scattered fragments, esp. of something wrecked or destroyed. **2** *Geol.* an accumulation of loose material, e.g. from rocks or plants. [F *débris* f. obs. *débriser* break down (as DE-, *briser* break)]

▪ **1** see WRECKAGE 1, 2, WASTE *n.* 2.

debt /det/ *n.* **1** something that is owed, esp. money. **2** a state of obligation to pay something owed (*in debt*; *out of debt*; *get into debt*). ▫ **debt-collector** a person who is employed to collect debts for creditors. **debt of honour** a debt not legally recoverable, esp. a sum lost in gambling. **in a person's debt** under an obligation to a person. [ME *det(te)* f. OF *dette* (later *debte*) ult. f. L *debitum* past part. of *debēre* owe]

▪ **2** obligation; due, indebtedness, liability, responsibility, accountability, encumbrance; (*in debt*) under obligation, owing, accountable, beholden, indebted; in arrears, straitened, in dire straits, in (financial) difficulty *or* difficulties, insolvent, in the red, *esp. US colloq.* in hock.

debtor /déttər/ *n.* a person who owes a debt, esp. money. [ME f. OF *det(t)or*, *-our* f. L *debitor* (as DEBT)]

debug /deebúg/ *v.tr.* (**debugged, debugging**) **1** *colloq.* trace and remove concealed listening devices from (a room etc.). **2** *colloq.* identify and remove defects from (a machine, computer program, etc.). **3** remove bugs from.

debunk /deebúngk/ *v.tr. colloq.* **1** show the good reputation or aspirations of (a person, institution, etc.) to be spurious. **2** expose the falseness of (a claim etc.). ▫▫ **debunker** *n.*

▪ see EXPLODE 4.

debus /deebúss/ *v.tr.* & *intr.* (**debussed, debussing**) esp. *Mil.* unload (personnel or stores) or alight from a motor vehicle.

début /dáy-byoo͞, -boo͞/ *n.* (*US* **debut**) **1** the first public appearance of a performer on stage etc., or the opening

performance of a show etc. **2** the first appearance of a débutante in society. [F f. *débuter* lead off]
■ **1** première, first night, opening (night). **2** appearance, coming out, introduction, initiation, inauguration, launch, launching.

débutante /débyootaant, dáy-/ *n.* (*US* **debutante**) a (usu. wealthy) young woman making her social début. [F, fem. part. of *débuter*: see DÉBUT]

Dec. *abbr.* December.

dec. *abbr.* **1** deceased. **2** declared.

deca- /dékkə/ *comb. form* (also **dec-** before a vowel) **1** having ten. **2** tenfold. **3** ten, esp. of a metric unit (*decagram*; *decalitre*). [Gk *deka* ten]

decade /dékkayd, *disp.* dikáyd/ *n.* **1** a period of ten years. **2** a set, series, or group of ten. □□ **decadal** /dékkəd'l/ *adj.* [ME f. F *décade* f. LL *decas -adis* f. Gk f. *deka* ten]

decadence /dékkəd'nss/ *n.* **1** moral or cultural deterioration, esp. after a peak or culmination of achievement. **2** decadent behaviour; a state of decadence. [F *décadence* f. med.L *decadentia* f. *decadere* DECAY]
■ **1** see DECAY *n.* 2.

decadent /dékkəd'nt/ *adj.* & *n.* ● *adj.* **1 a** in a state of moral or cultural deterioration; showing or characterized by decadence. **b** of a period of decadence. **2** self-indulgent. ● *n.* a decadent person. □□ **decadently** *adv.* [F *décadent* (as DECADENCE)]
■ *adj.* **1 a** debased, degenerating, degenerative; corrupt, degenerate, immoral, debauched, dissipated; see also DISSOLUTE. **2** see SELF-INDULGENT. ● *n.* see DEGENERATE *n.*

decaffeinate /deekáffinayt/ *v.tr.* **1** remove the caffeine from. **2** reduce the quantity of caffeine in (usu. coffee).

decagon /dékkəgən/ *n.* a plane figure with ten sides and angles. □□ **decagonal** /dikággən'l/ *adj.* [med.L *decagonum* f. Gk *dekagōnon* (as DECA-, -GON)]

decagynous /dikájinəss/ *adj.* *Bot.* having ten pistils. [mod.L *decagynus* (as DECA-, Gk *gūne* woman)]

decahedron /dékkəheédrən/ *n.* a solid figure with ten faces. □□ **decahedral** *adj.* [DECA- + -HEDRON after POLYHEDRON]

decal /deékal/ *n.* = DECALCOMANIA 2. [abbr.]

decalcify /deekálsifī/ *v.tr.* (**-ies, -ied**) remove lime or calcareous matter from (a bone, tooth, etc.). □□ **decalcification** /-fikáysh'n/ *n.* **decalcifier** *n.*

decalcomania /deekálkəmáyniə/ *n.* *US* **1** a process of transferring designs from specially prepared paper to the surface of glass, porcelain, etc. **2** a picture or design made by this process. [F *décalcomanie* f. *décalquer* transfer]

decalitre /dékkəleetər/ *n.* a metric unit of capacity, equal to 10 litres.

Decalogue /dékkəlog/ *n.* the Ten Commandments. [ME f. F *décalogue* or eccl.L *decalogus* f. Gk *dekalogos* (after *hoi deka logoi* the Ten Commandments)]

decametre /dékkəmeetər/ *n.* a metric unit of length, equal to 10 metres.

decamp /dikámp, dee-/ *v.intr.* **1** break up or leave a camp. **2** depart suddenly; abscond. □□ **decampment** *n.* [F *décamper* (as DE-, CAMP[1])]
■ *v.* **1** see LEAVE[1] *v.* 1b, 3, 4.

decanal /dikáyn'l, dékkə-/ *adj.* **1** of a dean or deanery. **2** of the south side of a choir, the side on which the dean sits (cf. CANTORIAL). [med.L *decanalis* f. LL *decanus* DEAN[1]]

decandrous /dikándrəss/ *adj.* *Bot.* having ten stamens. [DECA- + Gk *andr-* man (= male organ)]

decani /dikáynī/ *adj.* *Mus.* to be sung by the decanal side in antiphonal singing (cf. CANTORIS). [L, genit. of *decanus* DEAN[1]]

decant /dikánt/ *v.tr.* **1** gradually pour off (liquid, esp. wine or a solution) from one container to another, esp. without disturbing the sediment. **2** empty out; move as if by pouring. [med.L *decanthare* (as DE-, L *canthus* f. Gk *kanthos* canthus, used of the lip of a beaker)]

decanter /dikántər/ *n.* a stoppered glass container into which wine or spirit is decanted.
■ see JUG *n.* 1, 2.

decapitate /dikáppitayt, dee-/ *v.tr.* **1** behead (esp. as a form of capital punishment). **2** cut the head or end from. □□ **decapitation** /-táysh'n/ *n.* **decapitator** *n.* [LL *decapitare* (as DE-, *caput -itis* head)]
■ see BEHEAD.

decapod /dékkəpod/ *n.* **1** any crustacean of the chiefly marine order Decapoda, characterized by five pairs of walking legs, e.g. shrimps, crabs, and lobsters. **2** any of various molluscs of the class Cephalopoda, having ten tentacles, e.g. squids and cuttlefish. □□ **decapodan** /dikáppəd'n/ *adj.* [F *décapode* f. Gk *deka* ten + *pous podos* foot]

decarbonize /deekaárbənīz/ *v.tr.* (also **-ise**) remove carbon or carbonaceous deposits from (an internal-combustion engine etc.). □□ **decarbonization** /-záysh'n/ *n.*

decastyle /dékkəstīl/ *n.* & *adj.* *Archit.* ● *n.* a ten-columned portico. ● *adj.* having ten columns. [Gk *dekastulos* f. *deka* ten + *stulos* column]

decasyllable /dékkəsilləb'l/ *n.* a metrical line of ten syllables. □□ **decasyllabic** /-silábbik/ *adj.* & *n.*

decathlon /dikáthlən/ *n.* an athletic contest in which each competitor takes part in ten events. □□ **decathlete** /-leet/ *n.* [DECA- + Gk *athlon* contest]

decay /dikáy/ *v.* & *n.* ● *v.* **1 a** *intr.* rot, decompose. **b** *tr.* cause to rot or decompose. **2** *intr.* & *tr.* decline or cause to decline in quality, power, wealth, energy, beauty, etc. **3** *intr.* *Physics* **a** (usu. foll. by *to*) (of a substance etc.) undergo change by radioactivity. **b** undergo a gradual decrease in magnitude of a physical quantity. ● *n.* **1** a rotten or ruinous state; a process of wasting away. **2** decline in health, quality, etc. **3** *Physics* **a** change into another substance etc. by radioactivity. **b** a decrease in the magnitude of a physical quantity, esp. the intensity of radiation or amplitude of oscillation. **4** decayed tissue. □□ **decayable** *adj.* [ME f. OF *decair* f. Rmc (as DE-, L *cadere* fall)]
■ *v.* **1 a** rot, decompose, moulder, putrefy, spoil; turn, go bad, go off. **2** decline, degenerate, waste away, atrophy, weaken, wither, disintegrate, crumble, wane, ebb, dwindle, diminish, decrease; see also DETERIORATE. ● *n.* **1** rot, decomposition, mould, putrefaction, mortification. **2** decline, deterioration, decadence, degeneration, dilapidation, disintegration, collapse, wasting, atrophy; downfall.

decease /diseéss/ *n.* & *v.* *formal* esp. *Law* ● *n.* death. ● *v.intr.* die. [ME f. OF *deces* f. L *decessus* f. *decedere* (as DE-, *cedere cess-* go)]
■ *n.* see DEATH 1. ● *v.* see DIE[1] 1.

deceased /diseést/ *adj.* & *n.* *formal* ● *adj.* dead. ● *n.* (usu. prec. by *the*) a person who has died, esp. recently.
■ *adj.* see DEAD *adj.* 1.

decedent /diseéd'nt/ *n.* *US Law* a deceased person. [L *decedere* die: see DECEASE]

deceit /diseét/ *n.* **1** the act or process of deceiving or misleading, esp. by concealing the truth. **2** a dishonest trick or stratagem. **3** willingness to deceive. [ME f. OF f. past part. of *deceveir* f. L *decipere* deceive (as DE-, *capere* take)]
■ **1** deception, deceitfulness, fraud, fraudulence, cheating, trickery, chicanery, chicane, dissimulation, dishonesty, misrepresentation, double-dealing, dirty business *or* dealing, duplicity, hypocrisy, treachery, underhandedness, subterfuge, hocus-pocus, guile, craft, slyness, craftiness, cunning, knavery, flimflam, *archaic* covin, *colloq.* monkey business, gammon, *sl.* hanky-panky, funny business. **2** trick, subterfuge, stratagem, fraud, cheat, ruse, manoeuvre, artifice, wile, hoax, swindle, double-cross, pretence, imposture, sham, contrivance, shift, confidence trick *or US* game, blind, *colloq.* ploy, put-on, *formal* subreption, *sl.* con, con trick, *US sl.* scam.

deceitful /diseétfool/ *adj.* **1** (of a person) using deceit, esp. habitually. **2** (of an act, practice, etc.) intended to deceive. □□ **deceitfully** *adv.* **deceitfulness** *n.*
■ dishonest, underhand(ed), untrustworthy, misleading,

crooked, insincere, false, fraudulent, counterfeit, disingenuous, lying, mendacious, untruthful; wily, crafty, sly, cunning, scheming, guileful, artful, sneaky, double-dealing, two-faced, hypocritical, duplicitous.
□□ **deceitfulness** see DECEIT 1.

deceive /diseév/ *v.* **1** *tr.* make (a person) believe what is false, mislead purposely. **2** *tr.* be unfaithful to, esp. sexually. **3** *intr.* use deceit. **4** *tr. archaic* disappoint (esp. hopes). □ **be deceived** be mistaken or deluded. **deceive oneself** persist in a mistaken belief. □□ **deceivable** *adj.* **deceiver** *n.* [ME f. OF *deceivre* or *deceiv-* stressed stem of *deceveir* (as DECEIT)]
■ **1** mislead, delude, fool, hoax, trick, cheat, swindle, betray, double-cross, lead on, take in, lead up *or* down the garden path, lead astray, pull the wool over a person's eyes, *archaic* wilder, *colloq.* bamboozle, take for a ride, two-time, *literary* cozen, *sl.* con. **2** be unfaithful to, cuckold, *colloq.* cheat on. **3** see DISSIMULATE. **4** see DISAPPOINT 2. □ **be deceived** (*deceived*) see MISTAKEN.

decelerate /deesélərayt/ *v.* **1** *intr.* & *tr.* begin or cause to begin to reduce speed. **2** *tr.* make slower (*decelerated motion*). □□ **deceleration** /-ráysh'n/ *n.* **decelerator** *n.* **decelerometer** /-rómmitər/ *n.* [DE-, after ACCELERATE]
■ see SLOW *v.* 1, BRAKE¹ *v.* 2.

December /disémbər/ *n.* the twelfth month of the year. [ME f. OF *decembre* f. L *December* f. *decem* ten: orig. the tenth month of the Roman year]

decency /deéssənsi/ *n.* (*pl.* **-ies**) **1** correct and tasteful standards of behaviour as generally accepted. **2** conformity with current standards of behaviour or propriety. **3** avoidance of obscenity. **4** (in *pl.*) the requirements of correct behaviour. [L *decentia* f. *decēre* be fitting]
■ **1, 2** see PROPRIETY 2.

decennial /disénniəl/ *adj.* **1** lasting ten years. **2** recurring every ten years. □□ **decennially** *adv.* [L *decennis* of ten years f. *decem* ten + *annus* year]

decent /deéss'nt/ *adj.* **1 a** conforming with current standards of behaviour or propriety. **b** avoiding obscenity. **2** respectable. **3** acceptable, passable; good enough. **4** *Brit.* kind, obliging, generous (*was decent enough to apologize*). □□ **decently** *adv.* [F *décent* or L *decēre* be fitting]
■ **1 a** proper, seemly, fitting, becoming, suitable, appropriate, right, correct, acceptable. **b** clean, inoffensive. **2** respectable, proper, well-bred, well brought up, well-mannered, mannerly, nice, clean, presentable, acceptable, seemly, decorous, dignified; chaste, pure, virtuous, modest. **3** adequate, acceptable, passable, satisfactory, fair, competent, mediocre, middling, fair to middling, moderate, respectable, ordinary, so so, indifferent, not outstanding, unimpressive, average, neither here nor there, all right, *comme ci, comme ça*, reasonable, tolerable, good enough, *colloq.* OK, not bad. **4** courteous, proper, right, fair, honest, honourable, friendly, considerate, gracious, nice, thoughtful, obliging, kind, generous, accommodating.
□□ **decently** see PROPERLY 4.

decentralize /deeséntrəlīz/ *v.tr.* (also **-ise**) **1** transfer (powers etc.) from a central to a local authority. **2** reorganize (a centralized institution, organization, etc.) on the basis of greater local autonomy. □□ **decentralist** /-list/ *n.* & *adj.* **decentralization** /-záysh'n/ *n.*

deception /disépsh'n/ *n.* **1** the act or an instance of deceiving; the process of being deceived. **2** a thing that deceives; a trick or sham. [ME f. OF or LL *deceptio* f. *decipere* (as DECEIT)]
■ **1** see DECEIT 1. **2** see DECEIT 2.

deceptive /diséptiv/ *adj.* apt to deceive; easily mistaken for something else or as having a different quality. □□ **deceptively** *adv.* **deceptiveness** *n.* [OF *deceptif -ive* or LL *deceptivus* (as DECEPTION)]
■ misleading, false, illusory, deceiving, unreliable; fraudulent, deceitful, dishonest, untruthful, fake, false, *colloq.* shifty; tricky, dodgy, evasive, elusive, slippery.

decerebrate /deesérribrət/ *adj.* having had the cerebrum removed.

deci- /déssi/ *comb. form* one-tenth, esp. of a unit in the metric system (*decilitre*; *decimetre*). [L *decimus* tenth]

decibel /déssibel/ *n.* a unit (one-tenth of a bel) used in the comparison of two power levels relating to electrical signals or sound intensities, one of the pair usually being taken as a standard. ¶ Abbr.: **dB.**

decide /disīd/ *v.* **1 a** *intr.* (often foll. by *on, about*) come to a resolution as a result of consideration. **b** *tr.* (usu. foll. by *to* + infin., or *that* + clause) have or reach as one's resolution about something (*decided to stay*; *decided that we should leave*). **2** *tr.* **a** cause (a person) to reach a resolution (*was unsure about going but the weather decided me*). **b** resolve or settle (a question, dispute, etc.). **3** *intr.* (usu. foll. by *between, for, against, in favour of,* or *that* + clause) give a judgement concerning a matter. □□ **decidable** *adj.* [ME f. F *décider* or f. L *decidere* (as DE-, *cædere* cut)]
■ **1** take *or* reach *or* come to a decision *or* conclusion, make up one's mind, determine, resolve; conclude; (*decide on*) fix *or* fasten *or* settle on, choose, select, pick (out), elect, opt for, commit oneself to. **2 b** resolve, arbitrate, judge, adjudicate; see also SETTLE¹ 5–7, 8b.

decided /disīdid/ *adj.* **1** (usu. *attrib.*) definite, unquestionable (*a decided difference*). **2** (of a person, esp. as a characteristic) having clear opinions, resolute, not vacillating. □□ **decidedness** *n.*
■ **1** definite, pronounced, marked, unmistakable, unambiguous, unequivocal, certain, sure, absolute, obvious, clear, evident, unquestionable, unquestioned, indisputable, undisputed, undeniable, irrefutable, incontestable, unqualified, unconditional, incontrovertible, solid, real. **2** fixed, firm, resolute, determined, adamant, unhesitating, decisive, definite, unfaltering, assertive, asseverative, unswerving, uncompromising, unwavering.

decidedly /disīdidli/ *adv.* undoubtedly, undeniably.
■ see TRULY 2.

decider /disīdər/ *n.* **1** a game, race, etc., to decide between competitors finishing equal in a previous contest. **2** any person or thing that decides.

deciduous /disídyooəss/ *adj.* **1** (of a tree) shedding its leaves annually. **2** (of leaves, horns, teeth, etc.) shed periodically. **3** (of an ant etc.) shedding its wings after copulation. **4** fleeting, transitory. □□ **deciduousness** *n.* [L *deciduus* f. *decidere* f. *cadere* fall]

decigram /déssigram/ *n.* (also **decigramme**) a metric unit of mass, equal to 0.1 gram.

decile /déssil, -sīl/ *n. Statistics* any of the nine values of a random variable which divide a frequency distribution into ten groups, each containing one-tenth of the total population. [F *décile*, ult. f. L *decem* ten]

decilitre /déssileetər/ *n.* a metric unit of capacity, equal to 0.1 litre.

decimal /déssim'l/ *adj.* & *n.* ● *adj.* **1** (of a system of numbers, weights, measures, etc.) based on the number ten, in which the smaller units are related to the principal units as powers of ten (units, tens, hundreds, thousands, etc.). **2** of tenths or ten; reckoning or proceeding by tens. ● *n.* a decimal fraction. □ **decimal fraction** a fraction whose denominator is a power of ten, esp. when expressed positionally by units to the right of a decimal point. **decimal point** a full point or dot placed before a numerator in a decimal fraction. **decimal scale** a scale with successive places denoting units, tens, hundreds, etc. □□ **decimally** *adv.* [mod.L *decimalis* f. L *decimus* tenth]

decimalize /déssiməlīz/ *v.tr.* (also **-ise**) **1** express as a decimal. **2** convert to a decimal system (esp. of coinage). □□ **decimalization** /-záysh'n/ *n.*

decimate /déssimayt/ *v.tr.* **1** *disp.* destroy a large proportion of. ¶ Now the usual sense, although often deplored as an inappropriate use. **2** *orig. Mil.* kill or remove one in every

ten of. ▫▫ **decimation** /-máysh'n/ *n.* **decimator** *n.* [L *decimare* take the tenth man f. *decimus* tenth]
■ **1** see MASSACRE *v.* 2.

decimetre /déssimeetər/ *n.* a metric unit of length, equal to 0.1 metre.

decipher /disīfər/ *v.tr.* **1** convert (a text written in cipher) into an intelligible script or language. **2** determine the meaning of (anything obscure or unclear). ▫▫ **decipherable** *adj.* **decipherment** *n.*
■ **1** decode, decrypt. **2** decode, unravel, unscramble, disentangle, translate, work out, explain, solve, figure out, interpret, make out; understand.

decision /disízh'n/ *n.* **1** the act or process of deciding. **2** a conclusion or resolution reached, esp. as to future action, after consideration (*have made my decision*). **3** (often foll. by *of*) **a** the settlement of a question. **b** a formal judgement. **4** a tendency to decide firmly; resoluteness. [ME f. OF *decision* or L *decisio* (as DECIDE)]
■ **1** settlement, determination, resolution, arbitration. **2, 3** judgement, conclusion, resolution; verdict, sentence, ruling, finding, decree, settlement. **4** determination, firmness, decidedness, resolve, resolution, resoluteness, decisiveness, conclusiveness, steadfastness, purpose, purposefulness.

decisive /disīsiv/ *adj.* **1** that decides an issue; conclusive. **2** (of a person, esp. as a characteristic) able to decide quickly and effectively. ▫▫ **decisively** *adv.* **decisiveness** *n.* [F *décisif -ive* f. med.L *decisivus* (as DECIDE)]
■ **1** see ULTIMATE *adj.* 1, 2. **2** see FIRM[1] *adj.* 2a.

deck /dek/ *n.* & *v.* ● *n.* **1 a** a platform in a ship covering all or part of the hull's area at any level and serving as a floor. **b** the accommodation on a particular deck of a ship. **2** anything compared to a ship's deck, e.g. the floor or compartment of a bus. **3** a component, usu. a flat horizontal surface, that carries a particular recording medium (such as a disc or tape) in sound-reproduction equipment. **4** *US* **a** a pack of cards. **b** *sl.* a packet of narcotics. **5** *sl.* the ground. **6** any floor or platform, esp. the floor of a pier or a platform for sunbathing. ● *v.tr.* **1** (often foll. by *out*) decorate, adorn. **2** furnish with or cover as a deck. ▫ **below deck** (or **decks**) in or into the space below the main deck. **deck-chair** a folding chair of wood and canvas, of a kind used on deck on passenger ships. **deck-hand** a person employed in cleaning and odd jobs on a ship's deck. **deck quoits** a game in which rope quoits are aimed at a peg. **deck tennis** a game in which a quoit of rope, rubber, etc., is tossed to and fro over a net. **on deck 1** in the open air on a ship's main deck. **2** esp. *US* ready for action, work, etc. [ME, = covering f. MDu. *dec* roof, cloak]
■ *n.* **1a, 2** storey, level, floor. **4 a** pack, set, stack. ● *v.* **1** see DECORATE 1, 3.

-decker /dékkər/ *comb. form* having a specified number of decks or layers (*double-decker*).

deckle /dékk'l/ *n.* a device in a paper-making machine for limiting the size of the sheet. ▫ **deckle edge** the rough uncut edge formed by a deckle. **deckle-edged** having a deckle edge. [G *Deckel* dimin. of *Decke* cover]

declaim /dikláym/ *v.* **1** *intr.* & *tr.* speak or utter rhetorically or affectedly. **2** *intr.* practise oratory or recitation. **3** *intr.* (foll. by *against*) protest forcefully. **4** *intr.* deliver an impassioned (rather than reasoned) speech. ▫▫ **declaimer** *n.* [ME f. F *déclamer* or f. L *declamare* (as DE-, CLAIM)]
■ **1, 3, 4** see RANT *v.* 2, 3.

declamation /dékləmáysh'n/ *n.* **1** the act or art of declaiming. **2** a rhetorical exercise or set speech. **3** an impassioned speech; a harangue. ▫▫ **declamatory** /diklámmətəri, -tri/ *adj.* [F *déclamation* or L *declamatio* (as DECLAIM)]
■ **1** see ORATORY. **2** see ORATION. **3** see HARANGUE *n.*

declarant /dikláirənt/ *n.* a person who makes a legal declaration. [F *déclarant* part. of *déclarer* (as DECLARE)]

declaration /déklərάysh'n/ *n.* **1** the act or process of declaring. **2 a** a formal, emphatic, or deliberate statement or announcement. **b** a statement asserting or protecting a legal right. **3** a written public announcement of intentions, terms of an agreement, etc. **4** *Cricket* an act of declaring an innings closed. **5** *Cards* **a** the naming of trumps. **b** an announcement of a combination held. **6** *Law* **a** a plaintiff's statement of claim. **b** an affirmation made instead of taking an oath. **7** (in full **declaration of the poll**) a public official announcement of the votes cast for candidates in an election. [ME f. L *declaratio* (as DECLARE)]
■ **1, 2a** statement, assertion, attestation, deposition, asseveration, affirmation, avowal, announcement, proclamation, pronouncement, profession. **2b** proclamation, announcement, pronouncement, promulgation. **3** edict, manifesto, notice.

declare /dikláir/ *v.* **1** *tr.* announce openly or formally (*declare war; declare a dividend*). **2** *tr.* pronounce (a person or thing) to be something (*declared him to be an impostor; declared it invalid*). **3** *tr.* (usu. foll. by *that* + clause) assert emphatically; state explicitly. **4** *tr.* acknowledge possession of (dutiable goods, income, etc.). **5** *tr.* (as **declared** *adj.*) who admits to be such (*a declared atheist*). **6** *tr.* (also *absol.*) *Cricket* close (an innings) voluntarily before all the wickets have fallen. **7** *tr. Cards* **a** (also *absol.*) name (the trump suit). **b** announce that one holds (certain combinations of cards etc.). **8** *tr.* (of things) make evident, prove (*your actions declare your honesty*). **9** *intr.* (foll. by *for, against*) take the side of one party or another. ▫ **declare oneself** reveal one's intentions or identity. **well, I declare** (or **I do declare**) an exclamation of incredulity, surprise, or vexation. ▫▫ **declarable** *adj.* **declarative** /-klárrətiv/ *adj.* **declaratively** /-klárrətivli/ *adv.* **declaratory** /-klárrətəri/ *adj.* **declaredly** /-ridli/ *adv.* **declarer** *n.* [ME f. L *declarare* (as DE-, *clarare* f. *clarus* clear)]
■ **1, 2** announce, make known, pronounce, decree, rule, proclaim, herald, promulgate, publish, broadcast, trumpet (forth). **3** assert, affirm, state, asseverate, avow, profess, protest, swear, claim, proclaim, say, *archaic or rhet.* avouch, *formal* aver; confirm, certify. **5** (**declared**) avowed, professed, proclaimed, *archaic or rhet.* avouched. **8** see PROVE 1. **9** (*declare for*) see SIDE *v.*; (*declare against*) see OPPOSE 1–3. ▫ **declare oneself** see DECLARE 3 above. **well, I declare** (or **I do declare**) see *well I'm damned* (DAMN). ▫▫ **declarative, declaratory** see ASSERTIVE 1.

déclassé /dayklássay/ *adj.* (*fem.* ***déclassée***) that has fallen in social status. [F]

declassify /deeklássifī/ *v.tr.* (**-ies, -ied**) declare (information etc.) to be no longer secret. ▫▫ **declassification** /-fikáysh'n/ *n.*

declension /diklénsh'n/ *n.* **1** *Gram.* **a** the variation of the form of a noun, pronoun, or adjective, by which its grammatical case, number, and gender are identified. **b** the class in which a noun etc. is put according to the exact form of this variation. **2** deterioration, declining. ▫▫ **declensional** *adj.* [OF *declinaison* f. *decliner* DECLINE after L *declinatio*: assim. to ASCENSION etc.]

declination /déklináysh'n/ *n.* **1** a downward bend or turn. **2** *Astron.* the angular distance of a star etc. north or south of the celestial equator. **3** *Physics* the angular deviation of a compass needle from true north. **4** *US* a formal refusal. ▫▫ **declinational** *adj.* [ME f. L *declinatio* (as DECLINE)]

decline /diklīn/ *v.* & *n.* ● *v.* **1** *intr.* deteriorate; lose strength or vigour; decrease. **2 a** *tr.* reply with formal courtesy that one will not accept (an invitation, honour, etc.). **b** *tr.* refuse, esp. formally and courteously (*declined to be made use of; declined doing anything*). **c** *tr.* turn away from (a challenge, battle, discussion, etc.). **d** *intr.* give or send a refusal. **3** *intr.* slope downwards. **4** *intr.* bend down, droop. **5** *tr. Gram.* state the forms of (a noun, pronoun, or adjective) corresponding to cases, number, and gender. **6** *intr.* (of a day, life, etc.) draw to a close. **7** *intr.* decrease in price etc. **8** *tr.* bend down. ● *n.* **1** gradual loss of vigour or excellence (*on the decline*). **2** decay, deterioration. **3** setting; the last part of the course (of the sun, of life, etc.). **4** a fall in price. **5** *archaic* tuberculosis or a similar wasting disease. ▫ **declining years** old age. **on the decline** in a declining state. ▫▫ **declinable**

adj. **decliner** *n.* [ME f. OF *decliner* f. L *declinare* (as DE-, *clinare* bend)]

▪ *v.* **1, 7** deteriorate, degenerate, worsen; go down, drop, diminish, lessen, decrease, dip, sink, wane, flag, peter out, trail *or* tail off, fall *or* taper off, subside, ebb, abate, dwindle, shrink, fade. **2** refuse, turn down, say no to. **3** slope *or* slant (downwards), descend, drop *or* fall off, dip, sink. **4** see DROOP *v.* 1. **6** see STOP *v.* 2. ● *n.* **1, 4** diminution, decrease, lessening, ebb, downturn, fall-off, reduction, abatement, slump, descent, fall, slide, drop. **2** decay, degeneration, deterioration, weakening, debility, worsening. □ **declining years** see AGE *n.* 3. **on the decline** on the wane, in decline, waning, in eclipse, declining, falling, slipping, falling off, out of favour, losing ground, going downhill, *US* on the downgrade, *colloq.* on the skids.

declivity /diklívviti/ *n.* (*pl.* **-ies**) a downward slope, esp. a piece of sloping ground. □□ **declivitous** *adj.* [L *declivitas* f. *declivis* (as DE-, *clivus* slope)]

▪ see SLOPE *n.* 1–3.

declutch /deeklúch/ *v.intr.* disengage the clutch of a motor vehicle. □ **double-declutch** release and re-engage the clutch twice when changing gear.

Deco /dékkō/ *n.* (also **deco**) (usu. *attrib.*) = *art deco.* [F *décoratif* DECORATIVE]

decoct /dikókt/ *v.tr.* extract the essence from by decoction. [ME f. L *decoquere* boil down]

decoction /dikóksh'n/ *n.* **1** a process of boiling down so as to extract some essence. **2** the extracted liquor resulting from this. [ME f. OF *decoction* or LL *decoctio* (as DE-, L *coquere coct-* boil)]

▪ **2** see EXTRACT *n.* 2.

decode /deekṓd/ *v.tr.* convert (a coded message) into intelligible language. □□ **decodable** *adj.*

▪ see DECIPHER 1, 2.

decoder /deekṓdər/ *n.* **1** a person or thing that decodes. **2** an electronic device for analysing signals and feeding separate amplifier-channels.

decoke *v.* & *n. Brit. colloq.* ● *v.tr.* /deekṓk/ remove carbon or carbonaceous material from (an internal-combustion engine). ● *n.* /déekōk/ the process of decoking.

decollate /dikóllayt, dékkəlayt/ *v.tr. formal* **1** behead. **2** truncate. □□ **decollation** /déekoláysh'n/ *n.* [L *decollare decollat-* (as DE-, *collum* neck)]

▪ **1** see BEHEAD.

décolletage /dáykoltaázh/ *n.* a low neckline of a woman's dress etc. [F (as DE-, *collet* collar of a dress)]

décolleté /daykóltay/ *adj.* & *n.* ● *adj.* (also ***décolletée***) **1** (of a dress etc.) having a low neckline. **2** (of a woman) wearing a dress with a low neckline. ● *n.* a low neckline. [F (as DÉCOLLETAGE)]

decolonize /deekóllənīz/ *v.tr.* (also **-ise**) (of a State) withdraw from (a colony), leaving it independent. □□ **decolonization** /-záysh'n/ *n.*

decolorize /deekúllərīz/ *v.* (also **-ise**) **1** *tr.* remove the colour from. **2** *intr.* lose colour. □□ **decolorization** /-záysh'n/ *n.*

decommission /déekəmísh'n/ *v.tr.* **1** close down (a nuclear reactor etc.). **2** take (a ship) out of service.

decompose /déekəmpṓz/ *v.* **1** *intr.* decay, rot. **2** *tr.* separate (a substance, light, etc.) into its elements or simpler constituents. **3** *intr.* disintegrate; break up. □□ **decomposition** /déekompəzísh'n/ *n.* [F *décomposer* (as DE-, COMPOSE)]

▪ **1** rot, disintegrate, decay, moulder, putrefy, break down; spoil, go off *or* bad. **2** separate, break up *or* down, take apart, dissect, anatomize, atomize, resolve, analyse. **3** break up *or* down, fall *or* come apart; see also DISINTEGRATE. □□ **decomposition** see DECAY *n.* 1.

decompress /déekəmprés/ *v.tr.* subject to decompression; relieve or reduce the compression on.

decompression /déekəmprésh'n/ *n.* **1** release from compression. **2** a gradual reduction of air pressure on a person who has been subjected to high pressure (esp. underwater). □ **decompression chamber** an enclosed space for subjecting a person to decompression. **decompression sickness** a condition caused by the sudden lowering of air pressure and formation of bubbles in the blood: also called *caisson disease, the bends* (*see* BEND[1] *n.* 4).

decompressor /déekəmpréssər/ *n.* a device for reducing pressure in the engine of a motor vehicle.

decongestant /déekənjéstənt/ *adj.* & *n.* ● *adj.* that relieves (esp. nasal) congestion. ● *n.* a medicinal agent that relieves nasal congestion.

deconsecrate /deekónsikrayt/ *v.tr.* transfer (esp. a building) from sacred to secular use. □□ **deconsecration** /-kráysh'n/ *n.*

deconstruct /déekənstrúkt/ *v.tr.* subject to deconstruction. □□ **deconstructive** *adj.* [back-form. f. DECONSTRUCTION]

deconstruction /déekənstrúksh'n/ *n.* a method of critical analysis of philosophical and literary language. □□ **deconstructionism** *n.* **deconstructionist** *adj.* & *n.* [F *déconstruction* (as DE-, CONSTRUCTION)]

decontaminate /déekəntámminayt/ *v.tr.* remove contamination from (an area, person, clothes, etc.). □□ **decontamination** /-náysh'n/ *n.*

▪ see DISINFECT.

decontrol /déekəntrṓl/ *v.* & *n.* ● *v.tr.* (**decontrolled, decontrolling**) release (a commodity etc.) from controls or restrictions, esp. those imposed by the State. ● *n.* the act of decontrolling.

▪ *v.* deregulate, derestrict. ● *n.* see LAISSEZ-FAIRE.

décor /dáykor, dék-/ *n.* **1** the furnishing and decoration of a room etc. **2** the decoration and scenery of a stage. [F f. *décorer* (as DECORATE)]

decorate /dékkərayt/ *v.tr.* **1** provide with adornments. **2** provide (a room or building) with new paint, wallpaper, etc. **3** serve as an adornment to. **4** confer an award or distinction on. □ **Decorated style** *Archit.* the second stage of English Gothic (14th c.), with increasing use of decoration and geometrical tracery. [L *decorare decorat-* f. *decus -oris* beauty]

▪ **1, 3** bedeck, deck (out), trim, dress (up), spruce *or* smarten up, beautify, caparison, *Brit. colloq.* tart up; adorn, ornament, garnish, embroider; see also EMBELLISH 1. **2** paint, wallpaper, redecorate, furbish, refurbish, renovate, fix up.

decoration /dékkəráysh'n/ *n.* **1** the process or art of decorating. **2** a thing that decorates or serves as an ornament. **3** a medal etc. conferred and worn as an honour. **4** (in *pl.*) flags etc. put up on an occasion of public celebration. □ **Decoration Day** *US* Memorial Day. [F *décoration* or LL *decoratio* (as DECORATE)]

▪ **2** garnish, trim, trimming, adornment, embellishment, ornament, ornamentation, garnishment. **3** medal, laurel, award, badge, colours, order, ribbon, Garter.

decorative /dékkərətiv/ *adj.* serving to decorate. □□ **decoratively** *adv.* **decorativeness** *n.* [F *décoratif* (as DECORATE)]

▪ see FANCY *adj.* 1.

decorator /dékkəraytər/ *n.* a person who decorates, esp. one who paints or papers houses professionally.

decorous /dékkərəss/ *adj.* **1** respecting good taste or propriety. **2** dignified and decent. □□ **decorously** *adv.* **decorousness** *n.* [L *decorus* seemly]

▪ becoming, dignified, decent, correct, proper, mannerly, seemly, refined, elegant, polite, well-behaved, well-mannered, well-bred, genteel, demure, polished, gentlemanly, ladylike, *joc.* couth. □□ **decorousness** see DECORUM 1–3.

decorticate /deekórtikayt/ *v.tr.* **1** remove the bark, rind, or husk from. **2** remove the outside layer from (the kidney, brain, etc.). [L *decorticare decorticat-* (as DE-, *cortex -icis* bark)]

▪ **1** see PEEL[1] *v.* 1, 2.

decortication /déekortikáysh'n/ *n.* **1** the removal of the outside layer from an organ (e.g. the kidney) or structure. **2**

an operation removing the blood clot and scar tissue formed after bleeding in the chest cavity.

decorum /dikórəm/ *n.* **1 a** seemliness, propriety. **b** behaviour required by politeness or decency. **2** a particular requirement of this kind. **3** etiquette. [L, neut. of *decorus* seemly]
■ **1** seemliness, propriety, correctness, protocol, punctilio, form, formality, conformity. **2** civility, courtesy, politeness, formality. **3** etiquette, *politesse*, good form, propriety, mannerliness, politeness, dignity, gentility, good manners, *convenance(s)*, respectability, courtliness, deportment.

découpage /dáykoopaázh/ *n.* the decoration of surfaces with paper cut-outs. [F, = the action of cutting out]

decouple /deekúpp'l/ *v.tr.* **1** *Electr.* make the interaction between (oscillators etc.) so weak that there is little transfer of energy between them. **2** separate, disengage, dissociate.

decoy /deékoy, dikóy/ *n.* & *v.* ● *n.* **1 a** a person or thing used to lure an animal or person into a trap or danger. **b** a bait or enticement. **2** a pond with narrow netted arms into which wild duck may be tempted in order to catch them. ● *v.tr.* (often foll. by *into, out of*) allure or entice, esp. by means of a decoy. [17th c.: perh. f. Du. *de kooi* the decoy f. *de* THE + *kooi* f. L *cavea* cage]
■ *n.* **1** bait, lure, trap, attraction, enticement, inducement; stool-pigeon, *US* shill, stool, *Brit. sl.* nark. ● *v.* lure, entice, allure, attract, induce, coax, seduce, bait, trick, inveigle, persuade, draw (in).

decrease *v.* & *n.* ● *v.tr.* & *intr.* /dikreéss/ make or become smaller or fewer. ● *n.* /deékreess/ **1** the act or an instance of decreasing. **2** the amount by which a thing decreases. ▫▫ **decreasingly** *adv.* [ME f. OF *de(s)creiss-*, pres. stem of *de(s)creistre* ult. f. L *decrescere* (as DE-, *crescere cret-* grow)]
■ *v.* diminish, decline, lessen, go down, drop (off *or* away), fall, abate, fall off, shrink, contract, dwindle, ebb, subside, wane, taper off, trail *or* tail off, slacken, let up, ease (off *or* up); bring down, reduce, shorten, lower, de-escalate, curtail, cut (down *or* back), step down, mark down, slash, *US* roll back, *colloq.* knock down. ● *n.* diminution, reduction, decline, lessening, lowering, abatement, decrement, dwindling, ebb, subsidence, wane, de-escalation, slackening, easing (off *or* up), curtailment, cut, cut-back, drop, fall, fall-off, tail-off, slash, *US* roll-back.

decree /dikreé/ *n.* & *v.* ● *n.* **1** an official order issued by a legal authority. **2** a judgement or decision of certain lawcourts, esp. in matrimonial cases. ● *v.tr.* (**decrees, decreed, decreeing**) ordain by decree. ▫ **decree absolute** a final order for divorce, enabling either party to remarry. **decree nisi** a provisional order for divorce, made absolute unless cause to the contrary is shown within a fixed period. [ME f. OF *decré* f. L *decretum* neut. past part. of *decernere* decide (as DE-, *cernere* sift)]
■ *n.* **1** order, mandate, directive, ordinance, edict, law, statute, regulation, enactment, act, ruling, dictum, dictate, injunction, sanction, proclamation, announcement, promulgation, determination, rescript, prescription, firman, decretal. **2** see JUDGEMENT 4. ● *v.* order, command, direct, rule, mandate, ordain, dictate, charge, enjoin, proclaim, pronounce, prescribe, decide, determine, adjudge.

decrement /dékrimənt/ *n.* **1** *Physics* the ratio of the amplitudes in successive cycles of a damped oscillation. **2** the amount lost by diminution or waste. **3** the act of decreasing. [L *decrementum* (as DECREASE)]
■ **2, 3** see DECREASE *n.*

decrepit /dikréppit/ *adj.* **1** weakened or worn out by age and infirmity. **2** worn out by long use; dilapidated. ▫▫ **decrepitude** *n.* [ME f. L *decrepitus* (as DE-, *crepitus* past part. of *crepare* creak)]
■ **1** aged, old, elderly, ancient, superannuated, senescent, senile, feeble, enfeebled, weak, weakened, frail, infirm, wasted, worn out, unfit, debilitated, enervated, disabled, incapacitated, bedridden, doddering, broken-down, time-worn; out of shape, in bad shape, *sl.* gaga. **2** dilapidated, crumbling, decayed, decaying, withered, wasted, antiquated, tumbledown, broken-down, rickety, unstable, shaky, ramshackle, derelict, creaking, creaky, run-down, *Austral. sl.* warby, *Brit. sl.* clapped out. ▫▫ **decrepitude** feebleness, weakness, frailness, frailty, infirmity, debilitation, enervation, incapacity, incapacitation, old age, superannuation, senescence, senility, dotage; dilapidation, deterioration, decay, ruin.

decrepitate /dikréppitayt/ *v.* **1** *tr.* roast or calcine (a mineral or salt) until it stops crackling. **2** *intr.* crackle under heat. ▫▫ **decrepitation** /-táysh'n/ *n.* [prob. mod.L *decrepitare* f. DE- + L *crepitare* crackle]

decrescendo /deékrishéndō, dáy-/ *adv.*, *adj.*, & *n.* (*pl.* **-os**) = DIMINUENDO . [It., part. of *decrescere* DECREASE]

decrescent /dikréss'nt/ *adj.* (usu. of the moon) waning, decreasing. [L *decrescere*: see DECREASE]

decretal /dikreét'l/ *n.* **1** a papal decree. **2** (in *pl.*) a collection of these, forming part of canon law. [ME f. med.L *decretale* f. LL (*epistola*) *decretalis* (letter) of decree f. L *decernere*: see DECREE]

decriminalize /deekrímminəlīz/ *v.tr.* (also **-ise**) cease to treat (an action etc.) as criminal. ▫▫ **decriminalization** /-záysh'n/ *n.*

decry /dikrī́/ *v.tr.* (**-ies, -ied**) disparage, belittle. ▫▫ **decrial** *n.* **decrier** *n.* [after F *décrier*: cf. *cry down*]
■ see DISPARAGE 1.

decrypt /deekrípt/ *v.tr.* decipher (a cryptogram), with or without knowledge of its key. ▫▫ **decryption** *n.* [DE- + CRYPTOGRAM]

decumbent /dikúmb'nt/ *adj. Bot.* & *Zool.* (of a plant, shoot, or bristles) lying along the ground or a surface. [L *decumbere decumbent-* lie down]

decurve /deekúrv/ *v.tr.* & *intr. Zool.* & *Bot.* (esp. as **decurved** *adj.*) curve or bend down (*a decurved bill*). ▫▫ **decurvature** *n.*

decussate /deekússayt/ *adj.* & *v.* ● *adj.* **1** X-shaped. **2** *Bot.* with pairs of opposite leaves etc. each at right angles to the pair below. ● *v.tr.* & *intr.* **1** arrange or be arranged in a decussate form. **2** intersect. ▫▫ **decussation** /-sáysh'n/ *n.* [L *decussatus* past part. of *decussare* divide in a cross shape f. *decussis* the numeral ten or the shape X f. *decem* ten]

dedans /dədóɴ/ *n.* **1** (in real tennis) the open gallery at the end of the service side of a court. **2** the spectators watching a match. [F, = inside]

dedicate /déddikayt/ *v.tr.* **1** (foll. by *to*) devote (esp. oneself) to a special task or purpose. **2** (foll. by *to*) address (a book, piece of music, etc.) as a compliment to a friend, patron, etc. **3** (often foll. by *to*) devote (a building etc.) to a deity or a sacred person or purpose. **4** (as **dedicated** *adj.*) **a** (of a person) devoted to an aim or vocation; having single-minded loyalty or integrity. **b** (of equipment, esp. a computer) designed for a specific purpose. ▫▫ **dedicatee** /-kəteé/ *n.* **dedicative** *adj.* **dedicator** *n.* **dedicatory** *adj.* [L *dedicare* (DE-, *dicare* declare, dedicate)]
■ **1** devote, consecrate, give (up *or* over), offer (up), surrender, commit, pledge, assign. **2** inscribe; address, assign. **4 a** (**dedicated**) see DEVOTED.

dedication /déddikáysh'n/ *n.* **1** the act or an instance of dedicating; the quality or process of being dedicated. **2** the words with which a book etc. is dedicated. **3** a dedicatory inscription. [ME f. OF *dedicacion* or L *dedicatio* (as DEDICATE)]
■ **1** devotion, commitment, allegiance, adherence, faithfulness, fidelity, loyalty, devotedness, wholeheartedness, single-mindedness, fixedness, fealty; consecration, sanctification, hallowing. **2** inscription, address; message.

deduce /didyoóss/ *v.tr.* **1** (often foll. by *from*) infer; draw as a logical conclusion. **2** *archaic* trace the course or derivation of. ▫▫ **deducible** *adj.* [L *deducere* (as DE-, *ducere duct-* lead)]
■ **1** conclude, infer, draw the conclusion, understand, gather, assume, presume, derive, work out, divine, glean, take it, suppose, surmise, *Brit. sl.* suss (out).

deduct /didúkt/ *v.tr.* (often foll. by *from*) subtract, take away, withhold (an amount, portion, etc.). [L (as DEDUCE)]
■ subtract, take away *or* out *or* off, take, remove, withdraw, withhold, knock off.

deductible /didúktib'l/ *adj.* & *n.* ● *adj.* that may be deducted, esp. from tax to be paid or taxable income. ● *n.* *US* = EXCESS *n.* 6.

deduction /didúksh'n/ *n.* **1 a** the act of deducting. **b** an amount deducted. **2 a** the inferring of particular instances from a general law (cf. INDUCTION). **b** a conclusion deduced. [ME f. OF *deduction* or L *deductio* (as DEDUCE)]
■ **1 a** subtraction, withdrawal, removal, abstraction. **2 b** conclusion, inference, supposition, assumption, finding, reasoning, result; surmise, divination, guess, conjecture.

deductive /didúktiv/ *adj.* of or reasoning by deduction. □□ **deductively** *adv.* [med.L *deductivus* (as DEDUCE)]
■ see LOGICAL 1.

dee /dee/ *n.* **1** the letter D. **2 a** a thing shaped like this. **b** *Physics* either of two hollow semicircular electrodes in a cyclotron. [the name of the letter]

deed /deed/ *n.* & *v.* ● *n.* **1** a thing done intentionally or consciously. **2** a brave, skilful, or conspicuous act. **3** actual fact or performance (*kind in word and deed*; *in deed and not in name*). **4** *Law* a written or printed document often used for a legal transfer of ownership and bearing the disposer's signature. ● *v.tr.* *US* convey or transfer by legal deed. □ **deed-box** a strong box for keeping deeds and other documents. **deed of covenant** an agreement to pay a specified amount regularly to a charity etc., enabling the recipient to recover the tax paid by the donor on an equivalent amount of income. **deed poll** a deed made and executed by one party only, esp. to change one's name (the paper being polled or cut even, not indented). [OE *dēd* f. Gmc: cf. DO[1]]
■ *n.* **1** see ACT *n.* 1. **2** exploit, feat, achievement, accomplishment, attainment. **4** title-deed, document, instrument, contract, agreement.

deejay /deéjáy/ *n. sl.* a disc jockey. [abbr. *DJ*]

deem /deem/ *v.tr. formal* regard, consider, judge (*deem it my duty*; *was deemed sufficient*). [OE *dēman* f. Gmc, rel. to DOOM]
■ see CONSIDER 6.

de-emphasize /dee-émfəsīz/ *v.tr.* (also **-ise**) **1** remove emphasis from. **2** reduce emphasis on.
■ see MINIMIZE 2.

deemster /deémstər/ *n.* a judge in the Isle of Man. [DEEM + -STER]

deep /deep/ *adj.*, *n.*, & *adv.* ● *adj.* **1 a** extending far down from the top (*deep hole*; *deep water*). **b** extending far in from the surface or edge (*deep wound*; *deep plunge*; *deep shelf*; *deep border*). **2** (*predic.*) **a** extending to or lying at a specified depth (*water 6 feet deep*; *ankle-deep in mud*). **b** in a specified number of ranks one behind another (*soldiers drawn up six deep*). **3** situated far down or back or in (*hands deep in his pockets*). **4** coming or brought from far down or in (*deep breath*; *deep sigh*). **5** low-pitched, full-toned, not shrill (*deep voice*; *deep note*; *deep bell*). **6** intense, vivid, extreme (*deep disgrace*; *deep sleep*; *deep colour*; *deep secret*). **7** heartfelt, absorbing (*deep affection*; *deep feelings*; *deep interest*). **8** (*predic.*) fully absorbed or overwhelmed (*deep in a book*; *deep in debt*). **9** profound, penetrating, not superficial; difficult to understand (*deep thinker*; *deep thought*; *deep insight*; *deep learning*). **10** *Cricket* distant from the batsman (*deep mid-off*). **11** *Football* distant from the front line of one's team. **12** *sl.* cunning or secretive (*a deep one*). ● *n.* **1** (prec. by *the*) *poet.* the sea. **2** a deep part of the sea. **3** an abyss, pit, or cavity. **4** (prec. by *the*) *Cricket* the position of a fielder distant from the batsman. **5** a deep state (*deep of the night*). **6** *poet.* a mysterious region of thought or feeling. ● *adv.* deeply; far down or in (*dig deep*; *read deep into the night*). □ **deep breathing** breathing with long breaths, esp. as a form of exercise. **deep-drawn** (of metal etc.) shaped by forcing through a die when cold. **deep-fry** (**-fries**, **-fried**) fry (food) in an amount of fat or oil sufficient to cover it. **deep kiss** a kiss with contact between tongues. **deep-laid** (of a scheme) secret and elaborate. **deep mourning** mourning expressed by wearing only black clothes. **deep-mouthed** (esp. of a dog) having a deep voice. **deep-rooted** (esp. of convictions) firmly established. **deep sea** the deeper parts of the ocean. **deep-seated** (of emotion, disease, etc.) firmly established, profound. **Deep South** the States of the US bordering the Gulf of Mexico. **deep space** the regions beyond the solar system or the earth's atmosphere. **deep therapy** curative treatment with short-wave X-rays of high penetrating power. **go off** (or **go in off**) **the deep end** *colloq.* give way to anger or emotion. **in deep water** (or **waters**) in trouble or difficulty. **jump** (or **be thrown**) **in at the deep end** face a difficult problem, undertaking, etc., with little experience of it. □□ **deeply** *adv.* **deepness** *n.* [OE *dēop* (adj.), *dīope*, *dēope* (adv.), f. Gmc: rel. to DIP]
■ *adj.* **1** extensive, bottomless, abyssal, unfathomed, unfathomable, profound; yawning, chasmic. **3** far *or* deep *or* way down, far *or* way back. **5** low, low-pitched, resonant, booming, resounding, sonorous, rumbling. **6** rich, dark, strong; see also INTENSE 1, 3; VIVID 1. **7** profound, intense, sincere, serious, heartfelt, deep-seated, earnest, ardent, fervent, poignant, deep-rooted; see also ABSORBING. **8** rapt, absorbed, engrossed, occupied, preoccupied, intent, intense, involved, engaged, immersed, lost, overwhelmed, steeped. **9** profound, weighty, serious, heavy, arcane, recondite, abstruse, esoteric; obscure, unfathomable, inscrutable, incomprehensible, difficult, beyond *or* past comprehension; impenetrable, mysterious, mystic, mystical, occult; wise, learned, sage, sagacious, astute, perspicacious, discerning, acute, intense, penetrating, knowledgeable, knowing. **12** secretive, devious, cunning, shrewd, crafty, canny, clever, knowing, scheming, artful, designing. ● *n.* **1** (*the deep*) the ocean, the sea, the waters, the high seas, *archaic or poet.* the main, *poet.* the wave(s), *Brit. sl.* the briny (deep). **3** see ABYSS 1. **5** dead, middle. ● *adv.* see *deeply* below, *profoundly* (PROFOUND). □ **deep kiss** French kiss. **deep-rooted, deep-seated** see INGRAINED 1, DEEP *adj.* 7 above. **go off** (or **go in off**) **the deep end** see RAGE *v.* □□ **deeply** deep, (far) downwards *or* inwards, way down, deep down; profoundly, intensely, strongly, powerfully, very (much), really, acutely, keenly, gravely, greatly, to a great extent, extremely, thoroughly, completely, entirely, seriously, severely, irrevocably, unreservedly; passionately, heavily, emotionally. **deepness** see DEPTH 1, 4.

deepen /deép'n/ *v.tr.* & *intr.* make or become deep or deeper.
■ dig out, scoop (out); intensify, increase, grow, concentrate, strengthen, expand, magnify, extend.

deepening / deép'ning/ *n.* the act or process of making deeper, esp. the implementation of measures (such as economic and monetary union) to deepen and strengthen the ties among EC countries.

deep-freeze /deépfreéz/ *n.* & *v.* ● *n.* **1** a refrigerator in which food can be quickly frozen and kept for long periods at a very low temperature. **2** a suspension of activity. ● *v.tr.* (**-froze, -frozen**) freeze or store (food) in a deep-freeze.
■ *n.* **2** see PAUSE *n.*

deer /deer/ *n.* (*pl.* same) any four-hoofed grazing animal of the family Cervidae, the males of which usu. have deciduous branching antlers. □ **deer fly** any bloodsucking fly of the genus *Chrysops*. **deer-forest** an extensive area of wild land reserved for the stalking of deer. **deer-hound** a large rough-haired greyhound. **deer-lick** a spring or damp spot impregnated with salt etc. where deer come to lick. [OE *dēor* animal, deer]

deerskin /deérskin/ *n.* & *adj.* ● *n.* leather from a deer's skin. ● *adj.* made from a deer's skin.

deerstalker /deérstawkər/ *n.* **1** a soft cloth cap with peaks in front and behind and ear-flaps often joined at the top. **2** a person who stalks deer.

de-escalate /dee-éskəlayt/ *v.tr.* reduce the level or intensity of. □□ **de-escalation** /-láysh'n/ *n.*

■ see DECREASE *v.*

def /def/ *adj. sl.* excellent. [corrupt. of DEATH or shortened f. DEFINITIVE]

deface /difáyss/ *v.tr.* **1** spoil the appearance of; disfigure. **2** make illegible. □□ **defaceable** *adj.* **defacement** *n.* **defacer** *n.* [ME f. F *défacer* f. OF *desfacier* (as DE-, FACE)]

■ **1** mar, disfigure, spoil, ruin, deform, blemish, damage, mutilate, harm, impair, injure, destroy.

de facto /dee fáktō, day/ *adv., adj.,* & *n.* ● *adv.* in fact, whether by right or not. ● *adj.* that exists or is such in fact (*a de facto ruler*). ● *n.* (in full **de facto wife** or **husband**) a person living with another as if married. [L]

■ *adv.* see REALLY 1.

defalcate /deéfalkayt/ *v.intr. formal* misappropriate property in one's charge, esp. money. □□ **defalcator** *n.* [med.L *defalcare* lop (as DE-, L *falx -cis* sickle)]

defalcation /deéfalkáysh'n/ *n.* **1** *Law* **a** a misappropriation of money. **b** an amount misappropriated. **2** *formal* a shortcoming. **3** *formal* defection. [ME f. med.L *defalcatio* (as DEFALCATE)]

defame /difáym/ *v.tr.* attack the good reputation of; speak ill of. □□ **defamation** /déffəmáysh'n, deéfə-/ *n.* **defamatory** /difámmətəri, -tri/ *adj.* **defamer** *n.* [ME f. OF *diffamer* etc. f. L *diffamare* spread evil report (as DIS-, *fama* report)]

defat /deéfát/ *v.tr.* (**defatted, defatting**) remove fat or fats from.

default /difáwlt, -fólt/ *n.* & *v.* ● *n.* **1** failure to fulfil an obligation, esp. to appear, pay, or act in some way. **2** lack, absence. **3** a preselected option adopted by a computer program when no alternative is specified by the user or programmer. ● *v.* **1** *intr.* fail to fulfil an obligation, esp. to pay money or to appear in a lawcourt. **2** *tr.* declare (a party) in default and give judgement against that party. □ **go by default 1** be ignored because of absence. **2** be absent. **in default of** because of the absence of. **judgement by default** judgement given for the plaintiff on the defendant's failure to plead. **win by default** win because an opponent fails to be present. [ME f. OF *defaut(e)* f. *defaillir* fail f. Rmc (as DE-, L *fallere* deceive): cf. FAIL]

■ *n.* **1** failure, fault, defect, neglect, negligence, dereliction, lapse, oversight, non-performance, non-fulfilment, delinquency, inaction; non-payment. **2** see LACK *n.* ● *v.* **1** fail, lapse, fall short, come (up) short; (*default on*) neglect.

defaulter /difáwltər, -fóltər/ *n.* a person who defaults, esp. *Brit.* a soldier guilty of a military offence.

defeasance /difeéz'nss/ *n.* the act or process of rendering null and void. [ME f. OF *defesance* f. *de(s)faire* undo (as DE-, *faire* make f. L *facere*)]

defeasible /difeézib'l/ *adj.* **1** capable of annulment. **2** liable to forfeiture. □□ **defeasibility** /-bílliti/ *n.* **defeasibly** *adv.* [AF (as DEFEASANCE)]

defeat /difeét/ *v.* & *n.* ● *v.tr.* **1** overcome in a battle or other contest. **2** frustrate, baffle. **3** reject (a motion etc.) by voting. **4** *Law* annul. ● *n.* the act or process of defeating or being defeated. [ME f. OF *deffait, desfait* past part. of *desfaire* f. med.L *disfacere* (as DIS-, L *facere* do)]

■ *v.* **1** overcome, conquer, be victorious over, get the better *or* best of, subdue, overwhelm, overpower, prevail over, triumph over, surpass, bring down, worst, thrash, rout, repulse, overthrow, trounce, whip, crush, destroy, do in, best, *literary* vanquish, *sl.* whop; see also BEAT *v.* 3a. **2** thwart, frustrate, baffle, disappoint, check, baulk, stop, terminate, end, finish, destroy; see also FOIL[1] *v.* **3** see *throw out* 6. **4** see CANCEL *v.* 4. ● *n.* conquest, overthrow, beating, repulse, trouncing, rout, *literary* vanquishment; frustration, end.

defeatism /difeétiz'm/ *n.* **1** an excessive readiness to accept defeat. **2** conduct conducive to this. □□ **defeatist** *n.* & *adj.* [F *défaitisme* f. *défaite* DEFEAT]

■ see *desperation* (DESPERATE).

defecate /déffikayt/ *v.intr.* discharge faeces from the body. □□ **defecation** /-káysh'n/ *n.* [earlier as adj., = purified, f. L *defaecare* (as DE-, *faex faecis* dregs)]

■ move the bowels, excrete, void, evacuate the bowels, have a (bowel) movement, open the bowels, relieve oneself, pass a motion, *colloq.* mess. □□ **defecation** see *bowel movement* 1.

defect *n.* & *v.* ● *n.* /deéfekt, difékt/ **1** lack of something essential or required; imperfection. **2** a shortcoming or failing. **3** a blemish. **4** the amount by which a thing falls short. ● *v.intr.* /difékt/ abandon one's country or cause in favour of another. □□ **defector** *n.* [L *defectus* f. *deficere* desert, fail (as DE-, *facere* do)]

■ *n.* **1, 2** imperfection, deficiency, inadequacy, insufficiency, shortcoming, shortfall, failure, failing, weakness, frailty, weak point, irregularity. **3** blemish, imperfection, irregularity, flaw, fault, mark, stain, mistake, error. ● *v.* desert, change sides *or* loyalties, turn traitor, go over. □□ **defector** deserter, turncoat, traitor, renegade, rat.

defection /diféksh'n/ *n.* **1** the abandonment of one's country or cause. **2** ceasing in allegiance to a leader, party, religion, or duty. [L *defectio* (as DEFECT)]

■ see SECESSION.

defective /diféktiv/ *adj.* & *n.* ● *adj.* **1** having a defect or defects; incomplete, imperfect, faulty. **2** often *offens.* mentally subnormal. **3** (usu. foll. by *in*) lacking, deficient. **4** *Gram.* not having all the usual inflections. ● *n.* often *offens.* a mentally defective person. □□ **defectively** *adv.* **defectiveness** *n.* [ME f. OF *defectif -ive* or LL *defectivus* (as DEFECT)]

■ *adj.* **1** imperfect, faulty, flawed, deficient, incomplete, broken, out of order, impaired, marred, *sl.* on the blink, *US sl.* on the fritz. **2** retarded, simple, feeble-minded, simple-minded, (mentally) deficient *or* incompetent, backward, subnormal, slow, ESN, educationally subnormal. **3** see DEFICIENT 1. □□ **defectiveness** see *inadequacy* (INADEQUATE).

defence /difénss/ *n.* (*US* **defense**) **1** the act of defending from or resisting attack. **2 a** a means of resisting attack. **b** a thing that protects. **c** the military resources of a country. **3** (in *pl.*) fortifications. **4 a** justification, vindication. **b** a speech or piece of writing used to this end. **5 a** the defendant's case in a lawsuit. **b** the counsel for the defendant. **6 a** the action or role of defending one's goal etc. against attack. **b** the players in a team who perform this role. □ **defence mechanism 1** the body's reaction against disease organisms. **2** a usu. unconscious mental process to avoid conscious conflict or anxiety. □□ **defenceless** *adj.* **defencelessly** *adv.* **defencelessness** *n.* [ME f. OF *defens(e)* f. LL *defensum, -a*, past part. of *defendere*: see DEFEND]

■ **2 a, b** shelter, cover, guard, safeguard, shield; see also PROTECTION 1b, c. **3** (*defences*) fortifications, armour, barricades, screen, bulwark(s), ramparts. **4 a** excuse, apology, reason, apologia, explanation; justification, vindication, argument, plea, advocacy, support. □□ **defenceless** unprotected, exposed, vulnerable, unguarded; helpless, weak, powerless, impotent. **defencelessness** susceptibility, vulnerability, insecurity, exposure; helplessness, weakness, frailty, impotence.

defend /difénd/ *v.tr.* (also *absol.*) **1** (often foll. by *against, from*) resist an attack made on; protect (a person or thing) from harm or danger. **2** support or uphold by argument; speak or write in favour of. **3** conduct the case for (a defendant in a lawsuit). □□ **defendable** *adj.* **defender** *n.* [ME f. OF *defendre* f. L *defendere*: cf. OFFEND]

■ **1** fortify, arm, secure; protect, watch over, guard, safeguard, keep (safe), shelter, shield, screen, preserve; fight for. **2, 3** plead for, speak *or* stand up for, stick up for, support, uphold, stand by, champion, back, stand with *or* behind *or* beside, argue for *or* in favour of, hold a brief for.

defendant /diféndənt/ *n.* a person etc. sued or accused in a court of law. [ME f. OF, part. of *defendre*: see DEFEND]
■ see LITIGANT *n.*

defenestration /deefenistráysh'n/ *n. formal* or *joc.* the action of throwing (esp. a person) out of a window. □□ **defenestrate** /deefénnistrayt/ *v.tr.* [mod.L *defenestratio* (as DE-, L *fenestra* window)]

defense *US* var. of DEFENCE.

defensible /difénsib'l/ *adj.* **1** justifiable; supportable by argument. **2** that can be easily defended militarily. □□ **defensibility** /-bílliti/ *n.* **defensibly** *adv.* [ME f. LL *defensibilis* (as DEFEND)]
■ **1** see TENABLE.

defensive /difénsiv/ *adj.* **1** done or intended for defence or to defend. **2** (of a person or attitude) concerned to challenge criticism. □ **on the defensive 1** expecting criticism. **2** in an attitude or position of defence. □□ **defensively** *adv.* **defensiveness** *n.* [ME f. F *défensif -ive* f. med.L *defensivus* (as DEFEND)]
■ **1** see PROTECTIVE *adj.* 1a.

defer[1] /difér/ *v.tr.* (**deferred, deferring**) **1** put off to a later time; postpone. **2** *US* postpone the conscription of (a person). □ **deferred payment** payment by instalments. □□ **deferment** *n.* **deferrable** *adj.* **deferral** *n.* [ME, orig. the same as DIFFER]
■ **1** put off, postpone, delay, shelve, stay, lay *or* put aside, table, carry *or* hold over, remit, shunt, *US* put over. □□ **deferment, deferral** see *postponement* (POSTPONE), STAY[1] *n.* 2.

defer[2] /difér/ *v.intr.* (**deferred, deferring**) (foll. by *to*) yield or make concessions in opinion or action. □□ **deferrer** *n.* [ME f. F *déférer* f. L *deferre* (as DE-, *ferre* bring)]
■ give in, give ground *or* way, yield, submit, bow, capitulate, accede, acquiesce; comply, agree.

deference /déffərənss/ *n.* **1** courteous regard, respect. **2** compliance with the advice or wishes of another (*pay deference to*). □ **in deference to** out of respect for. [F *déférence* (as DEFER[2])]
■ **1** respect, regard, politeness, civility, courtesy, consideration, esteem. **2** obeisance, submission, acquiescence, obedience, compliance.

deferential /déffərénsh'l/ *adj.* showing deference; respectful. □□ **deferentially** *adv.* [DEFERENCE, after PRUDENTIAL etc.]
■ see RESPECTFUL.

defiance /difíənss/ *n.* **1** open disobedience; bold resistance. **2** a challenge to fight or maintain a cause, assertion, etc. □ **in defiance of** disregarding; in conflict with. [ME f. OF (as DEFY)]
■ **1** see RESISTANCE 1. **2** see CHALLENGE *n.* 1.

defiant /difíənt/ *adj.* **1** showing defiance. **2** openly disobedient. □□ **defiantly** *adv.*
■ **1** challenging, bold, brazen, daring, self-willed, stubborn, unyielding, headstrong, recalcitrant, pugnacious, belligerent, antagonistic; see also AUDACIOUS 2. **2** rebellious, disobedient, recalcitrant, obstinate, refractory, insubordinate, mutinous, unruly, contumacious.

defibrillation /deefibriláysh'n/ *n. Med.* the stopping of the fibrillation of the heart. □□ **defibrillator** /deefíbrilaytər/ *n.*

deficiency /difíshənsi/ *n.* (*pl.* **-ies**) **1** the state or condition of being deficient. **2** (usu. foll. by *of*) a lack or shortage. **3** a thing lacking. **4** the amount by which a thing, esp. revenue, falls short. □ **deficiency disease** a disease caused by the lack of some essential or important element in the diet.
■ **1, 2** see ABSENCE 3. **3** see DEFECT *n.* 1, 2; OMISSION *n.* 2. **4** see DEFICIT.

deficient /difísh'nt/ *adj.* **1** (usu. foll. by *in*) incomplete; not having enough of a specified quality or ingredient. **2** insufficient in quantity, force, etc. **3** (in full **mentally deficient**) incapable of adequate social or intellectual behaviour through imperfect mental development. □□ **deficiently** *adv.* [L *deficiens* part. of *deficere* (as DEFECT)]
■ **1** wanting, lacking, short, defective; see also INCOMPLETE. **2** faulty, impaired, flawed, inadequate, insufficient, imperfect, incomplete, defective, inferior, unsatisfactory; sparse, sketchy, skimpy, scarce. **3** see DEFECTIVE *adj.* 2.

deficit /déffisit/ *n.* **1** the amount by which a thing (esp. a sum of money) is too small. **2** an excess of liabilities over assets in a given period, esp. a financial year (opp. SURPLUS). □ **deficit financing** financing of (esp. State) spending by borrowing. **deficit spending** spending, esp. by the State, financed by borrowing. [F *déficit* f. L *deficit* 3rd sing. pres. of *deficere* (as DEFECT)]
■ **1** shortfall, shortage, default, loss, deficiency.

defier /difíər/ *n.* a person who defies.

defilade /déffiláyd/ *v.* & *n.* ● *v.tr.* secure (a fortification) against enfilading fire. ● *n.* this precaution or arrangement. [DEFILE[2] + -ADE[1]]

defile[1] /difíl/ *v.tr.* **1** make dirty; pollute, befoul. **2** corrupt. **3** desecrate, profane. **4** deprive (esp. a woman) of virginity. **5** make ceremonially unclean. □□ **defilement** *n.* **defiler** *n.* [ME *defoul* f. OF *defouler* trample down, outrage (as DE-, *fouler* tread, trample) altered after obs. *befile* f. OE *befȳlan* (BE-, *fūl* FOUL)]
■ **1** see FOUL *v.* 1. **2** see POISON *v.* 3, 5. **3, 5** see DESECRATE. **4** see DISHONOUR *v.* 4.

defile[2] /difíl/ *n.* & *v.* ● *n.* /also deefíl/ **1** a narrow way through which troops can only march in file. **2** a gorge. ● *v.intr.* march in file. [F *défiler* and *défilé* past part. (as DE-, FILE[2])]
■ *n.* **1, 2** see GORGE *n.* 2.

define /difín/ *v.tr.* **1** give the exact meaning of (a word etc.). **2** describe or explain the scope of (*define one's position*). **3** make clear, esp. in outline (*well-defined image*). **4** mark out the boundary or limits of. **5** (of properties) make up the total character of. □□ **definable** *adj.* **definer** *n.* [ME f. OF *definer* ult. f. L *definire* (as DE-, *finire* finish, f. *finis* end)]
■ **1** give the meaning of, explain. **2, 3** describe, explain, spell out, detail, delineate, expand on, expatiate on *or* upon; characterize, state, name; see also CLARIFY 1. **4** demarcate, mark off *or* out, delimit, fix, circumscribe, specify, identify, delineate, describe, decide on, determine, establish.

definite /déffinit/ *adj.* **1** having exact and discernible limits. **2** clear and distinct; not vague. ¶ See the note at *definitive*. □ **definite article** see ARTICLE. **definite integral** see INTEGRAL. □□ **definiteness** *n.* [L *definitus* past part. of *definire* (as DEFINE)]
■ **1** specific, particular, exact, pronounced, explicit, express, precise, certain; firm. **2** clear, plain, well-defined, unambiguous, unequivocal, distinct, clear-cut, obvious, evident.

definitely /déffinitli/ *adv.* & *int.* ● *adv.* **1** in a definite manner. **2** certainly; without doubt (*they were definitely there*). ● *int. colloq.* yes, certainly.
■ *adv.* **1** see *expressly* (EXPRESS[2]). **2** positively, absolutely, surely, to be sure, assuredly, certainly, indubitably, undoubtedly, without doubt, categorically, unequivocally, unquestionably, decidedly, plainly, clearly, obviously, patently. ● *int.* see ABSOLUTELY 6.

definition /déffinísh'n/ *n.* **1 a** the act or process of defining. **b** a statement of the meaning of a word or the nature of a thing. **2 a** the degree of distinctness in outline of an object or image (esp. of an image produced by a lens or shown in a photograph or on a cinema or television screen). **b** making or being distinct in outline. [ME f. OF f. L *definitio* (as DEFINE)]
■ **1** description, explanation, explication, clarification; statement *or* outline (of meaning). **2** delineation, delimitation, demarcation; acutance, acuteness, resolution, distinctness, clarity, sharpness, focus, precision.

definitive /difínnitiv/ *adj.* **1** (of an answer, treaty, verdict, etc.) decisive, unconditional, final. ¶ Often confused in this sense with *definite*, which does not have connotations of authority and conclusiveness: *a definite no* is a firm refusal,

whereas *a definitive no* is an authoritative judgement or decision that something is not the case. **2** (of an edition of a book etc.) most authoritative. **3** *Philately* (of a series of stamps) for permanent use, not commemorative etc. ▫▫ **definitively** *adv.* [ME f. OF *definitif -ive* f. L *definitivus* (as DEFINE)]
■ **1** clarifying, unambiguous, categorical, absolute, unqualified; see also FINAL *adj.* 2. **2** consummate, authoritative, reliable, dependable, complete; see also AUTHORITATIVE 1, 3.

deflagrate /défləgrayt, déé-/ *v.tr.* & *intr.* burn away with sudden flame. ▫▫ **deflagration** /-gráysh'n/ *n.* **deflagrator** *n.* [L *deflagrare* (as DE-, *flagrare* blaze)]

deflate /difláyt/ *v.* **1 a** *tr.* let air or gas out of (a tyre, balloon, etc.). **b** *intr.* be emptied of air or gas. **2 a** *tr.* cause to lose confidence or conceit. **b** *intr.* lose confidence. **3** *Econ.* **a** *tr.* subject (a currency or economy) to deflation. **b** *intr.* pursue a policy of deflation. **4** *tr.* reduce the importance of, depreciate. ▫▫ **deflator** *n.* [DE- + INFLATE]
■ **2a** see MORTIFY 1.

deflation /difláysh'n/ *n.* **1** the act or process of deflating or being deflated. **2** *Econ.* reduction of the amount of money in circulation to increase its value as a measure against inflation. **3** *Geol.* the removal of particles of rock etc. by the wind. ▫▫ **deflationary** *adj.* **deflationist** *n.*

deflect /diflékt/ *v.* **1** *tr.* & *intr.* bend or turn aside from a straight course or intended purpose. **2** (often foll. by *from*) **a** *tr.* cause to deviate. **b** *intr.* deviate. [L *deflectere* (as DE-, *flectere flex-* bend)]
■ avert, turn away *or* aside, divert, sidetrack, *Cricket* glance, snick, *Physics* scatter, refract; fend off; deviate, swerve, veer, bend, swing away, turn off.

deflection /difléksh'n/ *n.* (also **deflexion**) **1** the act or process of deflecting or being deflected. **2** a lateral bend or turn; a deviation. **3** *Physics* the displacement of a pointer on an instrument from its zero position. [LL *deflexio* (as DEFLECT)]
■ **1, 2** see SHIFT *n.* 1a.

deflector /difléktər/ *n.* a thing that deflects, esp. a device for deflecting a flow of air etc.

defloration /déefloráysh'n/ *n.* deflowering. [ME f. OF or f. LL *defloratio* (as DEFLOWER)]
■ see RAPE[1] *n.* 1.

deflower /diflówr/ *v.tr.* **1** deprive (esp. a woman) of virginity. **2** ravage, spoil. **3** strip of flowers. [ME f. OF *deflourer*, *des-*, ult. f. LL *deflorare* (as DE-, L *flos floris* flower)]
■ **1** see DISHONOUR *v.* 4.

defocus /deefṓkəss/ *v.tr.* & *intr.* (**defocused, defocusing** or **defocussed, defocussing**) put or go out of focus.

defoliate /deefṓliayt/ *v.tr.* remove leaves from, esp. as a military tactic. ▫▫ **defoliant** *n.* & *adj.* **defoliation** /-áysh'n/ *n.* **defoliator** *n.* [LL *defoliare* f. *folium* leaf]
■ see BARE *v.* 1.

deforest /deefórrist/ *v.tr.* clear of forests or trees. ▫▫ **deforestation** /-stáysh'n/ *n.*

deform /difórm/ *v.* **1** *tr.* make ugly, deface. **2** *tr.* put out of shape, misshape. **3** *intr.* undergo deformation; be deformed. ▫▫ **deformable** *adj.* [ME f. OF *deformer* etc. f. med.L *difformare* ult. f. L *deformare* (as DE-, *formare* f. *forma* shape)]
■ **1** see DEFACE. **2** see DISTORT 1a.

deformation /déeformáysh'n/ *n.* **1** disfigurement. **2** *Physics* **a** (often foll. by *of*) change in shape. **b** a quantity representing the amount of this change. **3** a perverted form of a word (e.g. *dang* for *damn*). ▫▫ **deformational** *adj.* [ME f. OF *deformation* or L *deformatio* (as DEFORM)]
■ **1** see BLEMISH *n.*, WARP *n.* 1.

deformed /difórmd/ *adj.* (of a person or limb) misshapen.
■ misshapen, malformed, distorted, twisted, grotesque, gnarled, crooked, contorted, awry, warped, bent; disfigured.

deformity /difórmiti/ *n.* (*pl.* **-ies**) **1** the state of being deformed; ugliness, disfigurement. **2** a malformation, esp. of body or limb. **3** a moral defect; depravity. [ME f. OF *deformité* etc. f. L *deformitas -tatis* f. *deformis* (as DE-, *forma* shape)]
■ **2** see ABNORMALITY 2.

defraud /difráwd/ *v.tr.* (often foll. by *of*) cheat by fraud. ▫▫ **defrauder** *n.* [ME f. OF *defrauder* or L *defraudare* (as DE-, FRAUD)]
■ cheat, swindle, trick, beguile, dupe, delude, fool, fleece, take in, deceive, humbug, hoodwink, flimflam, rook, *colloq.* do, diddle, put one over on, pull a fast one on, rip off, do a person in the eye, *literary* cozen, *sl.* take for a ride, bilk, clean out, take to the cleaners, gyp, con; (*defraud of*) do a person out of. ▫▫ **defrauder** see FRAUD 3.

defray /difráy/ *v.tr.* provide money to pay (a cost or expense). ▫▫ **defrayable** *adj.* **defrayal** *n.* **defrayment** *n.* [F *défrayer* (as DE-, obs. *frai(t)* cost, f. med.L *fredum, -us* fine for breach of the peace)]
■ pay, settle, meet, discharge, liquidate, clear, cover, reimburse; (*defray the cost*) pick up the bill, foot the bill, *US colloq.* pick up the tab *or* check. ▫▫ **defrayment** see PAY[1] *n.*

defrock /deefrók/ *v.tr.* deprive (a person, esp. a priest) of ecclesiastical status. [F *défroquer* (as DE-, FROCK)]

defrost /deefróst/ *v.* **1** *tr.* **a** free (the interior of a refrigerator) of excess frost, usu. by turning it off for a period. **b** remove frost or ice from (esp. the windscreen of a motor vehicle). **2** *tr.* unfreeze (frozen food). **3** *intr.* become unfrozen. ▫▫ **defroster** *n.*
■ **1a, 2, 3** see THAW *v.* 1, 5.

deft /deft/ *adj.* neatly skilful or dexterous; adroit. ▫▫ **deftly** *adv.* **deftness** *n.* [ME, var. of DAFT in obs. sense 'meek']
■ see DEXTEROUS.

defunct /difúngkt/ *adj.* **1** no longer existing. **2** no longer used or in fashion. **3** dead or extinct. ▫▫ **defunctness** *n.* [L *defunctus* dead, past part. of *defungi* (as DE-, *fungi* perform)]
■ **1, 2** inoperative, inapplicable, unused, unusable, invalid, expired, obsolete, *passé*, non-existent, outmoded, out. **3** see DEAD *adj.* 1.

defuse /deefyóoz/ *v.tr.* **1** remove the fuse from (an explosive device). **2** reduce the tension or potential danger in (a crisis, difficulty, etc.).
■ **2** see MODERATE *v.* 1.

defy /difí/ *v.tr.* (**-ies, -ied**) **1** resist openly; refuse to obey. **2** (of a thing) present insuperable obstacles to (*defies solution*). **3** (foll. by *to* + infin.) challenge (a person) to do or prove something. **4** *archaic* challenge to combat. [ME f. OF *defier* f. Rmc (as DIS-, L *fidus* faithful)]
■ **1** resist; disobey, flout, go against, thumb one's nose at, *sl.* cock a snook at. **2** frustrate, thwart, baffle, confound; resist, withstand. **3** challenge, dare; invite, summon.

deg. *abbr.* degree.

dégagé /daygaázhay/ *adj.* (*fem.* ***dégagée***) easy, unconstrained. [F, past part. of *dégager* set free]
■ see EASY *adj.* 3.

degas /deegáss/ *v.tr.* (**degassed, degassing**) remove unwanted gas from.

degauss /deegówss/ *v.tr.* neutralize the magnetism in (a thing) by encircling it with a current-carrying conductor. ▫▫ **degausser** *n.* [DE- + GAUSS]

degenerate *adj.*, *n.*, & *v.* ● *adj.* /dijénnərət/ **1** having lost the qualities that are normal and desirable or proper to its kind; fallen from former excellence. **2** *Biol.* having changed to a lower type. ● *n.* /dijénnərət/ a degenerate person or animal. ● *v.intr.* /dijénnərayt/ become degenerate. ▫▫ **degeneracy** *n.* **degenerately** *adv.* [L *degeneratus* past part. of *degenerare* (as DE-, *genus -eris* race)]
■ *adj.* **1** debased, degraded, corrupt, corrupted, vitiated, decadent, depraved, reprobate, dissolute; ignoble, base, low, inferior, vile. ● *n.* reprobate, debauchee, wastrel, profligate, rake, roué; pervert, deviate, deviant. ● *v.* decline, deteriorate, decay, worsen, degrade; backslide,

regress, retrogress, go to rack and ruin, *colloq.* go to pot, *sl.* go to the dogs.

degeneration /dijénnəráysh'n/ *n.* **1 a** the process of becoming degenerate. **b** the state of being degenerate. **2** *Med.* morbid deterioration of tissue or change in its structure. [ME f. F *dégénération* or f. LL *degeneratio* (as DEGENERATE)]
■ **1** see DECAY *n.* 2.

degenerative /dijénnərətiv/ *adj.* **1** of or tending to degeneration. **2** (of disease) characterized by progressive often irreversible deterioration.

degrade /digráyd/ *v.* **1** *tr.* reduce to a lower rank, esp. as a punishment. **2** *tr.* bring into dishonour or contempt. **3** *tr. Chem.* reduce to a simpler molecular structure. **4** *tr. Physics* reduce (energy) to a less convertible form. **5** *tr. Geol.* wear down (rocks etc.) by disintegration. **6** *intr.* degenerate. **7** *intr. Chem.* disintegrate. ▫▫ **degradable** *adj.* **degradation** /dégrədáysh'n/ *n.* **degradative** /-dətiv/ *adj.* **degrader** *n.* [ME f. OF *degrader* f. eccl.L *degradare* (as DE-, L *gradus* step)]
■ **1** see DOWNGRADE *v.* 1. **2** reduce, lower, debase, abase, demean, dishonour, disgrace, humble, shame; humiliate, mortify, belittle, deprecate, depreciate, cheapen. **5** see ERODE. **6** see DEGENERATE *v.* ▫▫ **degradation** degeneracy, degeneration, deterioration, corruptness, corruption, vitiation, baseness, depravity, *formal* turpitude; disrepute, discredit, shame, humiliation, ignominy, dishonour, disgrace, abasement, debasement.

degrading /digráyding/ *adj.* humiliating; causing a loss of self-respect. ▫▫ **degradingly** *adv.*
■ demeaning, humiliating, shameful, debasing, lowering, ignominious, inglorious, unedifying; menial.

degrease /deégreéss/ *v.tr.* remove unwanted grease or fat from.

degree /digreé/ *n.* **1** a stage in an ascending or descending scale, series, or process. **2** a stage in intensity or amount (*to a high degree; in some degree*). **3** relative condition (*each is good in its degree*). **4** *Math.* a unit of measurement of angles, one-ninetieth of a right angle or the angle subtended by one-three-hundred-and-sixtieth of the circumference of a circle. ¶ Symb.: ° (as in *45°*). **5** *Physics* a unit in a scale of temperature, hardness, etc. ¶ Abbr.: **deg.** (or omitted in the Kelvin scale of temperature). **6** *Med.* an extent of burns on a scale characterized by the destruction of the skin. **7** an academic rank conferred by a college or university after examination or after completion of a course, or conferred as an honour on a distinguished person. **8** a grade of crime or criminality (*murder in the first degree*). **9** a step in direct genealogical descent. **10** social or official rank. **11** *Math.* the highest power of unknowns or variables in an equation etc. (*equation of the third degree*). **12** a masonic rank. **13** a thing placed like a step in a series; a tier or row. **14** *Mus.* the classification of a note by its position in the scale. ▫ **by degrees** a little at a time; gradually. **degree of freedom 1** *Physics* the independent direction in which motion can occur. **2** *Chem.* the number of independent factors required to specify a system at equilibrium. **3** *Statistics* the number of independent values or quantities which can be assigned to a statistical distribution. **degrees of comparison** see COMPARISON. **forbidden** (or **prohibited**) **degrees** a number of degrees of descent too few to allow of marriage between two related persons. **to a degree** *colloq.* considerably. ▫▫ **degreeless** *adj.* [ME f. OF *degré* f. Rmc (as DE-, L *gradus* step)]
■ **1** see STAGE *n.* 1. **2** measure, magnitude, extent, limit; amount, intensity. **10** grade, level, class, caste, rank, order, standing, status, station, position, situation, condition, *archaic or literary* estate. ▫ **by degrees** gradually, little by little, bit by bit, step by step, inch by inch, piecemeal, inchmeal, slowly. **to a degree** substantially, considerably, quite, decidedly, to a considerable extent.

degressive /digréssiv/ *adj.* **1** (of taxation) at successively lower rates on low amounts. **2** reducing in amount. [L *degredi* (as DE-, *gradi* walk)]

de haut en bas /də ōt on baá/ *adv.* in a condescending or superior manner. [F, = from above to below]

dehire / deehír/ *v.tr. US colloq.* dismiss (a person) from employment; sack.

dehisce /dihíss/ *v.intr.* gape or burst open (esp. of a pod or seed-vessel or of a cut or wound). ▫▫ **dehiscence** *n.* **dehiscent** *adj.* [L *dehiscere* (as DE-, *hiscere* incept. of *hiare* gape)]

dehorn /deéhórn/ *v.tr.* remove the horns from (an animal).

dehumanize /deehyoómənīz/ *v.tr.* (also **-ise**) **1** deprive of human characteristics. **2** make impersonal or machine-like. ▫▫ **dehumanization** /-záysh'n/ *n.*

dehumidify /deéhyoomíddifī/ *v.tr.* (**-ies, -ied**) reduce the degree of humidity of; remove moisture from (a gas, esp. air). ▫▫ **dehumidification** /-fikáysh'n/ *n.* **dehumidifier** *n.*

dehydrate /deéhīdráyt/ *v.* **1** *tr.* **a** remove water from (esp. foods for preservation and storage in bulk). **b** make dry, esp. make (the body) deficient in water. **c** render lifeless or uninteresting. **2** *intr.* lose water. ▫▫ **dehydration** /-dráysh'n/ *n.* **dehydrator** *n.*
■ **1a, b, 2** see DRY *v.*

dehydrogenate /deéhīdrójinayt/ *v.tr. Chem.* remove a hydrogen atom or atoms from (a compound). ▫▫ **dehydrogenation** /-náysh'n/ *n.*

de-ice /dee-íss/ *v.tr.* **1** remove ice from. **2** prevent the formation of ice on.
■ **1** see THAW *v.* 1, 5.

de-icer /dee-ísər/ *n.* a device or substance for de-icing, esp. a windscreen or ice on an aircraft.

deicide /deé-isīd, dáy-/ *n.* **1** the killer of a god. **2** the killing of a god. [eccl.L *deicida* f. L *deus* god + -CIDE]

deictic /díktik/ *adj.* & *n. Philol.* & *Gram.* ● *adj.* pointing, demonstrative. ● *n.* a deictic word. [Gk *deiktikos* f. *deiktos* capable of proof f. *deiknumi* show]

deify /deé-ifī, dáyi-/ *v.tr.* (**-ies, -ied**) **1** make a god of. **2** regard or worship as a god. ▫▫ **deification** /-fikáysh'n/ *n.* [ME f. OF *deifier* f. eccl.L *deificare* f. *deus* god]
■ see IDOLIZE.

deign /dayn/ *v.* **1** *intr.* (foll. by *to* + infin.) think fit, condescend. **2** *tr.* (usu. with *neg.*) *archaic* condescend to give (an answer etc.). [ME f. OF *degnier, deigner, daigner* f. L *dignare, -ari* deem worthy f. *dignus* worthy]
■ condescend, stoop, lower oneself, think fit, *formal* vouchsafe.

Dei gratia /dáyi graátiə, graáshiə/ *adv.* by the grace of God. [L]

deinstitutionalize /deé-instityoóshənəlīz/ *v.tr.* (also **-ise**) (usu. as **deinstitutionalized** *adj.*) remove from an institution or from the effects of institutional life. ▫▫ **deinstitutionalization** /-záysh'n/ *n.*

deionize /dee-ī́ənīz/ *v.tr.* (also **-ise**) remove the ions or ionic constituents from (water, air, etc.). ▫▫ **deionization** /-záysh'n/ *n.* **deionizer** *n.*

deipnosophist /dīpnóssəfist/ *n.* a person skilled in dining and table talk. [Gk *deipnosophistēs* (in pl. as title of a work by Athenaeus (3rd c.) describing long discussions at a banquet) f. *deipnon* dinner + *sophistēs* wise man: see SOPHIST]
■ see CONVERSATIONALIST.

deism /deé-iz'm, dáy-/ *n.* belief in the existence of a supreme being arising from reason rather than revelation (cf. THEISM). ▫▫ **deist** *n.* **deistic** /-ístik/ *adj.* **deistical** /-ístik'l/ *adj.* [L *deus* god + -ISM]

deity /deé-iti, *disp.* dáy-/ *n.* (*pl.* **-ies**) **1** a god or goddess. **2** divine status, quality, or nature. **3** (**the Deity**) the Creator, God. [ME f. OF *deité* f. eccl.L *deitas -tatis* transl. Gk *theotēs* f. *theos* god]
■ **1** goddess, supreme being, creator, divinity; see also GOD *n.* 1. **3** the Creator, God, the Supreme Being.

déjà vu /dáyzhaa voó/ *n.* **1** *Psychol.* an illusory feeling of having already experienced a present situation. **2** something tediously familiar. [F, = already seen]

deject /dijékt/ *v.tr.* (usu. as **dejected** *adj.*) make sad or dispirited; depress. □□ **dejectedly** *adv.* [ME f. L *dejicere* (DE-, *jacĕre* throw)]
■ (**dejected**) downcast, downhearted, depressed, dispirited, discouraged, despondent, down, low, chap-fallen, crestfallen; melancholy, sad, unhappy, gloomy, glum, miserable, blue, low-spirited, in low spirits, forlorn, woebegone, disconsolate, sorrowful, morose, heartbroken, heavy-hearted, in the doldrums, *colloq.* down in the dumps, down in the mouth. □□ **dejectedly** see *sadly* (SAD).

dejection /dijéksh'n/ *n.* a dejected state; low spirits. [ME f. L *dejectio* (as DEJECT)]
■ see DEPRESSION 1b.

de jure /dee jóori, day jóoray/ *adj.* & *adv.* ● *adj.* rightful. ● *adv.* rightfully; by right. [L]
■ *adj.* see LEGITIMATE *adj.* 1, 2.

dekko /dékkō/ *n.* (*pl.* **-os**) *Brit. sl.* a look or glance (*took a quick dekko*). [Hindi *dekho*, imper. of *dekhnā* look]
■ see GLANCE *n.* 1.

Del. *abbr.* Delaware.

delate /diláyt/ *v.tr. archaic* **1** inform against; impeach (a person). **2** report (an offence). □□ **delation** /-láysh'n/ *n.* **delator** *n.* [L *delat-* (as DE-, *lat-* past part. stem of *ferre* carry)]

delay /diláy/ *v.* & *n.* ● *v.* **1** *tr.* postpone; defer. **2** *tr.* make late (*was delayed at the traffic lights*). **3** *intr.* loiter; be late (*don't delay!*). ● *n.* **1** the act or an instance of delaying; the process of being delayed. **2** time lost by inaction or the inability to proceed. **3** a hindrance. □ **delayed-action** (*attrib.*) (esp. of a bomb, camera, etc.) operating some time after being primed or set. **delay line** *Electr.* a device producing a desired delay in the transmission of a signal. □□ **delayer** *n.* [ME f. OF *delayer* (v.), *delai* (n.), prob. f. *des-* DIS- + *laier* leave: see RELAY]
■ *v.* **1** postpone, put off *or* aside, defer, break off, suspend, shelve, hold off *or* up (on), cut off *or* short, put on hold, hold in abeyance, table, pigeon-hole, *colloq.* put on the back burner, put on ice. **2** hold up *or* back, detain, retard, keep, set back, slow (up *or* down), impede, hinder, bog down. **3** loiter, procrastinate, temporize, hesitate, drag (along), drag one's feet *or* heels, wait, lag (behind), dawdle, hang back *or* about, stall, linger, dither, dally, mark time, shilly-shally, potter, *archaic or literary* tarry, *colloq.* dilly-dally. ● *n.* **1, 2** postponement, deferral, deferment, hold-up, set-back, hitch, snag, lull, interlude, hiatus, interruption, gap, interval, lacuna, stop, stoppage, wait, waiting, suspension. **3** see HINDRANCE.

dele /déeli/ *v.* & *n. Printing* ● *v.tr.* (**deled, deleing**) delete or mark for deletion (a letter, word, etc., struck out of a text). ● *n.* a sign marking something to be deleted; a deletion. [L, imper. of *delēre*: see DELETE]

delectable /diléktəb'l/ *adj.* esp. *literary* delightful, pleasant. □□ **delectability** /-bílliti/ *n.* **delectably** *adv.* [ME f. OF f. L *delectabilis* f. *delectare* DELIGHT]
■ see PLEASANT.

delectation /déelektáysh'n/ *n. literary* pleasure, enjoyment (*sang for his delectation*). [ME f. OF (as DELECTABLE)]
■ delight, enjoyment, amusement, entertainment, diversion, pleasure, satisfaction.

delegacy /délligəsi/ *n.* (*pl.* **-ies**) **1** a system of delegating. **2** **a** an appointment as a delegate. **b** a body of delegates; a delegation.

delegate *n.* & *v.* ● *n.* /délligət/ **1** an elected representative sent to a conference. **2** a member of a committee. **3** a member of a deputation. ● *v.tr.* /délligayt/ **1** (often foll. by *to*) **a** commit (authority, power, etc.) to an agent or deputy. **b** entrust (a task) to another person. **2** send or authorize (a person) as a representative; depute. □□ **delegable** /délligəb'l/ *adj.* [ME f. L *delegatus* (as DE-, *legare* depute)]
■ *n.* **1, 3** envoy, agent, representative, ambassador, plenipotentiary, minister, emissary, commissioner, (papal) nuncio, spokesperson, spokesman, spokeswoman, go-between, *archaic* legate. **2** committee member. ● *v.* **1** assign, give, hand over *or* on, pass over *or* on, depute, transfer, entrust. **2** depute, commission, appoint, designate, assign, name, nominate, accredit, authorize, empower, mandate.

delegation /délligáysh'n/ *n.* **1** a body of delegates; a deputation. **2** the act or process of delegating or being delegated. [L *delegatio* (as DELEGATE)]
■ **1** see MISSION 3.

delete /diléet/ *v.tr.* remove or obliterate (written or printed matter), esp. by striking out. □□ **deletion** /-léesh'n/ *n.* [L *delēre delet-* efface]
■ erase, cancel, rub out *or* off, cross out *or* off, remove, blot out, expunge, efface, eliminate, obliterate, wipe out, eradicate, strike out, cut *or* edit (out), *US* blue-pencil, *Printing* dele.

deleterious /délliteériəss/ *adj.* harmful (to the mind or body). □□ **deleteriously** *adv.* [med.L *deleterius* f. Gk *dēlētērios* noxious]
■ see HARMFUL.

delft /delft/ *n.* (also **delftware** /délftwair/) glazed, usu. blue and white, earthenware, made in Delft in Holland.

deli /délli/ *n.* (*pl.* **delis**) esp. *US colloq.* a delicatessen shop. [abbr.]

deliberate *adj.* & *v.* ● *adj.* /dilíbbərət/ **1** **a** intentional (*a deliberate foul*). **b** fully considered; not impulsive (*made a deliberate choice*). **2** slow in deciding; cautious (*a ponderous and deliberate mind*). **3** (of movement etc.) leisurely and unhurried. ● *v.* /dilíbbərayt/ **1** *intr.* think carefully; take counsel (*the jury deliberated for an hour*). **2** *tr.* consider, discuss carefully (*deliberated the question*). □□ **deliberately** /dilíbbərətli/ *adv.* **deliberateness** /dilíbbərətniss/ *n.* **deliberator** /dilíbbəraytər/ *n.* [L *deliberatus* past part. of *deliberare* (as DE-, *librare* weigh f. *libra* balance)]
■ *adj.* **1 a** intentional, planned, studied, wilful, intended, premeditated, calculated, conscious, purposeful, preconceived, considered. **1b, 2** confident, considered, calm, dispassionate, composed; careful, prudent, cautious, painstaking, considered, considerate, thoughtful, well-thought-out, thorough, methodical, systematic, fastidious, orderly, punctilious. **3** slow, methodical, careful, unhurried, paced, measured, regular, even, steady, sure, unhesitating, unfaltering, leisurely. ● *v.* **1** ponder, take counsel, think, meditate, reflect, cogitate, ruminate. **2** consider, discuss, think about *or* over, weigh up, debate, meditate on *or* over, reflect on *or* over, cogitate on *or* over, ruminate on *or* over, study. □□ **deliberately** intentionally, on purpose, purposely, wilfully, consciously, wittingly, calculatedly, calculatingly, knowingly, pointedly, of one's (own) free will, with one's eyes (wide) open.

deliberation /dilíbbəráysh'n/ *n.* **1** careful consideration. **2** **a** the discussion of reasons for and against. **b** a debate or discussion. **3** **a** caution and care. **b** (of action or behaviour) purposefulness, deliberateness. **c** (of movement) slowness or ponderousness. [ME f. OF f. L *deliberatio -onis* (as DELIBERATE)]
■ **1** see CONSIDERATION 1. **2** see DISCUSSION 2.

deliberative /dilíbbərətiv/ *adj.* of, or appointed for the purpose of, deliberation or debate (*a deliberative assembly*). □□ **deliberatively** *adv.* **deliberativeness** *n.* [F *délibératif -ive* or L *deliberativus* (as DELIBERATE)]

delicacy /déllikəsi/ *n.* (*pl.* **-ies**) **1** (esp. in craftsmanship or artistic or natural beauty) fineness or intricacy of structure or texture; gracefulness. **2** susceptibility to injury or disease; weakness. **3** the quality of requiring discretion or sensitivity (*a situation of some delicacy*). **4** a choice or expensive food. **5** **a** consideration for the feelings of others. **b** avoidance of immodesty or vulgarity. **6** (esp. in a person, a sense, or an instrument) accuracy of perception; sensitiveness. [ME f. DELICATE + -ACY]
■ **1** fineness, delicateness, grace, gracefulness, exquisiteness, daintiness; see also BEAUTY 1. **2** fragility, frailty, frailness, weakness, infirmity, feebleness, delicateness, tenderness. **3** sensitivity, sensitiveness,

delicateness, difficulty, ticklishness, nicety, trickiness, awkwardness. **4** luxury, sweetmeat, dainty, titbit, treat, morsel, *archaic* comfit. **5** consideration, tactfulness, tact, considerateness, thoughtfulness, discretion, discernment, sensitivity, sensibility, delicateness, finesse, artfulness, care. **6** sensitivity, sensitiveness; see also ACCURACY.

delicate /déllikət/ *adj.* **1 a** fine in texture or structure; soft, slender, or slight. **b** of exquisite quality or workmanship. **c** (of colour) subtle or subdued; not bright. **d** subtle, hard to appreciate. **2 a** (of a person) easily injured; susceptible to illness. **b** (of a thing) easily spoiled or damaged. **3 a** requiring careful handling; tricky (*a delicate situation*). **b** (of an instrument) highly sensitive. **4** deft (*a delicate touch*). **5** (of a person) avoiding the immodest or offensive. **6** (esp. of actions) considerate. **7** (of food) dainty; suitable for an invalid. □ **in a delicate condition** *archaic* pregnant. □□ **delicately** *adv.* **delicateness** *n.* [ME f. OF *delicat* or L *delicatus*, of unkn. orig.]

■ **1 a** fine, exquisite, dainty, graceful, slender, slight, airy, elegant, subtle, soft. **c** subtle, subdued, muted, soft, faint, pale, light, pastel. **d** see SUBTLE 2. **2 a** feeble, weak, sickly, frail, debilitated, weakened, unhealthy. **b** fragile, breakable, frail, tender, frangible, dainty, flimsy. **3 a** ticklish, sensitive, tricky, difficult, touchy, awkward, *colloq.* sticky, *sl.* hairy. **5, 6** tactful, considerate, thoughtful, discreet, sensitive, discriminating, discerning, proper. □ **in a delicate condition** see PREGNANT 1. □□ **delicateness** see DELICACY 1–3, 5–6.

delicatessen /déllikətéss'n/ *n.* **1** a shop selling cooked meats, cheeses, and unusual or foreign prepared foods. **2** (often *attrib.*) such foods collectively (*a delicatessen counter*). [G *Delikatessen* or Du. *delicatessen* f. F *délicatesse* f. *délicat* (as DELICATE)]

delicious /dilíshəss/ *adj.* **1** highly delightful and enjoyable to the taste or sense of smell. **2** (of a joke etc.) very witty. □□ **deliciously** *adv.* **deliciousness** *n.* [ME f. OF f. LL *deliciosus* f. L *deliciae* delight]

■ **1** luscious, ambrosial, savoury, mouth-watering, toothsome, choice, flavourful, tasty, appetizing, palatable, *colloq.* scrumptious, scrummy, yummy, *literary* delectable.

delict /dilíkt, déelikt/ *n. archaic* a violation of the law; an offence. [L *delictum* neut. past part. of *delinquere* offend (as DE-, *linquere* leave)]

delight /dilīt/ *v.* & *n.* ● *v.* **1** *tr.* (often foll. by *with*, or *that* + clause, or *to* + infin.) please greatly (*the gift delighted them; was delighted with the result; was delighted that you won; would be delighted to help*). **2** *intr.* (often foll. by *in*, or *to* + infin.) take great pleasure; be highly pleased (*he delighted in her success; they delight to humour him*). ● *n.* **1** great pleasure. **2** something giving pleasure (*her singing is a delight*). □□ **delighted** *adj.* **delightedly** *adv.* [ME f. OF *delitier, delit*, f. L *delectare* frequent. of *delicere*: alt. after *light* etc.]

■ *v.* **1** please, gratify, satisfy, gladden, cheer, tickle, amuse, entertain, divert, excite, thrill, captivate, entrance, fascinate. **2** (*delight in*) relish, revel in, glory in, love, adore, enjoy, appreciate, like, savour, *colloq.* get a kick from *or* out of. ● *n.* **1** pleasure, gratification, joy, satisfaction, enjoyment, *literary* delectation; bliss, ecstasy, rapture. □□ **delighted** pleased, happy, charmed, thrilled, enchanted, *colloq.* tickled pink *or* to death.

delightful /dilītfŏŏl/ *adj.* causing great delight; pleasant, charming. □□ **delightfully** *adv.* **delightfulness** *n.*

■ pleasing, agreeable, pleasurable, enjoyable, joyful, pleasant, lovely, amusing, entertaining, diverting, thrilling; attractive, congenial, winning, winsome, charming, engaging; captivating, ravishing, fascinating, entrancing, enchanting.

Delilah /dilīlə/ *n.* a seductive and wily temptress. [*Delilah*, betrayer of Samson (Judges 16)]

delimit /dilímmit/ *v.tr.* (**delimited, delimiting**) **1** determine the limits of. **2** fix the territorial boundary of. □□ **delimitation** /-táysh'n/ *n.* [F *délimiter* f. L *delimitare* (as DE-, *limitare* f. *limes -itis* boundary)]

■ **1** see RESTRICT.

delimitate /dilímmitayt/ *v.tr.* = DELIMIT.

delineate /dilínniayt/ *v.tr.* portray by drawing etc. or in words (*delineated her character*). □□ **delineation** /-áysh'n/ *n.* **delineator** *n.* [L *delineare delineat-* (as DE-, *lineare* f. *linea* line)]

delinquency /dilíngkwənsi/ *n.* (*pl.* **-ies**) **1 a** a crime, usu. not of a serious kind; a misdeed. **b** minor crime in general, esp. that of young people (*juvenile delinquency*). **2** wickedness (*moral delinquency; an act of delinquency*). **3** neglect of one's duty. [eccl. L *delinquentia* f. L *delinquens* part. of *delinquere* (as DELICT)]

■ **1 a** see MISDEED. **b** see *misbehaviour* (MISBEHAVE). **3** see DEFAULT *n.* 1.

delinquent /dilíngkwənt/ *n.* & *adj.* ● *n.* an offender (*juvenile delinquent*). ● *adj.* **1** guilty of a minor crime or a misdeed. **2** failing in one's duty. **3** *US* in arrears. □□ **delinquently** *adv.*

■ *n.* malefactor, (young *or* youthful) offender, wrongdoer, lawbreaker, criminal, miscreant; hooligan, ruffian. ● *adj.* **2** neglectful, negligent, derelict, remiss, failing. **3** in arrears, overdue, past due, late, unpaid, behindhand.

deliquesce /déllikwéss/ *v.intr.* **1** become liquid, melt. **2** *Chem.* dissolve in water absorbed from the air. □□ **deliquescence** *n.* **deliquescent** *adj.* [L *deliquescere* (as DE-, *liquescere* incept. of *liquēre* be liquid)]

■ **1** see MELT *v.* 1, 2, 4.

delirious /dilírriəss/ *adj.* **1** affected with delirium; temporarily or apparently mad; raving. **2** wildly excited, ecstatic. **3** (of behaviour) betraying delirium or ecstasy. □□ **deliriously** *adv.*

■ **1** wild, hysterical, distracted, incoherent, rambling, irrational, raving, ranting, frenzied, frantic, crazed, disturbed, demented, deranged, unhinged; mad, *colloq.* crazy. **2** wild, excited, thrilled; see also ECSTATIC *adj.* 1, 2.

delirium /dilírriəm/ *n.* **1** an acutely disordered state of mind involving incoherent speech, hallucinations, and frenzied excitement, occurring in metabolic disorders, intoxication, fever, etc. **2** great excitement, ecstasy. □ **delirium tremens** /tréemenz/ a psychosis of chronic alcoholism involving tremors and hallucinations. [L f. *delirare* be deranged (as DE-, *lira* ridge between furrows)]

deliver /dilívvər/ *v.tr.* **1 a** distribute (letters, parcels, ordered goods, etc.) to the addressee or the purchaser. **b** (often foll. by *to*) hand over (*delivered the boy safely to his teacher*). **2** (often foll. by *from*) save, rescue, or set free (*delivered him from his enemies*). **3 a** give birth to (*delivered a girl*). **b** (in *passive*; often foll. by *of*) give birth (*was delivered of a child*). **c** assist at the birth of (*delivered six babies that week*). **d** assist in giving birth (*delivered the patient successfully*). **4 a** (often *refl.*) utter or recite (an opinion, a speech, etc.) (*delivered himself of the observation; delivered the sermon well*). **b** (of a judge) pronounce (a judgement). **5** (often foll. by *up*, *over*) abandon; resign; hand over (*delivered his soul up to God*). **6** present or render (an account). **7** launch or aim (a blow, a ball, or an attack). **8** *Law* hand over formally (esp. a sealed deed to a grantee). **9** *colloq.* = *deliver the goods*. **10** *US* cause (voters etc.) to support a candidate. □ **deliver the goods** *colloq.* carry out one's part of an agreement. □□ **deliverable** *adj.* **deliverer** *n.* [ME f. OF *delivrer* f. Gallo-Roman (as DE-, LIBERATE)]

■ **1 a** carry, bring, convey, distribute, give *or* hand out, take round, cart, transport; purvey. **2** set free, liberate, extricate, release, save, rescue, emancipate, redeem, disencumber, disburden, *hist.* enfranchise, manumit. **3 a** bring forth, bear, give birth to, bring into the world, have; drop. **4 a** give, present, utter, recite, read, broadcast, give out; set forth, communicate, publish, hand over, hand out. **b** set forth, make known, express, promulgate, pronounce, *US* hand down. **5** hand over, give, surrender, cede, yield, make over, relinquish, give up *or* over, commit, transfer, turn over, resign, abandon.

7 give, administer, inflict, deal, direct, aim, send, launch, impart, throw; cast, hurl, shoot, discharge, fire.
□ **deliver the goods** perform, do one's bit, fulfil one's side of the bargain.

deliverance /dilívvərənss/ *n.* **1 a** the act or an instance of rescuing; the process of being rescued. **b** a rescue. **2** a formally expressed opinion. [ME f. OF *delivrance* (as DELIVER)]
■ **1** liberation, release, delivery, emancipation, relief, rescue; salvation.

delivery /dilívvəri/ *n.* (*pl.* **-ies**) **1 a** the delivering of letters etc. **b** a regular distribution of letters etc. (*two deliveries a day*). **c** something delivered. **2 a** the process of childbirth. **b** an act of this. **3** deliverance. **4 a** an act of throwing, esp. of a cricket ball. **b** the style of such an act (*a good delivery*). **5** the act of giving or surrendering (*delivery of the town to the enemy*). **6 a** the uttering of a speech etc. **b** the manner or style of such a delivery (*a measured delivery*). **7** *Law* **a** the formal handing over of property. **b** the transfer of a deed to a grantee or a third party. □ **take delivery of** receive (something purchased). [ME f. AF *delivree* fem. past part. of *delivrer* (as DELIVER)]
■ **1 a** distribution, conveyance, transportation, transport. **2** childbirth, *formal* parturition. **3** see DELIVERANCE 1. **4** see THROW *n.* 1. **5** donation, presentation, bestowal; see also SURRENDER *n.* **6 b** presentation, performance, execution; utterance, enunciation, articulation, pronunciation, expression. □ **take delivery of** see RECEIVE 1, 2.

dell /del/ *n.* a small usu. wooded hollow or valley. [OE f. Gmc]
■ see VALLEY.

Della Cruscan /déllə krúskən/ *adj.* & *n.* ● *adj.* **1** of or relating to the Academy della Crusca in Florence, concerned with the purity of Italian. **2** of or concerning a late 18th–c. school of English poets with an artificial style. ● *n.* a member of the Academy della Crusca or the late 18th–c. school of English poets. [It. (*Accademia*) *della Crusca* (Academy) of the bran (with ref. to sifting)]

delocalize /deelṓkəlīz/ *v.tr.* (also **-ise**) **1 a** detach or remove (a thing) from its place. **b** not limit to a particular location. **2** (as **delocalized** *adj.*) *Chem.* (of electrons) shared among more than two atoms in a molecule. □□ **delocalization** /-záysh'n/ *n.*

delouse /deelówss/ *v.tr.* rid (a person or animal) of lice.

Delphic /délfik/ *adj.* (also **Delphian** /-fiən/) **1** (of an utterance, prophecy, etc.) obscure, ambiguous, or enigmatic. **2** of or concerning the ancient Greek oracle at Delphi.

delphinium /delfínniəm/ *n.* any ranunculaceous garden plant of the genus *Delphinium*, with tall spikes of usu. blue flowers. [mod.L f. Gk *delphinion* larkspur f. *delphin* dolphin]

delphinoid /délfinoyd/ *adj.* & *n.* ● *adj.* **1** of the family that includes dolphins, porpoises, grampuses, etc. **2** dolphin-like. ● *n.* **1** a member of the delphinoid family of aquatic mammals. **2** a dolphin-like animal. [Gk *delphinoeidēs* f. *delphin* dolphin]

delta /déltə/ *n.* **1** a triangular tract of deposited earth, alluvium, etc., at the mouth of a river, formed by its diverging outlets. **2 a** the fourth letter of the Greek alphabet (Δ, δ). **b** a fourth-class mark given for a piece of work or in an examination. **3** *Astron.* the fourth star in a constellation. **4** *Math.* an increment of a variable. □ **delta connection** *Electr.* a triangular arrangement of three-phase windings with circuit wire from each angle. **delta rays** *Physics* rays of low penetrative power consisting of slow electrons ejected from an atom by the impact of ionizing radiation. **delta rhythm** (or **wave**) low-frequency electrical activity of the brain during sleep. **delta wing** the triangular swept-back wing of an aircraft. □□ **deltaic** /deltáyik/ *adj.* [ME f. Gk f. Phoen. *daleth*]

deltiology /déltióllәji/ *n.* the collecting and study of postcards. □□ **deltiologist** *n.* [Gk *deltion* dimin. of *deltos* writing-tablet + -LOGY]

deltoid /déltoyd/ *adj.* & *n.* ● *adj.* triangular; like a river delta. ● *n.* (in full **deltoid muscle**) a thick triangular muscle covering the shoulder joint and used for raising the arm away from the body. [F *deltoïde* or mod.L *deltoides* f. Gk *deltoeidēs* (as DELTA, -OID)]

delude /dilo͞od, -lyo͞od/ *v.tr.* deceive or mislead (*deluded by false optimism*). □□ **deluder** *n.* [ME f. L *deludere* mock (as DE-, *ludere lus-* play)]
■ see DECEIVE 1.

deluge /délyo͞oj/ *n.* & *v.* ● *n.* **1** a great flood. **2** (**the Deluge**) the biblical Flood (Gen. 6-8). **3** a great outpouring (of words, paper, etc.). **4** a heavy fall of rain. ● *v.tr.* **1** flood. **2** inundate with a great number or amount (*deluged with complaints*). [ME f. OF f. L *diluvium*, rel. to *lavare* wash]
■ *n.* **1** see FLOOD *n.* 1. **3** see FLOOD *n.* 2b. **4** see DOWNPOUR. ● *v.* **1** see FLOOD *v.* 1. **2** see DROWN.

delusion /dilo͞ozh'n, -lyo͞ozh'n/ *n.* **1** a false belief or impression. **2** *Psychol.* this as a symptom or form of mental disorder. □ **delusions of grandeur** a false idea of oneself as being important, noble, famous, etc. □□ **delusional** *adj.* [ME f. LL *delusio* (as DELUDE)]
■ **1** misapprehension, false *or* mistaken impression, illusion, mistake, error, misconception, misbelief, hallucination, misjudgement.

delusive /dilo͞ossiv, dilyo͞o-/ *adj.* **1** deceptive or unreal. **2** disappointing. □□ **delusively** *adv.* **delusiveness** *n.*
■ **1** see NON-EXISTENT.

delusory /dilo͞ossəri, dilyo͞o-/ *adj.* = DELUSIVE. [LL *delusorius* (as DELUSION)]

delustre /deelústər/ *v.tr.* (*US* **deluster**) remove the lustre from (a textile).

de luxe /də lúks, lo͝oks/ *adj.* **1** luxurious or sumptuous. **2** of a superior kind. [F, = of luxury]
■ see LUXURIOUS 1.

delve /delv/ *v.* **1** *intr.* (often foll. by *in*, *into*) **a** search energetically (*delved into his pocket*). **b** make a laborious search in documents etc.; research (*delved into his family history*). **2** *tr.* & *intr. poet.* dig. □□ **delver** *n.* [OE *delfan* f. WG]
■ **1** see ROOT^2 *v.* 2a. **2** see TILL^3.

Dem. *abbr. US* Democrat.

demagnetize /deemágnitīz/ *v.tr.* (also **-ise**) remove the magnetic properties of. □□ **demagnetization** /-záysh'n/ *n.* **demagnetizer** *n.*

demagogue /démmәgog/ *n.* (*US* **-gog**) **1** a political agitator appealing to the basest instincts of a mob. **2** *hist.* a leader of the people, esp. in ancient times. □□ **demagogic** /-góggik/ *adj.* **demagoguery** /-góggәri/ *n.* **demagogy** /-góggi/ *n.* [Gk *dēmagōgos* f. *dēmos* the people + *agōgos* leading]
■ **1** see AGITATOR 1.

demand /dimaánd/ *n.* & *v.* ● *n.* **1** an insistent and peremptory request, made as of right. **2** *Econ.* the desire of purchasers or consumers for a commodity (*no demand for solid tyres these days*). **3** an urgent claim (*care of her mother makes demands on her*). ● *v.tr.* **1** (often foll. by *of*, *from*, or *to* + infin., or *that* + clause) ask for (something) insistently and urgently, as of right (*demanded to know*; *demanded five pounds from him*; *demanded that his wife be present*). **2** require or need (*a task demanding skill*). **3** insist on being told (*demanded her business*). **4** (as **demanding** *adj.*) making demands; requiring skill, effort, etc. (*a demanding but worthwhile job*). □ **demand feeding** the practice of feeding a baby when it cries for a feed rather than at set times. **demand note 1** a written request for payment. **2** *US* a bill payable at sight. **demand pull** *Econ.* available money as a factor causing economic inflation. **in demand** sought after. **on demand** as soon as a demand is made (*a cheque payable on demand*). □□ **demandable** *adj.* **demander** *n.* **demandingly** *adv.* [ME f. OF *demande* (n.), *demander* (v.) f. L *demandare* entrust (as DE-, *mandare* order: see MANDATE)]
■ *n.* **1** request, order, command, insistence, call, bidding, requisition, *archaic* hest, *archaic or literary* bid, *literary* behest. **2** want, need, requirement, call, desire, market.

3 see CLAIM *n.* 1. ● *v.* **1** require, order, call for, *archaic or literary* bid; insist (on), command, ask (for), request; requisition. **2** require, call for, need, want, necessitate, cry out for. **4** (**demanding**) insistent, clamorous, nagging, persistent; difficult, hard, exigent, tough, exacting, trying, taxing. □ **in demand** sought after, wanted, needed, coveted, popular, desired, desirable. **on demand** on call, on request, on presentation, when requested *or* required; at once, immediately, without delay.

demantoid /dimántoyd/ *n.* a lustrous green garnet. [G]

demarcation /déemaarkáysh'n/ *n.* **1** the act of marking a boundary or limits. **2** the trade-union practice of strictly assigning specific jobs to different unions. □ **demarcation dispute** an inter-union dispute about who does a particular job. □□ **demarcate** *v.tr.* **demarcator** *n.* [Sp. *demarcación* f. *demarcar* mark the bounds of (as DE-, MARK[1])]
■ **1** see DEFINITION 2.

démarche /daymaarsh/ *n.* a political step or initiative. [F f. *démarcher* take steps (as DE-, MARCH[1])]

dematerialize /déemətéeriəlīz/ *v.tr.* & *intr.* (also **-ise**) make or become non-material or spiritual (esp. of psychic phenomena etc.). □□ **dematerialization** /-záysh'n/ *n.*
■ □□ **dematerialization** see *evaporation* (EVAPORATE).

deme /deem/ *n.* **1 a** a political division of Attica in ancient Greece. **b** an administrative division in modern Greece. **2** *Biol.* a local population of closely related plants or animals. [Gk *dēmos* the people]

demean[1] /diméen/ *v.tr.* (usu. *refl.*) lower the dignity of (*would not demean myself to take it*). [DE- + MEAN[2], after *debase*]
■ see LOWER[2] 4.

demean[2] /diméen/ *v.refl.* (with *adv.*) behave (*demeaned himself well*). [ME f. OF *demener* f. Rmc (as DE-, L *minare* drive animals f. *minari* threaten)]
■ (*demean oneself*) see BEHAVE 1a.

demeanour /diméenər/ *n.* (*US* **demeanor**) outward behaviour or bearing. [DEMEAN[2], prob. after obs. *havour* behaviour]
■ see BEARING 1.

dement /dimént/ *n. archaic* a demented person. [orig. adj. f. F *dément* or L *demens* (as DEMENTED)]

demented /diméntid/ *adj.* mad; crazy. □□ **dementedly** *adv.* **dementedness** *n.* [past part. of *dement* verb f. OF *dementer* or f. LL *dementare* f. *demens* out of one's mind (as DE-, *mens mentis* mind)]
■ see MAD *adj.* 1.

démenti /daymónti/ *n.* an official denial of a rumour etc. [F f. *démentir* accuse of lying]

dementia /diménshə/ *n. Med.* a chronic or persistent disorder of the mental processes marked by memory disorders, personality changes, impaired reasoning, etc., due to brain disease or injury. □ **dementia praecox** /préekoks/ schizophrenia. [L f. *demens* (as DEMENTED)]

demerara /démmərairə/ *n.* light-brown cane sugar coming orig. and chiefly from Demerara. [*Demerara* in Guyana]

demerit /deémérrit/ *n.* **1** a quality or action deserving blame; a fault. **2** *US* a mark given to an offender. □□ **demeritorious** /-tóriəss/ *adj.* [ME f. OF *de(s)merite* or L *demeritum* neut. past part. of *demerēri* deserve]
■ **2** see STIGMA 1.

demersal /dimérs'l/ *adj.* (of a fish etc.) being or living near the sea-bottom (cf. PELAGIC). [L *demersus* past part. of *demergere* (as DE-, *mergere* plunge)]

demesne /diméen, -máyn/ *n.* **1 a** a sovereign's or State's territory; a domain. **b** land attached to a mansion etc. **c** landed property; an estate. **2** (usu. foll. by *of*) a region or sphere. **3** *Law hist.* possession (of real property) as one's own. □ **held in demesne** (of an estate) occupied by the owner, not by tenants. [ME f. AF, OF *demeine* (later AF *demesne*) belonging to a lord f. L *dominicus* (as DOMINICAL)]

demi- /démmi/ *prefix* **1** half; half-size. **2** partially or imperfectly such (*demigod*). [ME f. F f. med.L *dimedius* half, for L *dimidius*]

demigod /démmigod/ *n.* (*fem.* **-goddess** /-goddiss/) **1 a** a partly divine being. **b** the offspring of a god or goddess and a mortal. **2** *colloq.* a person of compelling beauty, powers, or personality.
■ **1** see GOD *n.* 1a.

demijohn /démmijon/ *n.* a bulbous narrow-necked bottle holding from 3 to 10 gallons and usu. in a wicker cover. [prob. corrupt. of F *dame-jeanne* Lady Jane, assim. to DEMI- + the name *John*]

demilitarize /deemíllitərīz/ *v.tr.* (also **-ise**) remove a military organization or forces from (a frontier, a zone, etc.). □□ **demilitarization** /-záysh'n/ *n.*

demi-mondaine /démmimondayn, -mondayn/ *n.* a woman of a *demi-monde*.

demi-monde /démmimond, -mónd/ *n.* **1 a** *hist.* a class of women in 19th-c. France considered to be of doubtful social standing and morality. **b** a similar class of women in any society. **2** any group considered to be on the fringes of respectable society. [F, = half-world]

demineralize /deemínnərəlīz/ *v.tr.* (also **-ise**) remove salts from (sea water etc.). □□ **demineralization** /-záysh'n/ *n.*

demi-pension /dəmipónsyon/ *n.* hotel accommodation with bed, breakfast, and one main meal per day. [F (as DEMI-, PENSION[2])]

demirep /démmirep/ *n. archaic* a woman of doubtful sexual reputation. [abbr. of *demi-reputable*]

demise /dimīz/ *n.* & *v.* ● *n.* **1** death (*left a will on her demise; the demise of the agreement*). **2** *Law* conveyance or transfer (of property, a title, etc.) by demising. ● *v.tr. Law* **1** convey or grant (an estate) by will or lease. **2** transmit (a title etc.) by death. [AF use of past part. of OF *de(s)mettre* DISMISS, in refl. abdicate]
■ *n.* **1** see DEATH 1. ● *v.* **1** see LEASE *v.*, *make over* 1.

demisemiquaver /démmisémmikwayvər/ *n. Mus.* a note having the time value of half a semiquaver and represented by a large dot with a three-hooked stem. Also called *thirty-second note.*

demist /deemíst/ *v.tr.* clear mist from (a windscreen etc.). □□ **demister** *n.*

demit /dimit/ *v.tr.* (**demitted, demitting**) (often *absol.*) resign or abdicate (an office etc.). □□ **demission** /-mísh'n/ *n.* [F *démettre* f. L *demittere* (as DE-, *mittere miss-* send)]

demitasse /démmitass, dəmitáss/ *n.* **1** a small coffee-cup. **2** its contents. [F, = half-cup]

demiurge /démmiurj/ *n.* **1** (in the philosophy of Plato) the creator of the universe. **2** (in Gnosticism etc.) a heavenly being subordinate to the Supreme Being. □□ **demiurgic** /-úrjik/ *adj.* [eccl.L f. Gk *dēmiourgos* craftsman f. *dēmios* public f. *dēmos* people + *-ergos* working]

demo /démmō/ *n.* (*pl.* **-os**) *colloq.* = DEMONSTRATION 2, 3. [abbr.]

demob /deemób/ *v.* & *n. Brit. colloq.* ● *v.tr.* (**demobbed, demobbing**) demobilize. ● *n.* demobilization. [abbr.]

demobilize /deemṓbilīz/ *v.tr.* (also **-ise**) disband (troops, ships, etc.). □□ **demobilization** /-záysh'n/ *n.* [F *démobiliser* (as DE-, MOBILIZE)]
■ see DISBAND.

democracy /dimókrəsi/ *n.* (*pl.* **-ies**) **1 a** a system of government by the whole population, usu. through elected representatives. **b** a State so governed. **c** any organization governed on democratic principles. **2** a classless and tolerant form of society. **3** *US* **a** the principles of the Democratic Party. **b** its members. [F *démocratie* f. LL *democratia* f. Gk *dēmokratia* f. *dēmos* the people + -CRACY]

democrat /démmәkrat/ *n.* **1** an advocate of democracy. **2** (**Democrat**) (in the US) a member of the Democratic Party. □□ **democratism** /dimókrətiz'm/ *n.* [F *démocrate* (as DEMOCRACY), after *aristocrate*]

democratic /démmәkráttik/ *adj.* **1** of, like, practising, advocating, or constituting democracy or a democracy. **2**

favouring social equality. □ **democratic centralism** an organizational system in which policy is decided centrally and is binding on all members. **Democratic Party** one of the two main US political parties, considered to support social reform and international commitment (cf. *Republican Party*). □□ **democratically** *adv.* [F *démocratique* f. med.L *democraticus* f. Gk *dēmokratikos* f. *dēmokratia* DEMOCRACY]
■ **1** representative, popular; elected. **2** egalitarian, classless.

democratize /dimókrətīz/ *v.tr.* (also **-ise**) make (a State, institution, etc.) democratic. □□ **democratization** /-záysh'n/ *n.*

démodé /dáymodáy/ *adj.* out of fashion. [F, past part. of *démoder* (as DE-, *mode* fashion)]
■ see OUT *adv.* 16.

demodulate /deemódyoolayt/ *v.tr. Physics* extract (a modulating signal) from its carrier. □□ **demodulation** /deémodyooláysh'n/ *n.* **demodulator** *n.*

demography /dimógrəfi/ *n.* the study of the statistics of births, deaths, disease, etc., as illustrating the conditions of life in communities. □□ **demographer** *n.* **demographic** /démməgráffik/ *adj.* **demographical** /démməgráffik'l/ *adj.* **demographically** /démməgráffikəli/ *adv.* [Gk *dēmos* the people + -GRAPHY]

demoiselle /démwazél/ *n.* **1** *Zool.* a small crane, *Anthropoides virgo*, native to Asia and N. Africa. **2 a** a damselfly. **b** a damselfish. **3** *archaic* a young woman. [F, = DAMSEL]

demolish /dimóllish/ *v.tr.* **1 a** pull down (a building). **b** completely destroy or break. **2** overthrow (an institution). **3** refute (an argument, theory, etc.). **4** *joc.* eat up completely and quickly. □□ **demolisher** *n.* **demolition** /démməlish'n/ *n.* **demolitionist** /démməlíshənist/ *n.* [F *démolir* f. L *demoliri* (as DE-, *moliri molit-* construct f. *moles* mass)]
■ **1 a** tear *or* pull down, knock down, dismantle, reduce to ruin(s), pull to pieces, raze, topple, destroy, level. **b** see DESTROY 1. **2** bring to an end, make an end of, put an end to; see also OVERTHROW *v.* **3** refute, disprove, dispose of; destroy, overturn, crush, defeat, suppress, squelch, quash. **4** see DEVOUR 1.

demon[1] /deémən/ *n.* **1 a** an evil spirit or devil, esp. one thought to possess a person. **b** the personification of evil passion. **2** a malignant supernatural being; the Devil. **3** (often *attrib.*) a forceful, fierce, or skilful performer (*a demon on the tennis court; a demon player*). **4** a cruel or destructive person. **5** (also **daemon**) **a** an inner or attendant spirit; a genius (*the demon of creativity*). **b** a supernatural being in ancient Greece. □ **demon bowler** *Cricket* a very fast bowler. **a demon for work** *colloq.* a person who works strenuously. [ME f. med.L *demon* f. L *daemon* f. Gk *daimōn* deity]
■ **1 a** devil, evil spirit, fiend, cacodemon; monster, ghoul, ogre, beast, hell-hound. **2** see DEVIL *n.* 1, 2. **3** expert, master, maestro, wizard, adept, genius, talent, old hand, professional, virtuoso, *esp. Brit. colloq.* dab hand, *sl.* ace; (*attrib.*) see *first-rate adj.*

demon[2] / deémən/ *n. Austral. sl.* a police officer. [app. f. Van *Diemen*'s Land, early name for Tasmania, after DEMON[1]]
■ see *police officer*.

demonetize /deemúnnitīz/ *v.tr.* (also **-ise**) withdraw (a coin etc.) from use as money. □□ **demonetization** /-záysh'n/ *n.* [F *démonétiser* (as DE-, L *moneta* MONEY)]

demoniac /dimṓniak/ *adj.* & *n.* ● *adj.* **1** fiercely energetic or frenzied. **2 a** supposedly possessed by an evil spirit. **b** of or concerning such possession. **3** of or like demons. ● *n.* a person possessed by an evil spirit. □□ **demoniacal** /deémənī́ək'l/ *adj.* **demoniacally** /deémənī́əkəli/ *adv.* [ME f. OF *demoniaque* f. eccl.L *daemoniacus* f. *daemonium* f. Gk *daimonion* dimin. of *daimōn*: see DEMON[1]]

demonic /dimónnik/ *adj.* (also **daemonic**) **1** = DEMONIAC. **2** having or seeming to have supernatural genius or power. [LL *daemonicus* f. Gk *daimonikos* (as DEMON[1])]
■ **2** clairvoyant, telepathic, psychic, divinatory; witch-like.

demonism /deéməniz'm/ *n.* belief in the power of demons.

demonize /deémənīz/ *v.tr.* (also **-ise**) **1** make into or like a demon. **2** represent as a demon.

demonolatry /deémənóllətri/ *n.* the worship of demons.

demonology /deémənólləji/ *n.* the study of demons etc. □□ **demonologist** *n.*

demonstrable /démmənstrəb'l, dimónstrəb'l/ *adj.* capable of being shown or logically proved. □□ **demonstrability** /-bílliti/ *n.* **demonstrably** *adv.* [ME f. L *demonstrabilis* (as DEMONSTRATE)]
■ provable, confirmable, attestable, verifiable; evident, self-evident, obvious, undeniable, apparent, manifest, indisputable, unquestionable, positive, certain, conclusive.

demonstrate /démmənstrayt/ *v.* **1** *tr.* show evidence of (feelings etc.). **2** *tr.* describe and explain (a scientific proposition, machine, etc.) by experiment, practical use, etc. **3** *tr.* **a** logically prove the truth of. **b** be proof of the existence of. **4** *intr.* take part in or organize a public demonstration. **5** *intr.* act as a demonstrator. [L *demonstrare* (as DE-, *monstrare* show)]
■ **1, 3** show, make evident, establish, evince, evidence, exhibit, manifest; see also PROVE 1. **2** display, describe, present, report, illustrate; see also EXPLAIN 1. **4** march, parade, rally, protest.

demonstration /démmənstráysh'n/ *n.* **1** (foll. by *of*) **a** the outward showing of feeling etc. **b** an instance of this. **2** a public meeting, march, etc., for a political or moral purpose. **3 a** the exhibiting or explaining of specimens or experiments as a method of esp. scientific teaching. **b** an instance of this. **4** proof provided by logic, argument, etc. **5** *Mil.* a show of military force. □□ **demonstrational** *adj.* [ME f. OF *demonstration* or L *demonstratio* (as DEMONSTRATE)]
■ **1** show, manifestation, exhibition, display. **2** march, parade, protest, rally, sit-in, *colloq.* demo. **3** presentation, display, show, explanation, description, exposition, *colloq.* demo. **4** proof, evidence, testimony, indication, confirmation, verification, substantiation.

demonstrative /dimónstrətiv/ *adj.* & *n.* ● *adj.* **1** given to or marked by an open expression of feeling, esp. of affection (*a very demonstrative person*). **2** (usu. foll. by *of*) logically conclusive; giving proof (*the work is demonstrative of their skill*). **3 a** serving to point out or exhibit. **b** involving esp. scientific demonstration (*demonstrative technique*). **4** *Gram.* (of an adjective or pronoun) indicating the person or thing referred to (e.g. *this, that, those*). ● *n. Gram.* a demonstrative adjective or pronoun. □□ **demonstratively** *adv.* **demonstrativeness** *n.* [ME f. OF *demonstratif -ive* f. L *demonstrativus* (as DEMONSTRATION)]
■ *adj.* **1** open, expressive, unrestrained, unconstrained, unreserved, expansive, effusive, emotional; affectionate. **2** illustrative, indicative, representative, probative, evidential; conclusive.

demonstrator /démmənstraytər/ *n.* **1** a person who takes part in a political demonstration etc. **2** a person who demonstrates, esp. machines, equipment, etc., to prospective customers. **3** a person who teaches by demonstration, esp. in a laboratory etc. [L (as DEMONSTRATE)]
■ **1** protestor, activist, agitator.

demoralize /dimórrəlīz/ *v.tr.* (also **-ise**) **1** destroy (a person's) morale; make hopeless. **2** *archaic* corrupt (a person's) morals. □□ **demoralization** /-záysh'n/ *n.* **demoralizing** *adj.* **demoralizingly** *adv.* [F *démoraliser* (as DE-, MORAL)]
■ **1** dispirit, daunt, dishearten, discourage, demotivate, defeat; devitalize, depress, subdue, crush. **2** corrupt, pervert, deprave, vitiate, debase, debauch.

demote /dimṓt/ *v.tr.* reduce to a lower rank or class. □□ **demotion** /-mṓsh'n/ *n.* [DE- + PROMOTE]
■ see DOWNGRADE *v.* 1.

demotic /dimóttik/ *n.* & *adj.* ● *n.* **1** the popular colloquial form of a language. **2** a popular simplified form of ancient Egyptian writing (cf. HIERATIC). ● *adj.* **1** (esp. of language) popular, colloquial, or vulgar. **2** of or concerning the ancient Egyptian or modern Greek demotic. [Gk *dēmotikos* f. *dēmotēs* one of the people (*dēmos*)]

demotivate /deémṓtivayt/ *v.tr.* (also *absol.*) cause to lose motivation; discourage. □□ **demotivation** /-váysh'n/ *n.*

demount /deemównt/ *v.tr.* **1** take (apparatus, a gun, etc.) from its mounting. **2** dismantle for later reassembly. □□ **demountable** *adj.* & *n.* [F *démonter*: cf. DISMOUNT]

demulcent /dimúls'nt/ *adj.* & *n.* ● *adj.* soothing. ● *n.* an agent that forms a protective film soothing irritation or inflammation in the mouth. [L *demulcēre* (as DE-, *mulcēre* soothe)]

demur /dimúr/ *v.* & *n.* ● *v.intr.* (**demurred, demurring**) **1** (often foll. by *to, at*) raise scruples or objections. **2** *Law* put in a demurrer. ● *n.* (also **demurral** /dimúrrəl/) (usu. in *neg.*) **1** an objection (*agreed without demur*). **2** the act or process of objecting. □□ **demurrant** /dimúrrənt/ *n.* (in sense 2 of *v.*). [ME f. OF *demeure* (n.), *demeurer* (v.) f. Rmc (as DE-, L *morari* delay)]
■ *v.* **1** see PROTEST *v.* 1. ● *n.* **1** see OBJECTION.

demure /dimyo͝or/ *adj.* (**demurer, demurest**) **1** composed, quiet, and reserved; modest. **2** affectedly shy and quiet; coy. **3** decorous (*a demure high collar*). □□ **demurely** *adv.* **demureness** *n.* [ME, perh. f. AF *demuré* f. OF *demoré* past part. of *demorer* remain, stay (as DEMUR): infl. by OF *meür* f. L *maturus* ripe]
■ **1** see MODEST 1, 2. **2** see COY 3, *prudish* (PRUDE). **3** see DECOROUS, SEEMLY.

demurrable /dimúrrəb'l/ *adj.* esp. *Law* open to objection.

demurrage /dimúrrij/ *n.* **1 a** a rate or amount payable to a shipowner by a charterer for failure to load or discharge a ship within the time agreed. **b** a similar charge on railway trucks or goods. **2** such a detention or delay. [OF *demo(u)rage* f. *demorer* (as DEMUR)]

demurrer /dimúrrər/ *n. Law* an objection raised or exception taken. [AF (infin. as noun), = DEMUR]

demy /dimī́/ *n. Printing* a size of paper, 564 x 444 mm. [ME, var. of DEMI-]

demystify /deemístifī/ *v.tr.* (**-ies, -ied**) **1** clarify (obscure beliefs or subjects etc.). **2** reduce or remove the irrationality in (a person). □□ **demystification** /-fikáysh'n/ *n.*

demythologize /deemithólləjīz/ *v.tr.* (also **-ise**) **1** remove mythical elements from (a legend, famous person's life, etc.). **2** reinterpret what some consider to be the mythological elements in (the Bible).

den /den/ *n.* **1** a wild animal's lair. **2** a place of crime or vice (*den of iniquity; opium den*). **3** a small private room for pursuing a hobby etc. [OE *denn* f. Gmc, rel. to DEAN[2]]
■ **1** see LAIR *n.* 1a. **3** see SANCTUM 2.

denarius /dináiriəss/ *n.* (*pl.* **denarii** /-ri-ī/) an ancient Roman silver coin. [L, = (coin) of ten asses (as DENARY: see AS[2])]

denary /deenəri/ *adj.* of ten; decimal. □ **denary scale** = *decimal scale.* [L *denarius* containing ten (*deni* by tens)]

denationalize /deenáshənəlīz/ *v.tr.* (also **-ise**) **1** transfer (a nationalized industry or institution etc.) from public to private ownership. **2 a** deprive (a nation) of its status or characteristics as a nation. **b** deprive (a person) of nationality or national characteristics. □□ **denationalization** /-záysh'n/ *n.* [F *dénationaliser* (as DE-, NATIONAL)]

denaturalize /deenáchərəlīz/ *v.tr.* (also **-ise**) **1** change the nature or properties of; make unnatural. **2** deprive of the rights of citizenship. **3** = DENATURE *v.* 1. □□ **denaturalization** /-záysh'n/ *n.*

denature /deenáychər/ *v.tr.* **1** change the properties of (a protein etc.) by heat, acidity, etc. **2** make (alcohol) unfit for drinking esp. by the addition of another substance. □□ **denaturant** *n.* **denaturation** /deenachəráysh'n/ *n.* [F *dénaturer* (as DE-, NATURE)]

dendrite /déndrīt/ *n.* **1 a** a stone or mineral with natural treelike or mosslike markings. **b** such marks on stones or minerals. **2** *Chem.* a crystal with branching treelike growth. **3** *Zool.* & *Anat.* a branching process of a nerve-cell conducting signals to a cell body. [F f. Gk *dendritēs* (adj.) f. *dendron* tree]

dendritic /dendríttik/ *adj.* **1** of or like a dendrite. **2** treelike in shape or markings. □□ **dendritically** *adv.*

dendrochronology /déndrōkrənólləji/ *n.* **1** a system of dating using the characteristic patterns of annual growth rings of trees to assign dates to timber. **2** the study of these growth rings. □□ **dendrochronological** /-krónnəlójik'l/ *adj.* **dendrochronologist** *n.* [Gk *dendron* tree + CHRONOLOGY]

dendroid /déndroyd/ *adj.* tree-shaped. [Gk *dendrōdēs* treelike + -OID]

dendrology /dendrólləji/ *n.* the scientific study of trees. □□ **dendrological** /-drəlójik'l/ *adj.* **dendrologist** *n.* [Gk *dendron* tree + -LOGY]

dene[1] /deen/ *n.* (also **dean**) *Brit.* **1** a narrow wooded valley. **2** a vale (esp. as the ending of place-names). [OE *denu*, rel. to DEN]

dene[2] /deen/ *n. Brit.* a bare sandy tract, or a low sand-hill, by the sea. [orig. unkn.: cf. DUNE]

dengue /déngi/ *n.* an infectious viral disease of the tropics causing a fever and acute pains in the joints. [W. Ind. Sp., f. Swahili *denga, dinga*, with assim. to Sp. *dengue* fastidiousness, with ref. to the stiffness of the patient's neck and shoulders]

deniable /dinī́əb'l/ *adj.* that may be denied. □□ **deniability** *n.*

denial /dinī́əl/ *n.* **1** the act or an instance of denying. **2** a refusal of a request or wish. **3** a statement that a thing is not true; a rejection (*denial of the accusation*). **4** a disavowal of a person as one's leader etc. **5** = SELF-DENIAL.
■ **1** contradiction, negation, repudiation, refutation, disavowal, disclaimer, disaffirmation. **2** refusal, rejection, rebuff. **3** rejection, repudiation, *démenti*; renunciation, retraction, recantation, negation, withdrawal.

denier /dényər/ *n.* a unit of weight by which the fineness of silk, rayon, or nylon yarn is measured. [orig. the name of a small coin: ME f. OF f. L *denarius*]

denigrate /dénnigrayt/ *v.tr.* defame or disparage the reputation of (a person); blacken. □□ **denigration** /-gráysh'n/ *n.* **denigrator** *n.* **denigratory** /-gráytəri/ *adj.* [L *denigrare* (as DE-, *nigrare* f. *niger* black)]
■ see VILIFY.

denim /dénnim/ *n.* **1** (often *attrib.*) a usu. blue hard-wearing cotton twill fabric used for jeans, overalls, etc. (*a denim skirt*). **2** (in *pl.*) *colloq.* jeans, overalls, etc. made of this. [for *serge de Nim* f. *Nîmes* in S. France]

denitrify /deenī́trifī/ *v.tr.* (**-ies, -ied**) remove the nitrates or nitrites from (soil etc.). □□ **denitrification** /-fikáysh'n/ *n.*

denizen /dénniz'n/ *n.* **1** a foreigner admitted to certain rights in his or her adopted country. **2** a naturalized foreign word, animal, or plant. **3** (usu. foll. by *of*) *poet.* an inhabitant or occupant. □□ **denizenship** *n.* [ME f. AF *deinzein* f. OF *deinz* within f. L *de* from + *intus* within + *-ein* f. L *-aneus*: see -ANEOUS]
■ **1** see ALIEN *n.* 1. **3** inhabitant, dweller, occupant, frequenter, resident.

denominate /dinómminayt/ *v.tr.* **1** give a name to. **2** call or describe (a person or thing) as. [L *denominare* (as DE-, NOMINATE)]
■ see CALL *v.* 7.

denomination /dinómmináysh'n/ *n.* **1** a Church or religious sect. **2** a class of units within a range or sequence of numbers, weights, money, etc. (*money of small denominations*). **3 a** a name or designation, esp. a characteristic or class name. **b** a class or kind having a specific name. **4** the rank of a playing-card within a suit, or of a suit relative to others. □ **denominational education** education according to the principles of a Church or sect. □□ **denominational** *adj.* [ME f. OF *denomination* or L *denominatio* (as DENOMINATE)]
■ **1** sect, persuasion, school, church, order. **2** unit, size, value; see also CLASS *n.* 1. **3 a** designation, name, identification, style, title, tag, term, *formal* appellation. **b** sort, kind, type, nature, variety; grade, class, genus, species, order, classification.

denominative /dinómminətiv/ *adj.* serving as or giving a name. [LL *denominativus* (as DENOMINATION)]

denominator /dinómminaytər/ *n. Math.* the number below the line in a vulgar fraction; a divisor. ▫ **common denominator 1** a common multiple of the denominators of several fractions. **2** a common feature of members of a group. **least** (or **lowest**) **common denominator** the lowest common multiple as above. [F *dénominateur* or med.L *denominator* (as DE-, NOMINATE)]

de nos jours /də nō zhoór/ *adj.* (placed after noun) of the present time. [F, = of our days]
■ latter-day, contemporary, modern.

denote /dinṓt/ *v.tr.* **1** be a sign of; indicate (*the arrow denotes direction*). **2** (usu. foll. by *that* + clause) mean, convey. **3** stand as a name for; signify. ▫▫ **denotation** /deénətáysh'n/ *n.* **denotative** /-tətiv/ *adj.* [F *dénoter* or f. L *denotare* (as DE-, *notare* mark f. *nota* NOTE)]
■ **1** specify, signify, mark; see also INDICATE 2. **2** mean, convey. **3** name, symbolize, represent, betoken, signify.

denouement /daynoṓmon/ *n.* (also **dénouement**) **1** the final unravelling of a plot or complicated situation. **2** the final scene in a play, novel, etc., in which the plot is resolved. [F *dénouement* f. *dénouer* unknot (as DE-, L *nodare* f. *nodus* knot)]

denounce /dinównss/ *v.tr.* **1** accuse publicly; condemn (*denounced him as a traitor*). **2** inform against (*denounced her to the police*). **3** give notice of the termination of (an armistice, treaty, etc.). ▫▫ **denouncement** *n.* **denouncer** *n.* [ME f. OF *denoncier* f. L *denuntiare* (as DE-, *nuntiare* make known f. *nuntius* messenger)]
■ **1** accuse, brand, stigmatize, charge, blame, incriminate, implicate, complain about; criticize, condemn, decry, denunciate, attack, assail, censure, impugn, declaim *or* rail (against), vituperate, revile, vilify, inveigh against; (hold up to) shame, pillory, (heap) scorn (upon), cast a slur on. **2** betray, report, reveal, *archaic* delate; see also INFORM 2. ▫▫ **denouncement** see ACCUSATION.

de nouveau /də noōvṓ/ *adv.* starting again; anew. [F]

de novo /dee nṓvō, day/ *adv.* starting again; anew. [L]

dense /denss/ *adj.* **1** closely compacted in substance; thick (*dense fog*). **2** crowded together (*the population is less dense on the outskirts*). **3** *colloq.* stupid. ▫▫ **densely** *adv.* **denseness** *n.* [F *dense* or L *densus*]
■ **1** compact, thick, compressed, condensed, close, solid, heavy, impenetrable. **2** crowded, packed, tight, congested, teeming, populous, jammed, crammed. **3** slow, slow-witted, thickheaded, dull, thick-witted, obtuse, *colloq.* thick, dim, dim-witted, *esp. US colloq.* dumb; see also STUPID *adj.* 1, 5.

densitometer /dénsitómmitər/ *n.* an instrument for measuring the photographic density of an image on a film or photographic print.

density /dénsiti/ *n.* (*pl.* **-ies**) **1** the degree of compactness of a substance. **2** *Physics* degree of consistency measured by the quantity of mass per unit volume. **3** the opacity of a photographic image. **4** a crowded state. **5** stupidity. [F *densité* or L *densitas* (as DENSE)]
■ **1** see BODY *n.* 8.

dent /dent/ *n.* & *v.* ● *n.* **1** a slight mark or hollow in a surface made by, or as if by, a blow with a hammer etc. **2** a noticeable effect (*lunch made a dent in our funds*). ● *v.tr.* **1** mark with a dent. **2** have (esp. an adverse) effect on (*the news dented our hopes*). [ME, prob. f INDENT[1]]
■ *n.* **1** see IMPRESSION 4. ● *v.* **1** see MARK[1] *v.* 1a.

dental /dént'l/ *adj.* **1** of the teeth; of or relating to dentistry. **2** *Phonet.* (of a consonant) produced with the tongue-tip against the upper front teeth (as *th*) or the ridge of the teeth (as *n*, *s*, *t*). ▫ **dental floss** a thread of floss silk etc. used to clean between the teeth. **dental mechanic** a person who makes and repairs artificial teeth. **dental surgeon** a dentist. ▫▫ **dentalize** *v.tr.* (also **-ise**). [LL *dentalis* f. L *dens dentis* tooth]

dentalium /dentáyliəm/ *n.* (*pl.* **dentalia** /-liə/) **1** any marine mollusc of the genus *Dentalium*, having a conical foot protruding from a tusklike shell. **2** this shell used as an ornament or as a form of currency. [mod.L f. LL *dentalis*: *see* DENTAL]

dentate /déntayt/ *adj. Bot.* & *Zool.* toothed; with toothlike notches; serrated. [L *dentatus* f. *dens dentis* tooth]
■ see *notched* (NOTCH).

denticle /déntik'l/ *n. Zool.* a small tooth or toothlike projection, scale, etc. ▫▫ **denticulate** /dentíkyoolət/ *adj.* [ME f. L *denticulus* dimin. of *dens dentis* tooth]

dentifrice /déntifriss/ *n.* a paste or powder for cleaning the teeth. [F f. L *dentifricium* f. *dens dentis* tooth + *fricare* rub]

dentil /déntil/ *n. Archit.* each of a series of small rectangular blocks as a decoration under the moulding of a cornice in classical architecture. [obs. F *dentille* dimin. of *dent* tooth f. L *dens dentis*]

dentilingual /déntilínggwəl/ *adj. Phonet.* formed by the teeth and the tongue.

dentine /dénteen/ *n.* (*US* **dentin** /-tin/) a hard dense bony tissue forming the bulk of a tooth. ▫▫ **dentinal** /déntin'l/ *adj.* [L *dens dentis* tooth + -INE[4]]

dentist /déntist/ *n.* a person who is qualified to treat the diseases and conditions that affect the mouth, jaws, teeth, and their supporting tissues, esp. the repair and extraction of teeth and the insertion of artificial ones. ▫▫ **dentistry** *n.* [F *dentiste* f. *dent* tooth]

dentition /dentísh'n/ *n.* **1** the type, number, and arrangement of teeth in a species etc. **2** the cutting of teeth; teething. [L *dentitio* f. *dentire* to teethe]

denture /dénchər/ *n.* a removable artificial replacement for one or more teeth carried on a removable plate or frame. [F f. *dent* tooth]

denuclearize /deenyoókliərīz/ *v.tr.* (also **-ise**) remove nuclear armaments from (a country etc.). ▫▫ **denuclearization** /-záysh'n/ *n.*

denude /dinyoód/ *v.tr.* **1** make naked or bare. **2** (foll. by *of*) **a** strip of clothing, a covering, etc. **b** deprive of a possession or attribute. **3** *Geol.* lay (rock or a formation etc.) bare by removing what lies above. ▫▫ **denudation** /deényoodáysh'n/ *n.* **denudative** /-dətiv/ *adj.* [L *denudare* (as DE-, *nudus* naked)]
■ **1** see BARE *v.* 1.

denumerable /dinyoómərəb'l/ *adj. Math.* countable by correspondence with the infinite set of integers. ▫▫ **denumerability** /-bílliti/ *n.* **denumerably** *adv.* [LL *denumerare* (as DE-, *numerare* NUMBER)]

denunciation /dinúnsiáysh'n/ *n.* **1** the act of denouncing (a person, policy, etc.); public condemnation. **2** an instance of this. ▫▫ **denunciate** /-siayt/ *v.tr.* **denunciative** /-siətiv/ *adj.* **denunciator** /-siaytər/ *n.* **denunciatory** /-siətəri/ *adj.* [F *dénonciation* or L *denunciatio* (as DENOUNCE)]
■ see ACCUSATION.

deny /dinī́/ *v.tr.* (**-ies, -ied**) **1** declare untrue or non-existent (*denied the charge*; *denied that it is so*; *denied having lied*). **2** repudiate or disclaim (*denied his faith*; *denied his signature*). **3** (often foll. by *to*) refuse (a person or thing, or something to a person) (*this was denied to me*; *denied him the satisfaction*). **4** refuse access to (a person sought) (*denied him his son*). ▫ **deny oneself** be abstinent. ▫▫ **denier** *n.* [ME f. OF *denier* f. L *denegare* (as DE-, *negare* say no)]
■ **1** contradict, controvert, disaffirm, disclaim, dispute, challenge, *archaic or literary* gainsay; negate, rebut, confute, *disp.* refute. **2** disavow, repudiate, renounce, disown, forswear, disclaim. **3** reject, refuse, withhold, forbid, turn down, decline, disallow; recall, revoke, recant.

deoch an doris /dókh ən dórriss, dók/ *n.* (also **doch an dorris**) *Sc.* & *Ir.* a drink taken at parting; a stirrup-cup. [Gael. *deoch an doruis* drink at the door]

deodar /deéədaar/ *n.* the Himalayan cedar *Cedrus deodara*, the tallest of the cedar family, with drooping branches bearing large barrel-shaped cones. [Hindi *dē' odār* f. Skr. *deva-dāru* divine tree]

deodorant /dee-ṓdərənt/ *n.* (often *attrib.*) a substance sprayed or rubbed on to the body or sprayed into the air to remove or conceal unpleasant smells (*a roll-on deodorant; has a deodorant effect*). [as DEODORIZE + -ANT]

deodorize /dee-ṓdərīz/ *v.tr.* (also **-ise**) remove or destroy the (usu. unpleasant) smell of. ◻◻ **deodorization** /-záysh'n/ *n.* **deodorizer** *n.* [DE- + L *odor* smell]

▪ see FRESHEN 1.

Deo gratias /dáyō gráatiəss, gráashiəss/ *int.* thanks be to God. [L, = (we give) thanks to God]

deontic /dee-óntik/ *adj. Philos.* of or relating to duty and obligation as ethical concepts. [Gk *deont-* part. stem of *dei* it is right]

deontology /dee-ontólləji/ *n. Philos.* the study of duty. ◻◻ **deontological** /-təlójik'l/ *adj.* **deontologist** *n.*

Deo volente /dáyō vəléntay/ *adv.* God willing; if nothing prevents it. [L]

deoxygenate /dee-óksijənayt/ *v.tr.* remove oxygen, esp. free oxygen, from. ◻◻ **deoxygenation** /-náysh'n/ *n.*

deoxyribonucleic acid /dee-oksirībōnyookláyik/ *n.* see DNA. [DE- + OXYGEN + RIBONUCLEIC (ACID)]

dep. *abbr.* **1** departs. **2** deputy.

depart /dipaárt/ *v.* **1** *intr.* **a** (usu. foll. by *from*) go away; leave (*the train departs from this platform*). **b** (usu. foll. by *for*) start; set out (*trains depart for Crewe every hour*). **2** *intr.* (usu. foll. by *from*) diverge; deviate (*departs from standard practice*). **3 a** *intr.* leave by death; die. **b** *tr. formal* or *literary* leave by death (*departed this life*). [ME f. OF *departir* ult. f. L *dispertire* divide]

▪ **1** go, go away *or* out *or* off, leave, walk off, exit, set out *or* forth *or* off, start; take one's leave, check out, retire, retreat, withdraw. **2** deviate, diverge, turn (aside *or* away), differ, vary, break away, stray, veer; (*depart from*) leave, abandon. **3 a** see DIE[1] 1.

departed /dipaártid/ *adj.* & *n.* ● *adj.* bygone (*departed greatness*). ● *n.* (prec. by *the*) *euphem.* a particular dead person or dead people (*we are here to mourn the departed*).

department /dipaártmənt/ *n.* **1** a separate part of a complex whole, esp.: **a** a branch of municipal or State administration (*Housing Department; Department of Social Security*). **b** a branch of study and its administration at a university, school, etc. (*the physics department*). **c** a specialized section of a large store (*hardware department*). **2** *colloq.* an area of special expertise. **3** an administrative district in France and other countries. ◻ **department store** a large shop stocking many varieties of goods in different departments. [F *département* (as DEPART)]

▪ **1 a** division, subdivision, branch, office, bureau, section, segment, unit, part. **2** responsibility, concern, worry, sphere, jurisdiction, domain, control, area *or* sphere of influence *or* activity, *colloq.* thing, *joc.* bailiwick.

departmental /deepaartmént'l/ *adj.* of or belonging to a department. ◻ **departmental store** = *department store*. ◻◻ **departmentalism** *n.* **departmentalize** *v.tr.* (also **-ise**). **departmentalization** /-līzáysh'n/ *n.* **departmentally** *adv.*

departure /dipaárchər/ *n.* **1** the act or an instance of departing. **2** (often foll. by *from*) a deviation (from the truth, a standard, etc.). **3** (often *attrib.*) the starting of a train, an aircraft, etc. (*the departure was late; departure lounge*). **4** a new course of action or thought (*driving a car is rather a departure for him*). **5** *Naut.* the amount of a ship's change of longitude. [OF *departeüre* (as DEPART)]

▪ **1** see EXIT *n.* 2a. **2** see DIVERSION 1. **3** see *take-off* 1.

depasture /deepaáss-chər/ *v.* **1 a** *tr.* (of cattle) graze upon. **b** *intr.* graze. **c** *tr.* put (cattle) to graze. **2** *tr.* (of land) provide pasturage for (cattle). ◻◻ **depasturage** /-chərij/ *n.*

dépaysé /daypáyzay/ *adj.* (*fem.* ***dépaysée*** *pronunc.* same) removed from one's habitual surroundings. [F, = removed from one's own country]

depend /dipénd/ *v.intr.* **1** (often foll. by *on, upon*) be controlled or determined by (*success depends on hard work; it depends on whether they agree; it depends how you tackle the problem*). **2** (foll. by *on, upon*) **a** be unable to do without (*depends on her mother*). **b** rely on (*I'm depending on you to come*). **3** (foll. by *on, upon*) be grammatically dependent on. **4** (often foll. by *from*) *archaic poet.* hang down. ◻ **depend upon it!** you may be sure! **it** (or **it all** or **that**) **depends** expressing uncertainty or qualification in answering a question (*Will they come? It depends*). [ME f. OF *dependre* ult. f. L *dependēre* (as DE-, *pendēre* hang)]

▪ **1** (*depend on* or *upon*) be contingent *or* dependent *or* conditional on, turn on, hinge on, pivot on, hang on, be subject to, rest on, be influenced *or* determined *or* conditioned *or* controlled by. **2 b** (*depend on* or *upon*) trust (in), rely on, count on, reckon on, bank on, put one's faith *or* trust in. **4** hang down, be suspended.

dependable /dipéndəb'l/ *adj.* reliable. ◻◻ **dependability** /-bílliti/ *n.* **dependableness** *n.* **dependably** *adv.*

▪ see RELIABLE.

dependant /dipéndənt/ *n.* (*US* **dependent**) **1** a person who relies on another esp. for financial support. **2** a servant. [F *dépendant* pres. part. of *dépendre* (as DEPEND)]

▪ **1** see WARD *n.* 3.

dependence /dipéndənss/ *n.* **1** the state of being dependent, esp. on financial or other support. **2** reliance; trust; confidence (*shows great dependence on his judgement*). [F *dépendance* (as DEPEND)]

▪ **2** see TRUST *n.* 1, 5.

dependency /dipéndənsi/ *n.* (*pl.* **-ies**) **1** a country or province controlled by another. **2** anything subordinate or dependent.

▪ **1** see PROVINCE 1.

dependent /dipéndənt/ *adj.* & *n.* ● *adj.* **1** (usu. foll. by *on*) depending, conditional, or subordinate. **2** unable to do without (esp. a drug). **3** maintained at another's cost. **4** *Math.* (of a variable) having a value determined by that of another variable. **5** *Gram.* (of a clause, phrase, or word) subordinate to a sentence or word. ● *n. US* var. of DEPENDANT. ◻◻ **dependently** *adv.* [ME, earlier *-ant* = DEPENDANT]

depersonalization /deepérsənəlīzáysh'n/ *n.* (also **-isation**) esp. *Psychol.* the loss of one's sense of identity.

depersonalize /deepérsənəlīz/ *v.tr.* (also **-ise**) **1** make impersonal. **2** deprive of personality.

depict /dipíkt/ *v.tr.* **1** represent in a drawing or painting etc. **2** portray in words; describe (*the play depicts him as vain and petty*). ◻◻ **depicter** *n.* **depiction** /-píksh'n/ *n.* **depictive** *adj.* **depictor** *n.* [L *depingere depict-* (as DE-, *pingere* paint)]

▪ **2** see CHARACTERIZE 1, 2.

depilate /déppilayt/ *v.tr.* remove the hair from. ◻◻ **depilation** /-láysh'n/ *n.* [L *depilare* (as DE-, *pilare* f. *pilus* hair)]

depilatory /dipíllətəri, -tri/ *adj.* & *n.* ● *adj.* that removes unwanted hair. ● *n.* (*pl.* **-ies**) a depilatory substance.

deplane /deepláyn/ *v.* esp. *US* **1** *intr.* disembark from an aeroplane. **2** *tr.* remove from an aeroplane.

deplete /dipleét/ *v.tr.* (esp. in *passive*) **1** reduce in numbers or quantity (*depleted forces*). **2** empty out; exhaust (*their energies were depleted*). ◻◻ **depletion** /-pleésh'n/ *n.* [L *deplēre* (as DE-, *plēre plet-* fill)]

▪ **1** see DIMINISH 1. **2** see CONSUME 4.

deplorable /diplórəb'l/ *adj.* **1** exceedingly bad (*a deplorable meal*). **2** that can be deplored. ◻◻ **deplorably** *adv.*

▪ **1** bad, execrable, *colloq.* terrible, dreadful, abominable, appalling; see also AWFUL 1a, b. **2** shameful, disgraceful, scandalous, reprehensible, lamentable, regrettable.

deplore /diplór/ *v.tr.* **1** grieve over; regret. **2** be scandalized by; find exceedingly bad. ◻◻ **deploringly** *adv.* [F *déplorer* or It. *deplorare* f. L *deplorare* (as DE-, *plorare* bewail)]

▪ **1** see MOURN. **2** see DISAPPROVE.

deploy /diplóy/ *v.* **1** *Mil.* **a** *tr.* cause (troops) to spread out from a column into a line. **b** *intr.* (of troops) spread out in this way. **2** *tr.* bring (arguments, forces, etc.) into effective action. ◻◻ **deployment** *n.* [F *déployer* f. L *displicare* (as DIS-, *plicare* fold) & LL *deplicare* explain]

■ **1** see *draw up* 2.

deplume /deeplóóm/ *v.tr.* **1** strip of feathers, pluck. **2** deprive of honours etc. [ME f. F *déplumer* or f. med.L *deplumare* (as DE-, L *pluma* feather)]

depolarize /deepṓlərīz/ *v.tr.* (also **-ise**) *Physics* reduce or remove the polarization of. □□ **depolarization** /-záysh'n/ *n.*

depoliticize /deépəlíttisīz/ *v.tr.* (also **-ise**) **1** make (a person, an organization, etc.) non-political. **2** remove from political activity or influence. □□ **depoliticization** /-záysh'n/ *n.*

depolymerize /deepóllimərīz/ *v.tr.* & *intr.* (also **-ise**) *Chem.* break down into monomers or other smaller units. □□ **depolymerization** /-záysh'n/ *n.*

deponent /dipṓnənt/ *adj.* & *n.* ● *adj. Gram.* (of a verb, esp. in Latin or Greek) passive or middle in form but active in meaning. ● *n.* **1** *Gram.* a deponent verb. **2** *Law* **a** a person making a deposition under oath. **b** a witness giving written testimony for use in court etc. [L *deponere* (as DE-, *ponere posit-* place): adj. from the notion that the verb had laid aside the passive sense]

depopulate /deepópyoolayt/ *v.* **1** *tr.* reduce the population of. **2** *intr.* decline in population. □□ **depopulation** /-láysh'n/ *n.* [L *depopulari* (as DE-, *populari* lay waste f. *populus* people)]

■ **1** see DESOLATE *v.* 1.

deport /dipórt/ *v.tr.* **1 a** remove (an immigrant or foreigner) forcibly to another country; banish. **b** exile (a native) to another country. **2** *refl.* conduct (oneself) or behave (in a specified manner) (*deported himself well*). □□ **deportable** *adj.* **deportation** /deéportáysh'n/ *n.* [OF *deporter* and (sense 1) F *déporter* (as DE-, L *portare* carry)]

■ **1** see BANISH 1. **2** (*deport oneself*) see ACT *v.* 1.

deportee /deéporteé/ *n.* a person who has been or is being deported.

■ see EXILE *n.* 3.

deportment /dipórtmənt/ *n.* bearing, demeanour, or manners, esp. of a cultivated kind. [F *déportement* (as DEPORT)]

■ see CONDUCT *n.* 1.

depose /dipṓz/ *v.* **1** *tr.* remove from office, esp. dethrone. **2** *intr. Law* (usu. foll. by *to*, or *that* + clause) bear witness, esp. on oath in court. [ME f. OF *deposer* after L *deponere*: see DEPONENT, POSE[1]]

■ **1** see OVERTHROW *v.* **2** see ATTEST 1, 3.

deposit /dipózzit/ *n.* & *v.* ● *n.* **1 a** *Brit.* a sum of money kept in an account in a bank. **b** anything stored or entrusted for safe keeping, usu. in a bank. **2 a** a sum payable as a first instalment on an item bought on hire purchase, or as a pledge for a contract. **b** a returnable sum payable on the short-term hire of a car, boat, etc. **3 a** a natural layer of sand, rock, coal, etc. **b** a layer of precipitated matter on a surface, e.g. fur on a kettle. ● *v.tr.* (**deposited, depositing**) **1 a** put or lay down in a (usu. specified) place (*deposited the book on the floor*). **b** (of water, wind, etc.) leave (matter etc.) lying in a displaced position. **2 a** store or entrust for keeping. **b** pay (a sum of money) into a bank account, esp. a deposit account. **3** pay (a sum) as a first instalment or as a pledge for a contract. □ **deposit account** *Brit.* a bank account that pays interest but from which money cannot usu. be withdrawn without notice or loss of interest. **on deposit** (of money) placed in a deposit account. [L *depositum* (n.), med.L *depositare* f. L *deponere deposit-* (as DEPONENT)]

■ *n.* **2 a** down payment, part *or* partial payment, advance payment; see also EARNEST[2] 1. **3** sediment, accumulation, deposition, alluvium, *Chem.* precipitate. ● *v.* **1 a** place, leave, set *or* lay (down); see also PUT[1] *v.* 1. **2** entrust, leave, lodge, consign, keep, place, put; store, save, set *or* put aside, bank, lay *or* put away, pay in, stow, *colloq.* stash (away).

depositary /dipózzitəri, -tri/ *n.* (*pl.* **-ies**) a person to whom something is entrusted; a trustee. [LL *depositarius* (as DEPOSIT)]

deposition /deépəzísh'n, dép-/ *n.* **1** the act or an instance of deposing, esp. a monarch; dethronement. **2** *Law* **a** the process of giving sworn evidence; allegation. **b** an instance of this. **c** evidence given under oath; a testimony. **3** the act or an instance of depositing. **4** (**the Deposition**) **a** the taking down of the body of Christ from the Cross. **b** a representation of this. [ME f. OF f. L *depositio -onis* f. *deponere*: see DEPOSIT]

■ **1** see REMOVAL 3a. **2** see ALLEGATION, TESTIMONY 1, 2.

depositor /dipózzitər/ *n.* a person who deposits money, property, etc.

depository /dipózzitəri, -tri/ *n.* (*pl.* **-ies**) **1 a** a storehouse for furniture etc. **b** a store (of wisdom, knowledge, etc.) (*the book is a depository of wit*). **2** = DEPOSITARY. [LL *depositorium* (as DEPOSIT)]

■ **1 a** see STOREHOUSE. **b** see MINE[2] *n.* 2.

depot /déppō/ *n.* **1** a storehouse. **2** *Mil.* **a** a storehouse for equipment etc. **b** the headquarters of a regiment. **3 a** a building for the servicing, parking, etc. of esp. buses, trains, or goods vehicles. **b** *US* a railway or bus station. [F *dépôt*, OF *depost* f. L (as DEPOSIT)]

■ **1** see WAREHOUSE *n.* **2 b** see BASE[1] *n.* 3. **3** workshop, machine shop; see also STATION *n.* 1.

deprave /dipráyv/ *v.tr.* pervert or corrupt, esp. morally. □□ **depravation** /déprəváysh'n/ *n.* [ME f. OF *depraver* or L *depravare* (as DE-, *pravare* f. *pravus* crooked)]

■ see CORRUPT *v.* 1.

depravity /diprávviti/ *n.* (*pl.* **-ies**) **1 a** moral corruption; wickedness. **b** an instance of this; a wicked act. **2** *Theol.* the innate corruptness of human nature. [DE- + obs. *pravity* f. L *pravitas* (as DEPRAVE)]

■ **1** see VICE[1] 1, 2.

deprecate /déprikayt/ *v.tr.* **1** express disapproval of or a wish against; deplore (*deprecate hasty action*). ¶ Often confused with *depreciate*. **2** plead earnestly against. **3** *archaic* pray against. □□ **deprecatingly** *adv.* **deprecation** /-káysh'n/ *n.* **deprecative** /déprikətiv/ *adj.* **deprecator** *n.* **deprecatory** /-káytəri/ *adj.* [L *deprecari* (as DE-, *precari* pray)]

■ **1** see DISAPPROVE. **2** see IMPEACH 3.

depreciate /dipreéshiayt, -siayt/ *v.* **1** *tr.* & *intr.* diminish in value (*the car has depreciated*). **2** *tr.* disparage; belittle (*they are always depreciating his taste*). **3** *tr.* reduce the purchasing power of (money). □□ **depreciatingly** *adv.* **depreciatory** /dipreéshiətəri/ *adj.* [LL *depretiare* (as DE-, *pretiare* f. *pretium* price)]

■ **1** devalue, lessen, reduce, bring down, lower, depress, cheapen, mark down; go down, decrease, diminish. **2** disparage, deride, decry, underrate, undervalue, underestimate, minimize, belittle, slight, deprecate, discredit, denigrate, run down, play down, talk down from, *formal* derogate.

depreciation /dipreéshiáysh'n, -siáysh'n/ *n.* **1** the amount of wear and tear (of a property etc.) for which a reduction may be made in a valuation, an estimate, or a balance sheet. **2** *Econ.* a decrease in the value of a currency. **3** the act or an instance of depreciating; belittlement.

■ **2** see SLUMP *n.* **3** see MOCKERY 1a, *humiliation* (HUMILIATE).

depredation /dépridáysh'n/ *n.* (usu. in *pl.*) **1** despoiling, ravaging, or plundering. **2** an instance or instances of this. [F *déprédation* f. LL *depraedatio* (as DE-, *praedatio -onis* f. L *praedari* plunder)]

■ plunder, plundering, pillage, pillaging, despoliation, despoiling, ravaging, sacking, laying waste, devastation, destruction; ransacking, robbery, looting; ravages.

depredator /dépridaytər/ *n.* a despoiler or pillager. □□ **depredatory** /dépridaytəri, diprédditəri, -tri/ *adj.* [LL *depraedator* (as DEPREDATION)]

depress /diprés/ *v.tr.* **1** push or pull down; lower (*depressed the lever*). **2** make dispirited or dejected. **3** *Econ.* reduce the activity of (esp. trade). **4** (as **depressed** *adj.*) **a** dispirited or miserable. **b** *Psychol.* suffering from depression. □ **depressed area** an area suffering from economic depression. □□ **depressible** *adj.* **depressing** *adj.* **depressingly**

adv. [ME f. OF *depresser* f. LL *depressare* (as DE-, *pressare* frequent. of *premere* press)]
■ **1** press (down), push *or* pull down (on), push, pull, lower. **2** deject, dispirit, oppress, sadden, grieve, cast down, bring down, dishearten, discourage, dampen, cast a gloom *or* pall over, burden, weigh down. **3** weaken, dull, sap; depreciate; lower, bring down, reduce. **4 a** (**depressed**) see MISERABLE 1. □□ **depressing** see OPPRESSIVE 1, 2; SAD 2.

depressant /diprés'nt/ *adj.* & *n.* ● *adj.* **1** that depresses. **2** *Med.* sedative. ● *n.* **1** *Med.* an agent, esp. a drug, that sedates. **2** an influence that depresses.
■ *n.* **1** see SEDATIVE *n.*

depression /dipresh'n/ *n.* **1 a** *Psychol.* a state of extreme dejection or morbidly excessive melancholy; a mood of hopelessness and feelings of inadequacy, often with physical symptoms. **b** a reduction in vitality, vigour, or spirits. **2 a** a long period of financial and industrial decline; a slump. **b** (**the Depression**) the depression of 1929–34. **3** *Meteorol.* a lowering of atmospheric pressure, esp. the centre of a region of minimum pressure or the system of winds round it. **4** a sunken place or hollow on a surface. **5 a** a lowering or sinking (often foll. by *of*: *depression of freezing-point*). **b** pressing down. **6** *Astron.* & *Geog.* the angular distance of an object below the horizon or a horizontal plane. [ME f. OF or L *depressio* (as DE-, *premere press-* press)]
■ **1 b** dejection, despair, gloom, downheartedness, sadness, melancholy, discouragement, despondency, gloominess, glumness, the blues, unhappiness; see also MELANCHOLY *n.* **2 a** recession, slump, (economic) decline, downturn. **3** low-pressure area, cyclone, col. **4** indentation, dent, dimple, impression, pit, hollow, recess, cavity, concavity, dip.

depressive /diprésiv/ *adj.* & *n.* ● *adj.* **1** tending to depress. **2** *Psychol.* involving or characterized by depression. ● *n.* *Psychol.* a person suffering or with a tendency to suffer from depression. [F *dépressif -ive* or med.L *depressivus* (as DEPRESSION)]

depressor /diprésser/ *n.* **1** *Anat.* **a** (in full **depressor muscle**) a muscle that causes the lowering of some part of the body. **b** a nerve that lowers blood pressure. **2** *Surgery* an instrument for pressing down an organ etc. [L (as DEPRESSION)]

depressurize /deeprésherīz/ *v.tr.* (also **-ise**) cause an appreciable drop in the pressure of the gas inside (a container), esp. to the ambient level. □□ **depressurization** /-záysh'n/ *n.*

deprivation /déprivàysh'n, deeprī-/ *n.* **1** (usu. foll. by *of*) the act or an instance of depriving; the state of being deprived (*deprivation of liberty*; *suffered many deprivations*). **2 a** deposition from esp. an ecclesiastical office. **b** an instance of this. [med.L *deprivatio* (as DEPRIVE)]
■ **1** see PRIVATION 1.

deprive /diprīv/ *v.tr.* **1** (usu. foll. by *of*) strip, dispossess; debar from enjoying (*illness deprived him of success*). **2** (as **deprived** *adj.*) **a** (of a child etc.) suffering from the effects of a poor or loveless home. **b** (of an area) with inadequate housing, facilities, employment, etc. **3** *archaic* depose (esp. a clergyman) from office. □□ **deprivable** *adj.* **deprival** *n.* [ME f. OF *depriver* f. med.L *deprivare* (as DE-, L *privare* deprive)]
■ **1** deny, refuse; strip, dispossess, debar; mulct; see also DIVEST 2. **2** (**deprived**) needy, in want, in need, impoverished, badly off, destitute, poor, poverty-stricken, underprivileged, disadvantaged.

de profundis /dáy prəfoondiss/ *adv.* & *n.* ● *adv.* from the depths (of sorrow etc.). ● *n.* a cry from the depths. [opening L words of Ps. 130]

Dept. *abbr.* Department.

depth /depth/ *n.* **1 a** deepness (*the depth is not great at the edge*). **b** the measurement from the top down, from the surface inwards, or from the front to the back (*depth of the drawer is 12 inches*). **2** difficulty; abstruseness. **3 a** sagacity; wisdom. **b** intensity of emotion etc. (*the poem has little depth*). **4** an intensity of colour, darkness, etc. **5** (in *pl.*) **a** deep water, a deep place; an abyss. **b** a low, depressed state. **c** the lowest or inmost part (*the depths of the country*). **6** the middle (*in the depth of winter*). □ **depth-bomb** (or **-charge**) a bomb capable of exploding under water, esp. for dropping on a submerged submarine etc. **depth psychology** psychoanalysis to reveal hidden motives etc. **in depth** comprehensively, thoroughly, or profoundly. **in-depth** *adj.* thorough; done in depth. **out of one's depth 1** in water over one's head. **2** engaged in a task or on a subject too difficult for one. [ME (as DEEP, -TH[2])]
■ **1** deepness, profundity, profoundness; see also MEASUREMENT 2. **2** difficulty, profundity, profoundness, abstruseness, obscurity, reconditeness, complexity, intricacy. **3 a** profundity, wisdom, sagacity, sageness, understanding, perception, astuteness, perspicacity, perspicaciousness, insight, intuition, acumen, penetration. **b** see INTENSITY 1. **4** intensity, strength, deepness; vividness, brilliance, brilliancy, brightness, richness. **5 a, c** (*depths*) deep(s), abyss, chasm, bowels of the earth, (bottomless) pit, nethermost reaches *or* regions, nadir. **6** see MIDDLE *n.* 1. □ **in depth** thoroughly, comprehensively, in detail, profoundly, deeply, extensively, intensively, concentratedly, probingly. **in-depth** see THOROUGH 1.

depthless /dépthliss/ *adj.* **1** extremely deep; fathomless. **2** shallow, superficial.

depurate /dépyoorayt/ *v.tr.* & *intr.* make or become free from impurities. □□ **depuration** /-ráysh'n/ *n.* **depurative** /dipyóorətiv/ *adj.* & *n.* **depurator** *n.* [med.L *depurare* (as DE-, *purus* pure)]

deputation /dépyootáysh'n/ *n.* a group of people appointed to represent others, usu. for a specific purpose; a delegation. [ME f. LL *deputatio* (as DEPUTE)]
■ see MISSION 3.

depute *v.* & *n.* ● *v.tr.* /dipyóot/ (often foll. by *to*) **1** appoint as a deputy. **2** delegate (a task, authority, etc.) (*deputed the leadership to her*). ● *n.* /dépyoot/ *Sc.* a deputy. [ME f. OF *deputé* past part. of *deputer* f. L *deputare* regard as, allot (as DE-, *putare* think)]
■ *v.* **2** see DELEGATE *v.* 1.

deputize /dépyootīz/ *v.intr.* (also **-ise**) (usu. foll. by *for*) act as a deputy or understudy.
■ see COVER *v.* 8b.

deputy /dépyooti/ *n.* (*pl.* **-ies**) **1** a person appointed or delegated to act for another or others (also *attrib.*: *deputy manager*). **2** *Polit.* a parliamentary representative in certain countries, e.g. France. **3** a coalmine official responsible for safety. □ **by deputy** by proxy. **Chamber of Deputies** the lower legislative assembly in some parliaments. **deputy lieutenant** *Brit.* the deputy of the Lord Lieutenant of a county. □□ **deputyship** *n.* [ME var. of DEPUTE *n.*]
■ **1** substitute, replacement, surrogate, stand-in, reserve, proxy; agent, operative, representative, go-between, intermediary, spokesperson, spokesman, spokeswoman, delegate, ambassador, minister, emissary, envoy, (papal) nuncio, *Sc.* depute, *esp. US* alternate, *archaic* legate, *Austral. colloq.* offsider.

deracinate /dee-rássinayt/ *v.tr. literary* **1** tear up by the roots. **2** obliterate, expunge. □□ **deracination** /-náysh'n/ *n.* [F *déraciner* (as DE-, *racine* f. LL *radicina* dimin. of *radix* root)]
■ **2** see ABOLISH.

derail /diráyl, dee-/ *v.tr.* (usu. in *passive*) cause (a train etc.) to leave the rails. □□ **derailment** *n.* [F *dérailler* (as DE-, RAIL[1])]

derange /diráynj/ *v.tr.* **1** throw into confusion; disorganize; cause to act irregularly. **2** (esp. as **deranged** *adj.*) make insane (*deranged by the tragic events*). **3** disturb; interrupt. □□ **derangement** *n.* [F *déranger* (as DE-, *rang* RANK[1])]
■ **1** see UPSET *v.* 3. **2** (**deranged**) mad, insane, demented, lunatic, unhinged, unbalanced, berserk, crazy, crazed, psychotic, irrational, *non compos* (*mentis*), out of one's mind *or* senses, of unsound mind, mad as a hatter *or*

March hare, off the rails, *colloq.* touched, mental, crack-brained, not all there, dotty, *sl.* out of one's head *or* skull, cracked, bats, cuckoo, bonkers, dippy, batty, screwy, loony, nuts, nutty, off one's rocker *or* chump, (plumb) loco, *Brit. sl.* potty, barmy.

derate /déé-ráyt/ *v.* **1** *tr.* remove part or all of the burden of rates from. **2** *intr.* diminish or remove rates.

deration /déé-rásh'n/ *v.tr.* free (food etc.) from rationing.

Derby /daárbi/ *n.* (*pl.* **-ies**) **1 a** an annual horse-race run on the flat at Epsom. **b** a similar race elsewhere (*Kentucky Derby*). **2** any important sporting contest. **3** (**derby**) *US* a bowler hat. □ **Derby Day** the day on which the Derby is run. **local Derby** a match between two teams from the same district. [the 12th Earl of *Derby* d. 1834, founder of the horse-race]

deregister /dee-réjistər/ *v.tr.* remove from a register. □□ **deregistration** /-stráysh'n/ *n.*

de règle /də régla/ *predic.adj.* customary; proper. [F, = of rule]

deregulate /dee-régyoolayt/ *v.tr.* remove regulations or restrictions from. □□ **deregulation** /-láysh'n/ *n.*

■ decontrol, derestrict.

derelict /dérrilikt/ *adj.* & *n.* ● *adj.* **1** abandoned, ownerless (esp. of a ship at sea or an empty decrepit property). **2** (esp. of property) ruined; dilapidated. **3** *US* negligent (of duty etc.). ● *n.* **1** a social outcast; a person without a home, a job, or property. **2** abandoned property, esp. a ship. [L *derelictus* past part. of *derelinquere* (as DE-, *relinquere* leave)]

■ *adj.* **1** deserted, abandoned, forsaken, ownerless, neglected. **2** ruined, dilapidated, run-down, tumbledown. **3** negligent, remiss, neglectful, delinquent, dilatory, careless, heedless, lax, slack, irresponsible, slipshod, slovenly, sloppy. ● *n.* **1** vagrant, tramp, outcast, pariah, loafer, wastrel, good-for-nothing, ne'er-do-well, malingerer, vagabond, slacker, down-and-out, *US* hobo, *US sl.* bum.

dereliction /dérrilíksh'n/ *n.* **1** (usu. foll. by *of*) **a** neglect; failure to carry out one's obligations (*dereliction of duty*). **b** an instance of this. **2** the act or an instance of abandoning; the process of being abandoned. **3 a** the retreat of the sea exposing new land. **b** the land so exposed. [L *derelictio* (as DERELICT)]

■ **1** see NEGLECT *n.* 1.

derequisition /dee-rékwizísh'n/ *v.tr.* return (requisitioned property) to its former owner.

derestrict /déé-ristríkt/ *v.tr.* **1** remove restrictions from. **2** remove speed restrictions from (a road, area, etc.). □□ **derestriction** *n.*

deride /diríd/ *v.tr.* laugh scornfully at; mock. □□ **derider** *n.* **deridingly** *adv.* [L *deridēre* (as DE-, *ridēre ris-* laugh)]

■ mock (at), ridicule, scoff at, jeer at, laugh at, make fun *or* sport of, tease, taunt, twit, poke fun at, make a laughing-stock of, sneer at, scorn, flout at, disdain, pooh-pooh, belittle, diminish, disparage, rally, *archaic* hold *or* have in derision, *sl.* knock, take the mickey out of.

de rigueur /də rigṓr/ *predic.adj.* required by custom or etiquette (*evening dress is de rigueur*). [F, = of strictness]

■ see CORRECT *adj.* 2, 3.

derision /dirízh'n/ *n.* ridicule; mockery (*bring into derision*). □ **hold** (or **have**) **in derision** *archaic* mock at. □□ **derisible** /dirízzib'l/ *adj.* [ME f. OF f. LL *derisio -onis* (as DERIDE)]

■ ridicule, mockery, raillery, sarcasm, contempt, scorn, contumely, disrespect, *Austral. or dial.* mullock. □ **hold** (or **have**) **in derision** see DERIDE.

derisive /dirísiv/ *adj.* = DERISORY. □□ **derisively** *adv.* **derisiveness** *n.*

derisory /dirísəri/ *adj.* **1** scoffing; ironical; scornful (*derisory cheers*). **2** so small or unimportant as to be ridiculous (*derisory offer*; *derisory costs*). [LL *derisorius* (as DERISION)]

■ **1** mocking, scoffing, scornful, derisive, disdainful, contemptuous, taunting, insulting, contumelious, jeering; sardonic, sarcastic, ironic, ironical.

derivation /dérriváysh'n/ *n.* **1** the act or an instance of deriving or obtaining from a source; the process of being derived. **2 a** the formation of a word from another word or from a root. **b** a derivative. **c** the tracing of the origin of a word. **d** a statement or account of this. **3** extraction, descent. **4** *Math.* a sequence of statements showing that a formula, theorem, etc., is a consequence of previously accepted statements. □□ **derivational** *adj.* [F *dérivation* or L *derivatio* (as DERIVE)]

■ **2c, d, 3** origin, descent, extraction, source, beginning, foundation, ancestry, genealogy; etymology, root.

derivative /dirívvətiv/ *adj.* & *n.* ● *adj.* derived from another source; not original (*his music is derivative and uninteresting*). ● *n.* **1** something derived from another source, esp.: **a** a word derived from another or from a root (e.g. *quickly* from *quick*). **b** *Chem.* a chemical compound that is derived from another. **2** *Math.* a quantity measuring the rate of change of another. □□ **derivatively** *adv.* [F *dérivatif -ive* f. L *derivativus* (as DERIVE)]

■ *adj.* derived, borrowed, unoriginal, second-hand, copied, imitative, plagiarized, plagiaristic. ● *n.* **1** derivation, development; spin-off, by-product, offshoot.

derive /dirív/ *v.* **1** *tr.* (usu. foll. by *from*) get, obtain, or form (*derived satisfaction from work*). **2** *intr.* (foll. by *from*) arise from, originate in, be descended or obtained from (*happiness derives from many things*). **3** *tr.* gather or deduce (*derived the information from the clues*). **4** *tr.* **a** trace the descent of (a person). **b** show the origin of (a thing). **5** *tr.* (usu. foll. by *from*) show or state the origin or formation of (a word etc.) (*derived the word from Latin*). **6** *tr. Math.* obtain (a function) by differentiation. □□ **derivable** *adj.* [ME f. OF *deriver* or f. L *derivare* (as DE-, *rivus* stream)]

■ **1** draw, extract, get, obtain, acquire, procure, receive, secure, gain, collect, harvest, glean, cull. **2** (*derive from*) arise from *or* out of, originate in *or* with *or* from, emerge from *or* out of, come (forth) from *or* out of, arrive from, issue from, proceed from, develop from, spring from, flow from, emanate from, stem from, be traceable to. **3** elicit, educe, infer, gather; see also DEDUCE.

derm (also **derma**) var. of DERMIS.

dermatitis /dérmətítiss/ *n.* inflammation of the skin. [Gk *derma -atos* skin + -ITIS]

dermatoglyphics /dérmətōglíffiks/ *n.* the science or study of skin markings or patterns, esp. of the fingers, hands, and feet. □□ **dermatoglyphic** *adj.* **dermatoglyphically** *adv.* [as DERMATITIS + Gk *gluphē* carving: see GLYPH]

dermatology /dérmətólləji/ *n.* the study of the diagnosis and treatment of skin disorders. □□ **dermatological** /-təlójik'l/ *adj.* **dermatologist** *n.* [as DERMATITIS + -LOGY]

dermis /dérmiss/ *n.* (also **derm** /derm/ or **derma** /dérmə/) **1** (in general use) the skin. **2** *Anat.* the true skin, the thick layer of living tissue below the epidermis. □□ **dermal** *adj.* **dermic** *adj.* [mod.L, after EPIDERMIS]

dernier cri /dáirniay kréé/ *n.* the very latest fashion. [F, = last cry]

derogate /dérrəgayt/ *v.intr.* (foll. by *from*) *formal* **1 a** take away a part from; detract from (a merit, a right, etc.). **b** disparage. **2** deviate from (correct behaviour etc.). □□ **derogative** /diróggətiv/ *adj.* [L *derogare* (as DE-, *rogare* ask)]

■ **1 a** (*derogate from*) see DETRACT.

derogation /dérrəgáysh'n/ *n.* **1** (foll. by *of*) a lessening or impairment of (a law, authority, position, dignity, etc.). **2** deterioration; debasement. [ME f. F *dérogation* or L *derogatio* (as DEROGATE)]

■ **1** see *impairment* (IMPAIR).

derogatory /diróggətəri, -tri/ *adj.* (often foll. by *to*) involving disparagement or discredit; insulting, depreciatory (*made a derogatory remark*; *derogatory to my position*). □□ **derogatorily** *adv.* [LL *derogatorius* (as DEROGATE)]

■ depreciatory, depreciative, disparaging, uncomplimentary, offensive, insulting, abasing, debasing, denigrating, belittling, demeaning.

derrick /dérrik/ *n.* **1** a kind of crane for moving or lifting heavy weights, having a movable pivoted arm. **2** the framework over an oil well or similar excavation, holding the drilling machinery. [obs. senses *hangman, gallows*, f. the name of a London hangman *c.*1600]

derrière /dérriáir/ *n. colloq. euphem.* the buttocks. [F, = behind]
■ see BUM[1].

derring-do /dérringdóō/ *n. literary joc.* heroic courage or action. [ME, = *daring to do*, misinterpreted by Spenser and by Scott]
■ see DARING *n.*

derringer /dérrinjər/ *n.* a small large-bore pistol. [H. *Deringer*, Amer. inventor d. 1868]

derris /dérriss/ *n.* **1** any woody tropical climbing leguminous plant of the genus *Derris*, bearing leathery pods. **2** an insecticide made from the powdered root of some kinds of derris. [mod.L f. Gk, = leather covering (with ref. to its pod)]

derry /dérri/ *n.* □ **have a derry on** *Austral.* & *NZ colloq.* be prejudiced against (a person). [app. f. the song-refrain *derry down*]

derv /derv/ *n. Brit.* diesel oil for road vehicles. [f. *d*iesel-*e*ngined *r*oad-*v*ehicle]

dervish /dérvish/ *n.* a member of any of several Muslim fraternities vowed to poverty and austerity. □ **whirling** (or **dancing** or **howling**) **dervish** a dervish performing a wild dance, or howling, according to which sect he belongs to. [Turk. *derviş* f. Pers. *darvēsh* poor, a mendicant]

DES *abbr.* (in the UK) Department of Education and Science.

desalinate /deesállinayt/ *v.tr.* remove salt from (esp. sea water). □□ **desalination** /-náysh'n/ *n.*

desalt /deesáwlt/ *v.tr.* = DESALINATE.

desaparecido /dézzaparəsèedō/ *n.* a person who has 'disappeared' in a totalitarian state, esp. in South America. [Sp., lit. 'disappeared']

descale /deeskáyl/ *v.tr.* remove the scale from.
■ see PEEL[1] *v.* 1, 2.

descant *n.* & *v.* ● *n.* /déskant/ **1** *Mus.* an independent treble melody usu. sung or played above a basic melody, esp. of a hymn tune. **2** *poet.* a melody; a song. ● *v.intr.* /diskánt/ **1** (foll. by *on, upon*) talk lengthily and prosily, esp. in praise of. **2** *Mus.* sing or play a descant. □ **descant recorder** the most common size of recorder, with a range of two octaves. [ME f. OF *deschant* f. med.L *discantus* (as DIS-, *cantus* song, CHANT)]

descend /disénd/ *v.* **1** *tr.* & *intr.* go or come down (a hill, stairs, etc.). **2** *intr.* (of a thing) sink, fall (*rain descended heavily*). **3** *intr.* slope downwards, lie along a descending slope (*fields descended to the beach*). **4** *intr.* (usu. foll. by *on*) **a** make a sudden attack. **b** make an unexpected and usu. unwelcome visit (*hope they don't descend on us at the weekend*). **5** *intr.* (usu. foll. by *from, to*) (of property, qualities, rights, etc.) be passed by inheritance (*the house descends from my grandmother; the property descended to me*). **6** *intr.* **a** sink in rank, quality, etc. **b** (foll. by *to*) degrade oneself morally to (an unworthy act) (*descend to violence*). **7** *intr. Mus.* (of sound) become lower in pitch. **8** *intr.* (usu. foll. by *to*) proceed (in discourse or writing): **a** in time (to a subsequent event etc.). **b** from the general (to the particular) (*now let's descend to details*). **9** *tr.* go along (a river etc.) to the sea etc. **10** *intr. Printing* (of a letter) have its tail below the line. □ **be descended from** have as an ancestor. □□ **descendent** *adj.* [ME f. OF *descendre* f. L *descendere* (as DE-, *scandere* climb)]
■ **1** come *or* go down, move down, climb down, get down (off *or* from). **2** see SINK *v.* 1, FALL *v.* 1. **3** go down, decline, incline (downwards), slope down, slant down, dip, drop, fall, plunge. **4 a** (*descend on*) attack, assault, invade, pounce on *or* upon, swoop down on *or* upon. **6 b** sink, stoop, lower *or* abase *or* debase *or* humble *or* degrade oneself.

descendant /diséndənt/ *n.* (often foll. by *of*) a person or thing descended from another (*a descendant of Charles I*). [F, part. of *descendre* (as DESCEND)]
■ heir, scion; offshoot; (*descendants*) offspring, progeny, *Law* issue.

descender /diséndər/ *n. Printing* a part of a letter that extends below the line.

descendible /diséndib'l/ *adj.* **1** (of a slope etc.) that may be descended. **2** *Law* capable of descending by inheritance. [OF *descendable* (as DESCEND)]

descent /disént/ *n.* **1 a** the act of descending. **b** an instance of this. **c** a downward movement. **2 a** a way or path etc. by which one may descend. **b** a downward slope. **3 a** being descended; lineage, family origin (*traces his descent from William the Conqueror*). **b** the transmission of qualities, property, privileges, etc., by inheritance. **4 a** a decline; a fall. **b** a lowering (of pitch, temperature, etc.). **5** a sudden violent attack. [ME f. OF *descente* f. *descendre* DESCEND]
■ **1** see DROP *n.* 2a, b. **2** see SLOPE *n.* 1–3. **3** see LINEAGE. **4** see DECLINE *n.* 1, 4; DECREASE *n.* **5** see SWOOP *n.*

descramble /deeskrámb'l/ *v.tr.* **1** convert or restore (a signal) to intelligible form. **2** counteract the effects of (a scrambling device). **3** recover an original signal from (a scrambled signal). □□ **descrambler** *n.*

describe /diskrīb/ *v.tr.* **1 a** state the characteristics, appearance, etc. of, in spoken or written form (*described the landscape*). **b** (foll. by *as*) assert to be; call (*described him as a habitual liar*). **2 a** mark out or draw (esp. a geometrical figure) (*described a triangle*). **b** move in (a specified way, esp. a curve) (*described a parabola through the air*). □□ **describable** *adj.* **describer** *n.* [L *describere* (as DE-, *scribere script-* write)]
■ **1 a** tell (of), recount, relate, give an account of, narrate, recite, report, chronicle, retail; detail. **b** characterize, portray, paint, depict, identify, label, style. **2 a** mark out, outline, draw; see also TRACE[1] *v.* 3.

description /diskrípsh'n/ *n.* **1 a** the act or an instance of describing; the process of being described. **b** a spoken or written representation (of a person, object, or event). **2** a sort, kind, or class (*no food of any description*). □ **answers** (or **fits**) **the description** has the qualities specified. [ME f. OF f. L *descriptio -onis* (as DESCRIBE)]
■ **1 a** see *narration* (NARRATE). **b** account, narrative, story, report, representation, statement, definition; explanation, commentary; portrayal, characterization, depiction, (thumbnail) sketch, portrait; chronicle, history, record, narration; memoir. **2** sort, kind, nature, character, type, variety, brand, breed, species, category, genus, genre, class, *colloq. disp.* ilk; stripe, kidney.

descriptive /diskríptiv/ *adj.* **1** serving or seeking to describe (*a descriptive writer*). **2** describing or classifying without expressing feelings or judging (*a purely descriptive account*). **3** *Linguistics* describing a language without comparing, endorsing, or condemning particular usage, vocabulary, etc. **4** *Gram.* (of an adjective) describing the noun, rather than its relation, position, etc., e.g. *blue* as distinct from *few*. □□ **descriptively** *adv.* **descriptiveness** *n.* [LL *descriptivus* (as DESCRIBE)]
■ **1** see GRAPHIC *adj.* 1.

descriptor /diskríptər/ *n. Linguistics* a word or expression etc. used to describe or identify. [L, = describer (as DESCRIBE)]

descry /diskrī́/ *v.tr.* (**-ies, -ied**) *literary* catch sight of; discern (*descried him in the crowd; descries no glimmer of light in her situation*). [ME (earlier senses 'proclaim, DECRY') f. OF *descrier*: prob. confused with var. of obs. *descrive* f. OF *descrivre* DESCRIBE]
■ see SIGHT *v.* 1–3.

desecrate /déssikrayt/ *v.tr.* **1** violate (a sacred place or thing) with violence, profanity, etc. **2** deprive (a church, a sacred object, etc.) of sanctity; deconsecrate. □□ **desecration** /-kráysh'n/ *n.* **desecrator** *n.* [DE- + CONSECRATE]

■ **1** profane, violate, defile, blaspheme (against), dishonour, degrade, debase, contaminate, pollute, corrupt, vitiate, *poet.* befoul.

deseed /deesééd/ *v.tr.* remove the seeds from (a plant, vegetable, etc.).

desegregate /deeségrigayt/ *v.tr.* abolish racial segregation in (schools etc.) or of (people etc.). ▫▫ **desegregation** /-gáysh'n/ *n.*

■ see INTEGRATE *v.*

deselect /déessilékt/ *v.tr. Polit.* decline to select or retain as a constituency candidate in an election. ▫▫ **deselection** *n.*

desensitize /deesénsitīz/ *v.tr.* (also **-ise**) reduce or destroy the sensitiveness of (photographic materials, an allergic person, etc.). ▫▫ **desensitization** /-záysh'n/ *n.* **desensitizer** *n.*

■ see DEADEN 2.

desert[1] /dizért/ *v.* **1** *tr.* abandon, give up, leave (*deserted the sinking ship*). **2** *tr.* forsake or abandon (a cause or a person, people, etc., having claims on one) (*deserted his wife and children*). **3** *tr.* fail (*his presence of mind deserted him*). **4** *intr. Mil.* run away (esp. from military service). **5** *tr.* (as **deserted** *adj.*) empty, abandoned (*a deserted house*). ▫▫ **deserter** *n.* (in sense 4 of *v.*). **desertion** /-zérsh'n/ *n.* [F *déserter* f. LL *desertare* f. L *desertus* (as DESERT[2])]

■ **1** forsake, leave, abandon, give up. **2** forsake, leave, abandon, give up; jilt, throw over; maroon, strand, run *or* walk out on, leave in the lurch, leave high and dry, turn one's back on, *colloq.* dump, *sl.* ditch. **4** abscond, quit, run away, defect, *colloq.* go AWOL. **5** (**deserted**) abandoned, desolate, forsaken, neglected, uninhabited, unpeopled, vacant, vacated, unfrequented, unvisited, unoccupied, empty; God-forsaken, isolated, solitary, lonely; friendless, stranded, rejected, left in the lurch. ▫▫ **deserter** runaway, fugitive, escapee, escaper, absconder, defector, renegade; traitor, turncoat, rat.

desert[2] /dézzərt/ *n.* & *adj.* ● *n.* a dry barren often sand-covered area of land, characteristically desolate, waterless, and without vegetation; an uninteresting or barren subject, period, etc. (*a cultural desert*). ● *adj.* **1** uninhabited, desolate. **2** uncultivated, barren. ▫ **desert boot** a suede etc. boot reaching to or extending just above the ankle. **desert island** a remote (usu. tropical) island presumed to be uninhabited. **desert rat** *Brit. colloq.* a soldier of the 7th British armoured division (with the jerboa as a badge) in the N. African desert campaign of 1941–2. [ME f. OF f. L *desertus*, eccl.L *desertum* (n.), past part. of *deserere* leave, forsake]

■ *n.* waste, wilderness, wasteland, dust bowl; badlands, barrens, wilds; emptiness, void. ● *adj.* barren, desolate, uninhabited, unpeopled, lonely, deserted; arid, bare, vacant, empty, wild, uncultivated.

desert[3] /dizért/ *n.* **1** (in *pl.*) **a** acts or qualities deserving reward or punishment. **b** such reward or punishment (*has got his deserts*). **2** the fact of being worthy of reward or punishment; deservingness. [ME f. OF f. *deservir* DESERVE]

■ **1 b** (*deserts*) payment, recompense, requital, compensation, due, right, reward; retribution, justice, punishment, *colloq.* comeuppance.

desertification /dizértifikáysh'n/ *n.* the process of making or becoming a desert.

deserve /dizérv/ *v.tr.* **1** (often foll. by *to* + infin.) show conduct or qualities worthy of (reward, punishment, etc.) (*deserves to be imprisoned*; *deserves a prize*). **2** (as **deserved** *adj.*) rightfully merited or earned (*a deserved win*). ▫ **deserve well** (or **ill**) **of** be worthy of good (or bad) treatment at the hands of (*deserves well of the electorate*). ▫▫ **deservedly** /-vidli/ *adv.* **deservedness** /-vidnis/ *n.* **deserver** *n.* [ME f. OF *deservir* f. L *deservire* (as DE-, *servire* serve)]

■ **1** merit, earn, be entitled to, be worthy of, rate, warrant, justify. **2** (**deserved**) merited, well-earned, earned, well-deserved, just, rightful, fitting, fit, proper, fair, meet, warranted, condign.

deserving /dizérving/ *adj.* meritorious. ▫ **deserving of** showing conduct or qualities worthy of (praise, blame, help, etc.). ▫▫ **deservingly** *adv.* **deservingness** *n.*

■ meritorious, worthy, commendable, laudable, praiseworthy, creditable, estimable.

desex /deeséks/ *v.tr.* **1** castrate or spay (an animal). **2** deprive of sexual qualities or attractions.

■ **1** see NEUTER *v.*

desexualize /deeséksyooəlīz, -sékshooəlīz/ *v.tr.* (also **-ise**) deprive of sexual character or of the distinctive qualities of a sex.

■ desex, unsex.

déshabillé /dézzabée-ay/ *n.* (also ***déshabille*** /dáyzabéel/, ***dishabille*** /dissabéel/) a state of being only partly or carelessly clothed. [F, = undressed]

desiccant /déssikənt/ *n. Chem.* a hygroscopic substance used as a drying agent.

desiccate /déssikayt/ *v.tr.* remove the moisture from, dry (esp. food for preservation) (*desiccated coconut*). ▫▫ **desiccation** /-káysh'n/ *n.* **desiccative** /-kətiv/ *adj.* [L *desiccare* (as DE-, *siccus* dry)]

■ dry, dehydrate.

desiccator /déssikaytər/ *n.* **1** an apparatus for desiccating. **2** *Chem.* an apparatus containing a drying agent to remove the moisture from specimens.

desiderate /dizíddərayt/ *v.tr. archaic* feel to be missing; regret the absence of; wish to have. [L *desiderare* (as DE-, *siderare* as in CONSIDER)]

desiderative /dizíddərətiv/ *adj.* & *n.* ● *adj.* **1** *Gram.* (of a verb, conjugation, etc.) formed from another verb etc. and denoting a desire to perform the action of that verb etc. **2** desiring. ● *n. Gram.* a desiderative verb, conjugation, etc. [LL *desiderativus* (as DESIDERATE)]

desideratum /dizíddəraatəm, disíd-/ *n.* (*pl.* **desiderata** /-tə/) something lacking but needed or desired. [L neut. past part.: see DESIDERATE]

■ see *requirement* (REQUIRE).

design /dizīn/ *n.* & *v.* ● *n.* **1 a** a preliminary plan or sketch for the making or production of a building, machine, garment, etc. **b** the art of producing these. **2** a scheme of lines or shapes forming a pattern or decoration. **3** a plan, purpose, or intention. **4 a** the general arrangement or layout of a product. **b** an established version of a product (*one of our most popular designs*). ● *v.* **1** *tr.* produce a design for (a building, machine, picture, garment, etc.). **2** *tr.* intend, plan, or purpose (*the remark was designed to offend*; *a course designed for beginners*; *designed an attack*). **3** *absol.* be a designer. ▫ **argument from design** *Theol.* the argument that God's existence is provable by the evidence of design in the universe. **by design** on purpose. **have designs on** plan to harm or appropriate. [F *désigner* appoint or obs. F *desseing* ult. f. L *designare* DESIGNATE]

■ *n.* **1 a** plan, scheme, conception, study, project, proposal; blueprint, draft, sketch, model, pattern, chart, diagram, layout, map, drawing, prototype. **2, 4** form, shape, configuration, pattern, style, motif, format, layout, make-up, delineation, arrangement, organization, composition, structure, construction. **3** plan, aim, purpose, intention, objective, object, goal, point, target, intent. ● *v.* **1** plan, invent, contrive, create, devise, originate, visualize, envisage, envision; sketch out, pattern, set up, delineate, lay out, draw up, think of *or* up, conceive (of), outline, work *or* map *or* block out; develop, organize, frame, shape, mould, form, forge, make, construct, fashion, sketch, draft, draw. **2** mean, plan, hope, aim, purpose, destine; (*designed for*) see INTEND 4a. ▫ **by design** see *on purpose* (PURPOSE).

designate *v.* & *adj.* ● *v.tr.* /dézzignayt/ **1** (often foll. by *as*) appoint to an office or function (*designated him as postmaster general*; *designated his own successor*). **2** specify or particularize (*receives guests at designated times*). **3** (often foll. by *as*) describe as; entitle, style. **4** serve as the name or distinctive mark of (*English uses French words to designate ballet steps*). ● *adj.* /dézzignət/ (placed after noun) appointed to an office but not yet installed (*bishop designate*). ▫▫ **designator** /-naytər/ *n.* [L *designare*, past part. *designatus* (as DE-, *signare* f. *signum* mark)]

■ *v.* **1** appoint, nominate, name, identify, select, pick, choose, elect, assign, delegate, depute. **2** indicate, specify, pinpoint, particularize, delineate, point out, identify, state, set forth, write *or* put down, name. **3** call, name, style, term, label, christen, dub, nickname, describe as, *archaic* entitle. **4** mean, stand for, symbolize, denote, represent, indicate, name, distinguish.

designation /dézzignáysh'n/ *n.* **1** a name, description, or title. **2** the act or process of designating. [ME f. OF *designation* or L *designatio* (as DESIGNATE)]

■ **1** see DENOMINATION 3a. **2** see APPOINTMENT 2c.

designedly /dizínidli/ *adv.* by design; on purpose.

designer /dizínər/ *n.* **1** a person who makes artistic designs or plans for construction, e.g. for clothing, machines, theatre sets; a draughtsman. **2** (*attrib.*) (of clothing etc.) bearing the name or label of a famous designer; prestigious. □ **designer drug** a synthetic analogue, not itself illegal, of an illegal drug.

■ **1** creator, originator, architect, artificer, author, deviser, inventor; (interior) decorator, artist; draughtsman. **2** (*attrib.*) top-class, top-quality; see also STYLISH.

designing /dizíning/ *adj.* crafty, artful, or scheming. □□ **designingly** *adv.*

■ scheming, conniving, calculating, wily, tricky, cunning, sly, underhand, underhanded, crafty, artful, shrewd, machiavellian, guileful, deceitful, double-dealing, devious, treacherous, unscrupulous.

desirable /dizírəb'l/ *adj.* **1** worth having or wishing for (*it is desirable that nobody should smoke*). **2** arousing sexual desire; very attractive. □□ **desirability** /-bílliti/ *n.* **desirableness** *n.* **desirably** *adv.* [ME f. OF (as DESIRE)]

■ **1** sought-after, wanted, coveted, longed-for, looked-for, desired; profitable, worthwhile, beneficial, advantageous, valuable, worthy, estimable, commendable. **2** seductive, alluring, fetching, attractive, captivating, winning, winsome; sexy.

desire /dizír/ *n.* & *v.* ● *n.* **1 a** an unsatisfied longing or craving. **b** an expression of this; a request (*expressed a desire to rest*). **2** lust. **3** something desired (*achieved his heart's desire*). ● *v.tr.* **1** (often foll. by *to* + infin., or *that* + clause) long for; crave. **2** request (*desires a cup of tea*). **3** *archaic* pray, entreat, or command (*desire him to wait*). [ME f. OF *desir* f. *desirer* f. L *desiderare* DESIDERATE]

■ *n.* **1 a** longing, craving, yearning, hankering, hunger, thirst, appetite, *colloq.* yen. **b** wish, request, urge, requirement, requisition, demand. **2** passion, lust, libido, lustfulness, lecherousness, lechery, lasciviousness, salaciousness, prurience, *formal* concupiscence. **3** desideratum, whim; see also WISH *n.* ● *v.* **1** crave, want, fancy, covet, wish for, hope for, long *or* yearn for, pine *or* sigh for, hanker after, have an eye *or* taste for, hunger *or* thirst for *or* after, die for, have one's heart set on, *archaic* desiderate, *colloq.* have a yen for, *sl.* have the hots for. **2** ask for, request, order, demand, solicit, importune, summon, require.

desirous /dizírəss/ *predic.adj.* **1** (usu. foll. by *of*) ambitious, desiring (*desirous of stardom*; *desirous of doing well*). **2** (usu. foll. by *to* + infin., or *that* + clause) wishful; hoping (*desirous to do the right thing*). [ME f. AF *desirous*, OF *desireus* f. Rmc (as DESIRE)]

■ **1** see INTENT *adj.* 1a. **2** wishful, longing, yearning, hopeful, hoping, anxious, concerned.

desist /dizíst/ *v.intr.* (often foll. by *from*) *literary* abstain; cease (*please desist from interrupting*; *when requested, he desisted*). [OF *desister* f. L *desistere* (as DE-, *sistere* stop, redupl. f. *stare* stand)]

■ see CEASE *v.*

desk /desk/ *n.* **1** a piece of furniture or a portable box with a flat or sloped surface for writing on, and often drawers. **2** a counter in a hotel, bank, etc., which separates the customer from the assistant. **3** a section of a newspaper office etc. dealing with a specified topic (*the sports desk*; *the features desk*). **4** *Mus.* a music stand in an orchestra regarded as a unit of two players. □ **desk-bound** obliged to remain working at a desk. [ME f. med.L *desca* f. L DISCUS disc]

■ **1** see BUREAU 1. **2** counter, table, bar. **3** see BUREAU 2.

desktop /désktop/ *n.* **1** the working surface of a desk. **2** (*attrib.*) (esp. of a microcomputer) suitable for use at an ordinary desk. □ **desktop publishing** the production of printed matter with a desktop computer and printer.

desman /désmən/ *n.* (*pl.* **desmans**) any aquatic flesh-eating shrewlike mammal of two species, one originating in Russia (*Desmana moschata*) and one in the Pyrenees (*Galemys pyrenaicus*). [F & G f. Sw. *desman-råtta* musk-rat]

desolate *adj.* & *v.* ● *adj.* /déssələt/ **1** left alone; solitary. **2** (of a building or place) uninhabited, ruined, neglected, barren, dreary, empty (*a desolate moor*). **3** forlorn; wretched; miserable (*was left desolate and weeping*). ● *v.tr.* /déssəlayt/ **1** depopulate or devastate; lay waste to. **2** (esp. as **desolated** *adj.*) make wretched or forlorn (*desolated by grief*; *inconsolable and desolated*). □□ **desolately** /-lətli/ *adv.* **desolateness** /-lətniss/ *n.* **desolator** /-laytər/ *n.* [ME f. L *desolatus* past part. of *desolare* (as DE-, *solare* f. *solus* alone)]

■ *adj.* **1** solitary, lonely, isolated, deserted, alone, abandoned, neglected. **2** ruined, neglected, desert, uninhabited, empty, unfrequented, bare, barren, bleak, dreary, remote. **3** wretched, dreary, forsaken, friendless, wretched, joyless, cheerless, comfortless, miserable, unhappy, down, disconsolate, sad, melancholy, sorrowful, forlorn, mournful, woebegone, gloomy, broken-hearted, heavy-hearted, inconsolable, dejected, downcast, downhearted, dispirited, low-spirited, depressed, melancholy, spiritless, despondent, distressed, discouraged, hopeless, dismal. ● *v.* **1** depopulate; destroy, devastate, ruin, lay waste, ravage, demolish, obliterate, annihilate, raze, gut, *literary* despoil. **2** dismay, dishearten, depress, daunt, devastate, dispirit, sadden, deject, discourage; (**desolated**) see WRETCHED 1.

desolation /déssəláysh'n/ *n.* **1 a** the act of desolating. **b** the process of being desolated. **2** loneliness, grief, or wretchedness, esp. caused by desertion. **3** a neglected, ruined, barren, or empty state. [ME f. LL *desolatio* (as DESOLATE)]

■ **2** grief, sorrow, dreariness, despair, gloom, distress, melancholy, sadness, misery, anguish, wretchedness, dolefulness, unhappiness, *archaic or literary* woe, *literary* dolour; loneliness. **3** desolateness, destruction, ruin, devastation, waste, spoliation, despoliation, depredation, extirpation, barrenness, havoc, chaos.

desorb /dizórb/ *v.* **1** *tr.* cause the release of (an adsorbed substance) from a surface. **2** *intr.* (of an adsorbed substance) become released. □□ **desorbent** *adj.* & *n.* **desorption** *n.* [DE-, after ADSORB]

despair /dispáir/ *n.* & *v.* ● *n.* the complete loss or absence of hope. ● *v.intr.* **1** (often foll. by *of*) lose or be without hope (*despaired of ever seeing her again*). **2** (foll. by *of*) lose hope about (*his life is despaired of*). □ **be the despair of** be the cause of despair by badness or unapproachable excellence (*he's the despair of his parents*). □□ **despairingly** *adv.* [ME f. OF *desespeir*, *desperer* f. L *desperare* (as DE-, *sperare* hope)]

■ *n.* hopelessness, desperation, discouragement, disheartenment, despondency, despondence, dejection, depression, gloom, gloominess, misery, melancholy, wretchedness, distress, miserableness, anguish, *archaic* despond. ● *v.* **1** give up *or* lose hope, despond.

despatch var. of DISPATCH.

desperado /déspərаádō/ *n.* (*pl.* **-oes** or *US* **-os**) a desperate or reckless person, esp. a criminal. [after DESPERATE (obs. n.) & words in -ADO]

■ see CRIMINAL *n.*

desperate /déspərət/ *adj.* **1** reckless from despair; violent and lawless. **2 a** extremely dangerous or serious (*a desperate situation*). **b** staking all on a small chance (*a desperate remedy*). **3** very bad (*a desperate night*; *desperate poverty*). **4** (usu. foll. by *for*) needing or desiring very much (*desperate for recognition*). □□ **desperately** *adv.* **desperateness** *n.*

desperation /-ráysh'n/ *n.* [ME f. L *desperatus* past part. of *desperare* (as DE-, *sperare* hope)]

■ **1** reckless, foolhardy, rash, impetuous, frantic, frenzied, panic-stricken; careless, hasty, devil-may-care, wild, mad, frenetic, furious; at one's wit's end, forlorn, despairing, despondent, wretched, at the end of one's tether. **2 a** urgent, pressing, compelling, serious, grave, acute, critical, crucial, great; precarious, perilous, life-threatening, hazardous, dangerous, hopeless, beyond hope *or* help. **3** see TERRIBLE 1. **4** anxious, craving, hungry, thirsty, needful, desirous, covetous, eager, longing, yearning, wishing, hoping, aching, pining. □□ **desperately** see *extremely* (EXTREME), AWFULLY 2. **desperation** desperateness, recklessness, impetuosity, rashness, foolhardiness, imprudence, heedlessness; despair, anguish, despondency, depression, dejection, discouragement, defeatism, pessimism, hopelessness, distress, misery, melancholy, wretchedness, gloom, sorrow.

despicable /déspikəb'l, dispík-/ *adj.* vile; contemptible, esp. morally. □□ **despicably** *adv.* [LL *despicabilis* f. *despicari* (as DE-, *specere* look at)]

■ contemptible, below *or* beneath contempt, mean, detestable, base, low, scurvy, vile, sordid, wretched, miserable, ignoble, ignominious, shabby; shameful, shameless, reprehensible.

despise /dispíz/ *v.tr.* look down on as inferior, worthless, or contemptible. □□ **despiser** *n.* [ME f. *despis-* pres. stem of OF *despire* f. L *despicere* (as DE-, *specere* look at)]

■ disdain, disesteem, scorn, look down on *or* upon, look down one's nose at, be contemptuous of, sneer at, spurn, *literary* contemn; hate, loathe, detest, abhor.

despite /dispít/ *prep.* & *n.* ● *prep.* in spite of. ● *n. archaic* or *literary* **1** outrage, injury. **2** malice, hatred (*died of mere despite*). □ **despite** (or **in despite**) **of** *archaic* in spite of. □□ **despiteful** *adj.* [ME f. OF *despit* f. L *despectus* noun f. *despicere* (as DESPISE)]

■ *prep.* in spite of, notwithstanding, undeterred by, regardless of, in defiance of, without considering, without thought *or* consideration *or* regard for, ignoring, *archaic* despite of. ● *n.* **2** see ANIMOSITY.

despoil /dispóyl/ *v.tr. literary* (often foll. by *of*) plunder; rob; deprive (*despoiled the roof of its lead*). □□ **despoiler** *n.* **despoilment** *n.* **despoliation** /dispōliáysh'n/ *n.* [ME f. OF *despoill(i)er* f. L *despoliare* (as DE-, *spoliare* SPOIL)]

■ see PILLAGE *v.*

despond /dispónd/ *v.* & *n.* ● *v.intr.* lose heart or hope; be dejected. ● *n. archaic* despondency. [L *despondēre* give up, abandon (as DE-, *spondēre* promise)]

despondent /dispóndənt/ *adj.* in low spirits, dejected. □□ **despondence** *n.* **despondency** *n.* **despondently** *adv.*

■ dejected, sad, sorrowful, unhappy, melancholy, blue, depressed, down, downcast, downhearted, low, morose, miserable, disheartened, discouraged, dispirited, low-spirited, *colloq.* down in the dumps, down in the mouth, down on one's luck.

despot /déspot/ *n.* **1** an absolute ruler. **2** a tyrant or oppressor. □□ **despotic** /-spóttik/ *adj.* **despotically** /-spóttikəli/ *adv.* [F *despote* f. med.L *despota* f. Gk *despotēs* master, lord]

■ **1** absolute ruler *or* monarch, dictator, autocrat, overlord. **2** dictator, oppressor, autocrat, tyrant, bully. □□ **despotic** dictatorial, tyrannical, oppressive, authoritarian, imperious, domineering, totalitarian, absolute, autocratic, arbitrary.

despotism /déspətiz'm/ *n.* **1 a** rule by a despot. **b** a country ruled by a despot. **2** absolute power or control; tyranny.

■ autocracy, monocracy, autarchy, totalitarianism, absolutism, dictatorship, tyranny, oppression, suppression, repression.

desquamate /déskwəmayt/ *v.intr. Med.* (esp. of the skin) come off in scales (as in some diseases). □□ **desquamation** /-máysh'n/ *n.* **desquamative** /diskwámmətiv/ *adj.* **desquamatory** /diskwámmətəri, -tri/ *adj.* [L *desquamare* (as DE-, *squama* scale)]

des res /dez réz/ *n. sl.* a desirable residence. [abbr.]

dessert /dizért/ *n.* **1** the sweet course of a meal, served at or near the end. **2** *Brit.* a course of fruit, nuts, etc., served after a meal. □ **dessert wine** usu. sweet wine drunk with or following dessert. [F, past part. of *desservir* clear the table (as DIS-, *servir* SERVE)]

■ **1** sweet, pudding, *colloq.* pud, *Brit. colloq.* afters.

dessertspoon /dizértspōōn/ *n.* **1** a spoon used for dessert, smaller than a tablespoon and larger than a teaspoon. **2** the amount held by this. □□ **dessertspoonful** *n.* (*pl.* **-fuls**).

destabilize /deestáybilīz/ *v.tr.* (also **-ise**) **1** render unstable. **2** subvert (esp. a foreign government). □□ **destabilization** /-záysh'n/ *n.*

destination /déstináysh'n/ *n.* a place to which a person or thing is going. [OF *destination* or L *destinatio* (as DESTINE)]

■ journey's end, terminus, stop, stopping-place; goal, end, objective, target.

destine /déstin/ *v.tr.* (often foll. by *to*, *for*, or *to* + infin.) set apart; appoint; preordain; intend (*destined him for the navy*). □ **be destined to** be fated or preordained to (*was destined to become a great man*). [ME f. F *destiner* f. L *destinare* (as DE-, *stanare* (unrecorded) settle f. *stare* stand)]

■ fate, predetermine, predestine, ordain, foreordain, preordain; doom; design, intend, mean, devote, assign, appoint, designate, purpose, mark, earmark, set aside *or* apart. □ **be destined to** (*destined*) meant, intended, designed, foreordained, preordained, predestined, fated, doomed; sure, bound, certain.

destiny /déstini/ *n.* (*pl.* **-ies**) **1 a** the predetermined course of events; fate. **b** this regarded as a power. **2** what is destined to happen to a particular person etc. (*it was their destiny to be rejected*). [ME f. OF *destinée* f. Rmc, past part. of *destinare*: see DESTINE]

■ **1** fate, fortune. **2** fate, doom, fortune, lot, portion, kismet, *Hinduism* & *Buddhism* karma.

destitute /déstityōōt/ *adj.* **1** without food, shelter, etc.; completely impoverished. **2** (usu. foll. by *of*) lacking (*destitute of friends*). □□ **destitution** /-tyōōsh'n/ *n.* [ME f. L *destitutus* past part. of *destituere* forsake (as DE-, *statuere* place)]

■ **1** in want, impoverished, poverty-stricken, poor, indigent, down and out, needy, badly off, penniless, penurious, impecunious, insolvent, hard up, bankrupt, *US* on skid row *or* road, *colloq.* broke, on one's uppers, strapped (for cash). **2** (*destitute of*) bereft of, deficient in, deprived of, devoid of, lacking (in), wanting (in), in need of, needful of, without, hard up for.

destrier /déstriər/ *n. hist.* a war-horse. [ME f. AF *destrer*, OF *destrier* ult. f. L DEXTER[1] right (as the knight's horse was led by the squire with the right hand)]

destroy /distróy/ *v.tr.* **1** pull or break down; demolish (*destroyed the bridge*). **2** end the existence of (*the accident destroyed her confidence*). **3** kill (esp. a sick or savage animal). **4** make useless; spoil utterly. **5** ruin financially, professionally, or in reputation. **6** defeat (*destroyed the enemy*). [ME f. OF *destruire* ult. f. L *destruere* (as DE-, *struere struct-* build)]

■ **1** demolish, tear *or* pull down, raze, wipe out, ravage, wreck, smash, ruin, break up *or* down, *esp. US Astronaut.* destruct; annihilate, crush, eradicate, extirpate, exterminate, devastate, lay waste; vandalize, *esp. US colloq.* trash. **2** ruin, do away with, end, dash, make an end of, bring to an end, bring *or* put an end to, terminate, finish, kill. **3** kill, put down, put to sleep, exterminate, finish off. **4** negate, overturn, overthrow, ruin, spoil, undermine, weaken, enfeeble, devitalize, exhaust, disable, cripple; demolish, disprove, refute, confute, contradict. **5** see RUIN *v.* 1a, DISGRACE *v.* **6** see DEFEAT *v.* 1.

destroyer /distróyər/ *n.* **1** a person or thing that destroys. **2** *Naut.* a fast warship with guns and torpedoes used to protect other ships.

destruct /distrúkt/ *v.* & *n.* *US* esp. *Astronaut.* ● *v.* **1** *tr.* destroy (one's own rocket etc.) deliberately, esp. for safety reasons. **2** *intr.* be destroyed in this way. ● *n.* an act of destructing. [L *destruere* (as DESTROY) or as back-form. f. DESTRUCTION]

destructible /distrúktib'l/ *adj.* able to be destroyed. □□ **destructibility** /-billiti/ *n.* [F *destructible* or LL *destructibilis* (as DESTROY)]

destruction /distrúksh'n/ *n.* **1** the act or an instance of destroying; the process of being destroyed. **2** a cause of ruin; something that destroys (*greed was their destruction*). [ME f. OF f. L *destructio -onis* (as DESTROY)]

■ **1** demolition, ruin, ruining, ruination, breaking up *or* down, devastation, tearing *or* knocking down, laying waste, wiping out; rack and ruin; slaughter, annihilation, killing, eradication, murder, extermination, holocaust, liquidation, massacre, extinction, genocide, slaying; termination, breakup, breakdown, collapse. **2** undoing, end, ruination, downfall; see also RUIN *n.* 2a.

destructive /distrúktiv/ *adj.* **1** (often foll. by *to*, *of*) destroying or tending to destroy (*destructive of her peace of mind; is destructive to organisms; a destructive child*). **2** negative in attitude or criticism; refuting without suggesting, helping, amending, etc. (opp. CONSTRUCTIVE) (*has only destructive criticism to offer*). □□ **destructively** *adv.* **destructiveness** *n.* [ME f. OF *destructif -ive* f. LL *destructivus* (as DESTROY)]

■ **1** harmful, injurious, pernicious, dangerous, hurtful, toxic, poisonous, virulent, noxious, bad, malignant, baleful, unwholesome, damaging, detrimental, deleterious, devastating, baneful. **2** negative, adverse, opposed, contrary, contradictory, antithetical, conflicting, unfavourable, condemnatory, derogatory, disparaging, disapproving, critical.

destructor /distrúktər/ *n. Brit.* a refuse-burning furnace.

desuetude /disyóo-ityood, déswi-/ *n.* a state of disuse (*the custom fell into desuetude*). [F *désuétude* or L *desuetudo* (as DE-, *suescere suet-* be accustomed)]

desultory /dézzəltəri, -tri/ *adj.* **1** going constantly from one subject to another, esp. in a half-hearted way. **2** disconnected; unmethodical; superficial. □□ **desultorily** *adv.* **desultoriness** *n.* [L *desultorius* superficial f. *desultor* vaulter f. *desult-* (as DE-, *salt-* past part. stem of *salire* leap)]

■ shifting, unsteady, irregular, wavering, inconstant, fitful, spasmodic, unmethodical, disconnected, unsystematic, disorderly, disordered, unorganized, disorganized, inconsistent, random, haphazard, chaotic, erratic; see also SUPERFICIAL 2.

detach /ditách/ *v.tr.* **1** (often foll. by *from*) unfasten or disengage and remove (*detached the buttons; detached himself from the group*). **2** *Mil.* send (a ship, regiment, officer, messenger, etc.) on a separate mission. **3** (as **detached** *adj.*) **a** impartial; unemotional (*a detached viewpoint*). **b** (esp. of a house) not joined to another or others; separate. □□ **detachable** *adj.* **detachedly** /ditáchidli/ *adv.* [F *détacher* (as DE-, ATTACH)]

■ **1** separate, uncouple, decouple, part, disjoin, disengage, disunite, disconnect, disentangle, free, unfasten, undo, cut off, remove. **3** (**detached**) **a** disinterested, aloof, uninvolved, unemotional, dispassionate, equanimous, *dégagé*, nonchalant, indifferent, impersonal, impartial, neutral, objective, unbiased, unprejudiced. **b** disconnected, unattached, separated, separate, free, free-standing, isolated, disentangled, unfastened, removed, cut off, divided, disjoined.

detachment /ditáchmənt/ *n.* **1 a** a state of aloofness from or indifference to other people, one's surroundings, public opinion, etc. **b** disinterested independence of judgement. **2 a** the act or process of detaching or being detached. **b** an instance of this. **3** *Mil.* a separate group or unit of an army etc. used for a specific purpose. [F *détachement* (as DETACH)]

■ **1 a** aloofness, unconcern, indifference, coolness, nonchalance, inattention, insouciance; see also DISTANCE *n.* 4. **b** see *objectivity* (OBJECTIVE). **2** separation, disconnection, disengagement, dissociation, dissassociation, segregation. **3** see SQUAD.

detail /deétayl/ *n.* & *v.* ● *n.* **1 a** a small or subordinate particular; an item. **b** such a particular, considered (ironically) to be unimportant (*the truth of the statement is just a detail*). **2 a** small items or particulars (esp. in an artistic work) regarded collectively (*has an eye for detail*). **b** the treatment of them (*the detail was insufficient and unconvincing*). **3** (often in *pl.*) a number of particulars; an aggregate of small items (*filled in the details on the form*). **4 a** a minor decoration on a building, in a picture, etc. **b** a small part of a picture etc. shown alone. **5** *Mil.* **a** the distribution of orders for the day. **b** a small detachment of soldiers etc. for special duty. ● *v.tr.* **1** give particulars of (*detailed the plans*). **2** relate circumstantially (*detailed the anecdote*). **3** *Mil.* assign for special duty. **4** (as **detailed** *adj.*) **a** (of a picture, story, etc.) having many details. **b** itemized (*a detailed list*). □ **go into detail** give all the items or particulars. **in detail** item by item, minutely. [F *détail*, *détailler* (as DE-, *tailler* cut, formed as TAIL[2])]

■ *n.* **1** particular, element, factor, point, fact, technicality, component, item, feature; aspect, respect, count; (*details*) minutiae, niceties, fine points, specifics, technicalities. **5 b** detachment, party, group, unit; see also SQUAD. ● *v.* **1, 2** specify, spell out, itemize, delineate, catalogue, list, tabulate, enumerate, particularize, recount, cite, relate; describe, outline. **3** assign, appoint, charge, delegate, name, specify, send. **4** (**detailed**) itemized, exhaustive, comprehensive, thorough, full, complete, inclusive, particularized, precise, exact, blow-by-blow, circumstantial; intricate, complex, complicated, elaborate, ornate. □ **in detail** minutely, specifically, particularly, thoroughly, in depth, item by item, point by point, exhaustively, comprehensively, inside out, perfectly.

detain /ditáyn/ *v.tr.* **1** keep in confinement or under restraint. **2** keep waiting; delay. □□ **detainment** *n.* [ME f. OF *detenir* ult. f. L *detinēre detent-* (as DE-, *tenēre* hold)]

■ **1** see IMPRISON 2. **2** see DELAY *v.* 2.

detainee /deétaynée/ *n.* a person detained in custody, esp. for political reasons.

■ see PRISONER.

detainer /ditáynər/ *n. Law* **1** the wrongful detaining of goods taken from the owner for distraint etc. **2** the detention of a person in prison etc. [AF *detener* f. OF *detenir* (as DETAIN)]

detect /ditékt/ *v.tr.* **1 a** (often foll. by *in*) reveal the guilt of; discover (*detected him in his crime*). **b** discover (a crime). **2** discover or perceive the existence or presence of (*detected a smell of burning; do I detect a note of sarcasm?*). **3** *Physics* use an instrument to observe (a signal, radiation, etc.). □□ **detectable** *adj.* **detectably** *adv.* [L *detegere detect-* (as DE-, *tegere* cover)]

■ **2** uncover, find (out), discover, locate, learn of, ascertain, determine, dig up, unearth; perceive, note, notice, identify, spot, observe, sense, read, scent, smell (out), sniff (out), discern, feel, catch, find.

detection /ditéksh'n/ *n.* **1 a** the act or an instance of detecting; the process of being detected. **b** an instance of this. **2** the work of a detective. **3** *Physics* the extraction of a desired signal; a demodulation. [LL *detectio* (as DETECT)]

■ **1** see IDENTIFICATION 1a, DISCOVERY 1.

detective /ditéktiv/ *n.* & *adj.* ● *n.* (often *attrib.*) a person, esp. a member of a police force, employed to investigate crime. ● *adj.* serving to detect. □ **private detective** a usu. freelance detective carrying out investigations for a private employer. [DETECT]

■ *n.* (private) investigator, private detective, CID man, policeman, constable, *Brit.* inquiry agent, *US* operative, *colloq.* private eye, eye, sleuth-hound, sleuth, snoop, snooper, tec, *US colloq.* G-man, *sl.* dick, jack, cop, busy, *Brit. sl.* copper, *US sl.* gumshoe, peeper, shamus. □ **private detective** see DETECTIVE *n.* above, *inquiry agent*.

detector /ditéktər/ *n.* **1** a person or thing that detects. **2** *Physics* a device for the detection or demodulation of signals.

detent /ditént/ *n.* **1** a catch by the removal of which machinery is allowed to move. **2** (in a clock etc.) a catch that regulates striking. [F *détente* f. OF *destente* f. *destendre* slacken (as DE-, L *tendere*)]

détente /daytóNT/ *n.* an easing of strained relations esp. between States. [F, = relaxation]
■ see *reconciliation* (RECONCILE).

detention /diténsh'n/ *n.* **1** detaining or being detained. **2 a** being kept in school after hours as a punishment. **b** an instance of this. **3** custody; confinement. □ **detention centre** *Brit.* an institution for the brief detention of young offenders. [F *détention* or LL *detentio* (as DETAIN)]
■ **3** custody, confinement, imprisonment, captivity, internment, incarceration, restraint, *archaic* durance.

deter /ditér/ *v.tr.* (**deterred**, **deterring**) **1** (often foll. by *from*) discourage or prevent (a person) through fear or dislike of the consequences. **2** discourage, check, or prevent (a thing, process, etc.). □□ **determent** *n.* [L *deterrēre* (as DE-, *terrēre* frighten)]
■ dissuade, discourage, inhibit, intimidate, daunt, frighten off *or* away, scare off; prevent, stop, obstruct, check, hinder, impede.

detergent /ditérjənt/ *n.* & *adj.* ● *n.* a cleansing agent, esp. a synthetic substance (usu. other than soap) used with water as a means of removing dirt etc. ● *adj.* cleansing, esp. in the manner of a detergent. [L *detergēre* (as DE-, *tergēre ters-* wipe)]
■ *n.* cleaner, cleanser, soap (powder *or* flakes), liquid soap; surfactant, surface-active agent. ● *adj.* cleaning, cleansing, washing, purifying.

deteriorate /diteéeriərayt/ *v.tr.* & *intr.* make or become bad or worse (*food deteriorates in hot weather*; *his condition deteriorated after the operation*). □□ **deterioration** /-ráysh'n/ *n.* **deteriorative** /-rətiv/ *adj.* [LL *deteriorare deteriorat-* f. L *deterior* worse]
■ worsen, get worse, decline, degenerate, degrade, spoil, depreciate, slip, slide, *colloq.* go to pot, go downhill, *sl.* go to the dogs; decay, disintegrate, fall apart, crumble.

determinant /ditérminənt/ *adj.* & *n.* ● *adj.* serving to determine or define. ● *n.* **1** a determining factor, element, word, etc. **2** *Math.* a quantity obtained by the addition of products of the elements of a square matrix according to a given rule. [L *determinare* (as DETERMINE)]
■ *n.* **1** see FACTOR *n.* 1.

determinate /ditérminət/ *adj.* **1** limited in time, space, or character. **2** of definite scope or nature. □□ **determinacy** *n.* **determinately** *adv.* **determinateness** *n.* [ME f. L *determinatus* past part. (as DETERMINE)]
■ fixed, definite, exact, precise, distinct, determined, predetermined, ascertained, identified; limited.

determination /ditérmináysh'n/ *n.* **1** firmness of purpose; resoluteness. **2** the process of deciding, determining, or calculating. **3 a** the conclusion of a dispute by the decision of an arbitrator. **b** the decision reached. **4** *Law* the cessation of an estate or interest. **5** *Law* a judicial decision or sentence. **6** *archaic* a tendency to move in a fixed direction. [ME (in sense 4) f. OF f. L *determinatio -onis* (as DETERMINE)]
■ **1** resoluteness, resolution, firmness, resolve, steadfastness, tenacity, perseverance, fortitude, doggedness, persistence, constancy, single-mindedness, will, will-power, determinedness, *colloq.* grit, guts. **2** fixing, settling, determining, calculating, deciding, decision-making, ascertainment. **3** settlement, resolution, decision, solution, arbitration, judgement, verdict, outcome, result, upshot, conclusion, end, termination.

determinative /ditérminətiv/ *adj.* & *n.* ● *adj.* serving to define, qualify, or direct. ● *n.* a determinative thing or circumstance. □□ **determinatively** *adv.* [F *déterminatif -ive* (as DETERMINE)]

determine /ditérmin/ *v.* **1** *tr.* find out or establish precisely (*have to determine the extent of the problem*). **2** *tr.* decide or settle (*determined who should go*). **3** *tr.* be a decisive factor in regard to (*demand determines supply*). **4** *intr.* & *tr.* make or cause (a person) to make a decision (*we determined to go at once*; *what determined you to do it?*). **5** *tr.* & *intr.* esp. *Law* bring or come to an end. **6** *tr. Geom.* fix or define the position of. □ **be determined** be resolved (*was determined not to give up*). □□ **determinable** *adj.* [ME f. OF *determiner* f. L *determinare* (as DE-, *terminus* end)]
■ **1** ascertain, decide, find out, discover, learn, detect. **2, 4** settle (on *or* upon), fix on *or* upon, choose, select, resolve; make up one's mind; see also DECIDE 1. **3** affect, influence, act on, shape, condition, govern, regulate, dictate. **5** conclude, terminate; see also END *v.* 1.

determined /ditérmind/ *adj.* **1** showing determination; resolute, unflinching. **2** fixed in scope or character; settled; determinate. □□ **determinedly** *adv.* **determinedness** *n.*
■ **1** decided, resolute, resolved, purposeful, dogged, strong-willed, strong-minded, single-minded, tenacious, intent, firm, unflinching, unwavering, fixed, constant, persistent, persevering, steady, unfaltering, unhesitating, unyielding, stubborn, obstinate, adamant. **2** see DETERMINATE.

determiner /ditérminər/ *n.* **1** a person or thing that determines. **2** *Gram.* any of a class of words (e.g. *a*, *the*, *every*) that determine the kind of reference a noun or noun-substitute has.

determinism /ditérminiz'm/ *n. Philos.* the doctrine that all events, including human action, are determined by causes regarded as external to the will. □□ **determinist** *n.* **deterministic** /-nístik/ *adj.* **deterministically** /-nístikəli/ *adv.*

deterrent /ditérrənt/ *adj.* & *n.* ● *adj.* that deters. ● *n.* a deterrent thing or factor, esp. a nuclear weapon regarded as deterring an enemy from attack. □□ **deterrence** *n.*
■ *n.* hindrance, impediment, discouragement, disincentive, dissuasion, check, hitch, obstacle, obstruction, stumbling-block; catch, snag, rub, fly in the ointment, bar, drawback.

detest /ditést/ *v.tr.* hate, loathe. □□ **detester** *n.* [L *detestari* (as DE-, *testari* call to witness f. *testis* witness)]
■ despise, loathe, hate, abhor, execrate, abominate, be nauseated by, *literary* contemn.

detestable /ditéstəb'l/ *adj.* intensely disliked; hateful. □□ **detestably** *adv.*
■ see HATEFUL.

detestation /deétestáysh'n/ *n.* **1** intense dislike, hatred. **2** a detested person or thing. [ME f. OF f. L *detestatio -onis* (as DETEST)]
■ **1** see DISLIKE *n.* 1.

dethrone /deethrṓn/ *v.tr.* **1** remove from the throne, depose. **2** remove from a position of authority or influence. □□ **dethronement** *n.*
■ **1** see OVERTHROW *v.* 1–3. **2** see DOWNGRADE *v.* 1.

detonate /déttənayt/ *v.intr.* & *tr.* explode with a loud noise. □□ **detonative** *adj.* [L *detonare detonat-* (as DE-, *tonare* thunder)]
■ see EXPLODE 1.

detonation /déttənáysh'n/ *n.* **1 a** the act or process of detonating. **b** a loud explosion. **2** the premature combustion of fuel in an internal-combustion engine, causing it to pink. [F *détonation* f. *détoner* (as DETONATE)]
■ **1** see EXPLOSION 1, 2.

detonator /déttənaytər/ *n.* **1** a device for detonating an explosive. **2** a fog-signal that detonates, e.g. as used on railways.

detour /deétoor/ *n.* & *v.* ● *n.* a divergence from a direct or intended route; a roundabout course. ● *v.intr.* & *tr.* make or cause to make a detour. [F *détour* change of direction f. *détourner* turn away (as DE-, TURN)]
■ *n.* diversion, deviation, circuitous route *or* way, roundabout way, bypass. ● *v.* deviate (from), turn away (from), divert (from); see also BYPASS *v.*

detoxicate /deetóksikayt/ *v.tr.* = DETOXIFY. □□ **detoxication** /-káysh'n/ *n.* [DE- + L *toxicum* poison, after *intoxicate*]

detoxify /deetóksifī/ *v.tr.* remove the poison from. □□ **detoxification** /-fikáysh'n/ *n.* [DE- + L *toxicum* poison]

detract /ditrákt/ *v.tr.* (usu. foll. by *from*) take away (a part of something); reduce, diminish (*self-interest detracted nothing from their achievement*). □□ **detraction** *n.* **detractive** *adj.* **detractor** *n.* [L *detrahere detract-* (as DE-, *trahere* draw)]
■ (*detract from*) diminish, reduce, take (away) from, subtract from, lessen, depreciate, disparage.

detrain /deetráyn/ *v.intr.* & *tr.* alight or cause to alight from a train. □□ **detrainment** *n.*
■ see DISEMBARK.

detribalize /deetríbəlīz/ *v.tr.* (also **-ise**) **1** make (a person) no longer a member of a tribe. **2** destroy the tribal habits of. □□ **detribalization** /-záysh'n/ *n.*

detriment /détrimənt/ *n.* **1** harm, damage. **2** something causing this. [ME f. OF *detriment* or L *detrimentum* (as DE-, *terere trit-* rub, wear)]
■ disadvantage, drawback; damage, harm, ill, impairment, injury, hurt, loss.

detrimental /détrimént'l/ *adj.* harmful; causing loss. □□ **detrimentally** *adv.*
■ disadvantageous, harmful, injurious, hurtful, damaging, deleterious, destructive, prejudicial, adverse, unfavourable, inimical, pernicious.

detrition /ditrísh'n/ *n.* wearing away by friction. [med.L *detritio* (as DETRIMENT)]

detritus /ditrítəss/ *n.* **1** matter produced by erosion, such as gravel, sand, silt, rock-debris, etc. **2** debris of any kind; rubbish, waste. □□ **detrital** /ditrít'l/ *adj.* [after F *détritus* f. L *detritus* (n.) = wearing down (as DETRIMENT)]
■ **2** see JUNK[1] *n.* 1, 2.

de trop /də trṓ/ *predic.adj.* not wanted, unwelcome, in the way. [F, = excessive]
■ see NEEDLESS.

detumescence /déetyooméss'nss/ *n.* subsidence from a swollen state. [L *detumescere* (as DE-, *tumescere* swell)]

deuce[1] /dyōōss/ *n.* **1** the two on dice or playing cards. **2** (in lawn tennis) the score of 40 all, at which two consecutive points are needed to win. [OF *deus* f. L *duo* (accus. *duos*) two]

deuce[2] /dyōōss/ *n.* misfortune, the Devil, used esp. *colloq.* as an exclamation of surprise or annoyance (*who the deuce are you?*). □ **a** (or **the**) **deuce of a** a very bad or remarkable (*a deuce of a problem*; *a deuce of a fellow*). **the deuce to pay** trouble to be expected. [LG *duus*, formed as DEUCE[1], two aces at dice being the worst throw]
■ see DEVIL *n.* 1, 2; (**the deuce**) see *the devil* (DEVIL *n.* 7).

deuced /dyóōssid, dyōōst/ *adj.* & *adv. archaic* damned, confounded (*a deuced liar*). □□ **deucedly** /dyóōssidli/ *adv.*

deus ex machina /dáyōōss eks mákkinə, déeəss/ *n.* an unexpected power or event saving a seemingly hopeless situation, esp. in a play or novel. [mod.L transl. of Gk *theos ek mēkhanēs*, = god from the machinery (by which in the Greek theatre the gods were suspended above the stage)]

Deut. *abbr.* Deuteronomy (Old Testament).

deuteragonist /dyōōtərággənist/ *n.* the person second in importance to the protagonist in a drama. [Gk *deuteragōnistēs* (as DEUTERO-, *agōnistēs* actor)]

deuterate /dyóōtərayt/ *v.tr.* replace the usual isotope of hydrogen in (a substance) by deuterium. □□ **deuteration** /-ráysh'n/ *n.*

deuterium /dyootéeriəm/ *n. Chem.* a stable isotope of hydrogen with a mass about double that of the usual isotope. [mod.L, formed as DEUTERO- + -IUM]

deutero- /dyóōtərō/ *comb.form* second. [Gk *deuteros* second]

Deutero-Isaiah /dyóōtərō-īzíə/ *n.* the supposed later author of Isaiah 40–55.

deuteron /dyóōtəron/ *n. Physics* the nucleus of a deuterium atom, consisting of a proton and a neutron. [DEUTERIUM + -ON]

Deutschmark /dóychmaark/ *n.* (also **Deutsche Mark** /dóychə maark/) the chief monetary unit of Germany. [G, = German mark (see MARK[2])]

deutzia /dyóōtsiə, dóytsiə/ *n.* any ornamental shrub of the genus *Deutzia*, with usu. white flowers. [J. *Deutz* 18th-c. Du. patron of botany]

devalue /deeválуōō/ *v.tr.* (**devalues, devalued, devaluing**) **1** reduce the value of. **2** *Econ.* reduce the value of (a currency) in relation to other currencies or to gold (opp. REVALUE). □□ **devaluation** /-vályoo-áysh'n/ *n.*
■ see DEBASE.

Devanagari /dáyvənaágəri/ *n.* the alphabet used for Sanskrit, Hindi, and other Indian languages. [Skr., = divine town script]

devastate /dévvəstayt/ *v.tr.* **1** lay waste; cause great destruction to. **2** (often in *passive*) overwhelm with shock or grief; upset deeply. □□ **devastation** /-stáysh'n/ *n.* **devastator** *n.* [L *dēvastare devastat-* (as DE-, *vastare* lay waste)]
■ **1** lay waste, ravage, destroy, waste, sack, raze, ruin, desolate, spoil, wreck, demolish, level, flatten, gut, obliterate. **2** disconcert, discomfit, take aback, shatter, overwhelm; see also SHOCK[1] *v.* 1.

devastating /dévvəstayting/ *adj.* **1** crushingly effective; overwhelming. **2** *colloq.* **a** incisive, savage (*devastating accuracy, devastating wit*). **b** extremely impressive or attractive (*she wore a devastating black silk dress*). □□ **devastatingly** *adv.*
■ **1** overpowering, powerful, potent, awesome; see also OVERWHELMING. **2 a** keen, incisive, mordant, penetrating, trenchant, telling; brilliant, coruscating; sardonic, sarcastic, bitter, acid, satirical, virulent, savage, vitriolic. **b** spectacular, marvellous, splendid; ravishing, captivating, enthralling, bewitching, spellbinding, *colloq.* terrific; see also STUNNING.

develop /divélləp/ *v.* (**developed, developing**) **1** *tr.* & *intr.* **a** make or become bigger or fuller or more elaborate or systematic (*the new town developed rapidly*). **b** bring or come to an active or visible state or to maturity (*developed a plan of action*). **2 a** *tr.* begin to exhibit or suffer from (*developed a rattle*). **b** *intr.* come into existence; originate, emerge (*a fault developed in the engine*). **3** *tr.* **a** construct new buildings on (land). **b** convert (land) to a new purpose so as to use its resources more fully. **4** *tr.* treat (photographic film etc.) to make the latent image visible. **5** *tr. Mus.* elaborate (a theme) by modification of the melody, harmony, rhythm, etc. **6** *tr. Chess* bring (a piece) into position for effective use. □ **developing country** a poor or undeveloped country that is becoming more advanced economically and socially. □□ **developer** *n.* [F *développer* f. Rmc (as DIS-, orig. of second element unknown)]
■ **1** bring out *or* forth, advance, expand (on *or* upon), broaden, enlarge (on *or* upon), amplify, evolve, expatiate (on *or* upon), elaborate (on *or* upon), reveal, lay open, expose, unfold, disclose, bare, (cause to) grow, realize the potential (of); cultivate, improve, promote, exploit, strengthen; mature, ripen, age; flower, blossom, bloom. **2 a** exhibit, display, show, demonstrate, manifest; go *or* come down with; see also CONTRACT *v.* 3. **b** emerge, arise, appear, come out, come to light, evolve, originate, begin, happen, occur, come about, *formal* commence; come forth, result. □ **developing country** underdeveloped country, third world country. □□ **developer** builder, construction company.

developable /divélləpəb'l/ *adj.* that can be developed. □ **developable surface** *Geom.* a surface that can be flattened into a plane without overlap or separation, e.g. a cylinder.

development /divélləpmənt/ *n.* **1** the act or an instance of developing; the process of being developed. **2 a** a stage of growth or advancement. **b** a thing that has developed, esp. an event or circumstance (*the latest developments*). **3** a full-grown state. **4** the process of developing a photograph. **5** a developed area of land. **6** *Mus.* the elaboration of a theme or themes, esp. in the middle section of a sonata movement. **7** *Chess* the developing of pieces from their original position. □ **development area** *Brit.* one where new industries are encouraged in order to counteract unemployment.

■ **1** evolution, growth, evolvement, maturation, unfolding, increase, expansion, enlargement, increment; advance, advancement, progress; improvement; building, construction (work). **2 b** occurrence, happening, event, incident, circumstance, situation, condition, phenomenon.

developmental /divélləpmént'l/ *adj.* **1** incidental to growth (*developmental diseases*). **2** evolutionary. □□ **developmentally** *adv.*

deviant /deéviənt/ *adj.* & *n.* ● *adj.* that deviates from the normal, esp. with reference to sexual practices. ● *n.* a deviant person or thing. □□ **deviance** *n.* **deviancy** *n.* [ME (as DEVIATE)]

■ *adj.* deviating, divergent, different, strange, uncommon, unusual, odd, peculiar, curious, eccentric, idiosyncratic, queer, quirky, weird, bizarre, offbeat, singular, freaky, freakish; perverse, aberrant, abnormal, unnatural, degenerate, depraved, *colloq.* kinky, *sl.* bent. ● *n.* see ECCENTRIC *n.*

deviate *v.* & *n.* ● *v.intr.* /deéviayt/ (often foll. by *from*) turn aside or diverge (from a course of action, rule, truth, etc.); digress. ● *n.* /déeviət/ a deviant, esp. a sexual pervert. □□ **deviator** *n.* **deviatory** /-viətəri/ *adj.* [LL *deviare deviat-* (as DE-, *via* way)]

■ *v.* turn aside *or* away, swerve, veer, wander, stray, drift, digress, diverge; divert. ● *n.* pervert, deviant, degenerate, debauchee.

deviation /deéviáysh'n/ *n.* **1 a** deviating, digressing. **b** an instance of this. **2** *Polit.* a departure from accepted (esp. Communist) party doctrine. **3** *Statistics* the amount by which a single measurement differs from the mean. **4** *Naut.* the deflection of a ship's compass-needle caused by iron in the ship etc. □ **standard deviation** *Statistics* a quantity calculated to indicate the extent of deviation for a group as a whole. □□ **deviational** *adj.* **deviationism** *n.* **deviationist** *n.* [F *déviation* f. med.L *deviatio -onis* (as DEVIATE)]

■ **1** see *digression* (DIGRESS).

device /divī́ss/ *n.* **1 a** a thing made or adapted for a particular purpose, esp. a mechanical contrivance. **b** an explosive contrivance, a bomb. **2** a plan, scheme, or trick. **3 a** an emblematic or heraldic design. **b** a drawing or design. **4** *archaic* make, look (*things of rare device*). □ **leave a person to his** or **her own devices** leave a person to do as he or she wishes. [ME f. OF *devis* ult. f. L (as DIVIDE)]

■ **1 a** contrivance, mechanism, machine, machinery, implement, utensil, apparatus, instrument, appliance, tool, gadget, *Brit.* gubbins, *colloq.* widget, doodah, thingumajig, thingummy, thingy, *US colloq.* hickey, *derog. or joc.* contraption, *sl.* jigger, gismo. **b** see BOMB *n.* 1. **2** stratagem, trick, artifice, ruse, plot, gambit, strategy, manoeuvre, machination, plan, *colloq.* ploy; see also SCHEME *n.* 2. **3** emblem, figure, *Heraldry* charge, cognizance, (heraldic) bearing; insignia, hallmark, badge, signet, coat of arms, seal, crest; design, drawing, symbol, colophon, logotype, monogram, *colloq.* logo. **4** look, make, appearance, aspect.

devil /dévv'l/ *n.* & *v.* ● *n.* **1** (usu. **the Devil**) (in Christian and Jewish belief) the supreme spirit of evil; Satan. **2 a** an evil spirit; a demon; a superhuman malignant being. **b** a personified evil force or attribute. **3 a** a wicked or cruel person. **b** a mischievously energetic, clever, or self-willed person. **4** *colloq.* a person, a fellow (*lucky devil*). **5** fighting spirit, mischievousness (*the devil is in him tonight*). **6** *colloq.* something difficult or awkward (*this door is a devil to open*). **7** (**the devil** or **the Devil**) *colloq.* used as an exclamation of surprise or annoyance (*who the devil are you?*). **8** a literary hack exploited by an employer. **9** *Brit.* a junior legal counsel. **10** = *Tasmanian devil.* **11** applied to various instruments and machines, esp. when used for destructive work. **12** *S.Afr.* = *dust devil.* ● *v.* (**devilled, devilling;** *US* **deviled, deviling**) **1** *tr.* cook (food) with hot seasoning. **2** *intr.* act as a devil for an author or barrister. **3** *tr. US* harass, worry. □ **between the devil and the deep blue sea** in a dilemma. **devil-may-care** cheerful and reckless. **a devil of** *colloq.* a considerable, difficult, or remarkable. **devil a one** not even one. **devil ray** any cartilaginous fish of the family Mobulidae, esp. the manta. **devil's advocate** a person who tests a proposition by arguing against it. **devil's bit** any of various plants whose roots look bitten off, esp. a kind of scabious (*Succisa pratensis*). **devil's coach-horse** *Brit.* a large rove-beetle, *Staphylinus olens.* **devil's darning-needle** a dragonfly or damselfly. **devil's dozen** thirteen. **devils-on-horseback** a savoury of prune or plum wrapped in slices of bacon. **devil's own** *colloq.* very difficult or unusual (*the devil's own job*). **devil take the hindmost** a motto of selfish competition. **the devil to pay** trouble to be expected. **go to the devil 1** be damned. **2** (in *imper.*) depart at once. **like the devil** with great energy. **play the devil with** cause severe damage to. **printer's devil** *hist.* an errand-boy in a printing office. **speak** (or **talk**) **of the devil** said when a person appears just after being mentioned. **the very devil** (*predic.*) *colloq.* a great difficulty or nuisance. [OE *dēofol* f. LL *diabolus* f. Gk *diabolos* accuser, slanderer f. *dia* across + *ballō* to throw]

■ *n.* **1, 2** Satan, Lucifer, Mephistopheles, Beelzebub, Abaddon, Belial, Prince of Darkness, Tempter, deuce, arch-enemy, evil one, *colloq.* Old Nick; fiend, spirit of evil, evil spirit, demon, cacodemon, bogey, bugaboo, gremlin, *archaic* bugbear. **3 a** brute, fiend, demon, beast, ogre, monster, rogue, scoundrel, knave, villain, ghoul, hell-hound, barbarian. **b** imp, fox, mischief-maker, gamin, trickster, (little) monkey, *archaic or joc.* rapscallion, *colloq.* scamp, slyboots, *joc.* rogue, *often joc.* rascal. **4** fellow, person, chap, wretch, *colloq.* guy, beggar, *Brit. colloq.* blighter, *sl.* geezer, bastard, *Brit. sl.* bloke, toerag. **5** see MISCHIEF 1–3. **6** see PROBLEM 1, 2, BITCH *n.* 3. **7** (**the devil**) in heaven's name, in the world, in God's name, in the name of God, *colloq.* on earth, the dickens, the deuce. ● *v.* **3** see WORRY *v.* 2.

□ **devil-may-care** see RECKLESS. **a devil of** see CONSIDERABLE 1, 2, DIFFICULT 1, REMARKABLE 1. **devil's own** fiendish, *colloq.* beastly; see also DIFFICULT 1, UNUSUAL 2. **go to the devil 2** see *beat it.* **like the devil** rapidly, very fast, at a gallop, *colloq.* at the rate of knots, like a dose of salts, like thunder, like greased lightning, like the wind, *literary* apace, *Brit. sl.* like the clappers; see also *vigorously* (VIGOROUS).

devilfish /dévv'lfish/ *n.* (*pl.* same or **-fishes**) **1** = *devil ray.* **2** any of various fish, esp. the stonefish. **3** *hist.* an octopus.

devilish /dévvəlish/ *adj.* & *adv.* ● *adj.* **1** of or like a devil; wicked. **2** mischievous. ● *adv. colloq.* very, extremely. □□ **devilishly** *adv.* **devilishness** *n.*

■ *adj.* **1** diabolical, diabolic, wicked, evil, satanic, Mephistophelian, fiendish, demonic, demoniacal, demoniac, infernal, hellish, villainous, sinister, iniquitous, sinful, flagitious, heinous, malign, malevolent, malignant, cruel. **2** impish, prankish, naughty; see also MISCHIEVOUS 1, 2. ● *adv.* see VERY *adv.*

devilment /dévvəlmənt/ *n.* mischief, wild spirits.

■ see MISCHIEF 1–3.

devilry /dévvilri/ *n.* (also **deviltry**) (*pl.* **-ies**) **1 a** wickedness; reckless mischief. **b** an instance of this. **2 a** black magic. **b** the Devil and his works. [OF *diablerie*: *-try* wrongly after *harlotry* etc.]

■ **1 a** devilishness, wickedness, evil, fiendishness, cruelty, malice, malevolence, viciousness, perversity, iniquity, hellishness, villainy; mischief, diablerie, mischievousness, roguery, naughtiness, roguishness, knavery, knavishness, *often joc.* rascality.

devious /deéviəss/ *adj.* **1** (of a person etc.) not straightforward, underhand. **2** winding, circuitous. **3** erring, straying. □□ **deviously** *adv.* **deviousness** *n.* [L *devius* f. DE- + *via* way]

■ **1** deceitful, underhanded, underhand, insincere, deceptive, misleading, sneaky, furtive, surreptitious, secretive, double-dealing, treacherous, dishonest, smooth, slick, cunning, slippery, scheming, plotting, designing, foxy, vulpine, wily, sly, crafty, tricky, *colloq.* shifty. **2** winding, indirect, roundabout, zigzag, evasive, circuitous, crooked, rambling, serpentine, tortuous, sinuous, anfractuous.

devise /divīz/ *v.* & *n.* • *v.tr.* **1** plan or invent by careful thought. **2** *Law* leave (real estate) by the terms of a will (cf. BEQUEATH). • *n.* **1** the act or an instance of devising. **2** *Law* a devising clause in a will. □□ **devisable** *adj.* **devisee** /-zeé/ *n.* (in sense 2 of *v.*). **deviser** *n.* **devisor** *n.* (in sense 2 of *v.*). [ME f. OF *deviser* ult. f. L *dividere divis-* DIVIDE: (n.) f. OF *devise* f. med.L *divisa* fem. past part. of *dividere*]

▪ *v.* **1** concoct, make up, conceive, scheme, contrive, dream up, design, draft, frame, form, formulate, plan, work out, think up, originate, invent, create, *colloq.* cook up. **2** bequeath, will, convey, hand down, give, assign, dispose of, transfer, bestow.

devitalize /deevītəlīz/ *v.tr.* (also **-ise**) take away strength and vigour from. □□ **devitalization** /-záysh'n/ *n.*

▪ see ENERVATE *v.*

devitrify /deevítrifī/ *v.tr.* (**-ies, -ied**) deprive of vitreous qualities; make (glass or vitreous rock) opaque and crystalline. □□ **devitrification** /-fikáysh'n/ *n.*

devoid /divóyd/ *predic.adj.* (foll. by *of*) quite lacking or free from (*a book devoid of all interest*). [ME, past part. of obs. *devoid* f. OF *devoidier* (as DE-, VOID)]

devoir /devwaár/ *n. archaic* **1** duty, one's best (*do one's devoir*). **2** (in *pl.*) courteous or formal attentions; respects (*pay one's devoirs to*). [ME f. AF *dever* = OF *deveir* f. L *debēre* owe]

devolute /deévəlōōt, -lyōōt/ *v.tr.* transfer by devolution. [as DEVOLVE]

devolution /deévəlōōsh'n, -lyōōsh'n/ *n.* **1** the delegation of power, esp. by central government to local or regional administration. **2 a** descent or passing on through a series of stages. **b** descent by natural or due succession from one to another of property or qualities. **3** the lapse of an unexercised right to an ultimate owner. **4** *Biol.* degeneration. □□ **devolutionary** *adj.* **devolutionist** *n.* [LL *devolutio* (as DEVOLVE)]

devolve /divólv/ *v.* **1** (foll. by *on, upon*, etc.) **a** *tr.* pass (work or duties) to (a deputy etc.). **b** *intr.* (of work or duties) pass to (a deputy etc.). **2** *intr.* (foll. by *on, to, upon*) *Law* (of property etc.) descend or fall by succession to. □□ **devolvement** *n.* [ME f. L *devolvere devolut-* (as DE-, *volvere* roll)]

Devonian /divṓniən/ *adj.* & *n.* • *adj.* **1** of or relating to Devon in SW England. **2** *Geol.* of or relating to the fourth period of the Palaeozoic era with evidence of the first amphibians and tree forests. ¶ Cf. Appendix VII. • *n.* **1** this period or system. **2** a native of Devon. [med.L *Devonia* Devonshire]

dévot /dayvṓ/ *n.* (*fem.* ***dévote*** /-vŏt/) a devotee. [F f. OF (as DEVOUT)]

devote /divṓt/ *v.tr.* & *refl.* **1** (foll. by *to*) apply or give over (resources etc. or oneself) to (a particular activity or purpose or person) (*devoted their time to reading; devoted himself to his guests*). **2** *archaic* doom to destruction. □□ **devotement** *n.* [L *devovēre devot-* (as DE-, *vovēre* vow)]

▪ **1** apply, appropriate, assign, allot, commit, give up, allocate, set aside *or* apart, put aside, dedicate, consecrate; pledge.

devoted /divṓtid/ *adj.* very loving or loyal (*a devoted husband*). □□ **devotedly** *adv.* **devotedness** *n.*

▪ faithful, true, dedicated, committed, devout, loyal, loving, doting, staunch, tender, steadfast, constant; ardent, caring, fond, earnest, zealous, enthusiastic.

devotee /dévvəteé/ *n.* **1** (usu. foll. by *of*) a zealous enthusiast or supporter. **2** a zealously pious or fanatical person.

▪ **1** fan, aficionado, adherent, votary, enthusiast, energumen, addict; hound, *colloq.* buff, *sl.* nut, freak, fiend. **2** *dévot, dévote*, energumen.

devotion /divṓsh'n/ *n.* **1** (usu. foll. by *to*) enthusiastic attachment or loyalty (to a person or cause); great love. **2 a** religious worship. **b** (in *pl.*) prayers. **c** devoutness, religious fervour. □□ **devotional** *adj.* [ME f. OF *devotion* or L *devotio* (as DEVOTE)]

▪ **1** zeal, ardour, fervour, ardency, intensity, fanaticism, eagerness, enthusiasm, earnestness, readiness, willingness; love, passion, infatuation, fondness, affection, attachment, adherence, loyalty, allegiance; dedication, devotedness. **2 a** worship, prayer(s), praying, observance(s), ritual. **c** devotedness, devoutness, fervour, reverence, religiousness, piety, religiosity, pietism, godliness, holiness, spirituality, saintliness.

devour /divówr/ *v.tr.* **1** eat hungrily or greedily. **2** (of fire etc.) engulf, destroy. **3** take in greedily with the eyes or ears (*devoured book after book*). **4** absorb the attention of (*devoured by anxiety*). □□ **devourer** *n.* **devouringly** *adv.* [ME f. OF *devorer* f. L *devorare* (as DE-, *vorare* swallow)]

▪ **1** wolf (down), gulp (down), bolt, swallow (up), gorge, gobble (up), gormandize, *colloq.* kill. **2** consume, destroy, wipe out, ravage, annihilate, demolish, ruin, wreak havoc (up)on, devastate, obliterate, eradicate; engulf, swamp, overcome, overwhelm. **3** absorb, be absorbed by; engulf, consume, drink in, eat up, swallow up, take in. **4** consumed, absorbed, obsessed.

devout /divówt/ *adj.* **1** earnestly religious. **2** earnestly sincere (*devout hope*). □□ **devoutly** *adv.* **devoutness** *n.* [ME f. OF *devot* f. L *devotus* past part. (as DEVOTE)]

▪ **1** devoted, pious, religious, reverent, faithful, dedicated, staunch, churchgoing, *archaic* worshipful, *Brit. sl.* pi; holy, godly, saintly, pure; devotional, reverential. **2** earnest, sincere, genuine, hearty, heartfelt, devoted, ardent, zealous, true.

DEW *abbr.* distant early warning.

dew /dyōō/ *n.* & *v.* • *n.* **1** atmospheric vapour condensing in small drops on cool surfaces at night. **2** beaded or glistening moisture resembling this, e.g. tears. **3** freshness, refreshing quality. • *v.tr.* wet with or as with dew. □ **dew-claw 1** a rudimentary inner toe found on some dogs. **2** a false hoof on a deer etc. **dew-fall 1** the time when dew begins to form. **2** evening. **dew-point** the temperature at which dew forms. **dew-pond** a shallow usu. artificial pond once supposed to have been fed by atmospheric condensation. [OE *dēaw* f. Gmc]

▪ *v.* bedew, damp, dampen, moisten; see also WET *v.*

dewan /diwaán/ *n.* the prime minister or finance minister of an Indian state. [Arab. & Pers. *dīwān* fiscal register]

dewar /dyōōər/ *n. Physics* a double-walled flask with a vacuum between the walls to reduce the transfer of heat. [Sir James *Dewar*, Brit. physicist d. 1923]

dewberry /dyōōbəri/ *n.* (*pl.* **-ies**) **1** a bluish fruit like the blackberry. **2** the shrub, *Rubus caesius*, bearing this.

dewdrop /dyōōdrop/ *n.* a drop of dew.

Dewey system /dyōō-i/ *n.* a decimal system of library classification. [M. *Dewey*, Amer. librarian d. 1931, its deviser]

dewlap /dyōōlap/ *n.* **1** a loose fold of skin hanging from the throat of cattle, dogs, etc. **2** similar loose skin round the throat of an elderly person. [ME f. DEW + LAP[1], perh. after ON (unrecorded) *döggleppr*]

dewy /dyōō-i/ *adj.* (**dewier, dewiest**) **1 a** wet with dew. **b** moist as if with dew. **2** of or like dew. □ **dewy-eyed** innocently trusting; naïvely sentimental. □□ **dewily** *adv.* **dewiness** *n.* [OE *dēawig* (as DEW, -Y[1])]

▪ **1** see MOIST 1a.

dexter[1] /dékstər/ *adj.* esp. *Heraldry* on or of the right-hand side (the observer's left) of a shield etc. [L, = on the right]

dexter[2] /dékstər/ *n.* **1** an animal of a small hardy breed of Irish cattle. **2** this breed. [19th c.: perh. f. the name of a breeder]

dexterity /dekstérriti/ *n.* **1** skill in handling. **2** manual or mental adroitness. **3** right-handedness, using the right hand. [F *dextérité* f. L *dexteritas* (as DEXTER[1])]

▪ **1** touch, nimbleness, adroitness, deftness, facility, knack, skill, proficiency; sleight of hand. **2** adroitness, cleverness, ingenuity, ingeniousness, tact, astuteness, keenness, sharpness, shrewdness, canniness, artfulness.

dexterous /dékstrəss/ *adj.* (also **dextrous**) having or showing dexterity. □□ **dexterously** *adv.* **dexterousness** *n.* [L DEXTER[1] + -OUS]
■ deft, lithe, nimble, supple, agile, quick, skilful, slick; clever, ingenious, astute, keen, sharp, shrewd, canny, artful, crafty.

dextral /dékstrəl/ *adj.* & *n.* ● *adj.* **1** (of a person) right-handed. **2** of or on the right. **3** *Zool.* (of a spiral shell) with whorls rising to the right and coiling in an anticlockwise direction. **4** *Zool.* (of a flat-fish) with the right side uppermost. ● *n.* a right-handed person. □□ **dextrality** /-strálliti/ *n.* **dextrally** *adv.* [med.L *dextralis* f. L *dextra* right hand]

dextran /dékstran/ *n. Chem.* & *Pharm.* **1** an amorphous gum formed by the fermentation of sucrose etc. **2** a degraded form of this used as a substitute for blood-plasma. [G (as DEXTRO- + *-an* as in Chem. names)]

dextrin /dékstrin/ *n. Chem.* a soluble gummy substance obtained from starch and used as an adhesive. [F *dextrine* f. L *dextra*: see DEXTRO-, -IN]

dextro- /dékstrō/ *comb. form* on or to the right (*dextrorotatory*; *dextrose*). [L *dexter*, *dextra* on or to the right]

dextrorotatory /dékstrō-rōtáytəri/ *adj. Chem.* having the property of rotating the plane of a polarized light ray to the right (cf. LAEVOROTATORY). □□ **dextrorotation** *n.*

dextrorse /dékstrorss/ *adj.* rising towards the right, esp. of a spiral stem. [L *dextrorsus* (as DEXTRO-)]

dextrose /dékstrōss/ *n. Chem.* the dextrorotatory form of glucose. [formed as DEXTRO- + -OSE[2]]

dextrous var. of DEXTEROUS.

DF *abbr.* **1** Defender of the Faith. **2** direction-finder. [in sense 1 f. L *Defensor Fidei*]

DFC *abbr. Brit.* Distinguished Flying Cross.

DFM *abbr. Brit.* Distinguished Flying Medal.

DG *abbr.* **1** *Dei gratia.* **2** *Deo gratias.* **3** director-general.

dhal /daal/ *n.* (also **dal**) **1** a kind of split pulse, a common foodstuff in India. **2** a dish made with this. [Hindi]

dharma /daármə/ *n. Ind.* **1** social custom; the right behaviour. **2** the Buddhist truth. **3** the Hindu social or moral law. [Skr., = decree, custom]

dhobi /dṓbi/ *n.* (*pl.* **dhobis**) *Ind.* etc. a washerman or washerwoman. □ **dhobi** (or **dhobi's**) **itch** a tropical skin disease; an allergic dermatitis. [Hindi *dhobī* f. *dhob* washing]

dhoti /dṓti/ *n.* (*pl.* **dhotis**) the loincloth worn by male Hindus. [Hindi *dhotī*]

dhow /dow/ *n.* a lateen-rigged ship used on the Arabian sea. [19th c.: orig. unkn.]

DHSS *abbr. hist.* (in the UK) Department of Health and Social Security (cf. DoH, DSS).

dhurra var. of DURRA.

DI *abbr. Brit.* Defence Intelligence.

di-[1] /dī/ *comb. form* **1** twice, two-, double. **2** *Chem.* containing two atoms, molecules, or groups of a specified kind (*dichromate*; *dioxide*). [Gk f. *dis* twice]

di-[2] /dī, di/ *prefix* form of DIS- occurring before *l*, *m*, *n*, *r*, *s* (foll. by a consonant), *v*, usu. *g*, and sometimes *j*. [L var. of *dis*-]

di-[3] /dī/ *prefix* form of DIA- before a vowel.

dia. *abbr.* diameter.

dia- /dīə/ *prefix* (also **di-** before a vowel) **1** through (*diaphanous*). **2** apart (*diacritical*). **3** across (*diameter*). [Gk f. *dia* through]

diabetes /dīəbeéteez/ *n.* **1** any disorder of the metabolism with excessive thirst and the production of large amounts of urine. **2** (in full **diabetes mellitus**) the commonest form of diabetes in which sugar and starch are not properly absorbed from the blood, with thirst, emaciation, and excessive excretion of urine with glucose. □ **diabetes insipidus** a rare metabolic disorder due to a pituitary deficiency, with excessive urination and thirst. [orig. = siphon: L f. Gk f. *diabainō* go through]

diabetic /dīəbéttik/ *adj.* & *n.* ● *adj.* **1** of or relating to or having diabetes. **2** for use by diabetics. ● *n.* a person suffering from diabetes.

diablerie /dīaábləri/ *n.* **1** the devil's work; sorcery. **2** wild recklessness. **3** the realm of devils; devil-lore. [F f. *diable* f. L *diabolus* DEVIL]
■ **2** see DEVILRY.

diabolic /dīəbóllik/ *adj.* (also **diabolical** /-bóllik'l/) **1** of the Devil. **2** devilish; inhumanly cruel or wicked. **3** fiendishly clever or cunning or annoying. **4** *colloq.* disgracefully bad or defective; outrageous, atrocious. □□ **diabolically** *adv.* [ME f. OF *diabolique* or LL *diabolicus* f. L *diabolus* (as DEVIL)]
■ **1** devilish, satanic, Mephistophelian, demonic, demoniacal, demoniac, fiendish, hellish, infernal. **2** devilish, cruel, wicked, iniquitous, evil, fiendish, appalling, dreadful, inhuman, atrocious, execrable, abominable, awful, terrible, damnable, accursed, horrid, horrible, hideous, monstrous, odious, vile, base, corrupt, foul, depraved, flagitious, heinous, malicious, malevolent, malign, sinister, sinful, impious, bad, *literary* maleficent. **4** see DISGRACEFUL.

diabolism /dīábbəliz'm/ *n.* **1 a** belief in or worship of the Devil. **b** sorcery. **2** devilish conduct or character. □□ **diabolist** *n.* [Gk *diabolos* DEVIL]
■ **1 b** see *sorcery* (SORCERER).

diabolize /dīábbəlīz/ *v.tr.* (also **-ise**) make into or represent as a devil.

diabolo /diábbəlō, dī-/ *n.* (*pl.* **-os**) **1** a game in which a two-headed top is thrown up and caught with a string stretched between two sticks. **2** the top itself. [It., = DEVIL: formerly called *devil on two sticks*]

diachronic /dīəkrónnik/ *adj. Linguistics* etc. concerned with the historical development of a subject (esp. a language) (opp. SYNCHRONIC). □□ **diachronically** *adv.* **diachronism** /dīákrəniz'm/ *n.* **diachronistic** /dīákrənístik/ *adj.* **diachronous** /dīákrənəss/ *adj.* **diachrony** /dīákrəni/ *n.* [F *diachronique* (as DIA-, CHRONIC)]

diaconal /dīákkən'l/ *adj.* of a deacon. [eccl.L *diaconalis* f. *diaconus* DEACON]

diaconate /dīákkənayt, -nət/ *n.* **1 a** the office of deacon. **b** a person's time as deacon. **2** a body of deacons. [eccl.L *diaconatus* (as DIACONAL)]

diacritic /dīəkríttik/ *n.* & *adj.* ● *n.* a sign (e.g. an accent, diaeresis, cedilla) used to indicate different sounds or values of a letter. ● *adj.* = DIACRITICAL. [Gk *diakritikos* (as DIA-, CRITIC)]

diacritical /dīəkríttik'l/ *adj.* & *n.* ● *adj.* distinguishing, distinctive. ● *n.* (in full **diacritical mark** or **sign**) = DIACRITIC.

diadelphous /dīədélfəss/ *adj. Bot.* with the stamens united in two bundles (cf. MONADELPHOUS, POLYADELPHOUS). [DI-[1] + Gk *adelphos* brother]

diadem /dīədem/ *n.* & *v.* ● *n.* **1** a crown or headband worn as a sign of sovereignty. **2** a wreath of leaves or flowers worn round the head. **3** sovereignty. **4** a crowning distinction or glory. ● *v.tr.* (esp. as **diademed** *adj.*) adorn with or as with a diadem. [ME f. OF *diademe* f. L *diadema* f. Gk *diadēma* (as DIA-, *deō* bind)]
■ *n.* **1** see CROWN *n.* 1. **2** see GARLAND *n.* 1.

diaeresis /dī-éerəsiss/ *n.* (*US* **dieresis**) (*pl.* **-ses** /-seez/) **1** a mark (as in *naïve*) over a vowel to indicate that it is sounded separately. **2** *Prosody* a break where a foot ends at the end of a word. [L f. Gk, = separation]

diagenesis /dīəjénnisiss/ *n. Geol.* the transformation occurring during the conversion of sedimentation to sedimentary rock.

diagnose /dīəgnṓz/ *v.tr.* make a diagnosis of (a disease, a mechanical fault, etc.) from its symptoms. □□ **diagnosable** *adj.*
■ identify, name, determine, recognize, distinguish, pinpoint, interpret; analyse.

diagnosis /dīəgnṓsiss/ *n.* (*pl.* **diagnoses** /-seez/) **1 a** the identification of a disease by means of a patient's symptoms.

b an instance or formal statement of this. **2 a** the identification of the cause of a mechanical fault etc. **b** an instance of this. **3 a** the distinctive characterization in precise terms of a genus, species, etc. **b** an instance of this. [mod.L f. Gk (as DIA-, *gignōskō* recognize)]

■ **1, 2** see *interpretation* (INTERPRET).

diagnostic /dīəgnóstik/ *adj.* & *n.* ● *adj.* of or assisting diagnosis. ● *n.* a symptom. □□ **diagnostically** *adv.* **diagnostician** /-nostísh'n/ *n.* [Gk *diagnōstikos* (as DIAGNOSIS)]

diagnostics /dīəgnóstiks/ *n.* **1** (treated as *pl.*) *Computing* programs and other mechanisms used to detect and identify faults in hardware or software. **2** (treated as *sing.*) the science or study of diagnosing disease.

diagonal /dīággən'l/ *adj.* & *n.* ● *adj.* **1** crossing a straight-sided figure from corner to corner. **2** slanting, oblique. ● *n.* a straight line joining two non-adjacent corners. □□ **diagonally** *adv.* [L *diagonalis* f. Gk *diagōnios* (as DIA-, *gōnia* angle)]

■ *adj.* see OBLIQUE *adj.* 1.

diagram /dīəgram/ *n.* & *v.* ● *n.* **1** a drawing showing the general scheme or outline of an object and its parts. **2** a graphic representation of the course or results of an action or process. **3** *Geom.* a figure made of lines used in proving a theorem etc. ● *v.tr.* (**diagrammed, diagramming**; *US* **diagramed, diagraming**) represent by means of a diagram. □□ **diagrammatic** /-grəmáttik/ *adj.* **diagrammatically** /-grəmáttikəli/ *adv.* [L *diagramma* f. Gk (as DIA-, -GRAM)]

■ *n.* **1, 2** see PLAN *n.* 2.

diagrid /dīəgrid/ *n. Archit.* a supporting structure of diagonally intersecting ribs of metal etc. [DIAGONAL + GRID]

diakinesis /dīəkinéessiss, -kīnéessiss/ *n.* (*pl.* **diakineses** /-seez/) *Biol.* a stage during the prophase of meiosis when the separation of homologous chromosomes is complete and crossing over has occurred. [mod.L f. G *Diakinese* (as DIA-, Gk *kinēsis* motion)]

dial /dīəl/ *n.* & *v.* ● *n.* **1** the face of a clock or watch, marked to show the hours etc. **2** a similar flat plate marked with a scale for measuring weight, volume, pressure, consumption, etc., indicated by a pointer. **3** a movable disc on a telephone, with finger-holes and numbers for making a connection. **4 a** a plate or disc etc. on a radio or television set for selecting wavelength or channel. **b** a similar selecting device on other equipment, e.g. a washing machine. **5** *Brit. sl.* a person's face. ● *v.* (**dialled, dialling**; *US* **dialed, dialing**) **1** *tr.* (also *absol.*) select (a telephone number) by means of a dial or set of buttons (*dialled 999*). **2** *tr.* measure, indicate, or regulate by means of a dial. □ **dialling code** a sequence of numbers dialled to connect a telephone with the exchange of the telephone being called. **dialling tone** (*US* **dial tone**) a sound indicating that a caller may start to dial. □□ **dialler** *n.* [ME, = sundial, f. med.L *diale* clock-dial ult. f. L *dies* day]

■ *n.* **1, 2** see INDICATOR 2, 3. **4** see CONTROL *n.* 5. **5** see MUG[1] *n.* 2. ● *v.* **1** see CALL *v.* 2.

dialect /dīəlekt/ *n.* **1** a form of speech peculiar to a particular region. **2** a subordinate variety of a language with non-standard vocabulary, pronunciation, or grammar. □□ **dialectal** /-léktəl/ *adj.* **dialectology** /-tólləji/ *n.* **dialectologist** /-tólləjist/ *n.* [F *dialecte* or L *dialectus* f. Gk *dialektos* discourse f. *dialegomai* converse]

■ **1** speech (pattern), phraseology, idiom, accent, pronunciation, patois, brogue, vernacular. **2** jargon, cant, slang, argot, language, tongue, *colloq.* lingo.

dialectic /dīəléktik/ *n.* & *adj.* ● *n.* **1** (often in *pl.*) **a** the art of investigating the truth of opinions; the testing of truth by discussion. **b** logical disputation. **2** *Philos.* **a** inquiry into metaphysical contradictions and their solutions, esp. in the thought of Kant and Hegel. **b** the existence or action of opposing social forces etc. ● *adj.* **1** of or relating to logical disputation. **2** fond of or skilled in logical disputation. [ME f. OF *dialectique* or L *dialectica* f. Gk *dialektikē* (*tekhnē*) (art) of debate (as DIALECT)]

■ *n.* **1** (*dialectics*) see LOGIC.

dialectical /dīəléktik'l/ *adj.* of dialectic or dialectics. □ **dialectical materialism** the Marxist theory that political and historical events are due to a conflict of social forces caused by man's material needs. □□ **dialectically** *adv.*

dialectician /dīəlektísh'n/ *n.* a person skilled in dialectic. [F *dialecticien* f. L *dialecticus*]

dialectics /dīəléktiks/ *n.* (treated as *sing.* or *pl.*) = DIALECTIC *n.*

dialogic /dīəlójik/ *adj.* of or in dialogue. [LL *dialogicus* f. Gk *dialogikos* (as DIALOGUE)]

dialogist /dīálləjist/ *n.* a speaker in or writer of dialogue. [LL *dialogista* f. Gk *dialogistēs* (as DIALOGUE)]

dialogue /dīəlog/ *n.* (*US* **dialog**) **1 a** conversation. **b** conversation in written form; this as a form of composition. **2 a** a discussion, esp. one between representatives of two political groups. **b** a conversation, a talk (*long dialogues between the two main characters*). [ME f. OF *dialoge* f. L *dialogus* f. Gk *dialogos* f. *dialegomai* converse]

■ **1 a** see CONVERSATION. **2 a** duologue, conversation, discussion, meeting, conference, colloquy, communication, *colloq.* huddle. **b** conversation, parley, talk, chat, conference, colloquy, confabulation, *US* bull session, *colloq.* confab, *sl.* rap (session), chin-wag.

dialyse /dīəlīz/ *v.tr.* (*US* **dialyze**) separate by means of dialysis.

dialysis /dīállisiss/ *n.* (*pl.* **dialyses** /-seez/) **1** *Chem.* the separation of particles in a liquid by differences in their ability to pass through a membrane into another liquid. **2** *Med.* the clinical purification of blood by this technique. □□ **dialytic** /dīəlíttik/ *adj.* [L f. Gk *dialusis* (as DIA-, *luō* set free)]

diamagnetic /dīəmagnéttik/ *adj.* & *n.* ● *adj.* tending to become magnetized in a direction at right angles to the applied magnetic field. ● *n.* a diamagnetic body or substance. □□ **diamagnetically** *adv.* **diamagnetism** /-mágnitiz'm/ *n.*

diamanté /diəmóntay/ *adj.* & *n.* ● *adj.* decorated with powdered crystal or another sparkling substance. ● *n.* fabric or costume jewellery so decorated. [F, past part. of *diamanter* set with diamonds f. *diamant* DIAMOND]

diamantiferous /dīəmantiffərəss/ *adj.* diamond-yielding. [F *diamantifère* f. *diamant* DIAMOND]

diamantine /dīəmántīn/ *adj.* of or like diamonds. [F *diamantin* (as DIAMANTIFEROUS)]

diameter /dīámmitər/ *n.* **1 a** a straight line passing from side to side through the centre of a body or figure, esp. a circle or sphere. **b** the length of this line. **2** a transverse measurement; width, thickness. **3** a unit of linear measurement of magnifying power (*a lens magnifying 2000 diameters*). □□ **diametral** *adj.* [ME f. OF *diametre* f. L *diametrus* f. Gk *diametros* (*grammē*) (line) measuring across f. *metron* measure]

■ **1, 2** see WIDTH 1.

diametrical /dīəmétrik'l/ *adj.* (also **diametric**) **1** of or along a diameter. **2** (of opposition, difference, etc.) complete, like that between opposite ends of a diameter. □□ **diametrically** *adv.* [Gk *diametrikos* (as DIAMETER)]

diamond /dīəmənd/ *n.*, *adj.*, & *v.* ● *n.* **1** a precious stone of pure carbon crystallized in octahedrons etc., the hardest naturally-occurring substance. **2** a figure shaped like the cross-section of a diamond; a rhombus. **3 a** a playing-card of a suit denoted by a red rhombus. **b** (in *pl.*) this suit. **4** a glittering particle or point (of frost etc.). **5** a tool with a small diamond for glass-cutting. **6** *Baseball* **a** the space delimited by the bases. **b** the entire field. ● *adj.* **1** made of or set with diamonds or a diamond. **2** rhombus-shaped. ● *v.tr.* adorn with or as with diamonds. □ **diamond cut diamond** wit or cunning is met by its like. **diamond jubilee** the 60th (or 75th) anniversary of an event, esp. a sovereign's accession. **diamond wedding** a 60th (or 75th) wedding anniversary. □□ **diamondiferous** /-diffərəss/ *adj.*

[ME f. OF *diamant* f. med.L *diamas diamant-* var. of L *adamas* ADAMANT f. Gk]

diamondback /dī́əməndbak/ *n.* **1** an edible freshwater terrapin, *Malaclemys terrapin*, native to N. America, with lozenge-shaped markings on its shell. **2** any rattlesnake of the genus *Crotalus*, native to N. America, with diamond-shaped markings.

diandrous /dīándrəss/ *adj.* having two stamens. [DI-[1] + Gk *anēr andr-* man]

dianthus /dīánthəss/ *n.* any flowering plant of the genus *Dianthus*, e.g. a carnation or pink. [Gk *Dios* of Zeus + *anthos* flower]

diapason /dī́əpáyz'n, -páys'n/ *n. Mus.* **1** the compass of a voice or musical instrument. **2** a fixed standard of musical pitch. **3** (in full **open** or **stopped diapason**) either of two main organ-stops extending through the organ's whole compass. **4 a** a combination of notes or parts in a harmonious whole. **b** a melodious succession of notes, esp. a grand swelling burst of harmony. **5** an entire compass, range, or scope. [ME in sense 'octave' f. L *diapason* f. Gk *dia pasōn (khordōn)* through all (notes)]

diapause /dī́əpawz/ *n.* a period of retarded or suspended development in some insects.

diaper /dī́əpər/ *n.* & *v.* ● *n.* **1** *US* a baby's nappy. **2 a** a linen or cotton fabric with a small diamond pattern. **b** this pattern. **3** a similar ornamental design of diamonds etc. for panels, walls, etc. ● *v.tr.* decorate with a diaper pattern. [ME f. OF *diapre* f. med.L *diasprum* f. med.Gk *diaspros* (adj.) (as DIA-, *aspros* white)]

diaphanous /dīáffənəss/ *adj.* (of fabric etc.) light and delicate, and almost transparent. ▫▫ **diaphanously** *adv.* [med.L *diaphanus* f. Gk *diaphanes* (as DIA-, *phainō* show)]
■ see FILMY 1.

diaphoresis /dī́əfəréessiss/ *n. Med.* sweating, esp. artificially induced. [LL f. Gk f. *diaphoreō* carry through]

diaphoretic /dī́əfəréttik/ *adj.* & *n.* ● *adj.* inducing perspiration. ● *n.* an agent inducing perspiration. [LL *diaphoreticus* f. Gk *diaphorētikos* (formed as DIAPHORESIS)]

diaphragm /dī́əfram/ *n.* **1** a muscular partition separating the thorax from the abdomen in mammals. **2** a partition in animal and plant tissues. **3** a disc pierced by one or more holes in optical and acoustic systems etc. **4** a device for varying the effective aperture of the lens in a camera etc. **5** a thin contraceptive cap fitting over the cervix. **6** a thin sheet of material used as a partition etc. ▫ **diaphragm pump** a pump using a flexible diaphragm in place of a piston. ▫▫ **diaphragmatic** /-fragmáttik/ *adj.* [ME f. LL *diaphragma* f. Gk (as DIA-, *phragma -atos* f. *phrassō* fence in)]

diapositive /dī́əpózzitiv/ *n.* a positive photographic slide or transparency.

diarchy /dī́aarki/ *n.* (also **dyarchy**) (*pl.* **-ies**) **1** government by two independent authorities (esp. in India 1921–37). **2** an instance of this. ▫▫ **diarchal** /dīaárk'l/ *adj.* **diarchic** /dīaárkik/ *adj.* [DI-[1] + Gk *-arkhia* rule, after *monarchy*]

diarist /dī́ərist/ *n.* a person who keeps a diary. ▫▫ **diaristic** /-rístik/ *adj.*

diarize /dī́ərīz/ *v.* (also **-ise**) **1** *intr.* keep a diary. **2** *tr.* enter in a diary.

diarrhoea /dī́əréeə/ *n.* (esp. *US* **diarrhea**) a condition of excessively frequent and loose bowel movements. ▫▫ **diarrhoeal** *adj.* **diarrhoeic** *adj.* [ME f. LL f. Gk *diarrhoia* (as DIA-, *rheō* flow)]
■ loose bowels *or* motions, runny motions *or* tummy *colloq.* gippy tummy, *sl.* the trots *or* runs.

diary /dī́əri/ *n.* (*pl.* **-ies**) **1** a daily record of events or thoughts. **2** a book for this or for noting future engagements, usu. printed and with a calendar and other information. [L *diarium* f. *dies* day]
■ **1** journal, chronicle, memoirs, log, record, annal(s). **2** appointment book, date-book, calendar, engagement book.

diascope /dī́əskōp/ *n.* an optical projector giving images of transparent objects.

Diaspora /dīáspərə/ *n.* **1** (prec. by *the*) **a** the dispersion of the Jews among the Gentiles mainly in the 8th–6th c. BC. **b** Jews dispersed in this way. **2** (also **diaspora**) **a** any group of people similarly dispersed. **b** their dispersion. [Gk f. *diaspeirō* (as DIA-, *speirō* scatter)]

diastase /dī́əstayz/ *n. Biochem.* = AMYLASE. ▫▫ **diastasic** /-stáyzik/ *adj.* **diastatic** /-státtik/ *adj.* [F f. Gk *diastasis* separation (as DIA-, *stasis* placing)]

diastole /dīástəli/ *n. Physiol.* the period between two contractions of the heart when the heart muscle relaxes and allows the chambers to fill with blood (cf. SYSTOLE). ▫▫ **diastolic** /dī́əstóllik/ *adj.* [LL f. Gk *diastellō* (as DIA-, *stellō* place)]

diathermancy /dī́əthérmənsi/ *n.* the quality of transmitting radiant heat. ▫▫ **diathermic** *adj.* **diathermous** *adj.* [F *diathermansie* f. Gk *dia* through + *thermansis* heating: assim. to -ANCY]

diathermy /dī́əthermi/ *n.* the application of high-frequency electric currents to produce heat in the deeper tissues of the body. [G *Diathermie* f. Gk *dia* through + *thermon* heat]

diathesis /dīáthisiss/ *n. Med.* a constitutional predisposition to a certain state, esp. a diseased one. [mod.L f. Gk f. *diatithēmi* arrange]

diatom /dī́ətəm/ *n.* a microscopic unicellular alga with a siliceous cell-wall, found as plankton and forming fossil deposits. ▫▫ **diatomaceous** /-máyshəss/ *adj.* [mod.L *Diatoma* (genus-name) f. Gk *diatomos* (as DIA-, *temnō* cut)]

diatomic /dī́ətómmik/ *adj.* consisting of two atoms. [DI-[1] + ATOM]

diatomite /dīáttəmīt/ *n.* a deposit composed of the siliceous skeletons of diatoms.

diatonic /dī́ətónnik/ *adj. Mus.* **1** (of a scale, interval, etc.) involving only notes proper to the prevailing key without chromatic alteration. **2** (of a melody or harmony) constructed from such a scale. [F *diatonique* or LL *diatonicus* f. Gk *diatonikos* at intervals of a tone (as DIA-, TONIC)]

diatribe /dī́ətrīb/ *n.* a forceful verbal attack; a piece of bitter criticism. [F f. L *diatriba* f. Gk *diatribē* spending of time, discourse f. *diatribō* (as DIA-, *tribō* rub)]
■ see HARANGUE *n.*

diazepam /dīázzipam/ *n.* a tranquillizing muscle-relaxant drug with anticonvulsant properties used to relieve anxiety, tension, etc. [benzo*diazep*ine + *am*]

diazo /dīáyzō/ *n.* (in full **diazotype**) a copying or colouring process using a diazo compound decomposed by light. ▫ **diazo compound** *Chem.* a chemical compound containing two usu. multiply-bonded nitrogen atoms, often highly coloured and used as dyes. [DI-[1] + AZO-]

dib /dib/ *v.intr.* (**dibbed, dibbing**) = DAP. [var. of DAB[1]]

dibasic /dībáysik/ *adj. Chem.* having two replaceable protons. [DI-[1] + BASE[1] 6]

dibber /dibbər/ *n.* = DIBBLE.

dibble /dibb'l/ *n.* & *v.* ● *n.* a hand-tool for making holes in the ground for seeds or young plants. ● *v.* **1** *tr.* sow or plant with a dibble. **2** *tr.* prepare (soil) with a dibble. **3** *intr.* use a dibble. [ME: perh. rel. to DIB]

dibs /dibz/ *n.pl. sl.* money. [earlier sense 'pebbles for game', also *dib-stones*, perh. f. DIB]

dice /dīss/ *n.* & *v.* ● *n.pl.* **1 a** small cubes with faces bearing 1–6 spots used in games of chance. **b** (treated as *sing.*) one of these cubes (see DIE[2]). **2** a game played with one or more such cubes. **3** food cut into small cubes for cooking. ● *v.* **1 a** *intr.* play dice. **b** *intr.* take great risks, gamble (*dicing with death*). **c** *tr.* (foll. by *away*) gamble away. **2** *tr.* cut (food) into small cubes. **3** *tr. Austral. sl.* reject; leave alone. **4** *tr.* chequer, mark with squares. ▫ **no dice** *sl.* no success or prospect of it. ▫▫ **dicer** *n.* (in sense 1 of *v.*). [pl. of DIE[2]]
■ *v.* **2** see CHOP[1] *v.* 2.

dicey /dī́si/ *adj.* (**dicier, diciest**) *sl.* risky, unreliable. [DICE + -Y[1]]

■ risky, tricky, chancy, dangerous, difficult, ticklish, unpredictable, uncertain, unsure, doubtful, *colloq.* iffy, *sl.* hairy; see also UNRELIABLE.

dichotomy /dīkóttəmi/ *n.* (*pl.* **-ies**) **1 a** a division into two, esp. a sharply defined one. **b** the result of such a division. **2** binary classification. **3** *Bot.* & *Zool.* repeated bifurcation. □□ **dichotomic** /-kətómmik/ *adj.* **dichotomize** *v.* **dichotomous** *adj.* [mod.L *dichotomia* f. Gk *dikhotomia* f. *dikho-* apart + -TOMY]

■ **1** see SPLIT *n.* 3.

dichroic /dīkrṓ-ik/ *adj.* (esp. of doubly refracting crystals) showing two colours. □□ **dichroism** *n.* [Gk *dikhroos* (as DI-[1], *khrōs* colour)]

dichromatic /dīkrōmáttik/ *adj.* **1** two-coloured. **2 a** (of animal species) having individuals that show different colorations. **b** having vision sensitive to only two of the three primary colours. □□ **dichromatism** /dīkrṓmətiz'm/ *n.* [DI-[1] + Gk *khrōmatikos* f. *khrōma -atos* colour]

dick[1] /dik/ *n.* **1** *Brit. colloq.* (in certain set phrases) fellow; person (*clever dick*). **2** *coarse sl.* the penis. ¶ In sense 2 usually considered a taboo word. [pet form of the name *Richard*]

dick[2] /dik/ *n. sl.* a detective. [perh. abbr.]

■ see *inquiry agent* (INQUIRY).

dick[3] /dik/ *n.* □ **take one's dick** (often foll. by *that* + clause) *sl.* swear, affirm. [abbr. of *declaration*]

dicken /díkkən/ *int. Austral. sl.* an expression of disgust or disbelief. [usu. assoc. with DICKENS or the name *Dickens*]

dickens /díkinz/ *n.* (usu. prec. by *how, what, why*, etc., *the*) *colloq.* (esp. in exclamations) deuce; the Devil (*what the dickens are you doing here?*). [16th c.: prob. a use of the surname *Dickens*]

■ see *the devil* (DEVIL *n.* 7).

Dickensian /dikénziən/ *adj.* & *n.* ● *adj.* **1** of or relating to Charles Dickens, Engl. novelist d. 1870, or his work. **2** resembling or reminiscent of the situations, poor social conditions, or comically repulsive characters described in Dickens's work. ● *n.* an admirer or student of Dickens or his work. □□ **Dickensianly** *adv.*

dicker /díkkər/ *v.* & *n.* esp. *US* ● *v.* **1 a** *intr.* bargain, haggle. **b** *tr.* barter, exchange. **2** *intr.* dither, hesitate. ● *n.* a deal, a barter. □□ **dickerer** *n.* [perh. f. *dicker* set of ten (hides), as a unit of trade]

■ *v.* **1** bargain, deal, haggle, negotiate, trade, barter, exchange. **2** see HESITATE 1. ● *n.* bargain, deal, haggle, barter; transaction, contract.

dickhead /dík-hed/ *n. coarse sl.* a stupid or obnoxious person.

dicky[1] /díkki/ *n.* (also **dickey**) (*pl.* **-ies** or **-eys**) *colloq.* **1** a false shirt-front. **2** (in full **dicky-bird**) a child's word for a little bird. **3** *Brit.* a driver's seat in a carriage. **4** *Brit.* an extra folding seat at the back of a vehicle. **5** (in full **dicky bow**) *Brit.* a bow-tie. [some senses f. *Dicky* (as DICK[1])]

dicky[2] /díkki/ *adj.* (**dickier, dickiest**) *Brit. sl.* unsound, likely to collapse or fail. [19th c.: perh. f. 'as queer as Dick's hatband']

■ shaky, unreliable, unsteady, unsound, faulty, *colloq.* dodgy.

dicot /dīkot/ *n.* = DICOTYLEDON. [abbr.]

dicotyledon /dīkotileéd'n/ *n.* any flowering plant having two cotyledons. □□ **dicotyledonous** *adj.* [mod.L *dicotyledones* (as DI-[1], COTYLEDON)]

dicrotic /dīkróttik/ *adj.* (of the pulse) having a double beat. [Gk *dikrotos*]

dicta *pl.* of DICTUM.

Dictaphone /díktəfōn/ *n. propr.* a machine for recording and playing back dictated words. [DICTATE + PHONE]

dictate *v.* & *n.* ● *v.* /diktáyt/ **1** *tr.* say or read aloud (words to be written down or recorded). **2 a** *tr.* prescribe or lay down authoritatively (terms, things to be done). **b** *intr.* lay down the law; give orders. ● *n.* /díktayt/ (usu. in *pl.*) an authoritative instruction (*dictates of conscience*). [L *dictare dictat-* frequent. of *dicere dict-* say]

■ *v.* **2** say, prescribe, ordain, decree, demand, command, order, pronounce; lay down the law, give orders. ● *n.* decree, demand, command, order, direction, instruction, charge, pronouncement, edict, fiat, mandate, caveat, injunction, requirement, bidding, *literary* behest.

dictation /diktáysh'n/ *n.* **1 a** the saying of words to be written down or recorded. **b** an instance of this, esp. as a school exercise. **c** the material that is dictated. **2 a** authoritative prescription. **b** an instance of this. **c** a command. □ **dictation speed** a slow rate of speech suitable for dictation.

dictator /diktáytər/ *n.* **1** a ruler with (often usurped) unrestricted authority. **2** a person with supreme authority in any sphere. **3** a domineering person. **4** a person who dictates for transcription. **5** *Rom.Hist.* a chief magistrate with absolute power, appointed in an emergency. [ME f. L (as DICTATE)]

■ **1, 2** autocrat, absolute ruler *or* monarch, despot, overlord, tyrant, Führer, tsar, Big Brother. **3** tyrant, despot, bully, slave-driver, *colloq.* bossy-boots.

dictatorial /díktətóriəl/ *adj.* **1** of or like a dictator. **2** imperious, overbearing. □□ **dictatorially** *adv.* [L *dictatorius* (as DICTATOR)]

■ **1** absolute, arbitrary, totalitarian, authoritarian, autocratic, all-powerful, omnipotent, unlimited. **2** despotic, tyrannical, authoritarian, iron-handed, domineering, imperious, overbearing, high-handed, lordly, *colloq.* bossy.

dictatorship /diktáytərship/ *n.* **1** a State ruled by a dictator. **2 a** the position, rule, or period of rule of a dictator. **b** rule by a dictator. **3** absolute authority in any sphere.

■ see DESPOTISM.

diction /díksh'n/ *n.* **1** the manner of enunciation in speaking or singing. **2** the choice of words or phrases in speech or writing. [F *diction* or L *dictio* f. *dicere dict-* say]

■ **1** articulation, pronunciation, enunciation, delivery, elocution, oratory, presentation, speech, intonation, inflection. **2** language, wording, style, expression, usage, terminology, vocabulary, phraseology, phrasing, rhetoric, oratory, presentation.

dictionary /díkshənri, -nəri/ *n.* (*pl.* **-ies**) **1** a book that lists (usu. in alphabetical order) and explains the words of a language or gives equivalent words in another language. **2** a reference book on any subject, the items of which are arranged in alphabetical order (*dictionary of architecture*). [med.L *dictionarium* (*manuale* manual) & *dictionarius* (*liber* book) f. L *dictio* (as DICTION)]

■ **1** lexicon, glossary, wordbook, thesaurus, wordfinder. **2** encyclopedia, cyclopedia, reference (book), compendium, thesaurus.

dictum /díktəm/ *n.* (*pl.* **dicta** /-tə/ or **dictums**) **1** a formal utterance or pronouncement. **2** a saying or maxim. **3** *Law* = OBITER DICTUM. [L, = neut. past part. of *dicere* say]

■ **1** see DECREE *n.* 1. **2** see MAXIM.

dicty /dikti/ *adj. US sl.* **1** conceited, snobbish. **2** elegant, stylish. [20th c.: orig. unkn.]

did *past* of DO[1].

didactic /dīdáktik, di-/ *adj.* **1** meant to instruct. **2** (of a person) tediously pedantic. □□ **didactically** *adv.* **didacticism** /-tisiz'm/ *n.* [Gk *didaktikos* f. *didaskō* teach]

■ **1** see INSTRUCTIVE. **2** see *pedantic* (PEDANT).

didakai var. of DIDICOI.

diddicoy var. of DIDICOI.

diddle /dídd'l/ *v. colloq.* **1** *tr.* cheat, swindle. **2** *intr. US* waste time. □□ **diddler** *n.* [prob. back-form. f. Jeremy *Diddler* in Kenney's 'Raising the Wind' (1803)]

■ **1** see CHEAT *v.* 1a.

diddums /díddəmz/ *int.* expressing commiseration esp. to a child. [= *did 'em*, i.e. did they (tease you etc.)?]

didgeridoo /díjəridoó/ *n.* (also **didjeridoo**) an Australian Aboriginal musical wind instrument of long tubular shape. [imit.]

didicoi /díddikoy/ *n.* (also **didakai, diddicoy**) *sl.* a gypsy; an itinerant tinker. [Romany]

didn't /dídd'nt/ *contr.* did not.

dido /dīdō/ *n.* (*pl.* **-oes** or **-os**) *US colloq.* an antic, a caper, a prank. □ **cut** (or **cut up**) **didoes** play pranks. [19th c.: orig. unkn.]

didst /didst/ *archaic 2nd sing. past* of DO[1].

didymium /didímmiəm/ *n.* a mixture of praesodymium and neodymium, orig. regarded as an element. [mod.L f. Gk *didumos* twin (from being closely associated with lanthanum)]

die[1] /dī/ *v.* (**dies, died, dying** /dī-ing/) **1** *intr.* (often foll. by *of*) (of a person, animal, or plant) cease to live; expire, lose vital force (*died of hunger*). **2** *intr.* **a** come to an end, cease to exist, fade away (*the project died within six months*). **b** cease to function; break down (*the engine died*). **c** (of a flame) go out. **3** *intr.* (foll. by *on*) die or cease to function while in the presence or charge of (a person). **4** *intr.* (usu. foll. by *of, from, with*) be exhausted or tormented (*nearly died of boredom; was dying from the heat*). **5** *tr.* suffer (a specified death) (*died a natural death*). □ **be dying** (foll. by *for*, or *to* + infin.) wish for longingly or intently (*was dying for a drink; am dying to see you*). **die away** become weaker or fainter to the point of extinction. **die-away** *adj.* languishing. **die back** (of a plant) decay from the tip towards the root. **die down** become less loud or strong. **die hard** die reluctantly, not without a struggle (*old habits die hard*). **die-hard** *n.* a conservative or stubborn person. **die off** die one after another until few or none are left. **die out** become extinct, cease to exist. **never say die** keep up courage, not give in. [ME, prob. f. ON *deyja* f. Gmc]

■ **1** lose one's life, lay down one's life, perish, expire, suffer death, breathe one's last, be no more, close one's eyes, go (off), drop, drop dead, exit, fall, (go to) meet one's Maker, quit the scene, go to the happy hunting-grounds, go to one's final *or* last resting-place, pass through the Pearly Gates, go the way of all flesh, *archaic or colloq.* give up the ghost, *colloq.* turn up one's toes, pop off, cash in one's chips *or* checks, conk out, *Brit. colloq.* pip out, *euphem.* pass away *or* on *or* over, *formal esp. Law* decease, *formal or literary* depart (this life), *sl.* go west, peg out, bite the dust, go to glory, hop the twig *or* stick, buy it, kick the bucket, pop one's clogs, croak, *Austral. & NZ sl.* go bung, *Brit. sl.* snuff it, go for a burton. **2 a** come to an end, expire, end, stop, cease; die away, die out *or* down, dwindle, lessen, diminish, decrease, ebb, decline, wane, subside, wither (away), wilt, dissolve, peter out, fail, weaken, deteriorate, disintegrate, degenerate, fade (away), sink, vanish, disappear. **b** break down, fail. **c** see *go out* 3 (GO[1]). **4** see SUFFER 1a. □ **be dying** long, pine, yearn, hanker, hunger, ache; (*be dying for*) want, desire, crave. **die away** see DIE[1] 2a above. **die down** see DIE[1] 2a above. **die-hard** see REACTIONARY *n.*, stick-in-the-mud (STICK[2]). **die out** become extinct, perish. **never say die** (keep a) stiff upper lip, don't give in *or* up, be brave, *colloq.* chin up.

die[2] /dī/ *n.* **1** *sing.* of DICE *n.* 1a. ¶ *Dice* is now standard in general *Brit.* use in this sense. **2** (*pl.* **dies**) **a** an engraved device for stamping a design on coins, medals, etc. **b** a device for stamping, cutting, or moulding material into a particular shape. **3** (*pl.* **dice** /dīss/) *Archit.* the cubical part of a pedestal between the base and the cornice; a dado or plinth. □ **as straight** (or **true**) **as a die 1** quite straight. **2** entirely honest or loyal. **die-cast** cast (hot metal) in a die or mould. **die-casting** the process or product of casting from metal moulds. **the die is cast** an irrevocable step has been taken. **die-sinker** an engraver of dies. **die-stamping** embossing paper etc. with a die. [ME f. OF *de* f. L *datum* neut. past part. of *dare* give, play]

dieldrin /di-éldrin/ *n.* a crystalline insecticide produced by the oxidation of aldrin. [O. *Diels*, Ger. chemist d. 1954 + ALDRIN]

dielectric /dī-iléktrik/ *adj.* & *n.* *Electr.* ● *adj.* insulating. ● *n.* an insulating medium or substance. □ **dielectric constant** permittivity. □□ **dielectrically** *adv.* [DI-[3] + ELECTRIC = through which electricity is transmitted (without conduction)]

diene /dī-een/ *n.* *Chem.* any organic compound possessing two double bonds between carbon atoms. [DI-[1] + -ENE]

dieresis *US* var. of DIAERESIS.

diesel /deéz'l/ *n.* **1** (in full **diesel engine**) an internal-combustion engine in which the heat produced by the compression of air in the cylinder ignites the fuel. **2** a vehicle driven by a diesel engine. **3** fuel for a diesel engine. □ **diesel-electric** *n.* a vehicle driven by the electric current produced by a diesel-engined generator. ● *adj.* of or powered by this means. **diesel oil** a heavy petroleum fraction used as fuel in diesel engines. □□ **dieselize** *v.tr.* (also **-ise**). [R. *Diesel*, Ger. engineer d. 1913]

Dies irae /deé-ayz eérī/ *n.* a Latin hymn sung in a Mass for the dead. [L (its first words), = day of wrath]

dies non /dī-eez nón/ *n.* *Law* **1** a day on which no legal business can be done. **2** a day that does not count for legal purposes. [L, short for *dies non juridicus* non-judicial day]

diet[1] /dīət/ *n.* & *v.* ● *n.* **1** the kinds of food that a person or animal habitually eats. **2** a special course of food to which a person is restricted, esp. for medical reasons or to control weight. **3** a regular occupation or series of activities to which one is restricted or which form one's main concern, usu. for a purpose (*a diet of light reading and fresh air*). ● *v.* (**dieted, dieting**) **1** *intr.* restrict oneself to small amounts or special kinds of food, esp. to control one's weight. **2** *tr.* restrict (a person or animal) to a special diet. □□ **dieter** *n.* [ME f. OF *diete* (n.), *dieter* (v.) f. L *diaeta* f. Gk *diaita* a way of life]

■ *n.* **1** (food) intake, consumption; fare, food, nourishment, nutriment, sustenance, subsistence, victuals, *formal* aliment. **2** dietary, regime, *Med.* regimen. **3** see SYSTEM 4a. ● *v.* **1** fast, abstain, starve (oneself); be on a diet, slim.

diet[2] /dīət/ *n.* **1** a legislative assembly in certain countries. **2** *hist.* a national or international conference, esp. of a federal State or confederation. **3** *Sc. Law* a meeting or session of a court. [ME f. med.L *dieta* day's work, wages, etc.]

■ **1** council, congress, parliament, senate, legislature, house, chamber, assembly. **2** see CONFERENCE 2.

dietary /dīətri/ *adj.* & *n.* ● *adj.* of or relating to a diet. ● *n.* (*pl.* **-ies**) a regulated or restricted diet. [ME f. med.L *dietarium* (as DIET[1])]

dietetic /dīətéttik/ *adj.* of or relating to diet. □□ **dietetically** *adv.* [L *dieteticus* f. Gk *diaitētikos* (as DIET[1])]

dietetics /dīətéttiks/ *n.pl.* (usu. treated as *sing.*) the scientific study of diet and nutrition.

diethyl ether /dī-eéthīl/ *n.* *Chem.* = ETHER 1.

dietitian /dīətísh'n/ *n.* (also **dietician**) an expert in dietetics.

dif- /dif/ *prefix* assim. form of DIS- before *f.* [L var. of DIS-]

differ /díffər/ *v.intr.* **1** (often foll. by *from*) be unlike or distinguishable. **2** (often foll. by *with*) disagree; be at variance (with a person). [ME f. OF *differer* f. L *differre*, differ, DEFER[1], (as DIS-, *ferre* bear, tend)]

■ **1** diverge, deviate, be separate *or* distinct, be dissimilar *or* different, contrast; depart. **2** disagree, conflict, be at variance *or* odds, take issue, part company, fall out, quarrel, argue.

difference /dífrənss/ *n.* & *v.* ● *n.* **1** the state or condition of being different or unlike. **2** a point in which things differ; a distinction. **3** a degree of unlikeness. **4 a** the quantity by which amounts differ; a deficit (*will have to make up the difference*). **b** the remainder left after subtraction. **5 a** a disagreement, quarrel, or dispute. **b** the grounds of disagreement (*put aside their differences*). **6** a notable change (*the difference in his behaviour is remarkable*). **7** *Heraldry* an alteration in a coat of arms distinguishing members of a family. ● *v.tr.* *Heraldry* alter (a coat of arms) to distinguish members of a family. □ **make a** (or **all the** etc.) **difference** (often foll. by *to*) have a significant effect or influence (on a person, situation, etc.). **make no difference** (often foll. by *to*) have no effect (on a person, situation, etc.). **with a difference** having a new or unusual feature. [ME f. OF f. L *differentia* (as DIFFERENT)]

■ *n.* **1** dissimilarity, discrepancy, unlikeness, disagreement, inconsistency, diversity, variation, imbalance, inequality, dissimilitude, incongruity, contrast, contrariety. **2** distinction, contradistinction, contrast, dissimilarity, disparity. **4 a** see DEFICIT. **b** rest, remainder, leftovers, balance, excess, surplus, residue, residuum. **5** dispute, argument, disagreement, conflict; see also QUARREL[1] *n.* 1. **6** change, alteration, metamorphosis, reformation, transformation, conversion, adjustment, modification.

different /dífrənt/ *adj.* **1** (often foll. by *from, to, than*) unlike, distinguishable in nature, form, or quality (from another). ¶ *Different from* is generally regarded as the most acceptable collocation; *to* is common in less formal use; *than* is established in US use and also found in British use, esp. when followed by a clause, e.g. *I am a different person than I was a year ago.* **2** distinct, separate; not the same one (as another). **3** *colloq.* unusual (*wanted to do something different*). **4** of various kinds; assorted, several, miscellaneous (*available in different colours*). □□ **differently** *adv.* **differentness** *n.* [ME f. OF *different* f. L *different-* (as DIFFER)]

■ **1, 2** unlike, unalike, dissimilar, conflicting; distinct, opposite, separate, contrary, discrete, contrastive, contrasting, disparate, divergent, diverse, distinguishable; another. **3** unique, unusual, peculiar, odd, offbeat, singular, particular, distinctive, personalized, individual, alternative, unorthodox, extraordinary, special, remarkable, bizarre, rare, weird, strange, unconventional, original, out of the ordinary, exceptional, *colloq.* way-out, *sl.* wacky; new, novel, unheard-of, original. **4** assorted, miscellaneous, multifarious, numerous, abundant, sundry, various, varied, many, several, *archaic or literary* divers, *literary* manifold.

differentia /dífərénshiə/ *n.* (*pl.* **differentiae** /-shi-ee/) a distinguishing mark, esp. between species within a genus. [L: see DIFFERENCE]

differential /dífərénsh'l/ *adj.* & *n.* ● *adj.* **1 a** of, exhibiting, or depending on a difference. **b** varying according to circumstances. **2** *Math.* relating to infinitesimal differences. **3** constituting a specific difference; distinctive; relating to specific differences (*differential diagnosis*). **4** *Physics* & *Mech.* concerning the difference of two or more motions, pressures, etc. ● *n.* **1** a difference between individuals or examples of the same kind. **2** *Brit.* a difference in wage or salary between industries or categories of employees in the same industry. **3** a difference between rates of interest etc. **4** *Math.* **a** an infinitesimal difference between successive values of a variable. **b** a function expressing this as a rate of change with respect to another variable. **5** (in full **differential gear**) a gear allowing a vehicle's driven wheels to revolve at different speeds in cornering. □ **differential calculus** *Math.* a method of calculating rates of change, maximum or minimum values, etc. (cf. INTEGRAL). **differential coefficient** *Math.* = DERIVATIVE. **differential equation** *Math.* an equation involving differentials among its quantities. □□ **differentially** *adv.* [med. & mod.L *differentialis* (as DIFFERENCE)]

differentiate /dífərénshiayt/ *v.* **1** *tr.* constitute a difference between or in. **2** *tr.* & (often foll. by *between*) *intr.* find differences (between); discriminate. **3** *tr.* & *intr.* make or become different in the process of growth or development (species, word-forms, etc.). **4** *tr. Math.* transform (a function) into its derivative. □□ **differentiation** /-áysh'n/ *n.* **differentiator** *n.* [med.L *differentiare differentiat-* (as DIFFERENCE)]

■ **2** distinguish, discriminate, contradistinguish, separate, contrast, set off *or* apart, tell apart. **3** modify, specialize, change, alter, transform, transmute, convert, adapt, adjust, develop.

difficult /dífikəlt/ *adj.* **1 a** needing much effort or skill. **b** troublesome, perplexing. **2** (of a person): **a** not easy to please or satisfy. **b** uncooperative, troublesome. **3** characterized by hardships or problems (*a difficult period in his life*). □□ **difficultly** *adv.* **difficultness** *n.* [ME, back-form. f. DIFFICULTY]

■ **1 a** hard, arduous, toilsome, strenuous, tough, laborious, burdensome, onerous, demanding. **b** puzzling, perplexing, troublesome, baffling, complex, thorny, intricate, knotty, problematical, problematic, ticklish, scabrous, sensitive, delicate, awkward, tricky, *colloq.* sticky; profound, abstruse, obscure, recondite. **2** intractable, recalcitrant, obstructive, uncooperative, stubborn, unmanageable, obstinate, contrary, unaccommodating, refractory, unyielding, uncompromising, troublesome, awkward, *archaic* froward, *colloq.* bloody-minded, *sl.* Bolshie, *US sl.* feisty; naughty, ill-behaved; fussy, particular, demanding. **3** troubled, troubling, tough, burdensome, onerous, demanding, trying, hard, grim, unfavourable, straitening.

difficulty /dífikəlti/ *n.* (*pl.* **-ies**) **1** the state or condition of being difficult. **2 a** a difficult thing; a problem or hindrance. **b** (often in *pl.*) a cause of distress or hardship (*in financial difficulties; there was someone in difficulties in the water*). □ **make difficulties** be intransigent or unaccommodating. **with difficulty** not easily. [ME f. L *difficultas* (as DIS-, *facultas* FACULTY)]

■ **1** strain, hardship; hardness, toughness, arduousness, laboriousness, formidableness, painfulness; awkwardness, delicacy, trickiness, complexity, thorniness, knottiness, ticklishness. **2 a** hardship, obstacle, problem, hindrance, pitfall, predicament, tribulation, snag, *disp.* dilemma. **b** (*difficulties*) embarrassment, plight, problems, predicament, mess, (dire) strait(s), trouble, scrape, *colloq.* hot water, jam, pickle, fix. □ **make difficulties** cause *or* stir up trouble, stir things up, put *or* set a cat amongst the pigeons, throw a spanner in the works, *esp. Austral. colloq.* stir.

diffident /díffid'nt/ *adj.* **1** shy, lacking self-confidence. **2** excessively modest and reticent. □□ **diffidence** *n.* **diffidently** *adv.* [L *diffidere* (as DIS-, *fidere* trust)]

■ see SHY[1] *adj.* 1.

diffract /difrákt/ *v.tr. Physics* (of the edge of an opaque body, a narrow slit, etc.) break up (a beam of light) into a series of dark or light bands or coloured spectra, or (a beam of radiation or particles) into a series of alternately high and low intensities. □□ **diffraction** *n.* **diffractive** *adj.* **diffractively** *adv.* [L *diffringere diffract-* (as DIS-, *frangere* break)]

diffractometer /dífraktómmitər/ *n.* an instrument for measuring diffraction, esp. in crystallographic work.

diffuse *adj.* & *v.* ● *adj.* /difyo͞oss/ **1** (of light, inflammation, etc.) spread out, diffused, not concentrated. **2** (of prose, speech, etc.) not concise, long-winded, verbose. ● *v.tr.* & *intr.* /difyo͞oz/ **1** disperse or be dispersed from a centre. **2** spread or be spread widely; reach a large area. **3** *Physics* (esp. of fluids) intermingle by diffusion. □□ **diffusely** /difyo͞osli/ *adv.* **diffuseness** /difyo͞osniss/ *n.* **diffusible** /difyo͞ozib'l/ *adj.* **diffusive** /difyo͞ossiv/ *adj.* [ME f. F *diffus* or L *diffusus* extensive (as DIS-, *fusus* past part. of *fundere* pour)]

■ *adj.* **1** spread out, diffused, scattered, dispersed, widespread; light. **2** wordy, verbose, prolix, long-winded, loquacious, discursive, digressive, rambling, circumlocutory, circumlocutionary, circumlocutional, meandering, roundabout, circuitous, periphrastic, diffusive. ● *v.* **1, 2** spread, circulate, distribute, dispense, disperse, dispel, scatter, broadcast, sow, disseminate, dissipate; spread out.

diffuser /difyo͞ozər/ *n.* (also **diffusor**) **1** a person or thing that diffuses, esp. a device for diffusing light. **2** *Engin.* a duct for broadening an airflow and reducing its speed.

diffusion /difyo͞ozh'n/ *n.* **1** the act or an instance of diffusing; the process of being diffused. **2** *Physics* & *Chem.* the interpenetration of substances by the natural movement of

their particles. **3** *Anthropol.* the spread of elements of culture etc. to another region or people. □□ **diffusionist** *n.* [ME f. L *diffusio* (as DIFFUSE)]
■ **1** see RADIATION. **3** see CIRCULATION 2a.

dig /dig/ *v.* & *n.* ● *v.* (**digging**; *past* and *past part.* **dug** /dug/) **1** *intr.* break up and remove or turn over soil, ground, etc., with a tool, one's hands, (of an animal) claws, etc. **2** *tr.* **a** break up and displace (the ground etc.) in this way. **b** (foll. by *up*) break up the soil of (fallow land). **3** *tr.* make (a hole, grave, tunnel, etc.) by digging. **4** *tr.* (often foll. by *up, out*) **a** obtain or remove by digging. **b** find or discover after searching. **5** *tr.* (also *absol.*) excavate (an archaeological site). **6** *tr. sl.* like, appreciate, or understand. **7** *tr.* & *intr.* (foll. by *in, into*) thrust or poke into or down into. **8** *intr.* make one's way by digging (*dug through the mountainside*). **9** *intr.* (usu. foll. by *into*) investigate or study closely; probe. ● *n.* **1** a piece of digging. **2** a thrust or poke (*a dig in the ribs*). **3** *colloq.* (often foll. by *at*) a pointed or critical remark. **4** an archaeological excavation. **5** (in *pl.*) *Brit. colloq.* lodgings. □ **dig one's feet** (or **heels** or **toes**) **in** be obstinate. **dig in** *colloq.* begin eating. **dig oneself in 1** prepare a defensive trench or pit. **2** establish one's position. [ME *digge*, of uncert. orig.: cf. OE *dīc* ditch]
■ *v.* **1** see EXCAVATE 1, BURROW *v.* 1, 2. **2 b** (*dig up*) break up, work; see also PLOUGH *v.* 1. **3** gouge (out), scoop (out), hollow out, spoon out, cut, dig out, excavate; make. **4** (*dig out* or *up*) unearth, disinter, disentomb, exhume, bring up, find, obtain, extract, ferret out, discover, bring to light, expose, dredge up, extricate, come up with, *esp. Brit.* winkle out. **6** appreciate, enjoy, like, understand, go for, *colloq.* be into; see also LIKE[2] *v.* 1. **7** thrust, stab, jab, plunge, force, prod, nudge, poke. **9** (*dig into*) probe (into), delve into, go deeply into, enquire *or* inquire into, investigate, explore, look into, research, study. ● *n.* **2** thrust, poke, jab, stab, nudge, elbow. **3** insult, insinuation, gibe, slur, affront, taunt, jeer, slap in the face, *colloq.* crack. **5** (*digs*) see ACCOMMODATION 1. □ **dig in** help oneself, set to, *colloq.* dive in, tuck in, get stuck in, *Austral.* & *NZ sl.* hoe in.

digamma /dīgámmə/ *n.* the sixth letter (Ϝ, ϝ) of the early Greek alphabet (prob. pronounced w), later disused. [L f. Gk (as DI-[1], GAMMA)]

digastric /dīgástrik/ *adj.* & *n.* *Anat.* ● *adj.* (of a muscle) having two wide parts with a tendon between. ● *n.* the muscle that opens the jaw. [mod.L *digastricus* (as DI-[1], Gk *gastēr* belly)]

digest *v.* & *n.* ● *v.tr.* /dījést, di-/ **1** assimilate (food) in the stomach and bowels. **2** understand and assimilate mentally. **3** *Chem.* treat (a substance) with heat, enzymes, or a solvent in order to decompose it, extract the essence, etc. **4 a** reduce to a systematic or convenient form; classify; summarize. **b** think over; arrange in the mind. **5** bear without resistance; brook, endure. ● *n.* /dījest/ **1 a** a methodical summary esp. of a body of laws. **b** (**the Digest**) the compendium of Roman law compiled in the reign of Justinian (6th c. AD). **2 a** a compendium or summary of information; a résumé. **b** a regular or occasional synopsis of current literature or news. □□ **digester** *n.* **digestible** *adj.* **digestibility** /-jéstibilliti/ *n.* [ME f. L *digerere digest-* distribute, dissolve, digest (as DI-[2], *gerere* carry)]
■ *v.* **2** assimilate, take in, swallow; comprehend, grasp, get hold of, get, understand. **4 a** abbreviate, cut, condense, abridge, compress, epitomize, summarize, reduce, shorten; systematize; classify. **b** consider, study, ponder, meditate on *or* over, reflect on, think over. **5** bear, stand, endure, survive, accept, tolerate, swallow, stomach, *literary* brook. ● *n.* **2 a** condensation, abridgement, précis, résumé, compendium, summary, abbreviation. **b** abstract, synopsis, conspectus, survey, outline; see also SUMMARY *n.* □□ **digestible** palatable, easy to understand; see also INTELLIGIBLE, BEARABLE.

digestion /dījéss-chən/ *n.* **1** the process of digesting. **2** the capacity to digest food (*has a weak digestion*). **3** digesting a substance by means of heat, enzymes, or a solvent. [ME f. OF f. L *digestio -onis* (as DIGEST)]

digestive /dijéstiv, dī-/ *adj.* & *n.* ● *adj.* **1** of or relating to digestion. **2** aiding or promoting digestion. ● *n.* **1** a substance that aids digestion. **2** (in full **digestive biscuit**) *Brit.* a usu. round semi-sweet wholemeal biscuit. □□ **digestively** *adv.* [ME f. OF *digestif -ive* or L *digestivus* (as DIGEST)]

digger /diggər/ *n.* **1** a person or machine that digs, esp. a mechanical excavator. **2** a miner, esp. a gold-digger. **3** *colloq.* an Australian or New Zealander, esp. a private soldier. **4** *Austral.* & *NZ colloq.* (as a form of address) mate, fellow.

diggings /díggingz/ *n.pl.* **1 a** a mine or goldfield. **b** material dug out of a mine etc. **2** *Brit. colloq.* lodgings, accommodation.

dight /dīt/ *adj. archaic* clothed, arrayed. [past part. of *dight* (v.) f. OE *dihtan* f. L *dictare* DICTATE]

digit /díjit/ *n.* **1** any numeral from 0 to 9, esp. when forming part of a number. **2** *Anat.* & *Zool.* a finger, thumb, or toe. [ME f. L *digitus*]
■ **1** see FIGURE *n.* 6a.

digital /díjit'l/ *adj.* **1** of or using a digit or digits. **2** (of a clock, watch, etc.) that gives a reading by means of displayed digits instead of hands. **3** (of a computer) operating on data represented as a series of usu. binary digits or in similar discrete form. **4 a** (of a recording) with sound-information represented in digits for more reliable transmission. **b** (of a recording medium) using this process. □ **digital audio tape** magnetic tape on which sound is recorded digitally. **digital to analog converter** *Computing* a device for converting digital values to analog form. □□ **digitalize** *v.tr.* (also **-ise**). **digitally** *adv.* [L *digitalis* (as DIGIT)]

digitalin /díjitáylin/ *n.* the pharmacologically active constituent(s) of the foxglove. [DIGITALIS + -IN]

digitalis /díjitáyliss/ *n.* a drug prepared from the dried leaves of foxgloves and containing substances that stimulate the heart muscle. [mod.L, genus-name of foxglove after G *Fingerhut* thimble: see DIGITAL]

digitate /díjitayt/ *adj.* **1** *Zool.* having separate fingers or toes. **2** *Bot.* having deep radiating divisions. □□ **digitately** *adv.* **digitation** /-táysh'n/ *n.* [L *digitatus* (as DIGIT)]

digitigrade /díjitigrayd/ *adj.* & *n.* *Zool.* ● *adj.* (of an animal) walking on its toes and not touching the ground with its heels, e.g. dogs, cats, and rodents. ● *n.* a digitigrade animal (cf. PLANTIGRADE). [F f. L *digitus* + *-gradus* -walking]

digitize /díjitīz/ *v.tr.* (also **-ise**) convert (data etc.) into digital form, esp. for processing by a computer. □□ **digitization** /-záysh'n/ *n.*

dignified /dígnifīd/ *adj.* having or expressing dignity; noble or stately in appearance or manner. □□ **dignifiedly** *adv.*
■ stately, noble, majestic, formal, solemn, serious, sober, grave, distinguished, honourable, *distingué*, elegant, august, sedate, reserved; regal, courtly, lordly, lofty, exalted, grand.

dignify /dígnifī/ *v.tr.* (**-ies, -ied**) **1** give dignity or distinction to. **2** ennoble; make worthy or illustrious. **3** give the form or appearance of dignity to (*dignified the house with the name of mansion*). [obs. F *dignifier* f. OF *dignefier* f. LL *dignificare* f. *dignus* worthy]
■ distinguish, ennoble, elevate, raise, exalt, glorify, upraise, lift, uplift, enhance, improve, better, upgrade.

dignitary /dígnitəri, -tri/ *n.* (*pl.* **-ies**) a person holding high rank or office. [DIGNITY + -ARY[1], after PROPRIETARY]
■ personage, official, notable, worthy, magnate, VIP, power, big name, *Austral.* joss, *colloq.* bigwig, higher-up, big shot, hot stuff, big noise, *esp. US colloq.* hotshot, *sl.* big cheese, big gun, Big Chief, Big Daddy, *Austral. sl.* fat cat, *US sl.* Mr Big, big wheel; celebrity, lion, luminary.

dignity /dígniti/ *n.* (*pl.* **-ies**) **1** a composed and serious manner or style. **2** the state of being worthy of honour or respect. **3** worthiness, excellence (*the dignity of work*). **4** a high or honourable rank or position. **5** high regard or estimation. **6** self-respect. □ **beneath one's dignity** not considered worthy enough for one to do. **stand on one's dignity** insist (esp. by one's manner) on being treated with due respect. [ME f. OF *digneté*, *dignité* f. L *dignitas -tatis* f. *dignus* worthy]

■ **1** stateliness, formality, nobility, majesty, gravity, seriousness, *gravitas*, solemnity, courtliness, grandeur, grandness; hauteur, loftiness; composure, control. **3** worth, worthiness, nobility, nobleness, excellence, honour, honourableness, respectability, respectableness, importance, greatness, glory. **4** standing, station, status, rank, honour, level, position. **6** self-respect, self-regard, *amour propre*, self-confidence, self-esteem, pride.

digraph /dígraaf/ *n.* a group of two letters representing one sound, as in *ph* and *ey*. □□ **digraphic** /-gráffik/ *adj.*

digress /dīgréss/ *v.intr.* depart from the main subject temporarily in speech or writing. □□ **digresser** *n.* **digression** *n.* **digressive** *adj.* **digressively** *adv.* **digressiveness** *n.* [L *digredi digress-* (as DI-[2], *gradi* walk)]

■ get off the point, go off the track, go off at a tangent, get sidetracked, ramble, drift, wander, stray, diverge, deviate. □□ **digression** aside, departure, excursus, deviation, detour, *obiter dictum*, parenthesis, apostrophe.

digs see DIG *n.* 5.

dihedral /dīheédrəl/ *adj.* & *n.* ● *adj.* having or contained by two plane faces. ● *n.* = *dihedral angle*. □ **dihedral angle** an angle formed by two plane surfaces, esp. by an aircraft wing with the horizontal. [*dihedron* f. DI-[1] + -HEDRON]

dihydric /dīhídrik/ *adj.* *Chem.* containing two hydroxyl groups. [DI-[1] + HYDRIC]

dik-dik /díkdik/ *n.* any dwarf antelope of the genus *Madoqua*, native to Africa. [name in E. Africa and in Afrik.]

dike[1] var. of DYKE[1].

dike[2] var. of DYKE[2].

diktat /díktat/ *n.* a categorical statement or decree, esp. terms imposed after a war by a victor. [G, = DICTATE]

dilapidate /diláppidayt/ *v.intr.* & *tr.* fall or cause to fall into disrepair or ruin. [L *dilapidare* demolish, squander (as DI-[2], *lapis lapid-* stone)]

dilapidated /diláppidaytid/ *adj.* in a state of disrepair or ruin, esp. as a result of age or neglect.

■ ruined, broken-down, in ruins, gone to rack and ruin, wrecked, destroyed, falling apart, decrepit, derelict, battered, tumbledown, run-down, ramshackle, crumbling, decayed, decaying, rickety, shaky, *colloq.* beat-up, *Austral. sl* warby.

dilapidation /diláppidáysh'n/ *n.* **1 a** the process of dilapidating. **b** a state of disrepair. **2** (in *pl.*) repairs required at the end of a tenancy or lease. **3** *Eccl.* a sum charged against an incumbent for wear and tear during a tenancy. [ME f. LL *dilapidatio* (as DILAPIDATE)]

■ **1b** see DISREPAIR.

dilatation /dīlətáysh'n/ *n.* **1** the widening or expansion of a hollow organ or cavity. **2** the process of dilating. □ **dilatation and curettage** an operation in which the cervix is expanded and the womb-lining scraped off with a curette.

dilate /dīláyt/ *v.* **1** *tr.* & *intr.* make or become wider or larger (esp. of an opening in the body) (*dilated pupils*). **2** *intr.* (often foll. by *on*, *upon*) speak or write at length. □□ **dilatable** *adj.* **dilation** *n.* [ME f. OF *dilater* f. L *dilatare* spread out (as DI-[2], *latus* wide)]

■ see EXPAND 1.

dilator /dīláytər/ *n.* **1** *Anat.* a muscle that dilates an organ. **2** *Surgery* an instrument for dilating a tube or cavity in the body.

dilatory /díllətəri, -tri/ *adj.* given to or causing delay. □□ **dilatorily** *adv.* **dilatoriness** *n.* [LL *dilatorius* (as DI-[2], *dilat-* past part. stem of *differre* DEFER[1])]

■ see TARDY 1.

dildo /díldō/ *n.* (*pl.* **-os**) an object shaped like an erect penis and used, esp. by women, for sexual stimulation. [17th c.: orig. unkn.]

dilemma /dīlémmə, di-/ *n.* **1** a situation in which a choice has to be made between two equally undesirable alternatives. **2** a state of indecision between two alternatives. **3** *disp.* a difficult situation. **4** an argument forcing an opponent to choose either of two unfavourable alternatives. [L f. Gk (as DI-[1], *lēmma* premiss)]

■ **1** double bind, *colloq.* catch-22. **3** predicament, quandary, impasse, deadlock, stalemate; plight, difficulty, stymie, *esp. US* bind, *colloq.* fix, jam, spot, pickle, squeeze.

dilettante /díllitánti/ *n.* & *adj.* ● *n.* (*pl.* **dilettanti** /-ti/ or **dilettantes**) **1** a person who studies a subject or area of knowledge superficially. **2** a person who enjoys the arts. ● *adj.* trifling, not thorough; amateurish. □□ **dilettantish** *adj.* **dilettantism** *n.* [It. f. pres. part. of *dilettare* delight f. L *delectare*]

■ *n.* **1** dabbler, trifler, amateur, tinkerer. **2** see AESTHETE. ● *adj.* see SUPERFICIAL 1, 4, AMATEUR *adj.*

diligence[1] /díllijənss/ *n.* **1** careful and persistent application or effort. **2** (as a characteristic) industriousness. [ME f. OF f. L *diligentia* (as DILIGENT)]

■ see APPLICATION 4.

diligence[2] /díllijənss, déeleezhónss/ *n.* *hist.* a public stage-coach, esp. in France. [F, for *carrosse de diligence* coach of speed]

diligent /díllijənt/ *adj.* **1** careful and steady in application to one's work or duties. **2** showing care and effort. □□ **diligently** *adv.* [ME f. OF f. L *diligens* assiduous, part. of *diligere* love, take delight in (as DI-[2], *legere* choose)]

■ industrious, assiduous, attentive, conscientious, hard-working, sedulous, intent, steady, steadfast, focused, concentrated, earnest, constant; painstaking, careful, thorough, scrupulous, meticulous, punctilious.

dill[1] /dil/ *n.* **1** an umbelliferous herb, *Anethum graveolens*, with yellow flowers and aromatic seeds. **2** the leaves or seeds of this plant used for flavouring and medicinal purposes. □ **dill pickle** pickled cucumber etc. flavoured with dill. **dill-water** a distillate of dill used as a carminative. [OE *dile*]

dill[2] /dil/ *n.* *Austral. sl.* **1** a fool or simpleton. **2** the victim of a trickster. [app. back-form. f. DILLY[2]]

■ **1** see SILLY *n.*

dilly[1] /dílli/ *n.* (*pl.* **-ies**) esp. *US sl.* a remarkable or excellent person or thing. [*dilly* (adj.) f. DELIGHTFUL or DELICIOUS]

dilly[2] /dílli/ *adj.* *Austral. sl.* **1** odd or eccentric. **2** foolish, stupid, mad. [perh. f. DAFT, SILLY]

■ **1** see ECCENTRIC *adj.* 1. **2** see STUPID *adj.* 1, 5.

dillybag /díllibag/ *n.* *Austral.* a small bag or basket. [Aboriginal *dilly* + BAG]

dilly-dally /díllidálli/ *v.intr.* (**-ies, -ied**) *colloq.* **1** dawdle, loiter. **2** vacillate. [redupl. of DALLY]

■ **1** see DELAY *v.* 3.

diluent /dílyooənt/ *adj.* & *n.* *Chem.* & *Biochem.* ● *adj.* that serves to dilute. ● *n.* a diluting agent. [L *diluere diluent-* DILUTE]

dilute /dīlyóot/ *v.* & *adj.* ● *v.tr.* **1** reduce the strength of (a fluid) by adding water or another solvent. **2** weaken or reduce the strength or forcefulness of, esp. by adding something. ● *adj.* /also dī-/ **1** (esp. of a fluid) diluted, weakened. **2** (of a colour) washed out; low in saturation. **3** *Chem.* **a** (of a solution) having relatively low concentration of solute. **b** (of a substance) in solution (*dilute sulphuric acid*). □□ **diluter** *n.* **dilution** *n.* [L *diluere dilut-* (as DI-[2], *luere* wash)]

■ *v.* water (down), thin (down *or* out), weaken, deplete, reduce, lessen, diminish, decrease, impoverish, *US colloq.* split. ● *adj.* **1** weak, weakened, watered down, diluted, thinned out. **2** washed out, faded, bleached.

diluvial /dīlóoviəl, di-, -lyóoviəl/ *adj.* **1** of a flood, esp. of the Flood in Genesis. **2** *Geol.* of the Glacial Drift formation (see DRIFT *n.* 8). [LL *diluvialis* f. *diluvium* DELUGE]

diluvium /dīlóoviəm, di-, -lyóoviəm/ *n.* (*pl.* **diluvia** /-viə/) *Geol.* = DRIFT *n.* 8. [L: see DILUVIAL]

dim /dim/ *adj.* & *v.* ● *adj.* (**dimmer, dimmest**) **1 a** only faintly luminous or visible; not bright. **b** obscure; ill-defined. **2** not clearly perceived or remembered. **3** *colloq.* stupid; slow to understand. **4** (of the eyes) not seeing clearly. ● *v.* (**dimmed, dimming**) **1** *tr.* & *intr.* make or become dim or less bright. **2** *tr. US* dip (headlights). □ **dim-wit** *colloq.* a stupid person. **dim-witted** *colloq.* stupid, unintelligent. **take a dim view of** *colloq.* **1** disapprove of. **2** feel gloomy about. □□ **dimly** *adv.* **dimmish** *adj.* **dimness** *n.* [OE *dim*, *dimm*, of unkn. orig.]

■ *adj.* **1 a** faint, weak, weakened, pale, imperceptible, indiscernible, indistinguishable; dark, shadowy, murky, gloomy, sombre, dusky, crepuscular, *literary* tenebrous. **b** obscure, obscured, vague, fuzzy, indistinct, ill-defined, undefined, foggy, clouded, cloudy, nebulous, blurred, blurry, unclear, dull, hazy, misty. **3** obtuse, doltish, dull, dull-witted, foolish, slow-witted, *colloq.* thick, dense, dim-witted, *esp. US colloq.* dumb; see also STUPID *adj.* 1, 5. ● *v.* **1** obscure, dull, becloud, cloud; darken, shroud, shade; weaken. □ **dim-wit** see FOOL[1] *n.* 1. **dim-witted** see STUPID *adj.* 1, 5. **take a dim view of 1** object to, resent, take exception to, mind; see also DISAPPROVE.

dim. *abbr.* diminuendo.

dime /dīm/ *n. US* & *Can.* **1** a ten-cent coin. **2** *colloq.* a small amount of money. □ **a dime a dozen** very cheap or commonplace. **dime novel** a cheap popular novel. **turn on a dime** *US colloq.* make a sharp turn in a vehicle. [ME (orig. = tithe) f. OF *disme* f. L *decima pars* tenth part]

dimension /dīménsh'n, di-/ *n.* & *v.* ● *n.* **1** a measurable extent of any kind, as length, breadth, depth, area, and volume. **2** (in *pl.*) size, scope, extent. **3** an aspect or facet of a situation, problem, etc. **4** *Algebra* one of a number of unknown or variable quantities contained as factors in a product (x^3, x^2y, xyz, are all of three dimensions). **5** *Physics* the product of mass, length, time, etc., raised to the appropriate power, in a derived physical quantity. ● *v.tr.* (usu. as **dimensioned** *adj.*) mark the dimensions on (a diagram etc.). □□ **dimensional** *adj.* (also in *comb.*). **dimensionless** *adj.* [ME f. OF f. L *dimensio -onis* (as DI-[2], *metiri mensus* measure)]

■ *n.* **1** see MEASUREMENT 2.

dimer /dīmər/ *n. Chem.* a compound consisting of two identical molecules linked together (cf. MONOMER). □□ **dimeric** /-mérrik/ *adj.* [DI-[1] + *-mer* after POLYMER]

dimerous /dīmərəss/ *adj.* (of a plant) having two parts in a whorl etc. [mod.L *dimerus* f. Gk *dimerēs* bipartite]

dimeter /dímmitər/ *n. Prosody* a line of verse consisting of two metrical feet. [LL *dimetrus* f. Gk *dimetros* (as DI-[1], METER)]

diminish /dimínnish/ *v.* **1** *tr.* & *intr.* make or become smaller or less. **2** *tr.* lessen the reputation or influence of (a person). □ **law of diminishing returns** *Econ.* the fact that the increase of expenditure, investment, taxation, etc., beyond a certain point ceases to produce a proportionate yield. □□ **diminishable** *adj.* [ME, blending of earlier *minish* f. OF *menusier* (formed as MINCE) and *diminue* f. OF *diminuer* f. L *diminuere diminut-* break up small]

■ **1** decrease, decline, abate, shrink, contract; lessen, reduce, lower, curtail, compress, condense, pare (down), scale down; wane, fade, dwindle, ebb (away), die out *or* away, peter out, recede, subside; slacken, let up, wind down, slow (down), ease (off). **2** belittle, disparage, degrade, downgrade, discredit, detract from, vitiate, debase, deprecate, demean, depreciate, devalue, cheapen, *colloq.* put down, *formal* derogate.

diminished /dimínnisht/ *adj.* **1** reduced; made smaller or less. **2** *Mus.* (of an interval, usu. a seventh or fifth) less by a semitone than the corresponding minor or perfect interval. □ **diminished responsibility** *Law* the limitation of criminal responsibility on the ground of mental weakness or abnormality.

■ **1** see SMALL *adj.* 3–5.

diminuendo /dimínyoo-éndō/ *adv.* & *n. Mus.* ● *adv.* with a gradual decrease in loudness. ● *n.* (*pl.* **-os**) a passage to be played in this way. [It., part. of *diminuire* DIMINISH]

diminution /dímminyoosh'n/ *n.* **1 a** the act or an instance of diminishing. **b** the amount by which something diminishes. **2** *Mus.* the repetition of a passage in notes shorter than those originally used. [ME f. OF f. L *diminutio -onis* (as DIMINISH)]

■ **1** see DECREASE *n.*

diminutive /dimínyootiv/ *adj.* & *n.* ● *adj.* **1** remarkably small; tiny. **2** *Gram.* (of a word or suffix) implying smallness, either actual or imputed in token of affection, scorn, etc. (e.g. *-let*, *-kins*). ● *n. Gram.* a diminutive word or suffix. □□ **diminutival** /-tīv'l/ *adj.* **diminutively** *adv.* **diminutiveness** *n.* [ME f. OF *diminutif*, *-ive* f. LL *diminutivus* (as DIMINISH)]

■ *adj.* **1** small, tiny, little, miniature, petite, minute, minuscule, mini-, compact, undersized, pocket, pocket-sized, lilliputian, midget, *esp. Sc.* wee, *colloq.* teeny.

dimissory /dimíssəri/ *adj.* **1** ordering or permitting to depart. **2** *Eccl.* granting permission for a candidate to be ordained outside the bishop's own see (*dimissory letters*). [ME f. LL *dimissorius* f. *dimittere dimiss-* send away (as DI-[2], *mittere* send)]

dimity /dímmiti/ *n.* (*pl.* **-ies**) a cotton fabric woven with stripes or checks. [ME f. It. *dimito* or med.L *dimitum* f. Gk *dimitos* (as DI-[1], *mitos* warp-thread)]

dimmer /dímmər/ *n.* **1** a device for varying the brightness of an electric light. **2** *US* **a** (in *pl.*) small parking lights on a motor vehicle. **b** a headlight on low beam.

dimorphic /dīmórfik/ *adj.* (also **dimorphous** /dīmórfəss/) *Biol.*, *Chem.*, & *Mineral.* exhibiting, or occurring in, two distinct forms. □□ **dimorphism** *n.* [Gk *dimorphos* (as DI-[1], *morphē* form)]

dimple /dímp'l/ *n.* & *v.* ● *n.* a small hollow or dent in the flesh, esp. in the cheeks or chin. ● *v.* **1** *intr.* produce or show dimples. **2** *tr.* produce dimples in (a cheek etc.). □□ **dimply** *adj.* [ME prob. f. OE *dympel* (unrecorded) f. a Gmc root *dump-*, perh. a nasalized form rel. to DEEP]

■ *n.* hollow, depression, dent, indentation.

dim sum /dim súm/ *n.* (also **dim sim** /sim/) **1** a meal or course of savoury Cantonese-style snacks. **2** (usu. **dim sim**) *Austral.* a dish of Cantonese origin, consisting of steamed or fried meat cooked in thin dough. [Cantonese *dim-sām*, lit. 'dot of the heart']

DIN /din/ *n.* any of a series of technical standards originating in Germany and used internationally, esp. to designate electrical connections, film speeds, and paper sizes. [G, f. *D*eutsche *I*ndustrie-*N*orm]

din /din/ *n.* & *v.* ● *n.* a prolonged loud and distracting noise. ● *v.* (**dinned, dinning**) **1** *tr.* (foll. by *into*) instil (something to be learned) by constant repetition. **2** *intr.* make a din. [OE *dyne*, *dynn*, *dynian* f. Gmc]

■ *n.* noise, clamour, uproar, shouting, screaming, yelling, babel, clangour, clatter, commotion, racket, hullabaloo, hubbub, brouhaha, charivari, hurly-burly, *colloq.* row. ● *v.* **1** instil, drum, hammer, inculcate; implant, engrain.

dinar /deénaar/ *n.* **1** the chief monetary unit of the former Yugoslavia. **2** the chief monetary unit of certain countries of the Middle East and N. Africa. [Arab. & Pers. *dīnār* f. Gk *dēnarion* f. L *denarius*: see DENIER]

dine /dīn/ *v.* **1** *intr.* eat dinner. **2** *tr.* give dinner to. □ **dine out 1** dine away from home. **2** (foll. by *on*) be entertained to dinner etc. on account of (one's ability to relate an interesting event, story, etc.). **dining-car** a railway carriage equipped as a restaurant. **dining-room** a room in which meals are eaten. [ME f. OF *diner*, *disner*, ult. f. DIS- + LL *jejunare* f. *jejunus* fasting]

■ **1** have dinner, eat, banquet, feast, *archaic* sup, *colloq.* feed.

diner /dīnər/ *n.* **1** a person who dines, esp. in a restaurant. **2** a railway dining-car. **3** *US* a small restaurant. **4** a small dining-room.

■ **3** see CAFÉ 1.

dinette /dīnét/ *n.* a small room or part of a room used for eating meals.

ding[1] /ding/ *v.* & *n.* ● *v.intr.* make a ringing sound. ● *n.* a ringing sound, as of a bell. [imit.: infl. by DIN]

ding[2] /ding/ *n. Austral. sl.* a party or celebration, esp. a wild one. [perh. f. DING-DONG or WINGDING]

Ding an sich /díng an zíkh/ *n. Philos.* a thing in itself. [G]

dingbat /díngbat/ *n. sl.* **1** *US* & *Austral.* a stupid or eccentric person. **2** (in *pl.*) *Austral.* & *NZ* **a** madness. **b** discomfort, unease (*gives me the dingbats*). [19th c.: perh. f. *ding* to beat + BAT[1]]
▪ **1** see SILLY *n.*

ding-dong /díngdong/ *n.*, *adj.*, & *adv.* ● *n.* **1** the sound of alternate chimes, as of two bells. **2** *colloq.* an intense argument or fight. **3** *colloq.* a riotous party. ● *adj.* (of a contest etc.) evenly matched and intensely waged; thoroughgoing. ● *adv.* with vigour and energy (*hammer away at it ding-dong*). [16th c.: imit.]
▪ *n.* **1** see CHIME[1] *n.* 1b.

dinge /dinj/ *n.* & *v.* ● *n.* a dent or hollow caused by a blow. ● *v.tr.* make such a dent in. [17th c.: orig. unkn.]

dinghy /díngi, dínggi/ *n.* (*pl.* **-ies**) **1** a small boat carried by a ship. **2** a small pleasure-boat. **3** a small inflatable rubber boat (esp. for emergency use). [orig. a rowing-boat used on Indian rivers, f. Hindi *ḍīngī*, *ḍēngī*]
▪ **1, 2** see TENDER[3].

dingle /dínggʼl/ *n.* a deep wooded valley or dell. [ME: orig. unkn.]
▪ see VALLEY.

dingo /dínggō/ *n.* (*pl.* **-oes**) **1** a wild or half-domesticated Australian dog, *Canis dingo*. **2** *Austral. sl.* a coward or scoundrel. [Aboriginal]

dingy /dínji/ *adj.* (**dingier**, **dingiest**) dirty-looking, drab, dull-coloured. □□ **dingily** *adv.* **dinginess** *n.* [perh. ult. f. OE *dynge* DUNG]
▪ dark, dull, gloomy, dim, lacklustre, faded, discoloured, dusky, drab, dreary, dismal, cheerless, depressing, shadowy, grey-brown, *literary* tenebrous; grimy, dirty, soiled.

dink /dingk/ *n.* & *v. Austral. sl.* ● *n.* a lift on the handlebar of a bicycle etc. ● *v.tr.* carry (a person) in this way. [20th c.: orig. unkn.]

dinkum /díngkəm/ *adj.* & *n. Austral.* & *NZ colloq.* ● *adj.* genuine, right. ● *n.* work, toil. □ **dinkum oil** the honest truth. [19th c.: orig. unkn.]

dinky[1] /díngki/ *adj.* (**dinkier**, **dinkiest**) *colloq.* **1** *Brit. colloq.* (esp. of a thing) neat and attractive; small, dainty. **2** *US* trifling, insignificant. [Sc. *dink* neat, trim, of unkn. orig.]
▪ **1** see NEAT[1] 1, ADORABLE 2.

dinky[2] /díngki/ *n.* (*pl.* **-ies**) *colloq.* **1** a well-off young working couple with no children. **2** either partner of this. [contr. of *d*ouble *i*ncome *n*o *k*ids + -Y[2]]

dinner /dínnər/ *n.* **1** the main meal of the day, taken either at midday or in the evening. **2** a formal evening meal, often in honour of a person or event. □ **dinner-dance** a formal dinner followed by dancing. **dinner-jacket** a man's short usu. black formal jacket for evening wear. **dinner lady** a woman who supervises children's lunch in a school. **dinner service** a set of usu. matching crockery for serving a meal. [ME f. OF *diner*, *disner*: see DINE]
▪ **1** see MEAL[1]. **2** see BANQUET *n.*

dinosaur /dī́nəsawr/ *n.* **1** an extinct reptile of the Mesozoic era, often of enormous size. **2** a large unwieldy system or organization, esp. one not adapting to new conditions. □□ **dinosaurian** /-sáwriən/ *adj.* & *n.* [mod.L *dinosaurus* f. Gk *deinos* terrible + *sauros* lizard]

dinothere /dī́nətheer/ *n.* any elephant-like animal of the extinct genus *Deinotherium*, having downward curving tusks. [mod.L *dinotherium* f. Gk *deinos* terrible + *thērion* wild beast]

dint /dint/ *n.* & *v.* ● *n.* **1** a dent. **2** *archaic* a blow or stroke. ● *v.tr.* mark with dints. □ **by dint of** by force or means of. [ME f. OE *dynt*, and partly f. cogn. ON *dyntr*: ult. orig. unkn.]

diocesan /dīóssis'n/ *adj.* & *n.* ● *adj.* of or concerning a diocese. ● *n.* the bishop of a diocese. [ME f. F *diocésain* f. LL *diocesanus* (as DIOCESE)]

diocese /dī́əsiss/ *n.* a district under the pastoral care of a bishop. [ME f. OF *diocise* f. LL *diocesis* f. L *dioecesis* f. Gk *dioikēsis* administration (as DI-[3], *oikeō* inhabit)]

diode /dī́ōd/ *n. Electronics* **1** a semiconductor allowing the flow of current in one direction only and having two terminals. **2** a thermionic valve having two electrodes. [DI-[1] + ELECTRODE]

dioecious /dī-éeshəss/ *adj.* **1** *Bot.* having male and female organs on separate plants. **2** *Zool.* having the two sexes in separate individuals (cf. MONOECIOUS). [DI-[1] + Gk *-oikos* -housed]

diol /dī́ol/ *n. Chem.* any alcohol containing two hydroxyl groups in each molecule. [DI-[1] + -OL[1]]

Dionysiac /dī́ənissiak/ *adj.* (also **Dionysian** /-siən/) **1** wildly sensual; unrestrained. **2** (in Greek mythology) of or relating to Dionysus, the Greek god of wine, or his worship. [LL *Dionysiacus* f. L *Dionysus* f. Gk *Dionusos*]

Diophantine equation /dī́əfántin, -tīn/ *n. Math.* an equation with integral coefficients for which integral solutions are required. [*Diophantus* of Alexandria, mathematician of uncert. date]

dioptre /dīóptə/ *n.* (*US* **diopter**) *Optics* a unit of refractive power of a lens, equal to the reciprocal of its focal length in metres. [F *dioptre* f. L *dioptra* f. Gk *dioptra*: see DIOPTRIC]

dioptric /dīóptrik/ *adj. Optics* **1** serving as a medium for sight; assisting sight by refraction (*dioptric glass*; *dioptric lens*). **2** of refraction; refractive. [Gk *dioptrikos* f. *dioptra* a kind of theodolite]

dioptrics /dīóptriks/ *n. Optics* the part of optics dealing with refraction.

diorama /dī́əraámə/ *n.* **1** a scenic painting in which changes in colour and direction of illumination simulate a sunrise etc. **2** a small representation of a scene with three-dimensional figures, viewed through a window etc. **3** a small-scale model or film-set. □□ **dioramic** /-rámmik/ *adj.* [DI-[3] + Gk *horama* *-atos* f. *horaō* see]

diorite /dī́ərīt/ *n.* a coarse-grained plutonic igneous rock containing quartz. □□ **dioritic** /-ríttik/ *adj.* [F f. Gk *diorizō* distinguish]

dioxan /dīóks'n/ *n.* (also **dioxane** /-óksayn/) *Chem.* a colourless toxic liquid used as a solvent. ¶ Chem. formula: $C_4H_8O_2$.

dioxide /dīóksīd/ *n. Chem.* an oxide containing two atoms of oxygen which are not linked together (*carbon dioxide*).

DIP /dip/ *n. Computing* a form of integrated circuit consisting of a small plastic or ceramic slab with two parallel rows of pins. □ **DIP-switch** an arrangement of switches on a printer for selecting a printing mode. [abbr. of *d*ual *i*n-line *p*ackage]

Dip. *abbr.* Diploma.

dip /dip/ *v.* & *n.* ● *v.* (**dipped**, **dipping**) **1** *tr.* put or let down briefly into liquid etc.; immerse. **2** *intr.* **a** go below a surface or level (*the sun dipped below the horizon*). **b** (of a level of income, activity, etc.) decline slightly, esp. briefly (*profits dipped in May*). **3** *intr.* extend downwards; take or have a downward slope (*the road dips after the bend*). **4** *intr.* go under water and emerge quickly. **5** *intr.* (foll. by *into*) **a** read briefly from (a book etc.). **b** take a cursory interest in (a subject). **6** (foll. by *into*) **a** *intr.* put a hand, ladle, etc., into a container to take something out. **b** *tr.* put (a hand etc.) into a container to do this. **c** *intr.* spend from or make use of one's resources (*dipped into our savings*). **7** *tr.* & *intr.* lower or be lowered, esp. in salute. **8** *tr. Brit.* lower the beam of (a vehicle's headlights) to reduce dazzle. **9** *tr.* colour (a fabric) by immersing it in dye. **10** *tr.* wash (sheep) by immersion in a vermin-killing liquid. **11** *tr.* make (a candle) by immersing a wick briefly in hot tallow. **12** *tr.* baptize by immersion. **13** *tr.* (often foll. by *up*, *out of*) remove or scoop up (liquid, grain, etc., or something from liquid). ● *n.* **1** an act of dipping or being dipped. **2** a liquid into which something is dipped. **3** a brief bathe in the sea, river, etc. **4** a brief downward slope, followed by an upward one, in a road etc. **5** a sauce or dressing into which food is dipped before eating. **6** a depression in the skyline. **7** *Astron.* & *Surveying* the apparent depression of the horizon from the line of observation, due to the curvature of the earth. **8** *Physics* the angle made with the horizontal at any point by the earth's magnetic field. **9** *Geol.* the angle a stratum makes with the horizon. **10** *sl.* a pickpocket. **11** a quantity dipped up. **12** a candle made by dipping. □ **dip-switch** a switch for dipping a vehicle's headlight beams. [OE *dyppan* f. Gmc: rel. to DEEP]

■ *v.* **1** immerse, plunge, duck, dunk, douse, bathe, submerge. **2 b** decline, drop, go down, fall, descend, sag, sink, subside, slump. **5** (*dip into*) **a** skim (through), scan, look over, run one's eyes over, flick *or* thumb *or* leaf *or* flip through, peruse. **b** dabble in, trifle with, play at, trifle *or* toy *or* tinker *or* flirt with. **7** let *or* put down, lower, drop; be let *or* put down, be lowered *or* dropped. ● *n.* **1** lowering, fall, depression, drop, slump, decline; immersion. **3** swim, plunge, bathe, duck. **4** see SLOPE *n.* 1–3.

Dip. A.D. *abbr. Brit.* Diploma in Art and Design.

Dip. Ed. *abbr.* Diploma in Education.

dipeptide /dīpéptīd/ *n. Biochem.* a peptide formed by the combination of two amino acids.

Dip. H.E. *abbr. Brit.* Diploma of Higher Education.

diphtheria /dif-theériə, *disp.* dip-/ *n.* an acute infectious bacterial disease with inflammation of a mucous membrane esp. of the throat, resulting in the formation of a false membrane causing difficulty in breathing and swallowing. □□ **diphtherial** *adj.* **diphtheric** /-thérrik/ *adj.* **diphtheritic** /-thərittik/ *adj.* **diphtheroid** /dif-thəroyd, *disp.* dip-/ *adj.* [mod.L f. F *diphthérie*, earlier *diphthérite* f. Gk *diphthera* skin, hide]

diphthong /dif-thong, dip-/ *n.* **1** a speech sound in one syllable in which the articulation begins as for one vowel and moves as for another (as in *coin*, *loud*, and *side*). **2 a** a digraph representing the sound of a diphthong or single vowel (as in *feat*). **b** a compound vowel character; a ligature (as *æ*). □□ **diphthongal** /-thóngg'l/ *adj.* [F *diphtongue* f. LL *diphthongus* f. Gk *diphthoggos* (as DI-[1], *phthoggos* voice)]

diphthongize /dif-thongīz, dip-/ *v.tr.* (also **-ise**) pronounce as a diphthong. □□ **diphthongization** /-záysh'n/ *n.*

diplo- /díplō/ *comb. form* double. [Gk *diplous* double]

diplococcus /dipləkókkəss/ *n.* (*pl.* **diplococci** /-kī/) *Biol.* any coccus that occurs mainly in pairs.

diplodocus /diplóddəkəss, díplōdṓkəss/ *n.* a giant plant-eating dinosaur of the order Sauropoda, with a long neck and tail. [DIPLO- + Gk *dokos* wooden beam]

diploid /díployd/ *adj.* & *n. Biol.* ● *adj.* (of an organism or cell) having two complete sets of chromosomes per cell. ● *n.* a diploid cell or organism. [G (as DIPLO-, -OID)]

diploidy /díploydi/ *n. Biol.* the condition of being diploid.

diploma /diplṓmə/ *n.* **1** a certificate of qualification awarded by a college etc. **2** a document conferring an honour or privilege. **3** a State paper; an official document; a charter. □□ **diplomaed** /-məd/ *adj.* (also **diploma'd**). [L f. Gk *diplōma -atos* folded paper f. *diploō* to fold f. *diplous* double]

diplomacy /diplṓməsi/ *n.* **1 a** the management of international relations. **b** expertise in this. **2** adroitness in personal relations; tact. [F *diplomatie* f. *diplomatique* DIPLOMATIC after *aristocratic*]

■ **1** international relations, foreign affairs, statecraft, statesmanship, negotiation. **2** tact, tactfulness, adroitness, discretion, delicacy, discernment.

diplomat /dípləmat/ *n.* **1** an official representing a country abroad; a member of a diplomatic service. **2** a tactful person. [F *diplomate*, back-form. f. *diplomatique*: see DIPLOMATIC]

■ **1** see AMBASSADOR. **2** see PEACEMAKER.

diplomate /dípləmayt/ *n.* esp. *US* a person who holds a diploma, esp. in medicine.

diplomatic /dipləmáttik/ *adj.* **1 a** of or involved in diplomacy. **b** skilled in diplomacy. **2** tactful; adroit in personal relations. **3** (of an edition etc.) exactly reproducing the original. □ **diplomatic bag** a container in which official mail etc. is dispatched to or from an embassy, not usu. subject to customs inspection. **diplomatic corps** the body of diplomats representing other countries at a seat of government. **diplomatic immunity** the exemption of diplomatic staff abroad from arrest, taxation, etc. **diplomatic service** *Brit.* the branch of public service concerned with the representation of a country abroad. □□ **diplomatically** *adv.* [mod.L *diplomaticus* and F *diplomatique* f. L DIPLOMA]

■ **2** tactful, discreet, prudent, wise, sensitive, politic, courteous, polite, discerning, perceptive, perspicacious, thoughtful.

diplomatist /diplṓmətist/ *n.* = DIPLOMAT.

diplont /díplənt/ *n. Biol.* an animal or plant which has a diploid number of chromosomes in its somatic cells. [DIPLO- + Gk *ont-* stem of *ōn* being]

diplotene /díplōteen/ *n. Biol.* a stage during the prophase of meiosis where paired chromosomes begin to separate. [DIPLO- + Gk *tainia* band]

dipolar /dīpṓlər/ *adj.* having two poles, as in a magnet.

dipole /dīpōl/ *n.* **1** *Physics* two equal and oppositely charged or magnetized poles separated by a distance. **2** *Chem.* a molecule in which a concentration of positive charges is separated from a concentration of negative charges. **3** an aerial consisting of a horizontal metal rod with a connecting wire at its centre.

dipper /díppər/ *n.* **1** a diving bird, *Cinclus cinclus.* Also called *water ouzel.* **2** a ladle. **3** *colloq.* an Anabaptist or Baptist.

■ **2** see SCOOP *n.* 1b.

dippy /díppi/ *adj.* (**dippier**, **dippiest**) *sl.* crazy, silly. [20th c.: orig. uncert.]

■ see INANE 1.

dipso /dípsō/ *n.* (*pl.* **-os**) *colloq.* a dipsomaniac. [abbr.]

dipsomania /dipsəmáyniə/ *n.* an abnormal craving for alcohol. □□ **dipsomaniac** /-máyniak/ *n.* [Gk *dipso-* f. *dipsa* thirst + -MANIA]

■ see *drunkenness* (DRUNKEN).

dipstick /dípstik/ *n.* a graduated rod for measuring the depth of a liquid, esp. in a vehicle's engine.

dipteral /díptərəl/ *adj. Archit.* having a double peristyle. [L *dipteros* f. Gk (as DI-[1], *pteron* wing)]

dipteran /díptərən/ *n.* & *adj.* ● *n.* a dipterous insect. ● *adj.* = DIPTEROUS 1. [mod.L *diptera* f. Gk *diptera* neut. pl. of *dipterous* two-winged (as DI-[2], *pteron* wing)]

dipterous /díptərəss/ *adj.* **1** (of an insect) of the order Diptera, having two membranous wings, e.g. the fly, gnat, or mosquito. **2** *Bot.* having two winglike appendages. [mod.L *dipterus* f. Gk *dipteros*: see DIPTERAN]

diptych /díptik/ *n.* **1** a painting, esp. an altarpiece, on two hinged usu. wooden panels which may be closed like a book. **2** an ancient writing-tablet consisting of two hinged leaves with waxed inner sides. [LL *diptycha* f. Gk *diptukha* (as DI-[1], *ptukhē* fold)]

dire /dīr/ *adj.* **1 a** calamitous, dreadful (*in dire straits*). **b** ominous (*dire warnings*). **2** urgent (*in dire need*). □□ **direly** *adv.* **direness** *n.* [L *dirus*]

■ **1 a** see *calamitous* (CALAMITY). **b** see FEARFUL 2, 3. **2** see SORE *adj.* 4.

direct /dīrékt, di-/ *adj.*, *adv.*, & *v.* ● *adj.* **1** extending or moving in a straight line or by the shortest route; not crooked or circuitous. **2 a** straightforward; going straight to the point. **b** frank; not ambiguous. **3** without intermediaries or the intervention of other factors (*direct rule*; *the direct result*; *made a direct approach*). **4** (of descent) lineal, not collateral. **5** exact, complete, greatest possible (esp. where contrast is implied) (*the direct opposite*). **6** *Mus.* (of an interval or chord) not inverted. **7** *Astron.* (of planetary etc. motion) proceeding from East to West; not retrograde. ● *adv.* **1** in a direct way or manner; without an intermediary or intervening factor (*dealt with them direct*). **2** frankly; without evasion. **3** by a direct route (*send it direct to London*).

• *v.tr.* **1** control, guide; govern the movements of. **2** (foll. by *to* + infin., or *that* + clause) give a formal order or command to. **3** (foll. by *to*) **a** address or give indications for the delivery of (a letter etc.). **b** tell or show (a person) the way to a destination. **4** (foll. by *at, to, towards*) **a** point, aim, or cause (a blow or missile) to move in a certain direction. **b** point or address (one's attention, a remark, etc.). **5** guide as an adviser, as a principle, etc. (*I do as duty directs me*). **6 a** (also *absol.*) supervise the performing, staging, etc., of (a film, play, etc.). **b** supervise the performance of (an actor etc.). **7** (also *absol.*) guide the performance of (a group of musicians), esp. as a participant. □ **direct access** the facility of retrieving data immediately from any part of a computer file. **direct action** action such as a strike or sabotage directly affecting the community and meant to reinforce demands on a government, employer, etc. **direct address** *Computing* an address (see ADDRESS *n.* 1c) which specifies the location of data to be used in an operation. **direct current** (¶ Abbr.: **DC, d.c.**) an electric current flowing in one direction only. **direct debit** an arrangement for the regular debiting of a bank account at the request of the payee. **direct-grant school** *hist.* (in the UK) a school receiving funds from the Government and not from a local authority. **direct method** a system of teaching a foreign language using only that language and without the study of formal grammar. **direct object** *Gram.* the primary object of the action of a transitive verb. **direct proportion** a relation between quantities whose ratio is constant. **direct speech** (or **oration**) words actually spoken, not reported in the third person. **direct tax** a tax levied on the person who ultimately bears the burden of it, esp. on income. □□ **directness** *n.* [ME f. L *directus* past part. of *dirigere direct-* (as DI-[2], *regere* put straight)]

▪ *adj.* **1** straight, unswerving, shortest, undeviating, through. **2** honest, open, uninhibited, unreserved, forthright, sincere, unequivocal; tactless; unmitigated, outright, categorical, plain, clear, unambiguous, unmistakable, to the point, unqualified, unequivocal, point-blank, explicit, express; see also BLUNT *adj.* 2. **3** uninterrupted, without interference, unobstructed; straight. **4** unbroken, lineal. **5** exact, complete; polar, diametrical. • *v.* **1** control, manage, handle, conduct, pilot, steer, guide, look after, be at the helm, run, administer, govern, regulate, operate, superintend, supervise, command, head up, mastermind, rule. **2** rule, command, order, require, instruct, charge, dictate, enjoin, appoint, ordain, *literary* bid. **3 a** send, address, dispatch, deliver, post, *esp. US* mail. **b** guide, lead, show *or* point (the way), give directions; usher, escort. **4** aim, focus, level, point, target, train, turn; address. **5** advise, counsel, instruct, *literary* bid; see also COMMAND *v.* 1.

direction /dīréksh'n, di-/ *n.* **1** the act or process of directing; supervision. **2** (usu. in *pl.*) an order or instruction, esp. each of a set guiding use of equipment etc. **3 a** the course or line along which a person or thing moves or looks, or which must be taken to reach a destination (*sailed in an easterly direction*). **b** (in *pl.*) guidance on how to reach a destination. **c** the point to or from which a person or thing moves or looks. **4** the tendency or scope of a theme, subject, or inquiry. □ **direction-finder** a device for determining the source of radio waves, esp. as an aid in navigation. □□ **directionless** *adj.* [ME f. F *direction* or L *directio* (as DIRECT)]

▪ **1** guidance, managing, management, administration, government, supervision, operation, running, leadership, directorship, directorate, control, captaincy, handling, regulation, rule, charge. **2** (*directions*) instruction(s), information, guidelines, guide, order. **3 a** bearing, route, avenue; see also COURSE *n.* 2, WAY *n.* 1, 2.

directional /dīrékshən'l, di-/ *adj.* **1** of or indicating direction. **2** *Electronics* **a** concerned with the transmission of radio or sound waves in a particular direction. **b** (of equipment) designed to receive radio or sound waves most effectively from a particular direction or directions and not others. □□ **directionality** /-nálliti/ *n.* **directionally** *adv.*

directive /dīréktiv, di-/ *n.* & *adj.* • *n.* a general instruction from one in authority. • *adj.* serving to direct. [ME f. med.L *directivus* (as DIRECT)]

▪ *n.* see INSTRUCTION 1.

directly /dīréktli, di-/ *adv.* & *conj.* • *adv.* **1 a** at once; without delay. **b** presently, shortly. **2** exactly, immediately (*directly opposite*; *directly after lunch*). **3** in a direct manner. • *conj. colloq.* as soon as (*will tell you directly they come*).

▪ *adv.* **1 a** immediately, at once, straight away, right away, quickly, promptly, without delay, instantly, speedily, *US* momentarily. **b** soon, later (on), presently, in a (little) while, shortly, *archaic or literary* anon. **2** exactly, precisely, just, immediately; completely, entirely; diametrically. **3** straight, in a beeline, unswervingly, undeviatingly; frankly, straightforwardly, openly, plainly, bluntly, unreservedly, forthrightly; tactlessly. • *conj.* as soon as, when; see also IMMEDIATELY *conj.*

Directoire /dírrektwaár/ *adj. Needlework* & *Art* in imitation of styles prevalent during the French Directory. □ **Directoire drawers** (or **knickers**) knickers which are straight, full, and knee-length. [F (as DIRECTORY)]

director /dīréktər, di-/ *n.* **1** a person who directs or controls something. **2** a member of the managing board of a commercial company. **3** a person who directs a film, play, etc., esp. professionally. **4** a person acting as spiritual adviser. **5** esp. *US* = CONDUCTOR 1. □ **director-general** the chief executive of a large (esp. public) organization. **director of public prosecutions** *Brit.* = *public prosecutor*. □□ **directorial** /-tóriəl/ *adj.* **directorship** *n.* (esp. in sense 2). [AF *directour* f. LL *director* governor (as DIRECT)]

▪ **1** guide, leader, controller; steersman, helmsman, pilot, skipper, commander, commandant, captain; impresario. **2** executive, administrator, official, principal, governor, head, chief, manager, superintendent, supervisor, overseer, kingpin, *colloq.* top dog, *Brit. colloq.* gaffer, *sl.* big cheese, *US sl.* honcho, Mr Big; see also BOSS[1] *n.* **5** maestro, concert-master, conductor, *US* leader.

directorate /dīréktərət, di-/ *n.* **1** a board of directors. **2** the office of director.

▪ **1** see COUNCIL 1a.

directory /dīréktəri, di-, -tri/ *n.* (*pl.* **-ies**) **1** a book listing alphabetically or thematically a particular group of individuals (e.g. telephone subscribers) or organizations with various details. **2 a** (**Directory**) *hist.* the revolutionary executive of five persons in power in France 1795–9. **b** a body of directors. **3** a book of rules, esp. for the order of private or public worship. [LL *directorium* (as DIRECT)]

▪ **1** see INDEX *n.* 1. **2 b** see COUNCIL 1a.

directress /dīréktriss, di-/ *n.* (also **directrice**) a woman director. [DIRECTOR, F *directrice* (as DIRECTRIX)]

directrix /dīréktriks, di-/ *n.* (*pl.* **directrices** /-triseez/) *Geom.* a fixed line used in describing a curve or surface. [med.L f. LL *director*: see DIRECTOR, -TRIX]

direful /dīrfŏŏl/ *adj. literary* terrible, dreadful. □□ **direfully** *adv.* [DIRE + -FUL]

dirge /durj/ *n.* **1** a lament for the dead, esp. forming part of a funeral service. **2** any mournful song or lament. □□ **dirgeful** *adj.* [ME f. L *dirige* (imper.) direct, the first word in the Latin antiphon (from Ps. 5:8) in the Matins part of the Office for the Dead]

▪ see LAMENT *n.* 2.

dirham /dúrham/ *n.* the principal monetary unit of Morocco and the United Arab Emirates. [Arab. f. L DRACHMA]

dirigible /dírrijib'l, diríj-/ *adj.* & *n.* • *adj.* capable of being guided. • *n.* a dirigible balloon or airship. [L *dirigere* arrange, direct: see DIRECT]

diriment /dírrimənt/ *adj. Law* nullifying. □ **diriment impediment** a factor (e.g. the existence of a prior marriage) rendering a marriage null and void from the beginning. [L *dirimere* f. *dir-* = DIS- + *emere* take]

dirk /durk/ *n.* a long dagger, esp. as formerly worn by Scottish Highlanders. [17th-c. *durk*, of unkn. orig.]
■ see DAGGER.

dirndl /dúrnd'l/ *n.* **1** a woman's dress styled in imitation of Alpine peasant costume, with close-fitting bodice, tight waistband, and full skirt. **2** a full skirt of this kind. [G dial., dimin. of *Dirne* girl]

dirt /durt/ *n.* **1** unclean matter that soils. **2 a** earth, soil. **b** earth, cinders, etc., used to make a surface for a road etc. (usu. *attrib.*: *dirt track*; *dirt road*). **3 a** foul or malicious words or talk. **b** scurrilous information, scandal; gossip, the low-down. **4** excrement. **5** a dirty condition. **6** a person or thing considered worthless. □ **dirt bike** a motor cycle designed for use on unmade roads and tracks, esp. in scrambling. **dirt cheap** *colloq.* extremely cheap. **dirt-track** a course made of rolled cinders, soil, etc., for motor-cycle racing or flat racing. **do a person dirt** *sl.* harm or injure a person's reputation maliciously. **eat dirt 1** suffer insults etc. without retaliating. **2** *US* make a humiliating confession. **treat like dirt** treat (a person) contemptuously; abuse. [ME f. ON *drit* excrement]
■ **1** soil, mud, mire, grime, slime, scum, sludge, dust, soot, filth, *colloq.* muck, *Austral.* & *NZ colloq.* scunge, *Brit. colloq.* gunge, *esp. US sl.* grunge. **2 a** soil, earth, loam, ground, clay, sod, mould. **3** indecency, obscenity, smut, pornography, foulness, corruption, filth, vileness; gossip, scandal, rumour, inside information, *colloq.* low-down, dope, scuttlebutt. *Brit. sl.* the gen. **4** excrement, ordure, manure; see also DUNG *n.*, *bowel movement* 2. **6** waste, refuse, trash, garbage, rubbish, junk, dross, sweepings, leavings; *colloq.* scum. □ **do a person dirt** see BLACKEN 2, *run down* 6. **treat like dirt** see ABUSE *v.* 3.

dirty /dúrti/ *adj.*, *adv.*, & *v.* ● *adj.* (**dirtier**, **dirtiest**) **1** soiled, unclean. **2** causing one to become dirty (*a dirty job*). **3** sordid, lewd; morally illicit or questionable (*dirty joke*). **4** unpleasant, nasty. **5** dishonest, dishonourable, unfair (*dirty play*). **6** (of weather) rough, squally. **7** (of a colour) not pure or clear, dingy. **8** *colloq.* (of a nuclear weapon) producing considerable radioactive fallout. ● *adv. sl.* (with adjectives expressing magnitude) very (*a dirty great diamond*). ● *v.tr.* & *intr.* (**-ies**, **-ied**) make or become dirty. □ **dirty dog** *colloq.* a scoundrel; a despicable person. **the dirty end of the stick** *colloq.* the difficult or unpleasant part of an undertaking, situation, etc. **dirty linen** (or **washing**) *colloq.* intimate secrets, esp. of a scandalous nature. **dirty look** *colloq.* a look of disapproval, anger, or disgust. **dirty money** extra money paid to those who handle dirty materials. **dirty trick 1** a dishonourable and deceitful act. **2** (in *pl.*) underhand political activity, esp. to discredit an opponent. **dirty weekend** *colloq.* a weekend spent clandestinely with a lover. **dirty word 1** an offensive or indecent word. **2** a word for something which is disapproved of (*profit is a dirty word*). **dirty work** dishonourable or illegal activity, esp. done clandestinely. **do the dirty on** *colloq.* play a mean trick on. □□ **dirtily** *adv.* **dirtiness** *n.*
■ *adj.* **1** foul, unclean, muddy, grubby, soiled, begrimed, sooty, black, grimy, filthy, mucky, polluted, squalid, sullied, messy, stained, unwashed, scummy, muddied, Augean, impure, insanitary, unsanitary, bedraggled, *colloq.* crummy, manky, *Austral.* & *NZ colloq.* scungy, *Brit. colloq.* gungy, *poet.* befouled, *Brit. sl.* grot, grotty, *esp. US sl.* grungy. **3** sordid, smutty, indecent, obscene, crude, rude, coarse, ribald, prurient, risqué, salacious, lewd, lascivious, pornographic, licentious, blue, scabrous, *US* off colour. **4** unpleasant, nasty, horrible; bitter, malicious, malevolent, resentful, angry, furious, *literary* wrathful; sordid, base, mean, despicable, contemptible, scurvy, low, low-down, ignominious, vile. **5** unfair, unscrupulous, unsporting, dishonest, mean, rotten, underhanded, underhand, unsportsmanlike, dishonourable, ignoble, deceitful, corrupt, treacherous, perfidious, villainous, disloyal. **6** rough, bad, foul, nasty, stormy, squally, rainy, windy, blowy. ● *adv.* huge, *colloq.* whacking; see also ENORMOUS. ● *v.* stain, soil, begrime, besmirch, pollute, muddy, smear, defile, blacken, tarnish, drabble, foul, muck, *poet.* sully, befoul. □ **dirty dog** see SCOUNDREL. **dirty word 1** see EXPLETIVE *n.* 1.

dis- /diss/ *prefix* forming nouns, adjectives, and verbs: **1** expressing negation (*dishonest*). **2** indicating reversal or absence of an action or state (*disengage*; *disbelieve*). **3** indicating removal of a thing or quality (*dismember*; *disable*). **4** indicating separation (*distinguish*; *dispose*). **5** indicating completeness or intensification of the action (*disembowel*; *disgruntled*). **6** indicating expulsion from (*disbar*). [L *dis*-, sometimes through OF *des*-]

disability /díssəbílliti/ *n.* (*pl.* **-ies**) **1** physical incapacity, either congenital or caused by injury, disease, etc. **2** a lack of some asset, quality, or attribute, that prevents one's doing something. **3** a legal disqualification.
■ **1** handicap, impairment, defect, infirmity, disablement. **2** inability, incapacity, unfitness, inadequacy, impotence, powerlessness, helplessness.

disable /disáyb'l/ *v.tr.* **1** render unable to function; deprive of an ability. **2** (often as **disabled** *adj.*) deprive of or reduce the power to walk or do other normal activities, esp. by crippling. □□ **disablement** *n.*
■ **2** see CRIPPLE *v.*; (**disabled**) handicapped, incapacitated, crippled, lame; game, *archaic* halt; invalid.

disabuse /díssəbyóoz/ *v.tr.* **1** (foll. by *of*) free from a mistaken idea. **2** disillusion, undeceive.
■ see DISILLUSION *v.*

disaccord /díssəkórd/ *n.* & *v.* ● *n.* disagreement, disharmony. ● *v.intr.* (usu. foll. by *with*) disagree; be at odds. [ME f. F *désaccorder* (as ACCORD)]
■ *n.* see *disagreement* (DISAGREE).

disadvantage /díssədvaáantij/ *n.* & *v.* ● *n.* **1** an unfavourable circumstance or condition. **2** damage to one's interest or reputation. ● *v.tr.* cause disadvantage to. □ **at a disadvantage** in an unfavourable position or aspect. [ME f. OF *desavantage*: see ADVANTAGE]
■ *n.* **1** set-back, drawback, liability, handicap, defect, flaw, shortcoming, weakness, weak spot, fault; problem. **2** detriment, harm, loss, hurt, disservice; see also INJURY 3.

disadvantaged /díssədvaáantijd/ *adj.* placed in unfavourable circumstances (esp. of a person lacking the normal social opportunities).
■ see *deprived* (DEPRIVE 2).

disadvantageous /disádvəntáyjəss/ *adj.* **1** involving disadvantage or discredit. **2** derogatory. □□ **disadvantageously** *adv.*
■ **1** see DETRIMENTAL.

disaffected /díssəféktid/ *adj.* **1** disloyal, esp. to one's superiors. **2** estranged; no longer friendly; discontented. □□ **disaffectedly** *adv.* [past part. of *disaffect* (v.), orig. = dislike, disorder (as DIS-, AFFECT[2])]

disaffection /díssəféksh'n/ *n.* **1** disloyalty. **2** political discontent.

disaffiliate /díssəfílliayt/ *v.* **1** *tr.* end the affiliation of. **2** *intr.* end one's affiliation. **3** *tr.* & *intr.* detach. □□ **disaffiliation** /-áysh'n/ *n.*

disaffirm /díssəfúrm/ *v.tr. Law* **1** reverse (a previous decision). **2** repudiate (a settlement). □□ **disaffirmation** /disáffərmáysh'n/ *n.*
■ see REVERSE *v.* 2, 5.

disafforest /díssəfórrist/ *v.tr. Brit.* **1** clear of forests or trees. **2** reduce from the legal status of forest to that of ordinary land. □□ **disafforestation** /-stáysh'n/ *n.* [ME f. AL *disafforestare* (as DIS-, AFFOREST)]

disagree /díssəgrée/ *v.intr.* (**-agrees**, **-agreed**, **-agreeing**) (often foll. by *with*) **1** hold a different opinion. **2** quarrel. **3** (of factors or circumstances) not correspond. **4** have an adverse effect upon (a person's health, digestion, etc.). □□ **disagreement** *n.* [ME f. OF *desagreer* (as DIS-, AGREE)]
■ **1** dissent, diverge; see also DIFFER 2. **2** dispute, quarrel, argue, contend, contest, bicker, fight, fall out, squabble, wrangle, debate. □□ **disagreement** difference,

discrepancy, disparity, discord, discordance, discordancy, dissimilarity, disaccord, diversity, incongruity, nonconformity, incompatibility; dissent, opposition, conflict, strife, controversy, contention, dissension; quarrel, argument, dispute, altercation, debate, clash, *archaic* velitation, *US sl.* rhubarb.

disagreeable /dissəgréeəb'l/ *adj.* **1** unpleasant, not to one's liking. **2** quarrelsome; rude or bad-tempered. □□ **disagreeableness** *n.* **disagreeably** *adv.* [ME f. OF *desagreable* (as DIS-, AGREEABLE)]

■ **1** unpleasant, offensive, distasteful, disgusting, repugnant, obnoxious, repellent, repulsive, objectionable, revolting, odious, noxious, unsavoury, unpalatable, nauseating, nauseous, nasty, sickening, repellent. **2** quarrelsome, bad-tempered, ill-tempered, disobliging, uncooperative, unfriendly, uncivil, abrupt, blunt, curt, brusque, short, uncourtly, impolite, bad-mannered, ill-mannered, discourteous, rude, testy, splenetic, cross, ill-humoured, peevish, morose, sulky, sullen, *colloq.* grouchy.

disallow /dissəlów/ *v.tr.* refuse to allow or accept as valid; prohibit. □□ **disallowance** *n.* [ME f. OF *desalouer* (as DIS-, ALLOW)]

■ see PROHIBIT 1.

disambiguate /dissambígyoo-ayt/ *v.tr.* remove ambiguity from. □□ **disambiguation** /-áysh'n/ *n.*

disamenity /dissəméeniti, -ménniti/ *n.* (*pl.* **-ies**) an unpleasant feature (of a place etc.); a disadvantage.

disappear /dissəpéer/ *v.intr.* **1** cease to be visible; pass from sight. **2** cease to exist or be in circulation or use (*trams had all but disappeared*). □□ **disappearance** *n.*

■ **1** vanish, evaporate, vaporize, fade (away *or* out), evanesce. **2** die (out *or* off), become extinct, cease (to exist), perish (without a trace).

disappoint /dissəpóynt/ *v.tr.* **1** (also *absol.*) fail to fulfil a desire or expectation of (a person). **2** frustrate (hopes etc.); cause the failure of (a plan etc.). □ **be disappointed** (foll. by *with*, *at*, *in*, or *to* + infin., or *that* + clause) fail to have one's expectation etc. fulfilled in some regard (*was disappointed with you*; *disappointed at the result*; *am disappointed to be last*). □□ **disappointed** *adj.* **disappointedly** *adv.* **disappointing** *adj.* **disappointingly** *adv.* [ME f. F *désappointer* (as DIS-, APPOINT)]

■ **1** let down, fail, dissatisfy, disenchant, disillusion. **2** foil, thwart, balk, defeat; see also FRUSTRATE *v.* 2. □ **be disappointed** see *disappointed* below. □□ **disappointed** frustrated, dissatisfied, disenchanted, disillusioned, discouraged, disheartened, discontent(ed), *colloq.* choked; saddened, unhappy, dejected, downcast. **disappointing** discouraging, dissatisfying, unsatisfactory, unsatisfying, disconcerting; poor, second-rate, bad, sorry, inadequate, insufficient, inferior, *Brit. colloq.* pathetic.

disappointment /dissəpóyntmənt/ *n.* **1** an event, thing, or person that disappoints. **2** a feeling of distress, vexation, etc., resulting from this (*I cannot hide my disappointment*).

■ **1** set-back, let-down, comedown, one in the eye, failure, defeat, blow, calamity, disaster, anticlimax, non-event, *colloq.* wash-out. **2** frustration, dissatisfaction, vexation, discouragement, disenchantment, distress, regret, mortification, chagrin.

disapprobation /disáprəbáysh'n/ *n.* strong (esp. moral) disapproval.

■ see *disapproval* (DISAPPROVE).

disapprove /dissəpróov/ *v.* **1** *intr.* (usu. foll. by *of*) have or express an unfavourable opinion. **2** *tr.* be displeased with. □□ **disapproval** *n.* **disapprover** *n.* **disapproving** *adj.* **disapprovingly** *adv.*

■ **1** (*disapprove of*) condemn, criticize, disfavour, censure, object to, decry, denounce, put *or* run down, deplore, deprecate, belittle, look down on, look down one's nose at, frown on *or* upon, *sl.* knock; see also CRITICIZE 1. □□ **disapproval** disapprobation, condemnation, censure, criticism, reproof, reproach, objection, exception, disfavour, displeasure, dissatisfaction. **disapproving** see CRITICAL 1.

disarm /disaárm/ *v.* **1** *tr.* **a** take weapons away from (a person, State, etc.) (often foll. by *of*: *were disarmed of their rifles*). **b** *Fencing* etc. deprive of a weapon. **2** *tr.* deprive (a ship etc.) of its means of defence. **3** *intr.* (of a State etc.) disband or reduce its armed forces. **4** *tr.* remove the fuse from (a bomb etc.). **5** *tr.* deprive of the power to injure. **6** *tr.* pacify or allay the hostility or suspicions of; mollify; placate. □□ **disarmer** *n.* **disarming** *adj.* (esp. in sense 6). **disarmingly** *adv.* [ME f. OF *desarmer* (as DIS-, ARM[2])]

■ **4, 5** deactivate, defuse, incapacitate, put out of action. **6** win over, put *or* set at ease, mollify, appease, placate, pacify, reconcile, conciliate, propitiate, charm, *Austral.* square off. □□ **disarming** conciliatory; charming; see also *enchanting* (ENCHANT).

disarmament /disaármәmənt/ *n.* the reduction by a State of its military forces and weapons.

disarrange /dissəráynj/ *v.tr.* bring into disorder. □□ **disarrangement** *n.*

■ see DISORDER *v.*

disarray /dissəráy/ *n.* & *v.* ● *n.* (often prec. by *in*, *into*) disorder, confusion (esp. among people). ● *v.tr.* throw into disorder.

■ *n.* see DISORDER *n.* 1. ● *v.* see DISORDER *v.*

disarticulate /dissaartíkyoolayt/ *v.tr.* & *intr.* separate at the joints. □□ **disarticulation** /-láysh'n/ *n.*

disassemble /dissəsémb'l/ *v.tr.* take (a machine etc.) to pieces. □□ **disassembly** *n.*

■ see SEPARATE *v.* 1.

disassociate /dissəsóshiayt, -siayt/ *v.tr.* & *intr.* = DISSOCIATE. □□ **disassociation** /-áysh'n/ *n.*

disaster /dizaástər/ *n.* **1** a great or sudden misfortune. **2 a** a complete failure. **b** a person or enterprise ending in failure. □□ **disastrous** *adj.* **disastrously** *adv.* [orig. 'unfavourable aspect of a star', f. F *désastre* or It. *disastro* (as DIS-, *astro* f. L *astrum* star)]

■ **1** catastrophe, calamity, cataclysm, tragedy, misfortune, accident, mishap, act of God, trouble, reverse. **2 a** débâcle, collapse, downfall, breakdown, failure, *colloq.* wash-out. **b** failure, *colloq.* dead loss, *sl.* dead duck, no-hoper. □□ **disastrous** calamitous, catastrophic, cataclysmic, tragic, destructive, ruinous, devastating, appalling, harrowing, terrible, dire, horrendous, horrible, horrifying, dreadful, *colloq.* awful; unlucky, unfortunate, detrimental, grievous, harmful.

disavow /dissəvów/ *v.tr.* disclaim knowledge of, responsibility for, or belief in. □□ **disavowal** *n.* [ME f. OF *desavouer* (as DIS-, AVOW)]

■ see DENY 2.

disband /disbánd/ *v.* **1** *intr.* (of an organized group etc.) cease to work or act together; disperse. **2** *tr.* cause (such a group) to disband. □□ **disbandment** *n.* [obs. F *desbander* (as DIS-, BAND[1] *n.* 6)]

■ disperse, scatter, break up, dissolve, retire; demobilize, disarm, unarm.

disbar /disbaár/ *v.tr.* (**disbarred**, **disbarring**) deprive (a barrister) of the right to practise; expel from the Bar. □□ **disbarment** *n.*

disbelieve /disbiléev/ *v.* **1** *tr.* be unable or unwilling to believe (a person or statement). **2** *intr.* have no faith. □□ **disbelief** *n.* **disbeliever** *n.* **disbelievingly** *adv.*

■ **1** see DISTRUST *v.*

disbound /disbównd/ *adj.* (of a pamphlet etc.) removed from a bound volume.

disbud /disbúd/ *v.tr.* (**disbudded**, **disbudding**) remove (esp. superfluous) buds from.

disburden /disbúrd'n/ *v.tr.* **1** (often foll. by *of*) relieve (a person, one's mind, etc.) of a burden. **2** get rid of, discharge (a duty, anxiety, etc.).

■ (*disburden of*) see RELIEVE *v.* 6.

disburse /disbúrss/ *v.* **1** *tr.* expend (money). **2** *tr.* defray (a cost). **3** *intr.* pay money. □□ **disbursal** *n.* **disbursement** *n.* **disburser** *n.* [OF *desbourser* (as DIS-, BOURSE)]

■ **1** see SPEND 1. **2** see DEFRAY.

disc /disk/ *n.* (also **disk** esp. *US* and in sense 4a) **1 a** a flat thin circular object. **b** a round flat or apparently flat surface (*the sun's disc*). **c** a mark of this shape. **2** a layer of cartilage between vertebrae. **3** a gramophone record. **4 a** (usu. **disk**; in full **magnetic disk**) a computer storage device consisting of several flat circular magnetically coated plates formed into a rotatable disc. **b** (in full **optical disc**) a smooth non-magnetic disc with large storage capacity for data recorded and read by laser. **5** a device with a pointer or rotating disc indicating time of arrival or latest permitted time of departure, for display in a parked motor vehicle. □ **disc brake** a brake employing the friction of pads against a disc. **disk drive** *Computing* a mechanism for rotating a disk and reading or writing data from or to it. **disc harrow** a harrow with cutting edges consisting of a row of concave discs set at an oblique angle. **disc jockey** the presenter of a selection of gramophone records of popular music, esp. in a broadcast. [F *disque* or L *discus*: see DISCUS]

■ **1 a** see COUNTER[1] 2a, b. **c** circle, ring, round. **3** see RECORD *n.* 3a.

discalced /diskálst/ *adj.* (of a friar or a nun) barefoot or wearing only sandals. [var. of *discalceated* (after F *déchaux*) f. L *discalceatus* (as DIS-, *calceatus* f. *calceus* shoe)]

discard *v.* & *n.* ● *v.tr.* /diskaárd/ **1** reject or get rid of as unwanted or superfluous. **2** (also *absol.*) *Cards* remove or put aside (a card) from one's hand. ● *n.* /dískaard/ (often in *pl.*) a discarded item, esp. a card in a card-game. □□ **discardable** /-kaárdəb'l/ *adj.* [DIS- + CARD[1]]

■ *v.* **1** get rid of, dispense with, reject, dispose of, throw away *or* out, toss out *or* away, abandon, jettison, scrap, dump, *colloq.* bin, *esp. US colloq.* trash, *sl.* ditch. ● *n.* reject, cast-off; (*discards*) scraps, leavings, left-overs.

discarnate /diskaárnət/ *adj.* having no physical body; separated from the flesh. [DIS-, L *caro carnis* flesh]

discern /disérn/ *v.tr.* **1** perceive clearly with the mind or the senses. **2** make out by thought or by gazing, listening, etc. □□ **discerner** *n.* **discernible** *adj.* **discernibly** *adv.* [ME f. OF *discerner* f. L (as DIS-, *cernere cret-* separate)]

■ **1** see PERCEIVE. **2** see *make out* 1, 2. □□ **discernible** perceptible, visible, seeable, perceivable, apparent, clear, observable, plain, detectable, conspicuous, noticeable, distinguishable, recognizable, identifiable, distinct, real, tangible, actual, palpable.

discerning /disérning/ *adj.* having or showing good judgement or insight. □□ **discerningly** *adv.*

■ see JUDICIOUS.

discernment /disérnmənt/ *n.* good judgement or insight.

■ see DISCRIMINATION 2, 3.

discerptible /disérptib'l/ *adj. literary* able to be plucked apart; divisible. □□ **discerptibility** /-bílliti/ *n.* [L *discerpere discerpt-* (as DIS-, *carpere* pluck)]

discerption /disérpsh'n/ *n. archaic* **1 a** pulling apart; severance. **b** an instance of this. **2** a severed piece. [LL *discerptio* (as DISCERPTIBLE)]

discharge *v.* & *n.* ● *v.* /dischaárj/ **1** *tr.* **a** let go, release, esp. from a duty, commitment, or period of confinement. **b** relieve (a bankrupt) of residual liability. **2** *tr.* dismiss from office, employment, army commission, etc. **3** *tr.* **a** fire (a gun etc.). **b** (of a gun etc.) fire (a bullet etc.). **4 a** *tr.* (also *absol.*) pour out or cause to pour out (pus, liquid, etc.) (*the wound was discharging*). **b** *tr.* throw; eject (*discharged a stone at the cat*). **c** *tr.* utter (abuse etc.). **d** *intr.* (foll. by *into*) (of a river etc.) flow into (esp. the sea). **5** *tr.* **a** carry out, perform (a duty or obligation). **b** relieve oneself of (a financial commitment) (*discharged his debt*). **6** *tr.* *Law* cancel (an order of court). **7** *tr.* *Physics* release an electrical charge from. **8** *tr.* **a** relieve (a ship etc.) of its cargo. **b** unload (a cargo) from a ship. ● *n.* /dischaarj, dischaárj/ **1** the act or an instance of discharging; the process of being discharged. **2** a dismissal, esp. from the armed services. **3 a** a release, exemption, acquittal, etc. **b** a written certificate of release etc. **4** an act of firing a gun etc. **5 a** an emission (of pus, liquid, etc.). **b** the liquid or matter so discharged. **6** (usu. foll. by *of*) **a** the payment (of a debt). **b** the performance (of a duty etc.). **7** *Physics* **a** the release of a quantity of electric charge from an object. **b** a flow of electricity through the air or other gas esp. when accompanied by the emission of light. **c** the conversion of chemical energy in a cell into electrical energy. **8** the unloading (of a ship or a cargo). □□ **dischargeable** *adj.* **discharger** *n.* (in sense 7 of *v.*). [ME f. OF *descharger* (as DIS-, CHARGE)]

■ *v.* **1 a** let out, dismiss, let go, send away; liberate, (set) free; see also RELEASE *v.* 1. **b** relieve, acquit, let off, absolve; see also EXCUSE *v.* 4. **2** expel, oust, cashier, eject, give a person notice, give a person the brush-off, *colloq.* sack, give a person the boot *or* sack *or* chop, *sl.* fire, kick out; see also DISMISS 2. **3** shoot, fire (off); set *or* let off, detonate, explode. **4 a** emit, send out *or* forth, pour out *or* forth, exude; ooze, leak. **b** see THROW *v.* 1, 2. **5 a** carry out, perform, fulfil, accomplish, do, execute. **b** pay, settle, liquidate, clear, honour, meet, square. **8 b** unload, offload, empty. ● *n.* **2** expulsion, dismissal, ejection, *esp. US* ouster. **3 a** acquittal, exoneration; see also *exemption* (EXEMPT), RELEASE *n.* 1. **4** shooting, firing; salvo, fusillade, volley; detonation, explosion, burst. **5** emission, release, excretion, seepage, exudate, exudation; ooze, pus, suppuration, secretion, *Physiol.* matter. **6 a** payment, settlement, clearance. **b** performance, fulfilment, accomplishment, execution, observance. **8** unloading, offloading, emptying.

disciple /disíp'l/ *n.* **1** a follower or pupil of a leader, teacher, philosophy, etc. (*a disciple of Zen Buddhism*). **2** any early believer in Christ, esp. one of the twelve Apostles. □□ **discipleship** *n.* **discipular** /disípyoolər/ *adj.* [OE *discipul* f. L *discipulus* f. *discere* learn]

■ **1** apprentice, pupil, student, proselyte, learner, chela; follower, adherent, devotee, votary.

disciplinarian /díssiplináiriən/ *n.* a person who upholds or practises firm discipline (*a strict disciplinarian*).

■ (hard) taskmaster, taskmistress, martinet, slave-driver, drill-sergeant; tyrant, despot, dictator, authoritarian.

disciplinary /díssiplinnəri/ *adj.* of, promoting, or enforcing discipline. [med.L *disciplinarius* (as DISCIPLINE)]

■ regulatory; correctional, punitive, penal.

discipline /díssiplin/ *n.* & *v.* ● *n.* **1 a** control or order exercised over people or animals, esp. children, prisoners, military personnel, church members, etc. **b** the system of rules used to maintain this control. **c** the behaviour of groups subjected to such rules (*poor discipline in the ranks*). **2 a** mental, moral, or physical training. **b** adversity as used to bring about such training (*left the course because he couldn't take the discipline*). **3** a branch of instruction or learning (*philosophy is a hard discipline*). **4** punishment. **5** *Eccl.* mortification by physical self-punishment, esp. scourging. ● *v.tr.* **1** punish, chastise. **2** bring under control by training in obedience; drill. □□ **disciplinable** *adj.* **disciplinal** /díssiplín'l, díssiplin'l/ *adj.* [ME f. OF *discipliner* or LL & med.L *disciplinare*, *disciplina* f. *discipulus* DISCIPLE]

■ *n.* **1 a** order, direction, rule, regulation, government, authority, control, subjection, restriction, restraint, routine. **b** see CODE 4, 5. **c** behaviour, conduct, attitude. **2 a** training, drilling, exercise, practice, drill, inculcation, indoctrination, instruction, schooling, *esp. Med.* regimen. **3** subject, course, branch of knowledge, area, field, speciality. **4** chastisement, castigation, *archaic* correction; see also PUNISHMENT 1, 2. ● *v.* **1** punish, chastise, correct, penalize, reprove, criticize, reprimand, rebuke; see also CASTIGATE. **2** train, break in, condition, drill, exercise, instruct, coach, teach, tutor, school, indoctrinate, inculcate; check, curb, restrain, bridle, control, govern, direct, run, supervise, manage, regulate, hold *or* keep in check, *US* ride herd on.

disclaim /diskláym/ *v.tr.* **1** deny or disown (*disclaim all responsibility*). **2** (often *absol.*) *Law* renounce a legal claim to (property etc.). [ME f. AF *desclaim-* stressed stem of *desclamer* (as DIS-, CLAIM)]

■ see DENY 1, 2.

disclaimer /diskláymər/ *n.* a renunciation or disavowal, esp. of responsibility. [ME f. AF (= DISCLAIM as noun)]

■ see DENIAL 1.

disclose /disklṓz/ *v.tr.* **1** make known; reveal (*disclosed the truth*). **2** remove the cover from; expose to view. □□ **discloser** *n.* [ME f. OF *desclos-* stem of *desclore* f. Gallo-Roman (as DIS-, CLOSE²)]

■ **1** reveal, make known, impart, divulge, release, report, tell, blurt out, blab, leak, let slip, betray. **2** bare, reveal, expose, uncover, show, unveil.

disclosure /disklṓzhər/ *n.* **1** the act or an instance of disclosing; the process of being disclosed. **2** something disclosed; a revelation. [DISCLOSE + -URE after *closure*]

■ see REVELATION 2.

disco /dískō/ *n.* & *v. colloq.* ● *n.* (*pl.* **-os**) = DISCOTHÈQUE. ● *v.intr.* (**-oes, -oed**) **1** attend a discothèque. **2** dance to disco music (*discoed the night away*). □ **disco music** popular dance music characterized by a heavy bass rhythm. [abbr.]

discobolus /diskóbbələss/ *n.* (*pl.* **discoboli** /-lī/) **1** a discus-thrower in ancient Greece. **2** a statue of a discobolus. [L f. Gk *diskobolos* f. *diskos* DISCUS + *-bolos* -throwing f. *ballō* to throw]

discography /diskógrəfi/ *n.* (*pl.* **-ies**) **1** a descriptive catalogue of gramophone records, esp. of a particular performer or composer. **2** the study of gramophone records. □□ **discographer** *n.* [DISC + -GRAPHY after *biography*]

discoid /dískoyd/ *adj.* disc-shaped. [Gk *diskoeidēs* (as DISCUS, -OID)]

discolour /diskúllər/ *v.tr.* & *intr.* (*US* **discolor**) spoil or cause to spoil the colour of; stain; tarnish. □□ **discoloration** /-ráysh'n/ *n.* (also **discolouration**). [ME f. OF *descolorer* or med.L *discolorare* (as DIS-, COLOUR)]

■ see STAIN *v.* 1.

discombobulate /dískəmbóbyoolayt/ *v.tr. US joc.* disturb; disconcert. [prob. based on *discompose* or *discomfit*]

■ see DISTURB 1.

discomfit /diskúmfit/ *v.tr.* (**discomfited, discomfiting**) **1 a** disconcert or baffle. **b** thwart. **2** *archaic* defeat in battle. □□ **discomfiture** *n.* [ME f. *disconfit* f. OF past part. of *desconfire* f. Rmc (as DIS-, L *conficere* put together: see CONFECTION)]

■ **1 a** embarrass, abash, disconcert, disturb, make uneasy *or* uncomfortable, discompose, fluster, ruffle, perturb, upset, worry, unsettle, unnerve, *colloq.* rattle, faze, *US joc.* discombobulate; baffle, confuse, confound. **b** frustrate, foil, check, defeat, outdo, outwit, overcome, *colloq.* trump; see also THWART *v.*

discomfort /diskúmfərt/ *n.* & *v.* ● *n.* **1 a** a lack of ease; slight pain (*tight collar caused discomfort*). **b** mental uneasiness (*his presence caused her discomfort*). **2** a lack of comfort. ● *v.tr.* make uneasy. [ME f. OF *desconfort(er)* (as DIS-, COMFORT)]

■ *n.* **1 a** pain, soreness, irritation; bother, inconvenience. **b** uneasiness, difficulty, trouble, care, worry, distress, vexation. ● *v.* see DISCOMFIT 1a.

discommode /dískəmṓd/ *v.tr.* inconvenience (a person etc.). □□ **discommodious** *adj.* [obs. F *discommoder* var. of *incommoder* (as DIS-, INCOMMODE)]

■ see INCONVENIENCE *v.*

discompose /dískəmpṓz/ *v.tr.* disturb the composure of; agitate; disturb. □□ **discomposure** /-pṓzhər/ *n.*

■ see UPSET *v.* 2.

disconcert /dískənsért/ *v.tr.* **1** (often as **disconcerted** *adj.*) disturb the composure of; agitate; fluster (*disconcerted by his expression*). **2** spoil or upset (plans etc.). □□ **disconcertedly** *adv.* **disconcerting** *adj.* **disconcertingly** *adv.* **disconcertion** /-sérsh'n/ *n.* **disconcertment** *n.* [obs. F *desconcerter* (as DIS-, CONCERT)]

■ **1** see AGITATE. **2** see UPSET *v.* 3. □□ **disconcerting** awkward, upsetting, unnerving, unsettling, disturbing, *Brit.* off-putting; confusing, bewildering, perplexing, baffling, puzzling.

disconfirm /dískənfúrm/ *v.tr. formal* disprove or tend to disprove (a hypothesis etc.). □□ **disconfirmation** /-konfərmáysh'n/ *n.*

■ disprove, invalidate.

disconformity /dískənfórmiti/ *n.* (*pl.* **-ies**) **1 a** lack of conformity. **b** an instance of this. **2** *Geol.* a difference of plane between two parallel, approximately horizontal sets of strata.

disconnect /dískənékt/ *v.tr.* **1** (often foll. by *from*) break the connection of (things, ideas, etc.). **2** put (an electrical device) out of action by disconnecting the parts, esp. by pulling out the plug.

■ **1** separate, disjoin, disunite, uncouple, decouple, detach, unhook, undo, disengage, unhitch, cut *or* break off, cut *or* pull apart, part, divide, sever. **2** turn off, switch off, shut off, stop, deactivate.

disconnected /dískənéktid/ *adj.* **1** not connected; detached; separated. **2** (of speech, writing, argument, etc.) incoherent and illogical. □□ **disconnectedly** *adv.* **disconnectedness** *n.*

■ **1** separate, apart, detached, unattached; split, separated. **2** unconnected, incoherent, irrational, confused, illogical, garbled, disjointed, rambling, mixed-up, unintelligible, uncoordinated, random.

disconnection /dískənéksh'n/ *n.* (also **disconnexion**) the act or an instance of disconnecting; the state of being disconnected.

■ see DETACHMENT 2.

disconsolate /diskónsələt/ *adj.* **1** forlorn or inconsolable. **2** unhappy or disappointed. □□ **disconsolately** *adv.* **disconsolateness** *n.* **disconsolation** /-láysh'n/ *n.* [ME f. med.L *disconsolatus* (as DIS-, *consolatus* past part. of L *consolari* console)]

■ see WOEBEGONE.

discontent /dískəntént/ *n., adj.,* & *v.* ● *n.* lack of contentment; restlessness, dissatisfaction. ● *adj.* dissatisfied (*was discontent with his lot*). ● *v.tr.* (esp. as **discontented** *adj.*) make dissatisfied. □□ **discontentedly** *adv.* **discontentedness** *n.* **discontentment** *n.*

■ *n.* displeasure, unhappiness, dissatisfaction, discontentedness, discontentment, uneasiness, restlessness; malaise. ● *adj.* see *discontented* below. ● *v.* (**discontented**) displeased, dissatisfied, discontent, annoyed, vexed, irritated, piqued, disgruntled, exasperated, fed up, fed to death, *sl.* brassed off, hacked off, *Brit. sl.* browned off, cheesed off.

discontinue /dískəntínyoo/ *v.* (**-continues, -continued, -continuing**) **1** *intr.* & *tr.* cease or cause to cease to exist or be made (*a discontinued line*). **2** *tr.* give up, cease from (*discontinued his visits*). **3** *tr.* cease taking or paying (a newspaper, a subscription, etc.). □□ **discontinuance** *n.* **discontinuation** /-tínyoo-áysh'n/ *n.* [ME f. OF *discontinuer* f. med.L *discontinuare* (as DIS-, CONTINUE)]

■ **1** stop, put an end to; interrupt; see also STOP *v.* 1c.

discontinuous /dískəntínyooəss/ *adj.* lacking continuity in space or time; intermittent. □□ **discontinuity** /-kontinyóo-iti/ *n.* **discontinuously** *adv.* [med.L *discontinuus* (as DIS-, CONTINUOUS)]

■ see INTERMITTENT.

discord *n.* & *v.* ● *n.* /dískord/ **1** disagreement; strife. **2** harsh clashing noise; clangour. **3** *Mus.* **a** a lack of harmony between notes sounding together. **b** an unpleasing or unfinished chord needing to be completed by another. **c** any interval except unison, an octave, a perfect fifth and fourth, a major and minor third and sixth, and their octaves. **d** a single note dissonant with another. ● *v.intr.* /diskórd/ **1** (usu. foll. by *with*) **a** disagree or quarrel. **b** be different or inconsistent. **2** jar, clash, be dissonant. [ME f. OF *descord,* (n.), *descorder* (v.) f. L *discordare* f. *discors* discordant (as DIS-, *cor cord-* heart)]

■ *n.* **1** strife, dissension, disagreement, conflict, disharmony, contention, disunity, discordance, division, incompatibility. **2** see NOISE *n.* 1, 2. ● *v.* **1 a** see

DISAGREE. **b** see DIFFER 1. **2** grate, jangle, jar, clash, disharmonize.

discordant /diskórd'nt/ *adj.* (usu. foll. by *to*, *from*, *with*) **1** disagreeing; at variance. **2** (of sounds) not in harmony; dissonant. □□ **discordance** *n.* **discordancy** *n.* **discordantly** *adv.* [ME f. OF, part. of *discorder*: see DISCORD]

■ **1** contrary, disagreeing, divergent, opposite, opposed, adverse, contradictory, incompatible, differing, different, conflicting, at odds, incongruous, inconsonant, in conflict, in disagreement, at variance. **2** inharmonious, unharmonious, dissonant, jarring, cacophonous, unmelodious, unmusical, harsh, strident, jangling, grating.

discothèque /dískəték/ *n.* **1** a club etc. for dancing to recorded popular music. **2 a** the professional lighting and sound equipment used at a discothèque. **b** a business that provides this. **3** a party with dancing to popular music, esp. using such equipment. [F, = record-library]

discount *n.* & *v.* ● *n.* /dískownt/ **1** a deduction from a bill or amount due given esp. in consideration of prompt or advance payment or to a special class of buyers. **2** a deduction from the amount of a bill of exchange etc. by a person who gives value for it before it is due. **3** the act or an instance of discounting. ● *v.tr.* /diskównt/ **1** disregard as being unreliable or unimportant (*discounted his story*). **2** reduce the effect of (an event etc.) by previous action. **3** detract from; lessen; deduct (esp. an amount from a bill etc.). **4** give or get the present worth of (a bill not yet due). □ **at a discount 1** below the nominal or usual price (cf. PREMIUM). **2** not in demand; depreciated. **discount house 1** *Brit.* a firm that discounts bills. **2** *US* = *discount store*. **discount rate** *US* the minimum lending rate. **discount store** esp. *US* a shop etc. that sells goods at less than the normal retail price. □□ **discountable** /-kówntəb'l/ *adj.* **discounter** /-kówntər/ *n.* [obs. F *descompte*, *-conte*, *descompter* or It. (*di*)*scontare* (as DIS-, COUNT[1])]

■ *n.* **1, 2** reduction, mark-down, deduction; rebate, allowance. ● *v.* **1** disregard, omit, pass *or* gloss *or* gloze over, overlook, pay no attention to, dismiss, ignore. **3** reduce, mark down, deduct, lower, knock down; diminish, lessen, minimize, detract from, take away from.

discountenance /diskówntinənss/ *v.tr.* **1** (esp. in *passive*) disconcert (*was discountenanced by his abruptness*). **2** refuse to countenance; show disapproval of.

■ **1** see DISCOMFIT 1a. **2** see FROWN *v.* 2.

discourage /diskúrrij/ *v.tr.* **1** deprive of courage, confidence, or energy. **2** (usu. foll. by *from*) dissuade (*discouraged him from going*). **3** inhibit or seek to prevent (an action, etc.) by showing disapproval; oppose (*smoking is discouraged*). □□ **discouragement** *n.* **discouragingly** *adv.* [ME f. OF *descouragier* (as DIS-, COURAGE)]

■ **1** dispirit, dishearten, depress, daunt, unman, dismay, unnerve; see also DEMORALIZE 1. **2** deter, dissuade; (*discourage from*) put off, advise against, talk out of, divert from. **3** disapprove of, inhibit, hinder, slow, suppress; see also OPPOSE 1–3.

discourse *n.* & *v.* ● *n.* /dískorss, -kórss/ **1** *literary* **a** conversation; talk. **b** a dissertation or treatise on an academic subject. **c** a lecture or sermon. **2** *Linguistics* a connected series of utterances; a text. ● *v.* /diskórss/ **1** *intr.* talk; converse. **2** *intr.* (usu. foll. by *of*, *on*, *upon*) speak or write learnedly or at length (on a subject). **3** *tr. archaic* give forth (music etc.). [ME f. L *discursus* (as DIS-, COURSE): (v.) partly after F *discourir*]

■ *n.* **1 a** see CONVERSATION. **b, c** see LECTURE *n.* 1. ● *v.* **1** see CONVERSE *v.* **2** see LECTURE *v.* 1.

discourteous /diskúrtiəss/ *adj.* impolite; rude. □□ **discourteously** *adv.* **discourteousness** *n.*

■ uncivil, impolite, rude, unmannerly, ill-mannered, bad-mannered, disrespectful, boorish, abrupt, curt, brusque, short, blunt, ungentlemanly, unladylike, insolent, impertinent, ungracious.

discourtesy /diskúrtəsi/ *n.* (*pl.* **-ies**) **1** bad manners; rudeness. **2** an impolite act or remark.

■ **1** see INCIVILITY *n.* 1, 2. **2** see INSULT *n.* 1.

discover /diskúvvər/ *v.tr.* **1** (often foll. by *that* + clause) **a** find out or become aware of, whether by research or searching or by chance (*discovered a new entrance*; *discovered that they had been overpaid*). **b** be the first to find or find out (*who discovered America?*). **c** devise or pioneer (*discover new techniques*). **2** give (check) in a game of chess by removing one's own obstructing piece. **3** (in show business) find and promote as a new singer, actor, etc. **4** *archaic* **a** make known. **b** exhibit; manifest. **c** disclose; betray. **d** catch sight of; espy. □□ **discoverable** *adj.* **discoverer** *n.* [ME f. OF *descovrir* f. LL *discooperire* (as DIS-, COVER)]

■ **1 a, b** find (out), locate, unearth, become aware of, uncover, bring to light, turn *or* dig up, track down, come *or* chance *or* stumble upon, root *or* ferret out; determine, detect, discern, ascertain, identify; realize, notice, perceive, learn, *sl.* dope out. **c** originate, conceive (of), devise, contrive, invent, make up, design, pioneer. **4 d** see, spot, catch sight *or* a glimpse of, lay eyes on, view, encounter, meet (with), *literary* espy, descry, behold. □□ **discoverer** explorer, voyager; see also PIONEER *n.* 2.

discovery /diskúvvəri/ *n.* (*pl.* **-ies**) **1 a** the act or process of discovering or being discovered. **b** an instance of this (*the discovery of a new planet*). **2** a person or thing discovered. **3** *Law* the compulsory disclosure, by a party to an action, of facts or documents on which the other party wishes to rely. [DISCOVER after *recover*, *recovery*]

■ **1** finding, uncovering, unearthing, determining; exploration, disclosure, detection, identification, revelation; realization, recognition, perception. **2** find, catch, revelation; see also INVENTION 2.

discredit /diskréddit/ *n.* & *v.* ● *n.* **1** harm to reputation (*brought discredit on the enterprise*). **2** a person or thing causing this (*he is a discredit to his family*). **3** lack of credibility; doubt; disbelief (*throws discredit on her story*). **4** the loss of commercial credit. ● *v.tr.* (**-credited**, **-crediting**) **1** harm the good reputation of. **2** cause to be disbelieved. **3** refuse to believe.

■ *n.* **1** dishonour, degradation, disfavour, disrepute, ill repute, disgrace, ignominy, infamy, stigma, shame, scandal, obloquy, opprobrium, odium, humiliation, defamation; damage, harm, blot, brand, tarnish, blemish, taint. **3** doubt, suspicion, scepticism, dubiousness, doubtfulness, incredulity, distrust, mistrust, disbelief. ● *v.* **1** disparage, defame, dishonour, disgrace, degrade, bring into disfavour *or* disrepute, bring down, deprecate, demean, lower, devalue, depreciate, devaluate, belittle, diminish, reduce; slander, vilify, calumniate, sully, soil, mark, smear, blacken, taint, tarnish, besmirch, smirch, stigmatize, asperse, malign, libel, *archaic or US* slur. **2** detract from, *colloq.* debunk; see also EXPLODE 4. **3** disbelieve, deny, dispute, doubt, question, raise doubts about, distrust, mistrust, give no credit *or* credence to; reject; mock, ridicule.

discreditable /diskrédditəb'l/ *adj.* bringing discredit; shameful. □□ **discreditably** *adv.*

■ see SHAMEFUL.

discreet /diskréet/ *adj.* (**discreeter**, **discreetest**) **1 a** circumspect in speech or action, esp. to avoid social disgrace or embarrassment. **b** tactful; trustworthy. **2** unobtrusive (*a discreet touch of rouge*). □□ **discreetly** *adv.* **discreetness** *n.* [ME f. OF *discret -ete* f. L *discretus* separate (as DIS-, *cretus* past part. of *cernere* sift), with LL sense f. its derivative *discretio* discernment]

■ **1** careful, cautious, prudent, circumspect, wary, chary, heedful, guarded; judicious, tactful, diplomatic, considerate, trustworthy, thoughtful. **2** see UNOBTRUSIVE.

discrepancy /diskréppənsi/ *n.* (*pl.* **-ies**) **1** difference; failure to correspond; inconsistency. **2** an instance of this. □□ **discrepant** *adj.* [L *discrepare* be discordant (as DIS-, *crepare* creak)]

■ difference, disparity, dissimilarity, deviation, divergence, disagreement, incongruity, incompatibility, inconsistency, variance, conflict, discordance, discordancy, opposition, disaccord, contrariety, contradiction, contradictoriness, irreconcilability; gap, lacuna.

discrete /diskréet/ *adj.* individually distinct; separate, discontinuous. □□ **discretely** *adv.* **discreteness** *n.* [ME f. L *discretus*: see DISCREET]

■ separate, individual, disconnected, distinct, unattached, discontinuous; see also DISTINCT 1a.

discretion /diskrésh'n/ *n.* **1** being discreet; discreet behaviour (*treats confidences with discretion*). **2** prudence; self-preservation. **3** the freedom to act and think as one wishes, usu. within legal limits (*it is within his discretion to leave*). **4** *Law* a court's freedom to decide a sentence etc. □ **at discretion** as one pleases. **at the discretion of** to be settled or disposed of according to the judgement or choice of. **discretion is the better part of valour** reckless courage is often self-defeating. **use one's discretion** act according to one's own judgement. **years** (or **age**) **of discretion** the esp. legal age at which a person is able to manage his or her own affairs. □□ **discretionary** *adj.* [ME f. OF f. L *discretio -onis* (as DISCREET)]

■ **1** tact, diplomacy, discernment, tactfulness, delicacy, sound judgement, sagacity, common sense, good sense, wisdom, discrimination. **2** care, circumspection, carefulness; see also *prudence* (PRUDENT). **3** choice, option, judgement, preference, disposition, volition, *formal* pleasure; wish, will, liking, inclination.

discriminate /diskrímminayt/ *v.* **1** *intr.* (often foll. by *between*) make or see a distinction; differentiate (*cannot discriminate between right and wrong*). **2** *intr.* make a distinction, esp. unjustly and on the basis of race, colour, or sex. **3** *intr.* (foll. by *against*) select for unfavourable treatment. **4** *tr.* (usu. foll. by *from*) make or see or constitute a difference in or between (*many things discriminate one person from another*). **5** *intr.* (esp. as **discriminating** *adj.*) observe distinctions carefully; have good judgement. **6** *tr.* mark as distinctive; be a distinguishing feature of. □□ **discriminately** /-nətli/ *adv.* **discriminative** /-nətiv/ *adj.* **discriminator** *n.* **discriminatory** /-nətəri/ *adj.* [L *discriminare* f. *discrimen -minis* distinction f. *discernere* DISCERN]

■ **1** distinguish, separate, differentiate, discern, draw a distinction, tell the difference. **3** (*discriminate against*) disfavour, show favour *or* prejudice *or* bias against, be intolerant towards. **4** distinguish, differentiate, separate, mark out, set aside *or* apart, segregate. **5** be thoughtful, have discernment, be discerning, show diplomacy; (**discriminating**) see DISCRIMINATING.

discriminating /diskrímminayting/ *adj.* **1** able to discern, esp. distinctions. **2** having good taste. □□ **discriminatingly** *adv.*

■ discerning, discriminative, perceptive, thoughtful, critical, keen, selective, particular, refined, cultivated.

discrimination /diskrímmináysh'n/ *n.* **1** unfavourable treatment based on prejudice, esp. regarding race, colour, age, or sex. **2** good taste or judgement in artistic matters etc. **3** the power of discriminating or observing differences. **4** a distinction made with the mind or in action.

■ **1** bigotry, prejudice, bias, intolerance, favouritism, one-sidedness, unfairness, inequity. **2, 3** (good) taste, perception, perceptiveness, discernment, refinement, acumen, insight, penetration, keenness, (good) judgement, sensitivity; connoisseurship, aestheticism.

discursive /diskúrsiv/ *adj.* **1** rambling or digressive. **2** *Philos.* proceeding by argument or reasoning (opp. INTUITIVE). □□ **discursively** *adv.* **discursiveness** *n.* [med.L *discursivus* f. L *discurrere discurs-* (as DIS-, *currere* run)]

■ **1** extensive, long, lengthy, prolix; wandering, digressive, rambling, circuitous, roundabout, diffuse, long-winded, verbose, wordy, *colloq.* windy.

discus /diskəss/ *n.* (*pl.* **discuses**) **1** a heavy thick-centred disc thrown in ancient Greek games. **2** a similar disc thrown in modern field events. [L f. Gk *diskos*]

discuss /diskúss/ *v.tr.* **1** hold a conversation about (*discussed their holidays*). **2** examine by argument, esp. written; debate. □□ **discussable** *adj.* **discussant** *n.* **discusser** *n.* **discussible** *adj.* [ME f. L *discutere discuss-* disperse (as DIS-, *quatere* shake)]

■ **1** converse about, talk over *or* of *or* about, chat about, deliberate (over), review, examine, consult on, *US* bat around, *colloq.* kick about *or* around. **2** argue, thrash out; see also DEBATE *v.*

discussion /diskúsh'n/ *n.* **1** a conversation, esp. on specific subjects; a debate (*had a discussion about what they should do*). **2** an examination by argument, written or spoken. [ME f. OF f. LL *discussio -onis* (as DISCUSS)]

■ **1** conversation, talk, chat, dialogue, colloquy, exchange, confabulation, conference, parley, powwow, *US* bull session, *US sl.* skull session; debate, argument. **2** deliberation, examination, scrutiny, analysis, review.

disdain /disdáyn/ *n.* & *v.* ● *n.* scorn; contempt. ● *v.tr.* **1** regard with disdain. **2** think oneself superior to; reject (*disdained his offer*; *disdained to enter*; *disdained answering*). [ME f. OF *desdeign(ier)* ult. f. L *dedignari* (as DE-, *dignari* f. *dignus* worthy)]

■ *n.* see CONTEMPT 1. ● *v.* see DESPISE.

disdainful /disdáynfŏŏl/ *adj.* showing disdain or contempt. □□ **disdainfully** *adv.* **disdainfulness** *n.*

■ contemptuous, scornful, contumelious, derisive, sneering, superior, supercilious, pompous, arrogant, haughty, snobbish, snobby, lordly, regal, *colloq.* hoity-toity, high and mighty, uppity, highfalutin, stuck-up, snotty; jeering, mocking, insulting.

disease /dizéez/ *n.* **1** an unhealthy condition of the body (or a part of it) or the mind; illness, sickness. **2** a corresponding physical condition of plants. **3** a particular kind of disease with special symptoms or location. [ME f. OF *desaise*]

■ **1** sickness, affliction, ailment, malady, illness, infection, complaint, disorder, condition, affection. **2** blight, infestation, *archaic* murrain. **3** cancer, virus, plague; contagion, infection.

diseased /dizéezd/ *adj.* **1** affected with disease. **2** abnormal, disordered. [ME, past part. of *disease* (v.) f. OF *desaisier* (as DISEASE)]

■ **1** unhealthy, unwell, ill, sick, ailing, unsound, infirm, infected, contaminated, afflicted. **2** abnormal; unwholesome, morbid; see also ILL *adj.* 2.

diseconomy /díssikónnəmi/ *n. Econ.* the absence or reverse of economy, esp. the increase of costs in a large-scale operation.

disembark /díssimbáark/ *v.tr.* & *intr.* put or go ashore or land from a ship or an aircraft. □□ **disembarkation** /-káysh'n/ *n.* [F *désembarquer* (as DIS-, EMBARK)]

■ land, alight, go *or* put ashore, get *or* step off, get *or* step out, leave; debark, detrain, *esp. US* deplane.

disembarrass /díssimbárrəss/ *v.tr.* **1** (usu. foll. by *of*) relieve (of a load etc.). **2** free from embarrassment. □□ **disembarrassment** *n.*

disembody /díssimbóddi/ *v.tr.* (**-ies, -ied**) **1** (esp. as **disembodied** *adj.*) separate or free (esp. the soul) from the body or a concrete form (*disembodied spirit*). **2** *archaic* disband (troops). □□ **disembodiment** *n.*

■ **1** (**disembodied**) bodiless, incorporeal, discarnate; intangible, immaterial, insubstantial, unsubstantial, unreal; spiritual, ghostly, spectral, wraithlike.

disembogue /díssimbṓg/ *v.tr.* & *intr.* (**disembogues, disembogued, disemboguing**) (of a river etc.) pour forth (waters) at the mouth. [Sp. *desembocar* (as DIS-, *en* in, *boca* mouth)]

disembowel /díssimbówəl/ *v.tr.* (**-embowelled, -embowelling**; *US* **-emboweled, -emboweling**) remove the bowels or entrails of. □□ **disembowelment** *n.*

■ draw, gut.

disembroil /díssimbróyl/ *v.tr.* extricate from confusion or entanglement.

disenchant /díssincháant/ *v.tr.* free from enchantment; disillusion. □□ **disenchantingly** *adv.* **disenchantment** *n.* [F *désenchanter* (as DIS-, ENCHANT)]

■ see DISILLUSION *v.*

disencumber /dissinkúmbər/ *v.tr.* free from encumbrance.
■ (*disencumber of*) see RELIEVE 6.

disendow /dissindów/ *v.tr.* strip (esp. the Church) of endowments. □□ **disendowment** *n.*

disenfranchise /díssinfránchīz/ *v.tr.* (also **disfranchise** /disfránchīz/) **1 a** deprive (a person) of the right to vote. **b** deprive (a place) of the right to send a representative to parliament. **2** deprive (a person) of rights as a citizen or of a franchise held. □□ **disenfranchisement** *n.*

disengage /díssingáyj/ *v.* & *n.* ● *v.* **1 a** *tr.* detach, free, loosen, or separate (parts etc.) (*disengaged the clutch*). **b** *refl.* detach oneself; get loose (*disengaged ourselves from their company*). **2** *tr. Mil.* remove (troops) from a battle or a battle area. **3** *intr.* become detached. **4** *intr. Fencing* pass the point of one's sword to the other side of one's opponent's. **5** *intr.* (as **disengaged** *adj.*) **a** unoccupied; free; vacant. **b** uncommitted, esp. politically. ● *n. Fencing* a disengaging movement.
■ *v.* **1** loose, loosen, unloose, detach, unfasten, release, disconnect, disjoin, undo, disunite, unjoint, uncouple, extricate, unbuckle, unhitch, unclasp, unlatch, unbolt, unlock, unleash, unfetter, unchain, unlace, unhook, unbind, untie; (set) free, liberate, disentangle; divide, separate, part; throw off, shake (off), cut loose, get rid of; (*disengage oneself*) get out, get away, break away. **3** come off *or* away, separate, part, divide. **5** (**disengaged**) **a** unoccupied, vacant; see also FREE *adj.* 8b. **b** see NEUTRAL *adj.* 1, 2.

disengagement /díssingáyjmənt/ *n.* **1 a** the act of disengaging. **b** an instance of this. **2** freedom from ties; detachment. **3** the dissolution of an engagement to marry. **4** ease of manner or behaviour. **5** *Fencing* = DISENGAGE.

disentail /díssintáyl/ *v.tr. Law* free (property) from entail; break the entail of.

disentangle /díssintángg'l/ *v.* **1** *tr.* **a** unravel, untwist. **b** free from complications; extricate (*disentangled her from the difficulty*). **2** *intr.* become disentangled. □□ **disentanglement** *n.*
■ see STRAIGHTEN, EXTRICATE.

disenthral /díssinthráwl/ *v.tr.* (*US* **disenthrall**) (**-enthralled, -enthralling**) *literary* free from enthralment. □□ **disenthralment** *n.*

disentitle /díssintī́t'l/ *v.tr.* (usu. foll. by *to*) deprive of any rightful claim.

disentomb /díssintoōm/ *v.tr. literary* **1** remove from a tomb; disinter. **2** unearth. □□ **disentombment** /-toōm-mənt/ *n.*

disequilibrium /dísseekwilíbriəm/ *n.* a lack or loss of equilibrium; instability.

disestablish /díssistáblish/ *v.tr.* **1** deprive (a Church) of State support. **2** depose from an official position. **3** terminate the establishment of. □□ **disestablishment** *n.*

disesteem /díssisteém/ *v.* & *n.* ● *v.tr.* have a low opinion of; despise. ● *n.* low esteem or regard.

diseuse /deezṓz/ *n.* (*masc.* ***diseur*** /deezṓr/) a female artiste entertaining with spoken monologues. [F, = talker f. *dire dis-* say]

disfavour /disfáyvər/ *n.* & *v.* (*US* **disfavor**) ● *n.* **1** disapproval or dislike. **2** the state of being disliked (*fell into disfavour*). ● *v.tr.* regard or treat with disfavour.
■ *n.* **1** disapproval, dislike, displeasure, disapprobation, dissatisfaction. **2** low esteem *or* regard, disesteem, discredit, dishonour, disgrace, disrepute; see also DISCREDIT *n.* 1. ● *v.* dislike, discountenance, frown on *or* upon; see also DISAPPROVE.

disfigure /disfíggər/ *v.tr.* spoil the beauty of; deform; deface. □□ **disfigurement** *n.* [ME f. OF *desfigurer* f. Rmc (as DIS-, FIGURE)]
■ mar, damage, scar, deface, mutilate, injure, impair, deform, distort, spoil, ruin.

disforest /disfórrist/ *v.tr. Brit.* = DISAFFOREST. □□ **disforestation** /-stáysh'n/ *n.*

disfranchise var. of DISENFRANCHISE.

disfrock /disfrók/ *v.tr.* unfrock.

disgorge /disgórj/ *v.tr.* **1** eject from the throat or stomach. **2** pour forth, discharge (contents, ill-gotten gains, etc.). □□ **disgorgement** *n.* [ME f. OF *desgorger* (as DIS-, GORGE)]
■ **1** see REGURGITATE 1.

disgrace /disgráyss/ *n.* & *v.* ● *n.* **1** the loss of reputation; shame; ignominy (*brought disgrace on his family*). **2** a dishonourable, inefficient, or shameful person, thing, state of affairs, etc. (*the bus service is a disgrace*). ● *v.tr.* **1** bring shame or discredit on; be a disgrace to. **2** degrade from a position of honour; dismiss from favour. □ **in disgrace** having lost respect or reputation; out of favour. [F *disgrâce*, *disgracier* f. It. *disgrazia*, *disgraziare* (as DIS-, GRACE)]
■ *n.* **1** ignominy, shame, humiliation, embarrassment, degradation, debasement, dishonour, discredit, disfavour, disrepute, vitiation, infamy, stigma, scandal, vilification, disesteem, contempt, odium, obloquy, opprobrium. ● *v.* **1** shame, humiliate, embarrass, mortify; degrade, debase, dishonour, discredit, disfavour, vitiate, defame, disparage, scandalize, stain, taint, stigmatize, sully, besmirch, smirch, tarnish, smear, asperse, calumniate, vilify, blacken, drag through the mud, *archaic or US* slur. □ **in disgrace** out of favour, *sl.* on the mat, in the doghouse; see also UNPOPULAR.

disgraceful /disgráysfool/ *adj.* shameful; dishonourable; degrading. □□ **disgracefully** *adv.*
■ shameful, humiliating, embarrassing, dishonourable, disreputable, infamous, ignominious, degrading, debased, base, vile, corrupt, bad, wrong, evil, low, mean, despicable, contemptible, awful, terrible, shameless, outrageous, shocking, scandalous, improper, unseemly, unworthy, objectionable.

disgruntled /disgrúnt'ld/ *adj.* discontented; moody; sulky. □□ **disgruntlement** *n.* [DIS- + *gruntle* obs. frequent. of GRUNT]
■ discontented, displeased, unhappy, dissatisfied, irritated, vexed, cross, exasperated, annoyed, disappointed, put out, malcontent, discontent(ed), testy, peevish, grumpy, moody, sullen, sulky, crotchety, fractious, out of temper, in a bad temper, crabby, ill-humoured, bad-tempered, ill-tempered, *esp. US* cranky, *colloq.* fed up, peeved, grouchy, *Brit. sl.* browned off, cheesed off.

disguise /disgī́z/ *v.* & *n.* ● *v.tr.* **1** (often foll. by *as*) alter the appearance, sound, smell, etc., of so as to conceal the identity; make unrecognizable (*disguised herself as a policewoman*; *disguised the taste by adding sugar*). **2** misrepresent or cover up (*disguised the truth*; *disguised their intentions*). ● *n.* **1 a** a costume, false beard, make-up, etc., used to alter the appearance so as to conceal or deceive. **b** any action, manner, etc., used for deception. **2 a** the act or practice of disguising; the concealment of reality. **b** an instance of this. □ **in disguise 1** wearing a concealing costume etc. **2** appearing to be the opposite (*a blessing in disguise*). □□ **disguisement** *n.* [ME f. OF *desguis(i)er* (as DIS-, GUISE)]
■ *v.* **1** camouflage, cover up, conceal, hide, mask. **2** misrepresent, falsify, counterfeit, distort, twist, fake. ● *n.* **1** guise, false identity, camouflage, appearance, semblance, form; outfit, costume. **2 a** pretence, deception, dissimulation, semblance, concealment; see also DECEIT 1. **b** cover-up, façade, front, bluff, pretence; see also MASQUERADE *n.* 1.

disgust /disgúst/ *n.* & *v.* ● *n.* (usu. foll. by *at*, *for*) **1** strong aversion, repugnance; profound indignation. **2** strong distaste for (some item of) food, drink, medicine, etc.; nausea. ● *v.tr.* cause disgust in (*their behaviour disgusts me*; *was disgusted to find a slug*). □ **in disgust** as a result of disgust (*left in disgust*). □□ **disgustedly** *adv.* [OF *degoust*, *desgouster*, or It. *disgusto*, *disgustare* (as DIS-, GUSTO)]
■ *n.* **1** loathing, contempt, hatred, abhorrence, repugnance, aversion, odium, animus, animosity, enmity, antagonism, antipathy, dislike; outrage, indignation. **2** revulsion, nausea, sickness, repugnance, distaste, aversion. ● *v.* sicken, offend, nauseate, repel, revolt, put off, appal, *US sl.* gross out; outrage.

disgustful /disgústfŏŏl/ *adj.* **1** disgusting; repulsive. **2** (of curiosity etc.) caused by disgust.

disgusting /disgústing/ *adj.* arousing aversion or indignation (*disgusting behaviour*). □□ **disgustingly** *adv.* **disgustingness** *n.*

■ nauseating, sickening, offensive, repulsive, disgustful, revolting, repugnant, repellent, objectionable, distasteful, obnoxious, loathsome, gross, vile, foul, nasty, horrible, *Brit.* off-putting, *colloq.* sick-making; unappetizing, unsavoury; outrageous.

dish /dish/ *n.* & *v.* ● *n.* **1 a** a shallow, usu. flat-bottomed container for cooking or serving food, made of glass, ceramics, metal, etc. **b** the food served in a dish (*all the dishes were delicious*). **c** a particular kind of food (*a meat dish*). **2** (in *pl.*) dirty plates, cutlery, cooking pots, etc. after a meal. **3 a** a dish-shaped receptacle, object, or cavity. **b** = *satellite dish*. **4** *sl.* a sexually attractive person. ● *v.tr.* **1** put (food) into a dish ready for serving. **2** *colloq.* **a** outmanoeuvre. **b** *Brit.* destroy (one's hopes, chances, etc.). **3** make concave or dish-shaped. □ **dish out** *sl.* distribute, esp. carelessly or indiscriminately. **dish up 1** serve or prepare to serve (food). **2** *colloq.* seek to present (facts, argument, etc.) attractively. □□ **dishful** *n.* (*pl.* **-fuls**). **dishlike** *adj.* [OE *disc* plate, bowl (with Gmc and ON cognates) f. L *discus* DISC]

■ *n.* **1 a** see PLATE *n.* 1a. **b** see PLATE *n.* 1b.

dishabille var. of DÉSHABILLÉ.

disharmony /diss-haármәni/ *n.* a lack of harmony; discord. □□ **disharmonious** /-mṓniәss/ *adj.* **disharmoniously** /-mṓniәsli/ *adv.* **disharmonize** /-nīz/ *v.tr.*

■ see DISCORD *n.* 1.

dishcloth /díshkloth/ *n.* a usu. open-weave cloth for washing dishes. □ **dishcloth gourd** a loofah.

dishearten /diss-haárt'n/ *v.tr.* cause to lose courage or confidence; make despondent. □□ **dishearteningly** *adv.* **disheartenment** *n.*

■ see DISCOURAGE 1.

dishevelled /dishévv'ld/ *adj.* (*US* **disheveled**) (of the hair, a person, etc.) untidy; ruffled; disordered. □□ **dishevel** *v.tr.* (**dishevelled, dishevelling**; *US* **disheveled, disheveling**). **dishevelment** *n.* [ME *dischevelee* f. OF *deschevelé* past part. (as DIS-, *chevel* hair f. L *capillus*)]

■ see UNTIDY.

dishonest /disónnist/ *adj.* (of a person, act, or statement) fraudulent or insincere. □□ **dishonestly** *adv.* [ME f. OF *deshoneste* (as DIS-, HONEST)]

■ untrustworthy, underhanded, underhand, shady, dishonourable, fraudulent, deceptive, unfair, double-dealing, thievish, knavish, cheating, deceitful, lying, untruthful, mendacious, treacherous, perfidious, corrupt, unscrupulous, unprincipled, *colloq.* crooked, *sl.* bent, *Austral. sl.* shonky; insincere, two-faced, hypocritical.

dishonesty /disónnisti/ *n.* (*pl.* **-ies**) **1 a** a lack of honesty. **b** deceitfulness, fraud. **2** a dishonest or fraudulent act. [ME f. OF *deshon(n)esté* (as DISHONEST)]

dishonour /disónnәr/ *n.* & *v.* (*US* **dishonor**) ● *n.* **1** a state of shame or disgrace; discredit. **2** something that causes dishonour (*a dishonour to his profession*). ● *v.tr.* **1** treat without honour or respect. **2** disgrace (*dishonoured his name*). **3** refuse to accept or pay (a cheque or a bill of exchange). **4** *archaic* violate the chastity of; rape. [ME f. OF *deshonor*, *deshonorer* f. med.L *dishonorare* (as DIS-, HONOUR)]

■ *n.* **1** discredit, disesteem, disrespect, ignominy, disgrace, shame, disrepute, indignity, loss of face. **2** disgrace, slight, insult, offence, affront, embarrassment. ● *v.* **1** insult, abuse, affront, slight, offend, injure. **2** degrade, discredit, shame, debase, humiliate, mortify, abase; see also DISGRACE *v.* 1. **4** defile, violate, ravish, rape, deflower, sexually assault, *euphem.* assault.

dishonourable /disónnәrәb'l/ *adj.* (*US* **dishonorable**) **1** causing disgrace; ignominious. **2** unprincipled. □□ **dishonourableness** *n.* **dishonourably** *adv.*

■ **1** disgraceful, degrading, inglorious, ignominious, shameful, discreditable, humiliating. **2** unprincipled, shameless, corrupt, unscrupulous, untrustworthy, treacherous, traitorous, perfidious, disloyal, unfaithful, faithless, dishonest, hypocritical, two-faced, duplicitous, disreputable, base, despicable; improper, unseemly, unbecoming, unworthy, objectionable, reprehensible, flagrant, bad, evil, vile, low, mean, contemptible, below *or* beneath contempt, foul, heinous, dirty, filthy.

dishrag /díshrag/ *n.* = DISHCLOTH.

dishwasher /díshwoshәr/ *n.* **1** a machine for automatically washing dishes. **2** a person employed to wash dishes.

dishwater /díshwawtәr/ *n.* water in which dishes have been washed.

dishy /díshi/ *adj.* (**dishier, dishiest**) *Brit. colloq.* sexually attractive. [DISH *n.* 4 + -Y[1]]

disillusion /díssilŏŏzh'n, -lyŏŏzh'n/ *n.* & *v.* ● *n.* freedom from illusions; disenchantment. ● *v.tr.* rid of illusions; disenchant. □□ **disillusionize** *v.tr.* (also **-ise**). **disillusionment** *n.*

■ *n.* disillusionment, disenchantment, disappointment, *literary* disenthralment. ● *v.* disabuse, disappoint, disenchant, *literary* disenthral; enlighten, set straight, undeceive, put right.

disincentive /díssinséntiv/ *n.* & *adj.* ● *n.* **1** something that tends to discourage a particular action etc. **2** *Econ.* a source of discouragement to productivity or progress. ● *adj.* tending to discourage.

■ *n.* **1** see DETERRENT *n.*

disinclination /díssinklináysh'n/ *n.* (usu. foll. by *for*, or *to* + infin.) the absence of willingness; a reluctance (*a disinclination for work*; *disinclination to go*).

■ see *reluctance* (RELUCTANT).

disincline /díssinklīn/ *v.tr.* (usu. foll. by *to* + infin. or *for*) **1** make unwilling or reluctant. **2** (as **disinclined** *adj.*) unwilling, averse.

■ **2** (**disinclined**) unwilling, reluctant, hesitant, loath, opposed, averse.

disincorporate /díssinkórpәrayt/ *v.tr.* dissolve (a corporate body).

disinfect /díssinfékt/ *v.tr.* cleanse (a wound, a room, clothes, etc.) of infection, esp. with a disinfectant. □□ **disinfection** *n.* [F *désinfecter* (as DIS-, INFECT)]

■ clean, purify, purge, sanitize, fumigate, decontaminate, sterilize, *usu. formal* cleanse.

disinfectant /díssinféktәnt/ *n.* & *adj.* ● *n.* a usu. commercially produced chemical liquid that destroys germs etc. ● *adj.* causing disinfection.

■ *n.* germicide, antiseptic, sterilizer, bactericide, sanitizer, fumigant, purifier, cleaner, cleanser.

disinfest /díssinfést/ *v.tr.* rid (a person, a building, etc.) of vermin, infesting insects, etc. □□ **disinfestation** /-stáysh'n/ *n.*

disinflation /díssinfláysh'n/ *n. Econ.* a policy designed to counteract inflation without causing deflation. □□ **disinflationary** *adj.*

disinformation /díssinfәrmáysh'n/ *n.* false information, intended to mislead.

■ see LIE[2] *n.*

disingenuous /díssinjényooәss/ *adj.* having secret motives; dishonest, insincere. □□ **disingenuously** *adv.* **disingenuousness** *n.*

■ insincere, false, dishonest, tricky, devious, deceitful, underhanded, underhand, guileful, double-dealing, two-faced, duplicitous, hypocritical, calculating, designing, *colloq.* shifty.

disinherit /díssinhérrit/ *v.tr.* (**disinherited, disinheriting**) reject as one's heir; deprive of the right of inheritance. □□ **disinheritance** *n.* [ME f. DIS- + INHERIT in obs. sense 'make heir']

■ disown, cut off, reject.

disintegrate /disíntigrayt/ *v.* **1** *tr.* & *intr.* **a** separate into component parts or fragments. **b** lose or cause to lose cohesion. **2** *intr. colloq.* deteriorate mentally or physically; decay. **3** *intr.* & *tr. Physics* undergo or cause to undergo disintegration. ▫▫ **disintegrator** *n.*

■ **1** break up *or* apart, shatter, come *or* fall apart, come *or* go *or* fall to pieces, crumble, fragment, fall to bits. **2** break down, collapse, go to pieces, have a (nervous) breakdown, *colloq.* crack up. **3** decompose, rot, decay, moulder.

disintegration /disíntigráysh'n/ *n.* **1** the act or an instance of disintegrating. **2** *Physics* any process in which a nucleus emits a particle or particles or divides into smaller nuclei.

■ **1** see DECAY *n.* 2.

disinter /díssintér/ *v.tr.* (**disinterred, disinterring**) **1** remove (esp. a corpse) from the ground; unearth; exhume. **2** find after a protracted search (*disinterred the letter from the back of the drawer*). ▫▫ **disinterment** *n.* [F *désenterrer* (as DIS-, INTER)]

■ see DIG *v.* 4.

disinterest /dissíntrist/ *n.* **1** impartiality. **2** *disp.* lack of interest; unconcern.

■ **1** see *objectivity* (OBJECTIVE). **2** see INDIFFERENCE 1.

disinterested /dissíntristid/ *adj.* **1** not influenced by one's own advantage; impartial. **2** *disp.* uninterested. ▫▫ **disinterestedly** *adv.* **disinterestedness** *n.* [past part. of *disinterest* (v.) divest of interest]

■ **1** unbiased, impartial, unprejudiced, objective, fair, neutral, open-minded, equitable, just, dispassionate, detached, even-handed, impersonal, uninvolved. **2** see INDIFFERENT 4.

disinvest /díssinvést/ *v.intr.* (foll. by *from*, or *absol.*) reduce or dispose of one's investment (in a place, company, etc.). ▫▫ **disinvestment** *n.*

disjecta membra /disjéktə mémbrə/ *n.pl.* scattered remains; fragments, esp. of written work. [L, alt. of *disjecti membra poetae* (Horace) limbs of a dismembered poet]

disjoin /disjóyn/ *v.tr.* separate or disunite; part. [ME f. OF *desjoindre* f. L *disjungere* (as DIS-, *jungere junct-* join)]

disjoint /disjóynt/ *v.* & *adj.* ● *v.tr.* **1** take apart at the joints. **2** (as **disjointed** *adj.*) (esp. of conversation) incoherent; desultory. **3** disturb the working or connection of; dislocate. ● *adj.* (of two or more sets) having no elements in common. ▫▫ **disjointedly** *adv.* **disjointedness** *n.* [ME f. obs. *disjoint* (adj.) f. past part. of OF *desjoindre* (as DISJOIN)]

■ *v.* **1** disjoin, separate, take apart *or* to bits, disconnect, divide, split (up). **2** (**disjointed**) loose, incoherent, confused, aimless, directionless, rambling, muddled, jumbled, mixed up, fitful, discontinuous, disorganized, unorganized, disorderly, disordered, desultory, disconnected, unmethodical, inconsistent, unsystematic.

disjunction /disjúngksh'n/ *n.* **1** the process of disjoining; separation. **2** an instance of this. [ME f. OF *disjunction* or L *disjunctio* (as DISJOIN)]

■ see SEPARATION.

disjunctive /disjúngktiv/ *adj.* & *n.* ● *adj.* **1** involving separation; disjoining. **2** *Gram.* (esp. of a conjunction) expressing a choice between two words etc., e.g. *or* in *asked if he was going or staying* (cf. COPULATIVE). **3** *Logic* (of a proposition) expressing alternatives. ● *n.* **1** *Gram.* a disjunctive conjunction or other word. **2** *Logic* a disjunctive proposition. ▫▫ **disjunctively** *adv.* [ME f. L *disjunctivus* (as DISJOIN)]

disk var. of DISC (esp. *US* & *Computing*).

diskette /diskét/ *n. Computing* = *floppy disk*.

dislike /dislīk/ *v.* & *n.* ● *v.tr.* have an aversion or objection to; not like. ● *n.* **1** a feeling of repugnance or not liking. **2** an object of dislike. ▫▫ **dislikable** *adj.* (also **dislikeable**).

■ *v.* **1** be averse to, mind, have no time *or* use for, turn from, disfavour, be put *or* turned off by, disrelish, *archaic* mislike; loathe, scorn, despise, disesteem, detest, abominate, execrate, *colloq.* hate, *literary* contemn. ● *n.* **1** aversion, displeasure, distaste, disfavour, disesteem, disrelish, disinclination, *Sc.* scunner, *archaic* mislike; loathing, hate, hatred, animus, animosity, antipathy, detestation, contempt, execration, ill will; disgust, repugnance; hostility, antagonism. **2** see AVERSION 2.

dislocate /dísləkayt/ *v.tr.* **1** disturb the normal connection of (esp. a joint in the body). **2** disrupt; put out of order. **3** displace. [prob. back-form. f. DISLOCATION]

■ **1** see DISJOINT *v.* 1. **2, 3** see DISRUPT 1, DISPLACE.

dislocation /disləkáysh'n/ *n.* **1** the act or result of dislocating. **2** *Crystallog.* the displacement of part of a crystal lattice structure. [ME f. OF *dislocation* or med.L *dislocatio* f. *dislocare* (as DIS-, *locare* place)]

dislodge /dislój/ *v.tr.* remove from an established or fixed position (*was dislodged from his directorship*). ▫▫ **dislodgement** *n.* (also **dislodgment**). [ME f. OF *deslog(i)er* (as DIS-, LODGE)]

■ see EXPEL 2, 3.

disloyal /dislóyəl/ *adj.* (often foll. by *to*) **1** not loyal; unfaithful. **2** untrue to one's allegiance; treacherous to one's government etc. ▫▫ **disloyalist** *n.* **disloyally** *adv.* **disloyalty** *n.* [ME f. OF *desloial* (as DIS-, LOYAL)]

■ unfaithful, faithless, untrue, false, untrustworthy; treasonable, treasonous, treacherous, traitorous, unpatriotic, subversive, perfidious, deceitful; renegade, apostate, heretical, *literary* recreant.

dismal /dízm'l/ *adj.* **1** causing or showing gloom; miserable. **2** dreary or sombre (*dismal brown walls*). **3** *colloq.* feeble or inept (*a dismal performance*). ▫ **the dismals** *colloq.* melancholy. **the dismal science** *joc.* economics. ▫▫ **dismally** *adv.* **dismalness** *n.* [orig. noun = unlucky days: ME f. AF *dis mal* f. med.L *dies mali* two days in each month held to be unpropitious]

■ **1, 2** depressing, gloomy, cheerless, melancholy, sombre, dreary, sad, bleak, funereal, solemn, dark, grim; lugubrious, mournful, forlorn, miserable, morose, wretched, woebegone, woeful, black, blue, joyless, doleful, unhappy, pessimistic, *literary or joc.* dolorous. **3** see FEEBLE 2. ▫ **the dismals** see GLOOM *n.* 2.

dismantle /dismánt'l/ *v.tr.* **1** take to pieces; pull down. **2** deprive of defences or equipment. **3** (often foll. by *of*) strip of covering or protection. ▫▫ **dismantlement** *n.* **dismantler** *n.* [OF *desmanteler* (as DIS-, MANTLE)]

■ **1** see DEMOLISH 1a.

dismast /dismaást/ *v.tr.* deprive (a ship) of masts; break down the mast or masts of.

dismay /dismáy/ *v.* & *n.* ● *v.tr.* fill with consternation or anxiety; discourage or depress; reduce to despair. ● *n.* **1** consternation or anxiety. **2** depression or despair. [ME f. OF *desmaiier* (unrecorded) ult. f. a Gmc root = deprive of power (as DIS-, MAY)]

■ *v.* alarm, frighten, scare, terrify, appal, panic, horrify, petrify, startle, shock, take aback, intimidate, disconcert, unnerve, unsettle, discompose, upset, discourage, depress. ● *n.* **1** consternation, alarm, anxiety, agitation, terror, panic, horror, shock, fright, fear, trepidation, apprehension, dread, awe. **2** see DEPRESSION 1b, DESPAIR *n.*

dismember /dismémbər/ *v.tr.* **1** tear or cut the limbs from. **2** partition or divide up (an empire, country, etc.). ▫▫ **dismemberment** *n.* [ME f. OF *desmembrer* f. Rmc (as DIS-, L *membrum* limb)]

■ **1** see MUTILATE 1. **2** see PARTITION *v.* 1.

dismiss /dismíss/ *v.* **1 a** *tr.* send away, cause to leave one's presence, disperse; disband (an assembly or army). **b** *intr.* (of an assembly etc.) disperse; break ranks. **2** *tr.* discharge from employment, office, etc., esp. dishonourably. **3** *tr.* put out of one's thoughts; cease to feel or discuss (*dismissed him from memory*). **4** *tr.* treat (a subject) summarily (*dismissed his application*). **5** *tr. Law* refuse further hearing to (a case); send out of court. **6** *tr. Cricket* put (a batsman or a side) out (*was dismissed for 75 runs*). **7** *intr.* (in *imper.*) *Mil.* a word of command at the end of drilling. ▫▫ **dismissal** *n.* **dismissible** *adj.* **dismission** *n.* [ME, orig. as past part. after OF *desmis* f. med.L *dismissus* (as DIS-, L *mittere miss-* send)]

■ **1** disperse, disband; release, send away, discharge, let go; break ranks. **2** discharge, oust, release, give notice, let go, lay off, throw out, remove, send a person about his *or* her business, give a person his *or* her cards, boot (out), *esp. Mil.* cashier, *Mil.* drum out, *colloq.* send packing, kick out, give a person the push, turn off, sack, give a person the sack *or* boot, give a person his *or* her walking papers, give a person his *or* her marching orders, *Austral. colloq.* tramp, *sl.* fire, give a person the (old) heave-ho, *Brit. sl.* give a person the chop. **4** reject, set aside, repudiate, spurn, discount, disregard, lay aside, wave aside, put out of one's mind, think no more of, write off, have *or* be done with, scorn, discard, ignore, shrug off, brush aside, laugh off, *Austral. & NZ sl.* wipe; belittle, pooh-pooh. ▫▫ **dismissal** dismission, discharge, expulsion, notice, *colloq.* marching orders, walking papers, the sack, the boot, *sl.* the (old) heave-ho, *Brit. sl.* chop; discharge, release, disbandment, dispersal; *congé*.

dismissive /dismíssiv/ *adj.* tending to dismiss from consideration; disdainful. ▫▫ **dismissively** *adv.* **dismissiveness** *n.*

■ see DISDAINFUL.

dismount /dismównt/ *v.* **1 a** *intr.* alight from a horse, bicycle, etc. **b** *tr.* (usu. in *passive*) throw from a horse, unseat. **2** *tr.* remove (a thing) from its mounting (esp. a gun from its carriage).

■ **1 a** see *get down* 1.

disobedient /dìssəbeédiənt/ *adj.* disobeying; rebellious, rule-breaking. ▫▫ **disobedience** *n.* **disobediently** *adv.* [ME f. OF *desobedient* (as DIS-, OBEDIENT)]

■ insubordinate, unruly, rebellious, naughty, mischievous, bad, ill-behaved, badly behaved, obstreperous, unmanageable, refractory, fractious, ungovernable, unsubmissive, wayward, non-compliant, intractable, defiant, delinquent, contrary, perverse, wilful, headstrong, stubborn, recalcitrant, obdurate, obstinate, contumacious, cross-grained, opposed, mutinous.

disobey /dìssəbáy/ *v.tr.* (also *absol.*) fail or refuse to obey; disregard (orders); break (rules) (*disobeyed his mother; how dare you disobey!*). ▫▫ **disobeyer** *n.* [ME f. OF *desobeir* f. Rmc (as DIS-, OBEY)]

■ defy, break, contravene, flout, disregard, ignore, resist, oppose, violate, transgress, overstep, go counter to, fly in the face of, infringe, thumb one's nose at, snap one's fingers at, *sl.* cock a snook at; mutiny, rebel, revolt.

disoblige /dìssəblíj/ *v.tr.* **1** refuse to consider the convenience or wishes of. **2** (as **disobliging** *adj.*) uncooperative. [F *désobliger* f. Rmc (as DIS-, OBLIGE)]

disorder /disórdər/ *n.* & *v.* ● *n.* **1** a lack of order; confusion. **2** a riot; a commotion. **3** *Med.* a usu. minor ailment or disease. ● *v.tr.* **1** throw into confusion; disarrange. **2** *Med.* put out of good health; upset. [ME, alt. after ORDER *v.* of earlier *disordain* f. OF *desordener* (as DIS-, ORDAIN)]

■ *n.* **1** disarray, confusion, chaos, disorderliness, disorganization, untidiness; derangement, mess, muddle, jumble, tangle, clutter, *colloq.* shambles. **2** tumult, riot, disturbance, pandemonium, upheaval, ferment, fuss, unrest, uproar, hubbub, hullabaloo, commotion, clamour, turbulence, turmoil, bedlam, free-for-all, brouhaha, fracas, mêlée, affray, fray, scuffle, brawl, breach of the peace, battle royal, Donnybrook, *colloq.* rumpus, *esp. Brit. colloq.* kerfuffle; *archaic* distemper. **3** ailment, illness, sickness, affliction, malady, affection, complaint, disease. ● *v.* **1** upset, disarrange, muddle, confuse, confound, unsettle, disorganize, discompose, shake up, disturb, mix (up), befuddle, jumble, scramble, tangle.

disorderly /dissórdərli/ *adj.* **1** untidy; confused. **2** irregular; unruly; riotous. **3** *Law* contrary to public order or morality. ▫ **disorderly house** *Law* a brothel. ▫▫ **disorderliness** *n.*

■ **1** confused, chaotic, scrambled, muddled, disordered, irregular, untidy, messy, messed-up, disarranged, disorganized, unorganized, jumbled, cluttered, haphazard, in disarray, back to front, pell-mell, helter-skelter, topsy-turvy, higgledy-piggledy. **2** unruly, uncontrolled, riotous, undisciplined, ungoverned, disobedient, mutinous, rebellious, lawless, obstreperous, refractory, turbulent, violent, tumultuous, unrestrained, boisterous, noisy, rowdy, wild, unmanageable, ungovernable, uncontrollable, intractable; irregular. ▫ **disorderly house** see BROTHEL.

disorganize /disórgənīz/ *v.tr.* (also **-ise**) **1** destroy the system or order of; throw into confusion. **2** (as **disorganized** *adj.*) lacking organization or system. ▫▫ **disorganization** /-záysh'n/ *n.* [F *désorganiser* (as DIS-, ORGANIZE)]

■ **1** see JUMBLE *v.* 1.

disorient /disóriənt/ *v.tr.* = DISORIENTATE. [F *désorienter* (as DIS-, ORIENT *v.*)]

disorientate /disóriəntayt/ *v.tr.* **1** confuse (a person) as to his or her whereabouts or bearings. **2** (often as **disorientated** *adj.*) confuse (a person) (*disorientated by his unexpected behaviour*). ▫▫ **disorientation** /-táysh'n/ *n.*

■ (**disorientated**) confused, bewildered, lost, adrift, disoriented.

disown /disṓn/ *v.tr.* **1** refuse to recognize; repudiate; disclaim. **2** renounce one's connection with or allegiance to. ▫▫ **disowner** *n.*

■ see REPUDIATE 1a.

disparage /dispárrij/ *v.tr.* **1** speak slightingly of; depreciate. **2** bring discredit on. ▫▫ **disparagement** *n.* **disparagingly** *adv.* [ME f. OF *desparagier* marry unequally (as DIS-, *parage* equality of rank ult. f. L *par* equal)]

■ **1** belittle, diminish, depreciate, cheapen, run down, talk down, decry, demean, criticize, speak ill of, traduce, denigrate, deprecate, backbite, underrate, undervalue, downgrade, reduce, minimize, *formal* derogate, *Austral. sl.* bag. **2** slander, libel, discredit, dishonour, defame, malign, vilify, insult, stab in the back, *US* bad-mouth.

disparate /dispərət/ *adj.* & *n.* ● *adj.* essentially different in kind; without comparison or relation. ● *n.* (in *pl.*) things so unlike that there is no basis for their comparison. ▫▫ **disparately** *adv.* **disparateness** *n.* [L *disparatus* separated (as DIS-, *paratus* past part. of *parare* prepare), infl. in sense by L *dispar* unequal]

■ *adj.* see DIVERGENT.

disparity /dispárriti/ *n.* (*pl.* **-ies**) **1** inequality; difference; incongruity. **2** an instance of this. [F *disparité* f. LL *disparitas -tatis* (as DIS-, PARITY[1])]

■ difference, discrepancy, gap, inequality, unevenness, imbalance, dissimilarity, contrast, imparity, inconsistency, incongruity.

dispassionate /dispáshənət/ *adj.* free from passion; calm; impartial. ▫▫ **dispassionately** *adv.* **dispassionateness** *n.*

■ cool, calm, composed, self-possessed, unemotional, unexcited, unexcitable, level-headed, sober, self-controlled, even-tempered, unruffled, unmoved, tranquil, equable, equanimous, placid, peaceful, serene, *colloq.* unflappable; fair, impartial, neutral, disinterested, detached, equitable, even-handed, unbiased, just, objective, unprejudiced, open-minded.

dispatch /dispách/ *v.* & *n.* (also **despatch**) ● *v.tr.* **1** send off to a destination or for a purpose (*dispatched him with the message, dispatched the letter yesterday*). **2** perform (business, a task, etc.) promptly; finish off. **3** kill, execute (*dispatched him with the revolver*). **4** *colloq.* eat (food, a meal, etc.) quickly. ● *n.* **1** the act or an instance of sending (a messenger, letter, etc.). **2** the act or an instance of killing; execution. **3 a** an official written message on State or esp. military affairs. **b** a report sent in by a newspaper's correspondent, usu. from a foreign country. **4** promptness, efficiency (*done with dispatch*). ▫ **dispatch-box** (or **-case**) a container for esp. official State or military documents or dispatches. **dispatch-rider** a motor cyclist or rider on horseback carrying (esp. military) dispatches. ▫▫ **dispatcher** *n.* [It. *dispacciare* or Sp. *despachar* expedite (as DIS-, It. *impacciare* and Sp. *empachar* hinder, of uncert. orig.)]

■ *v.* **1** send off *or* away *or* out, send on one's way; send, mail, post, transmit, forward, ship, express, remit, convey, *esp. US* freight. **2** hasten *or* hurry *or* speed through, get done, accomplish, get through, conclude, finish off, complete, execute, do, *colloq.* knock off. **3** murder, dispose of, eliminate, put to death, execute, assassinate, liquidate, put an end to, put away (for good), *colloq.* polish off, do away with, *literary or joc.* slay, *sl.* finish (off), do in, bump off, knock off, zap, *esp. US sl.* take for a ride, hit, *US sl.* rub out, ice, waste; see also KILL[1] *v.* 1a. **4** see GULP *v.* 1. ● *n.* **1** see TRANSMISSION 1. **2** execution, killing, murder, disposal, assassination. **3 b** communiqué, report, bulletin, story, news (item), communication, message, piece; document, instruction, *joc.* missive. **4** haste, speed, promptness, quickness, efficiency, expedition, expeditiousness, alacrity, swiftness, rapidity, *archaic or literary* celerity.

dispel /dispél/ *v.tr.* (**dispelled, dispelling**) dissipate; disperse; scatter (*the dawn dispelled their fears*). □□ **dispeller** *n.* [L *dispellere* (as DIS-, *pellere* drive)]

■ see DISSIPATE 1a.

dispensable /dispénsəb'l/ *adj.* **1** able to be done without; unnecessary. **2** (of a law etc.) able to be relaxed in special cases. □□ **dispensability** /-bílliti/ *n.* [med.L *dispensabilis* (as DISPENSE)]

■ **1** disposable, non-essential, unessential, inessential, unnecessary, unneeded, expendable, superfluous, needless, useless, incidental.

dispensary /dispénsəri/ *n.* (*pl.* **-ies**) **1** a place where medicines etc. are dispensed. **2** a public or charitable institution for medical advice and the dispensing of medicines. [med.L *dispensarius* (as DISPENSE)]

■ **1** see PHARMACY 2. **2** see INFIRMARY 1.

dispensation /díspensáysh'n/ *n.* **1 a** the act or an instance of dispensing or distributing. **b** (foll. by *with*) the state of doing without (a thing). **c** something distributed. **2** (usu. foll. by *from*) **a** exemption from a penalty or duty; an instance of this. **b** permission to be exempted from a religious observance; an instance of this. **3** a religious or political system obtaining in a nation etc. (*the Christian dispensation*). **4 a** the ordering or management of the world by Providence. **b** a specific example of such ordering (of a community, a person, etc.). □□ **dispensational** *adj.* [ME f. OF *dispensation* or L *dispensatio* (as DISPENSE)]

■ **1 a** see ADMINISTRATION 6. **c** see SHARE *n.* 1. **2 a** see *exemption* (EXEMPT).

dispense /dispénss/ *v.* **1** *tr.* distribute; deal out. **2** *tr.* administer (a sacrament, justice, etc.). **3** *tr.* make up and give out (medicine etc.) according to a doctor's prescription. **4** *tr.* (usu. foll. by *from*) grant a dispensation to (a person) from an obligation, esp. a religious observance. **5** *intr.* (foll. by *with*) **a** do without; render needless. **b** give exemption from (a rule). □ **dispensing chemist** a chemist qualified to make up and give out medicine etc. [ME f. OF *despenser* f. L *dispensare* frequent. of *dispendĕre* weigh or pay out (as DIS-, *pendĕre pens-* weigh)]

■ **1** distribute, give out, hand *or* pass out, supply, provide, give away, deal out, dole out, parcel out, share (out), issue, apportion, allocate, allot, assign, *literary* mete out, *sl.* dish out. **2** administer, discharge, apply, implement, enforce, carry out, execute, conduct, direct, operate, superintend, supervise. **4** (*dispense from*) see EXEMPT *v.* **5 a** (*dispense with*) manage *or* do without, forgo, give up, relinquish, waive, forswear, abstain from, renounce, reject, *literary* eschew; do away with, get rid of, eliminate, dispose of, abolish, remove, cancel, ignore, render *or* make unnecessary *or* superfluous.

dispenser /dispénsər/ *n.* **1** a person or thing that dispenses something, e.g. medicine, good advice. **2** an automatic machine that dispenses an item or a specific amount of something (e.g. cash).

dispersant /dispérs'nt/ *n. Chem.* an agent used to disperse small particles in a medium.

disperse /dispérss/ *v.* **1** *intr.* & *tr.* go, send, drive, or distribute in different directions or over a wide area. **2 a** *intr.* (of people at a meeting etc.) leave and go their various ways. **b** *tr.* cause to do this. **3** *tr.* send to or station at separate points. **4** *tr.* put in circulation; disseminate. **5** *tr. Chem.* distribute (small particles) uniformly in a medium. **6** *tr. Physics* divide (white light) into its coloured constituents. □□ **dispersable** *adj.* **dispersal** *n.* **disperser** *n.* **dispersible** *adj.* **dispersive** *adj.* [ME f. L *dispergere dispers-* (as DIS-, *spargere* scatter)]

■ **1** spread, scatter, broadcast, distribute; diffuse, dissipate, dispel, break up, spread out. **2 a** disband, scatter, break up, leave, go (away). **b** dismiss, rout, send off *or* away, disband, scatter. **4** disseminate, broadcast, send; see also CIRCULATE 2a, b.

dispersion /dispérsh'n/ *n.* **1** the act or an instance of dispersing; the process of being dispersed. **2** *Chem.* a mixture of one substance dispersed in another. **3** *Physics* the separation of white light into colours or of any radiation according to wavelength. **4** *Statistics* the extent to which values of a variable differ from the mean. **5** (**the Dispersion**) the Jews dispersed among the Gentiles after the Captivity in Babylon. [ME f. LL *dispersio* (as DISPERSE), transl. Gk *diaspora*: see DIASPORA]

■ **1** see SPREAD *n.* 1.

dispirit /dispírrit/ *v.tr.* **1** (esp. as **dispiriting** *adj.*) make despondent; discourage. **2** (as **dispirited** *adj.*) dejected; discouraged. □□ **dispiritedly** *adv.* **dispiritedness** *n.* **dispiritingly** *adv.*

■ **1** see DEMORALIZE 1. **2** (**dispirited**) see MISERABLE 1.

displace /displáyss/ *v.tr.* **1** shift from its accustomed place. **2** remove from office. **3** take the place of; oust. □ **displaced person** a person who is forced to leave his or her home country because of war, persecution, etc.; a refugee.

■ **1** move, transfer, shift, relocate, resettle, dislocate; disturb, unsettle. **2** expel, unseat, eject, evict, exile, banish, throw out, boot out, depose, remove, oust, discharge, *esp. Mil.* cashier, *colloq.* kick out, sack, *sl.* fire; see also DISMISS 2. **3** take the place of, oust, supplant, replace, supersede, succeed, take over from. □ **displaced person** see REFUGEE.

displacement /displáysmənt/ *n.* **1 a** the act or an instance of displacing; the process of being displaced. **b** an instance of this. **2** *Physics* the amount of a fluid displaced by a solid floating or immersed in it (*a ship with a displacement of 11,000 tons*). **3** *Psychol.* **a** the substitution of one idea or impulse for another. **b** the unconscious transfer of strong unacceptable emotions from one object to another. **4** the amount by which a thing is shifted from its place.

display /displáy/ *v.* & *n.* ● *v.tr.* **1** expose to view; exhibit; show. **2** show ostentatiously. **3** allow to appear; reveal; betray (*displayed his ignorance*). ● *n.* **1** the act or an instance of displaying. **2** an exhibition or show. **3** ostentation; flashiness. **4** the distinct behaviour of some birds and fish, esp. used to attract a mate. **5 a** the presentation of signals or data on a visual display unit etc. **b** the information so presented. **6** *Printing* the arrangement and choice of type in order to attract attention. □□ **displayer** *n.* [ME f. OF *despleier* f. L *displicare* (as DIS-, *plicare* fold): cf. DEPLOY]

■ *v.* **1** show, exhibit, air, put *or* set forth, present; advertise, publicize. **2** show off, flaunt, boast about, parade, flourish, *colloq.* flash, *literary* vaunt. **3** betray, reveal, unveil, disclose, uncover, make visible, expose, evince, manifest, demonstrate. ● *n.* **1** show, demonstration, exposition, manifestation, revelation. **2** show, exhibition, exhibit, demonstration, presentation, array, panoply, spectacle, parade. **3** ostentation, showiness, flashiness, ceremony, pageantry, pageant, splendour, magnificence, grandeur, pomp, éclat, *élan*, dash.

displease /displéez/ *v.tr.* make indignant or angry; offend; annoy. □ **be displeased** (often foll. by *at*, *with*) be indignant or dissatisfied; disapprove. □□ **displeasing** *adj.* **displeasingly** *adv.* [ME f. OF *desplaisir* (as DIS-, L *placēre* please)]

■ offend, put out, dissatisfy, ruffle, upset, exasperate, worry, trouble, vex, annoy, irritate, pique, nettle, chafe, anger, infuriate, frustrate, *colloq.* miff, peeve, get a person's goat, rile, *sl.* bug; see also IRK. □ **be displeased** (*be displeased at* or *with*) see DISAPPROVE.

displeasure /displézhər/ *n.* & *v.* ● *n.* disapproval; anger; dissatisfaction. ● *v.tr. archaic* cause displeasure to; annoy. [ME f. OF (as DISPLEASE): assim. to PLEASURE]
■ *n.* dissatisfaction, disapproval, disfavour, discontentment, distaste, dislike; annoyance, anger, irritation, vexation, chagrin, indignation, resentment, dudgeon, exasperation, *literary* ire. ● *v.* see IRK.

disport /dispórt/ *v.* & *n.* ● *v.intr.* & *refl.* frolic; gambol; enjoy oneself (*disported on the sand*; *disported themselves in the sea*). ● *n. archaic* **1** relaxation. **2** a pastime. [ME f. AF & OF *desporter* (as DIS-, *porter* carry f. L *portare*)]
■ *v.* see PLAY *v.* 1.

disposable /dispṓzəb'l/ *adj.* & *n.* ● *adj.* **1** intended to be used once and then thrown away (*disposable nappies*). **2** that can be got rid of, made over, or used. **3** (esp. of financial assets) at the owner's disposal. ● *n.* a thing designed to be thrown away after one use. □ **disposable income** income after tax etc. □□ **disposability** /-bílliti/ *n.*
■ *adj.* **1** discardable, throw-away, non-returnable, biodegradable; paper, plastic. **2, 3** usable, obtainable; available, liquid, spendable.

disposal /dispṓz'l/ *n.* (usu. foll. by *of*) **1** the act or an instance of disposing of something. **2** the arrangement, disposition, or placing of something. **3** control or management (of a person, business, etc.). **4** (esp. as **waste disposal**) the disposing of rubbish. □ **at one's disposal 1** available for one's use. **2** subject to one's orders or decisions.
■ **2** see DISPOSITION 2b. **3** see DISPOSITION 4b.

dispose /dispṓz/ *v.* **1** *tr.* (usu. foll. by *to*, or *to* + infin.) **a** make willing; incline (*disposed him to the idea*; *was disposed to release them*). **b** give a tendency to (*the wheel was disposed to buckle*). **2** *tr.* place suitably or in order (*disposed the pictures in sequence*). **3** *tr.* (as **disposed** *adj.*) have a specified mental inclination (usu. in *comb.*: *ill-disposed*). **4** *intr.* determine the course of events (*man proposes, God disposes*). □ **dispose of 1 a** deal with. **b** get rid of. **c** finish. **d** kill. **e** distribute, dispense; bestow. **2** sell. **3** prove (a claim, an argument, an opponent, etc.) to be incorrect. **4** consume (food). □□ **disposer** *n.* [ME f. OF *disposer* (as DIS-, POSE[1]) after L *disponere disposit-*]
■ **1** incline, influence, persuade, induce, bend, tempt, move, motivate, lead, prompt, urge; (*be disposed*) be inclined *or disp.* liable *or* apt, tend, lean, be prone *or* subject *or* given, be willing. **2** place, arrange, adjust, order, array, organize, set up, situate, group, distribute, put. □ **dispose of 1 a, c** deal with, settle, sort out, take care of, attend to, see to, handle, decide, determine, conclude, finish (with), complete. **b** throw away *or* out, discard, get rid of, dump, do away with, jettison, scrap, junk, *colloq.* bin, *esp. US colloq.* trash. **d** see KILL[1] *v.* 1a. **e** distribute, give out, deal out, give (away), dispense, apportion, parcel out, allot, part with, transfer, make over, bestow. **2** see SELL *v.*1. **3** see DISPROVE. **4** consume, devour, eat (up), put away, gobble (up), *joc.* demolish.

disposition /díspəzísh'n/ *n.* **1 a** (often foll. by *to*) a natural tendency; an inclination (*a disposition to overeat*). **b** a person's temperament or attitude, esp. as displayed in dealings with others. (*a happy disposition*). **2 a** setting in order; arranging. **b** the relative position of parts; an arrangement. **3** (usu. in *pl.*) **a** *Mil.* the stationing of troops ready for attack or defence. **b** preparations; plans. **4 a** a bestowal by deed or will. **b** control; the power of disposing. **5** ordinance, dispensation. [ME f. OF f. L *dispositio* (as DIS-, *ponere posit-* place)]
■ **1 a** inclination, tendency; predisposition, susceptibility, partiality, predilection, leaning, preference, proclivity, penchant, bent, propensity. **b** character, temper, attitude, temperament, nature, personality, bent, frame of mind, humour, make-up, spirit. **2 b** arrangement, organization, placement, disposal, grouping. **4 a** bestowal, transfer, transference, dispensation, disposal, assignment, settlement, determination, distribution. **b** determination, choice, disposal, power, command, control, management, discretion, decision, regulation, dispensation.

dispossess /díspəzés/ *v.tr.* **1** dislodge; oust (a person). **2** (usu. foll. by *of*) deprive. □□ **dispossession** /-zésh'n/ *n.* [OF *despossesser* (as DIS-, POSSESS)]
■ **1** evict, expel, oust, eject, turn *or* drive out, dislodge, throw *or* push out, kick out, boot out. **2** deny, disallow; see also DIVEST 2.

dispraise /dispráyz/ *v.* & *n.* ● *v.tr.* express disapproval or censure of. ● *n.* disapproval, censure. [ME f. OF *despreisier* ult. f. LL *depretiare* DEPRECIATE]

disproof /disprṓōf/ *n.* **1** something that disproves. **2 a** refutation. **b** an instance of this.

disproportion /dísprəpórsh'n/ *n.* **1** a lack of proportion. **2** an instance of this. □□ **disproportional** *adj.* **disproportionally** *adv.*
■ inequality, unevenness, disparity, imbalance, asymmetry, irregularity, lopsidedness, dissimilarity, inconsistency, incongruity.

disproportionate /dísprəpórshənət/ *adj.* **1** lacking proportion. **2** relatively too large or small, long or short, etc. □□ **disproportionately** *adv.* **disproportionateness** *n.*
■ unbalanced, out of proportion, asymmetrical, irregular, lopsided; inconsistent, incommensurate, incongruous; unfair, unequal, uneven.

disprove /disprṓōv/ *v.tr.* prove false; refute. □□ **disprovable** *adj.* **disproval** *n.* [ME f. OF *desprover* (as DIS-, PROVE)]
■ refute, confute, invalidate, contradict, negate, rebut, discredit, controvert, puncture, demolish, destroy, disconfirm, shoot down.

disputable /dispyṓōtəb'l/ *adj.* open to question; uncertain. □□ **disputably** *adv.* [F or f. L *disputabilis* (as DISPUTE)]
■ debatable, moot, doubtful, in doubt, uncertain, dubious, questionable, open to question, undecided, unsettled, unsure, controversial, arguable, unresolved, in the balance, (up) in the air.

disputation /díspyootáysh'n/ *n.* **1 a** disputing, debating. **b** an argument; a controversy. **2** a formal debate. [ME f. F *disputation* or L *disputatio* (as DISPUTE)]
■ **1 b** see CONTROVERSY.

disputatious /díspyootáyshəss/ *adj.* fond of or inclined to argument. □□ **disputatiously** *adv.* **disputatiousness** *n.*
■ see ARGUMENTATIVE 1.

dispute *v.* & *n.* ● *v.* /dispyṓōt/ **1** *intr.* (usu. foll. by *with*, *against*) **a** debate, argue (*was disputing with them about the meaning of life*). **b** quarrel. **2** *tr.* discuss, esp. heatedly (*disputed whether it was true*). **3** *tr.* question the truth or correctness or validity of (a statement, alleged fact, etc.) (*I dispute that number*). **4** *tr.* contend for; strive to win (*disputed the crown*; *disputed the field*). **5** *tr.* resist (a landing, advance, etc.). ● *n.* /dispyṓōt, *disp.* dís-/ **1** a controversy; a debate. **2** a quarrel. **3** a disagreement between management and employees, esp. one leading to industrial action. **4** *archaic* a fight or altercation; a struggle. □ **beyond** (or **past** or **without**) **dispute 1** certainly; indisputably. **2** certain, indisputable. **in dispute 1** being argued about. **2** (of a workforce) involved in industrial action. □□ **disputant** /-spyṓōt'nt/ *n.* **disputer** *n.* [ME f. OF *desputer* f. L *disputare* estimate (as DIS-, *putare* reckon)]
■ *v.* **1** see ARGUE 1. **2** argue about, debate, quarrel about, wrangle over; see also DISCUSS. **3** argue with *or* against, question, challenge, impugn, deny, oppose, fight (against), object to, take exception to, disagree with, contest, quarrel with, doubt, raise doubts about, dissent from, *archaic or literary* gainsay. **4** see AIM *v.* 1, 4. ● *n.* **1, 2** argument, debate, disagreement, difference (of opinion), controversy, polemic, conflict, quarrel, wrangle, discussion, *archaic* velitation, *joc.* argy-bargy. **4** conflict, disturbance, fight, altercation, disagreement, brawl, Donnybrook, feud, fracas, *colloq.* row, rumpus; strife, discord; tiff, *archaic* velitation, *US colloq.* spat. □ **beyond** (or **past** or **without**) **dispute 1** see

undoubtedly (UNDOUBTED). **2** see UNDISPUTED. **in dispute 1** see UNCERTAIN 1.

disqualification /diskwóllifikáysh'n/ *n.* **1** the act or an instance of disqualifying; the state of being disqualified. **2** something that disqualifies.

disqualify /diskwóllifī/ *v.tr.* (**-ies, -ied**) **1** (often foll. by *from*) debar from a competition or pronounce ineligible as a winner because of an infringement of the rules etc. (*disqualified from the race for taking drugs*). **2** (often foll. by *for, from*) make or pronounce ineligible or unsuitable (*his age disqualifies him for the job; a criminal record disqualified him from applying*). **3** (often foll. by *from*) incapacitate legally; pronounce unqualified (*disqualified from practising as a doctor*).
■ declare ineligible *or* unqualified, turn down *or* away, reject, exclude, bar, debar, rule out, outlaw.

disquiet /diskwī́ət/ *v.* & *n.* ● *v.tr.* deprive of peace; worry. ● *n.* anxiety; unrest. □□ **disquieting** *adj.* **disquietingly** *adv.*
■ *v.* see PERTURB 2. ● *n.* see ANXIETY 1, 2.

disquietude /diskwī́ətyōōd/ *n.* a state of uneasiness; anxiety.
■ see CONCERN *n.* 1a.

disquisition /dískwizísh'n/ *n.* a long or elaborate treatise or discourse on a subject. □□ **disquisitional** *adj.* [F f. L *disquisitio* (as DIS-, *quaerere quaesit-* seek)]
■ see LECTURE *n.* 1.

disrate /disráyt/ *v.tr. Naut.* reduce (a sailor) to a lower rating or rank.

disregard /dísrigaárd/ *v.* & *n.* ● *v.tr.* **1** pay no attention to; ignore. **2** treat as of no importance. **3** *archaic* neglect contemptuously; slight, snub. ● *n.* (often foll. by *of, for*) indifference; neglect. □□ **disregardful** *adj.* **disregardfully** *adv.*
■ *v.* **1** ignore, overlook, pay no heed *or* attention to, take no notice *or* account of, dismiss from one's mind *or* thoughts, turn a blind eye *or* deaf ear to, brush aside, pass over, wink *or* blink at, let go, gloss over, bury. **2** make light of, underrate, underestimate, undervalue, minimize, dismiss, brush off, write off, shrug off, trivialize. **3** snub, slight, turn up one's nose at, disparage, despise, disdain, scorn, (give the) cold shoulder (to), cut, *literary* contemn; give the go-by. ● *n.* indifference, inattention, non-observance, neglect, heedlessness, *formal* pretermission; disrespect, contempt, disdain, low regard, disesteem.

disrelish /disréllish/ *n.* & *v.* ● *n.* dislike; distaste. ● *v.tr.* regard with dislike or distaste.
■ *n.* see DISTASTE.

disremember /dísrimémbər/ *v.tr.* & *intr.* esp. *US* or *dial.* fail to remember; forget.

disrepair /dísripáir/ *n.* poor condition due to neglect (*in disrepair; in a state of disrepair*).
■ decay, ruin, collapse, dilapidation, deterioration, ruination.

disreputable /disrépyootəb'l/ *adj.* **1** of bad reputation; discreditable. **2** not respectable in appearance; dirty, untidy. □□ **disreputableness** *n.* **disreputably** *adv.*
■ **1** low, base, abject, unworthy, discreditable, dishonourable, disgraceful, reprehensible, shameful, despicable, ugly, ignominious, bad, raffish, misbegotten, vile, *louche*, questionable, dubious, shady, seamy, *sl.* ragtime. **2** dishevelled, unkempt, slovenly, untidy, shabby, disordered, messy, dirty, bedraggled, scruffy, seedy, threadbare, tattered, down at heel, raddled, sloppy, *Brit. sl.* grotty.

disrepute /dísripyóōt/ *n.* a lack of good reputation or respectability; discredit (esp. *fall into disrepute*).

disrespect /dísrispékt/ *n.* a lack of respect; discourtesy. □□ **disrespectful** *adj.* **disrespectfully** *adv.*
■ rudeness, impoliteness, discourtesy, incivility, unmannerliness, indecorum; irreverence, impudence, insolence, cheek; see also *impertinence* (IMPERTINENT). □□ **disrespectful** impolite, rude, discourteous, uncivil, unmannerly, ill-mannered, bad-mannered, irreverent, impudent, insolent, indecorous, pert, saucy, forward, cheeky, *colloq.* fresh; see also IMPERTINENT 1.

disrobe /disrṓb/ *v.tr.* & *refl.* (also *absol.*) **1** divest (oneself or another) of a robe or a garment; undress. **2** divest (oneself or another) of office, authority, etc.
■ **1** undress, bare oneself; see also STRIP[1] *v.* 1, 2.

disrupt /disrúpt/ *v.tr.* **1** interrupt the flow or continuity of (a meeting, speech, etc.); bring disorder to. **2** separate forcibly; shatter. □□ **disrupter** *n.* (also **disruptor**). **disruption** *n.* **disruptive** *adj.* **disruptively** *adv.* **disruptiveness** *n.* [L *disrumpere disrupt-* (as DIS-, *rumpere* break)]
■ **1** disorder, upset, disorganize, disturb, unsettle, shake up, disconcert, agitate; interrupt, break in on, break into, interfere with, butt in on, cut in on, intrude on. **2** see SEVER 2, SHATTER 1, 2. □□ **disruptive** see UNRULY.

diss /diss/ *v.tr. US sl.* put (a person) down verbally; bad-mouth. [shortened f. DISRESPECT]

dissatisfy /dissáttisfī/ *v.tr.* (**-ies, -ied**) (often as **dissatisfied** *adj.*) make discontented; fail to satisfy (*dissatisfied with the accommodation; dissatisfied to find him gone*). □□ **dissatisfaction** /-fáksh'n/ *n.* **dissatisfactory** /-fáktəri/ *adj.* **dissatisfiedly** *adv.*
■ see DISPLEASE; (**dissatisfied**) discontent(ed), displeased, unsatisfied, discontent, disgruntled, unhappy, frustrated. □□ **dissatisfaction** discontent, discontentment, unhappiness, displeasure, non-fulfilment, disappointment, frustration, discomfort, uneasiness, disquiet, malaise; annoyance, irritation.

dissect /disékt/ *v.tr.* **1** cut into pieces. **2** cut up (a plant or animal) to examine its parts, structure, etc., or (a corpse) for a post mortem. **3** analyse; criticize or examine in detail. □□ **dissection** *n.* **dissector** *n.* [L *dissecare dissect-* (as DIS-, *secare* cut)]
■ see ANALYSE 1, 2b, 3.

dissemble /disémb'l/ *v.* **1** *intr.* conceal one's motives; talk or act hypocritically. **2** *tr.* **a** disguise or conceal (a feeling, intention, act, etc.). **b** simulate (*dissembled grief in public*). □□ **dissemblance** *n.* **dissembler** *n.* **dissemblingly** *adv.* [ME, alt. after *semblance* of obs. *dissimule* f. OF *dissimuler* f. L *dissimulare* (as DIS-, SIMULATE)]
■ see DISSIMULATE.

disseminate /disémminayt/ *v.tr.* scatter about, spread (esp. ideas) widely. □ **disseminated sclerosis** = SCLEROSIS 2. □□ **dissemination** /-náysh'n/ *n.* **disseminator** *n.* [L *disseminare* (as DIS-, *semen -inis* seed)]
■ see SPREAD *v.* 3.

dissension /disénsh'n/ *n.* disagreement giving rise to discord. [ME f. OF f. L *dissensio* (as DIS-, *sentire sens-* feel)]
■ disagreement, dissent, discord, contention, strife, conflict, discordance, friction, opposition, disaccord, discordancy.

dissent /disént/ *v.* & *n.* ● *v.intr.* (often foll. by *from*) **1** think differently, disagree; express disagreement. **2** differ in religious opinion, esp. from the doctrine of an established or orthodox church. ● *n.* **1 a** a difference of opinion. **b** an expression of this. **2** the refusal to accept the doctrines of an established or orthodox church; nonconformity. □□ **dissenting** *adj.* **dissentingly** *adv.* [ME f. L *dissentire* (as DIS-, *sentire* feel)]
■ *v.* **1** see DIFFER 2. ● *n.* **1** see DISSENSION.

dissenter /diséntər/ *n.* **1** a person who dissents. **2** (**Dissenter**) *Brit.* a member of a non-established church; a Nonconformist.
■ **1** see NONCONFORMIST.

dissentient /disénsh'nt/ *adj.* & *n.* ● *adj.* disagreeing with a majority or official view. ● *n.* a person who dissents. [L *dissentire* (as DIS-, *sentire* feel)]

dissertation /díssərtáysh'n/ *n.* a detailed discourse on a subject, esp. one submitted in partial fulfilment of the requirements of a degree or diploma. □□ **dissertational** *adj.* [L *dissertatio* f. *dissertare* discuss, frequent. of *disserere dissert-* examine (as DIS-, *serere* join)]

■ see ESSAY *n.* 1.

disservice /diss-sérviss/ *n.* an ill turn; an injury, esp. done when trying to help. □□ **disserve** *v.tr. archaic.*

■ injury, wrong, unkindness, bad turn, disfavour, injustice; harm, damage. □□ **disserve** see HARM *v.*

dissever /disévvər/ *v.tr.* & *intr.* sever; divide into parts. □□ **disseverance** *n.* **disseverment** *n.* [ME f. AF *dis(c)everer*, OF *dessevrer* f. LL *disseparare* (as DIS-, SEPARATE)]

■ see SEVER 1.

dissidence /díssid'nss/ *n.* disagreement; dissent. [F *dissidence* or L *dissidentia* (as DISSIDENT)]

dissident /díssid'nt/ *adj.* & *n.* ● *adj.* disagreeing, esp. with an established government, system, etc. ● *n.* a dissident person. [F or f. L *dissidēre* disagree (as DIS-, *sedēre* sit)]

■ *adj.* disagreeing, nonconformist, dissenting, dissentient, discordant, conflicting, heterodox, unorthodox; see also REBELLIOUS 1. ● *n.* dissenter, nonconformist, dissentient, protester, heretic, rebel, apostate, recusant; revolutionary, insurgent.

dissimilar /disímmilər/ *adj.* (often foll. by *to*) unlike, not similar. □□ **dissimilarity** /-lárriti/ *n.* (*pl.* **-ies**). **dissimilarly** *adv.*

■ different, unlike, unalike, distinct, separate, contrasting, diverse, unrelated, differing. □□ **dissimilarity** difference, dissimilitude, unlikeness, disparity, distinction, contrast; discrepancy.

dissimilate /disímmilayt/ *v.* (often foll. by *to*) *Phonet.* **1** *tr.* change (a sound or sounds in a word) to another when the word originally had the same sound repeated, as in *cinnamon*, orig. *cinnamom.* **2** *intr.* (of a sound) be changed in this way. □□ **dissimilation** /-láysh'n/ *n.* **dissimilatory** /-lətəri/ *adj.* [L *dissimilis* (as DIS-, *similis* like), after *assimilate*]

dissimilitude /díssimíllityōōd/ *n.* unlikeness, dissimilarity. [L *dissimilitudo* (as DISSIMILATE)]

dissimulate /disímyoolayt/ *v.tr.* & *intr.* dissemble. □□ **dissimulation** /-láysh'n/ *n.* **dissimulator** *n.* [L *dissimulare* (as DIS-, SIMULATE)]

■ dissemble, feign, disguise, camouflage, cover up, conceal, misrepresent, fake, counterfeit; pretend, deceive. □□ **dissimulation** deception, misrepresentation, dissembling, deceit, hypocrisy, pretence, duplicity, double-dealing.

dissipate /díssipayt/ *v.* **1 a** *tr.* cause (a cloud, vapour, fear, darkness, etc.) to disappear or disperse. **b** *intr.* disperse, scatter, disappear. **2** *intr.* & *tr.* break up; bring or come to nothing. **3** *tr.* squander or fritter away (money, energy, etc.). **4** *intr.* (as **dissipated** *adj.*) given to dissipation, dissolute. □□ **dissipater** *n.* **dissipative** *adj.* **dissipator** *n.* [L *dissipare dissipat-* (as DIS-, *sipare* (unrecorded) throw)]

■ **1 a** scatter, disperse, spread, dispel, break up, dissolve; shed. **b** scatter, spread out, disperse, be dispelled, diffuse, break up, move apart, separate; evaporate, vanish, disappear, vaporize, clear, go, dissolve, lift. **3** squander, waste, fritter away, throw away, burn up, use up, exhaust, run *or* go through. **4** (**dissipated**) see DISSOLUTE.

dissipation /díssipáysh'n/ *n.* **1** intemperate, dissolute, or debauched living. **2** (usu. foll. by *of*) wasteful expenditure (*dissipation of resources*). **3** scattering, dispersion, or disintegration. **4** a frivolous amusement. [F *dissipation* or L *dissipatio* (as DISSIPATE)]

■ **1** intemperance, dissoluteness, dissolution, abandon, abandonment, self-indulgence, self-gratification, overindulgence, hedonism, *dolce vita*, excess(es), wantonness, debauchery, carousing, rakishness, voluptuousness, sensualism, sybaritism. **2** waste, wastefulness, profligacy, recklessness, extravagance, prodigality. **3** disappearance, dispersion, dispersal, diffusion, scattering, vanishing, disintegration, evaporation. **4** distraction, amusement; see also DIVERSION 3.

dissociate /disṓshiayt, -siayt/ *v.* **1** *tr.* & *intr.* (usu. foll. by *from*) disconnect or become disconnected; separate (*dissociated her from their guilt*). **2** *tr. Chem.* decompose, esp. reversibly. **3** *tr. Psychol.* cause (a person's mind) to develop more than one centre of consciousness. □ **dissociated personality** *Psychol.* the pathological coexistence of two or more distinct personalities in the same person. **dissociate oneself from 1** declare oneself unconnected with. **2** decline to support or agree with (a proposal etc.). □□ **dissociative** /-shiətiv, -siətiv/ *adj.* [L *dissociare* (as DIS-, *socius* companion)]

■ **1** separate, cut off, sever, disassociate, disjoin, disconnect, abstract, disengage, detach, isolate, distance, break off *or* away, divorce, set apart, segregate.

dissociation /disṓsiáysh'n, -shiáysh'n/ *n.* **1** the act or an instance of dissociating. **2** *Psychol.* the state of suffering from dissociated personality.

■ **1** see SEPARATION.

dissoluble /disólyoob'l/ *adj.* able to be disintegrated, loosened, or disconnected; soluble. □□ **dissolubility** /-billiti/ *n.* **dissolubly** *adv.* [F *dissoluble* or L *dissolubilis* (as DIS-, SOLUBLE)]

dissolute /díssəlōōt, -lyōōt/ *adj.* lax in morals; licentious. □□ **dissolutely** *adv.* **dissoluteness** *n.* [ME f. L *dissolutus* past part. of *dissolvere* DISSOLVE]

■ dissipated, debauched, abandoned, corrupt, degenerate, rakish, profligate, wanton, intemperate, incontinent, loose, lax, licentious, overindulgent, self-indulgent, hedonistic, amoral, libidinous, unrestrained, depraved; see also IMMORAL 3.

dissolution /díssəlṓōsh'n, -lyṓōsh'n/ *n.* **1** disintegration; decomposition. **2** (usu. foll. by *of*) the undoing or relaxing of a bond, esp.: **a** a marriage. **b** a partnership. **c** an alliance. **3** the dismissal or dispersal of an assembly, esp. of a parliament at the end of its term. **4** death. **5** bringing or coming to an end; fading away; disappearance. **6** dissipation; debauchery. [ME f. OF *dissolution* or L *dissolutio* (as DISSOLVE)]

■ **1** disintegration, separation, breakup, breakdown, collapse, discontinuation; decomposition, decay, destruction, ruin. **2** annulment, nullification, rescission, cancellation, rescindment, repeal, repudiation, abrogation, reversal, revocation, disavowal, retraction; divorce. **3** dismissal, dispersal, adjournment, dissolving, disbandment. **4** see DEATH 4a. **5** ending, end, termination, conclusion, finish; recess, cessation; see also DISSIPATION 3. **6** see DISSIPATION 1.

dissolve /dizólv/ *v.* & *n.* ● *v.* **1** *tr.* & *intr.* make or become liquid, esp. by immersion or dispersion in a liquid. **2** *intr.* & *tr.* disappear or cause to disappear gradually. **3 a** *tr.* dismiss or disperse (an assembly, esp. parliament). **b** *intr.* (of an assembly) be dissolved (cf. DISSOLUTION³). **4** *tr.* annul or put an end to (a partnership, marriage, etc.). **5** *intr.* (of a person) become enfeebled or emotionally overcome (*completely dissolved when he saw her*; *dissolved into tears*). **6** *intr.* (often foll. by *into*) *Cinematog.* change gradually (from one picture into another). ● *n. Cinematog.* the act or process of dissolving a picture. □□ **dissolvable** *adj.* [ME f. L *dissolvere dissolut-* (as DIS-, *solvere* loosen)]

■ *v.* **1** melt, liquefy, disperse, disintegrate, diffuse, decompose, deliquesce. **2** vanish, disappear, fade (away), diminish, decline, peter out; see also ERODE. **3 a** break up, disperse, dismiss, adjourn, disband, wind up, *US* & *Austral.* recess; terminate, finish, conclude. **b** adjourn, break up, disperse, disband, *US* & *Austral.* recess. **4** see CANCEL *v.* 4. **5** be overcome, collapse, break down; (*dissolve into*) break (down) into, melt into. **6** see MERGE.

dissolvent /dizólv'nt/ *adj.* & *n.* ● *adj.* tending to dissolve or dissipate. ● *n.* a dissolvent substance. [L *dissolvere* (as DISSOLVE)]

dissonant /díssənənt/ *adj.* **1** *Mus.* harsh-toned; inharmonious. **2** incongruous; clashing. □□ **dissonance** *n.* **dissonantly** *adv.* [ME f. OF *dissonant* or L *dissonare* (as DIS-, *sonare* sound)]

■ see INCONGRUOUS.

dissuade /diswáyd/ *v.tr.* (often foll. by *from*) discourage (a person); persuade against (*dissuaded him from continuing*; *was dissuaded from his belief*). □□ **dissuader** *n.* **dissuasion**

/-swáyzh'n/ *n.* **dissuasive** /-swáysiv/ *adj.* [L *dissuadēre* (as DIS-, *suadēre suas-* persuade)]
■ see DISCOURAGE 2.

dissyllable var. of DISYLLABLE.

dissymmetry /dissímmitri/ *n.* (*pl.* **-ies**) **1 a** lack of symmetry. **b** an instance of this. **2** symmetry as of mirror images or the left and right hands (esp. of crystals with two corresponding forms). □□ **dissymmetrical** /díssimétrik'l/ *adj.*

distaff /dístaaf/ *n.* **1 a** a cleft stick holding wool or flax wound for spinning by hand. **b** the corresponding part of a spinning-wheel. **2** women's work. □ **distaff side** the female branch of a family. [OE *distæf* (as STAFF[1]), the first element being app. rel. to LG *diesse*, MLG *dise(ne)* bunch of flax]

distal /díst'l/ *adj. Anat.* situated away from the centre of the body or point of attachment; terminal. □□ **distally** *adv.* [DISTANT + -AL]

distance /dístənss/ *n.* & *v.* ● *n.* **1** the condition of being far off; remoteness. **2 a** a space or interval between two things. **b** the length of this (*a distance of twenty miles*). **3** a distant point or place (*came from a distance*). **4** the avoidance of familiarity; aloofness; reserve (*there was a certain distance between them*). **5** a remoter field of vision (*saw him in the distance*). **6** an interval of time (*can't remember what happened at this distance*). **7 a** the full length of a race etc. **b** *Brit. Racing* a length of 240 yards from the winning-post on a racecourse. **c** *Boxing* the scheduled length of a fight. ● *v.tr.* (often *refl.*) **1** place far off (*distanced herself from them*; *distanced the painful memory*). **2** leave far behind in a race or competition. □ **at a distance** far off. **distance-post** *Racing* a post at the distance on a racecourse, used to disqualify runners who have not reached it by the end of the race. **distance runner** an athlete who competes in long- or middle-distance races. **go the distance 1** *Boxing* complete a fight without being knocked out. **2** complete, esp. a hard task; endure an ordeal. **keep one's distance** maintain one's reserve. **middle distance** the part of a landscape or painting between the foreground and the furthest part. **within hailing** (or **walking**) **distance** near enough to reach by hailing or walking. [ME f. OF *distance*, *destance* f. L *distantia* f. *distare* stand apart (as DI-[2], *stare* stand)]
■ *n.* **2** space, gap, interval, mileage, footage, stretch. **4** aloofness, detachment, reserve, coolness, guardedness, reticence, remoteness; haughtiness, hauteur, stiffness, rigidity, coldness, standoffishness. ● *v.* **1** separate, detach, dissociate, disassociate, set apart. □ **at a distance** see DISTANT 1a. **go the distance 2** get there, make it, bring it off; see also ENDURE 3. **within hailing** (or **walking**) **distance** see NEARBY *adv.*

distant /dístənt/ *adj.* **1 a** far away in space or time. **b** (usu. *predic.*; often foll. by *from*) at a specified distance (*three miles distant from them*). **2** remote or far apart in position, time, resemblance, etc. (*a distant prospect*; *a distant relation*; *a distant likeness*). **3** not intimate; reserved; cool (*a distant nod*). **4** remote; abstracted (*a distant stare*). **5** faint, vague (*he was a distant memory to her*). □ **distant early warning** *US* a radar system for the early detection of a missile attack. **distant signal** *Railways* a railway signal preceding a home signal to give warning. □□ **distantly** *adv.* [ME f. OF *distant* or L *distant-* part. stem of *distare*: see DISTANCE]
■ **1 a** far, far-off, remote, far-away, far-removed, outlying, far-flung. **b** away, off. **3** aloof, detached, reserved, cool, cold, haughty, standoffish, unapproachable, inaccessible, withdrawn, reticent, ceremonious, formal, stiff, rigid, frigid, unfriendly. **4** remote, abstracted, distracted, absent, far-away, detached, *distrait*. **5** see VAGUE 1.

distaste /distáyst/ *n.* (usu. foll. by *for*) dislike; repugnance; aversion, esp. slight (*a distaste for prunes*; *a distaste for polite company*). □□ **distasteful** *adj.* **distastefully** *adv.* **distastefulness** *n.*
■ dislike, disfavour, antipathy, aversion, disrelish, disinclination; dissatisfaction, displeasure, discontent(ment). □□ **distasteful** nasty, disagreeable, off-putting, unpalatable, obnoxious, objectionable, offensive, unpleasing, unpleasant, displeasing; disgusting, revolting, nauseating, nauseous, *colloq.* sick-making.

distemper[1] /distémpər/ *n.* & *v.* ● *n.* **1** a kind of paint using glue or size instead of an oil-base, for use on walls or for scene-painting. **2** a method of mural and poster painting using this. ● *v.tr.* paint (walls etc.) with distemper. [earlier as verb, f. OF *destremper* or LL *distemperare* soak, macerate: see DISTEMPER[2]]

distemper[2] /distémpər/ *n.* **1** a disease of some animals, esp. dogs, causing fever, coughing, and catarrh. **2** *archaic* political disorder. [earlier as verb, = upset, derange: ME f. LL *distemperare* (as DIS-, *temperare* mingle correctly)]

distend /disténd/ *v.tr.* & *intr.* swell out by pressure from within (*distended stomach*). □□ **distensible** /-sténsib'l/ *adj.* **distensibility** /-sténsibílliti/ *n.* **distension** /-sténsh'n/ *n.* [ME f. L *distendere* (as DIS-, *tendere tens-* stretch)]
■ see SWELL *v.* 3, INFLATE 1, 2.

distich /dístik/ *n. Prosody* a pair of verse lines; a couplet. [L *distichon* f. Gk *distikhon* (as DI-[1], *stikhos* line)]

distichous /dístikəss/ *adj. Bot.* arranged in two opposite vertical rows. [L *distichus* (as DISTICH)]

distil /distíl/ *v.* (*US* **distill**) (**distilled**, **distilling**) **1** *tr. Chem.* purify (a liquid) by vaporizing it with heat, then condensing it with cold and collecting the result. **2** *tr.* **a** *Chem.* extract the essence of (a plant etc.) usu. by heating it in a solvent. **b** extract the essential meaning or implications of (an idea etc.). **3** *tr.* make (whisky, essence, etc.) by distilling raw materials. **4** *tr.* (foll. by *off*, *out*) *Chem.* drive (the volatile constituent) off or out by heat. **5** *tr.* & *intr.* come as or give forth in drops; exude. **6** *intr.* undergo distillation. □□ **distillatory** *adj.* [ME f. L *distillare* f. *destillare* (as DE-, *stilla* drop)]
■ **2 b** see EXTRACT *v.* 8.

distillate /dístilayt/ *n.* a product of distillation.
■ see EXTRACT *n.* 2.

distillation /dístiláysh'n/ *n.* **1** the process of distilling or being distilled (in various senses). **2** something distilled.
■ **1** see REFINEMENT 1. **2** see EXTRACT *n.* 2.

distiller /distíllər/ *n.* a person who distils, esp. a manufacturer of alcoholic liquor.

distillery /distílləri/ *n.* (*pl.* **-ies**) a place where alcoholic liquor is distilled.

distinct /distíngkt/ *adj.* **1** (often foll. by *from*) **a** not identical; separate; individual. **b** different in kind or quality; unlike. **2 a** clearly perceptible; plain. **b** clearly understandable; definite. **3** unmistakable, decided (*had a distinct impression of being watched*). □□ **distinctly** *adv.* **distinctness** *n.* [ME f. L *distinctus* past part. of *distinguere* DISTINGUISH]
■ **1 a** separate, discrete, different, distinguishable, individual, *sui generis*, unique, special, singular. **b** dissimilar, different, unlike, unalike, contrastive, contrasting. **2** clear, perceptible, plain, vivid, sharp, definite, well-defined, marked, noticeable, recognizable, obvious, precise, exact; understandable, manifest, evident, apparent, explicit, unambiguous, patent, clear-cut, palpable, unequivocal, lucid, pellucid, limpid, transparent. **3** unmistakable, decided; see also DEFINITE 2.

distinction /distíngksh'n/ *n.* **1 a** the act or an instance of discriminating or distinguishing. **b** an instance of this. **c** the difference made by distinguishing. **2 a** something that differentiates, e.g. a mark, name, or title. **b** the fact of being different. **3** special consideration or honour. **4** distinguished character; excellence; eminence (*a film of distinction*; *shows distinction in his bearing*). **5** a grade in an examination denoting great excellence (*passed with distinction*). □ **distinction without a difference** a merely nominal or artificial distinction. [ME f. OF f. L *distinctio -onis* (as DISTINGUISH)]
■ **1 a** differentiation, discrimination, separation, division. **c** see CONTRAST *n.* **2 b** distinctiveness, distinctness, difference, differentness; uniqueness, individuality. **3** see

HONOUR *n.* 1, PRESTIGE. **4** honour, credit, prominence, eminence, pre-eminence, superiority, greatness, excellence, quality, merit, worth, value, prestige, note, importance, significance, consequence, renown, fame, repute, reputation, celebrity, glory, account.

distinctive /distíngktiv/ *adj.* distinguishing, characteristic. □□ **distinctively** *adv.* **distinctiveness** *n.*
▪ distinguishing, characteristic, unique, singular, distinct, individual, personal, typical, idiosyncratic, peculiar.

distingué /distángay, distaNGáy/ *adj.* (*fem.* ***distinguée*** *pronunc.* same) having a distinguished air, features, manner, etc. [F, past part. of *distinguer*: see DISTINGUISH]
▪ see DISTINGUISHED 2.

distinguish /distínggwish/ *v.* **1** *tr.* (often foll. by *from*) **a** see or point out the difference of; draw distinctions between (*cannot distinguish one from the other*). **b** constitute such a difference (*the mole distinguishes him from his twin*). **c** draw distinctions between; differentiate. **2** *tr.* be a mark or property of; characterize (*distinguished by his greed*). **3** *tr.* discover by listening, looking, etc. (*could distinguish two voices*). **4** *tr.* (usu. *refl.*; often foll. by *by*) make prominent or noteworthy (*distinguished himself by winning first prize*). **5** *tr.* (often foll. by *into*) divide; classify. **6** *intr.* (foll. by *between*) make or point out a difference between. □□ **distinguishable** *adj.* [F *distinguer* or L *distinguere* (as DIS-, *stinguere stinct-* extinguish): cf. EXTINGUISH]
▪ **1** differentiate, tell apart, separate; set apart, single out. **2** characterize, individualize, individuate, particularize, mark (out), identify, indicate; define, designate, denote. **3** sense, make out, perceive, discern, pick out, recognize, identify, detect, notice, *literary* descry; see, *literary* espy; hear. **4** (*distinguish oneself*) see *stand out* 1. **5** classify, categorize, grade, group, separate, segregate; see also DIVIDE *v.* 3c. **6** differentiate, discriminate, draw a distinction, tell the difference, judge, decide, tell who's who *or* what's what.

distinguished /distínggwisht/ *adj.* **1** (often foll. by *for, by*) of high standing; eminent; famous. **2** = DISTINGUÉ.
▪ **1** celebrated, famous, illustrious, noted, renowned, notable, noteworthy, pre-eminent, eminent, prominent, honoured, respected, honourable. **2** dignified, noble, grand, stately, *distingué*, royal, regal, aristocratic.

distort /distórt/ *v.tr.* **1 a** put out of shape; make crooked or unshapely. **b** distort the appearance of, esp. by curved mirrors etc. **2** misrepresent (motives, facts, statements, etc.). □□ **distortedly** *adv.* **distortedness** *n.* [L *distorquēre distort-* (as DIS-, *torquēre* twist)]
▪ **1 a** twist, warp, deform, misshape, contort, gnarl, bend, disfigure; alter, change. **2** misrepresent, twist, warp, slant, tamper with, colour, torture, pervert, falsify, misstate, bend.

distortion /distórsh'n/ *n.* **1** the act or an instance of distorting; the process of being distorted. **2** *Electronics* a change in the form of a signal during transmission etc. usu. with some impairment of quality. □□ **distortional** *adj.* **distortionless** *adj.* [L *distortio* (as DISTORT)]
▪ see TWIST *n.* 6c, GLOSS[2] *n.* 2.

distract /distrákt/ *v.tr.* **1** (often foll. by *from*) draw away the attention of (a person, the mind, etc.). **2** bewilder, perplex. **3** (as **distracted** *adj.*) troubled or distraught (*distracted by grief; distracted with worry*). **4** amuse, esp. in order to take the attention from pain or worry. □□ **distractedly** *adv.* [ME f. L *distrahere distract-* (as DIS-, *trahere* draw)]
▪ **1** divert, deflect, sidetrack, turn aside, draw away; (*be distracted*) lose concentration, day-dream, be miles away, be in a world of one's own, be preoccupied. **2** bewilder, confuse, confound, perplex, puzzle, discompose, befuddle, mystify, disconcert, fluster, rattle, bemuse, daze. **3** (**distracted**) see DISTRAUGHT. **4** divert, amuse, entertain, occupy, interest.

distraction /distráksh'n/ *n.* **1 a** the act of distracting, esp. the mind. **b** something that distracts; an interruption. **2** a relaxation from work; an amusement. **3** a lack of concentration. **4** confusion; perplexity. **5** frenzy; madness. □ **to distraction** almost to a state of madness. [ME f. OF *distraction* or L *distractio* (as DISTRACT)]
▪ **1 b** see *interruption* (INTERRUPT). **2** diversion, entertainment, amusement, pastime, recreation, divertissement; relaxation, break, *colloq.* breather. **3** see *absent-mindedness* (ABSENT-MINDED). **4** confusion, perplexity, bewilderment, befuddlement, puzzlement, mystification, bemusement; disorder, disturbance, upset, confusion, agitation, discomposure. **5** see *madness* (MAD), FRENZY *n.* 1.

distrain /distráyn/ *v.intr. Law* (usu. foll. by *upon*) impose distraint (on a person, goods, etc.). □□ **distrainee** /-neé/ *n.* **distrainer** *n.* **distrainment** *n.* **distrainor** *n.* [ME f. OF *destreindre* f. L *distringere* (as DIS-, *stringere strict-* draw tight)]

distraint /distráynt/ *n. Law* the seizure of chattels to make a person pay rent etc. or meet an obligation, or to obtain satisfaction by their sale. [DISTRAIN, after *constraint*]

distrait /distráy/ *adj.* (*fem.* ***distraite*** /-stráyt/) not paying attention; absent-minded; distraught. [ME f. OF *destrait* past part. of *destraire* (as DISTRACT)]
▪ see ABSENT-MINDED.

distraught /distráwt/ *adj.* distracted with worry, fear, etc.; extremely agitated. [ME, alt. of obs. *distract* (adj.) (as DISTRACT), after *straught* obs. past part. of STRETCH]
▪ distracted, agitated, troubled, disturbed, beside oneself, upset, perturbed, worked up, excited, frantic, at one's wits' end, overwrought, frenetic, nervous, frenzied, feverish, wild, hysterical, delirious, irrational; mad, insane, berserk.

distress /distréss/ *n.* & *v.* ● *n.* **1** severe pain, sorrow, anguish, etc. **2** the lack of money or comforts. **3** *Law* = DISTRAINT. **4** breathlessness; exhaustion. ● *v.tr.* **1** subject to distress; exhaust, afflict. **2** cause anxiety to; make unhappy; vex. □ **distress-signal** a signal from a ship in danger. **distress-warrant** *Law* a warrant authorizing distraint. **in distress 1** suffering or in danger. **2** (of a ship, aircraft, etc.) in danger or damaged. □□ **distressful** *adj.* **distressingly** *adv.* [ME f. OF *destresse* etc., AF *destresser*, OF *-ecier* f. Gallo-Roman (as DISTRAIN)]
▪ *n.* **1** anguish, anxiety, affliction, *angst*, grief, misery, torment, ache, pain, suffering, agony, torture, woefulness, wretchedness, *archaic or literary* woe; unhappiness, sorrow, sadness, depression, heartache, desolation. **2** misfortune, difficulty, trouble, hardship, adversity, straits. **4** see EXHAUSTION *n.* 2. ● *v.* bother, disturb, perturb, upset, trouble, worry, harrow, harry, vex, harass, plague, oppress, grieve, torment, torture, afflict; see also TIRE[1] 1. □ **in distress** in jeopardy, in danger, in trouble; see also *in pain* (PAIN).

distressed /distrést/ *adj.* **1** suffering from distress. **2** impoverished (*distressed gentlefolk; in distressed circumstances*). **3** (of furniture, leather, etc.) having simulated marks of age and wear. □ **distressed area** *Brit.* a region of high unemployment and poverty.
▪ **1** see WORRY *v.* 4. **2** see STRAITEN *v.* 2.

distributary /distríbyootəri/ *n.* (*pl.* **-ies**) a branch of a river or glacier that does not return to the main stream after leaving it (as in a delta).

distribute /distríbyoot, *disp.* dístribyoot/ *v.tr.* **1** give shares of; deal out. **2** spread about; scatter (*distributed the seeds evenly over the garden*). **3** divide into parts; arrange; classify. **4** *Printing* separate (type that has been set up) and return the characters to their separate boxes. **5** *Logic* use (a term) to include every individual of the class to which it refers. □□ **distributable** *adj.* [ME f. L *distribuere distribut-* (as DIS-, *tribuere* assign)]
▪ **1** deal *or* dole out, parcel out, give (out), dispense, apportion, allot, share (out), partition, divide up, assign, issue, pass out, pass round, hand out, deliver, convey, *literary* mete out, *sl.* dish out. **2** disperse, scatter, strew, spread (about), diffuse, disseminate. **3** sort, classify, class, categorize, assort, arrange, group, file, order; see also DIVIDE *v.* 3c.

distribution /dístribyo͞osh'n/ *n.* **1** the act or an instance of distributing; the process of being distributed. **2** *Econ.* **a** the dispersal of goods etc. among consumers, brought about by commerce. **b** the extent to which different groups, classes, or individuals share in the total production or wealth of a community. **3** *Statistics* the way in which a characteristic is spread over members of a class. □□ **distributional** *adj.* [ME f. OF *distribution* or L *distributio* (as DISTRIBUTE)]
■ **1, 2a** apportionment, allotment, allocation, assignment, sharing; issuance, dissemination, giving (out), dispersal, dispensation; deployment. **3** arrangement, disposition, grouping, ordering.

distributive /distríbyootiv/ *adj.* & *n.* ● *adj.* **1** of, concerned with, or produced by distribution. **2** *Logic* & *Gram.* (of a pronoun etc.) referring to each individual of a class, not to the class collectively (e.g. *each*, *either*). ● *n. Gram.* a distributive word. □□ **distributively** *adv.* [ME f. F *distributif -ive* or LL *distributivus* (as DISTRIBUTE)]

distributor /distríbyootər/ *n.* **1** a person or thing that distributes. **2** an agent who supplies goods. **3** *Electr.* a device in an internal-combustion engine for passing current to each spark-plug in turn.
■ **2** see DEALER.

district /dístrikt/ *n.* & *v.* ● *n.* **1 a** (often *attrib.*) a territory marked off for special administrative purposes. **b** *Brit.* a division of a county or region electing its own councillors. **2** an area which has common characteristics; a region (*the wine-growing district*). ● *v.tr. US* divide into districts. □ **district attorney** (in the US) the prosecuting officer of a district. **district court** (in the US) the Federal court of first instance. **district heating** a supply of heat or hot water from one source to a district or a group of buildings. **district nurse** *Brit.* a peripatetic nurse serving a rural or urban area. **district visitor** *Brit.* a person working for a member of the clergy in a section of a parish. [F f. med.L *districtus* (territory of) jurisdiction (as DISTRAIN)]
■ *n.* territory, region, locality, area, locale; section, sector, part, precinct, department, province, community, quarter, neighbourhood, ward.

distrust /distrúst/ *n.* & *v.* ● *n.* a lack of trust; doubt; suspicion. ● *v.tr.* have no trust or confidence in; doubt. □□ **distruster** *n.* **distrustful** *adj.* **distrustfully** *adv.*
■ *n.* mistrust, doubt, doubtfulness, uncertainty, misgiving(s), scepticism, suspicion, disbelief, incredulity, incredulousness. ● *v.* mistrust, doubt, question, be sceptical of, suspect, be suspicious *or* wary of, discredit, disbelieve, take with a pinch *or* grain of salt. □□ **distrustful** distrusting, untrusting, mistrustful, incredulous, doubting, suspicious, sceptical, doubtful, dubious, cynical, disbelieving, unbelieving, questioning.

disturb /distúrb/ *v.tr.* **1** break the rest, calm, or quiet of; interrupt. **2 a** agitate; worry (*your story disturbs me*). **b** irritate. **3** move from a settled position, disarrange (*the papers had been disturbed*). **4** (as **disturbed** *adj.*) *Psychol.* emotionally or mentally unstable or abnormal. □□ **disturber** *n.* **disturbing** *adj.* **disturbingly** *adv.* [ME f. OF *desto(u)rber* f. L *disturbare* (as DIS-, *turbare* f. *turba* tumult)]
■ **1** agitate, stir *or* churn (up), shake (up), unsettle, upset, ruffle; interrupt, disrupt, intrude on, interfere with; inconvenience, discommode, put out. **2 a** agitate, worry, trouble, disconcert, discomfit, perturb, ruffle, fluster, upset, put off, bother, concern, put out, unsettle, distress, alarm, shake (up). **b** annoy, irritate, irk, bother, pester, plague, hector, harry, harass, provoke, pique, get on a person's nerves, *colloq.* hassle, peeve, get under a person's skin, get in a person's hair, drive a person crazy *or* up the wall, *sl.* drive a person nuts *or* bats *or* batty *or* bananas, bug. **3** disorder, upset, disarrange, confuse, change, move. **4** (**disturbed**) unstable, psychoneurotic, neurotic, unbalanced, maladjusted. □□ **disturbing** upsetting, off-putting, perturbing, troubling, unsettling, worrying, disconcerting, disquieting, alarming, distressing.

disturbance /distúrb'nss/ *n.* **1** the act or an instance of disturbing; the process of being disturbed. **2** a tumult; an uproar. **3** agitation; worry. **4** an interruption. **5** *Law* interference with rights or property; molestation. [ME f. OF *desto(u)rbance* (as DISTURB)]
■ **1, 4** disruption, upset, disorder, disorganization, disarrangement, disarray, confusion; upheaval, interruption, intrusion, interference; turmoil, turbulence, trouble, agitation. **2** commotion, disorder, upset, outburst, tumult, hubbub, hullabaloo, hurly-burly, uproar, brouhaha, brawl, mêlée, breach of the peace, Donnybrook, fray, affray, fracas, *esp. US* ruckus, *colloq.* row, rumpus, *esp. Brit. colloq.* kerfuffle, *Brit. sl.* (spot of) bovver. **3** see ANXIETY 1, 2.

disulphide /dīsúlfīd/ *n.* (*US* **disulfide**) *Chem.* a binary chemical containing two atoms of sulphur in each molecule.

disunion /disyo͞oniən/ *n.* a lack of union; separation; dissension. □□ **disunite** /díssyoonīt/ *v.tr.* & *intr.* **disunity** *n.*
■ see DIVISION *n.* 3.

disuse *n.* & *v.* ● *n.* /disyo͞oss/ **1** lack of use or practice; discontinuance. **2** a disused state. ● *v.tr.* /disyo͞oz/ (esp. as **disused** *adj.*) cease to use. □ **fall into disuse** cease to be used. [ME f. OF *desuser* (as DIS-, USE)]
■ *v.* (**disused**) neglected, unused; see also ABANDONED 1b.

disutility /díssyootílliti/ *n.* (*pl.* **-ies**) **1** harmfulness, injuriousness. **2** a factor tending to nullify the utility of something; a drawback.

disyllable /disílləb'l, dī-/ *n.* (also **dissyllable** /disíl-/) *Prosody* a word or metrical foot of two syllables. □□ **disyllabic** /-lábbik/ *adj.* [F *disyllabe* f. L *disyllabus* f. Gk *disullabos* (as DI-[1], SYLLABLE)]

dit /dit/ *n. Telegraphy* (in the Morse system) = DOT (cf. DAH). [imit.]

ditch /dich/ *n.* & *v.* ● *n.* **1** a long narrow excavated channel esp. for drainage or to mark a boundary. **2** a watercourse, stream, etc. ● *v.* **1** *intr.* make or repair ditches (*hedging and ditching*). **2** *tr.* provide with ditches; drain. **3** *tr. sl.* leave in the lurch; abandon. **4** *tr. colloq.* **a** bring (an aircraft) down on the sea in an emergency. **b** drive (a vehicle) into a ditch. **5** *intr. colloq.* (of an aircraft) make a forced landing on the sea. **6** *tr. sl.* defeat; frustrate. **7** *tr. US* derail (a train). □ **ditch-water** stagnant water in a ditch. **dull as ditch-water** extremely dull. **last ditch** see LAST. □□ **ditcher** *n.* [OE *dīc*, of unkn. orig.: cf. DIKE[1]]
■ *n.* see CHANNEL[1] 5a, 6. ● *v.* **3** see DESERT[1] 2.

ditheism /dīthee-iz'm/ *n. Theol.* **1** a belief in two gods; dualism. **2** a belief in equal independent ruling principles of good and evil. □□ **ditheist** *n.*

dither /díthər/ *v.* & *n.* ● *v.intr.* **1** hesitate; be indecisive. **2** *dial.* tremble; quiver. ● *n. colloq.* **1** a state of agitation or apprehension. **2** a state of hesitation; indecisiveness. □ **all of a dither** *colloq.* in a state of extreme agitation or vacillation. □□ **ditherer** *n.* **dithery** *adj.* [var. of *didder*, DODDER[1]]
■ *v.* **1** see HESITATE 1. **2** see FLUTTER *v.* 7. ● *n.* **1** see SWEAT *n.* 3.

dithyramb /díthiram, -ramb/ *n.* **1 a** a wild choral hymn in ancient Greece, esp. to Dionysus. **b** a Bacchanalian song. **2** any passionate or inflated poem, speech, etc. □□ **dithyrambic** /-rámbik/ *adj.* [L *dithyrambus* f. Gk *dithurambos*, of unkn. orig.]

dittany /díttəni/ *n.* (*pl.* **-ies**) any herb of the genus *Dictamnus*, formerly used medicinally. [ME f. OF *dita(i)n* f. med.L *dictamus* f. L *dictamnus* f. Gk *diktamnon* perh. f. *Diktē*, a mountain in Crete]

ditto /díttō/ *n.* & *v.* ● *n.* (*pl.* **-os**) **1** (in accounts, inventories, lists, etc.) the aforesaid, the same. ¶ Often represented by " under the word or sum to be repeated. **2** *colloq.* (replacing a word or phrase to avoid repetition) the same (*came in late last night and ditto the night before*). **3** a similar thing; a duplicate. ● *v.tr.* (**-oes**, **-oed**) repeat (another's action or words). □ **ditto marks** inverted commas etc. representing 'ditto'. **say ditto to** *colloq.* agree with; endorse. [It. dial. f. L *dictus* past part. of *dicere* say]

dittography /dítógrəfi/ *n.* (*pl.* **-ies**) **1** a copyist's mistaken repetition of a letter, word, or phrase. **2** an example of this. ▫▫ **dittographic** /díttəgráffik/ *adj.* [Gk *dittos* double + -GRAPHY]

ditty /ditti/ *n.* (*pl.* **-ies**) a short simple song. [ME f. OF *dité* composition f. L *dictatum* neut. past part. of *dictare* DICTATE]
▪ see SONG.

ditty-bag /díttibag/ *n.* (also **ditty-box** /-boks/) a sailor's or fisherman's receptacle for odds and ends. [19th c.: orig. unkn.]

diuresis /dī́yooréessiss/ *n. Med.* an increased excretion of urine. [mod.L f. Gk (as DI-[3], *ourēsis* urination)]

diuretic /dī́yoeréttik/ *adj.* & *n.* ● *adj.* causing increased output of urine. ● *n.* a diuretic drug. [ME f. OF *diuretique* or LL *diureticus* f. Gk *diourētikos* f. *dioureō* urinate]

diurnal /dīúrn'l/ *adj.* **1** of or during the day; not nocturnal. **2** daily; of each day. **3** *Astron.* occupying one day. **4** *Zool.* (of animals) active in the daytime. **5** *Bot.* (of plants) open only during the day. ▫▫ **diurnally** *adv.* [ME f. LL *diurnalis* f. L *diurnus* f. *dies* day]
▪ **1, 2** daily, daytime, *Physiol.* circadian; day-to-day, regular, everyday, quotidian.

Div. *abbr.* Division.

diva /déevə/ *n.* (*pl.* **divas**) a great or famous woman singer; a prima donna. [It. f. L, = goddess]
▪ see STAR *n.* 8a.

divagate /dī́vəgayt/ *v.intr. literary* stray; digress. ▫▫ **divagation** /-gáysh'n/ *n.* [L *divagari* (as DI-[2], *vagari* wander)]
▪ see STRAY *v.* 1.

divalent /dīváylənt/ *adj. Chem.* **1** having a valency of two; bivalent. **2** having two valencies. ▫▫ **divalency** *n.* [DI-[1] + *valent-* part. stem (as VALENCY)]

divan /diván, dī-/ *n.* **1 a** a long, low, padded seat set against a room-wall; a backless sofa. **b** a bed consisting of a base and mattress, usu. with no board at either end. **2** an oriental State legislative body, council-chamber, or court of justice. **3** *archaic* **a** a cigar-shop. **b** a smoking-room attached to such a shop. [F *divan* or It. *divano* f. Turk. *dīvān* f. Arab. *dīwān* f. Pers. *dīvān* anthology, register, court, bench]
▪ **1 a** see COUCH[1] *n.*

divaricate /dīvárrikayt, di-/ *v.intr.* diverge, branch; separate widely. ▫▫ **divaricate** /-kət/ *adj.* **divarication** /-káysh'n/ *n.* [L *divaricare* (as DI-[2], *varicus* straddling)]

dive /dīv/ *v.* & *n.* ● *v.* (**dived** or *US* **dove** /dōv/) **1** *intr.* plunge head first into water, esp. as a sport. **2** *intr.* **a** *Aeron.* (of an aircraft) plunge steeply downwards at speed. **b** *Naut.* (of a submarine) submerge. **c** (of a person) plunge downwards. **3** *intr.* (foll. by *into*) *colloq.* **a** put one's hand into (a pocket, handbag, vessel, etc.) quickly and deeply. **b** occupy oneself suddenly and enthusiastically with (a subject, meal, etc.). **4** *tr.* (foll. by *into*) plunge (a hand etc.) into. ● *n.* **1** an act of diving; a plunge. **2 a** the submerging of a submarine. **b** the steep descent of an aircraft. **3** a sudden darting movement. **4** *colloq.* a disreputable nightclub etc.; a drinking-den (*found themselves in a low dive*). **5** *Boxing sl.* a pretended knockout (*took a dive in the second round*). ▫ **dive-bomb** bomb (a target) while diving in an aircraft. **dive-bomber** an aircraft designed to dive-bomb. **dive in** *colloq.* help oneself (to food). **diving-bell** an open-bottomed box or bell, supplied with air, in which a person can descend into deep water. **diving-board** an elevated board used for diving from. **diving-suit** a watertight suit usu. with a helmet and an air-supply, worn for working under water. [OE *dūfan* (v.intr.) dive, sink, and *dȳfan* (v.tr.) immerse, f. Gmc: rel. to DEEP, DIP]
▪ *v.* **1, 2** plunge, nosedive, jump, leap, duck (down), descend, dip, swoop, plummet; submerge, go under, sink. **3 b** plunge; launch oneself; immerse oneself, involve oneself, bury oneself. ● *n.* **1, 2** plunge, nosedive; descent. **3** see DASH *n.* 1. **4** bar, saloon, club, nightclub, drinking-den, nightspot, *colloq.* honky-tonk, *sl.* joint, drum. ▫ **dive in** help oneself, set to, *colloq.* tuck in, dig in, *sl.* get stuck in, *Austral.* & *NZ sl.* hoe in.

diver /dī́vər/ *n.* **1** a person who dives. **2 a** a person who wears a diving-suit to work under water for long periods. **b** a pearl-diver etc. **3** any of various diving birds, esp. large water-birds of the family Gaviidae.

diverge /dīvérj/ *v.* **1** *intr.* **a** proceed in a different direction or in different directions from a point (*diverging rays; the path diverges here*). **b** take a different course or different courses (*their interests diverged*). **2** *intr.* **a** (often foll. by *from*) depart from a set course (*diverged from the track; diverged from his parents' wishes*). **b** differ markedly (*they diverged as to the best course*). **3** *tr.* cause to diverge; deflect. **4** *intr. Math.* (of a series) increase indefinitely as more of its terms are added. [med.L *divergere* (as DI-[2], L *vergere* incline)]
▪ **1 a** divide, subdivide, fork, branch (off *or* out), ramify, split, separate, radiate (out), spread (apart *or* out), divaricate. **b** see PART *v.* 1, 3; 2. **2 a** deviate, turn aside *or* away, wander, digress, stray, depart, drift, *literary* divagate; (*diverge from*) go off, get off, turn off.

divergent /dīvérjənt/ *adj.* **1** diverging. **2** *Psychol.* (of thought) tending to reach a variety of possible solutions when analysing a problem. **3** *Math.* (of a series) increasing indefinitely as more of its terms are added; not convergent. ▫▫ **divergence** *n.* **divergency** *n.* **divergently** *adv.*
▪ **1** differing, different, diverse, dissimilar, disparate, separate, diverging, disagreeing, conflicting, discrepant.

divers /dī́vərz/ *adj. archaic* or *literary* more than one; sundry; several. [ME f. OF f. L *diversus* DIVERSE (as DI-[2], *versus* past part. of *vertere* turn)]
▪ various, several, sundry; miscellaneous, varied, assorted.

diverse /dīvérss, di-/ *adj.* unlike in nature or qualities; varied. ▫▫ **diversely** *adv.* [ME (as DIVERS)]
▪ varied, diversified, divergent, heterogeneous, multiform, various, varying, mixed, miscellaneous, assorted, *archaic or literary* divers; distinctive, different, distinct, separate, discrete, dissimilar, differing.

diversify /dīvérsifī/ *v.* (**-ies, -ied**) **1** *tr.* make diverse; vary; modify. **2** *tr. Commerce* **a** spread (investment) over several enterprises or products, esp. to reduce the risk of loss. **b** introduce a spread of investment in (an enterprise etc.). **3** *intr.* (often foll. by *into*) esp. *Commerce* (of a firm etc.) expand the range of products handled. ▫▫ **diversification** /-fikáysh'n/ *n.* [ME f. OF *diversifier* f. med.L *diversificare* (as DIVERS)]
▪ **1** vary, variegate, change, mix, modify. **3** expand, extend, spread out, branch out.

diversion /dīvérsh'n, di-/ *n.* **1 a** the act of diverting; deviation. **b** an instance of this. **2 a** the diverting of attention deliberately. **b** a stratagem for this purpose (*created a diversion to secure their escape*). **3** a recreation or pastime. **4** *Brit.* an alternative route when a road is temporarily closed to traffic. ▫▫ **diversional** *adj.* **diversionary** *adj.* [LL *diversio* (as DIVERT)]
▪ **1** deviation, redirection, deflection, digression, departure; modification, change. **2 b** distraction, interruption, interlude. **3** amusement, distraction, entertainment, pastime, recreation, divertissement, game; relaxation. **4** detour, sidetrack, deviation, bypass.

diversionist /dīvérshənist, di-/ *n.* **1** a person who engages in disruptive or subversive activities. **2** *Polit.* (esp. used by communists) a conspirator against the State; a saboteur.

diversity /dīvérsiti, di-/ *n.* (*pl.* **-ies**) **1** being diverse; variety. **2** a different kind; a variety. [ME f. OF *diversité* f. L *diversitas -tatis* (as DIVERS)]
▪ **1** variety, diverseness, variation, heterogeneity, multiplicity, multifariousness, variegation, multiformity; difference, disparity, divergence, contrast, differentiation; distinctiveness, individuality.

divert /dīvért, di-/ *v.tr.* **1** (often foll. by *from, to*) **a** turn aside; deflect. **b** draw the attention of; distract. **2** (often as **diverting** *adj.*) entertain; amuse. ▫▫ **divertingly** *adv.* [ME f. F *divertir* f. L *divertere* (as DI-[2], *vertere* turn)]
▪ **1 a** switch, rechannel, redirect, deflect, siphon (off), hive off, set aside, turn away, turn aside, avert, re-route, sidetrack; change, alter, shift. **2** entertain, amuse, distract, interest, beguile, engage, occupy, absorb.

diverticular /dīvertíkyoolər/ *adj. Med.* of or relating to a diverticulum. □ **diverticular disease** a condition with abdominal pain as a result of muscle spasms in the presence of diverticula.

diverticulitis /dīvertíkyoolītiss/ *n. Med.* inflammation of a diverticulum.

diverticulum /dīvertíkyooləm/ *n.* (*pl.* **diverticula** /-lə/) *Anat.* a blind tube forming at weak points in a cavity or passage esp. of the alimentary tract. □□ **diverticulosis** /-lōsiss/ *n.* [med.L, var. of L *deverticulum* byway f. *devertere* (as DE-, *vertere* turn)]

divertimento /divértiméntō, diváir-/ *n.* (*pl.* **divertimenti** /-ti/ or **-os**) *Mus.* a light and entertaining composition, often in the form of a suite for chamber orchestra. [It., = diversion]

divertissement /deévairteésmon/ *n.* **1** a diversion; an entertainment. **2** a short ballet etc. between acts or longer pieces. [F, f. *divertiss-* stem of *divertir* DIVERT]
■ **1** see AMUSEMENT 1.

Dives /dīveez/ *n.* a rich man. [L, in Vulgate transl. of Luke 16]

divest /dīvést/ *v.tr.* **1** (usu. foll. by *of*; often *refl.*) unclothe; strip (*divested himself of his jacket*). **2** deprive, dispossess; free, rid (*cannot divest himself of the idea*). □□ **divestiture** *n.* **divestment** *n.* **divesture** *n.* [earlier *devest* f. OF *desvestir* etc. (as DIS-, L *vestire* f. *vestis* garment)]
■ **1** (*divest oneself of*) take *or* put off, remove, *literary* doff. **2** deprive, dispossess, strip, rid, rob, relieve, free, disencumber, *literary* despoil.

divi var. of DIVVY.

divide /divīd/ *v.* & *n.* ● *v.* **1** *tr.* & *intr.* (often foll. by *in, into*) separate or be separated into parts; break up; split (*the river divides into two*; *the road divides*; *divided them into three groups*). **2** *tr.* & *intr.* (often foll. by *out*) distribute; deal; share (*divided it out between them*). **3** *tr.* **a** cut off; separate; part (*divide the sheep from the goats*). **b** mark out into parts (*a ruler divided into inches*). **c** specify different kinds of, classify (*people can be divided into two types*). **4** *tr.* cause to disagree; set at variance (*religion divided them*). **5** *Math.* **a** *tr.* find how many times (a number) contains another (*divide 20 by 4*). **b** *intr.* (of a number) be contained in (a number) without a remainder (*4 divides into 20*). **c** *intr.* be susceptible of division (*10 divides by 2 and 5*). **d** *tr.* find how many times (a number) is contained in another (*divide 4 into 20*). **6** *intr. Math.* do division (*can divide well*). **7** *Parl.* **a** *intr.* (of a legislative assembly etc.) part into two groups for voting (*the House divided*). **b** *tr.* so divide (a Parliament etc.) for voting. ● *n.* **1** a dividing or boundary line (*the divide between rich and poor*). **2** a watershed. □ **divided against itself** formed into factions. **divided highway** *US* a dual carriageway. **divided skirt** culottes. **the Great Divide** the boundary between life and death. [ME f. L *dividere divis-* (as DI-[2], *vid-* separate)]
■ *v.* **1, 3a** separate, split (up), break up, cut up, partition, segregate, subdivide, cut off, *literary* cleave; disconnect, disjoin, detach, sever, part, *archaic or literary* sunder; branch (out), ramify. **2** distribute, share (out), measure out, parcel out, partition, dole (out), deal (out), allocate, allot, apportion, dispense, give (out), *literary* mete out. **3 c** categorize, classify, sort, assort, grade, group, order, rank, organize, arrange. **4** separate, split, cause to disagree, part, alienate, disunite, set at odds, sow dissension among, pit *or* set against one another, set at variance, estrange. ● *n.* **1** see BOUNDARY.

dividend /dívvidend/ *n.* **1 a** a sum of money to be divided among a number of persons, esp. that paid by a company to shareholders. **b** a similar sum payable to winners in a football pool, to members of a cooperative, or to creditors of an insolvent estate. **c** an individual's share of a dividend. **2** *Math.* a number to be divided by a divisor. **3** a benefit from any action (*their long training paid dividends*). □ **dividend stripping** the evasion of tax on dividends by arrangement between the company liable to pay tax and another able to claim repayment of tax. **dividend warrant** *Brit.* the documentary authority for a shareholder to receive a dividend. **dividend yield** a dividend expressed as a percentage of a current share price. [AF *dividende* f. L *dividendum* (as DIVIDE)]
■ **1** see CUT *n.* 9.

divider /divīdər/ *n.* **1** a screen, piece of furniture, etc., dividing a room into two parts. **2** (in *pl.*) a measuring-compass, esp. with a screw for setting small intervals.
■ **1** see PARTITION *n.* 2.

divi-divi /dívvidivvi/ *n.* (*pl.* **divi-divis**) **1** a small tree, *Caesalpinia coriaria*, native to tropical Africa, bearing curved pods. **2** this pod used as a source of tannin. [Carib]

divination /dívvináysh'n/ *n.* **1** supposed insight into the future or the unknown gained by supernatural means. **2 a** a skilful and accurate forecast. **b** a good guess. □□ **divinatory** *adj.* [ME f. OF *divination* or L *divinatio* (as DIVINE)]
■ **1** see PROPHECY 2.

divine /divīn/ *adj.*, *v.*, & *n.* ● *adj.* (**diviner, divinest**) **1 a** of, from, or like God or a god. **b** devoted to God; sacred (*divine service*). **2 a** more than humanly excellent, gifted, or beautiful. **b** *colloq.* excellent; delightful. ● *v.* **1** *tr.* discover by guessing, intuition, inspiration, or magic. **2** *tr.* foresee, predict, conjecture. **3** *intr.* practise divination. ● *n.* **1** a cleric, usu. an expert in theology. **2** (**the Divine**) providence or God. □ **divine office** see OFFICE. **divine right of kings** the doctrine that kings derive their sovereignty and authority from God, not from their subjects. **divining-rod** = *dowsing-rod* (see DOWSE[1]) . □□ **divinely** *adv.* **divineness** *n.* **diviner** *n.* **divinize** /dívvinīz/ *v.tr.* (also **-ise**). [ME f. OF *devin -ine* f. L *divinus* f. *divus* godlike]
■ *adj.* **1 a** godlike, godly, holy; heavenly, celestial. **b** sacred, sanctified, hallowed, consecrated, religious, spiritual. **2 a** superhuman, supernatural, saintly, pre-eminent, superior, supreme, exalted, transcendent, extraordinary. **b** marvellous, splendid, delightful, superlative, admirable, wonderful, perfect, excellent, beautiful, *colloq.* great, superb, glorious, super, terrific, smashing, fantastic, magic, brilliant, fabulous, A1, brill, ripsnorting, *colloq. or joc.* splendiferous, *sl.* ace, awesome, *Austral.* & *NZ sl.* beaut, *US sl.* bad. ● *v.* **1, 2** intuit, imagine, conjecture, guess, assume, presume, infer, suppose, hypothesize, surmise, suspect, theorize; determine, discover; predict, speculate, foretell, have foreknowledge of, foresee. ● *n.* **1** holy man, priest, clergyman, cleric, ecclesiastic, minister, pastor, reverend, churchman, churchwoman; theologian. **2** (**the Divine**) see *the Creator* (CREATOR 2).

divinity /divínniti/ *n.* (*pl.* **-ies**) **1** the state or quality of being divine. **2 a** a god; a divine being. **b** (as **the Divinity**) God. **3** the study of religion; theology. [ME f. OF *divinité* f. L *divinitas -tatis* (as DIVINE)]
■ **1** see SANCTITY 1. **2 a** see GOD *n.* 1a.

divisible /divízzib'l/ *adj.* **1** capable of being divided, physically or mentally. **2** (foll. by *by*) *Math.* containing (a number) a number of times without a remainder (*15 is divisible by 3 and 5*). □□ **divisibility** /-bílliti/ *n.* [F *divisible* or LL *divisibilis* (as DIVIDE)]
■ **1** see SEPARABLE.

division /divízh'n/ *n.* **1** the act or an instance of dividing; the process of being divided. **2** *Math.* the process of dividing one number by another (see also *long division* (see LONG[1]), *short division*). **3** disagreement or discord (*division of opinion*). **4** *Parl.* the separation of members of a legislative body into two sets for counting votes for and against. **5 a** one of two or more parts into which a thing is divided. **b** the point at which a thing is divided. **6** a major unit of administration or organization, esp.: **a** a group of army brigades or regiments. **b** *Sport* a grouping of teams within a league, usu. by ability. **7 a** a district defined for administrative purposes. **b** *Brit.* a part of a county or borough returning a Member of Parliament. **8 a** *Bot.* a major taxonomic grouping. **b** *Zool.* a subsidiary category between major levels of classification. **9** *Logic* a classification of kinds, parts, or senses. □ **division of labour** the improvement of efficiency by giving different parts of a manufacturing process etc. to different people. **division sign** the sign (÷) indicating that one quantity is to be divided by another. □□ **divisional** *adj.* **divisionally** *adv.* **divisionary** *adj.* [ME f. OF *divisiun* f. L *divisio -onis* (as DIVIDE)]

■ **1** dividing, splitting, separation, segmentation, segmenting; compartmentation, compartmentalization; split, partition. **3** discord, disagreement, conflict, argument, strife, disunity, disunion, dissension, disharmony, discordance, incompatibility. **5 a** section, compartment, segment, sector, unit; partition; part, space, chamber, cell. **b** boundary (line), border, borderline, frontier, margin, line, dividing line. **6** branch, department, sector, section, unit, group, arm. **7** see DISTRICT.

divisive /divī́siv/ *adj.* tending to divide, esp. in opinion; causing disagreement. □□ **divisively** *adv.* **divisiveness** *n.* [LL *divisivus* (as DIVIDE)]

■ see SCHISMATIC *adj.*

divisor /divī́zər/ *n. Math.* **1** a number by which another is to be divided. **2** a number that divides another without a remainder. [ME f. F *diviseur* or L *divisor* (as DIVIDE)]

divorce /divórss/ *n.* & *v.* ● *n.* **1 a** the legal dissolution of a marriage. **b** a legal decree of this. **2** a severance or separation (*a divorce between thought and feeling*). ● *v.* **1 a** *tr.* (usu. as **divorced** *adj.*) (often foll. by *from*) legally dissolve the marriage of (*a divorced couple; he wants to get divorced from her*). **b** *intr.* separate by divorce (*they divorced last year*). **c** *tr.* end one's marriage with (*divorced him for neglect*). **2** *tr.* (often foll. by *from*) detach, separate (*divorced from reality*). **3** *tr. archaic* dissolve (a union). □□ **divorcement** *n.* [ME f. OF *divorce* (n.), *divorcer* (v.) f. LL *divortiare* f. L *divortium* f. *divortere* (as DI-[2], *vertere* turn)]

■ *n.* **1 a** separation, break-up, split, split-up; severance; see also DISSOLUTION 2. **2** see SEPARATION. ● *v.* **2** separate, cut off, break off, divide, split (off), part, sever, detach, dissociate, disassociate.

divorcee /divvorseé/ *n.* (also *masc.* **divorcé**, *fem.* **divorcée** /-sáy/) a divorced person.

divot /dívvət/ *n.* **1** a piece of turf cut out by a golf club in making a stroke. **2** esp. *Sc.* a piece of turf; a sod. [16th c.: orig. unkn.]

divulge /dīvúlj, di-/ *v.tr.* disclose; reveal (a secret etc.). □□ **divulgation** /-vulgáysh'n/ *n.* **divulgement** *n.* **divulgence** *n.* [L *divulgare* (as DI-[2], *vulgare* publish f. *vulgus* common people)]

■ see DISCLOSE 1.

divvy /dívvi/ *n.* & *v.* (also **divi**) *colloq.* ● *n.* (*pl.* **-ies**) **1** *Brit.* a dividend; a share, esp. of profits earned by a cooperative. **2** a distribution. ● *v.tr.* (**-ies**, **-ied**) (often foll. by *up*) share out; divide. [abbr. of DIVIDEND]

■ *v.* see PARCEL *v.* 2.

Diwali /deewáali/ *n.* a Hindu festival with illuminations, held between September and November. [Hind. *dīwalī* f. Skr. *dīpāvalī* row of lights f. *dīpa* lamp]

Dixie /díksi/ *n.* the southern States of the US. [19th c.: orig. uncert.]

dixie /díksi/ *n.* a large iron cooking pot used by campers etc. [Hind. *degchī* cooking pot f. Pers. *degcha* dimin. of *deg* pot]

Dixieland /díksiland/ *n.* **1** = DIXIE. **2** a kind of jazz with a strong two-beat rhythm and collective improvisation. [DIXIE]

DIY *abbr. Brit.* do-it-yourself.

dizzy /dízzi/ *adj.* & *v.* ● *adj.* (**dizzier**, **dizziest**) **1 a** giddy, unsteady. **b** lacking mental stability; confused. **2** causing giddiness (*dizzy heights; dizzy speed*). ● *v.tr.* **1** make dizzy. **2** bewilder. □□ **dizzily** *adv.* **dizziness** *n.* [OE *dysig* f. WG]

■ *adj.* **1 a** giddy, unsteady, vertiginous, light-headed, light (in the head), faint, dazed, *colloq.* woozy. **b** confused, silly, giddy, empty-headed, muddled, befuddled, flighty, absent-minded, simple-minded, light-headed, wrong-headed, feather-headed, feather-brained, hare-brained, bird-brained, scatterbrained; see also *in a daze* (DAZE *n.*). ● *v.* **2** see BEWILDER, DISORDER *v.*

DJ *abbr.* **1** *Brit.* dinner-jacket. **2** disc jockey.

djellaba /jélləbə/ *n.* (also **djellabah, jellaba**) a loose hooded woollen cloak worn or as worn by Arab men. [Arab. *jallaba, jallābīya*]

djibba (also **djibbah**) var. of JIBBA.

djinn var. of JINNEE.

DL *abbr.* Deputy Lieutenant.

dl *abbr.* decilitre(s).

D-layer /deélayər/ *n.* the lowest layer of the ionosphere able to reflect low-frequency radio waves. [*D* (arbitrary)]

D.Litt. *abbr.* Doctor of Letters. [L *Doctor Litterarum*]

DM *abbr.* (also **D-mark**) Deutschmark.

dm *abbr.* decimetre(s).

D.Mus. *abbr.* Doctor of Music.

DMZ *abbr. US* demilitarized zone.

DNA *abbr.* deoxyribonucleic acid, the self-replicating material present in nearly all living organisms, esp. as a constituent of chromosomes, which is the carrier of genetic information.

DNB *abbr.* Dictionary of National Biography.

D-notice /deénōtiss/ *n. Brit.* a government notice to news editors not to publish items on specified subjects, for reasons of security. [*defence* + NOTICE]

do[1] /dōō, də/ *v.* & *n.* ● *v.* (*3rd sing. present* **does** /duz/; *past* **did** /did/; *past part.* **done** /dun/) **1** *tr.* perform, carry out, achieve, complete (work etc.) (*did his homework; there's a lot to do; he can do anything*). **2** *tr.* **a** produce, make (*she was doing a painting; I did a translation; decided to do a casserole*). **b** provide (*do you do lunches?*). **3** *tr.* bestow, grant; have a specified effect on (*a walk would do you good; do me a favour*). **4** *intr.* act, behave, proceed (*do as I do; she would do well to accept the offer*). **5** *tr.* work at, study; be occupied with (*what does your father do?; he did chemistry at university; we're doing Chaucer next term*). **6 a** *intr.* be suitable or acceptable; suffice (*this dress won't do for a wedding; a sandwich will do until we get home; that will never do*). **b** *tr.* satisfy; be suitable for (*that hotel will do me nicely*). **7** *tr.* deal with; put in order (*the garden needs doing; the barber will do you next; I must do my hair before we go*). **8** *intr.* **a** fare; get on (*the patients were doing excellently; he did badly in the test*). **b** perform, work (*could do better*). **9** *tr.* **a** solve; work out (*we did the puzzle*). **b** (prec. by *can* or *be able to*) be competent at (*can you do cartwheels?; I never could do maths*). **10** *tr.* **a** traverse (a certain distance) (*we did fifty miles today*). **b** travel at a specified speed (*he overtook us doing about eighty*). **11** *tr. colloq.* **a** act or behave like (*did a Houdini*). **b** play the part of (*she was asked to do hostess*). **12** *intr.* **a** *colloq.* finish (*have you done annoying me?; I've done in the bathroom*). **b** (as **done** *adj.*) be over (*the day is done*). **13** *tr.* produce or give a performance of (*the school does many plays and concerts; we've never done 'Pygmalion'*). **14** *tr.* cook, esp. to the right degree (*do it in the oven; the potatoes aren't done yet*). **15** *intr.* be in progress (*what's doing?*). **16** *tr. colloq.* visit; see the sights of (*we did all the art galleries*). **17** *tr. colloq.* **a** (often as **done** *adj.*; often foll. by *in*) exhaust; tire out (*the climb has completely done me*). **b** beat up, defeat, kill. **c** ruin (*now you've done it*). **18** *tr.* (foll. by *into*) translate or transform (*the book was done into French*). **19** *tr. colloq.* (with qualifying adverb) provide food etc. for in a specified way (*they do one very well here*). **20** *tr. sl.* **a** rob (*they did a shop in Soho*). **b** swindle (*I was done at the market*). **21** *tr. sl.* prosecute, convict (*they were done for shoplifting*). **22** *tr. sl.* undergo (a specified term of imprisonment) (*he did two years for fraud*). **23** *tr. coarse sl.* have sexual intercourse with. **24** *tr. sl.* take (a drug). ● *v.aux.* **1 a** (except with *be, can, may, ought, shall, will*) in questions and negative statements (*do you understand?; I don't smoke*). **b** (except with *can, may, ought, shall, will*) in negative commands (*don't be silly*; *do not come tomorrow*). **2** *ellipt.* or in place of verb or verb and object (*you know her better than I do*; *I wanted to go and I did so*; *tell me, do!*). **3** forming emphatic present and past tenses (*I do want to*; *do tell me*; *they did go but she was out*). **4** in inversion for emphasis (*rarely does it happen*; *did he but know it*). ● *n.* (*pl.* **dos** or **do's**) **1** *colloq.* an elaborate event, party, or operation. **2** *Brit. sl.* a swindle or hoax. □ **be done with** see DONE. **be nothing to do with 1** be no business or concern of (*his financial situation is nothing to do with me*). **2** be unconnected with (*his depression is nothing to do with his father's death*). **be to do with** be concerned or connected with (*the argument was to do with money*). **do about** see ABOUT *prep.* 1d. **do away with** *colloq.* **1** abolish. **2** kill. **do battle** enter into combat. **do one's best** see BEST. **do one's bit** see BIT. **do by** treat or deal with in a specified way (*do as you would be done by*). **do credit to** see CREDIT. **do down** *colloq.* **1** cheat, swindle. **2** get the better of; overcome. **do for 1** be satisfactory or sufficient for. **2** *colloq.* (esp. as **done for** *adj.*) destroy, ruin, kill (*he knew he was done for*). **3** *colloq.* act as housekeeper for. **do one's head** (or **nut**) *sl.* be extremely angry or agitated. **do the honours** see HONOUR. **do in 1** *sl.* **a** kill. **b** ruin, do injury to. **2** *colloq.* exhaust, tire out. **do-it-yourself** *adj.* (of work, esp. building, painting, decorating, etc.) done or to be done by an amateur at home. ● *n.* such work. **do justice to** see JUSTICE. **do nothing for** (or **to**) *colloq.* detract from the appearance or quality of (*such behaviour does nothing for our reputation*). **do or die** persist regardless of danger. **do out** *colloq.* clean or redecorate (a room). **do a person out of** *colloq.* unjustly deprive a person of; swindle out of (*he was done out of his holiday*). **do over 1** *sl.* attack; beat up. **2** *colloq.* redecorate, refurbish. **3** *US colloq.* do again. **do proud** see PROUD. **dos and don'ts** rules of behaviour. **do something for** (or **to**) *colloq.* enhance the appearance or quality of (*that carpet does something for the room*). **do one's stuff** see STUFF. **do to** (*archaic* **unto**) = *do by*. **do to death** see DEATH. **do the trick** see TRICK. **do up 1** fasten, secure. **2** *colloq.* **a** refurbish, renovate. **b** adorn, dress up. **3** *sl.* **a** ruin, get the better of. **b** beat up. **do well for oneself** prosper. **do well out of** profit by. **do with** (prec. by *could*) would be glad to have; would profit by (*I could do with a rest*; *you could do with a wash*). **do without** manage without; forgo (also *absol.*: *we shall just have to do without*). **have nothing to do with 1** have no connection or dealings with (*our problem has nothing to do with the latest news*; *after the disagreement he had nothing to do with his father*). **2** be no business or concern of (*the decision has nothing to do with him*). **have to do** (or **something to do**) **with** be connected with (*his limp has to do with a car accident*). [OE *dōn* f. Gmc: rel. to Skr *dádhāmi* put, Gk *tithemi* place, L *facere* do]

■ *v.* **1** see EFFECT *v.* 1, 2. **2 a** see MAKE *v.* 1. **b** see PROVIDE 1. **4** see ACT *v.* 1. **5** see STUDY *v.* 1, 3. **6** see SERVE *v.* 5a–c. **7** see *see about* 1 (SEE[1]). **8 a** see FARE *v.* 1. **10** see MAKE *v.* 15. **13** see PERFORM 2. **17 b** see ATTACK *v.* 1. ● *n.* **1** see PARTY *n.* 1.

do[2] var. of DOH.

do. *abbr.* ditto.

DOA *abbr.* dead on arrival (at hospital etc.).

doable /dŏŏəb'l/ *adj.* that can be done.

■ see PRACTICABLE.

dob /dob/ *v.tr.* (**dobbed, dobbing**) (foll. by *in*) *Austral. sl.* inform against; implicate; betray. [var. of DAB[1]]

dobbin /dóbbin/ *n.* a draught-horse; a farm horse. [pet-form of the name *Robert*]

■ farm horse, draught-horse, jade, *colloq.* nag.

dobe /dōbi/ *n. US colloq.* adobe. [abbr.]

Dobermann /dōbərmən/ *n.* (in full **Dobermann pinscher** /pínshər/) **1** a large dog of a German breed with a smooth coat. **2** this breed. [L. *Dobermann*, 19th-c. Ger. dog-breeder + G *Pinscher* terrier]

doc /dok/ *n. colloq.* doctor. [abbr.]

■ see DOCTOR *n.* 1.

doch an dorris var. of DEOCH AN DORIS.

docile /dōsīl/ *adj.* **1** submissive, easily managed. **2** *archaic* teachable. □□ **docilely** /dōsīl-li/ *adv.* **docility** /-sílliti/ *n.* [ME f. L *docilis* f. *docēre* teach]

■ **1** see SUBMISSIVE.

dock[1] /dok/ *n.* & *v.* ● *n.* **1** an artificially enclosed body of water for the loading, unloading, and repair of ships. **2** (in *pl.*) a range of docks with wharves and offices; a dockyard. **3** *US* a ship's berth, a wharf. **4** = *dry dock.* **5** *Theatr.* = *scene-dock.* ● *v.* **1** *tr.* & *intr.* bring or come into a dock. **2 a** *tr.* join (spacecraft) together in space. **b** *intr.* (of spacecraft) be joined. **3** *tr.* provide with a dock or docks. □ **dock-glass** a large glass for wine-tasting. **in dock** *Brit. colloq.* in hospital or (of a vehicle) laid up for repairs. [MDu. *docke*, of unkn. orig.]

■ *n.* **2, 3** pier, wharf, jetty, quay; (*docks*) harbour, dockyard. ● *v.* **1** (drop) anchor, berth, tie up, moor, land, put in.

dock[2] /dok/ *n.* the enclosure in a criminal court for the accused. □ **dock brief** a brief handed direct to a barrister selected by a prisoner in the dock. **in the dock** on trial. [16th c.: prob. orig. cant = Flem. *dok* cage, of unkn. orig.]

dock[3] /dok/ *n.* any weed of the genus *Rumex*, with broad leaves. [OE *docce*]

dock[4] /dok/ *v.* & *n.* ● *v.tr.* **1 a** cut short (an animal's tail). **b** cut short the tail of (an animal). **2 a** (often foll. by *from*) deduct (a part) from wages, supplies, etc. **b** reduce (wages etc.) in this way. ● *n.* **1** the solid bony part of an animal's tail. **2** the crupper of a saddle or harness. □ **dock-tailed** having a docked tail. [ME, of uncert. orig.]

dockage /dókkij/ *n.* **1** the charge made for using docks. **2** dock accommodation. **3** the berthing of vessels in docks.

docker /dókkər/ *n.* a person employed to load and unload ships.

■ stevedore, *US* longshoreman.

docket /dókkit/ *n.* & *v.* ● *n.* **1** *Brit.* **a** a document or label listing goods delivered or the contents of a package, or recording payment of customs dues etc. **b** a voucher; an order form. **2** *US* a list of causes for trial or persons having causes pending. **3** *US* a list of things to be done. ● *v.tr.* (**docketed, docketing**) label with a docket. [15th c.: orig. unkn.]

■ *n.* **1 a** see TAG[1] *n.* 1, PAPER *n.* 4. ● *v.* see LABEL *v.* 1.

dockland /dóklənd/ *n.* a district near docks. [DOCK[1]]

dockyard /dókyaard/ *n.* an area with docks and equipment for building and repairing ships, esp. for naval use.

doctor /dóktər/ *n.* & *v.* ● *n.* **1 a** a qualified practitioner of medicine; a physician. **b** *US* a qualified dentist or veterinary surgeon. **2** a person who holds a doctorate (*Doctor of Civil Law*). **3** *colloq.* a person who carries out repairs. **4** *archaic* a teacher or learned man. **5** *sl.* a cook on board a ship or in a camp. **6** (in full **doctor-blade**) *Printing* a blade for removing surplus ink etc. **7** an artificial fishing-fly. ● *v.* *colloq.* **1 a** *tr.* treat medically. **b** *intr.* (esp. as **doctoring** *n.*) practise as a physician. **2** *tr.* castrate or spay. **3** *tr.* patch up (machinery etc.); mend. **4** *tr.* adulterate. **5** *tr.* tamper with, falsify. **6** *tr.* confer a degree of doctor on. □ **Doctor of the Church** any of several early Christian Fathers of the Church. **Doctor of Philosophy** a doctorate in any faculty except law, medicine, or sometimes theology. **go for the doctor** *Austral. sl.* **1** make an all-out effort. **2** bet all one has. **what the doctor ordered** *colloq.* something beneficial or desirable. □□ **doctorhood** *n.* **doctorial** /-tóriəl/ *adj.* **doctorly** *adj.* **doctorship** *n.* [ME f. OF *doctour* f. L *doctor* f. *docēre doct-* teach]

■ *n.* **1 a** physician, medical practitioner, MD, general practitioner, GP, *colloq.* medic, medico, doc, *sl.* sawbones. **3** repairman, technician, engineer, fixer. **4** see TEACHER. ● *v.* **1** treat, attend, medicate; cure, heal; practise (medicine). **2** see NEUTER *v.* **3** mend, repair, patch (up), fix. **4** adulterate, dilute, water (down), *US* cut; spike, drug, poison, contaminate, pollute. **5** falsify, tamper with, meddle with, interfere with, tinker with, disguise, change, modify, alter. □ **go for the doctor** **1** see *go for broke* (BROKE).

doctoral /dóktərəl/ *adj.* of or for a degree of doctor.

doctorate /dóktərət/ *n.* the highest university degree in any faculty, often honorary.

doctrinaire /dóktrináir/ *adj.* & *n.* ● *adj.* seeking to apply a theory or doctrine in all circumstances without regard to practical considerations; theoretical and impractical. ● *n.* a doctrinaire person; a pedantic theorist. □□ **doctrinairism** *n.* **doctrinarian** *n.* [F f. *doctrine* DOCTRINE + *-aire* -ARY[1]]
■ *adj.* see *pedantic* (PEDANT).

doctrinal /doktrī́n'l, dóktrin'l/ *adj.* of or inculcating a doctrine or doctrines. □□ **doctrinally** *adv.* [LL *doctrinalis* (as DOCTRINE)]
■ see ORTHODOX.

doctrine /dóktrin/ *n.* **1** what is taught; a body of instruction. **2 a** a principle of religious or political etc. belief. **b** a set of such principles; dogma. □□ **doctrinism** *n.* **doctrinist** *n.* [ME f. OF f. L *doctrina* teaching (as DOCTOR)]
■ **1** teaching, body of instruction. **2** principle, precept, tenet, belief, opinion, idea, concept, theory, proposition, thesis, conviction, postulate; credo, dogma, article of faith, canon, creed.

docudrama /dókyoodraamə/ *n.* a dramatized television film based on real events. [DOCUMENTARY + DRAMA]

document *n.* & *v.* ● *n.* /dókyoomənt/ a piece of written or printed matter that provides a record or evidence of events, an agreement, ownership, identification, etc. ● *v.tr.* /dókyooment/ **1** prove by or provide with documents or evidence. **2** record in a document. □□ **documental** /-ment'l/ *adj.* [ME f. OF f. L *documentum* proof f. *docēre* teach]
■ *n.* paper, certificate, instrument, report, chronicle, record. ● *v.* record, chronicle, particularize, detail, describe; verify, validate, certify, authenticate, corroborate, substantiate.

documentalist /dókyooméntəlist/ *n.* a person engaged in documentation.

documentary /dókyooméntəri, -tri/ *adj.* & *n.* ● *adj.* **1** consisting of documents (*documentary evidence*). **2** providing a factual record or report. ● *n.* (*pl.* **-ies**) a documentary film etc. □□ **documentarily** *adv.*

documentation /dókyoomentáysh'n/ *n.* **1** the accumulation, classification, and dissemination of information. **2** the material collected or disseminated. **3** the collection of documents relating to a process or event, esp. the written specification and instructions accompanying a computer program.
■ **2** see MATERIAL *n.* 5.

DOD *abbr. US* Department of Defense.

dodder[1] /dóddər/ *v.intr.* tremble or totter, esp. from age. □ **dodder-grass** quaking-grass. □□ **dodderer** *n.* **doddering** *adj.* [17th c.: var. of obs. dial. *dadder*]
■ see TOTTER *v.* □□ **doddering** feeble, weak, infirm, frail; doddery, shambling, faltering, shaky, unsteady, trembly; see also AGED 2.

dodder[2] /dóddər/ *n.* any climbing parasitic plant of the genus *Cuscuta*, with slender leafless threadlike stems. [ME f. Gmc]

doddered /dóddərd/ *adj.* (of a tree, esp. an oak) having lost its top or branches. [prob. f. obs. *dod* poll, lop]

doddery /dóddəri/ *adj.* tending to tremble or totter, esp. from age. □□ **dodderiness** *n.* [DODDER[1] + -Y[1]]
■ see *doddering* (DODDER[1]).

doddle /dódd'l/ *n. Brit. colloq.* an easy task. [perh. f. *doddle* = TODDLE]
■ see PUSHOVER 1.

dodeca- /dṓdekə/ *comb. form* twelve. [Gk *dōdeka* twelve]

dodecagon /dōdékkəgən/ *n.* a plane figure with twelve sides.

dodecahedron /dṓdekəheédrən/ *n.* a solid figure with twelve faces. □□ **dodecahedral** *adj.*

dodecaphonic /dṓdekəfónnik/ *adj. Mus.* = *twelve-note.*

dodge /doj/ *v.* & *n.* ● *v.* **1** *intr.* (often foll. by *about, behind, round*) move quickly to one side or quickly change position, to elude a pursuer, blow, etc. (*dodged behind the chair*). **2** *tr.* **a** evade by cunning or trickery (*dodged paying the fare*). **b** elude (a pursuer, opponent, blow, etc.) by a sideward movement etc. **3** *tr. Austral. sl.* acquire dishonestly. **4** *intr.* (of a bell in change-ringing) move one place contrary to the normal sequence. ● *n.* **1** a quick movement to avoid or evade something. **2** a clever trick or expedient. **3** the dodging of a bell in change-ringing. □ **dodge the column** see COLUMN. [16th c.: orig. unkn.]
■ *v.* **1** dart, shift, move aside, sidestep, duck, bob, weave, swerve, veer. **2 a** evade, sidestep, *colloq.* duck. **b** avoid, elude, evade, escape from, sidestep; duck. ● *n.* **2** trick, expedient, subterfuge, scheme, ruse, device, stratagem, plan, plot, machination, deception, prevarication, contrivance, evasion, *colloq.* ploy, *Austral. colloq.* lurk, *Brit. colloq.* wheeze, *sl.* racket.

dodgem /dójəm/ *n.* each of a number of small electrically-driven cars in an enclosure at a funfair, driven round and bumped into each other. [DODGE + 'EM]

dodger /dójər/ *n.* **1** a person who dodges, esp. an artful or elusive person. **2** a screen on a ship's bridge etc. as protection from spray etc. **3** *US* a small handbill. **4** *US* a maize-flour cake. **5** *sl.* a sandwich; bread; food.

dodgy /dóji/ *adj.* (**dodgier, dodgiest**) **1** *colloq.* awkward, unreliable, tricky. **2** *Brit.* cunning, artful.
■ **1** tricky, dangerous, perilous, risky, chancy, difficult, ticklish, sensitive, delicate, touchy, awkward, *colloq.* iffy, *sl.* hairy, dicey; uncertain, doubtful, dubious, unreliable, unsound, rickety, *Brit. sl.* dicky. **2** see ARTFUL 1.

dodo /dṓdō/ *n.* (*pl.* **-os** or **-oes**) **1** any large flightless bird of the extinct family Raphidae, formerly native to Mauritius. **2** an old-fashioned, stupid, or inactive person. □ **as dead as the** (or **a**) **dodo** **1** completely or unmistakably dead. **2** entirely obsolete. [Port. *doudo* simpleton]
■ **2** see *stick-in-the-mud* (STICK[2]), SILLY *n.*

DoE *abbr.* (in the UK) Department of the Environment.

doe /dō/ *n.* a female fallow deer, reindeer, hare, or rabbit. [OE *dā*]

doek /dŏŏk/ *n. S.Afr.* a cloth, esp. a head-cloth. [Afrik.]

doer /dŏŏər/ *n.* **1** a person who does something. **2** one who acts rather than merely talking or thinking. **3** (in full **hard doer**) *Austral.* an eccentric or amusing person.

does *3rd sing. present* of DO[1].

doeskin /dṓskin/ *n.* **1 a** the skin of a doe fallow deer. **b** leather made from this. **2** a fine cloth resembling it.

doesn't /dúzz'nt/ *contr.* does not.

doest /dŏŏ-ist/ *archaic 2nd sing. present* of DO[1].

doeth /dŏŏ-ith/ *archaic* = DOTH.

doff /dof/ *v.tr. literary* take off (one's hat, clothing). [ME, = *do off*]
■ see *take off* 1a.

dog /dog/ *n.* & *v.* ● *n.* **1** any four-legged flesh-eating animal of the genus *Canis*, of many breeds domesticated and wild, kept as pets or for work or sport. **2** the male of the dog, or of the fox (also **dog-fox**) or wolf (also **dog-wolf**). **3 a** *colloq.* a despicable person. **b** *colloq.* a person or fellow of a specified kind (*a lucky dog*). **c** *US* & *Austral. sl.* an informer; a traitor. **d** *sl.* a horse that is difficult to handle. **e** *sl. derog.* an unattractive or slovenly woman. **4** a mechanical device for gripping. **5** *US sl.* something poor; a failure. **6** = FIREDOG. **7** (in *pl.*; prec. by *the*) *Brit. colloq.* greyhound-racing. ● *v.tr.* (**dogged, dogging**) **1** follow closely and persistently; pursue, track. **2** *Mech.* grip with a dog. □ **die like a dog** die miserably or shamefully. **dog-biscuit** a hard thick biscuit for feeding dogs. **dog-box** *Austral. sl.* a compartment in a railway carriage without a corridor. **dog-clutch** *Mech.* a device for coupling two shafts in the transmission of power, one member having teeth which engage with slots in another. **dog-collar 1** a collar for a dog. **2 a** *colloq.* a clerical collar. **b** a straight high collar. **dog days** the hottest period of the year (reckoned in antiquity from the heliacal rising of the dog-star). **dog-eared** (of a book etc.) with the corners worn or battered with use. **dog-eat-dog** *colloq.* ruthlessly competitive. **dog-end** *sl.* a cigarette-end. **dog-fall** a fall in which wrestlers touch the ground together. **dog in the manger** a person who prevents others from using something, although that person has no use for it. **dog-leg** (or **-legged**) bent like a dog's hind leg. **dog-leg hole** *Golf* a hole at which a player cannot aim directly at the green from the tee. **dog-paddle** *n.* an elementary swimming-stroke like that of a dog. ● *v.intr.* swim using this stroke. **dog-rose** a wild hedge-rose, *Rosa canina*: also called *brier-rose*. **dog's breakfast** (or **dinner**) *colloq.* a mess. **dog's disease** *Austral. sl.* influenza. **dog's life** a life of misery or harassment. **dog's meat** horse's or other flesh as food for dogs; carrion. **dogs of war** *poet.* the havoc accompanying war. **dog's-** (or **dog-**)**tail** any grass of the genus *Cynosurus*, esp. *C. cristatus*, a common pasture grass. **dog-star** the chief star of the constellation Canis Major or Minor, esp. Sirius. **dog's tooth** (in full **dog's tooth violet**) **1** any liliaceous plant of the genus *Erythronium*, esp. *E. dens-canis* with speckled leaves, purple flowers, and a toothed perianth. **2** = *dog-tooth* 2. **dog-tired** tired out. **dog-tooth 1** a small pointed ornament or moulding esp. in Norman and Early English architecture. **2** a broken check pattern used esp. in cloth for suits. **dog trials** *Austral.* & *NZ* a public competitive display of the skills of sheepdogs. **dog-violet** any of various scentless wild violets, esp. *Viola riviniana*. **go to the dogs** *sl.* deteriorate, be ruined. **hair of the dog** further drink to cure the effects of drink. **like a dog's dinner** *colloq.* smartly or flashily (dressed, arranged, etc.). **not a dog's chance** no chance at all. **put on dog** *colloq.* behave pretentiously. □□ **doglike** *adj.* [OE *docga*, of unkn. orig.]

■ *n.* **3 a** see VILLAIN 1, 3. **c** see TRAITOR. **d** see JADE[2] 1. **e** see BAG *n.* 5. ● *v.* **1** see PURSUE 1.

dogberry /dógbəri/ *n.* (*pl.* **-ies**) the fruit of the dogwood.

dogcart /dógkaart/ *n.* a two-wheeled driving-cart with cross seats back to back.

doge /dōj/ *n. hist.* the chief magistrate of Venice or Genoa. [F f. It. f. Venetian *doze* f. L *dux ducis* leader]

dogfight /dógfīt/ *n.* **1** a close combat between fighter aircraft. **2** uproar; a fight like that between dogs.

dogfish /dógfish/ *n.* (*pl.* same or **dogfishes**) any of various small sharks esp. of the families Scyliorhinidae or Squalidae.

dogged /dóggid/ *adj.* tenacious; grimly persistent. □ **it's dogged as does it** *colloq.* persistence succeeds. □□ **doggedly** *adv.* **doggedness** *n.* [ME f. DOG + -ED[1]]

dogger[1] /dóggər/ *n.* a two-masted bluff-bowed Dutch fishing-boat. [ME f. MDu., = fishing-boat]

dogger[2] /dóggər/ *n. Geol.* a large spherical concretion occurring in sedimentary rock. [dial., = kind of iron-stone, perh. f. DOG]

doggerel /dóggərəl/ *n.* poor or trivial verse. [ME, app. f. DOG: cf. -REL]

doggie var. of DOGGY *n.*

doggish /dóggish/ *adj.* **1** of or like a dog. **2** currish, malicious, snappish. □□ **doggishly** *adv.* **doggishness** *n.*

doggo /dóggō/ *adv.* □ **lie doggo** *sl.* lie motionless or hidden, making no sign. [prob. f. DOG: cf. -O]

doggone /dóggon/ *adj.*, *adv.*, & *int.* esp. *US sl.* ● *adj.* & *adv.* damned. ● *int.* expressing annoyance. [prob. f. *dog on it* = *God damn it*]

doggy /dóggi/ *adj.* & *n.* ● *adj.* **1** of or like a dog. **2** devoted to dogs. ● *n.* (also **doggie**) (*pl.* **-ies**) a little dog; a pet name for a dog. □ **doggy bag** a bag given to a customer in a restaurant or to a guest at a party etc. for putting leftovers in to take home. □□ **dogginess** *n.*

doghouse /dóg-howss/ *n. US* a dog's kennel. □ **in the doghouse** *sl.* in disgrace or disfavour.

dogie /dṓgi/ *n. US* a motherless or neglected calf. [19th c.: orig. unkn.]

dogma /dógmə/ *n.* **1 a** a principle, tenet, or system of these, esp. as laid down by the authority of a Church. **b** such principles collectively. **2** an arrogant declaration of opinion. [L f. Gk *dogma -matos* opinion f. *dokeō* seem]

■ **1** see PRINCIPLE 1, CODE *n.* 4.

dogman /dógmən/ *n.* (*pl.* **-men**) *Austral.* a person giving directional signals to the operator of a crane, often while sitting on the crane's load.

dogmatic /dogmáttik/ *adj.* **1 a** (of a person) given to asserting or imposing personal opinions; arrogant. **b** intolerantly authoritative. **2 a** of or in the nature of dogma; doctrinal. **b** based on a priori principles, not on induction. □□ **dogmatically** *adv.* [LL *dogmaticus* f. Gk *dogmatikos* (as DOGMA)]

■ **1** arbitrary, categorical, dictatorial, pontifical, imperious, peremptory, overbearing, authoritarian, autocratic, uncompromising, high-handed, self-assertive, emphatic, insistent, assertive, arrogant, domineering, obdurate, stubborn, intolerant, opinionated, pushful, *colloq.* pushy.

dogmatics /dogmáttiks/ *n.* **1** the study of religious dogmas; dogmatic theology. **2** a system of dogma. [DOGMATIC]

dogmatism /dógmətiz'm/ *n.* a tendency to be dogmatic. □□ **dogmatist** *n.* [F *dogmatisme* f. med.L *dogmatismus* (as DOGMA)]

■ see *intolerance* (INTOLERANT).

dogmatize /dógmətīz/ *v.* (also **-ise**) **1** *intr.* make positive unsupported assertions; speak dogmatically. **2** *tr.* express (a principle etc.) as a dogma. [F *dogmatiser* or f. LL *dogmatizare* f. Gk (as DOGMA)]

do-gooder /dṓōgŏŏddər/ *n.* a well-meaning but unrealistic philanthropist or reformer. □□ **do-good** /dṓōgŏŏd/ *adj.* & *n.* **do-goodery** *n.* **do-goodism** *n.*

dogsbody /dógzboddi/ *n.* (*pl.* **-ies**) **1** *colloq.* a drudge. **2** *Naut. sl.* a junior officer.

■ **1** see SLAVE *n.* 2.

dogshore /dógshor/ *n.* a temporary wooden support for a ship just before launching.

dogskin /dógskin/ *n.* leather made of or imitating dog's skin, used for gloves.

dogtrot /dógtrot/ *n.* a gentle easy trot.

■ see JOG *n.* 2.

dogwatch /dógwoch/ *n. Naut.* either of two short watches (4–6 or 6–8 p.m.).

dogwood /dógwŏŏd/ *n.* **1** any of various shrubs of the genus *Cornus*, esp. the wild cornel with dark red branches, greenish-white flowers, and purple berries, found in woods and hedgerows. **2** any of various similar trees. **3** the wood of the dogwood.

DoH *abbr.* (in the UK) Department of Health.

doh /dō/ *n.* (also **do**) *Mus.* **1** (in tonic sol-fa) the first and eighth note of a major scale. **2** the note C in the fixed-doh system. [18th c.: f. It. *do*]

doily /dóyli/ *n.* (also **doyley**) (*pl.* **-ies** or **-eys**) a small ornamental mat of paper, lace, etc., on a plate for cakes etc. [orig. the name of a fabric: f. *Doiley*, the name of a draper]

doing /dṓō-ing/ *n.* **1 a** (usu. in *pl.*) an action; the performance of a deed (*famous for his doings*; *it was my doing*). **b** activity, effort (*it takes a lot of doing*). **2** *colloq.* a scolding; a beating. **3** (in *pl.*) *sl.* things needed; adjuncts; things whose names are not known (*have we got all the doings?*).

■ **1 a** see ACTION *n.* 4.

doit /doyt/ *n. archaic* a very small amount of money. [MLG *doyt*, MDu. *duit*, of unkn. orig.]

dojo /dṓjō/ *n.* (*pl.* **-os**) **1** a room or hall in which judo and other martial arts are practised. **2** a mat on which judo etc. is practised. [Jap.]

dol. *abbr.* dollar(s).

Dolby /dólbi/ *n. propr.* an electronic noise-reduction system used esp. in tape-recording to reduce hiss. [R. M. *Dolby*, US inventor]

dolce far niente /dólchay faár ni-énti/ *n.* pleasant idleness. [It., = sweet doing nothing]

dolce vita /dólchay veétə/ *n.* a life of pleasure and luxury. [It., = sweet life]
■ see DISSIPATION 1.

doldrums /dóldrəmz/ *n.pl.* (usu. prec. by *the*) **1** low spirits; a feeling of boredom or depression. **2** a period of inactivity or state of stagnation. **3** an equatorial ocean region of calms, sudden storms, and light unpredictable winds. [prob. after *dull* and *tantrum*]
■ **1** see GLOOM *n.* 2.

dole[1] /dōl/ *n.* & *v.* ● *n.* **1** (usu. prec. by *the*) *Brit. colloq.* benefit claimable by the unemployed from the State. **2 a** charitable distribution. **b** a charitable (esp. sparing, niggardly) gift of food, clothes, or money. **3** *archaic* one's lot or destiny. ● *v.tr.* (usu. foll. by *out*) deal out sparingly. □ **dole-bludger** *Austral. sl.* one who allegedly prefers the dole to work. **on the dole** *Brit. colloq.* receiving State benefit for the unemployed. [OE *dāl* f. Gmc]
■ *n.* **1** (unemployment) benefit, welfare *colloq.* social. **2 a** distribution, apportionment, allocation, dispensation. **b** portion, allotment, share, quota, lot, allowance, parcel; donation, gift, gratuity, hand-out, *hist.* alms. **3** see LOT *n.* 4. ● *v.* give (out), deal (out), distribute, hand out, share (out), dispense, allot, allocate, apportion, *literary* mete out, *sl.* dish out.

dole[2] /dōl/ *n. poet.* grief, woe; lamentation. [ME f. OF *do(e)l* etc. f. pop.L *dolus* f. L *dolēre* grieve]

doleful /dṓlfŏŏl/ *adj.* **1** mournful, sad. **2** dreary, dismal. □□ **dolefully** *adv.* **dolefulness** *n.* [ME f. DOLE[2] + -FUL]
■ **1** sad, sorrowful, melancholy, gloomy, mournful, depressed, disconsolate, blue, down, distressed, dejected, downhearted, forlorn, unhappy, lugubrious, wretched, miserable, woebegone, woeful, *colloq.* down in the mouth, (down) in the dumps, *literary or joc.* dolorous; distressing, funereal, depressing, grievous, harrowing. **2** dreary, cheerless, joyless, sombre, gloomy; see also DISMAL 1, 2.

dolerite /dóllərīt/ *n.* a coarse basaltic rock. [F *dolérite* f. Gk *doleros* deceptive (because it is difficult to distinguish from diorite)]

dolichocephalic /dóllikṓsifállik/ *adj.* (also **dolichocephalous** /-séffələss/) having a long or narrow head. [Gk *dolikhos* long + -CEPHALIC, -CEPHALOUS]

dolina /dəleénə/ *n.* (also **doline** /dəleén/) *Geol.* an extensive depression or basin. [Russ. *dolina* valley]

doll /dol/ *n.* & *v.* ● *n.* **1** a small model of a human figure, esp. a baby or a child, as a child's toy. **2 a** *colloq.* a pretty but silly young woman. **b** *sl.* a young woman, esp. an attractive one. **3** a ventriloquist's dummy. ● *v.tr.* & *intr.* (foll. by *up*; often *refl.*) dress up smartly. □ **doll's house 1** a miniature toy house for dolls. **2** a very small house. [pet form of the name *Dorothy*]

dollar /dóllər/ *n.* **1** the chief monetary unit in the US, Canada, and Australia. **2** the chief monetary unit of certain countries in the Pacific, West Indies, SE Asia, Africa, and S. America. □ **dollar area** the area in which currency is linked to the US dollar. **dollar diplomacy** diplomatic activity aimed at advancing a country's international influence by furthering its financial and commercial interests abroad. **dollar gap** the excess of a country's import trade with the dollar area over the corresponding export trade. **dollar mark** (or **sign**) the sign $, representing a dollar. **dollar spot 1** a fungal disease of lawns etc. **2** a discoloured patch caused by this. [LG *daler* f. G *Taler*, short for *Joachimstaler*, a coin from the silver-mine of *Joachimstal*, now *Jáchymov* in the Czech Republic]

dollhouse /dólhowss/ *n. US* = *doll's house* (see DOLL).

dollop /dólləp/ *n.* & *v.* ● *n.* a shapeless lump of food etc. ● *v.tr.* (**dolloped**, **dolloping**) (usu. foll. by *out*) serve out in large shapeless quantities. [perh. f. Scand.]
■ *n.* see HELPING.

dolly /dólli/ *n.*, *v.*, & *adj.* ● *n.* (*pl.* **-ies**) **1** a child's name for a doll. **2** a movable platform for a cine-camera. **3** *Cricket colloq.* an easy catch or hit. **4** a stick for stirring in clothes-washing. **5** = *corn dolly* (see CORN[1]). **6** *colloq.* = *dolly-bird*. ● *v.* (**-ies**, **-ied**) **1** *tr.* (foll. by *up*) dress up smartly. **2** *intr.* (foll. by *in*, *up*) move a cine-camera in or up to a subject, or out from it. ● *adj.* (**dollier**, **dolliest**) **1** *Brit. colloq.* (esp. of a girl) attractive, stylish. **2** *Cricket colloq.* easily hit or caught. □ **dolly-bird** *Brit. colloq.* an attractive and stylish young woman. **dolly mixture** any of a mixture of small variously shaped and coloured sweets.

Dolly Varden /dólli vaárd'n/ *n.* **1** a woman's large hat with one side drooping and with a floral trimming. **2** a brightly spotted char, *Salvelinus malma*, of western N. America. [a character in Dickens's *Barnaby Rudge*]

dolma /dólmə/ *n.* (*pl.* **dolmas** or **dolmades** /-maáthez/) a SE European delicacy of spiced rice or meat etc. wrapped in vine or cabbage leaves. [Turk. f. *dolmak* fill, be filled: *dolmades* f. mod.Gk]

dolman /dólmən/ *n.* **1** a long Turkish robe open in front. **2** a hussar's jacket worn with the sleeves hanging loose. **3** a woman's mantle with capelike or dolman sleeves. □ **dolman sleeve** a loose sleeve cut in one piece with the body of the coat etc. [ult. f. Turk. *dolama*]

dolmen /dólmən/ *n.* a megalithic tomb with a large flat stone laid on upright ones. [F, perh. f. Cornish *tolmēn* hole of stone]

dolomite /dólləmīt/ *n.* a mineral or rock of calcium magnesium carbonate. □□ **dolomitic** /dólləmíttik/ *adj.* [F f. D. de *Dolomieu*, Fr. geologist d. 1801]

dolorous /dóllərəss/ *adj. literary* or *joc.* **1** distressing, painful; doleful, dismal. **2** distressed, sad. □□ **dolorously** *adv.* [ME f. OF *doleros* f. LL *dolorosus* (as DOLOUR)]
■ see DISMAL 1, 2.

dolour /dóllər/ *n.* (*US* **dolor**) *literary* sorrow, distress. [ME f. OF f. L *dolor -oris* pain, grief]
■ see SORROW *n.* 1.

dolphin /dólfin/ *n.* **1** any of various porpoise-like sea mammals of the family Delphinidae having a slender beaklike snout. **2** (in general use) = DORADO 1. **3** a bollard, pile, or buoy for mooring. **4** a structure for protecting the pier of a bridge. **5** a curved fish in heraldry, sculpture, etc. [ME, also *delphin* f. L *delphinus* f. Gk *delphis -inos*]

dolphinarium /dólfináiriəm/ *n.* (*pl.* **dolphinariums**) an aquarium for dolphins, esp. one open to the public.

dolt /dōlt/ *n.* a stupid person. □□ **doltish** *adj.* **doltishly** *adv.* **doltishness** *n.* [app. related to *dol*, *dold*, obs. var. of DULL]
■ fool, ass, blockhead, dunce, dullard, ignoramus, numskull, nincompoop, ninny, simpleton, dunderhead, *colloq.* moron, imbecile, idiot, fat-head, donkey, nitwit, dim-wit, chump, dummy, halfwit, birdbrain, pinhead, muggins, chucklehead, knucklehead, *Brit. colloq.* clot, *US colloq.* lame-brain, *sl.* jerk, dope, dumb-bell, bonehead, goon, clod, clodhopper, *Austral. sl.* alec, boofhead, dill, *Austral.* & *NZ sl.* dingbat, *Austral.* & *NZ sl. derog.* drongo, *esp. Brit. sl.* twit.

Dom /dom/ *n.* **1** a title prefixed to the names of some Roman Catholic dignitaries, and Benedictine and Carthusian monks. **2** the Portuguese equivalent of Don (see DON[1]). [L *dominus* master: sense 2 through Port.]

-dom /dəm/ *suffix* forming nouns denoting: **1** state or condition (*freedom*). **2** rank or status (*earldom*). **3** domain (*kingdom*). **4** a class of people (or the attitudes etc. associated with them) regarded collectively (*officialdom*). [OE *-dōm*, orig. = DOOM]

domain /dəmáyn/ *n.* **1** an area under one rule; a realm. **2** an estate or lands under one control. **3** a sphere of control or influence. **4** *Math.* the set of possible values of an independent variable. **5** *Physics* a discrete region of magnetism in ferromagnetic material. □□ **domanial** /dəmáyniəl/ *adj.* [ME f. F *domaine*, OF *demeine* DEMESNE, assoc. with L *dominus* lord]
■ **1** realm, dominion, territory, property, land(s), province,

kingdom, empire. **3** province, territory, field, area, department, sphere, discipline, speciality, specialization, concern, *formal esp. Law* realm, *joc.* bailiwick.

domaine /dəmáyn/ *n.* a vineyard. [F: see DOMAIN]

dome /dōm/ *n.* & *v.* ● *n.* **1 a** a rounded vault as a roof, with a circular, elliptical, or polygonal base; a large cupola. **b** the revolving openable hemispherical roof of an observatory. **2 a** a natural vault or canopy (of the sky, trees, etc.). **b** the rounded summit of a hill etc. **3** *Geol.* a dome-shaped structure. **4** *sl.* the head. **5** *poet.* a stately building. ● *v.tr.* (usu. as **domed** *adj.*) cover with or shape as a dome. □□ **domelike** *adj.* [F *dôme* f. It. *duomo* cathedral, dome f. L *domus* house]

■ **4** see HEAD *n.* 1.

Domesday /dóōmzday/ *n.* (in full **Domesday Book**) a record of the lands of England made in 1086 by order of William I. [ME var. of doomsday, as being a book of final authority]

domestic /dəméstik/ *adj.* & *n.* ● *adj.* **1** of the home, household, or family affairs. **2 a** of one's own country, not foreign or international. **b** home-grown or home-made. **3** (of an animal) kept by or living with man. **4** fond of home life. ● *n.* a household servant. □ **domestic science** the study of household management. □□ **domestically** *adv.* [F *domestique* f. L *domesticus* f. *domus* home]

■ *adj.* **1** home, private, family, familial; residential, household. **2 a** home, native, indigenous, internal; home-grown. **3** tame, domesticated, house-trained, house-broken, trained. **4** home-loving. ● *n.* servant, (hired) help, housekeeper, cleaner; major-domo, steward.

domesticate /dəméstikayt/ *v.tr.* **1** tame (an animal) to live with humans. **2** accustom to home life and management. **3** naturalize (a plant or animal). □□ **domesticable** /-kəb'l/ *adj.* **domestication** /-káysh'n/ *n.* [med.L *domesticare* (as DOMESTIC)]

■ **1** see TAME *v.* 1.

domesticity /dómməstíssiti, dō-/ *n.* **1** the state of being domestic. **2** domestic or home life.

domicile /dómmisīl, -sil/ *n.* & *v.* (also **domicil** /-sil/) ● *n.* **1** a dwelling-place; one's home. **2** *Law* **a** a place of permanent residence. **b** the fact of residing. **3** the place at which a bill of exchange is made payable. ● *v.tr.* **1** (usu. as **domiciled** *adj.*) (usu. foll. by *at*, *in*) establish or settle in a place. **2** (usu. foll. by *at*) make (a bill of exchange) payable at a certain place. [ME f. OF f. L *domicilium* f. *domus* home]

■ *n.* **1** residence, abode, home, house, habitation, (living) quarters, housing, rooms, accommodation(s), lodging(s), *colloq.* pad, *Brit. colloq.* digs, diggings, *formal* dwelling(-place). ● *v.* **1** house, locate, lodge, settle, establish, situate; (**domiciled**) see RESIDENT *adj.* 1.

domiciliary /dómmisilliəri/ *adj.* of a dwelling-place (esp. of a doctor's, official's, etc., visit to a person's home). [F *domiciliaire* f. med.L *domiciliarius* (as DOMICILE)]

dominance /dómminənss/ *n.* **1** the state of being dominant. **2** control, authority.

■ see POWER *n.* 3a, 5.

dominant /dómminənt/ *adj.* & *n.* ● *adj.* **1** dominating, prevailing, most influential. **2** (of a high place) prominent, overlooking others. **3 a** (of an allele) expressed even when inherited from only one parent. **b** (of an inherited characteristic) appearing in an individual even when its allelic counterpart is also inherited (cf. RECESSIVE). ● *n.* *Mus.* the fifth note of the diatonic scale of any key. □□ **dominantly** *adv.* [F f. L *dominari* (as DOMINATE)]

■ *adj.* **1** dominating, commanding, authoritative, controlling, governing, ruling, leading, influential, assertive, supreme, superior, ascendant; predominant, chief, main, principal, primary, prevailing, outstanding, pre-eminent, paramount.

dominate /dómminayt/ *v.* **1** *tr.* & (foll. by *over*) *intr.* have a commanding influence on; exercise control over (*fear dominated them for years*; *dominates over his friends*). **2** *intr.* (of a person, sound, feature of a scene, etc.) be the most influential or conspicuous. **3** *tr.* & (foll. by *over*) *intr.* (of a building etc.) have a commanding position over; overlook. □□ **dominator** *n.* [L *dominari dominat-* f. *dominus* lord]

■ **1** command, control, govern, rule, direct, lead, reign over, exercise command *or* authority *or* control *or* rule over, have under one's thumb; have the whip *or* upper hand (over), be in control, rule the roost *or* roast, call the shots *or* tune, be in the driver's seat, pull the strings, be in the saddle, wear the trousers, be at the wheel, *colloq.* run the show. **2** predominate, preponderate, stand out, stick out. **3** overlook, look (out) over, tower over *or* above, rise above, overshadow.

domination /dómmináysh'n/ *n.* **1 a** command, control. **b** oppression, tyranny. **2** the act or an instance of dominating; the process of being dominated. **3** (in *pl.*) angelic beings of the fourth order of the celestial hierarchy. [ME f. OF f. L *dominatio -onis* (as DOMINATE)]

■ **1 a** authority, control, rule, power, command, influence, sway, supremacy, ascendancy, hegemony, pre-eminence, mastery. **b** oppression, subjection, repression, suppression, subordination, enslavement, enthralment; dictatorship, despotism, tyranny.

domineer /dómmineér/ *v.intr.* (often as **domineering** *adj.*) behave in an arrogant and overbearing way. □□ **domineeringly** *adv.* [Du. *dominieren* f. F *dominer*]

■ throw one's weight about; dominate over, tyrannize over; (**domineering**) overbearing, imperious, officious, arrogant, autocratic, authoritarian, high-handed, high and mighty, masterful, arbitrary, peremptory, dictatorial, despotic, tyrannical, oppressive, strict, hard, harsh, tough, *colloq.* bossy, pushy.

dominical /dəmínnik'l/ *adj.* **1** of the Lord's day, of Sunday. **2** of the Lord (Jesus Christ). □ **dominical letter** the one of the seven letters A–G indicating the dates of Sundays in a year. [F *dominical* or L *dominicalis* f. L *dominicus* f. *dominus* lord]

Dominican /dəmínnikən/ *adj.* & *n.* ● *adj.* **1** of or relating to St Dominic or the order of preaching friars which he founded in 1215–16. **2** of or relating to either of the two orders of female religious founded on Dominican principles. ● *n.* a Dominican friar, nun, or sister (see also *Black Friar*). [med.L *Dominicanus* f. *Dominicus* L name of *Domingo* de Guzmán (St Dominic)]

dominie /dómmini/ *n.* *Sc.* a schoolmaster. [later spelling of *domine* sir, voc. of L *dominus* lord]

dominion /dəmínyən/ *n.* **1** sovereignty, control. **2** the territory of a sovereign or government; a domain. **3** *hist.* the title of each of the self-governing territories of the British Commonwealth. [ME f. OF f. med.L *dominio -onis* f. L *dominium* f. *dominus* lord]

■ **1** rule, authority, control, dominance, domination, grasp, mastery, grip, command, jurisdiction, power, sovereignty, sway, ascendancy, pre-eminence, primacy, supremacy, hegemony. **2** domain, territory, region, area, country, kingdom, *formal esp. Law* realm.

domino /dómminō/ *n.* (*pl.* **-oes**) **1 a** any of 28 small oblong pieces marked with 0–6 pips in each half. **b** (in *pl.*, usu. treated as *sing.*) a game played with these. **2** a loose cloak with a mask for the upper part of the face, worn at masquerades. □ **domino theory** the theory that a political event etc. in one country will cause similar events in neighbouring countries, like a row of falling dominoes. [F, prob. f. L *dominus* lord, but unexplained]

don[1] /don/ *n.* **1** a university teacher, esp. a senior member of a college at Oxford or Cambridge. **2** (**Don**) **a** a Spanish title prefixed to a forename. **b** a Spanish gentleman; a Spaniard. [Sp. f. L *dominus* lord]

■ **1** see TEACHER.

don[2] /don/ *v.tr.* (**donned, donning**) put on (clothing). [= *do on*]

■ see *put on* 1 (PUT[1]).

dona /dṓnə/ *n.* (also **donah**) *Brit. sl.* a woman; a sweetheart. [Sp. *doña* or Port. *dona* f. L (as DONNA)]

donate /dōnáyt/ *v.tr.* give or contribute (money etc.), esp. voluntarily to a fund or institution. □□ **donator** *n.* [back-form. f. DONATION]

■ give, provide, supply, present, contribute, subscribe (to *or* for), pledge, award, bestow, confer, grant, will, bequeath, *formal* vouchsafe.

donation /dōnáysh'n/ *n.* **1** the act or an instance of donating. **2** something, esp. an amount of money, donated. [ME f. OF f. L *donatio -onis* f. *donare* give f. *donum* gift]

■ **1** giving, contribution, bestowal, allotment. **2** gift, contribution, present, dole, grant, offer, award, offering, bequest, *hist.* alms.

donative /dṓnətiv, dón-/ *n.* & *adj.* ● *n.* a gift or donation, esp. one given formally or officially as a largess. ● *adj.* **1** given as a donation or bounty. **2** *hist.* (of a benefice) given directly, not presentative. [ME f. L *donativum* gift, largesse f. *donare*: see DONATION]

done /dun/ *past part.* of DO[1]. ● *adj.* **1** *colloq.* socially acceptable (*the done thing*; *it isn't done*). **2** (often with *in*, *up*) *colloq.* tired out. **3** (esp. as *int.* in reply to an offer etc.) accepted. □ **be done with** have finished with, be finished with. **done for** *colloq.* in serious trouble. **have done** have ceased or finished. **have done with** be rid of; have finished dealing with.

■ **1** see CORRECT *adj.* 2, 3.

donee /dōnée/ *n.* the recipient of a gift. [DONOR + -EE]

dong[1] /dong/ *v.* & *n.* ● *v.* **1** *intr.* make the deep sound of a large bell. **2** *tr. Austral.* & *NZ colloq.* hit, punch. ● *n.* **1** the deep sound of a large bell. **2** *Austral.* & *NZ colloq.* a heavy blow. [imit.]

■ *v.* **2** see HIT *v.* 1a. ● *n.* **2** see PUNCH *n.* 1.

dong[2] /dong/ *n.* the chief monetary unit of Vietnam. [Vietnamese]

donga /dónggə/ *n. S.Afr.* & *Austral.* **1** a dry watercourse. **2** a ravine caused by erosion. [Zulu]

dongle /dóngg'l/ *n. Computing* a security attachment required by a computer to enable protected software to be used. [arbitrary form.]

donjon /dónjən, dún-/ *n.* the great tower or innermost keep of a castle. [archaic spelling of DUNGEON]

■ see DUNGEON *n.* 2.

Don Juan /don jóōən, don waán/ *n.* a seducer of women; a libertine. [name of a legendary Sp. nobleman celebrated in fiction, e.g. by Byron]

■ see LIBERTINE *n.* 1.

donkey /dóngki/ *n.* (*pl.* **-eys**) **1** a domestic ass. **2** *colloq.* a stupid or foolish person. □ **donkey engine** a small auxiliary engine. **donkey jacket** a thick weatherproof jacket worn by workers and as a fashion garment. **donkey's years** *colloq.* a very long time. **donkey-work** the laborious part of a job; drudgery. [earlier with pronunc. as *monkey*: perh. f. DUN[1], or the Christian name *Duncan*]

■ **2** see DOLT.

donna /dónnə/ *n.* **1** an Italian, Spanish, or Portuguese lady. **2** (**Donna**) the title of such a lady. [It. f. L *domina* mistress fem. of *dominus*: cf. DON[1]]

donnée /dónnay/ *n.* (also ***donné***) **1** the subject or theme of a story etc. **2** a basic fact or assumption. [F, fem. or masc. past part. of *donner* give]

■ **2** see GIVEN *n.*

donnish /dónnish/ *adj.* like or resembling a college don, esp. in supposed pedantry. □□ **donnishly** *adv.* **donnishness** *n.*

■ see *pedantic* (PEDANT).

Donnybrook /dónnibrŏŏk/ *n.* a scene of uproar; a free fight. [*Donnybrook* near Dublin, Ireland, formerly site of annual fair]

donor /dṓnər/ *n.* **1** a person who gives or donates something (e.g. to a charity). **2** one who provides blood for a transfusion, semen for insemination, or an organ or tissue for transplantation. **3** *Chem.* an atom or molecule that provides a pair of electrons in forming a coordinate bond. **4** *Physics* an impurity atom in a semiconductor which contributes a conducting electron to the material. □ **donor card** an official card authorizing use of organs for transplant, carried by the donor. [ME f. AF *donour*, OF *doneur* f. L *donator -oris* f. *donare* give]

■ **1** giver, provider, supplier, benefactor, contributor, supporter, backer, patron.

don't /dōnt/ *contr.* do not. ● *n.* a prohibition (*dos and don'ts*).

donut *US* var. of DOUGHNUT.

doodad /dóōdad/ *n. US* = DOODAH. [20th c.: orig. unkn.]

doodah /dóōdaa/ *n.* **1** a fancy article; a trivial ornament. **2** a gadget or 'thingummy'. □ **all of a doodah** excited, dithering. [from the refrain of the song *Camptown Races*]

■ **1** see TRIFLE *n.* 1. **2** see THING 2, 3.

doodle /dóōd'l/ *v.* & *n.* ● *v.intr.* scribble or draw, esp. absent-mindedly. ● *n.* a scrawl or drawing made. □ **doodle-bug 1** *US* any of various insects, esp. the larva of an ant-lion. **2** *US* an unscientific device for locating minerals. **3** *colloq.* a flying bomb. □□ **doodler** *n.* [orig. = foolish person; cf. LG *dudelkopf*]

doohickey /dóōhikki/ *n.* (*pl.* **-eys**) *US colloq.* a small object, esp. mechanical. [DOODAD + HICKEY]

■ see GADGET.

doom /dōōm/ *n.* & *v.* ● *n.* **1 a** a grim fate or destiny. **b** death or ruin. **2 a** a condemnation; a judgement or sentence. **b** the Last Judgement (*the crack of doom*). **3** *hist.* a statute, law, or decree. ● *v.tr.* **1** (usu. foll. by *to*) condemn or destine (*a city doomed to destruction*). **2** (esp. as **doomed** *adj.*) consign to misfortune or destruction. [OE *dōm* statute, judgement f. Gmc: rel. to DO[1]]

■ *n.* **1** fate, destiny, fortune, lot, kismet; downfall, destruction, death, ruin, extinction, annihilation, end, termination, terminus. **2 a** see SENTENCE *n.* ● *v.* **1** see DESTINE. **2** (**doomed**) fated, cursed, condemned, damned; accursed, bedevilled, ill-fated, luckless, bewitched, *archaic* star-crossed; see also INAUSPICIOUS 1.

doomsday /dóōmzday/ *n.* the day of the Last Judgement. □ **till doomsday** for ever (cf. DOMESDAY). [OE *dōmes dæg*: see DOOM]

■ □ **till doomsday** see EVER 1.

doomwatch /dóōmwoch/ *n.* organized vigilance or observation to avert danger, esp. from environmental pollution. □□ **doomwatcher** *n.*

door /dor/ *n.* **1 a** a hinged, sliding, or revolving barrier for closing and opening an entrance to a building, room, cupboard, etc. **b** this as representing a house etc. (*lives two doors away*). **2 a** an entrance or exit; a doorway. **b** a means of access or approach. □ **close the door to** exclude the opportunity for. **door-case** (or **-frame**) the structure into which a door is fitted. **door-head** the upper part of a door-case. **door-keeper** = DOORMAN. **door-plate** a plate on the door of a house or room bearing the name of the occupant. **door-to-door** (of selling etc.) done at each house in turn. **lay** (or **lie**) **at the door of** impute (or be imputable) to. **leave the door open** ensure that an option remains available. **next door** in or to the next house or room. **next door to 1** in the next house to. **2** nearly, almost, near to. **open the door to** create an opportunity for. **out of doors** in or into the open air. □□ **doored** *adj.* (also in *comb.*). [OE *duru*, *dor* f. Gmc]

■ **1a, 2** see ENTRY 3a.

doorbell /dórbel/ *n.* a bell in a house etc. rung by visitors outside to signal their arrival.

doorknob /dórnob/ *n.* a knob for turning to release the latch of a door.

doorman /dórmən/ *n.* (*pl.* **-men**) a person on duty at the door to a large building; a janitor or porter.

doormat /dórmat/ *n.* **1** a mat at an entrance for wiping mud etc. from the shoes. **2** a feebly submissive person.
■ **2** see DRIP *n.* 2.

doornail /dórnayl/ *n.* a nail with which doors were studded for strength or ornament. □ **dead as a doornail** completely or unmistakably dead.

doorpost /dórpōst/ *n.* each of the uprights of a door-frame, on one of which the door is hung.

doorstep /dórstep/ *n.* & *v.* ● *n.* **1** a step leading up to the outer door of a house etc. **2** *sl.* a thick slice of bread. ● *v.intr.* (**-stepped**, **-stepping**) go from door to door selling, canvassing, etc. □ **on one's** (or **the**) **doorstep** very close.
■ *n.* **1** see THRESHOLD 1.

doorstop /dórstop/ *n.* a device for keeping a door open or to prevent it from striking a wall etc. when opened.

doorway /dórway/ *n.* an opening filled by a door.
■ see THRESHOLD 1.

dooryard /dóryaard/ *n.* *US* a yard or garden near a house-door.

dop /dop/ *n.* *S.Afr.* **1** a cheap kind of brandy. **2** a tot of liquor. [Afrik.]

dopa /dṓpə/ *n.* *Pharm.* a crystalline amino acid derivative used in the treatment of Parkinsonism. [G f. *D*ioxy*p*henyl*a*lanine, former name of the compound]

dopant /dṓp'nt/ *n.* *Electronics* a substance used in doping a semiconductor.

dope /dōp/ *n.* & *v.* ● *n.* **1** a varnish applied to the cloth surface of aeroplane parts to strengthen them, keep them airtight, etc. **2** a thick liquid used as a lubricant etc. **3** a substance added to petrol etc. to increase its effectiveness. **4 a** *sl.* a narcotic; a stupefying drug. **b** a drug etc. given to a horse or greyhound, or taken by an athlete, to affect performance. **5** *sl.* a stupid person. **6** *sl.* **a** information about a subject, esp. if not generally known. **b** misleading information. ● *v.* **1** *tr.* administer dope to, drug. **2** *tr.* *Electronics* add an impurity to (a semiconductor) to produce a desired electrical characteristic. **3** *tr.* smear, daub; apply dope to. **4** *intr.* take addictive drugs. □ **dope out** *sl.* discover. □□ **doper** *n.* [Du. *doop* sauce f. *doopen* to dip]
■ *n.* **4 a** narcotic, drug, opiate, hallucinogen, psychedelic, *sl.* upper, downer. **5** see DOLT. **6 a** information, data, facts, news, details, story, message, *colloq.* info, low-down, score, *literary* tidings, *Brit. sl.* gen, *US sl.* poop. ● *v.* **3** see SMEAR *v.* 1. □ **dope out** see DISCOVER 1a, b.

dopey /dṓpi/ *adj.* (also **dopy**) (**dopier**, **dopiest**) *colloq.* **1 a** half asleep. **b** stupefied by or as if by a drug. **2** stupid, silly. □□ **dopily** *adv.* **dopiness** *n.*
■ **1 b** see GROGGY. **2** see STUPID *adj.* 1, 5.

doppelgänger /dópp'lgengər/ *n.* an apparition or double of a living person. [G, = double-goer]
■ see DOUBLE *n.*, GHOST *n.* 1.

Dopper /dóppər/ *n.* *S.Afr.* a member of the Gereformeerde Kerk, a strictly orthodox Calvinistic denomination, usu. regarded as old-fashioned in ideas etc. [Afrik.: orig. unkn.]

Doppler effect /dóplər/ *n.* (also **Doppler shift**) *Physics* an increase (or decrease) in the frequency of sound, light, or other waves as the source and observer move towards (or away) from each other. [C. J. *Doppler*, Austrian physicist d. 1853]

dopy var. of DOPEY.

dorado /dəraádō/ *n.* (*pl.* **-os**) **1** a blue and silver marine fish, *Coryphaena hippurus*, showing brilliant colours when dying out of water. **2** a brightly coloured freshwater-fish, *Salminus maxillosus*, native to S. America. [Sp. f. LL *deauratus* gilt f. *aurum* gold]

Dorian /dóriən/ *n.* & *adj.* ● *n.* (in *pl.*) a Greek-speaking people thought to have entered Greece from the north *c.*1100 BC and settled in parts of Central and S. Greece. ● *adj.* of or relating to the Dorians or to Doris in Central Greece. □ **Dorian mode** *Mus.* the mode represented by the natural diatonic scale D–D. [L *Dorius* f. Gk *Dōrios* f. *Dōros*, the mythical ancestor]

Doric /dórrik/ *adj.* & *n.* ● *adj.* **1** (of a dialect) broad, rustic. **2** *Archit.* of the oldest, sturdiest, and simplest of the Greek orders. ● *n.* **1** rustic English or esp. Scots. **2** *Archit.* the Doric order. **3** the dialect of the Dorians in ancient Greece. [L *Doricus* f. Gk *Dōrikos* (as DORIAN)]

dorm /dorm/ *n.* *colloq.* dormitory. [abbr.]

dormant /dórmənt/ *adj.* **1** lying inactive as in sleep; sleeping. **2 a** (of a volcano etc.) temporarily inactive. **b** (of potential faculties etc.) in abeyance. **3** (of plants) alive but not actively growing. **4** *Heraldry* (of a beast) lying with its head on its paws. □□ **dormancy** *n.* [ME f. OF, pres. part. of *dormir* f. L *dormire* sleep]
■ **1** asleep, sleeping, resting, at rest, quiet, inactive, still, inert, unmoving, motionless, stationary, immobile, quiescent, comatose, torpid, hibernating, slumberous, *poet. rhet.* slumbering. **2 b** latent, potential, hidden, concealed, undisclosed, unrevealed, unexpressed; see also ABEYANCE.

dormer /dórmər/ *n.* (in full **dormer window**) a projecting upright window in a sloping roof. [OF *dormëor* (as DORMANT)]

dormitory /dórmitəri, -tri/ *n.* (*pl.* **-ies**) **1** a sleeping-room with several beds, esp. in a school or institution. **2** (in full **dormitory town** etc.) a small town or suburb from which people travel to work in a city etc. **3** *US* a university or college hall of residence or hostel. [ME f. L *dormitorium* f. *dormire dormit-* sleep]

Dormobile /dórməbeel/ *n.* *propr.* a type of motor caravan with a rear compartment convertible for sleeping and eating in. [blend of DORMITORY, AUTOMOBILE]

dormouse /dórmowss/ *n.* (*pl.* **dormice**) any small mouselike hibernating rodent of the family Gliridae, having a long bushy tail. [ME: orig. unkn., but assoc. with F *dormir*, L *dormire*: see DORMANT]

dormy /dórmi/ *adj.* *Golf* (of a player or side) ahead by as many holes as there are holes left to play (*dormy five*). [19th c.: orig. unkn.]

doronicum /dərónnikəm/ *n.* = *leopard's bane* (see LEOPARD). [mod.L (Linnaeus) ult. f. Arab. *darānaj*]

dorp /dorp/ *n.* *S.Afr.* a village or small township. [Du. (as THORP)]

dorsal /dórs'l/ *adj.* *Anat.*, *Zool.*, & *Bot.* **1** of, on, or near the back (cf. VENTRAL). **2** ridge-shaped. □□ **dorsally** *adv.* [F *dorsal* or LL *dorsalis* f. L *dorsum* back]

dory[1] /dóri/ *n.* (*pl.* **-ies**) any of various marine fish having a compressed body and flat head, esp. the John Dory, used as food. [ME f. F *dorée* fem. past part. of *dorer* gild (as DORADO)]

dory[2] /dóri/ *n.* (*pl.* **-ies**) *US* a flat-bottomed fishing-boat with high sides. [Miskito *dóri* dugout]

DOS /doss/ *n.* *Computing* a program for manipulating information on a disk. [abbr. of *d*isk *o*perating *s*ystem]

dos-à-dos /dṓzaadṓ/ *adj.* & *n.* ● *adj.* (of two books) bound together with a shared central board and facing in opposite directions. ● *n.* (*pl.* same) a seat, carriage, etc., in which the occupants sit back to back (cf. DO-SE-DO). [F, = back to back]

dosage /dṓsij/ *n.* **1** the giving of medicine in doses. **2** the size of a dose.

dose /dōss/ *n.* & *v.* ● *n.* **1** an amount of a medicine or drug for taking or taken at one time. **2** a quantity of something administered or allocated (e.g. work, praise, punishment, etc.). **3** the amount of ionizing radiation received by a person or thing. **4** *sl.* a venereal infection. ● *v.tr.* **1** treat (a person or animal) with doses of medicine. **2** give a dose or doses to. **3** adulterate or blend (esp. wine with spirit). □ **like a dose of salts** *colloq.* very fast and efficiently. [F f.

LL *dosis* f. Gk *dosis* gift f. *didōmi* give]
■ *n.* **2** portion, quantity, amount, measure, allotment. ● *v.* **1** see TREAT *v.* 3. □ **like a dose of salts** see *like a shot* (SHOT[1]).

do-se-do /dṓzidṓ, dṓsi-/ *n.* (also **do-si-do**) (*pl.* **-os**) a figure in which two dancers pass round each other back to back and return to their original positions. [corrupt. of DOS-À-DOS]

dosh /dosh/ *n. sl.* money. [20th c.: orig. unkn.]
■ see MONEY 1.

dosimeter /dōsímmitər/ *n.* a device used to measure an absorbed dose of ionizing radiation. □□ **dosimetric** /-métrik/ *adj.* **dosimetry** *n.*

doss /doss/ *v.* & *n. Brit. sl.* ● *v.intr.* (often foll. by *down*) sleep, esp. roughly or in cheap lodgings. ● *n.* a bed, esp. in cheap lodgings. □ **doss-house** a cheap lodging-house, esp. for vagrants. [prob. = *doss* ornamental covering for a seat-back etc. f. OF *dos* ult. f. L *dorsum* back]

dossal /dóss'l/ *n.* a hanging cloth behind an altar or round a chancel. [med.L *dossale* f. LL *dorsalis* DORSAL]

dosser /dóssər/ *n. Brit. sl.* **1** a person who dosses. **2** = *doss-house.*
■ **1** see TRAMP *n.* 1.

dossier /dóssiər, -iay/ *n.* a set of documents, esp. a collection of information about a person, event, or subject. [F, so called from the label on the back, f. *dos* back f. L *dorsum*]
■ file, papers, document.

dost /dust/ *archaic 2nd sing. present* of DO[1].

DoT *abbr.* (in the UK) Department of Transport.

dot[1] /dot/ *n.* & *v.* ● *n.* **1 a** a small spot, speck, or mark. **b** such a mark written or printed as part of an *i* or *j*, as a diacritical mark, as one of a series of marks to signify omission, or as a full stop. **c** a decimal point. **2** *Mus.* a dot used to denote the lengthening of a note or rest, or to indicate staccato. **3** the shorter signal of the two used in Morse code (cf. DASH *n.* 6). **4** a tiny or apparently tiny object (*a dot on the horizon*). ● *v.tr.* (**dotted, dotting**) **1 a** mark with a dot or dots. **b** place a dot over (a letter). **2** *Mus.* mark (a note or rest) to show that the time value is increased by half. **3** (often foll. by *about*) scatter like dots. **4** partly cover as with dots (*a sea dotted with ships*). **5** *sl.* hit (*dotted him one in the eye*). □ **dot the i's and cross the t's** *colloq.* **1** be minutely accurate, emphasize details. **2** add the final touches to a task, exercise, etc. **dot matrix printer** *Computing* a printer with characters formed from dots printed by configurations of the tips of small wires. **dotted line** a line of dots on a document, esp. to show a place left for a signature. **on the dot** exactly on time. **the year dot** *Brit. colloq.* far in the past. □□ **dotter** *n.* [OE *dott* head of a boil, perh. infl. by Du. *dot* knot]
■ *n.* **1** spot, speck, mark; decimal point, full stop, *esp. US* period. **4** spot, speck, point, mark, fleck. ● *v.* **1a, 4** spot, fleck, speckle, stipple. **5** see HIT *v.* 1a. □ **dot the i's and cross the t's 1** be pedantic *or* fussy *or* meticulous *or* precise *or* accurate *or* exact *or* fastidious *or* scrupulous *or* punctilious *or* finicky *or* perfectionist, *colloq.* be pernickety. **on the dot** on time, promptly, punctually, *Austral.* & *NZ colloq.* on the knocker. **the year dot** time immemorial, time out of mind, *colloq.* way back.

dot[2] /dot/ *n.* a woman's dowry. [F f. L *dos dotis*]

dotage /dṓtij/ *n.* feeble-minded senility (*in his dotage*).
■ see *decrepitude* (DECREPIT).

dotard /dṓtərd/ *n.* a person who is feeble-minded, esp. from senility. [ME f. DOTE + -ARD]

dote /dōt/ *v.intr.* **1** (foll. by *on*, *upon*) be foolishly or excessively fond of. **2** be silly or feeble-minded, esp. from old age. □□ **doter** *n.* **dotingly** *adv.* [ME, corresp. to MDu. *doten* be silly]
■ **1** (*dote on* or *upon*) be fond of, be infatuated with, love, idolize, hold dear, adore, make much of; coddle, pamper, spoil, indulge.

doth /duth/ *archaic 3rd sing. present* of DO[1].

dotterel /dóttərəl/ *n.* a small migrant plover, *Eudromias morinellus.* [ME f. DOTE + -REL, named from the ease with which it is caught, taken to indicate stupidity]

dottle /dótt'l/ *n.* a remnant of unburnt tobacco in a pipe. [DOT[1] + -LE[1]]

dotty /dótti/ *adj.* (**dottier, dottiest**) *colloq.* **1** feeble-minded, silly. **2** eccentric. **3** absurd. **4** (foll. by *about, on*) infatuated with; obsessed by. □□ **dottily** *adv.* **dottiness** *n.* [earlier = unsteady: f. DOT[1] + -Y[1]]
■ **1–3** see CRAZY 1. **4** see CRAZY 2.

douane /dōō-áan/ *n.* a foreign custom-house. [F f. It. *do(g)ana* f. Turk. *duwan*, Arab. *dīwān*: cf. DIVAN]

Douay Bible /dōō-ay, dóway/ *n.* (also **Douay version**) an English translation of the Bible formerly used in the Roman Catholic Church, completed at Douai in France early in the seventeenth century.

double /dúbb'l/ *adj., adv., n.,* & *v.* ● *adj.* **1 a** consisting of two usu. equal parts or things; twofold. **b** consisting of two identical parts. **2** twice as much or many (*double the amount; double the number; double thickness*). **3** having twice the usual size, quantity, strength, etc. (*double whisky*). **4** designed for two people (*double bed*). **5 a** having some part double. **b** (of a flower) having more than one circle of petals. **c** (of a domino) having the same number of pips on each half. **6** having two different roles or interpretations, esp. implying confusion or deceit (*double meaning; leads a double life*). **7** *Mus.* lower in pitch by an octave (*double bassoon*). ● *adv.* **1** at or to twice the amount etc. (*counts double*). **2** two together (*sleep double*). ● *n.* **1 a** a double quantity or thing; twice as much or many. **b** *colloq.* a double measure of spirits. **2 a** a counterpart of a person or thing; a person who looks exactly like another. **b** an understudy. **c** a wraith. **3** (in *pl.*) *Sport* (in lawn tennis) a game between two pairs of players. **4** *Sport* a pair of victories over the same team, a pair of championships at the same game, etc. **5** a system of betting in which the winnings and stake from the first bet are transferred to a second. **6** *Bridge* the doubling of an opponent's bid. **7** *Darts* a hit on the narrow ring enclosed by the two outer circles of a dartboard, scoring double. **8** a sharp turn, esp. of the tracks of a hunted animal, or the course of a river. ● *v.* **1** *tr.* & *intr.* make or become twice as much or many; increase twofold; multiply by two. **2** *tr.* amount to twice as much as. **3 a** *tr.* fold or bend (paper, cloth, etc.) over on itself. **b** *intr.* become folded. **4 a** *tr.* (of an actor) play (two parts) in the same piece. **b** *intr.* (often foll. by *for*) be understudy etc. **5** *intr.* (usu. foll. by *as*) play a twofold role. **6** *intr.* turn sharply in flight or pursuit; take a tortuous course. **7** *tr. Naut.* sail round (a headland). **8** *tr. Bridge* make a call increasing the value of the points to be won or lost on (an opponent's bid). **9** *Mus.* **a** *intr.* (often foll. by *on*) play two or more musical instruments (*the clarinettist doubles on tenor sax*). **b** *tr.* add the same note in a higher or lower octave to (a note). **10** *tr.* clench (a fist). **11** *intr.* move at twice the usual speed; run. **12** *Billiards* **a** *intr.* rebound. **b** *tr.* cause to rebound. □ **at the double** running, hurrying. **bent double** folded, stooping. **double acrostic** see ACROSTIC. **double agent** one who spies simultaneously for two rival countries etc. **double axe** an axe with two blades. **double back** take a new direction opposite to the previous one. **double-banking 1** double-parking. **2** *Austral.* & *NZ* riding two on a horse etc. **double-barrelled 1** (of a gun) having two barrels. **2** *Brit.* (of a surname) having two parts joined by a hyphen. **3** twofold. **double-bass 1** the largest and lowest-pitched instrument of the violin family. **2** its player. **double bill** a programme with two principal items. **double bind** a dilemma. **double-blind** *adj.* (of a test or experiment) in which neither the tester nor the subject has knowledge of identities etc. that might lead to bias. ● *n.* such a test or experiment. **double bluff** an action or statement intended to appear as a bluff, but in fact genuine. **double boiler** a saucepan with a detachable upper compartment heated by boiling water in the lower one. **double bond** *Chem.* a pair of bonds between two atoms in a molecule. **double-book** accept two reservations simultaneously for (the same seat, room, etc.). **double-breasted** (of a coat etc.) having two fronts overlapping across the body. **double-check** verify twice or in two ways. **double chin** a chin with a fold of loose flesh below it. **double-chinned** having a double chin. **double concerto** a concerto for two solo instruments. **double cream** thick cream with a high fat-content. **double-cross** *v.tr.* deceive or betray (a person one is supposedly helping). ● *n.* an act of doing this. **double-crosser** a person who double-crosses. **double dagger** *Printing* = *double obelus.* **double-dealer** a deceiver. **double-dealing** *n.* deceit, esp. in business. ● *adj.* deceitful; practising deceit. **double-decker 1** esp. *Brit.* a bus having an upper and lower deck. **2** *colloq.* anything consisting of two layers. **double-declutch** see DECLUTCH. **double decomposition** *Chem.* a chemical reaction involving exchange of radicals between two reactants: also called METATHESIS. **double density** *Computing* designating a storage device, esp. a disk, having twice the basic capacity. **double dummy** *Bridge* play with two hands exposed, allowing every card to be located. **double Dutch** *Brit. colloq.* incomprehensible talk. **double-dyed** deeply affected with guilt. **double eagle 1** a figure of a two-headed eagle. **2** *US Golf* = ALBATROSS. **3** *US* a coin worth twenty dollars. **double-edged 1** having two functions or (often contradictory) applications. **2** (of a knife etc.) having two cutting-edges. **double entry** a system of bookkeeping in which each transaction is entered as a debit in one account and a credit in another. **double exposure** *Photog.* the accidental or deliberate repeated exposure of a plate, film, etc. **double-faced 1** insincere. **2** (of a fabric or material) finished on both sides so that either may be used as the right side. **double fault** (in lawn tennis) two consecutive faults in serving. **double feature** a cinema programme with two full-length films. **double figures** the numbers from 10 to 99. **double first** *Brit.* **1** first-class honours in two subjects or examinations at a university. **2** a person achieving this. **double-fronted** (of a house) with principal windows on either side of the front door. **double-ganger** = DOPPELGÄNGER. **double glazing 1** a window consisting of two layers of glass with a space between them, designed to reduce loss of heat and exclude noise. **2** the provision of this. **double Gloucester** a kind of hard cheese orig. made in Gloucestershire. **double header 1** a train pulled by two locomotives coupled together. **2** *US* two games etc. in succession between the same opponents. **3** *Austral. colloq.* a coin with a head on both sides. **double helix** a pair of parallel helices with a common axis, esp. in the structure of the DNA molecule. **double-jointed** having joints that allow unusual bending of the fingers, limbs, etc. **double-lock** lock by a double turn of the key. **double negative** *Gram.* a negative statement containing two negative elements (e.g. *didn't say nothing*). ¶ Considered ungrammatical in standard English. **double obelus** (or **obelisk**) *Printing* a sign (‡) used to introduce a reference. **double or quits** a gamble to decide whether a player's loss or debt be doubled or cancelled. **double-park** park (a vehicle) alongside one that is already parked at the roadside. **double play** *Baseball* putting out two runners. **double pneumonia** pneumonia affecting both lungs. **double-quick** very quick or quickly. **double refraction** *Optics* refraction forming two separate rays from a single incident ray. **double rhyme** a rhyme including two syllables. **double salt** *Chem.* a salt composed of two simple salts and having different crystal properties from either. **double saucepan** *Brit.* = *double boiler.* **double shuffle** *Dancing* a shuffle executed twice with one foot and then twice with the other. **double standard 1** a rule or principle applied more strictly to some people than to others (or to oneself). **2** bimetallism. **double star** two stars actually or apparently very close together. **double-stopping** *Mus.* the sounding of two strings at once on a violin etc. **double take** a delayed reaction to a situation etc. immediately after one's first reaction. **double-talk** verbal expression that is (usu. deliberately) ambiguous or misleading. **double-think** the mental capacity to accept contrary opinions or beliefs at the same time esp. as a result of political indoctrination. **double time 1** payment of an employee at twice the normal rate. **2** *Mil.* the regulation running-pace. **double-tonguing** rapid articulation in playing a wind instrument. **double top** *Darts* a score of double twenty. **double up 1 a** bend or curl up. **b** cause to do this, esp. by a blow. **2** be overcome with pain or laughter. **3** share or assign to a room, quarters, etc., with another or others. **4** fold or become folded. **5** use winnings from a bet as stake for another. □□ **doubler** *n.* **doubly** *adv.* [ME f. OF *doble, duble* (n.), *dobler, dubler* (v.) f. L *duplus* DUPLE]

■ *adj.* **1** paired, coupled, duplicate(d), doubled; twofold. **2** twice. **6** dual, twofold, ambiguous; deceitful, dishonest, treacherous, traitorous, insincere, hypocritical, double-dealing, false. ● *n.* **2 a, b** twin, duplicate, copy, replica, facsimile, clone, counterpart, *doppelgänger*, look-alike, *colloq.* spitting image, the very spit; stand-in, understudy, reserve. ● *v.* **3 a** bend, fold, double up. **11** see RUN *v.* 1, 3. □ **at the double** quickly, briskly, chop-chop, on the run, at a run, double-quick, at full speed *or* tilt, *colloq.* p.d.q.; immediately, at once, without delay; see also *instantaneously* (INSTANTANEOUS). **bent double** see BENT[1] *adj.* 1. **double bind** dilemma, *colloq.* catch-22. **double-cross** (*v.*) defraud, swindle, hoodwink, trick, deceive, mislead, play false with, *colloq.* two-time; see also BETRAY 2, CHEAT *v.* 1a. (*n.*) see *betrayal* (BETRAY). **double-crosser** see *swindler* (SWINDLE). **double-dealer** see *swindler* (SWINDLE). **double-dealing** (*n.*) see DECEIT 1. (*adj.*) see DECEITFUL. **double Dutch** see GIBBERISH. **double-faced 1** see INSINCERE. **double-quick** see IMMEDIATELY *adv.* 1, *at the double* above. **double-talk** see AMBIGUITY 1a. **double up 1** see STOOP[1] *v.* 1. **2** see FLINCH[1] *v.*, LAUGH *v.* 1.

double entendre /do͞ob'l aantaándrə/ *n.* **1** a word or phrase open to two interpretations, one usu. *risqué* or indecent. **2** humour using such words or phrases. [obs. F, = double understanding]

■ see AMBIGUITY 1b.

doublet /dúblit/ *n.* **1** either of a pair of similar things, esp. either of two words of the same derivation but different sense (e.g. *fashion* and *faction*, *cloak* and *clock*). **2** *hist.* a man's short close-fitting jacket, with or without sleeves. **3** a historical or biblical account occurring twice in differing contexts, usu. traceable to different sources. **4** (in *pl.*) the same number on two dice thrown at once. **5** a pair of associated lines close together in a spectrum. **6** a combination of two simple lenses. [ME f. OF f. *double*: see DOUBLE]

doubloon /dublo͞on/ *n.* **1** *hist.* a Spanish gold coin. **2** (in *pl.*) *sl.* money. [F *doublon* or Sp. *doblón* (as DOUBLE)]

doublure /dooblyo͝or/ *n.* an ornamental lining, usu. leather, inside a book-cover. [F, = lining (*doubler* to line)]

doubt /dowt/ *n.* & *v.* ● *n.* **1** a feeling of uncertainty; an undecided state of mind (*be in no doubt about*; *have no doubt that*). **2** (often foll. by *of*, *about*) an inclination to disbelieve (*have one's doubts about*). **3** an uncertain state of things. **4** a lack of full proof or clear indication (*benefit of the doubt*). ● *v.* **1** *tr.* (often foll. by *whether*, *if*, *that* + clause; also foll. (after *neg.* or *interrog.*) by *but*, *but that*) feel uncertain or undecided about (*I doubt that you are right*; *I do not doubt but that you are wrong*). **2** *tr.* hesitate to believe or trust. **3** *intr.* (often foll. by *of*) feel uncertain or undecided; have doubts (*never doubted of success*). **4** *tr.* call in question. **5** *tr. Brit. archaic* or *dial.* rather think that; suspect or fear that (*I doubt we are late*). □ **beyond doubt** certainly. **doubting Thomas** an incredulous or sceptical person (after John 20: 24–29). **in doubt** uncertain; open to question. **no doubt** certainly; probably; admittedly. **without doubt** (or **a doubt**) certainly. □□ **doubtable** *adj.* **doubter** *n.* **doubtingly** *adv.* [ME *doute* f. OF *doute* (n.), *douter* (v.) f. L *dubitare* hesitate; mod. spelling after L]

■ *n.* **1** uncertainty, hesitation, misgiving, reservation(s), qualm(s), anxiety, worry, apprehension, disquiet, fear; indecision, indecisiveness, incertitude, irresolution; dubiousness, *literary* dubitation, dubiety. **2** distrust, mistrust, suspicion, incredulity, scepticism, doubtfulness, lack of faith *or* conviction. ● *v.* **2** disbelieve, discredit, mistrust, distrust, have misgivings about, question, suspect. **3** hesitate, be uncertain, entertain doubts, have reservations. **5** see SUSPECT *v.* 3. □ **beyond doubt** see *undoubtedly* (UNDOUBTED). **doubting Thomas** see NON-BELIEVER. **in doubt** see UNCERTAIN 1. **no doubt** see *undoubtedly* (UNDOUBTED), *probably* (PROBABLE). **without doubt** see *undoubtedly* (UNDOUBTED).

doubtful /dówtfo͝ol/ *adj.* **1** feeling doubt or misgivings; unsure or guarded in one's opinion. **2** causing doubt; ambiguous; uncertain in meaning etc. **3** unreliable (*a doubtful ally*). □□ **doubtfully** *adv.* **doubtfulness** *n.*
■ **1** sceptical, unconvinced, distrustful, mistrustful, suspicious, uncertain, unsure, undecided, hesitant, indecisive, *literary* dubitative. **2** in doubt, dubious, questionable, open to question, problematic, debatable, disputable, uncertain; unpredictable, indeterminate, unsettled, unresolved, conjectural; indefinite, unclear, obscure, vague, anybody's guess, up in the air. **3** see UNRELIABLE.

doubtless /dówtliss/ *adv.* (often qualifying a sentence) **1** certainly; no doubt. **2** probably. □□ **doubtlessly** *adv.*
■ **1** certainly, doubtlessly, undoubtedly, no doubt, indubitably, indisputably, unquestionably, surely, for certain, naturally, without (a) doubt, beyond *or* without (a shadow of) a doubt, truly, positively, absolutely, *colloq.* for sure. **2** probably, most *or* very likely, in all probability *or* likelihood, presumably.

douce /do͞oss/ *adj. Sc.* sober, gentle, sedate. [ME f. OF *dous douce* f. L *dulcis* sweet]

douche /do͞osh/ *n.* & *v.* ● *n.* **1** a jet of liquid applied to part of the body for cleansing or medicinal purposes. **2** a device for producing such a jet. ● *v.* **1** *tr.* treat with a douche. **2** *intr.* use a douche. [F f. It. *doccia* pipe f. *docciare* pour by drops ult. f. L *ductus*: see DUCT]

dough /dō/ *n.* **1** a thick mixture of flour etc. and liquid (usu. water), for baking into bread, pastry, etc. **2** *sl.* money. [OE *dāg* f. Gmc]
■ **2** see MONEY 1.

doughboy /dṓboy/ *n.* **1** a boiled dumpling. **2** *US colloq.* a United States infantryman, esp. in the war of 1914–18.
■ **2** see SOLDIER *n.*

doughnut /dṓnut/ *n.* (*US* **donut**) **1** a small fried cake of sweetened dough, usu. in the shape of a ball or ring. **2** a ring-shaped object, esp. *Physics* a vacuum chamber for acceleration of particles in a betatron or synchrotron.

doughty /dówti/ *adj.* (**doughtier**, **doughtiest**) *archaic* or *joc.* valiant, stout-hearted. □□ **doughtily** *adv.* **doughtiness** *n.* [OE *dohtig* var. of *dyhtig* f. Gmc]
■ see STOUT *adj.* 3.

doughy /dṓ-i/ *adj.* (**doughier**, **doughiest**) **1** having the form or consistency of dough. **2** pale and sickly in colour. □□ **doughiness** *n.*

Douglas fir /dúgləss/ *n.* (also **Douglas pine** or **spruce**) any large conifer of the genus *Pseudotsuga*, of Western N. America. [D. *Douglas*, Sc. botanist d. 1834]

doum /dowm, do͞om/ *n.* (in full **doum-palm**) a palm-tree, *Hyphaene thebaica*, with edible fruit. [Arab. *dawm*, *dūm*]

dour /door/ *adj.* severe, stern, or sullenly obstinate in manner or appearance. □□ **dourly** *adv.* **dourness** *n.* [ME (orig. Sc.), prob. f. Gael. *dúr* dull, obstinate, perh. f. L *durus* hard]
■ sullen, sour, unfriendly, forbidding, hard, tough, austere, severe, hardy, inflexible, obstinate, stubborn, unyielding, uncompromising, strict, rigid, obdurate, stern, harsh, *colloq.* hard-nosed; gloomy, morose, grim.

douroucouli /do͝orooko͞oli/ *n.* (*pl.* **douroucoulis**) any nocturnal monkey of the genus *Aotus*, native to S. America, having large staring eyes. [Indian name]

douse /dowss/ *v.tr.* (also **dowse**) **1 a** throw water over. **b** plunge into water. **2** extinguish (a light). **3** *Naut.* **a** lower (a sail). **b** close (a porthole). [16th c.: perh. rel. to MDu., LG *dossen* strike]
■ **1** see SOAK *v.* 1. **2** see QUENCH 2.

dove[1] /duv/ *n.* **1** any bird of the family Columbidae, with short legs, small head, and large breast. **2** a gentle or innocent person. **3** *Polit.* an advocate of peace or peaceful policies (cf. HAWK[1]). **4** (**Dove**) *Relig.* a representation of the Holy Spirit (John 1:32). **5** a soft grey colour. □ **dove's-foot** a cranesbill, *Geranium molle*. **dove-tree** a tree with dovelike flowers, *Davidia involucrata*, native to China. □□ **dovelike** *adj.* [ME f. ON *dúfa* f. Gmc]

dove[2] *US past* and *past part.* of DIVE.

dovecote /dúvkot/ *n.* (also **dovecot**) a shelter with nesting-holes for domesticated pigeons.

dovetail /dúvtayl/ *n.* & *v.* ● *n.* **1** a joint formed by a mortise with a tenon shaped like a dove's spread tail or a reversed wedge. **2** such a tenon. ● *v.* **1** *tr.* join together by means of a dovetail. **2** *tr.* & *intr.* (often foll. by *into*, *with*) fit readily together; combine neatly or compactly.
■ *v.* **2** see COMBINE *v.* 1, FIT[1] *v.* 1c.

dowager /dówəjər/ *n.* **1** a widow with a title or property derived from her late husband (*Queen dowager*; *dowager duchess*). **2** *colloq.* a dignified elderly woman. [OF *douag(i)ere* f. *douage* (as DOWER)]

dowdy /dówdi/ *adj.* & *n.* ● *adj.* (**dowdier**, **dowdiest**) **1** (of clothes) unattractively dull; unfashionable. **2** (of a person, esp. a woman) dressed in dowdy clothes. ● *n.* (*pl.* **-ies**) a dowdy woman. □□ **dowdily** *adv.* **dowdiness** *n.* [ME *dowd* slut, of unkn. orig.]
■ *adj.* **1** drab, dull, shabby, tatty, unseemly, unbecoming, *esp. US colloq.* tacky; old-fashioned, unfashionable. **2** frowzy, frumpy, frumpish. ● *n.* frump.

dowel /dówəl/ *n.* & *v.* ● *n.* a headless peg of wood, metal, or plastic for holding together components of a structure. ● *v.tr.* (**dowelled**, **dowelling**; *US* **doweled**, **doweling**) fasten with a dowel or dowels. [ME f. MLG *dovel*: cf. THOLE[1]]
■ *n.* see PEG *n.*

dowelling /dówəling/ *n.* (*US* **doweling**) round rods for cutting into dowels.

dower /dowr/ *n.* & *v.* ● *n.* **1** a widow's share for life of her husband's estate. **2** *archaic* a dowry. **3** a natural gift or talent. ● *v.tr.* **1** *archaic* give a dowry to. **2** (foll. by *with*) endow with talent etc. □ **dower house** *Brit.* a smaller house near a big one, forming part of a widow's dower. □□ **dowerless** *adj.* [ME f. OF *douaire* f. med.L *dotarium* f. L *dos dotis*]

Dow–Jones index /dowjṓnz/ *n.* (also **Dow–Jones average**) a figure based on the average price of selected stocks, indicating the relative price of shares on the New York Stock Exchange. [C. H. *Dow* d. 1902 & E. D. *Jones* d. 1920, Amer. economists]

down[1] /down/ *adv.*, *prep.*, *adj.*, *v.*, & *n.* ● *adv.* (*superl.* **downmost**) **1** into or towards a lower place, esp. to the ground (*fall down*; *knelt down*). **2** in a lower place or position (*blinds were down*). **3** to or in a place regarded as lower, esp.: **a** southwards. **b** *Brit.* away from a major city or a university. **4 a** in or into a low or weaker position, mood, or condition (*hit a man when he's down*; *many down with colds*). **b** *Brit.* in a position of lagging or loss (*our team was three goals down*; *£5 down on the transaction*). **c** (of a computer system) out of action or unavailable for use (esp. temporarily). **5** from an earlier to a later time (*customs handed down*; *down to 1600*). **6** to a finer or thinner consistency or a smaller amount or size (*grind down*; *water down*; *boil down*). **7** cheaper; lower in price or value (*bread is down*; *shares are down*). **8** into a more settled state (*calm down*). **9** in writing; in or into recorded or listed form (*copy it down*; *I got it* *down on tape; you are down to speak next*). **10** (of part of a larger whole) paid, dealt with (*£5 down, £20 to pay; three down, six to go*). **11** *Naut.* **a** with the current or wind. **b** (of a ship's helm) with the rudder to windward. **12** inclusively of the lower limit in a series (*read down to the third paragraph*). **13** (as *int.*) lie down, put (something) down, etc. **14** (of a crossword clue or answer) read vertically (*cannot do five down*). **15** downstairs, esp. after rising (*is not down yet*). **16** swallowed (*could not get the pill down*). **17** *Amer. Football* (of the ball) out of play. ● *prep.* **1** downwards along, through, or into. **2** from top to bottom of. **3** along (*walk down the road; cut down the middle*). **4** at or in a lower part of (*situated down the river*). ● *adj.* (*superl.* **downmost**) **1** directed downwards. **2** *Brit.* of travel away from a capital or centre (*the down train; the down platform*). **3** *colloq.* unhappy, depressed. ● *v.tr. colloq.* **1** knock or bring down. **2** swallow (a drink). ● *n.* **1** an act of putting down (esp. an opponent in wrestling, or the ball in American football). **2** a reverse of fortune (*ups and downs*). **3** *colloq.* a period of depression. **4** the play of the first piece in dominoes. □ **be** (or **have a**) **down on** *colloq.* disapprove of; show animosity towards. **be down to 1** be attributable to. **2** be the responsibility of. **3** have used up everything except (*down to their last tin of rations*). **down and out 1** penniless, destitute. **2** *Boxing* unable to resume the fight. **down-and-out** *n.* a destitute person. **down at heel 1** (of a shoe) with the heel worn down. **2** (of a person) wearing such shoes; shabby, slovenly. **down draught** a downward draught, esp. one down a chimney into a room. **down grade 1** a descending slope of a road or railway. **2** a deterioration (see also DOWNGRADE). **down in the mouth** *colloq.* looking unhappy. **down-market** *adj.* & *adv. colloq.* towards or relating to the cheaper or less affluent sector of the market. **down on one's luck** *colloq.* **1** temporarily unfortunate. **2** dispirited by misfortune. **down payment** a partial payment made at the time of purchase. **down stage** *Theatr.* at or to the front of the stage. **down-stroke** a stroke made or written downwards. **down time** time during which a machine, esp. a computer, is out of action or unavailable for use. **down-to-earth** practical, realistic. **down to the ground** *colloq.* completely. **down tools** *colloq.* cease work, esp. to go on strike. **down town 1** into a town from a higher or outlying part. **2** *US* to or in the business part of a city (see also DOWNTOWN). **down under** *colloq.* in the antipodes, esp. Australia. **down wind** in the direction in which the wind is blowing (see also DOWNWIND). **down with** *int.* expressing strong disapproval or rejection of a specified person or thing. [OE *dūn*(*e*) f. *adūne* ADOWN]

■ *adv.* **1** see DOWNWARD *adv.* **7** cheaper, lower, reduced. ● *adj.* **3** see MISERABLE 1. ● *v.* **1** see *knock down* 1. **2** see SWALLOW[1] *v.* 1. ● *n.* **2** nadir, low point; (*downs*) bad times, hard times; misfortunes. **3** see DEPRESSION 1b. □ **be** (or **have a**) **down on** see DISAPPROVE. **be down to 1, 2** be up to; see also *attributable* (ATTRIBUTE). **down and out 1** indigent, poverty-stricken, poor, penniless, destitute, impoverished, *colloq.* on the skids, *US colloq.* on skid row *or* road, *Brit. sl.* skint, *US sl.* on the bum; see also BROKE. **down-and-out** derelict, beggar, outcast, tramp, vagrant, vagabond; see also BUM[2] *n.* **down at heel 2** see SHABBY 1, 2. **down grade 2** see DECLINE *n.* 2. **down in the mouth** see UNHAPPY 1. **down-market** see CHEAP *adj.* 1, 2, INFERIOR *adj.* 2. **down on one's luck** see UNFORTUNATE *adj.* 1. **down-to-earth** see PRACTICAL *adj.* 3. **down to the ground** see *completely* (COMPLETE). **down tools** stop work; go on strike, strike, go out, walk out, *Brit.* come out.

down[2] /down/ *n.* **1 a** the first covering of young birds. **b** a bird's under-plumage, used in cushions etc. **c** a layer of fine soft feathers. **2** fine soft hair esp. on the face. **3** short soft hairs on some leaves, fruit, seeds, etc. **4** a fluffy substance, e.g. thistledown. [ME f. ON *dúnn*]

■ **1, 4** see FLUFF *n.* 1.

down[3] /down/ *n.* **1** an area of open rolling land. **2** (in *pl.*; usu. prec. by *the*) **a** undulating chalk and limestone uplands esp. in S. England, with few trees and used mainly for pasture. **b** (**Downs**) a part of the sea (opposite the North Downs) off E. Kent. □□ **downy** *adj.* [OE *dūn* perh. f. OCelt.]

■ **1** see PLAIN *n.*

downbeat /dównbeet/ *n.* & *adj.* ● *n. Mus.* an accented beat, usu. the first of the bar. ● *adj.* **1** pessimistic, gloomy. **2** relaxed.

■ *n.* see RHYTHM 1, 2.

downcast /dównkaast/ *adj.* & *n.* ● *adj.* **1** (of eyes) looking downwards. **2** (of a person) dejected. ● *n.* a shaft dug in a mine for extra ventilation.

■ *adj.* **2** see *dejected* (DEJECT).

downcomer /dównkummər/ *n.* a pipe for downward transport of water or gas.

downer /dównər/ *n. sl.* **1** a depressant or tranquillizing drug, esp. a barbiturate. **2** a depressing person or experience; a failure. **3** = DOWNTURN.

■ **1** see TRANQUILLIZER.

downfall /dównfawl/ *n.* **1 a** a fall from prosperity or power. **b** the cause of this. **2** a sudden heavy fall of rain etc.

■ **1** fall, collapse; ruin, undoing, débâcle, degradation, defeat, overthrow, breakdown.

downfold /dównfōld/ *n. Geol.* a syncline.

downgrade *v.* & *n.* & *v.tr.* ● *v.tr.* /dówngráyd/ **1** make lower in rank or status. **2** speak disparagingly of. ● *n.* /dówngrayd/ *US* a downward grade. □ **on the downgrade** *US* in decline.

■ *v.* **1** demote, dethrone, humble, lower, reduce, displace, depose, dispossess, *Naut.* disrate, *colloq.* bring *or* take down a peg (or two), *esp. US colloq.* bust. **2** belittle, minimize, play down, decry, denigrate, run down, downplay; see also DISPARAGE 1. ● *n.* descent, decline, declination, (downward) slope, gradient. □ **on the downgrade** see *on the decline* (DECLINE).

downhearted /dównhaártid/ *adj.* dejected; in low spirits. □□ **downheartedly** *adv.* **downheartedness** *n.*

■ discouraged, depressed, low-spirited, dispirited, miserable, blue, downcast, dejected *colloq.* down in the mouth; see also SAD 1.

downhill *adv.*, *adj.*, & *n.* ● *adv.* /dównhíl/ in a descending direction, esp. towards the bottom of an incline. ● *adj.* /dównhíl/ **1** sloping down, descending. **2** declining; deteriorating. ● *n.* /dównhil/ **1** *Skiing* a downhill race. **2** a downward slope. **3** a decline. □ **go downhill** *colloq.* decline, deteriorate (in health, state of repair, moral state, etc.).

■ □ **go downhill** see DETERIORATE.

downland /dównlənd/ *n.* = DOWN[3].

download /dównlōd/ *v.tr. Computing* transfer (data) from one storage device or system to another (esp. smaller remote one).

downmost /dównmōst/ *adj.* & *adv.* the furthest down.

downpipe /dównpīp/ *n. Brit.* a pipe to carry rainwater from a roof to a drain or to ground level.

■ see SPOUT *n.* 1a.

downplay /dównpláy/ *v.tr.* play down; minimize the importance of.

■ see MINIMIZE 2.

downpour /dównpor/ *n.* a heavy fall of rain.

■ rainstorm, deluge, inundation, downfall, cloudburst, thunderstorm, torrent, *chiefly US* thunder-shower.

downright /dównrīt/ *adj.* & *adv.* ● *adj.* **1** plain, definite, straightforward, blunt. **2** utter, complete (*a downright lie; downright nonsense*). ● *adv.* thoroughly, completely, positively (*downright rude*). □□ **downrightness** *n.*

■ *adj.* **1** direct, straightforward, plain, frank, open, candid, plain-spoken, explicit, blunt, brash, bluff, outspoken, unreserved, unabashed, unrestrained, unconstrained, bold. **2** utter, unambiguous, out-and-out, outright, absolute; see also COMPLETE *adj.* 3. ● *adv.* completely, totally, thoroughly, certainly, (most) assuredly, positively, definitely, absolutely, unconditionally, unequivocally; very, extremely, unqualifiedly, uncompromisingly, unmitigatedly, utterly, unquestionably, undoubtedly, indubitably; see also *profoundly* (PROFOUND).

downscale /dównskáyl/ *v.* & *adj. US* ● *v.tr.* reduce or restrict in size, scale, or extent. ● *adj.* at the lower end of a scale, esp. a social scale; inferior.

downside /dównsīd/ *n.* a downward movement of share prices etc.

downspout /dównspowt/ *n. US* = DOWNPIPE.

Down's syndrome /downz/ *n. Med.* a congenital disorder due to a chromosome defect, characterized by mental retardation and physical abnormalities (cf. MONGOLISM). [J. L. H. *Down*, Engl. physician d. 1896]

downstairs *adv., adj.,* & *n.* ● *adv.* /downstáirz/ **1** down a flight of stairs. **2** to or on a lower floor. ● *adj.*/dównstairz/ (also **downstair**) situated downstairs. ● *n.*/downstáirz/ the lower floor.
■ *adv.* see BELOW *adv.* 2a.

downstate /dównstáyt/ *adj., n.,* & *adv. US* ● *adj.* of or in a part of a state remote from large cities, esp. the southern part. ● *n.* a downstate area. ● *adv.* in a downstate area.

downstream /dównstréem/ *adv.* & *adj.* ● *adv.* in the direction of the flow of a stream etc. ● *adj.* moving downstream.

downthrow /dównthrō/ *n. Geol.* a downward dislocation of strata.

downtown /dówntówn/ *adj., n.,* & *adv. US* ● *adj.* of or in the lower or more central part, or the business part, of a town or city. ● *n.* a downtown area. ● *adv.* in or into a downtown area.

downtrodden /dówntródd'n/ *adj.* oppressed; badly treated; kept under.
■ subjugated, oppressed, burdened, afflicted, exploited, overwhelmed, cowed, overcome, beaten, abused, mistreated, maltreated, tyrannized.

downturn /dównturn/ *n.* a decline, esp. in economic or business activity.
■ see DECLINE *n.* 1, 4.

downward /dównwərd/ *adv.* & *adj.* ● *adv.* (also **downwards**) towards what is lower, inferior, less important, or later. ● *adj.* moving, extending, pointing, or leading downward. □□ **downwardly** *adv.*
■ *adv.* down, below, lower, downwardly. ● *adj.* declining, descending.

downwarp /dównwawrp/ *n. Geol.* a broad surface depression; a syncline.

downwind /dównwínd/ *adj.* & *adv.* in the direction in which the wind is blowing.

downy /dówni/ *adj.* (**downier, downiest**) **1 a** of, like, or covered with down. **b** soft and fluffy. **2** *Brit. sl.* aware, knowing. □□ **downily** *adv.* **downiness** *n.*
■ **1** see SOFT *adj.* 2.

dowry /dówri/ *n.* (*pl.* **-ies**) **1** property or money brought by a bride to her husband. **2** a talent, a natural gift. [ME f. AF *dowarie*, OF *douaire* DOWER]
■ **1** *dot; archaic* dower. **2** see ENDOWMENT 2.

dowse[1] /dowz/ *v.intr.* search for underground water or minerals by holding a Y-shaped stick or rod which dips abruptly when over the right spot. □ **dowsing-rod** such a stick or rod. □□ **dowser** *n.* [17th c.: orig. unkn.]

dowse[2] var. of DOUSE.

doxology /doksólləji/ *n.* (*pl.* **-ies**) a liturgical formula of praise to God. □□ **doxological** /-səlójik'l/ *adj.* [med.L *doxologia* f. Gk *doxologia* f. *doxa* glory + -LOGY]

doxy /dóksi/ *n.* (*pl.* **-ies**) *literary* **1** a lover or mistress. **2** a prostitute. [16th-c. cant: orig. unkn.]
■ **1** see MISTRESS 5. **2** see TART[2] *n.*

doyen /dóyən, dwaáyaN/ *n.* (*fem.* **doyenne** /doyén, dwaayén/) the senior member of a body of colleagues, esp. the senior ambassador at a court. [F (as DEAN[1])]
■ see LEADER 1.

doyley var. of DOILY.

doz. *abbr.* dozen.

doze /dōz/ *v.* & *n.* ● *v.intr.* sleep lightly; be half asleep. ● *n.* a short light sleep. □ **doze off** fall lightly asleep. □□ **dozer** *n.* [17th c.: cf. Da. *døse* make drowsy]
■ *v.* (take *or* have a) nap, catnap, drowse, sleep, *colloq.* snooze, have forty winks, grab some shut-eye, (have *or* take a) zizz, *Brit. sl.* kip, *poet. rhet.* slumber. ● *n.* nap, catnap, siesta, sleep, lie-down, *colloq.* snooze, forty winks, shut-eye, zizz, *Brit. sl.* kip. □ **doze off** fall asleep, *colloq.* drop *or* nod off; see also NOD *v.* 2.

dozen /dúzz'n/ *n.* **1** (prec. by *a* or a number) (*pl.* **dozen**) twelve, regarded collectively (*a dozen eggs; two dozen packets; ordered three dozen*). **2** a set or group of twelve (*packed in dozens*). **3** *colloq.* about twelve, a fairly large indefinite number. **4** (in *pl.*; usu. foll. by *of*) *colloq.* very many (*made dozens of mistakes*). **5** (**the dozens**) a Black American game or ritualized exchange of verbal insults. □ **by the dozen** in large quantities. **talk nineteen to the dozen** *Brit.* talk incessantly. □□ **dozenth** *adj.* & *n.* [ME f. OF *dozeine*, ult. f. L *duodecim* twelve]
■ **4** (*dozens*) see SCORE *n.* 3.

dozer /dṓzər/ *n. colloq.* = BULLDOZER. [abbr.]

dozy /dṓzi/ *adj.* (**dozier, doziest**) **1** drowsy; tending to doze. **2** *Brit. colloq.* stupid or lazy. □□ **dozily** *adv.* **doziness** *n.*
■ **1** see SLEEPY 1. **2** see STUPID *adj.* 1, 5.

DP *abbr.* **1** data processing. **2** displaced person.
■ **2** see OUTCAST *n.*

D.Phil. *abbr.* Doctor of Philosophy.

DPP *abbr.* (in the UK) Director of Public Prosecutions.

Dr *abbr.* **1** Doctor. **2** Drive. **3** debtor.

dr. *abbr.* **1** drachm(s). **2** drachma(s). **3** dram(s).

drab[1] /drab/ *adj.* & *n.* ● *adj.* (**drabber, drabbest**) **1** dull, uninteresting. **2** of a dull brownish colour. ● *n.* **1** drab colour. **2** monotony. □□ **drably** *adv.* **drabness** *n.* [prob. f. obs. *drap* cloth f. OF f. LL *drappus*, perh. of Celt. orig.]
■ *adj.* **1** dull, colourless, dreary, dingy, lacklustre, lustreless, dismal, cheerless, grey, sombre; see also BORING. ● *n.* **2** see TEDIUM 1.

drab[2] see DRIBS AND DRABS.

drab[3] /drab/ *n.* **1** a slut; a slattern. **2** a prostitute. [perh. rel. to LG *drabbe* mire, Du. *drab* dregs]

drabble /drább'l/ *v.intr.* & *tr.* become or make dirty and wet with water or mud. [ME f. LG *drabbelen* paddle in water or mire: cf. DRAB[3]]

drachm /dram/ *n. Brit.* a weight or measure formerly used by apothecaries, equivalent to 60 grains or one eighth of an ounce, or (in full **fluid drachm**) 60 minims, one eighth of a fluid ounce. [ME *dragme* f. OF *dragme* or LL *dragma* f. L *drachma* f. Gk *drakhmē* Attic weight and coin]

drachma /drákmə/ *n.* (*pl.* **drachmas** or **drachmae** /-mee/) **1** the chief monetary unit of Greece. **2** a silver coin of ancient Greece. [L f. Gk *drakhmē*]

drack /drak/ *adj. Austral. sl.* **1** (esp. of a woman) unattractive. **2** dismal, dull. [20th c.: orig. unkn.]

dracone /drákkōn/ *n.* a large flexible container for liquids, towed on the surface of the sea. [L *draco -onis* (as DRAGON)]

Draconian /drəkṓniən, dray-/ *adj.* (also **Draconic** /-kónnik/) very harsh or severe (esp. of laws and their application). [*Drakōn*, 7th-c. BC Athenian legislator]
■ see HARSH 2.

draff /draf, draaf/ *n.* **1** dregs, lees. **2** refuse. [ME, perh. repr. OE *dræf* (unrecorded)]

draft /draaft/ *n.* & *v.* ● *n.* **1 a** a preliminary written version of a speech, document, etc. **b** a rough preliminary outline of a scheme. **c** a sketch of work to be carried out. **2 a** a written order for payment of money by a bank. **b** the drawing of money by means of this. **3** (foll. by *on*) a demand made on a person's confidence, friendship, etc. **4 a** a party detached from a larger group for a special duty or purpose. **b** the selection of this. **5** *US* compulsory military service. **6** a reinforcement. **7** *US* = DRAUGHT. ● *v.tr.* **1** prepare a draft of (a document, scheme, etc.). **2** select for a special duty or purpose. **3** *US* conscript for military service. ▫▫ **draftee** /-tée/ *n.* **drafter** *n.* [phonetic spelling of DRAUGHT]

■ *n.* **1** plan, sketch, drawing, outline, blueprint, diagram. **2 a** bill of exchange, cheque, money order, postal order; letter of credit. **3** claim, demand. **4 a** division, unit; see also SQUAD. **5** military service, conscription, call-up, *Brit. hist.* national service, *US hist.* selective service. ● *v.* **1** sketch (out), delineate, outline, design, plan, frame, block out, draw (up). **2** see APPOINT 1. **3** recruit, call up, conscript, *US* induct.

draftsman /dráaftsmən/ *n.* (*pl.* **-men**) **1** a person who drafts documents. **2** = DRAUGHTSMAN 1. [phonetic spelling of DRAUGHTSMAN]

drafty *US* var. of DRAUGHTY.

drag /drag/ *v.* & *n.* ● *v.* (**dragged, dragging**) **1** *tr.* pull along with effort or difficulty. **2 a** *tr.* allow (one's feet, tail, etc.) to trail along the ground. **b** *intr.* trail along the ground. **c** *intr.* (of time etc.) go or pass heavily or slowly or tediously. **3 a** *intr.* (usu. foll. by *for*) use a grapnel or drag (to find a drowned person or lost object). **b** *tr.* search the bottom of (a river etc.) with grapnels, nets, or drags. **4** *tr.* (often foll. by *to*) *colloq.* take (a person to a place etc., esp. against his or her will). **5** *intr.* (foll. by *on, at*) draw on (a cigarette etc.). **6** *intr.* (often foll. by *on*) continue at tedious length. ● *n.* **1 a** an obstruction to progress. **b** *Aeron.* the longitudinal retarding force exerted by air. **c** slow motion; impeded progress. **d** an iron shoe for retarding a horse-drawn vehicle downhill. **2** *colloq.* a boring or dreary person, duty, performance, etc. **3 a** a strong-smelling lure drawn before hounds as a substitute for a fox. **b** a hunt using this. **4** an apparatus for dredging or recovering drowned persons etc. from under water. **5** = *drag-net*. **6** *sl.* a draw on a cigarette etc. **7** *sl.* **a** women's clothes worn by men. **b** a party at which these are worn. **c** clothes in general. **8** an act of dragging. **9 a** *sl.* a motor car. **b** (in full **drag race**) an acceleration race between cars usu. for a quarter of a mile. **10** *US sl.* influence, pull. **11** *US sl.* a street or road (*the main drag*). **12** *hist.* a private vehicle like a stagecoach, drawn by four horses. ▫ **drag anchor** (of a ship) move from a moored position when the anchor fails to hold. **drag-anchor** *n.* = *sea anchor*. **drag one's feet** (or **heels**) be deliberately slow or reluctant to act. **drag-hound** a hound used to hunt with a drag. **drag in** introduce (a subject) irrelevantly. **drag-line** an excavator with a bucket pulled in by a wire rope. **drag-net 1** a net drawn through a river or across ground to trap fish or game. **2** a systematic hunt for criminals etc. **drag out** protract. **drag queen** *sl.* a male homosexual transvestite. **drag through the mud** see MUD. **drag up** *colloq.* **1** deliberately mention (an unwelcome subject). **2** rear (a child) roughly and without proper training. [ME f. OE *dragan* or ON *draga* DRAW]

■ *v.* **1** pull (along), haul, tow, tug, trail, lug. **6** go on, last, continue, be prolonged, be extended, be drawn out. ● *n.* **2** bore, nuisance, annoyance, pest, irritant, *colloq.* pain (in the neck), headache, bind, hassle, *disp.* aggravation; see also BOTHER *n.* 1. **8** pull, draw, tug. **10** see INFLUENCE *n.* **11** street, road, thoroughfare. ▫ **drag one's feet** (or **heels**) delay, procrastinate, hang back, stall, go slow, hold back. **drag in** drag up, bring up. **drag out** see *string out*. **drag through the mud** see SMEAR *v.* 3.

dragée /draázhay/ *n.* **1** a sugar-coated almond etc. **2** a small silver ball for decorating a cake. **3** a chocolate-coated sweet. [F: see DREDGE[2]]

draggle /drágg'l/ *v.* **1** *tr.* make dirty or wet or limp by trailing. **2** *intr.* hang trailing. **3** *intr.* lag; straggle in the rear. ▫ **draggle-tailed** (of a woman) with untidily trailing skirts. [DRAG + -LE[4]]

■ **3** see LAG[1] *v.*

draggy /drággi/ *adj.* (**draggier, draggiest**) *colloq.* **1** tedious. **2** unpleasant.

dragoman /drággəmən/ *n.* (*pl.* **dragomans** or **dragomen**) an interpreter or guide, esp. in countries speaking Arabic, Turkish, or Persian. [F f. It. *dragomano* f. med.Gk *dragomanos* f. Arab. *tarjumān* f. *tarjama* interpret, f. Aram. *targēm* f. Assyr. *targumânu* interpreter]

dragon /drággən/ *n.* **1** a mythical monster like a reptile, usu. with wings and claws and able to breathe out fire. **2** a fierce person, esp. a woman. **3** (in full **flying dragon**) a lizard, *Draco volans*, with a long tail and membranous winglike structures. Also called *flying lizard*. ▫ **dragon's blood** a red gum that exudes from the fruit of some palms and the dragon-tree. **dragon's teeth** *Mil. colloq.* obstacles resembling teeth pointed upwards, used esp. against tanks. **dragon-tree** a tree, *Dracaena draco*, native to the Canary Isles. [ME f. OF f. L *draco -onis* f. Gk *drakōn* serpent]

■ **1** see MONSTER 1. **2** see SHREW.

dragonet /drággənit/ *n.* any marine spiny fish of the family Callionymidae, the males of which are brightly coloured. [ME f. F, dimin. of DRAGON]

dragonfish /drággənfish/ *n.* (*pl.* same or **-fishes**) any marine deep-water fish of the family Stomiatidae, having a long slender body and a barbel on the chin with luminous tissue, serving to attract prey.

dragonfly /drággənflī/ *n.* (*pl.* **-ies**) any of various insects of the order Odonata, having a long slender body and two pairs of large transparent wings usu. spread while resting.

dragonnade /drággənáyd/ *n.* & *v.* ● *n.* a persecution by use of troops, esp. (in *pl.*) of French Protestants under Louis XIV by quartering dragoons on them. ● *v.tr.* subject to a dragonnade. [F f. *dragon*: see DRAGOON]

dragoon /drəgóon/ *n.* & *v.* ● *n.* **1** a cavalryman (orig. a mounted infantryman armed with a carbine). **2** a rough fierce fellow. **3** a variety of pigeon. ● *v.tr.* **1** (foll. by *into*) coerce into doing something, esp. by use of strong force. **2** persecute, esp. with troops. [orig. = carbine (thought of as breathing fire) f. F *dragon* DRAGON]

dragster /drágstər/ *n.* a car built or modified to take part in drag races.

drail /drayl/ *n.* a fish-hook and line weighted with lead for dragging below the surface of the water. [app. var. of TRAIL]

drain /drayn/ *v.* & *n.* ● *v.* **1** *tr.* draw off liquid from, esp.: **a** make (land etc.) dry by providing an outflow for moisture. **b** (of a river) carry off the superfluous water of (a district). **c** remove purulent matter from (an abscess). **2** *tr.* (foll. by *off, away*) draw off (liquid) esp. by a pipe. **3** *intr.* (foll. by *away, off, through*) flow or trickle away. **4** *intr.* (of a wet cloth, a vessel, etc.) become dry as liquid flows away (*put it there to drain*). **5** *tr.* (often foll. by *of*) exhaust or deprive (a person or thing) of strength, resources, property, etc. **6** *tr.* **a** drink (liquid) to the dregs. **b** empty (a vessel) by drinking the contents. ● *n.* **1 a** a channel, conduit, or pipe carrying off liquid, esp. an artificial conduit for water or sewage. **b** a tube for drawing off the discharge from an abscess etc. **2** a constant outflow, withdrawal, or expenditure (*a great drain on my resources*). ▫ **down the drain** *colloq.* lost, wasted. **laugh like a drain** laugh copiously; guffaw. [OE *drē(a)hnian* f. Gmc]

■ *v.* **2** (*drain off* or *away*) draw off, tap, extract, remove, take away, withdraw, pump off *or* out. **3** seep, trickle (away), drip, flow from *or* out of, disappear, ebb, leach (away). **4** dry, dry off, get *or* become dry. **5** sap, exhaust, deplete, bleed (white); weaken, debilitate, impair, cripple; see also DEPRIVE 1. **6 a** drink up *or* down, swallow, finish, *literary* quaff. ● *n.* **1 a** ditch, channel, trench, culvert, conduit, pipe, drainpipe, gutter, outlet, watercourse; sewer, cloaca, soil pipe. **2** depletion, reduction, sap, strain, drag; outflow, withdrawal, expenditure, disbursement. □ **down the drain** wasted, gone, thrown away, lost, *sl.* up the spout. **laugh like a drain** see LAUGH *v.* 1.

drainage /dráynij/ *n.* **1** the process or means of draining (*the land has poor drainage*). **2** a system of drains, artificial or natural. **3** what is drained off, esp. sewage.

drainboard /dráynbord/ *n. US* = DRAINING-BOARD.

drainer /dráynər/ *n.* **1** a device for draining; anything on which things are put to drain, e.g. a draining-board. **2** a person who drains.

draining-board /dráyningbord/ *n.* a sloping usu. grooved surface beside a sink, on which washed dishes etc. are left to drain.

drainpipe /dráynpīp/ *n.* **1** a pipe for carrying off water, sewage, etc., from a building. **2** (*attrib.*) (of trousers etc.) very narrow. **3** (in *pl.*) very narrow trousers.

drake /drayk/ *n.* a male duck. [ME prob. f. Gmc]

Dralon /dráylon/ *n. propr.* **1** a synthetic acrylic fibre used in textiles. **2** a fabric made from this. [after NYLON]

dram /dram/ *n.* **1** a small drink of spirits. **2** = DRACHM. [ME f. OF *drame* or med.L *drama, dragma*: cf. DRACHM]

■ **1** see DRINK *n.* 2b.

drama /draáamə/ *n.* **1** a play for acting on stage or for broadcasting. **2** (often prec. by *the*) the art of writing and presenting plays. **3** an exciting or emotional event, set of circumstances, etc. **4** dramatic quality (*the drama of the situation*). [LL f. Gk *drama -atos* f. *draō* do]

■ **1** play, stage play, (stage) show, (theatrical) piece, (stage) production. **2** dramaturgy, stagecraft, dramatics, theatre art(s), acting, theatre, dramatic art(s), the stage. **3** event, *colloq.* (big) thing; theatricals; see also FUSS *n.* 1, 2a. **4** theatricalism, theatricality, histrionics, dramatics, staginess, theatrics.

dramatic /drəmáttik/ *adj.* **1** of drama or the study of drama. **2** (of an event, circumstance, etc.) sudden and exciting or unexpected. **3** vividly striking. **4** (of a gesture etc.) theatrical, overdone, absurd. □ **dramatic irony** = *tragic irony*. □□ **dramatically** *adv.* [LL *dramaticus* f. Gk *dramatikos* (as DRAMA)]

■ **1** theatrical, dramaturgical, dramaturgic, Thespian, histrionic, stage. **2, 3** vivid, sensational, startling, breathtaking, striking, noticeable, extraordinary, impressive, marked, shocking, graphic, effective, radical, drastic, serious; see also EXCITING, SUDDEN *adj.* **4** flamboyant, melodramatic, colourful, showy, stirring, spectacular; large, big; theatrical, absurd, histrionic, exaggerated, overdone.

dramatics /drəmáttiks/ *n.pl.* (often treated as *sing.*) **1** the production and performance of plays. **2** exaggerated or showy behaviour.

■ **1** see THEATRE 2a. **2** see DRAMA 4.

dramatis personae /drámmətiss persṓnī, -nee/ *n.pl.* (often treated as *sing.*) **1** the characters in a play. **2** a list of these. [L, = persons of the drama]

dramatist /drámmətist/ *n.* a writer of dramas.

■ playwright, dramaturge, screenwriter, scriptwriter, scenarist.

dramatize /drámmətīz/ *v.* (also **-ise**) **1 a** *tr.* adapt (a novel etc.) to form a stage play. **b** *intr.* admit of such adaptation. **2** *tr.* make a drama or dramatic scene of. **3** *tr.* (also *absol.*) express or react to in a dramatic way. □□ **dramatization** /-záysh'n/ *n.*

■ **3** exaggerate, overplay, overstate, overdo, overpitch, *colloq.* make a (big) thing (out) of, make a song and dance about; put it on, make a mountain out of a molehill, *colloq.* lay it on (thick), lay it on with a trowel, pile it on, go it strong, *sl.* ham (it) up.

dramaturge /drámmətürj/ *n.* **1** a specialist in theatrical production. **2** a dramatist. [F f. Gk *dramatourgos* (as DRAMA, *-ergos* worker)]

■ **2** see PLAYWRIGHT.

dramaturgy /drámmətürji/ *n.* **1** the art of theatrical production; the theory of dramatics. **2** the application of this. □□ **dramaturgic** /-túrjik/ *adj.* **dramaturgical** /-túrjik'l/ *adj.*

■ see DRAMA 2.

Drambuie /drambyóō-i, -bóō-i/ *n. propr.* a Scotch whisky liqueur. [Gael. *dram buidheach* satisfying drink]

drank *past* of DRINK.

drape /drayp/ *v.* & *n.* ● *v.tr.* **1** hang, cover loosely, or adorn with cloth etc. **2** arrange (clothes or hangings) carefully in folds. ● *n.* **1** (often in *pl.*) a curtain or drapery. **2** a piece of drapery. **3** the way in which a garment or fabric hangs. [ME f. OF *draper* f. *drap* f. LL *drappus* cloth]

■ *v.* **1** hang, festoon, swathe, deck, array, bedeck, adorn, ornament, decorate. ● *n.* **1** drapery, curtain.

draper /dráypər/ *n. Brit.* a retailer of textile fabrics. [ME f. AF, OF *drapier* (as DRAPE)]

drapery /dráypəri/ *n.* (*pl.* **-ies**) **1** clothing or hangings arranged in folds. **2** (often in *pl.*) a curtain or hanging. **3** *Brit.* cloth; textile fabrics. **4** *Brit.* the trade of a draper. **5** the arrangement of clothing in sculpture or painting. [ME f. OF *draperie* f. *drap* cloth]

■ **2** drapes, curtains; hanging, valance, tapestry, *portière*, *Theatr.* drop, *US* lambrequin, *hist.* arras.

drastic /drástik, draá-/ *adj.* having a strong or far-reaching effect; severe. □□ **drastically** *adv.* [Gk *drastikos* f. *draō* do]

■ serious, violent, severe, extreme, strong, powerful, all-embracing, sweeping, thorough, exhaustive, potent, fierce, forceful, vigorous, rigorous, harsh, radical, desperate, dire, *literary or archaic* puissant.

drat /drat/ *v.* & *int. colloq.* ● *v.tr.* (**dratted, dratting** (usu. as an exclam.)) curse, confound (*drat the thing!*). ● *int.* expressing anger or annoyance. □□ **dratted** *adj.* [for *'od* (= God) *rot*]

draught /draaft/ *n.* & *v.* (*US* **draft**) ● *n.* **1** a current of air in a confined space (e.g. a room or chimney). **2** pulling, traction. **3** *Naut.* the depth of water needed to float a ship. **4** the drawing of liquor from a cask etc. **5 a** a single act of drinking. **b** the amount drunk in this. **c** a dose of liquid medicine. **6** (in *pl.*; usu. treated as *sing.*) *Brit.* a game for two played with 12 pieces each on a draughtboard. **7 a** the drawing in of a fishing-net. **b** the fish taken at one drawing. **8** = DRAFT. ● *v.tr.* = DRAFT. □ **draught beer** beer drawn from a cask, not bottled. **draught-horse** a horse used for pulling heavy loads, esp. a cart or plough. **feel the draught** *colloq.* suffer from adverse (usu. financial) conditions. [ME *draht*, perh. f. ON *drahtr, dráttr* f. Gmc, rel. to DRAW]

■ *n.* **1** breeze, breath (of air), (light) wind, current (of air), puff (of air *or* wind). **5** drink, swallow, sip, gulp, potation, *colloq.* swig, *joc.* libation; nip, tot, dram, *colloq.* tipple; dose, portion, measure, quantity. □ **feel the draught** feel the pinch; see also BROKE.

draughtboard /draáftbord/ *n.* a chequered board, identical to a chessboard, used in draughts.

draughtsman /draáftsmən/ *n.* (*pl.* **-men**) **1** a person who makes drawings, plans, or sketches. **2** /draáftsman/ a piece in the game of draughts. **3** = DRAFTSMAN. □□ **draughtsmanship** *n.* [*draught's* + MAN]

■ **1** see DESIGNER 1. **2** see PIECE *n.* 5.

draughty /draáfti/ *adj.* (*US* **drafty**) (**-ier, -iest**) (of a room etc.) letting in sharp currents of air. □□ **draughtily** *adv.* **draughtiness** *n.*

■ see BREEZY 1.

Dravidian /drəvíddiən/ *n.* & *adj.* ● *n.* **1** a member of a dark-skinned aboriginal people of S. India and Sri Lanka (including the Tamils and Kanarese). **2** any of the group of languages spoken by this people. ● *adj.* of or relating to this people or group of languages. [Skr. *Dravida*, a province of S. India]

draw /draw/ *v.* & *n.* ● *v.* (*past* **drew** /drōō/; *past part.* **drawn** /drawn/) **1** *tr.* pull or cause to move towards or after one. **2** *tr.* pull (a thing) up, over, or across. **3** *tr.* pull (curtains etc.) open or shut. **4** *tr.* take (a person) aside, esp.

to talk to. **5** *tr.* attract; bring to oneself or to something; take in (*drew a deep breath; I felt drawn to her; drew my attention to the matter; draw him into conversation; the match drew large crowds*). **6** *intr.* (foll. by *at, on*) suck smoke from (a cigarette, pipe, etc.). **7** *tr.* **a** (also *absol.*) take out; remove (e.g. a tooth, a gun from a holster, etc.). **b** select by taking out (e.g. a card from a pack). **8** *tr.* obtain or take from a source (*draw a salary; draw inspiration; drew £100 from my account*). **9** *tr.* trace (a line, mark, furrow, or figure). **10 a** *tr.* produce (a picture) by tracing lines and marks. **b** *tr.* represent (a thing) by this means. **c** *absol.* make a drawing. **11** *tr.* (also *absol.*) finish (a contest or game) with neither side winning. **12** *intr.* make one's or its way, proceed, move, come (*drew near the bridge; draw to a close; the second horse drew level; drew ahead of the field; the time draws near*). **13** *tr.* infer, deduce (a conclusion). **14** *tr.* **a** elicit, evoke. **b** bring about, entail (*draw criticism; draw ruin upon oneself*). **c** induce (a person) to reveal facts, feelings, or talent (*refused to be drawn*). **d** (foll. by *to* + infin.) induce (a person) to do something. **e** *Cards* cause to be played (*drew all the trumps*). **15** *tr.* haul up (water) from a well. **16** *tr.* bring out (liquid from a vessel or blood from a wound). **17** *tr.* extract a liquid essence from. **18** *intr.* (of a chimney or pipe) promote or allow a draught. **19** *intr.* (of tea) infuse. **20 a** *tr.* obtain by lot (*drew the winner*). **b** *absol.* draw lots. **21** *intr.* (foll. by *on*) make a demand on a person, a person's skill, memory, imagination, etc. **22** *tr.* write out (a bill, cheque, or draft) (*drew a cheque on the bank*). **23** *tr.* frame (a document) in due form, compose. **24** *tr.* formulate or perceive (a comparison or distinction). **25** *tr.* (of a ship) require (a specified depth of water) to float in. **26** *tr.* disembowel (*hang, draw, and quarter; draw the fowl before cooking it*). **27** *tr. Hunting* search (cover) for game. **28** *tr.* drag (a badger or fox) from a hole. **29** *tr.* **a** protract, stretch, elongate (*long-drawn agony*). **b** make (wire) by pulling a piece of metal through successively smaller holes. **30** *tr.* **a** *Golf* drive (the ball) to the left (or, of a left-handed player, the right) esp. purposely. **b** *Bowls* cause (a bowl) to travel in a curve to the desired point. **31** *intr.* (of a sail) swell tightly in the wind. ● *n.* **1** an act of drawing. **2 a** a person or thing that draws custom, attention, etc. **b** the power to attract attention. **3** the drawing of lots, esp. a raffle. **4** a drawn game. **5** a suck on a cigarette etc. **6** the act of removing a gun from its holster in order to shoot (*quick on the draw*). **7** strain, pull. **8** *US* the movable part of a drawbridge. □ **draw back** withdraw from an undertaking. **draw a bead on** see BEAD. **draw bit** = *draw rein.* **draw a blank** see BLANK. **draw bridle** = *draw rein.* **draw a person's fire** attract hostility, criticism, etc., away from a more important target. **draw in 1 a** (of successive days) become shorter because of the changing seasons. **b** (of a day) approach its end. **c** (of successive evenings or nights) start earlier because of the changing seasons. **2** persuade to join, entice. **3** (of a train etc.) arrive at a station. **draw in one's horns** become less assertive or ambitious; draw back. **draw the line at** set a limit (of tolerance etc.) at. **draw lots** see LOT. **draw off 1** withdraw (troops). **2** drain off (a liquid), esp. without disturbing sediment. **draw on 1** approach, come near. **2** lead to, bring about. **3** allure. **4** put (gloves, boots, etc.) on. **draw out 1** prolong. **2** elicit. **3** induce to talk. **4** (of successive days) become longer because of the changing seasons. **5** (of a train etc.) leave a station etc. **6** write out in proper form. **7** lead out, detach, or array (troops). **draw rein** see REIN. **draw-sheet** a sheet that can be taken from under a patient without remaking the bed. **draw-string** a string that can be pulled to tighten the mouth of a bag, the waist of a garment, etc. **draw stumps** *Cricket* take the stumps out of the ground at the close of play. **draw one's sword against** attack. **draw up 1** compose or draft (a document etc.). **2** bring or come into regular order. **3** come to a halt. **4** make (oneself) stiffly erect. **5** (foll. by *with, to*) gain on or overtake. **draw-well** a deep well with a rope and a bucket. **quick on the draw** quick to act or react. [OE *dragan* f. Gmc]

■ *v.* **1** pull, tug, tow, drag, haul, lug. **5** attract, allure, lure; bring out *or* forth, elicit, pull. **6** take in, inhale, breathe (in), inspire, pull, suck in. **7 a** pull *or* take out, bring out, extract, remove; unsheathe. **b** choose, pick, select, take. **8** draw out, withdraw, take (out); receive, get, acquire, obtain, secure, procure. **9** see TRACE[1] *v.* 3. **10** sketch, paint; depict, portray, represent, outline, delineate, design, *archaic* limn. **12** see PROCEED *v.* 1. **13** (*draw the conclusion*) see INFER 1. **14 a** see ELICIT. **15** draw off, haul up. **16** draw off *or* out, bring out. **21** (*draw on*) employ, use, make use of, exploit, have resort *or* recourse to, resort to, fall back on, rely *or* depend on. **23** see *draw up* 1 below. **24** see PERCEIVE 2. **29** see *draw out* 1 below. ● *n.* **1** pull, tug, drag. **2 b** magnetism, attraction, lure, enticement, *colloq.* pull. **4** tie, stalemate, dead heat, deadlock. □ **draw back** retreat, recoil, shrink back, draw off, draw *or* pull in one's horns; see WITHDRAW 5. **draw in 1 a** shorten, get shorter. **2** see LURE[1] *v.* **3** arrive, pull in, come in. **draw off 1** see WITHDRAW 3. **2** tap, pour, decant. **draw on 1** come close *or* near, near, approach, advance, *archaic or dial.* draw nigh. **3** see ATTRACT 2. **draw out 1** extend, drag out, prolong, protract, lengthen, stretch, spin out. **2** see ELICIT. **4** lengthen, get longer. **5** leave, pull out, depart, go, set off, get away. **draw one's sword against** see ATTACK *v.* 1. **draw up 1** draft, compose, prepare, put down (in writing), frame, compile, put together, formulate, devise, contrive, draw. **2** arrange, deploy, position, order, rank, marshal. **3** halt, stop, pull up *or* over, come to a halt *or* stop.

drawback /dráwbak/ *n.* **1** a thing that impairs satisfaction; a disadvantage. **2** (foll. by *from*) a deduction. **3** an amount of excise or import duty paid back or remitted on goods exported. □ **drawback lock** a lock with a spring bolt that can be drawn back by an inside knob.

■ **1** disadvantage, hindrance, stumbling-block, obstacle, impediment, hurdle, obstruction, snag, problem, difficulty, hitch, catch, handicap, flaw, defect, *colloq.* fly in the ointment.

drawbridge /dráwbrij/ *n.* a bridge, esp. over water, hinged at one end so that it may be raised to prevent passage or to allow ships etc. to pass.

drawee /draweé/ *n.* the person on whom a draft or bill is drawn.

drawer *n.* **1** /dráwər/ a person or thing that draws, esp. a person who draws a cheque etc. **2** /drawr/ a boxlike storage compartment without a lid, sliding in and out of a frame, table, etc. (*chest of drawers*). **3** (in *pl.*) /drawrz/ an undergarment worn next to the body below the waist. □□ **drawerful** *n.* (*pl.* **-fuls**).

drawing /dráwing/ *n.* **1 a** the art of representing by line. **b** delineation without colour or with a single colour. **c** the art of representing with pencils, pens, crayons, etc., rather than paint. **2** a picture produced in this way. □ **back to the drawing-board** *colloq.* back to begin afresh (after earlier failure). **drawing-board** a board for spreading drawing-paper on. **drawing-paper** stout paper for drawing pictures etc. on. **drawing-pin** *Brit.* a flat-headed pin for fastening paper etc. (orig. drawing-paper) to a surface. **out of drawing** incorrectly depicted.

■ **2** picture, depiction, representation, sketch, plan, outline, design, composition, monochrome, cartoon.

drawing-room /dráwingro͝om, -ro͞om/ *n.* **1** a room for comfortable sitting or entertaining in a private house. **2** (*attrib.*) restrained; observing social proprieties (*drawing-room conversation*). **3** *US* a private compartment in a train. **4** *hist.* a levee, a formal reception esp. at court. [earlier *withdrawing-room*, because orig. used for women to withdraw to after dinner]

■ **1** see PARLOUR.

drawl /drawl/ *v.* & *n.* ● *v.* **1** *intr.* speak with drawn-out vowel sounds. **2** *tr.* utter in this way. ● *n.* a drawling utterance or way of speaking. □□ **drawler** *n.* [16th c.: prob. orig. cant, f. LG, Du. *dralen* delay, linger]

drawn /drawn/ *past part.* of DRAW. ● *adj.* **1** looking strained from fear, anxiety, or pain. **2** (of butter) melted. **3** (of a position in chess etc.) that will result in a draw if both players make the best moves available. □ **drawn-work** (or **drawn-thread-work**) ornamental work on linen etc., done by drawing out threads, usu. with additional needlework.
■ **1** haggard, worn out, tired, fatigued, strained, pinched, tense, exhausted.

dray[1] /dray/ *n.* **1** a low cart without sides for heavy loads, esp. beer-barrels. **2** *Austral.* & *NZ* a two-wheeled cart. □ **dray-horse** a large, powerful horse. [ME f. OE *dræge* drag-net, *dragan* DRAW]

dray[2] var. of DREY.

drayman /dráymən/ *n.* (*pl.* **-men**) a brewer's driver.

dread /dred/ *v.*, *n.*, & *adj.* ● *v.tr.* **1** (foll. by *that*, or *to* + infin.) fear greatly. **2** shrink from; look forward to with great apprehension. **3** be in great fear of. ● *n.* **1** great fear, apprehension, awe. **2** an object of fear or awe. ● *adj.* **1** dreaded. **2** *archaic* awe-inspiring, revered. [OE *ādrǣdan*, *ondrǣdan*]
■ *v.* **2, 3** fear, be afraid of, be in fear of, apprehend, flinch from, shrink *or* recoil from, cringe *or* quail *or* blench *or* wince at, view with horror *or* alarm. ● *n.* **1** fear, fright, fearfulness, trepidation, apprehension, apprehensiveness, awe, uneasiness, alarm, nervousness, qualm(s), queasiness, misgiving(s), dismay, worry, anxiety, consternation, concern, distress, perturbation, disquiet, aversion, horror, terror, panic. **2** see TERROR 1. ● *adj.* **1** feared, dreaded, dreadful, terrifying, terrible. **2** see AWESOME 1.

dreadful /drédfŏŏl/ *adj.* & *adv.* ● *adj.* **1** terrible; inspiring fear or awe. **2** *colloq.* troublesome, disagreeable; very bad. ● *adv.* *US colloq.* dreadfully, very. □□ **dreadfully** *adv.* **dreadfulness** *n.*
■ *adj.* **1** grievous, dire, horrible, horrendous, horrifying, horrid, monstrous, fearful, feared, frightful, dread, dreaded, frightening, shocking, alarming, appalling, fearsome, hideous, ghastly, atrocious, *poet.* awful. **2** bad, disagreeable, *colloq.* lousy, terrible, *sl.* rotten; see also AWFUL 1a, b, TROUBLESOME. □□ **dreadfully** see AWFULLY.

dreadlocks /drédloks/ *n.pl.* **1** a Rastafarian hairstyle in which the hair is twisted into tight braids or ringlets hanging down on all sides. **2** hair dressed in this way.

dreadnought /drédnawt/ *n.* **1** (usu. **Dreadnought**) *hist.* a type of battleship greatly superior in armament to all its predecessors (from the name of the first, launched in 1906). **2** *archaic* a fearless person. **3** *archaic* **a** a thick coat for stormy weather. **b** the cloth used for such coats.

dream /dreem/ *n.* & *v.* ● *n.* **1 a** a series of pictures or events in the mind of a sleeping person. **b** the act or time of seeing this. **c** (in full **waking dream**) a similar experience of one awake. **2** a day-dream or fantasy. **3** an ideal, aspiration, or ambition, esp. of a nation. **4** a beautiful or ideal person or thing. **5** a state of mind without proper perception of reality (*goes about in a dream*). ● *v.* (*past* and *past part.* **dreamt** /dremt, drempt/ or **dreamed**) **1** *intr.* experience a dream. **2** *tr.* imagine in or as if in a dream. **3** (usu. with *neg.*) **a** *intr.* (foll. by *of*) contemplate the possibility of, have any conception or intention of (*would not dream of upsetting them*). **b** *tr.* (often foll. by *that* + clause) think of as a possibility (*never dreamt that he would come*). **4** *tr.* (foll. by *away*) spend (time) unprofitably. **5** *intr.* be inactive or unpractical. **6** *intr.* fall into a reverie. □ **dream-time** *Austral.* the alcheringa. **dream up** imagine, invent. **like a dream** *colloq.* easily, effortlessly. □□ **dreamful** *adj.* **dreamless** *adj.* **dreamlike** *adj.* [ME f. OE *drēam* joy, music]
■ *n.* **2** reverie, day-dream, delusion, fantasy, hallucination, illusion, mirage, pipedream, (flight of) fancy, cloud-castle. **3** ideal, ambition, vision; see also ASPIRATION. **5** cloud, day-dream, different world, another world; cloud-land, cloud-cuckoo-land, dreamland. ● *v.* **1, 2** imagine, fancy, conjure up, hallucinate. **3 a** (*dream of*) think of, contemplate, entertain the thought of. **4** (*dream away*) see FRITTER[1]. □ **dream up** see *think up*. **like a dream** easily, effortlessly, without difficulty, without a hitch *or* hiccup, like a dream come true, like a charm; wonderfully, perfectly, successfully. □□ **dreamlike** unreal, fantastic, unbelievable, phantasmagorical, phantasmagoric, hallucinatory, surreal, illusional, delusive, delusory, illusory, illusive, insubstantial, unsubstantial, dreamy, imaginary, chimerical, fanciful, visionary.

dreamboat /dreémbōt/ *n.* *colloq.* **1** a very attractive or ideal person, esp. of the opposite sex. **2** a very desirable or ideal thing.
■ **1** see BEAUTY 3.

dreamer /dreémər/ *n.* **1** a person who dreams. **2** a romantic or unpractical person.
■ **2** fantasist, fantasizer, visionary, idealist, romantic, idealizer, Utopian; day-dreamer, escapist.

dreamland /dreémland/ *n.* an ideal or imaginary land.
■ see FAIRYLAND.

dreamy /dreémi/ *adj.* (**dreamier, dreamiest**) **1** given to day-dreaming; fanciful; unpractical. **2** dreamlike; vague; misty. **3** *colloq.* delightful; marvellous. **4** *poet.* full of dreams. □□ **dreamily** *adv.* **dreaminess** *n.*
■ **1** absent-minded, absent, far-away, abstracted, pensive, thoughtful; day-dreaming, musing, occupied; sleepy, drowsy, lazy; see also *idealistic* (IDEALISM). **2** dreamlike, vague, indefinite, indistinct, undefined, intangible, misty, shadowy, faint. **3** see DELIGHTFUL.

drear /dreer/ *adj. poet.* = DREARY. [abbr.]

dreary /dreéri/ *adj.* (**drearier, dreariest**) dismal, dull, gloomy. □□ **drearily** *adv.* **dreariness** *n.* [OE *drēorig* f. *drēor* gore: rel. to *drēosan* to drop f. Gmc]
■ dismal, joyless, cheerless, gloomy, bleak, sombre, doleful, depressing, melancholy, miserable, *poet.* drear; boring, lifeless, colourless, drab, dull, arid, dry, uninteresting, dead, monotonous, prosaic, tedious, tiresome, tiring, wearisome, wearying, humdrum, ordinary, vapid, run-of-the-mill, unstimulating, unexciting, banal, pedestrian, uninspired.

dreck /drek/ *n.* esp. *US sl.* rubbish, trash. [Yiddish *drek* f. G *Dreck* filth, dregs]

dredge[1] /drej/ *v.* & *n.* ● *v.* **1** *tr.* **a** (often foll. by *up*) bring up (lost or hidden material) as if with a dredge (*don't dredge all that up again*). **b** (often foll. by *away*, *up*, *out*) bring up or clear (mud etc.) from a river, harbour, etc. with a dredge. **2** *tr.* clean (a harbour, river, etc.) with a dredge. **3** *intr.* use a dredge. ● *n.* an apparatus used to scoop up oysters, specimens, etc., or to clear mud etc., from a river or sea bed. [15th-c. Sc. *dreg*, perh. rel. to MDu. *dregghe*]
■ *v.* **1 b** see WASH *v.* 10a.

dredge[2] /drej/ *v.tr.* **1** sprinkle with flour, sugar, etc. **2** (often foll. by *over*) sprinkle (flour, sugar, etc.) on. [obs. *dredge* sweetmeat f. OF *dragie*, *dragee*, perh. f. L *tragemata* f. Gk *tragēmata* spices]
■ powder, dust, flour.

dredger[1] /dréjər/ *n.* **1** a machine used for dredging rivers etc.; a dredge. **2** a boat containing this.

dredger[2] /dréjər/ *n.* a container with a perforated lid used for sprinkling flour, sugar, etc.

dree /dree/ *v.tr.* (**drees, dreed, dreeing**) *Sc.* or *archaic* endure. □ **dree one's weird** submit to one's destiny. [OE *drēogan* f. Gmc]

dreg /dreg/ *n.* **1** (usu. in *pl.*) **a** a sediment; grounds, lees, etc. **b** a worthless part; refuse (*the dregs of humanity*). **2** a small remnant (*not a dreg*). □ **drain** (or **drink**) **to the dregs** consume leaving nothing (*drained life to the dregs*). □□ **dreggy** *adj. colloq.* [ME prob. f. ON *dreggjar*]
■ **1** (*dregs*) **a** sediment, grounds, lees, deposit, draff, residue, solids, remains; precipitate. **b** outcasts, pariahs, losers; riff-raff, scum. **2** see BIT[1] 1.

drench /drench/ *v.* & *n.* ● *v.tr.* **1 a** wet thoroughly (*was drenched by the rain*). **b** saturate; soak (in liquid). **2** force (an animal) to take medicine. **3** *archaic* cause to drink. ● *n.* **1** a soaking; a downpour. **2** medicine administered to an animal. **3** *archaic* a medicinal or poisonous draught. [OE *drencan, drenc* f. Gmc: rel. to DRINK]

▪ *v.* **1** soak, saturate, wet, inundate, immerse, drown.

Dresden china /drézdən/ *n.* (also **Dresden porcelain**) **1** delicate and elaborate chinaware orig. made at Dresden in Germany, now made at nearby Meissen. **2** (*attrib.*) delicately pretty.

dress /dress/ *v.* & *n.* ● *v.* **1 a** *tr.* clothe; array (*dressed in rags; dressed her quickly*). **b** *intr.* wear clothes of a specified kind or in a specified way (*dresses well*). **2** *intr.* **a** put on clothes. **b** put on formal or evening clothes, esp. for dinner. **3** *tr.* decorate or adorn. **4** *tr. Med.* **a** treat (a wound) with ointment etc. **b** apply a dressing to (a wound). **5** *tr.* trim, comb, brush, or smooth (the hair). **6** *tr.* **a** clean and prepare (poultry, a crab, etc.) for cooking or eating. **b** add a dressing to (a salad etc.). **7** *tr.* apply manure etc. to a field, garden, etc. **8** *tr.* finish the surface of (fabric, building-stone, etc.). **9** *tr.* groom (a horse). **10** *tr.* curry (leather etc.). **11** *Mil.* **a** *tr.* correct the alignment of (troops etc.). **b** *intr.* (of troops) come into alignment. **12** *tr.* make (an artificial fly) for use in fishing. ● *n.* **1** a one-piece woman's garment consisting of a bodice and skirt. **2** clothing, esp. a whole outfit etc. (*fussy about his dress; wore the dress of a highlander*). **3** formal or ceremonial costume (*evening dress; morning dress*). **4** an external covering; the outward form (*birds in their winter dress*). □ **dress circle** the first gallery in a theatre, in which evening dress was formerly required. **dress coat** a man's swallow-tailed evening coat. **dress down** *colloq.* reprimand or scold. **dress length** a piece of material sufficient to make a dress. **dress out** attire conspicuously. **dress parade 1** *Mil.* a military parade in full dress uniform. **2** a display of clothes worn by models. **dress rehearsal** the final rehearsal of a play etc., wearing costume. **dress-shield** (or **-preserver**) a piece of waterproof material fastened in the armpit of a dress to protect it from sweat. **dress-shirt** a man's usu. starched white shirt worn with evening dress. **dress up 1** dress (oneself or another) elaborately for a special occasion. **2** dress in fancy dress. **3** disguise (unwelcome facts) by embellishment. [ME f. OF *dresser* ult. f. L *directus* DIRECT]

▪ *v.* **1 a** clothe, robe, outfit, fit out, garb, accoutre, array, deck out, bedeck, rig out, *archaic* apparel, *formal* attire, *poet.* bedizen. **2** get dressed, dress oneself; dress up, robe. **3** adorn, array, equip, deck out, bedeck, arrange; see also DECORATE 1, 3. **4** treat, medicate, *colloq.* doctor; bandage, swathe, bind (up). **6** clean; prepare, make ready. **9** see GROOM *v.* 1. ● *n.* **1** frock, gown. **2** outfit, costume, garb, garments, clothing, clothes, vestments, robes, *archaic* raiment, *colloq.* get-up, gear, *formal* attire, apparel, *Austral.* & *NZ sl.* mocker. □ **dress down** reprimand, scold, berate, rebuke, reprove, upbraid, haul (*or* call) over the coals, *colloq.* tell off, tear a person off a strip, *US colloq.* chew out; see also CASTIGATE. **dress up 1** dress, put on one's best bib and tucker, *colloq.* put on one's glad rags, *joc.* put on one's (Sunday) best. **2** put on a costume, disguise oneself, masquerade, camouflage oneself, put on fancy dress. **3** see EMBELLISH 2, MASK *v.* 2.

dressage /dréssaazh, -saaj/ *n.* the training of a horse in obedience and deportment, esp. for competition. [F f. *dresser* to train]

dresser[1] /dréssər/ *n.* **1** a kitchen sideboard with shelves above for displaying plates etc. **2** *US* a dressing-table or chest of drawers. [ME f. OF *dresseur* f. *dresser* prepare: cf. med.L *directorium*]

▪ **2** see BUREAU 1.

dresser[2] /dréssər/ *n.* **1** a person who assists actors to dress, takes care of their costumes, etc. **2** *Med.* a surgeon's assistant in operations. **3** a person who dresses elegantly or in a specified way (*a snappy dresser*).

dressing /dréssing/ *n.* **1** in senses of DRESS *v.* **2 a** an accompaniment to salads, usu. a mixture of oil with other ingredients; a sauce or seasoning (*French dressing*). **b** *US* stuffing. **3 a** a bandage for a wound. **b** ointment etc. used to dress a wound. **4** size or stiffening used to finish fabrics. **5** compost etc. spread over land (*a top dressing of peat*). □ **dressing-case** a case containing toiletries etc. **dressing-down** *colloq.* a scolding; a severe reprimand. **dressing-gown** a loose usu. belted robe worn over nightwear or while resting. **dressing-room 1** a room for changing the clothes etc. in a theatre, sports-ground, etc. **2** a small room attached to a bedroom, containing clothes. **dressing-station** esp. *Mil.* a place for giving emergency treatment to wounded people. **dressing-table** a table with a mirror, drawers, etc., used while applying make-up etc.

▪ **3 b** see SALVE *n.* 1.

dressmaker /drésmaykər/ *n.* a woman who makes clothes professionally. □□ **dressmaking** *n.*

▪ seamstress, tailor, couturier, couturière, modiste, clothier, outfitter, garment-maker, costumier.

dressy /dréssi/ *adj.* (**dressier, dressiest**) **1 a** fond of smart clothes. **b** overdressed. **c** (of clothes) stylish or elaborate. **2** over-elaborate (*the design is rather dressy*). □□ **dressiness** *n.*

▪ **1 b** formal, overdressed, dressed-up, *colloq.* over-the-top, OTT. **c** elegant, smart, stylish, fancy, chic, elaborate, fashionable, *colloq.* classy, ritzy, swish. **2** over-elaborate, *colloq.* over-the-top, OTT.

drew *past* of DRAW.

drey /dray/ *n.* (also **dray**) a squirrel's nest. [17th c.: orig. unkn.]

dribble /dríbb'l/ *v.* & *n.* ● *v.* **1** *intr.* allow saliva to flow from the mouth. **2** *intr.* & *tr.* flow or allow to flow in drops or a trickling stream. **3** *tr.* (also *absol.*) esp. *Football* & *Hockey* move (the ball) forward with slight touches of the feet, the stick, etc. ● *n.* **1** the act or an instance of dribbling. **2** a small trickling stream. □□ **dribbler** *n.* **dribbly** *adj.* [frequent. of obs. *drib*, var. of DRIP]

▪ *v.* **1** see SLAVER[2] *v.* **2** see TRICKLE *v.* ● *n.* **1** see SLAVER[2] *n.* 1. **2** see TRICKLE *n.*

driblet /dríblit/ *n.* **1 a** a small quantity. **b** a petty sum. **2** a thin stream; a dribble. [*drib* (see DRIBBLE) + -LET]

dribs and drabs /dríbz ənd drábz/ *n.pl. colloq.* small scattered amounts (*did the work in dribs and drabs*). [as DRIBBLE + *drab* redupl.]

dried *past* and *past part.* of DRY.

drier[1] *compar.* of DRY.

drier[2] /drīər/ *n.* (also **dryer**) **1** a machine for drying the hair, laundry, etc. **2** a substance mixed with oil-paint or ink to promote drying.

driest *superl.* of DRY.

drift /drift/ *n.* & *v.* ● *n.* **1 a** slow movement or variation. **b** such movement caused by a slow current. **2** the intention, meaning, scope, etc. of what is said etc. (*didn't understand his drift*). **3** a large mass of snow, sand, etc., accumulated by the wind. **4** esp. *derog.* a state of inaction. **5 a** *Naut.* a ship's deviation from its course, due to currents. **b** *Aeron.* an aircraft's deviation due to side winds. **c** a projectile's deviation due to its rotation. **d** a controlled slide of a racing car etc. **6** *Mining* a horizontal passage following a mineral vein. **7** a large mass of esp. flowering plants (*a drift of bluebells*). **8** *Geol.* **a** material deposited by the wind, a current of water, etc. **b** (**Drift**) Pleistocene ice detritus, e.g. boulder clay. **9** the movement of cattle, esp. a gathering on an appointed day to determine ownership etc. **10** a tool for enlarging or shaping a hole in metal. **11** *S.Afr.* a ford. ● *v.* **1** *intr.* be carried by or as if by a current of air or water. **2** *intr.* move or progress passively, casually, or aimlessly (*drifted into teaching*). **3 a** *tr.* & *intr.* pile or be piled by the wind into drifts. **b** *tr.* cover (a field, a road, etc.) with drifts. **4** *tr.* form or enlarge (a hole) with a drift. **5** *tr.* (of a current) carry. □ **drift-ice** ice driven or deposited by water. **drift-net** a large net for herrings etc., allowed to drift with the tide. □□ **driftage** *n.* [ME f. ON & MDu., MHG *trift* movement of cattle: rel. to DRIVE]

■ *n.* **1** see CURRENT *n.* **2** trend, tendency, direction, course, current, bias, inclination, flow, sweep, bent; intention, meaning, purport, essence, gist, purpose, import, aim, object; tenor, tone, spirit, colour. **3** accumulation, pile, heap, mass, bank, mound. **5** see TURN *n.* 2. **7** mass, host, bank, carpet. ● *v.* **1, 2** coast, float, waft, bob; wander, roam, meander, stray, rove, ramble, *sl.* mosey.

drifter /driftər/ *n.* **1** an aimless or rootless person. **2** a boat used for drift-net fishing.

■ **1** rambler, wanderer, itinerant, nomad, ranger, rover, vagrant, tramp, vagabond, *US* hobo, *colloq.* knight of the road, drop-out, *Austral.* & *NZ sl.* overlander.

driftwood /dríftwŏŏd/ *n.* wood etc. driven or deposited by water or wind.

drill[1] /dril/ *n.* & *v.* ● *n.* **1** a pointed, esp. revolving, steel tool or machine used for boring cylindrical holes, sinking wells, etc. **2 a** esp. *Mil.* instruction or training in military exercises. **b** rigorous discipline or methodical instruction, esp. when learning or performing tasks. **c** routine procedure to be followed in an emergency (*fire-drill*). **d** a routine or exercise (*drills in irregular verb patterns*). **3** *colloq.* a recognized procedure (*I expect you know the drill*). **4** any of various molluscs, esp. *Urosalpinx cinera*, that bore into the shells of young oysters. ● *v.* **1** *tr.* (also *absol.*) **a** (of a person or a tool) make a hole with a drill through or into (wood, metal, etc.). **b** make (a hole) with a drill. **2** *tr.* & *intr.* esp. *Mil.* subject to or undergo discipline by drill. **3** *tr.* impart (knowledge etc.) by a strict method. **4** *tr. sl.* shoot with a gun (*drilled him full of holes*). □ **drill-sergeant 1** *Mil.* a non-commissioned officer who trains soldiers in drill. **2** a strict disciplinarian. □□ **driller** *n.* [earlier as verb, f. MDu. *drillen* bore, of unkn. orig.]

■ *n.* **1** auger, (brace and) bit, gimlet, bradawl. **2** training, instruction, repetition, exercise, practice, rehearsal; discipline. **3** procedure, pattern, form, formula, practice, method, approach, strategy, routine, custom. ● *v.* **1 a** penetrate, pierce, cut a hole in, perforate. **b** bore. **2** train, discipline, exercise, teach, instruct, school, tutor, coach, indoctrinate. **3** drive, bang, knock, force.

drill[2] /dril/ *n.* & *v.* ● *n.* **1** a machine used for making furrows, sowing, and covering seed. **2** a small furrow for sowing seed in. **3** a ridge with such furrows on top. **4** a row of plants so sown. ● *v.tr.* **1** sow (seed) with a drill. **2** plant (the ground) in drills. [perh. f. obs. *drill* rill (17th c., of unkn. orig.)]

drill[3] /dril/ *n.* a W. African baboon, *Papio leucophaeus*, related to the mandrill. [prob. a native name: cf. MANDRILL]

drill[4] /dril/ *n.* a coarse twilled cotton or linen fabric. [earlier *drilling* f. G *Drillich* f. L *trilix -licis* f. *tri-* three + *licium* thread]

drily /drīli/ *adv.* (also **dryly**) **1** (said) in a dry manner; humorously. **2** in a dry way or condition.

drink /dringk/ *v.* & *n.* ● *v.* (*past* **drank** /drangk/; *past part.* **drunk** /drungk/) **1 a** *tr.* swallow (a liquid). **b** *tr.* swallow the liquid contents of (a vessel). **c** *intr.* swallow liquid, take draughts (*drank from the stream*). **2** *intr.* take alcohol, esp. to excess (*I have heard that he drinks*). **3** *tr.* (of a plant, porous material, etc.) absorb (moisture). **4** *refl.* bring (oneself etc.) to a specified condition by drinking (*drank himself into a stupor*). **5** *tr.* (usu. foll. by *away*) spend (wages etc.) on drink (*drank away the money*). **6** *tr.* wish (a person's good health, luck, etc.) by drinking (*drank his health*). ● *n.* **1 a** a liquid for drinking (*milk is a sustaining drink*). **b** a draught or specified amount of this (*had a drink of milk*). **2 a** alcoholic liquor (*got the drink in for Christmas*). **b** a portion, glass, etc. of this (*have a drink*). **c** excessive indulgence in alcohol (*drink is his vice*). **3** (as **the drink**) *colloq.* the sea. □ **drink deep** take a large draught or draughts. **drink-driver** a person who drives a vehicle with an excess of alcohol in the blood. **drink-driving** the act or an instance of this. **drink in** listen to closely or eagerly (*drank in his every word*). **drinking-song** a song sung while drinking, usu. concerning drink. **drinking-up time** *Brit.* a short period legally allowed for finishing drinks bought before closing time in a public house. **drinking-water** water pure enough for drinking. **drink off** drink the whole (contents) of at once. **drink to** toast; wish success to. **drink a person under the table** remain sober longer than one's drinking companion. **drink up** drink the whole of; empty. **in drink** drunk. **strong drink** alcohol, esp. spirits. □□ **drinkable** *adj.* **drinker** *n.* [OE *drincan* (v.), *drinc(a)* (n.) f. Gmc]

■ *v.* **1** sip, gulp, swallow, lap (up), *literary* quaff, *Brit. sl.* knock back; swill, guzzle, *colloq.* swig; imbibe, *colloq.* wet one's whistle. **2** tipple, nip, indulge, carouse, imbibe, fuddle, sot, *archaic or literary* tope, *colloq.* booze, have a few, drown one's sorrows, *Brit. colloq.* go on a pub-crawl, *N.Engl. colloq.* sup, *sl.* hit the bottle, go on a binge *or* bender, binge, *Brit. sl.* knock it back, *esp. US sl.* lush. ● *n.* **1 a** potation, liquid refreshment, *formal* beverage; liquid. **b** draught, sip, taste, gulp, swallow, *esp. US* slug, *colloq.* swig. **2 a** alcohol, spirits, strong drink, (hard) liquor, *colloq.* booze, the bottle, mother's ruin, fire-water, plonk, *US colloq.* hooch, *sl.* gut-rot, rot-gut, hard stuff, bevvy, gargle, *Brit. sl.* wallop, *esp. US sl.* lush, *US sl.* red-eye, juice. **b** tot, nip, draught, jigger, glass, (wee) dram, *colloq.* snort, tipple, *Brit. colloq.* pint, *sl.* snifter, *Austral. sl.* nobbler; eye-opener, nightcap, stirrup-cup, *Sc.* & *Ir.* deoch an doris, *Brit. colloq.* sundowner. **3** (**the drink**) the sea, the ocean, *archaic or poet.* the main, *joc.* the pond, *poet.* the deep, *sl.* Davy Jones's locker, *Brit. sl.* the briny. □ **drink off** empty, drain (off). **drink to** toast, salute, celebrate. **in drink** see DRUNK *adj.* 1. **strong drink** spirit(s), hard liquor, drink, *colloq.* fire-water, *sl.* hard stuff.

drip /drip/ *v.* & *n.* ● *v.* (**dripped, dripping**) **1** *intr.* & *tr.* fall or let fall in drops. **2** *intr.* (often foll. by *with*) be so wet as to shed drops (*dripped with blood*). ● *n.* **1 a** the act or an instance of dripping (*the steady drip of rain*). **b** a drop of liquid (*a drip of paint*). **c** a sound of dripping. **2** *colloq.* a stupid, dull, or ineffective person. **3** (*Med.* **drip-feed**) the drip-by-drip intravenous administration of a solution of salt, sugar, etc. **4** *Archit.* a projection, esp. from a window-sill, keeping the rain off the walls. □ **drip-dry** *v.* (**-dries, -dried**) **1** *intr.* (of fabric etc.) dry crease-free when hung up to drip. **2** *tr.* leave (a garment etc.) hanging up to dry. ● *adj.* able to be drip-dried. **drip-mat** a small mat under a glass. **drip-moulding** (or **-stone**) *Archit.* a stone etc. projection that deflects rain etc. from walls. **dripping wet** very wet. [MDa. *drippe* f. Gmc (cf. DROP)]

■ *v.* **1** see TRICKLE *v.* **2** be soaked, be sopping, be saturated, be wet through, be drenched, be sodden, be streaming, be wringing *or* dripping wet. ● *n.* **1** dribble, trickle, drop, dripping. **2** milksop, bore, weed, *colloq.* wimp, drag, cream puff, *Brit. colloq.* wet, chinless wonder, *sl.* dud, *Austral. sl.* droob. □ **dripping wet** soaked, sopping, saturated, wet through, drenched, sodden, streaming, wringing wet.

dripping /dripping/ *n.* **1** fat melted from roasted meat and used for cooking or as a spread. **2** (in *pl.*) water, grease, etc., dripping from anything.

drippy /dríppi/ *adj.* (**drippier, drippiest**) **1** tending to drip. **2** *sl.* (of a person) ineffectual; sloppily sentimental. □□ **drippily** *adv.* **drippiness** *n.*

■ **2** see SENTIMENTAL.

drive /drīv/ *v.* & *n.* ● *v.* (*past* **drove** /drōv/; *past part.* **driven** /drívv'n/) **1** *tr.* (usu. foll. by *away, back, in, out, to*, etc.) urge in some direction, esp. forcibly (*drove back the wolves*). **2** *tr.* **a** (usu. foll. by *to* + infin., or *to* + verbal noun) compel or constrain forcibly (*was driven to complain; drove her to stealing*). **b** (often foll. by *to*) force into a specified state (*drove him mad; driven to despair*). **c** (often *refl.*) urge to overwork (*drives himself too hard*). **3 a** *tr.* (also *absol.*) operate and direct the course of (a vehicle, a locomotive, etc.) (*drove a sports car*; *drives well*). **b** *tr.* & *intr.* convey or be conveyed in a vehicle (*drove them to the station*; *drove to the station in a bus*) (cf. RIDE). **c** *tr.* (also *absol.*) be licensed or competent to drive (a vehicle) (*does he drive?*). **d** *tr.* (also *absol.*) urge and direct the course of (an animal drawing a vehicle or plough). **4** *tr.* (of wind, water, etc.) carry along, propel, send, or cause to go in some direction (*pure as the driven snow*). **5** *tr.* **a** (often foll. by *into*) force (a stake, nail, etc.) into place by blows (*drove the nail home*). **b** *Mining* bore (a tunnel, horizontal cavity, etc.). **6** *tr.* effect or conclude forcibly (*drove a hard bargain*; *drove his point home*). **7** *tr.* (of steam or other power) set or keep (machinery) going. **8** *intr.* (usu. foll. by *at*) work hard; dash, rush, or hasten. **9** *tr. Cricket* & *Tennis* hit (the ball) hard from a freely swung bat or racket. **10** *tr.* (often *absol.*) *Golf* strike (a ball) with a driver from the tee. **11** *tr.* chase or frighten (game, wild beasts, an enemy in warfare, etc.) from a large area to a smaller, to kill or capture; corner. **12** *tr. Brit.* hold a drift in (a forest etc.) (see DRIFT *n.* 9). ● *n.* **1** an act of driving in a motor vehicle; a journey or excursion in such a vehicle (*went for a pleasant drive*; *lives an hour's drive from us*). **2 a** the capacity for achievement; motivation and energy (*lacks the drive needed to succeed*). **b** *Psychol.* an inner urge to attain a goal or satisfy a need (*unconscious emotional drives*). **3 a** a usu. landscaped street or road. **b** a usu. private road through a garden or park to a house. **4** *Cricket*, *Golf*, & *Tennis* a driving stroke of the bat etc. **5** an organized effort to achieve a usu. charitable purpose (*a famine-relief drive*). **6 a** the transmission of power to machinery, the wheels of a motor vehicle, etc. (*belt drive*; *front-wheel drive*). **b** the position of a steering-wheel in a motor vehicle (*left-hand drive*). **c** *Computing* = *disk drive* (see DISC). **7** *Brit.* an organized competition, for many players, of whist, bingo, etc. **8** an act of driving game or an enemy. **9** *Austral.* & *NZ* a line of partly cut trees on a hillside felled when the top one topples on the others. □ **drive at** seek, intend, or mean (*what is he driving at?*). **drive-by** (of a crime etc.) carried out from a moving vehicle. **drive-in** *attrib.adj.* (of a bank, cinema, etc.) able to be used while sitting in one's car. ● *n.* such a bank, cinema, etc. **drive-on** (of a ship) on to which motor vehicles may be driven. **drive out** take the place of; oust; exorcize, cast out (evil spirits etc.). **driving-licence** a licence permitting a person to drive a motor vehicle. **driving rain** an excessive windblown downpour. **driving-range** *Golf* an area for practising drives. **driving test** an official test of a motorist's competence which must be passed to obtain a driving licence. **driving-wheel 1** the large wheel of a locomotive. **2** a wheel communicating motive power in machinery. **let drive** aim a blow or missile. □□ **drivable** *adj.* [OE *drīfan* f. Gmc]

■ *v.* **1** force, urge, push, propel, thrust, press, prod, send; herd, shepherd. **2 a** push, compel, constrain, coerce, impel, force, pressure, make, press, move, motivate, actuate, pressurize; spur, goad, incite. **3 a** operate, conduct, manoeuvre, manipulate, handle, steer, control; pilot. **b** convey, take, bring, give a person a lift; ride, travel, motor, go, move, proceed, journey, tour, *sl.* tool along. **5 a** force, plunge, thrust, sink, push, send, ram. **7** see ACTIVATE. **8** see LABOUR *v.* 1, 2, DASH *v.* 1. ● *n.* **1** ride, trip, outing, journey, run, tour, excursion, *colloq.* spin. **2 a** energy, motivation, effort, impetus, vigour, vim, push, enterprise, industry, initiative, ambition, ambitiousness, determination, persistence, urgency, zeal, enthusiasm, keenness, aggressiveness, aggression, *colloq.* get-up-and-go, spunk, pep, zip, go. **b** see URGE *n.* **3** driveway, approach, road, street, avenue, boulevard, lane, route, way. **5** campaign, effort, appeal, crusade. **7** see COMPETITION 2. □ **drive at** hint (at), suggest, imply, intimate, allude *or* refer to, intend, mean, have in mind, indicate, *colloq.* get at; seek. **drive out** see LAY[1] *v.* 6b, *cast out*.

drivel /drívv'l/ *n.* & *v.* ● *n.* silly nonsense; twaddle. ● *v.* (**drivelled, drivelling**; *US* **driveled, driveling**) **1** *intr.* run at the mouth or nose; dribble. **2** *intr.* talk childishly or idiotically. **3** *tr.* (foll. by *away*) fritter; squander away. □□ **driveller** *n.* (*US* **driveler**). [OE *dreflian* (v.)]

■ *n.* gibberish, rubbish, (stuff and) nonsense, twaddle, garbage, balderdash, blarney, bunkum, slaver, claptrap, pap, fandangle, fandango, flummery, *Sc.* haver, *colloq.* hogwash, piffle, tripe, malarkey, tosh, flapdoodle, mouthwash, *Brit. dial.* squit, *sl.* hooey, tommy-rot, hot air, bosh, boloney, eyewash, bull, bilge, poppycock, rhubarb, rot, bunk, cod, guff, kibosh, *Brit. sl.* codswallop, (load of old) cobblers, cock, flannel. ● *v.* **1** dribble, drool, slobber, slaver. **2** prate, prattle, gibber, jabber, burble, gabble, chatter, blather, *colloq.* gab, witter, natter, *Brit. colloq.* rabbit on, *esp. Brit. colloq.* waffle; see also BABBLE *v.* 1a, b. **3** (*drivel away*) see FRITTER[1].

driven *past part.* of DRIVE.

driver /drī́vər/ *n.* **1** (often in *comb.*) a person who drives a vehicle (*bus-driver*; *engine-driver*). **2** *Golf* a club with a flat face and wooden head, used for driving from the tee. **3** *Electr.* a device or part of a circuit providing power for output. **4** *Mech.* a wheel etc. receiving power directly and transmitting motion to other parts. □ **in the driver's seat** in charge. □□ **driverless** *adj.*

■ **1** see OPERATOR 1.

driveway /drī́vway/ *n.* = DRIVE *n.* 3b.

drizzle /drízz'l/ *n.* & *v.* ● *n.* very fine rain. ● *v.intr.* (esp. of rain) fall in very fine drops (*it's drizzling again*). □□ **drizzly** *adj.* [prob. f. ME *drēse*, OE *drēosan* fall]

■ *n.* mizzle; rain, rainfall, precipitation. ● *v.* mizzle, spit; rain.

drogue /drōg/ *n.* **1** *Naut.* **a** a buoy at the end of a harpoon line. **b** a sea anchor. **2** *Aeron.* a truncated cone of fabric used as a brake, a target for gunnery, a wind-sock, etc. [18th c.: orig. unkn.]

droit /droyt/ *n. Law* a right or due. [ME f. OF f. L *directum* (n.) f. *directus* DIRECT]

droit de seigneur /drwaá də senyṓr/ *n. hist.* the alleged right of a feudal lord to have sexual intercourse with a vassal's bride on her wedding night. [F, = lord's right]

droll /drōl/ *adj.* & *n.* ● *adj.* **1** quaintly amusing. **2** strange; odd; surprising. ● *n. archaic* **1** a jester; an entertainer. **2** a quaintly amusing person. □□ **drollery** *n.* (*pl.* **-ies**). **drolly** /drṓl-li/ *adv.* **drollness** *n.* [F *drôle*, perh. f. MDu. *drolle* little man]

■ *adj.* **1** see COMIC *adj.* ● *n.* see JOKER 1.

drome /drōm/ *n. colloq. archaic* aerodrome. [abbr.]

-drome /drōm/ *comb. form* forming nouns denoting: **1** a place for running, racing, or other forms of movement (*aerodrome*; *hippodrome*). **2** a thing that runs or proceeds in a certain way (*palindrome*; *syndrome*). [Gk *dromos* course, running]

dromedary /drómmidəri, drúm-, -dri/ *n.* (*pl.* **-ies**) a one-humped camel, *Camelus dromedarius*, bred for riding and racing. Also called *Arabian camel*. [ME f. OF *dromedaire* or LL *dromedarius* ult. f. Gk *dromas -ados* runner]

dromond /drómmənd, drúm-/ *n. hist.* a large medieval ship used for war or commerce. [ME f. OF *dromon(t)* f. LL *dromo -onis* f. late Gk *dromōn* light vessel]

drone /drōn/ *n.* & *v.* ● *n.* **1** a non-working male of the honey-bee, whose sole function is to mate with fertile females. **2** an idler. **3** a deep humming sound. **4** a monotonous speech or speaker. **5 a** a pipe, esp. of a bagpipe, sounding a continuous note of fixed low pitch. **b** the note emitted by this. **6** a remote-controlled pilotless aircraft or missile. ● *v.* **1** *intr.* make a deep humming sound. **2** *intr.* & *tr.* speak or utter monotonously. **3 a** *intr.* be idle. **b** *tr.* (often foll. by *away*) idle away (one's time etc.). [OE *drān*, *drǣn* prob. f. WG]

■ *n.* **2** see IDLER. **3, 4** see HUM[1] *n.* 1. ● *v.* **1** see HUM[1] *v* 1. **2** see MURMUR *v.* 1, 2.

drongo /drónggō/ *n.* (*pl.* **-os** or **-oes**) **1** any black bird of the family Dicruridae, native to India, Africa, and Australia, having a long forked tail. **2** *Austral.* & *NZ sl. derog.* a simpleton. [Malagasy]

■ **2** see SILLY *n.*

droob /dro͞ob/ *n. Austral. sl.* a hopeless-looking ineffectual person. [perh. f. DROOP]

drool /dro͞ol/ *v.* & *n.* ● *v.intr.* **1** drivel; slobber. **2** (often foll. by *over*) show much pleasure or infatuation. ● *n.* slobbering; drivelling. [contr. of *drivel*]

■ *v.* **1** see SLAVER² *v.* ● *n.* see SLAVER² *n* 1.

droop /dro͞op/ *v.* & *n.* ● *v.* **1** *intr.* & *tr.* hang or allow to hang down; languish, decline, or sag, esp. from weariness. **2** *intr.* **a** (of the eyes) look downwards. **b** *poet.* (of the sun) sink. **3** *intr.* lose heart; be dejected; flag. ● *n.* **1** a drooping attitude. **2** a loss of spirit or enthusiasm. □ **droop-snoot** *colloq.* ● *adj.* (of an aircraft) having an adjustable nose or leading-edge flap. ● *n.* such an aircraft. [ME f. ON *drúpa* hang the head f. Gmc: cf. DROP]

■ *v.* **1** sag, hang (down), wilt, dangle; languish, weaken, flag, wilt, decline, wither, be limp, slump, sag. **2 b** sink, go down, drop, set.

droopy /dro͞opi/ *adj.* (**droopier**, **droopiest**) **1** drooping. **2** dejected, gloomy. □□ **droopily** *adv.* **droopiness** *n.*

drop /drop/ *n.* & *v.* ● *n.* **1 a** a small round or pear-shaped portion of liquid that hangs or falls or adheres to a surface (*drops of dew*; *tears fell in large drops*). **b** a very small amount of usu. drinkable liquid (*just a drop left in the glass*). **c** a glass etc. of alcoholic liquor (*take a drop with us*). **2 a** an abrupt fall or slope. **b** the amount of this (*a drop of fifteen feet*). **c** an act of falling or dropping (*had a nasty drop*). **d** a reduction in prices, temperature, etc. **e** a deterioration or worsening (*a drop in status*). **3** something resembling a drop, esp.: **a** a pendant or earring. **b** a crystal ornament on a chandelier etc. **c** (often in *comb.*) a sweet or lozenge (*pear-drop*; *cough drop*). **4** something that drops or is dropped, esp.: **a** *Theatr.* a painted curtain or scenery let down on to the stage. **b** a platform or trapdoor on a gallows, the opening of which causes the victim to fall. **5** *Med.* **a** the smallest separable quantity of a liquid. **b** (in *pl.*) liquid medicine to be measured in drops (*eye drops*). **6** a minute quantity (*not a drop of pity*). **7** *sl.* **a** a hiding-place for stolen or illicit goods. **b** a secret place where documents etc. may be left or passed on in espionage. **8** *sl.* a bribe. **9** *US* a box for letters etc. ● *v.* (**dropped**, **dropping**) **1** *intr.* & *tr.* fall or let fall in drops (*tears dropped on to the book*; *dropped the soup down his shirt*). **2** *intr.* & *tr.* fall or allow to fall; relinquish; let go (*dropped the box*; *the egg dropped from my hand*). **3 a** *intr.* & *tr.* sink or cause to sink or fall to the ground from exhaustion, a blow, a wound, etc. **b** *intr.* die. **4 a** *intr.* & *tr.* cease or cause to cease; lapse or let lapse; abandon (*the connection dropped*; *dropped the friendship*; *drop everything and come at once*). **b** *tr. colloq.* cease to associate with. **5** *tr.* set down (a passenger etc.) (*drop me at the station*). **6** *tr.* & *intr.* utter or be uttered casually (*dropped a hint*; *the remark dropped into the conversation*). **7** *tr.* send casually (*drop me a postcard*). **8 a** *intr.* & *tr.* fall or allow to fall in direction, amount, condition, degree, pitch, etc. (*his voice dropped*; *the wind dropped*; *we dropped the price by £20*; *the road dropped southwards*). **b** *intr.* (of a person) jump down lightly; let oneself fall. **c** *tr.* remove (clothes, esp. trousers) rapidly, allowing them to fall to the ground. **9** *tr. colloq.* lose (money, esp. in gambling). **10** *tr.* **a** omit (*drop this article*). **b** omit (a letter, esp. aitch, a syllable etc.) in speech. **11** *tr.* (as **dropped** *adj.*) in a lower position than usual (*dropped handlebars*; *dropped waist*). **12** *tr.* give birth to (esp. a lamb, a kitten, etc.). **13 a** *intr.* (of a card) be played in the same trick as a higher card. **b** *tr.* play or cause (a card) to be played in this way. **14** *tr. Sport* lose (a game, a point, a contest, a match, etc.). **15** *tr. Aeron.* deliver (supplies etc.) by parachute. **16** *tr. Football* **a** send (a ball) by a drop-kick. **b** score (a goal) by a drop-kick. **17** *tr. colloq.* dismiss or exclude (*was dropped from the team*). □ **at the drop of a hat** given the slightest excuse. **drop anchor** anchor ship. **drop asleep** fall gently asleep. **drop away** decrease or depart gradually. **drop back** (or **behind** or **to the rear**) fall back; get left behind. **drop back into** return to (a habit etc.). **drop a brick** *colloq.* make an indiscreet or embarrassing remark. **drop-curtain** (or **-scene**) *Theatr.* a painted curtain or scenery (cf. sense 4 of *n.*). **drop a curtsy** make a curtsy. **drop dead!** *sl.* an exclamation of intense scorn. **drop down** descend a hill etc. **drop-forging** a method of forcing white-hot metal through an open-ended die by a heavy weight. **drop-hammer** a heavy weight raised mechanically and allowed to drop, as used in drop-forging and pile-driving. **drop-head** *Brit.* the adjustable fabric roof of a car. **drop in** (or **by**) *colloq.* call casually as a visitor. **drop-in centre** a meeting-place where people may call casually for advice, conversation, etc. **a drop in the ocean** (or **a bucket**) a very small amount, esp. compared with what is needed or expected. **drop into** *colloq.* **1** call casually at (a place). **2** fall into (a habit etc.). **drop it!** *sl.* stop that! **drop-kick** *Football* a kick made by dropping the ball and kicking it on the bounce. **drop-leaf** (of a table etc.) having a hinged flap. **drop off 1** decline gradually. **2** *colloq.* fall asleep. **3** = sense 5 of *v.* **drop on** reprimand or punish. **drop out** *colloq.* cease to participate, esp. in a race, a course of study, or in conventional society. **drop-out** *n.* **1** *colloq.* a person who has dropped out. **2** the restarting of a game by a drop-kick. **drop scone** *Brit.* a small thick pancake made by dropping batter into a frying pan etc. **drop-shot** (in lawn tennis) a shot dropping abruptly over the net. **drop a stitch** let a stitch fall off the end of a knitting-needle. **drop-test** *Engin. n.* a test done by dropping under standard conditions. ● *v.tr.* carry out a drop-test on. **drop to** *sl.* become aware of. **fit** (or **ready**) **to drop** extremely tired. **have the drop on** *colloq.* have the advantage over. **have had a drop too much** *colloq.* be slightly drunk. □□ **droplet** *n.* [OE *dropa*, *drop(p)ian* ult. f. Gmc: cf. DRIP, DROOP]

■ *n.* **1 a** globule, bead, drip, droplet, tear. **b** bit, spot, dot, taste, dram, sip, nip, pinch, dash, dab, *colloq.* smidgen. **2 a, b** descent, fall; decline, slope, fall-off, drop-off, declivity. **d** see DECREASE *n.* **e** see DECLINE *n.* 2. **6** see TRACE¹ 1b. **8** see BRIBE *n.* ● *v.* **1** drip, trickle, dribble, fall. **2** release, let go (of), relinquish; fall. **3 a** fall (down), collapse, sink (down), go down. **b** see DIE¹ 1. **4** desert, forsake, give up, abandon, leave, quit, throw over, jilt, discard, get rid of, leave in the lurch, reject, repudiate, renounce, *colloq.* chuck, dump, *sl.* ditch; relinquish, shed, cast off, let go; discontinue, lapse, stop, cease, end, terminate. **5** drop off, set down, let off *or* out, leave. **8 a** fall, descend, sink, go down, drop away *or* down *or* off, dive, plunge, plummet, decline, collapse, decrease, fall off, diminish, slacken, slack *or* taper off, subside, lessen, wane, ebb, let up, ease (off *or* up); put *or* bring down, lower. **9** see WASTE *v.* 1. **10** omit, leave out, exclude, eliminate, delete. **14** lose, concede, let slip. **17** dismiss, let go, discharge, oust, *colloq.* sack, give a person the sack, *sl.* fire; see also DISMISS 2, OMIT 1. □ **drop asleep** see NOD *v.* 2. **drop away** see DECREASE *v.* **drop back into** return *or* revert to, fall back into, go back to. **drop a brick** drop a clanger, make a *faux pas*, *colloq.* put one's foot in it. **drop dead!** *colloq.* shut up, *sl.* (go) take a running jump, get lost. **drop in** (or **by**) visit, call in *or* round, pay a visit, pop in *or* by, come by, stop in *or* by. **drop off 1** see DIMINISH 1. **2** see NOD *v.* 2. **drop on** see CASTIGATE. **drop out** see WITHDRAW 5. **drop to** see REALIZE 2. **fit to drop** see *exhausted* (EXHAUST *v.* 2). **have the drop on** see *have the bulge on* (BULGE).

dropper /dróppər/ *n.* **1** a device for administering liquid, esp. medicine, in drops. **2** *Austral.*, *NZ*, & *S.Afr.* a light vertical stave in a fence.

droppings /dróppingz/ *n.pl.* **1** the dung of animals or birds. **2** something that falls or has fallen in drops, e.g. wax from candles.

■ **1** see DUNG *n.*

dropsy /drópsi/ *n.* (*pl.* **-ies**) **1** = OEDEMA. **2** *sl.* a tip or bribe. □□ **dropsical** *adj.* (in sense 1). [ME f. *idrop(e)sie* f. OF *idropesie* ult. f. L *hydropisis* f. Gk *hudrōps* dropsy (as HYDRO-)]

dropwort /drópwurt/ *n.* a plant, *Filipendula vulgaris*, with tuberous root fibres.

droshky /dróshki/ *n.* (*pl.* **-ies**) a Russian low four-wheeled open carriage. [Russ. *drozhki* dimin. of *drogi* wagon f. *droga* shaft]

drosophila /drəsóffilə/ *n.* any fruit fly of the genus *Drosophila*, used extensively in genetic research. [mod.L f. Gk *drosos* dew, moisture + *philos* loving]

dross /dross/ *n.* **1** rubbish, refuse. **2 a** the scum separated from metals in melting. **b** foreign matter mixed with anything; impurities. □□ **drossy** *adj.* [OE *drōs*: cf. MLG *drōsem*, OHG *truosana*]
■ **1** see RUBBISH *n.* 1.

drought /drowt/ *n.* **1** the continuous absence of rain; dry weather. **2** the prolonged lack of something. **3** *archaic* a lack of moisture; thirst; dryness. □□ **droughty** *adj.* [OE *drūgath* f. *drȳge* DRY]

drouth /drowth/ *n. Sc., Ir., US, & poet.* var. of DROUGHT.

drove[1] *past* of DRIVE.

drove[2] /drōv/ *n.* **1 a** a large number (of people etc.) moving together; a crowd; a multitude; a shoal. **b** (in *pl.*) *colloq.* a great number (*people arrived in droves*). **2** a herd or flock being driven or moving together. □ **drove-road** an ancient cattle track. [OE *drāf* f. *drīfan* DRIVE]
■ see THRONG *n.*

drover /drṓvər/ *n.* a person who drives herds to market; a cattle-dealer. □□ **drove** *v.tr.* **droving** *n.*

drown /drown/ *v.* **1** *tr.* & *intr.* kill or be killed by submersion in liquid. **2** *tr.* submerge; flood; drench (*drowned the fields in six feet of water*). **3** *tr.* (often foll. by *in*) deaden (grief etc.) with drink (*drowned his sorrows in drink*). **4** *tr.* (often foll. by *out*) make (a sound) inaudible by means of a louder sound. □ **drowned valley** a valley partly or wholly submerged by a change in land-levels. **drown out** drive out by flood. **like a drowned rat** *colloq.* extremely wet and bedraggled. [ME (orig. north.) *drun(e)*, *droun(e)*, perh. f. OE *drūnian* (unrecorded), rel. to DRINK]
■ **2** flood, inundate, swamp, deluge, drench, immerse, submerge, engulf; overwhelm, overcome, overpower.

drowse /drowz/ *v.* & *n.* ● *v.* **1** *intr.* be dull and sleepy or half asleep. **2** *tr.* **a** (often foll. by *away*) pass (the time) in drowsing. **b** make drowsy. **3** *intr. archaic* be sluggish. ● *n.* a condition of sleepiness. [back-form. f. DROWSY]
■ *v.* **1** see SLEEP *v.*

drowsy /drówzi/ *adj.* (**drowsier**, **drowsiest**) **1** half asleep; dozing. **2** soporific; lulling. **3** sluggish. □□ **drowsily** *adv.* **drowsiness** *n.* [prob. rel. to OE *drūsian* be languid or slow, *drēosan* fall: cf. DREARY]
■ **1, 3** sleepy, heavy-lidded, half asleep, dozy, dozing, groggy, somnolent, yawning; torpid, sluggish, tired, weary, listless, lethargic, lazy.

drub /drub/ *v.tr.* (**drubbed**, **drubbing**) **1** thump; belabour. **2** beat in a fight. **3** (usu. foll. by *into*, *out of*) beat (an idea, attitude, etc.) into or out of a person. □□ **drubbing** *n.* [ult. f. Arab. *ḍaraba* beat]
■ **1** see BEAT *v.* 1. **2** see OVERCOME *v.* 1.

drudge /druj/ *n.* & *v.* ● *n.* a servile worker, esp. at menial tasks; a hack. ● *v.intr.* (often foll. by *at*) work slavishly (at menial, hard, or dull work). □□ **drudgery** /drújəri/ *n.* [15th c.: perh. rel. to DRAG]
■ *n.* hack, plodder, toiler; see also MENIAL *n.* 1. ● *v.* see SLAVE *v.* 1, LABOUR *v.* 1, 2. □□ **drudgery** toil, labour, (hack) work, donkey-work, slog, slogging, *archaic* moil, *colloq.* grind, sweat, *literary* travail.

drug /drug/ *n.* & *v.* ● *n.* **1** a medicinal substance. **2** a narcotic, hallucinogen, or stimulant, esp. one causing addiction. ● *v.* (**drugged**, **drugging**) **1** *tr.* add a drug to (food or drink). **2** *tr.* **a** administer a drug to. **b** stupefy with a drug. **3** *intr.* take drugs as an addict. □ **drug addict** a person who is addicted to a narcotic drug. **drug on the market** a commodity that is plentiful but no longer in demand. **drug peddler** (*colloq.* **pusher**) a person who sells esp. addictive drugs illegally. **drug squad** a division of a police force investigating crimes involving illegal drugs. [ME *drogges*, *drouges* f. OF *drogue*, of unkn. orig.]
■ *n.* **1** medicine, medicament, pharmaceutical, remedy, cure, treatment. **2** opiate, narcotic, stimulant, hallucinogen, psychedelic, *sl.* dope, downer, upper. ● *v.* **2 a** dose, medicate, treat. **b** anaesthetize, dope, narcotize, knock out, sedate, stupefy, numb, benumb, dull; poison. □ **drug addict** see ADDICT *n.* 1.

drugget /drúggit/ *n.* **1** a coarse woven fabric used as a floor or table covering. **2** such a covering. [F *droguet*, of unkn. orig.]

druggist /drúggist/ *n.* esp. *US* a pharmacist. [F *droguiste* (as DRUG)]
■ pharmacist, dispensing chemist, *Brit.* chemist, *archaic* apothecary.

druggy /drúggi/ *n.* & *adj. colloq.* ● *n.* (also **druggie**) (*pl.* **-ies**) a drug addict. ● *adj.* of or associated with narcotic drugs.

drugstore /drúgstor/ *n. US* a chemist's shop also selling light refreshments and other articles.
■ see PHARMACY 2.

Druid /drṓō-id/ *n.* (*fem.* **Druidess**) **1** an ancient Celtic priest, magician, or soothsayer of Gaul, Britain, or Ireland. **2** a member of a Welsh etc. Druidic order, esp. the Gorsedd. □□ **Druidism** *n.* **Druidic** /-íddik/ *adj.* **Druidical** /-íddik'l/ *adj.* [F *druide* or L pl. *druidae*, *-des*, Gk *druidai* f. Gaulish *druides*]

drum[1] /drum/ *n.* & *v.* ● *n.* **1 a** a percussion instrument or toy made of a hollow cylinder or hemisphere covered at one or both ends with stretched skin or parchment and sounded by striking (*bass drum*; *kettledrum*). **b** (often in *pl.*) a drummer or a percussion section (*the drums are playing too loud*). **c** a sound made by or resembling that of a drum. **2** something resembling a drum in shape, esp.: **a** a cylindrical container or receptacle for oil, dried fruit, etc. **b** a cylinder or barrel in machinery on which something is wound etc. **c** *Archit.* the solid part of a Corinthian or composite capital. **d** *Archit.* a stone block forming a section of a shaft. **e** *Austral.* & *NZ* swag, a bundle. **3** *Zool.* & *Anat.* the membrane of the middle ear; the eardrum. **4** *sl.* **a** a house. **b** a nightclub. **c** a brothel. **5** (in full **drum-fish**) any marine fish of the family Sciaenidae, having a swim-bladder that produces a drumming sound. **6** *hist.* an evening or afternoon tea party. **7** *Austral. sl.* a piece of reliable information, esp. a racing tip. ● *v.* (**drummed**, **drumming**) **1** *intr.* & *tr.* play on a drum. **2** *tr.* & *intr.* beat, tap, or thump (knuckles, feet, etc.) continuously (on something) (*drummed on the table*; *drummed his feet*; *drumming at the window*). **3** *intr.* (of a bird or an insect) make a loud, hollow noise with quivering wings. **4** *tr. Austral. sl.* provide with reliable information. □ **drum brake** a brake in which shoes on a vehicle press against the drum on a wheel. **drum into** drive (a lesson) into (a person) by persistence. **drum machine** an electronic device that imitates the sound of percussion instruments. **drum major 1** the leader of a marching band. **2** *archaic* an NCO commanding the drummers of a regiment. **drum majorette** esp. *US* a member of a female baton-twirling parading group. **drum out** *Mil.* cashier (a soldier) by the beat of a drum; dismiss with ignominy. **drum up** summon, gather, or call up (*needs to drum up more support*). [obs. *drombslade*, *drombyllsclad*, f. LG *trommelslag* drum-beat f. *trommel* drum + *slag* beat]
■ *n.* **1 c** see PATTER[1] *n.* **2 b** see ROLLER 1a. ● *v.* **2** see TAP[2] *v.* 1, 2.

drum[2] /drum/ *n.* (also **drumlin** /drúmlin/) *Geol.* a long oval mound of boulder clay moulded by glacial action. □□ **drumlinoid** *n.* [Gael. & Ir. *druim* ridge: *-lin* perh. for -LING[1]]

drumbeat /drúmbeet/ *n.* the sound of a drum or drums being beaten.

drumfire /drúmfīr/ *n.* **1** *Mil.* heavy continuous rapid artillery fire, usu. heralding an infantry attack. **2** a barrage of criticism etc.

drumhead /drúmhed/ *n.* **1** the skin or membrane of a drum. **2** an eardrum. **3** the circular top of a capstan. **4** (*attrib.*) improvised (*drumhead court martial*).

drumlin var. of DRUM².

drummer /drúmmər/ *n.* **1** a person who plays a drum or drums. **2** esp. *US colloq.* a commercial traveller. **3** *sl.* a thief.

▪ **2** see SELLER.

drumstick /drúmstik/ *n.* **1** a stick used for beating a drum. **2** the lower joint of the leg of a cooked chicken, turkey, etc.

drunk /drungk/ *adj.* & *n.* ● *adj.* **1** rendered incapable by alcohol (*blind drunk*; *dead drunk*; *drunk as a lord*). **2** (often foll. by *with*) overcome or elated with joy, success, power, etc. ● *n.* **1** a habitually drunk person. **2** *sl.* a drinking-bout; a period of drunkenness. [past part. of DRINK]

▪ *adj.* **1** drunken, intoxicated, inebriated, besotted, mellow, tipsy, sotted, crapulent, crapulous, in one's cups, in drink, pixilated, soaked, one over the eight, roaring drunk, the worse for drink, *colloq.* soused, under the influence, under the weather, high (as a kite), tight, boozy, well-oiled, cock-eyed, sozzled, tiddly, well away, woozy, lit (up), stewed, happy, jolly, elevated, shot, out (cold), under the table, tanked (up), *Austral. colloq.* umpty-doo, *Brit. colloq.* merry, *joc.* the worse for wear, *sl.* pie-eyed, blind, bottled, canned, fried, full, legless, loaded, paralytic, stoned, pickled, squiffed, out of it, plastered, screwed, stinko, zonked, smashed, blotto, *Austral. sl.* full as a goog, inked, shicker, shickered, *esp. Brit. sl.* squiffy, *Brit. sl.* half-seas-over, cut, half-cut, sloshed, (feeling) queer. **2** overcome, inspired, exhilarated, excited, exuberant, invigorated, inspirited, animated, ecstatic; elated, flushed, feverish, inflamed, imbued, aflame, fervent, fervid, delirious. ● *n.* **1** drunkard, drinker, tippler, sot, winebibber; dipsomaniac, alcoholic, problem *or* serious *or* hard drinker, guzzler, *archaic* bibber, *archaic or literary* toper, *colloq.* soak, souse, swiller, boozer, dipso, barfly, sponge, *sl.* wino, *Austral. sl.* metho, *Austral.* & *NZ sl.* hophead, *esp. US sl.* lush, *US sl.* juicer. **2** see BENDER.

drunkard /drúngkərd/ *n.* a person who is drunk, esp. habitually.

▪ see DRUNK *n.* 1.

drunken /drúngkən/ *adj.* (usu. *attrib.*) **1** = DRUNK. **2** caused by or exhibiting drunkenness (*a drunken brawl*). **3** fond of drinking; often drunk. □□ **drunkenly** *adv.* **drunkenness** *n.*

▪ **1** see DRUNK *adj.* 1. **3** bibulous, crapulent, crapulous. □□ **drunkenness** intoxication, insobriety, intemperance, bibulousness, inebriety, crapulence, tipsiness; dipsomania, alcoholism.

drupe /dro͞op/ *n.* any fleshy or pulpy fruit enclosing a stone containing one or a few seeds, e.g. an olive, plum, or peach. □□ **drupaceous** /-páyshəss/ *adj.* [L *drupa* f. Gk *druppa* olive]

drupel /dro͞op'l/ *n.* (also **drupelet** /dro͞oplit/) a small drupe usu. in an aggregate fruit, e.g. a blackberry or raspberry.

Druse /dro͞oz/ *n.* (often *attrib.*) a member of a political or religious sect linked with Islam and living near Mt. Lebanon (*Druse militia*). [F f. Arab. *durūz* (pl.), prob. f. their founder *al-Darazī* (11th c.)]

druse /dro͞oz/ *n.* **1** a crust of crystals lining a rock-cavity. **2** a cavity lined with this. [F f. G, = weathered ore]

dry /drī/ *adj.*, *v.*, & *n.* ● *adj.* (**drier** /dríər/; **driest** /drí-ist/) **1** free from moisture, not wet, esp.: **a** with any moisture having evaporated, drained, or been wiped away (*the clothes are not dry yet*). **b** (of the eyes) free from tears. **c** (of a climate etc.) with insufficient rainfall; not rainy (*a dry spell*); (of land etc.) receiving little rain. **d** (of a river, well, etc.) dried up; not yielding water. **e** (of a liquid) having disappeared by evaporation etc. **f** not connected with or for use without moisture (*dry shampoo*). **g** (of a shave) with an electric razor. **2** (of wine etc.) not sweet (*dry sherry*). **3 a** meagre, plain, or bare (*dry facts*). **b** uninteresting; dull (*dry as dust*). **4** (of a sense of humour, a joke, etc.) subtle, ironic, and quietly expressed; not obvious. **5** (of a country, of legislation, etc.) prohibiting the sale of alcoholic drink. **6** (of toast, bread, etc.) without butter, margarine, etc. **7** (of provisions, groceries, etc.) solid, not liquid (*dry goods*). **8** impassive, unsympathetic; hard; cold. **9** (of a cow etc.) not yielding milk. **10** *colloq.* thirsty or thirst-making (*feel dry*; *this is dry work*). **11** *Polit. colloq.* of or being a political 'dry'. ● *v.* (**dries, dried**) **1** *tr.* & *intr.* make or become dry by wiping, evaporation, draining, etc. **2** *tr.* (usu. as **dried** *adj.*) preserve (food etc.) by removing the moisture (*dried egg*; *dried fruit*; *dried flowers*). **3** *intr.* (often foll. by *up*) *Theatr. colloq.* forget one's lines. **4** *tr.* & *intr.* (often foll. by *off*) cease or cause (a cow etc.) to cease yielding milk. ● *n.* (*pl.* **dries**) **1** the process or an instance of drying. **2** *sl.* a politician, esp. a Conservative, who advocates individual responsibility, free trade, and economic stringency, and opposes high government spending. **3 a** (prec. by *the*) esp. *Austral. colloq.* the dry season. **b** *Austral.* a desert area, waterless country. **4 a** dry ginger ale. **b** dry wine, sherry, etc. □ **dry battery** *Electr.* an electric battery consisting of dry cells. **dry cell** *Electr.* a cell in which the electrolyte is absorbed in a solid and cannot be spilled. **dry-clean** clean (clothes etc.) with organic solvents without using water. **dry-cleaner** a firm that specializes in dry-cleaning. **dry cough** a cough not producing phlegm. **dry-cure** cure (meat etc.) without pickling in liquid. **dry dock** an enclosure for the building or repairing of ships, from which water can be pumped out. **dry-fly** *adj.* (of fishing) with an artificial fly floating on the surface. ● *v.intr.* (**-flies, -flied**) fish by such a method. **dry ice** solid carbon dioxide. **dry land** land as opposed to the sea, a river, etc. **dry measure** a measure of capacity for dry goods. **dry milk** *US* dried milk. **dry-nurse** a nurse for young children, not required to breast-feed. **dry out 1** become fully dry. **2** (of a drug addict, alcoholic, etc.) undergo treatment to cure addiction. **dry-plate** *Photog.* a photographic plate with sensitized film hard and dry for convenience of keeping, developing at leisure, etc. **dry-point 1** a needle for engraving on a bare copper plate without acid. **2** an engraving produced with this. **dry rot 1** a decayed state of wood when not ventilated, caused by certain fungi. **2** these fungi. **dry run** *colloq.* a rehearsal. **dry-salt** = *dry-cure*. **dry-salter** a dealer in dyes, gums, drugs, oils, pickles, tinned meats, etc. **dry-shod** without wetting the shoes. **dry up 1** make utterly dry. **2** dry dishes. **3** (of moisture) disappear utterly. **4** (of a well etc.) cease to yield water. **5** *colloq.* (esp. in *imper.*) cease talking. **go dry** enact legislation for the prohibition of alcohol. □□ **dryish** *adj.* **dryness** *n.* [OE *drȳge*, *drygan*, rel. to MLG *dröge*, MDu. *dröghe*, f. Gmc]

▪ *adj.* **1 a** waterless, moistureless, dehydrated, desiccated. **c** arid, parched, waterless, *literary* sear; barren, bare. **3 a** unadorned, unembellished, meagre; see also PLAIN¹ *adj.* 3, BARE *adj.* 4. **b** dreary, boring, tiresome, wearisome, wearying, tiring, dull, uninteresting, monotonous, prosaic, commonplace, stale, uninspired; see also TEDIOUS. **4** subtle, ironic, droll, wry, cynical, biting, sarcastic, cutting, keen. **8** see COLD *adj.* 4. ● *v.* **1** dehydrate, desiccate, parch, dry up; dry out *or* off, drain; wither, shrivel, shrink, wilt. □ **dry run** see REHEARSAL 2. **dry up 5** see *wrap up* 3.

dryad /dríad, dríəd/ *n.* *Mythol.* a nymph inhabiting a tree; a wood nymph. [ME f. OF *dryade* f. L f. Gk *druas -ados* f. *drus* tree]

dryer var. of DRIER².

dryly var. of DRILY.

drystone /drístōn/ *adj.* (of a wall etc.) built without mortar.

DS *abbr.* **1** dal segno. **2** disseminated sclerosis.

DSC *abbr.* Distinguished Service Cross.

D.Sc. *abbr.* Doctor of Science.

DSM *abbr.* Distinguished Service Medal.

DSO *abbr.* (in the UK) Distinguished Service Order.

DSS *abbr.* (in the UK) Department of Social Security (formerly DHSS).

DT *abbr.* (also **DT's** /deeteez/) delirium tremens.
■ see *the jumps* (JUMP *n.* 2b).

DTI *abbr.* (in the UK) Department of Trade and Industry.

DTP *abbr.* desktop publishing.

dual /dyoōəl/ *adj.*, *n.*, & *v.* ● *adj.* **1** of two; twofold. **2** divided in two; double (*dual ownership*). **3** *Gram.* (in some languages) denoting two persons or things (additional to singular and plural). ● *n.* (also **dual number**) *Gram.* a dual form of a noun, verb, etc. ● *v.tr.* (**dualled, dualling**) *Brit.* convert (a road) into a dual carriageway. □ **dual carriageway** *Brit.* a road with a dividing strip between the traffic in opposite directions. **dual control** (of a vehicle or an aircraft) having two sets of controls, one of which is used by the instructor. **dual in-line package** *Computing* see DIP. **dual-purpose** (of a vehicle) usable for passengers or goods. □□ **duality** /dyoo-álliti/ *n.* **dualize** *v.tr.* (also **-ise**). **dually** *adv.* [L *dualis* f. *duo* two]
■ *adj.* **1** see DOUBLE *adj.* 6.

dualism /dyoōəliz'm/ *n.* **1** being twofold; duality. **2** *Philos.* the theory that in any domain of reality there are two independent underlying principles, e.g. mind and matter, form and content (cf. IDEALISM, MATERIALISM). **3** *Theol.* **a** the theory that the forces of good and evil are equally balanced in the universe. **b** the theory of the dual (human and divine) personality of Christ. □□ **dualist** *n.* **dualistic** /-lístik/ *adj.* **dualistically** /-lístikəli/ *adv.*

dub[1] /dub/ *v.tr.* (**dubbed, dubbing**) **1** make (a person) a knight by touching his shoulders with a sword. **2** give (a person) a name, nickname, or title (*dubbed him a crank*). **3** *Brit.* dress (an artificial fishing-fly). **4** smear (leather) with grease. [OE f. AF *duber*, *aduber*, OF *adober* equip with armour, repair, of unkn. orig.]
■ **2** see NAME *v.* 1.

dub[2] /dub/ *v.tr.* (**dubbed, dubbing**) **1** provide (a film etc.) with an alternative soundtrack, esp. in a different language. **2** add (sound effects or music) to a film or a broadcast. **3** combine (soundtracks) into one. **4** transfer or make a copy of (a soundtrack). [abbr. of DOUBLE]

dub[3] /dub/ *n.* esp. *US sl.* an inexperienced or unskilful person. [perh. f. DUB[1] in sense 'beat flat']

dub[4] /dub/ *v.intr.* (**dubbed, dubbing**) *sl.* (foll. by *in*, *up*) pay up; contribute money. [19th c.: orig. uncert.]

dubbin /dúbbin/ *n.* & *v.* ● *n.* (also **dubbing** /dúbbing/) prepared grease for softening and waterproofing leather. ● *v.tr.* (**dubbined, dubbining**) apply dubbin to (boots etc.). [see DUB[1] 4]

dubbing /dúbbing/ *n.* an alternative soundtrack to a film etc.

dubiety /dyoobíəti/ *n.* (*pl.* **-ies**) *literary* **1** a feeling of doubt. **2** a doubtful matter. [LL *dubietas* f. *dubium* doubt]
■ **1** see DOUBT *n.* 2.

dubious /dyoōbiəss/ *adj.* **1** hesitating or doubting (*dubious about going*). **2** of questionable value or truth (*a dubious claim*). **3** unreliable; suspicious (*dubious company*). **4** of doubtful result (*a dubious undertaking*). □□ **dubiously** *adv.* **dubiousness** *n.* [L *dubiosus* f. *dubium* doubt]
■ **1** see SCEPTICAL. **2** see DEBATABLE. **3** see UNRELIABLE, SHADY 3. **4** see SPECULATIVE 2.

dubitation /dyoōbitáysh'n/ *n.* *literary* doubt, hesitation. [ME f. OF *dubitation* or L *dubitatio* f. *dubitare* DOUBT]

dubitative /dyoōbitətiv/ *adj.* *literary* of, expressing, or inclined to doubt or hesitation. □□ **dubitatively** *adv.* [F *dubitatif -ive* or LL *dubitativus* (as DUBITATION)]

Dublin Bay prawn /dúblin/ *n.* **1** the Norway lobster. **2** (in *pl.*) scampi. [*Dublin* in Ireland]

Dubonnet /dyoobónnay/ *n.propr.* **1** a sweet French aperitif. **2** a glass of this. [name of a family of French wine-merchants]

ducal /dyoōk'l/ *adj.* of, like, or bearing the title of a duke. [F f. *duc* DUKE]

ducat /dúkkət/ *n.* **1** *hist.* a gold coin, formerly current in most European countries. **2 a** a coin. **b** (in *pl.*) money. [ME f. It. *ducato* or med.L *ducatus* DUCHY]

Duce /doōchay/ *n.* a leader, esp. (**Il Duce**) the title assumed by Mussolini (d. 1945). [It., = leader]

duchess /dúchiss/ *n.* (as a title usu. **Duchess**) **1** a duke's wife or widow. **2** a woman holding the rank of duke in her own right. [ME f. OF *duchesse* f. med.L *ducissa* (as DUKE)]
■ see PEER[2] *n.* 1.

duchesse /dooshéss, dúchiss/ *n.* **1** a soft heavy kind of satin. **2** a dressing-table with a pivoting mirror. □ **duchesse lace** a kind of Brussels pillow-lace. **duchesse potatoes** mashed potatoes mixed with egg, baked or fried, and served as small cakes. **duchesse set** a cover or a set of covers for a dressing-table. [F, = DUCHESS]

duchy /dúchi/ *n.* (*pl.* **-ies**) **1** the territory of a duke or duchess; a dukedom. **2** (often as **the Duchy**) the royal dukedom of Cornwall or Lancaster, each with certain estates, revenues, and jurisdiction of its own. [ME f. OF *duché(e)* f. med.L *ducatus* f. L *dux ducis* leader]
■ **1** see REALM 1.

duck[1] /duk/ *n.* (*pl.* same or **ducks**) **1 a** any of various swimming-birds of the family Anatidae, esp. the domesticated form of the mallard or wild duck. **b** the female of this (opp. DRAKE). **c** the flesh of a duck as food. **2** *Cricket* (in full **duck's-egg**) the score of a batsman dismissed for nought. **3** (also **ducks**) *Brit. colloq.* (esp. as a form of address) dear, darling. □ **duck-hawk 1** *Brit.* a marsh-harrier. **2** *US* a peregrine. **ducks and drakes** a game of making a flat stone skim along the surface of water. **duck's arse** *sl.* a haircut with the hair on the back of the head shaped like a duck's tail. **duck soup** *US sl.* an easy task. **like a duck to water** adapting very readily. **like water off a duck's back** *colloq.* (of remonstrances etc.) producing no effect. **play ducks and drakes with** *colloq.* squander. [OE *duce*, *dūce*: rel. to DUCK[2]]

duck[2] /duk/ *v.* & *n.* ● *v.* **1** *intr.* & *tr.* plunge, dive, or dip under water and emerge (*ducked him in the pond*). **2** *intr.* & *tr.* bend (the head or the body) quickly to avoid a blow or being seen, or as a bow or curtsy; bob (*ducked out of sight*; *ducked his head under the beam*). **3** *tr.* & *intr. colloq.* avoid or dodge; withdraw (from) (*ducked out of the engagement*; *ducked the meeting*). **4** *intr. Bridge* lose a trick deliberately by playing a low card. ● *n.* **1** a quick dip or swim. **2** a quick lowering of the head etc. □ **ducking-stool** *hist.* a chair fastened to the end of a pole, which could be plunged into a pond, used formerly for ducking scolds etc. □□ **ducker** *n.* [OE *dūcan* (unrecorded) f. Gmc]
■ *v.* **1** dunk, push under, submerge, immerse, dip; plunge (in), dive. **2** bob, dodge, dip, dive, stoop, bow, bend, crouch. **3** avoid, sidestep, evade, dodge, elude, shun, steer clear of, shy away from, shirk, withdraw (from). ● *n.* **1** swim, plunge, bathe, dip.

duck[3] /duk/ *n.* **1** a strong untwilled linen or cotton fabric used for small sails and the outer clothing of sailors. **2** (in *pl.*) trousers made of this (*white ducks*). [MDu. *doek*, of unkn. orig.]

duck[4] /duk/ *n. colloq.* an amphibious landing-craft. [*DUKW*, its official designation]

duckbill /dúkbil/ *n.* (also **duck-billed platypus**) = PLATYPUS.

duckboard /dúkbord/ *n.* (usu. in *pl.*) a path of wooden slats placed over muddy ground or in a trench.

duckling /dúkling/ *n.* **1** a young duck. **2** its flesh as food.

duckweed /dúkweed/ *n.* any of various aquatic plants, esp. of the genus *Lemna*, growing on the surface of still water.

ducky /dúkki/ *n.* & *adj. Brit. colloq.* ● *n.* (*pl.* **-ies**) darling, dear. ● *adj.* sweet, pretty; splendid.

duct /dukt/ *n.* & *v.* ● *n.* **1** a channel or tube for conveying fluid, cable, etc. **2 a** a tube in the body conveying secretions such as tears etc. **b** *Bot.* a tube formed by cells that have lost their intervening end walls, holding air, water, etc.

• *v.tr.* convey through a duct. [L *ductus* leading, aqueduct f. *ducere duct-* lead]
▪ *n.* **1** see PIPE *n.* 1.

ductile /dúktīl/ *adj.* **1** (of a metal) capable of being drawn into wire; pliable, not brittle. **2** (of a substance) easily moulded. **3** (of a person) docile, gullible. □□ **ductility** /-tílliti/ *n.* [ME f. OF *ductile* or L *ductilis* f. *ducere duct-* lead]
▪ **2** see PLASTIC *adj.* 1a. **3** see ADAPTABLE 2.

ducting /dúkting/ *n.* **1** a system of ducts. **2** material in the form of a duct or ducts.

ductless /dúktliss/ *adj.* lacking or not using a duct or ducts. □ **ductless gland** a gland secreting directly into the bloodstream: also called *endocrine gland*.

dud /dud/ *n.* & *adj. sl.* • *n.* **1** a futile or ineffectual person or thing (*a dud at the job*). **2** a counterfeit article. **3** a shell etc. that fails to explode. **4** (in *pl.*) clothes. • *adj.* **1** useless, worthless, unsatisfactory or futile. **2** counterfeit. [ME: orig. unkn.]
▪ *n.* **1** failure, *colloq.* washout, *sl.* flop. **2** fake, counterfeit, sham; forgery, imitation. **4** (*duds*) see CLOTHES. • *adj.* **1** worthless, valueless, broken, unusable, useless, inoperative, non-functioning, malfunctioning, unsatisfactory, *colloq.* bust, busted, *Austral.* & *NZ colloq.* crook, *sl.* kaput, up the spout, *Austral.* & *NZ sl.* bung, *Brit. sl.* duff. **2** see COUNTERFEIT *adj.* 1.

dude /dyōōd, dōōd/ *n. US sl.* **1** a fastidious aesthetic person, usu. male; a dandy. **2** a holiday-maker on a ranch in the western US, esp. when unused to ranch life. **3** a fellow; a guy. □ **dude ranch** a cattle ranch converted to a holiday centre for tourists etc. □□ **dudish** *adj.* [19th c.: prob. f. G dial. *dude* fool]
▪ **1** dandy, fop, fancy dresser, popinjay, man about town, coxcomb, *colloq.* swell, *hist.* macaroni, *Brit. sl.* toff. **3** see FELLOW 1.

dudgeon /dújən/ *n.* a feeling of offence; resentment. □ **in high dudgeon** very angry or angrily. [16th c.: orig. unkn.]
▪ see DISPLEASURE *n.*

due /dyōō/ *adj.*, *n.*, & *adv.* • *adj.* **1** (*predic.*) owing or payable as a debt or an obligation (*our thanks are due to him; £500 was due on the 15th*). **2** (often foll. by *to*) merited; appropriate; fitting (*his due reward; received the applause due to a hero*). **3** rightful; proper; adequate (*after due consideration*). **4** (*predic.*; foll. by *to*) to be ascribed to (a cause, an agent, etc.) (*the discovery was due to Newton*). **5** (*predic.*) intended to arrive at a certain time (*a train is due at 7.30*). **6** (foll. by *to* + infin.) under an obligation or agreement to do something (*due to speak tonight*). • *n.* **1** a person's right; what is owed to a person (*a fair hearing is my due*). **2** (in *pl.*) **a** what one owes (*pays his dues*). **b** a legally demandable toll or fee (*harbour dues; university dues*). • *adv.* (of a point of the compass) exactly, directly (*went due east; a due north wind*). □ **due to** *disp.* because of, owing to (*was late due to an accident*) (cf. sense 4 of *adj.*). **fall** (or **become**) **due** (of a bill etc.) be immediately payable. **in due course 1** at about the appropriate time. **2** in the natural order. [ME f. OF *deü* ult. f. L *debitus* past part. of *debēre* owe]
▪ *adj.* **1** payable, owed, owing, unpaid, outstanding, in arrears. **2, 3** fitting, right, rightful, correct, proper, appropriate, apropos, apposite, suitable, apt, meet; deserved, well-earned, merited, just, justified; necessary, needed, adequate, sufficient, enough, satisfactory, ample. **4** (*due to*) owing to, down to. **5** expected, *disp.* anticipated. • *n.* **1** see PREROGATIVE. **2 b** (*dues*) (membership) fee, charge(s), toll. • *adv.* directly, exactly, precisely, straight. □ **due to** because of, owing to, on account of, by reason of, thanks to, through, as a result of, resulting from, by virtue of, in consequence of. **in due course 1** see PRESENTLY 1.

duel /dyōōəl/ *n.* & *v.* • *n.* **1** *hist.* a contest with deadly weapons between two people, in the presence of two seconds, to settle a point of honour. **2** any contest between two people, parties, causes, animals, etc. (*a duel of wits*). • *v.intr.* (**duelled, duelling**; *US* **dueled, dueling**) fight a duel or duels. □□ **dueller** *n.* (*US* **dueler**). **duellist** *n.* (*US* **duelist**). [It. *duello* or L *duellum* (archaic form of *bellum* war), in med.L = single combat]
▪ *n.* **2** see BATTLE *n.* 2. • *v.* see COMBAT *v.* 1.

duende /doo-éndi/ *n.* **1** an evil spirit. **2** inspiration. [Sp.]
▪ **2** see INSPIRATION 1a.

duenna /dyoo-énnə/ *n.* an older woman acting as a governess and companion in charge of girls, esp. in a Spanish family; a chaperon. [Sp. *dueña* f. L *domina* mistress]
▪ chaperon, companion, attendant; see also ESCORT *n.* 1.

duet /dyoo-ét/ *n.* **1** *Mus.* **a** a performance by two voices, instrumentalists, etc. **b** a composition for two performers. **2** a dialogue. □□ **duettist** *n.* [G *Duett* or It. *duetto* dimin. of *duo* duet f. L *duo* two]

duff[1] /duf/ *n.* a boiled pudding. [N.Engl. form of DOUGH]

duff[2] /duf/ *adj. Brit. sl.* **1** worthless, counterfeit. **2** useless, broken. [perh. = DUFF[1]]
▪ **1** fake, false, sham, *colloq.* phoney, *sl.* dud; see also COUNTERFEIT *adj.* 1. **2** bad, useless, worthless, unworkable, inoperable, inoperative, broken, unusable, *colloq.* bust, busted, *sl.* kaput.

duff[3] /duf/ *v.tr. sl.* **1** *Brit. Golf* mishit (a shot, a ball); bungle. **2** *Austral.* steal and alter brands on (cattle). □ **duff up** *sl.* beat; thrash. [perh. back-form. f. DUFFER]

duffer /dúffər/ *n. sl.* **1** an inefficient, useless, or stupid person. **2** *Austral.* a person who duffs cattle. **3** *Austral.* an unproductive mine. [perh. f. Sc. *doofart* stupid person f. *douf* spiritless]
▪ **1** incompetent, blunderer, bungler, oaf, *US colloq.* lummox, *Austral. sl.* droob; see also CLOD 2.

duffle /dúff'l/ *n.* (also **duffel**) **1** a coarse woollen cloth with a thick nap. **2** *US* a sportsman's or camper's equipment. □ **duffle bag** a cylindrical canvas bag closed by a draw-string and carried over the shoulder. **duffle-coat** a hooded overcoat of duffle, usu. fastened with toggles. [*Duffel* in Belgium]

dug[1] *past* and *past part.* of DIG.

dug[2] /dug/ *n.* **1** the udder, breast, teat, or nipple of a female animal. **2** *derog.* the breast of a woman. [16th c.: orig. unkn.]

dugong /dōōgong/ *n.* (*pl.* same or **dugongs**) a marine mammal, *Dugong dugon*, of Asian seas and coasts. Also called *sea cow*. [ult. f. Malay *dūyong*]

dugout /dúggowt/ *n.* **1 a** a roofed shelter esp. for troops in trenches. **b** an underground air-raid or nuclear shelter. **2** a canoe made from a hollowed tree-trunk. **3** *sl.* a retired officer etc. recalled to service.

duiker /dīkər/ *n.* **1** (also **duyker**) any African antelope of the genus *Cephalophus*, usu. having a crest of long hair between its horns. **2** *S.Afr.* the long-tailed cormorant, *Phalacrocorax africanus*. [Du. *duiker* diver: in sense 1, from plunging through bushes when pursued]

duke /dyōōk/ *n.* (as a title usu. **Duke**) **1 a** a person holding the highest hereditary title of the nobility. **b** a sovereign prince ruling a duchy or small State. **2** (usu. in *pl.*) *sl.* the hand; the fist (*put up your dukes!*). **3** *Bot.* a kind of cherry, neither very sweet nor very sour. □ **royal duke** a duke who is also a royal prince. [ME f. OF *duc* f. L *dux ducis* leader]
▪ **1 a** see PEER[2] *n.* 1.

dukedom /dyōōkdəm/ *n.* **1** a territory ruled by a duke. **2** the rank of duke.

dulcet /dúlsit/ *adj.* (esp. of sound) sweet and soothing. [ME, earlier *doucet* f. OF dimin. of *doux* f. L *dulcis* sweet]
▪ see SWEET *adj.* 3.

dulcify /dúlsifī/ *v.tr.* (**-ies, -ied**) *literary* **1** make gentle. **2** sweeten. □□ **dulcification** /-fikáysh'n/ *n.* [L *dulcificare* f. *dulcis* sweet]

dulcimer /dúlsimər/ *n.* a musical instrument with strings of graduated length stretched over a sounding-board or box, played by being struck with hammers. [OF *doulcemer*, said to repr. L *dulce* sweet, *melos* song]

dulcitone /dúlsitōn/ *n. Mus.* a keyboard instrument with steel tuning-forks which are struck by hammers. [L *dulcis* sweet + TONE]

dulia /dyo͞oliə/ *n. RC Ch.* the reverence accorded to saints and angels. [med.L f. Gk *douleia* servitude f. *doulos* slave]

dull /dul/ *adj.* & *v.* ● *adj.* **1** slow to understand; stupid. **2** tedious; boring. **3** (of the weather) overcast; gloomy. **4 a** (esp. of a knife edge etc.) blunt. **b** (of colour, light, sound, or taste) not bright, shining, vivid, or keen. **5** (of a pain etc.) usu. prolonged and indistinct; not acute (*a dull ache*). **6 a** (of a person, an animal, trade, etc.) sluggish, slow-moving, or stagnant. **b** (of a person) listless; depressed (*he's a dull fellow since the accident*). **7** (of the ears, eyes, etc.) without keen perception. ● *v.tr.* & *intr.* make or become dull. □ **dull the edge of** make less sensitive, interesting, effective, amusing, etc.; blunt. **dull-witted** = DULL *adj.* 1. □□ **dullish** *adj.* **dullness** *n.* (also **dulness**). **dully** /dúl-li/ *adv.* [ME f. MLG, MDu. *dul*, corresp. to OE *dol* stupid]

■ *adj.* **1** dull-witted, slow-witted, unintelligent, bovine, cloddish, backward, slow, obtuse, doltish, *colloq.* thick, dense, dim, dim-witted, *esp. US colloq.* dumb; see also STUPID *adj.* 1, 5. **2** boring, tiresome, monotonous, uninspired, uninspiring, unoriginal, uninteresting, humdrum; see also TEDIOUS. **3** overcast, dismal, dreary, depressing, sombre, grey, dark, murky, gloomy, cloudy, clouded, sunless. **4 a** blunted; obtuse; see also BLUNT *adj.* 1. **b** hazy, blurry, opaque; drab, dingy, lacklustre, lustreless, grey, sombre; muffled. **5** numbing, numb, muted. **6** stagnant, slow-moving, sluggish, slow; lifeless, indifferent, unresponsive, inactive, torpid, depressed, down; see also LISTLESS. **7** insensitive, numb, insensible, impercipient, unresponsive. ● *v.* allay, assuage, relieve, mitigate, lessen, reduce; dim, tarnish, obscure, blur, cloud, becloud, *poet.* bedim; stupefy, narcotize, numb, benumb, desensitize, deaden, blunt, obtund. □ **dull the edge of** see DAMPEN 2, BLUNT *v.*

dullard /dúllərd/ *n.* a stupid person.

■ see DOLT.

dulse /dulss/ *n.* an edible seaweed, *Rhodymenia palmata*, with red wedge-shaped fronds. [Ir. & Gael. *duileasg*]

duly /dyo͞oli/ *adv.* **1** in due time or manner. **2** rightly, properly, fitly.

■ **1** punctually, on time; see also *promptly* (PROMPT). **2** properly, fittingly, fitly, deservedly, appropriately, suitably, befittingly, rightly, correctly, accordingly.

duma /do͞omə/ *n. hist.* a Russian council of State, esp. the elected body existing between 1905 and 1917. [Russ.: orig. an elective municipal council]

dumb /dum/ *adj.* **1 a** (of a person) unable to speak, usu. because of a congenital defect or deafness. **b** (of an animal) naturally unable to speak (*our dumb friends*). **2** silenced by surprise, shyness, etc. (*struck dumb by this revelation*). **3** taciturn or reticent, esp. insultingly (*dumb insolence*). **4** (of an action etc.) performed without speech. **5** (often in *comb.*) giving no sound; without voice or some other property normally belonging to things of the name (*a dumb piano*). **6** esp. *US colloq.* stupid; ignorant. **7** (usu. of a class, population, etc.) having no voice in government; inarticulate (*the dumb masses*). **8** (of a computer terminal etc.) able only to transmit data to or receive data from a computer; not programmable (opp. INTELLIGENT). □ **dumb animals** animals, esp. as objects of pity. **dumb-bell 1** a short bar with a weight at each end, used for exercise, muscle-building, etc. **2** *sl.* a stupid person, esp. a woman. **dumb blonde** a pretty but stupid blonde woman. **dumb cluck** *sl.* a stupid person. **dumb crambo** see CRAMBO. **dumb-iron** the curved side-piece of a motor-vehicle chassis, joining it to the front springs. **dumb piano** *Mus.* a silent or dummy keyboard. **dumb show 1** significant gestures or mime, used when words are inappropriate. **2** a part of a play in early drama, acted in mime. **dumb waiter 1** a small lift for carrying food, plates, etc., between floors. **2** a movable table, esp. with revolving shelves, used in a dining-room. □□ **dumbly** /dúmli/ *adv.* **dumbness** /dúmniss/ *n.* [OE: orig. unkn.: sense 6 f. G *dumm*]

■ **1, 2** mute, speechless, voiceless, wordless; silent, quiet, *colloq.* mum; inarticulate. **3** see TACITURN. **4** silent, unspeaking, mute, speechless, voiceless, wordless; mimed. **6** dull, *colloq.* thick, dense, dim; see also STUPID *adj.* 1, 5. □ **dumb-bell 2** see MISS[2], FOOL *n.* 1. **dumb blonde** see MISS[2], FOOL *n.* 1. **dumb cluck** see FOOL[1] *n.* 1.

dumbfound /dúmfównd/ *v.tr.* (also **dumfound**; esp. as **dumbfounded** *adj.*) strike dumb; confound; nonplus. [DUMB, CONFOUND]

■ strike dumb, make speechless, amaze, shock, surprise, startle, take aback, astonish, astound, bewilder, stagger, stun, nonplus, confuse, bewilder, confound, *colloq.* flabbergast, knock for six, floor, bowl over, knock sideways, *sl.* knock out; (*be dumbfounded*) be at a loss for words, be speechless, be thunderstruck, be dumbstruck, *colloq.* be flabbergasted, *sl.* be gobsmacked.

dumbhead /dúmhed/ *n.* esp. *US sl.* a stupid person.

dumbo /dúmbō/ *n.* (*pl.* **-os**) *sl.* a stupid person; a fool. [DUMB + -O]

dumbstruck /dúmstruk/ *adj.* greatly shocked or surprised and so lost for words.

■ see SPEECHLESS 1.

dumdum /dúmdum/ *n.* (in full **dumdum bullet**) a kind of soft-nosed bullet that expands on impact and inflicts laceration. [*Dum-Dum* in India, where it was first produced]

dummy /dúmmi/ *n.*, *adj.*, & *v.* ● *n.* (*pl.* **-ies**) **1** a model of a human being, esp.: **a** a ventriloquist's doll. **b** a figure used to model clothes in a shop window etc. **c** a target used for firearms practice. **2** (often *attrib.*) **a** a counterfeit object used to replace or resemble a real or normal one. **b** a prototype, esp. in publishing. **3** *colloq.* a stupid person. **4** a person taking no significant part; a figurehead. **5** *Brit.* a rubber or plastic teat for a baby to suck on. **6** an imaginary fourth player at whist, whose hand is turned up and played by a partner. **7** *Bridge* **a** the partner of the declarer, whose cards are exposed after the first lead. **b** this player's hand. **8** *Mil.* a blank round of ammunition. **9** *colloq.* a dumb person. ● *adj.* sham; counterfeit. ● *v.intr.* (**-ies, -ied**) *Football* make a pretended pass or swerve etc. □ **dummy run 1** a practice attack, etc.; a trial run. **2** a rehearsal. **dummy up** *US sl.* keep quiet; give no information. **sell the** (or **a**) **dummy** *Rugby Football colloq.* deceive (an opponent) by pretending to pass the ball. [DUMB + -Y[2]]

■ *n.* **1 b** mannequin, model, figure. **2 a** copy, reproduction, likeness, imitation, mock-up, simulation; counterfeit, *colloq.* phoney. **3** fool, idiot, dunce, blockhead, ninny, ass, dolt, numskull, simpleton, *colloq.* dim-wit; see also FOOL[1] *n.* 1. **4** see FIGUREHEAD. **5** *US* pacifier. ● *adj.* see SHAM *adj.* □ **dummy run** trial run, dry run, rehearsal, practice, run-through. **dummy up** keep quiet, lie low, keep one's lips sealed, *colloq.* keep mum, play one's cards close to one's chest.

dump /dump/ *n.* & *v.* ● *n.* **1 a** a place for depositing rubbish. **b** a heap of rubbish. **2** *colloq.* an unpleasant or dreary place. **3** *Mil.* a temporary store of ammunition, provisions, etc. **4** an accumulated pile of ore, earth, etc. **5** *Computing* **a** a printout of stored data. **b** the process or result of dumping data. ● *v.tr.* **1** put down firmly or clumsily (*dumped the shopping on the table*). **2** deposit or dispose of (rubbish etc.). **3** *colloq.* abandon, desert. **4** *Mil.* leave (ammunition etc.) in a dump. **5** *Econ.* send (goods unsaleable at a high price in the home market) to a foreign market for sale at a low price, to keep up the price at home, and to capture a new market. **6** *Computing* **a** copy (stored data) to a different location. **b** reproduce the contents of (a store) externally. □ **dump on** esp. *US sl.* criticize or abuse; get the better of. **dump truck** a truck with a body that tilts or opens at the back for unloading. □□ **dumping** *n.* [ME perh. f. Norse; cf. Da. *dumpe*, Norw. *dumpa* fall suddenly]

■ *n.* **1 a** *Brit.* rubbish dump, (rubbish) tip, *US* garbage dump. **b** see HEAP *n.* 1, REFUSE[2]. **2** see HOLE *n.* 4a. ● *v.* **1** put down, unload, offload, drop, deposit, throw *or* fling down. **2** get rid of, throw away, scrap, discard, jettison, dispose of, toss out *or* away, junk, *colloq.* chuck out *or* away, bin, unload, *US colloq.* trash, *sl.* ditch. **3** see DESERT[1] 1, 2. □ **dump on** see CRITICIZE 1, DEFEAT *v.* 1.

dumper /dúmpər/ *n.* **1** a person or thing that dumps. **2** *Austral.* & *NZ* a large wave that breaks and hurls the swimmer or surfer on to the beach.

dumpling /dúmpling/ *n.* **1 a** a small ball of usu. suet, flour, and water, boiled in stew or water, and eaten. **b** a pudding consisting of apple or other fruit enclosed in dough and baked. **2** a small fat person. [app. dimin., of *dump* small round object, but recorded much earlier]

dumps /dumps/ *n.pl. colloq.* depression; melancholy (*in the dumps*). [prob. f. LG or Du., fig. use of MDu. *domp* exhalation, haze, mist: rel. to DAMP]
■ (*in the dumps*) see DESPONDENT.

dumpy /dúmpi/ *adj.* (**dumpier, dumpiest**) short and stout. □□ **dumpily** *adv.* **dumpiness** *n.* [*dump* (cf. DUMPLING) + -Y[1]]
■ stocky, squat, chunky, chubby, heavy, tubby, stout, plump, portly, fat, thickset, *colloq.* pudgy, *Austral. colloq.* poddy.

dun[1] /dun/ *adj.* & *n.* ● *adj.* **1** dull greyish-brown. **2** *poet.* dark, dusky. ● *n.* **1** a dun colour. **2** a dun horse. **3** a dark fishing-fly. □ **dun-bird** a pochard. **dun diver** a female or young male goosander. [OE *dun, dunn*]

dun[2] /dun/ *n.* & *v.* ● *n.* **1** a debt-collector; an importunate creditor. **2** a demand for payment. ● *v.tr.* (**dunned, dunning**) importune for payment of a debt; pester. [abbr. of obs. *dunkirk* privateer, f. *Dunkirk* in France]
■ *v.* press, importune, solicit; plague, nag, harass; see also PESTER.

dunce /dunss/ *n.* a person slow at learning; a dullard. □ **dunce's cap** a paper cone formerly put on the head of a dunce at school as a mark of disgrace. [John *Duns* Scotus, scholastic theologian d. 1308, whose followers were ridiculed by 16th-c. humanists and reformers as enemies of learning]
■ see FOOL[1] *n.* 1.

Dundee cake /dundeé/ *n.* esp. *Brit.* a rich fruit cake usu. decorated with almonds. [*Dundee* in Scotland]

dunderhead /dúndərhed/ *n.* a stupid person. □□ **dunderheaded** *adj.* [17th c.: perh. rel. to dial. *dunner* resounding noise]
■ see DOLT.

dune /dyo͞on/ *n.* a mound or ridge of loose sand etc. formed by the wind, esp. beside the sea or in a desert. □ **dune buggy** = *beach buggy*. [F f. MDu. *dūne*: cf. DOWN[3]]
■ see MOUND *n.* 3.

dung /dung/ *n.* & *v.* ● *n.* the excrement of animals; manure. ● *v.tr.* apply dung to; manure (land). □ **dung-beetle** any of a family of beetles whose larvae develop in dung. **dung-fly** any of various flies feeding on dung. **dung-worm** any of various worms found in cow-dung and used as bait. [OE, rel. to OHG *tunga*, Icel. *dyngja*, of unkn. orig.]
■ *n.* manure, muck, droppings, guano, excrement, faeces.

dungaree /dúnggəreé/ *n.* **1** a coarse Indian calico. **2** (in *pl.*) **a** overalls etc. made of dungaree or similar material, worn esp. by workers. **b** trousers with a bib worn by children or as a fashion garment. [Hindi *dungrī*]

dungeon /dúnjən/ *n.* & *v.* ● *n.* **1** a strong underground cell for prisoners. **2** *archaic* a donjon. ● *v.tr. archaic* (usu. foll. by *up*) imprison in a dungeon. [orig. = *donjon*: ME f. OF *donjon* ult. f. L *dominus* lord]
■ *n.* **1** cell, prison, oubliette. **2** donjon, keep, tower, fortress, stronghold, fastness. ● *v.* see IMPRISON.

dunghill /dúng-hil/ *n.* a heap of dung or refuse, esp. in a farmyard.

dunk /dungk/ *v.tr.* **1** dip (bread, a biscuit, etc.) into soup, coffee, etc. while eating. **2** immerse, dip (*was dunked in the river*). [Pennsylvanian G *dunke* to dip f. G *tunken*]
■ see DIP *v.* 1.

dunlin /dúnlin/ *n.* a long-billed sandpiper, *Calidris alpina*. [prob. f. DUN[1] + -LING[1]]

dunnage /dúnnij/ *n. Naut.* **1** mats, brushwood, etc., stowed under or among cargo to prevent wetting or chafing. **2** *colloq.* miscellaneous baggage. [AL *dennagium*, of unkn. orig.]

dunno /dənṓ/ *colloq.* (I) do not know. [corrupt.]

dunnock /dúnnək/ *n. Brit.* the hedge sparrow. [app. f. DUN[1] + -OCK, from its brown and grey plumage]

dunny /dúnni/ *n.* (*pl.* **-ies**) **1** *Sc.* an underground passage or cellar, esp. in a tenement. **2** esp. *Austral.* & *NZ sl.* an earth-closet; an outdoor privy. [20th c.: orig. uncert.]

duo /dyo͞o-ō/ *n.* (*pl.* **-os**) **1** a pair of actors, entertainers, singers, etc. (*a comedy duo*). **2** *Mus.* a duet. [It. f. L, = two]
■ see PAIR *n.* 1.

duodecimal /dyo͞o-ōdéssim'l/ *adj.* & *n.* ● *adj.* relating to or using a system of numerical notation that has 12 as a base. ● *n.* **1** the duodecimal system. **2** duodecimal notation. □□ **duodecimally** *adv.* [L *duodecimus* twelfth f. *duodecim* twelve]

duodecimo /dyo͞o-ōdéssimō/ *n.* (*pl.* **-os**) *Printing* **1** a book-size in which each leaf is one-twelfth of the size of the printing-sheet. **2** a book of this size. [L (*in*) *duodecimo* in a twelfth (as DUODECIMAL)]

duodenary /dyo͞o-ōdeénəri/ *adj.* proceeding by twelves or in sets of twelve. [L *duodenarius* f. *duodeni* distrib. of *duodecim* twelve]

duodenum /dyo͞o-ōdeénəm/ *n. Anat.* the first part of the small intestine immediately below the stomach. □□ **duodenal** *adj.* **duodenitis** /-nītiss/ *n.* [ME f. med.L f. *duodeni* (see DUODENARY) from its length of about 12 fingers' breadth]

duologue /dyo͞oəlog/ *n.* **1** a conversation between two people. **2** a play or part of a play for two actors. [irreg. f. L *duo* or Gk *duo* two, after *monologue*]
■ **1** see CONVERSATION.

duomo /dwṓmō/ *n.* (*pl.* **-os**) an Italian cathedral. [It., = DOME]

duopoly /dyoo-óppəli/ *n.* (*pl.* **-ies**) *Econ.* the possession of trade in a commodity etc. by only two sellers. [Gk *duo* two + *pōleō* sell, after *monopoly*]

duotone /dyo͞oətōn/ *n.* & *adj. Printing* ● *n.* **1** a half-tone illustration in two colours from the same original with different screen angles. **2** the process of making a duotone. ● *adj.* in two colours. [L *duo* two + TONE]

dupe /dyo͞op/ *n.* & *v.* ● *n.* a victim of deception. ● *v.tr.* make a fool of; cheat; gull. □□ **dupable** *adj.* **duper** *n.* **dupery** *n.* [F f. dial. F *dupe* hoopoe, from the bird's supposedly stupid appearance]
■ *n.* fool, gull, victim, pigeon, cat's-paw, pawn, tool, puppet, *colloq.* stooge, *sl.* fall guy, sucker, sap, mark, *Brit. sl.* mug, *esp. US sl.* patsy. ● *v.* deceive, fool, outwit, trick, take in, defraud, humbug, hoax, swindle, hoodwink, flimflam, rook, gull, delude, mislead, make a fool of, *colloq.* bamboozle, rip off, put one over on, pull a fast one on, *literary* cozen, *sl.* con, bilk, *US sl.* snow, do a snow job on; see also CHEAT *v.* 1a.

dupion /dyo͞opiən/ *n.* **1** a rough silk fabric woven from the threads of double cocoons. **2** an imitation of this with other fibres. [F *doupion* f. It. *doppione* f. *doppio* double]

duple /dyo͞op'l/ *adj.* of two parts. □ **duple ratio** *Math.* a ratio of 2 to 1. **duple time** *Mus.* that with two beats to the bar. [L *duplus* f. *duo* two]

duplex /dyo͞opleks/ *n.* & *adj.* ● *n.* esp. *US* **1** a flat or maisonette on two levels. **2** a house subdivided for two families. ● *adj.* **1** having two elements; twofold. **2** esp. *US* **a** (of a flat) two-storeyed. **b** (of a house) for two families. **3** *Computing* (of a circuit) allowing the transmission of signals in both directions simultaneously (opp. SIMPLEX). □ **half-duplex** *Computing* (of a circuit) allowing the transmission of signals in both directions but not simultaneously. [L *duplex duplicis* f. *duo* two + *plic-* fold]

duplicate *adj.*, *n.*, & *v.* ● *adj.* /dyo͞oplikət/ **1** exactly like something already existing; copied (esp. in large numbers). **2 a** having two corresponding parts. **b** existing in two examples; paired. **c** twice as large or many; doubled. ● *n.* /dyŏŏplikət/ **1 a** one of two identical things, esp. a copy of an original. **b** one of two or more specimens of a thing exactly or almost identical. **2** *Law* a second copy of a letter or document. **3** (in full **duplicate bridge** or **whist**) a form of bridge or whist in which the same hands are played successively by different players. **4** *archaic* a pawnbroker's ticket. ● *v.tr.* /dyŏŏplikayt/ **1** multiply by two; double. **2 a** make or be an exact copy of. **b** make or supply copies of (*duplicated the leaflet for distribution*). **3** repeat (an action etc.), esp. unnecessarily. □ **duplicate ratio** *Math.* the proportion of the squares of two numbers. **in duplicate** consisting of two exact copies. □□ **duplicable** /-kəb'l/ *adj.* **duplication** /-káysh'n/ *n.* [L *duplicatus* past part. of *duplicare* (as DUPLEX)]

■ *adj.* **1** identical, twin, matching; copied. ● *n.* **1** (exact *or* carbon) copy, double, clone, (perfect) match, look-alike, twin, reproduction, replica, facsimile, replication; photocopy, machine copy, *propr.* Xerox. ● *v.* **2** match, replicate, imitate, reproduce; copy, photocopy, *propr.* Xerox. **3** see REPEAT *v.* 1, REPRODUCE 1, 2.

duplicator /dyŏŏplikaytər/ *n.* **1** a machine for making copies of a document, leaflet, etc. **2** a person or thing that duplicates.

duplicity /dyooplíssiti/ *n.* **1** double-dealing; deceitfulness. **2** *archaic* doubleness. □□ **duplicitous** *adj.* [ME f. OF *duplicité* or LL *duplicitas* (as DUPLEX)]

■ **1** see DECEIT 1.

duppy /dúppi/ *n.* (*pl.* **-ies**) *W.Ind.* a malevolent spirit or ghost. [perh. of Afr. orig.]

dura var. of DURRA.

durable /dyóorəb'l/ *adj.* & *n.* ● *adj.* **1** capable of lasting; hard-wearing. **2** (of goods) not for immediate consumption; able to be kept. ● *n.* (in *pl.*) durable goods. □□ **durability** /-bílliti/ *n.* **durableness** *n.* **durably** *adv.* [ME f. OF f. L *durabilis* f. *durare* endure f. *durus* hard]

■ *adj.* **1** hard-wearing, wear-resistant, heavy-duty, sturdy, tough, stout, strong, firm, sound, dependable, reliable, substantial. **2** enduring, long-lasting.

Duralumin /dyoorályoomin/ *n. propr.* a light hard alloy of aluminium with copper etc. [perh. f. *Düren* in the Rhineland or L *durus* hard + ALUMINIUM]

dura mater /dyóorə máytər/ *n. Anat.* the tough outermost membrane enveloping the brain and spinal cord (see MENINX). [med.L = hard mother, transl. Arab. *al-'umm al-jāfiya* ('mother' in Arab. indicating the relationship of things)]

duramen /dyooráymen/ *n.* = HEARTWOOD. [L f. *durare* harden]

durance /dyóorənss/ *n. archaic* imprisonment (*in durance vile*). [ME f. F f. *durer* last f. L *durare*: see DURABLE]

■ see CAPTIVITY.

duration /dyooráysh'n/ *n.* **1** the length of time for which something continues. **2** a specified length of time (*after the duration of a minute*). □ **for the duration 1** until the end of the war. **2** for a very long time. □□ **durational** *adj.* [ME f. OF f. med.L *duratio -onis* (as DURANCE)]

■ see TIME *n.* 4, 6.

durative /dyóorətiv/ *adj. Gram.* denoting continuing action.

durbar /dúrbaar/ *n. hist.* **1** the court of an Indian ruler. **2** a public levee of an Indian prince or an Anglo-Indian governor or viceroy. [Urdu f. Pers. *darbār* court]

durchkomponiert /dóorkhkomponeert/ *adj. Mus.* (of a song) having different music for each verse. [G f. *durch* through + *komponiert* composed]

duress /dyooréss/ *n.* **1** compulsion, esp. imprisonment, threats, or violence, illegally used to force a person to act against his or her will (*under duress*). **2** forcible restraint or imprisonment. [ME f. OF *duresse* f. L *duritia* f. *durus* hard]

■ **1** coercion, threat, pressure, constraint, compulsion, force. **2** confinement, incarceration, captivity, restraint, *archaic* durance; see also *imprisonment* (IMPRISON).

Durex /dyóoreks/ *n. propr.* a contraceptive sheath; a condom. [20th c.: orig. uncert.]

durian /dóoriən/ *n.* **1** a large tree, *Durio zibethinus*, native to SE Asia, bearing oval spiny fruits containing a creamy pulp with a fetid smell and an agreeable taste. **2** this fruit. [Malay *durīan* f. *dūrī* thorn]

during /dyóoring/ *prep.* **1** throughout the course or duration of (*read during the meal*). **2** at some point in the duration of (*came in during the evening*). [ME f. OF *durant* ult. f. L *durare* last, continue]

■ **1** see THROUGHOUT *prep.*

durmast /dúrmaast/ *n.* an oak tree, *Quercus petraea*, having sessile flowers. [*dur-* (perh. erron. for DUN[1]) + MAST[2]]

durn *US* var. of DARN[2].

durned *US* var. of DARNED.

durra /dúrrə/ *n.* (also **dura**, **dhurra**) a kind of sorghum, *Sorghum vulgare*, native to Asia, Africa, and the US. [Arab. *dura*, *durra*]

durst /durst/ *archaic past* of DARE.

durum /dyóorəm/ *n.* a kind of wheat, *Triticum turgidum*, having hard seeds and yielding a flour used in the manufacture of spaghetti etc. [L, neut. of *durus* hard]

durzi /dúrzi/ *n.* (*pl.* **durzis**) an Indian tailor. [Hindi f. Pers. *darzī* f. *darz* sewing]

dusk /dusk/ *n.*, *adj.*, & *v.* ● *n.* **1** the darker stage of twilight. **2** shade; gloom. ● *adj. poet.* shadowy; dim; dark-coloured. ● *v.tr.* & *intr. poet.* make or become shadowy or dim. [ME *dosk*, *dusk* f. OE *dox* dark, swarthy, *doxian* darken in colour]

■ *n.* **1** twilight, sundown, nightfall, evening, sunset, *archaic or poet.* eventide. **2** see GLOOM 1. ● *adj.* see SHADOWY 1, 2, DARK *adj.* 1. ● *v.* see DIM *v.*

dusky /dúski/ *adj.* (**duskier**, **duskiest**) **1** shadowy; dim. **2** dark-coloured, darkish. □□ **duskily** *adv.* **duskiness** *n.*

■ **1** shadowy, shady, dim, dark, dull, unilluminated, unlit, murky, gloomy, obscure, black, fuliginous, umber, *formal* subfusc, *poet.* dun. **2** dark, black, fuscous, umber; swarthy, dark-complexioned, *archaic* swart.

dust /dust/ *n.* & *v.* ● *n.* **1 a** a finely powdered earth, dirt, etc., lying on the ground or on surfaces, and blown about by the wind. **b** fine powder of any material (*pollen dust*; *gold-dust*). **c** a cloud of dust. **2** a dead person's remains (*honoured dust*). **3** confusion or turmoil (*raised quite a dust*). **4** *archaic* or *poet.* the mortal human body (*we are all dust*). **5** the ground; the earth (*kissed the dust*). ● *v.* **1** *tr.* (also *absol.*) clear (furniture etc.) of dust etc. by wiping, brushing, etc. **2** *tr.* **a** sprinkle (esp. a cake) with powder, dust, sugar, etc. **b** sprinkle or strew (sugar, powder, etc.). **3** *tr.* make dusty. **4** *intr. archaic* (of a bird) take a dust-bath. □ **dust and ashes** something very disappointing. **dust-bath** a bird's rolling in dust to freshen its feathers. **dust bowl** an area denuded of vegetation by drought or erosion and reduced to desert. **dust cover 1** = *dust-sheet*. **2** = *dust-jacket*. **dust devil** *S.Afr.* a whirlwind visible as a column of dust. **dust down 1** dust the clothes of (a person). **2** *colloq.* reprimand. **3** = *dust off*. **dusting-powder 1** talcum powder. **2** any dusting or drying powder. **dust-jacket** a usu. decorated paper cover used to protect a book from dirt etc. **dust off 1** remove the dust from (an object on which it has long been allowed to settle). **2** use and enjoy again after a long period of neglect. **dust-sheet** *Brit.* a cloth put over furniture to protect it from dust. **dust-shot** the smallest size of shot. **dust-storm** a storm with clouds of dust carried in the air. **dust-trap** something on, in, or under which dust gathers. **dust-up** *colloq.* a fight. **dust-wrapper** = *dust-jacket*. **in the dust 1** humiliated. **2** dead. **when the dust settles** when things quieten down. □□ **dustless** *adj.* [OE *dūst*: cf. LG *dunst* vapour]

■ *n.* **1 a** see DIRT 1. ● *v.* **1** see CLEAN *v.* 1. **2** powder, dredge, flour.

dustbin /dústbin/ *n. Brit.* a container for household refuse, esp. one kept outside.

dustcart /dústkaart/ *n. Brit.* a vehicle used for collecting household refuse.

duster /dústər/ *n.* **1 a** a cloth for dusting furniture etc. **b** a person or contrivance that dusts. **2** a woman's light, loose, full-length coat.

dustman /dústmən/ *n.* (*pl.* **-men**) *Brit.* **1** a man employed to clear household refuse. **2** the sandman.

dustpan /dústpan/ *n.* a small pan into which dust etc. is brushed from the floor.

dusty /dústi/ *adj.* (**dustier, dustiest**) **1** full of, covered with, or resembling dust. **2** dry as dust; uninteresting. **3** (of a colour) dull or muted. □ **dusty answer** a curt rejection of a request. **dusty miller 1** any of various plants, esp. *Artemisia stelleriana*, having white dust on the leaves and flowers. **2** an artificial fishing-fly. **not so dusty** *Brit. sl.* fairly good. □□ **dustily** *adv.* **dustiness** *n.* [OE *dūstig* (as DUST)]

Dutch /duch/ *adj.* & *n.* ● *adj.* **1** of, relating to, or associated with the Netherlands. **2** *US sl.* German. **3** *S.Afr.* of Dutch descent. **4** *archaic* of Germany including the Netherlands. ● *n.* **1 a** the language of the Netherlands. **b** *S.Afr.* usu. *derog.* Afrikaans. **2** (prec. by *the*; treated as *pl.*) **a** the people of the Netherlands. **b** *S.Afr.* Afrikaans-speakers. **3** *archaic* the language of Germany including the Netherlands. □ **beat the Dutch** *US colloq.* do something remarkable. **Dutch auction** see AUCTION. **Dutch bargain** a bargain concluded by drinking together. **Dutch barn** *Brit.* a barn roof over hay etc., set on poles and having no walls. **Dutch cap 1** a contraceptive diaphragm. **2** a woman's lace cap with triangular flaps on each side. **Dutch courage** false courage gained from alcohol. **Dutch doll** a jointed wooden doll. **Dutch door** a door divided into two parts horizontally allowing one part to be shut and the other open. **Dutch elm disease** a disease affecting elms caused by the fungus *Ceratocystis ulmi*, first found in the Netherlands. **Dutch hoe** a hoe pushed forward by the user. **Dutch interior** a painting of Dutch domestic life, esp. by P. de Hooch (d. 1683). **Dutch metal** a copper-zinc alloy imitating gold leaf. **Dutch oven 1** a metal box the open side of which is turned towards a fire. **2** a covered cooking pot for braising etc. **Dutch treat** a party, outing, etc. to which each person makes a contribution. **Dutch uncle** a person giving advice with benevolent firmness. **Dutch wife** a framework of cane etc., or a bolster, used for resting the legs in bed. **go Dutch** share expenses equally. [MDu. *dutsch* etc. Hollandish, Netherlandish, German, OHG *diutisc* national]

dutch /duch/ *n. Brit. sl.* a wife (esp. *old dutch*). [abbr. of *duchess* (also in this sense)]

Dutchman /dúchmən/ *n.* (*pl.* **-men**; *fem.* **Dutchwoman**, *pl.* **-women**) **1 a** a native or national of the Netherlands. **b** a person of Dutch descent. **2** a Dutch ship. **3** *US sl.* a German. □ **Dutchman's breeches** *US* a plant, *Dicentra cucullaria*, with white flowers and finely divided leaves. **Flying Dutchman 1** a ghostly ship. **2** its captain. **I'm a Dutchman** expression of disbelief or refusal.

duteous /dyóotiəss/ *adj. literary* (of a person or conduct) dutiful; obedient. □□ **duteously** *adv.* **duteousness** *n.* [DUTY + -OUS: cf. *beauteous*]

■ see DUTIFUL.

dutiable /dyóotiəb'l/ *adj.* liable to customs or other duties.

dutiful /dyóotifōol/ *adj.* doing or observant of one's duty; obedient. □□ **dutifully** *adv.* **dutifulness** *n.*

■ obedient, responsible, diligent, attentive, punctilious, respectful, pious, polite, considerate, deferential, submissive, acquiescent, compliant, filial, faithful, conscientious, reliable, *literary* duteous.

duty /dyóoti/ *n.* (*pl.* **-ies**) **1 a** a moral or legal obligation; a responsibility (*his duty to report it*). **b** the binding force of what is right (*strong sense of duty*). **c** what is required of one (*do one's duty*). **2** payment to the public revenue, esp.: **a** that levied on the import, export, manufacture, or sale of goods (*customs duty*). **b** that levied on the transfer of property, licences, the legal recognition of documents, etc. (*death duty*; *probate duty*). **3** a job or function (*his duties as caretaker*). **4** the behaviour due to a superior; deference, respect. **5** the measure of an engine's effectiveness in units of work done per unit of fuel. **6** *Eccl.* the performance of church services. □ **do duty for** serve as or pass for (something else). **duty-bound** obliged by duty. **duty-free** (of goods) on which duty is not leviable. **duty-free shop** a shop at an airport etc. at which duty-free goods can be bought. **duty-officer** the officer currently on duty. **duty-paid** (of goods) on which duty has been paid. **duty visit** a visit paid from obligation, not from pleasure. **on** (or **off**) **duty** engaged (or not engaged) in one's work. [AF *deweté, dueté* (as DUE)]

■ **1 a** see OBLIGATION 2. **b** see MORALITY 1, 2, 6, RESPONSIBILITY 1a. **c** office, work, assignment, job, occupation, charge; part, bit, stint. **2** tax, excise, tariff, impost, levy, customs. **3** job, function, role, task, chore. **4** respect, deference, loyalty, fealty, fidelity, faithfulness, allegiance. □ **do duty for** pass for, serve as, act as. **duty-bound** (*be duty-bound*) see SUPPOSE 7a, MUST[1] *v.* **off duty** off, free, on leave, on holiday, unoccupied, unengaged.

duumvir /dyoo-úmvər, dyóoəm-/ *n. Rom.Hist.* one of two coequal magistrates or officials. □□ **duumvirate** /-virət/ *n.* [L f. *duum virum* of the two men]

duvet /dóovay/ *n.* a thick soft quilt with a detachable cover, used instead of an upper sheet and blankets. [F]

■ see SPREAD *n.* 10.

dux /duks/ *n. Sc., Austral., NZ,* & *S.Afr.* the top pupil in a class or in a school. [L, = leader]

duyker var. of DUIKER 1.

DV *abbr. Deo volente.*

Dvr. *abbr.* Driver.

dwale /dwayl/ *n.* = BELLADONNA 1. [prob. f. Scand.]

dwarf /dwawrf/ *n.* & *v.* ● *n.* (*pl.* **dwarfs** or **dwarves** /dwawrvz/) **1 a** a person of abnormally small stature, esp. one with a normal-sized head and body but short limbs. ¶ The term *person of restricted growth* is now often preferred. **b** an animal or plant much below the ordinary size for the species. **2** a small mythological being with supernatural powers. **3** (in full **dwarf star**) a small usu. dense star. **4** (*attrib.*) **a** of a kind very small in size (*dwarf bean*). **b** puny, stunted. ● *v.tr.* **1** stunt in growth. **2** cause (something similar or comparable) to seem small or insignificant (*efforts dwarfed by their rivals' achievements*). □□ **dwarfish** *adj.* [OE *dweorg* f. Gmc]

■ *n.* **4 b** see PUNY 1, 2. ● *v.* **1** see STUNT[1] 2. **2** overshadow, dominate; diminish, minimize, lessen, make small, dim.

dwarfism /dwáwrfiz'm/ *n.* the condition of being a dwarf.

dweeb /dweeb/ *n. US sl.* a studious or tedious person. [orig. unkn.]

■ *Brit. colloq.* swot, *US colloq.* grind; see also FOOL[1] *n.* 1.

dwell /dwel/ *v.* & *n.* ● *v.intr.* (*past* and *past part.* **dwelt** or **dwelled**) **1** *literary* (usu. foll. by *in*, *at*, *near*, *on*, etc.) live, reside (*dwelt in the forest*). **2** (of a horse) be slow in raising its feet; pause before taking a fence. ● *n.* a slight, regular pause in the motion of a machine. □ **dwell on** (or **upon**) **1** spend time on, linger over; write, brood, or speak at length on (a specified subject) (*always dwells on his grievances*). **2** prolong (a note, a syllable, etc.). □□ **dweller** *n.* [OE *dwellan* lead astray, later 'continue in a place', f. Gmc]

■ *v.* **1** reside, live, lodge, stay, remain, rest, be domiciled, *archaic* abide. □ **dwell on** (or **upon**) **1** harp on, emphasize, stress, belabour, focus on, linger over, brood on *or* over, elaborate (on), talk about, *colloq.* go on about.

dwelling /dwélling/ *n.* (also **dwelling-place**) *formal* a house; a residence; an abode. □ **dwelling-house** a house used as a residence, not as an office etc.

■ habitation, house, domicile, lodging, quarters, home, residence, homestead; see also ABODE[1].

dwindle /dwínd'l/ *v.intr.* **1** become gradually smaller; shrink; waste away. **2** lose importance; decline; degenerate. [*dwine* fade away f. OE *dwīnan*, ON *dvína*]

■ **1** diminish, decrease, shrink, lessen, wane, fade, contract, condense, reduce, peter out, waste away, die out *or* down *or* away, ebb, decline, subside, taper off, shrivel (up *or* away). **2** see DEGENERATE *v.*

dwt. *abbr. hist.* pennyweight.

d.w.t. *abbr.* dead-weight tonnage.

Dy *symb. Chem.* the element dysprosium.

dyad /díad/ *n. Math.* an operator which is a combination of two vectors. □□ **dyadic** /-áddik/ *adj.* [LL *dyas dyad-* f. Gk *duas duados* f. *duo* two]

Dyak /díak/ *n.* (also **Dayak**) an aboriginal of Borneo or Sarawak. [Malay *dayak* up-country]

dyarchy var. of DIARCHY.

dybbuk /díbbŏŏk/ *n.* (*pl.* **dybbukim** /-kim/ or **dybbuks**) a malevolent spirit in Jewish folklore. [Heb. *dibbūḳ* f. *dāḇaḳ* cling]

dye /dī/ *n.* & *v.* ● *n.* **1 a** a substance used to change the colour of hair, fabric, wood, etc. **b** a colour produced by this. **2** (in full **dyestuff**) a substance yielding a dye, esp. for colouring materials in solution. ● *v.tr.* (**dyeing**) **1** impregnate with dye. **2** make (a thing) a specified colour with dye (*dyed it yellow*). □ **dyed in the wool** (or **grain**) **1** out and out; unchangeable, inveterate. **2** (of a fabric) made of yarn dyed in its raw state. **dye-line** a print made by the diazo process. □□ **dyeable** *adj.* [OE *deag*, *deagian*]

■ *n.* see COLOUR *n.* 3. ● *v.* see COLOUR *v.* 1.

dyer /díər/ *n.* a person who dyes cloth etc. □ **dyer's broom** (or **greenweed** or **oak** etc.) names of various plants yielding dyes.

dying /dí-ing/ *adj.* about to die, mortally ill; connected with, or at the time of, death (*his dying words*). □ **dying oath** an oath made at, or with the solemnity proper to, death. **to one's dying day** for the rest of one's life. [pres. part. of DIE[1]]

■ at death's door, on one's deathbed, with one foot in the grave, on one's last legs, breathing one's last, *in extremis*, moribund; last, final. □ **to one's dying day** see ALWAYS 4.

dyke[1] /dīk/ *n.* & *v.* (also **dike**) ● *n.* **1** a long wall or embankment built to prevent flooding, esp. from the sea. **2 a** a ditch or artificial watercourse. **b** *Brit.* a natural watercourse. **3 a** a low wall, esp. of turf. **b** a causeway. **4** a barrier or obstacle; a defence. **5** *Geol.* an intrusion of igneous rock across sedimentary strata. **6** esp. *Austral. sl.* a lavatory. ● *v.tr.* provide or defend with a dyke or dykes. [ME f. ON *dík* or MLG *dīk* dam, MDu. *dijc* ditch, dam: cf. DITCH]

■ **4** see PROTECTION 1b. **6** see PRIVY *n.* 1.

dyke[2] /dīk/ *n.* (also **dike**) *sl.* a lesbian. [20th c.: orig. unkn.]

dyn *abbr.* dyne.

dynamic /dīnámmik/ *adj.* & *n.* ● *adj.* (also **dynamical**) **1** energetic; active; potent. **2** *Physics* **a** concerning motive force (opp. STATIC). **b** concerning force in actual operation. **3** of or concerning dynamics. **4** *Mus.* relating to the volume of sound. **5** *Philos.* relating to dynamism. **6** (as **dynamical**) *Theol.* (of inspiration) endowing with divine power, not impelling mechanically. ● *n.* **1** an energizing or motive force. **2** *Mus.* = DYNAMICS 3. □ **dynamic equilibrium** see EQUILIBRIUM. **dynamic viscosity** see VISCOSITY. □□ **dynamically** *adv.* [F *dynamique* f. Gk *dunamikos* f. *dunamis* power]

■ *adj.* **1** vigorous, active, forceful, potent, powerful, high-powered, lively, spry, vital, electric, spirited, zealous, eager; see also ENERGETIC 1, 2. ● *n.* **1** see ENERGY 1.

dynamics /dīnámmiks/ *n.pl.* **1** (usu. treated as *sing.*) **a** *Mech.* the branch of mechanics concerned with the motion of bodies under the action of forces (cf. STATICS). **b** the branch of any science in which forces or changes are considered (*aerodynamics*; *population dynamics*). **2** the motive forces, physical or moral, affecting behaviour and change in any sphere. **3** *Mus.* the varying degree of volume of sound in musical performance. □□ **dynamicist** /-misist/ *n.* (in sense 1).

dynamism /dīnəmiz'm/ *n.* **1** energizing or dynamic action or power. **2** *Philos.* the theory that phenomena of matter or mind are due to the action of forces (rather than to motion or matter). □□ **dynamist** *n.* [Gk *dunamis* power + -ISM]

■ **1** vigour, vitality, liveliness, spirit, vim, spiritedness, forcefulness, power, drive, initiative, enterprise, *colloq.* get-up-and-go, pep, zip, push, go; see also ENERGY 1.

dynamite /dīnəmīt/ *n.* & *v.* ● *n.* **1** a high explosive consisting of nitroglycerine mixed with an absorbent. **2** a potentially dangerous person, thing, or situation. **3** *sl.* a narcotic, esp. heroin. ● *v.tr.* charge or shatter with dynamite. □□ **dynamiter** *n.* [formed as DYNAMISM + -ITE[1]]

■ *n.* **1** see EXPLOSIVE *n.* ● *v.* see BLAST *v.* 1.

dynamo /dīnəmō/ *n.* (*pl.* **-os**) **1** a machine converting mechanical into electrical energy, esp. by rotating coils of copper wire in a magnetic field. **2** *colloq.* an energetic person. [abbr. of *dynamo-electric machine* f. Gk *dunamis* power, force]

dynamometer /dīnəmómmitər/ *n.* an instrument measuring energy expended. [F *dynamomètre* f. Gk *dunamis* power, force]

dynast /dínnast, dī-/ *n.* **1** a ruler. **2** a member of a dynasty. [L f. Gk *dunastēs* f. *dunamai* be able]

dynasty /dínnəsti/ *n.* (*pl.* **-ies**) **1** a line of hereditary rulers. **2** a succession of leaders in any field. □□ **dynastic** /-nástik/ *adj.* **dynastically** /-nástikəli/ *adv.* [F *dynastie* or LL *dynastia* f. Gk *dunasteia* lordship (as DYNAST)]

■ **1** line, ancestry, family, house.

dynatron /dīnətron/ *n. Electronics* a thermionic valve, used to generate continuous oscillations. [Gk *dunamis* power + -TRON]

dyne /dīn/ *n. Physics* a unit of force that, acting on a mass of one gram, increases its velocity by one centimetre per second every second along the direction that it acts. ¶ Abbr.: **dyn.** [F f. Gk *dunamis* force, power]

dys- /diss/ *comb. form* esp. *Med.* bad, difficult. [Gk *dus-* bad]

dysentery /díssəntəri, -tri/ *n.* a disease with inflammation of the intestines, causing severe diarrhoea with blood and mucus. □□ **dysenteric** /-térrik/ *adj.* [OF *dissenterie* or L *dysenteria* f. Gk *dusenteria* (as DYS-, *enteria* f. *entera* bowels)]

dysfunction /disfúngksh'n/ *n.* an abnormality or impairment of function. □□ **dysfunctional** *adj.*

dysgraphia /disgráffiə/ *n.* an inability to write coherently. □□ **dysgraphic** *adj.* [DYS- + Gk *graphia* writing]

dyslexia /disléksiə/ *n.* an abnormal difficulty in reading and spelling, caused by a condition of the brain. □□ **dyslexic** *adj.* & *n.* **dyslectic** /-léktik/ *adj.* & *n.* [G *Dyslexie* (as DYS-, Gk *lexis* speech)]

dysmenorrhoea /dísmenəréeə/ *n.* painful or difficult menstruation.

dyspepsia /dispépsiə/ *n.* indigestion. [L *dyspepsia* f. Gk *duspepsia* (as DYS-, *peptos* cooked, digested)]

■ see INDIGESTION.

dyspeptic /dispéptik/ *adj.* & *n.* ● *adj.* of or relating to dyspepsia or the resulting depression. ● *n.* a person suffering from dyspepsia.

■ *adj.* see TOUCHY 1.

dysphasia /disfáyziə/ *n. Med.* lack of coordination in speech, owing to brain damage. □□ **dysphasic** *adj.* [Gk *dusphatos* hard to utter (as DYS-, PHATIC)]

dysphoria /disfóriə/ *n.* a state of unease or mental discomfort. □□ **dysphoric** /-fórrik/ *adj.* [Gk *dusphoria* f. *dusphoros* hard to bear (as DYS-, *pherō* bear)]

dysplasia /displáyziə/ *n. Med.* abnormal growth of tissues etc. □□ **dysplastic** /-plástik/ *adj.* [mod.L, formed as DYS- + Gk *plasis* formation]

dyspnoea /dispnéeə/ *n.* (*US* **dyspnea**) *Med.* difficult or laboured breathing. □□ **dyspnoeic** *adj.* [L f. Gk *duspnoia* (as DYS-, *pneō* breathe)]

dysprosium /disprōziəm/ *n. Chem.* a naturally occurring soft metallic element of the lanthanide series, used as a component in certain magnetic alloys. ¶ Symb.: **Dy**. [mod.L f. Gk *dusprositos* hard to get at + -IUM]

dystocia /distōshə/ *n. Med.* difficult or prolonged childbirth. [DYS- + Gk *tokos* childbirth]

dystrophy /dístrəfi/ *n.* defective nutrition. □ **muscular dystrophy** a hereditary progressive weakening and wasting of the muscles. □□ **dystrophic** /distróffik/ *adj.* [mod.L *dystrophia* formed as DYS- + Gk *-trophia* nourishment]

dysuria /disyoóriə/ *n.* painful or difficult urination. [LL f. Gk *dusouria* (as DYS-, *ouron* urine)]

dzho /zō/ *n.* (also **dzo, zho**) (*pl.* same or **-os**) a hybrid of a cow and a yak. [Tibetan *mdso*]

Ee

E[1] /ee/ *n.* (also **e**) (*pl.* **Es** or **E's**) **1** the fifth letter of the alphabet. **2** *Mus.* the third note of the diatonic scale of C major.

E[2] *abbr.* (also **E.**) **1** East, Eastern. **2** Egyptian (*£E*). **3** Engineering (*M.I.Mech.E.* etc.). **4** see E-NUMBER.

e *symb.* **1** *Math.* the base of natural logarithms, equal to approx. 2.71828. **2** used on packaging (in conjunction with specification of weight, size, etc.) to indicate compliance with EEC regulations.

e- /i, e/ *prefix* form of EX-[1] 1 before some consonants.

ea. *abbr.* each.

each /eech/ *adj.* & *pron.* ● *adj.* every one of two or more persons or things, regarded separately (*each person*; *five in each class*). ● *pron.* each person or thing (*each of us*; *have two books each*; *cost a penny each*). □ **each and every** every single. **each other** one another (used as a compound reciprocal pron.: *they hate each other*; *they wore each other's hats*). **each way** *Brit.* (of a bet) backing a horse etc. for both a win and a place. [OE *ǣlc* f. WG (as AYE[2], ALIKE)]

eager /éegər/ *adj.* **1 a** full of keen desire, enthusiastic. **b** (of passions etc.) keen, impatient. **2** keen, impatient, strongly desirous (*eager to learn*; *eager for news*). □ **eager beaver** *colloq.* a very or excessively diligent person. □□ **eagerly** *adv.* **eagerness** *n.* [ME f. AF *egre*, OF *aigre* keen, ult. f. L *acer acris*]

■ **1** avid, zealous, ardent, earnest, keen, enthusiastic, hot, hungry, fervent, fervid, passionate, spirited, energetic, energized, animated, excited, stimulated, impatient. **2** keen, desirous, yearning, desiring, craving, longing, itchy, impatient, anxious, itching, dying. □ **eager beaver** fanatic, zealot, workaholic, *colloq.* buff, freak, maniac, *sl.* fiend, nut. □□ **eagerness** avidity, zeal, earnestness, keenness, enthusiasm, fervour, hunger, vehemence, animation, vitality, appetite, zest, relish, spirit, spiritedness, gusto, verve, dash, *élan*, vim, vigour, energy, *archarnement*, *colloq.* get-up-and-go, zip, go; desire, longing, yearning, craving.

eagle /éeg'l/ *n.* **1 a** any of various large birds of prey of the family Accipitridae, with keen vision and powerful flight. **b** a figure of an eagle, esp. as a symbol of the US, or formerly as a Roman or French ensign. **2** *Golf* a score of two strokes under par at any hole. **3** *US* a coin worth ten dollars. □ **eagle eye** keen sight, watchfulness. **eagle-eyed** keen-sighted, watchful. **eagle owl** any large owl of the genus *Bubo*, with long ear tufts. [ME f. AF *egle*, OF *aigle* f. L *aquila*]

■ □ **eagle-eyed** sharp-eyed, sharp-sighted, keen-eyed, keen-sighted, lynx-eyed, hawk-eyed, lyncean; perceptive, perspicacious, discerning, sharp, watchful, vigilant, Argus-eyed; see also ALERT *adj.* 1.

eaglet /éeglit/ *n.* a young eagle.

eagre /áygər, éegər/ *n.* = BORE[3]. [17th c.: orig. unkn.]

-ean /éeən, iən/ *suffix* var. of -AN.

E. & O. E. *abbr.* errors and omissions excepted.

ear[1] /eer/ *n.* **1 a** the organ of hearing and balance in man and vertebrates, esp. the external part of this. **b** an organ sensitive to sound in other animals. **2** the faculty for discriminating sounds (*an ear for music*). **3** an ear-shaped thing, esp. the handle of a jug. **4** listening, attention. □ **all ears** listening attentively. **bring about one's ears** bring down upon oneself. **ear-drops 1** medicinal drops for the ear. **2** hanging earrings. **ear lobe** the lower soft pendulous external part of the ear. **ear-piercing** loud and shrill. **ear-splitting** excessively loud. **ear-trumpet** a trumpet-shaped device formerly used as a hearing-aid. **give ear to** listen to. **have a person's ear** receive a favourable hearing. **have** (or **keep**) **an ear to the ground** be alert to rumours or the trend of opinion. **in one ear and out the other** heard but disregarded or quickly forgotten. **out on one's ear** dismissed ignominiously. **up to one's ears** (often foll. by *in*) *colloq.* deeply involved or occupied. □□ **eared** *adj.* (also in *comb.*). **earless** *adj.* [OE *ēare* f. Gmc: rel. to L *auris*, Gk *ous*]

■ **2** sensitivity, appreciation, taste, discrimination. **4** attention, heed, notice, regard, consideration. □ **all ears** intent, heedful; see also OBSERVANT *adj.* 1a. **ear-piercing** see SHRILL *adj.* **ear-splitting** see SHRILL *adj.*, LOUD *adj.* 1. **give ear to** see HEED *v.* **have** (or **keep**) **an ear to the ground** watch out, be on the alert, keep one's eyes open *or* peeled *or* skinned. **out on one's ear** (*be out on one's ear*) see GO[1] *v.* 13a. **up to one's ears** see ENGAGED 2a.

ear[2] /eer/ *n.* the seed-bearing head of a cereal plant. [OE *ēar* f. Gmc]

earache /éerayk/ *n.* a (usu. prolonged) pain in the ear.

earbash /éerbash/ *v.tr.* esp. *Austral. sl.* talk inordinately to; harangue. □□ **earbasher** *n.* **earbashing** *n.*

eardrum /éerdrum/ *n.* the membrane of the middle ear (= *tympanic membrane*).

earful /éerfŏŏl/ *n.* (*pl.* **-fuls**) *colloq.* **1** a copious or prolonged amount of talking. **2** a strong reprimand.

earl /erl/ *n.* a British nobleman ranking between a marquess and a viscount (cf. COUNT[2]). □ **Earl Marshal** (in the UK) the officer presiding over the College of Heralds, with ceremonial duties on various royal occasions. **Earl Palatine** *hist.* an earl having royal authority within his country or domain. □□ **earldom** *n.* [OE *eorl*, of unkn. orig.]

■ see PEER[2] *n.* 1.

early /érli/ *adj.*, *adv.*, & *n.* ● *adj.* & *adv.* (**earlier**, **earliest**) **1** before the due, usual, or expected time (*was early for my appointment*; *the train arrived early*). **2 a** not far on in the day or night, or in time (*early evening*; *at the earliest opportunity*). **b** prompt (*early payment appreciated*; *at your earliest convenience*). **3 a** not far on in a period, development, or process of evolution; being the first stage (*Early English architecture*; *the early Christians*; *early Spring*). **b** of the distant past (*early man*). **c** not far on in a sequence or serial order (*the early chapters*; *appears early in the list*). **4 a** of childhood, esp. the preschool years (*early learning*). **b** (of a piece of writing, music, etc.) immature, youthful (*an early work*). **5** forward in flowering, ripening, etc. (*early peaches*). ● *n.* (*pl.* **-ies**) (usu. in *pl.*) an early fruit or vegetable, esp. potatoes. □ **at the earliest** (often placed after a specified time) not before (*will arrive on Monday at the earliest*). **early bird** *colloq.* one who arrives, gets up, etc. early. **early closing** *Brit.* the shutting of business premises on the afternoon of one particular day of the week. **early days** early in time for something to happen etc. **early grave** an untimely or premature death. **early hours** the very early morning, usu. before dawn. **early** (or **earlier**) **on** at an early (or earlier) stage. **early warning** advance warning of an imminent (esp. nuclear) attack. ▫▫ **earliness** *n.* [orig. as adv., f. OE *ǣrlīce*, *ārlīce* (*ǣr* ERE)]

■ *adj.* & *adv.* **1** beforehand, ahead (of time), in advance, before, prematurely; in good time, *literary* betimes. **2 a** at cock crow *or* cock's-crow, at (the crack *or* break of) dawn, at daybreak; first, soonest. **b** see PROMPT *adj.* 1b. **3 a** initially, originally, at *or* near the start, at *or* near the beginning; first, initial, original, advanced. **b** primeval, primitive, primordial, ancient, old, prehistoric, antediluvian; antique, antiquated. **4 b** see IMMATURE 1. **5** untimely; premature, precocious, forward.

earmark /éermaark/ *n.* & *v.* ● *n.* **1** an identifying mark. **2** an owner's mark on the ear of an animal. ● *v.tr.* **1** set aside (money etc.) for a special purpose. **2** mark (sheep etc.) with such a mark.

■ *n.* **1** see HALLMARK *n.* 2. ● *v.* **1** see ASSIGN *v.* 1a. **2** see LABEL *v.* 1.

earmuff /éermuf/ *n.* a wrap or cover for the ears, protecting them from cold, noise, etc.

earn /ern/ *v.tr.* **1** (also *absol.*) **a** (of a person) obtain (income) in the form of money in return for labour or services (*earn a weekly wage*; *happy to be earning at last*). **b** (of capital invested) bring in as interest or profit. **2 a** deserve; be entitled to; obtain as the reward for hard work or merit (*have earned a holiday*; *earned our admiration*; *earn one's keep*). **b** incur (a reproach, reputation, etc.). ▫ **earned income** income derived from wages etc. (opp. *unearned income*). [OE *earnian* f. WG, rel. to Gmc roots assoc. with reaping]

■ **1** make, gross, net, clear, receive, get, collect, reap, bring in, take home, draw, *colloq.* pull down, *Austral.*, *NZ*, & *US sl.* knock out; realize, amass; yield. **2 a** merit, deserve, be worthy of, be entitled to, win, warrant, rate, qualify for, have a claim *or* right to. **b** see INCUR.

earner /érnər/ *n.* **1** a person or thing that earns (often in *comb.*: *wage-earner*). **2** *sl.* a lucrative job or enterprise.

earnest[1] /érnist/ *adj.* & *n.* ● *adj.* ardently or intensely serious; zealous; not trifling or joking. ● *n.* seriousness. ▫ **in** (or **in real**) **earnest** serious(ly), not joking(ly); with determination. ▫▫ **earnestly** *adv.* **earnestness** *n.* [OE *eornust*, *eornost* (with Gmc cognates): cf. ON *ern* vigorous]

■ *adj.* serious, solemn, grave, sober, intense, steady, resolute, resolved, firm, determined, assiduous, diligent, assiduous, industrious, hard-working, sincere, dedicated, committed, devoted, thoughtful, conscientious; zealous, ardent, eager, keen, fervent, fervid, enthusiastic, passionate. ● *n.* see FERVOUR 1, SOLEMNITY 1. ▫ **in earnest** serious, sincere, earnest, determined; earnestly, sincerely, seriously, determinedly, fervently, fervidly, passionately, enthusiastically, eagerly, ardently, zealously.

earnest[2] /érnist/ *n.* **1** money paid as an instalment, esp. to confirm a contract etc. **2** a token or foretaste (*in earnest of what is to come*). [ME *ernes*, prob. var. of *erles*, *arles* prob. f. med.L *arrhula* (unrecorded) f. *arr(h)a* pledge]

■ **1** deposit, down payment, handsel, guarantee, security, pledge. **2** token, foretaste; anticipation.

earnings /érningz/ *n.pl.* money earned. ▫ **earnings-related** (of benefit, a pension, etc.) calculated on the basis of past or present income.

■ wages, salary, income, pay, stipend, emolument; proceeds, return, revenue, yield, takings, *esp. US* take.

earphone /éerfōn/ *n.* a device applied to the ear to aid hearing or receive radio or telephone communications.

earpiece /éerpeess/ *n.* the part of a telephone etc. applied to the ear during use.

earplug /éerplug/ *n.* a piece of wax etc. placed in the ear to protect against cold air, water, or noise.

earring /éering/ *n.* a piece of jewellery worn in or on (esp. the lobe of) the ear.

earshot /éershot/ *n.* the distance over which something can be heard (esp. *within* or *out of earshot*).

■ hearing, reach, range, call.

earth /erth/ *n.* & *v.* ● *n.* **1 a** (also **Earth**) one of the planets of the solar system orbiting about the sun between Venus and Mars; the planet on which we live. **b** land and sea, as distinct from sky. **2 a** dry land; the ground (*fell to earth*). **b** soil, clay, mould. **c** bodily matter (*earth to earth*). **3** *Relig.* the present abode of mankind, as distinct from heaven or hell; the world. **4** *Brit. Electr.* the connection to the earth as an arbitrary reference voltage in an electrical circuit. **5** the hole of a badger, fox, etc. **6** (prec. by *the*) *colloq.* a huge amount; everything (*cost the earth*; *want the earth*). ● *v.* **1** *tr.* (foll. by *up*) cover (the roots and lower stems of plants) with heaped-up earth. **2 a** *tr.* drive (a fox) to its earth. **b** *intr.* (of a fox etc.) run to its earth. **3** *tr. Brit. Electr.* connect to the earth. ▫ **come back** (or **down**) **to earth** return to realities. **earth-closet** a lavatory with dry earth used to cover excreta. **earth-hog** (or **-pig**) = AARDVARK. **earth mother 1** *Mythol.* a spirit or deity symbolizing the earth. **2** a sensual and maternal woman. **earth-nut** any of various plants, or its edible roundish tuber, esp.: **1** an umbelliferous woodland plant, *Conopodium majus*. **2** the peanut. **earth sciences** the sciences concerned with the earth or part of it, or its atmosphere (e.g. geology, oceanography, meteorology). **earth-shattering** *colloq.* having a traumatic or devastating effect. **earth-shatteringly** *colloq.* devastatingly, remarkably. **earth tremor** see TREMOR *n.* 3. **gone to earth** in hiding. **on earth** *colloq.* **1** existing anywhere (*the happiest man on earth*; *looked like nothing on earth*. **2** as an intensifier (*what on earth?*). ▫▫ **earthward** *adj.* & *adv.* **earthwards** *adv.* [OE *eorthe* f. Gmc]

■ *n.* **1 a** globe, mother earth, planet, world. **2 b** soil, dirt, loam, sod, clay, ground, mould. **6** see PILE[1] *n.* 3a. ▫ **earth-shattering** see OVERWHELMING. **gone to earth** in hiding, gone underground, gone to ground, hiding out, lying low, *US colloq.* holed up, *sl.* lying doggo. **on earth 2** see DEVIL *n.* 7.

earthbound /érthbownd/ *adj.* **1** attached to the earth or earthly things. **2** moving towards the earth.

■ **1** see TERRESTRIAL *adj.* 1, 2.

earthen /érthən/ *adj.* **1** made of earth. **2** made of baked clay.

earthenware /érthənwair/ *n.* & *adj.* ● *n.* pottery, vessels, etc., made of clay fired to a porous state which can be made impervious to liquids by the use of a glaze (cf. PORCELAIN). ● *adj.* made of fired clay. [EARTHEN + WARE[1]]

■ *n.* see POTTERY.

earthling /érthling/ *n.* an inhabitant of the earth, esp. as regarded in fiction by outsiders.

■ terrestrial, tellurian, mortal, human.

earthly /érthli/ *adj.* **1 a** of the earth; terrestrial. **b** of human life on earth; worldly, material; carnal. **2** (usu. with *neg.*) *colloq.* remotely possible or conceivable (*is no earthly use*; *there wasn't an earthly reason*). ▫ **not an earthly** *colloq.* no chance whatever. ▫▫ **earthliness** *n.*

■ **1 a** terrestrial, terrene, telluric. **b** physical, material, worldly, non-spiritual, sensual, carnal, fleshly, corporeal, base, natural, human, temporal, sublunary, secular, profane, mortal. **2** conceivable, imaginable, feasible, possible. ▫ **not an earthly** not a chance, no chance, *colloq.* not a hope in hell, not a hope, *Austral.* & *NZ colloq.* not a Buckley's.

earthquake /érthkwayk/ *n.* **1** a convulsion of the superficial parts of the earth due to the release of accumulated stress as a result of faults in strata or volcanic action. **2** a social etc. disturbance.

■ **1** quake, tremor.

earthshine /érthshīn/ *n. Astron.* **1** the unilluminated portion of a crescent moon shining faintly because of sunlight reflected from the earth on to the moon. **2** illumination on the moon's surface caused by this.

earthstar /érthstaar/ *n.* any woodland fungus of the genus *Geastrum*, esp. *G. triplex*, with a spherical spore-containing fruit body surrounded by a fleshy star-shaped structure.

earthwork /érthwurk/ *n.* **1** an artificial bank of earth in fortification or road-building etc. **2** the process of excavating soil in civil engineering work.

■ **1** see RAMPART *n.* 1a.

earthworm /érthwurm/ *n.* any of various annelid worms, esp. of the genus *Lumbricus* or *Allolobophora*, living and burrowing in the ground.

earthy /érthi/ *adj.* (**earthier, earthiest**) **1** of or like earth or soil. **2** somewhat coarse or crude; unrefined (*earthy humour*). □□ **earthily** *adv.* **earthiness** *n.*

■ **2** unrefined, coarse, vulgar, rough, dirty, indecent, obscene, ribald, bawdy, rude, shameless, wanton, uninhibited; see also CRUDE *adj.* 2a.

earwax /éerwaks/ *n.* a yellow waxy secretion produced by the ear, = CERUMEN.

earwig /éerwig/ *n.* & *v.* ● *n.* **1** any small elongate insect of the order Dermaptera, with a pair of terminal appendages in the shape of forceps. **2** *US* a small centipede. ● *v.tr.* (**earwigged, earwigging**) *archaic* influence (a person) by secret communication. [OE *ēarwicga* f. *ēare* EAR[1] + *wicga* earwig, prob. rel. to *wiggle*: once thought to enter the head through the ear]

ease /eez/ *n.* & *v.* ● *n.* **1** absence of difficulty; facility, effortlessness (*did it with ease*). **2 a** freedom or relief from pain, anxiety, or trouble. **b** freedom from embarrassment or awkwardness. **c** freedom or relief from constraint or formality. **d** freedom from poverty. ● *v.* **1** *tr.* **a** relieve from pain or anxiety etc. (often foll. by *of*: *eased my mind*; *eased me of the burden*). **b** make easy or easier; help, facilitate. **2** *intr.* (often foll. by *off*, *up*) **a** become less painful or burdensome. **b** relax; begin to take it easy. **c** slow down; moderate one's behaviour, habits, etc. **3** *tr. joc.* rob or extract money etc. from (*let me ease you of your loose change*). **4** *intr. Meteorol.* become less severe (*the wind will ease tonight*). **5 a** *tr.* relax; slacken; make a less tight fit. **b** *tr.* & *intr.* (foll. by *through*, *into*, etc.) move or be moved carefully into place (*eased it into the hole*). **6** *intr.* (often foll. by *off*) *Stock Exch.* (of shares etc.) descend in price or value. □ **at ease 1** free from anxiety or constraint. **2** *Mil.* **a** in a relaxed attitude, with the feet apart. **b** the order to stand in this way. **at one's ease** free from embarrassment, awkwardness, or undue formality. **ease away** (or **down** or **off**) *Naut.* slacken (a rope, sail, etc.). □□ **easer** *n.* [ME f. AF *ese*, OF *eise*, ult. f. L *adjacens* ADJACENT]

■ *n.* **1** easiness, simplicity, facility, effortlessness. **2 a** comfort, repose, relief, well-being, relaxation, leisure, rest, contentment, calmness, tranquillity, serenity, peacefulness, peace, peace and quiet. **b, c** naturalness, informality, unaffectedness, ingenuousness, casualness, artlessness, insouciance, nonchalance, aplomb, *savoir faire*. **d** affluence, wealth, prosperity, luxury, opulence, abundance, plenty. ● *v.* **1 a** relieve, comfort, relax, calm, tranquillize, quiet, still, pacify, soothe, disburden, *Brit.* quieten; mitigate, reduce, allay, alleviate, assuage, mollify, appease, palliate. **b** facilitate, expedite, simplify, smooth, further, clear, assist, aid, advance, forward, help. **2 a** lessen, diminish, abate, decrease. **b** see RELAX 1c. **c** calm down, relax, slacken off, remit, *colloq.* let up; see also SLOW *v.* 2. **4** drop, calm, remit, slacken, moderate; see also WANE *v.* **5 b** manoeuvre, manipulate, inch, guide, steer, slip. **6** see DROP *v.* 8a. □ **at ease 1** see TRANQUIL, EASY *adj.* 2a, 3. **at one's ease** see COMFORTABLE *adj.* 2, EASY *adj.* 3.

easel /éez'l/ *n.* **1** a standing frame, usu. of wood, for supporting an artist's work, a blackboard, etc. **2** an artist's work collectively. [Du. *ezel* = G *Esel* ASS[1]]

easement /éezmənt/ *n. Law* a right of way or a similar right over another's land. [ME f. OF *aisement*]

easily /éezili/ *adv.* **1** without difficulty. **2** by far (*easily the best*). **3** very probably (*it could easily snow*).

■ **1** effortlessly, readily, simply, smoothly, comfortably, cleanly; without difficulty, hands down, without even trying, with one's eyes closed, with one's hands tied behind one's back; without a hitch, like a charm *or* dream, like a bird. **2** by far, without doubt *or* question, beyond doubt, indisputably, indubitably, undoubtedly, doubtlessly, doubtless, unquestionably, clearly, far and away, definitely, conclusively, certainly, surely, undeniably, obviously, patently. **3** probably, most *or* very likely, well, almost certainly.

east /eest/ *n.*, *adj.*, & *adv.* ● *n.* **1 a** the point of the horizon where the sun rises at the equinoxes (cardinal point 90° to the right of north). **b** the compass point corresponding to this. **c** the direction in which this lies. **2** (usu. **the East**) **a** the regions or countries lying to the east of Europe. **b** the Communist States of eastern Europe. **3** the eastern part of a country, town, etc. **4** (**East**) *Bridge* a player occupying the position designated 'east'. ● *adj.* **1** towards, at, near, or facing east. **2** coming from the east (*east wind*). ● *adv.* **1** towards, at, or near the east. **2** (foll. by *of*) further east than. □ **East End** the part of London east of the City as far as the River Lea. **East Ender** an inhabitant of the East End. **East Indiaman** *hist.* a large ship engaged in trade with the East Indies. **East Indies** the islands etc. east of India, esp. the Malay archipelago. **east-north** (or **-south**) **-east** the direction or compass point midway between east and north-east (or south-east). **to the east** (often foll. by *of*) in an easterly direction. [OE *ēast-* f. Gmc]

■ *n.* **2 a** (**the East**) the Orient.

eastbound /éestbownd/ *adj.* travelling or leading eastwards.

Easter /éestər/ *n.* **1** (also **Easter Day** or **Sunday**) the festival (held on a variable Sunday in March or April) commemorating Christ's resurrection. **2** the season in which this occurs, esp. the weekend from Good Friday to Easter Monday. □ **Easter egg** an artificial usu. chocolate egg given at Easter, esp. to children. **Easter week** the week beginning on Easter Sunday. [OE *ēastre* app. f. *Ēostre*, a goddess associated with spring, f. Gmc]

easterly /éestərli/ *adj.*, *adv.*, & *n.* ● *adj.* & *adv.* **1** in an eastern position or direction. **2** (of a wind) blowing from the east. ● *n.* (*pl.* **-ies**) a wind blowing from the east.

eastern /éestərn/ *adj.* **1** of or in the east; inhabiting the east. **2** lying or directed towards the east. **3** (**Eastern**) of or in the Far, Middle, or Near East. □ **Eastern Church** the Orthodox Church. **Eastern hemisphere** the half of the earth containing Europe, Asia, and Africa. **Eastern Time** standard time used in eastern Canada and the US or in eastern Australia. □□ **easternmost** *adj.* [OE *ēasterne* (as EAST, -ERN)]

■ **3** (**Eastern**) orient, oriental.

easterner /éestərnər/ *n.* a native or inhabitant of the east.

Eastertide /éestərtīd/ *n.* the period including Easter.

■ see SPRING *n.* 5a.

easting /éesting/ *n. Naut.* etc. the distance travelled or the angle of longitude measured eastward from either a defined north–south grid line or a meridian.

eastward /éestwərd/ *adj.*, *adv.*, & *n.* ● *adj.* & *adv.* (also **eastwards**) towards the east. ● *n.* an eastward direction or region. □□ **eastwardly** *adj.* & *adv.*

easy /éezi/ *adj.*, *adv.*, & *int.* (**easier, easiest**) ● *adj.* **1** not difficult; achieved without great effort. **2 a** free from pain, discomfort, anxiety, etc. **b** comfortably off, affluent (*easy circumstances*). **3** free from embarrassment, awkwardness, constraint, or pressure; relaxed and pleasant (*an easy manner*). **4 a** not strict; tolerant. **b** compliant, obliging; easily persuaded (*an easy touch*). **5** *Stock Exch.* (of goods, money on loan, etc.) not much in demand. ● *adv.* with ease; in an effortless or relaxed manner. ● *int.* go carefully; move gently. □ **easy as pie** see PIE[1]. **easy chair** a large comfortable chair, usu. an armchair. **easy come easy go** *colloq.* what is easily got is soon lost or spent. **easy does it** *colloq.* go carefully. **easy money** money got without effort (esp. of dubious legality). **easy of access** easily entered or approached. **easy on the eye** (or **ear** etc.) *colloq.* pleasant to look at (or listen to etc.). **easy-peasy** *sl.* very simple. **Easy Street** *colloq.* affluence. **easy terms** payment by instalments. **go easy** (foll. by *with*, *on*) be sparing or cautious. **I'm easy** *colloq.* I have no preference. **of easy**

virtue (of a woman) sexually promiscuous. **stand easy!** *Brit. Mil.* permission to a squad standing at ease to relax their attitude further. **take it easy 1** proceed gently or carefully. **2** relax; avoid overwork. □□ **easiness** *n.* [ME f. AF *aisé*, OF *aisié* past part. of *aisier* EASE]
▪ *adj.* **1** simple, effortless, straightforward, elementary, rudimentary, basic, uncomplicated, undemanding, foolproof, plain, clear, *colloq.* soft, cushy, *sl.* easy-peasy; easy as pie, child's play, easy as can be, *colloq.* as easy as winking. **2 a** carefree, easygoing, relaxed, untroubled, quiet, serene, restful, relaxing, tranquil, peaceful, undisturbed, unoppressive, gentle, mild, calm, comfortable, cosy, unhurried, leisurely, *colloq.* cushy. **3** relaxed, unstrained, gentle, moderate, unhurried, leisurely, even, steady, flowing, undemanding, comfortable; affable, unconstrained, friendly, pleasant, amiable, amicable, agreeable, outgoing, informal, unstudied, *dégagé*, unceremonious, down-to-earth, unreserved, relaxing, natural, easygoing, approachable. **4 a** tolerant, indulgent, lenient, flexible, undemanding. **b** tractable, pliant, compliant, obliging, submissive, acquiescent, amenable, accommodating, soft, suggestible, credulous, trusting, weak. ● *adv.* effortlessly; calmly, unexcitedly, temperately, peacefully, tranquilly, serenely, nonchalantly, casually. □ **I'm easy** I don't mind, it's all the same to me, whatever you like. **of easy virtue** see PROMISCUOUS 1a. **take it easy 1** go easy, be careful, take care, look out. **2** see RELAX 4.

easygoing /éezigóing/ *adj.* **1** placid and tolerant; relaxed in manner; accepting things as they are. **2** (of a horse) having an easy gait.
▪ **1** relaxed, casual, mellow, carefree, undemanding, placid, even-tempered, forbearing, lenient, live-and-let-live, tolerant, permissive, *colloq.* laid-back; see also EASY *adj.* 3.

eat /eet/ *v.* (*past* **ate** /et, ayt/; *past part.* **eaten** /éet'n/) **1 a** *tr.* take into the mouth, chew, and swallow (food). **b** *intr.* consume food; take a meal. **c** *tr.* devour (*eaten by a lion*). **2** *intr.* (foll. by (*away*) *at*, *into*) **a** destroy gradually, esp. by corrosion, erosion, disease, etc. **b** begin to consume or diminish (resources etc.). **3** *tr. colloq.* trouble, vex (*what's eating you?*). □ **eat dirt** see DIRT. **eat one's hat** *colloq.* admit one's surprise in being wrong (only as a proposition unlikely to be fulfilled: *said he would eat his hat*). **eat one's heart out** suffer from excessive longing or envy. **eat humble pie** see HUMBLE. **eat out** have a meal away from home, esp. in a restaurant. **eat out of a person's hand** be entirely submissive to a person. **eat salt with** see SALT. **eat up 1** (also *absol.*) eat or consume completely. **2** use or deal with rapidly or wastefully (*eats up petrol*; *eats up the miles*). **3** encroach upon or annex (*eating up the neighbouring States*). **4** absorb, preoccupy (*eaten up with pride*). **eat one's words** admit that one was wrong. [OE *etan* f. Gmc]
▪ **1 a** consume, devour, take, have, ingest, munch, nibble, put away, eat up, gobble, guzzle, gormandize, *Ind.* tiffin, *colloq.* dispatch, partake of, tuck into, *joc.* demolish, *literary* manducate, *sl.* nosh, get outside (of), *sl. archaic* walk into, *Austral.* & *NZ sl.* hoe in, *Brit. sl.* knock back. **b** have a meal, dine, have a bite, *Ind.* tiffin, *archaic* sup, *colloq.* feed, *sl.* nosh. **2 a** see ERODE. **3** see TROUBLE *v.* 1, 3. □ **eat out of a person's hand** be under a person's thumb *or* control, be wrapped *or* twisted round a person's little finger, be in the palm of a person's hand, be at a person's beck and call. **eat up 4** see CONSUME 3.

eatable /éetəb'l/ *adj.* & *n.* ● *adj.* that is in a condition to be eaten (cf. EDIBLE). ● *n.* (usu. in *pl.*) food.
▪ *adj.* see EDIBLE *adj.* ● *n.* see FOOD 1.

eater /éetər/ *n.* **1** a person who eats (*a big eater*). **2** *Brit.* an eating apple etc.

eatery /éetəri/ *n. US* (*pl.* **-ies**) *colloq.* a restaurant or eating-place.
▪ see CAFÉ 1.

eating /éeting/ *adj.* **1** suitable for eating (*eating apple*). **2** used for eating (*eating-house*).

eats /eets/ *n.pl. colloq.* food.
▪ see FOOD 1.

eau-de-Cologne /ṓdəkəlṓn/ *n.* an alcohol-based perfume of a kind made orig. at Cologne. [F, lit. 'water of Cologne']
▪ see PERFUME *n.* 2.

eau-de-Nil /ṓdəneél/ *n.* a pale greenish colour. [F, lit. 'water of the Nile' (from the supposed resemblance)]

eau-de-vie /ṓdəvée/ *n.* spirits, esp. brandy. [F, lit. 'water of life']

eaves /eevz/ *n.pl.* the underside of a projecting roof. [orig. sing., f. OE *efes*: prob. rel. to OVER]

eavesdrop /éevzdrop/ *v.intr.* (**-dropped, -dropping**) listen secretly to a private conversation. □□ **eavesdropper** *n.* [*eavesdropper* orig. 'one who listens under walls' prob. f. ON *upsardropi* (cf. OE *yfæsdrypæ*): *eavesdrop* by back-form.]
▪ listen in, spy, pry, *colloq.* snoop; tap, *sl.* bug.

ebb /eb/ *n.* & *v.* ● *n.* **1** the movement of the tide out to sea (also *attrib.*: *ebb tide*). **2** the process of draining away of flood-water etc. **3** the process of declining or diminishing; the state of being in decline. ● *v.intr.* (often foll. by *away*) **1** (of tidewater) flow out to sea; recede; drain away. **2** decline; run low (*his life was ebbing away*). □ **at a low ebb** in a poor condition or state of decline. **ebb and flow** a continuing process of decline and upturn in circumstances. **on the ebb** in decline. [OE *ebba*, *ebbian*]
▪ *n.* **3** decline, decay, decrease, diminution, wane, drop, slackening (off), dwindling, lessening, deterioration, degeneration. ● *v.* **1** recede, flow back, subside, go out, go down, drain away, fall back *or* away, retreat, retrocede, retire. **2** decline, flag, decay, wane, diminish, decrease, lessen, drop, slacken, fade (away), drain away, dwindle, peter out, waste away, deteriorate, fall off *or* away, die out *or* down *or* away, run low. □ **at a low ebb** see *on the decline* (DECLINE). **on the ebb** see *on the decline* (DECLINE).

ebonite /ébbənīt/ *n.* = VULCANITE. [EBONY + -ITE[1]]

ebony /ébbəni/ *n.* & *adj.* ● *n.* (*pl.* **-ies**) **1** a heavy hard dark wood used for furniture. **2** any of various trees of the genus *Diospyros* producing this. ● *adj.* **1** made of ebony. **2** black like ebony. [earlier *hebeny* f. (*h*)*eben*(*e*) = *ebon*, perh. after *ivory*]
▪ *adj.* **2** see BLACK *adj.* 1.

ebullient /ibúlliənt, *disp.* ibŏŏl-/ *adj.* **1** exuberant, high-spirited. **2** *Chem.* boiling. □□ **ebullience** *n.* **ebulliency** *n.* **ebulliently** *adv.* [L *ebullire ebullient-* bubble out (as E-, *bullire* boil)]
▪ **1** high-spirited, buoyant, exuberant, enthusiastic, zestful, effervescent, excited, effusive, exhilarated, elated, animated, ecstatic, rapturous, rapt.

EC *abbr.* **1** East Central (London postal district). **2** executive committee. **3 a** European Community. **b** European Commission.

ecad /éekad/ *n. Ecol.* an organism modified by its environment. [Gk *oikos* house + -AD[1]]

écarté /aykaártay/ *n.* **1** a card-game for two persons in which cards from a player's hand may be exchanged for others from the pack. **2** a position in classical ballet with one arm and leg extended. [F, past part. of *écarter* discard]

Ecce Homo /ékkay hómmō/ *n. Art* one of the subjects of the Passion cycle: in Renaissance painting typically a depiction of Christ wearing the crown of thorns. [L, = 'behold the man', the words of Pilate to the Jews after the crowning with thorns (John 19:5)]

eccentric /iksséntrik/ *adj.* & *n.* ● *adj.* **1** odd or capricious in behaviour or appearance; whimsical. **2 a** not placed, not having its axis etc. placed centrally. **b** (often foll. by *to*) (of a circle) not concentric (to another). **c** (of an orbit) not circular. ● *n.* **1** an eccentric person. **2** *Mech.* an eccentric contrivance for changing rotatory into backward-and-forward motion, e.g. the cam used in an internal-combustion engine. □□ **eccentrically** *adv.* **eccentricity** /-trissiti/ *n.* (*pl.* **-ies**). [LL *eccentricus* f. Gk *ekkentros* f. *ek* out of + *kentros* CENTRE]
▪ *adj.* **1** unconventional, unusual, odd, peculiar, strange,

curious, bizarre, outlandish, queer, quaint, far-out, quirky, offbeat, kinky, uncommon, abnormal, idiosyncratic, unorthodox, whimsical, capricious, out of the ordinary, irregular, atypical, errant, aberrant, exceptional, individual, singular, unique, *colloq.* weird, cranky, oddball. ● *n.* **1** original, individualist, nonconformist, crank, *Austral.* (hard) doer, *Austral.* & *NZ* hard case, *colloq.* character, odd fish, freak, oddball, weirdo, weirdie, *Austral.* & *NZ sl.* dag, *Brit. sl.* oner. □□ **eccentricity** unconventionality, strangeness, oddness, bizarreness, bizarrerie, nonconformity, individuality, individualism, singularity, uniqueness, distinctiveness, capriciousness, weirdness; idiosyncrasy, quirk, peculiarity, whim, mannerism, crotchet, aberration, anomaly, oddity, curiosity, caprice.

Eccles. *abbr.* Ecclesiastes (Old Testament).

Eccles cake /ékk'lz/ *n.* a round flat cake made of pastry filled with currants etc. [*Eccles* in N. England]

ecclesial /ikleéziəl/ *adj.* of or relating to a Church. [Gk *ekklesia* assembly, church f. *ekklētos* summoned out f. *ek* out + *kaleō* call]

ecclesiastic /ikleéziástik/ *n.* & *adj.* ● *n.* a priest or clergyman. ● *adj.* = ECCLESIASTICAL. □□ **ecclesiasticism** /-tisiz'm/ *n.* [F *ecclésiastique* or LL *ecclesiasticus* f. Gk *ekklēsiastikos* f. *ekklēsia* assembly, church: see ECCLESIAL]
■ *n.* see CLERGYMAN.

ecclesiastical /ikleéziástik'l/ *adj.* of the Church or the clergy. □□ **ecclesiastically** *adv.*
■ see CLERICAL 1.

ecclesiology /ikleéziólləji/ *n.* **1** the study of churches, esp. church building and decoration. **2** theology as applied to the nature and structure of the Christian Church. □□ **ecclesiological** /-ziəlójik'l/ *adj.* **ecclesiologist** *n.* [Gk *ekklēsia* assembly, church (see ECCLESIAL) + -LOGY]

Ecclus. /ékləss/ *abbr.* Ecclesiasticus (Apocrypha).

eccrine /ékreen/ *adj.* (of a gland, e.g. a sweat gland) secreting without loss of cell material. [Gk *ek* out of + *krinō* sift]

ecdysis /ekdísiss/ *n.* the action of casting off skin or shedding an exoskeleton etc. [mod.L f. Gk *ekdusis* f. *ekduō* put off]

ECG *abbr.* electrocardiogram.

echelon /éshəlon, áyshəlon/ *n.* & *v.* ● *n.* **1** a level or rank in an organization, in society, etc.; those occupying it (often in *pl.*: *the upper echelons*). **2** *Mil.* a formation of troops, ships, aircraft, etc., in parallel rows with the end of each row projecting further than the one in front (*in echelon*). ● *v.tr.* arrange in an echelon. [F *échelon* f. *échelle* ladder f. L *scala*]
■ *n.* **1** see GRADE *n.* 1a, CATEGORY.

echeveria /échəveériə/ *n.* any succulent plant of the genus *Echeveria*, native to Central and S. America. [M. *Echeveri*, 19th-c. Mex. botanical draughtsman]

echidna /ikídnə/ *n.* any of several egg-laying pouch-bearing mammals native to Australia and New Guinea, with a covering of spines, and having a long snout and long claws. Also called *spiny anteater*. [mod.L f. Gk *ekhidna* viper]

echinoderm /ikínəderm, ékkin-/ *n.* any marine invertebrate of the phylum Echinodermata, usu. having a spiny skin, e.g. starfish and sea urchins. [ECHINUS + Gk *derma -atos* skin]

echinoid /ikínoyd, ékkin-/ *n.* a sea urchin.

echinus /ikínəss/ *n.* **1** any sea urchin of the genus *Echinus*, including the common European edible urchin, *E. esculentus*. **2** *Archit.* a rounded moulding below an abacus on a Doric or Ionic capital. [ME f. L f. Gk *ekhinos* hedgehog, sea urchin]

echo /ékkō/ *n.* & *v.* ● *n.* (*pl.* **-oes**) **1 a** the repetition of a sound by the reflection of sound waves. **b** the secondary sound produced. **2** a reflected radio or radar beam. **3** a close imitation or repetition of something already done. **4** a person who slavishly repeats the words or opinions of another. **5** (often in *pl.*) circumstances or events reminiscent of or remotely connected with earlier ones. **6** *Bridge* etc. a conventional mode of play to show the number of cards held in the suit led etc. ● *v.* (**-oes, -oed**) **1** *intr.* **a** (of a place) resound with an echo. **b** (of a sound) be repeated; resound. **2** *tr.* repeat (a sound) by an echo. **3** *tr.* **a** repeat (another's words). **b** imitate the words, opinions, or actions of (a person). □ **echo chamber** an enclosure with sound-reflecting walls. **echo location** the location of objects by reflected sound. **echo-sounder** sounding apparatus for determining the depth of the sea beneath a ship by measuring the time taken for an echo to be received. **echo-sounding** the use of an echo-sounder. **echo verse** a verse form in which a line repeats the last syllables of the previous line. □□ **echoer** *n.* **echoless** *adj.* [ME f. OF or L f. Gk *ēkhō*, rel. to *ēkhē* a sound]
■ *n.* **1** reverberation, repercussion, repetition, iteration, reiteration. **3** imitation, copy, replica, replication, repetition, duplication, reproduction; reflection, mirror image. ● *v.* **1 a** resound, reverberate, ring. **3** imitate, ape, parrot, mimic, copy, duplicate, reproduce, simulate, repeat, emulate, mirror, reflect.

echocardiogram /ékkōkaárdiəgram/ *n. Med.* a record produced by echocardiography.

echocardiography /ékkōkaárdiógrəfi/ *n. Med.* the use of ultrasound waves to investigate the action of the heart. □□ **echocardiograph** /ékkōkaárdiəgraaf/ *n.* **echocardiographer** *n.*

echoencephalogram /ékko-enséffəlōgram/ *n. Med.* a record produced by echoencephalography.

echoencephalography /ékko-enséffəlógrəfi/ *n. Med.* the use of ultrasound waves to investigate intracranial structures.

echogram /ékkōgram/ *n.* a record made by an echo-sounder.

echograph /ékkōgraaf/ *n.* a device for automatically recording echograms.

echoic /ekṓ-ik/ *adj. Phonet.* (of a word) imitating the sound it represents; onomatopoeic. □□ **echoically** *adv.*

echoism /ékkō-iz'm/ *n.* = ONOMATOPOEIA.

echolalia /ékkōláyliə/ *n.* **1** the meaningless repetition of another person's spoken words. **2** the repetition of speech by a child learning to talk. [mod.L f. Gk *ēkhō* echo + *lalia* talk]

echovirus /ékkōvīrəss/ *n.* (also **ECHO virus**) any of a group of enteroviruses sometimes causing mild meningitis, encephalitis, etc. [f. *e*nteric *c*ytopathogenic *h*uman *o*rphan (because not originally assignable to any known disease) + VIRUS]

echt /ekht/ *adj.* authentic, genuine, typical. [G]

éclair /aykláir/ *n.* a small elongated cake of choux pastry filled with cream and iced with chocolate or coffee icing. [F, lit. lightning, flash]

éclaircissement /áyklairseésmon/ *n. archaic* an enlightening explanation of something hitherto inexplicable (e.g. conduct etc.). [F f. *éclaircir* clear up]

eclampsia /iklámpsiə/ *n.* a condition involving convulsions leading to coma, occurring esp. in pregnant women. □□ **eclamptic** *adj.* [mod.L f. F *eclampsie* f. Gk *eklampsis* sudden development f. *eklampō* shine forth]

éclat /ayklaá/ *n.* **1** brilliant display; dazzling effect. **2** social distinction; conspicuous success; universal approbation (*with great éclat*). [F f. *éclater* burst out]
■ **1** see PANACHE. **2** see RENOWN.

eclectic /ikléktik/ *adj.* & *n.* ● *adj.* **1** deriving ideas, tastes, style, etc., from various sources. **2** *Philos.* & *Art* selecting one's beliefs etc. from various sources; attached to no particular school of philosophy. ● *n.* **1** an eclectic person. **2** a person who subscribes to an eclectic school of thought. □□ **eclectically** *adv.* **eclecticism** /-tisiz'm/ *n.* [Gk *eklektikos* f. *eklegō* pick out]
■ *adj.* **1** see CATHOLIC *adj.* 2.

eclipse /iklíps/ *n.* & *v.* ● *n.* **1** the obscuring of the reflected light from one celestial body by the passage of another between it and the eye or between it and its source of illumination. **2 a** a deprivation of light or the period of this. **b** obscuration or concealment; a period of this. **3** a rapid or

sudden loss of importance or prominence, esp. in relation to another or a newly-arrived person or thing. ● *v.tr.* **1** (of a celestial body) obscure the light from or to (another). **2** intercept (light, esp. of a lighthouse). **3** deprive of prominence or importance; outshine, surpass. □ **in eclipse 1** surpassed; in decline. **2** (of a bird) having lost its courting plumage. □□ **eclipser** *n.* [ME f. OF f. L f. Gk *ekleipsis* f. *ekleipō* fail to appear, be eclipsed f. *leipō* leave]
■ *n.* **2** darkening, shading, dimming, concealment, covering, hiding, blocking, blockage, occultation, obscuring, obscuration. **3** downturn, slump, deterioration; see also PLUNGE *n.* ● *v.* **1** conceal, hide, blot out, obscure, block, veil, shroud, cover. **3** overshadow, obscure, surpass, top, outshine. □ **in eclipse 1** see *on the decline* (DECLINE).

ecliptic /iklíptik/ *n.* & *adj.* ● *n.* the sun's apparent path among the stars during the year. ● *adj.* of an eclipse or the ecliptic. [ME f. L f. Gk *ekleiptikos* (as ECLIPSE)]

eclogue /éklog/ *n.* a short poem, esp. a pastoral dialogue. [L *ecloga* f. Gk *eklogē* selection f. *eklegō* pick out]
■ pastoral, idyll.

eclosion /iklṓzh'n/ *n.* the emergence of an insect from a pupa-case or of a larva from an egg. [F *éclosion* f. *éclore* hatch (as EX-[1], L *claudere* to close)]

eco- /éekō/ *comb. form* ecology, ecological.

ecoclimate /éekōklīmit/ *n.* climate considered as an ecological factor.

ecology /ikólləji/ *n.* **1** the branch of biology dealing with the relations of organisms to one another and to their physical surroundings. **2** (in full **human ecology**) the study of the interaction of people with their environment. □□ **ecological** /éekəlójik'l/ *adj.* **ecologically** /éekəlójikəli/ *adv.* **ecologist** *n.* [G *Ökologie* f. Gk *oikos* house]
■ □□ **ecologist** see CONSERVATIONIST, NATURALIST.

Econ. *abbr.* Economics.

econometrics /ikónnəmétriks/ *n.pl.* (usu. treated as *sing.*) a branch of economics concerned with the application of mathematical economics to economic data by the use of statistics. □□ **econometric** *adj.* **econometrical** *adj.* **econometrician** /-mətrísh'n/ *n.* **econometrist** *n.* [ECONOMY + METRIC]

economic /éekənómmik, ék-/ *adj.* **1** of or relating to economics. **2** maintained for profit; on a business footing. **3** adequate to repay or recoup expenditure with some profit (*not economic to run buses on Sunday*; *an economic rent*). **4** practical; considered or studied with regard to human needs (*economic geography*). [ME f. OF *economique* or L *oeconomicus* f. Gk *oikonomikos* (as ECONOMY)]
■ **1** financial, fiscal, pecuniary, monetary, budgetary; commercial, mercantile, *attrib.* trade. **3** profitable, cost-effective, money-making, remunerative, productive. **4** see PRACTICAL *adj.* 1, 2.

economical /éekənómmik'l, ék-/ *adj.* sparing in the use of resources; avoiding waste. □□ **economically** *adv.*
■ cost-effective, money-saving; cheap, inexpensive, reasonable, economic; provident, thrifty, sparing, prudent, conservative, frugal, careful.

economics /éekənómmiks, ék-/ *n.pl.* (often treated as *sing.*) **1 a** the science of the production and distribution of wealth. **b** the application of this to a particular subject (*the economics of publishing*). **2** the condition of a country etc. as regards material prosperity.
■ **1b, 2** see FINANCE *n.* 1.

economist /ikónnəmist/ *n.* **1** an expert in or student of economics. **2** a person who manages financial or economic matters. [Gk *oikonomos* (as ECONOMY) + -IST]

economize /ikónnəmīz/ *v.intr.* (also **-ise**) **1** be economical; make economies; reduce expenditure. **2** (foll. by *on*) use sparingly; spend less on. □□ **economization** /-záysh'n/ *n.* **economizer** *n.*
■ **1** tighten one's belt, cut costs, scrimp (and save), pinch pennies. **2** save, cut back, retrench, skimp, scrimp, spend less.

economy /ikónnəmi/ *n.* (*pl.* **-ies**) **1 a** the wealth and resources of a community, esp. in terms of the production and consumption of goods and services. **b** a particular kind of this (*a capitalist economy*). **c** the administration or condition of an economy. **2 a** the careful management of (esp. financial) resources; frugality. **b** (often in *pl.*) an instance of this (*made many economies*). **3** sparing or careful use (*economy of language*). **4** (also **economy class**) the cheapest class of air travel. **5** (*attrib.*) (also **economy-size**) (of goods) consisting of a large quantity for a proportionally lower cost. [F *économie* or L *oeconomia* f. Gk *oikonomia* household management f. *oikos* house + *nemō* manage]
■ **2 a** thrift, husbandry, thriftiness, frugality, conservation, conservatism, restraint, control. **b** saving, cut-back, reduction, cut. **3** brevity, briefness, succinctness, sparingness, terseness, curtness, conciseness, concision, compactness, restraint.

ecosphere /éekōsfeer/ *n.* the region of space including planets where conditions are such that living things can exist.

écossaise /áykosáyz/ *n.* **1** an energetic dance in duple time. **2** the music for this. [F, fem. of *écossais* Scottish]

ecosystem /éekōsistəm/ *n.* a biological community of interacting organisms and their physical environment.
■ see ENVIRONMENT 3.

ecru /áykroo͞/ *n.* the colour of unbleached linen; light fawn. [F *écru* unbleached]

ecstasize /ékstəsīz/ *v.tr.* & *intr.* (also **-ise**) throw or go into ecstasies.

ecstasy /ékstəsi/ *n.* (*pl.* **-ies**) **1** an overwhelming feeling of joy or rapture. **2** *Psychol.* an emotional or religious frenzy or trancelike state. **3** *sl.* methylenedioxymethamphetamine, a powerful stimulant and hallucinatory drug (see MDMA). [ME f. OF *extasie* f. LL *extasis* f. Gk *ekstasis* standing outside oneself f. *ek* out + *histēmi* to place]
■ **1** delight, joy, rapture, bliss, transport, exaltation, thrill, elation, excitement, nympholepsy, happiness, gladness, pleasure, enjoyment, gratification; heaven on earth.

ecstatic /ikstáttik/ *adj.* & *n.* ● *adj.* **1** in a state of ecstasy. **2** very enthusiastic or excited (*was ecstatic about his new job*). **3** producing ecstasy; sublime (*an ecstatic embrace*). ● *n.* a person subject to (usu. religious) ecstasy. □□ **ecstatically** *adv.* [F *extatique* f. Gk *ekstatikos* (as ECSTASY)]
■ *adj.* **1, 2** exhilarated, thrilled, exultant, euphoric, rapturous, enraptured, nympholeptic, enchanted, transported, excited, elated, delighted, joyful, gleeful, overjoyed, happy, glad, beside oneself, cock-a-hoop, delirious, over the moon, in seventh heaven, *colloq.* on cloud nine *or* seven. **3** blissful, sublime, heavenly, rhapsodic, delightful, orgasmic; see also EXQUISITE *adj.*

ECT *abbr.* electroconvulsive therapy.

ecto- /éktō/ *comb. form* outside. [Gk *ekto-* stem of *ektos* outside]

ectoblast /éktōblast/ *n.* = ECTODERM. □□ **ectoblastic** /-blástik/ *adj.*

ectoderm /éktōderm/ *n. Biol.* the outermost layer of an animal embryo in early development. □□ **ectodermal** /-dérm'l/ *adj.*

ectogenesis /éktōjénnisiss/ *n. Biol.* the production of structures outside the organism. □□ **ectogenetic** /-jinéttik/ *adj.* **ectogenic** /-jénnik/ *adj.* **ectogenous** /ektójinəss/ *adj.* [mod.L (as ECTO-, GENESIS)]

ectomorph /éktōmorf/ *n.* a person with a lean and delicate build of body and large skin surface in comparison with weight (cf. ENDOMORPH, MESOMORPH). □□ **ectomorphic** /-mórfik/ *adj.* **ectomorphy** *n.* [ECTO- + Gk *morphē* form]

-ectomy /éktəmi/ *comb. form* denoting a surgical operation in which a part of the body is removed (*appendectomy*). [Gk *ektomē* excision f. *ek* out + *temnō* cut]

ectopic /ektópik/ *adj. Med.* in an abnormal place or position. □ **ectopic pregnancy** a pregnancy occurring outside the womb. [mod.L *ectopia* f. Gk *ektopos* out of place]

ectoplasm /éktōplaz'm/ *n.* **1** the dense outer layer of the cytoplasm (cf. ENDOPLASM). **2** the supposed viscous substance exuding from the body of a spiritualistic medium during a trance. ▫▫ **ectoplasmic** /-plázmik/ *adj.*

ectozoon /éktōzṓ-on/ *n. Biol.* a parasite that lives on the outside of its host.

ECU *abbr.* (also **ecu** /ékyōō/) European currency unit.

ecumenical /éekyooménnik'l, ék-/ *adj.* **1** of or representing the whole Christian world. **2** seeking or promoting worldwide Christian unity. ▫▫ **ecumenically** *adv.* [LL *oecumenicus* f. Gk *oikoumenikos* of the inhabited earth (*oikoumenē*)]

▪ see BROAD *adj.* 8.

ecumenicalism /éekyooménnikəliz'm, ék-/ *n.* (also **ecumenism** /eekyōōməniz'm/) the principle or aim of the unity of Christians worldwide.

eczema /éksimə/ *n.* inflammation of the skin, with itching and discharge from blisters. ▫▫ **eczematous** /ekséemətəss, eksém-/ *adj.* [mod.L f. Gk *ekzema -atos* f. *ek* out + *zeō* boil]

ed. *abbr.* **1** edited by. **2** edition. **3** editor. **4** educated; education.

-ed[1] /əd, id/ *suffix* forming adjectives: **1** from nouns, meaning 'having, wearing, affected by, etc.' (*talented*; *trousered*; *diseased*). **2** from phrases of adjective and noun (*good-humoured*; *three-cornered*). [OE *-ede*]

-ed[2] /əd, id/ *suffix* forming: **1** the past tense and past participle of weak verbs (*needed*; *risked*). **2** participial adjectives (*escaped prisoner*; *a pained look*). [OE *-ed*, *-ad*, *-od*]

edacious /idáyshəss/ *adj. literary* or *joc.* **1** greedy. **2** of eating. ▫▫ **edacity** *n.* /idássity/ [L *edax -acis* f. *edere* eat]

Edam /éedam/ *n.* a round Dutch cheese, usu. pale yellow with a red rind. [*Edam* in Holland]

edaphic /idáffik/ *adj.* **1** *Bot.* of the soil. **2** *Ecol.* produced or influenced by the soil. [G *edaphisch* f. Gk *edaphos* floor]

Edda /éddə/ *n.* **1** (also **Elder Edda, Poetic Edda**) a collection of medieval Icelandic poems on Norse legends. **2** (also **Younger Edda, Prose Edda**) a 13th-c. miscellaneous handbook to Icelandic poetry. [perh. a name in a Norse poem or f. ON *óthr* poetry]

▪ **1** see LEGEND 1a–c.

eddo /éddō/ *n.* (*pl.* **-oes**) = TARO. [Afr. word]

eddy /éddi/ *n.* & *v.* ● *n.* (*pl.* **-ies**) **1** a circular movement of water causing a small whirlpool. **2** a movement of wind, fog, or smoke resembling this. ● *v.tr.* & *intr.* (**-ies, -ied**) whirl round in eddies. ▫ **eddy current** *Electr.* a localized current induced in a conductor by a varying magnetic field. [prob. OE *ed-* again, back, perh. of Scand. orig.]

▪ *n.* swirl, whirl, vortex, whirlpool; whirlwind, *S.Afr.* dust devil, devil; waterspout, *US* twister. ● *v.* swirl, whirl, turn, spin.

edelweiss /áyd'lvīss/ *n.* an Alpine plant, *Leontopodium alpinum*, with woolly white bracts around the flower-heads, growing in rocky places. [G f. *edel* noble + *weiss* white]

edema *US* var. of OEDEMA.

Eden /éed'n/ *n.* (also **Garden of Eden**) a place or state of great happiness; paradise (with reference to the abode of Adam and Eve in the biblical account of the Creation). [ME f. LL f. Gk *Ēdēn* f. Heb. *'ēḏen*, orig. = delight]

▪ see HEAVEN 2.

edentate /idéntayt/ *adj.* & *n.* ● *adj.* having no or few teeth. ● *n.* any mammal, esp. of the order Edentata, having no or few teeth, e.g. an anteater or sloth. [L *edentatus* (as E-, *dens dentis* tooth)]

edge /ej/ *n.* & *v.* ● *n.* **1** a boundary line or margin of an area or surface. **2** a narrow surface of a thin object. **3** the meeting-line of two surfaces of a solid. **4 a** the sharpened side of the blade of a cutting instrument or weapon. **b** the sharpness of this (*the knife has lost its edge*). **5** the area close to a steep drop (*along the edge of the cliff*). **6** anything compared to an edge, esp. the crest of a ridge. **7 a** effectiveness, force; incisiveness, **b** keenness, excitement (esp. as an element in an otherwise routine situation). **8** an advantage, superiority. ● *v.* **1** *tr.* & *intr.* (often foll. by *in*, *into*, *out*, etc.) move gradually or furtively towards an objective (*edged it into the corner*; *they all edged towards the door*). **2** *tr.* **a** provide with an edge or border. **b** form a border to. **c** trim the edge of. **3** *tr.* sharpen (a knife, tool, etc.). **4** *tr. Cricket* strike (the ball) with the edge of the bat. ▫ **have the edge on** (or **over**) have a slight advantage over. **on edge 1** tense and restless or irritable. **2** eager, excited. **on the edge of** almost involved in or affected by. **set a person's teeth on edge** (of a taste or sound) cause an unpleasant nervous sensation. **take the edge off** dull, weaken; make less effective or intense. ▫▫ **edgeless** *adj.* **edger** *n.* [OE *ecg* f. Gmc]

▪ *n.* **1** brink, verge, border, side, rim, lip, brim; fringe, margin, boundary, bound, limit, perimeter, periphery, *archaic* bourn. **4 b** acuteness, sharpness, keenness. **7 a** urgency, force, effectiveness; incisiveness, harshness, sharpness, acrimony, pungency. **b** see ANIMATION. **8** advantage, head start, superiority, lead, upper hand. ● *v.* **1** inch, move, sidle, crawl, creep, steal, worm, work one's way. **2 b** see BORDER *v.* 1, 2. **c** see TRIM *v.* 1b. ▫ **on edge 1** on tenterhooks, tense, nervous, touchy, sensitive, prickly, irascible, crabbed, crabby, peevish, apprehensive, edgy, anxious, ill at ease, restive, restless, fidgety, like a cat on a hot tin roof *or* on hot bricks, *colloq.* uptight; (*be on edge*) have one's heart in one's mouth; see also IRRITABLE 1. **2** see EAGER 1. **take the edge off** tarnish, dim, cloud, becloud; see also MITIGATE.

edgeways /éjwayz/ *adv.* (also **edgewise** /-wīz/) **1** with the edge uppermost or towards the viewer. **2** edge to edge. ▫ **get a word in edgeways** contribute to a conversation when the dominant speaker pauses briefly.

▪ **1** see SIDEWAYS *adv.*

edging /éjing/ *n.* **1** something forming an edge or border, e.g. a fringe or lace. **2** the process of making an edge. ▫ **edging-shears** shears for trimming the edges of a lawn.

▪ **1** see BORDER *n.* 3.

edgy /éji/ *adj.* (**edgier, edgiest**) **1** irritable; nervously anxious. **2** disjointed (*edgy rhythms*). ▫▫ **edgily** *adv.* **edginess** *n.*

▪ **1** see ANXIOUS 1, TESTY.

edh var. of ETH.

edible /éddib'l/ *adj.* & *n.* ● *adj.* fit or suitable to be eaten (cf. EATABLE). ● *n.* (in *pl.*) food. ▫▫ **edibility** /-bílliti/ *n.* [LL *edibilis* f. *edere* eat]

▪ *adj.* esculent, palatable, good *or* fit to eat, wholesome, *formal or joc.* comestible.

edict /éedikt/ *n.* an order proclaimed by authority. ▫▫ **edictal** /idíktəl/ *adj.* [ME f. L *edictum* f. *edicere* proclaim]

▪ see LAW 1a.

edifice /éddifiss/ *n.* **1** a building, esp. a large imposing one. **2** a complex organizational or conceptual structure. [ME f. OF f. L *aedificium* f. *aedis* dwelling + *-ficium* f. *facere* make]

▪ **1** see BUILDING.

edify /éddifī/ *v.tr.* (**-ies, -ied**) (of a circumstance, experience, etc.) instruct and improve morally or intellectually. ▫▫ **edification** /-fikáysh'n/ *n.* **edifying** *adj.* **edifyingly** *adv.* [ME f. OF *edifier* f. L *aedificare* (as EDIFICE)]

▪ see EDUCATE 1, 2. ▫▫ **edification** enlightenment, improvement, guidance, education, information, tuition, teaching, schooling, instruction. **edifying** see INFORMATIVE.

edit /éddit/ *v.* & *n.* ● *v.tr.* (**edited, editing**) **1 a** assemble, prepare, modify, or condense (written material, esp. the work of another or others) for publication. **b** prepare an edition of (an author's work). **2** be in overall charge of the content and arrangement of (a newspaper, journal, etc.). **3** take extracts from and collate (films, tape-recordings, etc.) to form a unified sequence. **4 a** prepare (data) for processing by a computer. **b** alter (a text entered in a word processor etc.). **5 a** reword to correct, or to alter the emphasis. **b** (foll. by *out*) remove (part) from a text etc. ● *n.* **1 a** a piece of editing. **b** an edited item. **2** a facility for editing. [F *éditer* (as EDITION): partly a back-form. f. EDITOR]

▪ *v.* **1** redact, copy-edit, copyread, *Brit.* sub-edit, *colloq.* sub; prepare, compile, assemble, select, arrange, organize, order, reorganize, reorder; modify, alter, adapt, change, revise, style, restyle; cut, condense, compress, shorten, crop, reduce. **5 a** rewrite, rephrase, reword, restyle, correct, emend; bowdlerize, expurgate, clean up. **b** (*edit out*) blue-pencil, cut (out), delete, censor, erase.

edition /idísh'n/ *n.* **1 a** one of the particular forms in which a literary work etc. is published (*paperback edition*; *pocket edition*). **b** a copy of a book in a particular form (*a first edition*). **2** a whole number of copies of a book, newspaper, etc., issued at one time. **3** a particular version or instance of a broadcast, esp. of a regular programme or feature. **4** a person or thing similar to or resembling another (*a miniature edition of her mother*). [F *édition* f. L *editio -onis* f. *edere edit-* put out (as E-, *dare* give)]

▪ **1, 2** number, issue, copy; printing, print run; version.

editio princeps /idíshiō prínseps/ *n.* (*pl.* ***editiones principes*** /idíshiōneez prínsipeez/) the first printed edition of a book, text, etc. [L]

editor /éddítər/ *n.* **1** a person who edits material for publication or broadcasting. **2** a person who directs the preparation of a newspaper or periodical, or a particular section of one (*sports editor*). **3** a person who selects or commissions material for publication. **4** a person who edits film, sound track, etc. **5** a computer program for modifying data. ▫▫ **editorship** *n.* [LL, = producer (of games), publisher (as EDIT)]

▪ **1** writer, columnist, journalist, rewrite man *or* woman, rewriter, copy editor, copyreader, redactor, reviser, *Brit.* sub-editor, *colloq.* sub. **2** editorial writer, *Brit.* leader-writer. **3** commissioner, compiler, collector, selector; publisher.

editorial /édditóriəl/ *adj.* & *n.* ● *adj.* **1** of or concerned with editing or editors. **2** written or approved by an editor. ● *n.* a newspaper article written by or on behalf of an editor, esp. one giving an opinion on a topical issue. ▫▫ **editorialist** *n.* **editorialize** *v.intr.* (also **-ise**). **editorially** *adv.*

▪ *n.* essay, article, column, leading article, *Brit.* leader.

-edly /idli/ *suffix* forming adverbs from verbs, meaning 'in a manner characterized by performance of or undergoing of the verbal action' (*allegedly*; *disgustedly*; *hurriedly*).

EDP *abbr.* electronic data processing.

EDT *abbr.* *US* Eastern Daylight Time.

educate /édyookayt/ *v.tr.* (also *absol.*) **1** give intellectual, moral, and social instruction to (a pupil, esp. a child), esp. as a formal and prolonged process. **2** provide education for. **3** (often foll. by *in*, or *to* + infin.) train or instruct for a particular purpose. **4** advise; give information to. ▫▫ **educable** /-kəb'l/ *adj.* **educability** /-kəbílliti/ *n.* **educatable** *adj.* **educative** /-kətiv/ *adj.* **educator** *n.* [L *educare educat-*, rel. to *educere* EDUCE]

▪ **1, 2** teach, train, instruct, edify, tutor, school, form, inform, enlighten, cultivate, develop, civilize. **3** train, instruct, coach, drill, prepare, ready. **4** see INFORM 1.

educated /édyookaytid/ *adj.* **1** having had an education, esp. to a higher level than average. **2** resulting from a (good) education (*an educated accent*). **3** based on experience or study (*an educated guess*).

▪ **1** erudite, well-read, lettered, literary, scholarly, learned, well-informed, knowledgeable; cultivated, cultured, enlightened. **2** refined, polished, cultivated, civilized, cultured, *colloq.* posh.

education /édyookáysh'n/ *n.* **1 a** the act or process of educating or being educated; systematic instruction. **b** the knowledge gained from this. **2** a particular kind of or stage in education (*further education*; *a classical education*). **3 a** development of character or mental powers. **b** a stage in or aspect of this (*travel will be an education for you*). ▫▫ **educational** *adj.* **educationalist** *n.* **educationally** *adv.* **educationist** *n.* [F *éducation* or L *educatio* (as EDUCATE)]

▪ **1 a** teaching, schooling, training, instruction, tuition, tutelage, edification, tutoring, cultivation, drilling; learning. **b** lore, knowledge, information, erudition. ▫▫ **educational** academic, scholastic, instructional, *archaic or derog.* pedagogical; informative, instructive, enlightening, edifying, eye-opening, revelatory, educative.

educe /idyóoss/ *v.tr.* **1** bring out or develop from latent or potential existence; elicit. **2** infer; elicit a principle, number, etc., from data. ▫▫ **educible** *adj.* **eduction** /idúksh'n/ *n.* **eductive** /idúktiv/ *adj.* [ME f. L *educere educt-* lead out (as E-, *ducere* lead)]

▪ **1** see DERIVE 1. **2** see DERIVE 3.

Edw. *abbr.* Edward.

Edwardian /edwáwrdiən/ *adj.* & *n.* ● *adj.* of, characteristic of, or associated with the reign of King Edward VII (1901–10). ● *n.* a person belonging to this period.

-ee /ee/ *suffix* forming nouns denoting: **1** the person affected by the verbal action (*addressee*; *employee*; *lessee*). **2** a person concerned with or described as (*absentee*; *bargee*; *refugee*). **3** an object of smaller size (*bootee*). [from or after AF past part. in *-é* f. L *-atus*]

EEC *abbr.* European Economic Community.

EEG *abbr.* electroencephalogram.

eel /eel/ *n.* **1** any of various snakelike fish, with slender body and poorly developed fins. **2** a slippery or evasive person or thing. ▫ **eel-grass 1** any marine plant of the genus *Zostera*, with long ribbon-like leaves. **2** any submerged freshwater plant of the genus *Vallisneria*. ▫▫ **eel-like** *adj.* **eely** *adj.* [OE *ǣl* f. Gmc]

eelpout /éelpowt/ *n.* **1** any fish of the family Zoarcidae, with slender body and dorsal and anal fins meeting to fuse with the tail. Also called POUT[2]. **2** = BURBOT. [OE *ǣleputa* (as EEL, POUT[2])]

eelworm /éelwurm/ *n.* any of various small nematode worms infesting plant roots.

e'en[1] /een/ *archaic* or *poet.* var. of EVEN[1].

e'en[2] /een/ *Sc.* var. of EVEN[2].

-een /een/ *suffix Ir.* forming diminutive nouns (*colleen*). [Ir. *-in* dimin. suffix]

e'er /air/ *poet.* var. of EVER.

-eer /eer/ *suffix* forming: **1** nouns meaning 'person concerned with or engaged in' (*auctioneer*; *mountaineer*; *profiteer*). **2** verbs meaning 'be concerned with' (*electioneer*). [from or after F *-ier* f. L *-arius*: cf. -IER, -ARY[1]]

eerie /éeri/ *adj.* (**eerier**, **eeriest**) gloomy and strange; weird, frightening (*an eerie silence*). ▫▫ **eerily** *adv.* **eeriness** *n.* [orig. N.Engl. and Sc. *eri*, of obscure orig.: cf. OE *earg* cowardly]

▪ frightening, weird, strange, uncanny, ghostly, spectral, dreadful, unearthly, mysterious, frightful, *Sc.* eldritch, *colloq.* scary, creepy, spooky.

EETPU *abbr.* (in the UK) Electrical, Electronic, Telecommunications, and Plumbing Union.

ef- /if, ef/ *prefix* assim. form of EX-[1] 1 before *f*.

eff /ef/ *v. sl. euphem.* **1** *tr.* & *intr.* (often foll. by *off*) = FUCK (in expletive use). **2** *intr.* say *fuck* or similar coarse slang words. ▫ **effing and blinding** using coarse slang. [name of the letter *F*, as a euphemistic abbr.]

efface /ifáyss/ *v.* **1** *tr.* rub or wipe out (a mark etc.). **2** *tr.* (in abstract senses) obliterate; wipe out (*effaced it from his memory*). **3** *tr.* utterly surpass; eclipse (*success has effaced all previous attempts*). **4** *refl.* treat or regard oneself as unimportant (*self-effacing*). ▫▫ **effacement** *n.* [F *effacer* (as EX-[1], FACE)]

▪ **1** see ERASE 1. **2** see ERASE 2.

effect /ifékt/ *n.* & *v.* ● *n.* **1** the result or consequence of an action etc.; the significance or implication of this. **2** efficacy (*had little effect*). **3** an impression produced on a spectator, hearer, etc. (*lights had a pretty effect*; *my words had no effect*). **4** (in *pl.*) property, luggage. **5** (in *pl.*) the lighting, sound, etc., used to accompany a play, film, broadcast, etc. **6** *Physics* a physical phenomenon, usually named after its discoverer (*Doppler effect*). **7** the state of being operative. ● *v.tr.* **1** bring about; accomplish. **2** cause to exist or occur. □ **bring** (or **carry**) **into effect** accomplish. **for effect** to create an impression. **give effect to** make operative. **in effect** for practical purposes; in reality. **take effect** become operative. **to the effect that** the general substance or gist being. **to that effect** having that result or implication. **with effect from** coming into operation at or on (a stated time or day). [ME f. OF *effect* or L *effectus* (as EX-[1], *facere* make)]

■ *n.* **1** result, consequence, outcome, conclusion, upshot; significance, meaning, signification, purport, sense, essence, drift, implication, import, tenor, purpose, intent, intention, object, objective. **2** effectiveness, efficacy, force, power, potency, influence, impression, impact, power, *colloq.* punch. **4** (*effects*) belongings, (personal) property, possessions, stuff, things, paraphernalia, chattels, goods, *colloq.* gear, *Brit. sl.* clobber; baggage, luggage, bags, cases. ● *v.* bring *or* carry into effect, bring about, cause, make happen *or* take place, effectuate, achieve, accomplish, succeed in, secure, obtain, make, execute, carry out, produce, create. □ **bring into effect** see ACCOMPLISH. **in effect** effectively, virtually, for (all) practical purposes, more or less; actually, in (point of) fact, really, in reality, essentially, basically, at bottom, truly, to all intents and purposes, at the end of the day, whichever way you look at it, *disp.* in actual fact, *literary* in truth. **take effect** become operative *or* operational, come into operation, come into force, begin to operate, start to operate.

effective /iféktiv/ *adj.* & *n.* ● *adj.* **1** having a definite or desired effect. **2** powerful in effect; impressive. **3 a** actual; existing in fact rather than officially or theoretically (*took effective control in their absence*). **b** actually usable; realizable; equivalent in its effect (*effective money*; *effective demand*). **4** coming into operation (*effective as from 1 May*). **5** (of manpower) fit for work or service. ● *n.* a soldier available for service. □□ **effectively** *adv.* **effectiveness** *n.* [ME f. L *effectivus* (as EFFECT)]

■ *adj.* **1** effectual, efficacious, productive; capable, useful, serviceable, competent, operative, able, functional, efficient. **2** impressive, outstanding, striking, powerful. **3** real, actual, true; realizable, usable. **4** operative, operational, in operation, functioning.

effector /iféktər/ *adj.* & *n. Biol.* ● *adj.* acting in response to a stimulus. ● *n.* an effector organ.

effectual /iféktyooəl/ *adj.* **1** capable of producing the required result or effect; answering its purpose. **2** valid. □□ **effectuality** /-tyoo-álliti/ *n.* **effectually** *adv.* **effectualness** *n.* [ME f. med.L *effectualis* (as EFFECT)]

■ **1** effective, efficacious, efficient, functional, productive, useful, influential, powerful, adequate. **2** in force, valid, legal, lawful, binding, sound.

effectuate /iféktyoo-ayt/ *v.tr.* cause to happen; accomplish. □□ **effectuation** /-áysh'n/ *n.* [med.L *effectuare* (as EFFECT)]

■ bring about, effect, cause, make happen, carry out, implement, accomplish, do, execute, realize, achieve.

effeminate /ifémminət/ *adj.* (of a man) feminine in appearance or manner; unmasculine. □□ **effeminacy** *n.* **effeminately** *adv.* [ME f. L *effeminatus* past part. of *effeminare* (as EX-[1], *femina* woman)]

■ unmanly, womanish, womanly, unmasculine, feminine, emasculate, epicene, effete, milky; affected, *colloq.* camp, campy, sissy, *sl.* limp-wristed, nancy, *Brit. sl. derog.* poofy.

effendi /eféndi/ *n.* (*pl.* **effendis**) **1** a man of education or standing in Eastern Mediterranean or Arab countries. **2** a former title of respect or courtesy in Turkey. [f. Turk. *efendi* f. mod. Gk *afentēs* f. Gk *authentēs* lord, master: see AUTHENTIC]

efferent /éffərənt/ *adj. Physiol.* conducting outwards (*efferent nerves*; *efferent vessels*) (opp. AFFERENT). □□ **efference** *n.* [L *efferre* (as EX-[1], *ferre* carry)]

effervesce /éffərvéss/ *v.intr.* **1** give off bubbles of gas; bubble. **2** (of a person) be lively or energetic. □□ **effervescence** *n.* **effervescency** *n.* **effervescent** *adj.* [L *effervescere* (as EX-[1], *fervēre* be hot)]

■ **1** see FIZZ *v.* 2. □□ **effervescent** bubbling, fizzy, carbonated, sparkling, fizzing, gassy; foaming, foamy, frothing, frothy, bubbly; high-spirited, sparkly, sparkling, vivacious, ebullient, lively, exuberant, buoyant, animated, lively, exhilarated, excited, enthusiastic, irrepressible; see also ENERGETIC 1, 2.

effete /ifeét/ *adj.* **1 a** feeble and incapable. **b** effeminate. **2** worn out; exhausted of its essential quality or vitality. □□ **effeteness** *n.* [L *effetus* worn out by bearing young (as EX-[1], FOETUS)]

■ see WEAK 2.

efficacious /éffikáyshəss/ *adj.* (of a thing) producing or sure to produce the desired effect. □□ **efficaciously** *adv.* **efficaciousness** *n.* **efficacy** /éffikəsi/ *n.* [L *efficax* (as EFFICIENT)]

■ effective, effectual, productive, competent, successful, efficient, useful, serviceable.

efficiency /ifíshənsi/ *n.* (*pl.* **-ies**) **1** the state or quality of being efficient. **2** *Mech.* & *Physics* the ratio of useful work performed to the total energy expended or heat taken in. □ **efficiency bar** a point on a salary scale requiring evidence of efficiency for further promotion. [L *efficientia* (as EFFICIENT)]

■ **1** effectiveness, efficacy, efficaciousness, competence, productiveness, capability, proficiency.

efficient /ifísh'nt/ *adj.* **1** productive with minimum waste or effort. **2** (of a person) capable; acting effectively. □ **efficient cause** *Philos.* an agent that brings a thing into being or initiates a change. □□ **efficiently** *adv.* [ME f. L *efficere* (as EX-[1], *facere* make, accomplish)]

■ **1** economic, thrifty; effective, efficacious, effectual, productive. **2** competent, proficient; see also CAPABLE 1.

effigy /éffiji/ *n.* (*pl.* **-ies**) a sculpture or model of a person. □ **in effigy** in the form of a (usu. crude) representation of a person. [L *effigies* f. *effingere* to fashion]

■ see IMAGE *n.* 1.

effleurage /éflöraázh/ *n.* & *v.* ● *n.* a form of massage involving a circular inward stroking movement made with the palm of the hand, used esp. during childbirth. ● *v.intr.* massage with a circular stroking movement. [F f. *effleurer* to skim]

effloresce /éfloréss/ *v.intr.* **1** burst out into flower. **2** *Chem.* **a** (of a substance) turn to a fine powder on exposure to air. **b** (of salts) come to the surface and crystallize on it. **c** (of a surface) become covered with salt particles. □□ **efflorescence** *n.* **efflorescent** *adj.* [L *efflorescere* (as EX-[1], *florēre* to bloom f. *flos floris* flower)]

■ **1** see FLOWER *v.* 1.

effluence /éflooənss/ *n.* **1** a flowing out (of light, electricity, etc.). **2** that which flows out. [F *effluence* or med.L *effluentia* f. L *effluere efflux-* flow out (as EX-[1], *fluere* flow)]

■ see STREAM *n.* 2.

effluent /éflooənt/ *adj.* & *n.* ● *adj.* flowing forth or out. ● *n.* **1** sewage or industrial waste discharged into a river, the sea, etc. **2** a stream or lake flowing from a larger body of water.

effluvium /iflóoviəm/ *n.* (*pl.* **effluvia** /-viə/) an unpleasant or noxious odour or exhaled substance affecting the lungs or the sense of smell etc. [L (as EFFLUENT)]

■ see SMELL *n.* 3.

efflux /éfluks/ *n.* = EFFLUENCE. □□ **effluxion** /eflúksh'n/ *n.* [med.L *effluxus* (as EFFLUENT)]

effort /éffərt/ *n.* **1** strenuous physical or mental exertion. **2** a vigorous or determined attempt. **3** *Mech.* a force exerted. **4** *colloq.* the result of an attempt; something accomplished (*not bad for a first effort*). □□ **effortful** *adj.* [F f. OF *esforcier* ult. f. L *fortis* strong]

■ **1** exertion, energy, striving, struggle, strain, labour, pains, toil, trouble, work, *colloq.* elbow-grease. **2** endeavour, try, venture, *formal* essay; see also ATTEMPT *n.* **4** achievement, feat, deed, attainment, exploit; see also ACCOMPLISHMENT 3.

effortless /éffərtliss/ *adj.* **1** seemingly without effort; natural, easy. **2** requiring no effort (*effortless contemplation*). ▫▫ **effortlessly** *adv.* **effortlessness** *n.*

■ simple, painless, smooth, trouble-free, uncomplicated; see also EASY *adj.* 1.

effrontery /ifrúntəri/ *n.* (*pl.* **-ies**) **1** shameless insolence; impudent audacity (esp. *have the effrontery to*). **2** an instance of this. [F *effronterie* f. *effronté* ult. f. LL *effrons -ontis* shameless (as EX-[1], *frons* forehead)]

■ **1** insolence, impertinence, impudence, audacity, presumption, presumptuousness, brazenness, boldness, temerity, brashness, arrogance, front, face, cheek, *colloq.* brass, nerve, lip, mouth, *esp. Austral.* & *NZ colloq.* hide, *Brit. colloq.* brass neck, *sl.* gall, chutzpah, *Brit. sl.* side.

effulgent /ifúljənt/ *adj. literary* radiant; shining brilliantly. ▫▫ **effulgence** *n.* **effulgently** *adv.* [L *effulgēre* shine forth (as EX-[1], *fulgēre* shine)]

■ see RADIANT *adj.* 1.

effuse *adj.* & *v.* ● *adj.* /ifyo͞oss/ *Bot.* (of an inflorescence etc.) spreading loosely. ● *v.tr.* /ifyo͞oz/ **1** pour forth (liquid, light, etc.). **2** give out (ideas etc.). [ME f. L *effusus* past part. of *effundere effus-* pour out (as EX-[1], *fundere* pour)]

effusion /ifyo͞ozh'n/ *n.* **1** a copious outpouring. **2** usu. *derog.* an unrestrained flow of speech or writing. [ME f. OF *effusion* or L *effusio* (as EFFUSE)]

■ see OUTPOURING.

effusive /ifyo͞ossiv/ *adj.* **1** gushing, demonstrative, exuberant (*effusive praise*). **2** *Geol.* (of igneous rock) poured out when molten and later solidified, volcanic. ▫▫ **effusively** *adv.* **effusiveness** *n.*

■ **1** demonstrative, gushing, enthusiastic, over-enthusiastic, expansive, emotional, exuberant, rhapsodic, ebullient, lavish, voluble, profuse, *disp.* fulsome.

EFL *abbr.* English as a foreign language.

eft /eft/ *n.* a newt. [OE *efeta*, of unkn. orig.]

Efta /éftə/ *n.* (also **EFTA**) European Free Trade Association. [abbr.]

EFTPOS /éftpoz/ *abbr.* electronic funds transfer at point-of-sale.

e.g. *abbr.* for example. [L *exempli gratia*]

■ see *for example* (EXAMPLE).

egad /eegád/ *int. archaic* or *joc.* by God. [prob. orig. *a* ah + GOD]

egalitarian /igállitáiriən/ *adj.* & *n.* ● *adj.* **1** of or relating to the principle of equal rights and opportunities for all (*an egalitarian society*). **2** advocating this principle. ● *n.* a person who advocates or supports egalitarian principles. ▫▫ **egalitarianism** *n.* [F *égalitaire* f. *égal* EQUAL]

■ *adj.* **1** democratic, classless.

egg[1] /eg/ *n.* **1 a** the spheroidal reproductive body produced by females of animals such as birds, reptiles, fish, etc., enclosed in a protective layer and capable of developing into a new individual. **b** the egg of the domestic hen, used for food. **2** *Biol.* the female reproductive cell in animals and plants. **3** *colloq.* a person or thing qualified in some way (*a tough egg*). **4** anything resembling or imitating an egg, esp. in shape or appearance. ▫ **as sure as eggs is** (or **are**) **eggs** *colloq.* without any doubt. **egg-beater 1** a device for beating eggs. **2** *US sl.* a helicopter. **egg-custard** = CUSTARD[1]. **egg-flip** (or **-nog**) a drink of alcoholic spirit with beaten egg, milk, etc. **eggs** (or **egg**) **and bacon** any of various yellow- and orange-shaded plants, esp. the snapdragon or toadflax. **egg-spoon** a small spoon for eating a boiled egg. **egg-timer** a device for timing the cooking of an egg. **egg-tooth** a projection of an embryo bird or reptile used for breaking out of the shell. **egg-white** the white of an egg. **have** (or **put**) **all one's eggs in one basket** *colloq.* risk everything on a single venture. **with egg on one's face** *colloq.* made to look foolish. ▫▫ **eggless** *adj.* **eggy** *adj.* (**eggier, eggiest**). [ME f. ON, rel. to OE *ǣg*]

■ **2** see SEED *n.* 1a. ▫ **egg-white** albumen, glair.

egg[2] /eg/ *v.tr.* (foll. by *on*) urge (*egged us on to it; egged them on to do it*). [ME f. ON *eggja* = EDGE]

■ see MOTIVATE.

eggcup /égkup/ *n.* a cup for holding a boiled egg.

egger /éggər/ *n.* (also **eggar**) any of various large moths of the family Lasiocampidae, esp. *Lasiocampa quercus*, with an egg-shaped cocoon. [prob. f. EGG[1] + -ER[1]]

egghead /ég-hed/ *n. colloq.* an intellectual; an expert.

■ see INTELLECTUAL *n.*

eggplant /égplaant/ *n.* = AUBERGINE.

eggshell /égshel/ *n.* & *adj.* ● *n.* **1** the shell of an egg. **2** anything very fragile. ● *adj.* **1** (of china) thin and fragile. **2** (of paint) with a slight gloss finish.

eglantine /églǝntīn/ *n.* sweet-brier. [ME f. F *églantine* f. OF *aiglent* ult. f. L *acus* needle]

ego /éegō/ *n.* (*pl.* **-os**) **1** *Metaphysics* a conscious thinking subject. **2** *Psychol.* the part of the mind that reacts to reality and has a sense of individuality. **3** self-esteem. ▫ **ego-ideal 1** *Psychol.* the part of the mind developed from the ego by an awareness of social standards. **2** (in general use) idealization of oneself. **ego-trip** *colloq.* activity etc. devoted entirely to one's own interests or feelings. [L, = I]

egocentric /éegōséntrik/ *adj.* **1** centred in the ego. **2** self-centred, egoistic. ▫▫ **egocentrically** *adv.* **ego-centricity** /-trissiti/ *n.* [EGO + -CENTRIC after *geocentric* etc.]

■ **2** see *egoistic, egoistical* (EGOISM).

egoism /éegō-iz'm/ *n.* **1** an ethical theory that treats self-interest as the foundation of morality. **2** systematic selfishness. **3** self-opinionatedness. **4** = EGOTISM. ▫▫ **egoist** *n.* **egoistic** /-ístik/ *adj.* **egoistical** /-ístik'l/ *adj.* [F *égoïsme* ult. f. mod.L *egoismus* (as EGO)]

■ **2** self-centredness, self-absorption, self-love, self-interest, self-indulgence, selfishness, egocentricity, egomania; see also EGOTISM 2, INTEREST *n.* 7. **3** see *intolerance* (INTOLERANT). ▫▫ **egoistic, egoistical** self-centred, egocentric, narcissistic, self-seeking, self-absorbed, egomaniacal, selfish, self-serving, self-indulgent, self-important, self-opinionated, self-aggrandizing; see also *egotistic, egotistical* (EGOTISM).

egomania /éegōmáyniə/ *n.* morbid egotism. ▫▫ **egomaniac** /-máyniak/ *n.* **egomaniacal** /-mənīək'l/ *adj.*

egotism /éegətiz'm/ *n.* **1** excessive use of 'I' and 'me'. **2** the practice of talking about oneself. **3** an exaggerated opinion of oneself. **4** selfishness. ▫▫ **egotist** *n.* **egotistic** /-tístik/ *adj.* **egotistical** /-tístik'l/ *adj.* **egotistically** /-tístikəli/ *adv.* **egotize** *v.intr.* (also **-ise**). [EGO + -ISM with intrusive *-t-*]

■ **2** self-obsession, self-absorption, self-love, self-centredness, egocentricity, egomania. **3** see VANITY 1. **4** see INTEREST *n.* 7. ▫▫ **egotistic, egotistical** conceited, proud, overweening, arrogant, boastful, boasting, *colloq.* swelled-headed, swollen-headed; vain, self-worshipping, self-admiring, self-important, egocentric, selfish, egomaniacal, *literary* vainglorious; see also *egoistic, egoistical* (EGOISM).

egregious /igréejəss/ *adj.* **1** outstandingly bad; shocking (*egregious folly; an egregious ass*). **2** *archaic* or *joc.* remarkable. ▫▫ **egregiously** *adv.* **egregiousness** *n.* [L *egregius* illustrious, lit. 'standing out from the flock' f. *grex gregis* flock]

■ **1** see TERRIBLE 1.

egress /éegress/ *n.* **1 a** a going out. **b** the right of going out. **2** an exit; a way out. **3** *Astron.* the end of an eclipse or transit. ▫▫ **egression** /eegrésh'n/ *n.* (in senses 1, 2). [L *egressus* f. *egredi egress-* (as E-, *gradi* to step)]

■ **2** exit, way out, door, gate.

egret /éegrit/ *n.* any of various herons of the genus *Egretta* or *Bulbulcus*, usu. having long white feathers in the breeding season. [ME, var. of AIGRETTE]

Egyptian /ijípsh'n/ *adj.* & *n.* ● *adj.* **1** of or relating to Egypt in NE Africa. **2** of or for Egyptian antiquities (e.g. in a museum) (*Egyptian room*). ● *n.* **1** a native of ancient or modern Egypt; a national of the Arab Republic of Egypt. **2**

the Hamitic language used in ancient Egypt until the 3rd c. AD. □□ **Egyptianize** *v.tr.* (also **-ise**) **Egyptianization** /-nīzáysh'n/ *n.*

Egyptology /éejiptólləji/ *n.* the study of the language, history, and culture of ancient Egypt. □□ **Egyptologist** *n.*

eh /ay/ *int. colloq.* **1** expressing enquiry or surprise. **2** inviting assent. **3** asking for something to be repeated or explained. [ME *ey*, instinctive exclam.]

-eian /iən/ *suffix* corresp. to *-ey* (or *-y*) + *-an* (*Bodleian*; *Rugbeian*).

Eid /eed/ *n.* a Muslim week-long festival celebrating the end of the fast of Ramadan. [Arab. *'īd* feast]

eider /ídər/ *n.* **1** (in full **eider duck**) any of various large northern ducks, esp. of the genus *Somateria*. **2** (in full **eider-down**) small soft feathers from the breast of the eider duck. [Icel. *aethr*]

eiderdown /ídərdown/ *n.* a quilt stuffed with down (orig. from the eider) or some other soft material, esp. as the upper layer of bedclothes.
■ see SPREAD *n.* 10.

eidetic /īdéttik/ *adj.* & *n.* ● *adj. Psychol.* (of a mental image) having unusual vividness and detail, as if actually visible. ● *n.* a person able to see eidetic images. □□ **eidetically** *adv.* [G *eidetisch* f. Gk *eidētikos* f. *eidos* form]

eidolon /īdṓlon/ *n.* (*pl.* **eidolons** or **eidola** /-lə/) **1** a spectre; a phantom. **2** an idealized figure. [Gk *eidōlon*: see IDOL]
■ **1** see VISION *n.* 2.

eigen- /ígən/ *comb. form Math.* & *Physics* proper, characteristic. [G *eigen* OWN]

eigenfrequency /ígənfreekwənsi/ *n.* (*pl.* **-ies**) *Math.* & *Physics* one of the natural resonant frequencies of a system.

eigenfunction /ígənfungksh'n/ *n. Math.* & *Physics* that function which under a given operation generates some multiple of itself.

eigenvalue /ígənvalyoo/ *n. Math.* & *Physics* that value by which an eigenfunction of an operation is multiplied after the eigenfunction has been subjected to that operation.

eight /ayt/ *n.* & *adj.* ● *n.* **1** one more than seven, or two less than ten; the product of two units and four units. **2** a symbol for this (8, viii, VIII). **3** a figure resembling the form of 8. **4** a size etc. denoted by eight. **5** an eight-oared rowing-boat or its crew. **6** the time of eight o'clock (*is it eight yet?*). **7** a card with eight pips. ● *adj.* that amount to eight. □ **have one over the eight** *sl.* get slightly drunk. [OE *ehta*, *eahta*]

eighteen /áytéen/ *n.* & *adj.* ● *n.* **1** one more than seventeen, or eight more than ten; the product of two units and nine units. **2** a symbol for this (18, xviii, XVIII). **3** a size etc. denoted by eighteen. **4** a set or team of eighteen individuals. **5** (**18**) *Brit.* (of films) classified as suitable for persons of 18 years and over. ● *adj.* that amount to eighteen. □□ **eighteenth** *adj.* & *n.* [OE *ehtatēne*, *eaht-*]
■ *n.* **4** see SIDE 5a.

eighteenmo /áytéenmō/ *n.* = OCTODECIMO.

eightfold /áytfōld/ *adj.* & *adv.* **1** eight times as much or as many. **2** consisting of eight parts. **3** amounting to eight.

eighth /aytth/ *n.* & *adj.* ● *n.* **1** the position in a sequence corresponding to the number 8 in the sequence 1–8. **2** something occupying this position. **3** one of eight equal parts of a thing. ● *adj.* that is the eighth. □ **eighth note** esp. *US Mus.* = QUAVER. □□ **eighthly** *adv.*

eightsome /áytsəm/ *n.* **1** (in full **eightsome reel**) a lively Scottish reel for eight dancers. **2** the music for this.

eighty /áyti/ *n.* & *adj.* ● *n.* (*pl.* **-ies**) **1** the product of eight and ten. **2** a symbol for this (80, lxxx, LXXX). **3** (in *pl.*) the numbers from 80 to 89, esp. the years of a century or of a person's life. ● *adj.* that amount to eighty. □ **eighty-first, -second**, etc. the ordinal numbers between eightieth and ninetieth. **eighty-one, -two**, etc. the cardinal numbers between eighty and ninety. □□ **eightieth** *adj.* & *n.* **eightyfold** *adj.* & *adv.* [OE *-eahtatig* (as EIGHT, -TY²)]

einkorn /ínkorn/ *n.* a kind of wheat (*Triticum monococcum*). [G f. *ein* one + *Korn* seed]

einsteinium /īnstíniəm/ *n. Chem.* a transuranic radioactive metallic element produced artificially from plutonium. ¶ Symb.: **Es**. [A. *Einstein*, Ger.-Amer. physicist d. 1955]

eirenic var. of IRENIC.

eirenicon /īréenikon/ *n.* (also **irenicon**) a proposal made as a means of achieving peace. [Gk, neut. of *eirēnikos* (adj.) f. *eirēnē* peace]

eisteddfod /īstéthvod, -stédfəd/ *n.* (*pl.* **eisteddfods** or **eisteddfodau** /-dī/) a congress of Welsh bards; a national or local festival for musical competitions etc. □□ **eisteddfodic** /-fóddik/ *adj.* [Welsh, lit. = session, f. *eistedd* sit]

either /íthər, éethər/ *adj.*, *pron.*, *adv.*, & *conj.* ● *adj.* & *pron.* **1** one or the other of two (*either of you can go*; *you may have either book*). **2** each of two (*houses on either side of the road*; *either will do*). ● *adv.* & *conj.* **1** as one possibility (*is either black or white*). **2** as one choice or alternative; which way you will (*either come in or go out*). **3** (with *neg.* or *interrog.*) **a** any more than the other (*I didn't like it either*; *if you do not go, I shall not either*). **b** moreover (*there is no time to lose, either*). □ **either-or** *n.* an unavoidable choice between alternatives. ● *adj.* involving such a choice. **either way** in either case or event. [OE *ǣgther* f. Gmc]

ejaculate *v.* & *n.* ● *v.tr.* /ijákyoolayt/ (also *absol.*) **1** utter suddenly (words esp. of prayer or other emotion). **2** eject (fluid etc., esp. semen) from the body. ● *n.* /ijákyoolət/ semen that has been ejaculated from the body. □□ **ejaculation** /-láysh'n/ *n.* **ejaculator** /ijákyoolaytər/ *n.* **ejaculatory** /ijákyoolaytəri/ *adj.* [L *ejaculari* to dart (as E-, *jaculum* javelin)]
■ *v.* **1** see EXCLAIM.

eject /ijékt/ *v.tr.* **1 a** send or drive out precipitately or by force, esp. from a building or other property; compel to leave. **b** dismiss from employment or office. **2 a** cause (the pilot etc.) to be propelled from an aircraft or spacecraft in an emergency. **b** (*absol.*) (of the pilot etc.) be ejected in this way (*they both ejected at 1,000 feet*). **3** cause to be removed or drop out (e.g. a spent cartridge from a gun). **4** dispossess (a tenant etc.) by legal process. **5** dart forth; emit. □□ **ejective** *adj.* **ejectment** *n.* [L *ejicere eject-* (as E-, *jacere* throw)]
■ **1 a** force *or* drive out, cast out, fling out, expel, oust, remove, get rid of, evict, throw out, boot out, *colloq.* kick out, *Brit. colloq.* turf out, *sl.* bounce. **b** discharge, dismiss, cashier, drum out, lay off, *colloq.* fire, sack, boot out, axe, give the sack *or* boot *or* axe, give a person his *or* her marching orders *or US also* walking papers, send packing. **5** emit, throw up *or* out, spew (forth), discharge, spout, disgorge, vomit (up *or* forth), send out *or* forth, dart forth; ooze, exude, extravasate.

ejection /ijéksh'n/ *n.* the act or an instance of ejecting; the process of being ejected. □ **ejection seat** = *ejector seat*.
■ expulsion, disgorgement, discharge, emission; banishment, deportation, ejectment, ouster, removal, eviction; dismissal, discharge, *congé*, cashiering, lay-off, *colloq.* firing, sacking, *sl.* the sack, the boot, the axe, the (old) heave-ho, the bounce.

ejector /ijéktər/ *n.* a device for ejecting. □ **ejector seat** a device for the automatic ejection of the pilot etc. of an aircraft or spacecraft in an emergency.

eke /eek/ *v.tr.* □ **eke out 1** (foll. by *with*, *by*) supplement; make the best use of (defective means etc.). **2** contrive to make (a livelihood) or support (an existence). [OE *ēacan*, rel. to L *augēre* increase]

ekka /ékkə/ *n. Ind.* a small one-horse vehicle. [Hindi *ekkā* unit]

-el var. of -LE².

elaborate *adj.* & *v.* ● *adj.* /ilábbərət/ **1** carefully or minutely worked out. **2** highly developed or complicated. ● *v.* /ilábbərayt/ **1 a** *tr.* work out or explain in detail. **b** *tr.* make more intricate or ornate. **c** *intr.* (often foll. by *on*) go into details (*I need not elaborate*). **2** *tr.* produce by labour. **3** *tr.* (of a natural agency) produce (a substance etc.) from its elements or sources. □□ **elaborately** /-rətli/ *adv.* **elaborateness** /-rətniss/ *n.* **elaboration** /-ráysh'n/ *n.* **elaborative** /-rətiv/ *adj.* **elaborator** /-raytər/ *n.* [L *elaboratus* past part. of *elaborare* (as E-, *labor* work)]

■ *adj.* **1** detailed, painstaking, meticulous, punctilious, comprehensive, thorough, complete, exhaustive, intricate, involved, minute, precise, exact. **2** complicated, complex, convoluted, ornate, fancy, Byzantine, extravagant, showy, baroque, rococo, highly ornamented, florid, busy, fussy. ● *v.* **1** work out, enlarge, expand (upon *or* on), amplify, flesh out, enhance, develop; go into detail, expatiate; see also EMBELLISH. □□ **elaboration** enlargement, development, amplification, expansion, enhancement, embellishment, garnishment, refinement, adornment.

élan /aylóN/ *n.* vivacity, dash. [F f. *élancer* launch]

■ see VERVE.

eland /éelənd/ *n.* any antelope of the genus *Taurotragus*, native to Africa, having spirally twisted horns, esp. the largest of living antelopes *T. derbianus*. [Du., = elk]

elapse /iláps/ *v.intr.* (of time) pass by. [L *elabor elaps-* slip away]

■ pass (by), go (by), slip by *or* away, pass away, slide by, glide by.

elasmobranch /ilázməbrangk/ *n. Zool.* any cartilaginous fish of the subclass Chondrichthyes, e.g. sharks, skates, rays. [mod.L *elasmobranchii* f. Gk *elasmos* beaten metal + *bragkhia* gills]

elasmosaurus /ilázməsáwrəss/ *n.* a large extinct marine reptile with paddle-like limbs and tough crocodile-like skin. [mod.L f. Gk *elasmos* beaten metal + *sauros* lizard]

elastic /ilástik/ *adj.* & *n.* ● *adj.* **1** able to resume its normal bulk or shape spontaneously after contraction, dilatation, or distortion. **2** springy. **3** (of a person or feelings) buoyant. **4** flexible, adaptable (*elastic conscience*). **5** *Econ.* (of demand) variable according to price. **6** *Physics* (of a collision) involving no decrease of kinetic energy. ● *n.* elastic cord or fabric, usu. woven with strips of rubber. □ **elastic band** = *rubber band* (see RUBBER[1]). □□ **elastically** *adv.* **elasticity** /íllastíssiti/ *n.* **elasticize** /ilástisīz/ *v.tr.* (also **-ise**). [mod.L *elasticus* f. Gk *elastikos* propulsive f. *elaunō* drive]

■ *adj.* **1, 2** flexible, stretchable, stretchy, bendable, pliable, springy, plastic, extensile, extensible, extendable, expansible, expandable, contractile, resilient, bouncy, compressible, *colloq.* bendy. **3** see BUOYANT 2. **4** adjustable, adaptable, accommodating, flexible, variable. □□ **elasticity** flexibility, resilience, rubberiness, plasticity, ductility, springiness, stretchability, stretchiness, suppleness, pliancy, give; adaptability, tolerance.

elasticated /ilástikaytid/ *adj.* (of a fabric) made elastic by weaving with rubber thread.

elastomer /ilástəmər/ *n.* a natural or synthetic rubber or rubber-like plastic. □□ **elastomeric** /-mérrik/ *adj.* [ELASTIC, after *isomer*]

elate /iláyt/ *v.* & *adj.* ● *v.tr.* **1** (esp. as **elated** *adj.*) inspirit, stimulate. **2** make proud. ● *adj. archaic* in high spirits; exultant, proud. □□ **elatedly** *adv.* **elatedness** *n.* **elation** *n.* [ME f. L *efferre elat-* raise]

■ *v.* **1** see INTOXICATE 2; (**elated**) exhilarated, uplifted, inspirited, stimulated, elevated, gleeful, joyful, jubilant, joyous, exultant, ecstatic, blissful, happy, delighted, euphoric, overjoyed, excited, thrilled, transported, pleased as Punch, delirious, over the moon, in seventh heaven, in raptures, *colloq.* tickled to death, on top of the world, tickled pink, on cloud nine, *Brit. sl.* chuffed. □□ **elation** see JOY *n.* 1.

elater /éllətər/ *n.* a click beetle. [mod.L f. Gk *elatēr* driver f. *elaunō* drive]

E-layer /éelayər/ *n.* a layer of the ionosphere able to reflect medium-frequency radio waves. [*E* (arbitrary) + LAYER]

elbow /élbō/ *n.* & *v.* ● *n.* **1 a** the joint between the forearm and the upper arm. **b** the part of the sleeve of a garment covering the elbow. **2** an elbow-shaped bend or corner; a short piece of piping bent through a right angle. ● *v.tr.* (foll. by *in*, *out*, *aside*, etc.) **1** thrust or jostle (a person or oneself). **2** make (one's way) by thrusting or jostling. **3** nudge or poke with the elbow. □ **at one's elbow** close at hand. **elbow-grease** *colloq.* vigorous polishing; hard work. **elbow-room** plenty of room to move or work in. **give a person the elbow** *colloq.* send a person away; dismiss or reject a person. **out at elbows 1** (of a coat) worn out. **2** (of a person) ragged, poor. [OE *elboga*, *elnboga*, f. Gmc (as ELL, BOW[1])]

■ *v.* **1, 2** see HUSTLE *v.* 1. **3** see DIG *v.* 7.

eld /eld/ *n. archaic* or *poet.* **1** old age. **2** olden time. [OE *(i)eldu* f. Gmc: cf. OLD]

elder[1] /éldər/ *adj.* & *n.* ● *attrib.adj.* (of two indicated persons, esp. when related) senior; of a greater age (*my elder brother*). ● *n.* (often prec. by *the*) **1** the older or more senior of two indicated (esp. related) persons (*which is the elder?*; *is my elder by ten years*). **2** (in *pl.*) **a** persons of greater age or seniority (*respect your elders*). **b** persons venerable because of age. **3** a person advanced in life. **4** *hist.* a member of a senate or governing body. **5** an official in the early Christian, Presbyterian, or Mormon Churches. □ **elder brother** (*pl.* **elder brethren**) *Brit.* each of thirteen senior members of Trinity House. **elder hand** *Cards* the first player. **elder statesman** an influential experienced person, esp. a politician, of advanced age. □□ **eldership** *n.* [OE *eldra*, rel. to OLD]

■ *attrib.adj.* older, senior; venerable, veteran. ● *n.* **2** (*elders*) superiors, seniors; patriarchs, matriarchs, elder statesmen, doyens, deans.

elder[2] /éldər/ *n.* any shrub or tree of the genus *Sambucus*, with white flowers and usu. blue-black or red berries. [OE *ellærn*]

elderberry /éldərbəri/ *n.* (*pl.* **-ies**) the berry of the elder, esp. common elder (*Sambucus nigra*) used for making jelly, wine, etc.

elderly /éldərli/ *adj.* & *n.* ● *adj.* **1** somewhat old. **2** (of a person) past middle age. ● *n.* (*collect.*) (prec. by *the*) elderly people. □□ **elderliness** *n.*

■ *adj.* **2** old, past middle age, oldish, advanced in years, of advanced age, grey, ageing, aged, venerable, hoary, ancient, long in the tooth, senescent; decrepit, superannuated, infirm; senile; *colloq.* over the hill, past it. ● *n.* (*the elderly*) the retired, the old, senior citizens, pensioners, OAPs, old-age pensioners, golden-agers, *colloq.* old-timers, (old) geezers, (old) fogies *or* fogeys, *sl. offens.* wrinklies.

eldest /éldist/ *adj.* & *n.* ● *adj.* first-born or oldest surviving (member of a family, son, daughter, etc.). ● *n.* (often prec. by *the*) the eldest of three or more indicated (*who is the eldest?*). □ **eldest hand** *Cards* the first player. [OE (as ELDER[1])]

eldorado /éldəraádō/ *n.* (*pl.* **-os**) **1** any imaginary country or city abounding in gold. **2** a place of great abundance. [Sp. *el dorado* the gilded]

eldritch /éldrich/ *adj. Sc.* **1** weird. **2** hideous. [16th c.: perh. f. OE *elfrīce* (unrecorded) 'fairy realm']

■ **1** see WEIRD *adj.* 1, 2.

elecampane /éllikampáyn/ *n.* **1** a sunflower-like plant, *Inula helenium*, with bitter aromatic leaves and roots, used in herbal medicine and cookery. **2** an esp. candied sweetmeat flavoured with this. [corrupt. of med.L *enula* (for L *inula* f. Gk *helenion*) *campana* (prob. = of the fields)]

elect /ilékt/ *v.* & *adj.* ● *v.tr.* (usu. foll. by *to* + infin.) **1** choose (*the principles they elected to follow*). **2** choose (a person) by vote (*elected a new chairman*). **3** *Theol.* (of God) choose (persons) in preference to others for salvation. ● *adj.* **1** chosen. **2** select, choice. **3** *Theol.* chosen by God. **4** (after a noun designating office) chosen but not yet in office (*president elect*). [ME f. L *electus* past part. of *eligere elect-* (as E-, *legere* pick)]

■ *v.* **1, 2** select, pick, determine, designate; see also

CHOOSE 1, 3, VOTE *v.* 1. ● *adj.* **1** chosen, elected, selected. **2** see CHOICE *adj.*

election /iléksh'n/ *n.* **1** the process of electing or being elected, esp. of members of a political body. **2** the act or an instance of electing. [ME f. OF f. L *electio -onis* (as ELECT)]
■ **1** selection, choice, nomination, designation, appointment. **2** poll, vote, referendum, plebiscite.

electioneer /iléksh əneér/ *v.* & *n.* ● *v.intr.* take part in an election campaign. ● *n.* a person who electioneers.
■ *v.* canvass, campaign, *Brit.* stand, *US* stump.

elective /iléktiv/ *adj.* & *n.* ● *adj.* **1 a** (of an office or its holder) filled or appointed by election. **b** (of authority) derived from election. **2** (of a body) having the power to elect. **3** having a tendency to act on or be concerned with some things rather than others (*elective affinity*). **4** (of a course of study) chosen by the student; optional. **5** (of a surgical operation etc.) optional; not urgently necessary. ● *n. US* an elective course of study. ▫▫ **electively** *adv.* [F *électif -ive* f. LL *electivus* (as ELECT)]
■ *adj.* **4, 5** see OPTIONAL.

elector /iléktər/ *n.* **1** a person who has the right of voting to elect an MP etc. **2** (**Elector**) *hist.* a German prince entitled to take part in the election of the Emperor. **3** *US* a member of an electoral college. ▫▫ **electorship** *n.* [ME f. F *électeur* f. L *elector* (as ELECT)]

electoral /iléktərəl/ *adj.* relating to or ranking as electors. ▫ **electoral college 1** a body of persons representing the States of the US, who cast votes for the election of the President. **2** a body of electors. ▫▫ **electorally** *adv.*

electorate /iléktərət/ *n.* **1** a body of electors. **2** *Austral.* & *NZ* an area represented by one member of parliament. **3** *hist.* the office or territories of a German Elector.

Electra complex /iléktrə/ *n. Psychol.* a daughter's subconscious sexual attraction to her father and hostility towards her mother, corresponding to the Oedipus complex in a son. [*Electra* in Gk tragedy, who caused her mother to be murdered for having murdered Electra's father]

electret /iléktrit/ *n. Physics* a permanently polarized piece of dielectric material, analogous to a permanent magnet. [ELECTRICITY + MAGNET]

electric /iléktrik/ *adj.* & *n.* ● *adj.* **1** of, worked by, or charged with electricity; producing or capable of generating electricity. **2** causing or charged with sudden and dramatic excitement (*the news had an electric effect*; *the atmosphere was electric*). ● *n.* **1** an electric light, vehicle, etc. **2** (in *pl.*) electrical equipment. ▫ **electric blanket** a blanket that can be heated electrically by an internal element. **electric blue** a steely or brilliant light blue. **electric chair** (in the US) an electrified chair used for capital punishment. **electric eel** an eel-like freshwater fish, *Electrophorus electricus*, native to S. America, that kills its prey by electric shock. **electric eye** *colloq.* a photoelectric cell operating a relay when the beam of light illuminating it is obscured. **electric fence** a fence charged with electricity, often consisting of one strand. **electric field** a region of electrical influence. **electric fire** an electrically operated incandescent or convector heater, usu. portable and for domestic use. **electric guitar** a guitar with a built-in electrical sound pick-up rather than a soundbox. **electric organ 1** *Biol.* the organ in some fishes giving an electric shock. **2** *Mus.* an electrically-operated organ. **electric ray** any of several rays which can give an electric shock (see RAY²). **electric shaver** (or **razor**) an electrical device for shaving, with oscillating blades behind a metal guard. **electric shock** the effect of a sudden discharge of electricity on a person or animal, usually with stimulation of the nerves and contraction of the muscles. **electric storm** a violent disturbance of the electrical condition of the atmosphere. ▫▫ **electrically** *adv.* [mod.L *electricus* f. L *electrum* f. Gk *ēlektron* amber, the rubbing of which causes electrostatic phenomena]
■ *adj.* **2** charged, alive, electrical, buzzing, astir, tense, energized, stimulating, exciting, thrilling, electrifying, moving, stirring, dynamic.

electrical /iléktrik'l/ *adj.* **1** of or concerned with or of the nature of electricity. **2** operating by electricity. **3** suddenly or dramatically exciting (*the effect was electrical*).

electrician /íllektrísh'n/ *n.* a person who installs or maintains electrical equipment, esp. professionally.

electricity /íllektríssiti, él-/ *n.* **1** a form of energy resulting from the existence of charged particles (electrons, protons, etc.), either statically as an accumulation of charge or dynamically as a current. **2** the branch of physics dealing with electricity. **3** a supply of electric current for heating, lighting, etc. **4** a state of heightened emotion; excitement, tension.
■ **4** excitement, verve, energy, tension, tenseness, fervency, intensity, ardour.

electrify /iléktrifī/ *v.tr.* (**-ies, -ied**) **1** charge (a body) with electricity. **2** convert (machinery or the place or system employing it) to the use of electric power. **3** cause dramatic or sudden excitement in. ▫▫ **electrification** /-fikáysh'n/ *n.* **electrifier** *n.*
■ **3** excite, galvanize, animate, move, rouse, stir, stimulate, vitalize, fire, thrill, arouse, charge, energize.

electro /iléktrō/ *n.* & *v.* ● *n.* (*pl.* **-os**) **1** = ELECTROTYPE *n.* **2** = ELECTROPLATE *n.* ● *v.tr.* (**-oes, -oed**) *colloq.* **1** = ELECTROTYPE *v.* **2** = ELECTROPLATE *v.* [abbr.]

electro- /iléktrō/ *comb. form Electr.* of, relating to, or caused by electricity (*electrocute*; *electromagnet*). [Gk *ēlektron* amber: see ELECTRIC]

electrobiology /iléktrōbīólləji/ *n.* the study of the electrical phenomena of living things.

electrocardiogram /iléktrōkaárdiəgram/ *n.* a record of the heartbeat traced by an electrocardiograph. [G *Elektrocardiogramm* (as ELECTRO-, CARDIO-, -GRAM)]

electrocardiograph /iléktrōkaárdiəgraaf/ *n.* an instrument recording the electric currents generated by a person's heartbeat. ▫▫ **electrocardiographic** /-gráffik/ *adj.* **electrocardiography** /-diógrəfi/ *n.*

electrochemical /iléktrōkémmik'l/ *adj.* involving electricity as applied to or occurring in chemistry. ▫▫ **electrochemist** *n.* **electrochemistry** *n.*

electroconvulsive /iléktrōkənvúlsiv/ *adj.* (of a therapy) employing the use of the convulsive response to the application of electric shocks.

electrocute /iléktrəkyōōt/ *v.tr.* **1** kill by electricity (as a form of capital punishment). **2** cause death of by electric shock. ▫▫ **electrocution** /-kyōōsh'n/ *n.* [ELECTRO-, after EXECUTE]

electrode /iléktrōd/ *n.* a conductor through which electricity enters or leaves an electrolyte, gas, vacuum, etc. [ELECTRIC + Gk *hodos* way]

electrodialysis /iléktrōdīállisiss/ *n.* dialysis in which electrodes are placed on either side of a semi-permeable membrane, as used in obtaining pure water from salt water.

electrodynamics /iléktrōdīnámmiks/ *n.pl.* (usu. treated as *sing.*) the branch of mechanics concerned with electric current applied to motive forces. ▫▫ **electrodynamic** *adj.*

electroencephalogram /iléktrō-inséffələgram/ *n.* a record of the brain's activity traced by an electroencephalograph. [G *Elektrenkephalogramm* (as ELECTRO-, ENCEPHALO-, -GRAM)]

electroencephalograph /iléktrō-inséffələgraaf/ *n.* an instrument recording the electrical activity of the brain. ▫▫ **electroencephalography** /-lógrəfi/ *n.*

electroluminescence /iléktrōlōōminéss'nss/ *n. Chem.* luminescence produced electrically, esp. by the application of a voltage. ▫▫ **electroluminescent** *adj.*

electrolyse /iléktrəlīz/ *v.tr.* (*US* **-yze**) subject to or treat by electrolysis. ▫▫ **electrolyser** *n.* [ELECTROLYSIS after *analyse*]

electrolysis /íllektróllisiss, él-/ *n.* **1** *Chem.* the decomposition of a substance by the application of an electric current. **2** *Surgery* this process applied to the destruction of tumours, hair-roots, etc. ▫▫ **electrolytic** /iléktrōlíttik/ *adj.*

electrolytical /-líttik'l/ *adj.* **electrolytically** /-líttikəli/ *adv.* [ELECTRO- + -LYSIS]

electrolyte /iléktrəlīt/ *n.* **1** a substance which conducts electricity when molten or in solution, esp. in an electric cell or battery. **2** a solution of this. [ELECTRO- + Gk *lutos* released f. *luō* loosen]

electromagnet /iléktrōmágnit/ *n.* a soft metal core made into a magnet by the passage of electric current through a coil surrounding it.

electromagnetic /iléktrōmagnéttik/ *adj.* having both an electrical and a magnetic character or properties. □ **electromagnetic radiation** a kind of radiation including visible light, radio waves, gamma rays, X-rays, etc., in which electric and magnetic fields vary simultaneously. **electromagnetic spectrum** the range of wavelengths over which electromagnetic radiation extends. **electromagnetic units** a system of units derived primarily from the magnetic properties of electric currents. □□ **electromagnetically** /-kəli/ *adv.*

electromagnetism /iléktrōmágnitiz'm/ *n.* **1** the magnetic forces produced by electricity. **2** the study of this.

electromechanical /iléktrōmikánnik'l/ *adj.* relating to the application of electricity to mechanical processes, devices, etc.

electrometer /illektrómmitər, él-/ *n.* an instrument for measuring electrical potential without drawing any current from the circuit. □□ **electrometric** /-métrik/ *adj.* **electrometry** *n.*

electromotive /iléktrōmṓtiv/ *adj.* producing or tending to produce an electric current. □ **electromotive force** a force set up in an electric circuit by a difference in potential.

electron /iléktron/ *n.* a stable elementary particle with a charge of negative electricity, found in all atoms and acting as the primary carrier of electricity in solids. □ **electron beam** a stream of electrons in a gas or vacuum. **electron diffraction** the diffraction of a beam of electrons by atoms or molecules, used for determining crystal structures etc. **electron gun** a device for producing a narrow stream of electrons from a heated cathode. **electron lens** a device for focusing a stream of electrons by means of electric or magnetic fields. **electron microscope** a microscope with high magnification and resolution, employing electron beams in place of light and using electron lenses. **electron pair** an electron and a positron. **electron spin resonance** a spectroscopic method of locating electrons within the molecules of a paramagnetic substance. ¶ Abbr.: **ESR.** [ELECTRIC + -ON]

electronegative /iléktrōnéggətiv/ *adj.* **1** electrically negative. **2** *Chem.* (of an element) tending to acquire electrons.

electronic /illektrónnik, él-/ *adj.* **1 a** produced by or involving the flow of electrons. **b** of or relating to electrons or electronics. **2** (of a device) using electronic components. **3 a** (of music) produced by electronic means and usu. recorded on tape. **b** (of a musical instrument) producing sounds by electronic means. □ **electronic flash** a flash from a gas-discharge tube, used in high-speed photography. **electronic mail** messages distributed by electronic means esp. from one computer system to one or more recipients: also called EMAIL. **electronic publishing** the publication of books etc. in machine-readable form rather than on paper. □□ **electronically** *adv.*

electronics /illektrónniks, él-/ *n.pl.* (usu. treated as *sing.*) **1** a branch of physics and technology concerned with the behaviour and movement of electrons in a vacuum, gas, semiconductor, etc. **2** the circuits used in this.

electronvolt /iléktronvōlt/ *n.* a unit of energy equal to the work done on an electron in accelerating it through a potential difference of one volt. ¶ Abbr.: **eV**.

electrophilic /iléktrōfillik/ *adj. Chem.* having an affinity for electrons. □□ **electrophile** /iléktrōfīl/ *n.*

electrophoresis /iléktrōforeéssiss/ *n. Physics* & *Chem.* the movement of colloidal particles in a fluid under the influence of an electric field. □□ **electrophoretic** /-fəréttik/ *adj.* [ELECTRO- + Gk *phorēsis* being carried]

electrophorus /illektróffərəss, él-/ *n.* a device for repeatedly generating static electricity by induction. [mod.L f. ELECTRO- + Gk *-phoros* bearing]

electroplate /iléktrəplayt/ *v.* & *n.* ● *v.tr.* coat (a utensil etc.) by electrolytic deposition with chromium, silver, etc. ● *n.* electroplated articles. □□ **electroplater** *n.*

electroplexy /iléktrəpleksi/ *n. Brit.* electroconvulsive therapy. [ELECTRO- + APOPLEXY]

electropositive /iléktrōpózzitiv/ *adj.* **1** electrically positive. **2** *Chem.* (of an element) tending to lose electrons.

electroscope /iléktrəskōp/ *n.* an instrument for detecting and measuring electricity, esp. as an indication of the ionization of air by radioactivity. □□ **electroscopic** /-skóppik/ *adj.*

electro-shock /iléktrōshok/ *attrib.adj.* (of medical treatment) by means of electric shocks.

electrostatic /iléktrōstáttik/ *adj.* of electricity at rest. □ **electrostatic units** a system of units based primarily on the forces between electric charges. [ELECTRO- + STATIC after *hydrostatic*]

electrostatics /iléktrōstáttiks/ *n.pl.* (treated as *sing.*) the study of electricity at rest.

electrotechnology /iléktrōteknólləji/ *n.* the science of the application of electricity in technology. □□ **electrotechnic** /-téknik/ *adj.* **electrotechnical** /-téknik'l/ *adj.* **electrotechnics** /-tékniks/ *n.*

electrotherapy /iléktrōthérrəpi/ *n.* the treatment of diseases by the use of electricity. □□ **electrotherapeutic** /-pyṓotik/ *adj.* **electrotherapeutical** /-pyṓotik'l/ *adj.* **electrotherapist** *n.*

electrothermal /iléktrōthérm'l/ *adj.* relating to heat electrically derived.

electrotype /iléktrōtīp/ *v.* & *n.* ● *v.tr.* copy by the electrolytic deposition of copper on a mould, esp. for printing. ● *n.* a copy so formed. □□ **electrotyper** *n.*

electrovalent /iléktrōváylənt/ *adj. Chem.* linking ions by a bond resulting from electrostatic attraction. □□ **electrovalence** *n.* **electrovalency** *n.* [ELECTRO- + *-valent* after *trivalent* etc.]

electrum /iléktrəm/ *n.* **1** an alloy of silver and gold used in ancient times. **2** native argentiferous gold ore. [ME f. L f. Gk *ēlektron* amber, electrum]

electuary /iléktyoori/ *n.* (*pl.* **-ies**) medicinal powder etc. mixed with honey or other sweet substance. [ME f. LL *electuarium*, prob. f. Gk *ekleikton* f. *ekleikhō* lick up]

eleemosynary /élli-eemóssinəri, -mózzinəri/ *adj.* **1** of or dependent on alms. **2** charitable. **3** gratuitous. [med.L *eleemosynarius* f. LL *eleemosyna*: see ALMS]

■ **2** see CHARITABLE 1.

elegant /élligənt/ *adj.* **1** graceful in appearance or manner. **2** tasteful, refined. **3** (of a mode of life etc.) of refined luxury. **4** ingeniously simple and pleasing. **5** *US* excellent. □□ **elegance** *n.* **elegantly** *adv.* [F *élégant* or L *elegant-*, rel. to *eligere*: see ELECT]

■ **1, 2** tasteful, exquisite, handsome, graceful, superior, fine, select, refined; delicate, discerning, dignified, genteel, sophisticated, cultivated, polished, urbane, suave, *soigné*, well-groomed, debonair, well-bred. **3** luxurious, sumptuous, grand, opulent, plush, swanky, smart, high-class, *colloq.* ritzy, *esp. US colloq.* swank. **4** apt, clever, ingenious, neat. **5** see EXCELLENT. □□ **elegance** refinement, grace, tastefulness, good taste, gentility, polish, culture, propriety, dignity; luxury, grandeur, luxuriousness, opulence, sumptuousness, exquisiteness, plushness, splendour, beauty, handsomeness, smartness, swankiness, *colloq.* ritziness.

elegiac /éllijī́ək/ *adj.* & *n.* ● *adj.* **1** (of a metre) used for elegies. **2** mournful. ● *n.* (in *pl.*) verses in an elegiac metre. □ **elegiac couplet** a pair of lines consisting of a dactylic hexameter and a pentameter, esp. in Greek and Latin verse.

□□ **elegiacally** *adv.* [F *élégiaque* or f. LL *elegiacus* f. Gk *elegeiakos*: see ELEGY]

elegize /éllijīz/ *v.* (also **-ise**) **1** *intr.* (often foll. by *upon*) write an elegy. **2** *intr.* write in a mournful strain. **3** *tr.* write an elegy upon. □□ **elegist** *n.*

elegy /élliji/ *n.* (*pl.* **-ies**) **1** a song of lament, esp. for the dead (sometimes vaguely used of other poems). **2** a poem in elegiac metre. [F *élégie* or L *elegia* f. Gk *elegeia* f. *elegos* mournful poem]

■ **1** see LAMENT *n.* 2.

element /éllimənt/ *n.* **1** a component part or group; a contributing factor or thing. **2** *Chem.* & *Physics* any of the hundred or so substances that cannot be resolved by chemical means into simpler substances. **3 a** any of the four substances (earth, water, air, and fire) in ancient and medieval philosophy. **b** any of these as a being's natural abode or environment. **c** a person's appropriate or preferred sphere of operation. **4** *Electr.* a resistance wire that heats up in an electric heater, cooker, etc.; an electrode. **5** (in *pl.*) atmospheric agencies, esp. wind and storm. **6** (in *pl.*) the rudiments of learning or of a branch of knowledge. **7** (in *pl.*) the bread and wine of the Eucharist. **8** *Math.* & *Logic* an entity that is a single member of a set. □ **in** (or **out of**) **one's element** in (or out of) one's accustomed or preferred surroundings. **reduced to its elements** analysed. [ME f. OF f. L *elementum*]

■ **1** component, constituent, ingredient, part, unit, piece, segment, feature, detail, particular; factor; sector, group. **3 c** environment, surroundings, atmosphere, situation, locale, territory, sphere, habitat, medium, domain. **5** (*elements*) (adverse *or* unfavourable) weather; outdoors. **6** (*elements*) rudiments, basics, fundamentals, foundations, essentials, principles. □ **reduced to its elements** (*reduce to its elements*) see ANALYSE 1, 2.

elemental /élliméntʼl/ *adj.* & *n.* ● *adj.* **1** of the four elements. **2** of the powers of nature (*elemental worship*). **3** comparable to a force of nature (*elemental grandeur*; *elemental tumult*). **4** uncompounded (*elemental oxygen*). **5** essential. ● *n.* an entity or force thought to be physically manifested by occult means. □□ **elementalism** *n.* (in senses 1, 2). [med.L *elementalis* (as ELEMENT)]

■ *adj.* **2, 3** primal, original, primordial, primitive. **5** basic, fundamental, key, main; see also INTRINSIC.

elementary /élliméntəri, -tri/ *adj.* **1 a** dealing with or arising from the simplest facts of a subject; rudimentary, introductory. **b** simple. **2** *Chem.* not decomposable. □ **elementary particle** *Physics* any of several subatomic particles supposedly not decomposable into simpler ones. **elementary school** a school in which elementary subjects are taught to young children. □□ **elementarily** *adv.* **elementariness** *n.* [ME f. L *elementarius* (as ELEMENT)]

■ **1 a** rudimentary, basic, fundamental, primary, introductory, initial, beginning, elemental. **b** simple, straightforward, uncomplicated, clear, understandable, plain; see also EASY *adj.* 1. □ **elementary school** primary school, *Brit.* first school, *US* grade school.

elenchus /iléngkəss/ *n.* (*pl.* **elenchi** /-kī/) *Logic* logical refutation. □ **Socratic elenchus** an attempted refutation of an opponent's position by short question and answer. □□ **elenctic** *adj.* [L f. Gk *elegkhos*]

elephant /éllifənt/ *n.* (*pl.* same or **elephants**) **1** the largest living land animal, of which two species survive, the larger African (*Loxodonta africana*) and the smaller Indian (*Elephas maximus*), both with a trunk and long curved ivory tusks. **2** a size of paper (711 x 584 mm). □ **elephant grass** any of various tall African grasses, esp. *Pennisetum purpureum*. **elephant seal** = *sea elephant*. **elephant shrew** any small insect-eating mammal of the family Macroscelididae, native to Africa, having a long snout and long hind limbs. □□ **elephantoid** /-fántoyd/ *adj.* [ME *olifaunt* etc. f. OF *oli-*, *elefant* ult. f. L *elephantus*, *elephans* f. Gk *elephas -antos* ivory, elephant]

elephantiasis /éllifəntī́əsiss/ *n.* gross enlargement of the body, esp. the limbs, due to lymphatic obstruction esp. by a nematode parasite. [L f. Gk (as ELEPHANT)]

elephantine /éllifántīn/ *adj.* **1** of elephants. **2 a** huge. **b** clumsy, unwieldy (*elephantine movements*; *elephantine humour*). [L *elephantinus* f. Gk *elephantinos* (as ELEPHANT)]

■ **2 a** see HUGE 1. **b** see PONDEROUS 1.

Eleusinian /élyoosínniən/ *adj.* of or relating to Eleusis near Athens. □ **Eleusinian mysteries** *Gk Hist.* the annual celebrations held at ancient Eleusis in honour of Demeter. [L *Eleusinius* f. Gk *Eleusinios*]

elevate /éllivayt/ *v.tr.* **1** bring to a higher position. **2** *Eccl.* hold up (the Host or the chalice) for adoration. **3** raise, lift (one's eyes etc.). **4** raise the axis of (a gun). **5** raise (a railway etc.) above ground level. **6** exalt in rank etc. **7** (usu. as **elevated** *adj.*) **a** raise the spirits of, elate. **b** raise morally or intellectually (*elevated style*). **8** (as **elevated** *adj.*) *colloq.* slightly drunk. □□ **elevatory** *adj.* [L *elevare* raise (as E-, *levis* light)]

■ **3** raise, upraise, uplift, lift (up). **6** see EXALT 1. **7 a** (**elevated**) elated, cheerful, happy, exhilarated, animated, joyful, glad. **b** see CIVILIZE; (**elevated**) uplifted, noble, lofty, high, grand, exalted, dignified, eminent, pre-eminent, ennobled, notable, illustrious, distinguished, imposing, impressive, sublime. **8** (**elevated**) see JOLLY[1] *adj.* 3.

elevation /élliváyshʼn/ *n.* **1 a** the process of elevating or being elevated. **b** the angle with the horizontal, esp. of a gun or of the direction of a heavenly body. **c** the height above a given level, esp. sea level. **d** a raised area; a swelling on the skin. **2** loftiness, grandeur, dignity. **3 a** a drawing or diagram made by projection on a vertical plane (cf. PLAN). **b** a flat drawing of the front, side, or back of a house etc. **4** *Ballet* **a** the capacity of a dancer to attain height in springing movements. **b** the action of tightening the muscles and uplifting the body. □□ **elevational** *adj.* (in sense 2). [ME f. OF *elevation* or L *elevatio*: see ELEVATE]

■ **1 a** advancement, promotion, advance; exaltation; uplifting, raising. **c** altitude, height. **d** hill, height, rise, hillock, prominence; swelling, lump, wen. **2** grandeur, nobleness, loftiness, exaltation, sublimity, distinction, dignity, refinement, cultivation.

elevator /éllivaytər/ *n.* **1** a hoisting machine. **2** *Aeron.* the movable part of a tailplane for changing the pitch of an aircraft. **3** *US* **a** = LIFT *n.* 3. **b** a place for lifting and storing quantities of grain. **4** that which elevates, esp. a muscle that raises a limb. [mod.L (as ELEVATE)]

eleven /ilévvʼn/ *n.* & *adj.* ● *n.* **1** one more than ten; the sum of six units and five units. **2** a symbol for this (11, xi, XI). **3** a size etc. denoted by eleven. **4** a set or team of eleven individuals. **5** the time of eleven o'clock (*is it eleven yet?*). ● *adj.* that amount to eleven. □ **eleven-plus** esp. *hist.* (in the UK) an examination taken at the age of 11–12 to determine the type of secondary school a child should enter. [OE *endleofon* f. Gmc]

elevenfold /ilévvʼnfōld/ *adj.* & *adv.* **1** eleven times as much or as many. **2** consisting of eleven parts.

elevenses /ilévvʼnziz/ *n.* (usu. in *pl.*) *Brit. colloq.* light refreshment, usu. with tea or coffee, taken about 11 a.m.

■ see SNACK *n.* 1, 2.

eleventh /ilévvʼnth/ *n.* & *adj.* ● *n.* **1** the position in a sequence corresponding to the number 11 in the sequence 1–11. **2** something occupying this position. **3** one of eleven equal parts of a thing. **4** *Mus.* **a** an interval or chord spanning an octave and a third in the diatonic scale. **b** a note separated from another by this interval. ● *adj.* that is the eleventh. □ **the eleventh hour** the last possible moment.

elevon /éllivon/ *n.* *Aeron.* the movable part of the trailing edge of a delta wing. [ELEVATOR + AILERON]

elf /elf/ *n.* (*pl.* **elves** /elvz/) **1** a mythological being, esp. one that is small and mischievous. **2** a sprite or little creature. □ **elf-lock** a tangled mass of hair. □□ **elfish** *adj.* **elvish** *adj.* [OE f. Gmc]

■ sprite, fairy, puck, *literary* fay; see also GOBLIN.

elfin /élfin/ *adj.* & *n.* ● *adj.* of elves; elflike; tiny, dainty. ● *n. archaic* a dwarf; a child. [ELF, perh. infl. by ME *elvene* genit. pl. of *elf*, and by *Elphin* in Arthurian romance]
▪ *adj.* elvish, elfish, elflike, impish, puckish; frolicsome, sprightly, playful, mischievous; small, diminutive, tiny, little, dainty, Lilliputian, *esp. Sc. or colloq.* wee.

elicit /ilíssit/ *v.tr.* (**elicited, eliciting**) **1** draw out, evoke (an admission, response, etc.). **2** draw forth (what is latent). ▫▫ **elicitation** /-táysh'n/ *n.* **elicitor** *n.* [L *elicere elicit-* (as E-, *lacere* entice)]
▪ **1** draw out *or* forth, call forth, evoke, bring out *or* forth, bring to light, extract, get, wring, wrest, wrench.

elide /ilíd/ *v.tr.* omit (a vowel or syllable) by elision. [L *elidere elis-* crush out (as E-, *laedere* knock)]

eligible /éllijib'l/ *adj.* **1** (often foll. by *for*) fit or entitled to be chosen (*eligible for a rebate*). **2** desirable or suitable, esp. as a partner in marriage. ▫▫ **eligibility** /-bílliti/ *n.* **eligibly** *adv.* [F *éligible* f. LL *eligibilis* (as ELECT)]
▪ **1** fit, worthy, entitled, qualified, suitable, appropriate, fitting. **2** desirable, suitable, available, free.

eliminate /ilímminayt/ *v.tr.* **1 a** remove, get rid of. **b** kill, murder. **2** exclude from consideration; ignore as irrelevant. **3** exclude from further participation in a competition etc. on defeat. **4** *Physiol.* discharge (waste matter). **5** *Chem.* remove (a simpler substance) from a compound. **6** *Algebra* remove (a quantity) by combining equations. ▫▫ **eliminable** /-nəb'l/ *adj.* **elimination** /-náysh'n/ *n.* **eliminator** *n.* **eliminatory** /-nətəri, -tri/ *adj.* [L *eliminare* (as E-, *limen liminis* threshold)]
▪ **1 a** remove, get rid of, dispose of, take out *or* away, erase, eradicate, expel, stamp out, expunge, obliterate; strike (out), cross out *or* off, cut (out), excise, delete, edit (out). **b** kill, murder, assassinate, terminate, exterminate, dispose of, liquidate, finish off, annihilate, destroy, *colloq.* polish off, *literary or joc.* slay, *sl.* bump off, *US sl.* rub out, take for a ride, bury, ice, waste. **2** exclude, rule out, drop, leave out, omit. **3** exclude, knock out; defeat, trounce.

elision /ilízh'n/ *n.* **1** the omission of a vowel or syllable in pronouncing (as in *I'm, let's, e'en*). **2** the omission of a passage in a book etc. [LL *elisio* (as ELIDE)]

élite /ayléet/ *adj.* & *n.* ● *n.* **1** (prec. by *the*) the best or choice part of a larger body or group. **2** a select group or class. **3** a size of letter in typewriting (12 per inch). ● *adj.* of or belonging to an élite; exclusive. [F f. past part. of *élire* f. Rmc: rel. to ELECT]
▪ *n.* **1** best, *crème de la crème*; see also CHOICE *n.* 3. **2** cream, gentry, aristocracy, aristocrats, elect, upper classes, nobility, privileged classes, *US* four hundred, *colloq.* upper crust, beautiful people, *esp. iron.* superior persons. ● *adj.* aristocratic, elect, upper-class, privileged, blue-blooded, noble, exclusive, choice, best, top.

élitism /ayléetiz'm/ *n.* **1** advocacy of or reliance on leadership or dominance by a select group. **2** a sense of belonging to an élite. ▫▫ **élitist** *n.* & *adj.*

elixir /ilíkseer/ *n.* **1** *Alchemy* **a** a preparation supposedly able to change metals into gold. **b** (in full **elixir of life**) a preparation supposedly able to prolong life indefinitely. **c** a supposed remedy for all ills. **2** *Pharm.* an aromatic solution used as a medicine or flavouring. **3** the quintessence or kernel of a thing. [ME f. med.L f. Arab. *al-iksīr* f. *al* the + *iksīr* prob. f. Gk *xērion* powder for drying wounds f. *xēros* dry]
▪ **1 c** panacea, cure-all, heal-all, wonder drug, miracle drug, sovereign remedy. **3** pith, core, kernel, heart, essence, quintessence, principle, extract, base, basis, soul, *Philos.* quiddity.

Elizabethan /ilizzəbeéthən/ *adj.* & *n.* ● *adj.* of the time of Queen Elizabeth I (1558–1603) or of Queen Elizabeth II (1952–). ● *n.* a person, esp. a writer, of the time of Queen Elizabeth I or II.

elk /elk/ *n.* (*pl.* same or **elks**) **1** a large deer, *Alces alces*, of N. Europe and Asia, with palmate antlers and a growth of skin hanging from the neck; a moose. **2** *US* a wapiti. ▫ **elk-hound** a large Scandinavian hunting dog with a shaggy coat. [ME, prob. repr. OE *elh*, *eolh*]

ell /el/ *n. hist.* a former measure of length, about 45 inches. [OE *eln*, rel. to L *ulna*: see ULNA]

ellipse /ilíps/ *n.* a regular oval, traced by a point moving in a plane so that the sum of its distances from two other points is constant, or resulting when a cone is cut by a plane which does not intersect the base and makes a smaller angle with the base than the side of the cone makes (cf. HYPERBOLA). [F f. L *ellipsus* f. Gk *elleipsis* f. *elleipō* come short f. *en* in + *leipō* leave]

ellipsis /ilípsiss/ *n.* (also **ellipse**) (*pl.* **ellipses** /-seez/) **1** the omission from a sentence of words needed to complete the construction or sense. **2** the omission of a sentence at the end of a paragraph. **3** a set of three dots etc. indicating an omission.

ellipsoid /ilípsoyd/ *n.* a solid of which all the plane sections normal to one axis are circles and all the other plane sections are ellipses. ▫▫ **ellipsoidal** /éllipsóyd'l/ *adj.*
▪ ▫▫ **ellipsoidal** see OVAL *adj.*

elliptic /ilíptik/ *adj.* (also **elliptical**) of, relating to, or having the form of an ellipse or ellipsis. ▫▫ **elliptically** *adv.* **ellipticity** /éllíptíssiti/ *n.* [Gk *elleiptikos* defective f. *elleipō* (as ELLIPSE)]

elm /elm/ *n.* **1** any tree of the genus *Ulmus*, esp. *U. procera* with rough serrated leaves. **2** (in full **elmwood**) the wood of the elm. ▫▫ **elmy** *adj.* [OE, rel. to L *ulmus*]

elocution /élləkyoósh'n/ *n.* **1** the art of clear and expressive speech, esp. of distinct pronunciation and articulation. **2** a particular style of speaking. ▫▫ **elocutionary** *adj.* **elocutionist** *n.* [L *elocutio* f. *eloqui elocut-* speak out (as E-, *loqui* speak)]
▪ see SPEECH 3.

elongate /eélonggayt/ *v.* & *adj.* ● *v.* **1** *tr.* lengthen, prolong. **2** *intr. Bot.* be of slender or tapering form. ● *adj. Bot.* & *Zool.* long in proportion to width. [LL *elongare* (as E-, L *longus* long)]
▪ *v.* **1** see LENGTHEN.

elongation /eélonggáysh'n/ *n.* **1** the act or an instance of lengthening; the process of being lengthened. **2** a part of a line etc. formed by lengthening. **3** *Mech.* the amount of extension under stress. **4** *Astron.* the angular separation of a planet from the sun or of a satellite from a planet. [ME f. LL *elongatio* (as ELONGATE)]

elope /ilóp/ *v.intr.* **1** run away to marry secretly, esp. without parental consent. **2** run away with a lover. ▫▫ **elopement** *n.* **eloper** *n.* [AF *aloper* perh. f. a ME form *alope*, rel. to LEAP]

eloquence /élləkwənss/ *n.* **1** fluent and effective use of language. **2** rhetoric. [ME f. OF f. L *eloquentia* f. *eloqui* speak out (as E-, *loqui* speak)]
▪ see RHETORIC 1.

eloquent /élləkwənt/ *adj.* **1** possessing or showing eloquence. **2** (often foll. by *of*) clearly expressive or indicative. ▫▫ **eloquently** *adv.* [ME f. OF f. L *eloqui* (as ELOQUENCE)]
▪ **1** articulate, silver-tongued, fluent, well-spoken, effective, persuasive, impressive, convincing, cogent, incisive; smooth, oratorical, rhetorical. **2** expressive, suggestive, indicative.

Elsan /élsan/ *n. Brit. propr.* a type of transportable chemical lavatory. [app. f. *E. L.* Jackson (its manufacturer) + SANITATION]

else /elss/ *adv.* **1** (prec. by indef. or interrog. pron.) besides; in addition (*someone else*; *nowhere else*; *who else*). **2** instead; other, different (*what else could I say?*; *he did not love her, but someone else*). **3** otherwise; if not (*run, (or) else you will be late*). [OE *elles*, rel. to L *alius*, Gk *allos*]

elsewhere /élswáir/ *adv.* in or to some other place. [OE *elles hwǣr* (as ELSE, WHERE)]
▪ somewhere else, to another place, abroad; in another place, absent, away.

eluant var. of ELUENT.

eluate /élyoo-ayt/ *n. Chem.* a solution or gas stream obtained by elution. [formed as ELUENT]

elucidate /ilóossidayt, ilyóo-/ *v.tr.* throw light on; explain. ▫▫ **elucidation** /-dáysh'n/ *n.* **elucidative** *adj.* **elucidator** *n.* **elucidatory** *adj.* [LL *elucidare* (as E-, LUCID)]
■ see EXPLAIN 1.

elude /ilóod, ilyóod/ *v.tr.* **1** escape adroitly from (a danger, difficulty, pursuer, etc.); dodge. **2** avoid compliance with (a law, request, etc.) or fulfilment of (an obligation). **3** (of a fact, solution, etc.) escape from or baffle (a person's memory or understanding). ▫▫ **elusion** /ilóozh'n, ilyóo-/ *n.* **elusory** *adj.* [L *eludere elus-* (as E-, *ludere* play)]
■ **1** evade, escape, avoid, dodge, slip away from, give the slip, shake off. **2** avoid, *colloq.* duck (out of); see also SIDESTEP *v.* **3** evade, escape; baffle, puzzle, confuse, bewilder, confound; frustrate, stump, thwart; see also FLOOR *v.* 3.

eluent /élyooənt/ *n.* (also **eluant**) *Chem.* a fluid used for elution. [L *eluere* wash out (as E-, *luere lut-* wash)]

elusive /ilóossiv, ilyóo-/ *adj.* **1** difficult to find or catch; tending to elude. **2** difficult to remember or recall. **3** (of an answer etc.) avoiding the point raised; seeking to elude. ▫▫ **elusively** *adv.* **elusiveness** *n.*
■ **1** evasive, elusory, slippery, fugitive; indefinable, intangible, impalpable. **3** evasive, equivocal, indirect.

elute /ilóot/ *v.tr. Chem.* remove (an adsorbed substance) by washing. ▫▫ **elution** *n.* [G *eluieren* (as ELUENT)]

elutriate /ilóotriayt, ilyóo-/ *v.tr. Chem.* separate (lighter and heavier particles in a mixture) by suspension in an upward flow of liquid or gas. ▫▫ **elutriation** /-áysh'n/ *n.* [L *elutriare elutriat-* (as E-, *lutriare* wash)]

elver /élvər/ *n.* a young eel. [var. of *eel-fare* (see FARE) = a brood of young eels]

elves *pl.* of ELF.

elvish see ELF.

Elysium /ilízziəm/ *n.* **1** (also **Elysian Fields**) (in Greek mythology) the abode of the blessed after death. **2** a place or state of ideal happiness. ▫▫ **Elysian** *adj.* [L f. Gk *Elusion* (*pedion* plain)]

elytron /éllitron/ *n.* (*pl.* **elytra** /-trə/) the outer hard usu. brightly coloured wing-case of a coleopterous insect. [Gk *elutron* sheath]

em /em/ *n. Printing* **1** a unit for measuring the amount of printed matter in a line, usually equal to the nominal width of capital M. **2** a unit of measurement equal to 12 points. ▫ **em rule** (or **dash**) a long dash used in punctuation. [name of the letter *M*]

em- /im, em/ *prefix* assim. form of EN-[1], EN-[2] before *b, p.*

'em /əm/ *pron. colloq.* them (*let 'em all come*). [orig. a form of ME *hem*, dative and accus. 3rd pers. pl. pron.: now regarded as an abbr. of THEM]

emaciate /imáysiayt, -shiayt/ *v.tr.* (esp. as **emaciated** *adj.*) make abnormally thin or feeble. ▫▫ **emaciation** /-áysh'n/ *n.* [L *emaciare emaciat-* (as E-, *macies* leanness)]
■ waste away, shrink, enfeeble, get thin; (**emaciated**) atrophied, shrivelled, wizened, shrunken, haggard, gaunt, drawn, pinched, bony, skeletal, cadaverous, withered, wasted, consumptive, scrawny, skinny, thin, spare, undernourished, underfed, starved, half-starved, anorexic, anorectic, *Med.* phthisic.

email /éemayl/ *n.* (also **e-mail**) = *electronic mail.*

emanate /émmənayt/ *v.* **1** *intr.* (usu. foll. by *from*) (of an idea, rumour, etc.) issue, originate (from a source). **2** *intr.* (usu. foll. by *from*) (of gas, light, etc.) proceed, issue. **3** *tr.* emit; send forth. [L *emanare* flow out]
■ **1** see ORIGINATE 2. **2** issue, come (out), emerge, proceed, flow, ooze, exude; radiate, disperse. **3** radiate, give off *or* out, send out *or* forth, disseminate, discharge, put out, emit; ooze, exude.

emanation /émmənáysh'n/ *n.* **1** the act or process of emanating. **2** something that emanates from a source (esp. of virtues, qualities, etc.). **3** *Chem.* a radioactive gas formed by radioactive decay. ▫▫ **emanative** *adj.* [LL *emanatio* (as EMANATE)]
■ **1** see OUTPOURING. **2** see AURA 1.

emancipate /imánsipayt/ *v.tr.* **1** free from restraint, esp. legal, social, or political. **2** (usu. as **emancipated** *adj.*) cause to be less inhibited by moral or social convention. **3** free from slavery. ▫▫ **emancipation** /-páysh'n/ *n.* **emancipator** *n.* **emancipatory** *adj.* [L *emancipare* transfer property (as E-, *manus* hand + *capere* take)]
■ **1, 3** release, liberate, deliver, loose, let loose, free, let go, set free; unfetter, unchain, unshackle, *hist.* enfranchise, manumit, *literary* disenthral. **2** (**emancipated**) liberated, liberalized; uninhibited, free and easy, free.

emasculate *v.* & *adj.* ● *v.tr.* /imáskyoolayt/ **1** deprive of force or vigour; make feeble or ineffective. **2** castrate. ● *adj.* /imáskyoolət/ **1** deprived of force or vigour. **2** castrated. **3** effeminate. ▫▫ **emasculation** /-láysh'n/ *n.* **emasculator** *n.* **emasculatory** /-lətəri/ *adj.* [L *emasculatus* past part. of *emasculare* (as E-, *masculus* dimin. of *mas* male)]
■ *v.* **1** see WEAKEN 1. **2** see NEUTER *v.*

embalm /imbaám/ *v.tr.* **1** preserve (a corpse) from decay orig. with spices, now by means of arterial injection. **2** preserve from oblivion. **3** endue with balmy fragrance. ▫▫ **embalmer** *n.* **embalmment** *n.* [ME f. OF *embaumer* (as EN-[1], BALM)]

embank /imbángk/ *v.tr.* shut in or confine (a river etc.) with an artificial bank.

embankment /imbángkmənt/ *n.* an earth or stone bank for keeping back water, or for carrying a road or railway.
■ see WALL *n.* 1.

embargo /embaárgō/ *n.* & *v.* ● *n.* (*pl.* **-oes**) **1** an order of a State forbidding foreign ships to enter, or any ships to leave, its ports. **2** an official suspension of commerce or other activity (*be under an embargo*). **3** an impediment. ● *v.tr.* (**-oes**, **-oed**) **1** place (ships, trade, etc.) under embargo. **2** seize (a ship, goods) for State service. [Sp. f. *embargar* arrest f. Rmc (as IN-[2], BAR[1])]
■ *n.* **1–3** restraint, block, blockage, bar, ban, stoppage, proscription, prohibition, interdiction, check, restriction, barrier; hindrance, impediment. ● *v.* **1** restrain, block, bar, ban, stop, cease, proscribe, prohibit, interdict, prevent, restrict, hold back.

embark /imbaárk/ *v.* **1** *tr.* & *intr.* (often foll. by *for*) put or go on board a ship or aircraft (to a destination). **2** *intr.* (foll. by *on*, *upon*) engage in an activity or undertaking. ▫▫ **embarkation** /émbaarkáysh'n/ *n.* (in sense 1). [F *embarquer* (as IN-[2], BARK[3])]
■ **1** board, go aboard, get on; emplane. **2** (*embark on*) begin, enter (upon), undertake, initiate, launch on, start, go into, set about, take up *or* on, assume, tackle, *formal* commence.

embarras de choix /óNbaraá də shwaá/ *n.* (also ***embarras de richesse(s)*** /reeshéss/) more choices than one needs or can deal with. [F, = embarrassment of choice, riches]

embarrass /imbárrəss/ *v.tr.* **1 a** cause (a person) to feel awkward or self-conscious or ashamed. **b** (as **embarrassed** *adj.*) having or expressing a feeling of awkwardness or self-consciousness. **2** (as **embarrassed** *adj.*) encumbered with debts. **3** encumber, impede. **4** complicate (a question etc.). **5** perplex. ▫▫ **embarrassedly** *adv.* **embarrassing** *adj.* **embarrassingly** *adv.* **embarrassment** *n.* [F *embarrasser* (orig. = hamper) f. Sp. *embarazar* f. It. *imbarrare* bar in (as IN-[2], BAR[1])]
■ **1 b** (**embarrassed**) ashamed, self-conscious, uncomfortable, red-faced, shamefaced.
▫▫ **embarrassing** awkward, uncomfortable, humiliating. **embarrassment** awkwardness, discomposure, discomfort, self-consciousness, mortification, chagrin; excess, superfluity, superabundance, surplus, profusion, *embarras de richesse(s)*.

embassy /émbəsi/ *n.* (*pl.* **-ies**) **1 a** the residence or offices of an ambassador. **b** the ambassador and staff attached to an embassy. **2** a deputation or mission to a foreign country.

[earlier *ambassy* f. OF *ambassée* etc. f. med.L *ambasciata* f. Rmc (as AMBASSADOR)]

embattle /imbátt'l/ *v.tr.* **1 a** set (an army etc.) in battle array. **b** fortify against attack. **2** provide (a building or wall) with battlements. **3** (as **embattled** *adj.*) **a** prepared or arrayed for battle. **b** involved in a conflict or difficult undertaking. **c** *Heraldry* like battlements in form. [ME f. OF *embataillier* (as EN-[1], BATTLE): see BATTLEMENT]

embay /imbáy/ *v.tr.* **1** enclose in or as in a bay; shut in. **2** form (a coast) into bays. ◻◻ **embayment** *n.*

embed /imbéd/ *v.tr.* (also **imbed**) (**-bedded, -bedding**) **1** (esp. as **embedded** *adj.*) fix firmly in a surrounding mass (*embedded in concrete*). **2** (of a mass) surround so as to fix firmly. **3** place in or as in a bed. ◻◻ **embedment** *n.*

■ **1, 2** see IMPLANT *v.* 1.

embellish /imbéllish/ *v.tr.* **1** beautify, adorn. **2** add interest to (a narrative) with fictitious additions. ◻◻ **embellisher** *n.* **embellishment** *n.* [ME f. OF *embellir* (as EN-[1], *bel* handsome f. L *bellus*)]

■ **1** beautify, adorn, dress (up), trick out *or* up, enhance, elaborate, enrich, embroider, gild, garnish, decorate, ornament, deck (out), bedeck, trim, caparison, *colloq.* titivate. **2** elaborate, embroider, exaggerate, enhance, dress up. ◻◻ **embellishment** decoration, ornamentation, elaboration, adornment, embroidery, garnishment, gilding, enrichment, beautification; exaggeration; ornament, enhancement, frill, trimming, extra, garnish.

ember[1] /émbər/ *n.* **1** (usu. in *pl.*) a small piece of glowing coal or wood in a dying fire. **2** an almost extinct residue of a past activity, feeling, etc. [OE *ǣmyrge* f. Gmc]

■ **2** remains, remnant, residue; see also VESTIGE 1.

ember[2] /émbər/ *n.* (in full **ember-goose**) = *great northern diver*. [Norw. *emmer*]

ember days /émbər/ *n.pl.* any of the days traditionally reserved for fasting and prayer in the Christian Church, now associated with ordinations. [OE *ymbren* (n.), perh. f. *ymbryne* period f. *ymb* about + *ryne* course]

embezzle /imbézz'l/ *v.tr.* (also *absol.*) divert (money etc.) fraudulently to one's own use. ◻◻ **embezzlement** *n.* **embezzler** *n.* [AF *embesiler* (as EN-[1], OF *besillier* maltreat, ravage, of unkn. orig.)]

■ misappropriate, peculate, misapply, misuse, make off *or* away with, *formal* defalcate; *colloq.* have one's hand in the till.

embitter /imbíttər/ *v.tr.* **1** arouse bitter feelings in (a person). **2** make more bitter or painful. **3** render (a person or feelings) hostile. ◻◻ **embitterment** *n.*

■ **1** sour, poison, envenom, aggrieve, pain, dispirit, make bitter; make angry *or* resentful *or* rancorous. **3** see EXASPERATE 1.

emblazon /imbláyz'n/ *v.tr.* **1 a** portray conspicuously, as on a heraldic shield. **b** adorn (a shield) with heraldic devices. **2** adorn brightly and conspicuously. **3** celebrate, extol. ◻◻ **emblazonment** *n.*

■ **1, 2** see ILLUMINATE 3.

emblem /émbləm/ *n.* **1** a symbol or representation typifying or identifying an institution, quality, etc. **2** (foll. by *of*) (of a person) the type (*the very emblem of courage*). **3** a heraldic device or symbolic object as a distinctive badge. ◻◻ **emblematic** /-máttik/ *adj.* **emblematical** /-máttik'l/ *adj.* **emblematically** /-máttikəli/ *adv.* [ME f. L *emblema* f. Gk *emblēma -matos* insertion f. *emballō* throw in (as EN-[1], *ballō* throw)]

■ **1, 3** badge, symbol, representation, device, seal, crest, token, sign; trade mark, logotype, *colloq.* logo. **2** see TYPE *n.* 2. ◻◻ **emblematic, emblematical** symbolical, representational; see also REPRESENTATIVE *adj.* 4.

emblematize /imblémmətīz/ *v.tr.* (also **-ise**) **1** serve as an emblem of. **2** represent by an emblem.

emblements /émblimənts/ *n.pl.* *Law* crops normally harvested annually, regarded as personal property. [ME f. OF *emblaement* f. *emblaier* (as EN-[1], *blé* corn)]

embody /imbóddi/ *v.tr.* (**-ies, -ied**) **1** give a concrete or discernible form to (an idea, concept, etc.). **2** (of a thing or person) be an expression of (an idea etc.). **3** express tangibly (*courage embodied in heroic actions*). **4** form into a body. **5** include, comprise. **6** provide (a spirit) with bodily form. ◻◻ **embodiment** *n.*

■ **1, 3** concretize, realize, materialize, reify, actualize, incarnate, body forth; manifest, express, personify, demonstrate, epitomize. **2** typify, represent; see also EXEMPLIFY. **5** incorporate, comprise; see also INCLUDE 1. ◻◻ **embodiment** incarnation, realization, concretization, manifestation, expression, personification, epitome, materialization, actualization, reification, substantiation; incorporation, inclusion.

embolden /imbṓldən/ *v.tr.* (often foll. by *to* + infin.) make bold; encourage.

■ see ENCOURAGE 1.

embolism /émbəliz'm/ *n.* an obstruction of any artery by a clot of blood, air-bubble, etc. [ME, = 'intercalation' f. LL *embolismus* f. Gk *embolismos* f. *emballō* (as EMBLEM)]

■ see STROKE *n.* 2.

embolus /émbələss/ *n.* (*pl.* **emboli** /-lī/) an object causing an embolism. [L, = piston, f. Gk *embolos* peg, stopper]

embonpoint /ónbonpwán/ *n.* plumpness (of a person). [F *en bon point* in good condition]

■ see *fatness* (FAT).

embosom /imbŏŏzz'm/ *v.tr.* *literary* **1** embrace. **2** enclose, surround.

emboss /imbóss/ *v.tr.* **1** carve or mould in relief. **2** form figures etc. so that they stand out on (a surface). **3** make protuberant. ◻◻ **embosser** *n.* **embossment** *n.* [ME, f. OF (as EN-[1], BOSS[2])]

■ **2** chase.

embouchure /ómbooshoor/ *n.* **1** *Mus.* **a** the mode of applying the mouth to the mouthpiece of a brass or wind instrument. **b** the mouthpiece of some instruments. **2** the mouth of a river. **3** the opening of a valley. [F f. *s'emboucher* discharge itself by the mouth (as EN-[1], *bouche* mouth)]

■ **2, 3** see MOUTH *n.* 3.

embowel /imbówəl/ *v.tr.* (**embowelled, embowelling**; *US* **emboweled, emboweling**) *archaic* = DISEMBOWEL. [OF *emboweler* f. *esbouele*r (as EX-[1], BOWEL)]

embower /imbówr/ *v.tr.* *literary* enclose as in a bower.

embrace /imbráyss/ *v.* & *n.* • *v.tr.* **1 a** hold (a person) closely in the arms, esp. as a sign of affection. **b** (*absol.*, of two people) hold each other closely. **2** clasp, enclose. **3** accept eagerly (an offer, opportunity, etc.). **4** adopt (a course of action, doctrine, cause, etc.). **5** include, comprise. **6** take in with the eye or mind. • *n.* an act of embracing; holding in the arms. ◻◻ **embraceable** *adj.* **embracement** *n.* **embracer** *n.* [ME f. OF *embracer*, ult. f. L *in-* IN-[1] + *bracchium* arm]

■ *v.* **1** hug, clasp, grasp, hold, enfold, cuddle, enclasp, *archaic* clip, *colloq.* clinch, *literary* embosom, *poet.* fold. **2** see CLASP *v.* 2, ENCLOSE 1, 6. **3** see ACCEPT 2. **4** adopt, espouse, support, welcome, advocate. **5** include, comprise, embody, incorporate, comprehend, encompass. **6** see COMPREHEND 1. • *n.* hug, squeeze, cuddle, clasp, *colloq.* clinch.

embranchment /imbraánchmənt/ *n.* a branching-out (of the arm of a river etc.). [F *embranchement* BRANCH (as EN-[1], BRANCH)]

embrasure /imbráyzhər/ *n.* **1** the bevelling of a wall at the sides of a door or window; splaying. **2** a small opening in a parapet of a fortified building, splayed on the inside. ◻◻ **embrasured** *adj.* [F f. *embraser* splay, of unkn. orig.]

embrittle /imbrítt'l/ *v.tr.* make brittle. ◻◻ **embrittlement** *n.*

embrocation /émbrōkáysh'n/ *n.* a liquid used for rubbing on the body to relieve muscular pain etc. [F *embrocation* or med.L *embrocatio* ult. f. Gk *embrokhē* lotion]

■ see LOTION.

embroider /imbróydər/ *v.tr.* **1** (also *absol.*) **a** decorate (cloth etc.) with needlework. **b** create (a design) in this way. **2** add interest to (a narrative) with fictitious additions. □□ **embroiderer** *n.* [ME f. AF *enbrouder* (as EN-[1], OF *brouder*, *broisder* f. Gmc)]
▪ **1** see ORNAMENT *v.* **2** see EMBELLISH 2.

embroidery /imbróydəri/ *n.* (*pl.* **-ies**) **1** the art of embroidering. **2** embroidered work; a piece of this. **3** unnecessary or extravagant ornament. [ME f. AF *enbrouderie* (as EMBROIDER)]
▪ **3** see ORNAMENT *n.* 1, 2.

embroil /imbróyl/ *v.tr.* **1** (often foll. by *with*) involve (a person) in conflict or difficulties. **2** bring (affairs) into a state of confusion. □□ **embroilment** *n.* [F *embrouiller* (as EN-[1], BROIL[2])]
▪ **1** see ENTANGLE 3. **2** see ENTANGLE 4.

embryo /émbriō/ *n.* (*pl.* **-os**) **1 a** an unborn or unhatched offspring. **b** a human offspring in the first eight weeks from conception. **2** a rudimentary plant contained in a seed. **3** a thing in a rudimentary stage. **4** (*attrib.*) undeveloped, immature. □ **in embryo** undeveloped. □□ **embryoid** *adj.* **embryonal** /émbriən'l/ *adj.* **embryonic** /émbriónnik/ *adj.* **embryonically** /-ónnikəli/ *adv.* [LL *embryo -onis* f. Gk *embruon* foetus (as EN-[2], *bruō* swell, grow)]
▪ **3** see GERM 3.

embryo- /émbriō/ *comb. form* embryo.

embryogenesis /émbriōjénnisiss/ *n.* the formation of an embryo.

embryology /émbriólləji/ *n.* the study of embryos. □□ **embryologic** /-briəlójik/ *adj.* **embryological** /-briəlójik'l/ *adj.* **embryologically** /-briəlójikəli/ *adv.* **embryologist** *n.*

embus /imbúss/ *v.* (**embused**, **embusing** or **embussed**, **embussing**) *Mil.* **1** *tr.* put (men or equipment) into a motor vehicle. **2** *intr.* board a motor vehicle.

emcee /émseé/ *n.* & *v. colloq.* ● *n.* a master of ceremonies or compère. ● *v.tr.* & *intr.* (**emcees**, **emceed**) compère. [the letters *MC*]
▪ *n.* see MODERATOR 2. ● *v.* see PRESENT[2] *v.* 3b.

-eme /eem/ *suffix Linguistics* forming nouns denoting units of structure etc. (*grapheme*; *morpheme*). [F *-ème* unit f. Gk *-ēma*]

emend /iménd/ *v.tr.* edit (a text etc.) to remove errors and corruptions. □□ **emendation** /éemendáysh'n/ *n.* **emendator** /éemendaytər/ *n.* **emendatory** *adj.* [ME f. L *emendare* (as E-, *menda* fault)]
▪ see REVISE *v.* 1.

emerald /émmərəld/ *n.* **1** a bright-green precious stone, a variety of beryl. **2** (also **emerald green**) the colour of this. □ **Emerald Isle** *literary* Ireland. □□ **emeraldine** /-dīn, -din/ *adj.* [ME f. OF *emeraude*, *esm-*, ult. f. Gk *smaragdos*]

emerge /imérj/ *v.intr.* (often foll. by *from*) **1** come up or out into view, esp. when formerly concealed. **2** come up out of a liquid. **3** (of facts, circumstances, etc.) come to light, become known, esp. as a result of inquiry etc. **4** become recognized or prominent (*emerged as a leading contender*). **5** (of a question, difficulty, etc.) become apparent. **6** survive (an ordeal etc.) with a specified result (*emerged unscathed*). □□ **emergence** *n.* [L *emergere emers-* (as E-, *mergere* dip)]
▪ **1** appear, come out, come forth, come up, rise; arise, surface, come into view, be revealed. **3, 5** be revealed, come to light, turn out, become known, become apparent, transpire. **6** see SURVIVE 1. □□ **emergence** emersion, surfacing; materialization, manifestation; see also APPEARANCE 1.

emergency /imérjənsi/ *n.* (*pl.* **-ies**) **1** a sudden state of danger, conflict, etc., requiring immediate action. **2 a** a medical condition requiring immediate treatment. **b** a patient with such a condition. **3** (*attrib.*) characterized by or for use in an emergency. **4** *Austral. Sport* a reserve player. □ **state of emergency** a condition of danger or disaster affecting a country, esp. with normal constitutional procedures suspended. [med.L *emergentia* (as EMERGE)]
▪ **1** crisis, exigency, danger, predicament, difficulty.

emergent /imérjənt/ *adj.* **1** becoming apparent; emerging. **2** (of a nation) newly formed or made independent.

emeritus /imérritəss/ *adj.* **1** retired and retaining one's title as an honour (*emeritus professor*; *professor emeritus*). **2** honourably discharged from service. [L, past part. of *emerēri* (as E-, *merēri* earn)]
▪ see OUTGOING *adj.* 2, 3.

emersion /imérsh'n/ *n.* **1** the act or an instance of emerging. **2** *Astron.* the reappearance of a celestial body after its eclipse or occultation. [LL *emersio* (as EMERGE)]

emery /émməri/ *n.* **1** a coarse rock of corundum and magnetite or haematite used for polishing metal or other hard materials. **2** (*attrib.*) covered with emery. □ **emery-board** a strip of thin wood or board coated with emery or another abrasive, used as a nail-file. **emery-paper** cloth or paper covered with emery, used for polishing or cleaning metals etc. [F *émeri(l)* f. It. *smeriglio* ult. f. Gk *smuris*, *smēris* polishing powder]

emetic /iméttik/ *adj.* & *n.* ● *adj.* that causes vomiting. ● *n.* an emetic medicine. [Gk *emetikos* f. *emeō* vomit]
▪ *adj.* see NAUSEOUS 2, 3.

EMF *abbr.* electromotive force.

-emia *US* var. of -AEMIA.

emigrant /émmigrənt/ *n.* & *adj.* ● *n.* a person who emigrates. ● *adj.* emigrating.
▪ *n.* émigré, expatriate, settler, displaced person, DP, refugee, exile.

emigrate /émmigrayt/ *v.* **1** *intr.* leave one's own country to settle in another. **2** *tr.* assist (a person) to emigrate. □□ **emigration** /-gráysh'n/ *n.* **emigratory** *adj.* [L *emigrare emigrat-* (as E-, *migrare* depart)]
▪ **1** migrate, move, relocate, resettle; (*emigrate from*) leave, quit, depart.

émigré /émmigray/ *n.* an emigrant, esp. a political exile. [F, past part. of *émigrer* EMIGRATE]
▪ see EXILE *n.* 3.

eminence /émminənss/ *n.* **1** distinction; recognized superiority. **2** a piece of rising ground. **3** (**Eminence**) a title used in addressing or referring to a cardinal (*Your Eminence*; *His Eminence*). **4** an important person. [L *eminentia* (as EMINENT)]
▪ **1** see DISTINCTION *n.* 4. **2** see RISE *n.* 2. **4** see WORTHY *n.* 2.

éminence grise /áyminónss greéz/ *n.* **1** a person who exercises power or influence without holding office. **2** a confidential agent. [F, = grey cardinal (see EMINENCE): orig. applied to Cardinal Richelieu's private secretary, Père Joseph d. 1638]

eminent /émminənt/ *adj.* **1** distinguished, notable. **2** (of qualities) remarkable in degree. □ **eminent domain** sovereign control over all property in a State, with the right of expropriation. □□ **eminently** *adv.* [ME f. L *eminēre eminent-* jut]
▪ **1** distinguished, esteemed, exalted, respected, revered, honoured, notable, noteworthy, important, noted, outstanding, prominent, pre-eminent, conspicuous, superior, great, illustrious, famous, renowned, well-known, celebrated. **2** remarkable, conspicuous, outstanding, marked, singular. □□ **eminently** very, exceedingly, extremely, exceptionally, remarkably, singularly, signally.

emir /emeér/ *n.* **1** a title of various Muslim rulers. **2** *archaic* a male descendant of Muhammad. [F *émir* f. Arab. *'amīr*: cf. AMIR]

emirate /émmeerət/ *n.* the rank, domain, or reign of an emir.

emissary /émmisəri/ *n.* (*pl.* **-ies**) a person sent on a special mission (usu. diplomatic, formerly usu. odious or underhand). [L *emissarius* scout, spy (as EMIT)]
▪ see ENVOY[1].

emission /imísh'n/ *n.* **1** (often foll. by *of*) the process or an act of emitting. **2** a thing emitted. [L *emissio* (as EMIT)]
■ **2** see DISCHARGE *n.* 5.

emissive /imíssiv/ *adj.* having the power to radiate light, heat, etc. □□ **emissivity** /éemisívviti/ *n.*

emit /imít/ *v.tr.* (**emitted, emitting**) **1 a** send out (heat, light, vapour, etc.). **b** discharge from the body. **2** utter (a cry etc.). [L *emittere emiss-* (as E-, *mittere* send)]
■ **1** discharge, eject, expel, emanate, send out *or* forth, pour out *or* forth, give off *or* out, vent, radiate; exude, ooze. **2** see VOICE *v.*

emitter /imíttər/ *n.* that which emits, esp. a region in a transistor producing carriers of current.

Emmental /émməntaal/ *n.* (also **Emmenthal**) a kind of hard Swiss cheese with many holes in it, similar to Gruyère. [G *Emmentaler* f. *Emmental* in Switzerland]

emmer /émmər/ *n.* a kind of wheat, *Triticum dicoccum*, grown mainly for fodder. [G dial.]

emmet /émmit/ *n.* *archaic* or *dial.* an ant. [OE *ǣmete*: see ANT]

Emmy /émmi/ *n.* (*pl.* **-ies**) (in the US) a statuette awarded annually to an outstanding television programme or performer. [perh. f. *Immy* = *image orthicon tube*]

emollient /imólliənt/ *adj.* & *n.* ● *adj.* that softens or soothes the skin. ● *n.* an emollient agent. □□ **emollience** *n.* [L *emollire* (as E-, *mollis* soft)]
■ *adj.* see *soothing* (SOOTHE). ● *n.* see OINTMENT.

emolument /imólyoomənt/ *n.* a salary, fee, or profit from employment or office. [ME f. OF *emolument* or L *emolumentum*, orig. prob. 'payment for corn-grinding', f. *emolere* (as E-, *molere* grind)]
■ see SALARY *n.*

emote /imṓt/ *v.intr.* *colloq.* show excessive emotion. □□ **emoter** *n.* [back-form. f. EMOTION]

emotion /imṓsh'n/ *n.* a strong mental or instinctive feeling such as love or fear. [earlier = agitation, disturbance of the mind, f. F *émotion* f. *émouvoir* excite]
■ feeling, passion, sentiment, sensation.

emotional /imṓshən'l/ *adj.* **1** of or relating to the emotions. **2** (of a person) liable to excessive emotion. **3** expressing or based on emotion (*an emotional appeal*). **4** likely to excite emotion (*an emotional issue*). □□ **emotionalism** *n.* **emotionalist** *n.* **emotionality** /-nálliti/ *n.* **emotionalize** *v.tr.* (also **-ise**). **emotionally** *adv.*
■ **2** excitable, highly-strung, high-strung, temperamental, volatile, hotheaded, demonstrative, irrational, hysterical, sentimental. **3** passionate, impassioned, ardent, enthusiastic, heated, zealous, heartfelt, excited, fervent, fervid. **4** sensitive, moving, poignant, stirring, emotive, affective, touching.

emotive /imṓtiv/ *adj.* **1** of or characterized by emotion. **2** tending to excite emotion. **3** arousing feeling; not purely descriptive. □□ **emotively** *adv.* **emotiveness** *n.* **emotivity** /éemōtívviti/ *n.* [L *emovēre emot-* (as E-, *movēre* move)]
■ see MOVING 2.

empanel /impánn'l/ *v.tr.* (also **impanel**) (**-panelled, -panelling**; *US* **-paneled, -paneling**) enrol or enter on a panel (those eligible for jury service). □□ **empanelment** *n.* [AF *empaneller* (as EN-[1], PANEL)]

empathize /émpəthīz/ *v.* *Psychol.* **1** *intr.* (usu. foll. by *with*) exercise empathy. **2** *tr.* treat with empathy.
■ (*empathize with*) see IDENTIFY 5.

empathy /émpəthi/ *n.* *Psychol.* the power of identifying oneself mentally with (and so fully comprehending) a person or object of contemplation. □□ **empathetic** /-théttik/ *adj.* **empathetically** /-théttikəli/ *adv.* **empathic** /empáthik/ *adj.* **empathically** /empáthikəli/ *adv.* **empathist** *n.* [transl. G *Einfühlung* f. *ein* in + *Fühlung* feeling, after Gk *empatheia*: see SYMPATHY]
■ see FEELING *n.* 3.

empennage /empénnij/ *n.* *Aeron.* an arrangement of stabilizing surfaces at the tail of an aircraft. [F f. *empenner* to feather (an arrow)]

emperor /émpərər/ *n.* **1** the sovereign of an empire. **2** a sovereign of higher rank than a king. □ **emperor moth** a large moth, *Saturnia pavonia*, of the silk-moth family, with eye-spots on all four wings. **emperor penguin** the largest known penguin, *Aptenodytes forsteri*, of the Antarctic. □□ **emperorship** *n.* [ME f. OF *emperere*, *empereor* f. L *imperator -oris* f. *imperare* command]
■ see SOVEREIGN *n.* 1.

emphasis /émfəsiss/ *n.* (*pl.* **emphases** /-seez/) **1** special importance or prominence attached to a thing, fact, idea, etc. (*emphasis on economy*). **2** stress laid on a word or words to indicate special meaning or importance. **3** vigour or intensity of expression, feeling, action, etc. **4** prominence, sharpness of contour. [L f. Gk f. *emphainō* exhibit (as EN-[2], *phainō* show)]
■ **1** importance, stress, significance, prominence, attention, weight, gravity, force, pre-eminence, priority. **3** force, vigour; see also INTENSITY 1.

emphasize /émfəsīz/ *v.tr.* (also **-ise**) **1** bring (a thing, fact, etc.) into special prominence. **2** lay stress on (a word in speaking).
■ **1** stress, accentuate, accent, underscore, point up, underline, call *or* draw attention to, highlight, play up, spotlight, feature.

emphatic /imfáttik/ *adj.* **1** (of language, tone, or gesture) forcibly expressive. **2** of words: **a** bearing the stress. **b** used to give emphasis. **3** expressing oneself with emphasis. **4** (of an action or process) forcible, significant. □□ **emphatically** *adv.* [LL *emphaticus* f. Gk *emphatikos* (as EMPHASIS)]
■ **1, 3** expressive, demonstrative, pronounced, strong, clear, definite; firm, uncompromising, determined, decided, resolute, dogged; earnest, unequivocal, unambiguous, distinct, categorical, explicit, insistent, affirmative, positive, sure, certain, unmistakable, specific, definitive, direct; forceful, vigorous, energetic, assertive, intense.

emphysema /émfiséemə/ *n.* **1** enlargement of the air sacs of the lungs causing breathlessness. **2** a swelling caused by the presence of air in the connective tissues of the body. [LL f. Gk *emphusēma* f. *emphusaō* puff up]

empire /émpīr/ *n.* **1** an extensive group of States or countries under a single supreme authority, esp. an emperor. **2 a** supreme dominion. **b** (often foll. by *over*) *archaic* absolute control. **3** a large commercial organization etc. owned or directed by one person or group. **4** (**the Empire**) *hist.* **a** the British Empire. **b** the Holy Roman Empire. **5** a type or period of government in which the sovereign is called emperor. **6** (**Empire**) (*attrib.*) **a** denoting a style of furniture or dress fashionable during the first (1804–14) or second (1852–70) French Empire. **b** *Brit.* denoting produce from the Commonwealth. □ **empire-builder** a person who deliberately acquires extra territory, authority, etc. esp. unnecessarily. **Empire Day** *hist.* the former name of Commonwealth Day, orig. 24 May. [ME f. OF f. L *imperium* rel. to *imperare*: see EMPEROR]
■ **1** see DOMAIN 1.

empiric /impírrik/ *adj.* & *n.* ● *adj.* = EMPIRICAL. ● *n.* *archaic* **1** a person relying solely on experiment. **2** a quack doctor. □□ **empiricism** *n.* **empiricist** *n.* [L *empiricus* f. Gk *empeirikos* f. *empeiria* experience f. *empeiros* skilled]

empirical /impírrik'l/ *adj.* **1** based or acting on observation or experiment, not on theory. **2** *Philos.* regarding sense-data as valid information. **3** deriving knowledge from experience alone. □ **empirical formula** *Chem.* a formula showing the constituents of a compound but not their configuration. □□ **empirically** *adv.*
■ **1** empiric, experiential, observational, practical, observed, pragmatic, experimental.

emplacement /impláysmənt/ *n.* **1** the act or an instance of putting in position. **2** a platform or defended position where a gun is placed for firing. **3** situation, position. [F (as EN-[1], PLACE)]
■ **1, 3** see *placement* (PLACE).

emplane /impláyn/ *v.intr.* & *tr.* (also **enplane** /in-/) go or put on board an aeroplane.
■ see EMBARK 1.

employ /implóy/ *v.* & *n.* ● *v.tr.* **1** use the services of (a person) in return for payment; keep (a person) in one's service. **2** (often foll. by *for, in, on*) use (a thing, time, energy, etc.) esp. to good effect. **3** (often foll. by *in*) keep (a person) occupied. ● *n.* the state of being employed, esp. for wages. □ **in the employ of** employed by. □□ **employable** *adj.* **employability** /-plóyəbílliti/ *n.* **employer** *n.* [ME f. OF *employer* ult. f. L *implicari* be involved f. *implicare* enfold: see IMPLICATE]
■ *v.* **1** hire, engage, enlist, recruit, enrol, sign (up), take on, contract; keep, retain. **2** use, make use of, utilize, apply. **3** occupy, engage, involve, engross. □□ **employer** proprietor, owner, patron, manager, director, chief, head, *colloq.* boss, *Brit. colloq.* gaffer, *sl.* governor, guv'nor, *Brit. sl* guv; company, firm, corporation, business, establishment, organization.

employee /émployeé, -plóyi/ *n.* (*US* **employe**) a person employed for wages or salary, esp. at non-executive level.
■ worker, member of staff, wage-earner; hand; (*employees*) staff, workforce.

employment /implóymənt/ *n.* **1** the act of employing or the state of being employed. **2** a person's regular trade or profession. □ **employment agency** a business that finds employers or employees for those seeking them. **employment office** (formerly **employment exchange**) *Brit.* any of a number of government offices concerned with advising and finding work for the unemployed.
■ **1** hire, hiring, engagement, enlistment; use, utilization, application, operation, implementation. **2** occupation, job, trade, work, business, profession, vocation, *métier*, skill, craft, *Austral. sl.* grip. □ **employment office** *Brit.* jobcentre, *Brit. colloq. or hist.* Labour Exchange.

empolder var. of IMPOLDER.

emporium /empóriəm/ *n.* (*pl.* **emporia** /-riə/ or **-ums**) **1** a large retail store selling a wide variety of goods. **2** a centre of commerce, a market. [L f. Gk *emporion* f. *emporos* merchant]

empower /impówr/ *v.tr.* (foll. by *to* + infin.) **1** authorize, license. **2** give power to; make able. □□ **empowerment** *n.*
■ **1** see AUTHORIZE.

empress /émpriss/ *n.* **1** the wife or widow of an emperor. **2** a woman emperor. [ME f. OF *emperesse* fem. of *emperere* EMPEROR]
■ see SOVEREIGN *n.* 1.

empty /émpti/ *adj., v.,* & *n.* ● *adj.* (**emptier, emptiest**) **1** containing nothing. **2** (of a space, place, house etc.) unoccupied, uninhabited, deserted; unfurnished. **3** (of a transport vehicle etc.) without a load, passengers, etc. **4 a** meaningless, hollow, insincere (*empty threats; an empty gesture*). **b** without substance or purpose (*an empty existence*). **c** (of a person) lacking sense or knowledge; vacant, foolish. **5** *colloq.* hungry. **6** (foll. by *of*) devoid, lacking. ● *v.* (**-ies, -ied**) **1** *tr.* **a** make empty; remove the contents of. **b** (foll. by *of*) deprive of certain contents (*emptied the room of its chairs*). **c** remove (contents) from a container etc. **2** *tr.* (often foll. by *into*) transfer (the contents of a container). **3** *intr.* become empty. **4** *intr.* (usu. foll. by *into*) (of a river) discharge itself (into the sea etc.). ● *n.* (*pl.* **-ies**) *colloq.* a container (esp. a bottle) left empty of its contents. □ **empty-handed 1** bringing or taking nothing. **2** having achieved or obtained nothing. **empty-headed** foolish; lacking common sense. **empty-nester** *US* either of a couple whose children have grown up and left home. **on an empty stomach** see STOMACH. □□ **emptily** *adv.* **emptiness** *n.* [OE *ǣmtig, ǣmetig* f. *ǣmetta* leisure]
■ *adj.* **1** void, unfilled, hollow, bare, barren, vacant, blank; clean, new, unused, clear; emptied, drained, spent, exhausted. **2** vacant, unoccupied, untenanted, uninhabited, deserted, unpeopled; desolate, wild, waste, bare, barren, forsaken; unfurnished. **4 a** trivial, shallow, insincere, hypocritical, hollow, cheap, worthless, valueless, meaningless, insignificant, insubstantial, vain, idle. **b** see PURPOSELESS. **c** vacant, blank; vacuous, fatuous, stupid, foolish, inane. **6** (*empty of*) devoid of, lacking (in), wanting, in want of, deficient in, destitute of, without, *archaic or joc.* sans. ● *v.* **1 a, b** clear (out), vacate, evacuate; drain, exhaust; void; see also DIVEST 2. **c** take out *or* away, put out, cast *or* throw out, eject, remove; dump, pour out, **2** see TRANSFER *v.* 1a. **4** discharge, unload. □ **empty-headed** see FOOLISH. □□ **emptiness** voidness, hollowness, vacantness, vacancy, vacuity, blankness, bareness, barrenness, desertedness; senselessness, meaninglessness, pointlessness, aimlessness, purposelessness, futility, uselessness, worthlessness, hollowness; vacuousness, expressionlessness, emotionlessness.

empurple /impúrp'l/ *v.tr.* **1** make purple or red. **2** make angry.

empyema /émpī-eémə, émpi-/ *n.* a collection of pus in a cavity, esp. in the pleura. [LL f. Gk *empuēma* f. *empueō* suppurate (as EN-[2], *puon* pus)]

empyrean /émpīreéən, empírriən/ *n.* & *adj.* ● *n.* **1** the highest heaven, as the sphere of fire in ancient cosmology or as the abode of God in early Christianity. **2** the visible heavens. ● *adj.* of the empyrean. □□ **empyreal** /émpīreéəl, empírriəl/ *adj.* [med.L *empyreus* f. Gk *empurios* (as EN-[2], *pur* fire)]
■ *n.* **2** see SKY *n.* 1. ● *adj.* see CELESTIAL 1.

EMS *abbr.* European Monetary System.

EMU /eé-emyōō, eémyōō , / *abbr.* economic and monetary union (of the EC); European monetary union.

emu /eémyōō/ *n.* a large flightless bird, *Dromaius novaehollandiae*, native to Australia, and capable of running at high speed. [earlier *emia, eme* f. Port. *ema*]

e.m.u. *abbr.* electromagnetic unit(s).

emulate /émyoolayt/ *v.tr.* **1** try to equal or excel. **2** imitate zealously. **3** rival. □□ **emulation** /-láysh'n/ *n.* **emulative** /-lətiv/ *adj.* **emulator** *n.* [L *aemulari* (as EMULOUS)]
■ see IMITATE 1, 2.

emulous /émyooləss/ *adj.* **1** (usu. foll. by *of*) seeking to emulate. **2** actuated by a spirit of rivalry. □□ **emulously** *adv.* [ME f. L *aemulus* rival]

emulsifier /imúlsifīər/ *n.* **1** any substance that stabilizes an emulsion, esp. a food additive used to stabilize processed foods. **2** an apparatus used for producing an emulsion.

emulsify /imúlsifī/ *v.tr.* (**-ies, -ied**) convert into an emulsion. □□ **emulsifiable** *adj.* **emulsification** /-fikáysh'n/ *n.*

emulsion /imúlsh'n/ *n.* **1** a fine dispersion of one liquid in another, esp. as paint, medicine, etc. **2** a mixture of a silver compound suspended in gelatin etc. for coating plates or films. □ **emulsion paint** a water-thinned paint containing a non-volatile substance, e.g. synthetic resin, as its binding medium. □□ **emulsionize** *v.tr.* (also **-ise**). **emulsive** *adj.* [F *émulsion* or mod.L *emulsio* f. *emulgēre* (as E-, *mulgēre muls-* to milk)]
■ **1** see SOLUTION 2.

en /en/ *n. Printing* a unit of measurement equal to half an em. □ **en rule** (or **dash**) a short dash used in punctuation. [name of the letter *N*]

en-[1] /en, in/ *prefix* (also **em-** before *b, p*) forming verbs, = IN-[1]: **1** from nouns, meaning 'put into or on' (*engulf; entrust; embed*). **2** from nouns or adjectives, meaning 'bring into the condition of' (*enslave*); often with the suffix *-en* (*enlighten*). **3** from verbs: **a** in the sense 'in, into, on' (*enfold*). **b** as an intensive (*entangle*). [from or after F *en-* f. L *in-*]

en-[2] /en, in/ *prefix* (also **em-** before *b, p*) in, inside (*energy; enthusiasm*). [Gk]

-en[1] /ən/ *suffix* forming verbs: **1** from adjectives, usu. meaning 'make or become so or more so' (*deepen; fasten; moisten*). **2** from nouns (*happen; strengthen*). [OE *-nian* f. Gmc]

-en[2] /ən/ *suffix* (also **-n**) forming adjectives from nouns, meaning: **1** made or consisting of (often with extended and figurative senses) (*wooden*). **2** resembling; of the nature of (*golden*; *silvern*). [OE f. Gmc]

-en[3] /ən/ *suffix* (also **-n**) forming past participles of strong verbs: **1** as a regular inflection (*spoken*; *sworn*). **2** with restricted sense (*drunken*). [OE f. Gmc]

-en[4] /ən/ *suffix* forming the plural of a few nouns (*children*; *brethren*; *oxen*). [ME reduction of OE *-an*]

-en[5] /ən/ *suffix* forming diminutives of nouns (*chicken*; *maiden*). [OE f. Gmc]

-en[6] /ən/ *suffix* **1** forming feminine nouns (*vixen*). **2** forming abstract nouns (*burden*). [OE f. Gmc]

enable /ináyb'l/ *v.tr.* **1** (foll. by *to* + infin.) give (a person etc.) the means or authority to do something. **2** make possible. **3** esp. *Computing* make (a device) operational; switch on. □ **enabling act 1** a statute empowering a person or body to take certain action. **2** *US* a statute legalizing something otherwise unlawful. □□ **enabler** *n.*

■ **1** qualify, authorize, entitle, permit, allow, sanction, approve, empower, license; capacitate, facilitate, help, aid, assist. **3** see *turn on* 1 (TURN).

enact /inákt/ *v.tr.* **1 a** (often foll. by *that* + clause) ordain, decree. **b** make (a bill etc.) law. **2** play (a part or scene on stage or in life). □□ **enactable** *adj.* **enaction** *n.* **enactive** *adj.* **enactor** *n.* **enactory** *adj.*

■ **1 a** ordain, decree, rule, command, order, authorize. **b** pass, ratify; see also APPROVE. **2** act (out), represent, play, portray, depict, perform, appear as.

enactment /ináktmənt/ *n.* **1** a law enacted. **2** the process of enacting.

■ **1** see LAW 1a. **2** see PASSAGE[1] *n.* 7.

enamel /inámm'l/ *n.* & *v.* ● *n.* **1** a glasslike opaque or semi-transparent coating on metallic or other hard surfaces for ornament or as a preservative lining. **2 a** a smooth hard coating. **b** a cosmetic simulating this. **3** the hard glossy natural coating over the crown of a tooth. **4** painting done in enamel. **5** *poet.* a smooth bright surface colouring, verdure, etc. ● *v.tr.* (**enamelled, enamelling**; *US* **enameled, enameling**) **1** inlay or encrust (a metal etc.) with enamel. **2** portray (figures etc.) with enamel. **3** *archaic* adorn with varied colours. □ **enamel paint** a paint that dries to give a smooth hard coat. □□ **enameller** *n.* **enamelwork** *n.* [ME f. AF *enameler*, *enamailler* (as EN-[1], OF *esmail* f. Gmc)]

■ *n.* **1, 2** see GLAZE *n.*

enamelware /inámm'lwair/ *n.* enamelled kitchenware.

enamour /inámmər/ *v.tr.* (*US* **enamor**) (usu. in *passive*; foll. by *of*) **1** inspire with love or liking. **2** charm, delight. [ME f. OF *enamourer* f. *amourer* (as EN-[1], AMOUR)]

■ see CAPTIVATE.

enanthema /énnantheéémə/ *n.* *Med.* an eruption occurring on a mucus-secreting surface such as the inside of the mouth. [mod.L f. Gk *enanthēma* eruption (as EN-[1], EXANTHEMA)]

enantiomer /enántiəmər/ *n.* *Chem.* a molecule with a mirror image. □□ **enantiomeric** /-mérrik/ *adj.* [Gk *enantios* opposite + -MER]

enantiomorph /enántiəmorf/ *n.* a mirror image; a form (esp. of a crystal structure etc.) related to another as an object is to its mirror image. □□ **enantiomorphic** /-mórfik/ *adj.* **enantiomorphism** /-mórfiz'm/ *n.* **enantiomorphous** /-mórfəss/ *adj.* [G f. Gk *enantios* opposite + *morphē* form]

enarthrosis /énnaarthrṓsiss/ *n.* (*pl.* **enarthroses** /-seez/) *Anat.* a ball-and-socket joint. [Gk f. *enarthros* jointed (as EN-[2], *arthron* joint)]

en bloc /ON blók/ *adv.* in a block; all at the same time; wholesale. [F]

en brosse /ON bróss/ *adj.* (of hair) cut short and bristly. [F]

encaenia /enseéniə/ *n.* **1** (at Oxford University) an annual celebration in memory of founders and benefactors. **2** a dedication festival. [L f. Gk *egkainia* (as EN-[2], *kainos* new)]

encage /inkáyj/ *v.tr.* confine in or as in a cage.

encamp /inkámp/ *v.tr.* & *intr.* **1** settle in a military camp. **2** lodge in the open in tents.

■ see CAMP[1] *v.* 1.

encampment /inkámpmənt/ *n.* **1** a place where troops etc. are encamped. **2** the process of setting up a camp.

■ see CAMP[1] *n.* 1a, 2.

encapsulate /inkápsyoolayt/ *v.tr.* **1** enclose in or as in a capsule. **2** summarize; express the essential features of. **3** isolate. □□ **encapsulation** /-láysh'n/ *n.* [EN-[1] + L *capsula* CAPSULE]

■ **2** see *sum up* 1 (SUM).

encase /inkáyss/ *v.tr.* (also **incase**) **1** put into a case. **2** surround as with a case. □□ **encasement** *n.*

■ see CASE[2] *v.* 1.

encash /inkásh/ *v.tr.* *Brit.* **1** convert (bills etc.) into cash. **2** receive in the form of cash; realize. □□ **encashable** *adj.* **encashment** *n.*

encaustic /inkáwstik/ *adj.* & *n.* ● *adj.* **1** (in painting, ceramics, etc.) using pigments mixed with hot wax, which are burned in as an inlay. **2** (of bricks and tiles) inlaid with differently coloured clays burnt in. ● *n.* **1** the art of encaustic painting. **2** a painting done with this technique. [L *encausticus* f. Gk *egkaustikos* (as EN-[2], CAUSTIC)]

-ence /ənss/ *suffix* forming nouns expressing: **1** a quality or state or an instance of one (*patience*; *an impertinence*). **2** an action (*reference*; *reminiscence*). [from or after F *-ence* f. L *-entia*, *-antia* (cf. -ANCE) f. pres. part. stem *-ent-*, *-ant-*]

enceinte /ONSÁNT/ *n.* & *adj.* ● *n.* an enclosure, esp. in fortification. ● *adj.* *archaic* pregnant. [F, ult. f. L *cingere cinct-* gird: see CINCTURE]

■ *adj.* see *be expecting* (EXPECT).

encephalic /énkifállik, énsi-/ *adj.* of or relating to the brain. [Gk *egkephalos* brain (as EN-[2], *kephalē* head)]

encephalin var. of ENKEPHALIN.

encephalitis /enkéffəlītiss, enséf-/ *n.* inflammation of the brain. □ **encephalitis lethargica** /lithaárjikə/ an infectious encephalitis caused by a virus, with headache and drowsiness leading to coma; sleepy sickness. □□ **encephalitic** /-líttik/ *adj.*

encephalo- /enkéffəlō, enséf-/ *comb. form* brain. [Gk *egkephalos* brain]

encephalogram /enkéffəlōgram, enséf-/ *n.* an X-ray photograph of the brain.

encephalograph /enkéffəlōgraaf, enséf-/ *n.* an instrument for recording the electrical activity of the brain.

encephalon /enkéffəlon, enséf-/ *n.* *Anat.* the brain.

encephalopathy /enkéffəlóppəthi, enséf-/ *n.* disease of the brain.

enchain /incháyn/ *v.tr.* **1** chain up, fetter. **2** hold fast (the attention, emotions, etc.). □□ **enchainment** *n.* [ME f. F *enchaîner* ult. f. L *catena* chain]

■ **1** see ENSLAVE.

enchant /inchaánt/ *v.tr.* **1** charm, delight. **2** bewitch. □□ **enchantedly** *adv.* **enchanting** *adj.* **enchantingly** *adv.* **enchantment** *n.* [ME f. F *enchanter* f. L *incantare* (as IN-[2], *canere cant-* sing)]

■ **1** charm, fascinate, delight, beguile, captivate, enthral, enrapture, attract, allure, entrance, spellbind. **2** bewitch, cast a spell on, spellbind, hypnotize, mesmerize, voodoo, bedevil, charm, *Brit.* magic, *esp. US* hoodoo, *US* hex, *archaic* witch, *poet.* glamour. □□ **enchanting** charming, fascinating, captivating, intriguing, enthralling, alluring, delightful, hypnotic, attractive, appealing, winsome, ravishing, seductive; beguiling, bewitching, entrancing, spellbinding, *archaic* witching. **enchantment** witchcraft, sorcery, magic, wizardry, thaumaturgy; charm, beguilement, allure, fascination, attraction; conjuration; spell, charm, *US* hex, *colloq.* jinx.

enchanter /inchaántər/ *n.* (*fem.* **enchantress**) a person who enchants, esp. by supposed use of magic. □ **enchanter's nightshade** a small plant, *Circaea lutetiana*, with white flowers.

■ see MAGICIAN 1, *charmer* (CHARM).

enchase /incháyss/ *v.tr.* **1** (foll. by *in*) place (a jewel) in a setting. **2** (foll. by *with*) set (gold etc.) with gems. **3** inlay

with gold etc. **4** adorn with figures in relief. **5** engrave. [ME f. F *enchâsser* (as EN-[1], CHASE[2])]
■ **5** see SCRIBE *v.*

enchilada /énchilaádə/ *n.* a tortilla with chilli sauce and usu. a filling, esp. meat. [Amer. Sp., fem. past part. of *enchilar* season with chilli]

enchiridion /énkīríddiən/ *n.* (*pl.* **enchiridions** or **enchiridia** /-diə/) *formal* a handbook. [LL f. Gk *egkheiridion* (as EN-[2], *kheir* hand, *-idion* dimin. suffix)]
■ see MANUAL *n.*

encipher /insífər/ *v.tr.* **1** write (a message etc.) in cipher. **2** convert into coded form using a cipher. □□ **encipherment** *n.*
■ code, encode, encrypt.

encircle /insúrk'l/ *v.tr.* **1** (usu. foll. by *with*) surround, encompass. **2** form a circle round. □□ **encirclement** *n.*
■ **1** surround, circle, enclose, ring, encompass, *literary* gird; confine, hem *or* hold in. **2** see CIRCLE *v.* 2.

encl. *abbr.* **1** enclosed. **2** enclosure.

en clair /ON kláir/ *adj.* & *adv.* (of a telegram, official message, etc.) in ordinary language (not in code or cipher). [F, lit. 'in clear']

enclasp /inklaásp/ *v.tr.* hold in a clasp or embrace.

enclave /énklayv/ *n.* **1** a portion of territory of one State surrounded by territory of another or others, as viewed by the surrounding territory (cf. EXCLAVE). **2** a group of people who are culturally, intellectually, or socially distinct from those surrounding them. [F f. *enclaver* ult. f. L *clavis* key]

enclitic /enklíttik/ *adj.* & *n. Gram.* ● *adj.* (of a word) pronounced with so little emphasis that it forms part of the preceding word. ● *n.* such a word, e.g. *not* in *cannot.* □□ **enclitically** *adv.* [LL *encliticus* f. Gk *egklitikos* (as EN-[2], *klinō* lean)]

enclose /inklṓz/ *v.tr.* (also **inclose**) **1** (often foll. by *with, in*) **a** surround with a wall, fence, etc. **b** shut in on all sides. **2** fence in (common land) so as to make it private property. **3** put in a receptacle (esp. in an envelope together with a letter). **4** (usu. as **enclosed** *adj.*) seclude (a religious community) from the outside world. **5** esp. *Math.* bound on all sides; contain. **6** hem in on all sides. [ME f. OF *enclos* past part. of *enclore* ult. f. L *includere* (as INCLUDE)]
■ **1, 6** surround, pen, encircle, encompass, bound, envelop, hedge in, ring, circle, wall in, immure, fence in *or* off, corral; lock, confine, shut in, close *or* hem in. **3** insert, include.

enclosure /inklṓzhər/ *n.* (also **inclosure**) **1** the act of enclosing, esp. of common land. **2** *Brit.* an enclosed space or area, esp. for a special class of persons at a sporting event. **3** a thing enclosed with a letter. **4** an enclosing fence etc. [AF & OF (as ENCLOSE)]
■ **2** fold, pen, cote, run, sty, yard, *US* corral; quadrangle, square, compound, close, *colloq.* quad. **4** fence, wall, rail, railing, barrier, hedge, barricade, boundary.

encode /inkṓd/ *v.tr.* put (a message etc.) into code or cipher. □□ **encoder** *n.*
■ code, encipher, encrypt.

encomiast /enkṓmiast/ *n.* **1** the composer of an encomium. **2** a flatterer. □□ **encomiastic** /-ástik/ *adj.* [Gk *egkōmiastēs* (as ENCOMIUM)]

encomium /enkṓmiəm/ *n.* (*pl.* **encomiums** or **encomia** /-miə/) a formal or high-flown expression of praise. [L f. Gk *egkōmion* (as EN-[2], *kōmos* revelry)]
■ see EULOGY.

encompass /inkúmpəss/ *v.tr.* **1** surround or form a circle about, esp. to protect or attack. **2** contain. □□ **encompassment** *n.*
■ **1** see CIRCLE *v.* 2. **2** see INCLUDE 1.

encore /óngkor/ *n., v., & int.* ● *n.* **1** a call by an audience or spectators for the repetition of an item, or for a further item. **2** such an item. ● *v.tr.* **1** call for the repetition of (an item). **2** call back (a performer) for this. ● *int.* /also -kór/ again, once more. [F, = again]

encounter /inkówntər/ *v.* & *n.* ● *v.tr.* **1** meet by chance or unexpectedly. **2** meet as an adversary. **3** meet with, experience (problems, opposition, etc.). ● *n.* **1** a meeting by chance. **2** a meeting in conflict. **3** participation in an encounter group. □ **encounter group** a group of persons seeking psychological benefit through close contact with one another. [ME f. OF *encontrer, encontre* ult. f. L *contra* against]
■ *v.* **1** meet, come upon, run into *or* across, happen upon, chance upon, stumble upon, *colloq.* bump into. **2** come into conflict with, contend with, assail, cross swords with, grapple with, engage, do battle with, confront, clash with, *hist.* joust with. **3** face, experience, meet with, contend with, be faced with, come into contact with, wrestle with. ● *n.* **2** confrontation, brush, quarrel, disagreement, dispute, altercation, engagement, action, fight, clash, conflict, skirmish, contest, competition, duel, struggle, run-in, tussle, to-do, wrangle, *colloq.* dust-up, scrap, set-to.

encourage /inkúrrij/ *v.tr.* **1** give courage, confidence, or hope to. **2** (foll. by *to* + infin.) urge, advise. **3** stimulate by help, reward, etc. **4** promote or assist (an enterprise, opinion, etc.). □□ **encouragement** *n.* **encourager** *n.* **encouraging** *adj.* **encouragingly** *adv.* [ME f. F *encourager* (as EN[1], COURAGE)]
■ **1** hearten, embolden, reassure, buoy (up), stimulate, animate, support, inspirit, inspire, cheer (up), *colloq.* pep up. **2** spur (on), incite, egg on; see also URGE *v.* 2, ADVISE. **4** promote, advance, aid, support, help, assist, abet, foster, forward, *colloq.* boost, give a shot in the arm. □□ **encouragement** reassurance, stimulation, support, promotion, inspiration; exhortation, incitement; stimulus, help, aid, support, *colloq.* pep talk, boost, shot in the arm.

encroach /inkrṓch/ *v.intr.* **1** (foll. by *on, upon*) intrude, esp. on another's territory or rights. **2** advance gradually beyond due limits. □□ **encroacher** *n.* **encroachment** *n.* [ME f. OF *encrochier* (as EN-[1], *crochier* f. *croc* hook: see CROOK)]
■ **1** intrude, trespass, make inroads; (*encroach on* or *upon*) invade, infringe. **2** invade, penetrate, infiltrate, permeate; enter, advance.

encrust /inkrúst/ *v.* (also **incrust**) **1** *tr.* cover with a crust. **2** *tr.* overlay with an ornamental crust of precious material. **3** *intr.* form a crust. □□ **encrustment** *n.* [F *incruster* f. L *incrustare* (as IN-[2], *crustare* f. *crusta* CRUST)]
■ **3** see CAKE *v.* 2.

encrustation var. of INCRUSTATION.

encrypt /inkrípt/ *v.tr.* **1** convert (data) into code, esp. to prevent unauthorized access. **2** conceal by this means. □□ **encryption** *n.* [EN-[1] + Gk *kruptos* hidden]
■ code, encode, encipher.

encumber /inkúmbər/ *v.tr.* **1** be a burden to. **2** hamper, impede. **3** burden (a person or estate) with debts, esp. mortgages. **4** fill or block (a place) esp. with lumber. □□ **encumberment** *n.* [ME f. OF *encombrer* block up f. Rmc]
■ **1** burden, weigh down, load (up *or* down), overload, overburden, strain, oppress, saddle, tax, overtax. **2** hamper, impede, hinder, handicap, inconvenience, trammel, retard, slow (down), *literary* cumber.

encumbrance /inkúmbrənss/ *n.* **1** a burden. **2** an impediment. **3** a mortgage or other charge on property. **4** an annoyance. □ **without encumbrance** having no children. [ME f. OF *encombrance* (as ENCUMBER)]
■ **1** weight, burden, onus, cross (to bear), load, albatross, millstone, encumberment, cumber. **2** handicap, impediment, hindrance, obstacle, obstruction, liability, disadvantage. **4** *colloq.* drag, bind; see also NUISANCE. □ **without encumbrance** childless, *Law* without issue, issueless.

-ency /ənsi/ *suffix* forming nouns denoting a quality (*efficiency; fluency*) or state (*presidency*) but not action (cf. -ENCE). [L *-entia* (cf. -ANCY)]

encyclical /ensíklik'l/ *n.* & *adj.* ● *n.* a papal letter sent to all bishops of the Roman Catholic Church. ● *adj.* (of a letter) for wide circulation. [LL *encyclicus* f. Gk *egkuklios* (as EN-^{2}, *kuklos* circle)]

encyclopedia /ensīkləpeédiə/ *n.* (also **encyclopaedia**) a book, often in several volumes, giving information on many subjects, or on many aspects of one subject, usu. arranged alphabetically. [mod.L f. spurious Gk *egkuklopaideia* for *egkuklios paideia* all-round education: cf. ENCYCLICAL]

encyclopedic /ensīkləpeédik/ *adj.* (also **encyclopaedic**) (of knowledge or information) comprehensive.
■ comprehensive, inclusive, broad, extensive, universal, thorough, exhaustive, wide-ranging, complete.

encyclopedism /ensīkləpeédiz'm/ *n.* (also **encyclopaedism**) encyclopedic learning.

encyclopedist /ensīkləpeédist/ *n.* (also **encyclopaedist**) a person who writes, edits, or contributes to an encyclopedia.

encyst /insíst/ *v.tr.* & *intr. Biol.* enclose or become enclosed in a cyst. □□ **encystation** /-táysh'n/ *n.* **encystment** *n.*

end /end/ *n.* & *v.* ● *n.* **1 a** the extreme limit; the point beyond which a thing does not continue. **b** an extremity of a line, or of the greatest dimension of an object. **c** the furthest point (*to the ends of the earth*). **2** the surface bounding a thing at either extremity; an extreme part (*a strip of wood with a nail in one end*). **3 a** conclusion, finish (*no end to his misery*). **b** the latter or final part. **c** death, destruction, downfall (*met an untimely end*). **d** result, outcome. **e** an ultimate state or condition. **4 a** a thing one seeks to attain; a purpose (*will do anything to achieve his ends; to what end?*). **b** the object for which a thing exists. **5** a remnant; a piece left over (*cigarette-end*). **6** (prec. by *the*) *colloq.* the limit of endurability. **7** the half of a sports pitch or court occupied by one team or player. **8** the part or share with which a person is concerned (*no problem at my end*). **9** *Bowls* a unit of play in which play is from one side of the green towards the other. **10** *US Football* a player at the extremity of a line or team. ● *v.* **1** *tr.* & *intr.* bring or come to an end. **2** *tr.* put an end to; destroy. **3** *intr.* (foll. by *in*) have as its result (*will end in tears*). **4** *intr.* (foll. by *by*) do or achieve eventually (*ended by marrying an heiress*). □ **all ends up** completely. **at an end** exhausted or completed. **at the end of one's tether** see TETHER. **come to a bad** (or **sticky**) **end** meet with ruin or disgrace. **come to an end 1** be completed or finished. **2** become exhausted. **end-around** *n. US Football* an offensive play in which an end carries the ball round the opposite end. ● *adj. Computing* involving the transfer of a digit from one end of a register to the other. **end-game** the final stage of a game (esp. chess), when few pieces remain. **end it all** (or **end it**) *colloq.* commit suicide. **end of the road** the point at which a hope or endeavour has to be abandoned. **end of the world** the cessation of mortal life. **end on** with the end facing one, or with the end adjoining the end of the next object. **end-play** *Bridge* a method of play in the last few tricks to force an opponent to make a disadvantageous lead. **end-point** the final stage of a process, esp. the point at which an effect is observed in titration, dilution, etc. **end-product** the final product of manufacture, radioactive decay, etc. **end result** final outcome. **end run** *US* **1** *Football* an attempt by the ball-carrier to run round his or her own end. **2** an evasive tactic esp. in war or politics. **end standard** a standard of length in the form of a metal bar or block with the end faces the standard distance apart. **end-stopped** (of verse) having a pause at the end of each line. **end to end** with the end of each of a series adjoining the end of the next. **end up** reach a specified state, action, or place eventually (*ended up a drunkard; ended up making a fortune*). **end-user** the person, customer, etc., who is the ultimate user of a product. **in the end** finally; after all. **keep one's end up** do one's part despite difficulties. **make an end of** put a stop to. **make ends** (or **both ends**) **meet** live within one's income. **no end** *colloq.* to a great extent, very much. **no end of** *colloq.* much or many of. **on end 1** upright (*hair stood on end*). **2** continuously (*for three weeks on end*). **put an end to 1** stop (an activity etc.). **2** abolish, destroy. □□ **ender** *n.* [OE *ende*, *endian*, f. Gmc]
■ *n.* **1** extremity, extreme, extent, bounds, tip, end-point, limit, terminus. **3 a, b** termination, conclusion, cessation, finish, completion; close, finale, ending, wind-up, denouement. **c** destruction, expiration, expiry, ruin, extermination, annihilation; see DEATH 4a. **d** consequence, result, outcome, effect, upshot. **4** aim, purpose, intention, intent, objective, object, goal, aspiration; point, reason, *raison d'être*; destination. **5** see REMNANT. **6** (*the end*) the worst, the last straw, the final blow, *colloq.* the limit, too much. ● *v.* **1** terminate, conclude, bring to an end, stop, halt, cease, wind up *or* down, discontinue, break off, cut off, close, finish; come to an end, die (out), expire, peter out, vanish. **2** put an end to, put a stopper on, get rid of, annihilate, terminate, extinguish; destroy, ruin. **3** see RESULT *v.* 2. **4** end up, culminate, finish (up) by. □ **all ends up** see *completely* (COMPLETE). **end it all** commit suicide, suicide, take one's own life, *sl.* top oneself. **end-product** result, outcome, product. **end run 2** see SUBTERFUGE 1. **end up** finish up, turn out, end. **in the end** see *finally* (FINAL). **make an end of** see STOP *v.* 1a, c. **make ends meet** see MANAGE *v.* 2, 3, 5a. **no end** see HIGHLY 1. **no end of** see ENDLESS 3. **on end 1** upright, erect, standing. **2** continuously, uninterruptedly, unceasingly, incessantly, running, consecutively, without a break, *colloq.* without let-up. **put an end to 1** see STOP *v.* 1. **2** see ABOLISH.

-end /end, ənd/ *suffix* forming nouns in the sense 'person or thing to be treated in a specified way' (*dividend; reverend*). [L gerundive ending *-endus*]

endanger /indáynjər/ *v.tr.* place in danger. □ **endangered species** a species in danger of extinction. □□ **endangerment** *n.*
■ imperil, jeopardize, put in jeopardy, threaten, expose (to danger); risk, put at risk, hazard; chance, venture.

endear /indeer/ *v.tr.* (usu. foll. by *to*) make dear to or beloved by.

endearing /indeéring/ *adj.* inspiring affection. □□ **endearingly** *adv.*
■ attractive, engaging, likeable, appealing, pleasing, winsome, captivating, winning, lovable.

endearment /indeérmənt/ *n.* **1** an expression of affection. **2** liking, affection.

endeavour /indévvər/ *v.* & *n.* (*US* **endeavor**) ● *v.* **1** *tr.* (foll. by *to* + infin.) try earnestly. **2** *intr.* (foll. by *after*) *archaic* strive. ● *n.* (often foll. by *at*, or *to* + infin.) effort directed towards a goal; an earnest attempt. [ME f. *put oneself in* DEVOIR]
■ *v.* **1** try, attempt, strive, make an effort, struggle, do one's best, *formal* essay; exert oneself, *colloq.* take a stab at, have a go *or* crack *or* whack *or* shot at; aim, aspire. ● *n.* effort, pains, attempt, try, striving, struggle, venture, enterprise, *formal* essay.

endemic /endémmik/ *adj.* & *n.* ● *adj.* regularly or only found among a particular people or in a certain region. ● *n.* an endemic disease or plant. □□ **endemically** *adv.* **endemicity** /éndimíssiti/ *n.* **endemism** /éndimiz'm/ *n.* [F *endémique* or mod.L *endemicus* f. Gk *endēmos* native (as EN-^{2}, *dēmos* the people)]
■ *adj.* native, indigenous, local.

endermic /endérmik/ *adj.* acting on or through the skin. □□ **endermically** *adv.* [EN-^{2} + Gk *derma* skin]

ending /énding/ *n.* **1** an end or final part, esp. of a story. **2** an inflected final part of a word. [OE (as END, -ING^1)]
■ **1** see END *n.* 3a, b. **2** termination, suffix.

endive /éndīv, -div/ *n.* **1** a curly-leaved plant, *Cichorium endivia*, used in salads. **2** *US* a chicory crown. [ME f. OF f. LL *endivia* ult. f. Gk *entubon*]

endless /éndliss/ *adj.* **1** infinite; without end; eternal. **2** continual, incessant (*tired of their endless complaints*). **3** *colloq.* innumerable. **4** (of a belt, chain, etc.) having the ends joined for continuous action over wheels etc. □ **endless screw** a short length of screw revolving to turn a cog-wheel.

□□ **endlessly** *adv.* **endlessness** *n.* [OE *endelēas* (as END, -LESS)]
■ **1** infinite, immeasurable, illimitable, limitless, measureless, unlimited, boundless, unbounded, unending; eternal, perpetual, ceaseless, without end *or* cease, everlasting, perennial. **2** continual, incessant, ceaseless, unceasing, unending, constant, never-ending, perpetual, everlasting, interminable, non-stop, continuous, uninterrupted, unremitting, relentless, persistent. **3** innumerable, countless, numerous, numberless, uncounted, untold, infinite, *literary* myriad. □□ **endlessly** ceaselessly, incessantly, constantly, eternally, perpetually, everlastingly, continually, continuously, interminably, relentlessly. **endlessness** ceaselessness, unendingness, everlastingness, eternity, perpetuity.

endmost /éndmōst/ *adj.* nearest the end.
■ see EXTREME *adj.* 3.

endnote /éndnōt/ *n.* a note printed at the end of a book or section of a book.

endo- /éndō/ *comb. form* internal. [Gk *endon* within]

endocarditis /éndōkaardī́tiss/ *n.* inflammation of the endocardium. □□ **endocarditic** /-díttik/ *adj.*

endocardium /éndōkaárdiəm/ *n.* the lining membrane of the heart. [ENDO- + Gk *kardia* heart]

endocarp /éndōkaarp/ *n.* the innermost layer of the pericarp. □□ **endocarpic** /-kaárpik/ *adj.* [ENDO- + PERICARP]

endocrine /éndōkrīn, -krin/ *adj.* (of a gland) secreting directly into the blood; ductless. [ENDO- + Gk *krinō* sift]

endocrinology /éndōkrinólləji/ *n.* the study of the structure and physiology of endocrine glands. □□ **endocrinological** /-nəlójik'l/ *adj.* **endocrinologist** *n.*

endoderm /éndōderm/ *n. Biol.* the innermost layer of an animal embryo in early development. □□ **endodermal** /-dérm'l/ *adj.* **endodermic** /-dérmik/ *adj.* [ENDO- + Gk *derma* skin]

endogamy /endóggəmi/ *n.* **1** *Anthropol.* marrying within the same tribe. **2** *Bot.* pollination from the same plant. □□ **endogamous** *adj.* [ENDO- + Gk *gamos* marriage]

endogenous /endójinəss/ *adj.* growing or originating from within. □□ **endogenesis** /éndəjénnisiss/ *n.* **endogeny** /endójini/ *n.*

endolymph /éndōlimf/ *n.* the fluid in the membranous labyrinth of the ear.

endometrium /éndōmeétriəm/ *n. Anat.* the membrane lining the womb. □□ **endometritis** /éndōmitrī́tiss/ *n.* [ENDO- + Gk *mētra* womb]

endomorph /éndōmorf/ *n.* **1** a person with a soft round build of body and a high proportion of fat tissue (cf. ECTOMORPH, MESOMORPH). **2** *Mineral.* a mineral enclosed within another. □□ **endomorphic** /-mórfik/ *adj.* **endomorphy** *n.* [ENDO- + Gk *morphē* form]

endoparasite /éndōpárrəsīt/ *n.* a parasite that lives on the inside of its host. Also called ENTOPARASITE.

endoplasm /éndōplaz'm/ *n.* the inner fluid layer of the cytoplasm.

endoplasmic reticulum /éndōplázmik/ *n. Biol.* a system of membranes within the cytoplasm of a eukaryotic cell forming a link between the cell and nuclear membranes and usu. having ribosomes attached to its surface.

endorphin /endórfin/ *n. Biochem.* any of a group of peptide neurotransmitters occurring naturally in the brain and having pain-relieving properties. [F *endorphine* f. *endogène* endogenous + MORPHINE]

endorse /indórss/ *v.tr.* (also **indorse**) **1 a** confirm (a statement or opinion). **b** declare one's approval of. **2** sign or write on the back of (a document), esp. the back of (a bill, cheque, etc.) as the payee or to specify another as payee. **3** write (an explanation or comment) on the back of a document. **4** *Brit.* enter details of a conviction for a motoring offence on (a driving licence). □□ **endorsable** *adj.* **endorsee** /éndorseé/ *n.* **endorser** *n.* [med.L *indorsare* (as IN-², L *dorsum* back)]
■ **1 a** confirm, ratify, sustain, support, back (up), second, subscribe to. **b** approve, sanction, authorize, advocate, countenance, agree to, assent to, rubber-stamp, put one's stamp *or* seal (of approval) on, set one's seal (of approval) to, give the go-ahead *or* thumbs up to, give one's imprimatur *or* blessing to, *colloq.* OK, okay, give the green light to. **2** ratify, countersign.

endorsement /indórsmənt/ *n.* (also **indorsement**) **1** the act or an instance of endorsing. **2** something with which a document etc. is endorsed, esp. a signature. **3** a record in a driving licence of a conviction for a motoring offence.
■ **1** approval, sanction, authorization, confirmation, ratification, support, backing, consent, agreement, approbation, go-ahead, seal *or* stamp of approval, imprimatur, rubber stamp, thumbs up, blessing, *colloq.* OK, okay, green light. **2** counter-signature, rubber stamp.

endoscope /éndōskōp/ *n. Surgery* an instrument for viewing the internal parts of the body. □□ **endoscopic** /-skóppik/ *adj.* **endoscopically** /-skóppikəli/ *adv.* **endoscopist** /endóskəpist/ *n.* **endoscopy** /endóskəpi/ *n.*

endoskeleton /éndōskellit'n/ *n.* an internal skeleton, as found in vertebrates.

endosperm /éndōsperm/ *n.* albumen enclosed with the germ in seeds.

endospore /éndōspor/ *n.* **1** a spore formed by certain bacteria. **2** the inner coat of a spore.

endothelium /éndōtheéliəm/ *n. Anat.* a layer of cells lining the blood-vessels, heart, and lymphatic vessels. [ENDO- + Gk *thēlē* teat]

endothermic /éndōthérmik/ *adj.* occurring or formed with the absorption of heat.

endow /indów/ *v.tr.* **1** bequeath or give a permanent income to (a person, institution, etc.). **2** (esp. as **endowed** *adj.*) (usu. foll. by *with*) provide (a person) with talent, ability, etc. □□ **endower** *n.* [ME f. AF *endouer* (as EN-¹, OF *douer* f. L *dotare* f. *dos dotis* DOWER)]
■ **1** see AWARD *v.* **2** see BLESS 5.

endowment /indówmənt/ *n.* **1** the act or an instance of endowing. **2** assets, esp. property or income with which a person or body is endowed. **3** (usu. in *pl.*) skill, talent, etc., with which a person is endowed. **4** (*attrib.*) denoting forms of life insurance involving payment by the insurer of a fixed sum on a specified date, or on the death of the insured person if earlier. □ **endowment mortgage** a mortgage linked to endowment insurance of the mortgagor's life, the capital being paid from the sum insured.
■ **1** presentation, bestowal, giving, award, allocation, apportionment, allotment, settlement; bequeathal. **2** grant, (financial) aid, award, funding, funds, subsidy, subvention, allowance, allotment, contribution, donation, gift, present; bequest, inheritance, dowry. **3** (*endowments*) talent(s), gift(s), abilities, aptitude(s), powers, capabilities, capacities, qualifications, strengths, qualities.

endpaper /éndpaypər/ *n.* a usu. blank leaf of paper at the beginning and end of a book, fixed to the inside of the cover.

endue /indyoō/ *v.tr.* (also **indue**) (foll. by *with*) invest or provide (a person) with qualities, powers, etc. [earlier = induct, put on clothes: ME f. OF *enduire* f. L *inducere* lead in, assoc. in sense with L *induere* put on (clothes)]
■ see CLOTHE 3.

endurance /indyoórənss/ *n.* **1** the power or habit of enduring (*beyond endurance*). **2** the ability to withstand prolonged strain (*endurance test*). **3** the act of enduring. **4** ability to last; enduring quality. [OF f. *endurer*: see ENDURE]
■ **1** see BEARING 3. **2** stamina, resilience, stay, staying power, robustness, hardiness; perseverance, persistence, resolution, fortitude, tenacity, patience, tolerance, *colloq.* grit. **3** survival, duration, persistence. **4** lasting *or* enduring quality, durability, longevity.

endure /indyoór/ *v.* **1** *tr.* undergo (a difficulty, hardship, etc.). **2** *tr.* **a** tolerate (a person) (*cannot endure him*). **b** (esp. with *neg.*; foll. by *to* + infin.) bear. **3** *intr.* (often as **enduring** *adj.*) remain in existence; last. **4** *tr.* submit to. □□ **endurable** *adj.* **endurability** /-rəbílliti/ *n.* **enduringly** *adv.* [ME f. OF *endurer* f. L *indurare* harden (as IN-[2], *durus* hard)]
■ **1** undergo, face, brave, go through with, survive, stand, bear, tolerate, abide, take, support, withstand, weather, suffer, stomach, hold out (against), last through, cope with, hold up *or* bear up *or* stand up under, *colloq.* stick *or* sweat out, *literary* brook. **2** bear, stand, put up with, submit to, abide, tolerate, support, stomach, cope with, handle, face, *literary* brook. **3** remain, last, stay, persist, carry on, linger, survive, live (on), continue, be left, hold, *archaic* abide; (**enduring**) lasting, continuing, persisting, persistent, durable, abiding, long-standing, permanent; steady. **4** submit to, bow to; see also ENDURE 1 above.

enduro /indyoórō/ *n.* (*pl.* **-os**) a long-distance race for motor vehicles, designed to test endurance.

endways /éndwayz/ *adv.* **1** with its end uppermost or foremost or turned towards the viewer. **2** end to end.

endwise /éndwīz/ *adv.* = ENDWAYS.

ENE *abbr.* east-north-east.

-ene /een/ *suffix* **1** forming names of inhabitants of places (*Nazarene*). **2** *Chem.* forming names of unsaturated hydrocarbons containing a double bond (*benzene*; *ethylene*). [from or after Gk *-ēnos*]

enema /énnimə/ *n.* (*pl.* **enemas** or **enemata** /inémmətə/) **1** the injection of liquid or gas into the rectum, esp. to expel its contents. **2** a fluid or syringe used for this. [LL f. Gk *enema* f. *eniēmi* inject (as EN-[2], *hiēmi* send)]

enemy /énnəmi/ *n.* (*pl.* **-ies**) **1** a person or group actively opposing or hostile to another, or to a cause etc. **2 a** a hostile nation or army, esp. in war. **b** a member of this. **c** a hostile ship or aircraft. **3** (usu. foll. by *of*, *to*) an adversary or opponent. **4** a thing that harms or injures. **5** (*attrib.*) of or belonging to an enemy (*destroyed by enemy action*). [ME f. OF *enemi* f. L *inimicus* (as IN-[1], *amicus* friend)]
■ **1–3** opponent, antagonist, rival, opposition, other side, adversary, *esp. poet. or formal* foe. **4** foe, opponent, hostile *or* harmful influence.

energetic /ennərjéttik/ *adj.* **1** strenuously active. **2** forcible, vigorous. **3** powerfully operative. □□ **energetically** *adv.* [Gk *energētikos* f. *energeō* (as EN-[2], *ergon* work)]
■ **1, 2** lively, active, vigorous, dynamic, alive, animated, spirited, untiring, tireless, indefatigable, sprightly, brisk, racy, vibrant, spry, zesty, zestful, zealous, enthusiastic, eager, go-ahead, enterprising, ambitious, *colloq.* peppy, full of pep, full of get-up-and-go, zippy, zingy, full of beans. **3** vital, invigorating, life-giving, vitalizing, energizing, powerful, high-powered.

energetics /ennərjéttiks/ *n.pl.* the science of energy.

energize /énnərjīz/ *v.tr.* (also **-ise**) **1** infuse energy into (a person or work). **2** provide energy for the operation of (a device). □□ **energizer** *n.*
■ stimulate, enliven, animate, liven up, invigorate, vitalize, vivify, inspire, inspirit, rouse, stir, arouse, awaken, waken, rally, excite, *colloq.* enthuse, pep up; activate, actuate, move, impel, drive, motivate, galvanize, spark, electrify, switch *or* turn on, fire (up), kick-start.

energumen /ennərgyoómen/ *n.* an enthusiast or fanatic. [LL *energumenus* f. Gk *energoumenos* passive part. of *energeō*: see ENERGETIC]

energy /énnərji/ *n.* (*pl.* **-ies**) **1** force, vigour; capacity for activity. **2** (in *pl.*) individual powers in use (*devote your energies to this*). **3** *Physics* the capacity of matter or radiation to do work. **4** the means of doing work by utilizing matter or radiation. [F *énergie* or LL *energia* f. Gk *energeia* f. *ergon* work]
■ **1** force, power, strength, might, forcefulness, *archaic* puissance; vigour, drive, dynamism, push, *élan*, dash, bounce, brio, zip, go, vim, vim and vigour, *colloq.* get-up-and-go, pep, zing, *sl.* zap, *Austral.* & *NZ sl.* toe; vitality, liveliness, vivacity, animation, vivaciousness, spirit, spiritedness, exuberance, zest, gusto, enthusiasm, verve, zeal, *sl.* oomph, pizazz. **2** (*energies*) see POWER *n.* 2.

enervate *v.* & *adj.* ● *v.tr.* /énnərvayt/ deprive of vigour or vitality. ● *adj.* /inérvət/ enervated. □□ **enervation** /ennərváysh'n/ *n.* [L *enervatus* past part. of *enervare* (as E-, *nervus* sinew)]
■ *v.* weaken, tire (out), weary, drain, tax, exhaust, sap, debilitate, enfeeble, fatigue, wear out, dull, subdue, devitalize, take it out of, strain, break, crush, depress, dispirit, *Brit sl.* knacker. ● *adj.* see TIRED 1.

en famille /ON faméey/ *adv.* **1** in or with one's family. **2** at home. [F, = in family]

enfant gâté /óNfoN gatáy/ *n.* a person given undue flattery or indulgence. [F, = spoilt child]

enfant terrible /óNfoN tereéblə/ *n.* a person who causes embarrassment by indiscreet or unruly behaviour. [F, = terrible child]

enfeeble /inféeb'l/ *v.tr.* make feeble. □□ **enfeeblement** *n.* [ME f. OF *enfeblir* (as EN-[1], FEEBLE)]
■ see WEAKEN 1.

en fête /ON fáyt/ *adv.* & *predic.adj.* holding or ready for a holiday or celebration. [F, = in festival]

enfetter /inféttər/ *v.tr. literary* **1** bind in or as in fetters. **2** (foll. by *to*) enslave.
■ **1** fetter, bind, tie up, shackle, manacle.

enfilade /énfiláyd/ *n.* & *v.* ● *n.* gunfire directed along a line from end to end. ● *v.tr.* direct an enfilade at (troops, a road, etc.). [F f. *enfiler* (as EN-[1], *fil* thread)]

enfold /infṓld/ *v.tr.* (also **infold**) **1** (usu. foll. by *in*, *with*) wrap up; envelop. **2** clasp, embrace.
■ **1** see WRAP *v.* 1. **2** see EMBRACE *v.* 1.

enforce /infórss/ *v.tr.* **1** compel observance of (a law etc.). **2** (foll. by *on*, *upon*) impose (an action, conduct, one's will). **3** persist in (a demand or argument). □□ **enforceable** *adj.* **enforceability** /-səbílliti/ *n.* **enforcedly** /-sidli/ *adv.* **enforcer** *n.* [ME f. OF *enforcir*, *-ier* ult. f. L *fortis* strong]
■ **1** insist upon *or* on, impose, implement, put into effect, apply, administer, bring to bear, prosecute, carry out, discharge, maintain,uphold, support, reinforce. **2** inflict, force; see also IMPOSE 1, 2, 4. **3** persist in, persevere with, keep to, be staunch *or* steadfast in, adhere *or* stick to, force, press, lay stress upon *or* on.

enforcement /infórsmənt/ *n.* the act or an instance of enforcing. □ **enforcement notice** *Brit.* an official notification to remedy a breach of planning legislation. [ME f. OF, as ENFORCE + -MENT]
■ see IMPOSITION 1.

enfranchise /infránchīz/ *v.tr.* **1** give (a person) the right to vote. **2** give (a town) municipal rights, esp. that of representation in parliament. **3** *hist.* free (a slave, villein, etc.). □□ **enfranchisement** /-chizmənt/ *n.* [OF *enfranchir* (as EN-[1], *franc franche* FRANK)]
■ **3** see FREE *v.* 1.

ENG *abbr.* electronic news gathering.

engage /in-gáyj/ *v.* **1** *tr.* employ or hire (a person). **2** *tr.* **a** (usu. in *passive*) employ busily; occupy (*are you engaged tomorrow?*). **b** hold fast (a person's attention). **3** *tr.* (usu. in *passive*) bind by a promise, esp. of marriage. **4** *tr.* (usu. foll. by *to* + infin.) bind by a contract. **5** *tr.* arrange beforehand to occupy (a room, seat, etc.). **6** (usu. foll. by *with*) *Mech.* **a** *tr.* interlock (parts of a gear etc.); cause (a part) to interlock. **b** *intr.* (of a part, gear, etc.) interlock. **7 a** *intr.* (usu. foll. by *with*) (of troops etc.) come into battle. **b** *tr.* bring (troops) into battle. **c** *tr.* come into battle with (an enemy etc.). **8** *intr.* take part (*engage in politics*). **9** *intr.* (foll. by *that* + clause or *to* + infin.) pledge oneself. **10** *tr.* (usu. as **engaged** *adj.*) *Archit.* attach (a column) to a wall. **11** *tr.* (of fencers etc.) interlock (weapons). □□ **engager** *n.* [F *engager*, rel. to GAGE[1]]
■ **1** employ, hire, recruit, take on, appoint, sign up *or* on,

put under contract, retain, enlist, *hist.* indenture. **2 a** occupy, keep busy, absorb, involve, preoccupy, take up, tie up. **b** attract, hold, capture, absorb, catch, draw; involve, interest, intrigue, engross, rivet, fascinate. **3** betroth, *literary* affiance. **4** contract, put under contract, commit, bind. **5** book, reserve, save, set *or* put aside, earmark, secure, bespeak, take, rent, hire. **7 a, c** join in battle *or* combat (with), battle *or* struggle *or* war (against), contend (with), wage war (against), take up arms (against), clash (with), skirmish; meet (with), fight (against); encounter. **8** (*engage in*) participate *or* take part in, be *or* become *or* get involved in, join *or* partake in, be *or* become associated with, enter into. **9** pledge, agree, undertake, promise, commit oneself, guarantee, contract, covenant.

engagé /ON-gázhay/ *adj.* (of a writer etc.) morally committed. [F, past part. of *engager*: see ENGAGE]

engaged /in-gáyjd/ *adj.* **1** under a promise to marry. **2 a** occupied, busy. **b** reserved, booked. **3** *Brit.* (of a telephone line) unavailable because already in use. □ **engaged signal** (or **tone**) *Brit.* a sound indicating that a telephone line is engaged.
■ **1** betrothed, pledged, *archaic* promised, plighted, *literary* affianced; spoken for. **2 a** busy, occupied, tied up, wrapped up, employed, involved, absorbed, preoccupied. **b** reserved, booked, occupied, taken, spoken for.

engagement /in-gáyjmənt/ *n.* **1** the act or state of engaging or being engaged. **2** an appointment with another person. **3** a betrothal. **4** an encounter between hostile forces. **5** a moral commitment. **6** a period of paid employment, a job. □ **engagement ring** a finger-ring given by a man to a woman when they promise to marry. [F f. *engager*: see ENGAGE]
■ **1** employment, hire, recruitment, appointment, enlistment. **2** appointment, meeting, rendezvous, arrangement, commitment, assignation, *archaic* tryst, *colloq.* date. **4** fight, battle, war, conflict, struggle, clash, fray, encounter, meeting, skirmish. **5** agreement, commitment, obligation, bond, promise, pledge, guarantee, covenant, contract, undertaking. **6** job, position, post, commission, booking; employment, work; *colloq.* spot, gig.

engaging /in-gáyjing/ *adj.* attractive, charming. □□ **engagingly** *adv.* **engagingness** *n.*
■ attractive, charming, pleasant, genial, sociable, delightful, prepossessing, enchanting, endearing, winsome, appealing, winning, agreeable, pleasing, likeable.

engender /injéndər/ *v.tr.* **1** give rise to; bring about (a feeling etc.). **2** *archaic* beget. [ME f. OF *engendrer* f. L *ingenerare* (as IN-², *generare* GENERATE)]
■ see CREATE 1.

engine /énjin/ *n.* **1** a mechanical contrivance consisting of several parts working together, esp. as a source of power. **2 a** a railway locomotive. **b** = *fire-engine*. **c** = *steam engine*. **3** *archaic* a machine or instrument, esp. a contrivance used in warfare. □ **engine-driver** the driver of an engine, esp. a railway locomotive. **engine-room** a room containing engines (esp. in a ship). □□ **engined** *adj.* (also in *comb.*). **engineless** *adj.* [OF *engin* f. L *ingenium* talent, device: cf. INGENIOUS]
■ **1** motor, machine, mechanism, appliance, apparatus, contrivance, device, *often derog. or joc.* contraption.

engineer /énjinéer/ *n.* & *v.* ● *n.* **1** a person qualified in a branch of engineering, esp. as a professional. **2** = *civil engineer*. **3** a person who makes or is in charge of engines. **4** *US* an engine-driver. **5** a person who designs and constructs military works; a soldier trained for this purpose. **6** (foll. by *of*) a skilful or artful contriver. ● *v.* **1** *tr.* arrange, contrive, or bring about, esp. artfully. **2** *intr.* act as an engineer. **3** *tr.* construct or manage as an engineer. □□ **engineership** *n.* [ME f. OF *engigneor* f. med.L *ingeniator -oris* f. *ingeniare* (as ENGINE)]
■ **4** engine-driver, driver, motorman. **6** designer, inventor, conceiver, originator, author, creator, contriver, architect, planner, mastermind, *colloq.* brain(s). ● *v.* **1** arrange, plan, organize, orchestrate, contrive, mastermind, manage, manoeuvre, plot, rig, bring about *or* off, set up, work out, develop, achieve, effect, settle, accomplish, *US* put over, *colloq.* wangle, swing, fix, work it, finagle.

engineering /énjinéering/ *n.* the application of science to the design, building, and use of machines, constructions, etc. □ **engineering science** engineering as a field of study.

enginery /énjinri/ *n.* engines and machinery generally.

engird /in-gúrd/ *v.tr.* surround with or as with a girdle.
■ see ENCIRCLE 1.

engirdle /in-gúrd'l/ *v.tr.* engird.

English /ínglish/ *adj.* & *n.* ● *adj.* of or relating to England or its people or language. ● *n.* **1** the language of England, now used in many varieties in the British Isles, the United States, and most Commonwealth or ex-Commonwealth countries, and often internationally. **2** (prec. by *the*; treated as *pl.*) the people of England. **3** *US Billiards* = SIDE *n.* 10. □ **English bond** *Building* a bond of brickwork arranged in alternate courses of stretchers and headers. **English horn** = COR ANGLAIS. **the Queen's** (or **King's**) **English** the English language as correctly written or spoken in Britain. □□ **Englishness** *n.* [OE *englisc*, *ænglisc* (as ANGLE, -ISH¹)]

Englishman /ínglishmən/ *n.* (*pl.* **-men**) a man who is English by birth or descent.

Englishwoman /ínglishwoomən/ *n.* (*pl.* **-women**) a woman who is English by birth or descent.

engorge /in-górj/ *v.tr.* **1** (in *passive*) **a** be crammed. **b** *Med.* be congested with blood. **2** devour greedily. □□ **engorgement** *n.* [F *engorger* (as EN-¹, GORGE)]
■ **2** see DEVOUR 1.

engraft /in-graaft/ *v.tr.* (also **ingraft**) **1** *Bot.* (usu. foll. by *into*, *upon*) insert (a scion of one tree into another). **2** (usu. foll. by *in*) implant (principles etc.) in a person's mind. **3** (usu. foll. by *into*) incorporate permanently. □□ **engraftment** *n.*

engrail /in-gráyl/ *v.tr.* (usu. as **engrailed** *adj.*) esp. *Heraldry* indent the edge of; give a serrated appearance to. [ME f. OF *engresler* (as EN-¹, *gresle* hail)]

engrain /in-gráyn/ *v.tr.* **1** implant (a habit, belief, or attitude) ineradicably in a person (see also INGRAINED). **2** cause (dye etc.) to sink deeply into a thing. [ME f. OF *engrainer* dye in grain (*en graine*): see GRAIN]
■ **1** see INSTIL 1.

engrained /in-gráynd/ *adj.* inveterate (see also INGRAINED).

engram /éngram/ *n.* a memory-trace, a supposed permanent change in the brain accounting for the existence of memory. □□ **engrammatic** /-grəmáttik/ *adj.* [G *Engramm* f. Gk *en* in + *gramma* letter of the alphabet]

engrave /in-gráyv/ *v.tr.* **1** (often foll. by *on*) inscribe, cut, or carve (a text or design) on a hard surface. **2** (often foll. by *with*) inscribe or ornament (a surface) in this way. **3** cut (a design) as lines on a metal plate, block, etc., for printing. **4** (often foll. by *on*) impress deeply on a person's memory etc. □□ **engraver** *n.* [EN-¹ + GRAVE³]
■ **1, 2** inscribe, cut, carve, chisel, incise, score, etch, *archaic* grave; chase, enchase. **4** impress, stamp, imprint, print, engrain, fix, set, lodge, record, embed.

engraving /in-gráyving/ *n.* a print made from an engraved plate, block or other surface.
■ print, impression, etching, dry-point, lithograph; woodcut, linocut, wood *or* steel engraving, anaglyph, block, cut.

engross /in-grṓss/ *v.tr.* **1** absorb the attention of; occupy fully (*engrossed in studying*). **2** make a fair copy of a legal document. **3** reproduce (a document etc.) in larger letters or larger format. **4** *archaic* monopolize (a conversation etc.). □□ **engrossing** *adj.* (in sense 1). **engrossment** *n.* [ME f.

AF *engrosser*: senses 2 and 3 f. *en* in + *grosse* large writing: senses 1 and 4 f. *en gros* wholesale]
■ **1** see OCCUPY 6.

engulf /in-gúlf/ *v.tr.* (also **ingulf**) **1** flow over and swamp; overwhelm. **2** swallow or plunge into a gulf. ▫▫ **engulfment** *n.*
■ **1** see DROWN. **2** see SWALLOW *v.* 6.

enhance /inhaánss/ *v.tr.* heighten or intensify (qualities, powers, value, etc.); improve (something already of good quality). ▫▫ **enhancement** *n.* **enhancer** *n.* [ME f. AF *enhauncer*, prob. alt. f. OF *enhaucier* ult. f. L *altus* high]
■ heighten, intensify, raise, increase, augment, add to, deepen, strengthen, reinforce, sharpen, develop, amplify, magnify, enlarge, expand, maximize, lift, swell, elevate, exalt, *colloq.* boost; improve, refine, better, polish, upgrade, enrich, *formal* ameliorate.

enharmonic /énhaarmónnik/ *adj. Mus.* of or having intervals smaller than a semitone (esp. such intervals as that between G sharp and A flat, these notes being made the same in a scale of equal temperament). ▫▫ **enharmonically** *adv.* [LL *enharmonicus* f. Gk *enarmonikos* (as EN-[2], *harmonia* HARMONY)]

enigma /inígmə/ *n.* **1** a puzzling thing or person. **2** a riddle or paradox. ▫▫ **enigmatic** /énnigmáttik/ *adj.* **enigmatical** /énnigmáttik'l/ *adj.* **enigmatically** /énnigmáttikəli/ *adv.* **enigmatize** *v.tr.* (also **-ise**). [L *aenigma* f. Gk *ainigma -matos* f. *ainissomai* speak allusively f. *ainos* fable]
■ **1** puzzle, mystery, riddle, problem. **2** riddle, conundrum, paradox, poser, puzzler, problem, *colloq.* teaser, brain-twister, brain-teaser. ▫▫ **enigmatic** see *puzzling* (PUZZLE *v.* 3).

enjambment /enjámmənt/ *n.* (also **enjambement**) *Prosody* the continuation of a sentence without a pause beyond the end of a line, couplet, or stanza. [F *enjambement* f. *enjamber* (as EN-[1], *jambe* leg)]

enjoin /injóyn/ *v.tr.* **1 a** (foll. by *to* + infin.) command or order (a person). **b** (foll. by *that* + clause) issue instructions. **2** (often foll. by *on*) impose or prescribe (an action or conduct). **3** (usu. foll. by *from*) *Law* prohibit (a person) by order. ▫▫ **enjoinment** *n.* [ME f. OF *enjoindre* f. L *injungere* (as IN-[2], *jungere* join)]
■ **1 a** see COMMAND *v.* 1. **1b, 2** see ORDER *v.* 1, 2, 5, 6.

enjoy /injóy/ *v.tr.* **1** take delight or pleasure in. **2** have the use or benefit of. **3** experience (*enjoy poor health*). ▫ **enjoy oneself** experience pleasure. ▫▫ **enjoyer** *n.* **enjoyment** *n.* [ME f. OF *enjoier* give joy to or *enjoïr* enjoy, ult. f. L *gaudēre* rejoice]
■ **1** (take) delight in, take pleasure in, like, derive pleasure *or* satisfaction from, be partial to, appreciate, have a taste *or* preference *or* passion for, admire, cherish, be fond of, be keen on, relish (in), savour, revel *or* glory in, take to, *colloq.* be into, get a kick from *or* out of, *sl.* dig, get a lift from *or* out of, get a buzz out of, get high on, get off on, *US sl.* get a bang from *or* out of; love, adore. **2** have the use *or* benefit of, benefit *or* profit from, take advantage of, use to advantage, use, utilize, make use of, have, possess, command, have at one's disposal. **3** experience, have, possess; suffer with *or* from. ▫ **enjoy oneself** have a good *or* great *or* super time, make merry, have fun, have the time of one's life, revel, indulge oneself, disport oneself, go wild *or* crazy *or* out of one's mind, *colloq.* have a whale of a time, paint the town red, rave it up, live it up, *sl.* groove, have a ball. ▫▫ **enjoyment** pleasure, delight, joy, gratification, satisfaction, relish, zest, recreation, entertainment, diversion, amusement, *literary* delectation; use, utilization, exercise, possession, benefit, advantage.

enjoyable /injóyəb'l/ *adj.* pleasant; giving enjoyment. ▫▫ **enjoyability** /-bílliti/ *n.* **enjoyableness** *n.* **enjoyably** *adv.*
■ see PLEASANT.

enkephalin /enkéffəlin/ *n.* (also **encephalin** /enséf-/) *Biochem.* either of two morphine-like peptides occurring naturally in the brain and thought to control levels of pain. [Gk *egkephalos* brain]

enkindle /inkínd'l/ *v.tr. literary* **1 a** cause (flames) to flare up. **b** stimulate (feeling, passion, etc.). **2** inflame with passion.
■ **1b, 2** see INFLAME *v.* 1.

enlace /inláyss/ *v.tr.* **1** encircle tightly. **2** entwine. **3** enfold. ▫▫ **enlacement** *n.* [ME f. OF *enlacier* ult. f. L *laqueus* noose]

enlarge /inlaárj/ *v.* **1** *tr.* & *intr.* make or become larger or wider. **2 a** *tr.* describe in greater detail. **b** *intr.* (usu. foll. by *upon*) expatiate. **3** *tr. Photog.* produce an enlargement of (a negative). [ME f. OF *enlarger* (as EN-[1], LARGE)]
■ **1, 3** make *or* become larger *or* greater *or* bigger *or* wider, magnify, elongate, add to, supplement; expand, increase, extend, develop, widen, broaden, lengthen, stretch, *colloq.* blow up. **2 a** detail, amplify, expound, embellish, embroider, refine, explain, flesh out. **b** expatiate, expand, go into detail, elaborate.

enlargement /inlaárjmənt/ *n.* **1** the act or an instance of enlarging; the state of being enlarged. **2** *Photog.* a print that is larger than the negative from which it is produced.
■ **1** see INCREASE *n.* 1, 2.

enlarger /inlaárjər/ *n. Photog.* an apparatus for enlarging or reducing negatives or positives.

enlighten /inlīt'n/ *v.tr.* **1 a** (often foll. by *on*) instruct or inform (a person) about a subject. **b** (as **enlightened** *adj*) well-informed, knowledgeable. **2** (esp. as **enlightened** *adj.*) free from prejudice or superstition. **3** *rhet.* or *poet.* **a** shed light on (an object). **b** give spiritual insight to (a person). ▫▫ **enlightener** *n.*
■ **1 a** instruct, inform, educate, teach, illuminate, edify, civilize, make aware, raise a person's consciousness, apprise, guide, direct, advise, counsel, school, train. **b** (**enlightened**) well-informed, informed, educated, aware, knowledgeable, literate, cultivated, civilized, sophisticated, *colloq.* in the know. **2** (**enlightened**) unprejudiced, sensible, rational, reasonable, commonsensical, sound, level-headed, fair-minded, clear-headed, sane, broad-minded, open-minded, liberal, emancipated, liberated; common-sense. **3 a** see ILLUMINATE 1. **b** illuminate, make a person see the light, guide, teach.

enlightenment /inlīt'nmənt/ *n.* **1** the act or an instance of enlightening; the state of being enlightened. **2** (**the Enlightenment**) the 18th-c. philosophy emphasizing reason and individualism rather than tradition.
■ **1** see *illumination* (ILLUMINATE).

enlist /inlíst/ *v.* **1** *intr.* & *tr.* enrol in the armed services. **2** *tr.* secure as a means of help or support. ▫ **enlisted man** *US* a soldier or sailor below the rank of officer. ▫▫ **enlister** *n.* **enlistment** *n.*
■ **1** join up, volunteer; enrol, sign up *or* on, register; recruit, call up, conscript, *US* draft. **2** secure, obtain, get, procure, employ, rally, drum up, muster (up), mobilize, gather, organize; retain.

enliven /inlīv'n/ *v.tr.* **1** give life or spirit to. **2** make cheerful, brighten (a picture or scene). ▫▫ **enlivener** *n.* **enlivenment** *n.*
■ **1** invigorate, stimulate, energize, vivify, breathe life into, put (some) life into, bring to life, vitalize, quicken, liven up, shake up, stir (up), get going, kindle, fire (up), spark (off), galvanize, electrify, activate, motivate, rally, revitalize, refresh, revive, *colloq.* pep up, *literary* enkindle; inspirit, animate, inspire, (a)wake, (a)waken, wake up, arouse, rouse, excite. **2** make cheerful, cheer *or* brighten (up), liven up, (up)lift, warm, lift up.

en masse /ON máss/ *adv.* **1** all together. **2** in a mass. [F]

enmesh /inmésh/ *v.tr.* entangle in or as in a net. ▫▫ **enmeshment** *n.*
■ see ENTANGLE 1, 2.

enmity /énmiti/ *n.* (*pl.* **-ies**) **1** the state of being an enemy. **2** a feeling of hostility. [ME f. OF *enemitié* f. Rmc (as ENEMY)]
■ **2** see HOSTILITY 1.

ennead /énniad/ *n.* a group of nine. [Gk *enneas enneados* f. *ennea* nine]

ennoble /inṓb'l/ *v.tr.* **1** make (a person) a noble. **2** make noble; elevate. □□ **ennoblement** *n.* [F *ennoblir* (as EN-[1], NOBLE)]
■ **2** see LIFT *v.* 4a.

ennui /onwéé/ *n.* mental weariness from lack of occupation or interest; boredom. [F f. L *in odio*: cf. ODIUM]
■ see BOREDOM.

enology *US* var. of OENOLOGY.

enormity /inórmiti/ *n.* (*pl.* **-ies**) **1** extreme wickedness. **2** an act of extreme wickedness. **3** a serious error. **4** *disp.* great size; enormousness. [ME f. F *énormité* f. L *enormitas -tatis* f. *enormis* (as ENORMOUS)]
■ **1** wickedness, evil, heinousness, viciousness, atrociousness, monstrousness, brutality, barbarity, savagery, cruelty, violence, horribleness, horridness, flagitiousness, outrageousness, inhumanity. **2** atrocity, horror, barbarity, evil, iniquity, infamy, crime, offence, villainy, outrage. **4** see SIZE *n.*

enormous /inórməss/ *adj.* very large; huge (*enormous animals; an enormous difference*). □□ **enormously** *adv.* **enormousness** *n.* [L *enormis* (as E-, *norma* pattern, standard)]
■ big, large, huge, immense, vast, massive, gigantic, mammoth, colossal, great, giant, *colloq.* whacking, thumping, socking, *sl.* humongous, whopping, *Brit. sl.* ginormous; gross, obese, gargantuan, monstrous, elephantine, monumental, monolithic, titanic, behemoth, leviathan, strapping, bulky, king-sized, prodigious, *colloq.* hulking, jumbo; tremendous, stupendous, thundering, *sl.* walloping. □□ **enormousness** see SIZE *n.*

enosis /énnōsiss/ *n.* the political union of Cyprus and Greece, as an ideal or proposal. [mod. Gk *enōsis* f. *ena* one]

enough /inúf/ *adj.*, *n.*, *adv.*, & *int.* ● *adj.* as much or as many as required (*we have enough apples; we do not have enough sugar; earned enough money to buy a house*). ● *n.* an amount or quantity that is enough (*we have enough of everything now; enough is as good as a feast*). ● *adv.* **1** to the required degree, adequately (*are you warm enough?*). **2** fairly (*she sings well enough*). **3** very, quite (*you know well enough what I mean; oddly enough*). ● *int.* that is enough (in various senses, esp. to put an end to an action, thing said, etc.). □ **have had enough of** want no more of; be satiated with or tired of. [OE *genog* f. Gmc]
■ *adj.* sufficient, adequate, ample. ● *n.* plenty; ample supply, abundance, (one's) fill; sufficiency, adequacy. ● *adv.* **1, 2** adequately, sufficiently, reasonably, fairly, satisfactorily. **3** very, quite, perfectly, full, *archaic* right, *colloq.* jolly, damn(ed), darned, *US sl.* plumb. ● *int.* stop, halt, no more, hold it, *colloq.* that's it.

en passant /ón pasón/ *adv.* **1** by the way. **2** *Chess* used with reference to the permitted capture of an opponent's pawn that has just advanced two squares in its first move with a pawn that could have taken it if it had advanced only one square. [F, = in passing]
■ **1** see *in passing* (PASS[1]).

en pension /ón ponsyón/ *adv.* as a boarder or resident. [F: see PENSION[2]]

enplane var. of EMPLANE.

enprint /énprint/ *n.* a standard-sized photographic print. [*en*larged *print*]

enquire /inkwī́r/ *v.* **1** *intr.* (often foll. by *of*) seek information; ask a question (of a person). **2** *intr.* = INQUIRE. **3** *intr.* (foll. by *about*, *after*, *for*) ask about a person, a person's health, etc. **4** *intr.* (foll. by *for*) ask about the availability of. **5** *tr.* ask for information as to (*enquired my name; enquired whether we were coming*). **6** *tr.* (foll. by *into*) investigate, look into. □□ **enquirer** *n.* [ME *enquere* f. OF *enquerre* ult. f. L *inquirere* (as IN-[2], *quaerere quaesit-* seek)]
■ **1, 3–5** inquire, ask; (*enquire of*) question. **2** see INQUIRE 1. **6** (*enquire into*) see INVESTIGATE 1.

enquiry /inkwī́ri/ *n.* (*pl.* **-ies**) **1** the act or an instance of asking or seeking information. **2** = INQUIRY.

enrage /inráyj/ *v.tr.* (often foll. by *at*, *by*, *with*) make furious. □□ **enragement** *n.* [F *enrager* (as EN-[1], RAGE)]
■ anger, infuriate, madden, incense, provoke, inflame, make a person's blood boil, get *or* put a person's back up, make a person's hackles rise, raise a person's hackles, make a person see red, empurple, excite a person to (a) frenzy *or* rage, *Brit.* get a person's blood up, get on a person's nerves, mad, *colloq.* get a person's dander up, drive crazy *or* up the wall *or* round the bend, wind up, drive round the twist, *US sl.* burn up.

en rapport /ón rapór/ *adv.* (usu. foll. by *with*) in harmony or rapport. [F: see RAPPORT]
■ see SYMPATHIZE 1.

enrapture /inrápchər/ *v.tr.* give intense delight to.
■ thrill, delight, electrify, transport, carry away, intoxicate; charm, enchant, bewitch, spellbind, enthral, captivate, beguile, fascinate, rivet, transfix, mesmerize, entrance, hypnotize.

enrich /inrích/ *v.tr.* **1** make rich or richer. **2** make richer in quality, flavour, nutritive value, etc. **3** add to the contents of (a collection, museum, or book). **4** increase the content of an isotope in (material) esp. enrich uranium with isotope U-235. □□ **enrichment** *n.* [ME f. OF *enrichir* (as EN-[1], RICH)]
■ **1, 2** enhance, improve, upgrade, better, raise, increase, intensify, elevate, refine, add to, *formal* ameliorate. **3** add to, expand, enlarge, extend; revise, improve, elaborate, develop, lengthen. □□ **enrichment** enhancement, improvement, embellishment.

enrobe /inrṓb/ *v.intr.* put on a robe, vestment, etc.
■ see ROBE *v.* 2.

enrol /inrṓl/ *v.* (*US* **enroll**) (**enrolled, enrolling**) **1** *intr.* enter one's name on a list, esp. as a commitment to membership. **2** *tr.* **a** write the name of (a person) on a list. **b** (usu. foll. by *in*) incorporate (a person) as a member of a society etc. **3** *tr. hist.* enter (a deed etc.) among the rolls of a court of justice. **4** *tr.* record. □□ **enrollee** /-léé/ *n.* **enroller** *n.* [ME f. OF *enroller* (as EN-[1], *rolle* ROLL)]
■ **1** register, sign up *or* on, give one's name; enlist, join. **2** write *or* note *or* put down, register, sign up *or* on *or* in, list; enlist, recruit. **4** record, chronicle, set *or* put down, register, note, list, inscribe, catalogue.

enrolment /inrṓlmənt/ *n.* (*US* **enrollment**) **1** the act or an instance of enrolling; the state of being enrolled. **2** *US* the number of persons enrolled, esp. at a school or college.
■ **1** see *initiation* (INITIATE).

en route /on rōōt/ *adv.* (usu. foll. by *to*, *for*) on the way. [F]

ensconce /inskónss/ *v.tr.* (usu. *refl.* or in *passive*) establish or settle comfortably, safely, or secretly.
■ see ESTABLISH 1, 2.

ensemble /onsómb'l/ *n.* **1 a** a thing viewed as the sum of its parts. **b** the general effect of this. **2** a set of clothes worn together; an outfit. **3** a group of actors, dancers, musicians, etc., performing together, esp. subsidiary dancers in ballet etc. **4** *Mus.* **a** a concerted passage for an ensemble. **b** the manner in which this is performed (*good ensemble*). **5** *Math.* a group of systems with the same constitution but possibly in different states. [F, ult. f. L *insimul* (as IN-[2], *simul* at the same time)]
■ **1** composite, aggregate; collection, set, assemblage, agglomeration, conglomeration, body, group, grouping. **2** outfit, costume, suit, equipage, uniform, *colloq.* get-up, *Brit. colloq.* rig-out, *poet.* array. **3** band, group, orchestra, chorus, choir, *sl.* combo; company, troupe, cast.

enshrine /inshrī́n/ *v.tr.* **1** enclose in or as in a shrine. **2** serve as a shrine for. **3** preserve or cherish. □□ **enshrinement** *n.*
■ **3** see REVERE.

enshroud /inshrówd/ *v.tr. literary* **1** cover with or as with a shroud. **2** cover completely; hide from view.
■ see ENVELOP 1.

ensign /énsīn, -s'n/ *n.* **1 a** a banner or flag, esp. the military or naval flag of a nation. **b** *Brit.* a flag with the union in the corner. **2** a standard-bearer. **3 a** *hist.* the lowest commissioned infantry officer. **b** *US* the lowest com-

missioned officer in the navy. □ **blue ensign** the ensign of government departments and formerly of the naval reserve etc. **red ensign** the ensign of the merchant service. **white ensign** the ensign of the Royal Navy and the Royal Yacht Squadron. □□ **ensigncy** *n.* [ME f. OF *enseigne* f. L *insignia*: see INSIGNIA]
■ **1 a** see FLAG[1] *n.*

ensilage /énsilij/ *n.* & *v.* ● *n.* = SILAGE. ● *v.tr.* treat (fodder) by ensilage. [F (as ENSILE)]

ensile /insíl/ *v.tr.* **1** put (fodder) into a silo. **2** preserve (fodder) in a silo. [F *ensiler* f. Sp. *ensilar* (as EN-[1], SILO)]

enslave /insláyv/ *v.tr.* make (a person) a slave. □□ **enslavement** *n.* **enslaver** *n.*
■ enthral, bind, yoke, fetter, enchain, shackle, trammel, *literary* enfetter; subjugate, oppress, dominate, overpower, subject, put down, humiliate, reduce. □□ **enslavement** see SLAVERY 1.

ensnare /insnáir/ *v.tr.* catch in or as in a snare; entrap. □□ **ensnarement** *n.*
■ see TRAP[1] *v.* 1.

ensue /insyóó/ *v.intr.* **1** happen afterwards. **2** (often foll. by *from, on*) occur as a result. [ME f. OF *ensuivre* ult. f. L *sequi* follow]
■ see RESULT *v.* 1.

en suite /ON sweét/ *adv.* forming a single unit (*bedroom with bathroom en suite*). [F, = in sequence]

ensure /inshóor/ *v.tr.* **1** (often foll. by *that* + clause) make certain. **2** (usu. foll. by *to, for*) secure (a thing for a person etc.). **3** (usu. foll. by *against*) make safe. □□ **ensurer** *n.* [ME f. AF *enseürer* f. OF *aseürer* ASSURE]
■ **1** make sure *or* certain, guarantee; see (to it), *US* insure. **3** make safe, protect, guard, shelter, shield, safeguard, secure, *US* insure.

enswathe /insway̱th/ *v.tr.* bind or wrap in or as in a bandage. □□ **enswathement** *n.*
■ swathe, bind, wrap, bandage.

ENT *abbr.* ear, nose, and throat.

-ent /ənt, ent/ *suffix* **1** forming adjectives denoting attribution of an action (*consequent*) or state (*existent*). **2** forming nouns denoting an agent (*coefficient*; *president*). [from or after F *-ent* or L *-ent-* pres. part. stem of verbs (cf. -ANT)]

entablature /intáblәchәr/ *n. Archit.* the upper part of a classical building supported by columns or a colonnade, comprising architrave, frieze, and cornice. [It. *intavolatura* f. *intavolare* board up (as IN-[2], *tavola* table)]

entablement /intáyb'lmənt/ *n.* a platform supporting a statue, above the dado and base. [F, f. *entabler* (as EN-[1], TABLE)]

entail /intáyl/ *v.* & *n.* ● *v.tr.* **1 a** necessitate or involve unavoidably (*the work entails much effort*). **b** give rise to, involve. **2** *Law* bequeath (property etc.) so that it remains within a family. **3** (usu. foll. by *on*) bestow (a thing) inalienably. ● *n. Law* **1** an entailed estate. **2** the succession to such an estate. □□ **entailment** *n.* [ME, f. EN-[1] + AF *taile* TAIL[2]]
■ *v.* **1b** necessitate, involve, mean, require, call for, demand; presuppose, imply. **2** give rise to, occasion, lead to, cause, create.

entangle /intángg'l/ *v.tr.* **1** cause to get caught in a snare or among obstacles. **2** cause to become tangled. **3** involve in difficulties or illicit activities. **4** make (a thing) tangled or intricate; complicate.
■ **1, 2** tangle (up), mesh, enmesh, snarl, ensnarl, catch (up), entwine, intertwine, entrammel, trammel, ravel (up), snag, foul (up), knot (up), twist (up), intertwist, coil, entrap, trap, lock, jam. **3** involve, embroil, mix up, entwine, catch up, tangle (up), tie up, draw *or* drag in, ensnare, enmesh, snarl, ensnarl, implicate, associate. **4** make involved *or* intricate, confuse, throw into confusion *or* perplexity, blur, muddle, confound, befuddle, mix up, jumble (up); complicate, make complicated *or* complex, compound.

entanglement /intángg'lmənt/ *n.* **1** the act or condition of entangling or being entangled. **2 a** a thing that entangles. **b** *Mil.* an extensive barrier erected to obstruct an enemy's movements (esp. one made of stakes and interlaced barbed wire). **3** a compromising (esp. amorous) relationship.
■ **1, 2a** see TANGLE *n.* 1. **3** see LIAISON 2.

entasis /éntəsiss/ *n. Archit.* a slight convex curve in a column shaft to correct the visual illusion that straight sides give of curving inwards. [mod.L f. Gk f. *enteinō* to stretch]

entellus /intélləss/ *n.* = HANUMAN. [name of a Trojan in Virgil's *Aeneid*]

entente /ontónt/ *n.* **1** = ENTENTE CORDIALE. **2** a group of States in such a relation. [F, = understanding (as INTENT)]

entente cordiale /ONTÓNT kordiaál/ *n.* a friendly understanding between States, esp. (often **Entente Cordiale**) that reached in 1904 between Britain and France. [F, = cordial understanding: see ENTENTE]

enter /éntər/ *v.* **1 a** *intr.* (often foll. by *into*) go or come in. **b** *tr.* go or come into. **c** *intr.* come on stage (as a direction: *enter Macbeth*). **2** *tr.* penetrate; go through; spread through (*a bullet entered his chest*; *a smell of toast entered the room*). **3** *tr.* (often foll. by *up*) write (a name, details, etc.) in a list, book, etc. **4 a** *intr.* register or announce oneself as a competitor (*entered for the long jump*). **b** *tr.* become a competitor in (an event). **c** *tr.* record the name of (a person etc.) as a competitor (*entered two horses for the Derby*). **5** *tr.* **a** become a member of (a society etc.). **b** enrol as a member or prospective member of a society, school, etc.; admit or obtain admission for. **6** *tr.* make known; present for consideration (*entered a protest*). **7** *tr.* put into an official record. **8** *intr.* (foll. by *into*) **a** engage in (conversation, relations, an undertaking, etc.). **b** subscribe to; bind oneself by (an agreement etc.). **c** form part of (one's calculations, plans, etc.). **d** sympathize with (feelings etc.). **9** *intr.* (foll. by *on, upon*) **a** begin, undertake; begin to deal with (a subject). **b** assume the functions of (an office). **c** assume possession of (property). **10** *intr.* (foll. by *up*) complete a series of entries in (account-books etc.). □□ **enterer** *n.* [ME f. OF *entrer* f. L *intrare*]
■ **1 a** go *or* come in, go *or* come into. **b** go *or* come into, pass into. **c** come *or* go on (stage), make an entrance. **2** penetrate, pierce, lance, spear, stab, stick (into), bore (into), go *or* pass through, go *or* pass into, puncture, perforate, riddle; spread *or* seep through(out), pervade, permeate, invade; infiltrate. **3** write *or* put *or* note (down), make a note of, set down, inscribe, take (down), jot down, record, register, list; log, document, chronicle, minute. **4** put in (for), put oneself forward (for), register (for). **5** enrol in, join, become a member of, sign up for; admit, let in, allow to enter, take *or* allow in. **6** make known, communicate, inform of; present, submit, tender, offer, proffer, lodge, file, prefer, put forward, advance, propose. **7** file, submit, register, record. **8** (*enter into*) **a** engage *or* participate *or* take part *or* partake in. **b** subscribe to, sign, be (a) party to, co-sign, countersign. **c** form part of, come into, play a part in, feature in. **9 a** (*enter on* or *upon*) begin, start, set about, undertake, *formal* commence; take up *or* on, go *or* launch into, embark on, pursue, investigate, analyse, discuss, tackle, proceed to, touch on. **b** take up, begin, start. **c** see ACQUIRE 2.

enteric /entérrik/ *adj.* & *n.* ● *adj.* of the intestines. ● *n.* (in full **enteric fever**) typhoid. □□ **enteritis** /éntərītiss/ *n.* [Gk *enterikos* (as ENTERO-)]

entero- /éntərō/ *comb. form* intestine. [Gk *enteron* intestine]

enterostomy /éntəróstəmi/ *n.* (*pl.* **-ies**) *Surgery* a surgical operation in which the small intestine is brought through the abdominal wall and opened, in order to bypass the stomach or the colon.

enterotomy /éntəróttəmi/ *n.* (*pl.* **-ies**) *Surgery* the surgical cutting open of the intestine.

enterovirus /éntərōvīrəss/ *n.* a virus infecting the intestines and sometimes spreading to other parts of the body, esp. the central nervous system.

enterprise /éntərprīz/ *n.* **1** an undertaking, esp. a bold or difficult one. **2** (as a personal attribute) readiness to engage in such undertakings (*has no enterprise*). **3** a business firm. □ **enterprise zone** *Brit.* a depressed (usu. urban) area where State incentives such as tax concessions are designed to encourage investment. □□ **enterpriser** *n.* [ME f. OF *entreprise* fem. past part. of *entreprendre* var. of *emprendre* ult. f. L *prendere*, *prehendere* take]

■ **1** undertaking, project, venture, adventure, initiative, speculation, plan, scheme, design, programme, activity, endeavour, effort, operation, task, concern. **2** initiative, resourcefulness, adventurousness, assertiveness, boldness, daring, nerve, audacity, verve, courage, pluck, mettle, spirit, vigour, energy, zip, drive, dynamism, go, dash, push, ambition, determination, resolve, purposefulness, purpose, motivation, will-power, aggressiveness, zeal, enthusiasm, keenness, *colloq.* get-up-and-go, gumption, guts, grit, spunk, pep, vim, zing. **3** business, firm, company, practice, house, concern, establishment, institution, organization, *colloq.* outfit; corporation, partnership.

enterprising /éntərprīzing/ *adj.* **1** ready to engage in enterprises. **2** resourceful, imaginative, energetic. □□ **enterprisingly** *adv.*

■ go-ahead, progressive, venturesome, forward-looking, adventurous, daring, courageous, bold, brave, plucky, mettlesome, audacious, clever, resourceful, ingenious, imaginative, inspired, inventive, innovative, original, creative, aspiring, ambitious, confident, fearless, intrepid, high-flying, goal-oriented, determined, persevering, resolved, resolute, purposeful, purposive, eager, keen, zealous, enthusiastic, spirited, vigorous, aggressive, assertive, energetic, indefatigable, tireless, *colloq.* pushy, go-getting, on the make, gutsy. □□ **enterprisingly** adventurously, resourcefully, imaginatively, energetically.

entertain /éntərtáyn/ *v.tr.* **1** amuse; occupy agreeably. **2 a** receive or treat as a guest. **b** (*absol.*) receive guests (*they entertain a great deal*). **3** give attention or consideration to (an idea, feeling, or proposal). [ME f. F *entretenir* ult. f. L *tenēre* hold]

■ **1** amuse, make laugh, tickle, cheer, delight, please, thrill, titillate, *colloq.* tickle pink *or* to death; beguile, divert, distract, absorb, engross, interest, engage, occupy. **2 a** receive, accommodate, treat, feed, regale. **b** have people round, have visitors *or* guests. **3** contemplate, consider, ponder, dwell on; harbour, experience; tolerate, allow; foster, encourage, nurse.

entertainer /éntərtáynər/ *n.* a person who entertains, esp. professionally on stage etc.

■ see PLAYER 3.

entertaining /éntərtáyning/ *adj.* amusing, diverting.

■ amusing, funny, comic, humorous, comical, witty, hilarious, droll, *colloq.* hysterical; diverting, engaging, beguiling, absorbing, interesting, delightful, enjoyable, pleasant, fun, pleasing, pleasurable, charming, agreeable.

entertainment /éntərtáynmənt/ *n.* **1** the act or an instance of entertaining; the process of being entertained. **2** a public performance or show. **3** diversions or amusements for guests etc. **4** amusement (*much to my entertainment*). **5** hospitality.

■ **1** amusement, diversion, distraction, pleasure, play, sport, interest; divertissement, beguilement, fun, enjoyment, recreation, leisure, relaxation, R and R, rest and recreation, relief, *literary* delectation. **2, 3** performance, show, production, presentation, piece, extravaganza, spectacular, pageant, spectacle. **4** see AMUSEMENT 2.

enthalpy /énthəlpi, enthálpi/ *n. Physics* the total thermodynamic heat content of a system. [Gk *enthalpō* warm in (as EN-[1], *thalpō* to heat)]

enthral /inthráwl/ *v.tr.* (*US* **enthrall, inthrall**) (**-thralled, -thralling**) **1** (often as **enthralling** *adj.*) captivate, please greatly. **2** enslave. □□ **enthralment** *n.* (*US* **enthrallment**). [EN-[1] + THRALL]

■ **1** see CAPTIVATE; (**enthralling**) captivating, mesmerizing, spellbinding, hypnotizing, fascinating, gripping, absorbing, riveting, entrancing, enchanting, bewitching, intriguing, beguiling. **2** see ENSLAVE.

enthrone /inthrṓn/ *v.tr.* **1** install (a king, bishop, etc.) on a throne, esp. ceremonially. **2** exalt. □□ **enthronement** *n.*

■ **1** see INSTALL 2.

enthuse /inthyóoz, -thóoz/ *v.intr.* & *tr. colloq.* be or make enthusiastic. [back-form. f. ENTHUSIASM]

■ see ENERGIZE.

enthusiasm /inthyóoziaz'm, -thóoziaz'm/ *n.* **1** (often foll. by *for*, *about*) **a** strong interest or admiration. **b** great eagerness. **2** an object of enthusiasm. **3** *archaic* extravagant religious emotion. [F *enthousiasme* or LL *enthusiasmus* f. Gk *enthousiasmos* f. *entheos* possessed by a god, inspired (as EN-[2], *theos* god)]

■ **1** interest, passion, *entrain*, fascination, infatuation, obsession, mania, fanaticism, rage, devotion, devotedness, admiration, liking, predilection, love; eagerness, keenness, appetite, relish, avidity, (burning) desire, fervour, earnestness, ardour, feeling, zeal, gusto, *acharnement*, zest, excitement. **2** passion, craze, mania, fad, obsession, *colloq.* thing, *sl.* bag; interest, hobby, pastime.

enthusiast /inthyóoziast, -thóoziast/ *n.* **1** (often foll. by *for*) a person who is full of enthusiasm. **2** a visionary; a self-deluded person. [F *enthousiaste* or eccl.L *enthusiastes* f. Gk (as ENTHUSIASM)]

■ **1** fan, devotee, aficionado, admirer, lover, *colloq.* buff; fanatic, zealot, energumen, addict, hound, faddist, hobbyist, *colloq.* freak, maniac, *sl.* fiend, nut, bug; champion.

enthusiastic /inthyóoziástik, -thóoziástik/ *adj.* having or showing enthusiasm. □□ **enthusiastically** *adv.* [Gk *enthousiastikos* (as ENTHUSIASM)]

■ eager, keen, obsessive, avid, fervent, compulsive, fervid, ardent, *literary* perfervid; vehement, animated, spirited, impassioned, enthused, fiery, exuberant, zestful, excited; hearty, vigorous; passionate, earnest, dedicated, committed, devoted, active, devout, zealous, mad, maniacal, rabid, fanatic, fanatical, wild, hotheaded, extreme.

enthymeme /énthimeem/ *n. Logic* a syllogism in which one premiss is not explicitly stated. [L *enthymema* f. Gk *enthumēma* f. *enthumeomai* consider (as EN-[2], *thumos* mind)]

entice /intī́ss/ *v.tr.* (often foll. by *from*, *into*, or *to* + infin.) persuade by the offer of pleasure or reward. □□ **enticement** *n.* **enticer** *n.* **enticingly** *adv.* [ME f. OF *enticier* prob. f. Rmc]

■ lure, tempt, wile away, allure, attract, draw (on), decoy, seduce, charm, coax, persuade, prevail (up)on, induce, beguile, cajole, blandish, coax, wheedle, lead on, inveigle, *colloq.* sweet-talk, soft-soap. □□ **enticement** temptation, allurement, beguilement, seduction, cajolery, wheedling, blandishment, coaxing, persuasion, *colloq.* soft soap; lure, bait, decoy, trap, inducement, attraction, temptation, *colloq.* come-on. **enticingly** seductively, temptingly, persuasively, beguilingly,

entire /intī́r/ *adj.* & *n.* ● *adj.* **1** whole, complete. **2** not broken or decayed. **3** unqualified, absolute (*an entire success*). **4** in one piece; continuous. **5** not castrated. **6** *Bot.* without indentation. **7** pure, unmixed. ● *n.* an uncastrated animal. [ME f. AF *enter*, OF *entier* f. L *integer* (as IN-[2], *tangere* touch)]

■ *adj.* **1** whole, complete, total, full, undivided; uncut, unabridged, undiminished, uncensored. **2** intact, whole, perfect, unbroken, undamaged, unharmed, inviolate, sound, unscathed, unblemished; in one piece, without a scratch. **3** see ABSOLUTE *adj.* 1. **4** continuous, full, whole, complete, total, uninterrupted, unbroken, unrelieved. **7** unmixed, unalloyed; see also PURE 1, 2.

entirely /intī́rli/ *adv.* **1** wholly, completely (*the stock is entirely exhausted*). **2** solely, exclusively (*did it entirely for my benefit*).

■ **1** completely, wholly, altogether, fully, perfectly, totally, utterly, thoroughly, absolutely, quite, a *or* one hundred per cent; lock, stock, and barrel; in every respect, in all respects, in every way, *in toto*, in full, in its entirety, every inch, to the nth degree, unreservedly, without exception *or* reservation, unqualifiedly, unequivocally; clear, clean; from head to toe *or* foot; (right) down to the ground; from A to Z, from beginning to end, from cover to cover, from start to finish; hook, line, and sinker; heart and soul, body and soul; root and branch; head over heels. **2** solely, exclusively, only, merely.

entirety /intīrəti/ *n.* (*pl.* **-ies**) **1** completeness. **2** (usu. foll. by *of*) the sum total. □ **in its entirety** in its complete form; completely. [ME f. OF *entiereté* f. L *integritas -tatis* f. *integer*: see ENTIRE]
■ **1** completeness, totality, whole(ness), fullness; perfection, togetherness, unity, integrity. **2** whole, sum total, aggregate, *colloq.* the (whole *or* entire) lot, the whole shooting match, *sl.* the whole (kit and) caboodle. □ **in its entirety** see *in full* (FULL[1]).

entitle /intīt'l/ *v.tr.* **1 a** (usu. foll. by *to*) give (a person etc.) a just claim. **b** (foll. by *to* + infin.) give (a person etc.) a right. **2 a** give (a book etc.) the title of. **b** *archaic* give (a person) the title of (*entitled him sultan*). □□ **entitlement** *n.* [ME f. AF *entitler*, OF *entiteler* f. LL *intitulare* (as IN-[2], TITLE)]
■ **1 a** allow, permit; make eligible, qualify. **b** allow, permit, authorize, give leave *or* permission, empower, qualify, fit; license. **2 a** name, title, call. **b** see CALL *v.* 7.

entity /éntiti/ *n.* (*pl.* **-ies**) **1** a thing with distinct existence, as opposed to a quality or relation. **2** a thing's existence regarded distinctly; a thing's essential nature. □□ **entitative** /-titətiv/ *adj.* [F *entité* or med.L *entitas* f. LL *ens* being]
■ **1** thing, object, phenomenon, element, unit, quantity, being; organism, specimen, creature, individual, body. **2** life, being, existence; essence, quintessence, *Philos.* quiddity.

ento- /éntō/ *comb. form* within. [Gk *entos* within]

entomb /intóom/ *v.tr.* **1** place in or as in a tomb. **2** serve as a tomb for. □□ **entombment** *n.* [OF *entomber* (as EN-[1], TOMB)]

entomo- /éntəmō/ *comb. form* insect. [Gk *entomos* cut up (in neut. = INSECT) f. EN-[2] + *temnō* cut]

entomology /éntəmólləji/ *n.* the study of the forms and behaviour of insects. □□ **entomological** /-məlójik'l/ *adj.* **entomologist** *n.* [F *entomologie* or mod.L *entomologia* (as ENTOMO-, -LOGY)]

entomophagous /éntəmóffəgəss/ *adj. Zool.* insect-eating.

entomophilous /éntəmóffiləss/ *adj. Biol.* pollinated by insects.

entoparasite /éntōpárrəsīt/ *n. Biol.* = ENDOPARASITE.

entophyte /éntōfīt/ *n. Bot.* a plant growing inside a plant or animal.

entourage /óntooraazh/ *n.* **1** people attending an important person. **2** surroundings. [F f. *entourer* surround]
■ **1** see RETINUE.

entr'acte /óntrakt/ *n.* **1** an interval between two acts of a play. **2** a piece of music or a dance performed during this. [F f. *entre* between + *acte* act]
■ see INTERLUDE 1, 2.

entrails /éntraylz/ *n.pl.* **1** the bowels and intestines of a person or animal. **2** the innermost parts (*entrails of the earth*). [ME f. OF *entrailles* f. med.L *intralia* alt. f. L *interaneus* internal f. *inter* among]
■ see GUT *n.* 1, 2.

entrain[1] /intráyn/ *v.intr.* & *tr.* go or put on board a train. □□ **entrainment** *n.*

entrain[2] /intráyn/ *v.tr.* **1** (of a fluid) carry (particles etc.) along in its flow. **2** drag along. □□ **entrainment** *n.* [F *entraîner* (as EN-[1], *traîner* drag, formed as TRAIN)]

entrain[3] /ONTRÁN/ *n.* enthusiasm, animation. [F]

entrammel /intrámm'l/ *v.tr.* (**entrammelled, entrammelling;** *US* **entrammeled, entrammeling**) entangle, hamper.

entrance[1] /éntrənss/ *n.* **1** the act or an instance of going or coming in. **2** a door, passage, etc., by which one enters. **3** right of admission. **4** the coming of an actor on stage. **5** *Mus.* = ENTRY 8. **6** (foll. by *into, upon*) entering into office etc. **7** (in full **entrance fee**) a fee paid for admission to a society, club, exhibition, etc. [OF (as ENTER, -ANCE)]
■ **1, 4** going *or* coming in, going *or* coming on, coming, entry, arrival, appearance; ingress. **2** entry, entrance-way, entry-way, door, doorway, gate, way in, access, inlet, ingress; opening. **3** (right of) entry, access, admission, admittance, entrée, leave *or* permission to enter. **6** start, arrival, entry, inception, *formal* commencement. **7** see CHARGE *n.* 1a.

entrance[2] /intraanss/ *v.tr.* **1** enchant, delight. **2** put into a trance. **3** (often foll. by *with*) overwhelm with strong feeling. □□ **entrancement** *n.* **entrancing** *adj.* **entrancingly** *adv.*
■ **1** enchant, bewitch, spellbind, fascinate, transport, carry away, delight, enrapture, intoxicate, thrill, electrify, ravish, charm, attract, allure, beguile, mesmerize, hypnotize, stun, transfix, captivate, enthral, take a person's breath away, overpower, *US* hex, *archaic* witch, *colloq.* bowl over, send, *poet.* trance. **2** hypnotize, mesmerize, *poet.* trance. **3** see OVERWHELM 1.

entrant /éntrənt/ *n.* a person who enters (esp. an examination, profession, etc.). [F, part. of *entrer*: see ENTER]
■ see ENTRY 7a.

entrap /intráp/ *v.tr.* (**entrapped, entrapping**) **1** catch in or as in a trap. **2** (often foll. by *into* + verbal noun) beguile or trick (a person). □□ **entrapper** *n.* [OF *entraper* (as EN-[1], TRAP[1])]
■ **1** see TRAP[1] *v.* 1. **2** see BEGUILE 3, SEDUCE 2.

entrapment /intrápmənt/ *n.* **1** the act or an instance of entrapping; the process of being entrapped. **2** *Law* inducement to commit a crime, esp. by the authorities to secure a prosecution.

entreat /intreét/ *v.tr.* **1 a** (foll. by *to* + infin. or *that* + clause) ask (a person) earnestly. **b** ask earnestly for (a thing). **2** *archaic* treat; act towards (a person). □□ **entreatingly** *adv.* [ME f. OF *entraiter* (as EN-[1], *traiter* TREAT)]
■ **1** see ASK 2.

entreaty /intreéti/ *n.* (*pl.* **-ies**) an earnest request; a supplication. [ENTREAT, after TREATY]
■ see REQUEST *n.* 1, 2.

entrechat /óntrəshaa/ *n.* a leap in ballet, with one or more crossings of the legs while in the air. [F f. It. (*capriola*) *intrecciata* complicated (caper)]

entrecôte /óntrəkōt/ *n.* a boned steak cut off the sirloin. [F f. *entre* between + *côte* rib]

entrée /óntray, óNtray/ *n.* **1** *Cookery* **a** *Brit.* a dish served between the fish and meat courses. **b** esp. *US* the main dish of a meal. **2** the right or privilege of admission, esp. at Court. [F, = ENTRY]
■ **2** see ADMISSION 2a.

entremets /óntrəmáy/ *n.* **1** a sweet dish. **2** any light dish served between two courses. [F f. *entre* between + *mets* dish]

entrench /intrénch/ *v.* (also **intrench**) **1** *tr.* establish firmly (in a defensible position, in office, etc.). **2** *tr.* surround (a post, army, town, etc.) with a trench as a fortification. **3** *tr.* apply extra safeguards to (rights etc. guaranteed by legislation). **4** *intr.* entrench oneself. **5** *intr.* (foll. by *upon*) encroach, trespass. □ **entrench oneself** adopt a well-defended position. □□ **entrenchment** *n.*
■ **1** fix, establish, root, embed, plant, set. **5** encroach, trespass, intrude, make inroads; (*entrench upon*) invade, infringe.

entre nous /óntrə nóo/ *adv.* **1** between you and me. **2** in private. [F, = between ourselves]

entrepôt /óntrəpō/ *n.* **1** a warehouse for temporary storage of goods in transit. **2** a commercial centre for import and export, and for collection and distribution. [F f. *entreposer* store f. *entre-* INTER- + *poser* place]

entrepreneur /óntrəprənőr/ *n.* **1** a person who undertakes an enterprise or business, with the chance of profit or loss. **2** a contractor acting as an intermediary. **3** the person in effective control of a commercial undertaking. **4** a person who organizes entertainments, esp. musical performances. □□ **entrepreneurial** /-nőriəl, -nyóoriəl/ *adj.* **entrepreneurialism** /-nőriəliz'm, -nyóoriəliz'm/ *n.* (also **entrepreneurism**). **entrepreneurially** /-nőriəli, -nyóoriəli/ *adv.* **entrepreneurship** *n.* [F f. *entreprendre* undertake: see ENTERPRISE]
■ **1** see ADVENTURER 2. **2** see INTERMEDIARY. **3** see EXECUTIVE *n.* 1.

entresol /óntrəsol/ *n.* a low storey between the first and the ground floor; a mezzanine floor. [F f. *entre* between + *sol* ground]

entrism var. of ENTRYISM.

entropy /éntrəpi/ *n.* **1** *Physics* a measure of the unavailability of a system's thermal energy for conversion into mechanical work. **2** *Physics* a measure of the disorganization or degradation of the universe. **3** a measure of the rate of transfer of information in a message etc. □□ **entropic** /-tróppik/ *adj.* **entropically** /-tróppikəli/ *adv.* [G *Entropie* (as EN-[2], Gk *tropē* transformation)]

entrust /intrúst/ *v.tr.* (also **intrust**) **1** (foll. by *to*) give responsibility for (a person or a thing) to a person in whom one has confidence. **2** (foll. by *with*) assign responsibility for a thing to (a person). □□ **entrustment** *n.*
■ **1** assign, delegate, depute, leave, consign, commit, give. **2** trust, charge, burden.

entry /éntri/ *n.* (*pl.* **-ies**) **1 a** the act or an instance of going or coming in. **b** the coming of an actor on stage. **c** ceremonial entrance. **2** liberty to go or come in. **3 a** a place of entrance; a door, gate, etc. **b** a lobby. **4** *Brit.* a passage between buildings. **5** the mouth of a river. **6 a** an item entered (in a diary, list, account-book, etc.). **b** the recording of this. **7 a** a person or thing competing in a race, contest, etc. **b** a list of competitors. **8** the start or resumption of music for a particular instrument in an ensemble. **9** *Law* the act of taking possession. **10** *Bridge* **a** the transfer of the lead to one's partner's hand. **b** a card providing this. □ **entry form** an application form for a competition. **entry permit** an authorization to enter a particular country etc. [ME f. OF *entree* ult. f. L *intrare* ENTER]
■ **1** going *or* coming in, going *or* coming on, coming, entrance, arrival, appearance; ingress. **2** access, entrance, entrée, admittance, admission, leave *or* permission to enter. **3 a** entrance, entrance-way, entry-way, door, doorway, gate, way in, access, inlet, ingress. **b** see LOBBY *n.* 1. **4** passage(way), alley(-way), back alley, **6 a** record, item, note, point, **b** recording, registration, listing. **7 a** competitor, entrant, contestant, participant, player, candidate.

entryism /éntri-iz'm/ *n.* (also **entrism**) infiltration into a political organization to change or subvert its policies or objectives. □□ **entrist** *n.* **entryist** *n.*

Entryphone /éntrifōn/ *n. propr.* an intercom device at an entrance to a building by which callers may identify themselves to gain admission.

entwine /intwīn/ *v.* (also **intwine**) **1** *tr.* & *intr.* (foll. by *with, about, round*) twine together (a thing with or round another). **2** *tr.* (as **entwined** *adj.*) entangled. **3** *tr.* interweave. □□ **entwinement** *n.*
■ **1** interlace, braid, weave, intertwine, twine, plait, wreathe, twist, wind, splice, pleach, tie, knit, criss-cross. **2** (**entwined**) entangled, tangled. **3** interweave, interlace, wreathe.

enucleate /inyóokliayt/ *v.tr. Surgery* extract (a tumour etc.). □□ **enucleation** /-áysh'n/ *n.* [L *enucleare* (as E-, NUCLEUS)]

E-number /éenumbər/ *n.* the letter E followed by a code number, designating food additives according to EEC directives.

enumerate /inyóoməravt/ *v.tr.* **1** specify (items); mention one by one. **2** count; establish the number of. □□ **enumerable** *adj.* **enumeration** /-ráysh'n/ *n.* **enumerative** /-rətiv/ *adj.* [L *enumerare* (as E-, NUMBER)]
■ **1** specify, mention, name, identify, cite, list, itemize, catalogue, recite, tick *or* check off, reel *or* rattle off, run through. **2** count (up), calculate, figure (up), compute, reckon (up), work out, tally, tot (up), total (up) add (up), sum, number, quantify. □□ **enumeration** see ACCOUNT *n.* 6.

enumerator /inyóoməraytər/ *n.* **1** a person who enumerates. **2** a person employed in census-taking.

enunciate /inúnsiayt/ *v.tr.* **1** pronounce (words) clearly. **2** express (a proposition or theory) in definite terms. **3** proclaim. □□ **enunciation** /-áysh'n/ *n.* **enunciative** /-siətiv/ *adj.* **enunciator** *n.* [L *enuntiare* (as E-, *nuntiare* announce f. *nuntius* messenger)]
■ **1** pronounce, articulate, say, speak, utter, voice, deliver, vocalize, sound. **2** see EXPRESS[1] 1, 2. **3** proclaim, state, declare, assert, pronounce, affirm, *formal* aver; promulgate, announce, make public, communicate, make known, broadcast, advertise, publicize, publish, trumpet, herald, circulate. □□ **enunciation** see SPEECH 3.

enure /inyóor/ *v.intr. Law* take effect. [var. of INURE]

enuresis /ényooreéssiss/ *n. Med.* involuntary urination. □□ **enuretic** /-réttik/ *adj.* & *n.* [mod.L f. Gk *enoureō* urinate in (as EN-[2], *ouron* urine)]

envelop /invéllәp/ *v.tr.* (**enveloped, enveloping**) **1** (often foll. by *in*) **a** wrap up or cover completely. **b** make obscure; conceal (*was enveloped in mystery*). **2** *Mil.* completely surround (an enemy). □□ **envelopment** *n.* [ME f. OF *envoluper* (as EN-[1]: cf. DEVELOP)]
■ **1 a** wrap, enfold, clothe, cover, swathe, swaddle, bind, mantle, shroud, engulf, enclose, sheathe, cocoon, encase, *literary* enwrap, enshroud. **b** (make) obscure, conceal, hide, disguise, screen, shield, veil, mask, cloak, clothe, mantle, shroud, cover, surround, bury, *literary* enshroud.

envelope /énvəlōp, ón-/ *n.* **1** a folded paper container, usu. with a sealable flap, for a letter etc. **2** a wrapper or covering. **3** the structure within a balloon or airship containing the gas. **4** the outer metal or glass housing of a vacuum tube, electric light, etc. **5** *Electr.* a curve joining the successive peaks of a modulated wave. **6** *Bot.* any enveloping structure esp. the calyx or corolla (or both). **7** *Math.* a line or curve tangent to each line or curve of a given family. [F *enveloppe* (as ENVELOP)]
■ **1, 2** see WRAPPER 1, 2.

envenom /invénnəm/ *v.tr.* **1** put poison on or into; make poisonous. **2** infuse venom or bitterness into (feelings, words, or actions). [ME f. OF *envenimer* (as EN-[1], *venim* VENOM)]
■ see POISON *v.* 3.

enviable /énviəb'l/ *adj.* (of a person or thing) exciting or likely to excite envy. □□ **enviably** *adv.*
■ desirable, desired, sought-after, covetable, coveted.

envious /énviəss/ *adj.* (often foll. by *of*) feeling or showing envy. □□ **enviously** *adv.* [ME f. AF *envious*, OF *envieus* f. *envie* ENVY]
■ jealous, green-eyed, covetous, desirous, resentful, jaundiced, begrudging; green (with envy).

environ /invīrən/ *v.tr.* encircle, surround (esp. hostilely or protectively). [ME f. OF *environer* f. *environ* surroundings f. *en* in + *viron* circuit f. *virer* turn, VEER[1]]

environment /invīrənmənt/ *n.* **1** physical surroundings and conditions, esp. as affecting people's lives. **2** conditions or circumstances of living. **3** *Ecol.* external conditions affecting the growth of plants and animals. **4** a structure designed to be experienced from inside as a work of art. **5** *Computing* the overall structure within which a user, computer, or program operates. □ **environment-friendly** not harmful to the environment. □□ **environmental** /-mént'l/ *adj.* **environmentalist** /-méntəlist/ *n.* **environmentally** /-méntəli/ *adv.*
■ **1, 2** surroundings, environs, ambience, conditions,

atmosphere, climate, circumstances; habitat, quarters, medium, milieu, element, territory; sphere, setting, context, situation, background, backdrop. **3** conditions, climate, biosphere, ecosystem; habitat, environs; nature, countryside.

environmentalist /invīrənméntəlist/ *n.* **1** a person who is concerned with or advocates the protection of the environment. **2** a person who considers that environment has the primary influence on the development of a person or group. ▫▫ **environmentalism** *n.*

■ **1** ecologist, conservationist, green, naturalist, nature-lover.

environs /invīrənz, énvirənz/ *n.pl.* a surrounding district, esp. round an urban area.

■ see NEIGHBOURHOOD.

envisage /invízzij/ *v.tr.* **1** have a mental picture of (a thing or conditions not yet existing). **2** contemplate or conceive, esp. as a possibility or desirable future event. **3** *archaic* **a** face (danger, facts, etc.). **b** look in the face of. ▫▫ **envisagement** *n.* [F *envisager* (as EN-[1], VISAGE)]

■ **1** visualize, imagine, picture, form a picture of, envision, see (in one's mind's eye) have (a) vision(s) of, fancy, conceive (of), dream *or* conjure up, concoct, create, devise, *colloq.* think up. **2** contemplate, conceive (of), picture, imagine, visualize, have (a) vision(s) of, see, foresee, predict, forecast, prophesy, anticipate, look forward to, dream of, fantasize about. **3** see FACE *v.* 3.

envision /invízh'n/ *v.tr.* envisage, visualize.

■ see ENVISAGE 1, 2.

envoy[1] /énvoy/ *n.* **1** a messenger or representative, esp. on a diplomatic mission. **2** (in full **envoy extraordinary**) a minister plenipotentiary, ranking below ambassador and above chargé d'affaires. ▫▫ **envoyship** *n.* [F *envoyé*, past part. of *envoyer* send f. *en voie* on the way f. L *via*]

■ **1** messenger, representative, emissary, agent, ambassador, minister, delegate, deputy, proxy, substitute, surrogate, factor, stand-in, spokeswoman, spokesman, spokesperson, attaché, diplomat, *RC Ch.* (papal) nuncio, *archaic* legate.

envoy[2] /énvoy/ *n.* (also **envoi**) **1** a short stanza concluding a ballade etc. **2** *archaic* an author's concluding words. [ME f. OF *envoi* f. *envoyer* (as ENVOY[1])]

envy /énvi/ *n.* & *v.* ● *n.* (*pl.* **-ies**) **1** a feeling of discontented or resentful longing aroused by another's better fortune etc. **2** the object or ground of this feeling (*their house is the envy of the neighbourhood*). ● *v.tr.* (**-ies, -ied**) feel envy of (a person, circumstances, etc.) (*I envy you your position*). ▫▫ **envier** *n.* [ME f. OF *envie* f. L *invidia* f. *invidēre* envy (as IN-[1], *vidēre* see)]

■ *n.* **1** jealousy, enviousness, resentment, bitterness, indignation, animosity, antipathy; covetousness, desire, longing, craving, yearning, hankering. ● *v.* resent, begrudge, grudge; covet, desire, crave, long *or* yearn for, hanker after *or* for.

enweave var. of INWEAVE.

enwrap /inráp/ *v.tr.* (also **inwrap**) (**-wrapped, -wrapping**) (often foll. by *in*) *literary* wrap or enfold.

■ see WRAP *v.* 1.

enwreathe /inreéth/ *v.tr.* (also **inwreathe**) *literary* surround with or as with a wreath.

Enzed /énzéd/ *n. Austral.* & *NZ colloq.* a popular written form of: **1** New Zealand. **2** a New Zealander. ▫▫ **Enzedder** *n.* [pronunc. of *NZ*]

enzootic /énzō-óttik/ *adj.* & *n.* ● *adj.* regularly affecting animals in a particular district or at a particular season (cf. ENDEMIC, EPIZOOTIC). ● *n.* an enzootic disease. [Gk *en* in + *zōion* animal]

enzyme /énzīm/ *n. Biochem.* a protein acting as a catalyst in a specific biochemical reaction. ▫▫ **enzymatic** /-zīmáttik/ *adj.* **enzymic** /-zímik/ *adj.* **enzymology** /-zīmólləji/ *n.* [G *Enzym* f. med. Gk *enzumos* leavened f. Gk *en* in + *zumē* leaven]

EOC *abbr.* Equal Opportunities Commission.

Eocene /eé-ōseen/ *adj.* & *n. Geol.* ● *adj.* of or relating to the second epoch of the Tertiary period with evidence of an abundance of mammals including horses, bats, and whales. ¶ Cf. Appendix VII. ● *n.* this epoch or system. [Gk *ēōs* dawn + *kainos* new]

eolian *US* var. of AEOLIAN.

eolith /eéəlith/ *n. Archaeol.* any of various flint objects found in Tertiary strata and thought to be early artefacts. [Gk *ēōs* dawn + *lithos* stone]

eolithic /eéəlíthik/ *adj. Archaeol.* of the period preceding the palaeolithic age, thought to include the earliest use of flint tools. [F *éolithique* (as EOLITH)]

eon var. of AEON.

eosin /eéəsin/ *n.* a red fluorescent dyestuff used esp. as a stain in optical microscopy. [Gk *ēōs* dawn + -IN]

eosinophil /eéəsínnəfil/ *n.* a white blood cell readily stained by eosin.

-eous /iəss/ *suffix* forming adjectives meaning 'of the nature of' (*erroneous*; *gaseous*).

EP *abbr.* **1** electroplate. **2** extended-play (gramophone record).

Ep. *abbr.* Epistle.

e.p. *abbr. Chess en passant.*

ep- /ep, ip, eep/ *prefix* form of EPI- before a vowel or *h.*

EPA *abbr.* (in the US) Environmental Protection Agency.

epact /eépakt/ *n.* the number of days by which the solar year exceeds the lunar year. [F *épacte* f. LL *epactae* f. Gk *epaktai (hēmerai)* intercalated (days) f. *epagō* intercalate (as EPI-, *agō* bring)]

eparch /éppaark/ *n.* the chief bishop of an eparchy. [Gk *eparkhos* (as EPI-, *arkhos* ruler)]

eparchy /éppaarki/ *n.* (*pl.* **-ies**) a province of the Orthodox Church. [Gk *eparkhia* (as EPARCH)]

epaulette /éppələt, éppawlét/ *n.* (*US* **epaulet**) an ornamental shoulder-piece on a coat, dress, etc., esp. on a uniform. [F *épaulette* dimin. of *épaule* shoulder f. L *spatula*: see SPATULA]

épée /éppay/ *n.* a sharp-pointed duelling-sword, used (with the end blunted) in fencing. ▫▫ **épéeist** *n.* [F, = sword, f. OF *espee*: see SPAY]

epeirogenesis /ipīrōjénnisiss/ *n.* (also **epeirogeny** /éppīrójəni/) *Geol.* the regional uplift of extensive areas of the earth's crust. ▫▫ **epeirogenic** /-jénnik/ *adj.* [Gk *ēpeiros* mainland + -GENESIS, -GENY]

epenthesis /epénthisiss/ *n.* (*pl.* **epentheses** /-seez/) the insertion of a letter or sound within a word, e.g. *b* in *thimble*. ▫▫ **epenthetic** /éppenthéttik/ *adj.* [LL f. Gk f. *epentithēmi* insert (as EPI- + EN-[2] + *tithēmi* place)]

epergne /ipérn/ *n.* an ornament (esp. in branched form) for the centre of a dinner-table, holding flowers or fruit. [18th c.: perh. a corrupt. of F *épargne* saving, economy]

epexegesis /epéksijeéssiss/ *n.* (*pl.* **epexegeses** /-seez/) **1** the addition of words to clarify meaning (e.g. *to do* in *difficult to do*). **2** the words added. ▫▫ **epexegetic** /-jéttik/ *adj.* **epexegetical** /-jéttik'l/ *adj.* **epexegetically** /-jéttikəli/ *adv.* [Gk *epexēgēsis* (as EPI-, EXEGESIS)]

Eph. *abbr.* Ephesians (New Testament).

ephebe /éffeeb/ *n. Gk Hist.* a young man of 18–20 undergoing military training. ▫▫ **ephebic** /ifeébik/ *adj.* [L *ephebus* f. Gk *ephēbos* (as EPI-, *hēbē* early manhood)]

ephedra /ifédrə/ *n.* any evergreen shrub of the genus *Ephedra*, with trailing stems and scalelike leaves. [mod.L f. Gk *ephedra* sitting upon]

ephedrine /éffədrin/ *n.* an alkaloid drug found in some ephedras, causing constriction of the blood-vessels and widening of the bronchial passages, used to relieve asthma, etc. [EPHEDRA + -INE[4]]

ephemera[1] /ifémmərə, ifeém-/ *n.* (*pl.* **ephemeras** or **ephemerae** /-ree/) **1 a** an insect living only a day or a few days. **b** any insect of the order Ephemeroptera, e.g. the mayfly. **2** = EPHEMERON. [mod.L f. Gk *ephēmeros* lasting only a day (as EPI-, *hēmera* day)]

ephemera[2] *pl.* of EPHEMERON 1.

ephemeral /ifémmərəl, ifeém-/ *adj.* **1** lasting or of use for only a short time; transitory. **2** lasting only a day. **3** (of an insect, flower, etc.) lasting a day or a few days. □□ **ephemerality** /-rálliti/ *n.* **ephemerally** *adv.* **ephemeralness** *n.* [Gk *ephēmeros*: see EPHEMERA]

■ *adj.* **1** see TRANSIENT *adj.* 1.

ephemeris /ifémməriss, ifeém-/ *n.* (*pl.* **ephemerides** /éffimérrideez/) *Astron.* an astronomical almanac or table of the predicted positions of celestial bodies. [L f. Gk *ephēmeris* diary (as EPHEMERAL)]

ephemerist /ifémmərist, ifeém-/ *n.* a collector of ephemera.

ephemeron /ifémmərən, ifeém-/ *n.* **1** (*pl.* **ephemera** /-rə/) (usu. in *pl.*) **a** a thing (esp. a printed item) of short-lived interest or usefulness. **b** a short-lived thing. **2** (*pl.* **ephemerons**) = EPHEMERA[1] 1. [as EPHEMERA[1]]

ephod /eéfod, éffod/ *n.* a Jewish priestly vestment. [ME f. Heb. *'ēpôd*]

ephor /éffor/ *n.* *Gk Hist.* any of five senior magistrates in ancient Sparta. □□ **ephorate** *n.* [Gk *ephoros* overseer (as EPI-, *horaō* see)]

epi- /éppi-/ *prefix* (usu. **ep-** before a vowel or *h*) **1** upon (*epicycle*). **2** above (*epicotyl*). **3** in addition (*epiphenomenon*). [Gk *epi* (prep.)]

epiblast /éppiblast/ *n.* *Biol.* the outermost layer of a gastrula etc.; the ectoderm. [EPI- + -BLAST]

epic /éppik/ *n.* & *adj.* ● *n.* **1** a long poem narrating the adventures or deeds of one or more heroic or legendary figures, e.g. the *Iliad*, *Paradise Lost*. **2** an imaginative work of any form, embodying a nation's conception of its past history. **3** a book or film based on an epic narrative or heroic in type or scale. **4** a subject fit for recital in an epic. ● *adj.* **1** of or like an epic. **2** grand, heroic. □□ **epical** *adj.* **epically** *adv.* [L *epicus* f. Gk *epikos* f. *epos* word, song]

■ *n.* **1–3** see LEGEND 1a–c. ● *adj.* see HEROIC *adj.* 2b.

epicarp /éppikaarp/ *n.* *Bot.* the outermost layer of the pericarp. [EPI- + Gk *karpos* fruit]

epicedium /éppiseédiəm/ *n.* (*pl.* **epicedia** /-diə/) a funeral ode. □□ **epicedian** *adj.* [L f. Gk *epikēdeion* (as EPI-, *kēdos* care)]

■ see KEEN[2] *n.*

epicene /éppiseen/ *adj.* & *n.* ● *adj.* **1** *Gram.* denoting either sex without change of gender. **2** of, for, or used by both sexes. **3** having characteristics of both sexes. **4** having no characteristics of either sex. **5** effete, effeminate. ● *n.* an epicene person. [ME f. LL *epicoenus* f. Gk *epikoinos* (as EPI-, *koinos* common)]

■ **3** see BISEXUAL *adj.* **4** see NEUTER 3.

epicentre /éppisentər/ *n.* (*US* **epicenter**) **1** *Geol.* the point at which an earthquake reaches the earth's surface. **2** the central point of a difficulty. □□ **epicentral** /-séntrəl/ *adj.* [Gk *epikentros* (adj.) (as EPI-, CENTRE)]

epicontinental /éppikóntinént'l/ *adj.* (of the sea) over the continental shelf.

epicotyl /éppikóttil/ *n.* *Bot.* the region of an embryo or seedling stem above the cotyledon(s).

epicure /éppikyoor/ *n.* a person with refined tastes, esp. in food and drink. □□ **epicurism** *n.* [med.L *epicurus* one preferring sensual enjoyment: see EPICUREAN]

■ gourmet, connoisseur, gastronome, *colloq.* foodie, *disp.* gourmand.

Epicurean /éppikyooreéən/ *n.* & *adj.* ● *n.* **1** a disciple or student of the Greek philosopher Epicurus (d. 270 BC), who taught that the highest good is personal happiness. **2** (**epicurean**) a person devoted to (esp. sensual) enjoyment. ● *adj.* **1** of or concerning Epicurus or his ideas. **2** (**epicurean**) characteristic of an epicurean. □□ **Epicureanism** *n.* [F *épicurien* or L *epicureus* f. Gk *epikoureios* f. *Epikouros* Epicurus]

■ *n.* **2** (**epicurean**) see SYBARITE *n.* ● *adj.* **2** (**epicurean**) pleasure-seeking, hedonistic, pleasure-orientated, voluptuous, voluptuary, sybarite, sybaritic(al), pampered, luxurious, sensual, carnal, orgiastic, libidinous, wild, Bacchanalian, saturnalian, extravagant, immoderate, unrestrained, debauched, dissolute, dissipated, licentious, profligate, intemperate, overindulgent, crapulent, crapulous, gluttonous, greedy, self-indulgent, porcine, *colloq.* piggish.

epicycle /éppisīk'l/ *n.* *Geom.* a small circle moving round the circumference of a larger one. □□ **epicyclic** /-sīklik, -síklik/ *adj.* [ME f. OF or LL *epicyclus* f. Gk *epikuklos* (as EPI-, *kuklos* circle)]

epicycloid /éppisīkloyd/ *n.* *Math.* a curve traced by a point on the circumference of a circle rolling on the exterior of another circle. □□ **epicycloidal** /-klóyd'l/ *adj.*

epideictic /éppidīktik/ *adj.* meant for effect or display, esp. in speaking. [Gk *epideiktikos* (as EPI-, *deiknumi* show)]

epidemic /éppidémmik/ *n.* & *adj.* ● *n.* **1** a widespread occurrence of a disease in a community at a particular time. **2** such a disease. **3** (foll. by *of*) a wide prevalence of something usu. undesirable. ● *adj.* in the nature of an epidemic (cf. ENDEMIC). □□ **epidemically** *adv.* [F *épidémique* f. *épidémie* f. LL *epidemia* f. Gk *epidēmia* prevalence of disease f. *epidēmios* (adj.) (as EPI-, *dēmos* the people)]

■ *n.* **1, 2** plague, pestilence, disease; outbreak, spread; scourge. **3** see *prevalence* (PREVALENT). ● *adj.* widespread, common, pandemic, rampant, rife, flourishing, mushrooming, nationwide, worldwide, international, universal, ubiquitous, general, prevalent; prevailing.

epidemiology /éppideemiólləji/ *n.* the study of the incidence and distribution of diseases, and of their control and prevention. □□ **epidemiological** /-miəlójik'l/ *adj.* **epidemiologist** *n.*

epidermis /éppidérmiss/ *n.* **1** the outer cellular layer of the skin. **2** *Bot.* the outer layer of cells of leaves, stems, roots, etc. □□ **epidermal** *adj.* **epidermic** *adj.* **epidermoid** *adj.* [LL f. Gk (as EPI-, DERMIS)]

■ **1** skin, dermis.

epidiascope /éppidīəskōp/ *n.* an optical projector capable of giving images of both opaque and transparent objects. [EPI- + DIA- + -SCOPE]

epididymis /éppidíddimiss/ *n.* (*pl.* **epididymides** /-didímmideez/) *Anat.* a convoluted duct behind the testis, along which sperm passes to the vas deferens. [Gk *epididumis* (as EPI-, *didumoi* testicles)]

epidural /éppidyoórəl/ *adj.* & *n.* ● *adj.* **1** *Anat.* on or around the dura mater. **2** (of an anaesthetic) introduced into the space around the dura mater of the spinal cord. ● *n.* an epidural anaesthetic, used esp. in childbirth to produce loss of sensation below the waist. [EPI- + DURA (MATER)]

epifauna /éppifawnə/ *n.* animals living on the seabed, either attached to animals, plants, etc., or free-living. [Da. (as EPI-, FAUNA)]

epigastrium /éppigástriəm/ *n.* (*pl.* **epigastria** /-riə/) *Anat.* the part of the abdomen immediately over the stomach. □□ **epigastric** *adj.* [LL f. Gk *epigastrion* (neut. adj.) (as EPI-, *gastēr* belly)]

epigeal /éppijeéəl/ *adj.* *Bot.* **1** having one or more cotyledons above the ground. **2** growing above the ground. [Gk *epigeios* (as EPI-, *gē* earth)]

epigene /éppijeen/ *adj.* *Geol.* produced on the surface of the earth. [F *épigène* f. Gk *epigenēs* (as EPI-, *genēs* born)]

epiglottis /éppiglóttiss/ *n.* *Anat.* a flap of cartilage at the root of the tongue, which is depressed during swallowing to cover the windpipe. □□ **epiglottal** *adj.* **epiglottic** *adj.* [Gk *epiglōttis* (as EPI-, *glōtta* tongue)]

epigone /éppigōn/ *n.* (*pl.* **epigones** or **epigoni** /ipíggənī/) one of a later (and less distinguished) generation. [pl. f. F *épigones* f. L *epigoni* f. Gk *epigonoi* those born afterwards (as EPI-, root of *gignomai* be born)]

epigram /éppigram/ *n.* **1** a short poem with a witty ending. **2** a saying or maxim, esp a proverbial one. **3 a** a pointed remark or expression, esp. a witty one. **b** the use of concise witty remarks. □□ **epigrammatic** /-grəmáttik/ *adj.* **epigrammatically** /-grəmáttikəli/ *adv.* **epigrammatist** /-grámmətist/ *n.* **epigrammatize** /-grámmətīz/ *v.tr.* & *intr.* (also **-ise**). [F *épigramme* or L *epigramma* f. Gk *epigramma -atos* (as EPI-, -GRAM)]
■ **2** (old) saying, proverb, aphorism, maxim, gnome, saw, adage, byword, catch-phrase, catchword, motto, slogan, apophthegm, *colloq.* (old) chestnut. **3 a** *bon mot*, quip, sally, *mot*, nice turn of phrase, atticism; witticism, pun, *double entendre*, paronomasia, equivoque, *colloq.* wisecrack. □□ **epigrammatic** pithy, terse, succinct, piquant, pungent, trenchant, sententious, witty, pointed, proverbial, aphoristic, apophthegmatic, *colloq.* snappy, punchy.

epigraph /éppigraaf/ *n.* an inscription on a statue or coin, at the head of a chapter, etc. [Gk *epigraphē* f. *epigraphō* (as EPI-, *graphō* write)]

epigraphy /ipígrəfi/ *n.* the study of (esp. ancient) inscriptions. □□ **epigraphic** /éppigráffik/ *adj.* **epigraphical** /éppigráffik'l/ *adj.* **epigraphically** /éppigráffikəli/ *adv.* **epigraphist** *n.*

epilate /éppilayt/ *v.tr.* remove hair from. □□ **epilation** /-láysh'n/ *n.* [F *épiler* (cf. DEPILATE)]

epilepsy /éppilepsi/ *n.* a nervous disorder with convulsions and often loss of consciousness. [F *épilepsie* or LL *epilepsia* f. Gk *epilēpsia* f. *epilambanō* attack (as EPI-, *lambanō* take)]

epileptic /éppiléptik/ *adj.* & *n.* ● *adj.* of or relating to epilepsy. ● *n.* a person with epilepsy. [F *épileptique* f. LL *epilepticus* f. Gk *epilēptikos* (as EPILEPSY)]

epilimnion /éppilímniən/ *n.* (*pl.* **epilimnia** /-niə/) the upper layer of water in a stratified lake. [EPI- + Gk *limnion* dimin. of *limnē* lake]

epilogist /ipílləjist/ *n.* the writer or speaker of an epilogue.

epilogue /éppilog/ *n.* **1 a** the concluding part of a literary work. **b** an appendix. **2** a speech or short poem addressed to the audience by an actor at the end of a play. **3** *Brit.* a short piece at the end of a day's broadcasting (cf. PROLOGUE). [ME f. F *épilogue* f. L *epilogus* f. Gk *epilogos* (as EPI-, *logos* speech)]
■ **1, 2** see SUPPLEMENT *n.* 1, 2.

epimer /éppimər/ *n.* *Chem.* either of two isomers with different configurations of atoms about one of several asymmetric carbon atoms present. □□ **epimeric** /-mérrik/ *adj.* **epimerism** /ipímməriz'm/ *n.* [G (as EPI-, -MER)]

epimerize /ipímmərīz/ *v.tr.* (also **-ise**) *Chem.* convert (one epimer) into the other.

epinasty /éppinasti/ *n.* *Bot.* a tendency in plant-organs to grow more rapidly on the upper side. [EPI- + Gk *nastos* pressed]

epinephrine /éppinéfrin/ *n.* *Biochem.* = ADRENALIN. [EPI + *nephros* kidney]

epiphany /ipíffəni/ *n.* (*pl.* **-ies**) **1** (**Epiphany**) **a** the manifestation of Christ to the Magi according to the biblical account. **b** the festival commemorating this on 6 January. **2** any manifestation of a god or demigod. □□ **epiphanic** /éppifánnik/ *adj.* [ME f. Gk *epiphaneia* manifestation f. *epiphainō* reveal (as EPI-, *phainō* show): sense 1 through OF *epiphanie* and eccl.L *epiphania*]

epiphenomenon /éppifinómminən/ *n.* (*pl.* **epiphenomena** /-nə/) **1** a secondary symptom, which may occur simultaneously with a disease etc. but is not regarded as its cause or result. **2** *Psychol.* consciousness regarded as a by-product of brain activity. □□ **epiphenomenal** *adj.*

epiphysis /ipíffisiss/ *n.* (*pl.* **epiphyses** /-seez/) *Anat.* **1** the end part of a long bone, initially growing separately from the shaft. **2** = *pineal body*. [mod.L f. Gk *epiphusis* (as EPI-, *phusis* growth)]

epiphyte /éppifīt/ *n.* a plant growing but not parasitic on another, e.g. a moss. □□ **epiphytal** /-fīt'l/ *adj.* **epiphytic** /-fittik/ *adj.* [EPI- + Gk *phuton* plant]

episcopacy /ipískəpəsi/ *n.* (*pl.* **-ies**) **1** government of a Church by bishops. **2** (prec. by *the*) the bishops.

episcopal /ipískəp'l/ *adj.* **1** of a bishop or bishops. **2** (of a Church) constituted on the principle of government by bishops. □ **Episcopal Church** the Anglican Church in Scotland and the US, with elected bishops. □□ **episcopalism** *n.* **episcopally** *adv.* [ME f. F *épiscopal* or eccl.L *episcopalis* f. *episcopus* BISHOP]
■ **1** see CLERICAL 1.

episcopalian /ipískəpáyliən/ *adj.* & *n.* ● *adj.* **1** of or advocating government of a Church by bishops. **2** of or belonging to an episcopal Church or (**Episcopalian**) the Episcopal Church. ● *n.* **1** an adherent of episcopacy. **2** (**Episcopalian**) a member of the Episcopal Church. □□ **episcopalianism** *n.*

episcopate /ipískəpət/ *n.* **1** the office or tenure of a bishop. **2** (prec. by *the*) the bishops collectively. [eccl.L *episcopatus* f. *episcopus* BISHOP]

episcope /éppiskōp/ *n.* an optical projector giving images of opaque objects.

episematic /éppisimáttik/ *adj.* *Zool.* (of coloration, markings, etc.) serving to help recognition by animals of the same species. [EPI- + Gk *sēma sēmatos* sign]

episiotomy /ipeéezióttəmi/ *n.* (*pl.* **-ies**) a surgical cut made at the opening of the vagina during childbirth, to aid delivery. [Gk *epision* pubic region]

episode /éppisōd/ *n.* **1** one event or a group of events as part of a sequence. **2** each of the parts of a serial story or broadcast. **3** an incident or set of incidents in a narrative. **4** an incident that is distinct but contributes to a whole (*a romantic episode in her life*). **5** *Mus.* a passage containing distinct material or introducing a new subject. **6** the part between two choric songs in Greek tragedy. [Gk *epeisodion* (as EPI- + *eisodos* entry f. *eis* into + *hodos* way)]
■ **1, 3, 4** event, incident, occurrence, happening, circumstance, occasion, experience, adventure, escapade, ordeal, trial, affair, matter. **2** instalment, part, chapter.

episodic /éppisóddik/ *adj.* (also **episodical** /-sóddik'l/) **1** in the nature of an episode. **2** sporadic; occurring at irregular intervals. □□ **episodically** *adv.*
■ **2** see OCCASIONAL 1.

epistaxis /éppistáksiss/ *n.* *Med.* a nosebleed. [mod.L f. Gk (as EPI-, *stazō* drip)]

epistemic /éppisteémik, -stémmik/ *adj.* *Philos.* relating to knowledge or to the degree of its validation. □□ **epistemically** *adv.* [Gk *epistēmē* knowledge]

epistemology /ipístimólləji/ *n.* the theory of knowledge, esp. with regard to its methods and validation. □□ **epistemological** /-məlójik'l/ *adj.* **epistemologically** /-məlójikəli/ *adv.* **epistemologist** *n.*

epistle /ipíss'l/ *n.* **1** *formal* or *joc.* a letter, esp. a long one on a serious subject. **2** (**Epistle**) **a** any of the letters of the apostles in the New Testament. **b** an extract from an Epistle read in a church service. **3** a poem or other literary work in the form of a letter or series of letters. [ME f. OF f. L *epistola* f. Gk *epistolē* f. *epistellō* send news (as EPI-, *stellō* send)]
■ **1** see LETTER 2.

epistolary /ipístələri/ *adj.* **1** in the style or form of a letter or letters. **2** of, carried by, or suited to letters. [F *épistolaire* or L *epistolaris* (as EPISTLE)]

epistrophe /ipístrəfi/ *n.* the repetition of a word at the end of successive clauses. [Gk (as EPI-, *strophē* turning)]

epistyle /éppistīl/ *n.* *Archit.* = ARCHITRAVE. [F *épistyle* or L *epistylium* f. Gk *epistulion* (as EPI-, *stulos* pillar)]

epitaph /éppitaaf/ *n.* words written in memory of a person who has died, esp. as a tomb inscription. [ME f. OF *epitaphe* f. L *epitaphium* f. Gk *epitaphion* funeral oration (as EPI-, *taphos* tomb)]

epitaxy /éppitaksi/ *n.* *Crystallog.* the growth of a thin layer on a single-crystal substrate that determines the lattice-structure of the layer. □□ **epitaxial** /-táksiəl/ *adj.* [F *épitaxie* (as EPI-, Gk *taxis* arrangement)]

epithalamium /éppithəláymiəm/ *n.* (*pl.* **epithalamiums** or **epithalamia** /-miə/) a song or poem celebrating a marriage. □□ **epithalamial** *adj.* **epithalamic** /-lámmik/ *adj.* [L f. Gk *epithalamion* (as EPI-, *thalamos* bridal chamber)]

epithelium /éppithéeliəm/ *n.* (*pl.* **epitheliums** or **epithelia** /-liə/) the tissue forming the outer layer of the body surface and lining many hollow structures. □□ **epithelial** *adj.* [mod.L f. EPI- + Gk *thēlē* teat]

epithet /éppithet/ *n.* **1** an adjective or other descriptive word expressing a quality or attribute, esp. used with or as a name. **2** such a word as a term of abuse. □□ **epithetic** /-théttik/ *adj.* **epithetical** /-théttik'l/ *adj.* **epithetically** /-théttikəli/ *adv.* [F *épithète* or L *epitheton* f. Gk *epitheton* f. *epitithēmi* add (as EPI-, *tithēmi* place)]
■ **1** see TITLE *n.* 5. **2** see EXPLETIVE *n.* 1.

epitome /ipíttəmi/ *n.* **1** a person or thing embodying a quality, class, etc. **2** a thing representing another in miniature. **3** a summary of a written work; an abstract. □□ **epitomist** *n.* [L f. Gk *epitomē* f. *epitemnō* abridge (as EPI-, *temnō* cut)]
■ **1** embodiment, incarnation, personification, image, picture, essence, quintessence, model, paragon, ideal, *beau idéal*, standard, criterion, measure, yardstick, (typical) example, archetype, exemplar, prototype. **3** summary, abstract, résumé, précis, outline, synopsis, *aperçu*, abbreviation, conspectus, condensation, abridgement, digest, potted version, compendium, concise edition *or* version, cut edition *or* version, *RC Ch.* syllabus.

epitomize /ipíttəmīz/ *v.tr.* (also **-ise**) **1** be a perfect example of (a quality etc.); typify. **2** make an epitome of (a work). □□ **epitomization** /-záysh'n/ *n.*
■ **1** see EXEMPLIFY.

epizoon /éppizṓ-on/ *n.* (*pl.* **epizoa** /-zṓə/) an animal living on another animal. [mod.L (as EPI-, Gk *zōion* animal)]

epizootic /éppizō-óttik/ *adj.* & *n.* ● *adj.* (of a disease) temporarily prevalent among animals (cf. ENZOOTIC). ● *n.* an outbreak of such a disease. [F *épizootique* f. *épizootie* (as EPIZOON)]

EPNS *abbr.* electroplated nickel silver.

epoch /éepok/ *n.* **1** a period of history or of a person's life marked by notable events. **2** the beginning of an era. **3** *Geol.* a division of a period, corresponding to a set of strata. □ **epoch-making** remarkable, historic; of major importance. □□ **epochal** /éppək'l/ *adj.* [mod.L *epocha* f. Gk *epokhē* stoppage]
■ **1** see ERA 1, 2.

epode /éppōd/ *n.* **1** a form of lyric poem written in couplets each of a long line followed by a shorter one. **2** the third section of an ancient Greek choral ode or of one division of it. [F *épode* or L *epodos* f. Gk *epōidos* (as EPI-, ODE)]

eponym /éppənim/ *n.* **1** a person (real or imaginary) after whom a discovery, invention, place, institution, etc., is named or thought to be named. **2** the name given. □□ **eponymous** /ipónniməss/ *adj.* [Gk *epōnumos* (as EPI-, *-ōnumos* f. *onoma* name)]

EPOS /éeposs/ *abbr.* electronic point-of-sale (of retail outlets recording information electronically).

epoxide /ipóksīd/ *n.* *Chem.* a compound containing an oxygen atom bonded in a triangular arrangement to two carbon atoms. [EPI- + OXIDE]

epoxy /ipóksi/ *adj.* *Chem.* relating to or derived from an epoxide. □ **epoxy resin** a synthetic thermosetting resin containing epoxy groups. [EPI- + OXY-^{2}]

epsilon /épsilon/ *n.* the fifth letter of the Greek alphabet (E, ϵ). [ME f. Gk, = bare E f. *psilos* bare]

Epsom salts /épsəm/ *n.* a preparation of magnesium sulphate used as a purgative etc. [*Epsom* in Surrey, where it was first found occurring naturally]

epyllion /epílliən/ *n.* (*pl.* **epyllia** /-liə/) a miniature epic poem. [Gk *epullion* dimin. of *epos* word, song]

equable /ékwəb'l/ *adj.* **1** even; not varying. **2** uniform and moderate (*an equable climate*). **3** (of a person) not easily disturbed or angered. □□ **equability** /-bílliti/ *n.* **equably** *adv.* [L *aequabilis* (as EQUATE)]
■ **1, 2** even, unvarying, stable, steady, regular, unchanging, constant, invariable, consistent, unvaried, uniform. **3** even-tempered, easygoing, imperturbable, unexcitable, serene, calm, placid, composed, equanimous, self-possessed, dispassionate, cool, level-headed, collected, tranquil, peaceful, *colloq.* unflappable.

equal /éekwəl/ *adj.*, *n.*, & *v.* ● *adj.* **1** (often foll. by *to*, *with*) the same in quantity, quality, size, degree, rank, level, etc. **2** evenly balanced (*an equal contest*). **3** having the same rights or status (*human beings are essentially equal*). **4** uniform in application or effect. ● *n.* a person or thing equal to another, esp. in rank, status, or characteristic quality (*their treatment of the subject has no equal*; *is the equal of any man*). ● *v.tr.* (**equalled**, **equalling**; *US* **equaled**, **equaling**) **1** be equal to in number, quality, etc. **2** achieve something that is equal to (an achievement) or to the achievement of (a person). □ **be equal to** have the ability or resources for. **equal opportunity** (often in *pl.*) the opportunity or right to be employed, paid, etc., without discrimination on grounds of sex, race, etc. **equal** (or **equals**) **sign** the symbol =. [ME f. L *aequalis* f. *aequus* even]
■ *adj.* **1, 3, 4** identical, mirror-image, the same, one and the same, interchangeable, level, fifty-fifty, on a par, *archaic or literary* coequal; similar, equivalent, commensurate; alike; like; (*equal to*) tantamount to. **2** (evenly) balanced, (evenly) matched, corresponding, symmetrical, *archaic* correspondent; equivalent, even, commensurate, comparable, proportionate, proportional; fifty-fifty, neck and neck, tied, *Brit.* level pegging, *US* nip and tuck, *colloq.* even Stephens. ● *n.* peer, match, compeer, counterpart, equivalent, fellow. ● *v.* **1** see AMOUNT *v.* 1. **2** (be a) match (for), compete with, rival, challenge, compare with, touch, come *or* get near, come *or* get close to, parallel, be on a par with, be in the same league *or* class as *or* with; even, come up to, approach; hold a candle to, copy, imitate, repeat. □ **be equal to** be up to, be capable of, measure up to, be suited to, be qualified for, be fit(ted) for.

equalitarian /eekwóllitáiriən/ *n.* = EGALITARIAN. □□ **equalitarianism** *n.* [EQUALITY, after *humanitarian* etc.]

equality /ikwólliti/ *n.* the state of being equal. [ME f. OF *equalité* f. L *aequalitas -tatis* (as EQUAL)]
■ parity, sameness, identity, uniformity, equivalence, similarity, *archaic or literary* coequality; impartiality, fairness, justice; egalitarianism.

equalize /éekwəlīz/ *v.* (also **-ise**) **1** *tr.* & *intr.* make or become equal. **2** *intr.* reach one's opponent's score in a game, after being behind. □□ **equalization** /-záysh'n/ *n.*
■ **1** make equal, counterbalance, counterpoise, equilibrate, offset, compensate, regularize, standardize; even up, match (up), balance. **2** draw level, catch up, even up, draw even.

equalizer /éekwəlīzər/ *n.* **1** an equalizing score or goal etc. in a game. **2** *sl.* a weapon, esp. a gun. **3** *Electr.* a connection in a system which compensates for any undesirable frequency or phase response with the system.

equally /éekwəli/ *adv.* **1** in an equal manner (*treated them all equally*). **2** to an equal degree (*is equally important*). ¶ In sense 2 construction with *as* (*equally as important*) is often found, but is *disp.*).
■ see ALIKE *adv.*

equanimity /ékwənímmiti, éek-/ *n.* mental composure, evenness of temper, esp. in misfortune. □□ **equanimous** /ikwánniməss/ *adj.* [L *aequanimitas* f. *aequanimis* f. *aequus* even + *animus* mind]
■ see TEMPER *n.* 4.

equate /ikwáyt/ *v.* **1** *tr.* (usu. foll. by *to*, *with*) regard as equal or equivalent. **2** *intr.* (foll. by *with*) **a** be equal or equivalent to. **b** agree or correspond. □□ **equatable** *adj.* [ME f. L *aequare aequat-* f. *aequus* equal]
■ **1** see IDENTIFY 4. **2** (*equate with*) see PARALLEL *v.* 1.

equation /ikwáyzh'n/ *n.* **1** the process of equating or making equal; the state of being equal. **2** *Math.* a statement that two mathematical expressions are equal (indicated by the sign =). **3** *Chem.* a formula indicating a chemical reaction by means of symbols for the elements taking part. □ **equation of the first order, second order**, etc. an equation involving only the first derivative, second derivative, etc. □□ **equational** *adj.* [ME f. OF *equation* or L *aequatio* (as EQUATE)]

equator /ikwáytər/ *n.* **1** an imaginary line round the earth or other body, equidistant from the poles. **2** *Astron.* = *celestial equator.* [ME f. OF *equateur* or med.L *aequator* (as EQUATION)]

equatorial /ékwətóriəl, éek-/ *adj.* of or near the equator. □ **equatorial telescope** a telescope attached to an axis perpendicular to the plane of the equator. □□ **equatorially** *adv.*

equerry /ékwəri, ikwérri/ *n.* (*pl.* **-ies**) **1** an officer of the British royal household attending members of the royal family. **2** *hist.* an officer of a prince's or noble's household having charge over the horses. [earlier *esquiry* f. OF *esquierie* company of squires, prince's stables, f. OF *esquier* ESQUIRE: perh. assoc. with L *equus* horse]

■ **2** see GROOM *n.* 1.

equestrian /ikwéstriən/ *adj.* & *n.* ● *adj.* **1** of or relating to horses and horse-riding. **2** on horseback. ● *n.* (*fem.* **equestrienne** /-tri-én/) a rider or performer on horseback. □□ **equestrianism** *n.* [L *equestris* f. *eques* horseman, knight, f. *equus* horse]

equi- /éekwi/ *comb. form* equal. [L *aequi-* f. *aequus* equal]

equiangular /éekwiánggyoolər/ *adj.* having equal angles.

equidistant /éekwidístənt/ *adj.* at equal distances. □□ **equidistantly** *adv.*

equilateral /éekwiláttərəl/ *adj.* having all its sides equal in length.

■ regular, equiangular.

equilibrate /ikwíllibrayt, éekwilíbrayt/ *v.* **1** *tr.* cause (two things) to balance. **2** *intr.* be in equilibrium; balance. □□ **equilibration** /-bráysh'n/ *n.* **equilibrator** /ikwíllibraytər/ *n.* [LL *aequilibrare aequilibrat-* (as EQUI-, *libra* balance)]

equilibrist /ikwíllibrist/ *n.* an acrobat, esp. on a high rope.

■ funambulist, (tight)rope-walker, high-wire walker.

equilibrium /éekwilíbriəm/ *n.* (*pl.* **equilibria** /-riə/ or **equilibriums**) **1** a state of physical balance. **2** a state of mental or emotional equanimity. **3** a state in which the energy in a system is evenly distributed and forces, influences, etc., balance each other. [L (as EQUI-, *libra* balance)]

■ **1, 3** see BALANCE *n.* 3.

equine /ékwīn/ *adj.* of or like a horse. [L *equinus* f. *equus* horse]

equinoctial /éekwinóksh'l/ *adj.* & *n.* ● *adj.* **1** happening at or near the time of an equinox (*equinoctial gales*). **2** of or relating to equal day and night. **3** at or near the (terrestrial) equator. ● *n.* (in full **equinoctial line**) = *celestial equator.* □ **equinoctial point** the point at which the ecliptic cuts the celestial equator (twice each year at an equinox). **equinoctial year** see YEAR. [ME f. OF *equinoctial* or L *aequinoctialis* (as EQUINOX)]

equinox /éekwinoks, ék-/ *n.* **1** the time or date (twice each year) at which the sun crosses the celestial equator, when day and night are of equal length. **2** = *equinoctial point.* □ **autumn** (or **autumnal**) **equinox** about 22 Sept. **spring** (or **vernal**) **equinox** about 20 March. [ME f. OF *equinoxe* or med.L *equinoxium* for L *aequinoctium* (as EQUI-, *nox noctis* night)]

equip /ikwíp/ *v.tr.* (**equipped**, **equipping**) supply with what is needed. □□ **equipper** *n.* [F *équiper*, prob. f. ON *skipa* to man (a ship) f. *skip* SHIP]

■ supply, furnish, provide, stock (up), outfit, fit (out *or* up), rig (out *or* up), fix up, accoutre, deck (out), caparison, kit (out *or* up), provision.

equipage /ékwipij/ *n.* **1 a** requisites for an undertaking. **b** an outfit for a special purpose. **2** a carriage and horses with attendants. [F *équipage* (as EQUIP)]

■ **1 a** see EQUIPMENT. **b** see ROBE *n.* 4.

equipment /ikwípmənt/ *n.* **1** the necessary articles, clothing, etc., for a purpose. **2** the process of equipping or being equipped. [F *équipement* (as EQUIP)]

■ **1** gear, apparatus, paraphernalia, kit, material, accoutrements, *matériel*, equipage, outfit, panoply, rig, rigging, gadgetry, tackle, tack, impedimenta, baggage, luggage, stuff, *Brit. sl.* clobber.

equipoise /ékwipoyz/ *n.* & *v.* ● *n.* **1** equilibrium; a balanced state. **2** a counterbalancing thing. ● *v.tr.* counterbalance.

equipollent /éekwipóllənt/ *adj.* & *n.* ● *adj.* **1** equal in power, force, etc. **2** practically equivalent. ● *n.* an equipollent thing. □□ **equipollence** *n.* **equipollency** *n.* [ME f. OF *equipolent* f. L *aequipollens -entis* of equal value (as EQUI-, *pollēre* be strong)]

equipotential /éekwipəténsh'l/ *adj.* & *n. Physics* ● *adj.* (of a surface or line) having the potential of a force the same or constant at all its points. ● *n.* an equipotential line or surface.

equiprobable /éekwipróbbəb'l/ *adj. Logic* equally probable. □□ **equiprobability** /-bílliti/ *n.*

equitable /ékwitəb'l/ *adj.* **1** fair, just. **2** *Law* valid in equity as distinct from law. □□ **equitableness** *n.* **equitably** *adv.* [F *équitable* (as EQUITY)]

■ **1** fair, just, fair-minded, right, square, decent, good, correct, rightful, even-handed, impartial, dispassionate, detached, objective, unbiased, neutral, uncoloured, non-partisan, disinterested, unprejudiced, non-prejudicial, unjaundiced, open-minded, unbigoted, reasonable, judicious, ethical, principled, moral, (right and) proper, upright, sound, respectable, regular, honest, clean, open, valid, honourable, righteous, scrupulous, conscientious, straight, straightforward, upstanding, right-minded, *colloq.* fair and square, upfront; (open and) above-board; *colloq.* on the level, *esp. US colloq.* on the up and up.

equitation /ékwitáysh'n/ *n.* the art and practice of horsemanship and horse-riding. [F *équitation* or L *equitatio* f. *equitare* ride a horse f. *eques equitis* horseman f. *equus* horse]

equity /ékwiti/ *n.* (*pl.* **-ies**) **1** fairness. **2** the application of the principles of justice to correct or supplement the law. **3 a** the value of the shares issued by a company. **b** (in *pl.*) stocks and shares not bearing fixed interest. **4** the net value of a mortgaged property after the deduction of charges. **5** (**Equity**) *Brit.* the actors' trade union. [ME f. OF *equité* f. L *aequitas -tatis* f. *aequus* fair]

■ **1, 2** fairness, justice, rightfulness, justness, even-handedness, equitableness, fair play, fair-mindedness, objectivity, objectiveness, disinterest, dispassionateness, disinterestedness, neutrality, impartiality, open-mindedness, tolerance, judiciousness.

equivalent /ikwívvələnt/ *adj.* & *n.* ● *adj.* **1** (often foll. by *to*) equal in value, amount, importance, etc. **2** corresponding. **3** (of words) having the same meaning. **4** having the same result. **5** *Chem.* (of a substance) equal in combining or displacing capacity. ● *n.* **1** an equivalent thing, amount, word, etc. **2** (in full **equivalent weight**) *Chem.* the weight of a substance that can combine with or displace one gram of hydrogen or eight grams of oxygen. □□ **equivalence** *n.* **equivalency** *n.* **equivalently** *adv.* [ME f. OF f. LL *aequivalēre* (as EQUI-, *valēre* be worth)]

■ *adj.* **1** equal, (virtually *or* nearly *or* (pretty) much) the same, one and the same, identical, interchangeable, comparable, analogous, similar, parallel, not unlike, *archaic* or *literary* coequal; like; alike, close, akin, along the same lines; commensurate, of a piece *or* kind, consistent, in keeping *or* line, tantamount. **2** see COORDINATE *adj.* 1. **3** see SYNONYMOUS 1. ● *n.* **1** match, counterpart, coordinate, twin; equal, peer, fellow, *archaic or literary* coequal; parallel, analogue, replica, copy.

equivocal /ikwívvək'l/ *adj.* **1** of double or doubtful meaning; ambiguous. **2** of uncertain nature. **3** (of a person, character, etc.) questionable, suspect. ▫▫ **equivocality** /-kálliti/ *n.* **equivocally** *adv.* **equivocalness** *n.* [LL *aequivocus* (as EQUI-, *vocare* call)]

■ **1, 2** equivocating, dubious, doubtful; ambiguous, vague, obscure, hazy, misty, foggy, muddy, murky, blurry, blurred, ill-defined, indistinct, obscure, fuzzy, unclear, indefinite, imprecise, inexact, undefined, unspecified, non-specific, inexplicit, indistinct, indeterminate, uncertain, confused, confusing, mysterious, mystifying, enigmatic(al), cryptic, puzzling, oracular, Delphic, Delphian. **3** see SUSPECT *adj.* ▫▫ **equivocality, equivocalness** see AMBIGUITY 1a. **equivocally** ambiguously; see also *vaguely* (VAGUE).

equivocate /ikwívvəkayt/ *v.intr.* use ambiguity to conceal the truth. ▫▫ **equivocacy** *n.* **equivocation** /-káysh'n/ *n.* **equivocator** *n.* **equivocatory** *adj.* [ME f. LL *aequivocare* (as EQUIVOCAL)]

■ prevaricate, quibble, hedge, fence, tergiversate, double-talk, palter, be evasive, beat about the bush. ▫▫ **equivocacy, equivocation** see AMBIGUITY 1a, b.

equivoque /ékwivōk/ *n.* (also **equivoke**) a pun or ambiguity. [ME in the sense 'equivocal' f. OF *equivoque* or LL *aequivocus* EQUIVOCAL]

■ see PUN[1] *n.*

ER *abbr.* **1** Queen Elizabeth. **2** King Edward. [L *Elizabetha Regina, Edwardus Rex*]

Er *symb. Chem.* the element erbium.

er /er/ *int.* expressing hesitation or a pause in speech. [imit.]

-er[1] /ər/ *suffix* forming nouns from nouns, adjectives, and many verbs, denoting: **1** a person, animal, or thing that performs a specified action or activity (*cobbler*; *lover*; *executioner*; *poker*; *computer*; *eye-opener*). **2** a person or thing that has a specified attribute or form (*foreigner*; *four-wheeler*; *second-rater*). **3** a person concerned with a specified thing or subject (*hatter*; *geographer*). **4** a person belonging to a specified place or group (*villager*; *New Zealander*; *sixth-former*). [orig. 'one who has to do with': OE *-ere* f. Gmc]

-er[2] /ər/ *suffix* forming the comparative of adjectives (*wider*; *hotter*) and adverbs (*faster*). [OE *-ra* (adj.), *-or* (adv.) f. Gmc]

-er[3] /ər/ *suffix* used in slang formations usu. distorting the root word (*rugger*; *soccer*). [prob. an extension of -ER[1]]

-er[4] /ər/ *suffix* forming iterative and frequentative verbs (*blunder*; *glimmer*; *twitter*). [OE *-erian*, *-rian* f. Gmc]

-er[5] /ər/ *suffix* **1** forming nouns and adjectives through OF or AF, corresponding to: **a** L *-aris* (*sampler*) (cf. -AR[1]). **b** L *-arius*, *-arium* (*butler*; *carpenter*; *danger*). **c** (through OF *-eüre*) L *-atura* or (through OF *-eör*) L *-atorium* (see COUNTER[1], FRITTER[2]). **2** = -OR.

-er[6] /ər/ *suffix* esp. *Law* forming nouns denoting verbal action or a document effecting this (*cesser*; *disclaimer*; *misnomer*). ¶ The same ending occurs in *dinner* and *supper*. [AF infin. ending of verbs]

era /éerə/ *n.* **1** a system of chronology reckoning from a noteworthy event (*the Christian era*). **2** a large distinct period of time, esp. regarded historically (*the pre-Roman era*). **3** a date at which an era begins. **4** *Geol.* a major division of time. [LL *aera* number expressed in figures (pl. of *aes aeris* money, treated as fem. sing.)]

■ **1, 2** age, period, time(s), day(s), epoch; aeon.

eradicate /iráddikayt/ *v.tr.* root out; destroy completely; get rid of. ▫▫ **eradicable** *adj.* **eradication** /-káysh'n/ *n.* **eradicator** *n.* [ME f. L *eradicare* tear up by the roots (as E-, *radix -icis* root)]

■ see REMOVE *v.* 2b.

erase /iráyz/ *v.tr.* **1** rub out; obliterate. **2** remove all traces of (*erased it from my memory*). **3** remove recorded material from (a magnetic tape or medium). ▫▫ **erasable** *adj.* **erasure** *n.* [L *eradere eras-* (as E-, *radere* scrape)]

■ **1** rub *or* wipe out, wipe, efface, delete, blot out, obliterate, cancel, scratch out, cross *or* rule out, strike out *or* off, cut (out), expunge, censor, expurgate, *Printing* dele *colloq.* scrub. **2** remove, efface, obliterate, eradicate, eliminate, destroy, annihilate, do away with, get rid of.

eraser /iráyzər/ *n.* a thing that erases, esp. a piece of rubber or plastic used for removing pencil and ink marks.

erbium /érbiəm/ *n. Chem.* a soft silvery metallic element of the lanthanide series, occurring naturally in apatite and xenotine. ¶ Symb.: **Er**. [mod.L f. *Ytterby* in Sweden]

ere /air/ *prep.* & *conj. poet.* or *archaic* before (of time) (*ere noon*; *ere they come*). [OE *ǣr* f. Gmc]

erect /iréckt/ *adj.* & *v.* ● *adj.* **1** upright, vertical. **2** (of the penis, clitoris, or nipples) enlarged and rigid, esp. in sexual excitement. **3** (of hair) bristling, standing up from the skin. ● *v.tr.* **1** raise; set upright. **2** build. **3** establish (*erect a theory*). ▫▫ **erectable** *adj.* **erectly** *adv.* **erectness** *n.* **erector** *n.* [ME f. L *erigere erect-* set up (as E-, *regere* direct)]

■ *adj.* **1** (bolt) upright, vertical, standing (up), upstanding, straight, plumb, *joc.* perpendicular; on one's feet. **2** enlarged, rigid, swollen, tumescent, stiff, hard. **3** bristling, upright, (standing) on end. ● *v.* **1, 2** raise, set up, assemble, put together, fabricate, manufacture, frame, make, build, put up, construct; pitch. **3** establish, found, set up, put together, frame, formulate, institute, form, devise, create.

erectile /iréktīl/ *adj.* that can be erected or become erect. ▫ **erectile tissue** *Physiol.* animal tissue that is capable of becoming rigid, esp. with sexual excitement. [F *érectile* (as ERECT)]

erection /iréksh'n/ *n.* **1** the act or an instance of erecting; the state of being erected. **2** a building or structure. **3** *Physiol.* an enlarged and erect state of erectile tissue, esp. of the penis. [F *érection* or L *erectio* (as ERECTILE)]

■ **1** see FABRICATION 1. **2** see BUILDING.

E-region var. of E-LAYER.

eremite /érrimīt/ *n.* a hermit or recluse (esp. Christian). ▫▫ **eremitic** /-míttik/ *adj.* **eremitical** /-míttik'l/ *adj.* **eremitism** *n.* [ME f. OF, var. of *hermite*, *ermite* HERMIT]

■ see HERMIT.

erethism /érrithiz'm/ *n.* **1** an excessive sensitivity to stimulation of any part of the body, esp. the sexual organs. **2** a state of abnormal mental excitement or irritation. [F *éréthisme* f. Gk *erethismos* f. *erethizō* irritate]

erg[1] /erg/ *n. Physics* a unit of work or energy, equal to the work done by a force of one dyne when its point of application moves one centimetre in the direction of action of the force. [Gk *ergon* work]

erg[2] /erg/ *n.* (*pl.* **ergs** or **areg** /aáreg/) an area of shifting sand-dunes in the Sahara. [F f. Arab. *ʿirj*]

ergo /érgō/ *adv.* therefore. [L]

■ see THEREFORE.

ergocalciferol /érgōkalsíffərol/ *n.* = CALCIFEROL. [ERGOT + CALCIFEROL]

ergonomics /érgənómmiks/ *n.* the study of the efficiency of persons in their working environment. ▫▫ **ergonomic** *adj.* **ergonomist** /ergónnəmist/ *n.* [Gk *ergon* work: cf. ECONOMICS]

ergosterol /ergóstərol/ *n. Biochem.* a plant sterol that is converted to vitamin D_2 when irradiated with ultraviolet light. [ERGOT, after CHOLESTEROL]

ergot /érgət/ *n.* **1** a disease of rye and other cereals caused by the fungus *Claviceps purpurea*. **2 a** this fungus. **b** the dried spore-containing structures of this, used as a medicine to aid childbirth. [F f. OF *argot* cock's spur, from the appearance produced]

ergotism /érgətiz'm/ *n.* poisoning produced by eating food affected by ergot.

erica /érrikə/ *n.* any shrub or heath of the genus *Erica*, with small leathery leaves and bell-like flowers. ▫▫ **ericaceous** /-káyshəss/ *adj.* [L f. Gk *ereikē* heath]

erigeron /iriggəron/ *n.* any hardy composite herb of the genus *Erigeron*, with daisy-like flowers. [Gk *ērigerōn* f. *ēri* early + *gerōn* old man, because some species bear grey down]

Erin /érrin, éerin/ *n. archaic* or *poet.* Ireland. [Ir.]

Erinys /erínniss/ *n.* (*pl.* **Erinyes** /-ni-eez/) *Mythol.* a Fury. [Gk]

eristic /erístik/ *adj.* & *n.* ● *adj.* **1** of or characterized by disputation. **2** (of an argument or arguer) aiming at winning rather than at reaching the truth. ● *n.* **1** the practice of disputation. **2** an exponent of disputation. □□ **eristically** *adv.* [Gk *eristikos* f. *erizō* wrangle f. *eris* strife]

erk /erk/ *n. Brit. sl.* **1** a naval rating. **2** an aircraftman. **3** a disliked person. [20th c.: orig. unkn.]

erl-king /érl-king/ *n.* (in Germanic mythology) a bearded giant or goblin who lures little children to the land of death. [G *Erlkönig* alder-king, a mistransl. of Da. *ellerkonge* king of the elves]

ERM *abbr.* exchange-rate mechanism (of the European monetary system).

ermine /érmin/ *n.* (*pl.* same or **ermines**) **1** the stoat, esp. when in its white winter fur. **2** its white fur, used as trimming for the robes of judges, peers, etc. **3** *Heraldry* a white fur marked with black spots. □□ **ermined** *adj.* [ME f. OF (*h*)*ermine* prob. f. med.L (*mus*) *Armenius* Armenian (mouse)]

ern *US* var. of ERNE.

-ern /ərn/ *suffix* forming adjectives (*northern*). [OE *-erne* f. Gmc]

erne /ern/ *n.* (*US* **ern**) *poet.* a sea eagle. [OE *earn* f. Gmc]

Ernie /érni/ *n.* (in the UK) a device for drawing prize-winning numbers of Premium Bonds. [initial letters of *electronic random number indicator equipment*]

erode /irṓd/ *v.* **1** *tr.* & *intr.* wear away, destroy or be destroyed gradually. **2** *tr. Med.* (of ulcers etc.) destroy (tissue) little by little. □□ **erodible** *adj.* [F *éroder* or L *erodere eros-* (as E-, *rodere ros-* gnaw)]

■ **1** wear (away *or* down), eat away (at), gnaw away, consume, devour, corrode, grind down, abrade, rub down *or* away, whittle (away), pare (down *or* away), wash away; reduce, diminish, destroy.

erogenous /irójinəss/ *adj.* **1** (esp. of a part of the body) sensitive to sexual stimulation. **2** giving rise to sexual desire or excitement. [as EROTIC + -GENOUS]

■ **2** see EROTIC.

erosion /irṓzh'n/ *n.* **1** *Geol.* the wearing away of the earth's surface by the action of water, wind, etc. **2** the act or an instance of eroding; the process of being eroded. □□ **erosional** *adj.* **erosive** *adj.* [F *érosion* f. L *erosio* (as ERODE)]

■ wearing (away *or* down), eating away, gnawing away, corrosion, corroding, grinding down, washing away, abrasion, abrading, fraying, wear (and tear), attrition, damage, weathering.

erotic /iróttik/ *adj.* of or causing sexual love, esp. tending to arouse sexual desire or excitement. □□ **erotically** *adv.* [F *érotique* f. Gk *erōtikos* f. *erōs erōtos* sexual love]

■ sensual, suggestive, titillating, risqué, bawdy, ribald, seductive, voluptuous, lustful, sexy; amatory, sexual, venereal, amorous, anacreontic; erogenous, erotogenic, carnal, arousing, rousing, aphrodisiac, libidinous, lubricious, prurient, lascivious, lewd, salacious, obscene, indecent, pornographic, dirty, filthy, blue, *formal* concupiscent, *colloq.* or *joc.* naughty.

erotica /iróttikə/ *n.pl.* erotic literature or art.

■ see PORNOGRAPHY *n.*

eroticism /iróttisiz'm/ *n.* **1** erotic nature or character. **2** the use of or reponse to erotic images or stimulation.

erotism /érrətiz'm/ *n.* sexual desire or excitement; eroticism.

eroto- /iróttō, irṓtō/ *comb. form* erotic, eroticism. [Gk *erōs erōtos* sexual love]

erotogenic /iróttəjénnik/ *adj.* (also **erotogenous** /érrətójinəss/) = EROGENOUS.

erotology /érrətólləji/ *n.* the study of sexual love.

erotomania /iróttəmáyniə/ *n.* **1** excessive or morbid erotic desire. **2** a preoccupation with sexual passion. □□ **erotomaniac** /-niak/ *n.*

err /er/ *v.intr.* **1** be mistaken or incorrect. **2** do wrong; sin. □ **err on the right side** act so that the least harmful of possible errors is the most likely to occur. **err on the side of** act with a specified bias (*errs on the side of generosity*). [ME f. OF *errer* f. L *errare* stray: rel. to Goth. *airzei* error, *airzjan* lead astray]

■ **1** be wrong, be in error, be mistaken, be inaccurate, be incorrect, be in the wrong, go wrong, go astray, make a mistake, miscalculate, (make a) blunder, make a mess, make a *faux pas*, *colloq.* slip (up), drop a brick, *sl.* drop a clanger, goof (up), *Brit. sl.* boob. **2** do wrong, sin, misbehave, lapse, fall, *literary or archaic* trespass.

errand /érrənd/ *n.* **1** a short journey, esp. on another's behalf, to take a message, collect goods, etc. **2** the object of such a journey. □ **errand of mercy** a journey to relieve suffering etc. [OE *ǣrende* f. Gmc]

■ **1** see JOURNEY *n.* **2** object, assignment, charge, task, duty, commission; see also MISSION 1a.

errant /érrənt/ *adj.* **1** erring; deviating from an accepted standard. **2** *literary* or *archaic* travelling in search of adventure (*knight errant*). □□ **errancy** *n.* (in sense 1). **errantry** *n.* (in sense 2). [ME: sense 1 formed as ERR: sense 2 f. OF *errer* ult. f. LL *itinerare* f. *iter* journey]

■ **1** see ECCENTRIC *adj.* 1. **2** see *travelling* (TRAVEL), VENTURESOME 1.

erratic /iráttik/ *adj.* **1** inconsistently variable in conduct, opinions, etc.; unpredictable, eccentric. **2** uncertain in movement. □ **erratic block** *Geol.* a large rock carried from a distance by glacial action. □□ **erratically** *adv.* [ME f. OF *erratique* f. L *erraticus* (as ERR)]

■ **1** inconsistent, variable, irregular, unpredictable, random, haphazard, capricious, wayward, changeable, flighty, unreliable, unstable; peculiar, abnormal, wayward, odd, eccentric, outlandish, strange, unusual, unorthodox, extraordinary, queer, quaint, bizarre, weird, unconventional. **2** wandering, meandering, planetary, directionless, aimless, haphazard.

erratum /iraátəm/ *n.* (*pl.* **errata** /-tə/) an error in printing or writing, esp. (in *pl.*) a list of corrected errors attached to a book etc. [L, neut. past part. (as ERR)]

■ see MISPRINT *n.*

erroneous /irṓniəss/ *adj.* incorrect; arising from error. □□ **erroneously** *adv.* **erroneousness** *n.* [ME f. OF *erroneus* or L *erroneus* f. *erro -onis* vagabond (as ERR)]

■ incorrect, wrong, mistaken, false, unsound, invalid, untrue, faulty, misleading, flawed, fallacious, spurious, inaccurate, inexact, imprecise; amiss, awry, off course, *colloq.* off the mark, off (the) beam.

error /érrər/ *n.* **1** a mistake. **2** the condition of being wrong in conduct or judgement (*led into error*). **3** a wrong opinion or judgement. **4** the amount by which something is incorrect or inaccurate in a calculation or measurement. □□ **errorless** *adj.* [ME f. OF *errour* f. L *error -oris* (as ERR)]

■ **1** mistake, inaccuracy, fault, flaw, solecism, slip, blunder, gaffe, foul-up, *colloq.* slip-up, howler, *sl.* clanger, bloomer, booboo, fluff, boner, goof, *Brit. sl.* boob; erratum, misprint, *Printing* literal, *colloq.* typo. **2** sin, transgression, indiscretion, wrongdoing, misconduct, iniquity, evil, wickedness, flagitiousness; (*in error*) wrong, mistaken, incorrect, at fault; mistakenly, incorrectly, by mistake, erroneously.

ersatz /érzats, áir-/ *adj.* & *n.* ● *adj.* substitute, imitation (esp. of inferior quality). ● *n.* an ersatz thing. [G, = replacement]

■ *adj.* see IMITATION *adj.*

Erse /erss/ *adj.* & *n.* ● *adj.* Irish or Highland Gaelic. ● *n.* the Gaelic language. [early Sc. form of IRISH]

erst /erst/ *adv. archaic* formerly; of old. [OE *ǣrest* superl. of *ǣr*: see ERE]

erstwhile /érstwīl/ *adj.* & *adv.* ● *adj.* former, previous. ● *adv. archaic* = ERST.

■ *adj.* see FORMER[1] 2.

erubescent /érroobéss'nt/ *adj.* reddening, blushing. [L *erubescere* (as E-, *rubescere* f. *rubēre* be red)]

eructation /éeruktáysh'n/ *n.* the act or an instance of belching. [L *eructatio* f. *eructare* (as E-, *ructare* belch)]

erudite /érroodīt/ *adj.* **1** (of a person) learned. **2** (of writing etc.) showing great learning. □□ **eruditely** *adv.* **erudition** /-dish'n/ *n.* [ME f. L *eruditus* past part. of *erudire* instruct, train (as E-, *rudis* untrained)]
■ see LEARNED 1.

erupt /irúpt/ *v.intr.* **1** break out suddenly or dramatically. **2** (of a volcano) become active and eject lava etc. **3 a** (of a rash, boil, etc.) appear on the skin. **b** (of the skin) produce a rash etc. **4** (of the teeth) break through the gums in normal development. □□ **eruption** *n.* **eruptive** *adj.* [L *erumpere erupt-* (as E-, *rumpere* break)]
■ **2** spout, gush, explode, blow up, vomit, spit, *colloq.* throw up. **3** break out, come out, appear, flare up. □□ **eruption** outbreak, outburst, discharge, emission, bursting forth, expulsion, explosion, spouting, vomiting (up *or* forth), belching forth; rash.

-ery /əri/ *suffix* forming nouns denoting: **1** a class or kind (*greenery*; *machinery*; *citizenry*). **2** employment; state or condition (*archery*; *dentistry*; *slavery*; *bravery*). **3** a place of work or cultivation or breeding (*brewery*; *orangery*; *rookery*). **4** behaviour (*mimicry*). **5** often *derog.* all that has to do with (*knavery*; *popery*; *tomfoolery*). [ME, from or after F *-erie*, *-ere* ult. f. L *-ario-*, *-ator*]

erysipelas /érrisíppiləss/ *n. Med.* a streptococcal infection producing inflammation and a deep red colour on the skin, esp. of the face and scalp. [ME f. L f. Gk *erusipelas*, perh. rel. to *eruthros* red + a root *pel-* skin]

erythema /érritheémə/ *n.* a superficial reddening of the skin, usu. in patches. □□ **erythemal** *adj.* **erythematic** /-thimáttik/ *adj.* [mod.L f. Gk *eruthēma* f. *eruthainō* be red f. *eruthros* red]

erythro- /iríthrō/ *comb. form* red. [Gk *eruthros* red]

erythroblast /iríthrōblast/ *n.* an immature erythrocyte. [G]

erythrocyte /iríthrōsīt/ *n.* a red blood cell, which contains the pigment haemoglobin and transports oxygen and carbon dioxide to and from the tissues. □□ **erythrocytic** /-síttik/ *adj.*

erythroid /érrithroyd/ *adj.* of or relating to erythrocytes.

Es *symb. Chem.* the element einsteinium.

-es[1] /iz/ *suffix* forming plurals of nouns ending in sibilant sounds (such words in *-e* dropping the *e*) (*kisses*; *cases*; *boxes*; *churches*). [var. of -s[1]]

-es[2] /iz, z/ *suffix* forming the 3rd person sing. present of verbs ending in sibilant sounds (such words in *-e* dropping the *e*) and ending in *-o* (but not *-oo*) (*goes*; *places*; *pushes*). [var. of -s[2]]

ESA *abbr.* European Space Agency.

escadrille /éskədríl/ *n.* a French squadron of aeroplanes. [F]

escalade /éskəláyd/ *n.* the scaling of fortified walls with ladders, as a military attack. [F f. Sp. *escalada*, *-ado* f. med.L *scalare* f. *scala* ladder]

escalate /éskəlayt/ *v.* **1** *intr.* & *tr.* increase or develop (usu. rapidly) by stages. **2** *tr.* cause (an action, activity, or process) to become more intense. □□ **escalation** /-láysh'n/ *n.* [back-form. f. ESCALATOR]
■ see INTENSIFY.

escalator /éskəlaytər/ *n.* a moving staircase consisting of a circulating belt forming steps. [f. the stem of *escalade* 'climb a wall by ladder' + -ATOR]

escallonia /éskəlṓniə/ *n.* any evergreen shrub of the genus *Escallonia*, bearing rose-red flowers. [*Escallon*, 18th-c. Sp. traveller]

escallop /iskálləp/ *n.* **1** = SCALLOP 1, 2. **2** = ESCALOPE. **3** (in *pl.*) = SCALLOP 3. **4** *Heraldry* a scallop shell as a device. [formed as ESCALOPE]

escalope /éskəlop/ *n.* a thin slice of meat without any bone, esp. from a leg of veal. [F (in OF = shell): see SCALLOP]
■ see SLICE *n.* 1.

escapade /éskəpáyd/ *n.* a piece of daring or reckless behaviour. [F f. Prov. or Sp. *escapada* (as ESCAPE)]
■ see ADVENTURE *n.* 2.

escape /iskáyp/ *v.* & *n.* ● *v.* **1** *intr.* (often foll. by *from*) get free of the restriction or control of a place, person, etc. **2** *intr.* (of a gas, liquid, etc.) leak from a container or pipe etc. **3** *intr.* succeed in avoiding danger, punishment, etc.; get off safely. **4** *tr.* get completely free of (a person, grasp, etc.). **5** *tr.* avoid or elude (a commitment, danger, etc.). **6** *tr.* elude the notice or memory of (*nothing escapes you*; *the name escaped me*). **7** *tr.* (of words etc.) issue unawares from (a person, a person's lips). ● *n.* **1** the act or an instance of escaping; avoidance of danger, injury, etc. **2** the state of having escaped (*was a narrow escape*). **3** a means of escaping (often *attrib.*: *escape hatch*). **4** a leakage of gas etc. **5** a temporary relief from reality or worry. **6** a garden plant running wild. □ **escape clause** *Law* a clause specifying the conditions under which a contracting party is free from an obligation. **escape road** a road for a vehicle to turn into if unable to negotiate a bend, descent, etc., safely (esp. on a racetrack). **escape velocity** the minimum velocity needed to escape from the gravitational field of a body. **escape wheel** a toothed wheel in the escapement of a watch or clock. □□ **escapable** *adj.* **escaper** *n.* [ME f. AF, ONF *escaper* ult. f. med.L (as EX-[1], *cappa* cloak)]
■ *v.* **1** get away, break out *or* free *or* loose, bolt, flee, fly, run away *or* off, decamp, abscond, steal *or* slip off, steal *or* slip away, take off, take to one's heels, take French leave, disappear, vanish, *Brit.* levant, *colloq.* clear out, make oneself scarce, skedaddle, do a moonlight flit, skip (it), scram, *US colloq.* hightail (it), *sl.* blow, cut and run, cut, take a powder, *Austral.* & *NZ sl.* shoot through, *Brit sl.* do a bunk, mizzle off, *US sl.* vamoose, go on the lam. **2** leak, drain, issue, seep, discharge, emanate. **5** avoid, elude, evade, dodge. **6** elude, evade, baffle, stump, mystify, puzzle. ● *n.* **1** getaway, flight, departure, decampment, bolt, jailbreak, prison-break, break, break-out. **4** leakage, leaking, seepage, seeping, drainage, draining, leak, discharge, outpouring, outflow, effluence, efflux, effluxion. **5** relief, distraction, diversion, recreation.

escapee /iskaypeé/ *n.* a person, esp. a prisoner, who has escaped.
■ see RUNAWAY 1.

escapement /iskáypmənt/ *n.* **1** the part of a clock or watch that connects and regulates the motive power. **2** the part of the mechanism in a piano that enables the hammer to fall back immediately it has struck the string. **3** *archaic* a means of escape. [F *échappement* f. *échapper* ESCAPE]

escapism /iskáypiz'm/ *n.* the tendency to seek distraction and relief from reality, esp. in the arts or through fantasy. □□ **escapist** *n.* & *adj.*

escapology /éskəpólləji/ *n.* the methods and techniques of escaping from confinement, esp. as a form of entertainment. □□ **escapologist** *n.*

escargot /eskaárgō/ *n.* an edible snail. [F]

escarpment /iskaárpmənt/ *n.* (also **escarp**) *Geol.* a long steep slope at the edge of a plateau etc. [F *escarpement* f. *escarpe* SCARP]
■ see CLIFF.

-esce /ess/ *suffix* forming verbs, usu. initiating action (*effervesce*; *fluoresce*). [from or after L *-escere*]

-escent /éss'nt/ *suffix* forming adjectives denoting the beginning of a state or action (*effervescent*; *fluorescent*). □□ **-escence** *suffix* forming nouns. [from or after F *-escent* or L *-escent-*, pres. part. stem of verbs in *-escere*]

eschatology /éskətólləji/ *n.* the part of theology concerned with death and final destiny. □□ **eschatological** /-təlójik'l/ *adj.* **eschatologist** *n.* [Gk *eskhatos* last + -LOGY]

escheat /iss-cheét/ *n.* & *v. hist.* ● *n.* **1** the reversion of property to the State, or (in feudal law) to a lord, on the owner's dying without legal heirs. **2** property affected by this. ● *v.* **1** *tr.* hand over (property) as an escheat. **2** *tr.* confiscate. **3** *intr.* revert by escheat. [ME f. OF *eschete*, ult. f. L *excidere* (as EX-[1], *cadere* fall)]

eschew /iss-chóō/ *v.tr. literary* avoid; abstain from. ▫▫ **eschewal** *n.* [ME f. OF *eschiver*, ult. f. Gmc: rel. to SHY[1]]
■ see AVOID 1.

eschscholtzia /iskólshə, eshóltsiə/ *n.* any yellow-flowering plant of the genus *Eschscholtzia*, esp. the Californian poppy (see POPPY). [J. F. von *Eschscholtz*, Ger. botanist d. 1831]

escort *n.* & *v.* ● *n.* /éskort/ **1** one or more persons, vehicles, ships, etc., accompanying a person, vehicle, etc., esp. for protection or security or as a mark of rank or status. **2** a person accompanying a person of the opposite sex socially. **3** a person or group acting as a guide or leader, esp. on a journey. ● *v.tr.* /iskórt/ act as an escort to. [F *escorte*, *escorter* f. It. *scorta* fem. past part. of *scorgere* conduct]
■ *n.* **1** guard, bodyguard, convoy, safe conduct, protection; guardian, protector, chaperon, companion, cortège, retinue, entourage, *Brit.* usher. **2** companion, boyfriend, partner, beau; *US colloq.* date; gigolo. **3** guide, attendant, conductor, leader, cicerone. ● *v.* accompany, shepherd, squire, usher, conduct, guide, attend; guard, convoy, protect, watch over.

escritoire /éskritwaár/ *n.* a writing-desk with drawers etc. [F f. L *scriptorium* writing-room: see SCRIPTORIUM]

escrow /éskrō/ *n.* & *v. Law* ● *n.* **1** money, property, or a written bond, kept in the custody of a third party until a specified condition has been fulfilled. **2** the status of this (*in escrow*). ● *v.tr.* place in escrow. [AF *escrowe*, OF *escroe* scrap, scroll, f. med.L *scroda* f. Gmc]

escudo /eskyóōdō/ *n.* (*pl.* **-os**) the principal monetary unit of Portugal and Chile. [Sp. & Port. f. L *scutum* shield]

esculent /éskyoolənt/ *adj.* & *n.* ● *adj.* fit to eat; edible. ● *n.* an edible substance. [L *esculentus* f. *esca* food]
■ *adj.* see EDIBLE *adj.*

escutcheon /iskúchən/ *n.* **1** a shield or emblem bearing a coat of arms. **2** the middle part of a ship's stern where the name is placed. **3** the protective plate around a keyhole or door-handle. ▫▫ **escutcheoned** *adj.* [AF & ONF *escuchon* ult. f. L *scutum* shield]
■ **1** see SYMBOL *n.*

Esd. *abbr.* Esdras (Apocrypha).

ESE *abbr.* east-south-east.

-ese /eez/ *suffix* forming adjectives and nouns denoting: **1** an inhabitant or language of a country or city (*Japanese*; *Milanese*; *Viennese*). ¶ Plural forms are the same. **2** often *derog.* character or style, esp. of language (*officialese*). [OF *-eis* ult. f. L *-ensis*]

esker /éskər/ *n.* (also **eskar**) *Geol.* a long ridge of post-glacial gravel in river valleys. [Ir. *eiscir*]

Eskimo /éskimō/ *n.* & *adj.* ● *n.* (*pl.* same or **-os**) **1** a member of a people inhabiting N. Canada, Alaska, Greenland, and E. Siberia. **2** the language of this people. ● *adj.* of or relating to the Eskimos or their language. ¶ The term *Inuit* is preferred by the people themselves. [Da. f. F *Esquimaux* (pl.) f. Algonquian]

Esky /éski/ *n.* (*pl.* **-ies**) *Austral. propr.* a portable insulated container for keeping food or drink cool. [prob. f. ESKIMO, with ref. to their cold climate]

ESN *abbr.* educationally subnormal.
■ see DEFECTIVE *adj.* 2.

esophagus *US* var. of OESOPHAGUS.

esoteric /éessōtérrik, éssō-/ *adj.* **1** intelligible only to those with special knowledge. **2** (of a belief etc.) intended only for the initiated. ▫▫ **esoterical** *adj.* **esoterically** *adv.* **esotericism** /-risiz'm/ *n.* **esotericist** /-risist/ *n.* [Gk *esōterikos* f. *esōterō* compar. of *esō* within]
■ see OCCULT *adj.* 2.

ESP *abbr.* extrasensory perception.

espadrille /éspədril/ *n.* a light canvas shoe with a plaited fibre sole. [F f. Prov. *espardillo* f. *espart* ESPARTO]

espalier /ispálliər/ *n.* **1** a lattice-work along which the branches of a tree or shrub are trained to grow flat against a wall etc. **2** a tree or shrub trained in this way. [F f. It. *spalliera* f. *spalla* shoulder]

esparto /espaártō/ *n.* (*pl.* **-os**) (in full **esparto grass**) a coarse grass, *Stipa tenacissima*, native to Spain and N. Africa, with tough narrow leaves, used to make ropes, wickerwork, and good-quality paper. [Sp. f. L *spartum* f. Gk *sparton* rope]

especial /ispésh'l/ *adj.* **1** notable, exceptional. **2** attributed or belonging chiefly to one person or thing (*your especial charm*). [ME f. OF f. L *specialis* special]
■ **1** see SPECIAL *adj.* 1a. **2** see SPECIAL *adj.* 1b, 2.

especially /ispéshəli, ispéshli/ *adv.* chiefly; much more than in other cases.
■ chiefly, mainly, predominantly, primarily, principally, first, first and foremost, firstly, first of all, above all; particularly, specially, specifically, exceptionally, conspicuously, singularly, remarkably, extraordinarily, unusually, uncommonly, peculiarly, outstandingly, notably, strikingly, noticeably, markedly, signally; *abbr.* esp.

Esperanto /éspəránto/ *n.* an artificial universal language devised in 1887, based on roots common to the chief European languages. ▫▫ **Esperantist** *n.* [the pen-name (f. L *sperare* hope) of its inventor, L. L. Zamenhof, Polish physician d. 1917]

espial /ispíəl/ *n.* **1** the act or an instance of catching sight of or of being seen. **2** *archaic* spying. [ME f. OF *espiaille* f. *espier*: see ESPY]

espionage /éspiənaazh/ *n.* the practice of spying or of using spies, esp. by governments. [F *espionnage* f. *espionner* f. *espion* SPY]
■ see *spying* (SPY).

esplanade /éspləna̋yd/ *n.* **1** a long open level area for walking on, esp. beside the sea. **2** a level space separating a fortress from a town. [F f. Sp. *esplanada* f. *esplanar* make level f. L *explanare* (as EX-[1], *planus* level)]
■ see PROMENADE *n.* 1.

espousal /ispówz'l/ *n.* **1** (foll. by *of*) the espousing of a cause etc. **2** *archaic* a marriage or betrothal. [ME f. OF *espousailles* f. L *sponsalia* neut. pl. of *sponsalis* (as ESPOUSE)]
■ **1** see *promotion* (PROMOTE).

espouse /ispówz/ *v.tr.* **1** adopt or support (a cause, doctrine, etc.). **2** *archaic* **a** (usu. of a man) marry. **b** (usu. foll. by *to*) give (a woman) in marriage. ▫▫ **espouser** *n.* [ME f. OF *espouser* f. L *sponsare* f. *sponsus* past part. of *spondēre* betroth]
■ **1** see PROMOTE 2. **2 a** see WED 1.

espresso /esprésso/ *n.* (also **expresso** /eksprésso/) (*pl.* **-os**) **1** strong concentrated black coffee made under steam pressure. **2** a machine for making this. [It., = pressed out]

esprit /espreé/ *n.* sprightliness, wit. ▫ ***esprit de corps*** /də kór/ a feeling of devotion to and pride in the group one belongs to. ***esprit de l'escalier*** /də leskályay/ an apt retort or clever remark that comes to mind after the chance to make it is gone. [F f. L *spiritus* SPIRIT (+ *corps* body, *escalier* stairs)]
■ see VERVE.

espy /ispí/ *v.tr.* (**-ies, -ied**) *literary* catch sight of; perceive. [ME f. OF *espier*: see SPY]
■ see PERCEIVE 1.

Esq. *abbr.* Esquire.

-esque /esk/ *suffix* forming adjectives meaning 'in the style of' or 'resembling' (*romanesque*; *Schumannesque*; *statuesque*). [F f. It. *-esco* f. med.L *-iscus*]

Esquimau /éskimō/ *n.* (*pl.* **-aux** /-mōz/) = ESKIMO . [F]

esquire /iskwír/ *n.* **1** (usu. as abbr. **Esq.**) *Brit.* a title appended to a man's surname when no other form of address is used, esp. as a form of address for letters. **2** *archaic* = SQUIRE. [ME f. OF *esquier* f. L *scutarius* shield-bearer f. *scutum* shield]

ESR *abbr. Physics* electron spin resonance .

-ess[1] /iss/ *suffix* forming nouns denoting females (*actress*; *lioness*; *mayoress*). [from or after F *-esse* f. LL *-issa* f. Gk *-issa*]

-ess[2] /ess/ *suffix* forming abstract nouns from adjectives (*duress*). [ME f. F *-esse* f. L *-itia*; cf. -ICE]

essay *n.* & *v.* ● *n.* /éssay/ **1** a composition, usu. short and in prose, on any subject. **2** (often foll. by *at*, *in*) *formal* an attempt. ● *v.tr.* /essáy/ *formal* attempt, try. □□ **essayist** *n.* [ME f. ASSAY, assim. to F *essayer* ult. f. LL *exagium* weighing f. *exigere* weigh: see EXACT]

■ *n.* **1** composition, article, paper, piece, *US* theme; tract; thesis, dissertation. **2** attempt, try, effort, endeavour, venture; *colloq.* go, shot. ● *v.* attempt, try, undertake, tackle, test, go about, *colloq.* have a shot *or* go at, have *or* take a crack at, have *or* take a stab at, *sl.* have a whack *or* bash at.

essence /éss'nss/ *n.* **1** the indispensable quality or element identifying a thing or determining its character; fundamental nature or inherent characteristics. **2 a** an extract obtained by distillation etc., esp. a volatile oil. **b** a perfume or scent, esp. made from a plant or animal substance. **3** the constituent of a plant that determines its chemical properties. **4** an abstract entity; the reality underlying a phenomenon or all phenomena. □ **in essence** fundamentally. **of the essence** indispensable, vital. [ME f. OF f. L *essentia* f. *esse* be]

■ **1** quintessence, substance, core, heart, pith, kernel, marrow, soul, crux, cornerstone, *Philos.* quiddity; nature, spirit, being, *colloq.* bottom line. **2 a** extract, concentrate, distillate, distillation, quintessence, elixir, tincture, decoction, attar. **b** see PERFUME *n.* 2. **4** see NATURE 1, 7. □ **in essence** fundamentally, essentially, basically, at bottom, in the final analysis, *au fond.* **of the essence** indispensable, vital, essential, critical, crucial, requisite, important.

Essene /ésseen, eséen/ *n.* a member of an ancient Jewish ascetic sect living communally. [L pl. *Esseni* f. Gk pl. *Essēnoi*]

essential /isénsh'l/ *adj.* & *n.* ● *adj.* **1** absolutely necessary; indispensable. **2** fundamental, basic. **3** of or constituting the essence of a person or thing. **4** (of a disease) with no known external stimulus or cause; idiopathic. ● *n.* (esp. in *pl.*) a basic or indispensable element or thing. □ **essential element** any of various elements required by living organisms for normal growth. **essential oil** a volatile oil derived from a plant etc. with its characteristic odour. □□ **essentiality** /-shiálliti/ *n.* **essentially** *adv.* **essentialness** *n.* [ME f. LL *essentialis* (as ESSENCE)]

■ *adj.* **1** indispensable, imperative, vital, necessary, requisite, required, important, material. **2** fundamental, basic, primary, key, main, leading, chief, principal, elementary, quintessential, intrinsic, elemental. **3** see INTRINSIC. **4** idiopathic, spontaneous. ● *n.* see NECESSITY 1a.

EST *abbr.* **1** *US* Eastern Standard Time. **2** electro-shock treatment.

-est[1] /ist/ *suffix* forming the superlative of adjectives (*widest*; *nicest*; *happiest*) and adverbs (*soonest*). [OE *-ost-*, *-ust-*, *-ast-*]

-est[2] /ist/ *suffix* (also **-st**) *archaic* forming the 2nd person sing. of verbs (*canst*; *findest*; *gavest*). [OE *-est*, *-ast*, *-st*]

establish /istáblish/ *v.tr.* **1** set up or consolidate (a business, system, etc.) on a permanent basis. **2** (foll. by *in*) settle (a person or oneself) in some capacity. **3** (esp. as **established** *adj.*) achieve permanent acceptance for (a custom, belief, practice, institution, etc.). **4** validate; place beyond dispute (a fact etc.). □ **Established Church** the Church recognized by the State as the national Church. □□ **establisher** *n.* [ME f. OF *establir* (stem *establiss-*) f. L *stabilire* f. *stabilis* STABLE[1]]

■ **1** set up, found, create, form, institute, start, begin, inaugurate, organize; constitute; decree, enact, introduce. **2** settle, secure, fix, entrench, install, ensconce. **3** (**established**) see STANDARD *adj.* 2–4. **4** validate, prove, verify, certify, confirm, corroborate, determine, authenticate, affirm, demonstrate, show, substantiate, support, back up.

establishment /istáblishmənt/ *n.* **1** the act or an instance of establishing; the process of being established. **2 a** a business organization or public institution. **b** a place of business. **c** a residence. **3 a** the staff or equipment of an organization. **b** a household. **4** any organized body permanently maintained for a purpose. **5** a Church system organized by law. **6** (**the Establishment**) **a** the group in a society exercising authority or influence, and seen as resisting change. **b** any influential or controlling group (*the literary Establishment*).

■ **1** foundation, founding, formation, construction, institution, inauguration, setting up, creation, organization. **2 a** business, concern, firm, company, enterprise, institution, organization; office. **b** office, workplace, consulting-room, business, premises, shop, store, market. **c** see RESIDENCE 2. **3 a** see STAFF[1] *n.* 2, APPARATUS. **b** household, family, ménage. **6 a** (**the Establishment**) the system, the government, the authorities, the administration, the power structure, the ruling class, the (established) order, the powers that be.

establishmentarian /istáblishməntáiriən/ *adj.* & *n.* ● *adj.* adhering to or advocating the principle of an established Church. ● *n.* a person adhering to or advocating this. □□ **establishmentarianism** *n.*

estaminet /estámminay/ *n.* a small French café etc. selling alcoholic drinks. [F f. Walloon *staminé* byre f. *stamo* a pole for tethering a cow, prob. f. G *Stamm* stem]

estate /istáyt/ *n.* **1** a property consisting of an extensive area of land usu. with a large house. **2** *Brit.* a modern residential or industrial area with integrated design or purpose. **3** all of a person's assets and liabilities, esp. at death. **4** a property where rubber, tea, grapes, etc., are cultivated. **5** (in full **estate of the realm**) an order or class forming (or regarded as) a part of the body politic. **6** *archaic* or *literary* a state or position in life (*the estate of holy matrimony*; *poor man's estate*). **7** *colloq.* = *estate car*. □ **estate agent** *Brit.* **1** a person whose business is the sale or lease of buildings and land on behalf of others. **2** the steward of an estate. **estate car** *Brit.* a car with the passenger area extended and combined with space for luggage, usu. with an extra door at the rear. **estate duty** *Brit. hist.* death duty levied on property. ¶ Replaced in 1975 by *capital transfer tax* and in 1986 by *inheritance tax*. **the Three Estates** Lords Spiritual (the heads of the Church), Lords Temporal (the peerage), and the Commons. [ME f. OF *estat* (as STATUS)]

■ **1** property, holding, domain, demesne, land, manor. **2** development, housing estate, *Brit.* new town; *Brit.* industrial *or* trading estate, business park. **3** assets, liabilities, property, holding(s), capital, resources, wealth, fortune; belongings, possessions, chattels. **4** plantation, farm, holding. **5** see ORDER *n.* 4. **6** state, position, standing, (social) status, station, place, situation, stratum, level, rank. □ **estate agent** **1** *US* real-estate agent, realtor.

esteem /istéem/ *v.* & *n.* ● *v.tr.* **1** (usu. in *passive*) have a high regard for; greatly respect; think favourably of. **2** *formal* consider, deem (*esteemed it an honour*). ● *n.* high regard; respect; favour (*held them in esteem*). [ME f. OF *estimer* f. L *aestimare* fix the price of]

■ *v.* **1** respect, value, treasure, prize, cherish, hold dear, appreciate, admire, look up to, regard highly, venerate, revere, reverence, honour, defer to; like, love, adore. **2** consider, view as, judge, regard as, hold, account, believe, think, reckon, *formal* deem. ● *n.* high regard, (high) opinion; respect, admiration; favour, approval, approbation.

ester /éstər/ *n. Chem.* any of a class of organic compounds produced by replacing the hydrogen of an acid by an alkyl, aryl, etc. radical, many of which occur naturally as oils and fats. □□ **esterify** /estérrifī/ *v.tr.* (**-ies**, **-ied**). [G, prob. f. *Essig* vinegar + *Äther* ether]

Esth. *abbr.* Esther (Old Testament & Apocrypha).

esthete *US* var. of AESTHETE.

esthetic *US* var. of AESTHETIC.

estimable /éstiməb'l/ *adj.* worthy of esteem. □□ **estimably** *adv.* [F f. L *aestimabilis* (as ESTEEM)]
▪ esteemed, respected, admired, valued, worthy, honoured, excellent, good; respectable, admirable, valuable, creditable, meritorious, reputable, honourable, laudable, praiseworthy, commendable.

estimate *n.* & *v.* ● *n.* /éstimət/ **1** an approximate judgement, esp. of cost, value, size, etc. **2** a price specified as that likely to be charged for work to be undertaken. **3** opinion, judgement, estimation. ● *v.tr.* (also *absol.*) /éstimayt/ **1** form an estimate or opinion of. **2** (foll. by *that* + clause) make a rough calculation. **3** (often foll. by *at*) form an estimate; adjudge. **4** fix (a price etc.) by estimate. □□ **estimative** /-mətiv/ *adj.* **estimator** /-maytər/ *n.* [L *aestimare aestimat-* fix the price of]
▪ *n.* **1, 2** reckoning, calculation, approximation, guess, conjecture, *colloq.* guestimate, *US colloq.* ballpark figure; evaluation, assessment, appraisal. **3** estimation, belief, opinion, judgement, thinking, feeling, sentiment, sense, (point of) view, viewpoint. ● *v.* **1** consider, think, believe, guess, conjecture, judge. **2, 3** guess, calculate, reckon, work out, gauge; judge, determine; assess, appraise, value, evaluate, adjudge. **4** price, evaluate, value, rate, cost, assess.

estimation /éstimáysh'n/ *n.* **1** the process or result of estimating. **2** judgement or opinion of worth (*in my estimation*). **3** *archaic* esteem (*hold in estimation*). [ME f. OF *estimation* or L *aestimatio* (as ESTIMATE)]
▪ **1** estimate, guess, approximation. **2** judgement, opinion, (way of) thinking; see also VIEW *n.* 5. **3** esteem, regard, respect; see also ADMIRATION 2.

estival *US* var. of AESTIVAL.

estivate *US* var. of AESTIVATE.

Estonian /istṓniən/ *n.* & *adj* ● *n.* **1 a** a native of Estonia, a Baltic republic. **b** a person of Estonian descent. **2** the Finno-Ugric language of Estonia. ● *adj.* of or relating to Estonia or its people or language.

estop /istóp/ *v.tr.* (**estopped, estopping**) (foll. by *from*) *Law* bar or preclude, esp. by estoppel. □□ **estoppage** *n.* [ME f. AF, OF *estoper* f. LL *stuppare* stop up f. L *stuppa* tow: cf. STOP, STUFF]

estoppel /istópp'l/ *n. Law* the principle which precludes a person from asserting something contrary to what is implied by a previous action or statement of that person or by a previous pertinent judicial determination. [OF *estouppail* bung f. *estoper* (as ESTOP)]

estovers /istṓvərz/ *n.pl. hist.* necessaries allowed by law to a tenant (esp. fuel, or wood for repairs). [AF *estover*, OF *estoveir* be necessary, f. L *est opus*]

estrange /istráynj/ *v.tr.* (usu. in *passive*; often foll. by *from*) cause (a person or group) to turn away in feeling or affection; alienate. □□ **estrangement** *n.* [ME f. AF *estraunger*, OF *estranger* f. L *extraneare* treat as a stranger f. *extraneus* stranger]
▪ (*estranged*) alienated, divided, separated, driven apart, disassociated; see also ALIENATE.

estreat /istréet/ *n.* & *v. Law* ● *n.* **1** a copy of a court record of a fine etc. for use in prosecution. **2** the enforcement of a fine or forfeiture of a recognizance. ● *v.tr.* enforce the forfeit of (a fine etc., esp. surety for bail). [ME f. AF *estrete*, OF *estraite* f. *estraire* f. L *extrahere* EXTRACT]

estrogen *US* var. of OESTROGEN.

estrus etc. *US* var. of OESTRUS etc.

estuary /éstyoori/ *n.* (*pl.* **-ies**) a wide tidal mouth of a river. □□ **estuarine** /-rīn/ *adj.* [L *aestuarium* tidal channel f. *aestus* tide]

e.s.u. *abbr.* electrostatic unit(s).

esurient /isyoóriənt/ *adj. archaic* or *joc.* **1** hungry. **2** impecunious and greedy. □□ **esuriently** *adv.* [L *esurire* (v.) hunger f. *edere es-* eat]
▪ see GREEDY 1.

ET *abbr.* extraterrestrial.

-et[1] /it/ *suffix* forming nouns (orig. diminutives) (*baronet*; *bullet*; *sonnet*). [OF *-et -ete*]

-et[2] /it/ *suffix* (also **-ete** /eet/) forming nouns usu. denoting persons (*comet*; *poet*; *athlete*). [Gk *-ētēs*]

ETA[1] *abbr.* estimated time of arrival.

ETA[2] /éttə/ *n.* a Basque separatist movement. [Basque abbr., f. *Euzkadi ta Azkatasuna* Basque homeland and liberty]

eta /éetə/ *n.* the seventh letter of the Greek alphabet (*H*, *η*). [Gk]

et al. /et ál/ *abbr.* and others. [L *et alii*, *et alia*, etc.]

etalon /éttəlon/ *n. Physics* a device consisting of two reflecting plates, for producing interfering light-beams. [F *étalon* standard]

etc. *abbr.* = ET CETERA.

et cetera /et séttərə, sétrə/ *adv.* & *n.* (also **etcetera**) ● *adv.* **1 a** and the rest; and similar things or people. **b** or similar things or people. **2** and so on. ● *n.* (in *pl.*) the usual sundries or extras. [ME f. L]

etch /ech/ *v.* & *n.* ● *v.* **1 a** *tr.* reproduce (a picture etc.) by engraving a design on a metal plate with acid (esp. to print copies). **b** *tr.* engrave (a plate) in this way. **2** *intr.* practise this craft. **3** *tr.* (foll. by *on*, *upon*) impress deeply (esp. on the mind). ● *n.* the action or process of etching. □□ **etcher** *n.* [Du. *etsen* f. G *ätzen* etch f. OHG *azzen* cause to eat or to be eaten f. Gmc]
▪ *v.* **1 a** print, reproduce. **b** engrave, carve, incise, inscribe, cut, score, scratch, *archaic* grave. **3** impress, imprint, engrave, grave. ● *n.* engraving, etching; photogravure, gravure.

etchant /échənt/ *n.* a corrosive used in etching.

etching /éching/ *n.* **1** a print made from an etched plate. **2** the art of producing these plates.
▪ see ENGRAVING.

-ete *suffix* var. of -ET[2].

eternal /itérn'l/ *adj.* **1** existing always; without an end or (usu.) beginning in time. **2** essentially unchanging (*eternal truths*). **3** *colloq.* constant; seeming not to cease (*your eternal nagging*). □ **the Eternal** God. **Eternal City** Rome. **eternal triangle** a relationship of three people involving sexual rivalry. □□ **eternality** /-nálliti/ *n.* **eternalize** *v.tr.* (also **-ise**). **eternally** *adv.* **eternalness** *n.* **eternize** *v.tr.* (also **-ise**). [ME f. OF f. LL *aeternalis* f. L *aeternus* f. *aevum* age]
▪ **1** everlasting, timeless, infinite, endless, limitless, immortal. **2** unchanging, unchangeable, immutable, unchanged, invariable, unvarying, unalterable, permanent, fixed, constant, everlasting, enduring, lasting. **3** constant, continuous, unending, endless, ceaseless, unceasing, incessant, perpetual, interminable, uninterrupted, non-stop, unremitting, persistent, relentless; continual, recurrent. □ **the Eternal** see LORD *n.* 4. □□ **eternally** see ALWAYS 4.

eternity /itérniti/ *n.* (*pl.* **-ies**) **1** infinite or unending (esp. future) time. **2** *Theol.* endless life after death. **3** the state of being eternal. **4** *colloq.* (often prec. by *an*) a very long time. **5** (in *pl.*) eternal truths. □ **eternity ring** a finger-ring set with gems all round, usu. given as a token of lasting affection. [ME f. OF *eternité* f. L *aeternitas -tatis* f. *aeternus*: see ETERNAL]
▪ **1, 3** infinity, endlessness, perpetuity, everlastingness, unendingness, boundlessness, timelessness. **2** see *immortality* (IMMORTAL). **4** see AGE *n.* 2a.

Etesian /itéezh'n/ *adj.* □ **Etesian winds** NW winds blowing each summer in the E. Mediterranean. [L *etesius* f. Gk *etēsios* annual f. *etos* year]

eth /eth/ *n.* (also **edh** /eth/) the name of an Old English and Icelandic letter, = th. [Icel.]

-eth[1] var. of -TH[1].

-eth[2] /ith/ *suffix* (also **-th**) *archaic* forming the 3rd person sing. present of verbs (*doeth*; *saith*). [OE *-eth*, *-ath*, *-th*]

ethanal /éthənal/ *n.* = ACETALDEHYDE. [ETHANE + ALDEHYDE]

ethane /éethayn, éethayn/ *n. Chem.* a gaseous hydrocarbon of the alkane series, occurring in natural gas. ¶ Chem. formula: C_2H_6. [ETHER + -ANE[2]]

ethanediol /éthaynd̄iol, éethayn-/ *n. Chem.* = *ethylene glycol.* [ETHANE + DIOL]

ethanol /éthənol, éethə-/ *n. Chem.* = ALCOHOL 1. [ETHANE + ALCOHOL]

ethene /étheen, éetheen/ *n. Chem.* = ETHYLENE. [ETHER + -ENE]

ether /éethər/ *n.* **1** *Chem.* **a** a colourless volatile organic liquid used as an anaesthetic or solvent. Also called DIETHYL ETHER, ETHOXYETHANE. ¶ Chem. formula: $C_2H_5OC_2H_5$. **b** any of a class of organic compounds with a similar structure to this, having an oxygen joined to two alkyl etc. groups. **2** a clear sky; the upper regions of air beyond the clouds. **3** *hist.* **a** a medium formerly assumed to permeate space and fill the interstices between particles of matter. **b** a medium through which electromagnetic waves were formerly thought to be transmitted. □□ **etheric** /eethérrik/ *adj.* [ME f. OF *ether* or L *aether* f. Gk *aithēr* f. root of *aithō* burn, shine]
■ **2, 3a** see SKY *n.*

ethereal /itheériəl/ *adj.* (also **etherial**) **1** light, airy. **2** highly delicate, esp. in appearance. **3** heavenly, celestial. **4** *Chem.* of or relating to ether. □□ **ethereality** /-riálliti/ *n.* **ethereally** *adv.* [L *aethereus, -ius* f. Gk *aitherios* (as ETHER)]
■ **1, 2** see IMMATERIAL 2. **3** see CELESTIAL 1.

etherial var. of ETHEREAL.

etherize /éethərīz/ *v.tr.* (also **-ise**) *hist.* treat or anaesthetize with ether. □□ **etherization** /-záysh'n/ *n.*

ethic /éthik/ *n.* & *adj.* ● *n.* a set of moral principles (*the Quaker ethic*). ● *adj.* = ETHICAL. [ME f. OF *éthique* or L *ethicus* f. Gk *ēthikos* (as ETHOS)]

ethical /éthik'l/ *adj.* **1** relating to morals, esp. as concerning human conduct. **2** morally correct; honourable. **3** (of a medicine or drug) not advertised to the general public, and usu. available only on a doctor's prescription. □ **ethical investment** investment in companies that meet ethical and moral criteria specified by the investor. □□ **ethicality** /-kálliti/ *n.* **ethically** *adv.*
■ **2** moral, correct, right, proper, just, righteous; honourable, decent, upright, principled, fair, honest, good, virtuous, noble.

ethics /éthiks/ *n.pl.* (also treated as *sing.*) **1** the science of morals in human conduct. **2 a** moral principles; rules of conduct. **b** a set of these (*medical ethics*). □□ **ethicist** /éthisist/ *n.*
■ **2 a, b** see MORAL *n.* 2.

Ethiopian /éethiṓpiən/ *n.* & *adj.* ● *n.* **1 a** a native or national of Ethiopia in NE Africa. **b** a person of Ethiopian descent. **2** *archaic* a Black person. ● *adj.* of or relating to Ethiopia. [*Ethiopia* f. L *Aethiops* f. Gk *Aithiops* f. *aithō* burn + *ōps* face]

Ethiopic /éethióppik, -ṓpik/ *n.* & *adj.* ● *n.* the Christian liturgical language of Ethiopia. ● *adj.* of or in this language. [L *aethiopicus* f. Gk *aithiopikos*: see ETHIOPIAN]

ethmoid /éthmoyd/ *adj.* sievelike. □ **ethmoid bone** a square bone at the root of the nose, with many perforations through which the olfactory nerves pass to the nose. □□ **ethmoidal** /-móyd'l/ *adj.* [Gk *ēthmoeidēs* f. *ēthmos* sieve]

ethnic /éthnik/ *adj.* & *n.* ● *adj.* **1 a** (of a social group) having a common national or cultural tradition. **b** (of clothes etc.) resembling those of a non-European exotic people. **2** denoting origin by birth or descent rather than nationality (*ethnic Turks*). **3** relating to race or culture (*ethnic group; ethnic origins*). **4** *archaic* pagan, heathen. ● *n.* **1** *US* a member of an (esp. minority) ethnic group. **2** (in *pl.*, usu. treated as *sing.*) = ETHNOLOGY. □ **ethnic cleansing** *euphem.* the practice of mass expulsion or killing of people from opposing ethnic or religious groups within a certain area. **ethnic minority** a (usu. identifiable) group differentiated from the main population of a community by racial origin or cultural background. □□ **ethnically** *adv.* **ethnicity** /-níssiti/ *n.* [ME f. eccl.L *ethnicus* f. Gk *ethnikos* heathen f. *ethnos* nation]
■ *adj.* **1 a** see RACIAL. **3** see NATIVE *adj.* 2, 5.

ethnical /éthnik'l/ *adj.* relating to ethnology.

ethno- /éthnō/ *comb. form* ethnic, ethnological. [Gk *ethnos* nation]

ethnoarchaeology /éthnō-aárkióllәji/ *n.* the study of a society's institutions based on examination of its material attributes. □□ **ethnoarchaeological** /-kiəlójik'l/ *adj.* **ethnoarchaeologist** *n.*

ethnocentric /éthnōséntrik/ *adj.* evaluating other races and cultures by criteria specific to one's own. □□ **ethnocentrically** *adv.* **ethnocentricity** /-tríssiti/ *n.* **ethnocentrism** *n.*

ethnography /ethnógrəfi/ *n.* the scientific description of races and cultures of mankind. □□ **ethnographer** *n.* **ethnographic** /-nəgráffik/ *adj.* **ethnographical** /-nəgráffik'l/ *adj.*

ethnology /ethnólləji/ *n.* the comparative scientific study of human peoples. □□ **ethnologic** /-nəlójik/ *adj.* **ethnological** /-nəlójik'l/ *adj.* **ethnologist** *n.*

ethnomusicology /éthnōmyōōzikólləji/ *n.* the study of the music of one or more (esp. non-European) cultures. □□ **ethnomusicologist** *n.*

ethogram /éethəgram/ *n. Zool.* a list of the kinds of behaviour or activity observed in an animal. [Gk *ēthо-* (see ETHOS) + -GRAM]

ethology /eethólləji/ *n.* **1** the science of animal behaviour. **2** the science of character-formation in human behaviour. □□ **ethological** /éethəlójik'l/ *adj.* **ethologist** *n.* [L *ethologia* f. Gk *ēthologia* (as ETHOS)]

ethos /éethoss/ *n.* the characteristic spirit or attitudes of a community, people, or system, or of a literary work etc. [mod.L f. Gk *ēthos* nature, disposition]

ethoxyethane /eethóksi-éethayn/ *n. Chem.* = ETHER 1a. [ETHER + OXY- + ETHANE]

ethyl /éethīl, éthil/ *n.* (*attrib.*) *Chem.* the univalent radical derived from ethane by removal of a hydrogen atom (*ethyl alcohol*). [G (as ETHER, -YL)]

ethylene /éthileen/ *n. Chem.* a gaseous hydrocarbon of the alkene series, occurring in natural gas and used in the manufacture of polythene. Also called ETHENE. ¶ Chem. formula: C_2H_4. □ **ethylene glycol** *Chem.* a colourless viscous hygroscopic liquid used as an antifreeze and in the manufacture of polyesters. ¶ Chem. formula: $C_2H_6O_2$.: also called ETHANEDIOL. □□ **ethylenic** /-léenik/ *adj.*

-etic /éttik/ *suffix* forming adjectives and nouns (*ascetic; emetic; genetic; synthetic*). [Gk *-ētikos* or *-ētikos*: cf. -IC]

etiolate /éetiōlayt/ *v.tr.* **1** make (a plant) pale by excluding light. **2** give a sickly hue to (a person). □□ **etiolation** /-láysh'n/ *n.* [F *étioler* f. Norman F *étieuler* make into haulm f. *éteule* ult. f. L *stipula* straw]

etiology *US* var. of AETIOLOGY.

etiquette /éttiket/ *n.* **1** the conventional rules of social behaviour. **2 a** the customary behaviour of members of a profession towards each other. **b** the unwritten code governing this (*medical etiquette*). [F *étiquette* label, etiquette]
■ **1** rules, code (of behaviour), form, convention, *convenance(s)*, protocol, ceremony, formalities, custom(s), decorum, (good) manners, propriety, *politesse*, politeness, courtesy, civility, seemliness. **2** see FORM *n.* 7.

Eton collar /éet'n/ *n.* a broad stiff collar worn outside the coat-collar, esp. of an Eton jacket.

Etonian /eetṓniən/ *n.* a past or present member of Eton College in S. England.

Eton jacket /éet'n/ *n.* a short jacket reaching only to the waist, as formerly worn by pupils of Eton College.

étrier /áytriay/ *n. Mountaineering* a short rope ladder with a few rungs of wood or metal. [F, = stirrup]

Etruscan /itrúskən/ *adj.* & *n.* ● *adj.* of ancient Etruria in Italy, esp. its pre-Roman civilization and physical remains. ● *n.* **1** a native of Etruria. **2** the language of Etruria. □□ **Etruscology** /-kólləji/ *n.* [L *Etruscus*]

et seq. *abbr.* (also **et seqq.**) and the following (pages etc.). [L *et sequentia*]

-ette /et/ *suffix* forming nouns meaning: **1** small (*kitchenette*; *cigarette*). **2** imitation or substitute (*leatherette*; *flannelette*). **3** female (*usherette*; *suffragette*). [from or after OF *-ette*, fem. of -ET[1]]

étude /áytyōōd, aytyōōd/ *n.* a short musical composition or exercise, usu. for one instrument, designed to improve the technique of the player. [F, = study]

étui /etwée/ *n.* a small case for needles etc. [F *étui* f. OF *estui* prison]

-etum /éetəm/ *suffix* forming nouns denoting a collection of trees or other plants (*arboretum*; *pinetum*). [L]

etymologize /éttimólləjīz/ *v.* (also **-ise**) **1** *tr.* give or trace the etymology of. **2** *intr.* study etymology. [med.L *etymologizare* f. L *etymologia* (as ETYMOLOGY)]

etymology /éttimólləji/ *n.* (*pl.* **-ies**) **1 a** the historically verifiable sources of the formation of a word and the development of its meaning. **b** an account of these. **2** the branch of linguistic science concerned with etymologies. □□ **etymological** /-məlójik'l/ *adj.* **etymologically** /-məlójikəli/ *adv.* **etymologist** *n.* [OF *ethimologie* f. L *etymologia* f. Gk *etumologia* (as ETYMON, -LOGY)]

▪ **1a** see DERIVATION.

etymon /éttimən/ *n.* (*pl.* **etyma** /-mə/) the word that gives rise to a derivative or a borrowed or later form. [L f. Gk *etumon* (neut. of *etumos* true), the literal sense or original form of a word]

Eu *symb. Chem.* the element europium.

eu- /yōō/ *comb. form* well, easily. [Gk]

eucalyptus /yōōkəlíptəss/ *n.* (also **eucalypt**) (*pl.* **eucalyptuses** or **eucalypti** /-tī/ or **eucalypts**) **1** any tree of the genus *Eucalyptus*, native to Australasia, cultivated for its timber and for the oil from its leaves. **2** (in full **eucalyptus oil**) this oil used as an antiseptic etc. [mod.L f. EU- + Gk *kaluptos* covered f. *kaluptō* to cover, the unopened flower being protected by a cap]

eucaryote var. of EUKARYOTE.

eucharis /yōōkəriss/ *n.* any bulbous plant of the genus *Eucharis*, native to S. America, with white umbellate flowers. [Gk *eukharis* pleasing (as EU-, *kharis* grace)]

Eucharist /yōōkərist/ *n.* **1** the Christian sacrament commemorating the Last Supper, in which bread and wine are consecrated and consumed. **2** the consecrated elements, esp. the bread (*receive the Eucharist*). □□ **Eucharistic** /-rístik/ *adj.* **Eucharistical** /-rístik'l/ *adj.* [ME f. OF *eucariste*, ult. f. eccl.Gk *eukharistia* thanksgiving f. Gk *eukharistos* grateful (as EU-, *kharizomai* offer willingly)]

▪ **1** (Holy) Communion, Mass, Lord's Supper, (Blessed *or* Holy) Sacrament, *archaic* mystery.

euchre /yōōkər/ *n.* & *v.* ● *n.* an American card-game for two, three, or four players. ● *v.tr.* **1** (in euchre) gain the advantage over (another player) when that player fails to take three tricks. **2** deceive, outwit. **3** *Austral.* exhaust, ruin. [19th c.: orig. unkn.]

▪ *v.* **2** see CHEAT *v.* 1a. **3** see WRECK *v.* 2.

Euclidean /yōōklíddiən/ *adj.* of or relating to Euclid, 3rd-c. BC Alexandrian geometrician, esp. the system of geometry based on his principles. □ **Euclidean space** space for which Euclidean geometry is valid. [L *Euclideus* f. Gk *Eukleideios*]

eudemonic /yōōdimónnik/ *adj.* (also **eudaemonic**) conducive to happiness. [Gk *eudaimonikos* (as EUDEMONISM)]

eudemonism /yōōdéemənizʹm/ *n.* (also **eudaemonism**) a system of ethics that bases moral obligation on the likelihood of actions producing happiness. □□ **eudemonist** *n.* **eudemonistic** /-nístik/ *adj.* [Gk *eudaimonismos* system of happiness f. *eudaimōn* happy (as EU-, *daimōn* guardian spirit)]

eudiometer /yōōdiómmitər/ *n. Chem.* a graduated glass tube in which gases may be chemically combined by an electric spark, used to measure changes in volume of gases during chemical reactions. □□ **eudiometric** /-diəmétrik/ *adj.* **eudiometrical** /-diəmétrik'l/ *adj.* **eudiometry** *n.* [Gk *eudios* clear (weather): orig. used to measure the amount of oxygen, thought to be greater in clear air]

eugenics /yōōjénniks/ *n.pl.* (also treated as *sing.*) the science of improving the (esp. human) population by controlled breeding for desirable inherited characteristics. □□ **eugenic** *adj.* **eugenically** *adv.* **eugenicist** /yōōjénnisist/ *n.* **eugenist** /yōōjinist/ *n.*

eukaryote /yōōkárriot/ *n.* (also **eucaryote**) *Biol.* an organism consisting of a cell or cells in which the genetic material is contained within a distinct nucleus (cf. PROKARYOTE). □□ **eukaryotic** /-óttik/ *adj.* [EU- + KARYO- + *-ote* as in ZYGOTE]

eulogium /yōōlōjiəm/ *n.* (*pl.* **eulogia** /-jiə/ or **-ums**) = EULOGY. [med.L: see EULOGY]

eulogize /yōōləjīz/ *v.tr.* (also **-ise**) praise in speech or writing. □□ **eulogist** *n.* **eulogistic** /-jístik/ *adj.* **eulogistically** /-jístikəli/ *adv.*

▪ praise, extol, laud, applaud, compliment, sing the praises of, sound the praises of, acclaim, panegyrize.

□□ **eulogistic** see COMPLIMENTARY 1.

eulogy /yōōləji/ *n.* (*pl.* **-ies**) **1 a** speech or writing in praise of a person. **b** an expression of praise. **2** *US* a funeral oration in praise of a person. [med.L *eulogium* f. (app. by confusion with L *elogium* epitaph) LL *eulogia* praise f. Gk]

▪ praise, encomium, accolade, paean, panegyric, acclaim, acclamation, commendation, tribute, homage, plaudits; see also ORATION.

eunuch /yōōnək/ *n.* **1** a castrated man, esp. one formerly employed at an oriental harem or court. **2** a person lacking effectiveness (*political eunuch*). [ME f. L *eunuchus* f. Gk *eunoukhos* lit. bedchamber attendant f. *eunē* bed + second element rel. to *ekhō* hold]

euonymus /yōō-ónniməss/ *n.* any tree of the genus *Euonymus*, e.g. the spindle tree. [L f. Gk *euōnumos* of lucky name (as EU-, *onoma* name)]

eupeptic /yōōpéptik/ *adj.* of or having good digestion. [Gk *eupeptos* (as EU-, *peptō* digest)]

euphemism /yōōfimizʹm/ *n.* **1** a mild or vague expression substituted for one thought to be too harsh or direct (e.g. *pass over* for *die*). **2** the use of such expressions. □□ **euphemist** *n.* **euphemistic** /-místik/ *adj.* **euphemistically** /-místikəli/ *adv.* **euphemize** *v.tr.* & *intr.* (also **-ise**). [Gk *euphēmismos* f. *euphēmos* (as EU-, *phēmē* speaking)]

euphonious /yōōfṓniəss/ *adj.* **1** sounding pleasant, harmonious. **2** concerning euphony. □□ **euphoniously** *adv.*

▪ **1** see MELODIOUS 2.

euphonium /yōōfṓniəm/ *n.* a brass wind instrument of the tuba family. [mod.L f. Gk *euphōnos* (as EUPHONY)]

euphony /yōōfəni/ *n.* (*pl.* **-ies**) **1 a** pleasantness of sound, esp. of a word or phrase; harmony. **b** a pleasant sound. **2** the tendency to make a phonetic change for ease of pronunciation. □□ **euphonic** /-fónnik/ *adj.* **euphonize** *v.tr.* (also **-ise**). [F *euphonie* f. LL *euphonia* f. Gk *euphōnia* (as EU-, *phōnē* sound)]

▪ **1 a** see MELODY 4. **2** haplology, *Gram.* metathesis, *Phonet.* assimilation.

euphorbia /yōōfórbiə/ *n.* any plant of the genus *Euphorbia*, including spurges. [ME f. L *euphorbea* f. *Euphorbus*, 1st-c. Gk physician]

euphoria /yōōfóriə/ *n.* a feeling of well-being, esp. one based on over-confidence or over-optimism. □□ **euphoric** /-fórrik/ *adj.* **euphorically** /-fórrikəli/ *adv.* [Gk f. *euphoros* well-bearing (as EU-, *pherō* bear)]

▪ see RAPTURE.

euphoriant /yōōfóriənt/ *adj.* & *n.* ● *adj.* inducing euphoria. ● *n.* a euphoriant drug.

euphuism /yōōfyoo-izʹm/ *n.* an affected or high-flown style of writing or speaking. □□ **euphuist** *n.* **euphuistic** /-ístik/ *adj.* **euphuistically** /-ístikəli/ *adv.* [Gk *euphuēs* well endowed by nature: orig. of writing imitating Lyly's *Euphues* (1578–80)]

Eurasian /yooráyzh'n/ *adj.* & *n.* ● *adj.* **1** of mixed European and Asian (esp. Indian) parentage. **2** of Europe and Asia. ● *n.* a Eurasian person.

Euratom /yoorátt əm/ *n.* European Atomic Energy Community. [abbr.]

eureka /yoore͞ekə/ *int.* & *n.* ● *int.* I have found it! (announcing a discovery etc.). ● *n.* the exultant cry of 'eureka'. [Gk *heurēka* 1st pers. sing. perfect of *heuriskō* find: attributed to Archimedes]

eurhythmic /yooríthmik/ *adj.* of or in harmonious proportion (esp. of architecture). [*eurhythmy* harmony of proportions f. L *eur(h)ythmia* f. Gk *eurhuthmia* (as EU-, *rhuthmos* proportion, rhythm)]

eurhythmics /yooríthmiks/ *n.pl.* (also treated as *sing.*) (*US* **eurythmics**) harmony of bodily movement, esp. as developed with music and dance into a system of education.

euro /yo͝orō/ *n.* (*pl.* **-os**) *Austral.* a large reddish kangaroo. [Aboriginal]

Euro- /yo͝orō/ *comb. form* Europe, European. [abbr.]

Eurocommunism /yo͝orōkómyooniz'm/ *n.* a form of Communism in Western European countries independent of the former Soviet Communist Party. ▫▫ **Eurocommunist** *adj.* & *n.*

Eurocrat /yo͝orōkrat/ *n.* usu. *derog.* a bureaucrat in the administration of the European Economic Community.

Eurodollar /yo͝orōdollər/ *n.* a dollar held in a bank in Europe.

European /yo͝orəpe͞eən/ *adj.* & *n.* ● *adj.* **1** of or in Europe. **2 a** descended from natives of Europe. **b** originating in or characteristic of Europe. **3 a** happening in or extending over Europe. **b** concerning Europe as a whole rather than its individual countries. **4** of or relating to the European Economic Community. ● *n.* **1 a** a native or inhabitant of Europe. **b** a person descended from natives of Europe. **c** a White person. **2** a person concerned with European matters. ▫ **European Economic Community** (or **European Community**) an economic and political association of certain European countries as a unit with internal free trade and common external tariffs. **European plan** *US* a system of charging for a hotel room only without meals. ▫▫ **Europeanism** *n.* **Europeanize** *v.tr.* & *intr.* (also **-ise**). **Europeanization** /-nīzáysh'n/ *n.* [F *européen* f. L *europaeus* f. L *Europa* f. Gk *Eurōpē* Europe]

europium /yoorṓpiəm/ *n. Chem.* a soft silvery metallic element of the lanthanide series, occurring naturally in small quantities. ¶ Symb.: **Eu.** [mod.L f. *Europe*]

Eurovision /yo͝orōvizh'n/ *n.* a network of European television production administered by the European Broadcasting Union.

eurythmics *US* var. of EURHYTHMICS.

Eustachian tube /yōōstáysh'n/ *n. Anat.* a tube leading from the pharynx to the cavity of the middle ear and equalizing the pressure on each side of the eardrum. [L *Eustachius* = B. *Eustachio*, It. anatomist d. 1574]

eustasy /yōōstəsi/ *n.* a change in sea level throughout the world caused by tectonic movements, melting of glaciers, etc. ▫▫ **eustatic** /-státtik/ *adj.* [back-form. f. G *eustatisch* (adj.) (as EU-, STATIC)]

eutectic /yōōtéktik/ *adj.* & *n. Chem.* ● *adj.* (of a mixture, alloy, etc.) having the lowest freezing-point of any possible proportions of its constituents. ● *n.* a eutectic mixture. ▫ **eutectic point** (or **temperature**) the minimum freezing-point for a eutectic mixture. [Gk *eutēktos* (as EU-, *tēkō* melt)]

euthanasia /yōōthənáyziə/ *n.* **1** the bringing about of a gentle and easy death in the case of incurable and painful disease. **2** such a death. [Gk (as EU-, *thanatos* death)]

eutrophic /yōōtróffik, -trṓfik/ *adj.* (of a lake etc.) rich in nutrients and therefore supporting a dense plant population, which kills animal life by depriving it of oxygen. ▫▫ **eutrophicate** *v.tr.* **eutrophication** /-káysh'n/ *n.* **eutrophy** /yōōtrəfi/ *n.* [*eutrophy* f. Gk *eutrophia* (as EU-, *trephō* nourish)]

eV *abbr.* electronvolt.

EVA *abbr. Astronaut.* extravehicular activity.

evacuate /ivákyoo-ayt/ *v.tr.* **1 a** remove (people) from a place of danger to stay elsewhere for the duration of the danger. **b** empty or leave (a place) in this way. **2** make empty (a vessel of air etc.). **3** (of troops) withdraw from (a place). **4 a** empty (the bowels or other bodily organ). **b** discharge (faeces etc.). ▫▫ **evacuant** *n.* & *adj.* **evacuation** /-áysh'n/ *n.* **evacuative** /ivákyooətiv/ *adj.* & *n.* **evacuator** *n.* [L *evacuare* (as E-, *vacuus* empty)]

■ **1 a** remove, move, relocate, transfer. **b** empty, vacate, leave, quit, go away from, depart (from), withdraw *or* retire from, decamp from, move out of *or* from, pull out of *or* from, abandon, desert. **2** see EMPTY *v.* 1. **3** pull out from *or* of, withdraw from; see also EVACUATE 1b above. **4 a** empty, clear (out), drain, purge. **b** discharge, excrete, void.

evacuee /ivákyoo-e͞e/ *n.* a person evacuated from a place of danger.

evade /iváyd/ *v.tr.* **1 a** escape from, avoid, esp. by guile or trickery. **b** avoid doing (one's duty etc.). **c** avoid answering (a question) or yielding to (an argument). **2 a** fail to pay (tax due). **b** defeat the intention of (a law etc.), esp. while complying with its letter. **3** (of a thing) elude or baffle (a person). ▫▫ **evadable** *adj.* **evader** *n.* [F *évader* f. L *evadere* (as E-, *vadere vas-* go)]

■ **1, 2** escape (from), get away from, avoid, elude, dodge, get out of, sidestep, duck (out of), circumvent, shirk, shuffle out of, weasel out of; see also FENCE *v.* 7. **3** see ELUDE 3.

evaginate /ivájinayt/ *v.tr. Med.* & *Physiol.* turn (a tubular organ) inside out. ▫▫ **evagination** /-náysh'n/ *n.* [L *evaginare* (as E-, *vaginare* as VAGINA)]

evaluate /ivályoo-ayt/ *v.tr.* **1** assess, appraise. **2 a** find or state the number or amount of. **b** find a numerical expression for. ▫▫ **evaluation** /-áysh'n/ *n.* **evaluative** /ivályooətiv/ *adj.* **evaluator** *n.* [back-form. f. *evaluation* f. F *évaluation* f. *évaluer* (as E-, VALUE)]

■ **1** assess, appraise, value. **2** estimate, gauge, calculate, figure, reckon, compute, judge; rate, rank; quantify. ▫▫ **evaluation** appraisal, valuation, assessment; estimate, estimation, judgement, reckoning, figuring, calculation, computation, rating, ranking.

evanesce /e͞evənéss, évvə-/ *v.intr.* **1** fade from sight; disappear. **2** become effaced. [L *evanescere* (as E-, *vanus* empty)]

■ see DISAPPEAR 1.

evanescent /e͞evənéss'nt, évvə-/ *adj.* (of an impression or appearance etc.) quickly fading. ▫▫ **evanescence** *n.* **evanescently** *adv.*

■ see FLEETING.

evangel /ivánjəl/ *n.* **1** *archaic* **a** the gospel. **b** any of the four Gospels. **2** a basic doctrine or set of principles. **3** *US* = EVANGELIST. [ME f. OF *evangile* f. eccl.L *evangelium* f. Gk *euaggelion* good news (as EU-, ANGEL)]

evangelic /e͞evanjéllik/ *adj.* = EVANGELICAL.

evangelical /e͞evanjéllik'l/ *adj.* & *n.* ● *adj.* **1** of or according to the teaching of the gospel or the Christian religion. **2** of the Protestant school maintaining that the doctrine of salvation by faith in the Atonement is the essence of the gospel. ● *n.* a member of the evangelical school. ▫▫ **evangelicalism** *n.* **evangelically** *adv.* [eccl.L *evangelicus* f. eccl.Gk *euaggelikos* (as EVANGEL)]

evangelism /ivánjəliz'm/ *n.* **1** the preaching or promulgation of the gospel. **2** evangelicalism.

evangelist /ivánjəlist/ *n.* **1** any of the writers of the four Gospels (Matthew, Mark, Luke, John). **2** a preacher of the gospel. **3** a lay person doing missionary work.

■ **2, 3** see MINISTER *n.* 2.

evangelistic /ivánjəlístik/ *adj.* **1** = EVANGELICAL. **2** of preachers of the gospel. **3** of the four evangelists.

evangelize /ivánjəlīz/ *v.tr.* (also **-ise**) **1** (also *absol.*) preach the gospel to. **2** convert (a person) to Christianity. ▫▫ **evangelization** /-záysh'n/ *n.* **evangelizer** *n.* [ME f. eccl.L *evangelizare* f. Gk *euaggelizomai* (as EVANGEL)]

evaporate /iváppərayt/ *v.* **1** *intr.* turn from solid or liquid into vapour. **2** *intr.* & *tr.* lose or cause to lose moisture as vapour. **3** *intr.* & *tr.* disappear or cause to disappear (*our courage evaporated*). □ **evaporated milk** milk concentrated by partial evaporation. □□ **evaporable** *adj.* **evaporation** /-ráysh'n/ *n.* **evaporative** /-rətiv/ *adj.* **evaporator** *n.* [L *evaporare* (as E-, *vaporare* as VAPOUR)]

■ **1** vaporize; steam. **2** vaporize, boil off *or* away; dehydrate, desiccate. **3** disappear, vanish, evanesce, fade (away), melt away, dissolve; dispel, dissipate, disperse. □□ **evaporation** vaporization, drying (up *or* out), dehydration, desiccation, parching; disappearance, evanescence, dematerialization, dissolution, fading (away), melting (away); dispersion, dispelling, dissipation.

evasion /iváyzh'n/ *n.* **1** the act or a means of evading. **2 a** subterfuge or a prevaricating excuse. **b** an evasive answer. [ME f. OF f. L *evasio -onis* (as EVADE)]

■ **1** escape, avoidance, shirking, dodging. **2** subterfuge, deceit, deception, chicanery, chicane, artifice, cunning, trickery, lying, sophistry; prevarication, dodging, fudging, evasiveness, quibbling, equivocation.

evasive /iváysiv/ *adj.* **1** seeking to evade something. **2** not direct in one's answers etc. **3** enabling or effecting evasion (*evasive action*). **4** (of a person) tending to evasion; habitually practising evasion. □□ **evasively** *adv.* **evasiveness** *n.*

■ **1, 3, 4** equivocal, ambiguous; devious, dissembling, cunning, tricky, deceitful, *colloq.* shifty, *often offens.* Jesuitical. **2** indirect, oblique, equivocating, equivocal, ambiguous, *colloq.* cagey; devious, sophistical, casuistic, misleading.

eve /eev/ *n.* **1** the evening or day before a church festival or any date or event (*Christmas Eve*; *the eve of the funeral*). **2** the time just before anything (*the eve of the election*). **3** *archaic* evening. [ME, = EVEN²]

■ **1** evening *or* day *or* night before. **2** time *or* period before; *Eccl.* vigil.

evection /iváksh'n/ *n. Astron.* a perturbation of the moon's motion caused by the sun's attraction. [L *evectio* (as E-, *vehere vect-* carry)]

even¹ /éev'n/ *adj.*, *adv.*, & *v.* ● *adj.* (**evener**, **evenest**) **1** level; flat and smooth. **2 a** uniform in quality; constant. **b** equal in number or amount or value etc. **c** equally balanced. **3** (usu. foll. by *with*) in the same plane or line. **4** (of a person's temper etc.) equable, calm. **5 a** (of a number such as 4, 6) divisible by two without a remainder. **b** bearing such a number (*no parking on even dates*). **c** not involving fractions; exact (*in even dozens*). ● *adv.* **1** used to invite comparison of the stated assertion, negation, etc., with an implied one that is less strong or remarkable (*never even opened* [let alone read] *the letter*; *does he even suspect* [not to say realize] *the danger?*; *ran even faster* [not just as fast as before]; *even if my watch is right we shall be late* [later if it is slow]). **2** used to introduce an extreme case (*even you must realize it*; *it might even cost £100*). **3** (sometimes foll. by *with* or *though*) in spite of, notwithstanding (*even with the delays, we arrived on time*). ● *v.* **1** *tr.* & *intr.* (often foll. by *up* or *out*) make or become even. **2** *tr.* (often foll. by *to*) *archaic* treat as equal or comparable. □ **even as** at the very moment that. **even break** *colloq.* an equal chance. **even chance** an equal chance of success or failure. **even money 1** betting odds offering the gambler the chance of winning the amount he or she staked. **2** equally likely to happen or not (*it's even money he'll fail to arrive*). **even now 1** now as well as before. **2** at this very moment. **even so 1** notwithstanding that; nevertheless. **2** quite so. **3** in that case as well as in others. **even Stephens** (or **Stevens**) *colloq.* even, equal, level. **get** (or **be**) **even with** have one's revenge on. **of even date** *Law* & *Commerce* of the same date. **on an even keel 1** (of a ship or aircraft) not listing. **2** (of a plan or person) untroubled. □□ **evenly** *adv.* **evenness** *n.* [OE *efen*, *efne*]

■ *adj.* **1** level, flat, smooth, plane, regular, uniform, flush, straight. **2 a** uniform, regular, steady, consistent; constant, unvaried, unvarying,unchanging, set, stable; measured, orderly, ordered, monotonous, unbroken, uninterrupted. **b** equal, balanced, the same, identical, level, fifty-fifty, *archaic or literary* coequal; drawn, on a par, tied, neck and neck, *Brit.* level pegging, *colloq.* even Stephens. **3** level, uniform, coextensive, flush, parallel. **4** equable, calm, even-tempered, composed, placid, serene, peaceful, cool, tranquil, imperturbable, impassive, steady, temperate, equanimous, self-possessed, sober, staid, sedate. **5 c** exact, precise, round; rounded off *or* out *or* up *or* down. ● *adv.* **3** (*even with* or *though*) notwithstanding, despite, in spite of, disregarding. ● *v.* **1** smooth, flatten, level; align; equalize, balance (out). □ **even break** see CHANCE *n.* 4. **even so** notwithstanding (that), nevertheless, none the less, still, yet, all the same, in spite of that, despite that. **get even with** have one's revenge on, revenge oneself on, be revenged on, repay, settle accounts with, settle a *or* the score with; requite. **be even with** be square with, be quits with, be equal with. **on an even keel** **1** balanced, stable, level. **2** see LEVEL *adj.* 4, STABLE ¹ 2.

even² /éev'n/ *n. poet.* evening. [OE *ǣfen*]

even-handed /éev'nhándid/ *adj.* impartial, fair. □□ **even-handedly** *adv.* **even-handedness** *n.*

evening /éevning/ *n.* & *int.* ● *n.* **1** the end part of the day, esp. from about 6 p.m. to bedtime (*this evening*; *during the evening*; *evening meal*). **2** this time spent in a particular way (*had a lively evening*). **3** a time compared with this, esp. the last part of a person's life. ● *int.* = *good evening* (see GOOD *adj.* 14). □ **evening dress** formal dress for evening wear. **evening primrose** any plant of the genus *Oenothera* with pale yellow flowers that open in the evening. **evening star** a planet, esp. Venus, conspicuous in the west after sunset. [OE *ǣfnung*, rel. to EVEN²]

■ *n.* **1** nightfall, dusk, twilight, sunset, sundown, p.m., night, *archaic or poet.* eventide, *poet.* gloaming. **3** autumn, twilight, waning; see also AGE *n.* 3.

evens /éev'nz/ *n.pl. Brit.* = *even money*.

evensong /éev'nsong/ *n.* a service of evening prayer in the Church of England. [EVEN² + SONG]

event /ivént/ *n.* **1** a thing that happens or takes place, esp. one of importance. **2 a** the fact of a thing's occurring. **b** a result or outcome. **3** an item in a sports programme, or the programme as a whole. **4** *Physics* a single occurrence of a process, e.g. the ionization of one atom. **5** something on the result of which money is staked. □ **at all events** (or **in any event**) whatever happens. **event horizon** *Astron.* the gravitational boundary enclosing a black hole, from which no light escapes. **in the event** as it turns (or turned) out. **in the event of** if (a specified thing) happens. **in the event that** *disp.* if it happens that. [L *eventus* f. *evenire event-* happen (as E-, *venire* come)]

■ **1** occurrence, happening, incident, episode, occasion, circumstance, affair, experience. **2** result, outcome, issue, consequence, conclusion, upshot, effect, end. **3** see HEAT *n.* 6, CONTEST *n.* 1. □ **at all events** (or **in any event**) whatever happens, come what may, in any case, at any rate, anyhow, anyway; regardless. **in the event** as it turns *or* turned out, as things turn *or* turned out, as it happens, when it happened, in reality *or* actuality.

eventful /ivéntfōōl/ *adj.* marked by noteworthy events. □□ **eventfully** *adv.* **eventfulness** *n.*

■ busy, full, active, lively, exciting, interesting; important, significant, signal, notable, noteworthy, momentous, memorable.

eventide /éev'ntīd/ *n. archaic* or *poet.* = EVENING. □ **eventide home** a home for the elderly, orig. one run by the Salvation Army. [OE *ǣfentīd* (as EVEN², TIDE)]

■ see EVENING *n.* 1.

eventing /ivénting/ *n. Brit.* participation in equestrian competitions, esp. dressage and showjumping. [EVENT 3 as in *three-day event*]

eventless /ivéntliss/ *adj.* without noteworthy or remarkable events. □□ **eventlessly** *adv.*

eventual /ivéntyooəl/ *adj.* occurring or existing in due course or at last; ultimate. □□ **eventually** *adv.* [as EVENT, after *actual*]
■ due, expected, consequent, resultant, resulting, unavoidable, inevitable, ineluctable, foreordained, preordained, predestined, likely, probable, *disp.* anticipated; ultimate, final, last, concluding, resulting. □□ **eventually** ultimately, finally, in the end *or* long run, at the end of the day, sooner or later, at last, when all is said and done, in the final analysis, in due course, in (the course of) time, after all.

eventuality /ivéntyoo-álliti/ *n.* (*pl.* **-ies**) a possible event or outcome.
■ possibility, likelihood, chance, probability; circumstance, contingency, event, occurrence, happening, case.

eventuate /ivéntyoo-ayt/ *v.intr. formal* **1** turn out in a specified way as the result. **2** (often foll. by *in*) result. □□ **eventuation** /-áysh'n/ *n.* [as EVENT, after *actuate*]
■ see *turn out* 9 (TURN).

ever /évvər/ *adv.* **1** at all times; always (*ever hopeful*; *ever after*). **2** at any time (*have you ever been to Paris?*; *nothing ever happens*; *as good as ever*). **3** as an emphatic word: **a** in any way; at all (*how ever did you do it?*; *when will they ever learn?*). **b** (prec. by *as*) in any manner possible (*be as quick as ever you can*). **4** (in *comb.*) constantly (*ever-present*; *ever-recurring*). **5** (foll. by *so*, *such*) *Brit. colloq.* very; very much (*is ever so easy*; *was ever such a nice man*; *thanks ever so*). **6** (foll. by compar.) constantly, increasingly (*grew ever larger*). □ **did you ever?** *colloq.* did you ever hear or see the like? **ever since** throughout the period since. **for ever 1** for all future time. **2** *colloq.* for a long time (cf. FOREVER). [OE *ǣfre*]
■ **1** at all times, always, all the time, for ever, eternally, perpetually, endlessly, everlastingly, constantly, continuously, continually, for ever and a day, till the end of time, till doomsday, *colloq.* till the cows come home, till kingdom come; yet, still, even. **2** (at) any time, at all, at any point, at any period, on any occasion; by any chance. □ **for ever 1** see ALWAYS 4.

evergreen /évvərgreen/ *adj.* & *n.* ● *adj.* **1** always green or fresh. **2** (of a plant) retaining green leaves throughout the year. ● *n.* an evergreen plant (cf. DECIDUOUS).

everlasting /évvərláasting/ *adj.* & *n.* ● *adj.* **1** lasting for ever. **2** lasting for a long time, esp. so as to become unwelcome. **3** (of flowers) keeping their shape and colour when dried. ● *n.* **1** eternity. **2** = IMMORTELLE. □□ **everlastingly** *adv.* **everlastingness** *n.*
■ *adj.* **1** eternal, perpetual, immortal, undying, deathless, infinite, timeless. **2** never-ending, perpetual, eternal, constant, continual, continuous, permanent, unceasing, incessant, interminable, endless. ● *n.* **1** see ETERNITY.

evermore /évvərmór/ *adv.* for ever; always.
■ see ALWAYS 1.

evert /ivért/ *v.tr. Physiol.* turn (an organ etc.) outwards or inside out. □□ **eversion** *n.* [L *evertere* (as E-, *vertere vers-* turn)]

every /évri/ *adj.* **1** each single (*heard every word*; *watched her every movement*). **2** each at a specified interval in a series (*take every third one*; *comes every four days*). **3** all possible; the utmost degree of (*there is every prospect of success*). □ **every bit as** *colloq.* (in comparisons) quite as (*every bit as good*). **every now and again** (or **now and then**) from time to time. **every one** each one (see also EVERYONE). **every other** each second in a series (*every other day*). **every so often** at intervals; occasionally. **every time** *colloq.* **1** without exception. **2** without hesitation. **every which way** *US colloq.* **1** in all directions. **2** in a disorderly manner. [OE *ǣfre ǣlc* ever each]

everybody /évriboddi/ *pron.* every person.
■ see EVERYONE.

everyday /évridáy/ *adj.* **1** occurring every day. **2** suitable for or used on ordinary days. **3** commonplace, usual. **4** mundane; mediocre, inferior.
■ **1** daily, day-to-day; quotidian, diurnal; *Physiol.* circadian. **2, 3** ordinary, common, usual, customary, familiar, regular, habitual, routine, commonplace, run-of-the-mill; unexceptional, conventional; accustomed. **4** prosaic, mundane, dull, unimaginative, unexciting, mediocre, inferior.

Everyman /évriman/ *n.* the ordinary or typical human being; the 'man in the street'. [the principal character in a 15th-c. morality play]
■ see PEOPLE *n.* 2.

everyone /évriwun/ *pron.* every person; everybody.
■ everybody, all (and sundry), one and all, each and every one *or* person, the whole world, everybody under the sun, every man jack, *usu. derog.* every Tom, Dick, and Harry.

everything /évrithing/ *pron.* **1** all things; all the things of a group or class. **2** *colloq.* a great deal (*gave me everything*). **3** an essential consideration (*speed is everything*). □ **have everything** *colloq.* possess all the desired attributes etc.
■ **1** all things, all, the (whole *or* entire) lot, the entirety, *sl.* the whole (kit and) caboodle, the whole shooting match, everything but the kitchen sink, *US sl.* the whole shebang; the total, the aggregate. **2** see LOT *n.* 1. **3** see ESSENTIAL *adj.*

everywhere /évriwair/ *adv.* **1** in every place. **2** *colloq.* in many places.
■ in each *or* every place, to each *or* every place, in all places, in every nook and cranny, high and low, far and wide, near and far; ubiquitously, universally, globally; all over.

evict /ivíkt/ *v.tr.* expel (a tenant) from a property by legal process. □□ **eviction** *n.* **evictor** *n.* [L *evincere evict-* (as E-, *vincere* conquer)]
■ expel, turn out (of house and home), oust, remove, eject, dispossess, put out, kick *or* throw *or* boot out, *colloq.* toss out, *Brit. colloq.* turf out. □□ **eviction** expulsion, removal, ejection, ouster, dispossession.

evidence /évvid'nss/ *n.* & *v.* ● *n.* **1** (often foll. by *for*, *of*) the available facts, circumstances, etc. supporting or otherwise a belief, proposition, etc., or indicating whether or not a thing is true or valid. **2** *Law* **a** information given personally or drawn from a document etc. and tending to prove a fact or proposition. **b** statements or proofs admissible as testimony in a lawcourt. **3** clearness, obviousness. ● *v.tr.* be evidence of; attest. □ **call in evidence** *Law* summon (a person) as a witness. **in evidence** noticeable, conspicuous. **Queen's** (or **King's** or **State's**) **evidence** *Law* evidence for the prosecution given by a participant in or accomplice to the crime at issue. [ME f. OF f. L *evidentia* (as EVIDENT)]
■ *n.* **1** facts, circumstances, proof, grounds, data, documentation, support; indication, sign(s), hint, marks, traces, manifestation(s), suggestion(s), token(s), clue(s). **2** testimony, attestation, deposition, affidavit, averment, statement, assertion. **3** see CLARITY. ● *v.* attest, demonstrate, show, manifest, evince, display, signify, exhibit, reveal, denote, prove, testify, bear witness to, witness. □ **in evidence** see NOTICEABLE 1.

evident /évvid'nt/ *adj.* **1** plain or obvious (visually or intellectually); manifest. **2** seeming, apparent (*his evident anxiety*). [ME f. OF *evident* or L *evidēre evident-* (as E-, *vidēre* see)]
■ plain, obvious, clear, apparent, patent; manifest, perceptible, perceivable, discernible, noticeable, conspicuous; palpable, unmistakable, recognizable; express.

evidential /évvidénsh'l/ *adj.* of or providing evidence. □□ **evidentially** *adv.*
■ see DEMONSTRATIVE *adj.* 2.

evidentiary /évvidénshəri/ *adj.* = EVIDENTIAL.

evidently /évvidəntli/ *adv.* **1** as shown by evidence. **2** seemingly; as it appears (*was evidently unwilling to go*).
■ **1** clearly, obviously, plainly, manifestly, palpably, patently, indubitably, undoubtedly, doubtless(ly), without a doubt, indisputably, incontestably,

incontrovertibly, undeniably, unquestionably, certainly. **2** seemingly, apparently, outwardly, it would seem (so), so it seems, as far as one can tell, to all appearances, ostensibly.

evil /éev'l/ *adj.* & *n.* ● *adj.* **1** morally bad; wicked. **2** harmful or tending to harm, esp. intentionally or characteristically. **3** disagreeable or unpleasant (*has an evil temper*). **4** unlucky; causing misfortune (*evil days*). ● *n.* **1** an evil thing; an instance of something evil. **2** evil quality; wickedness, harm. □ **evil eye** a gaze or stare superstitiously believed to be able to cause material harm. **speak evil of** slander. **evil-minded** having evil intentions. □□ **evilly** *adv.* **evilness** *n.* [OE *yfel* f. Gmc]

■ *adj.* **1** bad, wicked, awful, wrong, immoral, sinful, nefarious, iniquitous, heinous, base, corrupt, vile, damnable, villainous, flagitious, foul, nasty, abominable, infamous, atrocious, horrible, horrid, ghastly, grisly, dreadful, depraved, vicious, malevolent, evil-minded, *colloq.* accursed. **2** harmful, hurtful, destructive, pernicious, injurious, mischievous, detrimental, ruinous, deleterious, disastrous, catastrophic, noxious, malignant, malign, poisonous, deadly, lethal, black-hearted, *literary* malefic; virulent, toxic; treacherous, traitorous, perfidious, insidious, unscrupulous, unprincipled, dishonest, knavish, dishonourable, crooked, criminal, felonious, sinister, *literary* maleficent. **3** disagreeable, unpleasant, bad, disgusting, repulsive, awful, nasty, foul, vile, offensive, noxious; putrid, mephitic. **4** unlucky, unfortunate, ominous, inauspicious, dire, unpropitious, infelicitous. ● *n.* **1** sin, vice, iniquity, crime. **2** wickedness, badness, evildoing, wrongdoing, iniquity, immorality, devilry, villainy, nefariousness, viciousness, vileness, heinousness, flagitiousness, foulness, baseness, corruption, degradation, depravity, degeneracy, *formal* turpitude; harm, hurt, injury, mischief, damage; ruin, calamity, misfortune, catastrophe, destruction, disaster; misery, suffering, pain, sorrow, agony, anguish, *archaic or literary* woe. □ **evil eye** see JINX *n.* **speak evil of** see DISCREDIT *v.* 1. **evil-minded** vicious, hateful, malicious, spiteful, malevolent, evil, wicked, bad.

evildoer /éev'ldōōər/ *n.* a person who does evil. □□ **evil-doing** *n.*

evince /ivínss/ *v.tr.* **1** indicate or make evident. **2** show that one has (a quality). □□ **evincible** *adj.* **evincive** *adj.* [L *evincere*: see EVICT]

■ see DEMONSTRATE 1, 3.

eviscerate /ivíssərayt/ *v.tr. formal* **1** disembowel. **2** empty or deprive of essential contents. □□ **evisceration** /-ráysh'n/ *n.* [L *eviscerare eviscerat-* (as E-, VISCERA)]

■ see GUT *v.* 2.

evocative /ivókkətiv/ *adj.* tending to evoke (esp. feelings or memories). □□ **evocatively** *adv.* **evocativeness** *n.*

■ see SUGGESTIVE 1.

evoke /ivṓk/ *v.tr.* **1** inspire or draw forth (memories, feelings, a response, etc.). **2** summon (a supposed spirit from the dead). □□ **evocation** /évvəkáysh'n/ *n.* **evoker** *n.* [L *evocare* (as E-, *vocare* call)]

■ **1** see *call forth*. **2** summon (up), call up *or* forth, conjure (up), invoke, recall; wake, awake, waken, rouse, arouse, raise, reawaken.

evolute /évvəlyōōt, -lōōt/ *n.* (in full **evolute curve**) *Math.* a curve which is the locus of the centres of curvature of another curve that is its involute. [L *evolutus* past part. (as EVOLVE)]

evolution /éevəlōōsh'n, -lyōōsh'n/ *n.* **1** gradual development, esp. from a simple to a more complex form. **2** a process by which species develop from earlier forms, as an explanation of their origins. **3** the appearance or presentation of events etc. in due succession (*the evolution of the plot*). **4** a change in the disposition of troops or ships. **5** the giving off or evolving of gas, heat, etc. **6** an opening out. **7** the unfolding of a curve. **8** *Math.* the extraction of a root from any given power (cf. INVOLUTION). □□ **evolutional** *adj.* **evolutionally** *adv.* **evolutionary** *adj.* **evolutionarily** *adv.* [L *evolutio* unrolling (as EVOLVE)]

■ **1–3** development, growth, advance, progress, progression, evolvement, maturation; phylogeny, phylogenesis.

evolutionist /éevəlōōshənist, -lyōōshənist/ *n.* a person who believes in evolution as explaining the origin of species. □□ **evolutionism** *n.* **evolutionistic** /-nístik/ *adj.*

evolve /ivólv/ *v.* **1** *intr.* & *tr.* develop gradually by a natural process. **2** *tr.* work out or devise (a theory, plan, etc.). **3** *intr.* & *tr.* unfold; open out. **4** *tr.* give off (gas, heat, etc.). □□ **evolvable** *adj.* **evolvement** *n.* [L *evolvere evolut-* (as E-, *volvere* roll)]

■ **1–3** see DEVELOP 1.

evzone /évzōn/ *n.* a member of a select Greek infantry regiment. [mod. Gk *euzōnos* f. Gk, = dressed for exercise (as EU-, *zōnē* belt)]

ewe /yōō/ *n.* a female sheep. □ **ewe lamb** one's most cherished possession (2 Sam. 12). **ewe-necked** (of a horse) having a thin concave neck. [OE *ēowu* f. Gmc]

ewer /yōōər/ *n.* a large pitcher or water-jug with a wide mouth. [ME f. ONF *eviere*, OF *aiguiere*, ult. f. L *aquarius* of water f. *aqua* water]

■ see JUG *n.* 1, 2.

ex[1] /eks/ *prep.* **1** (of goods) sold from (*ex-works*). **2** (of stocks or shares) without, excluding. [L, = out of]

ex[2] /eks/ *n. colloq.* a former husband or wife. [absol. use of EX-[1] 2]

ex-[1] /eks/ *prefix* (also **e-** before some consonants, **ef-** before *f*) **1** forming verbs meaning: **a** out, forth (*exclude*; *exit*). **b** upward (*extol*). **c** thoroughly (*excruciate*). **d** bring into a state (*exasperate*). **e** remove or free from (*expatriate*; *exonerate*). **2** forming nouns from titles of office, status, etc., meaning 'formerly' (*ex-convict*; *ex-president*; *ex-wife*). [L f. *ex* out of]

ex-[2] /eks/ *prefix* out (*exodus*). [Gk f. *ex* out of]

exa- /éksə/ *comb. form* denoting a factor of 10^{18}. [perh. f. HEXA-]

exacerbate /igzássərbayt/ *v.tr.* **1** make (pain, anger, etc.) worse. **2** irritate (a person). □□ **exacerbation** /-báysh'n/ *n.* [L *exacerbare* (as EX-[1], *acerbus* bitter)]

■ **1** see AGGRAVATE 1. **2** see AGGRAVATE 2.

exact /igzákt/ *adj.* & *v.* ● *adj.* **1** accurate; correct in all details (*an exact description*). **2 a** precise. **b** (of a person) tending to precision. ● *v.tr.* (often foll. by *from*, *of*) **1** demand and enforce payment of (money, fees, etc.) from a person. **2 a** demand; insist on. **b** (of circumstances) require urgently. □ **exact science** a science admitting of absolute or quantitative precision. □□ **exactable** *adj.* **exactitude** *n.* **exactness** *n.* **exactor** *n.* [L *exigere exact-* (as EX-[1], *agere* drive)]

■ *adj.* **1, 2a** accurate, correct, precise, faithful, true, identical, literal, perfect. **2 b** careful, meticulous, strict, rigorous, fastidious, severe, scrupulous, thorough, painstaking, accurate, punctilious, rigid. ● *v.* demand, extort, enforce, insist on *or* upon, wrest, require; claim, compel, call for, requisition.

exacting /igzákting/ *adj.* **1** making great demands. **2** calling for much effort. □□ **exactingly** *adv.* **exactingness** *n.*

■ demanding, challenging, hard, tough, severe, rigid, stern, stringent, harsh, unsparing, merciless, rigorous; difficult, burdensome, taxing; oppressive, tyrannical.

exaction /igzáksh'n/ *n.* **1** the act or an instance of exacting; the process of being exacted. **2 a** an illegal or exorbitant demand; an extortion. **b** a sum or thing exacted. [ME f. L *exactio* (as EXACT)]

■ **2 a** see TRIBUTE 2. **b** see TOLL[1] 2.

exactly /igzáktli/ *adv.* **1** accurately, precisely; in an exact manner (*worked it out exactly*). **2** in exact terms (*exactly when did it happen?*). **3** (said in reply) quite so; I quite agree. **4** just; in all respects. □ **not exactly** *colloq.* **1** by no means. **2** not precisely.

■ **1** accurately, precisely, perfectly, correctly, faultlessly, faithfully, scrupulously, strictly, literally, to the letter, *literatim*, word for word, verbatim, closely; methodically, systematically. **3** see ABSOLUTELY 6. **4** absolutely, undeniably, certainly, unequivocally, completely, in every respect, in all respects, particularly, specifically, explicitly, just, quite, expressly, precisely, truly, *Brit. colloq.* bang on.

exaggerate /igzájərayt/ *v.tr.* **1** (also *absol.*) give an impression of (a thing), esp. in speech or writing, that makes it seem larger or greater etc. than it really is. **2** enlarge or alter beyond normal or due proportions (*spoke with exaggerated politeness*). □□ **exaggeratedly** *adv.* **exaggeratingly** *adv.* **exaggeration** /-ráysh'n/ *n.* **exaggerative** /-rətiv/ *adj.* **exaggerator** *n.* [L *exaggerare* (as EX-[1], *aggerare* heap up f. *agger* heap)]

■ **1** overstate, magnify, inflate, overdraw, stretch, enlarge, overemphasize, overstress, overplay, overdo; *colloq.* lay it on thick, lay (it) on with a trowel, pile (it) on, *sl.* stick it on. **2** see AMPLIFY 2. □□ **exaggeration** overstatement, extravagance, overemphasis, hyperbole; magnification; excess; empty talk, bombast, puffery, *sl.* hot air, bull.

exalt /igzáwlt/ *v.tr.* **1** raise in rank or power etc. **2** praise highly. **3** (usu. as **exalted** *adj.*) **a** make lofty or noble (*exalted aims*; *an exalted style*). **b** make rapturously excited. **4** (as **exalted** *adj.*) elevated in rank or character; eminent, celebrated. **5** stimulate (a faculty, etc.) to greater activity; intensify, heighten. □□ **exaltedly** *adv.* **exaltedness** *n.* **exalter** *n.* [ME f. L *exaltare* (as EX-[1], *altus* high)]

■ **1** elevate, raise (up *or* on high), lift (up *or* on high), upraise, uplift, upgrade, promote, advance, *colloq.* boost. **2** praise, honour, extol, glorify, idolize, dignify, ennoble, revere, reverence, venerate, pay homage *or* tribute to, celebrate; lionize. **3** (**exalted**) **a** lofty, noble, elevated, uplifting, grand, high-flown, exaggerated, overblown, inflated, heightened, superior. **b** elated, excited, exultant, ecstatic, jubilant, overjoyed, joyful, rapturous, transported, blissful, happy, joyous, uplifted; over the moon, in seventh heaven, *colloq.* on cloud nine. **4** (**exalted**) elevated, lofty, high, eminent, notable, noted, prominent, famous, famed, celebrated, distinguished, dignified, honoured, prestigious, glorified, sublime, grand. **5** stimulate, excite, animate, rouse, arouse, fire, inspire, electrify, awaken, spur, stir (up), inspirit; intensify, heighten.

exaltation /égzawltáysh'n/ *n.* **1** the act or an instance of exalting; the state of being exalted. **2** elation; rapturous emotion. [ME f. OF *exaltation* or LL *exaltatio* (as EXALT)]

■ **1** see GLORY *n.* 1, 3. **2** see JOY *n.* 1.

exam /igzám/ *n.* = EXAMINATION 3.

examination /igzámmináysh'n/ *n.* **1** the act or an instance of examining; the state of being examined. **2** a detailed inspection. **3** the testing of the proficiency or knowledge of students or other candidates for a qualification by oral or written questions. **4** an instance of examining or being examined medically. **5** *Law* the formal questioning of the accused or of a witness in court. □ **examination paper 1** the printed questions in an examination. **2** a candidate's set of answers. □□ **examinational** *adj.* [ME f. OF f. L *examinatio -onis* (as EXAMINE)]

■ **1, 2** investigation, study, analysis, inspection, inquiry, exploration, research, appraisal, assessment; scrutiny; probe, search, survey, check-up, check, *US* checkout, *colloq.* going-over. **3** testing, quiz, exam, test, trial; viva voce, *colloq.* oral, *Brit. colloq.* viva. **4** check-up, check, *colloq.* going-over. **5** questioning, interrogation, inquisition, inquiry, catechism, cross-examination, *colloq.* third degree, grilling.

examine /igzámmin/ *v.* **1** *tr.* inquire into the nature or condition etc. of. **2** *tr.* look closely or analytically at. **3** *tr.* test the proficiency of, esp. by examination (see EXAMINATION 3). **4** *tr.* check the health of (a patient) by inspection or experiment. **5** *tr. Law* formally question (the accused or a witness) in court. **6** *intr.* (foll. by *into*) inquire. □□ **examinable** *adj.* **examinee** /-neé/ *n.* **examiner** *n.* [ME f. OF *examiner* f. L *examinare* weigh, test f. *examen* tongue of a balance, ult. f. *exigere* examine, weigh: see EXACT]

■ **1, 2** inquire into, investigate, look over *or* into, inspect, go over *or* through *or* into, scrutinize, analyse, research, study, peruse, scan, pore over, sift, probe, search, explore, survey, check up on, check, appraise, assess, weigh, vet, *US* check out. **3** see TEST[1] *v.* 1. **5** interrogate, quiz, cross-examine, question, grill, pump, sound out. **6** see INQUIRE 1.

example /igzaámp'l/ *n.* & *v.* ● *n.* **1** a thing characteristic of its kind or illustrating a general rule. **2** a person, thing, or piece of conduct, regarded in terms of its fitness to be imitated (*must set him an example*; *you are a bad example*). **3** a circumstance or treatment seen as a warning to others; a person so treated (*shall make an example of you*). **4** a problem or exercise designed to illustrate a rule. ● *v.tr.* (usu. in *passive*) serve as an example of. □ **for example** by way of illustration. [ME f. OF f. L *exemplum* (as EXEMPT)]

■ *n.* **1** instance, case, sample, specimen, illustration, exemplum. **2** model, standard, exemplar, prototype, archetype, pattern, benchmark, norm, criterion. **3** warning, admonition; see also LESSON 4. **4** illustration, application; problem; exercise. □ **for example** for instance, by way of illustration, by way of example, as an illustration, as an example, as a case in point, to illustrate, e.g.

exanimate /igzánnimət/ *adj.* **1** dead, lifeless (esp. in appearance); inanimate. **2** lacking animation or courage. [L *exanimatus* pa. pple of *exanimare* deprive of life, f. EX-[1] + *anima* breath of life]

exanthema /éksantheémə/ *n. Med.* a skin rash accompanying any eruptive disease or fever. [LL f. Gk *exanthēma* eruption f. *exantheō* (as EX-[2], *anthos* blossom)]

exarch /éksaark/ *n.* in the Orthodox Church, a bishop lower in rank than a patriarch and having jurisdiction wider than the metropolitan of a diocese. □□ **exarchate** *n.* [eccl.L f. Gk *exarkhos* (as EX-[2], *arkhos* ruler)]

exasperate /igzaáspərayt/ *v.tr.* **1** (often as **exasperated** *adj.* or **exasperating** *adj.*) irritate intensely; infuriate, enrage. **2** make (a pain, ill feeling, etc.) worse. □□ **exasperatedly** *adv.* **exasperatingly** *adv.* **exasperation** /-ráysh'n/ *n.* [L *exasperare exasperat-* (as EX-[1], *asper* rough)]

■ **1** irritate, irk, annoy, bother, harass, pique, gall, nettle, provoke, vex, pester, torment, plague, rub up the wrong way, *colloq.* needle, peeve (off), get, get under a person's skin, *disp.* aggravate, *sl.* bug, get a person's goat; anger, infuriate, enrage, incense, madden, rile, drive mad; embitter; inflame, *colloq.* drive crazy, drive up the wall. **2** see AGGRAVATE 1. □□ **exasperation** see ANNOYANCE 1.

ex cathedra /éks kətheédrə/ *adj.* & *adv.* with full authority (esp. of a papal pronouncement, implying infallibility as doctrinally defined). [L, = from the (teacher's) chair]

excavate /ékskəvayt/ *v.tr.* **1 a** make (a hole or channel) by digging. **b** dig out material from (the ground). **2** reveal or extract by digging. **3** (also *absol.*) *Archaeol.* dig systematically into the ground to explore (a site). □□ **excavation** /-váysh'n/ *n.* **excavator** *n.* [L *excavare* (as EX-[1], *cavus* hollow)]

■ **1** dig (out *or* up), hollow *or* gouge (out), scoop out, burrow, cut (out). **2, 3** reveal, unearth, uncover, expose, lay bare, dig up, disinter, exhume; clear, dredge up. □□ **excavation** cavity, hole, pit, crater, ditch, trench, trough, burrow, hollow; shaft, tunnel; mine, quarry; *Archaeol.* dig.

exceed /ikseéd/ *v.tr.* **1** (often foll. by *by* an amount) be more or greater than (in number, extent, etc.). **2** go beyond or do more than is warranted by (a set limit, esp. of one's instructions or rights). **3** surpass, excel (a person or achievement). [ME f. OF *exceder* f. L *excedere* (as EX-[1], *cedere cess-* go)]

■ **1, 3** surpass, be superior to, beat, go beyond, better, outdistance, overtake, outstrip, outrank, outrun, outdo, outpace; excel, top, pass; outshine, outreach, transcend, overshadow, eclipse. **2** go beyond, overstep; overdo.

exceeding /ikséeding/ *adj.* & *adv.* ● *adj.* **1** surpassing in amount or degree. **2** pre-eminent. ● *adv. archaic* = EXCEEDINGLY 2.
■ *adj.* great, huge, enormous, outstanding, extraordinary, excessive, exceptional, surpassing; see also PRE-EMINENT 2.

exceedingly /ikséedingli/ *adv.* **1** very; to a great extent. **2** surpassingly, pre-eminently.
■ **1** very, extremely, exceptionally, extraordinarily, remarkably, incomparably, immeasurably; excessively, greatly, hugely, enormously. **2** see *pre-eminently* (PRE-EMINENT).

excel /iksél/ *v.* (**excelled, excelling**) (often foll. by *in, at*) **1** *tr.* be superior to. **2** *intr.* be pre-eminent or the most outstanding (*excels at games*). □ **excel oneself** surpass one's previous performance. [ME f. L *excellere* (as EX-[1], *celsus* lofty)]
■ **1** surpass, be superior to, beat, exceed, go beyond, outdo, outstrip, outrank, outpace, outshine, eclipse, top, *sl.* whip. **2** dominate, shine, stand out, be pre-eminent, be superior, be excellent, be outstanding.

excellence /éksələnss/ *n.* **1** the state of excelling; surpassing merit or quality. **2** the activity etc. in which a person excels. [ME f. OF *excellence* or L *excellentia* (as EXCEL)]
■ **1** superiority, merit, distinction, greatness, prominence, eminence, pre-eminence, supremacy; (high) quality, value, worth. **2** see SPECIALITY.

Excellency /éksələnsi/ *n.* (*pl.* **-ies**) (usu. prec. by *Your, His, Her, Their*) a title used in addressing or referring to certain high officials, e.g. ambassadors and governors, and (in some countries) senior Church dignitaries. [ME f. L *excellentia* (as EXCEL)]

excellent /éksələnt/ *adj.* extremely good; pre-eminent. □□ **excellently** *adv.* [ME f. OF (as EXCEL)]
■ superb, splendid, great, marvellous, remarkable, sterling, exceptional, superior, supreme, superlative, prime, choice, select, *colloq.* smashing, super, terrific, fantastic, magic, brilliant, brill, ripsnorting, *sl.* wicked, *esp. US sl.* bad, cool; distinguished, noteworthy, notable, worthy, admirable; pre-eminent, outstanding, capital, first-class, first-rate, matchless, peerless, unequalled, nonpareil, *colloq.* tiptop, A1, *colloq. or dial.* champion, *esp. Brit. colloq.* slap-up, *Brit. colloq.* top-hole, *US colloq.* A-OK, *sl.* crucial, *Austral. sl.* bonzer, grouse; without equal.

excelsior /iksélsior/ *int.* & *n.* ● *int.* higher, outstanding (esp. as a motto or trade mark). ● *n.* soft wood shavings used for stuffing, packing, etc. [L, compar. of *excelsus* lofty]

excentric var. of ECCENTRIC (in technical senses).

except /iksépt/ *v., prep.,* & *conj.* ● *v.tr.* (often as **excepted** *adj.* placed after object) exclude from a general statement, condition, etc. (*excepted him from the amnesty; present company excepted*). ● *prep.* (often foll. by *for* or *that*) not including; other than (*all failed except him; all here except for John; is all right except that it is too long*). ● *conj. archaic* unless (*except he be born again*). [ME f. L *excipere except-* (as EX-[1], *capere* take)]
■ *v.* exclude; omit, leave out, excuse. ● *prep.* not including, not counting, other than, excepting, barring, bar, with the exception of, apart from, but for, saving, excluding, exclusive of; but for the fact that, *archaic or poet.* save (that); but.

excepting /iksépting/ *prep.* & *conj.* ● *prep.* = EXCEPT *prep.* ● *conj. archaic* = EXCEPT *conj.*

exception /iksépsh'n/ *n.* **1** the act or an instance of excepting; the state of being excepted (*made an exception in my case*). **2** a thing that has been or will be excepted. **3** an instance that does not follow a rule. □ **take exception** (often foll. by *to*) object; be resentful (about). **with the exception of** except; not including. [ME f. OF f. L *exceptio -onis* (as EXCEPT)]
■ **3** anomaly, irregularity, special case, departure; oddity, rarity, peculiarity, quirk. □ **take exception (to)** object (to), make an objection (to *or* against), raise an objection (to *or* against), raise objections (to *or* against), demur (to *or* at), find fault (with), take offence *or* umbrage (at), be offended (by); (call into) question, challenge, oppose, disagree (with).

exceptionable /iksépshənəb'l/ *adj.* open to objection. □□ **exceptionably** *adv.*
■ objectionable, unsatisfactory, criticizable; see also UNACCEPTABLE.

exceptional /iksépshən'l/ *adj.* **1** forming an exception. **2** unusual; not typical (*exceptional circumstances*). **3** unusually good; outstanding. □□ **exceptionality** /-nálliti/ *n.* **exceptionally** *adv.*
■ **1, 2** special, especial; unusual, out of the ordinary, untypical, atypical, uncommon, rare, extraordinary, singular, strange, irregular, aberrant, anomalous, odd, peculiar. **3** outstanding, gifted, talented, above average, excellent, superior, prodigious, extraordinary.

excerpt *n.* & *v.* ● *n.* /ékserpt/ a short extract from a book, film, piece of music, etc. ● *v.tr.* /iksérpt/ (also *absol.*) **1** take an excerpt or excerpts from (a book etc.). **2** take (an extract) from a book etc. □□ **excerptible** /-sérptib'l/ *adj.* **excerption** /-sérpsh'n/ *n.* [L *excerpere excerpt-* (as EX-[1], *carpere* pluck)]
■ *n.* extract, passage, quotation, selection, citation, pericope. ● *v.* extract, select; quote, cite; take, cull.

excess /ikséss, éksess/ *n.* & *adj.* ● *n.* **1** the state or an instance of exceeding. **2** the amount by which one quantity or number exceeds another. **3** exceeding of a proper or permitted limit. **4 a** the overstepping of the accepted limits of moderation, esp. intemperance in eating or drinking. **b** (in *pl.*) outrageous or immoderate behaviour. **5** an extreme or improper degree or extent (*an excess of cruelty*). **6** part of an insurance claim to be paid by the insured, esp. by prior agreement. ● *attrib.adj.* /usu. éksess/ **1** that exceeds a limited or prescribed amount (*excess weight*). **2** required as extra payment (*excess postage*). □ **excess baggage** (or **luggage**) that exceeding a weight allowance and liable to an extra charge. **in** (or **to**) **excess** exceeding the proper amount or degree. **in excess of** more than; exceeding. [ME f. OF *exces* f. L *excessus* (as EXCEED)]
■ *n.* **1** over-abundance, overflow, superabundance, superfluity, redundancy; surplus, surfeit, plethora, glut, leftovers; overkill; supererogation. **2** balance, difference, discrepancy. **4 a** (*excesses*) debauchery, immoderation, profligacy, overindulgence, intemperance, dissipation, dissoluteness, extravagance. ● *attrib.adj.* **1** surplus, extra, superfluous, excessive, leftover, remaining, residual. **2** further, extra; see also SUPPLEMENTARY. □ **in excess of** more than, exceeding; see also OVER *prep.* 10.

excessive /iksésiv/ *adj.* **1** too much or too great. **2** more than what is normal or necessary. □□ **excessively** *adv.* **excessiveness** *n.*
■ immoderate, inordinate, disproportionate, exorbitant, superfluous, extravagant, excess, undue, enormous, extreme, overdone, unreasonable, unwarranted, unjustifiable, outrageous, unconscionable, *colloq.* over-the-top; fulsome, cloying, nauseating, disgusting.

exchange /ikscháynj/ *n.* & *v.* ● *n.* **1** the act or an instance of giving one thing and receiving another in its place. **2 a** the giving of money for its equivalent in the money of the same or another country. **b** the fee or percentage charged for this. **3** the central telephone office of a district, where connections are effected. **4 a** a place where merchants, bankers, etc. gather to transact business. **b** (**the Exchange**) = *Stock Exchange.* **5 a** an office where certain information is given or a service provided, usu. involving two parties. **b** an employment office. **6** a system of settling debts between persons (esp. in different countries) without the use of money, by bills of exchange (see BILL[1]). **7 a** a short conversation, esp. a disagreement or quarrel. **b** a sequence of letters between correspondents. **8** *Chess* the capture of an important piece (esp. a rook) by one player at the loss of a minor piece to the opposing player. **9** (*attrib.*) forming part of an exchange, e.g. of personnel between institutions (*an exchange student*). ● *v.* **1** *tr.* (often foll. by *for*) give or receive (one thing) in place of another. **2** *tr.* give and receive as equivalents (e.g. things or people, blows, information, etc.); give one and receive another of. **3** *intr.* (often foll. by *with*) make an exchange. □ **exchange rate** the value of one currency in terms of another. **in exchange** (often foll. by *for*) as a thing exchanged (for). □□ **exchangeable** *adj.* **exchangeability** /-jəbílliti/ *n.* **exchanger** *n.* [ME f. OF *eschangier* f. Rmc (as EX-[1], CHANGE)]

■ *n.* **1** trade, barter, traffic, truck, change, transfer, interchange, switch, swap; reciprocity, reciprocation; quid pro quo, tit for tat. **4** market, stock market, Stock Exchange, securities exchange, the Exchange, Bourse, *Brit.* the Market, *US* Wall Street, *US colloq.* Big Board. **5** see BUREAU 2. **7a** conversation, altercation, argument, disagreement, dispute; see also QUARREL[1] *n.* 1. ● *v.* **1, 2** trade, barter, switch, change, interchange, reciprocate, swap.

exchequer /ikschékkər/ *n.* **1** *Brit.* the former government department in charge of national revenue. ¶ Its functions now belong to the Treasury, although the name formally survives, esp. in the title *Chancellor of the Exchequer*. **2** a royal or national treasury. **3** the money of a private individual or group. [ME f. AF *escheker*, OF *eschequier* f. med.L *scaccarium* chessboard (its orig. sense, with ref. to keeping accounts on a chequered cloth)]

■ see TREASURY 2.

excise[1] /éksīz/ *n.* & *v.* ● *n.* **1 a** a duty or tax levied on goods and commodities produced or sold within the country of origin. **b** a tax levied on certain licences. **2** *Brit.* a former government office collecting excise. ¶ Now the *Board of Customs and Excise*. ● *v.tr.* **1** charge excise on (goods). **2** force (a person) to pay excise. [MDu. *excijs*, *accijs*, perh. f. Rmc: rel. to CENSUS]

■ *n.* **1** see CUSTOM 4a.

excise[2] /iksīz/ *v.tr.* **1** remove (a passage of a book etc.). **2** cut out (an organ etc.) by surgery. □□ **excision** /iksízh'n/ *n.* [L *excidere excis-* (as EX-[1], *caedere* cut)]

■ **1** see *cut out* 3. **2** see *cut out* 1 .

exciseman /éksīzman/ *n.* (*pl.* **-men**) *Brit. hist.* an officer responsible for collecting excise duty.

excitable /iksītəb'l/ *adj.* **1** (esp. of a person) easily excited. **2** (of an organism, tissue, etc.) responding to a stimulus, or susceptible to stimulation. □□ **excitability** /-bílliti/ *n.* **excitably** *adv.*

■ **1** emotional, nervous, jumpy, restive, restless, fidgety, edgy, touchy, testy, highly-strung, high-strung, volatile, mercurial, quick-tempered, hot-blooded, feverish, hysterical, *colloq.* on a short fuse. **2** see SENSITIVE 3, 4, 6.

excitation /éksitáysh'n/ *n.* **1 a** the act or an instance of exciting. **b** the state of being excited; excitement. **2** the action of an organism, tissue, etc., resulting from stimulation. **3** *Electr.* **a** the process of applying current to the winding of an electromagnet to produce a magnetic field. **b** the process of applying a signal voltage to the control electrode of an electron tube or the base of a transistor. **4** *Physics* the process in which an atom etc. acquires a higher energy state.

■ **1 b** see *excitement* (EXCITE).

excite /iksīt/ *v.tr.* **1 a** rouse the feelings or emotions of (a person). **b** bring into play; rouse up (feelings, faculties, etc.). **c** arouse sexually. **2** provoke; bring about (an action or active condition). **3** promote the activity of (an organism, tissue, etc.) by stimulus. **4** *Electr.* **a** cause (a current) to flow in the winding of an electromagnet. **b** supply a signal. **5** *Physics* **a** cause the emission of (a spectrum). **b** cause (a substance) to emit radiation. **c** put (an atom etc.) into a state of higher energy. □□ **excitant** /éksit'nt, iksīt'nt/ *adj.* & *n.* **excitative** /-tətiv/ *adj.* **excitatory** /-tətəri/ *adj.* **excitedly** *adv.* **excitedness** *n.* **excitement** *n.* **exciter** *n.* (esp. in senses 4, 5). [ME f. OF *exciter* or L *excitare* frequent. of *exciēre* (as EX-[1], *ciēre* set in motion)]

■ **1 a, b** rouse, arouse, stir (up), awake, wake, awaken, waken, inspire, stimulate, rally, galvanize; foment, fire, inflame, kindle, ignite; rouse up, call forth; summon up, elicit; inspirit, electrify, animate, enliven, activate, motivate, invigorate, energize, *colloq.* enthuse. **c** arouse, thrill, titillate, *colloq.* turn on. **2** provoke, stir up, stimulate, inspire, call forth, prod; bring about, cause, incite, spur (on), instigate, generate, occasion, begin, start, initiate, effect, set in motion, spark (off). □□ **excitedness, excitement** agitation, restlessness, jumpiness, nervousness, excitation, tension, unrest, disquiet, disquietude; perturbation, upset, action, ado, activity, ferment, furore, turmoil, tumult, to-do, stir, commotion, hubbub, brouhaha, fuss, hurly-burly, fireworks; animation, eagerness, enthusiasm, exhilaration, ebullience.

exciting /iksīting/ *adj.* arousing great interest or enthusiasm; stirring. □□ **excitingly** *adv.* **excitingness** *n.*

■ rousing, stimulating, inspiring, stirring, moving; seductive, sensuous, voluptuous, ravishing, captivating, charming, tempting, enticing, alluring, provocative, titillating, sexy; intoxicating, heady, thrilling, exhilarating, stirring, electrifying, galvanizing, energizing, invigorating; overwhelming, overpowering, astounding, astonishing, amazing, *colloq.* mind-boggling, *sl.* mind-blowing.

exciton /eksīton, éksiton/ *n.* *Physics* a combination of an electron with a hole in a crystalline solid. [EXCITATION + -ON]

exclaim /ikskláym/ *v.* **1** *intr.* cry out suddenly, esp. in anger, surprise, pain, etc. **2** *tr.* (foll. by *that*) utter by exclaiming. [F *exclamer* or L *exclamare* (as EX-[1]: cf. CLAIM)]

■ **1** call *or* cry (out), shout, yell, bawl, bellow, burst out, blurt out, *US colloq.* holler. **2** call *or* cry (out), proclaim, declare, shout, yell, bawl, bellow, *US colloq.* holler.

exclamation /èkskləmáysh'n/ *n.* **1** the act or an instance of exclaiming. **2** words exclaimed; a strong sudden cry. □ **exclamation mark** (*US* **point**) a punctuation mark (!) indicating an exclamation. [ME f. OF *exclamation* or L *exclamatio* (as EXCLAIM)]

■ call, cry, utterance, ejaculation, interjection, outcry, vociferation, shout, yell, bellow, *US colloq.* holler.

exclamatory /iksklámmətəri, -tri/ *adj.* of or serving as an exclamation.

exclave /éksklayv/ *n.* a portion of territory of one State completely surrounded by territory of another or others, as viewed by the home territory (cf. ENCLAVE). [EX-[1] + ENCLAVE]

exclosure /eksklṓzhər/ *n.* *Forestry* etc. an area from which unwanted animals are excluded. [EX-[1] + ENCLOSURE]

exclude /iksklṓōd/ *v.tr.* **1** shut or keep out (a person or thing) from a place, group, privilege, etc. **2** expel and shut out. **3** remove from consideration (*no theory can be excluded*). **4** prevent the occurrence of; make impossible (*excluded all doubt*). □ **excluded middle** *Logic* the principle that of two contradictory propositions one must be true. □□ **excludable** *adj.* **excluder** *n.* [ME f. L *excludere exclus-* (as EX-[1], *claudere* shut)]

■ **1** shut *or* lock out, keep out *or* away, ban, bar, debar, prohibit, interdict, forbid, proscribe. **2** expel, shut out, eject, evict, oust, get rid of, remove, throw out, *sl.* bounce. **3** leave out, eliminate, reject, omit, except, preclude, *colloq.* count out. **4** see STOP *v.* 1b.

exclusion /iksklṓōzh'n/ *n.* the act or an instance of excluding; the state of being excluded. □ **exclusion order** *Brit.* an official order preventing a person (esp. a suspected terrorist) from entering the UK. **exclusion principle** *Physics* see PAULI EXCLUSION PRINCIPLE. **to the exclusion of** so as to exclude. □□ **exclusionary** *adj.* [L *exclusio* (as EXCLUDE)]

■ ban, banning, bar, prohibition, interdiction, proscription, forbiddance, lockout; expulsion, ejection, eviction, ouster, removal, riddance; elimination, rejection, omission, exception, preclusion.

exclusionist /iksklṓōzhənist/ *adj.* & *n.* ● *adj.* favouring exclusion, esp. from rights or privileges. ● *n.* a person favouring exclusion.

exclusive /iksklṓōssiv/ *adj.* & *n.* ● *adj.* **1** excluding other things. **2** (*predic.*; foll. by *of*) not including; except for. **3** tending to exclude others, esp. socially; select. **4** catering for few or select customers; high-class. **5 a** (of a commodity) not obtainable elsewhere. **b** (of a newspaper article) not published elsewhere. **6** (*predic.*; foll. by *to*) restricted or limited to; existing or available only in. **7** (of terms etc.) excluding all but what is specified. **8** employed or followed or held to the exclusion of all else (*my exclusive occupation*; *exclusive rights*). ● *n.* an article or story published by only one newspaper or periodical. □ **Exclusive Brethren** a more exclusive section of the Plymouth Brethren. □□ **exclusively** *adv.* **exclusiveness** *n.* **exclusivity** /ékskloosívviti/ *n.* [med.L *exclusivus* (as EXCLUDE)]

■ *adj.* **2** (*exclusive of*) not including, not counting, excluding, omitting, ignoring, apart from, leaving aside, barring; except for, excepting. **3, 4** select, choice, closed, restricted, restrictive, private, snobbish, *usu. derog.* clannish; chic, fashionable, elegant, stylish, upper-class, high-class, aristocratic, *colloq.* classy, *colloq. often derog.* trendy. **5, 6** unique, restricted, limited. **8** only, single, one, sole, unique, singular. ● *n.* scoop, special; *colloq.* one-off.

excogitate /ekskójitayt/ *v.tr.* think out; contrive. □□ **excogitation** /-táysh'n/ *n.* [L *excogitare excogitat-* (as EX-[1], *cogitare* COGITATE)]

excommunicate *v.*, *adj.*, & *n.* *Eccl.* ● *v.tr.* /ékskəmyóonikayt/ officially exclude (a person) from participation in the sacraments, or from formal communion with the Church. ● *adj.* /ékskəmyóonikət/ excommunicated. ● *n.* /ékskəmyóonikət/ an excommunicated person. □□ **excommunication** /-káysh'n/ *n.* **excommunicative** /-kətiv/ *adj.* **excommunicator** *n.* **excommunicatory** /-káytəri/ *adj.* [L *excommunicare -atus* (as EX-[1], *communis* COMMON)]

■ *v.* unchurch, curse; see also BANISH 1.

ex-con /ékskón/ *n. colloq.* an ex-convict; a former inmate of a prison. [abbr.]

excoriate /ekskóriayt/ *v.tr.* **1 a** remove part of the skin of (a person etc.) by abrasion. **b** strip or peel off (skin). **2** censure severely. □□ **excoriation** /-áysh'n/ *n.* [L *excoriare excoriat-* (as EX-[1], *corium* hide)]

■ **1 a** see SKIN *v.* 1. **b** see PARE 1. **2** see BERATE.

excrement /ékskrimənt/ *n.* (in *sing.* or *pl.*) faeces. □□ **excremental** /-mént'l/ *adj.* [F *excrément* or L *excrementum* (as EXCRETE)]

excrescence /ikskréss'nss/ *n.* **1** an abnormal or morbid outgrowth on the body or a plant. **2** an ugly addition. □□ **excrescent** *adj.* **excrescential** /ékskrisénsh'l/ *adj.* [L *excrescentia* (as EX-[1], *crescere* grow)]

■ **1** see GROWTH 4.

excreta /ikskréetə/ *n.pl.* waste discharged from the body, esp. faeces and urine. [L neut. pl.: see EXCRETE]

■ see FILTH 1.

excrete /ikskréet/ *v.tr.* (also *absol.*) (of an animal or plant) separate and expel (waste matter) as a result of metabolism. □□ **excreter** *n.* **excretion** *n.* **excretive** *adj.* **excretory** *adj.* [L *excernere excret-* (as EX-[1], *cernere* sift)]

■ see DEFECATE.

excruciate /ikskróoshiayt/ *v.tr.* (esp. as **excruciating** *adj.*) torment acutely (a person's senses); torture mentally. □□ **excruciatingly** *adv.* **excruciation** /-áysh'n/ *n.* [L *excruciare excruciat-* (as EX-[1], *cruciare* torment f. *crux crucis* cross)]

■ (**excruciating**) tormenting, torturing, torturous, agonizing, painful, racking, intense, extreme, unbearable, unendurable, insufferable, severe, acute, harrowing, distressful, distressing.

exculpate /ékskulpayt/ *v.tr. formal* **1** free from blame. **2** (foll. by *from*) clear (a person) of a charge. □□ **exculpation** /-páysh'n/ *n.* **exculpatory** /-kúlpətəri/ *adj.* [med.L *exculpare exculpat-* (as EX-[1], *culpa* blame)]

■ see VINDICATE 1.

excursion /ikskúrsh'n/ *n.* **1** a short journey or ramble for pleasure, with return to the starting-point. **2** a digression. **3** *Astron.* a deviation from a regular path. **4** *archaic* a sortie (see ALARUM). □□ **excursional** *adj.* **excursionary** *adj.* **excursionist** *n.* [L *excursio* f. *excurrere excurs-* (as EX-[1], *currere* run)]

■ **1** journey, trip, tour, outing, expedition, voyage, cruise, junket, jaunt; detour, side-trip; ramble, stroll, walk, hike, trek, drive, ride, sail. **2** digression, deviation, excursus, diversion.

excursive /ikskúrsiv/ *adj.* digressive; diverse. □□ **excursively** *adv.* **excursiveness** *n.*

excursus /ikskúrsəss/ *n.* **1** a detailed discussion of a special point in a book, usu. in an appendix. **2** a digression in a narrative. [L, verbal noun formed as EXCURSION]

■ **2** see *digression* (DIGRESS).

excuse *v.* & *n.* ● *v.tr.* /ikskyóoz/ **1** attempt to lessen the blame attaching to (a person, act, or fault). **2** (of a fact or circumstance) serve in mitigation of (a person or act). **3** obtain exemption for (a person or oneself). **4** (foll. by *from*) release (a person) from a duty etc. (*excused from supervision duties*). **5** overlook or forgive (a fault or offence). **6** (foll. by *for*) forgive (a person) for a fault. **7** not insist upon (what is due). **8** *refl.* apologize for leaving. ● *n.* /ikskyóoss/ **1** a reason put forward to mitigate or justify an offence, fault, etc. **2** an apology (*made my excuses*). **3** (foll. by *for*) a poor or inadequate example of. **4** the action of excusing; indulgence, pardon. □ **be excused** be allowed to leave a room etc., e.g. to go to the lavatory. **excuse me** a polite apology for lack of ceremony, for an interruption etc., or for disagreeing. **excuse-me** a dance in which dancers may interrupt other pairs to change partners. □□ **excusable** /-kyóozəb'l/ *adj.* **excusably** /-kyóozəbli/ *adv.* **excusatory** /-kyóozətəri/ *adj.* [ME f. OF *escuser* f. L *excusare* (as EX-[1], *causa* CAUSE, accusation)]

■ *v.* **1** condone, justify, vindicate, defend, mitigate, extenuate, palliate, warrant, allow, permit, explain, rationalize; apologize for. **2** see *explain away*. **4** (*excuse from*) release from, let off, liberate from, free from *or* of, relieve of, exempt from, absolve of *or* from, *colloq.* let off the hook for. **5** overlook, forgive, pardon, disregard, ignore, wink at, pass over, be blind to, pay no attention *or* heed to, turn a blind eye to, turn a deaf ear to. **7** see WAIVE. **8** see LEAVE[1] 1b, 3, 4. ● *n.* **1, 2** reason, explanation, story, argument; apology, justification, defence, plea, vindication, rationalization; basis, ground(s), foundation, cause. **3** see APOLOGY 4. **4** forgiveness, remission, pardon, indulgence, reprieve, clearing, absolution, exoneration, acquittal, vindication, clearance, acquittance, *formal* exculpation.

ex-directory /éksdīréktəri, -diréktəri/ *adj. Brit.* not listed in a telephone directory, at the wish of the subscriber.

ex div. *abbr.* ex dividend.

ex dividend /eks dívvidend/ *adj.* & *adv.* (of stocks or shares) not including the next dividend.

exeat /éksiat/ *n. Brit.* permission granted to a student by a college for temporary absence or permission granted to a priest by a bishop to move to another diocese. [L, 3rd sing. pres. subjunctive of *exire* go out (as EX-[1], *ire* go)]

exec /igzék/ *n.* an executive. [abbr.]

execrable /éksikrəb'l/ *adj.* abominable, detestable. □□ **execrably** *adv.* [ME f. OF f. L *execrabilis* (as EXECRATE)]

■ see ABOMINABLE 1.

execrate /éksikrayt/ *v.* **1** *tr.* express or feel abhorrence for. **2** *tr.* curse (a person or thing). **3** *intr.* utter curses. □□ **execration** /-kráysh'n/ *n.* **execrative** *adj.* **execratory** *adj.* [L *exsecrare* (as EX-[1], *sacrare* devote f. *sacer* sacred, accursed)]

■ **1** see ABHOR. **2, 3** see CURSE *v.* 1a.

executant /igzékyoot'nt/ *n. formal* **1** a performer, esp. of music. **2** one who carries something into effect. [F *exécutant* pres. part. (as EXECUTE)]

execute /éksikyoot/ *v.tr.* **1 a** carry out a sentence of death on (a condemned person). **b** kill as a political act. **2** carry into effect, perform (a plan, duty, command, operation, etc.). **3 a** carry out a design for (a product of art or skill). **b** perform (a musical composition, dance, etc.). **4** make (a legal instrument) valid by signing, sealing, etc. **5** put into effect (a judicial sentence, the terms of a will, etc.). □□ **executable** *adj.* [ME f. OF *executer* f. med.L *executare* f. L *exsequi exsecut-* (as EX-[1], *sequi* follow)]

■ **1 a** put to death, kill. **b** assassinate, kill, liquidate, murder, snuff out, *colloq.* remove, *sl.* bump off, wipe out, knock off, *esp. US sl.* rub out, *US sl.* waste, ice. **2** effect, perform, fulfil, accomplish, do, carry out *or* through, discharge, dispatch, implement, engineer, cut, pull off, carry off, *colloq.* swing. **3 a** carry out, complete, finish, deliver. **b** perform, present, put on. **4** effect; sign, seal, validate, ratify, countersign. **5** see *carry out* (CARRY).

execution /éksikyóosh'n/ *n.* **1** the carrying out of a sentence of death. **2** the act or an instance of carrying out or performing something. **3** technique or style of performance in the arts, esp. music. **4 a** seizure of the property or person of a debtor in default of payment. **b** a judicial writ enforcing a judgement. □□ **executionary** *adj.* [ME f. OF f. L *executio -onis* (as EXECUTE)]

■ **1** killing; assassination, murder, liquidation, removal. **2** carrying out, performance, accomplishment, doing, discharge, dispatch, implementation, prosecution, realization, enactment; completion, fulfilment, achievement, attainment, implementation. **3** technique, style, rendering, rendition, manner, touch, approach, delivery, production, skill, art, mastery. **4 a** see SEIZURE 1.

executioner /éksikyóoshənər/ *n.* an official who carries out a sentence of death.

■ hangman, headsman.

executive /igzékyootiv/ *n.* & *adj.* ● *n.* **1** a person or body with managerial or administrative responsibility in a business organization etc.; a senior businessman. **2** a branch of a government or organization concerned with executing laws, agreements, etc., or with other administration or management. ● *adj.* **1** concerned with executing laws, agreements, etc., or with other administration or management. **2** relating to or having the function of executing. □ **Executive Council** the Australian constitutional body which gives legal form to Cabinet decisions. **executive session** *US* a usu. private meeting of a legislative body for executive business. □□ **executively** *adv.* [med.L *executivus* (as EXECUTE)]

■ *n.* **1** chairman (of the board), chairperson, chairwoman, director, managing director, chief, chief executive, president, manager, head, leader, principal, administrator, official; supervisor, superintendent, overseer, master, kingpin, *colloq.* top dog, boss, *sl.* top banana, (big) cheese, *US sl.* (head) honcho, Mr Big. **2** administration, management, directorship, directorate, government, leadership. ● *adj.* administrative, managerial, supervisory, official, governing, governmental.

executor /igzékyootər/ *n.* (*fem.* **executrix** /-triks/) a person appointed by a testator to carry out the terms of his or her will. □ **literary executor** a person entrusted with a writer's papers, unpublished works, etc. □□ **executorial** /-tóriəl/ *adj.* **executorship** *n.* **executory** *adj.* [ME f. AF *executor, -our* f. L *executor -oris* (as EXECUTE)]

exegesis /éksijéessiss/ *n.* (*pl.* **exegeses** /-seez/) critical explanation of a text, esp. of Scripture. □□ **exegete** /éksijeet/ *n.* **exegetic** /-jéttik/ *adj.* **exegetical** /-jéttik'l/ *adj.* **exegetist** /-jéetist/ *n.* [Gk *exēgēsis* f. *exēgeomai* interpret (as EX-[2], *hēgeomai* lead)]

■ see GLOSS[2] *n.* 1, 3b.

exemplar /igzémplər, -plaar/ *n.* **1** a model or pattern. **2** a typical instance of a class of things. **3** a parallel instance. [ME f. OF *exemplaire* f. LL *exemplarium* (as EXAMPLE)]

■ **1** see EXAMPLE *n.* 2. **2** see EPITOME 1.

exemplary /igzémpləri/ *adj.* **1** fit to be imitated; outstandingly good. **2 a** serving as a warning. **b** *Law* (of damages) exceeding the amount needed for simple compensation. **3** illustrative, representative. □□ **exemplarily** *adv.* **exemplariness** *n.* [LL *exemplaris* (as EXAMPLE)]

■ **1** model; outstanding, excellent, meritorious, admirable, commendable, praiseworthy, noteworthy, superior. **2 a** cautionary, admonitory, warning, *literary* monitory. **3** illustrative, representative, typical, characteristic; archetypal; paradigmatic.

exemplify /igzémplifī/ *v.tr.* (**-ies, -ied**) **1** illustrate by example. **2** be an example of. **3** *Law* make an attested copy of (a document) under an official seal. □□ **exemplification** /-fikáysh'n/ *n.* [ME f. med.L *exemplificare* (as EXAMPLE)]

■ **1, 2** illustrate, typify, represent, epitomize, instance, instantiate; embody, personify; demonstrate, display, show, exhibit, model, depict.

exemplum /igzémpləm/ *n.* (*pl.* **exempla** /-plə/) an example or model, esp. a moralizing or illustrative story. [L: see EXAMPLE]

exempt /igzémpt/ *adj.*, *n.*, & *v.* ● *adj.* **1** free from an obligation or liability etc. imposed on others. **2** (foll. by *from*) not liable to. ● *n.* **1** a person who is exempt, esp. from payment of tax. **2** *Brit.* = EXON. ● *v.tr.* (usu. foll. by *from*) free from an obligation, esp. one imposed on others. □□ **exemption** *n.* [ME f. L *exemptus* past part. of *eximere exempt-* (as EX-[1], *emere* take)]

■ *adj.* **1** exempted, free, let off, excepted, excused, immune, *colloq.* off the hook. **2** (*exempt from*) exempted from, free from *or* of, liberated from, released from, excused from, relieved of, spared, let off, excepted from. ● *v.* spare, let off, *colloq.* let off the hook; (*exempt from*) free *or* release from, excuse *or* relieve from, absolve from *or* of. □□ **exemption** exception, immunity, freedom, release, impunity, dispensation, exclusion.

exequies /éksikwiz/ *n.pl. formal* funeral rites. [ME f. OF f. L *exsequiae* (as EX-[1], *sequi* follow)]

■ see FUNERAL *n.*

exercise /éksərsīz/ *n.* & *v.* ● *n.* **1** activity requiring physical effort, done esp. as training or to sustain or improve health. **2** mental or spiritual activity, esp. as practice to develop a skill. **3** (often in *pl.*) a particular task or set of tasks devised as exercise, practice in a technique, etc. **4 a** the use or application of a mental faculty, right, etc. **b** practice of an ability, quality, etc. **5** (often in *pl.*) military drill or manoeuvres. **6** (foll. by *in*) a process directed at or concerned with something specified (*was an exercise in public relations*). ● *v.* **1** *tr.* use or apply (a faculty, right, influence, restraint, etc.). **2** *tr.* perform (a function). **3 a** *intr.* take (esp. physical) exercise; do exercises. **b** *tr.* provide (an animal) with exercise. **c** *tr.* train (a person). **4** *tr.* **a** tax the powers of. **b** perplex, worry. □ **exercise book 1** a book containing exercises. **2** a book for writing school work, notes, etc., in. □□ **exercisable** *adj.* **exerciser** *n.* [ME f. OF *exercice* f. L *exercitium* f. *exercere exercit-* keep at work (as EX-[1], *arcēre* restrain)]

■ *n.* **1** activity, movement, working-out, warming up; training, drilling; see also PRACTICE *n.* 3. **2** see PRACTICE *n.* 3. **3** (*exercises*) keep-fit, workout, warm-up, practice, drill; callisthenics, aerobics, isometrics, gymnastics. **4** use, utilization, employment, application, practice, operation, performance. **5** see MANOEUVRE *n.* 2. ● *v.* **1** use, employ, apply, practise, bring to bear, put to *or* into use, put to effect; exert, wield, execute. **2** see PERFORM 1. **3 a** work out, limber up, warm up, train, drill. **b** see WALK *v.* 4. **c** see TRAIN *v.* 1a. **4 b** perplex, worry, concern, distress, burden, try, trouble, perturb, disturb, agitate, make nervous, harry, harass, vex, *colloq.* drive crazy, drive up the wall.

exergue /ekság/ *n.* **1** a small space usu. on the reverse of a coin or medal, below the principal device. **2** an inscription on this space. [F f. med.L *exergum* f. Gk *ex-* (as EX-[2]) + *ergon* work]

exert /igzért/ *v.tr.* **1** exercise, bring to bear (a quality, force, influence, etc.). **2** *refl.* (often foll. by *for*, or *to* + infin.) use one's efforts or endeavours; strive. □□ **exertion** *n.* [L *exserere exsert-* put forth (as EX-[1], *serere* bind)]

■ **1** exercise, bring to bear, use, bring into play, utilize, put to use, put to work *or* effect, employ, wield, deploy, expend. **2** (*exert oneself*) try, make an effort, apply oneself, strive, do one's best, work, strain, struggle, toil, push (oneself), drive oneself, go all out, give one's all, cudgel one's brains, *colloq.* knock oneself out, beat one's brains out, do one's damnedest, bust a gut. ▫▫ **exertion** effort, striving, strain, work, struggle, toil, drive, push, diligence, industry, action, assiduity, assiduousness, sedulousness, sedulity.

exeunt /éksiunt/ *v.intr.* (as a stage direction) (actors) leave the stage. ▫ ***exeunt omnes*** all leave the stage. [L, = they go out: 3rd pl. pres. of *exire* go out: see EXIT]

exfiltrate /éksfiltrayt/ *v.tr.* (also *absol.*) withdraw (troops, spies, etc.) surreptitiously, esp. from danger. ▫▫ **exfiltration** /-tráysh'n/ *n.*

exfoliate /eksfṓliayt/ *v.intr.* **1** (of bone, the skin, a mineral, etc.) come off in scales or layers. **2** (of a tree) throw off layers of bark. ▫▫ **exfoliation** /-áysh'n/ *n.* **exfoliative** /-liətiv/ *adj.* [LL *exfoliare exfoliat-* (as EX-[1], *folium* leaf)]

▪ **1** see FLAKE[1] *v.*

ex gratia /eks gráyshə/ *adv.* & *adj.* ● *adv.* as a favour rather than from an (esp. legal) obligation. ● *adj.* granted on this basis. [L, = from favour]

exhalation /éks-həláysh'n/ *n.* **1 a** an expiration of air. **b** a puff of breath. **2** a mist, vapour. **3** an emanation or effluvium. [ME f. L *exhalatio* (as EXHALE)]

▪ **1** expiration, exhaling, breath; breathing (out), respiration. **2, 3** mist, vapour, whiff, emission, gas, fume; emanation, effluvium.

exhale /eks-háyl/ *v.* **1** *tr.* (also *absol.*) breathe out (esp. air or smoke) from the lungs. **2** *tr.* & *intr.* give off or be given off in vapour. ▫▫ **exhalable** *adj.* [ME f. OF *exhaler* f. L *exhalare* (as EX-[1], *halare* breathe)]

▪ **1** breathe (out), blow *or* puff out, discharge, emit, give forth, eject, expel. **2** breathe (out), blow out, puff (out); evaporate; emanate, issue (forth), blow off; pass, discharge, emit, give forth, eject, expel.

exhaust /igzáwst/ *v.* & *n.* ● *v.tr.* **1** consume or use up the whole of. **2** (often as **exhausted** *adj.* or **exhausting** *adj.*) use up the strength or resources of (a person); tire out. **3** study or expound on (a subject) completely. **4** (often foll. by *of*) empty (a vessel etc.) of its contents. **5** (often as **exhausted** *adj.*) drain of strength or resources; (of land) make barren. ● *n.* **1 a** waste gases etc. expelled from an engine after combustion. **b** (also **exhaust-pipe**) the pipe or system by which these are expelled. **c** the process of expulsion of these gases. **2 a** the production of an outward current of air by the creation of a partial vacuum. **b** an apparatus for this. ▫▫ **exhauster** *n.* **exhaustible** *adj.* **exhaustibility** /-stəbílliti/ *n.* **exhaustibly** *adv.* [L *exhaurire exhaust-* (as EX-[1], *haurire* draw (water), drain)]

▪ *v.* **1** consume, use (up), expend, finish, deplete, spend, run through, fritter away, squander, waste, *sl.* blow. **2** use up, sap, tire out, take it out of; (**exhausted**) (dead) tired, tired out, fatigued, weary, wearied, worn out, shattered, enervated, debilitated, drained, overtired, strained, taxed, weak, weakened, prostrate, fagged out, burnt-out, spent, dog-tired, *colloq.* frazzled, all in, dead, knocked out, done in, *US colloq.* pooped, *sl.* (dead) beat, *Brit. sl.* knackered, cooked; (**exhausting**) tiring, fatiguing, wearying, enervating, wearing, debilitating; arduous, laborious, back-breaking, strenuous, hard, gruelling, burdensome, onerous. **3** see RANSACK 2, AMPLIFY 2. **4** empty, drain, evacuate, void, clean *or* clear out. **5** (**exhausted**) spent, worn out, depleted, impoverished, poor, infertile, barren. ● *n.* **1 a** gases, fumes, emissions; waste.

exhaustion /igzáwss-chən/ *n.* **1** the action or process of draining or emptying something; the state of being depleted or emptied. **2** a total loss of strength or vitality. **3** the process of establishing a conclusion by eliminating alternatives. [LL *exhaustio* (as EXHAUST)]

▪ **1** emptying, draining, evacuation, voiding, depletion. **2** tiredness, fatigue, enervation, debilitation, weariness, lassitude. **3** elimination, rejection, exclusion.

exhaustive /igzáwstiv/ *adj.* **1** thorough, comprehensive. **2** tending to exhaust a subject. ▫▫ **exhaustively** *adv.* **exhaustiveness** *n.*

▪ thorough, comprehensive, complete, all-inclusive, all-embracing, all-encompassing, encyclopedic, extensive, far-reaching, sweeping, full-scale, in-depth, maximal; thoroughgoing, definitive.

exhibit /igzíbbit/ *v.* & *n.* ● *v.tr.* (**exhibited, exhibiting**) **1** show or reveal publicly (for amusement, in competition, etc.). **2 a** show, display. **b** manifest (a quality). **3** submit for consideration. ● *n.* **1** a thing or collection of things forming part or all of an exhibition. **2** a document or other item or object produced in a lawcourt as evidence. ▫▫ **exhibitory** *adj.* [L *exhibēre exhibit-* (as EX-[1], *habēre* hold)]

▪ *v.* **1, 2a** show, reveal, present, display, offer, demonstrate, betray, manifest, exemplify, evince, evidence, disclose, express. **2b** manifest, show, reveal, display, expose, betray, demonstrate, exemplify, evince, evidence, disclose, express. **3** see SUBMIT 2. ● *n.* **1** see DISPLAY 2. **2** see EVIDENCE 2.

exhibition /éksibísh'n/ *n.* **1** a display (esp. public) of works of art, industrial products, etc. **2** the act or an instance of exhibiting; the state of being exhibited. **3** *Brit.* a scholarship, esp. from the funds of a school, college, etc. ▫ **make an exhibition of oneself** behave so as to appear ridiculous or foolish. [ME f. OF f. LL *exhibitio -onis* (as EXHIBIT)]

▪ **1** exposition, fair, show, showing, display, presentation, exhibit, Expo, demonstration, *colloq.* demo. **2** see DEMONSTRATION 3. **3** see SCHOLARSHIP 2. ▫ **make an exhibition of oneself** see *show off* (SHOW).

exhibitioner /éksibíshənər/ *n. Brit.* a student who has been awarded an exhibition.

exhibitionism /éksibíshəniz'm/ *n.* **1** a tendency towards display or extravagant behaviour. **2** *Psychol.* a mental condition characterized by the compulsion to display one's genitals indecently in public. ▫▫ **exhibitionist** *n.* **exhibitionistic** /-nístik/ *adj.* **exhibitionistically** /-nístikəli/ *adv.*

▪ **1** see OSTENTATION.

exhibitor /igzíbbitər/ *n.* a person who provides an item or items for an exhibition.

exhilarate /igzíllərayt/ *v.tr.* (often as **exhilarating** *adj.* or **exhilarated** *adj.*) affect with great liveliness or joy; raise the spirits of. ▫▫ **exhilarant** *adj.* & *n.* **exhilaratingly** *adv.* **exhilaration** /-ráysh'n/ *n.* **exhilarative** /-rətiv/ *adj.* [L *exhilarare* (as EX-[1], *hilaris* cheerful)]

▪ (**exhilarating**) invigorating, bracing, stimulating, vivifying, enlivening, rejuvenating, refreshing, vitalizing, fortifying, restorative, tonic; cheering, uplifting, gladdening, elating, inspiriting, heartening, comforting, reassuring; (**exhilarated**) see ECSTATIC 1, 2.

exhort /igzórt/ *v.tr.* (often foll. by *to* + infin.) urge or advise strongly or earnestly. ▫▫ **exhortative** /-tətiv/ *adj.* **exhortatory** /-tətəri/ *adj.* **exhorter** *n.* [ME f. OF *exhorter* or L *exhortari* (as EX-[1], *hortari* exhort)]

▪ see URGE *v.* 2.

exhortation /égzortáysh'n/ *n.* **1** the act or an instance of exhorting; the state of being exhorted. **2** a formal or liturgical address. [ME f. OF *exhortation* or L *exhortatio* (as EXHORT)]

▪ **1** inducement, persuasion, influence; see also *encouragement* (ENCOURAGE). **2** see SERMON 1.

exhume /eks-hyóom, igzyóom/ *v.tr.* dig out, unearth (esp. a buried corpse). ▫▫ **exhumation** /-máysh'n/ *n.* [F *exhumer* f. med.L *exhumare* (as EX-[1], *humus* ground)]

▪ see DIG *v.* 4.

ex hypothesi /éks hīpóthəsi/ *adv.* according to the hypothesis proposed. [mod.L]

exigency /éksijənsi, igzij-/ *n.* (*pl.* **-ies**) (also **exigence** /éksijənss/) **1** an urgent need or demand. **2** an emergency. [F *exigence* & LL *exigentia* (as EXIGENT)]

▪ **1** see NEED *n.* 3, 4. **2** see EMERGENCY.

exigent /éksijənt/ *adj.* **1** requiring much; exacting. **2** urgent, pressing. [ME f. L *exigere* EXACT]
■ **1** see SEVERE 1, 5. **2** see URGENT 1.

exiguous /igzígyooəss/ *adj.* scanty, small. □□ **exiguity** /éksigyōō-iti/ *n.* **exiguously** *adv.* **exiguousness** *n.* [L *exiguus* scanty f. *exigere* weigh exactly: see EXACT]
■ see MEAGRE 1.

exile /éksīl, égzīl/ *n.* & *v.* ● *n.* **1** expulsion, or the state of being expelled, from one's native land or (**internal exile**) native town etc. **2** long absence abroad, esp. enforced. **3** a person expelled or long absent from his or her native country. **4** (**the Exile**) the captivity of the Jews in Babylon in the 6th c. BC. ● *v.tr.* (foll. by *from*) officially expel (a person) from his or her native country or town etc. □□ **exilic** /-síllik, -zíllik/ *adj.* (esp. in sense 4 of *n.*). [ME f. OF *exil*, *exiler* f. L *exilium* banishment]
■ *n.* **1** expulsion, expatriation, banishment, deportation, *hist.* transportation. **3** expatriate, émigré, emigrant, deportee, displaced person, DP; alien, outsider. ● *v.* expel, deport, expatriate, banish, oust, displace, eject, transport, drive *or* cast out, exclude, bar, ban; extradite.

exist /igzíst/ *v.intr.* **1** have a place as part of objective reality. **2 a** have being under specified conditions. **b** (foll. by *as*) exist in the form of. **3** (of circumstances etc.) occur; be found. **4** live with no pleasure under adverse conditions (*felt he was merely existing*). **5** continue in being; maintain life (*can hardly exist on this salary*). **6** be alive, live. [prob. back-form. f. EXISTENCE; cf. LL *existere*]
■ **1, 2a** be, prevail, endure, continue, *archaic* abide; live, breathe. **2 b** see FORM *v.* 3. **3** occur, be found, be present; obtain, prevail. **4** see ENDURE 3. **5** survive, subsist, eke out a living *or* an existence, stay alive, *colloq.* get by. **6** see LIVE[1] 1–4.

existence /igzístənss/ *n.* **1** the fact or condition of being or existing. **2** continued being; the manner of one's existing or living, esp. under adverse conditions (*a wretched existence*). **3** an existing thing. **4** all that exists. [ME f. OF *existence* or LL *existentia* f. L *exsistere* (as EX-[1], *stare* stand)]
■ **1** fact, being, presence, actuality, essence; *Philos.* quiddity. **2** continuance, continuation, persistence, permanence, duration, endurance; see also LIFE 5. **3** being, entity, creature. **4** see WORLD 2a.

existent /igzístənt/ *adj.* existing, actual, current.

existential /égzisténsh'l/ *adj.* **1** of or relating to existence. **2** *Logic* (of a proposition etc.) affirming or implying the existence of a thing. **3** *Philos.* concerned with existence, esp. with human existence as viewed by existentialism. □□ **existentially** *adv.* [LL *existentialis* (as EXISTENCE)]

existentialism /égzisténshəliz'm/ *n.* a philosophical theory emphasizing the existence of the individual person as a free and responsible agent determining his or her own development. □□ **existentialist** *n.* [G *Existentialismus* (as EXISTENTIAL)]

exit /éksit, égzit/ *n.* & *v.* ● *n.* **1** a passage or door by which to leave a room, building, etc. **2 a** the act of going out. **b** the right to go out. **3** a place where vehicles can leave a motorway or major road. **4** the departure of an actor from the stage. **5** death. ● *v.intr.* (**exited, exiting**) **1** go out of a room, building, etc. **2** (as a stage direction) (an actor) leaves the stage (*exit Macbeth*). **3** die. □ **exit permit** (or **visa** etc.) authorization to leave a particular country. [L, 3rd sing. pres. of *exire* go out (as EX-[1], *ire* go): cf. L *exitus* going out]
■ *n.* **1** way out, egress, door, gate. **2 a** departure, leave-taking, withdrawal, leaving, retreat, retirement; flight, exodus, escape. **3** see *turn-off* 1. **5** see DEATH 1. ● *v.* **1** go (out *or* away), (take one's) leave, depart, take *or* make one's departure, retire, (beat a) retreat, withdraw, walk out, escape, take to one's heels, take off, vanish, disappear, *colloq.* show a clean pair of heels, skedaddle, run, *sl.* beat it, take a powder, *US sl.* go on the lam. **3** see DIE[1] 1.

ex-libris /ekslēébriss/ *n.* (*pl.* same) a usu. decorated bookplate or label bearing the owner's name, pasted into the front of a book. [L *ex libris* among the books of]

ex nihilo /eks nīhilō/ *adv.* out of nothing (*creation ex nihilo*). [L]

exo- /éksō/ *comb. form* external. [Gk *exō* outside]

exobiology /éksōbīólləji/ *n.* the study of life outside the earth. □□ **exobiologist** *n.*

Exocet /éksəset/ *n. propr.* a short-range guided missile used esp. in sea warfare. [F *exocet* flying fish]

exocrine /éksōkrīn/ *adj.* (of a gland) secreting through a duct (cf. ENDOCRINE). [EXO- + Gk *krinō* sift]

Exod. *abbr.* Exodus (Old Testament).

exoderm /éksōderm/ *n. Biol.* = ECTODERM.

exodus /éksədəss/ *n.* **1** a mass departure of people (esp. emigrants). **2** (**Exodus**) *Bibl.* **a** the departure of the Israelites from Egypt. **b** the book of the Old Testament relating this. [eccl.L f. Gk *exodos* (as EX-[2], *hodos* way)]
■ **1** see FLIGHT[2].

ex officio /éks əfíshiō/ *adv.* & *adj.* by virtue of one's office or status. [L]

exogamy /eksóggəmi/ *n.* **1** *Anthropol.* marriage of a man outside his own tribe. **2** *Biol.* the fusion of reproductive cells from distantly related or unrelated individuals. □□ **exogamous** *adj.*

exogenous /eksójinəss/ *adj. Biol.* growing or originating from outside. □□ **exogenously** *adv.*

exon /ékson/ *n. Brit.* each of the four officers acting as commanders of the Yeomen of the Guard. [repr. F pronunc. of EXEMPT]

exonerate /igzónnərayt/ *v.tr.* (often foll. by *from*) **1** free or declare free from blame etc. **2** release from a duty etc. □□ **exoneration** /-ráysh'n/ *n.* **exonerative** /-rətiv/ *adj.* [L *exonerare exonerat-* (as EX-[1], *onus*, *oneris* burden)]
■ **1** see VINDICATE 1.

exophthalmos /éksof-thálməss/ *n.* (also **exophthalmus, exophthalmia** /-miə/) *Med.* abnormal protrusion of the eyeball. □□ **exophthalmic** *adj.* [mod.L f. Gk *exophthalmos* having prominent eyes (as EX-[2], *ophthalmos* eye)]

exoplasm /éksōplaz'm/ *n. Biol.* = ECTOPLASM.

exor. *abbr.* executor.

exorbitant /igzórbit'nt/ *adj.* (of a price, demand, etc.) grossly excessive. □□ **exorbitance** *n.* **exorbitantly** *adv.* [LL *exorbitare* (as EX-[1], *orbita* ORBIT)]
■ excessive, outrageous, extortionate, unreasonable, unconscionable, extravagant, immoderate, extreme, inordinate, disproportionate, preposterous, unwarranted, unjustifiable, unjustified.

exorcize /éksorsīz/ *v.tr.* (also **-ise**) **1** expel (a supposed evil spirit) by invocation or by use of a holy name. **2** (often foll. by *of*) free (a person or place) of a supposed evil spirit. □□ **exorcism** *n.* **exorcist** *n.* **exorcization** /-záysh'n/ *n.* [F *exorciser* or eccl.L *exorcizare* f. Gk *exorkizō* (as EX-[2], *horkos* oath)]

exordium /eksórdiəm/ *n.* (*pl.* **exordiums** or **exordia** /-diə/) the beginning or introductory part, esp. of a discourse or treatise. □□ **exordial** *adj.* **exordially** *adv.* [L f. *exordiri* (as EX-[1], *ordiri* begin)]
■ see PREFACE *n.*

exoskeleton /éksōskéllit'n/ *n.* a rigid external covering for the body in certain animals, esp. arthropods, providing support and protection. □□ **exoskeletal** *adj.*

exosphere /éksōsfeer/ *n.* the layer of atmosphere furthest from the earth.

exothermic /éksōthérmik/ *adj.* (also **exothermal** /-m'l/) esp. *Chem.* occurring or formed with the evolution of heat. □□ **exothermally** *adv.* **exothermically** *adv.*

exotic /igzóttik/ *adj.* & *n.* ● *adj.* **1** introduced from or originating in a foreign (esp. tropical) country (*exotic fruits*). **2** attractively or remarkably strange or unusual; bizarre. **3** (of a fuel, metal, etc.) of a kind newly brought into use. ● *n.* an exotic person or thing. □ **exotic dancer** a striptease

dancer. □□ **exotically** *adv.* **exoticism** /-tisiz'm/ *n.* [L *exoticus* f. Gk *exōtikos* f. *exō* outside]
▪ *adj.* **1** foreign, alien, non-native, imported. **2** strange, unusual, unique, singular; bizarre, extraordinary, remarkable, out of the ordinary, odd, peculiar, different, outlandish, *colloq.* weird, crazy. ● *n.* see WONDER *n.* 2.

exotica /igzóttikə/ *n.pl.* remarkably strange or rare objects. [L, neut. pl. of *exoticus*: see EXOTIC]

expand /ikspánd/ *v.* **1** *tr.* & *intr.* increase in size or bulk or importance. **2** *intr.* (often foll. by *on*) give a fuller description or account. **3** *intr.* become more genial or effusive; discard one's reserve. **4** *tr.* set or write out in full (something condensed or abbreviated). **5** *tr.* & *intr.* spread out flat. □ **expanded metal** sheet metal slit and stretched into a mesh, used to reinforce concrete and other brittle materials. □□ **expandable** *adj.* **expander** *n.* **expansible** /ikpánsib'l/ *adj.* **expansibility** /ikpánsibílliti/ *n.* [ME f. L *expandere expans-* spread out (as EX-[1], *pandere* spread)]
▪ **1** increase, enlarge, extend, stretch, inflate, distend, dilate; spread (out), open out, swell, amplify, magnify, broaden, widen, augment, heighten, develop. **2** (*expand on* or *upon*) enlarge on, develop, amplify, expatiate on *or* upon, elaborate (on), flesh out. **5** see SPREAD *v.* 1a.

expanse /ikspánss/ *n.* **1** a wide continuous area or extent of land, space, etc. **2** an amount of expansion. [mod.L *expansum* neut. past part. (as EXPAND)]
▪ **1** area, space, stretch, extent, range, sweep, reach, spread.

expansile /ikspánsīl/ *adj.* **1** of expansion. **2** capable of expansion.

expansion /ikspánsh'n/ *n.* **1** the act or an instance of expanding; the state of being expanded. **2** enlargement of the scale or scope of (esp. commercial) operations. **3** increase in the amount of a State's territory or area of control. **4** an increase in the volume of fuel etc. on combustion in the cylinder of an engine. **5** the action of making or becoming greater in area, bulk, capacity, etc.; dilatation; the degree of this (*alternate expansion and contraction of the muscle*). □□ **expansionary** *adj.* **expansionism** *n.* **expansionist** *n.* **expansionistic** /-shənístik/ *adj.* (all in senses 2, 3). [LL *expansio* (as EXPAND)]
▪ **1, 2** development, increase, augmentation, enlargement, extension, growth, flourishing, spread, *literary* burgeoning. **5** stretching; dilatation, dilation, distension; inflation, swelling.

expansive /ikspánsiv/ *adj.* **1** able or tending to expand. **2** extensive, wide-ranging. **3** (of a person, feelings, or speech) effusive, open. □□ **expansively** *adv.* **expansiveness** *n.* **expansivity** /-sívviti/ *n.*
▪ **1** expansible, expandable, extensible, extendible, extendable; extending, expanding. **2** extensive; wide-ranging, broad, far-reaching, comprehensive, widespread. **3** effusive, open, free, easy, genial, amiable, friendly, warm, affable, sociable, outgoing, communicative, outspoken, extrovert, extroverted, talkative, loquacious, garrulous, frank, unreserved.

ex parte /eks paárti/ *adj.* & *adv.* *Law* in the interests of one side only or of an interested outside party. [L]

expat /ékspát/ *n.* & *adj. colloq.* = EXPATRIATE. [abbr.]

expatiate /ikspáyshiayt/ *v.intr.* (usu. foll. by *on, upon*) speak or write at length or in detail. □□ **expatiation** /-áysh'n/ *n.* **expatiatory** /-shiətəri/ *adj.* [L *exspatiari* digress (as EX-[1], *spatium* SPACE)]
▪ (*expatiate on*) see EXPLAIN 1.

expatriate *adj.*, *n.*, & *v.* ● *adj.* /ékspátriət, -páytriət/ **1** living abroad, esp. for a long period. **2** expelled from one's country; exiled. ● *n.* /ekspátriət, -páytriət/ an expatriate person. ● *v.tr.* /ekspátriayt, -páytriayt/ **1** expel or remove (a person) from his or her native country. **2** *refl.* withdraw (oneself) from one's citizenship or allegiance. □□ **expatriation** /-áysh'n/ *n.* [med.L *expatriare* (as EX-[1], *patria* native country)]
▪ *n.* see EXILE *n.* 3. ● *v.* **1** see EXILE *v.*

expect /ikspékt/ *v.tr.* **1** (often foll. by *to* + infin., or *that* + clause) **a** regard as likely; assume as a future event or occurrence. **b** (often foll. by *of*) look for as appropriate or one's due (from a person) (*I expect cooperation; expect you to be here; expected better of you*). **2** *colloq.* (often foll. by *that* + clause) think, suppose (*I expect we'll be on time*). **3** be shortly to have (a baby) (*is expecting twins*). □ **be expecting** *colloq.* be pregnant. □□ **expectable** *adj.* [L *exspectare* (as EX-[1], *spectare* look, frequent. of *specere* see)]
▪ **1 a** look forward *or* ahead to, envisage, contemplate, foresee, envision, *disp.* anticipate; await, watch *or* look for, wait for. **b** look for, want, require, need, demand, reckon on *or* upon, calculate *or* count on, calculate *or* count upon, hope for. **2** think, suppose, guess, assume, presume, imagine, believe, trust, surmise, conjecture; foresee. □ **be expecting** be pregnant, *archaic* be enceinte, *colloq.* be in a *or* the family way, *literary* be with child, *literary or Zool.* be gravid, *sl.* have a bun in the oven, *Brit. sl.* be in the club.

expectancy /ikspéktənsi/ *n.* (*pl.* **-ies**) **1** a state of expectation. **2** a prospect, esp. of future possession. **3** (foll. by *of*) a prospective chance. [L *exspectantia, exp-* (as EXPECT)]
▪ **1** see EXPECTATION 1.

expectant /ikspéktənt/ *adj.* & *n.* ● *adj.* **1** (often foll. by *of*) expecting. **2** having the expectation of possession, status, etc. **3** (*attrib.*) expecting a baby (said of the mother or father). ● *n.* **1** one who expects. **2** a candidate for office etc. □□ **expectantly** *adv.*
▪ *adj.* **1** waiting, ready, eager, apprehensive, anxious, hopeful, watchful; (*expectant of*) expecting. **2** see HOPEFUL *adj.* 1. ● *n.* **2** see CANDIDATE 1, 3.

expectation /ékspektáysh'n/ *n.* **1** the act or an instance of expecting or looking forward. **2** something expected or hoped for. **3** (foll. by *of*) the probability of an event. **4** (in *pl.*) one's prospects of inheritance. [L *expectatio* (as EXPECT)]
▪ **1** expectancy, confidence, hopefulness, watchfulness, apprehension, apprehensiveness, suspense, *disp.* anticipation. **2** belief, assumption, presumption, surmise, supposition, conjecture, guess, hope; wish, desire, want, demand, requirement. **3** see PROBABILITY. **4** (*expectations*) see PROSPECT *n.* 1a.

expectorant /ikspéktərənt/ *adj.* & *n.* ● *adj.* causing the coughing out of phlegm etc. ● *n.* an expectorant medicine.

expectorate /ikspéktərayt/ *v.tr.* (also *absol.*) cough or spit out (phlegm etc.) from the chest or lungs. □□ **expectoration** /-ráysh'n/ *n.* **expectorator** *n.* [L *expectorare expectorat-* (as EX-[1], *pectus -oris* breast)]
▪ see SPIT[1] *v.* 2a.

expedient /ikspeédiənt/ *adj.* & *n.* ● *adj.* **1** advantageous; advisable on practical rather than moral grounds. **2** suitable, appropriate. ● *n.* a means of attaining an end; a resource. □□ **expedience** *n.* **expediency** *n.* **expediently** *adv.* [ME f. L *expedire*: see EXPEDITE]
▪ *adj.* **1** advantageous, beneficial, useful, practical, utilitarian, helpful, effective, desirable; advisable, recommended, prudent, politic, wise, propitious, opportune. **2** suitable, appropriate, fitting, fit, befitting, proper, apropos, right, correct, pertinent, applicable, practical, *archaic* meet. ● *n.* means, measure, contrivance, resort, recourse; resource, device.

expedite /ékspidīt/ *v.tr.* **1** assist the progress of; hasten (an action, process, etc.). **2** accomplish (business) quickly. □□ **expediter** *n.* [L *expedire expedit-* extricate, put in order (as EX-[1], *pes pedis* foot)]
▪ **1** assist, enable, facilitate, ease, advance, promote, forward; hasten, rush, hurry, speed up, step up, accelerate. **2** dispatch, despatch; see also COMPLETE *v.* 1.

expedition /ékspidísh'n/ *n.* **1** a journey or voyage for a particular purpose, esp. exploration, scientific research, or war. **2** the personnel or ships etc. undertaking this. **3** promptness, speed. □□ **expeditionist** *n.* [ME f. OF f. L *expeditio -onis* (as EXPEDITE)]

■ **1** journey, voyage, exploration, (field) trip, tour, excursion; mission, quest. **2** see PARTY[1] *n.* 2. **3** promptness, speed, alacrity, dispatch, haste, rapidity, swiftness, quickness, *archaic or literary* celerity.

expeditionary /ékspidíshənəri, -shənri/ *adj.* of or used in an expedition, esp. military.

expeditious /ékspidíshəss/ *adj.* **1** acting or done with speed and efficiency. **2** suited for speedy performance. ▫▫ **expeditiously** *adv.* **expeditiousness** *n.* [EXPEDITION + -OUS]
■ ready, quick, rapid, swift, fast, brisk, speedy, efficient, *poet. or literary* fleet.

expel /ikspél/ *v.tr.* (**expelled**, **expelling**) (often foll. by *from*) **1** deprive (a person) of the membership of or involvement in (a school, society, etc.). **2** force out or eject (a thing from its container etc.). **3** order or force to leave a building etc. ▫▫ **expellable** *adj.* **expellee** /-lée/ *n.* **expellent** *adj.* **expeller** *n.* [ME f. L *expellere expuls-* (as EX-[1], *pellere* drive)]
■ **1** deprive, proscribe, ban, bar, debar, dismiss, exclude, cashier, discharge, oust, *Mil.* drum out. **2, 3** throw *or* cast out, force *or* drive out, eject, push out, remove, dislodge, displace, evict, show the door, dismiss, *colloq.* turf out; banish, deport, exile, expatriate.

expend /ikspénd/ *v.tr.* spend or use up (money, time, etc.). [ME f. L *expendere expens-* (as EX-[1], *pendere* weigh)]
■ spend, use up, finish (off), consume, exhaust, dissipate, drain; pay out, disburse, use, employ, lay out, *colloq.* shell out, *sl.* dish *or* fork out.

expendable /ikspéndəb'l/ *adj.* **1** that may be sacrificed or dispensed with, esp. to achieve a purpose. **2 a** not regarded as worth preserving or saving. **b** unimportant, insignificant. **3** not normally reused. ▫▫ **expendability** /-bílliti/ *n.* **expendably** *adv.*
■ **1, 2** dispensable, disposable, non-essential, inessential, unessential, unnecessary, replaceable; unimportant, insignificant. **3** see DISPOSABLE *adj.* 1.

expenditure /ikspéndichər/ *n.* **1** the process or an instance of spending or using up. **2** a thing (esp. a sum of money) expended. [EXPEND, after obs. *expenditor* officer in charge of expenditure, f. med.L f. *expenditus* irreg. past part. of L *expendere*]
■ **2** outlay, disbursement, spending, expense, cost; outgoings; price, charge, fee.

expense /ikspénss/ *n.* **1** cost incurred; payment of money. **2** (usu. in *pl.*) **a** costs incurred in doing a particular job etc. (*will pay your expenses*). **b** an amount paid to reimburse this (*offered me £40 per day expenses*). **3** a thing that is a cause of much expense (*the house is a real expense to run*). ▫ **at the expense of** so as to cause loss or damage or discredit to. **expense account** a list of an employee's expenses payable by the employer. [ME f. AF, alt. of OF *espense* f. LL *expensa* (money) spent, past part. of L *expendere* EXPEND]
■ **1** payment, outlay, disbursement; price, charge, fee, rate; expenditure, spending; cost(s); sacrifice. **2** costs, out-of-pocket expenses, outlays, outgoings; expenditure, spending. **3** see BURDEN *n.* 1, 2.

expensive /ikspénsiv/ *adj.* **1** costing much. **2** making a high charge. **3** causing much expense (*has expensive tastes*). ▫▫ **expensively** *adv.* **expensiveness** *n.*
■ **1** costly, dear, high-priced, up-market, overpriced; valuable, precious, priceless; see also EXTRAVAGANT 2. **3** see EXTRAVAGANT 1.

experience /ikspéeriənss/ *n.* & *v.* ● *n.* **1** actual observation of or practical acquaintance with facts or events. **2** knowledge or skill resulting from this. **3 a** an event regarded as affecting one (*an unpleasant experience*). **b** the fact or process of being so affected (*learnt by experience*). ● *v.tr.* **1** have experience of; undergo. **2** feel or be affected by (an emotion etc.). ▫▫ **experienceable** *adj.* [ME f. OF f. L *experientia* f. *experiri expert-* try]
■ *n.* **1, 3b** observation, participation, contact, involvement, practice, exposure; acquaintance, familiarity, knowledge. **2** knowledge, common sense, wisdom, sagacity, know-how, *savoir faire*, *savoir vivre*, sophistication, skill, judgement, *sl.*savvy. **3 a** event, incident, happening, affair, episode, occurrence, circumstance, adventure, encounter; trial, test, ordeal. ● *v.* **1** undergo, live through, go through, suffer, endure, sustain, face, encounter, meet (with). **2** feel, sense, taste, sample, be familiar with, know.

experienced /ikspéeriənst/ *adj.* **1** having had much experience. **2** skilled from experience (*an experienced driver*).
■ **1** mature, seasoned, sophisticated, battle-scarred, seasoned, veteran. **2** skilled, adept, skilful, accomplished, practised, proficient, knowledgeable, knowing, wise, sage, sagacious, shrewd, (well-)informed, trained, (well-)versed, expert, master, masterly, qualified, prepared, professional; *colloq.* in the know, *au fait*, *US sl.* savvy.

experiential /ikspéeri-énsh'l/ *adj.* involving or based on experience. ▫ **experiential philosophy** a philosophy that treats all knowledge as based on experience. ▫▫ **experientialism** *n.* **experientialist** *n.* **experientially** *adv.*
■ see EMPIRICAL.

experiment /iksperrimənt/ *n.* & *v.* ● *n.* **1** a procedure adopted on the chance of its succeeding, for testing a hypothesis etc., or to demonstrate a known fact. **2** (foll. by *of*) a test or trial of. ● *v.intr.* (often foll. by *on*, *with*) make an experiment. ▫▫ **experimentation** /-mentáysh'n/ *n.* **experimenter** *n.* [ME f. OF *experiment* or L *experimentum* (as EXPERIENCE)]
■ *n.* procedure, policy; test, trial, investigation, inquiry, enquiry, examination, experimentation, research. ● *v.* test, try, examine, investigate, research, probe.

experimental /ikspérriméent'l/ *adj.* **1** based on or making use of experiment (*experimental psychology*). **2 a** used in experiments. **b** serving or resulting from (esp. incomplete) experiment; tentative, provisional. **3** based on experience, not on authority or conjecture. ▫▫ **experimentalism** *n.* **experimentalist** *n.* **experimentalize** *v.intr.* (also **-ise**). **experimentally** *adv.* [ME f. med.L *experimentalis* (as EXPERIMENT)]
■ **1, 3** empirical; experiential. **2 b** tentative, speculative, conjectural, hypothetical, theoretical; exploratory.

expert /ékspert/ *adj.* & *n.* ● *adj.* **1** (often foll. by *at*, *in*) having special knowledge or skill in a subject. **2** involving or resulting from this (*expert evidence*; *an expert piece of work*). ● *n.* (often foll. by *at*, *in*) a person having special knowledge or skill. ▫▫ **expertly** *adv.* **expertness** *n.* [ME f. OF f. L *expertus* past part. of *experiri*: see EXPERIENCE]
■ *adj.* **1** skilful, skilled, trained, knowledgeable, learned, experienced, practised, qualified, adept, proficient, accomplished, adroit, dexterous, masterful, masterly, first-rate, excellent, superb, wonderful, superior, *colloq.* A 1, top-notch, *colloq. or dial.* champion, *esp. Brit. sl.* wizard, *US sl.* crackerjack; virtuoso, *colloq.* crack; *au fait*; see also KNOWLEDGEABLE. **2** see *first-rate*. ● *n.* authority, professional, specialist, scholar, master, connoisseur, wizard, ace, *colloq.* whiz, pro, *esp. Brit. colloq.* dab hand, boffin, *US colloq.* maven, *often iron.* pundit.

expertise /éksperteéz/ *n.* expert skill, knowledge, or judgement. [F (as EXPERT)]
■ expertness, skill, dexterity, adroitness, knowledge, know-how, mastery, judgement, *sl.* savvy.

expertize /ékspertīz/ *v.* (also **-ise**) **1** *intr.* give an expert opinion. **2** *tr.* give an expert opinion concerning.

expiate /ékspiayt/ *v.tr.* **1** pay the penalty for (wrongdoing). **2** make amends for. ▫▫ **expiable** /ékspiəb'l/ *adj.* **expiatory** /-piətəri, -piaytəri/ *adj.* **expiation** /-áysh'n/ *n.* **expiator** *n.* [L *expiare expiat-* (as EX-[1], *pius* devout)]
■ **2** see COMPENSATE 2.

expiration /ékspiráysh'n/ *n.* **1** breathing out. **2** expiry. [L *expiratio* (as EXPIRE)]
■ **1** exhalation, exhaling, breath, respiration, breathing (out). **2** expiry, finish, end, termination, conclusion, concluding, close, closing, discontinuation, discontinuance.

expire /ikspī́r/ *v.* **1** *intr.* (of a period of time, validity, etc.) come to an end. **2** *intr.* (of a document, authorization, etc.) cease to be valid; become void. **3** *intr.* (of a person) die. **4** *tr.* (usu. foll. by *from*; also *absol.*) exhale (air etc.) from the lungs. □□ **expiratory** *adj.* (in sense 4). [ME f. OF *expirer* f. L *exspirare* (as EX-[1], *spirare* breathe)]
■ **1, 2** (come to an) end, cease, finish, terminate; run out, close. **3** breathe one's last, perish, pass away, *formal esp. Law* decease; see also DIE[1] 1. **4** exhale, breathe out, expel.

expiry /ikspī́ri/ *n.* **1** the end of the validity or duration of something. **2** death.
■ **1** see EXPIRATION 2. **2** see DEATH.

explain /ikspláyn/ *v.tr.* **1** make clear or intelligible with detailed information etc. (also *absol.*: *let me explain*). **2** (foll. by *that* + clause) say by way of explanation. **3** account for (one's conduct etc.). □ **explain away** minimize the significance of (a difficulty or mistake) by explanation. **explain oneself 1** make one's meaning clear. **2** give an account of one's motives or conduct. □□ **explainable** *adj.* **explainer** *n.* [L *explanare* (as EX-[1], *planus* flat, assim. to PLAIN[1])]
■ **1** make clear, define, explicate, detail, delineate, make plain, get across, clarify, spell out, simplify, interpret, elucidate, expound, describe, clear up, unravel, untangle. **2** see SAY *v.* 1b. **3** see *account for* 2b. □ **explain away** justify, account for, excuse, rationalize; extenuate, palliate; see also *account for* 2b.

explanation /éksplənáysh'n/ *n.* **1** the act or an instance of explaining. **2** a statement or circumstance that explains something. **3** a declaration made with a view to mutual understanding or reconciliation. [ME f. L *explanatio* (as EXPLAIN)]
■ **1** interpretation, definition, explication, delineation, description, exposition, account; exegesis, commentary, criticism, analysis. **2** cause, motive, reason, key. **3** excuse, rationalization, justification, vindication.

explanatory /iksplánnətəri, -tri/ *adj.* serving or intended to serve to explain. □□ **explanatorily** *adv.* [LL *explanatorius* (as EXPLAIN)]
■ elucidative, interpretive, interpretative, expository, exegetic, exegetical.

explant /ekspla̋ant/ *v.* & *n. Biol.* ● *v.tr.* transfer (living cells, tissues, or organs) from animals or plants to a nutrient medium. ● *n.* a piece of explanted tissue etc. □□ **explantation** /-táysh'n/ *n.* [mod.L *explantare* (as EX-[1], *plantare* PLANT)]

expletive /ikspleétiv/ *n.* & *adj.* ● *n.* **1** an oath, swear-word, or other expression, used in an exclamation. **2** a word used to fill out a sentence etc., esp. in verse. ● *adj.* serving to fill out (esp. a sentence, line of verse, etc.). [LL *expletivus* (as EX-[1], *plēre plet-* fill)]
■ *n.* **1** oath, swear-word, curse, obscenity, epithet, dirty word, four-letter word, *US* cuss-word. ● *adj.* wordy, verbose, prolix, tautological, pleonastic; redundant, unnecessary, superfluous.

explicable /iksplíkkəb'l, éksplik-/ *adj.* that can be explained.

explicate /éksplikayt/ *v.tr.* **1** develop the meaning or implication of (an idea, principle, etc.). **2** make clear, explain (esp. a literary text). □□ **explication** /-káysh'n/ *n.* **explicative** /iksplíkkətiv, éksplikaytiv/ *adj.* **explicator** *n.* **explicatory** /iksplíkkətəri, -tri, éksplikaytəri/ *adj.* [L *explicare explicat-* unfold (as EX-[1], *plicare plicat-* or *plicit-* fold)]
■ see EXPLAIN 1.

explicit /iksplíssit/ *adj.* **1** expressly stated, leaving nothing merely implied; stated in detail. **2** (of knowledge, a notion, etc.) definite, clear. **3** (of a person, book, etc.) expressing views unreservedly; outspoken. □□ **explicitly** *adv.* **explicitness** *n.* [F *explicite* or L *explicitus* (as EXPLICATE)]
■ **1** express, clear, plain, overt, manifest, definite, positive, unmistakable, categorical, distinct, unambiguous, unequivocal; specific, well-defined, precise, exact. **2** see DEFINITE. **3** unreserved, open, outspoken, forthright, definite; unrestrained, candid, frank, direct, straightforward.

explode /iksplṓd/ *v.* **1 a** *intr.* (of gas, gunpowder, a bomb, a boiler, etc.) expand suddenly with a loud noise owing to a release of internal energy. **b** *tr.* cause (a bomb etc.) to explode. **2** *intr.* give vent suddenly to emotion, esp. anger. **3** *intr.* (of a population etc.) increase suddenly or rapidly. **4** *tr.* show (a theory etc.) to be false or baseless. **5** *tr.* (as **exploded** *adj.*) (of a drawing etc.) showing the components of a mechanism as if separated by an explosion but in the normal relative positions. □□ **exploder** *n.* [earliest in sense 4: L *explodere* hiss off the stage (as EX-[1], *plodere plos-* = *plaudere* clap)]
■ **1** blow up, fly apart, go off, erupt, burst; blast; set off, detonate. **2** lose one's temper, throw a tantrum, rant, rave, rage, storm, *colloq.* get into a tizzy, blow one's top, fly off the handle, go through *or* hit *or* raise the roof, hit the ceiling, lose one's cool, go up the wall, freak (out), *Austral.* & *NZ colloq.* go crook, *US colloq.* blow one's stack, *sl.* flip (one's lid), *US sl.* blow *or* lose one's cool. **3** see GROW 1. **4** discredit, disprove, reject, repudiate, pick holes in, refute, belie, give the lie to, *colloq.* debunk.

exploit *n.* & *v.* ● *n.* /éksployt/ a bold or daring feat. ● *v.tr.* /iksplóyt/ **1** make use of (a resource etc.); derive benefit from. **2** usu. *derog.* utilize or take advantage of (esp. a person) for one's own ends. □□ **exploitable** /iksplóytəb'l/ *adj.* **exploitation** /éksploytáysh'n/ *n.* **exploitative** /iksplóytətiv/ *adj.* **exploiter** *n.* **exploitive** /iksplóytiv/ *adj.* [ME f. OF *esploit*, *exploiter* ult. f. L *explicare*: see EXPLICATE]
■ *n.* feat, achievement, attainment, accomplishment, deed. ● *v.* use, take advantage of, utilize, turn to account, make capital out of, profit from; work; manipulate.

exploration /éksploráysh'n/ *n.* **1** an act or instance of exploring. **2** the process of exploring. □□ **explorational** *adj.*
■ examination, investigation, inquiry, study, analysis, review, scrutiny, inspection, survey, observation; search, probe; reconnaissance, expedition; research.

exploratory /iksplórrətəri, -tri/ *adj.* **1** (of discussion etc.) preliminary, serving to establish procedure etc. **2** of or concerning exploration or investigation (*exploratory surgery*).
■ **1** see PRELIMINARY *adj.* **2** see EXPERIMENTAL 2b.

explore /iksplór/ *v.tr.* **1** travel extensively through (a country etc.) in order to learn or discover about it. **2** inquire into; investigate thoroughly. **3** *Surgery* examine (a part of the body) in detail. □□ **explorative** /iksplórrətiv/ *adj.* [F *explorer* f. L *explorare*]
■ **1** travel, tour, traverse; survey, reconnoitre. **2** inquire into, examine, look into, inspect, search, investigate, probe; research, study, analyse, review. **3** see INSPECT.

explorer /iksplórər/ *n.* a traveller into undiscovered or uninvestigated territory, esp. to get scientific information.
■ see PIONEER *n.* 2.

explosion /iksplṓzh'n/ *n.* **1** the act or an instance of exploding. **2** a loud noise caused by something exploding. **3 a** a sudden outburst of noise. **b** a sudden outbreak of feeling, esp. anger. **4** a rapid or sudden increase, esp. of population. [L *explosio* scornful rejection (as EXPLODE)]
■ **1** burst, eruption. **2** blast, bang, report, boom, clap, crack, crash; detonation. **3 a** outburst, blast, crash. **b** outburst, outbreak, paroxysm, flare-up, eruption, burst, spasm, *colloq.* fit. **4** increase, expansion, mushrooming, blossoming, *literary* burgeoning.

explosive /iksplṓsiv/ *adj.* & *n.* ● *adj.* **1** able or tending or likely to explode. **2** likely to cause a violent outburst etc.; (of a situation etc.) dangerously tense. ● *n.* an explosive substance. □□ **explosively** *adv.* **explosiveness** *n.*
■ *adj.* **2** volatile, tense, fraught, (highly) charged, inflammable, precarious, dangerous, perilous, hazardous, chancy, unstable, shaky, uncertain, unpredictable, critical, touch-and-go, sensitive, delicate, nasty, ugly, *colloq.* iffy, *sl.* dicey. ● *n.* dynamite, gelignite, gunpowder, TNT.

Expo /ékspō/ *n.* (also **expo**) (*pl.* **-os**) a large international exhibition. [abbr. of EXPOSITION 4]
■ see EXHIBITION 1.

exponent /ikspṓnənt/ *n.* & *adj.* ● *n.* **1** a person who favours or promotes an idea etc. **2** a representative or practitioner of an activity, profession, etc. **3** a person who explains or interprets something. **4** an executant (of music etc.). **5** a type or representative. **6** *Math.* a raised symbol or expression beside a numeral indicating how many times it is to be multiplied by itself (e.g. $2^3 = 2 \times 2 \times 2$). ● *adj.* that sets forth or interprets. [L *exponere* (as EX-[1], *ponere posit-* put)]
■ *n.* **1** see PROPONENT *n.*

exponential /ékspənénsh'l/ *adj.* **1** *Math.* of or indicated by a mathematical exponent. **2** (of an increase etc.) more and more rapid. □ **exponential function** *Math.* a function which increases as a quantity raised to a power determined by the variable on which the function depends. **exponential growth** *Biol.* a form of population growth in which the rate of growth is related to the number of individuals present. □□ **exponentially** *adv.* [F *exponentiel* (as EXPONENT)]

export *v.* & *n.* ● *v.tr.* /ekspórt, éks-/ send out (goods or services) esp. for sale in another country. ● *n.* /éksport/ **1** the process of exporting. **2 a** an exported article or service. **b** (in *pl.*) an amount exported (*exports exceeded £50m.*). **3** (*attrib.*) suitable for export, esp. of better quality. □ **export reject** an article sold in its country of manufacture, as being below the standard for export. □□ **exportable** *adj.* **exportability** /-təbílliti/ *n.* **exportation** /-táysh'n/ *n.* **exporter** /-pórtər/ *n.* [L *exportare* (as EX-[1], *portare* carry)]

expose /ikspṓz/ *v.tr.* **1** leave uncovered or unprotected, esp. from the weather. **2** (foll. by *to*) **a** cause to be liable to or in danger of (*was exposed to great danger*). **b** lay open to the action or influence of; introduce to (*exposed to bad influences, exposed to Chaucer at a young age*). **3** (as **exposed** *adj.*) **a** (foll. by *to*) open to; unprotected from (*exposed to the east*). **b** vulnerable, risky. **4** *Photog.* subject (a film) to light, esp. by operation of a camera. **5** reveal the identity or fact of (esp. a person or thing disapproved of or guilty of crime etc.). **6** disclose; make public. **7** exhibit, display. **8** put up for sale. □ **expose oneself** display one's body, esp. the genitals, publicly and indecently. □□ **exposer** *n.* [ME f. OF *exposer* after L *exponere*: see EXPONENT, POSE[1]]
■ **2 a** see SUBJECT *v.* 1. **b** (*expose to*) introduce to, acquaint with, bring into contact with. **3** (**exposed**) **b** see VULNERABLE 1. **5** reveal, disclose, divulge, unveil, unmask, lay bare, uncover, let out, leak, betray, bring to light, make known, *archaic* discover. **6** make public, make known; see also DISCLOSE 1. **7** exhibit, display, show, reveal, bare, uncover. □ **expose oneself** see DISPLAY *v.* 2.

exposé /ekspṓzay/ *n.* **1** an orderly statement of facts. **2** the act or an instance of revealing something discreditable. [F, past part. of *exposer* (as EXPOSE)]
■ **1** see RECORD *n.* 1, REPORT *n.* 1, 2. **2** see REVELATION.

exposition /ékspəzísh'n/ *n.* **1** an explanatory statement or account. **2** an explanation or commentary; an interpretative article or treatise. **3** *Mus.* the part of a movement, esp. in sonata form, in which the principal themes are first presented. **4** a large public exhibition. **5** *archaic* exposure. □□ **expositional** *adj.* **expositive** /-pózzitiv/ *adj.* [ME f. OF *exposition*, or L *expositio* (as EXPONENT)]
■ **1, 2** statement, account; explanation, description, commentary, interpretation, exegesis; explication, clarification; paper, theme, article, essay, thesis, dissertation, treatise, disquisition, study, critique. **4** exhibition, show, showing, exhibit, display, Expo; presentation, demonstration. **5** see EXPOSURE 3.

expositor /ikspózzitər/ *n.* an expounder or interpreter. □□ **expository** *adj.*

ex post facto /éks pōst fáktō/ *adj.* & *adv.* with retrospective action or force. [L *ex postfacto* in the light of subsequent events]

expostulate /ikspóstyoolayt/ *v.intr.* (often foll. by *with* a person) make a protest; remonstrate earnestly. □□ **expostulation** /-láysh'n/ *n.* **expostulatory** /-lətəri, -tri/ *adj.* [L *expostulare expostulat-* (as EX-[1], *postulare* demand)]
■ see PROTEST *v.* 1.

exposure /ikspṓzhər/ *n.* **1** (foll. by *to*) the act or condition of exposing or being exposed (to air, cold, danger, etc.). **2** the condition of being exposed to the elements, esp. in severe conditions (*died from exposure*). **3** the revelation of an identity or fact, esp. when concealed or likely to find disapproval. **4** *Photog.* **a** the action of exposing a film etc. to the light. **b** the duration of this action. **c** the area of film etc. affected by it. **5** an aspect or outlook (*has a fine southern exposure*). **6** experience, esp. of a specified kind of work. □ **exposure meter** *Photog.* a device for measuring the strength of the light to determine the correct duration of exposure. [EXPOSE after *enclosure* etc.]
■ **3** revelation, disclosure, revealing, uncovering, disclosing, exposé, unmasking, unveiling, baring, laying open, leak, leaking, divulging; publication, publishing. **5** aspect, view, outlook, orientation, frontage; setting, location, direction. **6** familiarity, knowledge, acquaintance, experience, contact, conversancy.

expound /ikspównd/ *v.tr.* **1** set out in detail (a doctrine etc.). **2** explain or interpret (esp. Scripture). □□ **expounder** *n.* [ME f. OF *espondre* (as EXPONENT)]
■ see EXPLAIN 1.

express[1] /iksprés/ *v.tr.* **1** represent or make known (thought, feelings, etc.) in words or by gestures, conduct, etc. **2** *refl.* say what one thinks or means. **3** esp. *Math.* represent by symbols. **4** squeeze out (liquid or air). □□ **expresser** *n.* **expressible** *adj.* [ME f. OF *expresser* f. Rmc (as EX-[1], PRESS[1])]
■ **1, 2** articulate, verbalize, utter, voice, state, put into words, enunciate, set forth, put forward, put *or* get across, communicate, *formal* put forth; phrase, word, put; say; show, indicate, demonstrate, manifest, exhibit, evince, evidence, reveal, expose, disclose, divulge, make known, intimate, denote, convey, betoken, signify; embody, depict. **3** symbolize, represent, signify, denote. **4** squeeze *or* press *or* wring *or* force out, extract, expel.

express[2] /iksprés/ *adj.*, *adv.*, *n.*, & *v.* ● *adj.* **1** operating at high speed. **2** /also ékspress/ **a** definitely stated, not merely implied. **b** *archaic* (of a likeness) exact. **3 a** done, made, or sent for a special purpose. **b** (of messages or goods) delivered by a special messenger or service. ● *adv.* **1** at high speed. **2** by express messenger or train. ● *n.* **1 a** an express train or messenger. **b** an express rifle. **2** *US* a company undertaking the transport of parcels etc. ● *v.tr.* send by express messenger or delivery. □ **express rifle** a rifle that discharges a bullet at high speed. **express train** a fast train, stopping at few intermediate stations. □□ **expressly** *adv.* (in senses 2 and 3a of *adj.*) [ME f. OF *expres* f. L *expressus* distinctly shown, past part. of *exprimere* (as EX-[1], *premere* press)]
■ *adj.* **1** speedy, quick, swift, fast, rapid, prompt, direct. **2** explicit, definite, clear, plain, unambiguous, direct, straightforward, outright, specific, categorical, unmistakable, well-defined, distinct, exact. **3 a** special, specific, particular; marked, customized. ● *adv.* **1** see *promptly* (PROMPT). □□ **expressly** definitely, categorically, distinctly, explicitly, directly, unambiguously, unequivocally, unmistakably, plainly, pointedly, clearly, positively; purposely, especially, purposefully, particularly, specifically, specially; on purpose.

expression /ikspréshʼn/ *n.* **1** the act or an instance of expressing. **2 a** a word or phrase expressed. **b** manner or means of expressing in language; wording, diction. **3** *Math.* a collection of symbols expressing a quantity. **4** a person's facial appearance or intonation of voice, esp. as indicating feeling. **5** depiction of feeling, movement, etc., in art. **6** conveying of feeling in the performance of a piece of music. □ **expression-mark** *Mus.* a sign or word indicating the required manner of performance. □□ **expressional** *adj.*

expressionless *adj.* **expressionlessly** *adv.* **expressionlessness** *n.* [ME f. OF *expression* or L *expressio* f. *exprimere*: see EXPRESS[1]]
■ **1** verbalization, representation, declaration, utterance, assertion, asseveration, pronouncement, communication, announcement; voicing, airing; manifestation, sign, show, demonstration, indication, evidence, token, symbol. **2 a** word, term, phrase, idiom, turn of phrase, locution, saying. **b** wording, phrasing, phraseology, language, style, diction, usage, speech, delivery. **4** look, air, appearance, face, aspect, countenance, *literary* mien; intonation, tone, note. **6** tone, intonation, touch, shading; expressiveness, emotion, feeling, sensitivity, passion, spirit, depth, ardour, intensity, pathos.

expressionism /ikspréshəniz'm/ *n.* a style of painting, music, drama, etc., in which an artist or writer seeks to express emotional experience rather than impressions of the external world. □□ **expressionist** *n.* & *adj.* **expressionistic** /-nístik/ *adj.* **expressionistically** /-nístikəli/ *adv.*

expressive /ikspréssiv/ *adj.* **1** full of expression (*an expressive look*). **2** (foll. by *of*) serving to express (*words expressive of contempt*). □□ **expressively** *adv.* **expressiveness** *n.* **expressivity** /-sívviti/ *n.* [ME f. F *expressif -ive* or med.L *expressivus* (as EXPRESSION)]
■ **1** vivid, striking, loaded, forceful, moving, emotional, poignant, provocative, pointed, explicit, pithy, telling, eloquent, meaningful, significant, pregnant. **2** indicative, suggestive, revealing, denotative.

expresso var. of ESPRESSO.

expressway /ikspréswαy/ *n. US* an urban motorway.
■ see ROAD[1] 1.

expropriate /eksprṓpriayt/ *v.tr.* **1** (esp. of the State) take away (property) from its owner. **2** (foll. by *from*) dispossess. □□ **expropriation** /-áysh'n/ *n.* **expropriator** *n.* [med.L *expropriare expropriat-* (as EX-[1], *proprium* property: see PROPER)]
■ see APPROPRIATE *v.* 1.

expulsion /ikspúlsh'n/ *n.* the act or an instance of expelling; the process of being expelled. □□ **expulsive** /-púlsiv/ *adj.* [ME f. L *expulsio* (as EXPEL)]
■ ejection, expelling, *sl.* the bounce; removal, dismissal, discharge, *esp. US* ouster, *colloq.* the boot, the sack, sacking; eviction.

expunge /ikspúnj/ *v.tr.* (foll. by *from*) erase, remove (esp. a passage from a book or a name from a list). □□ **expunction** /ikspúngksh'n/ *n.* **expunger** *n.* [L *expungere expunct-* (as EX-[1], *pungere* prick)]
■ see REMOVE *v.* 2b.

expurgate /ékspərgayt/ *v.tr.* **1** remove matter thought to be objectionable from (a book etc.). **2** remove (such matter). □□ **expurgation** /-gáysh'n/ *n.* **expurgator** *n.* **expurgatorial** /ékspərgətóriəl/ *adj.* **expurgatory** /ekspúrgətəri, -tri/ *adj.* [L *expurgare expurgat-* (as EX-[1], *purgare* cleanse)]
■ see EDIT *v.* 5.

exquisite /ékskwizit, *disp.* ikskwízzit/ *adj.* & *n.* ● *adj.* **1** extremely beautiful or delicate. **2** acute; keenly felt (*exquisite pleasure*). **3 a** keen; highly sensitive or discriminating (*exquisite taste*). **b** elaborately devised or accomplished; consummate, perfect. ● *n.* a person of refined (esp. affected) tastes. □□ **exquisitely** *adv.* **exquisiteness** *n.* [ME f. L *exquirere exquisit-* (as EX-[1], *quaerere* seek)]
■ *adj.* **1** beautiful, perfect, lovely, attractive, handsome; comely, good-looking; smart, chic, striking, elegant; delicate, fine, graceful, excellent, choice, well-crafted, well-made, well-executed, refined. **2** acute, sharp, keen, excruciating, agonizing, intense. **3** superb, superior, peerless, matchless, incomparable, unequalled, rare, consummate, outstanding, superlative, excellent, flawless, perfect, wonderful, splendid, marvellous; see also ACUTE *adj.* 1a. ● *n.* aesthete, connoisseur, art-lover, lover of beauty, epicure, gourmet, dilettante.

exsanguinate /iksánggwinayt/ *Med. v.tr.* drain of blood. □□ **exsanguination** /-náysh'n/ *n.* [L *exsanguinatus* (as EX-[1], *sanguis -inis* blood)]

exsert /iksért/ *v.tr. Biol.* put forth. [L *exserere*: see EXERT]

ex-service /éks-sérviss/ *adj.* **1** having formerly been a member of the armed forces. **2** relating to former servicemen and -women.

ex-serviceman /éks-sérvismən/ *n.* (*pl.* **-men**) a former member of the armed forces.

ex-servicewoman /éks-sérviswo͝omən/ *n.* (*pl.* **-women**) a former woman member of the armed forces.

ex silentio /éks silénshiō/ *adv.* by the absence of contrary evidence. [L, = from silence]

ext. *abbr.* **1** exterior. **2** external.

extant /ekstánt, ékstənt/ *adj.* (esp. of a document etc.) still existing, surviving. [L *exstare exstant-* (as EX-[1], *stare* stand)]
■ see ACTUAL 2.

extemporaneous /ikstémpəráyniəss/ *adj.* spoken or done without preparation. □□ **extemporaneously** *adv.* **extemporaneousness** *n.*
■ impromptu, improvised, spontaneous, unrehearsed, extemporized, extempore, extemporary, unprepared, unstudied, unplanned, unpremeditated, unscripted, offhand, ad lib, *colloq.* off the cuff.

extemporary /ikstémpərəri/ *adj.* = EXTEMPORANEOUS. □□ **extemporarily** *adv.* **extemporariness** *n.*

extempore /ikstémpəri/ *adj.* & *adv.* **1** without preparation. **2** offhand. [L *ex tempore* on the spur of the moment, lit. out of the time f. *tempus* time]
■ see EXTEMPORANEOUS.

extemporize /ikstémpərīz/ *v.tr.* (also **-ise**) (also *absol.*) compose or produce (music, a speech, etc.) without preparation; improvise. □□ **extemporization** /-záysh'n/ *n.*
■ see IMPROVISE 1.

extend /iksténd/ *v.* **1** *tr.* & *intr.* lengthen or make larger in space or time. **2 a** *tr.* stretch or lay out at full length. **b** *tr.* & *intr.* (often foll. by *over*) (cause to) stretch or span over a period of time. **3** *intr.* & *tr.* (foll. by *to, over*) reach or be or make continuous over a certain area. **4** *intr.* (foll. by *to*) have a certain scope (*the permit does not extend to camping*). **5** *tr.* offer or accord (an invitation, hospitality, kindness, etc.). **6** *tr.* (usu. *refl.* or in *passive*) tax the powers of (an athlete, horse, etc.) to the utmost. □ **extended family** a family including relatives living near. **extended-play** (of a gramophone record) playing for longer than most singles, usu. at 45 r.p.m. □□ **extendable** *adj.* **extendability** /-dəbílliti/ *n.* **extendible** *adj.* **extendibility** *n.* **extensible** /-sténsib'l/ *adj.* **extensibility** /-sténsibílliti/ *n.* [ME f. L *extendere extens-* or *extent-* stretch out (as EX-[1], *tendere* stretch)]
■ **1** lengthen, elongate, add to, increase, augment; widen, broaden, enlarge, stretch (out). **2 a** stretch *or* lay out, hold out, stretch forth, offer, proffer, give, tender, present; see also SPREAD *v.* 1a. **b** last, stretch, continue, go *or* carry on, drag on; perpetuate, drag out, prolong. **3** stretch *or* spread (out); reach, range; carry on, continue. **4** (*extend to*) see INCLUDE 1. **5** offer, bestow, accord, grant, impart, confer, advance. **6** see CHALLENGE *v.* 3a.

extender /iksténdər/ *n.* **1** a person or thing that extends. **2** a substance added to paint, ink, glue, etc., to dilute its colour or increase its bulk.

extensile /iksténsīl/ *adj.* capable of being stretched out or protruded.
■ see ELASTIC *adj.* 1.

extension /iksténsh'n/ *n.* **1** the act or an instance of extending; the process of being extended. **2** prolongation; enlargement. **3** a part enlarging or added on to a main structure or building. **4** an additional part of anything. **5 a** a subsidiary telephone on the same line as the main one. **b** its number. **6 a** an additional period of time, esp. extending allowance for a project etc. **b** permission for the sale of alcoholic drinks until later than usual, granted to licensed premises on special occasions. **7** extramural instruction by a university or college (*extension course*). **8** extent, range. **9**

Logic a group of things denoted by a term. □□ **extensional** *adj.* [ME f. LL *extensio* (as EXTEND)]
■ **1, 2** enlargement, expansion, increase, augmentation, development, amplification, broadening, widening, lengthening, stretching. **3** annexe, wing, addition. **4** addition, appendage, adjunct, supplement. **6 a** see RESPITE *n.* 2. **8** extent, range, scope, magnitude, sweep, reach, extensiveness, capacity, span, compass, gauge, size, dimensions; breadth, width, height, length, spread, stretch, volume.

extensive /iksténsiv/ *adj.* **1** covering a large area in space or time. **2** having a wide scope; far-reaching, comprehensive (*an extensive knowledge of music*). **3** *Agriculture* involving cultivation from a large area, with a minimum of special resources (cf. INTENSIVE). □□ **extensively** *adv.* **extensiveness** *n.* [F *extensif -ive* or LL *extensivus* (as EXTENSION)]
■ **1** large, big, great, huge, substantial, considerable, sizeable, immense, enormous, vast, gigantic, massive; spacious, voluminous, commodious, capacious. **2** wide, broad; far-reaching, far-ranging, wide-ranging, sweeping, widespread, far-flung; comprehensive, catholic, all-embracing; national, nationwide, international, intercontinental, cosmopolitan, worldwide, global, universal; cosmic.

extensometer /ékstensómmitər/ *n.* **1** an instrument for measuring deformation of metal under stress. **2** an instrument using such deformation to record elastic strains in other materials. [L *extensus* (as EXTEND) + -METER]

extensor /iksténsər/ *n.* (in full **extensor muscle**) *Anat.* a muscle that extends or straightens out part of the body (cf. FLEXOR). [mod.L (as EXTEND)]

extent /ikstént/ *n.* **1** the space over which a thing extends. **2** the width or limits of application; scope (*to a great extent*; *to the full extent of their power*). [ME f. AF *extente* f. med.L *extenta* past part. of L *extendere*: see EXTEND]
■ **1** space, magnitude, dimensions, compass, size, range, scale, sweep, scope, amplitude; expanse, area, region, tract, territory. **2** limits, lengths; scope; see also RANGE *n.* 1a–c.

extenuate /ikstényoo-ayt/ *v.tr.* (often as **extenuating** *adj.*) lessen the seeming seriousness of (guilt or an offence) by reference to some mitigating factor. □□ **extenuatingly** *adv.* **extenuation** /-áysh'n/ *n.* **extenuatory** /-yooətəri/ *adj.* [L *extenuare extenuat-* (as EX-[1], *tenuis* thin)]
■ (**extenuating**) mitigating, tempering, palliating, qualifying, moderating, lessening.

exterior /ikstéeriər/ *adj.* & *n.* ● *adj.* **1 a** of or on the outer side (opp. INTERIOR). **b** (foll. by *to*) situated on the outside of (a building etc.). **c** coming from outside. **2** *Cinematog.* outdoor. ● *n.* **1** the outward aspect or surface of a building etc. **2** the outward or apparent behaviour or demeanour of a person. **3** *Cinematog.* an outdoor scene. □ **exterior angle** the angle between the side of a rectilinear figure and the adjacent side extended outward. □□ **exteriority** /-riórriti/ *n.* **exteriorize** *v.tr.* (also **-ise**). **exteriorly** *adv.* [L, compar. of *exterus* outside]
■ *adj.* **1 a** outer, outside, external, outward; surface, superficial. **c** outside, external, extrinsic, extraneous, foreign, alien, exotic. **2** see OUTDOOR. ● *n.* **1** aspect, surface, outside, front, face, façade; skin, shell, covering, coating. **2** see BEARING 1.

exterminate /ikstérminayt/ *v.tr.* **1** destroy utterly (esp. something living). **2** get rid of; eliminate (a pest, disease, etc.). □□ **extermination** /-náysh'n/ *n.* **exterminator** *n.* **exterminatory** /-nətəri/ *adj.* [L *exterminare exterminat-* (as EX-[1], *terminus* boundary)]
■ destroy, eradicate, extirpate, annihilate, eliminate, root out, get rid of, wipe out, obliterate, put an end to, terminate, liquidate, kill off, *US sl.* rub out, waste.

external /ikstérn'l/ *adj.* & *n.* ● *adj.* **1 a** of or situated on the outside or visible part (opp. INTERNAL). **b** coming or derived from the outside or an outside source. **2** relating to a country's foreign affairs. **3** outside the conscious subject (*the external world*). **4** (of medicine etc.) for use on the outside of the body. **5** for or concerning students taking the examinations of a university without attending it. ● *n.* (in *pl.*) **1** the outward features or aspect. **2** external circumstances. **3** inessentials. □ **external evidence** evidence derived from a source independent of the thing discussed. □□ **externality** /éksternálliti/ *n.* (*pl.* **-ies**). **externally** *adv.* [med.L f. L *externus* f. *exterus* outside]
■ *adj.* **1a, 3** outside, outward, exterior, visible, apparent, perceptible. **1 b** outside, exterior, extrinsic, extraneous, alien, foreign, exotic. **2** international, overseas, foreign. ● *n.* (*externals*) **1** see ASPECT 2b. **2** see ENVIRONMENT 1, 2. **3** see ACCESSORY *n.* 2.

externalize /ikstérnəlīz/ *v.tr.* (also **-ise**) give or attribute external existence to. □□ **externalization** /-záysh'n/ *n.*

exteroceptive /ékstərōséptiv/ *adj.* *Biol.* relating to stimuli produced outside an organism. [irreg. f. L *externus* exterior + RECEPTIVE]

exterritorial /éksterritóriəl/ *adj.* = EXTRATERRITORIAL. □□ **exterritoriality** /-riálliti/ *n.*

extinct /ikstíngkt/ *adj.* **1** (of a family, class, or species) that has died out. **2 a** (of fire etc.) no longer burning. **b** (of a volcano) that no longer erupts. **3** (of life, hope, etc.) terminated, quenched. **4** (of an office etc.) obsolete. **5** (of a title of nobility) having no qualified claimant. [ME f. L *exstinguere exstinct-* (as EX-[1], *stinguere* quench)]
■ **1** dead, departed, vanished; defunct, died out, gone. **2** inactive, dormant; extinguished, quenched, burnt-out. **3** see DEAD *adj.* 1. **4** dated, outmoded, old-fashioned, antiquated, obsolete, archaic, out of date, ancient, *passé*, *démodé*, *colloq.* antediluvian, old hat.

extinction /ikstíngksh'n/ *n.* **1** the act of making extinct; the state of being or process of becoming extinct. **2** the act of extinguishing; the state of being extinguished. **3** total destruction or annihilation. **4** the wiping out of a debt. **5** *Physics* a reduction in the intensity of radiation by absorption, scattering, etc. □□ **extinctive** *adj.* [L *extinctio* (as EXTINCT)]
■ **1, 3** see DESTRUCTION 1. **2** see *suppression* (SUPPRESS).

extinguish /ikstínggwish/ *v.tr.* **1** cause (a flame, light, etc.) to die out; put out. **2** make extinct; annihilate, destroy (*a programme to extinguish disease*). **3** put an end to; terminate; obscure utterly (a feeling, quality, etc.). **4 a** abolish; wipe out (a debt). **b** *Law* render void. **5** *colloq.* reduce to silence (*the argument extinguished the opposition*). **6** *archaic* surpass by superior brilliance. □□ **extinguishable** *adj.* **extinguishment** *n.* [irreg. f. L *extinguere* (as EXTINCT): cf. *distinguish*]
■ **1** put *or* snuff *or* blow out, quench; turn off *or* out. **2, 3** annihilate, destroy, exterminate, kill (off), eliminate, end, finish, nullify, obliterate, terminate, eradicate, extirpate, remove, wipe *or* blot *or* root out, obscure, *colloq.* do away with. **4** see ABOLISH. **5** see SILENCE *v.* **6** obscure, eclipse, dim, outdo, put in the shade, overshadow, adumbrate, *colloq.* show up.

extinguisher /ikstínggwishər/ *n.* a person or thing that extinguishes, esp. = *fire extinguisher*.

extirpate /ékstərpayt/ *v.tr.* root out; destroy completely. □□ **extirpation** /-páysh'n/ *n.* **extirpator** *n.* [L *exstirpare exstirpat-* (as EX-[1], *stirps* stem)]
■ see *root out* (ROOT[1]).

extol /ikstṓl, ikstól/ *v.tr.* (**extolled**, **extolling**) praise enthusiastically. □□ **extoller** *n.* **extolment** *n.* [L *extollere* (as EX-[1], *tollere* raise)]
■ praise, laud, applaud, commend, acclaim, celebrate, pay tribute *or* homage to, exalt, sing the praises of, make much of, glorify, honour, compliment.

extort /ikstórt/ *v.tr.* obtain by force, threats, persistent demands, etc. □□ **extorter** *n.* **extortive** *adj.* [L *extorquēre extort-* (as EX-[1], *torquēre* twist)]
■ obtain, exact, extract, force, wring, wrest.

extortion /ikstórsh'n/ *n.* **1** the act or an instance of extorting, esp. money. **2** illegal exaction. □□ **extortioner** *n.* **extortionist** *n.* [ME f. LL *extortio* (as EXTORT)]
■ see BLACKMAIL *n.* 2.

extortionate /ikstórshənət/ *adj.* **1** (of a price etc.) exorbitant. **2** using or given to extortion (*extortionate methods*). ▫▫ **extortionately** *adv.*
■ **1** see EXORBITANT. **2** see RAPACIOUS.

extra /ékstrə/ *adj.*, *adv.*, & *n.* ● *adj.* additional; more than is usual or necessary or expected. ● *adv.* **1** more than usually. **2** additionally (*was charged extra*). ● *n.* **1** an extra thing. **2** a thing for which an extra charge is made; such a charge. **3** a person engaged temporarily to fill out a scene in a film or play, esp. as one of a crowd. **4** a special issue of a newspaper etc. **5** *Cricket* a run scored other than from a hit with the bat. ▫ **extra cover** *Cricket* **1** a fielding position on a line between cover-point and mid-off, but beyond these. **2** a fielder at this position. **extra size** outsize. **extra time** *Sport* a further period of play at the end of a match when the scores are equal. [prob. a shortening of EXTRAORDINARY]
■ *adj.* additional, added, further; accessory, supplementary, supplemental; adventitious; auxiliary, subsidiary, collateral. ● *adv.* **1** unusually, exceptionally, extraordinarily, uncommonly, unexpectedly, surprisingly, amazingly, remarkably, notably, strikingly, very, particularly, especially, extremely. **2** additionally, more, again, in addition. ● *n.* **1** see ADDITION 2. **2** supplement, mark-up, surcharge. **3** supernumerary, walk-on, *Theatr.* super. **4** special, one-off; exclusive.

extra- /ékstrə/ *comb. form* **1** outside, beyond (*extragalactic*). **2** beyond the scope of (*extracurricular*). [med.L f. L *extra* outside]

extracellular /ékstrəsélyoolər/ *adj.* situated or taking place outside a cell or cells.

extract *v.* & *n.* ● *v.tr.* /ikstrákt/ **1** remove or take out, esp. by effort or force (anything firmly rooted). **2** obtain (money, an admission, etc.) with difficulty or against a person's will. **3** obtain (a natural resource) from the earth. **4** select or reproduce for quotation or performance (a passage of writing, music, etc.). **5** obtain (juice etc.) by suction, pressure, distillation, etc. **6** derive (pleasure etc.). **7** *Math.* find (the root of a number). **8** *archaic* deduce (a principle etc.). ● *n.* /ékstrakt/ **1** a short passage taken from a book, piece of music, etc.; an excerpt. **2** a preparation containing the active principle of a substance in concentrated form (*malt extract*). ▫▫ **extractable** *adj.* **extractability** /-təbílliti/ *n.* [L *extrahere extract-* (as EX-[1], *trahere* draw)]
■ *v.* **1** remove, take *or* pluck out, draw *or* pull (out), withdraw, draw forth, extricate. **2** obtain, wrench, wring, wrest, extort, extricate; worm out, prise out, *esp. Brit.* winkle out, force out. **3** see MINE[2] *v.* 1, 2. **4** select, choose, glean, cull, abstract, quote, cite; reproduce, copy. **6** see DERIVE 1. **8** deduce, derive, glean, draw, distil, get, obtain. ● *n.* **1** passage, excerpt, quotation, citation, clipping, cutting, selection. **2** concentrate, essence, distillation, distillate, quintessence, decoction.

extraction /ikstráksh'n/ *n.* **1** the act or an instance of extracting; the process of being extracted. **2** the removal of a tooth. **3** origin, lineage, descent (*of Indian extraction*). **4** something extracted; an extract. [ME f. F f. LL *extractio -onis* (as EXTRACT)]
■ **1** removal, extrication, uprooting, withdrawal. **2** removal, pulling. **3** origin, birth, lineage, ancestry, descent, derivation, blood, parentage, race, stock, pedigree. **4** extract, concentrate, distillate, essence, distillation, quintessence, concentration, decoction.

extractive /ikstráktiv/ *adj.* of or involving extraction, esp. extensive extracting of natural resources without provision for their renewal.

extractor /ikstráktər/ *n.* **1** a person or machine that extracts. **2** (*attrib.*) (of a device) that extracts bad air etc. or ventilates a room (*extractor fan*; *extractor hood*).

extracurricular /ékstrəkəríkyoolər/ *adj.* (of a subject of study) not included in the normal curriculum.

extraditable /ékstrədītəb'l/ *adj.* **1** liable to extradition. **2** (of a crime) warranting extradition.

extradite /ékstrədīt/ *v.tr.* hand over (a person accused or convicted of a crime) to the foreign State etc. in which the crime was committed.
■ see BANISH 1.

extradition /ékstrədísh'n/ *n.* **1** the extraditing of a person accused or convicted of a crime. **2** *Psychol.* the localizing of a sensation at a distance from the centre of sensation.

extrados /ekstráydoss/ *n.* *Archit.* the upper or outer curve of an arch (opp. INTRADOS). [EXTRA- + *dos* back f. L *dorsum*]

extragalactic /ékstrəgəláktik/ *adj.* occurring or existing outside the Galaxy.

extrajudicial /ékstrəjoodísh'l/ *adj.* **1** not legally authorized. **2** (of a confession) not made in court. ▫▫ **extrajudicially** *adv.*

extramarital /ékstrəmárrit'l/ *adj.* (esp. of sexual relations) occurring outside marriage. ▫▫ **extramaritally** *adv.*

extramundane /ékstrəmúndayn/ *adj.* outside or beyond the physical world.
■ see SUPERNATURAL *adj.*

extramural /ékstrəmyŏŏrəl/ *adj.* & *n.* ● *adj.* **1** taught or conducted off the premises of a university, college, or school. **2** additional to normal teaching or studies, esp. for non-resident students. **3** outside the walls or boundaries of a town or city. ● *n.* an extramural lesson, course, etc. ▫▫ **extramurally** *adv.* [L *extra muros* outside the walls]

extraneous /ikstráyniəss/ *adj.* **1** of external origin. **2** (often foll. by *to*) **a** separate from the object to which it is attached etc. **b** external to; irrelevant or unrelated to. **c** inessential, superfluous. ▫▫ **extraneously** *adv.* **extraneousness** *n.* [L *extraneus*]
■ **1** see EXTERNAL *adj.* 1b. **2 b** irrelevant, unrelated, inapposite, unconnected, impertinent, inapplicable, inapt, unapt, unfitting, inappropriate, remote, foreign, alien, strange, outlandish, external, extrinsic; out of place, beside *or* off the point, beside *or* off *or* wide of the mark, off the subject. **c** unessential, non-essential, inessential, peripheral, superfluous, unnecessary, unneeded, extra, added, additional, supernumerary, incidental, needless.

extraordinary /ikstrórdinəri, -dinri, ékstrəórdinəri/ *adj.* **1** unusual or remarkable; out of the usual course. **2** unusually great (*an extraordinary talent*). **3** so exceptional as to provoke astonishment or admiration. **4 a** (of an official etc.) additional; specially employed (*envoy extraordinary*). **b** (of a meeting) specially convened. ▫▫ **extraordinarily** *adv.* **extraordinariness** *n.* [L *extraordinarius* f. *extra ordinem* outside the usual order]
■ **1, 2** unusual, remarkable, exceptional, uncommon, outstanding, rare, special, singular, signal, particular, abnormal, unprecedented, unparalleled, *disp.* unique; unheard-of, curious, peculiar, odd, bizarre, strange, queer. **3** amazing, surprising, astonishing, astounding, remarkable, notable, noteworthy, marvellous, fantastic, incredible, unbelievable, impressive, fabulous, miraculous, unparalleled, far-out, *colloq.* super, smashing, lovely, gorgeous, *US* & *Austral. sl.* unreal. **4** see SPECIAL *adj.* 2.

extrapolate /ikstráppəlayt/ *v.tr.* (also *absol.*) **1** *Math.* & *Philos.* **a** calculate approximately from known values, data, etc. (others which lie outside the range of those known). **b** calculate on the basis of (known facts) to estimate unknown facts, esp. extend (a curve) on a graph. **2** infer more widely from a limited range of known facts. ▫▫ **extrapolation** /-láysh'n/ *n.* **extrapolative** /-lətiv/ *adj.* **extrapolator** *n.* [EXTRA- + INTERPOLATE]

extrasensory /ékstrəsénsəri/ *adj.* regarded as derived by means other than the known senses, e.g. by telepathy, clairvoyance, etc. ▫ **extrasensory perception** a person's supposed faculty of perceiving by such means.
■ see PSYCHIC *adj.* 1b.

extraterrestrial /ékstrətiréstriəl/ *adj.* & *n.* ● *adj.* **1** outside the earth or its atmosphere. **2** (in science fiction) from outer space. ● *n.* (in science fiction) a being from outer space.

■ *adj.* see UNEARTHLY 3. ● *n.* alien, ET, Martian.

extraterritorial /ékstrətérritóriəl/ *adj.* **1** situated or (of laws etc.) valid outside a country's territory. **2** (of an ambassador etc.) free from the jurisdiction of the territory of residence. □□ **extraterritoriality** /-riálliti/ *n.* [L *extra territorium* outside the territory]

extravagance /ikstrávvəgənss/ *n.* **1** excessive spending or use of resources; being extravagant. **2** an instance or item of this. **3** unrestrained or absurd behaviour, speech, thought, or writing. □□ **extravagancy** *n.* (*pl.* **-ies**). [F (as EXTRAVAGANT)]
■ **1** overspending, excess, thriftlessness, improvidence, dissipation, wastefulness, waste, lavishness, squandering, profligacy, prodigality, recklessness. **2** see SPLURGE *n.* 2. **3** immoderation, immoderateness, excessiveness, outrageousness, unrestraint, superfluity, superfluousness, preposterousness, unreasonableness, irrationality, absurdity; capriciousness, whimsicality, flightiness.

extravagant /ikstrávvəgənt/ *adj.* **1** spending (esp. money) excessively; immoderate or wasteful in use of resources. **2** exorbitant; costing much. **3** exceeding normal restraint or sense; unreasonable, absurd (*extravagant claims*). □□ **extravagantly** *adv.* [ME f. med.L *extravagari* (as EXTRA-, *vagari* wander)]
■ **1** lavish, improvident, spendthrift, immoderate, wasteful, profligate, prodigal, reckless. **2** exorbitant, expensive, costly, extortionate, unreasonable, overpriced; dear, *colloq.* steep. **3** unrestrained, wild, outrageous, immoderate; unreasonable, absurd, preposterous, ridiculous, fanciful, flamboyant, high-sounding, exaggerated; undeserved, unjustified, unjustifiable.

extravaganza /ikstrávvəgánzə/ *n.* **1** a fanciful literary, musical, or dramatic composition. **2** a spectacular theatrical or television production, esp. of light entertainment. [It. *estravaganza* extravagance]
■ **1** see FANCY *n.* 2. **2** spectacular, spectacle, pageant, production, show.

extravasate /ikstrávvəsayt/ *v.* **1** *tr.* force out (a fluid, esp. blood) from its proper vessel. **2** *intr.* (of blood, lava, etc.) flow out. □□ **extravasation** /-sáysh'n/ *n.* [L *extra* outside + *vas* vessel]
■ **1** see EJECT 4. **2** see LEAK *v.* 1b.

extravehicular /ékstrəvihíkyoolər/ *adj.* outside a vehicle, esp. a spacecraft.

extrema *pl.* of EXTREMUM.

extreme /ikstréem/ *adj.* & *n.* ● *adj.* **1** reaching a high or the highest degree; exceedingly great or intense; exceptional (*extreme old age*; *in extreme danger*). **2 a** severe, stringent; lacking restraint or moderation (*take extreme measures*; *an extreme reaction*). **b** (of a person, opinion, etc.) going to great lengths; advocating immoderate measures. **3** outermost; furthest from the centre; situated at either end (*the extreme edge*). **4** *Polit.* on the far left or right of a party. **5** utmost; last. ● *n.* **1** (often in *pl.*) one or other of two things as remote or as different as possible. **2** a thing at either end of anything. **3** the highest degree of anything. **4** *Math.* the first or the last term of a ratio or series. **5** *Logic* the subject or predicate in a proposition; the major or the minor term in a syllogism. □ **extreme unction** the last rites in the Roman Catholic and Orthodox Churches. **go to extremes** take an extreme course of action. **go to the other extreme** take a diametrically opposite course of action. **in the extreme** to an extreme degree. □□ **extremely** *adv.* **extremeness** *n.* [ME f. OF f. L *extremus* superl. of *exterus* outward]
■ *adj.* **1** unusual, uncommon, exceptional, extraordinary, abnormal, remarkable, outstanding; see also GREAT *adj.* 1a. **2 a** severe, acute, intense; stringent, rigid, stern, strict, harsh, Draconian, stiff, uncompromising, drastic; immoderate, excessive; inordinate, extravagant, outrageous; beyond the pale, beyond the limits *or* bounds; unconventional, radical, outrageous, wild. **b** immoderate, unconventional, radical, outrageous, wild, far-out, bizarre, queer, offbeat, exotic, eccentric, *outré*, *colloq.* weird, different, way-out, *sl.* kooky. **3** outermost, endmost, farthest, very, remotest. **5** utmost, uttermost, final, last, ultimate. ● *n.* **1, 3** limit, bounds, maximum; extremity, height, apex, apogee, peak, acme, zenith, pinnacle, summit; depth, nadir. □ **in the extreme** extremely, very, exceptionally, exceedingly, extraordinarily, unusually. □□ **extremely** very, exceedingly, not a little, exceptionally, extraordinarily, unusually, uncommonly, outrageously, *colloq.* damned, darned, *Brit. colloq.* hellishly; to the nth degree.

extremist /ikstréemist/ *n.* (also *attrib.*) a person who holds extreme or fanatical political or religious views and esp. resorts to or advocates extreme action. □□ **extremism** *n.*
■ radical, revolutionary, fanatic, zealot, militant, ultra(ist).

extremity /ikstrémmiti/ *n.* (*pl.* **-ies**) **1** the extreme point; the very end. **2** (in *pl.*) the hands and feet. **3** a condition of extreme adversity or difficulty. **4** excessiveness; extremeness. [ME f. OF *extremité* or L *extremitas* (as EXTREME)]
■ **1** extreme; end, limit, edge, boundary, bound, margin, periphery; border, frontier; maximum. **2** (*extremities*) hands, feet; fingers, fingertips, toes; arms, legs, limbs. **3** see CALAMITY 2. **4** see EXCESS *n.* 1, 4a.

extremum /ikstréeməm/ *n.* (*pl.* **extremums** or **extrema** /-mə/) *Math.* the maximum or minimum value of a function. □□ **extremal** *adj.* [L, neut. of *extremus* EXTREME]

extricate /ékstrikayt/ *v.tr.* (often foll. by *from*) free or disentangle from a constraint or difficulty. □□ **extricable** *adj.* **extrication** /-káysh'n/ *n.* [L *extricare extricat-* (as EX-[1], *tricae* perplexities)]
■ (set) free, disentangle, disengage, liberate, release, rescue, save, deliver.

extrinsic /ekstrínsik/ *adj.* **1** not inherent or intrinsic; not essential (opp. INTRINSIC). **2** (often foll. by *to*) extraneous; lying outside; not belonging (to). **3** originating or operating from without. □□ **extrinsically** *adv.* [LL *extrinsicus* outward f. L *extrinsecus* (adv.) f. *exter* outside + *secus* beside]
■ **1** see IRRELEVANT. **2, 3** extraneous, outside, external, exterior, outer, outward; unrelated, irrelevant.

extrovert /ékstrəvert/ *n.* & *adj.* ● *n.* **1** *Psychol.* a person predominantly concerned with external things or objective considerations. **2** an outgoing or sociable person. ● *adj.* typical or characteristic of an extrovert. □□ **extroversion** /-vérsh'n/ *n.* **extroverted** *adj.* [*extro-* = EXTRA- (after *intro-*) + L *vertere* turn]

extrude /ikstro͞od/ *v.tr.* **1** (foll. by *from*) thrust or force out. **2** shape metal, plastics, etc. by forcing them through a die. □□ **extrusion** /-tro͞ozh'n/ *n.* **extrusile** /-tro͞ossīl/ *adj.* **extrusive** /-tro͞ossiv/ *adj.* [L *extrudere extrus-* (as EX-[1], *trudere* thrust)]

exuberant /igzyo͞obərənt/ *adj.* **1** lively, high-spirited. **2** (of a plant etc.) prolific; growing copiously. **3** (of feelings etc.) abounding, lavish, effusive. □□ **exuberance** *n.* **exuberantly** *adv.* [F *exubérant* f. L *exuberare* (as EX-[1], *uberare* be fruitful f. *uber* fertile)]
■ **1** lively, high-spirited, buoyant, animated, spirited, spry, sprightly, vivacious, energetic, vigorous, ebullient, effervescent, cheerful, joyful, happy, glad, delighted, overjoyed, ecstatic, enthusiastic, zealous; in seventh heaven, *colloq.* on cloud nine. **2** see PROLIFIC 3. **3** see EFFUSIVE. □□ **exuberance** liveliness, buoyancy, animation, spirit, spiritedness, sprightliness, vitality, vivacity, cheerfulness, joy, joyfulness, ebullience, effervescence, exhilaration, enthusiasm, excitement, zeal, zest, energy, vigour; abundance, copiousness, superabundance, superfluity, excess, profusion, prodigality; lavishness, flamboyance.

exuberate /igzyo͞obərayt/ *v.intr.* be exuberant.

exude /igzyo͞od/ *v.* **1** *tr.* & *intr.* (of a liquid, moisture, etc.) escape or cause to escape gradually; ooze out; give off. **2** *tr.* emit (a smell). **3** *tr.* display (an emotion etc.) freely or abundantly (*exuded displeasure*). □□ **exudate** /égzyoodayt/ *n.* **exudation** /-dáysh'n/ *n.* **exudative** /igzyo͞odətiv/ *adj.* [L *exsudare* (as EX-[1], *sudare* sweat)]
■ **1, 2** see EMANATE 2, 3.

exult /igzúlt/ *v.intr.* (often foll. by *at, in, over,* or *to* + infin.) **1** be greatly joyful. **2** (often foll. by *over*) have a feeling of triumph (over a person). □□ **exultancy** *n.* **exultation** /égzultáysh'n/ *n.* **exultant** *adj.* **exultantly** *adv.* **exultingly** *adv.* [L *exsultare* (as EX-[1], *saltare* frequent. of *salire salt-* leap)]
■ **1** rejoice, revel, glory, triumph, delight, jump for joy; celebrate, make merry. □□ **exultant** delighted, jubilant, triumphant, overjoyed, elated, joyful, gleeful, glad, ecstatic, exuberant; in seventh heaven, cock-a-hoop, over the moon, *colloq.* on cloud nine.

exurb /éksurb/ *n.* a district outside a city or town, esp. a prosperous area beyond the suburbs. □□ **exurban** /eksúrb'n/ *adj.* **exurbanite** /eksúrbənīt/ *n.* [L *ex* out of + *urbs* city, or back-form. f. *exurban* (as EX-[1] + URBAN, after *suburban*)]
■ see MUNICIPALITY.

exurbia /eksúrbiə/ *n.* the exurbs collectively; the region beyond the suburbs. [EX-[1], after *suburbia*]

exuviae /igzyóōvi-ee/ *n.pl.* (also treated as *sing.*) an animal's cast skin or covering. □□ **exuvial** *adj.* [L, = animal's skins, spoils of the enemy, f. *exuere* divest oneself of]

exuviate /igzyóōviayt/ *v.tr.* shed (a skin etc.). □□ **exuviation** /-áysh'n/ *n.*

ex voto /eks vṓtō/ *n.* (*pl.* **-os**) an offering made in pursuance of a vow. [L, = out of a vow]

-ey /i/ *suffix* var. of -Y[2].

eyas /íəss/ *n.* a young hawk, esp. one taken from the nest for training in falconry. [orig. *nyas* f. F *niais* ult. f. L *nidus* nest: for loss of *n-* cf. ADDER]

eye /ī/ *n.* & *v.* ● *n.* **1 a** the organ of sight in man and other animals. **b** the light-detecting organ in some invertebrates. **2** the eye characterized by the colour of the iris (*has blue eyes*). **3** the region round the eye (*eyes red from weeping*). **4** a glass or plastic ball serving as an artificial eye (*his eye fell out*). **5** (in *sing.* or *pl.*) sight; the faculty of sight (*demonstrate to the eye; need perfect eyes to be a pilot*). **6** a particular visual faculty or talent; visual appreciation; perspicacity (*a straight eye; cast an expert eye over*). **7 a** (in *sing.* or *pl.*) a look, gaze, or glance, esp. as indicating the disposition of the viewer (*a friendly eye*). **b** (**the eye**) a flirtatious or sexually provocative glance. **8** mental awareness; consciousness. **9** a person or animal etc. that sees on behalf of another. **10 a** = *electric eye*. **b** = *private eye*. **11** a thing like an eye, esp.: **a** a spot on a peacock's tail (cf. EYELET *n.* 3). **b** the leaf bud of a potato. **12** the centre of something circular, e.g. a flower or target. **13** the relatively calm region at the centre of a storm or hurricane. **14** an aperture in an implement, esp. a needle, for the insertion of something, e.g. thread. **15** a ring or loop for a bolt or hook etc. to pass through. ● *v.tr.* (**eyes, eyed, eyeing** or **eying**) watch or observe closely, esp. admiringly or with curiosity or suspicion. □ **all eyes 1** watching intently. **2** general attention (*all eyes were on us*). **before one's** (or **one's very**) **eyes** right in front of one. **do a person in the eye** *colloq.* defraud or thwart a person. **eye-bolt** a bolt or bar with an eye at the end for a hook etc. **eye-catching** *colloq.* striking, attractive. **eye contact** looking directly into another person's eyes. **an eye for an eye** retaliation in kind (Exodus 21:24). **eye language** the process of communication by the expression of the eyes. **eye-level** the level seen by the eyes looking horizontally (*eye-level grill*). **eye-liner** a cosmetic applied as a line round the eye. **eye mask 1** a covering of soft material saturated with a lotion for refreshing the eyes. **2** a covering for the eyes. **eye-opener** *colloq.* **1** an enlightening experience; an unexpected revelation. **2** *US* an alcoholic drink taken on waking up. **eye-rhyme** a correspondence of words in spelling but not in pronunciation (e.g. *love* and *move*). **eyes front** (or **left** or **right**) *Mil.* a command to turn the head in the direction stated. **eye-shade** a device to protect the eyes, esp. from strong light. **eye-shadow** a coloured cosmetic applied to the skin round the eyes. **eye-spot 1 a** a light-sensitive area on the bodies of some invertebrate animals, e.g. flatworms, starfish, etc.; an ocellus. **b** *Bot.* an area of light-sensitive pigment found in some algae etc. **2** any of several fungus diseases of plants characterized by yellowish oval spots on the leaves and stems. **eye-stalk** *Zool.* a movable stalk carrying the eye, esp. in crabs, shrimps, etc. **eye strain** fatigue of the (internal or external) muscles of the eye. **eye-tooth** a canine tooth just under or next to the eye, esp. in the upper jaw. **eye-worm** a nematode worm, *Loa loa*, parasitic on man and other primates in Central and West Africa. **get** (or **keep**) **one's eye in** *Sport* accustom oneself (or keep oneself accustomed) to the conditions of play so as to judge speed, distance, etc. **have one's eye on** wish or plan to procure. **have an eye for 1** be quick to notice. **2** be partial to. **have an eye to** have as one's objective; prudently consider. **have eyes for** be interested in; wish to acquire. **have an eye to** have as one's objective; prudently consider. **hit a person in the eye** (or **between the eyes**) *colloq.* be very obvious or impressive. **keep an eye on 1** pay attention to. **2** look after; take care of. **keep an eye open** (or **out**) (often foll. by *for*) watch carefully. **keep one's eyes open** (or **peeled** or **skinned**) watch out; be on the alert. **lower one's eyes** look modestly or sheepishly down or away. **make eyes** (or **sheep's eyes**) (foll. by *at*) look amorously or flirtatiously at. **my** (or **all my**) **eye** *sl.* nonsense. **one in the eye** (foll. by *for*) a disappointment or set-back. **open a person's eyes** be enlightening or revealing to a person. **raise one's eyes** look upwards. **see eye to eye** (often foll. by *with*) be in full agreement. **set eyes on** catch sight of. **take one's eyes off** (usu. in *neg.*) stop watching; stop paying attention to. **under the eye of** under the supervision or observation of. **up to the** (or **one's**) **eyes in 1** deeply engaged or involved in; inundated with (*up to the eyes in work*). **2** to the utmost limit (*mortgaged up to the eyes*). **with one's eyes open** deliberately; with full awareness. **with one's eyes shut** (or **closed**) **1** easily; with little effort. **2** without awareness; unobservant (*goes around with his eyes shut*). **with an eye to** with a view to; prudently considering. **with a friendly** (or **jealous** etc.) **eye** with a feeling of friendship, jealousy, etc. **with one eye on** directing one's attention partly to. **with one eye shut** *colloq.* easily; with little effort (*could do this with one eye shut*). □□ **eyed** *adj.* (also in *comb.*). **eyeless** *adj.* [OE *ēage* f. Gmc]
■ *n.* **1** eyeball, *archaic or joc.* optic, *poet.* orb. **5** (eye)sight, vision, visual acuity. **6** discernment, perception, taste, judgement, discrimination, percipience, perspicacity, appreciation, sensitivity, comprehension. **7 a** gaze, glance, look, regard, stare. **b** ogle, leer, look, wink, sidelong glance, *colloq.* glad eye. **8** see UNDERSTANDING *n.* 1. **12** see MIDDLE *n.* 1. **13** see HEART 5a. **14, 15** slit, slot; see also APERTURE. see LOOP *n.* ● *v.* watch, observe, contemplate, study, look *or* gaze *or* peer at, look *or* gaze upon, regard, view, inspect, examine, scrutinize, *literary* behold. □ **all eyes** see ALERT *adj.* 1. **do a person in the eye** see SWINDLE *v.*, THWART *v.* **eye-catching** see ATTRACTIVE. **an eye for an eye** *lex talionis*, tit for tat, measure for measure; retaliation. **eye-opener 1** discovery, revelation; see also SURPRISE *n.* 1. **have an eye for 1** see APPRECIATE 1a, c. **2** like, be fond of, be partial to, appreciate, have a liking *or* affection *or* fondness for. **have an eye to** concentrate *or* focus on, be concentrated *or* centred on, pinpoint; see also HEED *v.* **have eyes for** see DESIRE *v.* 1. **keep an eye on 1, 2** see WATCH *v.* 2a, 4; 2b. **keep an eye open** (or **out**) see WATCH *v.* 2a, 4; 2b. **keep one's eyes open** (or **peeled** or **skinned**) see *watch out*. **make eyes** (or **sheep's eyes**) see FLIRT *v.* 1. **my** (or **all my**) **eye** see NONSENSE. **one in the eye** see DISAPPOINTMENT 1. **open a person's eyes** see EDUCATE 1, 2. **see eye to eye** see AGREE 1. **set eyes on** see *catch sight of* (SIGHT). **under the eye of** under the supervision *or* observation *or* scrutiny of. **up to the** (or **one's**) **eyes in 1** see DEEP *adj.* 8. **with one's eyes open** see *deliberately* (DELIBERATE). **with one's eyes shut** (or **closed**) **1** see EASILY 1. **2** see BLIND 2. **with an eye to** with a view to, with the aim *or* intention *or* purpose *or*

plan *or* idea *or* notion of. **with one eye shut** see EASILY 1.

eyeball /íbawl/ *n.* & *v.* ● *n.* the ball of the eye within the lids and socket. ● *v. US sl.* **1** *tr.* look or stare at. **2** *intr.* look or stare. □ **eyeball to eyeball** *colloq.* confronting closely. **to** (or **up to**) **the eyeballs** *colloq.* completely (permeated, soaked, etc.).
■ *v.* see LOOK *v.* 1a, 2b.

eyebath /íbaath/ *n.* (also **eyecup** /íkup/) a small glass or vessel for applying lotion etc. to the eye.

eyeblack /íblak/ *n.* = MASCARA.

eyebright /íbrīt/ *n.* any plant of the genus *Euphrasia*, formerly used as a remedy for weak eyes.

eyebrow /íbrow/ *n.* the line of hair growing on the ridge above the eye-socket. □ **raise one's eyebrows** show surprise, disbelief, or mild disapproval.

eyeful /ífōōl/ *n.* (*pl.* **-fuls**) *colloq.* **1** a long steady look. **2** a visually striking person or thing. **3** anything thrown or blown into the eye.

eyeglass /íglaass/ *n.* **1 a** a lens for correcting or assisting defective sight. **b** (in *pl.*) a pair of these held in the hand or kept in position on the nose by means of a frame or a spring. **2** a small glass vessel for applying lotion etc. to the eye.
■ **1b** (*eyeglasses*) see SPECTACLES.

eyehole /íhōl/ *n.* a hole to look through.

eyelash /ílash/ *n.* each of the hairs growing on the edges of the eyelids. □ **by an eyelash** by a very small margin.

eyelet /ílit/ *n.* & *v.* ● *n.* **1** a small hole in paper, leather, cloth, etc., for string or rope etc. to pass through. **2** a metal ring reinforcement for this. **3** a small eye, esp. the ocellus on a butterfly's wing (cf. EYE *n.* 11a). **4** a form of decoration in embroidery. **5** a small hole for observation, shooting through, etc. ● *v.tr.* (**eyeleted**, **eyeleting**) provide with eyelets. [ME f. OF *oillet* dimin. of *oil* eye f. L *oculus*]

eyelid /ílid/ *n.* the upper or lower fold of skin closing to cover the eye.

eyepiece /ípeess/ *n.* the lens or lenses to which the eye is applied at the end of a microscope, telescope, etc.

eyeshot /íshot/ *n.* seeing-distance (*out of eyeshot*).
■ see SIGHT *n.* 4.

eyesight /ísīt/ *n.* the faculty or power of seeing.
■ see SIGHT *n.* 1a.

eyesore /ísor/ *n.* a visually offensive or ugly thing, esp. a building.
■ see SIGHT *n.* 7.

Eyetie /ítī/ *n.* & *adj. sl. offens.* Italian. [joc. pronunc. of *Italian*]

eyewash /íwosh/ *n.* **1** lotion for the eye. **2** *sl.* nonsense, bunkum; pretentious or insincere talk.
■ **1** see WASH *n.* 7, 10. **2** see NONSENSE.

eyewitness /íwitniss/ *n.* a person who has personally seen a thing done or happen and can give evidence of it.
■ witness, observer, spectator, viewer, watcher; bystander, onlooker.

eyot var. of AIT.

eyra /áirə/ *n. Zool.* a red form of jaguarundi. [Tupi (*e*)*irara*]

eyrie /íri, éeri, éri/ *n.* (also **aerie**) **1** a nest of a bird of prey, esp. an eagle, built high up. **2** a house etc. perched high up. [med.L *aeria*, *aerea*, etc., prob. f. OF *aire* lair ult. f. L *agrum* piece of ground]
■ **1** nest, roost, perch.

Ezek. *abbr.* Ezekiel (Old Testament).

Ff

F[1] /ef/ *n.* (also **f**) (*pl.* **Fs** or **F's**) **1** the sixth letter of the alphabet. **2** *Mus.* the fourth note of the diatonic scale of C major.

F[2] *abbr.* (also **F.**) **1** Fahrenheit. **2** farad(s). **3** female. **4** fine (pencil-lead). **5** *Biol.* filial generation (as F_1 for the first filial generation, F_2 for the second, etc.).

F[3] *symb. Chem.* the element fluorine.

F *abbr. Electr.* faraday.

f *abbr.* (also **f.**) **1** female. **2** feminine. **3** following page etc. **4** *Mus.* forte. **5** folio. **6** focal length (cf. F-NUMBER). **7** femto-. **8** filly. **9** foreign. **10** frequency.

FA *abbr.* **1** (in the UK) Football Association. **2** = FANNY ADAMS 1.

fa var. of FAH.

FAA *abbr.* Fleet Air Arm.

fab /fab/ *adj. colloq.* fabulous, marvellous. [abbr.]
■ see FABULOUS 2.

Fabian /fáybiən/ *n.* & *adj.* ● *n.* a member or supporter of the Fabian Society, an organization of socialists aiming at a gradual rather than revolutionary achievement of socialism. ● *adj.* **1** relating to or characteristic of the Fabians. **2** employing a cautiously persistent and dilatory strategy to wear out an enemy (*Fabian tactics*). □□ **Fabianism** *n.* **Fabianist** *n.* [L *Fabianus* f. the name of Q. *Fabius* Maximus Cunctator (= delayer), Roman general of the 3rd c. BC, noted for cautious strategies]

fable /fáyb'l/ *n.* & *v.* ● *n.* **1 a** a story, esp. a supernatural one, not based on fact. **b** a tale, esp. with animals as characters, conveying a moral. **2** (*collect.*) myths and legendary tales (*in fable*). **3 a** a false statement; a lie. **b** a thing only supposed to exist. ● *v.* **1** *intr.* tell fictitious tales. **2** *tr.* describe fictitiously. **3** *tr.* (as **fabled** *adj.*) celebrated in fable; famous, legendary. □□ **fabler** /fáyblər/ *n.* [ME f. OF *fabler* f. L *fabulari* f. *fabula* discourse f. *fari* speak]
■ *n.* **1, 2** see MYTH 4. **3** see FABRICATION 3. ● *v.* **3** (**fabled**) see LEGENDARY 3.

fabliau /fábliō/ *n.* (*pl.* **fabliaux** /-ōz/) a metrical tale in early French poetry, often coarsely humorous. [F f. OF dialect *fabliaux*, *-ax* pl. of *fablel* dimin. (as FABLE)]

fabric /fábrik/ *n.* **1 a** a woven material; a textile. **b** other material resembling woven cloth. **2** a structure or framework, esp. the walls, floor, and roof of a building. **3** (in abstract senses) the essential structure or essence of a thing (*the fabric of society*). [ME f. F *fabrique* f. L *fabrica* f. *faber* metal-worker etc.]
■ **1** material, cloth; textile. **2** see STRUCTURE *n.* 1b. **3** structure, constitution, construction, make-up, foundation, framework, organization; essence, core, heart.

fabricate /fábrikayt/ *v.tr.* **1** construct or manufacture, esp. from prepared components. **2** invent or concoct (a story, evidence, etc.). **3** forge (a document). □□ **fabricator** *n.* [L *fabricare fabricat-* (as FABRIC)]
■ **1** construct, manufacture, build, erect, frame, raise, put *or* set up, assemble, fashion, form, make, produce. **2** invent, concoct, create, originate, devise, make up, manufacture, hatch, *colloq.* think up, cook up. **3** forge, counterfeit, fake.

fabrication /fábrikáysh'n/ *n.* **1** the action or process of manufacturing or constructing something. **2** the invention of a lie, forging of a document, etc. **3** an invention or falsehood; a forgery. [L *fabricatio* (as FABRICATE)]
■ **1** construction, manufacture, building, constructing, erection, framing, putting together, assembly, assemblage, fashioning, formation, forming, making, production. **2** invention, concoction, creation, origination, making up, manufacture, hatching, contrivance. **3** falsehood, lie, tale, fable, untruth, fiction, cock-and-bull story, fairy story, fairy tale, *colloq.* story; forgery, falsification, fake, sham.

fabulist /fábyoolist/ *n.* **1** a composer of fables. **2** a liar. [F *fabuliste* f. L *fabula*: see FABLE]

fabulous /fábyooləss/ *adj.* **1** incredible, exaggerated, absurd (*fabulous wealth*). **2** *colloq.* marvellous (*looking fabulous*). **3 a** celebrated in fable. **b** legendary, mythical. □□ **fabulosity** /-lóssiti/ *n.* **fabulously** *adv.* **fabulousness** *n.* [F *fabuleux* or L *fabulosus* (as FABLE)]
■ **1** incredible, unbelievable, inconceivable, astounding, astonishing, amazing, fantastic, extraordinary, phenomenal, exaggerated, absurd. **2** marvellous, wonderful, far-out, *colloq.* superb, terrific, great, super, smashing, keen, fab, magic, *sl.* hot, groovy, ace, *esp. US sl.* cool, *US sl.* copacetic, neat. **3** fabled, mythic, mythical, legendary, celebrated, fictitious, fictional, imaginary, fanciful, *literary* storied; story-book, fairy-tale.

façade /fəsaád/ *n.* **1** the face of a building, esp. its principal front. **2** an outward appearance or front, esp. a deceptive one. [F (as FACE)]
■ see FACE *n.* 4e.

face /fayss/ *n.* & *v.* ● *n.* **1** the front of the head from the forehead to the chin. **2 a** the expression of the facial features (*had a happy face*). **b** an expression of disgust; a grimace (*make a face*). **3** composure, coolness, effrontery. **4** the surface of a thing, esp. as regarded or approached, esp.: **a** the visible part of a celestial body. **b** a side of a mountain etc. (*the north face*). **c** the (usu. vertical) surface of a coal-seam. **d** *Geom.* each surface of a solid. **e** the façade of a building. **f** the plate of a clock or watch bearing the digits, hands, etc. **5 a** the functional or working side of a tool etc. **b** the distinctive side of a playing card. **c** the obverse of a coin. **6** = TYPEFACE. **7 a** the outward appearance or aspect (*the unacceptable face of capitalism*). **b** outward show; disguise, pretence (*put on a brave face*). **8** a person, esp. conveying some quality or association (*a face from the past*; *some young faces for a change*). **9** credibility or respect; good reputation; dignity (*lose face*). ● *v.* **1** *tr.* & *intr.* look or be positioned towards or in a certain direction (*face towards the window*; *facing the window*; *the room faces north*). **2** *tr.* be opposite (*facing page 20*). **3** *tr.* **a** (often foll. by *out*) meet resolutely or defiantly; confront (*face one's critics*). **b** not shrink from (*face the facts*). **4** *tr.* present itself to; confront (*the problem that faces us*; *faces us with a problem*). **5** *tr.* **a** cover the surface of (a thing) with a coating, extra layer, etc. **b** put a facing on (a garment). **6** *intr.* & *tr.* turn or cause to turn in a certain direction. □ **face-ache 1** neuralgia. **2** *sl.* a mournful-looking person. **face-card** = *court-card*.

face-cloth 1 a cloth for washing one's face. **2** a smooth-surfaced woollen cloth. **face-cream** a cosmetic cream applied to the face to improve the complexion. **face down** (or **downwards**) with the face or surface turned towards the ground, floor, etc. **face a person down** overcome a person by a show of determination or by browbeating. **face facts** (or **the facts**) recognize the truth. **face-flannel** = *face-cloth* 1. **face-lift 1** (also **face-lifting**) cosmetic surgery to remove wrinkles etc. by tightening the skin of the face. **2** a procedure to improve the appearance of a thing. **face the music** *colloq.* put up with or stand up to unpleasant consequences, esp. criticism. **face-pack** a preparation beneficial to the complexion, spread over the face and removed when dry. **face-powder** a cosmetic powder for reducing the shine on the face. **face-saving** preserving one's reputation, credibility, etc. **face to face** (often foll. by *with*) facing; confronting each other. **face up** (or **upwards**) with the face or surface turned upwards to view. **face up to** accept bravely; confront; stand up to. **face value 1** the nominal value as printed or stamped on money. **2** the superficial appearance or implication of a thing. **face-worker** a miner who works at the coalface. **have the face** be shameless enough. **in one's** (or **the**) **face 1** straight against one; as one approaches. **2** confronting. **in face** (or **the face**) **of 1** despite. **2** confronted by. **let's face it** *colloq.* we must be honest or realistic about it. **on the face of it** as it would appear. **put a bold** (or **brave**) **face on it** accept difficulty etc. cheerfully or with courage. **put one's face on** *colloq.* apply make-up to one's face. **put a good face on** make (a matter) look well. **put a new face on** alter the aspect of. **save face** preserve esteem; avoid humiliation. **save a person's face** enable a person to save face; forbear from humiliating a person. **show one's face** see SHOW. **set one's face against** oppose or resist with determination. **to a person's face** openly in a person's presence. □□ **faced** *adj.* (also in *comb.*). **facing** *adj.* (also in *comb.*). [ME f. OF ult. f. L *facies*]

■ *n.* **1** countenance, physiognomy, *Brit. colloq.* phiz, *literary* visage, *sl.* mug, mush, *Brit. sl.* dial, clock, *US sl.* pan. **2 a** expression, look, appearance, aspect, *literary* mien. **3** effrontery, boldness, daring, audacity, impudence, coolness, impertinence, presumption, brashness, cheek, *colloq.* brass, nerve, guts, gutsiness, *Brit. colloq.* brass neck, *sl.* gall; composure; see also POISE[1] *n.* 1. **4 e** façade, exterior, front, outside; surface, cover, facing. **7** front, guise, appearance, aspect, look, exterior; mask, veneer, façade, camouflage, pretence, disguise, (false) impression, semblance, masquerade, show. **8** see FIGURE *n.* 2b. **9** credibility, respect, self-respect, dignity, standing, status, reputation, name, honour. ● *v.* **1** look out on *or* over *or* towards, give (out) on to, front on *or* to *or* towards *or* upon, overlook. **2** see FRONT *v.* 1, 5a. **3 a** meet (with), encounter, confront, brave, deal *or* cope with, face up to; appear before; experience, come up against, go up against. **b** confront, brave, deal *or* cope with, face up to. **4** see CHALLENGE *v.* 3a. **5 a** cover, coat, overlay; finish, surface, veneer. **b** overlay; finish. **6** see TURN *v.* 3b. □ **face-ache 2** see KILLJOY. **face a person down** confront, intimidate, cow, subdue, overawe, browbeat. **face to face** facing (each other), *vis-à-vis*, tête-à-tête, *à deux*, *colloq.* eyeball to eyeball. **face up to** accept, admit, acknowledge, allow, confess; confront, stand up to, deal *or* cope with, brave, go up against; bite (on) the bullet, grasp the nettle; see also FACE *v.* 3a, b above. **in face** (or **the face**) **of 1** despite, in spite of, notwithstanding. **on the face of it** to all appearances, to outward appearances, seemingly, apparently, as far as can be seen, superficially. **set one's face against** see OPPOSE 1–3. **to a person's face** openly, face to face, directly, brazenly, candidly, frankly.

faceless /fáysliss/ *adj.* **1** without identity; purposely not identifiable. **2** lacking character. **3** without a face. □□ **facelessly** *adv.* **facelessness** *n.*

facer /fáysər/ *n. colloq.* **1** a sudden difficulty or obstacle. **2** a blow in the face.

■ **1** see PROBLEM 1, 2.

facet /fássit/ *n.* **1** a particular aspect of a thing. **2** one side of a many-sided body, esp. of a cut gem. **3** one segment of a compound eye. □□ **faceted** *adj.* (also in *comb.*). [F *facette* dimin. (as FACE, -ETTE)]

■ **1** see ASPECT 1a. **2** see SIDE *n.* 1a.

facetiae /fəseéshi-ee/ *n.pl.* **1** pleasantries, witticisms. **2** (in bookselling) pornography. [L, pl. of *facetia* jest f. *facetus* witty]

facetious /fəseéshəss/ *adj.* **1** characterized by flippant or inopportune humour. **2** (of a person) intending to be amusing, esp. inopportunely. □□ **facetiously** *adv.* **facetiousness** *n.* [F *facétieux* f. *facétie* f. L *facetia* jest]

■ **1** see FLIPPANT.

facia var. of FASCIA.

facial /fáysh'l/ *adj.* & *n.* ● *adj.* of or for the face. ● *n.* a beauty treatment for the face. □□ **facially** *adv.* [med.L *facialis* (as FACE)]

-facient /fáysh'nt/ *comb. form* forming adjectives and nouns indicating an action or state produced (*abortifacient*). [from or after L *-faciens -entis* part. of *facere* make]

facies /fáysheez/ *n.* (*pl.* same) **1** *Med.* the appearance or facial expression of an individual. **2** *Geol.* the character of rock etc. expressed by its composition, fossil content, etc. [L, = FACE]

facile /fássīl/ *adj.* usu. *derog.* **1** easily achieved but of little value. **2** (of speech, writing, etc.) fluent, ready, glib. □□ **facilely** *adv.* **facileness** *n.* [F *facile* or L *facilis* f. *facere* do]

■ **2** see GLIB.

facilitate /fəsíllitayt/ *v.tr.* make easy or less difficult or more easily achieved. □□ **facilitation** /-táysh'n/ *n.* **facilitative** /-tətiv/ *adj.* **facilitator** *n.* [F *faciliter* f. It. *facilitare* f. *facile* easy f. L *facilis*]

■ ease, expedite, smooth, assist, aid, help, further, promote, advance.

facility /fəsílliti/ *n.* (*pl.* **-ies**) **1** ease; absence of difficulty. **2** fluency, dexterity, aptitude (*facility of expression*). **3** (esp. in *pl.*) an opportunity, the equipment, or the resources for doing something. **4** *US* a plant, installation, or establishment. **5** *euphem.* (in *pl.*) a (public) lavatory. [F *facilité* or L *facilitas* (as FACILE)]

■ **1, 2** ease, fluency, effortlessness, skill, skilfulness, deftness, dexterity, adroitness, ability, aptitude, expertise, expertness, proficiency, mastery, masterfulness, masterliness; efficiency, smoothness, quickness, alacrity, swiftness, speed, *archaic or literary* celerity. **3** (*facilities*) opportunity, potential, capacity; see also APPARATUS. **4** plant, installation, establishment, system, buildings, structure, complex. **5** (*facilities*) WC, water-closet, lavatory, toilet, powder-room, men's room, ladies' room, *Brit.* convenience, the ladies, *esp. US* rest room, *US or archaic* privy, *Brit. colloq.* loo, the Gents, *Brit sl.* bog, *US sl.* john.

facing /fáysing/ *n.* **1 a** a layer of material covering part of a garment etc. for contrast or strength. **b** (in *pl.*) the cuffs, collar, etc., of a military jacket. **2** an outer layer covering the surface of a wall etc.

■ **1 a** overlay. **2** façade, surface, front, cladding.

facsimile /faksímmili/ *n.* & *v.* ● *n.* **1** an exact copy, esp. of writing, printing, a picture, etc. (often *attrib.*: *facsimile edition*). **2 a** production of an exact copy of a document etc. by electronic scanning and transmission of the resulting data (see also FAX). **b** a copy produced in this way. ● *v.tr.* (**facsimiled, facsimileing**) make a facsimile of. □ **in facsimile** as an exact copy. [mod.L f. L *fac* imper. of *facere* make + *simile* neut. of *similis* like]

■ *n.* **1** copy, reproduction, carbon copy, duplicate, replica. **2** photocopy, duplicate, fax, *US colloq.* dupe, *propr.* Xerox (copy), Photostat. ● *v.* see DUPLICATE *v.* 2.

fact /fakt/ *n.* **1** a thing that is known to have occurred, to exist, or to be true. **2** a datum of experience (often foll. by an explanatory clause or phrase: *the fact that fire burns; the fact of my having seen them*). **3** (usu. in *pl.*) an item of verified information; a piece of evidence. **4** truth, reality. **5** a thing assumed as the basis for argument or inference. □ **before** (or **after**) **the fact** before (or after) the committing of a crime. **a fact of life** something that must be accepted. **facts and figures** precise details. **fact-sheet** a paper setting out relevant information. **the facts of life** information about sexual functions and practices. **in** (or **in point of**) **fact 1** in reality; as a matter of fact. **2** (in summarizing) in short. [L *factum* f. *facere* do]

■ **1** occurrence, event, happening, incident, experience. **2, 4** truth, reality, actuality, certainty. **3** data, information, particular, detail, point, item, factor, inside information, *colloq.* low-down, info, score, *Brit. sl.* gen, *US sl.* poop. **5** see BASIS. □ **facts and figures** see PARTICULAR *n.* **in** (or **in point of**) **fact 1** in reality, as a matter of fact, actually, really, indeed, to be sure, truly, truthfully, factually, *literary* in truth. **2** see *in short* (SHORT).

factice /fáktiss/ *n. Chem.* a rubber-like substance obtained by vulcanizing unsaturated vegetable oils. [G *Faktis* f. L *facticius* FACTITIOUS]

faction[1] /fáksh'n/ *n.* **1** a small organized dissentient group within a larger one, esp. in politics. **2** a state of dissension within an organization. [F f. L *factio -onis* f. *facere fact-* do, make]

■ **1** group, cabal, cadre, camp, splinter group, circle, camarilla, clique, set, coterie, lobby, pressure group, junta, ring, *Brit.* ginger group. **2** dissension, disharmony, discord, disagreement, quarrelling, infighting, contention, controversy, sedition, intrigue, strife, schism.

faction[2] /fáksh'n/ *n.* a book, film, etc., using real events as a basis for a fictional narrative or dramatization. [blend of FACT and FICTION]

-faction /fáksh'n/ *comb. form* forming nouns of action from verbs in *-fy* (*petrifaction; satisfaction*). [from or after L *-factio -factionis* f. *-facere* do, make]

factional /fákshən'l/ *adj.* **1** of or characterized by faction. **2** belonging to a faction. □□ **factionalism** *n.* **factionalize** *v.tr.* & *intr.* (also **-ise**). **factionally** *adv.* [FACTION[1]]

■ see SECTARIAN *adj.* 1.

factious /fákshəss/ *adj.* of, characterized by, or inclined to faction. □□ **factiously** *adv.* **factiousness** *n.*

■ divisive, conflicting, discordant, contentious, disputatious, argumentative, quarrelsome, seditious, mutinous, refractory, rebellious; at odds, at loggerheads.

factitious /faktíshəss/ *adj.* **1** specially contrived, not genuine (*factitious value*). **2** artificial, not natural (*factitious joy*). □□ **factitiously** *adv.* **factitiousness** *n.* [L *facticius* f. *facere fact-* do, make]

■ contrived, manufactured, fabricated, engineered, unauthentic; artificial, insincere, unreal, fake, false, bogus, falsified, spurious, sham, simulated, imitation, counterfeit, synthetic, *colloq.* phoney; mock.

factitive /fáktitiv/ *adj. Gram.* (of a verb) having a sense of regarding or designating, and taking a complement as well as an object (e.g. *appointed me captain*). [mod.L *factitivus*, irreg. f. L *factitare* frequent. of *facere fact-* do, make]

factoid /fáktoyd/ *n.* & *adj.* ● *n.* an assumption or speculation that is reported and repeated so often that it becomes accepted as fact; a simulated or imagined fact. ● *adj.* being or having the character of a factoid; containing factoids.

factor /fáktər/ *n.* & *v.* ● *n.* **1** a circumstance, fact, or influence contributing to a result. **2** *Math.* a whole number etc. that when multiplied with another produces a given number or expression. **3** *Biol.* a gene etc. determining hereditary character. **4** (foll. by identifying number) *Med.* any of several substances in the blood contributing to coagulation (*factor eight*). **5 a** a business agent; a merchant buying and selling on commission. **b** *Sc.* a land-agent or steward. **c** an agent or a deputy. **6** an agent or company that buys a manufacturer's invoices and takes responsibility for collecting the payments due on them; a backer. ● *v.tr.* **1** *Math.* resolve into factors or components. **2** *tr.* sell (one's receivable debts) to a factor. □ **factor analysis** *Statistics* a process by which the relative importance of variables in the study of a sample is assessed by mathematical techniques. □□ **factorable** *adj.* [F *facteur* or L *factor* f. *facere fact-* do, make]

■ *n.* **1** circumstance, fact, ingredient, element, consideration, particular, aspect, influence, determinant, cause. **5 a** agent, representative, middleman, intermediary, deputy, go-between. **6** banker, financier, backer, moneylender, lender.

factorage /fáktərij/ *n.* commission or charges payable to a factor.

factorial /faktóriəl/ *n.* & *adj. Math.* ● *n.* **1** the product of a number and all the whole numbers below it (*factorial four = 4 x 3 x 2 x 1*). ¶ Symb.: ! (as in 4!). **2** the product of a series of factors in an arithmetical progression. ● *adj.* of a factor or factorial. □□ **factorially** *adv.*

factorize /fáktərīz/ *v.* (also **-ise**) *Math.* **1** *tr.* resolve into factors. **2** *intr.* be capable of resolution into factors. □□ **factorization** /-záysh'n/ *n.*

factory /fáktəri, -tri/ *n.* (*pl.* **-ies**) **1** a building or buildings containing plant or equipment for manufacturing machinery or goods. **2** *hist.* a merchant company's foreign trading station. □ **factory farm** a farm employing factory farming. **factory farming** a system of rearing livestock using industrial or intensive methods. **factory floor** workers in industry as distinct from management. **factory ship** *Brit.* a fishing ship with facilities for immediate processing of the catch. [Port. *feitoria* and LL *factorium*]

■ **1** plant, mill, works, workshop. □ **factory floor** see LABOUR *n.* 2a.

factotum /faktṓtəm/ *n.* (*pl.* **factotums**) an employee who does all kinds of work. [med.L f. L *fac* imper. of *facere* do, make + *totum* neut. of *totus* whole]

■ see SERVANT.

factual /fáktyooəl/ *adj.* **1** based on or concerned with fact or facts. **2** actual, true. □□ **factuality** /-tyoo-álliti/ *n.* **factually** *adv.* **factualness** *n.* [FACT, after *actual*]

■ real, true, actual, authentic, verifiable, genuine, realistic, true to life; faithful, bona fide, accurate, precise; objective, unbiased, unprejudiced, undistorted, unvarnished, straightforward.

factum /fáktəm/ *n.* (*pl.* **factums** or **facta** /-tə/) *Law* **1** an act or deed. **2** a statement of the facts. [F f. L: see FACT]

facture /fákchər/ *n.* the quality of execution esp. of the surface of a painting. [ME f. OF f. L *factura* f. *facere fact-* do, make]

facula /fákyoolə/ *n.* (*pl.* **faculae** /-lee/) *Astron.* a bright spot or streak on the sun. □□ **facular** *adj.* **faculous** *adj.* [L, dimin. of *fax facis* torch]

facultative /fákkəltətiv/ *adj.* **1** *Law* enabling an act to take place. **2** that may occur. **3** *Biol.* not restricted to a particular function, mode of life, etc. **4** of a faculty. □□ **facultatively** *adv.* [F *facultatif -ive* (as FACULTY)]

faculty /fákkəlti/ *n.* (*pl.* **-ies**) **1** an aptitude or ability for a particular activity. **2** an inherent mental or physical power. **3 a** a department of a university etc. teaching a specific branch of learning (*faculty of modern languages*). **b** *US* the staff of a university or college. **c** a branch of art or science; those qualified to teach it. **4** the members of a particular profession, esp. medicine. **5** authorization, esp. by a Church authority. □ **Faculty of Advocates** *Law* the society constituting the Scottish Bar. [ME f. OF *faculté* f. L *facultas -tatis* f. *facilis* easy]

■ **1, 2** aptitude, ability, capacity, capability, skill, talent, flair, knack, gift, genius, cleverness; potential. **3 a** division, department, school. **b, c** staff, personnel, members; dons; see also BRANCH *n.* 2, 3. **4** membership; associates, fellows, members. **5** authorization, power, sanction, licence, prerogative, privilege, right, permission, liberty.

FAD *abbr.* flavin adenine dinucleotide.

fad /fad/ *n.* **1** a craze. **2** a peculiar notion or idiosyncrasy. □□ **faddish** *adj.* **faddishly** *adv.* **faddishness** *n.* **faddism** *n.* **faddist** *n.* [19th c. (orig. dial.): prob. f. *fidfad* f. FIDDLE-FADDLE]
■ **1** craze, mania, rage, fashion, trend, vogue. **2** see *eccentricity* (ECCENTRIC).

faddy /fáddi/ *adj.* (**faddier**, **faddiest**) having arbitrary likes and dislikes, esp. about food. □□ **faddily** *adv.* **faddiness** *n.*

fade /fayd/ *v.* & *n.* ● *v.* **1** *intr.* & *tr.* lose or cause to lose colour. **2** *intr.* lose freshness or strength; (of flowers etc.) droop, wither. **3** *intr.* **a** (of colour, light, etc.) disappear gradually; grow pale or dim. **b** (of sound) grow faint. **4** *intr.* (of a feeling etc.) diminish. **5** *intr.* (foll. by *away*, *out*) (of a person etc.) disappear or depart gradually. **6** *tr.* (foll. by *in*, *out*) *Cinematog.* & *Broadcasting* **a** cause (a picture) to come gradually in or out of view on a screen, or to merge into another shot. **b** make (the sound) more or less audible. **7** *intr.* (of a radio signal) vary irregularly in intensity. **8** *intr.* (of a brake) temporarily lose effectiveness. **9** *Golf* **a** *intr.* (of a ball) deviate from a straight course, esp. in a deliberate slice. **b** *tr.* cause (a ball) to fade. ● *n.* the action or an instance of fading. □ **do a fade** *sl.* depart. **fade away** *colloq.* languish, grow thin. **fade-in** *Cinematog.* & *Broadcasting* the action or an instance of fading in a picture or sound. **fade-out 1** *colloq.* disappearance, death. **2** *Cinematog.* & *Broadcasting* the action or an instance of fading out a picture or sound. □□ **fadeless** *adj.* **fader** *n.* (in sense 6 of *v.*). [ME f. OF *fader* f. *fade* dull, insipid prob. ult. f. L *fatuus* silly + *vapidus* VAPID]
■ *v.* **1, 3a** (grow) dim *or* pale, cloud (over); grow faint, blanch; discolour. **2, 3b** ebb, flag, fade away, wane, waste away, diminish, dwindle; decline, languish, deteriorate; die out *or* away, peter out *or* away; droop, wilt, wither, shrivel, perish. **4** see DIMINISH 1. **6 a** see MERGE. **9** see TURN *v.* 3b. ● *n.* see DECREASE *n.* □ **do a fade** see LEAVE[1] *v.* 1b, 3, 4. **fade away** see FLAG[1] *v.* 1a, WASTE *v.* 4. **fade-out 1** see PASSING *n.*

fadge /faj/ *n. Austral.* & *NZ* **1** a limp package of wool. **2** a loosely packed wool bale. [16th-c. Engl. dial.: orig. uncert.]

faeces /féesseez/ *n.pl.* (*US* **feces**) waste matter discharged from the bowels. □□ **faecal** /féek'l/ *adj.* [L, pl. of *faex* dregs]
■ see DUNG *n.*

faerie /fáiri/ *n.* (also **faery**) *archaic* **1** Fairyland; the fairies esp. as represented by Spenser (*the Faerie Queene*). **2** (*attrib.*) visionary, fancied. [var. of FAIRY]

Faeroese /fáirō-éez/ *adj.* & *n.* (also **Faroese**) ● *adj.* of or relating to the Faeroes, an island group in the N. Atlantic between Norway and Iceland. ● *n.* (*pl.* same) **1** a native of the Faeroes; a person of Faeroese descent. **2** the Norse language of this people.

faff /faf/ *v.* & *n. Brit. colloq.* ● *v.intr.* (often foll. by *about*, *around*) fuss, dither. ● *n.* a fuss. [imit.]

fag[1] /fag/ *n.* & *v.* ● *n.* **1** esp. *Brit. colloq.* a piece of drudgery; a wearisome or unwelcome task. **2** *sl.* a cigarette. **3** *Brit.* (at public schools) a junior pupil who runs errands for a senior. ● *v.* (**fagged**, **fagging**) **1** *colloq.* **a** *tr.* (often foll. by *out*) tire out; exhaust. **b** *intr.* toil. **2** *intr. Brit.* (in public schools) act as a fag. **3** *tr. Naut.* (often foll. by *out*) fray (the end of a rope etc.). □ **fag-end** *sl.* **1** *Brit.* a cigarette-end. **2** an inferior or useless remnant. [orig. unkn.: cf. FLAG[1]]
■ *n.* **1** chore, bore, nuisance, pain, *colloq.* drag. **2** see CIGARETTE 1. **3** servant, menial, drudge, *usu. derog.* underling. ● *v.* **1 a** tire (out), exhaust, wear out, weary, fatigue, *US colloq.* poop, *Brit. sl.* knacker. **b** see LABOUR *v.* 1, 2. □ **fag-end 1** see STUB *n.* 1, 4. **2** see REMNANT 2.

fag[2] /fag/ *n. US sl.* often *offens.* a male homosexual. [abbr. of FAGGOT]

faggot /fággət/ *n.* & *v.* (*US* **fagot**) ● *n.* **1** (usu. in *pl.*) a ball or roll of seasoned chopped liver etc., baked or fried. **2** a bundle of sticks or twigs bound together as fuel. **3** a bundle of iron rods for heat treatment. **4** a bunch of herbs. **5** *sl. derog.* **a** an unpleasant woman. **b** *US* often *offens.* a male homosexual. ● *v.tr.* (**faggoted**, **faggoting**) **1** bind in or make into faggots. **2** join by faggoting (see FAGGOTING). □□ **faggoty** *adj.* [ME f. OF *fagot*, of uncert. orig.]

faggoting /fággəting/ *n.* **1** embroidery in which threads are fastened together like a faggot. **2** the joining of materials in a similar manner.

fagot *US* var. of FAGGOT.

fah /faa/ *n.* (also **fa**) *Mus.* **1** (in tonic sol-fa) the fourth note of a major scale. **2** the note F in the fixed-doh system. [ME *fa* f. L *famuli*: see GAMUT]

Fahr. *abbr.* Fahrenheit.

Fahrenheit /fárrənhīt/ *adj.* of or measured on a scale of temperature on which water freezes at 32° and boils at 212° under standard conditions. [G. *Fahrenheit*, Ger. physicist d. 1736]

faience /fíonss/ *n.* decorated and glazed earthenware and porcelain, e.g. delft or majolica. [F *faïence* f. *Faenza* in Italy]

fail /fayl/ *v.* & *n.* ● *v.* **1** *intr.* not succeed (*failed in persuading*; *failed to qualify*; *tried but failed*). **2 a** *tr.* & *intr.* be unsuccessful in (an examination, test, interview, etc.); be rejected as a candidate. **b** *tr.* (of a commodity etc.) not pass (a test of quality). **c** *tr.* reject (a candidate etc.); adjudge unsuccessful. **3** *intr.* be unable to; neglect to; choose not to (*I fail to see the reason*; *he failed to appear*). **4** *tr.* disappoint; let down; not serve when needed. **5** *intr.* (of supplies, crops, etc.) be or become lacking or insufficient. **6** *intr.* become weaker; cease functioning; break down (*her health is failing*; *the engine has failed*). **7** *intr.* **a** (of an enterprise) collapse; come to nothing. **b** become bankrupt. ● *n.* a failure in an examination or test. □ **fail-safe** reverting to a safe condition in the event of a breakdown etc. **without fail** for certain, whatever happens. [ME f. OF *faillir* (v.), *fail(l)e* (n.) ult. f. L *fallere* deceive]
■ *v.* **1, 2a** be unsuccessful (in); not succeed; come to grief; fall through, come to naught *or* nothing, founder, run aground, miscarry, abort, go wrong, misfire, meet with disaster, *colloq.* go up in smoke, *sl.* flop; *US colloq.* flunk, go belly up; fall short, be (found) lacking *or* wanting, be deficient, be *or* prove inadequate. **2 c** see REJECT *v.* 1. **4** disappoint, let down, dissatisfy. **5** see *run out* 1. **6** weaken, decline, wane, diminish, deteriorate, dwindle, flag, ebb, sink, languish, disappear, fade *or* die (away); give out, peter out, stop, *colloq.* pack up. **7 a** see COLLAPSE *v.* **b** go bankrupt, crash, go out of business, go under, go into receivership, become insolvent, close up, close down, cease operation(s), *Brit.* go to the wall, *colloq.* fold (up), go broke, go bust. □ **without fail** see *for a certainty* (CERTAINTY).

failed /fayld/ *adj.* **1** unsuccessful; not good enough (*a failed actor*). **2** weak, deficient; broken down (*a failed crop*; *a failed battery*).
■ **1** see UNSUCCESSFUL.

failing /fáyling/ *n.* & *prep.* ● *n.* a fault or shortcoming; a weakness, esp. in character. ● *prep.* in default of; if not.
■ *n.* fault, shortcoming, weakness, flaw, defect, foible, weak point *or* spot, blind spot, imperfection. ● *prep.* in default of, in the absence of, without, *archaic or joc.* sans.

failure /fáylyər/ *n.* **1** lack of success; failing. **2** an unsuccessful person, thing, or attempt. **3** non-performance, non-occurrence. **4** breaking down or ceasing to function (*heart failure*; *engine failure*). **5** running short of supply etc. **6** bankruptcy, collapse. [earlier *failer* f. AF, = OF *faillir* FAIL]
■ **1** see IMPERFECTION 2. **2** incompetent, *colloq.* lemon; also-ran, loser, nonentity, *colloq.* non-starter, *sl.* flop, dud, dead duck; damp squib, washout, lead balloon, *Austral. colloq.* gutzer, *Austral. sl.* fizzer, shicer. **3** non-performance, neglect, dereliction; default, remissness, failing, deficiency; non-occurrence. **4** breakdown, collapse, decline, failing, decay, deterioration, loss. **5** see SLACK[1] *n.* 2. **6** bankruptcy, collapse, ruin, insolvency, crash, *colloq.* folding.

fain /fayn/ *adj.* & *adv. archaic* ● *predic.adj.* (foll. by *to* + infin.) **1** willing under the circumstances to. **2** left with no alternative but to. ● *adv.* gladly (esp. *would fain*). [OE *fægen* f. Gmc]

fainéant /fáynayon/ *n.* & *adj.* ● *n.* an idle or ineffective person. ● *adj.* idle, inactive. □□ **fainéancy** *n.* [F f. *fait* does + *néant* nothing]

faint /faynt/ *adj.*, *v.*, & *n.* ● *adj.* **1** indistinct, pale, dim; quiet; not clearly perceived. **2** (of a person) weak or giddy; inclined to faint. **3** slight, remote, inadequate (*a faint chance*). **4** feeble, half-hearted (*faint praise*). **5** timid (*a faint heart*). **6** (also **feint**) (of ruled paper) with inconspicuous lines to guide writing. ● *v.intr.* **1** lose consciousness. **2** become faint. ● *n.* a sudden loss of consciousness; fainting. □ **faint-hearted** cowardly, timid. **faint-heartedly** in a faint-hearted manner. **faint-heartedness** cowardliness, timidity. **not have the faintest** *colloq.* have no idea. □□ **faintness** *n.* [ME f. OF, past part. of *faindre* FEIGN]

■ *adj.* **1** indistinct, pale, dim, feeble, weak, subdued, flickering, blurred, ill-defined, blurry, dull, vague, muzzy, hazy; faded; imperceptible, indiscernible, unclear; low, soft, quiet, slight, hushed, muffled, muted, stifled, inaudible. **2** weak, giddy, dizzy, light-headed, unsteady, *colloq.* woozy. **3** see REMOTE 4, INADEQUATE 1. **4** see FEEBLE 2. **5** see TIMID. ● *v.* **1** lose consciousness, pass out, black out, collapse, keel over, *literary* swoon. **2** see SUBSIDE 1. ● *n.* loss of consciousness, blackout, collapse, *Med.* syncope, *literary* swoon. □ **faint-hearted** cowardly, weak, feeble, timorous, afraid, frightened, scared, faint, lily-livered, chicken, chicken-hearted, chicken-livered, *colloq.* yellow, yellow-bellied; timid, pusillanimous, shy, diffident. **not have the faintest** have no idea, *colloq.* not have a clue; (*I haven't the faintest*) see *ask me another*.

faintly /fáyntli/ *adv.* **1** very slightly (*faintly amused*). **2** indistinctly, feebly.

fair[1] /fair/ *adj.*, *adv.*, *n.*, & *v.* ● *adj.* **1** just, unbiased, equitable; in accordance with the rules. **2** blond; light or pale in colour or complexion. **3 a** of (only) moderate quality or amount; average. **b** considerable, satisfactory (*a fair chance of success*). **4** (of weather) fine and dry; (of the wind) favourable. **5** clean, clear, unblemished (*fair copy*). **6** beautiful, attractive. **7** *archaic* kind, gentle. **8 a** specious (*fair speeches*). **b** complimentary (*fair words*). **9** *Austral.* & *NZ* complete, unquestionable. **10** unobstructed, open. ● *adv.* **1** in a fair manner (*play fair*). **2** exactly, completely (*was hit fair on the jaw*). ● *n.* **1** a fair thing. **2** *archaic* a beautiful woman. ● *v.* **1** *tr.* make (the surface of a ship, aircraft, etc.) smooth and streamlined. **2** *intr. dial.* (of the weather) become fair. □ **fair and square** *adv.* & *adj.* **1** exactly. **2** straightforward, honest, above-board. **fair crack of the whip** see CRACK. **a fair deal** equitable treatment. **fair dos** /dooz/ *colloq.* fair shares. **fair enough** *colloq.* that is reasonable or acceptable. **fair game** a thing or person one may legitimately pursue, exploit, etc. **fair-minded** just, impartial. **fair-mindedly** justly, impartially. **fair-mindedness** a sense of justice; impartiality. **fair name** a good reputation. **fair play** reasonable treatment or behaviour. **fair rent** the amount of rent which a tenant may reasonably be expected to pay according to established guidelines. **the fair sex** women. **fair's fair** *colloq.* all involved should act fairly. **fair-spoken** courteous. **a fair treat** *colloq.* a very enjoyable or attractive thing or person. **fair-weather friend** a friend or ally who is unreliable in times of difficulty. **for fair** *US sl.* completely. **in a fair way to** likely to. □□ **fairish** *adj.* **fairness** *n.* [OE *fæger* f. Gmc]

■ *adj.* **1** just, equitable, unbiased, impartial, fair-minded, unprejudiced, objective, disinterested, even-handed; square, fair and square, honest, straightforward, above-board, upright, proper, honourable, lawful, legitimate, trustworthy. **2** blond(e), fair-haired, flaxen-haired, tow-headed, tow-coloured; light, pale, light-complexioned, peaches and cream. **3 a** see MEDIOCRE 1. **b** considerable, satisfactory, adequate, respectable, pretty good, tolerable, passable, average, decent, reasonable, middling, mediocre, indifferent, *colloq.* OK; so so, *comme ci, comme ça*, all right, not bad. **4** fine, dry, sunny, bright, clear, cloudless, pleasant, halcyon; favourable, benign. **5** clean, clear, unblemished, spotless, immaculate. **6** beautiful, attractive, pretty, lovely, comely, good-looking, handsome, *literary* pulchritudinous, *poet.* beauteous. **7** see GENTLE *adj.* 1. **8 a** see SPECIOUS. **b** civil, courteous, polite, gracious, complimentary, agreeable. **10** unobstructed, open, clear, free. ● *adv.* **1** see FAIRLY 1. **2** see *completely* (COMPLETE). □ **fair and square** (*adv. & adj.*) **1** see EXACTLY 4. **2** see HONEST 3. **fair-minded** see IMPARTIAL. **fair-mindedly** see FAIRLY 1. **fair-mindedness** see *objectivity* (OBJECTIVE). **fair play** see JUSTICE 1–3. **the fair sex** see WOMAN 2. **fair-spoken** see COURTEOUS. **for fair** see *completely* (COMPLETE).

fair[2] /fair/ *n.* **1** a gathering of stalls, amusements, etc., for public (usu. outdoor) entertainment. **2** a periodical gathering for the sale of goods, often with entertainments. **3** an exhibition, esp. to promote particular products. [ME f. OF *feire* f. LL *feria* sing. f. L *feriae* holiday]

■ **1** fête, festival, *Austral.* Mardi Gras, *US* carnival. **2** market, fête, bazaar, mart, kermis. **3** exhibition, exposition, show, exhibit.

fairground /fáirgrownd/ *n.* an outdoor area where a fair is held.

fairing[1] /fáiring/ *n.* **1** a streamlining structure added to a ship, aircraft, vehicle, etc. **2** the process of streamlining. [FAIR[1] *v.* 1 + -ING[1]]

fairing[2] /fáiring/ *n. Brit. archaic* a present bought at a fair.

Fair Isle /fáirīl/ *n.* (also *attrib.*) a piece of knitwear knitted in a characteristic particoloured design. [*Fair Isle* in the Shetlands, where the design was first devised]

fairlead /fáirleed/ *n. Naut.* a device to guide rope etc., e.g. to prevent cutting or chafing.

fairly /fáirli/ *adv.* **1** in a fair manner; justly. **2** moderately, acceptably (*fairly good*). **3** to a noticeable degree (*fairly narrow*). **4** utterly, completely (*fairly beside himself*). **5** actually (*fairly jumped for joy*). □ **fairly and squarely** = *fair and square* (see FAIR[1]).

■ **1** justly, equitably, properly, honestly, impartially, objectively; fair. **2** moderately, acceptably, tolerably, passably, quite, rather, sufficiently, adequately, *colloq.* pretty. **3** see SOMEWHAT *adv.* **4** utterly, completely, absolutely, totally, positively. **5** actually, veritably, really, positively.

fairwater /fáirwawtər/ *n.* a structure on a ship etc. assisting its passage through water.

fairway /fáirway/ *n.* **1** a navigable channel; a regular course or track of a ship. **2** the part of a golf-course between a tee and its green, kept free of rough grass.

fairy /fáiri/ *n.* & *adj.* ● *n.* (*pl.* **-ies**) **1** a small imaginary being with magical powers. **2** *sl. derog.* a male homosexual. ● *adj.* of fairies, fairy-like, delicate, small. □ **fairy cake** a small individual iced sponge cake. **fairy cycle** a small bicycle for a child. **fairy godmother** a benefactress. **fairy lights** small coloured lights esp. for outdoor decoration. **fairy ring** a ring of darker grass caused by fungi. **fairy story** (or **tale**) **1** a tale about fairies. **2** an incredible story; a fabrication. □□ **fairy-like** *adj.* [ME f. OF *faerie* f. *fae* FAY]

■ *n.* **1** see IMP *n.* 2.

fairyland /fáiriland/ *n.* **1** the imaginary home of fairies. **2** an enchanted region.

■ dreamland, wonderland, never-never land, paradise, cloud-land, cloud-cuckoo-land, Shangri-La.

fait accompli /fáyt əkómplee, əkónplee/ *n.* a thing that has been done and is past arguing against or altering. [F]

■ see *all over bar the shouting* (SHOUT).

faith /fayth/ *n.* **1** complete trust or confidence. **2** firm belief, esp. without logical proof. **3 a** a system of religious belief (*the Christian faith*). **b** belief in religious doctrines. **c** spiritual apprehension of divine truth apart from proof. **d** things believed or to be believed. **4** duty or commitment to fulfil a trust, promise, etc.; obligation, allegiance (*keep faith*). **5** (*attrib.*) concerned with a supposed ability to cure by faith rather than treatment (*faith-healing*). □ **bad faith** intent to deceive. **good faith** honesty or sincerity of intention. [ME f. AF *fed* f. OF *feid* f. L *fides*]

■ **1, 2** belief, trust, confidence; certainty, conviction, certitude. **3 a** religion, creed, persuasion; teaching, doctrine, dogma; denomination, sect. **b, c** see BELIEF. **4** duty, commitment, obligation, promise; allegiance, faithfulness, loyalty, fidelity, devotion, consecration, dedication, fealty, obedience. □ **bad faith** see CANT[1] *n.* 1. **good faith** see *sincerity* (SINCERE).

faithful /fáythfŏŏl/ *adj.* **1** showing faith. **2** (often foll. by *to*) loyal, trustworthy, constant. **3** accurate; true to fact (*a faithful account*). **4** thorough in performing one's duty; conscientious. **5** (**the Faithful**) the believers in a religion, esp. Muslims and Christians. □□ **faithfulness** *n.*

■ **2** loyal, true, constant, devoted, dedicated; steadfast; staunch, *archaic* trusty; trustworthy, reliable, dependable; trusted. **3** accurate, close, exact, precise, perfect; literal; true, valid. **4** conscientious, dutiful, scrupulous, careful, meticulous, thorough, punctilious, finicky, finical, fastidious, rigorous, rigid, severe, particular.

faithfully /fáythfŏŏli/ *adv.* in a faithful manner. □ **yours faithfully** a formula for ending a business or formal letter.

■ see *consistently* (CONSISTENT), EXACTLY 1.

faithless /fáythliss/ *adj.* **1** false, unreliable, disloyal. **2** without religious faith. □□ **faithlessly** *adv.* **faithlessness** *n.*

■ **1** false, insincere, hypocritical, untrustworthy, crooked, unscrupulous, *colloq.* shifty; unreliable; disloyal, unfaithful, inconstant, fickle, treacherous, traitorous, perfidious. **2** sceptical, doubting, unbelieving, disbelieving, agnostic, atheistic, atheistical, freethinking.

fake[1] /fayk/ *n., adj., & v.* ● *n.* **1** a thing or person that is not genuine. **2** a trick. ● *adj.* counterfeit; not genuine. ● *v.tr.* **1** make (a false thing) appear genuine; forge, counterfeit. **2** make a pretence of having (a feeling, illness, etc.). □□ **faker** *n.* **fakery** *n.* [obs. *feak*, *feague* thrash f. G *fegen* sweep, thrash]

■ *n.* **1** forgery, imitation, counterfeit; sham; faker, impostor, charlatan, fraud, mountebank, cheat, humbug, quack, pretender, *colloq.* phoney. **2** see HOAX *n.* ● *adj.* counterfeit, forged, fraudulent; imitation, pinchbeck; false, bogus; sham, spurious, factitious, *colloq.* phoney. ● *v.* **1** forge, counterfeit, fabricate, manufacture; doctor, tamper with, falsify, alter. **2** pretend, feign, make a pretence of, dissemble, sham, simulate, affect.

fake[2] /fayk/ *n.* & *v. Naut.* ● *n.* one round of a coil of rope. ● *v.tr.* coil (rope). [ME: cf. Scottish *faik* fold]

fakir /fáykeer, fəkéer/ *n.* (also **faquir**) a Muslim or (rarely) Hindu religious mendicant or ascetic. [Arab. *fakīr* needy man]

falafel var. of FELAFEL.

Falange /falánj/ *n.* the Fascist movement in Spain, founded in 1933. □□ **Falangism** *n.* **Falangist** *n.* [Sp., = PHALANX]

falcate /fálkayt/ *adj. Anat.* curved like a sickle. [L *falcatus* f. *falx falcis* sickle]

falchion /fáwlchən/ *n. hist.* a broad curved sword with a convex edge. [ME *fauchoun* f. OF *fauchon* ult. f. L *falx falcis* sickle]

falciform /fálsiform/ *adj. Anat.* curved like a sickle. [L *falx falcis* sickle]

falcon /fáwlkən, fól-/ *n.* **1** any diurnal bird of prey of the family Falconidae, having long pointed wings, and sometimes trained to hunt small game for sport. **2** (in falconry) a female falcon (cf. TERCEL). [ME f. OF *faucon* f. LL *falco -onis*, perh. f. L *falx* scythe or f. Gmc]

falconer /fáwlkənər, fól-/ *n.* **1** a keeper and trainer of hawks. **2** a person who hunts with hawks. [ME f. AF *fauconer*, OF *fauconier* (as FALCON)]

falconet /fáwlkənit, fól-/ *n.* **1** *hist.* a light cannon. **2** *Zool.* a small falcon. [sense 1 f. It. *falconetto* dimin. of *falcone* FALCON: sense 2 f. FALCON + -ET[1]]

falconry /fáwlkənri, fól-/ *n.* the breeding and training of hawks; the sport of hawking. [F *fauconnerie* (as FALCON)]

falderal /fáldəral/ *n.* (also **folderol** /fóldərol/) **1** a gewgaw or trifle. **2** a nonsensical refrain in a song. [perh. f. *falbala* trimming on a dress]

faldstool /fáwldstōōl/ *n.* **1** a bishop's backless folding chair. **2** *Brit.* a small movable desk for kneeling at prayer. [OE *fældestōl* f. med.L *faldistolium* f. WG (as FOLD[1], STOOL)]

fall /fawl/ *v.* & *n.* ● *v.intr.* (*past* **fell** /fel/; *past part.* **fallen** /fáwlən/) **1 a** go or come down freely; descend rapidly from a higher to a lower level (*fell from the top floor*; *rain was falling*). **b** drop or be dropped (*supplies fell by parachute*; *the curtain fell*). **2 a** (often foll. by *over* or *down*) cease to stand; come suddenly to the ground from loss of balance etc. **b** collapse forwards or downwards esp. of one's own volition (*fell into my arms*). **3** become detached and descend or disappear. **4** take a downward direction: **a** (of hair, clothing, etc.) hang down. **b** (of ground etc.) slope. **c** (foll. by *into*) (of a river etc.) discharge into. **5 a** find a lower level; sink lower. **b** subside, abate. **6** (of a barometer, thermometer, etc.) show a lower reading. **7** occur; become apparent or present (*darkness fell*). **8** decline, diminish (*demand is falling*; *standards have fallen*). **9 a** (of the face) show dismay or disappointment. **b** (of the eyes or a glance) look downwards. **10 a** lose power or status (*the government will fall*). **b** lose esteem, moral integrity, etc. **11** commit sin; yield to temptation. **12** take or have a particular direction or place (*his eye fell on me*; *the accent falls on the first syllable*). **13 a** find a place; be naturally divisible (*the subject falls into three parts*). **b** (foll. by *under*, *within*) be classed among. **14** occur at a specified time (*Easter falls early this year*). **15** come by chance or duty (*it fell to me to answer*). **16 a** pass into a specified condition (*fall into decay*; *fell ill*). **b** become (*fall asleep*). **17 a** (of a position etc.) be overthrown or captured; succumb to attack. **b** be defeated; fail. **18** die (*fall in battle*). **19** (foll. by *on*, *upon*) **a** attack. **b** meet with. **c** embrace or embark on avidly. **20** (foll. by *to* + verbal noun) begin (*fell to wondering*). **21** (foll. by *to*) lapse, revert (*revenues fall to the Crown*). ● *n.* **1** the act or an instance of falling; a sudden rapid descent. **2** that which falls or has fallen, e.g. snow, rocks, etc. **3** the recorded amount of rainfall etc. **4** a decline or diminution; depreciation in price, value, demand, etc. **5** overthrow, downfall (*the fall of Rome*). **6 a** succumbing to temptation. **b** (**the Fall**) the sin of Adam and its consequences, as described in Genesis. **7** (of material, land, light, etc.) a downward direction; a slope. **8** (also **Fall**) *US* autumn. **9** (esp. in *pl.*) a waterfall, cataract, or cascade. **10** *Mus.* a cadence. **11 a** a wrestling-bout; a throw in wrestling which keeps the opponent on the ground for a specified time. **b** a controlled act of falling, esp. as a stunt or in judo etc. **12 a** the birth of young of certain animals. **b** the number of young born. **13** a rope of a hoisting-tackle. □ **fall about** *colloq.* be helpless, esp. with laughter. **fall apart** (or **to pieces**) **1** break into pieces. **2** (of a situation etc.) disintegrate; be reduced to chaos. **3** lose one's capacity to cope. **fall away 1** (of a surface) incline abruptly. **2** become few or thin; gradually vanish. **3** desert, revolt; abandon one's principles. **fall back** retreat. **fall-back** (*attrib.*) emergency, esp. (of wages) the minimum paid when no work is available. **fall back on** have recourse to in difficulty. **fall behind 1** be outstripped by one's competitors etc.; lag. **2** be in arrears. **fall down** (often foll. by *on*) *colloq.* fail; perform poorly; fail to deliver (payment etc.). **fall flat** fail to achieve expected success or evoke a desired response. **fall for** *colloq.* **1** be captivated or deceived by. **2** yield to the charms or merits of. **fall foul of** come into conflict with; quarrel with. **fall guy** *sl.* **1** an easy victim. **2** a scapegoat. **fall in 1 a** take one's place in military formation. **b** (as *int.*) the order to do this. **2** collapse inwards. **falling star** a meteor. **fall in love** see LOVE. **fall into line 1** take one's place in the ranks. **2** conform or collaborate with others. **fall into place** begin to make sense or cohere. **fall in with 1** meet or become involved with by chance. **2** agree with; accede to; humour. **3** coincide with. **fall off 1** (of demand etc.) decrease, deteriorate. **2** withdraw. **fall-off** *n.* a decrease, deterioration, withdrawal, etc. **fall out 1** quarrel. **2** (of the hair, teeth, etc.) become detached. **3** *Mil.* come out of formation. **4** result; come to pass; occur. **fall out of** gradually discontinue (a habit etc.). **fall over oneself** *colloq.* **1** be eager or competitive. **2** be awkward, stumble through haste, confusion, etc. **fall-pipe** a downpipe. **fall short 1** be or become deficient or inadequate. **2** (of a missile etc.) not reach its target. **fall short of** fail to reach or obtain. **fall through** fail; come to nothing; miscarry. **fall to** begin an activity, e.g. eating or working. [OE *fallan*, *feallan* f. Gmc]

■ *v.* **1 a** descend, plummet, plunge, dive, nosedive; come down, cascade. **b** drop (down), come down. **2 a** tumble, topple (over *or* down), keel over; trip, stumble, overbalance. **b** collapse, slump, drop. **4 a** see HANG *v.* 10. **b** slope (away *or* down), fall away. **5 a** see SUBSIDE 4, SINK *v.* 1. **b** see SUBSIDE 1. **6** see DROP *v.* 8a. **7, 14** see OCCUR 1. **8** decline; come *or* go down, (become) lower, drop, sink; fall *or* drop off, decrease, diminish, dwindle, subside. **10 a** see *give way* 1 (WAY). **11** see SIN[1] *v.* 1. **16** see BECOME 1. **17** be overthrown, be captured, be taken, be defeated *or* conquered, be lost, be destroyed; succumb, surrender, yield, give up *or* in, capitulate. **18** die, perish, be killed, *literary or joc.* be slain. **19** (*fall on* or *upon*) **a** attack, assault, assail, set upon. **b** see MEET[1] *v.* 1. **c** see EMBARK 2. **20** (*fall to*) see COMMENCE. **21** (*fall to*) see REVERT. ● *n.* **1** descent, drop, dive, nosedive, plunge, tumble. **2** covering, coating, layer. **4** decline, diminution, decrease, downturn, down-swing, drop, drop-off, lowering, sinking, abatement, slump, collapse; depreciation. **5** overthrow, downfall, capture, taking, seizure, defeat, conquest, ruin, destruction; surrender, capitulation, submission; decline, collapse, eclipse. **6 a** see SIN[1]. **7** slope, sloping, drop, descent; decline. **9** cataract, cascade; see also WATERFALL. □ **fall about** see STAGGER *v.* 1a, LAUGH *v.* 1. **fall apart** (or **to pieces**) **1** break into pieces, disintegrate, break apart, fragment, shatter. **2** collapse, break up; see also DISINTEGRATE. **3** disintegrate, crumble, go to pieces, collapse, have a nervous breakdown. **fall away 1** see INCLINE *v.* 3, 4. **2** see DISAPPEAR. **3** see REVOLT *v.* 1a. **fall back** retreat, withdraw, draw back; retire. **fall back on** have recourse to, rely *or* depend on, rely *or* depend upon, return to, count on *or* upon, resort to, call on *or* upon, make use of, use, employ. **fall behind 1** lag, trail (behind), drop back *or* behind *or* to the rear. **2** be in arrears, be behind. **fall down** be found wanting *or* lacking, be unsuccessful, be *or* prove inadequate, be *or* prove disappointing; see also FAIL *v.* 1, 2a. **fall flat** collapse, fail, *sl.* flop, *US sl.* bomb, go down like a lead balloon. **fall for 1** be captivated *or* deceived by, be fooled *or* duped *or* taken in by, swallow, *sl.* be a sucker for, *US sl.* be a patsy for. **2** fall in love with, become infatuated with. **fall guy 1** see FOOL[1] *n.* 3. **2** see SCAPEGOAT *n.* **fall in 2** collapse (inwards), sink inwards; see also *cave in* 1a (CAVE[1]). **fall into line 1** see *line up* 1 (LINE[1]). **2** see CONFORM 2. **fall into place** see *add up* 3. **fall in with 1** become associated *or* allied with, befriend, join, associate with. **2** agree with, go along with, concur with, support, accept; cooperate with; accede to; humour. **fall off 1** decrease, diminish, deteriorate; see also DECLINE *v.* 1, 7. **2** see WITHDRAW 5. **fall out 1** quarrel, disagree, differ, clash, squabble, wrangle, dispute, fight. **4** see RESULT *v.* 1. **fall out of** see DISCONTINUE. **fall over oneself 1** see RUSH *v.* 1. **2** see STUMBLE *v.* 1. **fall short 1** be *or* prove deficient, be *or* prove inadequate, be *or* prove insufficient, be *or* prove lacking, be *or* prove disappointing; disappoint, fail. **fall through** come to nothing *or* naught, miscarry, die, *colloq.* fizzle (out); see also FAIL *v.* 1, 2a. **fall to** begin, start, *formal* commence; get moving, *colloq.* get the show on the road, get cracking, get a move on, *US colloq.* move it, *US sl.* get a wiggle on.

fallacy /fálləsi/ *n.* (*pl.* **-ies**) **1** a mistaken belief, esp. based on unsound argument. **2** faulty reasoning; misleading or unsound argument. **3** *Logic* a flaw that vitiates an argument. □□ **fallacious** /fəláyshəss/ *adj.* **fallaciously** /fəláyshəsli/ *adv.* **fallaciousness** /fəláyshəsniss/ *n.* [L *fallacia* f. *fallax -acis* deceiving f. *fallere* deceive]

■ **1, 2** misconception, misjudgement, miscalculation, mistake, error; *non sequitur*, *Logic* paralogism. □□ **fallacious** see UNSOUND 3a.

fallen *past part.* of FALL *v.* ● *adj.* **1** (*attrib.*) having lost one's honour or reputation. **2** killed in war. □□ **fallenness** *n.*

■ **2** see *lost* (LOSE 14b).

fallfish /fáwlfish/ *n. US* a N. American freshwater fish like the chub.

fallible /fállib'l/ *adj.* **1** capable of making mistakes. **2** liable to be erroneous. □□ **fallibility** /-bílliti/ *n.* **fallibly** *adv.* [med.L *fallibilis* f. L *fallere* deceive]

Fallopian tube /fəlṓpiən/ *n. Anat.* either of two tubes in female mammals along which ova travel from the ovaries to the uterus. [*Fallopius*, Latinized name of G. *Fallopio*, It. anatomist d. 1562]

fallout /fáwlowt/ *n.* **1** radioactive debris caused by a nuclear explosion or accident. **2** the adverse side-effects of a situation etc.

■ **2** see UPSHOT.

fallow[1] /fállō/ *adj.*, *n.*, & *v.* ● *adj.* **1 a** (of land) ploughed and harrowed but left unsown for a year. **b** uncultivated. **2** (of an idea etc.) potentially useful but not yet in use. **3** inactive. **4** (of a sow) not pregnant. ● *n.* fallow or uncultivated land. ● *v.tr.* break up (land) for sowing or to destroy weeds. □□ **fallowness** *n.* [ME f. OE *fealh* (n.), *fealgian* (v.)]

fallow[2] /fállō/ *adj.* of a pale brownish or reddish yellow. □ **fallow deer** any small deer of the genus *Dama*, having a white-spotted reddish-brown coat in the summer. [OE *falu*, *fealu* f. Gmc]

false /folss, fawlss/ *adj.* & *adv.* ● *adj.* **1** not according with fact; wrong, incorrect (*a false idea*). **2 a** spurious, sham, artificial (*false gods*; *false teeth*; *false modesty*). **b** acting as such; appearing to be such, esp. deceptively (*a false lining*). **3** illusory; not actually so (*a false economy*). **4** improperly so called (*false acacia*). **5** deceptive. **6** (foll. by *to*) deceitful, treacherous, or unfaithful. **7** illegal (*false imprisonment*). ● *adv.* in a false manner (esp. *play false*). □ **false acacia** see ACACIA. **false alarm** an alarm given needlessly. **false bedding** *Geol.* = CROSS-BEDDING. **false colours** deceitful pretence. **false dawn** a transient light in the east before dawn. **false gharial** see GHARIAL. **false pretences** misrepresentations made with intent to deceive (esp. *under false pretences*). **false rib** = *floating rib*. **false start 1** an invalid or disallowed start in a race. **2** an unsuccessful attempt to begin something. **false step** a slip; a mistake. **false topaz** = CITRINE. □□ **falsely** *adv.* **falseness** *n.* **falsity** *n.* (*pl.* **-ies**). [OE *fals* and OF *fals*, *faus* f. L *falsus* past part. of *fallere* deceive]

■ *adj.* **1** untrue, inaccurate, inexact, imprecise, untruthful, unfactual, invalid, unsound, fictitious, spurious, unreal; wrong, incorrect, mistaken, fallacious, erroneous, faulty, flawed. **2 a** spurious, sham, artificial, feigned, affected, insincere, fake, faked, simulated, synthetic, pseudo, factitious, unnatural, bogus, ersatz, counterfeit, imitation, forged; mock; *colloq.* phoney. **b** deceptive, misleading, untrue, untrustworthy, fraudulent, deceitful, deceiving, treacherous, *colloq.* phoney. **3** see ILLUSORY. **5** see DECEPTIVE. **6** see DISLOYAL. **7** see ILLEGAL 1. □ **false colours** see DISGUISE *n.* 1. **false step** see SLIP[1] *n.* □□ **falseness, falsity** untruthfulness, falsehood, mendacity, mendaciousness, insincerity, dishonesty, spuriousness, speciousness, deceptiveness, deceit, deceitfulness, fraudulence; casuistry, sophistry; hypocrisy; treachery, perfidy.

falsehood /fóls-hōōd, fáwls-/ *n.* **1** the state of being false, esp. untrue. **2** a false or untrue thing. **3 a** the act of lying. **b** a lie or lies.
■ **1** see *falseness*, *falsity* (FALSE). **2, 3b** untruth, fiction, fabrication, distortion; lie, fib, tale, story, fairy tale *or* story, *colloq.* cock-and-bull story.

falsetto /folséttō, fawl-/ *n.* (*pl.* **-os**) **1** a method of voice production used by male singers, esp. tenors, to sing notes higher than their normal range. **2** a singer using this method. [It., dimin. of *falso* FALSE]

falsework /fólswurk, fáwls-/ *n.* a temporary framework or support used during building to form arches etc.

falsies /fólsiz, fáwls-/ *n.pl. colloq.* padded material to increase the apparent size of the breasts.

falsify /fólsifī, fáwls-/ *v.tr.* (**-ies, -ied**) **1** fraudulently alter or make false (a document, evidence, etc.). **2** misrepresent. **3** make wrong; pervert. **4** show to be false. **5** disappoint (a hope, fear, etc.). □□ **falsifiable** *adj.* **falsifiability** /-fīəbílliti/ *n.* **falsification** /-fikáysh'n/ *n.* [ME f. F *falsifier* or med.L *falsificare* f. L *falsificus* making false f. *falsus* false]
■ **1** alter, massage, *colloq.* cook. **2** distort, twist; see also MISREPRESENT. **3** see PERVERT *v.* 1–3. **4** see EXPOSE 5. **5** see FRUSTRATE *v.* 4.

falter /fóltər, fáwl-/ *v.* **1** *intr.* stumble, stagger; go unsteadily. **2** *intr.* waver; lose courage. **3** *tr.* & *intr.* stammer; speak hesitatingly. □□ **falterer** *n.* **falteringly** *adv.* [ME: orig. uncert.]
■ **1** see HOBBLE *v.* 1. **2** see HESITATE 1, DOUBT *v.* 3. **3** see STAMMER *v.*

fame /faym/ *n.* **1** renown; the state of being famous. **2** reputation. **3** *archaic* public report; rumour. □ **house of ill fame** *archaic* a brothel. **ill fame** disrepute. [ME f. OF f. L *fama*]
■ **1, 2** renown, reputation, celebrity, stardom, name, illustriousness, (pre-)eminence, prominence, repute; notoriety, notoriousness. **3** see RUMOUR *n.* 1. □ **house of ill fame** see BROTHEL. **ill fame** see DISCREDIT *n.* 1.

famed /faymd/ *adj.* **1** (foll. by *for*) famous; much spoken of (*famed for its good food*). **2** *archaic* currently reported.
■ **1** see FAMOUS 1.

familial /fəmílliəl/ *adj.* of, occurring in, or characteristic of a family or its members. [F f. L *familia* FAMILY]
■ see DOMESTIC *adj.* 1.

familiar /fəmílliər/ *adj.* & *n.* ● *adj.* **1 a** (often foll. by *to*) well known; no longer novel. **b** common, usual; often encountered or experienced. **2** (foll. by *with*) knowing a thing well or in detail (*am familiar with all the problems*). **3** (often foll. by *with*) **a** well-acquainted (with a person); in close friendship; intimate. **b** sexually intimate. **4** excessively informal; impertinent. **5** unceremonious, informal. ● *n.* **1** a close friend or associate. **2** *RC Ch.* a person rendering certain services in a pope's or bishop's household. **3** (in full **familiar spirit**) a demon supposedly attending and obeying a witch etc. □□ **familiarly** *adv.* [ME f. OF *familier* f. L *familiaris* (as FAMILY)]
■ *adj.* **1** commonplace, common, usual, customary, habitual, routine, everyday, ordinary, traditional; see also *well-known* 2 (WELL[1]). **2** (*familiar with*) knowledgeable about *or* of *or* in, conversant *or* acquainted with, up on *or* in, (well-)versed in, (well-)informed about, *au fait* with, *au courant* with, *colloq.* in the know about; aware *or* conscious *or* cognizant of, no stranger to.
3 well-acquainted, friendly, close, *colloq.* chummy; see also INTIMATE[1] *adj.* 1. **4** over-friendly, informal, over-free, over-familiar, free, unrestrained, free and easy, bold, forward, presumptuous, presuming, disrespectful, impudent, insolent, impertinent. **5** casual, unceremonious, unstructured, unofficial, relaxed, informal. ● *n.* **1** see ASSOCIATE *n.* 2, FRIEND *n.* 1. **3** see DEMON 1a.

familiarity /fəmílliárriti/ *n.* (*pl.* **-ies**) **1** the state of being well known (*the familiarity of the scene*). **2** (foll. by *with*) close acquaintance. **3** a close relationship. **4 a** sexual intimacy. **b** (in *pl.*) acts of physical intimacy. **5** familiar or informal behaviour, esp. excessively so. [ME f. OF *familiarité* f. L *familiaritas -tatis* (as FAMILIAR)]
■ **2** (*familiarity with*) knowledge of, cognizance of, acquaintance with, conversance *or* conversancy with, experience of; awareness of. **3** see FRIENDSHIP 1.
5 informality, unceremoniousness; over-familiarity, boldness, presumptuousness, presumption, impudence, insolence, impertinence, impropriety.

familiarize /fəmílliərīz/ *v.tr.* (also **-ise**) **1** (foll. by *with*) make (a person) conversant or well acquainted. **2** make (a thing) well known. □□ **familiarization** /-záysh'n/ *n.* [F *familiariser* f. *familiaire* (as FAMILIAR)]
■ **1** (*familiarize with*) accustom to, make familiar *or* acquaint with, initiate in *or* into, inform about *or* on, enlighten about *or* as to, teach about, educate *or* instruct *or* tutor in. **2** see PUBLICIZE.

famille /faméey/ *n.* a Chinese enamelled porcelain with a predominant colour: (***famille jaune*** /zhōn/) yellow, (***famille noire*** /nwaar/) black, (***famille rose*** /rōz/) red, (***famille verte*** /vairt/) green. [F, = family]

family /fámmili, fámli/ *n.* (*pl.* **-ies**) **1** a set of parents and children, or of relations, living together or not. **2 a** the members of a household, esp. parents and their children. **b** a person's children. **c** (*attrib.*) serving the needs of families (*family butcher*). **3 a** all the descendants of a common ancestor; a house, a lineage. **b** a race or group of peoples from a common stock. **4** all the languages ultimately derived from a particular early language, regarded as a group. **5** a brotherhood of persons or nations united by political or religious ties. **6** a group of objects distinguished by common features. **7** *Math.* a group of curves etc. obtained by varying one quantity. **8** *Biol.* a group of related genera of organisms within an order in taxonomic classification. □ **family allowance** *Brit.* a former name for *child benefit*. **family credit** (or **income supplement**) (in the UK) a regular payment by the State to a family with an income below a certain level. **Family Division** (in the UK) a division of the High Court dealing with adoption, divorce, etc. **family man** a man having a wife and children, esp. one fond of family life. **family name** a surname. **family planning** birth control. **family tree** a chart showing relationships and lines of descent. **in the** (or **a**) **family way** *colloq.* pregnant. [ME f. L *familia* household f. *famulus* servant]
■ **1** (kith and) kin, kinsmen, kindred, kinsfolk, next of kin, relatives, relations, folks, people, one's own flesh and blood, one's nearest and dearest, household, ménage, *US* kinfolk. **2 a** household, ménage. **b** children, offspring, progeny, *Law* issue, *colloq.* brood, *sl.* kids. **3 a** ancestors, forebears, forefathers, progenitors; ancestry, parentage, descent, extraction, derivation, lineage, pedigree, genealogy, family tree, house, line, bloodline, dynasty; blood, stock, strain. **b** see LINE[1] *n.* 18, RACE[2]. **4** group, set, division, subdivision, class, type, kind, order, species, genus. **5** see BROTHERHOOD 2. **6** see GROUP *n.* 1. □ **in the** (or **a**) **family way** see PREGNANT 1.

famine /fámmin/ *n.* **1 a** extreme scarcity of food. **b** a shortage of something specified (*water famine*). **2** *archaic* hunger, starvation. [ME f. OF f. *faim* f. L *fames* hunger]
■ **1 b** shortage, scarcity, dearth, paucity, exiguity, lack. **2** see *starvation* (STARVE).

famish /fámmish/ *v.tr.* & *intr.* (usu. in *passive*) **1** reduce or be reduced to extreme hunger. **2** *colloq.* (esp as **famished** *adj.*) feel very hungry. [ME f. obs. *fame* f. OF *afamer* ult. f. L *fames* hunger]
■ **2** (**famished**) hungry, ravenous, empty, *colloq.* starving, starved.

famous /fáyməss/ *adj.* **1** (often foll. by *for*) celebrated; well known. **2** *colloq.* excellent. □□ **famousness** *n.* [ME f. AF, OF *fameus* f. L *famosus* f. *fama* fame]
■ **1** celebrated, well-known, renowned, famed, (pre-)eminent, prominent, illustrious, noted, notable, acclaimed, venerable, distinguished; legendary. **2** see EXCELLENT.

famously /fáyməsli/ *adv.* **1** *colloq.* excellently (*got on famously*). **2** notably.
■ **1** excellently, (very) well, superbly, marvellously, splendidly, capitally, spectacularly, superlatively. **2** see *notably* (NOTABLE).

famulus /fámyooləss/ *n.* (*pl.* **famuli** /-lī/) *hist.* an attendant on a magician or scholar. [L, = servant]

fan[1] /fan/ *n.* & *v.* ● *n.* **1** an apparatus, usu. with rotating blades, giving a current of air for ventilation etc. **2** a device, usu. folding and forming a semicircle when spread out, for agitating the air to cool oneself. **3** anything spread out like a fan, e.g. a bird's tail or kind of ornamental vaulting (*fan tracery*). **4** a device for winnowing grain. **5** a fan-shaped deposit of alluvium esp. where a stream begins to descend a gentler slope. **6** a small sail for keeping the head of a windmill towards the wind. ● *v.* (**fanned**, **fanning**) **1** *tr.* **a** blow a current of air on, with or as with a fan. **b** agitate (the air) with a fan. **2** *tr.* (of a breeze) blow gently on; cool. **3** *tr.* **a** winnow (grain). **b** winnow away (chaff). **4** *tr.* sweep away by or as by the wind from a fan. **5** *intr.* & *tr.* (usu. foll. by *out*) spread out in the shape of a fan. □ **fan belt** a belt that drives a fan to cool the radiator in a motor vehicle. **fan dance** a dance in which the dancer is (apparently) nude and partly concealed by fans. **fan heater** an electric heater in which a fan drives air over an element. **fan-jet** = TURBOFAN. **fan palm** a palm-tree with fan-shaped leaves. □□ **fanlike** *adj.* **fanner** *n.* [OE *fann* (in sense 4 of *n.*) f. L *vannus* winnowing-fan]

fan[2] /fan/ *n.* a devotee of a particular activity, performer, etc. (*film fan*; *football fan*). □ **fan club** an organized group of devotees. **fan mail** letters from fans. □□ **fandom** *n.* [abbr. of FANATIC]
■ devotee, admirer, enthusiast, lover, adherent, follower, supporter, aficionado, fanatic, zealot, *colloq.* buff, addict, freak, *sl.* fiend, bug, nut, groupie.

fanatic /fənáttik/ *n.* & *adj.* ● *n.* a person filled with excessive and often misguided enthusiasm for something. ● *adj.* excessively enthusiastic. □□ **fanatical** *adj.* **fanatically** *adv.* **fanaticism** /-tisiz'm/ *n.* **fanaticize** /-tisīz/ *v.intr.* & *tr.* (also **-ise**). [F *fanatique* or L *fanaticus* f. *fanum* temple (orig. in religious sense)]
■ *n.* extremist, maniac, zealot, *sl.* nut, *Austral. sl.* wowser. ● *adj.* see ENTHUSIASTIC. □□ **fanatical** fanatic, extreme, maniacal, mad, rabid, compulsive, monomaniacal, obsessive, frenzied, feverish, frantic, frenetic, zealous, excessive, immoderate, passionate. **fanaticism** extremism, hysteria, franticness, frenzy, zeal; monomania, obsessiveness, single-mindedness, mania, madness.

fancier /fánsiər/ *n.* a connoisseur or follower of some activity or thing (*dog-fancier*).

fanciful /fánsifŏŏl/ *adj.* **1** existing only in the imagination or fancy. **2** indulging in fancies; whimsical, capricious. **3** fantastically designed, ornamented, etc.; odd-looking. □□ **fancifully** *adv.* **fancifulness** *n.*
■ **1** extravagant, fantastic, chimerical, fabulous, unreal, illusory, visionary, imaginary; make-believe, fairy-tale. **2** capricious, impulsive, fickle; see also WHIMSICAL 1. **3** odd, curious, peculiar, bizarre, unusual, original; see also FANTASTIC 2, 3.

fancy /fánsi/ *n.*, *adj.*, & *v.* ● *n.* (*pl.* **-ies**) **1** an individual taste or inclination (*take a fancy to*). **2** a caprice or whim. **3** a thing favoured, e.g. a horse to win a race. **4** an arbitrary supposition. **5 a** the faculty of using imagination or of inventing imagery. **b** a mental image. **6** delusion; unfounded belief. **7** (prec. by *the*) those who have a certain hobby; fanciers, esp. patrons of boxing. ● *adj.* (usu. *attrib.*) (**fancier**, **fanciest**) **1** ornamental; not plain. **2** capricious, whimsical, extravagant (*at a fancy price*). **3** based on imagination, not fact. **4** *US* (of foods etc.) above average quality. **5** (of flowers etc.) particoloured. **6** (of an animal) bred for particular points of beauty etc. ● *v.tr.* (**-ies**, **-ied**) **1** (foll. by *that* + clause) be inclined to suppose; rather think. **2** *Brit. colloq.* feel a desire for (*do you fancy a drink?*). **3** *Brit. colloq.* find sexually attractive. **4** *colloq.* have an unduly high opinion of (oneself, one's ability, etc.). **5** (in *imper.*) an exclamation of surprise (*fancy their doing that!*). **6 a** picture to oneself; conceive, imagine. **b** (as **fancied** *adj.*) having no basis in fact; imaginary. □ **catch** (or **take**) **the fancy of** please; appeal to. **fancy dress** fanciful costume, esp. for masquerading as a different person or as an animal etc. at a party. **fancy-free** without (esp. emotional) commitments. **fancy goods** ornamental novelties etc. **fancy man** *sl. derog.* **1** a woman's lover. **2** a pimp. **fancy woman** *sl. derog.* a mistress. **fancy-work** ornamental sewing etc. □□ **fanciable** *adj.* (in sense 3 of *v.*). **fancily** *adv.* **fanciness** *n.* [contr. of FANTASY]
■ *n.* **1** taste, inclination, penchant, preference, partiality, predilection, liking, fondness, attraction. **2** caprice, whim, idea, whimsy, notion, vagary, quirk, crotchet, peculiarity, impulse. **3** see PREFERENCE 2. **4** see SUPPOSITION 1. **5 a** imagination, inventiveness, creativity, creativeness. **b** see IMAGE *n.* 8. **6** delusion, illusion, fantasy, make-believe, unreality, hallucination. ● *adj.* **1** ornamental, decorative, ornate, decorated, ornamented, elaborate, embellished, embroidered, fanciful, extravagant, rococo, baroque, Byzantine, intricate; gingerbread. **2** capricious, whimsical, fanciful, fantastic, far-fetched, visionary, grandiose, delusive, illusory, unrealistic; extravagant; high, exorbitant, inflated, outrageous. **3** see IMAGINARY. **4** de luxe, luxury, luxurious, choice, select, superior, high-class, special; quality, prime; *colloq.* posh. ● *v.* **1** suppose, think, guess, conjecture, presume, surmise, assume, take it, infer, reckon, imagine, believe, suspect, understand. **2** see WANT *v.* 1a. **3** like, be attracted to, take (a liking) to, have an eye for, desire, want, crave, have a craving for, hunger for, favour, prefer, lust after; *colloq.* have a yen for. **4** see PRIDE *v.* **5** just imagine. **6 a** picture, imagine, visualize, envisage, envision, think *or* dream about. **b** (**fancied**) imaginary, unreal, fanciful, imagined, illusory, make-believe, fairy-tale. □ **catch** (or **take**) **the fancy of** see ATTRACT 2. **fancy-free** see FREE *adj.* 3d. **fancy goods** see BAUBLE. **fancy man 1** see SUITOR 1. **2** see PIMP *n.* **fancy woman** see MISTRESS 5. **fancy-work** see *embellishment* (EMBELLISH).

fandangle /fandángg'l/ *n.* **1** a fantastic ornament. **2** nonsense, tomfoolery. [perh. f. FANDANGO after *newfangle*]

fandango /fandánggō/ *n.* (*pl.* **-oes** or **-os**) **1 a** a lively Spanish dance for two. **b** the music for this. **2** nonsense, tomfoolery. [Sp.: orig. unkn.]

fane /fayn/ *n. poet.* = TEMPLE[1]. [ME f. L *fanum*]

fanfare /fánfair/ *n.* **1** a short showy or ceremonious sounding of trumpets, bugles, etc. **2** an elaborate display; a burst of publicity. [F, imit.]
■ **1** flourish, fanfaronade, trumpet-blast, blast, trumpet-blare, blare. **2** fuss, commotion, stir, ado, to-do, ballyhoo, hullabaloo, hubbub, brouhaha.

fanfaronade /fánfarənáyd/ *n.* **1** arrogant talk; brag. **2** a fanfare. [F *fanfaronnade* f. *fanfaron* braggart (as FANFARE)]

fang /fang/ *n.* **1** a canine tooth, esp. of a dog or wolf. **2** the tooth of a venomous snake, by which poison is injected. **3** the root of a tooth or its prong. **4** *Brit. colloq.* a person's tooth. □□ **fanged** *adj.* (also in *comb.*). **fangless** *adj.* [OE f. ON *fang* f. a Gmc root = to catch]

fanlight /fánlīt/ *n.* a small, orig. semicircular window over a door or another window.

fanny /fánni/ *n.* (*pl.* **-ies**) **1** *Brit. coarse sl.* the female genitals. **2** *US sl.* the buttocks. ¶ Usually considered a taboo word in *Brit.* use. □ **fanny pack** *US sl.* = *bum-bag*. [20th c.: orig. unkn.]
■ **2** see BUTTOCK.

Fanny Adams /fánni áddəmz/ *n. Brit. sl.* **1** (also **sweet Fanny Adams**) nothing at all. ¶ Sometimes understood as a euphemism for *fuck all*. **2** *Naut.* **a** tinned meat. **b** stew. [name of a murder victim *c.*1870]

fantail /fántayl/ *n.* **1** a pigeon with a broad-shaped tail. **2** any flycatcher of the genus *Rhipidura*, with a fan-shaped tail. **3** a fan-shaped tail or end. **4** the fan of a windmill. **5** the projecting part of a boat's stern. ▫▫ **fantailed** *adj*.

fan-tan /fántan/ *n*. **1** a Chinese gambling game in which players try to guess the remainder after the banker has divided a number of hidden objects into four groups. **2** a card-game in which players build on sequences of sevens. [Chin., = repeated divisions]

fantasia /fantáyziə, fántəzéeə/ *n*. a musical or other composition free in form and often in improvisatory style, or which is based on several familiar tunes. [It., = FANTASY]

fantasize /fántəsīz/ *v*. (also **phantasize, -ise**) **1** *intr*. have a fantasy or fanciful vision. **2** *tr*. imagine; create a fantasy about. ▫▫ **fantasist** *n*.

▪ **1** dream, day-dream, speculate, *literary* muse; build castles in the air *or* in Spain; hallucinate. **2** see IMAGINE 1.

fantast /fántast/ *n*. (also **phantast**) a visionary; a dreamer. [med.L f. Gk *phantastēs* boaster f. *phantazomai* make a show f. *phainō* show]

fantastic /fantástik/ *adj*. (also **fantastical**) **1** *colloq*. excellent, extraordinary. **2** extravagantly fanciful; capricious, eccentric. **3** grotesque or quaint in design etc. ▫▫ **fantasticality** /-kálliti/ *n*. **fantastically** *adv*. [ME f. OF *fantastique* f. med.L *fantasticus* f. LL *phantasticus* f. Gk *phantastikos* (as FANTAST)]

▪ **1** marvellous, spectacular, splendid, wonderful, tremendous, overwhelming, *colloq*. great, fabulous, terrific; extraordinary; see also EXCELLENT. **2** extravagant, fanciful, imaginary, illusory, imagined, illusive, unreal, irrational, visionary; capricious, eccentric, extraordinary, unbelievable, incredible, preposterous, implausible, absurd, unlikely. **3** grotesque, eccentric, outlandish, fanciful, remarkable, strange, peculiar, odd, queer, bizarre, quaint, exotic, extravagant, *colloq*. weird.

fantasticate /fantástikayt/ *v.tr*. make fantastic. ▫▫ **fantastication** /-káysh'n/ *n*.

fantasy /fántəsi, -zi/ *n*. & *v*. (also **phantasy**) ● *n*. (*pl*. **-ies**) **1** the faculty of inventing images, esp. extravagant or visionary ones. **2** a fanciful mental image; a day-dream. **3** a whimsical speculation. **4** a fantastic invention or composition; a fantasia. **5** fabrication, pretence; make-believe (*his account was pure fantasy*). ● *v.tr*. (**-ies, -ied**) imagine in a visionary manner. [ME f. OF *fantasie* f. L *phantasia* appearance f. Gk (as FANTAST)]

▪ *n*. **1** imagination, fancy, creativity, inventiveness, originality. **2** vision, hallucination, mirage, illusion, delusion, chimera; day-dream, dream, (flight of) fancy, pipedream. **3** see HOPE *n*. 1, 3. **5** invention, make-believe, fiction, fabrication, fable, concoction, pretence.

Fanti /fánti/ *n*. (also **Fante** /fántee/) (*pl*. same or **Fantis**) **1** a member of a Black tribe native to Ghana. **2** the language of this tribe. [native name]

FAO *abbr*. Food and Agriculture Organization (of the United Nations).

far /faar/ *adv*. & *adj*. (**further, furthest** or **farther, farthest**) ● *adv*. **1** at or to or by a great distance (*far away*; *far off*; *far out*). **2** a long way (off) in space or time (*are you travelling far?*; *we talked far into the night*). **3** to a great extent or degree; by much (*far better*; *far the best*; *far too early*). ● *adj*. **1** situated at or extending over a great distance in space or time; remote (*a far cry*; *a far country*). **2** more distant (*the far end of the hall*). ▫ **as far as 1** to the distance of (a place). **2** to the extent that (*travel as far as you like*). **by far 1** by a great amount. **2** (as an intensifier) without doubt. **far and away** by a very large amount. **far and near** everywhere. **far and wide** over a large area. **far-away 1** remote; long-past. **2** (of a look) dreamy. **3** (of a voice) sounding as if from a distance. **far be it from me** (foll. by *to* + infin.) I am reluctant to (esp. express criticism etc.). **far cry** a long way. **the Far East** China, Japan, and other countries of E. Asia. **Far Eastern** of or in the Far East. **far-fetched** (of an explanation etc.) strained, unconvincing. **far-flung 1** extending far; widely distributed. **2** remote, distant. **far from** very different from being; tending to the opposite of (*the problem is far from being solved*). **far gone 1** advanced in time. **2** *colloq*. in an advanced state of illness, drunkenness, etc. **3** *colloq*. in a dilapidated state; beyond help. **far-off** remote. **far-out 1** distant. **2** avant-garde, unconventional, excellent. **far-reaching 1** widely applicable. **2** having important consequences or implications. **far-seeing** shrewd in judgement; prescient. **go far 1** achieve much. **2** contribute greatly. **3** be adequate. **go too far** go beyond the limits of what is reasonable, polite, etc. **how far** to what extent. **so far 1** to such an extent or distance; to this point. **2** until now. **so** (or **in so**) **far as** (or **that**) to the extent that. **so far so good** progress has been satisfactory up to now. ▫▫ **farness** *n*. [OE *feorr*]

▪ *adv*. **1, 2** far away, far off, a good *or* great *or* long way (off *or* away); afar, far out, a good *or* great *or* long distance (off *or* away). **3** (very) much, considerably, decidedly, incomparably. ● *adj*. **1** remote *or* distant, far-away, far-off. **2** extreme, farthest, further; other, opposite. ▫ **by far** much, considerably, incomparably, immeasurably; far and away, easily, *Brit*. by a long chalk; definitely, undoubtedly, indubitably, without (a) doubt, unquestionably, beyond (the shadow of a) doubt. **far and away** see *undoubtedly* (UNDOUBTED). **far and near** see *far and wide*. **far and wide** near and far, far and near, extensively, widely, high and low; here, there, and everywhere; see also EVERYWHERE. **far-away 1** distant, far-off, far-flung; see also REMOTE 1, 2. **2** dreamy, detached, absent, absent-minded, preoccupied, abstracted. **3** see FAINT *adj*. 1. **far-fetched** strained, forced, unconvincing, unbelievable, incredible, improbable, implausible, unlikely, doubtful, dubious, questionable, unrealistic, fantastic, preposterous; difficult *or* hard to believe; *sl*. fishy. **far-flung 1** see EXTENSIVE 2. **2** see REMOTE 1. **far gone 2** see DRUNK *adj*. 1; seriously *or* acutely *or* dangerously *or* critically *or* terminally ill. **3** beyond *or* past help, deteriorated, worn out, dilapidated, near the end. **far-off** see REMOTE 1, 4. **far-out 1** see DISTANT 1a. **2** see AVANT-GARDE *adj*. **far-reaching 1** see EXTENSIVE 2. **2** see IMPORTANT 1. **far-seeing** see SHREWD. **go far 1** succeed, get ahead, rise in the world, make a name for oneself, become successful, set the world *or* Thames on fire, *colloq*. go places. **2** contribute, help, aid, play a part. **go too far** go overboard, go over the top, not know when to stop, go to extremes. **so far 1** to such an extent *or* distance, to a certain extent *or* limit *or* point. **2** until *or* till *or* up to now *or* then, until *or* till *or* up to the present, until *or* till *or* up to this *or* that point, to date, to this *or* that point in time, *formal* thus far; see also YET *adv*. 2.

farad /fárrəd/ *n*. *Electr*. the SI unit of capacitance, such that one coulomb of charge causes a potential difference of one volt. ¶ Abbr.: **F.** [shortening of FARADAY]

faradaic /fárrədáyik/ *adj*. (also **faradic** /fəráddik/) *Electr*. inductive, induced. [see FARADAY]

faraday /fárrəday/ *n*. (also **Faraday's constant**) *Electr*. the quantity of electric charge carried by one mole of electrons. ¶ Abbr.: F. ▫ **Faraday cage** *Electr*. an earthed metal screen used for excluding electrostatic influences. **Faraday effect** *Physics* the rotation of the plane of polarization of electromagnetic waves in certain substances in a magnetic field. [M. *Faraday*, Engl. physicist d. 1867]

farandole /fárrəndól/ *n*. **1** a lively Provençal dance. **2** the music for this. [F f. mod. Prov. *farandoulo*]

farce /faarss/ *n*. **1 a** a coarsely comic dramatic work based on ludicrously improbable events. **b** this branch of drama. **2** absurdly futile proceedings; pretence, mockery. [F, orig. = stuffing, f. OF *farsir* f. L *farcire* to stuff, used metaph. of interludes etc.]

▪ **2** see MOCKERY 2.

farceur /faarsőr/ *n*. **1** a joker or wag. **2** an actor or writer of farces. [F f. *farcer* act farces]

farcical /faársik'l/ *adj*. **1** extremely ludicrous or futile. **2** of

or like farce. □□ **farcicality** /-kálliti/ *n.* **farcically** *adv.*
■ **1** ludicrous, futile, laughable, ridiculous, absurd, risible, funny, comical, humorous, droll, amusing, silly, foolish.

farcy /faársi/ *n.* glanders with inflammation of the lymph vessels. □ **farcy bud** (or **button**) a small lymphatic tumour as a result of farcy. [ME f. earlier & OF *farcin* f. LL *farciminum* f. *farcire* to stuff]

farded /faárdid/ *adj. archaic* (of a face etc.) painted with cosmetics. [past part. of obs. *fard* f. OF *farder*]

fare /fair/ *n.* & *v.* ● *n.* **1 a** the price a passenger has to pay to be conveyed by bus, train, etc. **b** a passenger paying to travel in a public vehicle. **2** a range of food provided by a restaurant etc. ● *v.intr. literary* **1** progress; get on (*how did you fare?*). **2** happen; turn out. **3** journey, go, travel. □ **fare-stage** *Brit.* **1** a section of a bus etc. route for which a fixed fare is charged. **2** a stop marking this. [OE *fær*, *faru* journeying, *faran* (v.), f. Gmc]
■ *n.* **1 a** see CHARGE *n.* 1a. **b** see PASSENGER. **2** food, meals, victuals, provisions, eatables, *formal* viands. ● *v.* **1** get on *or* along, manage, do, make one's way, survive, *colloq.* make out. **2** see *turn out* 9. **3** see TRAVEL *v.* 1.

farewell /fáirwél/ *int.* & *n.* ● *int.* goodbye, adieu. ● *n.* **1** leave-taking, departure (also *attrib.*: *a farewell kiss*). **2** parting good wishes. [ME f. imper. of FARE + WELL¹]
■ *int.* **1** goodbye, adieu, adios, Godspeed, God bless, vale, *au revoir*, *Austral.* & *NZ* hooray, *colloq.* toodle-oo, toodle-pip, so long, ciao, bye, bye-bye, see you, see you later, *Brit. colloq.* ta-ta. ● *n.* **1** leave-taking, departure, *congé*, parting, send-off, goodbye.

farina /fərīnə, -reénə/ *n.* **1** the flour or meal of cereal, nuts, or starchy roots. **2** a powdery substance. **3** *Brit.* starch. □□ **farinaceous** /fárrináyshəss/ *adj.* [L f. *far* corn]

farl /faarl/ *n. Sc.* a thin cake, orig. quadrant-shaped, of oatmeal or flour. [obs. *fardel* quarter (as FOURTH, DEAL¹)]

farm /faarm/ *n.* & *v.* ● *n.* **1** an area of land and its buildings used under one management for growing crops, rearing animals, etc. **2** a place or establishment for breeding a particular type of animal, growing fruit, etc. (*trout-farm*; *mink-farm*). **3** = FARMHOUSE. **4** a place for the storage of oil or oil products. **5** = *sewage farm*. ● *v.* **1 a** *tr.* use (land) for growing crops, rearing animals, etc. **b** *intr.* be a farmer; work on a farm. **2** *tr.* breed (fish etc.) commercially. **3** *tr.* (often foll. by *out*) **a** delegate or subcontract (work) to others. **b** contract (the collection of taxes) to another for a fee. **c** arrange for (a person, esp. a child) to be looked after by another, with payment. **4** *tr.* let the labour of (a person) for hire. **5** *tr.* contract to maintain and care for (a person, esp. a child) for a fixed sum. □ **farm-hand** a worker on a farm. □□ **farmable** *adj.* **farming** *n.* [ME f. OF *ferme* f. med.L *firma* fixed payment f. L *firmus* FIRM¹: orig. applied only to leased land]
■ *n.* **1** farmstead, smallholding, grange, *Austral.* & *NZ* station, *Brit.* croft, steading; see also SPREAD *n.* 12. ● *v.* **1 a** cultivate, work, till. **b** work the land. **3 a** subcontract, give; see also DELEGATE *v.* 1. **4** (*farm out*) see JOB¹ *v.* 1b. □□ **farming** agriculture, cultivation, husbandry; agribusiness.

farmer /faármər/ *n.* **1** a person who cultivates a farm. **2** a person to whom the collection of taxes is contracted for a fee. **3** a person who looks after children for payment. [ME f. AF *fermer*, OF *fermier* f. med.L *firmarius*, *firmator* f. *firma* FIRM²]
■ **1** *Brit.* smallholder, *esp. hist.* yeoman. **3** see *child-minder*.

farmhouse /faármhowss/ *n.* a dwelling-place (esp. the main one) attached to a farm.

farmstead /faármsted/ *n.* a farm and its buildings regarded as a unit.
■ see FARM *n.*

farmyard /faármyaard/ *n.* a yard or enclosure attached to a farmhouse.

faro /fáirō/ *n.* a gambling card-game in which bets are placed on the order of appearance of the cards. [F *pharaon* PHARAOH (said to have been the name of the king of hearts)]

Faroese var. of FAEROESE.

farouche /fəro͞osh/ *adj.* sullen, shy. [F f. OF *faroche*, *forache* f. med.L *forasticus* f. L *foras* out of doors]

farrago /fəraágō/ *n.* (*pl.* **-os** or *US* **-oes**) a medley or hotchpotch. □□ **farraginous** /-raájinəss/ *adj.* [L *farrago farraginis* mixed fodder f. *far* corn]
■ see MEDLEY *n.*

farrier /fárriər/ *n. Brit.* **1** a smith who shoes horses. **2** a horse-doctor. □□ **farriery** *n.* [OF *ferrier* f. L *ferrarius* f. *ferrum* iron, horseshoe]

farrow /fárrō/ *n.* & *v.* ● *n.* **1** a litter of pigs. **2** the birth of a litter. ● *v.tr.* (also *absol.*) (of a sow) produce (pigs). [OE *fearh*, *færh* pig f. WG]

farruca /fəro͞okə/ *n.* a type of flamenco dance. [Sp.]

Farsi /faársee/ *n.* the modern Persian language. [Pers.: cf. PARSEE]

far-sighted /faársītid/ *adj.* **1** having foresight, prudent. **2** esp. *US* = LONG-SIGHTED. □□ **far-sightedly** *adv.* **far-sightedness** *n.*
■ **1** foresighted, prescient, far-seeing, provident; prudent, wise, sensible; imaginative; see also SHREWD.
2 long-sighted, hypermetropic, hyperopic, presbyopic.

fart /faart/ *v.* & *n. coarse sl.* ● *v.intr.* **1** emit wind from the anus. **2** (foll. by *about*, *around*) behave foolishly; waste time. ● *n.* **1** an emission of wind from the anus. **2** an unpleasant person. ¶ Usually considered a taboo word. [OE (recorded in *feorting* verbal noun) f. Gmc]

farther var. of FURTHER (esp. with ref. to physical distance).

farthest var. of FURTHEST (esp. with ref. to physical distance).

farthing /faár<u>th</u>ing/ *n.* **1** (in the UK) a coin and monetary unit formerly worth a quarter of an old penny. ¶ Withdrawn in 1961. **2** the least possible amount (*it doesn't matter a farthing*). [OE *fēorthing* f. *fēortha* fourth]

farthingale /faár<u>th</u>inggayl/ *n. hist.* a hooped petticoat or a stiff curved roll to extend a woman's skirt. [earlier *vardingale*, *verd-* f. F *verdugale* f. Sp. *verdugado* f. *verdugo* rod]

fartlek /faártlek/ *n. Athletics* a method of training for middle- and long-distance running, mixing fast with slow work. [Sw. f. *fart* speed + *lek* play]

fasces /fásseez/ *n.pl.* **1** *Rom.Hist.* a bundle of rods with a projecting axe-blade, carried by a lictor as a symbol of a magistrate's power. **2** *hist.* (in Fascist Italy) emblems of authority. [L, pl. of *fascis* bundle]

fascia /fáyshə/ *n.* (also **facia**) **1** *Brit.* **a** the instrument panel of a motor vehicle. **b** any similar panel or plate for operating machinery. **2** the upper part of a shop-front with the proprietor's name etc. **3** *Archit.* **a** a long flat surface between mouldings on the architrave in classical architecture. **b** a flat surface, usu. of wood, covering the ends of rafters. **4** a stripe or band. **5** /fáshə/ *Anat.* a thin sheath of fibrous tissue. □□ **fascial** *adj.* [L, = band, door-frame, etc.]

fasciate /fáshiayt/ *adj.* (also **fasciated**) **1** *Bot.* (of contiguous parts) compressed or growing into one. **2** striped or banded. □□ **fasciation** /-áysh'n/ *n.* [L *fasciatus* past part. of *fasciare* swathe (as FASCIA)]

fascicle /fássik'l/ *n.* **1** (also **fascicule** /-kyo͞ol/) a separately published instalment of a book, usu. not complete in itself. **2** a bunch or bundle. **3** (also **fasciculus** /fasíkyooləss/) *Anat.* a bundle of fibres. □□ **fascicled** *adj.* **fascicular** /fasíkyoolər/ *adj.* **fasciculate** /fasíkyoolət/ *adj.* **fasciculation** /fasíkyooláysh'n/ *n.* [L *fasciculus* bundle, dimin. of *fascis*: see FASCES]

fascinate /fássinayt/ *v.tr.* **1** capture the interest of; attract irresistibly. **2** (esp. of a snake) paralyse (a victim) with fear. □□ **fascinated** *adj.* **fascinating** *adj.* **fascinatingly** *adv.* **fascination** /-náysh'n/ *n.* **fascinator** *n.* [L *fascinare* f. *fascinum* spell]
■ **1** intrigue, beguile, absorb, engross, enthral, captivate, spellbind, hold spellbound, cast a spell on *or* over, put *or* have under a spell, bewitch, enchant, charm, hypnotize, mesmerize, transfix, entrance; see also ENTICE. **2** see PARALYSE. □□ **fascination** enchantment, entrancement,

attraction, attractiveness, draw, pull, magnetism, charm, allure, influence, sorcery, magic, witchcraft.

fascine /faseén/ *n.* a long faggot used for engineering purposes and (esp. in war) for lining trenches, filling ditches, etc. [F f. L *fascina* f. *fascis* bundle: see FASCES]

Fascism /fáshiz'm/ *n.* **1** the totalitarian principles and organization of the extreme right-wing nationalist movement in Italy (1922–43). **2** (also **fascism**) **a** any similar nationalist and authoritarian movement. **b** *disp.* any system of extreme right-wing or authoritarian views. ▫▫ **Fascist** *n.* & *adj.* (also **fascist**). **Fascistic** /-shístik/ *adj.* (also **fascistic**). [It. *fascismo* f. *fascio* political group f. L *fascis* bundle: see FASCES]

■ **2b** see TYRANNY.

fashion /fásh'n/ *n.* & *v.* ● *n.* **1** the current popular custom or style, esp. in dress or social conduct. **2** a manner or style of doing something (*in a peculiar fashion*). **3** (in *comb.*) in a specified manner (*walk crab-fashion*). **4** fashionable society (*a woman of fashion*). ● *v.tr.* (often foll. by *into*) make into a particular or the required form. ▫ **after** (or **in**) **a fashion** as well as is practicable, though not satisfactorily. **in** (or **out of**) **fashion** fashionable (or not fashionable) at the time in question. ▫▫ **fashioner** *n.* [ME f. AF *fasun*, OF *façon*, f. L *factio -onis* f. *facere fact-* do, make]

■ *n.* **1** custom, style, mode, vogue, trend, look, fad, mania, craze, rage; the latest thing, *dernier cri*. **2** manner, style, mode, way. ● *v.* make, model, style, shape, form, mould, forge, create, construct, work, manufacture. ▫ **in fashion** see FASHIONABLE. **out of fashion** see PASSÉ.

fashionable /fáshnəb'l/ *adj.* **1** following, suited to, or influenced by the current fashion. **2** characteristic of or favoured by those who are leaders of social fashion. ▫▫ **fashionableness** *n.* **fashionably** *adv.*

■ in fashion, chic, à la mode, modish, voguish, in vogue, in, *colloq.* with it, all the go, *colloq. often derog.* trendy; stylish.

fast[1] /faast/ *adj.* & *adv.* ● *adj.* **1** rapid, quick-moving. **2** capable of high speed (*a fast car*). **3** enabling or causing or intended for high speed (*a fast road*; *fast lane*). **4** (of a clock etc.) showing a time ahead of the correct time. **5** (of a pitch or ground etc. in a sport) likely to make the ball bounce or run quickly. **6 a** (of a photographic film) needing only a short exposure. **b** (of a lens) having a large aperture. **7 a** firmly fixed or attached. **b** secure; firmly established (*a fast friendship*). **8** (of a colour) not fading in light or when washed. **9** (of a person) immoral, dissipated. ● *adv.* **1** quickly; in quick succession. **2** firmly, fixedly, tightly, securely (*stand fast*; *eyes fast shut*). **3** soundly, completely (*fast asleep*). **4** close, immediately (*fast on their heels*). **5** in a dissipated manner; extravagantly, immorally. ▫ **fast breeder** (or **fast breeder reactor**) a reactor using fast neutrons to produce the same fissile material as it uses. **fast buck** see BUCK[2]. **fast food** food that can be prepared and served quickly and easily, esp. in a snack bar or restaurant. **fast neutron** a neutron with high kinetic energy, esp. not slowed by a moderator etc. **fast reactor** a nuclear reactor using mainly fast neutrons. **fast-talk** *US colloq.* persuade by rapid or deceitful talk. **fast-wind** wind (magnetic tape) rapidly backwards or forwards. **fast worker** *colloq.* a person who achieves quick results, esp. in love affairs. **pull a fast one** (often foll. by *on*) *colloq.* try to deceive or gain an unfair advantage. [OE *fæst* f. Gmc]

■ *adj.* **1, 2** rapid, quick-moving, quick, swift, speedy, brisk, *colloq.* zippy, nippy, *poet. or literary* fleet; hurried, hasty, high-speed, expeditious, express. **7 a** fixed, attached, fastened, secured, tied, bound, connected; firm, secure. **b** secure, firm, stable, solid, immovable, unshakeable, settled; steadfast, staunch, unwavering, constant, lasting, close, loyal, devoted, faithful, permanent. **9** immoral, dissipated, loose, profligate, dissolute, unrestrained, wild, extravagant, intemperate, irresponsible, indecorous, licentious, wanton, rakish, self-indulgent, promiscuous, lecherous. ● *adv.* **1** quick, quickly, swiftly, rapidly, speedily, briskly, hastily, hurriedly, presto, with all speed *or* haste, expeditiously, post-haste, in a flash, in a wink, in a trice, in no time (at all), like a bat out of hell, *colloq.* before you can say Jack Robinson, like a shot, p.d.q., lickety-split, *literary* apace, *Brit. sl.* like the clappers. **2** soundly, firmly, fixedly, tightly, tight, securely, immovably, solidly, unshakeably. **3** see *completely* (COMPLETE). **4** closely, close, immediately, near, right. **5** loosely, wildly, recklessly, irresponsibly, fecklessly, extravagantly, intemperately, sybaritically, self-indulgently, dissolutely, unrestrainedly, indecorously, rakishly, licentiously, promiscuously, immorally, wantonly, lecherously, lustfully. ▫ **pull a fast one** (*pull a fast one on*) see SWINDLE *v.*

fast[2] /faast/ *v.* & *n.* ● *v.intr.* abstain from all or some kinds of food or drink, esp. as a religious observance. ● *n.* an act or period of fasting. ▫▫ **faster** *n.* [ON *fasta* f. Gmc (as FAST[1])]

■ *v.* abstain, go hungry, deny oneself, diet, starve (oneself). ● *n.* diet; hunger strike; sacrifice.

fastback /faástbak/ *n.* **1** a motor car with the rear sloping continuously down to the bumper. **2** such a rear.

fasten /faáss'n/ *v.* **1** *tr.* make or become fixed or secure. **2** *tr.* (foll. by *in*, *up*) lock securely; shut in. **3** *tr.* **a** (foll. by *on*, *upon*) direct (a look, thoughts, etc.) fixedly or intently. **b** focus or direct the attention fixedly upon (*fastened him with her eyes*). **4** *tr.* (foll. by *on*, *upon*) fix (a designation or imputation etc.). **5** *intr.* (foll. by *on*, *upon*) **a** take hold of. **b** single out. ▫▫ **fastener** *n.* [OE *fæstnian* f. Gmc]

■ **1** fix, attach, bind, bond, stick, affix, anchor; tie, lock, hook (up), secure; join, connect, link, fuse, cement, clamp. **2** (*fasten in* or *up*) see LOCK *v.* 2. **3 a** fix, rivet, focus, concentrate, direct, aim, point. **5** (*fasten on* or *upon*) **a** see HOLD *v.* 1a, c. **b** see SINGLE *v.*

fastening /faásning/ *n.* a device that fastens something; a fastener.

■ fastener, catch, clasp, clip, lock, tie.

fastidious /fastíddiəss/ *adj.* **1** very careful in matters of choice or taste; fussy. **2** easily disgusted; squeamish. ▫▫ **fastidiously** *adv.* **fastidiousness** *n.* [ME f. L *fastidiosus* f. *fastidium* loathing]

■ **1** fussy, meticulous, finicky, finical, nice, particular, difficult, critical, hypercritical, over-precise, punctilious, *colloq.* pernickety, picky, nit-picking. **2** see SQUEAMISH 1.

fastigiate /fastíjiət/ *adj. Bot.* **1** having a conical or tapering outline. **2** having parallel upright branches. [L *fastigium* gable-top]

fastness /faástniss/ *n.* **1** a stronghold or fortress. **2** the state of being secure. [OE *fæstnes* (as FAST[1])]

fat /fat/ *n.*, *adj.*, & *v.* ● *n.* **1** a natural oily or greasy substance occurring esp. in animal bodies. **2** the part of anything containing this. **3** excessive presence of fat in a person or animal; corpulence. **4** *Chem.* any of a group of natural esters of glycerol and various fatty acids existing as solids at room temperature. ● *adj.* (**fatter**, **fattest**) **1** (of a person or animal) having excessive fat; corpulent. **2** (of an animal) made plump for slaughter; fatted. **3** containing much fat. **4** greasy, oily, unctuous. **5** (of land or resources) fertile, rich; yielding abundantly. **6 a** thick, substantial in content (*a fat book*). **b** substantial as an asset or opportunity (*a fat cheque*; *was given a fat part in the play*). **7 a** (of coal) bituminous. **b** (of clay etc.) sticky. **8** *colloq. iron.* very little; not much (*a fat chance*; *a fat lot*). ● *v.tr.* & *intr.* (**fatted**, **fatting**) make or become fat. ▫ **fat cat** *sl.* **1** *US* a wealthy person, esp. as a benefactor. **2** *Austral.* a highly paid executive or official. **fat-head** *colloq.* a stupid person. **fat-headed** stupid. **fat-headedness** stupidity. **fat hen** the white goosefoot, *Chenopodium album*. **the fat is in the fire** trouble is imminent. **kill the fatted calf** celebrate, esp. at a prodigal's return (Luke 15). **live off** (or **on**) **the fat of the land** have the best of everything. ▫▫ **fatless** *adj.* **fatly** *adv.* **fatness** *n.* **fattish** *adj.* [OE *fæt* (adj.), *fǣttian* (v.) f. Gmc]

■ *n.* **3** corpulence, obesity, stoutness, heaviness, plumpness, rotundity, portliness, chubbiness, podginess, tubbiness, fleshiness, paunchiness, flabbiness, *colloq.*

pudginess. ● *adj.* **1** obese, stout, overweight, corpulent, portly, rotund, heavy, bulky, well-fed, plump, chubby, podgy, roly-poly, tubby, fleshy, paunchy, pot-bellied, overfed, flabby, elephantine, broad in the beam, *colloq.* beefy, porky, pudgy. **4** greasy, oily, unctuous, oleaginous, fatty, sebaceous, adipose, *formal or joc.* pinguid. **5** fertile, abundant, fruitful, profitable; rich. **6 a** see BULKY. **b** see SUBSTANTIAL 1. □ **fat cat 1** see TYCOON. **2** see DIGNITARY. **fat-head** see DOLT. **fat-headed** see STUPID *adj.* 1, 5. **kill the fatted calf** see CELEBRATE 4. **live off** (or **on**) **the fat of the land** see PROSPER. □□ **fatness** obesity, stoutness, corpulence, *embonpoint*, portliness, plumpness, chubbiness, rotundity, podginess, *colloq.* pudginess.

fatal /fáyt'l/ *adj.* **1** causing or ending in death (*a fatal accident*). **2** (often foll. by *to*) destructive; ruinous; ending in disaster (*was fatal to their chances*; *made a fatal mistake*). **3** fateful, decisive. □□ **fatally** *adv.* **fatalness** *n.* [ME f. OF *fatal* or L *fatalis* (as FATE)]

■ **1** deadly, lethal, mortal, murderous, final, terminal; poisonous, toxic, baneful. **2** destructive, ruinous, fateful, calamitous, disastrous, catastrophic, devastating, cataclysmic, harmful, damaging, dreadful. **3** fateful, decisive, fated, destined, predestined, decreed, ordained, foreordained, preordained, predetermined, inevitable, unavoidable, necessary, essential, inescapable, ineluctable.

fatalism /fáytəliz'm/ *n.* **1** the belief that all events are predetermined and therefore inevitable. **2** a submissive attitude to events as being inevitable. □□ **fatalist** *n.* **fatalistic** /-lístik/ *adj.* **fatalistically** /-lístikəli/ *adv.*

fatality /fətálləti/ *n.* (*pl.* **-ies**) **1 a** an occurrence of death by accident or in war etc. **b** a person killed in this way. **2** a fatal influence. **3** a predestined liability to disaster. **4** subjection to or the supremacy of fate. **5** a disastrous event; a calamity. [F *fatalité* or LL *fatalitas* f. L *fatalis* FATAL]

■ **1 a** death, casualty, killing. **b** see CASUALTY 1. **5** catastrophe, disaster, calamity, cataclysm.

fate /fayt/ *n.* & *v.* ● *n.* **1** a power regarded as predetermining events unalterably. **2 a** the future regarded as determined by such a power. **b** an individual's appointed lot. **c** the ultimate condition or end of a person or thing (*that sealed our fate*). **3** death, destruction. **4** (usu. **Fate**) a goddess of destiny, esp. one of three Greek or Scandinavian goddesses. ● *v.tr.* **1** (usu. in *passive*) preordain (*was fated to win*). **2** (as **fated** *adj.*) **a** doomed to destruction. **b** unavoidable, preordained; fateful. □ **fate worse than death** see DEATH. [ME f. It. *fato* & L *fatum* that which is spoken, f. *fari* speak]

■ *n.* **1** fortune, luck, chance, life, destiny, providence, a person's lot, kismet, *Buddhism* & *Hinduism* karma, *archaic* God's will, *US colloq.* the way the cookie crumbles. **2** future, end, outcome; see also DESTINY. **3** death, destruction, doom, downfall, undoing, ruin, disaster, nemesis, end, finish. ● *v.* **1** preordain, foreordain, predestine, predetermine, destine, ordain, doom; (*be fated*) be sure *or* certain. **2** (**fated**) doomed, damned, cursed; fatal, fateful, unavoidable, inescapable, inevitable, ineluctable.

fateful /fáytfŏŏl/ *adj.* **1** important, decisive; having far-reaching consequences. **2** controlled as if by fate. **3** causing or likely to cause disaster. **4** prophetic. □□ **fatefully** *adv.* **fatefulness** *n.*

■ **1** important, significant, major, consequential, momentous, critical, crucial, weighty, portentous, earth-shaking, decisive, pivotal. **3** disastrous, catastrophic, fatal, ruinous, cataclysmic, lethal, deadly, destructive. **4** see PROPHETIC.

father /faáthər/ *n.* & *v.* ● *n.* **1 a** a man in relation to a child or children born from his fertilization of an ovum. **b** (in full **adoptive father**) a man who has continuous care of a child, esp. by adoption. **2** any male animal in relation to its offspring. **3** (usu. in *pl.*) a progenitor or forefather. **4** an originator, designer, or early leader. **5** a person who deserves special respect (*the father of his country*). **6** (**Fathers** or **Fathers of the Church**) early Christian theologians whose writings are regarded as especially authoritative. **7** (also **Father**) **a** (often as a title or form of address) a priest, esp. of a religious order. **b** a religious leader. **8** (**the Father**) (in Christian belief) the first person of the Trinity. **9** (**Father**) a venerable person, esp. as a title in personifications (*Father Time*). **10** the oldest member or doyen (*Father of the House*). **11** (usu. in *pl.*) the leading men or elders in a city or State (*city fathers*). ● *v.tr.* **1** beget; be the father of. **2** behave as a father towards. **3** originate (a scheme etc.). **4** appear as or admit that one is the father or originator of. **5** (foll. by *on*) assign the paternity of (a child, book) to a person. □ **father-figure** an older man who is respected like a father; a trusted leader. **father-in-law** (*pl.* **fathers-in-law**) the father of one's husband or wife. **father of chapel** see CHAPEL. **Father's Day** a day (usu. the third Sunday in June) established for a special tribute to fathers. **Father Time** see TIME. □□ **fatherhood** *n.* **fatherless** *adj.* **fatherlessness** *n.* **fatherlike** *adj.* & *adv.* **fathership** *n.* [OE *fæder* with many Gmc cognates: rel. to L *pater*, Gk *patēr*]

■ *n.* **1 a** paterfamilias, *archaic* papa, *archaic poet.* sire, *colloq.* dad, daddy, old man, pa, *esp. US colloq.* pop, *sl.* governor, *Brit. sl.* pater. **3** progenitor, forefather, forebear, ancestor, primogenitor. **4** originator, creator, founder, initiator, inventor, author, architect, designer, framer. **5** see LEADER 1. **7 a** priest, confessor, *curé*, abbé, minister, pastor, parson, chaplain, padre, *sl.* sky pilot. **8** see CREATOR 2. **10** see SAGE² *n.* 1. **11** (*fathers*) see ELDER *n.* ● *v.* **1** procreate, sire, *archaic* get, engender, *literary* beget. **3** originate, found, invent, establish, initiate, institute, create, frame, *disp.* author. □ **father-figure** see SAGE² *n.* 1, LEADER 1.

fatherland /faáthərland/ *n.* one's native country.

■ native country, native land, motherland, homeland, birthplace; mother country, (old) country.

fatherly /faáthərli/ *adj.* **1** like or characteristic of a father in affection, care, etc. (*fatherly concern*). **2** of or proper to a father. □□ **fatherliness** *n.*

■ **1** fatherlike, paternal, protective, kindly, kind, warm, friendly, affectionate, amiable, benevolent, well-meaning, benign, caring, sympathetic, indulgent, understanding. **2** paternal, fatherlike.

fathom /fáthəm/ *n.* & *v.* ● *n.* (*pl.* often **fathom** when prec. by a number) **1** a measure of six feet, esp. used in taking depth soundings. **2** *Brit.* a quantity of wood six feet square in cross-section. ● *v.tr.* **1** grasp or comprehend (a problem or difficulty). **2** measure the depth of (water) with a sounding-line. □□ **fathomable** *adj.* **fathomless** *adj.* [OE *fæthm* outstretched arms f. Gmc]

■ *v.* **1** grasp, comprehend, understand, penetrate, divine, determine, ascertain, work out, get to the bottom of, sound out. **2** measure, gauge, plumb, sound.

Fathometer /fəthómmitər/ *n.* a type of echo-sounder.

fatigue /fəteég/ *n.* & *v.* ● *n.* **1** extreme tiredness after exertion. **2** weakness in materials, esp. metal, caused by repeated variations of stress. **3** a reduction in the efficiency of a muscle, organ, etc., after prolonged activity. **4** an activity that causes fatigue. **5 a** a non-military duty in the army, often as a punishment. **b** (in full **fatigue-party**) a group of soldiers ordered to do fatigues. ● *v.tr.* (**fatigues**, **fatigued**, **fatiguing**) **1** cause fatigue in; tire, exhaust. **2** (as **fatigued** *adj.*) weary; listless. □□ **fatiguable** *adj.* (also **fatigable**). **fatiguability** /-gəbílliti/ *n.* (also **fatigability**). **fatigueless** *adj.* [F *fatigue*, *fatiguer* f. L *fatigare* tire out]

■ *n.* **1** tiredness, weariness, exhaustion, lassitude, weakness, enervation, lethargy, languor, sluggishness, listlessness. **2, 3** see WEAKNESS 1, 2. **4** see *exertion* (EXERT). ● *v.* **1** tire, weary, exhaust, weaken, drain, enervate, *colloq.* fag (out). **2** (**fatigued**) weary, wearied, tired, overtired, dead tired, weak, weakened, exhausted, listless, lethargic, languorous, sluggish, enervated, strained; dead, *Brit.* knackered, *colloq.* knocked out, all in, *esp. Brit. colloq.* whacked, *US colloq.* pooped, bushed, tuckered (out), *sl.* beat, dead beat, *Austral.* & *NZ* stonkered.

Fatiha /faátihaa/ *n.* (also **Fatihah**) the short first sura of the Koran, used by Muslims as a prayer. [Arab. *fātiḥa* opening f. *fataḥa* to open]

Fatimid /fáttimid/ *n.* (also **Fatimite** /-mīt/) **1** a descendant of Fatima, the daughter of Muhammad. **2** a member of a dynasty ruling in N. Africa in the 10th–12th c.

fatling /fátling/ *n.* a young fatted animal.

fatso /fátsō/ *n.* (*pl.* **-oes**) *sl. joc.* or *offens.* a fat person. [prob. f. FAT or the designation *Fats*]

fatstock /fátstok/ *n.* livestock fattened for slaughter.

fatten /fátt'n/ *v.* **1** *tr.* & *intr.* (esp. with ref. to meat-producing animals) make or become fat. **2** *tr.* enrich (soil).

fatty /fátti/ *adj.* & *n.* ● *adj.* (**fattier**, **fattiest**) **1** like fat; oily, greasy. **2** consisting of or containing fat; adipose. **3** marked by abnormal deposition of fat, esp. in fatty degeneration. ● *n.* (*pl.* **-ies**) *colloq.* a fat person (esp. as a nickname). □ **fatty acid** *Chem.* any of a class of organic compounds consisting of a hydrocarbon chain and a terminal carboxyl group, esp. those occurring as constituents of lipids. **fatty oil** = *fixed oil.* □□ **fattily** *adv.* **fattiness** *n.*

■ *adj.* **1** see GREASY 1.

fatuous /fátyooəss/ *adj.* vacantly silly; purposeless, idiotic. □□ **fatuity** /fətyoō-iti/ *n.* (*pl.* **-ies**). **fatuously** *adv.* **fatuousness** *n.* [L *fatuus* foolish]

■ see SENSELESS 2, 3.

fatwa /fátwaa/ *n.* (in Islamic countries) an authoritative ruling on a religious matter. [Arab. *fatwa*]

faubourg /fōboorg/ *n.* a suburb, esp. of Paris. [F: cf. med.L *falsus burgus* not the city proper]

fauces /fáwseez/ *n.pl. Anat.* a cavity at the back of the mouth. □□ **faucial** /fáwsh'l/ *adj.* [L, = throat]

faucet /fáwsit/ *n.* esp. *US* a tap. ¶ In Brit. use only in special applications. [ME f. OF *fausset* vent-peg f. Prov. *falset* f. *falsar* to bore]

■ see TAP[1] *n.* 1.

fault /folt, fawlt/ *n.* & *v.* ● *n.* **1** a defect or imperfection of character or of structure, appearance, etc. **2** a break or other defect in an electric circuit. **3** a transgression, offence, or thing wrongly done. **4 a** *Tennis* etc. a service of the ball not in accordance with the rules. **b** (in showjumping) a penalty for an error. **5** responsibility for wrongdoing, error, etc. (*it will be your own fault*). **6** a defect regarded as the cause of something wrong (*the fault lies in the teaching methods*). **7** *Geol.* an extended break in the continuity of strata or a vein. ● *v.* **1** *tr.* find fault with; blame. **2** *tr.* declare to be faulty. **3** *tr. Geol.* break the continuity of (strata or a vein). **4** *intr.* commit a fault. **5** *intr. Geol.* show a fault. □ **at fault** guilty; to blame. **fault-finder** a person given to continually finding fault. **fault-finding** continual criticism. **find fault** (often foll. by *with*) make an adverse criticism; complain. **to a fault** (usu. of a commendable quality etc.) excessively (*generous to a fault*). [ME *faut(e)* f. OF ult. f. L *fallere* FAIL]

■ *n.* **1** defect, imperfection, blemish, flaw, deficiency, shortcoming, failing, weakness; frailty, foible, peccadillo. **2** see BREAK[1] *n.* 1a. **3** transgression, offence, sin, trespass, misdeed, misdemeanour, vice, indiscretion; mistake, error, lapse, failure, oversight, gaffe, blunder, gaucherie, *faux pas*, *colloq.* slip-up, howler, *sl.* goof, boner, clanger, booboo, *Brit. sl.* boob. **5** blame, culpability, accountability, liability, answerability; see also RESPONSIBILITY 1a. **6** see REASON *n.* 1, 2. **7** see BREAK[1] *n.* 1a. ● *v.* **1** find fault with, blame, censure, criticize; call to account, hold a person responsible *or* accountable, hold a person to blame, lay at a person's door, accuse. **2** see CRITICIZE 1. **3** see BREAK[1] *v.* 1a. **4** see ERR 2. □ **at fault** guilty, to blame, culpable, in the wrong, blameable, blameworthy; responsible, accountable, answerable, liable. **fault-finder** nag, *colloq.* fusspot, nit-picker. **fault-finding** criticism, censure, carping, cavilling, captiousness, quibbling, fussiness, hair-splitting, pettifogging, *colloq.* nit-picking. **find fault** (*find fault with*) complain about, criticize, censure, take exception to, pick on, *sl.* knock; pick at, carp at, cavil at *or* about, pick apart, pick holes in. **to a fault** excessively, extremely, to an extreme, in the extreme, exceedingly, unduly, disproportionately, immoderately, irrationally, *esp. US* & *Sc.* overly.

faultless /fóltliss, fáwlt-/ *adj.* without fault; free from defect or error. □□ **faultlessly** *adv.* **faultlessness** *n.*

■ flawless, immaculate; perfect, ideal, exemplary, irreproachable, unimpeachable, *Brit. colloq.* bang on, spot on.

faulty /fólti, fáwlti/ (**faultier**, **faultiest**) *adj.* having faults; imperfect, defective. □□ **faultily** *adv.* **faultiness** *n.*

■ flawed, unsound, imperfect; defective, impaired; out of order, malfunctioning, broken, bad; damaged; *sl.* on the blink, *US sl.* on the fritz.

faun /fawn/ *n.* a Latin rural deity with a human face and torso and a goat's horns, legs, and tail. [ME f. OF *faune* or L *Faunus*, a Latin god identified with Gk Pan]

fauna /fáwnə/ *n.* (*pl.* **faunae** /-nee/ or **faunas**) **1** the animal life of a region or geological period (cf. FLORA). **2** a treatise on or list of this. □□ **faunal** *adj.* **faunist** *n.* **faunistic** /-nístik/ *adj.* [mod.L f. the name of a rural goddess, sister of Faunus: see FAUN]

faute de mieux /fōt də myő/ *adv.* for want of a better alternative. [F]

fauteuil /fōtő-i/ *n.* a kind of wooden seat in the form of an armchair with open sides and upholstered arms. [F f. OF *faudestuel*, *faldestoel* FALDSTOOL]

fauve /fōv/ *n.* a person who practises or favours fauvism.

fauvism /fōviz'm/ *n.* a style of painting with vivid use of colour. □□ **fauvist** *n.* [F *fauve* wild beast, applied to painters of the school of Matisse]

faux pas /fō paá/ *n.* (*pl.* same /paaz/) **1** a tactless mistake; a blunder. **2** a social indiscretion. [F, = false step]

■ **1** see MISTAKE *n.* **2** see PECCADILLO.

fave /fayv/ *n.* & *adj. sl.* = FAVOURITE (esp. in show business). [abbr.]

favela /fəvéllə/ *n.* a Brazilian shack, slum, or shanty town. [Port.]

favour /fáyvər/ *n.* & *v.* (*US* **favor**) ● *n.* **1** an act of kindness beyond what is due or usual (*did it as a favour*). **2** esteem, liking, approval, goodwill; friendly regard (*gained their favour; look with favour on*). **3** partiality; too lenient or generous treatment. **4** aid, support (*under favour of night*). **5** a thing given or worn as a mark of favour or support, e.g. a badge or a knot of ribbons. **6** *archaic* leave, pardon (*by your favour*). **7** *Commerce archaic* a letter (*your favour of yesterday*). ● *v.tr.* **1** regard or treat with favour or partiality. **2** give support or approval to; promote, prefer. **3 a** be to the advantage of (a person). **b** facilitate (a process etc.). **4** tend to confirm (an idea or theory). **5** (foll. by *with*) oblige (*favour me with a reply*). **6** (as **favoured** *adj.*) **a** having special advantages. **b** preferred; favourite. **7** *colloq.* resemble in features. □ **in favour 1** meeting with approval. **2** (foll. by *of*) **a** in support of. **b** to the advantage of. **out of favour** lacking approval. □□ **favourer** *n.* [ME f. OF f. L *favor -oris* f. *favēre* show kindness to]

■ *n.* **1** kindness, courtesy, good *or* kind deed, good turn, gesture, *beau geste*. **2** esteem, regard, (good) opinion, consideration, grace; goodwill, approval, liking, approbation; (*in a person's favour*) in a person's good *or* bad books. **3** partiality, favouritism, preference, bias, prejudice; lenience, leniency. **4** see SHELTER *n.* 1, 3, SUPPORT *n.* 1. **5** see DECORATION 3. **6** see PARDON *n.* ● *v.* **1, 2** have a liking *or* preference for, be partial to, like, side with, take the side of, take the part of; incline to *or* towards, go for, opt for, choose, adopt, go in for; support, back, approve, promote, endorse, champion, advocate, prefer, espouse, recommend. **3 a** see BENEFIT *v.* 1. **b** facilitate, help, benefit, aid, assist, expedite, promote, encourage, smile upon, advance, forward. **4** see SUPPORT *v.* 5. **5** see OBLIGE 3. **6** (**favoured**)

a advantaged, privileged, blessed, prosperous, wealthy, rich, affluent, well off. **b** preferred, chosen, choice, selected, popular, favourite, *often joc.* pet. **7** see RESEMBLE. □ **in favour 2** (*in favour of*) in support of, for, pro; on the side of, behind, in back of, at the back of; *US* at a person's back. **out of favour** see UNPOPULAR.

favourable /fáyvərəb'l/ *adj.* (*US* **favorable**) **1 a** well-disposed; propitious. **b** commendatory, approving. **2** giving consent (*a favourable answer*). **3** promising, auspicious, satisfactory (*a favourable aspect*). **4** (often foll. by *to*) helpful, suitable. □□ **favourableness** *n.* **favourably** *adv.* [ME f. OF *favorable* f. L *favorabilis* (as FAVOUR)]

▪ **1a, 3** well-disposed, propitious, promising, auspicious, fair, encouraging; satisfactory, advantageous, beneficial, helpful, convenient, useful, suitable, appropriate. **1 b** commendatory, approving, laudatory, enthusiastic, eager, good, positive, encouraging, reassuring, sympathetic, promising, affirmative. **2** see WILLING *adj.* **4** see *advantageous* (ADVANTAGE). □□ **favourably** enthusiastically, positively, sympathetically, agreeably; genially, graciously, indulgently; advantageously, affirmatively.

favourite /fáyvərit/ *adj.* & *n.* (*US* **favorite**) ● *adj.* preferred to all others (*my favourite book*). ● *n.* **1** a specially favoured person. **2** *Sport* a competitor thought most likely to win. □ **favourite son** *US* a person preferred as the presidential candidate by delegates from the candidate's home State. [obs. F *favorit* f. It. *favorito* past part. of *favorire* favour]

▪ *adj.* preferred, beloved, best-liked, most-liked, chosen, favoured, *often joc.* pet. ● *n.* **1** darling, pet, apple of one's eye, ideal, preference, *Brit. colloq. usu. derog.* blue-eyed boy.

favouritism /fáyvəritiz'm/ *n.* (*US* **favoritism**) the unfair favouring of one person or group at the expense of another.

▪ partiality, bias, prepossession, prejudice, predisposition, partisanship, nepotism.

fawn[1] /fawn/ *n.*, *adj.*, & *v.* ● *n.* **1** a young deer in its first year. **2** a light yellowish brown. ● *adj.* fawn-coloured. ● *v.tr.* (also *absol.*) (of a deer) bring forth (young). □ **in fawn** (of a deer) pregnant. [ME f. OF *faon* etc. ult. f. L *fetus* offspring: cf. FOETUS]

fawn[2] /fawn/ *v.intr.* **1** (often foll. by *on*, *upon*) (of a person) behave servilely, cringe. **2** (of an animal, esp. a dog) show extreme affection. □□ **fawner** *n.* **fawning** *adj.* **fawningly** *adv.* [OE *fagnian*, *fægnian* (as FAIN)]

▪ **1** see CRINGE *v.* 2.

fax /faks/ *n.* & *v.* ● *n.* **1** facsimile transmission (see FACSIMILE *n.* 2). **2 a** a copy produced by this. **b** a machine for transmitting and receiving these. ● *v.tr.* transmit (a document) in this way. [abbr. of FACSIMILE]

▪ *n.* see FACSIMILE *n.* 2. ● *v.* see TRANSMIT 1a.

fay /fay/ *n. literary* a fairy. [ME f. OF *fae*, *faie* f. L *fata* (pl.) the Fates]

faze /fayz/ *v.tr.* (often as **fazed** *adj.*) *colloq.* disconcert, perturb, disorientate. [var. of *feeze* drive off, f. OE *fēsian*, of unkn. orig.]

▪ see DISCOMFIT 1a.

FBA *abbr.* Fellow of the British Academy.

FBI *abbr.* (in the US) Federal Bureau of Investigation.

FC *abbr.* Football Club.

FCC *abbr.* (in the US) Federal Communications Commission.

FCO *abbr.* (in the UK) Foreign and Commonwealth Office.

fcp. *abbr.* foolscap.

FD *abbr.* Defender of the Faith. [L *Fidei Defensor*]

FDA *abbr.* **1** (in the US) Food and Drugs Administration. **2** (in the UK) First Division (Civil Servants) Association (cf. AFDCS).

Fe *symb. Chem.* the element iron.

fealty /féeəlti/ *n.* (*pl.* **-ies**) **1** *hist.* **a** a feudal tenant's or vassal's fidelity to a lord. **b** an acknowledgement of this. **2** allegiance. [ME f. OF *feaulté* f. L *fidelitas -tatis* f. *fidelis* faithful f. *fides* faith]

fear /feer/ *n.* & *v.* ● *n.* **1 a** an unpleasant emotion caused by exposure to danger, expectation of pain, etc. **b** a state of alarm (*be in fear*). **2** a cause of fear (*all fears removed*). **3** (often foll. by *of*) dread or fearful respect (towards) (*had a fear of heights*). **4** anxiety for the safety of (*in fear of their lives*). **5** danger; likelihood (of something unwelcome) (*there is little fear of failure*). ● *v.* **1 a** *tr.* feel fear about or towards (a person or thing). **b** *intr.* feel fear. **2** *intr.* (foll. by *for*) feel anxiety or apprehension about (*feared for my life*). **3** *tr.* apprehend; have uneasy expectation of (*fear the worst*). **4** *tr.* (usu. foll. by *that* + clause) apprehend with fear or regret (*I fear that you are wrong*). **5** *tr.* **a** (foll. by *to* + infin.) hesitate. **b** (foll. by verbal noun) shrink from; be apprehensive about (*he feared meeting his ex-wife*). **6** *tr.* show reverence towards. □ **for fear of** (or **that**) to avoid the risk of (or that). **never fear** there is no danger of that. **no fear** *colloq.* expressing strong denial or refusal. **without fear or favour** impartially. [OE f. Gmc]

▪ *n.* **1 a** dread, terror, horror; panic, fright, timidity. **b** alarm, dread, terror, horror, panic, fright, trepidation, apprehension, fearfulness, apprehensiveness, consternation, dismay. **2** horror, spectre, nightmare, bogey, phobia, bugbear, *bête noir*, misgivings, forebodings. **3** dread, terror, horror; awe, respect, reverence, veneration. **4** anxiety, solicitude, *angst*, foreboding, distress, concern, apprehension, worry, uneasiness, unease. **5** see DANGER. ● *v.* **1 a** be afraid *or* scared *or* fearful *or* frightened of; dread, shrink from; tremble *or* shudder at. **b** be afraid *or* scared *or* fearful *or* frightened; quiver, tremble, shudder, quail, quake. **2** see WORRY *v.* 1. **3** expect, suspect, imagine, foresee, *disp.* anticipate. **5 a** see HESITATE 2. **b** see DREAD *v.* **6** respect, venerate, be *or* stand in awe of; see also REVERE. □ **no fear** see *by no means* (MEANS). **without fear or favour** see FAIRLY 1.

fearful /féerfool/ *adj.* **1** (usu. foll. by *of*, or *that* + clause) afraid. **2** terrible, awful. **3** *colloq.* extremely unwelcome or unpleasant (*a fearful row*). □□ **fearfully** *adv.* **fearfulness** *n.*

▪ **1** afraid, scared, frightened, terrified, alarmed, panic-stricken, terror-stricken, terror-struck, intimidated, jumpy, nervous, edgy, panicky, anxious, apprehensive; cowardly, pusillanimous, hesitant, timid, timorous, shy, diffident, *colloq.* yellow, jittery. **2, 3** terrible, awful, dire, dreadful, frightful, appalling, ghastly, atrocious, horrific, horrible, horrendous, hideous, gruesome, grisly, grim, unspeakable; terrifying, frightening, horrifying, fearsome, monstrous, loathsome, repugnant, repulsive, revolting, disgusting, nauseating, nauseous. □□ **fearfully** apprehensively, anxiously, edgily, nervously, hesitantly, timidly, timorously, shyly, diffidently; frightfully, awfully, terribly, very, extremely, exceedingly, tremendously.

fearless /féerliss/ *adj.* **1** courageous, brave. **2** (foll. by *of*) without fear. □□ **fearlessly** *adv.* **fearlessness** *n.*

▪ **1** courageous, brave, bold, intrepid, valorous, dauntless, valiant, plucky, daring, audacious, heroic, venturesome, gallant, chivalrous. **2** (*fearless of*) see *heedless* (HEED).

fearsome /féersəm/ *adj.* appalling or frightening, esp. in appearance. □□ **fearsomely** *adv.* **fearsomeness** *n.*

▪ appalling, frightening, terrifying, menacing, terrible, dreadful, awesome, formidable, frightful, daunting, intimidating.

feasibility /féezibílliti/ *n.* the state or degree of being feasible. □ **feasibility study** a study of the practicability of a proposed project.

▪ practicability, workability, workableness, viability, practicality.

feasible /féezib'l/ *adj.* **1** practicable, possible; easily or conveniently done. **2** *disp.* likely, probable (*it is feasible that it will rain*). □□ **feasibly** *adv.* [ME f. OF *faisable*, *-ible* f. *fais-* stem of *faire* f. L *facere* do, make]

▪ **1** practicable, workable, doable, viable, practical, realizable, possible, achievable, attainable, realistic. **2** see LIKELY *adj.* 1.

feast /feest/ *n.* & *v.* ● *n.* **1** a large or sumptuous meal. **2** a gratification to the senses or mind. **3 a** an annual religious celebration. **b** a day dedicated to a particular saint. **4** an annual village festival. ● *v.* **1** *intr.* partake of a feast; eat and drink sumptuously. **2** *tr.* **a** regale. **b** pass (time) in feasting. □ **feast-day** a day on which a feast (esp. in sense 3) is held. **feast one's eyes on** take pleasure in beholding. **feast of reason** intellectual talk. □□ **feaster** *n.* [ME f. OF *feste, fester* f. L *festus* joyous]

■ *n.* **1** banquet, (lavish) dinner, *colloq.* spread, blow-out. **2** treat, delight, pleasure; see also *gratification* (GRATIFY). **3** celebration, feast-day, holy day, holiday, festival, fête; saint's day. **4** see FESTIVAL *n.* ● *v.* **1** dine, wine and dine; gorge (oneself), gormandize, eat one's fill; wine, indulge, overindulge. **2 a** regale, entertain, feed; see also BANQUET *v.* □ **feast-day** see FEAST *n.* 3 above.

feat /feet/ *n.* a noteworthy act or achievement. [ME f. OF *fait, fet* (as FACT)]

■ achievement, accomplishment, exploit, deed, act, *tour de force*.

feather /féthər/ *n.* & *v.* ● *n.* **1** any of the appendages growing from a bird's skin, with a horny hollow stem and fine strands. **2** one or more of these as decoration etc. **3** (*collect.*) **a** plumage. **b** game-birds. ● *v.* **1** *tr.* cover or line with feathers. **2** *tr. Rowing* turn (an oar) so that it passes through the air edgeways. **3** *tr. Aeron.* & *Naut.* **a** cause (the propeller blades) to rotate in such a way as to lessen the air or water resistance. **b** vary the angle of incidence of (helicopter blades). **4** *intr.* float, move, or wave like feathers. □ **feather bed** a bed with a mattress stuffed with feathers. **feather-bed** *v.tr.* (**-bedded, -bedding**) provide with (esp. financial) advantages. **feather-bedding** the employment of excess staff. **feather-brain** (or **-head**) a silly or absent-minded person. **feather-brained** (or **-headed**) silly, absent-minded. **feather-edge** the fine edge of a wedge-shaped board. **a feather in one's cap** an achievement to one's credit. **feather one's nest** enrich oneself. **feather-stitch** ornamental zigzag sewing. **in fine** (or **high**) **feather** *colloq.* in good spirits. □□ **feathered** *adj.* (also in *comb.*). **featherless** *adj.* **feathery** *adj.* **featheriness** *n.* [OE *fether, gefithrian,* f. Gmc]

feathering /féthəring/ *n.* **1** bird's plumage. **2** the feathers of an arrow. **3** a feather-like structure in an animal's coat. **4** *Archit.* cusps in tracery.

featherweight /féthərwayt/ *n.* **1 a** a weight in certain sports intermediate between bantamweight and lightweight, in the amateur boxing scale 54–7kg but differing for professionals, wrestlers, and weightlifters. **b** a sportsman of this weight. **2** a very light person or thing. **3** (usu. *attrib.*) a trifling or unimportant thing.

feature /féechər/ *n.* & *v.* ● *n.* **1** a distinctive or characteristic part of a thing. **2** (usu. in *pl.*) (a distinctive part of) the face, esp. with regard to shape and visual effect. **3 a** a distinctive or regular article in a newspaper or magazine. **b** a special attraction at an event etc. **4 a** (in full **feature film**) a full-length film intended as the main item in a cinema programme. **b** (in full **feature programme**) a broadcast devoted to a particular topic. ● *v.* **1** *tr.* make a special display or attraction of; give special prominence to. **2** *tr.* & *intr.* have as or be an important actor, participant, or topic in a film, broadcast, etc. **3** *intr.* be a feature. □□ **featured** *adj.* (also in *comb.*). **featureless** *adj.* [ME f. OF *feture, faiture* form f. L *factura* formation: see FACTURE]

■ *n.* **1** characteristic, attribute, trait, mark, hallmark, earmark, property, character, quality, aspect, facet, peculiarity, quirk, idiosyncrasy. **2** (*features*) face, physiognomy, countenance, looks, *literary* visage, *sl.* mug, kisser. **3 a** column, article, piece. **b** (main) attraction, draw, special attraction, high point, best *or* memorable part, *sl.* high spot. **4 a** see FILM *n.* 3a, b. **b** see BROADCAST. ● *v.* **1** promote, publicize, advertise, *sl.* hype; stress, emphasize, highlight, call attention to, spotlight, put into the limelight. **2** (*intr.*) act, perform, take a role *or* part, star; have a role *or* part, be involved.

Feb. *abbr.* February.

febrifuge /fébrifyooj/ *n.* a medicine or treatment that reduces fever; a cooling drink. □□ **febrifugal** /fibrífyoog'l, fébrifyóog'l/ *adj.* [F *fébrifuge* f. L *febris* fever + -FUGE]

febrile /féebrīl/ *adj.* of or relating to fever; feverish. □□ **febrility** /fibrílliti/ *n.* [F *fébrile* or med.L *febrilis* f. L *febris* fever]

■ see FEVERISH 1.

February /fébroori/ *n.* (*pl.* **-ies**) the second month of the year. [ME f. OF *feverier* ult. f. L *februarius* f. *februa* a purification feast held in this month]

feces *US* var. of FAECES.

feckless /fékliss/ *adj.* **1** feeble, ineffective. **2** unthinking, irresponsible (*feckless gaiety*). □□ **fecklessly** *adv.* **fecklessness** *n.* [Sc. *feck* f. *effeck* var. of EFFECT]

■ **1** see FEEBLE 2. **2** see IRRESPONSIBLE 1.

feculent /fékyoolənt/ *adj.* **1** murky; filthy. **2** containing sediments or dregs. □□ **feculence** *n.* [F *féculent* or L *faeculentus* (as FAECES)]

■ **1** see MUDDY *adj.* 2.

fecund /féekənd, fék-/ *adj.* **1** prolific, fertile. **2** fertilizing. □□ **fecundability** /fikúndəbílliti/ *n.* **fecundity** /fikúnditi/ *n.* [ME f. F *fécond* or L *fecundus*]

■ **1** see PROLIFIC 1.

fecundate /féekəndayt, fék-/ *v.tr.* **1** make fruitful. **2** = FERTILIZE 2. □□ **fecundation** /-dáysh'n/ *n.* [L *fecundare* f. *fecundus* fruitful]

Fed /fed/ *n. US sl.* a federal official, esp. a member of the FBI. [abbr. of FEDERAL]

fed *past* and *past part.* of FEED. □ **fed up** (or **fed to death**) (often foll. by *with*) discontented or bored, esp. from a surfeit of something (*am fed up with the rain*). **fed-upness** the state of being fed up.

fedayeen /féddəyéen/ *n.pl.* Arab guerrillas operating esp. against Israel. [colloq. Arab. *fidā'iyīn* pl. f. Arab. *fidā'ī* adventurer]

federal /féddərəl/ *adj.* **1** of a system of government in which several States form a unity but remain independent in internal affairs. **2** relating to or affecting such a federation (*federal laws*). **3** relating to or favouring centralized government. **4** (**Federal**) *US* of the Northern States in the Civil War. **5** comprising an association of largely independent units. □ **federal reserve** (in the US) a national system of reserve cash available to banks. □□ **federalism** *n.* **federalist** *n.* **federalize** *v.tr.* (also **-ise**). **federalization** /-līzáysh'n/ *n.* **federally** *adv.* [L *foedus -eris* league, covenant]

■ **1, 2** see NATIONAL *adj.*

federate *v.* & *adj.* ● *v.tr.* & *intr.* /féddərayt/ organize or be organized on a federal basis. ● *adj.* /féddərət/ having a federal organization. □□ **federative** /féddərətiv/ *adj.* [LL *foederare foederat-* (as FEDERAL)]

■ *v.* see BAND[2] *v.*

federation /féddəráysh'n/ *n.* **1** a federal group of States. **2** a federated society or group. **3** the act or an instance of federating. □□ **federationist** *n.* [F *fédération* f. LL *foederatio* (as FEDERAL)]

■ **1** confederacy, confederation. **2** society, group, association, league. **3** amalgamation, alliance, union, unification.

fedora /fidórə/ *n.* a low soft felt hat with a crown creased lengthways. [*Fédora*, drama by V. Sardou (1882)]

fee /fee/ *n.* & *v.* ● *n.* **1** a payment made to a professional person or to a professional or public body in exchange for advice or services. **2** money paid as part of a special transaction, for a privilege, admission to a society, etc. (*enrolment fee*). **3** (in *pl.*) money regularly paid (esp. to a school) for continuing services. **4** *Law* an inherited estate, unlimited (**fee simple**) or limited (**fee tail**) as to the category of heir. **5** *hist.* a fief; a feudal benefice. ● *v.tr.* (**fee'd** or **feed**) **1** pay a fee to. **2** engage for a fee. [ME f. AF, = OF *feu, fieu,* etc. f. med.L *feodum, feudum,* perh. f. Frank.: cf. FEUD[2], FIEF]

■ *n.* **1** payment, wage, rate, stipend, salary,

US compensation; honorarium; pay. **2** charge, price, cost, bill, payment. ● *v.* **1** see PAY[1] *v.* 1. **2** see ENGAGE 1.

feeble /fē′b'l/ *adj.* **1** weak, infirm. **2** lacking energy, force, or effectiveness. **3** dim, indistinct. **4** deficient in character or intelligence. □□ **feebleness** *n.* **feeblish** *adj.* **feebly** *adv.* [ME f. AF & OF *feble, fieble, fleible* f. L *flebilis* lamentable f. *flēre* weep]

■ **1** weak, infirm, frail, puny, slight, decrepit, *Brit. sl.* wonky; debilitated, enfeebled, exhausted, weakened, effete; delicate, fragile, languid, spiritless, sickly, ailing. **2** weak, effete, half-baked, lame, flimsy, unconvincing, poor, unsatisfactory, insufficient, inadequate; shoddy, thin, insubstantial, meagre, paltry, insignificant; ineffectual, effete, feckless, ineffective, impotent, impuissant, namby-pamby, wishy-washy, *Brit. colloq.* wet. **3** dim, indistinct, weak, obscure, imperceptible, faint, unclear. **4** see WEAK 3a, DEFECTIVE *adj.* 2.

feeble-minded /fē′b'lmīndid/ *adj.* **1** unintelligent. **2** mentally deficient. □□ **feeble-mindedly** *adv.* **feeble-mindedness** *n.*

■ **1** unintelligent, stupid, simple, dull, dull-witted, witless, simple-minded, imbecile, slow, slow-witted, obtuse, soft-headed, empty-headed, vacant, *colloq.* halfwitted, moronic, idiotic, imbecile, cretinous, dim-witted, slow on the uptake, thick, *esp. Brit. colloq.* gormless, *esp. US colloq.* dumb, *sl.* boneheaded. **2** mentally defective, weak-minded, (mentally) deficient, deficient, subnormal, retarded, ESN, halfwitted, soft-headed, moronic, idiotic, imbecile, imbecilic, cretinous, simple-minded.

feed /fēed/ *v.* & *n.* ● *v.* (*past* and *past part.* **fed** /fed/) **1** *tr.* **a** supply with food. **b** put food into the mouth of. **2** *tr.* **a** give as food, esp. to animals. **b** graze (cattle). **3** *tr.* serve as food for. **4** *intr.* (usu. foll. by *on*) (esp. of animals, or *colloq.* of people) take food; eat. **5** *tr.* nourish; make grow. **6 a** *tr.* maintain supply of raw material, fuel, etc., to (a fire, machine, etc.). **b** *tr.* (foll. by *into*) supply (material) to a machine etc. **c** *intr.* (often foll. by *into*) (of a river etc.) flow into another body of water. **d** *tr.* insert further coins into (a meter) to continue its function, validity, etc. **7** *intr.* (foll. by *on*) **a** be nourished by. **b** derive benefit from. **8** *tr.* use (land) as pasture. **9** *tr. Theatr. sl.* supply (an actor etc.) with cues. **10** *tr. Sport* send passes to (a player) in a ball-game. **11** *tr.* gratify (vanity etc.). **12** *tr.* provide (advice, information, etc.) to. ● *n.* **1** an amount of food, esp. for animals or infants. **2** the act or an instance of feeding; the giving of food. **3** *colloq.* a meal. **4** pasturage; green crops. **5 a** a supply of raw material to a machine etc. **b** the provision of this or a device for it. **6** the charge of a gun. **7** *Theatr. sl.* an actor who supplies another with cues. □ **feed back** produce feedback. **feed the fishes 1** meet one's death by drowning. **2** be seasick. **feeding-bottle** a bottle with a teat for feeding infants. **feed up 1** fatten. **2** satiate (cf. *fed up* (see FED)). □□ **feedable** *adj.* [OE *fēdan* f. Gmc]

■ *v.* **1 a** supply, provision, cater *or* provide for, victual; maintain, board. **4** graze, pasture; see also EAT *v.* 1b; (*feed on*) see EAT *v.* 1a. **5** make grow, nurture; sustain; see also NOURISH 1. **6 a** maintain, fuel; stoke. **7** (*feed on*) **a** be nourished by, subsist *or* survive *or* depend on. **b** benefit from, thrive on *or* upon. **11** see PANDER *v.* **12** see ADVISE 3. ● *n.* **1** food; fodder, provender, forage, silage. **3** see MEAL[1]. **4** see PASTURE *n.* □ **feed up 2** see SATE 2.

feedback /fē′edbak/ *n.* **1** information about the result of an experiment etc.; response. **2** *Electronics* **a** the return of a fraction of the output signal from one stage of a circuit, amplifier, etc., to the input of the same or a preceding stage. **b** a signal so returned. **3** *Biol.* etc. the modification or control of a process or system by its results or effects, esp. by the difference between the desired and the actual result.

■ **1** see RESPONSE 1, INFORMATION 1.

feeder /fē′edər/ *n.* **1** a person or thing that feeds. **2** a person who eats in a specified manner. **3** a child's feeding-bottle. **4** *Brit.* a bib for an infant. **5** a tributary stream. **6** a branch road, railway line, etc., linking outlying districts with a main communication system. **7** *Electr.* a main carrying electricity to a distribution point. **8** a hopper or feeding apparatus in a machine.

■ **5** see TRIBUTARY *n.* **6** see *turn-off* 1.

feel /fēel/ *v.* & *n.* ● *v.* (*past* and *past part.* **felt** /felt/) **1** *tr.* **a** examine or search by touch. **b** (*absol.*) have the sensation of touch (*was unable to feel*). **2** *tr.* perceive or ascertain by touch; have a sensation of (*could feel the warmth*; *felt that it was cold*). **3** *tr.* **a** undergo, experience (*shall feel my anger*). **b** exhibit or be conscious of (an emotion, sensation, conviction, etc.). **4 a** *intr.* have a specified feeling or reaction (*felt strongly about it*). **b** *tr.* be emotionally affected by (*felt the rebuke deeply*). **5** *tr.* (foll. by *that* + clause) have a vague or unreasoned impression (*I feel that I am right*). **6** *tr.* consider, think (*I feel it useful to go*). **7** *intr.* seem; give an impression of being; be perceived as (*the air feels chilly*). **8** *intr.* be consciously; consider oneself (*I feel happy*; *do not feel well*). **9** *intr.* **a** (foll. by *with*) have sympathy with. **b** (foll. by *for*) have pity or compassion for. **10** *tr.* (often foll. by *up*) *sl.* fondle the genitals of. ● *n.* **1** the act or an instance of feeling; testing by touch. **2** the sensation characterizing a material, situation, etc. **3** the sense of touch. □ **feel free** (often foll. by *to* + infin.) not be reluctant or hesitant (*do feel free to criticize*). **feel like** have a wish for; be inclined towards. **feel one's oats** see OAT. **feel oneself** be fit or confident etc. **feel out** investigate cautiously. **feel strange** see STRANGE. **feel up to** be ready to face or deal with. **feel one's way** proceed carefully; act cautiously. **get the feel of** become accustomed to using. **make one's influence** (or **presence etc.**) **felt** assert one's influence; make others aware of one's presence etc. [OE *fēlan* f. WG]

■ *v.* **1 a** touch, handle, manipulate, finger. **2** perceive, note; see also SENSE *v.* **3 a** undergo. experience, suffer, bear, endure, withstand, stand, tolerate, go through. **b** sense, be conscious of, be aware *or* sensible of, experience. **5, 6** sense, believe, think, perceive, judge, consider, know, discern, intuit, have a (funny) feeling, get *or* have the impression, *archaic* trow, *colloq.* have a hunch, feel in one's bones, *formal* deem; see also THINK *v.* 2. **7** seem, appear; give an impression of being, strike one as, have a *or* the feeling of being. **8** seem to be, be, consider oneself, regard *or* characterize oneself as. **9** (*feel with* or *for*) have sympathy with *or* for, sympathize *or* empathize with, commiserate with, be sorry for, pity, have compassion for. **10** see FONDLE. ● *n.* **2** texture, touch, sensation; feeling, air, atmosphere, climate, ambience, sense, note, tone, quality. □ **feel like** have a wish for, want, desire, crave, *Brit. colloq.* fancy; be inclined to *or* towards. **get the feel of** see ACCUSTOM.

feeler /fē′elər/ *n.* **1** an organ in certain animals for testing things by touch or for searching for food. **2** a tentative proposal or suggestion, esp. to elicit a response (*put out feelers*). **3** a person or thing that feels. □ **feeler gauge** a gauge equipped with blades for measuring narrow gaps etc.

■ **1** antenna, tentacle, palp. **3** prober, tester; probe, sensor.

feeling /fē′eling/ *n.* & *adj.* ● *n.* **1 a** the capacity to feel; a sense of touch (*lost all feeling in his arm*). **b** a physical sensation. **2 a** (often foll. by *of*) a particular emotional reaction, an atmosphere (*a feeling of despair*). **b** (in *pl.*) emotional susceptibilities or sympathies (*hurt my feelings*; *had strong feelings about it*). **c** intense emotion (*said it with such feeling*). **3** a particular sensitivity (*had a feeling for literature*). **4 a** an opinion or notion, esp. a vague or irrational one (*my feelings on the subject*; *had a feeling she would be there*). **b** vague awareness (*had a feeling of safety*). **c** sentiment (*the general feeling was against it*). **5** readiness to feel sympathy or compassion. **6 a** the general emotional response produced by a work of art, piece of music, etc. **b** emotional commitment or sensibility in artistic execution (*played with feeling*). ● *adj.* **1** sensitive, sympathetic. **2** showing emotion or sensitivity. □□ **feelingless** *adj.* **feelingly** *adv.*

■ *n.* **1** sense of touch, sensibility, sensitivity, sensation, sense; feel. **2 a** feel, mood, atmosphere, climate, sense, air, ambience; see also EMOTION. **b** (*feelings*) susceptibilities, sympathies, emotions, sensibilities. **c** ardour, warmth, passion, fervency, fervour, ardency, intensity, heat, sentiment, emotion, vehemence. **3** sensitivity, appreciation, sympathy, empathy, identification, compassion, tenderness, concern, regard, understanding. **4 a** opinion, view; notion, idea, intuition, instinct, inkling, suspicion, belief, hunch, sense; premonition, presentiment, sense of foreboding, impression, sensation. **b** awareness, consciousness; see also IMPRESSION 1. **c** see ATTITUDE 1. **5, 6b** see SENSITIVITY. **6 a** see IMPRESSION 1. ● *adj.* **1** sensitive, sympathetic, tender-hearted, compassionate; see also TENDER[1] 5. **2** see DEMONSTRATIVE *adj.* 1, DELICATE 5, 6.

feet *pl.* of FOOT.

feign /fayn/ *v.* **1** *tr.* simulate; pretend to be affected by (*feign madness*). **2** *tr. archaic* invent (an excuse etc.). **3** *intr.* indulge in pretence. [ME f. *feign-* stem of OF *feindre* f. L *fingere* mould, contrive]
■ **1, 3** see DISSIMULATE.

feijoa /fayjṓə, fī-/ *n.* **1** any evergreen shrub or tree of the genus *Feijoa*, bearing edible guava-like fruit. **2** this fruit. [mod.L f. J. da Silva *Feijo*, 19th-c. Sp. naturalist]

feint[1] /faynt/ *n.* & *v.* ● *n.* **1** a sham attack or blow etc. to divert attention or fool an opponent or enemy. **2** pretence. ● *v.intr.* make a feint. [F *feinte*, fem. past part. of *feindre* FEIGN]
■ *n.* **1** sham *or* mock attack, distraction, diversion; see also MANOEUVRE *n.* 1, 3. **2** pretence, bluff, ruse, subterfuge, deception, gambit, artifice, *colloq.* ploy. ● *v.* see ATTACK *v.* 6, MANOEUVRE *v.* 3.

feint[2] /faynt/ *adj.* esp. *Printing* = FAINT *adj.* 6 (*feint lines*). [ME f. OF (as FEINT[1]): see FAINT]

feisty /fīsti/ *adj.* (**feistier, feistiest**) *US sl.* **1** aggressive, exuberant. **2** touchy. □□ **feistiness** *n.* [*feist* (= fist) small dog]

felafel /feláaf'l/ *n.* (also **falafel**) (in Near Eastern countries) a spicy dish of fried rissoles made from mashed chick peas or beans. [Arab. *falāfil*]

feldspar /féldspaar/ *n.* (also **felspar** /félspaar/) *Mineral.* any of a group of aluminium silicates of potassium, sodium, or calcium, which are the most abundant minerals in the earth's crust. □□ **feldspathic** /-spáthik/ *adj.* **feldspathoid** /féldspəthoyd, félspə-/ *n.* [G *Feldspat*, *-spath* f. *Feld* FIELD + *Spat*, *Spath* SPAR[3]: *felspar* by false assoc. with G *Fels* rock]

felicitate /fəlíssitayt/ *v.tr.* (usu. foll. by *on*) congratulate. □□ **felicitation** /-táysh'n/ *n.* (usu. in *pl.*). [LL *felicitare* make happy f. L *felix -icis* happy]
■ see COMPLIMENT *v.*

felicitous /fəlíssitəss/ *adj.* (of an expression, quotation, civilities, or a person making them) strikingly apt; pleasantly ingenious. □□ **felicitously** *adv.* **felicitousness** *n.*
■ see APPROPRIATE *adj.*

felicity /fəlíssiti/ *n.* (*pl.* **-ies**) **1** intense happiness; being happy. **2** a cause of happiness. **3 a** a capacity for apt expression; appropriateness. **b** an appropriate or well-chosen phrase. **4** a fortunate trait. [ME f. OF *felicité* f. L *felicitas -tatis* f. *felix -icis* happy]
■ **1** see *happiness* (HAPPY). **3 a** see *fitness* (FIT[1]).

feline /féelīn/ *adj.* & *n.* ● *adj.* **1** of or relating to the cat family. **2** catlike, esp. in beauty or slyness. ● *n.* an animal of the cat family Felidae. □□ **felinity** /filínniti/ *n.* [L *felinus* f. *feles* cat]

fell[1] *past* of FALL *v.*

fell[2] /fel/ *v.* & *n.* ● *v.tr.* **1** cut down (esp. a tree). **2** strike or knock down (a person or animal). **3** stitch down (the edge of a seam) to lie flat. ● *n.* an amount of timber cut. □□ **feller** *n.* [OE *fellan* f. Gmc, rel. to FALL]
■ *v.* **1** cut down, hew (down). **2** cut *or* knock *or* strike down, floor, prostrate, *colloq.* flatten.

fell[3] /fel/ *n. N.Engl.* **1** a hill. **2** a stretch of hills or moorland. [ME f. ON *fjall*, *fell* hill]

fell[4] /fel/ *adj. poet.* or *rhet.* **1** fierce, ruthless. **2** terrible, destructive. □ **at** (or **in**) **one fell swoop** in a single (orig. deadly) action. [ME f. OF *fel* f. Rmc FELON[1]]

fell[5] /fel/ *n.* an animal's hide or skin with its hair. [OE *fel*, *fell* f. Gmc]

fellah /féllə/ *n.* (*pl.* **fellahin** /-ləhéen/) an Egyptian peasant. [Arab. *fallāḥ* husbandman f. *falaḥa* till the soil]

fellatio /filáyshiō, feláatiō/ *n.* oral stimulation of the penis. □□ **fellate** /filáyt/ *v.tr.* **fellator** /filáytər/ *n.* [mod.L f. L *fellare* suck]

feller /féllər/ *n.* = FELLOW 1, 2. [repr. an affected or sl. pronunc.]

felloe /féllō/ *n.* (also **felly** /félli/) (*pl.* **-oes** or **-ies**) the outer circle (or a section of it) of a wheel, to which the spokes are fixed. [OE *felg*, of unkn. orig.]

fellow /féllō/ *n.* **1** *colloq.* a man or boy (*poor fellow!*; *my dear fellow*). **2** *derog.* a person regarded with contempt. **3** (usu. in *pl.*) a person associated with another; a comrade (*were separated from their fellows*). **4** a counterpart or match; the other of a pair. **5** an equal; one of the same class. **6** a contemporary. **7 a** an incorporated senior member of a college. **b** an elected graduate receiving a stipend for a period of research. **c** a member of the governing body in some universities. **8** a member of a learned society. **9** (*attrib.*) belonging to the same class or activity (*fellow soldier*; *fellow-countryman*). □ **fellow-feeling** sympathy from common experience. **fellow-traveller 1** a person who travels with another. **2** a sympathizer with, or a secret member of, the Communist Party. [OE *fēolaga* f. ON *félagi* f. *fé* cattle, property, money: see LAY[1]]
■ **1** man, boy, gentleman, person, individual, *archaic* wight, *colloq.* guy, chap, *sl.* geezer, *Brit. sl.* bloke, *sl. often derog.* gink. **2** *sl.* bastard, jerk, git, son of a bitch, *sl. often derog.* gink; see also WRETCH 2. **3** associate, companion, colleague, ally; see also COMRADE. **4** counterpart, match, complement, mate, partner. **5** see EQUAL *n.* **6** contemporary, peer, compeer. **9** associate(d), affiliate(d), allied, related; co-, joint.

fellowship /féllōship/ *n.* **1** companionship, friendliness. **2** participation, sharing; community of interest. **3** a body of associates; a company. **4** a brotherhood or fraternity. **5** a guild or corporation. **6** the status or emoluments of a fellow of a college or society.
■ **1** companionship, friendship, amity, comradeship, brotherhood, fraternization, association; friendliness, amicability, sociability, companionability, camaraderie, affability, kindliness, cordiality, congeniality, warmth, hospitality, familiarity, affinity, intimacy, togetherness. **2** see RAPPORT. **3–5** company, circle, community, order, organization, society, club, association, alliance, guild, corporation, league, union, sisterhood, brotherhood, fraternity, *US* sorority, clan; see also ASSOCIATION 1.

felly var. of FELLOE.

felon[1] /féllən/ *n.* & *adj.* ● *n.* a person who has committed a felony. ● *adj. archaic* cruel, wicked. □□ **felonry** *n.* [ME f. OF f. med.L *felo -onis*, of unkn. orig.]
■ *n.* criminal, outlaw, lawbreaker, offender, miscreant, malefactor, wrongdoer. ● *adj.* see WICKED 1, 2.

felon[2] /féllən/ *n.* an inflammatory sore on the finger near the nail. [ME, perh. as FELON[1]: cf. med.L *felo*, *fello* in the same sense]

felonious /filṓniəss/ *adj.* **1** criminal. **2** *Law* **a** of or involving felony. **b** who has committed felony. □□ **feloniously** *adv.*
■ **1, 2a** see ILLEGAL 2. **2 b** see MISCREANT *adj.*

felony /félləni/ *n.* (*pl.* **-ies**) a crime regarded by the law as grave, and usu. involving violence. [ME f. OF *felonie* (as FELON[1])]
■ see CRIME 1a.

felspar var. of FELDSPAR.

felt[1] /felt/ *n.* & *v.* ● *n.* **1** a kind of cloth made by rolling and pressing wool etc., or by weaving and shrinking it. **2** a similar material made from other fibres. ● *v.* **1** *tr.* make into felt; mat together. **2** *tr.* cover with felt. **3** *intr.* become matted. □ **felt-tipped** (or **felt-tip**) **pen** a pen with a writing-point made of felt or fibre. □□ **felty** *adj.* [OE f. WG]

felt[2] *past* and *past part.* of FEEL.

felucca /filúkkə/ *n.* a small Mediterranean coasting vessel with oars or lateen sails or both. [It. *felucca* f. obs. Sp. *faluca* f. Arab. *fulk*, perh. f. Gk *epholkion* sloop]

felwort /félwurt/ *n.* a purple-flowered gentian, *Gentianella amarella*. [OE *feldwyrt* (as FIELD, WORT)]

female /féemayl/ *adj.* & *n.* ● *adj.* **1** of the sex that can bear offspring or produce eggs. **2** (of plants or their parts) fruit-bearing; having a pistil and no stamens. **3** of or consisting of women or female animals or female plants. **4** (of a screw, socket, etc.) manufactured hollow to receive a corresponding inserted part. ● *n.* a female person, animal, or plant. □ **female impersonator** a male performer impersonating a woman. □□ **femaleness** *n.* [ME f. OF *femelle* (n.) f. L *femella* dimin. of *femina* a woman, assim. to *male*]
■ *n.* see WOMAN 1.

feme /feem/ *n. Law* a woman or wife. □ **feme covert** a married woman. **feme sole** a woman without a husband (esp. if divorced). [ME f. AF & OF f. L *femina* woman]

feminal /fémmin'l/ *adj. archaic* womanly. □□ **feminality** /-nálliti/ *n.* [med.L *feminalis* f. L *femina* woman]

femineity /fémminée-iti/ *n. archaic* womanliness; womanishness. [L *femineus* womanish f. *femina* woman]

feminine /fémminin/ *adj.* & *n.* ● *adj.* **1** of or characteristic of women. **2** having qualities associated with women. **3** womanly, effeminate. **4** *Gram.* of or denoting the gender proper to women's names. ● *n. Gram.* a feminine gender or word. □□ **femininely** *adv.* **feminineness** *n.* **femininity** /-nínniti/ *n.* [ME f. OF *feminin -ine* or L *femininus* f. *femina* woman]
■ *adj.* **1** female, womanlike, womanly, ladylike, *archaic* feminal. **3** effeminate, unmanly, unmasculine, effete, *colloq.* sissy, sissified, *usu. derog.* womanish.

feminism /fémminiz'm/ *n.* **1** the advocacy of women's rights on the ground of the equality of the sexes. **2** *Med.* the development of female characteristics in a male person. □□ **feminist** *n.* (in sense 1). [L *femina* woman (in sense 1 after F *féminisme*)]

feminity /feminniti/ *n.* = FEMININITY (see FEMININE). [ME f. OF *feminité* f. med.L *feminitas -tatis* f. L *femina* woman]

feminize /fémmintz/ *v.tr.* & *intr.* (also **-ise**) make or become feminine or female. □□ **feminization** /-záysh'n/ *n.*

femme fatale /fám fataál/ *n.* (*pl.* ***femmes fatales*** *pronunc.* same) a seductively attractive woman. [F]
■ see SIREN 4a.

femto- /fémtō/ *comb. form* denoting a factor of 10^{-15} (*femtometre*). [Da. or Norw. *femten* fifteen]

femur /féemər/ *n.* (*pl.* **femurs** or **femora** /fémmərə/) **1** *Anat.* the thigh-bone, the thick bone between the hip and the knee. **2** the corresponding part of an insect. □□ **femoral** /fémmərəl/ *adj.* [L *femur femoris* thigh]

fen /fen/ *n.* **1** a low marshy or flooded area of land. **2** (**the Fens**) flat low-lying areas in and around Cambridgeshire. □ **fen-berry** (*pl.* **-berries**) a cranberry. **fen-fire** will-o'-the-wisp. □□ **fenny** *adj.* [OE *fenn* f. Gmc]
■ **1** see MARSH.

fence /fenss/ *n.* & *v.* ● *n.* **1** a barrier or railing or other upright structure enclosing an area of ground, esp. to prevent or control access. **2** a large upright obstacle in steeplechasing or showjumping. **3** *sl.* a receiver of stolen goods. **4** a guard or guide in machinery. ● *v.* **1** *tr.* surround with or as with a fence. **2** *tr.* **a** (foll. by *in*, *off*) enclose or separate with or as with a fence. **b** (foll. by *up*) seal with or as with a fence. **3** *tr.* (foll. by *from*, *against*) screen, shield, protect. **4** *tr.* (foll. by *out*) exclude with or as with a fence; keep out. **5** *tr.* (also *absol.*) *sl.* deal in (stolen goods). **6** *intr.* practise the sport of fencing; use a sword. **7** *intr.* (foll. by *with*) evade answering (a person or question). **8** *intr.* (of a horse etc.) leap fences. □ **sit on the fence** remain neutral or undecided in a dispute etc. □□ **fenceless** *adj.* **fencer** *n.* [ME f. DEFENCE]
■ *n.* **1** barrier, railing, palisade, enclosure, barricade; confine, wall, rampart. **2** see JUMP *n.* 4. **4** shield, guard, safeguard, screen, cover; guide. ● *v.* **1** surround, enclose, encircle, circumscribe, hedge, bound. **2 a** enclose, separate, coop (up *or* in), confine, hedge in. **b** (*fence up*) see *close off* (CLOSE[2]). **3** see SHIELD *v.* **4** (*fence out*) see *shut out* 1. **5** see DEAL[1] *v.* 2. **7** hedge; (*fence with*) parry, avoid, fend off, sidestep, dodge, evade; see also DUCK[2] *v.* 3. **8** see JUMP *v.* 1, 2. □ **sit on the fence** remain neutral *or* undecided *or* indecisive *or* uncommitted *or* uncertain *or* irresolute *or* impartial *or* unaligned *or* non-aligned *or* independent; vacillate.

fencible /fénsib'l/ *n. hist.* a soldier liable only for home service. [ME f. DEFENSIBLE]

fencing /fénsing/ *n.* **1** a set or extent of fences. **2** material for making fences. **3** the art or sport of swordplay.

fend /fend/ *v.* **1** *intr.* (foll. by *for*) look after (esp. oneself). **2** *tr.* (usu. foll. by *off*) keep away; ward off (an attack etc.). [ME f. DEFEND]
■ **1** (*fend for oneself*) look after oneself, get along (on one's own), make do, shift for oneself, *colloq.* get by, take care of oneself. **2** (*fend off*) keep away, keep *or* hold at bay, stave *or* ward *or* fight off, parry, resist, repel, deflect.

fender /féndər/ *n.* **1** a low frame bordering a fireplace to keep in falling coals etc. **2** *Naut.* a piece of old cable, matting, etc., hung over a vessel's side to protect it against impact. **3 a** a thing used to keep something off, prevent a collision, etc. **b** *US* a wing or mudguard of a motor vehicle.

fenestella /fénnistéllə/ *n. Archit.* a niche in a wall south of an altar, holding the piscina and often the credence. [L, dimin. of *fenestra* window]

fenestra /finéstrə/ *n.* (*pl.* **fenestrae** /-tree/) **1** *Anat.* a small hole or opening in a bone etc., esp. one of two (**fenestra ovalis, fenestra rotunda**) in the inner ear. **2** a perforation in a surgical instrument. **3** a hole made by surgical fenestration. [L, = window]

fenestrate /finéstrayt/ *adj. Bot.* & *Zool.* having small window-like perforations or transparent areas. [L *fenestratus* past part. of *fenestrare* f. *fenestra* window]

fenestrated /finéstraytid/ *adj.* **1** *Archit.* having windows. **2** perforated. **3** = FENESTRATE. **4** *Surgery* having fenestrae.

fenestration /fénnistráysh'n/ *n.* **1** *Archit.* the arrangement of windows in a building. **2** *Bot.* & *Zool.* being fenestrate. **3** a surgical operation in which a new opening is formed, esp. in the bony labyrinth of the inner ear, as a form of treatment in some cases of deafness.

Fenian /féeniən/ *n.* & *adj.* ● *n. hist.* a member of a 19th-c. league among the Irish in the US & Ireland for promoting revolution and overthrowing British government in Ireland. ● *adj.* of or relating to the Fenians. □□ **Fenianism** *n.* [OIr. *féne* name of an ancient Irish people, confused with *fiann* guard of legendary kings]

fennec /fénnik/ *n.* a small fox, *Vulpes zerda*, native to N. Africa, having large pointed ears. [Arab. *fanak*]

fennel /fénn'l/ *n.* **1** a yellow-flowered fragrant umbelliferous plant, *Foeniculum vulgare*, with leaves or leaf-stalks used in salads, soups, etc. **2** the seeds of this used as flavouring. [OE *finugl* etc. & OF *fenoil* f. L *feniculum* f. *fenum* hay]

fenugreek /fényoogreek/ *n.* **1** a leguminous plant, *Trigonella foenum-graecum*, having aromatic seeds. **2** these seeds used as flavouring, esp. ground and used in curry powder. [OE *fenogrecum*, superseded in ME f. OF *fenugrec* f. L *faenugraecum* (*fenum graecum* Greek hay), used by the Romans as fodder]

feoffment /féfmənt, féef-/ *n. hist.* a mode of conveying a freehold estate by a formal transfer of possession. □□ **feoffee** /feféé/ *n.* **feoffor** *n.* [ME f. AF *feoffement*, rel. to FEE]

feral /féerəl, férrəl/ *adj.* **1** (of an animal or plant) wild, untamed, uncultivated. **2 a** (of an animal) in a wild state after escape from captivity. **b** born in the wild of such an animal. **3** brutal. [L *ferus* wild]
■ **1, 2a** see WILD *adj.* 1. **3** see VICIOUS 1.

fer de lance /fáir də laánss/ *n.* a large highly venomous snake, *Bothrops atrox*, native to Central and S. America. [F, = iron (head) of a lance]

feretory /férritəri/ *n.* (*pl.* **-ies**) **1** a shrine for a saint's relics. **2** a chapel containing such a shrine. [ME f. OF *fiertre* f. L *feretrum* f. Gk *pheretron* f. *pherō* bear]

ferial /féeriəl, férriəl/ *adj. Eccl.* **1** (of a day) ordinary; not appointed for a festival or fast. **2** (of a service etc.) for use on a ferial day. [ME f. OF *ferial* or med.L *ferialis* f. L *feriae*: see FAIR²]

fermata /fərmaátə/ *n.* (*pl.* **fermatas**) *Mus.* **1** an unspecified prolongation of a note or rest. **2** a sign indicating this. [It.]

ferment *n.* & *v.* ● *n.* /férment/ **1** agitation, excitement, tumult. **2 a** fermenting, fermentation. **b** a fermenting-agent or leaven. ● *v.* /fərmént/ **1** *intr.* & *tr.* undergo or subject to fermentation. **2** *intr.* & *tr.* effervesce or cause to effervesce. **3** *tr.* excite; stir up; foment. □□ **fermentable** /-méntəb'l/ *adj.* **fermenter** /-méntər/ *n.* [ME f. OF *ferment* or L *fermentum* f. L *fervēre* boil]
■ *n.* **1** see AGITATION 1. ● *v.* **1** leaven, brew; stir up, simmer, seethe. **2** effervesce, bubble, foam, froth; boil, seethe. **3** excite, agitate, inflame, rouse; stir up, foment, incite, instigate, provoke.

fermentation /férmentáysh'n/ *n.* **1** the breakdown of a substance by micro-organisms, such as yeasts and bacteria, usu. in the absence of oxygen, esp. of sugar to ethyl alcohol in making beers, wines, and spirits. **2** agitation, excitement. □□ **fermentative** /-méntətiv/ *adj.* [ME f. LL *fermentatio* (as FERMENT)]

fermi /férmi/ *n.* (*pl.* **fermis**) a unit of length equal to 10^{-15} metre, formerly used in nuclear physics. [E. *Fermi*, Ital.-Amer. physicist d. 1954]

fermion /férmion/ *n. Physics* any of several elementary particles with half-integral spin, e.g. nucleons (cf. BOSON). [as FERMI + -ON]

fermium /férmiəm/ *n. Chem.* a transuranic radioactive metallic element produced artificially. ¶ Symb.: **Fm**. [as FERMI + -IUM]

fern /fern/ *n.* (*pl.* same or **ferns**) any flowerless plant of the order Filicales, reproducing by spores and usu. having feathery fronds. □□ **fernery** *n.* (*pl.* **-ies**). **fernless** *adj.* **ferny** *adj.* [OE *fearn* f. WG]

ferocious /fərṓshəss/ *adj.* fierce, savage; wildly cruel. □□ **ferociously** *adv.* **ferociousness** *n.* [L *ferox -ocis*]
■ fierce, savage, wild, feral, cruel, vicious, brutal, bestial, merciless, ruthless, pitiless, inhuman, barbaric, barbarous, violent, destructive, murderous, bloodthirsty, sanguinary, predatory, fiendish, diabolic, devilish, hellish, monstrous, *poet. or rhet.* fell.

ferocity /fəróssiti/ *n.* (*pl.* **-ies**) a ferocious nature or act. [F *férocité* or L *ferocitas* (as FEROCIOUS)]
■ see VIOLENCE 1.

-ferous /fərəss/ *comb. form* (usu. **-iferous**) forming adjectives with the sense 'bearing', 'having' (*auriferous*; *odoriferous*). □□ **-ferously** *suffix* forming adverbs. **-ferousness** *suffix* forming nouns. [from or after F *-fère* or L *-fer* producing f. *ferre* bear]

ferrate /férrayt/ *n. Chem.* a salt of (the hypothetical) ferric acid. [L *ferrum* iron]

ferrel var. of FERRULE.

ferret /férrit/ *n.* & *v.* ● *n.* **1** a small half-domesticated polecat, *Mustela putorius furo*, used in catching rabbits, rats, etc. **2** a person who searches assiduously. ● *v.* **1** *intr.* hunt with ferrets. **2** *intr.* rummage; search about. **3** *tr.* (often foll. by *about*, *away*, *out*, etc.) **a** clear out (holes or an area of ground) with ferrets. **b** take or drive away (rabbits etc.) with ferrets. **4** *tr.* (foll. by *out*) search out (secrets, criminals, etc.). □□ **ferreter** *n.* **ferrety** *adj.* [ME f. OF *fu(i)ret* alt. f. *fu(i)ron* f. LL *furo -onis* f. L *fur* thief]

ferri- /férri/ *comb. form Chem.* containing iron, esp. in ferric compounds. [L *ferrum* iron]

ferriage /férri-ij/ *n.* **1** conveyance by ferry. **2** a charge for using a ferry.

ferric /férrik/ *adj.* **1** of iron. **2** *Chem.* containing iron in a trivalent form (cf. FERROUS).

ferrimagnetism /férrimágnitiz'm/ *n. Physics* a form of ferromagnetism with non-parallel alignment of neighbouring atoms or ions. □□ **ferrimagnetic** /-magnéttik/ *adj.* [F *ferrimagnétisme* (as FERRI-, MAGNETISM)]

Ferris wheel /férriss/ *n.* a fairground ride consisting of a tall revolving vertical wheel with passenger cars suspended on its outer edge. [G. W. G. *Ferris*, Amer. engineer d. 1896]

ferrite /férrīt/ *n. Chem.* **1** a salt of (the hypothetical) ferrous acid $H_2Fe_2O_4$, often with magnetic properties. **2** an allotrope of pure iron occurring in low-carbon steel. □□ **ferritic** /ferríttik/ *adj.* [L *ferrum* iron]

ferro- /férrō/ *comb. form Chem.* **1** iron, esp. in ferrous compounds (*ferrocyanide*). **2** (of alloys) containing iron (*ferromanganese*). [L *ferrum* iron]

ferroconcrete /férrōkónkreet/ *n.* & *adj.* ● *n.* concrete reinforced with steel. ● *adj.* made of reinforced concrete.

ferroelectric /férrō-iléktrik/ *adj.* & *n. Physics* ● *adj.* exhibiting permanent electric polarization which varies in strength with the applied electric field. ● *n.* a ferroelectric substance. □□ **ferroelectricity** /-trissiti/ *n.* [ELECTRIC after *ferromagnetic*]

ferromagnetism /férrōmágnitiz'm/ *n. Physics* a phenomenon in which there is a high susceptibility to magnetization, the strength of which varies with the applied magnetizing field, and which may persist after removal of the applied field. □□ **ferromagnetic** /-magnéttik/ *adj.*

ferrous /férrəss/ *adj.* **1** containing iron (*ferrous and non-ferrous metals*). **2** *Chem.* containing iron in a divalent form (cf. FERRIC). [L *ferrum* iron]

ferruginous /fəróōjinəss/ *adj.* **1** of or containing iron-rust, or iron as a chemical constituent. **2** rust-coloured; reddish-brown. [L *ferrugo -ginis* rust f. *ferrum* iron]

ferrule /férrōōl/ *n.* (also **ferrel** /férrəl/) **1** a ring or cap strengthening the end of a stick or tube. **2** a band strengthening or forming a joint. [earlier *verrel* etc. f. OF *virelle*, *virol(e)*, f. L *viriola* dimin. of *viriae* bracelet: assim. to L *ferrum* iron]

ferry /férri/ *n.* & *v.* ● *n.* (*pl.* **-ies**) **1** a boat or aircraft etc. for conveying passengers and goods, esp. across water and as a regular service. **2** the service itself or the place where it operates. ● *v.* (**-ies, -ied**) **1** *tr.* & *intr.* convey or go in a boat etc. across water. **2** *intr.* (of a boat etc.) pass to and fro across water. **3** *tr.* transport from one place to another, esp. as a regular service. □□ **ferryman** *n.* (*pl.* **-men**). [ME f. ON *ferja* f. Gmc]
■ *v.* **3** see SHIP *v.* 1, 4.

fertile /fértīl/ *adj.* **1 a** (of soil) producing abundant vegetation or crops. **b** fruitful. **2 a** (of a seed, egg, etc.) capable of becoming a new individual. **b** (of animals and plants) able to conceive young or produce fruit. **3** (of the mind) inventive. **4** (of nuclear material) able to become fissile by the capture of neutrons. □ **Fertile Crescent** the fertile region extending in a crescent shape from the E. Mediterranean to the Persian Gulf. □□ **fertility** /-tílliti/ *n.* [ME f. F f. L *fertilis*]
■ **1** productive, fructuous; see also FRUITFUL 1. **2 b** fecund; productive, prolific. **3** inventive, fecund, generative, luxuriant, teeming, prolific, rich.

fertilization /fértilīzáysh'n/ *n.* (also **-isation**) **1** *Biol.* the fusion of male and female gametes during sexual reproduction to form a zygote. **2 a** the act or an instance of fertilizing. **b** the process of being fertilized.

fertilize /fértilīz/ *v.tr.* (also **-ise**) **1** make (soil etc.) fertile or productive. **2** cause (an egg, female animal, or plant) to develop a new individual by introducing male reproductive material. □□ **fertilizable** *adj.*
■ **1** manure, mulch, feed, nourish, enrich, dress, compost. **2** impregnate, inseminate, fecundate, fructify, pollinate.

fertilizer /fértilīzər/ *n.* a chemical or natural substance added to soil to make it more fertile.

ferula /féryoolə/ *n.* **1** any plant of the genus *Ferula*, esp. the giant fennel (*F. communis*), having a tall sticklike stem and thick roots. **2** = FERULE. [ME f. L, = giant fennel, rod]

ferule /férrool/ *n.* & *v.* ● *n.* a flat ruler with a widened end formerly used for beating children. ● *v.tr.* beat with a ferule. [ME (as FERULA)]

fervent /férv'nt/ *adj.* **1** ardent, impassioned, intense (*fervent admirer*; *fervent hatred*). **2** hot, glowing. □□ **fervency** *n.* **fervently** *adv.* [ME f. OF f. L *fervēre* boil]
■ **1** ardent, eager, earnest, enthusiastic, zealous, animated, intense, impassioned, passionate, emotional, fervid, fiery, hotheaded, fanatical, fanatic; ecstatic, rapturous, rapt, heartfelt. **2** hot, glowing, inflamed, burning, *poet.* fervid.

fervid /férvid/ *adj.* **1** ardent, intense. **2** *poet.* hot, glowing. □□ **fervidly** *adv.* [L *fervidus* (as FERVENT)]
■ **1** see *on fire* 2 (FIRE). **2** see INCANDESCENT.

fervour /férvər/ *n.* (*US* **fervor**) **1** vehemence, passion, zeal. **2** a glowing condition; intense heat. [ME f. OF f. L *fervor -oris* (as FERVENT)]
■ **1** vehemence, passion, zeal, fervency, ardour, eagerness, earnestness, enthusiasm, animation, glow, gusto, ebullience, spirit, verve, intensity, warmth. **2** see *incandescence* (INCANDESCENT).

fescue /féskyoo/ *n.* any grass of the genus *Festuca*, valuable for pasture and fodder. [ME *festu(e)* f. OF *festu* ult. f. L *festuca* stalk, straw]

fess /fess/ *n.* (also **fesse**) *Heraldry* a horizontal stripe across the middle of a shield. □ **fess point** a point at the centre of a shield. **in fess** arranged horizontally. [ME f. OF f. L *fascia* band]

festal /fést'l/ *adj.* **1** joyous, merry. **2** engaging in holiday activities. **3** of a feast. □□ **festally** *adv.* [OF f. LL *festalis* (as FEAST)]

fester /féstər/ *v.* **1** *tr.* & *intr.* make or become septic. **2** *intr.* cause continuing annoyance. **3** *intr.* rot, stagnate. [ME f. obs. *fester* (n.) or OF *festrir*, f. OF *festre* f. L *fistula*: see FISTULA]
■ **1** suppurate, decompose; see also ROT *v.* 1a. **2** see RANKLE 1. **3** putrefy, necrose, mortify, rot, decay, decompose; stagnate.

festival /féstiv'l/ *n.* & *adj.* ● *n.* **1** a day or period of celebration, religious or secular. **2** a concentrated series of concerts, plays, etc., held regularly in a town etc. (*Bath Festival*). ● *attrib.adj.* of or concerning a festival. [earlier as adj.: ME f. OF f. med.L *festivalis* (as FESTIVE)]
■ *n.* **1** holiday, holy day, fête, *fête champêtre*, fiesta, feast, anniversary, entertainment, carnival, red-letter day, gala (day), event.

festive /féstiv/ *adj.* **1** of or characteristic of a festival. **2** joyous. **3** fond of feasting, jovial. □□ **festively** *adv.* **festiveness** *n.* [L *festivus* f. *festum* (as FEAST)]
■ **1** see GALA *adj.* 1. **2** see JOLLY[1] *adj.* 1, 2.

festivity /festívviti/ *n.* (*pl.* **-ies**) **1** gaiety, rejoicing. **2 a** a festive celebration. **b** (in *pl.*) festive proceedings. [ME f. OF *festivité* or L *festivitas* (as FESTIVE)]
■ **1** gaiety, rejoicing, mirth, jubilation, conviviality, merriment, revelry, merrymaking, glee, jollity, jollification, felicity, joyfulness. **2** festival, party, fun and games, entertainment; see also *celebration* (CELEBRATE).

festoon /festoón/ *n.* & *v.* ● *n.* **1** a chain of flowers, leaves, ribbons, etc., hung in a curve as a decoration. **2** a carved or moulded ornament representing this. ● *v.tr.* (often foll. by *with*) adorn with or form into festoons; decorate elaborately. □□ **festoonery** *n.* [F *feston* f. It. *festone* f. *festa* FEAST]
■ *n.* **1** see GARLAND *n.* 1. ● *v.* see GARLAND *v.*

Festschrift /féstshrift/ *n.* (also **festschrift**) (*pl.* **-schriften** or **-schrifts**) a collection of writings published in honour of a scholar. [G f. *Fest* celebration + *Schrift* writing]

feta /féttə/ *n.* (also **fetta**) a soft white ewe's-milk or goat's-milk cheese made esp. in Greece. [mod.Gk *pheta*]

fetch[1] /fech/ *v.* & *n.* ● *v.tr.* **1** go for and bring back (a person or thing) (*fetch a doctor*). **2** be sold for; realize (a price) (*fetched £10*). **3** cause (blood, tears, etc.) to flow. **4** draw (breath), heave (a sigh). **5** *colloq.* give (a blow, slap, etc.) (usu. with recipient stated: *fetched him a slap on the face*). **6** excite the emotions of, delight or irritate. ● *n.* **1** an act of fetching. **2** a dodge or trick. **3** *Naut.* **a** the distance travelled by wind or waves across open water. **b** the distance a vessel must sail to reach open water. □ **fetch and carry** run backwards and forwards with things, be a mere servant. **fetch up** *colloq.* **1** arrive, come to rest. **2** vomit. □□ **fetcher** *n.* [OE *fecc(e)an* var. of *fetian*, prob. rel. to a Gmc root = grasp]
■ *v.* **1** go for *or* after, get, bring (back), retrieve, obtain; summon, call, bring *or* draw forth. **2** sell for, go for, bring in, yield, earn, make. ● *n.* **2** see DODGE *n.* **3** reach; stretch, extent; see also RANGE *n.* 1a–c.

fetch[2] /fech/ *n.* a person's wraith or double. [18th c.: orig. unkn.]

fetching /féching/ *adj.* attractive. □□ **fetchingly** *adv.*
■ attractive, alluring, taking, winsome, winning, *colloq. esp. US* cute.

fête /fayt/ *n.* & *v.* ● *n.* **1** an outdoor function with the sale of goods, amusements, etc., esp. to raise funds for charity. **2** a great entertainment; a festival. **3** a saint's day. ● *v.tr.* honour or entertain lavishly. [F *fête* (as FEAST)]
■ *n.* **2** entertainment, celebration, party, frolic, festivities, reception, *colloq.* get-together, social, *archaic or US* levee, *colloq.* shindig, *sl.* bash, blast, do, *sl. esp. US* wingding; festival, jamboree, carnival. ● *v.* honour, celebrate, lionize, make a fuss of *or* over, kill the fatted calf for, roll *or* bring out the red carpet for; entertain.

fête champêtre /fáyt shoNpáytrə/ *n.* an outdoor entertainment; a rural festival. [F (as FÊTE, *champêtre* rural)]

fetid /féttid, féetid/ *adj.* (also **foetid**) stinking. □□ **fetidly** *adv.* **fetidness** *n.* [L *fetidus* f. *fetēre* stink]
■ see STINKING *adj.* 1.

fetish /féttish/ *n.* **1** *Psychol.* a thing abnormally stimulating or attracting sexual desire. **2 a** an inanimate object worshipped by primitive peoples for its supposed inherent magical powers or as being inhabited by a spirit. **b** a thing evoking irrational devotion or respect. □□ **fetishism** *n.* **fetishist** *n.* **fetishistic** /-shístik/ *adj.* [F *fétiche* f. Port. *feitiço* charm: orig. adj. = made by art, f. L *factitius* FACTITIOUS]
■ **2 a** charm, amulet, talisman, totem, periapt. **b** obsession, mania, compulsion, fixation, *idée fixe*.

fetlock /fétlok/ *n.* part of the back of a horse's leg above the hoof where a tuft of hair grows. [ME *fetlak* etc. rel. to G *Fessel* fetlock f. Gmc]

fetor /féetər/ *n.* a stench. [L (as FETID)]

fetta var. of FETA.

fetter /féttər/ *n.* & *v.* ● *n.* **1 a** a shackle for holding a prisoner by the ankles. **b** any shackle or bond. **2** (in *pl.*) captivity. **3** a restraint or check. ● *v.tr.* **1** put into fetters. **2** restrict, restrain, impede. [OE *feter* f. Gmc]
■ *n.* **1, 3** see TETHER *n.* ● *v.* see CHAIN *v.*

fetterlock /féttərlok/ *n.* **1** a D-shaped fetter for tethering a horse by the leg. **2** a heraldic representation of this.

fettle /fétt'l/ *n.* & *v.* ● *n.* condition or trim (*in fine fettle*). ● *v.tr.* trim or clean (the rough edge of a metal casting, pottery before firing, etc.). [earlier as verb, f. dial. *fettle* (n.) = girdle, f. OE *fetel* f. Gmc]
■ *n.* see CONDITION *n.* 2a.

fettler /fétlər/ *n.* **1** *Brit.* & *Austral.* a railway maintenance worker. **2** a person who fettles.

fetus *US* var. of FOETUS.

feu /fyoo/ *n.* & *v. Sc.* ● *n.* **1** a perpetual lease at a fixed rent. **2** a piece of land so held. ● *v.tr.* (**feus, feued, feuing**) grant (land) on feu. [OF: see FEE]

feud[1] /fyood/ *n.* & *v.* ● *n.* **1** prolonged mutual hostility, esp. between two families, tribes, etc., with murderous assaults in revenge for a previous injury (*a family feud*; *be at feud with*). **2** a prolonged or bitter quarrel or dispute. ● *v.intr.* conduct a feud. [ME *fede* f. OF *feide*, *fede* f. MDu., MLG *vēde* f. Gmc, rel. to FOE]
■ *n.* **1** vendetta, blood feud. **2** quarrel, dispute,

disagreement, argument, squabble, falling out. ● *v.* quarrel, fall out, dispute, disagree, clash, conflict, fight, be at odds, be at daggers drawn, *colloq.* row.

feud[2] /fyōōd/ *n.* a piece of land held under the feudal system or in fee; a fief. [med.L *feudum*: see FEE]

feudal /fyōōd'l/ *adj.* **1** of, according to, or resembling the feudal system. **2** of a feud or fief. **3** outdated (*had a feudal attitude*). □ **feudal system** the social system in medieval Europe whereby a vassal held land from a superior in exchange for allegiance and service. □□ **feudalism** *n.* **feudalist** *n.* **feudalistic** /-dəlístik/ *adj.* **feudalize** *v.tr.* (also **-ise**). **feudalization** /-dəlīzáysh'n/ *n.* **feudally** *adv.* [med.L *feudalis, feodalis* f. *feudum, feodum* FEE, perh. f. Gmc]

feudality /fyoodálliti/ *n.* (*pl.* **-ies**) **1** the feudal system or its principles. **2** a feudal holding, a fief. [F *féodalité* f. *féodal* (as FEUDAL)]

feudatory /fyōōdətəri/ *adj.* & *n.* ● *adj.* (often foll. by *to*) feudally subject, under overlordship. ● *n.* (*pl.* **-ies**) a feudal vassal. [med.L *feudatorius* f. *feudare* enfeoff (as FEUD[2])]

feu de joie /fō də zhwaá/ *n.* (*pl.* ***feux*** *pronunc.* same) a salute by firing rifles etc. on a ceremonial occasion. [F, = fire of joy]

feudist /fyōōdist/ *n.* *US* a person who is conducting a feud.

feuilleton /fō-itóɴ/ *n.* **1** a part of a newspaper etc. devoted to fiction, criticism, light literature, etc. **2** an item printed in this. [F, = leaflet]

fever /féevər/ *n.* & *v.* ● *n.* **1 a** an abnormally high body temperature, often with delirium etc. **b** a disease characterized by this (*scarlet fever*; *typhoid fever*). **2** nervous excitement; agitation. ● *v.tr.* (esp. as **fevered** *adj.*) affect with fever or excitement. □ **fever pitch** a state of extreme excitement. [OE *fēfor* & AF *fevre*, OF *fievre* f. L *febris*]

■ *n.* **2** see FRENZY *n.* 1. ● *v.* (**fevered**) see IMPASSIONED.

feverfew /féevərfyōō/ *n.* an aromatic bushy plant, *Tenacetum parthenium*, with feathery leaves and white daisy-like flowers, formerly used to reduce fever. [OE *feferfuge* f. L *febrifuga* (as FEBRIFUGE)]

feverish /féevərish/ *adj.* **1** having the symptoms of a fever. **2** excited, fitful, restless. **3** (of a place) infested by fever; feverous. □□ **feverishly** *adv.* **feverishness** *n.*

■ **1** flushed, hot; febrile, pyretic, *Med.* pyrexic. **2** excited, frenzied, frantic, frenetic; fitful, restless; ardent, fervent, passionate, burning, fiery, heated, hot, inflamed; flushed, hot-blooded.

feverous /féevərəss/ *adj.* **1** infested with or apt to cause fever. **2** *archaic* feverish.

few /fyōō/ *adj.* & *n.* ● *adj.* not many (*few doctors smoke*; *visitors are few*). ● *n.* (as *pl.*) **1** (prec. by *a*) some but not many (*a few words should be added*; *a few of his friends were there*). **2** a small number, not many (*many are called but few are chosen*). **3** (prec. by *the*) **a** the minority. **b** the elect. **4** (**the Few**) *colloq.* the RAF pilots who took part in the Battle of Britain. □ **every few** once in every small group of (*every few days*). **few and far between** scarce. **a good few** *colloq.* a fairly large number. **have a few** *colloq.* take several alcoholic drinks. **no fewer than** as many as (a specified number). **not a few** a considerable number. **some few** some but not at all many. □□ **fewness** *n.* [OE *fēawe, fēawa* f. Gmc]

■ *adj.* not many, hardly *or* scarcely any; infrequent, occasional. ● *n.* **1** (*a few*) some, not many, one or two; a handful, a scattering, a small number. **2** not many, (only) one or two, (only) a handful *or* a scattering *or* a small number. □ **few and far between** see SCARCE *adj.* 2.

fey /fay/ *adj.* **1 a** strange, other-worldly; elfin; whimsical. **b** clairvoyant. **2** *Sc.* **a** fated to die soon. **b** overexcited or elated, as formerly associated with the state of mind of a person about to die. □□ **feyly** *adv.* **feyness** *n.* [OE *fǣge* f. Gmc]

■ **1 a** see WHIMSICAL 2, 3.

fez /fez/ *n.* (*pl.* **fezzes**) a flat-topped conical red cap with a tassel, worn by men in some Muslim countries. □□ **fezzed** *adj.* [Turk., perh. f. *Fez* (now *Fès*) in Morocco]

ff *abbr. Mus.* fortissimo.

ff. *abbr.* **1** following pages etc. **2** folios.

fiacre /fiaákər/ *n. hist.* a small four-wheeled cab. [the Hôtel de St *Fiacre*, Paris]

fiancé /fiónsay/ *n.* (*fem.* **fiancée** *pronunc.* same) a person to whom another is engaged to be married. [F, past part. of *fiancer* betroth f. OF *fiance* a promise, ult. f. L *fidere* to trust]

■ betrothed, wife-to-be, bride-to-be, husband-to-be, intended.

fianchetto /féeənchéttō/ *n.* & *v.* *Chess* ● *n.* (*pl.* **-oes**) the development of a bishop to a long diagonal of the board. ● *v.tr.* (**-oes, -oed**) develop (a bishop) in this way. [It., dimin. of *fianco* FLANK]

fiasco /fiáskō/ *n.* (*pl.* **-os**) a ludicrous or humiliating failure or breakdown (orig. in a dramatic or musical performance); an ignominious result. [It., = bottle (with unexplained allusion): see FLASK]

■ failure, disaster, muddle, mess, botch, *Austral. colloq.* gutzer, *sl.* flop, *Austral. sl.* fizzer.

fiat /fíat, fíət/ *n.* **1** an authorization. **2** a decree or order. □ **fiat money** *US* inconvertible paper money made legal tender by a Government decree. [L, = let it be done]

fib /fib/ *n.* & *v.* ● *n.* a trivial or venial lie. ● *v.intr.* (**fibbed, fibbing**) tell a fib. □□ **fibber** *n.* **fibster** *n.* [perh. f. obs. *fible-fable* nonsense, redupl. of FABLE]

■ *n.* (little) white lie, tale, fairy story *or* tale, untruth, falsehood, fabrication, invention, story, fiction, lie. ● *v.* see LIE[2] *v.* 1a.

fiber *US* var. of FIBRE.

Fibonacci series /fibbənaáchi/ *n. Math.* a series of numbers in which each number (**Fibonacci number**) is the sum of the two preceding numbers, esp. 1, 1, 2, 3, 5, 8, etc. [L. *Fibonacci*, It. mathematician *fl.* 1200]

fibre /fíbər/ *n.* (*US* **fiber**) **1** *Biol.* any of the threads or filaments forming animal or vegetable tissue and textile substances. **2** a piece of glass in the form of a thread. **3 a** a substance formed of fibres. **b** a substance that can be spun, woven, or felted. **4** the structure, grain, or character of something (*lacks moral fibre*). **5** dietary material that is resistant to the action of digestive enzymes; roughage. □ **fibre optics** optics employing thin glass fibres, usu. for the transmission of light, esp. modulated to carry signals. □□ **fibred** *adj.* (also in *comb.*). **fibreless** *adj.* **fibriform** /fíbriform/ *adj.* [ME f. F f. L *fibra*]

■ **1** thread, filament, strand, fibril. **4** structure, texture, mould, cast, composition, constitution, make-up, grain, material, substance, fabric, character, essence, nature, quality.

fibreboard /fíbərbord/ *n.* (*US* **fiberboard**) a building material made of wood or other plant fibres compressed into boards.

fibreglass /fíbərglaass/ *n.* (*US* **fiberglass**) **1** a textile fabric made from woven glass fibres. **2** a plastic reinforced by glass fibres.

fibril /fíbril/ *n.* **1** a small fibre. **2** a subdivision of a fibre. □□ **fibrillar** *adj.* **fibrillary** *adj.* [mod.L *fibrilla* dimin. of L *fibra* fibre]

fibrillate /fíbrilayt, fí-/ *v.* **1** *intr.* **a** (of a fibre) split up into fibrils. **b** (of a muscle, esp. in the heart) undergo a quivering movement in fibrils. **2** *tr.* break (a fibre) into fibrils. □□ **fibrillation** /-láysh'n/ *n.*

fibrin /fíbrin/ *n.* an insoluble protein formed during blood-clotting from fibrinogen. □□ **fibrinoid** *adj.* [FIBRE + -IN]

fibrinogen /fibrínnəjən/ *n.* a soluble blood-plasma protein which produces fibrin when acted upon by the enzyme thrombin.

fibro /fíbrō/ *n.* (*pl.* **-os**) *Austral.* **1** fibro-cement. **2** a house constructed mainly of this. [abbr.]

fibro- /fíbrō/ *comb. form* fibre.

fibro-cement /fíbrōsimént/ *n.* a mixture of any of various fibrous materials, such as glass fibre, cellulose fibre, etc. and cement, used in sheets for building etc.

fibroid /fíbroyd/ *adj.* & *n.* ● *adj.* **1** of or characterized by fibrous tissue. **2** resembling or containing fibres. ● *n.* a benign tumour of muscular and fibrous tissues, one or more of which may develop in the wall of the womb.

fibroin /fíbrō-in/ *n.* a protein which is the chief constituent of silk. [FIBRO- + -IN]

fibroma /fibrṓmə/ *n.* (*pl.* **fibromas** or **fibromata** /-mətə/) a fibrous tumour. [mod.L f. L *fibra* fibre + -OMA]

fibrosis /fibrṓsiss/ *n. Med.* a thickening and scarring of connective tissue, usu. as a result of injury. □□ **fibrotic** /-bróttik/ *adj.* [mod.L f. L *fibra* fibre + -OSIS]

fibrositis /fíbrəsítiss/ *n.* an inflammation of fibrous connective tissue, usu. rheumatic and painful. □□ **fibrositic** /-síttik/ *adj.* [mod.L f. L *fibrosus* fibrous + -ITIS]

fibrous /fíbrəss/ *adj.* consisting of or like fibres. □□ **fibrously** *adv.* **fibrousness** *n.*
■ see STRINGY 2.

fibula /fíbyoolə/ *n.* (*pl.* **fibulae** /-lee/ or **fibulas**) **1** *Anat.* the smaller and outer of the two bones between the knee and the ankle in terrestrial vertebrates. **2** *Antiq.* a brooch or clasp. □□ **fibular** *adj.* [L, perh. rel. to *figere* fix]

-fic /fik/ *suffix* (usu. as **-ific**) forming adjectives meaning 'producing', 'making' (*prolific*; *pacific*). □□ **-fically** *suffix* forming adverbs. [from or after F *-fique* or L *-ficus* f. *facere* do, make]

-fication /fikáysh'n/ *suffix* (usu. as **-ification**) forming nouns of action from verbs in *-fy* (*acidification*; *purification*; *simplification*). [from or after F *-fication* or L *-ficatio -onis* f. *-ficare*: see -FY]

fiche /feesh/ *n.* (*pl.* same or **fiches**) a microfiche. [F, = slip of paper]

fichu /físhoo, féeshoo/ *n.* a woman's small triangular shawl of lace etc. for the shoulders and neck. [F]

fickle /fikk'l/ *adj.* inconstant, changeable, esp. in loyalty. □□ **fickleness** *n.* **fickly** *adv.* [OE *ficol*: cf. *befician* deceive, *fǣcne* deceitful]
■ inconstant, unfaithful, faithless, disloyal, changeable, changeful, unsteady, unsteadfast, wavering, indecisive, uncertain, unsure, wishy-washy, vacillating, erratic, flighty, capricious, unpredictable, moody, whimsical, fitful, unstable, unreliable, *literary* mutable.

fictile /fiktīl/ *adj.* **1** made of earth or clay by a potter. **2** of pottery. [L *fictilis* f. *fingere fict-* fashion]

fiction /fiksh'n/ *n.* **1** an invented idea or statement or narrative; an imaginary thing. **2** literature, esp. novels, describing imaginary events and people. **3** a conventionally accepted falsehood (*legal fiction*; *polite fiction*). **4** the act or process of inventing imaginary things. □□ **fictional** *adj.* **fictionality** /-nálliti/ *n.* **fictionalize** *v.tr.* (also **-ise**). **fictionalization** /-nəlīzáysh'n/ *n.* **fictionally** *adv.* **fictionist** *n.* [ME f. OF f. L *fictio -onis* (as FICTILE)]
■ **1, 3** see INVENTION 3. **2** see WRITING 4. □□ **fictional** unreal, imaginary, invented, made-up, fanciful, mythical, fictitious.

fictitious /fiktíshəss/ *adj.* **1** imaginary, unreal. **2** counterfeit; not genuine. **3** (of a name or character) assumed. **4** of or in novels. **5** regarded as what it is called by a legal or conventional fiction. □□ **fictitiously** *adv.* **fictitiousness** *n.* [L *ficticius* (as FICTILE)]
■ **1** imaginary, unreal, imagined, fictive, fanciful, fictional, fancied, non-existent, made-up, invented, fabricated, mythical, apocryphal, untrue. **2** counterfeit, false, bogus, spurious, made-up, invented, *colloq.* phoney; make-believe, imaginary. **3** false, adopted, improvised, *colloq.* phoney; see also ASSUMED 1.

fictive /fiktiv/ *adj.* **1** creating or created by imagination. **2** not genuine. □□ **fictively** *adv.* **fictiveness** *n.* [F *fictif -ive* or med.L *fictivus* (as FICTILE)]
■ see FICTITIOUS.

fid /fid/ *n.* **1** a small thick piece or wedge or heap of anything. **2** *Naut.* **a** a square wooden or iron bar to support the topmast. **b** a conical wooden pin used in splicing. [17th c.: orig. unkn.]

Fid. Def. *abbr. Brit.* Defender of the Faith. [L *Fidei Defensor*]

fiddle /fidd'l/ *n.* & *v.* ● *n.* **1** *colloq.* or *derog.* a stringed instrument played with a bow, esp. a violin. **2** *colloq.* an instance of cheating or fraud. **3** *Naut.* a contrivance for stopping things from rolling or sliding off a table in bad weather. ● *v.* **1** *intr.* **a** (often foll. by *with*, *at*) play restlessly. **b** (often foll. by *about*) move aimlessly. **c** act idly or frivolously. **d** (usu. foll. by *with*) make minor adjustments; tinker (esp. in an attempt to make improvements). **2** *tr. sl.* **a** cheat, swindle. **b** falsify. **c** get by cheating. **3 a** *intr.* play the fiddle. **b** *tr.* play (a tune etc.) on the fiddle. □ **as fit as a fiddle** in very good health. **face as long as a fiddle** a dismal face. **fiddle-back** a fiddle-shaped back of a chair or front of a chasuble. **fiddle-head** a scroll-like carving at a ship's bows. **fiddle pattern** the pattern of spoons and forks with fiddle-shaped handles. **play second** (or **first**) **fiddle** take a subordinate (or leading) role. [OE *fithele* f. Gmc f. a Rmc root rel. to VIOL]
■ *n.* **1** violin, viola, viol, cello, *formal* violoncello, *hist.* kit. **2** fraud, *sl.* racket, funny business, *US sl.* skin game; see also SWINDLE *n.* 1, 3. ● *v.* **1 a** (*fiddle with*) play with, twiddle; see also TOY *v.* 1. **b** see FIDGET *v.* 1. **c** fool *or* fuss *or* mess about *or* around, *Brit. colloq.* muck about *or* around, frivol, trifle, monkey (around *or* about). **d** see TINKER *v.* **2 a** cheat, flimflam, *colloq.* finagle; see also SWINDLE *v.* **b** falsify, alter, meddle *or* tamper *or* interfere with, *colloq.* fix, wangle. **c** *colloq.* wangle. □ **play first fiddle** see *call the shots.*

fiddle-de-dee /fidd'ldidée/ *int.* & *n.* nonsense.

fiddle-faddle /fidd'lfadd'l/ *n.*, *v.*, *int.*, & *adj.* ● *n.* trivial matters. ● *v.intr.* fuss, trifle. ● *int.* nonsense! ● *adj.* (of a person or thing) petty, fussy. [redupl. of FIDDLE]

fiddler /fidlər/ *n.* **1** a fiddle-player. **2** *sl.* a swindler, a cheat. **3** any small N. American crab of the genus *Uca*, the male having one of its claws held in a position like a violinist's arm. [OE *fithelere* (as FIDDLE)]

fiddlestick /fidd'lstik/ *n.* **1** (in *pl.*; as *int.*) nonsense! **2** *colloq.* a bow for a fiddle.
■ **1** (*fiddlesticks!*) nonsense, rubbish, fiddle-de-dee, fiddle-faddle, balderdash, stuff and nonsense, moonshine, rot, *colloq.* hogwash, *sl.* bosh, poppycock, tommy-rot, eyewash, boloney, bilge-water, humbug, bull, *Brit. sl.* codswallop.

fiddling /fidling/ *adj.* **1 a** petty, trivial. **b** contemptible, futile. **2** *colloq.* = FIDDLY. **3** that fiddles.

fiddly /fidli/ *adj.* (**fiddlier**, **fiddliest**) *colloq.* intricate, awkward, or tiresome to do or use.

fideism /fídi-iz'm, féeday-/ *n.* the doctrine that all or some knowledge depends on faith or revelation. □□ **fideist** *n.* **fideistic** /-ístik/ *adj.* [L *fides* faith + -ISM]

fidelity /fidélliti/ *n.* **1** (often foll. by *to*) faithfulness, loyalty. **2** strict conformity to truth or fact. **3** exact correspondence to the original. **4** precision in reproduction of sound (*high fidelity*). □ **fidelity insurance** insurance taken out by an employer against losses incurred through an employee's dishonesty etc. [F *fidélité* or L *fidelitas* (as FEALTY)]
■ **1** see ATTACHMENT 2.

fidget /fíjit/ *v.* & *n.* ● *v.* (**fidgeted**, **fidgeting**) **1** *intr.* move or act restlessly or nervously, usu. while maintaining basically the same posture. **2** *intr.* be uneasy, worry. **3** *tr.* make (a person) uneasy or uncomfortable. ● *n.* **1** a person who fidgets. **2** (usu. in *pl.*) **a** bodily uneasiness seeking relief in spasmodic movements; such movements. **b** a restless mood. □□ **fidgety** *adj.* **fidgetiness** *n.* [obs. or dial. *fidge* to twitch]
■ *v.* **1** squirm, twitch, shuffle, wriggle, jig about, fiddle, fuss, *colloq.* have ants in one's pants, wiggle. **2** see FRET[1] *v.* 1a. ● *n.* **1** *colloq.* cat on hot bricks, cat on a hot tin roof. **2 a** (*the fidgets*) see JITTER *n.* **b** restlessness, fidgetiness, uneasiness, nervousness, itchiness, *colloq.* jim-jams, *sl.* the heebie-jeebies.

Fido /fídō/ *n.* a device enabling aircraft to land by dispersing fog by means of petrol-burners on the ground. [initials of *Fog Intensive Dispersal Operation*]

fiducial /fidyóōsh'l/ *adj. Surveying, Astron.*, etc. (of a line, point, etc.) assumed as a fixed basis of comparison. [LL *fiducialis* f. *fiducia* trust f. *fidere* to trust]

fiduciary /fidyóōshəri/ *adj.* & *n.* ● *adj.* **1 a** of a trust, trustee, or trusteeship. **b** held or given in trust. **2** (of a paper currency) depending for its value on public confidence or securities. ● *n.* (*pl.* **-ies**) a trustee. [L *fiduciarius* (as FIDUCIAL)]

fidus Achates /fídəss əkáyteez/ *n.* a faithful friend; a devoted follower. [L, = faithful Achates (a companion of Aeneas in Virgil's *Aeneid*)]

fie /fī/ *int.* expressing disgust, shame, or a pretence of outraged propriety. [ME f. OF f. L *fi* exclam. of disgust at a stench]

fief /feef/ *n.* **1** a piece of land held under the feudal system or in fee. **2** a person's sphere of operation or control. [F (as FEE)]

fiefdom /féefdəm/ *n.* a fief.

field /feeld/ *n.* & *v.* ● *n.* **1** an area of open land, esp. one used for pasture or crops, often bounded by hedges, fences, etc. **2** an area rich in some natural product (*gas field*; *diamond field*). **3** a piece of land for a specified purpose, esp. an area marked out for games (*football field*). **4 a** the participants in a contest or sport. **b** all the competitors in a race or all except those specified. **5** *Cricket* **a** the side fielding. **b** a fielder. **6** an expanse of ice, snow, sea, sky, etc. **7 a** the ground on which a battle is fought; a battlefield (*left his rival in possession of the field*). **b** the scene of a campaign. **c** (*attrib.*) (of artillery etc.) light and mobile for use on campaign. **d** a battle. **8** an area of operation or activity; a subject of study (*each supreme in his own field*). **9 a** the region in which a force is effective (*gravitational field*; *magnetic field*). **b** the force exerted in such an area. **10** a range of perception (*field of view*; *wide field of vision*; *filled the field of the telescope*). **11** *Math.* a system subject to two operations analogous to those for the multiplication and addition of real numbers. **12** (*attrib.*) **a** (of an animal or plant) found in the countryside, wild (*field mouse*). **b** carried out or working in the natural environment, not in a laboratory etc. (*field test*). **13 a** the background of a picture, coin, flag, etc. **b** *Heraldry* the surface of an escutcheon or of one of its divisions. **14** *Computing* a part of a record, representing an item of data. ● *v.* **1** *Cricket, Baseball*, etc. **a** *intr.* act as a fielder. **b** *tr.* stop (and return) (the ball). **2** *tr.* select (a team or individual) to play in a game. **3** *tr.* deal with (a succession of questions etc.). □ **field-book** a book used in the field by a surveyor for technical notes. **field-cornet** *S.Afr. hist.* a minor magistrate. **field-day 1** wide scope for action or success; a time occupied with exciting events (*when crowds form, pickpockets have a field-day*). **2** *Mil.* an exercise, esp. in manoeuvring; a review. **3** a day spent in exploration, scientific investigation, etc., in the natural environment. **field events** athletic sports other than races (e.g. shot-putting, jumping, discus-throwing). **field-glasses** binoculars for outdoor use. **field goal** *US Football* & *Basketball* a goal scored when the ball is in normal play. **field hockey** *US* = HOCKEY[1]. **field hospital** a temporary hospital near a battlefield. **Field Marshal** *Brit.* an army officer of the highest rank. **field mouse** a small rodent, *Apodemus sylvaticus*, with beady eyes, prominent ears, and a long tail. **field mushroom** the edible fungus *Agaricus campestris*. **field mustard** charlock. **field officer** an army officer of field rank. **field of honour** the place where a duel or battle is fought. **field rank** any rank in the army above captain and below general. **field sports** outdoor sports, esp. hunting, shooting, and fishing. **field telegraph** a movable telegraph for use on campaign. **hold the field** not be superseded. **in the field 1** campaigning. **2** working etc. away from one's laboratory, headquarters, etc. **keep the field** continue a campaign. **play the field** *colloq.* avoid exclusive attachment to one person or activity etc. **take the field 1** begin a campaign. **2** (of a sports team) go on to a pitch to begin a game. [OE *feld* f. WG]

■ *n.* **1** pasture, meadow, grassland, clearing, acreage, common, *Austral.* & *NZ* paddock, *poet.* lea, *poet. or archaic* mead. **3** playing-field, pitch, court, ground, *US* gridiron; airfield. **4** participants, competitors, players, entrants, contestants, competition. **7 a, b** battlefield, battleground. **8** area, domain, realm, territory, sphere, line, province, subject, division, department, *métier*, discipline, speciality, specialization, *esp. US* specialty, *joc.* bailiwick; forte, strength. ● *v.* **1 b** stop, catch, return, retrieve. **3** deal *or* cope with, handle, answer, reply to, respond *or* react to.

fielder /féeldər/ *n. Cricket* etc. a member (other than the bowler) of the side that is fielding.

fieldfare /féeldfair/ *n.* a thrush, *Turdus pilaris*, having grey plumage with a speckled breast. [ME *feldefare*, perh. as FIELD + FARE]

fieldsman /féeldzmən/ *n.* (*pl.* **-men**) *Cricket* = FIELDER.

fieldstone /féeldstōn/ *n.* stone used in its natural form.

fieldwork /féeldwurk/ *n.* **1** the practical work of a surveyor, collector of scientific data, sociologist, etc., conducted in the natural environment rather than a laboratory, office, etc. **2** a temporary fortification. □□ **fieldworker** *n.*

fiend /feend/ *n.* **1 a** an evil spirit, a demon. **b** (prec. by *the*) the Devil. **2 a** a very wicked or cruel person. **b** a person causing mischief or annoyance. **3** (with a qualifying word) *sl.* a devotee or addict (*a fitness fiend*). **4** something difficult or unpleasant. □□ **fiendish** *adj.* **fiendishly** *adv.* **fiendishness** *n.* **fiendlike** *adj.* [OE *fēond* f. Gmc]

■ **1** see DEVIL *n.* 1, 2. **3** fan, enthusiast, devotee, aficionado, follower, fanatic, *colloq.* addict, maniac, buff, freak, *sl.* nut. □□ **fiendish** wicked, cruel, malignant, malevolent, malicious, evil, bad, black-hearted, satanic, devilish, Mephistophelian, demonic, demoniac(al), diabolic(al), hellish, infernal, savage, inhuman, ghoulish, monstrous.

fierce /feerss/ *adj.* (**fiercer**, **fiercest**) **1** vehemently aggressive or frightening in temper or action, violent. **2** eager, intense, ardent. **3** unpleasantly strong or intense; uncontrolled (*fierce heat*). **4** (of a mechanism) not smooth or easy in action. □□ **fiercely** *adv.* **fierceness** *n.* [ME f. AF *fers*, OF *fiers fier* proud f. L *ferus* savage]

■ **1** ferocious, savage, wild, truculent, violent, brutish, feral, bestial, tigerish, brutal, barbaric, barbarous, inhuman, dangerous, aggressive, cruel, murderous, bloodthirsty, sanguinary, homicidal, *poet. or rhet.* fell. **2** eager, intense, ardent, fiery, vehement, furious. **3** intense, frenzied, stormy, turbulent, tempestuous, tumultuous, uncontrollable; uncontrolled, severe, keen, dire, raging, wild, merciless, bitter, biting, *colloq.* awful, dreadful. □□ **fiercely** very, extremely, exceedingly, intensely, furiously, ferociously; vehemently, violently, savagely, viciously.

fieri facias /fírī fáyshass/ *n. Law* a writ to a sheriff for executing a judgement. [L, = cause to be made or done]

fiery /fíri/ *adj.* (**fierier**, **fieriest**) **1 a** consisting of or flaming with fire. **b** (of an arrow etc.) fire-bearing. **2** like fire in appearance, bright red. **3 a** hot as fire. **b** acting like fire; producing a burning sensation. **4 a** flashing, ardent (*fiery eyes*). **b** eager, pugnacious, spirited, irritable (*fiery temper*). **c** (of a horse) mettlesome. **5** (of gas, a mine, etc.) inflammable; liable to explosions. **6** *Cricket* (of a pitch) making the ball rise dangerously. □ **fiery cross** a wooden cross charred or set on fire as a symbol. □□ **fierily** *adv.* **fieriness** *n.*

■ **1 a** flaming, burning, blazing; afire, on fire, in flames, ablaze. **2** glowing, red, incandescent, brilliant, luminous, glaring, gleaming, radiant; aglow, afire. **3 a** hot, red-hot, white-hot, overheated. **4 a** see ARDENT, BRIGHT *adj.* 1. **b** eager, pugnacious, spirited, passionate, excited, excitable, peppery, irascible, touchy, irritable, edgy, hotheaded, fierce.

fiesta /fi-éstə/ *n.* **1** a holiday or festivity. **2** a religious festival in Spanish-speaking countries. [Sp., = feast]

■ **1** see FESTIVAL *n.*

FIFA /féefə/ *abbr.* International Football Federation. [F *Fédération Internationale de Football Association*]

fi. fa. *abbr.* fieri facias.

fife /fīf/ *n.* & *v.* ● *n.* **1** a kind of small shrill flute used with the drum in military music. **2** its player. ● *v.* **1** *intr.* play the fife. **2** *tr.* play (an air etc.) on the fife. □□ **fifer** *n.* [G *Pfeife* PIPE, or F *fifre* f. Swiss G *Pfifre* piper]

fife-rail /fífrayl/ *n. Naut.* a rail round the mainmast with belaying-pins. [18th c.: orig. unkn.]

fifteen /fifteén/ *n.* & *adj.* ● *n.* **1** one more than fourteen, or five more than ten; the product of three units and five units. **2** a symbol for this (15, xv, XV). **3** a size etc. denoted by fifteen. **4** a team of fifteen players, esp. in Rugby football. **5** (**the Fifteen**) *hist.* the Jacobite rebellion of 1715. **6** (**15**) *Brit.* (of films) classified as suitable for persons of 15 years and over. ● *adj.* that amount to fifteen. □□ **fifteenth** *adj.* & *n.* [OE *fīftēne* (as FIVE, -TEEN)]

fifth /fifth/ *n.* & *adj.* ● *n.* **1** the position in a sequence corresponding to that of the number 5 in the sequence 1–5. **2** something occupying this position. **3** the fifth person etc. in a race or competition. **4** any of five equal parts of a thing. **5** *Mus.* **a** an interval or chord spanning five consecutive notes in the diatonic scale (e.g. C to G). **b** a note separated from another by this interval. **6** *US colloq.* **a** a fifth of a gallon of liquor. **b** a bottle containing this. ● *adj.* that is the fifth. □ **fifth column** a group working for an enemy within a country at war etc. (from General Mola's reference to such support in besieged Madrid in 1936). **fifth-columnist** a member of a fifth column; a traitor or spy. **fifth generation** *Computing* a stage in computer design involving machines that make use of artificial intelligence. **Fifth Monarchy** the last of the five great kingdoms predicted in Daniel 2:44. **Fifth-monarchy-man** *hist.* a 17th-c. zealot expecting the immediate second coming of Christ and repudiating all other government. **fifth part** = sense 4 of *n.* **fifth wheel 1** an extra wheel of a coach. **2** a superfluous person or thing. **3** a horizontal turntable over the front axle of a carriage as an extra support to prevent its tipping. **take the fifth** (in the US) exercise the right guaranteed by the Fifth Amendment to the Constitution of refusing to answer questions in order to avoid incriminating oneself. □□ **fifthly** *adv.* [earlier and dial. *fift* f. OE *fīfta* f. Gmc, assim. to FOURTH]

fifty /fifti/ *n.* & *adj.* ● *n.* (*pl.* **-ies**) **1** the product of five and ten. **2** a symbol for this (50, l (letter), L). **3** (in *pl.*) the numbers from 50 to 59, esp. the years of a century or of a person's life. **4** a set of fifty persons or things. **5** a large indefinite number (*have fifty things to tell you*). ● *adj.* that amount to fifty. □ **fifty-fifty** *adj.* equal, with equal shares or chances (*on a fifty-fifty basis*). ● *adv.* equally, half and half (*go fifty-fifty*). **fifty-first, -second**, etc. the ordinal numbers between fiftieth and sixtieth. **fifty-one, -two**, etc. the cardinal numbers between fifty and sixty. □□ **fiftieth** *adj.* & *n.* **fiftyfold** *adj.* & *adv.* [OE *fīftig* (as FIVE, -TY²)]

fig¹ /fig/ *n.* **1 a** a soft pear-shaped fruit with many seeds, eaten fresh or dried. **b** (in full **fig-tree**) any deciduous tree of the genus *Ficus*, esp. *F. carica*, having broad leaves and bearing figs. **2** a valueless thing (*don't care a fig for*). □ **fig-leaf 1** a leaf of a fig-tree. **2** a device for concealing something, esp. the genitals (Gen. 3:7). [ME f. OF *figue* f. Prov. *fig(u)a* ult. f. L *ficus*]

fig² /fig/ *n.* & *v.* ● *n.* **1** dress or equipment (*in full fig*). **2** condition or form (*in good fig*). ● *v.tr.* (**figged, figging**) **1** (foll. by *out*) dress up (a person). **2** (foll. by *out, up*) make (a horse) lively. [var. of obs. *feague* (v.) f. G *fegen*: see FAKE¹]

■ *v.* **1** (*fig out*) see PRIMP 2.

fig. *abbr.* figure.

fight /fīt/ *v.* & *n.* ● *v.* (*past* and *past part.* **fought** /fawt/) **1** *intr.* **a** (often foll. by *against, with*) contend or struggle in war, battle, single combat, etc. **b** (often foll. by *with*) argue, quarrel. **2** *tr.* contend with (an opponent) in this way. **3** *tr.* take part or engage in (a battle, war, duel, etc.). **4** *tr.* contend about (an issue, an election); maintain (a lawsuit, cause, etc.) against an opponent. **5** *intr.* campaign or strive determinedly to achieve something. **6** *tr.* strive to overcome (disease, fire, fear, etc.). **7** *tr.* make (one's way) by fighting. **8** *tr.* cause (cocks or dogs) to fight. **9** *tr.* handle (troops, a ship, etc.) in battle. ● *n.* **1 a** a combat, esp. unpremeditated, between two or more persons, animals, or parties. **b** a boxing-match. **c** a battle. **d** an argument. **2** a conflict or struggle; a vigorous effort in the face of difficulty. **3** power or inclination to fight (*has no fight left*; *showed fight*). □ **fight back 1** counter-attack. **2** suppress (one's feelings, tears, etc.). **fight down** suppress (one's feelings, tears, etc.). **fight for 1** fight on behalf of. **2** fight to secure (a thing). **fighting chair** *US* a fixed chair on a boat for use when catching large fish. **fighting chance** an opportunity of succeeding by great effort. **fighting fish** (in full **Siamese fighting fish**) a freshwater fish, *Betta splendens*, native to Thailand, the males of which sometimes kill each other during fights for territory. **fighting fit** fit enough to fight; at the peak of fitness. **fighting fund** money raised to support a campaign. **fighting-top** *Naut.* a circular gun-platform high on a warship's mast. **fighting words** *colloq.* words indicating a willingness to fight. **fight off** repel with effort. **fight out** (usu. **fight it out**) settle (a dispute etc.) by fighting. **fight shy of** avoid; be unwilling to approach (a person, task, etc.). **make a fight of it** (or **put up a fight**) offer resistance. [OE *feohtan, feoht(e)*, f. WG]

■ *v.* **1 a** contend, struggle, battle, conflict, war, engage, clash, feud, combat, bear *or* take up arms, brawl, strive, cross swords, lock horns, close, come to *or* exchange blows, go to *or* wage war, grapple, wrestle, skirmish, tussle, scuffle, *hist.* joust, *Austral. sl.* go to the knuckle. **b** argue, dispute, bicker, quarrel, have words, wrangle, squabble, tiff, fall out, disagree, altercate, *colloq.* row, *US colloq.* spat. **2** contend with, encounter, engage; see also TACKLE *v.* 2, 4. **3** see ENGAGE 8. **4** argue about *or* against, dispute, question, challenge; contest; maintain, argue, put, plead, claim, protest, try to prove, assert. **5** campaign, strive, rise up, make *or* take a stand, struggle, take up arms. **6** oppose, defy, resist, rail *or* struggle against, make *or* take a stand against, withstand, confront. ● *n.* **1 a** (single) combat, brawl, Donnybrook, fray, riot, affray, fracas, disturbance, broil, mêlée, tussle, scuffle, scrimmage, skirmish, brush, free-for-all, *colloq.* set-to, scrap, row, scrum, *US sl.* rumble, *hist.* duel. **b** see BOUT 2a. **c** battle, conflict, clash, war, struggle; engagement, encounter. **d** argument, altercation, quarrel, feud, dispute, run-in, disagreement, difference (of opinion), squabble, misunderstanding, *esp. US* ruckus, *colloq.* row, *US colloq.* spat. **3** power, pugnacity, militancy, belligerence, truculence, mettle, spirit, pluck, zeal, enthusiasm, zest, *US* feistiness. □ **fight back 1** see RETALIATE 1. **2** see SUPPRESS 2. **fight down** see SUPPRESS 2. **fight off** see REPULSE *v.* 1. **fight shy of** keep away from, keep *or* remain aloof from, keep *or* remain aloof of; be wary *or* cautious *or* watchful of; be unwilling *or* reluctant *or* averse *or* loath *or* disinclined *or* not disposed to; see also AVOID. **make a fight of it** struggle, battle; see also FIGHT *v.* 1a above.

fighter /fítər/ *n.* **1** a person or animal that fights. **2** a fast military aircraft designed for attacking other aircraft. □ **fighter-bomber** an aircraft serving as both fighter and bomber.

■ **1** see BRUISER 2, SOLDIER *n.*

figment /figmənt/ *n.* a thing invented or existing only in the imagination. [ME f. L *figmentum*, rel. to *fingere* fashion]

■ see ILLUSION 4.

figura /figyóorə/ *n.* **1** a person or thing representing or symbolizing a fact etc. **2** *Theol.* a type of a person etc. [mod.L f. L, = FIGURE]

figural /figyoorəl/ *adj.* **1** figurative. **2** relating to figures or shapes. **3** *Mus.* florid in style. [OF *figural* or LL *figuralis* f. *figura* FIGURE]

figurant /figyoorənt/ *n.* (*fem.* ***figurante*** *pronunc.* same) a ballet-dancer appearing only in a group. [F, pres. part. of *figurer* FIGURE]

figurante /figyoorànti/ *n.* (*pl.* ***figuranti*** /-tee/) = FIGURANT. [It., pres. part. of *figurare* FIGURE]

figuration /figyooráysh'n/ *n.* **1 a** the act of formation. **b** a mode of formation; a form. **c** a shape or outline. **2 a** ornamentation by designs. **b** *Mus.* ornamental patterns of scales, arpeggios, etc., often derived from an earlier motif. **3** allegorical representation. [ME f. F or f. L *figuratio* (as FIGURE)]

figurative /figyoorətiv, figgər-/ *adj.* **1 a** metaphorical, not literal. **b** metaphorically so called. **2** characterized by or addicted to figures of speech. **3** of pictorial or sculptural representation. **4** emblematic, serving as a type. ▫▫ **figuratively** *adv.* **figurativeness** *n.* [ME f. LL *figurativus* (as FIGURE)]

■ **1a, 2** see *metaphoric, metaphorical* (METAPHOR).

figure /figgər/ *n.* & *v.* ● *n.* **1 a** the external form or shape of a thing. **b** bodily shape (*has a well-developed figure*). **2 a** a person as seen in outline but not identified (*saw a figure leaning against the door*). **b** a person as contemplated mentally (*a public figure*). **3** appearance as giving a certain impression (*cut a poor figure*). **4 a** a representation of the human form in drawing, sculpture, etc. **b** an image or likeness. **c** an emblem or type. **5** *Geom.* a two-dimensional space enclosed by a line or lines, or a three-dimensional space enclosed by a surface or surfaces; any of the classes of these, e.g. the triangle, the sphere. **6 a** a numerical symbol, esp. any of the ten in Arabic notation. **b** a number so expressed. **c** an amount of money, a value (*cannot put a figure on it*). **d** (in *pl.*) arithmetical calculations. **7** a diagram or illustrative drawing. **8** a decorative pattern. **9 a** a division of a set dance, an evolution. **b** (in skating) a prescribed pattern of movements from a stationary position. **10** *Mus.* a short succession of notes producing a single impression, a brief melodic or rhythmic formula out of which longer passages are developed. **11** (in full **figure of speech**) a recognized form of rhetorical expression giving variety, force, etc., esp. metaphor or hyperbole. **12** *Gram.* a permitted deviation from the usual rules of construction, e.g. ellipsis. **13** *Logic* the form of a syllogism, classified according to the position of the middle term. **14** a horoscope. ● *v.* **1** *intr.* appear or be mentioned, esp. prominently. **2** *tr.* represent in a diagram or picture. **3** *tr.* imagine; picture mentally. **4** *tr.* **a** embellish with a pattern (*figured satin*). **b** *Mus.* embellish with figures. **5** *tr.* mark with numbers (*figured bass*) or prices. **6 a** *tr.* calculate. **b** *intr.* do arithmetic. **7** *tr.* be a symbol of, represent typically. **8** esp. *US* **a** *tr.* understand, ascertain, consider. **b** *intr.* *colloq.* be likely or understandable (*that figures*). ▫ **figured bass** *Mus.* = CONTINUO. **figure of fun** a ridiculous person. **figure on** *US* count on, expect. **figure out 1** work out by arithmetic or logic. **2** estimate. **3** understand. **figure-skater** a person who practises figure-skating. **figure-skating** skating in prescribed patterns from a stationary position. ▫▫ **figureless** *adj.* [ME f. OF *figure* (n.), *figurer* (v.) f. L *figura*, *figurare*, rel. to *fingere* fashion]

■ *n.* **1 a** form, shape; outline, silhouette; cut, cast; conformation. **b** shape, form, physique, build, body, outline. **2 a** form, person, individual, being. **b** person, personality, presence, force, character, individual. **3** see APPEARANCE 2. **4 a** representation, statue, effigy, sculpture, bust, mould, cast, image, icon. **b** image, likeness, representation, semblance. **c** emblem, symbol, device; design, pattern, motif; type. **6 a** number, numeral, cipher, digit; symbol, character, sign. **7** diagram, drawing, illustration, picture, sketch, plate. ● *v.* **1** appear, feature, have a place, take *or* play a part, take *or* play a role; be mentioned *or* included, be featured *or* conspicuous. **3** imagine, picture, think, reckon, consider, judge, believe; assume, presume, suppose; take. **6 a** calculate, figure out, compute, reckon, work out; count, total (up), tot (up), enumerate, tally, sum. ▫ **figure on** count on, rely *or* depend on, trust in, put faith in; expect, plan on *or* upon, take into consideration *or* account, consider, make allowance for. **figure out 1** calculate, reckon, compute, work out; see also SOLVE. **3** understand, decipher, interpret, translate, grasp, solve, fathom, see, perceive, *colloq.* get, make head or tail of, get the hang of, get the drift of, catch on (to), twig, *sl.* suss (out).

figurehead /figgərhed/ *n.* **1** a nominal leader or head without real power. **2** a carving, usu. a bust or a full-length figure, at a ship's prow.

■ **1** puppet, dummy, mouthpiece, front man, man of straw.

figurine /figyooréen/ *n.* a statuette. [F f. It. *figurina* dimin. of *figura* FIGURE]

■ see STATUE.

figwort /figwurt/ *n.* any aromatic green-flowered plant of the genus *Scrophularia*, once believed to be useful against scrofula.

filagree var. of FILIGREE.

filament /filləmənt/ *n.* **1** a slender threadlike body or fibre (esp. in animal or vegetable structures). **2** a conducting wire or thread with a high melting-point in an electric bulb or thermionic valve, heated or made incandescent by an electric current. **3** *Bot.* the part of the stamen that supports the anther. **4** *archaic* (of air, light, etc.) a notional train of particles following each other. ▫▫ **filamentary** /-méntəri/ *adj.* **filamented** *adj.* **filamentous** /-méntəss/ *adj.* [F *filament* or mod.L *filamentum* f. LL *filare* spin f. L *filum* thread]

■ **1** see FIBRE 1.

filaria /filáiriə/ *n.* (*pl.* **filariae** /-ri-ee/) any threadlike parasitic nematode worm of the family Filariidae introduced into the blood by certain biting flies and mosquitoes. ▫▫ **filarial** *adj.* [mod.L f. L *filum* thread]

filariasis /fillərī́əsiss, filáiriáysiss/ *n.* a disease common in the tropics, caused by the presence of filarial worms in the lymph vessels.

filature /filləchər/ *n.* an establishment for or the action of reeling silk from cocoons. [F f. It. *filatura* f. *filare* spin]

filbert /filbərt/ *n.* **1** the cultivated hazel, *Corylus maxima*, bearing edible ovoid nuts. **2** this nut. [ME *philliberd* etc. f. AF *philbert*, dial. F *noix de filbert*, a nut ripe about St Philibert's day (20 Aug.)]

filch /filch/ *v.tr.* pilfer, steal. ▫▫ **filcher** *n.* [16th-c. thieves' sl.: orig. unkn.]

■ see STEAL *v.* 1.

file[1] /fīl/ *n.* & *v.* ● *n.* **1** a folder, box, etc., for holding loose papers, esp. arranged for reference. **2** a set of papers kept in this. **3** *Computing* a collection of (usu. related) data stored under one name. **4** a series of issues of a newspaper etc. in order. **5** a stiff pointed wire on which documents etc. are impaled for keeping. ● *v.tr.* **1** place (papers) in a file or among (esp. public) records; classify or arrange (papers etc.). **2** submit (a petition for divorce, an application for a patent, etc.) to the appropriate authority. **3** (of a reporter) send (a story, information, etc.) to a newspaper. ▫ **filing cabinet** a case with drawers for storing documents. ▫▫ **filer** *n.* [F *fil* f. L *filum* thread]

■ *n.* **1** portfolio, folder, box, case. **2** document, dossier, papers. ● *v.* **1** classify, organize, systematize, categorize, alphabetize, chronologize, order, arrange, pigeon-hole, interfile, put *or* place in order, record, register, enter. **2** submit, send in, complete, fill in, *US* fill out, enter.

file[2] /fīl/ *n.* & *v.* ● *n.* **1** a line of persons or things one behind another. **2** (foll. by *of*) *Mil.* a small detachment of men (now usu. two). **3** *Chess* a line of squares from player to player (cf. RANK[1]). ● *v.intr.* walk in a file. ▫ **file off** (or **away**) *Mil.* go off by files. [F *file* f. LL *filare* spin or L *filum* thread]

■ *n.* **1** line, column, row, rank, *esp. Brit.* queue. ● *v.* walk, march, troop, parade.

file[3] /fīl/ *n.* & *v.* ● *n.* a tool with a roughened surface or surfaces, usu. of steel, for smoothing or shaping wood, fingernails, etc. ● *v.tr.* **1** smooth or shape with a file. **2** elaborate or improve (a thing, esp. a literary work). ▫ **file away** remove (roughness etc.) with a file. **file-fish** any fish of the family Ostracionidae, with sharp dorsal fins and usu. bright coloration. ▫▫ **filer** *n.* [OE *fīl* f. WG]

filet /fillit/ *n.* **1** a kind of net or lace with a square mesh. **2** a fillet of meat. □ **filet mignon** /féelay méenyon/ a small tender piece of beef from the end of the undercut. [F, = thread]

filial /filliəl/ *adj.* **1** of or due from a son or daughter. **2** *Biol.* bearing the relation of offspring (cf. F² 5). □□ **filially** *adv.* [ME f. OF *filial* or LL *filialis* f. *filius* son, *filia* daughter]
■ **1** see DUTIFUL.

filiation /filliáysh'n/ *n.* **1** being the child of one or two specified parents. **2** (often foll. by *from*) descent or transmission. **3** the formation of offshoots. **4** a branch of a society or language. **5** a genealogical relation or arrangement. [F f. LL *filiatio* -*onis* f. L *filius* son]

filibeg /fillibeg/ *n.* (also **philabeg** /fillə-/) *Sc.* a kilt. [Gael. *feileadh-beag* little fold]

filibuster /fillibustər/ *n.* & *v.* ● *n.* **1 a** the obstruction of progress in a legislative assembly, esp. by prolonged speaking. **b** esp. *US* a person who engages in a filibuster. **2** esp. *hist.* a person engaging in unauthorized warfare against a foreign State. ● *v.* **1** *intr.* act as a filibuster. **2** *tr.* act in this way against (a motion etc.). □□ **filibusterer** *n.* [ult. f. Du. *vrijbuiter* FREEBOOTER, infl. by F *flibustier*, Sp. *filibustero*]

filigree /filligree/ *n.* (also **filagree** /fillə-/) **1** ornamental work of gold or silver or copper as fine wire formed into delicate tracery; fine metal openwork. **2** anything delicate resembling this. □□ **filigreed** *adj.* [earlier *filigreen*, *filigrane* f. F *filigrane* f. It. *filigrana* f. L *filum* thread + *granum* seed]
■ **2** see LACE *n.* 1.

filing /fíling/ *n.* (usu. in *pl.*) a particle rubbed off by a file.

Filipino /fillipéenō/ *n.* & *adj.* ● *n.* (*pl.* **-os**; *fem.* **Filipina** /-nə/) a native or national of the Philippines, a group of islands in the SW Pacific. ● *adj.* of or relating to the Philippines or the Filipinos. [Sp., = Philippine]

fill /fil/ *v.* & *n.* ● *v.* **1** *tr.* & *intr.* (often foll. by *with*) make or become full. **2** *tr.* occupy completely; spread over or through; pervade. **3** *tr.* block up (a cavity or hole in a tooth) with cement, amalgam, gold, etc.; drill and put a filling into (a decayed tooth). **4** *tr.* appoint a person to hold (a vacant post). **5** *tr.* hold (a position); discharge the duties of (an office). **6** *tr.* carry out or supply (an order, commission, etc.). **7** *tr.* occupy (vacant time). **8** *intr.* (of a sail) be distended by wind. **9** *tr.* (usu. as **filling** *adj.*) (esp. of food) satisfy, satiate. **10** *tr.* satisfy, fulfil (a need or requirement). **11** *tr. Poker* etc. complete (a holding) by drawing the necessary cards. **12** *tr.* stock abundantly. ● *n.* **1** (prec. by possessive) as much as one wants or can bear (*eat your fill*). **2** enough to fill something (*a fill of tobacco*). **3** earth etc. used to fill a cavity. □ **fill the bill** be suitable or adequate. **fill in 1** add information to complete (a form, document, blank cheque, etc.). **2 a** complete (a drawing etc.) within an outline. **b** fill (an outline) in this way. **3** fill (a hole etc.) completely. **4** (often foll. by *for*) act as a substitute. **5** occupy oneself during (time between other activities). **6** *colloq.* inform (a person) more fully. **7** *sl.* thrash, beat. **fill out 1** enlarge to the required size. **2** become enlarged or plump. **3** *US* fill in (a document etc.). **fill up 1** make or become completely full. **2** fill in (a document etc.). **3** fill the petrol tank of (a car etc.). **4** provide what is needed to occupy vacant parts or places or deal with deficiencies in. **5** do away with (a pond etc.) by filling. **fill-up** *n.* a thing that fills something up. [OE *fyllan* f. Gmc, rel. to FULL¹]
■ *v.* **1** make full, fill up; *esp. Brit.* top up. **2** occupy, crowd (into), stuff, cram (into), pack (into), squeeze into; jam, load; pervade, abound in, overflow, be abundant *or* plentiful in. **3** block, stop (up), close, stuff, seal, plug, fill in. **5** hold, occupy, take over; discharge, carry out, do, execute. **8** distend, inflate, swell, stretch, blow up, expand. **9** satisfy, satiate, bloat, sate, gorge, stuff. **10** satisfy, meet, fulfil, answer. **12** supply, stock, furnish, fill up. □ **fill in 1** complete, answer, make out, fill up, *US* fill out. **3** see FILL *v.* 3 above. **4** (*fill in for*) take the place of, take a person's place, stand in for; see also SUBSTITUTE *v.* 1. **5** see OCCUPY 2. **6** inform, tell, advise, let in on, bring up to date. **7** see BEAT *v.* 1. **fill out 1** see PAD¹ *v.* 2. **2** swell, expand, grow; distend, stretch; fatten, increase. **3** see *fill in* 1 above. **fill up 1** see FILL *v.* 1 above. **2** see *fill in* 1 above.

fille de joie /féey də zwaá/ *n.* a prostitute. [F, lit. 'daughter of joy']

filler /fillər/ *n.* **1** material or an object used to fill a cavity or increase bulk. **2** an item filling space in a newspaper etc. **3** a person or thing that fills. □ **filler cap** a cap closing the filling-pipe leading to the petrol tank of a motor vehicle.
■ **2** see ITEM *n.* 3.

fillet /fillit/ *n.* & *v.* ● *n.* **1 a** a fleshy boneless piece of meat from near the loins or the ribs. **b** (in full **fillet steak**) the undercut of a sirloin. **c** a boned longitudinal section of a fish. **2 a** a headband, ribbon, string, or narrow band, for binding the hair or worn round the head. **b** a band or bandage. **3 a** a thin narrow strip of anything. **b** a raised rim or ridge on any surface. **4** *Archit.* **a** a narrow flat band separating two mouldings. **b** a small band between the flutes of a column. **5** *Carpentry* an added triangular piece of wood to round off an interior angle. **6 a** a plain line impressed on the cover of a book. **b** a roller used to impress this. **7** *Heraldry* a horizontal division of a shield, a quarter of the depth of a chief. ● *v.tr.* (**filleted, filleting**) **1 a** remove bones from (fish or meat). **b** divide (fish or meat) into fillets. **2** bind or provide with a fillet or fillets. **3** encircle with an ornamental band. □□ **filleter** *n.* [ME f. OF *filet* f. Rmc dimin. of L *filum* thread]
■ *n.* **2 a** see BAND¹ *n.* 1. **3 a** see STRIP².

filling /filling/ *n.* **1** any material that fills or is used to fill, esp.: **a** a piece of material used to fill a cavity in a tooth. **b** the edible substance between the bread in a sandwich or between the pastry in a pie. **2** *US* weft. □ **filling-station** an establishment selling petrol etc. to motorists.
■ **1 a** filler, stuffing, padding, wadding; contents.

fillip /fillip/ *n.* & *v.* ● *n.* **1** a stimulus or incentive. **2 a** a sudden release of a finger or thumb when it has been bent and checked by a thumb or finger. **b** a slight smart stroke given in this way. ● *v.* (**filliped, filliping**) **1** *tr.* stimulate (*fillip one's memory*). **2** *tr.* strike slightly and smartly. **3** *tr.* propel (a coin, marble, etc.) with a fillip. **4** *intr.* make a fillip. [imit.]
■ *n.* **1** see STIMULANT *n.* 2.

fillis /filliss/ *n. Hort.* loosely-twisted string used as a tying material. [F *filasse* tow]

fillister /fillistər/ *n.* a rabbet or rabbet plane for window-sashes etc. [19th c.: perh. f. F *feuilleret*]

filly /filli/ *n.* (*pl.* **-ies**) **1** a young female horse, usu. before it is four years old. **2** *colloq.* a girl or young woman. [ME, prob. f. ON *fylja* f. Gmc (as FOAL)]
■ **2** see GIRL 2.

film /film/ *n.* & *v.* ● *n.* **1** a thin coating or covering layer. **2** *Photog.* a strip or sheet of plastic or other flexible base coated with light-sensitive emulsion for exposure in a camera, either as individual visual representations or as a sequence which form the illusion of movement when shown in rapid succession. **3 a** a representation of a story, episode, etc., on a film, with the illusion of movement. **b** a story represented in this way. **c** (in *pl.*) the cinema industry. **4** a slight veil or haze etc. **5** a dimness or morbid growth affecting the eyes. **6** a fine thread or filament . ● *v.* **1 a** *tr.* make a photographic film of (a scene, person, etc.). **b** *tr.* (also *absol.*) make a cinema or television film of (a book etc.). **c** *intr.* be (well or ill) suited for reproduction on film. **2** *tr.* & *intr.* cover or become covered with or as with a film. □ **film-goer** a person who frequents the cinema. **film star** a celebrated actor or actress in films. **film-strip** a series of transparencies in a strip for projection. [OE *filmen* membrane f. WG, rel. to FELL⁵]
■ *n.* **1** coating, layer, covering, sheet, overlay; skin, coat, membrane, integument, cover, pellicle. **3 a, b** picture, moving picture, motion picture, *colloq.* pic, *Brit. colloq.* flick, *esp. US colloq.* movie; videotape, video. **4** veil, haze, dusting, murkiness, blur, mist, haziness, mistiness,

vapour, fog. ● *v.* **1** photograph, shoot, take. **2** (*film over*) become coated *or* covered *or* veiled *or* dimmed *or* glazed *or* blurred *or* bleary *or* misty *or* cloudy.

filmic /filmik/ *adj.* of or relating to films or cinematography.
■ cinematic, pictorial, photographic.

filmography /filmógrəfi/ *n.* (*pl.* **-ies**) a list of films by one director etc. or on one subject. [FILM + -GRAPHY after *bibliography*]

filmset /filmset/ *v.tr.* (**-setting**; *past* and *past part.* **-set**) *Printing* set (material for printing) by filmsetting. ▫▫ **filmsetter** *n.*

filmsetting /filmsetting/ *n.* *Printing* typesetting using characters on photographic film.

filmy /filmi/ *adj.* (**filmier**, **filmiest**) **1** thin and translucent. **2** covered with or as with a film. ▫▫ **filmily** *adv.* **filminess** *n.*
■ **1** gauzy, thin, sheer, gossamer(-like), cobwebby, diaphanous, delicate, flimsy, light, insubstantial, transparent, translucent, see-through, peekaboo. **2** murky, blurry, cloudy, hazy, misty, bleary, blurred, dim, clouded, milky, pearly, opalescent.

filo / féelō/ *n.* dough that can be stretched into very thin layers; pastry made from this dough. [mod.Gk *phullo* leaf]

Filofax /fīlōfaks/ *n. propr.* a portable loose-leaf filing system for personal or office use. [FILE[1] + *facts* pl. of FACT]

filoselle /filləsel/ *n.* floss silk. [F]

fils /feess/ *n.* (added to a surname to distinguish a son from a father) the son, junior (cf. PÈRE). [F, = son]

filter /filtər/ *n.* & *v.* ● *n.* **1** a porous device for removing impurities or solid particles from a liquid or gas passed through it. **2** = *filter tip.* **3** a screen or attachment for absorbing or modifying light, X-rays, etc. **4** a device for suppressing electrical or sound waves of frequencies not required. **5** *Brit.* **a** an arrangement for filtering traffic. **b** a traffic-light signalling this. ● *v.* **1** *tr.* & *intr.* pass or cause to pass through a filter. **2** *tr.* (foll. by *out*) remove (impurities etc.) by means of a filter. **3** *intr.* (foll. by *through*, *into*, etc.) make way gradually. **4** *intr.* (foll. by *out*) leak or cause to leak. **5** *tr.* & *intr.* *Brit.* allow (traffic) or (of traffic) be allowed to pass to the left or right at a junction while traffic going straight ahead is halted (esp. at traffic lights). ▫ **filter-bed** a tank or pond containing a layer of sand etc. for filtering large quantities of liquid. **filter-paper** porous paper for filtering. **filter tip 1** a filter attached to a cigarette for removing impurities from the inhaled smoke. **2** a cigarette with this. **filter-tipped** having a filter tip. [F *filtre* f. med.L *filtrum* felt used as a filter, f. WG]
■ *n.* **1** strainer, sieve, riddle. ● *v.* **1** filtrate, pass *or* run through, strain, drain; percolate, leach; clarify, refine, purify, clean. **2** screen, sift, winnow; separate, weed out, exclude, eliminate.

filterable /filtərəb'l/ *adj.* (also **filtrable** /filtrəb'l/) **1** *Med.* (of a virus) able to pass through a filter that retains bacteria. **2** that can be filtered.

filth /filth/ *n.* **1** repugnant or extreme dirt; excrement, refuse. **2** vileness, corruption, obscenity. **3** foul or obscene language. **4** (prec. by *the*) *sl. derog.* the police. [OE *fȳlth* (as FOUL, -TH[2])]
■ **1** dirt, slime, filthiness, *colloq.* muck, *Brit. colloq.* gunge, *sl.* crud, *esp. US sl.* grunge; excrement, faeces, excreta, night-soil, manure, dung, droppings, ordure, guano; sewage, sullage, sludge; rubbish, garbage, refuse, offal, soil, *esp. US* trash. **2** vileness, corruption, baseness, foulness, rottenness, debasement, defilement; pollution, adulteration, perversion, degradation, sullying, besmirchment, putrescence, putrefaction; obscenity, vulgarity, indecency, grossness, pornography. **3** see DIRT 3.

filthy /filthi/ *adj.* & *adv.* ● *adj.* (**filthier**, **filthiest**) **1** extremely or disgustingly dirty. **2** obscene. **3** *colloq.* (of weather) very unpleasant. **4** vile; disgraceful. ● *adv.* **1** filthily (*filthy dirty*). **2** *colloq.* extremely (*filthy rich*). ▫ **filthy lucre 1** dishonourable gain (Tit. 1:11). **2** *joc.* money. ▫▫ **filthily** *adv.* **filthiness** *n.*
■ *adj.* **1** dirty, unclean, begrimed, soiled, stained, grimy, mucky, disgusting; scummy, slimy, sordid, squalid, shabby, *sl.* cruddy, *Brit. colloq.* gungy, *esp. US sl.* grungy; putrid, fetid, maggotty, fly-blown, purulent, feculent, faecal. **2** obscene, indecent, immoral, gross, impure, smutty, coarse, bawdy, ribald, depraved, corrupt, dirty, lewd, lascivious, licentious, offensive, foul-mouthed, dirty-minded, filthy-minded, blue, pornographic, taboo. **4** see DISGRACEFUL, VILE 1.

filtrable var. of FILTERABLE.

filtrate /filtrayt/ *v.* & *n.* ● *v.tr.* filter. ● *n.* filtered liquid. ▫▫ **filtration** /-tráysh'n/ *n.* [mod.L *filtrare* (as FILTER)]
■ *v.* see FILTER *v.* 1.

fimbriate /fimbriayt/ *adj.* (also **fimbriated**) **1** *Bot.* & *Zool.* fringed or bordered with hairs etc. **2** *Heraldry* having a narrow border. [L *fimbriatus* f. *fimbriae* fringe]

fin /fin/ *n.* & *v.* ● *n.* **1** an organ on various parts of the body of many aquatic vertebrates and some invertebrates, including fish and cetaceans, for propelling, steering, and balancing (*dorsal fin*; *anal fin*). **2** a small projecting surface or attachment on an aircraft, rocket, or motor car for ensuring aerodynamic stability. **3** an underwater swimmer's flipper. **4** a sharp lateral projection on the share or coulter of a plough. **5** a finlike projection on any device, for improving heat transfer etc. ● *v.* (**finned**, **finning**) **1** *tr.* provide with fins. **2** *intr.* swim under water. ▫ **fin-back** (or **fin whale**) a rorqual, *Balaenoptera physalus*. ▫▫ **finless** *adj.* **finned** *adj.* (also in *comb.*). [OE *fin(n)*]

finable see FINE[2].

finagle /fináyg'l/ *v.intr.* & *tr. colloq.* act or obtain dishonestly. ▫▫ **finagler** *n.* [dial. *fainaigue* cheat]
■ see CHEAT *v.* 1a.

final /fīn'l/ *adj.* & *n.* ● *adj.* **1** situated at the end, coming last. **2** conclusive, decisive, unalterable, putting an end to doubt. **3** concerned with the purpose or end aimed at. ● *n.* **1** the last or deciding heat or game in sports or in a competition (*Cup Final*). **2** the edition of a newspaper published latest in the day. **3** (usu. in *pl.*) the series of examinations at the end of a degree course. **4** *Mus.* the principal note in any mode. ▫ **final cause** *Philos.* the end towards which a thing naturally develops or at which an action aims. **final clause** *Gram.* a clause expressing purpose, introduced by *in order that*, *lest*, etc. **final drive** the last part of the transmission system in a motor vehicle. **final solution** the Nazi policy (1941–5) of exterminating European Jews. ▫▫ **finally** *adv.* [ME f. OF or f. L *finalis* f. *finis* end]
■ *adj.* **1** last, closing, concluding, finishing, terminating, ultimate. **2** conclusive, decisive, definitive, unalterable, unchangeable, immutable, irreversible, irrevocable; incontrovertible, irrefutable, indisputable; settled, fixed, absolute, certain, sure. ▫▫ **finally** lastly; at (long) last, eventually, in the end, ultimately, at length; when all is said and done, in the long run, at the end of the day; conclusively, once (and) for all, decisively, irrevocably, completely, absolutely, definitively, definitely, for good, for ever, for all time.

finale /finaáli, -lay/ *n.* **1 a** the last movement of an instrumental composition. **b** a piece of music closing an act in an opera. **2** the close of a drama etc. **3** a conclusion. [It. (as FINAL)]
■ **2, 3** see END *n.* 3a, b.

finalism /fīnəliz'm/ *n.* the doctrine that natural processes (e.g. evolution) are directed towards some goal. ▫▫ **finalistic** /-lístik/ *adj.*

finalist /fīnəlist/ *n.* a competitor in the final of a competition etc.

finality /fīnálliti/ *n.* (*pl.* **-ies**) **1** the quality or fact of being final. **2** the belief that something is final. **3** a final act, state, or utterance. **4** the principle of final cause viewed as operative in the universe. [F *finalité* f. LL *finalitas -tatis* (as FINAL)]
■ **1** conclusiveness, decisiveness, unalterability,

unchangeability, immutability, irreversibility, irrevocableness, incontrovertibility, irrefutability, indisputability; certainty, certitude, sureness, fixedness.

finalize /fínəlīz/ *v.tr.* (also **-ise**) **1** put into final form. **2** complete; bring to an end. **3** approve the final form or details of. □□ **finalization** /-záysh'n/ *n.*

■ **2** complete, conclude, settle, decide, wrap up, clinch, *colloq.* sew up.

finance /fínanss, finánss, fínánss/ *n.* & *v.* ● *n.* **1** the management of (esp. public) money. **2** monetary support for an enterprise. **3** (in *pl.*) the money resources of a State, company, or person. ● *v.tr.* provide capital for (a person or enterprise). □ **finance company** (or **house**) a company concerned mainly with providing money for hire-purchase transactions. [ME f. OF f. *finer* settle a debt f. *fin* end: see FINE²]

■ *n.* **1** (money) management, financial affairs, business, commerce, economics, resources. **2** see SUPPORT *n.* 1. **3** (*finances*) money, resources, capital, cash, funds, assets, holdings, wealth; *colloq.* wherewithal. ● *v.* fund, invest in, back, capitalize, underwrite, subsidize, pay for, *US colloq.* bankroll, stake.

financial /fínánsh'l, fi-/ *adj.* **1** of finance. **2** *Austral.* & *NZ sl.* possessing money. □ **financial year** a year as reckoned for taxing or accounting (e.g. the British tax year, reckoned from 6 April). □□ **financially** *adv.*

■ **1** monetary, pecuniary, fiscal, economic. **2** see WEALTHY.

financier *n.* & *v.* ● *n.* /finánsiər, fi-/ a person engaged in large-scale finance. ● *v.intr.* /fínanseér, fi-/ usu. *derog.* conduct financial operations. [F (as FINANCE)]

■ *n.* capitalist, banker, backer, *derog.* or *joc.* plutocrat, *US* money-man, *sl.* angel.

finch /finch/ *n.* any small seed-eating passerine bird of the family Fringillidae (esp. one of the genus *Fringilla*), including crossbills, canaries, and chaffinches. [OE *finc* f. WG]

find /find/ *v.* & *n.* ● *v.tr.* (*past* and *past part.* **found** /fownd/) **1 a** discover by chance or effort (*found a key*). **b** become aware of. **c** (*absol.*) discover game, esp. a fox. **2 a** get possession of by chance (*found a treasure*). **b** obtain, receive (*idea found acceptance*). **c** succeed in obtaining (*cannot find the money; can't find time to read*). **d** summon up (*found courage to protest*). **e** *sl.* steal. **3 a** seek out and provide (*will find you a book*). **b** supply, furnish (*each finds his own equipment*). **4** ascertain by study or calculation or inquiry (*could not find the answer*). **5 a** perceive or experience (*find no sense in it; find difficulty in breathing*). **b** (often in *passive*) recognize or discover to be present (*the word is not found in Shakespeare*). **c** regard or discover from experience (*finds England too cold; you'll find it pays; find it impossible to reply*). **6** *Law* (of a jury, judge, etc.) decide and declare (*found him guilty; found that he had done it; found it murder*). **7** reach by a natural or normal process (*water finds its own level*). **8 a** (of a letter) reach (a person). **b** (of an address) be adequate to enable a letter etc. to reach (a person). **9** *archaic* reach the conscience of. ● *n.* **1 a** a discovery of treasure, minerals, etc. **b** *Hunting* the finding of a fox. **2** a thing or person discovered, esp. when of value. □ **all found** (of an employee's wages) with board and lodging provided free. **find against** *Law* decide against (a person), judge to be guilty. **find fault** see FAULT. **find favour** prove acceptable. **find one's feet 1** become able to walk. **2** develop one's independent ability. **find for** *Law* decide in favour of (a person), judge to be innocent. **find it in one's heart** (esp. with *neg.*; foll. by *to* + infin.) prevail upon oneself, be willing. **find oneself 1** discover that one is (*woke to find myself in hospital; found herself agreeing*). **2** discover one's vocation. **3** provide for one's own needs. **find out 1** discover or detect (a wrongdoer etc.). **2** (often foll. by *about*) get information (*find out about holidays abroad*). **3** discover (*find out where we are*). **4** (often foll. by *about*) discover the truth, a fact, etc. (*he never found out*). **5** devise. **6** solve. **find-spot** *Archaeol.* the place where an object is found. **find one's way 1** (often foll. by *to*) manage to reach a place. **2** (often foll. by *into*) be brought or get. □□ **findable** *adj.* [OE *findan* f. Gmc]

■ *v.* **1a, 2a** discover, come across, happen on *or* upon, come on *or* upon, hit on *or* upon, chance on *or* upon, light on *or* upon, stumble on *or* upon; recover, get back, repossess, recoup, *disp.* locate. **2 b** see RECEIVE 1, 2. **c** secure, get, procure, acquire, win, gain; set aside, allot, assign, manage. **d** summon up, command, gather (up), muster (up). **e** see STEAL *v.* 1. **3 b** see SUPPLY *v.* 1, 2. **4** ascertain, find out, discover, learn, calculate, determine, work out. **5 a** perceive, see, notice, note, mark, remark, discern, distinguish; experience. **b** see SPOT *v.* 1. **c** regard, consider, think, view, feel *or* discover to be. **6** judge, decide *or* determine to be, pronounce, declare, *formal* deem. **8** see REACH *v.* 4. ● *n.* **1a, 2** discovery, catch; bargain. □ **find out 1** discover, detect, lay one's hand(s) on, track down, turn up, identify, determine, ascertain, put one's finger on, point to, *US sl.* finger. **2** see LEARN 4. **3** discover, light on *or* upon, catch sight of, see, detect, learn, spot, locate, identify, become aware of, determine, ascertain, put one's finger on, point to, *literary* espy, descry. **4** *colloq.* twig, catch on (to); (*find out about*) *Brit. sl.* rumble, suss. **5** see DEVISE *v.* 1. **6** see SOLVE.

finder /findər/ *n.* **1** a person who finds. **2** a small telescope attached to a large one to locate an object for observation. **3** the viewfinder of a camera. □ **finders keepers** *colloq.* whoever finds a thing is entitled to keep it.

fin de siècle /fán də syéklə/ *adj.* **1** characteristic of the end of the nineteenth century. **2** decadent. [F, = end of century]

finding /fínding/ *n.* **1** (often in *pl.*) a conclusion reached by an inquiry. **2** (in *pl.*) *US* small parts or tools used by workmen.

■ **1** (*findings*) conclusion, judgement, verdict, decree, decision, pronouncement, declaration.

fine¹ /fin/ *adj.*, *n.*, *adv.*, & *v.* ● *adj.* **1** of high quality (*they sell fine fabrics*). **2 a** excellent; of notable merit (*a fine painting*). **b** good, satisfactory (*that will be fine*). **c** fortunate (*has been a fine thing for him*). **d** well conceived or expressed (*a fine saying*). **3 a** pure, refined. **b** (of gold or silver) containing a specified proportion of pure metal. **4** of handsome appearance or size; imposing, dignified (*fine buildings; a person of fine presence*). **5** in good health (*I'm fine, thank you*). **6** (of weather etc.) bright and clear with sunshine; free from rain. **7 a** thin; sharp. **b** in small particles. **c** worked in slender thread. **d** (esp. of print) small. **e** (of a pen) narrow-pointed. **8** *Cricket* behind the wicket and near the line of flight of the ball. **9** tritely complimentary; euphemistic (*say fine things about a person; call things by fine names*). **10** ornate, showy, smart. **11** fastidious, dainty, pretending refinement; (of speech or writing) affectedly ornate. **12 a** capable of delicate perception or discrimination. **b** perceptible only with difficulty (*a fine distinction*). **13 a** delicate, subtle, exquisitely fashioned. **b** (of feelings) refined, elevated. **14** (of wine or other goods) of a high standard; conforming to a specified grade. ● *n.* **1** fine weather (*in rain or fine*). **2** (in *pl.*) very small particles in mining, milling, etc. ● *adv.* **1** finely. **2** *colloq.* very well (*suits me fine*). ● *v.* **1** (often foll. by *down*) **a** *tr.* make (beer or wine) clear. **b** *intr.* (of liquid) become clear. **2** *tr.* & *intr.* (often foll. by *away*, *down*, *off*) make or become finer, thinner, or less coarse; dwindle or taper, or cause to do so. □ **cut** (or **run**) **it fine** allow very little margin of time etc. **fine arts** those appealing to the mind or to the sense of beauty, as poetry, music, and esp. painting, sculpture, and architecture. **fine chemicals** see CHEMICAL. **fine-draw** sew together (two pieces of cloth, edges of a tear, parts of a garment) so that the join is imperceptible. **fine-drawn 1** extremely thin. **2** subtle. **fine print** detailed printed information, esp. in legal documents, instructions, etc. **fine-spun 1** delicate. **2** (of a theory etc.) too subtle, unpractical. **fine-tooth comb** a comb with narrow close-set teeth. **fine-tune** make small adjustments to (a mechanism etc.) in order to obtain the best possible results. **fine up** *Austral. colloq.* (of the weather) become fine. **go over with a fine-tooth comb** check or search thoroughly. **not to put too fine a point on it** (as a parenthetic remark) to speak bluntly. □□ **finely** *adv.* **fineness** *n.* [ME f. OF *fin* ult. f. L *finire* finish]

■ *adj.* **1, 14** superior, supreme, first-class, first-rate, prime, choice, select, top-grade, high-grade, *colloq.* quality. **2 a** excellent, magnificent, marvellous, exquisite, splendid, admirable, super, brilliant, outstanding, exceptional, consummate, great, commendable, meritorious, good; enjoyable, entertaining, amusing, satisfying, interesting; (*of an artist or a performance*) masterly, virtuoso, accomplished, skilful. **b** good, satisfactory, pleasant, nice, *Sc.* braw, *colloq.* out of this world, great, OK, peachy, keen, *colloq. or dial.* champion, *Brit. colloq.* tickety-boo, *US colloq.* swell, *Austral. sl.* bonzer, *Brit. archaic sl.* ripping, *esp. US sl.* cool, *US sl.* neat. **3 a** see PURE 1, 2. **4** handsome, attractive, striking, beautiful, pretty, lovely; fair, good-looking, comely, *esp. Sc. & N.Engl.* bonny, *esp. US colloq.* cute; imposing, dignified, impressive. **5** in good health, well, all right, healthy, *colloq.* OK. **6** bright, clear, sunny, fair, cloudless, pleasant, dry, balmy, nice. **7 a** thin, diaphanous, gauzy, sheer, gossamer, flimsy, delicate; sharp, keen, keen-edged, razor-sharp, pointed. **b** powdery, powdered, pulverized, crushed, fine-grained; comminuted. **c** slender, thin, gossamer, filamentous, threadlike. **9** see *flattering* (FLATTER). **10** see ELEGANT 1–3. **11** see DAINTY *adj.* 4, FLOWERY. **12 b** subtle, refined, nice, hair-splitting, delicate, close. **13 a** delicate, subtle, exquisite, well-made, dainty, elegant. **b** see REFINED 1.

fine[2] /fīn/ *n.* & *v.* ● *n.* **1** a sum of money exacted as a penalty. **2** *hist.* a sum of money paid by an incoming tenant in return for the rent's being small. ● *v.tr.* punish by a fine (*fined him £5*). □ **in fine** to sum up; in short. □□ **finable** /fīnəb'l/ *adj.* [ME f. OF *fin* f. med.L *finis* sum paid on settling a lawsuit f. L *finis* end]

■ *n.* **1** penalty, charge, fee, mulct, forfeit, forfeiture, *Law* amercement. ● *v.* penalize, charge, mulct, *Law* amerce.

fine[3] /feen/ *n.* = FINE CHAMPAGNE. [abbr.]

fine champagne /feén shonpaányə/ *n.* old liqueur brandy. [F, = fine (brandy from) Champagne (vineyards in Charente)]

finery[1] /fīnəri/ *n.* showy dress or decoration. [FINE[1] + -ERY, after BRAVERY]

■ decoration(s), ornaments, trappings, trinkets, frippery, showy dress, best bib and tucker, *colloq.* glad rags, *joc.* Sunday best.

finery[2] /fīnəri/ *n.* (*pl.* **-ies**) *hist.* a hearth where pig iron was converted into wrought iron. [F *finerie* f. *finer* refine, FINE[1]]

fines herbes /feenz áirb/ *n.pl.* mixed herbs used in cooking, esp. chopped as omelette-flavouring. [F, = fine herbs]

finesse /finéss/ *n.* & *v.* ● *n.* **1** refinement. **2** subtle or delicate manipulation. **3** artfulness, esp. in handling a difficulty tactfully. **4** *Cards* an attempt to win a trick with a card that is not the highest held. ● *v.* **1** *intr.* & *tr.* use or achieve by finesse. **2** *Cards* **a** *intr.* make a finesse. **b** *tr.* play (a card) by way of finesse. **3** *tr.* evade or trick by finesse. [F, rel. to FINE[1]]

■ *n.* **1** refinement, grace, tact, diplomacy, discretion, taste, polish, delicacy, elegance. **2** trick(s), artifice(s), manipulation(s), stratagem(s), wile(s), ruse(s), scheme(s), machination(s), intrigue(s), device(s), expedient(s), manoeuvre(s), deception(s), deceit(s). **3** artfulness, subtlety, cunning, craftiness, cleverness, shrewdness, skill; style, dash, *élan*, panache; skilfulness, adroitness, expertness, expertise, adeptness, proficiency, ability, facility. ● *v.* **1** see MANOEUVRE *v.* 3. **3** evade, trick, bluff, delude, deceive, fool, hoodwink, *colloq.* finagle, *sl.* con.

finger /finggər/ *n.* & *v.* ● *n.* **1** any of the terminal projections of the hand (including or excluding the thumb). **2** the part of a glove etc. intended to cover a finger. **3 a** a finger-like object (*fish finger*). **b** a long narrow structure. **4** *colloq.* a measure of liquor in a glass, based on the breadth of a finger. **5** *sl.* **a** an informer. **b** a pickpocket. **c** a policeman. ● *v.tr.* **1** touch, feel, or turn about with the fingers. **2** *Mus.* **a** play (a passage) with fingers used in a particular way. **b** mark (music) with signs showing which fingers are to be used. **c** play upon (an instrument) with the fingers. **3** *US sl.* indicate (a victim, or a criminal to the police). □ **all fingers and thumbs** clumsy. **finger alphabet** a form of sign language using the fingers. **finger-board** a flat strip at the top end of a stringed instrument, against which the strings are pressed to determine tones. **finger-bowl** (or **-glass**) a small bowl for rinsing the fingers during a meal. **finger-dry** dry and style (the hair) by running one's fingers through it. **finger language** language expressed by means of the finger alphabet. **finger-mark** a mark left on a surface by a finger. **finger-paint** *n.* paint that can be applied with the fingers. ● *v.intr.* apply paint with the fingers. **finger-plate** a plate fixed to a door above the handle to prevent finger-marks. **finger-post** a signpost at a road junction. **one's fingers itch** (often foll. by *to* + infin.) one is longing or impatient. **finger-stall** a cover to protect a finger, esp. when injured. **get** (or **pull**) **one's finger out** *sl.* cease prevaricating and start to act. **have a finger in** (or **in the pie**) be (esp. officiously) concerned in (the matter). **lay a finger on** touch however slightly. **point the finger at** *colloq.* accuse, blame. **put one's finger on** locate or identify exactly. **put the finger on** *sl.* **1** inform against. **2** identify (an intended victim). **slip through one's fingers** escape. **twist** (or **wind**) **round one's finger** (or **little finger**) persuade (a person) without difficulty, dominate (a person) completely. **work one's fingers to the bone** see BONE. □□ **fingered** *adj.* (also in *comb.*). **fingerless** *adj.* [OE f. Gmc]

■ *n.* **1** digit. **5 a** see INFORMER 1. **b** see THIEF. **c** see CONSTABLE 1a. ● *v.* **1** touch, feel, handle; toy *or* play *or* fiddle with. **3** indicate, identify, point out, *sl.* put the finger on. □ **all fingers and thumbs** see CLUMSY 1. **get** (or **pull**) **one's finger out** get on with it, stop delaying *or* procrastinating, *colloq.* get cracking. **have a finger in** be *or* become *or* get involved in, figure in, have a hand in, influence; interfere in, tamper *or* meddle *or* tinker *or* monkey with. **lay a finger on** (so much as) touch; strike, hit, punch. **point the finger at** see ACCUSE 2. **put one's finger on** locate, find, discover, unearth, lay *or* put one's hands on, track down, get hold of, come by, acquire; identify, indicate, point to, pin down, zero in on; recall, remember, recollect, bring *or* call to mind, think of. **put the finger on 1** inform on *or* against, tell on, tattle on, betray, bear witness against, *colloq.* peach on *or* against, *sl.* snitch on, squeal on, *Austral. & NZ sl.* put a person's pot on, *US sl.* finger. **slip through one's fingers** escape, get away, vanish, disappear. **twist** (or **wind**) **around one's finger** (or **little finger**) persuade, control, dominate, have under control, manipulate, manoeuvre, wield power *or* authority over, have under a person's thumb, have the upper hand over, be master of, influence.

fingering[1] /finggəring/ *n.* **1** a manner or technique of using the fingers, esp. to play an instrument. **2** an indication of this in a musical score.

fingering[2] /finggəring/ *n.* fine wool for knitting. [earlier *fingram*, perh. f. F *fin grain*, as GROGRAM f. *gros grain*]

fingerling /finggərling/ *n.* a parr.

fingernail /finggərnayl/ *n.* the nail at the tip of each finger.

fingerprint /finggərprint/ *n.* & *v.* ● *n.* **1** an impression made on a surface by the fingertips, esp. as used for identifying individuals. **2** a distinctive characteristic. ● *v.tr.* record the fingerprints of (a person).

■ *n.* **2** see MARK[1] *n.* 2a, 3, 4a.

fingertip /finggərtip/ *n.* the tip of a finger. □ **have at one's fingertips** be thoroughly familiar with (a subject etc.).

finial /finniəl/ *n. Archit.* **1** an ornament finishing off the apex of a roof, pediment, gable, tower-corner, canopy, etc. **2** the topmost part of a pinnacle. [ME f. OF *fin* f. L *finis* end]

finical /finnik'l/ *adj.* = FINICKY. □□ **finicality** /-kálliti/ *n.* **finically** *adv.* **finicalness** *n.* [16th c.: prob. orig. university sl. f. FINE[1] + -ICAL]

finicking /finniking/ *adj.* = FINICKY. [FINICAL + -ING[2]]

finicky /finniki/ *adj.* **1** over-particular, fastidious. **2** needing much attention to detail; fiddly. □□ **finickiness** *n.*

■ **1** over-particular, fastidious, particular, finical, finicking, over-nice, fussy, nice, critical, hard to please, difficult, meticulous, over-precise, precise, punctilious, over-scrupulous, scrupulous, *colloq.* choosy, pernickety, nit-picking, picky. **2** fiddly, fussy, elaborate, detailed, fine.

finis /finniss, féeniss, fíniss/ *n.* **1** (at the end of a book) the end. **2** the end of anything, esp. of life. [L]

finish /finnish/ *v.* & *n.* ● *v.* **1** *tr.* **a** (often foll. by *off*) bring to an end; come to the end of; complete. **b** (usu. foll. by *off*) *colloq.* kill; overcome completely. **c** (often foll. by *off, up*) consume or get through the whole or the remainder of (food or drink) (*finish up your dinner*). **2** *intr.* **a** come to an end, cease. **b** reach the end, esp. of a race. **c** = *finish up*. **3** *tr.* **a** complete the manufacture of (cloth, woodwork, etc.) by surface treatment. **b** put the final touches to; make perfect or highly accomplished (*finished manners*). **c** prepare (a girl) for entry into fashionable society. ● *n.* **1 a** the end, the last stage. **b** the point at which a race etc. ends. **c** the death of a fox in a hunt (*be in at the finish*). **2** a method, material, or texture used for surface treatment of wood, cloth, etc. (*mahogany finish*). **3** what serves to give completeness. **4** an accomplished or completed state. □ **fight to a finish** fight till one party is completely beaten. **finishing-school** a private college where girls are prepared for entry into fashionable society. **finish off** provide with an ending. **finish up** (often foll. by *in, by*) end in something, end by doing something (*he finished up last in the race*; *the plan finished up in the waste-paper basket*; *finished up by apologizing*). **finish with** have no more to do with, complete one's use of or association with. [ME f. OF *fenir* f. L *finire* f. *finis* end]

■ *v.* **1 a** bring to an end, come to the end of, complete, accomplish, perfect, achieve, carry out, fulfil, consummate, clinch, wrap up. **b** kill, exterminate, finish off, annihilate, destroy, get rid of, dispose of, dispatch, put an end to, administer *or* deliver *or* give the *coup de grâce* to, *colloq.* polish off, *sl.* bump off, *esp. US sl.* rub out, *US sl.* waste, ice. **c** consume, dispose of, finish off *or* up, eat *or* drink (up), use (up), devour, drain, polish off. **2 a** come to an end, cease, end, stop, conclude, close, finish up, terminate, wind up; culminate. **3 b** put the final touches to, finish off; perfect, polish, put a finish on. ● *n.* **1 a** end, conclusion, termination, close, closing, completion, ending, finale, culmination, winding up, wind-up; death, killing, annihilation, extermination, downfall, destruction, defeat. **2** surface, polish; see also TEXTURE *n.* 1, 2. □ **finish up** see *wind up* 6 (WIND[2]). **finish with** have *or* be done with, *colloq.* be through with.

finisher /finnishər/ *n.* **1** a person who finishes something. **2** a worker or machine doing the last operation in manufacture. **3** *colloq.* a discomfiting thing, a crushing blow, etc.

finite /fínīt/ *adj.* **1** limited, bounded; not infinite. **2** *Gram.* (of a part of a verb) having a specific number and person. **3** not infinitely small. □□ **finitely** *adv.* **finiteness** *n.* **finitude** /finnityōōd/ *n.* [L *finitus* past part. of *finire* FINISH]

■ **1** limited, bounded, restricted, delimited, numerable, countable.

finitism /fínītiz'm/ *n.* belief in the finiteness of the world, God, etc. □□ **finitist** *n.*

fink /fingk/ *n.* & *v.* *US sl.* ● *n.* **1** an unpleasant person. **2** an informer. **3** a strikebreaker; a blackleg. ● *v.intr.* (foll. by *on*) inform on. [20th c.: orig. unkn.]

■ *n.* **2** see SNEAK *n.* ● *v.* see INFORM 2.

Finn /fin/ *n.* a native or national of Finland; a person of Finnish descent. [OE *Finnas* pl.]

finnan /finnən/ *n.* (in full **finnan haddock**) a haddock cured with the smoke of green wood, turf, or peat. [*Findhorn* or *Findon* in Scotland]

finnesko /finnəskō/ *n.* (*pl.* same) a boot of tanned reindeer-skin with the hair on the outside. [Norw. *finnsko* (as FINN, *sko* SHOE)]

Finnic /finnik/ *adj.* **1** of the group of peoples related to the Finns. **2** of the group of languages related to Finnish.

Finnish /finnish/ *adj.* & *n.* ● *adj.* of the Finns or their language. ● *n.* the language of the Finns.

Finno-Ugric /finnō-óōgrik, -yóōgrik/ *adj.* & *n.* (also **Finno-Ugrian** /-óōgriən, -yóōgriən/) ● *adj.* belonging to the group of Ural-Altaic languages including Finnish, Estonian, Lapp, and Magyar. ● *n.* this group.

finny /finni/ *adj.* **1** having fins; like a fin. **2** *poet.* of or teeming with fish.

fino /féenō/ *n.* (*pl.* **-os**) a light-coloured dry sherry. [Sp., = fine]

fiord /fyord/ *n.* (also **fjord**) a long narrow inlet of sea between high cliffs, as in Norway. [Norw. f. ON *fjörthr* f. Gmc: cf. FIRTH, FORD]

■ see GULF *n.* 1.

fioritura /fióritōōrə/ *n.* (*pl.* **fioriture** *pronunc.* same) *Mus.* the usu. improvised decoration of a melody. [It., = flowering f. *fiorire* to flower]

fipple /fipp'l/ *n.* a plug at the mouth-end of a wind instrument. □ **fipple flute** a flute played by blowing endwise, e.g. a recorder. [17th c.: orig. unkn.]

fir /fur/ *n.* **1** (in full **fir-tree**) any evergreen coniferous tree, esp. of the genus *Abies*, with needles borne singly on the stems (cf. PINE[1]). **2** the wood of the fir. □ **fir-cone** the fruit of the fir. □□ **firry** *adj.* [ME, prob. f. ON *fyri-* f. Gmc]

fire /fīr/ *n.* & *v.* ● *n.* **1 a** the state or process of combustion, in which substances combine chemically with oxygen from the air and usu. give out bright light and heat. **b** the active principle operative in this. **c** flame or incandescence. **2** a conflagration, a destructive burning (*forest fire*). **3 a** burning fuel in a grate, furnace, etc. **b** = *electric fire*. **c** = *gas fire*. **4** firing of guns (*open fire*). **5 a** fervour, spirit, vivacity. **b** poetic inspiration, lively imagination. **c** vehement emotion. **6** burning heat, fever. **7** luminosity, glow (*St Elmo's fire*). ● *v.* **1 a** *tr.* discharge (a gun etc.). **b** *tr.* propel (a missile) from a gun etc. **c** *intr.* (often foll. by *at, into, on*) fire a gun or missile. **d** *tr.* produce (a broadside, salute, etc.) by discharge of guns. **e** *intr.* (of a gun etc.) be discharged. **2** *tr.* cause (explosive) to explode. **3** *tr.* deliver or utter in rapid succession (*fired insults at us*). **4** *tr. sl.* dismiss (an employee) from a job. **5** *tr.* **a** set fire to with the intention of destroying. **b** kindle (explosives). **6** *intr.* catch fire. **7** *intr.* (of an internal-combustion engine, or a cylinder in one) undergo ignition of its fuel. **8** *tr.* supply (a furnace, engine, boiler, or power station) with fuel. **9** *tr.* **a** stimulate (the imagination or emotion). **b** fill (a person) with enthusiasm. **10** *tr.* **a** bake or dry (pottery, bricks, etc.). **b** cure (tea or tobacco) by artificial heat. **11** *intr.* become heated or excited. **12** *tr.* cause to glow or redden. □ **catch fire** begin to burn. **fire-alarm** a device for giving warning of fire. **fire and brimstone** the supposed torments of hell. **fire away** *colloq.* begin; go ahead. **fire-ball 1** a large meteor. **2** a ball of flame, esp. from a nuclear explosion. **3** an energetic person. **4** ball lightning. **5** *Mil. hist.* a ball filled with combustibles. **fire-balloon** a balloon made buoyant by the heat of a fire burning at its mouth. **fire-blight** a disease of plants, esp. hops and fruit trees, causing a scorched appearance. **fire-bomb** an incendiary bomb. **fire-break** an obstacle to the spread of fire in a forest etc., esp. an open space. **fire-brick** a fireproof brick used in a grate. **fire brigade** esp. *Brit.* an organized body of firemen trained and employed to extinguish fires. **fire-bug** *colloq.* a pyromaniac. **fire company 1** = *fire brigade*. **2** a fire-insurance company. **fire-control** a system of regulating the fire of a ship's or a fort's guns. **fire department** *US* = *fire brigade*. **fire door** a fire-resistant door to prevent the spread of fire. **fire-drake** (in Germanic mythology) a fiery dragon. **fire-drill 1** a rehearsal of the procedures to be used in case of fire. **2** a primitive device for kindling fire with a stick and wood. **fire-eater 1** a conjuror who appears to swallow fire. **2** a person fond of quarrelling or fighting. **fire-engine** a vehicle carrying equipment for fighting large fires. **fire-escape** an emergency staircase or apparatus for escape from a building on fire. **fire extinguisher** an apparatus with a jet for discharging liquid chemicals, water, or foam to extinguish a fire. **fire-fighter** a person whose task is to extinguish fires. **fire-guard 1** a protective screen or grid placed in front of a fireplace. **2** *US* a fire-watcher. **3** *US* a fire-break. **fire-hose** a hose-pipe used in extinguishing fires. **fire-irons** tongs, poker, and shovel, for tending a domestic fire. **fire-lighter** *Brit.* a piece of inflammable material to help start a fire in a grate. **fire-office** a fire-insurance company. **fire-opal** girasol. **fire-plug** a hydrant for a fire-hose. **fire-power 1** the destructive capacity of guns etc. **2** financial, intellectual, or emotional strength. **fire-practice** a fire-drill. **fire-raiser** *Brit.* an arsonist. **fire-raising** *Brit.* arson. **fire-screen 1** a screen to keep off the direct heat of a fire. **2** a fire-guard. **3** an ornamental screen for a fireplace. **fire-ship** *hist.* a ship loaded with combustibles and set adrift to ignite an enemy's ships etc. **fire station** the headquarters of a fire brigade. **fire-step** = *firing-step*. **fire-stone** stone that resists fire, used for furnaces etc. **fire-storm** a high wind or storm following a fire caused by bombs. **fire-tongs** tongs for picking up pieces of coal etc. in tending a fire. **fire-trap** a building without proper provision for escape in case of fire. **fire up** show sudden anger. **fire-walking** the (often ceremonial) practice of walking barefoot over white-hot stones, wood-ashes, etc. **fire warden** *US* a person employed to prevent or extinguish fires. **fire-watcher** a person keeping watch for fires, esp. those caused by bombs. **fire-water** *colloq.* strong alcoholic liquor. **go on fire** *Sc.* & *Ir.* catch fire. **go through fire and water** face all perils. **on fire 1** burning. **2** excited. **set fire to** (or **set on fire**) ignite, kindle, cause to burn. **set the world** (or **Thames**) **on fire** do something remarkable or sensational. **take fire** catch fire. **under fire 1** being shot at. **2** being rigorously criticized or questioned. □□ **fireless** *adj.* **firer** *n.* [OE *fȳr*, *fȳrian*, f. WG]

■ *n.* **1 c** flame, blaze; see also *incandescence* (INCANDESCENT). **2** conflagration, holocaust, inferno, blaze. **4** firing, gunfire, fusillade, volley, barrage, bombardment, salvo, cannonade, shelling, broadside, flak. **5** fervour, spirit, feeling, passion, ardour, ardency, fervency, intensity, vigour, energy, vivacity, animation, liveliness, verve, *élan*, éclat, dash, vitality, enthusiasm, fever, feverishness, *colloq.* vim, pep; inspiration, imagination. **6** heat, torridity, fieriness, fever, feverishness. **7** see *radiance* (RADIANT). ● *v.* **1 a** see DISCHARGE *v.* 3. **b** propel, launch; throw, catapult, hurl. **c** open fire, shoot, blaze away, *colloq.* blast. **2** detonate, set *or* let off. **4** dismiss, discharge, oust, give a person notice, ask for (*or* get) one's cards, boot out, show a person the door, axe, give a person the axe, give a person his *or* her marching orders, *Brit.* make *or* declare redundant, *colloq.* sack, give a person the sack, give a person the boot, give a person his *or* her walking papers, *sl.* bounce, give a person the bounce. **5 a** set fire to, set afire *or* alight, set on fire, ignite, put to the torch, burn, *US sl.* torch. **b** see KINDLE 1. **9 a** see STIMULATE. **b** excite, motivate, animate, inspire, energize, inspirit, vitalize, vivify, rouse, stir, awaken, move. □ **catch fire** burn, kindle, ignite, take fire, *Sc.* & *Ir.* go on fire. **fire away** see BEGIN 5b, *go ahead* (GO[1]). **fire-bomb** see BOMB *n.* 1. **fire up** see FLARE *v.* 3. **on fire 1** burning, blazing, flaming; afire, alight, aflame. **2** excited, enthusiastic, eager, ardent, passionate, fervent, fervid, fired up, aroused, stirred, stimulated, inspired, intense. **set fire to** (or **set on fire**) see FIRE *v.* 5a above.

firearm /fīraarm/ *n.* (usu. in *pl.*) a gun, esp. a pistol or rifle.
■ see REVOLVER.

fireback /fīrbak/ *n.* **1 a** the back wall of a fireplace. **b** an iron sheet for this. **2** a SE Asian pheasant of the genus *Lophura*.

firebox /fīrboks/ *n.* the fuel-chamber of a steam engine or boiler.

firebrand /fīrbrand/ *n.* **1** a piece of burning wood. **2** a cause of trouble, esp. a person causing unrest.
■ **2** see AGITATOR 1.

fireclay /fīrklay/ *n.* clay capable of withstanding high temperatures, often used to make fire-bricks.

firecracker /fīrkrakkər/ *n.* *US* an explosive firework.

firecrest /fīrkrest/ *n.* a warbler, *Regulus ignicapillus*, with red and orange crown feathers which may be erected.

firedamp /fīrdamp/ *n.* a miners' name for methane, which is explosive when mixed in certain proportions with air.

firedog /fīrdog/ *n.* a metal support for burning wood or for a grate or fire-irons.

firefly /fīrflī/ *n.* (*pl.* **-flies**) any soft-bodied beetle of the family Lampyridae, emitting phosphorescent light, including glow-worms.

firehouse /fīrhowss/ *n.* *US* a fire station.

firelight /fīrlīt/ *n.* light from a fire in a fireplace. [OE *fyr-leoht* (as FIRE, LIGHT[1])]
■ see LIGHT[1] *n.* 2.

firelock /fīrlok/ *n.* *hist.* a musket in which the priming was ignited by sparks.

fireman /fīrmən/ *n.* (*pl.* **-men**) **1** a member of a fire brigade; a person employed to extinguish fires. **2** a person who tends a furnace or the fire of a steam engine or steamship.

fireplace /fīrplayss/ *n.* *Archit.* **1** a place for a domestic fire, esp. a grate or hearth at the base of a chimney. **2** a structure surrounding this. **3** the area in front of this.

fireproof /fīrproof/ *adj.* & *v.* ● *adj.* able to resist fire or great heat. ● *v.tr.* make fireproof.
■ *adj.* see INCOMBUSTIBLE.

fireside /fīrsīd/ *n.* **1** the area round a fireplace. **2** a person's home or home-life. □ **fireside chat** an informal talk.

firewood /fīrwood/ *n.* wood for use as fuel.

firework /fīrwurk/ *n.* **1** a device containing combustible chemicals that cause explosions or spectacular effects. **2** (in *pl.*) **a** an outburst of passion, esp. anger. **b** a display of wit or brilliance.
■ **2 a** see *excitement* (EXCITE).

firing /fīring/ *n.* **1** the discharging of guns. **2** material for a fire, fuel. **3** the heating process which hardens clay into pottery etc. □ **firing-line 1** the front line in a battle. **2** the leading part in an activity etc. **firing-party** a group detailed to fire the salute at a military funeral. **firing-squad 1** a group detailed to shoot a condemned person. **2** a firing-party. **firing-step** a step on which soldiers in a trench stand to fire.
■ **1** see FIRE *n.* 4.

firkin /fúrkin/ *n.* **1** a small cask for liquids, butter, fish, etc. **2** *Brit.* (as a measure) half a kilderkin (8 or 9 gallons). [ME *ferdekyn*, prob. f. MDu. *vierdekijn* (unrecorded) dimin. of *vierde* fourth]

firm[1] /furm/ *adj.*, *adv.*, & *v.* ● *adj.* **1 a** of solid or compact structure. **b** fixed, stable. **c** steady; not shaking. **2 a** resolute, determined. **b** not easily shaken (*firm belief*). **c** steadfast, constant (*a firm friend*). **3 a** (of an offer etc.) not liable to cancellation after acceptance. **b** (of a decree, law, etc.) established, immutable. **4** *Commerce* (of prices or goods) maintaining their level or value. ● *adv.* firmly (*stand firm*; *hold firm to*). ● *v.* **1** *tr.* & *intr.* make or become firm, secure, compact, or solid. **2** *tr.* fix (plants) firmly in the soil. □□ **firmly** *adv.* **firmness** *n.* [ME f. OF *ferme* f. L *firmus*]
■ *adj.* **1 a** solid, compact, dense, compressed, rigid, stiff, hard, unyielding, inelastic, inflexible. **b** fixed, stable, fast, secure, tight, stationary, anchored, moored, unmovable, immovable. **c** steady, strong, sturdy, unwavering, unshakeable. **2 a** resolute, determined, persistent, dogged, definite, positive, decisive, unflinching. **b** staunch, unshaken, unshakeable, unwavering, immovable, inflexible, rigid, undeviating, unswerving, unchanging, unchangeable, obstinate, obdurate, stubborn, strict, unyielding, unbending, unalterable,

inalterable. **c** constant, staunch; see also STEADFAST. **3 b** established, immutable; see also FINAL *adj.* 2. ● *v.* **1** secure, settle, establish, consolidate, solidify, determine, set up. ▫▫ **firmly** solidly, strongly; securely, tightly, rigidly, fast, immovably; resolutely, steadfastly, determinedly, staunchly, unwaveringly, decisively, unhesitatingly, constantly.

firm[2] /furm/ *n.* **1 a** a business concern. **b** the partners in such a concern. **2** a group of persons working together, esp. of hospital doctors and assistants. [earlier = signature, style: Sp. & It. *firma* f. med.L, f. L *firmare* confirm f. *firmus* FIRM[1]]

■ **1** company, organization, business, enterprise, concern, house, partnership, corporation, *colloq.* outfit. **2** see TEAM *n.* 2.

firmament /fúrməmənt/ *n. literary* the sky regarded as a vault or arch. ▫▫ **firmamental** /-mént'l/ *adj.* [ME f. OF f. L *firmamentum* f. *firmare* (as FIRM[2])]

■ sky, skies, heaven, vault (of heaven), empyrean, *poet.* welkin, *esp. poet.* heavens.

firman /furmaán, fúrmən/ *n.* **1** an oriental sovereign's edict. **2** a grant or permit. [Pers. *fermān*, Skr. *pramāṇam* right measure]

firmware /fúrmwair/ *n. Computing* a permanent kind of software programmed into a read-only memory.

firry see FIR.

first /furst/ *adj.*, *n.*, & *adv.* ● *adj.* **1 a** earliest in time or order. **b** coming next after a specified or implied time (*shall take the first train*; *the first cuckoo*). **2** foremost in position, rank, or importance (*First Lord of the Treasury*; *first mate*). **3** *Mus.* performing the highest or chief of two or more parts for the same instrument or voice. **4** most willing or likely (*should be the first to admit the difficulty*). **5** basic or evident (*first principles*). ● *n.* **1** (prec. by *the*) the person or thing first mentioned or occurring. **2** the first occurrence of something notable. **3 a** a place in the first class in an examination. **b** a person having this. **4** the first day of a month. **5** first gear. **6 a** first place in a race. **b** the winner of this. **7** (in *pl.*) goods of the best quality. ● *adv.* **1** before any other person or thing (*first of all*; *first and foremost*; *first come first served*). **2** before someone or something else (*must get this done first*). **3** for the first time (*when did you first see her?*). **4** in preference; rather (*will see him damned first*). **5** first-class (*I usually travel first*). ▫ **at first** at the beginning. **at first hand** directly from the original source. **first aid** help given to an injured person until proper medical treatment is available. **first and last** taking one thing with another, on the whole. **first blood** see BLOOD. **first-born** *adj.* eldest. ● *n.* the eldest child of a person. **First Cause** the Creator of the universe. **first class 1** a set of persons or things grouped together as the best. **2** the best accommodation in a train, ship, etc. **3** the class of mail given priority in handling. **4 a** the highest division in an examination list. **b** a place in this. **first-class** *adj.* **1** belonging to or travelling by the first class. **2** of the best quality; very good. ● *adv.* by the first class (*travels first-class*). **first cousin** see COUSIN. **first-day cover** an envelope with stamps postmarked on their first day of issue. **first-degree** *Med.* denoting burns that affect only the surface of the skin, causing reddening. **first finger** the finger next to the thumb. **first floor** see FLOOR. **first-foot** *Sc. n.* the first person to cross a threshold in the New Year. ● *v.intr.* be a first-foot. **first-fruit** (usu. in *pl.*) **1** the first agricultural produce of a season, esp. as offered to God. **2** the first results of work etc. **3** *hist.* a payment to a superior by the new holder of an office. **first gear** see GEAR. **first intention** see INTENTION. **First Lady** (in the US) the wife of the President. **first lesson** the first of several passages from the Bible read at a service in the Church of England. **first lieutenant** *US* an army or air force officer next below captain. **first light** the time when light first appears in the morning. **first mate** (on a merchant ship) the officer second in command to the master. **first name** a personal or Christian name. **first night** the first public performance of a play etc. **first-nighter** a habitual attender of first nights. **first off** *US colloq.* at first, first of all. **first offender** a criminal against whom no previous conviction is recorded. **first officer** the mate on a merchant ship. **first or last** sooner or later. **first past the post 1** winning a race etc. by being the first to reach the finishing line. **2** (of an electoral system) selecting a candidate or party by simple majority (see also *proportional representation*, *single transferable vote*). **first person** see PERSON. **first post** see POST[3]. **first-rate** *adj.* of the highest class, excellent. ● *adv. colloq.* **1** very well (*feeling first-rate*). **2** excellently. **first reading** the occasion when a Bill is presented to a legislature to permit its introduction. **first refusal** see REFUSAL. **first school** *Brit.* a school for children from 5 to 9 years old. **first sergeant** *US* the highest-ranking non-commissioned officer in a company. **first-strike** denoting a first aggressive attack with nuclear weapons. **first thing** *colloq.* before anything else; very early in the morning (*shall do it first thing*). **the first thing** even the most elementary fact or principle (*does not know the first thing about it*). **first things first** the most important things before any others (*we must do first things first*). **first up** *Austral.* first of all; at the first attempt. **from the first** from the beginning. **from first to last** throughout. **get to first base** *US* achieve the first step towards an objective. **in the first place** as the first consideration. **of the first water** see WATER. [OE *fyrst* f. Gmc]

■ *adj.* **1 a** earliest, oldest, original; initial, maiden, opening. **2** foremost, leading, principal, pre-eminent, primary, chief, head, premier, prime. **3** chief, head, lead, principal. **5** basic, fundamental, elementary, primary, cardinal, key, essential, evident. ● *n.* **6 a** first place, gold (medal); see also WIN *n.* **b** see WINNER 1. ● *adv.* **1** before, in front, earliest, foremost; firstly, in the first place, before all, before anything else, to begin *or* start with, from the start, *sl.* for starters. **2** before, beforehand, ahead, sooner. **4** see RATHER 1. ▫ **at first** at *or* in the beginning, initially, at the start *or* outset, *US colloq.* first off; see also *in the first instance* (INSTANCE). **first-class 2** see EXCELLENT. **first light** see DAWN *n.* 1. **first off** see *at first* (FIRST) above. **first-rate** (*adj.*) first-class, excellent, high-grade, prime, superior, superb, great, remarkable, admirable, fine, exceptional, outstanding, extraordinary, unparalleled, matchless, unsurpassed, top, *colloq.* A1, top-notch, tiptop, *sl.* ace, *esp. Brit. sl.* wizard. **from the first** see *originally* (ORIGINAL). **from first to last** see THROUGHOUT *adv.* **in the first place** see FIRST *adv.* 1 above.

firsthand /fúrst-hánd/ *attrib. adj.* & *adv.* from the original source; direct.

firstling /fúrstling/ *n.* (usu. in *pl.*) **1** the first result of anything, first-fruits. **2** the first offspring; the first born in a season.

firstly /fúrstli/ *adv.* (in enumerating topics, arguments, etc.) in the first place, first (cf. FIRST *adv.*).

■ see FIRST *adv.* 1.

firth /furth/ *n.* (also **frith** /frith/) **1** a narrow inlet of the sea. **2** an estuary. [ME (orig. Sc.) f. ON *fjörthr* FIORD]

■ see GULF *n.* 1.

fisc /fisk/ *n. Rom.Hist.* the public treasury; the emperor's privy purse. [F *fisc* or L *fiscus* rush-basket, purse, treasury]

fiscal /fisk'l/ *adj.* & *n.* ● *adj.* of public revenue; esp. *US* of financial matters. ● *n.* **1** a legal official in some countries. **2** *Sc.* = *procurator fiscal.* ▫ **fiscal year** = *financial year.* ▫▫ **fiscally** *adv.* [F *fiscal* or L *fiscalis* (as FISC)]

■ *adj.* financial, economic, budgetary, pecuniary, monetary.

fiscality /fiskálliti/ *n.* (*pl.* **-ies**) **1** (in *pl.*) fiscal matters. **2** excessive regard for these.

fish[1] /fish/ *n.* & *v.* ● *n.* (*pl.* same or **fishes**) **1 a** vertebrate cold-blooded animal with gills and fins living wholly in water. **2** any animal living wholly in water, e.g. cuttlefish, shellfish, jellyfish. **3** the flesh of fish as food. **4** *colloq.* a person remarkable in some way (usu. unfavourable) (*an odd* *fish*). **5** (**the Fish** or **Fishes**) the zodiacal sign or constellation Pisces. **6** *Naut. sl.* a torpedo; a submarine. ● *v.* **1** *intr.* try to catch fish, esp. with a line or net. **2** *tr.* fish for (a certain kind of fish) or in (a certain stretch of water). **3** *intr.* (foll. by *for*) **a** search for in water or a concealed place. **b** seek by indirect means (*fishing for compliments*). **4** *tr.* (foll. by *up*, *out*, etc.) retrieve with careful or awkward searching. □ **drink like a fish** drink excessively. **fish-bowl** a usu. round glass bowl for keeping pet fish in. **fish cake** a cake of shredded fish and mashed potato, usu. eaten fried. **fish eagle 1** any large eagle of the genus *Haliaeetus*, with long broad wings, strong legs, and a strong tail. **2** any of several other eagles catching and feeding on fish. **fish-eye lens** a very wide-angle lens with a curved front. **fish farm** a place where fish are bred for food. **fish finger** *Brit.* a small oblong piece of fish in batter or breadcrumbs. **fish-glue** isinglass. **fish-hawk** an osprey, *Pandion haliaeetus*. **fish-hook** a barbed hook for catching fish. **fish-kettle** an oval pan for boiling fish. **fish-knife** a knife for eating or serving fish. **fish-meal** ground dried fish used as fertilizer or animal feed. **fish out of water** a person in an unsuitable or unwelcome environment or situation. **fish-pond** (or **-pool**) a pond or pool in which fish are kept. **fish-slice** a flat utensil for lifting fish and fried foods during and after cooking. **other fish to fry** other matters to attend to. □□ **fishlike** *adj.* [OE *fisc*, *fiscian* f. Gmc]

■ *v.* **1–3** see ANGLE[2] *v.* 2. **4** (*fish up* or *out*) see DIG *v.* 4.

fish[2] /fish/ *n.* & *v.* ● *n.* **1** a flat plate of iron, wood, etc., to strengthen a beam or joint. **2** *Naut.* a piece of wood, convex and concave, used to strengthen a mast etc. ● *v.tr.* **1** mend or strengthen (a spar etc.) with a fish. **2** join (rails) with a fish-plate. □ **fish-bolt** a bolt used to fasten fish-plates and rails together. **fish-plate a** a flat piece of iron etc. connecting railway rails. **b** a flat piece of metal with ends like a fish's tail, used to position masonry. [orig. as verb: f. F *ficher* fix ult. f. L *figere*]

fish[3] /fish/ *n.* a piece of ivory etc. used as a counter in games. [F *fiche* (*ficher*; see FISH[2])]

fisher /fishər/ *n.* **1** an animal that catches fish, esp. a pekan. **2** *archaic* a fisherman. [OE *fiscere* f. Gmc (as FISH[1])]

fisherman /fishərmən/ *n.* (*pl.* **-men**) **1** a person who catches fish as a livelihood or for sport. **2** a fishing-boat.

fishery /fishəri/ *n.* (*pl.* **-ies**) **1** a place where fish are caught or reared. **2** the occupation or industry of catching or rearing fish.

fishing /fishing/ *n.* the activity of catching fish, esp. for food or as a sport. □ **fishing-line** a long thread of silk etc. with a baited hook, sinker, float, etc., used for catching fish. **fishing-rod** a long tapering usu. jointed rod to which a fishing-line is attached. **fishing story** *Brit. colloq.* an exaggerated account.

fishmonger /fishmunggər/ *n.* esp. *Brit.* a dealer in fish.

fishnet /fishnet/ *n.* (often *attrib.*) an open-meshed fabric (*fishnet stockings*).

fishpot /fishpot/ *n.* a wicker trap for eels, lobsters, etc.

fishtail /fishtayl/ *n.* & *v.* ● *n.* a device etc. shaped like a fish's tail. ● *v.intr.* move the tail of a vehicle from side to side. □ **fishtail burner** a kind of burner producing a broadening jet of flame.

fishwife /fishwīf/ *n.* (*pl.* **-wives**) **1** a coarse-mannered or noisy woman. **2** a woman who sells fish.

■ **1** see SCOLD *n.*

fishy /fishi/ *adj.* (**fishier**, **fishiest**) **1 a** smelling or tasting like fish. **b** like that of a fish. **c** (of an eye) dull, vacant-looking. **d** consisting of fish (*a fishy repast*). **e** *joc.* or *poet.* abounding in fish. **2** *sl.* of dubious character, questionable, suspect. □□ **fishily** *adv.* **fishiness** *n.*

■ **1 b** piscine, fishlike. **c** see VACANT 2. **2** dubious, questionable, doubtful, suspect, suspicious, not kosher, shady, funny, odd, peculiar, strange, queer; improbable, implausible, unlikely, far-fetched.

fisk /fisk/ *n. Sc.* the State treasury, the exchequer. [var. of FISC]

fissile /fissīl/ *adj.* **1** capable of undergoing nuclear fission. **2** cleavable; tending to split. □□ **fissility** /-sílliti/ *n.* [L *fissilis* (as FISSURE)]

■ **2** see SEPARABLE.

fission /fish'n/ *n.* & *v.* ● *n.* **1** *Physics* the spontaneous or impact-induced splitting of a heavy atomic nucleus, accompanied by a release of energy. **2** *Biol.* the division of a cell etc. into new cells etc. as a mode of reproduction. ● *v.intr.* & *tr.* undergo or cause to undergo fission. □ **fission bomb** an atomic bomb. □□ **fissionable** *adj.* [L *fissio* (as FISSURE)]

■ *n.* **2** see SEPARATION.

fissiparous /fisíppərəss/ *adj.* **1** *Biol.* reproducing by fission. **2** tending to split. □□ **fissiparity** /fissipárriti/ *n.* **fissiparously** *adv.* **fissiparousness** *n.* [L *fissus* past part. (as FISSURE) after *viviparous*]

fissure /fishər/ *n.* & *v.* ● *n.* **1** an opening, usu. long and narrow, made esp. by cracking, splitting, or separation of parts. **2** *Bot.* & *Anat.* a narrow opening in an organ etc., esp. a depression between convolutions of the brain. **3** a cleavage. ● *v.tr.* & *intr.* split or crack. [ME f. OF *fissure* or L *fissura* f. *findere fiss-* cleave]

■ *n.* **1, 3** see CRACK *n.* 2. ● *v.* see CRACK *v.* 1.

fist /fist/ *n.* & *v.* ● *n.* **1** a tightly closed hand. **2** *sl.* handwriting (*writes a good fist*; *I know his fist*). **3** *sl.* a hand (*give us your fist*). ● *v.tr.* **1** strike with the fist. **2** *Naut.* handle (a sail, an oar, etc.). □ **make a good** (or **poor** etc.) **fist** (foll. by *at*, *of*) *colloq.* make a good (or poor etc.) attempt at. □□ **fisted** *adj.* (also in *comb.*). **fistful** *n.* (*pl.* **-fuls**). [OE *fȳst* f. WG]

fistic /fistik/ *adj.* (also **fistical**) *joc.* pugilistic.

fisticuffs /fistikufs/ *n.pl.* fighting with the fists. [prob. obs. *fisty* adj. = FISTIC, + CUFF[2]]

■ boxing, pugilism, prizefighting.

fistula /fistyoolə/ *n.* (*pl.* **fistulas** or **fistulae** /-lee/) **1** an abnormal or surgically made passage between a hollow organ and the body surface or between two hollow organs. **2** a natural pipe or spout in whales, insects, etc. □□ **fistular** *adj.* **fistulous** *adj.* [L, = pipe, flute]

fit[1] /fit/ *adj.*, *v.*, *n.*, & *adv.* ● *adj.* (**fitter**, **fittest**) **1 a** (usu. foll. by *for*, or *to* + infin.) well adapted or suited. **b** (foll. by *to* + infin.) qualified, competent, worthy. **c** (foll. by *for*, or *to* + infin.) in a suitable condition, ready. **d** (foll. by *for*) good enough (*a dinner fit for a king*). **e** (foll. by *to* + infin.) sufficiently exhausted, troubled, or angry (*fit to drop*). **2** in good health or athletic condition. **3** proper, becoming, right (*it is fit that*). ● *v.* (**fitted**, **fitting**) **1 a** *tr.* (also *absol.*) be of the right shape and size for (*the dress fits her*; *the key doesn't fit the lock*; *these shoes don't fit*). **b** *tr.* make, fix, or insert (a thing) so that it is of the right size or shape (*fitted shelves in the alcoves*). **c** *intr.* (often foll. by *in*, *into*) (of a component) be correctly positioned (*that bit fits here*). **d** *tr.* find room for (*can't fit another person on the bench*). **2** *tr.* (foll. by *for*, or *to* + infin.) **a** make suitable; adapt. **b** make competent (*fitted him to be a priest*). **3** *tr.* (usu. foll. by *with*) supply, furnish (*fitted the boat with a new rudder*). **4** *tr.* fix in place (*fit a lock on the door*). **5** *tr.* = *fit on*. **6** *tr.* be in harmony with, befit, become (*it fits the occasion*; *the punishment fits the crime*). ● *n.* the way in which a garment, component, etc., fits (*a bad fit*; *a tight fit*). ● *adv.* (foll. by *to* + infin.) *colloq.* in a suitable manner, appropriately (*was laughing fit to bust*). □ **fit the bill** = *fill the bill*. **fit in 1** (often foll. by *with*) be (esp. socially) compatible or accommodating (*doesn't fit in with the rest of the group*; *tried to fit in with their plans*). **2** find space or time for (an object, engagement, etc.) (*the dentist fitted me in at the last minute*). **fit on** try on (a garment). **fit out** (or **up**) (often foll. by *with*) equip. **fit-up** *Theatr. sl.* **1** a temporary stage etc. **2** a travelling company. **see** (or **think**) **fit** (often foll. by *to* + infin.) decide or choose (a specified course of action). □□ **fitly** *adv.* **fitness** *n.* [ME: orig. unkn.]

■ *adj.* **1 a** (well) adapted *or* suited, suitable, appropriate, fitted; apt. **b** (*fit to*) qualified to, competent to, prepared to, ready to, able to, adequate to, capable of, worthy of *or* to. **c** see READY *adj.* 1, 2. **e** (*fit to*) ready to, sufficiently exhausted, troubled *or* angry to, disposed to, likely to, about to. **2** in good health *or* condition *or* shape *or* trim, in fine fettle; healthy, well, hale, vigorous, strong, sturdy, robust, strapping, able-bodied, abled. **3** proper, becoming, right, correct, fitting, applicable, apropos, *archaic* meet. ● *v.* **1 c** go together, join, match, correspond, dovetail. **d** see ACCOMMODATE 1. **2 a** adapt, adjust, modify, change, alter, shape. **b** see TRAIN *v.* 1a. **3** supply, furnish, equip, provide, fit out *or* up, install, rig out, gear up. **6** befit, suit, become, be suited to, be suitable *or* appropriate for; answer, satisfy. □ **fit in 1** harmonize, find one's place *or* niche, fit; (*fit in with*) see CONFORM 4. **fit on** try (on), put on. **fit out** (or **up**) see EQUIP. □□ **fitness** aptness, appropriateness, pertinence, seemliness, suitability, suitableness; competence, eligibility, adequacy, qualification; health, healthiness, good (physical) condition, vigour, well-being, good shape, fine fettle, tone; wholesomeness, salubriousness, salubrity.

fit[2] /fit/ *n.* **1** a sudden seizure of epilepsy, hysteria, apoplexy, fainting, or paralysis, with unconsciousness or convulsions. **2** a sudden brief attack of an illness or of symptoms (*fit of coughing*). **3** a sudden short bout or burst (*fit of energy; fit of giggles*). **4** *colloq.* an attack of strong feeling (*fit of rage*). **5** a capricious impulse; a mood (*when the fit was on him*). □ **by** (or **in**) **fits and starts** spasmodically. **give a person a fit** *colloq.* surprise or outrage him or her. **have a fit** *colloq.* be greatly surprised or outraged. **in fits** laughing uncontrollably. [ME, = position of danger, perh. = OE *fitt* conflict (?)]

■ **1** seizure, attack, convulsion, paroxysm, spasm; *Med.* ictus. **2** attack, assault, bout. **3** bout, burst, outburst, outbreak, paroxysm, spell, period. **4** see OUTBURST. □ **by** (or **in**) **fits and starts** spasmodically, sporadically, occasionally, fitfully, intermittently, erratically, haphazardly, off and on, now and then, irregularly. **give a person a fit** see SURPRISE *v.* 1, 2. **in fits** (*be in fits*) see KILL *v.* 3b.

fit[3] /fit/ *n.* (also **fytte**) *archaic* a section of a poem. [OE *fitt*]

fitch /fich/ *n.* **1** a polecat. **2 a** the hair of a polecat. **b** a brush made from this or similar hair. [MDu. *fisse* etc.: cf. FITCHEW]

fitchew /fichoo/ *n.* a polecat. [14th c. f. OF *ficheau, fissel* dimin. of MDu. *fisse*]

fitful /fitfool/ *adj.* active or occurring spasmodically or intermittently. □□ **fitfully** *adv.* **fitfulness** *n.*

■ spasmodic, intermittent, sporadic, occasional, periodic, erratic, haphazard, irregular, capricious; varying, fluctuating, variable, uneven.

fitment /fitmənt/ *n.* (usu. in *pl.*) a fixed item of furniture.

■ see FIXTURE 1.

fitted /fittid/ *adj.* **1** made or shaped to fill a space or cover something closely or exactly (*a fitted carpet*). **2** provided with appropriate equipment, fittings, etc. (*a fitted kitchen*). **3** built-in; filling an alcove etc. (*fitted cupboards*).

■ **1** custom-made, tailor-made, tailored, bespoke. **3** built-in, integral.

fitter /fittər/ *n.* **1** a person who supervises the cutting, fitting, altering, etc. of garments. **2** a mechanic who fits together and adjusts machinery.

fitting /fitting/ *n.* & *adj.* ● *n.* **1** the process or an instance of having a garment etc. fitted (*needed several fittings*). **2 a** (in *pl.*) the fixtures and fitments of a building. **b** a piece of apparatus or furniture. ● *adj.* proper, becoming, right. □ **fitting-shop** a place where machine parts are put together. □□ **fittingly** *adv.* **fittingness** *n.*

■ *n.* **2 a** (*fittings*) fixtures, fitments, attachments, pieces, parts, units, furniture, appointments, furnishings, equipment, trappings, accoutrements, paraphernalia, trimmings; accessories, extras, installations. ● *adj.* proper, becoming, right, fit, befitting, suitable, appropriate, seemly, apt, apropos, apposite, germane, relevant, *archaic* meet; *comme il faut*.

FitzGerald contraction /fitsjérrəld/ *n.* (also **FitzGerald effect**) (in full **FitzGerald-Lorentz**) *Physics* the shortening of a moving body in the direction of its motion esp. at speeds close to that of light. [G. F. *FitzGerald*, Ir. physicist d. 1901 and H. A. *Lorentz*, Du. physicist d. 1928]

five /fīv/ *n.* & *adj.* ● *n.* **1** one more than four or one half of ten; the sum of three units and two units. **2** a symbol for this (5, v, V). **3** a size etc. denoted by five. **4** a set or team of five individuals. **5** the time of five o'clock (*is it five yet?*). **6** a card with five pips. **7** *Cricket* a hit scoring five runs. ● *adj.* that amount to five. □ **bunch of fives** *Brit. sl.* a hand or fist. **five-corner** (or **-corners**) *Austral.* **1** a shrub of the genus *Styphelia*. **2** the pentagonal fruit of this. **five-eighth** *Austral.* & *NZ Rugby Football* either of two players between the scrum-half and the centre three-quarter. **five-finger exercise 1** an exercise on the piano involving all the fingers. **2** an easy task. **five hundred** a form of euchre in which 500 points make a game. **five o'clock shadow** beard-growth visible on a man's face in the latter part of the day. **five-star** of the highest class. **five-year plan 1** (in the former USSR) a government plan for economic development over five years, inaugurated in 1928. **2** a similar plan in another country. [OE *fīf* f. Gmc]

fivefold /fīvfōld/ *adj.* & *adv.* **1** five times as much or as many. **2** consisting of five parts. **3** amounting to five.

fiver /fīvər/ *n. colloq.* **1** *Brit.* a five-pound note. **2** *US* a five-dollar bill.

fives /fīvz/ *n.* a game in which a ball is hit with a gloved hand or a bat against the walls of a court with three walls (**Eton fives**) or four walls (**Rugby fives**). [*pl.* of FIVE used as *sing.*: significance unkn.]

fivestones /fīvstōnz/ *n. Brit.* jacks played with five pieces of metal etc. and usu. without a ball.

fix /fiks/ *v.* & *n.* ● *v.* **1** *tr.* make firm or stable; fasten, secure (*fixed a picture to the wall*). **2** *tr.* decide, settle, specify (a price, date, etc.). **3** *tr.* mend, repair. **4** *tr.* implant (an idea or memory) in the mind (*couldn't get the rules fixed in his head*). **5** *tr.* **a** (foll. by *on, upon*) direct steadily, set (one's eyes, gaze, attention, or affection). **b** attract and hold (a person's attention, eyes, etc.). **c** (foll. by *with*) single out with one's eyes etc. **6** *tr.* place definitely or permanently, establish, station. **7** *tr.* determine the exact nature, position, etc., of; refer (a thing or person) to a definite place or time; identify, locate. **8 a** *tr.* make (eyes, features, etc.) rigid. **b** *intr.* (of eyes, features, etc.) become rigid. **9** *tr. US colloq.* prepare (food or drink) (*fixed me a drink*). **10 a** *tr.* deprive of fluidity or volatility; congeal. **b** *intr.* lose fluidity or volatility, become congealed. **11** *tr. colloq.* punish, kill, silence, deal with, take revenge on (a person). **12** *tr. colloq.* **a** secure the support of (a person) fraudulently, esp. by bribery. **b** arrange the result of (a race, match, etc.) fraudulently (*the competition was fixed*). **13** *sl.* **a** *tr.* inject (a person, esp. oneself) with a narcotic. **b** *intr.* take an injection of a narcotic. **14** *tr.* make (a colour, photographic image, or microscope-specimen) fast or permanent. **15** *tr.* (of a plant or micro-organism) assimilate (nitrogen or carbon dioxide) by forming a non-gaseous compound. **16** *tr.* castrate or spay (an animal). **17** *tr.* arrest changes or development in (a language or literature). **18** *tr.* determine the incidence of (liability etc.). **19** *intr. archaic* take up one's position. **20** (as **fixed** *adj.*) **a** permanently placed, stationary. **b** without moving, rigid; (of a gaze, etc.) steady or intent. **c** definite. **d** *sl.* dishonest, fraudulent. ● *n.* **1** *colloq.* a position hard to escape from; a dilemma or predicament. **2 a** the act of finding one's position by bearings or astronomical observations (*get a fix on that star*). **b** a position found in this way. **3** *sl.* a dose of a narcotic drug to which one is addicted. **4** *US sl.* bribery. □ **be fixed** (usu. foll. by *for*) be disposed or affected (regarding) (*how is he fixed for money?; how are you fixed for Friday?*). **fixed capital** machinery etc. that remains in the owner's use. **fixed-doh** *Mus.* applied to a system of sight-singing in which C is called 'doh', D is called 'ray', etc., irrespective of the key in which they occur (cf. *movable-doh*). **fixed focus** a camera focus at a distance from a lens that is not adjustable. **fixed idea** = IDÉE FIXE. **fixed income** income deriving from a pension, investment at fixed interest, etc. **fixed odds** predetermined odds in racing etc. (opp. *starting price*). **fixed oil** an oil of animal or plant origin used in varnishes, lubricants, illuminants, soaps, etc. **fixed point** *Physics* a well-defined reproducible temperature. **fixed star** *Astron.* a star so far from the earth as to appear motionless. **fix on** (or **upon**) choose, decide on. **fix up 1** arrange, organize, prepare. **2** accommodate. **3** (often foll. by *with*) provide (a person) (*fixed me up with a job*). □□ **fixable** *adj.* **fixedly** /fíksidli/ *adv.* **fixedness** /fíksidniss/ *n.* [ME, partly f. obs. *fix* fixed f. OF *fix* or L *fixus* past part. of *figere* fix, fasten, partly f. med.L *fixare* f. *fixus*]

■ *v.* **1** make firm *or* stable; fasten, secure, affix, anchor, retain, attach, make fast, set. **2** decide, resolve, settle, specify, establish, set, agree on, organize, arrange, prearrange, cement, conclude, arrive at. **3** mend, repair, fix up, patch up, remedy, rectify, correct, emend, adjust, regulate, put *or* set to rights, straighten out, *colloq.* doctor. **4** see IMPLANT *v.* 2. **5 a** (*fix on* or *upon*) direct at, fasten on *or* upon, focus on, rivet on, concentrate on. **b** attract, hold, rivet. **c** see SINGLE *v.* **6** place, establish, station, settle, install, situate, locate, position. **7** determine, specify, establish, identify, locate; assign, allocate, attribute, ascribe, specify, pin, attach, fasten. **9** see PREPARE 2. **10** congeal, harden, thicken, set, solidify, rigidify, stiffen, freeze; become congealed *or* hard. **11** punish, deal with, take care of, see to, *colloq.* settle a person's hash, sort out; retaliate against, wreak vengeance on, hit *or* strike *or* get back at, get even with, even the score with, make reprisals against, avenge oneself against, take revenge on, take retribution against, repay, pay back. **12 a** bribe, buy, *colloq.* grease the palm of, *Brit. sl.* nobble. **b** arrange, rig; prearrange, pre-determine, set up, contrive, *sl.* fiddle. **13 a** see INJECT 1. **16** see STERILIZE 2. **17** set, settle, freeze, stabilize, solidify. **18** see DETERMINE 1, 2, 4. **20** (**fixed**) **a** fastened, attached, anchored, set, secure, secured, firm; immovable, immobile, stationary, rooted, solid, immobilized, stuck. **b** rigid, unchangeable, unchanging, unfluctuating, unwavering, undeviating, unflinching, unblinking, steady; intent. **c** definite, settled, firm, secure, established, decided, prearranged, unalterable. **d** crooked, dishonest, put-up, *sl.* bent. ● *n.* **1** dilemma, predicament, difficulty, corner, double bind, quandary, mess, bad situation, dire *or* desperate straits, *colloq.* pickle, catch-22, jam, hole, tight spot, tough spot, *esp. US colloq.* bind. **4** bribery, subornation. □ **fix on** (or **upon**) decide (on *or* upon), set, agree (on *or* upon), choose, select, settle (on), determine, finalize. **fix up 1** see ARRANGE 2, 3. **2** see ACCOMMODATE 1. **3 c** provide, furnish, supply, accommodate, set up; lay on.

fixate /fiksáyt/ *v.tr.* **1** direct one's gaze on. **2** *Psychol.* **a** (usu. in *passive*; often foll. by *on*, *upon*) cause (a person) to acquire an abnormal attachment to persons or things (*was fixated on his son*). **b** arrest (part of the libido) at an immature stage, causing such attachment. [L *fixus* (see FIX) + -ATE[3]]

fixation /fiksáysh'n/ *n.* **1** the act or an instance of being fixated. **2** an obsession, concentration on a single idea. **3** fixing or being fixed. **4** the process of rendering solid; coagulation. **5** the process of assimilating a gas to form a solid compound. [ME f. med.L *fixatio* f. *fixare*: see FIX]

■ **1, 2** mania, obsession, compulsion, fixed idea, *idée fixe*, monomania, preoccupation, fetish, *colloq.* thing.

fixative /fíksətiv/ *adj.* & *n.* ● *adj.* tending to fix or secure. ● *n.* a substance used to fix colours, hair, microscope-specimens, etc.

fixer /fíksər/ *n.* **1** a person or thing that fixes. **2** *Photog.* a substance used for fixing a photographic image etc. **3** *colloq.* a person who makes arrangements, esp. of an illicit kind.

fixings /fíksingz/ *n.pl. US* **1** apparatus or equipment. **2** the trimmings for a dish. **3** the trimmings of a dress etc.

fixity /fíksiti/ *n.* **1** a fixed state. **2** stability; permanence. [obs. *fix* fixed: see FIX]

fixture /fíks-chər/ *n.* **1 a** something fixed or fastened in position. **b** (usu. *predic.*) *colloq.* a person or thing confined to or established in one place (*he seems to be a fixture*). **2 a** a sporting event, esp. a match, race, etc. **b** the date agreed for this. **3** (in *pl.*) *Law* articles attached to a house or land and regarded as legally part of it. [alt. of obs. *fixure* f. LL *fixura* f. L *figere fix-* fix]

■ **1** appliance, fitting, fitment, appendage. **2 a** event, meet, match, occasion, occurrence.

fizgig /fízgig/ *n.* & *adj.* ● *n.* **1** *archaic* a silly or flirtatious young woman. **2** *archaic* a kind of small firework; a cracker. **3** *Austral. sl.* a police informer. ● *adj. archaic* flighty. [prob. f. FIZZ + obs. *gig* flighty girl]

fizz /fiz/ *v.* & *n.* ● *v.intr.* **1** make a hissing or spluttering sound. **2** (of a drink) make bubbles; effervesce. ● *n.* **1** effervescence. **2** *colloq.* an effervescent drink, esp. champagne. [imit.]

■ *v.* **1** hiss, sputter, sizzle, splutter, fizzle. **2** bubble, effervesce, sparkle, froth. ● *n.* **1** effervescence, sparkle, carbonation, bubbling, froth, fizziness. **2** champagne, *sl.* champers; soda water, seltzer, tonic, *esp. US* soda.

fizzer / fízzər/ *n.* **1** an excellent or first-rate thing. **2** *Cricket colloq.* a very fast ball, or one that deviates with unexpected speed. **3** *Austral. sl.* a disappointing failure or fiasco.

fizzle /fízz'l/ *v.* & *n.* ● *v.intr.* make a feeble hissing or spluttering sound. ● *n.* such a sound. □ **fizzle out** end feebly (*the party fizzled out at 10 o'clock*). [formed as FIZZ + -LE[4]]

■ *v.* see FIZZ *v.* 1. □ **fizzle out** die (out *or* away), expire, peter out, come to nothing *or* naught, fail, fall through, miscarry, abort, come to grief, misfire, collapse, cave in.

fizzy /fízzi/ *adj.* (**fizzier, fizziest**) effervescent. □□ **fizzily** *adv.* **fizziness** *n.*

■ see *effervescent* (EFFERVESCE).

FJI *abbr.* Fellow of the Institute of Journalists.

fjord var. of FIORD.

FL *abbr. US* Florida (in official postal use).

fl. *abbr.* **1** floor. **2** floruit. **3** fluid.

Fla. *abbr.* Florida.

flab /flab/ *n. colloq.* fat; flabbiness. [imit., or back-form. f. FLABBY]

flabbergast /flábbərgaast/ *v.tr.* (esp. as **flabbergasted** *adj.*) *colloq.* overwhelm with astonishment; dumbfound. [18th c.: perh. f. FLABBY + AGHAST]

■ see ASTONISH.

flabby /flábbi/ *adj.* (**flabbier, flabbiest**) **1** (of flesh etc.) hanging down; limp; flaccid. **2** (of language or character) feeble. □□ **flabbily** *adv.* **flabbiness** *n.* [alt. of earlier *flappy* f. FLAP]

■ **1** limp, flaccid, loose, slack, floppy, sagging, drooping, baggy, pendulous, soft. **2** feeble, weak, spineless, impotent, ineffective, ineffectual.

flaccid /fláksid, flássid/ *adj.* **1 a** (of flesh etc.) hanging loose or wrinkled; limp, flabby. **b** (of plant tissue) soft; less rigid. **2** relaxed, drooping. **3** lacking vigour; feeble. □□ **flaccidity** /-sídditi/ *n.* **flaccidly** *adv.* [F *flaccide* or L *flaccidus* f. *flaccus* flabby]

■ **1a, 2** see FLABBY 1.

flack[1] /flak/ *n. US sl.* a publicity agent. [20th c.: orig. unkn.]

flack[2] var. of FLAK.

flag[1] /flag/ *n.* & *v.* ● *n.* **1 a** a piece of cloth, usu. oblong or square, attachable by one edge to a pole or rope and used as a country's emblem or as a standard, signal, etc. **b** a small toy, device, etc., resembling a flag. **2** *Brit.* an oblong strip of metal etc. that can be raised or lowered to indicate whether a taxi is for hire or occupied. **3** *Naut.* a flag carried by a flagship as an emblem of an admiral's rank afloat. ● *v.* (**flagged, flagging**) **1** *intr.* **a** grow tired; lose vigour; lag (*his energy flagged after the first lap*). **b** hang down; droop; become limp. **2** *tr.* **a** place a flag on or over. **b** mark out with or as if with a flag or flags. **3** *tr.* (often foll. by *that*) **a**

inform (a person) by flag-signals. **b** communicate (information) by flagging. □ **black flag 1** a pirate's ensign. **2** *hist.* a flag hoisted outside a prison to announce an execution. **flag-boat** a boat serving as a mark in sailing-matches. **flag-captain** the captain of a flagship. **flag-day** *Brit.* a day on which money is raised for a charity by the sale of small paper flags etc. in the street. **Flag Day** *US* 14 June, the anniversary of the adoption of the Stars and Stripes in 1777. **flag down** signal to (a vehicle or driver) to stop. **flag-lieutenant** *Naut.* an admiral's ADC. **flag-list** *Naut.* a roll of flag-officers. **flag of convenience** a foreign flag under which a ship is registered, usu. to avoid financial charges etc. **flag-officer** *Naut.* an admiral, vice admiral, or rear admiral, or the commodore of a yacht-club. **flag of truce** a white flag indicating a desire for a truce. **flag-pole** = FLAGSTAFF. **flag-rank** *Naut.* the rank attained by flag-officers. **flag-station** a station at which trains stop only if signalled. **flag-wagging** *sl.* **1** signalling with hand-held flags. **2** = *flag-waving*. **flag-waver** a populist agitator; a chauvinist. **flag-waving** populist agitation, chauvinism. **keep the flag flying** continue the fight. **put the flag out** celebrate victory, success, etc. **show the flag 1** make an official visit to a foreign port etc. **2** ensure that notice is taken of one's country, oneself, etc.; make a patriotic display. □□ **flagger** *n.* [16th c.: perh. f. obs. *flag* drooping]

■ *n.* **1 a** banner, ensign, standard, pennant, pennon, streamer, jack, gonfalon, *Eccl.* vexillum. ● *v.* **1 a** grow tired, tire, weaken, languish, falter, fail, dwindle, fade, deteriorate, waste away, degenerate, decline, diminish, decrease, lessen, abate, peter out, die, taper (off), ease (up), subside, slump, fall off, wane, ebb, sink, lag, *colloq.* let up. **b** hang down, droop, sag, dangle, swag. **2 b** mark (out), tag, label, tab, identify. **3** inform; communicate; see also SIGNAL *v.* 1, 2a. □ **flag down** hail, stop. **flag-waver** see AGITATOR 1. **flag-waving** activism, agitation, militancy, chauvinism, *sl.* flag-wagging.

flag[2] /flag/ *n.* & *v.* ● *n.* (also **flagstone**) **1** a flat usu. rectangular stone slab used for paving. **2** (in *pl.*) a pavement made of these. ● *v.tr.* (**flagged, flagging**) pave with flags. [ME, = sod: cf. Icel. *flag* spot from which a sod has been cut out, ON *flaga* slab of stone, and FLAKE[1]]

flag[3] /flag/ *n.* **1** any plant with a bladed leaf (esp. several of the genus *Iris*) growing on moist ground. **2** the long slender leaf of such a plant. [ME: cf. MDu. *flag*, Da. *flæg*]

flag[4] /flag/ *n.* (in full **flag-feather**) a quill-feather of a bird's wing. [perh. rel. to obs. *fag* loose flap: cf. FLAG[1] *v.*]

flagellant /flájələnt, fləjéllənt/ *n.* & *adj.* ● *n.* **1** a person who scourges himself or herself or others as a religious discipline. **2** a person who engages in flogging as a sexual stimulus. ● *adj.* of or concerning flagellation. [L *flagellare* to whip f. FLAGELLUM]

flagellate[1] /flájəlayt/ *v.tr.* scourge, flog (cf. FLAGELLANT). □□ **flagellation** /-láysh'n/ *n.* **flagellator** *n.* **flagellatory** /-lətəri/ *adj.*

■ see FLOG 1a.

flagellate[2] /flájilit/ *adj.* & *n.* ● *adj.* having flagella (see FLAGELLUM). ● *n.* a protozoan having one or more flagella.

flagellum /fləjélləm/ *n.* (*pl.* **flagella** /-lə/) **1** *Biol.* a long lashlike appendage found principally on microscopic organisms. **2** *Bot.* a runner; a creeping shoot. □□ **flagellar** *adj.* **flagelliform** *adj.* [L, = whip, dimin. of *flagrum* scourge]

flageolet[1] /flájəlét/ *n.* **1** a small flute blown at the end, like a recorder but with two thumb-holes. **2** an organ stop having a similar sound. [F, dimin. of OF *flag(e)ol* f. Prov. *flajol*, of unkn. orig.]

flageolet[2] /flájōláy, -lét/ *n.* a kind of French kidney bean. [F]

flagitious /fləjíshəss/ *adj.* deeply criminal; utterly villainous. □□ **flagitiously** *adv.* **flagitiousness** *n.* [ME f. L *flagitiosus* f. *flagitium* shameful crime]

flagman /flágmən/ *n.* (*pl.* **-men**) a person who signals with or as with a flag, e.g. at races.

flagon /flággən/ *n.* **1** a large bottle in which wine, cider, etc., are sold, usu. holding 1.13 litres. **2 a** a large vessel usu. with a handle, spout, and lid, to hold wine etc. **b** a similar vessel used for the Eucharist. [ME *flakon* f. OF *flacon* ult. f. LL *flasco -onis* FLASK]

■ **1, 2a** see JAR[1] 1.

flagrant /fláygrənt/ *adj.* (of an offence or an offender) glaring; notorious; scandalous. □□ **flagrancy** /-grənsi/ *n.* **flagrantly** *adv.* [F *flagrant* or L *flagrant-* part. stem of *flagrare* blaze]

■ glaring, blatant, conspicuous, gross, obvious, out and out, utter, complete, brazen, rank, bold, barefaced, open, defiant, audacious; notorious, scandalous, infamous, arrant, outrageous, shocking, egregious, shameless, atrocious, monstrous, heinous, villainous, treacherous, nefarious, awful, reprehensible, contemptible.

flagship /flágship/ *n.* **1** a ship having an admiral on board. **2** something that is held to be the best or most important of its kind; a leader.

flagstaff /flágstaaf/ *n.* a pole on which a flag may be hoisted.

■ staff, pole, flag-pole.

flagstone /flágstōn/ *n.* = FLAG[2].

flail /flayl/ *n.* & *v.* ● *n.* a threshing-tool consisting of a wooden staff with a short heavy stick swinging from it. ● *v.* **1** *tr.* beat or strike with or as if with a flail. **2** *intr.* wave or swing wildly or erratically (*went into the fight with arms flailing*). [OE prob. f. L FLAGELLUM]

■ *v.* **1** see LASH *v.* 1, 2. **2** see FLAP *v.* 1.

flair /flair/ *n.* **1** an instinct for selecting or performing what is excellent, useful, etc.; a talent (*has a flair for knowing what the public wants; has a flair for languages*). **2** talent or ability, esp. artistic or stylistic. [F *flairer* to smell ult. f. L *fragrare*: see FRAGRANT]

■ instinct; talent, ability, aptitude, feel, forte, knack, genius, brilliance, skill, mind, gift, faculty, propensity, bent, proclivity, facility, capacity, virtuosity, ingenuity; see also STYLE *n.* 5a, VERVE.

flak /flak/ *n.* (also **flack**) **1** anti-aircraft fire. **2** adverse criticism; abuse. □ **flak jacket** a protective jacket of heavy camouflage fabric reinforced with metal, worn by soldiers etc. [abbr. of G *Fliegerabwehrkanone*, lit. aviator-defence-gun]

■ **2** criticism, censure, abuse, disapproval, disapprobation, condemnation, blame, complaints, brickbats.

flake[1] /flayk/ *n.* & *v.* ● *n.* **1 a** a small thin light piece of snow. **b** a similar piece of another material. **2** a thin broad piece of material peeled or split off. **3** *Archaeol.* a piece of hard stone chipped off and used as a tool. **4** a natural division of the flesh of some fish. **5** the dogfish or other shark as food. **6** esp. *US sl.* a crazy or eccentric person. ● *v.tr.* & *intr.* (often foll. by *away*, *off*) **1** take off or come away in flakes. **2** sprinkle with or fall in snowlike flakes. □ **flake out** *colloq.* fall asleep or drop from exhaustion; faint. [ME: orig. unkn.: cf. ON *flakna* flake off]

■ *n.* **1 a** snowflake. **b** piece, chip, bit, scrap, scale, particle, tuft, flock, fragment, shaving, sliver, lamina, squama. ● *v.* **1** scale (off), chip (off), *Med.* desquamate, exfoliate; see also PEEL[1] *v.* 1, 2. □ **flake out** collapse, go to sleep, fall asleep, *colloq.* drop off (to sleep); faint, pass out, black out, lose consciousness, *literary* swoon.

flake[2] /flayk/ *n.* **1** a stage for drying fish etc. **2** a rack for storing oatcakes etc. [ME, perh. f. ON *flaki*, *fleki* wicker shield]

flaky /fláyki/ *adj.* (**flakier, flakiest**) **1** of or like flakes; separating easily into flakes. **2** esp. *US sl.* crazy, eccentric. □ **flaky pastry** pastry consisting of thin light layers. □□ **flakily** *adv.* **flakiness** *n.*

■ **2** see CRAZY 1.

flambé /flómbay/ *adj.* (of food) covered with alcohol and set alight briefly. [F, past part. of *flamber* singe (as FLAMBEAU)]

flambeau /flámbō/ *n.* (*pl.* **flambeaus** or **flambeaux** /-bōz/) **1** a flaming torch, esp. composed of several thick waxed wicks. **2** a branched candlestick. [F f. *flambe* f. L *flammula* dimin. of *flamma* flame]

flamboyant /flambóyənt/ *adj.* **1** ostentatious; showy. **2** floridly decorated. **3** gorgeously coloured. **4** *Archit.* (of decoration) marked by wavy flamelike lines. □□ **flamboyance** *n.* **flamboyancy** *n.* **flamboyantly** *adv.* [F (in Archit. sense), pres. part. of *flamboyer* f. *flambe*: see FLAMBEAU]

■ **1** ostentatious, showy, extravagant, gaudy, flashy, dazzling, brilliant, splendid; high, wide, and handsome; dashing, rakish, swashbuckling. **2** florid, decorated, elaborate, ornamented, ornate, embellished, baroque, rococo.

flame /flaym/ *n.* & *v.* ● *n.* **1 a** ignited gas (*the fire burnt with a steady flame*). **b** one portion of this (*the flame flickered and died*). **c** (usu. in *pl.*) visible combustion (*burst into flames*). **2 a** a bright light; brilliant colouring. **b** a brilliant orange-red colour. **3 a** strong passion, esp. love (*fan the flame*). **b** *colloq.* a boyfriend or girlfriend. ● *v.* **1** *intr.* & *tr.* (often foll. by *away*, *forth*, *out*, *up*) emit or cause to emit flames. **2** *intr.* (often foll. by *out*, *up*) **a** (of passion) break out. **b** (of a person) become angry. **3** *intr.* shine or glow like flame (*leaves flamed in the autumn sun*). **4** *intr. poet.* move like flame. **5** *tr.* send (a signal) by means of flame. **6** *tr.* subject to the action of flame. □ **flame gun** a device for throwing flames to destroy weeds etc. **flame out** (of a jet engine) lose power through the extinction of the flame in the combustion chamber. **flame-proof** (esp. of a fabric) treated so as to be non-flammable. **flame-thrower** (or **-projector**) a weapon for throwing a spray of flame. **flame-tree** any of various trees with brilliant red flowers esp. flame-of-the-forest, *Delonix regia*. **go up in flames** be consumed by fire. □□ **flameless** *adj.* **flamelike** *adj.* **flamy** *adj.* [ME f. OF *flame*, *flam(m)er* f. L *flamma*]

■ *n.* **2** see *incandescence* (INCANDESCENT). **3 a** passion, fervour, ardour, zeal, enthusiasm, eagerness, feverishness. **b** boyfriend, girlfriend, lover, sweetheart, *esp. US* beau, *colloq.* heartthrob. ● *v.* **1** see BURN[1] *v.* 2. **2 a** burn, flare up; see also *break out* 2. **b** see FLARE *v.* 3. **3** see SHINE *v.* 1.

flamen /fláymən/ *n. Rom.Hist.* a priest serving a particular deity. [ME f. L]

flamenco /fləméngkō/ *n.* (*pl.* **-os**) **1** a style of music played (esp. on the guitar) and sung by Spanish gypsies. **2** a dance performed to this music. [Sp., = Flemish]

flaming /fláyming/ *adj.* **1** emitting flames. **2** very hot (*flaming June*). **3** *colloq.* **a** passionate; intense (*a flaming row*). **b** expressing annoyance, or as an intensifier (*that flaming dog*). **4** bright-coloured (*flaming red hair*).

■ **1** see ABLAZE *adj.* 1. **2** see HOT *adj.* 1. **3 a** see INTENSE 1, 3. **b** blasted, *colloq.* damn(ed), *Austral.* & *NZ sl.* plurry, *Brit. sl.* blooming, blinking, bally. **4** see BRIGHT *adj.* 2.

flamingo /fləmínggō/ *n.* (*pl.* **-os** or **-oes**) any tall long-necked web-footed wading bird of the family Phoenicopteridae, with crooked bill and pink, scarlet, and black plumage. [Port. *flamengo* f. Prov. *flamenc* f. *flama* flame + *-enc* = -ING[3]]

flammable /flámməb'l/ *adj.* inflammable. ¶ Often used because *inflammable* can be mistaken for a negative (the true negative being *non-flammable*). □□ **flammability** /-bílliti/ *n.* [L *flammare* f. *flamma* flame]

■ inflammable, combustible, ignitable.

flan /flan/ *n.* **1 a** a pastry case with a savoury or sweet filling. **b** a sponge base with a sweet topping. **2** a disc of metal from which a coin etc. is made. [F (orig. = round cake) f. OF *flaon* f. med.L *flado -onis* f. Frank.]

■ **1** see TART[1] 1.

flanch /flaanch/ *v.tr.* & *intr.* (also **flaunch** /flawnch/) (esp. with ref. to a chimney) slope inwards or cause to slope inwards towards the top. □□ **flanching** *n.* [perh. f. OF *flanchir* f. *flanche*, *flanc* FLANK]

flânerie /flanree/ *n.* idling, idleness. [F f. *flâner* lounge]

flâneur /flanőr/ *n.* an idler; a lounger. [F (as FLÂNERIE)]

flange /flanj/ *n.* & *v. Engin.* ● *n.* a projecting flat rim, collar, or rib, used for strengthening or attachment. ● *v.tr.* provide with a flange. □□ **flangeless** *n.* [17th c.: perh. f. *flange* widen out f. OF *flangir* (as FLANCH)]

flank /flangk/ *n.* & *v.* ● *n.* **1 a** the side of the body between the ribs and the hip. **b** the side of an animal carved as meat (*flank of beef*). **2** the side of a mountain, building, etc. **3** the right or left side of an army or other body of persons. ● *v.tr.* **1** (often in *passive*) be situated at both sides of (*a road flanked by mountains*). **2** *Mil.* **a** guard or strengthen on the flank. **b** menace the flank of. **c** rake with sweeping gunfire; enfilade. □ **flank forward** *Rugby Football* a wing forward. **in flank** at the side. [ME f. OF *flanc* f. Frank.]

■ *n.* **1** side, loin. **2** see SIDE *n.* 1. ● *v.* **1** edge, border, line. **2 c** rake, enfilade.

flanker /flángkər/ *n.* **1** *Mil.* a fortification guarding or menacing the flank. **2** anything that flanks another thing. **3** (in Rugby and American Football) a flank forward. **4** *sl.* a trick; a swindle (*pulled a flanker*).

flannel /flánn'l/ *n.* & *v.* ● *n.* **1 a** a kind of woven woollen fabric, usu. without a nap. **b** (in *pl.*) flannel garments, esp. trousers. **2** *Brit.* a small usu. towelling cloth, used for washing oneself. **3** *Brit. sl.* nonsense; flattery. ● *v.* (**flannelled**, **flannelling**; *US* **flanneled**, **flanneling**) **1** *Brit. sl.* **a** *tr.* flatter. **b** *intr.* use flattery. **2** *tr.* wash or clean with a flannel. □ **flannel-mouth** *US sl.* a flatterer; a braggart. □□ **flannelly** *adj.* [perh. f. Welsh *gwlanen* f. *gwlān* wool]

■ *n.* **2** face-flannel, face-cloth, *Austral.* washer. **3** nonsense, rubbish, slaver, *colloq.* hogwash, *sl.* eyewash, bull, boloney, *Brit. sl.* cock, codswallop; flattery, humbug, blarney, *colloq.* soft soap, weasel words, sweet talk. ● *v.* **1 a** see FLATTER 1. □ **flannel-mouth** see *flatterer* (FLATTER), BRAGGART *n.*

flannelboard /flánn'lbord/ *n.* a piece of flannel as a base for paper or cloth cut-outs, used as a toy or a teaching aid.

flannelette /flánnəlét/ *n.* a napped cotton fabric imitating flannel. [FLANNEL]

flannelgraph /flánn'lgraaf/ *n.* = FLANNELBOARD.

flannelled /flánn'ld/ *adj.* (*US* also **flanneled**) wearing flannel trousers. [FLANNEL]

flap /flap/ *v.* & *n.* ● *v.* (**flapped**, **flapping**) **1 a** *tr.* move (wings, the arms, etc.) up and down when flying, or as if flying. **b** *intr.* (of wings, the arms, etc.) move up and down; beat. **2** *intr. colloq.* be agitated or panicky. **3** *intr.* (esp. of curtains, loose cloth, etc.) swing or sway about; flutter. **4** *tr.* (usu. foll. by *away*, *off*) strike (flies etc.) with something broad; drive. **5** *intr. colloq.* (of ears) listen intently. ● *n.* **1** a piece of cloth, wood, paper, etc. hinged or attached by one side only and often used to cover a gap, e.g. a pocket-cover, the folded part of an envelope, a table-leaf. **2** one up-and-down motion of a wing, an arm, etc. **3** *colloq.* a state of agitation; panic (*don't get into a flap*). **4** a hinged or sliding section of a wing used to control lift; an aileron. **5** a light blow with something broad. **6** an open mushroom-top. □□ **flappy** *adj.* [ME, prob. imit.]

■ *v.* **1** move, flap, flail, wave, wag, flutter, thrash, oscillate, vibrate, *colloq.* waggle; thresh, thrash about *or* around, beat. **3** see SWING *v.* 1, 2a, c. ● *n.* **1** fold, fly, lappet, lap. **2** beat, flutter, wave, wag, oscillation, *colloq.* waggle. **3** upset, to-do, commotion, fuss, *esp. Brit. colloq.* kerfuffle; (*in a flap*) in a panic *or* flurry, *colloq.* in a state *or* tizzy *or* sweat.

flapdoodle /flápdōōd'l/ *n. colloq.* nonsense. [19th c.: orig. unkn.]

flapjack /flápjak/ *n.* **1** a cake made from oats and golden syrup etc. **2** esp. *US* a pancake. [FLAP + JACK[1]]

flapper /fláppər/ *n.* **1** a person or thing that flaps. **2** an instrument that is flapped to kill flies, scare birds, etc. **3** a person who panics easily or is easily agitated. **4** *sl.* (in the 1920s) a young unconventional or lively woman. **5** a young mallard or partridge.

flare /flair/ *v.* & *n.* ● *v.* **1** *intr.* & *tr.* widen or cause to widen gradually towards the top or bottom (*flared trousers*). **2** *intr.* & *tr.* burn or cause to burn suddenly with a bright unsteady flame. **3** *intr.* burst into anger; burst forth. ● *n.* **1 a** a dazzling irregular flame or light, esp. in the open air. **b** a sudden outburst of flame. **2 a** a signal light used at sea. **b** a bright light used as a signal. **c** a flame dropped from an aircraft to illuminate a target etc. **3** *Astron.* a sudden burst of radiation from a star. **4 a** a gradual widening, esp. of a skirt or trousers. **b** (in *pl.*) wide-bottomed trousers. **5** an outward bulge in a ship's sides. **6** *Photog.* unnecessary illumination on a lens caused by internal reflection etc. □ **flare-path** an area illuminated to enable an aircraft to land or take off. **flare up 1** burst into a sudden blaze. **2** become suddenly angry or active. **flare-up** *n.* an outburst of flame, anger, activity, etc. [16th c.: orig. unkn.]

■ *v.* **1** widen, flare out, spread (out *or* outwards), broaden, expand, increase, enlarge, bulge, swell. **2** blaze *or* flame (up), flare up, flash; see also BURN[1] *v.* 1, 2. **3** explode, erupt, lose one's temper, flare up, flash out *or* up, throw a tantrum, become incensed *or* angry, see red, get worked up, get hot under the collar, *colloq.* blow up, blow one's top, fly off the handle, lose one's cool. ● *n.* **1** flame, blaze, flash, light, glare, dazzle, incandescence, brilliance, luminosity. **2** beacon, light, signal, torch. **4 a** widening, broadening, spread, expansion, increase, enlargement, bulge, swelling. □ **flare up 1** blaze, flame, flash, burn, flare. **2** see FLARE *v.* 3 above. **flare-up** see OUTBURST.

flash /flash/ *v.*, *n.*, & *adj.* ● *v.* **1** *intr.* & *tr.* emit or reflect or cause to emit or reflect light briefly, suddenly, or intermittently; gleam or cause to gleam. **2** *intr.* break suddenly into flame; give out flame or sparks. **3** *tr.* send or reflect like a sudden flame or blaze (*his eyes flashed fire*). **4** *intr.* **a** burst suddenly into view or perception (*the explanation flashed upon me*). **b** move swiftly (*the train flashed through the station*). **5** *tr.* **a** send (news etc.) by radio, telegraph, etc. (*flashed a message to her*). **b** signal to (a person) by shining lights or headlights briefly. **6** *tr. colloq.* show ostentatiously (*flashed her engagement ring*). **7** *intr.* (of water) rush along; rise and flow. **8** *intr. sl.* indecently expose oneself. ● *n.* **1** a sudden bright light or flame, e.g. of lightning. **2** a very brief time; an instant (*all over in a flash*). **3 a** a brief, sudden burst of feeling (*a flash of hope*). **b** a sudden display (of wit, understanding, etc.). **4** = NEWSFLASH. **5** *Photog.* = FLASHLIGHT 1. **6 a** a rush of water, esp. down a weir to take a boat over shallows. **b** a contrivance for producing this. **7** *Brit. Mil.* a coloured patch of cloth on a uniform etc. as a distinguishing emblem. **8** vulgar display, ostentation. **9** a bright patch of colour. **10** *Cinematog.* the momentary exposure of a scene. **11** excess plastic or metal oozing from a mould during moulding. ● *adj. colloq.* **1** gaudy; showy; vulgar (*a flash car*). **2** counterfeit (*flash notes*). **3** connected with thieves, the underworld, etc. □ **flash-board** a board used for sending more water from a mill-dam into a mill-race. **flash bulb** *Photog.* a bulb for a flashlight. **flash burn** a burn caused by sudden intense heat, esp. from a nuclear explosion. **flash card** a card containing a small amount of information, held up for pupils to see, as an aid to learning. **flash-cube** *Photog.* a set of four flash bulbs arranged as a cube and operated in turn. **flash-flood** a sudden local flood due to heavy rain etc. **flash-gun** *Photog.* a device used to operate a camera flashlight. **flashing-point** = FLASHPOINT. **flash in the pan** a promising start followed by failure (from the priming of old guns). **flash-lamp** a portable flashing electric lamp. **flash out** (or **up**) show sudden passion. **flash over** *Electr.* make an electric circuit by sparking across a gap. **flash-over** *n.* an instance of this. [ME orig. with ref. to the rushing of water: cf. SPLASH]

■ *v.* **1, 3** scintillate, sparkle, dazzle, glitter, coruscate, twinkle, flicker, shimmer, glimmer; gleam, beam, shine, glare. **2** flare (up), blaze, flame (up), spark, burn. **4 b** rush, race, speed, dash, streak, tear, hurry, hasten, flick, fly, zoom, shoot, run, sprint, dart; *colloq.* whiz. **6** see FLAUNT. ● *n.* **1** flare, burst, blaze, dazzle, spark, sparkle, coruscation, fulguration, glitter, twinkle, twinkling, flicker, flickering, scintilla, scintillation, glint, shimmer, glimmer, gleam, light, flame. **2** moment, (split) second, instant, twinkle, twinkling (of an eye), trice, minute, two shakes (of a lamb's *or* dog's tail), *colloq.* jiffy; before you can say Jack Robinson. **3 a** burst, outbreak; see also OUTBURST. **b** (sudden *or* momentary) display, stroke, flicker, spark. **8** see OSTENTATION. ● *adj.* **1** gaudy, showy, ostentatious, vulgar, flashy, *colloq.* swish, *sl.* snazzy. **2** see COUNTERFEIT *adj.* 1. □ **flash out** (or **up**) see FLARE *v.* 3.

flashback /fláshbak/ *n. Cinematog.* a scene set in a time earlier than the main action.

flasher /fláshər/ *n.* **1** *Brit. sl.* a man who indecently exposes himself. **2 a** an automatic device for switching lights rapidly on and off. **b** a sign or signal using this. **3** a person or thing that flashes.

flashing /fláshing/ *n.* a usu. metallic strip used to prevent water penetration at the junction of a roof with a wall etc. [dial. *flash* seal with lead sheets or obs. *flash* flashing]

flashlight /fláshlīt/ *n.* **1 a** a light giving an intense flash, used for photographing by night, indoors, etc. **b** a picture so taken. **2** *US* an electric torch. **3** a flashing light used for signals and in lighthouses.

flashpoint /fláshpoynt/ *n.* **1** the temperature at which vapour from oil etc. will ignite in air. **2** the point at which anger, indignation, etc. becomes uncontrollable.

flashy /fláshi/ *adj.* (**flashier**, **flashiest**) showy; gaudy; cheaply attractive. □□ **flashily** *adv.* **flashiness** *n.*

■ showy, ostentatious, *colloq.* flash; gaudy, loud, garish, glaring; cheap, vulgar, meretricious, pretentious, tawdry, tasteless, *esp. US colloq.* tacky, *sl.* glitzy.

flask /flaask/ *n.* **1** a narrow-necked bulbous bottle for wine etc. or as used in chemistry. **2** = *hip-flask* (see HIP[1]). **3** = *vacuum flask*. **4** *hist.* = *powder-flask*. [F *flasque* & (prob.) It. *fiasco* f. med.L *flasca*, *flasco*: cf. FLAGON]

■ **1** see JAR 1.

flat[1] /flat/ *adj.*, *adv.*, *n.*, & *v.* ● *adj.* (**flatter**, **flattest**) **1 a** horizontally level (*a flat roof*). **b** even; smooth; unbroken; without projection or indentation (*a flat stomach*). **c** with a level surface and little depth; shallow (*a flat cap*; *a flat heel*). **2** unqualified; plain; downright (*a flat refusal*; *a flat denial*). **3 a** dull; lifeless; monotonous (*spoke in a flat tone*). **b** without energy; dejected. **4** (of a fizzy drink) having lost its effervescence; stale. **5** (of an accumulator, a battery, etc.) having exhausted its charge. **6** *Mus.* **a** below true or normal pitch (*the violins are flat*). **b** (of a key) having a flat or flats in the signature. **c** (as **B, E,** etc. **flat**) a semitone lower than B, E, etc. **7** *Photog.* lacking contrast. **8 a** (of paint etc.) not glossy; matt. **b** (of a tint) uniform. **9** (of a tyre) punctured; deflated. **10** (of a market, prices, etc.) inactive; sluggish. **11** of or relating to flat-racing. ● *adv.* **1** lying at full length; spread out, esp. on another surface (*lay flat on the floor*; *the ladder was flat against the wall*). **2** *colloq.* **a** completely, absolutely (*turned it down flat*; *flat broke*). **b** exactly (*in five minutes flat*). **3** *Mus.* below the true or normal pitch (*always sings flat*). ● *n.* **1** the flat part of anything; something flat (*the flat of the hand*). **2** level ground, esp. a plain or swamp. **3** *Mus.* **a** a note lowered a semitone below natural pitch. **b** the sign (♭) indicating this. **4** (as **the flat**) *Brit.* **a** flat racing. **b** the flat racing season. **5** *Theatr.* a flat section of scenery mounted on a frame. **6** esp. *US colloq.* a flat tyre. **7** *sl.* a foolish person. ● *v.tr.* (**flatted**, **flatting**) **1** make flat, flatten (esp. in technical use). **2** *US Mus.* make (a note) flat. □ **fall flat** fail to live up to expectations; not win applause. **flat arch** *Archit.* an arch with a flat lower or inner curve. **flat** (or **flat-bottomed**) **boat** a boat with a flat bottom for transport in shallow water. **flat-fish** any marine fish of various families having an asymmetric appearance with both eyes on one side of a flattened body, including sole, turbot, plaice, etc. **flat foot** a foot with a less than normal arch. **flat-four** (of an engine) having four cylinders all horizontal, two on each side of the crankshaft. **flat-head 1** any marine fish of the family Platycephalidae, having a flattened body with both eyes on the top side. **2** *sl.* a foolish person. **flat-iron** *hist.* an iron heated externally and used for pressing clothes etc. **flat out 1** at top speed. **2** without hesitation or delay. **3** using all one's strength, energy, or resources. **flat race** a horse race over level ground, as opposed to a steeplechase or hurdles. **flat-racing** the racing of horses in flat races. **flat rate** a rate that is the same in all cases, not proportional. **flat spin 1** *Aeron.* a nearly horizontal spin. **2** *colloq.* a state of agitation or panic. **flat-top 1** *US Aeron. sl.* an aircraft-carrier. **2** *sl.* a man's short flat haircut. **that's flat** *colloq.* let there be no doubt about it. ▫▫ **flatly** *adv.* **flatness** *n.* **flattish** *adj.* [ME f. ON *flatr* f. Gmc]

■ *adj.* **1 a** level, horizontal, plane. **b** even, smooth; unbroken, uninterrupted. **2** unqualified, unreserved, unconditional, absolute, categorical; plain, direct, unequivocal, unambiguous; downright, outright, irrevocable, definite, firm, certain, sure, peremptory, positive, out-and-out, complete, total. **3 a** dull, insipid, bland, lifeless, spiritless, lacklustre, prosaic, uninteresting, unexciting, dry, jejune, boring, dead, monotonous; tired, stale; two-dimensional, unrealistic. **b** see LISTLESS. **4** non-effervescent, decarbonated, dead; stale, insipid, tasteless, flavourless, unpalatable. **8 a** matt, non-gloss(y), dull. **9** punctured, deflated, blown out. **10** inactive, sluggish, slow, depressed, dull. ● *adv.* **1** spread out, prostrate, prone, supine, stretched out, recumbent, outstretched, lying (down), reclining, spread-eagled, outspread. **2 a** completely, absolutely, categorically, utterly, wholly, uncompromisingly, irrevocably, positively, definitely, directly, flatly. **b** exactly, precisely. ● *n.* **2** plain, lowland, tundra, steppe, savannah, heath; pampas; swamp, marsh, bog, fen; mud-flat. **7** see FOOL[1] *n.* 1. ▫ **fall flat** disappoint; founder, *esp. US sl.* bomb; see also FAIL *v.* 1, 2a. **flat-head 2** see FOOL[1] *n.* 1. **flat out 1** at top *or* maximum *or* full *or* breakneck speed, speedily, quickly, rapidly, swiftly, at full gallop, post-haste, hell for leather, like a bat out of hell, *colloq.* like (greased) lightning, like the wind, *literary* apace. **2** unhesitatingly, directly, at once, immediately, forthwith, without delay; plainly, openly, flatly, baldly. **flat rate** standard *or* fixed rate. **flat spin 2** see FLURRY *n.* 3.

flat[2] /flat/ *n.* & *v.* ● *n.* a set of rooms, usu. on one floor, used as a residence. ● *v.intr.* (**flatted**, **flatting**) (often foll. by *with*) *Austral.* share a flat with. ▫▫ **flatlet** *n.* [alt. f. obs. *flet* floor, dwelling f. Gmc (as FLAT[1])]

■ *n.* set *or* suite of rooms, tenement, *US* apartment.

flatcar /flátkaar/ *n.* a railway wagon without raised sides or ends.

flatfoot /flátfo͝ot/ *n.* (*pl.* **-foots** or **-feet**) *sl.* a policeman.

■ see *police officer*.

flat-footed /flátfo͝ottid/ *adj.* **1** having flat feet. **2** *colloq.* downright, positive. **3** *colloq.* unprepared; off guard (*was caught flat-footed*). ▫▫ **flat-footedly** *adv.* **flat-footedness** *n.*

flatmate /flátmayt/ *n. Brit.* a person in relation to one or more others living in the same flat.

flatten /flátt'n/ *v.* **1** *tr.* & *intr.* make or become flat. **2** *tr. colloq.* **a** humiliate. **b** knock down. ▫ **flatten out** bring an aircraft parallel to the ground. ▫▫ **flattener** *n.*

■ **1** level (off *or* out), even (off *or* out). **2 b** knock down *or* over, knock out, floor, fell; level, raze (to the ground), tear down, demolish.

flatter /fláttər/ *v.tr.* **1** compliment unduly; overpraise, esp. for gain or advantage. **2** (usu. *refl.*; usu. foll. by *that* + clause) please, congratulate, or delude (oneself etc.) (*I flatter myself that I can sing*). **3 a** (of a colour, a style, etc.) make (a person) appear to the best advantage (*that blouse flatters you*). **b** (esp. of a portrait, a painter, etc.) represent too favourably. **4** gratify the vanity of; make (a person) feel honoured. **5** inspire (a person) with hope, esp. unduly (*was flattered into thinking himself invulnerable*). **6** please or gratify (the ear, the eye, etc.). ▫ **flattering unction** a salve that one administers to one's own conscience or self-esteem (Shakesp. esp. *Hamlet* III. iv. 136). ▫▫ **flatterer** *n.* **flattering** *adj.* **flatteringly** *adv.* [ME, perh. rel. to OF *flater* to smooth]

■ **1** compliment, overpraise, toady (to), truckle to, fawn (on *or* upon), court, curry favour with, *colloq.* butter up, soft-soap, suck up to, sweet-talk, *Brit. sl.* flannel. **2** see FOOL[1] *v.* 1, 3. **3 a** see SUIT *v.* 1. **b** show to advantage, compliment, favour. ▫▫ **flatterer** toady, sycophant, fawner, backscratcher, truckler, lickspittle, *colloq.* sweet-talker, yes-man, bootlicker, *sl.* bum-sucker. **flattering** becoming, enhancing; complimentary, adulatory, laudatory, fulsome, fawning, ingratiating, unctuous, slimy, sugary, *colloq.* smarmy.

flattery /fláttəri/ *n.* (*pl.* **-ies**) **1** exaggerated or insincere praise. **2** the act or an instance of flattering.

■ adulation, cajolery, blandishment, toadying, sycophancy, *colloq.* sweet talk, soft soap, bootlicking, *sl.* bum-sucking, *Brit. sl.* flannel.

flattie /flátti/ *n.* (also **flatty**) (*pl.* **-ies**) *colloq.* **1** a flat-heeled shoe. **2** a flat-bottomed boat. **3** a policeman.

flatulent /flátyoolənt/ *adj.* **1 a** causing formation of gas in the alimentary canal. **b** caused by or suffering from this. **2** (of speech etc.) inflated, pretentious. ▫▫ **flatulence** *n.* **flatulency** *n.* **flatulently** *adv.* [F f. mod.L *flatulentus* (as FLATUS)]

■ **2** see POMPOUS 2.

flatus /fláytəss/ *n.* wind in or from the stomach or bowels. [L, = blowing f. *flare* blow]

■ see WIND[1] *n.* 4.

flatware /flátwair/ *n.* **1** plates, saucers, etc. (opp. HOLLOWWARE). **2** *US* domestic cutlery.

flatworm /flátwurm/ *n.* any worm of the phylum Platyhelminthes, having a flattened body and no body-cavity or blood vessels, including turbellaria, flukes, etc.

flaunch var. of FLANCH.

flaunt /flawnt/ *v.* & *n.* ● *v.tr.* & *intr.* **1** (often *refl.*) display ostentatiously (oneself or one's finery); show off; parade (*liked to flaunt his gold cuff-links*; *flaunted themselves before the crowd*). ¶ Often confused with *flout*. **2** wave or cause to wave proudly (*flaunted the banner*). ● *n.* an act or instance of flaunting. ▫▫ **flaunter** *n.* **flaunty** *adj.* [16th c.: orig. unkn.]

■ *v.* **1** display, show (off), parade, flourish, exhibit, sport, spotlight.

flautist /fláwtist/ *n.* a flute-player. [It. *flautista* f. *flauto* FLUTE]

flavescent /fləvéss'nt/ *adj.* turning yellow; yellowish. [L *flavescere* f. *flavus* yellow]

flavin /fláyvin/ *n.* (also **flavine** /-veen/) **1** the chemical compound forming the nucleus of various natural yellow pigments. **2** a yellow dye obtained from dyer's oak. ▫ **flavin adenine dinucleotide** a coenzyme derived from riboflavin, important in various biochemical reactions. ¶ Abbr.: **FAD**. [L *flavus* yellow + -IN]

flavine /fláyveen/ *n. Pharm.* an antiseptic derived from acridine. [as FLAVIN + -INE[4]]

flavone /fláyvōn/ *n. Biochem.* any of a group of naturally occurring white or yellow pigments found in plants. [as FLAVINE + -ONE]

flavoprotein /fláyvōprō̆teen/ *n. Biochem.* any of a group of conjugated proteins containing flavin that are involved in oxidation reactions in cells. [FLAVINE + PROTEIN]

flavorous /fláyvərəss/ *adj.* having a pleasant or pungent flavour.

■ see TASTY.

flavour /fláyvər/ *n.* & *v.* (*US* **flavor**) ● *n.* **1** a distinctive mingled sensation of smell and taste (*has a cheesy flavour*). **2** an indefinable characteristic quality (*music with a romantic flavour*). **3** (usu. foll. by *of*) a slight admixture of a usu. undesirable quality (*the flavour of failure hangs over the enterprise*). **4** esp. *US* = FLAVOURING. ● *v.tr.* give flavour to; season. ▫ **flavour of the month** (or **week**) a temporary trend or fashion. ▫▫ **flavourful** *adj.* **flavourless** *adj.* **flavoursome** *adj.* [ME f. OF *flaor* perh. f. L *flatus* blowing & *foetor* stench: assim. to *savour*]

■ *n.* **1** taste, tastiness, savour, tang, piquancy, zest, sapor.

2 quality, character, spirit, nature, property, mark, stamp, style, taste, feel, feeling, sense, tinge, aroma, air, atmosphere, hint, suggestion, soupçon, touch. ● *v.* season, spice.

flavouring /fláyvəring/ *n.* a substance used to flavour food or drink.

flaw[1] /flaw/ *n.* & *v.* ● *n.* **1** an imperfection; a blemish (*has a character without a flaw*). **2** a crack or similar fault (*the cup has a flaw*). **3** *Law* an invalidating defect in a legal matter. ● *v.tr.* & *intr.* crack; damage; spoil. ▫▫ **flawed** *adj.* **flawless** *adj.* **flawlessly** *adv.* **flawlessness** *n.* [ME perh. f. ON *flaga* slab f. Gmc: cf. FLAKE[1], FLAG[2]]

■ *n.* **1** imperfection, fault, defect, error, mistake, blemish, blot, stain, taint, chink, (black) mark, disfigurement, failing, weakness, weak spot. **2** crack, break, chip, fracture; split, cleft, slit, cut, gash, rent, rift, tear, rip; puncture, hole, perforation. ● *v.* crack, damage, harm, spoil, ruin, mark, disfigure; discredit, stigmatize, hurt, taint, mar, blot. ▫▫ **flawed** damaged, harmed; tainted, stained, tarnished; defective, imperfect, unsound, faulty; marred, weakened. **flawless** perfect, pristine, pure, uncorrupted, chaste, virgin, clean, immaculate, unsullied, unspoiled, unspoilt, unsoiled, spotless, untarnished, impeccable, unblemished, faultless; undamaged, intact, whole, unimpaired; unassailable, unimpeachable, unquestionable, irrefutable, undeniable, foolproof, sound, demonstrable.

flaw[2] /flaw/ *n.* a squall of wind; a short storm. [prob. f. MDu. *vlāghe*, MLG *vlāge*, perh. = stroke]

flax /flaks/ *n.* **1 a** a blue-flowered plant, *Linum usitatissimum*, cultivated for its textile fibre and its seeds (see LINSEED). **b** a plant resembling this. **2 a** dressed or undressed flax fibres. **b** *archaic* linen, cloth of flax. ▫ **flax-lily** (*pl.* **-ies**) *NZ* any plant of the genus *Phormium*, yielding valuable fibre. **flax-seed** linseed. [OE *flæx* f. WG]

flaxen /fláks'n/ *adj.* **1** of flax. **2** (of hair) coloured like dressed flax; pale yellow.

■ **2** see GOLDEN 2.

flay /flay/ *v.tr.* **1** strip the skin or hide off, esp. by beating. **2** criticize severely (*the play was flayed by the critics*). **3** peel off (skin, bark, peel, etc.). **4** strip (a person) of wealth by extortion or exaction. ▫▫ **flayer** *n.* [OE *flēan* f. Gmc]

■ **1** see FLOG 1a. **2** see LAMBASTE 2. **3** see PEEL[1] *v.* 1, 2.

F-layer /éflayər/ *n.* the highest and most strongly ionized region of the ionosphere. [*F* (arbitrary) + LAYER]

flea /flee/ *n.* **1** a small wingless jumping insect of the order Siphonaptera, feeding on human and other blood. **2 a** (in full **flea beetle**) a small jumping beetle infesting hops, cabbages, etc. **b** (in full **water flea**) daphnia. ▫ **flea-bite 1** the bite of a flea. **2** a trivial injury or inconvenience. **flea-bitten 1** bitten by or infested with fleas. **2** shabby. **flea-bug** *US* = FLEA 2a. **flea-circus** a show of performing fleas. **flea-collar** an insecticidal collar for pets. **a flea in one's ear** a sharp reproof. **flea market** a street market selling second-hand goods etc. **flea-pit** a dingy dirty place, esp. a run-down cinema. **flea-wort** any of several plants supposed to drive away fleas. [OE *flēa*, *flēah* f. Gmc]

fleabag /fléebag/ *n. sl.* a shabby or unattractive person or thing.

fleabane /fléebayn/ *n.* any of various composite plants of the genus *Inula* or *Pulicaria*, supposed to drive away fleas.

flèche /flaysh, flesh/ *n.* a slender spire, often perforated with windows, esp. at the intersection of the nave and the transept of a church. [F, orig. = arrow]

fleck /flek/ *n.* & *v.* ● *n.* **1** a small patch of colour or light (*eyes with green flecks*). **2** a small particle or speck, esp. of dust. **3** a spot on the skin; a freckle. ● *v.tr.* mark with flecks; dapple; variegate. [perh. f. ON *flekkr* (n.), *flekka* (v.), or MLG, MDu. *vlecke*, OHG *flec*, *fleccho*]

■ *n.* see SPOT *n.* 1a, b. ● *v.* see DOT[1] *v.* 4; (*flecked*) dappled, spotted, pied, speckled, sprinkled, dotted, marked, stippled, dusted, specked, spattered, freckled.

flection *US* var. of FLEXION.

fled *past* and *past part.* of FLEE.

fledge /flej/ *v.* **1** *intr.* (of a bird) grow feathers. **2** *tr.* provide (an arrow) with feathers. **3** *tr.* bring up (a young bird) until it can fly. **4** *tr.* (as **fledged** *adj.*) **a** able to fly. **b** independent; mature. **5** *tr.* deck or provide with feathers or down. [obs. *fledge* (adj.) 'fit to fly', f. OE *flycge* (recorded in *unfligge*) f. a Gmc root rel. to FLY[1]]

fledgling /fléjling/ *n.* (also **fledgeling**) **1** a young bird. **2** an inexperienced person. [FLEDGE + -LING[1]]

■ **2** see NOVICE.

flee /flee/ *v.* (*past* and *past part.* **fled** /fled/) **1** *intr.* (often foll. by *from*, *before*) **a** run away. **b** seek safety by fleeing. **2** *tr.* run away from; leave abruptly; shun (*fled the room*; *fled his attentions*). **3** *intr.* vanish; cease; pass away. ▫▫ **fleer** /fléeər/ *n.* [OE *flēon* f. Gmc]

■ **1** run away *or* off, escape, get away, fly, take (to) flight, bolt, go (away), decamp, abscond, make off *or* away, make an exit, make (good) one's escape, make a (clean) getaway, beat a (hasty) retreat, take to one's heels, take off, turn tail, vanish, disappear, make a run for it, take to the hills *or* woods, *Brit.* levant, *colloq.* show a clean pair of heels, make tracks, scoot, make oneself scarce, clear out, skedaddle, scram, do a (moonlight) flit, skip, *US colloq.* hightail it, *sl.* cut and run, beat it, take a powder, split, blow, take a powder, *sl.* do a runner, *Austral. and NZ sl.* shoot through, *Brit. sl.* scarper, do a bunk, *US sl.* skiddoo, vamoose, go on the lam. **2** run away from, quit, *colloq.* skip, *sl.* blow; avoid, evade, shun, escape from, *literary* eschew. **3** see DISAPPEAR.

fleece /fleess/ *n.* & *v.* ● *n.* **1 a** the woolly covering of a sheep or a similar animal. **b** the amount of wool sheared from a sheep at one time. **2** something resembling a fleece, esp.: **a** a woolly or rough head of hair. **b** a soft warm fabric with a pile, used for lining coats etc. **c** a white cloud, a blanket of snow, etc. **3** *Heraldry* a representation of a fleece suspended from a ring. ● *v.tr.* **1** (often foll. by *of*) strip (a person) of money, valuables, etc.; swindle. **2** remove the fleece from (a sheep etc.); shear. **3** cover as if with a fleece (*a sky fleeced with clouds*). ▫ **fleece-picker** *Austral.* & *NZ* = FLEECY. **Golden Fleece** see GOLDEN. ▫▫ **fleeceable** *adj.* **fleeced** *adj.* (also in *comb.*). [OE *flēos*, *flēs* f. WG]

■ *v.* **1** swindle, cheat, defraud, overcharge, plunder, milk, rob, rook, soak, flimflam, bleed, pluck, *colloq.* diddle, rip off, *sl.* bilk, skin, take, gyp, take to the cleaners, chisel. **2** shear, shave, crop, strip, clip.

fleecy /fléessi/ *adj.* & *n.* ● *adj.* (**fleecier**, **fleeciest**) **1** of or like a fleece. **2** covered with a fleece. ● *n.* (also **fleecie**) (*pl.* **-ies**) *Austral.* & *NZ* a person whose job is to pick up fleeces in a shearing shed. ▫▫ **fleecily** *adv.* **fleeciness** *n.*

■ *adj.* **1** see WOOLLY *adj.* 2.

fleer /fleer/ *v.* & *n.* ● *v.intr.* laugh impudently or mockingly; sneer; jeer. ● *n.* a mocking look or speech. [ME, prob. f. Scand.: cf. Norw. & Sw. dial. *flira* to grin]

fleet[1] /fleet/ *n.* **1 a** a number of warships under one commander-in-chief. **b** (prec. by *the*) all the warships and merchant-ships of a nation. **2** a number of ships, aircraft, buses, lorries, taxis, etc. operating together or owned by one proprietor. ▫ **Fleet Admiral** see ADMIRAL. **Fleet Air Arm** *hist.* the aviation service of the Royal Navy. [OE *flēot* ship, shipping f. *flēotan* float, FLEET[5]]

■ **1 a** armada, flotilla, naval task force, squadron, convoy, *poet.* navy.

fleet[2] /fleet/ *adj. poet.* or *literary* swift; nimble. ▫▫ **fleetly** *adv.* **fleetness** *n.* [prob. f. ON *fljótr* f. Gmc: cf. FLEET[5]]

■ swift, nimble, rapid, fast, speedy, quick, expeditious, agile.

fleet[3] /fleet/ *n. dial.* a creek; an inlet. ▫ **Fleet Street 1** the London press. **2** British journalism or journalists. [OE *flēot* f. Gmc: cf. FLEET[5]]

fleet[4] /fleet/ *adj.* & *adv. dial.* ● *adj.* (of water) shallow. ● *adv.* at or to a small depth (*plough fleet*). [orig. uncert.: perh. f. OE *flēat* (unrecorded), rel. to FLEET[5]]

fleet[5] /fleet/ *v.intr. archaic* **1** glide away; vanish; be transitory. **2** (usu. foll. by *away*) (of time) pass rapidly; slip away. **3** move swiftly; fly. [OE *flēotan* float, swim f. Gmc]

fleeting /fleéting/ *adj.* transitory; brief. ▫▫ **fleetingly** *adv.* [FLEET[5] + -ING[2]]
■ transitory, fugitive, transient, temporary, passing, ephemeral, evanescent, momentary, short-lived, short, brief, *literary* fugacious.

Fleming /flémming/ *n.* **1** a native of medieval Flanders in the Low Countries. **2** a member of a Flemish-speaking people inhabiting N. and W. Belgium (see also WALLOON). [OE f. ON *Flæmingi* & MDu. *Vlāming* f. root of *Vlaanderen* Flanders]

Flemish /flémmish/ *adj.* & *n.* ● *adj.* of or relating to Flanders. ● *n.* the language of the Flemings. ▫ **Flemish bond** *Building* a bond in which each course consists of alternate headers and stretchers. [MDu. *Vlāmisch* (as FLEMING)]

flense /flenz/ *v.tr.* (also **flench** /flench/, **flinch** /flinch/) **1** cut up (a whale or seal). **2** flay (a seal). [Da. *flense*: cf. Norw. *flinsa*, *flunsa* flay]

flesh /flesh/ *n.* & *v.* ● *n.* **1 a** the soft, esp. muscular, substance between the skin and bones of an animal or a human. **b** plumpness; fat (*has put on flesh*). **c** *archaic* meat, esp. excluding poultry, game, and offal. **2** the body as opposed to the mind or the soul, esp. considered as sinful. **3** the pulpy substance of a fruit or a plant. **4 a** the visible surface of the human body with ref. to its colour or appearance. **b** (also **flesh-colour**) a yellowish pink colour. **5** animal or human life. ● *v.tr.* **1** embody in flesh. **2** incite (a hound etc.) by the taste of blood. **3** initiate, esp. by aggressive or violent means, esp.: **a** use (a sword etc.) for the first time on flesh. **b** use (wit, the pen, etc.) for the first time. **c** inflame (a person) by the foretaste of success. ▫ **all flesh** all human and animal creation. **flesh and blood** ● *n.* **1** the body or its substance. **2** humankind. **3** human nature, esp. as being fallible. ● *adj.* actually living, not imaginary or supernatural. **flesh-fly** (*pl.* **-flies**) any fly of the family Sarcophagidae that deposits eggs or larvae in dead flesh. **flesh out** make or become substantial. **flesh side** the side of a hide that adjoined the flesh. **flesh tints** flesh-colours as rendered by a painter. **flesh-wound** a wound not reaching a bone or a vital organ. **in the flesh** in bodily form, in person. **lose** (or **put on**) **flesh** grow thinner or fatter. **make a person's flesh creep** frighten or horrify a person, esp. with tales of the supernatural etc. **one flesh** (of two people) intimately united, esp. by virtue of marriage (Gen. 2:24). **one's own flesh and blood** near relatives; descendants. **sins of the flesh** unchastity. **the way of all flesh** experience common to all mankind. ▫▫ **fleshless** *adj.* [OE *flǣsc* f. Gmc]
■ *n.* **1 a** muscle, tissue. **b** see FAT *n.* **2** body, corporeality; flesh and blood. ▫ **flesh and blood** (*n.*) **2** humankind, mankind, humanity; people. (*adj.*) living, real, corporeal, physical, human. **flesh out** give *or* lend substance to, fill out, enlarge *or* expand on, develop, amplify, expatiate on, elaborate on. **in the flesh** bodily, in person, *in propria persona*, personally, really, physically, alive, living. **make a person's flesh creep** see FRIGHTEN 1. **one flesh** married, *archaic* espoused; see ATTACHED 2. **one's own flesh and blood** relatives, kin, kinsfolk, family, stock, blood, kith and kin, relations.

flesher /fléshər/ *n. Sc.* a butcher.

fleshings /fléshingz/ *n.pl.* an actor's flesh-coloured tights.

fleshly /fléshli/ *adj.* (**fleshlier**, **fleshliest**) **1** (of desire etc.) bodily; lascivious; sensual. **2** mortal, not divine. **3** worldly. ▫▫ **fleshliness** *n.* [OE *flǣsclic* (as FLESH)]
■ **1** see SENSUAL. **2** see MORTAL *adj.* 1. **3** see WORLDLY 1.

fleshpots /fléshpots/ *n.pl.* luxurious living (Exod. 16:3).

fleshy /fléshi/ *adj.* (**fleshier**, **fleshiest**) **1** plump, fat. **2** of flesh, without bone. **3** (of plant or fruit tissue) pulpy. **4** like flesh. ▫▫ **fleshiness** *n.*
■ **1** see FAT *adj.*

fletcher /fléchər/ *n. archaic* a maker or seller of arrows. [ME f. OF *flech(i)er* f. *fleche* arrow]

fleur-de-lis /flőrdəleé/ *n.* (also **fleur-de-lys**) (*pl.* **fleurs-** *pronunc.* same) **1** the iris flower. **2** *Heraldry* **a** a lily composed of three petals bound together near their bases. **b** the former royal arms of France. [ME f. OF *flour de lys* flower of lily]

fleuret /flooréṫ/ *n.* an ornament like a small flower. [F *fleurette* f. *fleur* flower]

fleuron /flőróN/ *n.* a flower-shaped ornament on a building, a coin, a book, etc. [ME f. OF *floron* f. *flour* FLOWER]

fleury /floori/ *adj.* (also **flory** /flóri/) *Heraldry* decorated with fleurs-de-lis. [ME f. OF *flo(u)ré* (as FLEURON)]

flew *past* of FLY[1].

flews /flooz/ *n.pl.* the hanging lips of a bloodhound etc. [16th c.: orig. unkn.]

flex[1] /fleks/ *v.* **1** *tr.* & *intr.* bend (a joint, limb, etc.) or be bent. **2** *tr.* & *intr.* move (a muscle) or (of a muscle) be moved to bend a joint. **3** *tr. Geol.* bend (strata). **4** *tr. Archaeol.* place (a corpse) with the legs drawn up under the chin. [L *flectere flex-* bend]
■ **1** see BEND[1] *v.* 1. **2** move, exercise, tense, tighten, contract.

flex[2] /fleks/ *n. Brit.* a flexible insulated cable used for carrying electric current to an appliance. [abbr. of FLEXIBLE]
■ cable, wire, lead, cord, extension.

flexible /fléksib'l/ *adj.* **1** able to bend without breaking; pliable; pliant. **2** easily led; manageable; docile. **3** adaptable; versatile; variable (*works flexible hours*). ▫▫ **flexibility** /-bílliti/ *n.* **flexibly** *adv.* [ME f. OF *flexible* or L *flexibilis* (as FLEX[1])]
■ **1** pliable, pliant, elastic, resilient, supple, bendable, limber, lithe, stretchy, stretchable, springy, extensible, extensile, ductile, tensile, yielding, willowy, *archaic* flexile. **2** persuadable, persuasible; manageable, tractable, malleable, cooperative, amenable, modifiable, conformable; docile, compliant, obedient, submissive. **3** versatile; variable; see also ADAPTABLE 1. ▫▫ **flexibility** pliability, pliancy, elasticity, resilience, resiliency, suppleness, flexibleness, limberness, give, stretch, spring, springiness, ductility; manageability, compliance, tractability, tractableness, malleability, conformability, adjustability; docility, obedience, submissiveness, agreeability, conformity; adaptability, versatility.

flexile /fléksīl/ *adj. archaic* **1** supple; mobile. **2** tractable; manageable. **3** versatile. ▫▫ **flexility** /-sílliti/ *n.* [L *flexilis* (as FLEX[1])]

flexion /fléksh'n/ *n.* (*US* **flection**) **1 a** the act of bending or the condition of being bent, esp. of a limb or joint. **b** a bent part; a curve. **2** *Gram.* inflection. **3** *Math.* = FLEXURE. ▫▫ **flexional** *adj.* (in sense 2). **flexionless** *adj.* (in sense 2). [L *flexio* (as FLEX[1])]

flexitime /fléksitīm/ *n. Brit.* **1** a system of working a set number of hours with the starting and finishing times chosen within agreed limits by the employee. **2** the hours worked in this way. [FLEXIBLE + TIME]

flexography /fleksógrəfi/ *n. Printing* a rotary letterpress technique using rubber or plastic plates and synthetic inks or dyes for printing on fabrics, plastics, etc., as well as on paper. ▫▫ **flexographic** /-səgráffik/ *adj.* [L *flexus* a bending f. *flectere* bend + -GRAPHY]

flexor /fléksər/ *n.* (in full **flexor muscle**) a muscle that bends part of the body (cf. EXTENSOR). [mod.L (as FLEX[1])]

flexuous /fléksyooəss/ *adj.* full of bends; winding. ▫▫ **flexuosity** /-yoo-óssiti/ *n.* **flexuously** *adv.* [L *flexuosus* f. *flexus* bending formed as FLEX[1]]

flexure /flékshər/ *n.* **1 a** the act of bending or the condition of being bent. **b** a bend, curve, or turn. **2** *Math.* the curving of a line, surface, or solid, esp. from a straight line, plane, etc. **3** *Geol.* the bending of strata under pressure. ▫▫ **flexural** *adj.* [L *flexura* (as FLEX[1])]

flibbertigibbet /flíbbərtijíbbit/ *n.* a gossiping, frivolous, or restless person. [imit. of chatter]
▪ see GOSSIP *n.* 3.

flick /flik/ *n.* & *v.* ● *n.* **1 a** a light, sharp, quickly retracted blow with a whip etc. **b** the sudden release of a bent finger or thumb, esp. to propel a small object. **2** a sudden movement or jerk. **3** a quick turn of the wrist in playing games, esp. in throwing or striking a ball. **4** a slight, sharp sound. **5** *Brit. colloq.* **a** a cinema film. **b** (in *pl.*; prec. by *the*) the cinema. ● *v.* **1** *tr.* (often foll. by *away*, *off*) strike or move with a flick (*flicked the ash off his cigar*; *flicked away the dust*). **2** *tr.* give a flick with (a whip, towel, etc.). **3** *intr.* make a flicking movement or sound. □ **flick-knife** a weapon with a blade that springs out from the handle when a button is pressed. **flick through 1** turn over (cards, pages, etc.). **2 a** turn over the pages etc. of, by a rapid movement of the fingers. **b** look cursorily through (a book etc.). [ME, imit.]
▪ *n.* **2, 3** see WHISK *n.* 1. **5 a** see FILM *n.* 3a, b. ● *v.* **1** flip, brush, sweep, toss. □ **flick through** see BROWSE *v.* 1.

flicker[1] /flíkkər/ *v.* & *n.* ● *v.intr.* **1** (of light) shine unsteadily or fitfully. **2** (of a flame) burn unsteadily, alternately flaring and dying down. **3 a** (of a flag, a reptile's tongue, an eyelid, etc.) move or wave to and fro; quiver; vibrate. **b** (of the wind) blow lightly and unsteadily. **4** (of hope etc.) increase and decrease unsteadily and intermittently. ● *n.* a flickering movement or light. □ **flicker out** die away after a final flicker. [OE *flicorian, flycerian*]
▪ *v.* **1** glimmer, shimmer, blink, twinkle, sparkle. **2** waver, flare; see also BLINK *v.* 5. **3 a** flap, flutter; quiver, vibrate, shake, tremble, fluctuate, oscillate. ● *n.* glimmer, glimmering, twinkle, twinkling, sparkle, flare; (of recognition) hint, spark.

flicker[2] /flíkkər/ *n.* any woodpecker of the genus *Colaptes*, native to N. America. [imit. of its note]

flier var. of FLYER.

flight[1] /flīt/ *n.* & *v.* ● *n.* **1 a** the act or manner of flying through the air (*studied swallows' flight*). **b** the swift movement or passage of a projectile etc. through the air (*the flight of an arrow*). **2 a** a journey made through the air or in space. **b** a timetabled journey made by an airline. **c** an RAF unit of about six aircraft. **3 a** a flock or large body of birds, insects, etc., esp. when migrating. **b** a migration. **4** (usu. foll. by *of*) a series, esp. of stairs between floors, or of hurdles across a race track (*lives up six flights*). **5** an extravagant soaring, a mental or verbal excursion or sally (of wit etc.) (*a flight of fancy*; *a flight of ambition*). **6** the trajectory and pace of a ball in games. **7** the distance that a bird, aircraft, or missile can fly. **8** (usu. foll. by *of*) a volley (*a flight of arrows*). **9** the tail of a dart. **10** the pursuit of game by a hawk. **11** swift passage (of time). ● *v.tr.* **1** vary the trajectory and pace of (a cricket-ball etc.). **2** provide (an arrow) with feathers. **3** shoot (wildfowl etc.) in flight. □ **flight bag** a small, zipped, shoulder bag carried by air travellers. **flight control** an internal or external system directing the movement of aircraft. **flight-deck 1** the deck of an aircraft-carrier used for take-off and landing. **2** the accommodation for the pilot, navigator, etc. in an aircraft. **flight-feather** a bird's wing or tail feather. **flight lieutenant** an RAF officer next in rank below squadron leader. **flight officer** a rank in the WRAF, corresponding to flight lieutenant. **flight path** the planned course of an aircraft or spacecraft. **flight-recorder** a device in an aircraft to record technical details during a flight, that may be used in the event of an accident to discover its cause. **flight sergeant** *Mil.* an RAF rank next above sergeant. **flight-test** test (an aircraft, rocket, etc.) during flight. **in the first** (or **top**) **flight** taking a leading place. **take** (or **wing**) **one's flight** fly. [OE *flyht* f. WG: rel to FLY[1]]
▪ *n.* **1a, 5** flying, soaring; winging. **2 a** (air *or* space) journey, (air *or* space) voyage, (air *or* space) trip. **3 a** flock, swarm, cloud; covey (of grouse *or* partridge), bevy (of quail *or* larks), skein (of geese). **b** see MOVEMENT 1. **8** see VOLLEY *n.* 1. **9** tail, feather.

flight[2] /flīt/ *n.* **1 a** the act or manner of fleeing. **b** a hasty retreat. **2** *Econ.* the selling of currency, investments, etc. in anticipation of a fall in value (*flight from sterling*). □ **put to flight** cause to flee. **take** (or **take to**) **flight** flee. [OE f. Gmc: rel. to FLEE]
▪ **1** retreat, escape, departure, exit, exodus, getaway, fleeing, bolting. □ **put to flight** chase (off *or* away), drive (off *or* away), disperse, send off *or* away, *colloq.* send packing, dismiss, rout, stampede. **take** (or **take to**) **flight** see FLEE 1.

flightless /flītliss/ *adj.* (of a bird etc.) naturally unable to fly.

flighty /flīti/ *adj.* (**flightier, flightiest**) **1** (usu. of a girl) frivolous, fickle, changeable. **2** crazy. □□ **flightily** *adv.* **flightiness** *n.* [FLIGHT[1] + -Y[1]]
▪ **1** frivolous, fickle, inconstant, capricious, fanciful, changeable, variable, unstable, unsteady. **2** mad, silly, hare-brained, reckless, irresponsible, *sl.* nutty, screwy, dippy, *colloq.* dotty, crazy.

flimflam /flímflam/ *n.* & *v.* ● *n.* **1** a trifle; nonsense; idle talk. **2** humbug; deception. ● *v.tr.* (**flimflammed, flimflamming**) cheat; deceive. □□ **flimflammer** *n.* **flimflammery** *n.* (*pl.* **-ies**). [imit. redupl.]
▪ *n.* **2** see DECEIT 1. ● *v.* see CHEAT *v.* 1a.

flimsy /flímzi/ *adj.* & *n.* ● *adj.* (**flimsier, flimsiest**) **1** lightly or carelessly assembled; insubstantial, easily damaged (*a flimsy structure*). **2** (of an excuse etc.) unconvincing (*a flimsy pretext*). **3** paltry; trivial; superficial (*a flimsy play*). **4** (of clothing) thin (*a flimsy blouse*). ● *n.* (*pl.* **-ies**) **1 a** very thin paper. **b** a document, esp. a copy, made on this. **2** a flimsy thing, esp. women's underwear. □□ **flimsily** *adv.* **flimsiness** *n.* [17th c.: prob. f. FLIMFLAM: cf. TIPSY]
▪ **1** makeshift, jerry-built, rickety, ramshackle, dilapidated; insubstantial, slight, unsubstantial, fragile, weak, delicate, frail, feeble, frangible, breakable; gimcrack. **2** unconvincing, feeble, weak, lame, implausible, unbelievable, unsatisfactory, poor, inadequate, makeshift, insubstantial, unsubstantial. **3** see PALTRY, SUPERFICIAL 4. **4** thin, delicate, light, gossamer, sheer; gauzy, transparent, see-through, filmy, diaphanous.

flinch[1] /flinch/ *v.* & *n.* ● *v.intr.* **1** draw back in pain or expectation of a blow etc.; wince. **2** (often foll. by *from*) give way; shrink, turn aside (*flinched from his duty*). ● *n.* an act or instance of flinching. □□ **flincher** *n.* **flinchingly** *adv.* [OF *flenchir, flainchir* f. WG]
▪ *v.* **1** draw back, wince, cower, withdraw, cringe, recoil, start, quail, shrink, shy (away); dodge, duck.

flinch[2] var. of FLENSE.

flinders /flíndərz/ *n.pl.* fragments; splinters. [ME, prob. f. Scand.]

fling /fling/ *v.* & *n.* ● *v.* (*past* and *past part.* **flung** /flung/) **1** *tr.* throw or hurl (an object) forcefully. **2** *refl.* **a** (usu. foll. by *into*) rush headlong (into a person's arms, a train, etc.). **b** (usu. foll. by *into*) embark wholeheartedly (on an enterprise). **c** (usu. foll. by *on*) throw (oneself) on a person's mercy etc. **3** *tr.* utter (words) forcefully. **4** *tr.* (usu. foll. by *out*) suddenly spread (the arms). **5** *tr.* (foll. by *on*, *off*) put on or take off (clothes) carelessly or rapidly. **6** *intr.* go angrily or violently; rush (*flung out of the room*). **7** *tr.* put or send suddenly or violently (*was flung into jail*). **8** *tr.* (foll. by *away*) discard or put aside thoughtlessly or rashly (*flung away their reputation*). **9** *intr.* (usu. foll. by *out*) (of a horse etc.) kick and plunge. **10** *tr. archaic* send, emit (sound, light, smell). ● *n.* **1** an act or instance of flinging; a throw; a plunge. **2 a** a spell of indulgence or wild behaviour (*he's had his fling*). **b** *colloq.* an attempt (*give it a fling*). **3** an impetuous, whirling Scottish dance, esp. the Highland fling. □ **have a fling at 1** make an attempt at. **2** jeer at. □□ **flinger** *n.* [ME, perh. f. ON]
▪ *v.* **1** throw, hurl, toss, pitch, cast, heave, sling, *colloq.* lob, chuck. **4** see OPEN *v.* 6a. **6** see STORM *v.* 2. **7, 8** see THROW *v.* 1, 2. ● *n.* **1** see THROW *n.* 1. **2 a** indulgence, debauch, spree, *sl.* binge. **b** gamble, risk, venture, attempt, try,

colloq. go, shot, crack, whirl, *sl.* bash. □ **have a fling at** **1** see TRY *v.* 1, 2. **2** see MOCK *v.* 1, 3.

flint /flint/ *n.* **1 a** a hard grey stone of nearly pure silica occurring naturally as nodules or bands in chalk. **b** a piece of this esp. as flaked or ground to form a primitive tool or weapon. **2** a piece of hard alloy of rare-earth metals used to give an igniting spark in a cigarette-lighter etc. **3** a piece of flint used with steel to produce fire, esp. in a flintlock gun. **4** anything hard and unyielding. □ **flint corn** a variety of maize having hard translucent grains. **flint glass** a pure lustrous kind of glass orig. made with flint. □□ **flinty** *adj.* (**flintier, flintiest**). **flintily** *adv.* **flintiness** *n.* [OE]

flintlock /flíntlok/ *n. hist.* **1** an old type of gun fired by a spark from a flint. **2** the lock producing such a spark.

flip[1] /flip/ *v., n., & adj.* ● *v.* (**flipped, flipping**) **1** *tr.* **a** flick or toss (a coin, pellet, etc.) with a quick movement so that it spins in the air. **b** remove (a small object) from a surface with a flick of the fingers. **2** *tr.* **a** strike or flick (a person's ear, cheek, etc.) lightly or smartly. **b** move (a fan, whip, etc.) with a sudden jerk. **3** *tr.* turn (a small object) over. **4** *intr.* **a** make a fillip or flicking noise with the fingers. **b** (foll. by *at*) strike smartly at. **5** *intr.* move about with sudden jerks. **6** *intr. sl.* become suddenly angry, excited, or enthusiastic. ● *n.* **1** a smart light blow; a flick. **2** *colloq.* **a** a short pleasure flight in an aircraft. **b** a quick tour etc. **3** an act of flipping over (*gave the stone a flip*). ● *adj. colloq.* glib; flippant. □ **flip chart** a large pad erected on a stand and bound so that one page can be turned over at the top to reveal the next. **flip one's lid** *sl.* **1** lose self-control. **2** go mad. **flip side** *colloq.* the less important side of something (orig. of a gramophone record). **flip through** = *flick through*. [prob. f. FILLIP]

■ *v.* **1** toss, spin; flick. **3** see TURN *v.* 2. **6** become angry *or* furious, go berserk, go out of one's head, *colloq.* go mad, go crazy, go (in) off the deep end, lose one's cool, freak (out), *sl.* flip one's lid, go ape. ● *n.* **1** see RAP[1] *n.* 1. ● *adj.* see FLIPPANT. □ **flip one's lid** see FLIP[1] *v.* 6 above.

flip[2] /flip/ *n.* **1** a drink of heated beer and spirit. **2** = *egg-flip*. [perh. f. FLIP[1] in the sense *whip up*]

flip-flop /flípflop/ *n.* & *v.* ● *n.* **1** a usu. rubber sandal with a thong between the big and second toe. **2** esp. *US* a backward somersault. **3** an electronic switching circuit changed from one stable state to another, or through an unstable state back to its stable state, by a triggering pulse. ● *v.intr.* (**-flopped, -flopping**) move with a sound or motion suggested by 'flip-flop'. [imit.]

flippant /flípp'nt/ *adj.* lacking in seriousness; treating serious things lightly; disrespectful. □□ **flippancy** *n.* **flippantly** *adv.* [FLIP[1] + -ANT]

■ frivolous, facetious, light-hearted, jocular, unserious; disrespectful, impudent, impertinent, irreverent, saucy, discourteous, pert, insolent, brash, rude, brazen, cheeky, *colloq.* flip. □ **flippancy** frivolousness, frivolity, facetiousness, levity, light-heartedness, jocularity, unseriousness; disrespect, disrespectfulness, impudence, impertinence, irreverence, sauciness, discourtesy, brashness, pertness, insolence, rudeness, brazenness, cheek, cheekiness, *colloq.* lip, mouth.

flipper /flíppər/ *n.* **1** a broadened limb of a turtle, penguin, etc., used in swimming. **2** a flat rubber etc. attachment worn on the foot for underwater swimming. **3** *sl.* a hand.

flipping /flípping/ *adj.* & *adv. Brit. sl.* expressing annoyance, or as an intensifier (*where's the flipping towel?*; *he flipping beat me*). [FLIP[1] + -ING[2]]

flirt /flurt/ *v.* & *n.* ● *v.* **1** *intr.* (usu. foll. by *with*) behave in a frivolously amorous or sexually enticing manner. **2** *intr.* (usu. foll. by *with*) **a** superficially interest oneself (with an idea etc.). **b** trifle (with danger etc.) (*flirted with disgrace*). **3** *tr.* wave or move (a fan, a bird's tail, etc.) briskly. **4** *intr.* & *tr.* move or cause to move with a jerk. ● *n.* **1** a person who indulges in flirting. **2** a quick movement; a sudden jerk. □□ **flirtation** /-táysh'n/ *n.* **flirtatious** /-táyshəss/ *adj.* **flirtatiously** /-táyshəsli/ *adv.* **flirtatiousness** /-táyshəsniss/ *n.* **flirty** *adj.* (**flirtier, flirtiest**). [imit.]

■ *v.* **1** play *or* act the coquette, philander, play the field, womanize, carry on, dally, tease, toy, *colloq.* gallivant; (*flirt with*) make eyes at, *Brit. colloq.* chat up. **2** (*flirt with*) trifle *or* play with, entertain, think about *or* of; see also TOY *v.* 1. ● *n.* **1** coquette, tease, *colloq.* vamp, minx; playboy, lady-killer, *sl.* wolf; see also *philanderer* (PHILANDER). □□ **flirtatious** coquettish, seductive, flirty, philandering, provocative, enticing, alluring, amorous, *colloq.* come-hither.

flit /flit/ *v.* & *n.* ● *v.intr.* (**flitted, flitting**) **1** move lightly, softly, or rapidly (*flitted from one room to another*). **2** fly lightly; make short flights (*flitted from branch to branch*). **3** *Brit. colloq.* leave one's house etc. secretly to escape creditors or obligations. **4** esp. *Sc.* & *N.Engl.* change one's home; move. ● *n.* **1** an act of flitting. **2** (also **moonlight flit**) a secret change of abode in order to escape creditors etc. □□ **flitter** *n.* [ME f. ON *flytja*: rel. to FLEET[5]]

■ *v.* **1** move, go, fly, skip, hop, dart, flick, whisk, flash. **2** flitter, flutter, fly. **3** see FLEE 1.

flitch /flich/ *n.* **1** a side of bacon. **2** a slab of timber from a tree-trunk, usu. from the outside. **3** (in full **flitch-plate**) a strengthening plate in a beam etc. □ **flitch-beam** a compound beam, esp. of an iron plate between two slabs of wood. [OE *flicce* f. Gmc]

flitter /flíttər/ *v.intr.* flit about; flutter. □ **flitter-mouse** = BAT[2]. [FLIT + -ER[4]]

■ see FLUTTER *v.* 3, 4.

flivver /flívvər/ *n. US sl.* **1** a cheap car or aircraft. **2** a failure. [20th c.: orig. uncert.]

flixweed /flíksweed/ *n.* a cruciferous plant, *Descurainia sophia*, formerly thought to cure dysentery. [earlier *fluxweed*]

float /flōt/ *v.* & *n.* ● *v.* **1** *intr.* & *tr.* **a** rest or move or cause (a buoyant object) to rest or move on the surface of a liquid without sinking. **b** get afloat or set (a stranded ship) afloat. **2** *intr.* move with a liquid or current of air; drift (*the clouds floated high up*). **3** *intr. colloq.* **a** move in a leisurely or casual way (*floated about humming quietly*). **b** (often foll. by *before*) hover before the eye or mind (*the prospect of lunch floated before them*). **4** *intr.* (often foll. by *in*) move or be suspended freely in a liquid or a gas. **5** *tr.* **a** bring (a company, scheme, etc.) into being; launch. **b** offer (stock, shares, etc.) on the stock market. **6** *Commerce* **a** *intr.* (of currency) be allowed to have a fluctuating exchange rate. **b** *tr.* cause (currency) to float. **c** *intr.* (of an acceptance) be in circulation. **7** *tr.* (of water etc.) support; bear along (a buoyant object). **8** *intr.* & *tr.* circulate or cause (a rumour or idea) to circulate. **9** *tr.* waft (a buoyant object) through the air. **10** *tr. archaic* cover with liquid; inundate. ● *n.* **1** a thing that floats, esp.: **a** a raft. **b** a cork or quill on a fishing-line as an indicator of a fish biting. **c** a cork supporting the edge of a fishing-net. **d** the hollow or inflated part or organ supporting a fish etc. in the water; an air bladder. **e** a hollow structure fixed underneath an aircraft enabling it to float on water. **f** a floating device on the surface of water, petrol, etc., controlling the flow. **2** a small vehicle or cart, esp. one powered by electricity (*milk float*). **3** a platform mounted on a lorry and carrying a display in a procession etc. **4 a** a sum of money used at the beginning of a period of selling in a shop, a fête, etc. to provide change. **b** a small sum of money for minor expenditure; petty cash. **5** *Theatr.* (in *sing.* or *pl.*) footlights. **6** a tool used for smoothing plaster. □ **float-board** one of the boards of a water-wheel or paddle-wheel. **float glass** a kind of glass made by drawing the molten glass continuously on to a surface of molten metal for hardening. **float process** the process used to make float glass. **float-stone** a light, porous stone that floats. □□ **floatable** *adj.* **floatability** /-təbílliti/ *n.* [OE *flot*, *flotian* float, OE *flota* ship, ON *flota*, *floti* rel. to FLEET[5]: in ME infl. by OF *floter*]

■ *v.* **1 a** hover, bob, waft, hang, be suspended *or* poised. **2** bob, coast, drift; waft. **5 a** launch, establish, set up, organize, found, initiate, get going *or* moving. **8** see SPREAD *v.* 3. ● *n.* **1 a** raft, pontoon.

floatage /flṓtij/ *n.* **1** the act or state of floating. **2** *Brit.* **a** floating objects or masses; flotsam. **b** the right of appropriating flotsam. **3 a** ships etc. afloat on a river. **b** the part of a ship above the water-line. **4** buoyancy; floating power.

floatation var. of FLOTATION.

floater /flṓtər/ *n.* **1** a person or thing that floats. **2** a floating voter. **3** *sl.* a mistake; a gaffe. **4** a person who frequently changes occupation. **5** *Stock Exch.* a government stock certificate etc. recognized as a security.

floating /flṓting/ *adj.* not settled in a definite place; fluctuating; variable (*the floating population*). □ **floating anchor** a sea anchor. **floating bridge 1** a bridge on pontoons etc. **2** a ferry working on chains. **floating debt** a debt repayable on demand, or at a stated time. **floating dock** a floating structure usable as a dry dock. **floating kidney 1** an abnormal condition in which the kidneys are unusually movable. **2** such a kidney. **floating light 1** a lightship. **2** a lifebuoy with a lantern. **floating point** *Computing* a decimal etc. point that does not occupy a fixed position in the numbers processed. **floating rib** any of the lower ribs, which are not attached to the breastbone. **floating voter** a voter without allegiance to any political party. □□ **floatingly** *adv.*

■ see VARIABLE *adj.* 2.

floaty /flṓti/ *adj.* (esp. of a woman's garment or a fabric) light and airy. [FLOAT]

floc /flok/ *n.* a flocculent mass of fine particles. [abbr. of FLOCCULUS]

flocculate /flókyoolayt/ *v.tr.* & *intr.* form into flocculent masses. □□ **flocculation** /-láysh'n/ *n.*

floccule /flókyōōl/ *n.* a small portion of matter resembling a tuft of wool.

flocculent /flókyoolənt/ *adj.* **1** like tufts of wool. **2** consisting of or showing tufts, downy. **3** *Chem.* (of precipitates) loosely massed. □□ **flocculence** *n.* [L *floccus* FLOCK[2]]

flocculus /flókyooləss/ *n.* (*pl.* **flocculi** /-lī/) **1** a floccule. **2** *Anat.* a small ovoid lobe in the under-surface of the cerebellum. **3** *Astron.* a small cloudy wisp on the sun's surface. [mod.L, dimin. of FLOCCUS]

floccus /flókkəss/ *n.* (*pl.* **flocci** /flóksī/) a tuft of woolly hairs or filaments. [L, = FLOCK[2]]

flock[1] /flok/ *n.* & *v.* ● *n.* **1 a** a number of animals of one kind, esp. birds, feeding or travelling together. **b** a number of domestic animals, esp. sheep, goats, or geese, kept together. **2** a large crowd of people. **3 a** a Christian congregation or body of believers, esp. in relation to one minister. **b** a family of children, a number of pupils, etc. ● *v.intr.* **1** congregate; mass. **2** (usu. foll. by *to, in, out, together*) go together in a crowd; troop (*thousands flocked to Wembley*). [OE *flocc*]

■ *n.* **1** flight, gaggle, bevy, covey; pride, pack, troop, school, swarm, horde, host; herd, drove, *Austral.* mob. **2** crowd, body, company, group, band, bunch, troop, set, collection, assembly, gathering, mass, mob, throng, gang, multitude, number, quantity, host, horde, swarm, drove. **3 b** see BROOD *n.* 2. ● *v.* **1** congregate, assemble, meet, collect, gather, mass, mob. **2** crowd, throng, herd, band together; pour, flood, swarm; troop.

flock[2] /flok/ *n.* **1** a lock or tuft of wool, cotton, etc. **2 a** (also in *pl.*; often *attrib.*) material for quilting and stuffing made of wool-refuse or torn-up cloth (*a flock pillow*). **b** powdered wool or cloth. □ **flock-paper** (or **-wallpaper**) wallpaper sized and sprinkled with powdered wool to make a raised pattern. □□ **flocky** *adj.* [ME f. OF *floc* f. L *floccus*]

floe /flō/ *n.* a sheet of floating ice. [prob. f. Norw. *flo* f. ON *fló* layer]

flog /flog/ *v.* (**flogged, flogging**) **1** *tr.* **a** beat with a whip, stick, etc. (as a punishment or to urge on). **b** make work through violent effort (*flogged the engine*). **2** *tr. Brit. sl.* sell. **3** *tr.* (usu. foll. by *into, out of*) drive (a quality, knowledge, etc.) into or out of a person, esp. by physical punishment. **4** *intr.* & *refl. sl.* proceed by violent or painful effort. □ **flog a dead horse** waste energy on something unalterable. **flog to death** *colloq.* talk about or promote at tedious length. □□ **flogger** *n.* [17th-c. cant: prob. imit. or f. L *flagellare* to whip]

■ **1 a** beat, whip, lash, horsewhip, strap, flagellate, flay, scourge, thrash, thresh; chastise. **2** promote, advertise, publicize; see also SELL *v.* 2.

flong /flong/ *n. Printing* prepared paper for making stereotype moulds. [F *flan* FLAN]

flood /flud/ *n.* & *v.* ● *n.* **1 a** an overflowing or influx of water beyond its normal confines, esp. over land; an inundation. **b** the water that overflows. **2 a** an outpouring of water; a torrent (*a flood of rain*). **b** something resembling a torrent (*a flood of tears; a flood of relief*). **c** an abundance or excess. **3** the inflow of the tide (also in *comb.*: *flood-tide*). **4** *colloq.* a floodlight. **5** (**the Flood**) the flood described in Genesis. **6** *poet.* a river; a stream; a sea. ● *v.* **1** *tr.* **a** cover with or overflow in a flood (*rain flooded the cellar*). **b** overflow as if with a flood (*the market was flooded with foreign goods*). **2** *tr.* irrigate (*flooded the paddy fields*). **3** *tr.* deluge (a burning house, a mine, etc.) with water. **4** *intr.* (often foll. by *in, through*) arrive in great quantities (*complaints flooded in; fear flooded through them*). **5** *intr.* become inundated (*the bathroom flooded*). **6** *tr.* overfill (a carburettor) with petrol. **7** *intr.* experience a uterine haemorrhage. **8** *tr.* (of rain etc.) fill (a river) to overflowing. □ **flood and field** sea and land. **flood out** drive out (of one's home etc.) with a flood. **flood-tide** the periodical exceptional rise of the tide because of lunar or solar attraction. [OE *flōd* f. Gmc]

■ *n.* **1** overflowing, inundation, deluge, overflow, débâcle. **2 a** outpouring, torrent, cataract, stream, spate; freshet. **b** torrent, surge, outpouring, stream, rush, flow, deluge, overflowing, tide, tidal wave. **c** abundance, glut, surfeit, satiety, profusion, over-abundance, superabundance, plethora, excess, surplus, superfluity. ● *v.* **1** cover, pour over *or* into *or* through(out); overflow, inundate, deluge, submerge, swamp, drown, engulf, fill. **2** irrigate, inundate, water. **4** sweep, flow, pour, surge, rush, crowd, swarm.

floodgate /flúdgayt/ *n.* **1** a gate opened or closed to admit or exclude water, esp. the lower gate of a lock. **2** (usu. in *pl.*) a last restraint holding back tears, rain, anger, etc.

floodlight /flúdlīt/ *n.* & *v.* ● *n.* **1** a large powerful light (usu. one of several) to illuminate a building, sportsground, stage, etc. **2** the illumination so provided. ● *v.tr.* illuminate with floodlight.

floor /flor/ *n.* & *v.* ● *n.* **1 a** the lower surface of a room. **b** the boards etc. of which it is made. **2 a** the bottom of the sea, a cave, a cavity, etc. **b** any level area. **3** all the rooms etc. on the same level of a building; a storey (*lives on the ground floor; walked up to the sixth floor*). **4 a** (in a legislative assembly) the part of the house in which members sit and from which they speak. **b** the right to speak next in debate (*gave him the floor*). **5** *Stock Exch.* the large central hall where trading takes place. **6** the minimum of prices, wages, etc. **7** *colloq.* the ground. ● *v.tr.* **1** furnish with a floor; pave. **2** bring to the ground; knock (a person) down. **3** *colloq.* confound, baffle (*was floored by the puzzle*). **4** *colloq.* get the better of; overcome. **5** serve as the floor of (*leopard skins floored the hall*). □ **first** (*US* **second**) **floor** the floor above the ground floor. **floor-lamp** *US* a standard lamp. **floor-leader** *US* the leader of a party in a legislative assembly. **floor manager 1** the stage-manager of a television production. **2** a shopwalker. **floor plan** a diagram of the rooms etc. on one storey of a building. **floor-polish** a manufactured substance used for polishing floors. **floor show** an entertainment presented on the floor (as opposed to the stage) of a nightclub etc. **floor-walker** *US* a shopwalker. **from the floor** (of a speech etc.) given by a member of the audience, not by those on the platform etc. **take the floor 1** begin to dance on a dance-floor etc. **2** speak in a debate. □□ **floorless** *adj.* [OE *flōr* f. Gmc]

■ *n.* **1 b** flooring, boarding, planking, parquet. **2 a** see BOTTOM *n.* 4. **3** storey, level; deck. **6** minimum, base, lower limit, bottom. **7** ground, earth, *sl.* deck. ● *v.* **1** see

PAVE 1. **2** bring to the ground, knock down *or* over, bowl over, fell, bring down. **3** confound, baffle, stump, bewilder, dumbfound, confuse, perplex, puzzle, nonplus, disconcert. **4** overcome, beat, defeat, conquer, destroy, rout, overwhelm, crush, trounce, thrash, drub, best, worst, *sl.* whip. □ **take the floor 2** debate, speak; see also LECTURE *v.* 1.

floorboard /flórbord/ *n.* a long wooden board used for flooring.

floorcloth /flórkloth/ *n.* a cloth for washing the floor.

flooring /flóring/ *n.* the boards etc. of which a floor is made.
■ floor, parquet, planking.

floozie /flóozi/ *n.* (also **floozy**) (*pl.* **-ies**) *colloq.* a girl or a woman, esp. a disreputable one. [20th c.: cf. FLOSSY and dial. *floosy* fluffy]
■ see TART[2] *n.*

flop /flop/ *v.*, *n.*, & *adv.* ● *v.intr.* (**flopped**, **flopping**) **1** sway about heavily or loosely (*hair flopped over his face*). **2** move in an ungainly way (*flopped along the beach in flippers*). **3** (often foll. by *down*, *on*, *into*) sit, kneel, lie, or fall awkwardly or suddenly (*flopped down on to the bench*). **4** *sl.* (esp. of a play, film, book, etc.) fail; collapse (*flopped on Broadway*). **5** *sl.* sleep. **6** make a dull sound as of a soft body landing, or of a flat thing slapping water. ● *n.* **1 a** a flopping movement. **b** the sound made by it. **2** *sl.* a failure. **3** *sl.* esp. *US* a bed. ● *adv.* with a flop. □ **flop-house** *sl.* esp. *US* a doss-house. [var. of FLAP]
■ *v.* **1** dangle, hang (down), droop, drop, tumble down; swing, wave, flap. **2** pad, tramp; see also PLOD *v.* **3** collapse, drop *or* fall *or* tumble (down), topple, plop down, plump (down), flounce down. **4** fall flat, founder, *esp. US sl.* bomb; see also FAIL *v.* 1, 2a. ● *n.* **2** failure, fiasco, disaster, non-starter, débâcle, lead balloon, damp squib, *colloq.* lemon, *Austral. colloq.* gutzer, *US colloq.* bomb, *sl.* wash-out, dud, *Austral. sl.* fizzer, *US sl.* turkey.

floppy /flóppi/ *adj.* & *n.* ● *adj.* (**floppier**, **floppiest**) tending to flop; not firm or rigid. ● *n.* (*pl.* **-ies**) (in full **floppy disk**) *Computing* a flexible removable magnetic disc for the storage of data. □□ **floppily** *adv.* **floppiness** *n.*
■ *adj.* see LIMP[2] 1.

flor. *abbr.* floruit.

flora /flórə/ *n.* (*pl.* **floras** or **florae** /-ree/) **1** the plants of a particular region, geological period, or environment. **2** a treatise on or list of these. [mod.L f. the name of the goddess of flowers f. L *flos floris* flower]

floral /flórəl, flórrəl/ *adj.* **1** of flowers. **2** decorated with or depicting flowers. **3** of flora or floras. □□ **florally** *adv.* [L *floralis* or *flos floris* flower]

floreat /flórriat/ *v.intr.* may (he, she, or it) flourish. [L, 3rd sing. pres. subj. of *florēre* flourish]

Florentine /flórrəntīn/ *adj.* & *n.* ● *adj.* **1** of or relating to Florence in Italy. **2** (**florentine** /-teen/) (of a dish) served on a bed of spinach. ● *n.* a native or citizen of Florence. [F *Florentin -ine* or L *Florentinus* f. *Florentia* Florence]

florescence /floréss'nss/ *n.* the process, state, or time of flowering. [mod.L *florescentia* f. L *florescere* f. *florēre* bloom]

floret /flórit/ *n. Bot.* **1** each of the small flowers making up a composite flower-head. **2** each of the flowering stems making up a head of cauliflower, broccoli, etc. **3** a small flower. [L *flos floris* flower]

floriate /flóriayt/ *v.tr.* decorate with flower-designs etc.

floribunda /flórribúndə/ *n.* a plant, esp. a rose, bearing dense clusters of flowers. [mod.L f. *floribundus* freely flowering f. L *flos floris* flower, infl. by L *abundus* copious]

floriculture /flórikulchər/ *n.* the cultivation of flowers. □□ **floricultural** /-kúlchərəl/ *adj.* **floriculturist** /-kúlchərist/ *n.* [L *flos floris* flower + CULTURE, after *horticulture*]

florid /flórrid/ *adj.* **1** ruddy; flushed; high-coloured (*a florid complexion*). **2** (of a book, a picture, music, architecture, etc.) elaborately ornate; ostentatious; showy. **3** adorned with or as with flowers; flowery. □□ **floridity** /-ríddit/ *n.* **floridly** *adv.* **floridness** *n.* [F *floride* or L *floridus* f. *flos floris* flower]
■ **1** see ROSY 1. **2** see ORNATE.

floriferous /floríffərəss/ *adj.* (of a seed or plant) producing many flowers. [L *florifer* f. *flos floris* flower]

florilegium /flórileéjiəm/ *n.* (*pl.* **florilegia** /-leéjiə/ or **florilegiums**) an anthology. [mod.L f. L *flos floris* flower + *legere* gather, transl. of Gk *anthologion* ANTHOLOGY]

florin /flórrin/ *n. hist.* **1 a** a British silver or alloy two-shilling coin of the 19th–20th c. (worth 10 pence at face value). **b** an English gold coin of the 14th c., worth 6s. 8d. (33 pence). **2** a foreign coin of gold or silver, esp. a Dutch guilder. [ME f. OF f. It. *fiorino* dimin. of *fiore* flower f. L *flos floris*, the orig. coin having a figure of a lily on it]

florist /flórrist/ *n.* a person who deals in or grows flowers. □□ **floristry** *n.* [L *flos floris* flower + -IST]

floristic /florístik/ *adj.* relating to the study of the distribution of plants. □□ **floristically** *adv.* **floristics** *n.*

floruit /flórroo-it/ *v.* & *n.* ● *v.intr.* (he or she) was alive and working; flourished (used of a person, esp. a painter, a writer, etc., whose exact dates are unknown). ● *n.* the period or date at which a person lived or worked. [L, = he or she flourished]

flory var. of FLEURY.

floscular /flóskyoolər/ *adj.* (also **flosculous** /-kyooləss/) having florets or composite flowers. [L *flosculus* dimin. of *flos* flower]

floss /floss/ *n.* & *v.* ● *n.* **1** the rough silk enveloping a silkworm's cocoon. **2** untwisted silk thread used in embroidery. **3** = *dental floss*. ● *v.tr.* (also *absol.*) clean (the teeth) with dental floss. □ **floss silk** a rough silk used in cheap goods. [F (*soie*) *floche* floss(-silk) f. OF *flosche* down, nap of velvet]

flossy /flóssi/ *adj.* (**flossier**, **flossiest**) **1** of or like floss. **2** *colloq.* fancy, showy.

flotation /flōtáysh'n/ *n.* (also **floatation**) **1** the process of launching or financing a commercial enterprise. **2** the separation of the components of crushed ore etc. by their different capacities to float. **3** the capacity to float. □ **centre of flotation** the centre of gravity in a floating body. [alt. of *floatation* f. FLOAT, after *rotation* etc.]

flotilla /flətíllə/ *n.* **1** a small fleet. **2** a fleet of boats or small ships. [Sp., dimin. of *flota* fleet, OF *flote* multitude]
■ see FLEET[1].

flotsam /flótsəm/ *n.* wreckage found floating. □ **flotsam and jetsam 1** odds and ends; rubbish. **2** vagrants etc. [AF *floteson* f. *floter* FLOAT]

flounce[1] /flownss/ *v.* & *n.* ● *v.intr.* (often foll. by *away*, *about*, *off*, *out*) go or move with an agitated, violent, or impatient motion (*flounced out in a huff*). ● *n.* a flouncing movement. [16th c.: orig. unkn.: perh. imit., as *bounce*, *pounce*]
■ *v.* strut, march, storm, stamp, stomp, bounce; fling, *esp. US colloq.* sashay.

flounce[2] /flownss/ *n.* & *v.* ● *n.* a wide ornamental strip of material gathered and sewn to a skirt, dress, etc.; a frill. ● *v.tr.* trim with a flounce or flounces. [alt. of earlier *frounce* fold, pleat, f. OF *fronce* f. *froncir* wrinkle]
■ *n.* frill, valance, furbelow, peplum; ruffle.

flounder[1] /flówndər/ *v.* & *n.* ● *v.intr.* **1** struggle in mud, or as if in mud, or when wading. **2** perform a task badly or without knowledge; be out of one's depth. ● *n.* an act of floundering. □□ **flounderer** *n.* [imit.: perh. assoc. with *founder*, *blunder*]
■ *v.* struggle, grope, blunder, stumble, tumble, stagger, plunge about.

flounder[2] /flówndər/ *n.* **1** an edible flat-fish, *Pleuronectes flesus*, native to European shores. **2** any of various flat-fish native to N. American shores. [ME f. AF *floundre*, OF *flondre*, prob. of Scand. orig.]

flour /flowr/ *n.* & *v.* ● *n.* **1** a meal or powder obtained by grinding and usu. sifting cereals, esp. wheat. **2** any fine powder. ● *v.tr.* **1** sprinkle with flour. **2** *US* grind into flour.

□□ **floury** *adj.* (**flourier, flouriest**). **flouriness** *n.* [ME, different. spelling of FLOWER in the sense 'finest part']

flourish /flúrrish/ *v.* & *n.* ● *v.* **1** *intr.* **a** grow vigorously; thrive. **b** prosper; be successful. **c** be in one's prime. **d** be in good health. **e** (as **flourishing** *adj.*) successful, prosperous. **2** *intr.* (usu. foll. by *in, at, about*) spend one's life; be active (at a specified time) (*flourished in the Middle Ages*) (cf. FLORUIT). **3** *tr.* show ostentatiously (*flourished his cheque-book*). **4** *tr.* wave (a weapon, one's limbs, etc.) vigorously. ● *n.* **1** an ostentatious gesture with a weapon, a hand, etc. (*removed his hat with a flourish*). **2** an ornamental curving decoration of handwriting. **3** a florid verbal expression; a rhetorical embellishment. **4** *Mus.* **a** a fanfare played by brass instruments. **b** an ornate musical passage. **c** an extemporized addition played esp. at the beginning or end of a composition. **5** *archaic* an instance of prosperity; a flourishing. □□ **flourisher** *n.* **flourishy** *adj.* [ME f. OF *florir* ult. f. L *florēre* f. *flos floris* flower]

■ *v.* **1 a, d** thrive, bloom, blossom, flower, *literary* burgeon. **b** prosper, boom, succeed, get ahead, do well, go up *or* rise in the world, *colloq.* go great guns, *literary* fare well; bear fruit. **c** mature, develop, ripen, mellow, come of age. **e** (**flourishing**) successful, prosperous, booming, thriving, prospering. **4** wave, wield, brandish, wag, swing, twirl, flaunt, shake, swish, flap, *literary* vaunt. ● *n.* **1** gesture, gesturing, wave; show, display. **2** curl, curlicue. **3** embellishment, decoration, ornament(ation), adornment, frill. **4 a** see FANFARE 1.

flout /flowt/ *v.* & *n.* ● *v.* **1** *tr.* express contempt for (the law, rules, etc.) by word or action; mock; insult (*flouted convention by shaving her head*). ¶ Often confused with *flaunt*. **2** *intr.* (often foll. by *at*) mock or scoff. ● *n.* a flouting speech or act. [perh. f. Du. *fluiten* whistle, hiss: cf. FLUTE]

■ *v.* **1** mock, deride, scorn, jeer, disdain, spurn, guy, ridicule, disparage, decry, denigrate, belittle, depreciate, degrade, abase, deprecate, blaspheme, denounce, fly in the face of, *colloq.* put down, *literary* contemn, misprize; insult, affront. **2** mock, scoff, jeer, sneer, gibe, fleer, blaspheme.

flow /flō/ *v.* & *n.* ● *v.intr.* **1** glide along as a stream (*the Thames flows under London Bridge*). **2 a** (of a liquid, esp. water) gush out; spring. **b** (of blood, liquid, etc.) be spilt. **3** (of blood, money, electric current, etc.) circulate. **4** (of people or things) come or go in large numbers or smoothly (*traffic flowed down the hill*). **5** (of talk, literary style, etc.) proceed easily and smoothly. **6** (of a garment, hair, etc.) hang easily or gracefully; undulate. **7** (often foll. by *from*) result from; be caused by (*his failure flows from his diffidence*). **8** (esp. of the tide) be in flood; run full. **9** (of wine) be poured out copiously. **10** (of a rock or metal) undergo a permanent change of shape under stress. **11** (foll. by *with*) *archaic* be plentifully supplied with (*land flowing with milk and honey*). ● *n.* **1 a** a flowing movement in a stream. **b** the manner in which a thing flows (*a sluggish flow*). **c** a flowing liquid (*couldn't stop the flow*). **d** a copious outpouring; a stream (*a continuous flow of complaints*). **2** the rise of a tide or a river (*ebb and flow*). **3** the gradual deformation of a rock or metal under stress. **4** *Sc.* a bog or morass. □ **flow chart** (or **diagram** or **sheet**) **1** a diagram of the movement or action of things or persons engaged in a complex activity. **2** a graphical representation of a computer program in relation to its sequence of functions (as distinct from the data it processes). **flow of spirits** habitual cheerfulness. **flow-on** *Austral.* a wage or salary adjustment made as a consequence of one already made in a similar or related occupation. [OE *flōwan* f. Gmc, rel. to FLOOD]

■ *v.* **1** glide, run, course, stream, trickle, go, move, proceed, progress; purl. **2 a** gush *or* rush (out), surge, well forth *or* out *or* up, stream (out), spout, spurt, squirt, spew (out), flood (out), cascade; spring, issue, originate, come, emanate; (*flow over or on to*) spread over *or* on to, overspread, cover. **3** see CIRCULATE 1. **7** see STEM[1] *v.* 1. **11** (*flow with*) see ABOUND 2. ● *n.* **1 a** movement, current, course, stream, drift. **c, d** rush, gush, surge, outpouring; flood, overflow, overflowing, deluge, tide; see also STREAM *n.* 2a.

flower /flowr/ *n.* & *v.* ● *n.* **1** the part of a plant from which the fruit or seed is developed. **2** the reproductive organ in a plant containing one or more pistils or stamens or both, and usu. a corolla and calyx. **3** a blossom, esp. on a stem and used in bunches for decoration. **4** a plant cultivated or noted for its flowers. **5** (in *pl.*) ornamental phrases (*flowers of speech*). ● *v.* **1** *intr.* (of a plant) produce flowers; bloom or blossom. **2** *intr.* reach a peak. **3** *tr.* cause or allow (a plant) to flower. **4** *tr.* decorate with worked flowers or a floral design. □ **flower-bed** a garden bed in which flowers are grown. **flower-girl** a woman who sells flowers, esp. in the street. **flower-head** = HEAD *n.* 4d. **the flower of** the best or best part of. **flower people** hippies carrying or wearing flowers as symbols of peace and love. **flower power** the ideas of the flower people regarded as an instrument in changing the world. **flowers of sulphur** *Chem.* a fine powder produced when sulphur evaporates and condenses. **in flower** with the flowers out. □□ **flowered** *adj.* (also in *comb.*). **flowerless** *adj.* **flowerlike** *adj.* [ME f. AF *flur*, OF *flour, flor*, f. L *flos floris*]

■ *n.* **3** blossom, bloom, efflorescence, floweret, floret. ● *v.* **1** bloom, blossom, come out, open, effloresce, unfold, *literary* burgeon. **2** see PEAK *v.* □ **the flower (of)** the cream *or* best *or* pick *or* élite *or crème de la crème or* finest *or* choicest (of).

flowerer /flówərər/ *n.* a plant that flowers at a specified time (*a late flowerer*).

floweret /flówərit/ *n.* a small flower.

■ see FLOWER *n.*

flowering /flówəring/ *adj.* (of a plant) capable of producing flowers.

flowerpot /flówrpot/ *n.* a pot in which a plant may be grown.

flowery /flówəri/ *adj.* **1** decorated with flowers or floral designs. **2** (of literary style, manner of speech, etc.) high-flown; ornate. **3** full of flowers (*a flowery meadow*). □□ **floweriness** *n.*

■ **2** high-flown, florid, fancy, showy, grandiloquent, bombastic, inflated, pompous; ornate, elaborate(d), decorated, ornamented, overwrought, embellished, rococo, euphuistic, affected, artificial.

flowing /flṓ-ing/ *adj.* **1** (of literary style etc.) fluent; easy. **2** (of a line, a curve, or a contour) smoothly continuous, not abrupt. **3** (of hair, a garment, a sail, etc.) unconfined. □□ **flowingly** *adv.*

■ **1** see FLUENT 1a. **3** see LOOSE *adj.* 3–5.

flown *past part.* of FLY[1].

flowstone /flṓstōn/ *n.* rock deposited in a thin sheet by a flow of water.

FLQ *abbr.* Front de Libération du Québec.

Flt. Lt. *abbr.* Flight Lieutenant.

Flt. Off. *abbr.* Flight Officer.

Flt. Sgt. *abbr.* Flight Sergeant.

flu /floo/ *n. colloq.* influenza. [abbr.]

■ see COLD *n.* 2.

flub /flub/ *v.* & *n.* *US colloq.* ● *v.tr.* & *intr.* (**flubbed, flubbing**) botch; bungle. ● *n.* something badly or clumsily done. [20th c.: orig. unkn.]

■ *v.* see FUMBLE *v.* 2a, BOTCH *v.* 1, BUNGLE *v.* 2. ● *n.* see MISTAKE *n.*

fluctuate /flúktyoo-ayt/ *v.intr.* vary irregularly; be unstable, vacillate; rise and fall, move to and fro. □□ **fluctuation** /-áysh'n/ *n.* [L *fluctuare* f. *fluctus* flow, wave f. *fluere fluct-* flow]

■ vary, change, shift, alternate, see-saw, yo-yo, swing, vacillate, oscillate, waver, undulate. □□ **fluctuation** variation(s), change(s), alternation(s), swing(s), vacillation(s), wavering(s), oscillation(s), undulation(s), up(s) and down(s); instability, unsteadiness, inconstancy, variability.

flue /floo/ *n.* **1** a smoke-duct in a chimney. **2** a channel for conveying heat, esp. a hot-air passage in a wall; a tube for heating water in some kinds of boiler. □ **flue-cure** cure (tobacco) by artificial heat from flues. **flue-pipe** an organ pipe into which the air enters directly, not striking a reed. [16th c.: orig. unkn.]
■ see VENT[1] *n.* 8.

fluence /flóoənss/ *n. colloq.* influence. □ **put the fluence on** apply hypnotic etc. power to (a person). [shortening of INFLUENCE]

fluency /flóoənsi/ *n.* **1** a smooth, easy flow, esp. in speech or writing. **2** a ready command of words or of a specified foreign language.
■ flow, articulateness, eloquence, control, command, ease, effortlessness, facility, smoothness, polish, slickness, glibness, volubility, felicity.

fluent /flóoənt/ *adj.* **1 a** (of speech or literary style) flowing naturally and readily. **b** having command of a foreign language (*is fluent in German*). **c** able to speak quickly and easily. **2** flowing easily or gracefully (*the fluent line of her arabesque*). **3** *archaic* liable to change; unsettled. □□ **fluently** *adv.* [L *fluere* flow]
■ **1 a** flowing, natural, facile, effortless, ready, smooth, polished. **c** articulate, eloquent, well-spoken, felicitous, voluble, glib, slick.

fluff /fluf/ *n.* & *v.* ● *n.* **1** soft, light, feathery material coming off blankets etc. **2** soft fur or feathers. **3** *sl.* **a** a mistake in delivering theatrical lines, in playing music, etc. **b** a mistake in playing a game. ● *v.* **1** *tr.* & *intr.* (often foll. by *up*) shake into or become a soft mass. **2** *tr.* & *intr. colloq.* make a mistake in (a theatrical part, a game, playing music, a speech, etc.); blunder (*fluffed his opening line*). **3** *tr.* make into fluff. **4** *tr.* put a soft surface on (the flesh side of leather). □ **bit of fluff** *sl. offens.* a woman regarded as an object of sexual desire. [prob. dial. alt. of *flue* fluff]
■ *n.* **1** down, fuzz, lint, dust. **3** mistake, error, slip; *colloq.* howler, *esp. US colloq.* blooper. ● *v.* **1** shake out *or* up, puff up; aerate. **2** ruin, make a mess of, spoil, bungle, botch, foul up, mess up, *sl.* screw up, *Brit. sl.* cock up; blunder. □ **bit of fluff** girl, girlfriend, mistress, *Brit. joc. or offens.* (bit of) crumpet, *sl.* bit of all right, *sl. offens.* (bit of) skirt, bit of stuff.

fluffy /flúffi/ *adj.* (**fluffier**, **fluffiest**) **1** of or like fluff. **2** covered in fluff; downy. □□ **fluffily** *adv.* **fluffiness** *n.*
■ **1** downy, soft, puffy, light, lightweight, airy, feathery, thin, insubstantial, gossamer. **2** downy, woolly, linty.

flugelhorn /floog'lhorn/ *n.* a valved brass wind instrument like a cornet but with a broader tone. [G *Flügelhorn* f. *Flügel* wing + *Horn* horn]

fluid /floo-id/ *n.* & *adj.* ● *n.* **1** a substance, esp. a gas or liquid, lacking definite shape and capable of flowing and yielding to the slightest pressure. **2** a fluid part or secretion. ● *adj.* **1** able to flow and alter shape freely. **2** constantly changing or fluctuating (*the situation is fluid*). **3** (of a clutch, coupling, etc.) in which liquid is used to transmit power. □ **fluid drachm** see DRACHM. **fluid ounce** see OUNCE[1]. □□ **fluidify** /-íddifī/ *v.tr.* (**-ies**, **-ied**). **fluidity** /-íddit i/ *n.* **fluidly** *adv.* **fluidness** *n.* [F *fluide* or L *fluidus* f. *fluere* flow]
■ *n.* **1** liquid, solution, liquor; ichor; gas, vapour. ● *adj.* **1** liquid, flowing, runny, watery, aqueous. **2** changeable, variable, flexible, adjustable, unfixed, non-static, liquid, mercurial, mobile, unstable, shifting, uncertain, indefinite, unsettled, *literary* mutable.

fluidics /floo-íddiks/ *n.pl.* (usu. treated as *sing.*) the study and technique of using small interacting flows and fluid jets for functions usu. performed by electronic devices. □□ **fluidic** *adj.*

fluidize /floo-idīz/ *v.tr.* (also **-ise**) cause (a finely divided solid) to acquire the characteristics of a fluid by the upward passage of a gas etc. □□ **fluidization** /-záysh'n/ *n.*

fluidounce /floo-idownss/ *n. US* a fluid ounce (see OUNCE[1]).

fluidram /floo-idram/ *n. US* a fluid drachm (see DRACHM).

fluke[1] /flook/ *n.* & *v.* ● *n.* **1** a lucky accident (*won by a fluke*). **2** a chance breeze. ● *v.tr.* achieve by a fluke (*fluked that shot*). [19th c.: perh. f. dial. *fluke* guess]
■ *n.* **1** stroke of (good) luck, lucky *or* successful stroke, (happy) accident, quirk *or* twist of fate, *colloq.* lucky *or* big break.

fluke[2] /flook/ *n.* **1** any parasitic flatworm of the class Digenea or Monogenea, including liver flukes and blood flukes. **2** a flat-fish, esp. a flounder. [OE *flōc*]

fluke[3] /flook/ *n.* **1** *Naut.* a broad triangular plate on the arm of an anchor. **2** the barbed head of a lance, harpoon, etc. **3** *Zool.* either of the lobes of a whale's tail. [16th c.: perh. f. FLUKE[2]]

fluky /flóoki/ *adj.* (**flukier**, **flukiest**) of the nature of a fluke; obtained more by chance than skill. □□ **flukily** *adv.* **flukiness** *n.*

flume /floom/ *n.* & *v.* ● *n.* **1 a** an artificial channel conveying water etc. for industrial use. **b** a water-slide into a swimming-pool etc. **2** a ravine with a stream. ● *v.* **1** *intr.* build flumes. **2** *tr.* convey down a flume. [ME f. OF *flum*, *flun* f. L *flumen* river f. *fluere* flow]

flummery /flúmməri/ *n.* (*pl.* **-ies**) **1** empty compliments; trifles; nonsense. **2** a sweet dish made with beaten eggs, sugar, etc. [Welsh *llymru*, of unkn. orig.]
■ **1** see NONSENSE.

flummox /flúmməks/ *v.tr. colloq.* bewilder, confound, disconcert. [19th c.: prob. dial., imit.]
■ bewilder, confound, disconcert, confuse, baffle, perplex, throw into confusion, stump, puzzle, mystify, nonplus, fox.

flump /flump/ *v.* & *n.* ● *v.* (often foll. by *down*) **1** *intr.* fall or move heavily. **2** *tr.* set or throw down with a heavy thud. ● *n.* the action or sound of flumping. [imit.]

flung *past* and *past part.* of FLING.

flunk /flungk/ *v.* & *n. US colloq.* ● *v.* **1** *tr.* **a** fail (an examination etc.). **b** fail (an examination candidate). **2** *intr.* (often foll. by *out*) fail utterly; give up. ● *n.* an instance of flunking. □ **flunk out** be dismissed from school etc. after failing an examination. [cf. FUNK[1] and obs. *flink* be a coward]
■ *v.* see FAIL *v.* 1, 2a.

flunkey /flúngki/ *n.* (also **flunky**) (*pl.* **-eys** or **-ies**) usu. *derog.* **1** a liveried servant; a footman. **2** a toady; a snob. **3** *US* a cook, waiter, etc. □□ **flunkeyism** *n.* [18th c. (orig. Sc.): perh. f. FLANK with the sense 'sidesman, flanker']
■ **1** servant, lackey, footman, menial, subordinate, inferior, *colloq.* jackal, dogsbody, *derog.* minion, *usu. derog.* hireling, underling, *hist.* retainer, *esp. US sl.* gofer; slave. **2** toady, hanger-on, sycophant, *colloq.* lickspittle, *derog.* lackey; see also *yes-man*.

fluoresce /flooréss/ *v.intr.* be or become fluorescent.

fluorescence /flooréss'nss/ *n.* **1** the visible or invisible radiation produced from certain substances as a result of incident radiation of a shorter wavelength as X-rays, ultraviolet light, etc. **2** the property of absorbing light of short (invisible) wavelength and emitting light of longer (visible) wavelength. [FLUORSPAR (which fluoresces) after *opalescence*]

fluorescent /flooréss'nt/ *adj.* (of a substance) having or showing fluorescence. □ **fluorescent lamp** (or **bulb**) a lamp or bulb radiating largely by fluorescence, esp. a tubular lamp in which phosphor on the inside surface of the tube is made to fluoresce by ultraviolet radiation from mercury vapour. **fluorescent screen** a screen coated with fluorescent material to show images from X-rays etc.

fluoridate /flóoridayt/ *v.tr.* add traces of fluoride to (drinking-water etc.).

fluoridation /flóoridáysh'n/ *n.* (also **fluoridization** /-dīzáysh'n/) the addition of traces of fluoride to drinking-water in order to prevent or reduce tooth-decay.

fluoride /flóorīd/ *n.* any binary compound of fluorine.

fluorinate /flóorinayt/ *v.tr.* **1** = FLUORIDATE. **2** introduce fluorine into (a compound) (*fluorinated hydrocarbons*). □□ **fluorination** /-náysh'n/ *n.*

fluorine /flóoreen/ *n.* a poisonous pale-yellow gaseous element of the halogen group occurring naturally in fluorite and cryolite, and the most reactive of all elements. ¶ Symb.: F. [F (as FLUORSPAR)]

fluorite /flóorīt/ *n.* a mineral form of calcium fluoride. [It. (as FLUORSPAR)]

fluoro- /flóorō/ *comb. form* **1** fluorine (*fluorocarbon*). **2** fluorescence (*fluoroscope*). [FLUORINE, FLUORESCENCE]

fluorocarbon /flóorōkaárb'n/ *n.* a compound formed by replacing one or more of the hydrogen atoms in a hydrocarbon with fluorine atoms.

fluoroscope /flóorəskōp/ *n.* an instrument with a fluorescent screen on which X-ray images may be viewed without taking and developing X-ray photographs.

fluorosis /floorṓsiss/ *n.* poisoning by fluorine or its compounds. [F *fluorose* (as FLUORO- 1)]

fluorspar /flóorspaar/ *n.* = FLUORITE. [*fluor* a flow, any of the minerals used as fluxes, fluorspar, f. L *fluor* f. *fluere* flow + SPAR[3]]

flurry /flúrri/ *n.* & *v.* ● *n.* (*pl.* **-ies**) **1** a gust or squall (of snow, rain, etc.). **2** a sudden burst of activity. **3** a commotion; excitement; nervous agitation (*a flurry of speculation; the flurry of the city*). ● *v.tr.* (**-ies, -ied**) confuse by haste or noise; agitate. [imit.: cf. obs. *flurr* ruffle, *hurry*]

■ *n.* **2** see STIR[1] *n.* 2. **3** commotion, to-do, fuss, upset, stir, disturbance, tumult, whirl, furore, flutter, fluster, *literary* pother; excitement, activity, agitation, ado, hustle, bustle, hurry. ● *v.* confuse, bewilder, agitate, put out, disturb, excite, fluster, disconcert, upset, perturb, unsettle, shake (up), *colloq.* rattle.

flush[1] /flush/ *v.* & *n.* ● *v.* **1** *intr.* **a** blush, redden (*he flushed with embarrassment*). **b** glow with a warm colour (*sky flushed pink*). **2** *tr.* (usu. as **flushed** *adj.*) cause to glow, blush, or be elated (often foll. by *with*: *flushed with pride*). **3** *tr.* **a** cleanse (a drain, lavatory, etc.) by a rushing flow of water. **b** (often foll. by *away, down*) dispose of (an object) in this way (*flushed away the cigarette*). **4** *intr.* rush out, spurt. **5** *tr.* flood (*the river flushed the meadow*). **6** *intr.* (of a plant) throw out fresh shoots. ● *n.* **1 a** a blush. **b** a glow of light or colour. **2 a** a rush of water. **b** the cleansing of a drain, lavatory, etc. by flushing. **3 a** a rush of emotion. **b** the elation produced by a victory etc. (*the flush of triumph*). **4** sudden abundance. **5** freshness; vigour (*in the first flush of womanhood*). **6 a** (also **hot flush**) a sudden feeling of heat during the menopause. **b** a feverish temperature. **c** facial redness, esp. caused by fever, alcohol, etc. **7** a fresh growth of grass etc. □□ **flusher** *n.* [ME, perh. = FLUSH[4] infl. by *flash* and *blush*]

■ *v.* **1 a** blush, redden, crimson, burn, colour (up); glow. **2** (**flushed**) glowing; elated, delighted, thrilled, cheered. **3 a** rinse, flush out, wash (out *or* away), douse, hose down, flood, drench, clean out, *usu. formal* cleanse. **b** wash away, sluice away. **4** see SPURT *v.* 1a. **5** see FLOOD *v.* 1. ● *n.* **1** blush, redness, pinkness; glow, radiance, rosiness. **2 a** rush *or* gush *or* surge of water, stream, flow; flood, deluge, drenching, soaking, inundation. **3 b** elation, euphoria, thrill, excitement, delight, tingle. **5** see VIGOUR 1.

flush[2] /flush/ *adj.* & *v.* ● *adj.* **1** (often foll. by *with*) in the same plane; level; even (*the sink is flush with the cooker; fitted it flush with the wall*). **2** (usu. *predic.*) *colloq.* **a** having plenty of money. **b** (of money) abundant, plentiful. **3** full to overflowing; in flood. ● *v.tr.* **1** make (surfaces) level. **2** fill in (a joint) level with a surface. □□ **flushness** *n.* [prob. f. FLUSH[1]]

■ *adj.* **1** in the same plane, level, even, square, true. **2 a** wealthy, rich, prosperous, affluent, moneyed, well-to-do, well off, *colloq.* well-heeled, on Easy Street, in the money, rolling (in money *or* it), *sl.* in the chips, loaded. **b** see PLENTIFUL. **3** full, brimming, brim-full, overflowing, replete, in flood.

flush[3] /flush/ *n.* a hand of cards all of one suit, esp. in poker. □ **royal flush** a straight poker flush headed by an ace. **straight flush** a flush that is a numerical sequence. [OF *flus, flux* f. L *fluxus* FLUX]

flush[4] /flush/ *v.* **1** *tr.* cause (esp. a game bird) to fly up. **2** *intr.* (of a bird) fly up and away. □ **flush out 1** reveal. **2** drive out. [ME, imit.: cf. *fly, rush*]

fluster /flústər/ *v.* & *n.* ● *v.* **1** *tr.* & *intr.* make or become nervous or confused; flurry (*was flustered by the noise; he flusters easily*). **2** *tr.* confuse with drink; half-intoxicate. **3** *intr.* bustle. ● *n.* a confused or agitated state. [ME: orig. unkn.: cf. Icel. *flaustr(a)* hurry, bustle]

■ *v.* **1** make nervous, flurry, agitate, stir up, discompose, discomfit, discomfort, disconcert, shake (up), upset, disquiet, discommode, bother, put out *or* off, disturb, perturb, flutter, *colloq.* throw (out), rattle, hassle, faze, *US joc.* discombobulate; confuse, baffle, confound, puzzle, perplex, befuddle, bewilder, distract, daze. ● *n.* agitation, upset, nervousness, discomfort, disquiet, bother, disturbance, commotion, perturbation, flurry, flutter, *colloq.* dither; confusion, bafflement, befuddlement, perplexity, bewilderment, distraction.

flute /flo͞ot/ *n.* & *v.* ● *n.* **1 a** a high-pitched woodwind instrument of metal or wood, having holes along it stopped by the fingers or keys, and held across the body. **b** an organ stop having a similar sound. **c** any of various wind instruments resembling a flute. **d** a flute-player. **2 a** *Archit.* an ornamental vertical groove in a column. **b** a trumpet-shaped frill on a dress etc. **c** any similar cylindrical groove. **3** a tall narrow wineglass. ● *v.* **1** *intr.* play the flute. **2** *intr.* speak, sing, or whistle in a fluting way. **3** *tr.* make flutes or grooves in. **4** *tr.* play (a tune etc.) on a flute. □□ **flutelike** *adj.* **fluting** *n.* **flutist** *n. US* (cf. FLAUTIST). **fluty** *adj.* (in sense 1a of *n.*). [ME f. OF *fleüte, flaüte, flahute*, prob. f. Prov. *flaüt*]

flutter /flúttər/ *v.* & *n.* ● *v.* **1 a** *intr.* flap the wings in flying or trying to fly (*butterflies fluttered in the sunshine*). **b** *tr.* flap (the wings). **2** *intr.* fall with a quivering motion (*leaves fluttered to the ground*). **3** *intr.* & *tr.* move or cause to move irregularly or tremblingly (*the wind fluttered the flag*). **4** *intr.* go about restlessly; flit; hover. **5** *tr.* agitate, confuse. **6** *intr.* (of a pulse or heartbeat) beat feebly or irregularly. **7** *intr.* tremble with excitement or agitation. ● *n.* **1 a** the act of fluttering. **b** an instance of this. **2** a tremulous state of excitement; a sensation (*was in a flutter; caused a flutter with his behaviour*). **3** *Brit. sl.* a small bet, esp. on a horse. **4** an abnormally rapid but regular heartbeat. **5** *Aeron.* an undesired oscillation in a part of an aircraft etc. under stress. **6** *Mus.* a rapid movement of the tongue (as when rolling one's *rs*) in playing a wind instrument. **7** *Electronics* a rapid variation of pitch, esp. of recorded sound (cf. WOW[2]). **8** a vibration. □ **flutter the dovecots** cause alarm among normally imperturbable people. □□ **flutterer** *n.* **fluttery** *adj.* [OE *floterian, flotorian*, frequent. form rel. to FLEET[5]]

■ *v.* **3** flap, flop, wave, oscillate. **4** flit, flicker, flitter; hover, dance about; fuss. **5** see AGITATE 1. **7** tremble, shake, quiver, jump, twitch, *dial.* dither. ● *n.* **1** fluttering, flapping, flopping, wave, waving, oscillation, oscillating, trembling, quiver, quivering. **2** flurry, stir, whirl, *literary* pother; see also SENSATION 2a. **8** see QUAVER *n.*

fluvial /flo͞oviəl/ *adj.* of or found in a river or rivers. [ME f. L *fluvialis* f. *fluvius* river f. *fluere* flow]

fluviatile /flo͞oviətīl/ *adj.* of, found in, or produced by a river or rivers. [F f. L *fluviatilis* f. *fluviatus* moistened f. *fluvius*]

fluvio- /flo͞oviō/ *comb. form* river (*fluviometer*). [L *fluvius* river f. *fluere* flow]

fluvioglacial /flo͞oviōgláysh'l, -gláysiəl/ *adj.* of or caused by streams from glacial ice, or the combined action of rivers and glaciers.

fluviometer /flo͞ooviómmitər/ *n.* an instrument for measuring the rise and fall of rivers.

flux /fluks/ *n.* & *v.* ● *n.* **1** a process of flowing or flowing out. **2** an issue or discharge. **3** continuous change (*in a state of flux*). **4** *Metallurgy* a substance mixed with a metal etc. to promote fusion. **5** *Physics* **a** the rate of flow of any fluid across a given area. **b** the amount of fluid crossing an area in a given time. **6** *Physics* the amount of radiation or particles incident on an area in a given time. **7** *Electr.* the total electric or magnetic field passing through a surface. **8** *Med.* an abnormal discharge of blood or excrement from the body. ● *v.* **1** *tr.* & *intr.* make or become fluid. **2** *tr.* **a** fuse. **b** treat with a fusing flux. [ME f. OF *flux* or L *fluxus* f. *fluere flux-* flow]

■ *n.* **3** fluctuation, instability, unrest, swing, swinging, wavering, movement, motion, oscillation, mutation, modification; see also CHANGE *n.* 1.

fluxion /flúksh'n/ *n. Math.* the rate at which a variable quantity changes; a derivative. [F *fluxion* or L *fluxio* (as FLUX)]

fly[1] /flī/ *v.* & *n.* ● *v.* (**flies**; *past* **flew** /flōō/; *past part.* **flown** /flōn/) **1** *intr.* move through the air under control, esp. with wings. **2** (of an aircraft or its occupants): **a** *intr.* travel through the air or through space. **b** *tr.* traverse (a region or distance) (*flew the Channel*). **3** *tr.* **a** control the flight of (esp. an aircraft). **b** transport in an aircraft. **4 a** *tr.* cause to fly or remain aloft. **b** *intr.* (of a flag, hair, etc.) wave or flutter. **5** *intr.* pass or rise quickly through the air or over an obstacle. **6** *intr.* go or move quickly; pass swiftly (*time flies*). **7** *intr.* **a** flee. **b** *colloq.* depart hastily. **8** *intr.* be driven or scattered; be forced off suddenly (*sent me flying; the door flew open*). **9** *intr.* (foll. by *at, upon*) **a** hasten or spring violently. **b** attack or criticize fiercely. **10** *tr.* flee from; escape in haste. ● *n.* (*pl.* **-ies**) **1** (usu. in *pl.*) **a** a flap on a garment, esp. trousers, to contain or cover a fastening. **b** this fastening. **2** a flap at the entrance of a tent. **3** (in *pl.*) the space over the proscenium in a theatre. **4** the act or an instance of flying. **5** (*pl.* usu. **flys**) *Brit. hist.* a one-horse hackney carriage. **6** a speed-regulating device in clockwork and machinery. □ **fly-away** (of hair etc.) tending to fly out or up; streaming. **fly-by** (*pl.* **-bys**) a flight past a position, esp. the approach of a spacecraft to a planet for observation. **fly-by-night** *adj.* **1** unreliable. **2** short-lived. ● *n.* an unreliable person. **fly-half** *Rugby Football* a stand-off half. **fly high 1** pursue a high ambition. **2** excel, prosper. **fly in the face of** openly disregard or disobey; conflict roundly with (probability, the evidence, etc.). **fly into a rage** (or **temper** etc.) become suddenly or violently angry. **fly a kite 1** try something out; test public opinion. **2** raise money by an accommodation bill. **fly off the handle** *colloq.* lose one's temper suddenly and unexpectedly. **fly-past** a ceremonial flight of aircraft past a person or a place. **fly-pitcher** *sl.* a street-trader. **fly-pitching** *sl.* street-trading. □□ **flyable** *adj.* [OE *flēogan* f. Gmc]

■ *v.* **1** take wing, take to the air, wing, soar. **3 a** see PILOT *v.* **b** see TRANSPORT *v.* 1. **4 b** see FLAP *v.* 1. **6** hurry, make haste, hasten, sprint, *colloq.* tear; rush (by), run (on), dash *or* race (by). **7** see FLEE 1. **10** see FLEE 2. ● *n.* **1** flap, fly front, *esp. Brit.* zip, *esp. US* zipper. **4** see FLIGHT[1] *n.* 1a, 5; 2a. □ **fly-by-night** (*adj.*) **1** unreliable, untrustworthy, irresponsible; disreputable, shady, dubious, questionable; dishonest, sharp, *colloq.* shifty, crooked. **2** temporary, short-lived, transitory, fugitive, ephemeral, transient, fleeting, passing, brief, impermanent. **fly high 2** see EXCEL 2. **fly in the face of** flout, defy, go against, scorn, oppose, go *or* run counter to, counter, counteract, countervail, countermine, contradict, contravene, thumb one's nose at, *sl.* cock a snook at, *literary* contemn. **fly into a rage** (or **temper** etc.) see FLARE *v.* 3, *fly off the handle* (FLY[1]) below. **fly off the handle** fly into a rage *or* fury *or* temper *or* passion, lose one's temper, go berserk, explode, get worked up, *colloq.* have a fit *or* tantrum, go crazy, go mad, lose one's cool, blow one's top, hit *or* go through *or* raise the roof, *US colloq.* blow one's stack, *sl.* blow a a gasket, flip (one's lid).

fly[2] /flī/ *n.* (*pl.* **flies**) **1** any insect of the order Diptera with two usu. transparent wings. **2** any other winged insect, e.g. a firefly or mayfly. **3** a disease of plants or animals caused by flies. **4** a natural or artificial fly used as bait in fishing. □ **fly agaric** a poisonous fungus *Amanita Muscaria*, forming bright-red mushrooms with white flecks. **fly-blow** flies' eggs contaminating food, esp. meat. **fly-blown** *adj.* tainted, esp. by flies. **fly-fish** *v.intr.* fish with a fly. **fly in the ointment** a minor irritation that spoils enjoyment. **fly on the wall** an unnoticed observer. **fly-paper** sticky treated paper for catching flies. **fly-post** display (posters etc.) rapidly in unauthorized places. **fly-tip** illegally dump (waste). **fly-tipper** a person who engages in fly-tipping. **fly-trap** any of various plants that catch flies, esp. the Venus fly-trap. **like flies** in large numbers (usu. of people dying in an epidemic etc.). **no flies on** *colloq.* nothing to diminish (a person's) astuteness. [OE *flȳge, flēoge* f. WG]

■ □ **fly in the ointment** hitch, snag, impediment, obstacle, obstruction, problem, difficulty, drawback, detraction, rub, hindrance, bogey, bugaboo.

fly[3] /flī/ *adj. Brit. sl.* knowing, clever, alert. □□ **flyness** *n.* [19th c.: orig. unkn.]

flycatcher /flīkachər/ *n.* any bird of the families Tyrannidae and Muscicapidae, catching insects esp. in short flights from a perch.

flyer /flīər/ *n.* (also **flier**) *colloq.* **1** an airman or airwoman. **2** a thing that flies in a specified way (*a poor flyer*). **3** a fast-moving animal or vehicle. **4** an ambitious or outstanding person. **5** *US* a small handbill. **6** *US* a speculative investment. **7** a flying jump.

■ **5** see LEAFLET *n.*

flying /flī-ing/ *adj.* & *n.* ● *adj.* **1** fluttering or waving in the air; hanging loose. **2** hasty, brief (*a flying visit*). **3** designed for rapid movement. **4** (of an animal) able to make very long leaps by using winglike membranes etc. ● *n.* flight, esp. in an aircraft. □ **flying boat** a seaplane with a boatlike fuselage. **flying bomb** a pilotless aircraft with an explosive warhead. **flying buttress** a buttress slanting from a separate column, usu. forming an arch with the wall it supports. **flying doctor** a doctor (esp. in a large sparsely populated area) who visits distant patients by aircraft. **flying fish** any tropical fish of the family Exocoetidae, with winglike pectoral fins for gliding through the air. **flying fox** any of various fruit-eating bats esp. of the genus *Pteropus*, with a fox-like head. **flying lemur** either of two mammals of the genus *Cyanocephalus* of S. Asia, with a lemur-like appearance and having a membrane between the fore and hind limbs for gliding from tree to tree. **flying lizard** any lizard of the genus *Draco*, having membranes on elongated ribs for gliding. **flying officer** the RAF rank next below flight lieutenant. **flying phalanger** any of various phalangers having a membrane between the fore and hind limbs for gliding. **flying picket** an industrial picket that can be moved rapidly from one site to another, esp. to reinforce local pickets. **flying saucer** any unidentified, esp. circular, flying object, popularly supposed to have come from space. **flying squad** a police detachment or other body organized for rapid movement. **flying squirrel** any of various squirrels, esp. of the genus *Pteromys*, with skin joining the fore and hind limbs for gliding from tree to tree. **flying start 1** a start (of a race etc.) in which the starting-point is passed at full speed. **2** a vigorous start giving an initial advantage. **flying wing** an aircraft with little or no fuselage and no tailplane. **with flying colours** with distinction.

■ *n.* see FLIGHT[1] *n.* 1a, 5.

flyleaf /flīleef/ *n.* (*pl.* **-leaves**) a blank leaf at the beginning or end of a book.

flyover /flīōvər/ *n.* **1** *Brit.* a bridge carrying one road or railway over another. **2** *US* = *fly-past* (see FLY[1]).

flysheet /flīsheet/ *n.* **1** a tract or circular of two or four pages. **2** a canvas cover pitched outside and over a tent to give extra protection against bad weather.

flyweight /flīwayt/ *n.* **1** a weight in certain sports intermediate between light flyweight and bantamweight, in the amateur boxing scale 48-51 kg but differing for professionals, wrestlers, and weightlifters. **2** a sportsman of this weight. □ **light flyweight 1** a weight in amateur boxing up to 48 kg. **2** an amateur boxer of this weight.

flywheel /flīweel/ *n.* a heavy wheel on a revolving shaft used to regulate machinery or accumulate power.

FM *abbr.* **1** Field Marshal. **2** frequency modulation.

Fm *symb. Chem.* the element fermium.

fm. *abbr.* (also **fm**) fathom(s).

f-number /éfnumbər/ *n. Photog.* the ratio of the focal length to the effective diameter of a lens (e.g. *f5*, indicating that the focal length is five times the diameter). [*f* (denoting focal length) + NUMBER]

FO *abbr.* **1** Flying Officer. **2** *hist.* (in the UK) Foreign Office.

fo. *abbr.* folio.

foal /fōl/ *n.* & *v.* ● *n.* the young of a horse or related animal. ● *v.tr.* (of a mare etc.) give birth to (a foal). □ **in** (or **with**) **foal** (of a mare etc.) pregnant. [OE *fola* f. Gmc: cf. FILLY]

foam /fōm/ *n.* & *v.* ● *n.* **1** a mass of small bubbles formed on or in liquid by agitation, fermentation, etc. **2** a froth of saliva or sweat. **3** a substance resembling these, e.g. rubber or plastic in a cellular mass. ● *v.intr.* **1** emit foam; froth. **2** run with foam. **3** (of a vessel) be filled and overflow with foam. □ **foam at the mouth** be very angry. □□ **foamless** *adj.* **foamy** *adj.* (**foamier, foamiest**). [OE *fām* f. WG]

■ *n.* **1** froth, spume, lather; bubbles, suds; head, effervescence, carbonation, fizz. ● *v.* **1, 2** bubble, froth, spume, lather, suds. □ **foam at the mouth** see RAGE *v.*

fob[1] /fob/ *n.* & *v.* ● *n.* **1** (in full **fob-chain**) a chain attached to a watch for carrying in a waistcoat or waistband pocket. **2** a small pocket for carrying a watch. **3** a tab on a key-ring. ● *v.tr.* (**fobbed, fobbing**) put in one's fob; pocket. [orig. cant, prob. f. G]

fob[2] /fob/ *v.tr.* (**fobbed, fobbing**) □ **fob off 1** (often foll. by *with* a thing) deceive into accepting something inferior. **2** (often foll. by *on to* a person) palm or pass off (an inferior thing). [16th c.: cf. obs. *fop* to dupe, G *foppen* to banter]

f.o.b. *abbr.* free on board.

focal /fṓk'l/ *adj.* of, at, or in terms of a focus. □ **focal distance** (or **length**) the distance between the centre of a mirror or lens and its focus. **focal plane** the plane through the focus perpendicular to the axis of a mirror or lens. **focal point** = FOCUS *n.* 1. [mod.L *focalis* (as FOCUS)]

focalize /fṓkəlīz/ *v.tr.* (also **-ise**) = FOCUS *v.* □□ **focalization** /-záysh'n/ *n.*

fo'c's'le var. of FORECASTLE.

focus /fṓkəss/ *n.* & *v.* ● *n.* (*pl.* **focuses** or **foci** /fṓsī/) **1** *Physics* **a** the point at which rays or waves meet after reflection or refraction. **b** the point from which diverging rays or waves appear to proceed. Also called *focal point*. **2 a** *Optics* the point at which an object must be situated for an image of it given by a lens or mirror to be well defined (*bring into focus*). **b** the adjustment of the eye or a lens necessary to produce a clear image (*the binoculars were not in focus*). **c** a state of clear definition (*the photograph was out of focus*). **3** the centre of interest or activity (*focus of attention*). **4** *Geom.* one of the points from which the distances to any point of a given curve are connected by a linear relation. **5** *Med.* the principal site of an infection or other disease. **6** *Geol.* the place of origin of an earthquake. ● *v.* (**focused, focusing** or **focussed, focussing**) **1** *tr.* bring into focus. **2** *tr.* adjust the focus of (a lens, the eye, etc.). **3** *tr.* & *intr.* (often foll. by *on*) concentrate or be concentrated on. **4** *intr.* & *tr.* converge or make converge to a focus. □□ **focuser** *n.* [L, = hearth]

■ *n.* **2c** (*in focus*) clear, clear-cut, distinct, sharp, well- *or* sharply defined; (*out of focus*) unclear, indistinct, blurred, blurry, fuzzy. **3** centre, focal point, heart, core, hub; cynosure. ● *v.* **3** concentrate, centre, direct, bring to bear; be concentrated, be centred, be directed, be brought to bear; (*focus on*) zero in on, pinpoint. **4** converge, merge, meet; come *or* bring into focus.

fodder /fóddər/ *n.* & *v.* ● *n.* dried hay or straw etc. for cattle, horses, etc. ● *v.tr.* give fodder to. [OE *fōdor* f. Gmc, rel. to FOOD]

■ *n.* see FEED *n.* 1.

foe /fō/ *n.* esp. *poet.* or *formal* an enemy or opponent. [OE *fāh* hostile, rel. to FEUD[1]]

■ see ENEMY 1–3.

foehn var. of FÖHN.

foetid var. of FETID.

foetus /féetəss/ *n.* (*US* **fetus**) an unborn or unhatched offspring of a mammal esp. a human one more than eight weeks after conception. □□ **foetal** *adj.* **foeticide** /-tisīd/ *n.* [ME f. L *fetus* offspring]

fog[1] /fog/ *n.* & *v.* ● *n.* **1 a** a thick cloud of water droplets or smoke suspended in the atmosphere at or near the earth's surface restricting or obscuring visibility. **b** obscurity in the atmosphere caused by this. **2** *Photog.* cloudiness on a developed negative etc. obscuring the image. **3** an uncertain or confused position or state. ● *v.* (**fogged, fogging**) **1** *tr.* **a** (often foll. by *up*) cover with fog or condensed vapour. **b** bewilder or confuse as if with a fog. **2** *intr.* (often foll. by *up*) become covered with fog or condensed vapour. **3** *tr. Photog.* make (a negative etc.) obscure or cloudy. □ **fog-bank** a mass of fog at sea. **fog-bound** unable to proceed because of fog. **fog-bow** a manifestation like a rainbow, produced by light on fog. **fog-lamp** a lamp used to improve visibility in fog. **fog-signal** a detonator placed on a railway line in fog to warn train drivers. **in a fog** puzzled; at a loss. [perh. back-form. f. FOGGY]

■ *n.* **1** mist, haze, vapour, cloud, smog, *Brit. colloq.* pea-souper. **3** see DISTRACTION 4. ● *v.* **1a, 2** fog up, mist up *or* over, cloud up *or* over. **1b** bewilder, confuse, obscure, cloud, becloud, muddle. □ **in a fog** see DAZE *n.*

fog[2] /fog/ *n.* & *v.* esp. *Brit.* ● *n.* **1** a second growth of grass after cutting; aftermath. **2** long grass left standing in winter. ● *v.tr.* (**fogged, fogging**) **1** leave (land) under fog. **2** feed (cattle) on fog. [ME: orig. unkn.]

fogey var. of FOGY.

foggy /fóggi/ *adj.* (**foggier, foggiest**) **1** (of the atmosphere) thick or obscure with fog. **2** of or like fog. **3** vague, confused, unclear. □ **not have the foggiest** *colloq.* have no idea at all. □□ **foggily** *adv.* **fogginess** *n.*

■ **1** see MISTY. **3** see VAGUE 1.

foghorn /fóg-horn/ *n.* **1** a deep-sounding instrument for warning ships in fog. **2** *colloq.* a loud penetrating voice.

■ **1** see SIREN 1.

fogy /fṓgi/ *n.* (also **fogey**) (*pl.* **-ies** or **-eys**) a dull old-fashioned person (esp. *old fogy*). □□ **fogydom** *n.* **fogyish** *adj.* [18th c.: rel. to sl. *fogram*, of unkn. orig.]

■ old fogy, conservative, *colloq.* fossil, stick-in-the-mud, *sl.* fuddy-duddy, back number, square.

föhn /fön/ *n.* (also **foehn**) **1** a hot southerly wind on the northern slopes of the Alps. **2** a warm dry wind on the lee side of mountains. [G, ult. f. L *Favonius* mild west wind]

foible /fóyb'l/ *n.* **1** a minor weakness or idiosyncrasy. **2** *Fencing* the part of a sword-blade from the middle to the point. [F, obs. form of *faible* (as FEEBLE)]

■ **1** weakness, imperfection, weak point, fault, frailty, shortcoming, flaw, defect, failing, blemish, infirmity; idiosyncrasy, peculiarity, quirk, crotchet, eccentricity, kink.

foie gras /fwaa graá/ *n. colloq.* = *pâté de foie gras*.

foil[1] /foyl/ *v.* & *n.* ● *v.tr.* **1** frustrate, baffle, defeat. **2** *Hunting* **a** run over or cross (ground or a scent) to confuse the hounds. **b** (*absol.*) (of an animal) spoil the scent in this way. ● *n.* **1** *Hunting* the track of a hunted animal. **2** *archaic* a repulse or defeat. [ME, = trample down, perh. f. OF *fouler* to full cloth, trample, ult. f. L *fullo* FULLER[1]]

■ *v.* **1** frustrate, outwit, baffle, defeat, thwart, offset, baulk, check, impede, hamper, discomfit, circumvent, *Brit.* put a spoke in a person's wheel.

foil[2] /foyl/ *n.* **1 a** metal hammered or rolled into a thin sheet (*tin foil*). **b** a sheet of this, or of tin amalgam, attached to mirror glass as a reflector. **c** a leaf of foil placed under a precious stone etc. to brighten or colour it. **2** a person or thing that enhances the qualities of another by contrast. **3**

Archit. a leaf-shaped curve formed by the cusping of an arch or circle. [ME f. OF f. L *folium* leaf, and f. OF *foille* f. L *folia* (pl.)]

foil[3] /foyl/ *n.* a light blunt-edged sword with a button on its point used in fencing. □□ **foilist** *n.* [16th c.: orig. unkn.]

foil[4] /foyl/ *n.* = HYDROFOIL. [abbr.]

foist /foyst/ *v.tr.* **1** (foll. by *on, upon*) impose (an unwelcome person or thing). **2** (foll. by *on, upon*) falsely fix the authorship of (a composition). **3** (foll. by *in, into*) introduce surreptitiously or unwarrantably. [orig. of palming a false die, f. Du. dial. *vuisten* take in the hand f. *vuist* FIST]
■ **1** impose, thrust, force, press, *often joc.* inflict; (*foist on* or *upon*) saddle *or* lumber a person with.

fol. *abbr.* folio.

folacin /fṓləsin/ *n.* = FOLIC ACID. [*fol*ic *ac*id + -IN]

fold[1] /fōld/ *v.* & *n.* ● *v.* **1** *tr.* **a** bend or close (a flexible thing) over upon itself. **b** (foll. by *back, over, down*) bend a part of (a flexible thing) in the manner specified (*fold down the flap*). **2** *intr.* become or be able to be folded. **3** *tr.* (foll. by *away, up*) make compact by folding. **4** *intr.* (often foll. by *up*) *colloq.* **a** collapse, disintegrate. **b** (of an enterprise) fail; go bankrupt. **5** *tr. poet.* embrace (esp. *fold in the arms* or *to the breast*). **6** *tr.* (foll. by *about, round*) clasp (the arms); wrap, envelop. **7** *tr.* (foll. by *in*) mix (an ingredient with others) using a gentle cutting and turning motion. ● *n.* **1** the act or an instance of folding. **2** a line made by or for folding. **3** a folded part. **4** a hollow among hills. **5** *Geol.* a curvature of strata. □ **fold one's arms** place one's arms across the chest, side by side or entwined. **fold one's hands** clasp them. **folding door** a door with jointed sections, folding on itself when opened. **folding money** esp. *US colloq.* banknotes. **fold-out** an oversize page in a book etc. to be unfolded by the reader. □□ **foldable** *adj.* [OE *falden, fealden* f. Gmc]
■ *v.* **1** bend, double (over *or* up), crease, pleat, gather, crimp. **4 a** see *give way* 3 (WAY). **b** fail, go out of business, go bankrupt, go under, go to the wall, close down, shut down, *colloq.* go broke, go bust. **5, 6** embrace, hug; clasp, gather, wrap, enfold, enclose, envelop, *literary* enwrap. ● *n.* **3** crease, pleat, gather, crimp.

fold[2] /fōld/ *n.* & *v.* ● *n.* **1** = SHEEPFOLD. **2** a body of believers or members of a Church. ● *v.tr.* enclose (sheep) in a fold. [OE *fald*]

-fold /fōld/ *suffix* forming adjectives and adverbs from cardinal numbers, meaning: **1** in an amount multiplied by (*repaid tenfold*). **2** consisting of so many parts (*threefold blessing*). [OE *-fald, -feald*, rel. to FOLD[1]: orig. sense 'folded in so many layers']

foldaway /fṓldəway/ *adj.* adapted or designed to be folded away.

folder /fṓldər/ *n.* **1** a folding cover or holder for loose papers. **2** a folded leaflet.
■ **1** see FILE[1] *n.* 1. **2** see LEAFLET *n.*

folderol var. of FALDERAL.

foliaceous /fṓliáyshəss/ *adj.* **1** of or like leaves. **2** having organs like leaves. **3** laminated. [L *foliaceus* leafy f. *folium* leaf]

foliage /fṓli-ij/ *n.* **1** leaves, leafage. **2** a design in art resembling leaves. □ **foliage leaf** a leaf excluding petals and other modified leaves. [ME f. F *feuillage* f. *feuille* leaf f. OF *foille*: see FOIL[2]]

foliar /fṓliər/ *adj.* of or relating to leaves. □ **foliar feed** feed supplied to leaves of plants. [mod.L *foliaris* f. L *folium* leaf]

foliate *adj.* & *v.* ● *adj.* /fṓliət/ **1** leaflike. **2** having leaves. **3** (in *comb.*) having a specified number of leaflets (*trifoliate*). ● *v.* /fṓliayt/ **1** *intr.* split into laminae. **2** *tr.* decorate (an arch or door-head) with foils. **3** *tr.* number leaves (not pages) of (a volume) consecutively. □□ **foliation** /-áysh'n/ *n.* [L *foliatus* leaved f. *folium* leaf]

folic acid /fṓlik/ *n.* a vitamin of the B complex, found in leafy green vegetables, liver, and kidney, a deficiency of which causes pernicious anaemia. Also called FOLACIN or PTEROYLGLUTAMIC ACID. [L *folium* leaf (because found esp. in green leaves) + -IC]

folio /fṓliō/ *n.* & *adj.* ● *n.* (*pl.* **-os**) **1** a leaf of paper etc., esp. one numbered only on the front. **2** a leaf-number of a book. **3** a sheet of paper folded once making two leaves of a book. **4** a book made of such sheets. ● *adj.* (of a book) made of folios, of the largest size. □ **in folio** made of folios. [L, ablat. of *folium* leaf, = *on leaf* (as specified)]
■ *n.* **1, 3** page, leaf, sheet.

foliole /fṓliōl/ *n.* a division of a compound leaf; a leaflet. [F f. LL *foliolum* dimin. of L *folium* leaf]

folk /fōk/ *n.* (*pl.* **folk** or **folks**) **1** (treated as *pl.*) people in general or of a specified class (*few folk about; townsfolk*). **2** (in *pl.*) (usu. **folks**) one's parents or relatives. **3** (treated as *sing.*) a people. **4** (treated as *sing.*) *colloq.* traditional music. **5** (*attrib.*) of popular origin; traditional (*folk art*). □ **folk-dance 1** a dance of popular origin. **2** the music for such a dance. **folk etymology** a popular modifying of the form of a word or phrase to make it seem to be derived from a more familiar word (e.g. *forlorn hope*). **folk memory** recollection of the past persisting among a people. **folk-singer** a singer of folk-songs. **folk-song** a song of popular or traditional origin or style. **folk-tale** a popular or traditional story. **folk-ways** the traditional behaviour of a people. [OE *folc* f. Gmc]
■ **1** people, society, the nation, the (general) public, the populace, the population, the citizenry. **2** (*folks*) parents; relatives; see also FAMILY 1. **3** people, tribe, (ethnic) group, clan, race.

folkish /fṓkish/ *adj.* of the common people; traditional, unsophisticated.

folklore /fṓklor/ *n.* the traditional beliefs and stories of a people; the study of these. □□ **folkloric** *adj.* **folklorist** *n.* **folkloristic** /-rístik/ *adj.*
■ see LORE[1].

folksy /fṓksi/ *adj.* (**folksier, folksiest**) **1** friendly, sociable, informal. **2 a** having the characteristics of folk art, culture, etc. **b** ostensibly or artificially folkish. □□ **folksiness** *n.*
■ **1** see INFORMAL.

folkweave /fṓkweev/ *n.* a rough loosely woven fabric.

folky /fṓki/ *adj.* (**folkier, folkiest**) **1** = FOLKSY 2. **2** = FOLKISH. □□ **folkiness** *n.*

follicle /fóllik'l/ *n.* **1** a small sac or vesicle. **2** a small sac-shaped secretory gland or cavity. **3** *Bot.* a single-carpelled dry fruit opening on one side only to release its seeds. □□ **follicular** /folíkyoolər/ *adj.* **folliculate** /folíkyoolət/ *adj.* **folliculated** /folíkyoolaytid/ *adj.* [L *folliculus* dimin. of *follis* bellows]

follow /fóllō/ *v.* **1** *tr.* or (foll. by *after*) *intr.* go or come after (a person or thing proceeding ahead). **2** *tr.* go along (a route, path, etc.). **3** *tr.* & *intr.* come after in order or time (*Nero followed Claudius; dessert followed; my reasons are as follows*). **4** *tr.* take as a guide or leader. **5** *tr.* conform to (*follow your example*). **6** *tr.* practise (a trade or profession). **7** *tr.* undertake (a course of study etc.). **8** *tr.* understand the meaning or tendency of (a speaker or argument). **9** *tr.* maintain awareness of the current state or progress of (events etc. in a particular sphere). **10** *tr.* (foll. by *with*) provide with a sequel or successor. **11** *intr.* happen after something else; ensue. **12** *intr.* **a** be necessarily true as a result of something else. **b** (foll. by *from*) be a result of. **13** *tr.* strive after; aim at; pursue (*followed fame and fortune*). □ **follow-my-leader** a game in which players must do as the leader does. **follow one's nose** trust to instinct. **follow on 1** continue. **2** (of a cricket team) have to bat again immediately after the first innings. **follow-on** *n.* an instance of this. **follow out** carry out; adhere precisely to (instructions etc.). **follow suit 1** *Cards* play a card of the suit led. **2** conform to another person's actions. **follow through 1** continue (an action etc.) to its conclusion. **2** *Sport* continue the movement of a stroke after the ball has been struck. **follow-through** *n.* the action of following through. **follow up 1** (foll. by *with*) pursue, develop, supplement. **2** make further investigation of. **follow-up** *n.* a subsequent or continued action, measure, experience, etc. [OE *folgian* f. Gmc]

■ **1** go *or* come after, go *or* walk *or* tread *or* move behind; string *or* tag along (with), go along (with); go *or* come next. **2** trace, keep to, pursue, continue *or* proceed along. **3** come after, succeed, supersede, take the place of, replace, supplant. **5** conform to, adhere to, comply with, obey, be guided by, be modelled after *or* on, observe, heed, mind, go along with, reflect, mirror, echo, imitate, *literary* cleave to. **6** see PURSUE 2, 9. **7** see UNDERTAKE 1. **8** understand, fathom, comprehend, grasp, see, appreciate, take in, catch, keep up with, *colloq.* get, *sl.* dig. **9** keep up with, keep abreast of, take an interest in, be a fan *or* aficionado of, pursue, watch. **11** ensue, arise, develop; see also RESULT *v.* 1. **12 b** (*follow from*) be a result *or* consequence of, result *or* develop from, issue *or* flow from. **13** see AIM *v.* 1, 4. □ **follow through 1** persist *or* persevere with, continue, conclude, realize, consummate, pursue, carry out, see through, make good, fulfil, effect, discharge. **follow-through** see EXECUTION 2. **follow up 1** pursue, develop, supplement, reinforce, consolidate, support, buttress, bolster, augment. **2** pursue, investigate, check (out), check up, inquire about, make inquiries into *or* about, look into, track down. **follow-up** reinforcement, support, backup, consolidation.

follower /fóllōər/ *n.* **1** an adherent or devotee. **2** a person or thing that follows.

■ **1** adherent, disciple, student, pupil, protégé(e); devotee, supporter, fan, aficionado, enthusiast, advocate, champion, *sl.* groupie, *US sl.* rooter.

following /fólloing/ *prep., n.,* & *adj.* ● *prep.* coming after in time; as a sequel to. ● *n.* a body of adherents or devotees. ● *adj.* that follows or comes after.

■ *prep.* see SUBSEQUENT. ● *n.* see RETINUE. ● *adj.* see ATTENDANT *adj* 1.

folly /fólli/ *n.* (*pl.* **-ies**) **1** foolishness; lack of good sense. **2** a foolish act, behaviour, idea, etc. **3** an ornamental building, usu. a tower or mock Gothic ruin. **4** (in *pl.*) *Theatr.* **a** a revue with glamorous female performers, esp. scantily-clad. **b** the performers. [ME f. OF *folie* f. *fol* mad, FOOL[1]]

■ **1** foolishness, nonsense, absurdity, silliness, preposterousness, absurdness, senselessness, fatuousness, fatuity, stupidity, asininity, inanity, idiocy, imbecility, lunacy, insanity, madness, craziness, eccentricity, weak-mindedness, feeble-mindedness, simple-mindedness, muddle-headedness, thickheadedness, obtuseness, brainlessness, *colloq.* dopiness, *esp. Brit. colloq.* daftness, *esp. US colloq.* dumbness, *sl.* nuttiness, kookiness. **2** absurdity, brainstorm, blunder, *faux pas*, gaffe, *sl.* goof.

foment /fəmént, fō-/ *v.tr.* **1** instigate or stir up (trouble, sedition, etc.). **2 a** bathe with warm or medicated liquid. **b** apply warmth to. □□ **fomenter** *n.* [ME f. F *fomenter* f. LL *fomentare* f. L *fomentum* poultice, lotion f. *fovēre* heat, cherish]

■ **1** instigate, stir *or* whip up, provoke, incite, initiate, prompt, start, inspire, work up, inflame, fan the flames of, kindle, galvanize, rally, excite, stimulate, encourage, promote, foster, cultivate, sow the seed *or* seeds of.

fomentation /fōmentáysh'n/ *n.* **1** the act or an instance of fomenting. **2** materials prepared for application to a wound etc. [ME f. OF or LL *fomentatio* (as FOMENT)]

fond /fond/ *adj.* **1** (foll. by *of*) having affection or a liking for. **2** affectionate, loving, doting. **3** (of beliefs etc.) foolishly optimistic or credulous; naïve. □□ **fondly** *adv.* **fondness** *n.* [ME f. obs. *fon* fool, be foolish]

■ **1** (*fond of*) partial to, having affection *or* a liking for, affectionate towards, attached to, having a taste for, predisposed to *or* towards, inclined to *or* towards. **2** tender, loving, doting, affectionate, warm, adoring, caring. **3** foolish, credulous; see also NAÏVE. □□ **fondly** affectionately, lovingly, tenderly, warmly, adoringly, caressingly; foolishly, credulously, naïvely.

fondant /fóndənt/ *n.* a soft sweet of flavoured sugar. [F, pres. part. of *fondre* melt f. L *fundere* pour]

fondle /fónd'l/ *v.tr.* touch or stroke lovingly; caress. □□ **fondler** *n.* [back-form. f. *fondling* fondled person (as FOND, -LING[1])]

■ caress, stroke, pet, pat, touch, feel, cuddle.

fondue /fóndyōō, -dōō/ *n.* a dish of flavoured melted cheese. [F, fem. past part. of *fondre* melt f. L *fundere* pour]

font[1] /font/ *n.* **1** a receptacle in a church for baptismal water. **2** the reservoir for oil in a lamp. □□ **fontal** *adj.* (in sense 1). [OE *font*, *fant* f. OIr. *fant*, *font* f. L *fons fontis* fountain, baptismal water]

font[2] var. of FOUNT[2].

fontanel *US* var. of FONTANELLE.

fontanelle /fóntənél/ *n.* (*US* **fontanel**) a membranous space in an infant's skull at the angles of the parietal bones. [F *fontanelle* f. mod.L *fontanella* f. OF *fontenelle* dimin. of *fontaine* fountain]

food /fōōd/ *n.* **1** a nutritious substance, esp. solid in form, that can be taken into an animal or a plant to maintain life and growth. **2** ideas as a resource for or stimulus to mental work (*food for thought*). □ **food additive** a substance added to food to enhance its colour, flavour, or presentation, or for any other non-nutritional purpose. **food-chain** *Ecol.* a series of organisms each dependent on the next for food. **food poisoning** illness due to bacteria or other toxins in food. **food processor** a machine for chopping and mixing food materials. **food value** the relative nourishing power of a food. [OE *fōda* f. Gmc: cf. FEED]

■ **1** nourishment, nutriment, sustenance, *formal* aliment; foodstuffs, edibles, eatables, bread, victuals, provisions, commons, *colloq.* grub, eats, scoff, tuck, *formal* viands, *formal or joc.* comestibles, *sl.* chow. **2** ideas, stimuli; inspiration, stimulation.

foodie /fōōdi/ *n.* (also **foody**) (*pl.* **-ies**) *colloq.* a person who is particular about food; a gourmet.

foodstuff /fōōdstuf/ *n.* any substance suitable as food.

fool[1] /fōōl/ *n., v.,* & *adj.* ● *n.* **1** a person who acts unwisely or imprudently; a stupid person. **2** *hist.* a jester; a clown. **3** a dupe. ● *v.* **1** *tr.* deceive so as to cause to appear foolish. **2** *tr.* (foll. by *into* + verbal noun, or *out of*) trick; cause to do something foolish. **3** *tr.* play tricks on; dupe. **4** *intr.* act in a joking, frivolous, or teasing way. **5** *intr.* (foll. by *about*, *around*) behave in a playful or silly way. ● *adj. US colloq.* foolish, silly. □ **act** (or **play**) **the fool** behave in a silly way. **fool's errand** a fruitless venture. **fool's gold** iron pyrites. **fool's paradise** happiness founded on an illusion. **fool's parsley** a species of hemlock resembling parsley. **make a fool of** make (a person or oneself) look foolish; trick or deceive. **no** (or **nobody's**) **fool** a shrewd or prudent person. [ME f. OF *fol* f. L *follis* bellows, empty-headed person]

■ *n.* **1** simpleton, ninny, nincompoop, ass, jackass, dunce, dolt, halfwit, numskull, greenhorn, oaf, blockhead, feather-brain, booby, mooncalf, pigeon, *US* retardate, *colloq.* pinhead, silly, loon, goose, idiot, dim-wit, nitwit, birdbrain, imbecile, moron, chump, fat-head, chucklehead, knucklehead, *sl.* bonehead, goon, clod, clodpoll, jerk, dumb-bell, twerp, sap, dope, *Austral. sl.* boofhead, hoon, alec, *esp. Brit. sl.* twit, buffer, *Brit. sl.* nit, pillock, git, mug. **2** (court) jester, clown, comic, comedian, comedienne, entertainer, zany, buffoon, merry andrew, *farceur*, joker, Punch, Punchinello, pierrot, harlequin, *archaic* droll. **3** butt, dupe, gull, victim, cat's-paw, *colloq.* stooge, *sl.* mark, fall guy, pigeon, sucker, *Brit. sl.* mug. ● *v.* **1, 3** trick, deceive, take in, hoax, hoodwink, bluff, dupe, gull, humbug, make a fool of, pull the wool over a person's eyes, pull a person's leg, tease, *colloq.* have on, kid, bamboozle, pull a fast one on, *sl.* josh, *esp. US sl.* do a snow job on, snow-job, *US sl.* snow. **2** trick, gull, dupe, delude, mislead, *colloq.* kid, *literary* cozen, *sl.* con. **4** joke, jest, banter, tease, *colloq.* kid. **5** (*fool around* or *about*) play around *or* about, mess around *or* about, gambol, frolic, romp, *colloq.* footle (about), *sl.* cavort. □ **act** (or **play**)

the fool see FOOL[1] *v.* 4, 5 above. **make a fool of** see FOOL[1] *v.* 1, 3 above.

fool[2] /fōōl/ *n.* a dessert of usu. stewed fruit crushed and mixed with cream, custard, etc. [16th c.: perh. f. FOOL[1]]

foolery /fōōləri/ *n.* (*pl.* **-ies**) **1** foolish behaviour. **2** a foolish act.

foolhardy /fōōlhaardi/ *adj.* (**foolhardier, foolhardiest**) rashly or foolishly bold; reckless. □□ **foolhardily** *adv.* **foolhardiness** *n.* [ME f. OF *folhardi* f. *fol* foolish + *hardi* bold]

■ rash, imprudent, impetuous, reckless, brash, venturesome, bold, daring, audacious, adventurous, daredevil, incautious, hotheaded, careless, heedless, devil-may-care, hasty, thoughtless, unthinking, irresponsible, wild, madcap, *US* nervy, *colloq.* gutsy, *literary* temerarious.

foolish /fōōlish/ *adj.* (of a person, action, etc.) lacking good sense or judgement; unwise. □□ **foolishly** *adv.* **foolishness** *n.*

■ senseless, incautious, imprudent, impolitic, indiscreet, unwise, absurd, preposterous, ridiculous, ludicrous, injudicious, ill-considered, ill-advised, misguided, short-sighted, impetuous, headlong, rash, brash, reckless, heedless, unwary, foolhardy, nonsensical, stupid, asinine, inane, silly, fatuous, obtuse, scatterbrained, feather-brained, hare-brained, demented, irrational, simple-minded, light-headed, muddle-headed, bemused, feeble-minded, halfwitted, slow-witted, witless, brainless, empty-headed, blockheaded, *colloq.* dim-witted, dopey, crazy, mad, insane, crack-brained, birdbrained, confused, moronic, idiotic, imbecilic, thickheaded, dotty, dim, thick, *esp. Brit. colloq.* daft, *esp. US colloq.* dumb, *sl.* boneheaded, balmy, nuts, nutty, dippy, goofy, screwy, wacky, cuckoo, *esp. Brit. sl.* barmy, batty, loony, *Brit. sl.* potty.

foolproof /fōōlprōōf/ *adj.* (of a procedure, mechanism, etc.) so straightforward or simple as to be incapable of misuse or mistake.

■ safe, certain, sure, trustworthy, dependable, reliable, infallible, unfailing, guaranteed, *colloq.* sure-fire.

foolscap /fōōlskap/ *n. Brit.* a size of paper, about 330 x 200 (or 400) mm. [named from the former watermark representing a fool's cap]

foot /fŏŏt/ *n.* & *v.* ● *n.* (*pl.* **feet** /feet/) **1 a** the lower extremity of the leg below the ankle. **b** the part of a sock etc. covering the foot. **2 a** the lower or lowest part of anything, e.g. a mountain, a page, stairs, etc. **b** the lower end of a table. **c** the end of a bed where the user's feet normally rest. **3** the base, often projecting, of anything extending vertically. **4** a step, pace, or tread; a manner of walking (*fleet of foot*). **5** (*pl.* **feet** or **foot**) a unit of linear measure equal to 12 inches (30.48 cm). **6** *Prosody* **a** a group of syllables (one usu. stressed) constituting a metrical unit. **b** a similar unit of speech etc. **7** *Brit. hist.* infantry (*a regiment of foot*). **8** *Zool.* the locomotive or adhesive organ of invertebrates. **9** *Bot.* the part by which a petal is attached. **10** a device on a sewing-machine for holding the material steady as it is sewn. **11** (*pl.* **foots**) **a** dregs; oil refuse. **b** coarse sugar. ● *v.tr.* **1** (usu. as **foot it**) **a** traverse (esp. a long distance) by foot. **b** dance. **2** pay (a bill, esp. one considered large). □ **at a person's feet** as a person's disciple or subject. **feet of clay** a fundamental weakness in a person otherwise revered. **foot-and-mouth disease** a contagious viral disease of cattle etc. **foot-fault** (in lawn tennis) incorrect placement of the feet while serving. **foot-pound** the amount of energy required to raise 1 lb. a distance of 1 foot. **foot-pound-second system** a system of measurement with these as basic units. **foot-rot** a bacterial disease of the feet in sheep and cattle. **foot-rule** a ruler 1 foot long. **foot-soldier** a soldier who fights on foot. **get one's feet wet** begin to participate. **have one's** (or **both**) **feet on the ground** be practical. **have a foot in the door** have a prospect of success. **have one foot in the grave** be near death or very old. **my foot!** *int.* expressing strong contradiction. **not put a foot wrong** make no mistakes. **off one's feet** so as to be unable to stand, or in a state compared with this (*was rushed off my feet*). **on one's feet** standing or walking. **on foot** walking, not riding etc. **put one's best foot forward** make every effort; proceed with determination. **put one's feet up** *colloq.* take a rest. **put one's foot down** *colloq.* **1** be firmly insistent or repressive. **2** accelerate a motor vehicle. **put one's foot in it** *colloq.* commit a blunder or indiscretion. **set foot on** (or **in**) enter; go into. **set on foot** put (an action, process, etc.) in motion. **under one's feet** in the way. **under foot** on the ground. □□ **footed** *adj.* (also in *comb.*). **footless** *adj.* [OE *fōt* f. Gmc]

footage /fŏŏttij/ *n.* **1** length or distance in feet. **2** an amount of film made for showing, broadcasting, etc.

■ **1** see DISTANCE *n.* 2.

football /fŏŏtbawl/ *n.* & *v.* ● *n.* **1** any of several outdoor games between two teams played with a ball on a pitch with goals at each end, esp. = *Association Football.* **2** a large inflated ball of a kind used in these. **3** a topical issue or problem that is the subject of continued argument or controversy. ● *v.intr.* play football. □ **football pool** (or **pools**) a form of gambling on the results of football matches, the winners receiving sums accumulated from entry money. □□ **footballer** *n.*

footboard /fŏŏtbord/ *n.* **1** a board to support the feet or a foot. **2** an upright board at the foot of a bed.

footbrake /fŏŏtbrayk/ *n.* a brake operated by the foot in a motor vehicle.

footbridge /fŏŏtbrij/ *n.* a bridge for use by pedestrians.

footer[1] /fŏŏttər/ *n.* (in *comb.*) a person or thing of so many feet in length or height (*six-footer*).

footer[2] /fŏŏttər/ *n. Brit. colloq.* = FOOTBALL 1.

footfall /fŏŏtfawl/ *n.* the sound of a footstep.

■ step, footstep, tread.

foothill /fŏŏt-hil/ *n.* (often in *pl.*) any of the low hills around the base of a mountain.

■ see HILL *n.* 1.

foothold /fŏŏt-hōld/ *n.* **1** a place, esp. in climbing, where a foot can be supported securely. **2** a secure initial position or advantage.

■ **1** footing, toe-hold. **2** see OPENING *n.* 2.

footing /fŏŏtting/ *n.* **1** a foothold; a secure position (*lost his footing*). **2** the basis on which an enterprise is established or operates; the position or status of a person in relation to others (*on an equal footing*). **3** the foundations of a wall, usu. with a course of brickwork wider than the base of the wall.

■ **1** foothold, toe-hold. **2** foundation, basis, base; level, position, state, rank; terms.

footle /fŏŏt'l/ *v.intr.* (usu. foll. by *about*) *colloq.* behave foolishly or trivially. [19th c.: perh. f. dial. *footer* idle]

footlights /fŏŏtlīts/ *n.pl.* a row of lights along the front of a stage at the level of the actors' feet.

footling /fŏŏtling/ *adj. colloq.* trivial, silly.

footloose /fŏŏtlōōss/ *adj.* free to go where or act as one pleases.

footman /fŏŏtmən/ *n.* (*pl.* **-men**) **1** a liveried servant attending at the door, at table, or on a carriage. **2** *hist.* an infantryman.

■ **1** see SERVANT 1.

footmark /fŏŏtmaark/ *n.* a footprint.

footnote /fŏŏtnōt/ *n.* & *v.* ● *n.* a note printed at the foot of a page. ● *v.tr.* supply with a footnote or footnotes.

■ *n.* see NOTE *n.* 2, 5.

footpad /fŏŏtpad/ *n. hist.* an unmounted highwayman.

■ see THIEF.

footpath /fŏŏtpaath/ *n.* a path for pedestrians; a pavement.

■ see PATH 1.

footplate /fŏŏtplayt/ *n.* esp. *Brit.* the platform in the cab of a locomotive for the crew.

footprint /fŏŏtprint/ *n.* **1** the impression left by a foot or shoe. **2** *Computing* the area of desk space etc. occupied by a microcomputer or other piece of hardware. **3** the ground

area covered by a communications satellite or affected by noise etc. from aircraft.
■ **1** see STEP *n.* 6.

footrest /fŏŏtrest/ *n.* a support for the feet or a foot.

footsie /fŏŏtsi/ *n. colloq.* amorous play with the feet. [joc. dimin. of FOOT]

footslog /fŏŏtslog/ *v.* & *n.* ● *v.intr.* (**-slogged, -slogging**) walk or march, esp. laboriously for a long distance. ● *n.* a laborious walk or march. ▫▫ **footslogger** *n.*

footsore /fŏŏtsor/ *adj.* having sore feet, esp. from walking.

footstalk /fŏŏtstawk/ *n.* **1** *Bot.* a stalk of a leaf or peduncle of a flower. **2** *Zool.* an attachment of a barnacle etc.

footstep /fŏŏtstep/ *n.* **1** a step taken in walking. **2** the sound of this. ▫ **follow** (or **tread**) **in a person's footsteps** do as another person did before.
■ **1** step, tread, pace, stride. **2** footfall, step, tread. ▫ **follow** (or **tread**) **in a person's footsteps** follow a person's example *or* way of life *or* tradition.

footstool /fŏŏtstōōl/ *n.* a stool for resting the feet on when sitting.

footway /fŏŏtway/ *n.* a path or way for pedestrians.
■ see PATH 1.

footwear /fŏŏtwair/ *n.* shoes, socks, etc.

footwork /fŏŏtwurk/ *n.* the use of the feet, esp. skilfully, in sports, dancing, etc.

fop /fop/ *n.* an affectedly elegant or fashionable man; a dandy. ▫▫ **foppery** *n.* **foppish** *adj.* **foppishly** *adv.* **foppishness** *n.* [17th c.: perh. f. earlier *fop* fool]
■ see DANDY *n.*

for /fər, for/ *prep.* & *conj.* ● *prep.* **1** in the interest or to the benefit of; intended to go to (*these flowers are for you; wish to see it for myself; did it all for my country; silly for you to go*). **2** in defence, support, or favour of (*fight for one's rights*). **3** suitable or appropriate to (*a dance for beginners; not for me to say*). **4** in respect of or with reference to; regarding; so far as concerns (*usual for ties to be worn; don't care for him at all; ready for bed; MP for Lincoln*). **5** representing or in place of (*here for my uncle*). **6** in exchange against (*swopped it for a bigger one*). **7 a** as the price of (*give me £5 for it*). **b** at the price of (*bought it for £5*). **c** to the amount of (*a bill for £100; all out for 45*). **8** as the penalty of (*fined them heavily for it*). **9** in requital of (*that's for upsetting my sister*). **10** as a reward for (*here's £5 for your trouble*). **11 a** with a view to; in the hope or quest of; in order to get (*go for a walk; run for a doctor; did it for the money*). **b** on account of (*could not speak for laughing*). **12** corresponding to (*word for word*). **13** to reach; in the direction of; towards (*left for Rome; ran for the end of the road*). **14** conducive or conducively to; in order to achieve (*take the pills for a sound night's sleep*). **15** so as to start promptly at (*the meeting is at seven-thirty for eight*). **16** through or over (a distance or period); during (*walked for miles; sang for two hours*). **17** in the character of; as being (*for the last time; know it for a lie; I for one refuse*). **18** because of; on account of (*could not see for tears*). **19** in spite of; notwithstanding (*for all we know; for all your fine words*). **20** considering or making due allowance in respect of (*good for a beginner*). **21** in order to be (*gone for a soldier*). ● *conj.* because, since, seeing that. ▫ **be for it** *Brit. colloq.* be in imminent danger of punishment or other trouble. **for ever** see EVER; (cf. FOREVER). **o** (or **oh**) **for** I wish I had. [OE, prob. a reduction of Gmc *fora* (unrecorded) BEFORE (of place and time)]
■ *prep.* **1** in the interest of, to the benefit of, for the sake of, on (*US* in) behalf of. **2** in defence *or* support *or* favour of, on the side of, pro, in the service of, as a service to, on (*US* in) behalf of. **3** suitable *or* appropriate for, suited to, fit *or* fitting for, proper for; for the treatment of, as a remedy for, against. **4** in respect of, regarding, in *or* with regard to, as regards, respecting, concerning, as far as (a person) is concerned, (so far) as concerns, with reference to. **5** instead of, in place of, representing, as a replacement for, on (*US* in) behalf of. **9, 10** in return *or* exchange for, in compensation *or* recompense *or* payment *or* repayment for, in requital of, as a reward for, as recompense for. **11 a** in search *or* quest *or* pursuit of, in the hope of, seeking, looking for *or* after, after, with a view *or* an eye to. **b** because of, on account of, by reason of, owing to. **13** in the direction of, to, towards, into; to go to, bound *or* destined for. **14** conducive *or* conducively to, for the purpose of, with the object of, in the interest of, for the sake of. **16** for the duration of, through, over, during, in the course of, throughout. **19** despite, in spite of, notwithstanding, allowing for. ● *conj.* because, since, as, inasmuch as, seeing that, owing to the fact that, *disp.* due to the fact that, *archaic* forasmuch as.

f.o.r. *abbr.* free on rail.

for- /for, fər/ *prefix* forming verbs and their derivatives meaning: **1** away, off, apart (*forget; forgive*). **2** prohibition (*forbid*). **3** abstention or neglect (*forgo; forsake*). **4** excess or intensity (*forlorn*). [OE *for-, fær-*]

forage /fórrij/ *n.* & *v.* ● *n.* **1** food for horses and cattle. **2** the act or an instance of searching for food. ● *v.* **1** *intr.* go searching; rummage (esp. for food). **2** *tr.* obtain food from; plunder. **3** *tr.* **a** get by foraging. **b** supply with food. ▫ **forage cap** an infantry undress cap. ▫▫ **forager** *n.* [ME f. OF *fourrage, fourrager*, rel. to FODDER]
■ *n.* **1** see FEED *n.* 1. ● *v.* **1** see LOOK *v.* 2a, 3a.

foramen /foráymen/ *n.* (*pl.* **foramina** /-rámminə/) *Anat.* an opening, hole, or passage, esp. in a bone. ▫▫ **foraminate** /-rámminət/ *adj.* [L *foramen -minis* f. *forare* bore a hole]

foraminifer /fórrəmínnifər/ *n.* (also **foraminiferan** /-nífførən/) any protozoan of the order Foraminifera, having a perforated shell through which amoeba-like pseudopodia emerge. ▫▫ **foraminiferous** /-nífførəss/ *adj.*

foraminiferan var. of FORAMINIFER.

forasmuch as /fórəzmúch/ *conj. archaic* because, since. [= for as much]

foray /fórray/ *n.* & *v.* ● *n.* a sudden attack; a raid or incursion. ● *v.intr.* make or go on a foray. [ME, prob. earlier as verb: back-form. f. *forayer* f. OF *forrier* forager, rel. to FODDER]
■ *n.* see INROAD 2.

forbade (also **forbad**) *past* of FORBID.

forbear[1] /fórbáir/ *v.intr.* & *tr.* (*past* **forbore** /-bór/; *past part.* **forborne** /-bórn/) (often foll. by *from*, or *to* + infin.) *literary* abstain or desist (from) (*could not forbear (from) speaking out; forbore to mention it*). [OE *forberan* (as FOR-, BEAR[1])]
■ (*forbear from*) see REFRAIN[1].

forbear[2] var. of FOREBEAR.

forbearance /forbáirənss/ *n.* patient self-control; tolerance.
■ see TOLERANCE 1.

forbearing /forbáiring/ *adj.* patient, long-suffering. ▫▫ **forbearingly** *adv.*
■ patient, long-suffering, tolerant, forgiving, lenient, accommodating.

forbid /fərbíd/ *v.tr.* (**forbidding**; *past* **forbade** /-bád, -báyd/ or **forbad** /-bád/; *past part.* **forbidden** /-bídd'n/) **1** (foll. by *to* + infin.) order not (*I forbid you to go*). **2** refuse to allow (a thing, or a person to have a thing) (*I forbid it; was forbidden any wine*). **3** refuse a person entry to (*the gardens are forbidden to children*). ▫ **forbidden degrees** see DEGREE. **forbidden fruit** something desired or enjoyed all the more because not allowed. **God forbid!** may it not happen! ▫▫ **forbiddance** *n.* [OE *forbēodan* (as FOR-, BID)]
■ **1** (*forbid to*) direct *or* command *or* instruct *or* charge *or* tell *or* bid *or* require not to, prohibit *or* ban *or* debar from, hinder *or* stop *or* prevent from, preclude *or* exclude from, *archaic or literary* bid not to. **2** prohibit, ban, outlaw, interdict, disallow, proscribe, taboo; veto.

forbidding /fərbídding/ *adj.* uninviting, repellent, stern. ▫▫ **forbiddingly** *adv.*
■ uninviting, repellent, repulsive, odious, abhorrent, offensive; stern, hostile, unfriendly, harsh, menacing, threatening, ominous, dangerous, nasty, ugly, unpleasant, *Brit.* off-putting.

forbore *past* of FORBEAR[1].

forborne *past part.* of FORBEAR[1].

forbye /forbī/ *prep.* & *adv. archaic* or *Sc.* ● *prep.* besides. ● *adv.* in addition.

force[1] /forss/ *n.* & *v.* ● *n.* **1** power; exerted strength or impetus; intense effort. **2** coercion or compulsion, esp. with the use or threat of violence. **3 a** military strength. **b** (in *pl.*) troops; fighting resources. **c** an organized body of people, esp. soldiers, police, or workers. **4** binding power; validity. **5** effect; precise significance (*the force of their words*). **6 a** mental or moral strength; influence, efficacy (*force of habit*). **b** vividness of effect (*described with much force*). **7** *Physics* **a** an influence tending to cause the motion of a body. **b** the intensity of this equal to the mass of the body and its acceleration. **8** a person or thing regarded as exerting influence (*is a force for good*). ● *v.* **1** *tr.* constrain (a person) by force or against his or her will. **2** *tr.* make a way through or into by force; break open by force. **3** *tr.* (usu. with prep. or adv.) drive or propel violently or against resistance (*forced it into the hole*; *the wind forced them back*). **4** *tr.* (foll. by *on*, *upon*) impose or press (on a person) (*forced their views on us*). **5** *tr.* **a** cause or produce by effort (*forced a smile*). **b** attain by strength or effort (*forced an entry*; *must force a decision*). **6** *tr.* strain or increase to the utmost; overstrain. **7** *tr.* artificially hasten the development or maturity of (a plant). **8** *tr.* seek or demand quick results from; accelerate the process of (*force the pace*). **9** *intr. Cards* make a play that compels another particular play. □ **by force of** by means of. **force the bidding** (at an auction) make bids to raise the price rapidly. **forced labour** compulsory labour, esp. under harsh conditions. **forced landing** the unavoidable landing of an aircraft in an emergency. **forced march** a long and vigorous march esp. by troops. **force-feed** force (esp. a prisoner) to take food. **force field** (in science fiction) an invisible barrier of force. **force a person's hand** make a person act prematurely or unwillingly. **force the issue** render an immediate decision necessary. **force-land** land an aircraft in an emergency. **force-pump** a pump that forces water under pressure. **in force 1** valid, effective. **2** in great strength or numbers. **join forces** combine efforts. □□ **forceable** *adj.* **forcer** *n.* [ME f. OF *force*, *forcer* ult. f. L *fortis* strong]

■ *n.* **1** power, might, energy, strength, potency, vigour, intensity, violence, impact; effort, strain, exertion. **2** coercion, pressure, *force majeure*, constraint, duress, compulsion, *colloq.* arm-twisting. **3 b** (*forces*) troops, soldiers, armed forces; see also SERVICE[1] *n.* 8. **4** power, weight, persuasiveness, cogency, effectiveness, strength, validity. **5** effect, meaning, import; see also SIGNIFICANCE 1. **6 a** strength, influence, efficacy; see also STRENGTH 1. **b** see INTENSITY 2. **8** see INFLUENCE *n.* ● *v.* **1** make, oblige, require, compel, coerce, constrain, impel, pressure, pressurize, press, dragoon, *colloq.* bulldoze, put the squeeze on, twist a person's arm. **2** prise (*US* pry) *or* wrench open, break open *or* down, jemmy, *US* jimmy. **3** push, drive, thrust, propel. **4** see THRUST *v.* 2. **5b** see WRENCH *v.* 3, *insist on.* **6** see STRETCH *v.* 6. **8** see HURRY *v.* 2, QUICKEN 1. □ **by force of** see *by means of* (MEANS). **in force 1** in effect, effective, in operation, operative, valid, binding, current. **join forces** see COOPERATE.

force[2] /forss/ *n. N.Engl.* a waterfall. [ON *fors*]

forced /forst/ *adj.* **1** obtained or imposed by force (*forced entry*). **2** (of a gesture, etc.) produced or maintained with effort; affected, unnatural (*a forced smile*).

■ **2** artificial, unnatural, contrived, stilted, laboured, strained, stiff, false, feigned, affected, mannered, self-conscious, *colloq.* phoney.

forceful /fórsfōōl/ *adj.* **1** vigorous, powerful. **2** (of speech) compelling, impressive. □□ **forcefully** *adv.* **forcefulness** *n.*

■ **1** vigorous, energetic, dynamic, aggressive, potent, strong, mighty, powerful, weighty, effective, convincing, compelling. **2** compelling, effective, efficacious, cogent, impressive, telling, convincing, persuasive, strong, forcible, powerful, irresistible; pithy.

force majeure /fórss ma<u>zh</u>ốr/ *n.* **1** irresistible compulsion or coercion. **2** an unforeseeable course of events excusing a person from the fulfilment of a contract. [F, = superior strength]

forcemeat /fórsmeet/ *n.* meat etc. chopped and seasoned for use as a stuffing or a garnish. [obs. *force*, *farce* stuff f. OF *farsir*: see FARCE]

forceps /fórseps/ *n.* (*pl.* same) **1** surgical pincers, used for grasping and holding. **2** *Bot.* & *Zool.* an organ or structure resembling forceps. □□ **forcipate** /-sipət/ *adj.* [L *forceps forcipis*]

forcible /fórsib'l/ *adj.* done by or involving force; forceful. □□ **forcibleness** *n.* **forcibly** *adv.* [ME f. AF & OF (as FORCE[1])]

■ drastic, coercive, severe, stringent, aggressive, violent; forced; see also FORCEFUL.

ford /ford/ *n.* & *v.* ● *n.* a shallow place where a river or stream may be crossed by wading or in a vehicle. ● *v.tr.* cross (water) at a ford. □□ **fordable** *adj.* **fordless** *adj.* [OE f. WG]

■ *v.* see WADE *v.* 5.

fore /for/ *adj.*, *n.*, *int.*, & *prep.* ● *adj.* situated in front. ● *n.* the front part, esp. of a ship; the bow. ● *int. Golf* a warning to a person in the path of a ball. ● *prep. archaic* (in oaths) in the presence of (*fore God*). □ **come to the fore** take a leading part. **fore and aft** at bow and stern; all over the ship. **fore-and-aft** *adj.* (of a sail or rigging) set lengthwise, not on the yards. **to the fore** in front; conspicuous. [OE f. Gmc.: (adj. & n.) ME f. compounds with FORE-]

■ *n.* see FRONT *n.* 1.

fore- /for/ *prefix* forming: **1** verbs meaning: **a** in front (*foreshorten*). **b** beforehand; in advance (*foreordain*; *forewarn*). **2** nouns meaning: **a** situated in front of (*forecourt*). **b** the front part of (*forehead*). **c** of or near the bow of a ship (*forecastle*). **d** preceding (*forerunner*).

forearm[1] /fóraarm/ *n.* **1** the part of the arm from the elbow to the wrist or the fingertips. **2** the corresponding part in a foreleg or wing.

forearm[2] /foráarm/ *v.tr.* prepare or arm beforehand.

forebear /fórbair/ *n.* (also **forbear**) (usu. in *pl.*) an ancestor. [FORE + obs. *bear*, *beer* (as BE, -ER[1])]

■ see ANCESTOR 1.

forebode /forbṓd/ *v.tr.* **1** betoken; be an advance warning of (an evil or unwelcome event). **2** have a presentiment of (usu. evil).

■ **1** see BODE. **2** see PREDICT.

foreboding /forbṓding/ *n.* an expectation of trouble or evil; a presage or omen. □□ **forebodingly** *adv.*

■ premonition, presentiment, foreshadowing; omen, sign, portent, intimation, forewarning, presage, warning, foretoken, augury, prophecy, prediction, prognostication; apprehension, apprehensiveness, misgiving, dread, suspicion, anxiety, fear.

forecast /fórkaast/ *v.* & *n.* ● *v.tr.* (*past* and *past part.* **-cast** or **-casted**) predict; estimate or calculate beforehand. ● *n.* a calculation or estimate of something future, esp. coming weather. □□ **forecaster** *n.*

■ *v.* predict, foretell, prophesy, prognosticate, foresee, augur, presage, *disp.* anticipate, *formal* vaticinate; estimate, calculate. ● *n.* calculation, estimate, prediction, prophecy, prognosis, prognostication, augury, anticipation, *formal* vaticination.

forecastle /fṓks'l/ *n.* (also **fo'c's'le**) *Naut.* **1** the forward part of a ship where the crew has quarters. **2** *hist.* a short raised deck at the bow.

foreclose /forklṓz/ *v.tr.* **1** (also *absol.*; foll. by *on*) stop (a mortgage) from being redeemable or (a mortgager) from redeeming, esp. as a result of defaults in payment. **2** exclude, prevent. **3** shut out; bar. □□ **foreclosure** *n.* [ME f. OF *forclos* past part. of *forclore* f. *for-* out f. L *foras* + CLOSE[2]]

forecourt /fórkort/ *n.* **1** an enclosed space in front of a building. **2** the part of a filling-station where petrol is supplied. **3** (in lawn tennis) the part of a tennis-court between the service line and the net.

foredoom /fordóòm/ *v.tr.* (often foll. by *to*) doom or condemn beforehand.

fore-edge /fórej/ *n.* (also **foredge**) the front or outer edge (esp. of the pages of a book).

forefather /fórfaathər/ *n.* (usu. in *pl.*) **1** an ancestor. **2** a member of a past generation of a family or people.
■ see ANCESTOR 1.

forefinger /fórfinggər/ *n.* the finger next to the thumb.

forefoot /fórfòot/ *n.* (*pl.* **-feet**) **1** either of the front feet of a four-footed animal. **2** *Naut.* the foremost section of a ship's keel.

forefront /fórfrunt/ *n.* **1** the foremost part. **2** the leading position.
■ **2** see FRONT *n.* 6.

foregather var. of FORGATHER.

forego[1] /fórgō/ *v.tr.* & *intr.* (**-goes**; *past* **-went** /-wént/; *past part.* **-gone** /-gón/) precede in place or time. □□ **foregoer** *n.* [OE *foregān*]

forego[2] var. of FORGO.

foregoing /fórgōing/ *adj.* preceding; previously mentioned.
■ preceding, former, previous, precedent, antecedent, earlier, preliminary, prior, anterior; above, aforementioned, aforesaid.

foregone /fórgón/ *past part.* of FOREGO[1]. ● *attrib.adj.* previous, preceding, completed. □ **foregone conclusion** an easily foreseen or predictable result.
■ previous, preceding; see also ABOVE *adj.*

foreground /fórgrownd/ *n.* **1** the part of a view, esp. in a picture, that is nearest the observer. **2** the most conspicuous position. [Du. *voorgrond* (as FORE-, GROUND[1])]

forehand /fórhand/ *n.* **1** *Tennis* etc. **a** a stroke played with the palm of the hand facing the opponent. **b** (*attrib.*) (also **forehanded**) of or made with a forehand. **2** the part of a horse in front of the seated rider.

forehead /fórrid, fórhed/ *n.* the part of the face above the eyebrows. [OE *forhēafod* (as FORE-, HEAD)]

forehock /fórhok/ *n.* a foreleg cut of pork or bacon.

foreign /fórrin/ *adj.* **1** of or from or situated in or characteristic of a country or a language other than one's own. **2** dealing with other countries (*foreign service*). **3** of another district, society, etc. **4** (often foll. by *to*) unfamiliar, strange, uncharacteristic (*his behaviour is foreign to me*). **5** coming from outside (*a foreign body lodged in my eye*). □ **foreign aid** money, food, etc. given or lent by one country to another. **foreign exchange 1** the currency of other countries. **2** dealings in these. **foreign legion** a body of foreign volunteers in an army (esp. the French army). **foreign minister** (or **secretary**) a government minister in charge of his or her country's relations with other countries. **foreign office** a government department dealing with other countries. □□ **foreignness** *n.* [ME f. OF *forein*, *forain* ult. f. L *foras*, *-is* outside: for *-g-* cf. *sovereign*]
■ **1** alien, imported, non-native; overseas, distant; tramontane. **2** external, international, overseas. **4** strange, outlandish, unfamiliar, peculiar, odd, uncharacteristic, curious, exotic, unknown, remote. **5** see EXTERNAL *adj.* 1b. □ **foreign minister** (or **secretary**) minister of the exterior, secretary of state for foreign affairs. **foreign office** foreign ministry, ministry for foreign affairs; Foreign and Commonwealth Office, State Department.

foreigner /fórrinər/ *n.* **1** a person born in or coming from a foreign country or place. **2** *dial.* a non-native of a place. **3 a** a foreign ship. **b** an imported animal or article.
■ **1** alien, non-native, immigrant, outsider, outlander, stranger. **2** non-native, outsider, stranger, newcomer, new arrival.

forejudge /fórjúj/ *v.tr.* judge or determine before knowing the evidence.

foreknow /fórnṓ/ *v.tr.* (*past* **-knew** /-nyóò/; *past part.* **-known** /-nṓn/) know beforehand; have prescience of. □□ **foreknowledge** /fórnóllij/ *n.*

forelady /fórlaydi/ *n.* (*pl.* **-ies**) *US* = FOREWOMAN.

foreland /fórland/ *n.* **1** a cape or promontory. **2** a piece of land in front of something.

foreleg /fórleg/ *n.* each of the front legs of a quadruped.

forelimb /fórlim/ *n.* any of the front limbs of an animal.

forelock /fórlok/ *n.* a lock of hair growing just above the forehead. □ **take time by the forelock** seize an opportunity.

foreman /fórmən/ *n.* (*pl.* **-men**) **1** a worker with supervisory responsibilities. **2** the member of a jury who presides over its deliberations and speaks on its behalf.
■ **1** superintendent, supervisor, overseer, manager, *Brit.* shopwalker, *US* floor-walker, straw boss, *colloq.* boss, super, *Brit. colloq.* gaffer, *Austral. sl.* pannikin boss.

foremast /fórmaast, -məst/ *n.* the forward (lower) mast of a ship.

foremost /fórmōst/ *adj.* & *adv.* ● *adj.* **1** the chief or most notable. **2** the most advanced in position; the front. ● *adv.* before anything else in position; in the first place (*first and foremost*). [earlier *formost*, *formest*, superl. of OE *forma* first, assim. to FORE, MOST]
■ *adj.* chief, first, primary, prime, leading, pre-eminent, supreme, paramount, main, best, superior. ● *adv.* first, firstly, primarily, in the first place, before anything else.

forename /fórnaym/ *n.* a first or Christian name.

forenoon /fórnòon/ *n. Naut.* or *Law* or *archaic* the part of the day before noon.

forensic /fərénsik/ *adj.* **1** of or used in connection with courts of law (*forensic science*). **2** *disp.* of or involving forensic science (*sent for forensic examination*). □ **forensic medicine** the application of medical knowledge to legal problems. □□ **forensically** *adv.* [L *forensis* f. FORUM]
■ see LEGAL 1.

foreordain /fórordáyn/ *v.tr.* predestinate; ordain beforehand. □□ **foreordination** /-dináysh'n/ *n.*

forepaw /fórpaw/ *n.* either of the front paws of a quadruped.

forepeak /fórpeek/ *n. Naut.* the end of the forehold in the angle of the bows.

foreplay /fórplay/ *n.* stimulation preceding sexual intercourse.

forerun /fór-rún/ *v.tr.* (**-running**; *past* **-ran** /-rán/; *past part.* **-run**) **1** go before. **2** indicate the coming of; foreshadow.

forerunner /fór-runnər/ *n.* **1** a predecessor. **2** an advance messenger.
■ **1** predecessor, precursor, foregoer, ancestor, progenitor. **2** herald, harbinger, envoy; see also MESSENGER.

foresail /fórsayl, -s'l/ *n. Naut.* the principal sail on a foremast (the lowest square sail, or the fore-and-aft bent on the mast, or the triangular before the mast).

foresee /fórsée/ *v.tr.* (*past* **-saw** /-sáw/; *past part.* **-seen** /-séen/) (often foll. by *that* + clause) see or be aware of beforehand. □□ **foreseeable** *adj.* **foreseeability** /-seeəbílliti/ *n.* **foreseer** /-séeər/ *n.* [OE *foresēon* (as FORE- + SEE[1])]
■ presage, foretell, envisage, forecast, predict, prophesy, augur, envision.

foreshadow /fórsháddō/ *v.tr.* be a warning or indication of (a future event).
■ presage, foretoken, portend, augur, indicate, bode.

foresheets /fórsheets/ *n.pl. Naut.* the inner part of the bows of a boat with gratings for the bowman to stand on.

foreshore /fórshor/ *n.* the part of the shore between high- and low-water marks, or between the water and cultivated or developed land.

foreshorten /fórshórt'n/ *v.tr.* show or portray (an object) with the apparent shortening due to visual perspective.

foreshow /fórshṓ/ *v.tr.* (*past part.* **-shown** /-shṓn/) **1** foretell. **2** foreshadow, portend, prefigure.

foresight /fórsīt/ *n.* **1** regard or provision for the future. **2** the process of foreseeing. **3** the front sight of a gun. **4** *Surveying* a sight taken forwards. □□ **foresighted** /-sītid/ *adj.* **foresightedly** /-sītidli/ *adv.* **foresightedness** /-sītidniss/ *n.* [ME, prob. after ON *forsjá, forsjó* (as FORE-, SIGHT)]
■ **1** providence, far-sightedness, long-sightedness. **2** prevision, vision, foreknowledge, prescience.

foreskin /fórskin/ *n.* the fold of skin covering the end of the penis. Also called PREPUCE.

forest /fórrist/ *n.* & *v.* ● *n.* **1 a** (often *attrib.*) a large area covered chiefly with trees and undergrowth. **b** the trees growing in it. **c** a large number or dense mass of vertical objects (*a forest of masts*). **2** a district formerly a forest but now cultivated (*Sherwood Forest*). **3** *hist.* an area usu. owned by the sovereign and kept for hunting. ● *v.tr.* **1** plant with trees. **2** convert into a forest. □ **forest-tree** a large tree suitable for a forest. [ME f. OF f. LL *forestis silva* wood outside the walls of a park f. L *foris* outside]
■ *n.* **1 a, b** see WOOD 2.

forestall /fórstáwl/ *v.tr.* **1** act in advance of in order to prevent. **2** anticipate (the action of another, or an event). **3** anticipate the action of. **4** deal with beforehand. **5** *hist.* buy up (goods) in order to profit by an enhanced price. □□ **forestaller** *n.* **forestalment** *n.* [ME in sense 5: cf. AL *forestallare* f. OE *foresteall* an ambush (as FORE-, STALL)]
■ **1** anticipate, prevent, obstruct, hinder, thwart, frustrate, avert, ward *or* stave *or* fend off, intercept, parry, stop, delay. **2, 3** see ANTICIPATE 4.

forestay /fórstay/ *n. Naut.* a stay from the head of the foremast to the ship's deck to support the foremast.

forester /fórristər/ *n.* **1** a person in charge of a forest or skilled in forestry. **2** a person or animal living in a forest. **3** (**Forester**) a member of the Ancient Order of Foresters (a friendly society). [ME f. OF *forestier* (as FOREST)]

forestry /fórristri/ *n.* **1** the science or management of forests. **2** wooded country; forests.

foretaste *n.* & *v.* ● *n.* /fórtayst/ partial enjoyment or suffering in advance; anticipation. ● *v.tr.* /fórtáyst/ taste beforehand; anticipate the experience of.
■ *n.* earnest, token; anticipation.

foretell /fórtél/ *v.tr.* (*past* and *past part.* **-told** /-tṓld/) **1** tell of (an event etc.) before it takes place; predict, prophesy. **2** presage; be a precursor of. □□ **foreteller** *n.*
■ **1** see PROPHESY.

forethought /fórthawt/ *n.* **1** care or provision for the future. **2** previous thinking or devising. **3** deliberate intention.
■ **1** far-sightedness, long-sightedness; preparation, planning, organization. **2** premeditation, pre-planning, planning.

foretoken *n.* & *v.* ● *n.* /fórtōkən/ a sign of something to come. ● *v.tr.* /fórtṓkən/ portend; indicate beforehand. [OE *foretācn* (as FORE-, TOKEN)]
■ *n.* see INDICATION 1b. ● *v.* see FORESHADOW.

foretold *past* and *past part.* of FORETELL.

foretop /fórtop/ *n. Naut.* a platform at the top of a foremast (see TOP¹ *n.* 9). □ **foretop-gallant mast** the mast above the fore-topmast. **foretop-gallant-sail** the sail above the fore-topsail.

fore-topmast /fortópmaast/ *n. Naut.* the mast above the foremast.

fore-topsail /fortópsayl, -s'l/ *n. Naut.* the sail above the foresail.

forever /fərévvər/ *adv.* continually, persistently (*is forever complaining*) (cf. *for ever*).
■ constantly, continually, continuously, always, all the time, unceasingly, persistently, perpetually.

forevermore /fərévvərmór/ *adv.* esp. *US* an emphatic form of FOREVER or *for ever* (see EVER).
■ see *permanently* (PERMANENT).

forewarn /fórwáwrn/ *v.tr.* warn beforehand. □□ **forewarner** *n.*

forewent *past* of FOREGO¹, FOREGO².

forewoman /fórwŏŏmmən/ *n.* (*pl.* **-women**) **1** a female worker with supervisory responsibilities. **2** a woman who presides over a jury's deliberations and speaks on its behalf.

foreword /fórwurd/ *n.* introductory remarks at the beginning of a book, often by a person other than the author. [FORE- + WORD after G *Vorwort*]
■ preface, prologue, preamble, prolegomenon, proem, introduction.

foreyard /fóryaard/ *n. Naut.* the lowest yard on a foremast.

forfeit /fórfit/ *n.*, *adj.*, & *v.* ● *n.* **1** a penalty for a breach of contract or neglect; a fine. **2 a** a trivial fine for a breach of rules in clubs etc. or in games. **b** (in *pl.*) a game in which forfeits are exacted. **3** something surrendered as a penalty. **4** the process of forfeiting. **5** *Law* property or a right or privilege lost as a legal penalty. ● *adj.* lost or surrendered as a penalty. ● *v.tr.* (**forfeited, forfeiting**) lose the right to, be deprived of, or have to pay as a penalty. □□ **forfeitable** *adj.* **forfeiter** *n.* **forfeiture** *n.* [ME (= crime) f. OF *forfet, forfait* past part. of *forfaire* transgress (f. L *foris* outside) + *faire* f. L *facere* do]
■ *n.* **1** penalty, fine, fee, charge, damages, mulct, *Law* amercement. **4** forfeiture, sequestration, confiscation, surrender, relinquishment, *Law* amercement. ● *v.* lose, yield, give up *or* over, relinquish, concede, surrender, cede, deliver up, turn *or* make over, be stripped *or* deprived of, forgo.

forfend /forfénd/ *v.tr.* **1** *US* protect by precautions. **2** *archaic* avert; keep off.

forgather /forgáthər/ *v.intr.* (also **foregather**) assemble; meet together; associate. [16th-c. Sc. f. Du. *vergaderen*, assim. to FOR-, GATHER]
■ see ASSEMBLE 1.

forgave *past* of FORGIVE.

forge¹ /forj/ *v.* & *n.* ● *v.tr.* **1 a** make (money etc.) in fraudulent imitation. **b** write (a document or signature) in order to pass it off as written by another. **2** fabricate, invent. **3** shape (esp. metal) by heating in a fire and hammering. ● *n.* **1** a blacksmith's workshop; a smithy. **2 a** a furnace or hearth for melting or refining metal. **b** a workshop containing this. □□ **forgeable** *adj.* **forger** *n.* [ME f. OF *forge* (n.), *forger* (v.) f. L *fabricare* FABRICATE]
■ *v.* **1** counterfeit, copy, reproduce; falsify, fake, fabricate. **2** see INVENT 1. **3** make, construct, fashion, fabricate, manufacture, shape, beat, hammer out.

forge² /forj/ *v.intr.* move forward gradually or steadily. □ **forge ahead 1** take the lead in a race. **2** move forward or make progress rapidly. [18th c.: perh. an aberrant pronunc. of FORCE¹]

forgery /fórjəri/ *n.* (*pl.* **-ies**) **1** the act or an instance of forging, counterfeiting, or falsifying a document etc. **2** a forged or spurious thing, esp. a document or signature.
■ **1** falsification, fraud, counterfeiting. **2** counterfeit, fake, sham, fraud, imitation, simulation, reproduction, *colloq.* phoney.

forget /fərgét/ *v.* (**forgetting**; *past* **forgot** /-gót/; *past part.* **forgotten** /-gótt'n/ or esp. *US* **forgot**) **1** *tr.* & (often foll. by *about*) *intr.* lose the remembrance of; not remember (a person or thing). **2** *tr.* (foll. by clause or *to* + infin.) not remember; neglect (*forgot to come; forgot how to do it*). **3** *tr.* inadvertently omit to bring or mention or attend to. **4** *tr.* (also *absol.*) put out of mind; cease to think of (*forgive and forget*). □ **forget-me-not** any plant of the genus *Myosotis*, esp. *M. alpestris* with small yellow-eyed bright blue flowers. **forget oneself 1** neglect one's own interests. **2** act unbecomingly or unworthily. □□ **forgettable** *adj.* **forgetter** *n.* [OE *forgietan* f. WG (as FOR-, GET)]
■ **1** fail to remember *or* recall, fail to think of, lose, lose sight of, draw a blank on, *esp. US or dial.* disremember. **2** omit, neglect, fail (in), overlook. **3** leave (behind), come *or* go without; overlook, miss, fail to notice, pass over. **4** ignore, disregard; dismiss from one's mind *or* thoughts, put out of one's mind, consign to oblivion, bury, sink, overlook, brush aside, gloss over, kiss goodbye.

forgetful /fərgétfŏŏl/ *adj.* **1** apt to forget, absent-minded. **2** (often foll. by *of*) forgetting, neglectful. ▫▫ **forgetfully** *adj.* **forgetfulness** *n.*

■ **1** absent-minded, *distrait*, thoughtless, inattentive, lax, dreamy, oblivious; amnesic; (*be forgetful*) be in dreamland, be (with one's head) in the clouds, be in cloud-land *or* cloud-cuckoo-land. **2** neglectful, negligent, heedless, unheeding, unheedful, unmindful, unthinking, remiss, careless, thoughtless.

forgive /fərgív/ *v.tr.* (also *absol.* or with double object) (*past* **forgave**; *past part.* **forgiven**) **1** cease to feel angry or resentful towards; pardon (an offender or offence) (*forgive us our mistakes*). **2** remit or let off (a debt or debtor). ▫▫ **forgivable** *adj.* **forgivably** *adv.* **forgiver** *n.* [OE *forgiefan* (as FOR-, GIVE)]

■ **1** pardon, excuse, allow, make allowance(s) for; overlook, condone, indulge, ignore, disregard, pay no attention to, pass over; clear, acquit, absolve, exonerate, vindicate, reprieve, let off, *formal* exculpate. **2** remit, cancel, waive, abolish, void, nullify, erase, delete; let off.

forgiveness /fərgívniss/ *n.* **1** the act of forgiving; the state of being forgiven. **2** readiness to forgive. [OE *forgiefenes* (as FORGIVE)]

■ **1** pardon, absolution, exoneration, reprieve, remission, acquittal, vindication, indulgence, allowance, *archaic* shrift, *formal* exculpation. **2** mercy, mercifulness, compassion, grace, leniency, clemency, indulgence, tolerance.

forgiving /fərgívving/ *adj.* inclined readily to forgive. ▫▫ **forgivingly** *adv.*

■ tolerant, lenient, forbearing, charitable, merciful, compassionate, conciliatory, magnanimous, indulgent, understanding, humane, soft-hearted, clement, placable.

forgo /fórgō/ *v.tr.* (also **forego**) (**-goes**; *past* **-went** /-wént/; *past part.* **-gone** /-gón/) **1** abstain from; go without; relinquish. **2** omit or decline to take or use (a pleasure, advantage, etc.). [OE *forgān* (as FOR-, GO[1])]

■ abstain from, do *or* go without, give up, turn down, deny oneself, sacrifice, cede, waive, decline, yield, surrender, relinquish, renounce, forswear, abdicate, forfeit, abandon, *colloq.* pass up, *literary* eschew.

forgot *past* of FORGET.

forgotten *past part.* of FORGET.

forint /fórrint/ *n.* the chief monetary unit of Hungary. [Magyar f. It. *fiorino*: see FLORIN]

fork /fork/ *n.* & *v.* ● *n.* **1** an instrument with two or more prongs used in eating or cooking. **2** a similar much larger instrument used for digging, lifting, etc. **3** any pronged device or component (*tuning-fork*). **4** a forked support for a bicycle wheel. **5 a** a divergence of anything, e.g. a stick or road, or *US* a river, into two parts. **b** the place where this occurs. **c** either of the two parts (*take the left fork*). **6** a flash of forked lightning. **7** *Chess* a simultaneous attack on two pieces by one. ● *v.* **1** *intr.* form a fork or branch by separating into two parts. **2** *intr.* take one or other road etc. at a fork (*fork left for Banbury*). **3** *tr.* dig or lift etc. with a fork. **4** *tr. Chess* attack (two pieces) simultaneously with one. ▫ **fork-lift truck** a vehicle with a horizontal fork in front for lifting and carrying loads. **fork lunch** (or **supper** etc.) a light meal eaten with a fork at a buffet etc. **fork out** (or **up**) *sl.* hand over or pay, usu. reluctantly. [OE *forca, force* f. L *furca*]

■ *v.* **1** see SEPARATE *v.* 3, 4.

forked /forkt/ *adj.* **1** having a fork or forklike end or branches. **2** divergent, cleft. **3** (in *comb.*) having so many prongs (*three-forked*). ▫ **forked lightning** a lightning-flash in the form of a zigzag or branching line.

forlorn /forlórn/ *adj.* **1** sad and abandoned or lonely. **2** in a pitiful state; of wretched appearance. ▫ **forlorn hope 1** a faint remaining hope or chance. **2** a desperate enterprise. ▫▫ **forlornly** *adv.* **forlornness** *n.* [past part. of obs. *forlese* f. OE *forlēosan* (as FOR-, LOSE): *forlorn hope* f. Du. *verloren hoop* lost troop, orig. of a storming-party etc.]

■ **1** lonely, lonesome, abandoned, forsaken, deserted, neglected, friendless, comfortless, bereft, solitary, isolated; desolate, inconsolable, despairing, broken-hearted, sad, woebegone, woeful, cheerless, joyless, unhappy, depressed, miserable, disconsolate, gloomy, lugubrious, glum, despondent, dismal, doleful, dejected, dispirited, low-spirited, melancholy, sorrowful, mournful, *literary or joc.* dolorous. **2** miserable, wretched, pitiable, pitiful, pathetic, sad, sorry, hapless, unfortunate, *colloq.* down in the mouth.

form /form/ *n.* & *v.* ● *n.* **1 a** a shape; an arrangement of parts. **b** the outward aspect (esp. apart from colour) or shape of a body. **2** a person or animal as visible or tangible (*the familiar form of the postman*). **3** the mode in which a thing exists or manifests itself (*took the form of a book*). **4** a species, kind, or variety. **5 a** a printed document with blank spaces for information to be inserted. **b** a regularly drawn document. **6** esp. *Brit.* a class in a school. **7** a customary method; what is usually done (*common form*). **8** a set order of words; a formula. **9** behaviour according to a rule or custom. **10** (prec. by *the*) correct procedure (*knows the form*). **11 a** (of an athlete, horse, etc.) condition of health and training (*is in top form*). **b** *Racing* details of previous performances. **12** general state or disposition (*was in great form*). **13** *sl.* a criminal record. **14** formality or mere ceremony. **15** *Gram.* **a** one of the ways in which a word may be spelt or pronounced or inflected. **b** the external characteristics of words apart from meaning. **16** arrangement and style in literary or musical composition. **17** *Philos.* the essential nature of a species or thing. **18** a long bench without a back. **19** esp. *US Printing* = FORME. **20** a hare's lair. **21** = FORMWORK. ● *v.* **1** *tr.* make or fashion into a certain shape or form. **2** *intr.* take a certain shape; be formed. **3** *tr.* be the material of; make up or constitute (*together form a unit*; *forms part of the structure*). **4** *tr.* train or instruct. **5** *tr.* develop or establish as a concept, institution, or practice (*form an idea*; *formed an alliance*; *form a habit*). **6** *tr.* (foll. by *into*) embody, organize. **7** *tr.* articulate (a word). **8** *tr.* & *intr.* (often foll. by *up*) esp. *Mil.* bring or be brought into a certain arrangement or formation. **9** *tr.* construct (a new word) by derivation, inflection, etc. ▫ **bad form** an offence against current social conventions. **form class** *Linguistics* a class of linguistic forms with grammatical or syntactical features in common. **form criticism** textual analysis of the Bible etc. by tracing the history of its content by forms (e.g. proverbs, myths). **form letter** a standardized letter to deal with frequently occurring matters. **good form** what complies with current social conventions. **in form** fit for racing etc. **off form** not playing or performing well. **on form** playing or performing well. **out of form** not fit for racing etc. [ME f. OF *forme* f. L *forma* mould, form]

■ *n.* **1 a** shape, figure; configuration, conformation, order, organization, arrangement, formation, construction, structure, composition. **b** build, shape, physique, body, cut, cast, mould, pattern, frame; silhouette, profile, contour(s); aspect, look, likeness, semblance, guise, appearance. **2** silhouette, figure, shape, image. **3** style, mode, character, manner, fashion, way, nature, state, stamp; aspect, look, likeness, semblance, guise, appearance. **4** type, kind, variety, version, sort, breed, species, genus, genre, make, brand, category, class, classification, order, strain, group, family. **6** class, year, *US* grade. **7** custom, convention, code, rule, procedure, routine, style, tradition, protocol, ritual, observance, practice, technique, way, means, approach, mode, style. **8** form of words; see also FORMULA 3a. **9** behaviour, manners, etiquette, conduct; propriety, seemliness, decency, decorum, convention(s). **10** protocol, practice, routine; see also PROCEDURE 1–3. **11 a** condition, state, order, shape, trim, fettle, health. **12** condition, shape, health; state, disposition, mood, temper. **14** see CEREMONY 2, 3. ● *v.* **1** make, fashion, fabricate, forge, shape, mould, turn, fashion, manufacture, construct, assemble, arrange, organize, cast, compose. **2** develop, grow, arise, appear, materialize, show up, take shape, emerge, spring up, brew; crystallize, *colloq.* jell. **3** make up, constitute, *disp.* comprise; serve as, function as, act as. **4** see INSTRUCT 1. **5** create, originate, establish, generate, devise, invent, design, compose, formulate, coin, concoct, conceive, contrive, dream up; acquire, develop, cultivate, contract. **6** embody; organize, arrange, assemble. **7** articulate, pronounce, utter, voice, vocalize, enunciate; say, speak. □ **bad form** see IMPROPER 1b. **good form** see CORRECT *adj.* 2, 3.

-form /form/ *comb. form* (usu. as **-iform**) forming adjectives meaning: **1** having the form of (*cruciform*; *cuneiform*). **2** having such a number of (*uniform*; *multiform*). [from or after F *-forme* f. L *-formis* f. *forma* FORM]

formal /fórm'l/ *adj.* & *n.* ● *adj.* **1** used or done or held in accordance with rules, convention, or ceremony (*formal dress*; *a formal occasion*). **2** ceremonial; required by convention (*a formal call*). **3** precise or symmetrical (*a formal garden*). **4** prim or stiff in manner. **5** perfunctory, having the form without the spirit. **6** valid or correctly so called because of its form; explicit and definite (*a formal agreement*). **7** in accordance with recognized forms or rules. **8** of or concerned with (outward) form or appearance, esp. as distinct from content or matter. **9** *Logic* concerned with the form and not the matter of reasoning. **10** *Philos.* of the essence of a thing; essential not material. ● *n. US* **1** evening dress. **2** an occasion on which evening dress is worn. □□ **formally** *adv.* **formalness** *n.* [ME f. L *formalis* (as FORM)]

▪ *adj.* **1, 2, 7** correct, proper, set, prescribed, pro forma, formulaic, official, civic, diplomatic, civil, polite, ceremonious; conventional, customary, established; stately, courtly, dignified, solemn, ceremonial; professional, literary, specialized. **3** precise, symmetrical, orderly, ordered, well-ordered. **4** prim, rigid, stiff, exact, punctilious, strict, stilted, starched, straight-laced, stuffy, *colloq.* straight; impersonal, reserved, controlled, measured, reticent; pedantic, hidebound, particular. **5** nominal, perfunctory, routine, official, standard, formulaic. **6** formalized, authorized, official, structured, fixed, valid, authentic, legal, lawful; explicit, express, definite, exact, specific.

formaldehyde /formáldihīd/ *n.* a colourless pungent gas used as a disinfectant and preservative and in the manufacture of synthetic resins. ¶ Chem. formula: CH_2O. Also called METHANAL. [FORMIC (ACID) + ALDEHYDE]

formalin /fórməlin/ *n.* a colourless solution of formaldehyde in water used as a preservative for biological specimens etc.

formalism /fórməliz'm/ *n.* **1 a** excessive adherence to prescribed forms. **b** the use of forms without regard to inner significance. **2** *derog.* an artist's concentration on form at the expense of content. **3** the treatment of mathematics as a manipulation of meaningless symbols. **4** *Theatr.* a symbolic and stylized manner of production. **5** *Physics* & *Math.* the mathematical description of a physical situation etc. □□ **formalist** *n.* **formalistic** /-listik/ *adj.*

formality /formálliti/ *n.* (*pl.* **-ies**) **1 a** a formal or ceremonial act, requirement of etiquette, regulation, or custom (often with an implied lack of real significance). **b** a thing done simply to comply with a rule. **2** the rigid observance of rules or convention. **3** ceremony; elaborate procedure. **4** being formal; precision of manners. **5** stiffness of design. [F *formalité* or med.L *formalitas* (as FORMAL)]

▪ **1** form, (social) convention, practice, procedure, custom, observance, protocol, rule(s), regulation(s), ceremony, rite, ritual; (*formalities*) niceties, proprieties, etiquette, appearances, motions; rigmarole. **2** formalness, strictness, punctilio, exactness, precision, preciseness, correctness, stringency, inflexibility, rigidity. **3** see CEREMONY 2, 3. **4** formalness, *politesse*, punctilio, conformity, propriety, correctness, properness, punctiliousness, niceness, ceremoniousness, courtliness, courtesy, decorum, stateliness, seriousness, stuffiness, stiffness, gravity.

formalize /fórməlīz/ *v.tr.* (also **-ise**) **1** give definite shape or legal formality to. **2** make ceremonious, precise, or rigid; imbue with formalism. □□ **formalization** /-záysh'n/ *n.*

formant /fórmənt/ *n.* **1** the characteristic pitch-constituent of a vowel. **2** a morpheme occurring only in combination in a word or word-stem. [G f. L *formare formant-* to form]

format /fórmat/ *n.* & *v.* ● *n.* **1** the shape and size of a book, periodical, etc. **2** the style or manner of an arrangement or procedure. **3** *Computing* a defined structure for holding data etc. in a record for processing or storage. ● *v.tr.* (**formatted, formatting**) **1** arrange or put into a format. **2** *Computing* prepare (a storage medium) to receive data. [F f. G f. L *formatus* (*liber*) shaped (book), past part. of *formare* FORM]

▪ *n.* **1** shape, size, form, dimension(s), appearance, look, aspect, layout, plan, design, style, pattern, contour(s), composition. **2** structure, method, plan, organization, composition, make-up, constitution, arrangement, configuration, form, framework, system, order, set-up, theme, character, style, manner. ● *v.* **1** see STRUCTURE *v.*

formate see FORMIC ACID.

formation /formáysh'n/ *n.* **1** the act or an instance of forming; the process of being formed. **2** a thing formed. **3** a structure or arrangement of parts. **4** a particular arrangement, e.g. of troops, aircraft in flight, etc. **5** *Geol.* an assemblage of rocks or series of strata having some common characteristic. □□ **formational** *adj.* [ME f. OF *formation* or L *formatio* (as FORM)]

▪ **1, 2** foundation, development, appearance, materialization, generation, creation, genesis, crystallization, origination, fabrication, invention, production, establishment, institution, founding, composition. **3** arrangement, structure, set-up, grouping, organization, configuration, disposition, pattern. **4** configuration, pattern, display, array.

formative /fórmətiv/ *adj.* & *n.* ● *adj.* **1** serving to form or fashion; of formation. **2** *Gram.* (of a flexional or derivative suffix or prefix) used in forming words. ● *n. Gram.* a formative element. □□ **formatively** *adv.* [ME f. OF *formatif -ive* or med.L *formativus* (as FORM)]

▪ *adj.* **1** see SEMINAL 4.

forme /form/ *n.* (*US* **form**: see FORM *n.* 19.) *Printing* **1** a body of type secured in a chase for printing at one impression. **2** a quantity of film arranged for making a plate etc. [var. of FORM]

former[1] /fórmər/ *attrib.adj.* **1** of or occurring in the past or an earlier period (*in former times*). **2** having been previously (*her former husband*). **3** (prec. by *the*; often *absol.*) the first or first mentioned of two (opp. LATTER). [ME f. *forme* first, after FOREMOST]

▪ **1** old, past, bygone, ancient, *archaic* olden; obsolete; earlier, previous, prior; quondam, of old, *literary* of yore. **2** previous, earlier, ex-, one-time, sometime, erstwhile, late, *ci-devant*, *archaic* whilom.

former[2] /fórmər/ *n.* **1** a person or thing that forms. **2** *Electr.* a frame or core for winding a coil on. **3** *Aeron.* a transverse strengthening member in a wing or fuselage. **4** (in *comb.*) a pupil of a specified form in a school (*fourth-former*).

formerly /fórmərli/ *adv.* in the past; in former times.

▪ once, before, previously, long ago, in the past, at one time, in the old days, once upon a time, in days gone by, hitherto, sometime, *ci-devant*, of old, *archaic* erst, erstwhile, *colloq.* way back, *US colloq.* way back when, *formal* heretofore, *literary* of yore.

Formica /formīkə/ *n. propr.* a hard durable plastic laminate used for working surfaces, cupboard doors, etc. [20th c.: orig. uncert.]

formic acid /fórmik/ *n.* a colourless irritant volatile acid (HCOOH) contained in the fluid emitted by some ants. Also called METHANOIC ACID. □□ **formate** /-mayt/ *n.* [L *formica* ant]

formication /fórmikáysh'n/ *n.* a sensation as of ants crawling over the skin. [L *formicatio* f. *formica* ant]

formidable /fórmidəb'l, *disp.* formíddəb'l/ *adj.* **1** inspiring fear or dread. **2** inspiring respect or awe. **3** likely to be hard to overcome, resist, or deal with. □□ **formidableness** *n.* **formidably** *adv.* [F *formidable* or L *formidabilis* f. *formidare* fear]
■ **1** dreadful, fearful, fearsome, frightful, daunting, intimidating, alarming, frightening, startling, appalling, menacing, horrifying, petrifying, terrifying, terrible, shocking, dire. **2** impressive, awesome, awe-inspiring, imposing, redoubtable, *poet.* awful; breathtaking, amazing, marvellous, incredible, unbelievable, astonishing, *colloq.* stunning, mind-boggling. **3** arduous, difficult, daunting, challenging, burdensome, onerous, tough; indomitable, overwhelming, powerful, potent, strong, mighty, forbidding.

formless /fórmliss/ *adj.* shapeless; without determinate or regular form. □□ **formlessly** *adv.* **formlessness** *n.*
■ see SHAPELESS 1, *chaotic* (CHAOS).

formula /fórmyoolə/ *n.* (*pl.* **formulas** or (esp. in senses 1, 2) **formulae** /-lee/) **1** *Chem.* a set of chemical symbols showing the constituents of a substance and their relative proportions. **2** *Math.* a mathematical rule expressed in symbols. **3 a** a fixed form of words, esp. one used on social or ceremonial occasions. **b** a rule unintelligently or slavishly followed; an established or conventional usage. **c** a form of words embodying or enabling agreement, resolution of a dispute, etc. **4 a** a list of ingredients; a recipe. **b** *US* an infant's food made up from a recipe. **5** a classification of racing car, esp. by the engine capacity. □□ **formulaic** /-láyik/ *adj.* **formularize** *v.tr.* (also **-ise**). **formulize** *v.tr.* (also **-ise**). [L, dimin. of *forma* FORM]
■ **3 a** liturgy, rubric, observance, formulation, code; rite, ritual, spell, incantation, chant. **b** rule, protocol, convention, custom, practice, prescription, instruction, direction, directive; plan, routine, method, procedure, convention, form, technique, way, pattern, system, *modus operandi*, code; principle, axiom, theorem. **4 a** recipe, prescription; contents, ingredients.

formulary /fórmyooləri/ *n.* & *adj.* ● *n.* (*pl.* **-ies**) **1** a collection of formulas or set forms, esp. for religious use. **2** *Pharm.* a compendium of formulae used in the preparation of medicinal drugs. ● *adj.* **1** using formulae. **2** in or of formulae. [(n.) F *formulaire* or f. med.L *formularius* (*liber* book) f. L (as FORMULA): (adj.) f. FORMULA]

formulate /fórmyoolayt/ *v.tr.* **1** express in a formula. **2** express clearly and precisely. **3** create or devise (a plan etc.). □□ **formulation** /-láysh'n/ *n.*
■ **1** programme, systematize, codify, shape, draft, develop, work out, form, frame, map out, block out, draw up; arrange, cast. **2** express, define, specify, particularize, articulate, vocalize, enunciate, pronounce, phrase, delineate. **3** devise, originate, initiate, create, dream up, hatch (up), conceive, concoct, invent, compose, improvise, *colloq.* think up, cook up.

formulism /fórmyooliz'm/ *n.* adherence to or dependence on conventional formulas. □□ **formulist** *n.* **formulistic** /-lístik/ *adj.*

formwork /fórmwurk/ *n.* = SHUTTERING 1.

fornicate /fórnikayt/ *v.intr. archaic* or *joc.* (of people not married or not married to each other) have sexual intercourse voluntarily. □□ **fornication** /-káysh'n/ *n.* **fornicator** *n.* [eccl.L *fornicari* f. L *fornix -icis* brothel]

forrader /fórrədər/ *colloq. compar.* of FORWARD.

forsake /fərsáyk/ *v.tr.* (*past* **forsook** /-sŏŏk/; *past part.* **forsaken** /-sáykən/) **1** give up; break off from; renounce. **2** withdraw one's help, friendship, or companionship from; desert, abandon. □□ **forsakenness** *n.* **forsaker** *n.* [OE *forsacan* deny, renounce, refuse, f. WG; cf. OE *sacan* quarrel]
■ **1** give up, abstain from, relinquish, yield, forgo, waive, forfeit, resign, abdicate, secede from, surrender; renounce, reject, jettison, repudiate; abandon, pull out of, withdraw from, break off with, break with, have *or* be done with, quit, leave, flee, depart from, vacate, *sl.* jack in. **2** abandon, desert, leave, maroon, jilt, reject, rebuff, snub, turn one's back on, leave in the lurch, brush off, drop, throw over, cast off *or* aside, *colloq.* dump, *sl.* ditch.

forsooth /fərsŏŏth/ *adv. archaic* or *joc.* truly; in truth; no doubt. [OE *forsōth* (as FOR, SOOTH)]

forswear /fórswáir/ *v.tr.* (*past* **forswore** /-swór/; *past part.* **forsworn** /-swórn/) **1** abjure; renounce on oath. **2** (in *refl.* or *passive*) swear falsely; commit perjury. [OE *forswerian* (as FOR-, SWEAR)]
■ **1** see FORGO, RECANT 1.

forsythia /forsīthiə/ *n.* any ornamental shrub of the genus *Forsythia* bearing bright-yellow flowers in early spring. [mod.L f. W. *Forsyth*, Engl. botanist d. 1804]

fort /fort/ *n.* **1** a fortified building or position. **2** *hist.* a trading-station, orig. fortified. [F *fort* or It. *forte* f. L *fortis* strong]

forte[1] /fórtay/ *n.* **1** a person's strong point; a thing in which a person excels. **2** *Fencing* the part of a sword-blade from the hilt to the middle (cf. FOIBLE 2). [F *fort* strong f. L *fortis*]
■ **1** strong point, speciality, long *or* strong suit, strength, *métier*, *esp. US* specialty; talent, gift, skill, knack, genius, flair, expertise.

forte[2] /fórti/ *adj.*, *adv.*, & *n. Mus.* ● *adj.* performed loudly. ● *adv.* loudly. ● *n.* a passage to be performed loudly. □ **forte piano** *adj.* & *adv.* loud and then immediately soft. [It., = strong, loud]

fortepiano /fórtipiánnō/ *n.* (*pl.* **-os**) *Mus.* = PIANOFORTE esp. with ref. to an instrument of the 18th to early 19th c. [FORTE[2] + PIANO[2]]

forth /forth/ *adv. archaic* except in set phrases and after certain verbs, esp. *bring*, *come*, *go*, and *set*. **1** forward; into view. **2** onwards in time (*from this time forth*; *henceforth*). **3** forwards. **4** out from a starting-point (*set forth*). □ **and so forth** and so on; and the like. [OE f. Gmc]
■ **1, 3** see FORWARD *adv.* 2. **2** see ONWARD *adv.*

forthcoming /fórthkúmming/ *attrib. adj.* **1 a** about or likely to appear or become available. **b** approaching. **2** produced when wanted (*no reply was forthcoming*). **3** (of a person) informative, responsive. □□ **forthcomingness** *n.*
■ **1** impending, approaching, coming, imminent, prospective, *esp. US* upcoming; near, pending, at hand, in the offing, on the horizon, in store, *archaic or dial.* nigh, *colloq.* just round the corner; likely, probable, possible, on (*US* in) the cards. **3** informative, responsive, outgoing, approachable, expansive, communicative, open, frank, candid, unreserved.

forthright *adj.* & *adv.* ● *adj.* /fórthrīt/ **1** direct and outspoken; straightforward. **2** decisive, unhesitating. ● *adv.* /forthrīt/ in a direct manner; bluntly. □□ **forthrightly** *adv.* **forthrightness** *n.* [OE *forthriht* (as FORTH, RIGHT)]
■ *adj.* **1** straightforward, straight, direct, blunt, outspoken, plain-spoken, plain, explicit, unequivocal, candid, frank, honest, ingenuous, above-board, open, truthful, *colloq.* upfront; uninhibited, unreserved, unconstrained, unrestrained. **2** see UNHESITATING.

forthwith /fórthwíth, -wíth/ *adv.* immediately; without delay. [earlier *forthwithal* (as FORTH, WITH, ALL)]

fortification /fórtifikáysh'n/ *n.* **1** the act or an instance of fortifying; the process of being fortified. **2** *Mil.* **a** the art or science of fortifying. **b** (usu. in *pl.*) defensive works fortifying a position. [ME f. F f. LL *fortificatio -onis* act of strengthening (as FORTIFY)]

fortify /fórtifī/ *v.tr.* (**-ies**, **-ied**) **1** provide or equip with defensive works so as to strengthen against attack. **2** strengthen or invigorate physically, mentally, or morally. **3** strengthen the structure of. **4** strengthen (wine) with alcohol. **5** increase the nutritive value of (food, esp. with vitamins). □□ **fortifiable** *adj.* **fortifier** *n.* [ME f. OF *fortifier* f. LL *fortificare* f. L *fortis* strong]
■ **1** arm, make ready; defend, strengthen, safeguard, secure, protect, shield, guard. **2** strengthen, invigorate, brace, stimulate, animate, vivify, quicken, enliven,

energize; steel, harden, support, buoy (up), prop (up), uphold, sustain, encourage, hearten, embolden, cheer (on *or* up), uplift, inspire, reassure, *colloq.* boost. **3** reinforce, strengthen, toughen, brace, harden, stay, prop (up), shore (up), buttress (up), brace, bolster (up), *literary* stay. **4, 5** supplement, enhance, enrich, augment, lace, *colloq.* boost, spike.

fortissimo /fortíssimō/ *adj.*, *adv.*, & *n. Mus.* ● *adj.* performed very loudly. ● *adv.* very loudly. ● *n.* (*pl.* **-os** or **fortissimi** /-mee/) a passage to be performed very loudly. [It., superl. of FORTE[2]]
■ *adj.* see LOUD *adj.* 1.

fortitude /fórtityo͞od/ *n.* courage in pain or adversity. [ME f. F f. L *fortitudo -dinis* f. *fortis* strong]
■ courage, bravery, daring, valour, boldness, intrepidity, stalwartness, stout-heartedness, resoluteness, resolution, pluck, nerve, mettle, *colloq.* grit, guts; stoicism, strength, backbone, endurance, will-power.

fortnight /fórtnīt/ *n.* **1** a period of two weeks. **2** (prec. by a specified day) two weeks after (that day) (*Tuesday fortnight*). [OE *fēowertīene niht* fourteen nights]

fortnightly /fórtnītli/ *adj.*, *adv.*, & *n.* ● *adj.* done, produced, or occurring once a fortnight. ● *adv.* every fortnight. ● *n.* (*pl.* **-ies**) a magazine etc. issued every fortnight.

Fortran /fórtran/ *n.* (also **FORTRAN**) *Computing* a high-level programming language used esp. for scientific calculations. [*for*mula *tran*slation]

fortress /fórtriss/ *n.* a military stronghold, esp. a strongly fortified town fit for a large garrison. [ME f. OF *forteresse*, ult. f. L *fortis* strong]
■ see STRONGHOLD 1.

fortuitous /fortyo͞o-itəss/ *adj.* due to or characterized by chance; accidental, casual. □□ **fortuitously** *adv.* **fortuitousness** *n.* [L *fortuitus* f. *forte* by chance]
■ see ACCIDENTAL *adj.* 1.

fortuity /fortyo͞o-iti/ *n.* (*pl.* **-ies**) **1** a chance occurrence. **2** accident or chance; fortuitousness.
■ **1** see COINCIDENCE 2. **2** see ACCIDENT 1, 3.

fortunate /fórtyoonət, fórchənət/ *adj.* **1** favoured by fortune; lucky, prosperous. **2** auspicious, favourable. [ME f. L *fortunatus* (as FORTUNE)]
■ **1** lucky, blessed, charmed, favoured; prosperous. **2** advantageous, promising, propitious, auspicious, providential, favourable, opportune, timely, well-timed, happy, serendipitous.

fortunately /fórtyoonətli, fórchənətli/ *adv.* **1** luckily, successfully. **2** (qualifying a whole sentence) it is fortunate that.
■ **1** see *happily* (HAPPY).

fortune /fórtyo͞on, fórcho͞on/ *n.* **1 a** chance or luck as a force in human affairs. **b** a person's destiny. **2** (**Fortune**) this force personified, often as a deity. **3** (in *sing.* or *pl.*) the good or bad luck that befalls a person or an enterprise. **4** good luck. **5** prosperity; a prosperous condition. **6** (also *colloq.* **small fortune**) great wealth; a huge sum of money. □ **fortune-hunter** *colloq.* a person seeking wealth by marriage. **fortune-teller** a person who claims to predict future events in a person's life. **fortune-telling** the practice of this. **make a** (or **one's**) **fortune** acquire wealth or prosperity. **tell a person's fortune** make predictions about a person's future. [ME f. OF f. L *fortuna* luck, chance]
■ **1 a** luck, chance, fate, destiny, hazard, accident, *US* happenstance. **b** destiny, lot, fate, portion, kismet, *Buddhism* & *Hinduism* karma. **2** Fate, Chance, Providence. **3** circumstance(s), experience(s), adventures. **4** good luck, serendipity; fluke, stroke of luck, *colloq.* break. **5** prosperity, wealth, money, affluence, opulence, riches, plenty, *literary* weal; success. **6** *colloq.* packet, pile, *Brit. sl.* bomb; see also MINT[2] *n.* 2. □ **fortune-teller** clairvoyant, soothsayer, psychic, oracle, prophet, diviner, augur, seer, sibyl, haruspex, palmist, prognosticator, *colloq. usu. derog. or joc.* star-gazer; futurologist.

forty /fórti/ *n.* & *adj.* ● *n.* (*pl.* **-ies**) **1** the product of four and ten. **2** a symbol for this (40, xl, XL). **3** (in *pl.*) the numbers from 40 to 49, esp. the years of a century or of a person's life. **4** (**the Forties**) *Brit.* the sea area between the NE coast of Scotland and the SW coast of Norway (so called from its depth of forty fathoms or more). ● *adj.* that amount to forty. □ **forty-first, -second**, etc. the ordinal numbers between fortieth and fiftieth. **forty-five** a gramophone record played at 45 r.p.m. **the Forty-five** the Jacobite rebellion of 1745. **forty-niner** *US* a seeker for gold etc., esp. in the Californian gold-rush of 1849. **forty-one, -two**, etc. the cardinal numbers between forty and fifty. **forty winks** *colloq.* a short sleep. □□ **fortieth** *adj.* & *n.* **fortyfold** *adj.* & *adv.* [OE *fēowertig* (as FOUR, -TY[2])]

forum /fórəm/ *n.* **1** a place of or meeting for public discussion. **2** a periodical etc. giving an opportunity for discussion. **3** a court or tribunal. **4** *hist.* a public square or market-place in an ancient Roman city used for judicial and other business. [L, in sense 4]
■ **1** see DISCUSSION 1. **2** see ORGAN 3.

forward /fórwərd/ *adj.*, *n.*, *adv.*, & *v.* ● *adj.* **1** lying in one's line of motion. **2 a** onward or towards the front. **b** *Naut.* belonging to the fore part of a ship. **3** precocious; bold in manner; presumptuous. **4** *Commerce* relating to future produce, delivery, etc. (*forward contract*). **5 a** advanced; progressing towards or approaching maturity or completion. **b** (of a plant etc.) well advanced or early. ● *n.* an attacking player positioned near the front of a team in football, hockey, etc. ● *adv.* **1** to the front; into prominence (*come forward*; *move forward*). **2** in advance; ahead (*sent them forward*). **3** onward so as to make progress (*not getting any further forward*). **4** towards the future; continuously onwards (*from this time forward*). **5** (also **forwards**) **a** towards the front in the direction one is facing. **b** in the normal direction of motion or of traversal. **c** with continuous forward motion (*backwards and forwards*; *rushing forward*). **6** *Naut.* & *Aeron.* in, near, or towards the bow or nose. ● *v.tr.* **1 a** send (a letter etc.) on to a further destination. **b** dispatch (goods etc.) (*forwarding agent*). **2** help to advance; promote. □ **forward-looking** progressive; favouring change. □□ **forwarder** *n.* **forwardly** *adv.* **forwardness** *n.* (esp. in sense 3 of *adj.*). [OE *forweard*, var. of *forthweard* (as FORTH, -WARD)]
■ *adj.* **1** (up) ahead, in front, *colloq.* up front. **2** advance, front, head, fore; foremost, leading, first; frontal. **3** precocious, presumptuous, presuming, familiar, confident, bold, brazen, audacious, saucy, *colloq.* fresh, pushy. **5** advanced, developed, well-developed, mature, ripe, precocious; early. ● *adv.* **1** ahead, in front, frontward(s), to the fore, up, out, (out) into the open, to the surface, into view, *colloq.* up front. **2** (up) ahead, in advance, in front, at the front, in the lead *or* vanguard, before, to the fore, *archaic* forth; onward(s). **3, 5** along, onward(s), forwards, ahead; in front. ● *v.* **1 a** send on. **b** dispatch, send (on), transmit, post, mail, consign, remit, speed. **2** advance, further, promote, back, champion, favour, foster, support, benefit, aid, assist, help; propose, move, submit, suggest, advocate, recommend. □ **forward-looking** see PROGRESSIVE *adj.* 3.

forwards var. of FORWARD *adv.* 5.

forwent *past* of FORGO.

fossa /fóssə/ *n.* (*pl.* **fossae** /-see/) *Anat.* a shallow depression or cavity. [L, = ditch, fem. past part. of *fodere* dig]

fosse /foss/ *n.* **1** a long narrow trench or excavation, esp. in a fortification. **2** *Anat.* = FOSSA. [ME f. OF f. L *fossa*: see FOSSA]

fossick /fóssik/ *v.intr. Austral.* & *NZ colloq.* **1** (foll. by *about*, *around*) rummage, search. **2** search for gold etc. in abandoned workings. □□ **fossicker** *n.* [19th c.: cf. dial. *fossick* bustle about]

fossil /fóss'l/ *n.* & *adj.* ● *n.* **1** the remains or impression of a (usu. prehistoric) plant or animal hardened in rock (often *attrib.*: *fossil bones*; *fossil shells*). **2** *colloq.* an antiquated or unchanging person or thing. **3** a word that has become

obsolete except in set phrases or forms, e.g. *hue* in *hue and cry*. ● *adj.* **1** of or like a fossil. **2** antiquated; out of date. □ **fossil fuel** a natural fuel such as coal or gas formed in the geological past from the remains of living organisms. **fossil ivory** see IVORY. □□ **fossiliferous** /fóssilíffərəss/ *adj.* **fossilize** *v.tr.* & *intr.* (also **-ise**). **fossilization** /-silīzáysh'n/ *n.* [F *fossile* f. L *fossilis* f. *fodere foss-* dig]
■ *n.* **2** see FOGY. ● *adj.* **2** see ANCIENT[1] *adj.* 2.

fossorial /fosóriəl/ *adj.* **1** (of animals) burrowing. **2** (of limbs etc.) used in burrowing. [med.L *fossorius* f. *fossor* digger (as FOSSIL)]

foster /fóstər/ *v.* & *adj.* ● *v.tr.* **1 a** promote the growth or development of. **b** encourage or harbour (a feeling). **2** (of circumstances) be favourable to. **3 a** bring up (a child that is not one's own by birth). **b** *Brit.* (of a local authority etc.) assign (a child) to be fostered. **4** cherish; have affectionate regard for (an idea, scheme, etc.). ● *adj.* **1** having a family connection by fostering and not by birth (*foster-brother*; *foster-child*; *foster-parent*). **2** involving or concerned with fostering a child (*foster care*; *foster home*). □□ **fosterage** *n.* (esp. in sense 3 of *v.*). **fosterer** *n.* [OE *fōstrian*, *fōster*, rel. to FOOD]
■ *v.* **1 a** promote, encourage, stimulate, favour, further, forward, advance, aid, help, assist. **b** harbour, nurture; encourage, stimulate, arouse, awaken, excite, incite, stir up, inspire, fuel. **2** create, produce, generate, cultivate, encourage, stimulate. **3 a** bring up, rear, raise, take care of, look after, care for. **4** cherish, nurse, harbour, indulge, incubate; see also ENTERTAIN 3.

fosterling /fóstərling/ *n.* a foster-child; a nursling or protégé. [OE *fōsterling* (as FOSTER)]

fouetté /fwetáy/ *n.* *Ballet* a quick whipping movement of the raised leg. [F, past part. of *fouetter* whip]

fought *past* and *past part.* of FIGHT.

foul /fowl/ *adj.*, *n.*, *adv.*, & *v.* ● *adj.* **1** offensive to the senses; loathsome, stinking. **2** dirty, soiled, filthy. **3** *colloq.* revolting, disgusting. **4 a** containing or charged with noxious matter (*foul air*). **b** clogged, choked. **5** morally polluted; disgustingly abusive or offensive (*foul language*; *foul deeds*). **6** unfair; against the rules of a game etc. (*by fair means or foul*). **7** (of the weather) wet, rough, stormy. **8** (of a rope etc.) entangled. **9** (of a ship's bottom) overgrown with weeds, barnacles, etc. ● *n.* **1** *Sport* an unfair or invalid stroke or piece of play. **2** a collision or entanglement, esp. in riding, rowing, or running. **3** a foul thing. ● *adv.* unfairly; contrary to the rules. ● *v.* **1** *tr.* & *intr.* make or become foul or dirty. **2** *tr.* (of an animal) make dirty with excrement. **3 a** *tr.* *Sport* commit a foul against (a player). **b** *intr.* commit a foul. **4 a** *tr.* (often foll. by *up*) cause (an anchor, cable, etc.) to become entangled or muddled. **b** *intr.* become entangled. **5** *tr.* jam or block (a crossing, railway line, or traffic). **6** *tr.* (usu. foll. by *up*) *colloq.* spoil or bungle. **7** *tr.* run foul of; collide with. **8** *tr.* pollute with guilt; dishonour. □ **foul brood** a fatal disease of larval bees caused by bacteria. **foul mouth** a person who uses foul language. **foul play 1** unfair play in games. **2** treacherous or violent activity, esp. murder. **foul-up** a muddled or bungled situation. □□ **foully** *adv.* **foulness** *n.* [OE *fūl* f. Gmc]
■ *adj.* **1** offensive, loathsome, vile, obnoxious, revolting, repulsive, repellent, repugnant, rank, sickening, nauseous, nauseating, *literary* noisome; stinking, malodorous, fetid, rancid, sour, putrid, rotten, smelly, rank. **2** filthy, dirty, grimy, mucky, unclean, squalid, sordid, soiled, *sl.* yucky. **3** revolting, disgusting, nauseating, sickening, repulsive, odious, execrable, detestable, hateful, abominable, hideous, horrid, distasteful, nasty, *colloq.* vile, horrible, beastly, *sl.* gross. **4 a** tainted, adulterated, contaminated, polluted, poisonous, impure, stale, musty, bad, mephitic. **b** choked, clogged (up), blocked, congested, obstructed; overgrown, rank. **5** vile, bad, base, depraved, reprobate, corrupt, squalid, sordid, seamy, shameful, low, sinful, immoral, nefarious, iniquitous, wicked, evil, diabolic, damnable, abominable, vicious, villainous, flagitious, atrocious, monstrous, disgraceful, ignominious; abusive, offensive, dirty, obscene, filthy, scatological, coarse, crude, gross, smutty, lewd, indecent, vulgar, rude, scurrilous, outrageous, profane, blasphemous. **6** dirty, dishonest, fraudulent, two-faced, dishonourable, unfair, unscrupulous, underhand, underhanded, unsporting, unsportsmanlike, double-dealing, *colloq.* crooked, *sl.* bent; illegal, forbidden, prohibited, interdicted. **7** wet, rough, stormy, nasty, violent, atrocious, *colloq.* vile; adverse, hostile. **8** tangly, entangled, tangled, snarled (up), muddled (up), twisted; snagged, enmeshed, ensnared, entrapped, trapped, caught (up). ● *n.* **1** violation, breach, abuse, contravention, professional foul, infringement, infraction. **2** collision, entanglement, *colloq.* snarl-up; see also TANGLE[1] *n.* 1. **3** horror, abomination, anathema; see also *infamy* (INFAMOUS). ● *adv.* foully, unfairly, meanly, dishonestly, fraudulently, shabbily, dirtily, unsportingly; in violation. ● *v.* **1** dirty, defile, soil, besmirch, pollute, contaminate, taint, *poet.* sully, befoul. **4** tangle, entangle, catch (up), snare, ensnare, snarl (up), jam, twist. **5** jam, block, impede, obstruct, choke, stop (up), clog (up). **6** spoil, ruin, bungle, mismanage, mishandle, botch (up), mess up, make a mess of, muff, *colloq.* muck (up), make a muck of, *sl.* louse up, screw up, goof, blow. **7** strike, hit, collide with, bang *or* bump (into), crash *or* run *or* smash *or* slam into, dash against. **8** pollute, shame, degrade, debase, demean, disparage, abase, humiliate, belittle, besmirch, defile, tarnish, smear, taint, blacken, discredit; defame, dishonour, disgrace, sully; desecrate, violate. □ **foul play 1** cheating, unfairness, dirty tricks, dirty work. **2** trickery, perfidy, chicanery, duplicity, deceitfulness, deceit, guile, skulduggery; deception, dirty trick, crime, conspiracy; murder, manslaughter, homicide. **foul-up** see BLUNDER *n.*

foulard /fo͞olaárd/ *n.* **1** a thin soft material of silk or silk and cotton. **2** an article made of this. [F]

foumart /fo͞omaart/ *n.* a polecat. [ME *fulmert* etc. (as FOUL, *mart* MARTEN)]

found[1] *past* and *past part.* of FIND.

found[2] /fownd/ *v.* **1** *tr.* **a** establish (esp. with an endowment). **b** originate or initiate (an institution). **2** *tr.* be the original builder or begin the building of (a town etc.). **3** *tr.* lay the base of (a building etc.). **4** (foll. by *on*, *upon*) **a** *tr.* construct or base (a story, theory, rule, etc.) according to a specified principle or ground. **b** *intr.* have a basis in. □ **founding father** a person associated with a founding, esp. an American statesman at the time of the Revolution. [ME f. OF *fonder* f. L *fundare* f. *fundus* bottom]
■ **1** establish, constitute, set up, originate, institute, initiate, float, launch, organize, inaugurate, pioneer, start, create, begin, bring about, father. **2** build, erect, raise, construct, develop, establish. **4 a** construct, ground, build; rest; see also BASE[1] *v.* 1.

found[3] /fownd/ *v.tr.* **1 a** melt and mould (metal). **b** fuse (materials for glass). **2** make by founding. □□ **founder** *n.* [ME f. OF *fondre* f. L *fundere fus-* pour]

foundation /fowndáysh'n/ *n.* **1 a** the solid ground or base, natural or artificial, on which a building rests. **b** (usu. in *pl.*) the lowest load-bearing part of a building, usu. below ground level. **2** a body or ground on which other parts are overlaid. **3** a basis or underlying principle; groundwork (*the report has no foundation*). **4 a** the act or an instance of establishing or constituting (esp. an endowed institution) on a permanent basis. **b** such an institution, e.g. a monastery, college, or hospital. **5** (in full **foundation garment**) a woman's supporting undergarment, e.g. a corset. □ **foundation cream** a cream used as a base for applying cosmetics. **foundation-stone 1** a stone laid with ceremony to celebrate the founding of a building. **2** the main ground or basis of something. □□ **foundational** *adj.* [ME f. OF *fondation* f. L *fundatio -onis* (as FOUND[2])]
■ **1** base, substructure. **2** background, body, ground, field, infrastructure. **3** basis, base, underlying principle, starting-point, fundamental(s), grounds, groundwork, rationale, justification, *raison d'être*. **4** establishment,

founding, instituting, institution, creation, origination, initiation, setting up, organizing, organization, inauguration, endowment.

founder[1] /fówndər/ *n.* a person who founds an institution. □□ **foundership** *n.*
▪ originator, creator, progenitor, author, framer, father, architect, designer, builder, initiator, establisher.

founder[2] /fówndər/ *v.* & *n.* ● *v.* **1 a** *intr.* (of a ship) fill with water and sink. **b** *tr.* cause (a ship) to founder. **2** *intr.* (of a plan etc.) fail. **3** *intr.* (of earth, a building, etc.) fall down or in, give way. **4 a** *intr.* (of a horse or its rider) fall to the ground, fall from lameness, stick fast in mud etc. **b** *tr.* cause (a horse) to break down, esp. with founder. ● *n.* **1** inflammation of a horse's foot from overwork. **2** rheumatism of the chest-muscles in horses. [ME f. OF *fondrer, esfondrer* submerge, collapse, ult. f. L *fundus* bottom]
▪ *v.* **1 a** sink, go down *or* under, go to Davy Jones's locker, be wrecked *or* destroyed. **2** fail, miscarry, collapse, come to nothing *or* naught, fall through, abort, break down, come to grief, die, *sl.* come a cropper. **3** see *give way* 3 (WAY). **4 a** trip, stumble, lurch, fall, topple (over *or* down), collapse; go lame.

foundling /fówndling/ *n.* an abandoned infant of unknown parentage. [ME, perh. f. obs. *funding* (as FIND, -ING[3]), assim. to -LING[1]]
▪ orphan, waif; stray, outcast.

foundry /fówndri/ *n.* (*pl.* **-ies**) a workshop for or a business of casting metal.
▪ see MILL[1] *n.* 3a.

fount[1] /fownt/ *n. poet.* a spring or fountain; a source. [back-form. f. FOUNTAIN after MOUNT[2]]
▪ see FOUNTAIN 1–3, SPRING *n.* 6.

fount[2] /fownt, font/ *n.* (also **font** /font/) *Printing* a set of type of one face or size. [F *fonte* f. *fondre* FOUND[3]]

fountain /fówntin/ *n.* **1 a** a jet or jets of water made to spout for ornamental purposes or for drinking. **b** a structure provided for this. **2** a structure for the constant public supply of drinking-water. **3** a natural spring of water. **4** a source (in physical or abstract senses). **5** = *soda-fountain.* **6** a reservoir for oil, ink, etc. □ **fountain-head** an original source. **fountain-pen** a pen with a reservoir or cartridge holding ink. □□ **fountained** *adj.* (also in *comb.*). [ME f. OF *fontaine* f. LL *fontana* fem. of L *fontanus* (adj.) f. *fons fontis* a spring]
▪ **1–3** spring, jet, spout, spray, well-spring, well-head, *archaic* well, *poet.* fount. **4** see SPRING *n.* 6, ORIGIN 1. □ **fountain-head** see SOURCE *n.* 1.

four /for/ *n.* & *adj.* ● *n.* **1** one more than three, or six less than ten; the product of two units and two units. **2** a symbol for this (4, iv, IV, rarely iiii, IIII). **3** a size etc. denoted by four. **4** a four-oared rowing-boat or its crew. **5** the time of four o'clock (*is it four yet?*). **6** a card with four pips. **7** a hit at cricket scoring four runs. ● *adj.* that amount to four. □ **four-eyes** *sl.* a person wearing glasses. **four-flush** *US Cards* a poker hand of little value, having four cards of the same suit and one of another. **four-flusher** *US* a bluffer or humbug. **four hundred** *US* the social élite of a community. **four-in-hand 1** a vehicle with four horses driven by one person. **2** *US* a necktie worn with a knot and two hanging ends superposed. **four-leaf** (or **-leaved**) **clover** a clover leaf with four leaflets thought to bring good luck. **four-letter word** any of several short words referring to sexual or excretory functions, regarded as coarse or offensive. **four o'clock** = *marvel of Peru.* **four-part** *Mus.* arranged for four voices to sing or instruments to play. **four-poster** a bed with a post at each corner supporting a canopy. **four-square** *adj.* **1** solidly based. **2** steady, resolute; forthright. **3** square-shaped. ● *adv.* steadily, resolutely. **four-stroke** (of an internal-combustion engine) having a cycle of four strokes (intake, compression, combustion, and exhaust). **four-wheel drive** drive acting on all four wheels of a vehicle. **on all fours** on hands and knees. [OE *fēower* f. Gmc]

fourchette /foorshét/ *n. Anat.* a thin fold of skin at the back of the vulva. [F, dimin. of *fourche* (as FORK)]

fourfold /fórfōld/ *adj.* & *adv.* **1** four times as much or as many. **2** consisting of four parts. **3** amounting to four.

Fourier analysis /fóoriay/ *n. Math.* the resolution of periodic data into harmonic functions using a Fourier series. [J. B. J. *Fourier*, Fr. mathematician d. 1830]

Fourier series /fóoriay/ *n. Math.* an expansion of a periodic function as a series of trigonometric functions.

fourpence /fórpənss/ *n. Brit.* the sum of four pence, esp. before decimalization.

fourpenny /fórpəni/ *adj. Brit.* costing four pence, esp. before decimalization. □ **fourpenny one** *colloq.* a hit or blow.

fourscore /fórskór/ *n. archaic* eighty.

foursome /fórsəm/ *n.* **1** a group of four persons. **2** a golf match between two pairs with partners playing the same ball.

fourteen /fórtéen/ *n.* & *adj.* ● *n.* **1** one more than thirteen, or four more than ten; the product of two units and seven units. **2** a symbol for this (14, xiv, XIV). **3** a size etc. denoted by fourteen. ● *adj.* that amount to fourteen. □□ **fourteenth** *adj.* & *n.* [OE *fēowertīene* (as FOUR, -TEEN)]

fourth /forth/ *n.* & *adj.* ● *n.* **1** the position in a sequence corresponding to that of the number 4 in the sequence 1–4. **2** something occupying this position. **3** the fourth person etc. in a race or competition. **4** each of four equal parts of a thing; a quarter. **5** the fourth (and often highest) in a sequence of gears. **6** *Mus.* **a** an interval or chord spanning four consecutive notes in the diatonic scale (e.g. C to F). **b** a note separated from another by this interval. ● *adj.* that is the fourth. □ **fourth dimension 1** a postulated dimension additional to those determining area and volume. **2** time regarded as equivalent to linear dimensions. **fourth estate** *joc.* the press; journalism. □□ **fourthly** *adv.* [OE *fēortha, fēowertha* f. Gmc]

fovea /fṓviə/ *n.* (*pl.* **foveae** /-vi-ee/) *Anat.* a small depression or pit, esp. the pit in the retina of the eye for focusing images. □□ **foveal** *adj.* **foveate** /-viayt/ *adj.* [L]

fowl /fowl/ *n.* & *v.* (*pl.* same or **fowls**) ● *n.* **1** any domestic cock or hen of various gallinaceous birds, kept for eggs and flesh. **2** the flesh of birds, esp. a domestic cock or hen, as food. **3** *archaic* (except in *comb.* or *collect.*) a bird (*guineafowl; wildfowl*). ● *v.intr.* catch or hunt wildfowl. □ **fowl cholera** see CHOLERA. **fowl pest** an infectious virus disease of fowls. **fowl-run 1** a place where fowls may run. **2** a breeding establishment for fowls. □□ **fowler** *n.* **fowling** *n.* [OE *fugol* f. Gmc]

fox /foks/ *n.* & *v.* ● *n.* **1 a** any of various wild flesh-eating mammals of the dog family, esp. of the genus *Vulpes*, with a sharp snout, bushy tail, and red or grey fur. **b** the fur of a fox. **2** a cunning or sly person. **3** *US sl.* an attractive young woman. ● *v.* **1 a** *intr.* act craftily. **b** *tr.* deceive, baffle, trick. **2** *tr.* (usu. as **foxed** *adj.*) discolour (the leaves of a book, engraving, etc.) with brownish marks. □ **fox-terrier 1** a terrier of a short-haired breed originally used for unearthing foxes. **2** this breed. □□ **foxing** *n.* (in sense 2 of *v.*). **foxlike** *adj.* [OE f. WG]
▪ *n.* **2** see DEVIL *n.* 3b. **3** see *temptress* (TEMPTER 1). ● *v.* **1 b** see FLUMMOX.

foxglove /fóksgluv/ *n.* any tall plant of the genus *Digitalis*, with erect spikes of purple or white flowers like glove-fingers.

foxhole /fóks-hōl/ *n.* **1** *Mil.* a hole in the ground used as a shelter against enemy fire or as a firing-point. **2** a place of refuge or concealment.

foxhound /fóks-hownd/ *n.* a kind of hound bred and trained to hunt foxes.

fox-hunt /fóks-hunt/ *n.* & *v.* ● *n.* **1** the hunting of foxes with hounds. **2** a particular group of people engaged in this. ● *v.intr.* engage in a fox-hunt. □□ **fox-hunter** *n.* **fox-hunting** *n.* & *adj.*

foxtail /fókstayl/ *n.* any of several grasses of the genus *Alopecurus*, with brushlike spikes.

foxtrot /fókstrot/ *n.* & *v.* ● *n.* **1** a ballroom dance with slow and quick steps. **2** the music for this. ● *v.intr.* (**foxtrotted, foxtrotting**) perform this dance.

foxy /fóksi/ *adj.* (**foxier, foxiest**) **1** of or like a fox. **2** sly or cunning. **3** reddish-brown. **4** (of paper) damaged, esp. by mildew. **5** *US sl.* (of a woman) sexually attractive. □□ **foxily** *adv.* **foxiness** *n.*
■ **1** foxlike, vulpine. **2** clever, sly, cunning, wily, crafty, tricky, guileful, devious, slippery, smooth, slick, artful, calculating, designing, plotting, scheming, disingenuous, knowing, shrewd, sharp, astute, *colloq.* shifty, *US colloq.* wise. **3** see RED *adj.* 4. **5** attractive, alluring, seductive, vampish, sexy.

foyer /fóyay/ *n.* the entrance hall or other large area in a hotel, theatre, etc. [F, = hearth, home, ult. f. L *focus* fire]
■ see HALL 1.

FP *abbr.* freezing-point.

fp *abbr.* forte piano.

FPA *abbr.* (in the UK) Family Planning Association.

FPS *abbr.* Fellow of the Pharmaceutical Society of Great Britain.

fps *abbr.* (also **f.p.s.**) **1** feet per second. **2** foot-pound-second.

Fr *symb. Chem.* the element francium.

Fr. *abbr.* (also **Fr**) **1** Father. **2** French.

fr. *abbr.* franc(s).

Fra /fraa/ *n.* a prefixed title given to an Italian monk or friar. [It., abbr. of *frate* brother]

frabjous /frábjəss/ *adj.* delightful, joyous. □□ **frabjously** *adv.* [devised by Lewis Carroll, app. to suggest *fair* and *joyous*]

fracas /frákkaa/ *n.* (*pl.* same /-kaaz/) a noisy disturbance or quarrel. [F f. *fracasser* f. It. *fracassare* make an uproar]
■ disturbance, commotion, fuss, spot of trouble *or* bother, hubbub, hullabaloo, uproar, scramble, turmoil, tumult, free-for-all, riot, fray, brouhaha, mêlée, affray, tussle, Donnybrook, brawl, scuffle, fight, *esp. US* ruckus, *colloq.* scrum, scrap, rumpus, *Brit. colloq.* punch-up, *sl.* rough house, *Brit. sl.* spot of bovver; argument, disagreement, quarrel, dispute, discord, wrangle, altercation, squabble, tiff, *colloq.* row, *Brit. colloq.* barney, *US colloq.* spat.

fraction /fráksh'n/ *n.* **1** a numerical quantity that is not a whole number (e.g. $^1/_2$, 0.5). **2** a small, esp. very small, part, piece, or amount. **3** a portion of a mixture separated by distillation etc. **4** *Polit.* any organized dissentient group, esp. a group of communists in a non-communist organization. **5** the division of the Eucharistic bread. □□ **fractionary** *adj.* **fractionize** *v.tr.* (also **-ise**). [ME f. OF f. LL *fractio -onis* f. L *frangere fract-* break]
■ **2** see SECTION *n.* 2.

fractional /frákshən'l/ *adj.* **1** of or relating to or being a fraction. **2** very slight; incomplete. **3** *Chem.* relating to the separation of parts of a mixture by making use of their different physical properties (*fractional crystallization; fractional distillation*). □□ **fractionalize** *v.tr.* (also **-ise**). **fractionally** *adv.* (esp. in sense 2).
■ **2** see LITTLE *adj.* 1, 2.

fractionate /frákshənayt/ *v.tr.* **1** break up into parts. **2** separate (a mixture) by fractional distillation etc. □□ **fractionation** /-náysh'n/ *n.*

fractious /frákshəss/ *adj.* **1** irritable, peevish. **2** unruly. □□ **fractiously** *adv.* **fractiousness** *n.* [FRACTION in obs. sense 'brawling', prob. after *factious* etc.]
■ **1** see IRRITABLE 1. **2** see UNRULY.

fracto- /fráktō/ *comb. form Meteorol.* (of a cloud form) broken or fragmentary (*fracto-cumulus; fracto-nimbus*). [L *fractus* broken: see FRACTION]

fracture /frákchər/ *n.* & *v.* ● *n.* **1 a** breakage or breaking, esp. of a bone or cartilage. **b** the result of breaking; a crack or split. **2** the surface appearance of a freshly broken rock or mineral. **3** *Linguistics* **a** the substitution of a diphthong for a simple vowel owing to an influence esp. of a following consonant. **b** a diphthong substituted in this way. ● *v.intr.* & *tr.* **1** *Med.* undergo or cause to undergo a fracture. **2** break or cause to break. [ME f. F *fracture* or f. L *fractura* (as FRACTION)]
■ *n.* **1 a** break, breakage, breaking, separation, division. **b** break, crack, split, rupture, breach, cleavage, rift. ● *v.* break, rupture, crack, split, breach, separate, *literary* cleave.

fraenulum /freényooləm/ *n.* (also **frenulum**) (*pl.* **-la** /-lə/) *Anat.* a small fraenum. [mod.L, dimin. of FRAENUM]

fraenum /freénəm/ *n.* (also **frenum**) (*pl.* **-na** /-nə/) *Anat.* a fold of mucous membrane or skin esp. under the tongue, checking the motion of an organ. [L, = bridle]

fragile /frájīl, -jil/ *adj.* **1** easily broken; weak. **2** of delicate frame or constitution; not strong. □□ **fragilely** *adv.* **fragility** /frəjílliti/ *n.* [F *fragile* or L *fragilis* f. *frangere* break]
■ **1** breakable, brittle, rickety, frangible, frail, flimsy, weak, feeble, infirm, decrepit; tenuous, shaky, insubstantial. **2** delicate, dainty, thin, light, slight; frail, weak; see also FEEBLE 2.

fragment *n.* & *v.* ● *n.* /frágmənt/ **1** a part broken off; a detached piece. **2** an isolated or incomplete part. **3** the remains of an otherwise lost or destroyed whole, esp. the extant remains or unfinished portion of a book or work of art. ● *v.tr.* & *intr.* /fragmént/ break or separate into fragments. □□ **fragmental** /-mént'l/ *adj.* **fragmentize** /frágməntīz/ *v.tr.* (also **-ise**). [ME f. F *fragment* or L *fragmentum* (as FRAGILE)]
■ *n.* **1, 2** piece, portion, part, chip, shard, splinter, sliver, scrap, bit, speck, snippet, morsel, crumb, particle, remnant, shred; snatch; (*fragments*) smithereens, debris, remains, *disjecta membra.* ● *v.* break (up), split (up), separate, shatter, splinter, explode, disintegrate; come apart.

fragmentary /frágməntəri, -tri/ *adj.* **1** consisting of fragments. **2** disconnected. **3** *Geol.* composed of fragments of previously existing rocks. □□ **fragmentarily** *adv.*
■ **1** piecemeal, incomplete, sketchy, bitty, scrappy, patchy, skimpy. **2** disconnected, scattered, disjointed; see also INCOHERENT 2.

fragmentation /frágməntáysh'n/ *n.* the process or an instance of breaking into fragments. □ **fragmentation bomb** a bomb designed to break up into small rapidly-moving fragments when exploded.
■ see SEPARATION.

fragrance /fráygrənss/ *n.* **1** sweetness of smell. **2** a sweet scent. [F *fragrance* or L *fragrantia* (as FRAGRANT)]
■ **1** fragrancy, redolence, perfume. **2** fragrancy, scent, aroma, redolence, perfume, balm; bouquet.

fragrancy /fráygrənsi/ *n.* (*pl.* **-ies**) = FRAGRANCE.

fragrant /fráygrənt/ *adj.* sweet-smelling. □□ **fragrantly** *adv.* [ME f. F *fragrant* or L *fragrare* smell sweet]
■ aromatic, redolent, perfumed, odoriferous, ambrosial, sweet-scented, sweet-smelling.

frail /frayl/ *adj.* & *n.* ● *adj.* **1** fragile, delicate. **2** in weak health. **3** morally weak; unable to resist temptation. **4** transient, insubstantial. ● *n. US sl.* a woman. □□ **frailly** *adv.* **frailness** *n.* [ME f. OF *fraile, frele* f. L *fragilis* FRAGILE]
■ *adj.* **1** see FRAGILE 1. **2** ailing, unwell, ill, sick, sickly, poorly, wasting *or* fading away, languishing, infirm, feeble, fragile. **3** susceptible, weak, venal, corruptible; bribable, buyable, purchasable. ● *n.* see WOMAN 1.

frailty /fráylti/ *n.* (*pl.* **-ies**) **1** the condition of being frail. **2** liability to err or yield to temptation. **3** a fault, weakness, or foible. [ME f. OF *frailete* f. L *fragilitas -tatis* (as FRAGILE)]
■ **1** frailness, weakness, infirmity, feebleness, fragility, delicacy. **2** susceptibility, suggestibility, impressionability, vulnerability; fallibility. **3** weakness, foible, flaw, fault, defect, imperfection.

Fraktur /fráktoor/ *n.* a German style of black-letter type. [G]

framboesia /frambeéziə/ *n.* (*US* **frambesia**) *Med.* = YAWS. [mod.L f. F *framboise* raspberry f. L *fraga ambrosia* ambrosial strawberry]

frame /fraym/ *n.* & *v.* ● *n.* **1** a case or border enclosing a picture, window, door, etc. **2** the basic rigid supporting structure of anything, e.g. of a building, motor vehicle, or aircraft. **3** (in *pl.*) the structure of spectacles holding the lenses. **4** a human or animal body, esp. with reference to its size or structure (*his frame shook with laughter*). **5** a framed work or structure (*the frame of heaven*). **6 a** an established order, plan, or system (*the frame of society*). **b** construction, constitution, build. **7** a temporary state (esp. in **frame of mind**). **8** a single complete image or picture on a cinema film or transmitted in a series of lines by television. **9 a** a triangular structure for positioning the balls in snooker etc. **b** the balls positioned in this way. **c** a round of play in snooker etc. **10** *Hort.* a boxlike structure of glass etc. for protecting plants. **11** a removable box of slats for the building of a honeycomb in a beehive. **12** *US sl.* = *frame-up*. ● *v.tr.* **1 a** set in or provide with a frame. **b** serve as a frame for. **2** construct by a combination of parts or in accordance with a design or plan. **3** formulate or devise the essentials of (a complex thing, idea, theory, etc.). **4** (foll. by *to, into*) adapt or fit. **5** *colloq.* concoct a false charge or evidence against; devise a plot with regard to. **6** articulate (words). □ **frame-house** a house constructed of a wooden skeleton covered with boards etc. **frame of reference 1** a set of standards or principles governing behaviour, thought, etc. **2** *Geom.* a system of geometrical axes for defining position. **frame-saw** a saw stretched in a frame to make it rigid. **frame-up** *colloq.* a conspiracy, esp. to make an innocent person appear guilty. □□ **framable** *adj.* **frameless** *adj.* **framer** *n.* [OE *framian* be of service f. *fram* forward: see FROM]

■ *n.* **1** border, casing, mount, edge, edging; setting. **2** framework, framing, body, structure, fabric, shell, form, skeleton, support; chassis; fuselage. **4** physique, build, bone structure, body, skeleton, figure. **6 a** system, form, pattern, scheme, schema, plan, order, organization, framework, scaffolding. **b** structure, construct, construction, build, arrangement, blueprint, design, layout, composition, constitution, context, make-up, configuration. **7** (**frame of mind**) mood, humour, state (of mind), condition, attitude, bent, disposition. ● *v.* **1** enclose, box (in). **2** construct, build, put together, make up, assemble, put up, erect, raise, elevate. **3** make, fashion, form, mould, carve out, forge, originate, set up, create, devise, compose, formulate, put together, conceive, draw up, draft, shape, block out, give form *or* shape to; contrive. **4** (*frame to* or *into*) see ADAPT 1a. □ **frame of reference 1** see CODE *n.* 5. **frame-up** see CONSPIRACY 1.

framework /fráymwurk/ *n.* **1** an essential supporting structure. **2** a basic system.

■ **1** see STRUCTURE *n.* 1b. **2** see FORMAT *n.* 2.

framing /fráyming/ *n.* a framework; a system of frames.

■ see FABRICATION 1.

franc /frangk/ *n.* the chief monetary unit of France, Belgium, Switzerland, Luxembourg, and several other countries. [ME f. OF f. *Francorum Rex* king of the Franks, the legend on the earliest gold coins so called (14th c.): see FRANK]

franchise /fránchīz/ *n.* & *v.* ● *n.* **1 a** the right to vote at State (esp. parliamentary) elections. **b** the principle of qualification for this. **2** full membership of a corporation or State; citizenship. **3** authorization granted to an individual or group by a company to sell its goods or services in a particular way. **4** *hist.* legal immunity or exemption from a burden or jurisdiction. **5** a right or privilege granted to a person or corporation. ● *v.tr.* grant a franchise to. □□ **franchisee** /-zeé/ *n.* **franchiser** *n.* (also **franchisor**). [ME f. OF f. *franc, franche* free: see FRANK]

■ *n.* **1** see SUFFRAGE. **3** see LICENCE 2. **5** see PRIVILEGE *n.* 1a. ● *v.* see CHARTER *v.* 1.

Franciscan /fransískən/ *n.* & *adj.* ● *n.* a friar, sister, or lay member of an order founded in 1209 by St Francis of Assisi (see also *Grey Friar*). ● *adj.* of St Francis or his order. [F *franciscain* f. mod.L *Franciscanus* f. *Franciscus* Francis]

francium /frángkiəm/ *n.* *Chem.* a radioactive metallic element occurring naturally in uranium and thorium ores. ¶ Symb.: **Fr**. [mod.L f. *France* (the discoverer's country)]

Franco- /frángkō/ *comb. form* **1** French; French and (*Franco-German*). **2** regarding France or the French (*Francophile*). [med.L *Francus* FRANK]

francolin /frángkōlin/ *n.* any medium-sized partridge of the genus *Francolinus*. [F f. It. *francolino*]

Francophile /frángkəfīl/ *n.* a person who is fond of France or the French.

francophone /frángkəfōn/ *n.* & *adj.* ● *n.* a French-speaking person. ● *adj.* French-speaking. [FRANCO- + Gk *phōnē* voice]

frangible /fránjib'l/ *adj.* breakable, fragile. [OF *frangible* or med.L *frangibilis* f. L *frangere* to break]

frangipane /fránjipayn/ *n.* **1 a** an almond-flavoured cream or paste. **b** a flan filled with this. **2** = FRANGIPANI. [F prob. f. Marquis *Frangipani*, 16th-c. It. inventor of the perfume]

frangipani /fránjipaáni/ *n.* (*pl.* **frangipanis**) **1** any tree or shrub of the genus *Plumeria*, native to tropical America, esp. *P. rubra* with clusters of fragrant white, pink, or yellow flowers. **2** the perfume from this plant. [var. of FRANGIPANE]

franglais /fróNglay/ *n.* a corrupt version of French using many words and idioms borrowed from English. [F f. *français* French + *anglais* English]

Frank /frangk/ *n.* **1** a member of the Germanic nation or coalition that conquered Gaul in the 6th c. **2** (in the Levant) a person of Western nationality. □□ **Frankish** *adj.* [OE *Franca*, OHG *Franko*, perh. f. the name of a weapon: cf. OE *franca* javelin]

frank /frangk/ *adj.*, *v.*, & *n.* ● *adj.* **1** candid, outspoken (*a frank opinion*). **2** undisguised, avowed (*frank admiration*). **3** ingenuous, open (*a frank face*). **4** *Med.* unmistakable. ● *v.tr.* **1** stamp (a letter) with an official mark (esp. other than a normal postage stamp) to record the payment of postage. **2** *hist.* superscribe (a letter etc.) with a signature ensuring conveyance without charge; send without charge. **3** *archaic* facilitate the coming and going of (a person). ● *n.* **1** a franking signature or mark. **2** a franked cover. □□ **frankable** *adj.* **franker** *n.* **frankness** *n.* [ME f. OF *franc* f. med.L *francus* free, f. FRANK (since only Franks had full freedom in Frankish Gaul)]

■ *adj.* **1** candid, direct, outspoken, blunt, plain-spoken, forthright, *colloq.* upfront; explicit, truthful, *colloq.* on the level. **2** undisguised, avowed, open, free, unreserved, uninhibited, unrestrained, unchecked, unconstrained, unrestricted, unabashed. **3** ingenuous, open, honest, sincere, genuine, candid, naïve, guileless, artless, innocent.

Frankenstein /frángkənstīn/ *n.* (in full **Frankenstein's monster**) a thing that becomes terrifying to its maker; a monster. [Baron *Frankenstein*, a character in and the title of a novel (1818) by Mary Shelley]

frankfurter /frángkfurtər/ *n.* a seasoned smoked sausage made of beef and pork. [G *Frankfurter Wurst* Frankfurt sausage]

frankincense /frángkinsenss/ *n.* an aromatic gum resin obtained from trees of the genus *Boswellia*, used for burning as incense. [ME f. OF *franc encens* pure incense]

franklin /frángklin/ *n.* *hist.* a landowner of free but not noble birth in the 14th and 15th c. in England. [ME *francoleyn* etc. f. AL *francalanus* f. *francalis* held without dues f. *francus* free: see FRANK]

frankly /frángkli/ *adv.* **1** in a frank manner. **2** (qualifying a whole sentence) to be frank.

■ **1** see OPENLY 1.

frantic /frántik/ *adj.* **1** wildly excited; frenzied. **2** characterized by great hurry or anxiety; desperate, violent. **3** *colloq.* extreme; very great. □□ **frantically** *adv.* **franticly** *adv.* **franticness** *n.* [ME *frentik, frantik* f. OF *frenetique* f. L *phreneticus*: see PHRENETIC]

■ **1** frenzied, excited, frenetic, hectic, hysterical, wild, mad, running amok, *literary* infuriate; *colloq.* in a state, all of a dither. **2** desperate, violent; upset, agitated, perturbed, at one's wit's end, disconcerted; overwrought, distraught, beside oneself, berserk, *colloq.* up the wall, in a tizzy.

frap /frap/ *v.tr.* (**frapped, frapping**) *Naut.* bind tightly. [F *frapper* bind, strike]

frappé /fráppay/ *adj.* & *n.* ● *adj.* (esp. of wine) iced, cooled. ● *n.* **1** an iced drink. **2** a soft water-ice. [F, past part. of *frapper* strike, ice (drinks)]

frass /frass/ *n.* **1** a fine powdery refuse left by insects boring. **2** the excrement of insect larvae. [G f. *fressen* devour (as FRET[1])]

fraternal /frətérn'l/ *adj.* **1** of a brother or brothers. **2** suitable to a brother; brotherly. **3** (of twins) developed from separate ova and not necessarily closely similar. **4** *US* of or concerning a fraternity (see FRATERNITY 3). □□ **fraternalism** *n.* **fraternally** *adv.* [med.L *fraternalis* f. L *fraternus* f. *frater* brother]

■ **2** friendly, comradely; see also *brotherly* (BROTHER).

fraternity /frətérniti/ *n.* (*pl.* **-ies**) **1** a religious brotherhood. **2** a group or company with common interests, or of the same professional class. **3** *US* a male students' society in a university or college. **4** being fraternal; brotherliness. [ME f. OF *fraternité* f. L *fraternitas -tatis* (as FRATERNAL)]

■ **1** brotherhood, sodality. **2** community, brotherhood, crowd, set, clique, coterie, circle, society, club, company, guild, clan, league, union, association. **4** brotherliness, fellowship, camaraderie, comradeship, friendship, companionship, association, solidarity, unity, *esprit de corps*, clannishness.

fraternize /fráttərnīz/ *v.intr.* (also **-ise**) (often foll. by *with*) **1** associate; make friends; behave as intimates. **2** (of troops) enter into friendly relations with enemy troops or the inhabitants of an occupied country. □□ **fraternization** /-záysh'n/ *n.* [F *fraterniser* & med.L *fraternizare* f. L *fraternus*: see FRATERNAL]

■ **1** consort, associate, hobnob, mingle, keep company, spend time (together), hang around (with), *sl.* hang out (with); (*fraternize with*) socialize with, go around with, spend time with, mix with, rub shoulders with; take up with, fall in with.

fratricide /frátrisīd/ *n.* **1** the killing of one's brother or sister. **2** a person who does this. □□ **fratricidal** /-sīd'l/ *adj.* [F *fratricide* or LL *fratricidium*, L *fratricida*, f. *frater fratris* brother]

Frau /frow/ *n.* (*pl.* **Frauen** /frówən/) (often as a title) a married or widowed German woman. [G]

fraud /frawd/ *n.* **1** criminal deception; the use of false representations to gain an unjust advantage. **2** a dishonest artifice or trick. **3** a person or thing not fulfilling what is claimed or expected of it. [ME f. OF *fraude* f. L *fraus fraudis*]

■ **1** deception, trickery, cheating, subterfuge, sharp practice, chicanery, deceit, swindling, double-dealing, duplicity, artifice, craft, guile, bluff, humbug, humbuggery, treachery, *colloq.* monkey business, *sl.* funny business, hanky-panky. **2** trick, hoax, swindle, scam, deception, cheat, wile, stratagem, dodge, ruse, sham, fake, flimflam, *colloq.* rip-off, *sl.* gyp, *Austral. sl.* rort, *US sl.* scam. **3** deceiver, trickster, cheat(er), impostor, swindler, charlatan, humbug, sharper, quack, mountebank, fake(r), pretender, bluffer, confidence man, confidence trickster, defrauder, flimflammer, *US* four-flusher, *colloq.* shark, phoney, *sl.* con man, bilker.

fraudulent /fráwdyoolənt/ *adj.* **1** characterized or achieved by fraud. **2** guilty of fraud; intending to deceive. □□ **fraudulence** *n.* **fraudulently** *adv.* [ME f. OF *fraudulent* or L *fraudulentus* (as FRAUD)]

■ **1** fake, counterfeit, forged, false, falsified, spurious, imitation, sham, misleading, pinchbeck, *colloq.* phoney. **2** deceitful, dishonest, deceptive, tricky, artful, crafty, double-dealing, duplicitous, guileful, sharp, shady, *colloq.* crooked, shifty, *sl.* bent.

fraught /frawt/ *adj.* **1** (foll. by *with*) filled or attended with (*fraught with danger*). **2** *colloq.* causing or affected by great anxiety or distress. [ME, past part. of obs. *fraught* (v.) load with cargo f. MDu. *vrachten* f. *vracht* FREIGHT]

■ **1** (*fraught with*) filled with, charged with, attended with, packed with, loaded with, replete with, overflowing with, abundant in. **2** tense, taut, stressed, strained, fretful, anxious; stressful, trying, distressing, distressful, upsetting, nerve-racking, traumatic.

Fräulein /fróylīn/ *n.* (often as a title or form of address) an unmarried (esp. young) German woman. [G, dimin. of FRAU]

Fraunhofer lines /frównhōfər/ *n.pl.* the dark lines visible in solar and stellar spectra. [J. von *Fraunhofer*, Bavarian physicist d. 1826]

fraxinella /fráksinéllə/ *n.* an aromatic plant *Dictamnus albus*, having foliage that emits an ethereal inflammable oil. Also called DITTANY, *gas plant*, *burning bush*. [mod.L, dimin. of L *fraxinus* ash-tree]

fray[1] /fray/ *v.* **1** *tr.* & *intr.* wear through or become worn, esp. (of woven material) unweave at the edges. **2** *intr.* (of nerves, temper, etc.) become strained; deteriorate. [F *frayer* f. L *fricare* rub]

■ **1** shred, wear thin, become threadbare, wear out, rub, unravel.

fray[2] /fray/ *n.* **1** conflict, fighting (*eager for the fray*). **2** a noisy quarrel or brawl. [ME f. *fray* to quarrel f. *affray* (v.) (as AFFRAY)]

■ **1** conflict, fight, fighting, action, battle, war. **2** see FRACAS.

frazil /fráyzil/ *n.* *US* ice crystals that form in a stream or on its bed. [Can.F *frasil* snow floating in the water; cf. F *fraisil* cinders]

frazzle /frázz'l/ *n.* & *v.* *colloq.* ● *n.* a worn or exhausted state (*burnt to a frazzle*). ● *v.tr.* (usu. as **frazzled** *adj.*) wear out; exhaust. [orig. uncert.]

freak /freek/ *n.* & *v.* ● *n.* **1** (also **freak of nature**) a monstrosity; an abnormally developed individual or thing. **2** (often *attrib.*) an abnormal, irregular, or bizarre occurrence (*a freak storm*). **3** *colloq.* **a** an unconventional person. **b** a person with a specified enthusiasm or interest (*health freak*). **c** a person who undergoes hallucinations; a drug addict (see sense 2 of *v.*). **4 a** a caprice or vagary. **b** capriciousness. ● *v.* (often foll. by *out*) *colloq.* **1** *intr.* & *tr.* become or make very angry. **2** *intr.* & *tr.* undergo or cause to undergo hallucinations or a strong emotional experience, esp. from use of narcotics. **3** *intr.* adopt a wildly unconventional lifestyle. □ **freak-out** *colloq.* an act of freaking out; a hallucinatory or strong emotional experience. [16th c.: prob. f. dial.]

■ *n.* **1** monstrosity, mutant, *lusus* (*naturae*); see also MONSTER 3, 4. **2** anomaly, rarity, abnormality, irregularity, oddity, curiosity, quirk, *rara avis*, rare bird, *colloq.* one-off; (*attrib.*) freakish, freaky, abnormal, anomalous, extraordinary, unique, rare, atypical, unusual, odd, queer, strange, exceptional, bizarre, weird, unparalleled, unforeseen, unexpected, unpredicted, unpredictable, *colloq.* one-off. **3 b** enthusiast, fan, devotee, aficionado, *colloq.* buff; fanatic, addict, *sl.* fiend, nut. **4 a** whim, caprice, vagary, crotchet, eccentricity, fancy, idiosyncrasy, peculiarity. ● *v.* **1** see RAGE *v.*, ANGER *v.* □ **freak-out** see TANTRUM, EXPERIENCE *n.* 3a.

freakish /fréekish/ *adj.* **1** of or like a freak. **2** bizarre, unconventional. □□ **freakishly** *adv.* **freakishness** *n.*

■ **1** see GROTESQUE *adj.* 1. **2** see BIZARRE.

freaky /fréeki/ *adj.* (**freakier, freakiest**) = FREAKISH. □□ **freakily** *adv.* **freakiness** *n.*

freckle /frékk'l/ *n.* & *v.* ● *n.* (often in *pl.*) a light brown spot on the skin, usu. caused by exposure to the sun. ● *v.* **1** *tr.* (usu. as **freckled** *adj.*) spot with freckles. **2** *intr.* be spotted with freckles. □□ **freckly** *adj.* [ME *fracel* etc. f. dial. *freken* f. ON *freknur* (pl.)]

free /free/ *adj.*, *adv.*, & *v.* ● *adj.* (**freer** /fréeər/; **freest** /frée-ist/) **1** not in bondage to or under the control of another; having personal rights and social and political liberty. **2** (of a State, or its citizens or institutions) subject neither to foreign domination nor to despotic government; having national and civil liberty (*a free press*; *a free society*). **3 a** unrestricted, unimpeded; not restrained or fixed. **b** at liberty; not confined or imprisoned. **c** released from ties or duties; unimpeded. **d** unrestrained as to action; independent (*set free*). **4** (foll. by *of, from*) **a** not subject to; exempt from (*free of tax*). **b** not containing or subject to a specified (usu. undesirable) thing (*free of preservatives*; *free from disease*). **5** (foll. by *to* + infin.) able or permitted to take a specified action (*you are free to choose*). **6** unconstrained (*free gestures*). **7 a** available without charge; costing nothing. **b** not subject to tax, duty, trade-restraint, or fees. **8 a** clear of engagements or obligations (*are you free tomorrow?*). **b** not occupied or in use (*the bathroom is free now*). **c** clear of obstructions. **9** spontaneous, unforced (*free compliments*). **10** open to all comers. **11** lavish, profuse; using or used without restraint (*very free with their money*). **12** frank, unreserved. **13** (of a literary style) not observing the strict laws of form. **14** (of a translation) conveying the broad sense; not literal. **15** forward, familiar, impudent. **16** (of talk, stories, etc.) slightly indecent. **17** *Physics* **a** not modified by an external force. **b** not bound in an atom or molecule. **18** *Chem.* not combined (*free oxygen*). **19** (of power or energy) disengaged or available. ● *adv.* **1** in a free manner. **2** without cost or payment. **3** *Naut.* not close-hauled. ● *v.tr.* **1** make free; set at liberty. **2** (foll. by *of, from*) relieve from (something undesirable). **3** disengage, disentangle. □ **free agent** a person with freedom of action. **free and easy** informal, unceremonious. **free association** *Psychol.* a method of investigating a person's unconscious by eliciting from him or her spontaneous associations with ideas proposed by the examiner. **free-born** inheriting a citizen's rights and liberty. **Free Church** a Church dissenting or seceding from an established Church. **free enterprise** a system in which private business operates in competition and largely free of State control. **free fall** movement under the force of gravity only, esp.: **1** the part of a parachute descent before the parachute opens. **2** the movement of a spacecraft in space without thrust from the engines. **free fight** a general fight in which all present join. **free-for-all** a free fight, unrestricted discussion, etc. **free-form** (*attrib.*) of an irregular shape or structure. **free hand** freedom to act at one's own discretion (see also FREEHAND). **free-handed** generous. **free-handedly** generously. **free-handedness** generosity. **free house** *Brit.* an inn or public house not controlled by a brewery and therefore not restricted to selling particular brands of beer or liquor. **free kick** *Football* a set kick allowed to be taken by one side without interference from the other. **free labour** the labour of workmen not in a trade union. **free-living 1** indulgence in pleasures, esp. that of eating. **2** *Biol.* living freely and independently; not attached to a substrate. **free love** sexual relations according to choice and unrestricted by marriage. **free market** a market in which prices are determined by unrestricted competition. **free on board** (or **rail**) without charge for delivery to a ship or railway wagon. **free pass** an authorization of free admission, travel, etc. **free port 1** a port area where goods in transit are exempt from customs duty. **2** a port open to all traders. **free radical** *Chem.* an unchanged atom or group of atoms with one or more unpaired electrons. **free-range** esp. *Brit.* (of hens etc.) kept in natural conditions with freedom of movement. **free rein** see REIN. **free school 1** a school for which no fees are charged. **2** a school run on the basis of freedom from restriction for the pupils. **free speech** the right to express opinions freely. **free-spoken** speaking candidly; not concealing one's opinions. **free-standing** not supported by another structure. **free trade** international trade left to its natural course without restriction on imports or exports. **free verse** = VERS LIBRE. **free vote** a Parliamentary vote not subject to party discipline. **free wheel** the driving wheel of a bicycle, able to revolve with the pedals at rest. **free-wheel** *v.intr.* **1** ride a bicycle with the pedals at rest, esp. downhill. **2** move or act without constraint or effort. **free will 1** the power of acting without the constraint of necessity or fate. **2** the ability to act at one's own discretion (*I did it of my own free will*). **free world** esp. *US* the non-Communist countries. □□ **freely** *adv.* **freeness** *n.* [OE *frēo, frēon* f. Gmc]

■ *adj.* **1** free-born. **2** independent, self-governing, self-governed, self-ruling, autonomous, democratic, sovereign. **3 a** unrestricted, unimpeded, unrestrained, untrammelled, unconstrained, uncontrolled, unencumbered; relaxed, casual, informal, free and easy, easy, natural, unceremonious, *colloq.* laid-back. **b** at liberty, at large, loose, out, unconfined, unfettered, unchained, unshackled, *sl.* sprung. **c** liberated, set free, let go, let off, emancipated, delivered, unshackled, unfettered, released, freed, *hist.* manumitted. **d** unattached, unconstrained, loose, independent, on the loose. **4** (*free of* or *from*) rid of, exempt(ed) from, relieved of, safe from, not liable *or* subject to, immune from, unaffected by, above, without, untouched by. **5** able, permitted, allowed, within one's rights. **6** unconstrained, unrestrained, relaxed. **7** cost-free, free of charge, complimentary, gratis, gratuitous, for nothing, without cost (or obligation), on the house, *Brit. sl.* buckshee. **8 a** at liberty; not busy, unoccupied, unengaged, available, accessible. **b** vacant, empty, not in use; unused, spare, extra; uninhabited, untenanted. **c** clear, empty; see also UNIMPEDED. **9** spontaneous, unforced, unasked for, unsolicited, unbidden, voluntary, unconditioned, unconditional; gratuitous. **10** see OPEN *adj.* 9–11. **11** generous, lavish, open, liberal, munificent, unstinting, bountiful, open-handed, unsparing; charitable. **12** frank, candid, plain, straight, unreserved, open, direct, outspoken, uninhibited. **15** forward, impudent; see also FAMILIAR *adj.* 4. **16** see INDECENT. ● *adv.* **1** freely, openly, at will, unrestrictedly, loose; loosely. **2** gratis, at no cost, free of charge, without charge. ● *v.* **1** set free, make free, set at liberty, release, let go, liberate, let out, let loose, emancipate, pardon, parole, furlough, *hist.* enfranchise, manumit, *literary* disenthral; unloose, unchain, unfetter, uncage. **2** relieve, rid, unburden, disburden, discharge, disencumber, unbosom; rescue, redeem. **3** disengage, disentangle, untie, unbind, unfasten, undo, unshackle, unlock, open, release, loose, loosen, detach, extricate. □ **free and easy** see INFORMAL. **free fight** see BRAWL *n.* **free-form** see IRREGULAR 1, 2. **free hand** see CARTE BLANCHE. **free-handed** see GENEROUS 1. **free-living 1** see DISSIPATION 1, GLUTTONY. **free pass** pass, complimentary ticket, *esp. US colloq.* freebie. **free school** non-fee-paying school, *US*, *Austral.*, & *Sc.* public school. **free-spoken** see CANDID 1. **free-wheel 2** coast, drift, idle. **free will 2** see VOLITION. □□ **freely** unrestrainedly, unrestrictedly, without restriction, without let or hindrance, without interference; easily, smoothly, cleanly, unobstructedly; willingly, spontaneously, readily, voluntarily, on one's own, independently, of one's own accord, of one's own volition *or* free will; liberally, lavishly, unreservedly, generously, unstintingly, open-handedly, ungrudgingly, munificently, amply, plentifully, abundantly; candidly, frankly, openly, directly, plainly, outspokenly.

-free /free/ *comb. form* free of or from (*duty-free*; *trouble-free*).

freebase /freebayss/ *n.* & *v. sl.* ● *n.* cocaine that has been purified by heating with ether, and is taken by inhaling the fumes or smoking the residue. ● *v.tr.* purify (cocaine) for smoking or inhaling.

freebie /freebi/ *n.* esp. *US colloq.* a thing provided free of charge. [arbitrary f. FREE]

freeboard /freebord/ *n.* the part of a ship's side between the water-line and the deck.

freebooter /freebōōtər/ *n.* a pirate or lawless adventurer. □□ **freeboot** *v.intr.* [Du. *vrijbuiter* (as FREE, BOOTY): cf. FILIBUSTER]

■ see THIEF.

freedman /freédmən/ *n.* (*pl.* **-men**) an emancipated slave.

freedom /freédəm/ *n.* **1** the condition of being free or unrestricted. **2** personal or civic liberty; absence of slave status. **3** the power of self-determination; the quality of not being controlled by fate or necessity. **4** the state of being free to act (often foll. by *to* + infin.: *we have the freedom to leave*). **5** frankness, outspokenness; undue familiarity. **6** (foll. by *from*) the condition of being exempt from or not subject to (a defect, burden, etc.). **7** (foll. by *of*) **a** full or honorary participation in (membership, privileges, etc.). **b** unrestricted use of (facilities etc.). **8** a privilege possessed by a city or corporation. **9** facility or ease in action. **10** boldness of conception. □ **the four freedoms** freedom of speech and religion, and freedom from fear and want. **freedom fighter** a person who takes part in violent resistance to an established political system etc. [OE *frēodōm* (as FREE, -DOM)]
■ **1, 2** freeness, liberty; release, deliverance, liberation, emancipation, independence, self-government, self-determination, self-direction, autonomy, *hist.* manumission. **3** self-determination, independence. **4** ability, facility, licence, permission, right, privilege, authority, discretion, authorization, power, free hand, *carte blanche*. **5** candour, honesty, openness, frankness, outspokenness, candidness, unconstraint, naturalness; boldness, audacity, audaciousness, forwardness, brazenness, impertinence, impudence, disrespect, arrogance, presumption, presumptuousness, *colloq.* brass, nerve, *sl.* gall. **6** exemption, immunity, deliverance, liberation, relief. **7** range, latitude, scope, play, run, liberty, free use. **9** facility, ease, easiness, effortlessness, simplicity. **10** see CONFIDENCE 2b. □ **freedom fighter** see GUERRILLA.

freehand /freéhand/ *adj.* & *adv.* ● *adj.* (of a drawing or plan etc.) done by hand without special instruments or guides. ● *adv.* in a freehand manner.

freehold /freéhōld/ *n.* & *adj.* ● *n.* **1** tenure of land or property in fee simple or fee tail or for life. **2** land or property or an office held by such tenure. ● *adj.* held by or having the status of freehold. □□ **freeholder** *n.*

freelance /freélaanss/ *n.*, *v.*, & *adv.* ● *n.* **1 a** (also **free-lancer**) a person, usu. self-employed, offering services on a temporary basis, esp. to several businesses etc. for particular assignments. **b** (*attrib.*) (*a freelance editor*). **2** (usu. **free lance**) *hist.* a medieval mercenary. ● *v.intr.* act as a freelance. ● *adv.* as a freelance. [19th c.: orig. in sense 2 of *n.*]

freeloader /freélōdər/ *n. US sl.* a person who eats or drinks at others' expense; a sponger. □□ **freeload** /-lṓd/ *v.intr.*
■ see PARASITE.

freeman /freémən/ *n.* (*pl.* **-men**) **1** a person who has the freedom of a city, company, etc. **2** a person who is not a slave or serf.

freemartin /freémaartin/ *n.* a hermaphrodite or imperfect female calf of oppositely sexed twins. [17th c.: orig. unkn.]

Freemason /freémays'n/ *n.* a member of an international fraternity for mutual help and fellowship (the *Free and Accepted Masons*), with elaborate secret rituals.

Freemasonry /freémaysənri/ *n.* **1** the system and institutions of the Freemasons. **2** (**freemasonry**) instinctive sympathy or understanding.

freepost /freépōst/ *n.* a system of sending business post in envelopes prepaid by the recipient.

freer *compar.* of FREE.

freesia /freézyə, -zhə/ *n.* any bulbous plant of the genus *Freesia*, native to Africa, having fragrant coloured flowers. [mod.L f. F. H. T. *Freese*, Ger. physician d. 1876]

freest *superl.* of FREE.

freestone /freéstōn/ *n.* **1** any fine-grained stone which can be cut easily, esp. sandstone or limestone. **2** a stone-fruit, esp. a peach, in which the stone is loose when the fruit is ripe (cf. CLINGSTONE).

freestyle /freéstīl/ *adj.* (of a race or contest) in which all styles are allowed, esp.: **1** *Swimming* in which any stroke may be used. **2** *Wrestling* with few restrictions on the holds permitted.

freethinker /freéthingkər/ *n.* a person who rejects dogma or authority, esp. in religious belief. □□ **freethinking** *n.* & *adj.*
■ see *individualist* (INDIVIDUALISM), LIBERAL *n.* 1, NON-BELIEVER.

freeware /freéwair/ *n. Computing* software that is distributed free and without technical support to users. [FREE + SOFTWARE]

freeway /freéway/ *n. US* **1** an express highway, esp. with controlled access. **2** a toll-free highway.

freeze /freez/ *v.* & *n.* ● *v.* (*past* **froze** /frōz/; *past part.* **frozen** /frṓz'n/) **1** *tr.* & *intr.* **a** turn or be turned into ice or another solid by cold. **b** (often foll. by *over*, *up*) make or become rigid or solid as a result of the cold. **2** *intr.* be or feel very cold. **3** *tr.* & *intr.* cover or become covered with ice. **4** *intr.* (foll. by *to*, *together*) adhere or be fastened by frost (*the curtains froze to the window*). **5** *tr.* preserve (food) by refrigeration below freezing-point. **6** *tr.* & *intr.* **a** make or become motionless or powerless through fear, surprise, etc. **b** react or cause to react with sudden aloofness or detachment. **7** *tr.* stiffen or harden, injure or kill, by chilling (*frozen to death*). **8** *tr.* make (credits, assets, etc.) temporarily or permanently unrealizable. **9** *tr.* fix or stabilize (prices, wages, etc.) at a certain level. **10** *tr.* arrest (an action) at a certain stage of development. **11** *tr.* arrest (a movement in a film) by repeating a frame or stopping the film at a frame. ● *n.* **1** a state of frost; a period or the coming of frost or very cold weather. **2** the fixing or stabilization of prices, wages, etc. **3** a film-shot in which movement is arrested by the repetition of a frame. □ **freeze-dry** (**-dries**, **-dried**) freeze and dry by the sublimation of ice in a high vacuum. **freeze-frame** = sense 3 of *n.* **freeze on to** *colloq.* take or keep tight hold of. **freeze out** *US colloq.* exclude from business, society, etc. by competition or boycott etc. **freeze up** obstruct or be obstructed by the formation of ice. **freeze-up** *n.* a period or conditions of extreme cold. **freezing-mixture** salt and snow or some other mixture used to freeze liquids. **freezing-point** the temperature at which a liquid, esp. water, freezes. **freezing works** *Austral.* & *NZ* a place where animals are slaughtered and carcasses frozen for export. **frozen mitt** *colloq.* a cool reception. □□ **freezable** *adj.* **frozenly** *adv.* [OE *frēosan* f. Gmc]
■ *v.* **1 a** ice; solidify, congeal, harden, stiffen. **b** ice. **2** be cold *or* icy *or* freezing *or* frozen *or* perished *or* perishing *or* chilled to the bone. **6 a** fix, immobilize, paralyse, stop (dead), pin, transfix, gorgonize, *archaic or literary* stay. **b** see *pull back*. **10** see ARREST *v.* 2. ● *n.* **1** frost, freeze-up. **2** immobilization, stabilization. □ **freeze on to** see CLUTCH[1] *v.* 1. **freeze out** exclude, debar, ban, reject, ostracize; eject, drive away *or* out, expel, force out. **freeze-up** freeze, frost. **frozen mitt** cold shoulder, spurning; see also REBUFF *n.*

freezer /freézər/ *n.* a refrigerated cabinet or room for preserving food at very low temperatures; = DEEP-FREEZE *n.*

freight /frayt/ *n.* & *v.* ● *n.* **1** the transport of goods in containers or by water or air or *US* by land. **2** goods transported; cargo. **3** a charge for transportation of goods. **4** the hire of a ship or aircraft for transporting goods. **5** a load or burden. ● *v.tr.* **1** transport (goods) as freight. **2** load with freight. **3** hire or let out (a ship) for the carriage of goods and passengers. □ **freight ton** see TON[1]. [MDu., MLG *vrecht* var. of *vracht*: cf. FRAUGHT]
■ *n.* **1** transport, transportation, carriage, conveyance, shipping, shipment, freightage. **2** goods, cargo, freightage; load, shipload, lorry-load, consignment, payload. **3** freightage, tonnage. **5** see LOAD *n.* 3. ● *v.* **1** see TRANSPORT *v.* 1. **2** see LOAD *v.* 1.

freightage /fráytij/ *n.* **1 a** the transportation of freight. **b** the cost of this. **2** freight transported.

■ **1 a** see FREIGHT *n.* 1. **b** see CARRIAGE 3b. **2** see FREIGHT *n.* 2.

freighter /fráytər/ *n.* **1** a ship or aircraft designed to carry freight. **2** *US* a wagon for freight. **3** a person who loads or charters and loads a ship. **4** a person who consigns goods for carriage inland. **5** a person whose business is to receive and forward freight.

freightliner /fráytlīnər/ *n.* a train carrying goods in containers.

French /french/ *adj.* & *n.* ● *adj.* **1** of or relating to France or its people or language. **2** having the characteristics attributed to the French people. ● *n.* **1** the language of France, also used in Belgium, Switzerland, Canada, and elsewhere. **2** (prec. by *the*; treated as *pl.*) the people of France. **3** *colloq.* bad language (*excuse my French*). **4** *colloq.* dry vermouth (*gin and French*). □ **French bean** *Brit.* **1** a beanplant, *Phaseolus vulgaris*, having many varieties cultivated for their pods and seeds. **2 a** the pod used as food. **b** the seed used as food: also called HARICOT, *kidney bean*. **French bread** white bread in a long crisp loaf. **French Canadian** *n.* a Canadian whose principal language is French. ● *adj.* of or relating to French-speaking Canadians. **French chalk** a kind of steatite used for marking cloth and removing grease and as a dry lubricant. **French cricket** an informal type of cricket without stumps and played with a soft ball. **French cuff** a double cuff formed by turning back a long cuff and fastening it. **French curve** a template used for drawing curved lines. **French door** = *French window*. **French dressing** a salad dressing of vinegar and oil, usu. seasoned. **French fried potatoes** (*US* **French fries**) potato chips. **French horn** a coiled brass wind instrument with a wide bell. **French kiss** a kiss with one partner's tongue inserted in the other's mouth. **French knickers** wide-legged knickers. **French leave** absence without permission. **French letter** *Brit. colloq.* a condom. **French mustard** *Brit.* a mild mustard mixed with vinegar. **French polish** shellac polish for wood. **French-polish** *v.tr.* polish with this. **French roof** a mansard. **French seam** a seam with the raw edges enclosed. **French toast 1** *Brit.* bread buttered on one side and toasted on the other. **2** bread dipped in egg and milk and fried. **French vermouth** dry vermouth. **French window** a glazed door in an outside wall, serving as a window and door. □□ **Frenchness** *n.* [OE *frencisc* f. Gmc]

Frenchify /frénchifī/ *v.tr.* (**-ies, -ied**) (usu. as **Frenchified** *adj.*) make French in form, character, or manners.

Frenchman /frénchmən/ *n.* (*pl.* **-men**) a man who is French by birth or descent.

Frenchwoman /frénchwŏŏmmən/ *n.* (*pl.* **-women**) a woman who is French by birth or descent.

frenetic /frənéttik/ *adj.* **1** frantic, frenzied. **2** fanatic. □□ **frenetically** *adv.* [ME f. OF *frenetique* f. L *phreneticus* f. Gk *phrenitikos* f. *phrenitis* delirium f. *phrēn phrenos* mind]

■ **1** see HECTIC *adj.* 1. **2** see *fanatical* (FANATIC).

frenulum var. of FRAENULUM.

frenum var. of FRAENUM.

frenzy /frénzi/ *n.* & *v.* ● *n.* (*pl.* **-ies**) **1** mental derangement; wild excitement or agitation. **2** delirious fury. ● *v.tr.* (**-ies, -ied**) (usu. as **frenzied** *adj.*) drive to frenzy; infuriate. □□ **frenziedly** *adv.* [ME f. OF *frenesie* f. med.L *phrenesia* f. L *phrenesis* f. Gk *phrēn* mind]

■ *n.* **1** excitement, agitation, fever, passion, turmoil, transport. **2** fury, distraction; paroxysm, outburst, furore, bout, fit. ● *v.* (**frenzied**) see FEVERISH 2.

Freon /fréé-on/ *n. propr.* any of a group of halogenated hydrocarbons containing fluorine, chlorine, and sometimes bromine, used in aerosols, refrigerants, etc. (see also CFC).

frequency /fréékwənsi/ *n.* (*pl.* **-ies**) **1** commonness of occurrence. **2 a** the state of being frequent; frequent occurrence. **b** the process of being repeated at short intervals. **3** *Physics* the rate of recurrence of a vibration, oscillation, cycle, etc.; the number of repetitions in a given time, esp. per second. ¶ Abbr.: *f.* **4** *Statistics* the ratio of the number of actual to possible occurrences of an event. □ **frequency band** *Electronics* = BAND[1] *n.* 3a. **frequency distribution** *Statistics* a measurement of the frequency of occurrence of the values of a variable. **frequency modulation** *Electronics* a modulation in which the frequency of the carrier wave is varied. ¶ Abbr.: **FM. frequency response** *Electronics* the dependence on signal-frequency of the output–input ratio of an amplifier etc. [L *frequentia* (as FREQUENT)]

■ *n.* **1** see INCIDENCE 1.

frequent *adj.* & *v.* ● *adj.* /fréékwənt/ **1** occurring often or in close succession. **2** habitual, constant (*a frequent caller*). **3** found near together; numerous, abundant. **4** (of the pulse) rapid. ● *v.tr.* /frikwént/ attend or go to habitually. □□ **frequentation** /fréékwentáysh'n/ *n.* **frequenter** /frikwéntər/ *n.* **frequently** /fréékwəntli/ *adv.* [F *fréquent* or L *frequens -entis* crowded]

■ *adj.* **1** reiterative, continual. **2** habitual, constant, continual, continuing, recurrent, recurring, regular, familiar, everyday, customary, usual, ordinary, normal, common; persistent. **3** many, numerous, abundant, countless, innumerable, untold, numberless, infinite, *literary* myriad; see also UMPTEEN *adj.* ● *v.* haunt, patronize, visit, resort to, go to *or* attend regularly, *sl.* hang out at. □□ **frequently** often, regularly, continually, repeatedly, over and over (again), again and again, many times, many a time, time after time, time and (time) again, *archaic or literary* oft-times; habitually, customarily, regularly, usually, ordinarily, generally, commonly, as often as not.

frequentative /frikwéntətiv/ *adj.* & *n. Gram.* ● *adj.* expressing frequent repetition or intensity of action. ● *n.* a verb or verbal form or conjugation expressing this (e.g. *chatter*, *twinkle*). [F *fréquentatif -ive* or L *frequentativus* (as FREQUENT)]

fresco /fréskō/ *n.* (*pl.* **-os** or **-oes**) **1** a painting done in water-colour on a wall or ceiling while the plaster is still wet. **2** this method of painting (esp. *in fresco*). □ **fresco secco** = SECCO. □□ **frescoed** *adj.* [It., = cool, fresh]

fresh /fresh/ *adj.*, *adv.*, & *n.* ● *adj.* **1** newly made or obtained (*fresh sandwiches*). **2 a** other, different; not previously known or used (*start a fresh page*; *we need fresh ideas*). **b** additional (*fresh supplies*). **3** (foll. by *from*) lately arrived from (a specified place or situation). **4** not stale or musty or faded (*fresh flowers*; *fresh memories*). **5** (of food) not preserved by salting, tinning, freezing, etc. **6** not salty (*fresh water*). **7 a** pure, untainted, refreshing, invigorating (*fresh air*). **b** bright and pure in colour (*a fresh complexion*). **8** (of the wind) brisk; of fair strength. **9** alert, vigorous, fit (*never felt fresher*). **10** *colloq.* **a** cheeky, presumptuous. **b** amorously impudent. **11** young and inexperienced. ● *adv.* newly, recently (esp. in *comb.*: *fresh-baked*; *fresh-cut*). ● *n.* the fresh part of the day, year, etc. (*in the fresh of the morning*). □□ **freshly** *adv.* **freshness** *n.* [ME f. OF *freis fresche* ult. f. Gmc]

■ *adj.* **1** new, today's, brand-new, most recent, latest. **2 a** new, modern, up to date, recent; novel, original, unusual, unconventional, different, alternative, unorthodox, *derog.* newfangled. **b** additional, new, further, renewed, extra, supplementary. **4** new, recent. **7 a** pure, clean, clear, cool, refreshing, invigorating, untainted, unpolluted; wholesome. **b** bright, pure, glowing, rosy, ruddy, blooming; peaches and cream. **8** moderate, fair, strong; see also BRISK 2. **9** alert, fit, well, refreshed, vigorous, energetic, invigorated, spry, lively, full of vim and vigour, keen, bright, brisk, active, sprightly, flourishing, *colloq.* bright-eyed and bushy-tailed. **10 a** bold, impudent, impertinent, brazen, brassy, forward, disrespectful, saucy, pert, cheeky, presumptuous, insolent, rude, *colloq.* flip, *esp. US colloq.* sassy. **b** see NAUGHTY 2. **11** young, raw, green, naïve, callow, immature, inexperienced, untested, unsophisticated, untried, unfledged, untrained, wet behind the ears. □□ **freshly** newly, recently, just now, (just) a moment ago, fresh.

freshen /frésh'n/ *v.* **1** *tr.* & *intr.* make or become fresh or fresher. **2** *intr.* & *tr.* (foll. by *up*) **a** wash, change one's clothes, etc. **b** revive, refresh, renew.
■ **1** ventilate, air out, deodorize, purify; strengthen, increase, blow harder. **2** (*freshen up*) **a** (have a) wash, *US* wash up; titivate. **b** revive, refresh, renew, enliven, (re)vitalize, stimulate, invigorate, rouse, *colloq.* liven (up).

fresher /fréshər/ *n. Brit. colloq.* = FRESHMAN.

freshet /fréshit/ *n.* **1** a rush of fresh water flowing into the sea. **2** the flood of a river from heavy rain or melted snow. [prob. f. OF *freschete* f. *frais* FRESH]

freshman /fréshmən/ *n.* (*pl.* **-men**) a first-year student at university or *US* at high school.
■ see NEWCOMER 2.

freshwater /fréshwawtər/ *adj.* **1** of or found in fresh water; not of the sea. **2** *US* (esp. of a school or college) rustic or provincial. □ **freshwater flea** = DAPHNIA.

fret[1] /fret/ *v.* & *n.* ● *v.* (**fretted, fretting**) **1** *intr.* **a** be greatly and visibly worried or distressed. **b** be irritated or resentful. **2** *tr.* **a** cause anxiety or distress to. **b** irritate, annoy. **3** *tr.* wear or consume by gnawing or rubbing. **4** *tr.* form (a channel or passage) by wearing away. **5** *intr.* (of running water) flow or rise in little waves. ● *n.* irritation, vexation, querulousness (esp. *in a fret*). [OE *fretan* f. Gmc, rel. to EAT]
■ *v.* **1 a** worry, agonize, grieve, brood, be concerned, be upset, be distressed, be anxious, be disturbed, be in a state, tear one's hair out, *colloq.* stew. **b** see RESENT. **2 a** worry, concern; see also DISTRESS *v.* **b** annoy, irritate, vex, torment, provoke, rankle. **3** see WEAR[1] *v.* 5. **4** furrow, groove, channel, plough, bore. ● *n.* see ANNOYANCE 1.

fret[2] /fret/ *n.* & *v.* ● *n.* **1** an ornamental pattern made of continuous combinations of straight lines joined usu. at right angles. **2** *Heraldry* a device of narrow bands and a diamond interlaced. ● *v.tr.* (**fretted, fretting**) **1** embellish or decorate with a fret. **2** adorn (esp. a ceiling) with carved or embossed work. [ME f. OF *frete* trellis-work and *freter* (v.)]

fret[3] /fret/ *n.* each of a sequence of bars or ridges on the finger-board of some stringed musical instruments (esp. the guitar) fixing the positions of the fingers to produce the desired notes. □□ **fretless** *adj.* [15th c.: orig. unkn.]

fretful /frétfŏŏl/ *adj.* visibly anxious, distressed, or irritated. □□ **fretfully** *adv.* **fretfulness** *n.*
■ anxious, nervous, on edge, edgy, distressed, troubled, bothered, vexed, irritated, irked, upset, cross.

fretsaw /frétsaw/ *n.* a saw consisting of a narrow blade stretched on a frame, for cutting thin wood in patterns.

fretwork /frétwurk/ *n.* ornamental work in wood, done with a fretsaw.

Freudian /fróydiən/ *adj.* & *n. Psychol.* ● *adj.* of or relating to the Austrian psychologist Sigmund Freud (d. 1939) or his methods of psychoanalysis, esp. with reference to the importance of sexuality in human behaviour. ● *n.* a follower of Freud or his methods. □ **Freudian slip** an unintentional error regarded as revealing subconscious feelings. □□ **Freudianism** *n.*

Fri. *abbr.* Friday.

friable /frīəb'l/ *adj.* easily crumbled. □□ **friability** /-bílliti/ *n.* **friableness** *n.* [F *friable* or L *friabilis* f. *friare* crumble]
■ see BRITTLE *adj.* 1.

friar /frīər/ *n.* a member of any of certain religious orders of men, esp. the four mendicant orders (Augustinians, Carmelites, Dominicans, and Franciscans). □ **friar's** (or **friars'**) **balsam** a tincture of benzoin etc. used esp. as an inhalant. □□ **friarly** *adj.* [ME & OF *frere* f. L *frater fratris* brother]
■ see MONK.

friary /frīəri/ *n.* (*pl.* **-ies**) a convent of friars.
■ see MONASTERY.

fricandeau /fríkkəndō/ *n.* & *v.* ● *n.* (*pl.* **fricandeaux** /-dōz/) **1** a cushion-shaped piece of meat, esp. veal, cut from the leg. **2** a dish made from this, usu. fried or stewed and served with a sauce. ● *v.tr.* (**fricandeaus, fricandeaued, fricandeauing**) make into fricandeaux. [F]

fricassee /fríkkəsée/ *n.* & *v.* ● *n.* a dish of stewed or fried pieces of meat served in a thick white sauce. ● *v.tr.* (**fricassees, fricasseed**) make a fricassee of. [F, fem. past part. of *fricasser* (v.)]

fricative /fríkkətiv/ *adj.* & *n. Phonet.* ● *adj.* made by the friction of breath in a narrow opening. ● *n.* a consonant made in this way, e.g. *f* and *th.* [mod.L *fricativus* f. L *fricare* rub]

friction /fríksh'n/ *n.* **1** the action of one object rubbing against another. **2** the resistance an object encounters in moving over another. **3** a clash of wills, temperaments, or opinions; mutual animosity arising from disagreement. **4** (in *comb.*) of devices that transmit motion by frictional contact (*friction-clutch*; *friction-disc*). □ **friction-ball** a ball used in bearings to lessen friction. □□ **frictional** *adj.* **frictionless** *adj.* [F f. L *frictio -onis* f. *fricare frict-* rub]
■ **1** rubbing, scraping, grating, chafing, fretting; abrasion, attrition, erosion. **2** grip. **3** clash, disagreement, discord, conflict, contention, argument, dispute, dissension, disharmony, controversy, wrangle, dissent, bickering, wrangling, ill feeling, ill will, bad feeling, bad blood, animosity, rivalry, hostility, antagonism, strife.

Friday /frīday, -di/ *n.* & *adv.* ● *n.* the sixth day of the week, following Thursday. ● *adv. colloq.* **1** on Friday. **2** (**Fridays**) on Fridays; each Friday. □ **girl** (or **man**) **Friday** a helper or follower (after *Man Friday* in Defoe's *Robinson Crusoe*). [OE *frīgedæg* f. Gmc (named after *Frigg* the wife of Odin)]

fridge /frij/ *n. Brit. colloq.* = REFRIGERATOR. □ **fridge-freezer** an upright unit comprising a refrigerator and a freezer, each self-contained. [abbr.]

friend /frend/ *n.* & *v.* ● *n.* **1** a person with whom one enjoys mutual affection and regard (usu. exclusive of sexual or family bonds). **2** a sympathizer, helper, or patron (*no friend to virtue*; *a friend of order*). **3** a person who is not an enemy or who is on the same side (*friend or foe?*). **4 a** a person already mentioned or under discussion (*my friend at the next table then left the room*). **b** a person known by sight. **c** used as a polite or ironic form of address. **5** (usu. in *pl.*) a regular contributor of money or other assistance to an institution. **6** (**Friend**) a member of the Society of Friends, a Quaker. **7** (in *pl.*) one's near relatives, those responsible for one. **8** a helpful thing or quality. ● *v.tr. archaic* or *poet.* befriend, help. □ **be** (or **keep**) **friends with** be friendly with. **friend at court** a friend whose influence may be made use of. **my honourable friend** *Brit.* used in the House of Commons to refer to another member of one's own party. **my learned friend** used by a lawyer in court to refer to another lawyer. **my noble friend** *Brit.* used in the House of Lords to refer to another member of one's own party. □□ **friended** *adj.* **friendless** *adj.* [OE *frēond* f. Gmc]
■ *n.* **1** (boon) companion, partner, comrade, crony, familiar, confidant, confidante, intimate, *fidus Achates*, *alter ego*, ally, compeer, mate, playmate, *colloq.* chum, pal, *Austral.* & *NZ colloq.* cobber, *esp. US colloq.* (bosom) buddy, *Brit. sl.* (old) cock; pen-friend, *colloq.* pen-pal; lover, sweetheart, escort; girl, girlfriend, lady friend, mistress, concubine; man, boy, boyfriend. **2** see SUPPORTER. **3** see *sympathizer* (SYMPATHIZE). **4 c** see DEAR *n.* **5** benefactor, patron, Maecenas, supporter, adherent, advocate. **7** (*friends*) see FAMILY 1. **8** asset, advantage, strength, benefit, plus, boon. □ **be friends with** see ASSOCIATE *v.* 5.

friendly /fréndli/ *adj.*, *n.*, & *adv.* ● *adj.* (**friendlier, friendliest**) **1** acting as or like a friend, well-disposed, kindly. **2 a** (often foll. by *with*) on amicable terms. **b** not hostile. **3** characteristic of friends, showing or prompted by kindness. **4** favourably disposed, ready to approve or help. **5 a** (of a thing) serviceable, convenient, opportune. **b** = *user-friendly*. ● *n.* (*pl.* **-ies**) = *friendly match*. ● *adv.* in a friendly manner. □ **friendly action** *Law* an action brought merely to get a point decided. **friendly fire** *Mil.* fire coming from one's own side in a conflict, esp. as the cause of accidental injury or damage to one's forces. **friendly match** a match played for enjoyment and not in competition for a cup etc. **Friendly Society** *Brit.* = *benefit society*. □□ **friendlily** *adv.* **friendliness** *n.*

■ *adj.* **1** well-disposed, kindly, kind, kind-hearted, warm-hearted, warm, affectionate, amiable, amicable, cordial, genial, sociable, agreeable, good-natured, pleasant, affable; approachable, accessible, unreserved, demonstrative, open. **2** congenial, companionable, comradely, convivial, familiar, close, on good terms, comfortable, at home, neighbourly, chummy, matey, *esp. US* clubby, *colloq.* pally, thick. **3** see KIND². **4** sympathetic, well-disposed, favourably disposed, supportive, approving, agreeable. **5** serviceable, convenient, useful, helpful, handy, expedient, suitable, *archaic* commodious; see also CONVENIENT 1.

friendship /fréndship/ *n.* **1** being friends, the relationship between friends. **2** a friendly disposition felt or shown. [OE *frēondscipe* (as FRIEND, -SHIP)]

■ **1** amity, harmony, alliance, companionability, comradeship, fellowship, neighbourliness, familiarity, closeness, rapport, intimacy. **2** friendliness, amiability, amicability, congeniality, conviviality, sociability, warmth, devotion, affection, fondness, attachment, esteem, regard.

frier var. of FRYER.

Friesian /fréezh'n, -ziən/ *n.* & *adj. Brit.* ● *n.* **1** a large animal of a usu. black and white breed of dairy cattle orig. from Friesland. **2** this breed. ● *adj.* of or concerning Friesians. [var. of FRISIAN]

frieze¹ /freez/ *n.* **1** *Archit.* the part of an entablature between the architrave and the cornice. **2** *Archit.* a horizontal band of sculpture filling this. **3** a band of decoration elsewhere, esp. along a wall near the ceiling. [F *frise* f. med.L *frisium*, *frigium* f. L *Phrygium* (*opus*) (work) of Phrygia]

■ **3** see BORDER *n.* 3.

frieze² /freez/ *n.* coarse woollen cloth with a nap, usu. on one side only. [ME f. F *frise*, prob. rel. to FRISIAN]

frig¹ /frig/ *v.* & *n. coarse sl.* ¶ Usually considered a taboo word. ● *v.* (**frigged**, **frigging**) **1 a** *tr.* & *intr.* have sexual intercourse (with). **b** masturbate. **2** *tr.* (usu. as an exclamation) = FUCK *v.* 3. **3** *intr.* (foll. by *about, around*) mess about; fool around. **4** *intr.* (foll. by *off*) go away. ● *n.* an act of frigging. [perh. imit.: orig. senses 'move about, rub']

frig² /frij/ *n. Brit. colloq.* = REFRIGERATOR. [abbr.]

frigate /fríggit/ *n.* **1 a** *Brit.* a naval escort-vessel between a corvette and a destroyer in size. **b** *US* a similar ship between a destroyer and a cruiser in size. **2** *hist.* a warship next in size to ships of the line. □ **frigate-bird** any marine bird of the family Fregatidae, found in tropical seas, with a wide wingspan and deeply forked tail: also called *hurricane-bird*. [F *frégate* f. It. *fregata*, of unkn. orig.]

fright /frīt/ *n.* & *v.* ● *n.* **1 a** sudden or extreme fear. **b** an instance of this (*gave me a fright*). **2** a person or thing looking grotesque or ridiculous. ● *v.tr. poet.* frighten. □ **take fright** become frightened. [OE *fryhto*, metathetic form of *fyrhto*, f. Gmc]

■ *n.* **1 a** fear, alarm, terror, horror, panic, trepidation, dread, apprehension, *sl.* (blue) funk. **b** scare, shock, surprise, start. **2** eyesore, mess, disaster, monstrosity, *colloq.* sight. ● *v.* see FRIGHTEN 1, 2.

frighten /frīt'n/ *v.* **1** *tr.* fill with fright; terrify (*was frightened at the bang*; *is frightened of dogs*). **2** *tr.* (foll. by *away, off, out of, into*) drive or force by fright (*frightened it out of the room*; *frightened them into submission*; *frightened me into agreeing*). **3** *intr.* become frightened (*I frighten easily*). □□ **frightening** *adj.* **frighteningly** *adv.*

■ **1** terrify, scare, alarm, intimidate, panic, petrify, horrify, startle, shock, daunt, cow, scare a person out of his *or* her wits, make a person's hair stand on end, scare the (living) daylights out of, scare stiff, *colloq.* put the wind up, *sl.* put the frighteners on, *poet.* fright. **2** scare, terrify, *poet.* fright; see also INTIMIDATE. **3** scare. □□ **frightening** terrifying, alarming, startling, shocking, petrifying, horrifying, daunting, intimidating, formidable, hair-raising, harrowing, dreadful, *colloq.* scary, spooky.

frightener /frīt'nər/ *n.* a person or thing that frightens. □ **put the frighteners on** *sl.* intimidate.

frightful /frītfōōl/ *adj.* **1 a** dreadful, shocking, revolting. **b** ugly, hideous. **2** *colloq.* extremely bad (*a frightful idea*). **3** *colloq.* very great, extreme. □□ **frightfully** *adv.*

■ **1** awful, dreadful, terrible, disagreeable, atrocious, abhorrent, loathsome, grisly, ghastly, lurid, horrible, horrifying, horrid, horrendous, nasty, hideous, vile, unspeakable, nauseating, nauseous, repugnant, repulsive, shocking, revolting, abominable, offensive, ugly. **2** see AWFUL 1a, b. **3** see GREAT *adj.* 1a. □□ **frightfully** very, extremely, *colloq.* awfully; amazingly, surprisingly.

frightfulness /frītfōōlniss/ *n.* **1** being frightful. **2** (transl. G *Schrecklichkeit*) the terrorizing of a civilian population as a military resource.

frigid /fríjid/ *adj.* **1 a** lacking friendliness or enthusiasm; apathetic, formal, forced. **b** dull, flat, insipid. **c** chilling, depressing. **2** (of a woman) sexually unresponsive. **3** (esp. of climate or air) cold. □ **frigid zones** the parts of the earth north of the Arctic Circle and south of the Antarctic Circle. □□ **frigidity** /-jídditi/ *n.* **frigidly** *adv.* **frigidness** *n.* [L *frigidus* f. *frigēre* be cold f. *frigus* (n.) cold]

■ **1 a** cold, cool, cold-hearted, forbidding, austere, unemotional, unfeeling, stiff, rigid, formal, prim, strait-laced, stony, callous, steely, obdurate, thick-skinned, inaccessible, remote, unapproachable, unfriendly, standoffish, haughty, aloof, reserved; apathetic, unenthusiastic; forced. **b** see FLAT¹ *adj.* 3a. **2** unresponsive, cold. **3** cold, frosty, frozen, glacial, icy, hyperborean, polar, boreal, Siberian, freezing, wintry, chilly, *colloq.* arctic, *literary* chill, *poet.* frore.

frijoles /freehōlayss/ *n.pl.* beans. [Sp., pl. of *frijol* bean ult. f. L *phaseolus*]

frill /fril/ *n.* & *v.* ● *n.* **1 a** a strip of material with one side gathered or pleated and the other left loose with a fluted appearance, used as an ornamental edging. **b** a similar paper ornament on a ham-knuckle, chop, etc. **c** a natural fringe of feathers, hair, etc., on an animal (esp. a bird) or a plant. **2** (in *pl.*) **a** unnecessary embellishments or accomplishments. **b** airs, affectation (*put on frills*). ● *v.tr.* **1** decorate with a frill. **2** form into a frill. □ **frill** (or **frilled**) **lizard** a large N. Australian lizard, *Chlamydosaurus kingii*, with an erectile membrane round the neck. □□ **frilled** *adj.* **frillery** *n.* [16th c.: orig. unkn.]

■ *n.* **1 a** trimming, edging, furbelow, flounce, ruffle, decoration, ornamentation. **2 a** (*frills*) embellishment(s), extras, additions, trimmings, gewgaws, *colloq.* bells and whistles; ornamentation, frippery, falderal, showiness, ostentation, superfluity.

frilling /frílling/ *n.* **1** a set of frills. **2** material for frills.

frilly /frílli/ *adj.* & *n.* ● *adj.* (**frillier**, **frilliest**) **1** having a frill or frills. **2** resembling a frill. ● *n.* (*pl.* **-ies**) (in *pl.*) *colloq.* frilled underwear. □□ **frilliness** *n.*

fringe /frinj/ *n.* & *v.* ● *n.* **1 a** an ornamental bordering of threads left loose or formed into tassels or twists. **b** such a bordering made separately. **c** any border or edging. **2 a** a portion of the front hair hanging over the forehead. **b** a natural border of hair etc. in an animal or plant. **3** an outer edge or margin; the outer limit of an area, population, etc. (often *attrib.*: *fringe theatre*). **4** a thing, part, or area of secondary or minor importance. **5 a** a band of contrasting brightness or darkness produced by diffraction or interference of light. **b** a strip of false colour in an optical image. **6** *US* a fringe benefit. ● *v.tr.* **1** adorn or encircle with a fringe. **2** serve as a fringe to. □ **fringe benefit** an employee's benefit supplementing a money wage or salary. **fringe medicine** systems of treatment of disease etc. not regarded as orthodox by the medical profession. **fringing reef** a coral reef that fringes the shore. □□ **fringeless** *adj.* **fringy**

adj. [ME & OF *frenge* ult. f. LL *fimbria* (earlier only in pl.) fibres, fringe]
■ *n.* **1** trimming, edge, edging, border, frill, flounce, ruffle, purfling, ruff, ruche, ricrac, decoration, furbelow, *archaic* purfle. **3** border, perimeter, edge, boundary, periphery, margin, limits, bounds, outskirts, *hist.* march(es). ● *v.* **1** bind, purfle, trim, edge, border. **2** edge, border, surround, ring, flank, skirt, circle.

fringing /frínjing/ *n.* material for a fringe or fringes.

frippery /fríppəri/ *n.* & *adj.* ● *n.* (*pl.* **-ies**) **1** showy, tawdry, or unnecessary finery or ornament, esp. in dress. **2** empty display in speech, literary style, etc. **3 a** knick-knacks, trifles. **b** a knick-knack or trifle. ● *adj.* **1** frivolous. **2** contemptible. [F *friperie* f. OF *freperie* f. *frepe* rag]
■ *n.* **1** see FINERY[1]. **3 b** see ORNAMENT *n.* 1, 2.

frippet /fríppit/ *n. sl.* a frivolous or showy young woman. [20th c.: orig. unkn.]

Frisbee /frízbi/ *n. propr.* a concave plastic disc for skimming through the air as an outdoor game. [perh. f. *Frisbie* bakery (Bridgeport, Conn.), whose pie-tins could be used similarly]

Frisian /frízziən/ *adj.* & *n.* ● *adj.* of Friesland (an area comprising the NW Netherlands and adjacent islands). ● *n.* **1** a native or inhabitant of Friesland. **2** the language of Friesland. [L *Frisii* pl. f. OFris. *Frīsa, Frēsa*]

frisk /frisk/ *v.* & *n.* ● *v.* **1** *intr.* leap or skip playfully. **2** *tr. sl.* feel over or search (a person) for a weapon etc. (usu. rapidly). ● *n.* **1** a playful leap or skip. **2** *sl.* the frisking of a person. ▫▫ **frisker** *n.* [obs. *frisk* (adj.) f. OF *frisque* lively, of unkn. orig.]
■ *v.* **1** caper, gambol, frolic, skip, trip, romp, leap, dance, prance, play, rollick, curvet, *sl.* cavort. **2** feel (over), search, inspect, check, examine, go over, *US* check out. ● *n.* **1** see CAPER[1] *n.* 1.

frisket /frískit/ *n. Printing* a thin iron frame keeping the sheet in position during printing on a hand-press. [F *frisquette* f. Prov. *frisqueto* f. Sp. *frasqueta*]

frisky /fríski/ *adj.* (**friskier, friskiest**) lively, playful. ▫▫ **friskily** *adv.* **friskiness** *n.*
■ lively, frolicsome, rollicking, playful, active, animated, (high-)spirited, coltish.

frisson /freésson/ *n.* an emotional thrill. [F, = shiver]

frit /frit/ *n.* & *v.* ● *n.* **1** a calcined mixture of sand and fluxes as material for glass-making. **2** a vitreous composition from which soft porcelain, enamel, etc., are made. ● *v.tr.* (**fritted, fritting**) make into frit, partially fuse, calcine. [It. *fritta* fem. past part. of *friggere* FRY[1]]

frit-fly /frítflī/ *n.* (*pl.* **-flies**) a small fly, *Oscinella frit*, of which the larvae are destructive to cereals. [19th c.: orig. unkn.]

frith var. of FIRTH.

fritillary /fritíllәri/ *n.* (*pl.* **-ies**) **1** any liliaceous plant of the genus *Fritillaria*, esp. snake's head, having pendent bell-like flowers. **2** any of various butterflies, esp. of the genus *Argynnis*, having red-brown wings chequered with black. [mod.L *fritillaria* f. L *fritillus* dice-box]

fritter[1] /fríttər/ *v.tr.* **1** (usu. foll. by *away*) waste (money, time, energy, etc.) triflingly, indiscriminately, or on divided aims. **2** *archaic* subdivide. [obs. n. *fritter(s)* fragments = obs. *fitters* (n.pl.), perh. rel. to MHG *vetze* rag]
■ **1** (*fritter away*) squander, waste, trifle away, idle away, frivol away, misspend, dissipate.

fritter[2] /fríttər/ *n.* a piece of fruit, meat, etc., coated in batter and deep-fried (*apple fritter*). [ME f. OF *friture* ult. f. L *frigere frict-* FRY[1]]

fritto misto /fríttō místō/ *n.* a mixed grill. [It., = mixed fry]

fritz /frits/ *n.* ▫ **on the fritz** *US sl.* out of order, unsatisfactory. [20th c.: orig. unkn.]

frivol /frívv'l/ *v.* (**frivolled, frivolling**; *US* **frivoled, frivoling**) **1** *intr.* be a trifler; trifle. **2** *tr.* (foll. by *away*) spend (money or time) foolishly. [back-form. f. FRIVOLOUS]

frivolous /frívvələss/ *adj.* **1** paltry, trifling, trumpery. **2** lacking seriousness; given to trifling; silly. ▫▫ **frivolity** /-vólliti/ *n.* (*pl.* **-ies**). **frivolously** *adv.* **frivolousness** *n.* [L *frivolus* silly, trifling]
■ **1** trifling, paltry, trumpery, inconsequential, unimportant, trivial, nugatory, insignificant, minor, petty, niggling, peripheral, superficial, worthless, two a penny, *Brit.* twopenny-halfpenny, *colloq.* small-time, *Brit. colloq.* twopenny, *US colloq.* two-bit. **2** scatterbrained, silly, feather-brained, irresponsible, flighty, giddy, puerile, flippant, superficial, casual, airy, light, slight, *colloq.* birdbrained, airy-fairy, flip.

frizz /friz/ *v.* & *n.* ● *v.tr.* **1** form (hair) into a mass of small curls. **2** dress (wash-leather etc.) with pumice or a scraping-knife. ● *n.* **1 a** a frizzed hair. **b** a row of curls. **2** a frizzed state. [F *friser*, perh. f. the stem of *frire* FRY[1]]

frizzle[1] /frízz'l/ *v.intr.* & *tr.* **1** fry, toast, or grill, with a sputtering noise. **2** (often foll. by *up*) burn or shrivel. [*frizz* (in the same sense) f. FRY[1], with imit. ending + -LE[4]]

frizzle[2] /frízz'l/ *v.* & *n.* ● *v.* **1** *tr.* form (hair) into tight curls. **2** *intr.* (often foll. by *up*) (of hair etc.) curl tightly. ● *n.* frizzled hair. [16th c.: orig. unkn. (earlier than FRIZZ)]

frizzly /frízli/ *adj.* in tight curls.

frizzy /frízzi/ *adj.* (**frizzier, frizziest**) in a mass of small curls. ▫▫ **frizziness** *n.*

Frl. *abbr.* Fräulein.

fro /frō/ *adv.* back (now only in *to and fro*: see TO). [ME f. ON *frá* FROM]

frock /frok/ *n.* & *v.* ● *n.* **1** a woman's or girl's dress. **2 a** a monk's or priest's long gown with loose sleeves. **b** priestly office. **3** a smock. **4 a** a frock-coat. **b** a military coat of similar shape. **5** a sailor's woollen jersey. ● *v.tr.* invest with priestly office (cf. UNFROCK). ▫ **frock-coat** a man's long-skirted coat not cut away in front. [ME f. OF *froc* f. Frank.]
■ *n.* **1** dress, gown. ● *v.* see INAUGURATE 1.

froe /frō/ *n.* (also **frow**) *US* a cleaving tool with a handle at right angles to the blade. [abbr. of *frower* f. FROWARD 'turned away']

Froebel system /frṓb'l, frṓb'l/ *n.* a system of education of children by means of kindergartens. ▫▫ **Froebelian** /-beélian/ *adj.* **Froebelism** *n.* [F. W. A. *Fröbel*, Ger. teacher d. 1852]

frog[1] /frog/ *n.* **1** any of various small amphibians of the order Anura, having a tailless smooth-skinned body with legs developed for jumping. **2** (**Frog**) *Brit. sl. offens.* a Frenchman. **3** a hollow in the top face of a brick for holding the mortar. **4** the nut of a violin-bow etc. ▫ **frog-fish** = *angler-fish*. **frog in the** (or **one's**) **throat** *colloq.* hoarseness. **frog-spawn** the spawn of a frog. [OE *frogga* f. Gmc]

frog[2] /frog/ *n.* an elastic horny substance in the sole of a horse's foot. [17th c.: orig. uncert. (perh. a use of FROG[1])]

frog[3] /frog/ *n.* **1** an ornamental coat-fastening of a spindle-shaped button and loop. **2** an attachment to a waist-belt to support a sword, bayonet, etc. ▫▫ **frogged** *adj.* **frogging** *n.* [18th c.: orig. unkn.]

frog[4] /frog/ *n.* a grooved piece of iron at a place in a railway where tracks cross. [19th c.: orig. unkn.]

froggy /fróggi/ *adj.* & *n.* ● *adj.* **1** of or like a frog or frogs. **2 a** cold as a frog. **b** abounding in frogs. **3** *Brit. sl. offens.* French. ● *n.* (**Froggy**) (*pl.* **-ies**) *sl. derog.* a Frenchman.

froghopper /fróg-hoppər/ *n.* any jumping insect of the family Cercopidae, sucking sap and as larvae producing a protective mass of froth (see *cuckoo-spit*).

frogman /frógmən/ *n.* (*pl.* **-men**) a person equipped with a rubber suit, flippers, and an oxygen supply for underwater swimming.

frogmarch /frógmaarch/ *v.* & *n.* esp. *Brit.* ● *v.tr.* **1** hustle (a person) forward holding and pinning the arms from behind. **2** carry (a person) in a frogmarch. ● *n.* the carrying of a person face downwards by four others each holding a limb.

frogmouth /frógmowth/ *n.* any of various birds of Australia and SE Asia, esp. of the family Podargidae, having large wide mouths.

frolic /fróllik/ *v.*, *n.*, & *adj.* ● *v.intr.* (**frolicked, frolicking**) play about cheerfully, gambol. ● *n.* **1** cheerful play. **2** a prank. **3** a merry party. **4** an outburst of gaiety. **5** merriment. ● *adj. archaic* **1** full of pranks, sportive. **2** joyous, mirthful. □□ **frolicker** *n.* [Du. *vrolijk* (adj.) f. *vro* glad + *-lijk* -LY[1]]
▪ *v.* frisk, caper, skylark, gambol, rollick, romp, cut a caper, play, skip, sport, have fun, party, horse around, *colloq.* make whoopee, *sl.* cavort. ● *n.* **1** play, horseplay, skylarking. **2** escapade, gambade, antic, caper; see also PRANK. **3** romp, party, revel, gambol, *colloq.* spree. **4** joke, laugh, *colloq.* lark, giggle, scream. **5** merriment, merrymaking, gaiety, sport, fun (and games), high jinks, jollity, mirth, jollification, festivity, celebration, revelry.

frolicsome /frólliksəm/ *adj.* merry, playful. □□ **frolicsomely** *adv.* **frolicsomeness** *n.*
▪ playful, merry, frisky, sportive, gay, lively, sprightly, animated, spirited, coltish.

from /frəm, from/ *prep.* expressing separation or origin, followed by: **1** a person, place, time, etc., that is the starting-point of motion or action, or of extent in place or time (*rain comes from the clouds*; *repeated from mouth to mouth*; *dinner is served from 8*; *from start to finish*). **2** a place, object, etc. whose distance or remoteness is reckoned or stated (*ten miles from Rome*; *I am far from admitting it*; *absent from home*; *apart from its moral aspect*). **3 a** a source (*dig gravel from a pit*; *a man from Italy*; *draw a conclusion from premisses*; *quotations from Shaw*). **b** a giver or sender (*presents from Father Christmas*; *have not heard from her*). **4 a** a thing or person avoided, escaped, lost, etc. (*released him from prison*; *cannot refrain from laughing*; *dissuaded from folly*). **b** a person or thing deprived (*took his gun from him*). **5** a reason, cause, or motive (*died from fatigue*; *suffering from mumps*; *did it from jealousy*; *from his looks you might not believe it*). **6** a thing distinguished or unlike (*know black from white*). **7** a lower limit (*saw from 10 to 20 boats*; *tickets from £5*). **8** a state changed for another (*from being the victim he became the attacker*; *raised the penalty from a fine to imprisonment*). **9** an adverb or preposition of time or place (*from long ago*; *from abroad*; *from under the bed*). **10** the position of a person who observes or considers (*saw it from the roof*; *from his point of view*). **11** a model (*painted it from nature*). □ **from a child** since childhood. **from day to day** (or **hour to hour** etc.) daily (or hourly etc.); as the days (or hours etc.) pass. **from home** out, away. **from now on** henceforward. **from time to time** occasionally. **from year to year** each year; as the years pass. [OE *fram*, *from* f. Gmc]

fromage frais /frómmaazh fráy/ *n.* a kind of smooth low-fat soft cheese. [Fr., lit. 'fresh cheese']

frond /frond/ *n.* **1** *Bot.* **a** a large usu. divided foliage leaf in various flowerless plants, esp. ferns and palms. **b** the leaflike thallus of some algae. **2** *Zool.* a leaflike expansion. □□ **frondage** *n.* **frondose** *adj.* [L *frons frondis* leaf]

frondeur /frondőr/ *n.* a political rebel. [F, = slinger, applied to a party (the Fronde) rebelling during the minority of Louis XIV of France]

front /frunt/ *n.*, *adj.*, & *v.* ● *n.* **1** the side or part normally nearer or towards the spectator or the direction of motion (*the front of the car*; *the front of the chair*; *the front of the mouth*). **2** any face of a building, esp. that of the main entrance. **3** *Mil.* **a** the foremost line or part of an army etc. **b** line of battle. **c** the part of the ground towards a real or imaginary enemy. **d** a scene of actual fighting (*go to the front*). **e** the direction in which a formed line faces (*change front*). **4 a** a sector of activity regarded as resembling a military front. **b** an organized political group. **5 a** demeanour, bearing (*show a bold front*). **b** outward appearance. **6** a forward or conspicuous position (*come to the front*). **7 a** a bluff. **b** a pretext. **8** a person etc. serving to cover subversive or illegal activities. **9** (prec. by *the*) the promenade of a seaside resort. **10** *Meteorol.* the forward edge of an advancing mass of cold or warm air. **11** (prec. by *the*) the auditorium of a theatre. **12 a** a face. **b** *poet.* or *rhet.* a forehead. **13 a** the breast of a man's shirt. **b** a false shirt-front. **14** impudence. ● *attrib.adj.* **1** of the front. **2** situated in front. **3** *Phonet.* formed at the front of the mouth. ● *v.* **1** *intr.* (foll. by *on*, *to*, *towards*, *upon*) have the front facing or directed. **2** *intr.* (foll. by *for*) *sl.* act as a front or cover for. **3** *tr.* furnish with a front (*fronted with stone*). **4** *tr.* lead (a band). **5** *tr.* **a** stand opposite to, front towards. **b** have its front on the side of (a street etc.). **6** *tr. archaic* confront, meet, oppose. □ **front bench** *Brit.* the foremost seats in Parliament, occupied by leading members of the government and opposition. **front-bencher** *Brit.* such a member. **front door 1** the chief entrance of a house. **2** a chief means of approach or access to a place, situation, etc. **front line** *Mil.* = sense 3 of *n.* **front-line States** countries in Southern Africa bordering on and opposed to South Africa. **front man** a person acting as a front or cover. **front matter** *Printing* the title-page, preface, etc. preceding the text proper. **front office** a main office, esp. police headquarters. **front page** the first page of a newspaper, esp. as containing important or remarkable news. **front passage** *colloq.* the vagina. **front runner 1** the contestant most likely to succeed. **2** an athlete or horse running best when in the lead. **in front 1** in an advanced position. **2** facing the spectator. **in front of 1** ahead of, in advance of. **2** in the presence of, confronting. **on the front burner** see BURNER. □□ **frontless** *adj.* **frontward** *adj.* & *adv.* **frontwards** *adv.* [ME f. OF *front* (n.), *fronter* (v.) f. L *frons frontis*]
▪ *n.* **1** face, fore-part, fore; obverse. **2** face, frontage, façade. **3** vanguard, van, formation, *Mil.* front line. **4 b** movement, organization, party, group, league; faction, wing. **5 a** bearing, demeanour, air, face, expression, countenance, *literary* mien. **b** façade, mask, show, guise, appearance, aspect, look, exterior. **6** beginning, head, forefront, fore. **7** bluff, disguise, guise, cover, show, pretext. **8** cover. **9** esplanade, *Brit.* promenade, prom. **12 a** see FACE *n.* 1. **14** impudence, haughtiness, overconfidence, effrontery. ● *attrib.adj.* **2** first, advance, leading, head, anterior. ● *v.* **1, 5a** overlook, face, look out on *or* over; be opposite. **2** (*front for*) act for, represent; substitute for, cover for, replace. **6** see FACE *v.* 3. □ **front matter** *colloq.* prelims. **in front 1** first, leading, in the lead, ahead, winning, in advance, in the vanguard *or* van, to the fore, in the forefront. **in front of 1** see *ahead of*.

frontage /frúntij/ *n.* **1** the front of a building. **2 a** land abutting on a street or on water. **b** the land between the front of a building and the road. **3** extent of front (*a shop with little frontage*). **4 a** the way a thing faces. **b** outlook. □ **frontage road** *US* a service road. □□ **frontager** *n.*
▪ **1** see FACE *n.* 4e. **4** see EXPOSURE 5.

frontal[1] /frúnt'l/ *adj.* **1 a** of, at, or on the front (*a frontal attack*). **b** of the front as seen by an onlooker (*a frontal view*). **2** of the forehead or front part of the skull (*frontal bone*). □□ **frontally** *adv.* [mod.L *frontalis* (as FRONT)]

frontal[2] /frúnt'l/ *n.* **1** a covering for the front of an altar. **2** the façade of a building. [ME f. OF *frontel* f. L *frontale* (as FRONT)]

frontier /frúntiər, -teér/ *n.* **1 a** the border between two countries. **b** the district on each side of this. **2** the limits of attainment or knowledge in a subject. **3** *US* the borders between settled and unsettled country. □□ **frontierless** *adj.* [ME f. AF *frounter*, OF *frontiere* ult. f. L *frons frontis* FRONT]
▪ **1** border, boundary, bound(s), pale, *archaic* bourn, *hist.* march(es). **2** limit(s), bound(s), extreme(s), *archaic* bourn.

frontiersman /frúntiərzmən, -teérzmən/ *n.* (*pl.* **-men**) a person living in the region of a frontier, esp. between settled and unsettled country.
▪ see PIONEER *n.* 2.

frontispiece /frúntispeess/ *n.* **1** an illustration facing the title-page of a book or of one of its divisions. **2** *Archit.* **a** the principal face of a building. **b** a decorated entrance. **c** a pediment over a door etc. [F *frontispice* or LL *frontispicium* façade f. L *frons frontis* FRONT + *-spicium* f. *specere* look: assim. to PIECE]

frontlet /frúntlit/ *n.* **1** a piece of cloth hanging over the upper part of an altar frontal. **2** a band worn on the forehead. **3** a phylactery. **4** an animal's forehead. [OF *frontelet* (as FRONTAL[2])]

fronton /frúntən/ *n.* a pediment. [F f. It. *frontone* f. *fronte* forehead]

frore /fror/ *adj. poet.* frozen, frosty. [archaic past part. of FREEZE]

frost /frost/ *n.* & *v.* ● *n.* **1 a** (also **white frost**) a white frozen dew coating esp. the ground at night (*windows covered with frost*). **b** a consistent temperature below freezing-point causing frost to form. **2** a chilling dispiriting atmosphere. **3** *sl.* a failure. ● *v.* **1** *intr.* (usu. foll. by *over, up*) become covered with frost. **2** *tr.* **a** cover with or as if with frost, powder, etc. **b** injure (a plant etc.) with frost. **3** *tr.* give a roughened or finely granulated surface to (glass, metal) (*frosted glass*). **4** *tr. US* cover or decorate (a cake etc.) with icing. □ **black frost** a frost without white dew. **degrees of frost** *Brit.* degrees below freezing-point (*ten degrees of frost tonight*). **frost-work** tracery made by frost on glass etc. □□ **frostless** *adj.* [OE f. Gmc]
■ *n.* **1 b** see FREEZE *n.* 1.

frostbite /fróstbīt/ *n.* injury to body tissues, esp. the nose, fingers, or toes, due to freezing and often resulting in gangrene.

frosting /frósting/ *n.* **1** *US* icing. **2** a rough surface on glass etc.

frosty /frósti/ *adj.* (**frostier, frostiest**) **1** cold with frost. **2** covered with or as with hoar-frost. **3** unfriendly in manner, lacking in warmth of feeling. □□ **frostily** *adv.* **frostiness** *n.*
■ **1** see COLD *adj.* 1. **3** see COLD *adj.* 4.

froth /froth/ *n.* & *v.* ● *n.* **1 a** a collection of small bubbles in liquid, caused by shaking, fermenting, etc.; foam. **b** impure matter on liquid, scum. **2 a** idle talk or ideas. **b** anything unsubstantial or of little worth. ● *v.* **1** *intr.* emit or gather froth (*frothing at the mouth*). **2** *tr.* cause (beer etc.) to foam. □ **froth-blower** *Brit. joc.* a beer-drinker (esp. as a designation of a member of a charitable organization). □□ **frothily** *adv.* **frothiness** *n.* **frothy** *adj.* (**frothier, frothiest**). [ME f. ON *frotha, frauth* f. Gmc]
■ *n.* **1 a** foam, spume, suds, lather, bubbles; head. **2** trivia, rubbish, nonsense, twaddle, babble, gibberish, drivel, *colloq.* gab, piffle, *sl.* hot air, gas. ● *v.* **1** foam, spume, bubble, fizz, effervesce; lather. **2** aerate.

frottage /frotaázh/ *n.* **1** *Psychol.* an abnormal desire for contact between the clothed bodies of oneself and another. **2** *Art* the technique or process of taking a rubbing from an uneven surface to form the basis of a work of art. [F, = rubbing f. *frotter* rub f. OF *froter*]

frou-frou /fróofroo/ *n.* a rustling, esp. of a dress. [F, imit.]

frow[1] /frow/ *n.* **1** a Dutchwoman. **2** a housewife. [ME f. Du. *vrouw* woman]

frow[2] var. of FROE.

froward /fróərd/ *adj. archaic* perverse; difficult to deal with. □□ **frowardly** *adv.* **frowardness** *n.* [ME f. FRO + -WARD]

frown /frown/ *v.* & *n.* ● *v.* **1** *intr.* wrinkle one's brows, esp. in displeasure or deep thought. **2** *intr.* (foll. by *at, on, upon*) express disapproval. **3** *intr.* (of a thing) present a gloomy aspect. **4** *tr.* compel with a frown (*frowned them into silence*). **5** *tr.* express (defiance etc.) with a frown. ● *n.* **1** an action of frowning; a vertically furrowed or wrinkled state of the brow. **2** a look expressing severity, disapproval, or deep thought. □□ **frowner** *n.* **frowningly** *adv.* [ME f. OF *frongnier, froignier* f. *froigne* surly look f. Celt.]
■ *v.* **1** scowl, glower, glare, knit one's brows, grimace, lour. **2** (*frown on* or *upon*) disapprove of, disfavour, discountenance, look askance at, not take kindly to, not think much of, look disapprovingly upon, *colloq.* take a dim view of. **3** look grim *or* gloomy. ● *n.* **2** scowl, glower, glare, grimace, lour, *colloq.* dirty look.

frowst /frowst/ *n.* & *v. Brit. colloq.* ● *n.* fusty warmth in a room. ● *v.intr.* stay in or enjoy frowst. □□ **frowster** *n.* [back-form. f. FROWSTY]

frowsty /frówsti/ *adj. Brit.* (**frowstier, frowstiest**) fusty, stuffy. □□ **frowstiness** *n.* [var. of FROWZY]
■ see STUFFY 1.

frowzy /frówzi/ *adj.* (also **frowsy**) (**-ier, -iest**) **1** fusty, musty, ill-smelling, close. **2** slatternly, unkempt, dingy. □□ **frowziness** *n.* [17th c.: orig. unkn.: cf. earlier *frowy*]
■ **1** see STUFFY 1. **2** see UNKEMPT 1.

froze *past* of FREEZE.

frozen *past part.* of FREEZE.

FRS *abbr.* (in the UK) Fellow of the Royal Society.

FRSE *abbr.* Fellow of the Royal Society of Edinburgh.

fructiferous /fruktíffərəss/ *adj.* bearing fruit. [L *fructifer* f. *fructus* FRUIT]

fructification /frúktifikáysh'n/ *n. Bot.* **1** the process of fructifying. **2** any spore-bearing structure esp. in ferns, fungi, and mosses. [LL *fructificatio* (as FRUCTIFY)]

fructify /frúktifī/ *v.* (**-ies, -ied**) **1** *intr.* bear fruit. **2** *tr.* make fruitful; impregnate. [ME f. OF *fructifier* f. L *fructificare* f. *fructus* FRUIT]
■ **2** see FERTILIZE 2.

fructose /frúktōz, -tōss, fróok-/ *n. Chem.* a simple sugar found in honey and fruits. Also called LAEVULOSE, *fruit sugar*. [L *fructus* FRUIT + -OSE[2]]

fructuous /frúktyooəss/ *adj.* full of or producing fruit. [ME f. OF *fructuous* or L *fructuosus* (as FRUIT)]

frugal /fróog'l/ *adj.* **1** (often foll. by *of*) sparing or economical, esp. as regards food. **2** sparingly used or supplied, meagre, costing little. □□ **frugality** /-gálliti/ *n.* **frugally** *adv.* **frugalness** *n.* [L *frugalis* f. *frugi* economical]
■ **1** thrifty, sparing, economical, careful, prudent, provident, moderate; abstemious. **2** meagre, paltry, poor, skimpy, scanty, scant, small, negligible, *colloq.* piddling.

frugivorous /froojívvərəss/ *adj.* feeding on fruit. [L *frux frugis* fruit + -VOROUS]

fruit /froot/ *n.* & *v.* ● *n.* **1 a** the usu. sweet and fleshy edible product of a plant or tree, containing seed. **b** (in *sing.*) these in quantity (*eats fruit*). **2** the seed of a plant or tree with its covering, e.g. an acorn, pea pod, cherry, etc. **3** (usu. in *pl.*) vegetables, grains, etc. used for food (*fruits of the earth*). **4** (usu. in *pl.*) the result of action etc., esp. as financial reward (*fruits of his labours*). **5** *sl.* esp. *US* a male homosexual. **6** *Bibl.* an offspring (*the fruit of the womb*; *the fruit of his loins*). ● *v.intr.* & *tr.* bear or cause to bear fruit. □ **fruit bar** a piece of dried and pressed fruit. **fruit-bat** any large bat of the suborder Megachiroptera, feeding on fruit. **fruit-** (or **fruiting-**) **body** (*pl.* **-ies**) the spore-bearing part of a fungus. **fruit cake 1** a cake containing dried fruit. **2** *sl.* an eccentric or mad person. **fruit cocktail** a finely-chopped usu. tinned fruit salad. **fruit fly** (*pl.* **flies**) any of various flies, esp. of the genus *Drosophila*, having larvae that feed on fruit. **fruit machine** *Brit.* a coin-operated gaming machine giving random combinations of symbols often representing fruit. **fruit salad 1** various fruits cut up and served in syrup, juice, etc. **2** *sl.* a display of medals etc. **fruit sugar** fructose. **fruit-tree** a tree grown for its fruit. **fruit-wood** the wood of a fruit-tree, esp. when used in furniture. □□ **fruitage** *n.* **fruited** *adj.* (also in *comb.*). [ME f. OF f. L *fructus* fruit, enjoyment f. *frui* enjoy]
■ *n.* **4** product(s), result(s), revenue(s), outcome, consequence(s), return(s), advantage(s), benefit(s), profit(s), emolument, payment, income, deserts. **6** see OFFSPRING. □ **fruit cake 2** see ECCENTRIC *n.*

fruitarian /frootáiriən/ *n.* a person who eats only fruit. [FRUIT, after *vegetarian*]

fruiter /frootər/ *n.* **1** a tree producing fruit, esp. with reference to its quality (*a poor fruiter*). **2** *Brit.* a fruit grower. **3** a ship carrying fruit. [ME f. OF *fruitier* (as FRUIT, -ER[5]): later f. FRUIT + -ER[1]]

fruiterer /frootərər/ *n.* esp. *Brit.* a dealer in fruit.

fruitful /fro͞otfo͝ol/ *adj.* **1** producing much fruit; fertile; causing fertility. **2** producing good results, successful; beneficial, remunerative. **3** producing offspring, esp. prolifically. □□ **fruitfully** *adv.* **fruitfulness** *n.*
■ **1** fertile, plentiful, abundant, fecund, copious, luxurious, rich, flourishing, bountiful, *poet.* plenteous, bounteous; fructiferous, fructuous. **2** successful, effective, beneficial, profitable, remunerative, productive, advantageous, worthwhile, useful, rewarding, well-spent. **3** productive, fertile, prolific, fecund.

fruition /fro͞o-ísh'n/ *n.* **1 a** the bearing of fruit. **b** the production of results. **2** the realization of aims or hopes. **3** enjoyment. [ME f. OF f. LL *fruitio -onis* f. *frui* enjoy, erron. assoc. with FRUIT]
■ **1b, 2** production, completion; achievement, success, attainment, accomplishment, fulfilment, realization, consummation, materialization, perfection. **3** see *enjoyment* (ENJOY).

fruitless /fro͞otliss/ *adj.* **1** not bearing fruit. **2** useless, unsuccessful, unprofitable. □□ **fruitlessly** *adv.* **fruitlessness** *n.*
■ **1** barren, unfruitful, unproductive, sterile, infertile. **2** worthless, futile, pointless, useless, vain, unavailing, ineffectual, ineffective, unprofitable, unsuccessful, unrewarding, abortive, *archaic* bootless; for naught, to no avail.

fruitlet /fro͞otlit/ *n.* = DRUPEL.

fruity /fro͞oti/ *adj.* (**fruitier, fruitiest**) **1 a** of fruit. **b** tasting or smelling like fruit, esp. (of wine) tasting of the grape. **2** (of a voice etc.) of full rich quality. **3** *colloq.* full of rough humour or (usu. scandalous) interest; suggestive. □□ **fruitily** *adv.* **fruitiness** *n.*
■ **1 b** see ROBUST 5.

frumenty /fro͞omənti/ *n.* (also **furmety** /fúrmiti/) hulled wheat boiled in milk and seasoned with cinnamon, sugar, etc. [ME f. OF *frumentee* f. *frument* f. L *frumentum* corn]

frump /frump/ *n.* a dowdy unattractive old-fashioned woman. □□ **frumpish** *adj.* **frumpishly** *adv.* [16th c.: perh. f. dial. *frumple* (v.) wrinkle f. MDu. *verrompelen* (as FOR-, RUMPLE)]

frumpy /frúmpi/ *adj.* (**frumpier, frumpiest**) dowdy, unattractive, and old-fashioned. □□ **frumpily** *adv.* **frumpiness** *n.*
■ see DOWDY *adj.* 2.

frustrate *v.* & *adj.* ● *v.tr.* /frustráyt, frús-/ **1** make (efforts) ineffective. **2** prevent (a person) from achieving a purpose. **3** (as **frustrated** *adj.*) **a** discontented because unable to achieve one's desire. **b** sexually unfulfilled. **4** disappoint (a hope). ● *adj.* /frústrayt/ *archaic* frustrated. □□ **frustratedly** *adv.* **frustrater** *n.* **frustrating** *adj.* **frustratingly** *adv.* **frustration** *n.* [ME f. L *frustrari frustrat-* f. *frustra* in vain]
■ *v.* **1** counteract, neutralize, nullify, counter, negate. **2** prevent, defeat, forestall, stop, halt, cripple, hinder, hamper, disrupt, impede, hamstring, thwart, upset, foil, stymie, obstruct, block, baffle, check, baulk; fight off, repel, repulse. **3** (**frustrated**) **a** see *discontented* (DISCONTENT). **b** unfulfilled, dissatisfied. **4** discourage, disappoint, foil, thwart, defeat, baulk.

frustule /frústyo͞ol/ *n. Bot.* the siliceous cell wall of a diatom. [F f. L *frustulum* (as FRUSTUM)]

frustum /frústəm/ *n.* (*pl.* **frusta** /-tə/ or **frustums**) *Geom.* **1** the remainder of a cone or pyramid whose upper part has been cut off by a plane parallel to its base. **2** the part of a cone or pyramid intercepted between two planes. [L, = piece cut off]

frutescent /fro͞otéss'nt/ *adj. Bot.* of the nature of a shrub. [irreg. f. L *frutex* bush]

frutex /fro͞oteks/ *n.* (*pl.* **frutices** /-tiseez/) *Bot.* a woody-stemmed plant smaller than a tree; a shrub. [L *frutex fruticis*]

fruticose /fro͞otikōz, -kōss/ *adj. Bot.* resembling a shrub. [L *fruticosus* (as FRUTEX)]

fry[1] /frī/ *v.* & *n.* ● *v.* (**fries, fried**) **1** *tr.* & *intr.* cook or be cooked in hot fat. **2** *tr.* & *intr. sl.* electrocute or be electrocuted. **3** *tr.* (as **fried** *adj.*) *sl.* drunk. **4** *intr. colloq.* be very hot. ● *n.* (*pl.* **fries**) **1** various internal parts of animals usu. eaten fried (*lamb's fry*). **2** a dish of fried food, esp. meat. **3** *US* a social gathering to eat fried food. □ **frying-** (*US* **fry-**) **pan** a shallow pan used in frying. **fry up** heat or reheat (food) in a frying-pan. **fry-up** *n. Brit. colloq.* a dish of miscellaneous fried food. **out of the frying-pan into the fire** from a bad situation to a worse one. [ME f. OF *frire* f. L *frigere*]
■ *v.* **3** (**fried**) see DRUNK *adj.* 1. **4** see BOIL[1] *v.* 3c.

fry[2] /frī/ *n.pl.* **1** young or newly hatched fishes. **2** the young of other creatures produced in large numbers, e.g. bees or frogs. □ **small fry** people of little importance; children. [ME f. ON *frjó*]

fryer /frīər/ *n.* (also **frier**) **1** a person who fries. **2** a vessel for frying esp. fish. **3** *US* a chicken suitable for frying.

FSA *abbr.* Fellow of the Society of Antiquaries.

FSH *abbr.* follicle-stimulating hormone.

Ft. *abbr.* Fort.

ft. *abbr.* foot, feet.

FTC *abbr. US* Federal Trade Commission.

fubsy /fúbzi/ *adj.* (**fubsier, fubsiest**) *Brit.* fat or squat. [obs. *fubs* small fat person + -Y[1]]

fuchsia /fyo͞oshə/ *n.* any shrub of the genus *Fuchsia*, with drooping red or purple or white flowers. [mod.L f. L. *Fuchs*, Ger. botanist d. 1566]

fuchsine /fo͞okseen, -sin/ *n.* a deep red aniline dye used in the pharmaceutical and textile-processing industries, rosaniline. [FUCHSIA (from its resemblance to the colour of the flower)]

fuck /fuk/ *v.*, *int.*, & *n. coarse sl.* ● *v.* **1** *tr.* & *intr.* have sexual intercourse (with). **2** *intr.* (foll. by *about*, *around*) mess about; fool around. **3** *tr.* (usu. as an exclam.) curse, confound (*fuck the thing!*). **4** *intr.* (as **fucking** *adj.*, *adv.*) used as an intensive to express annoyance etc. ● *int.* expressing anger or annoyance. ● *n.* **1 a** an act of sexual intercourse. **b** a partner in sexual intercourse. **2** the slightest amount (*don't give a fuck*). □ **fuck all** nothing. **fuck off** go away. **fuck up** make a mess of. **fuck-up** *n.* a mess or muddle. ¶ A highly taboo word. □□ **fucker** *n.* (often as a term of abuse). [16th c.: orig. unkn.]

fucus /fyo͞okəss/ *n.* (*pl.* **fuci** /fyo͞ossī/) any seaweed of the genus *Fucus*, with flat leathery fronds. □□ **fucoid** *adj.* [L, = rock-lichen, f. Gk *phukos*, of Semitic orig.]

fuddle /fúdd'l/ *v.* & *n.* ● *v.* **1** *tr.* confuse or stupefy, esp. with alcoholic liquor. **2** *intr.* tipple, booze. ● *n.* **1** confusion. **2** intoxication. **3** a spell of drinking (*on the fuddle*). [16th c.: orig. unkn.]

fuddy-duddy /fúddidúddi/ *adj.* & *n. sl.* ● *adj.* old-fashioned or quaintly fussy. ● *n.* (*pl.* **-ies**) a fuddy-duddy person. [20th c.: orig. unkn.]
■ *adj.* see SQUEAMISH 2, STUFFY 4. ● *n.* see FOGY.

fudge /fuj/ *n.*, *v.*, & *int.* ● *n.* **1** a soft toffee-like sweet made with milk, sugar, butter, etc. **2** nonsense. **3** a piece of dishonesty or faking. **4** a piece of late news inserted in a newspaper page. ● *v.* **1** *tr.* put together in a makeshift or dishonest way; fake. **2** *tr.* deal with incompetently. **3** *intr.* practise such methods. ● *int.* expressing disbelief or annoyance. [perh. f. obs. *fadge* (v.) fit]
■ *v.* **1** see FALSIFY 1.

fuehrer var. of FÜHRER.

fuel /fyo͞oəl/ *n.* & *v.* ● *n.* **1** material, esp. coal, wood, oil, etc., burnt or used as a source of heat or power. **2** food as a source of energy. **3** material used as a source of nuclear energy. **4** anything that sustains or inflames emotion or passion. ● *v.* (**fuelled, fuelling**; *US* **fueled, fueling**) **1** *tr.* supply with fuel. **2** *tr.* sustain or inflame (an argument, feeling, etc.) (*drink fuelled his anger*). **3** *intr.* take in or get fuel. □ **fuel cell** a cell producing an electric current direct from a chemical reaction. **fuel element** an element of nuclear fuel etc. for use in a reactor. **fuel injection**

the direct introduction of fuel under pressure into the combustion units of an internal-combustion engine. **fuel oil** oil used as fuel in an engine or furnace. [ME f. AF *fuaille*, *fewaile*, OF *fouaille*, ult. f. L *focus* hearth]

■ *n.* **2** nourishment, sustenance, nutriment, nutrition; food. **4** incitement, stimulus, stimulation, provocation; see also *encouragement* (ENCOURAGE), SPUR *n.* 2. ● *v.* **2** nourish, feed, sustain; stimulate, encourage, incite, provoke, inflame, exacerbate, excite.

fug /fug/ *n.* & *v. colloq.* ● *n.* stuffiness or fustiness of the air in a room. ● *v.intr.* (**fugged, fugging**) stay in or enjoy a fug. ▫▫ **fuggy** *adj.* [19th c.: orig. unkn.]

fugacious /fyoogáyshəss/ *adj. literary* fleeting, evanescent, hard to capture or keep. ▫▫ **fugaciously** *adv.* **fugaciousness** *n.* **fugacity** /-gássiti/ *n.* [L *fugax fugacis* f. *fugere* flee]

fugal /fyóōg'l/ *adj.* of the nature of a fugue. ▫▫ **fugally** *adv.*

-fuge /fyōōj/ *comb. form* forming adjectives and nouns denoting expelling or dispelling (*febrifuge*; *vermifuge*). [from or after mod.L *-fugus* f. L *fugare* put to flight]

fugitive /fyóōjitiv/ *adj.* & *n.* ● *adj.* **1** fleeing; that runs or has run away. **2** transient, fleeting; of short duration. **3** (of literature) of passing interest, ephemeral. **4** flitting, shifting. ● *n.* **1** (often foll. by *from*) a person who flees, esp. from justice, an enemy, danger, or a master. **2** an exile or refugee. ▫▫ **fugitively** *adv.* [ME f. OF *fugitif -ive* f. L *fugitivus* f. *fugere fugit-* flee]

■ *adj.* **1** fleeing, escaped, running away, runaway. **2, 3** fleeting, passing, short-lived, transitory, transient, ephemeral, evanescent, momentary, volatile, *literary* fugacious. ● *n.* **1** runaway, escapee, deserter. **2** refugee, deportee; see also EXILE *n.* 3.

fugle /fyóōg'l/ *v.intr.* act as a fugleman. [back-form. f. FUGLEMAN]

fugleman /fyóōg'lmən/ *n.* (*pl.* **-men**) **1** *hist.* a soldier placed in front of a regiment etc. while drilling to show the motions and time. **2** a leader, organizer, or spokesman. [G *Flügelmann* f. *Flügel* wing + *Mann* man]

fugue /fyōōg/ *n.* & *v.* ● *n.* **1** *Mus.* a contrapuntal composition in which a short melody or phrase (the subject) is introduced by one part and successively taken up by others and developed by interweaving the parts. **2** *Psychol.* loss of awareness of one's identity, often coupled with flight from one's usual environment. ● *v.intr.* (**fugues, fugued, fuguing**) *Mus.* compose or perform a fugue. ▫▫ **fuguist** *n.* [F or It. f. L *fuga* flight]

fugued /fyōōgd/ *adj.* in the form of a fugue.

führer /fyóorər/ *n.* (also **fuehrer**) a leader, esp. a tyrannical one. [G, = leader: part of the title assumed in 1934 by Hitler (see HITLER)]

-ful /fōōl/ *comb. form* forming: **1** adjectives from nouns, meaning: **a** full of (*beautiful*). **b** having the qualities of (*masterful*). **2** adjectives from adjectives or Latin stems with little change of sense (*direful*; *grateful*). **3** adjectives from verbs, meaning 'apt to', 'able to', 'accustomed to' (*forgetful*; *mournful*; *useful*). **4** nouns (*pl.* **-fuls**) meaning 'the amount needed to fill' (*handful*; *spoonful*).

fulcrum /fóōlkrəm, fúl-/ *n.* (*pl.* **fulcra** /-rə/ or **fulcrums**) **1** the point against which a lever is placed to get a purchase or on which it turns or is supported. **2** the means by which influence etc. is brought to bear. [L, = post of a couch, f. *fulcire* to prop]

■ **1** see PIVOT *n.* 1.

fulfil /fōōlfil/ *v.tr.* (*US* **fulfill**) (**fulfilled, fulfilling**) **1** bring to consummation, carry out (a prophecy or promise). **2** satisfy (a desire or prayer). **3 a** execute, obey (a command or law). **b** perform, carry out (a task). **4** comply with (conditions). **5** answer (a purpose). **6** bring to an end, finish, complete (a period or piece of work). ▫ **fulfil oneself** develop one's gifts and character to the full. ▫▫ **fulfillable** *adj.* **fulfiller** *n.* **fulfilment** *n.* (*US* **fulfillment**). [OE *fullfyllan* (as FULL[1], FILL)]

■ **1** bring about, consummate; see also REALIZE 4, KEEP *v.* 7a, b. **2** satisfy, live up to; see also ACHIEVE 2. **3 a** see OBEY. **b** perform, do, carry out, bring *or* carry off, see to, accomplish, effect, effectuate; implement. **4** abide by, comply with, conform to *or* with, observe, obey. **5** answer, satisfy, meet; see also SERVE *v.* 5a–c. **6** finish, complete, discharge, bring to an end, carry through, bring *or* carry to completion. ▫▫ **fulfilment** completion, realization, implementation, execution, consummation, accomplishment, carrying out *or* through, discharge; performance, achievement, satisfaction; compliance, conformity *or* conformance, meeting (with).

fulgent /fúljənt/ *adj. poet.* or *rhet.* shining, brilliant. [ME f. L *fulgēre* shine]

fulguration /fúlgyooráysh'n/ *n. Surgery* the destruction of tissue by means of high-voltage electric sparks. [L *fulguratio* sheet lightning f. *fulgur* lightning]

fulgurite /fúlgyoorīt/ *n. Geol.* a rocky substance of sand fused or vitrified by lightning. [L *fulgur* lightning]

fuliginous /fyoolijinəss/ *adj.* sooty, dusky. [LL *fuliginosus* f. *fuligo -ginis* soot]

full[1] /fōōl/ *adj.*, *adv.*, *n.*, & *v.* ● *adj.* **1** (often foll. by *of*) holding all its limits will allow (*the bucket is full*; *full of water*). **2** having eaten to one's limits or satisfaction. **3** abundant, copious, satisfying, sufficient (*a full programme of events*; *led a full life*; *turned it to full account*; *give full details*; *the book is very full on this point*). **4** (foll. by *of*) having or holding an abundance of, showing marked signs of (*full of vitality*; *full of interest*; *full of mistakes*). **5** (foll. by *of*) **a** engrossed in thinking about (*full of himself*; *full of his work*). **b** unable to refrain from talking about (*full of the news*). **6 a** complete, perfect, reaching the specified or usual or utmost limit (*full membership*; *full daylight*; *waited a full hour*; *it was full summer*; *in full bloom*). **b** *Bookbinding* used for the entire cover (*full leather*). **7 a** (of tone or colour) deep and clear, mellow. **b** (of light) intense. **c** (of motion etc.) vigorous (*a full pulse*; *at full gallop*). **8** plump, rounded, protuberant (*a full figure*). **9** (of clothes) made of much material arranged in folds or gathers. **10** (of the heart etc.) overcharged with emotion. **11** *sl.* drunk. **12** (foll. by *of*) *archaic* having had plenty of (*full of years and honours*). ● *adv.* **1** very (*you know full well*). **2** quite, fully (*full six miles*; *full ripe*). **3** exactly (*hit him full on the nose*). **4** more than sufficiently (*full early*). ● *n.* **1** height, acme (*season is past the full*). **2** the state or time of full moon. **3** the whole (*cannot tell you the full of it*). ● *v.intr.* & *tr.* be or become or make (esp. clothes) full. ▫ **at full length 1** lying stretched out. **2** without abridgement. **come full circle** see CIRCLE. **full age** adult status (esp. with ref. to legal rights and duties). **full and by** *Naut.* close-hauled but with sails filling. **full back** a defensive player, or a position near the goal, in football, hockey, etc. **full blood** pure descent. **full-blooded 1** vigorous, hearty, sensual. **2** not hybrid. **full-bloodedly** forcefully, wholeheartedly. **full-bloodedness** being full-blooded. **full-blown** fully developed, complete, (of flowers) quite open. **full board** provision of accommodation and all meals at a hotel etc. **full-bodied** rich in quality, tone, etc. **full-bottomed** (of a wig) long at the back. **full brother** a brother born of the same parents. **full-cream** of or made from unskimmed milk. **full dress** formal clothes worn on great occasions. **full-dress** *adj.* (of a debate etc.) of major importance. **full employment 1** the condition in which there is no idle capital or labour of any kind that is in demand. **2** the condition in which virtually all who are able and willing to work are employed. **full face** with all the face visible to the spectator. **full-fashioned** = *fully-fashioned*. **full-fledged** mature. **full-frontal 1** (of nudity or a nude figure) with full exposure at the front. **2** unrestrained, explicit; with nothing concealed. **full-grown** having reached maturity. **full hand** *Poker* a hand with three of a kind and a pair. **full-hearted** full of feeling; confident, zealous. **full-heartedly** in a full-hearted manner. **full-heartedness** fullness of feeling, ardour, zeal. **full house 1** a maximum or large attendance at a theatre, in Parliament, etc. **2** = *full hand*. **full-length 1** not shortened or abbreviated. **2** (of a mirror, portrait, etc.) showing the whole height of the human figure. **full lock** see LOCK[1]. **full marks** the maximum award in an examination, in assessment of a person, etc. **full measure** not less than the professed amount. **full moon 1** the moon with its whole disc illuminated. **2** the time when this occurs. **full-mouthed 1** (of cattle or sheep) having a full set of teeth. **2** (of a dog) baying loudly. **3** (of oratory etc.) sonorous, vigorous. **full out 1** *Printing* flush with the margin. **2** at full power. **3** complete. **full page** an entire page of a newspaper etc. **full pitch** = *full toss*. **full point** = *full stop* 1. **full professor** a professor of the highest grade in a university etc. **full-scale** not reduced in size, complete. **full score** *Mus.* a score giving the parts for all performers on separate staves. **full service** a church service performed by a choir without solos, or performed with music wherever possible. **full sister** a sister born of the same parents. **full speed** (or **steam**) **ahead!** an order to proceed at maximum speed or to pursue a course of action energetically. **full stop 1** a punctuation mark (.) used at the end of a sentence or an abbreviation. **2** a complete cessation. **full term** the completion of a normal pregnancy. **full tilt** see TILT. **full time 1** the total normal duration of work etc. **2** the end of a football etc. match. **full-time** *adj.* occupying or using the whole of the available working time. **full-timer** a person who does a full-time job. **full toss** *Cricket n.* a ball pitched right up to the batsman. ● *adv.* without the ball's having touched the ground. **full up** *colloq.* completely full. **in full 1** without abridgement. **2** to or for the full amount (*paid in full*). **in full swing** at the height of activity. **in full view** entirely visible. **on a full stomach** see STOMACH. **to the full** to the utmost extent. [OE f. Gmc]

■ *adj.* **1** filled, replete, brimming, brim-full, chock-a-block, chock-full, packed, loaded, crammed, crowded, stuffed, bursting, *colloq.* jam-packed; saturated. **2** gorged, sated, satiated, stuffed, replete, satisfied, filled up, *archaic* satiate. **3** copious, abundant, satisfying, sufficient, complete, thorough, detailed, broad, extensive, comprehensive, all-inclusive, all-encompassing, exhaustive, plenary. **4** (*be full of*) see TEEM[1] 2. **5** (*full of*) occupied in *or* with, engrossed in, absorbed in, immersed in, preoccupied with, obsessed with, consumed with, engaged with *or* in. **6** complete, maximum, top, unrestricted; entire, whole, unconditional, unqualified; greatest, highest, utmost; perfect. **7 b** unobscured, unshaded, undimmed, open, broad, bright, vivid, shining, brilliant, intense, blazing. **8** plump, rounded, protuberant, well-rounded, ample, shapely, buxom, busty, voluptuous, well-built, robust, *colloq.* curvaceous. **9** wide, ample, generous; see also LOOSE *adj.* 3–5. **10** overflowing. **11** see DRUNK *adj.* 1. ● *adv.* **1** very, exceedingly, extremely, perfectly, quite, *colloq.* damned. **2** fully, completely, entirely, wholly, thoroughly, altogether, quite. **3** square(ly), directly, precisely, exactly, right, slap, *colloq.* bang, smack. ● *n.* **1** height, acme, maximum, greatest degree, fullest. □ **at full length 1** fully, completely, to the fullest extent. **2** in full, complete; see also UNABRIDGED. **full-blooded 1** see VIGOROUS 1, 3, 4. **2** pedigree, thoroughbred, pure-bred. **full-bodied** see RICH 8. **full-fledged** see MATURE *adj.* 1. **full-frontal 2** see EXPLICIT 3. **full-grown** see ADULT *adj.* 1. **full-hearted** see CONFIDENT *adj.* 1, ENTHUSIASTIC. **full-heartedly** see *authoritatively* (AUTHORITATIVE). **full-heartedness** see CONFIDENCE 2b, ENTHUSIASM 1. **full-length 1** in full, complete; see also UNABRIDGED. **full-mouthed 3** see LOUD *adj.* 1, VIGOROUS 1, 3, 4. **full-scale** see COMPLETE *adj.* 1, 3. **in full 1** see UNABRIDGED. **2** completely, fully, entirely, wholly, thoroughly, in its entirety, totally, *in toto*. **in full swing** in (full) operation, under way, in progress, in business, animated, lively, on the move, moving, going, *colloq.* on the hop, cooking. **to the full** quite, to the utmost, to the greatest *or* fullest extent, a great deal; thoroughly, greatly, hugely, enormously.

full[2] /fo͝ol/ *v.tr.* cleanse and thicken (cloth). [ME, back-form. f. FULLER[1]: cf. OF *fouler* (FOIL[1])]

fuller[1] /fo͝olər/ *n.* a person who fulls cloth. □ **fuller's earth** a type of clay used in fulling cloth and as an adsorbent. [OE *fullere* f. L *fullo*]

fuller[2] /fo͝olər/ *n.* & *v.* ● *n.* **1** a grooved or rounded tool on which iron is shaped. **2** a groove made by this esp. in a horseshoe. ● *v.tr.* stamp with a fuller. [19th c.: orig. unkn.]

fullness /fo͝olniss/ *n.* (also **fulness**) **1** being full. **2** (of sound, colour, etc.) richness, volume, body. **3** all that is contained (in the world etc.). □ **the fullness of the heart** emotion, genuine feelings. **the fullness of time** the appropriate or destined time.

■ **2** see BODY *n.* 8. **3** see ENTIRETY 1.

fully /fo͝oli/ *adv.* **1** completely, entirely (*am fully aware*). **2** no less or fewer than (*fully 60*). □ **fully-fashioned** (of women's clothing) shaped to fit the body. **fully-fledged** mature. [OE *fullīce* (as FULL[1], -LY[2])]

■ **1** see *completely* (COMPLETE).

-fully /fo͝oli/ *comb. form* forming adverbs corresp. to adjectives in *-ful*.

fulmar /fo͝olmər/ *n.* any medium-sized sea bird of the genus *Fulmarus*, with stout body, robust bill, and rounded tail. [orig. Hebridean dial.: perh. f. ON *fúll* FOUL (with ref. to its smell) + *már* gull (cf. MEW[2])]

fulminant /fúlminənt, fo͝ol-/ *adj.* **1** fulminating. **2** *Med.* (of a disease or symptom) developing suddenly. [F *fulminant* or L *fulminant-* (as FULMINATE)]

fulminate /fúlminayt, fo͝ol-/ *v.* & *n.* ● *v.intr.* **1** (often foll. by *against*) express censure loudly and forcefully. **2** explode violently; flash like lightning (*fulminating mercury*). **3** *Med.* (of a disease or symptom) develop suddenly. ● *n. Chem.* a salt or ester of fulminic acid. □□ **fulmination** /-náysh'n/ *n.* **fulminatory** *adj.* [L *fulminare fulminat-* f. *fulmen -minis* lightning]

■ *v.* **1** (*fulminate against*) see RAIL[2].

fulminic acid /fulmínnik, fo͝ol-/ *n. Chem.* an isomer of cyanic acid that is stable only in solution. ¶ Chem. formula: HONC. [L *fulmen*: see FULMINATE]

fulness var. of FULLNESS.

fulsome /fo͝olsəm/ *adj.* **1** disgusting by excess of flattery, servility, or expressions of affection; excessive, cloying. **2** *disp.* copious. ¶ In *fulsome praise*, *fulsome* means 'excessive', not 'generous'. □□ **fulsomely** *adv.* **fulsomeness** *n.* [ME f. FULL[1] + -SOME[1]]

■ **1** see EXCESSIVE.

fulvous /fúlvəss/ *adj.* reddish-yellow, tawny. □□ **fulvescent** /-véss'nt/ *adj.* [L *fulvus*]

fumarole /fyo͞omərōl/ *n.* an opening in or near a volcano, through which hot vapours emerge. □□ **fumarolic** /-róllik/ *adj.* [F *fumarolle*]

fumble /fúmb'l/ *v.* & *n.* ● *v.* **1** *intr.* (often foll. by *at*, *with*, *for*, *after*) use the hands awkwardly, grope about. **2** *tr.* **a** handle or deal with clumsily or nervously. **b** *Sport* fail to stop (a ball) cleanly. ● *n.* an act of fumbling. □□ **fumbler** *n.* **fumblingly** *adv.* [LG *fummeln*, *fommeln*, Du. *fommelen*]

■ *v.* **1** grope, feel (about); (*fumble for*) search for, grope for, feel for, fish for. **2 a** mishandle, muff, bungle, botch, *US colloq.* flub. ● *n.* grope, feel.

fume /fyo͞om/ *n.* & *v.* ● *n.* **1** (usu. in *pl.*) exuded gas or smoke or vapour, esp. when harmful or unpleasant. **2** a fit of anger (*in a fume*). ● *v.* **1 a** *intr.* emit fumes. **b** *tr.* give off as fumes. **2** *intr.* (often foll. by *at*) be affected by (esp. suppressed) anger (*was fuming at their inefficiency*). **3** *tr.* **a** fumigate. **b** subject to fumes esp. those of ammonia (to darken tints in oak, photographic film, etc.). **4** *tr.* perfume with incense. □ **fume cupboard** (or **chamber** etc.) a ventilated structure in a laboratory, for storing or experimenting with noxious chemicals. □□ **fumeless** *adj.* **fumingly** *adv.* **fumy** *adj.* (in sense 1 of *n.*). [ME f. OF *fum* f. L *fumus* smoke & OF *fume* f. *fumer* f. L *fumare* to smoke]

■ *n.* **1** smell, odour, stench, stink; (*fumes*) smoke, vapour, gas, exhalation, exhaust, pollution, smog, effluvium, *archaic* miasma. **2** see TANTRUM. ● *v.* **1** smoke, reek, steam, give off smoke. **2** seethe, smoulder, chafe, rage, be hot under the collar, *colloq.* be steamed up, *Austral. sl.* spit chips. **3 a** see FUMIGATE 1.

fumigate /fyóomigayt/ *v.tr.* **1** disinfect or purify with fumes. **2** apply fumes to. ▫▫ **fumigant** *n.* **fumigation** /-gáysh'n/ *n.* **fumigator** *n.* [L *fumigare fumigat-* f. *fumus* smoke]

■ **1** disinfect, purify, sanitize, sterilize, *usu. formal* cleanse; fume. **2** fume.

fumitory /fyóomitəri, -tri/ *n.* any plant of the genus *Fumaria*, esp. *F. officinalis*, formerly used against scurvy. [ME f. OF *fumeterre* f. med.L *fumus terrae* earth-smoke]

fun /fun/ *n.* & *adj.* ● *n.* **1** amusement, esp. lively or playful. **2** a source of this. **3** (in full **fun and games**) exciting or amusing goings-on. ● *adj. disp. colloq.* amusing, entertaining, enjoyable (*a fun thing to do*). ▫ **be great** (or **good**) **fun** be very amusing. **for fun** (or **for the fun of it**) not for a serious purpose. **fun run** *colloq.* an uncompetitive run, esp. for sponsored runners in support of a charity. **have fun** enjoy oneself. **in fun** as a joke, not seriously. **like fun 1** vigorously, quickly. **2** much. **3** *iron.* not at all. **make fun of** tease, ridicule. **what fun!** how amusing! [obs. *fun* (v.) var. of *fon* befool: cf. FOND]

■ *n.* **1** amusement, enjoyment, merriment, *colloq.* whoopee; joy, pleasure, gaiety, glee, jollity, playfulness, mirth, cheer, delight. **2** joy, pleasure, delight. **3** merrymaking, sport, recreation, entertainment, high jinks, horseplay, *colloq.* whoopee; festivity, frolic, diversion, pastime, prank(s), tomfoolery, joking, clowning, jesting, jocularity, nonsense, fooling around *or* about, skylarking. ▫ **for fun** (or **for the fun of it**) on impulse, *colloq.* for the hell of it; see also *in fun* below. **have fun** see *enjoy oneself.* **in fun** jokingly, teasingly, in jest, facetiously, with tongue in cheek, playfully, for a joke *or* gag, for fun. **like fun 1** see *vigorously* (VIGOROUS). **3** in *or* under no circumstances, *colloq.* no way, like hell. **make fun of** poke fun at, tease, deride, (hold up to) ridicule, scoff at, lampoon, parody, satirize, make sport *or* game of, taunt, gibe, rag, *colloq.* kid, rib, *Brit. colloq.* send up, *Austral. sl.* mullock, *Austral.* & *NZ sl.* poke borak at, sling off at.

funambulist /fyoonámbyoolist/ *n.* a rope-walker. [F *funambule* or L *funambulus* f. *funis* rope + *ambulare* walk]

function /fúngksh'n/ *n.* & *v.* ● *n.* **1 a** an activity proper to a person or institution. **b** a mode of action or activity by which a thing fulfils its purpose. **c** an official or professional duty; an employment, profession, or calling. **2 a** a public ceremony or occasion. **b** a social gathering, esp. a large, formal, or important one. **3** *Math.* a variable quantity regarded in relation to another or others in terms of which it may be expressed or on which its value depends (*x is a function of y and z*). **4** a part of a program that corresponds to a single value. ● *v.intr.* fulfil a function, operate; be in working order. ▫▫ **functionless** *adj.* [F *fonction* f. L *functio -onis* f. *fungi funct-* perform]

■ *n.* **1 a, b** activity, task, chore, assignment, commission; purpose, aim, use, role, *raison d'être.* **c** duty, job, occupation, work, employment, profession, calling; responsibility, mission, charge, concern, business, province, office. **2** reception, gathering, party, gala, ceremony; occasion, event, affair. ● *v.* serve, operate, act, act the part, take the role; perform, behave, work, go, run.

functional /fúngkshən'l/ *adj.* **1** of or serving a function. **2** (esp. of buildings) designed or intended to be practical rather than attractive; utilitarian. **3** *Physiol.* **a** (esp. of disease) of or affecting only the functions of an organ etc., not structural or organic. **b** (of mental disorder) having no discernible organic cause. **c** (of an organ) having a function, not functionless or rudimentary. **4** *Math.* of a function. ▫ **functional group** *Chem.* a group of atoms that determine the reactions of a compound containing the group. ▫▫ **functionality** /-nálliti/ *n.* **functionally** *adv.*

■ **1** working, functioning, operating, running, going; operational. **2** utilitarian, practical, useful, serviceable, usable.

functionalism /fúngkshənəliz'm/ *n.* belief in or stress on the practical application of a thing. ▫▫ **functionalist** *n.*

functionary /fúngkshənəri, -shənri/ *n.* (*pl.* **-ies**) a person who has to perform official functions or duties; an official.

■ official, commissioner, bureaucrat, office-holder, officer, *apparatchik.*

fund /fund/ *n.* & *v.* ● *n.* **1** a permanent stock of something ready to be drawn upon (*a fund of knowledge*; *a fund of tenderness*). **2** a stock of money, esp. one set apart for a purpose. **3** (in *pl.*) money resources. **4** (in *pl.*; prec. by *the*) *Brit.* the stock of the National Debt (as a mode of investment). ● *v.tr.* **1** provide with money. **2** convert (a floating debt) into a more or less permanent debt at fixed interest. **3** put into a fund. ▫ **fund-raiser** a person who seeks financial support for a cause, enterprise, etc. **fund-raising** the seeking of financial support. **in funds** *colloq.* having money to spend. [L *fundus* bottom, piece of land]

■ *n.* **1** supply, stock, reserve, store, pool, reservoir, mine, repository. **2** stock, nest egg, endowment; see also CACHE *n.* 2. **3** (*funds*) assets, means, wealth, resources, capital, savings; money, ready money, (hard) cash, *colloq.* wherewithal, *derog. or joc.* pelf, *joc.* filthy lucre, *sl.* loot, dosh, green, bread, dough, scratch, the ready, *Brit. sl.* lolly. ● *v.* **1** finance, pay for, support, endow, subsidize, back, capitalize, *US colloq.* stake. ▫ **in funds** see *in the money* (MONEY).

fundament /fúndəmənt/ *n. joc.* the buttocks. [ME f. OF *fondement* f. L *fundamentum* (as FOUND[2])]

fundamental /fúndəmént'l/ *adj.* & *n.* ● *adj.* of, affecting, or serving as a base or foundation, essential, primary, original (*a fundamental change*; *the fundamental rules*; *the fundamental form*). ● *n.* **1** (usu. in *pl.*) a fundamental rule, principle, or article. **2** *Mus.* a fundamental note or tone. ▫ **fundamental note** *Mus.* the lowest note of a chord in its original (uninverted) form. **fundamental particle** *Physics* an elementary particle. **fundamental tone** *Mus.* the tone produced by vibration of the whole of a sonorous body (opp. HARMONIC). ▫▫ **fundamentality** /-tálliti/ *n.* **fundamentally** *adv.* [ME f. F *fondamental* or LL *fundamentalis* (as FUNDAMENT)]

■ *adj.* essential, inherent, intrinsic, quintessential, rudimentary, elementary, basic, underlying, gut; main, prime, primary, first, principal, central, cardinal, crucial, critical, vital; original. ● *n.* **1** principle, axiom, essential, law, rule, *sine qua non*, cornerstone, keystone; (*fundamentals*) basics.

fundamentalism /fúndəméntəliz'm/ *n.* **1** strict maintenance of traditional Protestant beliefs such as the inerrancy of Scripture and literal acceptance of the creeds as fundamentals of Christianity. **2** strict maintenance of ancient or fundamental doctrines of any religion, esp. Islam. ▫▫ **fundamentalist** *n.*

fundus /fúndəss/ *n.* (*pl.* **fundi** /-dī/) *Anat.* the base of a hollow organ; the part furthest from the opening. [L, = bottom]

funeral /fyóonərəl/ *n.* & *adj.* ● *n.* **1 a** the burial or cremation of a dead person with its ceremonies. **b** a burial or cremation procession. **c** *US* a burial or cremation service. **2** *sl.* one's (usu. unpleasant) concern (*that's your funeral*). ● *attrib.adj.* of or used etc. at a funeral (*funeral oration*). ▫ **funeral director** an undertaker. **funeral parlour** (*US* **home**) an establishment where the dead are prepared for burial or cremation. **funeral pile** (or **pyre**) a pile of wood etc. on which a corpse is burnt. **funeral urn** an urn holding the ashes of a cremated body. [ME f. OF *funeraille* f. med.L *funeralia* neut. pl. of LL *funeralis* f. L *funus -eris* funeral: (adj.) OF f. L *funeralis*]

■ *n.* **1** burial, interment, entombment, *literary* sepulture, inhumation; cremation; obsequies, exequies.

funerary /fyóonərəri/ *adj.* of or used at a funeral or funerals. [LL *funerarius* (as FUNERAL)]

funereal /fyooneériəl/ *adj.* **1** of or appropriate to a funeral. **2** gloomy, dismal, dark. □□ **funereally** *adv.* [L *funereus* (as FUNERAL)]
■ **2** gloomy, dismal, morose, sombre, lugubrious, mournful, doleful, sorrowful, grave, solemn, sad, unhappy, melancholy, depressing, dreary, woeful, dark, sepulchral.

funfair /fúnfair/ *n. Brit.* a fair, or part of one, consisting of amusements and sideshows.

fungi *pl.* of FUNGUS.

fungible /fúnjib'l/ *adj. Law* (of goods etc. contracted for, when an individual specimen is not meant) that can serve for, or be replaced by, another answering to the same definition. □□ **fungibility** /-bílliti/ *n.* [med.L *fungibilis* f. *fungi (vice)* serve (in place of)]

fungicide /fúnjisīd/ *n.* a fungus-destroying substance. □□ **fungicidal** /-sīd'l/ *adj.*

fungistatic /fúnjistáttik/ *adj.* inhibiting the growth of fungi. □□ **fungistatically** *adv.*

fungoid /fúnggoyd/ *adj.* & *n.* ● *adj.* **1** resembling a fungus in texture or in rapid growth. **2** *Brit.* of a fungus or fungi. ● *n.* a fungoid plant.

fungous /fúnggəss/ *adj.* **1** having the nature of a fungus. **2** springing up like a mushroom; transitory. [ME f. L *fungosus* (as FUNGUS)]

fungus /fúnggəss/ *n.* (*pl.* **fungi** /-gī, -jī/ or **funguses**) **1** any of a group of unicellular, multicellular, or multinucleate non-photosynthetic organisms feeding on organic matter, which include moulds, yeast, mushrooms, and toadstools. **2** anything similar usu. growing suddenly and rapidly. **3** *Med.* a spongy morbid growth. **4** *sl.* a beard. □□ **fungal** *adj.* **fungiform** /fúnggiform, fúnji-/ *adj.* **fungivorous** /funjívvərəss/ *adj.* [L, perh. f. Gk *sp(h)oggos* SPONGE]
■ **1** see MOULD[2].

funicular /fyoonikyoolər/ *adj.* & *n.* ● *adj.* **1** (of a railway, esp. on a mountainside) operating by cable with ascending and descending cars counterbalanced. **2** of a rope or its tension. ● *n.* a funicular railway. [L *funiculus* f. *funis* rope]

funk[1] /fungk/ *n.* & *v. sl.* ● *n.* **1** fear, panic. **2** a coward. ● *v. Brit.* **1** *intr.* flinch, shrink, show cowardice. **2** *tr.* try to evade (an undertaking), shirk. **3** *tr.* be afraid of. [18th-c. Oxford sl.: perh. f. sl. FUNK[2] = tobacco-smoke]
■ *n.* **1** see FRIGHT *n.* 1a.

funk[2] /fungk/ *n. sl.* **1** funky music. **2** *US* a strong smell. [*funk* blow smoke on, perh. f. F dial. *funkier* f. L (as FUMIGATE)]

funkia /fúngkiə/ *n.* = HOSTA. [mod.L f. H. C. *Funck*, Prussian botanist d. 1839]

funky[1] /fúngki/ *adj.* (**funkier, funkiest**) *sl.* **1** (esp. of jazz or rock music) earthy, bluesy, with a heavy rhythmical beat. **2** fashionable. **3** *US* having a strong smell. □□ **funkily** *adv.* **funkiness** *n.*

funky[2] /fúngki/ *adj.* (**funkier, funkiest**) *sl.* **1** terrified. **2** cowardly.

funnel /fúnn'l/ *n.* & *v.* ● *n.* **1** a narrow tube or pipe widening at the top, for pouring liquid, powder, etc., into a small opening. **2** a metal chimney on a steam engine or ship. **3** something resembling a funnel in shape or use. ● *v.tr.* & *intr.* (**funnelled, funnelling**; *US* **funneled, funneling**) guide or move through or as through a funnel. □□ **funnel-like** *adj.* [ME f. Prov. *fonilh* f. LL *fundibulum* f. L *infundibulum* f. *infundere* (as IN-[2], *fundere* pour)]
■ *n.* **2** see STACK *n.* 4.

funniosity /fúnnióssiti/ *n.* (*pl.* **-ies**) *joc.* **1** comicality. **2** a comical thing. [FUNNY + -OSITY]

funny /fúnni/ *adj.* & *n.* ● *adj.* (**funnier, funniest**) **1** amusing, comical. **2** strange, perplexing, hard to account for. **3** *colloq.* slightly unwell, eccentric, etc. ● *n.* (*pl.* **-ies**) (usu. in *pl.*) *colloq.* **1** a comic strip in a newspaper. **2** a joke. □ **funny-bone** the part of the elbow over which the ulnar nerve passes. **funny business 1** *sl.* misbehaviour or deception. **2** comic behaviour, comedy. **funny-face** *joc. colloq.* an affectionate form of address. **funny farm** *sl.* a mental hospital. **funny-ha-ha** *colloq.* = sense 1 of *adj.* **funny man** a clown or comedian, esp. a professional. **funny money** *colloq.* inflated currency. **funny paper** a newspaper etc. containing humorous matter. **funny-peculiar** *colloq.* = senses 2, 3 of *adj.* □□ **funnily** *adv.* **funniness** *n.* [FUN + -Y[1]]
■ *adj.* **1** comical, humorous, jocular, jocose, comic, droll, witty, zany; amusing, entertaining, diverting, side-splitting, hilarious, uproarious, *colloq.* hysterical; laughable, risible. **2** strange, peculiar, odd, queer, weird, bizarre, curious, mysterious, mystifying, puzzling, perplexing. **3** unwell, strange; unconventional, unusual, eccentric, *sl.* off-the-wall. ● *n.* **2** see JOKE *n.* 1. □ **funny business 1** see *misbehaviour* (MISBEHAVE), DECEIT 1. **2** see JOKE *n.* 2. **funny farm** mental home *or* hospital, (mental) asylum *or* institution, *archaic or colloq.* madhouse, *hist.* lunatic asylum, *sl.* loony-bin, nut-house. **funny man** see CLOWN *n.* 1.

fur /fur/ *n.* & *v.* ● *n.* **1 a** the short fine soft hair of certain animals, distinguished from the longer hair. **b** the skin of such an animal with the fur on it; a pelt. **2 a** the coat of certain animals as material for making, trimming, or lining clothes. **b** a trimming or lining made of the dressed coat of such animals, or of material imitating this. **c** a garment made of or trimmed or lined with fur. **3** (*collect.*) furred animals. **4 a** a coating formed on the tongue in sickness. **b** *Brit.* a coating formed on the inside surface of a pipe, kettle, etc., by hard water. **c** a crust adhering to a surface, e.g. a deposit from wine. **5** *Heraldry* a representation of tufts on a plain ground. ● *v.* (**furred, furring**) **1** *tr.* (esp. as **furred** *adj.*) **a** line or trim (a garment) with fur. **b** provide (an animal) with fur. **c** clothe (a person) with fur. **d** coat (a tongue, the inside of a kettle) with fur. **2** *intr.* (often foll. by *up*) (of a kettle etc.) become coated with fur. **3** *tr.* level (floor-timbers) by inserting strips of wood. □ **fur and feather** game animals and birds. **fur-seal** a sea lion with a valuable undercoat. **make the fur fly** *colloq.* cause a disturbance, stir up trouble. □□ **furless** *adj.* [ME (earlier as v.) f. OF *forrer* f. *forre, fuerre* sheath f. Gmc]
■ *n.* **1b, 2a** see PELT[2].

fur. *abbr.* furlong(s).

furbelow /fúrbilō/ *n.* & *v.* ● *n.* **1** a gathered strip or pleated border of a skirt or petticoat. **2** (in *pl.*) *derog.* showy ornaments. ● *v.tr.* adorn with a furbelow or furbelows. [18th-c. var. of *falbala* flounce, trimming]
■ *n.* **1** see FRILL *n.* 1a. **2** see ORNAMENT *n.* 1, 2.

furbish /fúrbish/ *v.tr.* (often foll. by *up*) **1** remove rust from, polish, burnish. **2** give a new look to, renovate, revive (something antiquated). □□ **furbisher** *n.* [ME f. OF *forbir* f. Gmc]
■ **1** see POLISH *v.* 1. **2** see DECORATE 2.

furcate /fúrkayt/ *adj.* & *v.* ● *adj.* /also fúrkət/ forked, branched. ● *v.intr.* form a fork, divide. □□ **furcation** /furkáysh'n/ *n.* [L *furca* fork: (adj.) f. LL *furcatus*]

furfuraceous /fúrfəráyshəss/ *adj.* **1** *Med.* (of skin) resembling bran or dandruff; scaly. **2** *Bot.* covered with branlike scales. [*furfur* scurf f. L *furfur* bran]

furious /fyóoriəss/ *adj.* **1** extremely angry. **2** full of fury. **3** raging, violent, intense. □ **fast and furious** *adv.* **1** rapidly. **2** eagerly, uproariously. ● *adj.* (of mirth etc.) eager, uproarious. □□ **furiously** *adv.* **furiousness** *n.* [ME f. OF *furieus* f. L *furiosus* (as FURY)]
■ **1, 2** angry, cross, irate, mad, enraged, infuriated, incensed, maddened, provoked, fuming, beside oneself, in high dudgeon, on the warpath, foaming at the mouth, *archaic* wroth, *colloq.* up the wall, steamed up, livid, wild, *literary* wrathful, infuriate, *Austral.* & *NZ sl.* ropeable. **3** fierce, wild, raging, violent, savage, intense; unrestrained, frantic, frenzied. □ **fast and furious** (*adv.*) **1** see *rapidly* (RAPID). **2** see *warmly* (WARM). (*adj.*) see EAGER 1, UPROARIOUS.

furl /furl/ *v.* **1** *tr.* roll up and secure (a sail, umbrella, flag, etc.). **2** *intr.* become furled. **3** *tr.* **a** close (a fan). **b** fold up (wings). **c** draw away (a curtain). **d** relinquish (hopes). □□

furlable *adj.* [F *ferler* f. OF *fer(m)* FIRM[1] + *lier* bind f. L *ligare*]
■ **1, 2** roll (up), wind up; see also WIND[2] *v.* 4.

furlong /fúrlong/ *n.* an eighth of a mile, 220 yards. [OE *furlang* f. *furh* FURROW + *lang* LONG[1]: orig. = length of a furrow in a common field]

furlough /fúrlō/ *n.* & *v.* ● *n.* leave of absence, esp. granted to a member of the services or to a missionary. ● *v. US* **1** *tr.* grant furlough to. **2** *intr.* spend furlough. [Du. *verlof* after G *Verlaub* (as FOR-, LEAVE[2])]
■ *n.* see HOLIDAY *n.* 1. ● *v.* **1** see FREE *v.* 1.

furmety var. of FRUMENTY.

furnace /fúrniss/ *n.* **1** an enclosed structure for intense heating by fire, esp. of metals or water. **2** a very hot place. [ME f. OF *fornais* f. L *fornax -acis* f. *fornus* oven]

furnish /fúrnish/ *v.tr.* **1** provide (a house, room, etc.) with all necessary contents, esp. movable furniture. **2** (foll. by *with*) cause to have possession or use of. **3** provide, afford, yield. [OF *furnir* ult. f. WG]
■ **1** see EQUIP. **2** equip, rig (out *or* up), kit (out *or* up); outfit, provision. **3** provide, afford, yield, give, supply.

furnished /fúrnisht/ *adj.* (of a house, flat, etc.) let with furniture.

furnisher /fúrnishər/ *n.* **1** a person who sells furniture. **2** a person who furnishes.

furnishings /fúrnishingz/ *n.pl.* the furniture and fitments in a house, room, etc.
■ see FURNITURE 1.

furniture /fúrnichər/ *n.* **1** the movable equipment of a house, room, etc., e.g. tables, chairs, and beds. **2** *Naut.* a ship's equipment, esp. tackle etc. **3** accessories, e.g. the handles and lock of a door. **4** *Printing* pieces of wood or metal placed round or between type to make blank spaces and fasten the matter in the chase. □ **furniture beetle** a beetle, *Anobium punctatum*, the larvae of which bore into wood (see WOODWORM). **furniture van** a large van used to move furniture from one house to another. **part of the furniture** *colloq.* a person or thing taken for granted. [F *fourniture* f. *fournir* (as FURNISH)]
■ **1** furnishings; goods, movables, chattels, effects, possessions, belongings. **2** tackle, apparatus, gear, tack. **3** fittings, fitments, fixtures, attachments, accessories, appliances, equipment. □ **furniture van** removal van, *Brit.* pantechnicon.

furore /fyoorórі/ *n.* (*US* **furor** /fyóoror/) **1** an uproar; an outbreak of fury. **2** a wave of enthusiastic admiration, a craze. [It. f. L *furor -oris* f. *furere* be mad]
■ **1** uproar, outburst, commotion, brouhaha, to-do, hubbub, stir, fuss, disturbance; tumult, turmoil, ado, excitement. **2** rage, craze, mania, vogue, enthusiasm, fad.

furphy /fúrfi/ *n.* (*pl.* **-ies**) *Austral. sl.* **1** a false report or rumour. **2** an absurd story. [water and sanitary *Furphy carts* of the war of 1914–18, made at a foundry set up by the Furphy family]

furrier /fúrriər/ *n.* a dealer in or dresser of furs. [ME *furrour* f. OF *forreor* f. *forrer* trim with fur, assim. to -IER]

furriery /fúrriəri/ *n.* the work of a furrier.

furrow /fúrrō/ *n.* & *v.* ● *n.* **1** a narrow trench made in the ground by a plough. **2** a rut, groove, or deep wrinkle. **3** a ship's track. ● *v.tr.* **1** plough. **2 a** make furrows, grooves, etc. in. **b** mark with wrinkles. □ **furrow-slice** the slice of earth turned up by the mould-board of a plough. □□ **furrowless** *adj.* **furrowy** *adj.* [OE *furh* f. Gmc]
■ *n.* **2** groove, channel, rut, trench, track, ditch, gutter, trough, fosse, fissure, sulcation, flute, score, cut, gash, scratch, line; wrinkle, crinkle, crease, corrugation, crow's-foot, *Anat.* sulcus. ● *v.* **1** plough, harrow, till, cultivate, rib. **2 a** groove, channel, flute, score, cut, gash, scratch. **b** wrinkle, crease, corrugate, knit, pucker, crinkle.

furry /fúri/ *adj.* (**furrier, furriest**) **1** of or like fur. **2** covered with or wearing fur. □□ **furriness** *n.*
■ **1** see SOFT *adj.* 2, WOOLLY *adj.* 1.

further /fúrthər/ *adv.*, *adj.*, & *v.* ● *adv.* (also **farther** /faárthər/ esp. with ref. to physical distance) **1** to or at a more advanced point in space or time (*unsafe to proceed further*). **2** at a greater distance (*nothing was further from his thoughts*). **3** to a greater extent, more (*will enquire further*). **4** in addition; furthermore (*I may add further*). ● *adj.* (also **farther** /faárthər/) **1** more distant or advanced (*on the further side*). **2** more, additional, going beyond what exists or has been dealt with (*threats of further punishment*). ● *v.tr.* promote, favour, help on (a scheme, undertaking, movement, or cause). □ **further education** *Brit.* education for persons above school age but usu. below degree level. **further to** *formal* following on from (esp. an earlier letter etc.). **till further notice** (or **orders**) to continue until explicitly changed. □□ **furtherer** *n.* **furthermost** *adj.* [OE *furthor* (adv.), *furthra* (adj.), *fyrthrian* (v.), formed as FORTH, -ER[3]]
■ *adv.* **4** furthermore, besides, moreover, too, also, additionally, in addition, what is more, to boot, yet, then (again), again. ● *adj.* **2** more, additional, other, new, supplemental, supplementary, accessory, auxiliary, extra, spare, fresh. ● *v.* advance, promote, favour, forward, foster, back, patronize, support, help, assist, aid. □ **further to** following, with reference *or* regard to.

furtherance /fúrthərənss/ *n.* furthering or being furthered; the advancement of a scheme etc.
■ promotion, advancement, championship, advocacy, patronage, backing, fostering, championing, advocating, *colloq.* boost(ing); support, help, aid, assistance.

furthermore /fúrthərmór/ *adv.* in addition, besides (esp. introducing a fresh consideration in an argument).
■ see *in addition* (ADDITION).

furthest /fúrthist/ *adj.* & *adv.* (also **farthest** /faárthist/ esp. with ref. to physical distance) ● *adj.* most distant. ● *adv.* to or at the greatest distance. □ **at the furthest** (or **at furthest**) at the greatest distance; at the latest; at most. [ME, superl. f. FURTHER]
■ *adj.* see ULTIMATE *adj.* 1, 2.

furtive /fúrtiv/ *adj.* **1** done by stealth, clandestine, meant to escape notice. **2** sly, stealthy. **3** stolen, taken secretly. **4** thievish, pilfering. □□ **furtively** *adv.* **furtiveness** *n.* [F *furtif -ive* or L *furtivus* f. *furtum* theft]
■ **1** secret, secretive, clandestine, conspiratorial, surreptitious, underhand(ed), covert, hidden, hugger-mugger, sneaky. **2** sly, foxy, cunning, crafty, wily, shifty, skulking, sneaky, untrustworthy, *colloq.* stealthy.

furuncle /fyóorungk'l/ *n. Med.* = BOIL[2]. □□ **furuncular** /-rúngkyoolər/ *adj.* **furunculous** /-rúngkyooləss/ *adj.* [L *furunculus* f. *fur* thief]

furunculosis /fyoorúngkyoolṓsiss/ *n.* **1** a diseased condition in which boils appear. **2** a bacterial disease of salmon and trout. [mod.L (as FURUNCLE)]

fury /fyóori/ *n.* (*pl.* **-ies**) **1 a** wild and passionate anger, rage. **b** a fit of rage (*in a blind fury*). **c** impetuosity in battle etc. **2** violence of a storm, disease, etc. **3** (**Fury**) (usu. in *pl.*) (in Greek mythology) each of three goddesses sent from Tartarus to avenge crime, esp. against kinship. **4** an avenging spirit. **5** an angry or malignant woman, a virago. □ **like fury** *colloq.* with great force or effect. [ME f. OF *furie* f. L *furia* f. *furere* be mad]
■ **1 a** rage, *literary* ire, wrath, *poet. or archaic* choler; see also ANGER *n.* **b** see TEMPER *n.* 2b. **c** impetuosity, vehemence; see also VIOLENCE 1. **2** ferocity, savagery, fierceness, tempestuousness, turbulence, violence. **5** virago, shrew, hell-cat, termagant, vixen, she-devil, hag, witch, *archaic* beldam, *sl. offens.* bitch.

furze /furz/ *n. Brit.* = GORSE. □□ **furzy** /fúrzi/ *adj.* [OE *fyrs*, of unkn. orig.]

fuscous /fúskəss/ *adj.* sombre, dark-coloured. [L *fuscus* dusky]

fuse[1] /fyōōz/ *v.* & *n.* ● *v.* **1** *tr.* & *intr.* melt with intense heat; liquefy. **2** *tr.* & *intr.* blend or amalgamate into one whole by or as by melting. **3** *tr.* provide (a circuit, plug, etc.) with a fuse. **4 a** *intr.* (of an appliance) cease to function when a fuse blows. **b** *tr.* cause (an appliance) to do this. ● *n.* a device or component for protecting an electric circuit, containing a strip of wire of easily melted metal and placed in the circuit so as to break it by melting when an excessive current passes through. □ **fuse-box** a box housing the fuses for circuits in a building. [L *fundere fus-* pour, melt]

■ *v.* **2** blend, merge, unite, combine, mix, amalgamate, mingle, *literary* commingle; compound, consolidate; coalesce.

fuse[2] /fyo͞oz/ *n.* & *v.* (also **fuze**) ● *n.* **1** a device for igniting a bomb or explosive charge, consisting of a tube or cord etc. filled or saturated with combustible matter. **2** a component in a shell, mine, etc., designed to detonate an explosive charge on impact, after an interval, or when subjected to a magnetic or vibratory stimulation. ● *v.tr.* fit a fuse to. □□ **fuseless** *adj.* [It. *fuso* f. L *fusus* spindle]

fusee /fyoozée/ *n.* (*US* **fuzee**) **1** a conical pulley or wheel esp. in a watch or clock. **2** a large-headed match for lighting a cigar or pipe in a wind. **3** *US* a railway signal-flare. [F *fusée* spindle ult. f. L *fusus*]

fuselage /fyo͞ozəlaazh, -lij/ *n.* the body of an aeroplane. [F f. *fuseler* cut into a spindle f. *fuseau* spindle f. OF *fusel* ult. f. L *fusus*]

■ see BODY *n.* 3a.

fusel oil /fyo͞oz'l/ *n.* a mixture of several alcohols, chiefly amyl alcohol, produced usu. in small amounts during alcoholic fermentation. [G *Fusel* bad brandy etc.: cf. *fuseln* to bungle]

fusible /fyo͞ozib'l/ *adj.* that can be easily fused or melted. □□ **fusibility** /-bílliti/ *n.*

fusiform /fyo͞oziform/ *adj. Bot.* & *Zool.* shaped like a spindle or cigar, tapering at both ends. [L *fusus* spindle + -FORM]

fusil /fyo͞ozil/ *n. hist.* a light musket. [F ult. f. L *focus* hearth, fire]

fusilier /fyo͞ozileér/ *n.* (*US* **fusileer**) **1** a member of any of several British regiments formerly armed with fusils. **2** *hist.* a soldier armed with a fusil. [F (as FUSIL)]

fusillade /fyo͞ozilάyd/ *n.* & *v.* ● *n.* **1 a** a continuous discharge of firearms. **b** a wholesale execution by this means. **2** a sustained outburst of criticism etc. ● *v.tr.* **1** assault (a place) by a fusillade. **2** shoot down (persons) with a fusillade. [F f. *fusiller* shoot]

■ *n.* **1 a** see DISCHARGE *n.* 4.

fusion /fyo͞ozh'n/ *n.* **1** the act or an instance of fusing or melting. **2** a fused mass. **3** the blending of different things into one. **4** a coalition. **5** *Physics* = *nuclear fusion.* □ **fusion bomb** a bomb involving nuclear fusion, esp. a hydrogen bomb. □□ **fusional** *adj.* [F *fusion* or L *fusio* (as FUSE[1])]

■ **1–4** see *amalgamation* (AMALGAMATE).

fuss /fuss/ *n.* & *v.* ● *n.* **1** excited commotion, bustle, ostentatious or nervous activity. **2 a** excessive concern about a trivial thing. **b** abundance of petty detail. **3** a sustained protest or dispute. **4** a person who fusses. ● *v.* **1** *intr.* **a** make a fuss. **b** busy oneself restlessly with trivial things. **c** (often foll. by *about, up and down*) move fussily. **2** *tr.* agitate, worry. □ **make a fuss** complain vigorously. **make a fuss of** (or **over**) treat (a person or animal) with great or excessive attention. □□ **fusser** *n.* [18th c.: perh. Anglo-Ir.]

■ *n.* **1, 2a** bother, fluster, flurry, commotion, bustle, to-do, furore, stir, uproar, disturbance, hubbub, brouhaha, excitement, ado, unrest, trouble, upset, agitation, *colloq.* flap, stink, *esp. Brit. colloq.* kerfuffle, *literary* pother, *sl.* hoo-ha, hoop-la. **4** see *perfectionist* (PERFECTIONISM). ● *v.* **1 a** make a fuss, kick up a fuss; see also COMPLAIN 1, 2b. **c** rush about *or* around, flutter *or* fly about *or* around, run round in circles, bustle; see also TEAR[1] *v.* 5. **2** see WORRY *v.* 2. □ **make a fuss** see COMPLAIN 1, 2b. **make a fuss of** (or **over**) see FÊTE *v.*

fusspot /fúspot/ *n. colloq.* a person given to fussing.

■ see BOTHER *n.* 1, *perfectionist* (PERFECTIONISM).

fussy /fússi/ *adj.* (**fussier, fussiest**) **1** inclined to fuss. **2** full of unnecessary detail or decoration. **3** fastidious. □□ **fussily** *adv.* **fussiness** *n.*

■ **1** see CHOOSY. **2** fancy, elaborate, over-decorated, rococo, ornate, *Archit.* & *Painting* Byzantine. **3** particular, finicky, finical, dainty, fastidious, *colloq.* picky, choosy, pernickety, nit-picking.

fustanella /fústənéllə/ *n.* a man's stiff white kilt worn in Albania and Greece. [It. dimin. of mod. Gk *phoustani* prob. f. It. *fustagno* FUSTIAN]

fustian /fústiən/ *n.* & *adj.* ● *n.* **1** thick twilled cotton cloth with a short nap, usu. dyed in dark colours. **2** turgid speech or writing, bombast. ● *adj.* **1** made of fustian. **2** bombastic. **3** worthless. [ME f. OF *fustaigne* f. med.L *fustaneus* (adj.) relating to cloth from *Fostat* a suburb of Cairo]

■ *n.* **2** see RHETORIC 2. ● *adj.* **2** see *bombastic* (BOMBAST).

fustic /fústik/ *n.* a yellow dye obtained from either of two kinds of wood, esp. old fustic. □ **old fustic 1** a tropical tree, *Chlorophora tinctoria*, native to America. **2** the wood of this tree. **young fustic 1** a sumac, *Cotinus coggyria*, native to Europe (also called *Venetian sumac*). **2** the wood of this tree. [F f. Sp. *fustoc* f. Arab. *fustuķ* f. Gk *pistakē* pistachio]

fusty /fústi/ *adj.* (**fustier, fustiest**) **1** stale-smelling, musty, mouldy. **2** stuffy, close. **3** antiquated, old-fashioned. □□ **fustily** *adv.* **fustiness** *n.* [ME f. OF *fusté* smelling of the cask f. *fust* cask, tree-trunk, f. L *fustis* cudgel]

■ **1** see MUSTY 1, 2. **2** see CLOSE[1] *adj.* 8.

futhorc /fo͞othork/ *n.* the Scandinavian runic alphabet. [its first six letters *f, u, th, ö, r, k*]

futile /fyo͞otīl/ *adj.* **1** useless, ineffectual, vain. **2** frivolous, trifling. □□ **futilely** *adv.* **futility** /-tílliti/ *n.* [L *futilis* leaky, futile, rel. to *fundere* pour]

■ **1** useless, vain, unavailing, unsuccessful, unprofitable, abortive, profitless, fruitless, unproductive, ineffective, ineffectual, *archaic* bootless, *Austral. colloq.* no good to gundy. **2** frivolous, trifling; see also WORTHLESS.

futon /fo͞oton/ *n.* a Japanese quilted mattress rolled out on the floor for use as a bed; a type of low-slung wooden bed using this kind of mattress. [Jap.]

futtock /fúttək/ *n.* each of the middle timbers of a ship's frame, between the floor and the top timbers. [ME *votekes* etc. pl. f. MLG f. *fōt* FOOT + *-ken* -KIN]

future /fyo͞ochər/ *adj.* & *n.* ● *adj.* **1 a** going or expected to happen or be or become (*his future career*). **b** that will be something specified (*my future wife*). **c** that will be after death (*a future life*). **2 a** of time to come (*future years*). **b** *Gram.* (of a tense or participle) describing an event yet to happen. ● *n.* **1** time to come (*past, present, and future*). **2** what will happen in the future (*the future is uncertain*). **3** the future condition of a person, country, etc. **4** a prospect of success etc. (*there's no future in it*). **5** *Gram.* the future tense. **6** (in *pl.*) *Stock Exch.* **a** goods and stocks sold for future delivery. **b** contracts for these. □ **for the future** = *in future.* **future perfect** *Gram.* a tense giving the sense *will have done.* **future shock** inability to cope with rapid progress. **in future** from now onwards. □□ **futureless** *adj.* [ME f. OF *futur -ure* f. L *futurus* future part. of *esse* be f. stem *fu-* be]

■ *adj.* **1 a** see PROSPECTIVE. **b** to be. **2 a** tomorrow's, coming; subsequent; to be, to come; see also PROSPECTIVE. ● *n.* **1** days *or* time to come; tomorrow; futurity. **3** see PROSPECT *n.* 1a. □ **in future** hence, henceforth, as of now, from now (on *or* onwards).

futurism /fyo͞ochəriz'm/ *n.* a movement in art, literature, music, etc., with violent departure from traditional forms so as to express movement and growth. [FUTURE + -ISM, after It. *futurismo*, F *futurisme*]

futurist /fyo͞ochərist/ *n.* (often *attrib.*) **1** an adherent of futurism. **2** a believer in human progress. **3** a student of the future. **4** *Theol.* one who believes that biblical prophecies, esp. those of the Apocalypse, are still to be fulfilled.

futuristic /fyo͞ochərístik/ *adj.* **1** suitable for the future; ultra-modern. **2** of futurism. **3** relating to the future. □□ **futuristically** *adv.*

futurity /fyootyo͝oriti/ *n.* (*pl.* **-ies**) **1** future time. **2** (in *sing.* or *pl.*) future events. **3** future condition; existence after death. □ **futurity stakes** *US* stakes raced for long after entries or nominations are made.

futurology /fyōōchərólləji/ *n.* systematic forecasting of the future esp. from present trends in society. □□ **futurologist** *n.*

fuze var. of FUSE².

fuzee *US* var. of FUSEE.

fuzz /fuz/ *n.* **1** fluff. **2** fluffy or frizzled hair. **3** *sl.* **a** the police. **b** a policeman. □ **fuzz-ball** a puff-ball fungus. [17th c.: prob. f. LG or Du.: sense 3 perh. a different word]

■ **1** see FLUFF *n.* 1. **3 a** see POLICE *n.* **b** see *police officer*.

fuzzy /fúzzi/ *adj.* (**fuzzier, fuzziest**) **1 a** like fuzz. **b** frayed, fluffy. **c** frizzy. **2** blurred, indistinct. □ **fuzzy-wuzzy** (*pl.* **-ies**) *offens.* **1** *colloq. hist.* a Sudanese soldier. **2** *sl.* a Coloured native of any country. □□ **fuzzily** *adv.* **fuzziness** *n.*

■ **1 a** woolly, furry, downy, flocculent, fluffy, linty. **b** see HAIRY 1. **c** see KINKY 3. **2** dim, faint, hazy, foggy, misty, blurred, blurry, indistinct, unclear, vague, shadowy, indefinite, obscure, ill-defined, woolly, distorted.

fwd *abbr.* forward.

f.w.d. *abbr.* **1** four-wheel drive. **2** front-wheel drive.

f.y. *abbr. US* fiscal year.

-fy /fī/ *suffix* forming: **1** verbs from nouns, meaning: **a** make, produce (*pacify*; *satisfy*). **b** make into (*deify*; *petrify*). **2** verbs from adjectives, meaning 'bring or come into such a state' (*Frenchify*; *solidify*). **3** verbs in causative sense (*horrify*; *stupefy*). [from or after F *-fier* f. L *-ficare*, *-facere* f. *facere* do, make]

fylfot /filfət/ *n.* a swastika. [perh. f. *fill-foot*, pattern to fill the foot of a painted window]

fyrd /furd/ *n. hist.* **1** the English militia before 1066. **2** the duty to serve in this. [OE f. Gmc (as FARE)]

fytte var. of FIT³.

Gg

G[1] /jee/ *n.* (also **g**) (*pl.* **Gs** or **G's**) **1** the seventh letter of the alphabet. **2** *Mus.* the fifth note in the diatonic scale of C major.

G[2] *abbr.* (also **G.**) **1** gauss. **2** giga-. **3** gravitational constant. **4** *US sl.* = GRAND *n.* 2.

g *abbr.* (also **g.**) **1** gelding. **2** gram(s). **3 a** gravity. **b** acceleration due to gravity.

GA *abbr. US* Georgia (in official postal use).

Ga *symb. Chem.* the element gallium.

Ga. *abbr.* Georgia (US).

gab /gab/ *n.* & *v. colloq.* ● *n.* talk, chatter, twaddle. ● *v.intr.* talk incessantly, trivially, or indiscreetly; chatter. □ **gift of the gab** the facility of speaking eloquently or profusely. □□ **gabber** *n.* [17th-c. var. of GOB[1]]

■ *n.* talk, chatter, prattle, jabber, blather, tittle-tattle, gossip, *colloq.* chit-chat; cackle, drivel, twaddle, moonshine, blarney, nonsense, rubbish, bunkum, balderdash, garbage, *colloq.* hogwash, piffle, tosh, *sl.* poppycock, bunk, eyewash, *Brit. sl.* codswallop. ● *v.* jabber, gabble, chatter, gibber, blather, prate, prattle, blab, gossip, *colloq.* natter, witter, jaw, *Austral. colloq.* yabber, *sl. derog.* yack.

gabardine /gábbərdeén/ *n.* (also **gaberdine**) **1** a smooth durable twill-woven cloth esp. of worsted or cotton. **2** a garment made of this, esp. a raincoat. [var. of GABERDINE]

gabble /gább'l/ *v.* & *n.* ● *v.* **1** *intr.* **a** talk volubly or inarticulately. **b** read aloud too fast. **2** *tr.* utter too fast, esp. in reading aloud. ● *n.* fast unintelligible talk. □□ **gabbler** *n.* [MDu. *gabbelen* (imit.)]

■ *v.* see PRATTLE *v.* ● *n.* see PRATTLE *n.*

gabbro /gábrō/ *n.* (*pl.* **-os**) a dark granular plutonic rock of crystalline texture. □□ **gabbroic** /-brṓ-ik/ *adj.* **gabbroid** *adv.* [It. f. *Gabbro* in Tuscany]

gabby /gábbi/ *adj.* (**gabbier, gabbiest**) *colloq.* talkative. [GAB + -Y[1]]

■ see TALKATIVE.

gaberdine /gábbərdeén/ *n.* **1** var. of GABARDINE. **2** *hist.* a loose long upper garment worn esp. by Jews and almsmen. [OF *gauvardine* perh. f. MHG *wallevart* pilgrimage]

gabion /gáybiən/ *n.* a cylindrical wicker or metal basket for filling with earth or stones, used in engineering or (formerly) in fortification. □□ **gabionage** *n.* [F f. It. *gabbione* f. *gabbia* CAGE]

gable /gáyb'l/ *n.* **1 a** the triangular upper part of a wall at the end of a ridged roof. **b** (in full **gable-end**) a gable-topped wall. **2** a gable-shaped canopy over a window or door. □□ **gabled** *adj.* (also in *comb.*). [ME *gable* f. ON *gafl*]

gad[1] /gad/ *v.* & *n.* ● *v.intr.* (**gadded, gadding**) (foll. by *about, abroad, around*) go about idly or in search of pleasure. ● *n.* idle wandering or adventure (esp. in **on the gad**). [back-form. f. obs. *gadling* companion f. OE *gædeling* f. *gæd* fellowship]

■ *v.*(*gad about* or *around*) run around, flit, *colloq.* gallivant; see also IDLE *v.* 2, PHILANDER.

gad[2] /gad/ *int.* (also **by gad**) an expression of surprise or emphatic assertion. [= *God*]

■ *archaic* gadzooks, *archaic or joc.* egad.

gadabout /gáddəbowt/ *n.* a person who gads about; an idle pleasure-seeker.

■ see ROVER[1].

Gadarene /gáddəreen/ *adj.* involving or engaged in headlong or suicidal rush or flight. [LL *Gadarenus* f. Gk *Gadarēnos* of Gadara in anc. Palestine, with ref. to Matthew 8:28–32]

gadfly /gádflī/ *n.* (*pl.* **-flies**) **1** a cattle-biting fly, esp. a warble fly, horsefly, or bot-fly. **2** an irritating or harassing person. [obs. *gad* goad, spike f. ON *gaddr*, rel. to YARD[1]]

■ **2** see TROUBLEMAKER.

gadget /gájit/ *n.* any small and usu. ingenious mechanical device or tool. □□ **gadgeteer** /-teér/ *n.* **gadgetry** *n.* **gadgety** *adj.* [19th-c. Naut.: orig. unkn.]

■ device, contrivance, appliance, apparatus, mechanism, machine, instrument, implement, utensil, tool, what-d'you-call-it, what's-its-name, doodah, *Brit.* gubbins, *US* doodad, *colloq.* widget, thingummy, thingy, *US colloq.* hickey, doohickey, *usu. derog. or joc.* contraption, *sl.* gismo. □□ **gadgetry** see APPARATUS.

gadoid /gáydoyd/ *n.* & *adj.* ● *n.* any marine fish of the cod family Gadidae, including haddock and whiting. ● *adj.* belonging to or resembling the Gadidae. [mod.L *gadus* f. Gk *gados* cod + -OID]

gadolinite /gáddəlinīt/ *n.* a dark crystalline mineral consisting of ferrous silicate of beryllium. [J. *Gadolin*, Finnish mineralogist d. 1852]

gadolinium /gáddəlinniəm/ *n. Chem.* a soft silvery metallic element of the lanthanide series, occurring naturally in gadolinite. ¶ Symb.: **Gd**. [mod.L f. GADOLINITE]

gadroon /gədrōōn/ *n.* a decoration on silverware etc., consisting of convex curves in a series forming an ornamental edge like inverted fluting. [F *godron*: cf. *goder* pucker]

gadwall /gádwawl/ *n.* a brownish-grey freshwater duck, *Anas strepera*. [17th c.: orig. unkn.]

gadzooks /gadzōōks/ *int. archaic* an expression of asseveration etc. [GAD[2] + *zooks* of unkn. orig.]

Gael /gayl/ *n.* **1** a Scottish Celt. **2** a Gaelic-speaking Celt. □□ **Gaeldom** *n.* [Gael. *Gaidheal*]

Gaelic /gáylik, gállik/ *n.* & *adj.* ● *n.* any of the Celtic languages spoken in Ireland, Scotland, and the Isle of Man. ● *adj.* of or relating to the Celts or the Celtic languages.

Gaeltacht /gáyltə<u>kh</u>t/ *n.* any of the regions in Ireland where the vernacular language is Irish. [Ir.]

gaff[1] /gaf/ *n.* & *v.* ● *n.* **1 a** a stick with an iron hook for landing large fish. **b** a barbed fishing-spear. **2** a spar to which the head of a fore-and-aft sail is bent. ● *v.tr.* seize (a fish) with a gaff. [ME f. Prov. *gaf* hook]

gaff[2] /gaf/ *n. Brit. sl.* □ **blow the gaff** let out a plot or secret. [19th c., = nonsense: orig. unkn.]

gaffe /gaf/ *n.* a blunder; an indiscreet act or remark. [F]

■ see BLUNDER *n.*

gaffer /gáffər/ *n.* **1** an old fellow; an elderly rustic. **2** *Brit. colloq.* a foreman or boss. **3** *colloq.* the chief electrician in a film or television production unit. [prob. contr. of GODFATHER]

■ **2** see BOSS[1] *n.*

gag /gag/ *n.* & *v.* ● *n.* **1** a piece of cloth etc. thrust into or held over the mouth to prevent speaking or crying out, or to hold it open in surgery. **2** a joke or comic scene in a play, film, etc., or as part of a comedian's act. **3** an actor's interpolation in a dramatic dialogue. **4** a thing or circumstance restricting free speech. **5 a** a joke or hoax. **b** a humorous action or situation. **6** an imposture or deception. **7** *Parl.* a closure or guillotine. ● *v.* (**gagged**, **gagging**) **1** *tr.* apply a gag to. **2** *tr.* silence; deprive of free speech. **3** *tr.* apply a gag-bit to (a horse). **4 a** *intr.* choke or retch. **b** *tr.* cause to do this. **5** *intr. Theatr.* make gags. □ **gag-bit** a specially powerful bit for horse-breaking. **gag man** a deviser or performer of theatrical gags. [ME, orig. as verb: orig. uncert.]

■ *n.* **1** muzzle. **4** restriction, ban, proscription; embargo, boycott. **5 a** joke, witticism, jest, quip, pun, *colloq.* wisecrack, crack; practical joke, hoax, prank, trick, *colloq.* fast one, *Austral.* goak. **b** joke, frolic, *colloq.* giggle, lark, scream, hoot, laugh. **6** see MASQUERADE *n.* 1. ● *v.* **2** silence, curb, put a lid on, suppress, repress, check, inhibit, restrain; stifle, still, muffle, muzzle. **4 a** retch, choke; see also HEAVE *v.* 6. **b** see CHOKE[1] *v.* 1. □ **gag man** see COMEDIAN.

gaga /gaágaa/ *adj. sl.* **1** senile. **2** fatuous; slightly crazy. [F, = senile]

■ **2** see CRAZY 1.

gage[1] /gayj/ *n.* & *v.* ● *n.* **1** a pledge; a thing deposited as security. **2 a** a challenge to fight. **b** a symbol of this, esp. a glove thrown down. ● *v.tr. archaic* stake, pledge; offer as a guarantee. [ME f. OF *gage* (n.), F *gager* (v.) ult. f. Gmc, rel. to WED]

■ *n.* **1** see PLEDGE *n.* 2. **2** see CHALLENGE *n.* 1.

gage[2] *US* var. of GAUGE.

gage[3] /gayj/ *n.* = GREENGAGE. [abbr.]

gaggle /gágg'l/ *n.* & *v.* ● *n.* **1** a flock of geese. **2** *colloq.* a disorderly group of people. ● *v.intr.* (of geese) cackle. [ME, imit.: cf. *gabble*, *cackle*]

gagster /gágstər/ *n.* = *gag man.*

gaiety /gáyəti/ *n.* (*US* **gayety**) **1** the state of being light-hearted or merry; mirth. **2** merrymaking, amusement. **3** a bright appearance. □ **gaiety of nations** the cheerfulness or pleasure of numerous people. [F *gaieté* (as GAY)]

■ **1** light-heartedness, cheerfulness, cheeriness, happiness, high spirits, *joie de vivre*, buoyancy, exhilaration, elation, glee, felicity, delight, pleasure, joy, joyfulness, joyousness, exultation, jubilation, merriment, mirth, mirthfulness, joviality, jollity, hilarity, *poet.* blitheness. **2** merrymaking, amusement, festivity, celebration, revelry, rejoicing, conviviality. **3** brightness, colourfulness, brilliance, glow; see also SPLENDOUR 2.

gaillardia /gayla ́ardiə/ *n.* any composite plant of the genus *Gaillardia*, with showy flowers. [mod.L f. *Gaillard* de Marentoneau, 18th-c. Fr. botanist]

gaily /gáyli/ *adv.* **1** in a gay or light-hearted manner. **2** with a bright or colourful appearance.

■ **1** light-heartedly, happily, cheerfully, cheerily, gleefully, joyously, joyfully, jubilantly, merrily, jauntily, insouciantly, *poet.* blithely. **2** brightly, brilliantly, colourfully.

gain /gayn/ *v.* & *n.* ● *v.* **1** *tr.* obtain or secure (usu. something desired or favourable) (*gain an advantage*; *gain recognition*). **2** *tr.* acquire (a sum) as profits or as a result of changed conditions; earn. **3** *tr.* obtain as an increment or addition (*gain momentum*; *gain weight*). **4** *tr.* **a** win (a victory). **b** reclaim (land from the sea). **5** *intr.* (foll. by *in*) make a specified advance or improvement (*gained in stature*). **6** *intr.* & *tr.* (of a clock etc.) become fast, or be fast by (a specified amount of time). **7** *intr.* (often foll. by *on*, *upon*) come closer to a person or thing pursued. **8** *tr.* **a** bring over to one's interest or views. **b** (foll. by *over*) win by persuasion etc. **9** *tr.* reach or arrive at (a desired place). ● *n.* **1** something gained, achieved, etc. **2** an increase of possessions etc.; a profit, advance, or improvement. **3** the acquisition of wealth. **4** (in *pl.*) sums of money acquired by trade etc., emoluments, winnings. **5** an increase in amount. **6** *Electronics* **a** the factor by which power etc. is increased. **b** the logarithm of this. □ **gain ground** see GROUND[1]. **gain time** improve one's chances by causing or accepting delay. □□ **gainable** *adj.* **gainer** *n.* **gainings** *n.pl.* [OF *gaigner*, *gaaignier* to till, acquire, ult. f. Gmc]

■ *v.* **1** get, obtain, acquire, procure, attain, achieve, secure, earn, win, capture, net, reap, glean, collect, gather, come by, pick up, *colloq.* bag. **2** make, get, realize, clear; see also EARN 1. **3** gather, acquire, pick up; put on. **4 a** see WIN *v.* 1. **5** improve, progress, advance, increase. **7** gain ground, narrow the gap; (*gain on*) catch up (with), approach, get nearer to, overtake, close in on. **8** proselytize, change, switch, convert, win over. **9** arrive at, get to, come to; see also REACH *v.* 4. ● *n.* **1** achievement, attainment, acquisition; see also ACCOMPLISHMENT 3, ADVANTAGE *n.* 1, 3. **2** profit, increase, advance, improvement, emolument, yield, return, dividend; proceeds, revenue, income, earnings, winnings, payout, *esp. US* take, *sl.* pay-off. **4** (*gains*) see FRUIT *n.* 4. **5** increase, increment, rise, addition, advance, enhancement, elevation, augmentation; upward *or* forward movement, progress.

gainful /gáynfŏŏl/ *adj.* **1** (of employment) paid. **2** lucrative, remunerative. □□ **gainfully** *adv.* **gainfulness** *n.*

■ **2** lucrative, remunerative, moneymaking, profitable, advantageous, productive, fruitful.

gainsay /gáynsáy/ *v.tr.* (*past* and *past part.* **gainsaid** /-séd/) *archaic* or *literary* deny, contradict. □□ **gainsayer** *n.* [ME f. obs. *gain-* against f. ON *gegn* straight f. Gmc + SAY]

'gainst /genst/ *prep. poet.* = AGAINST. [abbr.]

gait /gayt/ *n.* **1** a manner of walking; one's bearing or carriage as one walks. **2** the manner of forward motion of a runner, horse, vehicle, etc. □ **go one's** (or **one's own**) **gait** pursue one's own course. [var. of GATE[2]]

■ **1** see WALK *n.* 1.

gaiter /gáytər/ *n.* a covering of cloth, leather, etc. for the leg below the knee, for the ankle, for part of a machine, etc. □□ **gaitered** *adj.* [F *guêtre*, prob. rel. to WRIST]

Gal. *abbr.* Galatians (New Testament).

gal[1] /gal/ *n. sl.* a girl. [repr. var. pronunc.]

■ see GIRL 1.

gal[2] /gal/ *n. Physics* a unit of acceleration for a gravitational field, equal to one centimetre per second per second. [*Galileo*: see GALILEAN[1]]

gal. *abbr.* gallon(s).

gala /ga ́alə/ *n.* **1** (often *attrib.*) a festive or special occasion (*a gala performance*). **2** *Brit.* a festive gathering for sports, esp. swimming. [F or It. f. Sp. f. OF *gale* rejoicing f. Gmc]

■ **1** fête, festival, festivity, feast, celebration, holiday, carnival, pageant, party; (*attrib.*) festive, celebratory; special, commemorative. **2** event, meet.

galactagogue /gəláktəgog/ *adj.* & *n.* ● *adj.* inducing a flow of milk. ● *n.* a galactagogue substance. [Gk *gala galaktos* milk, + *agōgos* leading]

galactic /gəláktik/ *adj.* of or relating to a galaxy or galaxies, esp. the Galaxy. [Gk *galaktias*, var. of *galaxias*: see GALAXY]

galago /gəláygō/ *n.* (*pl.* **-os**) any small tree-climbing primate of the genus *Galago*, found in southern Africa, with large eyes and ears and a long tail. Also called *bush-baby*. [mod.L]

galah /gəla ́a/ *n. Austral.* **1** a small rose-breasted grey-backed cockatoo, *Cacatua roseicapilla*. **2** *sl.* a fool or simpleton. [Aboriginal]

Galahad /gálləhad/ *n.* a person characterized by nobility, integrity, courtesy, etc. [name of a knight of the Round Table in Arthurian legend]

galantine /gállənteen/ *n.* white meat or fish boned, cooked, pressed, and served cold in aspic etc. [ME f. OF, alt. f. *galatine* jellied meat f. med.L *galatina*]

galaxy /gálləksi/ *n.* (*pl.* **-ies**) **1** any of many independent systems of stars, gas, dust, etc., held together by gravitational attraction. **2** (**the Galaxy**) the galaxy of which the solar system is a part. **3** (**the Galaxy**) the irregular luminous band of stars indistinguishable to the naked eye encircling the heavens, the Milky Way. **4** (foll. by *of*) a brilliant company or gathering. [ME f. OF *galaxie* f. med.L *galaxia*, LL *galaxias* f. Gk f. *gala galaktos* milk]

galbanum /gálbənəm/ *n.* a bitter aromatic gum resin produced from kinds of ferula. [ME f. L f. Gk *khalbanē*, prob. of Semitic orig.]

gale[1] /gayl/ *n.* **1** a very strong wind, esp. (on the Beaufort scale) one of 32–54 m.p.h. **2** *Naut.* a storm. **3** an outburst, esp. of laughter. [16th c.: orig. unkn.]
■ **2** see STORM *n.* 1. **3** outburst, burst, explosion, eruption; peal, roar, scream, shout, howl, shriek, hoot.

gale[2] /gayl/ *n.* (in full **sweet-gale**) bog myrtle. [OE *gagel(le)*, MDu. *gaghel*]

galea /gáyliə/ *n.* (*pl.* **galeae** /-li-ee/ or **-as**) *Bot.* & *Zool.* a structure like a helmet in shape, form, or function. □□ **galeate** /-liət/ *adj.* **galeated** /-liaytid/ *adj.* [L, = helmet]

galena /gəle͞enə/ *n.* a bluish, grey or black mineral ore of lead sulphide. ¶ Chem. formula: PbS. [L, = lead ore (in a partly purified state)]

galenic /gəlénnik/ *adj.* & *n.* (also **galenical** /-lénnik'l/) ● *adj.* **1** of or relating to Galen, a Greek physician of the 2nd c. AD, or his methods. **2** made of natural as opposed to synthetic components. ● *n.* a drug or medicament produced directly from animal or vegetable tissues.

galenical var. of GALENIC.

Galilean[1] /gállile͞eən/ *adj.* of or relating to Galileo, Italian astronomer d. 1642, or his methods.

Galilean[2] /gállile͞eən/ *adj.* & *n.* ● *adj.* **1** of Galilee in Palestine. **2** Christian. ● *n.* **1** a native of Galilee. **2** a Christian. **3** (prec. by *the*) *derog.* Christ.

galingale /gállinggayl/ *n.* **1** an aromatic rhizome of an E. Asian plant of the genus *Alpinia*, formerly used in cookery and medicine. **2** (in full **English galingale**) a sedge (*Cyperus longus*) having a root with similar properties. [OE *gallengar* OF *galingal* f. Arab. *ḵalanjān* f. Chin. *ge-liang-jiang* mild ginger from Ge in Canton]

galiot var. of GALLIOT.

galipot /gállipot/ *n.* a hardened deposit of resin formed on the stem of the cluster pine. [F: orig. unkn.]

gall[1] /gawl/ *n.* **1** *sl.* impudence. **2** asperity, rancour. **3** bitterness; anything bitter (*gall and wormwood*). **4** the bile of animals. **5** the gall-bladder and its contents. □ **gall-bladder** the vessel storing bile after its secretion by the liver and before release into the intestine. [ON, corresp. to OE *gealla*, f. Gmc]
■ **1** impudence, insolence, impertinence, audacity, brashness, brazenness, sauciness, effrontery, temerity, cheek, front, *colloq.* brass, nerve, guts, sauce, *sl.* crust, chutzpah. **2, 3** asperity, acerbity, causticity, harshness, rancour, acrimony, vitriol, bile, spleen; see also *bitterness* (BITTER).

gall[2] /gawl/ *n.* & *v.* ● *n.* **1** a sore on the skin made by chafing. **2 a** mental soreness or vexation. **b** a cause of this. **3** a place rubbed bare. ● *v.tr.* **1** rub sore; injure by rubbing. **2** vex, annoy, humiliate. □□ **gallingly** *adv.* [ME f. LG or Du. *galle*, corresp. to OE *gealla* sore on a horse]
■ *n.* **1** sore (spot), abrasion, scrape, graze, scratch, chafe. **2 a** soreness, vexation, exasperation; see also ANNOYANCE 1. **b** nuisance, bother, *disp.* aggravation; see also ANNOYANCE 2. ● *v.* **1** irritate, chafe, abrade, fret, scrape, rub, scratch. **2** vex, bother, humiliate, annoy, irritate, irk, exasperate, provoke, nettle, ruffle, fret, *colloq.* needle; anger, enrage, inflame, infuriate, incense.

gall[3] /gawl/ *n.* **1** a growth produced by insects or fungus etc. on plants and trees, esp. on oak. **2** (*attrib.*) of insects producing galls (*gall-fly*). [ME f. OF *galle* f. L *galla*]

gall. *abbr.* gallon(s).

gallant *adj.*, *n.*, & *v.* ● *adj.* /gállənt/ **1** brave, chivalrous. **2 a** (of a ship, horse, etc.) grand, fine, stately. **b** *archaic* finely dressed. **3** /gállənt, gəlánt/ **a** markedly attentive to women. **b** concerned with sexual love; amatory. ● *n.* /gállənt, gəlánt/ **1** a ladies' man; a lover or paramour. **2** *archaic* a man of fashion; a fine gentleman. ● *v.* /gəlánt/ **1** *tr.* flirt with. **2** *tr.* escort; act as a cavalier to (a lady). **3** *intr.* **a** play the gallant. **b** (foll. by *with*) flirt. □□ **gallantly** /gállәntli/ *adv.* [ME f. OF *galant* part. of *galer* make merry]
■ *adj.* **1** brave, courageous, bold, valiant, daring, dauntless, intrepid, plucky, fearless, valorous, unafraid, undaunted, manful, mettlesome, stout-hearted, lion-hearted, heroic; chivalrous, gracious, honourable, manly, courtly, courteous, polite, attentive, considerate, mannerly. **2 a** fine, elegant, imposing, grand, noble, stately, dignified, glorious, splendid, majestic, magnificent. **b** see DAPPER 1. **3 b** see EROTIC. ● *n.* **1** lover, Romeo, ladies' man, seducer, *archaic or derog.* paramour; sweetheart, beloved, boyfriend, escort, suitor, admirer, *esp. US* beau, *poet.* swain. **2** see SWELL *n.* 4. ● *v.* **1** see *chat up* (CHAT[1]). **2** see ESCORT *v.* **3 a** see PHILANDER.

gallantry /gállәntri/ *n.* (*pl.* **-ies**) **1** bravery; dashing courage. **2** courtliness; devotion to women. **3** a polite act or speech. **4** the conduct of a gallant; sexual intrigue; immorality. [F *galanterie* (as GALLANT)]
■ **1** see BRAVERY. **2** see CHIVALRY 2.

galleon /gálliən/ *n. hist.* **1** a ship of war (usu. Spanish). **2** a large Spanish ship used in American trade. **3** a vessel shorter and higher than a galley. [MDu. *galjoen* f. F *galion* f. *galie* galley, or f. Sp. *galeón*]

galleria /gállәre͞eә/ *n.* a collection of small shops under a single roof; an arcade. [It.]

gallery /gálləri/ *n.* (*pl.* **-ies**) **1** a room or building for showing works of art. **2** a balcony, esp. a platform projecting from the inner wall of a church, hall, etc., providing extra room for spectators etc. or reserved for musicians etc. (*minstrels' gallery*). **3 a** the highest balcony in a theatre. **b** its occupants. **4 a** a covered space for walking in, partly open at the side; a portico or colonnade. **b** a long narrow passage in the thickness of a wall or supported on corbels, open towards the interior of the building. **5** a long narrow room, passage, or corridor. **6** *Mil.* & *Mining* a horizontal underground passage. **7** a group of spectators at a golf-match etc. □ **play to the gallery** seek to win approval by appealing to popular taste. □□ **galleried** *adj.* [F *galerie* f. It. *galleria* f. med.L *galeria*]
■ **4 a** see PORTICO.

galleryite /gálləri-īt/ *n.* a person occupying a seat in a gallery; a playgoer.

galley /gálli/ *n.* (*pl.* **-eys**) **1** *hist.* **a** a low flat single-decked vessel using sails and oars, and usu. rowed by slaves or criminals. **b** an ancient Greek or Roman warship with one or more banks of oars. **c** a large open rowing-boat, e.g. that used by the captain of a man-of-war. **2** a ship's or aircraft's kitchen. **3** *Printing* **a** an oblong tray for set type. **b** the corresponding part of a composing-machine. **c** (in full **galley proof**) a proof in the form of long single-column strips from type in a galley, not in sheets or pages. □ **galley-slave 1** *hist.* a person condemned to row in a galley. **2** a drudge. [ME f. OF *galie* f. med.L *galea*, med.Gk *galaia*]
■ **2** see KITCHEN.

galliard /gálliaard/ *n. hist.* **1** a lively dance usu. in triple time for two persons. **2** the music for this. [ME f. OF *gaillard* valiant]

Gallic /gállik/ *adj.* **1** French or typically French. **2** of the Gauls; Gaulish. □□ **Gallicize** /-lisīz/ *v.tr.* & *intr.* (also **-ise**). [L *Gallicus* f. *Gallus* a Gaul]

gallic acid /gállik/ *n. Chem.* an acid extracted from gallnuts etc., formerly used in making ink. [F *gallique* f. *galle* GALL[3]]

gallice /gállisee/ *adv.* in French. [L, = in Gaulish]

Gallicism /gállisiz'm/ *n.* a French idiom, esp. one adopted in another language. [F *gallicisme* (as GALLIC)]

galligaskins /gálligáskinz/ *n.pl. hist.* or *joc.* breeches, trousers. [orig. wide hose of the 16th–17th c., f. obs. F *garguesque* for *greguesque* f. It. *grechesca* fem. of *grechesco* Greek]

gallimaufry /gállimáwfri/ *n.* (*pl.* **-ies**) a heterogeneous mixture; a jumble or medley. [F *galimafrée*, of unkn. orig.]

gallinaceous /gállináyshəss/ *adj.* of or relating to the order Galliformes, which includes domestic poultry, pheasants, partridges, etc. [L *gallinaceus* f. *gallina* hen f. *gallus* cock]

gallinule /gállinyool/ *n.* **1** a moorhen. **2** any of various similar birds of the genus *Porphyrula* or *Porphyrio*. [mod.L *gallinula*, dimin. of L *gallina* hen f. *gallus* cock]

galliot /gálliət/ *n.* (also **galiot**) **1** a Dutch cargo-boat or fishing-vessel. **2** a small (usu. Mediterranean) galley. [ME f. OF *galiote* f. It. *galeotta* f. med.L *galea* galley]

gallipot /gállipot/ *n.* a small pot of earthenware, metal, etc., used for ointments etc. [prob. GALLEY + POT[1], because brought in galleys from the Mediterranean]

gallium /gálliəm/ *n. Chem.* a soft bluish-white metallic element occurring naturally in zinc blende, bauxite, and kaolin. ¶ Symb.: **Ga**. [mod.L f. L *Gallia* France (so named patriotically by its discoverer Lecoq de Boisbaudran d. 1912)]

gallivant /gállivant/ *v.intr. colloq.* **1** gad about. **2** flirt. [orig. uncert.]
■ **1** see JOURNEY *v.* **2** see PHILANDER.

galliwasp /gálliwosp/ *n.* a W. Indian lizard, *Diploglossus monotropis*. [18th c.: orig. unkn.]

gallnut /gáwlnut/ *n.* = GALL[3].

Gallo- /gállō/ *comb. form* **1** French; French and. **2** Gaul (*Gallo-Roman*). [L *Gallus* a Gaul]

gallon /gállən/ *n.* **1 a** (in full **imperial gallon**) *Brit.* a measure of capacity equal to eight pints and equivalent to 4546 cc, used for liquids and corn etc. **b** *US* a measure of capacity equivalent to 3785 cc, used for liquids. **2** (usu. in *pl.*) *colloq.* a large amount. □□ **gallonage** *n.* [ME f. ONF *galon*, OF *jalon*, f. base of med.L *gallēta*, *gallētum*, perh. of Celtic orig.]

galloon /gəlóon/ *n.* a narrow close-woven braid of gold, silver, silk, cotton, nylon, etc., for binding dresses etc. [F *galon* f. *galonner* trim with braid, of unkn. orig.]

gallop /gálləp/ *n.* & *v.* ● *n.* **1** the fastest pace of a horse or other quadruped, with all the feet off the ground together in each stride. **2** a ride at this pace. **3** a track or ground for this. ● *v.* (**galloped, galloping**) **1 a** *intr.* (of a horse etc. or its rider) go at the pace of a gallop. **b** *tr.* make (a horse etc.) gallop. **2** *intr.* (foll. by *through, over*) read, recite, or talk at great speed. **3** *intr.* move or progress rapidly (*galloping inflation*). □ **at a gallop** at the pace of a gallop. □□ **galloper** *n.* [OF *galop, galoper*: see WALLOP]
■ *v.* **1a, 3** see RUN *v.* 1, 3.

galloway /gálləway/ *n.* **1** an animal of a breed of hornless black beef cattle from Galloway in SW Scotland. **2** this breed.

gallows /gállōz/ *n.pl.* (usu. treated as *sing.*) **1** a structure, usu. of two uprights and a crosspiece, for the hanging of criminals. **2** (prec. by *the*) execution by hanging. □ **gallows humour** grim and ironical humour. [ME f. ON *gálgi*]
■ **1** gibbet, *hist.* scaffold.

gallstone /gáwlstōn/ *n.* a small hard mass forming in the gall-bladder.

Gallup poll /gálləp/ *n.* an assessment of public opinion by questioning a representative sample, esp. as the basis for forecasting the results of voting. [G. H. *Gallup*, Amer. statistician d. 1984]

galluses /gálləsiz/ *n.pl. dial.* & *US* trouser-braces. [pl. of *gallus* var. of GALLOWS]

galoot /gəlóot/ *n. colloq.* a person, esp. a strange or clumsy one. [19th-c. Naut. sl.: orig. unkn.]

galop /gálləp/ *n.* & *v.* ● *n.* **1** a lively dance in duple time. **2** the music for this. ● *v.intr.* (**galoped, galoping**) perform this dance. [F: see GALLOP]

galore /gəlór/ *adv.* in abundance (placed after noun: *flowers galore*). [Ir. *go leór* to sufficiency]
■ aplenty, in abundance, in large quantity *or* quantities *or* number(s) *or* amounts, in profusion, à gogo; everywhere, all over.

galosh /gəlósh/ *n.* (also **golosh**) (usu. in *pl.*) a waterproof overshoe, usu. of rubber. [ME f. OF *galoche* f. LL *gallicula* small Gallic shoe]

galumph /gəlúmf/ *v.intr. colloq.* **1** move noisily or clumsily. **2** go prancing in triumph. [coined by Lewis Carroll (in sense 2), perh. f. GALLOP + TRIUMPH]
■ **1** see PLOD *v.* 1. **2** see CAVORT.

galvanic /galvánnik/ *adj.* **1 a** sudden and remarkable (*had a galvanic effect*). **b** stimulating; full of energy. **2** of or producing an electric current by chemical action. □□ **galvanically** *adv.*

galvanism /gálvəniz'm/ *n. hist.* **1** electricity produced by chemical action. **2** the use of electricity for medical purposes. □□ **galvanist** *n.* [F *galvanisme* f. L. *Galvani*, It. physiologist d. 1798]

galvanize /gálvənīz/ *v.tr.* (also **-ise**) **1** (often foll. by *into*) rouse forcefully, esp. by shock or excitement (*was galvanized into action*). **2** stimulate by or as if by electricity. **3** coat (iron) with zinc (usu. without the use of electricity) as a protection against rust. □□ **galvanization** /-záysh'n/ *n.* **galvanizer** *n.* [F *galvaniser*: see GALVANISM]
■ **1** see ROUSE 2a.

galvanometer /gálvənómmitər/ *n.* an instrument for detecting and measuring small electric currents. □□ **galvanometric** /-nəmétrik/ *adj.*

gambade /gambáad/ *n.* (also **gambado** /-báadō/) (*pl.* **gambades; -os** or **-oes**) **1** a horse's leap or bound. **2** a fantastic movement. **3** an escapade. [F *gambade* & Sp. *gambado* f. It. & Sp. *gamba* leg]

gambier /gámbiər/ *n.* an astringent extract of an Eastern plant used in tanning etc. [Malay *gambir* name of the plant]

gambit /gámbit/ *n.* **1** a chess opening in which a player sacrifices a piece or pawn to secure an advantage. **2** an opening move in a discussion etc. **3** a trick or device. [earlier *gambett* f. It. *gambetto* tripping up f. *gamba* leg]
■ **3** see DEVICE 2.

gamble /gámb'l/ *v.* & *n.* ● *v.* **1** *intr.* play games of chance for money, esp. for high stakes. **2** *tr.* **a** bet (a sum of money) in gambling. **b** (often foll. by *away*) lose (assets) by gambling. **3** *intr.* take great risks in the hope of substantial gain. **4** *intr.* (foll. by *on*) act in the hope or expectation of (*gambled on fine weather*). ● *n.* **1** a risky undertaking or attempt. **2** a spell or an act of gambling. □□ **gambler** *n.* [obs. *gamel* to sport, *gamene* GAME[1]]
■ *v.* **1, 3** play, game, wager, bet, *Brit. colloq.* punt; try one's luck; see also SPECULATE 3. **2 a** risk, venture, hazard, bet, wager, stake; play; place, put, lay. **4** (*gamble on*) take a chance on, count on, bargain on, rely on. ● *n.* **1** risk, venture, chance; uncertainty, speculation, leap in the dark. **2** bet, wager, stake, *Brit. colloq.* punt, *Brit. sl.* flutter.

gamboge /gambṓzh, -bóozh/ *n.* a gum resin produced by various E. Asian trees and used as a yellow pigment and as a purgative. [mod.L *gambaugium* f. *Cambodia* in SE Asia]

gambol /gámb'l/ *v.* & *n.* ● *v.intr.* (**gambolled, gambolling**; *US* **gamboled, gamboling**) skip or frolic playfully. ● *n.* a playful frolic. [GAMBADE]
■ *v.* see SKIP[1] *v.* 1. ● *n.* see SKIP[1] *n.*

gambrel /gámbrəl/ *n.* (in full **gambrel roof**) **1** *Brit.* a roof like a hipped roof but with gable-like ends. **2** *US* = *curb roof*. [ONF *gamberel* f. *gambier* forked stick f. *gambe* leg (from the resemblance to the shape of a horse's hind leg)]

game[1] /gaym/ *n.*, *adj.*, & *v.* ● *n.* **1** a form or spell of play or sport, esp. a competitive one played according to rules and decided by skill, strength, or luck. **2** a single portion of play forming a scoring unit in some contests, e.g. bridge or tennis. **3** (in *pl.*) **a** athletics or sports as organized in a school etc. **b** a meeting for athletic etc. contests (*Olympic Games*). **4** a winning score in a game; the state of the score in a game (*the game is two all*). **5** the equipment for a game. **6** one's level of achievement in a game, as specified (*played a good game*). **7 a** a piece of fun; a jest (*was only playing a game with you*). **b** (in *pl.*) dodges, tricks (*none of your games!*). **8** a scheme or undertaking etc. regarded as a game (*so that's your game*). **9 a** a policy or line of action. **b** an occupation or profession (*the fighting game*). **10** (*collect.*) **a**

wild animals or birds hunted for sport or food. **b** the flesh of these. **11** a hunted animal; a quarry or object of pursuit or attack. **12** a kept flock of swans. ● *adj.* **1** spirited; eager and willing. **2** (foll. by *for*, or *to* + infin.) having the spirit or energy; eagerly prepared. ● *v.intr.* play at games of chance for money; gamble. □ **the game is up** the scheme is revealed or foiled. **game plan** esp. *US* **1** a winning strategy worked out in advance for a particular match. **2** a plan of campaign, esp. in politics. **game point** *Tennis* etc. a point which, if won, would win the game. **game** (or **games**) **theory** the mathematical analysis of conflict in war, economics, games of skill, etc. **game-warden** an official locally supervising game and hunting. **gaming-house** a place frequented for gambling; a casino. **gaming-table** a table used for gambling. **make game** (or **a game**) **of** mock, taunt. **off** (or **on**) **one's game** playing badly (or well). **on the game** *Brit. sl.* involved in prostitution or thieving. **play the game** behave fairly or according to the rules. □□ **gamely** *adv.* **gameness** *n.* **gamester** *n.* [OE *gamen*]

■ *n.* **1** amusement, pastime, diversion, distraction; recreation, sport. **2** round, bout; see also HEAT *n.* 6. **3 b** (*games*) contest, competition, meeting, meet, tournament, tourney, match, event. **7 a** see PRANK. **b** (*games*) dodges, tricks, ruses, ploys; mischief, horseplay, *colloq.* monkey business, shenanigans. **8** scheme, undertaking, plan, plot, design, stratagem, strategy, tactic, *sl.* racket. **9 a** policy, line of action, approach. **b** occupation, line (of work), field, business, trade, profession, *colloq.* racket. **11** quarry, prey; victim, target. ● *adj.* **1** spirited, high-spirited, devil-may-care, adventurous, plucky, daring, unflinching, courageous, brave, bold, *colloq.* gutsy. **2** eager, willing, ready, prepared; see also ENTHUSIASTIC. ● *v.* see SPECULATE 3. □ **game plan 2** see POLICY[1] 1. **make game** (or **a game**) **of** see MOCK *v.* 1, 3. **play the game** play fair, be a sport.

game[2] /gaym/ *adj.* (of a leg, arm, etc.) lame, crippled. [18th-c. dial.: orig. unkn.]

gamebook /gáymbo͝ok/ *n.* a book for recording game killed by a sportsman.

gamecock /gáymkok/ *n.* (also **gamefowl** /-fowl/) a cock bred and trained for cock-fighting.

gamekeeper /gáymkeepər/ *n.* a person employed to breed and protect game.

gamelan /gámməlan/ *n.* **1** a type of orchestra found in SE Asia (esp. Indonesia), with string and woodwind instruments, and a wide range of percussion instruments. **2** a kind of xylophone used in this. [Jav.]

gamesman /gáymzmən/ *n.* (*pl.* **-men**) an exponent of gamesmanship.

gamesmanship /gáymzmənship/ *n.* the art or practice of winning games or other contests by gaining a psychological advantage over an opponent.

gamesome /gáymsəm/ *adj.* merry, sportive. □□ **gamesomely** *adv.* **gamesomeness** *n.*

gametangium /gámmitánjiəm/ *n.* (*pl.* **gametangia** /-jiə/) *Bot.* an organ in which gametes are formed. [as GAMETE + *aggeion* vessel]

gamete /gámmeet, gəmeét/ *n. Biol.* a mature germ cell able to unite with another in sexual reproduction. □□ **gametic** /gəméttik/ *adj.* [mod.L *gameta* f. Gk *gametē* wife f. *gamos* marriage]

gameto- /gəmeétō/ *comb. form Biol.* gamete.

gametocyte /gəmeétōsīt/ *n. Biol.* any cell that is in the process of developing into one or more gametes.

gametogenesis /gəmeétōjénnisiss/ *n. Biol.* the process by which cells undergo meiosis to form gametes.

gametophyte /gəmeétōfīt/ *n.* the gamete-producing form of a plant that has alternation of generations between this and the asexual form. □□ **gametophytic** /-fittik/ *adj.*

gamin /gámmin/ *n.* **1** a street urchin. **2** an impudent child. [F]

■ **1** see GUTTERSNIPE. **2** see DEVIL *n.* 3b.

gamine /gameén/ *n.* **1** a girl gamin. **2** a girl with mischievous or boyish charm. [F]

gamma /gámmə/ *n.* **1** the third letter of the Greek alphabet (Γ, γ). **2** a third-class mark given for a piece of work or in an examination. **3** *Astron.* the third brightest star in a constellation. **4** the third member of a series. □ **gamma radiation** (or **rays**) electromagnetic radiation of very short wavelength emitted by some radioactive substances. [ME f. Gk]

gammer /gámmər/ *n. archaic* an old woman, esp. as a rustic name. [prob. contr. of GODMOTHER: cf. GAFFER]

gammon[1] /gámmən/ *n.* & *v.* ● *n.* **1** the bottom piece of a flitch of bacon including a hind leg. **2** the ham of a pig cured like bacon. ● *v.tr.* cure (bacon). [ONF *gambon* f. *gambe* leg: cf. JAMB]

■ *n.* see LEG *n.* 2.

gammon[2] /gámmən/ *n.* & *v.* ● *n.* a kind of victory scoring two games at backgammon. ● *v.tr.* defeat in this way. [app. = ME *gamen* GAME[1]]

gammon[3] /gámmən/ *n.* & *v. colloq.* ● *n.* humbug, deception. ● *v.* **1** *intr.* **a** talk speciously. **b** pretend. **2** *tr.* hoax, deceive. [18th c.: orig. uncert.]

■ *n.* see DECEIT 1. ● *v.* see TRICK *v.*

gammy /gámmi/ *adj.* (**gammier**, **gammiest**) *Brit. sl.* (esp. of a leg) lame; permanently injured. [dial. form of GAME[2]]

gamp /gamp/ *n. Brit. colloq.* an umbrella, esp. a large unwieldy one. [Mrs *Gamp* in Dickens's *Martin Chuzzlewit*]

gamut /gámmət/ *n.* **1** the whole series or range or scope of anything (*the whole gamut of crime*). **2** *Mus.* **a** the whole series of notes used in medieval or modern music. **b** a major diatonic scale. **c** a people's or a period's recognized scale. **d** a voice's or instrument's compass. **3** *Mus.* the lowest note in the medieval sequence of hexachords, = modern G on the lowest line of the bass staff. [med.L *gamma ut* f. GAMMA taken as the name for a note one tone lower than A of the classical scale + *ut* the first of six arbitrary names of notes forming the hexachord, being syllables (*ut*, *re*, *mi*, *fa*, *so*, *la*) of the Latin hymn beginning *Ut queant laxis*)]

■ **1** range, scale, spectrum, compass, spread, scope, sweep, field, series.

gamy /gáymi/ *adj.* (**gamier**, **gamiest**) **1** having the flavour or scent of game kept till it is high. **2** *US* scandalous, sensational. **3** = GAME[1] *adj.* □□ **gamily** *adv.* **gaminess** *n.*

gander /gándər/ *n.* & *v.* ● *n.* **1** a male goose. **2** *sl.* a look, a glance (*take a gander*). ● *v.intr.* look or glance. [OE *gandra*, rel. to GANNET]

■ *n.* **2** see GLANCE[1] *n.* 1. ● *v.* see PEEP *v.* 1.

gang[1] /gang/ *n.* & *v.* ● *n.* **1 a** a band of persons acting or going about together, esp. for criminal purposes. **b** *colloq.* such a band pursuing a purpose causing disapproval. **2** a set of workers, slaves, or prisoners. **3** a set of tools arranged to work simultaneously. ● *v.tr.* arrange (tools etc.) to work in coordination. □ **gang-bang** *sl.* an occasion on which several men successively have sexual intercourse with one woman. **gang up** *colloq.* **1** (often foll. by *with*) act in concert. **2** (foll. by *on*) combine against. [orig. = going, journey, f. ON *gangr*, *ganga* GOING, corresp. to OE *gang*]

■ *n.* **1** group, pack, mob, ring, company; crowd, band, set, party, team. □ **gang up 1** join together, join forces, get together, unite. **2** (*gang up on*) conspire *or* plot against, unite *or* unify against, club *or* band together against, join forces against.

gang[2] /gang/ *v.intr. Sc.* go. □ **gang agley** (of a plan etc.) go wrong. [OE *gangan*: cf. GANG[1]]

gangboard /gángbord/ *n.* = GANGPLANK.

ganger /gángər/ *n. Brit.* the foreman of a gang of workers, esp. navvies.

gangle /gángg'l/ *v.intr.* move ungracefully. [back-form. f. GANGLING]

gangling /gánggling/ *adj.* (of a person) loosely built; lanky. [frequent. of GANG[2]]

■ see LANKY.

ganglion /gángglian/ *n.* (*pl.* **ganglia** /-lia/ or **ganglions**) **1 a** an enlargement or knot on a nerve etc. containing an assemblage of nerve-cells. **b** a mass of grey matter in the central nervous system forming a nerve-nucleus. **2** *Med.* a cyst, esp. on a tendon sheath. **3** a centre of activity or interest. □□ **gangliar** *adj.* **gangliform** *adj.* **ganglionated** *adj.* **ganglionic** /-liónnik/ *adj.* [Gk *gagglion*]

gangly /gánggli/ *adj.* (**ganglier, gangliest**) = GANGLING.

gangplank /gángplangk/ *n.* a movable plank usu. with cleats nailed on it for boarding or disembarking from a ship etc.

gangrene /gánggreen/ *n.* & *v.* ● *n.* **1** *Med.* death and decomposition of a part of the body tissue, usu. resulting from obstructed circulation. **2** moral corruption. ● *v.tr.* & *intr.* affect or become affected with gangrene. □□ **gangrenous** /gánggrinəss/ *adj.* [F *gangrène* f. L *gangraena* f. Gk *gaggraina*]

■ *v.* see MORTIFY 3.

gangster /gángstər/ *n.* a member of a gang of violent criminals. □□ **gangsterism** *n.*

■ Mafioso, brigand, bandit, racketeer, *sl.* mobster, *esp. US sl.* goon, *US sl.* hood, gunsel; see also CRIMINAL *n.*

gangue /gang/ *n.* valueless earth etc. in which ore is found. [F f. G *Gang* lode = GANG[1]]

gangway /gángway/ *n.* & *int.* ● *n.* **1** *Brit.* a passage, esp. between rows of seats. **2 a** an opening in the bulwarks by which a ship is entered or left. **b** a bridge laid from ship to shore. **c** a passage on a ship, esp. a platform connecting the quarterdeck and forecastle. **3** a temporary bridge on a building site etc. ● *int.* make way!

ganister /gánnistər/ *n.* a close-grained hard siliceous stone found in the coal measures of northern England, and used for furnace-linings. [19th c.: orig. unkn.]

ganja /gánjə/ *n.* marijuana. [Hindi *gāṅjhā*]

gannet /gánnit/ *n.* **1** any sea bird of the genus *Sula*, esp. *Sula bassana*, catching fish by plunge-diving. **2** *sl.* a greedy person. □□ **gannetry** *n.* (*pl.* **-ies**). [OE *ganot* f. Gmc, rel. to GANDER]

■ **2** see GLUTTON 1.

ganoid /gánnoyd/ *adj.* & *n.* ● *adj.* **1** (of fish scales) enamelled; smooth and bright. **2** having ganoid scales. ● *n.* a fish having ganoid scales. [F *ganoïde* f. Gk *ganos* brightness]

gantlet *US* var. of GAUNTLET[2].

gantry /gántri/ *n.* (*pl.* **-ies**) **1** an overhead structure with a platform supporting a travelling crane, or railway or road signals. **2** a structure supporting a space rocket prior to launching. **3** (also **gauntry** /gáwntri/) a wooden stand for barrels. [prob. f. *gawn*, dial. form of GALLON + TREE]

gaol *Brit.* var. of JAIL.

gaoler *Brit.* var. of JAILER.

gap /gap/ *n.* **1** an unfilled space or interval; a blank; a break in continuity. **2** a breach in a hedge, fence, or wall. **3** a wide (usu. undesirable) divergence in views, sympathies, development, etc. (*generation gap*). **4** a gorge or pass. □ **fill** (or **close** etc.) **a gap** make up a deficiency. **gap-toothed** having gaps between the teeth. □□ **gapped** *adj.* **gappy** *adj.* [ME f. ON, = chasm, rel. to GAPE]

■ **1** interval, space, blank, void, gulf, lacuna; lull, pause, cessation, intermission, rest, respite; wait, delay, halt, stop, break, hiatus, disruption, interruption, discontinuity, suspension. **2** opening, space, aperture, hole, cavity, crevice, chink, crack, cleft, breach, rift. **3** difference, distinction, divergence, disparity, discrepancy, inconsistency; division, split. **4** see GORGE *n.* 1.

gape /gayp/ *v.* & *n.* ● *v.intr.* **1 a** open one's mouth wide, esp. in amazement or wonder. **b** be or become wide open. **2** (foll. by *at*) gaze curiously or wondrously. **3** split; part asunder. **4** yawn. ● *n.* **1** an open-mouthed stare. **2** a yawn. **3** (in *pl.*; prec. by *the*) **a** a disease of birds with gaping as a symptom, caused by infestation with gapeworm. **b** *joc.* a fit of yawning. **4 a** an expanse of open mouth or beak. **b** the part of a beak that opens. **5** a rent or opening. □□ **gapingly** *adv.* [ME f. ON *gapa*]

■ *v.* **1 b** yawn, open (wide), be (wide) open. **2** gaze, stare, goggle, *colloq.* gawk, rubberneck, *Brit. colloq.* gawp. **3** see SPLIT *v.* 1a. ● *n.* **1** stare, goggle, gaze. **5** see SPLIT *n.* 2.

gaper /gáypər/ *n.* **1** any bivalve mollusc of the genus *Mya*, with the shell open at one or both ends. **2** the comber fish, which gapes when dead. **3** a person who gapes.

gapeworm /gáypwurm/ *n.* a nematode worm, *Syngamus tracheae*, that infests the trachea and bronchi of birds and causes the gapes.

gar /gaar/ *n.* = GARFISH 2.

garage /gárraaj, -raazh, -rij/ *n.* & *v.* ● *n.* **1** a building or shed for the storage of a motor vehicle or vehicles. **2** an establishment selling petrol etc., or repairing and selling motor vehicles. ● *v.tr.* put or keep (a motor vehicle) in a garage. □ **garage sale** *US* a sale of miscellaneous household goods, usu. for charity, held in the garage of a private house. [F f. *garer* shelter]

garb /gaarb/ *n.* & *v.* ● *n.* **1** clothing, esp. of a distinctive kind. **2** the way a person is dressed. ● *v.tr.* **1** (usu. in *passive* or *refl.*) put (esp. distinctive) clothes on (a person). **2** attire. [obs. F *garbe* f. It. *garbo* f. Gmc, rel. to GEAR]

■ *n.* see DRESS *n.* 2. ● *v.* see CLOTHE 1, 2.

garbage /gaárbij/ *n.* **1 a** refuse, filth. **b** domestic waste. **2** foul or rubbishy literature etc. **3** nonsense. □ **garbage can** *US* a dustbin. [AF: orig. unkn.]

■ **1 a** filth, dross, rubbish, junk, refuse, litter, debris, detritus, waste, offal, *esp. US* trash, *colloq.* muck; sweepings, slops, scraps. **2** rubbish, trash, *colloq.* tripe. **3** see NONSENSE.

garble /gaárb'l/ *v.tr.* **1** unintentionally distort or confuse (facts, messages, etc.). **2 a** mutilate in order to misrepresent. **b** make (usu. unfair or malicious) selections from (facts, statements, etc.). □□ **garbler** *n.* [It. *garbellare* f. Arab. *ġarbala* sift, perh. f. LL *cribellare* to sieve f. L *cribrum* sieve]

■ **1** distort, confuse, mix up, misconstrue, misunderstand, misread, jumble (up). **2** warp, twist, mangle, mutilate, falsify, misrepresent, misstate, misquote, misreport, mistranslate, misrender, slant, corrupt, colour.

garboard /gaárbərd/ *n.* (in full **garboard strake**) the first range of planks or plates laid on a ship's bottom next to the keel. [Du. *gaarboord*, perh. f. *garen* GATHER + *boord* BOARD]

garçon /gaárson/ *n.* a waiter in a French restaurant, hotel, etc. [F, lit. 'boy']

Garda /gaárdə/ *n.* **1** the State police force of the Irish Republic. **2** (also **garda**) (*pl.* **-dai** /-dee/) a member of this. [Ir. *Garda Síochána* Civic Guard]

garden /gaárd'n/ *n.* & *v.* ● *n.* **1** esp. *Brit.* a piece of ground, usu. partly grassed and adjoining a private house, used for growing flowers, fruit, or vegetables, and as a place of recreation. **2** (esp. in *pl.*) ornamental grounds laid out for public enjoyment (*botanical gardens*). **3** a similar place with the service of refreshments (*tea garden*). **4** (*attrib.*) **a** (of plants) cultivated, not wild. **b** for use in a garden (*garden seat*). **5** (usu. in *pl.* prec. by a name) *Brit.* a street, square, etc. (*Onslow Gardens*). **6** an especially fertile region. **7** *US* a large public hall. **8** (**the Garden**) the philosophy or school of Epicurus. ● *v.intr.* cultivate or work in a garden. □ **garden centre** an establishment where plants and garden equipment etc. are sold. **garden city** an industrial or other town laid out systematically with spacious surroundings, parks, etc. **garden cress** a cruciferous plant, *Lepidium sativum*, used in salads. **garden party** a social event held on a lawn or in a garden. **garden suburb** *Brit.* a suburb laid out spaciously with open spaces, parks, etc. **garden warbler** a European woodland songbird, *Sylvia borin.* □□ **gardenesque** /-dənésk/ *adj.* **gardening** *n.* [ME f. ONF *gardin* (OF *jardin*) ult. f. Gmc: cf. YARD[2]]

gardener /gaárdnər/ *n.* a person who gardens or is employed to tend a garden. □ **gardener-bird** a bowerbird making a 'garden' of moss etc. in front of a bower. [ME ult. f. OF *jardinier* (as GARDEN)]

gardenia /gaardeéniə/ *n.* any tree or shrub of the genus *Gardenia*, with large white or yellow flowers and usu. a fragrant scent. [mod.L f. Dr A. *Garden*, Sc. naturalist d. 1791]

garfish /gaárfish/ *n.* (*pl.* same) **1** any mainly marine fish of the family *Belonidae*, esp. *Belone belone*, having long beaklike jaws with sharp teeth. Also called NEEDLEFISH. **2** *US* any similar freshwater fish of the genus *Lepisosteus*, with ganoid scales. Also called GAR or GARPIKE. **3** *NZ* & *Austral.* either of two marine fish of the genus *Hemiramphus*. Also called HALFBEAK. [app. f. OE *gār* spear + *fisc* FISH[1]]

garganey /gaárgəni/ *n.* (*pl.* **-eys**) a small duck, *Anas querquedula*, the drake of which has a white stripe from the eye to the neck. [It., dial. var. of *garganello*]

gargantuan /gaargántyooən/ *adj.* enormous, gigantic. [the name of a giant in Rabelais' book *Gargantua* (1534)]
■ see GIGANTIC.

garget /gaárgit/ *n.* **1** inflammation of a cow's or ewe's udder. **2** *US* pokeweed. [perh. f. obs. *garget* throat f. OF *gargate*, *-guete*]

gargle /gaárg'l/ *v.* & *n.* ● *v.* **1** *tr.* (also *absol.*) wash (one's mouth and throat), esp. for medicinal purposes, with a liquid kept in motion by breathing through it. **2** *intr.* make a sound as when doing this. ● *n.* **1** a liquid used for gargling. **2** *sl.* an alcoholic drink. [F *gargouiller* f. *gargouille*: see GARGOYLE]

gargoyle /gaárgoyl/ *n.* a grotesque carved human or animal face or figure projecting from the gutter of (esp. a Gothic) building usu. as a spout to carry water clear of a wall. [OF *gargouille* throat, gargoyle]

gargoylism /gaárgoyliz'm/ *n. Med.* = HURLER'S SYNDROME.

garibaldi /gárribáwldi/ *n.* (*pl.* **garibaldis**) **1** a kind of woman's or child's loose blouse, orig. of bright red material imitating the shirts worn by Garibaldi and his followers. **2** *Brit.* a biscuit containing a layer of currants. **3** *US* a small red Californian fish, *Hypsypops rubicundus*. [G. *Garibaldi*, It. patriot d. 1882]

garish /gáirish/ *adj.* **1** obtrusively bright; showy. **2** gaudy; over-decorated. ▫▫ **garishly** *adv.* **garishness** *n.* [16th-c. *gaurish* app. f. obs. *gaure* stare]
■ **1** bright, showy, florid, flashy, harsh, loud, obtrusive. **2** gaudy, tawdry, raffish, meretricious, Brummagem, showy, *colloq.* flash, *sl.* glitzy; over-decorated, over-elaborate, over-ornate.

garland /gaárlənd/ *n.* & *v.* ● *n.* **1** a wreath of flowers, leaves, etc., worn on the head or hung as a decoration. **2** a prize or distinction. **3** a literary anthology or miscellany. ● *v.tr.* **1** adorn with garlands. **2** crown with a garland. [ME f. OF *garlande*, of unkn. orig.]
■ *n.* **1** wreath, crown, chaplet, circlet; festoon. **2** see PRIZE[1] *n.* 2. ● *v.* wreathe, festoon, crown, decorate; encircle, ring, circle.

garlic /gaárlik/ *n.* **1** any of various alliaceous plants, esp. *Allium sativum*. **2** the strong-smelling pungent-tasting bulb of this plant, used as a flavouring in cookery. ▫▫ **garlicky** *adj.* [OE *gārleac* f. *gār* spear + *lēac* LEEK]

garment /gaármənt/ *n.* & *v.* ● *n.* **1 a** an article of dress. **b** (in *pl.*) clothes. **2** the outward and visible covering of anything. ● *v.tr.* (usu. in *passive*) *rhet.* attire. [ME f. OF *garnement* (as GARNISH)]
■ *n.* **1 a** item *or* piece of clothing. **b** (*garments*) clothes, vestments, *colloq.* togs, *joc.* habiliments, *sl.* duds, threads; outfit, costume; garb, clothing, dress, rig, *archaic* raiment, habit, *colloq.* gear, *formal* attire, apparel. ● *v.* see DRESS *v.* 1a.

garner /gaárnər/ *v.* & *n.* ● *v.tr.* **1** collect. **2** store, deposit. ● *n. literary* a storehouse or granary. [ME (orig. as noun) f. OF *gernier* f. L *granarium* GRANARY]
■ *v.* **1** gather, collect, assemble, amass, accumulate, heap up, pile up. **2** store (up), stock (up), lay in *or* up *or* down, put away, put by, stow (away), cache, store. ● *n.* see STOREHOUSE.

garnet /gaárnit/ *n.* a vitreous silicate mineral, esp. a transparent deep-red kind used as a gem. [ME f. OF *grenat* f. med.L *granatum* POMEGRANATE, from its resemblance to the pulp of the fruit]

garnish /gaárnish/ *v.* & *n.* ● *v.tr.* **1** decorate or embellish (esp. food). **2** *Law* **a** serve notice on (a person) for the purpose of legally seizing money belonging to a debtor or defendant. **b** summon (a person) as a party to litigation started between others. ● *n.* (also **garnishing**) a decoration or embellishment, esp. to food. ▫▫ **garnishment** *n.* (in sense 2). [ME f. OF *garnir* f. Gmc]
■ *v.* **1** see DECORATE 1, 3. ● *n.* see DECORATION 2.

garnishee /gaárnisheé/ *n.* & *v. Law* ● *n.* a person garnished. ● *v.tr.* (**garnishees**, **garnisheed**) **1** garnish (a person). **2** attach (money etc.) by way of garnishment.

garniture /gaárnichər/ *n.* **1** decoration or trimmings, esp. of food. **2** accessories, appurtenances. [F (as GARNISH)]

garotte var. of GARROTTE.

garpike /gaárpīk/ *n.* a gar or garfish (see GARFISH 2). [OE *gār* spear + PIKE[1]]

garret /gárrit/ *n.* **1** a top-floor or attic room, esp. a dismal one. **2** an attic. [ME f. OF *garite* watch-tower f. Gmc]

garrison /gárris'n/ *n.* & *v.* ● *n.* **1** the troops stationed in a fortress, town, etc., to defend it. **2** the building occupied by them. ● *v.tr.* **1** provide (a place) with or occupy as a garrison. **2** place on garrison duty. ▫ **garrison town** a town having a permanent garrison. [ME f. OF *garison* f. *garir* defend, furnish f. Gmc]
■ *n.* **2** see STRONGHOLD 1. ● *v.* **1** see OCCUPY 4. **2** see STATION *v.* 1.

garrotte /gərót/ *v.* & *n.* (also **garotte**; *US* **garrote**) ● *v.tr.* **1** execute or kill by strangulation, esp. with an iron or wire collar etc. **2** throttle in order to rob. ● *n.* **1 a** a Spanish method of execution by garrotting. **b** the apparatus used for this. **2** highway robbery in which the victim is throttled. [F *garrotter* or Sp. *garrotear* f. *garrote* a cudgel, of unkn. orig.]
■ *v.* **1** see CHOKE[1] *v.* 1.

garrulous /gárrooləss/ *adj.* **1** talkative, esp. on trivial matters. **2** loquacious, wordy. ▫▫ **garrulity** /gəro͞oliti/ *n.* **garrulously** *adv.* **garrulousness** *n.* [L *garrulus* f. *garrire* chatter]
■ see TALKATIVE.

garter /gaártər/ *n.* & *v.* ● *n.* **1** a band worn to keep a sock or stocking up. **2** (**the Garter**) *Brit.* **a** the highest order of English knighthood. **b** the badge of this. **c** membership of this. **3** *US* a suspender for a sock or stocking. ● *v.tr.* fasten (a stocking) or encircle (a leg) with a garter. ▫ **garter-belt** *US* a suspender belt. **Garter King of Arms** see *King of Arms*. **garter-snake** any water-snake of the genus *Thamnophis*, native to N. America, having lengthwise stripes. **garter stitch** a plain knitting stitch or pattern, forming ridges in alternate rows. [ME f. OF *gartier* f. *garet* bend of the knee]

garth /gaarth/ *n. Brit.* **1** an open space within cloisters. **2** *archaic* **a** a close or yard. **b** a garden or paddock. [ME f. ON *garthr* = OE *geard* YARD[2]]

gas /gass/ *n.* & *v.* ● *n.* (*pl.* **gases**) **1** any airlike substance which moves freely to fill any space available, irrespective of its quantity. **2 a** such a substance (esp. found naturally or extracted from coal) used as a domestic or industrial fuel (also *attrib.*: *gas cooker*; *gas fire*). **b** an explosive mixture of firedamp with air. **3** nitrous oxide or another gas used as an anaesthetic (esp. in dentistry). **4** a gas or vapour used as a poisonous agent to disable an enemy in warfare. **5** *US colloq.* petrol, gasoline. **6** *sl.* pointless idle talk; boasting. **7** *sl.* an enjoyable, attractive, or amusing thing or person. ● *v.* (**gases**, **gassed**, **gassing**) **1** *tr.* expose to gas, esp. to kill or make unconscious. **2** *intr.* give off gas. **3** *tr.* (usu. foll. by *up*) *US colloq.* fill (the tank of a motor vehicle) with petrol. **4** *intr. colloq.* talk idly or boastfully. ▫ **gas chamber** an airtight chamber that can be filled with poisonous gas to kill people or animals. **gas chromatography** chromatography employing gas as the eluent. **gas-cooled** (of a nuclear reactor etc.) cooled by a current of gas. **gas fire** a domestic fire using gas as its fuel. **gas-fired** using gas as the fuel. **gas gangrene** a rapidly spreading gangrene of injured tissue infected by a soil bacterium and accompanied by the evolution of gas. **gas mask** a respirator used as a defence against poison gas. **gas meter** an apparatus recording the amount of gas consumed. **gas oil** a type of fuel oil distilled from petroleum and heavier than paraffin oil. **gas-permeable** (esp. of a contact lens) allowing the diffusion of gases. **gas plant** *Bot.* fraxinella. **gas-proof** impervious to gas. **gas ring** a hollow ring perforated with gas jets, used esp. for cooking. **gas station** *US* a filling-station. **gas-tight** proof against the leakage of gas. **gas turbine** a turbine driven by a flow of gas or by gas from combustion. [invented by J. B. van Helmont, Belgian chemist d. 1644, after Gk *khaos* chaos]

■ *n.* **1** see FUME *n.* 1. **6** see *hot air.* **7** see GIGGLE *n.* 2. ● *v.* **4** see JABBER *v.* 1.

gasbag /gásbag/ *n.* **1** a container of gas, esp. for holding the gas for a balloon or airship. **2** *sl.* an idle talker.

■ **2** see *talker* (TALK).

Gascon /gáskən/ *n.* **1** a native of Gascony. **2** (**gascon**) a braggart. [F f. L *Vasco -onis*]

gaseous /gássiəss, gáys-/ *adj.* of or like gas. □□ **gaseousness** *n.*

gash[1] /gash/ *n.* & *v.* ● *n.* **1** a long and deep slash, cut, or wound. **2 a** a cleft such as might be made by a slashing cut. **b** the act of making such a cut. ● *v.tr.* make a gash in; cut. [var. of ME *garse* f. OF *garcer* scarify, perh. ult. f. Gk *kharassō*]

■ *n.* **1** cut, slash, wound, incision, laceration. **2 a** score, slit, groove, split, cleft. **b** cut, slash, slice. ● *v.* cut, slash, lacerate, wound; score, incise, slit, groove, split, *literary* cleave.

gash[2] /gash/ *adj. Brit. sl.* spare, extra. [20th-c. Naut. sl.: orig. unkn.]

gasholder /gáss-hōldər/ *n.* a large receptacle for storing gas; a gasometer.

gasify /gássifī/ *v.tr.* & *intr.* (**-ies**, **-ied**) convert or be converted into gas. □□ **gasification** /-fikáysh'n/ *n.*

gasket /gáskit/ *n.* **1** a sheet or ring of rubber etc., shaped to seal the junction of metal surfaces. **2** a small cord securing a furled sail to a yard. □ **blow a gasket** *sl.* lose one's temper. [perh. f. F *garcette* thin rope (orig. little girl)]

gaskin /gáskin/ *n.* the hinder part of a horse's thigh. [perh. erron. f. GALLIGASKINS]

gaslight /gáslīt/ *n.* **1** a jet of burning gas, usu. heating a mantle, to provide light. **2** light emanating from this.

■ see LIGHT[1] *n.* 2.

gasman /gásmən/ *n.* (*pl.* **-men**) a man who instals or services gas appliances, or reads gas meters.

gasolene var. of GASOLINE.

gasoline /gássəleén/ *n.* (also **gasolene**) **1** a volatile inflammable liquid distilled from petroleum and used for heating and lighting. **2** *US* petrol. [GAS + -OL[2] + -INE[4], -ENE]

gasometer /gasómmitər/ *n.* a large tank in which gas is stored for distribution by pipes to users. [F *gazomètre* f. *gaz* gas + *-mètre* -METER]

gasp /gaasp/ *v.* & *n.* ● *v.* **1** *intr.* catch one's breath with an open mouth as in exhaustion or astonishment. **2** *intr.* (foll. by *for*) strain to obtain by gasping (*gasped for air*). **3** *tr.* (often foll. by *out*) utter with gasps. ● *n.* a convulsive catching of breath. □ **at one's last gasp 1** at the point of death. **2** exhausted. [ME f. ON *geispa*: cf. *geip* idle talk]

■ *v.* **1** pant, catch one's breath, puff, huff, heave, wheeze. **2** (*gasp for*) gulp for, fight for, strain for. ● *n.* snort, puff, gulp, huff, heave, wheeze. □ **at one's last gasp 1** at death's door, on one's deathbed, with one foot in the grave, on one's last legs, *in extremis*, on the way out. **2** see *exhausted* (EXHAUST *v.* 2).

gasper /gaáspər/ *n.* **1** a person who gasps. **2** *Brit. sl.* a cigarette.

gasser /gássər/ *n.* **1** *colloq.* an idle talker. **2** *sl.* a very attractive or impressive person or thing.

gassy /gássi/ *adj.* (**gassier**, **gassiest**) **1 a** of or like gas. **b** full of gas. **2** *colloq.* (of talk etc.) pointless, verbose. □□ **gassiness** *n.*

gasteropod var. of GASTROPOD.

gasthaus /gást-howss/ *n.* a small inn or hotel in German-speaking countries. [G f. *Gast* GUEST + *Haus* HOUSE]

gastrectomy /gastréktəmi/ *n.* (*pl.* **-ies**) a surgical operation in which the whole or part of the stomach is removed. [GASTRO- + -ECTOMY]

gastric /gástrik/ *adj.* of the stomach. □ **gastric flu** a popular name for an intestinal disorder of unknown cause. **gastric juice** a thin clear virtually colourless acid fluid secreted by the stomach glands and active in promoting digestion. [mod.L *gastricus* f. Gk *gastēr gast(e)ros* stomach]

gastritis /gastrítiss/ *n.* inflammation of the lining of the stomach.

gastro- /gástrō/ *comb. form* (also **gastr-** before a vowel) stomach. [Gk *gastēr gast(e)ros* stomach]

gastro-enteric /gástrō-entérrik/ *adj.* of or relating to the stomach and intestines.

gastro-enteritis /gástrō-éntərītiss/ *n. Med.* inflammation of the stomach and intestines.

gastronome /gástrənōm/ *n.* a gourmet. [F f. *gastronomie* GASTRONOMY]

■ see GOURMET.

gastronomy /gastrónnəmi/ *n.* the practice, study, or art of eating and drinking well. □□ **gastronomic** /gástrənómmik/ *adj.* **gastronomical** /gástrənómmik'l/ *adj.* **gastronomically** /gástrənómmikəli/ *adv.* [F *gastronomie* f. Gk *gastronomia* (as GASTRO-, *-nomia* f. *nomos* law)]

gastropod /gástrəpod/ *n.* (also **gasteropod**) any mollusc of the class Gastropoda that moves along by means of a large muscular foot, e.g. a snail, slug, etc. □□ **gastropodous** /gastróppədəss/ *adj.* [F *gastéropode* f. mod.L *gasteropoda* (as GASTRO-, Gk *pous podos* foot)]

gastroscope /gástrəskōp/ *n.* an optical instrument used for inspecting the interior of the stomach.

gastrula /gástroolə/ *n.* (*pl.* **gastrulae** /-lee/) *Zool.* an embryonic stage developing from the blastula. [mod.L f. Gk *gastēr gast(e)ros* belly]

gasworks /gáswurks/ *n.* a place where gas is manufactured and processed.

gat[1] /gat/ *n. sl.* a revolver or other firearm. [abbr. of GATLING]

gat[2] /gat/ *archaic past* of GET *v.*

gate[1] /gayt/ *n.* & *v.* ● *n.* **1** a barrier, usu. hinged, used to close an opening made for entrance and exit through a wall, fence, etc. **2** such an opening, esp. in the wall of a city, enclosure, or large building. **3** a means of entrance or exit. **4** a numbered place of access to aircraft at an airport. **5** a mountain pass. **6** an arrangement of slots into which the gear lever of a motor vehicle moves to engage the required gear. **7** a device for holding the frame of a cine film momentarily in position behind the lens of a camera or projector. **8 a** an electrical signal that causes or controls the passage of other signals. **b** an electrical circuit with an output which depends on the combination of several inputs. **9** a device regulating the passage of water in a lock etc. **10 a** the number of people entering by payment at the gates of a sports ground etc. **b** (in full **gate-money**) the proceeds taken for admission. **11** *sl.* the mouth. **12** *US sl.* dismissal. **13** = *starting-gate.* ● *v.tr.* **1** *Brit.* confine to college or school entirely or after certain hours. **2** (as **gated** *adj.*) (of a road) having a gate or gates to control the movement of traffic or animals. [OE *gæt*, *geat*, pl. *gatu*, f. Gmc]

■ *n.* **2, 3** gateway, opening, entrance, exit, access; see also MOUTH *n.* 2a, b. **5** see GORGE *n.* 1. **10 a** admission(s), attendance, crowd, audience, assemblage. **b** see TAKE *n.* **11** see MOUTH *n.* 1. **12** see *dismissal* (DISMISS).

gate[2] /gayt/ *n.* (prec. or prefixed by a name) *Brit.* a street (*Westgate*). [ME f. ON *gata*, f. Gmc]

-gate /gayt/ *suffix* forming nouns denoting an actual or alleged scandal comparable in some way to the Watergate scandal of 1972 (*Irangate*). [f. (WATER)GATE]

gateau /gáttō/ *n.* (*pl.* **gateaus** or **gateaux** /-tōz/) any of various rich cakes, usu. containing cream or fruit. [F *gâteau* cake]

gatecrasher /gáytkrashər/ *n.* an uninvited guest at a party etc. □□ **gatecrash** *v.tr.* & *intr.*
■ see INTRUDER.

gatefold /gáytfōld/ *n.* a page in a book or magazine etc. that folds out to be larger than the page-format.

gatehouse /gáyt-howss/ *n.* **1** a house standing by a gateway, esp. to a large house or park. **2** *hist.* a room over a city gate, often used as a prison.

gatekeeper /gáytkeepər/ *n.* **1** an attendant at a gate, controlling entrance and exit. **2** any of several large brown species of butterfly, esp. *Maniola tithonus*, frequenting hedgerows and woodland.
■ **1** see PORTER[2].

gateleg /gáytleg/ *n.* (in full **gateleg table**) a table with folding flaps supported by legs swung open like a gate. □□ **gatelegged** *adj.*

gateman /gáytmən/ *n.* (*pl.* **-men**) = GATEKEEPER 1.

gatepost /gáytpōst/ *n.* a post on which a gate is hung or against which it shuts. □ **between you and me and the gatepost** in strict confidence.
■ □ **between you and me and the gatepost** between you and me, between ourselves, *entre nous*, in (strict) confidence.

gateway /gáytway/ *n.* **1** an entrance with or opening for a gate. **2** a frame or structure built over a gate.

gather /gáthər/ *v.* & *n.* ● *v.* **1** *tr.* & *intr.* bring or come together; assemble, accumulate. **2** *tr.* (usu. foll. by *up*) **a** bring together from scattered places or sources. **b** take up together from the ground, a surface, etc. **c** draw into a smaller compass. **3** *tr.* acquire by gradually collecting; amass. **4** *tr.* **a** pick a quantity of (flowers etc.). **b** collect (grain etc.) as a harvest. **5** *tr.* (often foll. by *that* + clause) infer or understand. **6** *tr.* be subjected to or affected by the accumulation or increase of (*unread books gathering dust*; *gather speed*; *gather strength*). **7** *tr.* (often foll. by *up*) summon up (one's thoughts, energy, etc.) for a purpose. **8** *tr.* gain or recover (one's breath). **9** *tr.* **a** draw (material, or one's brow) together in folds or wrinkles. **b** pucker or draw together (part of a dress) by running a thread through. **10** *intr.* come to a head; develop a purulent swelling. ● *n.* (in *pl.*) a part of a garment that is gathered or drawn in. □ **gather way** (of a ship) begin to move. □□ **gatherer** *n.* [OE *gaderian* f. WG]
■ *v.* **1** collect, assemble, muster, convene, meet, forgather, get *or* come together, congregate, group; heap *or* pile (up), stockpile, stock, accumulate, amass, assemble, bring together. **2 a** collect, assemble, muster, get *or* bring *or* draw together. **3** acquire, collect, accumulate, amass, garner, glean. **4 a** see PICK[1] *v.* 2. **b** collect, harvest, reap, glean. **5** understand, infer, deduce, conclude, be led to believe, take it; hear. **6** gain, acquire, accumulate, pick up, increase. **9 a** draw *or* pull together, contract, pleat, tuck, fold; see also WRINKLE *v.* 1. **b** shirr, ruffle, pucker. ● *n.* (*gathers*) pleats, folds, ruffles, tucks.

gathering /gáthəring/ *n.* **1** an assembly or meeting. **2** a purulent swelling. **3** a group of leaves taken together in bookbinding.
■ **1** assembly, meeting, convocation, convention, congress, assemblage, rally, conclave, meet, conference, *colloq.* get-together.

Gatling /gátling/ *n.* (in full **Gatling gun**) a machine-gun with clustered barrels. [R. J. *Gatling*, Amer. inventor d. 1903]

GATT /gat/ *abbr.* (also **Gatt**) General Agreement on Tariffs and Trade.

gauche /gōsh/ *adj.* **1** lacking ease or grace; socially awkward. **2** tactless. □□ **gauchely** *adv.* **gaucheness** *n.* [F, = left-handed, awkward]
■ **1** see AWKWARD 2. **2** see TACTLESS.

gaucherie /gṓshəree/ *n.* **1** gauche manners. **2** a gauche action. [F]

gaucho /gówchō/ *n.* (*pl.* **-os**) a cowboy from the S. American pampas. [Sp. f. Quechua]

gaud /gawd/ *n.* **1** a gaudy thing; a showy ornament. **2** (in *pl.*) showy ceremonies. [perh. through AF f. OF *gaudir* rejoice f. L *gaudēre*]

gaudy[1] /gáwdi/ *adj.* (**gaudier**, **gaudiest**) tastelessly or extravagantly bright or showy. □□ **gaudily** *adv.* **gaudiness** *n.* [prob. f. GAUD + -Y[1]]
■ garish, flashy, loud, ostentatious, florid, showy, tawdry, raffish, vulgar, crude, Brummagem, meretricious, tinselly, chintzy, trashy, tasteless, *colloq.* tarty *sl.* glitzy.

gaudy[2] /gáwdi/ *n.* (*pl.* **-ies**) *Brit.* an annual feast or entertainment, esp. a college dinner for old members etc. [L *gaudium* joy or *gaude* imper. of *gaudēre* rejoice]

gauge /gayj/ *n.* & *v.* (*US* **gage**: see also sense 7) ● *n.* **1** a standard measure to which certain things must conform, esp.: **a** the measure of the capacity or contents of a barrel. **b** the fineness of a textile. **c** the diameter of a bullet. **d** the thickness of sheet metal. **2** any of various instruments for measuring or determining this, or for measuring length, thickness, or other dimensions or properties. **3** the distance between a pair of rails or the wheels on one axle. **4** the capacity, extent, or scope of something. **5** a means of estimating; a criterion or test. **6** a graduated instrument measuring the force or quantity of rainfall, stream, tide, wind, etc. **7** (usu. **gage**) *Naut.* a relative position with respect to the wind. ● *v.tr.* **1** measure exactly (esp. objects of standard size). **2** determine the capacity or content of. **3** estimate or form a judgement of (a person, temperament, situation, etc.). **4** make uniform; bring to a standard size or shape. □ **gauge pressure** the amount by which a pressure exceeds that of the atmosphere. **take the gauge of** estimate. □□ **gaugeable** *adj.* **gauger** *n.* [ME f. ONF *gauge*, *gauger*, of unkn. orig.]
■ *n.* **1** yardstick, benchmark, measure, rule, pattern, guide. **4** scope, capacity, amount, extent, measure, size, dimension(s), magnitude, degree, limit. **5** criterion, standard, yardstick, measure, touchstone, model, guide-line, guide, rule, norm, example; test. ● *v.* **1, 2** measure, calculate, compute, figure, reckon, determine, weigh. **3** judge, evaluate, appraise, assess, rate, estimate, take the gauge of; guess. **4** standardize, regularize.

Gaul /gawl/ *n.* a native or inhabitant of ancient Gaul. [*Gaul* the country f. F *Gaule* f. Gmc]

gauleiter /gówlītər/ *n.* **1** an official governing a district under Nazi rule. **2** a local or petty tyrant. [G f. *Gau* administrative district + *Leiter* leader]

Gaulish /gáwlish/ *adj.* & *n.* ● *adj.* of or relating to the ancient Gauls. ● *n.* their language.

Gaullism /gṓliz'm/ *n.* **1** the principles and policies of Charles de Gaulle, French military and political leader (d. 1970), characterized by their conservatism, nationalism, and advocacy of centralized government. **2** adherence to these. □□ **Gaullist** *n.* [F *Gaullisme*]

gault /gawlt/ *n.* *Geol.* **1** a series of clay and marl beds between the upper and lower greensand in S. England. **2** clay obtained from these beds. [16th c.: orig. unkn.]

gaunt /gawnt/ *adj.* **1** lean, haggard. **2** grim or desolate in appearance. □□ **gauntly** *adv.* **gauntness** *n.* [ME: orig. unkn.]
■ **1** lean, thin, scrawny, skinny, scraggy, haggard, raw-boned, bony, angular, skeletal, cadaverous, hollow-cheeked, spare, pinched. **2** grim, dreary, dismal, bleak, deserted, forlorn, desolate, bare, stark, harsh, hostile, unfriendly, inimical, forbidding.

gauntlet[1] /gáwntlit/ *n.* **1** a stout glove with a long loose wrist. **2** *hist.* an armoured glove. **3** the part of a glove covering the wrist. **4** a challenge (esp. in **throw down the gauntlet**). [ME f. OF *gantelet* dimin. of *gant* glove f. Gmc]

gauntlet[2] /gáwntlit/ *n.* (*US* **gantlet** /gánt-/) □ **run the gauntlet 1** be subjected to harsh criticism. **2** pass between two rows of people and receive blows from them, as a punishment or ordeal. [earlier *gantlope* f. Sw. *gatlopp* f. *gata* lane, *lopp* course, assim. to GAUNTLET[1]]

gauntry var. of GANTRY 3.

gaur /gowr/ *n.* a wild species of Indian cattle, *Bos gaurus.* [Hind.]

gauss /gowss/ *n.* (*pl.* same or **gausses**) a unit of magnetic induction, equal to one ten-thousandth of a tesla. ¶ Abbr.: **G.** [K. *Gauss*, Ger. mathematician d. 1855]

Gaussian distribution /gówsiən/ *n. Statistics* = *normal distribution.* [as GAUSS]

gauze /gawz/ *n.* **1** a thin transparent fabric of silk, cotton, etc. **2** a fine mesh of wire etc. **3** a slight haze. [F *gaze* f. *Gaza* in Palestine]

gauzy /gáwzi/ *adj.* (**gauzier, gauziest**) **1** like gauze; thin and translucent. **2** flimsy, delicate. □□ **gauzily** *adv.* **gauziness** *n.*
▪ see FILMY 1.

gave *past* of GIVE.

gavel /gávv'l/ *n.* & *v.* ● *n.* a small hammer used by an auctioneer, or for calling a meeting to order. ● *v.* (**gavelled, gavelling;** *US* **gaveled, gaveling**) **1** *intr.* use a gavel. **2** *tr.* (often foll. by *down*) end (a meeting) or dismiss (a speaker) by use of a gavel. [19th c.: orig. unkn.]

gavial var. of GHARIAL.

gavotte /gəvót/ *n.* **1** an old French dance in common time beginning on the third beat of the bar. **2** the music for this, or a piece of music in the rhythm of this as a movement in a suite. [F f. Prov. *gavoto* f. *Gavot* native of a region in the Alps]

gawk /gawk/ *v.* & *n.* ● *v.intr. colloq.* stare stupidly. ● *n.* an awkward or bashful person. □□ **gawkish** *adj.* [rel. to obs. *gaw* gaze f. ON *gá* heed]
▪ *v.* stare, goggle, gape, *colloq.* rubberneck, *Brit. colloq.* gawp. ● *n.* lout, churl, dolt, dunderhead, ignoramus, fool, simpleton, ass, clodhopper, oaf, bumpkin, boor, bungler, bumbler, *colloq.* galoot, *Brit. colloq.* clot, *US colloq.* lummox, *sl.* clod, *Austral. sl.* galah, *esp. US sl.* lug.

gawky /gáwki/ *adj.* (**gawkier, gawkiest**) awkward or ungainly. □□ **gawkily** *adv.* **gawkiness** *n.*
▪ see CLUMSY 1.

gawp /gawp/ *v.intr. Brit. colloq.* stare stupidly or obtrusively. □□ **gawper** *n.* [earlier *gaup*, *galp* f. ME *galpen* yawn, rel. to YELP]
▪ see STARE *v.*

gay /gay/ *adj.* & *n.* ● *adj.* **1** light-hearted and carefree; mirthful. **2** characterized by cheerfulness or pleasure (*a gay life*). **3** brightly coloured; showy, brilliant (*a gay scarf*). **4** *colloq.* **a** homosexual. **b** intended for or used by homosexuals (*a gay bar*). ¶ Generally informal in use, but favoured by homosexuals with ref. to themselves. **5** *colloq.* dissolute, immoral. ● *n. colloq.* a homosexual, esp. male. □ **Gay Liberation** the advocacy of homosexuals' freedom from social and legal discrimination. □□ **gayness** *n.* [ME f. OF *gai*, of unkn. orig.]
▪ *adj.* **1** happy, jovial, light-hearted, debonair, cheerful, gleeful, bright, joyful, jubilant, high-spirited, gamesome, merry, mirthful, lively, carefree, vivacious, buoyant, effervescent, exuberant, bubbly, sparkling, *esp. US colloq.* chipper, *poet.* blithe. **2** see PLEASANT. **3** colourful, showy, bright, brilliant, vivid. **5** see DISSOLUTE.

gayal /gəyál/ *n.* a wild species of Indian cattle, *Bos fontalis.* [Hindi]

gayety *US* var. of GAIETY.

gazania /gəzáyniə/ *n.* any herbaceous plant of the genus *Gazania*, with showy yellow or orange daisy-shaped flowers. [18th c.: f. Theodore of *Gaza*, Greek scholar d. 1478]

gaze /gayz/ *v.* & *n.* ● *v.intr.* (foll. by *at, into, on, upon*, etc.) look fixedly. ● *n.* a fixed or intent look. □□ **gazer** *n.* [ME: orig. unkn.; cf. obs. *gaw* GAWK]
▪ *v.* gape, look; (*gaze at*) contemplate, regard, scrutinize, observe, watch, eye; see also STARE *v.* ● *n.* stare, look, goggle, fixed *or* intent *or* blank look.

gazebo /gəzeébō/ *n.* (*pl.* **-os** or **-oes**) a small building or structure such as a summer-house or turret, designed to give a wide view. [perh. joc. f. GAZE, in imitation of L futures in *-ēbo*: cf. LAVABO]

gazelle /gəzél/ *n.* any of various small graceful soft-eyed antelopes of Asia or Africa, esp. of the genus *Gazella.* [F prob. f. Sp. *gacela* f. Arab. *ġazāl*]

gazette /gəzét/ *n.* & *v.* ● *n.* **1** a newspaper, esp. the official one of an organization or institution (*University Gazette*). **2** *hist.* a news-sheet; a periodical publication giving current events. **3** *Brit.* an official journal with a list of government appointments, bankruptcies, and other public notices (*London Gazette*). ● *v.tr. Brit.* announce or publish in an official gazette. [F f. It. *gazzetta* f. *gazeta*, a Venetian small coin]
▪ *n.* see JOURNAL 1.

gazetteer /gázziteér/ *n.* a geographical index or dictionary. [earlier = journalist, for whom such an index was provided: f. F *gazettier* f. It. *gazzettiere* (as GAZETTE)]

gazpacho /gaspáchō/ *n.* (*pl.* **-os**) a Spanish soup made with oil, garlic, onions, etc., and served cold. [Sp.]

gazump /gəzúmp/ *v.tr.* (also *absol.*) *Brit. colloq.* **1** (of a seller) raise the price of a property after having accepted an offer by (an intending buyer). **2** swindle. □□ **gazumper** *n.* [20th c.: orig. uncert.]

gazunder /gəzúndər/ *v.tr.* (also *absol.*) *Brit. colloq.* (of a buyer) lower the amount of an offer made to (the seller) for a property, esp. just before exchange of contracts. [GAZUMP + UNDER]

GB *abbr.* Great Britain.

GBE *abbr.* (in the UK) Knight (or Dame) Grand Cross (of the Order) of the British Empire.

GBH *abbr.* grievous bodily harm.

GC *abbr.* (in the UK) George Cross.

GCB *abbr.* (in the UK) Knight (or Dame) Grand Cross (of the Order) of the Bath.

GCE *abbr.* (in the UK) General Certificate of Education.

GCHQ *abbr.* (in the UK) Government Communications Headquarters.

GCMG *abbr.* (in the UK) Knight (or Dame) Grand Cross (of the Order) of St Michael & St George.

GCSE *abbr.* (in the UK) General Certificate of Secondary Education.

GCVO *abbr.* (in the UK) Knight (or Dame) Grand Cross of the Royal Victorian Order.

Gd *symb. Chem.* the element gadolinium.

Gdn. *abbr.* Garden.

Gdns. *abbr.* Gardens.

GDP *abbr.* gross domestic product.

GDR *abbr. hist.* German Democratic Republic.

Ge *symb. Chem.* the element germanium.

gear /geer/ *n.* & *v.* ● *n.* **1** (often in *pl.*) **a** a set of toothed wheels that work together to transmit and control motion from an engine, esp. to the road wheels of a vehicle. **b** a mechanism for doing this. **2** a particular function or state of adjustment of engaged gears (*low gear; second gear*). **3** a mechanism of wheels, levers, etc., usu. for a special purpose (*winding-gear*). **4** a particular apparatus or mechanism, as specified (*landing-gear*). **5** equipment or tackle for a special purpose. **6** *colloq.* **a** clothing, esp. when modern or fashionable. **b** possessions in general. **7** goods; household utensils. **8** rigging. **9** a harness for a draught animal. ● *v.* **1** *tr.* (foll. by *to*) adjust or adapt to suit a special purpose or need. **2** *tr.* (often foll. by *up*) equip with gears. **3** *tr.* (foll. by *up*) make ready or prepared. **4** *tr.* put (machinery) in gear. **5** *intr.* **a** be in gear. **b** (foll. by *with*) work smoothly with. □ **be geared** (or **all geared**) **up** (often foll. by *for*, or *to* + infin.) *colloq.* be ready or enthusiastic. **first** (or **bottom**) **gear** the lowest gear in a series. **gear down** (or **up**) provide with a low (or high) gear. **gear lever** (or **shift**) a lever used to engage or change gear, esp. in a motor vehicle. **high** (or **low**) **gear** a gear such that the driven end of a transmission revolves faster (or slower) than the driving end. **in gear** with a gear engaged. **out of gear 1** with no gear engaged. **2** out of order. **top gear** the highest gear in a series. [ME f. ON *gervi* f. Gmc]

■ *n.* **1** (*gears*) **a** cog-wheels. **b** gearbox. **4, 5** apparatus, mechanism, outfit, appliance; equipment, machinery, tackle, material. **6 a** clothing, clothes, garments, *colloq.* togs, *formal* apparel, attire, *joc.* habiliments, *sl.* duds, *Brit. sl.* clobber. **b** possessions, belongings, things, effects, chattels, goods, impedimenta, baggage, accoutrements, stuff, kit. **7** goods, materials, supplies, utensils, implements, tools, accoutrements, paraphernalia. ● *v.* **1** adjust, adapt, tailor, fit, accommodate, suit, alter. **3** (*gear up*) ready, make *or* get ready, set, equip, *colloq.* psych up; see also PREPARE 3a. **5 b** (*gear with*) go together with, work well with, accord with, fit with. □ **be geared** (or **all geared**) **up** see READY *adj.* 1, 2.

gearbox /geérboks/ *n.* **1** the casing that encloses a set of gears. **2** a set of gears with its casing, esp. in a motor vehicle.

gearing /geéring/ *n.* **1** a set or arrangement of gears in a machine. **2** *Brit. Commerce* **a** the allocation of part of a dividend to preferred recipients. **b** the amount of this part.

gearwheel /geérweel/ *n.* **1** a toothed wheel in a set of gears. **2** (in a bicycle) the cog-wheel driven directly by the chain.

gecko /gékkō/ *n.* (*pl.* **-os** or **-oes**) any of various house lizards found in warm climates, with adhesive feet for climbing vertical surfaces. [Malay *chichak* etc., imit. of its cry]

gee[1] /jee/ *int.* (also **gee whiz** /wiz/) *US colloq.* a mild expression of surprise, discovery, etc. [perh. abbr. of JESUS]

gee[2] /jee/ *int.* (often foll. by *up*) a command to a horse etc., esp. to go faster. [17th c.: orig. unkn.]

gee[3] /jee/ *n. US sl.* (usu. in *pl.*) a thousand dollars. [the letter *G*, as initial of GRAND]

gee-gee /jeéjee/ *n. Brit. colloq.* a horse. [orig. a child's word, f. GEE[2]]

geek[1] /geek/ *n. Austral. sl.* a look. [E dial.]

■ see GLANCE[1] *n.* 1.

geek[2] /geek/ *n. US sl.* a person who is socially inept or tediously conventional; a dupe. [var. of dial. *geck* fool, dupe]

geese *pl.* of GOOSE.

gee-string var. of G-STRING 2.

geezer /geézər/ *n. sl.* a person, esp. an old man. [dial. pronunc. of *guiser* mummer]

■ see FELLOW 1.

Gehenna /gihénnə/ *n.* **1** (in the New Testament) hell. **2** a place of burning, torment, or misery. [eccl.L f. Gk f. Heb. *gē' hinnōm* hell, orig. the valley of Hinnom near Jerusalem, where children were sacrificed]

Geiger counter /gīgər/ *n.* a device for measuring radio-activity by detecting and counting ionizing particles. [H. *Geiger*, Ger. physicist d. 1945]

geisha /gáyshə/ *n.* (*pl.* same or **geishas**) **1** a Japanese hostess trained in entertaining men with dance and song. **2** a Japanese prostitute. [Jap.]

Geissler tube /gīslər/ *n.* a sealed tube of glass or quartz with a central constriction, filled with vapour for the production of a luminous electrical discharge. [H. *Geissler*, Ger. mechanic d. 1879]

gel /jel/ *n.* & *v.* ● *n.* a semi-solid colloidal suspension or jelly, of a solid dispersed in a liquid. ● *v.intr.* (**gelled**, **gelling**) form a gel. □□ **gelation** /jeláysh'n/ *n.* [abbr. of GELATIN]

■ *v.* see SET[1] *v.* 11, 26.

gelatin /jéllətin/ *n.* (also **gelatine** /-teen/) a virtually colourless tasteless transparent water-soluble protein derived from collagen and used in food preparation, photography, etc. □ **gelatin paper** a paper coated with sensitized gelatin for photography. □□ **gelatinize** /jiláttinīz/ *v.tr.* & *intr.* (also **-ise**). **gelatinization** /jiláttinīzáysh'n/ *n.* [F *gélatine* f. It. *gelatina* f. *gelata* JELLY]

gelatinous /jiláttinəss/ *adj.* **1** of or like gelatin. **2** of a jelly-like consistency. □□ **gelatinously** *adv.*

■ **2** see THICK *adj.* 5a.

gelation /jiláysh'n/ *n.* solidification by freezing. [L *gelatio* f. *gelare* freeze]

gelato / gəláatō/ *n. Austral.* a kind of ice-cream. [It.]

geld /geld/ *v.tr.* **1** deprive (usu. a male animal) of the ability to reproduce. **2** castrate or spay; excise the testicles or ovaries of. [ME f. ON *gelda* f. *geldr* barren f. Gmc]

■ see STERILIZE 2.

gelding /gélding/ *n.* a gelded animal, esp. a male horse. [ME f. ON *geldingr*: see GELD]

gelid /jéllid/ *adj.* **1** icy, ice-cold. **2** chilly, cool. [L *gelidus* f. *gelu* frost]

■ see COLD *adj.* 1.

gelignite /jéllignīt/ *n.* an explosive made from nitroglycerine, cellulose nitrate, sodium nitrate, and wood pulp. [GELATIN + L *ignis* fire + -ITE[1]]

gelly /jélli/ *n. Brit. sl.* gelignite. [abbr.]

gem /jem/ *n.* & *v.* ● *n.* **1** a precious stone, esp. when cut and polished or engraved. **2** an object or person of great beauty or worth. ● *v.tr.* (**gemmed**, **gemming**) adorn with or as with gems. □□ **gemlike** *adj.* **gemmy** *adj.* [ME f. OF *gemme* f. L *gemma* bud, jewel]

■ *n.* **1** gemstone, jewel, precious stone, stone, *sl.* rock. **2** pearl, marvel, treasure; nonpareil, ideal, prize, masterpiece, *chef-d'œuvre*. ● *v.* bejewel, bedeck, decorate, adorn.

Gemara /gimaárə/ *n.* a rabbinical commentary on the Mishnah, forming the second part of the Talmud. [Aram. *g^emārâ* completion]

geminal /jémmin'l/ *adj. Chem.* (of molecules) having two functional groups attached to the same atom. □□ **geminally** *adv.* [as GEMINATE + -AL]

geminate *adj.* & *v.* ● *adj.* /jémminət/ combined in pairs. ● *v.tr.* /jémminayt/ **1** double, repeat. **2** arrange in pairs. □□ **gemination** /-náysh'n/ *n.* [L *geminatus* past part. of *geminare* f. *geminus* twin]

Gemini /jémminī, -nee/ *n.* **1** a constellation, traditionally regarded as contained in the figures of twins. **2 a** the third sign of the zodiac (the Twins). **b** a person born when the sun is in this sign. □□ **Geminean** /jémmineéən/ *n.* & *adj.* [ME f. L, = twins]

gemma /jémmə/ *n.* (*pl.* **gemmae** /-mee/) a small cellular body in cryptogams that separates from the mother-plant and starts a new one; an asexual spore. [L: see GEM]

gemmation /jemáysh'n/ *n.* reproduction by gemmae. [F f. *gemmer* to bud, *gemme* bud]

gemmiferous /jemíffərəss/ *adj.* **1** producing precious stones. **2** bearing buds. [L *gemmifer* (as GEMMA, -FEROUS)]

gemmiparous /jemíppərəss/ *adj.* of or propagating by gemmation. [mod.L *gemmiparus* f. L *gemma* bud + *parere* bring forth]

gemmology /jemólləji/ *n.* the study of gems. □□ **gemmologist** *n.* [L *gemma* gem + -LOGY]

gemmule /jémyōōl/ *n.* an encysted embryonic cell-cluster in sponges. [F *gemmule* or L *gemmula* little bud (as GEM)]

gemstone /jémstōn/ *n.* a precious stone used as a gem.

■ see JEWEL *n.* 1a.

gemütlich /gəmōōtlikh/ *adj.* **1** pleasant and comfortable. **2** genial, agreeable. [G]

Gen. *abbr.* **1** General. **2** Genesis (Old Testament).

gen /jen/ *n.* & *v. Brit. sl.* ● *n.* information. ● *v.tr.* & *intr.* (**genned**, **genning**) (foll. by *up*) provide with or obtain information. [perh. f. first syll. of *general information*]

■ *n.* see INFORMATION 1.

-gen /jən/ *comb. form* **1** *Chem.* that which produces (*hydrogen*; *antigen*). **2** *Bot.* growth (*endogen*; *exogen*; *acrogen*). [F *-gène*

f. Gk *-genēs* -born, of a specified kind f. *gen-* root of *gignomai* be born, become]

gendarme /zhóndaarm/ *n.* **1** a soldier, mounted or on foot, employed in police duties esp. in France. **2** a rock-tower on a mountain, occupying and blocking an arête. [F f. *gens d'armes* men of arms]

■ **1** see *police officer*.

gendarmerie /zhondaármәri/ *n.* **1** a force of gendarmes. **2** the headquarters of such a force.

gender /jéndәr/ *n.* **1 a** the grammatical classification of nouns and related words, roughly corresponding to the two sexes and sexlessness. **b** each of the classes of nouns (see MASCULINE, FEMININE, NEUTER, COMMON *adj.* 6). **2** (of nouns and related words) the property of belonging to such a class. **3** *colloq.* a person's sex. [ME f. OF *gendre* ult. f. L GENUS]

gene /jeen/ *n.* a unit of heredity composed of DNA or RNA and forming part of a chromosome etc., that determines a particular characteristic of an individual. □ **gene therapy** *Med.* the introduction of normal genes into cells in place of defective or missing ones in order to correct genetic disorders. [G *Gen*: see -GEN]

genealogical /jeéniәlójik'l/ *adj.* **1** of or concerning genealogy. **2** tracing family descent. □ **genealogical tree** a chart like an inverted branching tree showing the descent of a family or of an animal species. □□ **genealogically** *adv.* [F *généalogique* f. Gk *genealogikos* (as GENEALOGY)]

genealogy /jeéniálәji/ *n.* (*pl.* **-ies**) **1 a** a line of descent traced continuously from an ancestor. **b** an account or exposition of this. **2** the study and investigation of lines of descent. **3** a plant's or animal's line of development from earlier forms. □□ **genealogist** *n.* **genealogize** *v.tr.* & *intr.* (also **-ise**). [ME f. OF *genealogie* f. LL *genealogia* f. Gk *genealogia* f. *genea* race]

■ **1** see LINEAGE.

genera *pl.* of GENUS.

general /jénnәrәl/ *adj.* & *n.* ● *adj.* **1 a** completely or almost universal. **b** including or affecting all or nearly all parts or cases of things. **2** prevalent, widespread, usual. **3** not partial, particular, local, or sectional. **4** not limited in application; relating to whole classes or all cases. **5** including points common to the individuals of a class and neglecting the differences (*a general term*). **6** not restricted or specialized (*general knowledge*). **7 a** roughly corresponding or adequate. **b** sufficient for practical purposes. **8** not detailed (*a general resemblance; a general idea*). **9** vague, indefinite (*spoke only in general terms*). **10** chief or principal; having overall authority (*general manager; Secretary-General*). ● *n.* **1 a** an army officer ranking next below Field Marshal or above lieutenant-general. **b** *US* = *lieutenant-general, major-general*. **2** a commander of an army. **3** a tactician or strategist of specified merit (*a great general*). **4** the head of a religious order, e.g. of the Jesuits or Dominicans or the Salvation Army. **5** (prec. by *the*) *archaic* the public. □ **as a general rule** in most cases. **General American** a form of US speech not markedly dialectal or regional. **General Certificate of Education 1** an examination set esp. for secondary-school pupils at advanced level in England and Wales. **2** the certificate gained by passing it. **General Certificate of Secondary Education** an examination replacing and combining the GCE ordinary level and CSE examinations. **general delivery** *US* the delivery of letters to callers at a post office. **general election** the election of representatives to a legislature (esp. in the UK to the House of Commons) from constituencies throughout the country. **general headquarters** the headquarters of a military commander. **general meeting** a meeting open to all the members of a society etc. **general of the army** (or **air force**) *US* the officer of the highest rank in the army or air force. **general practice** the work of a general practitioner. **general practitioner** a doctor working in the community and treating cases of all kinds in the first instance, as distinct from a consultant or specialist. **general staff** the staff assisting a military commander in planning and administration. **general strike** a strike of workers in all or most trades. **General Synod** the highest governing body in the Church of England. **in general 1** as a normal rule; usually. **2** for the most part. □□ **generalness** *n.* [ME f. OF f. L *generalis* (as GENUS)]

■ *adj.* **1** extensive, comprehensive, worldwide, global, ubiquitous; accepted, public, popular, shared, communal, well-known; see also UNIVERSAL *adj.* **2** common, usual, normal, regular, prevailing, prevalent, widespread, customary, habitual, everyday, familiar. **3** mixed, assorted, heterogeneous; see also MISCELLANEOUS. **4** inclusive, all-inclusive, non-exclusive, unrestricted; overall, across the board. **5** see SWEEPING *adj.* 1. **6** unspecialized, non-specialized, encyclopedic, broad, comprehensive, catholic; sweeping, panoramic. **8, 9** vague, indefinite, ill-defined, loose, inexact, imprecise, unspecific, undetailed, generalized; overall, approximate, rough. □ **general practitioner** see DOCTOR *n.* 1a. **in general** see *usually* (USUAL).

generalissimo /jénnәrәlíssimō/ *n.* (*pl.* **-os**) the commander of a combined military force consisting of army, navy, and air-force units. [It., superl. of *generale* GENERAL]

generalist /jénnәrәlist/ *n.* a person competent in several different fields or activities (opp. SPECIALIST).

generality /jénnәrálliti/ *n.* (*pl.* **-ies**) **1** a statement or principle etc. having general validity or force. **2** applicability to a whole class of instances. **3** vagueness; lack of detail. **4** the state of being general. **5** (foll. by *of*) the main body or majority. [F *généralité* f. LL *generalitas -tatis* (as GENERAL)]

■ **1** principle, law; generalization. **2** see *prevalence* (PREVALENT). **5** (*the generality of*) the great majority of, the vast majority of, the greater part of, most of.

generalization /jénnәrәlīzáysh'n/ *n.* (also **-isation**) **1** a general notion or proposition obtained by inference from (esp. limited or inadequate) particular cases. **2** the act or an instance of generalizing. [F *généralisation* (as GENERALIZE)]

generalize /jénnәrәlīz/ *v.* (also **-ise**) **1** *intr.* **a** speak in general or indefinite terms. **b** form general principles or notions. **2** *tr.* reduce to a general statement, principle, or notion. **3** *tr.* **a** give a general character to. **b** call by a general name. **4** *tr.* infer (a law or conclusion) by induction. **5** *tr. Math.* & *Philos.* express in a general form; extend the application of. **6** *tr.* (in painting) render only the typical characteristics of. **7** *tr.* bring into general use. □□ **generalizable** *adj.* **generalizability** /-līzәbílliti/ *n.* **generalizer** *n.* [F *généraliser* (as GENERAL)]

generally /jénnәrәli/ *adv.* **1** usually; in most cases. **2** in a general sense; without regard to particulars or exceptions (*generally speaking*). **3** for the most part; extensively (*not generally known*). **4** in most respects (*they were generally well-behaved*).

■ **1** usually, commonly, ordinarily, customarily, habitually, normally, typically; on average, as a rule, by and large, in general, for the most part, mostly, mainly, on the whole, predominantly. **2** roughly, broadly, loosely, approximately, unspecifically. **3** largely, extensively, widely. **4** see MAINLY.

generalship /jénnәrәlship/ *n.* **1** the art or practice of exercising military command. **2** military skill; strategy. **3** skilful management; tact, diplomacy.

■ **2** see TACTICS 1.

generate /jénnәrayt/ *v.tr.* **1** bring into existence; produce, evolve. **2** produce (electricity). **3** *Math.* (of a point or line or surface conceived as moving) make (a line or surface or solid). **4** *Math.* & *Linguistics* produce (a set or sequence of items) by the formulation and application of precise criteria. □□ **generable** /-rәb'l/ *adj.* [L *generare* beget (as GENUS)]

■ **1** create, originate, initiate, invent, devise, coin; produce, evolve, develop, form, forge, make, manufacture; give rise to, bring about, engender, *literary* beget. **4** yield, produce, give.

generation /jénnәráysh'n/ *n.* **1** all the people born at a particular time, regarded collectively (*my generation; the* *rising generation*). **2** a single step in descent or pedigree (*have known them for three generations*). **3** a stage in (esp. technological) development (*fourth-generation computers*). **4** the average time in which children are ready to take the place of their parents (usu. reckoned at about 30 years). **5** production by natural or artificial process, esp. the production of electricity or heat. **6 a** procreation; the propagation of species. **b** the act of begetting or being begotten. □ **generation gap** differences of outlook or opinion between those of different generations. □□ **generational** *adj.* [ME f. OF f. L *generatio -onis* (as GENERATE)]

■ **1** age (group), cohort; contemporaries, peers. **6 a** propagation, procreation, production, reproduction; breeding, spawning. **b** mothering, fathering, siring, *literary* begetting; conception.

generative /jénnərətiv/ *adj.* **1** of or concerning procreation. **2** able to produce, productive. □ **generative grammar** a set of rules whereby permissible sentences may be generated from the elements of a language. [ME f. OF *generatif* or LL *generativus* (as GENERATE)]

■ **2** see FERTILE 3.

generator /jénnəraytər/ *n.* **1** a machine for converting mechanical into electrical energy; a dynamo. **2** an apparatus for producing gas, steam, etc. **3** a person who generates an idea etc.; an originator.

generic /jinérrik/ *adj.* **1** characteristic of or relating to a class; general, not specific or special. **2** *Biol.* characteristic of or belonging to a genus. **3** (of goods, esp. a drug) having no brand name; not protected by a registered trade mark. □□ **generically** *adv.* [F *générique* f. L GENUS]

generous /jénnərəss/ *adj.* **1** giving or given freely. **2** magnanimous, noble-minded, unprejudiced. **3 a** ample, abundant, copious (*a generous portion*). **b** (of wine) rich and full. □□ **generosity** /-róssiti/ *n.* **generously** *adv.* **generousness** *n.* [OF *genereus* f. L *generosus* noble, magnanimous (as GENUS)]

■ **1** bountiful, charitable, lavish, open-handed, free, liberal, unstinting, ungrudging, munificent, handsome, *poet.* bounteous. **2** magnanimous, benevolent, charitable, beneficent, benevolent, big-hearted, unselfish, forgiving, humanitarian, philanthropic, humane, kindly, noble, noble-minded, good; disinterested, unprejudiced, unbiased, liberal-minded, broad-minded, tolerant, liberal. **3 a** ample, abundant, copious, plentiful, full, lavish, overflowing, bountiful, liberal; large, substantial, sizeable, substantial, considerable, biggish, big.

genesis /jénnisiss/ *n.* **1** the origin, or mode of formation or generation, of a thing. **2** (**Genesis**) the first book of the Old Testament, with an account of the creation of the world. [L f. Gk f. *gen-* be produced, root of *gignomai* become]

■ **1** see ORIGIN 1.

genet /jénnit/ *n.* (also **genette** /jinét/) **1** any catlike mammal of the genus *Genetta*, native to Africa and S. Europe, with spotted fur and a long ringed bushy tail. **2** the fur of the genet. [ME f. OF *genete* f. Arab. *jarnaiṭ*]

genetic /jinéttik/ *adj.* **1** of genetics or genes; inherited. **2** of, in, or concerning origin; causal. □ **genetic code** *Biochem.* the means by which genetic information is stored as sequences of nucleotide bases in the chromosomal DNA. **genetic engineering** the deliberate modification of the characters of an organism by the manipulation of DNA and the transformation of certain genes. **genetic fingerprinting** (or **profiling**) the analysis of characteristic patterns in DNA as a means of identifying individuals. □□ **genetically** *adv.* [GENESIS after *antithetic*]

■ **1** see HEREDITARY 1.

genetics /jinéttiks/ *n.pl.* (usu. treated as *sing.*) the study of heredity and the variation of inherited characteristics. □□ **geneticist** /-tisist/ *n.*

genette var. of GENET.

geneva /jineévə/ *n.* Hollands gin. [Du. *genever* f. OF *genevre* f. L *juniperus*, with assim. to the place name *Geneva*]

Geneva bands /jineévə/ *n.pl.* two white cloth strips attached to the collar of some Protestants' clerical dress. [*Geneva* in Switzerland, where orig. worn by Calvinists]

Geneva Convention /jineévə/ *n.* an international agreement first made at Geneva in 1864 and later revised, governing the status and treatment of captured and wounded military personnel in wartime.

genial[1] /jeéniəl/ *adj.* **1** jovial, sociable, kindly, cheerful. **2** (of the climate) mild and warm; conducive to growth. **3** cheering, enlivening. □□ **geniality** /-niálliti/ *n.* **genially** *adv.* [L *genialis* (as GENIUS)]

■ **1** jovial, good-humoured, cheerful, cheery, convivial, sociable, affable, amiable, cordial, warm, pleasant, nice, friendly, congenial, agreeable, hospitable, good-natured, kindly, kind. **2** see MILD 3. **3** cheering, good, enlivening, heartening, reassuring, uplifting, comforting, gladdening, refreshing.

genial[2] /jineéəl/ *adj.* *Anat.* of or relating to the chin. [Gk *geneion* chin f. *genus* jaw]

genic /jeénik/ *adj.* of or relating to genes.

-genic /jénnik/ *comb. form* forming adjectives meaning: **1** producing (*carcinogenic*; *pathogenic*). **2** well suited to (*photogenic*; *radiogenic*). **3** produced by (*iatrogenic*). □□ **-genically** *suffix* forming adverbs. [-GEN + -IC]

genie /jeéni/ *n.* (*pl.* usu. **genii** /jeéni-ī/) a jinnee, goblin, or familiar spirit of Arabian folklore. [F *génie* f. L GENIUS: cf. JINNEE]

genii *pl.* of GENIE, GENIUS.

genista /jinístə/ *n.* any almost leafless shrub of the genus *Genista*, with a profusion of yellow pea-shaped flowers, e.g. dyer's broom. [L]

genital /jénnit'l/ *adj.* & *n.* ● *adj.* of or relating to animal reproduction. ● *n.* (in *pl.*) the external reproductive organs. [OF *génital* or L *genitalis* f. *gignere genit-* beget]

■ *adj.* see SEXUAL. ● *n.* (*genitals*) genitalia, reproductive organs, sex organs, private parts, *colloq.* privates, parts.

genitalia /jénnitáyliə/ *n.pl.* the genitals. [L, neut. pl. of *genitalis*: see GENITAL]

genitive /jénnitiv/ *n.* & *adj.* *Gram.* ● *n.* the case of nouns and pronouns (and words in grammatical agreement with them) corresponding to *of*, *from*, and other prepositions and indicating possession or close association. ● *adj.* of or in the genitive. □□ **genitival** /-tīv'l/ *adj.* **genitivally** /-tīvəli/ *adv.* [ME f. OF *genetif*, *-ive* or L *genitivus* f. *gignere genit-* beget]

genito- /jénnitō/ *comb. form* genital.

genito-urinary /jénnitō-yoórinəri, -yoórinri/ *adj.* of the genital and urinary organs.

genius /jeéniəss/ *n.* (*pl.* **geniuses** or **genii** /-ni-ī/) **1** (*pl.* **geniuses**) **a** an exceptional intellectual or creative power or other natural ability or tendency. **b** a person having this. **2** the tutelary spirit of a person, place, institution, etc. **3** a person or spirit regarded as powerfully influencing a person for good or evil. **4** the prevalent feeling or associations etc. of a nation, age, etc. [L (in sense 2) f. the root of *gignere* beget]

■ **1 a** intellect, intelligence, brilliance; ingenuity, wit, brain(s); talent, gift, knack, flair, aptitude, forte; faculty, capacity, ability, capability. **b** mastermind, master, great, giant, luminary; virtuoso, maestro, adept, expert, wizard; *colloq.* brain, brain-box, whiz, whiz-kid, Einstein, *US colloq.* maven.

genizah /geneézə/ *n.* a room attached to a synagogue and housing damaged, discarded, or heretical books etc., and sacred relics. [Heb. *gĕnīzāh*, lit. hiding-place f. *gānaz* hide, set aside]

Genoa cake /jénnōə/ *n.* a rich fruit cake with almonds on top. [*Genoa* in Italy]

Genoa jib /jénnōə/ *n.* a large jib or foresail used esp. on yachts.

genocide /jénnəsīd/ *n.* the deliberate extermination of a people or nation. □□ **genocidal** /-sīd'l/ *adj.* [Gk *genos* race + -CIDE]

■ see MURDER *n.* 1.

genome /jeénōm/ *n.* **1** the haploid set of chromosomes of an organism. **2** the genetic material of an organism. [GENE + CHROMOSOME]

genotype /jeénətīp/ *n. Biol.* the genetic constitution of an individual. ▫▫ **genotypic** /-típpik/ *adj.* [G *Genotypus* (as GENE, TYPE)]

-genous /jénnəss/ *comb. form* forming adjectives meaning 'produced' (*endogenous*).

genre /zhóNrə/ *n.* **1** a kind or style, esp. of art or literature (e.g. novel, drama, satire). **2** (in full **genre painting**) the painting of scenes from ordinary life. [F, = a kind (as GENDER)]

■ **1** style, kind, genus, sort, type, class, category, variety, brand, species.

gens /jenz/ *n.* (*pl.* **gentes** /jénteez/) **1** *Rom.Hist.* a group of families sharing a name and claiming a common origin. **2** *Anthropol.* a number of people sharing descent through the male line. [L, f. the root of *gignere* beget]

gent /jent/ *n. colloq.* (often *joc.*) **1** a gentleman. **2** (in *pl.*) (in shop titles) men (*gents' outfitters*). **3** (**the Gents**) *Brit. colloq.* a men's public lavatory. [abbr. of GENTLEMAN]

genteel /jenteél/ *adj.* **1** affectedly or ostentatiously refined or stylish. **2** often *iron.* of or appropriate to the upper classes. ▫▫ **genteelly** *adv.* **genteelness** *n.* [earlier *gentile*, readoption of F *gentil* GENTLE]

■ **1** over-polite, over-refined, pretentious, affected, pompous, snobbish, *colloq.* posh, la-di-da, snooty, stuck-up, *esp. Brit. sl.* toffee-nosed. **2** well-bred, county, high-class, upper-class, aristocratic, thoroughbred, blue-blooded, patrician, gracious, refined, polished, sophisticated, debonair, suave, urbane, cultivated, cultured, elegant; courtly, polite, civil, well-mannered, courteous, ceremonious, mannerly, proper, respectable, decorous, *colloq.* classy, upper-crust, *US colloq.* tony.

genteelism /jenteéliz'm/ *n.* a word used because it is thought to be less vulgar than the commoner word (e.g. *perspire* for *sweat*).

gentes *pl.* of GENS.

gentian /jénsh'n/ *n.* **1** any plant of the genus *Gentiana* or *Gentianella*, found esp. in mountainous regions, and having usu. vivid blue flowers. **2** (in full **gentian bitter**) a liquor extracted from the root of the gentian. ▫ **gentian violet** a violet dye used as an antiseptic, esp. in the treatment of burns. [OE f. L *gentiana* f. *Gentius* king of Illyria]

gentile /jéntīl/ *adj.* & *n.* • *adj.* **1** (**Gentile**) not Jewish; heathen. **2** of or relating to a nation or tribe. **3** *Gram.* (of a word) indicating nationality. • *n.* **1** (**Gentile**) a person who is not Jewish. **2** *Gram.* a word indicating nationality. [ME f. L *gentilis* f. *gens gentis* family: see GENS]

■ *adj.* **1** (**Gentile**) heathen, *sl. derog.* goyish. • *n.* **1** (**Gentile**) heathen, *sl. derog.* goy.

gentility /jentílliti/ *n.* **1** social superiority. **2** good manners; habits associated with the nobility. **3** people of noble birth. [ME f. OF *gentilité* (as GENTLE)]

■ **2** see PROPRIETY 2. **3** see *upper crust* (UPPER[1]).

gentle /jént'l/ *adj.*, *v.*, & *n.* • *adj.* (**gentler**, **gentlest**) **1** not rough; mild or kind, esp. in temperament. **2** moderate; not severe or drastic (*a gentle rebuke*; *a gentle breeze*). **3** (of birth, pursuits, etc.) honourable, of or fit for people of good social position. **4** quiet; requiring patience (*gentle art*). **5** *archaic* generous, courteous. • *v.tr.* **1** make gentle or docile. **2** handle (a horse etc.) firmly but gently. • *n.* a maggot, the larva of the meat-fly or bluebottle used as fishing-bait. ▫▫ **gentleness** *n.* **gently** *adv.* [ME f. OF *gentil* f. L *gentilis*: see GENTILE]

■ *adj.* **1** kind, kindly, mild, tender, thoughtful, patient, indulgent, benign, gracious, compassionate, humane, tender-hearted, merciful, lenient; quiet, calm, still, temperate, unruffled, untroubled, undisturbed, tranquil, restful, peaceful, pacific, placid, smooth, soothing. **2** moderate, soft, light; balmy. **3** honourable, noble, high. **5** see COURTEOUS. • *v.* **1** see TAME *v.* 1.

gentlefolk /jént'lfōk/ *n.pl. literary* people of good family.

gentleman /jént'lmən/ *n.* (*pl.* **-men**) **1** a man (in polite or formal use). **2** a chivalrous or well-bred man. **3** a man of good social position or of wealth and leisure (*country gentleman*). **4** a man of gentle birth attached to a royal household (*gentleman in waiting*). **5** (in *pl.* as a form of address) a male audience or the male part of an audience. ▫ **gentleman-at-arms** one of a sovereign's bodyguard. **gentleman farmer** a country gentleman who farms. **gentleman's** (or **-men's**) **agreement** one which is binding in honour but not legally enforceable. [GENTLE + MAN after OF *gentilz hom*]

■ **1** see MAN *n.* 1. **3** see NOBLE *n.*

gentlemanly /jént'lmənli/ *adj.* like a gentleman in looks or behaviour; befitting a gentleman. ▫▫ **gentlemanliness** *n.*

■ see *well-bred* (WELL[1]).

gentlewoman /jént'lwŏŏmmən/ *n.* (*pl.* **-women**) *archaic* a woman of good birth or breeding.

■ see NOBLE *n.*

gentoo /jéntōō/ *n.* a penguin, *Pygoscelis papua*, esp. abundant in the Falkland Islands. [perh. f. Anglo-Ind. *Gentoo* = Hindu, f. Port. *gentio* GENTILE]

gentrification /jéntrifikáysh'n/ *n.* the social advancement of an inner urban area by the arrival of affluent middle-class residents. ▫▫ **gentrify** /-fī/ *v.tr.* (**-ies**, **-ied**).

gentry /jéntri/ *n.pl.* **1** the people next below the nobility in position and birth. **2** *derog.* people (*these gentry*). [prob. f. obs. *gentrice* f. OF *genterise* var. of *gentelise* nobility f. *gentil* GENTLE]

■ **1** landowners, squirearchy; ladies, gentlemen, *literary* gentlefolk. **2** see PEOPLE *n.* 2.

genuflect /jényooflekt/ *v.intr.* bend the knee, esp. in worship or as a sign of respect. ▫▫ **genuflection** /-fléksh'n/ *n.* (also **genuflexion**). **genuflector** *n.* [eccl.L *genuflectere genuflex-* f. L *genu* the knee + *flectere* bend]

■ see BEND[1] *v.* 8a.

genuine /jényoo-in/ *adj.* **1** really coming from its stated, advertised, or reputed source. **2** properly so called; not sham. **3** pure-bred. **4** (of a person) free from affectation or hypocrisy; honest. ▫▫ **genuinely** *adv.* **genuineness** *n.* [L *genuinus* f. *genu* knee, with ref. to a father's acknowledging a new-born child by placing it on his knee: later associated with GENUS]

■ **1, 2** authentic, veritable, real, bona fide, legitimate, true, proper, pukka, unfeigned; original. **4** candid, frank, open, sincere, honest; decent, honourable, principled.

genus /jeénəss, jén-/ *n.* (*pl.* **genera** /jénnərə/) **1** *Biol.* a taxonomic grouping of organisms having common characteristics distinct from those of other genera, usu. containing several or many species and being one of a series constituting a taxonomic family. **2** a kind or class having common characteristics. **3** *Logic* kinds of things including subordinate kinds or species. [L *genus -eris* birth, race, stock]

■ **1, 2** see SORT *n.* 1.

-geny /jəni/ *comb. form* forming nouns meaning 'mode of production or development of' (*anthropogeny*; *ontogeny*; *pathogeny*). [F *-génie* (as -GEN, -Y[3])]

Geo. *abbr.* George.

geo- /jeé-ō/ *comb. form* earth. [Gk *geō-* f. *gē* earth]

geobotany /jeé-ōbóttəni/ *n.* the study of the geographical distribution of plants. ▫▫ **geobotanist** *n.*

geocentric /jeé-ōséntrik/ *adj.* **1** considered as viewed from the centre of the earth. **2** having or representing the earth as the centre; not heliocentric. ▫ **geocentric latitude** the latitude at which a planet would appear if viewed from the centre of the earth. ▫▫ **geocentrically** *adv.*

geochemistry /jeé-ōkémmistri/ *n.* the chemistry of the earth and its rocks, minerals, etc. ▫▫ **geochemical** *adj.* **geochemist** *n.*

geochronology /jeé-ōkrənólləji/ *n.* **1** the study and measurement of geological time by means of geological events. **2**

the ordering of geological events. □□ **geochronological** /-krónnəlójik'l/ *adj.* **geochronologist** *n.*

geode /jée-ōd/ *n.* **1** a small cavity lined with crystals or other mineral matter. **2** a rock containing such a cavity. □□ **geodic** /jee-óddik/ *adj.* [L *geodes* f. Gk *geōdēs* earthy f. *gē* earth]

geodesic /jée-ōdéezik/ *adj.* (also **geodetic** /-déttik/) **1** of or relating to geodesy. **2** of, involving, or consisting of a geodesic line. □ **geodesic dome** a dome constructed of short struts along geodesic lines. **geodesic line** the shortest possible line between two points on a curved surface.

geodesy /jee-óddisi/ *n.* the branch of mathematics dealing with the shape and area of the earth or large portions of it. □□ **geodesist** *n.* [mod.L f. Gk *geōdaisia* (as GEO-, *daiō* divide)]

geodetic var. of GEODESIC.

geographic var. of GEOGRAPHICAL.

geographical /jéeəgráffik'l/ *adj.* (also **geographic** /-gráffik/) of or relating to geography. □ **geographical latitude** the angle made with the plane of the equator by a perpendicular to the earth's surface at any point. **geographical mile** a distance equal to one minute of longitude or latitude at the equator (about 1850 metres). □□ **geographically** *adv.* [*geographic* f. F *géographique* or LL *geographicus* f. Gk *geōgraphikos* (as GEO-, -GRAPHIC)]

geography /jiógrəfi/ *n.* **1** the study of the earth's physical features, resources, and climate, and the physical aspects of its population. **2** the main physical features of an area. **3** the layout or arrangement of rooms in a building. □□ **geographer** *n.* [F *géographie* or L *geographia* f. Gk *geōgraphia* (as GEO-, -GRAPHY)]

geoid /jée-oyd/ *n.* **1** the shape of the earth. **2** a shape formed by the mean sea level and its imagined extension under land areas. **3** an oblate spheroid. [Gk *geoeidēs* (as GEO-, -OID)]

geology /jiólləji/ *n.* **1** the science of the earth, including the composition, structure, and origin of its rocks. **2** this science applied to any other planet or celestial body. **3** the geological features of a district. □□ **geologic** /jéeəlójik/ *adj.* **geological** /jéeəlójik'l/ *adj.* **geologically** /jéeəlójikəli/ *adv.* **geologist** *n.* **geologize** *v.tr.* & *intr.* (also **-ise**). [mod.L *geologia* (as GEO-, -LOGY)]

geomagnetism /jée-ōmágnitiz'm/ *n.* the study of the magnetic properties of the earth. □□ **geomagnetic** /-magnéttik/ *adj.* **geomagnetically** /-magnéttikəli/ *adv.*

geomancy /jée-ōmansi/ *n.* divination from the configuration of a handful of earth or random dots. □□ **geomantic** /-mántik/ *adj.*

geometer /jiómmitər/ *n.* **1** a person skilled in geometry. **2** any moth, esp. of the family Geometridae, having twiglike larvae which move in a looping fashion, seeming to measure the ground. [ME f. LL *geometra* f. L *geometres* f. Gk *geōmetrēs* (as GEO-, *metrēs* measurer)]

geometric /jiəmétrik/ *adj.* (also **geometrical**) **1** of, according to, or like geometry. **2** (of a design, architectural feature, etc.) characterized by or decorated with regular lines and shapes. □ **geometric mean** the central number in a geometric progression, also calculable as the nth root of a product of n numbers (as 9 from 3 and 27). **geometric progression** a progression of numbers with a constant ratio between each number and the one before (as 1, 3, 9, 27, 81). **geometric tracery** tracery with openings of geometric form. □□ **geometrically** *adv.* [F *géometrique* f. L *geometricus* f. Gk *geōmetrikos* (as GEOMETER)]

geometry /jiómmitri/ *n.* **1** the branch of mathematics concerned with the properties and relations of points, lines, surfaces, and solids. **2** the relative arrangement of objects or parts. □□ **geometrician** /jéeəmitrísh'n/ *n.* [ME f. OF *geometrie* f. L *geometria* f. Gk (as GEO-, -METRY)]

geomorphology /jée-ōmorfólləji/ *n.* the study of the physical features of the surface of the earth and their relation to its geological structures. □□ **geomorphological** /-fəlójik'l/ *adj.* **geomorphologist** *n.*

geophagy /jióffəji/ *n.* the practice of eating earth. [GEO- + Gk *phagō* eat]

geophysics /jée-ōfízziks/ *n.* the physics of the earth. □□ **geophysical** *adj.* **geophysicist** /-zisist/ *n.*

geopolitics /jée-ōpóllitiks/ *n.* **1** the politics of a country as determined by its geographical features. **2** the study of this. □□ **geopolitical** /-pəlíttik'l/ *adj.* **geopolitically** /-pəlíttikəli/ *adv.* **geopolitician** /-tísh'n/ *n.*

Geordie /jórdi/ *n. Brit. colloq.* a native of Tyneside. [GEORGE + -IE]

George /jorj/ *n. Brit. sl.* the automatic pilot of an aircraft. [the name *George*]

George Cross /jorj/ *n.* (also **George Medal**) (in the UK) a decoration for bravery awarded esp. to civilians, instituted in 1940 by King George VI.

georgette /jorjét/ *n.* a thin silk or crêpe dress-material. [*Georgette* de la Plante, Fr. dressmaker]

Georgian[1] /jórjən/ *adj.* **1** of or characteristic of the time of Kings George I–IV (1714–1830). **2** of or characteristic of the time of Kings George V and VI (1910–52), esp. of the literature of 1910–20.

Georgian[2] /jórjən/ *adj.* & *n.* ● *adj.* of or relating to Georgia in the Caucasus. ● *n.* **1** a native of Georgia; a person of Georgian descent. **2** the language of Georgia.

Georgian[3] /jórjən/ *adj.* & *n.* ● *adj.* of or relating to Georgia in the US. ● *n.* a native of Georgia.

geosphere /jéeəsfeer/ *n.* **1** the solid surface of the earth. **2** any of the almost spherical concentric regions of the earth and its atmosphere.

geostationary /jée-ōstáyshənəri, -shənri/ *adj. Electronics* (of an artificial satellite of the earth) moving in such an orbit as to remain above the same point on the earth's surface (see also GEOSYNCHRONOUS).

geostrophic /jée-ōstróffik/ *adj. Meteorol.* depending upon the rotation of the earth. [GEO- + Gk *strophē* a turning f. *strephō* to turn]

geosynchronous /jée-ōsíngkrənəss/ *adj.* (of an artificial satellite of the earth) moving in an orbit equal to the earth's period of rotation (see also GEOSTATIONARY).

geothermal /jée-ōthérm'l/ *adj.* relating to, originating from, or produced by the internal heat of the earth.

geotropism /jiótrəpiz'm/ *n.* plant growth in relation to gravity. □ **negative geotropism** the tendency of stems etc. to grow away from the centre of the earth. **positive geotropism** the tendency of roots to grow towards the centre of the earth. □□ **geotropic** /jée-ōtróppik/ *adj.* [GEO- + Gk *tropikos* f. *tropē* a turning f. *trepō* to turn]

Ger. *abbr.* German.

geranium /jəráyniəm/ *n.* **1** any herb or shrub of the genus *Geranium* bearing fruit shaped like the bill of a crane, e.g. cranesbill. **2** (in general use) a cultivated pelargonium. **3** the colour of the scarlet geranium. [L f. Gk *geranion* f. *geranos* crane]

gerbera /jérbərə/ *n.* any composite plant of the genus *Gerbera* of Africa or Asia, esp. the Transvaal daisy. [T. *Gerber*, Ger. naturalist d. 1743]

gerbil /jérbil/ *n.* (also **jerbil**) a mouselike desert rodent of the subfamily Gerbillinae, with long hind legs. [F *gerbille* f. mod.L *gerbillus* dimin. of *gerbo* JERBOA]

gerenuk /jérrənōōk/ *n.* an antelope, *Litocranius walleri*, native to E. Africa, with a very long neck and small head. [Somali]

gerfalcon var. of GYRFALCON.

geri /jérri/ *n. Austral. colloq.* a geriatric person. [abbr.]

geriatric /jérriátrik/ *adj.* & *n.* ● *adj.* **1** of or relating to old people. **2** *colloq.* old, outdated. ● *n.* **1** an old person, esp. one receiving special care. **2** *colloq.* a person or thing considered as relatively old or outdated. [Gk *gēras* old age + *iatros* doctor]

geriatrics /jérriátriks/ *n.pl.* (usu. treated as *sing.*) a branch of medicine or social science dealing with the health and care of old people. □□ **geriatrician** /-riətrísh'n/ *n.*

germ /jerm/ *n.* **1** a micro-organism, esp. one which causes disease. **2 a** a portion of an organism capable of developing into a new one; the rudiment of an animal or plant. **b** an embryo of a seed (*wheat germ*). **3** an original idea etc. from which something may develop; an elementary principle. □ **germ-cell 1** a cell containing half the number of chromosomes of a somatic cell and able to unite with one from the opposite sex to form a new individual; a gamete. **2** any embryonic cell with the potential of developing into a gamete. **germ warfare** the systematic spreading of micro-organisms to cause disease in an enemy population. **in germ** not yet developed. □□ **germy** *adj.* [F *germe* f. L *germen germinis* sprout]
■ **1** micro-organism, microbe, bacterium, virus, *sl.* bug. **3** embryo, seed, source, root, origin, beginning, start, *poet.* fount; principle, base, basis, rudiments.

German /jérmən/ *n.* & *adj.* ● *n.* **1** a native or national of Germany; a person of German descent. **2** the language of Germany, also used in Austria and Switzerland. ● *adj.* of or relating to Germany or its people or language. □ **German measles** a contagious disease, rubella, with symptoms like mild measles. **German shepherd** (or **shepherd dog**) an Alsatian. **German silver** a white alloy of nickel, zinc, and copper. **High German** a literary and cultured form of German. **Low German** German dialects other than High German. [L *Germanus* with ref. to related peoples of Central and N. Europe, a name perh. given by Celts to their neighbours: cf. OIr. *gair* neighbour]

german /jérmən/ *adj.* (placed after *brother*, *sister*, or *cousin*) **1** having both parents the same (*brother german*). **2** having both grandparents the same on one side (*cousin german*). **3** *archaic* germane. [ME f. OF *germain* f. L *germanus* genuine, of the same parents]

germander /jermándər/ *n.* any plant of the genus *Teucrium*. □ **germander speedwell** a creeping plant, *Veronica chamaedrys*, with germander-like leaves and blue flowers. [ME f. med.L *germandra* ult. f. Gk *khamaidrus* f. *khamai* on the ground + *drus* oak]

germane /jermáyn/ *adj.* (usu. foll. by *to*) relevant (to a subject under consideration). □□ **germanely** *adv.* **germaneness** *n.* [var. of GERMAN]
■ see RELEVANT.

Germanic /jermánnik/ *adj.* & *n.* ● *adj.* **1** having German characteristics. **2** *hist.* of the Germans. **3** of the Scandinavians, Anglo-Saxons, or Germans. **4** of the languages or language group called Germanic. ● *n.* **1** the branch of Indo-European languages including English, German, Dutch, and the Scandinavian languages. **2** the (unrecorded) early language from which other Germanic languages developed. □ **East Germanic** an extinct group including Gothic. **North Germanic** the Scandinavian languages. **West Germanic** a group including High and Low German, English, Frisian, and Dutch. [L *Germanicus* (as GERMAN)]

germanic /jermánnik/ *adj. Chem.* of or containing germanium, esp. in its quadrivalent state.

Germanist /jérmənist/ *n.* an expert in or student of the language, literature, and civilization of Germany, or Germanic languages.

germanium /jermáyniəm/ *n. Chem.* a lustrous brittle semi-metallic element occurring naturally in sulphide ores and used in semiconductors. ¶ Symb.: **Ge**. [mod.L f. *Germanus* GERMAN]

Germanize /jérmənīz/ *v.tr.* & *intr.* (also **-ise**) make or become German; adopt or cause to adopt German customs etc. □□ **Germanization** /-záysh'n/ *n.* **Germanizer** *n.*

Germano- /jermánnō/ *comb. form* German; German and.

germanous /jermáynəss/ *adj. Chem.* containing germanium in the bivalent state.

germicide /jérmisīd/ *n.* a substance destroying germs, esp. those causing disease. □□ **germicidal** /-sīd'l/ *adj.*
■ see DISINFECTANT *n.*

germinal /jérmin'l/ *adj.* **1** relating to or of the nature of a germ or germs (see GERM 1). **2** in the earliest stage of development. **3** productive of new ideas. □□ **germinally** *adv.* [L *germen germin-* sprout: see GERM]
■ **2** see PRIMARY *adj.* 2.

germinate /jérminayt/ *v.* **1 a** *intr.* sprout, bud, or put forth shoots. **b** *tr.* cause to sprout or shoot. **2 a** *tr.* cause (ideas etc.) to originate or develop. **b** *intr.* come into existence. □□ **germination** /-náysh'n/ *n.* **germinative** /-nətiv/ *adj.* **germinator** *n.* [L *germinare germinat-* (as GERM)]
■ **1 a** see SPROUT *v.* 2.

germon /jérmən/ *n.* = ALBACORE 1. [F]

gerontology /jérrontólləji/ *n.* the scientific study of old age, the process of ageing, and the special problems of old people. □□ **gerontological** /-təlójik'l/ *adj.* **gerontologist** *n.* [Gk *gerōn -ontos* old man + -LOGY]

-gerous /jərəss/ *comb. form* forming adjectives meaning 'bearing' (*lanigerous*).

gerrymander /jérrimándər/ *v.* & *n.* (also **jerrymander**) ● *v.tr.* **1** manipulate the boundaries of (a constituency etc.) so as to give undue influence to some party or class. **2** manipulate (a situation etc.) to gain advantage. ● *n.* this practice. □□ **gerrymanderer** *n.* [the name of Governor *Gerry* of Massachusetts + (SALA)MANDER, from the shape of a district on a political map drawn when he was in office (1812)]

gerund /jérrənd/ *n. Gram.* a form of a verb functioning as a noun, orig. in Latin ending in *-ndum* (declinable), in English ending in *-ing* and used distinctly as a part of a verb (e.g. *do you mind my asking you?*). [LL *gerundium* f. *gerundum* var. of *gerendum*, the gerund of L *gerere* do]

gerundive /jerúndiv/ *n. Gram.* a form of a Latin verb, ending in *-ndus* (declinable) and functioning as an adjective meaning 'that should or must be done' etc. [LL *gerundivus* (*modus* mood) f. *gerundium*: see GERUND]

gesso /jéssō/ *n.* (*pl.* **-oes**) plaster of Paris or gypsum as used in painting or sculpture. [It. f. L *gypsum*: see GYPSUM]

gestalt /gəstaált/ *n. Psychol.* an organized whole that is perceived as more than the sum of its parts. □ **gestalt psychology** a system maintaining that perceptions, reactions, etc., are gestalts. □□ **gestaltism** *n.* **gestaltist** *n.* [G, = form, shape]

Gestapo /gestaápō/ *n.* **1** the German secret police under Nazi rule. **2** *derog.* an organization compared to this. [G, f. *Geheime Staatspolizei*]

gestate /jestáyt/ *v.tr.* **1** carry (a foetus) in gestation. **2** develop (an idea etc.).

gestation /jestáysh'n/ *n.* **1 a** the process of carrying or being carried in the womb between conception and birth. **b** this period. **2** the private development of a plan, idea, etc. [L *gestatio* f. *gestare* frequent. of *gerere* carry]

gesticulate /jestíkyoolayt/ *v.* **1** *intr.* use gestures instead of or in addition to speech. **2** *tr.* express with gestures. □□ **gesticulation** /-láysh'n/ *n.* **gesticulative** /-lətiv/ *adj.* **gesticulator** *n.* **gesticulatory** /-lətəri/ *adj.* [L *gesticulari* f. *gesticulus* dimin. of *gestus* GESTURE]
■ see SIGNAL[1] *v.* 1, 2a.

gesture /jéss-chər/ *n.* & *v.* ● *n.* **1** a significant movement of a limb or the body. **2** the use of such movements esp. to convey feeling or as a rhetorical device. **3** an action to evoke a response or convey intention, usu. friendly. ● *v.tr.* & *intr.* gesticulate. □□ **gestural** *adj.* **gesturer** *n.* [ME f. med.L *gestura* f. L *gerere gest-* wield]
■ *n.* **1** movement, motion, gesticulation, action, move. **2** gesturing, gesticulation, movement, body language, kinesics; mime. **3** token, signal, indication; gambit, device, *colloq.* ploy, *US colloq.* high sign. ● *v.* gesticulate, motion, signal, sign, indicate, *US colloq.* give (a person) the high sign.

gesundheit /gəzoont-hīt/ *int.* expressing a wish of good health, esp. before drinking or to a person who has sneezed. [G, = health]

get /get/ *v.* & *n.* ● *v.* (**getting**; *past* **got** /got/; *past part.* **got** or *US* (and in *comb.*) **gotten** /gótt'n/) **1** *tr.* come into the possession of; receive or earn (*get a job*; *got £200 a week*; *got* *first prize*). **2** *tr.* **a** fetch, obtain, procure, purchase (*get my book for me; got a new car*). **b** capture, get hold of (a person). **3** *tr.* go to reach or catch (a bus, train, etc.). **4** *tr.* prepare (a meal etc.). **5** *intr.* & *tr.* reach or cause to reach a certain state or condition; become or cause to become (*get rich; get one's feet wet; get to be famous; got them ready; got him into trouble; cannot get the key into the lock*). **6** *tr.* obtain as a result of calculation. **7** *tr.* contract (a disease etc.). **8** *tr.* establish or be in communication with via telephone or radio; receive (a radio signal). **9** *tr.* experience or suffer; have inflicted on one; receive as one's lot or penalty (*got four years in prison*). **10 a** *tr.* succeed in bringing, placing, etc. (*get it round the corner; get it on to the agenda; flattery will get you nowhere*). **b** *intr.* & *tr.* succeed or cause to succeed in coming or going (*will get you there somehow; got absolutely nowhere*). **11** *tr.* (prec. by *have*) **a** possess (*have not got a penny*). **b** (foll. by *to* + infin.) be bound or obliged (*have got to see you*). **12** *tr.* (foll. by *to* + infin.) induce; prevail upon (*got them to help me*). **13** *tr. colloq.* understand (a person or an argument) (*have you got that?; I get your point; do you get me?*). **14** *tr. colloq.* inflict punishment or retribution on, esp. in retaliation (*I'll get you for that*). **15** *tr. colloq.* **a** annoy. **b** move; affect emotionally. **c** attract, obsess. **d** amuse. **16** *tr.* (foll. by *to* + infin.) develop an inclination as specified (*am getting to like it*). **17** *intr.* (foll. by verbal noun) begin (*get going*). **18** *tr.* (esp. in *past* or *perfect*) catch in an argument; corner, puzzle. **19** *tr.* establish (an idea etc.) in one's mind. **20** *intr. sl.* be off; go away. **21** *tr. archaic* beget. **22** *tr. archaic* learn; acquire (knowledge) by study. ● *n.* **1 a** an act of begetting (of animals). **b** an offspring (of animals). **2** *sl.* a fool or idiot. □ **get about** (or **around**) **1** travel extensively or fast; go from place to place. **2** manage to walk, move about, etc. (esp. after illness). **3** (of news) be circulated, esp. orally. **get across 1** manage to communicate (an idea etc.). **2** (of an idea etc.) be communicated successfully. **3** *colloq.* annoy, irritate. **get ahead** be or become successful. **get along** (or **on**) **1** (foll. by *together*, *with*) live harmoniously, accord. **2** be off! nonsense! **3** leave, depart (*I must be getting along*). **get at 1** reach; get hold of. **2** *colloq.* imply (*what are you getting at?*). **3** *colloq.* annoy; try to upset or irritate. **get away 1** escape. **2** leave, esp. on holiday. **3** (as *imper.*) *colloq.* expressing disbelief or scepticism. **4** (foll. by *with*) escape blame or punishment for. **get back at** *colloq.* retaliate against. **get by** *colloq.* **1** just manage, even with difficulty. **2** be acceptable. **get down 1** alight, descend (from a vehicle, ladder, etc.). **2** record in writing. **get a person down** depress or deject him or her. **get down to** begin working on or discussing. **get even** (often foll. by *with*) **1** achieve revenge; act in retaliation. **2** equalize the score. **get his** (or **hers** etc.) *sl.* be killed. **get hold of 1** grasp (physically). **2** grasp (intellectually); understand. **3** make contact with (a person). **4** acquire. **get in 1** enter. **2** be elected. **get into** become interested or involved in. **get it** *sl.* be punished or in trouble. **get it into one's head** (foll. by *that* + clause) firmly believe or maintain; realize. **get off 1** *colloq.* be acquitted; escape with little or no punishment. **2** leave. **3** alight; alight from (a bus etc.). **4** go, or cause to go, to sleep. **5** (foll. by *with, together*) *Brit. colloq.* form an amorous or sexual relationship, esp. abruptly or quickly. **get a person off** *colloq.* cause a person to be acquitted. **get off on** *sl.* be excited or aroused by, enjoy. **get on 1** make progress; manage. **2** enter (a bus etc.). **3** = *get along* 1. **4** *colloq.* become more advanced in time, age, etc. **get on to** *colloq.* **1** make contact with. **2** understand; become aware of. **get out 1** leave or escape. **2** manage to go outdoors. **3** alight from a vehicle. **4** transpire; become known. **5** succeed in uttering, publishing, etc. **6** solve or finish (a puzzle etc.). **7** *Cricket* be dismissed. **get-out** *n.* a means of avoiding something. **get a person out 1** help a person to leave or escape. **2** *Cricket* dismiss (a batsman). **get out of 1** avoid or escape (a duty etc.). **2** abandon (a habit) gradually. **get a thing out of** manage to obtain it from (a person) esp. with difficulty. **get outside** (or **outside of**) *sl.* eat or drink. **get over 1** recover from (an illness, upset, etc.). **2** overcome (a difficulty). **3** manage to communicate (an idea etc.). **get a thing over** (or **over with**) complete (a tedious task) promptly. **get one's own back** *colloq.* have one's revenge. **get-rich-quick** *adj.* designed to make a lot of money fast. **get rid of** see RID. **get round** (*US* **around**) **1** successfully coax or cajole (a person) esp. to secure a favour. **2** evade (a law etc.). **get round to** deal with (a task etc.) in due course. **get somewhere** make progress; be initially successful. **get there** *colloq.* **1** succeed. **2** understand what is meant. **get through 1** pass or assist in passing (an examination, an ordeal, etc.). **2** finish or use up (esp. resources). **3** make contact by telephone. **4** (foll. by *to*) succeed in making (a person) listen or understand. **get a thing through** cause it to overcome obstacles, difficulties, etc. **get to 1** reach. **2** = *get down to*. **get together** gather, assemble. **get-together** *n. colloq.* a social gathering. **get up 1** rise or cause to rise from sitting etc., or from bed after sleeping or an illness. **2** ascend or mount, e.g. on horseback. **3** (of fire, wind, or the sea) begin to be strong or agitated. **4** prepare or organize. **5** enhance or refine one's knowledge of (a subject). **6** work up (a feeling, e.g. anger). **7** produce or stimulate (*get up steam; get up speed*). **8** (often *refl.*) dress or arrange elaborately; make presentable; arrange the appearance of. **9** (foll. by *to*) *colloq.* indulge or be involved in (*always getting up to mischief*). **get-up** *n. colloq.* **1** a style or arrangement of dress etc., esp. an elaborate one. **2** a style of production or finish, esp. of a book. **get-up-and-go** *colloq.* energy, vim, enthusiasm. **get the wind up** see WIND[1]. **get with child** *archaic* make pregnant. **have got it bad** (or **badly**) *sl.* be obsessed or affected emotionally. □□ **gettable** *adj.* [ME f. ON *geta* obtain, beget, guess, corresp. to OE *gietan* (recorded only in compounds), f. Gmc]

■ *v.* **1** obtain, secure, acquire, come by *or* into (the) possession of, pick up, collect, receive, be given, come by; earn, make, take (home), gross, clear, net, pocket, be paid, *colloq.* pull down; accede to, inherit, fall heir to, succeed to. **2 a** obtain, procure; fetch, go and get, go for *or* after, pick up; bring (back), retrieve; buy, purchase, engage; glean, absorb, take in. **b** capture, seize, arrest, take, apprehend, grab, lay *or* get hold of. **3** catch, take, make, come *or* go by, travel *or* journey by. **5** become, fall, turn, grow; put, place, set, fit, manoeuvre, manipulate; manage, arrange, come, succeed; contrive, fix it. **7** catch, contract, have, suffer from, come down with, fall ill *or* sick with, be afflicted with, become infected with, acquire, *Brit.* go down with. **8** reach, get in touch with, communicate with, get on *or* through to, contact; receive, pick up, tune in to *or* on to. **9** receive; suffer, endure, go through. **10 b** transport, carry, bear, bring, move; reach, arrive (at), come, go, travel, journey. **11 a** have, possess, own, be provided with. **b** (*have got to*) have to, be obliged to, be bound to, must, need to. **12** persuade, prevail upon, coax, induce, influence, cajole, wheedle, sway, bring round, cause. **13** understand, appreciate, see, grasp, apprehend, perceive, follow, comprehend, take in, work out, make head or tail of; catch, hear. **14** get even with, revenge oneself on, take vengeance on, pay back, settle *or* even the score with, get back at, get one's own back on. **15 a** get at, irritate, annoy, vex, irk, nettle, pique, provoke, anger, exasperate, bother, perturb, rile, rub up the wrong way, get *or* put a person's back up, *colloq.* get across, get a person's goat, get in a person's hair, *disp.* aggravate, *sl.* bug; see also ANNOY 1. **b** affect, stir, move, touch, have an impact *or* effect on, make an impression on, impress, leave a mark on, get to. **c** see ATTRACT 1, OBSESS. **d** see AMUSE 1. **16** start, begin, come. **17** see BEGIN 2, 4. **18** baffle, confound, puzzle, perplex, bewilder; see also CONFUSE 1a. **20** see RUN *v.* 2. **22** see LEARN 3. ● *n.* **2** see FOOL[1] *n.* 1. □ **get about** (or **around**) **1** be active, go *or* get out; run about *or* around, gad about, move about. **3** spread, become known, leak (out), circulate, be bruited about *or* around, be noised abroad, go about *or* around. **get across 1** get *or* put over, put across, get through, communicate, make clear, impart. **3** see ANNOY 1. **get ahead** succeed, prosper, be *or* become successful, do well, thrive, flourish, make good, (make) progress, go far, go a long way, get on, go *or* come up *or* rise (up) in the world, *colloq.* go places. **get along 1** be friendly *or* compatible, agree, accord, be agreeable *or* congenial, *colloq.* hit it off. **2** see *go on!* (GO[1]), RUBBISH *n.* 3. **3** leave, depart, go *or* move away, get going, get *or* be on one's way, go along, proceed. **get at 1** gain access to, access, reach, get hold of, put *or* lay one's hands on, get to. **2** intend, mean, suggest, hint (at), insinuate, imply, have in mind *or* view. **3** taunt, criticize, find fault with, carp, nag, pick on; see also TEASE *v.* **get away 1** escape, leave, break out *or* away, flee, depart, make good one's escape, elude one's captors, break free, disappear. **2** take a holiday *or* break, take a rest *or* respite. **3** see *go on!* (GO[1]). **get back at** see GET *v.* 14 above. **get by 1** make ends meet, keep the wolf from the door, make do, keep one's head above water; see also MANAGE *v.* 2, 3, 5a. **get down 1** dismount, alight, descend, come *or* go down, climb *or* step down; (*get down from*) get off. **2** write (down), note (down), record, make a note of. **get a person down** (*get down*) depress, bring down, dispirit, sadden, dishearten, discourage, deject. **get down to** concentrate *or* focus on, turn one's attention to, turn to, attend to. **get even 1** (*get even with*) see GET *v.* 14 above. **2** draw level, even up, draw even, equalize. **get hold of 1** see GRASP *v.* 1a. **2** see UNDERSTAND 1, 2. **3** see CONTACT *v.* **4** see ACQUIRE 1. **get in 1** enter, get into *or* on *or* on to, embark, get *or* go aboard; arrive, return, come *or* go in. **get into** be *or* become involved in, take up, pursue, become enthusiastic about, *sl.* get off on. **get it into one's head** see REALIZE 2. **get off 1** be acquitted *or* set free *or* released, escape, get away, *US sl.* walk. **2** leave, depart, go (off), set out *or* off, make a start, head off. **3** alight (from), disembark, dismount, descend (from); climb *or* step down off *or* from, get down from, get out of. **get on 1** manage, cope, shift, survive, make do, *colloq.* get by, make out, *literary* fare; make progress, proceed, advance, come on, move ahead *or* along *or* on. **4** age, get *or* become *or* grow older, advance; get *or* grow *or* become late. **get on to 1** see CONTACT *v.* **2** discover, learn about, become aware of, find out about, understand, *colloq.* twig, cotton on to. **get out 1** leave, depart, go out *or* away, be off, retire; escape, extricate *or* free oneself; be released. **4** see TRANSPIRE 1. **5** publish, put out, bring out; utter. **get out of 1** avoid, evade, sidestep, escape, shirk. **get over 1** recover *or* recuperate from, get better from, convalesce from. **2** overcome, surmount, hurdle, cope with; see also SOLVE. **3** see COMMUNICATE 1a. **get one's own back** see GET *v.* 14 above. **get round 1** cajole, wheedle, persuade, coax, win over. **2** bypass, circumvent, skirt, evade; see also AVOID 2. **get round to** get *or* come to, reach, arrive at (finally), find time for. **get there 1** see SUCCEED 1a. **2** see UNDERSTAND 7. **get somewhere** make progress, do well. **get through 1** succeed in, complete, pass. **2** see *use up* 1. **3** (*get through to*) reach, contact, get, make contact with, get in touch with, get hold of. **4** (*get through to*) make oneself clear to. **get to 1** arrive at, come to, reach; near, approach. **get together** gather, accumulate, collect, assemble, convene, meet, congregate, socialize. **get-together** see PARTY[1] *n.* 1. **get up 1** awaken, awake, wake (up), bestir oneself, rise, get out of bed, come to, *esp. archaic* & *poet.* arise, *colloq.* surface; stand (up); get dressed. **2** mount, climb (up), ascend, scale, go up. **4** create, devise, organize; see also PREPARE 1, ARRANGE 2, 3. **5** brush up (on), study, learn, bring up to date, *US* get up on, *Brit. colloq.* swot up (on), *Brit. sl.* gen up on. **8** dress, clothe, outfit, turn out, deck out, rig out, dress up, fit out *or* up, *archaic* apparel, *formal* attire. **9** (*get up to*) become *or* be involved in, be up to, indulge in, take part in. **get-up** see OUTFIT *n.* 1. **2** format, layout, arrangement, structure, look, style. **get-up-and-go** see ENERGY 1. **get with child** see IMPREGNATE *v.* 3.

get-at-able /getáttəb'l/ *adj. colloq.* accessible.

getaway /géttəway/ *n.* an escape, esp. after committing a crime.

■ flight, retreat; see also ESCAPE *n.* 1.

getter /géttər/ *n.* & *v.* ● *n.* **1** in senses of GET *v.* **2** *Physics* a substance used to remove residual gas from an evacuated vessel. ● *v.tr. Physics* remove (gas) or evacuate (a vessel) with a getter.

geum /jéeəm/ *n.* any rosaceous plant of the genus *Geum* including herb bennet, with rosettes of leaves and yellow, red, or white flowers. [mod.L, var. of L *gaeum*]

GeV *abbr.* gigaelectronvolt (equivalent to 10^9 electronvolts).

gewgaw /gyóogaw/ *n.* a gaudy plaything or ornament; a bauble. [ME: orig. unkn.]

■ bauble, ornament, gimcrack, trifle, bagatelle, kickshaw, trinket, falderal, *bijou*, knick-knack, plaything, toy, novelty; (*gewgaws*) bric-à-brac, frippery.

geyser /gízər, géé-/ *n.* **1** an intermittently gushing hot spring that throws up a tall column of water. **2** /géezər/ *Brit.* an apparatus for heating water rapidly for domestic use. [Icel. *Geysir*, the name of a particular spring in Iceland, rel. to *geysa* to gush]

■ **1** see STREAM *n.* 2.

GG *abbr.* Governor-General.

Ghanaian /gaanáyən/ *adj.* & *n.* ● *adj.* of or relating to Ghana in W. Africa. ● *n.* a native or national of Ghana; a person of Ghanaian descent.

gharial /gáiriəl, gárriəl/ *n.* (also **gavial** /gáyviəl/) a large Indian crocodile, *Gavialis gangeticus*, having a long narrow snout widening at the nostrils. □ **false gharial** a similar crocodile, *Tomistoma schlegelii*, of Indonesia and Malaya. [Hind.]

ghastly /gaástli/ *adj.* & *adv.* ● *adj.* (**ghastlier, ghastliest**) **1** horrible, frightful. **2** *colloq.* objectionable, unpleasant. **3** deathlike, pallid. ● *adv.* in a ghastly or sickly way (*ghastly pale*). □□ **ghastlily** *adv.* **ghastliness** *n.* [ME *gastlich* f. obs. *gast* terrify: *gh* after *ghost*]

■ *adj.* **1** horrible, horrendous, horrid, horrifying, frightful, shocking, appalling, dreadful, terrible, terrifying, grim, grisly, gruesome, loathsome, repulsive, repellent, hideous, ugly, *colloq.* scary. **2** objectionable, unpleasant, *sl.* gross; see also AWFUL 1a, b. **3** pallid, livid, ashen, wan, pale, pasty(-faced), ill, ailing, sick; deathlike, grim, cadaverous, haggard, drawn.

ghat /gaat/ *n.* (also **ghaut**) in India: **1** steps leading down to a river. **2** a landing-place. **3** a defile or mountain pass. [Hindi *ghāṭ*]

Ghazi /gaázi/ *n.* (*pl.* **Ghazis**) a Muslim fighter against non-Muslims. [Arab. *al-ġāzī* part. of *ġazā* raid]

ghee /gee/ *n.* (also **ghi**) Indian clarified butter esp. from the milk of a buffalo or cow. [Hindi *ghī* f. Skr. *ghṛitá-* sprinkled]

gherao /geróẃ/ *n.* (*pl.* **-os**) (in India and Pakistan) coercion of employers, by which their workers prevent them from leaving the premises until certain demands are met. [Hind. *gherna* besiege]

gherkin /gérkin/ *n.* **1** a small variety of cucumber, or a young green cucumber, used for pickling. **2 a** a trailing plant, *Cucumis sativus*, with cucumber-like fruits used for pickling. **b** this fruit. [Du. *gurkkijn* (unrecorded), dimin. of *gurk*, f. Slavonic, ult. f. med. Gk *aggourion*]

ghetto /géttō/ *n.* & *v.* ● *n.* (*pl.* **-os**) **1** a part of a city, esp. a slum area, occupied by a minority group or groups. **2** *hist.* the Jewish quarter in a city. **3** a segregated group or area. ● *v.tr.* (**-oes, -oed**) put or keep (people) in a ghetto. □ **ghetto-blaster** *sl.* a large portable radio, esp. used to play loud pop music. [perh. f. It. *getto* foundry (applied to the site of the first ghetto in Venice in 1516)]

■ *n.* **1** see SLUM *n.* 1.

ghi var. of GHEE.

ghillie var. of GILLIE.

ghost /gōst/ *n.* & *v.* ● *n.* **1** the supposed apparition of a dead person or animal; a disembodied spirit. **2** a shadow or mere semblance (*not a ghost of a chance*). **3** an emaciated or pale person. **4** a secondary or duplicated image produced by defective television reception or by a telescope. **5** *archaic* a spirit or soul. ● *v.* **1** *intr.* (often foll. by *for*) act as ghost-writer. **2** *tr.* act as ghost-writer of (a work). □ **ghost town** a deserted town with few or no remaining inhabitants. **ghost-write** *v.tr.* & *intr.* act as ghost-writer (of). **ghost-writer** a person who writes on behalf of the credited author of a work. □□ **ghostlike** *adj.* [OE *gāst* f. WG: *gh-* occurs first in Caxton, prob. infl. by Flem. *gheest*]

■ *n.* **1** apparition, phantom, spectre, phantasm, spirit, wraith, double-ganger, *doppelgänger*, ghoul, mane, poltergeist, *Ir.* & *Sc.* banshee; *colloq.* spook, *literary* shade. **2** shadow, semblance, suggestion, hint, trace, scintilla, glimmer.

ghosting /gṓsting/ *n.* the appearance of a 'ghost' (see GHOST *n.* 4) or secondary image in a television picture.

ghostly /gṓstli/ *adj.* (**ghostlier**, **ghostliest**) like a ghost; spectral. □□ **ghostliness** *n.* [OE *gāstlic* (as GHOST)]

■ spectral, ghostlike, wraithlike, phantasmal; eerie, unearthly, *colloq.* spooky, creepy.

ghoul /gōōl/ *n.* **1** a person morbidly interested in death etc. **2** an evil spirit or phantom. **3** a spirit in Muslim folklore preying on corpses. □□ **ghoulish** *adj.* **ghoulishly** *adv.* **ghoulishness** *n.* [Arab. *ġūl* protean desert demon]

■ **2** see GHOST *n.* 1. □□ **ghoulish** devilish, demonic, satanic, diabolic(al), fiendish, demoniac(al), Mephistophelian, malign; morbid, macabre, grisly, gruesome, *colloq.* sick.

GHQ *abbr.* General Headquarters.

ghyll *Brit.* var. of GILL³.

GI /jée-í/ *n.* & *adj.* ● *n.* a private soldier in the US Army. ● *adj.* of or for US servicemen. [abbr. of *government* (or *general*) *issue*]

■ *n.* see SOLDIER *n.*

giant /jíənt/ *n.* & *adj.* ● *n.* **1** an imaginary or mythical being of human form but superhuman size. **2** (in Greek mythology) one of such beings who fought against the gods. **3** an abnormally tall or large person, animal, or plant. **4** a person of exceptional ability, integrity, courage, etc. **5** a large star. ● *attrib.adj.* **1** of extraordinary size or force, gigantic; monstrous. **2** *colloq.* extra large (*giant packet*). **3** (of a plant or animal) of a very large kind. □ **giant-killer** a person who defeats a seemingly much more powerful opponent. **giant-killing** defeat of or victory over a seemingly much stronger opponent. □□ **giantism** *n.* **giant-like** *adj.* [ME *geant* (later infl. by L) f. OF, ult. f. L *gigas gigant-* f. Gk]

■ *n.* **1** superhuman, colossus, ogre, Goliath; amazon. **2** Titan. **3** leviathan, behemoth, monster; see also JUMBO *n.* **4** see PRODIGY 1, WONDER *n.* 2. ● *attrib.adj.* **1, 2** see GIGANTIC.

giaour /jówər/ *n.* *derog.* or *literary* a non-Muslim, esp. a Christian (orig. a Turkish name). [Pers. *gaur*, *gōr*]

Gib. /jib/ *n.* *colloq.* Gibraltar. [abbr.]

gib /jib, gib/ *n.* a wood or metal bolt, wedge, or pin for holding a machine part etc. in place. [18th c.: orig. unkn.]

gibber¹ /jíbbər/ *v.* & *n.* ● *v.intr.* speak fast and inarticulately; chatter incoherently. ● *n.* such speech or sound. [imit.]

■ *v.* see PRATTLE *v.* ● *n.* see PRATTLE *n.*

gibber² /gíbbər/ *n.* *Austral.* a boulder or large stone. [Aboriginal]

gibberellin /jíbbərélin/ *n.* one of a group of plant hormones that stimulate the growth of leaves and shoots. [*Gibberella* a genus of fungi, dimin. of genus-name *Gibbera* f. L *gibber* hump]

gibberish /jíbbərish/ *n.* unintelligible or meaningless speech; nonsense. [perh. f. GIBBER¹ (but attested earlier) + -ISH¹ as used in *Spanish*, *Swedish*, etc.]

■ gibber, gabble, jabber, blather, babble, jabberwocky, mumbo-jumbo; drivel, nonsense, rubbish, twaddle, balderdash, garbage, jargon, *colloq.* gobbledegook, tripe, piffle, *sl.* poppycock, bunk, *Brit. sl.* codswallop, bull; see also NONSENSE.

gibbet /jíbbit/ *n.* & *v.* ● *n.* *hist.* **1 a** a gallows. **b** an upright post with an arm on which the bodies of executed criminals were hung up. **2** (prec. by *the*) death by hanging. ● *v.tr.* (**gibbeted**, **gibbeting**) **1** put to death by hanging. **2 a** expose on a gibbet. **b** hang up as on a gibbet. **3** hold up to contempt. [ME f. OF *gibet* gallows dimin. of *gibe* club, prob. f. Gmc]

■ *v.* **1** see HANG *v.* 7a.

gibbon /gíbb'n/ *n.* any small ape of the genus *Hylobates*, native to SE Asia, having a slender body and long arms. [F f. a native name]

gibbous /gíbbəss/ *adj.* **1** convex or protuberant. **2** (of a moon or planet) having the bright part greater than a semicircle and less than a circle. **3** humped or humpbacked. □□ **gibbosity** /-bóssiti/ *n.* **gibbously** *adv.* **gibbousness** *n.* [ME f. LL *gibbosus* f. *gibbus* hump]

gibe /jīb/ *v.* & *n.* (also **jibe**) ● *v.intr.* (often foll. by *at*) jeer, mock. ● *n.* an instance of gibing; a taunt. □□ **giber** *n.* [perh. f. OF *giber* handle roughly]

■ *v.* jeer, scoff, mock, sneer, make fun, poke fun, chaff; (*gibe at*) gird at, deride, tease, ridicule, twit, taunt, rag, heckle, *colloq.* rib, *US sl.* razz. ● *n.* jeer, taunt, sneer, cutting remark, scoff, *colloq.* dig, crack, wisecrack; (*gibes*) mockery, raillery, derision, chaff, ridicule.

giblets /jíblits/ *n.pl.* the liver, gizzard, neck, etc., of a bird, usu. removed and kept separate when the bird is prepared for cooking. [OF *gibelet* game stew, perh. f. *gibier* game]

giddy /gíddi/ *adj.* & *v.* ● *adj.* (**giddier**, **giddiest**) **1** having a sensation of whirling and a tendency to fall, stagger, or spin round. **2 a** overexcited as a result of success, pleasurable emotion, etc.; mentally intoxicated. **b** excitable, frivolous. **3** tending to make one giddy. ● *v.tr.* & *intr.* (**-ies**, **-ied**) make or become giddy. □□ **giddily** *adv.* **giddiness** *n.* [OE *gidig* insane, lit. 'possessed by a god']

■ *adj.* **1** dizzy, reeling, light-headed, vertiginous, unsteady, *colloq.* woozy. **2 a** see OVERWROUGHT 1. **b** excitable, volatile, impulsive, capricious, whimsical, fickle, flighty, erratic; silly, frivolous, scatterbrained, irresponsible, reckless.

gie /gee/ *v.tr.* & *intr.* *Sc.* = GIVE.

gift /gift/ *n.* & *v.* ● *n.* **1** a thing given; a present. **2** a natural ability or talent. **3** the power to give (*in his gift*). **4** the act or an instance of giving. **5** *colloq.* an easy task. ● *v.tr.* **1** endow with gifts. **2 a** (foll. by *with*) give to as a gift. **b** bestow as a gift. □ **gift of tongues** see TONGUE. **gift token** (or **voucher**) a voucher used as a gift and exchangeable for goods. **gift-wrap** (**-wrapped**, **-wrapping**) wrap attractively as a gift. **look a gift-horse in the mouth** (usu. *neg.*) find fault with what has been given. [ME f. ON *gipt* f. Gmc, rel. to GIVE]

■ *n.* **1** present, donation, benefaction, offering; premium, bonus, hand-out, tip, gratuity, *pourboire*; (*gifts*) largesse, bounty, charity, *hist.* alms. **2** talent, ability, aptitude, facility, capability, capacity, flair, knack, forte, strength, bent; (*gifts*) powers. **4** see PRESENTATION 1. **5** see BREEZE¹ *n.* 5.

gifted /gíftid/ *adj.* exceptionally talented or intelligent. □□ **giftedly** *adv.* **giftedness** *n.*

■ talented, intelligent, capable, able, skilled, skilful; outstanding, excellent, superb, brilliant, expert, master, masterful, virtuoso, first-class, first-rate, top-flight, *colloq.* top-notch, crack, *sl.* ace, *US sl.* crackerjack.

gig¹ /gig/ *n.* **1** a light two-wheeled one-horse carriage. **2** a light ship's boat for rowing or sailing. **3** a rowing-boat esp. for racing. [ME in var. senses: prob. imit.]

■ **2** see TENDER³.

gig² /gig/ *n.* & *v.* *colloq.* ● *n.* an engagement of an entertainer, esp. of musicians to play jazz or dance music, usu. for a single appearance. ● *v.intr.* (**gigged**, **gigging**) perform a gig. [20th c.: orig. unkn.]

■ *n.* see PERFORMANCE 2.

gig³ /gig/ *n.* a kind of fishing-spear. [short for *fizgig*, *fishgig*: cf. Sp. *fisga* harpoon]

■ see LANCE *n.*

giga- /gígə, gíggə/ *comb. form* denoting a factor of 10^9. [Gk *gigas* giant]

gigametre /gíggəmeetər/ *n.* a metric unit equal to 10^9 metres.

gigantic /jīgántik/ *adj.* **1** very large; enormous. **2** like or suited to a giant. □□ **gigantesque** /-tésk/ *adj.* **gigantically** *adv.* [L *gigas gigantis* GIANT]
■ **1** huge, enormous, massive, immense, towering, vast, giant, colossal, mammoth, titanic, gargantuan, elephantine, *colloq.* jumbo, thumping, thundering, *sl.* walloping, whopping, humongous, *Brit. sl.* ginormous.

gigantism /jīgəntiz'm/ *n.* abnormal largeness, esp. *Med.* excessive growth due to hormonal imbalance, or to polyploidy in plants.

giggle /gígg'l/ *v.* & *n.* ● *v.intr.* laugh in half-suppressed spasms, esp. in an affected or silly manner. ● *n.* **1** such a laugh. **2** *colloq.* an amusing person or thing; a joke. □□ **giggler** *n.* **giggly** *adj.* (**gigglier, giggliest**). **giggliness** *n.* [imit.: cf. Du. *gichelen*, G *gickeln*]
■ *v.* laugh, chuckle, titter, cackle, snicker, snigger, *colloq.* chortle. ● *n.* **1** laugh, chuckle, chortle, titter, snicker, snigger, cackle, *colloq.* chortle. **2** joke, prank, frolic, *colloq.* hoot, card, gag, laugh, lark, riot, *sl.* gas, yell.

gigolo /zhíggəlō, jíg-/ *n.* (*pl.* **-os**) **1** a young man paid by an older woman to be her escort or lover. **2** a professional male dancing-partner or escort. [F, formed as masc. of *gigole* dance-hall woman]
■ **1** see PARAMOUR.

gigot /jíggət, zhéegō/ *n.* a leg of mutton or lamb. □ **gigot sleeve** a leg-of-mutton sleeve. [F, dimin. of dial. *gigue* leg]

gigue /zheeg/ *n.* **1** = JIG 1. **2** *Mus.* a lively dance usu. in a dotted rhythm with two sections each repeated. [F: see JIG[1]]

gild[1] /gild/ *v.tr.* (*past part.* **gilded** or as adj. in sense 1 **gilt**) **1** cover thinly with gold. **2** tinge with a golden colour or light. **3** give a specious or false brilliance to. □ **gilded cage** luxurious but restrictive surroundings. **gilded youth** young people of wealth, fashion, and flair. **gild the lily** try to improve what is already beautiful or excellent. □□ **gilder** *n.* [OE *gyldan* f. Gmc]
■ **1** see EMBELLISH 1.

gild[2] var. of GUILD.

gilding /gilding/ *n.* **1** the act or art of applying gilt. **2** material used in applying gilt.
■ **1** see *embellishment* (EMBELLISH).

gilet /jiláy/ *n.* a light often padded waistcoat, usu. worn for warmth by women. [F, = waistcoat]

gilgai /gílgī/ *n. Austral.* a saucer-like natural reservoir for rainwater. [Aboriginal]

gill[1] /gil/ *n.* & *v.* ● *n.* (usu. in *pl.*) **1** the respiratory organ in fishes and other aquatic animals. **2** the vertical radial plates on the underside of mushrooms and other fungi. **3** the flesh below a person's jaws and ears (*green about the gills*). **4** the wattles or dewlap of fowls. ● *v.tr.* **1** gut (a fish). **2** cut off the gills of (a mushroom). **3** catch in a gill-net. □ **gill-cover** a bony case protecting a fish's gills; an operculum. **gill-net** a net for entangling fishes by the gills. □□ **gilled** *adj.* (also in *comb.*). [ME f. ON *gil* (unrecorded) f. Gmc]

gill[2] /jil/ *n.* **1** a unit of liquid measure, equal to a quarter of a pint. **2** *Brit. dial.* half a pint. [ME f. OF *gille*, med.L *gillo* f. LL *gello, gillo* water-pot]

gill[3] /gil/ *n.* (also **ghyll**) *Brit.* **1** a deep usu. wooded ravine. **2** a narrow mountain torrent. [ME f. ON *gil* glen]

gill[4] /jil/ *n.* (also **Gill, jill, Jill**) **1** *derog.* a young woman. **2** *colloq.* or *dial.* a female ferret. [ME, abbr. of *Gillian* f. OF *Juliane* f. L *Juliana* (*Julius*)]

gillie /gílli/ *n.* (also **ghillie**) *Sc.* **1** a man or boy attending a person hunting or fishing. **2** *hist.* a Highland chief's attendant. [Gael. *gille* lad, servant]

gillion /jílliən/ *n.* **1** a thousand million. **2** a large number. ¶ Mainly used to avoid the ambiguity of *billion*. [GIGA- + MILLION]

gillyflower /jílliflowr/ *n.* **1** (in full **clove gillyflower**) a clove-scented pink (see CLOVE[1] 2). **2** any of various similarly scented flowers such as the wallflower or white stock. [ME *gilofre, gerofle* f. OF *gilofre, girofle*, f. med.L f. Gk *karuophullon* clove-tree f. *karuon* nut + *phullon* leaf, assim. to FLOWER]

gilt[1] /gilt/ *adj.* & *n.* ● *adj.* **1** covered thinly with gold. **2** gold-coloured. ● *n.* **1** gold or a goldlike substance applied in a thin layer to a surface. **2** (often in *pl.*) a gilt-edged security. □ **gilt-edged 1** (of securities, stocks, etc.) having a high degree of reliability as an investment. **2** having a gilded edge. [past part. of GILD[1]]
■ *adj.* see GOLDEN 1a.

gilt[2] /gilt/ *n.* a young unbred sow. [ME f. ON *gyltr*]

gimbals /jímb'lz/ *n.pl.* a contrivance, usu. of rings and pivots, for keeping instruments such as a compass and chronometer horizontal at sea, in the air, etc. [var. of earlier *gimmal* f. OF *gemel* double finger-ring f. L *gemellus* dimin. of *geminus* twin]

gimcrack /jímkrak/ *adj.* & *n.* ● *adj.* showy but flimsy and worthless. ● *n.* a cheap showy ornament; a knick-knack. □□ **gimcrackery** *n.* **gimcracky** *adj.* [ME *gibecrake* a kind of ornament, of unkn. orig.]
■ *adj.* see INFERIOR *adj.* 2. ● *n.* see GEWGAW.

gimlet /gímlit/ *n.* **1** a small tool with a screw-tip for boring holes. **2** a cocktail usu. of gin and lime-juice. □ **gimlet eye** an eye with a piercing glance. [ME f. OF *guimbelet*, dimin. of *guimble*]

gimmick /gímmik/ *n. colloq.* a trick or device, esp. to attract attention, publicity, or trade. □□ **gimmickry** *n.* **gimmicky** *adj.* [20th-c. US: orig. unkn.]
■ trick, stratagem, ruse, wile, dodge; device, contrivance, gadget, *colloq.* ploy, *derog.* or *joc.* contraption, *sl.* gismo; see also GADGET, TRICK *n.* 1.

gimp[1] /gimp/ *n.* (also **guimp, gymp**) **1** a twist of silk etc. with cord or wire running through it, used esp. as trimming. **2** fishing-line of silk etc. bound with wire. **3** a coarser thread outlining the design of lace. [Du.: orig. unkn.]

gimp[2] /gimp/ *n. sl.* a lame person or leg.

gin[1] /jin/ *n.* an alcoholic spirit distilled from grain or malt and flavoured with juniper berries. □ **gin rummy** a form of the card-game rummy. [abbr. of GENEVA]

gin[2] /jin/ *n.* & *v.* ● *n.* **1** a snare or trap. **2** a machine for separating cotton from its seeds. **3** a kind of crane and windlass. ● *v.tr.* (**ginned, ginning**) **1** treat (cotton) in a gin. **2** trap. □□ **ginner** *n.* [ME f. OF *engin* ENGINE]
■ *n.* **1** see TRAP[1] *n.* 1.

gin[3] /jin/ *n. Austral.* an Aboriginal woman. [Aboriginal]

ging / ging/ *n. Austral. colloq.* a catapult. [20th c.: orig. uncert.]

ginger /jínjər/ *n., adj.,* & *v.* ● *n.* **1 a** a hot spicy root usu. powdered for use in cooking, or preserved in syrup, or candied. **b** the plant, *Zingiber officinale*, of SE Asia, having this root. **2** a light reddish-yellow colour. **3** spirit, mettle. **4** stimulation. ● *adj.* of a ginger colour. ● *v.tr.* **1** flavour with ginger. **2** (foll. by *up*) rouse or enliven. **3** *Austral. colloq.* steal from (a person). □ **black ginger** unscraped ginger. **ginger ale** an effervescent non-alcoholic clear drink flavoured with ginger extract. **ginger beer** an effervescent mildly alcoholic cloudy drink, made by fermenting a mixture of ginger and syrup. **ginger group** *Brit.* a group within a party or movement that presses for stronger or more radical policy or action. **ginger-nut** a ginger-flavoured biscuit. **ginger-pop** *colloq.* = *ginger ale*. **ginger-snap** a thin brittle biscuit flavoured with ginger. **ginger wine** a drink of fermented sugar, water, and bruised ginger. □□ **gingery** *adj.* [ME f. OE *gingiber* & OF *gingi(m)bre*, both f. med.L *gingiber* ult. f. Skr. *śṛṅgaveram* f. *śṛṅgam* horn + *-vera* body, with ref. to the antler-shape of the root]

gingerbread /jínjərbred/ *n.* **1** a cake made with treacle or syrup and flavoured with ginger. **2** (often *attrib.*) a gaudy or tawdry decoration or ornament.
■ **2** see ORNAMENT *n.* 1, 2.

gingerly /jínjərli/ *adv.* & *adj.* ● *adv.* in a careful or cautious manner. ● *adj.* showing great care or caution. □□

gingerliness *n.* [perh. f. OF *gensor* delicate, compar. of *gent* graceful f. L *genitus* (well-)born]
■ *adv.* cautiously, carefully, charily, tentatively, warily, circumspectly, guardedly, timidly, timorously, watchfully; delicately, daintily. ● *adj.* careful, cautious, wary, chary, tentative, circumspect, guarded, watchful, timid; fastidious, delicate, dainty.

gingham /gingəm/ *n.* a plain-woven cotton cloth esp. striped or checked. [Du. *gingang* f. Malay *ginggang* (orig. adj. = striped)]

gingili /jinjili/ *n.* **1** sesame. **2** sesame oil. [Hindi *jinjalī* f. Arab. *juljulān*]

gingiva /jinjivə/ *n.* (*pl.* **gingivae** /-vee/) the gum. □□ **gingival** /-jīv'l/ *adj.* [L]

gingivitis /jinjivītiss/ *n.* inflammation of the gums.

gingko var. of GINKGO.

ginglymus /jingglimәss/ *n.* (*pl.* **ginglymi** /-mī/) *Anat.* a hingelike joint in the body with motion in one plane only, e.g. the elbow or knee. [mod.L f. Gk *gigglumos* hinge]

gink[1] /gingk/ *n. sl.* often *derog.* a fellow; a man. [20th-c. US: orig. unkn.]

gink[2] / gingk/ *n. Austral.* a scrutinising look. [prob. alt. of GEEK]
■ see LOOK *n.* 1.

ginkgo /gingkgō/ *n.* (also **gingko** /gingkō/) (*pl.* **-os** or **-oes**) an orig. Chinese and Japanese tree, *Ginkgo biloba*, with fan-shaped leaves and yellow flowers. Also called *maidenhair tree*. [Jap. *ginkyo* f. Chin. *yinxing* silver apricot]

ginormous /jīnórmәss/ *adj. Brit. sl.* very large; enormous. [GIANT + ENORMOUS]

ginseng /jinseng/ *n.* **1** any of several medicinal plants of the genus *Panax*, found in E. Asia and N. America. **2** the root of this. [Chin. *renshen* perh. = man-image, with allusion to its forked root]

gippy tummy /jippi/ *n.* (also **gyppy tummy**) *colloq.* diarrhoea affecting visitors to hot countries. [abbr. of EGYPTIAN]

gipsy var. of GYPSY.

giraffe /jiraáf, -ráf/ *n.* (*pl.* same or **giraffes**) a ruminant mammal, *Giraffa camelopardalis* of Africa, the tallest living animal, with a long neck and forelegs and a skin of dark patches separated by lighter lines. [F *girafe*, It. *giraffa*, ult. f. Arab. *zarāfa*]

girandole /jirrəndōl/ *n.* **1** a revolving cluster of fireworks. **2** a branched candle-bracket or candlestick. **3** an earring or pendant with a large central stone surrounded by small ones. [F f. It. *girandola* f. *girare* GYRATE]

girasol /jirrəsol/ *n.* (also **girasole** /-sōl/) a kind of opal reflecting a reddish glow; a fire-opal. [orig. = sunflower, f. F *girasol* or It. *girasole* f. *girare* (as GIRANDOLE) + *sole* sun]

gird[1] /gurd/ *v.tr.* (*past* and *past part.* **girded** or **girt**) *literary* **1** encircle, attach, or secure with a belt or band. **2** secure (clothes) on the body with a girdle or belt. **3** enclose or encircle. **4 a** (foll. by *with*) equip with a sword in a belt. **b** fasten (a sword) with a belt. **5** (foll. by *round*) place (cord etc.) round. □ **gird** (or **gird up**) **one's loins** prepare for action. [OE *gyrdan* f. Gmc (as GIRTH)]
■ **1** see BAND[1] *v.* 1. **3** see ENCIRCLE 1.

gird[2] /gurd/ *v.* & *n.* ● *v.intr.* (foll. by *at*) jeer or gibe. ● *n.* a gibe or taunt. [ME, = strike etc.: orig. unkn.]

girder /gúrdər/ *n.* a large iron or steel beam or compound structure for bearing loads, esp. in bridge-building. [GIRD[1] + -ER[1]]
■ see BEAM *n.* 1.

girdle[1] /gúrd'l/ *n.* & *v.* ● *n.* **1** a belt or cord worn round the waist. **2** a woman's corset extending from waist to thigh. **3** a thing that surrounds like a girdle. **4** the bony support for a limb (*pelvic girdle*). **5** the part of a cut gem dividing the crown from the base and embraced by the setting. **6** a ring round a tree made by the removal of bark. ● *v.tr.* **1** surround with a girdle. **2** remove a ring of bark from (a tree), esp. to make it more fruitful. [OE *gyrdel*: see GIRD[1]]
■ *n.* **1** see BELT *n.* 1.

girdle[2] /gúrd'l/ *n. Sc.* & *N.Engl.* a circular iron plate placed over a fire or otherwise heated for baking, toasting, etc. [var. of GRIDDLE]

girl /gurl/ *n.* **1** a female child or youth. **2** *colloq.* a young (esp. unmarried) woman. **3** *colloq.* a girlfriend or sweetheart. **4** a female servant. □ **girl Friday** see FRIDAY. □□ **girlhood** *n.* [ME *gurle*, *girle*, *gerle*, perh. rel. to LG *gör* child]
■ **1** female child, young lady, miss, mademoiselle, *Ir.* colleen, *esp. Sc.* & *N.Engl. or poet.* lass, *archaic or poet.* maid, maiden, *colloq.* lassie, *sl.* gal. **2** young woman, Fräulein, *archaic* demoiselle, *archaic or literary* damsel, *colloq.* filly, popsy, *joc.* wench, *sl.* chick, *Austral.* & *NZ sl.* sheila, *Brit. sl.* bird, *US sl.* frail, dame, broad. **3** girlfriend, sweetheart, lover, inamorata, *colloq.* popsy, *sl.* moll, squeeze; betrothed, fiancée.

girlfriend /gúrlfrend/ *n.* **1** a regular female companion or lover. **2** a female friend.
■ **1** see WOMAN 3.

girlie /gúrli/ *adj. colloq.* (of a magazine etc.) depicting nude or partially nude young women in erotic poses.

girlish /gúrlish/ *adj.* of or like a girl. □□ **girlishly** *adv.* **girlishness** *n.*
■ see YOUNG *adj.* 3.

giro /jīrō/ *n.* & *v.* ● *n.* (*pl.* **-os**) **1** a system of credit transfer between banks, post offices, etc. **2** a cheque or payment by giro. ● *v.tr.* (**-oes, -oed**) pay by giro. [G f. It., = circulation (of money)]

girt[1] *past part.* of GIRD[1].

girt[2] var. of GIRTH.

girth /gurth/ *n.* & *v.* (also **girt** /gurt/) ● *n.* **1** the distance around a thing. **2** a band round the body of a horse to secure the saddle etc. ● *v.* **1** *tr.* **a** secure (a saddle etc.) with a girth. **b** put a girth on (a horse). **2** *tr.* surround, encircle. **3** *intr.* measure (an amount) in girth. [ME f. ON *gjörth*, Goth. *gairda* f. Gmc]
■ *n.* **1** circumference, ambit, periphery, circuit. **2** belt, girdle, *esp. US* cinch, *archaic* zone, *literary* cincture.
● *v.* **2** surround, encompass, encircle, enclose, envelop.

gismo /gizmō/ *n.* (also **gizmo**) (*pl.* **-os**) *sl.* a gadget. [20th c.: orig. unkn.]
■ see GADGET.

gist /jist/ *n.* **1** the substance or essence of a matter. **2** *Law* the real ground of an action etc. [OF, 3rd sing. pres. of *gesir* lie f. L *jacēre*]
■ **1** substance, essence, pith, meat, marrow, core, heart, point, nub; significance, import, (main *or* basic) idea, meaning; direction, drift.

git /git/ *n. Brit. sl.* a silly or contemptible person. [var. of GET *n.*]
■ see FOOL[1] *n.* 1.

gîte /zheet/ *n.* a furnished holiday house in France, usu. small and in a rural district. [orig. = lodging: F f. OF *giste*, rel. to *gésir* lie]

gittern /gittərn/ *n.* a medieval stringed instrument, a forerunner of the guitar. [ME f. OF *guiterne*: cf. CITTERN, GUITAR]

give /giv/ *v.* & *n.* ● *v.* (*past* **gave** /gayv/; *past part.* **given** /givv'n/) **1** *tr.* (also *absol.*; often foll. by *to*) transfer the possession of freely; hand over as a present (*gave them her old curtains*; *gives to cancer research*). **2** *tr.* **a** transfer the ownership of with or without actual delivery; bequeath (*gave him £200 in her will*). **b** transfer, esp. temporarily or for safe keeping; hand over; provide with (*gave him the dog to hold*; *gave them a drink*). **c** administer (medicine). **d** deliver (a message) (*give her my best wishes*). **3** *tr.* (usu. foll. by *for*) **a** pay (*gave him £30 for the bicycle*). **b** sell (*gave him the bicycle for £30*) **4** *tr.* **a** confer; grant (a benefit, an honour, etc.). **b** accord; bestow (one's affections, confidence, etc.). **c** award; administer (one's approval, blame, etc.); tell, offer (esp. something unpleasant) (*gave him a talking-to*; *gave him my blessing*; *gave him the sack*). **d** pledge, assign as a guarantee (*gave his word*). **5** *tr.* **a** effect or perform (an action etc.) (*gave him a kiss; gave a jump*). **b** utter (*gave a shriek*). **6** *tr.* allot; assign; grant (*was given the contract*). **7** *tr.* (in *passive*; foll. by *to*) be inclined to or fond of (*is given to speculation*). **8** *tr.* yield as a product or result (*the lamp gives a bad light; the field gives fodder for twenty cows*). **9** *intr.* **a** yield to pressure; become relaxed; lose firmness (*this elastic doesn't give properly*). **b** collapse (*the roof gave under the pressure*). **10** *intr.* (usu. foll. by *of*) grant; bestow (*gave freely of his time*). **11** *tr.* **a** commit, consign, or entrust (*gave him into custody; give her into your care*). **b** sanction the marriage of (a daughter etc.). **12** *tr.* devote; dedicate (*gave his life to table tennis; shall give it my attention*). **13** *tr.* (usu. *absol.*) *colloq.* tell what one knows (*What happened? Come on, give!*). **14** *tr.* present; offer; show; hold out (*gives no sign of life; gave her his arm; give him your ear*). **15** *tr. Theatr.* read, recite, perform, act, etc. (*gave them Hamlet's soliloquy*). **16** *tr.* impart; be a source of (*gave him my sore throat; gave its name to the battle; gave them to understand; gives him a right to complain*). **17** *tr.* allow (esp. a fixed amount of time) (*can give you five minutes*). **18** *tr.* (usu. foll. by *for*) value (something) (*gives nothing for their opinions*). **19** *tr.* concede; yield (*I give you the victory*). **20** *tr.* deliver (a judgement etc.) authoritatively (*gave his verdict*). **21** *tr. Cricket* (of an umpire) declare (a batsman) out or not out. **22** *tr.* toast (a person, cause, etc.) (*I give you our President*). **23** *tr.* provide (a party, meal, etc.) as host (*gave a banquet*). ● *n.* **1** capacity to yield or bend under pressure; elasticity (*there is no give in a stone floor*). **2** ability to adapt or comply (*no give in his attitudes*). □ **give and take** *v.tr.* exchange (words, blows, or concessions). ● *n.* an exchange of words etc.; a compromise. **give as good as one gets** retort adequately in words or blows. **give away 1** transfer as a gift. **2** hand over (a bride) ceremonially to a bridegroom. **3** betray or expose to ridicule or detection. **4** *Austral.* abandon, desist from, give up, lose faith or interest in. **give-away** *n. colloq.* **1** an inadvertent betrayal or revelation. **2** an act of giving away. **3** a free gift; a low price. **give back** return (something) to its previous owner or in exchange. **give a person the best** see BEST. **give birth (to)** see BIRTH. **give chase** pursue a person, animal, etc.; hunt. **give down** (often *absol.*) (of a cow) let (milk) flow. **give forth** emit; publish; report. **give the game** (or **show**) **away** reveal a secret or intention. **give a hand** see HAND. **give a person** (or **the devil**) **his or her due** acknowledge, esp. grudgingly, a person's rights, abilities, etc. **give in 1** cease fighting or arguing; yield. **2** hand in (a document etc.) to an official etc. **give in marriage** sanction the marriage of (one's daughter etc.). **give it to a person** *colloq.* scold or punish. **give me** I prefer or admire (*give me the Greek islands*). **give off** emit (vapour etc.). **give oneself** (of a woman) yield sexually. **give oneself airs** act pretentiously or snobbishly. **give oneself up to 1** abandon oneself to an emotion, esp. despair. **2** addict oneself to. **give on to** (or **into**) (of a window, corridor, etc.) overlook or lead into. **give or take** *colloq.* add or subtract (a specified amount or number) in estimating. **give out 1** announce; emit; distribute. **2** cease or break down from exhaustion etc. **3** run short. **give over 1** *colloq.* cease from doing; abandon (a habit etc.); desist (*give over sniffing*). **2** hand over. **3** devote. **give rise to** cause, induce, suggest. **give tongue 1** speak one's thoughts. **2** (of hounds) bark, esp. on finding a scent. **give a person to understand** inform authoritatively. **give up 1** resign; surrender. **2** part with. **3** deliver (a wanted person etc.). **4** pronounce incurable or insoluble; renounce hope of. **5** renounce or cease (an activity). **give up the ghost** *archaic* or *colloq.* die. **give way** see WAY. **give a person what for** *colloq.* punish or scold severely. **give one's word** (or **word of honour**) promise solemnly. **not give a damn** (or **monkey's** or **toss** etc.) *colloq.* not care at all. **what gives?** *colloq.* what is the news?; what's happening? **would give the world** (or **one's ears, eyes,** etc.) **for** covet or wish for desperately. □□ **giveable** *adj.* **giver** *n.* [OE *g(i)efan* f. Gmc]

■ *v.* **1, 2a** provide, supply, present, offer, furnish; hand over, make over, contribute, grant, donate; see also BEQUEATH. **2 b** supply with, furnish with, provide with; transfer, hand over. **2 d** deliver, impart, pass on, transmit, send, convey, communicate, express. **3 b** sell, exchange, trade, barter, swap. **4** confer, grant, accord, bestow, pledge, award, offer. **5 b** utter, emit, give out. **6** see ASSIGN *v.* 1a. **7** (*be given*) be inclined, be prone, be liable. **8** yield, produce, make, furnish, provide. **9 b** give way, fail, collapse, buckle, break down, fall *or* come apart. **12** devote, dedicate; sacrifice, yield (up), surrender, give up, consign. **14** see SHOW *v.* 3. **15** present, offer, put on; recite, read, sing, act, perform. **16** cause, lead, induce, prompt, move, dispose; allow, provide with, furnish with, let have; impart, lend. **17** see ALLOW 2. **19** relinquish, concede, surrender, allow, cede, yield. ● *n.* **1** elasticity, flexibility, stretch, slack, play, leeway. **2** see *flexibility* (FLEXIBLE). □ **give and take** (*n.*) interaction, reciprocity, cooperation, teamwork, fair exchange; compromise. **give away 3** betray, inform on, *colloq.* blow the whistle on, *sl.* rat on, *US sl.* fink on; reveal, let out, divulge, disclose, expose, uncover, leak, let slip; (*give it away*) let the cat out of the bag, give the game *or* show away. **4** see ABANDON *v.* 1. **give-away 3** see BARGAIN *n.* 2. **give forth** see EMIT 1. **give in 1** yield, submit, give ground, back off *or* down; give up, capitulate, surrender, admit defeat. **give it to a person** see SCOLD *v.* 1. **give off** give out, emit, exude, discharge, send *or* throw out, release; exhale. **give out 1** publish, announce, make public, make known, broadcast; impart, issue, reveal; disseminate, spread; distribute, dispense, hand out, dole (out), deal (out), pass around, allot, apportion, allocate, assign, *literary* mete out, *sl.* dish out; emit. **2** become exhausted, fail, collapse, break down, cease; see also FLAG[1] *v.* 1a. **3** become depleted, run short; see also *run out* 1. **give over 1** see STOP *v.* 1c. **2** hand over, surrender, relinquish, pass over, give up. **give rise to** start, engender, generate, begin, produce, bring out, bring about, bring into being, *formal* commence; see also CAUSE *v.* 1. **give up 1** resign, surrender, capitulate, yield, cede, concede, give in, admit defeat, throw in the towel. **5** abandon, stop, cease, quit, leave off, *Austral.* give away, *literary* desist (from); forgo, forsake, renounce, abstain from, *colloq.* swear off, chuck (in). **give up the ghost** see DIE[1]. **give a person what for** see SCOLD *v.* 1. **give one's word** (or **word of honour**) see PROMISE *v.* 1. **not give a damn** (or **monkey's** or **toss**) not care *or* mind at all, *sl.* not give *or* care a hoot.

given /gívv'n/ *adj.* & *n.* ● *adj.* **1** as previously stated or assumed; granted; specified (*given that he is a liar, we cannot trust him; a given number of people*). **2** *Law* (of a document) signed and dated (*given this day the 30th June*). ● *n.* a known fact or situation. □ **given name** *US* a name given at, or as if at, baptism; a Christian name. [past part. of GIVE]

■ *adj.* **1** assumed, understood, acknowledged, allowed, granted; stated, delineated, specified, set, confirmed, accepted, agreed; (pre)arranged, preordained, foreordained. ● *n.* assumption, *donnée*; fact, certainty, reality, actuality, certainty.

gizmo var. of GISMO.

gizzard /gízzərd/ *n.* **1** the second part of a bird's stomach, for grinding food usu. with grit. **2** a muscular stomach of some fish, insects, molluscs, and other invertebrates. □ **stick in one's gizzard** *colloq.* be distasteful. [ME *giser* f. OF *giser, gesier* etc., ult. f. L *gigeria* cooked entrails of fowl]

glabella /gləbéllə/ *n.* (*pl.* **glabellae** /-lee/) the smooth part of the forehead above and between the eyebrows. □□ **glabellar** *adj.* [mod.L f. L *glabellus* (adj.) dimin. of *glaber* smooth]

glabrous /gláybrəss/ *adj.* free from hair or down; smooth skinned. [L *glaber glabri* hairless]

glacé /glássay/ *adj.* **1** (of fruit, esp. cherries) preserved in sugar, usu. resulting in a glossy surface. **2** (of cloth, leather, etc.) smooth; polished. □ **glacé icing** icing made with icing sugar and water. [F, past part. of *glacer* to ice, gloss f. *glace* ice: see GLACIER]

glacial /gláysh'l, gláysiəl/ *adj.* **1** of ice; icy. **2** *Geol.* characterized or produced by the presence or agency of ice. **3** *Chem.* forming icelike crystals upon freezing (*glacial acetic acid*). □ **glacial epoch** (or **period**) a period when ice-sheets were exceptionally extensive. □□ **glacially** *adv.* [F *glacial* or L *glacialis* icy f. *glacies* ice]
■ **1** see ICY 1, 2.

glaciated /gláysiaytid, gláss-/ *adj.* **1** marked or polished by the action of ice. **2** covered or having been covered by glaciers or ice sheets. □□ **glaciation** /-áysh'n/ *n.* [past part. of *glaciate* f. L *glaciare* freeze f. *glacies* ice]

glacier /glássiər/ *n.* a mass of land ice formed by the accumulation of snow on high ground. [F f. *glace* ice ult. f. L *glacies*]

glaciology /gláysióllәji/ *n.* the science of the internal dynamics and effects of glaciers. □□ **glaciological** /-siəlójik'l/ *adj.* **glaciologist** *n.* [L *glacies* ice + -LOGY]

glacis /glássiss, -see/ *n.* (*pl.* same /-siz, -seez/) a bank sloping down from a fort, on which attackers are exposed to the defenders' missiles etc. [F f. OF *glacier* to slip f. *glace* ice: see GLACIER]

glad[1] /glad/ *adj.* & *v.* ● *adj.* (**gladder, gladdest**) **1** (*predic.*; usu. foll. by *of*, *about*, or *to* + infin.) pleased; willing (*shall be glad to come*; *would be glad of a chance to talk about it*). **2 a** marked by, filled with, or expressing, joy (*a glad expression*). **b** (of news, events, etc.) giving joy (*glad tidings*). **3** (of objects) bright; beautiful. ● *v.tr.* (**gladded, gladding**) *archaic* make glad. □ **the glad eye** *colloq.* an amorous glance. **glad hand** the hand of welcome. **glad-hand** *v.tr.* greet cordially; welcome. **glad rags** *colloq.* best clothes; evening dress. □□ **gladly** *adv.* **gladness** *n.* **gladsome** *adj. poet.* [OE *glæd* f. Gmc]
■ *adj.* **1** pleased, willing, ready, keen, eager; thrilled, tickled, *colloq.* tickled pink *or* to death, pleased as Punch, *Brit. sl.* chuffed; see also HAPPY 1. **2 a** contented, gratified, satisfied; joyful, delighted. **b** joyful, satisfying, gratifying, delightful, cheering, *poet.* gladsome. □ **glad-hand** greet, welcome. □□ **gladly** cheerfully, happily, readily, with pleasure; see also *willingly* (WILLING).

glad[2] /glad/ *n.* (also *Austral.* **gladdie** /gláddi/) *colloq.* a gladiolus. [abbr.]

gladden /gládd'n/ *v.tr.* & *intr.* make or become glad. □□ **gladdener** *n.*
■ cheer (up), delight, enliven, brighten (up), hearten, buoy (up), exhilarate, elate, *archaic* glad.

gladdie *Austral.* var. of GLAD[2].

glade /glayd/ *n.* an open space in a wood or forest. [16th c.: orig. unkn.]

gladiator /gláddiaytər/ *n.* **1** *hist.* a man trained to fight with a sword or other weapons at ancient Roman shows. **2** a person defending or opposing a cause; a controversialist. □□ **gladiatorial** /-diətóriəl/ *adj.* [L f. *gladius* sword]

gladiolus /gláddiṓləss/ *n.* (*pl.* **gladioli** /-lī/ or **gladioluses**) any iridaceous plant of the genus *Gladiolus* with sword-shaped leaves and usu. brightly coloured flower-spikes. [L, dimin. of *gladius* sword]

Gladstone bag /gládstən/ *n.* a bag like a briefcase having two equal compartments joined by a hinge. [W. E. *Gladstone*, Engl. statesman d. 1898]

Glagolitic /glággəlíttik/ *adj.* of or relating to the alphabet ascribed to St Cyril and formerly used in writing some Slavonic languages. [mod.L *glagoliticus* f. Serbo-Croatian *glagolica* Glagolitic alphabet f. OSlav. *glagol* word]

glair /glair/ *n.* (also **glaire**) **1** white of egg. **2** an adhesive preparation made from this, used in bookbinding etc. □□ **glaireous** *adj.* **glairy** *adj.* [ME f. OF *glaire*, ult. f. L *clara* fem. of *clarus* clear]

glaire var. of GLAIR.

glaive /glayv/ *n. archaic poet.* **1** a broadsword. **2** any sword. [ME f. OF, app. f. L *gladius* sword]

Glam. *abbr.* Glamorgan.

glam /glam/ *adj.*, *n.*, & *v. colloq.* ● *adj.* glamorous. ● *n.* glamour. ● *v.tr.* (**glammed, glamming**) glamorize. [abbr.]

glamorize /glámmərīz/ *v.tr.* (also **glamourize, -ise**) make glamorous or attractive. □□ **glamorization** /-záysh'n/ *n.*

glamour /glámmər/ *n.* & *v.* (*US* **glamor**) ● *n.* **1** physical attractiveness, esp. when achieved by make-up etc. **2** alluring or exciting beauty or charm (*the glamour of New York*). ● *v.tr.* **1** *poet.* affect with glamour; bewitch; enchant. **2** *colloq.* make glamorous. □ **cast a glamour over** enchant. **glamour girl** (or **boy**) an attractive young woman (or man), esp. a model etc. □□ **glamorous** *adj.* **glamorously** *adv.* [18th c.: var. of GRAMMAR, with ref. to the occult practices associated with learning in the Middle Ages]
■ *n.* **1** see *elegance* (ELEGANT), BEAUTY 1. **2** allure, beauty, brilliance, glitter, attractiveness, fascination, charm, charisma, enchantment, magic. ● *v.* **2** see PRIMP 2. □ **cast a glamour over** see ENCHANT 1. **glamour girl** (or **boy**) sex symbol, *colloq.* sex kitten, *sl.* dish; model; see also BEAUTY 3. □□ **glamorous** alluring, fascinating, intriguing, beguiling, charming, attractive, desirable; chic, smart, stylish, fashionable.

glance[1] /glaanss/ *v.* & *n.* ● *v.* **1** *intr.* (often foll. by *down*, *up*, etc.) cast a momentary look (*glanced up at the sky*). **2** *intr.* (often foll. by *off*) (esp. of a weapon) glide or bounce (off an object). **3** *intr.* (usu. foll. by *over*, *off*, *from*) (of talk or a talker) pass quickly over a subject or subjects (*glanced over the question of payment*). **4** *intr.* (of a bright object or light) flash, dart, or gleam; reflect (*the sun glanced off the knife*). **5** *tr.* (esp. of a weapon) strike (an object) obliquely. **6** *tr.* *Cricket* deflect (the ball) with an oblique stroke. ● *n.* **1** (usu. foll. by *at*, *into*, *over*, etc.) a brief look (*took a glance at the paper*; *threw a glance over her shoulder*). **2 a** a flash or gleam (*a glance of sunlight*). **b** a sudden movement producing this. **3** a swift oblique movement or impact. **4** *Cricket* a stroke with the bat's face turned slantwise to deflect the ball. □ **at a glance** immediately upon looking. **glance at 1** give a brief look at. **2** make a passing and usu. sarcastic allusion to. **glance one's eye** (foll. by *at*, *over*, etc.) look at briefly (esp. a document). **glance over** (or **through**) read cursorily. □□ **glancingly** *adv.* [ME *glence* etc., prob. a nasalized form of obs. *glace* in the same sense, f. OF *glacier* to slip: see GLACIS]
■ *v.* **1** peek, look briefly; see also PEEP[1] *v.* 1. **2** glide, bounce, ricochet, rebound, *Billiards* cannon, *US Billiards* carom. **3** see *pass over* 1 (PASS[1]). **4** flash, dart, glint, sparkle, flicker, glitter, glisten, gleam, shimmer, twinkle; reflect. ● *n.* **1** peek, peep, look, *coup d'œil*, *Brit. colloq.* shufti, *sl.* gander, *Austral. sl.* geek, *Austral.* & *NZ sl.* squiz, *Brit. sl.* dekko. **2 a** gleam, glint, twinkle, sparkle, glitter, flicker, flash. □ **glance at 1** see SCAN *v.* 1.

glance[2] /glaanss/ *n.* any lustrous sulphide ore (*copper glance*; *lead glance*). [G *Glanz* lustre]

gland[1] /gland/ *n.* **1 a** an organ in an animal body secreting substances for use in the body or for ejection. **b** a structure resembling this, such as a lymph gland. **2** *Bot.* a secreting cell or group of cells on the surface of a plant-structure. [F *glande* f. OF *glandre* f. L *glandulae* throat-glands]

gland[2] /gland/ *n.* a sleeve used to produce a seal round a moving shaft. [19th c.: perh. var. of *glam*, *glan* a vice, rel. to CLAMP[1]]

glanders /glándərz/ *n.pl.* (also treated as *sing.*) **1** a contagious disease of horses, caused by a bacterium and characterized by swellings below the jaw and mucous discharge from the nostrils. **2** this disease in humans or other animals. □□ **glandered** *adj.* **glanderous** *adj.* [OF *glandre*: see GLAND[1]]

glandular /glándyoolər/ *adj.* of or relating to a gland or glands. □ **glandular fever** an infectious viral disease characterized by swelling of the lymph glands and prolonged lassitude, infectious mononucleosis (see MONONUCLEOSIS). [F *glandulaire* (as GLAND[1])]

glans /glanz/ *n.* (*pl.* **glandes** /glándeez/) the rounded part forming the end of the penis or clitoris. [L, = acorn]

glare[1] /glair/ *v.* & *n.* ● *v.* **1** *intr.* (usu. foll. by *at*, *upon*) look fiercely or fixedly. **2** *intr.* shine dazzlingly or disagreeably. **3** *tr.* express (hate, defiance, etc.) by a look. **4** *intr.* be over-conspicuous or obtrusive. ● *n.* **1 a** a strong fierce light, esp. sunshine. **b** oppressive public attention (*the glare of fame*). **2** a fierce or fixed look (*a glare of defiance*). **3** tawdry brilliance. □□ **glary** *adj.* [ME, prob. ult. rel. to GLASS: cf. MDu. and MLG *glaren* gleam, glare]

■ *v.* **1** frown, scowl, stare, glower, lour, look daggers. **2** dazzle, be blinding, be dazzling. **4** look out of place, stick out like a sore thumb, scream, stick out a mile. ● *n.* **1 a** brilliance, brightness, radiance, radiation, luminescence, fluorescence, luminosity; dazzle. **2** stare, frown, scowl, dirty look, black look, glower, lour. **3** garishness, tawdriness, gaudiness, floridity, flashiness.

glare[2] /glair/ *adj. US* (esp. of ice) smooth and glassy. [perh. f. *glare* frost (16th c., of uncert. orig.)]

glaring /gláiring/ *adj.* **1** obvious, conspicuous (*a glaring error*). **2** shining oppressively. **3** staring fiercely. □□ **glaringly** *adv.* **glaringness** *n.*

■ **1** obvious, conspicuous, obtrusive, prominent, patent, manifest, blatant, flagrant, gross. **2** dazzling, brilliant, blinding, blazing, vivid, harsh, strong.

glasnost /glàznost, glaàs-/ *n.* (in the former Soviet Union) the policy or practice of more open consultative government and wider dissemination of information. [Russ. *glasnost'*, lit. = publicity, openness]

glass /glaass/ *n.*, *v.*, & *adj.* ● *n.* **1 a** (often *attrib.*) a hard, brittle, usu. transparent, translucent, or shiny substance, made by fusing sand with soda and lime and sometimes other ingredients (*a glass jug*) (cf. *crown glass*, *flint glass*, *plate glass*). **b** a substance of similar properties or composition. **2** (often *collect.*) an object or objects made from, or partly from, glass, esp.: **a** a drinking vessel. **b** a mirror; a looking-glass. **c** an hour- or sand-glass. **d** a window. **e** a greenhouse (*rows of lettuce under glass*). **f** glass ornaments. **g** a barometer. **h** a glass disc covering a watch-face. **i** a magnifying lens. **j** a monocle. **3** (in *pl.*) **a** spectacles. **b** field-glasses; opera-glasses. **4** the amount of liquid contained in a glass; a drink (*he likes a glass*). ● *v.tr.* **1** (usu. as **glassed** *adj.*) fit with glass; glaze. **2** *poet.* reflect as in a mirror. **3** *Mil.* look at or for with field-glasses. ● *adj.* of or made from glass. □ **glass-blower** a person who blows semi-molten glass to make glassware. **glass-blowing** this occupation. **glass case** an exhibition display case made mostly from glass. **glass-cloth 1** a linen cloth for drying glasses. **2** a cloth covered with powdered glass or abrasive, like glass-paper. **glass cloth** a woven fabric of fine-spun glass. **glass-cutter 1** a worker who cuts glass. **2** a tool used for cutting glass. **glass eye** a false eye made from glass. **glass fibre 1** a filament or filaments of glass made into fabric. **2** such filaments embedded in plastic as reinforcement. **glass-gall** = SANDIVER. **glass-making** the manufacture of glass. **glass-paper** paper covered with glass-dust or abrasive and used for smoothing and polishing. **glass snake** any snakelike lizard of the genus *Ophisaurus*, with a very brittle tail. **glass wool** glass in the form of fine fibres used for packing and insulation. **has had a glass too much** is rather drunk. □□ **glassful** *n.* (*pl.* **-fuls**). **glassless** *adj.* **glasslike** *adj.* [OE *glæs* f. Gmc: cf. GLAZE]

■ *n.* **2 a** glassware; tumbler, flute, wineglass, goblet. **b** mirror, looking-glass, speculum, reflector. **d** window, pane, window-pane. **i** lens, magnifying glass. **3** (*glasses*) **a** spectacles, eyeglasses, lorgnette(s), *colloq.* specs, goggles. **b** field-glasses, binoculars; opera-glasses. **4** see DRINK *n.* 1b, 2b.

glasshouse /glaàss-howss/ *n.* **1** a greenhouse. **2** *Brit. sl.* a military prison. **3** a building where glass is made.

■ **1** see HOTHOUSE *n.* 1. **2** see PRISON *n.* 1.

glassie var. of GLASSY *n.*

glassine /glaàsseen/ *n.* a glossy transparent paper. [GLASS]

glassware /glaàswair/ *n.* articles made from glass, esp. drinking glasses, tableware, etc.

glasswort /glaàswurt/ *n.* any plant of the genus *Salicornia* or *Salsola* formerly burnt for use in glass-making.

glassy /glaàssi/ *adj.* & *n.* ● *adj.* (**glassier**, **glassiest**) **1** of or resembling glass, esp. in smoothness. **2** (of the eye, the expression, etc.) abstracted; dull; fixed (*fixed her with a glassy stare*). ● *n.* (also **glassie**) *Austral.* a glass marble. □ **the** (or **just the**) **glassy** *Austral.* the most excellent person or thing. □□ **glassily** *adv.* **glassiness** *n.*

■ *adj.* **1** smooth, gleaming, glossy, shining, shiny, slippery; icy. **2** fixed, staring, hypnotic, vacant, empty, abstracted, expressionless, blank, vacuous, dazed, dull, glazed, cold, lifeless.

Glaswegian /glazweéjən, glaaz-/ *adj.* & *n.* ● *adj.* of or relating to Glasgow in Scotland. ● *n.* a native of Glasgow. [*Glasgow* after *Norwegian* etc.]

Glauber's salt /glówbərz, gláw-/ *n.* (also **Glauber's salts**) a crystalline hydrated form of sodium sulphate used esp. as a laxative. [J. R. *Glauber*, Ger. chemist d. 1668]

glaucoma /glawkṓmə/ *n.* an eye-condition with increased pressure within the eyeball, causing gradual loss of sight. □□ **glaucomatous** *adj.* [L f. Gk *glaukōma -atos*, ult. f. *glaukos*: see GLAUCOUS]

glaucous /gláwkəss/ *adj.* **1** of a dull greyish green or blue. **2** covered with a powdery bloom as of grapes. [L *glaucus* f. Gk *glaukos*]

glaze /glayz/ *v.* & *n.* ● *v.* **1** *tr.* **a** fit (a window, picture, etc.) with glass. **b** provide (a building) with glass windows. **2** *tr.* **a** cover (pottery etc.) with a glaze. **b** fix (paint) on pottery with a glaze. **3** *tr.* cover (pastry, meat, etc.) with a glaze. **4** *intr.* (often foll. by *over*) (of the eyes) become fixed or glassy (*his eyes glazed over*). **5** *tr.* cover (cloth, paper, leather, a painted surface, etc.) with a glaze or other similar finish. **6** *tr.* give a glassy surface to, e.g. by rubbing. ● *n.* **1** a vitreous substance, usu. a special glass, used to glaze pottery. **2** a smooth shiny coating of milk, sugar, gelatine, etc., on food. **3** a thin topcoat of transparent paint used to modify the tone of the underlying colour. **4** a smooth surface formed by glazing. **5** *US* a thin coating of ice. □ **glazed frost** a glassy coating of ice caused by frozen rain or a sudden thaw succeeded by a frost. **glaze in** enclose (a building, a window frame, etc.) with glass. □□ **glazer** *n.* **glazy** *adj.* [ME f. an oblique form of GLASS]

■ *v.* **4** see MIST *v.* **6** polish, burnish, shine, gloss, brighten, buff, furbish; varnish, lacquer, shellac. ● *n.* **4** coat, coating, covering; polish, shine, gloss, lustre, patina.

glazier /gláyzyər/ *n.* a person whose trade is glazing windows etc. □□ **glaziery** *n.*

glazing /gláyzing/ *n.* **1** the act or an instance of glazing. **2** windows (see also *double glazing*). **3** material used to produce a glaze.

GLC *abbr. hist.* (in the UK) Greater London Council.

gleam /gleem/ *n.* & *v.* ● *n.* **1** a faint or brief light (*a gleam of sunlight*). **2** a faint, sudden, intermittent, or temporary show (*not a gleam of hope*). ● *v.intr.* **1** emit gleams. **2** shine with a faint or intermittent brightness. **3** (of a quality) be indicated (*fear gleamed in his eyes*). □□ **gleamingly** *adv.* **gleamy** *adj.* [OE *glǣm*: cf. GLIMMER]

■ *n.* **1** light, glimmer, glow, glint, flicker, shine, shimmer, glitter, twinkle, spark; beam, ray, shaft. **2** glimmer, ray, spark, flicker, hint, suggestion, indication, vestige, trace, scintilla. ● *v.* **2** glimmer, glint, shimmer, shine, twinkle, glitter, glisten.

glean /gleen/ *v.* **1** *tr.* collect or scrape together (news, facts, gossip, etc.) in small quantities. **2 a** *tr.* (also *absol.*) gather (ears of corn etc.) after the harvest. **b** *tr.* strip (a field etc.) after a harvest. □□ **gleaner** *n.* [ME f. OF *glener* f. LL *glennare*, prob. of Celt. orig.]

■ **1** see EXTRACT *v.* 4, 8. **2** see HARVEST *v.* 1.

gleanings /gleéningz/ *n.pl.* things gleaned, esp. facts.

glebe /gleeb/ *n.* **1** a piece of land serving as part of a clergyman's benefice and providing income. **2** *poet.* earth; land; a field. [ME f. L *gl(a)eba* clod, soil]

glee /glee/ *n.* **1** mirth; delight (*watched the enemy's defeat with glee*). **2** a song for three or more, esp. adult male, voices, singing different parts simultaneously, usu. unaccompanied. □ **glee club** a society for singing part-songs. □□ **gleesome** *adj.* [OE *glīo*, *glēo* minstrelsy, jest f. Gmc]
■ **1** mirth, merriment, mirthfulness, joviality, jollity, gaiety, high spirits, cheerfulness, good cheer, exuberance, exhilaration, elation, exultation, delight, joy, joyfulness, joyousness, jubilation; *schadenfreude*.

gleeful /gleéfo͝ol/ *adj.* joyful. □□ **gleefully** *adv.* **gleefulness** *n.*
■ joyful, delighted, merry, mirthful, exuberant, cheerful, high-spirited, gamesome, exhilarated, elated, exultant, jubilant.

Gleichschaltung /glī́kh-shalto͝ong/ *n.* the standardization of political, economic, and social institutions in authoritarian States. [G]

glen /glen/ *n.* a narrow valley. [Gael. & Ir. *gleann*]
■ see VALLEY.

glengarry /glengárri/ *n.* (*pl.* **-ies**) a brimless Scottish hat with a cleft down the centre and usu. two ribbons hanging at the back. [*Glengarry* in Scotland]

glenoid cavity /gleénoyd/ *n.* a shallow depression on a bone, esp. the scapula and temporal bone, receiving the projection of another bone to form a joint. [F *glénoïde* f. Gk *glēnoeidēs* f. *glēnē* socket]

gley /glay/ *n.* a tacky waterlogged soil grey to blue in colour. [Ukrainian, = sticky blue clay, rel. to CLAY]

glia /glī́ə/ *n.* = NEUROGLIA. □□ **glial** *adj.* [Gk, = glue]

glib /glib/ *adj.* (**glibber, glibbest**) **1** (of a speaker, speech, etc.) fluent and voluble but insincere and shallow. **2** *archaic* smooth; unimpeded. □□ **glibly** *adv.* **glibness** *n.* [rel. to obs. *glibbery* slippery f. Gmc: perh. imit.]
■ **1** smooth, suave, smooth-spoken, smooth-tongued, smooth-
talking, fast-talking; slick, superficial; ready, facile.

glide /glīd/ *v.* & *n.* ● *v.* **1** *intr.* (of a stream, bird, snake, ship, train, skater, etc.) move with a smooth continuous motion. **2** *intr.* (of an aircraft, esp. a glider) fly without engine-power. **3** *intr.* of time etc.: **a** pass gently and imperceptibly. **b** (often foll. by *into*) pass and change gradually and imperceptibly (*night glided into day*). **4** *intr.* move quietly or stealthily. **5** *tr.* cause to glide (*breezes glided the ship on its course*). **6** *tr.* cross in a glider. ● *n.* **1 a** the act of gliding. **b** an instance of this. **2** *Phonet.* a gradually changing sound made in passing from one position of the speech-organs to another. **3** a gliding dance or dance-step. **4** a flight in a glider. **5** *Cricket* = GLANCE *n.* 4. □ **glide clip** *Austral.* a paper fastener made of bent wire. **glide path** an aircraft's line of descent to land, esp. as indicated by ground radar. □□ **glidingly** *adv.* [OE *glīdan* f. WG]
■ *v.* **1** slide, slip, stream, flow, coast, sail, soar; skate. **3 a** slide by, pass by, disappear. **4** see SLITHER *v.*

glider /glī́dər/ *n.* **1 a** an aircraft that flies without an engine. **b** a glider pilot. **2** a person or thing that glides.

glim /glim/ *n.* **1** a faint light. **2** *archaic sl.* a candle; a lantern. [17th c.: perh. abbr. of GLIMMER or GLIMPSE]

glimmer /glímmər/ *v.* & *n.* ● *v.intr.* shine faintly or intermittently. ● *n.* **1** a feeble or wavering light. **2** (usu. foll. by *of*) a faint gleam (of hope, understanding, etc.). **3** a glimpse. □□ **glimmeringly** *adv.* [ME prob. f. Scand. f. WG: see GLEAM]
■ *v.* see FLICKER[1] *v.* 1. ● *n.* **1** see FLICKER[1] *n.* **2** see GLEAM *n.* 2.

glimmering /glímməring/ *n.* **1** = GLIMMER *n.* **2** an act of glimmering.

glimpse /glimps/ *n.* & *v.* ● *n.* (often foll. by *of*) **1** a momentary or partial view (*caught a glimpse of her*). **2** a faint and transient appearance (*glimpses of the truth*). ● *v.* **1** *tr.* see faintly or partly (*glimpsed his face in the crowd*). **2** *intr.* (often foll. by *at*) cast a passing glance. **3** *intr.* **a** shine faintly or intermittently. **b** *poet.* appear faintly; dawn. [ME *glimse* corresp. to MHG *glimsen* f. WG (as GLIMMER)]
■ *n.* **1** see SIGHT *n.* 1b. ● *v.* **1** see SIGHT *v.* 1–3.

glint /glint/ *v.* & *n.* ● *v.intr.* & *tr.* flash or cause to flash; glitter; sparkle; reflect (*eyes glinted with amusement*; *the sword glinted fire*). ● *n.* a brief flash of light; a sparkle. [alt. of ME *glent*, prob. of Scand. orig.]
■ *v.* see SPARKLE *v.* 1a. ● *n.* see FLASH *n.* 1.

glissade /glisaád, -sáyd/ *n.* & *v.* ● *n.* **1** an act of sliding down a steep slope of snow or ice, usu. on the feet with the support of an ice-axe etc. **2** a gliding step in ballet. ● *v.intr.* perform a glissade. [F f. *glisser* slip, slide]

glissando /glisándō/ *n.* (*pl.* **glissandi** /-di/ or **-os**) *Mus.* a continuous slide of adjacent notes upwards or downwards. [It. f. F *glissant* sliding (as GLISSADE)]

glissé /gleesáy/ *n.* (also ***pas glissé*** /paa/) *Ballet* a sliding step in which the flat of the foot is often used. [F, past part. of *glisser*: see GLISSADE]

glisten /gliss'n/ *v.* & *n.* ● *v.intr.* shine, esp. like a wet object, snow, etc.; glitter. ● *n.* a glitter; a sparkle. [OE *glisnian* f. *glisian* shine]
■ *v.* gleam, glint, sparkle, glitter; see also SHINE *v.* 1. ● *n.* see GLEAM *n.* 1.

glister /glístər/ *v.* & *n. archaic* ● *v.intr.* sparkle; glitter. ● *n.* a sparkle; a gleam. [ME f. MLG *glistern*, MDu *glisteren*, rel. to GLISTEN]

glitch /glich/ *n. colloq.* a sudden irregularity or malfunction (of equipment etc.). [20th c.: orig. unkn.]
■ see BUG *n.* 4.

glitter /glíttər/ *v.* & *n.* ● *v.intr.* **1** shine, esp. with a bright reflected light; sparkle. **2** (usu. foll. by *with*) **a** be showy or splendid (*glittered with diamonds*). **b** be ostentatious or flashily brilliant (*glittering rhetoric*). ● *n.* **1** a gleam; a sparkle. **2** showiness; splendour. **3** tiny pieces of sparkling material as on Christmas-tree decorations. □□ **glitteringly** *adv.* **glittery** *adj.* [ME f. ON *glitra* f. Gmc]
■ *v.* **1** see GLISTEN *v.* **2** see SHINE *v.* 1. ● *n.* **1** see GLEAM *n.* 1. **2** showiness, flashiness, splendour, brilliance, *colloq.* razzmatazz, *literary* refulgence, *sl.* pizazz, razzle-dazzle, glitz, glitziness.

glitterati /glíttəraáti/ *n.pl. sl.* the fashionable set of literary or show-business people. [GLITTER + LITERATI]

glitz /glits/ *n. sl.* extravagant but superficial display; show-business glamour. [back-form. f. GLITZY]
■ see GLITTER *n.* 2.

glitzy /glítsi/ *adj.* (**glitzier, glitziest**) *sl.* extravagant, ostentatious; tawdry, gaudy. □□ **glitzily** *adv.* **glitziness** *n.* [GLITTER, after RITZY: cf. G *glitzerig* glittering]
■ see GAUDY[1].

gloaming /glṓming/ *n. poet.* twilight; dusk. [OE *glōmung* f. *glōm* twilight, rel. to GLOW]

gloat /glōt/ *v.* & *n.* ● *v.intr.* (often foll. by *on*, *upon*, *over*) consider or contemplate with lust, greed, malice, triumph, etc. (*gloated over his collection*). ● *n.* **1** the act of gloating. **2** a look or expression of triumphant satisfaction. □□ **gloater** *n.* **gloatingly** *adv.* [16th c.: orig. unkn., but perh. rel. to ON *glotta* grin, MHG *glotzen* stare]
■ *v.* (*gloat over*) exult in, glory in, relish, revel in, delight in; crow over.

glob /glob/ *n.* a mass or lump of semi-liquid substance, e.g. mud. [20th c.: perh. f. BLOB and GOB[1]]

global /glṓb'l/ *adj.* **1** worldwide (*global conflict*). **2** relating to or embracing a group of items etc.; total. □ **global warming** the increase in temperature of the earth's atmosphere caused by the greenhouse effect. □□ **globally** *adv.* [F (as GLOBE)]
■ **1** worldwide, universal, international; cosmic. **2** broad, wide-ranging, far-reaching, all-embracing; total; see also EXTENSIVE 2.

globe /glōb/ *n.* & *v.* ● *n.* **1 a** (prec. by *the*) the planet earth. **b** a planet, star, or sun. **c** any spherical body; a ball. **2** a spherical representation of the earth or of the constellations with a map on the surface. **3** a golden sphere as an emblem of sovereignty; an orb. **4** any spherical glass vessel, esp. a fish bowl, a lamp, etc. **5** the eyeball. ● *v.tr.* & *intr.* make (usu. in *passive*) or become globular. □ **globe artichoke** the partly edible head of the artichoke plant. **globe-fish** any tropical fish of the family Tetraodontidae, able to inflate itself into a spherical form: also called PUFFER-FISH. **globe-flower** any ranunculaceous plant of the genus *Trollius* with globular usu. yellow flowers. **globe lightning** = *ball lightning* (see BALL[1]). **globe-trotter** a person who travels widely. **globe-trotting** such travel. □□ **globelike** *adj.* **globoid** *adj.* & *n.* **globose** *adj.* [F *globe* or L *globus*]

■ *n.* **1 a** world, (mother) earth, planet. **b** planet, sun; see also STAR *n.* 1. **c** sphere, ball, orb; globule, spherule, spheroid. □ **globe-trotter** see TRAVELLER 1.

globigerina /glōbíjərī́nə, -reénə/ *n.* any planktonic protozoan of the genus *Globigerina*, living near the surface of the sea. [mod.L f. L *globus* globe + *-ger* carrying + -INA]

globular /glóbyoolər/ *adj.* **1** globe-shaped, spherical. **2** composed of globules. □□ **globularity** /-lárriti/ *n.* **globularly** *adv.*

■ **1** see SPHERICAL.

globule /glóbyo͞ol/ *n.* **1** a small globe or round particle; a drop. **2** a pill. □□ **globulous** *adj.* [F *globule* or L *globulus* (as GLOBE)]

■ **1** see DROP *n.* 1a.

globulin /glóbyoolin/ *n.* any of a group of proteins found in plant and animal tissues and esp. responsible for the transport of molecules etc.

glockenspiel /glókkənspeel, -shpeel/ *n.* a musical instrument consisting of a series of bells or metal bars or tubes suspended or mounted in a frame and struck by hammers. [G, = bell-play]

glom /glom/ *v. US sl.* (**glommed, glomming**) **1** *tr.* steal; grab. **2** *intr.* (usu. foll. by *on to*) steal; grab. [var. of Sc. *glaum* (18th c., of unkn. orig.)]

glomerate /glómmərət/ *adj. Bot.* & *Anat.* compactly clustered. [L *glomeratus* past part. of *glomerare* f. *glomus -eris* ball]

glomerule /glómmərо͞ol/ *n.* a clustered flower-head.

glomerulus /gləmérrələss/ *n.* (*pl.* **glomeruli** /-lī/) a cluster of small organisms, tissues, or blood vessels, esp. of the capillaries of the kidney. □□ **glomerular** *adj.* [mod.L, dimin. of L *glomus -eris* ball]

gloom /glo͞om/ *n.* & *v.* ● *n.* **1** darkness; obscurity. **2** melancholy; despondency. **3** *poet.* a dark place. ● *v.* **1** *intr.* be gloomy or melancholy; frown. **2** *intr.* (of the sky etc.) be dull or threatening; lour. **3** *intr.* appear darkly or obscurely. **4** *tr.* cover with gloom; make dark or dismal. [ME *gloum(b)e*, of unkn. orig.: cf. GLUM]

■ *n.* **1** darkness, dark, dusk, shadow(s), shade, shadowiness, dimness, gloominess, murkiness, murk, obscurity. **2** melancholy, sadness, blackness, downheartedness, sorrow, dejection, despondency, moroseness, depression, desolation, despair, misery, low spirits, *archaic or literary* woe, *literary* dolour; blues, doldrums, *colloq.* dumps. ● *v.* **2** darken, threaten, menace, lour.

gloomy /glo͞omi/ *adj.* (**gloomier, gloomiest**) **1** dark; unlighted. **2** depressed; sullen. **3** dismal; depressing. □□ **gloomily** *adv.* **gloominess** *n.*

■ **1** dark, black, shadowy, shaded, shady, obscure, unlighted, murky, dim, dusky, *literary* Stygian; dull, cloudy, overcast. **2** depressed, dejected, morose, glum, lugubrious, cheerless, dismal, moody, down, downcast, desolate, doleful, downhearted, crestfallen, chap-fallen, forlorn, despondent, miserable, sullen, saturnine, joyless, dispirited, despairing, dreary, sorrowful, unhappy, melancholy, sad, distressed, blue, in the doldrums, *colloq.* down in the mouth, (down) in the dumps. **3** dismal, depressing, cheerless, dreary, dispiriting, sad, disheartening.

glop /glop/ *n. US sl.* a liquid or sticky mess, esp. inedible food. [imit.: cf. obs. *glop* swallow greedily]

Gloria /glóriə/ *n.* **1** any of various doxologies beginning with *Gloria*, esp. the hymn beginning with *Gloria in excelsis Deo* (Glory be to God in the highest). **2** an aureole. [L, = glory]

glorify /glórifī/ *v.tr.* (**-ies, -ied**) **1** exalt to heavenly glory; make glorious. **2** transform into something more splendid. **3** extol; praise. **4** (as **glorified** *adj.*) seeming or pretending to be more splendid than in reality (*just a glorified office boy*). □□ **glorification** /-fikáysh'n/ *n.* **glorifier** *n.* [ME f. OF *glorifier* f. eccl.L *glorificare* f. LL *glorificus* f. L *gloria* glory]

■ **2** elevate, exalt, raise (up), enhance, dignify, ennoble. **3** extol, praise, laud, lionize, applaud, commend, hail, acclaim, revere, venerate, pay tribute *or* homage to, honour, celebrate. **4** (**glorified**) exalted, high-flown, high-sounding, *colloq.* jumped-up.

gloriole /glóriōl/ *n.* an aureole; a halo. [F f. L *gloriola* dimin. of *gloria* glory]

glorious /glóriəss/ *adj.* **1** possessing glory; illustrious. **2** conferring glory; honourable. **3** *colloq.* splendid; magnificent; delightful (*a glorious day; glorious fun*). **4** *iron.* intense; unmitigated (*a glorious muddle*). **5** *colloq.* happily intoxicated. □□ **gloriously** *adv.* **gloriousness** *n.* [ME f. AF *glorious*, OF *glorios, -eus* f. L *gloriosus* (as GLORY)]

■ **1** illustrious, famed, famous, renowned, celebrated, distinguished, honoured, eminent, excellent. **2** outstanding, splendid, magnificent, marvellous, memorable, wonderful, spectacular, dazzling; honourable, estimable, admirable, excellent, superior. **3** splendid, superb, magnificent, marvellous, wonderful, gorgeous; delightful, fine, excellent, beautiful, *colloq.* heavenly, great, fabulous; see also BRILLIANT *adj.* 4. **5** see DRUNK *adj.* 1.

glory /glóri/ *n.* & *v.* ● *n.* (*pl.* **-ies**) **1** high renown or fame; honour. **2** adoring praise and thanksgiving (*Glory to the Lord*). **3** resplendent majesty or magnificence; great beauty (*the glory of Versailles; the glory of the rose*). **4** a thing that brings renown or praise; a distinction. **5** the bliss and splendour of heaven. **6** *colloq.* a state of exaltation, prosperity, happiness, etc. (*is in his glory playing with his trains*). **7** an aureole, a halo. **8** an anthelion. ● *v.intr.* (often foll. by *in*, or *to* + infin.) pride oneself; exult (*glory in their skill*). □ **glory be! 1** a devout ejaculation. **2** *colloq.* an exclamation of surprise or delight. **glory-box** *Austral.* & *NZ* a box for women's clothes etc., stored in preparation for marriage. **glory-hole 1** *colloq.* an untidy room, drawer, or receptacle. **2** *US* an open quarry. **glory-of-the-snow** = CHIONODOXA. **go to glory** *sl.* die; be destroyed. [ME f. AF & OF *glorie* f. L *gloria*]

■ *n.* **1** honour, dignity, prestige, renown, eminence, distinction, illustriousness, celebrity, fame, exaltation, immortality. **2** worship, adoration, glorification, exaltation, praise, homage, thanksgiving, gratitude, *formal* laudation. **3** majesty, magnificence, excellence, splendour, pomp, pageantry, grandeur, greatness, beauty, radiance, brilliance, *literary* effulgence, refulgence. **4** distinction, merit, quality, credit; see also ACCOMPLISHMENT 3. **7** aureole, nimbus, aura, halo, gloriole; crown, circlet, corona, radiance, *Art* vesica, mandorla. ● *v.* revel, relish, delight, exult, pride oneself, rejoice. □ **glory be! 2** see INDEED *int.* **glory-box** *Brit.* bottom drawer, *US* hope chest; trousseau.

Glos. /gloss/ *abbr.* Gloucestershire.

gloss[1] /gloss/ *n.* & *v.* ● *n.* **1 a** surface shine or lustre. **b** an instance of this; a smooth finish. **2 a** deceptively attractive appearance. **b** an instance of this. **3** (in full **gloss paint**) paint formulated to give a hard glossy finish (cf. MATT). ● *v.tr.* make glossy. □ **gloss over 1** seek to conceal beneath a false appearance. **2** conceal or evade by mentioning briefly or misleadingly. □□ **glosser** *n.* [16th c.: orig. unkn.]

■ *n.* **1** shine, sheen, lustre, gleam, glow; glaze, polish, burnish; brightness. **2** façade, mask, surface, veneer, false appearance, disguise, camouflage, show, front, semblance. ● *v.* glaze, polish, burnish, shine, buff, furbish, brighten, clean. □ **gloss over** veil, cover up, conceal, hide, disguise, camouflage, mask; evade, explain away, gloss, gloze (over), smooth over, whitewash.

gloss[2] /gloss/ *n.* & *v.* ● *n.* **1 a** an explanatory word or phrase inserted between the lines or in the margin of a text. **b** a comment, explanation, interpretation, or paraphrase. **2 a** misrepresentation of another's words. **3 a** a glossary. **b** an interlinear translation or annotation. ● *v.* **1** *tr.* **a** add a gloss or glosses to (a text, word, etc.). **b** read a different sense into; explain away. **2** *intr.* (often foll. by *on*) make (esp. unfavourable) comments. **3** *intr.* write or introduce glosses. ▫▫ **glosser** *n.* [alt. of GLOZE after med.L *glossa*]
■ *n.* **1, 3b** footnote; annotation, comment, commentary, critique, criticism, analysis; explanation, interpretation, exegesis, explication, definition, elucidation; paraphrase, translation. **2** falsification, misrepresentation, distortion, misstatement, misquotation, perversion. ● *v.* **1 a** explain, interpret, explicate, define, elucidate; comment on, annotate, criticize, analyse, review, critique; translate. **b** see *gloss over* (GLOSS[1]).

glossal /glóss'l/ *adj. Anat.* of the tongue; lingual. [Gk *glōssa* tongue]

glossary /glóssəri/ *n.* (*pl.* **-ies**) **1** (also **gloss**) an alphabetical list of terms or words found in or relating to a specific subject or text, esp. dialect, with explanations; a brief dictionary. **2** a collection of glosses. ▫▫ **glossarial** /glosáiriəl/ *adj.* **glossarist** *n.* [L *glossarium* f. *glossa* GLOSS[2]]
■ **1** word-list, dictionary, wordbook, wordfinder.

glossator /glosáytər/ *n.* **1** a writer of glosses. **2** *hist.* a commentator on, or interpreter of, medieval law-texts. [ME f. med.L f. *glossare* f. *glossa* GLOSS[2]]

glosseme /glósseem/ *n.* any meaningful feature of a language that cannot be analysed into smaller meaningful units. [Gk *glōssēma* f. *glōssa* GLOSS[2]]

glossitis /glosítiss/ *n.* inflammation of the tongue. [Gk *glōssa* tongue + -ITIS]

glossographer /glosógrəfər/ *n.* a writer of glosses or commentaries. [GLOSS[2] + -GRAPHER]

glossolalia /glóssəláyliə/ *n.* = *gift of tongues* (see TONGUE). [mod.L f. Gk *glōssa* tongue + *-lalia* speaking]

glosso-laryngeal /glóssōlarínjiəl/ *adj.* of the tongue and larynx. [Gk *glōssa* tongue + LARYNGEAL]

glossy /glóssi/ *adj.* & *n.* ● *adj.* (**glossier, glossiest**) **1** having a shine; smooth. **2** (of paper etc.) smooth and shiny. **3** (of a magazine etc.) printed on such paper; expensively produced and attractively presented, but sometimes lacking in content or depth. ● *n.* (*pl.* **-ies**) *colloq.* **1** a glossy magazine. **2** a photograph with a glossy surface. ▫▫ **glossily** *adv.* **glossiness** *n.*
■ *adj.* **1** shining, shiny, smooth, lustrous, sleek, glassy, glistening; polished, glazed, burnished, waxed. **3** coffee-table; upmarket; showy, *sl.* glitzy.

glottal /glótt'l/ *adj.* of or produced by the glottis. ▫ **glottal stop** a sound produced by the sudden opening or shutting of the glottis.

glottis /glóttiss/ *n.* the space at the upper end of the windpipe and between the vocal cords, affecting voice modulation through expansion or contraction. ▫▫ **glottic** *adj.* [mod.L f. Gk *glōttis* f. *glōtta* var. of *glōssa* tongue]

Gloucester /glóstər/ *n.* (usu. **double Gloucester**, orig. a richer kind) a kind of hard cheese orig. made in Gloucestershire in S. England.

glove /gluv/ *n.* & *v.* ● *n.* **1** a covering for the hand, of wool, leather, cotton, etc., worn esp. for protection against cold or dirt, and usu. having separate fingers. **2** a padded protective glove, esp.: **a** a boxing glove. **b** a wicket-keeper's glove. ● *v.tr.* cover or provide with a glove or gloves. ▫ **fit like a glove** fit exactly. **glove box 1** a box for gloves. **2** a closed chamber with sealed-in gloves for handling radioactive material etc. **3** = *glove compartment*. **glove compartment** a recess for small articles in the dashboard of a motor vehicle. **glove puppet** a small cloth puppet fitted on the hand and worked by the fingers. **throw down** (or **take up**) **the glove** issue (or accept) a challenge. **with the gloves off** mercilessly; unfairly; with no compunction. ▫▫ **gloveless** *adj.* **glover** *n.* [OE *glōf*, corresp. to ON *glófi*, perh. f. Gmc]

glow /glō/ *v.* & *n.* ● *v.intr.* **1 a** throw out light and heat without flame; be incandescent. **b** shine like something heated in this way. **2** (of the cheeks) redden, esp. from cold or exercise. **3** (often foll. by *with*) **a** (of the body) be heated, esp. from exertion; sweat. **b** express or experience strong emotion (*glowed with pride*; *glowing with indignation*). **4** show a warm colour (*the painting glows with warmth*). **5** (as **glowing** *adj.*) expressing pride or satisfaction (*a glowing report*). ● *n.* **1** a glowing state. **2** a bright warm colour, esp. the red of cheeks. **3** ardour; passion. **4** a feeling induced by good health, exercise, etc.; well-being. ▫ **glow discharge** a luminous sparkless electrical discharge from a pointed conductor in a gas at low pressure. **glow-worm** any beetle of the genus *Lampyris* whose wingless female emits light from the end of the abdomen. **in a glow** *colloq.* hot or flushed; sweating. ▫▫ **glowingly** *adv.* [OE *glōwan* f. Gmc]
■ *v.* **1** shine, glimmer, gleam, radiate, incandesce, phosphoresce. **2** flush, blush, colour (up), redden, go red, burn. **5** (**glowing**) laudatory, complimentary, enthusiastic, eulogistic, rhapsodic, favourable, encomiastic, panegyrical. ● *n.* **1** luminosity, phosphorescence, incandescence, light, lambency, lustre, brightness, gleam, luminousness, radiance. **2** flush, blush, redness, ruddiness; radiance, rosiness, bloom. **3** ardour, passion, excitement, warmth, fervour, fervency, enthusiasm, thrill. **4** well-being, (good) health.

glower /glowr/ *v.* & *n.* ● *v.intr.* (often foll. by *at*) stare or scowl, esp. angrily. ● *n.* a glowering look. ▫▫ **gloweringly** *adv.* [orig. uncert.: perh. Sc. var. of ME *glore* f. LG or Scand., or f. obs. (ME) *glow* stare + -ER[4]]
■ *v.* see SCOWL *v.* ● *n.* see GLARE[1] *n.* 2.

gloxinia /gloksínniə/ *n.* any tropical plant of the genus *Gloxinia*, native to S. America, with large bell flowers of various colours. [mod.L f. B. P. *Gloxin*, 18th-c. Ger. botanist]

gloze /glōz/ *v.* **1** *tr.* (also **gloze over**) explain away; extenuate; palliate. **2** *intr. archaic* **a** (usu. foll. by *on*, *upon*) comment. **b** talk speciously; fawn. [ME f. OF *gloser* f. *glose* f. med.L *glosa*, *gloza* f. L *glossa* tongue, GLOSS[2]]

glucagon /glóokəgən/ *n.* a polypeptide hormone formed in the pancreas, which aids the breakdown of glycogen. [Gk *glukus* sweet + *agōn* leading]

glucose /glóokōss, -kōz/ *n.* **1** a simple sugar containing six carbon atoms, found mainly in its dextrorotatory form (see DEXTROSE), which is an important energy source in living organisms and obtainable from some carbohydrates by hydrolysis. ¶ Chem. formula: $C_6H_{12}O_6$. **2** a syrup containing glucose sugars from the incomplete hydrolysis of starch. [F f. Gk *gleukos* sweet wine, rel. to *glukus* sweet]

glucoside /glóokəsīd/ *n.* a compound giving glucose and other products upon hydrolysis. ▫▫ **glucosidic** /-síddik/ *adj.*

glue /gloo/ *n.* & *v.* ● *n.* an adhesive substance used for sticking objects or materials together. ● *v.tr.* (**glues, glued, gluing** or **glueing**) **1** fasten or join with glue. **2** keep or put very close (*an eye glued to the keyhole*). ▫ **glue-pot 1** a pot with an outer vessel holding water to heat glue. **2** *colloq.* an area of sticky mud etc. **glue-sniffer** a person who inhales the fumes from adhesives as a drug. ▫▫ **gluelike** *adj.* **gluer** *n.* **gluey** /glóo-i/ *adj.* (**gluier, gluiest**). **glueyness** *n.* [ME f. OF *glu* (n.), *gluer* (v.), f. LL *glus glutis* f. L *gluten*]
■ *n.* adhesive, gum, paste, cement, *colloq.* sticky. ● *v.* **1** gum, paste, fix, affix, cement; see also STICK[2] 4.

glug /glug/ *n.* & *v.* ● *n.* a hollow, usu. repetitive gurgling sound. ● *v.intr.* make a gurgling sound as of water from a bottle. [imit.]

glum /glum/ *adj.* (**glummer, glummest**) looking or feeling dejected; sullen; displeased. ▫▫ **glumly** *adv.* **glumness** *n.* [rel. to dial. *glum* (v.) frown, var. of *gloume* GLOOM *v.*]
■ gloomy, dejected, dispirited, miserable, woebegone, crestfallen, doleful, down, lugubrious, morose, low, dismal, saturnine, sullen, sulky, dour, moody, displeased; see also SAD 1.

glume /gloom/ *n.* **1** a membranous bract surrounding the spikelet of grasses or the florets of sedges. **2** the husk of grain. ▫▫ **glumaceous** /-máyshəss/ *adj.* **glumose** *adj.* [L *gluma* husk]

gluon /gloo-on/ *n. Physics* any of a group of elementary particles that are thought to bind quarks together. [GLUE + -ON]

glut /glut/ *v.* & *n.* ● *v.tr.* (**glutted, glutting**) **1** feed (a person, one's stomach, etc.) or indulge (an appetite, a desire, etc.) to the full; satiate; cloy. **2** fill to excess; choke up. **3** *Econ.* overstock (a market) with goods. ● *n.* **1** *Econ.* supply exceeding demand; a surfeit (*a glut in the market*). **2** full indulgence; one's fill. [ME prob. f. OF *gloutir* swallow f. L *gluttire*: cf. GLUTTON]

■ *v.* **1** gorge, stuff, cram, overfeed, surfeit, satiate, sate; indulge; sicken, cloy. **2, 3** overfill, overload, oversupply, overstock; flood, saturate, swamp, inundate, deluge; clog, choke up. ● *n.* **1** surplus, excess, surfeit, saturation, oversupply, over-abundance, superabundance, superfluity.

glutamate /glootəmayt/ *n.* any salt or ester of glutamic acid, esp. a sodium salt used to enhance the flavour of food.

glutamic acid /glootámmik/ *n.* a naturally occurring amino acid, a constituent of many proteins. [GLUTEN + AMINE + -IC]

gluten /gloot'n/ *n.* **1** a mixture of proteins present in cereal grains. **2** *archaic* a sticky substance. [F f. L *gluten glutinis* glue]

gluteus /glootiəss/ *n.* (*pl.* **glutei** /-ti-ī/) any of the three muscles in each buttock. ▫▫ **gluteal** *adj.* [mod.L f. Gk *gloutos* buttock]

glutinous /glootinəss/ *adj.* sticky; like glue. ▫▫ **glutinously** *adv.* **glutinousness** *n.* [F *glutineux* or L *glutinosus* (as GLUTEN)]

■ see STICKY *adj.* 2.

glutton /glútt'n/ *n.* **1** an excessively greedy eater. **2** (often foll. by *for*) *colloq.* a person insatiably eager (*a glutton for work*). **3** a voracious animal *Gulo gulo*, of the weasel family. Also called WOLVERINE. ▫ **a glutton for punishment** a person eager to take on hard or unpleasant tasks. ▫▫ **gluttonize** *v.intr.* (also **-ise**). **gluttonous** *adj.* **gluttonously** *adv.* [ME f. OF *gluton, gloton* f. L *glutto -onis* f. *gluttire* swallow, *gluttus* greedy]

■ **1** gormandizer, gourmand, overeater, *colloq.* hog, pig, greedy-guts, *sl.* gannet. **2** see ADDICT *n.* 2. ▫ **a glutton for punishment** see SUCKER *n.* 2. ▫▫ **gluttonous** greedy, voracious, insatiable, *archaic or joc.* esurient, *colloq.* piggish, hoggish, swinish, piggy, *literary or joc.* edacious.

gluttony /glúttəni/ *n.* habitual greed or excess in eating. [OF *glutonie* (as GLUTTON)]

■ greed, greediness, gourmandism, voraciousness, voracity, insatiability, *colloq.* hoggishness, piggishness, pigginess.

glyceride /glíssərīd/ *n.* any fatty-acid ester of glycerol.

glycerine /glíssəreen/ *n.* (*US* **glycerin** /-rin/) = GLYCEROL. [F *glycerin* f. Gk *glukeros* sweet]

glycerol /glíssərol/ *n.* a colourless sweet viscous liquid formed as a by-product in the manufacture of soap, used as an emollient and laxative, in explosives, etc. ¶ Chem. formula: $C_3H_8O_3$. Also called GLYCERINE. [GLYCERINE + -OL[1]]

glycine /glíseen/ *n.* the simplest naturally occurring amino acid, a general constituent of proteins. [G *Glycin* f. Gk *glukus* sweet]

glyco- /glīkō/ *comb. form* sugar. [Gk *glukus* sweet]

glycogen /glīkəjən/ *n.* a polysaccharide serving as a store of carbohydrates, esp. in animal tissues, and yielding glucose on hydrolysis. ▫▫ **glycogenic** /-jénnik/ *adj.*

glycogenesis /glīkōjénnisiss/ *n. Biochem.* the formation of glycogen from sugar.

glycol /glīkol/ *n.* a diol, esp. ethylene glycol. ▫▫ **glycolic** /-kóllik/ *adj.* **glycollic** /-kóllik/ *adj.* [GLYCERINE + -OL[1], orig. as being intermediate between glycerine and alcohol]

glycolysis /glīkóllisiss/ *n. Biochem.* the breakdown of glucose by enzymes in most living organisms to release energy and pyruvic acid.

glycoprotein /glīkōprōteen/ *n.* any of a group of compounds consisting of a protein combined with a carbohydrate.

glycoside /glīkəsīd/ *n.* any compound giving sugar and other products on hydrolysis. ▫▫ **glycosidic** /-síddik/ *adj.* [GLYCO-, after GLUCOSIDE]

glycosuria /glīkəsyooriə/ *n.* a condition characterized by an excess of sugar in the urine, associated with diabetes, kidney disease, etc. ▫▫ **glycosuric** *adj.* [F *glycose* glucose + -URIA]

glyph /glif/ *n.* **1** a sculptured character or symbol. **2** a vertical groove, esp. that on a Greek frieze. ▫▫ **glyphic** *adj.* [F *glyphe* f. Gk *gluphē* carving f. *gluphō* carve]

glyptal /glíptal/ *n.* an alkyd resin, esp. one formed from glycerine and phthalic acid or anhydride. [perh. f. *gly*cerol + *pht*h*al*ic]

glyptic /glíptik/ *adj.* of or concerning carving, esp. on precious stones. [F *glyptique* or Gk *gluptikos* f. *gluptēs* carver f. *gluphō* carve]

glyptodont /glíptədont/ *n.* any extinct armadillo-like edentate animal of the genus *Glyptodon* native to S. America, having fluted teeth and a body covered in a hard thick bony shell. [mod.L f. Gk *gluptos* carved + *odous odontos* tooth]

glyptography /gliptógrəfi/ *n.* the art or scientific study of gem-engraving. [Gk *gluptos* carved + -GRAPHY]

GM *abbr.* **1** (in the UK) George Medal. **2** (in the US) General Motors. **3** general manager.

gm *abbr.* gram(s).

G-man /jeeman/ *n.* (*pl.* **G-men**) **1** *US colloq.* a federal criminal-investigation officer. **2** *Ir.* a political detective. [Government + MAN]

GMT *abbr.* Greenwich Mean Time.

GMWU *abbr.* (in the UK) General & Municipal Workers' Union.

gnamma /námmə/ *n.* (also **namma**) *Austral.* a natural hole in a rock, containing water; a water-hole. [Aboriginal]

gnarled /naarld/ *adj.* (also **gnarly** /naarli/) (of a tree, hands, etc.) knobbly, twisted, rugged. [var. of *knarled*, rel. to KNURL]

■ knobbly, knotty, knotted, lumpy, bumpy, rugged, twisted, bent, crooked, distorted, contorted, warped.

gnash /nash/ *v.* & *n.* ● *v.* **1** *tr.* grind (the teeth). **2** *intr.* (of the teeth) strike together; grind. ● *n.* an act of grinding the teeth. [var. of obs. *gnacche* or *gnast*, rel. to ON *gnastan* a gnashing (imit.)]

■ *v.* see GRIND *v.* 2b.

gnat /nat/ *n.* **1** any small two-winged biting fly of the genus *Culex*, esp. *C. pipiens*. **2** an insignificant annoyance. **3** a tiny thing. [OE *gnætt*]

■ **2** see PEST 1.

gnathic /náthik/ *adj.* of or relating to the jaws. [Gk *gnathos* jaw]

gnaw /naw/ *v.* (*past part.* **gnawed** or **gnawn**) **1 a** *tr.* (usu. foll. by *away, off, in two*, etc.) bite persistently; wear away by biting. **b** *intr.* (often foll. by *at, into*) bite, nibble. **2 a** *intr.* (often foll. by *at, into*) (of a destructive agent, pain, fear, etc.) corrode; waste away; consume; torture. **b** *tr.* corrode, consume, torture, etc. with pain, fear, etc. (*was gnawed by doubt*). **3** *tr.* (as **gnawing** *adj.*) persistent; worrying. ▫▫ **gnawingly** *adv.* [OE *gnagen*, ult. imit.]

■ **1** bite, chew, nibble, champ, munch, masticate, *literary* manducate. **2 a** (*gnaw at*) worry, bother, haunt, trouble, distress, plague, torment, torture; consume, devour, wear down *or* away; erode, corrode, waste away. **3** (**gnawing**) nagging, lingering, niggling, worrying, worrisome; see also PERSISTENT 2, 3, *disturbing* (DISTURB).

gneiss /nīss/ *n.* a usu. coarse-grained metamorphic rock foliated by mineral layers, principally of feldspar, quartz, and ferromagnesian minerals. □□ **gneissic** *adj.* **gneissoid** *adj.* **gneissose** *adj.* [G]

gnocchi /nókki, nyókki/ *n.pl.* an Italian dish of small dumplings usu. made from potato, semolina flour, etc., or from spinach and cheese. [It., pl. of *gnocco* f. *nocchio* knot in wood]

gnome[1] /nōm/ *n.* **1 a** a dwarfish legendary creature supposed to guard the earth's treasures underground; a goblin. **b** a figure of a gnome, esp. as a garden ornament. **2** (esp. in *pl.*) *colloq.* a person with sinister influence, esp. financial (*gnomes of Zurich*). □□ **gnomish** *adj.* [F f. mod.L *gnomus* (word invented by Paracelsus)]

■ **1 a** see GOBLIN.

gnome[2] /nṓmi, nōm/ *n.* a maxim; an aphorism. [Gk *gnōmē* opinion f. *gignōskō* know]

gnomic /nṓmik/ *adj.* **1** of, consisting of, or using gnomes or aphorisms; sententious (see GNOME[2]). **2** *Gram.* (of a tense) used without the implication of time to express a general truth, e.g. *men were deceivers ever.* □□ **gnomically** *adv.* [Gk *gnōmikos* (as GNOME[2])]

gnomon /nṓmon/ *n.* **1** the rod or pin etc. on a sundial that shows the time by the position of its shadow. **2** *Geom.* the part of a parallelogram left when a similar parallelogram has been taken from its corner. **3** *Astron.* a column etc. used in observing the sun's meridian altitude. □□ **gnomonic** /-mónnik/ *adj.* [F or L *gnomon* f. Gk *gnōmōn* indicator etc. f. *gignōskō* know]

gnosis /nṓsiss/ *n.* knowledge of spiritual mysteries. [Gk *gnōsis* knowledge (as GNOMON)]

gnostic /nóstik/ *adj.* & *n.* ● *adj.* **1** relating to knowledge, esp. esoteric mystical knowledge. **2** (**Gnostic**) concerning the Gnostics; occult; mystic. ● *n.* (**Gnostic**) (usu. in *pl.*) a Christian heretic of the 1st–3rd c. claiming gnosis. □□ **Gnosticism** /-tisiz'm/ *n.* **gnosticize** /-tisīz/ *v.tr.* & *intr.* [eccl.L *gnosticus* f. Gk *gnōstikos* (as GNOSIS)]

GNP *abbr.* gross national product.

Gnr. *abbr. Brit.* Gunner.

gns. *abbr. Brit. hist.* guineas.

gnu /nōō, nyōō/ *n.* any antelope of the genus *Connochaetes*, native to S. Africa, with a large erect head and brown stripes on the neck and shoulders. Also called WILDEBEEST. [Bushman *nqu*, prob. through Du. *gnoe*]

go[1] /gō/ *v.*, *n.*, & *adj.* ● *v.* (*3rd sing. present* **goes** /gōz/; *past* **went** /went/; *past part.* **gone** /gon/) **1** *intr.* **a** start moving or be moving from one place or point in time to another; travel, proceed. **b** (foll. by *to* + infin., or *and* + verb) proceed in order to (*went to find him; go and buy some bread*). **c** (foll. by *and* + verb) *colloq.* expressing annoyance (*you went and told him; they've gone and broken it; she went and won*). **2** *intr.* (foll. by verbal noun) make a special trip for; participate in; proceed to do (*went skiing; then went shopping; often goes running*). **3** *intr.* lie or extend in a certain direction; lead to (*the road goes to London; where does that door go?*). **4** *intr.* **a** leave; depart (*they had to go*). **b** *colloq.* disappear, vanish (*my bag has gone*). **5** *intr.* move, act, work, etc. (*the clock doesn't go; his brain is going all the time*). **6** *intr.* **a** make a specified movement (*go like this with your foot*). **b** make a sound (often of a specified kind) (*the gun went bang; the door bell went*). **c** *colloq.* say (*so he goes to me 'Why didn't you like it?'*). **d** (of an animal) make (its characteristic cry) (*the cow went 'moo'*). **7** *intr.* be in a specified state (*go hungry; went in fear of his life*). **8** *intr.* **a** pass into a specified condition (*gone bad; went mad; went to sleep*). **b** *colloq.* die. **c** proceed or escape in a specified condition (*the poet went unrecognized; the crime went unnoticed*). **9** *intr.* **a** (of time or distance) pass, elapse; be traversed (*ten days to go before Easter; the last mile went quickly*). **b** be finished (*the film went quickly*). **10** *intr.* **a** (of a document, verse, song, etc.) have a specified content or wording; run (*the tune goes like this*). **b** be current or accepted (*so the story goes*). **c** be suitable; fit; match (*the shoes don't go with the hat*). **d** be regularly kept or put (*the forks go here*). **e** find room; fit (*this won't go into the cupboard*). **11** *intr.* **a** turn out, proceed; take a course or view (*things went well; Liverpool went Labour*). **b** be successful (*make the party go; went like a bomb*). **c** progress (*we've still a long way to go*). **12** *intr.* **a** be sold (*went for £1; went cheap*). **b** (of money) be spent (*£200 went on a new jacket*). **13** *intr.* **a** be relinquished, dismissed, or abolished (*the car will have to go*). **b** fail, decline; give way, collapse (*his sight is going; the bulb has gone*). **14** *intr.* be acceptable or permitted; be accepted without question (*anything goes; what I say goes*). **15** *intr.* (often foll. by *by, with, on, upon*) be guided by; judge or act on or in harmony with (*have nothing to go on; a good rule to go by*). **16** *intr.* attend or visit or travel to regularly (*goes to church; goes to school; this train goes to Bristol*). **17** *intr.* (foll. by pres. part.) *colloq.* proceed (often foolishly) to do (*went running to the police; don't go making him angry*). **18** *intr.* act or proceed to a certain point (*will go so far and no further; went as high as £100*). **19** *intr.* (of a number) be capable of being contained in another (*6 into 12 goes twice; 6 into 5 won't go*). **20** *tr. Cards* bid; declare (*go nap; has gone two spades*). **21** *intr.* (usu. foll. by *to*) be allotted or awarded; pass (*first prize went to the girl; the job went to his rival*). **22** *intr.* (foll. by *to, towards*) amount to; contribute to (*12 inches go to make a foot; this will go towards your holiday*). **23** *intr.* (in *imper.*) begin motion (a starter's order in a race) (*ready, steady, go!*). **24** *intr.* (usu. foll. by *to*) refer or appeal (*go to him for help*). **25** *intr.* (often foll. by *on*) take up a specified profession (*went on the stage; gone soldiering; went to sea*). **26** *intr.* (usu. foll. by *by, under*) be known or called (*goes by the name of Droopy*). **27** *tr. colloq.* proceed to (*go jump in the lake*). **28** *intr.* (foll. by *for*) apply to; have relevance for (*that goes for me too*). ● *n.* (*pl.* **goes**) **1** the act or an instance of going. **2** mettle; spirit; dash; animation (*she has a lot of go in her*). **3** vigorous activity (*it's all go*). **4** *colloq.* a success (*made a go of it*). **5** *colloq.* a turn; an attempt (*I'll have a go; it's my go; all in one go*). **6** *colloq.* a state of affairs (*a rum go*). **7** *colloq.* an attack of illness (*a bad go of flu*). **8** *colloq.* a quantity of liquor, food, etc. served at one time. ● *adj. colloq.* **1** functioning properly (*all systems are go*). **2** fashionable; progressive. □ **all the go** *colloq.* in fashion. **as** (or **so**) **far as it goes** an expression of caution against taking a statement too positively (*the work is good as far as it goes*). **as** (**a person or thing**) **goes** as the average is (*a good actor as actors go*). **from the word go** *colloq.* from the very beginning. **give it a go** *colloq.* make an effort to succeed. **go about 1** busy oneself with; set to work at. **2** be socially active. **3** (foll. by pres. part.) make a habit of doing (*goes about telling lies*). **4** *Naut.* change to an opposite tack. **go ahead** proceed without hesitation. **go-ahead** *n.* permission to proceed. ● *adj.* enterprising. **go along with** agree to; take the same view as. **go around 1** (foll. by *with*) be regularly in the company of. **2** = *go about* 3. **3** = *go on* 4. **go-as-you-please** untrammelled; free. **go at** take in hand energetically; attack. **go away** depart, esp. from home for a holiday etc. **go back 1** return, revert. **2** extend backwards (in time or space). **3** (foll. by *to*) have a history extending back to. **go back on** fail to keep (one's word, promise, etc.). **go bail** see BAIL[1]. **go begging** see BEG. **go-between** an intermediary; a negotiator. **go by 1** pass. **2** be dependent on; be guided by. **go-by** *colloq.* a snub; a slight (*gave it the go-by*). **go by default** see DEFAULT. **go-cart 1** a handcart; a pushchair. **2** = *go-kart*. **3** *archaic* a baby-walker. **go-devil** *US* an instrument used to clean the inside of pipes etc. **go down 1 a** (of an amount) become less (*the coffee has gone down a lot*). **b** subside (*the flood went down*). **c** decrease in price; lose value. **2 a** (of a ship) sink. **b** (of the sun) set. **3** (usu. foll. by *to*) be continued to a specified point. **4** deteriorate; fail; (of a computer network etc.) cease to function. **5** be recorded in writing. **6** be swallowed. **7** (often foll. by *with*) be received (in a specified way). **8** *Brit. colloq.* leave university. **9** *colloq.* be sent to prison (*went down for ten years*). **10** (often foll. by *before*) fall (before a conqueror). **go down with** *Brit.* begin to suffer from (a disease). **go Dutch** see DUTCH. **go far** be very successful. **go for 1** go to fetch. **2** be accounted as or achieve (*went for nothing*). **3** prefer; choose (*that's the one I go for*). **4** *colloq.* strive to attain (*go for it!*). **5** *colloq.* attack (*the dog went for him*). **go-getter** *colloq.* an aggressively enterprising person, esp. a businessman. **go-go** *colloq.* **1** (of a dancer, music, etc.) in modern style, lively, and rhythmic. **2** unrestrained; energetic. **3** (of investment) speculative. **go great guns** see GUN. **go halves** (or **shares**) (often foll. by *with*) share equally. **go in 1** enter a room, house, etc. **2** (usu. foll. by *for*) enter as a competitor. **3** *Cricket* take or begin an innings. **4** (of the sun etc.) become obscured by cloud. **go in for** take as one's object, style, pursuit, principle, etc. **going!, gone!** an auctioneer's announcement that bidding is closing or closed. **go into 1** enter (a profession, Parliament, etc.). **2** take part in; be a part of. **3** investigate. **4** allow oneself to pass into (hysterics etc.). **5** dress oneself in (mourning etc.). **6** frequent (society). **go it** *colloq.* **1** act vigorously, furiously, etc. **2** indulge in dissipation. **go it alone** see ALONE. **go it strong** *colloq.* go to great lengths; exaggerate. **go-kart** a miniature racing car with a skeleton body. **go a long way 1** (often foll. by *towards*) have a great effect. **2** (of food, money, etc.) last a long time, buy much. **3** = *go far*. **go off 1** explode. **2 a** leave the stage. **b** leave, depart. **3** gradually cease to be felt. **4** (esp. of foodstuffs) deteriorate; decompose. **5** go to sleep; become unconscious. **6** be extinguished. **7** die. **8** be got rid of by sale etc. **9** *Brit. colloq.* begin to dislike (*I've gone off him*). **go-off** *colloq.* a start (*at the first go-off*). **go off at** *Austral.* & *NZ sl.* reprimand, scold. **go off well** (or **badly** etc.) (of an enterprise etc.) be received or accomplished well (or badly etc.). **go on 1** (often foll. by pres. part.) continue, persevere (*decided to go on with it*; *went on trying*; *unable to go on*). **2** *colloq.* **a** talk at great length. **b** (foll. by *at*) admonish (*went on and on at him*). **3** (foll. by *to* + infin.) proceed (*went on to become a star*). **4** happen. **5** conduct oneself (*shameful, the way they went on*). **6** *Theatr.* appear on stage. **7** *Cricket* begin bowling. **8** (of a garment) be large enough for its wearer. **9** take one's turn to do something. **10** (also **go upon**) *colloq.* use as evidence (*police don't have anything to go on*). **11** *colloq.* (esp. in *neg.*) **a** concern oneself about. **b** care for (*don't go much on red hair*). **12** become chargeable to (the parish etc.). **go on!** *colloq.* an expression of encouragement or disbelief. **go out 1** leave a room, house, etc. **2** be broadcast. **3** be extinguished. **4** (often foll. by *with*) be courting. **5** (of a government) leave office. **6** cease to be fashionable. **7** (usu. foll. by *to*) depart, esp. to a colony etc. **8** *colloq.* lose consciousness. **9** (of workers) strike. **10** (usu. foll. by *to*) (of the heart etc.) expand with sympathy etc. towards (*my heart goes out to them*). **11** *Golf* play the first nine holes in a round. **12** *Cards* be the first to dispose of one's hand. **13** (of a tide) turn to low tide. **14** mix socially; attend (social) events. **go over 1** inspect the details of; rehearse; retouch. **2** (often foll. by *to*) change one's allegiance or religion. **3** (of a play etc.) be received in a specified way (*went over well in Dundee*). **go round 1** spin, revolve. **2** be long enough to encompass. **3** (of food etc.) suffice for everybody. **4** (usu. foll. by *to*) visit informally. **5** = *go around*. **go slow** work slowly, as a form of industrial action. **go-slow** *Brit.* such industrial action. **go through 1** be dealt with or completed. **2** discuss in detail; scrutinize in sequence. **3** perform (a ceremony, a recitation, etc.). **4** undergo. **5** *colloq.* use up; spend (money etc.). **6** make holes in. **7** (of a book) be successively published (in so many editions). **8** *Austral. sl.* abscond. **go through with** not leave unfinished; complete. **go to!** *archaic* an exclamation of disbelief, impatience, admonition, etc. **go to the bar** become a barrister. **go to blazes** (or **hell** or **Jericho** etc.) *sl.* an exclamation of dismissal, contempt, etc. **go to the country** see COUNTRY. **go together 1** match; fit. **2** be courting. **go to it!** *colloq.* begin work! **go-to-meeting** (of a hat, clothes, etc.) suitable for going to church in. **go to show** (or **prove**) serve to demonstrate (or prove). **go under** sink; fail; succumb. **go up 1** increase in price. **2** *Brit. colloq.* enter university. **3** be consumed (in flames etc.); explode. **go up in the world** attain a higher social position. **go well** (or **ill** etc.) (often foll. by *with*) turn out well, (or ill etc.). **go with 1** be harmonious with; match. **2** agree to; take the same view as. **3 a** be a pair with. **b** be courting. **4** follow the drift of. **go without** manage without; forgo (also *absol.*: *we shall just have to go without*). **go with the tide** (or **times**) do as others do; follow the drift. **have a go at 1** attack, criticize. **2** attempt, try. **on the go** *colloq.* **1** in constant motion. **2** constantly working. **to go** *US* (of refreshments etc.) to be eaten or drunk off the premises. **who goes there?** a sentry's challenge. [OE *gān* f. Gmc: *went* orig. past of WEND]

■ *v.* **1 a** go off *or* along, move (ahead *or* forward *or* onwards), proceed, advance, pass, travel, voyage, make headway, *literary or archaic* wend; set off, start off. **3** lead, open to, give access to, communicate to *or* with, connect with *or* to; run, extend. **4 a** depart, go out *or* away, move (out *or* away), decamp, make off, withdraw, repair, retire, retreat, take off; see also LEAVE[1] *v.* 1b, 3, 4. **b** see DISAPPEAR 1. **5** function, operate, work, move, run, perform, act. **6 c** say, utter. **7** live, continue, go on, survive, last (out), endure. **8 a** become, turn, grow, get, fall. **b** see DIE[1] 1. **c** pass, escape, continue, proceed, go on. **9** pass, elapse, slip *or* tick away, fly, glide by. **10 b** be told, run. **c** fit, belong (together), agree *or* conform, harmonize, blend, match, tone, be appropriate *or* suitable, complement each other; (*go with*) set off. **d** belong, be kept *or* put, live. **11 b** swing, *colloq.* be a hit. **c** see PROGRESS *v.* 1. **13 a** be disposed of *or* discarded *or* thrown away, be relinquished, be dismissed, be got rid of *or* abolished, be given up, be cast *or* set *or* put aside, be done with. **b** fail, fade, decline, flag, weaken, deteriorate, get worse, worsen, degenerate, wear out, give (out); give way, collapse, fall *or* come *or* go to pieces, break, disintegrate, crack. **15** see JUDGE *v.* 2, BEHAVE 1a. **16** see TRAVEL *v.* 1; (*go to*) see ATTEND 1a, 2a, VISIT *v.* 1. **24** (*go to*) see REFER 4. **28** see APPLY 2. ● *n.* **2** see ENERGY 1. **3** action; change; see also STIR[1] *n.* 2. **4** see TRIUMPH *n.* 1b. **5** chance, turn, opportunity, try, attempt, *colloq.* crack, whirl, shot, stab, bid, *formal* essay, *sl.* bash. ● *adj.* **2** see FASHIONABLE, PROGRESSIVE *adj.* 3b. □ **all the go** in fashion, all the rage, fashionable, popular, modish, à la mode, in, in vogue, *colloq.* swish, the thing, *sl.* in the groove, groovy. **go about 1** approach, tackle, set about, undertake, begin, start. **go ahead** proceed, continue, move *or* go forward, advance, progress, go on. **go-ahead** (*n.*) permisssion, approval, leave, authorization, sanction, say-so, *colloq* OK, green light, *US* nod. (*adj.*) ambitious, enterprising, progressive, forward-looking, modern, advanced, resourceful, *colloq.* go. **go along with** agree to *or* with, concur with, acquiesce to *or* in, assent to. **go around 1** (*go around with*) socialize with, frequent *or* seek the company of, spend time with, associate with, hang around *or* about with, *sl.* hang out with. **go-as-you-please** see FREE *adj.* 3a, b. **go at** attack, assault, assail, go for; launch into, throw oneself into, embark on, get going on *or* with. **go away** go (off), depart, withdraw, exit; retreat, recede, decamp, disappear, vanish, *colloq.* up sticks; go on holiday, get away, take a break; see also LEAVE[1] *v.* 1b, 3, 4. **go back 3** (*go back to*) originate in, begin *or* start with, date back to. **go back on** renege (on), break, retract, repudiate, forsake, fail to keep. **go-between** intermediary, middleman, mediator, negotiator, intercessor, interceder, agent; messenger. **go by 1** pass (by), go past, move by *or* on, slip by *or* away, slide by, glide by; elapse. **2** rely *or* count *or* depend *or* bank on, put faith in, be guided by, judge from. **go-by** see INSULT *n.* **go down 1** decrease, decline, drop, sink, drop, fall; subside. **2 a** sink, go under, founder, become submerged, be engulfed, dive. **4** crash; see also DETERIORATE, FAIL *v.* 1, 2a. **5** be remembered *or* memorialized, *or* recalled *or* commemorated *or* recorded. **7** (*go down well*) find favour *or* acceptance *or* approval, be accepted. **go down with** see CONTRACT *v.* 3. **go for 1** fetch, get, run for, go after, bring (back), retrieve, obtain. **3** fancy, favour, like, admire, be attracted to, prefer, choose, *sl.* dig. **4** target, strive for, try for, set one's sights on, aim for, focus attention *or* effort(s) on. **5** attack, assault, assail, set upon, go at. **go-go 2** see ENERGETIC 1, 2. **3** see SPECULATIVE 2. **go in 1** enter, come in. **2** (*go in for*) enter, enrol for, sign up for, put one's name down for. **go in for** embark on, pursue, take up, embrace, espouse, undertake, follow, adopt, go into, *US* go out for; like, fancy, favour, practise, do, engage in. **go into 3** delve into, examine, pursue, investigate, analyse, probe, scrutinize, inquire into, study; touch on, discuss, mention, talk about. **go it 1** pull all the stops out, bend over backwards; see also SPEED *v.* **go it strong** see EXAGGERATE 1. **go off 1** explode, blow up, detonate, erupt, fly apart, burst; fire, be discharged. **2 a** leave, exit, walk off, go. **b** depart, leave, go (away), set out, exit, decamp, quit. **3** see DIMINISH 1. **4** deteriorate, rot, moulder, decompose, go mouldy, go stale, go bad, spoil, (go) sour, turn. **6** go out, cease to function, be extinguished, be put out *or* off. **7** see DIE[1] 1. **go off at** see REPRIMAND *v.* **go on 1** continue, proceed, keep (on), carry on; go, persist, last, endure, persevere. **2 a** gabble, chatter, drone on, *colloq.* natter, witter (on), rabbit on; see also CHATTER *v.* 1. **b** (*go on at*) see CRITICIZE 1. **4** occur, take place, come about; see also HAPPEN *v.* 1. **5** see BEHAVE 1a. **6** enter, make an *or* one's entrance, come on (stage), go on stage. **10** rely *or* depend on, use (as evidence). **11 b** see LIKE[2] *v.* 1. **go on!** you're having me on, you're kidding, you're not serious, get along, nonsense, rubbish, *archaic* go to, *colloq.* pull the other one (it's got bells on), come off it, get away, tell that to the (horse) marines, you don't say so, *Austral. sl.* dicken. **go out 1** depart, exit, go off; see also LEAVE[1] *v.* 1b, 3, 4. **3** fade *or* die (out), expire, cease functioning, go off, be extinguished. **4** court, go together, see (one another), *Brit. archaic* walk out, *colloq.* date. **9** see STRIKE *v.* 17a. **10** see SYMPATHIZE 1. **14** go about, socialize, mix. **go over 1** review, skim (through *or* over), go through, scan, look at, read, study; inspect, examine, scrutinize, investigate; rehearse, repeat, reiterate; retouch, redo. **2** convert, switch, change; (*go over to*) become, turn into. **3** go down, be received. **go round 1** rotate, spin, whirl, twirl; see also REVOLVE 1, 2. **2** fit, extend, reach, span, stretch; see also ENCIRCLE 1. **3** suffice, be sufficient *or* adequate *or* enough, satisfy. **4** see VISIT *v.* 1. **go through 1** be accepted *or* approved, pass (muster), be dealt with. **2** see *go over* 1 above. **4** experience, suffer, undergo, bear, take, stand, tolerate, put up with, submit to, endure, live through, brave, *literary* brook. **5** see *use up* 1. **8** see RUN *v.* 2. **go through with** follow through, finish; see also COMPLETE *v.* 1. **go to!** well I never, *colloq.* well I'm damned, well I'll be damned, you don't say, *sl.* well I'll be blowed; see also *go on!* above. **go to blazes** (or **hell** or **Jericho**) damn you; see also *drop dead!* **go together 1** match, harmonize, accord, agree, fit, go, suit each other, belong (with each other). **2** see *go out* 4 above. **go to it!** get cracking, buckle down; see also *jump to it*, *fall to*. **go to show** or (**prove**) see PROVE 1. **go under** sink, fail, collapse, subside, go bankrupt, succumb, go to the wall, *colloq.* fold, *US colloq.* go belly up. **go up 1** rise, increase, climb, ascend, *colloq.* go through the roof; see also SOAR 2. **3** see EXPLODE 1. **go with 1** go together with, harmonize with, blend with, be suitable *or* suited for, fit (in) with, accord *or* agree with, match, suit. **2** go along with, concur with, acquiesce to *or* in, assent to; see also AGREE 4, 5. **3 b** socialize with, associate with, accompany, court, *archaic* walk out with, *colloq.* date. **go without** do *or* manage *or* get by without, forgo; lack, be deprived of, need; abstain from, survive *or* live *or* continue without. **go with the tide** (or **times**) go with the flow, follow the crowd *or* herd. **have a go at 1** see ATTACK *v.* 3. **2** see ESSAY *v.* **to go** to take away, *esp. Sc.* to carry out.

go[2] /gō/ *n.* a Japanese board game of territorial possession and capture. [Jap.]

goad /gōd/ *n.* & *v.* ● *n.* **1** a spiked stick used for urging cattle forward. **2** anything that torments, incites, or stimulates. ● *v.tr.* **1** urge on with a goad. **2** (usu. foll. by *on*, *into*) irritate; stimulate (*goaded him into retaliating*; *goaded me on to win*). [OE *gād*, rel. to Lombard *gaida* arrowhead f. Gmc]

■ *n.* **2** see SPUR *n.* 2. ● *v.* **2** see SPUR *v.*

goak /gōk/ *n. Austral.* a practical joke. [prob. alt. of JOKE infl. by GOWK]

goal /gōl/ *n.* **1** the object of a person's ambition or effort; a destination; an aim (*fame is his goal*; *London was our goal*). **2 a** *Football* a pair of posts with a crossbar between which the ball has to be sent to score. **b** a cage or basket used similarly in other games. **c** a point won (*scored 3 goals*). **3** a point marking the end of a race. □ **goal average** *Football* the ratio of the numbers of goals scored for and against a team in a series of matches. **goal difference** *Football* the difference of goals scored for and against. **goal-kick 1** *Assoc. Football* a kick by the defending side after attackers send the ball over the goal-line without scoring. **2** *Rugby Football* an attempt to kick a goal. **goal-line** *Football* a line between each pair of goalposts, extended to form the end-boundary of a field of play (cf. *touch-line*). **goal-minder** (or **-tender**) *US* a goalkeeper at ice hockey. **goal-mouth** *Football* the space between or near the goalposts. **in goal** in the position of goalkeeper. □□ **goalless** *adj.* [16th c.: orig. unkn.: perh. identical with ME *gol* boundary]

■ **1** object, aim, purpose, end, objective, target; ambition, ideal, aspiration; destination.

goalball /gṓlbawl/ *n.* a team ball game for blind and visually handicapped players.

goalie /gṓli/ *n. colloq.* = GOALKEEPER.

goalkeeper /gṓlkeepər/ *n.* a player stationed to protect the goal in various sports.

goalpost /gṓlpōst/ *n.* either of the two upright posts of a goal. □ **move the goalposts** alter the basis or scope of a procedure during its course, so as to fit adverse circumstances encountered.

goanna /gō-ánnə/ *n. Austral.* a monitor lizard. [corrupt. of IGUANA]

goat /gōt/ *n.* **1 a** a hardy lively frisky short-haired domesticated mammal, *Capra aegagrus*, having horns and (in the male) a beard, and kept for its milk and meat. **b** either of two similar mammals, the mountain goat and the Spanish goat. **2** any other mammal of the genus *Capra*, including the ibex. **3** a lecherous man. **4** *colloq.* a foolish person. **5** (**the Goat**) the zodiacal sign or constellation Capricorn. **6** *US* a scapegoat. □ **get a person's goat** *colloq.* irritate a person. **goat-antelope** any antelope-like member of the goat family, including the chamois and goral. **goat-god** Pan. **goat moth** any of various large moths of the family Cossidae. **goat's-beard 1** a meadow plant, *Tragopogon pratensis*. **2** a herbaceous plant, *Aruncus dioicus*, with long plumes of white flowers. □□ **goatish** *adj.* **goaty** *adj.* [OE *gāt* she-goat f. Gmc]

■ **4** see SUCKER *n.* 2.

goatee /gōtée/ *n.* a small pointed beard like that of a goat.

goatherd /gṓt-herd/ *n.* a person who tends goats.

goatskin /gṓtskin/ *n.* **1** the skin of a goat. **2** a garment or bottle made out of goatskin.

goatsucker /gṓtsukkər/ *n.* = NIGHTJAR.

gob[1] /gob/ *n.* esp. *Brit. sl.* the mouth. □ **gob-stopper** a very large hard sweet. [perh. f. Gael. & Ir., = beak, mouth]

gob[2] /gob/ *n.* & *v. Brit. sl.* ● *n.* a clot of slimy matter. ● *v.intr.* (**gobbed**, **gobbing**) spit. [ME f. OF *go(u)be* mouthful]

■ *n.* clot, blob, lump, gobbet, morsel, chunk, piece, fragment.

gob[3] /gob/ *n. sl.* a US sailor. [20th c.: cf. GOBBY]

gobbet /góbbit/ *n.* **1** a piece or lump of raw meat, flesh, food, etc. **2** an extract from a text, esp. one set for translation or comment in an examination. [ME f. OF *gobet* (as GOB[2])]

■ **1** see MORSEL.

gobble[1] /góbb'l/ *v.tr.* & *intr.* eat hurriedly and noisily. □□ **gobbler** *n.* [prob. dial. f. GOB[2]]

■ see EAT 1a.

gobble[2] /góbb'l/ *v.intr.* **1** (of a turkeycock) make a characteristic swallowing sound in the throat. **2** make such a sound when speaking, esp. when excited, angry, etc. [imit.: perh. based on GOBBLE[1]]

gobbledegook /góbb'ldigōōk, -gōōk/ *n.* (also **gobbledygook**) *colloq.* pompous or unintelligible jargon. [prob. imit. of a turkeycock]
■ jargon, mumbo-jumbo, humbug, nonsense, gibberish, moonshine, rubbish, balderdash, drivel, garbage, *colloq.* hogwash, tosh, piffle, malarkey, *sl.* bull, poppycock, eyewash, tommy-rot, bunk, rot, bosh, bilge, *Brit. sl.* codswallop, (load of old) cobblers.

gobbler /góblər/ *n. colloq.* a turkeycock.

gobby /góbbi/ *n.* (*pl.* **-ies**) *sl.* **1** a coastguard. **2** an American sailor. [perh. f. GOB[2] + -Y[1]]

Gobelin /gṓbəlin, gobláN/ *n.* (in full **Gobelin tapestry**) **1** a tapestry made at the Gobelins factory. **2** a tapestry imitating this. [name of a State factory in Paris, called *Gobelins* after its orig. owners]

gobemouche /góbmōōsh/ *n.* (*pl.* **gobemouches** *pronunc.* same) a gullible listener. [F *gobe-mouches*, = fly-catcher f. *gober* swallow + *mouches* flies]

goblet /góblit/ *n.* **1** a drinking-vessel with a foot and a stem, usu. of glass. **2** *archaic* a metal or glass bowl-shaped drinking-cup without handles, sometimes with a foot and a cover. **3** *poet.* a drinking-cup. [ME f. OF *gobelet* dimin. of *gobel* cup, of unkn. orig.]
■ see GLASS *n.* 2a.

goblin /góblin/ *n.* a mischievous ugly dwarflike creature of folklore. [ME prob. f. AF *gobelin*, med.L *gobelinus*, prob. f. name dimin. of *Gobel*, rel. to G *Kobold*: see COBALT]
■ elf, gnome, hobgoblin, imp, kobold, leprechaun, demon, brownie, pixie, nix, nixie.

gobsmacked /góbsmakt/ *adj. sl.* flabbergasted; struck dumb with awe or amazement. [GOB[1] + SMACK[1]]

goby /gṓbi/ *n.* (*pl.* **-ies**) any small marine fish of the family Gobiidae, having ventral fins joined to form a sucker or disc. [L *gobius*, *cobius* f. Gk *kōbios* GUDGEON[1]]

GOC *abbr.* General Officer Commanding.

god /god/ *n.* & *int.* ● *n.* **1 a** (in many religions) a superhuman being or spirit worshipped as having power over nature, human fortunes, etc.; a deity. **b** an image, idol, animal, or other object worshipped as divine or symbolizing a god. **2** (**God**) (in Christian and other monotheistic religions) the creator and ruler of the universe; the supreme being. **3 a** an adored, admired, or influential person. **b** something worshipped like a god (*makes a god of success*). **4** *Theatr.* (in *pl.*) **a** the gallery. **b** the people sitting in it. ● *int.* (**God!**) an exclamation of surprise, anger, etc. □ **by God!** an exclamation of surprise etc. **for God's sake!** see SAKE[1]. **God-awful** *sl.* extremely unpleasant, nasty, etc. **God bless** an expression of good wishes on parting. **God bless me** (or **my soul**) see BLESS. **God damn** (**you, him**, etc.) may (you etc.) be damned. **god-damn** (or **-dam** or **-damned**) *sl.* accursed, damnable. **god-daughter** a female godchild. **God the Father, Son, and Holy Ghost** (in the Christian tradition) the Persons of the Trinity. **God-fearing** earnestly religious. **God forbid** (foll. by *that* + clause, or *absol.*) may it not happen! **God-forsaken** devoid of all merit; dismal; dreary. **God grant** (foll. by *that* + clause) may it happen. **God help** (**you, him**, etc.) an expression of concern for or sympathy with a person. **God knows 1** it is beyond all knowledge (*God knows what will become of him*). **2** I call God to witness that (*God knows we tried hard enough*). **God's Acre** a churchyard. **God's book** the Bible. **God's gift** often *iron.* a godsend. **God's own country** an earthly paradise, esp. the United States. **God squad** *sl.* **1** a religious organization, esp. an evangelical Christian group. **2** its members. **God's truth** the absolute truth. **God willing** if Providence allows. **good God!** an exclamation of surprise, anger, etc. **in God's name** an appeal for help. **in the name of God** an expression of surprise or annoyance. **my** (or **oh**) **God!** an exclamation of surprise, anger, etc. **play God** assume importance or superiority. **thank God!** an exclamation of pleasure or relief. **with God** dead and in Heaven. □□ **godhood** *n.* **godship** *n.* **godward** *adj.* & *adv.* **godwards** *adv.* [OE f. Gmc]
■ *n.* **1 a** deity, demigod, demiurge, divinity, spirit, power, numen; (*gods*) immortals. **b** see IDOL 1. **2** (**God**) the Creator, Supreme Being, the Deity, the Godhead; Allah, Jehovah, Yahweh. **3 a** see IDOL 3. ● *int.* (**God!**) by God, good God, my *or* oh god, Heavens, goodness, gracious, mercy, for Christ's *or* God's *or* goodness' *or* Heaven's *or* Pete's sake, good grief, *Ir.* begorra, *colloq.* hell, Jesus, *euphem.* my godfathers, *sl.* Christ; see also GRACIOUS *int.* □ **by God!** see GOD *int.* above. **God-awful** see NASTY 1, 5a, b; 3. **God damn** (**you, him** etc.) see CURSE *v.* 1b. **god-damn** see DAMNABLE. **God-fearing** see DEVOUT 1. **God-forsaken** see DISMAL 1, 2, BLEAK[1]. **God knows 1** Heaven (only) knows, God alone knows, goodness knows. **God's Acre** see GRAVEYARD. **God willing** *Deo volente*, DV, inshallah. **good God!** see GOD *int.* above. **my** (or **oh**) **God!** see GOD *int.* above. **thank God!** *Deo gratias*, phew, that was lucky, *colloq.* thank goodness *or* heavens.

godchild /gódchīld/ *n.* a person in relation to a godparent.

goddess /góddiss/ *n.* **1** a female deity. **2** a woman who is adored, esp. for her beauty.
■ **1** see DEITY 1.

godet /gṓday/ *n.* a triangular piece of material inserted in a dress, glove, etc. [F]

godetia /gədeeshə/ *n.* any plant of the genus *Godetia*, having showy rose-purple or reddish flowers. [mod.L f. C. H. *Godet*, Swiss botanist d. 1879]

godfather /gódfaathər/ *n.* **1** a male godparent. **2** esp. *US* a person directing an illegal organization, esp. the Mafia. □ **my godfathers!** *euphem.* my God!

godhead /gódhed/ *n.* (also **Godhead**) **1 a** the state of being God or a god. **b** divine nature. **2** a deity. **3** (**the Godhead**) God.
■ **1 a** godhood, godship, divinity. **3** (**the Godhead**) see GOD *n.* 2.

godless /gódliss/ *adj.* **1** impious; wicked. **2** without a god. **3** not recognizing God. □□ **godlessness** *n.*
■ **1** wicked, evil, sinful, unrighteous, unholy; impious, blasphemous, profane, sacrilegious, ungodly. **3** atheistic, nullifidian, agnostic, unbelieving, sceptical; see also FAITHLESS 2, *heretical* (HERETIC).

godlike /gódlīk/ *adj.* **1** resembling God or a god in some quality, esp. in physical beauty. **2** befitting or appropriate to a god.
■ **1** divine; saintly, angelic, seraphic, deific, deiform; blessed, sainted, *poet.* blest. **2** holy, godly, heavenly, celestial, beatific, ethereal; see also SACRED 1b.

godly /gódli/ *adj.* religious, pious, devout. □□ **godliness** *n.*
■ religious, pious, devout, God-fearing, holy, reverent, saintly, pietistic, devoted, faithful, righteous, good, virtuous, moral, pure.

godmother /gódmuthər/ *n.* a female godparent.

godown /gṓdown/ *n.* a warehouse in parts of E. Asia, esp. in India. [Port. *gudão* f. Malay *godong* perh. f. Telugu *giḍaṅgi* place where goods lie f. *kiḍu* lie]

godparent /gódpairənt/ *n.* a person who presents a child at baptism and responds on the child's behalf.

godsend /gódsend/ *n.* an unexpected but welcome event or acquisition.
■ gift, blessing, boon, windfall, bonanza, stroke of (good) fortune, stroke of (good) luck, piece *or* bit of luck.

godson /gódsun/ *n.* a male godchild.

Godspeed /gódspeed/ *int.* an expression of good wishes to a person starting a journey.

godwit /gódwit/ *n.* any wading bird of the genus *Limosa*, with long legs and a long straight or slightly upcurved bill. [16th c.: of unkn. orig.]

Godwottery /godwóttəri/ *n. joc.* affected, archaic, or excessively elaborate speech or writing, esp. regarding gardens. [*God wot* (in a poem on gardens, by T. E. Brown 1876)]

goer /gṓər/ *n.* **1** a person or thing that goes (*a slow goer*). **2** (often in *comb.*) a person who attends, esp. regularly (*a churchgoer*). **3** *colloq.* **a** a lively or persevering person. **b** a sexually promiscuous person. **4** *Austral. colloq.* a project likely to be accepted or to succeed.

goes *3rd sing. present* of GO[1].

goest /gṓ-ist/ *archaic 2nd sing. present* of GO[1].

goeth /gṓ-ith/ *archaic 3rd sing. present* of GO[1].

Goethean /gṓtiən/ *adj.* & *n.* (also **Goethian**) ● *adj.* of, relating to, or characteristic of the German writer J. W. von Goethe (d. 1832). ● *n.* an admirer or follower of Goethe.

gofer /gṓfər/ *n.* esp. *US sl.* a person who runs errands, esp. on a film set or in an office; a dogsbody. [*go for* (see GO[1])]

■ see MESSENGER.

goffer /gṓfər, gófˊ-/ *v.* & *n.* ● *v.tr.* **1** make wavy, flute, or crimp (a lace edge, a trimming, etc.) with heated irons. **2** (as **goffered** *adj.*) (of the edges of a book) embossed. ● *n.* **1** an iron used for goffering. **2** ornamental plaiting used for frills etc. [F *gaufrer* stamp with a patterned tool f. *gaufre* honeycomb, rel. to WAFER, WAFFLE[2]]

goggle /gógg'l/ *v.*, *adj.*, & *n.* ● *v.* **1** *intr.* **a** (often foll. by *at*) look with wide-open eyes. **b** (of the eyes) be rolled about; protrude. **2** *tr.* turn (the eyes) sideways or from side to side. ● *adj.* (usu. *attrib.*) (of the eyes) protuberant or rolling. ● *n.* **1** (in *pl.*) **a** spectacles for protecting the eyes from glare, dust, water, etc. **b** *colloq.* spectacles. **2** (in *pl.*) a sheep disease, the staggers. **3** a goggling expression. □ **goggle-box** *Brit. colloq.* a television set. **goggle-dive** an underwater dive in goggles. **goggle-eyed** having staring or protuberant eyes, esp. through astonishment or disbelief. [ME, prob. from a base *gog* (unrecorded) expressive of oscillating movement]

■ *v.* **1 a** see GAPE *v.* 2. **b** see PROTRUDE. ● *adj.* see PROTUBERANT. ● *n.* **1** (*goggles*) glasses, spectacles, eyeglasses, lorgnette(s), *colloq.* specs, *esp. US colloq.* shades; bifocals, trifocals. **3** gape, stare, gaze, ogle, fixed *or* blank look. □ **goggle-box** see TELEVISION 2, 3. **goggle-eyed** wide-eyed, staring, gawking, agape; open-mouthed, awestruck, thunderstruck, dumbfounded, astonished, astounded, amazed, stupefied, dazed, surprised.

goglet /góglit/ *n. Ind.* a long-necked usu. porous earthenware vessel used for keeping water cool. [Port. *gorgoleta*]

Goidel /góyd'l/ *n.* a Celt who speaks Irish Gaelic, Scottish Gaelic, or Manx. □□ **Goidelic** /-déllik/ *n.* [OIr. *Góidel*]

going /gṓing/ *n.* & *adj.* ● *n.* **1 a** the act or process of going. **b** an instance of this; a departure. **2 a** the condition of the ground for walking, riding, etc. **b** progress affected by this (*found the going hard*). ● *adj.* **1** in or into action (*set the clock going*). **2** existing, available; to be had (*there's cold beef going; one of the best fellows going*). **3** current, prevalent (*the going rate*). □ **get going** start steadily talking, working, etc. (*can't stop him when he gets going*). **going away** a departure, esp. on a honeymoon. **going concern** a thriving business. **going for one** *colloq.* acting in one's favour (*he has got a lot going for him*). **going on fifteen** etc. esp. *US* approaching one's fifteenth etc. birthday. **going on for** approaching (a time, an age, etc.) (*must be going on for 6 years*). **going-over 1** *colloq.* an inspection or overhaul. **2** *sl.* a thrashing. **3** *US colloq.* a scolding. **goings-on** /gṓingzón/ behaviour, esp. morally suspect. **going to** intending or intended to; about to; likely to (*it's going to sink!*). **heavy going** slow or difficult to progress with (*found Proust heavy going*). **to be going on with** to start with; for the time being. **while the going is good** while conditions are favourable. [GO[1]: in some senses f. earlier *a-going*: see A[2]]

■ *n.* **1** departure, leaving; see also RETREAT *n.* 1a. ● *adj.* **2** see AVAILABLE 2. **3** current, present, accepted, prevailing, prevalent, universal, common, usual, customary. □ **going concern** booming business; growth industry. **going on for** see ALMOST. **going-over 1** see CHECK[1] *n.* 1, OVERHAUL *n.* **2** see *thrashing* (THRASH). **3** see REPRIMAND *n.* **goings-on** see HANKY-PANKY. **heavy going** see TEDIOUS.

goitre /góytər/ *n.* (*US* **goiter**) *Med.* a swelling of the neck resulting from enlargement of the thyroid gland. □□ **goitred** *adj.* **goitrous** *adj.* [F, back-form. f. *goitreux* or f. Prov. *goitron*, ult. f. L *guttur* throat]

Golconda /golkóndə/ *n.* a mine or source of wealth, advantages, etc. [city near Hyderabad, India]

gold /gōld/ *n.* & *adj.* ● *n.* **1** a yellow malleable ductile high density metallic element resistant to chemical reaction, occurring naturally in quartz veins and gravel, and precious as a monetary medium, in jewellery, etc. ¶ Symb.: **Au. 2** the colour of gold. **3 a** coins or articles made of gold. **b** money in large sums, wealth. **4** something precious, beautiful, or brilliant (*all that glitters is not gold*). **5** = *gold medal.* **6** gold used for coating a surface or as a pigment, gilding. **7** the bull's-eye of an archery target (usu. gilt). ● *adj.* **1** made wholly or chiefly of gold. **2** coloured like gold. □ **age of gold** = *golden age.* **gold amalgam** an easily-moulded combination of gold with mercury. **gold-beater** a person who beats gold out into gold leaf. **gold-beater's skin** a membrane used to separate leaves of gold during beating, or as a covering for slight wounds. **gold bloc** a bloc of countries having a gold standard. **gold brick** *sl.* **1** a thing with only a surface appearance of value, a sham or fraud. **2** *US* a lazy person. **gold card** a kind of preferential charge card giving privileges and benefits not available to holders of the standard card. **gold-digger 1** *sl.* a woman who wheedles money out of men. **2** a person who digs for gold. **gold-dust 1** gold in fine particles as often found naturally. **2** a plant, *Alyssum saxatile*, with many small yellow flowers. **gold-field** a district in which gold is found as a mineral. **gold foil** gold beaten into a thin sheet. **gold leaf** gold beaten into a very thin sheet. **gold medal** a medal of gold, usu. awarded as first prize. **gold-mine 1** a place where gold is mined. **2** *colloq.* a source of wealth. **gold of pleasure** an annual yellow-flowered plant, *Camelina sativa.* **gold plate 1** vessels made of gold. **2** material plated with gold. **gold-plate** *v.tr.* plate with gold. **gold reserve** a reserve of gold coins or bullion held by a central bank etc. **gold-rush** a rush to a newly-discovered gold-field. **gold standard** a system by which the value of a currency is defined in terms of gold, for which the currency may be exchanged. **Gold Stick 1** (in the UK) a gilt rod carried on State occasions by the colonel of the Life Guards or the captain of the gentlemen-at-arms. **2** the officer carrying this rod. **gold thread 1** a thread of silk etc. with gold wire wound round it. **2** a bitter plant, *Coptis tinfolia.* [OE f. Gmc]

goldcrest /gṓldkrest/ *n.* a small bird, *Regulus regulus*, with a golden crest.

golden /gṓldən/ *adj.* **1 a** made or consisting of gold (*golden sovereign*). **b** yielding gold. **2** coloured or shining like gold (*golden hair*). **3** precious; valuable; excellent; important (*a golden memory; a golden opportunity*). □ **golden age 1** a supposed past age when people were happy and innocent. **2** the period of a nation's greatest prosperity, literary merit, etc. **golden-ager** *US* an old person. **golden balls** a pawnbroker's sign. **golden boy** (or **girl**) *colloq.* a popular or successful person. **golden calf** wealth as an object of worship (Exod. 32). **golden chain** the laburnum. **golden delicious** a variety of dessert apple. **golden disc** an award given to a performer after the sale of 500,000 copies of a record. **golden eagle** a large eagle, *Aquila chrysaetos*, with yellow-tipped head-feathers. **golden-eye** any marine duck of the genus *Bucephala*. **Golden Fleece** (in Greek mythology) a fleece of gold sought and won by Jason. **golden goose** a continuing source of wealth or profit. **golden hamster** a usu. tawny hamster, *Mesocricetus auratus*, kept as a pet or laboratory animal. **golden handshake** *colloq.* a payment given on redundancy or early retirement. **golden hello** *colloq.* a payment made by an employer to a keenly sought recruit. **Golden Horde** the Tartar horde that overran E. Europe in the 13th c. (from the richness of the leader's tent). **Golden Horn** the harbour of Istanbul. **golden jubilee 1** the fiftieth anniversary of a sovereign's accession. **2** any other fiftieth anniversary. **golden mean 1** the principle of moderation, as opposed to excess. **2** = *golden section*. **golden number** the number of a year in the Metonic lunar cycle, used to fix the date of Easter. **golden oldie** *colloq.* an old hit record or film etc. that is still well known and popular. **golden opinions** high regard. **golden oriole** a European oriole, *Oriolus oriolus*, of which the male has yellow and black plumage and the female has mainly green plumage. **golden perch** *Austral.* = CALLOP. **golden retriever** a retriever with a thick golden-coloured coat. **golden rod** any plant of the genus *Solidago* with a rodlike stem and a spike of small bright-yellow flowers. **golden rule** a basic principle of action, esp. 'do as you would be done by'. **golden section** the division of a line so that the whole is to the greater part as that part is to the smaller part. **golden share** the controlling interest in a company, esp. as retained by the government after a nationalized industry is privatized. **Golden State** *US* California. **golden syrup** *Brit.* a pale treacle. **golden wedding** the fiftieth anniversary of a wedding. ▫▫ **goldenly** *adv.* **goldenness** *n.*

■ **1 a** gold, gilded, gilt. **b** auriferous. **2** gold, aureate, blond, yellow, flaxen; bright, shining, gleaming, lustrous, shiny, brilliant, sunny, glittering, dazzling, resplendent, radiant, glowing, sparkling. **3** precious, valuable, important; excellent, outstanding; happy, blissful, delightful, joyful, glorious, joyous; flourishing, halcyon, prosperous, thriving, favourable, blessed, palmy; advantageous, propitious, auspicious, promising, opportune, favourable, rosy. ▫ **golden age 2** see PRIME[1] *n.* 1. **golden-ager** senior, oldster, old dear, *colloq.* old girl, old boy, oldie; see also *senior citizen*. **golden boy** (or **girl**) see FAVOURITE *n.* **golden rule** see MOTTO.

goldfinch /gṓldfinch/ *n.* any of various bright-coloured songbirds of the genus *Carduelis*, esp. the Eurasian *C. carduelis*, with a yellow band across each wing. [OE *goldfinc* (as GOLD, FINCH)]

goldfish /gṓldfish/ *n.* a small reddish-golden Chinese carp kept for ornament, *Carassius auratus*. ▫ **goldfish bowl 1** a globular glass container for goldfish. **2** a situation lacking privacy.

goldilocks /gṓldiloks/ *n.* **1** a person with golden hair. **2 a** a kind of buttercup, *Ranunculus auricomus*. **b** a composite plant, *Aster linosyris*, like the golden rod. [*goldy* f. GOLD + LOCK[2]]

goldsmith /gṓldsmith/ *n.* a worker in gold, a manufacturer of gold articles. [OE (as GOLD, SMITH)]

golem /gṓləm/ *n.* **1** a clay figure supposedly brought to life in Jewish legend. **2** an automaton; a robot. [Yiddish *goylem* f. Heb. *gōlem* shapeless mass]

golf /golf/ *n.* & *v.* ● *n.* a game played on a course set in open country, in which a small hard ball is driven with clubs into a series of 18 or 9 holes with the fewest possible strokes. ● *v.intr.* play golf. ▫ **golf-bag** a bag used for carrying clubs and balls. **golf ball 1** a ball used in golf. **2** *colloq.* a small ball used in some electric typewriters to carry the type. **golf cart 1** a trolley used for carrying clubs in golf. **2** a motorized cart for golfers and equipment. **golf club 1** a club used in golf. **2** an association for playing golf. **3** the premises used by a golf club. **golf-course** (or **-links**) the course on which golf is played. [15th-c. Sc.: orig. unkn.]

golfer /gólfər/ *n.* **1** a golf-player. **2** a cardigan.

Golgi body /gólji/ *n.* (also **Golgi apparatus**) *Biol.* an organelle of vesicles and folded membranes within the cytoplasm of most eukaryotic cells, involved esp. in the secretion of substances. [C. *Golgi*, It. cytologist d. 1926]

Goliath beetle /gəlī́əth/ *n.* any large beetle of the genus *Goliathus*, esp. *G. giganteus* native to Africa. [LL f. Heb. *golyat* giant slain by David (1 Sam. 17)]

golliwog /gólliwog/ *n.* a black-faced brightly dressed soft doll with fuzzy hair. [19th c.: perh. f. GOLLY[1] + POLLIWOG]

gollop /góllәp/ *v.* & *n. colloq.* ● *v.tr.* (**golloped, golloping**) swallow hastily or greedily. ● *n.* a hasty gulp. [perh. f. GULP, infl. by GOBBLE[1]]

golly[1] /gólli/ *int.* expressing surprise. [euphem. for GOD]

golly[2] /gólli/ *n.* (*pl.* **-ies**) *colloq.* = GOLLIWOG. [abbr.]

golosh *Brit.* var. of GALOSH.

GOM *abbr.* Grand Old Man (name orig. applied to W. E. Gladstone).

gombeen /gombeén/ *n. Ir.* usury. ▫ **gombeen-man** a moneylender. [Ir. *gaimbín* perh. f. the same OCelt. source as med.L *cambire* CHANGE]

-gon /gən/ *comb. form* forming nouns denoting plane figures with a specified number of angles (*hexagon*; *polygon*; *n-gon*). [Gk *-gōnos* -angled]

gonad /gṓnad/ *n.* an animal organ producing gametes, e.g. the testis or ovary. ▫▫ **gonadal** /gōnáyd'l/ *adj.* [mod.L *gonas gonad-* f. Gk *gonē*, *gonos* generation, seed]

gonadotrophic hormone /gṓnədōtrṓfik/ *n.* (also **gonadotropic** /-tróppik, -trṓpik/) *Biochem.* any of various hormones stimulating the activity of the gonads.

gonadotrophin /gṓnədōtrṓfin/ *n.* = GONADOTROPHIC HORMONE.

gondola /góndələ/ *n.* **1** a light flat-bottomed boat used on Venetian canals, with a central cabin and a high point at each end, worked by one oar at the stern. **2** a car suspended from an airship or balloon. **3** an island of shelves used to display goods in a supermarket. **4** (also **gondola car**) *US* a flat-bottomed open railway goods wagon. **5** a car attached to a ski-lift. [Venetian It., of obscure orig.]

gondolier /góndəleér/ *n.* the oarsman on a gondola. [F f. It. *gondoliere* (as GONDOLA)]

gone /gon/ *adj.* **1** (of time) past (*not until gone nine*). **2 a** lost; hopeless. **b** dead. **3** *colloq.* pregnant for a specified time (*already three months gone*). **4** *sl.* completely enthralled or entranced, esp. by rhythmic music, drugs, etc. ▫ **all gone** consumed, finished, used up. **be gone** depart; leave temporarily (cf. BEGONE). **gone away!** a huntsman's cry, indicating that a fox has been started. **gone goose** (or **gosling**) *colloq.* a person or thing beyond hope. **gone on** *sl.* infatuated with. [past part. of GO[1]]

■ **1** see PAST *adj.* 1. **2 b** see DEAD *adj.* 1.

goner /gónnər/ *n. sl.* a person or thing that is doomed, ended, irrevocably lost, etc.; a dead person.

gonfalon /gónfələn/ *n.* **1** a banner, often with streamers, hung from a crossbar. **2** *hist.* such a banner as the standard of some Italian republics. ▫▫ **gonfalonier** /gónfələneér/ *n.* [It. *gonfalone* f. Gmc (cf. VANE)]

gong /gong/ *n.* & *v.* ● *n.* **1** a metal disc with a turned rim, giving a resonant note when struck. **2** a saucer-shaped bell. **3** *Brit. sl.* a medal; a decoration. ● *v.tr.* **1** summon with a gong. **2** (of traffic police) sound a gong etc. to direct (a motorist) to stop. [Malay *gong*, *gung* of imit. orig.]

goniometer /gṓniómmitər/ *n.* an instrument for measuring angles. ▫▫ **goniometry** *n.* **goniometric** /-niəmétrik/ *adj.* **goniometrical** /-niəmétrik'l/ *adj.* [F *goniomètre* f. Gk *gōnia* angle]

gonococcus /gónnəkókkəss/ *n.* (*pl.* **gonococci** /-kī/) a bacterium causing gonorrhoea. ▫▫ **gonococcal** *adj.* [Gk *gonos* generation, semen + COCCUS]

gonorrhoea /gónnəreéə/ *n.* (*US* **gonorrhea**) a venereal disease with inflammatory discharge from the urethra or vagina. ▫▫ **gonorrhoeal** *adj.* [LL f. Gk *gonorrhoia* f. *gonos* semen + *rhoia* flux]

goo /goo/ *n.* **1** a sticky or slimy substance. **2** sickly sentiment. [20th c.: perh. f. *burgoo* (Naut. sl.) = porridge]

■ **1** see OOZE[2].

good /good/ *adj.*, *n.*, & *adv.* ● *adj.* (**better, best**) **1** having the right or desired qualities; satisfactory, adequate. **2 a** (of a person) efficient, competent (*good at French*; *a good driver*). **b** (of a thing) reliable, efficient (*good brakes*). **c** (of health etc.) strong (*good eyesight*). **3 a** kind, benevolent (*good of you to come*). **b** morally excellent; virtuous (*a good deed*). **c** charitable (*good works*). **d** well-behaved (*a good child*). **4**

enjoyable, agreeable (*a good party*). **5** thorough, considerable (*gave it a good wash*). **6 a** not less than (*waited a good hour*). **b** considerable in number, quality, etc. (*a good many people*). **7** healthy, beneficial (*milk is good for you*). **8 a** valid, sound (*a good reason*). **b** financially sound (*his credit is good*). **9** in exclamations of surprise (*good heavens!*). **10** right, proper, expedient (*thought it good to have a try*). **11** fresh, eatable, untainted (*is the meat still good?*). **12** (sometimes patronizing) commendable, worthy (*good old George*; *your good lady wife*; *good men and true*; *my good man*). **13** well shaped, attractive (*has good legs*; *good looks*). **14** in courteous greetings and farewells (*good afternoon*). **15** promising or favourable (*a good omen*; *good news*). **16** expressing approval; complimentary (*a good review*). ● *n.* **1** (only in *sing.*) that which is good; what is beneficial or morally right (*only good can come of it*; *did it for your own good*; *what good will it do?*). **2** (only in *sing.*) a desirable end or object; a thing worth attaining (*sacrificing the present for a future good*). **3** (in *pl.*) **a** movable property or merchandise. **b** *Brit.* things to be transported, as distinct from passengers. **c** (prec. by *the*) *colloq.* what one has undertaken to supply (esp. *deliver the goods*). **d** (prec. by *the*) *sl.* the real thing; the genuine article. **4** (as *pl.*; prec. by *the*) virtuous people. ● *adv. US colloq.* well (*doing pretty good*). □ **as good as** practically (*he as good as told me*). **be so good as** (or **be good enough**) **to** (often in a request) be kind and do (a favour) (*be so good as to open the window*). **be** (**a certain amount**) **to the good** have as net profit or advantage. **do good** show kindness, act philanthropically. **do a person good** be beneficial to. **for good** (**and all**) finally, permanently. **good and** *colloq.* used as an intensifier before an adj. or adv. (*raining good and hard*; *was good and angry*). **the good book** the Bible. **good breeding** correct or courteous manners. **good faith** see FAITH. **good for 1** beneficial to; having a good effect on. **2** able to perform; inclined for (*good for a ten-mile walk*). **3** able to be trusted to pay (*is good for £100*). **good form** see FORM. **good-for-nothing** (or **-nought**) *adj.* worthless. ● *n.* a worthless person. **good for you!** (or **him!**, **her!**, etc.) exclamation of approval towards a person. **Good Friday** the Friday before Easter Sunday commemorating the Crucifixion of Christ. **good-hearted** kindly, well-meaning. **good humour** a genial mood. **a good job** a fortunate state of affairs (*it's a good job you came early*). **good-looker** a handsome or attractive person. **good-looking** handsome; attractive. **good luck 1** good fortune, happy chance. **2** exclamation of well-wishing. **good money 1** genuine money; money that might usefully have been spent elsewhere. **2** *colloq.* high wages. **good nature** a friendly disposition. **good oil** *Austral. sl.* reliable information. **good on you!** (or **him!** etc.) = *good for you!* **goods and chattels** see CHATTEL. **good-time** recklessly pursuing pleasure. **good-timer** a person who recklessly pursues pleasure. **good times** a period of prosperity. **good will** the intention and hope that good will result (see also GOODWILL). **a good word** (often in phr. **put in a good word for**) words in recommendation or defence of a person. **good works** charitable acts. **have a good mind** see MIND. **have the goods on a person** *sl.* have advantageous information about a person. **have a good time** enjoy oneself. **in a person's good books** see BOOK. **in good faith** with honest or sincere intentions. **in good time 1** with no risk of being late. **2** (also **all in good time**) in due course but without haste. **make good 1** make up for, compensate for, pay (an expense). **2** fulfil (a promise); effect (a purpose or an intended action). **3** demonstrate the truth of (a statement); substantiate (a charge). **4** gain and hold (a position). **5** replace or restore (a thing lost or damaged). **6** (*absol.*) accomplish what one intended. **no good 1** mischief (*is up to no good*). **2** useless; to no advantage (*it is no good arguing*). **no-good** *adj.* useless. ● *n.* a useless thing or person. **take in good part** not be offended by. **to the good** having as profit or benefit. □□ **goodish** *adj.* [OE *gōd* f. Gmc]

■ *adj.* **1** commendable, acceptable, fair, adequate; see also SATISFACTORY. **2 a** efficient, competent, capable, accomplished, proficient, adept, adroit, skilled, skilful, gifted, talented, clever, admirable. **b** safe, secure, sound; efficient; see also RELIABLE. **c** see SOUND[2] *adj.* 1, HEALTHY 1. **3 a** kind, benevolent, beneficent, gracious, gentle, kindly, nice, considerate, friendly, solicitous, good-hearted, sympathetic, benign, charitable, humane, kind-hearted, well-disposed. **b** moral, high-minded, righteous, noble, honourable, ethical, upstanding, upright, virtuous, worthy, saintly, godly, godlike; lofty, elevated; honourable, esteemed, respected, respectable, well-thought-of, reputable. **d** obedient, well-mannered; angelic; see also *well-behaved* (BEHAVE). **4** enjoyable, agreeable, fine, exemplary, choice, *Sc.* braw, *US sl.* neat; welcome, propitious, favourable. **5** complete; penetrating, careful; see also THOROUGH 2.
6 b considerable, extensive, sizeable, large, substantial; ample, sufficient, adequate, fair. **7** healthy, salubrious, wholesome, healthful, salutary; see also BENEFICIAL.
8 genuine, valid, legitimate, authentic, proper, sensible, creditable, sound, solid, substantial, well-founded; credible, believable, convincing, compelling, cogent; reliable, secure, dependable, sound, safe. **10** right, proper, expedient; correct, decorous, orderly, seemly, fitting, suitable, appropriate; right, fit, all right, *Austral.* & *NZ* goodo, *archaic* meet. **11** fresh, palatable, eatable, edible, consumable; untainted, unspoilt. **13** see SHAPELY, ATTRACTIVE 2. **15** advantageous, propitious, promising, opportune, beneficial, profitable, favourable.
16 approving, complimentary, flattering, positive, favourable, enthusiastic, laudatory, eulogistic, encomiastic, praising. ● *n.* **1, 2** goodness, virtue, merit, right, worth; advantage, profit, use, gain; avail; see also BENEFIT *n.* 1. **3** (*goods*) **a** commodities, wares, assets; merchandise, stock, produce. **b** freight, movables; see also BELONGING 1. **d** (*the goods*) the real thing, the genuine article, *colloq.* the real McCoy. □ **for good** (**and all**) see *finally* (FINAL). **good breeding** see BREEDING 4. **good-for-nothing** (or **nought**) (*adj.*) worthless, useless. (*n.*) ne'er-do-well, wastrel, idler, loafer, layabout, sluggard, *archaic* slugabed, *colloq.* waster, lazybones, *US sl.* gold brick, goof-off. **good for you!** bravo, well done, congratulations. **good-hearted** see KIND[2]. **good-looker** see BEAUTY 3. **good-looking** see BEAUTIFUL 1. **good-timer** see SYBARITE *n.* **a good word** see *recommendation* (RECOMMEND). **have a good time** see *enjoy oneself*. **in good faith** see HONESTLY 1. **in good time 1** see EARLY *adj.* & *adv.* 1. **2** see PRESENTLY 1. **make good 1** see REDEEM 5, PAY[1] *v.* 1. **2** see KEEP *v.* 7b, EFFECT *v.* **3** see SUBSTANTIATE. **4** see *follow up* 1. **5** replace, put back; see also RESTORE 1, 3. **6** see SUCCEED 1a. **no good 1** see MISCHIEF 1–3, 4. **2** see POINTLESS. **no-good** (*adj.*) see USELESS 1. (*n.*) see *good-for-nothing n.* above.

goodbye /gŏŏdbī/ *int.* & *n.* (*US* **goodby**) ● *int.* expressing good wishes on parting, ending a telephone conversation, etc., or said with reference to a thing got rid of or irrevocably lost. ● *n.* (*pl.* **goodbyes** or *US* **goodbys**) the saying of 'goodbye'; a parting; a farewell. [contr. of *God be with you!* with *good* substituted after *good night* etc.]

■ *int.* farewell, adios, adieu, vale, *au revoir*, *Austral.* & *NZ* hooray, *colloq.* ciao, see you (later), bye, bye-bye, toodle-oo, toodle-pip, so long, *Brit. colloq.* ta-ta, cheers, cheerio. ● *n.* see FAREWELL.

good-humoured /gŏŏdhyōōmərd/ *adj.* genial, cheerful, amiable. □□ **good-humouredly** *adv.*

■ see GOOD-NATURED.

goodly /gŏŏdli/ *adj.* (**goodlier**, **goodliest**) **1** comely, handsome. **2** of imposing size etc. □□ **goodliness** *n.* [OE *gōdlic* (as GOOD, -LY[1])]

■ **1** see COMELY. **2** considerable, sizeable, substantial, ample, great, large, significant.

goodman /gŏŏdmən/ *n.* (*pl.* **-men**) *archaic* esp. *Sc.* the head of a household.

good-natured /gŏŏdnáychərd/ *adj.* kind, patient; easygoing. □□ **good-naturedly** *adv.*

■ kind, kindly, kind-hearted, tender-hearted, charitable,

tolerant, generous, good-humoured, cheerful, good-tempered, friendly, agreeable, genial, gracious, good-hearted, pleasant, mellow, easygoing, considerate, nice, courteous, cordial, warm, warm-hearted, amiable, amicable, cooperative, patient.

goodness /gŏŏdniss/ *n.* & *int.* ● *n.* **1** virtue; excellence, esp. moral. **2** kindness, generosity (*had the goodness to wait*). **3** what is good or beneficial in a thing (*vegetables with all the goodness boiled out*). ● *int.* (as a substitution for 'God') expressing surprise, anger, etc. (*goodness me!*; *goodness knows*; *for goodness' sake!*). [OE *gōdnes* (as GOOD, -NESS)]
■ *n.* **1** see VIRTUE 1. **2** see KINDNESS 1. ● *int.* see INDEED *int.*

goodo /gŏŏdō/ *adj. Austral.* & *NZ* = GOOD *adj.* 10.

good-tempered /gŏŏdtémpərd/ *adj.* having a good temper; not easily annoyed. □□ **good-temperedly** *adv.*

goodwife /gŏŏdwīf/ *n.* (*pl.* **-wives**) *archaic* esp. *Sc.* the mistress of a household.

goodwill /gŏŏdwíl/ *n.* **1** kindly feeling. **2** the established reputation of a business etc. as enhancing its value. **3** cheerful consent or acquiescence; readiness, zeal.
■ **1** see AFFECTION 1.

goody[1] /gŏŏddi/ *n.* & *int.* ● *n.* (also **goodie**) (*pl.* **-ies**) **1** *colloq.* a good or favoured person, esp. a hero in a story, film, etc. **2** (usu. in *pl.*) something good or attractive, esp. to eat. **3** = GOODY-GOODY *n.* ● *int.* expressing childish delight.

goody[2] /gŏŏddi/ *n.* (*pl.* **goodies**) *archaic* (often as a title prefixed to a surname) an elderly woman of humble station (*Goody Blake*). [for GOODWIFE: cf. HUSSY]

goody-goody /gŏŏddigŏŏddi/ *n.* & *adj. colloq.* ● *n.* a smug or obtrusively virtuous person. ● *adj.* obtrusively or smugly virtuous.
■ *n.* see PRIG, PHARISEE. ● *adj.* smug, sanctimonious, self-righteous, priggish, prim, hypocritical, *colloq.* holier-than-thou.

gooey /gōō-i/ *adj.* (**gooier, gooiest**) *sl.* **1** viscous, sticky. **2** sickly, sentimental. □□ **gooeyness** *n.* (also **gooiness**). [GOO + -Y[2]]
■ **1** viscous, gluey, sticky, tacky, glutinous, mucilaginous, gummy. **2** sickly, sentimental, sweet, sugary, saccharine, cloying, syrupy, sloppy, mushy, *colloq.* slushy; mawkish, maudlin.

goof /gōōf/ *n.* & *v. sl.* ● *n.* **1** a foolish or stupid person. **2** a mistake. ● *v.* **1** *tr.* bungle, mess up. **2** *intr.* blunder, make a mistake. **3** *intr.* (often foll. by *off*) idle. **4** *tr.* (as **goofed** *adj.*) stupefied with drugs. [var. of dial. *goff* f. F *goffe* f. It. *goffo* f. med.L *gufus* coarse]
■ *n.* **1** see SILLY *n.* **2** see MISTAKE *n.* ● *v.* **1, 2** see FOUL *v.* 6. **3** see IDLE *v.* 2.

goofy /gōōfi/ *adj.* (**goofier, goofiest**) *sl.* **1** stupid, silly, daft. **2** having protruding or crooked front teeth. □□ **goofily** *adv.* **goofiness** *n.*
■ **1** see CRAZY 1.

goog /gŏŏg/ *n. Austral. sl.* an egg. □ **full as a goog** very drunk. [20th c.: orig. unkn.]

googly /gōōgli/ *n.* (*pl.* **-ies**) *Cricket* an off-break ball bowled with apparent leg-break action. [20th c.: orig. unkn.]

googol /gōōgol/ *n.* ten raised to the hundredth power (10^{100}). ¶ Not in formal use. [arbitrary formation]

gook /gōōk, gŏŏk/ *n. US sl. offens.* a foreigner, esp. a coloured person from E. Asia. [20th c.: orig. unkn.]

goolie /gōōli/ *n.* (also **gooly**) (*pl.* **-ies**) **1** (usu. in *pl.*) *sl.* a testicle. **2** *Austral. sl.* a stone or pebble. [app. of Ind. orig.; cf. Hind. *golī* bullet, ball, pill]

goon /gōōn/ *n. sl.* **1** a stupid or playful person. **2** esp. *US* a person hired by racketeers etc. to terrorize political or industrial opponents. [perh. f. dial. *gooney* booby: infl. by the subhuman cartoon character 'Alice the *Goon*']
■ **1** see FOOL[1] *n.* 1. **2** see THUG.

goop /gōōp/ *n. sl.* a stupid or fatuous person. [20th c.: cf. GOOF]

goopy /gōōpi/ *adj. sl.* (**goopier, goopiest**) stupid, fatuous. □□ **goopiness** *n.*

goosander /gōōsándər/ *n.* a large diving duck, *Mergus merganser*, with a narrow serrated bill. [prob. f. GOOSE + *-ander* in *bergander* sheldrake]

goose /gōōss/ *n.* & *v.* ● *n.* (*pl.* **geese** /geess/) **1 a** any of various large water-birds of the family Anatidae, with short legs, webbed feet, and a broad bill. **b** the female of this (opp. GANDER). **c** the flesh of a goose as food. **2** *colloq.* a simpleton. **3** (*pl.* **gooses**) a tailor's smoothing-iron, having a handle like a goose's neck. ● *v.tr. sl.* poke (a person) in the bottom. □ **goose bumps** *US* = *goose-flesh*. **goose-egg** *US* a zero score in a game. **goose-flesh** (or **-pimples** or **-skin**) a bristling state of the skin produced by cold or fright. **goose-step** a military marching step in which the knees are kept stiff. [OE *gōs* f. Gmc]
■ *n.* **2** see FOOL[1] *n.* 1.

gooseberry /gŏŏzbəri/ *n.* (*pl.* **-ies**) **1** a round edible yellowish-green berry with a thin usu. translucent skin enclosing seeds in a juicy flesh. **2** the thorny shrub, *Ribes grossularia*, bearing this fruit. □ **play gooseberry** *Brit. colloq.* be an unwanted extra (usu. third) person. [perh. f. GOOSE + BERRY]

goosefoot /gōōsfŏŏt/ *n.* (*pl.* **-foots**) any plant of the genus *Chenopodium*, having leaves shaped like the foot of a goose.

goosegog /gŏŏzgog/ *n. Brit. colloq.* a gooseberry. [joc. corrupt.]

goosegrass /gōōsgraass/ *n.* cleavers.

GOP *abbr. US* Grand Old Party (the Republican Party).

gopher[1] /gṓfər/ *n.* **1** (in full **pocket gopher**) any burrowing rodent of the family Geomyidae, native to N. America, having external cheek pouches and sharp front teeth. **2** a N. American ground squirrel. **3** a tortoise, *Gopherus polyphemus*, native to the southern US, that excavates tunnels as shelter from the sun. □ **gopher snake** a cribo. [18th c.: orig. uncert.]

gopher[2] /gṓfər/ *n.* **1** *Bibl.* a tree from the wood of which Noah's ark was made. **2** (in full **gopher-wood**) a tree, *Cladrastis lutea*, yielding yellowish timber. [Heb. *gōper*]

goral /górəl/ *n.* a goat-antelope, *Nemorhaedus goral*, native to mountainous regions of N. India, having short horns curving to the rear. [native name]

gorblimey /gorblími/ *int.* & *n. Brit. sl.* ● *int.* an expression of surprise, indignation, etc. ● *n.* (*pl.* **-eys**) a soft service cap. [corrupt. of *God blind me*]

gorcock /górkok/ *n. Sc.* & *N.Engl.* the male of the red grouse. [*gor-* (of unkn. orig.) + COCK[1]]

Gordian knot /górdiən/ *n.* **1** an intricate knot. **2** a difficult problem or task. □ **cut the Gordian knot** solve a problem by force or by evasion. [*Gordius*, king of Phrygia, who tied an intricate knot that remained tied until cut by Alexander the Great]

gordo / górdō/ *n. Austral.* a popular variety of grape. [Sp. *gordo blanco* fat white]

Gordon setter /górd'n/ *n.* **1** a setter of a black and tan breed, used as a gun dog. **2** this breed. [4th Duke of *Gordon*, d. 1827, promoter of the breed]

gore[1] /gor/ *n.* **1** blood shed and clotted. **2** slaughter, carnage. [OE *gor* dung, dirt]
■ **2** carnage, butchery, slaughter, bloodshed, killing, murder, violence, *joc.* blood-letting.

gore[2] /gor/ *v.tr.* pierce with a horn, tusk, etc. [ME: orig. unkn.]
■ pierce, stab, poke, horn, penetrate, puncture, spear, gouge, spit, stick, impale.

gore[3] /gor/ *n.* & *v.* ● *n.* **1** a wedge-shaped piece in a garment. **2** a triangular or tapering piece in an umbrella etc. ● *v.tr.* shape with a gore. [OE *gāra* triangular piece of land, rel. to OE *gār* spear, a spearhead being triangular]

gorge /gorj/ *n.* & *v.* ● *n.* **1** a narrow opening between hills or a rocky ravine, often with a stream running through it. **2** an act of gorging; a feast. **3** the contents of the stomach; what has been swallowed. **4** the neck of a bastion or other outwork; the rear entrance to a work. **5** *US* a mass of ice etc. blocking a narrow passage. ● *v.* **1** *intr.* feed greedily. **2** *tr.* **a** (often *refl.*) satiate, glut. **b** swallow, devour greedily. □ **cast the gorge at** reject with loathing. **one's gorge rises at** one is sickened by. □□ **gorger** *n.* [ME f. OF *gorge* throat ult. f. L *gurges* whirlpool]

■ *n.* **1** ravine, canyon, defile, pass, chasm, fissure, crevasse, gully, gap, *Brit.* gill, *US* notch, gulch. **2** see FEAST *n.* 1. **3** vomit, *Brit. colloq.* sick, *sl.* puke, *Austral. sl.* chunder, *US sl.* upchuck. ● *v.* **1** feed, gormandize, gluttonize, overindulge, gobble, eat one's fill, guzzle, *sl.* nosh; see also OVEREAT. **2 a** satiate, glut, fill, stuff, cram, overfeed, surfeit, pall; (*gorge oneself*) gluttonize, *colloq.* make a hog of oneself; see also OVEREAT. **b** swallow, devour, gulp (down), gobble (down *or* up), bolt (down), wolf (down), gormandize.

gorgeous /górjəss/ *adj.* **1** richly coloured, sumptuous, magnificent. **2** *colloq.* very pleasant, splendid (*gorgeous weather*). **3** *colloq.* strikingly beautiful. □□ **gorgeously** *adv.* **gorgeousness** *n.* [earlier *gorgayse*, *-yas* f. OF *gorgias* fine, elegant, of unkn. orig.]

■ **1** rich, sumptuous, dazzling, radiant, brilliant, resplendent, splendid, magnificent, glorious, exquisite, beautiful, showy, colourful, *colloq. or joc.* splendiferous, *literary* refulgent. **2** splendid, wonderful, marvellous, glorious, spectacular, superb, excellent, *colloq.* great, terrific, fantastic, smashing, super, *US colloq.* swell. **3** see BEAUTIFUL 1.

gorget /górgit/ *n.* **1** *hist.* **a** a piece of armour for the throat. **b** a woman's wimple. **2** a patch of colour on the throat of a bird, insect, etc. [OF *gorgete* (as GORGE)]

Gorgio /górjiō/ *n.* (*pl.* **-os**) the Gypsy name for a non-Gypsy. [Romany]

gorgon /górgən/ *n.* **1** (in Greek mythology) each of three snake-haired sisters (esp. Medusa) with the power to turn anyone who looked at them to stone. **2** a frightening or repulsive person, esp. a woman. □□ **gorgonian** /gorgṓniən/ *adj.* [L *Gorgo -onis* f. Gk *Gorgō* f. *gorgos* terrible]

■ **2** see HAG[1] 2.

gorgonian /gorgṓniən/ *n.* & *adj.* ● *n.* a usu. brightly coloured horny coral of the order Gorgonacea, having a treelike skeleton bearing polyps, e.g. a sea fan. ● *adj.* of or relating to the Gorgonacea. [mod.L (as GORGON), with ref. to its petrifaction]

gorgonize /górgənīz/ *v.tr.* (also **-ise**) **1** stare at like a gorgon. **2** paralyse with terror etc.

Gorgonzola /górgənzṓlə/ *n.* a type of rich cheese with bluish-green veins. [*Gorgonzola* in Italy]

gorilla /gərillə/ *n.* the largest anthropoid ape, *Gorilla gorilla*, native to Central Africa, having a large head, short neck, and prominent mouth. [adopted as the specific name in 1847 f. Gk *Gorillai* an African tribe noted for hairiness]

gormandize /górməndīz/ *v.* & *n.* (also **-ise**) ● *v.* **1** *intr.* & *tr.* eat or devour voraciously. **2** *intr.* indulge in good eating. ● *n.* = GOURMANDISE. □□ **gormandizer** *n.* [as GOURMANDISE]

■ *v.* **1** see DEVOUR 1. **2** see FEAST *v.* 1.

gormless /górmliss/ *adj.* esp. *Brit. colloq.* foolish, lacking sense. □□ **gormlessly** *adv.* **gormlessness** *n.* [orig. *gaumless* f. dial. *gaum* understanding]

■ see DAFT 1.

gorse /gorss/ *n.* any spiny yellow-flowered shrub of the genus *Ulex*, esp. growing on European wastelands. Also called FURZE. □□ **gorsy** *adj.* [OE *gors(t)* rel. to OHG *gersta*, L *hordeum*, barley]

Gorsedd /górseth/ *n.* a meeting of Welsh etc. bards and druids (esp. as a daily preliminary to the eisteddfod). [Welsh, lit. 'throne']

gory /góri/ *adj.* (**gorier**, **goriest**) **1** involving bloodshed; bloodthirsty (*a gory film*). **2** covered in gore. □□ **gorily** *adv.* **goriness** *n.*

■ **1** bloodthirsty, bloody, sanguinary; gruesome, grisly, horrific, blood-curdling. **2** bloody, blood-soaked, bloodstained.

gosh /gosh/ *int.* expressing surprise. [euphem. for GOD]

goshawk /góss-hawk/ *n.* a large short-winged hawk, *Accipiter gentilis*. [OE *gōs-hafoc* (as GOOSE, HAWK[1])]

gosling /gózling/ *n.* a young goose. [ME, orig. *gesling* f. ON *gǽslingr*]

gospel /gósp'l/ *n.* **1** the teaching or revelation of Christ. **2** (**Gospel**) **a** the record of Christ's life and teaching in the first four books of the New Testament. **b** each of these books. **c** a portion from one of them read at a service. **3** a thing regarded as absolutely true (*take my word as gospel*). **4** a principle one acts on or advocates. **5** (in full **gospel music**) Black American evangelical religious singing. □ **Gospel side** the north side of the altar, at which the Gospel is read. **gospel truth** something as true as the Gospel. [OE *gōdspel* (as GOOD, *spel* news, SPELL[1]), rendering eccl.L *bona annuntiatio*, *bonus nuntius* = *evangelium* EVANGEL: assoc. with GOD]

■ **3** truth, fact, certainty, reality, actuality. **4** see PRINCIPLE 1.

gospeller /góspələr/ *n.* the reader of the Gospel in a Communion service. □ **hot gospeller** a zealous puritan; a rabid propagandist.

gossamer /góssəmər/ *n.* & *adj.* ● *n.* **1** a filmy substance of small spiders' webs. **2** delicate filmy material. **3** a thread of gossamer. ● *adj.* light and flimsy as gossamer. □□ **gossamered** *adj.* **gossamery** *adj.* [ME *gos(e)somer(e)*, app. f. GOOSE + SUMMER[1] (*goose summer* = St Martin's summer, i.e. early November when geese were eaten, gossamer being common then)]

■ *adj.* see FLIMSY 4.

gossip /góssip/ *n.* & *v.* ● *n.* **1 a** easy or unconstrained talk or writing esp. about persons or social incidents. **b** idle talk; groundless rumour. **2** an informal chat, esp. about persons or social incidents. **3** a person who indulges in gossip. ● *v.intr.* (**gossiped**, **gossiping**) talk or write gossip. □ **gossip column** a section of a newspaper devoted to gossip about well-known people. **gossip columnist** a regular writer of gossip columns. **gossip-monger** a perpetrator of gossip. □□ **gossiper** *n.* **gossipy** *adj.* [earlier sense 'godparent': f. OE *godsibb* person related to one in GOD: see SIB]

■ *n.* **1** talk, small talk, tittle-tattle, prattle, *colloq.* chit-chat; see also CHATTER *n.* **2** chat, conversation, talk, *colloq.* natter, *sl.* chin-wag. **3** rumour-monger, scandalmonger, gossip-monger, newsmonger, gossiper, busybody, blabber(mouth), blatherskite, tell-tale, talebearer, flibbertigibbet, *US* tattle-tale, *archaic* quidnunc, *colloq.* big-mouth, *esp. Brit. colloq.* Nosy Parker. ● *v.* tattle, whisper, blather, blab, tittle-tattle, tell tales, *colloq.* name names; see also *spill the beans* (SPILL[1]), BABBLE *v.* 1a, b. □ **gossip-monger** see GOSSIP *n.* 3. □□ **gossipy** see INDISCREET 1.

gossoon /gosṓōn/ *n.* *Ir.* a lad. [earlier *garsoon* f. F *garçon* boy]

got *past* and *past part.* of GET.

Goth /goth/ *n.* **1** a member of a Germanic tribe that invaded the Roman Empire in the 3rd–5th c. **2** an uncivilized or ignorant person. [LL *Gothi* (pl.) f. Gk *Go(t)thoi* f. Goth.]

goth /goth / *n.* **1** a style of rock music with an intense or droning blend of guitars, bass, and drums, often with apocalyptic or mystical lyrics. **2** a performer or devotee of this music, often dressing in black clothing and wearing black make-up.

Gothic /góthik/ *adj.* & *n.* ● *adj.* **1** of the Goths or their language. **2** in the style of architecture prevalent in W. Europe in the 12th–16th c., characterized by pointed arches. **3** (of a novel etc.) in a style popular in the 18th–19th c., with supernatural or horrifying events. **4** barbarous, uncouth. **5** *Printing* (of type) old-fashioned German, black letter, or sanserif. ● *n.* **1** the Gothic language. **2** Gothic architecture. **3** *Printing* Gothic type. □□ **Gothically** *adv.* **Gothicism** /-thisiz'm/ *n.* **Gothicize** /-thisīz/ *v.tr.* & *intr.* (also **-ise**). [F *gothique* or LL *gothicus* f. *Gothi*: see GOTH]

gotta /góttə/ *colloq.* have got a; have got to (*I gotta pain; we gotta go*). [corrupt.]

gotten *US past part.* of GET.

Götterdämmerung /gṓttərdémmərŏŏng/ *n.* **1** the twilight (i.e. downfall) of the gods. **2** the complete downfall of a regime etc. [G, esp. as the title of an opera by Wagner]

gouache /goo-aash, gwaash/ *n.* **1** a method of painting in opaque pigments ground in water and thickened with a gluelike substance. **2** these pigments. **3** a picture painted in this way. [F f. It. *guazzo*]

Gouda /gówdə/ *n.* a flat round usu. Dutch cheese with a yellow rind. [*Gouda* in Holland, where orig. made]

gouge /gowj/ *n.* & *v.* • *n.* **1 a** a chisel with a concave blade, used in carpentry, sculpture, and surgery. **b** an indentation or groove made with or as with this. **2** *US colloq.* a swindle. • *v.* **1** *tr.* cut with or as with a gouge. **2** *tr.* **a** (foll. by *out*) force out (esp. an eye with the thumb) with or as with a gouge. **b** force out the eye of (a person). **3** *tr. US colloq.* swindle; extort money from. **4** *intr. Austral.* dig for opal. □□ **gouger** *n.* [F f. LL *gubia*, perh. of Celt. orig.]

▪ *n.* **1 b** groove, furrow, scratch, gash, score, channel, flute, cut; indentation, hollow. **2** see SWINDLE *n.* 1, 3. • *v.* **1** chisel, gash, groove, incise, dig, scratch; scoop out, hollow out. **3** extort, extract, defraud, blackmail, cheat, swindle, squeeze, milk, bleed, fleece, *sl.* skin, bilk.

goulash /gōōlash/ *n.* **1** a highly-seasoned Hungarian dish of meat and vegetables, usu. flavoured with paprika. **2** (in contract bridge) a re-deal, several cards at a time, of the four hands (unshuffled, but with each hand arranged in suits and order of value) when no player has bid. [Magyar *gulyás-hús* f. *gulyás* herdsman + *hús* meat]

gourami /gŏŏrəmi, -raámi/ *n.* **1 a** a large freshwater fish, *Osphronemus goramy*, native to SE Asia, used as food. **b** any small fish of the family Osphronemidae, usu. kept in aquariums. **2** any small brightly coloured freshwater fish of the family Belontiidae, usu. kept in aquariums. Also called LABYRINTH FISH. [Malay *gurāmi*]

gourd /goord/ *n.* **1 a** any of various fleshy usu. large fruits with a hard skin, often used as containers, ornaments, etc. **b** any of various climbing or trailing plants of the family Cucurbitaceae bearing this fruit. Also called CUCURBIT. **2** the hollow hard skin of the gourd-fruit, dried and used as a drinking-vessel, water container, etc. □□ **gourdful** *n.* (*pl.* **-fuls**). [ME f. AF *gurde*, OF *gourde* ult. f. L *cucurbita*]

gourmand /gŏŏrmənd/ *n.* & *adj.* • *n.* **1** a glutton. **2** *disp.* a gourmet. • *adj.* gluttonous; fond of eating, esp. to excess. □□ **gourmandism** *n.* [ME f. OF, of unkn. orig.]

▪ *n.* **1** see GLUTTON 1. **2** see GOURMET.

gourmandise /gŏŏrmondéez/ *n.* the habits of a gourmand; gluttony. [F (as GOURMAND)]

gourmet /góormay/ *n.* a connoisseur of good or delicate food. [F, = wine-taster: sense infl. by GOURMAND]

▪ epicure, gastronome, *bon vivant*, *bon viveur*, *colloq.* foodie, *disp.* gourmand.

gout /gowt/ *n.* **1** a disease with inflammation of the smaller joints, esp. the toe, as a result of excess uric acid salts in the blood. **2** *archaic* **a** a drop, esp. of blood. **b** a splash or spot. □□ **gouty** *adj.* **goutily** *adv.* **goutiness** *n.* [ME f. OF *goute* f. L *gutta* drop, with ref. to the medieval theory of the flowing down of humours]

Gov. *abbr.* **1** Government. **2** Governor.

gov. *abbr.* governor.

govern /gúvvərn/ *v.* **1 a** *tr.* rule or control (a State, subject, etc.) with authority; conduct the policy and affairs of (an organization etc.). **b** *intr.* be in government. **2 a** *tr.* influence or determine (a person or a course of action). **b** *intr.* be the predominating influence. **3** *tr.* be a standard or principle for; constitute a law for; serve to decide (a case). **4** *tr.* check or control (esp. passions). **5** *tr. Gram.* (esp. of a verb or preposition) have (a noun or pronoun or its case) depending on it. **6** *tr.* be in military command of (a fort, town). □ **governing body** the managers of an institution. □□ **governable** *adj.* **governability** /-nəbílliti/ *n.* **governableness** *n.* [ME f. OF *governer* f. L *gubernare* steer, rule f. Gk *kubernaō*]

▪ **1 a** rule, control, direct, manage, run, steer, lead, captain, pilot, command, head (up), look after, be in charge of, hold sway over, reign over. **b** wield power, exercise power, hold sway, be in power, have *or* hold the whip hand, be in charge, *colloq.* run the show, be in the saddle *or* driver's seat; reign, sit on the throne, wield the sceptre, wear the crown. **2 a** see INFLUENCE *v.*, DETERMINE 3. **b** predominate, dominate, hold sway. **3** see DETERMINE 3. **4** control, check, bridle, curb, master, subdue, restrain, contain, hold, suppress, repress.

governance /gúvvərnənss/ *n.* **1** the act or manner of governing. **2** the office or function of governing. **3** sway, control. [ME f. OF (as GOVERN)]

▪ **1, 2** see MANAGEMENT 1.

governess /gúvvərniss/ *n.* a woman employed to teach children in a private household. [earlier *governeress* f. OF *governeresse* (as GOVERNOR)]

▪ see TEACHER.

governessy /gúvvərnisi/ *adj.* characteristic of a governess; prim.

government /gúvvərnmənt/ *n.* **1** the act or manner of governing. **2** the system by which a State or community is governed. **3 a** a body of persons governing a State. **b** (usu. **Government**) a particular ministry in office. **4** the State as an agent. **5** *Gram.* the relation between a governed and a governing word. □ **Government House** the official residence of a governor. **government issue** *US* (of equipment) provided by the government. **government paper** (or **securities**) bonds etc. issued by the government. **government surplus** unused equipment sold by the government. □□ **governmental** /-mént'l/ *adj.* **governmentally** /-méntəli/ *adv.* [ME f. OF *governement* (as GOVERN)]

▪ **1–3** rule, governance, command, regulation, control, management, administration, direction, supervision, superintendence, domination, guidance, charge, operation, running, leadership, directorate, governorate, ministry; see also REGIME 1.

governor /gúvvərnər/ *n.* **1** a person who governs; a ruler. **2 a** an official governing a province, town, etc. **b** a representative of the Crown in a colony. **3** the executive head of each State of the US. **4** an officer commanding a fortress or garrison. **5** the head or a member of a governing body of an institution. **6** the official in charge of a prison. **7 a** *sl.* one's employer. **b** *sl.* one's father. **c** *colloq.* (as a form of address) sir. **8** *Mech.* an automatic regulator controlling the speed of an engine etc. □ **Governor-General** the representative of the Crown in a Commonwealth country that regards the Queen as Head of State. □□ **governorate** /-rət/ *n.* **governorship** *n.* [ME f. AF *gouvernour*, OF *governëo(u)r* f. L *gubernator -oris* (as GOVERN)]

▪ **1–4** see LEADER 1. **5** see HEAD *n.* 6a. **6** see JAILER. **7 a** see *employer* (EMPLOY). **b** see FATHER *n.* 1a.

Govt. *abbr.* Government.

gowan /gówən/ *n. Sc.* **1** a daisy. **2** any white or yellow field-flower. [prob. var. of dial. *gollan* ranunculus etc., and rel. to *gold* in *marigold*]

gowk /gowk/ *n. dial.* **1** a cuckoo. **2** an awkward or halfwitted person; a fool. [ME f. ON *gaukr* f. Gmc]

gown /gown/ *n.* & *v.* • *n.* **1** a loose flowing garment, esp. a long dress worn by a woman. **2** the official robe of an alderman, judge, cleric, member of a university, etc. **3** a surgeon's overall. **4** the members of a university as distinct from the permanent residents of the university town (cf. TOWN). • *v.tr.* (usu. as **gowned** *adj.*) attire in a gown. [ME f. OF *goune*, *gon(n)e* f. LL *gunna* fur garment: cf. med. Gk *gouna* fur]

goy /goy/ *n.* (*pl.* **goyim** /góyim/ or **goys**) *sl. derog.* a Jewish name for a non-Jew. □□ **goyish** *adj.* (also **goyisch**). [Heb. *gōy* people, nation]

GP *abbr.* **1** general practitioner. **2** Grand Prix.

Gp. Capt. *abbr.* (in the RAF) Group Captain.

GPI *abbr.* general paralysis of the insane.

GPO *abbr.* **1** General Post Office. **2** *US* Government Printing Office.

GR *abbr.* King George. [L *Georgius Rex*]

gr *abbr.* (also **gr.**) **1** gram(s). **2** grains. **3** gross. **4** grey.

Graafian follicle /graáfiən/ *n.* a follicle in the mammalian ovary in which an ovum develops prior to ovulation. [R. de *Graaf*, Du. anatomist d. 1673]

grab /grab/ *v.* & *n.* ● *v.* (**grabbed, grabbing**) **1** *tr.* **a** seize suddenly. **b** capture, arrest. **2** *tr.* take greedily or unfairly. **3** *tr. sl.* attract the attention of, impress. **4** *intr.* (foll. by *at*) make a sudden snatch at. **5** *intr.* (of the brakes of a motor vehicle) act harshly or jerkily. ● *n.* **1** a sudden clutch or attempt to seize. **2** a mechanical device for clutching. **3** the practice of grabbing; rapacious proceedings esp. in politics and commerce. **4** a children's card-game in which certain cards may be snatched from the table. □ **grab-bag** *US* a lucky dip. **grab handle** (or **rail** etc.) a handle or rail etc. to steady passengers in a moving vehicle. **up for grabs** *sl.* easily obtainable; inviting capture. □□ **grabber** *n.* [MLG, MDu. *grabben*: cf. GRIP, GRIPE, GROPE]

■ *v.* **1 a** snatch, lay *or* catch hold of, fasten upon, grasp, seize, catch, grip, clutch, *US* snag. **b** seize, capture, catch, arrest, collar, apprehend, *sl.* nab, pinch. **2** appropriate, expropriate, arrogate, seize, commandeer, get one's hands *or* fingers on; usurp. **3** see IMPRESS[1] *v.* 1a. **4** (*grab at*) snatch at, make a grab for, *colloq.* go for. ● *n.* **1** snatch, clutch; grasp, grip. **3** money-grabbing, predaciousness; see also AVARICE. □ **up for grabs** see *on sale* (SALE).

grabble /grább'l/ *v.intr.* **1** grope about, feel for something. **2** (often foll. by *for*) sprawl on all fours, scramble (for something). [Du. & LG *grabbeln* scramble for a thing (as GRAB)]

■ **1** grope *or* feel about, *Austral.* & *NZ colloq.* fossick.

grabby /grábbi/ *adj. colloq.* tending to grab; greedy, grasping.

graben /graáb'n/ *n.* (*pl.* same or **grabens**) *Geol.* a depression of the earth's surface between faults. [G, orig. = ditch]

grace /grayss/ *n.* & *v.* ● *n.* **1** attractiveness, esp. in elegance of proportion or manner or movement; gracefulness. **2** courteous good will (*had the grace to apologize*). **3** an attractive feature; an accomplishment (*social graces*). **4 a** (in Christian belief) the unmerited favour of God; a divine saving and strengthening influence. **b** the state of receiving this. **c** a divinely given talent. **5** goodwill, favour (*fall from grace*). **6** delay granted as a favour (*a year's grace*). **7** a short thanksgiving before or after a meal. **8** (**Grace**) (in Greek mythology) each of three beautiful sister goddesses, bestowers of beauty and charm. **9** (**Grace**) (prec. by *His, Her, Your*) forms of description or address for a duke, duchess, or archbishop. ● *v.tr.* **1** lend or add grace to, enhance or embellish. **2** (often foll. by *with*) confer honour or dignity on (*graced us with his presence*). □ **days of grace** the time allowed by law for payment of a sum due. **grace and favour house** etc. *Brit.* a house etc. occupied by permission of a sovereign etc. **grace-note** *Mus.* an extra note as an embellishment not essential to the harmony or melody. **in a person's good** (or **bad**) **graces** regarded by a person with favour (or disfavour). **with good** (or **bad**) **grace** as if willingly (or reluctantly). [ME f. OF f. L *gratia* f. *gratus* pleasing: cf. GRATEFUL]

■ *n.* **1** elegance, gracefulness, attractiveness, finesse, refinement, polish, poise, suppleness, ease; tastefulness, cultivation, suavity, suaveness, culture, *savoir faire*, discrimination, breeding, propriety, decorum, etiquette. **2** good will, courtesy, (good) taste, discernment, (good) manners, politeness, consideration, decency, tact, mannerliness; kindness, kindliness, benevolence, generosity, goodness, graciousness. **3** accomplishment, skill, talent, gift, ability. **4 a** goodwill, goodness, indulgence, forgiveness, favour, mercy, mercifulness, leniency, compassion, clemency, charity. **7** thanksgiving, prayer; blessing, benediction. ● *v.* **1** enhance, adorn, embellish, set off, decorate, ornament, beautify. **2** dignify, enhance, distinguish, enrich, honour, favour. □ **with good grace** see *willingly* (WILLING), KINDLY[1] 1. **with bad grace** see *begrudgingly* (BEGRUDGE).

graceful /gráysfŏŏl/ *adj.* having or showing grace or elegance. □□ **gracefully** *adv.* **gracefulness** *n.*

■ fluid, flowing, supple, lissom, lithe, smooth, nimble, agile; elegant, courtly, urbane, polished, refined, suave.

graceless /gráysliss/ *adj.* lacking grace or elegance or charm. □□ **gracelessly** *adv.* **gracelessness** *n.*

■ see UNGRACEFUL.

gracile /grássīl, -sil/ *adj.* slender; gracefully slender. [L *gracilis* slender]

gracility /grəsílliti/ *n.* **1** slenderness. **2** (of literary style) unornamented simplicity.

gracious /gráyshəss/ *adj.* & *int.* ● *adj.* **1** kind; indulgent and beneficent to inferiors. **2** (of God) merciful, benign. **3** *poet.* kindly, courteous. **4** a polite epithet used of royal persons or their acts (*the gracious speech from the throne*). ● *int.* expressing surprise. □ **gracious living** an elegant way of life. □□ **graciosity** /graysiόssiti/ *n.* **graciously** *adv.* **graciousness** *n.* [ME f. OF f. L *gratiosus* (as GRACE)]

■ *adj.* **1, 3** kind, kindly, benevolent, beneficent, indulgent, kind-hearted, warm-hearted, cordial, warm, friendly, sociable, good-natured, amiable, affable, benign, accommodating, obliging, agreeable, considerate; courteous, polite, well-mannered, tactful, mannerly. **2** see MERCIFUL. **4** see ROYAL *adj.* 5. ● *int.* (upon) my word, by Jove, (well) I'm blessed, well I (do) declare, my (sainted) aunt, (my) goodness, (good) Lord, good heavens, well I never, mercy, *Brit.* I say, *colloq.* my stars, well I'm *or* I'll be damned, *Brit. sl.* crikey, lumme, (cor) blimey, gorblimey; see also GOD *int.*

grackle /grákk'l/ *n.* **1** any of various orioles, esp. of the genus *Quiscalus*, native to America, the males of which are shiny black with a blue-green sheen. Also called BLACKBIRD. **2** any of various minas, esp. of the genus *Gracula*, native to Asia. [mod.L *Gracula* f. L *graculus* jackdaw]

grad /grad/ *n. colloq.* = GRADUATE *n.* 1. [abbr.]

gradate /grədáyt/ *v.* **1** *v.intr.* & *tr.* pass or cause to pass by gradations from one shade to another. **2** *tr.* arrange in steps or grades of size etc. [back-form. f. GRADATION]

■ **1** see BLEND *v.* 4a.

gradation /grədáysh'n/ *n.* (usu. in *pl.*) **1** a stage of transition or advance. **2 a** a certain degree in rank, intensity, merit, divergence, etc. **b** such a degree; an arrangement in such degrees. **3** (of paint etc.) the gradual passing from one shade, tone, etc., to another. **4** *Philol.* ablaut. □□ **gradational** *adj.* **gradationally** *adv.* [L *gradatio* f. *gradus* step]

■ **1, 2** see GRADE *n.* 1a.

grade /grayd/ *n.* & *v.* ● *n.* **1 a** a certain degree in rank, merit, proficiency, quality, etc. **b** a class of persons or things of the same grade. **2 a** a mark indicating the quality of a student's work. **b** an examination, esp. in music. **3** *US* a class in school, concerned with a particular year's work and usu. numbered from the first upwards. **4 a** a gradient or slope. **b** the rate of ascent or descent. **5 a** a variety of cattle produced by crossing native stock with a superior breed. **b** a group of animals at a similar level of development. **6** *Philol.* a relative position in a series of forms involving ablaut. ● *v.* **1** *tr.* arrange in or allocate to grades; class, sort. **2** *intr.* (foll. by *up, down, off, into*, etc.) pass gradually between grades, or into a grade. **3** *tr.* give a grade to (a student). **4** *tr.* blend so as to affect the grade of colour with tints passing into each other. **5** *tr.* reduce (a road etc.) to easy gradients. **6** *tr.* (often foll. by *up*) cross (livestock) with a better breed. □ **at grade** *US* on the same level. **grade crossing** *US* = *level crossing*. **grade school** *US* elementary school. **make the grade** *colloq.* succeed; reach the desired standard. [F *grade* or L *gradus* step]

■ *n.* **1 a** degree, position, stage, station, gradation, echelon, class, level, category; rung, rank, status, standing. **b** see CATEGORY. **2 a** rating, mark, score, grading; result. **b** see EXAMINATION 3. **3** class, form, year. **4 a** slope, rise, gradient, acclivity, declivity, incline, decline, ascent, descent. ● *v.* **1** classify, class, order, organize, rank, sort, size, group, categorize. **3** mark, rate, evaluate, assess, judge; rank. □ **make the grade** measure up, succeed, qualify, pass muster, *colloq.* make it; see also PASS[1] *v.* 8a.

grader /gráydər/ *n.* **1** a person or thing that grades. **2** a wheeled machine for levelling the ground, esp. in road-making. **3** (in *comb.*) *US* a pupil of a specified grade in a school.

gradient /gráydiənt/ *n.* **1 a** a stretch of road, railway, etc., that slopes from the horizontal. **b** the amount of such a slope. **2** the rate of rise or fall of temperature, pressure, etc., in passing from one region to another. [prob. formed on GRADE after *salient*]
■ **1** see SLOPE *n.* 1–3.

gradine /gráydeen/ *n.* (also **gradin** /-din/) **1** each of a series of low steps or a tier of seats. **2** a ledge at the back of an altar. [It. *gradino* dimin. of *grado* GRADE]

gradual /grádyooəl/ *adj.* & *n.* ● *adj.* **1** taking place or progressing slowly or by degrees. **2** not rapid or steep or abrupt. ● *n. Eccl.* **1** a response sung or recited between the Epistle and Gospel in the Mass. **2** a book of music for the sung Mass service. □□ **gradually** *adv.* **gradualness** *n.* [med.L *gradualis*, *-ale* f. L *gradus* step, the noun referring to the altar-steps on which the response is sung]
■ *adj.* **1** piecemeal, inchmeal, steady; see also SLOW *adj.* 1. **2** easy, gentle, even, moderate, regular, steady. □□ **gradually** slowly, evenly, piecemeal, inchmeal, step by step, bit by bit, little by little, by degrees; cautiously, carefully.

gradualism /grádyooəliz'm/ *n.* a policy of gradual reform rather than sudden change or revolution. □□ **gradualist** *n.* **gradualistic** /-lístik/ *adj.*

graduand /grádyoo-and/ *n. Brit.* a person about to receive an academic degree. [med.L *graduandus* gerundive of *graduare* GRADUATE]

graduate *n.* & *v.* ● *n.* /grádyooət/ **1** a person who has been awarded an academic degree (also *attrib.*: *graduate student*). **2** *US* a person who has completed a school course. ● *v.* /grádyoo-ayt/ **1 a** *intr.* take an academic degree. **b** *tr. US* admit to an academic degree or a certificate of completion of School Studies. **2** *intr.* **a** (foll. by *from*) be a graduate of a specified university. **b** (foll. by *in*) be a graduate in a specified subject. **3** *tr. US* send out as a graduate from a university etc. **4** *intr.* **a** (foll. by *to*) move up to (a higher grade of activity etc.). **b** (foll. by *as*, *in*) gain specified qualifications. **5** *tr.* mark out in degrees or parts. **6** *tr.* arrange in gradations; apportion (e.g. tax) according to a scale. **7** *intr.* (foll. by *into*, *away*) pass by degrees. □ **graduated pension** (in the UK) a system of pension contributions by employees in proportion to their wages or salary. **graduate school** a department of a university for advanced work by graduates. □□ **graduator** *n.* [med.L *graduari* take a degree f. L *gradus* step]
■ *v.* **4 a** see ADVANCE *v.* 1, 2. **b** qualify, get *or* obtain qualifications, get a degree. **5** see CALIBRATE 1, 2. **6** gradate, scale, apportion; see also GRADE *v.* 1. **7** shade, merge, slip, blend, pass, move.

graduation /grádyoo-áysh'n/ *n.* **1** the act or an instance of graduating or being graduated. **2** a ceremony at which degrees are conferred. **3** each or all of the marks on a vessel or instrument indicating degrees of quantity etc.

Graecism /gréekiz'm, gréessiz'm/ *n.* (also **Grecism**) **1** a Greek idiom, esp. as imitated in another language. **2 a** the Greek spirit, style, mode of expression, etc. **b** the imitation of these. [F *grécisme* or med.L *Graecismus* f. *Graecus* GREEK]

Graecize /gréekīz/ *v.tr.* (also **Grecize**, **-ise**) give a Greek character or form to. [L *Graecizare* (as GRAECISM)]

Graeco- /gréekō/ *comb. form* (also **Greco-**) Greek; Greek and. [L *Graecus* GREEK]

Graeco-Roman /gréekō-rṓmən/ *adj.* **1** of or relating to the Greeks and Romans. **2** *Wrestling* denoting a style attacking only the upper part of the body.

graffito /grəféetō/ *n.* (*pl.* **graffiti** /-tee/) **1** (usu. in *pl.*) a piece of writing or drawing scribbled, scratched, or sprayed on a surface. ¶ Not a mass noun in this sense, and so a plural construction is needed, e.g. *graffiti are* (not *is*) *an art form*. **2** *Art* a form of decoration made by scratches on wet plaster, showing a different-coloured under-surface. [It. f. *graffio* a scratch]

graft[1] /graaft/ *n.* & *v.* ● *n.* **1** *Bot.* **a** a shoot or scion inserted into a slit of stock, from which it receives sap. **b** the place where a graft is inserted. **2** *Surgery* a piece of living tissue, organ, etc., transplanted surgically. **3** *sl.* hard work. ● *v.* **1** *tr.* **a** (often foll. by *into*, *on*, *together*, etc.) insert (a scion) as a graft. **b** insert a graft on (a stock). **2** *intr.* insert a graft. **3** *tr.* *Surgery* transplant (living tissue). **4** *tr.* (foll. by *in*, *on*) insert or fix (a thing) permanently to another. **5** *intr. sl.* work hard. □ **grafting-clay** (or **-wax**) a substance for covering the united parts of a graft and stock. □□ **grafter** *n.* [ME (earlier *graff*) f. OF *grafe*, *grefe* f. L *graphium* f. Gk *graphion* stylus f. *graphō* write]
■ *n.* **1 a** bud, scion; see also SHOOT *n.* **2** implantation, implant, transplant. **3** see LABOUR *n.* 1. ● *v.* **1 a** insert, implant, splice, join. **4** fix, affix, join, secure, fasten; see also ATTACH 1. **5** see SLAVE *v.*, LABOUR *v.* 1, 2.

graft[2] /graaft/ *n.* & *v. colloq.* ● *n.* **1** practices, esp. bribery, used to secure illicit gains in politics or business. **2** such gains. ● *v.intr.* seek or make such gains. □□ **grafter** *n.* [19th c.: orig. unkn.]
■ *n.* **1** corruption, jobbery, bribery, extortion, *esp. US* payola. **2** *esp. US* payola, *colloq.* kickback; see also BLACKMAIL *n.* 1.

Grail /grayl/ *n.* (in full **Holy Grail**) **1** (in medieval legend) the cup or platter used by Christ at the Last Supper, and in which Joseph of Arimathea received Christ's blood at the Cross, esp. as the object of quests by medieval knights. **2** any object of a quest. [ME f. OF *graal* etc. f. med.L *gradalis* dish, of unkn. orig.]

grain /grayn/ *n.* & *v.* ● *n.* **1** a fruit or seed of a cereal. **2 a** (*collect.*) wheat or any allied grass used as food, corn. **b** (*collect.*) their fruit. **c** any particular species of corn. **3 a** a small hard particle of salt, sand, etc. **b** a discrete particle or crystal, usu. small, in a rock or metal. **c** a piece of solid propellant for use in a rocket engine. **4** the smallest unit of weight in the troy system (equivalent to $^1/_{480}$ of an ounce), and in the avoirdupois system (equivalent to $^1/_{437.5}$ of an ounce). **5** the smallest possible quantity (*not a grain of truth in it*). **6 a** roughness of surface. **b** *Photog.* a granular appearance on a photograph or negative. **7** the texture of skin, wood, stone, textile, etc.; the arrangement and size of constituent particles. **8 a** a pattern of lines of fibre in wood or paper. **b** lamination or planes of cleavage in stone, coal, etc. **9** nature, temper, tendency. **10 a** *hist.* kermes or cochineal, or dye made from either of these. **b** *poet.* dye; colour. ● *v.* **1** *tr.* paint in imitation of the grain of wood or marble. **2** *tr.* give a granular surface to. **3** *tr.* dye in grain. **4** *tr.* & *intr.* form into grains. **5** *tr.* remove hair from (hides). □ **against the grain** (often in phr. **go against the grain**) contrary to one's natural inclination or feeling. **grain-leather** leather dressed with grain-side out. **grain-side** the side of a hide on which the hair was. **grains of Paradise** capsules of a W. African plant (*Aframomum melegueta*), used as a spice and a drug. **in grain** thorough, genuine, by nature, downright, indelible. □□ **grained** *adj.* (also in *comb.*). **grainer** *n.* **grainless** *adj.* [ME f. OF f. L *granum*]
■ *n.* **1** kernel, fruit; see also SEED *n.* 1a. **2** cereal, corn, grist; wheat, barley, rice, oats. **3 a** particle, bit, fragment, crumb, crystal, speck, granule, molecule. **5** iota, scrap, trace, scintilla, hint, suggestion, whit, jot, jot or tittle, soupçon, *colloq.* smidgen. **6** graininess, lumpiness, roughness; see also INEQUALITY 3. **7** texture, pattern, fibre, weave, nap. **8 b** see SHEET[1] *n.* 2a, 3. **9** see NATURE 1, 7, TENDENCY. □ **against the grain** see ALIEN *adj.* 1a.

grainy /gráyni/ *adj.* (**grainier**, **grainiest**) **1** granular. **2** resembling the grain of wood. **3** *Photog.* having a granular appearance. □□ **graininess** *n.*

■ **1** see GRANULAR.

grallatorial /grállətóriəl/ *adj. Zool.* of or relating to long-legged wading birds, e.g. storks, flamingos, etc. [mod.L *grallatorius* f. L *grallator* stilt-walker f. *grallae* stilts]

gram[1] /gram/ *n.* (also **gramme**) a metric unit of mass equal to one-thousandth of a kilogram. □ **gram-atom** *Chem.* the quantity of a chemical element equal to its relative atomic mass in grams (see MOLE[4]). **gram-equivalent** *Chem.* the quantity of a substance equal to its equivalent weight in grams. **gram-molecule** *Chem.* the quantity of a substance equal to its relative molecular mass in grams. [F *gramme* f. Gk *gramma* small weight]

gram[2] /gram/ *n.* any of various pulses used as food. [Port. *grão* f. L *granum* grain]

-gram /gram/ *comb. form* forming nouns denoting a thing written or recorded (often in a certain way) (*anagram*; *epigram*; *monogram*; *telegram*). □□ **-grammatic** /grəmáttik/ *comb. form* forming adjectives. [from or after Gk *gramma -atos* thing written, letter of the alphabet, f. *graphō* write]

graminaceous /grámmináyshəss/ *adj.* of or like grass; grassy. [L *gramen -inis* grass]

gramineous /grəmínniəss/ *adj.* = GRAMINACEOUS. [L *gramineus* f. *gramen -inis* grass]

graminivorous /grámminívvərəss/ *adj.* feeding on grass, cereals, etc. [L *gramen -inis* grass + -VOROUS]

grammalogue /grámməlog/ *n.* **1** a word represented by a single shorthand sign. **2** a logogram. [irreg. f. Gk *gramma* letter of the alphabet + *logos* word]

grammar /grámmər/ *n.* **1 a** the study or rules of a language's inflections or other means of showing the relation between words, including its phonetic system. **b** a body of form and usages in a specified language (*Latin grammar*). **2** a person's manner or quality of observance or application of the rules of grammar (*bad grammar*). **3** a book on grammar. **4** the elements or rudiments of an art or science. **5** *Brit. colloq.* = *grammar school*. □ **grammar school 1** *Brit.* esp. *hist.* a selective State secondary school with a mainly academic curriculum. **2** *Brit. hist.* a school founded in or before the 16th c. for teaching Latin, later becoming a secondary school teaching academic subjects. **3** *US* a primary school. □□ **grammarless** *adj.* [ME f. AF *gramere*, OF *gramaire* f. L *grammatica* f. Gk *grammatikē* (*tekhnē*) (art) of letters f. *gramma -atos* letter of the alphabet]

grammarian /grəmáiriən/ *n.* an expert in grammar or linguistics; a philologist. [ME f. OF *gramarien*]

grammatical /grəmáttik'l/ *adj.* **1 a** of or relating to grammar. **b** determined by grammar, esp. by form or inflection (*grammatical gender*). **2** conforming to the rules of grammar, or to the formal principles of an art, science, etc. □□ **grammatically** *adv.* **grammaticalness** *n.* [F *grammatical* or LL *grammaticalis* f. L *grammaticus* f. Gk *grammatikos* (as GRAMMAR)]

gramme var. of GRAM[1].

gramophone /grámməfōn/ *n.* an instrument reproducing recorded sound by a stylus resting on a rotating grooved disc. ¶ Now more usually called *record-player*. □□ **gramophonic** /-fónnik/ *adj.* [formed by inversion of PHONOGRAM]

■ record-player, *US* phonograph.

grampus /grámpəss/ *n.* (*pl.* **grampuses**) **1** a dolphin, *Grampus griseus*, with a blunt snout and long pointed black flippers. **2** a person breathing heavily and loudly. [earlier *graundepose*, *grapeys* f. OF *grapois* etc. f. med.L *craspiscis* f. L *crassus piscis* fat fish]

Gram's method /gramz/ *n. Biol.* a method of differentiating bacteria by staining with a dye, then attempting to remove the dye with a solvent, for purposes of identification. □ **Gram-positive** (or **negative**) (of bacteria) that do (or do not) retain the dye. [H. C. J. *Gram*, Da. physician d. 1938]

gran /gran/ *n. colloq.* grandmother (cf. GRANNY). [abbr.]

granadilla /grànnədíllə/ *n.* (also **grenadilla** /grén-/) a passion-fruit. [Sp., dimin. of *granada* pomegranate]

granary /grànnəri/ *n.* (*pl.* **-ies**) **1** a storehouse for threshed grain. **2** a region producing, and esp. exporting, much corn. [L *granarium* f. *granum* grain]

grand /grand/ *adj.* & *n.* ● *adj.* **1 a** splendid, magnificent, imposing, dignified. **b** solemn or lofty in conception, execution, or expression; noble. **2** main; of chief importance (*grand staircase*; *grand entrance*). **3** (**Grand**) of the highest rank, esp. in official titles (*Grand Cross*; *grand vizier*; *Grand Inquisitor*). **4** *colloq.* excellent, enjoyable (*had a grand time*; *in grand condition*). **5** belonging to high society; wealthy (*the grand folk at the big house*). **6** (in *comb.*) in names of family relationships, denoting the second degree of ascent or descent (*granddaughter*). **7** (**Grand**) (in French phrases or imitations) great (*grand army*; *Grand Monarch*; *Grand Hotel*). **8** *Law* serious, important (*grand larceny*) (cf. COMMON, PETTY). ● *n.* **1** = *grand piano*. **2** (*pl.* same) (usu. in *pl.*) esp. *US sl.* a thousand dollars or pounds. □ **grand aunt** a great-aunt (see GREAT *adj.* 11). **grand duchy** a State ruled by a grand duke or duchess. **grand duke** (or **duchess**) **1** a prince (or princess) or noble person ruling over a territory. **2** (**Grand Duke**) *hist.* the son or grandson of a Russian tsar. **grand jury** esp. *US Law* a jury selected to examine the validity of an accusation prior to trial. **grand master 1** a chess-player of the highest class. **2** the head of a military order of knighthood, of Freemasons, etc. **Grand National** a steeplechase held annually at Aintree, Liverpool. **grand nephew** (or **niece**) a great-nephew or -niece (see GREAT *adj.* 11). **grand opera** opera on a serious theme, or in which the entire libretto (including dialogue) is sung. **grand piano** a large full-toned piano standing on three legs, with the body, strings, and soundboard arranged horizontally and in line with the keys. **grand slam 1** *Sport* the winning of all of a group of championships. **2** *Bridge* the winning of 13 tricks. **grand total** the final amount after everything is added up; the sum of other totals. **grand tour** *hist.* a cultural tour of Europe, esp. in the 18th c. for educational purposes. □□ **grandly** *adv.* **grandness** *n.* [ME f. AF *graunt*, OF *grant* f. L *grandis* full-grown]

■ *adj.* **1 a** splendid, magnificent, imposing, impressive, fine, dignified, majestic, distinguished, stately, lofty, monumental, lavish, opulent, luxurious, palatial, sumptuous, *colloq.* posh; august, respected, eminent, pre-eminent, outstanding, celebrated, illustrious, renowned, notable, exalted, revered, venerable. **b** solemn, lofty; see also NOBLE *adj.* 3, 4. **2** principal, chief, main, head, leading, foremost, highest. **4** marvellous, wonderful, outstanding, first-class, first-rate, splendid, excellent, superb, admirable, *colloq.* great, smashing, terrific, fantastic, fabulous, super; see also SUPERB. **5** see POSH *adj.* 2, RICH 1.

grandad /grándad/ *n.* (also **grand-dad**) *colloq.* **1** grandfather. **2** an elderly man.

grandam /grándam/ *n.* **1** (also **grandame**) *archaic* grandmother. **2** an old woman. **3** an ancestress. [ME f. AF *graund dame* (as GRAND, DAME)]

grandchild /gránchīld, gránd-/ *n.* (*pl.* **-children**) a child of one's son or daughter.

granddaughter /grándawtər/ *n.* a female grandchild.

grande dame /groɴd daám/ *n.* a dignified lady of high rank. [F]

grandee /grandeé/ *n.* **1** a Spanish or Portuguese nobleman of the highest rank. **2** a person of high rank or eminence. [Sp. & Port. *grande*, assim. to -EE]

grandeur /grándyər, gránjər/ *n.* **1** majesty, splendour; dignity of appearance or bearing. **2** high rank, eminence. **3** nobility of character. [F f. *grand* great, GRAND]

■ **1** magnificence, majesty, pomp; see also SPLENDOUR 2. **2** see DISTINCTION 4. **3** see NOBILITY 1.

grandfather /gránfaa*th*ər, gránd-/ *n.* a male grandparent. □ **grandfather clock** a clock in a tall wooden case, driven by weights. □□ **grandfatherly** *adj.*

Grand Guignol /gróɴ geenyól/ *n.* a dramatic entertainment of a sensational or horrific nature. [the name (= Great Punch) of a theatre in Paris]

grandiflora /grándiflórə/ *adj.* bearing large flowers. [mod.L (often used in specific names of large-flowered plants) f. L *grandis* great + FLORA]

grandiloquent /grandílləkwənt/ *adj.* **1** pompous or inflated in language. **2** given to boastful talk. □□ **grandiloquence** *n.* **grandiloquently** *adv.* [L *grandiloquus* (as GRAND, *-loquus* -speaking f. *loqui* speak), after *eloquent* etc.]
■ see POMPOUS 2.

grandiose /grándiōss/ *adj.* **1** producing or meant to produce an imposing effect. **2** planned on an ambitious or magnificent scale. □□ **grandiosely** *adv.* **grandiosity** /-dióssiti/ *n.* [F f. It. *grandioso* (as GRAND, -OSE[1])]
■ **1** imposing, grand, monumental, magnificent; see also IMPRESSIVE 1. **2** ambitious, lofty, flamboyant, showy, bombastic, extravagant, pompous, high-flown, high-flying, melodramatic, flashy, *colloq.* highfalutin, flash.

grandma /gránmaa, gránd-/ *n. colloq.* grandmother.

grand mal /groN mál/ *n.* a serious form of epilepsy with loss of consciousness (cf. PETIT MAL). [F, = great sickness]

grandmama /gránməmaa, gránd-/ *n. archaic colloq.* = GRANDMA.

grandmother /gránmuthər, gránd-/ *n.* a female grandparent. □ **grandmother clock** a clock like a grandfather clock but in a smaller case. **teach one's grandmother to suck eggs** presume to advise a more experienced person. □□ **grandmotherly** *adj.*

grandpa /gránpaa, gránd-/ *n. colloq.* grandfather.

grandpapa /gránpəpaa, gránd-/ *n. archaic colloq.* = GRANDPA.

grandparent /gránpairənt, gránd-/ *n.* a parent of one's father or mother.

Grand Prix /groN preé/ *n.* any of several important international motor or motor-cycle racing events. [F, = great or chief prize]

grand siècle /gróN syéklə/ *n.* the classical or golden age, esp. the 17th c. in France. [F, = great century or age]

grandsire /gránsīr, gránd-/ *n. archaic* **1** grandfather, old man, ancestor. **2** *Bell-ringing* a method of change-ringing.

grandson /gránsun, gránd-/ *n.* a male grandchild.

grandstand /gránstand, gránd-/ *n.* the main stand, usu. roofed, for spectators at a racecourse etc. □ **grandstand finish** a close and exciting finish to a race etc.

grange /graynj/ *n.* **1** a country house with farm-buildings. **2** *archaic* a barn. [ME f. AF *graunge*, OF *grange* f. med.L *granica (villa)* ult. f. L *granum* GRAIN]

graniferous /grəníffərəss/ *adj.* producing grain or a grainlike seed. □□ **graniform** /gránniform/ *adj.* [L *granum* GRAIN]

granite /gránnit/ *n.* **1** a granular crystalline igneous rock of quartz, mica, feldspar, etc., used for building. **2** a determined or resolute quality, attitude, etc. □□ **granitic** /grəníttik/ *adj.* **granitoid** *adj.* & *n.* [It. *granito*, lit. grained f. *grano* f. L *granum* GRAIN]

graniteware /grännitwair/ *n.* **1** a speckled form of earthenware imitating the appearance of granite. **2** a kind of enamelled ironware.

granivorous /grənívvərəss/ *adj.* feeding on grain. □□ **granivore** /gránnivor/ *n.* [L *granum* GRAIN]

granny /gránni/ *n.* (also **grannie**) (*pl.* **-ies**) *colloq.* grandmother. □ **granny bond** *Brit. colloq.* a form of National Savings certificate orig. available only to pensioners. **granny flat** (or **annexe**) *Brit.* part of a house made into self-contained accommodation for an elderly relative. **granny knot** a reef-knot crossed the wrong way and therefore insecure. [obs. *grannam* for GRANDAM + -Y[2]]

Granny Smith /gránni smíth/ *n.* an Australian green variety of apple. [Maria Ann ('Granny') Smith d. 1870]

grant /graant/ *v.* & *n.* ● *v.tr.* **1 a** consent to fulfil (a request, wish, etc.) (*granted all he asked*). **b** allow (a person) to have (a thing) (*granted me my freedom*). **c** (as **granted**) *colloq.* apology accepted; pardon given. **2** give (rights, property, etc.) formally; transfer legally. **3** (often foll. by *that* + clause) admit as true; concede, esp. as a basis for argument. ● *n.* **1** the process of granting or a thing granted. **2** a sum of money given by the State for any of various purposes, esp. to finance education. **3** *Law* **a** a legal conveyance by written instrument. **b** formal conferment. □ **grant-in-aid** (*pl.* **grants-in-aid**) a grant by central government to local government or an institution. **take for granted 1** assume something to be true or valid. **2** cease to appreciate through familiarity. □□ **grantable** *adj.* **grantee** /-teé/ *n.* (esp. in sense 2 of *v.*). **granter** *n.* **grantor** /-tór/ *n.* (esp. in sense 2 of *v.*). [ME f. OF *gr(e)anter* var. of *creanter* ult. f. part. of L *credere* entrust]
■ *v.* **1 a** agree to, consent to, concur with, assent to, concede to, admit, allow, accept, approve of, conform to. **b** allow, permit; give, award, offer, confer a thing on a person, bestow a thing on a person; supply with, furnish with; donate, allocate, assign. **2** see *make over* 1. **3** see CONCEDE 1a. ● *n.* **1, 2** gift, presentation, endowment, bequest, award, donation, contribution, concession, allowance; subvention, subsidy, grant-in-aid.

Granth /grunt/ *n.* (also **Grunth**) the sacred scriptures of the Sikhs. [Hindi, = book, code f. Skr. *grantha* tying, literary composition]

gran turismo /grán toorízmō/ *n.* (*pl.* **-os**) a touring-car. [It., = great touring]

granular /grányoolər/ *adj.* **1** of or like grains or granules. **2** having a granulated surface or structure. □□ **granularity** /-lárriti/ *n.* **granularly** *adv.* [LL *granulum* GRANULE]
■ grainy, granulated, particulate, comminuted, sandy, gritty.

granulate /grányoolayt/ *v.* **1** *tr.* & *intr.* form into grains (*granulated sugar*). **2** *tr.* roughen the surface of. **3** *intr.* (of a wound etc.) form small prominences as the beginning of healing; heal, join. □□ **granulation** /-láysh'n/ *n.* **granulator** *n.*
■ **1** see GRIND *v.* 1a.

granule /grányōōl/ *n.* a small grain. [LL *granulum*, dimin. of L *granum* grain]
■ see GRAIN *n.* 3a.

granulocyte /grányooləsīt/ *n. Physiol.* any of various white blood cells having granules in their cytoplasm. □□ **granulocytic** /-síttik/ *adj.*

granulometric /grányooləmétrik/ *adj.* relating to the distribution of grain sizes in sand etc. [F *granulométrique* (as GRANULE, METRIC)]

grape /grayp/ *n.* **1** a berry (usu. green, purple, or black) growing in clusters on a vine, used as fruit and in making wine. **2** (prec. by *the*) *colloq.* wine. **3** = GRAPESHOT. **4** (in *pl.*) a diseased growth like a bunch of grapes on the pastern of a horse etc., or on a pleura in cattle. □ **grape hyacinth** any liliaceous plant of the genus *Muscari*, with clusters of usu. blue flowers. **grape-sugar** dextrose. □□ **grapey** *adj.* (also **grapy**). [ME f. OF *grape* bunch of grapes prob. f. *graper* gather (grapes) f. *grap(p)e* hook, ult. f. Gmc]

grapefruit /gráypfrōōt/ *n.* (*pl.* same) **1** a large round yellow citrus fruit with an acid juicy pulp. **2** the tree, *Citrus paradisi*, bearing this fruit.

grapeshot /gráypshot/ *n. hist.* small balls used as charge in a cannon and scattering when fired.

grapevine /gráypvīn/ *n.* **1** any of various vines of the genus *Vitis*, esp. *Vitis vinifera*. **2** *colloq.* the means of transmission of unofficial information or rumour (*heard it through the grapevine*).
■ **2** bush telegraph, network.

graph[1] /graaf, graf/ *n.* & *v.* ● *n.* **1** a diagram showing the relation between variable quantities, usu. of two variables, each measured along one of a pair of axes at right angles. **2** *Math.* a collection of points whose coordinates satisfy a given relation. ● *v.tr.* plot or trace on a graph. □ **graph paper** paper printed with a network of lines as a basis for drawing graphs. [abbr. of *graphic formula*]
■ *n.* **1** see CHART *n.* 2.

graph[2] /graaf, graf/ *n. Linguistics* a visual symbol, esp. a letter or letters, representing a unit of sound or other feature of speech. [Gk *graphē* writing]

-graph /graaf/ *comb. form* forming nouns and verbs meaning: **1** a thing written or drawn etc. in a specified way (*autograph*; *photograph*). **2** an instrument that records (*heliograph*; *seismograph*; *telegraph*).

grapheme /gráffeem/ *n. Linguistics* **1** a class of letters etc. representing a unit of sound. **2** a feature of a written expression that cannot be analysed into smaller meaningful units. □□ **graphematic** /-máttik/ *adj.* **graphemic** /grəféemik/ *adj.* **graphemically** /grəféemikəli/ *adv.* [GRAPH[2] + -EME]

-grapher /grəfər/ *comb. form* forming nouns denoting a person concerned with a subject (*geographer*; *radiographer*). [from or after Gk *-graphos* writer + -ER[1]]

graphic /gráffik/ *adj.* & *n.* ● *adj.* **1** of or relating to the visual or descriptive arts, esp. writing and drawing. **2** vividly descriptive; conveying all (esp. unwelcome or unpleasant) details; unequivocal. **3** (of minerals) showing marks like writing on the surface or in a fracture. **4** = GRAPHICAL. ● *n.* a product of the graphic arts (cf. GRAPHICS). □ **graphic arts** the visual and technical arts involving design, writing, drawing, printing, etc. **graphic equalizer** a device for the separate control of the strength and quality of selected frequency bands. **graphic novel** an adult novel in comic-strip format. □□ **graphically** *adv.* **graphicness** *n.* [L *graphicus* f. Gk *graphikos* f. *graphē* writing]
■ *adj.* **1** representational, visual, pictorial, descriptive. **2** vivid, picturesque, lifelike, telling, clear, explicit, realistic, true to life, descriptive, photographic, detailed, well-drawn; accurate, precise; clear, lucid, unambiguous, unequivocal.

-graphic /gráffik/ *comb. form* (also **-graphical**) forming adjectives corresponding to nouns in *-graphy* (see -GRAPHY). □□ **-graphically** *comb. form* forming adverbs. [from or after Gk *-graphikos* (as GRAPHIC)]

graphicacy /gráffikəsi/ *n.* the ability to read a map, graph, etc., or to present information by means of diagrams. [GRAPHIC, after *literacy*, *numeracy*]

graphical /gráffik'l/ *adj.* **1** of or in the form of graphs (see GRAPH[1]). **2** graphic. □□ **graphically** *adv.*

graphics /gráffiks/ *n.pl.* (usu. treated as *sing.*) **1** the products of the graphic arts, esp. commercial design or illustration. **2** the use of diagrams in calculation and design. **3** (in full **computer graphics**) *Computing* a mode of processing and output in which a significant part of the information is in pictorial form.

graphite /gráffīt/ *n.* a crystalline allotropic form of carbon used as a solid lubricant, in pencils, and as a moderator in nuclear reactors etc. Also called PLUMBAGO, *black lead.* □□ **graphitic** /-fittik/ *adj.* **graphitize** /-fitīz/ *v.tr.* & *intr.* (also **-ise**). [G *Graphit* f. Gk *graphō* write]

graphology /grəfólləji/ *n.* **1** the study of handwriting esp. as a supposed guide to character. **2** a system of graphic formulae; notation for graphs (see GRAPH[1]). **3** *Linguistics* the study of systems of writing. □□ **graphological** /gráffəlójik'l/ *adj.* **graphologist** *n.* [Gk *graphē* writing]

-graphy /grəfi/ *comb. form* forming nouns denoting: **1** a descriptive science (*bibliography*; *geography*). **2** a technique of producing images (*photography*; *radiography*). **3** a style or method of writing, drawing, etc. (*calligraphy*). [from or after F or G *-graphie* f. L *-graphia* f. Gk *-graphia* writing]

grapnel /grápnəl/ *n.* **1** a device with iron claws, attached to a rope and used for dragging or grasping. **2** a small anchor with several flukes. [ME f. AF f. OF *grapon* f. Gmc: cf. GRAPE]

grappa /gráppə/ *n.* a brandy distilled from the fermented residue of grapes after they have been pressed in wine-making. [It.]

grapple /grápp'l/ *v.* & *n.* ● *v.* **1** *intr.* (often foll. by *with*) fight at close quarters or in close combat. **2** *intr.* (foll. by *with*) try to manage or overcome a difficult problem etc. **3** *tr.* **a** grip with the hands; come to close quarters with. **b** seize with or as with a grapnel; grasp. ● *n.* **1 a** a hold or grip in or as in wrestling. **b** a contest at close quarters. **2** a clutching-instrument; a grapnel. □ **grappling-iron** (or **-hook**) = GRAPNEL. □□ **grappler** *n.* [OF *grapil* (n.) f. Prov., dimin. of *grapa* hook (as GRAPNEL)]
■ *v.* **1** fight, wrestle, tussle, scuffle, skirmish; see also FIGHT *v.* 1a. **2** (*grapple with*) struggle with, contend with, wrestle with, tackle, face, take on, do battle with, combat, fight. **3** grip, hold, clutch, clasp; grab, seize, catch, snatch, grasp. ● *n.* **1 a** grip, hold, grasp, clutch, handgrip, clasp, hand-clasp. **b** see BOUT 2a. **2** grapnel, grappling-iron *or* -hook, grab. □ **grappling-iron** (or **-hook**) grapnel, grab, grapple.

graptolite /gráptəlīt/ *n.* an extinct marine invertebrate animal found as a fossil in lower Palaeozoic rocks. [Gk *graptos* marked with letters + -LITE]

grasp /graasp/ *v.* & *n.* ● *v.* **1** *tr.* **a** clutch at; seize greedily. **b** hold firmly; grip. **2** *intr.* (foll. by *at*) try to seize; accept avidly. **3** *tr.* understand or realize (a fact or meaning). ● *n.* **1** a firm hold; a grip. **2** (foll. by *of*) **a** mastery or control (*a grasp of the situation*). **b** a mental hold or understanding (*a grasp of the facts*). **3** mental agility (*a quick grasp*). □ **grasp at a straw** see STRAW. **grasp the nettle** tackle a difficulty boldly. **within one's grasp** capable of being grasped or comprehended by one. □□ **graspable** *adj.* **grasper** *n.* [ME *graspe*, *grapse* perh. f. OE *grǣpsan* (unrecorded) f. Gmc, rel. to GROPE: cf. LG *grapsen*]
■ *v.* **1 a** clutch at, seize, grab, snatch, take *or* lay *or* catch *or* get hold of. **b** clutch, grip, hold, clasp. **2** (*grasp at*) grab *or* snatch *or* clutch at, reach for; latch on to, snap up; see also *jump at*. **3** understand, comprehend, catch, follow, make head or tail of, get the point *or* drift of, *colloq.* get, *sl.* dig; appreciate, see, realize. ● *n.* **1** hold, grip, clasp, embrace, lock; clutches. **2 a** (*grasp of*) possession of, control of *or* over, power over, mastery of, hold of *or* over. **b** understanding, comprehension, apprehension, awareness, perception, sense. **3** see INTELLIGENCE 1b. □ **within one's grasp** graspable, possible, attainable, realizable, achievable, reachable, accomplishable; understandable, comprehensible, accessible.

grasping /graásping/ *adj.* avaricious, greedy. □□ **graspingly** *adv.* **graspingness** *n.*
■ greedy, avaricious, acquisitive, rapacious.

grass /graass/ *n.* & *v.* ● *n.* **1 a** vegetation belonging to a group of small plants with green blades that are eaten by cattle, horses, sheep, etc. **b** any species of this. **c** any plant of the family Gramineae, which includes cereals, reeds, and bamboos. **2** pasture land. **3** grass-covered ground, a lawn (*keep off the grass*). **4** grazing (*be at grass*). **5** *sl.* marijuana. **6** *Brit. sl.* an informer, esp. a police informer. **7** the earth's surface above a mine; the pit-head. **8** *sl.* asparagus. ● *v.* **1** *tr.* cover with turf. **2** *tr. US* provide with pasture. **3** *Brit. sl.* **a** *tr.* betray, esp. to the police. **b** *intr.* inform the police. **4** *tr.* knock down; fell (an opponent). **5** *tr.* **a** bring (a fish) to the bank. **b** bring down (a bird) by a shot. □ **at grass** out of work, on holiday, etc. **grass bird** *Austral.* any of various warblers, esp. of the genus *Megalurus*, living among reeds. **grass-box** a receptacle for cut grass on a lawnmower. **grass-cloth** a linen-like cloth woven from ramie etc. **grass court** a grass-covered lawn-tennis court. **grass of Parnassus** a herbaceous plant, *Parnassia palustris*. **grass parakeet** *Austral.* a parakeet, esp. of the genus *Neophema*, frequenting grassland. **grass roots 1** a fundamental level or source. **2** ordinary people, esp. as voters; the rank and file of an organization, esp. a political party. **grass skirt** a skirt made of long grass and leaves fastened to a waistband. **grass snake 1** *Brit.* the common ringed snake, *Natrix natrix*. **2** *US* the common greensnake, *Opheodrys vernalis*. **grass tree** = BLACKBOY. **grass widow** (or **widower**) a person whose husband (or wife) is away for a prolonged period. **grass-wrack** eel-grass. **not let the grass grow under one's feet** be quick to act or to seize an opportunity. **out to grass 1** to pasture. **2** redundant, in retirement, on holiday. □□ **grassless** *adj.* **grasslike** *adj.* [OE *græs* f. Gmc, rel. to GREEN, GROW]
■ *n.* **2** see PASTURE *n.* **3** see LAWN[1]. **4** grazing, feeding, feed.

5 cannabis, marijuana, hemp, hashish, ganja, *colloq.* hash, *sl.* pot, green, dope, the weed. **6** traitor, informer, stool-pigeon, *sl.* squealer, snitch, *Austral. sl.* fizgig, *Brit. sl.* nark, *US sl.* stoolie. ● *v.* **3 a** betray, give away, sell out, *archaic* peach, *colloq.* rat on, *sl.* snitch on; see also INFORM 2. **b** *colloq.* peach, *sl.* squeal, squeak; see also INFORM 2. **4** see FELL[2] *v.* 2. □ **at grass** unemployed, jobless, out of a job, idle, between assignments, *Brit. colloq.* on the dole, *Brit. euphem.* resting; on holiday, off work. **grass roots 1** see BOTTOM *n.* 5. **2** see PEOPLE *n.* 2.

grasshopper /graáss-hoppər/ *n.* a jumping and chirping plant-eating insect of the order Saltatoria.

grassland /graásland/ *n.* a large open area covered with grass, esp. one used for grazing.
■ see PLAIN[1] *n.*

grassy /graássi/ *adj.* (**grassier**, **grassiest**) **1** covered with or abounding in grass. **2** resembling grass. **3** of grass. □□ **grassiness** *n.*
■ **1** see GREEN *adj.* 2a.

grate[1] /grayt/ *v.* **1** *tr.* reduce to small particles by rubbing on a serrated surface. **2** *intr.* (often foll. by *against*, *on*) rub with a harsh scraping sound. **3** *tr.* utter in a harsh tone. **4** *intr.* (often foll. by *on*) **a** sound harshly or discordantly. **b** have an irritating effect. **5** *tr.* grind (one's teeth). **6** *intr.* (of a hinge etc.) creak. [ME f. OF *grater* ult. f. WG]
■ **1** shred, rasp, scrape, rub. **2** scrape, rasp, rub, grind, scratch; stridulate. **3** croak, rasp, growl, bark, snap; see also BAWL 1. **4 a** see JAR[2] *v.* 1, 2. **b** jar, go against the grain, rub a person up the wrong way, *colloq.* get on a person's nerves; (*grate on*) annoy, vex, irk, irritate, fret, chafe. **5** grind, gnash, rub. **6** creak, squeak.

grate[2] /grayt/ *n.* **1** the recess of a fireplace or furnace. **2** a metal frame confining fuel in a grate. [ME, = grating f. OF ult. f. L *cratis* hurdle]

grateful /gráytfool/ *adj.* **1** thankful; feeling or showing gratitude (*am grateful to you for helping*). **2** pleasant, acceptable. □□ **gratefully** *adv.* **gratefulness** *n.* [obs. *grate* (adj.) f. L *gratus* + -FUL]
■ **1** thankful, appreciative; see also INDEBTED 1. **2** see PLEASANT.

grater /gráytər/ *n.* a device for reducing cheese or other food to small particles.

graticule /gráttikyool/ *n.* **1** fine lines or fibres incorporated in a telescope or other optical instrument as a measuring scale or as an aid in locating objects. **2** *Surveying* a network of lines on paper representing meridians and parallels. [F f. med.L *graticula* for *craticula* gridiron f. L *cratis* hurdle]

gratify /gráttifī/ *v.tr.* (**-fies**, **-fied**) **1 a** please, delight. **b** please by compliance; assent to the wish of. **2** indulge in or yield to (a feeling or desire). □□ **gratification** /-fikáysh'n/ *n.* **gratifier** *n.* **gratifying** *adj.* **gratifyingly** *adv.* [F *gratifier* or L *gratificari* do a favour to, make a present of, f. *gratus* pleasing]
■ **1 a** delight, cheer, gladden; see also PLEASE 1. **1b, 2** see SATISFY 2, 3. □□ **gratification** satisfaction, fulfilment, enjoyment, pleasure, delight; compensation, recompense, reward, return, requital.

grating[1] /gráyting/ *adj.* **1** sounding harsh or discordant (*a grating laugh*). **2** having an irritating effect. □□ **gratingly** *adv.*
■ **1** jarring, strident, raucous, harsh, shrill, discordant, dissonant, unharmonious; grinding, jangling, screeching, squawking, croaking, rasping. **2** irritating, offensive, irksome, annoying, vexatious, galling.

grating[2] /gráyting/ *n.* **1** a framework of parallel or crossed metal bars. **2** *Optics* a set of parallel wires, lines ruled on glass, etc., for producing spectra by diffraction.
■ **1** grate, grid, grille. **2** reticle, reticule; reticulation.

gratis /graátiss, gráy-/ *adv.* & *adj.* free; without charge. [L, contracted ablat. pl. of *gratia* favour]
■ see FREE *adj.* 7.

gratitude /gráttityood/ *n.* being thankful; readiness to show appreciation for and to return kindness. [F *gratitude* or med.L *gratitudo* f. *gratus* thankful]
■ thankfulness, appreciation, gratefulness, thanks, acknowledgement, recognition, thanksgiving.

gratuitous /grətyoó-itəss/ *adj.* **1** given or done free of charge. **2** uncalled-for; unwarranted; lacking good reason (*a gratuitous insult*). □□ **gratuitously** *adv.* **gratuitousness** *n.* [L *gratuitus* spontaneous: cf. *fortuitous*]
■ **1** see FREE *adj.* 7. **2** unrequested, unprovoked, unsolicited, wanton, unlooked-for, uncalled-for, unjustified, unwarranted, baseless, groundless, needless, unfounded, ungrounded, unjustifiable, unreasonable.

gratuity /grətyoó-iti/ *n.* (*pl.* **-ies**) money given in recognition of services; a tip. [OF *gratuité* or med.L *gratuitas* gift f. L *gratus* grateful]
■ see TIP[3] *n.* 1.

gratulatory /grátyoolətəri, -tri/ *adj.* expressing congratulation. [LL *gratulatorius* f. L *gratus* grateful]

graunch /grawnch/ *v.intr.* & *tr.* make or cause to make a crunching or grinding sound. [imit.]

gravamen /grəváymen/ *n.* (*pl.* **gravamens** or **gravamina** /-vámminə/) **1** the essence or most serious part of an argument. **2** a grievance. [LL, = inconvenience, f. L *gravare* to load f. *gravis* heavy]

grave[1] /grayv/ *n.* **1 a** a trench dug in the ground to receive a coffin on burial. **b** a mound or memorial stone placed over this. **2** (prec. by *the*) death, esp. as indicating mortal finality. **3** something compared to or regarded as a grave. □ **turn in one's grave** (of a dead person) be thought of in certain circumstances as likely to have been shocked or angry if still alive. □□ **graveless** *adj.* **graveward** *adv.* & *adj.* [OE *græf* f. WG]
■ **1 b** crypt, sepulchre, tomb, vault, mausoleum; tumulus, *Archaeol.* barrow; gravestone, headstone. **2** (*the grave*) see DEATH 1.

grave[2] /grayv/ *adj.* & *n.* ● *adj.* **1 a** serious, weighty, important (*a grave matter*). **b** dignified, solemn, sombre (*a grave look*). **2** extremely serious or threatening (*grave danger*). **3** /graav/ (of sound) low-pitched, not acute. ● *n.* /graav/ = *grave accent*. □ **grave accent** /graav/ a mark (`) placed over a vowel in some languages to denote pronunciation, length, etc., orig. indicating low or falling pitch. □□ **gravely** *adv.* **graveness** *n.* [F *grave* or L *gravis* heavy, serious]
■ *adj.* **1 a** weighty, important, critical; see also SERIOUS 2, 3, 7. **b** dignified, sombre, solemn, unsmiling, earnest, sober, gloomy, grim-faced, dour. **2** serious, vital, urgent, crucial, grim; perilous, dangerous, threatening, life-threatening.

grave[3] /grayv/ *v.tr.* (*past part.* **graven** or **graved**) **1** (foll. by *in*, *on*) fix indelibly (on one's memory). **2** *archaic* engrave, carve. □ **graven image** an idol. [OE *grafan* dig, engrave f. Gmc: cf. GROOVE]

grave[4] /grayv/ *v.tr.* clean (a ship's bottom) by burning off accretions and by tarring. □ **graving dock** = *dry dock*. [perh. F dial. *grave* = OF *greve* shore]

gravedigger /gráyvdiggər/ *n.* **1** a person who digs graves. **2** (in full **gravedigger beetle**) a sexton beetle.

gravel /grávv'l/ *n.* & *v.* ● *n.* **1 a** a mixture of coarse sand and small water-worn or pounded stones, used for paths and roads and as an aggregate. **b** *Geol.* a stratum of this. **2** *Med.* aggregations of crystals formed in the urinary tract. ● *v.tr.* (**gravelled**, **gravelling**; *US* **graveled**, **graveling**) **1** lay or strew with gravel. **2** perplex, puzzle, nonplus (from an obs. sense 'run (a ship) aground'). □ **gravel-blind** *literary* almost completely blind ('more than sand-blind', in Shakesp. *Merchant of Venice* II. ii. 33). [ME f. OF *gravel(e)* dimin. of *grave* (as GRAVE[4])]

gravelax / grávvəlaks/ *n.* (also **gravlax**) filleted salmon cured by marination in salt, sugar, and dill. [Sw.]

gravelly /grávvəli/ *adj.* **1** of or like gravel. **2** having or containing gravel. **3** (of a voice) deep and rough-sounding.
■ **1, 2** see *gritty* (GRIT). **3** see STRIDENT.

graven *past part.* of GRAVE[3].

graver /gráyvər/ *n.* **1** an engraving tool; a burin. **2** *archaic* an engraver; a carver.

Graves /graav/ *n.* a light usu. white wine from Graves in France.

Graves' disease /grayvz/ *n.* exophthalmic goitre with characteristic swelling of the neck and protrusion of the eyes, resulting from an overactive thyroid gland. [R. J. *Graves*, Ir. physician d. 1853]

gravestone /gráyvstōn/ *n.* a stone (usu. inscribed) marking a grave.
■ see MONUMENT 1–3.

graveyard /gráyvyaard/ *n.* a burial-ground, esp. by a church.
■ burial-ground, churchyard, cemetery, God's Acre, necropolis, potter's field, *sl.* bone-yard.

gravid /grávvid/ *adj. literary* or *Zool.* pregnant. [L *gravidus* f. *gravis* heavy]

gravimeter /grəvímmitər/ *n.* an instrument for measuring the difference in the force of gravity from one place to another. [F *gravimètre* f. L *gravis* heavy]

gravimetric /grávvimétrik/ *adj.* **1** of or relating to the measurement of weight. **2** denoting chemical analysis based on weight.

gravimetry /grəvímmitri/ *n.* the measurement of weight.

gravitas /grávvitass, -taass/ *n.* solemn demeanour; seriousness. [L f. *gravis* serious]

gravitate /grávvitayt/ *v.* **1** *intr.* (foll. by *to, towards*) move or be attracted to some source of influence. **2** *tr.* & *intr.* **a** move or tend by force of gravity towards. **b** sink by or as if by gravity. [mod.L *gravitare* GRAVITAS]
■ **1** see LEAN[1] *v.* 4. **2 b** see SETTLE[1] 13.

gravitation /grávvitáysh'n/ *n. Physics* **1** a force of attraction between any particle of matter in the universe and any other. **2** the effect of this, esp. the falling of bodies to the earth. [mod.L *gravitatio* (as GRAVITY)]
■ see ATTRACTION 2.

gravitational /grávvitáyshən'l/ *adj.* of or relating to gravitation. □ **gravitational constant** the constant in Newton's law of gravitation relating gravity to the masses and separation of particles. ¶ Symb.: **G. gravitational field** the region of space surrounding a body in which another body experiences a force of attraction. □□ **gravitationally** *adv.*

gravity /grávviti/ *n.* **1 a** the force that attracts a body to the centre of the earth or other celestial body. **b** the degree of intensity of this measured by acceleration. **c** gravitational force. **2** the property of having weight. **3 a** importance, seriousness; the quality of being grave. **b** solemnity, sobriety; serious demeanour. □ **gravity feed** the supply of material by its fall under gravity. [F *gravité* or L *gravitas* f. *gravis* heavy]
■ **1** gravitation; attraction. **2** see WEIGHT *n.* 2, 3.
3 a seriousness, acuteness, immediacy, importance, graveness, significance, magnitude, severity, urgency, exigency, momentousness, weight, weightiness.
b solemnity, dignity, sombreness, sobriety, *gravitas*, soberness, graveness.

gravure /grəvyóor/ *n.* = PHOTOGRAVURE. [abbr.]

gravy /gráyvi/ *n.* (*pl.* **-ies**) **1 a** the juices exuding from meat during and after cooking. **b** a dressing or sauce for food, made from these or from other materials, e.g. stock. **2** *sl.* unearned or unexpected money. □ **gravy-boat** a boat-shaped vessel for serving gravy. **gravy train** *sl.* a source of easy financial benefit. [ME, perh. from a misreading as *gravé* of OF *grané*, prob. f. *grain* spice: see GRAIN]

gray[1] /gray/ *n. Physics* the SI unit of the absorbed dose of ionizing radiation, corresponding to one joule per kilogram. ¶ Abbr.: **Gy.** [L. H. *Gray*, Engl. radiobiologist d. 1965]

gray[2] *US* var. of GREY.

grayling /gráyling/ *n.* **1** any silver-grey freshwater fish of the genus *Thymallus*, with a long high dorsal fin. **2** a butterfly, *Hipparchia semele*, having wings with grey undersides and bright eye-spots on the upper side. [*gray* var. of GREY + -LING[2]]

graywacke *US* var. of GREYWACKE.

graze[1] /grayz/ *v.* **1** *intr.* (of cattle, sheep, etc.) eat growing grass. **2** *tr.* **a** feed (cattle etc.) on growing grass. **b** feed on (grass). **3** *intr.* pasture cattle. □□ **grazer** *n.* [OE *grasian* f. *græs* GRASS]
■ **1** see FEED *v.* 4.

graze[2] /grayz/ *v.* & *n.* ● *v.* **1** *tr.* rub or scrape (a part of the body, esp. the skin) so as to break the surface without causing bleeding. **2 a** *tr.* touch lightly in passing. **b** *intr.* (foll. by *against, along*, etc.) move with a light passing contact. ● *n.* an act or instance of grazing. [perh. a specific use of GRAZE[1], as if 'take off the grass close to the ground' (of a shot etc.)]
■ *v.* **1** see SCRAPE *v.* 3b. **2 a** see KISS *v.* 4. ● *n.* see SCRAPE *n.* 2.

grazier /gráyziər/ *n.* **1** a person who feeds cattle for market. **2** *Austral.* a large-scale sheep-farmer or cattle-farmer. □□ **graziery** *n.* [GRASS + -IER]

grazing /gráyzing/ *n.* grassland suitable for pasturage.

grease /greess/ *n.* & *v.* ● *n.* **1** oily or fatty matter esp. as a lubricant. **2** the melted fat of a dead animal. **3** oily matter in unprocessed wool. ● *v.tr.* /also greez/ smear or lubricate with grease. □ **grease-gun** a device for pumping grease under pressure to a particular point. **grease the palm of** *colloq.* bribe. **like greased lightning** *colloq.* very fast. □□ **greaseless** *adj.* [ME f. AF *grece, gresse*, OF *graisse* ult. f. L *crassus* (adj.) fat]
■ *n.* see OIL *n.* ● *v.* see OIL *v.*

greasepaint /gréespaynt/ *n.* a waxy composition used as make-up for actors.

greaseproof /gréesproof/ *adj.* impervious to the penetration of grease.

greaser /gréessər/ *n.* **1** a person or thing that greases. **2** *sl.* a member of a gang of youths with long hair and riding motor cycles. **3** *US sl. offens.* a Mexican or Spanish-American. **4** *sl.* a gentle landing of an aircraft.

greasy /gréessi, gréezi/ *adj.* (**greasier, greasiest**) **1 a** of or like grease. **b** smeared or covered with grease. **c** containing or having too much grease. **2 a** slippery. **b** (of a person or manner) unpleasantly unctuous, smooth. **c** objectionable. □□ **greasily** *adv.* **greasiness** *n.*
■ **1** oily, sebaceous, fatty, fat, buttery, lardy, oleaginous, *formal or joc.* pinguid. **2 a** see SLIPPERY 1, 2. **b** unctuous, oily, slippery, fawning, slick, smooth, toadying, sycophantic, obsequious, *colloq.* smarmy.

great /grayt/ *adj.* & *n.* ● *adj.* **1 a** of a size, amount, extent, or intensity considerably above the normal or average; big (*made a great hole; take great care; lived to a great age*). **b** also with implied surprise, admiration, contempt, etc., esp. in exclamations (*you great idiot!; great stuff!; look at that great wasp*). **c** reinforcing other words denoting size, quantity, etc. (*a great big hole; a great many*). **2** important, pre-eminent; worthy or most worthy of consideration (*the great thing is not to get caught*). **3** grand, imposing (*a great occasion; the great hall*). **4 a** (esp. of a public or historic figure) distinguished; prominent. **b** (**the Great**) as a title denoting the most important of the name (*Alfred the Great*). **5 a** (of a person) remarkable in ability, character, achievement, etc. (*great men; a great thinker*). **b** (of a thing) outstanding of its kind (*the Great Fire*). **6** (foll. by *at, on*) competent, skilled, well-informed. **7** fully deserving the name of; doing a thing habitually or extensively (*a great reader; a great believer in tolerance; not a great one for travelling*). **8** (also **greater**) the larger of the name, species, etc. (*great auk; greater celandine*). **9** (**Greater**) (of a city etc.) including adjacent urban areas (*Greater Manchester*). **10** *colloq.* **a** very enjoyable or satisfactory; attractive, fine (*had a great time; it would be great if we won*). **b** (as an exclam.) fine, very good. **11** (in *comb.*) (in names of family relationships) denoting one degree further removed upwards or downwards (*great-uncle; great-great-grandmother*). ● *n.* **1** a great or outstanding person or thing. **2** (in *pl.*) (**Greats**) *colloq.* (at Oxford University) an honours course or final examinations in classics and philosophy. □ **great and small** all classes or types. **the Great Bear** see BEAR[2]. **Great**

Britain England, Wales, and Scotland. **great circle** see CIRCLE. **Great Dane** see DANE. **great deal** see DEAL[1]. **great-hearted** magnanimous; having a noble or generous mind. **great-heartedness** magnanimity. **the great majority** by far the most. **great northern diver** a diving sea bird, *Gavia immer*, of the northern hemisphere. **great organ** the chief manual in a large organ, with its related pipes and mechanism. **Great Russian** *n.* a member or the language of the principal East Slavonic ethnic group, inhabiting mainly the Russian Republic; (a) Russian. ● *adj.* of or relating to this people or language. **great tit** a Eurasian songbird, *Parus major*, with black and white head markings. **great toe** the big toe. **Great War** the world war of 1914–18. **to a great extent** largely. □□ **greatness** *n.* [OE *grēat* f. WG]

■ *adj.* **1 a** big, large, huge, immense, enormous, stupendous, grand, extensive, colossal, gigantic, monstrous, mammoth, massive, vast, prodigious, tremendous; extreme, considerable, a lot of; marked, pronounced, inordinate, extraordinary, *colloq.* terrific; significant, profound, basic, cardinal. **2** critical, important, pre-eminent, crucial, vital, major, main, chief. **3** grand, fine, imposing, lofty, elevated, exalted, noble, spectacular; momentous, significant, serious, weighty. **4 a** distinguished, prominent, important, eminent, celebrated, famous, famed, renowned, notable, illustrious, outstanding, well-known, weighty, influential. **5 a** gifted, talented, accomplished, skilled, excellent, brilliant, first-rate, outstanding, remarkable, exceptional, incomparable, matchless, peerless; leading. **b** extraordinary, outstanding. **6** (*great at* or *on*) competent at, well-informed on *or* about, expert at *or* in; talented at, skilled at, clever at, adept at, proficient at. **7** keen, zealous, eager, active, enthusiastic, devoted, ardent, passionate. **10** outstanding, first-rate, first-class, superior, marvellous, wonderful, splendid, *colloq.* tiptop, capital, super(-duper), smashing, A1, knockout, brill, brilliant, grand, fantastic, terrific, fab, fabulous, crucial, *Brit. colloq.* tickety-boo, *US colloq.* A-OK, *colloq. or dial.* champion, *sl.* cracking, ace, groovy, awesome, *Austral. sl.* grouse, *esp. US sl.* bad; see also SUPERB.
□ **great-hearted** see NOBLE *adj.* 2, GENEROUS 2. **to a great extent** see LARGELY.

greatcoat /gráytkōt/ *n.* a long heavy overcoat.

greatly /gráytli/ *adv.* by a considerable amount; much (*greatly admired; greatly superior*).
■ see EXCEEDINGLY 1.

greave /greev/ *n.* (usu. in *pl.*) armour for the shin. [ME f. OF *greve* shin, greave, of unkn. orig.]

grebe /greeb/ *n.* any diving bird of the family Podicipedidae, with a long neck, lobed toes, and almost no tail. □ **little grebe** a small water bird of the grebe family, *Tachybaptus ruficollis*. [F *grèbe*, of unkn. orig.]

Grecian /gre̍esh'n/ *adj.* (of architecture or facial outline) following Greek models or ideals. □ **Grecian nose** a straight nose that continues the line of the forehead without a dip. [OF *grecien* or med.L *graecianus* (unrecorded) f. L *Graecia* Greece]

Grecism var. of GRAECISM.

Grecize var. of GRAECIZE.

Greco- var. of GRAECO-.

greed /greed/ *n.* an excessive desire, esp. for food or wealth. [back-form. f. GREEDY]
■ greediness, avarice, avariciousness, covetousness, acquisitiveness, cupidity, avidity; gluttony, piggishness, voraciousness, voracity, gormandizing.

greedy /gre̍edi/ *adj.* (**greedier**, **greediest**) **1** having or showing an excessive appetite for food or drink. **2** wanting wealth or pleasure to excess. **3** (foll. by *for*, or *to* + infin.) very keen or eager; needing intensely (*greedy for affection; greedy to learn*). □ **greedy-guts** *colloq.* a glutton. □□ **greedily** *adv.* **greediness** *n.* [OE *grǣdig* f. Gmc]
■ **1** voracious, gluttonous, esurient, *colloq.* piggish, hoggish, swinish, gutsy, *literary or joc.* edacious. **2** avaricious, acquisitive, covetous, grasping, rapacious; materialistic, money-hungry, mercenary. **3** see EAGER 2.
□ **greedy-guts** see GLUTTON 1.

Greek /greek/ *n.* & *adj.* ● *n.* **1 a** a native or national of modern Greece; a person of Greek descent. **b** a native or citizen of any of the ancient States of Greece; a member of the Greek people. **2** the Indo-European language of Greece. ● *adj.* of Greece or its people or language; Hellenic. □ **Greek** (or **Greek Orthodox**) **Church** the national Church of Greece (see also *Orthodox Church*). **Greek cross** a cross with four equal arms. **Greek fire** *hist.* a combustible composition for igniting enemy ships etc. **Greek to me** *colloq.* incomprehensible to me. □□ **Greekness** *n.* [OE *Grēcas* (pl.) f. Gmc f. L *Graecus* Greek f. Gk *Graikoi*, the prehistoric name of the Hellenes (in Aristotle)]

green /green/ *adj.*, *n.*, & *v.* ● *adj.* **1** of the colour between blue and yellow in the spectrum; coloured like grass, emeralds, etc. **2 a** covered with leaves or grass. **b** mild and without snow (*a green Christmas*). **3** (of fruit etc. or wood) unripe or unseasoned. **4** not dried, smoked, or tanned. **5** inexperienced, naïve, gullible. **6 a** (of the complexion) pale, sickly-hued. **b** jealous, envious. **7** young, flourishing. **8** not withered or worn out (*a green old age*). **9** vegetable (*green food*; *green salad*). **10** (also **Green**) concerned with or supporting protection of the environment as a political principle. **11** *archaic* fresh; not healed (*a green wound*). ● *n.* **1** a green colour or pigment. **2** green clothes or material (*dressed in green*). **3 a** a piece of public or common grassy land (*village green*). **b** a grassy area used for a special purpose (*putting-green*; *bowling-green*). **c** *Golf* a putting-green. **d** *Golf* a fairway. **4** (in *pl.*) green vegetables. **5** vigour, youth, virility (*in the green*). **6** a green light. **7** a green ball, piece, etc., in a game or sport. **8** (also **Green**) a member or supporter of an environmentalist group or party. **9** (in *pl.*) *sl.* sexual intercourse. **10** *sl.* low-grade marijuana. **11** *sl.* money. **12** green foliage or growing plants. ● *v.* **1** *tr.* & *intr.* make or become green. **2** *tr. sl.* hoax; take in. □ **green belt** an area of open land round a city, designated for preservation. **Green Beret** *colloq.* a British or American commando. **green card** an international insurance document for motorists. **green cheese 1** cheese coloured green with sage. **2** whey cheese. **3** unripened cheese. **Green Cloth** (in full **Board of Green Cloth**) (in the UK) the Lord Steward's department of the Royal Household. **green crop** a crop used as fodder in a green state rather than as hay etc. **green drake** the common mayfly. **green earth** a hydrous silicate of potassium, iron, and other metals. **green-eyed** jealous. **the green-eyed monster** jealousy. **green fat** part of a turtle, highly regarded by gourmets. **green-fee** *Golf* a charge for playing one round on a course. **green fingers** skill in growing plants. **green goose** a goose killed under four months old and eaten without stuffing. **green in a person's eye** a sign of gullibility (*do you see any green in my eye?*). **green leek** any of several green-faced Australian parakeets. **green light 1** a signal to proceed on a road, railway, etc. **2** *colloq.* permission to go ahead with a project. **green linnet** = GREENFINCH. **green manure** growing plants ploughed into the soil as fertilizer. **green meat** grass and green vegetables as food. **Green Paper** (in the UK) a preliminary report of Government proposals, for discussion. **green plover** a lapwing. **green pound** the exchange rate for the pound for payments for agricultural produce in the EEC. **green revolution** greatly increased crop production in underdeveloped countries. **green-room** a room in a theatre for actors and actresses who are off stage. **green-stick fracture** a bone-fracture, esp. in children, in which one side of the bone is broken and one only bent. **green tea** tea made from steam-dried, not fermented, leaves. **green thumb** = *green fingers*. **green turtle** a green-shelled sea turtle, *Chelonia mydas*, highly regarded as food. **green vitriol** ferrous sulphate crystals.

□□ **greenish** *adj.* **greenly** *adv.* **greenness** *n.* [OE *grēne* (adj. & n.), *grēnian* (v.), f. Gmc, rel. to GROW]
■ *adj.* **1** emerald, jade, lime, lime-green, bottle-green, Lincoln-green. **2 a** verdant, fresh, grassy; rural, pastoral, country-like; see also LEAFY. **b** see MILD 3. **3** immature, unripe, unripened, unseasoned, unready. **5** naïve, callow, untested, untrained, unversed, inexperienced, new, raw, unsophisticated, *colloq.* wet behind the ears; gullible, amateur, unskilled, unskilful, amateurish, non-professional, inexpert. **6 a** see PALE[1] *adj.* 1. **b** see ENVIOUS. **7** young, youthful, flourishing, blooming, blossoming, thriving. **8** young, youthful; see also SPRIGHTLY. **10** (also **Green**) environmental, conservational, ecological, eco-, *attrib.* conservation. **11** fresh, new; see also RAW *adj.* 6a, b. ● *n.* **3 a** common, grassland; lawn(s), *archaic or literary* greensward, *literary* sward. **b** lawn, turf. **5** youth, youthfulness, salad days; see also VIGOUR 1, MANHOOD 2a. **8** (also **Green**) see CONSERVATIONIST. **9** (*greens*) see SEX *n.* 5. **10** see GRASS *n.* 5. **11** see MONEY 1. **12** foliage; plants, shrubs, trees. ● *v.* **2** see *take in* 5. □ **green-eyed** see ENVIOUS. **the green-eyed monster** see ENVY *n.* **green light 2** see *go-ahead n.* (GO[1]).

greenback /grēēnbak/ *n. US* **1** a US legal-tender note. **2** any of various green-backed animals.

greenbottle /grēēnbott'l/ *n.* any fly of the genus *Lucilia*, esp. *L. sericata* which lays eggs in the flesh of sheep.

greenery /grēēnəri/ *n.* green foliage or growing plants.

greenfeed /grēēnfeed/ *n. Austral.* & *NZ* forage grown to be fed fresh to livestock.

greenfield /grēēnfeeld/ *n.* (*attrib.*) (of a site, in terms of its potential development) having no previous building development on it.

greenfinch /grēēnfinch/ *n.* a finch, *Carduelis chloris*, with green and yellow plumage.

greenfly /grēēnflī/ *n.* (*pl.* **-flies**) *Brit.* **1** a green aphid. **2** these collectively.

greengage /grēēngayj/ *n.* a roundish green fine-flavoured variety of plum. [Sir W. *Gage* d. 1727]

greengrocer /grēēngrōsər/ *n. Brit.* a retailer of fruit and vegetables.

greengrocery /grēēngrōsəri/ *n.* (*pl.* **-ies**) *Brit.* **1** the business of a greengrocer. **2** goods sold by a greengrocer.

greenhead /grēēnhed/ *n.* **1** any biting fly of the genus *Chrysops*. **2** an Australian ant, *Chalcoponera metallica*, with a painful sting.

greenheart /grēēnhaart/ *n.* **1** any of several tropical American trees, esp. *Ocotea rodiaei*. **2** the hard greenish wood of one of these.

greenhide /grēēnhīd/ *n. Austral.* the untanned hide of an animal.

greenhorn /grēēnhorn/ *n.* an inexperienced or foolish person; a new recruit.
■ newcomer, beginner, novice, tiro, learner, tenderfoot, neophyte, initiate, (new) recruit, *sl.* rookie.

greenhouse /grēēnhowss/ *n.* a light structure with the sides and roof mainly of glass, for rearing delicate plants or hastening the growth of plants. □ **greenhouse effect** the trapping of the sun's warmth in the lower atmosphere of the earth caused by an increase in carbon dioxide, which is more transparent to solar radiation than to the reflected radiation from the earth. **greenhouse gas** any of various gases, esp. carbon dioxide, that contribute to the greenhouse effect.

greening /grēēning/ *n.* a variety of apple that is green when ripe. [prob. f. MDu. *groeninc* (as GREEN)]

greenkeeper /grēēnkeepər/ *n.* the keeper of a golf-course.

greenlet /grēēnlit/ *n.* = VIREO.

greensand /grēēnsand/ *n.* **1** a greenish kind of sandstone, often imperfectly cemented. **2** a stratum largely formed of this sandstone.

greenshank /grēēnshangk/ *n.* a large sandpiper, *Tringa nebularia*.

greensick /grēēnsik/ *adj.* affected with chlorosis. □□ **greensickness** *n.*

greenstone /grēēnstōn/ *n.* **1** a greenish igneous rock containing feldspar and hornblende. **2** a variety of jade found in New Zealand, used for tools, ornaments, etc.

greenstuff /grēēnstuf/ *n.* vegetation; green vegetables.

greensward /grēēnswawrd/ *n. archaic* or *literary* **1** grassy turf. **2** an expanse of this.

greenweed /grēēnweed/ *n.* (in full **dyer's greenweed**) a bushy plant, *Genista tinctoria*, with deep yellow flowers.

Greenwich Mean Time /grénnich, grínnij/ *n.* (also **Greenwich Time**) the local time on the meridian of Greenwich, used as an international basis of time-reckoning. [*Greenwich* in London, former site of the Royal Observatory]

greenwood /grēēnwŏŏd/ *n.* a wood in summer, esp. as the scene of outlaw life.

greeny /grēēni/ *adj.* greenish (*greeny-yellow*).

greenyard /grēēnyaard/ *n. Brit.* an enclosure for stray animals, a pound.

greet[1] /greet/ *v.tr.* **1** address politely or welcomingly on meeting or arrival. **2** receive or acknowledge in a specified way (*was greeted with derision*). **3** (of a sight, sound, etc.) become apparent to or noticed by. □□ **greeter** *n.* [OE *grētan* handle, attack, salute f. WG]
■ **1, 2** welcome, receive, hail, salute, meet; acknowledge.

greet[2] /greet/ *v.intr. Sc.* weep. [OE *grētan*, *grēotan*, of uncert. orig.]

greeting /grēēting/ *n.* **1** the act or an instance of welcoming or addressing politely. **2** words, gestures, etc., used to greet a person. **3** (often in *pl.*) an expression of goodwill. □ **greetings card** a decorative card sent to convey greetings.
■ **1** welcome, salutation, reception. **3** (*greetings*) regards, respects, best *or* good wishes, compliments, *archaic* devoirs.

gregarious /grigáiriəss/ *adj.* **1** fond of company. **2** living in flocks or communities. **3** growing in clusters. □□ **gregariously** *adv.* **gregariousness** *n.* [L *gregarius* f. *grex gregis* flock]
■ **1** see SOCIABLE.

Gregorian calendar /grigóriən/ *n.* the calendar introduced in 1582 by Pope Gregory XIII, as a correction of the Julian calendar. [med.L *Gregorianus* f. LL *Gregorius* f. Gk *Grēgorios* Gregory]

Gregorian chant /grigóriən/ *n.* plainsong ritual music, named after Pope Gregory I.

Gregorian telescope /grigóriən/ *n.* a reflecting telescope in which light reflected from a secondary mirror passes through a hole in a primary mirror. [J. *Gregory*, Sc. mathematician d. 1675, who devised it]

gregory-powder /gréggəri/ *n. hist.* a compound powder of rhubarb, magnesia, and ginger, used as a laxative. [J. *Gregory*, Sc. physician d. 1822]

gremlin /grémlin/ *n. colloq.* **1** an imaginary mischievous sprite regarded as responsible for mechanical faults, esp. in aircraft. **2** any similar cause of trouble. [20th c.: orig. unkn., but prob. after *goblin*]

grenade /grináyd/ *n.* **1** a small bomb thrown by hand (**hand-grenade**) or shot from a rifle. **2** a glass receptacle containing chemicals which disperse on impact, for testing drains, extinguishing fires, etc. [F f. OF *grenate* and Sp. *granada* POMEGRANATE]

grenadier /grénnədeér/ *n.* **1 a** *Brit.* (**Grenadiers** or **Grenadier Guards**) the first regiment of the royal household infantry. **b** *hist.* a soldier armed with grenades. **2** any deep-sea fish of the family Macrouridae, with a long tapering body and pointed tail, and secreting luminous bacteria when disturbed. [F (as GRENADE)]

grenadilla var. of GRANADILLA.

grenadine[1] /grénnədeén/ *n.* a French cordial syrup of pomegranates etc. [F f. *grenade*: see GRENADE]

grenadine[2] /grénnədeén/ *n.* a dress-fabric of loosely woven silk or silk and wool. [F, earlier *grenade* grained silk f. *grenu* grained]

Gresham's law /gréshəmz/ *n.* the tendency for money of lower intrinsic value to circulate more freely than money of higher intrinsic and equal nominal value. [Sir T. *Gresham*, Engl. financier d. 1579]

gressorial /gresóriəl/ *adj. Zool.* **1** walking. **2** adapted for walking. [mod.L *gressorius* f. L *gradi gress-* walk]

grew *past* of GROW.

grey /gray/ *adj., n., & v.* (*US* **gray**) ● *adj.* **1** of a colour intermediate between black and white, as of ashes or lead. **2 a** (of the weather etc.) dull, dismal; heavily overcast. **b** bleak, depressing; (of a person) depressed. **3 a** (of hair) turning white with age etc. **b** (of a person) having grey hair. **4** anonymous, nondescript, unidentifiable. ● *n.* **1 a** a grey colour or pigment. **b** grey clothes or material (*dressed in grey*). **2** a cold sunless light. **3** a grey or white horse. ● *v.tr. & intr.* make or become grey. □ **grey area 1** a situation or topic sharing features of more than one category and not clearly attributable to any one category. **2** *S.Afr.* an area where Black and Coloured people live (usu. illicitly) alongside White. **3** *Brit.* an area in economic decline. **grey eminence** = ÉMINENCE GRISE. **Grey Friar** a Franciscan friar. **grey goose** = GREYLAG. **grey-hen** the female of the black grouse (cf. BLACKCOCK). **grey matter 1** the darker tissues of the brain and spinal cord consisting of nerve-cell bodies and branching dendrites. **2** *colloq.* intelligence. **grey squirrel** an American squirrel, *Sciurus carolinensis*, brought to Europe in the 19th c. □□ **greyish** *adj.* **greyly** *adv.* **greyness** *n.* [OE *grǣg* f. Gmc]

■ *adj.* **1** ashen, leaden, livid, pearly, smoky, grizzly. **2** dark, murky, foggy, misty, cloudy, overcast, sunless; cheerless, gloomy, dull, dismal, drab, depressing, bleak, dreary, sombre; glum; see also MISERABLE 3. **4** anonymous, unidentifiable; colourless; see also NONDESCRIPT *adj.* □ **grey matter 2** see BRAIN *n.* 3a, b.

greybeard /gráybeerd/ *n. archaic* **1** an old man. **2** a large stoneware jug for spirits. **3** *Brit.* clematis in seed.

greyhound /gráyhownd/ *n.* **1** a dog of a tall slender breed having keen sight and capable of high speed, used in racing and coursing. **2** this breed. [OE *grīghund* f. *grīeg* bitch (unrecorded: cf. ON *grey*) + *hund* dog, rel. to HOUND]

greylag /gráylag/ *n.* (in full **greylag goose**) a wild goose, *Anser anser*, native to Europe. [GREY + LAG[1] (because of its late migration)]

greywacke /gráywakkə, -wak/ *n.* (*US* **graywacke**) *Geol.* a dark and coarse-grained sandstone, usu. with an admixture of clay. [Anglicized f. G *Grauwacke* f. *grau* grey: see WACKE]

grid /grid/ *n.* **1** a framework of spaced parallel bars; a grating. **2** a system of numbered squares printed on a map and forming the basis of map references. **3** a network of lines, electric-power connections, gas-supply lines, etc. **4** a pattern of lines marking the starting-places on a motor-racing track. **5** the wire network between the filament and the anode of a thermionic valve etc. **6** an arrangement of town streets in a rectangular pattern. □ **grid bias** *Electr.* a fixed voltage applied between the cathode and the control grid of a thermionic valve which determines its operating conditions. □□ **gridded** *adj.* [back-form. f. GRIDIRON]

■ **1** see GRATING[2] 1. **3** see NETWORK *n.* 2.

griddle /gríd'l/ *n. & v.* ● *n.* **1** = GIRDLE[2]. **2** a miner's wire-bottomed sieve. ● *v.tr.* **1** cook with a griddle; grill. **2** sieve with a griddle. [ME f. OF *gredil, gridil* gridiron ult. f. L *craticula* dimin. of *cratis* hurdle; cf. GRATE[2], GRILL[1]]

gridiron /gríddīrn/ *n.* **1** a cooking utensil of metal bars for broiling or grilling. **2** a frame of parallel beams for supporting a ship in dock. **3** *US* a football field (with parallel lines marking out the area of play). **4** *Theatr.* a plank structure over a stage supporting the mechanism for drop-scenes etc. **5** = GRID 6. [ME *gredire*, var. of *gredil* GRIDDLE, later assoc. with IRON]

gridlock /grídlok/ *n.* a traffic jam affecting a network of streets, caused by continuous queues of intersecting traffic.

grief /greef/ *n.* **1** deep or intense sorrow or mourning. **2** the cause of this. □ **come to grief** meet with disaster; fail. **good** (or **great**) **grief!** an exclamation of surprise, alarm, etc. [ME f. AF *gref*, OF *grief* f. *grever* GRIEVE[1]]

■ **1** anguish, suffering, agony, misery, distress, wretchedness, pain, hurt, sadness, sorrow, unhappiness, torment, desolation, heartbreak, heartache, *archaic or literary* woe; mourning. **2** tribulation, burden, ordeal, affliction, calamity, adversity, misfortune. □ **come to grief** fail, miscarry, meet with disaster, fall apart *or* to pieces, *colloq.* come unstuck, *sl.* come a cropper. **good grief!** see GRACIOUS *int.*

grievance /gréev'nss/ *n.* a real or fancied cause for complaint. [ME, = injury, f. OF *grevance* (as GRIEF)]

■ complaint, objection, charge, allegation, grudge, gravamen, *Brit. Law* plaint, *colloq.* gripe, *sl.* beef; injustice, disservice, unfairness, injury, insult, outrage, affront, indignity, wrongdoing; wrong, ill, damage, harm.

grieve[1] /greev/ *v.* **1** *tr.* cause grief or great distress to. **2** *intr.* suffer grief, esp. at another's death. □□ **griever** *n.* [ME f. OF *grever* ult. f. L *gravare* f. *gravis* heavy]

■ **1** see DISTRESS *v.* **2** mourn, suffer, sorrow, mope, eat one's heart out; weep, cry, moan, keen, shed tears; (*grieve over*) bemoan, lament, deplore, regret, rue, bewail.

grieve[2] /greev/ *n. Sc.* a farm-bailiff; an overseer. [OE *grǣfa*: cf. REEVE[1]]

grievous /gréevəss/ *adj.* **1** (of pain etc.) severe. **2** causing grief or suffering. **3** injurious. **4** flagrant, heinous. □ **grievous bodily harm** *Law* serious injury inflicted intentionally on a person. □□ **grievously** *adv.* **grievousness** *n.* [ME f. OF *grevos* (as GRIEVE[1])]

■ **1** severe, grave, serious; see also ACUTE *adj.* 1a. **2, 3** distressing, hurtful, harmful, wounding; injurious, damaging, wrongful. **4** flagrant, heinous, egregious, outrageous, atrocious, monstrous, deplorable, calamitous, lamentable, shameful, *colloq.* awful, appalling, terrible, shocking, dreadful.

griffin /gríffin/ *n.* (also **gryphon**) a fabulous creature with an eagle's head and wings and a lion's body. [ME f. OF *grifoun* ult. f. LL *gryphus* f. L *gryps* f. Gk *grups*]

griffon /gríff'n/ *n.* **1 a** a dog of a small terrier-like breed with coarse or smooth hair. **b** this breed. **2** (in full **griffon vulture**) a large vulture, *Gyps fulvus*. **3** = GRIFFIN. [F (in sense 1) or var. of GRIFFIN]

grig /grig/ *n.* **1** a small eel. **2** a grasshopper or cricket. □ **merry** (or **lively**) **as a grig** full of fun; extravagantly lively. [ME, orig. = dwarf: orig. unkn.]

grill[1] /gril/ *n. & v.* ● *n.* **1 a** a device on a cooker for radiating heat downwards. **b** = GRIDIRON 1. **2** a dish of food cooked on a grill. **3** (in full **grill room**) a restaurant serving grilled food. ● *v.* **1** *tr. & intr.* cook or be cooked under a grill or on a gridiron. **2** *tr. & intr.* subject or be subjected to extreme heat, esp. from the sun. **3** *tr.* subject to severe questioning or interrogation. □□ **griller** *n.* **grilling** *n.* (in sense 3 of *v.*). [F *gril* (n.), *griller* (v.), f. OF forms of GRILLE]

■ *v.* **1** see BROIL[1] 1. **3** see QUESTION *v.* 1, 2.

grill[2] var. of GRILLE.

grillage /grílij/ *n.* a heavy framework of cross-timbering or metal beams forming a foundation for building on difficult ground. [F (as GRILLE)]

grille /gril/ *n.* (also **grill**) **1** a grating or latticed screen, used as a partition or to allow discreet vision. **2** a metal grid protecting the radiator of a motor vehicle. [F f. OF *graïlle* f. med.L *graticula, craticula*: see GRIDDLE]

■ **1** see GRATING[2] 1.

grilse /grilss/ *n.* a young salmon that has returned to fresh water from the sea for the first time. [ME: orig. unkn.]

grim /grim/ *adj.* (**grimmer, grimmest**) **1** of a stern or forbidding appearance. **2 a** harsh, merciless, severe. **b** resolute, uncompromising (*grim determination*). **3** ghastly, joyless, sinister (*has a grim truth in it*). **4** unpleasant, unattractive. □ **like grim death** with great determination. □□ **grimly** *adv.* **grimness** *n.* [OE f. Gmc]

■ **1** see FORBIDDING. **2 a** harsh, merciless, stern, severe, unrelenting, stony, iron, implacable, inexorable, formidable, ferocious, fierce, heartless, ruthless, pitiless, cruel, savage, vicious, brutal. **b** resolute, uncompromising, unyielding, inflexible, adamant, unbending, firm, intractable, unflinching, unmoving, unmoved, determined, steadfast, set, fixed, decided, obstinate, headstrong, stubborn, obdurate, dogged, unwavering. **3** ghastly, joyless, dreadful, frightful, frightening, sinister, hideous, horrid, horrible, horrendous, terrible, dread, alarming, gruesome, eerie, macabre, *poet.* awful. **4** see AWFUL 1a, b.

grimace /grímməss, grimáyss/ *n.* & *v.* ● *n.* a distortion of the face made in disgust etc. or to amuse. ● *v.intr.* make a grimace. □□ **grimacer** *n.* [F f. Sp. *grimazo* f. *grima* fright]
■ *n.* see FROWN *n.* ● *v.* see FROWN *v.* 1.

grimalkin /grimálkin, -máwlkin/ *n. archaic* (esp. in fiction) **1** an old she-cat. **2** a spiteful old woman. [GREY + *Malkin* dimin. of the name *Matilda*]

grime /grīm/ *n.* & *v.* ● *n.* soot or dirt ingrained in a surface, esp. of buildings or the skin. ● *v.tr.* blacken with grime; befoul. [orig. as verb: f. MLG & MDu.]
■ *n.* filth, soot, *colloq.* muck; see also DIRT 1. ● *v.* blacken, dirty, soil, begrime, besmirch, muddy, defile, muck, *poet.* befoul.

grimy /grī́mi/ *adj.* (**grimier, grimiest**) covered with grime; dirty. □□ **grimily** *adv.* **griminess** *n.*
■ see DIRTY *adj.* 1.

grin /grin/ *v.* & *n.* ● *v.* (**grinned, grinning**) **1** *intr.* **a** smile broadly, showing the teeth. **b** make a forced, unrestrained, or stupid smile. **2** *tr.* express by grinning (*grinned his satisfaction*). ● *n.* the act or action of grinning. □ **grin and bear it** take pain or misfortune stoically. □□ **grinner** *n.* **grinningly** *adv.* [OE *grennian* f. Gmc]
■ □ **grin and bear it** see *bite the bullet*.

grind /grīnd/ *v.* & *n.* ● *v.* (*past* and *past part.* **ground** /grownd/) **1 a** *tr.* reduce to small particles or powder by crushing esp. by passing through a mill. **b** *intr.* (of a mill, machine, etc.) move with a crushing action. **2 a** *tr.* reduce, sharpen, or smooth by friction. **b** *tr.* & *intr.* rub or rub together gratingly (*grind one's teeth*). **3** *tr.* (often foll. by *down*) oppress; harass with exactions (*grinding poverty*). **4** *intr.* **a** (often foll. by *away*) work or study hard. **b** (foll. by *out*) produce with effort (*grinding out verses*). **c** (foll. by *on*) (of a sound) continue gratingly or monotonously. **5** *tr.* turn the handle of e.g. a coffee-mill, barrel-organ, etc. **6** *intr. sl.* (of a dancer) rotate the hips. **7** *intr. coarse sl.* have sexual intercourse. ● *n.* **1** the act or an instance of grinding. **2** *colloq.* hard dull work; a laborious task (*the daily grind*). **3** the size of ground particles. **4** *sl.* a dancer's rotary movement of the hips. **5** *coarse sl.* an act of sexual intercourse. □ **grind to a halt** stop laboriously. **ground glass 1** glass made non-transparent by grinding etc. **2** glass ground to a powder. □□ **grindingly** *adv.* [OE *grindan*, of unkn. orig.]
■ *v.* **1 a** pound, powder, pulverize, crush, mince, granulate, mill, kibble, triturate, *archaic* bray. **2 a** reduce; sharpen, whet; file, smooth, abrade, polish. **b** gnash, grate, rub. **3** (*grind down*) crush, wear down, oppress, harass, plague, subdue, suppress, tyrannize, persecute. **4 a** work, labour, toil, slave; study, burn the midnight oil, cram, *Brit. colloq.* swot, *literary* lucubrate. **b** (*grind out*) produce, generate, crank out. ● *n.* **2** work, toil, labour, drudgery, exertion, effort, *literary* travail; tasks, chores.

grinder /grī́ndər/ *n.* **1** a person or thing that grinds, esp. a machine (often in *comb.*: *coffee-grinder*; *organ-grinder*). **2** a molar tooth.
■ **1** see MILL[1] *n.* 1b, 2.

grindstone /grī́ndstōn/ *n.* **1** a thick revolving disc used for grinding, sharpening, and polishing. **2** a kind of stone used for this. □ **keep one's nose to the grindstone** work hard and continuously.

gringo /grínggō/ *n.* (*pl.* **-os**) *colloq.* a foreigner, esp. a British or N. American person, in a Spanish-speaking country. [Sp., = gibberish]

grip /grip/ *v.* & *n.* ● *v.* (**gripped, gripping**) **1 a** *tr.* grasp tightly; take a firm hold of. **b** *intr.* take a firm hold, esp. by friction. **2** *tr.* (of a feeling or emotion) deeply affect (a person) (*was gripped by fear*). **3** *tr.* compel the attention or interest of (*a gripping story*). ● *n.* **1 a** a firm hold; a tight grasp or clasp. **b** a manner of grasping or holding. **2** the power of holding attention. **3 a** mental or intellectual understanding or mastery. **b** effective control of a situation or one's behaviour etc. (*lose one's grip*). **4 a** a part of a machine that grips or holds something. **b** a part or attachment by which a tool, implement, weapon, etc., is held in the hand. **5** = HAIRGRIP. **6** a travelling bag. **7** an assistant in a theatre, film studio, etc. **8** *Austral. sl.* a job or occupation. □ **come** (or **get**) **to grips with** approach purposefully; begin to deal with. **get a grip** (**on oneself**) keep or recover one's self-control. **in the grip of** dominated or affected by (esp. an adverse circumstance or unpleasant sensation). **lose one's grip** lose control. □□ **gripper** *n.* **grippingly** *adv.* [OE *gripe*, *gripa* handful (as GRIPE)]
■ *v.* **1 a** grasp, clutch, clasp, hold. **b** hold, stay; see also STICK[2] 6. **2** see SEIZE 4, POSSESS 4b. **3** engross, engage, hold the attention of, fascinate, enthral, entrance, absorb, mesmerize, hypnotize, spellbind, rivet. ● *n.* **1** hold, grasp, clutch, handgrip, clasp, hand-clasp. **2** control, command, hold, mastery; authority, influence, power. **3 a** grasp, understanding, mastery, apprehension, comprehension, awareness, perception. **b** see SELF-CONTROL. **6** valise, bag, holdall, *US* carry-all; see also SUITCASE. **8** see JOB[1] *n.* 2. □ **come** (*or* **get**) **to grips with** tackle, confront, approach, meet head on, grapple with, deal with, cope with, handle, face, address. **in the grip of** under the control of, dominated *or* affected *or* controlled by; under the thumb of.

gripe /grīp/ *v.* & *n.* ● *v.* **1** *intr. colloq.* complain, esp. peevishly. **2** *tr.* affect with gastric or intestinal pain. **3** *tr. archaic* clutch, grip. **4** *Naut.* **a** *tr.* secure with gripes. **b** *intr.* turn to face the wind in spite of the helm. ● *n.* **1** (usu. in *pl.*) gastric or intestinal pain; colic. **2** *colloq.* **a** a complaint. **b** the act of griping. **3** a grip or clutch. **4** (in *pl.*) *Naut.* lashings securing a boat in its place. □ **Gripe Water** *propr.* a carminative solution to relieve colic and stomach ailments in infants. □□ **griper** *n.* **gripingly** *adv.* [OE *grīpan* f. Gmc: cf. GROPE]
■ *v.* **1** complain, moan, grumble, whine, bleat, nag, cavil, carp, *colloq.* grouse, whinge, bitch, *sl.* beef, bellyache. ● *n.* **1** stomach-ache, cramp, twinge, pang, pain, *colloq.* bellyache; colic. **2** complaint, grievance, objection, protest, grumble, moan, whine, *sl.* beef; nagging, carping, grousing, *colloq.* whinging, bitching, *sl.* bellyaching. **3** grip, clasp, clutch, hold.

grippe /grip/ *n. archaic* or *colloq.* influenza. [F f. *gripper* seize]

grisaille /grizáyl, -zīl/ *n.* **1** a method of painting in grey monochrome, often to imitate sculpture. **2** a painting or stained-glass window of this kind. [F f. *gris* grey]

griseofulvin /grízziōfŏŏlvin/ *n.* an antibiotic used against fungal infections of the hair and skin. [mod.L *griseofulvum* f. med.L *griseus* grey + L *fulvus* reddish-yellow]

grisette /greezét/ *n.* a young working-class Frenchwoman. [F, orig. a grey dress-material, f. *gris* grey]

grisly /grízli/ *adj.* (**grislier, grisliest**) causing horror, disgust, or fear. □□ **grisliness** *n.* [OE *grislic* terrifying]
■ gruesome, grim, gory, abhorrent, hideous, nasty, dreadful, repulsive, repellent, repugnant, disgusting, sickening, nauseating, horrific, horrendous, horrifying, awful, terrible, horrid, abominable, appalling.

grison /grízz'n/ *n.* any weasel-like mammal of the genus *Galictis*, with dark fur and a white stripe across the forehead. [F, app. f. *grison* grey]

grist /grist/ *n.* **1** corn to grind. **2** malt crushed for brewing. □ **grist to the** (or **a person's**) **mill** a source of profit or advantage. [OE f. Gmc, rel. to GRIND]

gristle /gríss'l/ *n.* tough flexible tissue in vertebrates; cartilage. □□ **gristly** /grísli/ *adj.* [OE *gristle*]

grit /grit/ *n.* & *v.* ● *n.* **1** particles of stone or sand, esp. as causing discomfort, clogging machinery, etc. **2** coarse sandstone. **3** *colloq.* pluck, endurance; strength of character. ● *v.* (**gritted, gritting**) **1** *tr.* spread grit on (icy roads etc.). **2** *tr.* clench (the teeth). **3** *intr.* make or move with a grating sound. □□ **gritter** *n.* **gritty** *adj.* (**grittier, grittiest**). **grittily** *adv.* **grittiness** *n.* [OE *grēot* f. Gmc: cf. GRITS, GROATS]

■ *n.* **3** pluck, courage, courageousness, valour, bravery, fortitude, endurance, resolution, resoluteness, resolve, toughness, mettle, spirit, backbone, nerve, gameness, intrepidity, dauntlessness, tenacity, determination, firmness, hardiness, staunchness, stalwartness, fearlessness, *archaic or joc.* doughtiness, *colloq.* guts, gutsiness, spunk, spunkiness, *Brit. sl.* bottle, *US sl.* moxie. □□ **gritty** sandy, gravelly, granular, grainy; rough, abrasive, rasping; courageous, valorous, brave, resolute, tough, mettlesome, plucky, spirited, game, intrepid, dauntless, tenacious, determined, persistent, firm, hardy, staunch, stalwart, fearless, *archaic or joc.* doughty, *colloq.* gutsy, spunky.

grits /grits/ *n.pl.* **1** coarsely ground grain, esp. oatmeal. **2** oats that have been husked but not ground. [OE *grytt(e)*: cf. GRIT, GROATS]

grizzle /grízz'l/ *v.intr. Brit. colloq.* **1** (esp. of a child) cry fretfully. **2** complain whiningly. □□ **grizzler** *n.* **grizzly** *adj.* [19th c.: orig. unkn.]

■ **1** see CRY *v.* 2a.

grizzled /grízz'ld/ *adj.* having, or streaked with, grey hair. [*grizzle* grey f. OF *grisel* f. *gris* grey]

grizzly /grízli/ *adj.* & *n.* ● *adj.* (**grizzlier, grizzliest**) grey, greyish, grey-haired. ● *n.* (*pl.* **-ies**) (in full **grizzly bear**) a large variety of brown bear found in N. America.

groan /grōn/ *v.* & *n.* ● *v.* **1 a** *intr.* make a deep sound expressing pain, grief, or disapproval. **b** *tr.* utter with groans. **2** *intr.* complain inarticulately. **3** *intr.* (usu. foll. by *under, beneath, with*) be loaded or oppressed. ● *n.* the sound made in groaning. □ **groan inwardly** be distressed. □□ **groaner** *n.* **groaningly** *adv.* [OE *grānian* f. Gmc, rel. to GRIN]

■ *v.* **1** moan, sigh, murmur, wail, whimper, whine. **2** complain, grumble, moan, object, protest, *colloq.* gripe, grouse, whinge, bitch, *colloq. or dial.* yammer, *sl.* beef. **3** be weighed down, be loaded *or* overloaded, be bowed down; be oppressed, be burdened *or* saddled *or* pressured *or* lumbered, be overwhelmed. ● *n.* moan, sigh, murmur, wail, whimper, whine.

groat /grōt/ *n. hist.* **1** a silver coin worth four old pence. **2** *archaic* a small sum (*don't care a groat*). [ME f. MDu. *groot*, orig. = great, i.e. thick (penny): cf. GROSCHEN]

groats /grōts/ *n.pl.* hulled or crushed grain, esp. oats. [OE *grotan* (pl.): cf. *grot* fragment, *grēot* GRIT, *grytt* bran]

grocer /grṓsər/ *n.* a dealer in food and household provisions. [ME & AF *grosser*, orig. one who sells in the gross, f. OF *grossier* f. med.L *grossarius* (as GROSS)]

grocery /grṓsəri/ *n.* (*pl.* **-ies**) **1** a grocer's trade or shop. **2** (in *pl.*) provisions, esp. food, sold by a grocer.

■ **2** see PROVISION *n.* 2.

grockle /grókk'l/ *n. dial.* & *sl.* a visitor or holiday-maker, esp. from the North or Midlands to SW England. [20th c.: orig. uncert.]

grog /grog/ *n.* **1** a drink of spirit (orig. rum) and water. **2** *Austral.* & *NZ colloq.* alcoholic liquor, esp. beer. [said to be from 'Old *Grog*', the reputed nickname (f. his GROGRAM cloak) of Admiral Vernon, who in 1740 first had diluted instead of neat rum served out to sailors]

■ **2** see LIQUOR *n.* 1.

groggy /gróggi/ *adj.* (**groggier, groggiest**) incapable or unsteady from being dazed or semi-conscious. □□ **groggily** *adv.* **grogginess** *n.*

■ unsteady, shaky, wobbly, weak, stupefied, dazed, stunned, dizzy, faint, reeling, punch-drunk, muddle-headed, addled, confused, bewildered, befuddled, muzzy, *colloq.* dopey, woozy.

grogram /grógrəm/ *n.* a coarse fabric of silk, mohair, and wool, or a mixture of these, often stiffened with gum. [F *gros grain* coarse grain (as GROSS, GRAIN)]

groin[1] /groyn/ *n.* & *v.* ● *n.* **1** the depression between the belly and the thigh. **2** *Archit.* **a** an edge formed by intersecting vaults. **b** an arch supporting a vault. ● *v.tr. Archit.* build with groins. [ME *grynde*, perh. f. OE *grynde* depression]

groin[2] *US* var. of GROYNE.

grommet /grómmit/ *n.* (also **grummet** /grúmmit/) **1** a metal, plastic, or rubber eyelet placed in a hole to protect or insulate a rope or cable etc. passed through it. **2** a tube passed through the eardrum in surgery to make a communication with the middle ear. [obs. F *grommette* f. *gourmer* to curb, of unkn. orig.]

gromwell /grómwəl/ *n.* any of various plants of the genus *Lithospermum*, with hard seeds formerly used in medicine. [ME f. OF *gromil*, prob. f. med.L *gruinum milium* (unrecorded) crane's millet]

groom /groom/ *n.* & *v.* ● *n.* **1** a person employed to take care of horses. **2** = BRIDEGROOM. **3** *Brit. Mil.* any of certain officers of the Royal Household. ● *v.tr.* **1 a** curry or tend (a horse). **b** give a neat appearance to (a person etc.). **2** (of an ape or monkey etc.) clean and comb the fur of (its fellow) with the fingers. **3** prepare or train (a person) for a particular purpose or activity (*was groomed for the top job*). [ME, orig. = boy: orig. unkn.]

■ *n.* **1** stable-boy, stable-girl, stableman, stable-lad, *hist.* equerry, *Brit. hist.* ostler. ● *v.* **1** spruce up, dress, tidy up, neaten *or* smarten up, preen, primp, *colloq.* titivate; tend; curry. **2** see CLEAN *v.* 1. **3** fit, train, prepare, coach, tutor, brief, drill, prime, (get *or* make) ready, shape.

groove /groov/ *n.* & *v.* ● *n.* **1 a** a channel or hollow, esp. one made to guide motion or receive a corresponding ridge. **b** a spiral track cut in a gramophone record. **2** an established routine or habit, esp. a monotonous one. ● *v.* **1** *tr.* make a groove or grooves in. **2** *intr. sl.* **a** enjoy oneself. **b** (often foll. by *with*) make progress; get on well. ¶ Often with ref. to popular music or jazz; now largely disused in general contexts. □ **in the groove** *sl.* **1** doing or performing well. **2** fashionable. [ME, = mine-shaft, f. obs. Du. *groeve* furrow f. Gmc]

■ *n.* **1 a** slot, cut, track, channel, furrow, flute, glyph, gouge, *Anat.*, *Biol.*, & *Geol.* stria, striation. **2** routine, habit, rut, grind, treadmill. ● *v.* **1** furrow, flute; see SCORE *v.* 3. **2 a** see *enjoy oneself*. □ **in the groove 2** see TRENDY *adj.*

groovy /gróovi/ *adj.* (**groovier, grooviest**) **1** *sl.* fashionable and exciting; enjoyable, excellent. **2** of or like a groove. □□ **groovily** *adv.* **grooviness** *n.*

■ **1** see MARVELLOUS 2.

grope /grōp/ *v.* & *n.* ● *v.* **1** *intr.* (usu. foll. by *for*) feel about or search blindly or uncertainly with the hands. **2** *intr.* (foll. by *for, after*) search mentally (*was groping for the answer*). **3** *tr.* feel (one's way) towards something. **4** *tr. sl.* fondle clumsily for sexual pleasure. ● *n.* the process or an instance of groping. □□ **groper** *n.* **gropingly** *adv.* [OE *grāpian* f. Gmc]

■ *v.* **1** fumble, feel about, *Austral.* & *NZ colloq.* fossick about *or* around; (*grope for*) search for, feel for, fish for. **2** (*grope for*) seek, look for, search for, hunt for, quest for, pursue, be after, try to find. **4** see FONDLE, MOLEST 2. ● *n.* feel, fumble, search; fumbling, searching. □□ **gropingly** with difficulty; uncertainly, hesitantly, tentatively.

groper /grṓpər/ *n.* esp. *Austral.* & *NZ* = GROUPER. [var. of GROUPER]

grosbeak /grṓsbeek/ *n.* any of various finches of the families Cardinalidae and Fringillidae, having stout conical bills and usu. brightly coloured plumage. [F *grosbec* (as GROSS)]

groschen /grṓsh'n/ *n.* **1** an Austrian coin and monetary unit, one hundredth of a schilling. **2** *colloq.* a German 10-pfennig piece. **3** *hist.* a small German silver coin. [G f. MHG *gros, grosse* f. med.L *(denarius) grossus* thick (penny): cf. GROAT]

grosgrain /grṓgrayn/ *n.* a corded fabric of silk etc. [F, = coarse grain (as GROSS, GRAIN)]

gros point /grō pwáN/ *n.* cross-stitch embroidery on canvas. [F (as GROSS, POINT)]

gross /grōss/ *adj., v., & n.* ● *adj.* **1** overfed, bloated; repulsively fat. **2** (of a person, manners, or morals) noticeably coarse, unrefined, or indecent. **3** flagrant; conspicuously wrong *(gross negligence)*. **4** total; without deductions; not net *(gross tonnage; gross income)*. **5 a** luxuriant, rank. **b** thick, solid, dense. **6** (of the senses etc.) dull; lacking sensitivity. **7** *sl.* repulsive, disgusting. ● *v.tr.* produce or earn as gross profit or income. ● *n.* (*pl.* same) an amount equal to twelve dozen. □ **by the gross** in large quantities; wholesale. **gross domestic product** the total value of goods produced and services provided in a country in one year. **gross national product** the gross domestic product plus the total of net income from abroad. **gross out** *US sl.* disgust, esp. by repulsive or obscene behaviour. **gross up** increase (a net amount) to its value before deductions. □□ **grossly** *adv.* **grossness** *n.* [ME f. OF *gros grosse* large f. LL *grossus*: (n.) f. F *grosse douzaine* large dozen]

■ *adj.* **1** overfed, bloated, fat, overweight, big, large, bulky, heavy, *Austral. colloq.* poddy; see also OBESE. **2** coarse, vulgar, crude, unsophisticated, uncultured, crass, indelicate, inappropriate, unseemly, improper, unrefined, bawdy, ribald, Rabelaisian, rude, offensive, obscene, indecent, lewd, dirty, smutty, earthy, pornographic, filthy. **3** outrageous, flagrant, glaring, blatant, monstrous; obvious, plain, manifest, evident. **4** total, entire, inclusive, overall, whole; pre-tax. **5 a** see LUXURIANT 2. **6** see DULL *adj.* 1. **7** disgusting, repulsive, repellent, revolting, nauseating, *sl.* yucky. ● *v.* **1** produce, bring in, make; see also EARN 1. □ **gross out** see DISGUST *v.*

grot /grot/ *n. & adj. Brit. sl.* ● *n.* rubbish, junk. ● *adj.* dirty . [back-form. f. GROTTY]

grotesque /grōtésk/ *adj. & n.* ● *adj.* **1** comically or repulsively distorted; monstrous, unnatural. **2** incongruous, ludicrous, absurd. ● *n.* **1** a decorative form interweaving human and animal features. **2** a comically distorted figure or design. **3** *Printing* a family of sanserif typefaces. □□ **grotesquely** *adv.* **grotesqueness** *n.* **grotesquerie** /-téskəri/ *n.* [earlier *crotesque* f. F *crotesque* f. It. *grottesca* grotto-like (painting etc.) fem. of *grottesco* (as GROTTO, -ESQUE)]

■ *adj.* **1** distorted, gnarled, misshapen, malformed, deformed, unnatural, freakish, monstrous, gruesome. **2** absurd, incongruous, ludicrous, ridiculous, farcical, preposterous, bizarre, weird, odd, fantastic, strange, queer, peculiar, curious, outlandish, offbeat, abnormal, aberrant, *colloq.* crazy, insane. ● *n.* **1, 2** gargoyle; caricature; cartoon.

grotto /gróttō/ *n.* (*pl.* **-oes** or **-os**) **1** a small picturesque cave. **2** an artificial ornamental cave, e.g. in a park or large garden. □□ **grottoed** *adj.* [It. *grotta* ult. f. L *crypta* f. Gk *kruptē* CRYPT]

■ see CAVE[1] *n.* 1.

grotty /grótti/ *adj.* (**grottier, grottiest**) *Brit. sl.* unpleasant, dirty, shabby, unattractive. □□ **grottiness** *n.* [shortening of GROTESQUE + -Y[1]]

■ see BAD *adj.* 1.

grouch /growch/ *v. & n. colloq.* ● *v.intr.* grumble. ● *n.* **1** a discontented person. **2** a fit of grumbling or the sulks. **3** a cause of discontent. [var. of *grutch*: see GRUDGE]

■ *v.* see COMPLAIN 1. ● *n.* **1** see MISERY 3. **2** see SQUAWK *n.* 2.

grouchy /grówchi/ *adj.* (**grouchier, grouchiest**) *colloq.* discontented, grumpy. □□ **grouchily** *adv.* **grouchiness** *n.*

■ see DISGRUNTLED.

ground[1] /grownd/ *n. & v.* ● *n.* **1 a** the surface of the earth, esp. as contrasted with the air around it. **b** a part of this specified in some way *(low ground)*. **2** the substance of the earth's surface; soil, earth *(stony ground; dug deep into the ground)*. **3 a** a position, area, or distance on the earth's surface. **b** the extent of activity etc. achieved or of a subject dealt with *(the book covers a lot of ground)*. **4** (often in *pl.*) a foundation, motive, or reason *(there is ground for concern; there are grounds for believing; excused on the grounds of ill-health)*. **5** an area of a special kind or designated for special use (often in *comb.*: *cricket-ground; fishing-grounds*). **6** (in *pl.*) an area of usu. enclosed land attached to a house etc. **7** an area or basis for consideration, agreement, etc. *(common ground; on firm ground)*. **8 a** (in painting) the prepared surface giving the predominant colour or tone. **b** (in embroidery, ceramics, etc.) the undecorated surface. **9** (in full **ground bass**) *Mus.* a short theme in the bass constantly repeated with the upper parts of the music varied. **10** (in *pl.*) solid particles, esp. of coffee, forming a residue. **11** *Electr.* = EARTH. **12** the bottom of the sea *(the ship touched ground)*. **13** *Brit.* the floor of a room etc. **14** a piece of wood fixed to a wall as a base for boards, plaster, or joinery. **15** (*attrib.*) **a** (of animals) living on or in the ground; (of fish) living at the bottom of water; (of plants) dwarfish or trailing. **b** relating to or concerned with the ground *(ground staff)*. ● *v.* **1** *tr.* refuse authority for (a pilot or an aircraft) to fly. **2 a** *tr.* run (a ship) aground; strand. **b** *intr.* (of a ship) run aground. **3** *tr.* (foll. by *in*) instruct thoroughly (in a subject). **4** *tr.* (often as **grounded** *adj.*) (foll. by *on*) base (a principle, conclusion, etc.) on. **5** *tr. Electr.* = EARTH *v.* **6** *intr.* alight on the ground. **7** *tr.* place or lay (esp. weapons) on the ground. □ **break new** (or **fresh**) **ground** treat a subject previously not dealt with. **cut the ground from under a person's feet** anticipate and pre-empt a person's arguments, plans, etc. **down to the ground** *Brit. colloq.* thoroughly; in every respect. **fall to the ground** (of a plan etc.) fail. **gain** (or **make**) **ground 1** advance steadily; make progress. **2** (foll. by *on*) catch (a person) up. **get in on the ground floor** become part of an enterprise in its early stages. **get off the ground** *colloq.* make a successful start. **give** (or **lose**) **ground 1** retreat, decline. **2** lose the advantage or one's position in an argument, contest, etc. **go to ground 1** (of a fox etc.) enter its earth or burrow etc. **2** (of a person) become inaccessible for a prolonged period. **ground-bait** bait thrown to the bottom of a fishing-ground. **ground control** the personnel directing the landing etc. of aircraft or spacecraft. **ground cover** plants covering the surface of the earth, esp. low-growing spreading plants that inhibit the growth of weeds. **ground elder** a garden weed, *Aegopodium podagraria*, spreading by means of underground stems. **ground floor** the floor of a building at ground level. **ground frost** frost on the surface of the ground or in the top layer of soil. **ground level 1** the level of the ground; the ground floor. **2** *Physics* the lowest energy state of an atom etc. **ground-plan 1** the plan of a building at ground level. **2** the general outline of a scheme. **ground-rent** rent for land leased for building. **ground rule** a basic principle. **ground speed** an aircraft's speed relative to the ground. **ground-squirrel 1** a squirrel-like rodent, e.g. a chipmunk, gopher, etc. **2** any squirrel of the genus *Spermophilus* living in burrows. **ground staff** the non-flying personnel of an airport or airbase. **ground state** *Physics* = *ground level* 2. **ground stroke** *Tennis* a stroke played near the ground after the ball has bounced. **ground swell 1** a heavy sea caused by a distant or past storm or an earthquake. **2** an increasingly forceful presence (esp. of public opinion). **ground zero** the point on the ground under an exploding (usu. nuclear) bomb. **hold one's ground** not retreat or give way. **on the ground** at the point of production or operation; in practical conditions. **on one's own ground** on one's own territory or subject; on one's own terms. **thin on the ground** not numerous. **work** (or **run** etc.) **oneself**

into the ground *colloq.* work etc. to the point of exhaustion. □□ **grounder** *n.* [OE *grund* f. Gmc]
■ *n.* **1 a** (dry) land, earth, (solid) ground, terra firma. **b** land, terrain, country, territory. **2** earth, soil, sod, loam, clay, mould, dirt. **3** position, area, distance, range, scope, compass, territory. **4** reason, justification, rationale, argument, cause, motive, excuse, foundation. **7** base, basis, foundation, footing, position. **10** (*grounds*) particles, dregs, lees, settlings, grouts; sediment, deposit. ● *v.* **3** instruct, teach, train, coach, tutor, inform, prepare, initiate. **4** establish, found, organize; see also BASE[1] *v.* 1. □ **break new** (or **fresh**) **ground** innovate, pioneer, blaze a trail. **down to the ground** see *thoroughly* (THOROUGH). **fall to the ground** see FAIL *v.* 1, 2a. **gain** (or **make**) **ground 1** see ADVANCE *v.* 1, 2, PROGRESS *v.* 1. **get off the ground** see START *v.* 1, 2. **give** (or **lose**) **ground 1** see RETREAT *v.* 1a **2** see LOSE 4, 5, 8, 10. **go to ground** see HIDE[1] *v.* 2. **ground rule** see PRINCIPLE 1. **ground swell 2** see WAVE *n.* 6a. **hold one's ground** stand firm, *esp. US* stand pat, *colloq.* stick to one's guns; see also PERSEVERE. **thin on the ground** rare, uncommon, few (and far between), hard to come by *or* find; see also SCANTY. **work oneself into the ground** see SLAVE *v.*

ground[2] *past* and *past part.* of GRIND.

groundage /grówndij/ *n. Brit.* duty levied on a ship entering a port or lying on a shore.

groundhog /grówndhog/ *n.* **1** = AARDVARK. **2** *US* a marmot; a woodchuck.

grounding /grównding/ *n.* basic training or instruction in a subject.
■ see BACKGROUND 3.

groundless /grówndliss/ *adj.* without motive or foundation. □□ **groundlessly** *adv.* **groundlessness** *n.* [OE *grundlēas* (as GROUND[1], -LESS)]
■ baseless, without foundation, unfounded, unsupported; suppositional, hypothetical, tenuous, flimsy, illusory, imaginary; unsound, unjustified, unjustifiable, unwarranted, uncalled-for, unreasoned, unreasonable; unmotivated.

groundling /grówndling/ *n.* **1 a** a creeping or dwarf plant. **b** an animal that lives near the ground, at the bottom of a lake, etc., esp. a ground-fish. **2** a person on the ground as opposed to one in an aircraft. **3** a spectator or reader of inferior taste (with ref. to Shakesp. *Hamlet* III. ii. 11).

groundnut /grówndnut/ *n.* **1** *Brit.* = PEANUT. **2 a** a N. American wild bean. **b** its edible tuber.

groundsel /grówns'l/ *n.* any composite plant of the genus *Senecio*, esp. *S. vulgaris*, used as a food for cage-birds. [OE *grundeswylige, gundæswelgiæ* (perh. = pus-absorber f. *gund* pus, with ref. to use for poultices)]

groundsheet /grówndsheet/ *n.* a waterproof sheet for spreading on the ground, esp. in a tent.

groundsman /grówndzmən/ *n.* (*pl.* **-men**) a person who maintains a sports ground.

groundwater /grówndwawtər/ *n.* water found in soil or in pores, crevices, etc., in rock.

groundwork /grówndwurk/ *n.* **1** preliminary or basic work. **2** a foundation or basis.
■ **1** spadework, preparation(s), preliminaries. **2** base, underpinning(s), cornerstone; see also FOUNDATION 3, BASIS 1, 2.

group /grōōp/ *n.* & *v.* ● *n.* **1** a number of persons or things located close together, or considered or classed together. **2** (*attrib.*) concerning or done by a group (*a group photograph; group sex*). **3** a number of people working together or sharing beliefs, e.g. part of a political party. **4** a number of commercial companies under common ownership. **5** an ensemble playing popular music. **6** a division of an air force or air-fleet. **7** *Math.* a set of elements, together with an associative binary operation, which contains an inverse for each element and an identity element. **8** *Chem.* **a** a set of ions or radicals giving a characteristic qualitative reaction. **b** a set of elements having similar properties. **c** a combination of atoms having a recognizable identity in a number of compounds. ● *v.* **1** *tr.* & *intr.* form or be formed into a group. **2** *tr.* (often foll. by *with*) place in a group or groups. **3** *tr.* form (colours, figures, etc.) into a well-arranged and harmonious whole. **4** *tr.* classify. □ **group captain** an RAF officer next below air commodore. **group dynamics** *Psychol.* the field of social psychology concerned with the nature, development, and interactions of human groups. **group practice** a medical practice in which several doctors are associated. **group therapy** therapy in which patients with a similar condition are brought together to assist one another psychologically. **group velocity** the speed of travel of the energy of a wave or wave-group. □□ **groupage** *n.* [F *groupe* f. It. *gruppo* f. Gmc, rel. to CROP]
■ *n.* **1** batch, set, grouping, classification, collection, assemblage, number, accumulation, conglomeration, agglomeration, assortment, series; assembly, gathering, congregation, company, crowd, body, *colloq.* bunch. **2** (*attrib.*) see JOINT *adj.* **3** alliance, union, association, organization, league, society, coterie, clique, set, band, circle, club, party, body, faction, team, corps, guild, troupe, unit, troop, platoon, squad, gang. **4** see TRUST *n.* 8c. **5** see BAND[2] *n.* 2. ● *v.* **1, 2** collect, assemble, gather; arrange, place, organize, order, bring *or* put together. **3** see ARRANGE 1. **4** classify, class, sort, bracket, rank, assort, categorize, catalogue.

grouper /grōōpər/ *n.* any marine fish of the family Serranidae, with heavy body, big head, and wide mouth. [Port. *garupa*, prob. f. native name in S. America]

groupie /grōōpi/ *n. sl.* an ardent follower of touring pop groups, esp. a young woman seeking sexual relations with them.
■ see FOLLOWER.

grouping /grōōping/ *n.* **1** a process or system of allocation to groups. **2** the formation or arrangement so produced.
■ **2** see ARRANGEMENT 1–3.

grouse[1] /growss/ *n.* (*pl.* same) **1** any of various game-birds of the family Tetraonidae, with a plump body and feathered legs. **2** the flesh of a grouse used as food. [16th c.: orig. uncert.]

grouse[2] /growss/ *v.* & *n. colloq.* ● *v.intr.* grumble or complain pettily. ● *n.* a complaint. □□ **grouser** *n.* [19th c.: orig. unkn.]
■ *v.* see COMPLAIN 1. ● *n.* see COMPLAINT 2.

grouse[3] / growss/ *adj. Austral. sl.* very good or excellent (*extra grouse*). [20th c.: orig. unkn.]

grout[1] /growt/ *n.* & *v.* ● *n.* a thin fluid mortar for filling gaps in tiling etc. ● *v.tr.* provide or fill with grout. □□ **grouter** *n.* [perh. f. GROUT[2], but cf. F dial. *grouter* grout a wall]

grout[2] /growt/ *n.* sediment, dregs. [OE *grūt*, rel. to GRITS, GROATS]

grouter /grówtər/ *n. Austral. sl.* an unfair advantage. [20th c.: orig. uncert.]

grove /grōv/ *n.* a small wood or group of trees. □□ **grovy** *adj.* [OE *grāf*, rel. to *grǣfa* brushwood]
■ see THICKET.

grovel /gróvv'l/ *v.intr.* (**grovelled, grovelling**; *US* **groveled, groveling**) **1** behave obsequiously in seeking favour or forgiveness. **2** lie prone in abject humility. □□ **groveller** *n.* **grovelling** *adj.* **grovellingly** *adv.* [back-form. f. obs. *grovelling* (adv.) f. *gruf* face down f. *on grufe* f. ON *á grúfu*, later taken as pres. part.]
■ **1** see TRUCKLE *v.* **2** see PROSTRATE *v.* 2. □□ **grovelling** obsequious, fawning, toadying, sycophantish, sycophantic, subservient, slavish, servile, submissive, cringing, cowering, snivelling, scraping, abject, crawling, *colloq.* bootlicking.

grow /grō/ *v.* (*past* **grew** /grōō/; *past part.* **grown** /grōn/) **1** *intr.* increase in size, height, quantity, degree, or in any way regarded as measurable (e.g. authority or reputation) (often foll. by *in*: *grew in stature*). **2** *intr.* **a** develop or exist as a living plant or natural product. **b** develop in a specific way or direction (*began to grow sideways*). **c** germinate, sprout; spring up. **3** *intr.* be produced; come naturally into existence; arise. **4** *intr.* (as **grown** *adj.*) fully matured; adult. **5** *intr.* **a** become gradually (*grow rich; grow less*). **b** (foll. by *to* + infin.) come by degrees (*grew to like it*). **6** *intr.* (foll. by *into*) **a** become, having grown or developed (*the acorn has grown into a tall oak; will grow into a fine athlete*). **b** become large enough for or suited to (*will grow into the coat; grew into her new job*). **7** *intr.* (foll. by *on*) become gradually more favoured by. **8** *tr.* **a** produce (plants, fruit, wood, etc.) by cultivation. **b** bring forth. **c** cause (a beard etc.) to develop. **9** *tr.* (in *passive*; foll. by *over, up*) be covered with a growth. □ **growing bag** a bag containing peat-based potting compost in which plants may be grown. **growing pains 1** early difficulties in the development of an enterprise etc. **2** neuralgic pain in children's legs due to fatigue etc. **grown-up** *adj.* adult. ● *n.* an adult person. **grow out of 1** become too large to wear (a garment). **2** become too mature to retain (a childish habit etc.). **3** be the result or development of. **grow together** coalesce. **grow up 1 a** advance to maturity. **b** (esp. in *imper.*) begin to behave sensibly. **2** (of a custom) arise, become common. □□ **growable** *adj.* [OE *grōwan* f. Gmc, rel. to GRASS, GREEN]

■ **1** develop, increase, enlarge, wax, swell, expand, extend, broaden, thicken, spread, lengthen, multiply, intensify. **2 a, b** develop; exist, live. **c** see SPRING *v.* 4. **3** develop, evolve, arise, spring (up), originate, begin, start; see also OCCUR 1. **4** (**grown**) see MATURE *adj.* 1. **5 a** become, get. **b** come, get; start, begin. **6 a** (*grow into*) see BECOME 1. **b** see ADAPT 2. **7** (*grow on*) become accepted by, become liked by, become more pleasing to, become more favoured by. **8 a** plant, sow, cultivate; breed, nurture, raise, propagate, produce. **9** (*be grown over*) be overgrown, be covered. □ **grown-up** (*adj.*) see MATURE *adj.* 1. **grow out of 3** be the result of, result *or* develop from, stem from, go back to, date back to, originate in, be caused by, start with. **grow up 1 a** mature, reach maturity *or* adulthood, come of age, reach the age of majority. **b** be sensible, behave, act one's age, stop acting like a child, stop being a baby. **2** see ARISE 1.

grower /grṓər/ *n.* **1** (often in *comb.*) a person growing produce (*fruit-grower*). **2** a plant that grows in a specified way (*a fast grower*).

growl /growl/ *v.* & *n.* ● *v.* **1** *intr.* **a** (often foll. by *at*) (esp. of a dog) make a low guttural sound, usu. of anger. **b** murmur angrily. **2** *intr.* rumble. **3** *tr.* (often foll. by *out*) utter with a growl. ● *n.* **1** a growling sound, esp. made by a dog. **2** an angry murmur; complaint. **3** a rumble. □□ **growlingly** *adv.* [prob. imit.]

■ *v.* **1, 3** see ROAR *v.* 3.

growler /grówlər/ *n.* **1** a person or thing that growls, esp. *sl.* a dog. **2** a small iceberg.

grown *past part.* of GROW.

growth /grōth/ *n.* **1** the act or process of growing. **2** an increase in size or value. **3** something that has grown or is growing. **4** *Med.* a morbid formation. **5** the cultivation of produce. **6** a crop or yield of grapes. □ **full growth** the size ultimately attained; maturity. **growth hormone** *Biol.* a substance which stimulates the growth of a plant or animal. **growth industry** an industry that is developing rapidly. **growth stock** etc. stock etc. that tends to increase in capital value rather than yield high income.

■ **1** development, evolution, evolvement; increase, expansion, broadening, extension, enlargement, spread, proliferation, flowering. **2** advance, advancement, increase, appreciation, improvement, expansion, rise, progress. **3** vegetation; see SPREAD *n.* 1. **4** excrescence, lump, tumour, swelling. **5** cultivation, culture, growing, farming. **6** crop, yield, harvest. □ **full growth** see *maturity* (MATURE).

groyne /groyn/ *n.* (*US* **groin**) a timber framework or low broad wall built out from a shore to check erosion of a beach. [dial. *groin* snout f. OF *groign* f. LL *grunium* pig's snout]

grub /grub/ *n.* & *v.* ● *n.* **1** the larva of an insect, esp. of a beetle. **2** *colloq.* food. ● *v.* (**grubbed, grubbing**) **1** *tr.* & *intr.* dig superficially. **2** *tr.* **a** clear (the ground) of roots and stumps. **b** clear away (roots etc.). **3** *tr.* (foll. by *up, out*) **a** fetch by digging (*grubbing up weeds*). **b** extract (information etc.) by searching in books etc. **4** *intr.* search, rummage. **5** *intr.* (foll. by *on, along, away*) toil, plod. □ **grub-screw** a small headless screw, esp. used to attach a handle etc. to a spindle. □□ **grubber** *n.* (also in *comb.*). [ME, (v.) perh. corresp. to OE *grybban* (unrecorded) f. Gmc]

■ *n.* **2** see FOOD 1. ● *v.* **5** see PLOD *v.* 2.

grubby /grúbbi/ *adj.* (**grubbier, grubbiest**) **1** dirty, grimy, slovenly. **2** of or infested with grubs. □□ **grubbily** *adv.* **grubbiness** *n.*

grubstake /grúbstayk/ *n.* & *v.* *US colloq.* ● *n.* material or provisions supplied to an enterprise in return for a share in the resulting profits (orig. in prospecting for ore). ● *v.tr.* provide with a grubstake. □□ **grubstaker** *n.*

Grub Street / grúb street/ *n.* (often *attrib.*) the world or class of literary hacks and impoverished authors. [name of a street (later Milton St.) in Moorgate, London, inhabited by these in the 17th c.]

grudge /gruj/ *n.* & *v.* ● *n.* a persistent feeling of ill will or resentment, esp. one due to an insult or injury (*bears a grudge against me*). ● *v.tr.* **1** be resentfully unwilling to give, grant, or allow (a thing). **2** (foll. by verbal noun or *to* + infin.) be reluctant to do (a thing) (*grudged paying so much*). □□ **grudger** *n.* [ME *grutch* f. OF *grouchier* murmur, of unkn. orig.]

■ *n.* bitterness, resentment, rancour, ill will, hard feelings, pique, dislike, antipathy, animosity, enmity, malice, malevolence, *esp. Austral.* & *NZ colloq.* set; grievance, aversion, animus. ● *v.* **1, 2** see BEGRUDGE 1, 2, MIND *v.* 1.

grudging /grújing/ *adj.* reluctant; not willing. □□ **grudgingly** *adv.* **grudgingness** *n.*

gruel /gróōəl/ *n.* a liquid food of oatmeal etc. boiled in milk or water chiefly for invalids. [ME f. OF, ult. f. Gmc, rel. to GROUT[1]]

gruelling /gróōəling/ *adj.* & *n.* (*US* **grueling**) ● *adj.* extremely demanding, severe, or tiring. ● *n.* a harsh or exhausting experience; punishment. □□ **gruellingly** *adv.* [GRUEL as verb, = exhaust, punish]

■ *adj.* see ARDUOUS.

gruesome /gróōssəm/ *adj.* horrible, grisly, disgusting. □□ **gruesomely** *adv.* **gruesomeness** *n.* [Sc. *grue* to shudder f. Scand. + -SOME[1]]

■ ghastly, repugnant, horrible, horrid, horrific, horrendous, grisly, hideous, revolting, disgusting, repellent, repulsive, loathsome, grim, grotesque, macabre, frightful, fearsome, shocking, terrible, *colloq.* awful.

gruff /gruf/ *adj.* **1 a** (of a voice) low and harsh. **b** (of a person) having a gruff voice. **2** surly, laconic, rough-mannered. □□ **gruffly** *adv.* **gruffness** *n.* [Du., MLG *grof* coarse f. WG (rel. to ROUGH)]

■ **1 a** low, throaty, harsh, rough, guttural, rasping, hoarse, husky, deep. **2** laconic, terse, rough-mannered, surly, crusty, grumpy, curmudgeonly, cantankerous, churlish, rude, uncivil, bearish, testy, irritable, cross, irascible, bluff, abrupt, curt, blunt, brusque, short, short-tempered, bad-tempered, crabbed, sullen, sulky, ill-humoured, *colloq.* grouchy, crotchety.

grumble /grúmb'l/ *v.* & *n.* ● *v.* **1** *intr.* **a** (often foll. by *at, about, over*) complain peevishly. **b** be discontented. **2** *intr.* **a** utter a dull inarticulate sound; murmur, growl faintly. **b** rumble. **3** *tr.* (often foll. by *out*) utter complainingly. **4** *intr.* (as **grumbling** *adj.*) *colloq.* giving intermittent discomfort without causing illness (*a grumbling appendix*). ● *n.* **1** a complaint. **2 a** a dull inarticulate sound; a murmur. **b** a rumble. □□ **grumbler** *n.* **grumbling** *adj.* **grumblingly** *adv.* **grumbly** *adj.* [obs. *grumme*: cf. MDu. *grommen*, MLG *grommelen*, f. Gmc]

■ *v.* **1, 3** see COMPLAIN 1. ● *n.* **1** see COMPLAINT 2.

grummet var. of GROMMET.

grump /grump/ *n. colloq.* **1** a grumpy person. **2** (in *pl.*) a fit of sulks. □□ **grumpish** *adj.* **grumpishly** *adv.* [imit.]
■ **1** see MISERY 3.

grumpy /grúmpi/ *adj.* (**grumpier, grumpiest**) morosely irritable; surly. □□ **grumpily** *adv.* **grumpiness** *n.*
■ see SURLY.

Grundy /grúndi/ *n.* (*pl.* **-ies**) (in full **Mrs Grundy**) a person embodying conventional propriety and prudery. □□ **Grundyism** *n.* [a person repeatedly mentioned in T. Morton's comedy *Speed the Plough* (1798)]

grunge / grunj/ *n.* esp. *US sl.* **1** grime, dirt. **2** an aggressive style of rock music characterized by a raucous guitar sound. □□ **grungy** *adj.* [app. after GRUBBY, DINGY, etc.]

grunion /grúnyən/ *n.* a slender Californian marine fish, *Leuresthes tenuis*, that comes ashore to spawn. [prob. f. Sp. *gruñón* grunter]

grunt /grunt/ *n.* & *v.* ● *n.* **1** a low guttural sound made by a pig. **2** a sound resembling this. **3** any fish of the genus *Haemulon* that grunts when caught. ● *v.* **1** *intr.* (of a pig) make a grunt or grunts. **2** *intr.* (of a person) make a low inarticulate sound resembling this, esp. to express discontent, dissent, fatigue, etc. **3** *tr.* utter with a grunt. [OE *grunnettan*, prob. orig. imit.]

grunter /grúntər/ *n.* **1** a person or animal that grunts, esp. a pig. **2** a grunting fish, esp. = GRUNT *n.* 3.

Grunth var. of GRANTH.

Gruyère /gro͞o-yair/ *n.* a firm pale cheese made from cow's milk. [*Gruyère*, a district in Switzerland where it was first made]

gryphon var. of GRIFFIN.

grysbok /grísbok/ *n.* any small antelope of the genus *Raphicerus*, native to S. Africa. [S.Afr. Du. f. Du. *grijs* grey + *bok* BUCK[1]]

gs. *abbr. Brit. hist.* guineas.

G-string /jéestring/ *n.* **1** *Mus.* a string sounding the note G. **2** (also **gee-string**) a narrow strip of cloth etc. covering only the genitals and attached to a string round the waist, as worn esp. by striptease artistes.

G-suit /jée-so͞ot, -syo͞ot/ *n.* a garment with inflatable pressurized pouches, worn by pilots and astronauts to enable them to withstand high acceleration. [*g* = gravity + SUIT]

GT /jéetée/ *n.* a high-performance saloon car. [abbr. f. It. *gran turismo* great touring]

Gt. *abbr.* Great.

guacamole /gwaákəmṓli/ *n.* a dish of mashed avocado pears mixed with chopped onion, tomatoes, chilli peppers, and seasoning. [Amer. Sp. f. Nahuatl *ahuacamolli* f. *ahuacatl* avocado + *molli* sauce]

guacharo /gwaáchərō/ *n.* (*pl.* **-os**) a nocturnal bird, *Steatornis caripensis*, native to S. America and feeding on fruit. Also called *oil-bird*. [S.Amer. Sp.]

guaiac var. of GUAIACUM 2.

guaiacum /gwī́əkəm/ *n.* **1** any tree of the genus *Guaiacum*, native to tropical America. **2** (also **guaiac** /gwī́ak/) **a** the hard dense oily timber of some of these, esp. *G. officinale*. Also called LIGNUM VITAE. **b** the resin from this used medicinally. [mod.L f. Sp. *guayaco* of Haitian orig.]

guan /gwaan/ *n.* any of various game-birds of the family Cracidae, of tropical America. [prob. f. a native name]

guanaco /gwənaákō/ *n.* (*pl.* **-os**) a llama-like camelid, *Lama guanicoe*, with a coat of soft pale-brown hair used for wool. [Quechua *huanaco*]

guanine /gwaáneen/ *n. Biochem.* a purine derivative found in all living organisms as a component base of DNA and RNA. [GUANO + -INE[4]]

guano /gwaánō/ *n.* & *v.* (*pl.* **-os**) ● *n.* **1** the excrement of sea birds, found esp. in the islands off Peru and used as manure. **2** an artificial manure, esp. that made from fish. ● *v.tr.* (**-oes, -oed**) fertilize with guano. [Sp. f. Quechua *huanu* dung]
■ **1** see DUNG *n.*

Guarani /gwaáranée/ *n.* **1 a** a member of a S. American Indian people. **b** the language of this people. **2** (**guarani**) the monetary unit of Paraguay. [Sp.]

guarantee /gárrəntée/ *n.* & *v.* ● *n.* **1 a** a formal promise or assurance, esp. that an obligation will be fulfilled or that something is of a specified quality and durability. **b** a document giving such an undertaking. **2** = GUARANTY. **3** a person making a guaranty or giving a security. ● *v.tr.* (**guarantees, guaranteed**) **1 a** give or serve as a guarantee for; answer for the due fulfilment of (a contract etc.) or the genuineness of (an article). **b** assure the permanence etc. of. **c** provide with a guarantee. **2** (foll. by *that* + clause, or *to* + infin.) give a promise or assurance. **3 a** (foll. by *to*) secure the possession of (a thing) for a person. **b** make (a person) secure against a risk or in possession of a thing. □ **guarantee fund** a sum pledged as a contingent indemnity for loss. [earlier *garante*, perh. f. Sp. *garante* = F *garant* WARRANT: later infl. by F *garantie* guaranty]
■ *n.* **1, 2** promise, assurance, word (of honour), oath, undertaking, pledge; guaranty, warranty, bond, security. **3** guarantor, assurer, insurer, warranter. ● *v.* **1** vouch for, answer for, stand behind, attest to; ensure, certify. **2** pledge, promise, undertake, make sure *or* certain, swear, attest. **3 a** see SECURE *v.* 3.

guarantor /gárrəntór, gárrəntər/ *n.* a person who gives a guarantee or guaranty.

guaranty /gárrənti/ *n.* (*pl.* **-ies**) **1** a written or other undertaking to answer for the payment of a debt or for the performance of an obligation by another person liable in the first instance. **2** a thing serving as security for a guaranty. [AF *guarantie*, var. of *warantie* WARRANTY]

guard /gaard/ *v.* & *n.* ● *v.* **1** *tr.* (often foll. by *from, against*) watch over and defend or protect from harm. **2** *tr.* keep watch by (a door etc.) so as to control entry or exit. **3** *tr.* supervise (prisoners etc.) and prevent from escaping. **4** *tr.* provide (machinery) with a protective device. **5** *tr.* keep (thoughts or speech) in check. **6** *tr.* provide with safeguards. **7** *intr.* (foll. by *against*) take precautions. **8** *tr.* (in various games) protect (a piece, card, etc.) with set moves. ● *n.* **1** a state of vigilance or watchfulness. **2** a person who protects or keeps watch. **3** a body of soldiers etc. serving to protect a place or person; an escort. **4** *US* a prison warder. **5** a part of an army detached for some purpose (*advance guard*). **6** (in *pl.*) (usu. **Guards**) any of various bodies of troops nominally employed to guard a monarch. **7** a thing that protects or defends. **8** (often in *comb.*) a device fitted to a machine, vehicle, weapon, etc., to prevent injury or accident to the user (*fire-guard*). **9** *Brit.* an official who rides with and is in general charge of a train. **10** in some sports: **a** a protective or defensive player. **b** a defensive posture or motion. □ **be on** (or **keep** or **stand**) **guard** (of a sentry etc.) keep watch. **guard cell** *Bot.* either of a pair of cells surrounding the stomata in plants. **guard-rail** a rail, e.g. a handrail, fitted as a support or to prevent an accident. **guard ring** *Electronics* a ring-shaped electrode used to limit the extent of an electric field, esp. in a capacitor. **guard's van** *Brit.* a coach or compartment occupied by a guard. **lower one's guard** reduce vigilance against attack. **off** (or **off one's**) **guard** unprepared for some surprise or difficulty. **on** (or **on one's**) **guard** prepared for all contingencies; vigilant. **raise one's guard** become vigilant against attack. □□ **guarder** *n.* **guardless** *adj.* [ME f. OF *garde*, *garder* ult. f. WG, rel. to WARD *n.*]
■ *v.* **1** protect, shield, defend; safeguard, watch over, look after, tend, mind, supervise. **2** see WATCH *v.* 2a, 4. **3** see SUPERVISE. **5** see CONTROL *v.* 3. **7** see PREPARE 1. **8** see DEFEND 1. ● *n.* **1** watch, alert, vigil, lookout. **2** sentinel, watchman, sentry, security guard, *hist.* watch; custodian, guardian, protector; bodyguard, *sl.* minder. **3** convoy, patrol; see also ESCORT *n.* 1. **4** *Brit.* warder, wardress, *sl.* screw; see also JAILER. **5** see SQUAD. **7** defence, protection, safeguard, shield, screen, safeguard, cover. **10 a** back, defender; *collect.* defence; see also BACK *n.* 4. □ **be on** (or

keep or **stand**) **guard** see PATROL *v.* 2, WATCH *v.* 3. **guard-rail** see RAIL[1] *n.* 1. **lower one's guard** relax, lower one's defences; see also *let up* 2 (LET[1]). **off** (or **off one's**) **guard** see UNPREPARED. **on** (or **on one's**) **guard** see VIGILANT. **raise one's guard** raise *or* put up one's defences.

guardant /gaárd'nt/ *adj. Heraldry* depicted with the body sideways and the face towards the viewer.

guarded /gaárdid/ *adj.* (of a remark etc.) cautious, avoiding commitment. ▫▫ **guardedly** *adv.* **guardedness** *n.*
■ careful, cautious, prudent, circumspect, wary, mindful, restrained, reticent, leery; noncommittal, *colloq.* cagey.

guardhouse /gaárdhowss/ *n.* a building used to accommodate a military guard or to detain prisoners.
■ see PRISON *n.* 1.

guardian /gaárdiən/ *n.* **1** a defender, protector, or keeper. **2** a person having legal custody of another person and his or her property when that person is incapable of managing his or her own affairs. **3** the superior of a Franciscan convent. ▫ **guardian angel** a spirit conceived as watching over a person or place. ▫▫ **guardianship** *n.* [ME f. AF *gardein*, OF *garden* f. Frank., rel. to WARD, WARDEN]
■ **1, 2** protector, defender, preserver, custodian, keeper, ward; trustee. ▫ **guardian angel** see PROTECTOR. ▫▫ **guardianship** see CARE *n.* 4a.

guardroom /gaárdrōōm, -rŏŏm/ *n.* a room with the same purpose as a guardhouse.

guardsman /gaárdzmən/ *n.* (*pl.* **-men**) **1** a soldier belonging to a body of guards. **2** (in the UK) a soldier of a regiment of Guards.

guava /gwaávə/ *n.* **1** a small tropical American tree, *Psidium guajava*, bearing an edible pale yellow fruit with pink juicy flesh. **2** this fruit. [Sp. *guayaba* prob. f. a S. Amer. name]

guayule /gwīyŏŏli/ *n.* **1** a silver-leaved shrub, *Parthenium argentatum*, native to Mexico. **2** a rubber substitute made from the sap of this plant. [Amer. Sp. f. Nahuatl *cuauhuli*]

gubbins /gúbbinz/ *n. Brit.* **1** a set of equipment or paraphernalia. **2** a gadget. **3** something of little value. **4** *colloq.* a foolish person (often with ref. to oneself). [orig. = fragments, f. obs. *gobbon*: perh. rel. to GOBBET]

gubernatorial /gyŏŏbərnətóriəl/ *adj.* esp. *US* of or relating to a governor. [L *gubernator* governor]

gudgeon[1] /gújən/ *n.* **1** a small European freshwater fish, *Gobio gobio*, often used as bait. **2** a credulous or easily fooled person. [ME f. OF *goujon* f. L *gobio -onis* GOBY]

gudgeon[2] /gújən/ *n.* **1** any of various kinds of pivot working a wheel, bell, etc. **2** the tubular part of a hinge into which the pin fits to effect the joint. **3** a socket at the stern of a boat, into which a rudder is fitted. **4** a pin holding two blocks of stone etc. together. ▫ **gudgeon-pin** (in an internal-combustion engine) a pin holding a piston-rod and a connecting-rod together. [ME f. OF *goujon* dimin. of *gouge* GOUGE]

guelder rose /géldər/ *n.* a deciduous shrub, *Viburnum opulus*, with round bunches of creamy-white flowers. Also called *snowball tree*. [Du. *geldersch* f. *Gelderland* a province in the Netherlands]

guenon /gənón/ *n.* any African monkey of the genus *Cercopithecus*, having a characteristic long tail, e.g. the vervet. [F: orig. unkn.]

guerdon /gérd'n/ *n.* & *v. poet.* ● *n.* a reward or recompense. ● *v.tr.* give a reward to. [ME f. OF *guerdon* f. med.L *widerdonum* f. WG *widarlōn* (as WITH, LOAN[1]), assim. to L *donum* gift]

Guernsey /gérnzi/ *n.* (*pl.* **-eys**) **1 a** an animal of a breed of dairy cattle from Guernsey in the Channel Islands. **b** this breed. **2** (**guernsey**) **a** a thick (usu. blue) woollen sweater of a distinctive pattern. **b** *Austral.* a football shirt. ▫ **get a guernsey** *Austral. colloq.* **1** be selected for a football team. **2** gain recognition. **guernsey lily** a kind of nerine orig. from S. Africa, with large pink lily-like flowers.

guerrilla /gərillə/ *n.* (also **guerilla**) a member of a small independently acting (usu. political) group taking part in irregular fighting, esp. against larger regular forces. ▫ **guerrilla war** (or **warfare**) fighting by or with guerrillas. [Sp. *guerrilla*, dimin. of *guerra* war]
■ partisan, freedom fighter, resistance *or* underground fighter, irregular; insurgent, revolutionary, saboteur, terrorist. ▫ **guerrilla war** (or **warfare**) terrorism, bush warfare, insurgency, freedom fighting.

guess /gess/ *v.* & *n.* ● *v.* **1** *tr.* (often *absol.*) estimate without calculation or measurement, or on the basis of inadequate data. **2** *tr.* (often foll. by *that* etc. + clause, or *to* + infin.) form a hypothesis or opinion about; conjecture; think likely (*cannot guess how you did it*; *guess them to be Italian*). **3** *tr.* conjecture or estimate correctly by guessing (*you have to guess the weight*). **4** *intr.* (foll. by *at*) make a conjecture about. ● *n.* an estimate or conjecture reached by guessing. ▫ **anybody's** (or **anyone's**) **guess** something very vague or difficult to determine. **I guess** *colloq.* I think it likely; I suppose. **keep a person guessing** *colloq.* withhold information. ▫▫ **guessable** *adj.* **guesser** *n.* [ME *gesse*, of uncert. orig.: cf. OSw. *gissa*, MLG, MDu. *gissen*: f. the root of GET *v.*]
■ *v.* **1, 4** estimate, make a guess (at), *colloq.* make a stab (at). **2** conjecture, surmise, infer, deduce, conclude, judge, suppose, assume; believe, reckon, think, fancy, feel, suspect, divine, *formal* deem; hypothesize, speculate. ● *n.* estimate, assumption, supposition, judgement, feeling, suspicion, conjecture, speculation, surmise, shot in the dark, *colloq.* guestimate. ▫ **anybody's** (or **anyone's**) **guess** poser, problem, moot point *or* issue, tricky one. **keep a person guessing** keep a person in the dark, not tell, not let on to.

guess-rope var. of GUEST-ROPE.

guesswork /géswurk/ *n.* the process of or results got by guessing.

guest /gest/ *n.* & *v.* ● *n.* **1** a person invited to visit another's house or have a meal etc. at the expense of the inviter. **2** a person lodging at a hotel, boarding-house, etc. **3 a** an outside performer invited to take part with a regular body of performers. **b** a person who takes part by invitation in a radio or television programme (often *attrib.*: *guest artist*). **4** (*attrib.*) **a** serving or set aside for guests (*guest-room*; *guest-night*). **b** acting as a guest (*guest speaker*). **5** an organism living in close association with another. ● *v.intr.* be a guest on a radio or television show or in a theatrical performance etc. ▫ **be my guest** *colloq.* make what use you wish of the available facilities. **guest-house** a private house offering paid accommodation. **guest of honour** the most important guest at an occasion. ▫▫ **guestship** *n.* [ME f. ON *gestr* f. Gmc]
■ *n.* **1** visitor, caller; (*guests*) company. **2** patron, customer, lodger, boarder, *US* roomer. **3b, 4b** (*attrib.*) visiting; outside, external.

guestimate /géstimət/ *n.* (also **guesstimate**) *colloq.* an estimate based on a mixture of guesswork and calculation. [GUESS + ESTIMATE]

guest-rope /géstrōp, gésrōp/ *n.* (also **guess-rope**) **1** a second rope fastened to a boat in tow to steady it. **2** a rope slung outside a ship to give a hold for boats coming alongside. [17th c.: orig. uncert.]

guff /guf/ *n. sl.* empty talk; nonsense. [19th c., orig. = 'puff': imit.]
■ see MOONSHINE 1.

guffaw /gufáw/ *n.* & *v.* ● *n.* a coarse or boisterous laugh. ● *v.* **1** *intr.* utter a guffaw. **2** *tr.* say with a guffaw. [orig. Sc.: imit.]
■ *n.* see LAUGH *n.* 1. ● *v.* see LAUGH *v.* 1.

guidance /gīd'nss/ *n.* **1 a** advice or information aimed at resolving a problem, difficulty, etc. **b** leadership or direction. **2** the process of guiding or being guided.
■ **1 a** advice, information, counsel, instruction, teaching, briefing. **b** leadership, direction, management, government, conduct, control, regulation, charge, handling, rule, auspices. **2** counselling, edification, preparation, guiding; see also INSTRUCTION 2.

guide /gīd/ *n.* & *v.* ● *n.* **1** a person who leads or shows the way, or directs the movements of a person or group. **2** a person who conducts travellers on tours etc. **3** a professional mountain-climber in charge of a group. **4** an adviser. **5** a directing principle or standard (*one's feelings are a bad guide*). **6** a book with essential information on a subject, esp. = GUIDEBOOK. **7** a thing marking a position or guiding the eye. **8** a soldier, vehicle, or ship whose position determines the movements of others. **9** *Mech.* **a** a bar, rod, etc., directing the motion of something. **b** a gauge etc. controlling a tool. **10** (**Guide**) *Brit.* a member of a girls' organization similar to the Scouts. ● *v.tr.* **1 a** act as guide to; lead or direct. **b** arrange the course of (events). **2** be the principle, motive, or ground of (an action, judgement, etc.). **3** direct the affairs of (a State etc.). □ **guided missile** a missile directed to its target by remote control or by equipment within itself. **guide-dog** a dog trained to guide a blind person. **guide-rope** a rope guiding the movement of a crane, airship, etc. **Queen's** (or **King's**) **Guide** a Guide (sense 10) who has reached the highest rank of proficiency. □□ **guidable** *adj.* **guider** *n.* [ME f. OF *guide* (n.), *guider* (v.), earlier *guier* ult. f. Gmc, rel. to WIT[2]]

▪ *n.* **1–3** leader, conductor, director, guider, chaperon; cicerone. **4** adviser, mentor, counsellor, guru, master, teacher. **5** principle, standard, model, criterion, exemplar, ideal, lodestar, inspiration. **6** guidebook, handbook, manual, vade-mecum, *formal* enchiridion; Baedeker. **7** beacon, light, lodestar, guiding light, signal, sign, landmark, marker, indicator, signpost. ● *v.* **1, 3** lead, conduct, shepherd, direct, usher, steer, manoeuvre, pilot, channel, navigate; instruct, show, teach, tutor, train, counsel, advise; supervise, oversee, handle, manage, superintend, direct, control, regulate, govern. **2** steer, instruct, influence, sway, govern; see also MOTIVATE.

guidebook /gīdbŏŏk/ *n.* a book of information about a place for visitors, tourists, etc.

guideline /gīdlīn/ *n.* a principle or criterion guiding or directing action.

▪ see STANDARD *n.* 1, 8.

guidepost /gīdpōst/ *n.* = SIGNPOST.

Guider /gīdər/ *n.* an adult leader of Guides (see GUIDE *n.* 10).

guideway /gīdway/ *n.* a groove or track that guides movement.

guidon /gīd'n/ *n.* a pennant narrowing to a point or fork at the free end, esp. one used as the standard of a regiment of dragoons. [F f. It. *guidone* f. *guida* GUIDE]

guild /gild/ *n.* (also **gild**) **1** an association of people for mutual aid or the pursuit of a common goal. **2** a medieval association of craftsmen or merchants. [ME prob. f. MLG, MDu. *gilde* f. Gmc: rel. to OE *gild* payment, sacrifice]

▪ see ASSOCIATION 1.

guilder /gíldər/ *n.* **1** the chief monetary unit of the Netherlands. **2** *hist.* a gold coin of the Netherlands and Germany. [ME, alt. of Du. *gulden*: see GULDEN]

guildhall /gíldháwl/ *n.* **1** the meeting-place of a guild or corporation; a town hall. **2** (**the Guildhall**) the hall of the Corporation of the City of London, used for ceremonial occasions.

guildsman /gíldzmən/ *n.* (*pl.* **-men**; *fem.* **guildswoman**, *pl.* **-women**) a member of a guild.

guile /gīl/ *n.* treachery, deceit; cunning or sly behaviour. □□ **guileful** *adj.* **guilefully** *adv.* **guilefulness** *n.* **guileless** *adj.* **guilelessly** *adv.* **guilelessness** *n.* [ME f. OF, prob. f. Gmc]

▪ see DECEIT 1.

guillemot /gíllimot/ *n.* any fast-flying sea bird of the genus *Uria* or *Cepphus*, nesting on cliffs or islands. [F f. *Guillaume* William]

guilloche /gilósh/ *n.* an architectural or metalwork ornament imitating braided ribbons. [F *guillochis* (or *guilloche* the tool used)]

guillotine /gíllətéen/ *n.* & *v.* ● *n.* **1** a machine with a heavy knife-blade sliding vertically in grooves, used for beheading. **2** a device for cutting paper, metal, etc. **3** a surgical instrument for excising the uvula etc. **4** *Parl.* a method of preventing delay in the discussion of a legislative bill by fixing times at which various parts of it must be voted on. ● *v.tr.* **1** use a guillotine on. **2** *Parl.* end discussion of (a bill) by applying a guillotine. □□ **guillotiner** *n.* [F f. J.-I. *Guillotin*, Fr. physician d. 1814, who recommended its use for executions in 1789]

▪ *n.* **4** closure, *US* cloture.

guilt /gilt/ *n.* **1** the fact of having committed a specified or implied offence. **2 a** culpability. **b** the feeling of this. □ **guilt complex** *Psychol.* a mental obsession with the idea of having done wrong. [OE *gylt*, of unkn. orig.]

▪ **1** sinfulness, feloniousness, wrongdoing, criminality, misconduct. **2 a** culpability, guiltiness, blameworthiness, blame; responsibility. **b** remorse, self-reproach, regret, sorrow, contrition, penitence, repentance, shame, contriteness, self-condemnation.

guiltless /gíltliss/ *adj.* **1** (often foll. by *of* an offence) innocent. **2** (foll. by *of*) not having knowledge or possession of. □□ **guiltlessly** *adv.* **guiltlessness** *n.* [OE *gyltlēas* (as GUILT, -LESS)]

▪ **1** see INNOCENT *adj.* 2.

guilty /gílti/ *adj.* (**guiltier**, **guiltiest**) **1** culpable of or responsible for a wrong. **2** conscious of or affected by guilt (*a guilty conscience*; *a guilty look*). **3** concerning guilt (*a guilty secret*). **4 a** (often foll. by *of*) having committed a (specified) offence. **b** *Law* adjudged to have committed a specified offence, esp. by a verdict in a trial. □□ **guiltily** *adv.* **guiltiness** *n.* [OE *gyltig* (as GUILT, -Y[1])]

▪ **1, 4** culpable, blameworthy; responsible, answerable; at fault. **2** guilt-ridden, shamefaced, sheepish, red-faced; remorseful, contrite, regretful, repentant, sorrowful, conscience-stricken, rueful, penitent, sorry, ashamed. **3** see SORDID 2.

guimp var. of GIMP[1].

guinea /gínni/ *n.* **1** *Brit. hist.* the sum of 21 old shillings (£1.05), used esp. in determining professional fees. **2** *hist.* a former British gold coin worth 21 shillings, first coined for the African trade. □ **guinea-fowl** any African fowl of the family Numididae, esp. *Numida meleagris*, with slate-coloured white-spotted plumage. **guinea-pig 1** a domesticated S. American cavy, *Cavia porcellus*, kept as a pet or for research in biology etc. **2** a person or thing used as a subject for experiment. [*Guinea* in W. Africa]

guipure /geepyoor/ *n.* a heavy lace of linen pieces joined by embroidery. [F f. *guiper* cover with silk etc. f. Gmc]

guise /gīz/ *n.* **1** an assumed appearance; a pretence (*in the guise of*; *under the guise of*). **2** external appearance. **3** *archaic* style of attire, garb. [ME f. OF ult. f. Gmc]

▪ **1** disguise, pretence, cloak, cover; see also MASK *n.* 4. **2** appearance, aspect, semblance, façade, front, look, image, likeness. **3** see DRESS *n.* 2.

guitar /gitaár/ *n.* a usu. six-stringed musical instrument with a fretted finger-board, played by plucking with the fingers or a plectrum. □□ **guitarist** *n.* [Sp. *guitarra* (partly through F *guitare*) f. Gk *kithara*: see CITTERN, GITTERN]

guiver /gīvər/ *n.* (also **gyver**) *Austral.* & *NZ sl.* **1** plausible talk. **2** affectation of speech or manner. [19th c.: orig. unkn.]

Gujarati /gŏŏjəraáti/ *n.* & *adj.* ● *n.* (*pl.* **Gujaratis**) **1** the language of Gujarat in W. India. **2** a native of Gujarat. ● *adj.* of or relating to Gujarat or its language. [Hind.: see -I[2]]

gulch /gulch/ *n.* *US* a ravine, esp. one in which a torrent flows. [perh. dial. *gulch* to swallow]

▪ see RAVINE.

gulden /gŏŏldən/ *n.* = GUILDER. [Du. & G, = GOLDEN]

gules /gyŏŏlz/ *n.* & *adj.* (usu. placed after noun) *Heraldry* red. [ME f. OF *goules* red-dyed fur neck ornaments f. *gole* throat]

gulf /gulf/ *n.* & *v.* ● *n.* **1** a stretch of sea consisting of a deep inlet with a narrow mouth. **2** (**the Gulf**) the Persian Gulf. **3** a deep hollow; a chasm or abyss. **4** a wide difference of feelings, opinion, etc. ● *v.tr.* engulf; swallow up. □ **Gulf Stream** an oceanic warm current flowing from the Gulf of Mexico to Newfoundland where it is deflected into the Atlantic Ocean. [ME f. OF *golfe* f. It. *golfo* ult. f. Gk *kolpos* bosom, gulf]

■ *n.* **1** cove, inlet, firth, fiord, *Brit.* creek, *Ir.* lough, *Sc.* loch; bay, bight. **3** hollow, deep, depths; chasm, abyss, rift, gap, split, *archaic or poet.* abysm; void, breach, space. **4** rift, gap; difference, disagreement, conflict, schism. ● *v.* see SWALLOW[1] *v.* 6.

gulfweed /gúlfweed/ *n.* = SARGASSO.

gull[1] /gul/ *n.* any of various long-winged web-footed sea birds of the family Laridae, usu. having white plumage with a mantle varying from pearly-grey to black, and a bright bill. □□ **gullery** *n.* (*pl.* **-ies**). [ME ult. f. OCelt.]

gull[2] /gul/ *v.tr.* (usu. in *passive*; foll. by *into*) dupe, fool. [perh. f. obs. *gull* yellow f. ON *gulr*]

■ see DUPE *n.*

Gullah /gúllə/ *n.* **1** a member of a Negro people living on the coast of S. Carolina or the nearby sea islands. **2** the Creole language spoken by them. [perh. a shortening of *Angola*, or f. a tribal name *Golas*]

gullet /gúllit/ *n.* **1** the food-passage extending from the mouth to the stomach; the oesophagus. **2** the throat. [ME f. OF dimin. of *go(u)le* throat f. L *gula*]

gullible /gúllib'l/ *adj.* easily persuaded or deceived, credulous. □□ **gullibility** /-bílliti/ *n.* **gullibly** *adv.* [GULL[2] + -IBLE]

■ credulous, persuadable, unsuspecting, unwary, unsuspicious; innocent, green, unsophisticated, naïve, wide-eyed, inexperienced.

gully /gúlli/ *n.* & *v.* ● *n.* (*pl.* **-ies**) **1** a water-worn ravine. **2** a deep artificial channel; a gutter or drain. **3** *Austral.* & *NZ* a river valley. **4** *Cricket* **a** the fielding position between point and slips. **b** a fielder in this position. ● *v.tr.* (**-ies, -ied**) **1** form (channels) by water action. **2** make gullies in. □ **gully-hole** an opening in a street to a drain or sewer. [F *goulet* bottle-neck (as GULLET)]

■ *n.* **1, 3** channel, river-bed, river valley, gorge, ravine, canyon, defile, *Brit.* gill, *US* notch, arroyo, gulch. **2** see DRAIN *n.* 1a. ● *v.* **1, 2** see FURROW *v.* 2a. □ **gully-hole** grating, grate, grid, grille.

gulp /gulp/ *v.* & *n.* ● *v.* **1** *tr.* (often foll. by *down*) swallow hastily, greedily, or with effort. **2** *intr.* swallow gaspingly or with difficulty; choke. **3** *tr.* (foll. by *down, back*) stifle, suppress (esp. tears). ● *n.* **1** an act of gulping (*drained it at one gulp*). **2** an effort to swallow. **3** a large mouthful of a drink. □□ **gulper** *n.* **gulpingly** *adv.* **gulpy** *adj.* [ME prob. f. MDu. *gulpen* (imit.)]

■ *v.* **1** bolt, gobble, wolf, devour, gorge, guzzle, swallow, *Brit. sl.* knock back; swill, *colloq.* swig, *literary* quaff. **2** choke, catch one's breath, gasp (for breath), heave. **3** see STIFLE 1. ● *n.* **1** swallow, slurp, sip, sup, drink, *colloq.* swig. **3** mouthful, draught, swallow, *colloq.* swig.

gum[1] /gum/ *n.* & *v.* ● *n.* **1 a** a viscous secretion of some trees and shrubs that hardens on drying but is soluble in water (cf. RESIN). **b** an adhesive substance made from this. **2** *US* chewing gum. **3** = GUMDROP. **4** = *gum arabic*. **5** = *gum-tree*. **6** a secretion collecting in the corner of the eye. **7** *US* = GUMBOOT. ● *v.* (**gummed, gumming**) **1** *tr.* smear or cover with gum. **2** *tr.* (usu. foll. by *down, together*, etc.) fasten with gum. **3** *intr.* exude gum. □ **gum arabic** a gum exuded by some kinds of acacia and used as glue and in incense. **gum benjamin** benzoin. **gum dragon** tragacanth. **gum juniper** sandarac. **gum resin** a vegetable secretion of resin mixed with gum, e.g. gamboge. **gum-tree** a tree exuding gum, esp. a eucalyptus. **gum up 1** (of a mechanism etc.) become clogged or obstructed with stickiness. **2** *colloq.* interfere with the smooth running of (*gum up the works*). **up a gum-tree** *colloq.* in great difficulties. [ME f. OF *gomme* ult. f. L *gummi, cummi* f. Gk *kommi* f. Egypt. *kemai*]

■ *n.* **1 b** see GLUE *n.* ● *v.* **2** see GLUE *v.* □ **up a gum-tree** see *in trouble* 1 (TROUBLE).

gum[2] /gum/ *n.* (usu. in *pl.*) the firm flesh around the roots of the teeth. □ **gum-shield** a pad protecting a boxer's teeth and gums. [OE *gōma* rel. to OHG *guomo*, ON *gómr* roof or floor of the mouth]

gum[3] /gum/ *n. colloq.* (in oaths) God (*by gum!*). [corrupt. of *God*]

gumbo /gúmbō/ *n.* (*pl.* **-os**) *US* **1** okra. **2** a soup thickened with okra pods. **3** (**Gumbo**) a patois of Blacks and Creoles spoken esp. in Louisiana. [of Afr. orig.]

gumboil /gúmboyl/ *n.* a small abscess on the gums.

gumboot /gúmbōōt/ *n.* a rubber boot; a wellington.

gumdrop /gúmdrop/ *n.* a soft coloured sweet made with gelatin or gum arabic.

gumma /gúmmə/ *n.* (*pl.* **gummas** or **gummata** /-mətə/) *Med.* a small soft swelling occurring in the connective tissue of the liver, brain, testes, and heart, and characteristic of the late stages of syphilis. □□ **gummatous** *adj.* [mod.L f. L *gummi* GUM[1]]

gummy[1] /gúmmi/ *adj.* (**gummier, gummiest**) **1** viscous, sticky. **2** abounding in or exuding gum. □□ **gumminess** *n.* [ME f. GUM[1] + -Y[1]]

■ **1** see STICKY *adj.* 2.

gummy[2] /gúmmi/ *adj.* & *n.* ● *adj.* (**gummier, gummiest**) toothless. ● *n.* (*pl.* **-ies**) **1** *Austral.* a small shark, *Mustelus antarcticus*, having rounded teeth with which it crushes hard-shelled prey. **2** *Austral.* & *NZ* a toothless sheep. □□ **gummily** *adv.* [GUM[2] + -Y[1]]

gumption /gúmpsh'n/ *n. colloq.* **1** resourcefulness, initiative; enterprising spirit. **2** common sense. [18th-c. Sc.: orig. unkn.]

■ **1** resourcefulness, enterprise, initiative, gameness, backbone, pluck, mettle, courage, boldness, audacity, nerve, daring, spirit, vigour, energy, stamina, *colloq.* grit, spunk, guts, get-up-and-go, *Brit. sl.* bottle. **2** (common) sense, shrewdness, cleverness, mother wit, astuteness, judgement, *colloq.* horse sense, nous.

gumshoe /gúmshōō/ *n. US* **1** a galosh. **2** *sl.* a detective.

gun /gun/ *n.* & *v.* ● *n.* **1** any kind of weapon consisting of a metal tube and often held in the hand with a grip at one end, from which bullets or other missiles are propelled with great force, esp. by a contained explosion. **2** any device imitative of this, e.g. a starting pistol. **3** a device for discharging insecticide, grease, electrons, etc., in the required direction (often in *comb.*: *grease-gun*). **4** a member of a shooting-party. **5** *US* a gunman. **6** the firing of a gun. **7** (in *pl.*) *Naut. sl.* a gunnery officer. ● *v.* (**gunned, gunning**) **1** *tr.* **a** (usu. foll. by *down*) shoot (a person) with a gun. **b** shoot at with a gun. **2** *tr. colloq.* accelerate (an engine or vehicle). **3** *intr.* go shooting. **4** *intr.* (foll. by *for*) seek out determinedly to attack or rebuke. □ **go great guns** *colloq.* proceed forcefully or vigorously or successfully. **gun-carriage** a wheeled support for a gun. **gun-cotton** an explosive used for blasting, made by steeping cotton in nitric and sulphuric acids. **gun crew** a team manning a gun. **gun dog** a dog trained to follow sportsmen using guns. **gun-shy** (esp. of a sporting dog) alarmed at the report of a gun. **gun-site** a (usu. fortified) emplacement for a gun. **jump the gun** *colloq.* start before a signal is given, or before an agreed time. **stick to one's guns** *colloq.* maintain one's position under attack. □□ **gunless** *adj.* **gunned** *adj.* [ME *gunne, gonne*, perh. f. the Scand. name *Gunnhildr*]

■ *n.* **1** see REVOLVER. **5** gunman, *sl.* hit man, *US sl.* hood, gunsel, *esp. US sl.* gunslinger. ● *v.* **2** accelerate, speed up, open out *or* up, quicken; (*gun it*) *colloq.* put one's foot down, step on it, step on the gas, *Austral. colloq.* give it the herbs. □ **stick to one's guns** see PERSEVERE.

gunboat /gúnbōt/ *n.* a small vessel of shallow draught and with relatively heavy guns. □ **gunboat diplomacy** political negotiation supported by the use or threat of military force.

gundy /gúndi/ *n. Austral. colloq.* □ **no good to gundy** no good at all. [20th c.: orig. unkn.]

gunfight /gúnfīt/ *n. US* a fight with firearms. □□ **gunfighter** *n.*

gunfire /gúnfīr/ *n.* **1** the firing of a gun or guns, esp. repeatedly. **2** the noise from this.

gunge /gunj/ *n.* & *v. Brit. colloq.* ● *n.* sticky or viscous matter, esp. when messy or indeterminate. ● *v.tr.* (usu. foll. by *up*) clog or obstruct with gunge. □□ **gungy** *adj.* [20th c.: orig. uncert.: cf. GOO, GUNK]
■ *n.* see MUCK *n.* 1, 2.

gung-ho /gúng-hṓ/ *adj.* enthusiastic, eager. [Chin. *gonghe* work together, slogan adopted by US Marines in 1942]

gunk /gungk/ *n. sl.* viscous or liquid material. [20th c.: orig. the name of a detergent (propr.)]
■ see MUCK *n.* 1, 2.

gunlock /gúnlok/ *n.* a mechanism by which the charge of a gun is exploded.

gunman /gúnmən/ *n.* (*pl.* **-men**) a man armed with a gun, esp. in committing a crime.

gun-metal /gúnmett'l/ *n.* **1** a dull bluish-grey colour. **2** an alloy of copper and tin or zinc (formerly used for guns).

gunnel[1] /gúnn'l/ *n.* any small eel-shaped marine fish of the family Pholidae, esp. *Pholis gunnellus.* Also called BUTTERFISH. [17th c.: orig. unkn.]

gunnel[2] var. of GUNWALE.

gunner /gúnnər/ *n.* **1** an artillery soldier (esp. as an official term for a private). **2** *Naut.* a warrant-officer in charge of a battery, magazine, etc. **3** a member of an aircraft crew who operates a gun. **4** a person who hunts game with a gun.

gunnera /gúnnərə/ *n.* any plant of the genus *Gunnera* from S. America and New Zealand, having large leaves and often grown for ornament. [J. E. *Gunnerus*, Norw. botanist d. 1773]

gunnery /gúnnəri/ *n.* **1** the construction and management of large guns. **2** the firing of guns.

gunny /gúnni/ *n.* (*pl.* **-ies**) **1** coarse sacking, usu. of jute fibre. **2** a sack made of this. [Hindi & Marathi *gōnī* f. Skr. *gōṇī* sack]

gunplay /gúnplay/ *n.* the use of guns.

gunpoint /gúnpoynt/ *n.* the point of a gun. □ **at gunpoint** threatened with a gun or an ultimatum etc.

gunpowder /gúnpowdər/ *n.* **1** an explosive made of saltpetre, sulphur, and charcoal. **2** a fine green tea of granular appearance.

gunpower /gúnpowr/ *n.* the strength or quantity of available guns.

gunroom /gúnrōōm, -rŏŏm/ *n. Brit.* **1** a room in a house for storing sporting-guns. **2** quarters for junior officers (orig. for gunners) in a warship.

gunrunner /gúnrunnər/ *n.* a person engaged in the illegal sale or importing of firearms. □□ **gunrunning** *n.*

gunsel /gúns'l/ *n. US sl.* a criminal, esp. a gunman. [Yiddish *gendzel* = G *Gänslein* gosling; infl. by GUN]

gunship /gúnship/ *n.* a heavily-armed helicopter or other aircraft.

gunshot /gúnshot/ *n.* **1** a shot fired from a gun. **2** the range of a gun (*within gunshot*).

gunslinger /gúnslingər/ *n.* esp. *US sl.* a gunman. □□ **gunslinging** *n.*

gunsmith /gúnsmith/ *n.* a person who makes, sells, and repairs small firearms.

gunstock /gúnstok/ *n.* the wooden mounting of the barrel of a gun.

Gunter's chain /gúntərz/ *n. Surveying* **1** a measuring chain of 66 ft. **2** this length as a unit. [E. *Gunter*, Engl. mathematician d. 1626]

gunwale /gúnn'l/ *n.* (also **gunnel**) the upper edge of the side of a boat or ship. [GUN + WALE (because formerly used to support guns)]

gunyah /gúnyaa/ *n. Austral.* an Aboriginal bush hut. [Aboriginal]

guppy /gúppi/ *n.* (*pl.* **-ies**) a freshwater fish, *Poecilia reticulata*, of the W. Indies and S. America, frequently kept in aquariums, and giving birth to live young. [R. J. L. *Guppy*, 19th-c. Trinidad clergyman who sent the first specimen to the British Museum]

gurdwara /gurdwaárə/ *n.* a Sikh temple. [Punjabi *gurduārā* f. Skr. *guru* teacher + *dvāra* door]

gurgle /gúrg'l/ *v.* & *n.* ● *v.* **1** *intr.* make a bubbling sound as of water from a bottle. **2** *tr.* utter with such a sound. ● *n.* a gurgling sound. □□ **gurgler** *n.* [imit., or f. Du. *gorgelen*, G *gurgeln*, or med.L *gurgulare* f. L *gurgulio* gullet]
■ *v.* **1** bubble, burble, babble, ripple, splash, plash, lap, murmur, purl, glug. ● *n.* burble, bubble, purl, glug.

Gurkha /gúrkə/ *n.* **1** a member of the dominant Hindu people in Nepal. **2** a Nepalese soldier serving in the British army. [native name, f. Skr. *gāus* cow + *raksh* protect]

gurnard /gúrnərd/ *n.* (also **gurnet** /gúrnit/) any marine fish of the family Triglidae, having a large spiny head with mailed sides, and three finger-like pectoral rays used for walking on the sea bed etc. [ME f. OF *gornart* f. *grondir* to grunt f. L *grunnire*]

guru /gŏŏrrōō, góorōō/ *n.* **1** a Hindu spiritual teacher or head of a religious sect. **2 a** an influential teacher. **b** a revered mentor. [Hindi *gurū* teacher f. Skr. *gurús* grave, dignified]
■ see TEACHER.

gush /gush/ *v.* & *n.* ● *v.* **1** *tr.* & *intr.* emit or flow in a sudden and copious stream. **2** *intr.* speak or behave with effusiveness or sentimental affectation. ● *n.* **1** a sudden or copious stream. **2** an effusive or sentimental manner. □□ **gushing** *adj.* **gushingly** *adv.* [ME *gosshe*, *gusche*, prob. imit.]
■ *v.* **1** cascade, rush, flood, stream, spurt, jet, spout, burst; run, flow. **2** effervesce, bubble over, be ebullient *or* effusive, *colloq.* enthuse; go over the top. ● *n.* **1** cascade, rush, flood, flow, stream, spurt, jet, spout, burst, torrent; outburst, effusion. **2** effusiveness, animation; see also *exuberance* (EXUBERANT).

gusher /gúshər/ *n.* **1** an oil well from which oil flows without being pumped. **2** an effusive person.

gushy /gúshi/ *adj.* (**gushier, gushiest**) excessively effusive or sentimental. □□ **gushily** *adv.* **gushiness** *n.*
■ gushing, effusive, (over-)sentimental, overenthusiastic, sloppy, *colloq.* slushy; fulsome, cloying, mawkish, excessive, over the top.

gusset /gússit/ *n.* **1** a piece let into a garment etc. to strengthen or enlarge a part. **2** a bracket strengthening an angle of a structure. □□ **gusseted** *adj.* [ME f. OF *gousset* flexible piece filling up a joint in armour f. *gousse* pod, shell]

gust /gust/ *n.* & *v.* ● *n.* **1** a sudden strong rush of wind. **2** a burst of rain, fire, smoke, or sound. **3** a passionate or emotional outburst. ● *v.intr.* blow in gusts. [ON *gustr*, rel. to *gjósa* to gush]
■ *n.* **1** rush, blast, puff, blow; see also BREEZE[1] *n.* 1. **2** burst, spurt, wave, surge, outbreak; see also OUTBURST. **3** see OUTBURST. ● *v.* **2** puff, waft, blow, blast.

gustation /gustáysh'n/ *n.* the act or capacity of tasting. □□ **gustative** /gústətiv/ *adj.* **gustatory** /gústətəri/ *adj.* [F *gustation* or L *gustatio* f. *gustare* f. *gustus* taste]

gusto /gústō/ *n.* (*pl.* **-oes**) **1** zest; enjoyment or vigour in doing something. **2** (foll. by *for*) *archaic* relish or liking. **3** *archaic* a style of artistic execution. [It. f. L *gustus* taste]
■ **1** zest, zeal, zealousness, *acharnement*, avidity, eagerness, relish, vigour, enjoyment, enthusiasm, pleasure, delight, satisfaction, appreciation. **2** relish, appetite, liking, taste, fancy, preference.

gusty /gústi/ *adj.* (**gustier, gustiest**) **1** characterized by or blowing in strong winds. **2** characterized by gusto. □□ **gustily** *adv.* **gustiness** *n.*
■ **1** see WINDY 1. **2** see EAGER 1.

gut /gut/ *n.* & *v.* ● *n.* **1** the lower alimentary canal or a part of this; the intestine. **2** (in *pl.*) the bowel or entrails, esp. of animals. **3** (in *pl.*) *colloq.* personal courage and determination; vigorous application and perseverance. **4** *colloq.* **a** (in *pl.*) the belly as the source of appetite. **b** the belly or abdomen. **5** (in *pl.*) **a** the contents of anything, esp. representing substantiality. **b** the essence of a thing, e.g. of an issue or problem. **6 a** material for violin or racket strings or surgical use made from the intestines of animals. **b** material for fishing-lines made from the silk-glands of silkworms. **7 a** a narrow water-passage; a sound, straits. **b** a defile or narrow passage. **8** (*attrib.*) **a** instinctive (*a gut reaction*). **b** fundamental (*a gut issue*). ● *v.tr.* (**gutted, gutting**) **1** remove or destroy (esp. by fire) the internal fittings of (a house etc.). **2** take out the guts of (a fish). **3** extract the essence of (a book etc.). □ **gut-rot** *sl.* **1** = *rot-gut.* **2** a stomach upset. **hate a person's guts** *colloq.* dislike a person intensely. **sweat** (or **work**) **one's guts out** *colloq.* work extremely hard. [OE *guttas* (pl.), prob. rel. to *gēotan* pour]

■ *n.* **1, 2** intestine, alimentary canal, bowel; (*guts*) entrails, viscera, vitals, *colloq.* insides, innards. **3** (*guts*) backbone, bravery, boldness, audacity, pluck, courage, daring, spirit, mettle, nerve, *colloq.* grit, gumption, spunk, gutsiness, *Brit. sl.* bottle; application, perseverance, determination, will-power, stamina, endurance. **4 a** (*guts*) belly, *colloq.* tummy; see also STOMACH *n.* 3b. **b** stomach, abdomen, belly, beer-belly, *joc.* corporation. **5** (*guts*) see SUBSTANCE 2a. **8** (*attrib.*) **a** basic, heartfelt, instinctive, instinctual, intuitive, visceral, deep-seated, deep-rooted, emotional; see also INSTINCTIVE 2. **b** see FUNDAMENTAL *adj.* ● *v.* **1** destroy, devastate, ravage, *literary* despoil; ransack, pillage, plunder, loot; strip, empty, *sl.* clean out. **2** disembowel, draw, dress, clean, *formal* eviscerate. **3** see DIGEST *v.* 4a. □ **gut-rot 2** see INDIGESTION. **hate a person's guts** see LOATHE. **sweat** (or **work**) **one's guts out** see LABOUR *v.* 1, 2, SLAVE *v.*

gutless /gútliss/ *adj. colloq.* lacking courage or determination; feeble. □ **gutless wonder** *Austral. colloq.* a person who lacks courage or determination. □□ **gutlessly** *adv.* **gutlessness** *n.*

■ see SPINELESS 2.

gutsy /gútsi/ *adj.* (**gutsier, gutsiest**) *colloq.* **1** courageous. **2** greedy. □□ **gutsily** *adv.* **gutsiness** *n.*

■ **1** see BRAVE *adj.* 1. **2** see GREEDY 1.

gutta-percha /gúttəpérchə/ *n.* a tough plastic substance obtained from the latex of various Malaysian trees. [Malay *getah* gum + *percha* name of a tree]

guttate /gúttayt/ *adj. Biol.* having droplike markings. [L *guttatus* speckled f. *gutta* drop]

gutted /gúttid/ *adj. sl.* utterly exhausted; devastated.

gutter /gúttər/ *n.* & *v.* ● *n.* **1** a shallow trough below the eaves of a house, or a channel at the side of a street, to carry off rainwater. **2** (prec. by *the*) a poor or degraded background or environment. **3** an open conduit along which liquid flows out. **4** a groove. **5** a track made by the flow of water. ● *v.* **1** *intr.* flow in streams. **2** *tr.* furrow, channel. **3** *intr.* (of a candle) melt away as the wax forms channels down the side. □ **gutter press** sensational journalism concerned esp. with the private lives of public figures. [ME f. AF *gotere*, OF *gotiere* ult. f. L *gutta* drop]

■ *n.* **1, 3** see DRAIN *n.* 1a.

guttering /gúttəring/ *n.* **1 a** the gutters of a building etc. **b** a section or length of a gutter. **2** material for gutters.

guttersnipe /gúttərsnīp/ *n.* a street urchin.

■ waif, (street) urchin, street Arab, ragamuffin, gamin, *hist.* mudlark.

guttural /gúttərəl/ *adj.* & *n.* ● *adj.* **1** throaty, harsh-sounding. **2 a** *Phonet.* (of a consonant) produced in the throat or by the back of the tongue and palate. **b** (of a sound) coming from the throat. **c** of the throat. ● *n. Phonet.* a guttural consonant (e.g. *k*, *g*). □□ **gutturally** *adv.* [F *guttural* or med.L *gutturalis* f. L *guttur* throat]

■ *adj.* **1** see GRUFF 1a.

gutzer / gútsər/ *n.* (also **gutser**) *Austral. colloq.* **1** a heavy fall. **2** a failure. [20th c.: orig. uncert.]

guv /guv/ *n. Brit. sl.* = GOVERNOR 7. [abbr.]

guy[1] /gī/ *n.* & *v.* ● *n.* **1** *colloq.* a man; a fellow. **2** (usu. in *pl.*) *US* a person of either sex. **3** *Brit.* an effigy of Guy Fawkes in ragged clothing, burnt on a bonfire on 5 Nov. **4** *Brit.* a grotesquely dressed person. ● *v.tr.* **1** ridicule. **2** exhibit in effigy. [*Guy* Fawkes, conspirator in the Gunpowder Plot to blow up Parliament in 1605]

■ *n.* **1** man, fellow, *colloq.* chap, *sl.* geezer, *Brit. sl.* bloke, *US sl.* dude, *sl. often derog.* gink. **2** person, individual, human (being), being, (living) soul, mortal, *Brit. colloq.* bod; (*guys*) people, folk(s). **4** scarecrow, mess, sight for sore eyes; see also SIGHT *n.* 7. ● *v.* **1** mock, ridicule, make fun of, caricature, satirize, poke fun at, lampoon, *colloq.* rib, *Brit. colloq.* send up; see also RIDICULE *v.*

guy[2] /gī/ *n.* & *v.* ● *n.* a rope or chain to secure a tent or steady a crane-load etc. ● *v.tr.* secure with a guy or guys. [prob. of LG orig.: cf. LG & Du. *gei* brail etc.]

guzzle /gúzz'l/ *v.tr.* & *intr.* eat, drink, or consume excessively or greedily. □□ **guzzler** *n.* [perh. f. OF *gosiller* chatter, vomit f. *gosier* throat]

■ see SCOFF[2] *v.*

Gy *abbr.* = GRAY[1].

gybe /jīb/ *v.* & *n.* (*US* **jibe**) ● *v.* **1** *intr.* (of a fore-and-aft sail or boom) swing across in wearing or running before the wind. **2** *tr.* cause (a sail) to do this. **3** *intr.* (of a ship or its crew) change course so that this happens. ● *n.* a change of course causing gybing. [obs. Du. *gijben*]

gym /jim/ *n. colloq.* **1** a gymnasium. **2** gymnastics. [abbr.]

gymkhana /jimkaánə/ *n.* **1** a meeting for competition or display in sport, esp. horse-riding. **2** a public place with facilities for athletics. [Hind. *gendkhāna* ball-house, racket-court, assim. to GYMNASIUM]

gymnasium /jimnáyziəm/ *n.* (*pl.* **gymnasiums** or **gymnasia** /-ziə/) **1** a room or building equipped for gymnastics. **2** a school in Germany or Scandinavia that prepares pupils for university entrance. □□ **gymnasial** *adj.* [L f. Gk *gumnasion* f. *gumnazō* exercise f. *gumnos* naked]

gymnast /jímnast/ *n.* an expert in gymnastics. [F *gymnaste* or Gk *gumnastēs* athlete-trainer f. *gumnazō*: see GYMNASIUM]

gymnastic /jimnástik/ *adj.* of or involving gymnastics. □□ **gymnastically** *adv.* [L *gymnasticus* f. Gk *gumnastikos* (as GYMNASIUM)]

gymnastics /jimnástiks/ *n.pl.* (also treated as *sing.*) **1** exercises developing or displaying physical agility and coordination, usu. in competition. **2** other forms of physical or mental agility.

■ **1** see EXERCISE *n.* 3.

gymno- /jímnō/ *comb. form Biol.* bare, naked. [Gk *gumnos* naked]

gymnosophist /jimnóssəfist/ *n.* a member of an ancient Hindu sect wearing little clothing and devoted to contemplation. □□ **gymnosophy** *n.* [ME f. F *gymnosophiste* f. L *gymnosophistae* (pl.) f. Gk *gumnosophistai*: see GYMNO-, SOPHIST]

gymnosperm /jímnōsperm/ *n.* any of various plants having seeds unprotected by an ovary, including conifers, cycads, and ginkgos (opp. ANGIOSPERM). □□ **gymnospermous** /-spérməss/ *adj.*

gymp var. of GIMP[1].

gymslip /jímslip/ *n.* a sleeveless tunic, usu. belted, worn by schoolgirls.

gynaeceum var. of GYNOECIUM.

gynaeco- /gī́nikō/ *comb. form* (*US* **gyneco-**) woman, women; female. [Gk *gunē gunaikos* woman]

gynaecology /gī́nikólləji/ *n.* (*US* **gynecology**) the science of the physiological functions and diseases of women and girls, esp. those affecting the reproductive system. □□ **gynaecological** /-kəlójik'l/ *adj.* **gynaecologically** /-kəlójikəli/ *adv.* **gynaecologist** *n.* **gynecologic** /-kəlójik/ *adj. US.*

gynaecomastia /gī́nikōmástiə/ *n.* (*US* **gynecomastia**) *Med.* enlargement of a man's breasts, usu. due to hormone imbalance or hormone therapy.

gynandromorph /gīnándrəmorf/ *n. Biol.* an individual, esp. an insect, having male and female characteristics. □□ **gynandromorphic** /-mórfik/ *adj.* **gynandromorphism** /-mórfiz'm/ *n.* [formed as GYNANDROUS + Gk *morphē* form]

gynandrous /gīnándrəss/ *adj. Bot.* with stamens and pistil united in one column as in orchids. [Gk *gunandros* of doubtful sex, f. *gunē* woman + *anēr andros* man]

gyneco- *comb. form US* var. of GYNAECO-.

gynoecium /gīnéessiəm/ *n.* (also **gynaecium**) (*pl.* **-cia** /-siə/) *Bot.* the carpels of a flower taken collectively. [mod.L f. Gk *gunaikeion* women's apartments (as GYNAECO-, Gk *oikos* house)]

-gynous /ginnəss, jinnəss/ *comb. form Bot.* forming adjectives meaning 'having specified female organs or pistils' (*monogynous*). [Gk *-gunos* f. *gunē* woman]

gyp[1] /jip/ *n. Brit. colloq.* **1** pain or severe discomfort. **2** a scolding (*gave them gyp*). [19th c.: perh. f. *gee-up* (see GEE[2])]

gyp[2] /jip/ *n. Brit.* a college servant at Cambridge and Durham. [perh. f. obs. *gippo* scullion, orig. a man's short tunic, f. obs. F *jupeau*]

gyp[3] /jip/ *v.* & *n. sl.* ● *v.tr.* (**gypped, gypping**) cheat, swindle. ● *n.* an act of cheating; a swindle. [19th c.: perh. f. GYP[2]]

gyppy tummy var. of GIPPY TUMMY.

gypsophila /jipsóffilə/ *n.* any plant of the genus *Gypsophila*, with a profusion of small usu. white composite flowers. [mod.L f. Gk *gupsos* chalk + *philos* loving]

gypsum /jípsəm/ *n.* a hydrated form of calcium sulphate occurring naturally and used to make plaster of Paris and in the building industry. □□ **gypseous** *adj.* **gypsiferous** /-sífərəss/ *adj.* [L f. Gk *gupsos*]

Gypsy /jípsi/ *n.* (also **Gipsy**) (*pl.* **-ies**) **1** a member of a nomadic people of Europe and N. America, of Hindu origin with dark skin and hair, and speaking a language related to Hindi. **2** (**gypsy**) a person resembling or living like a Gypsy. □ **gypsy moth** a kind of tussock moth, *Lymantria dispar*, of which the larvae are very destructive to foliage. □□ **Gypsydom** *n.* **Gypsyfied** *adj.* **Gypsyhood** *n.* **Gypsyish** *adj.* [earlier *gipcyan, gipsen* f. EGYPTIAN, from the supposed origin of Gypsies when they appeared in England in the early 16th c.]
■ **1** Romany, traveller. **2** (**gypsy**) see MIGRANT *n.*

gyrate *v.* & *adj.* ● *v.intr.* /jīráyt/ go in a circle or spiral; revolve, whirl. ● *adj.* /jīrət/ *Bot.* arranged in rings or convolutions. □□ **gyration** /-ráysh'n/ *n.* **gyrator** /jīráytər/ *n.* **gyratory** /-rətəri, -ráytəri/ *adj.* [L *gyrare gyrat-* revolve f. *gyrus* ring f. Gk *guros*]
■ *v.* rotate, spin, revolve, whirl, twirl, pirouette; swivel, turn round, turn, go round.

gyre /jīr/ *v.* & *n.* esp. *poet.* ● *v.intr.* whirl or gyrate. ● *n.* a gyration. [L *gyrus* ring f. Gk *guros*]

gyrfalcon /júrfawlkən, -folkən/ *n.* (also **gerfalcon**) a large falcon, *Falco rusticolus*, of the northern hemisphere. [ME f. OF *gerfaucon* f. Frank. *gērfalco* f. ON *geirfálki*: see FALCON]

gyro /jīrō/ *n.* (*pl.* **-os**) *colloq.* **1** = GYROSCOPE. **2** = GYROCOMPASS. [abbr.]

gyro- /jīrō/ *comb. form* rotation. [Gk *guros* ring]

gyrocompass /jīrōkumpəss/ *n.* a non-magnetic compass giving true north and bearings from it by means of a gyroscope.

gyrograph /jīrōgraaf/ *n.* an instrument for recording revolutions.

gyromagnetic /jīrōmagnéttik/ *adj.* **1** *Physics* of the magnetic and mechanical properties of a rotating charged particle. **2** (of a compass) combining a gyroscope and a normal magnetic compass.

gyropilot /jīrōpīlət/ *n.* a gyrocompass used for automatic steering.

gyroplane /jīrōplayn/ *n.* a form of aircraft deriving its lift mainly from freely rotating overhead vanes.

gyroscope /jīrəskōp/ *n.* a rotating wheel whose axis is free to turn but maintains a fixed direction unless perturbed, esp. used for stabilization or with the compass in an aircraft, ship, etc. □□ **gyroscopic** /-skóppik/ *adj.* **gyroscopically** /-skóppikəli/ *adv.* [F (as GYRO-, SCOPE[2])]

gyrostabilizer /jīrōstáybilīzər/ *n.* a gyroscopic device for maintaining the equilibrium of a ship, aircraft, platform, etc.

gyrus /jīrəss/ *n.* (*pl.* **gyri** /-ri/) a fold or convolution, esp. of the brain. [L f. Gk *guros* ring]

gyttja /yichə/ *n. Geol.* a lake deposit of a usu. black organic sediment. [Sw., = mud, ooze]

gyver var. of GUIVER.

Hh

H[1] /aych/ *n.* (also **h**) (*pl.* **Hs** or **H's**) **1** the eighth letter of the alphabet (see AITCH). **2** anything having the form of an H (esp. in *comb.*: *H-girder*).

H[2] *abbr.* (also **H.**) **1** hardness. **2** (of a pencil-lead) hard. **3** henry, henrys. **4** (water) hydrant. **5** *sl.* heroin.

H[3] *symb. Chem.* the element hydrogen.

h. *abbr.* **1** hecto-. **2** height. **3** horse. **4** hot. **5** hour(s). **6** husband. **7** Planck's constant.

Ha *symb. Chem.* the element hahnium.

ha[1] /haa/ *int.* & *v.* (also **hah**) ● *int.* expressing surprise, suspicion, triumph, etc. (cf. HA HA). ● *v.intr.* (in **hum and ha**: see HUM[1]) [ME]

ha[2] *abbr.* hectare(s).

haar /haar/ *n.* a cold sea-fog on the east coast of England or Scotland. [perh. f. ON *hárr* hoar, hoary]

Hab. *abbr.* Habakkuk (Old Testament).

habanera /hábbənáirə/ *n.* **1** a Cuban dance in slow duple time. **2** the music for this. [Sp., fem. of *habanero* of Havana in Cuba]

habeas corpus /háybiəss kórpəss/ *n.* a writ requiring a person to be brought before a judge or into court, esp. to investigate the lawfulness of his or her detention. [L, = you must have the body]

haberdasher /hábbərdashər/ *n.* **1** *Brit.* a dealer in dress accessories and sewing-goods. **2** *US* a dealer in men's clothing. □□ **haberdashery** *n.* (*pl.* **-ies**). [ME prob. ult. f. AF *hapertas* perh. the name of a fabric]

habergeon /hábbərjən/ *n. hist.* a sleeveless coat of mail. [ME f. OF *haubergeon* (as HAUBERK)]

habiliment /həbíllimənt/ *n.* (usu. in *pl.*) **1** clothes suited to a particular purpose. **2** *joc.* ordinary clothes. [ME f. OF *habillement* f. *habiller* fit out f. *habile* ABLE]

habilitate /həbíllitayt/ *v.intr.* qualify for office (esp. as a teacher in a German university). □□ **habilitation** /-táysh'n/ *n.* [med.L *habilitare* (as ABILITY)]

habit /hábbit/ *n.* & *v.* ● *n.* **1** a settled or regular tendency or practice (often foll. by *of* + verbal noun: *has a habit of ignoring me*). **2** a practice that is hard to give up. **3** a mental constitution or attitude. **4** *Psychol.* an automatic reaction to a specific situation. **5** *colloq.* an addictive practice, esp. of taking drugs. **6 a** the dress of a particular class, esp. of a religious order. **b** (in full **riding-habit**) a woman's riding-dress. **c** *archaic* dress, attire. **7** a bodily constitution. **8** *Biol.* & *Crystallog.* a mode of growth. ● *v.tr.* (usu. as **habited** *adj.*) clothe. □ **habit-forming** causing addiction. **make a habit of** do regularly. [ME f. OF *abit* f. L *habitus* f. *habēre habit-* have, be constituted]
▪ *n.* **1** tendency, disposition, inclination, bent, penchant, propensity, proclivity; second nature; custom, routine, practice, convention, usage, ritual, pattern, mode, rule, praxis, *formal or joc.* wont; way, mannerism, quirk, peculiarity, idiosyncrasy. **2, 5** addiction, compulsion, obsession, fixation, vice; dependence. **3** see ATTITUDE 1. **6 a, c** costume, uniform, livery, garb; clothing, dress, *archaic* raiment, *colloq.* gear, get-up, *formal* attire, apparel; clothes, garments, vestments, robe(s), *joc.* habiliments. **7** see SHAPE *n.* 6. ● *v.* see CLOTHE 1. □ **habit-forming** addictive, compulsive, (*of a drug*) hard; see also *obsessive* (OBSESS).

habitable /hábbitəb'l/ *adj.* that can be inhabited. □□ **habitability** /-bílliti/ *n.* **habitableness** *n.* **habitably** *adv.* [ME f. OF f. L *habitabilis* (as HABITANT)]
▪ liveable, inhabitable.

habitant *n.* **1** /hábbit'nt/ an inhabitant. **2** /ábbeetóN/ **a** an early French settler in Canada or Louisiana. **b** a descendant of these settlers. [F f. OF *habiter* f. L *habitare* inhabit (as HABIT)]

habitat /hábbitat/ *n.* **1** the natural home of an organism. **2** a habitation. [L, = it dwells: see HABITANT]
▪ **1** domain, range, terrain, territory, realm, element, environment, surroundings, haunt, home, *colloq.* stamping-ground, *joc.* bailiwick. **2** habitation, *formal* dwelling(-place); see also ABODE[1].

habitation /hábbitáysh'n/ *n.* **1** the process of inhabiting (*fit for human habitation*). **2** a house or home. [ME f. OF f. L *habitatio -onis* (as HABITANT)]
▪ **2** see HOME *n.* 1.

habitual /həbítyooəl/ *adj.* **1** done constantly or as a habit. **2** regular, usual. **3** given to a (specified) habit (*a habitual smoker*). □□ **habitually** *adv.* **habitualness** *n.* [med.L *habitualis* (as HABIT)]
▪ **1** persistent, constant, continual, perpetual; frequent; automatic, mechanical, compulsive, obsessive. **2** settled, set, rooted, ingrained, fixed, established, regular, standard, routine, ritual, traditional, normal, usual, common, customary, accustomed, everyday, familiar, *attrib.* wonted. **3** inveterate, confirmed, compulsive, obsessional, hardened, established, *colloq. disp.* chronic.

habituate /həbítyoo-ayt/ *v.tr.* (often foll. by *to*) accustom; make used to something. □□ **habituation** /-áysh'n/ *n.* [LL *habituare* (as HABIT)]
▪ see ACCUSTOM.

habitude /hábbityood/ *n.* **1** a mental or bodily disposition. **2** a custom or tendency. [ME f. OF f. L *habitudo -dinis* f. *habēre habit-* have]

habitué /həbítyoo-ay/ *n.* a habitual visitor or resident. [F, past part. of *habituer* (as HABITUATE)]
▪ frequent visitor, frequenter, patron, regular customer, *colloq.* regular; resident.

háček /háchek/ *n.* a diacritic mark (ˇ) placed over letters to modify the sound in some Slavonic and Baltic languages. [Czech, dimin. of *hák* hook]

hachures /hashyóor/ *n.pl.* parallel lines used in hill-shading on maps, their closeness indicating the steepness of gradient. [F f. *hacher* HATCH[3]]

hacienda /hássi-éndə/ *n.* in Spanish-speaking countries: **1** an estate or plantation with a dwelling-house. **2** a factory. [Sp. f. L *facienda* things to be done]

hack[1] /hak/ *v.* & *n.* ● *v.* **1** *tr.* cut or chop roughly; mangle. **2** *tr.* kick the shin of (an opponent at football). **3** *intr.* (often foll. by *at*) deliver cutting blows. **4** *tr.* cut (one's way) through thick foliage etc. **5** *tr. colloq.* gain unauthorized access to (data in a computer). **6** *tr. sl.* **a** manage, cope with. **b** tolerate. **c** (often foll. by *off* or as **hacked off** *adj.*) annoy, disconcert. ● *n.* **1** a kick with the toe of a boot. **2** a gash or wound, esp. from a kick. **3 a** a mattock. **b** a miner's pick. □ **hacking cough** a short dry frequent cough. [OE *haccian* cut in pieces f. WG]

■ *v.* **1** chop, cut, carve, hew; gash, slash; mangle, lacerate, mutilate, butcher; (*hack off*) lop (off), sever, amputate. **2** kick, *colloq.* boot. **3** (*hack at*) stab (at), jab (at), thrust at, strike out at; cut, carve up, maim, mutilate, destroy, damage, deface. **4** cut, chop, carve, hew. **6 a** see ACCOMPLISH. **b** see TOLERATE 1, 3, 6. **c** (**hacked off**) see *discontented* (DISCONTENT *v.*). ● *n.* **1** kick, *colloq.* boot. □ **hacking cough** bark, (dry) cough.

hack[2] /hak/ *n.*, *adj.*, & *v.* ● *n.* **1 a** a horse for ordinary riding. **b** a horse let out for hire. **c** = JADE[2] 1. **2** a writer of mediocre literary work or journalism; *colloq.* usu. *derog.* a journalist. **3** a person hired to do dull routine work. **4** *US* a taxi. ● *attrib.adj.* **1** used as a hack. **2** typical of a hack; commonplace (*hack work*). ● *v.* **1 a** *intr.* ride on horseback on a road at an ordinary pace. **b** *tr.* ride (a horse) in this way. **2** *tr.* make common or trite. [abbr. of HACKNEY]

■ *n.* **1** horse, saddle-horse, mount, hackney, *archaic* palfrey, *colloq.* nag; jade. **2** penny-a-liner, *often derog.* scribbler; see also WRITER 1. **3** drudge, plodder, toiler, menial, lackey, slave, *Brit.* fag, *usu. derog.* flunkey. **4** see TAXI *n.* ● *attrib. adj.* **2** commonplace, hackneyed, trite, banal, humdrum, mediocre, stereotyped, stock, unoriginal, run-of-the-mill; tired, stale, tedious, overworked, overdone, *colloq.* old hat. ● *v.* **2** see PROSTITUTE *v.* 2b.

hack[3] /hak/ *n.* **1** a board on which a hawk's meat is laid. **2** a rack holding fodder for cattle. □ **at hack** (of a young hawk) not yet allowed to prey for itself. [var. of HATCH[1]]

hackberry /hákbəri/ *n.* (*pl.* **-ies**) *US* **1** any tree of the genus *Celtis*, native to N. America, bearing purple edible berries. **2** the berry of this tree. [var. of *hagberry*, of Norse orig.]

hacker /hákkər/ *n.* **1** a person or thing that hacks or cuts roughly. **2** *colloq.* a person who uses computers for a hobby, esp. to gain unauthorized access to data.

hackle /hákk'l/ *n.* & *v.* ● *n.* **1** a long feather or series of feathers on the neck or saddle of a domestic cock and other birds. **2** *Fishing* an artificial fly dressed with a hackle. **3** a feather in a Highland soldier's bonnet. **4** (in *pl.*) the erectile hairs along the back of a dog, which rise when it is angry or alarmed. **5** a steel comb for dressing flax. ● *v.tr.* dress or comb with a hackle. □ **make a person's hackles rise** cause a person to be angry or indignant. [ME *hechele*, *hakele*, prob. f. OE f. WG]

hackney /hákni/ *n.* (*pl.* **-eys**) **1** a horse of average size and quality for ordinary riding. **2** (*attrib.*) designating any of various vehicles kept for hire. ¶ No longer used except in *hackney carriage*, still in official use as a term for 'taxi'. [ME, perh. f. *Hackney* (formerly *Hakenei*) in London, where horses were pastured]

■ **1** see HACK[2] *n.* 1. **2** (*hackney carriage*) see CAB.

hackneyed /háknid/ *adj.* (of a phrase etc.) made commonplace or trite by overuse.

■ see STALE[1] 2.

hacksaw /háksaw/ *n.* a saw with a narrow blade set in a frame, for cutting metal.

had *past* and *past part.* of HAVE.

haddock /háddək/ *n.* (*pl.* same) a marine fish, *Melanogrammus aeglefinus*, of the N. Atlantic, allied to cod, but smaller. [ME, prob. f. AF *hadoc*, OF *(h)adot*, of unkn. orig.]

hade /hayd/ *n.* & *v.* *Geol.* ● *n.* an incline from the vertical. ● *v.intr.* incline from the vertical. [17th c., perh. dial. form of *head*]

Hades /háydeez/ *n.* (in Greek mythology) the underworld, the abode of the spirits of the dead. □□ **Hadean** *adj.* [Gk *haidēs*, orig. a name of Pluto]

Hadith /háddith/ *n.* *Relig.* a body of traditions relating to Muhammad. [Arab. *ḥadīṯ* tradition]

hadj var. of HAJJ.

hadji var. of HAJJI.

hadn't /hádd'nt/ *contr.* had not.

hadron /hádron/ *n.* *Physics* any strongly interacting elementary particle. □□ **hadronic** /-drónnik/ *adj.* [Gk *hadros* bulky]

hadst /hadst/ *archaic 2nd sing. past* of HAVE.

haecceity /hekseé-iti/ *n.* *Philos.* **1** the quality of a thing that makes it unique or describable as 'this (one)'. **2** individuality. [med.L *haecceitas* f. *haec* fem. of *hic* this]

■ **1** see SUBSTANCE 4, 6.

haem /heem/ *n.* (also **heme**) a non-protein compound containing iron, and responsible for the red colour of haemoglobin. [Gk *haima* blood or f. HAEMOGLOBIN]

haemal /heém'l/ *adj.* (*US* **hemal**) *Anat.* **1** of or concerning the blood. **2 a** situated on the same side of the body as the heart and great blood-vessels. **b** ventral. [Gk *haima* blood]

haematic /heemáttik/ *adj.* (*US* **hematic**) *Med.* of or containing blood. [Gk *haimatikos* (as HAEMATIN)]

haematin /heémətin/ *n.* (*US* **hematin** /heém-, hém-/) *Anat.* a bluish-black derivative of haemoglobin, formed by removal of the protein part and oxidation of the iron atom. [Gk *haima -matos* blood]

haematite /heémətīt/ *n.* (*US* **hematite** /heém-, hém-/) a ferric oxide ore. [L *haematites* f. Gk *haimatitēs* (*lithos*) bloodlike (stone) (as HAEMATIN)]

haemato- /heémətō/ *comb. form* (*US* **hemato-** /heémətō-, hém-/) blood. [Gk *haima haimat-* blood]

haematocele /heémətōseel/ *n.* (*US* **hematocele** /heém-, hém-/) *Med.* a swelling caused by blood collecting in a body cavity.

haematocrit /heémətōkrit/ *n.* (*US* **hematocrit** /heém-, hém-/) *Physiol.* **1** the ratio of the volume of red blood-cells to the total volume of blood. **2** an instrument for measuring this. [HAEMATO- + Gk *kritēs* judge]

haematology /heémətólləji/ *n.* (*US* **hematology** /heém-, hém-/) the study of the physiology of the blood. □□ **haematologic** /-təlójik/ *adj.* **haematological** /-təlójik'l/ *adj.* **haematologist** *n.*

haematoma /heémətṓmə/ *n.* (*US* **hematoma** /heém-, hém-/) *Med.* a solid swelling of clotted blood within the tissues.

haematuria /heémətyoóriə/ *n.* (*US* **hematuria** /heém-, hém-/) *Med.* the presence of blood in urine.

-haemia var. of -AEMIA.

haemo- /heémō/ *comb. form* (*US* **hemo-** /heémo, hémmō/) = HAEMATO-. [abbr.]

haemocyanin /heéməsī́ənin/ *n.* (*US* **hemocyanin** /heém-, hém-/) an oxygen-carrying substance containing copper, present in the blood plasma of arthropods and molluscs. [HAEMO- + *cyanin* blue pigment (as CYAN)]

haemodialysis /heémōdīállisiss/ *n.* = DIALYSIS 2.

haemoglobin /heéməglṓbin/ *n.* (*US* **hemoglobin** /heém-, hém-/) a red oxygen-carrying substance containing iron, present in the red blood-cells of vertebrates. [shortened f. *haematoglobin*, compound of HAEMATIN + GLOBULIN]

haemolysis /heemóllisiss/ *n.* (*US* **hemolysis** /heem-, hem-/) the loss of haemoglobin from red blood-cells. □□ **haemolytic** /-məlíttik/ *adj.*

haemophilia /heéməfilliə/ *n.* (*US* **hemophilia** /heém-, hém-/) *Med.* a usu. hereditary disorder with a tendency to bleed severely from even a slight injury, through the failure of the blood to clot normally. □□ **haemophilic** *adj.* [mod.L (as HAEMO-, -PHILIA)]

haemophiliac /heéməfilliak/ *n.* (*US* **hemophiliac** /heém-, hém-/) a person suffering from haemophilia.

haemorrhage /hémmərij/ *n.* & *v.* (*US* **hemorrhage**) ● *n.* **1** an escape of blood from a ruptured blood-vessel, esp. when profuse. **2** an extensive damaging loss suffered by a State, organization, etc., esp. of people or assets. ● *v.intr.* undergo a haemorrhage. □□ **haemorrhagic** /hémmərájik/ *adj.* [earlier *haemorrhagy* f. F *hémorr(h)agie* f. L *haemorrhagia* f. Gk *haimorrhagia* f. *haima* blood + stem of *rhēgnumi* burst]

haemorrhoid /hémmәroyd/ *n.* (*US* **hemorrhoid**) (usu. in *pl.*) swollen veins at or near the anus; piles. □□ **haemorrhoidal** /-róyd'l/ *adj.* [ME *emeroudis* (Bibl. *emerods*) f. OF *emeroyde* f. L f. Gk *haimorrhoides* (*phlebes*) bleeding (veins) f. *haima* blood, *-rhoos* -flowing]

haemostasis /heémōstáysiss/ *n.* (*US* **hemostasis** /heém-, hém-/) the stopping of the flow of blood. □□ **haemostatic** /heémәstáttik/ *adj.*

haere mai /hīrә mī/ *int. NZ* welcome. [Maori, lit. 'come hither']

hafiz /haáfiz/ *n.* a Muslim who knows the Koran by heart. [Pers. f. Arab. *ḥāfiẓ* guardian]

hafnium /háfniәm/ *n. Chem.* a silvery lustrous metallic element occurring naturally with zirconium, used in tungsten alloys for filaments and electrodes. ¶ Symb.: **Hf**. [mod.L f. *Hafnia* Copenhagen]

haft /haaft/ *n.* & *v.* ● *n.* the handle of a dagger, knife etc. ● *v.tr.* provide with a haft. [OE *hæft* f. Gmc]
■ *n.* see HANDLE *n.* 1.

Hag. *abbr.* Haggai (Old Testament).

hag[1] /hag/ *n.* **1** an ugly old woman. **2** a witch. **3** = HAGFISH. □□ **haggish** *adj.* [ME *hegge*, *hagge*, perh. f. OE *hægtesse*, OHG *hagazissa*, of unkn. orig.]
■ **1** crone, fishwife, harridan, shrew, *archaic* beldam, *sl. derog.* (old) bag. **2** witch, fury, gorgon, harpy, sorceress, enchantress, magician, sibyl, pythoness.

hag[2] /hag/ *n. Sc.* & *N.Engl.* **1** a soft place on a moor. **2** a firm place in a bog. [ON *högg* gap, orig. 'cutting blow', rel. to HEW]

hagfish /hágfish/ *n.* any jawless fish of the family Myxinidae, with a rasp-like tongue used for feeding on dead or dying fish. [HAG[1]]

Haggadah /hәgaádә/ *n.* **1** a legend etc. used to illustrate a point of the Law in the Talmud; the legendary element of the Talmud. **2** a book recited at the Passover Seder service. □□ **Haggadic** /-gáddik, -gaádik/ *adj.* [Heb., = tale, f. *higgîḏ* tell]

haggard /hággәrd/ *adj.* & *n.* ● *adj.* **1** looking exhausted and distraught, esp. from fatigue, worry, privation, etc. **2** (of a hawk) caught and trained as an adult. ● *n.* a haggard hawk. □□ **haggardly** *adv.* **haggardness** *n.* [F *hagard*, of uncert. orig.: later infl. by HAG[1]]
■ *adj.* **1** gaunt, drawn, distraught, hollow-eyed, hollow-cheeked, pinched, scrawny, scraggy, run-down, weary(-looking), careworn, spent, played out, exhausted, toil-worn, worn out, worn(-looking); see also *emaciated* (EMACIATE).

haggis /hággiss/ *n.* a Scottish dish consisting of a sheep's or calf's offal mixed with suet, oatmeal, etc., and boiled in a bag made from the animal's stomach or in an artificial bag. [ME: orig. unkn.]

haggle /hágg'l/ *v.* & *n.* ● *v.intr.* (often foll. by *about*, *over*) dispute or bargain persistently. ● *n.* a dispute or wrangle. □□ **haggler** *n.* [earlier sense 'hack' f. ON *höggva* HEW]
■ *v.* wrangle, higgle, bicker, chaffer, palter, dispute, squabble, quibble; bargain, negotiate, barter, *esp. US* dicker. ● *n.* see ARGUMENT 1.

hagio- /hággiō/ *comb. form* of saints or holiness. [Gk *hagios* holy]

Hagiographa /hággiógrәfә/ *n. pl.* the twelve books comprising the last of the three major divisions of the Hebrew Scriptures, additional to the Law and the Prophets.

hagiographer /hággiógrәfәr/ *n.* **1** a writer of the lives of saints. **2** a writer of any of the Hagiographa.

hagiography /hággiógrәfi/ *n.* the writing of the lives of saints. □□ **hagiographic** /-giәgráffik/ *adj.* **hagiographical** /-giәgráffik'l/ *adj.*

hagiolatry /hággiόllәtri/ *n.* the worship of saints.

hagiology /hággiόllәji/ *n.* literature dealing with the lives and legends of saints. □□ **hagiological** /-giәlójik'l/ *adj.* **hagiologist** *n.*

hagridden /hágridd'n/ *adj.* afflicted by nightmares or anxieties.

hah var. of HA.

ha ha /haahaá/ *int.* repr. laughter. [OE: cf. HA]

ha-ha /haáhaa/ *n.* a ditch with a wall on its inner side below ground level, forming a boundary to a park or garden without interrupting the view. [F, perh. from the cry of surprise on encountering it]

hahnium /haániәm/ *n. Chem.* an artificially produced radioactive element. ¶ Symb.: **Ha**. [O. *Hahn*, Ger. chemist d. 1968 + -IUM]

haik /hīk, hayk/ *n.* (also **haick**) an outer covering for head and body worn by Arabs. [Moroccan Arab. *ḥā'ik*]

haiku /hīkoo/ *n.* (*pl.* same) **1** a Japanese three-part poem of usu. 17 syllables. **2** an English imitation of this. [Jap.]

hail[1] /hayl/ *n.* & *v.* ● *n.* **1** pellets of frozen rain falling in showers from cumulonimbus clouds. **2** (foll. by *of*) a barrage or onslaught (of missiles, curses, questions, etc.). ● *v.* **1** *intr.* (prec. by *it* as subject) hail falls (*it is hailing*; *if it hails*). **2 a** *tr.* pour down (blows, words, etc.). **b** *intr.* come down forcefully. [OE *hagol*, *hægl*, *hagalian* f. Gmc]
■ *n.* **1** sleet. **2** barrage, onslaught, volley, storm, shower, torrent, bombardment. ● *v.* **1** sleet. **2** rain, shower, pour, volley; pelt.

hail[2] /hayl/ *v.*, *int.*, & *n.* ● *v.* **1** *tr.* greet enthusiastically. **2** *tr.* signal to or attract the attention of (*hailed a taxi*). **3** *tr.* acclaim (*hailed him king*; *was hailed as a prodigy*). **4** *intr.* (foll. by *from*) have one's home or origins in (a place) (*hails from Mauritius*). ● *int. archaic* or *rhet.* expressing greeting. ● *n.* **1** a greeting or act of hailing. **2** distance as affecting the possibility of hailing (*was within hail*). □ **hail-fellow-well-met** intimate, esp. too intimate. **Hail Mary** the Ave Maria (see AVE). □□ **hailer** *n.* [ellipt. use of obs. *hail* (adj.) f. ON *heill* sound, WHOLE]
■ *v.* **1** salute, greet; welcome, receive, meet, acknowledge, address, accost. **2** call, flag down, stop. **3** acclaim, acknowledge, *archaic* salute; cheer, applaud, approve, glorify, praise, laud, honour. **4** (*hail from*) come *or* be from, be a native *or* inhabitant *or* product of, trace one's roots to. ● *int.* see HELLO. ● *n.* **1** greeting, salutation; welcome, reception. **2** hailing distance.
□ **hail-fellow-well-met** see FAMILIAR 4.

hailstone /háylstōn/ *n.* a pellet of hail.

hailstorm /háylstorm/ *n.* a period of heavy hail.
■ see STORM *n.* 1.

hair /hair/ *n.* **1 a** any of the fine threadlike strands growing from the skin of mammals, esp. from the human head. **b** these collectively (*his hair is falling out*). **c** a hairstyle or way of wearing the hair (*I like your hair today*). **2 a** an artificially produced hairlike strand, e.g. in a brush. **b** a mass of such hairs. **3** anything resembling a hair. **4** an elongated cell growing from the epidermis of a plant. **5** a very small quantity or extent (also *attrib.*: *a hair crack*). □ **get in a person's hair** *colloq.* encumber or annoy a person. **hair-drier** (or **-dryer**) an electrical device for drying the hair by blowing warm air over it. **hair-grass** any of various grasses, esp. of the genus *Deschampsia*, *Corynephous*, *Aira*, etc., with slender stems. **hair of the dog** see DOG. **hair-raising** extremely alarming; terrifying. **hair's breadth** a very small amount or margin. **hair shirt** a shirt of haircloth, worn formerly by penitents and ascetics. **hair-shirt** *adj.* (*attrib.*) austere, harsh, self-sacrificing. **hair-slide** *Brit.* a (usu. ornamental) clip for keeping the hair in position. **hair-splitter** a quibbler. **hair-splitting** *adj.* & *n.* making overfine distinctions; quibbling. **hair-trigger** a trigger of a firearm set for release at the slightest pressure. **keep one's hair on** *Brit. colloq.* remain calm; not get angry. **let one's hair down** *colloq.* abandon restraint; behave freely or wildly. **make a person's hair stand on end** alarm or horrify a person. **not turn a hair** remain apparently unmoved or unaffected. □□ **haired** *adj.* (also in *comb.*). **hairless** *adj.* **hairlike** *adj.* [OE *hǣr* f. Gmc]
■ **1 b** tresses, locks, head of hair, mop, *colloq.* mane. **c** hairstyle, haircut, *coiffure*, cut, *colloq.* hairdo. **3** fibre, thread, filament, strand, fibril. **5** trifle, fraction, narrow margin, *colloq.* whisker; hair's breadth, hairbreadth, skin

of one's teeth. □ **get in a person's hair** see ANNOY 1. **hair-raising** see *terrifying* (TERRIFY). **hair's breadth** see HAIR 5 above. **hair-shirt** self-sacrificing, self-immolating, self-punishing, masochistic, ascetic; see also HARSH 2. **hair-slide** hair-clip, clip, barrette, *Brit.* slide; grip, hairgrip, *Brit.* kirby-grip. **hair-splitting** (*adj.*) quibbling, (over-)fussy, hypercritical, petty, captious, finicky, niggling, *colloq.* nit-picking. **keep one's hair on** stay calm *or* cool, take it easy, relax, *colloq.* keep one's shirt on, *sl.* cool it; see also *not turn a hair* (HAIR) below. **let one's hair down** see REVEL *v.* 1, *enjoy oneself*. **make a person's hair stand on end** see SCARE *v.* 1. **not turn a hair** be *or* remain calm, keep one's head, *colloq.* not *or* never bat an eyelid; see also *keep one's hair on* (HAIR) above. □□ **hairless** bald, bald-headed, bald-pated, glabrous; see also SMOOTH *adj.* 2.

hairbreadth /háirbredth/ *n.* = *hair's breadth*; (esp. *attrib.*: *a hairbreadth escape*).

hairbrush /háirbrush/ *n.* a brush for arranging or smoothing the hair.

haircloth /háirkloth/ *n.* stiff cloth woven from hair, used e.g. in upholstery.

haircut /háirkut/ *n.* **1** a cutting of the hair. **2** the style in which the hair is cut.

hairdo /háirdoo/ *n.* (*pl.* **-dos**) *colloq.* the style or an act of styling a woman's hair.
■ hairstyle, haircut, *coiffure*, hair, cut.

hairdresser /háirdressər/ *n.* **1** a person who cuts and styles hair, esp. professionally. **2** the business or establishment of a hairdresser. □□ **hairdressing** *n.*

hairgrip /háirgrip/ *n. Brit.* a flat hairpin with the ends close together.

hairline /háirlīn/ *n.* **1** the edge of a person's hair, esp. on the forehead. **2** a very thin line or crack etc.

hairnet /háirnet/ *n.* a piece of fine mesh-work for confining the hair.

hairpiece /háirpeess/ *n.* a quantity or switch of detached hair used to augment a person's natural hair.

hairpin /háirpin/ *n.* a U-shaped pin for fastening the hair. □ **hairpin bend** a sharp U-shaped bend in a road.

hairspray /háirspray/ *n.* a solution sprayed on to the hair to keep it in place.

hairspring /háirspring/ *n.* a fine spring regulating the balance-wheel in a watch.

hairstreak /háirstreek/ *n.* a butterfly of the genus *Strymonidia* etc. with fine streaks or rows of spots on its wings.

hairstyle /háirstīl/ *n.* a particular way of arranging or dressing the hair. □□ **hairstyling** *n.* **hairstylist** *n.*
■ see HAIRDO.

hairy /háiri/ *adj.* (**hairier, hairiest**) **1** made of or covered with hair. **2** having the feel of hair. **3** *sl.* **a** alarmingly unpleasant or difficult. **b** crude, clumsy. □□ **hairily** *adv.* **hairiness** *n.*
■ **1** hirsute, shaggy, downy, fleecy, fluffy, woolly, bristly, fringy, strigose; whiskered, whiskery, bearded, unshaven; *Bot.* comose, *Bot.* & *Zool.* setaceous, hispid. **2** downy, fluffy, woolly; rough, bristly. **3 a** unpleasant, dangerous, perilous, risky, uncertain, precarious, hazardous, frightening, worrying, nerve-racking, *colloq.* scary; tricky, difficult, knotty, complex, complicated, problematic.

hajj /haj/ *n.* (also **hadj**) the Islamic pilgrimage to Mecca. [Arab. *ḥajj* pilgrimage]
■ see PILGRIMAGE *n.* 1.

hajji /háji/ *n.* (also **hadji**) (*pl.* **-is**) a Muslim who has been to Mecca as a pilgrim: also (**Hajji**) used as a title. [Pers. *ḥājī* (partly through Turk. *hacı*) f. Arab. *ḥājj*: see HAJJ]
■ see PILGRIM *n.*

haka /haákə/ *n. NZ* **1** a Maori ceremonial war-dance accompanied by chanting. **2** an imitation of this by members of a sports team before a match. [Maori]

hake /hayk/ *n.* any marine fish of the genus *Merluccius*, esp. *M. merluccius* with an elongate body and large head. [ME perh. ult. f. dial. *hake* hook + FISH[1]]

hakenkreuz /haákənkroyts/ *n.* a swastika, esp. as a Nazi symbol. [G f. *Haken* hook + *Kreuz* CROSS]

hakim[1] /hukeém/ *n.* (in India and Muslim countries) a physician. [Arab. *ḥakīm* wise man, physician]

hakim[2] /haákim/ *n.* (in India and Muslim countries) a judge, ruler, or governor. [Arab. *ḥākim* governor]

Halacha /həlaákhə/ *n.* (also **Halakah**) Jewish law and jurisprudence, based on the Talmud. □□ **Halachic** *adj.* [Aram. *hᵃlākāh* law]

halal /haalaál/ *v.* & *n.* (also **hallal**) ● *v.tr.* (**halalled, halalling**) kill (an animal) as prescribed by Muslim law. ● *n.* (often *attrib.*) meat prepared in this way; lawful food. [Arab. *ḥalāl* lawful]

halation /haláysh'n/ *n. Photog.* the spreading of light beyond its proper extent in a developed image, caused by internal reflection in the support of the emulsion. [irreg. f. HALO + -ATION]

halberd /hálbərd/ *n.* (also **halbert**) *hist.* a combined spear and battleaxe. [ME f. F *hallebarde* f. It *alabarda* f. MHG *helmbarde* f. *helm* handle + *barde* hatchet]

halberdier /hálbərdeér/ *n. hist.* a man armed with a halberd. [F *hallebardier* (as HALBERD)]

halcyon /hálsiən/ *adj.* & *n.* ● *adj.* **1** calm, peaceful (*halcyon days*). **2** (of a period) happy, prosperous. ● *n.* **1** any kingfisher of the genus *Halcyon*, native to Europe, Africa, and Australasia, with brightly-coloured plumage. **2** *Mythol.* a bird thought in antiquity to breed in a nest floating at sea at the winter solstice, charming the wind and waves into calm. [ME f. L (*h*)*alcyon* f. Gk (*h*)*alkuōn* kingfisher]
■ *adj.* **1** see CALM *adj.* 1. **2** see GOLDEN 3.

hale[1] /hayl/ *adj.* (esp. of an old person) strong and healthy (esp. in **hale and hearty**). □□ **haleness** *n.* [OE *hāl* WHOLE]
■ strong, healthy, hearty, fit (as a fiddle), sound, able-bodied, hardy, robust, flourishing, in good *or* fine fettle, spry, sprightly, *colloq.* in the pink.

hale[2] /hayl/ *v.tr.* drag or draw forcibly. [ME f. OF *haler* f. ON *hala*]

half /haaf/ *n.*, *adj.*, & *adv.* ● *n.* (*pl.* **halves** /haavz/) **1** either of two equal or corresponding parts or groups into which a thing is or might be divided. **2** *colloq.* = *half-back*. **3** *colloq.* half a pint, esp. of beer etc. **4** either of two equal periods of play in sports. **5** *colloq.* a half-price fare or ticket, esp. for a child. **6** *Golf* a score that is the same as one's opponent's. ● *adj.* **1** of an amount or quantity equal to a half, or loosely to a part thought of as roughly a half (*take half the men*; *spent half the time reading*; *half a pint*; *a half-pint*; *half-price*). **2** forming a half (*a half share*). ● *adv.* **1** (often in *comb.*) to the extent of half; partly (*only half cooked*; *half-frozen*; *half-laughing*). **2** to a certain extent; somewhat (esp. in idiomatic phrases: *half dead*; *am half inclined to agree*). **3** (in reckoning time) by the amount of half (an hour etc.) (*half past two*). □ **at half cock** see COCK[1]. **by half** (prec. by *too* + adj.) excessively (*too clever by half*). **by halves** imperfectly or incompletely (*never does things by halves*). **half-and-half** being half one thing and half another. **half-back** (in some sports) a player between the forwards and full backs. **half-baked 1** incompletely considered or planned. **2** (of enthusiasm etc.) only partly committed. **3** foolish. **half the battle** see BATTLE. **half-beak** any fish of the family Hemirhamphidae with the lower jaw projecting beyond the upper. **half-binding** a type of bookbinding in which the spine and corners are bound in one material (usu. leather) and the sides in another. **half-blood 1** a person having one parent in common with another. **2** this relationship. **3** = *half-breed*. **half-blooded** born from parents of different races. **half-blue** *Brit.* **1** a person who has represented a university, esp. Oxford or Cambridge, in a sport but who has not received a full blue. **2** this distinction (see BLUE[1] *n.* 3). **half board** provision of bed, breakfast, and one main meal at a hotel etc. **half-boot** a boot reaching up to the calf. **half-breed** often *offens.* a person of mixed race. **half-brother** a brother with only one parent in common. **half-caste** often *offens.* *n.* a person whose parents are of different races, esp. the offspring of a European father and an Indian mother. ● *adj.* of or relating to such a person. **half a chance** *colloq.* the slightest opportunity (esp. *given half a chance*). **half-crown** (or **half a crown**) (in the UK) a former coin and monetary unit worth 2s. 6d. ($12^1/_2$p). **half-cut** *Brit. sl.* fairly drunk. **half-deck** the quarters of cadets and apprentices on a merchant vessel. **half-dozen** (or **half a dozen**) *colloq.* six, or about six. **half-duplex** see DUPLEX. **half an eye** the slightest degree of perceptiveness. **half-hardy** (of a plant) able to grow in the open air at all times except in severe frost. **half hitch** a noose or knot formed by passing the end of a rope round its standing part and then through the loop. **half holiday** a day of which half (usu. the afternoon) is taken as a holiday. **half-hour 1** (also **half an hour**) a period of 30 minutes. **2** a point of time 30 minutes after any hour o'clock. **half-hourly** at intervals of 30 minutes. **half-hunter** a watch with a hinged cover in which a small opening allows identification of the approximate position of the hands. **half-inch** *n.* a unit of length half as large as an inch. ● *v.tr. rhyming sl.* steal (= *pinch*). **half-integral** equal to half an odd integer. **half-landing** a landing part of the way up a flight of stairs, whose length is twice the width of the flight plus the width of the well. **half-lap** the joining of rails, shafts, etc., by halving the thickness of each at one end and fitting them together. **half-length** a portrait of a person's upper half. **half-life** *Physics* & *Biochem.* etc. the time taken for the radioactivity or some other property of a substance to fall to half its original value. **half-light** a dim imperfect light. **half-mast** the position of a flag halfway down the mast, as a mark of respect for a person who has died. **half measures** an unsatisfactory compromise or inadequate policy. **half a mind** see MIND. **half moon 1** the moon when only half its illuminated surface is visible from earth. **2** the time when this occurs. **3** a semicircular object. **half nelson** *Wrestling* see NELSON. **half-note** esp. *US Mus.* = MINIM 1. **the half of it** *colloq.* the rest or more important part of something (usu. after *neg.*: *you don't know the half of it*). **half pay** reduced income, esp. on retirement. **half-pie** *NZ sl.* imperfect, mediocre. **half-plate 1** a photographic plate 16.5 by 10.8 cm. **2** a photograph reproduced from this. **half-seas-over** *Brit. sl.* partly drunk. **half-sister** a sister with only one parent in common. **half-sole** the sole of a boot or shoe from the shank to the toe. **half-sovereign** a former British gold coin and monetary unit worth ten shillings (50p). **half-starved** poorly or insufficiently fed; malnourished. **half-step** *Mus.* a semitone. **half-term** *Brit.* a period about halfway through a school term, when a short holiday is usually taken. **half-timbered** *Archit.* having walls with a timber frame and a brick or plaster filling. **half-time 1** the time at which half of a game or contest is completed. **2** a short interval occurring at this time. **half the time** see TIME. **half-title 1** the title or short title of a book, printed on the recto of the leaf preceding the title-page. **2** the title of a section of a book printed on the recto of the leaf preceding it. **half-tone 1** a reproduction printed from a block (produced by photographic means) in which the various tones of grey are produced from small and large black dots. **2** *US Mus.* a semitone. **half-track 1** a propulsion system for land vehicles with wheels at the front and an endless driven belt at the back. **2** a vehicle equipped with this. **half-truth** a statement that (esp. deliberately) conveys only part of the truth. **half-volley** (*pl.* **-eys**) (in ball games) the playing of a ball as soon as it bounces off the ground. **half-yearly** at intervals of six months. **not half 1** not nearly (*not half long enough*). **2** *colloq.* not at all (*not half bad*). **3** *Brit. sl.* to an extreme degree (*he didn't half get angry*). [OE *half*, *healf* f. Gmc, orig. = 'side']

half-hearted /haáfhaártid/ *adj.* lacking enthusiasm; feeble. □□ **half-heartedly** *adv.* **half-heartedness** *n.*

■ feeble, lukewarm, unenthusiastic, indifferent, unconcerned, uninterested, half-baked, lackadaisical.

halfpenny /háypni/ *n.* (also **ha'penny** /háypni/) (*pl.* **-pennies** or **-pence** /háyp'nss/) (in the UK) a former bronze coin worth half a penny. ¶ Withdrawn in 1984 (cf. FARTHING).

halfpennyworth /háypəth/ *n.* (also **ha'p'orth**) **1** as much as could be bought for a halfpenny. **2** *colloq.* a negligible amount (esp. after *neg.*: *doesn't make a halfpennyworth of difference*).

halfway /haáfwáy/ *adv.* & *adj.* ● *adv.* **1** at a point equidistant between two others (*we were halfway to Rome*). **2** *US* to some extent; more or less (*is halfway decent*). ● *adj.* situated halfway (*reached a halfway point*). □ **halfway house 1** a compromise. **2** the halfway point in a progression. **3** a centre for rehabilitating ex-prisoners, mental patients, or others unused to normal life. **4** an inn midway between two towns. **halfway line** a line midway between the ends of a pitch, esp. in football.

■ *adj.* see INTERMEDIATE *adj.*

halfwit /haáfwit/ *n.* **1** *colloq.* an extremely foolish or stupid person. **2** a person who is mentally deficient. □□ **halfwitted** /-wíttid/ *adj.* **halfwittedly** /-wíttidli/ *adv.* **halfwittedness** /-wíttidniss/ *n.*

■ **1** dunce, fool, idiot, simpleton, ninny, ass, dolt, dunderhead, nincompoop, dullard, numskull, *colloq.* moron, imbecile, nitwit, dim-wit, birdbrain, cretin, *Brit. sl.* nit, *esp. Brit. sl.* twit. □□ **halfwitted** stupid, foolish, silly, inane, asinine, doltish, feeble-minded, *non compos* (*mentis*), weak-minded, *colloq.* moronic, imbecilic, cretinous, thick, dotty, dim-witted, *esp. US colloq.* dumb, *sl.* balmy, *esp. Brit. sl.* barmy.

halibut /hállibət/ *n.* (also **holibut** /hól-/) (*pl.* same) a large marine flat-fish, *Hippoglossus vulgaris*, used as food. [ME f. *haly* HOLY + BUTT[3] flat-fish, perh. because eaten on holy days]

halide /hállīd, háyl-/ *n. Chem.* **1** a binary compound of a halogen with another group or element. **2** any organic compound containing a halogen.

halieutic /hálliyóotik/ *adj. formal* of or concerning fishing. [L *halieuticus* f. Gk *halieutikos* f. *halieutēs* fisherman]

haliotis /hálliốtiss/ *n.* any edible gastropod mollusc of the genus *Haliotis* with an ear-shaped shell lined with mother-of-pearl. [Gk *hals hali-* sea + *ous ōt-* ear]

halite /hállīt/ *n.* rock-salt. [mod.L *halites* f. Gk *hals* salt]

halitosis /hállitṓsiss/ *n.* = *bad breath.* [mod.L f. L *halitus* breath]

hall /hawl/ *n.* **1 a** a space or passage into which the front entrance of a house etc. opens. **b** *US* a corridor or passage in a building. **2 a** a large room or building for meetings, meals, concerts, etc. **b** (in *pl.*) music-halls. **3** a large country house, esp. with a landed estate. **4** (in full **hall of residence**) a university residence for students. **5 a** (in a college etc.) a common dining-room. **b** dinner in this. **6** the building of a guild (*Fishmongers' Hall*). **7 a** a large public room in a palace etc. **b** the principal living-room of a medieval house. □ **Hall of Fame** *US* a building with memorials of celebrated people. **hall porter** *Brit.* a porter who carries baggage etc. in a hotel. **hall-stand** a stand in the hall of a house, with a mirror, pegs, etc. [OE = *hall* f. Gmc, rel. to HELL]

■ **1** passage, hallway, passageway, corridor; entrance(-hall), entry(-way), lobby, vestibule; foyer. **2 a** auditorium, amphitheatre, theatre; lecture-room, lecture-hall, lecture-theatre, concert hall, ballroom; assembly rooms. **b** (*halls*) music-halls. **3** manor, landed estate; see also SEAT *n.* 10. **4** see ACCOMMODATION 1.

hallal var. of HALAL.

hallelujah var. of ALLELUIA.

halliard var. of HALYARD.

hallmark /háwlmaark/ *n.* & *v.* ● *n.* **1** a mark used at Goldsmiths' Hall (and by the UK assay offices) for marking the standard of gold, silver, and platinum. **2** any distinctive feature esp. of excellence. ● *v.tr.* **1** stamp with a hallmark. **2** designate as excellent.

■ *n.* **1** stamp, mark, sign, symbol; plate-mark, assay-mark. **2** feature, stamp, mark, trade mark, sign, characteristic.

hallo var. of HELLO.

halloo /həlóó/ *int., n.,* & *v.* ● *int.* **1** inciting dogs to the chase. **2** calling attention. **3** expressing surprise. ● *n.* the cry 'halloo'. ● *v.* (**halloos, hallooed**) **1** *intr.* cry 'halloo', esp. to dogs. **2** *intr.* shout to attract attention. **3** *tr.* urge on (dogs etc.) with shouts. [perh. f. *hallow* pursue with shouts f. OF *halloer* (imit.)]

hallow /hállō/ *v.* & *n.* ● *v.tr.* **1** make holy, consecrate. **2** honour as holy. ● *n. archaic* a saint or holy person. □ **All Hallows** All Saints' Day, 1 Nov. [OE *hālgian, hālga* f. Gmc]

■ *v.* **1** consecrate, bless, sanctify; dedicate. **2** venerate, worship, revere, reverence, respect, honour, pay homage to, exalt, glorify. ● *n.* saint, holy man *or* woman, man *or* woman of God.

Hallowe'en /hállō-éen/ *n.* the eve of All Saints' Day, 31 Oct. [HALLOW + EVEN[2]]

Hallstatt /haálshtaat/ *adj.* of or relating to the early Iron Age in Europe as attested by archaeological finds at Hallstatt in Upper Austria.

halluces *pl.* of HALLUX.

hallucinate /həlóósinayt/ *v.* **1** *tr.* produce illusions in the mind of (a person). **2** *intr.* experience hallucinations. □□ **hallucinant** *adj.* & *n.* **hallucinator** *n.* [L *(h)allucinari* wander in mind f. Gk *alussō* be uneasy]

■ **2** see TRIP *v.* 7.

hallucination /həlóóssináysh'n/ *n.* the apparent or alleged perception of an object not actually present. □□ **hallucinatory** /həlóóssinətəri, -tri/ *adj.* [L *hallucinatio* (as HALLUCINATE)]

■ mirage, illusion, vision, chimera, phantasm, phantom, figment, apparition. □□ **hallucinatory** dreamy, dreamlike, visionary; phantasmagorical, chimerical, fantastic, illusory, fanciful, fancied, imaginary, imagined, fictional, unreal, untrue, fallacious, false.

hallucinogen /həlóóssinəjən/ *n.* a drug causing hallucinations. □□ **hallucinogenic** /-jénnik/ *adj.*

■ see DRUG *n.* 2.

hallux /hálluks/ *n.* (*pl.* **halluces** /hályooseez/) **1** the big toe. **2** the innermost digit of the hind foot of vertebrates. [mod.L f. L *allex*]

hallway /háwlway/ *n.* an entrance-hall or corridor.

■ see HALL 1.

halm var. of HAULM.

halma /hálmə/ *n.* a game played by two or four persons on a board of 256 squares, with men advancing from one corner to the opposite corner by being moved over other men into vacant squares. [Gk, = leap]

halo /háylō/ *n.* & *v.* ● *n.* (*pl.* **-oes**) **1** a disc or circle of light shown surrounding the head of a sacred person. **2** the glory associated with an idealized person etc. **3** a circle of white or coloured light round a luminous body, esp. the sun or moon. **4** a circle or ring. ● *v.tr.* (**-oes, -oed**) surround with a halo. [med.L f. L f. Gk *halōs* threshing-floor, disc of the sun or moon]

■ *n.* **1, 3** nimbus, aura, aureole; corona, radiance, *Art* vesica, mandorla. **2** see GLORY *n.* 3. **4** ring, disc, circle; loop, wheel.

halogen /hálləjən/ *n. Chem.* any of the group of non-metallic elements: fluorine, chlorine, bromine, iodine, and astatine, which form halides (e.g. sodium chloride) by simple union with a metal. □□ **halogenic** /-jénnik/ *adj.* [Gk *hals halos* salt]

halogenation /hálləjináysh'n/ *n.* the introduction of a halogen atom into a molecule.

halon /háylon/ *n. Chem.* any of various gaseous compounds of carbon, bromine, and other halogens, used to extinguish fires. [as HALOGEN + -ON]

halt[1] /holt, hawlt/ *n.* & *v.* ● *n.* **1** a stop (usu. temporary); an interruption of progress (*come to a halt*). **2** a temporary stoppage on a march or journey. **3** *Brit.* a minor stopping-place on a local railway line, usu. without permanent buildings. ● *v.intr.* & *tr.* stop; come or bring to a halt. □ **call a halt** (**to**) decide to stop. [orig. in phr. *make halt* f. G *Halt machen* f. *halten* hold, stop]

■ *n.* **1** stop, standstill, stoppage, cessation, interruption, break; end, termination, close. **2** see PAUSE *n.*, *hold-up* 1 (HOLD[1]). **3** see STOP *n.* 2. ● *v.* end, terminate, finish, cease, call a halt (to), discontinue, conclude, shut *or* close down; check, stem; see also STOP *v.* 1, 2. □ **call a halt** (**to**) see HALT[1] *v.* above and STOP *v.* 1, 2.

halt[2] /holt, hawlt/ *v.* & *adj.* ● *v.intr.* **1** (esp. as **halting** *adj.*) lack smooth progress. **2** hesitate (*halt between two opinions*). **3** walk hesitatingly. **4** *archaic* be lame. ● *adj. archaic* lame or crippled. □□ **haltingly** *adv.* [OE *halt, healt, healtian* f. Gmc]

■ *v.* **1** (**halting**) hesitant, wavering, uneven, faltering, faulty, unsteady, awkward; stammering, stuttering. **2** see HESITATE 1. **3** dawdle, drag one's feet, scuff, shuffle, scrape along, shamble. ● *adj.* crippled, game; see also LAME *adj.* 1.

halter /hóltər, háwl-/ *n.* & *v.* ● *n.* **1** a rope or strap with a noose or headstall for horses or cattle. **2 a** a strap round the back of a woman's neck holding her dress-top and leaving her shoulders and back bare. **b** a dress-top held by this. **3 a** a rope with a noose for hanging a person. **b** death by hanging. ● *v.tr.* **1** put a halter on (a horse etc.). **2** hang (a person) with a halter. □ **halter-break** accustom (a horse) to a halter. [OE *hælftre*: cf. HELVE]

■ *n.* **1** see TETHER *n.*

halteres /halteéreez/ *n.pl.* the balancing-organs of dipterous insects. [Gk, = weights used to aid leaping f. *hallomai* to leap]

halva /hálvaa, -və/ *n.* (also **halvah**) a sweet confection of sesame flour and honey. [Yiddish f. Turk. *helva* f. Arab. *ḥalwa*]

halve /haav/ *v.tr.* **1** divide into two halves or parts. **2** reduce by half. **3** share equally (with another person etc.). **4** *Golf* use the same number of strokes as one's opponent in (a hole or match). **5** fit (crossing timbers) together by cutting out half the thickness of each. [ME *halfen* f. HALF]

■ **1–3** see SPLIT *v.* 1a.

halves *pl.* of HALF.

halyard /hályərd/ *n.* (also **halliard, haulyard** /háwlyərd/) *Naut.* a rope or tackle for raising or lowering a sail or yard etc. [ME *halier* f. HALE[2] + -IER, assoc. with YARD[1]]

ham /ham/ *n.* & *v.* ● *n.* **1 a** the upper part of a pig's leg salted and dried or smoked for food. **b** the meat from this. **2** the back of the thigh; the thigh and buttock. **3** *sl.* (often *attrib.*) an inexpert or unsubtle actor or piece of acting. **4** (in full **radio ham**) *colloq.* the operator of an amateur radio station. ● *v.intr.* & (often foll. by *up*) *tr.* (**hammed, hamming**) *sl.* overact; act or treat emotionally or sentimentally. [OE *ham, hom* f. a Gmc root meaning 'be crooked']

■ *n.* **1, 2** see LEG *n.* 1–3. **3** see THESPIAN *n.* ● *v.* see DRAMATIZE.

hamadryad /hámmədríad/ *n.* **1** (in Greek and Roman mythology) a nymph who lives in a tree and dies when it dies. **2** the king cobra, *Naja bungarus.* [ME f. L *hamadryas* f. Gk *hamadruas* f. *hama* with + *drus* tree]

hamadryas /hámmədríəss/ *n.* a large Arabian baboon, *Papio hamadryas*, with a silvery-grey cape of hair over the shoulders, held sacred in ancient Egypt.

hamamelis /hámməméeliss/ *n.* any shrub of the genus *Hamamelis*, e.g. wych-hazel. [mod.L f. Gk *hamamēlis* medlar]

hamba /hámbə/ *int. S.Afr.* be off; go away. [Nguni *-hambe* go]

hambone / hámbōn/ *n. Austral. colloq.* a male striptease show. [20th c.: orig. uncert.]

hamburger /hámburgər/ *n.* a cake of minced beef usu. fried or grilled and eaten in a soft bread roll. [G, = of Hamburg in Germany]

hames /haymz/ *n.pl.* two curved pieces of iron or wood forming the collar or part of the collar of a draught-horse, to which the traces are attached. [ME f. MDu. *hame*]

ham-fisted /hámfistid/ *adj. colloq.* clumsy, heavy-handed, bungling. □□ **ham-fistedly** *adv.* **ham-fistedness** *n.*
■ see CLUMSY 1.

ham-handed /hámhándid/ *adj. colloq.* = HAM-FISTED. □□ **ham-handedly** *adv.* **ham-handedness** *n.*

Hamitic /həmíttik/ *n.* & *adj.* ● *n.* a group of African languages including ancient Egyptian and Berber. ● *adj.* **1** of or relating to this group of languages. **2** of or relating to the Hamites, a group of peoples in Egypt and N. Africa, by tradition descended from Noah's son Ham (Gen. 10:6 ff.).

hamlet /hámlit/ *n.* a small village, esp. one without a church. [ME f. AF *hamelet(t)e*, OF *hamelet* dimin. of *hamel* dimin. of *ham* f. MLG *hamm*]
■ see SETTLEMENT 2.

hammer /hámmər/ *n.* & *v.* ● *n.* **1 a** a tool with a heavy metal head at right angles to the handle, used for breaking, driving nails, etc. **b** a machine with a metal block serving the same purpose. **c** a similar contrivance, as for exploding the charge in a gun, striking the strings of a piano, etc. **2** an auctioneer's mallet, indicating by a rap that an article is sold. **3 a** a metal ball of about 7 kg, attached to a wire for throwing in an athletic contest. **b** the sport of throwing the hammer. **4** a bone of the middle ear; the malleus. ● *v.* **1 a** *tr.* & *intr.* hit or beat with or as with a hammer. **b** *intr.* strike loudly; knock violently (esp. on a door). **2** *tr.* **a** drive in (nails) with a hammer. **b** fasten or secure by hammering (*hammered the lid down*). **3** *tr.* (often foll. by *in*) inculcate (ideas, knowledge, etc.) forcefully or repeatedly. **4** *tr. colloq.* utterly defeat; inflict heavy damage on. **5** *intr.* (foll. by *at*, *away at*) work hard or persistently at. **6** *tr. Stock Exch.* declare (a person or a firm) a defaulter. □ **come under the hammer** be sold at an auction. **hammer and sickle** the symbols of the industrial worker and the peasant used as the emblem of the former USSR and of international communism. **hammer and tongs** *colloq.* with great vigour and commotion. **hammer out 1** make flat or smooth by hammering. **2** work out the details of (a plan, agreement, etc.) laboriously. **3** play (a tune, esp. on the piano) loudly or clumsily. **hammer-toe** a deformity in which the toe is bent permanently downwards. □□ **hammering** *n.* (esp. in sense 4 of *v.*). **hammerless** *adj.* [OE *hamor*, *hamer*]
■ *v.* **1, 2a** see POUND[2] *v.* 1a, b. **3** see DIN *v.*

hammerbeam /hámmərbeem/ *n.* a wooden beam (often carved) projecting from a wall to support the principal rafter or the end of an arch.

hammerhead /hámmərhed/ *n.* **1** any shark of the family Sphyrinidae, with a flattened head and eyes in lateral extensions of it. **2** a long-legged African marsh-bird, *Scopus umbretta*, with a thick bill and an occipital crest.

hammerlock /hámmərlok/ *n. Wrestling* a hold in which the arm is twisted and bent behind the back.

hammock /hámmək/ *n.* a bed of canvas or rope network, suspended by cords at the ends, used esp. on board ship. [earlier *hamaca* f. Sp., of Carib orig.]

hammy /hámmi/ *adj.* (**hammier**, **hammiest**) **1** of or like ham. **2** *colloq.* (of an actor or acting) over-theatrical.
■ **2** see *melodramatic* (MELODRAMA).

hamper[1] /hámpər/ *n.* **1** a large basket usu. with a hinged lid and containing food (*picnic hamper*). **2** *Brit.* a selection of food, drink, etc., for an occasion. [ME f. obs. *hanaper*, AF f. OF *hanapier* case for a goblet f. *hanap* goblet]

hamper[2] /hámpər/ *v.* & *n.* ● *v.tr.* **1** prevent the free movement or activity of. **2** impede, hinder. ● *n. Naut.* necessary but cumbersome equipment on a ship. [ME: orig. unkn.]
■ *v.* encumber, obstruct, block, impede, prevent; baulk, thwart, hinder, delay, check, slow down, bog down, hold up, tie (up *or* down), retard, inhibit, interfere with, snarl (up), frustrate, restrict, curb, limit, handicap, trammel, bar, *archaic or literary* stay.

hamsin var. of KHAMSIN.

hamster /hámstər/ *n.* any of various rodents of the subfamily Cricetinae, esp. *Cricetus cricetus*, having a short tail and large cheek pouches for storing food, kept as a pet or laboratory animal. [G f. OHG *hamustro* corn-weevil]

hamstring /hámstring/ *n.* & *v. Anat.* ● *n.* **1** each of five tendons at the back of the knee in humans. **2** the great tendon at the back of the hock in quadrupeds. ● *v.tr.* (*past* and *past part.* **hamstrung** or **hamstringed**) **1** cripple by cutting the hamstrings of (a person or animal). **2** prevent the activity or efficiency of (a person or enterprise).
■ *v.* **1** see LAME *v.* **2** see FRUSTRATE *v.* 2.

hamulus /hámyooləss/ *n.* (*pl.* **hamuli** /-lī/) *Anat.*, *Zool.*, & *Bot.* a hooklike process. [L, dimin. of *hamus* hook]

hand /hand/ *n.* & *v.* ● *n.* **1 a** the end part of the human arm beyond the wrist, including the fingers and thumb. **b** in other primates, the end part of a forelimb, also used as a foot. **2 a** (often in *pl.*) control, management, custody, disposal (*is in good hands*). **b** agency or influence (*suffered at their hands*). **c** a share in an action; active support. **3** a thing compared with a hand or its functions, esp. the pointer of a clock or watch. **4** the right or left side or direction relative to a person or thing. **5 a** a skill, esp. in something practical (*a hand for making pastry*). **b** a person skilful in some respect. **6** a person who does or makes something, esp. distinctively (*a picture by the same hand*). **7** an individual's writing or the style of this; a signature (*a legible hand*; *in one's own hand*; *witness the hand of . . .*). **8** a person etc. as the source of information etc. (*at first hand*). **9** a pledge of marriage. **10** a person as a source of manual labour esp. in a factory, on a farm, or on board ship. **11 a** the playing-cards dealt to a player. **b** the player holding these. **c** a round of play. **12** *colloq.* applause (*got a big hand*). **13** the unit of measure of a horse's height, equal to 4 inches (10.16 cm). **14** a forehock of pork. **15** a bunch of bananas. **16** (*attrib.*) **a** operated or held in the hand (*hand-drill*; *hand-luggage*). **b** done by hand and not by machine (*hand-knitted*). ● *v.tr.* **1** (foll. by *in*, *to*, *over*, etc.) deliver; transfer by hand or otherwise. **2** convey verbally (*handed me a lot of abuse*). **3** *colloq.* give away too readily (*handed them the advantage*). □ **all hands 1** the entire crew of a ship. **2** the entire workforce. **at hand 1** close by. **2** about to happen. **by hand 1** by a person and not a machine. **2** delivered privately and not by the public post. **from hand to mouth** satisfying only one's immediate needs (also *attrib.*: *a hand-to-mouth existence*). **get** (or **have** or **keep**) **one's hand in** become (or be or remain) practised in something. **give** (or **lend**) **a hand** assist in an action or enterprise. **hand and foot** completely; satisfying all demands (*waited on them hand and foot*). **hand cream** an emollient for the hands. **hand down 1** pass the ownership or use of to another. **2 a** transmit (a decision) from a higher court etc. **b** *US* express (an opinion or verdict). **hand-grenade** see GRENADE. **hand in glove** in collusion or association. **hand in hand** in close association. **hand it to** *colloq.* acknowledge the merit of (a person). **hand-me-down** an article of clothing etc. passed on from another person. **hand off** *Rugby Football* push off (a tackling opponent) with the hand. **hand on** pass (a thing) to the next in a series or succession. **hand out 1** serve, distribute. **2** award, allocate (*the judges handed out stiff sentences*). **hand-out 1** something given free to a needy person. **2** a statement given to the press etc. **hand over** deliver; surrender possession of. **hand-over** *n.* the act or an instance of handing over. **hand-over-fist** *colloq.* with rapid progress. **hand-pick** choose carefully or personally. **hand-picked** carefully or personally chosen. **hand round** distribute. **hands down** (esp. of winning) with no difficulty. **hands off 1** a warning not to touch or interfere with something. **2** *Computing* etc. not requiring manual use of controls. **hands on 1** *Computing* of or requiring personal operation at a keyboard. **2** direct, practical; involving or offering active participation rather than theory. **hands up!** an instruction to raise one's hands in surrender or to signify assent or participation. **hand-to-hand** (of fighting) at close quarters. **have** (or **take**) **a hand** (often foll. by *in*) share or take part. **have one's hands full** be fully occupied. **have one's hands tied** *colloq.* be unable to act. **hold one's hand** =

stay one's hand (see HAND). **in hand 1** receiving attention. **2** in reserve; at one's disposal. **3** under one's control. **lay** (or **put**) **one's hands on** see LAY[1]. **off one's hands** no longer one's responsibility. **on every hand** (or **all hands**) to or from all directions. **on hand** available. **on one's hands** resting on one as a responsibility. **on the one** (or **the other**) **hand** from one (or another) point of view. **out of hand 1** out of control. **2** peremptorily (*refused out of hand*). **put** (or **set**) **one's hand to** start work on; engage in. **stay one's hand** *archaic* or *literary* refrain from action. **to hand 1** within easy reach. **2** (of a letter) received. **turn one's hand to** undertake (as a new activity). □□ **handed** *adj.* **handless** *adj.* [OE *hand, hond*]

■ *n.* **1 a** fist, *colloq.* paw, *sl.* mitt, flipper. **b** paw. **2 a** (*hands*) control, hold, grasp, possession, custody, charge, clutches, keeping, power, disposal, authority, supervision, management, care. **b** see AGENCY 2b, INFLUENCE *n.* **c** part, share; participation, involvement; see also SUPPORT *n.* 1. **3** pointer, indicator. **5 a** touch, skill; see also TALENT 1. **b** see EXPERT *n.*, VIRTUOSO 1a. **7** writing, handwriting; signature; style. **10** labourer, worker, workman, workwoman, man, drudge, employee, *colloq.* woman. **12** ovation, clap, (round of) applause. ● *v.* **1** (*hand in*) deliver, submit, give in, tender, present, proffer, offer; (*hand to*) pass to, give to, deliver to, present to *or* with; (*hand over*) deliver, submit, yield, give up, surrender, turn over; transfer. **2** give, convey; see also EXPRESS[1] 1, 2. □ **at hand 1** nearby, near, close, close by; handy, (readily) available, to *or* on hand, convenient, within reach, accessible, in sight. **2** imminent, impending, approaching, forthcoming, *esp. US* upcoming; in the offing, on the horizon, in store, on *or US* in the cards. **give** (or **lend**) **a hand** see ASSIST *v.* 1. **hand and foot** see *completely* (COMPLETE). **hand down 1** see BEQUEATH. **2 a** see TRANSMIT 1a. **b** see DELIVER 4. **hand in glove** hand in hand, in league, in collusion, *sl.* in cahoots. **hand in hand** side by side, hand in glove, in close association. **hand it to** see RESPECT *v.* 1. **hand out 1** distribute, disseminate, pass round, deal (out), dole (out); give out, disburse, serve. **2** award, allocate, dispense, *literary* mete. **hand-out 1** see GIFT *n.* 1. **2** statement, communiqué. **hand over** see DELIVER 5. **hand-over** transfer, delivery, presentation, bestowal, *esp. US* conferral. **hand-over-fist** quickly, speedily, rapidly, swiftly, steadily. **hand-pick** see SELECT *v.* **hand-picked** see SELECT *adj.* 1. **hand round** see *hand out* 1 above, DISTRIBUTE 1. **hands down** readily, effortlessly; see also EASILY 1. **hands off 1** keep away (from), do not touch *or* interfere (with). **hands on 2** see PRACTICAL *adj.* 1. **have** (or **take**) **a hand** (**in**) see *take part* (PART). **have one's hands full** be swamped, be snowed under, *colloq.* have a lot on one's plate, be up to one's ears. **in hand 1** see *under way*. **2** in reserve, ready, available, on call, at one's disposal, accessible, in readiness, in store, *colloq.* on tap. **3** under control, in good hands; under a person's thumb. **on hand** see *at hand* 1 above. **out of hand 1** out of control, messy; see also *chaotic* (CHAOS). **2** categorically, peremptorily, flat(ly); see also ABSOLUTELY 1. **to hand 1** see *at hand* 1 above. **turn one's hand to** see UNDERTAKE 1.

handbag /hándbag/ *n.* & *v.* ● *n.* a small bag for a purse etc., carried esp. by a woman. ● *v.tr.* (of a woman politician) treat (a person, idea, etc.) ruthlessly or insensitively.
■ *n.* see BAG *n.* 2b.

handball *n.* **1** /hándbawl/ a game with a ball thrown by hand among players or against a wall. **2** /hándbáwl/ *Football* intentional touching of the ball with the hand or arm by a player other than the goalkeeper in the goal area, constituting a foul.

handbell /hándbel/ *n.* a small bell, usu. tuned to a particular note and rung by hand, esp. one of a set giving a range of notes.

handbill /hándbil/ *n.* a printed notice distributed by hand.
■ see LEAFLET *n.*

handbook /hándbŏŏk/ *n.* a short manual or guidebook.
■ see MANUAL *n.*

handbrake /hándbrayk/ *n.* a brake operated by hand.

h. & c. *abbr.* hot and cold (water).

handcart /hándkaart/ *n.* a small cart pushed or drawn by hand.
■ see CART *n.* 2.

handclap /hándklap/ *n.* a clapping of the hands.

handcraft /hándkraaft/ *n.* & *v.* ● *n.* = HANDICRAFT. ● *v.tr.* make by handicraft.

handcuff /hándkuf/ *n.* & *v.* ● *n.* (in *pl.*) a pair of lockable linked metal rings for securing a prisoner's wrists. ● *v.tr.* put handcuffs on.
■ *n.* (*handcuffs*) manacles, shackle(s), *colloq.* cuffs, *sl.* bracelets, *Brit. sl.* darbies. ● *v.* see SHACKLE *v.*

-handed /hándid/ *adj.* (in *comb.*) **1** for or involving a specified number of hands (in various senses) (*two-handed*). **2** using chiefly the hand specified (*left-handed*). □□ **-handedly** *adv.* **-handedness** *n.* (both in sense 2).

handful /hándfŏŏl/ *n.* (*pl.* **-fuls**) **1** a quantity that fills the hand. **2** a small number or amount. **3** *colloq.* a troublesome person or task.
■ **1** fistful. **2** sprinkling, small number, small amount, scattering; a few. **3** see BOTHER *n.* 1.

handglass /hándglaass/ *n.* **1** a magnifying glass held in the hand. **2** a small mirror with a handle.

handgrip /hándgrip/ *n.* **1** a grasp with the hand. **2** a handle designed for easy holding.
■ **1** see GRIP *n.* 1. **2** see HANDLE *n.* 1.

handgun /hándgun/ *n.* a small firearm held in and fired with one hand.
■ see PISTOL *n.*

handhold /hándhōld/ *n.* something for the hands to grip on (in climbing, sailing, etc.).

handicap /hándikap/ *n.* & *v.* ● *n.* **1 a** a disadvantage imposed on a superior competitor in order to make the chances more equal. **b** a race or contest in which this is imposed. **2** the number of strokes by which a golfer normally exceeds par for the course. **3** a thing that makes progress or success difficult. **4** a physical or mental disability. ● *v.tr.* (**handicapped, handicapping**) **1** impose a handicap on. **2** place (a person) at a disadvantage. □□ **handicapper** *n.* [prob. from the phrase *hand i'* (= in) *cap* describing a kind of sporting lottery]
■ *n.* **3** hindrance, restraint, encumbrance, restriction, limitation, disability, disadvantage, impediment, barrier, bar, obstacle, block, stumbling-block, constraint, check, curb, trammel(s). **4** see DISABILITY 1. ● *v.* hinder, hamper, encumber, restrict, limit, impede, bar, block, check, curb, trammel, disadvantage.

handicapped /hándikapt/ *adj.* suffering from a physical or mental disability.
■ see *disabled* (DISABLE 2).

handicraft /hándikraaft/ *n.* work that requires both manual and artistic skill. [ME, alt. of earlier HANDCRAFT after HANDIWORK]

handiwork /hándiwurk/ *n.* work done or a thing made by hand, or by a particular person. [OE *handgeweorc*]
■ see WORK *n.* 3.

handkerchief /hángkərchif, -cheef/ *n.* (*pl.* **handkerchiefs** or **-chieves** /-cheevz/) a square of cotton, linen, silk, etc., usu. carried in the pocket for wiping one's nose, etc.

handle /hánd'l/ *n.* & *v.* ● *n.* **1** the part by which a thing is held, carried, or controlled. **2** a fact that may be taken advantage of (*gave a handle to his critics*). **3** *colloq.* a personal title. **4** the feel of goods, esp. textiles, when handled. ● *v.tr.* **1** touch, feel, operate, or move with the hands. **2** manage or deal with; treat in a particular or correct way (*knows how to handle people*; *unable to handle the situation*). **3** deal in (goods). **4** discuss or write about (a subject). □ **get a handle on** *colloq.* understand the basis of or reason for a situation, circumstance, etc. □□ **handleable** *adj.* **handleability**

/-ləbílliti/ *n.* **handled** *adj.* (also in *comb.*). [OE *handle*, *handlian* (as HAND)]
■ *n.* **1** grip, handgrip; hilt, haft, helve; lever, knob, switch, pull. **3** see TITLE *n.* 5. **4** see TEXTURE *n.* 1, 2. ● *v.* **1** feel, touch, finger; caress, fondle, pat; hold, move, operate, use. **2** manage, run, operate, direct, control; deal with, cope with, use, employ, utilize, manipulate; tackle, treat. **3** deal in, trade in, traffic in; market. **4** see TREAT *v.* 4. □ **get a handle on** see UNDERSTAND 1, 2.

handlebar /hánd'lbaar/ *n.* (often in *pl.*) the steering bar of a bicycle etc., with a handgrip at each end. □ **handlebar moustache** a thick moustache with curved ends.

handler /hándlər/ *n.* **1** a person who handles or deals in certain commodities. **2** a person who trains and looks after an animal (esp. a police dog).

handlist /hándlist/ *n.* a short list of essential reading, reference books, etc.

handmade /hándmáyd/ *adj.* made by hand and not by machine, esp. as designating superior quality.

handmaid /hándmayd/ *n.* (also **handmaiden** /-mayd'n/) *archaic* a female servant or helper.

handrail /hándrayl/ *n.* a narrow rail for holding as a support on stairs etc.

handsaw /hándsaw/ *n.* a saw worked by one hand.

handsel /háns'l/ *n.* & *v.* (also **hansel**) ● *n.* **1** a gift at the beginning of the new year, or on coming into new circumstances. **2** = EARNEST[2] 1. **3** a foretaste. ● *v.tr.* (**handselled**, **handselling**; *US* **handseled**, **handseling**) **1** give a handsel to. **2** inaugurate. **3** be the first to try. [ME, corresp. to OE *handselen* giving into a person's hands, ON *handsal* giving of the hand (esp. in promise), formed as HAND + OE *sellan* SELL]

handset /hándset/ *n.* a telephone mouthpiece and earpiece forming one unit.
■ see TELEPHONE *n.*

handshake /hándshayk/ *n.* the shaking of a person's hand with one's own as a greeting etc.

handsome /hánsəm/ *adj.* (**handsomer**, **handsomest**) **1** (of a person) good-looking. **2** (of a building etc.) imposing, attractive. **3 a** generous, liberal (*a handsome present*; *handsome treatment*). **b** (of a price, fortune, etc., as assets gained) considerable. □□ **handsomeness** *n.* [ME, = easily handled, f. HAND + -SOME[1]]
■ **1** good-looking, attractive, comely, goodly; see also BEAUTIFUL 1. **2** see IMPRESSIVE 1. **3 a** see GENEROUS 1. **b** sizeable, large, big, substantial, considerable, good, goodly, ample, abundant.

handsomely /hánsəmli/ *adv.* **1** generously, liberally. **2** finely, beautifully. **3** *Naut.* carefully.

handspike /hándspīk/ *n.* a wooden rod shod with iron, used on board ship and by artillery soldiers.

handspring /hándspring/ *n.* a somersault in which one lands first on the hands and then on the feet.

handstand /hándstand/ *n.* balancing on one's hands with the feet in the air or against a wall.

handwork /hándwurk/ *n.* work done with the hands, esp. as opposed to machinery. □□ **handworked** *adj.*

handwriting /hándrīting/ *n.* **1** writing with a pen, pencil, etc. **2** a person's particular style of writing. □□ **handwritten** /-rítt'n/ *adj.*
■ see WRITING 2.

handy /hándi/ *adj.* (**handier**, **handiest**) **1** convenient to handle or use; useful. **2** ready to hand; placed or occurring conveniently. **3** clever with the hands. □□ **handily** *adv.* **handiness** *n.*
■ **1** convenient, useful, clever, helpful, practical; usable, serviceable. **2** nearby, accessible, at *or* on *or* to hand, close by, convenient, within reach. **3** deft, dexterous, adroit, adept, skilled, skilful, proficient. □□ **handily** conveniently, readily, easily, comfortably; skilfully, capably, deftly, cleverly, dexterously, adroitly, expertly, proficiently, masterfully.

handyman /hándiman/ *n.* (*pl.* **-men**) a person able or employed to do occasional domestic repairs and minor renovations.

hang /hang/ *v.* & *n.* ● *v.* (*past* and *past part.* **hung** /hung/ except in sense 7) **1** *tr.* **a** secure or cause to be supported from above, esp. with the lower part free. **b** (foll. by *up*, *on*, *on to*, etc.) attach loosely by suspending from the top. **2** *tr.* set up (a door, gate, etc.) on its hinges so that it moves freely. **3** *tr.* place (a picture) on a wall or in an exhibition. **4** *tr.* attach (wallpaper) in vertical strips to a wall. **5** *tr.* (foll. by *on*) *colloq.* attach the blame for (a thing) to (a person) (*you can't hang that on me*). **6** *tr.* (foll. by *with*) decorate by hanging pictures or decorations etc. (*a hall hung with tapestries*). **7** *tr.* & *intr.* (*past* and *past part.* **hanged**) **a** suspend or be suspended by the neck with a noosed rope until dead, esp. as a form of capital punishment. **b** as a mild oath (*hang the expense*; *let everything go hang*). **8** *tr.* let droop (*hang one's head*). **9** *tr.* suspend (meat or game) from a hook and leave it until dry or tender or high. **10** *intr.* be or remain hung (in various senses). **11** *intr.* remain static in the air. **12** *intr.* (often foll. by *over*) be present or imminent, esp. oppressively or threateningly (*a hush hung over the room*). **13** *intr.* (foll. by *on*) **a** be contingent or dependent on (*everything hangs on the discussions*). **b** listen closely to (*hangs on their every word*). ● *n.* **1** the way a thing hangs or falls. **2** a downward droop or bend. □ **get the hang of** *colloq.* understand the technique or meaning of. **hang about** (or **around**) **1** loiter or dally; not move away. **2** (foll. by *with*) associate with (a person etc.). **hang back 1** show reluctance to act or move. **2** remain behind. **hang fire** be slow in taking action or in progressing. **hang heavily** (or **heavy**) (of time) pass slowly. **hang in** *US colloq.* **1** persist, persevere. **2** linger. **hang loose** *colloq.* relax, stay calm. **hang on** *colloq.* **1** continue or persevere, esp. with difficulty. **2** (often foll. by *to*) cling, retain one's grip. **3** (foll. by *to*) retain; fail to give back. **4 a** wait for a short time. **b** (in telephoning) continue to listen during a pause in the conversation. **hang out 1** hang from a window, clothes-line, etc. **2** protrude or cause to protrude downwards. **3** (foll. by *of*) lean out of (a window etc.). **4** *sl.* reside or be often present. **5** (foll. by *with*) *sl.* accompany, be friends with. **hang-out** *n. sl.* a place one lives in or frequently visits. **hang together 1** make sense. **2** remain associated. **hang up 1** hang from a hook, peg, etc. **2** (often foll. by *on*) end a telephone conversation, esp. abruptly (*then he hung up on me*). **3** cause delay or difficulty to. **4** (usu. in *passive*, foll. by *on*) *sl.* be a psychological or emotional obsession or problem to (*is really hung up on her father*). **hang-up** *n. sl.* an emotional problem or inhibition. **hung-over** *colloq.* suffering from a hangover. **hung parliament** a parliament in which no party has a clear majority. **let it all hang out** *sl.* be uninhibited or relaxed. **not care** (or **give**) **a hang** *colloq.* not care at all. [ON *hanga* (tr.) = OE *hōn*, & f. OE *hangian* (intr.), f. Gmc]
■ *v.* **1** suspend, hang *or* hook up, sling; attach, fasten. **3** put up, show, exhibit. **5** see BLAME *v.* 2. **6** see DECORATE 1, 3. **7 a** gibbet, string up; execute, kill, lynch, *sl.* top. **b** damn, *sl.* stuff; see also CURSE *v.* 1b. **8** droop, drop, let down *or* fall, move *or* bring *or* put down. **9** suspend, hang up, hook up. **10** drape, swing, fall, dangle; be suspended *or* poised. **11** hover, be suspended, hang in the air, float, poise. **12** fall, descend, come down. **13** (*hang on*) **a** depend on, be dependent *or* contingent on, be subject to, be conditional on. **b** see LISTEN 1, 2. ● *n.* **1** drape, fall. **2** droop, fall. □ **get the hang of** see GRASP *v.* 3. **hang about** (or **around**) **1** loiter, wait (around), linger, dally, idle, loaf about, *archaic or literary* tarry. **2** (*hang about* or *around with*) associate with, socialize with, hobnob with, rub elbows with, rub shoulders with, consort with, fraternize with, mix with, *sl.* hang out with. **hang back 1** be reluctant, hesitate, falter, demur, think twice. **2** see LINGER 1. **hang fire** see POSTPONE, STALL[2] *v.* 1. **hang heavily** see DRAG *v.* 6. **hang in 1** see PERSEVERE. **2** see LINGER 1. **hang loose** see *let it all hang out* (HANG)

below. **hang on 1** continue, persist, carry on, persevere, go on, hold out, endure. **2** (*hang on to*) hold on to, cling to, clutch, grip, grasp. **3** (*hang on to*) see RETAIN 1. **4** wait (a moment *or* minute *or* second), stay (here); hold on, hold the line. **hang out 1** put out *or* up, hang up, suspend, swing. **2** see PROTRUDE. **3** lean *or* bend out. **4** reside, live, be present; (*hang out at*) frequent, haunt, visit, spend time at. **5** (*hang out with*) see ASSOCIATE *v.* 5. **hang-out** see LAIR[1] *n.* 1b. **hang together 1** make sense, be logical, be consistent, correspond, match (up), cohere, be coherent. **2** be *or* remain united, be *or* remain as *or* at one, remain associated, stick together; unite, join forces, cooperate, act in concert *or* harmony. **hang up 1** see SUSPEND 1. **2** break the connection, put down the receiver, *Brit.* ring off; (*hang up on*) cut off. **4** (*be hung up on*) be obsessed by, *Psychol.* have a complex about, be fixated on, *colloq.* have a thing about. **hang-up** problem, difficulty, *Psychol.* complex, *colloq.* thing; see also INHIBITION 1, 2. **let it all hang out** open up, *colloq.* let one's hair down; relax, stay *or* keep calm *or* cool, cool off *or* down, sit back, take it easy, *colloq.* hang loose.

hangar /hángər/ *n.* a building with extensive floor area, for housing aircraft etc. □□ **hangarage** *n.* [F, of unkn. orig.]

hangdog /hángdog/ *adj.* having a dejected or guilty appearance; shamefaced.

hanger[1] /hángər/ *n.* **1** a person or thing that hangs. **2** (in full **coat-hanger**) a shaped piece of wood or plastic etc. from which clothes may be hung. □ **hanger-on** (*pl.* **hangers-on**) a follower or dependant, esp. an unwelcome one.

■ □ **hanger-on** follower, adherent, supporter, fan, dependant, parasite, toady, sycophant; *sl.* groupie, wannabe; see also *yes-man, scrounger* (SCROUNGE).

hanger[2] /hángər/ *n. Brit.* a wood on the side of a steep hill. [OE *hangra* f. *hangian* HANG]

hang-glider /hángglīdər/ *n.* a frame with a fabric aerofoil stretched over it, from which the operator is suspended and controls flight by body movement. □□ **hang-glide** *v.intr.* **hang-gliding** *n.*

hanging /hánging/ *n.* & *adj.* ● *n.* **1 a** the practice or an act of executing by hanging a person. **b** (*attrib.*) meriting or causing this (*a hanging offence*). **2** (usu. in *pl.*) draperies hung on a wall etc. ● *adj.* that hangs or is hung; suspended. □ **hanging gardens** gardens laid out on a steep slope. **hanging valley** a valley, usu. tributary, above the level of the valleys or plains it joins.

■ *n.* **2** see DRAPERY. ● *adj.* see PENDULOUS 1.

hangman /hángmən/ *n.* (*pl.* **-men**) **1** an executioner who hangs condemned persons. **2** a word-game for two players, in which the tally of failed guesses is kept by drawing a representation of a gallows.

hangnail /hángnayl/ *n.* = AGNAIL. [alt. of AGNAIL, infl. by HANG and taking *nail* as = NAIL *n.* 2a]

hangover /hángōvər/ *n.* **1** a severe headache or other after-effects caused by drinking an excess of alcohol. **2** a survival from the past.

hank /hangk/ *n.* **1** a coil or skein of wool or thread etc. **2** any of several measures of length of cloth or yarn, e.g. 840 yds. for cotton yarn and 560 yds. for worsted. **3** *Naut.* a ring of rope, iron, etc., for securing the staysails to the stays. [ME f. ON *hönk*: cf. Sw. *hank* string, Da. *hank* handle]

hanker /hángkər/ *v.intr.* (foll. by *to* + infin., *for*, or *after*) long for; crave. □□ **hankerer** *n.* **hankering** *n.* [obs. *hank*, prob. rel. to HANG]

■ (*hanker after* or *for* or *to*) crave, fancy, want (to), desire (to), yearn for *or* to, long for *or* to, thirst after *or* for, hunger after *or* for, pine for, lust after *or* for, have a hankering for, *colloq.* yen for, have a yen for; itch to.

hanky /hángki/ *n.* (also **hankie**) (*pl.* **-ies**) *colloq.* a handkerchief. [abbr.]

hanky-panky /hángkipángki/ *n. sl.* **1** naughtiness, esp. sexual misbehaviour. **2** dishonest dealing; trickery. [19th c.: perh. based on *hocus-pocus*]

■ **1** mischief, naughtiness, tomfoolery, goings-on, antics, *colloq.* monkey business, shenanigans. **2** trickery, double-dealing, deception, duplicity, deceit, legerdemain, chicanery, *Brit. colloq.* jiggery-pokery, *sl.* funny business.

Hanoverian /hánnəvéeriən/ *adj.* of or relating to the British sovereigns from George I to Victoria (1714–1901). [*Hanover* in Germany, whose Elector became George I in 1714]

Hansa /hánsə/ *n.* (also **Hanse**) **1 a** a medieval guild of merchants. **b** the entrance fee to a guild. **2** (also **Hanseatic League**) a medieval political and commercial league of Germanic towns. □□ **Hanseatic** /-siáttik/ *adj.* [MHG *hanse*, OHG, Goth. *hansa* company]

Hansard /hánsaard/ *n.* the official verbatim record of debates in the British Parliament. [T. C. *Hansard*, Engl. printer d. 1833, who first printed it]

hansel var. of HANDSEL.

Hansen's disease /hánsʼnz/ *n.* leprosy. [G. H. A. *Hansen*, Norw. physician d. 1912]

hansom /hánsəm/ *n.* (in full **hansom cab**) *hist.* a two-wheeled horse-drawn cab accommodating two inside, with the driver seated behind. [J. A. *Hansom*, Engl. architect d. 1882, who designed it]

Hants /hants/ *abbr.* Hampshire. [OE *Hantescire*]

Hanukkah /haánəkə, -khə/ *n.* (also **Chanukkah**) the Jewish festival of lights, commemorating the purification of the Temple in 165 BC. [Heb. *ḥănukkāh* consecration]

hanuman /hánnoomaán/ *n.* **1** an Indian langur venerated by Hindus. **2** (**Hanuman**) (in Hindu mythology) the monkey-god, a loyal helper of Rama. [Hindi]

hap /hap/ *n.* & *v. archaic* ● *n.* **1** chance, luck. **2** a chance occurrence. ● *v.intr.* (**happed, happing**) **1** come about by chance. **2** (foll. by *to* + infin.) happen to. [ME f. ON *happ*]

hapax legomenon /háppaks ligómminon/ *n.* (*pl.* ***hapax legomena*** /-minə/) a word of which only one instance of use is recorded. [Gk, = a thing said once]

ha'penny var. of HALFPENNY.

haphazard /háphàzzərd/ *adj.* & *adv.* ● *adj.* done etc. by chance; random. ● *adv.* at random. □□ **haphazardly** *adv.* **haphazardness** *n.* [HAP + HAZARD]

■ *adj.* random, arbitrary, chance, aleatoric, accidental, adventitious, fortuitous, serendipitous. ● *adv.* see *at random* (RANDOM).

hapless /hápliss/ *adj.* unlucky. □□ **haplessly** *adv.* **haplessness** *n.* [HAP + -LESS]

■ see UNHAPPY 2.

haplography /haplógrəfi/ *n.* the accidental omission of letters when these are repeated in a word (e.g. *philogy* for *philology*). [Gk *haplous* single + -GRAPHY]

haploid /háployd/ *adj.* & *n. Biol.* ● *adj.* (of an organism or cell) with a single set of chromosomes. ● *n.* a haploid organism or cell. [G f. Gk *haplous* single + *eidos* form]

haplology /haplólləji/ *n.* the omission of a sound when this is repeated within a word (e.g. *February* pronounced /fébri/). [Gk *haplous* + -LOGY]

ha'p'orth *Brit.* var. of HALFPENNYWORTH.

happen /hápp'n/ *v.* & *adv.* ● *v.intr.* **1** occur (by chance or otherwise). **2** (foll. by *to* + infin.) have the (good or bad) fortune to (*I happened to meet her*). **3** (foll. by *to*) be the (esp. unwelcome) fate or experience of (*what happened to you?; I hope nothing happens to them*). **4** (foll. by *on*) encounter or discover by chance. ● *adv. N.Engl. dial.* perhaps, maybe (*happen it'll rain*). □ **as it happens** in fact; in reality (*as it happens, it turned out well*). [ME f. HAP + -EN[1]]

■ *v.* **1** occur, take place, come about, go on, come to pass, come off, arise, *poet.* befall, betide; develop, materialize; *disp.* transpire. **2** chance. **3** (*happen to*) become of, come of, *archaic* hap to, *poet.* befall, betide. **4** (*happen on*) come upon, chance on *or* upon, hit on *or* upon, stumble on *or* upon *or* across, find; encounter, meet. ● *adv.* see PERHAPS. □ **as it happens** see *in fact* 1 (FACT).

happening /háppʼning/ *n.* & *adj.* ● **1** an event or occurrence. **2** an improvised or spontaneous theatrical etc. performance. ● *adj. sl.* exciting, fashionable, trendy.
■ *n.* **1** event, incident, occurrence, occasion, episode; phenomenon. **2** see *improvisation* (IMPROVISE). ● *adj.* see TRENDY *adj.*

happenstance /háppənstənss/ *n. US* a thing that happens by chance. [HAPPEN + CIRCUMSTANCE]
■ see COINCIDENCE 2.

happi /háppi/ *n.* (*pl.* **happis**) (also **happi-coat**) a loose informal Japanese coat. [Jap.]

happy /háppi/ *adj.* (**happier, happiest**) **1** feeling or showing pleasure or contentment. **2 a** fortunate; characterized by happiness. **b** (of words, behaviour, etc.) apt, pleasing. **3** *colloq.* slightly drunk. **4** (in *comb.*) *colloq.* inclined to use excessively or at random (*trigger-happy*). □ **happy as a sandboy** see SANDBOY. **happy event** *colloq.* the birth of a child. **happy families** a card-game the object of which is to acquire four members of the same 'family'. **happy-go-lucky** cheerfully casual. **happy hour** esp. *US* a period of the day when drinks are sold at reduced prices in bars, hotels, etc. **happy hunting-ground** a place where success or enjoyment is obtained. **happy medium** a compromise; the avoidance of extremes. □□ **happily** *adv.* **happiness** *n.* [ME f. HAP + -Y[1]]
■ **1** pleased, content(ed), glad, delighted, joyful, overjoyed, cheerful, cheery, light-hearted, thrilled, gleeful, elated, jubilant, exhilarated, exultant, exuberant, euphoric, ecstatic; pleased as Punch, in seventh heaven, over the moon, *colloq.* on top of the world, on cloud nine, tickled pink, *poet.* blithe. **2 a** lucky, fortunate; propitious, auspicious, favourable, blessed. **b** apt, pleasing, felicitous; see also APPROPRIATE *adj.* **3** see DRUNK *adj.* 2. □ **happy-go-lucky** see CAREFREE. **happy medium** balance, compromise, middle way *or* course, golden mean, *literary via media*; middle ground. □□ **happily** joyfully, delightedly, gleefully, cheerily, cheerfully, gaily, merrily, gladly, with pleasure, heartily, enthusiastically, willingly, contentedly, *poet.* blithely; luckily, propitiously, providentially, opportunely. **happiness** pleasure, delight, felicity, enjoyment, joy, joyousness, joyfulness, jubilation, cheerfulness, cheeriness, gladness, light-heartedness, exhilaration, elation, exuberance, high spirits, glee.

haptic /háptik/ *adj.* relating to the sense of touch. [Gk *haptikos* able to touch f. *haptō* fasten]

hara-kiri /hárrəkírri/ *n.* ritual suicide by disembowelment with a sword, formerly practised by Samurai to avoid dishonour. [colloq. Jap. f. *hara* belly + *kiri* cutting]

harangue /həráng/ *n.* & *v.* ● *n.* a lengthy and earnest speech. ● *v.tr.* lecture or make a harangue to. □□ **haranguer** *n.* [ME f. F f. OF *arenge* f. med.L *harenga*, perh. f. Gmc]
■ *n.* speech, address, oration, declamation, exhortation, screed, diatribe, tirade, philippic. ● *v.* preach, sermonize, *esp. Austral sl.* earbash; see also LECTURE *v.* 2.

harass /hárrəss, *disp.* hərа́ss/ *v.tr.* **1** trouble and annoy continually or repeatedly. **2** make repeated attacks on (an enemy or opponent). □□ **harasser** *n.* **harassingly** *adv.* **harassment** /hárrəsmənt, *disp.* hərа́ss-/ *n.* [F *harasser* f. OF *harer* set a dog on]
■ **1** badger, harry, trouble, torment, bother, hound, persecute, annoy, irritate, pester, worry, beset, bait, nag, pick on, chivvy, henpeck, *colloq.* hassle, plague, *Austral. colloq.* heavy, *disp.* aggravate, *sl.* ballyrag. **2** see MOLEST 2.

harbinger /ha̋arbinjər/ *n.* & *v.* ● *n.* **1** a person or thing that announces or signals the approach of another. **2** a forerunner. ● *v.tr.* announce the approach of. [earlier = 'one who provides lodging': ME *herbergere* f. OF f. *herberge* lodging f. Gmc]
■ *n.* omen, foretoken, sign, portent, augury; herald, forerunner, precursor. ● *v.* see ANNOUNCE 1.

harbour /ha̋arbər/ *n.* & *v.* (*US* **harbor**) ● *n.* **1** a place of shelter for ships. **2** a shelter; a place of refuge or protection. ● *v.* **1** *tr.* give shelter to (esp. a criminal or wanted person). **2** *tr.* keep in one's mind, esp. resentfully (*harbour a grudge*). **3** *intr.* come to anchor in a harbour. □ **harbour-master** an official in charge of a harbour. □□ **harbourless** *adj.* [OE *herebeorg* perh. f. ON, rel. to HARBINGER]
■ *n.* **1** port, seaport, haven, harbourage. **2** refuge, haven, asylum; see also SHELTER *n.* 1, 3. ● *v.* **1** shelter, protect, guard, shield; conceal, hide. **2** foster, nurture, cherish, nurse, retain, maintain, hold, cling to.

harbourage /ha̋arbərij/ *n.* (*US* **harborage**) a shelter or place of shelter, esp. for ships.

hard /haard/ *adj.*, *adv.*, & *n.* ● *adj.* **1** (of a substance, material, etc.) firm and solid; unyielding to pressure; not easily cut. **2 a** difficult to understand or explain (*a hard problem*). **b** difficult to accomplish (*a hard decision*). **c** (foll. by *to* + infin.) not easy (*hard to believe*; *hard to please*). **3** difficult to bear; entailing suffering (*a hard life*). **4** (of a person) unfeeling; severely critical. **5** (of a season or the weather) severe, harsh (*a hard winter*; *a hard frost*). **6** harsh or unpleasant to the senses (*a hard voice*; *hard colours*). **7 a** strenuous, enthusiastic, intense (*a hard worker*; *a hard fight*). **b** severe, uncompromising (*a hard blow*; *a hard bargain*; *hard words*). **c** *Polit.* extreme; most radical (*the hard right*). **8 a** (of liquor) strongly alcoholic. **b** (of drugs) potent and addictive. **c** (of radiation) highly penetrating. **d** (of pornography) highly suggestive and explicit. **9** (of water) containing mineral salts that make lathering difficult. **10** established; not disputable; reliable (*hard facts*; *hard data*). **11** *Stock Exch.* (of currency, prices, etc.) high; not likely to fall in value. **12** *Phonet.* (of a consonant) guttural (as *c* in *cat*, *g* in *go*). **13** (of a shape, boundary, etc.) clearly defined, unambiguous. ● *adv.* **1** strenuously, intensely, copiously; with one's full effort (*try hard*; *look hard at*; *is raining hard*; *hard-working*). **2** with difficulty or effort (*hard-earned*). **3** so as to be hard or firm (*hard-baked*; *the jelly set hard*). ● *n. Brit.* **1** a sloping roadway across a foreshore. **2** *sl.* = *hard labour* (*got two years hard*). □ **be hard on 1** be difficult for. **2** be severe in one's treatment or criticism of. **3** be unpleasant to (the senses). **be hard put to it** (usu. foll. by *to* + infin.) find it difficult. **go hard with** turn out to (a person's) disadvantage. **hard and fast** (of a rule or a distinction made) definite, unalterable, strict. **hard at it** *colloq.* busily working or occupied. **hard-boiled 1** (of an egg) boiled until the white and the yolk are solid. **2** (of a person) tough, shrewd. **hard by** near; close by. **a hard case 1** *colloq.* **a** an intractable person. **b** *Austral.* & *NZ* an amusing or eccentric person. **2** a case of hardship. **hard cash** negotiable coins and banknotes. **hard coal** anthracite. **hard copy** printed material produced by computer, usu. on paper, suitable for ordinary reading. **hard core 1** an irreducible nucleus. **2** *colloq.* **a** the most active or committed members of a society etc. **b** a conservative or reactionary minority. **3** *Brit.* solid material, esp. rubble, forming the foundation of a road etc. **hard-core** *adj.* blatant, uncompromising, esp.: **1** (of pornography) explicit, obscene. **2** (of drug addiction) relating to hard drugs, esp. heroin. **hard disk** *Computing* a large-capacity rigid usu. magnetic storage disk. **hard-done-by** harshly or unfairly treated. **hard error** *Computing* a permanent error. **hard feelings** feelings of resentment. **hard hat 1** a protective helmet worn on building sites etc. **2** *colloq.* a reactionary person. **hard hit** badly affected. **hard-hitting** aggressively critical. **hard labour** heavy manual work as a punishment, esp. in a prison. **hard landing 1** a clumsy or rough landing of an aircraft. **2** an uncontrolled landing in which a spacecraft is destroyed. **hard line** unyielding adherence to a firm policy. **hard-liner** a person who adheres rigidly to a policy. **hard lines** *Brit. colloq.* = *hard luck*. **hard luck** worse fortune than one deserves. **hard-nosed** *colloq.* realistic, uncompromising. **a hard nut** *sl.* a tough, aggressive person. **a hard nut to crack** *colloq.* **1** a difficult problem. **2** a person or thing not easily understood or influenced. **hard of hearing** somewhat deaf. **hard on** (or **upon**) close to in pursuit etc. **hard-on** *n. coarse sl.* an erection of the penis. **hard pad** a form of distemper in dogs etc. **hard palate**

the front part of the palate. **hard-paste** denoting a Chinese or 'true' porcelain made of fusible and infusible materials (usu. clay and stone) and fired at a high temperature. **hard-pressed 1** closely pursued. **2** burdened with urgent business. **hard rock** *colloq.* rock music with a heavy beat. **hard roe** see ROE[1]. **hard sauce** a sauce of butter and sugar, often with brandy etc. added. **hard sell** aggressive salesmanship or advertising. **hard shoulder** *Brit.* a hardened strip alongside a motorway for stopping on in an emergency. **hard stuff** *sl.* strong alcoholic drink, esp. whisky. **hard tack** a ship's biscuit. **hard up 1** short of money. **2** (foll. by *for*) at a loss for; lacking. **hard-wearing** able to stand much wear. **hard wheat** wheat with a hard grain rich in gluten. **hard-wired** involving or achieved by permanently connected circuits designed to perform a specific function. **hard-working** diligent. **put the hard word on** *Austral.* & *NZ sl.* ask a favour (esp. sexual or financial) of. □□ **hardish** *adj.* **hardness** *n.* [OE *hard, heard* f. Gmc]

■ *adj.* **1** rigid, stiff, solid, inflexible, tough, firm, dense, compressed, solidified, hardened; leathery, callous; stony, rocklike, flinty, steely, unyielding, adamantine, impenetrable, impervious. **2 a** perplexing, knotty, puzzling, baffling, enigmatic, intricate, complicated, complex, involved; see also DIFFICULT 1b. **b** thorny, problematic, tough, awkward, tricky; see also DIFFICULT 3. **c** difficult, tough, awkward, tricky. **3** difficult, laborious, arduous, back-breaking, burdensome, onerous, fatiguing, tiring, exhausting, wearying, strenuous, toilsome; bad, grievous, calamitous, racking, dark, grim, distressing, painful, unpleasant, severe, austere, rough, *colloq.* tough. **4** stern, cold, callous, intractable, adamant, exacting, strict, demanding, hard-hearted, stony-hearted, severe, tyrannical, despotic, dictatorial, oppressive, cruel, ruthless, pitiless, merciless, savage, brutal, inhuman, unfeeling, heartless, harsh, unkind, implacable, unsympathetic, obdurate, insensitive, stony, unsparing; see also HARD *adj.* 7b below. **5** see SEVERE 3, 4. **6** see SEVERE 1, 5. **7 a** strenuous, sedulous, assiduous, conscientious, diligent, industrious, indefatigable, untiring, persistent, dogged, intent, intense, eager, enthusiastic, zealous, ardent, energetic, keen, avid, devoted. **b** severe, penetrating, searching, uncompromising, calculating, critical, methodical, systematic, practical, cool, unemotional, pragmatic, businesslike, realistic, hard-headed, hard-boiled, *colloq.* hardbitten, hard-nosed, tough; see also HARD *adj.* 4 above. **8 a** alcoholic, spirituous, potent; see also STRONG *adj.* 14. **b** potent, addictive, habit-forming, hard-core. **10** established, reliable, real, plain, strict, straight, straightforward, cold, bare, unvarnished, unquestionable, verifiable, indisputable, undeniable, incontestable, incontrovertible, inescapable, ineluctable, unavoidable, unalterable, immutable. **13** sharp, well-defined, clearly defined, clear, distinct, stark, definite, unambiguous. ● *adv.* **1** vigorously, forcefully, copiously, energetically, arduously, laboriously, strenuously, earnestly; actively, dynamically, spiritedly, eagerly, intensely, ardently, heartily, zealously, intently, carefully, earnestly, diligently, assiduously, sedulously, studiously, determinedly, steadfastly, conscientiously, industriously, devotedly, urgently, persistently, untiringly, indefatigably, perseveringly, unfalteringly, relentlessly, doggedly, *colloq.* mightily. **2** well, thoroughly. **3** see FIRM[1] *adj.* 1a. □ **be hard on 1** see DIFFICULT 1a, 3. **2** keep in line, *colloq.* sit on; see also SEVERE 1, 5. **3** see HARSH 1. **hard and fast** see STRICT 2b. **hard at it** see BUSY *adj.* 1, 3. **hard-boiled 1** hard, firm, set. **2** see HARD *adj.* 7b above, TOUGH *adj.* 4a, SHREWD. **hard by** see NEAR *adj.* 1. **a hard case 1 a** mule, tartar, die-hard, *sl.* hard nut. **b** see CARD[1] *n.* 6, ECCENTRIC *n.* **hard cash** see MONEY 1. **hard-core 1** see OBSCENE 1. **2** hard, potent, addictive, habit-forming. **hard-done-by** abused, ill-treated, misused, mistreated, hurt. **hard feelings** see RESENTMENT. **hard hit** hurt, damaged, harmed, badly affected, *colloq.* knocked sideways. **hard-hitting** see *scathing* (SCATHE *v.*). **hard labour** see SLAVERY 2. **hard line** tough stance, firm position. **hard-liner** stickler, bigot, partisan, sectionalist, intransigent, *colloq.* stick in the mud. **hard luck** misfortune, bad luck, ill luck, ill fortune, infelicity, adversity. **hard-nosed** see REALISTIC 2, INFLEXIBLE 2. **a hard nut** see *a hard case* 1 above, TOUGH *n.* **a hard nut to crack 1** see PROBLEM 1, 2. **2** enigma, puzzle, mystery, problem, conundrum, riddle. **hard on** (or **upon**) close behind, right behind, on a person's tail, in hot pursuit of, at *or* on the heels of. **hard-pressed 1** see TRACK[1] *v.* 1. **2** busy, occupied, engaged, tied up, wrapped up. **hard rock** rock, heavy metal. **hard stuff** see SPIRIT *n.* 4a. **hard up 1** poor, indigent, needy, poverty-stricken, impoverished, penniless, impecunious, in the red, *colloq.* broke, on one's uppers, *Brit. sl.* skint. **2** (*hard up for*) see DESTITUTE 2. **hard-wearing** see DURABLE *adj.* 1. **hard-working** see DILIGENT.

hardback /haárdbak/ *adj.* & *n.* ● *adj.* (of a book) bound in stiff covers. ● *n.* a hardback book.

hardball /haárdbawl/ *n.* & *v. US* ● *n.* **1** = BASEBALL. **2** *sl.* uncompromising methods or dealings, esp. in politics (*play hardball*). ● *v.tr. sl.* pressure or coerce politically.

hardbitten /haárdbitt'n/ *adj. colloq.* tough and cynical.
■ see HARD *adj.* 7b.

hardboard /haárdbord/ *n.* stiff board made of compressed and treated wood pulp.

harden /haárd'n/ *v.* **1** *tr.* & *intr.* make or become hard or harder. **2** *intr.* & *tr.* become, or make (one's attitude etc.), uncompromising or less sympathetic. **3** *intr.* (of prices etc.) cease to fall or fluctuate. □ **harden off** inure (a plant) to cold by gradual increase of its exposure. □□ **hardener** *n.*
■ **1** set, solidify, stiffen, freeze. **2** intensify, strengthen, toughen, stiffen; brace, fortify, reinforce. **3** stabilize, become fixed; freeze; level off, bottom out. □□ **hardener** coagulant; thermoplastic.

hardening /haárd'ning/ *n.* **1** the process or an instance of becoming hard. **2** (in full **hardening of the arteries**) *Med.* = ARTERIOSCLEROSIS.

hard-headed /haárdhéddid/ *adj.* practical, realistic; not sentimental. □□ **hard-headedly** *adv.* **hard-headedness** *n.*
■ see HARD *adj.* 7b.

hard-hearted /haárdhaártid/ *adj.* unfeeling, unsympathetic. □□ **hard-heartedly** *adv.* **hard-heartedness** *n.*
■ see HARD *adj.* 4.

hardihood /haárdihood/ *n.* boldness, daring.

hardly /haárdli/ *adv.* **1** scarcely; only just (*we hardly knew them*). **2** only with difficulty (*could hardly speak*). **3** harshly.
■ **1, 2** scarcely, barely, only just; seldom, rarely; with difficulty, with effort. **3** see ROUGHLY 1.

hardpan /haárdpan/ *n. Geol.* a hardened layer of clay occurring in or below the soil profile.

hardshell /haárdshel/ *adj.* **1** having a hard shell. **2** esp. *US* rigid, orthodox, uncompromising.

hardship /haárdship/ *n.* **1** severe suffering or privation. **2** the circumstance causing this.
■ want, suffering, misery, distress, trouble, unhappiness; privation, deprivation, rigours, adversity, austerity, ill fortune, bad luck; affliction, misfortune, difficulty.

hardtop /haárdtop/ *n.* a motor car with a rigid (usu. detachable) roof.

hardware /haárdwair/ *n.* **1** tools and household articles of metal etc. **2** heavy machinery or armaments. **3** the mechanical and electronic components of a computer etc. (cf. SOFTWARE).
■ **1** tools, equipment, utensils, implements, kit, *Brit.* ironmongery, *colloq.* gear. **2** machinery, equipment; arms, munitions, armaments. **3** equipment, machinery; components, parts.

hardwood /haárdwood/ *n.* the wood from a deciduous broad-leaved tree as distinguished from that of conifers.

hardy /haárdi/ *adj.* (**hardier, hardiest**) **1** robust; capable of enduring difficult conditions. **2** (of a plant) able to grow in the open air all the year. □ **hardy annual 1** an annual plant that may be sown in the open. **2** *joc.* a subject that comes up at regular intervals. □□ **hardily** *adv.* **hardiness** *n.* [ME f. OF *hardi* past part. of *hardir* become bold, f. Gmc, rel. to HARD]
■ **1** robust, strong, tough, vigorous, husky, able-bodied, fit, hale, healthy, stalwart, stout, sturdy, sound.

hare /hair/ *n.* & *v.* ● *n.* **1** any of various mammals of the family Leporidae, esp. *Lepus europaeus*, like a large rabbit, with tawny fur, long ears, short tail, and hind legs longer than forelegs, inhabiting fields, hills, etc. **2** (in full **electric hare**) a dummy hare propelled by electricity, used in greyhound racing. ● *v.intr.* run with great speed. □ **hare and hounds** a paper-chase. **hare-brained** rash, foolish, wild. **hare's-foot** (in full **hare's-foot clover**) a clover, *Trifolium arvense*, with soft hair around the flowers. **run with the hare and hunt with the hounds** try to remain on good terms with both sides. **start a hare** raise a topic of conversation. [OE *hara* f. Gmc]
■ *v.* see TEAR[1] *v.* 5. □ **hare-brained** rash, foolhardy, foolish, stupid, silly, inane, asinine, witless, brainless, mindless, flighty, giddy, frivolous, scatterbrained; wild, madcap, reckless, *colloq.* airy-fairy, crackpot.

harebell /háirbel/ *n.* **1** a plant, *Campanula rotundifolia*, with slender stems and pale-blue bell-shaped flowers. **2** = BLUEBELL 2.

Hare Krishna /haári kríshnə/ *n.* **1** a sect devoted to the worship of the Hindu deity Krishna (an incarnation of Vishnu). **2** (*pl.* **Hare Krishnas**) a member of this sect. [the title of a mantra based on the name *Krishna*, f. Skr. *O Hari!* an epithet of Krishna]

harelip /háirlip/ *n.* often *offens.* a cleft lip. □□ **harelipped** *adj.*

harem /haáreem, haareém/ *n.* **1 a** the women of a Muslim household, living in a separate part of the house. **b** their quarters. **2** a group of female animals sharing a mate. [Arab. *ḥarām*, *ḥarīm*, orig. = prohibited, prohibited place, f. *ḥarama* prohibit]

harewood /háirwŏŏd/ *n.* stained sycamore-wood used for making furniture. [G dial. *Ehre* f. L *acer* maple + WOOD]

haricot /hárrikō/ *n.* **1** (in full **haricot bean**) a variety of French bean with small white seeds. **2** the dried seed of this used as a vegetable. [F]

Harijan /hárrijən/ *n.* a member of the class of untouchables in India. [Skr., = a person dedicated to Vishnu, f. *Hari* Vishnu, *jana* person]

hark /haark/ *v.intr.* (usu. in *imper.*) *archaic* listen attentively. □ **hark back** revert to a topic discussed earlier. [ME *herkien* f. OE *heorcian* (unrecorded): cf. HEARKEN: *hark back* was orig. a hunting call to retrace steps]
■ see LISTEN 1, 2.

harken var. of HEARKEN.

harl /haarl/ *n.* (also **harle, herl** /herl/) fibre of flax or hemp. [MLG *herle*, *harle* fibre of flax or hemp]

harlequin /haárlikwin/ *n.* & *adj.* ● *n.* **1** (**Harlequin**) **a** a mute character in pantomime, usu. masked and dressed in a diamond-patterned costume. **b** *hist.* a stock comic character in Italian *commedia dell'arte*. **2** (in full **harlequin duck**) an Icelandic duck, *Histrionicus histrionicus*, with variegated plumage. ● *adj.* in varied colours; variegated. [F f. earlier *Herlequin* leader of a legendary troup of demon horsemen]
■ *n.* **1** see FOOL[1] *n.* 2. ● *adj.* see *variegated* (VARIEGATE).

harlequinade /haárlikwináyd/ *n.* **1** the part of a pantomime featuring Harlequin. **2** a piece of buffoonery. [F *arlequinade* (as HARLEQUIN)]

harlot /haárlət/ *n.* *archaic* a prostitute. □□ **harlotry** *n.* [ME f. OF *harlot*, *herlot* lad, knave, vagabond]
■ see PROSTITUTE *n.* 1a.

harm /haarm/ *n.* & *v.* ● *n.* hurt, damage. ● *v.tr.* cause harm to. □ **out of harm's way** in safety. [OE *hearm*, *hearmian* f. Gmc]
■ *n.* hurt, injury, damage, mischief, abuse; see also SIN[1] *n.* 1, GRIEVANCE. ● *v.* hurt, damage, injure, abuse, maltreat, wound, impair, mar. □ **out of harm's way** see SAFE *adj.* 5.

harmattan /haarmátt'n/ *n.* a parching dusty land-wind of the W. African coast occurring from December to February. [Fanti or Twi *haramata*]
■ see STORM *n.* 1.

harmful /haármfŏŏl/ *adj.* causing or likely to cause harm. □□ **harmfully** *adv.* **harmfulness** *n.*
■ dangerous, pernicious, deleterious, destructive, damaging, bad, detrimental, injurious; unhealthy, noxious, baleful, toxic, poisonous, venomous, malign, malignant, baneful.

harmless /haármliss/ *adj.* **1** not able or likely to cause harm. **2** inoffensive. □□ **harmlessly** *adv.* **harmlessness** *n.*
■ **1** benign, innocuous, gentle, mild, safe, non-toxic, non-poisonous, non-venomous. **2** see INOFFENSIVE.

harmonic /haarmónnik/ *adj.* & *n.* ● *adj.* **1** of or characterized by harmony; harmonious. **2** *Mus.* **a** of or relating to harmony. **b** (of a tone) produced by vibration of a string etc. in an exact fraction of its length. **3** *Math.* of or relating to quantities whose reciprocals are in arithmetical progression (*harmonic progression*). ● *n.* **1** *Mus.* an overtone accompanying at a fixed interval (and forming a note with) a fundamental. **2** *Physics* a component frequency of wave motion. □ **harmonic motion** (in full **simple harmonic motion**) oscillatory motion under a retarding force proportional to the amount of displacement from an equilibrium position. **harmonic progression** (or **series**) *Math.* a series of quantities whose reciprocals are in arithmetical progression. □□ **harmonically** *adv.* [L *harmonicus* f. Gk *harmonikos* (as HARMONY)]
■ *adj.* **1, 2a** see TUNEFUL.

harmonica /haarmónnikə/ *n.* a small rectangular wind instrument with a row of metal reeds along its length, held against the lips and moved from side to side to produce different notes by blowing or sucking. [L, fem. sing. or neut. pl. of *harmonicus*: see HARMONIC]

harmonious /haarmṓniəss/ *adj.* **1** sweet-sounding, tuneful. **2** forming a pleasing or consistent whole; concordant. **3** free from disagreement or dissent. □□ **harmoniously** *adv.* **harmoniousness** *n.*
■ **1** see TUNEFUL. **2** congruous, compatible, concordant, consonant, consistent, in accord, complementary; congenial, sympathetic, agreeable, *simpatico*. **3** see PEACEFUL 1.

harmonist /haármənist/ *n.* a person skilled in musical harmony, a harmonizer. □□ **harmonistic** /-nístik/ *adj.*

harmonium /haarmṓniəm/ *n.* a keyboard instrument in which the notes are produced by air driven through metal reeds by bellows operated by the feet. [F f. L (as HARMONY)]

harmonize /haármənīz/ *v.* (also **-ise**) **1** *tr.* add notes to (a melody) to produce harmony. **2** *tr.* & *intr.* (often foll. by *with*) bring into or be in harmony. **3** *intr.* make or form a pleasing or consistent whole. □□ **harmonization** /-záysh'n/ *n.* [f. F *harmoniser* (as HARMONY)]
■ **2** see AGREE 3a. **3** see COORDINATE *v.* 1.

harmony /haárməni/ *n.* (*pl.* **-ies**) **1 a** a combination of simultaneously sounded musical notes to produce chords and chord progressions, esp. as having a pleasing effect. **b** the study of this. **2 a** an apt or aesthetic arrangement of parts. **b** the pleasing effect of this. **3** agreement, concord. **4** a collation of parallel narratives, esp. of the Gospels. □ **in harmony 1** (of singing etc.) producing chords; not discordant. **2** (often foll. by *with*) in agreement. **harmony of the spheres** see SPHERE. [ME f. OF *harmonie* f. L *harmonia* f. Gk *harmonia* joining, concord, f. *harmos* joint]
■ **1 a** euphony, melodiousness, tunefulness. **2** see UNITY 1. **3** consonance, congruity, balance, consistency, agreement, accord, concord, chime, rapport, unanimity, compatibility, suitability, harmoniousness; see also UNITY 2. □ **in harmony 1** in tune, harmonious; see also MUSICAL *adj.* **2** see AGREEABLE 2.

harness /haárniss/ *n.* & *v.* ● *n.* **1** the equipment of straps and fittings by which a horse is fastened to a cart etc. and controlled. **2** a similar arrangement for fastening a thing to a person's body, for restraining a young child, etc. ● *v.tr.* **1 a** put a harness on (esp. a horse). **b** (foll. by *to*) attach by a harness. **2** make use of (natural resources) esp. to produce energy. □ **in harness** in the routine of daily work. □□ **harnesser** *n.* [ME f. OF *harneis* military equipment f. ON *hernest* (unrecorded) f. *herr* army + *nest* provisions]
■ *n.* **1** see TACK². ● *v.* **1** see HITCH *v.* 1.

harp /haarp/ *n.* & *v.* ● *n.* a large upright roughly triangular musical instrument consisting of a frame housing a graduated series of vertical strings, played by plucking with the fingers. ● *v.intr.* **1** (foll. by *on, on about*) talk repeatedly and tediously about. **2** play on a harp. □ **harp-seal** a Greenland seal, *Phoca groenlandica*, with a harp-shaped dark mark on its back. □□ **harper** *n.* **harpist** *n.* [OE *hearpe* f. Gmc]

harpoon /haarpoón/ *n.* & *v.* ● *n.* a barbed spearlike missile with a rope attached, for catching whales etc. ● *v.tr.* spear with a harpoon. □ **harpoon-gun** a gun for firing a harpoon. □□ **harpooner** *n.* [F *harpon* f. *harpe* clamp f. L *harpa* f. Gk *harpē* sickle]

harpsichord /haárpsikord/ *n.* a keyboard instrument with horizontal strings which are plucked mechanically. □□ **harpsichordist** *n.* [obs. F *harpechorde* f. LL *harpa* harp, + *chorda* string, the -*s*- being unexplained]

harpy /haárpi/ *n.* (*pl.* **-ies**) **1** (in Greek and Roman mythology) a monster with a woman's head and body and bird's wings and claws. **2** a grasping unscrupulous person. □ **harpy eagle** a S. American crested bird of prey, *Harpia harpyja*, one of the largest of eagles. [F *harpie* or L *harpyia* f. Gk *harpuiai* snatchers (cf. *harpazō* snatch)]

harquebus /haárkwibəss/ *n.* (also **arquebus** /aárk-/) *hist.* an early type of portable gun supported on a tripod or on a forked rest. [F *(h)arquebuse* ult. f. MLG *hakebusse* or MHG *hakenbühse*, f. *haken* hook + *busse* gun]

harridan /hárrid'n/ *n.* a bad-tempered old woman. [17th-c. cant, perhaps f. F *haridelle* old horse]
■ see HAG¹ 1.

harrier¹ /hárriər/ *n.* a person who harries or lays waste.

harrier² /hárriər/ *n.* **1 a** a hound used for hunting hares. **b** (in *pl.*) a pack of these with huntsmen. **2** a group of cross-country runners. [HARE + -IER, assim. to HARRIER¹]

harrier³ /hárriər/ *n.* any bird of prey of the genus *Circus*, with long wings for swooping over the ground. [*harrower* f. *harrow* harry, rob, assim. to HARRIER¹]

Harris tweed /hárriss/ *n.* a kind of tweed woven by hand in Harris in the Outer Hebrides.

harrow /hárrō/ *n.* & *v.* ● *n.* a heavy frame with iron teeth dragged over ploughed land to break up clods, remove weeds, cover seed, etc. ● *v.tr.* **1** draw a harrow over (land). **2** (usu. as **harrowing** *adj.*) distress greatly. □□ **harrower** *n.* **harrowingly** *adv.* [ME f. ON *hervi*]
■ *v.* **1** see PLOUGH *v.* 1. **2** (**harrowing**) distressing, disturbing, upsetting, worrying, alarming, unnerving, frightening, terrifying, horrifying, horrible, painful, torturous, heart-rending, nerve-racking, traumatic, agonizing.

harrumph /hərúmf/ *v.intr. US* clear the throat or make a similar sound, esp. ostentatiously. [imit.]

harry /hárri/ *v.tr.* (**-ies, -ied**) **1** ravage or despoil. **2** harass, worry. [OE *herian, hergian* f. Gmc, rel. to OE *here* army]
■ **1** see OVERRUN *v.* **2** see WORRY *v.* 2.

harsh /haarsh/ *adj.* **1** unpleasantly rough or sharp, esp. to the senses. **2** severe, cruel. □□ **harshen** *v.tr.* & *intr.* **harshly** *adv.* **harshness** *n.* [MLG *harsch* rough, lit. 'hairy', f. *haer* HAIR]
■ **1** rough, coarse, bristly, scratchy; grating, raucous, rasping, clashing, discordant, cacophonous, strident, shrill, *Mus.* dissonant, *esp. Mus.* inharmonious; bitter, acrid, sour, sharp. **2** severe, stern, stringent, tyrannical, merciless, pitiless, ruthless, unkind, cruel, unfeeling, unfriendly, hard, brutal, *Austral.* & *NZ colloq.* solid; Draconian, punitive; austere, bleak, dour, comfortless, grim, Spartan, stark, inhuman.

harslet var. of HASLET.

hart /haart/ *n.* the male of the deer (esp. the red deer) usu. over five years old. □ **hart's tongue** a fern, *Phyllitis scolopendrium*, with narrow undivided fronds. [OE *heor(o)t* f. Gmc]

hartal /haárt'l/ *n.* the closing of shops and offices in India as a mark of protest or sorrow. [Hind. *hartāl*, *haṭṭāl* f. Skr. *haṭṭa* shop + *tālaka* lock]

hartebeest /haártibeest/ *n.* any large African antelope of the genus *Alcelaphus*, with ringed horns bent back at the tips. [Afrik. f. Du. *hert* HART + *beest* BEAST]

hartshorn /haárts-horn/ *n. archaic* **1** an ammonious substance got from the horns of a hart. **2** (in full **spirit of hartshorn**) an aqueous solution of ammonia. [OE (as HART, HORN¹)]

harum-scarum /háirəmskáirəm/ *adj.* & *n. colloq.* ● *adj.* wild and reckless. ● *n.* such a person. [rhyming form. on HARE, SCARE]

haruspex /hərŏŏspeks/ *n.* (*pl.* **haruspices** /-spiseez/) a Roman religious official who interpreted omens from the inspection of animals' entrails. □□ **haruspicy** /-spisi/ *n.* [L]
■ see *fortune-teller*.

harvest /haárvist/ *n.* & *v.* ● *n.* **1 a** the process of gathering in crops etc. **b** the season when this takes place. **2** the season's yield or crop. **3** the product or result of any action. ● *v.tr.* **1 a** gather as a harvest, reap. **b** earn, obtain as a result of harvesting. **2** experience (consequences). □ **harvest festival** a thanksgiving festival in church for the harvest. **harvest home** the close of harvesting or the festival to mark this. **harvest mite** any arachnid larvae of the genus *Trombicula*, a chigger. **harvest moon** the full moon nearest to the autumn equinox (22 or 23 Sept.). **harvest mouse** a small rodent, *Micromys minutus*, that nests in the stalks of growing grain. □□ **harvestable** *adj.* [OE *hærfest* f. Gmc]
■ *n.* **1 a** ingathering, reaping, gathering; gleaning. **b** autumn, harvest home; Lammas, Pentecost. **2** crop, yield, produce, fruit; vintage; *Law* emblements. **3** see OUTCOME. ● *v.* **1 a** reap, gather, pick, collect, garner, take in; glean. **b** earn, make, take in, collect, garner, get, receive, obtain, procure, net. **2** reap, experience; see also INCUR.

harvester /haárvistər/ *n.* **1** a reaper. **2** a reaping-machine, esp. with sheaf-binding.

harvestman /haárvistmən/ *n.* (*pl.* **-men**) any of various arachnids of the family Opilionidae, with very long thin legs, found in humus and on tree trunks.

has *3rd sing. present* of HAVE.

has-been /házbeen/ *n. colloq.* a person or thing that has lost a former importance or usefulness.

hash¹ /hash/ *n.* & *v.* ● *n.* **1** a dish of cooked meat cut into small pieces and recooked. **2 a** a mixture; a jumble. **b** a mess. **3** re-used or recycled material. ● *v.tr.* (often foll. by *up*) **1** make (meat etc.) into a hash. **2** recycle (old material). □ **make a hash of** *colloq.* make a mess of; bungle. **settle a person's hash** *colloq.* deal with and subdue a person. [F *hacher* f. *hache* HATCHET]
■ *n.* **2 a** mixture, hotchpotch, mishmash, gallimaufry, farrago, jumble, olio, *mélange*, medley. **b** mess, shambles, confusion, bungle, botch, foul-up, *sl.* snafu. □ **make a hash of** bungle, make a mess *or* shambles of, mess *or* muddle up, botch, mishandle, mismanage, ruin, spoil, muff, *colloq.* foul up, *sl.* louse up, screw up. **settle a person's hash** see *put a person in his* or *her place* (PLACE).

hash² /hash/ *n. colloq.* hashish. [abbr.]

hashish /hásheesh/ *n.* a resinous product of the top leaves and tender parts of hemp, smoked or chewed for its narcotic effects. [f. Arab. *ḥašīš* dry herb; powdered hemp leaves]

Hasid /hássid/ (*pl.* **Hasidim**) a member of any of several mystical Jewish sects esp. one founded in the 18th c. □□ **Hasidic** /-síddik/ *adj.* [Heb. *ḥasîd* pious]

haslet /házlit/ *n.* (also **harslet** /haáz-/) pieces of (esp. pig's) offal cooked together and usu. compressed into a meat loaf. [ME f. OF *hastelet* dimin. of *haste* roast meat, spit, f. OLG, OHG *harst* roast]

hasn't /házz'nt/ *contr.* has not.

hasp /haasp/ *n.* & *v.* • *n.* a hinged metal clasp that fits over a staple and can be secured by a padlock. • *v.tr.* fasten with a hasp. [OE *hæpse, hæsp*]
▪ *n.* see LOCK[1] *n.*

hassle /háss'l/ *n.* & *v.* *colloq.* • *n.* **1** a prolonged trouble or inconvenience. **2** an argument or involved struggle. • *v.* **1** *tr.* harass, annoy; cause trouble to. **2** *intr.* argue, quarrel. [20th c.: orig. dial.]
▪ *n.* **1** see BOTHER *n.* 1. • *v.* **1** see BOTHER *v.* 1a.

hassock /hássək/ *n.* **1** a thick firm cushion for kneeling on, esp. in church. **2** a tuft of matted grass etc. [OE *hassuc*]

hast /hast/ *archaic 2nd sing. present* of HAVE.

hastate /hástayt/ *adj.* *Bot.* triangular like the head of a spear. [L *hastatus* f. *hasta* spear]

haste /hayst/ *n.* & *v.* • *n.* **1** urgency of movement or action. **2** excessive hurry. • *v.intr.* *archaic* = HASTEN. □ **in haste** quickly, hurriedly. **make haste** hurry; be quick. [ME f. OF *haste, haster* f. WG]
▪ *n.* **1** swiftness, rapidity, quickness, speed, velocity, urgency, alacrity, briskness, *archaic or literary* celerity. **2** hurry, rush, rashness, hastiness, (hustle and) bustle, impetuousness, impetuosity, recklessness, precipitateness. □ **in haste** see *hastily* (HASTY). **make haste** see HURRY *v.* 1.

hasten /háys'n/ *v.* **1** *intr.* (often foll. by *to* + infin.) make haste; hurry. **2** *tr.* cause to occur or be ready or be done sooner.
▪ **1** hurry, rush, make haste, fly, flee, run, sprint, race, bolt, dash, scurry, scamper, scuttle, speed. **2** hurry (up), speed (up), quicken, accelerate, expedite, rush.

hasty /háysti/ *adj.* (**hastier, hastiest**) **1** hurried; acting quickly or hurriedly. **2** said, made, or done too quickly or too soon; rash, unconsidered. **3** quick-tempered. □□ **hastily** *adv.* **hastiness** *n.* [ME f. OF *hasti, hastif* (as HASTE, -IVE)]
▪ **1** rushed, hurried, brief, speedy, fleeting; quick, swift, rapid, fast, brisk. **2** cursory, superficial, careless, slapdash, perfunctory; rash, precipitate, impetuous, impulsive, reckless, thoughtless, unthinking, incautious, heedless, ill-considered, unconsidered. **3** irritable, quick-tempered, irascible, testy, impatient, hot-tempered, volatile, choleric, short-tempered. □□ **hastily** quickly, speedily, swiftly, rapidly, post-haste, hurriedly, in haste; precipitately, impetuously, impulsively, rashly, recklessly, unthinkingly, thoughtlessly, heedlessly, incautiously; see also IMMEDIATELY *adv.* 1.

hat /hat/ *n.* & *v.* • *n.* **1** a covering for the head, often with a brim and worn out of doors. **2** *colloq.* a person's occupation or capacity, esp. one of several (*wearing his managerial hat*). • *v.tr.* (**hatted, hatting**) cover or provide with a hat. □ **hat trick 1** *Cricket* the taking of three wickets by the same bowler with three successive balls. **2** the scoring of three goals, points, etc. in other sports. **keep it under one's hat** *colloq.* keep it secret. **out of a hat** by random selection. **pass the hat round** collect contributions of money. **take off one's hat to** *colloq.* acknowledge admiration for. **throw one's hat in the ring** take up a challenge. □□ **hatful** *n.* (*pl.* **-fuls**). **hatless** *adj.* [OE *hætt* f. Gmc]

hatband /hátband/ *n.* a band of ribbon etc. round a hat above the brim.

hatbox /hátboks/ *n.* a box to hold a hat, esp. for travelling.

hatch[1] /hach/ *n.* **1** an opening between two rooms, e.g. between a kitchen and a dining-room for serving food. **2** an opening or door in an aircraft, spacecraft, etc. **3** *Naut.* **a** = HATCHWAY. **b** a trapdoor or cover for this (often in *pl.*: *batten the hatches*). **4** a floodgate. □ **down the hatch** *sl.* (as a drinking toast) drink up, cheers! **under hatches 1** below deck. **2 a** down out of sight. **b** brought low; dead. [OE *hæcc* f. Gmc]

hatch[2] /hach/ *v.* & *n.* • *v.* **1** *intr.* **a** (often foll. by *out*) (of a young bird or fish etc.) emerge from the egg. **b** (of an egg) produce a young animal. **2** *tr.* incubate (an egg). **3** *tr.* (also foll. by *up*) devise (a plot etc.). • *n.* **1** the act or an instance of hatching. **2** a brood hatched. [ME *hacche*, of unkn. orig.]
▪ *v.* **2** incubate, brood, sit on. **3** devise, contrive, concoct, design, formulate, originate, invent, dream up, *colloq.* cook up.

hatch[3] /hach/ *v.tr.* mark (a surface, e.g. a map or drawing) with close parallel lines. [ME f. F *hacher* f. *hache* HATCHET]

hatchback /háchbak/ *n.* a car with a sloping back hinged at the top to form a door.

hatchery /háchəri/ *n.* (*pl.* **-ies**) a place for hatching eggs, esp. of fish or poultry.

hatchet /háchit/ *n.* a light short-handled axe. □ **hatchet-faced** *colloq.* sharp-featured or grim-looking. **hatchet job** *colloq.* a fierce verbal attack on a person, esp. in print. **hatchet man** *colloq.* **1** a hired killer. **2** a person employed to carry out a hatchet job. [ME f. OF *hachette* dimin. of *hache* axe f. med.L *hapia* f. Gmc]

hatching /háching/ *n.* *Art* & *Archit.* close parallel lines forming shading esp. on a map or an architectural drawing.

hatchling /háchling/ *n.* a bird or fish that has just hatched.

hatchment /háchmənt/ *n.* a large usu. diamond-shaped tablet with a deceased person's armorial bearings, affixed to that person's house, tomb, etc. [contr. of ACHIEVEMENT]

hatchway /háchway/ *n.* an opening in a ship's deck for lowering cargo into the hold.

hate /hayt/ *v.* & *n.* • *v.tr.* **1** dislike intensely; feel hatred towards. **2** *colloq.* **a** dislike. **b** (foll. by verbal noun or *to* + infin.) be reluctant (to do something) (*I hate to disturb you*). • *n.* **1** hatred. **2** *colloq.* a hated person or thing. □□ **hatable** *adj.* (also **hateable**). **hater** *n.* [OE *hatian* f. Gmc]
▪ *v.* **1** loathe, abhor, detest, have an aversion to, abominate, dislike, execrate, despise, scorn. **2 a** see DISLIKE *v.* **b** dislike, shrink from, be averse to, resist; (*hate to*) be loath to, be reluctant *or* unwilling *or* disinclined to. • *n.* **1** hatred, abhorrence, detestation, loathing; animosity, antipathy, hostility, enmity, aversion; odium, animus. **2** enemy, *bête noire*, *esp. poet. or formal* foe; see also AVERSION 2.

hateful /háytfŏŏl/ *adj.* arousing hatred. □□ **hatefully** *adv.* **hatefulness** *n.*
▪ loathsome, detestable, abhorrent, execrable, despicable, odious, abominable, obnoxious, heinous, foul, contemptible, repugnant, scurvy, repulsive, repellent, revolting, vile.

hath /hath/ *archaic 3rd sing. present* of HAVE.

hatha yoga /háthə/ *n.* a system of physical exercises and breathing control used in yoga. [Skr. *haṭha* force: see YOGA]

hatpin /hátpin/ *n.* a long pin, often decorative, for securing a hat to the head.

hatred /háytrid/ *n.* intense dislike or ill will. [ME f. HATE + *-red* f. OE *rǣden* condition]
▪ *n.* see DISLIKE *n.* 1.

hatstand /hátstand/ *n.* a stand with hooks on which to hang hats.

hatter /háttər/ *n.* **1** a maker or seller of hats. **2** *Austral.* & *NZ* a person (esp. a miner or bushman) who lives alone. □ **as mad as a hatter** wildly eccentric.
▪ □ **as mad as a hatter** see INSANE 1.

hauberk /háwberk/ *n.* *hist.* a coat of mail. [ME f. OF *hau(s)berc* f. Frank., = neck protection, f. *hals* neck + *berg-* f. *beorg* protection]

haughty /háwti/ *adj.* (**haughtier, haughtiest**) arrogantly self-admiring and disdainful. □□ **haughtily** *adv.* **haughtiness** *n.* [extension of *haught* (adj.), earlier *haut* f. OF *haut* f. L *altus* high]
▪ arrogant, proud, superior, self-important, self-admiring, pretentious, pompous, conceited, snobbish, lofty, aloof, supercilious, vain, disdainful, scornful, contemptuous,

hoity-toity, *colloq.* highfalutin, stuck-up, high and mighty, on one's high horse, snooty, la-di-da, snotty, uppity, *esp. Brit. colloq.* uppish.

haul /hawl/ *v.* & *n.* ● *v.* **1** *tr.* pull or drag forcibly. **2** *tr.* transport by lorry, cart, etc. **3** *intr.* turn a ship's course. **4** *tr. colloq.* (usu. foll. by *up*) bring for reprimand or trial. ● *n.* **1** the act or an instance of hauling. **2** an amount gained or acquired. **3** a distance to be traversed (*a short haul*). □ **haul over the coals** see COAL. [var. of HALE[2]]

■ *v.* **1** drag, pull, tug, tow, trail, lug, heave, draw. **2** cart, transport, carry, convey, truck, move. **4** summon, subpoena, *esp. Law* summons. ● *n.* **1** pull, tug, drag, draw, heave, tow. **2** gain, catch, take, takings, yield, harvest; bag. **3** see DISTANCE *n.* 2.

haulage /háwlij/ *n.* **1** the commercial transport of goods. **2** a charge for this.

■ **1** see TRANSPORT *n.* 1a.

hauler /háwlər/ *n.* **1** a person or thing that hauls. **2** a miner who takes coal from the workface to the bottom of the shaft. **3** a person or firm engaged in the transport of goods.

haulier /háwliər/ *n. Brit.* = HAULER.

haulm /hawm, haam/ *n.* (also **halm**) **1** a stalk or stem. **2** the stalks or stems collectively of peas, beans, potatoes, etc., without the pods etc. [OE *h(e)alm* f. Gmc]

haulyard var. of HALYARD.

haunch /hawnch/ *n.* **1** the fleshy part of the buttock with the thigh, esp. in animals. **2** the leg and loin of a deer etc. as food. **3** the side of an arch between the crown and the pier. [ME f. OF *hanche*, of Gmc orig.: cf. LG *hanke* hind leg of a horse]

■ **1, 2** see LEG *n.* 2.

haunt /hawnt/ *v.* & *n.* ● *v.* **1** *tr.* (of a ghost) visit (a place) regularly, usu. reputedly giving signs of its presence. **2** *tr.* (of a person or animal) frequent or be persistently in (a place). **3** *tr.* (of a memory etc.) be persistently in the mind of. **4** *intr.* (foll. by *with, in*) stay habitually. ● *n.* **1** (often in *pl.*) a place frequented by a person. **2** a place frequented by animals, esp. for food and drink. □□ **haunter** *n.* [ME f. OF *hanter* f. Gmc]

■ *v.* **2** visit, frequent, spend time at, *sl.* hang out at. **3** obsess, preoccupy, beset, harass, torment, trouble, possess, prey on, *colloq.* plague. ● *n.* **1** stamping-ground, territory, domain, preserve, *colloq.* patch, *joc.* bailiwick, *sl.* hang-out, turf.

haunting /háwnting/ *adj.* (of a memory, melody, etc.) poignant, wistful, evocative. □□ **hauntingly** *adv.*

Hausa /hówzə/ *n.* & *adj.* ● *n.* (*pl.* same or **Hausas**) **1 a** a people of W. Africa and the Sudan. **b** a member of this people. **2** the Hamitic language of this people, widely used in W. Africa. ● *adj.* of or relating to this people or language. [native name]

hausfrau /hówsfrow/ *n.* a German housewife. [G f. *Haus* house + *Frau* woman]

hautboy *archaic* var. of OBOE.

haute couture /ōt kootyŏŏr/ *n.* high fashion; the leading fashion houses or their products. [F, lit. = high dressmaking]

haute cuisine /ōt kwizeén/ *n.* cookery of a high standard, esp. of the French traditional school. [F, lit. = high cookery]

haute école /ōt aykól/ *n.* the art or practice of advanced classical dressage. [F, = high school]

hauteur /ōtőr/ *n.* haughtiness of manner. [F f. *haut* high]

■ see PRIDE *n.* 2.

haut monde /ō mond/ *n.* fashionable society. [F, lit. = high world]

■ see SOCIETY 5a.

Havana /həvánnə/ *n.* a cigar made at Havana or elsewhere in Cuba.

have /hav, həv/ *v.* & *n.* ● *v.* (*3rd sing. present* **has** /haz, hass/; *past* and *past part.* **had** /had/) ● *v.tr.* **1** hold in possession as one's property or at one's disposal; be provided with (*has a car; had no time to read; has nothing to wear*). **2** hold in a certain relationship (*has a sister; had no equals*). **3** contain as a part or quality (*house has two floors; has green eyes*). **4 a** undergo, experience, enjoy, suffer (*had a good time; had a shock; has a headache*). **b** be subjected to a specified state (*had my car stolen; the book has a page missing*). **c** cause, instruct, or invite (a person or thing) to be in a particular state or take a particular action (*had him dismissed; had us worried; had my hair cut; had a copy made; had them to stay*). **5 a** engage in (an activity) (*had an argument; had sex*). **b** hold (a meeting, party, etc.). **6** eat or drink (*had a beer*). **7** (usu. in *neg.*) accept or tolerate; permit to (*I won't have it; will not have you say such things*). **8 a** let (a feeling etc.) be present (*have no doubt; has a lot of sympathy for me; have nothing against them*). **b** show or feel (mercy, pity, etc.) towards another person (*have pity on him; have mercy!*). **c** (foll. by *to* + infin.) show by action that one is influenced by (a feeling, quality, etc.) (*have the goodness to leave now*). **9 a** give birth to or beget (offspring). **b** conceive mentally (an idea etc.). **10** receive, obtain (*had a letter from him; not a ticket to be had*). **11** be burdened with or committed to (*has a job to do; have my garden to attend to*). **12 a** have obtained (a qualification) (*has six O levels*). **b** know (a language) (*has no Latin*). **13** *sl.* **a** get the better of (*I had him there*). **b** (usu. in *passive*) *Brit.* cheat, deceive (*you were had*). **14** *coarse sl.* have sexual intercourse with. ● *v.aux.* (with *past part.* or *ellipt.*, to form the perfect, pluperfect, and future perfect tenses, and the conditional mood) (*have worked; had seen; will have been; had I known, I would have gone; have you met her? yes, I have*). ● *n.* **1** (usu. in *pl.*) *colloq.* a person who has wealth or resources. **2** *sl.* a swindle. □ **had best** see BEST. **had better** would find it prudent to. **had rather** see RATHER. **have a care** see CARE. **have done, have done with** see DONE. **have an eye for, have eyes for, have an eye to** see EYE. **have a good mind to** see MIND. **have got to** *colloq.* = *have to.* **have had it** *colloq.* **1** have missed one's chance. **2** (of a person) have passed one's prime; (of a thing) be worn out or broken. **3** have been killed, defeated, etc. **have it 1** (foll. by *that* + clause) express the view that. **2** win a decision in a vote etc. **3** *colloq.* have found the answer etc. **have it away** (or **off**) *Brit. coarse sl.* have sexual intercourse. **have it both ways** see BOTH. **have it in for** *colloq.* be hostile or ill-disposed towards. **have it out** (often foll. by *with*) *colloq.* attempt to settle a dispute by discussion or argument. **have it one's own way** see WAY. **have-not** (usu. in *pl.*) *colloq.* a person lacking wealth or resources. **have nothing to do with** see DO[1]. **have on 1** be wearing (clothes). **2** be committed to (an engagement). **3** *colloq.* tease, play a trick on. **have out** get (a tooth etc.) extracted (*had her tonsils out*). **have sex** (often foll. by *with*) *colloq.* have sexual intercourse. **have something** (or **nothing**) **on a person 1** know something (or nothing) discreditable or incriminating about a person. **2** have an (or no) advantage or superiority over a person. **have to** be obliged to, must. **have to do with** see DO[1]. **have up** *Brit. colloq.* bring (a person) before a court of justice, interviewer, etc. [OE *habban* f. Gmc, prob. rel. to HEAVE]

■ *v.* **1** possess, hold, own, keep, be provided with. **3** possess, bear, contain, include. **4 a** undergo, suffer, endure, experience, enjoy. **c** cause to do *or* be, instruct to do *or* be, invite to do *or* be, induce to do *or* be, make a person do *or* be, make a thing do *or* be, force to do *or* be, oblige to do *or* be, press to do *or* be, require to do *or* be, compel to do *or* be, get to do, get done. **5 a** see ENGAGE 8. **b** hold, give, arrange, plan, organize, set (up), fix, prearrange, prepare, throw. **6** partake of, have a share *or* portion *or* part *or* bit of, consume; eat; drink. **7** see ALLOW 1. **8 b** see SHOW *v.* 3. **9 a** give birth to, bear, deliver, bring into the world; procreate, sire, father, *literary* beget. **b** see CONCEIVE 3a. **10** receive, get, obtain, acquire, procure, secure; take, accept. **12 b** see KNOW *v.* 1a. **13 a** see BEAT *v.* 3a. **b** see DECEIVE 1. ● *n.* **1** (*haves*) winners, fortunate ones, the rich *or* affluent *or* prosperous *or* well off *or* moneyed *or* well-to-do *or* wealthy. **2** see SWINDLE *n.* 1, 3. □ **had better** ought to, must, should. **have had it 1** have missed the boat *or* bus, have missed one's chance, be too late. **2** see *on one's last* *legs* (LEG). **3** see DEAD *adj.* 1. **have it 1** see ARGUE 2. **2** see WIN *v.* 3a. **3** know, understand, see; *colloq.* get it, catch on, cotton on, twig. **have it in for** see DISLIKE *v.* **have it out** see NEGOTIATE 1. **have-not** (*have-nots*) losers, the poor *or* needy *or* destitute *or* poverty-stricken *or* badly off *or* hard up *or* down and out. **have on 1** wear, be wearing, be dressed *or* clothed in, *formal* be attired in. **2** be committed to, have in the offing *or* pipeline, plan; see also ARRANGE 2, 3. **3** trick, tease, deceive, fool, play a trick *or* joke on; pull a (person's) leg. **have sex** (**with**) see *make love* (LOVE). **have to** see MUST[1] *v.*

haven /háyv'n/ *n.* **1** a harbour or port. **2** a place of refuge. [OE *hæfen* f. ON *höfn*]
■ **1** see HARBOUR *n.* 1. **2** see REFUGE 1, 2.

haven't /hávv'nt/ *contr.* have not.

haver /háyvər/ *v.* & *n.* ● *v.intr. Brit.* **1** talk foolishly; babble. **2** vacillate, hesitate. ● *n.* (usu. in *pl.*) *Sc.* foolish talk; nonsense. [18th c.: orig. unkn.]
■ *v.* **2** see HESITATE 1. ● *n.* see DRIVEL *n.*

haversack /hávvərsak/ *n.* a stout bag for provisions etc., carried on the back or over the shoulder. [F *havresac* f. G *Habersack* f. *Haber* oats + *Sack* SACK[1]]
■ see PACK[1] *n.* 1.

haversine /hávvərsīn/ *n.* (also **haversin**) *Math.* half of a versed sine. [contr.]

havildar /hávvildaar/ *n.* an Indian NCO corresponding to an army sergeant. [Hind. *ḥavildār* f. Pers. *ḥawāldār* trust-holder]

havoc /hávvək/ *n.* & *v.* ● *n.* widespread destruction; great confusion or disorder. ● *v.tr.* (**havocked, havocking**) devastate. □ **play havoc with** *colloq.* cause great confusion or difficulty to. [ME f. AF *havok* f. OF *havo(t)*, of unkn. orig.]
■ *n.* devastation, destruction, desolation, damage, (rack and) ruin, *literary* despoliation; confusion, chaos, disorder, mayhem, disruption. □ **play havoc with** see DISRUPT 1.

haw[1] /haw/ *n.* the hawthorn or its fruit. [OE *haga* f. Gmc, rel. to HEDGE]

haw[2] /haw/ *n.* the nictitating membrane of a horse, dog, etc., esp. when inflamed. [16th c.: orig. unkn.]

haw[3] /haw/ *int.* & *v.* ● *int.* expressing hesitation. ● *v.intr.* (in **hum and haw**: see HUM[1]) [imit.: cf. HA]

Hawaiian /həwīən/ *n.* & *adj.* ● *n.* **1 a** a native of Hawaii, an island or island-group in the N. Pacific. **b** a person of Hawaiian descent. **2** the Malayo-Polynesian language of Hawaii. ● *adj.* of or relating to Hawaii or its people or language.

hawfinch /háwfinch/ *n.* any large stout finch of the genus *Coccothraustes*, with a thick beak for cracking seeds. [HAW[1] + FINCH]

hawk[1] /hawk/ *n.* & *v.* ● *n.* **1** any of various diurnal birds of prey of the family Accipitridae, having a characteristic curved beak, rounded short wings, and a long tail. **2** *Polit.* a person who advocates an aggressive or warlike policy, esp. in foreign affairs. **3** a rapacious person. ● *v.* **1** *intr.* hunt game with a hawk. **2** *intr.* (often foll. by *at*) & *tr.* attack, as a hawk does. **3** *intr.* (of a bird) hunt on the wing for food. □ **hawk-eyed** keen-sighted. **hawk moth** any darting and hovering moth of the family Sphingidae, having narrow forewings and a stout body. **hawk-nosed** having an aquiline nose. □□ **hawkish** *adj.* **hawkishness** *n.* **hawklike** *adj.* [OE *h(e)afoc*, *hæbuc* f. Gmc]
■ *n.* **2** see BELLIGERENT *n.*

hawk[2] /hawk/ *v.tr.* **1** carry about or offer around (goods) for sale. **2** (often foll. by *about*) relate (news, gossip, etc.) freely. [back-form. f. HAWKER[1]]
■ **1** see SELL *v.* 2.

hawk[3] /hawk/ *v.* **1** *intr.* clear the throat noisily. **2** *tr.* (foll. by *up*) bring (phlegm etc.) up from the throat. [prob. imit.]

hawk[4] /hawk/ *n.* a plasterer's square board with a handle underneath for carrying plaster or mortar. [17th c.: orig. unkn.]

hawker[1] /háwkər/ *n.* a person who travels about selling goods. [16th c.: prob. f. LG or Du.; cf. HUCKSTER]
■ see SELLER.

hawker[2] /háwkər/ *n.* a falconer. [OE *hafocere*]

hawksbill /háwksbil/ *n.* (in full **hawksbill turtle**) a small turtle, *Eretmochelys imbricata*, yielding tortoiseshell.

hawkweed /háwkweed/ *n.* any composite plant of the genus *Hieracium*, with yellow flowers.

hawse /hawz/ *n.* **1** the part of a ship's bows in which hawse-holes or hawse-pipes are placed. **2** the space between the head of an anchored vessel and the anchors. **3** the arrangement of cables when a ship is moored with port and starboard forward anchors. □ **hawse-hole** a hole in the side of a ship through which a cable or anchor-rope passes. **hawse-pipe** a metal pipe lining a hawse-hole. [ME *halse*, prob. f. ON *háls* neck, ship's bow]

hawser /háwzər/ *n. Naut.* a thick rope or cable for mooring or towing a ship. [ME f. AF *haucer*, *hauceour* f. OF *haucier* hoist ult. f. L *altus* high]
■ see ROPE *n.* 1a.

hawthorn /háwthorn/ *n.* any thorny shrub or tree of the genus *Crataegus*, esp. *C. monogyna*, with white, red, or pink blossom and small dark-red fruit or haws. [OE *hagathorn* (as HAW[1], THORN)]

hay[1] /hay/ *n.* & *v.* ● *n.* grass mown and dried for fodder. ● *v.* **1** *intr.* make hay. **2** *tr.* put (land) under grass for hay. **3** *tr.* make into hay. □ **hay fever** an allergy with catarrhal and other asthmatic symptoms, caused by pollen or dust. **make hay of** throw into confusion. **make hay** (**while the sun shines**) seize opportunities for profit or enjoyment. [OE *hēg*, *hīeg*, *hīg* f. Gmc]
■ *n.* see PROVENDER 1.

hay[2] /hay/ *n.* (also **hey**) **1** a country dance with interweaving steps. **2** a figure in this. [obs. F *haie*]

haybox /háyboks/ *n.* a box stuffed with hay, in which heated food is left to continue cooking.

haycock /háykok/ *n.* a conical heap of hay in a field.

hayfield /háyfeeld/ *n.* a field where hay is being or is to be made.

haymaker /háymaykər/ *n.* **1** a person who tosses and spreads hay to dry after mowing. **2** an apparatus for shaking and drying hay. **3** *sl.* a forceful blow or punch. □□ **haymaking** *n.*
■ **3** see PUNCH[1] *n.* 1.

haymow /háymō/ *n.* hay stored in a stack or barn.

hayrick /háyrik/ *n.* = HAYSTACK.

hayseed /háyseed/ *n.* **1** grass seed obtained from hay. **2** *US colloq.* a rustic or yokel.
■ **2** see PEASANT.

haystack /háystak/ *n.* a packed pile of hay with a pointed or ridged top.
■ see STACK *n.* 2.

haywire /háywīr/ *adj. colloq.* **1** badly disorganized, out of control. **2** (of a person) badly disturbed; erratic. [HAY[1] + WIRE, from the use of hay-baling wire in makeshift repairs]
■ **1** see *out of order* 1 (ORDER).

hazard /házzərd/ *n.* & *v.* ● *n.* **1** a danger or risk. **2** a source of this. **3** chance. **4** a dice game with a complicated arrangement of chances. **5** *Golf* an obstruction in playing a shot, e.g. a bunker, water, etc. **6** each of the winning openings in a real-tennis court. ● *v.tr.* **1** venture on (*hazard a guess*). **2** run the risk of. **3** expose to hazard. [ME f. OF *hasard* f. Sp. *azar* f. Arab. *az-zahr* chance, luck]
■ *n.* **1, 2** peril, endangerment, threat, jeopardy; danger, risk, pitfall. **3** chance, uncertainty, luck; see also FORTUNE 1a. ● *v.* **1** venture, dare, stake, wager; make, (take the) risk (of). **2** (run the) risk (of), stake, chance, gamble on. **3** jeopardize, threaten, imperil; see also ENDANGER.

hazardous /házzərdəss/ *adj.* **1** risky, dangerous. **2** dependent on chance. □□ **hazardously** *adv.* **hazardousness** *n.* [F *hasardeux* (as HAZARD)]
■ unsafe, unsound, risky, dangerous, shaky, questionable, unreliable, unpredictable, precarious, uncertain, chancy, *archaic or joc.* parlous, *sl.* dicey, hairy, *Brit. sl.* dicky.

haze[1] /hayz/ *n.* **1** obscuration of the atmosphere near the earth by fine particles of water, smoke, or dust. **2** mental obscurity or confusion. [prob. back-form. f. HAZY]
■ **1** see FOG[1] *n.* 1.

haze[2] /hayz/ *v.tr.* **1** *Naut.* harass with overwork. **2** *US* bully; seek to disconcert. [orig. uncert.: cf. obs. F *haser* tease, insult]

hazel /háyz'l/ *n.* **1** any shrub or small tree of the genus *Corylus*, esp. *C. avellana* bearing round brown edible nuts. **2 a** wood from the hazel. **b** a stick made of this. **3** a reddish-brown or greenish-brown colour (esp. of the eyes). □ **hazel-grouse** a woodland grouse, *Tetrastes bonasia*. [OE *hæsel* f. Gmc]

hazelnut /háyz'lnut/ *n.* the fruit of the hazel.

hazy /háyzi/ *adj.* (**hazier**, **haziest**) **1** misty. **2** vague, indistinct. **3** confused, uncertain. □□ **hazily** *adv.* **haziness** *n.* [17th c. in Naut. use: orig. unkn.]
■ **1** misty, foggy. **2** indistinct, unclear, blurred, blurry, fuzzy, vague, dim, dark, murky, opaque, shadowy, obscure, faint, nebulous. **3** uncertain, unclear, indefinite, muddled; see also *confused* (CONFUSE 4b).

HB *abbr.* hard black (pencil-lead).

Hb *symb.* haemoglobin.

HBM *abbr.* Her or His Britannic Majesty (or Majesty's).

H-bomb /áychbom/ *n.* = *hydrogen bomb*. [H[3] + BOMB]

HC *abbr.* **1** Holy Communion. **2** (in the UK) House of Commons.

h.c. *abbr. honoris causa.*

HCF *abbr.* **1** highest common factor. **2** *Brit.* Honorary Chaplain to the Forces.

HE *abbr.* **1** His or Her Excellency. **2** His Eminence. **3** high explosive.

He *symb. Chem.* the element helium.

he /hee, hi/ *pron.* & *n.* ● *pron.* (*obj.* **him** /him/; *poss.* **his** /hiz/; *pl.* **they** /thay/) **1** the man or boy or male animal previously named or in question. **2** a person etc. of unspecified sex, esp. referring to one already named or identified (*if anyone comes he will have to wait*). ● *n.* **1** a male; a man. **2** (in *comb.*) male (*he-goat*). **3** a children's chasing game, with the chaser designated 'he'. □ **he-man** (*pl.* **-men**) a masterful or virile man. [OE f. Gmc]

head /hed/ *n.*, *adj.*, & *v.* ● *n.* **1** the upper part of the human body, or the foremost or upper part of an animal's body, containing the brain, mouth, and sense-organs. **2 a** the head regarded as the seat of intellect or repository of comprehended information. **b** intelligence; imagination (*use your head*). **c** mental aptitude or tolerance (usu. foll. by *for*: *a good head for business*; *no head for heights*). **3** *colloq.* a headache, esp. resulting from a blow or from intoxication. **4** a thing like a head in form or position, esp.: **a** the operative part of a tool. **b** the flattened top of a nail. **c** the ornamented top of a pillar. **d** a mass of leaves or flowers at the top of a stem. **e** the flat end of a drum. **f** the foam on top of a glass of beer etc. **g** the upper horizontal part of a window frame, door frame, etc. **5** life when regarded as vulnerable (*it cost him his head*). **6 a** a person in charge; a director or leader (esp. the principal teacher at a school or college). **b** a position of leadership or command. **7** the front or forward part of something, e.g. a queue. **8** the upper end of something, e.g. a table or bed. **9** the top or highest part of something, e.g. a page, stairs, etc. **10** a person or individual regarded as a numerical unit (*£10 per head*). **11** (*pl.* same) **a** an individual animal as a unit. **b** (as *pl.*) a number of cattle or game as specified (*20 head*). **12 a** the side of a coin bearing the image of a head. **b** (usu. in *pl.*) this side as a choice when tossing a coin. **13 a** the source of a river or stream etc. **b** the end of a lake at which a river enters it. **14** the height or length of a head as a measure. **15** the component of a machine that is in contact with or very close to what is being processed or worked on, esp.: **a** the component on a tape recorder that touches the moving tape in play and converts the signals. **b** the part of a record-player that holds the playing cartridge and stylus. **c** = PRINTHEAD. **16 a** a confined body of water or steam in an engine etc. **b** the pressure exerted by this. **17** a promontory (esp. in place-names) (*Beachy Head*). **18** *Naut.* **a** the bows of a ship. **b** (often in *pl.*) a ship's latrine. **19** a main topic or category for consideration or discussion. **20** *Journalism* = HEADLINE *n.* **21** a culmination, climax, or crisis. **22** the fully developed top of a boil etc. **23** *sl.* a habitual taker of drugs; a drug addict. ● *attrib.adj.* chief or principal (*head gardener*; *head office*). ● *v.* **1** *tr.* be at the head or front of. **2** *tr.* be in charge of (*headed a small team*). **3** *tr.* **a** provide with a head or heading. **b** (of an inscription, title, etc.) be at the top of, serve as a heading for. **4 a** *intr.* face or move in a specified direction or towards a specified result (often foll. by *for*: *is heading for trouble*). **b** *tr.* direct in a specified direction. **5** *tr. Football* strike (the ball) with the head. **6 a** *tr.* (often foll. by *down*) cut the head off (a plant etc.). **b** *intr.* (of a plant etc.) form a head. □ **above** (or **over**) **one's head** beyond one's ability to understand. **come to a head** reach a crisis. **enter** (or **come into**) **one's head** *colloq.* occur to one. **from head to toe** (or **foot**) all over a person's body. **get one's head down** *sl.* **1** go to bed. **2** concentrate on the task in hand. **give a person his** or **her head** allow a person to act freely. **go out of one's head** go mad. **go to one's head** **1** (of liquor) make one dizzy or slightly drunk. **2** (of success) make one conceited. **head and shoulders** *colloq.* by a considerable amount. **head back 1** get ahead of so as to intercept and turn back. **2** return home etc. **head-banger** *sl.* **1** a young person shaking violently to the rhythm of pop music. **2** a crazy or eccentric person. **head-butt** *n.* a forceful thrust with the top of the head into the chin or body of another person. ● *v.tr.* attack (another person) with a head-butt. **head-dress** an ornamental covering or band for the head. **head first 1** with the head foremost. **2** precipitately. **head in the sand** refusal to acknowledge an obvious danger or difficulty. **head off 1** get ahead of so as to intercept and turn aside. **2** forestall. **a head of hair** the hair on a person's head, esp. as a distinctive feature. **head-on 1** with the front foremost (*a head-on crash*). **2** in direct confrontation. **head over heels 1** turning over completely in forward motion as in a somersault etc. **2** topsy-turvy. **3** utterly, completely (*head over heels in love*). **head-shrinker** *sl.* a psychiatrist. **head start** an advantage granted or gained at an early stage. **heads will roll** *colloq.* people will be disgraced or dismissed. **head teacher** the teacher in charge of a school. **head up** take charge of (a group of people). **head-up** *adj.* (of instrument readings in an aircraft, vehicle, etc.) shown so as to be visible without lowering the eyes. **head-voice** the high register of the voice in speaking or singing. **head wind** a wind blowing from directly in front. **hold up one's head** be confident or unashamed. **in one's head 1** in one's thoughts or imagination. **2** by mental process without use of physical aids. **keep one's head** remain calm. **keep one's head above water** *colloq.* **1** keep out of debt. **2** avoid succumbing to difficulties. **keep one's head down** *colloq.* remain inconspicuous in difficult or dangerous times. **lose one's head** lose self-control; panic. **make head or tail of** (usu. with *neg.* or *interrog.*) understand at all. **off one's head** *sl.* crazy. **off the top of one's head** *colloq.* impromptu; without careful thought or investigation. **on one's** (or **one's own**) **head** as one's sole responsibility. **out of one's head 1** *sl.* crazy. **2** from one's imagination or memory. **over one's head 1** beyond one's ability to understand. **2** without one's knowledge or involvement, esp. when one has a right to this. **3** with disregard for one's own (stronger) claim (*was promoted over their heads*). **put heads together** consult together. **put into a person's head** suggest to a person. **take** (or **get**) **it into one's head** (foll. by *that* + clause or *to* + infin.) form a definite idea or plan. **turn a person's head** make a person conceited. **with one's head in the clouds** see CLOUD. □□ **headed** *adj.* (also in *comb.*). **headless** *adj.* **headward** *adj.* & *adv.* [OE *hēafod* f. Gmc]
■ *n.* **1** *archaic or colloq.* pate, *colloq.* noddle, *sl.* dome, coconut, noggin, nut, noodle, conk, *archaic sl.* crumpet, *Austral. sl.* pannikin, *Brit. sl.* bonce, *US sl.* bean; skull,

cranium. **2** mind, brain(s), mentality, intellect, wit, intelligence, perception, imagination, *colloq.* grey matter, *sl.* loaf; aptitude, talent, faculty, flair, perceptiveness; tolerance. **4** see TIP[1] *n.* 1. **6 a** chief, leader, headman, director, managing director, MD, president, chairman, chairwoman, superintendent, governor, principal, head teacher, headmaster, headmistress, *colloq.* boss, *sl.* (big) cheese, governor, *Brit. sl.* guv, *US sl.* (chief) honcho, Mr Big. **b** top, first place, leading position, leadership, command, forefront. **7** front, vanguard, forefront, van. **9** see TOP[1] *n.* 1. **13 a** source, origin, fountain-head, well-spring, *poet.* fount. **17** promontory, headland; see also CLIFF. **21** crisis, (critical) point, (fever) pitch; climax, culmination, apex, peak, crest, conclusion, *disp.* crescendo. ● *attrib. adj.* first, leading, premier, chief, main, principal, foremost, prime, pre-eminent, cardinal, paramount, supreme; superior, senior. ● *v.* **1** top; see also LEAD[1] *v.* 5. **2** head up, be in charge of, direct, supervise, oversee, control, govern, run, lead, guide, manage, command, rule, conduct. **4 a** go, move, proceed, turn, steer, face, aim, point; (*head for*) make a beeline for, turn one's steps towards. **b** see DIRECT *v.* 3b. □ **above** (or **over**) **one's head** see INCOMPREHENSIBLE. **come to a head** reach a crisis *or* climax, *disp.* come to *or* reach a crescendo; peak, culminate, *colloq.* climax. **enter** (or **come into**) **one's head** see OCCUR 3. **from head to toe** (or **foot**) see *completely* (COMPLETE). **get one's head down 1** see *hit the hay*. **2** see CONCENTRATE *v.* 1. **go out of one's head** go mad, *sl.* go ape; see also CRAZY 1. **go to one's head 1** see INTOXICATE 1. **head and shoulders** see *substantially* (SUBSTANTIAL). **head-banger 2** see ECCENTRIC *n.* **head first 2** see *prematurely* (PREMATURE). **head off 1** intercept, divert. **2** stop, forestall, cut off, block, prevent, inhibit, avert, ward *or* fend off. **head-on 2** see BLUNT *adj.* 2, OPENLY. **head over heels 3** completely, entirely, deeply, utterly, wholly, fully, wildly, *colloq.* madly. **head-shrinker** see *therapist* (THERAPY). **head start** see ADVANTAGE *n.* 1, 3. **head up** see HEAD *v.* 2 above. **in one's head 2** mentally, in one's mind. **keep one's head** not turn a hair, stay calm *or* cool *or* calm and collected, not panic, *colloq.* not *or* never bat an eyelid. **lose one's head** see PANIC[1] *v.* **make head or tail of** see UNDERSTAND 1, 2. **off one's head** see CRAZY 1. **off the top of one's head** see OFFHAND *adv.* 2. **out of one's head 1** see CRAZY 1. **over one's head 1** see INCOMPREHENSIBLE. **2** see *behind a person's back*. **put heads together** see CONFER 2.

-head /hed/ *suffix* = -HOOD (*godhead*; *maidenhead*). [ME *-hed*, *-hede* = -HOOD]

headache /héddayk/ *n.* **1** a continuous pain in the head. **2** *colloq.* **a** a worrying problem. **b** a troublesome person. □□ **headachy** *adj.*

■ **2** worry, bother, vexation, inconvenience, nuisance, annoyance, problem, difficulty, trouble, bane; *colloq.* hassle, pain (in the neck), *esp. US sl.* pain in the butt.

headband /hédband/ *n.* a band worn round the head as decoration or to keep the hair off the face.

headboard /hédbord/ *n.* an upright panel placed behind the head of a bed.

headcount /hédkownt/ *n.* **1** a counting of individual people. **2** a total number of people, esp. the number of people employed in a particular organization.

header /héddər/ *n.* **1** *Football* a shot or pass made with the head. **2** *colloq.* a headlong fall or dive. **3** a brick or stone laid at right angles to the face of a wall. **4** (in full **header-tank**) a tank of water etc. maintaining pressure in a plumbing system.

■ **2** see TUMBLE *n.* 1.

headgear /hédgeer/ *n.* a hat or head-dress.

head-hunting /hédhunting/ *n.* **1** the practice among some peoples of collecting the heads of dead enemies as trophies. **2** the practice of filling a (usu. senior) business position by approaching a suitable person employed elsewhere. □□ **head-hunt** *v.tr.* (also *absol.*). **head-hunter** *n.*

heading /hédding/ *n.* **1 a** a title at the head of a page or section of a book etc. **b** a division or section of a subject of discourse etc. **2 a** a horizontal passage made in preparation for building a tunnel. **b** *Mining* = DRIFT *n.* 6. **3** material for making cask-heads. **4** the extension of the top of a curtain above the tape that carries the hooks or the pocket for a wire. **5** the course of an aircraft, ship, etc.

■ **1 b** see CATEGORY.

headlamp /hédlamp/ *n.* = HEADLIGHT.

headland *n.* **1** /hédlənd/ a promontory. **2** /hédland/ a strip left unploughed at the end of a field, for machinery to pass along.

■ **1** see CAPE[2].

headlight /hédlīt/ *n.* **1** a strong light at the front of a motor vehicle or railway engine. **2** the beam from this.

■ **1** see LIGHT[1] *n.* 4a.

headline /hédlīn/ *n.* & *v.* ● *n.* **1** a heading at the top of an article or page, esp. in a newspaper. **2** (in *pl.*) the most important items of news in a newspaper or broadcast news bulletin. ● *v.tr.* give a headline to. □ **hit** (or **make**) **the headlines** *colloq.* be given prominent attention as news.

■ *n.* **1** see TITLE *n.* 2.

headliner /hédlīnər/ *n.* *US* a star performer.

■ see STAR *n.* 8a.

headlock /hédlok/ *n.* *Wrestling* a hold with an arm round the opponent's head.

headlong /hédlóng/ *adv.* & *adj.* **1** with head foremost. **2** in a rush. [ME *headling* (as HEAD, -LING[2]), assim. to -LONG]

■ **2** see IMPULSIVE.

headman /hédmən/ *n.* (*pl.* **-men**) the chief man of a tribe etc.

■ see CHIEF *n.*

headmaster /hédmaástər/ *n.* (*fem.* **headmistress** /-místriss/) the principal teacher in charge of a school.

■ see PRINCIPAL *n.* 2.

headmost /hédmōst/ *adj.* (esp. of a ship) foremost.

headphone /hédfōn/ *n.* (usu. in *pl.*) a pair of earphones joined by a band placed over the head, for listening to audio equipment etc.

headpiece /hédpeess/ *n.* **1** an ornamental engraving at the head of a chapter etc. **2** a helmet. **3** *archaic* intellect.

headquarters /hédkwáwrtərz/ *n.* (as *sing.* or *pl.*) **1** the administrative centre of an organization. **2** the premises occupied by a military commander and the commander's staff.

■ **1** see SEAT *n.* 9. **2** see BASE[1] *n.* 3.

headrest /hédrest/ *n.* a support for the head, esp. on a seat or chair.

headroom /hédrōōm, -rŏŏm/ *n.* **1** the space or clearance between the top of a vehicle and the underside of a bridge etc. which it passes under. **2** the space above a driver's or passenger's head in a vehicle.

headscarf /hédskaarf/ *n.* a scarf worn round the head and tied under the chin, instead of a hat.

headset /hédset/ *n.* a set of headphones, often with a microphone attached, used esp. in telephony and radio communications.

headship /hédship/ *n.* the position of chief or leader, esp. of a headmaster or headmistress.

headsman /hédzmən/ *n.* (*pl.* **-men**) **1** *hist.* an executioner who beheads. **2** a person in command of a whaling boat.

headspring /hédspring/ *n.* **1** the main source of a stream. **2** a principal source of ideas etc.

headsquare /hédskwair/ *n.* a rectangular scarf for wearing on the head.

headstall /hédstawl/ *n.* the part of a halter or bridle that fits round a horse's head.

headstock /hédstok/ *n.* a set of bearings in a machine, supporting a revolving part.

headstone /hédstōn/ *n.* a (usu. inscribed) stone set up at the head of a grave.

■ see TOMBSTONE.

headstrong /hédstrong/ *adj.* self-willed and obstinate. ▫▫ **headstrongly** *adv.* **headstrongness** *n.*

■ see SELF-WILLED.

headwater /hédwawtər/ *n.* (in *sing.* or *pl.*) streams flowing from the sources of a river.

headway /hédway/ *n.* **1** progress. **2** the rate of progress of a ship. **3** = HEADROOM 1. ▫ **make headway** see MAKE.

■ **1** progress, improvement; see also ADVANCE *n.* 1, 2. **2** speed, rate of progress; knots.

headword /hédwurd/ *n.* a word forming a heading, e.g. of an entry in a dictionary or encyclopedia.

headwork /hédwurk/ *n.* mental work or effort.

heady /héddi/ *adj.* (**headier, headiest**) **1** (of liquor) potent, intoxicating. **2** (of success etc.) likely to cause conceit. **3** (of a person, thing, or action) impetuous, violent. ▫▫ **headily** *adv.* **headiness** *n.*

heal /heel/ *v.* **1** *intr.* (often foll. by *up*) (of a wound or injury) become sound or healthy again. **2** *tr.* cause (a wound, disease, or person) to heal or be healed. **3** *tr.* put right (differences etc.). **4** *tr.* alleviate (sorrow etc.). ▫ **heal-all 1** a universal remedy, a panacea. **2** a popular name of various medicinal plants. ▫▫ **healable** *adj.* **healer** *n.* [OE *hǣlan* f. Gmc, rel. to WHOLE]

■ **1** mend, improve, get better. **2** cure, restore (to health); mend. **3** reconcile, settle, patch up, put *or* set straight, put *or* set right, remedy, repair, mend, rectify, make good. **4** see RELIEVE 2. ▫ **heal-all 1** cure, cure-all, panacea, universal remedy.

heald /heeld/ *n.* = HEDDLE. [app. f. OE *hefel, hefeld,* f. Gmc]

health /helth/ *n.* **1** the state of being well in body or mind. **2** a person's mental or physical condition (*has poor health*). **3** soundness, esp. financial or moral (*the health of the nation*). **4** a toast drunk in someone's honour. ▫ **health centre** the headquarters of a group of local medical services. **health certificate** a certificate stating a person's fitness for work etc. **health farm** a residential establishment where people seek improved health by a regime of dieting, exercise, etc. **health food** natural food thought to have health-giving qualities. **health service** a public service providing medical care. **health visitor** *Brit.* a trained nurse who visits those in need of medical attention in their homes. [OE *hǣlth* f. Gmc]

■ **1** healthiness, haleness, wholeness, fitness, robustness, vigour, vitality, well-being, strength. **2** condition, fitness, trim, fettle, form; constitution. **3** see STRENGTH 1. **4** see TOAST *n.* 2b.

healthful /hélthfŏŏl/ *adj.* conducive to good health; beneficial. ▫▫ **healthfully** *adv.* **healthfulness** *n.*

healthy /hélthi/ *adj.* (**healthier, healthiest**) **1** having, showing, or promoting good health. **2** beneficial, helpful (*a healthy respect for experience*). ▫▫ **healthily** *adv.* **healthiness** *n.*

■ **1** well, fit, trim, in good *or* fine fettle, in good shape, in good health, whole, robust, hale (and hearty), sturdy, strong, vigorous, thriving, flourishing, *colloq.* in the pink; healthful, wholesome, salubrious, nourishing, nutritious, tonic, bracing, invigorating, *archaic* salutary. **2** see BENEFICIAL.

heap /heep/ *n.* & *v.* ● *n.* **1** a collection of things lying haphazardly one on another. **2** (esp. in *pl.*) *colloq.* a large number or amount (*there's heaps of time; is heaps better*). **3** *sl.* an old or dilapidated thing, esp. a motor vehicle or building. ● *v.* **1** *tr.* & *intr.* (foll. by *up, together,* etc.) collect or be collected in a heap. **2** *tr.* (foll. by *with*) load copiously or to excess. **3** *tr.* (foll. by *on, upon*) accord or offer copiously to (*heaped insults on them*). **4** *tr.* (as **heaped** *adj.*) (of a spoonful etc.) with the contents piled above the brim. ▫ **heap coals of fire on a person's head** cause a person remorse by returning good for evil. [OE *hēap, hēapian* f. Gmc]

■ *n.* **1** collection, pile, mound, stack, accumulation, agglomeration, congeries, conglomeration. **2** abundance, mass, lot, mountain, peck, sea, *colloq.* good *or* great deal, pile, raft, *esp. US colloq.* slew; (*heaps*) lots, scores, plenty, *colloq.* loads, oodles, *Brit. colloq.* lashings, tons, pots, *US colloq.* scads. **3** see WRECK *n.* 3. ● *v.* **1** collect, gather, accumulate, cumulate, amass, pile up, bank up. **2** see LOAD *v.* 3–5. **3** pile, pour; see also HURL *v.*

hear /heer/ *v.* (*past* and *past part.* **heard** /herd/) **1** *tr.* (also *absol.*) perceive (sound etc.) with the ear. **2** *tr.* listen to (*heard them on the radio*). **3** *tr.* listen judicially to and judge (a case, plaintiff, etc.). **4** *intr.* (foll. by *about, of,* or *that* + clause) be told or informed. **5** *intr.* (foll. by *from*) be contacted by, esp. by letter or telephone. **6** *tr.* be ready to obey (an order). **7** *tr.* grant (a prayer). ▫ **have heard of** be aware of; know of the existence of. **hear! hear!** *int.* expressing agreement (esp. with something said in a speech). **hear a person out** listen to all that a person says. **hear say** (or **tell**) (usu. foll. by *of,* or *that* + clause) be informed. **will not hear of** will not allow or agree to. ▫▫ **hearable** *adj.* **hearer** *n.* [OE *hīeran* f. Gmc]

■ **1** perceive, catch. **2** listen to, *archaic* hark at *or* to, *archaic or literary* hearken to. **3** see JUDGE *v.* 1a. **4** learn, discover, find out, be told *or* advised *or* informed; understand, gather; (*hear of*) get wind of, pick up rumours of, hear tell of, *colloq.* hear on the grapevine. **6** attend to, pay attention to; take note of, obey. **7** heed, grant, answer. ▫ **have heard of** know of, be aware of, be conscious of, be cognizant of, be informed of, be advised of, have knowledge of. **hear say** (or **tell**) see HEAR 4 above. **will not hear of** will not entertain *or* consider, will not sanction *or* condone, will not agree *or* consent *or* assent to.

hearing /heéring/ *n.* **1** the faculty of perceiving sounds. **2** the range within which sounds may be heard; earshot (*within hearing; in my hearing*). **3** an opportunity to state one's case (*give them a fair hearing*). **4** the listening to evidence and pleadings in a lawcourt. ▫ **hearing-aid** a small device to amplify sound, worn by a partially deaf person.

■ **3** see CHANCE *n.* 4. **4** see TRIAL 1.

hearken /haárkən/ *v.intr.* (also **harken**) *archaic* or *literary* (often foll. by *to*) listen. [OE *heorcnian* (as HARK)]

■ see LISTEN 1, 2.

hearsay /heérsay/ *n.* rumour, gossip. ▫ **hearsay evidence** *Law* evidence given by a witness based on information received from others rather than personal knowledge.

■ see RUMOUR *n.* 1.

hearse /herss/ *n.* a vehicle for conveying the coffin at a funeral. [ME f. OF *herse* harrow f. med.L *herpica* ult. f. L *hirpex -icis* large rake]

heart /haart/ *n.* **1** a hollow muscular organ maintaining the circulation of blood by rhythmic contraction and dilation. **2** the region of the heart; the breast. **3 a** the heart regarded as the centre of thought, feeling, and emotion (esp. love). **b** a person's capacity for feeling emotion (*has no heart*). **4 a** courage or enthusiasm (*take heart; lose heart*). **b** one's mood or feeling (*change of heart*). **5 a** the central or innermost part of something. **b** the vital part or essence (*the heart of the matter*). **6** the close compact head of a cabbage, lettuce, etc. **7 a** a heart-shaped thing. **b** a conventional representation of a heart with two equal curves meeting at a point at the bottom and a cusp at the top. **8 a** a playing-card of a suit denoted by a red figure of a heart. **b** (in *pl.*) this suit. **c** (in *pl.*) a card-game in which players avoid taking tricks containing a card of this suit. **9** condition of land as regards fertility (*in good heart*). ▫ **after one's own heart** such as one likes or desires. **at heart 1** in one's inmost feelings. **2** basically, essentially. **break a person's heart** overwhelm a person with sorrow. **by heart** in or from memory. **close to** (or **near**) **one's heart 1** dear to one. **2** affecting one deeply. **from the heart** (or **the bottom of one's heart**) sincerely, profoundly. **give** (or **lose**) **one's heart** (often foll. by *to*) fall in love (with). **have a heart** be merciful. **have the heart** (usu. with *neg.*; foll. by *to* + infin.) be insensitive or hard-hearted enough (*didn't have the heart to ask him*). **have** (or **put**) **one's heart in** be keenly involved in or committed to (an enterprise etc.). **have one's heart in one's mouth** be greatly alarmed or apprehensive. **have one's heart in the right place** be sincere or well-intentioned. **heart attack** a sudden occurrence of coronary thrombosis usu. resulting in the death of part of a heart muscle. **heart failure** a gradual failure of the heart to function properly, resulting in breathlessness, oedema, etc. **heart-lung machine** a machine that temporarily takes over the functions of the heart and lungs, esp. in surgery. **heart of gold** a generous nature. **heart of oak** a courageous nature. **heart of stone** a stern or cruel nature. **heart-rending** very distressing. **heart-rendingly** in a heart-rending way. **heart's-blood** lifeblood, life. **heart-searching** the thorough examination of one's own feelings and motives. **heart to heart** candidly, intimately. **heart-to-heart** *adj.* (of a conversation etc.) candid, intimate. ● *n.* a candid or personal conversation. **heart-warming** emotionally rewarding or uplifting. **in heart** in good spirits. **in one's heart of hearts** in one's inmost feelings. **out of heart** in low spirits. **take to heart** be much affected or distressed by. **to one's heart's content** see CONTENT[1]. **wear one's heart on one's sleeve** make one's feelings apparent. **with all one's heart** sincerely; with all goodwill. **with one's whole heart** with enthusiasm; without doubts or reservations. ▫▫ **-hearted** *adj.* [OE *heorte* f. Gmc]

■ **1** *colloq.* ticker. **2** breast, chest. **3 a** core, heart of hearts, blood, bosom; midst, interior, core, centre; see also SOUL 1, 2. **b** humanity, sympathy, kindness, kindliness, kind-heartedness, compassion, goodness, consideration, concern, tenderness, magnanimity, generosity, sensitivity, sensibility, feeling, pity, love. **4 a** courage, stomach, nerve, bravery, boldness, pluck, resolution, determination, mettle, will, *colloq.* guts, spunk; enthusiasm, spirit, verve. **b** see MOOD[1] 1, FEELING 4. **5 a** kernel, core, centre, hub, middle, marrow, nucleus. **b** essence, quintessence, nub, crux, pith; basics, fundamentals, *colloq.* bottom line, *sl.* nitty-gritty, brass tacks. ▫ **at heart 1** see INSIDE *adv.* 1. **2** see PRINCIPALLY. **close to** (or **near**) **one's heart 1** see DEAR *adj.* 3. **2** see IMPORTANT 1. **from the heart** (or **the bottom of one's heart**) see SINCERELY. **heart-rending** agonizing, heartbreaking, harrowing, tragic, distressing, painful. **heart's-blood** see LIFE 8. **heart-searching** soul-searching, introspection; psychoanalysis, *Psychol.* self-analysis; see also THOUGHT[1] 3a. **heart to heart** candidly, intimately, directly, frankly, freely, unrestrictedly; see also OPENLY 1. **heart-warming** moving, touching, affecting, uplifting, stirring, inspiriting, cheering, encouraging, rewarding; satisfying, gratifying, pleasing, comforting, pleasurable. **out of heart** see *dejected* (DEJECT). **with all one's heart** see SINCERELY. **with one's whole heart** see ABSOLUTELY 1.

heartache /haártayk/ *n.* mental anguish or grief.
■ see GRIEF 1.

heartbeat /haártbeet/ *n.* a pulsation of the heart.

heartbreak /haártbrayk/ *n.* overwhelming distress. ▫▫ **heartbreaker** *n.* **heartbreaking** *adj.* **heartbroken** *adj.*
■ see GRIEF 1. ▫▫ **heartbroken** broken-hearted, unhappy, grief-stricken, heartsick, disconsolate, distressed, doleful, sorrowful, mournful, crushed, devastated, *archaic or literary* heartsore, *sl.* gutted.

heartburn /haártburn/ *n.* a burning sensation in the chest resulting from indigestion; pyrosis.
■ see INDIGESTION.

hearten /haárt'n/ *v.tr.* & *intr.* make or become more cheerful. ▫▫ **hearteningly** *adv.*
■ see CHEER *v.* 3.

heartfelt /haártfélt/ *adj.* sincere; deeply felt.
■ sincere, honest, genuine, unfeigned, earnest, serious, wholehearted, deep, profound, ardent, fervent, fervid, hearty, passionate.

hearth /haarth/ *n.* **1 a** the floor of a fireplace. **b** the area in front of a fireplace. **2** this symbolizing the home. **3** the bottom of a blast-furnace where molten metal collects. [OE *heorth* f. WG]

hearthrug /haárthrug/ *n.* a rug laid before a fireplace.

hearthstone /haárthstōn/ *n.* **1** a flat stone forming a hearth. **2** a soft stone used to whiten hearths, doorsteps, etc.

heartily /haártili/ *adv.* **1** in a hearty manner; with goodwill, appetite, or courage. **2** very; to a great degree (esp. with ref. to personal feelings) (*am heartily sick of it*; *disliked him heartily*).
■ **1** see *happily* (HAPPY).

heartland /haártlənd/ *n.* the central or most important part of an area.

heartless /haártliss/ *adj.* unfeeling, pitiless. ▫▫ **heartlessly** *adv.* **heartlessness** *n.*
■ cruel, hard-hearted, pitiless, callous, unconcerned, inhuman, inhumane, unkind, unfeeling, unsympathetic, brutal, cold, merciless, ruthless, cold-blooded.

heartsease /haártseez/ *n.* (also **heart's-ease**) a pansy.

heartsick /haártsik/ *adj.* very despondent. ▫▫ **heartsickness** *n.*
■ see SAD 1.

heartsore /haártsor/ *adj. archaic* or *literary* grieving, heartsick.

heartstrings /haártstringz/ *n.pl.* one's deepest feelings or emotions.

heartthrob /haárt-throb/ *n.* **1** beating of the heart. **2** *colloq.* a person for whom one has (esp. immature) romantic feelings.
■ **2** see PASSION 3b.

heartwood /haártwŏŏd/ *n.* the dense inner part of a tree-trunk yielding the hardest timber.

hearty /haárti/ *adj.* & *n.* ● *adj.* (**heartier, heartiest**) **1** strong, vigorous. **2** spirited. **3** (of a meal or appetite) large. **4** warm, friendly. **5** genuine, sincere. ● *n.* **1** a hearty person, esp. one ostentatiously so. **2** (usu. in *pl.*) (as a form of address) fellows, esp. fellow sailors. ▫▫ **heartiness** *n.*
■ *adj.* **1** strong, healthy, hale, vigorous, robust, energetic, active. **2** spirited, enthusiastic, vigorous, eager, zealous, exuberant. **3** (*of a meal*) abundant, ample, substantial, solid, sizeable, satisfying, square; nourishing, invigorating, strengthening; (*of appetite*) healthy, robust, large, big, ample, good. **4** genial, warm, kind-hearted, affectionate, amiable, amicable, friendly, affable, cordial, open, convivial. **5** genuine, unfeigned, authentic, sincere, heartfelt, warm, wholehearted, honest, earnest, devout, stalwart, stout. ● *n.* **1** see ENTHUSIAST.

heat /heet/ *n.* & *v.* ● *n.* **1 a** the condition of being hot. **b** the sensation or perception of this. **c** high temperature of the body. **2** *Physics* **a** a form of energy arising from the random motion of the molecules of bodies, which may be transferred by conduction, convection, or radiation. **b** the amount of this needed to cause a specific process, or evolved in a process (*heat of formation*; *heat of solution*). **3** hot weather (*succumbed to the heat*). **4 a** warmth of feeling. **b** anger or excitement (*the heat of the argument*). **5** (foll. by *of*) the most intense part or period of an activity (*in the heat of the battle*). **6** a (usu. preliminary or trial) round in a race or contest. **7** the receptive period of the sexual cycle, esp. in female mammals. **8** redness of the skin with a sensation of heat (*prickly heat*). **9** pungency of flavour. **10** *sl.* intensive pursuit, e.g. by the police. ● *v.* **1** *tr.* & *intr.* make or become hot or warm. **2** *tr.* inflame; excite or intensify. ▫ **heat barrier** the limitation of the speed of an aircraft etc. by heat resulting from air friction. **heat capacity** thermal capacity. **heat death** *Physics* a state of uniform distribution of energy to which the universe is thought to be tending. **heat engine** a device for producing motive power from heat. **heat-exchanger** a device for the transfer of heat from one medium to another. **heat pump** a device for the transfer of heat from a colder area to a hotter area by using mechanical energy. **heat-resistant** = HEATPROOF. **heat-seeking** (of a missile etc.) able to detect infrared radiation to guide it to its target. **heat shield** a device for protection from excessive heat, esp. fitted to a spacecraft. **heat sink** a device or substance for absorbing excessive or unwanted heat. **heat-treat** subject to heat treatment. **heat treatment** the use of heat to modify the properties of a metal etc. **heat wave** a period of very hot weather. **in the heat of the moment** during or resulting from intense activity, without pause for thought. **on heat** (of mammals, esp. females) sexually receptive. **turn the heat on** *colloq.* concentrate an attack or criticism on (a person). [OE *hǣtu* f. Gmc]

▪ *n.* **1 a, b** warmth, warmness, hotness; torridity. **c** fever, temperature, fieriness, feverishness, *Med.* pyrexia. **4** passion, ardour, fervour, intensity, arousal, stimulation, enthusiasm, zeal, excitement, exhilaration; fury, vehemence; see also ANGER *n.* **5** see CLIMAX *n.* **6** round, trial, preliminary, qualifier; game, stage, level. **8** see RASH^2 1. **9** see SPICE *n.* 3a. ● *v.* **1** see WARM *v.* 1, THAW *v.* 1, 5. **2** excite, intensify, impassion, inflame; kindle, ignite, quicken, inspirit, rouse, waken, stir, animate, stimulate, activate, *Brit. colloq.* hot up. ▫ **turn the heat on** see ATTACK *v.* 3.

heated /heétid/ *adj.* **1** (of a person, discussions, etc.) angry; inflamed with passion or excitement. **2** made hot. ▫▫ **heatedly** *adv.*

▪ **1** angry, furious, stormy, tempestuous, violent, fiery, frenzied, frantic; impassioned, excited, inflamed, vehement, passionate, fervent, fervid, ardent, intense.

heater /heétər/ *n.* **1** a device for supplying heat to its environment. **2** a container with an element etc. for heating the contents (*water-heater*). **3** *sl.* a gun.

▪ **3** see PISTOL *n.*

heath /heeth/ *n.* **1** an area of flattish uncultivated land with low shrubs. **2** a plant growing on a heath, esp. of the genus *Erica* or *Calluna* (e.g. heather). ▫▫ **heathless** *adj.* **heathlike** *adj.* **heathy** *adj.* [OE *hǣth* f. Gmc]

▪ **1** see MOOR^1 1.

heathen /heéthən/ *n.* & *adj.* ● *n.* **1** a person who does not belong to a widely-held religion (esp. who is not Christian, Jew, or Muslim) as regarded by those that do. **2** an unenlightened person; a person regarded as lacking culture or moral principles. **3** (**the heathen**) heathen people collectively. **4** *Bibl.* a Gentile. ● *adj.* **1** of or relating to heathens. **2** having no religion. ▫▫ **heathendom** *n.* **heathenism** *n.* [OE *hǣthen* f. Gmc]

▪ *n.* **1** unbeliever, infidel, Gentile, pagan, idolater, idolatress, polytheist, atheist, nullifidian, sceptic, agnostic, heretic. **2** barbarian, savage, brute. ● *adj.* **1** polytheistic, pantheistic, infidel, Gentile, *hist.* heretical; savage, barbarian, barbaric, uncivilized, primitive, unenlightened. **2** pagan, atheistic, godless, nullifidian, sceptical, doubting, agnostic, irreligious.

heather /héthər/ *n.* **1** an evergreen shrub, *Calluna vulgaris*, with purple bell-shaped flowers. **2** any of various shrubs of the genus *Erica* or *Daboecia*, growing esp. on moors and heaths. ▫ **heather mixture 1** a fabric of mixed hues supposed to resemble heather. **2** the colour of this. ▫▫ **heathery** *adj.* [ME, Sc., & N.Engl. *hathir* etc., of unkn. orig.: assim. to *heath*]

Heath Robinson /heeth róbbins'n/ *adj.* absurdly ingenious and impracticable in design or construction. [W. *Heath Robinson*, Engl. cartoonist d. 1944 who drew such contrivances]

heating /heéting/ *n.* **1** the imparting or generation of heat. **2** equipment or devices used to provide heat, esp. to a building.

heatproof /heétproof/ *adj.* & *v.* ● *adj.* able to resist great heat. ● *v.tr.* make heatproof.

heatstroke /heétstrōk/ *n.* a feverish condition caused by excessive exposure to high temperature.

heatwave /heétwayv/ *n.* a prolonged period of abnormally hot weather.

heave /heev/ *v.* & *n.* ● *v.* (*past* and *past part.* **heaved** or esp. *Naut.* **hove** /hōv/) **1** *tr.* lift or haul (a heavy thing) with great effort. **2** *tr.* utter with effort or resignation (*heaved a sigh*). **3** *tr. colloq.* throw. **4** *intr.* rise and fall rhythmically or spasmodically. **5** *tr. Naut.* haul by rope. **6** *intr.* retch. ● *n.* **1** an instance of heaving. **2** *Geol.* a sideways displacement in a fault. **3** (in *pl.*) a disease of horses, with laboured breathing. ▫ **heave-ho 1** a sailors' cry, esp. on raising the anchor. **2** *sl.* (usu. prec. by *the* or *the old*) a dismissal or rejection. **heave in sight** *Naut.* or *colloq.* come into view. **heave to** esp. *Naut.* bring or be brought to a standstill. ▫▫ **heaver** *n.* [OE *hebban* f. Gmc, rel. to L *capere* take]

▪ *v.* **1** lift, hoist, raise; haul, pull, draw, tug; move. **2** breathe, utter. **3** hurl, throw, toss, fling, cast, pitch, *colloq.* sling, chuck, *Austral. sl.* hoy. **6** gag, retch, vomit, be sick, *colloq.* throw up, *sl.* puke, *US sl.* upchuck. ● *n.* **1** pull, draw, tug, jerk, wrench, *colloq.* yank.

heaven /hévv'n/ *n.* **1** a place regarded in some religions as the abode of God and the angels, and of the good after death, often characterized as above the sky. **2** a place or state of supreme bliss. **3** *colloq.* something delightful. **4** (usu. **Heaven**) **a** God, Providence. **b** (in *sing.* or *pl.*) an exclam. or mild oath (*by Heaven!*). **5** (**the heavens**) esp. *poet.* the sky as the abode of the sun, moon, and stars and regarded from earth. ▫ **heaven-sent** providential; wonderfully opportune. **in heaven's name** *colloq.* used as an exclamation of surprise or annoyance. **in seventh heaven** in a state of ecstasy. **move heaven and earth** (foll. by *to* + infin.) make extraordinary efforts. ▫▫ **heavenward** *adj.* & *adv.* **heavenwards** *adv.* [OE *heofon*]

▪ **1** paradise, empyrean, kingdom (of heaven); Canaan, Zion, Valhalla. **2** paradise, bliss, nirvana, Elysium, Eden, Utopia, heaven on earth, paradise on earth; happiness, joy, rapture, ecstasy. **3** see DELIGHT *n.* **4 a** (**Heaven**) God, Providence, Fate. **b** (**Heaven!** or **Heavens!**) God, *colloq.* Jesus, *sl.* Christ; see also BOY *int.* **5** (**the heavens**) sky, skies, the blue, empyrean, *literary* firmament, *poet.* welkin.

heavenly /hévvənli/ *adj.* **1** of heaven; divine. **2** of the heavens or sky. **3** *colloq.* very pleasing; wonderful. ▫ **heavenly bodies** the sun, stars, planets, etc. ▫▫ **heavenliness** *n.* [OE *heofonlic* (as HEAVEN)]

▪ **1** divine, celestial, ethereal, paradisaical, unearthly; holy, immortal, blessed, beatific, spiritual, *esp. poet.* supernal; angelic, seraphic. **2** celestial. **3** delightful, wonderful, marvellous, sublime, paradisaical, glorious, splendid, superb, exquisite, perfect, excellent, rapturous, entrancing, blissful, *colloq.* fantastic, gorgeous, divine, smashing, great.

Heaviside layer /hévvisīd/ *n.* (in full **Heaviside–Kennelly layer** /hévvisīdkénnəli/) = E-LAYER. [O. *Heaviside*, Engl. physicist d. 1925, and A. E. *Kennelly*, US physicist d. 1939]

heavy /hévvi/ *adj.*, *n.*, *adv.*, & *v.* ● *adj.* (**heavier, heaviest**) **1 a** of great or exceptionally high weight; difficult to lift. **b** (of a person) fat, overweight. **2 a** of great density. **b** *Physics* having a greater than the usual mass (esp. of isotopes and compounds containing them). **3** abundant, considerable (*a heavy crop*). **4** severe, intense, extensive, excessive (*heavy fighting*; *a heavy sleep*). **5** doing something to excess (*a heavy drinker*). **6 a** striking or falling with force (*heavy blows*; *heavy rain*). **b** (of the sea) having large powerful waves. **7** (of machinery, artillery, etc.) very large of its kind; large in calibre etc. **8** causing a strong impact (*a heavy fall*). **9** needing much physical effort (*heavy work*). **10** (foll. by *with*) laden. **11** carrying heavy weapons (*the heavy brigade*). **12 a** (of a person, writing, music, etc.) serious or sombre in tone or attitude; dull, tedious. **b** (of an issue etc.) grave; important, weighty. **13 a** (of food) hard to digest. **b** (of a literary work etc.) hard to read or understand. **14 a** (of temperament) dignified, stern. **b** intellectually slow. **15** (of bread etc.) too dense from not having risen. **16** (of ground) difficult to traverse or work. **17 a** oppressive; hard to endure (*a heavy fate*; *heavy demands*). **b** (of the atmosphere, weather, etc.) overcast; oppressive, sultry. **18 a** coarse, ungraceful (*heavy features*). **b** unwieldy. ● *n.* (*pl.* **-ies**) **1** *colloq.* a large violent person; a thug. **2** a villainous or tragic role or actor in a play etc. (usu. in *pl.*). **3** *colloq.* a serious newspaper. **4** anything large or heavy of its kind, e.g. a vehicle. ● *adv.* heavily (esp. in *comb.*: *heavy-laden*). ● *v.tr. colloq.* harass or pressurize (a person). □ **heavier-than-air** (of an aircraft) weighing more than the air it displaces. **heavy chemicals** see CHEMICAL. **heavy-duty** *adj.* intended to withstand hard use. **heavy-footed** awkward, ponderous. **heavy going** slow or difficult progress. **heavy-hearted** sad, doleful. **heavy hydrogen** = DEUTERIUM. **heavy industry** industry producing metal, machinery, etc. **heavy-lidded** sleepy. **heavy metal 1** heavy guns. **2** metal of high density. **3** *colloq.* (often *attrib.*) a type of highly-amplified rock music with a strong beat. **heavy petting** erotic fondling between two people, stopping short of intercourse. **heavy-set** stocky, thickset. **heavy sleeper** a person who sleeps deeply. **heavy water** a substance composed entirely or mainly of deuterium oxide. **make heavy weather of** see WEATHER. □□ **heavily** *adv.* **heaviness** *n.* **heavyish** *adj.* [OE *hefig* f. Gmc, rel. to HEAVE]

■ *adj.* **1 a** weighty, massive. **b** overweight, fat, obese, stout, chubby, plump, corpulent, portly, paunchy, tubby, podgy, thickset, *colloq.* pudgy, *Austral. colloq.* poddy. **2 a** dense, solid. **3** abundant, considerable, copious, prodigious, ample, profuse. **4** intense, severe, concentrated, extensive, excessive, forceful, violent. **5** see IMMODERATE. **6 a** see FORCEFUL 1; (*of rain*) torrential, pouring. **b** see ROUGH *adj.* 5. **7** see LARGE *adj.* 1, 2. **8** see CONSIDERABLE 1, 2. **9** see HARD *adj.* 3. **10** burdened, laden, encumbered, loaded, overloaded, weighed down. **12 a** serious, sombre, grave, ponderous; tedious, dull, dry, monotonous, dry as dust; prosaic, leaden, stodgy. **b** serious, grave, important, crucial, critical, acute; see also WEIGHTY 2. **13 a** see STODGY 1. **b** dense, weighty, difficult, complex, recondite, arcane, deep, profound, esoteric, impenetrable. **14 a** see DIGNIFIED, STERN[1]. **b** see SLOW *adj.* 5. **15** stodgy, indigestible, solid, dense, filling. **16** see ROUGH *adj.* 1a. **17 a** burdensome, onerous, weighty, severe; see also OPPRESSIVE 1, 2. **b** gloomy, cloudy, overcast, bleak, dismal, dreary, leaden, grey, dark, louring, threatening, oppressive; sultry, humid. **18 a** thick, coarse, broad, blunt, clumsy, ungraceful. **b** see UNWIELDY. ● *n.* **1** see THUG. ● *v.* see HARASS 1. □ **heavy-duty** see TOUGH *adj.* 1. **heavy-footed** see AWKWARD 2. **heavy-hearted** see SAD 1. **heavy-lidded** see DROWSY 1, 3. **heavy-set** see STOCKY.

heavy-handed /hévvihándid/ *adj.* **1** clumsy. **2** overbearing, oppressive. □□ **heavy-handedly** *adv.* **heavy-handedness** *n.*

■ **1** awkward, clumsy, inept, maladroit, ungraceful, graceless, bungling. **2** overbearing, oppressive, domineering, autocratic, imperious, magisterial, despotic, dictatorial, tyrannical, harsh, severe.

heavyweight /hévviwayt/ *n.* **1 a** a weight in certain sports, in the amateur boxing scale over 81 kg but differing for professional boxers, wrestlers, and weightlifters. **b** a sportsman of this weight. **2** a person, animal, or thing of above average weight. **3** *colloq.* a person of influence or importance. □ **light heavyweight 1** the weight in some sports between middleweight and heavyweight, in the amateur boxing scale 75-81 kg: also called CRUISERWEIGHT. **2** a sportsman of this weight.

Heb. *abbr.* **1** Hebrew. **2** Hebrews (New Testament).

hebdomadal /hebdómməd'l/ *adj. formal* weekly, esp. meeting weekly. [LL *hebdomadalis* f. Gk *hebdomas, -ados* f. *hepta* seven]

hebe /heébi/ *n.* any flowering shrub of the genus *Hebe*, with usu. overlapping scale-like leaves. [mod.L after the Gk goddess *Hēbē*]

hebetude /hébbityood/ *n. literary* dullness. [LL *hebetudo* f. *hebes, -etis* blunt]

■ see LETHARGY 1.

Hebraic /heebráyik/ *adj.* of Hebrew or the Hebrews. □□ **Hebraically** *adv.* [LL f. Gk *Hebraikos* (as HEBREW)]

Hebraism /heébrayiz'm/ *n.* **1** a Hebrew idiom or expression, esp. in the Greek of the Bible. **2** an attribute of the Hebrews. **3** the Hebrew system of thought or religion. □□ **Hebraistic** /-ístik/ *adj.* **Hebraize** *v.tr.* & *intr.* (also **-ise**). [F *hébraïsme* or mod.L *Hebraismus* f. late Gk *Hebraïsmos* (as HEBREW)]

Hebraist /heébrayist/ *n.* an expert in Hebrew.

Hebrew /heébroo/ *n.* & *adj.* ● *n.* **1** a member of a Semitic people orig. centred in ancient Palestine. **2 a** the language of this people. **b** a modern form of this used esp. in Israel. ● *adj.* **1** of or in Hebrew. **2** of the Hebrews or the Jews. [ME f. OF *Ebreu* f. med.L *Ebreus* f. L *hebraeus* f. Gk *Hebraios* f. Aram. *'ibray* f. Heb. *'ibrî* one from the other side (of the river)]

Hebridean /hébrideéən/ *adj.* & *n.* ● *adj.* of or relating to the Hebrides, an island group off the W. coast of Scotland. ● *n.* a native of the Hebrides.

hecatomb /hékkətoom/ *n.* **1** (in ancient Greece or Rome) a great public sacrifice, orig. of 100 oxen. **2** any extensive sacrifice. [L *hecatombe* f. Gk *hekatombē* f. *hekaton* hundred + *bous* ox]

■ see SLAUGHTER *n.* 2.

heck /hek/ *int. colloq.* a mild exclamation of surprise or dismay. [alt. f. HELL]

heckelphone /hékk'lfōn/ *n. Mus.* a bass oboe. [G *Heckelphon* f. W. *Heckel*, 20th-c. Ger. instrument-maker]

heckle /hékk'l/ *v.tr.* **1** interrupt and harass (a public speaker). **2** dress (flax or hemp). □□ **heckler** *n.* [ME, northern and eastern form of HACKLE[1]]

■ **1** interrupt, pester, bother, harass, harry, hector, taunt, *Brit.* barrack, *colloq.* hassle, plague.

hectare /héktair, -taar/ *n.* a metric unit of square measure, equal to 100 ares (2.471 acres or 10,000 square metres). □□ **hectarage** /héktərij/ *n.* [F (as HECTO-, ARE[2])]

hectic /héktik/ *adj.* & *n.* ● *adj.* **1** busy and confused; excited. **2** having a hectic fever; morbidly flushed. ● *n.* **1** a hectic fever or flush. **2** a patient suffering from this. □ **hectic fever** (or **flush**) *hist.* a fever which accompanies consumption and similar diseases, with flushed cheeks and hot dry skin. □□ **hectically** *adv.* [ME *etik* f. OF *etique* f. LL *hecticus* f. Gk *hektikos* habitual f. *hexis* habit, assim. to F *hectique* or LL]

■ *adj.* **1** feverish, excited, agitated, busy, bustling, over-active, rushed, frenzied, frantic, chaotic, confused, wild, frenetic, riotous. **2** flushed, feverish, hot; febrile, pyretic, *Med.* pyrexic.

hecto- /héktō/ *comb. form* a hundred, esp. of a unit in the metric system. ¶ Abbr.: **ha.** [F, irreg. f. Gk *hekaton* hundred]

hectogram /héktəgram/ *n.* (also **hectogramme**) a metric unit of mass, equal to one hundred grams.

hectograph /héktəgraaf/ *n.* an apparatus for copying documents by the use of a gelatin plate which receives an impression of the master copy.

hectolitre /héktəleetər/ *n.* (*US* **hectoliter**) a metric unit of capacity, equal to one hundred litres.

hectometre /héktəmeetər/ *n.* (*US* **hectometer**) a metric unit of length, equal to one hundred metres.

hector /héktər/ *v.* & *n.* ● *v.tr.* bully, intimidate. ● *n.* a bully. □□ **hectoringly** *adv.* [*Hector*, L f. Gk *Hektōr*, Trojan hero and son of Priam in Homer's *Iliad*, f. its earlier use to mean 'swaggering fellow']

■ *v.* see BULLY[1] *v.* 1. ● *n.* see BULLY[1] *n.*

he'd /heed, hid/ *contr.* **1** he had. **2** he would.

heddle /hédd'l/ *n.* one of the sets of small cords or wires between which the warp is passed in a loom before going through the reed. [app. f. OE *hefeld*]

hedge /hej/ *n.* & *v.* ● *n.* **1** a fence or boundary formed by closely growing bushes or shrubs. **2** a protection against possible loss or diminution. ● *v.* **1** *tr.* surround or bound with a hedge. **2** *tr.* (foll. by *in*) enclose. **3 a** *tr.* reduce one's risk of loss on (a bet or speculation) by compensating transactions on the other side. **b** *intr.* avoid a definite decision or commitment. **4** *intr.* make or trim hedges. □ **hedge-hop** fly at a very low altitude. **hedge sparrow** a common grey and brown bird, *Prunella modularis*; the dunnock. □□ **hedger** *n.* [OE *hegg* f. Gmc]

■ *n.* **1** see ENCLOSURE 4. ● *v.* **1, 2** see ENCLOSE 1, 6. **3 b** see EQUIVOCATE.

hedgehog /héjhog/ *n.* **1** any small nocturnal insect-eating mammal of the genus *Erinaceus*, esp. *E. europaeus*, having a piglike snout and a coat of spines, and rolling itself up into a ball for defence. **2** a porcupine or other animal similarly covered with spines. □□ **hedgehoggy** *adj.* [ME f. HEDGE (from its habitat) + HOG (from its snout)]

hedgerow /héjrō/ *n.* a row of bushes etc. forming a hedge.
■ see SHRUBBERY.

hedonic /heedónnik, hed-/ *adj.* **1** of or characterized by pleasure. **2** *Psychol.* of pleasant or unpleasant sensations. [Gk *hēdonikos* f. *hēdonē* pleasure]

hedonism /heédəniz'm, héd-/ *n.* **1** belief in pleasure as the highest good and mankind's proper aim. **2** behaviour based on this. □□ **hedonist** *n.* **hedonistic** /-nístik/ *adj.* [Gk *hēdonē* pleasure]
■ **2** see DISSIPATION 1.

-hedron /heédrən, hédrən/ *comb. form* (*pl.* **-hedra**) forming nouns denoting geometrical solids with various numbers or shapes of faces (*dodecahedron*; *rhombohedron*). □□ **-hedral** *comb. form* forming adjectives. [Gk *hedra* seat]

heebie-jeebies /heébeejeébeez/ *n.pl.* (prec. by *the*) *sl.* a state of nervous depression or anxiety. [20th c.: orig. unkn.]
■ see NERVE *n.* 3b.

heed /heed/ *v.* & *n.* ● *v.tr.* attend to; take notice of. ● *n.* careful attention. □□ **heedful** *adj.* **heedfully** *adv.* **heedfulness** *n.* **heedless** *adj.* **heedlessly** *adv.* **heedlessness** *n.* [OE *hēdan* f. WG]
■ *v.* pay attention to, attend to, take note *or* notice of, listen to, mark, mind, bear in mind, consider; take, follow, obey, abide by. ● *n.* attention, notice, consideration, thought. □□ **heedless** unobservant, uncaring, inattentive; (*heedless of*) unmindful of, neglectful of, regardless of, oblivious of *or* to, deaf to, blind to.

hee-haw /heéhaw/ *n.* & *v.* ● *n.* the bray of a donkey. ● *v.intr.* (of or like a donkey) emit a braying sound. [imit.]

heel[1] /heel/ *n.* & *v.* ● *n.* **1** the back part of the foot below the ankle. **2** the corresponding part in vertebrate animals. **3 a** the part of a sock etc. covering the heel. **b** the part of a shoe or boot supporting the heel. **4** a thing like a heel in form or position, e.g. the part of the palm next to the wrist, the end of a violin bow at which it is held, or the part of a golf club near where the head joins the shaft. **5** the crust end of a loaf of bread. **6** *colloq.* a person regarded with contempt or disapproval. **7** (as *int.*) a command to a dog to walk close to its owner's heel. ● *v.* **1** *tr.* fit or renew a heel on (a shoe or boot). **2** *intr.* touch the ground with the heel as in dancing. **3** *intr.* (foll. by *out*) *Rugby Football* pass the ball with the heel. **4** *tr.* *Golf* strike (the ball) with the heel of the club. □ **at heel 1** (of a dog) close behind. **2** (of a person etc.) under control. **at** (or **on**) **the heels of** following closely after (a person or event). **cool** (or **kick**) **one's heels** be kept waiting. **down at heel** see DOWN[1]. **take to one's heels** run away. **to heel 1** (of a dog) close behind. **2** (of a person etc.) under control. **turn on one's heel** turn sharply round. **well-heeled** *colloq.* wealthy. □□ **heelless** *adj.* [OE *hēla*, *hǣla* f. Gmc]
■ *n.* **5** end, crust; tail-end, stump. **6** cad, scoundrel, rogue, worm, knave, blackguard, *colloq.* swine, *colloq. or joc.* bounder, *sl.* bastard, *esp. Brit. sl.* rotter. □ **down at heel 2** shabby, slovenly, ragged; destitute, poor, impoverished, indigent, down and out, in straitened circumstances; *colloq.* broke, on one's uppers, strapped (for cash). **take to one's heels** take flight, flee, run off *or* away, do a moonlight flit, *colloq.* show a clean pair of heels, skedaddle, fly the coop, *sl.* split, take a powder, *Austral.* & *NZ sl.* shoot through; see also RUN *v.* 2. **well-heeled** see WEALTHY.

heel[2] /heel/ *v.* & *n.* ● *v.* **1** *intr.* (of a ship etc.) lean over owing to the pressure of wind or an uneven load (cf. LIST[2]). **2** *tr.* cause (a ship etc.) to do this. ● *n.* the act or amount of heeling. [prob. f. obs. *heeld*, *hield* incline, f. OE *hieldan*, OS *-heldian* f. Gmc]
■ *v.* **1** list, lean (over), tip, incline; see also TILT *v.* 1. ● *n.* see TILT *n.* 2.

heel[3] var. of HELE.

heelball /heélbawl/ *n.* **1** a mixture of hard wax and lampblack used by shoemakers for polishing. **2** this or a similar mixture used in brass-rubbing.

heeltap /heéltap/ *n.* **1** a layer of leather in a shoe heel. **2** liquor left at the bottom of a glass after drinking.

heft /heft/ *v.* & *n.* ● *v.tr.* lift (something heavy), esp. to judge its weight. ● *n. dial.* or *US* weight, heaviness. [prob. f. HEAVE after *cleft*, *weft*]
■ *n.* see WEIGHT *n.* 2, 3.

hefty /héfti/ *adj.* (**heftier, heftiest**) **1** (of a person) big and strong. **2** (of a thing) large, heavy, powerful; sizeable, considerable. □□ **heftily** *adv.* **heftiness** *n.*
■ **1** big, strong, powerful, strapping, robust, burly, husky, muscular, brawny, beefy, *colloq.* hunky. **2** big, large, enormous, huge, massive, bulky, substantial, heavy, powerful; considerable, sizeable, *colloq.* thumping.

Hegelian /haygeéliən/ *adj.* & *n.* ● *adj.* of or relating to the German philosopher G. W. F. Hegel (d. 1831) or his philosophy of objective idealism. ● *n.* an adherent of Hegel or his philosophy. □□ **Hegelianism** *n.*

hegemonic /héjimónnik, héggi-/ *adj.* ruling, supreme. [Gk *hēgemonikos* (as HEGEMONY)]

hegemony /hijémməni, -gémməni/ *n.* leadership esp. by one State of a confederacy. [Gk *hēgemonia* f. *hēgemōn* leader f. *hēgeomai* lead]
■ see *leadership* (LEADER).

hegira /héjirə/ *n.* (also **hejira, hijra** /híjrə/) **1** (**Hegira**) **a** Muhammad's departure from Mecca to Medina in AD 622. **b** the Muslim era reckoned from this date. **2** a general exodus or departure. [med.L *hegira* f. Arab. *hijra* departure from one's country f. *hajara* separate]

heifer /héffər/ *n.* **1 a** a young cow, esp. one that has not had more than one calf. **b** a female calf. **2** *sl. derog.* a woman. [OE *heahfore*]

heigh /hay/ *int.* expressing encouragement or enquiry. □ **heigh-ho** expressing boredom, resignation, etc. [imit.]

height /hīt/ *n.* **1** the measurement from base to top or (of a standing person) from head to foot. **2** the elevation above ground or a recognized level (usu. sea level). **3** any considerable elevation (*situated at a height*). **4 a** a high place or area. **b** rising ground. **5** the top of something. **6** *Printing* the distance from the foot to the face of type. **7 a** the most intense part or period of anything (*the battle was at its height*). **b** an extreme instance or example (*the height of fashion*). □ **height of land** *US* a watershed. [OE *hēhthu* f. Gmc]
■ **1** tallness, size. **2, 3** altitude, elevation, level. **4** elevation, mound, hill, tor, cliff, bluff, peak, summit, promontory, headland, *N.Eng.* fell; (*heights*) slopes. **5** crest, apex; see also TOP[1] *n.* 1. **7** pinnacle, acme, zenith, apogee, peak, high point, summit, climax, culmination; extreme.

heighten /hīt'n/ *v.tr.* & *intr.* make or become higher or more intense.
■ raise, elevate, lift, upraise, build up; intensify, deepen, strengthen, reinforce, amplify, magnify, enhance, augment, add to, supplement; see also RISE *v.* 2, INCREASE *v.* 1.

heinous /háynəss, heénəss/ *adj.* (of a crime or criminal) utterly odious or wicked. □□ **heinously** *adv.* **heinousness** *n.* [ME f. OF *haïneus* ult. f. *haïr* to hate f. Frank.]
■ see WICKED 1.

heir /air/ *n.* **1** a person entitled to property or rank as the legal successor of its former owner (often foll. by *to*: *heir to the throne*). **2** a person deriving or morally entitled to some thing, quality, etc., from a predecessor. □ **heir apparent** an heir whose claim cannot be set aside by the birth of another heir. **heir-at-law** (*pl.* **heirs-at-law**) an heir by right of blood, esp. to the real property of an intestate. **heir presumptive** an heir whose claim may be set aside by the

birth of another heir. □□ **heirdom** *n.* **heirless** *adj.* **heirship** *n.* [ME f. OF *eir* f. LL *herem* f. L *heres -edis*]
■ heiress, beneficiary, inheritor, successor, *esp. Sc. Law* heritor; legatee.

heiress /áiriss/ *n.* a female heir, esp. to wealth or high title.

heirloom /áirlōōm/ *n.* **1** a piece of personal property that has been in a family for several generations. **2** a piece of property received as part of an inheritance. [HEIR + LOOM[1] in the sense 'tool']
■ **1** see ANTIQUE *n.*

Heisenberg uncertainty principle see *uncertainty principle.*

heist /hīst/ *n.* & *v. US sl.* ● *n.* a robbery. ● *v.tr.* rob. [repr. a local pronunc. of HOIST]
■ *n.* see ROBBERY 1b. ● *v.* see STEAL *v.* 1.

hei-tiki /haytíkki/ *n. NZ* a greenstone neck-ornament worn by Maoris. [Maori f. *hei* hang, TIKI]

hejira var. of HEGIRA.

HeLa /héelə/ *adj.* of a strain of human epithelial cells maintained in tissue culture. [*He*nrietta *La*cks, whose cervical carcinoma provided the original cells]

held *past* and *past part.* of HOLD.

Heldentenor /héldəntennor/ *n.* **1** a powerful tenor voice suitable for heroic roles in opera. **2** a singer with this voice. [G f. *Held* a hero]

hele /heel/ *v.tr.* (also **heel**) (foll. by *in*) set (a plant) in the ground and cover its roots. [OE *helian* f. Gmc]

helenium /heléeniəm/ *n.* any composite plant of the genus *Helenium*, with daisy-like flowers having prominent central discs. [mod.L f. Gk *helenion*, possibly commemorating Helen of Troy]

heli- /hélli/ *comb. form* helicopter (*heliport*).

heliacal /hilīək'l/ *adj. Astron.* relating to or near the sun. □ **heliacal rising** (or **setting**) the first rising (or setting) of a star after (or before) a period of invisibility due to conjunction with the sun. [LL *heliacus* f. Gk *hēliakos* f. *hēlios* sun]

helianthemum /héeliánthəməm/ *n.* any evergreen shrub of the genus *Helianthemum*, with saucer-shaped flowers. Also called *rock rose*. [mod.L f. Gk *hēlios* sun + *anthemon* flower]

helianthus /héeliánthəss/ *n.* any plant of the genus *Helianthus*, including the sunflower and Jerusalem artichoke. [mod.L f. Gk *hēlios* sun + *anthos* flower]

helical /héllik'l/ *adj.* having the form of a helix. □□ **helically** *adv.* **helicoid** *adj.* & *n.*
■ see SPIRAL *adj.*

helices *pl.* of HELIX.

helichrysum /héllikrīz'm/ *n.* any composite plant of the genus *Helichrysum*, with flowers retaining their appearance when dried. [L f. Gk *helikhrusos* f. *helix* spiral + *khrusos* gold]

helicon /héllikən/ *n.* a large spiral bass tuba played encircling the player's head and resting on the shoulder. [L f. Gk *Helikōn* mountain sacred to the Muses: later assoc. with HELIX]

helicopter /héllikoptər/ *n.* & *v.* ● *n.* a type of aircraft without wings, obtaining lift and propulsion from horizontally revolving overhead blades or rotors, and capable of moving vertically and horizontally. ● *v.tr.* & *intr.* transport or fly by helicopter. [F *hélicoptère* f. Gk *helix* (see HELIX) + *pteron* wing]

helio- /héeliō/ *comb. form* the sun. [Gk *hēlios* sun]

heliocentric /héeliəséntrik/ *adj.* **1** regarding the sun as centre. **2** considered as viewed from the sun's centre. □□ **heliocentrically** *adv.*

heliogram /héeliəgram/ *n.* a message sent by heliograph.

heliograph /héeliəgraaf/ *n.* & *v.* ● *n.* **1 a** a signalling apparatus reflecting sunlight in flashes from a movable mirror. **b** a message sent by means of this; a heliogram. **2** an apparatus for photographing the sun. **3** an engraving obtained chemically by exposure to light. ● *v.tr.* send (a message) by heliograph. □□ **heliography** /-liógrəfi/ *n.*

heliogravure /héeliōgrəvyóor/ *n.* = PHOTOGRAVURE.

heliolithic /héeliəlíthik/ *adj.* (of a civilization) characterized by sun-worship and megaliths.

heliometer /héeliómmitər/ *n.* an instrument used for finding the angular distance between two stars (orig. used for measuring the diameter of the sun).

heliostat /héeliəstat/ *n.* an apparatus with a mirror driven by clockwork to reflect sunlight in a fixed direction. □□ **heliostatic** /-státtik/ *adj.*

heliotherapy /héeliōthérrəpi/ *n.* the use of sunlight in treating disease.

heliotrope /héeliətrōp, hél-/ *n.* **1 a** any plant of the genus *Heliotropium*, with fragrant purple flowers. **b** the scent of these. **2** a light purple colour. **3** bloodstone. [L *heliotropium* f. Gk *hēliotropion* plant turning its flowers to the sun, f. *hēlios* sun + *-tropos* f. *trepō* turn]

heliotropism /héeliótrəpiz'm/ *n.* the directional growth of a plant in response to sunlight (cf. PHOTOTROPISM). □□ **heliotropic** /-liətróppik/ *adj.*

heliotype /héeliətīp/ *n.* a picture obtained from a sensitized gelatin film exposed to light.

heliport /hélliport/ *n.* a place where helicopters take off and land. [HELI-, after *airport*]

helium /héeliəm/ *n. Chem.* a colourless light inert gaseous element occurring in deposits of natural gas, used in airships and as a refrigerant. ¶ Symb.: **He**. [Gk *hēlios* sun (having been first identified in the sun's atmosphere)]

helix /héeliks/ *n.* (*pl.* **helices** /-seez, hél-/) **1** a spiral curve (like a corkscrew) or a coiled curve (like a watch spring). **2** *Geom.* a curve that cuts a line on a solid cone or cylinder, at a constant angle with the axis. **3** *Archit.* a spiral ornament. **4** *Anat.* the rim of the external ear. [L *helix -icis* f. Gk *helix -ikos*]
■ **1, 3** see SPIRAL *n.*

hell /hel/ *n.* **1** a place regarded in some religions as the abode of the dead, or of condemned sinners and devils. **2** a place or state of misery or wickedness. **3** *colloq.* used as an exclamation of surprise or annoyance (*who the hell are you?*; *a hell of a mess*). **4** *US colloq.* fun; high spirits. □ **beat** (or **knock** etc.) **the hell out of** *colloq.* beat etc. without restraint. **come hell or high water** no matter what the difficulties. **for the hell of it** *colloq.* for fun; on impulse. **get** (or **catch**) **hell** *colloq.* be severely scolded or punished. **give a person hell** *colloq.* scold or punish or make things difficult for a person. **hell-bent** (foll. by *on*) recklessly determined. **hell-cat** a spiteful violent woman. **hell-fire** the fire or fires regarded as existing in hell. **hell for leather** at full speed. **hell-hole** *colloq.* an oppressive or unbearable place. **hell-hound** a fiend. **hell-raiser** a person who causes trouble or creates chaos. **hell's angel** a member of a gang of male motor-cycle enthusiasts notorious for outrageous and violent behaviour. **like hell** *colloq.* **1** not at all. **2** recklessly, exceedingly. **not a hope in hell** *colloq.* no chance at all. **play hell** (or **merry hell**) **with** *colloq.* be upsetting or disruptive to. **what the hell** *colloq.* it is of no importance. □□ **hell-like** *adj.* **hellward** *adv.* & *adj.* [OE *hel, hell* f. Gmc]
■ **1** underworld, abyss, inferno, (bottomless) pit, infernal regions, Hades, Tartarus, Gehenna, Abaddon, Sheol, abode of the damned, lower world, other place, *Bibl.* Tophet, *archaic* nether regions *or* world. **2** purgatory, chaos, misery, torment, agony. anguish, torture, pain; affliction, ordeal, nightmare, trial. **4** see FUN *n.* 3. □ **give a person hell** see SCOLD *v.* 1, PUNISH 1. **hell-bent on** intent *or* bent *or* set on, resolved *or* determined *or* decided on; keen on, enthusiastic *or* avid *or* passionate about. **hell-cat** see SHREW. **hell-hole** see HOLE *n.* 4a. **hell-hound** see DEVIL *n.* 3a. **like hell 2** see *dangerously* (DANGEROUS).

he'll /heel, hil/ *contr.* he will; he shall.

hellacious /heláyshəss/ *adj. US sl.* terrific, tremendous; remarkable, enormous. [HELL + -ACIOUS]

Helladic /heláddik/ *adj.* of or belonging to the Bronze Age culture of mainland Greece. [Gk *Helladikos* f. *Hellas -ados* Greece]

hellebore /héllibor/ *n.* **1** any evergreen plant of the genus *Helleborus*, having large white, green, or purplish flowers, e.g. the Christmas rose. **2** a liliaceous plant, *Veratrum album*. **3** *hist.* any of various plants supposed to cure madness. [ME f. OF *ellebre, elebore* or med.L *eleborus* f. L *elleborus* f. Gk (*h*)*elleboros*]

helleborine /héllibəreen/ *n.* any orchid of the genus *Epipactis* or *Cephalanthera*. [F or L *helleborine* or L f. Gk *helleborinē* plant like hellebore (as HELLEBORE)]

Hellene /hélleen/ *n.* **1** a native of modern Greece. **2** an ancient Greek. ▫▫ **Hellenic** /helénnik, -léenik/ *adj.* [Gk *Hellēn* a Greek]

Hellenism /hélliniz'm/ *n.* **1** Greek character or culture (esp. of ancient Greece). **2** the study or imitation of Greek culture. ▫▫ **Hellenize** *v.tr.* & *intr.* (also **-ise**). **Hellenization** /-nīzáysh'n/ *n.* [Gk *hellēnismos* f. *hellēnizō* speak Greek, make Greek (as HELLENE)]

Hellenist /héllinist/ *n.* an expert on or admirer of Greek language or culture. [Gk *Hellēnistēs* (as HELLENISM)]

Hellenistic /héllinístik/ *adj.* of or relating to Greek history, language, and culture from the death of Alexander the Great to the time of Augustus (4th–1st c. BC).

hellgrammite /hélgrəmīt/ *n.* *US* an aquatic larva of an American fly, *Corydalus cornutus*, often used as fishing bait. [19th c.: orig. unkn.]

hellion /hélliən/ *n.* *US colloq.* a mischievous or troublesome person, esp. a child. [perh. f. dial. *hallion* a worthless fellow, assim. to HELL]

hellish /héllish/ *adj.* & *adv.* ● *adj.* **1** of or like hell. **2** *colloq.* extremely difficult or unpleasant. ● *adv. Brit. colloq.* (as an intensifier) extremely (*hellish expensive*). ▫▫ **hellishly** *adv.* **hellishness** *n.*

■ *adj.* **1** see INFERNAL 1. **2** see ATROCIOUS 1.

hello /həlṓ/ *int.*, *n.*, & *v.* (also **hallo, hullo**) ● *int.* **1 a** an expression of informal greeting, or of surprise. **b** used to begin a telephone conversation. **2** a cry used to call attention. ● *n.* (*pl.* **-os**) a cry of 'hello'. ● *v.intr.* (**-oes, -oed**) cry 'hello'. [var. of earlier HOLLO]

■ *int.* hi, how do you do?, *US* howdy, *archaic or literary* hail, *colloq.* ciao, hiya, *Brit. sl.* wotcher.

helm[1] /helm/ *n.* & *v.* ● *n.* **1** a tiller or wheel by which a ship's rudder is controlled. **2** the amount by which this is turned (*more helm needed*). ● *v.tr.* steer or guide as if with a helm. ▫ **at the helm** in control; at the head (of an organization etc.). [OE *helma*, prob. related to HELVE]

■ *n.* **1** tiller, wheel, steering gear *or* apparatus. ● *v.* see STEER[1] *v.* 1. ▫ **at the helm** in control *or* command, in the chair *or* driver's seat *or* saddle; directing, presiding, leading, ruling.

helm[2] /helm/ *n. archaic* helmet. ▫▫ **helmed** *adj.* [OE f. Gmc]

helmet /hélmit/ *n.* **1** any of various protective head-coverings worn by soldiers, policemen, firemen, divers, motor cyclists, etc. **2** *Bot.* the arched upper part of the corolla in some flowers. **3** the shell of a gastropod mollusc of the genus *Cassis*, used in jewellery. ▫▫ **helmeted** *adj.* [ME f. OF, dimin. of *helme* f. WG (as HELM[2])]

helminth /hélminth/ *n.* any of various parasitic worms including flukes, tapeworms, and nematodes. ▫▫ **helminthic** /-mínthik/ *adj.* **helminthoid** /-mínthoyd/ *adj.* **helminthology** /-minthólləji/ *n.* [Gk *helmins -inthos* intestinal worm]

helminthiasis /hélminthī́əsiss/ *n.* a disease characterized by the presence of any of several parasitic worms in the body.

helmsman /hélmzmən/ *n.* (*pl.* **-men**) a steersman.

■ see PILOT *n.* 2, 5.

helot /héllət/ *n.* a serf (esp. **Helot**), of a class in ancient Sparta. ▫▫ **helotism** *n.* **helotry** *n.* [L *helotes* pl. f. Gk *heilōtes*, *-ōtai*, erron. taken as = inhabitants of *Helos*, a Laconian town]

■ see SLAVE *n.* 1.

help /help/ *v.* & *n.* ● *v.tr.* **1** provide (a person etc.) with the means towards what is needed or sought (*helped me with my work; helped me (to) pay my debts*). **2** (foll. by *up, down*, etc.) assist or give support to (a person) in moving etc. as specified (*helped her into the chair; helped him on with his coat*). **3** (often *absol.*) be of use or service to (a person) (*does that help?*). **4** contribute to alleviating (a pain or difficulty). **5** prevent or remedy (*it can't be helped*). **6** (usu. with *neg.*) **a** *tr.* refrain from (*can't help it; could not help laughing*). **b** *refl.* refrain from acting (*couldn't help himself*). **7** *tr.* (often foll. by *to*) serve (a person with food) (*shall I help you to greens?*). ● *n.* **1** the act of helping or being helped (*we need your help; came to our help*). **2** a person or thing that helps. **3** a domestic servant or employee, or several collectively. **4** a remedy or escape (*there is no help for it*). ▫ **helping hand** assistance. **help oneself** (often foll. by *to*) **1** serve oneself (with food). **2** take without seeking help; take without permission, steal. **help a person out** give a person help, esp. in difficulty. **so help me** (or **help me God**) (as an invocation or oath) I am speaking the truth. ▫▫ **helper** *n.* [OE *helpan* f. Gmc]

■ *v.* **1, 2** assist, aid, lend *or* give a hand; support. **3** serve, succour, aid, be of use *or* useful (to), be advantageous *or* of advantage (to), avail. **4, 5** relieve, alleviate, mitigate, ease, remedy, cure, make better, improve; prevent, avoid, obviate. **6 a** stop, refrain from, resist, keep from, *literary* forbear (from) *or* to do. **b** stop, control oneself. ● *n.* **1** aid, support, succour, assistance. **2** support; prop, helper, assistant, *esp. US* aide. **3** employee(s), worker(s), member(s) of staff, helper(s), hand(s), assistant(s), labourer(s), domestic(s), servant(s); *Brit. colloq.* daily help, daily; staff, *Brit. colloq.* daily helps, dailies. **4** relief, escape; remedy, cure, balm. ▫ **helping hand** see *assistance* (ASSIST). **help oneself 2** take; appropriate, commandeer, steal, *colloq.* lift, *formal or joc.* purloin, *sl.* pinch, *Brit. sl.* nick.

helpful /hélpfŏŏl/ *adj.* (of a person or thing) giving help; useful. ▫▫ **helpfully** *adv.* **helpfulness** *n.*

■ useful, serviceable, practical, beneficial, valuable, constructive, productive; supportive, reassuring, sympathetic, caring, kind, benevolent, considerate, cooperative, accommodating.

helping /hélping/ *n.* a portion of food esp. at a meal.

■ serving, portion, ration, plateful, dollop.

helpless /hélpliss/ *adj.* **1** lacking help or protection; defenceless. **2** unable to act without help. ▫▫ **helplessly** *adv.* **helplessness** *n.*

■ **1** vulnerable, dependent; see also *defenceless* (DEFENCE). **2** weak, feeble, infirm; confused, bewildered, muddled; incapable.

helpline /hélplīn/ *n.* a telephone service providing help with problems.

helpmate /hélpmayt/ *n.* a helpful companion or partner (usu. a husband or wife).

■ see PARTNER *n.* 1, 4.

helter-skelter /héltərskéltər/ *adv.*, *adj.*, & *n.* ● *adv.* in disorderly haste; confusedly. ● *adj.* characterized by disorderly haste or confusion. ● *n. Brit.* a tall spiral slide round a tower, at a fairground or funfair. [imit., orig. in a rhyming jingle, perh. f. ME *skelte* hasten]

■ *adv.* hastily, hurriedly, confusedly, recklessly, pell-mell, headlong, unsystematically, chaotically, erratically, higgledy-piggledy, *US colloq.* every which way. ● *adj.* hasty, hurried, reckless, headlong; disorderly, disorganized, confused, muddled, haphazard, careless, jumbled, random, topsy-turvy, higgledy-piggledy.

helve /helv/ *n.* the handle of a weapon or a tool. [OE *helfe* f. WG]

■ see HANDLE *n.* 1.

Helvetian /helvéesh'n/ *adj.* & *n.* ● *adj.* Swiss. ● *n.* a native of Switzerland. [L *Helvetia* Switzerland]

hem[1] /hem/ *n.* & *v.* ● *n.* the border of a piece of cloth, esp. a cut edge turned under and sewn down. ● *v.tr.* (**hemmed,**

hemming) turn down and sew in the edge of (a piece of cloth etc.). □ **hem in** confine; restrict the movement of. [OE, perh. rel. to dial. *ham* enclosure]
■ *n.* see BORDER *n.* 3. ● *v.* see SEW. □ **hem in** see BOX[1] *v.* 2.

hem[2] /hem, həm/ *int.*, *n.*, & *v.* ● *int.* calling attention or expressing hesitation by a slight cough or clearing of the throat. ● *n.* an utterance of this. ● *v.intr.* (**hemmed, hemming**) say *hem*; hesitate in speech. □ **hem and haw** = *hum and haw* (see HUM[1]). [imit.]

hemal etc. *US* var. of HAEMAL etc.

hemato- etc. *US* var. of HAEMATO- etc.

heme var. of HAEM.

hemerocallis /hémmərōkálliss/ *n.* = *day lily*. [L *hemerocalles* f. Gk *hēmerokalles* a kind of lily f. *hēmera* day + *kallos* beauty]

hemi- /hémmi/ *comb. form* half. [Gk *hēmi-* = L *semi-*: see SEMI-]

-hemia *comb. form US* var. of -AEMIA.

hemianopsia /hémmiənópsiə/ *n.* (also **hemianopia** /hémmiənṓpiə/) blindness over half the field of vision.

hemicellulose /hémmisélyoolōz/ *n.* any of various polysaccharides forming the matrix of plant cell walls in which cellulose is embedded. [G (as HEMI-, CELLULOSE)]

hemicycle /hémmisīk'l/ *n.* a semicircular figure.

hemidemisemiquaver /hémmidémmisémmikwayvər/ *n.* *Mus.* a note having the time value of half a demisemiquaver and represented by a large dot with a four-hooked stem. Also called *sixty-fourth note*.

hemihedral /hémmihéedrəl/ *adj. Crystallog.* having half the number of planes required for symmetry of the holohedral form.

hemiplegia /hémmipléejiə/ *n. Med.* paralysis of one side of the body. □□ **hemiplegic** *n.* & *adj.* [mod.L f. Gk *hēmiplēgia* paralysis (as HEMI-, *plēgē* stroke)]

hemipterous /hemíptərəss/ *adj.* of the insect order Hemiptera including aphids, bugs, and cicadas, with piercing or sucking mouthparts. [HEMI- + Gk *pteron* wing]

hemisphere /hémmisfeer/ *n.* **1** half of a sphere. **2** a half of the earth, esp. as divided by the equator (into *northern* and *southern hemisphere*) or by a line passing through the poles (into *eastern* and *western hemisphere*). □□ **hemispheric** /-sférrik/ *adj.* **hemispherical** /-sférrik'l/ *adj.* [OF *emisphere* & L *hemisphaerium* f. Gk *hēmisphaira* (as HEMI, SPHERE)]

hemistich /hémmistik/ *n.* half of a line of verse. [LL *hemistichium* f. Gk *hēmistikhion* (as HEMI-, *stikhion* f. *stikhos* line)]

hemline /hémlīn/ *n.* the line or level of the lower edge of a skirt, dress, or coat.

hemlock /hémlok/ *n.* **1 a** a poisonous umbelliferous plant, *Conium maculatum*, with fernlike leaves and small white flowers. **b** a poisonous potion obtained from this. **2** (in full **hemlock fir** or **spruce**) **a** any coniferous tree of the genus *Tsuga*, having foliage that smells like hemlock when crushed. **b** the timber or pitch of these trees. [OE *hymlic(e)*]

hemo- *comb. form US* var. of HAEMO-.

hemp /hemp/ *n.* **1** (in full **Indian hemp**) a herbaceous plant, *Cannabis sativa*, native to Asia. **2** its fibre extracted from the stem and used to make rope and stout fabrics. **3** any of several narcotic drugs made from the hemp plant (cf. CANNABIS, MARIJUANA). **4** any of several other plants yielding fibre, including Manila hemp and sunn hemp. □ **hemp agrimony** a composite plant, *Eupatorium cannabinum*, with pale-purple flowers and hairy leaves. **hemp-nettle** any of various nettle-like plants of the genus *Galeopsis*. [OE *henep*, *hænep* f. Gmc, rel. to Gk *kannabis*]

hempen /hémpən/ *adj.* made from hemp.

hemstitch /hémstich/ *n.* & *v.* ● *n.* a decorative stitch used in sewing hems. ● *v.tr.* hem with this stitch.

hen /hen/ *n.* **1 a** a female bird, esp. of a domestic fowl. **b** (in *pl.*) domestic fowls of either sex. **2** a female lobster or crab or salmon. □ **hen and chickens** any of several plants esp. the houseleek. **hen-coop** a coop for keeping fowls in. **hen-harrier** a common harrier, *Circus cyaneus*. **hen-house** a small shed for fowls to roost in. **hen-party** *colloq.* often *derog.* a social gathering of women. **hen-roost** a place where fowls roost at night. **hen-run** an enclosure for fowls. [OE *henn* f. WG]

henbane /hénbayn/ *n.* **1** a poisonous herbaceous plant, *Hyoscyamus niger*, with sticky hairy leaves and an unpleasant smell. **2** a narcotic drug obtained from this.

hence /henss/ *adv.* **1** from this time (*two years hence*). **2** for this reason; as a result of inference (*hence we seem to be wrong*). **3** *archaic* from here; from this place. [ME *hens*, *hennes*, *henne* f. OE *heonan* f. the root of HE]
■ **1** from now, in the future. **2** therefore, consequently, accordingly, *ergo*, as a result, for that *or* this reason, so, *formal* thus.

henceforth /hénsfórth/ *adv.* (also **henceforward** /-fórwərd/) from this time onwards.
■ hereafter, from now on, in future.

henchman /hénchmən/ *n.* (*pl.* **-men**) **1 a** a trusted supporter or attendant. **b** often *derog.* a political supporter; a partisan. **2** *hist.* a squire; a page of honour. **3** the principal attendant of a Highland chief. [ME *henxman*, *hengestman* f. OE *hengst* male horse]
■ **1** attendant, associate, supporter, partisan, confidant, crony, right-hand man, *US* cohort, *colloq.* sidekick.

hendeca- /hendékkə/ *comb. form* eleven. [Gk *hendeka* eleven]

hendecagon /hendékkəgon/ *n.* a plane figure with eleven sides and angles.

hendiadys /hendī́ədiss/ *n.* the expression of an idea by two words connected with 'and', instead of one modifying the other, e.g. *nice and warm* for *nicely warm*. [med.L f. Gk *hen dia duoin* one thing by two]

henequen /hénniken/ *n.* **1** a Mexican agave, *Agave fourcroydes*. **2** the sisal-like fibre obtained from this. [Sp. *jeniquen*]

henge /henj/ *n.* a prehistoric monument consisting of a circle of massive stone or wood uprights. [back-form. f. *Stonehenge*, such a monument in S. England]

henna /hénnə/ *n.* **1** a tropical shrub, *Lawsonia inermis*, having small pink, red, or white flowers. **2** the reddish dye from its shoots and leaves esp. used to colour hair. [Arab. *ḥinnā'*]

hennaed /hénnəd/ *adj.* treated with henna.

henotheism /hénnəthee-iz'm/ *n.* belief in or adoption of a particular god in a polytheistic system as the god of a tribe, class, etc. [Gk *heis henos* one + *theos* god]

henpeck /hénpek/ *v.tr.* (of a woman) constantly harass (a man, esp. her husband).
■ nag, harass, pester, torment, carp at, cavil at, *colloq.* go on at.

henry /hénri/ *n.* (*pl.* **-ies** or **henrys**) *Electr.* the SI unit of inductance which gives an electromotive force of one volt in a closed circuit with a uniform rate of change of current of one ampere per second. ¶ Abbr.: **H.** [J. *Henry*, Amer. physicist d. 1878]

heortology /hée-ortólləji/ *n.* the study of Church festivals. [G *Heortologie*, F *héortologie* f. Gk *heortē* feast]

hep[1] var. of HIP[3].

hep[2] var. of HIP[2].

heparin /héppərin/ *n. Biochem.* a substance produced in liver cells etc. which inhibits blood coagulation, and is used as an anticoagulant in the treatment of thrombosis. □□ **heparinize** *v.tr.* (also **-ise**). [L f. Gk *hēpar* liver]

hepatic /hipáttik/ *adj.* **1** of or relating to the liver. **2** dark brownish-red; liver-coloured. [ME f. L *hepaticus* f. Gk *hēpatikos* f. *hēpar -atos* liver]

hepatica /hipáttikə/ *n.* any plant of the genus *Hepatica*, with reddish-brown lobed leaves resembling the liver. [med.L fem. of *hepaticus*: see HEPATIC]

hepatitis /héppətī́tiss/ *n.* inflammation of the liver. [mod.L: see HEPATIC]

Hepplewhite /hépp'lwīt/ *n.* a light and graceful style of furniture. [G. *Hepplewhite*, Engl. cabinet-maker d. 1786]

hepta- /héptə/ *comb. form* seven. [Gk *hepta* seven]

heptad /héptad/ *n.* a group of seven. [Gk *heptas -ados* set of seven (*hepta*)]

heptagon /héptəgən/ *n.* a plane figure with seven sides and angles. □□ **heptagonal** /-tággən'l/ *adj.* [F *heptagone* or med.L *heptagonum* f. Gk (as HEPTA-, -GON)]

heptahedron /héptəhéedrən/ *n.* a solid figure with seven faces. □□ **heptahedral** *adj.* [HEPTA- + -HEDRON after POLYHEDRON]

heptameter /heptámmitər/ *n.* a line or verse of seven metrical feet. [L *heptametrum* f. Gk (as HEPTA-, -METER)]

heptane /héptayn/ *n. Chem.* a liquid hydrocarbon of the alkane series, obtained from petroleum. ¶ Chem. formula: C_7H_{16}. [HEPTA- + -ANE[2]]

heptarchy /héptaarki/ *n.* (*pl.* **-ies**) **1 a** government by seven rulers. **b** an instance of this. **2** *hist.* the supposed seven kingdoms of the Angles and the Saxons in Britain in the 7th–8th c. □□ **heptarchic** /-aárkik/ *adj.* **heptarchical** /-aárkik'l/ *adj.* [HEPTA- after *tetrarchy*]

Heptateuch /héptətyook/ *n.* the first seven books of the Old Testament. [L f. Gk f. *hepta* seven + *teukhos* book, volume]

heptavalent /héptəváylənt/ *adj. Chem.* having a valency of seven; septivalent.

her /her, hər/ *pron.* & *poss.pron.* ● *pron.* **1** *objective case* of SHE (*I like her*). **2** *colloq.* she (*it's her all right; am older than her*). **3** *archaic* herself (*she fell and hurt her*). ● *poss.pron.* (*attrib.*) **1** of or belonging to her or herself (*her house; her own business*). **2** (**Her**) (in titles) that she is (*Her Majesty*). □ **her indoors** *colloq.* or *joc.* one's wife. [OE *hi(e)re* dative & genit. of *hio, hēo* fem. of HE]

herald /hérrəld/ *n.* & *v.* ● *n.* **1** an official messenger bringing news. **2** a forerunner (*spring is the herald of summer*). **3 a** *hist.* an officer responsible for State ceremonial and etiquette. **b** *Brit.* an official of the Heralds' College. ● *v.tr.* proclaim the approach of; usher in (*the storm heralded trouble*). □ **Heralds' College** *Brit. colloq.* = *College of Arms.* [ME f. OF *herau(l)t, herauder* f. Gmc]

■ *n.* **1** see MESSENGER. **2** see FORERUNNER 2. ● *v.* see ANNOUNCE 1.

heraldic /heráldik/ *adj.* of or concerning heraldry. □□ **heraldically** *adv.* [HERALD]

heraldist /hérrəldist/ *n.* an expert in heraldry. [HERALD]

heraldry /hérrəldri/ *n.* **1** the science or art of a herald, esp. in dealing with armorial bearings. **2** heraldic pomp. **3** armorial bearings.

herb /herb/ *n.* **1** any non-woody seed-bearing plant which dies down to the ground after flowering. **2** any plant with leaves, seeds, or flowers used for flavouring, food, medicine, scent, etc. □ **give it the herbs** *Austral. colloq.* accelerate. **herb bennet** a common yellow-flowered plant, *Geum urbanum.* **herb Christopher** a white-flowered baneberry, *Actaea spicata.* **herb Gerard** a white-flowered plant, *Aegopodium podagraria.* **herb Paris** a plant, *Paris quadrifolia,* with a single flower and four leaves in a cross shape on an unbranched stem. **herb Robert** a common cranesbill, *Geranium robertianum,* with red-stemmed leaves and pink flowers. **herb tea** an infusion of herbs. **herb tobacco** a mixture of herbs smoked as a substitute for tobacco. □□ **herbiferous** /-bíffərəss/ *adj.* **herblike** *adj.* [ME f. OF *erbe* f. L *herba* grass, green crops, herb; *herb bennet* prob. f. med.L *herba benedicta* blessed herb (thought of as expelling the Devil)]

■ **2** see SPICE *n.* 1.

herbaceous /herbáyshəss/ *adj.* of or like herbs (see HERB 1). □ **herbaceous border** a garden border containing esp. perennial flowering plants. **herbaceous perennial** a plant whose growth dies down annually but whose roots etc. survive. [L *herbaceus* grassy (as HERB)]

herbage /hérbij/ *n.* **1** herbs collectively. **2** the succulent part of herbs, esp. as pasture. **3** *Law* the right of pasture on another person's land. [ME f. OF *erbage* f. med.L *herbaticum, herbagium* right of pasture, f. L *herba* herb]

herbal /hérb'l/ *adj.* & *n.* ● *adj.* of herbs in medicinal and culinary use. ● *n.* a book with descriptions and accounts of the properties of these. [med.L *herbalis* (as HERB)]

herbalist /hérbəlist/ *n.* **1** a dealer in medicinal herbs. **2** a person skilled in herbs, esp. an early botanical writer.

herbarium /herbáiriəm/ *n.* (*pl.* **herbaria** /-riə/) **1** a systematically arranged collection of dried plants. **2** a book, room, or building for these. [LL (as HERB)]

herbicide /hérbisīd/ *n.* a substance toxic to plants and used to destroy unwanted vegetation.

herbivore /hérbivor/ *n.* an animal that feeds on plants. □□ **herbivorous** /-bívvərəss/ *adj.* [L *herba* herb + -VORE (see -VOROUS)]

herby /hérbi/ *adj.* (**herbier, herbiest**) **1** abounding in herbs. **2** of the nature of a culinary or medicinal herb.

Herculean /hérkyooléeən, -kyoolíən/ *adj.* having or requiring great strength or effort. [L *Herculeus* (as HERCULES)]

■ see SUPERHUMAN 1.

Hercules /hérkyooleez/ *n.* a man of exceptional strength or size. □ **Hercules beetle** *Zool.* a large S. American beetle, *Dynastes hercules,* with two horns extending from the head. [ME f. L f. Gk *Hēraklēs* a hero noted for his great strength]

Hercynian /hersínniən/ *adj. Geol.* of a mountain-forming time in the E. hemisphere in the late Palaeozoic era. [L *Hercynia silva* forested mountains of central Germany]

herd /herd/ *n.* & *v.* ● *n.* **1** a large number of animals, esp. cattle, feeding or travelling or kept together. **2** (often prec. by *the*) *derog.* a large number of people; a crowd, a mob (*prefers not to follow the herd*). **3** (esp. in *comb.*) a keeper of herds; a herdsman (*cowherd*). ● *v.* **1** *intr.* & *tr.* go or cause to go in a herd (*herded together for warmth; herded the cattle into the field*). **2** *tr.* tend (sheep, cattle, etc.) (*he herds the goats*). □ **herd-book** a book recording the pedigrees of cattle or pigs. **the herd instinct** the tendency of associating or conforming with one's own kind for support etc. **ride herd on** *US* keep watch on. □□ **herder** *n.* [OE *heord,* (in sense 3) *hirdi,* f. Gmc]

■ *n.* **1** see FLOCK[1] *n.* 1. **2** group, flock, crowd, multitude, host, throng, mass, swarm; *usu. derog.* mob, horde, common herd, masses, *hoi polloi,* riff-raff, rabble, *colloq.* great unwashed. ● *v.* **1** gather (together), congregate, flock together, assemble, collect; round up, gather (together *or* up), *US* wrangle, corral. **2** shepherd, look after; see also TEND[2] 1.

herdsman /hérdzmən/ *n.* (*pl.* **-men**) the owner or keeper of herds (of domesticated animals).

Herdwick /hérdwik/ *n.* **1** an animal of a hardy breed of mountain sheep from N. England. **2** this breed. [obs. *herdwick* pasture-ground (as HERD, WICK[2]), perh. because this breed originated in Furness Abbey pastures]

here /heer/ *adv., n.,* & *int.* ● *adv.* **1** in or at or to this place or position (*put it here; has lived here for many years; comes here every day*). **2** indicating a person's presence or a thing offered (*here is your coat; my son here will show you*). **3** at this point in the argument, situation, etc. (*here I have a question*). ● *n.* this place (*get out of here; lives near here; fill it up to here*). ● *int.* **1** calling attention: short for *come here, look here,* etc. (*here, where are you going with that?*). **2** indicating one's presence in a roll-call: short for *I am here.* □ **here and now** at this very moment; immediately. **here and there** in various places. **here goes!** *colloq.* an expression indicating the start of a bold act. **here's to** I drink to the health of. **here we are** *colloq.* said on arrival at one's destination. **here we go again** *colloq.* the same, usu. undesirable, events are recurring. **here you are** said on handing something to somebody. **neither here nor there** of no importance or relevance. [OE *hēr* f. Gmc: cf. HE]

hereabouts /heérəbówts/ *adv.* (also **hereabout**) near this place.

hereafter /heeraáftər/ *adv.* & *n.* ● *adv.* **1** from now on; in the future. **2** in the world to come (after death). ● *n.* **1** the future. **2** life after death.

hereat /heérát/ *adv. archaic* as a result of this.

hereby /he͞erbī́/ *adv.* by this means; as a result of this.
hereditable /hiréddɪtəb'l/ *adj.* that can be inherited. [obs. F *héréditable* or med.L *hereditabilis* f. eccl.L *hereditare* f. L *heres -edis* heir]
hereditament /hérridíttəmənt, hiréddi-/ *n. Law* **1** any property that can be inherited. **2** inheritance. [med.L *hereditamentum* (as HEREDITABLE)]
hereditary /hiréddɪtəri, -tri/ *adj.* **1** (of disease, instinct, etc.) able to be passed down from one generation to another. **2 a** descending by inheritance. **b** holding a position by inheritance. **3** the same as or resembling what one's parents had (*a hereditary hatred*). **4** of or relating to inheritance. □□ **hereditarily** *adv.* **hereditariness** *n.* [L *hereditarius* (as HEREDITY)]
■ **1** inheritable, transmissible, *Biol.* heritable; inherited, genetic, inborn, innate, bred in the bone. **2 a** ancestral, inherited, traditional, handed down. **3** inherited, ingrained; see also INBORN.
heredity /hiréddɪti/ *n.* **1 a** the passing on of physical or mental characteristics genetically from one generation to another. **b** these characteristics. **2** the genetic constitution of an individual. [F *hérédité* or L *hereditas* heirship (as HEIR)]
Hereford /hérrifərd/ *n.* **1** an animal of a breed of red and white beef cattle. **2** this breed. [*Hereford* in England, where it originated]
herein /he͞erín/ *adv. formal* in this matter, book, etc.
hereinafter /he͞erinaáftər/ *adv.* esp. *Law formal* in a later part of this document etc.
hereinbefore /he͞erinbifór/ *adv.* esp. *Law formal* in a preceding part of this document etc.
hereof /he͞eróv/ *adv. formal* of this.
heresiarch /hereézi aark/ *n.* the leader or founder of a heresy. [eccl.L *haeresiarcha* f. Gk *hairesiarkhēs* (as HERESY + *arkhēs* ruler)]
heresy /hérrəsi/ *n.* (*pl.* **-ies**) **1 a** belief or practice contrary to the orthodox doctrine of the Christian Church. **b** an instance of this. **2 a** opinion contrary to what is normally accepted or maintained (*it's heresy to suggest that instant coffee is as good as the real thing*). **b** an instance of this. □□ **heresiology** /hérrisióllәji/ *n.* [ME f. OF (*h*)*eresie*, f. eccl.L *haeresis*, in L = school of thought, f. Gk *hairesis* choice, sect f. *haireomai* choose]
■ **1** see SACRILEGE.
heretic /hérrətik/ *n.* **1** the holder of an unorthodox opinion. **2** a person believing in or practising religious heresy. □□ **heretical** /hiréttik'l/ *adj.* **heretically** /hiréttikəli/ *adv.* [ME f. OF *heretique* f. eccl.L *haereticus* f. Gk *hairetikos* able to choose (as HERESY)]
■ **1** see NONCONFORMIST. **2** see INFIDEL *n.* □□ **heretical** unorthodox, heterodox, freethinking, iconoclastic; schismatic, apostatical, sceptical, agnostic, atheistic, infidel, idolatrous, heathen, pagan, godless; blasphemous, impious.
hereto /he͞ertóo/ *adv. formal* to this matter.
heretofore /he͞ertoofór/ *adv. formal* before this time.
■ see *previously* (PREVIOUS).
hereunder /he͞erúndər/ *adv. formal* below (in a book, legal document, etc.).
hereunto /he͞eruntóo/ *adv. archaic* to this.
hereupon /he͞erəpón/ *adv.* after this; in consequence of this.
herewith /he͞erwíth, -with/ *adv.* with this (esp. of an enclosure in a letter etc.).
heriot /hérriət/ *n. Brit. hist.* a tribute paid to a lord on the death of a tenant, consisting of a live animal, a chattel, or, orig., the return of borrowed equipment. [OE *heregeatwa* f. *here* army + *geatwa* trappings]
heritable /hérritəb'l/ *adj.* **1** *Law* **a** (of property) capable of being inherited by heirs-at-law (cf. MOVABLE). **b** capable of inheriting. **2** *Biol.* (of a characteristic) transmissible from parent to offspring. □□ **heritability** /-bílliti/ *n.* **heritably** *adv.* [ME f. OF f. *heriter* f. eccl.L *hereditare*: see HEREDITABLE]
■ **2** see HEREDITARY 1.
heritage /hérritij/ *n.* **1** anything that is or may be inherited. **2** inherited circumstances, benefits, etc. (*a heritage of confusion*). **3** a nation's historic buildings, monuments, countryside, etc., esp. when regarded as worthy of preservation. **4** *Bibl.* **a** the ancient Israelites. **b** the Church. [ME f. OF (as HERITABLE)]
■ **1** bequest, inheritance, legacy, patrimony; birthright. **2** legacy, inheritance.
heritor /hérritər/ *n.* (esp. in Scottish Law) a person who inherits. [ME f. AF *heriter*, OF *heritier* (as HEREDITARY), assim. to words in -OR[1]]
herl var. of HARL.
herm /herm/ *n. Gk Antiq.* a squared stone pillar with a head (esp. of Hermes) on top, used as a boundary-marker etc. (cf. TERMINUS 6). [L *Herma* f. Gk *Hermēs* messenger of the gods]
hermaphrodite /hermáfrədīt/ *n.* & *adj.* ● *n.* **1 a** *Zool.* an animal having both male and female sexual organs. **b** *Bot.* a plant having stamens and pistils in the same flower. **2** a human being in which both male and female sex organs are present, or in which the sex organs contain both ovarian and testicular tissue. **3** a person or thing combining opposite qualities or characteristics. ● *adj.* **1** combining both sexes. **2** combining opposite qualities or characteristics. □ **hermaphrodite brig** *hist.* a two-masted sailing ship rigged on the foremast as a brig and on the mainmast as a schooner. □□ **hermaphroditic** /-díttik/ *adj.* **hermaphroditical** /-díttik'l/ *adj.* **hermaphroditism** *n.* [L *hermaphroditus* f. Gk *hermaphroditos*, orig. the name of a son of Hermes and Aphrodite in Greek mythology, who became joined in one body with the nymph Salmacis]
■ *n.* **1, 2** see BISEXUAL *n.* ● *adj.* **1** see BISEXUAL *adj.*
hermeneutic /hérminyóotik/ *adj.* concerning interpretation, esp. of Scripture or literary texts. □□ **hermeneutical** *adj.* **hermeneutically** *adv.* [Gk *hermēneutikos* f. *hermēneuō* interpret]
hermeneutics /hérminyóotiks/ *n.pl.* (also treated as *sing.*) *Bibl.* interpretation, esp. of Scripture or literary texts.
hermetic /herméttik/ *adj.* (also **hermetical**) **1** with an airtight closure. **2** protected from outside agencies. **3 a** of alchemy or other occult sciences (*hermetic art*). **b** esoteric. □ **hermetic seal** an airtight seal (orig. as used by alchemists). □□ **hermetically** *adv.* **hermetism** /hérmitiz'm/ *n.* [mod.L *hermeticus* irreg. f. *Hermes Trismegistus* thrice-greatest Hermes (as the founder of alchemy)]
■ **1** airtight, sealed; see also TIGHT *adj.* 4. **2** enclosed, protected, secured, sheltered, shielded, safe, impregnable. **3 a** see OCCULT *adj.* 1, 3. **b** see OCCULT *adj.* 2.
hermit /hérmit/ *n.* **1** an early Christian recluse. **2** any person living in solitude. □ **hermit-crab** any crab of the family Paguridae that lives in a cast-off mollusc shell for protection. **hermit thrush** a migratory N. American thrush, *Catharus guttatus*. □□ **hermitic** /-míttik/ *adj.* [ME f. OF (*h*)*ermite* or f. LL *eremita* f. Gk *erēmitēs* f. *erēmia* desert f. *erēmos* solitary]
■ recluse, eremite, anchorite, anchoress, solitary.
hermitage /hérmitij/ *n.* **1** a hermit's dwelling. **2** a monastery. **3** a solitary dwelling. [ME f. OF (*h*)*ermitage* (as HERMIT)]
hernia /hérniə/ *n.* (*pl.* **hernias** or **herniae** /-ni-ee/) the displacement and protrusion of part of an organ through the wall of the cavity containing it, esp. of the abdomen. □□ **hernial** *adj.* **herniary** *adj.* **herniated** *adj.* [L]
hero /he͞erō/ *n.* (*pl.* **-oes**) **1 a** a man noted or admired for nobility, courage, outstanding achievements, etc. (*Newton, a hero of science*). **b** a great warrior. **2** the chief male character in a poem, play, story, etc. **3** *Gk Antiq.* a man of superhuman qualities, favoured by the gods; a demigod. □ **hero's welcome** a rapturous welcome, like that given to a successful warrior. **hero-worship** *n.* **1** idealization of an admired man. **2** *Gk Antiq.* worship of the ancient heroes. ● *v.tr.* (**-worshipped**, **-worshipping**; *US* **-worshiped**,

-worshiping) worship as a hero; idolize. **hero-worshipper** a person engaging in hero-worship. [ME f. L *heros* f. Gk *hērōs*]

■ **1 a** champion, exemplar, luminary, notable; celebrity, star, superstar, idol. **b** knight, warrior, *hist.* paladin. **2** protagonist; (male) lead, star, leading man, principal. □ **hero-worship** (*n.*) **1** idolization, idealization, adoration; cultism; see also WORSHIP *n.* (*v.*) see WORSHIP *v.*

heroic /hirṓ-ik/ *adj.* & *n.* ● *adj.* **1 a** (of an act or a quality) of or fit for a hero. **b** (of a person) like a hero. **2 a** (of language) grand, high-flown, dramatic. **b** (of a work of art) heroic in scale or subject; unusually large or impressive. **3** of the heroes of Greek antiquity; (of poetry) dealing with the ancient heroes. ● *n.* (in *pl.*) **1 a** high-flown language or sentiments. **b** unduly bold behaviour. **2** = *heroic verse*. □ **the heroic age** the period in Greek history before the return from Troy. **heroic couplet** two lines of rhyming iambic pentameters. **heroic verse** a type of verse used for heroic poetry, esp. the hexameter, the iambic pentameter, or the alexandrine. □□ **heroically** *adv.* [F *héroïque* or L *heroicus* f. Gk *hērōikos* (as HERO)]

■ *adj.* **1** brave, courageous, bold, valiant, valorous, dauntless, stout-hearted, noble, upstanding, honourable, virtuous, staunch, steadfast, stalwart, intrepid, gallant, daring, fearless, manly; majestic, grand, august, towering, eminent, distinguished, prominent. **2 a** grand, high-flown, dramatic, bombastic, exaggerated, magniloquent, grandiose, extravagant. **b** epic, Homeric, wonderful; prodigious, larger than life, enormous, huge, titanic, colossal, stupendous. **3** epic, mythological, legendary, classical, fabulous. ● *n.* **1 b** (*heroics*) see BRAVADO.

heroi-comic /hírrō-ikómmik/ *adj.* (also **heroi-comical**) combining the heroic with the comic. [F *héroï-comique* (as HERO, COMIC)]

heroin /hérrō-in/ *n.* a highly addictive white crystalline analgesic drug derived from morphine, often used as a narcotic. [G (as HERO, from its effects on the user's self-esteem)]

heroine /hérrō-in/ *n.* **1** a woman noted or admired for nobility, courage, outstanding achievements, etc. **2** the chief female character in a poem, play, story, etc. **3** *Gk Antiq.* a demigoddess. [F *héroïne* or L *heroina* f. Gk *hērōinē*, fem. of *hērōs* HERO]

■ **1** see HERO 1a. **2** protagonist; (female) lead, star, leading lady, principal; diva, prima donna.

heroism /hérrō-iz'm/ *n.* heroic conduct or qualities. [F *héroïsme* f. *héros* HERO]

■ see BRAVERY.

heroize /hérrō-īz/ *v.* (also **-ise**) **1** *tr.* **a** make a hero of. **b** make heroic. **2** *intr.* play the hero.

heron /hérrən/ *n.* any of various large wading birds of the family Ardeidae, esp. *Ardea cinerea*, with long legs and a long S-shaped neck. □□ **heronry** *n.* (*pl.* **-ies**). [ME f. OF *hairon* f. Gmc]

herpes /hérpeez/ *n.* a virus disease with outbreaks of blisters on the skin etc. □ **herpes simplex** a viral infection which may produce blisters or conjunctivitis. **herpes zoster** /zóstər/ = SHINGLES. □□ **herpetic** /-péttik/ *adj.* [ME f. L f. Gk *herpēs -ētos* shingles f. *herpō* creep: *zoster* f. Gk *zōstēr* belt, girdle]

herpetology /hérpitólləji/ *n.* the study of reptiles. □□ **herpetological** /-təlójik'l/ *adj.* **herpetologist** *n.* [Gk *herpeton* reptile f. *herpō* creep]

Herr /hair/ *n.* (*pl.* **Herren** /hérrən/) **1** the title of a German man; Mr. **2** a German man. [G f. OHG *hērro* compar. of *hēr* exalted]

Herrenvolk /hérrənfolk, -fōk/ *n.* **1** the German nation characterized by the Nazis as born to mastery. **2** a group regarding itself as naturally superior. [G, = master-race (as HERR, FOLK)]

herring /hérring/ *n.* a N. Atlantic fish, *Clupea harengus*, coming near the coast in large shoals to spawn. □ **herring-gull** a large gull, *Larus argentatus*, with dark wing-tips. [OE *hǣring*, *hēring* f. WG]

herring-bone /hérringbōn/ *n.* & *v.* ● *n.* **1** a stitch with a zigzag pattern, resembling the pattern of a herring's bones. **2** this pattern, or cloth woven in it. **3** any zigzag pattern, e.g. in building. **4** *Skiing* a method of ascending a slope with the skis pointing outwards. ● *v.* **1** *tr.* **a** work with a herring-bone stitch. **b** mark with a herring-bone pattern. **2** *intr. Skiing* ascend a slope using the herring-bone technique.

Herrnhuter /háirnhōōtər, hérrən-/ *n.* a member of a Christian Moravian sect (see MORAVIAN). [G f. *Herrnhut* (= the Lord's keeping), name of their first German settlement]

hers /herz/ *poss.pron.* the one or ones belonging to or associated with her (*it is hers; hers are over there*). □ **of hers** of or belonging to her (*a friend of hers*).

herself /hərsélf/ *pron.* **1 a** *emphat. form* of SHE or HER (*she herself will do it*). **b** *refl. form* of HER (*she has hurt herself*). **2** in her normal state of body or mind (*does not feel quite herself today*). □ **be herself** act in her normal unconstrained manner. **by herself** see *by oneself*. [OE *hire self* (as HER, SELF)]

Herts. /haarts/ *abbr.* Hertfordshire.

hertz /herts/ *n.* (*pl.* same) the SI unit of frequency, equal to one cycle per second. ¶ Abbr.: **Hz.** [H. R. *Hertz*, Ger. physicist d. 1894]

Hertzian wave /hértsiən/ *n.* an electromagnetic wave of a length suitable for use in radio.

he's /heez, hiz/ *contr.* **1** he is. **2** he has.

hesitant /hézzit'nt/ *adj.* **1** hesitating; irresolute. **2** (of speech) stammering, faltering. □□ **hesitance** *n.* **hesitancy** *n.* **hesitantly** *adv.*

■ **1** undecided, hesitating, irresolute, uncertain, unresolved, ambivalent, in two minds, *Brit.* havering; see also CAUTIOUS. **2** halting, stammering, stuttering, faltering.

hesitate /hézzitayt/ *v.intr.* **1** (often foll. by *about, over*) show or feel indecision or uncertainty; pause in doubt (*hesitated over her choice*). **2** (often foll. by *to* + infin.) be deterred by scruples; be reluctant (*I hesitate to inform against him*). **3** stammer or falter in speech. □□ **hesitater** *n.* **hesitatingly** *adv.* **hesitation** /-táysh'n/ *n.* **hesitative** *adj.* [L *haesitare* frequent. of *haerēre haes-* stick fast]

■ **1** vacillate, dither, shilly-shally, waver, be in two minds, *Brit.* haver, *colloq.* dilly-dally. **2** hang back, think twice, demur; (*hesitate to*) be reluctant to, hold back from, baulk at, jib at, shrink from, scruple to, *colloq.* boggle at. **3** stammer, stutter, falter, sputter, splutter, stumble, hum *or* hem and haw *or* ha.

Hesperian /hespeériən/ *adj. poet.* **1** western. **2** (in Greek mythology) of or concerning the Hesperides (nymphs who guarded the garden of golden apples at the western extremity of the earth). [L *Hesperius* f. Gk *Hesperios* (as HESPERUS)]

hesperidium /héspərídiəm/ *n.* (*pl.* **hesperidia** /-diə/) a fruit with sectioned pulp inside a separable rind, e.g. an orange or grapefruit. [Gk *Hesperides* daughters of Hesperus, nymphs in Greek mythology who guarded a tree of golden apples]

Hesperus /héspərəss/ *n.* the evening star, Venus. [ME f. L f. Gk *hesperos* (adj. & n.) western, evening (star)]

hessian /héssiən/ *n.* & *adj.* ● *n.* **1** a strong coarse sacking made of hemp or jute. **2** (**Hessian**) a native of Hesse in Germany. ● *adj.* (**Hessian**) of or concerning Hesse. □ **Hessian boot** a tasselled high boot first worn by Hessian troops. **Hessian fly** a midge, *Mayetiola destructor*, whose larva destroys growing wheat (thought to have been taken to America by Hessian troops). [*Hesse* in Germany]

hest /hest/ *n. archaic* behest. [OE *hǣs* (see HIGHT), assim. to ME nouns in *-t*]

hetaera /hiteérə/ *n.* (also **hetaira** /-tīrə/) (*pl.* **-as, hetaerae** /-teéree/, or **hetairai** /-tīrī/) a courtesan or mistress, esp. in ancient Greece. [Gk *hetaira*, fem. of *hetairos* companion]

■ see PROSTITUTE *n.* 1a.

hetaerism /hitéeriz'm/ *n.* (also **hetairism** /-tíriz'm/) **1** a recognized system of concubinage. **2** communal marriage in a tribe. [Gk *hetairismos* prostitution (as HETAERA)]

hetero /héttərō/ *n.* (*pl.* **-os**) *colloq.* a heterosexual. [abbr.]
■ see STRAIGHT *n.* 4b.

hetero- /héttərō/ *comb. form* other, different (often opp. HOMO-). [Gk *heteros* other]

heterochromatic /héttərōkrəmáttik/ *adj.* of several colours.

heteroclite /héttərōklīt/ *adj.* & *n.* ● *adj.* **1** abnormal. **2** *Gram.* (esp. of a noun) irregularly declined. ● *n.* **1** an abnormal thing or person. **2** *Gram.* an irregularly declined word, esp. a noun. [LL *heteroclitus* f. Gk (as HETERO-, *klitos* f. *klinō* bend, inflect)]
■ *adj.* **1** see UNORTHODOX.

heterocyclic /héttərōsíklik, -síklik/ *adj. Chem.* (of a compound) with a bonded ring of atoms of more than one kind.

heterodox /héttərōdoks/ *adj.* (of a person, opinion, etc.) not orthodox. □□ **heterodoxy** *n.* [LL *heterodoxus* f. Gk (as HETERO-, *doxos* f. *doxa* opinion)]
■ see *heretical* (HERETIC).

heterodyne /héttərōdīn/ *adj.* & *v. Radio* ● *adj.* relating to the production of a lower frequency from the combination of two almost equal high frequencies. ● *v.intr.* produce a lower frequency in this way.

heterogamous /héttəróggəməss/ *adj.* **1** *Bot.* irregular as regards stamens and pistils. **2** *Biol.* characterized by heterogamy or heterogony.

heterogamy /héttəróggəmi/ *n.* **1** the alternation of generations, esp. of a sexual and parthenogenic generation. **2** sexual reproduction by fusion of unlike gametes. **3** *Bot.* a state in which the flowers of a plant are of two types.

heterogeneous /héttərōjéeniəss/ *adj.* **1** diverse in character. **2** varied in content. **3** *Math.* incommensurable through being of different kinds or degrees. □□ **heterogeneity** /-jinée-iti/ *n.* **heterogeneously** *adv.* **heterogeneousness** *n.* [med.L *heterogeneus* f. Gk *heterogenēs* (as HETERO-, *genos* kind)]
■ **1, 2** see DIVERSE.

heterogenesis /héttərōjénnisiss/ *n.* **1** the birth of a living being otherwise than from parents of the same kind. **2** spontaneous generation from inorganic matter. □□ **heterogenetic** /-jinéttik/ *adj.*

heterogony /héttəróggəni/ *n.* the alternation of generations, esp. of a sexual and hermaphroditic generation. □□ **heterogonous** *adj.*

heterograft /héttərōgraaft/ *n.* living tissue grafted from one individual to another of a different species.

heterologous /héttəróllәgəss/ *adj.* not homologous. □□ **heterology** *n.*

heteromerous /héttərómmərəss/ *adj.* not isomerous.

heteromorphic /héttərōmórfik/ *adj.* (also **heteromorphous** /-mórfəss/) *Biol.* **1** of dissimilar forms. **2** (of insects) existing in different forms at different stages in their life cycle.

heteromorphism /héttərōmórfiz'm/ *n.* existing in various forms.

heteronomous /héttərónnəməss/ *adj.* **1** subject to an external law (cf. AUTONOMOUS). **2** *Biol.* subject to different laws (of growth etc.).

heteronomy /héttərónnəmi/ *n.* **1** the presence of a different law. **2** subjection to an external law.

heteropathic /héttərōpáthik/ *adj.* **1** allopathic. **2** differing in effect.

heterophyllous /héttərōfilləss/ *adj.* bearing leaves of different forms on the same plant. □□ **heterophylly** *n.* [HETERO- + Gk *phullon* leaf]

heteropolar /héttərōpṓlər/ *adj.* having dissimilar poles, esp. *Electr.* with an armature passing north and south magnetic poles alternately.

heteropteran /héttəróptərən/ *n.* any insect of the suborder Heteroptera, including bugs, with non-uniform fore-wings having a thickened base and membranous tip (cf. HOMOPTERAN). □□ **heteropterous** *adj.* [HETERO- + Gk *pteron* wing]

heterosexual /héttərōséksyooəl, -sékshooəl/ *adj.* & *n.* ● *adj.* **1** feeling or involving sexual attraction to persons of the opposite sex. **2** concerning heterosexual relations or people. **3** relating to the opposite sex. ● *n.* a heterosexual person. □□ **heterosexuality** /-séksyoo-álliti, -sékshoo-álliti/ *n.* **heterosexually** *adv.*
■ *adj.* **1, 2** see STRAIGHT *adj.* 9b. ● *n.* see STRAIGHT *n.* 4b.

heterosis /héttərṓsiss/ *n.* the tendency of a cross-bred individual to show qualities superior to those of both parents. [Gk f. *heteros* different]

heterotaxy /héttərōtaksi/ *n.* the abnormal disposition of organs or parts. [HETERO- + Gk *taxis* arrangement]

heterotransplant /héttərōtránzplaant, -tráanzplaant/ *n.* = HETEROGRAFT.

heterotrophic /héttərōtróffik/ *adj. Biol.* deriving its nourishment and carbon requirements from organic substances; not autotrophic. [HETERO- + Gk *trophos* feeder]

heterozygote /héttərōzígōt/ *n. Biol.* **1** a zygote resulting from the fusion of unlike gametes. **2** an individual with dominant and recessive alleles determining a particular characteristic. □□ **heterozygous** *adj.*

hetman /hétmən/ *n.* (*pl.* **-men**) a Polish or Cossack military commander. [Pol., prob. f. G *Hauptmann* captain]

het up /hét úp/ *adj. colloq.* excited, overwrought. [*het* dial. past part. of HEAT]
■ see JUMPY 1.

heuchera /hyṓōkərə, hóykərə/ *n.* any N. American herbaceous plant of the genus *Heuchera*, with dark-green round or heart-shaped leaves and tiny flowers. [mod.L f. J. H. von *Heucher*, Ger. botanist d. 1747]

heuristic /hyooristik/ *adj.* & *n.* ● *adj.* **1** allowing or assisting to discover. **2** *Computing* proceeding to a solution by trial and error. ● *n.* **1** the science of heuristic procedure. **2** a heuristic process or method. **3** (in *pl.*, usu. treated as *sing.*) *Computing* the study and use of heuristic techniques in data processing. □ **heuristic method** a system of education under which pupils are trained to find out things for themselves. □□ **heuristically** *adv.* [irreg. f. Gk *heuriskō* find]

hevea /héeviə/ *n.* any S. American tree of the genus *Hevea*, yielding a milky sap used for making rubber. [mod.L f. native name *hevé*]

HEW *abbr. US* Department of Health, Education, and Welfare.

hew /hyōō/ *v.* (*past part.* **hewn** /hyōōn/ or **hewed**) **1** *tr.* **a** (often foll. by *down*, *away*, *off*) chop or cut (a thing) with an axe, a sword, etc. **b** cut (a block of wood etc.) into shape. **2** *intr.* (often foll. by *at*, *among*, etc.) strike cutting blows. **3** *intr. US* (usu. foll. by *to*) conform. □ **hew one's way** make a way for oneself by hewing. [OE *hēawan* f. Gmc]
■ **1, 2** see CHOP[1] *v.* 1.

hewer /hyṓōər/ *n.* **1** a person who hews. **2** a person who cuts coal from a seam. □ **hewers of wood and drawers of water** menial drudges; labourers (Josh. 9:21).

hex /heks/ *v.* & *n. US* ● *v.* **1** *intr.* practise witchcraft. **2** *tr.* cast a spell on; bewitch. ● *n.* **1** a magic spell; a curse. **2** a witch. [Pennsylvanian G *hexe* (v.), *Hex* (n.), f. G *hexen*, *Hexe*]
■ *v.* **2** see BEWITCH 2. ● *n.* **1** see JINX *n.*

hexa- /héksə/ *comb. form* six. [Gk *hex* six]

hexachord /héksəkord/ *n.* a diatonic series of six notes with a semitone between the third and fourth, used at three different pitches in medieval music. [HEXA- + CHORD[1]]

hexad /héksad/ *n.* a group of six. [Gk *hexas -ados* f. *hex* six]

hexadecimal /héksədéssim'l/ *adj.* & *n.* esp. *Computing.* ● *adj.* relating to or using a system of numerical notation that has 16 rather than 10 as a base. ● *n.* the hexadecimal system; hexadecimal notation. □□ **hexadecimally** *adv.*

hexagon /héksəgən/ *n.* a plane figure with six sides and angles. ▫▫ **hexagonal** /-sággən'l/ *adj.* [LL *hexagonum* f. Gk (as HEXA-, -GON)]

hexagram /héksəgram/ *n.* **1** a figure formed by two intersecting equilateral triangles. **2** a figure of six lines. [HEXA- + Gk *gramma* line]

hexahedron /héksəhéedrən/ *n.* a solid figure with six faces. ▫▫ **hexahedral** *adj.* [Gk (as HEXA-, -HEDRON)]

hexameter /heksámmitər/ *n.* a line or verse of six metrical feet. ▫ **dactylic hexameter** a hexameter having five dactyls and a spondee or trochee, any of the first four feet, and sometimes the fifth, being replaceable by a spondee. ▫▫ **hexametric** /-səmétrik/ *adj.* **hexametrist** *n.* [ME f. L f. Gk *hexametros* (as HEXA-, *metron* measure)]

hexane /héksayn/ *n. Chem.* a liquid hydrocarbon of the alkane series. ¶ Chem. formula: C_6H_{14}. [HEXA- + -ANE[2]]

hexapla /héksəplə/ *n.* a sixfold text, esp. of the Old Testament, in parallel columns. [Gk neut. pl. of *hexaploos* (as HEXA-, *ploos* -fold), orig. of Origen's OT text]

hexapod /héksəpod/ *n.* & *adj.* ● *n.* any arthropod with six legs; an insect. ● *adj.* having six legs. [Gk *hexapous*, *hexapod-* (as HEXA-, *pous pod-* foot)]

hexastyle /héksəstīl/ *n.* & *adj.* ● *n.* a six-columned portico. ● *adj.* having six columns. [Gk *hexastulos* (as HEXA-, *stulos* column)]

Hexateuch /héksətyōōk/ *n.* the first six books of the Old Testament. [Gk *hex* six + *teukhos* book]

hexavalent /héksəváylənt/ *adj.* having a valency of six; sexivalent.

hexose /héksōz/ *n. Biochem.* a monosaccharide with six carbon atoms in each molecule, e.g. glucose or fructose. [HEXA- + -OSE[2]]

hey[1] /hay/ *int.* calling attention or expressing joy, surprise, inquiry, enthusiasm, etc. ▫ **hey presto!** a phrase of command, or indicating a successful trick, used by a conjuror etc. [ME: cf. OF *hay*, Du., G *hei*]

hey[2] var. of HAY[2].

heyday /háyday/ *n.* the flush or full bloom of youth, vigour, prosperity, etc. [archaic *heyday* expression of joy, surprise, etc.: cf. LG *heidi*, *heida*, excl. denoting gaiety]
■ see PRIME[1] *n.* 1.

HF *abbr.* high frequency.

Hf *symb. Chem.* the element hafnium.

hf. *abbr.* half.

HG *abbr.* **1** Her or His Grace. **2** Home Guard.

Hg *symb. Chem.* the element mercury. [mod.L *hydrargyrum*]

hg *abbr.* hectogram(s).

HGV *abbr. Brit.* heavy goods vehicle.

HH *abbr.* **1** Her or His Highness. **2** His Holiness. **3** double-hard (pencil-lead).

hh. *abbr.* hands (see HAND *n.* 13).

hhd. *abbr.* hogshead(s).

H-hour /áychowr/ *n.* the hour at which an operation is scheduled to begin. [*H* for *hour* + HOUR]

HI *abbr.* *US* **1** Hawaii (also in official postal use). **2** the Hawaiian Islands.

hi /hī/ *int.* calling attention or as a greeting. [parallel form to HEY[1]]

hiatus /hīáytəss/ *n.* (*pl.* **hiatuses**) **1** a break or gap, esp. in a series, account, or chain of proof. **2** *Prosody* & *Gram.* a break between two vowels coming together but not in the same syllable, as in *though oft the ear.* ▫▫ **hiatal** *adj.* [L, = gaping f. *hiare* gape]
■ **1** see SPACE *n.* 4.

hibernate /hībərnayt/ *v.intr.* **1** (of some animals) spend the winter in a dormant state. **2** remain inactive. ▫▫ **hibernation** /-náysh'n/ *n.* **hibernator** *n.* [L *hibernare* f. *hibernus* wintry]

Hibernian /hībérniən/ *adj.* & *n. archaic poet.* ● *adj.* of or concerning Ireland. ● *n.* a native of Ireland. [L *Hibernia*, *Iverna* f. Gk *Iernē* f. OCelt.]

Hibernicism /hībérnisiz'm/ *n.* an Irish idiom or expression; = BULL[3] 1. [as HIBERNIAN after *Anglicism* etc.]

Hiberno- /hībérnō/ *comb. form* Irish (*Hiberno-British*). [med.L *hibernus* Irish (as HIBERNIAN)]

hibiscus /hibískəss/ *n.* any tree or shrub of the genus *Hibiscus*, cultivated for its large bright-coloured flowers. Also called *rose-mallow*. [L f. Gk *hibiskos* marsh mallow]

hic /hik/ *int.* expressing the sound of a hiccup, esp. a drunken hiccup. [imit.]

hiccup /híkkup/ *n.* & *v.* (also **hiccough**) ● *n.* **1 a** an involuntary spasm of the diaphragm and respiratory organs, with sudden closure of the glottis and characteristic cough-like sound. **b** (in *pl.*) an attack of such spasms. **2** a temporary or minor stoppage or difficulty. ● *v.* **1** *intr.* make a hiccup or series of hiccups. **2** *tr.* utter with a hiccup. ▫▫ **hiccupy** *adj.* [imit.]
■ *n.* **2** see *set-back* 1 (SET[1]).

hic jacet /hik jáyset, heek jákket/ *n.* an epitaph. [L, = here lies]

hick /hik/ *n.* esp. *US colloq.* a country dweller; a provincial. [pet-form of the name *Richard*: cf. DICK[1]]
■ see PROVINCIAL *n.*

hickey /híkki/ *n.* (*pl.* **-eys**) *US colloq.* a gadget (cf. DOOHICKEY). [20th c.: orig. unkn.]
■ see GADGET.

hickory /híkkəri/ *n.* (*pl.* **-ies**) **1** any N. American tree of the genus *Carya*, yielding tough heavy wood and bearing nutlike edible fruits (see PECAN). **2 a** the wood of these trees. **b** a stick made of this. [native Virginian *pohickery*]

hid *past* of HIDE[1].

hidalgo /hidálgō/ *n.* (*pl.* **-os**) a Spanish gentleman. [Sp. f. *hijo dalgo* son of something]
■ caballero, don.

hidden *past part.* of HIDE[1] ▫▫ **hiddenness** *n.*

hide[1] /hīd/ *v.* & *n.* ● *v.* (*past* **hid**; *past part.* **hidden** /hídd'n/ or *archaic* **hid**) **1** *tr.* put or keep out of sight (*hid it under the cushion*; *hid her in the cupboard*). **2** *intr.* conceal oneself. **3** *tr.* (usu. foll. by *from*) keep (a fact) secret (*hid his real motive from her*). **4** *tr.* conceal (a thing) from sight intentionally or not (*trees hid the house*). ● *n. Brit.* a camouflaged shelter used for observing wildlife or hunting animals. ▫ **hidden agenda** a secret motivation behind a policy, statement, etc.; an ulterior motive. **hidden reserves** extra profits, resources, etc. kept concealed in reserve. **hide-and-seek 1** a children's game in which one or more players seek a child or children hiding. **2** a process of attempting to find an evasive person or thing. **hide one's head** keep out of sight, esp. from shame. **hide one's light under a bushel** conceal one's merits (Matthew 5:15). **hide out** (or **up**) remain in concealment. **hide-out** *colloq.* a hiding-place. ▫▫ **hidden** *adj.* **hider** *n.* [OE *hȳdan* f. WG]
■ *v.* **1** conceal, secrete, cache, squirrel away, cover up. **2** go underground, take cover, lie low, lurk, go to ground, drop out of sight, go into hiding, hide out *or* up, *US colloq.* hole up, *sl.* lie doggo. **3** conceal, cover (up), mask, camouflage, disguise, veil, shroud, screen, keep secret *or* quiet, suppress, hush (up), repress, silence; (*hide from*) keep from. **4** conceal, blot out; see also OBSCURE *v.* 3.
▫ **hide-out** see HIDEAWAY. ▫▫ **hidden** concealed, secret, obscure(d), occult, veiled, cryptic, recondite, arcane, covert, esoteric, unseen, private.

hide[2] /hīd/ *n.* & *v.* ● *n.* **1** the skin of an animal, esp. when tanned or dressed. **2** *colloq.* the human skin (*saved his own hide*; *I'll tan your hide*). **3** esp. *Austral.* & *NZ colloq.* impudence, effrontery, nerve. ● *v.tr. colloq.* flog. ▫▫ **hided** *adj.* (also in *comb.*). [OE *hȳd* f. Gmc]
■ *n.* **1** pelt, skin, fell. ● *v.* whip, lash, flail, beat, thrash; see also FLOG 1a.

hide[3] /hīd/ *n.* a former measure of land large enough to support a family and its dependants, usu. between 60 and 120 acres. [OE *hī(gi)d* f. *hīw-*, *hīg-* household]

hideaway /hīdəway/ *n.* a hiding-place or place of retreat.

■ refuge, haven, retreat, sanctuary, hiding-place, lair, den, hole, *colloq.* hidey-hole, hide-out.

hidebound /hīdbownd/ *adj.* **1 a** narrow-minded; bigoted. **b** (of the law, rules, etc.) constricted by tradition. **2** (of cattle) with the skin clinging close as a result of bad feeding. [HIDE[2] + BOUND[4]]

■ **1 a** narrow-minded, bigoted, illiberal, intolerant; strait-laced, conventional, conservative, reactionary, rigid, set in one's ways, inflexible, intractable. **b** bound, constricted, constrained, limited, restricted, hemmed in.

hideosity /híddióssiti/ *n.* (*pl.* **-ies**) **1** a hideous object. **2** hideousness.

hideous /híddiəss/ *adj.* **1** frightful, repulsive, or revolting, to the senses or the mind (*a hideous monster*; *a hideous pattern*). **2** *colloq.* unpleasant. □□ **hideously** *adv.* **hideousness** *n.* [ME *hidous* f. AF *hidous*, OF *hidos*, *-eus*, f. OF *hide*, *hisde* fear, of unkn. orig.]

■ **1** frightful, grotesque, ugly, repulsive, revolting, disgusting, horrible, repellent, monstrous, beastly, gorgonian, unsightly, ghastly, grisly, gruesome, foul, abhorrent, heinous, horrifying, appalling, outrageous, abominable, vile, shocking, loathsome, contemptible, hateful, odious, atrocious, horrific, damnable, execrable. **2** see REVOLTING.

hidey-hole /hīdihōl/ *n. colloq.* a hiding-place.

hiding[1] /hīding/ *n. colloq.* a thrashing. □ **on a hiding to nothing** in a position from which there can be no successful outcome. [HIDE[2] + -ING[1]]

■ see *thrashing* (THRASH).

hiding[2] /hīding/ *n.* **1** the act or an instance of hiding. **2** the state of remaining hidden (*go into hiding*). □ **hiding-place** a place of concealment. [ME, f. HIDE[1] + -ING[1]]

hidrosis /hidrṓsiss, hī-/ *n. Med.* perspiration. □□ **hidrotic** /-dróttik/ *adj.* [mod.L f. Gk f. *hidrōs* sweat]

hie /hī/ *v.intr.* & *refl.* (**hies, hied, hieing** or **hying**) *archaic* or *poet.* go quickly (*hie to your chamber*; *hied him to the chase*). [OE *hīgian* strive, pant, of unkn. orig.]

■ see RUN *v.* 1, 3.

hierarch /hīraark/ *n.* **1** a chief priest. **2** an archbishop. □□ **hierarchal** /-aárk'l/ *adj.* [med.L f. Gk *hierarkhēs* f. *hieros* sacred + *-arkhēs* ruler]

hierarchy /hīraarki/ *n.* (*pl.* **-ies**) **1 a** a system in which grades or classes of status or authority are ranked one above the other (*ranks third in the hierarchy*). **b** the hierarchical system (of government, management, etc.). **2 a** priestly government. **b** a priesthood organized in grades. **3 a** each of the three divisions of angels. **b** the angels. □□ **hierarchic** /-aárkik/ *adj.* **hierarchical** /-aárkik'l/ *adj.* **hierarchism** *n.* **hierarchize** *v.tr.* (also **-ise**). [ME f. OF *ierarchie* f. med.L (*h*)*ierarchia* f. Gk *hierarkhia* (as HIERARCH)]

■ **1** see ORDER *n.* 4.

hieratic /hīráttik/ *adj.* **1** of or concerning priests; priestly. **2** of the ancient Egyptian writing of abridged hieroglyphics as used by priests (opp. DEMOTIC). **3** of or concerning Egyptian or Greek traditional styles of art. □□ **hieratically** *adv.* [L f. Gk *hieratikos* f. *hieraomai* be a priest f. *hiereus* priest]

■ **1** see PRIESTLY.

hiero- /hīrō/ *comb. form* sacred, holy. [Gk *hieros* sacred + -o-]

hierocracy /hīrókrəsi/ *n.* (*pl.* **-ies**) **1** priestly rule. **2** a body of ruling priests. [HIERO- + -CRACY]

hieroglyph /hīrəglif/ *n.* **1 a** a picture of an object representing a word, syllable, or sound, as used in ancient Egyptian and other writing. **b** a writing consisting of characters of this kind. **2** a secret or enigmatic symbol. **3** (in *pl.*) *joc.* writing difficult to read. [back-form. f. HIEROGLYPHIC]

■ **1a, 2** see SIGN *n.* 2.

hieroglyphic /hīrəglíffik/ *adj.* & *n.* ● *adj.* **1** of or written in hieroglyphs. **2** symbolical. ● *n.* (in *pl.*) hieroglyphs; hieroglyphic writing. □□ **hieroglyphical** *adj.* **hieroglyphically** *adv.* [F *hiéroglyphique* or LL *hieroglyphicus* f. Gk *hieroglyphikos* (as HIERO-, *gluphikos* f. *gluphē* carving)]

hierogram /hīrōgram/ *n.* a sacred inscription or symbol.

hierograph /hīrōgraaf/ *n.* = HIEROGRAM.

hierolatry /hīróllətri/ *n.* the worship of saints or sacred things.

hierology /hīrólləji/ *n.* sacred literature or lore.

hierophant /hīrəfant/ *n.* **1** *Gk Antiq.* an initiating or presiding priest; an official interpreter of sacred mysteries. **2** an interpreter of sacred mysteries or any esoteric principle. □□ **hierophantic** /-fántik/ *adj.* [LL *hierophantes* f. Gk *hierophantēs* (as HIERO-, *phantēs* f. *phainō* show)]

hi-fi /hīfī/ *adj.* & *n. colloq.* ● *adj.* of high fidelity. ● *n.* (*pl.* **hi-fis**) a set of equipment for high-fidelity sound reproduction. [abbr.]

higgle /higg'l/ *v.intr.* dispute about terms; haggle. [var. of HAGGLE]

■ see HAGGLE *v.*

higgledy-piggledy /higg'ldipigg'ldi/ *adv.*, *adj.*, & *n.* ● *adv.* & *adj.* in confusion or disorder. ● *n.* a state of disordered confusion. [rhyming jingle, prob. with ref. to the irregular herding together of pigs]

■ *adv.* & *adj.* see *chaotic* (CHAOS). ● *n.* see CHAOS 1a.

high /hī/ *adj.*, *n.*, & *adv.* ● *adj.* **1 a** of great vertical extent (*a high building*). **b** (*predic.*; often in *comb.*) of a specified height (*one inch high*; *water was waist-high*). **2 a** far above ground or sea level etc. (*a high altitude*). **b** inland, esp. when raised (*High Asia*). **3** extending above the normal or average level (*high boots*; *jersey with a high neck*). **4** of exalted, esp. spiritual, quality (*high minds*; *high principles*; *high art*). **5 a** of exalted rank (*in high society*; *is high in the Government*). **b** important, serious, grave. **6 a** great; intense; extreme; powerful (*high praise*; *high temperature*). **b** greater than normal (*high prices*). **c** extreme in religious or political opinion (*high Tory*). **7** (of physical action, esp. athletics) performed at, to, or from a considerable height (*high diving*; *high flying*). **8 a** elated, merry. **b** *colloq.* (often foll. by *on*) intoxicated by alcohol or esp. drugs. **9** (of a sound or note) of high frequency; shrill; at the top end of the scale. **10** (of a period, an age, a time, etc.) at its peak (*high noon*; *high summer*; *High Renaissance*). **11 a** (of meat) beginning to go bad; off. **b** (of game) well-hung and slightly decomposed. **12** *Geog.* (of latitude) near the North or South Pole. **13** *Phonet.* (of a vowel) close (see CLOSE[1] *adj.* 14). ● *n.* **1** a high, or the highest, level or figure. **2** an area of high barometric pressure; an anticyclone. **3** *sl.* a euphoric drug-induced state. **4** top gear in a motor vehicle. **5** *US colloq.* high school. **6** (**the High**) *Brit. colloq.* a High Street, esp. that in Oxford. ● *adv.* **1** far up; aloft (*flew the flag high*). **2** in or to a high degree. **3** at a high price. **4** (of a sound) at or to a high pitch (*sang high*). □ **ace** (or **King** or **Queen** etc.) **high** (in card games) having the ace etc. as the highest-ranking card. **from on high** from heaven or a high place. **High Admiral** etc. a chief officer. **high altar** the chief altar of a church. **high and dry 1** out of the current of events; stranded. **2** (of a ship) out of the water. **high and low 1** everywhere (*searched high and low*). **2** (people) of all conditions. **high and mighty 1** *colloq.* arrogant. **2** *archaic* of exalted rank. **high-born** of noble birth. **high camp** sophisticated camp (cf. CAMP[2]). **high card** a card that outranks others, esp. the ace or a court-card. **high chair** an infant's chair with long legs and a tray, for use at meals. **High Church** *n.* a section of the Church of England emphasizing ritual, priestly authority, and sacraments. ● *adj.* of or relating to this section. **High Churchman** (*pl.* **-men**) an advocate of High Church principles. **high-class 1** of high quality. **2** characteristic of the upper class. **high colour** a flushed complexion. **high command** an army commander-in-chief and associated staff. **High Commission** an embassy from one Commonwealth country to another. **High Commissioner** the head of such an embassy. **High Court** (also in England **High Court of Justice**) a supreme court of justice for civil cases. **high day** a festal day. **High Dutch** see DUTCH. **high enema** an enema delivered into the colon. **higher animal** (or **plant**) an animal or plant evolved to a high degree. **higher court** *Law* a court that can overrule the decision of another.

the higher criticism see CRITICISM. **higher education** education at university etc., esp. to degree level. **higher mathematics** advanced mathematics as taught at university etc. **higher-up** *colloq.* a person of higher rank. **highest common factor** *Math.* the highest number that can be divided exactly into each of two or more numbers. **high explosive** an extremely explosive substance used in shells, bombs, etc. **high fashion** = HAUTE COUTURE. **high fidelity** the reproduction of sound with little distortion, giving a result very similar to the original. **high finance** financial transactions involving large sums. **high-flown** (of language etc.) extravagant, bombastic. **high-flyer** (or **-flier**) **1** an ambitious person. **2** a person or thing with great potential for achievement. **high-flying** reaching a great height; ambitious. **high frequency** a frequency, esp. in radio, of 3 to 30 megahertz. **high gear** see GEAR. **High German** see GERMAN. **high-grade** of high quality. **high hat 1** a tall hat; a top hat. **2** foot-operated cymbals. **3** a snobbish or overbearing person. **high-hat** ● *adj.* supercilious; snobbish. ● *v.* (**-hatted, -hatting**) *US* **1** *tr.* treat superciliously. **2** *intr.* assume a superior attitude. **high holiday** the Jewish New Year or the Day of Atonement. **high jinks** boisterous joking or merrymaking. **high jump 1** an athletic event consisting of jumping as high as possible over a bar of adjustable height. **2** *colloq.* a drastic punishment (*he's for the high jump*). **high-key** *Photog.* consisting of light tones only. **high kick** a dancer's kick high in the air. **high-level 1** (of negotiations etc.) conducted by high-ranking people. **2** *Computing* (of a programming language) that is not machine-dependent and is usu. at a level of abstraction close to natural language. **high life** (or **living**) a luxurious existence ascribed to the upper classes. **high-lows** *archaic* boots reaching over the ankles. **high mass** see MASS². **high-octane** (of petrol etc.) having good antiknock properties. **high old** *colloq.* most enjoyable (*had a high old time*). **high opinion of** a favourable opinion of. **high-pitched 1** (of a sound) high. **2** (of a roof) steep. **3** (of style etc.) lofty. **high places** the upper ranks of an organization etc. **high point** the maximum or best state reached. **high polymer** a polymer having a high molecular weight. **high-powered 1** having great power or energy. **2** important or influential. **high pressure 1** a high degree of activity or exertion. **2** a condition of the atmosphere with the pressure above average. **high priest 1** a chief priest, esp. Jewish. **2** the head of any cult. **high profile** exposure to attention or publicity. **high-profile** *adj.* (usu. *attrib.*) having a high profile. **high-ranking** of high rank, senior. **high relief** see RELIEF. **high-rise 1** (of a building) having many storeys. **2** such a building. **high-risk** (usu. *attrib.*) involving or exposed to danger (*high-risk sports*). **high road 1** a main road. **2** (usu. foll. by *to*) a direct route (*on the high road to success*). **high roller** *US sl.* a person who gambles large sums or spends freely. **high school 1** *Brit.* a grammar school. **2** *US* & *Sc.* a secondary school. **high sea** (or **seas**) open seas not within any country's jurisdiction. **high season** the period of the greatest number of visitors at a resort etc. **High Sheriff** see SHERIFF. **high sign** *US colloq.* a surreptitious gesture indicating that all is well or that the coast is clear. **high-sounding** pretentious, bombastic. **high-speed 1** operating at great speed. **2** (of steel) suitable for cutting-tools even when red-hot. **high-spirited** vivacious; cheerful. **high-spiritedness** = *high spirits*. **high spirits** vivacity; energy; cheerfulness. **high spot** *sl.* an important place or feature. **high-stepper 1** a horse that lifts its feet high when walking or trotting. **2** a stately person. **High Steward** see STEWARD *n.* 6. **high street** *Brit.* a main road, esp. the principal shopping street of a town. **high-strung** = *highly-strung*. **high table** a table on a platform at a public dinner or for the fellows of a college. **high tea** *Brit.* a main evening meal usu. consisting of a cooked dish, bread and butter, tea, etc. **high tech** *n.* = *high technology*. ● *adj.* **1** (of interior design etc.) imitating styles more usual in industry etc., esp. using steel, glass, or plastic in a functional way. **2** employing, requiring, or involved in high technology. **high technology** advanced technological development, esp. in electronics. **high-tensile** (of metal) having great tensile strength. **high tension** = *high voltage*. **high tide** the time or level of the tide at its flow. **high time** a time that is late or overdue (*it is high time they arrived*). **high-toned** stylish; dignified; superior. **high treason** see TREASON. **high-up** *colloq.* a person of high rank. **high voltage** electrical potential causing some danger of injury or damage. **high water 1** the tide at its fullest. **2** the time of this. **high-water mark 1** the level reached at high water. **2** the maximum recorded value or highest point of excellence. **high, wide, and handsome** *colloq.* in a carefree or stylish manner. **high wire** a high tightrope. **high words** angry talk. **high yellow** *US* a person of mixed race with a palish skin. **in high feather** see FEATHER. **the Most High** God. **on high** in or to heaven or a high place. **on one's high horse** *colloq.* behaving superciliously or arrogantly. **play high 1** play for high stakes. **2** play a card of high value. **run high 1** (of the sea) have a strong current with high tide. **2** (of feelings) be strong. [OE *hēah* f. Gmc]

■ *adj.* **1 a** tall, elevated, towering, *literary* lofty. **4** exalted, elevated, lofty, superior, great; high-class. **5 a** chief, leading, important, principal, foremost; see also SUPERIOR *adj.* 1. **b** important, consequential, grave, serious, weighty, momentous. **6 a** great, intense, huge, enormous, considerable, strong, extreme, powerful. **b** extreme, excessive; exorbitant, (*predic.*) *colloq.* stiff, steep. **c** hard-line, extreme; see also *fanatical* (FANATIC). **8 a** cheerful, exuberant, merry, elated, boisterous, exhilarated, excited, *colloq.* switched-on. **b** intoxicated, inebriated, drunk, drugged, tipsy, *colloq.* turned on, switched-on, on a trip, *sl.* loaded, stoned, spaced out, squiffed, *esp. Brit. sl.* squiffy; euphoric. **9** high-pitched, shrill, squeaky, sharp, penetrating, piercing, ear-splitting, acute; treble, soprano. **10** mid-; late. **11** off, tainted, gamy, ripe, *Brit. colloq.* pongy. ● *n.* **1** peak, record, height, high point, maximum, acme, apex. **3** see TRANCE *n.* ● *adv.* **1** far up, aloft; see also ABOVE *adv.* 1. **2** well, far, greatly, highly. **3** dear, (right) up, sky-high, *colloq.* through the roof. □ **high and dry** stranded, marooned, out on a limb, isolated, cut off. **high and low 1** see EVERYWHERE. **high and mighty 1** see ARROGANT. **high-born** see NOBLE *adj.* 1. **high-class** first-rate, superior, high-grade, *colloq.* top-drawer, tiptop, A1; aristocratic, upper-class, élite, select, exclusive, upper crust, county, *colloq.* classy, *US colloq.* tony. **high colour** flush, blush, redness; glow, radiance, rosiness, bloom. **high day** feast, feast-day, holy day, holiday, festal day, festival, celebration, fête, gala, red-letter day. **higher-up** see SUPERIOR *n.* **high-flown** see *bombastic* (BOMBAST). **high-flyer 1** high achiever, self-starter, *arriviste*, *colloq.* whiz-kid. **high-flying** see AMBITIOUS 1a. **high-grade** see SUPERIOR *adj.* 2a. **high-hat** (*adj.*) see HAUGHTY. **high jinks** see FROLIC *n.* 5. **high-pitched 1** see HIGH *adj.* 9 above. **2** see STEEP¹ *adj.* 1. **3** see REFINED 1. **high point** see ZENITH. **high-powered 1** see POWERFUL 1. **2** see POWERFUL 2. **high-profile** see PROMINENT 2. **high-ranking** see SENIOR *adj.* **high-risk** see DANGEROUS. **high-sounding** see PRETENTIOUS 2. **high-spirited** see VIVACIOUS. **high spirits** see VITALITY 1. **high spot** see SIGHT *n.* 2. **high-toned** see SUPERIOR *adj.* 2a. **high-up** see SUPERIOR *n.* **high, wide, and handsome** stylishly, with style; see also EASY *adv.*

highball /hī́bawl/ *n. US* **1** a drink of spirits and soda etc., served with ice in a tall glass. **2** a railway signal to proceed.

highbinder /hī́bīndər/ *n. US* a ruffian; a swindler; an assassin.

■ see THIEF.

highboy /hī́boy/ *n. US* a tall chest of drawers on legs.

■ see *chest of drawers*.

highbrow /hī́brow/ *adj.* & *n. colloq.* ● *adj.* intellectual; cultural. ● *n.* an intellectual or cultured person.

■ *adj.* scholarly, intellectual, learned, erudite, bookish, cultured, cultivated; cultural. ● *n.* scholar, *colloq.* egghead, brain; see also INTELLECTUAL *n.*

highfalutin /hīfəlóotin/ *adj.* & *n.* (also **highfaluting** /-ing/) *colloq.* ● *adj.* absurdly pompous or pretentious. ● *n.* highfalutin speech or writing. [HIGH + *-falutin*, of unkn. orig.]
■ *adj.* see POMPOUS 1.

high-handed /hīhándid/ *adj.* disregarding others' feelings; overbearing. □□ **high-handedly** *adv.* **high-handedness** *n.*
■ see *overbearing* (OVERBEAR).

highland /hīlənd/ *n.* & *adj.* ● *n.* (usu. in *pl.*) **1** an area of high land. **2** (**the Highlands**) the mountainous part of Scotland. ● *adj.* of or in a highland or the Highlands. □ **Highland cattle 1** cattle of a shaggy-haired breed with long curved widely-spaced horns. **2** this breed. **Highland dress** the kilt etc. **Highland fling** see FLING *n.* 3. □□ **highlander** *n.* (also **Highlander**). **Highlandman** *n.* (*pl.* **-men**). [OE *hēahlond* promontory (as HIGH, LAND)]
■ *n.* **1** see RISE *n.* 2.

highlight /hīlīt/ *n.* & *v.* ● *n.* **1** (in a painting etc.) a light area, or one seeming to reflect light. **2** a moment or detail of vivid interest; an outstanding feature. **3** (usu. in *pl.*) a bright tint in the hair produced by bleaching. ● *v.tr.* **1 a** bring into prominence; draw attention to. **b** mark with a highlighter. **2** create highlights in (the hair).
■ *n.* **2** see PIÈCE DE RÉSISTANCE. ● *v.* **1** see EMPHASIZE.

highlighter /hīlītər/ *n.* a marker pen which overlays colour on a printed word etc., leaving it legible and emphasized.

highly /hīli/ *adv.* **1** in a high degree (*highly amusing*; *highly probable*; *commend it highly*). **2** honourably; favourably (*think highly of him*). **3** in a high position or rank (*highly placed*). □ **highly-strung** very sensitive or nervous. [OE *hēalīce* (as HIGH)]
■ **1** greatly, tremendously, enthusiastically, warmly, immensely, hugely; extremely, exceptionally, extraordinarily, incomparably, decidedly; very, much, well, quite. **2** honourably, favourably, enthusiastically, approvingly, warmly, well. **3** well, influentially, powerfully, strongly, authoritatively, importantly.
□ **highly-strung** see NERVOUS 1–3, 5.

high-minded /hīmīndid/ *adj.* **1** having high moral principles. **2** *archaic* proud. □□ **high-mindedly** *adv.* **high-mindedness** *n.*
■ **1** see MORAL *adj.* 2.

high-muck-a-muck /hīmukəmuk/ *n.* *US* a person of great self-importance. [perh. f. Chinook *hiu* plenty + *muckamuck* food]

highness /hīniss/ *n.* **1** the state of being high (*highness of taxation*) (cf. HEIGHT). **2** (**Highness**) a title used in addressing and referring to a prince or princess (*Her Highness*; *Your Royal Highness*). [OE *hēanes* (as HIGH)]

hight /hīt/ *adj.* *archaic poet.*, or *joc.* called; named. [past part. (from 14th c.) of OE *hātan* command, call]

hightail /hītayl/ *v.intr.* *US colloq.* move at high speed.
■ see HURRY *v.* 1.

highway /hīway/ *n.* **1 a** a public road. **b** a main route (by land or water). **2** a direct course of action (*on the highway to success*). □ **Highway Code** *Brit.* the official booklet of guidance for road-users. **King's** (or **Queen's**) **highway** a public road, regarded as being under the sovereign's protection.
■ **1** see ROAD[1] 1.

highwayman /hīwaymən/ *n.* (*pl.* **-men**) *hist.* a robber of passengers, travellers, etc., usu. mounted. [HIGHWAY]
■ see ROBBER.

HIH *abbr.* Her or His Imperial Highness.

hijack /hījak/ *v.* & *n.* ● *v.tr.* **1** seize control of (a loaded lorry, an aircraft in flight, etc.), esp. to force it to a different destination. **2** seize (goods) in transit. **3** take over (an organization etc.) by force or subterfuge in order to redirect it. ● *n.* an instance of hijacking. □□ **hijacker** *n.* [20th c.: orig. unkn.]
■ *v.* **2** see STEAL *v.* 1.

hijra var. of HEGIRA.

hike /hīk/ *n.* & *v.* ● *n.* **1** a long country walk, esp. with rucksacks etc. **2** esp. *US* an increase (of prices etc.). ● *v.* **1** *intr.* walk, esp. across country, for a long distance, esp. with boots, rucksack, etc. **2** (usu. foll. by *up*) **a** *tr.* hitch up (clothing etc.); hoist; shove. **b** *intr.* work upwards out of place, become hitched up. **3** *tr.* esp. *US* increase (prices etc.). □□ **hiker** *n.* [19th-c. dial.: orig. unkn.]
■ *n.* **1** see WALK *n.* 2b. **2** see JUMP *n.* 3. ● *v.* **1** see WALK *v.* 1, 2. **2 a** see *hitch up*. **3** see *mark up* 1 (MARK[1]).

hila *pl.* of HILUM.

hilarious /hiláiriəss/ *adj.* **1** exceedingly funny. **2** boisterously merry. □□ **hilariously** *adv.* **hilariousness** *n.* **hilarity** /-lárriti/ *n.* [L *hilaris* f. Gk *hilaros* cheerful]
■ **1** funny, humorous, comical, amusing, entertaining, side-splitting, uproarious; *colloq.* hysterical, killing. **2** merry, gay, jolly, jovial, cheerful, cheery, joyous, joyful, mirthful, rollicking. □□ **hilariousness, hilarity** laughter, gaiety, joviality, jollity, merriment, mirth, exuberance, glee, cheerfulness, joyfulness, jubilation, elation, revelry, high spirits, vivacity.

Hilary term /hílləri/ *n.* *Brit.* the university term beginning in January, esp. at Oxford. [*Hilarius* bishop of Poitiers d. 367, with a festival on 13 Jan.]

hill /hil/ *n.* & *v.* ● *n.* **1 a** a naturally raised area of land, not as high as a mountain. **b** (as **the hills**) *Anglo-Ind.* = *hill-station*. **2** (often in *comb.*) a heap; a mound (*anthill*; *dunghill*). **3** a sloping piece of road. ● *v.tr.* **1** form into a hill. **2** (usu. foll. by *up*) bank up (plants) with soil. □ **hill and dale** (of a gramophone record) with groove-undulations in a vertical plane. **hill-billy** (*pl.* **-ies**) *US* **1** *colloq.*, often *derog.* a person from a remote rural area in a southern State (cf. HICK). **2** folk music of or like that of the southern US. **hill climb** a race for vehicles up a steep hill. **hill-fort** a fort built on a hill. **hill-station** *Anglo-Ind.* a government settlement, esp. for holidays etc. during the hot season, in the low mountains of N. India. **old as the hills** very ancient. **over the hill** *colloq.* **1** past the prime of life; declining. **2** past the crisis. **up hill and down dale** see UP. [OE *hyll*]
■ *n.* **1** elevation, rise, mound, knoll, hillock, hummock, foothill, tor, *N.Eng.* fell, *Sc.* brae, *US* butte, *archaic* mount; (*hills*) highlands, uplands, downs, downlands. **2** heap, pile, mound, stack; mountain. **3** slope, incline, acclivity, declivity, gradient. □ **hill-billy** see RUSTIC *n.*

hillock /hillək/ *n.* a small hill or mound. □□ **hillocky** *adj.*

hillside /hílsīd/ *n.* the sloping side of a hill.

hilltop /hiltop/ *n.* the summit of a hill.

hillwalking /hílwawking/ *n.* the pastime of walking in hilly country. □□ **hillwalker** *n.*

hilly /hílli/ *adj.* (**hillier, hilliest**) having many hills. □□ **hilliness** *n.*

hilt /hilt/ *n.* & *v.* ● *n.* **1** the handle of a sword, dagger, etc. **2** the handle of a tool. ● *v.tr.* provide with a hilt. □ **up to the hilt** completely. [OE *hilt(e)* f. Gmc]
■ *n.* see HANDLE *n.* 1.

hilum /hīləm/ *n.* (*pl.* **hila** /-lə/) **1** *Bot.* the point of attachment of a seed to its seed-vessel. **2** *Anat.* a notch or indentation where a vessel enters an organ. [L, = little thing, trifle]

HIM *abbr.* Her or His Imperial Majesty.

him /him/ *pron.* **1** *objective case* of HE (*I saw him*). **2** *colloq.* he (*it's him again*; *is taller than him*). **3** *archaic* himself (*fell and hurt him*). [OE, masc. and neut. dative sing. of HE, IT[1]]

Himalayan /himməláyən/ *adj.* of or relating to the Himalaya mountains in Nepal. [*Himalaya* Skr. f. *hima* snow + *ālaya* abode]

himation /himáttiən/ *n.* *hist.* the outer garment worn by the ancient Greeks over the left shoulder and under the right. [Gk]

himself /himsélf/ *pron.* **1 a** *emphat. form* of HE or HIM (*he himself will do it*). **b** *refl. form* of HIM (*he has hurt himself*). **2** in his normal state of body or mind (*does not feel quite himself today*). **3** esp. *Ir.* a third party of some importance; the master of the house. □ **be himself** act in his normal unconstrained manner. **by himself** see *by oneself*. [OE (as HIM, SELF)]

Hinayana /heénəyaánə/ *n.* = THERAVADA. [Skr. f. *hīna* lesser + *yāna* vehicle]

hind[1] /hīnd/ *adj.* (esp. of parts of the body) situated at the back, posterior (*hind leg*) (opp. FORE). □ **on one's hind legs** see LEG. [ME, perh. shortened f. OE *bihindan* BEHIND]
▪ see POSTERIOR *adj.* 2.

hind[2] /hīnd/ *n.* a female deer (usu. a red deer or sika), esp. in and after the third year. [OE f. Gmc]

hind[3] /hīnd/ *n. hist.* **1** esp. *Sc.* a skilled farm-worker, usu. married and with a tied cottage, and formerly having charge of two horses. **2** a steward on a farm. **3** a rustic, a boor. [ME *hine* f. OE *hīne* (pl.) app. f. *hī(g)na* genit. pl. of *hīgan*, *hīwan* 'members of a family' (cf. HIDE[3]): for *-d* cf. SOUND[1]]
▪ **1, 3** see PEASANT.

hinder[1] /híndər/ *v.tr.* (also *absol.*) impede; delay; prevent (*you will hinder him*; *hindered me from working*). [OE *hindrian* f. Gmc]
▪ hamper, delay, interrupt, hold back; thwart, frustrate, impede, interfere with, stymie, baulk, handicap, hobble, set back, put back, *archaic* let; stop, prevent, check, arrest, foil, forestall, bar, obstruct.

hinder[2] /hī́ndər/ *adj.* rear, hind (*the hinder part*). [ME, perh. f. OE *hinderweard* backward: cf. HIND[1]]

Hindi /híndi/ *n.* & *adj.* ● *n.* **1** a group of spoken dialects of N. India. **2** a literary form of Hindustani with a Sanskrit-based vocabulary and the Devanagari script, an official language of India. ● *adj.* of or concerning Hindi. [Urdu *hindī* f. *Hind* India]

hindmost /hī́ndmōst/ *adj.* furthest behind; most remote.
▪ see LAST[1] *adj.* 1, 5.

Hindoo *archaic* var. of HINDU.

hindquarters /hī́ndkwáwrtərz/ *n.pl.* the hind legs and adjoining parts of a quadruped.

hindrance /híndrənss/ *n.* **1** the act or an instance of hindering; the state of being hindered. **2** a thing that hinders; an obstacle.
▪ **2** obstruction, impediment, barrier, obstacle, restraint, encumbrance, *archaic* let; drawback, hitch, stumbling-block.

hindsight /hī́ndsīt/ *n.* **1** wisdom after the event (*realized with hindsight that they were wrong*) (opp. FORESIGHT). **2** the backsight of a gun.

Hindu /híndoo/ *n.* & *adj.* ● *n.* **1** a follower of Hinduism. **2** *archaic* an Indian. ● *adj.* **1** of or concerning Hindus or Hinduism. **2** *archaic* Indian. [Urdu f. Pers. f. *Hind* India]

Hinduism /híndoo-iz'm/ *n.* the main religious and social system of India, including belief in reincarnation, the worship of several gods, and a caste system as the basis of society. □□ **Hinduize** *v.tr.* (also **-ise**).

Hindustani /híndoostaáni/ *n.* & *adj.* ● *n.* **1** a language based on Western Hindi, with elements of Arabic, Persian, etc., used as a lingua franca in much of India. **2** *archaic* Urdu. ● *adj.* of or relating to Hindustan or its people, or Hindustani. [Urdu f. Pers. *hindūstānī* (as HINDU, *stān* country)]

hinge /hinj/ *n.* & *v.* ● *n.* **1 a** a movable, usu. metal, joint or mechanism such as that by which a door is hung on a side post. **b** *Biol.* a natural joint performing a similar function, e.g. that of a bivalve shell. **2** a central point or principle on which everything depends. ● *v.* **1** *intr.* (foll. by *on*) **a** depend (on a principle, an event, etc.) (*all hinges on his acceptance*). **b** (of a door etc.) hang and turn (on a post etc.). **2** *tr.* attach with or as if with a hinge. □ **stamp-hinge** a small piece of gummed transparent paper used for fixing postage stamps in an album etc. □□ **hinged** *adj.* **hingeless** *adj.* **hingewise** *adv.* [ME *heng* etc., rel. to HANG]
▪ *n.* **1 a** see PIVOT *n.* 1. ● *v.* **1 a** (*hinge on*) see DEPEND 1.

hinny[1] /hínni/ *n.* (*pl.* **-ies**) the offspring of a female donkey and a male horse. [L *hinnus* f. Gk *hinnos*]

hinny[2] /hínni/ *n.* (also **hinnie**) (*pl.* **-ies**) *Sc.* & *N.Engl.* (esp. as a form of address) darling, sweetheart. □ **singing hinny** a currant cake baked on a griddle. [var. of HONEY]

hint /hint/ *n.* & *v.* ● *n.* **1** a slight or indirect indication or suggestion (*took the hint and left*). **2** a small piece of practical information (*handy hints on cooking*). **3** a very small trace; a suggestion (*a hint of perfume*). ● *v.tr.* (often foll. by *that* + clause) suggest slightly (*hinted the contrary*; *hinted that they were wrong*). □ **hint at** give a hint of; refer indirectly to. [app. f. obs. *hent* grasp, lay hold of, f. OE *hentan*, f. Gmc, rel. to HUNT]
▪ *n.* **1** suggestion, clue, indication, tip, tip-off; intimation, allusion, innuendo, insinuation, implication, inkling; *colloq.* pointer. **2** clue, suggestion, tip, *colloq.* pointer; (*hints*) help, advice. **3** trace, suggestion, breath, whiff, undertone, tinge, whisper; taste, touch, dash, soupçon. ● *v.* suggest, imply, indicate, intimate, insinuate, mention. □ **hint at** allude to; see also REFER 7, 8.

hinterland /híntərland/ *n.* **1** the often deserted or uncharted areas beyond a coastal district or a river's banks. **2** an area served by a port or other centre. **3** a remote or fringe area. [G f. *hinter* behind + *Land* LAND]
▪ **1** see INTERIOR *n.* 2. **3** see STICK[1] *n.* 11.

hip[1] /hip/ *n.* **1** a projection of the pelvis and upper thigh-bone on each side of the body in human beings and quadrupeds. **2** (often in *pl.*) the circumference of the body at the buttocks. **3** *Archit.* the sharp edge of a roof from ridge to eaves where two sides meet. □ **hip-bath** a portable bath in which a person sits. **hip-bone** a bone forming the hip, esp. the ilium. **hip-flask** a flask for spirits etc., carried in a hip-pocket. **hip-joint** the articulation of the head of the thigh-bone with the ilium. **hip-length** (of a garment) reaching down to the hips. **hip-pocket** a trouser-pocket just behind the hip. **hip-** (or **hipped-**) **roof** a roof with the sides and the ends inclined. **on the hip** *archaic* at a disadvantage. □□ **hipless** *adj.* **hipped** *adj.* (also in comb.). [OE *hype* f. Gmc, rel. to HOP[1]]

hip[2] /hip/ *n.* (also **hep** /hep/) the fruit of a rose, esp. a wild kind. [OE *hēope*, *hīope* f. WG]

hip[3] /hip/ *adj.* (also **hep** /hep/) (**hipper, hippest** or **hepper, heppest**) *sl.* **1** following the latest fashion in esp. jazz music, clothes, etc.; stylish. **2** (often foll. by *to*) understanding, aware. □ **hip-cat** a hip person; a devotee of jazz or swing. **hip hop** a style of Black rock music or the street subculture that surrounds it (typically including graffiti art, rap, and break-dancing). □□ **hipness** *n.* [20th c.: orig. unkn.]
▪ **1** see STYLISH 1. **2** understanding, informed, aware, knowledgeable, knowing, perceptive, *esp. US* streetwise, *colloq.* with it; (*hip to*) alert to, in *or* up on, on to, *colloq.* wise to. □ **hip-cat** *sl.* cat, hipster; see also TRENDY *n.*

hip[4] /hip/ *int.* introducing a united cheer (*hip, hip, hooray*). [19th c.: orig. unkn.]

hippeastrum /hípiástrəm/ *n.* any S. American bulbous plant of the genus *Hippeastrum* with showy white or red flowers. [mod.L f. Gk *hippeus* horseman (the leaves appearing to ride on one another) + *astron* star (from the flower-shape)]

hipped /hipt/ *adj.* (usu. foll. by *on*) esp. *US sl.* obsessed, infatuated. [past part. of *hip* (v.) = make hip (HIP[3])]

hipper / híppər/ *n. Austral.* a soft pad used to protect the hip when sleeping on hard ground.

hippie /híppi/ *n.* (also **hippy**) (*pl.* **-ies**) *colloq.* **1** (esp. in the 1960s) a person of unconventional appearance, typically with long hair, jeans, beads, etc., often associated with hallucinogenic drugs and a rejection of conventional values. **2** = HIPSTER[2]. [HIP[3]]
▪ **1** bohemian, longhair, flower person, *colloq.* drop-out.

hippo /híppō/ *n.* (*pl.* **-os**) *colloq.* a hippopotamus. [abbr.]

hippocampus /híppəkámpəss/ *n.* (*pl.* **hippocampi** /-pī/) **1** any marine fish of the genus *Hippocampus*, swimming vertically and with a head suggestive of a horse; a sea horse. **2** *Anat.* the elongated ridges on the floor of each lateral ventricle of the brain, thought to be the centre of emotion and the autonomic nervous system. [L f. Gk *hippokampos* f. *hippos* horse + *kampos* sea monster]

hippocras /híppəkrass/ *n. hist.* wine flavoured with spices. [ME f. OF *ipocras* Hippocrates (see HIPPOCRATIC OATH), prob. because strained through a filter called 'Hippocrates' sleeve']

Hippocratic oath /híppəkráttik/ *n.* an oath formerly taken by doctors affirming their obligations and proper conduct. [med.L *Hippocraticus* f. *Hippocrates*, Gk physician of the 5th c. BC]

Hippocrene /híppəkreen/ *n. poet.* poetic or literary inspiration. [name of a fountain on Mount Helicon sacred to the Muses: L f. Gk f. *hippos* horse + *krēnē* fountain, as having been produced by a stroke of Pegasus' hoof]

hippodrome /híppədrōm/ *n.* **1** a music- or dancehall. **2** (in classical antiquity) a course for chariot races etc. **3** a circus. [F *hippodrome* or L *hippodromus* f. Gk *hippodromos* f. *hippos* horse + *dromos* race, course]
■ **1** see THEATRE 1a. **2** see STADIUM.

hippogriff /híppəgrif/ *n.* (also **hippogryph**) a mythical griffin-like creature with the body of a horse. [F *hippogriffe* f. It. *ippogrifo* f. Gk *hippos* horse + It. *grifo* GRIFFIN]

hippopotamus /híppəpóttəməss/ *n.* (*pl.* **hippopotamuses** or **hippopotami** /-mī/) **1** a large thick-skinned four-legged mammal, *Hippopotamus amphibius*, native to Africa, inhabiting rivers, lakes, etc. **2** (in full **pigmy hippopotamus**) a smaller related mammal, *Choeropsis liberiensis*, native to Africa, inhabiting forests and swamps. [ME f. L f. Gk *hippopotamos* f. *hippos* horse + *potamos* river]

hippy[1] var. of HIPPIE.

hippy[2] /híppi/ *adj.* having large hips.
■ see PLUMP[1] *adj.*

hipster[1] /hípstər/ *adj.* & *n. Brit.* ● *adj.* (of a garment) hanging from the hips rather than the waist. ● *n.* (in *pl.*) trousers hanging from the hips.

hipster[2] /hípstər/ *n. sl.* a person who is stylish or hip. □□ **hipsterism** *n.*

hiragana /he'erəgaánə/ *n.* the cursive form of Japanese syllabic writing or kana (cf. KATAKANA). [Jap., = plain kana]

hircine /húrsīn/ *adj.* goatlike. [L *hircinus* f. *hircus* he-goat]

hire /hīr/ *v.* & *n.* ● *v.tr.* **1** (often foll. by *from*) procure the temporary use of (a thing) for an agreed payment (*hired a van from them*). **2** esp. *US* employ (a person) for wages or a fee. **3** *US* borrow (money). ● *n.* **1** hiring or being hired. **2** payment for this. □ **for** (or **on**) **hire** ready to be hired. **hire-car** a car available for hire. **hired girl** (or **man**) *US* a domestic servant, esp. on a farm. **hire out** grant the temporary use of (a thing) for an agreed payment. **hire purchase** *Brit.* a system by which a person may purchase a thing by regular payments while having the use of it. □□ **hireable** *adj.* (*US* **hirable**). **hirer** *n.* [OE *hȳrian*, *hȳr* f. WG]
■ *v.* **1** rent, lease, hire out; charter (out). **2** engage, employ, appoint, enlist, take on, sign on. ● *n.* **1** rent, rental, lease, *Brit.* let; charter. **2** (hire) charge, cost, fee, price, rate, rent, rental. □ **hire out** rent (out), lease, *Brit.* let; charter.

hireling /hī́rling/ *n.* usu. *derog.* a person who works for hire. [OE *hȳrling* (as HIRE, -LING[1])]
■ see SUBORDINATE *n.*

hirsute /húrsyōōt/ *adj.* **1** hairy, shaggy. **2** untrimmed. □□ **hirsuteness** *n.* [L *hirsutus*]
■ **1** see HAIRY 1. **2** see SHAGGY.

hirsutism /húrsyootiz'm/ *n.* the excessive growth of hair on the face and body.

his /hiz/ *poss.pron.* **1** (*attrib.*) of or belonging to him or himself (*his house*; *his own business*). **2** (**His**) (*attrib.*) (in titles) that he is (*His Majesty*). **3** the one or ones belonging to or associated with him (*it is his*; *his are over there*). □ **his and hers** *joc.* (of matching items) for husband and wife, or men and women. **of his** of or belonging to him (*a friend of his*). [OE, genit. of HE, IT[1]]

Hispanic /hispánnik/ *adj.* & *n.* ● *adj.* **1** of or relating to Spain or to Spain and Portugal. **2** of Spain and other Spanish-speaking countries. ● *n.* a Spanish-speaking person, esp. one of Latin-American descent, living in the US. □□ **Hispanicize** /-nisīz/ *v.tr.* (also **-ise**). [L *Hispanicus* f. *Hispania* Spain]

Hispanist /híspənist/ *n.* (also **Hispanicist** /hispánnisist/) an expert in or student of the language, literature, and civilization of Spain.

Hispano- /hispánnō/ *comb. form* Spanish. [L *Hispanus* Spanish]

hispid /híspid/ *adj. Bot.* & *Zool.* **1** rough with bristles; bristly. **2** shaggy. [L *hispidus*]
■ see HAIRY 1.

hiss /hiss/ *v.* & *n.* ● *v.* **1** *intr.* (of a person, snake, goose, etc.) make a sharp sibilant sound, esp. as a sign of disapproval or derision (*audience booed and hissed*; *the water hissed on the hotplate*). **2** *tr.* express disapproval of (a person etc.) by hisses. **3** *tr.* whisper (a threat etc.) urgently or angrily (*'Where's the door?' he hissed*). ● *n.* **1** a sharp sibilant sound as of the letter *s*, esp. as an expression of disapproval or derision. **2** *Electronics* unwanted interference at audio frequencies. □ **hiss away** (or **down**) drive off etc. by hisses. **hiss off** hiss (actors etc.) so that they leave the stage. [ME: imit.]
■ *v.* **1** sizzle, splutter, spit; whistle; see also SCOFF[1] *v.* **2** catcall; see also JEER *v.* 1. ● *n.* **1** sibilance, hissing; catcall, jeer, boo, hoot, *colloq.* raspberry. **2** see INTERFERENCE 2.

hist /hist/ *int. archaic* used to call attention, enjoin silence, incite a dog, etc. [16th c.: natural excl.]

histamine /hístəmin, -meen/ *n. Biochem.* an organic compound occurring in injured body tissues etc., and also associated with allergic reactions. □□ **histaminic** /-mínnik/ *adj.* [HISTO- + AMINE]

histidine /hístideen/ *n. Biochem.* an amino acid from which histamine is derived. [Gk *histos* web, tissue]

histo- /hístō/ *comb. form* (before a vowel also **hist-**) *Biol.* tissue. [Gk *histos* web]

histochemistry /hístōkémmistri/ *n.* the study of the identification and distribution of the chemical constituents of tissues by means of stains, indicators, and microscopy. □□ **histochemical** *adj.*

histogenesis /hístōjénnisiss/ *n.* the formation of tissues. □□ **histogenetic** /-jinéttik/ *adj.*

histogeny /histójini/ *n.* = HISTOGENESIS. □□ **histogenic** /hístəjénnik/ *adj.*

histogram /hístəgram/ *n. Statistics* a chart consisting of rectangles (usu. drawn vertically from a base line) whose areas and positions are proportional to the value or range of a number of variables. [Gk *histos* mast + -GRAM]

histology /histólləji/ *n.* the study of the structure of tissues. □□ **histological** /hístəlójik'l/ *adj.* **histologist** /histólləjist/ *n.*

histolysis /históllisiss/ *n.* the breaking down of tissues. □□ **histolytic** /-təlíttik/ *adj.*

histone /hístōn/ *n. Biochem.* any of a group of proteins found in chromatin. [G *Histon* perh. f. Gk *histamai* arrest, or as HISTO-]

histopathology /hístōpəthólləji/ *n.* **1** changes in tissues caused by disease. **2** the study of these.

historian /histórian/ *n.* **1** a writer of history, esp. a critical analyst, rather than a compiler. **2** a person learned in or studying history (*English historian*; *ancient historian*). [F *historien* f. L (as HISTORY)]

historiated /históriaytid/ *adj.* = STORIATED. [med.L *historiare* (as HISTORY)]

historic /histórrik/ *adj.* **1** famous or important in history or potentially so (*a historic moment*). **2** *Gram.* (of a tense) normally used in the narration of past events (esp. Latin & Greek imperfect and pluperfect; (cf. PRIMARY)). **3** *archaic* or *disp.* = HISTORICAL. □ **historic infinitive** the infinitive when used instead of the indicative. **historic present** the present tense used instead of the past in vivid narration. [L *historicus* f. Gk *historikos* (as HISTORY)]

■ **1** momentous, important, noteworthy, significant, red-letter, notable, signal; celebrated, famous, distinguished, prominent, great, unforgettable, memorable.

historical /histórrik'l/ *adj.* **1** of or concerning history (*historical evidence*). **2** belonging to history, not to prehistory or legend. **3** (of the study of a subject) based on an analysis of its development over a period. **4** belonging to the past, not the present. **5** (of a novel, a film, etc.) dealing or professing to deal with historical events. **6** in connection with history, from the historian's point of view (*of purely historical interest*). □□ **historically** *adv.*

■ **1, 2** factual, true, verifiable, reliable, real, authentic, recorded, documented. **3** period; chronological. **4** see PAST *adj.* 1. **5** period.

historicism /histórrisiz'm/ *n.* **1 a** the theory that social and cultural phenomena are determined by history. **b** the belief that historical events are governed by laws. **2** the tendency to regard historical development as the most basic aspect of human existence. **3** an excessive regard for past styles etc. □□ **historicist** *n.* [HISTORIC after G *Historismus*]

historicity /histərissiti/ *n.* the historical genuineness of an event etc.

historiographer /histórióg rəfər/ *n.* **1** an expert in or student of historiography. **2** a writer of history, esp. an official historian. [ME f. F *historiographe* or f. LL *historiographus* f. Gk *historiographos* (as HISTORY, -GRAPHER)]

historiography /histórióg rəfi/ *n.* **1** the writing of history. **2** the study of history-writing. □□ **historiographic** /-riəgráffik/ *adj.* **historiographical** /-riəgráffik'l/ *adj.* [med.L *historiographia* f. Gk *historiographia* (as HISTORY, -GRAPHY)]

history /histəri, -tri/ *n.* (*pl.* **-ies**) **1** a continuous, usu. chronological, record of important or public events. **2 a** the study of past events, esp. human affairs. **b** the total accumulation of past events, esp. relating to human affairs or to the accumulation of developments connected with a particular nation, person, thing, etc. (*our island history*; *the history of astronomy*). **c** the past in general; antiquity. **3** an eventful past (*this house has a history*). **4 a** a systematic or critical account of or research into a past event or events etc. **b** a similar record or account of natural phenomena. **5** a historical play. □ **make history 1** influence the course of history. **2** do something memorable. [ME f. L *historia* f. Gk *historia* finding out, narrative, history f. *histōr* learned, wise man, rel. to WIT[2]]

■ **1** account, description, story, record, chronicle, narrative; annals. **2 b** tale, experience(s); biography, memoir; see also STORY[1] 2, 4. **c** ancient history, the past, yesterday, *archaic* olden days, antiquity, *literary* yesteryear. **3** past, reputation, background, life. **4** report; see also INQUIRY 1.

histrionic /histriónnik/ *adj.* & *n.* ● *adj.* **1** of or concerning actors or acting. **2** (of behaviour) theatrical, dramatic. ● *n.* **1** (in *pl.*) **a** insincere and dramatic behaviour designed to impress. **b** theatricals; theatrical art. **2** *archaic* an actor. □□ **histrionically** *adv.* [LL *histrionicus* f. L *histrio -onis* actor]

■ *adj.* **1** see DRAMATIC 1. **2** see DRAMATIC 4.

hit /hit/ *v.* & *n.* ● *v.* (**hitting**; *past* and *past part.* **hit**) **1** *tr.* **a** strike with a blow or a missile. **b** (of a moving body) strike (*the plane hit the ground*). **c** reach (a target, a person, etc.) with a directed missile (*hit the window with the ball*). **2** *tr.* cause to suffer or affect adversely; wound (*the loss hit him hard*). **3** *intr.* (often foll. by *at*, *against*, *upon*) direct a blow. **4** *tr.* (often foll. by *against*, *on*) knock (a part of the body) (*hit his head on the door-frame*). **5** *tr.* light upon; get at (a thing aimed at) (*he's hit the truth at last*; *tried to hit the right tone in his apology*) (see *hit on*). **6** *tr. colloq.* **a** encounter (*hit a snag*). **b** arrive at (*hit an all-time low*; *hit the town*). **c** indulge in, esp. liquor etc. (*hit the bottle*). **7** *tr.* esp. *US sl.* rob or kill. **8** *tr.* occur forcefully to (*the seriousness of the situation only hit him later*). **9** *tr. Sport* **a** propel (a ball etc.) with a bat etc. to score runs or points. **b** score (runs etc.) in this way. **c** (usu. foll. by *for*) strike (a ball or a bowler) for so many runs (*hit him for six*). **10** *tr.* represent exactly. **11** *tr. US*, *Austral.*, & *NZ sl.* (often foll. by *up*) ask (a person) for; beg. ● *n.* **1 a** a blow; a stroke. **b** a collision. **2** a shot etc. that hits its target. **3** *colloq.* a popular success in entertainment. **4** a stroke of sarcasm, wit, etc. **5** a stroke of good luck. **6** esp. *US sl.* **a** a murder or other violent crime. **b** a drug injection etc. **7** a successful attempt. □ **hit and run** cause (accidental or wilful) damage and escape or leave the scene before being discovered. **hit-and-run** *attrib.adj.* relating to or (of a person) committing an act of this kind. **hit back** retaliate. **hit below the belt 1** esp. *Boxing* give a foul blow. **2** treat or behave unfairly. **hit for six** *Brit.* defeat in argument. **hit the hay** (or **sack**) *colloq.* go to bed. **hit the headlines** see HEADLINE. **hit home** make a salutary impression. **hit it off** (often foll. by *with*, *together*) agree or be congenial. **hit list** *sl.* a list of prospective victims. **hit man** (*pl.* **hit men**) *sl.* a hired assassin. **hit the nail on the head** state the truth exactly. **hit on** (or **upon**) find (what is sought), esp. by chance. **hit-or-miss** aimed or done carelessly. **hit out** deal vigorous physical or verbal blows (*hit out at her enemies*). **hit-out** *n. Austral. sl.* a brisk gallop. **hit parade** *colloq.* a list of the current best-selling records of popular music. **hit the road** (*US* **trail**) *sl.* depart. **hit the roof** see ROOF. **hit up** *Cricket* score (runs) energetically. **hit wicket** *Cricket* be out by striking the wicket with the bat etc. **make a hit** (usu. foll. by *with*) be successful or popular. □□ **hitter** *n.* [ME f. OE *hittan* f. ON *hitta* meet with, of unkn. orig.]

■ *v.* **1 a** strike, cuff, smack, knock, bash, thump, punch, buffet, slap, swat, spank, beat, batter, belabour, clout, *archaic or literary* smite, *colloq.* thwack, whack, sock, clip, swipe, bop, lambaste, *Austral.* & *NZ colloq.* dong, *sl.* belt, wallop, whop, clobber, crown, conk, paste, zap, *Austral. sl.* quilt; bludgeon, club, cudgel, thrash, pummel, flog, scourge, birch, cane, lash, flagellate, whip, horsewhip. **b** strike, collide with, smash *or* crash into, bump *or* bang into. **2** wound, hurt, touch; see also AFFECT[1] 2. **3** lash out; (*hit at*) swing at, *colloq.* swipe at. **4** see BEAT *v.* 2a. **5** light upon, discover; see also FIND *v.* 1a, 2a. **6 a** encounter, meet (with); see also FACE *v.* 3a. **b** reach, arrive at, come *or* get to, attain. **7** see ROB 1, KILL[1] *v.* 1a. **8** dawn on, enter a person's mind, occur to, strike. **9 a** propel, strike, bat, drive, *colloq.* swipe. **11** importune, beseech, petition, beg, implore, entreat, ask. ● *n.* **1 a** blow, stroke, punch, knock, strike, swat, smack, bump, *esp. US* bust, *colloq.* whack, thwack, bop, sock, *sl.* conk. **b** impact, bump, bang; see also COLLISION 1. **2** shot, bull's-eye. **3** success, triumph, coup, winner, sensation, *colloq.* smash (hit), sell-out. **6 a** murder, killing, slaying, assassination. **b** *sl.* bang. **7** see ACCOMPLISHMENT 3. □ **hit back** see RETALIATE 1. **hit for six** shoot down, make mincemeat of, tear apart, *colloq.* tear to shreds; see also DEFEAT *v.* 1. **hit the hay** (or **sack**) retire, go to bed, *colloq.* turn in, *Brit. sl.* kip (down). **hit home** strike home, affect; see also TOUCH *v.* 4. **hit it off** see *get along* 1. **hit man** see THUG. **hit the nail on the head** be accurate, correct, right, *or* precise, put one's finger on it **hit on** (or **upon**) come upon, happen on, chance on *or* upon, light on *or* upon, discover, find, uncover, unearth, stumble upon, arrive at, see, perceive, detect, discern; devise, think up, invent, dream up, come up with, work out. **hit-or-miss** see CASUAL *adj.* 3a, CARELESS 1, 2. **hit parade** top ten, top twenty, etc., *colloq.* charts. **hit the road** (*US* **trail**) see *beat it*.

hitch /hich/ *v.* & *n.* ● *v.* **1 a** *tr.* fasten with a loop, hook, etc.; tether (*hitched the horse to the cart*). **b** *intr.* (often foll. by *in*, *on to*, etc.) become fastened in this way (*the rod hitched in to the bracket*). **2** *tr.* move (a thing) with a jerk; shift slightly (*hitched the pillow to a comfortable position*). **3** *colloq.* **a** *intr.* = HITCHHIKE. **b** *tr.* obtain (a lift) by hitchhiking. ● *n.* **1** an impediment; a temporary obstacle. **2** an abrupt pull or push; a jerk. **3** a noose or knot of various kinds. **4** *colloq.* a free ride in a vehicle. **5** *US sl.* a period of service. □ **get hitched** *colloq.* marry. **half hitch** a knot formed by

passing the end of a rope round its standing part and then through the bight. **hitch up** lift (esp. clothing) with a jerk. **hitch one's wagon to a star** make use of powers higher than one's own. ▫▫ **hitcher** *n.* [ME: orig. uncert.]
▪ *v.* **1** fasten, connect, attach, join, unite, hook (up), link, fix; harness, tether. **2** jerk, tug, shift, pull, wrench, *colloq.* yank, hoick. ● *n.* **1** impediment, obstacle, snag, catch, difficulty, problem, hindrance, obstruction. **2** see JERK[1] *n.* 1, 2. **3** knot, noose; see also LOOP *n.* **4** lift, ride. ▫ **get hitched** see MARRY 1, 2a. **hitch up** pull up, hike up, hoist, haul up, raise, lift (up).

hitchhike /hích-hīk/ *v.* & *n.* ● *v.intr.* travel by seeking free lifts in passing vehicles. ● *n.* a journey made by hitchhiking. ▫▫ **hitchhiker** *n.*
▪ *v.* hitchhike, thumb a lift *or* ride, *US sl.* bum a ride.

hi-tech /hīték/ *n.* = *high tech.* [abbr.]

hither /hí*th*ər/ *adv.* & *adj.* usu. *formal* or *literary* ● *adv.* to or towards this place. ● *adj.* situated on this side; the nearer (of two). ▫ **hither and thither** (or **yon**) in various directions; to and fro. [OE *hider*: cf. THITHER]

hitherto /hi*th*ərtōō/ *adv.* until this time, up to now.
▪ see *previously* (PREVIOUS).

hitherward /hí*th*ərwərd/ *adv. archaic* in this direction.

Hitler /hítlər/ *n.* a person who embodies the authoritarian characteristics of Adolf Hitler, Ger. dictator d. 1945. ▫▫ **Hitlerite** /-rīt/ *n.* & *adj.*
▪ see TYRANT.

Hitlerism /hítləriz'm/ *n.* the political principles or policy of the Nazi Party in Germany. [HITLER]

Hittite /híttīt/ *n.* & *adj.* ● *n.* **1** a member of an ancient people of Asia Minor and Syria. **2** the language of the Hittites. ● *adj.* of or relating to the Hittites or their language. [Heb. *Ḥittīm*]

HIV *abbr.* human immunodeficiency virus, either of two retroviruses causing Aids.

hive /hīv/ *n.* & *v.* ● *n.* **1 a** a beehive. **b** the bees in a hive. **2** a busy swarming place. **3** a swarming multitude. **4** a thing shaped like a hive in being domed. ● *v.* **1** *tr.* **a** place (bees) in a hive. **b** house (people etc.) snugly. **2** *intr.* **a** enter a hive. **b** live together like bees. ▫ **hive off 1** separate from a larger group. **2 a** form into or assign (work) to a subsidiary department or company. **b** denationalize or privatize (an industry etc.). **hive up** hoard. [OE *hȳf* f. Gmc]
▪ *n.* **3** see SWARM[1] *n.* 1–3.

hives /hīvz/ *n.pl.* **1** a skin-eruption, esp. nettle-rash. **2** inflammation of the larynx etc. [16th c. (orig. Sc.): orig. unkn.]

hiya /hīyə/ *int. colloq.* a word used in greeting. [corrupt. of *how are you?*]

HK *abbr.* Hong Kong.

HL *abbr.* (in the UK) House of Lords.

hl *abbr.* hectolitre(s).

HM *abbr.* **1** Her (or His) Majesty('s). **2 a** headmaster. **b** headmistress.

hm *abbr.* hectometre(s).

h'm /hm/ *int.* & *n.* (also **hmm**) = HEM[2], HUM[2].

HMG *abbr.* Her or His Majesty's Government.

HMI *abbr.* Her or His Majesty's Inspector (of Schools).

HMS *abbr.* Her or His Majesty's Ship.

HMSO *abbr.* Her or His Majesty's Stationery Office.

HMV *abbr.* (in the UK) His Master's Voice.

HNC *abbr.* (in the UK) Higher National Certificate.

HND *abbr.* (in the UK) Higher National Diploma.

Ho *symb. Chem.* the element holmium.

ho /hō/ *int.* **1 a** an expression of surprise, admiration, triumph, or (often repeated as **ho! ho!** etc.) derision. **b** (in *comb.*) (*heigh-ho*; *what ho*). **2** a call for attention. **3** (in *comb.*) *Naut.* an addition to the name of a destination etc. (*westward ho*). [ME, imit.: cf. ON *hó*]

ho. *abbr.* house.

hoar /hor/ *adj.* & *n. literary* ● *adj.* **1** grey-haired with age. **2** greyish-white. **3** (of a thing) grey with age. ● *n.* **1** = *hoar-frost.* **2** hoariness. ▫ **hoar-frost** frozen water vapour deposited in clear still weather on vegetation etc. [OE *hār* f. Gmc]

hoard /hord/ *n.* & *v.* ● *n.* **1** a stock or store (esp. of money) laid by. **2** an amassed store of facts etc. **3** *Archaeol.* an ancient store of treasure etc. ● *v.* **1** *tr.* (often *absol.*; often foll. by *up*) amass (money etc.) and put away; store. **2** *intr.* accumulate more than one's current requirements of food etc. in a time of scarcity. **3** *tr.* store in the mind. ▫▫ **hoarder** *n.* [OE *hord* f. Gmc]
▪ *n.* **1** supply, stock, store, stockpile, accumulation, collection; repertoire, fund, reserve, cache, reservoir. ● *v.* **1** amass, collect, accumulate, assemble, gather, stockpile, lay in, save (up); put away, store, reserve, set aside, squirrel away, *colloq.* stash (away). **3** see MEMORIZE.

hoarding /hórding/ *n.* **1** *Brit.* a large, usu. wooden, structure used to carry advertisements etc. **2** a board fence erected round a building site etc., often used for displaying posters etc. [obs. *hoard* f. AF *h(o)urdis* f. OF *hourd, hort*, rel. to HURDLE]

hoarhound var. of HOREHOUND.

hoarse /horss/ *adj.* **1** (of the voice) rough and deep; husky; croaking. **2** having such a voice. ▫▫ **hoarsely** *adv.* **hoarsen** *v.tr.* & *intr.* **hoarseness** *n.* [ME f. ON *hārs* (unrecorded) f. Gmc]
▪ see HUSKY[1] 1.

hoarstone /hórstōn/ *n. Brit.* an ancient boundary stone.

hoary /hóri/ *adj.* (**hoarier, hoariest**) **1 a** (of hair) grey or white with age. **b** having such hair; aged. **2** old and trite (*a hoary joke*). **3** *Bot.* & *Zool.* covered with short white hairs. ▫▫ **hoarily** *adv.* **hoariness** *n.*
▪ **1 a** see WHITE *adj.* 1. **b** see AGED 2. **2** see MUSTY 3.

hoatzin /hwatséen/ *n.* a tropical American bird, *Opisthocomus hoatzin*, whose young climb by means of hooked claws on their wings. [native name, imit.]

hoax /hōks/ *n.* & *v.* ● *n.* a humorous or malicious deception; a practical joke. ● *v.tr.* deceive (a person) with a hoax. ▫▫ **hoaxer** *n.* [18th c.: prob. contr. f. HOCUS]
▪ *n.* swindle, imposture, trick, (practical) joke, cheat, *sl.* con, gyp, *Brit. sl.* cod, *US sl.* scam, snow job; deception, fraud, flimflam, humbug. ● *v.* **2** deceive, defraud, cheat, swindle, trick, fool, dupe, take in, hoodwink, delude, gull, bluff, *colloq.* bamboozle, *literary* cozen, *sl.* con, gyp.

hob[1] /hob/ *n.* **1 a** a flat heating surface for a pan on a cooker. **b** a flat metal shelf at the side of a fireplace, having its surface level with the top of the grate, used esp. for heating a pan etc. **2** a tool used for cutting gear-teeth etc. **3** a peg or pin used as a mark in quoits etc. **4** = HOBNAIL. [perh. var. of HUB, orig. = lump]

hob[2] /hob/ *n.* **1** a male ferret. **2** a hobgoblin. ▫ **play** (or **raise**) **hob** *US* cause mischief. [ME, familiar form of *Rob*, short for *Robin* or *Robert*]

hobbit /hóbbit/ *n.* a member of an imaginary race of half-sized people in stories by Tolkien. ▫▫ **hobbitry** *n.* [invented by J. R. R. Tolkien, Engl. writer d. 1973, and said by him to mean 'hole-dweller']

hobble /hóbb'l/ *v.* & *n.* ● *v.* **1** *intr.* **a** walk lamely; limp. **b** proceed haltingly in action or speech (*hobbled lamely to his conclusion*). **2** *tr.* **a** tie together the legs of (a horse etc.) to prevent it from straying. **b** tie (a horse's etc. legs). **3** *tr.* cause (a person etc.) to limp. ● *n.* **1** an uneven or infirm gait. **2** a rope, clog, etc. used for hobbling a horse etc. ▫ **hobble skirt** a skirt so narrow at the hem as to impede walking. ▫▫ **hobbler** *n.* [ME, prob. f. LG: cf. HOPPLE and Du. *hobbelen* rock from side to side]
▪ *v.* **1** limp, dodder, totter, stumble, shuffle, falter, shamble. **2, 3** shackle, fetter, restrain, trammel, impede; see also HINDER[1]. ● *n.* **1** shuffle, shamble, totter; see also LIMP[1] *n.*

hobbledehoy /hóbb'ldihoy/ *n. colloq.* **1** a clumsy or awkward youth. **2** a hooligan. [16th c.: orig. unkn.]
▪ see BOOR 1, 2.

hobby[1] /hóbbi/ *n.* (*pl.* **-ies**) **1** a favourite leisure-time activity or occupation. **2** *archaic* a small horse. **3** *hist.* an early type of velocipede. □□ **hobbyist** *n.* [ME *hobyn, hoby*, f. pet-forms of *Robin*: cf. DOBBIN]

■ **1** pastime, occupation, activity, sideline, pursuit, recreation, diversion.

hobby[2] /hóbbi/ *n.* (*pl.* **-ies**) any of several small long-winged falcons, esp. *Falco subbuteo*, catching prey on the wing. [ME f. OF *hobé, hobet* dimin. of *hobe* small bird of prey]

hobby-horse /hóbbihorss/ *n.* **1** a child's toy consisting of a stick with a horse's head. **2** a preoccupation; a favourite topic of conversation. **3** a model of a horse, esp. of wicker, used in morris dancing etc. **4** a rocking horse. **5** a horse on a merry-go-round.

hobday /hóbday/ *v.tr.* operate on (a horse) to improve its breathing. [F. T. *Hobday*, veterinary surgeon d. 1939]

hobgoblin /hóbgoblin/ *n.* a mischievous imp; a bogy; a bugbear. [HOB[2] + GOBLIN]

■ see IMP *n.* 2.

hobnail /hóbnayl/ *n.* a heavy-headed nail used for boot-soles. □ **hobnail** (or **hobnailed**) **liver** a liver having many small knobbly projections due to cirrhosis. □□ **hobnailed** *adj.* [HOB[1] + NAIL]

hobnob /hóbnob/ *v.intr.* (**hobnobbed, hobnobbing**) **1** (usu. foll. by *with*) mix socially or informally. **2** drink together. [*hob or nob* = give or take, of alternate drinking; earlier *hab nab*, = have or not have]

■ **1** associate, fraternize, consort, mingle, mix, keep company; (*hobnob with*) hang about *or* around with, rub shoulders with.

hobo /hṓbō/ *n.* (*pl.* **-oes** or **-os**) *US* a wandering worker; a tramp. [19th c.: orig. unkn.]

■ see TRAMP *n.* 1.

Hobson's choice /hóbs'nz/ *n.* a choice of taking the thing offered or nothing. [T. *Hobson*, Cambridge carrier d. 1631, who let out horses on the basis that customers must take the one nearest the door]

hock[1] /hok/ *n.* **1** the joint of a quadruped's hind leg between the knee and the fetlock. **2** a knuckle of pork; the lower joint of a ham. [obs. *hockshin* f. OE *hōhsinu*: see HOUGH]

hock[2] /hok/ *n. Brit.* a German white wine from the Rhineland (properly that of Hochheim on the river Main). [abbr. of obs. *hockamore* f. G *Hochheimer*]

hock[3] /hok/ *v.* & *n.* esp. *US colloq.* ● *v.tr.* pawn; pledge. ● *n.* a pawnbroker's pledge. □ **in hock 1** in pawn. **2** in debt. **3** in prison. [Du. *hok* hutch, prison, debt]

■ *v.* see PAWN[2] *v.*

hockey[1] /hókki/ *n.* **1** a game played between two teams on a field with curved sticks and a small hard ball. **2** *US* = *ice hockey*. □□ **hockeyist** *n.* (in sense 2). [16th c.: orig. unkn.]

hockey[2] var. of OCHE.

Hocktide /hóktīd/ *n. hist.* a festival formerly kept on the second Monday and Tuesday after Easter, orig. for money-raising. [ME: orig. unkn.]

hocus /hṓkəss/ *v.tr.* (**hocussed, hocussing**; *US* **hocused, hocusing**) **1** take in; hoax. **2** stupefy (a person) with drugs. **3** drug (liquor). [obs. noun *hocus* = HOCUS-POCUS]

hocus-pocus /hṓkəspṓkəss/ *n.* & *v.* ● *n.* **1** deception; trickery. **2 a** a typical verbal formula used in conjuring. **b** language intended to mystify; mumbo-jumbo. **3** conjuring, sleight of hand. ● *v.* (**-pocussed, -pocussing**; *US* **-pocused, -pocusing**) **1** *intr.* (often foll. by *with*) play tricks. **2** *tr.* play tricks on, deceive. [17th-c. sham L]

■ *n.* **1** trickery, sophistry, legerdemain, chicanery, deceit, deception, artifice, duplicity, mischief, pretence, humbug, flimflam, *Brit. colloq.* jiggery-pokery, *sl.* hanky-panky; sleight of hand. **2 a** abracadabra, hey presto. **b** mumbo-jumbo, incantation, nonsense, rigmarole, gibberish, *colloq.* gobbledegook. **3** magic, conjuring, jugglery, *formal* prestidigitation. ● *v.* **2** see DECEIVE 1.

hod /hod/ *n.* **1** a V-shaped open trough on a pole used for carrying bricks, mortar, etc. **2** a portable receptacle for coal. [prob. = dial. *hot* f. OF *hotte* pannier, f. Gmc]

hodden /hódd'n/ *n. Sc.* a coarse woollen cloth. □ **hodden grey** grey hodden; typical rustic clothing. [16th c.: orig. unkn.]

hoddie / hóddi/ *n. Austral.* a bricklayer's labourer; a hodman. [HOD + -IE]

Hodge /hoj/ *n. Brit.* a typical English agricultural labourer. [pet-form of the name *Roger*]

hodgepodge /hójpoj/ *n.* = HOTCHPOTCH 1, 2. [ME, assim. to HODGE]

Hodgkin's disease /hójkinz/ *n.* a malignant disease of lymphatic tissues usu. characterized by enlargement of the lymph nodes. [T. *Hodgkin*, Engl. physician d. 1866]

hodiernal /hóddi-érnəl, hṓ-/ *adj. formal* of the present day. [L *hodiernus* f. *hodie* today]

hodman /hódman/ *n.* (*pl.* **-men**) **1** a labourer who carries a hod. **2** a literary hack. **3** a person who works mechanically.

hodograph /hóddəgraaf/ *n.* a curve in which the radius vector represents the velocity of a moving particle. [Gk *hodos* way + -GRAPH]

hodometer /hədómmitər/ var. of ODOMETER.

hoe /hō/ *n.* & *v.* ● *n.* a long-handled tool with a thin metal blade, used for weeding etc. ● *v.* (**hoes, hoed, hoeing**) **1** *tr.* weed (crops); loosen (earth); dig up or cut down with a hoe. **2** *intr.* use a hoe. □ **hoe-cake** *US* a coarse cake of maize flour orig. baked on the blade of a hoe. **hoe in** *Austral.* & *NZ sl.* eat eagerly. **hoe into** *Austral.* & *NZ sl.* attack (food, a person, a task). □□ **hoer** *n.* [ME *howe* f. OF *houe* f. Gmc]

■ *v.* see TILL[3].

hoedown /hṓdown/ *n. US* a lively dance or dance-party.

hog /hog/ *n.* & *v.* ● *n.* **1 a** a domesticated pig, esp. a castrated male reared for slaughter. **b** any of several other pigs of the family Suidae, e.g. a wart-hog. **2** *colloq.* a greedy person. **3** (also **hogg**) *Brit. dial.* a young sheep before the first shearing. ● *v.* (**hogged, hogging**) **1** *tr. colloq.* take greedily; hoard selfishly. **2** *tr.* & *intr.* raise (the back), or rise in an arch in the centre. □ **go the whole hog** *colloq.* do something completely or thoroughly. **hog-tie** *US* **1** secure by fastening the hands and feet or all four feet together. **2** restrain, impede. □□ **hogger** *n.* **hoggery** *n.* **hoggish** *adj.* **hoggishly** *adv.* **hoggishness** *n.* **hoglike** *adj.* [OE *hogg, hocg*, perh. of Celt. orig.]

■ *n.* **2** see GLUTTON 1. ● *v.* **1** see TAKE *v.* 1, MONOPOLIZE. □□ **hoggish** greedy, avaricious, insatiable; gluttonous, voracious, *colloq.* piggish, *literary or joc.* edacious; acquisitive, possessive, self-seeking, selfish.

hogan /hṓgən/ *n.* an American Indian hut of logs etc. [Navajo]

hogback /hógbak/ *n.* (also **hog's back**) a steep-sided ridge of a hill.

hogg var. of HOG *n.* 3.

hogget /hóggit/ *n. Brit.* a yearling sheep. [HOG]

hoggin /hóggin/ *n.* **1** a mixture of sand and gravel. **2** sifted gravel. [19th c.: orig. unkn.]

hogmanay /hógmənáy/ *n. Sc.* **1** New Year's Eve. **2** a celebration on this day. **3** a gift of cake etc. demanded by children at hogmanay. [17th c.: perh. f. Norman F *hoguinané* f. OF *aguillanneuf* (also = new year's gift)]

hog's back var. of HOGBACK.

hogshead /hógz-hed/ *n.* **1** a large cask. **2** a liquid or dry measure, usu. about 50 imperial gallons. [ME f. HOG, HEAD: reason for the name unkn.]

■ **1** see KEG.

hogwash /hógwosh/ *n.* **1** *colloq.* nonsense, rubbish. **2** kitchen swill etc. for pigs.

■ **1** see NONSENSE. **2** see SWILL *n.* 2, 4.

hogweed /hógweed/ *n.* any of various coarse weeds of the genus *Heracleum*, esp. *H. sphondylium*.

ho-ho /hōhṓ/ *int.* expressing surprise, triumph, or derision. [redupl. of HO]

ho-hum /hṓhúm/ *int.* expressing boredom. [imit. of yawn]

hoick[1] /hoyk/ *v.* & *n. colloq.* ● *v.tr.* (often foll. by *out*) lift or pull, esp. with a jerk. ● *n.* a jerky pull; a jerk. [perh. var. of HIKE]
▪ *v.* see HITCH *v.* 2.

hoick[2] /hoyk/ *v.intr. sl.* spit. [perh. var. of HAWK[3]]

hoicks var. of YOICKS.

hoi polloi /hóy pəlóy/ *n.* (often prec. by *the*: see note below) **1** the masses; the common people. **2** the majority. ¶ Use with *the* is strictly unnecessary, since *hoi* = 'the', but this construction is very common. [Gk, = the many]
▪ **1** masses, herd, common herd, riff-raff, rabble, *canaille*, common people, crowd, multitude, rank and file, silent majority, *colloq.* great unwashed, *colloq. derog.* proles, *colloq. usu. derog.* plebs, *derog.* populace, *esp. derog.* proletariat, *usu. derog.* mob.

hoist /hoyst/ *v.* & *n.* ● *v.tr.* **1** raise or haul up. **2** raise by means of ropes and pulleys etc. ● *n.* **1** an act of hoisting, a lift. **2** an apparatus for hoisting. **3 a** the part of a flag nearest the staff. **b** a group of flags raised as a signal. □ **hoist the flag** stake one's claim to discovered territory by displaying a flag. **hoist one's flag** signify that one takes command. **hoist with one's own petard** see PETARD. □□ **hoister** *n.* [16th c.: alt. of *hoise* f. (15th-c.) *hysse*, prob. of LG orig.: cf. LG *hissen*]
▪ *v.* **1, 2** lift (up), haul up, elevate, raise, heave up, uplift; winch. ● *n.* **2** crane, lift, davit, winch, tackle, *US* elevator.

hoity-toity /hóytitóyti/ *adj.*, *int.*, & *n.* ● *adj.* **1** haughty; petulant; snobbish. **2** *archaic* frolicsome. ● *int.* expressing surprised protest at presumption etc. ● *n. archaic* riotous or giddy conduct. [obs. *hoit* indulge in riotous mirth, of unkn. orig.]
▪ *adj.* **1** haughty, arrogant, snobbish, disdainful, supercilious, conceited, petulant, lofty, superior, self-important, *colloq.* high and mighty, stuck-up, snooty, uppity, snotty, *esp. Brit. colloq.* uppish, *esp. Brit. sl.* toffee-nosed.

hokey /hṓki/ *adj.* (also **hoky**) (**hokier**, **hokiest**) *US sl.* sentimental, melodramatic, artificial. □□ **hokeyness** *n.* (also **hokiness**). **hokily** *adv.* [HOKUM + -Y[2]]
▪ see *melodramatic* (MELODRAMA).

hokey-cokey /hṓkikṓki/ *n.* a communal dance performed in a circle with synchronized shaking of the limbs in turn. [perh. f. HOCUS-POCUS]

hokey-pokey /hṓkipṓki/ *n. colloq.* **1** = HOCUS-POCUS 1. **2** ice-cream formerly sold esp. by Italian street vendors. [HOCUS-POCUS: sense 2 of unkn. orig.]

hokku /hókkoo/ *n.* (*pl.* same) = HAIKU. [Jap.]

hokum /hṓkəm/ *n.* esp. *US sl.* **1** sentimental, popular, sensational, or unreal situations, dialogue, etc., in a film or play etc. **2** bunkum; rubbish. [20th c.: orig. unkn.]
▪ **2** see RUBBISH *n.* 3.

hoky var. of HOKEY.

Holarctic /həlaárktik/ *adj.* of or relating to the geographical distribution of animals in the whole northern or Arctic region. [HOLO- + ARCTIC]

hold[1] /hōld/ *v.* & *n.* ● *v.* (*past* and *past part.* **held** /held/) **1** *tr.* **a** keep fast; grasp (esp. in the hands or arms). **b** (also *refl.*) keep or sustain (a thing, oneself, one's head, etc.) in a particular position (*hold it to the light*; *held himself erect*). **c** grasp so as to control (*hold the reins*). **2** *tr.* (of a vessel etc.) contain or be capable of containing (*the jug holds two pints*; *the hall holds 900*). **3** *tr.* possess, gain, or have, esp.: **a** be the owner or tenant of (land, property, stocks, etc.) (*holds the farm from the trust*). **b** gain or have gained (a degree, record, etc.) (*holds the long-jump record*). **c** have the position of (a job or office). **d** have (a specified card) in one's hand. **e** keep possession of (a place, a person's thoughts, etc.) esp. against attack (*held the fort against the enemy*; *held his place in her estimation*). **4** *intr.* remain unbroken; not give way (*the roof held under the storm*). **5** *tr.* observe; celebrate; conduct (a meeting, festival, conversation, etc.). **6** *tr.* **a** keep (a person etc.) in a specified condition, place, etc. (*held him prisoner*; *held him at arm's length*). **b** detain, esp. in custody (*hold him until I arrive*). **7** *tr.* **a** engross (a person or a person's attention) (*the book held him for hours*). **b** dominate (*held the stage*). **8** *tr.* (foll. by *to*) make (a person etc.) adhere to (terms, a promise, etc.). **9** *intr.* (of weather) continue fine. **10** *tr.* (often foll. by *to* + infin., or *that* + clause) think; believe (*held it to be self-evident*; *held that the earth was flat*). **11** *tr.* regard with a specified feeling (*held him in contempt*). **12** *tr.* **a** cease; restrain (*hold your fire*). **b** *US colloq.* withhold; not use (*a burger please, and hold the onions!*). **13** *tr.* keep or reserve (*will you hold our seats please?*). **14** *tr.* be able to drink (liquor) without effect (*can't hold his drink*). **15** *tr.* (usu. foll. by *that* + clause) (of a judge, a court, etc.) lay down; decide. **16** *intr.* keep going (*held on his way*). **17** *tr. Mus.* sustain (a note). **18** *intr. archaic* restrain oneself. ● *n.* **1** a grasp (*catch hold of him*; *keep a hold on him*). **2** (often in *comb.*) a thing to hold by (*seized the handhold*). **3** (foll. by *on*, *over*) influence over (*has a strange hold over them*). **4** a manner of holding in wrestling etc. **5** *archaic* a fortress. □ **hold (a thing) against (a person)** resent or regard it as discreditable to (a person). **hold aloof** avoid communication with people etc. **hold back 1** impede the progress of; restrain. **2** keep (a thing) to or for oneself. **3** (often foll. by *from*) hesitate; refrain. **hold-back** *n.* a hindrance. **hold one's breath** see BREATH. **hold by** (or **to**) adhere to (a choice, purpose, etc.). **hold cheap** not value highly; despise. **hold the clock on** time (a sporting event etc.). **hold court** preside over one's admirers etc., like a sovereign. **hold dear** regard with affection. **hold down 1** repress. **2** *colloq.* be competent enough to keep (one's job etc.). **hold everything!** (or **it!**) cease action or movement. **hold the fort 1** act as a temporary substitute. **2** cope in an emergency. **hold forth 1** offer (an inducement etc.). **2** usu. *derog.* speak at length or tediously. **hold good** (or **true**) be valid; apply. **hold one's ground** see GROUND[1]. **hold one's hand** see HAND. **hold a person's hand** give a person guidance or moral support. **hold hands** grasp one another by the hand as a sign of affection or for support or guidance. **hold hard!** stop!; wait! **hold harmless** *Law* indemnify. **hold one's head high** behave proudly and confidently. **hold one's horses** *colloq.* stop; slow down. **hold in** keep in check, confine. **hold it good** think it advisable. **hold the line 1** not yield. **2** maintain a telephone connection. **hold one's nose** compress the nostrils to avoid a bad smell. **hold off 1** delay; not begin. **2** keep one's distance. **3** keep at a distance, fend off. **hold on 1** keep one's grasp on something. **2** wait a moment. **3** (when telephoning) not ring off. **hold out 1** stretch forth (a hand etc.). **2** offer (an inducement etc.). **3** maintain resistance. **4** persist or last. **hold out for** continue to demand. **hold out on** *colloq.* refuse something to (a person). **hold over 1** postpone. **2** retain. **hold-over** *n. US* a relic. **hold something over** threaten (a person) constantly with something. **hold one's own** see OWN. **hold to bail** *Law* bind by bail. **hold to a draw** manage to achieve a draw against (an opponent thought likely to win). **hold together 1** cohere. **2** cause to cohere. **hold one's tongue** *colloq.* be silent. **hold to ransom 1** keep (a person) prisoner until a ransom is paid. **2** demand concessions from by threats of esp. damaging action. **hold up 1 a** support; sustain. **b** maintain (the head etc.) erect. **c** last, endure. **2** exhibit; display. **3** arrest the progress of; obstruct. **4** stop and rob by violence or threats. **hold-up** *n.* **1** a stoppage or delay by traffic, fog, etc. **2** a robbery, esp. by the use of threats or violence. **hold water** (of reasoning) be sound; bear examination. **hold with** (usu. with *neg.*) *colloq.* approve of (*don't hold with motor bikes*). **left holding the baby** left with unwelcome responsibility. **on hold 1** in abeyance; temporarily deferred. **2** (of a telephone call or caller) holding on (see *hold on* 3 above). **take hold** (of a custom or habit) become established. **there is no holding him** (or **her** etc.) he (or she etc.) is restive, high-spirited, determined, etc. **with no holds barred** with no restrictions, all methods being permitted. □□ **holdable** *adj.* [OE *h(e)aldan*, *heald*]

■ *v.* **1 a, c** seize, grasp, grip, clench, clasp, clutch, keep, *colloq.* hang on to; carry, cradle, enfold, hug, embrace. **b** maintain, sustain, keep, put. **2** contain, accommodate, support, carry. **3** possess, have; gain, achieve; maintain, keep, sustain. **4** stay, stick, remain, survive. **5** observe, celebrate; call, convene, assemble, *formal* convoke; run, conduct, engage in, participate in, have. **6** confine, restrain, contain; keep; imprison, detain, shut up, jail. **7 a** engross, possess, keep, absorb, occupy, engage, involve, monopolize. **9** see *carry on* 1. **10, 11** believe, judge, consider, regard, take, assume, *formal* deem, esteem; think, maintain. **12 a** see CEASE *v.* **b** see WITHHOLD 1 **13** see RESERVE *v.* 2. **15** decide, rule; see also *lay down* 3, 7 (LAY[1]). **16** see PERSEVERE. ● *n.* **1** grasp, grip, clasp, clutch, purchase. **3** dominance, mastery, control, ascendancy, authority, influence, power; leverage, sway, pull, *colloq.* clout. □ **hold back 1** restrain, repress, suppress, curb, inhibit, control, check, hinder, impede. **2** withhold, reserve, deny, keep back, refuse. **3** see HESITATE 2. **hold-back** see HINDRANCE. **hold by** (or **to**) see KEEP *v.* 7a. **hold dear** see APPRECIATE 1a. **hold down 1** control, restrain, check; see also REPRESS 1. **2** keep, maintain, manage. **hold forth 1** hold out, offer, proffer, tender, submit, advance, propose, propound, extend. **2** lecture, declaim, preach, sermonize, discourse, expatiate, pontificate, *colloq.* go on, witter on, *Brit. colloq.* rabbit on, *joc. or derog.* speechify, *esp. joc. or derog.* orate. **hold good** apply, stand *or* hold up, hold *or* prove *or* be true, be the case, operate, be *or* remain *or* prove valid, be relevant *or* applicable *or* operative, hold water, wash. **hold in** control, curb, check, hold back, restrain, contain. **hold off 1** delay, defer, put off, postpone, avoid; (*hold off from*) refrain from. **3** repel, repulse, fend off, rebuff, resist, withstand. **hold on 1** (*hold on to*) grip, clutch (on to), cling to. **2** see WAIT *v.* 1a. **hold out 1, 2** offer, proffer, extend, present, hold up. **3** see RESIST *v.* 1, 2. **4** last, carry on, persist, persevere, continue, hang on, stand firm, *esp. US* stand pat. **hold over 1** postpone, delay, defer, put off, hold off, suspend, adjourn. **2** continue, retain, extend, prolong. **hold together 1** see JELL 2. **hold one's tongue** be *or* remain *or* keep silent, say nothing *or* naught, not breathe *or* say a word, keep one's counsel, *colloq.* keep mum, shut up. **hold up 1 a, b** see SUPPORT *v.* 1, 2. **c** last, survive, bear up, endure, hold out. **2** present, show, exhibit, display, hold out. **3** obstruct, delay, impede, hinder, slow (down *or* up), set back. **4** rob, waylay, mug, *colloq.* stick up. **hold-up 1** delay, set-back, hitch, snag, interruption, stoppage. **2** robbery, mugging, *colloq.* stick-up, *US sl.* heist. **hold water** be logical *or* sound *or* valid *or* sensible *or* consistent, be believable *or* credible *or* defensible *or* feasible *or* workable; make sense, ring true; hold up under scrutiny *or* examination, bear scrutiny *or* examination. **hold with** support, approve (of), subscribe to, condone, concur with.

hold[2] /hōld/ *n.* a cavity in the lower part of a ship or aircraft in which the cargo is stowed. [obs. *holl* f. OE *hol* (orig. adj. = hollow), rel. to HOLE, assim. to HOLD[1]]

holdall /hṓldawl/ *n.* a portable case for miscellaneous articles.
■ see SUITCASE.

holder /hṓldər/ *n.* **1** (often in *comb.*) a device or implement for holding something (*cigarette-holder*). **2 a** the possessor of a title etc. **b** the occupant of an office etc. **3** = SMALLHOLDER.
■ **1** see RECEPTACLE. **2** see INCUMBENT *n.*

holdfast /hṓldfaast/ *n.* **1** a firm grasp. **2** a staple or clamp securing an object to a wall etc. **3** the attachment-organ of an alga etc.
■ **2** see BRACE *n.* 1a.

holding /hṓlding/ *n.* **1 a** a land held by lease (cf. SMALLHOLDING). **b** the tenure of land. **2** stocks, property, etc. held. □ **holding company** a company created to hold the shares of other companies, which it then controls. **holding operation** a manoeuvre designed to maintain the *status quo*.
■ **1 a** see FARM *n.* **b** see TENURE 1, 2.

hole /hōl/ *n.* & *v.* ● *n.* **1 a** an empty space in a solid body. **b** an aperture in or through something. **2** an animal's burrow. **3** a cavity or receptacle for a ball in various sports or games. **4 a** *colloq.* a small, mean, or dingy abode. **b** a dungeon, a prison cell. **5** *colloq.* an awkward situation. **6** *Golf* **a** a point scored by a player who gets the ball from tee to hole with the fewest strokes. **b** the terrain or distance from tee to hole. **7** a position from which an electron is absent, esp. acting as a mobile positive particle in a semiconductor. ● *v.tr.* **1** make a hole or holes in. **2** pierce the side of (a ship). **3** put into a hole. **4** (also *absol.*; often foll. by *out*) send (a golf ball) into a hole. □ **hole-and-corner** secret; underhand. **hole in the heart** a congenital defect in the heart septum. **hole in one** *Golf* a shot that enters the hole from the tee. **hole in the wall** a small dingy place (esp. of business). **hole-proof** (of materials etc.) treated so as to be resistant to wear. **hole up** *US colloq.* hide oneself. **in holes** worn so much that holes have formed. **make a hole in** use a large amount of. **a round** (or **square**) **peg in a square** (or **round**) **hole** see PEG. □□ **holey** *adj.* [OE *hol*, *holian* (as HOLD[2])]
■ *n.* **1 a** cavity, pit, hollow, pocket, depression, indentation, dent, crater, recess, niche, nook. **b** aperture, opening, orifice, perforation, puncture, slit, slot, breach, rip, tear, rent, break, crack, fissure. **2** warren, burrow, tunnel; den, set, lair. **4 a** hole in the wall, shack, hovel, hut, shanty, slum, *colloq.* dump, hell-hole. **b** cell, prison, dungeon, donjon, keep, jail, oubliette, *US* brig. **5** difficulty, predicament, fix, plight, mess, muddle, cleft stick, tight corner *or* place *or* spot, *colloq.* scrape, pickle, *esp. US colloq.* bind, *disp.* dilemma; *colloq.* hot water, trouble. ● *v.* **1** puncture, pierce, perforate, prick, nick, penetrate, go through, rupture. □ **hole-and-corner** see SECRET *adj.* 1. **hole in the wall** see HOLE *n.* 4a above. **hole up** see HIDE[1] *v.* 2. **in holes** see TATTERED.

holibut var. of HALIBUT.

holiday /hólliday, -di/ *n.* & *v.* ● *n.* **1** esp. *Brit.* (often in *pl.*) an extended period of recreation, esp. away from home or in travelling; a break from work (cf. VACATION). **2** a day of festivity or recreation when no work is done, esp. a religious festival etc. **3** (*attrib.*) (of clothes etc.) festive. ● *v.intr.* esp. *Brit.* spend a holiday. □ **holiday camp** *Brit.* a camp for holiday-makers with accommodation, entertainment, and facilities on site. **holiday centre** a place with many tourist attractions. **holiday-maker** esp. *Brit.* a person on holiday. **on holiday** (or **one's holidays**) in the course of one's holiday. **take a** (or *archaic* **make**) **holiday** have a break from work. [OE *hāligdæg* (HOLY, DAY)]
■ *n.* **1** time off, break, recess, respite, leave (of absence), furlough, *US* vacation. **2** festival, feast, celebration, fête, fiesta, gala, red-letter day. **3** festive, best, Sunday. □ **holiday-maker** see TOURIST.

holily /hṓlili/ *adv.* in a holy manner. [OE *hāliglīce* (as HOLY)]

holiness /hṓliniss/ *n.* **1** sanctity; the state of being holy. **2** (**Holiness**) a title used when referring to or addressing the Pope. [OE *hālignes* (as HOLY)]
■ **1** see SANCTITY 1, 2.

holism /hólliz'm, hṓ-/ *n.* (also **wholism**) **1** *Philos.* the theory that certain wholes are to be regarded as greater than the sum of their parts (cf. REDUCTIONISM). **2** *Med.* the treating of the whole person including mental and social factors rather than just the symptoms of a disease. □□ **holistic** /-lístik/ *adj.* **holistically** /-lístikəli/ *adv.* [as HOLO- + -ISM]

holla /hóllə/ *int.*, *n.*, & *v.* ● *int.* calling attention. ● *n.* a cry of 'holla'. ● *v.* (**hollas, hollaed** or **holla'd, hollaing**) **1** *intr.* shout. **2** *tr.* call to (hounds). [F *holà* (as HO, *là* there)]

holland /hóllənd/ *n.* a smooth, hard-wearing, linen fabric. □ **brown holland** unbleached holland. [*Holland* = Netherlands: Du., earlier *Holtlant* f. *holt* wood + *-lant* land, describing the Dordrecht district]

hollandaise sauce /hólləndáyz/ *n.* a creamy sauce of melted butter, egg-yolks, vinegar, etc., served esp. with fish. [F, fem. of *hollandais* Dutch f. *Hollande* Holland]

Hollander /hólləndər/ *n.* **1** a native of Holland (the Netherlands). **2** a Dutch ship.

Hollands /hóllәndz/ *n.* gin made in Holland. [Du. *hollandsch genever* Dutch gin]

holler /hóllər/ *v.* & *n. US colloq.* ● *v.* **1** *intr.* make a loud cry or noise. **2** *tr.* express with a loud cry or shout. ● *n.* a loud cry, noise, or shout. [var. of HOLLO]
■ *v.* see BAWL 1. ● *n.* see BELLOW *n.*

hollo /hóllō/ *int.*, *n.*, & *v.* ● *int.* = HOLLA. ● *n.* (*pl.* **-os**) = HOLLA. ● *v.* (**-oes, -oed**) (also **hollow** *pronunc.* same) = HOLLA. [rel. to HOLLA]

hollow /hóllō/ *adj.*, *n.*, *v.*, & *adv.* ● *adj.* **1 a** having a hole or cavity inside; not solid throughout. **b** having a depression; sunken (*hollow cheeks*). **2** (of a sound) echoing, as though made in or on a hollow container. **3** empty; hungry. **4** without significance; meaningless (*a hollow triumph*). **5** insincere; cynical; false (*a hollow laugh*; *hollow promises*). ● *n.* **1** a hollow place; a hole. **2** a valley; a basin. ● *v.tr.* (often foll. by *out*) make hollow; excavate. ● *adv. colloq.* completely (*beaten hollow*). □ **hollow-eyed** with eyes deep sunk. **hollow-hearted** insincere. **hollow square** *Mil. hist.* a body of infantry drawn up in a square with a space in the middle. **in the hollow of one's hand** entirely subservient to one. □□ **hollowly** *adv.* **hollowness** *n.* [ME *holg*, *holu*, *hol(e)we* f. OE *holh* cave, rel. to HOLE]
■ *adj.* **1 a** vacant, void, unfilled; see also EMPTY *adj.* 1. **b** sunken, concave, indented, recessed. **2** echoing, muffled, low, sepulchral. **3** hungry, ravenous, starved, empty, famished. **4** empty, futile, pyrrhic, worthless, vain, unavailing, fruitless, profitless, unprofitable, valueless, ineffective, pointless, senseless, meaningless, *archaic* bootless. **5** insincere, false, cynical, hypocritical, sham, artificial, feigned, fraudulent, spurious, deceitful, mendacious, deceptive. ● *n.* **1** hole, cavity, crater, pit, trough, furrow, indentation, dent, impression, dip; excavation. **2** basin, depression, dip, valley, dale, dell, glen, *Brit.* coomb, combe. ● *v.* excavate, dig, gouge, furrow; (*hollow out*) scoop out. ● *adv.* see *completely* (COMPLETE). □ **hollow-hearted** see INSINCERE.

hollowware /hóllōwair/ *n.* hollow articles of metal, china, etc., such as pots, kettles, jugs, etc. (opp. FLATWARE).
■ see SILVER *n.* 5, 6.

holly /hólli/ *n.* (*pl.* **-ies**) **1** an evergreen shrub, *Ilex aquifolium*, with prickly usu. dark-green leaves, small white flowers, and red berries. **2** its branches and foliage used as decorations at Christmas. □ **holly oak** a holm-oak. [OE *hole(g)n*]

hollyhock /hóllihok/ *n.* a tall plant, *Alcea rosea*, with large showy flowers of various colours. [ME (orig. = marsh mallow) f. HOLY + obs. *hock* mallow, OE *hoc*, of unkn. orig.]

Hollywood /hólliwŏŏd/ *n.* the American cinema industry or its products, with its principal centre at Hollywood in California.

holm[1] /hōm/ *n.* (also **holme**) *Brit.* **1** an islet, esp. in a river or near a mainland. **2** a piece of flat ground by a river, which is submerged in time of flood. [ON *holmr*]
■ **1** see ISLAND.

holm[2] /hōm/ *n.* (in full **holm-oak**) an evergreen oak, *Quercus ilex*, with holly-like young leaves. [ME alt. of obs. *holin* (as HOLLY)]

holmium /hṓlmiəm/ *n. Chem.* a soft silvery metallic element of the lanthanide series occurring naturally in apatite. ¶ Symb.: **Ho.** [mod.L f. *Holmia* Stockholm]

holo- /hóllō/ *comb. form* whole (*Holocene*; *holocaust*). [Gk *holos* whole]

holocaust /hólləkawst/ *n.* **1** a case of large-scale destruction or slaughter, esp. by fire or nuclear war. **2** (**the Holocaust**) the mass murder of the Jews by the Nazis 1939–45. **3** a sacrifice wholly consumed by fire. [ME f. OF *holocauste* f. LL *holocaustum* f. Gk *holokauston* (as HOLO-, *kaustos* burnt f. *kaiō* burn)]
■ **1** destruction, devastation; slaughter, genocide, mass murder, massacre, blood bath, pogrom, butchery, carnage, annihilation, extinction, extermination, eradication, elimination; conflagration, fire-storm, inferno, fire.

Holocene /hólləseen/ *adj.* & *n. Geol.* ● *adj.* of or relating to the most recent epoch of the Quaternary period with evidence of human development and intervention, and the extinction of large mammals. ¶ Cf. Appendix VII. ● *n.* this period or system. Also called RECENT. [HOLO- + Gk *kainos* new]

holoenzyme /hóllō-énzīm/ *n. Biochem.* a complex enzyme consisting of several components.

hologram /hólləgram/ *n. Physics* **1** a three-dimensional image formed by the interference of light beams from a coherent light source. **2** a photograph of the interference pattern, which when suitably illuminated produces a three-dimensional image.

holograph /hólləgraaf/ *adj.* & *n.* ● *adj.* wholly written by hand by the person named as the author. ● *n.* a holograph document. [F *holographe* or LL *holographus* f. Gk *holographos* (as HOLO-, -GRAPH)]

holography /həlógrəfi/ *n. Physics* the study or production of holograms. □□ **holographic** /hólləgráffik/ *adj.* **holographically** /hólləgráffikəli/ *adv.*

holohedral /hólləhéedrəl/ *adj. Crystallog.* having the full number of planes required by the symmetry of a crystal system.

holophyte /hólləfīt/ *n.* an organism that synthesizes complex organic compounds by photosynthesis. □□ **holophytic** /-fíttik/ *adj.*

holothurian /hólləthyŏŏriən/ *n.* & *adj.* ● *n.* any echinoderm of the class Holothurioidea, with a wormlike body, e.g. a sea cucumber. ● *adj.* of or relating to this class. [mod.L *Holothuria* (n.pl.) f. Gk *holothourion*, a zoophyte]

holotype /hóllətīp/ *n.* the specimen used for naming and describing a species.

hols /holz/ *n.pl. Brit. colloq.* holidays. [abbr.]

Holstein /hólsteen/ *n.* & *adj. US* = FRIESIAN. [*Holstein* in NW Germany]

holster /hṓlstər/ *n.* a leather case for a pistol or revolver, worn on a belt or under an arm or fixed to a saddle. [17th c., synonymous with Du. *holster*: orig. unkn.]

holt[1] /hōlt/ *n.* **1** an animal's (esp. an otter's) lair. **2** *colloq.* or *dial.* grip, hold. [var. of HOLD[1]]

holt[2] /hōlt/ *n. archaic* or *dial.* **1** a wood or copse. **2** a wooded hill. [OE f. Gmc]

holus-bolus /hṓləsbṓləss/ *adv.* all in a lump, altogether. [app. sham L]

holy /hṓli/ *adj.* (**holier, holiest**) **1** morally and spiritually excellent or perfect, and to be revered. **2** belonging to, devoted to, or empowered by, God. **3** consecrated, sacred. **4** used in trivial exclamations (*holy cow!*; *holy mackerel!*; *holy Moses!*; *holy smoke!*). □ **holier-than-thou** *colloq.* self-righteous. **Holy City 1** a city held sacred by the adherents of a religion, esp. Jerusalem. **2** Heaven. **Holy Communion** see COMMUNION. **Holy Cross Day** the festival of the Exaltation of the Cross, 14 Sept. **holy day** a religious festival. **Holy Family** the young Jesus with his mother and St Joseph (often with St John the Baptist, St Anne, etc.) as grouped in pictures etc. **Holy Father** the Pope. **Holy Ghost** = *Holy Spirit*. **Holy Grail** see GRAIL. **holy Joe** *orig. Naut. sl.* **1** a clergyman. **2** a pious person. **Holy Land 1** W. Palestine, esp. Judaea. **2** a region similarly revered in non-Christian religions. **Holy Name** *RC Ch.* the name of Jesus as an object of formal devotion. **Holy Office** the Inquisition. **holy of holies 1** the inner chamber of the sanctuary in the Jewish temple, separated by a veil from the outer chamber. **2** an innermost shrine. **3** a thing regarded as most sacred. **holy orders** see ORDER. **holy place 1** (in *pl.*) places to which religious pilgrimage is made. **2** the outer chamber of the sanctuary in the Jewish temple. **holy roller** *sl.* a member of a religious group characterized by frenzied excitement or trances. **Holy Roman Empire** see ROMAN. **Holy Rood Day 1** the festival of the Invention of the Cross, 3 May. **2** = *Holy Cross Day*. **Holy Sacrament** see SACRAMENT. **Holy Saturday** Saturday in Holy Week. **Holy Scripture** the Bible. **Holy See** the papacy or the papal court. **Holy Spirit** the Third Person of the Trinity, God as spiritually acting. **holy terror** see TERROR. **Holy Thursday 1** *Anglican Ch.* Ascension Day. **2** *RC Ch.* Maundy Thursday. **Holy Trinity** see TRINITY. **holy war** a war waged in support of a religious cause. **holy water** water dedicated to holy uses, or blessed by a priest. **Holy Week** the week before Easter. **Holy Writ** holy writings collectively, esp. the Bible. **Holy Year** *RC Ch.* a period of remission from the penal consequences of sin, granted under certain conditions for a year usu. at intervals of 25 years. [OE *hālig* f. Gmc, rel. to WHOLE]

■ **1, 2** godly, godlike, saintly, saintlike, pious, devout, religious, reverent, faithful, God-fearing; chaste, pure, unsullied, clean, sinless, spotless, immaculate, undefiled, uncorrupted, untainted; sacred, divine, heavenly, celestial, *esp. poet.* supernal. **3** sacred, consecrated, sanctified, blessed, hallowed. □ **holier-than-thou** see SELF-RIGHTEOUS. **holy Joe** see CLERGYMAN. **holy of holies 1** sanctum sanctorum. **2** sanctuary, shrine. **3** fetish, *colloq.* sacred cow.

holystone /hṓlistōn/ *n.* & *v. Naut.* ● *n.* a piece of soft sandstone used for scouring decks. ● *v.tr.* scour with this. [19th c.: prob. f. HOLY + STONE: the stones were called *bibles* etc., perh. because used while kneeling]

hom /hōm/ *n.* (also **homa** /hṓmə/) **1** the soma plant. **2** the juice of this plant as a sacred drink of the Parsees. [Pers. *hōm*, *hūm*, Avestan *haoma*]

homage /hómmij/ *n.* **1** acknowledgement of superiority; respect, dutiful reverence (*pay homage to*; *do homage to*). **2** *hist.* formal public acknowledgement of feudal allegiance. [ME f. OF *(h)omage* f. med.L *hominaticum* f. L *homo -minis* man]

■ **1** obeisance, deference, reverence, veneration; respects, honour, tribute.

hombre /ómbray/ *n. US* a man. [Sp.]

Homburg /hómburg/ *n.* a man's felt hat with a narrow curled brim and a lengthwise dent in the crown. [*Homburg* in Germany, where first worn]

home /hōm/ *n.*, *adj.*, *adv.*, & *v.* ● *n.* **1 a** the place where one lives; the fixed residence of a family or household. **b** a dwelling-house. **2** the members of a family collectively; one's family background (*comes from a good home*). **3** the native land of a person or of a person's ancestors. **4** an institution for persons needing care, rest, or refuge (*nursing home*). **5** the place where a thing originates or is native or most common. **6 a** the finishing-point in a race. **b** (in games) the place where one is free from attack; the goal. **c** *Lacrosse* a player in an attacking position near the opponents' goal. **7** *Sport* a home match or win. ● *attrib.adj.* **1 a** of or connected with one's home. **b** carried on, done, or made, at home. **c** proceeding from home. **2 a** carried on or produced in one's own country (*home industries*; *the home market*). **b** dealing with the domestic affairs of a country. **3** *Sport* played on one's own ground etc. (*home match*; *home win*). **4** in the neighbourhood of home. ● *adv.* **1 a** to one's home or country (*go home*). **b** arrived at home (*is he home yet?*). **c** *US* at home (*stay home*). **2 a** to the point aimed at (*the thrust went home*). **b** as far as possible (*drove the nail home*; *pressed his advantage home*). ● *v.* **1** *intr.* (esp. of a trained pigeon) return home (cf. HOMING 1). **2** *intr.* (often foll. by *on*, *in on*) (of a vessel, missile, etc.) be guided towards a destination or target by a landmark, radio beam, etc. **3** *tr.* send or guide homewards. **4** *tr.* provide with a home. □ **at home 1** in one's own house or native land. **2** at ease as if in one's own home (*make yourself at home*). **3** (usu. foll. by *in*, *on*, *with*) familiar or well informed. **4** available to callers. **at-home** *n.* a social reception in a person's home. **come home to** become fully realized by. **come home to roost** see ROOST[1]. **home and dry** having achieved one's purpose. **home away from home** = *home from home*. **home-bird** a person who likes to stay at home. **home-brew** beer or other alcoholic drink brewed at home. **home-brewed** (of beer etc.) brewed at home. **home-coming** arrival at home. **Home Counties** the counties closest to London. **home economics** the study of household management. **home farm** *Brit.* a farm (one of several on an estate) set aside to provide produce for the owner. **home-felt** felt intimately. **home from home** a place other than one's home where one feels at home; a place providing homelike amenities. **home-grown** grown or produced at home. **Home Guard** *hist.* **1** the British citizen army organized in 1940 to defend the UK against invasion, and disbanded in 1957. **2** a member of this. **home help** *Brit.* a woman employed to help in a person's home, esp. one provided by a local authority. **home, James!** *joc.* drive home quickly! **home-made** made at home. **home-making** creation of a (pleasant) home. **home movie** a film made at home or of one's own activities. **Home Office 1** the British government department dealing with law and order, immigration, etc., in England and Wales. **2** the building used for this. **home of lost causes** Oxford University. **home-owner** a person who owns his or her own home. **home perm** a permanent wave made with domestic equipment. **home plate** *Baseball* a plate beside which the batter stands. **home port** the port from which a ship originates. **home rule** the government of a country or region by its own citizens. **home run** *Baseball* a hit that allows the batter to make a complete circuit of the bases. **Home Secretary** (in the UK) the Secretary of State in charge of the Home Office. **home signal** a signal indicating whether a train may proceed into a station or to the next section of the line. **home straight** (*US* **stretch**) the concluding stretch of a racecourse. **home town** the town of one's birth or early life or present fixed residence. **home trade** trade carried on within a country. **home truth** basic but unwelcome information concerning oneself. **home unit** *Austral.* a private residence, usu. occupied by the owner, as one of several in a building. **near home** affecting one closely. □□ **homelike** *adj.* [OE *hām* f. Gmc]

■ *n.* **1** residence, domicile, abode, address, (living) quarters; house, habitation, place, *formal* dwelling(-place), dwelling-house, *Austral. sl.* kipsie. **2** family, household, ménage, background. **3** country, territory, (native) land *or* soil, homeland, fatherland, motherland, mother country. **4** institution, rest-home, *Brit.* hospice, *hist.* almshouse, poorhouse; refuge, shelter, hostel. **5** see ENVIRONMENT 1, 2. ● *attrib.adj.* **1** family, domestic, household. **2** native, national, internal. **4** see NEIGHBOURHOOD. ● *v.* **2** (*home in on*) zero in on, make a beeline for, head for, aim at *or* for, target. □ **at home 2** comfortable, at ease, relaxed, composed, tranquil, serene, untroubled. **3** (*at home with* or *in*) comfortable with, conversant with, knowledgeable about, familiar with, well-versed in, competent in, expert in, proficient in, skilled in, up on, current in, adroit in, informed in *or* on *or* about, *sl.* clued up on. **4** in, accessible, available, welcoming. **at-home** see RECEPTION 3.

homebody /hṓmboddi/ *n.* (*pl.* **-ies**) a home-bird.

homeboy /hṓmboy/ *n. US colloq.* a person from one's own town or neighbourhood.

homeland /hṓmland/ *n.* **1** one's native land. **2** *hist.* an area in S. Africa formerly reserved for a particular African people (the official name for a Bantustan).

homeless /hṓmliss/ *adj.* & *n.* ● *adj.* lacking a home. ● *n.* (prec. by *the*) homeless people. □□ **homelessness** *n.*

■ *adj.* on the streets, sleeping out *or* rough, dispossessed.

homely /hṓmli/ *adj.* (**homelier, homeliest**) **1 a** simple, plain. **b** unpretentious. **c** primitive. **2** *US* (of people or their features) not attractive in appearance, ugly. **3** comfortable in the manner of a home, cosy. **4** skilled at housekeeping. □□ **homeliness** *n.*

■ **1 a** basic, plain, natural; see also SIMPLE *adj.* 2. **b** unpretentious, modest, unassuming, unaffected, informal, unsophisticated, homespun, commonplace, ordinary, familiar, everyday. **2** ugly, plain, uncomely, unattractive, unlovely, *Austral. sl.* drack. **3** homey, homelike, warm, cosy, snug, domestic, friendly, congenial, comfortable, easy.

homeopath etc. *US* var. of HOMOEOPATH etc.

homeostasis *US* var. of HOMOEOSTASIS.

homer /hṓmər/ *n.* **1** a homing pigeon. **2** *Baseball* a home run.

Homeric /hōmérrik/ *adj.* **1** of, or in the style of, Homer or the epic poems ascribed to him. **2** of Bronze Age Greece as described in these poems. **3** epic, large-scale, titanic (*Homeric conflict*). [L *Homericus* f. Gk *Homērikos* f. *Homēros* Homer, traditional author of the *Iliad* and the *Odyssey*]

■ **1, 3** see HEROIC *adj.* 2b.

homesick /hṓmsik/ *adj.* depressed by longing for one's home during absence from it. ▫▫ **homesickness** *n.*

■ depressed, longing, pining, lonely, lonesome; nostalgic, wistful.

homespun /hṓmspun/ *adj.* & *n.* ● *adj.* **1 a** (of cloth) made of yarn spun at home. **b** (of yarn) spun at home. **2** plain, simple, unsophisticated, homely. ● *n.* **1** homespun cloth. **2** anything plain or homely.

■ *adj.* **2** rustic, homely, plain, simple, unrefined, unpolished, unsophisticated, down-to-earth.

homestead /hṓmsted, -stid/ *n.* **1** a house, esp. a farmhouse, and outbuildings. **2** *Austral.* & *NZ* the owner's residence on a sheep or cattle station. **3** *US* an area of land (usu. 160 acres) granted to a settler as a home. ▫▫ **homesteader** *n.* [OE *hāmstede* (as HOME, STEAD)]

■ **1, 2** see HOUSE *n.* 1a.

homestyle /hṓmstīl/ *adj.* *US* (esp. of food) of a kind made or done at home, homely.

homeward /hṓmwərd/ *adv.* & *adj.* ● *adv.* (also **homewards** /-wərdz/) towards home. ● *adj.* going or leading towards home. ▫ **homeward-bound** (esp. of a ship) preparing to go, or on the way, home. [OE *hāmweard(es)* (as HOME, -WARD)]

homework /hṓmwurk/ *n.* **1** work to be done at home, esp. by a school pupil. **2** preparatory work or study.

■ see ASSIGNMENT 1.

homey /hṓmi/ *adj.* (also **homy**) (**homier**, **homiest**) suggesting home; cosy. ▫▫ **homeyness** *n.* (also **hominess**).

■ see HOMELY 3.

homicide /hómmisīd/ *n.* **1** the killing of a human being by another. **2** a person who kills a human being. ▫▫ **homicidal** /-sīd'l/ *adj.* [ME f. OF f. L *homicidium* (sense 1), *homicida* (sense 2) (HOMO man)]

■ **1** see MURDER *n.* 1. **2** see *murderer*, *murderess* (MURDER). ▫▫ **homicidal** murderous, bloodthirsty, sanguinary, ferocious, death-dealing.

homiletic /hómmiléttik/ *adj.* & *n.* ● *adj.* of homilies. ● *n.* (usu. in *pl.*) the art of preaching. [LL *homileticus* f. Gk *homilētikos* f. *homileō* hold converse, consort (as HOMILY)]

homiliary /homílliəri/ *n.* (*pl.* **-ies**) a book of homilies. [med.L *homeliarius* (as HOMILY)]

homily /hómmili/ *n.* (*pl.* **-ies**) **1** a sermon. **2** a tedious moralizing discourse. ▫▫ **homilist** *n.* [ME f. OF *omelie* f. eccl.L *homilia* f. Gk *homilia* f. *homilos* crowd]

■ see SERMON 1.

homing /hṓming/ *attrib.adj.* **1** (of a pigeon) trained to fly home, bred for long-distance racing. **2** (of a device) for guiding to a target etc. **3** that goes home. ▫ **homing instinct** the instinct of certain animals to return to the territory from which they have been moved.

hominid /hómminid/ *n.* & *adj.* ● *n.* any member of the primate family Hominidae, including humans and their fossil ancestors. ● *adj.* of or relating to this family. [mod.L *Hominidae* f. L *homo hominis* man]

hominoid /hómminoyd/ *adj.* & *n.* ● *adj.* **1** like a human. **2** hominid or pongid. ● *n.* an animal resembling a human.

■ *adj.* **1** see HUMAN *adj.* 1–3.

hominy /hómmini/ *n.* esp. *US* coarsely ground maize kernels esp. boiled with water or milk. [Algonquian]

Homo /hṓmō, hómmō/ *n.* any primate of the genus *Homo*, including modern humans and various extinct species. [L, =man]

homo /hṓmō/ *n.* (*pl.* **-os**) *colloq.* a homosexual. [abbr.]

homo- /hṓmō, hómmō/ *comb.form* same (often opp. HETERO-). [Gk *homos* same]

homocentric /hṓmōséntrik, hóm-/ *adj.* having the same centre.

homoeopath /hṓmiōpath, hóm-/ *n.* (*US* **homeopath**) a person who practises homoeopathy. [G *Homöopath* (as HOMOEOPATHY)]

homoeopathy /hṓmióppəthi, hóm-/ *n.* (*US* **homeopathy**) the treatment of disease by minute doses of drugs that in a healthy person would produce symptoms of the disease (cf. ALLOPATHY). ▫▫ **homoeopathic** /-miəpáthik/ *adj.* **homoeopathist** *n.* [G *Homöopathie* f. Gk *homoios* like + *patheia* -PATHY]

homoeostasis /hṓmiōstáysiss, hóm-/ *n.* (*US* **homeostasis**) (*pl.* **-stases** /-seez/) the tendency towards a relatively stable equilibrium between interdependent elements, esp. as maintained by physiological processes. ▫▫ **homoeostatic** /-státtik/ *adj.* [mod.L f. Gk *homoios* like + -STASIS]

homoeotherm /hómmiōtherm/ *n.* (also **homoiotherm**) an organism that maintains its body temperature at a constant level, usu. above that of the environment, by its metabolic activity; a warm-blooded organism (cf. POIKILOTHERM). ▫▫ **homoeothermal** /-thérm'l/ *adj.* **homoeothermic** /-thérmik/ *adj.* **homoeothermy** *n.* [mod.L f. Gk *homoios* like + *thermē* heat]

homoerotic /hṓmō-iróttik, hóm-/ *adj.* homosexual.

homogametic /hṓmōgəméetik, hóm-/ *adj.* *Biol.* (of a sex or individuals of a sex) producing gametes that carry the same sex chromosome.

homogamy /həmóggəmi/ *n.* *Bot.* **1** a state in which the flowers of a plant are hermaphrodite or of the same sex. **2** the simultaneous ripening of the stamens and pistils of a flower. ▫▫ **homogamous** *adj.* [Gk *homogamos* (as HOMO-, *gamos* marriage)]

homogenate /həmójinayt/ *n.* a suspension produced by homogenizing.

homogeneous /hṓmōjéeniəss, hóm-/ *adj.* **1** of the same kind. **2** consisting of parts all of the same kind; uniform. **3** *Math.* containing terms all of the same degree. ▫▫ **homogeneity** /-jinée-iti/ *n.* **homogeneously** *adv.* **homogeneousness** *n.* [med.L *homogeneus* f. Gk *homogenēs* (as HOMO-, *genēs* f. *genos* kind)]

■ **1** identical, alike, akin, similar, comparable. **2** uniform, constant, consistent, unvarying.

homogenetic /hṓmōjinéttik, hóm-/ *adj.* *Biol.* having a common descent or origin.

homogenize /həmójinīz/ *v.* (also **-ise**) **1** *tr.* & *intr.* make or become homogeneous. **2** *tr.* treat (milk) so that the fat droplets are emulsified and the cream does not separate. ▫▫ **homogenization** /-záysh'n/ *n.* **homogenizer** *n.*

■ **1** see STANDARDIZE.

homogeny /həmójini/ *n.* *Biol.* similarity due to common descent. ▫▫ **homogenous** *adj.*

homograft /hómməgraaft/ *n.* a graft of living tissue from one to another of the same species but different genotype.

homograph /hómməgraaf/ *n.* a word spelt like another but of different meaning or origin (e.g. POLE[1], POLE[2]).

homoiotherm var. of HOMOEOTHERM.

homoiousian /hómmoy-óossiən, -ówsiən/ *n.* *hist.* a person who held that God the Father and God the Son are of like but not identical substance (cf. HOMOOUSIAN). [eccl.L f. Gk *homoiousios* f. *homoios* like + *ousia* essence]

homolog *US* var. of HOMOLOGUE.

homologate /həmólləgayt/ *v.tr.* **1** acknowledge, admit. **2** confirm, accept. **3** approve (a car, boat, engine, etc.) for use in a particular class of racing. ▫▫ **homologation** /-gáysh'n/

n. [med.L *homologare* agree f. Gk *homologeō* (as HOMO-, *logos* word)]

homologize /həmóllǝjīz/ *v.* (also **-ise**) **1** *intr.* be homologous; correspond. **2** *tr.* make homologous.

homologous /həmóllǝgəss/ *adj.* **1 a** having the same relation, relative position, etc. **b** corresponding. **2** *Biol.* (of organs etc.) similar in position and structure but not necessarily in function. **3** *Biol.* (of chromosomes) pairing at meiosis and having the same structural features and pattern of genes. **4** *Chem.* (of a series of chemical compounds) having the same functional group but differing in composition by a fixed group of atoms. [med.L *homologus* f. Gk (as HOMO-, *logos* ratio, proportion)]

■ see LIKE[1] *adj.* 1a.

homologue /hómməlog/ *n.* (*US* **homolog**) a homologous thing. [F f. Gk *homologon* (neut. adj.) (as HOMOLOGOUS)]

■ see PARALLEL *n.* 1.

homology /həmólləji/ *n.* a homologous state or relation; correspondence. ◻◻ **homological** /hómməlójik'l/ *adj.*

homomorphic /hṓmōmórfik, hóm-/ *adj.* (also **homomorphous**) of the same or similar form. ◻◻ **homomorphically** *adv.* **homomorphism** *n.* **homomorphy** *n.*

homonym /hómmənim/ *n.* **1** a word of the same spelling or sound as another but of different meaning; a homograph or homophone. **2** a namesake. ◻◻ **homonymic** /-nímmik/ *adj.* **homonymous** /həmónniməss/ *adj.* [L *homonymum* f. Gk *homōnumon* (neut. adj.) (as HOMO-, *onoma* name)]

homoousian /hómmō-ṓōssiən, -ówsiən/ *n.* (also **homousian**) *hist.* a person who held that God the Father and God the Son are of the same substance (cf. HOMOIOUSIAN). [eccl.L *homoousianus* f. LL *homousius* f. Gk *homoousios* (as HOMO-, *ousia* essence)]

homophobia /hṓməfṓbiə/ *n.* a hatred or fear of homosexuals. ◻◻ **homophobe** /hṓm-/ *n.* **homophobic** /-fṓbik/ *adj.*

homophone /hómməfōn/ *n.* **1** a word having the same sound as another but of different meaning or origin (e.g. *pair*, *pear*). **2** a symbol denoting the same sound as another.

homophonic /hómmōfónnik/ *adj. Mus.* in unison; characterized by movement of all parts to the same melody. ◻◻ **homophonically** *adv.*

homophonous /həmóffənəss/ *adj.* **1** (of music) homophonic. **2** (of a word or symbol) that is a homophone. ◻◻ **homophony** *n.*

homopolar /hṓmōpṓlər, hóm-/ *adj.* **1** electrically symmetrical. **2** *Electr.* (of a generator) producing direct current without the use of commutators. **3** *Chem.* (of a covalent bond) in which one atom supplies both electrons.

homopteran /həmóptərən/ *n.* any insect of the suborder Homoptera, including aphids and cicadas, with wings of uniform texture (cf. HETEROPTERAN). ◻◻ **homopterous** *adj.* [HOMO- + Gk *pteron* wing]

Homo sapiens /hṓmō sáppi-enz/ *n.* modern humans regarded as a species. [L, = wise man]

■ see HUMANITY 1a, b.

homosexual /hṓmōséksyooəl, hóm-, -sékshooəl/ *adj.* & *n.* ● *adj.* **1** feeling or involving sexual attraction only to persons of the same sex. **2** concerning homosexual relations or people. **3** relating to the same sex. ● *n.* a homosexual person. ◻◻ **homosexuality** /-séksyoo-álliti, -sékshoo-álliti/ *n.* **homosexually** *adv.*

homousian var. of HOMOOUSIAN.

homozygote /hṓmōzígōt, hóm-/ *n. Biol.* **1** an individual with identical alleles determining a particular characteristic. **2** an individual that is homozygous and so breeds true. ◻◻ **homozygous** *adj.*

homunculus /həmúngkyooləss/ *n.* (also **homuncule** /-kyōōl/) (*pl.* **homunculi** /-lī/ or **homuncules**) a little man, a manikin. [L *homunculus* f. *homo -minis* man]

homy var. of HOMEY.

Hon. *abbr.* **1** Honorary. **2** Honourable.

hon /hun/ *n. colloq.* = HONEY 5. [abbr.]

honcho /hónchō/ *n.* & *v. US sl.* ● *n.* (*pl.* **-os**) **1** a leader or manager, the person in charge. **2** an admirable man. ● *v.tr.* (**-oes, -oed**) be in charge of, oversee. [Jap. *han'chō* group leader]

■ *n.* **1** see BOSS[1] *n.*

hone /hōn/ *n.* & *v.* ● *n.* **1** a whetstone, esp. for razors. **2** any of various stones used as material for this. ● *v.tr.* sharpen on or as on a hone. [OE *hān* stone f. Gmc]

■ *v.* see SHARPEN.

honest /ónnist/ *adj.* & *adv.* ● *adj.* **1** fair and just in character or behaviour, not cheating or stealing. **2** free of deceit and untruthfulness, sincere. **3** fairly earned (*an honest living*). **4** (of an act or feeling) showing fairness. **5** (with patronizing effect) blameless but undistinguished (cf. WORTHY). **6** (of a thing) unadulterated, unsophisticated. ● *adv. colloq.* genuinely, really. ◻ **earn** (or **turn**) **an honest penny** earn money fairly. **honest broker** a mediator in international, industrial, etc., disputes (orig. of Bismarck). **honest Injun** *colloq.* genuinely, really. **honest-to-God** (or **-goodness**) *colloq. adj.* genuine, real. ● *adv.* genuinely, really. **make an honest woman of** *colloq.* marry (esp. a pregnant woman). [ME f. OF (*h*)*oneste* f. L *honestus* f. *honos* HONOUR]

■ *adj.* **1** fair, just, trustworthy, truthful, honourable, decent, moral, virtuous, principled, upright, high-minded, *archaic* true, *archaic or joc.* trusty, *formal* veracious. **2** sincere, candid, frank, open, straightforward, forthright, direct, explicit, plain-spoken, unambiguous, unequivocal, *colloq.* upfront. **3** above-board, straight, square, square-dealing, proper, genuine, bona fide, legitimate, valid, rightful, sound, proper, *esp. US colloq* on the up and up. **4** fair, equitable; see also JUST *adj.* 2. **6** see UNSOPHISTICATED 2. ● *adv.* see REALLY 1. ◻ **honest-to-god** (or **goodness**) see GENUINE 1, 2.

honestly /ónnistli/ *adv.* **1** in an honest way. **2** really (*I don't honestly know*; *honestly, the cheek of it!*).

■ **1** truthfully, honourably, decently, morally, justly, fairly, equitably; in good faith, *colloq.* on the level; candidly, frankly, openly, straightforwardly, forthrightly, sincerely, unequivocally, plainly, simply; square, straight (out), in plain words *or* English. **2** see REALLY 1.

honesty /ónnisti/ *n.* **1** being honest. **2** truthfulness. **3** a plant of the genus *Lunaria* with purple or white flowers, so called from its flat round semi-transparent seed-pods. [ME f. OF (*h*)*onesté* f. L *honestas -tatis* (as HONEST)]

■ **1** trustworthiness, uprightness, rectitude, probity, integrity, virtue, virtuousness, honour; fairness, equity, equitableness, even-handedness, objectivity, impartiality, disinterestedness, justness, justice. **2** truthfulness, veracity, candour, openness, frankness, forthrightness, directness, straightforwardness, sincerity.

honey /húnni/ *n.* (*pl.* **-eys**) **1** a sweet sticky yellowish fluid made by bees and other insects from nectar collected from flowers. **2** the colour of this. **3 a** sweetness. **b** a sweet thing. **4** a person or thing excellent of its kind. **5** esp. *US* (usu. as a form of address) darling, sweetheart. ◻ **honey-badger** a ratel. **honey-bee** any of various bees of the genus *Apis*, esp. the common hive-bee (*A. mellifera*). **honey-bun** (or **-bunch**) (esp. as a form of address) darling. **honey-buzzard** any bird of prey of the genus *Pernis* feeding on the larvae of bees and wasps. **honey-eater** any Australasian bird of the family Meliphagidae with a long tongue that can take nectar from flowers. **honey-fungus** a parasitic fungus, *Armillaria mellea*, with honey-coloured edible toadstools. **honey-guide 1** any small bird of the family Indicatoridae which feeds on beeswax and insects. **2** a marking on the corolla of a flower thought to guide bees to nectar. **honey-parrot** a lorikeet. **honey-pot 1** a pot for honey. **2** a posture with the hands clasped under the hams. **3** something very attractive or tempting. **honey sac** an enlarged part of a bee's gullet where honey is formed. **honey-sweet** sweet as honey. [OE *hunig* f. Gmc]

■ **5** see DEAR *n.*

honeycomb /húnnikōm/ *n.* & *v.* ● *n.* **1** a structure of hexagonal cells of wax, made by bees to store honey and

eggs. **2 a** a pattern arranged hexagonally. **b** fabric made with a pattern of raised hexagons etc. **3** tripe from the second stomach of a ruminant. **4** a cavernous flaw in metalwork, esp. in guns. ● *v.tr.* **1** fill with cavities or tunnels, undermine. **2** mark with a honeycomb pattern. [OE *hunigcamb* (as HONEY, COMB)]
■ *v.* **1** see RIDDLE² *v.* 1.

honeydew /húnnidyoō/ *n.* **1** a sweet sticky substance found on leaves and stems, excreted by aphids. **2** a variety of melon with smooth pale skin and sweet green flesh. **3** an ideally sweet substance. **4** tobacco sweetened with molasses.

honeyed /húnnid/ *adj.* (also **honied**) **1** of or containing honey. **2** sweet.

honeymoon /húnnimoōn/ *n.* & *v.* ● *n.* **1** a holiday spent together by a newly married couple. **2** an initial period of enthusiasm or goodwill. ● *v.intr.* (usu. foll. by *in, at*) spend a honeymoon. □□ **honeymooner** *n.* [HONEY + MOON, orig. with ref. to waning affection, not to a period of a month]

honeysuckle /húnnisukk'l/ *n.* any climbing shrub of the genus *Lonicera* with fragrant yellow and pink flowers. [ME *hunisuccle, -soukel*, extension of *hunisuce, -souke*, f. OE *hunigsūce, -sūge* (as HONEY, SUCK)]

honied var. of HONEYED.

honk /hongk/ *n.* & *v.* ● *n.* **1** the cry of a wild goose. **2** the harsh sound of a car horn. ● *v.* **1** *intr.* emit or give a honk. **2** *tr.* cause to do this. [imit.]

honky /hóngki/ *n.* (*pl.* **-ies**) *US Black sl. offens.* **1** a White person. **2** White people collectively. [20th c.: orig. unkn.]

honky-tonk /hóngkitongk/ *n. colloq.* **1** ragtime piano music. **2** a cheap or disreputable nightclub, dancehall, etc. [20th c.: orig. unkn.]
■ **2** see DIVE *n.* 4.

honnête homme /ónnayt óm/ *n.* an honest and decent man. [F]

honor *US* var. of HONOUR.

honorable *US* var. of HONOURABLE.

honorand /ónnərand/ *n.* a person to be honoured, esp. with an honorary degree. [L *honorandus* (as HONOUR)]

honorarium /ónnəráiriəm/ *n.* (*pl.* **honorariums** or **honoraria** /-riə/) a fee, esp. a voluntary payment for professional services rendered without the normal fee. [L, neut. of *honorarius*: see HONORARY]
■ pay, payment, remuneration; emolument, fee.

honorary /ónnərəri/ *adj.* **1 a** conferred as an honour, without the usual requirements, functions, etc. (*honorary degree*). **b** holding such a title or position (*honorary colonel*). **2** (of an office or its holder) unpaid (*honorary secretaryship*; *honorary treasurer*). **3** (of an obligation) depending on honour, not legally enforceable. [L *honorarius* (as HONOUR)]
■ **1** see NOMINAL 1. **2** see UNPAID.

honorific /ónnəriffik/ *adj.* & *n.* ● *adj.* **1** conferring honour. **2** (esp. of Oriental forms of speech) implying respect. ● *n.* an honorific form of words. □□ **honorifically** *adv.* [L *honorificus* (as HONOUR)]

honoris causa /onóriss kówzə/ *adv.* (esp. of a degree awarded without examination) as a mark of esteem. [L, = for the sake of honour]

honour /ónnər/ *n.* & *v.* (*US* **honor**) ● *n.* **1** high respect; glory; credit, reputation, good name. **2** adherence to what is right or to a conventional standard of conduct. **3** nobleness of mind, magnanimity (*honour among thieves*). **4** a thing conferred as a distinction, esp. an official award for bravery or achievement. **5** (foll. by *of* + verbal noun, or *to* + infin.) privilege, special right (*had the honour of being invited*). **6 a** exalted position. **b** (**Honour**) (prec. by *your, his*, etc.) a title of a circuit judge, *US* a mayor, and *Ir.* or in rustic speech any person of rank. **7** (foll. by *to*) a person or thing that brings honour (*she is an honour to her profession*). **8 a** (of a woman) chastity. **b** the reputation for this. **9** (in *pl.*) **a** special distinction for proficiency in an examination. **b** a course of degree studies more specialized than for an ordinary pass. **10 a** *Bridge* the ace, king, queen, jack, and ten, esp. of trumps, or the four aces at no trumps. **b** *Whist* the ace, king, queen, and jack, esp. of trumps. **11** *Golf* the right of driving off first as having won the last hole (*it is my honour*). ● *v.tr.* **1** respect highly. **2** confer honour on. **3** accept or pay (a bill or cheque) when due. **4** acknowledge. □ **do the honours** perform the duties of a host to guests etc. **honour bright** *colloq.* = *on my honour.* **honour point** *Heraldry* the point halfway between the top of a shield and the fesse point. **honours are even** there is equality in the contest. **honours list** a list of persons awarded honours. **honours of war** privileges granted to a capitulating force, e.g. that of marching out with colours flying. **honour system** a system of examinations etc. without supervision, relying on the honour of those concerned. **honour-trick** = *quick trick.* **in honour bound** = *on one's honour.* **in honour of** as a celebration of. **on one's honour** (usu. foll. by *to* + infin.) under a moral obligation. **on** (or **upon**) **my honour** an expression of sincerity. [ME f. OF *(h)onor* (n.), *onorer* (v.) f. L *honor, honarare*]
■ *n.* **1** respect, esteem, reverence, veneration, homage, regard, renown, glory, celebrity, distinction, prestige, illustriousness, reputation, credit, *colloq.* kudos. **2, 3** probity, uprightness, decency, righteousness, rectitude, morality, justice, virtuousness, virtue; nobleness, magnanimity, integrity, honesty, fairness, justness, goodness. **4** see AWARD *n.* 1a. **5** privilege, distinction, special right; blessing. **6 a** see DIGNITY 4. **8** virginity, chastity, virtue, purity, innocence, chasteness; reputation, (good) name. ● *v.* **1** respect, esteem, revere, venerate, prize, value, pay homage to. **2** praise, laud, glorify, eulogize, salute, hail, acclaim, exalt. **3** pay, redeem, accept, clear, settle. **4** carry out, discharge, fulfil, observe, meet; acknowledge.

honourable /ónnərəb'l/ *adj.* (*US* **honorable**) **1 a** worthy of honour. **b** bringing honour to its possessor. **c** showing honour, not base. **d** consistent with honour. **e** *colloq.* (of the intentions of a man courting a woman) directed towards marriage. **2** (**Honourable**) a title indicating eminence or distinction, given to certain high officials, the children of certain ranks of the nobility, and MPs. □ **honourable mention** an award of merit to a candidate in an examination, a work of art, etc., not awarded a prize. □□ **honourableness** *n.* **honourably** *adv.* [ME f. OF *honorable* f. L *honorabilis* (as HONOUR)]
■ **1 a, b, c** upright, upstanding, trustworthy, honest, just, fair, moral, principled, uncorrupt, uncorrupted, incorruptible, high-minded, noble, virtuous, chivalrous, righteous, right-minded, good, scrupulous, worthy, sterling, laudable, creditable, commendable, glorious, equitable, *archaic or joc.* trusty. **d** right, correct, proper, fitting, appropriate, virtuous, ethical, worthy, respectable, reputable, decent.

Hon. Sec. *abbr.* Honorary Secretary.

hooch /hoōch/ *n.* (also **hootch**) *US colloq.* alcoholic liquor, esp. inferior or illicit whisky. [abbr. of Alaskan *hoochinoo*, name of a liquor-making tribe]
■ see DRINK *n.* 2a.

hood¹ /hŏŏd/ *n.* & *v.* ● *n.* **1 a** a covering for the head and neck, whether part of a cloak etc. or separate. **b** a separate hoodlike garment worn over a university gown or a surplice to indicate the wearer's degree. **2** *Brit.* a folding waterproof top of a motor car, pram, etc. **3** *US* the bonnet of a motor vehicle. **4** a canopy to protect users of machinery or to remove fumes etc. **5** the hoodlike part of a cobra, seal, etc. **6** a leather covering for a hawk's head. ● *v.tr.* cover with a hood. □ **hood-mould** (or **-moulding**) *Archit.* a dripstone. □□ **hoodless** *adj.* **hoodlike** *adj.* [OE *hōd* f. WG, rel. to HAT]

hood² /hŏŏd, hoōd/ *n. US sl.* a gangster or gunman. [abbr. of HOODLUM]
■ see GANGSTER.

-hood /hŏŏd/ *suffix* forming nouns: **1** of condition or state (*childhood*; *falsehood*). **2** indicating a collection or group (*sisterhood*; *neighbourhood*). [OE *-hād*, orig. an independent noun, = person, condition, quality]

hooded /hŏŏddid/ *adj.* having a hood; covered with a hood. □ **hooded crow** a piebald grey and black crow, *Corvus cornix*.

hoodie /hŏŏddi/ *n.* = *hooded crow*.

hoodlum /hŏŏdləm/ *n.* **1** a street hooligan, a young thug. **2** a gangster. [19th c.: orig. unkn.]

■ **1** thug, ruffian, tough, rowdy, knave, rogue, scoundrel, hooligan, *Austral.* larrikin, *colloq.* roughneck, *Brit. sl.* yob, yobbo, bovver boy, *US sl.* plug-ugly, mug; see also BARBARIAN *n.* 1. **2** gangster, racketeer, desperado, terrorist, apache, crook, *colloq.* baddy, *sl.* mobster, *esp. US sl.* goon, *US sl.* hood, gunsel.

hoodoo /hŏŏdōō/ *n.* & *v.* esp. *US* ● *n.* **1 a** bad luck. **b** a thing or person that brings or causes this. **2** voodoo. **3** a fantastic rock pinnacle or column of rock formed by erosion etc. ● *v.tr.* (**hoodoos, hoodooed**) **1** make unlucky. **2** bewitch. [alt. of VOODOO]

■ *n.* **1** see JINX *n.* ● *v.* **2** see BEWITCH 2.

hoodwink /hŏŏdwingk/ *v.tr.* deceive, delude. [orig. 'blindfold', f. HOOD[1] *n.* + WINK]

■ fool, trick, deceive, delude, mislead, dupe, gull, defraud, cheat, humbug, lead up *or* down the garden path, flimflam, take in, throw dust in a person's eyes, pull the wool over a person's eyes, beguile, *archaic* chicane, *colloq.* do, bamboozle, diddle, pull a fast one on, string along, finagle, rip off, put one over on, *sl.* take for a ride, chisel, cross, clip, bilk, rook, con, gyp, take to the cleaners.

hooey /hōō-i/ *n.* & *int. sl.* nonsense, humbug. [20th c.: orig. unkn.]

■ see NONSENSE.

hoof /hōōf/ *n.* & *v.* ● *n.* (*pl.* **hoofs** or **hooves** /hōōvz/) the horny part of the foot of a horse, antelope, and other ungulates. ● *v.* **1** *tr.* strike with a hoof. **2** *tr. sl.* kick or shove. □ **hoof it** *sl.* **1** go on foot. **2** dance. **on the hoof** (of cattle) not yet slaughtered. □□ **hoofed** *adj.* (also in *comb.*). [OE *hōf* f. Gmc]

hoofer /hōōfər/ *n. sl.* a professional dancer.

hoo-ha /hōōhaa/ *n. sl.* a commotion, a row; uproar, trouble. [20th c.: orig. unkn.]

■ see UPROAR.

hook /hŏŏk/ *n.* & *v.* ● *n.* **1 a** a piece of metal or other material bent back at an angle or with a round bend, for catching hold or for hanging things on. **b** (in full **fish-hook**) a bent piece of wire, usu. barbed and baited, for catching fish. **2** a curved cutting instrument (*reaping-hook*). **3 a** a sharp bend, e.g. in a river. **b** a projecting point of land (*Hook of Holland*). **c** a sand-spit with a curved end. **4 a** *Cricket* & *Golf* a hooking stroke (see sense 5 of *v.*). **b** *Boxing* a short swinging blow with the elbow bent and rigid. **5** a trap, a snare. **6 a** a curved stroke in handwriting, esp. as made in learning to write. **b** *Mus.* an added stroke transverse to the stem in the symbol for a quaver etc. **7** (in *pl.*) *sl.* fingers. ● *v.* **1** *tr.* **a** grasp with a hook. **b** secure with a hook or hooks. **2** (often foll. by *on, up*) **a** *tr.* attach with or as with a hook. **b** *intr.* be or become attached with a hook. **3** *tr.* catch with or as with a hook (*he hooked a fish*; *she hooked a husband*). **4** *tr. sl.* steal. **5** *tr.* **a** *Cricket* play (the ball) round from the off to the on side with an upward stroke. **b** (also *absol.*) *Golf* strike (the ball) so that it deviates towards the striker. **6** *tr. Rugby Football* secure (the ball) and pass it backward with the foot in the scrum. **7** *tr. Boxing* strike (one's opponent) with the elbow bent and rigid. □ **be hooked on** *sl.* be addicted to or captivated by. **by hook or by crook** by one means or another, by fair means or foul. **hook and eye** a small metal hook and loop as a fastener on a garment. **hook it** *sl.* make off, run away. **hook, line, and sinker** entirely. **hook-nose** an aquiline nose. **hook-nosed** having an aquiline nose. **hook-up** a connection, esp. an interconnection of broadcasting equipment for special transmissions. **off the hook 1** *colloq.* no longer in difficulty or trouble. **2** (of a telephone receiver) not on its rest, and so preventing incoming calls. **off the hooks** *sl.* dead. **on one's own hook** *sl.* on one's own account. **sling** (or **take**) **one's hook** *sl.* = *hook it*. □□ **hookless** *adj.* **hooklet** *n.* **hooklike** *adj.* [OE *hōc*: sense 3 of *n.* prob. influenced by Du. *hoek* corner]

■ *n.* **1 a** hanger, peg, holder; fastener, catch, clasp, clip, pin. **5** see TRAP[1] *n.* 1. ● *v.* **3** catch, trap, entrap, snare, ensnare, bag, land; grab, capture, collar, seize, *US* snag, *sl.* nab. **4** steal, pilfer, filch, *colloq.* lift, rip off, *sl.* snitch, pinch, liberate, *Brit. sl.* nick; see also APPROPRIATE *v.* 1. □ **be hooked on** be mad *or* crazy about, be addicted to; see also LOVE *v.* 2–4. **by hook or by crook** somehow (or other), some way, come what may, by fair means or foul, one way or another. **hook it** see RUN *v.* 2. **hook, line, and sinker** completely, entirely, all the way, through and through, thoroughly, totally, utterly, wholly. **off the hook 1** (set) free, (in the) clear, out of trouble, acquitted, exonerated, cleared. **off the hooks** see DEAD *adj.* 1.

hookah /hŏŏkkə/ *n.* an oriental tobacco-pipe with a long tube passing through water for cooling the smoke as it is drawn through. [Urdu f. Arab. *ḥukkah* casket]

■ see PIPE *n.* 2a.

hooked /hŏŏkt/ *adj.* **1** hook-shaped (*hooked nose*). **2** furnished with a hook or hooks. **3** in senses of HOOK *v.* **4** (of a rug or mat) made by pulling woollen yarn through canvas with a hook.

hooker[1] /hŏŏkkər/ *n.* **1** *Rugby Football* the player in the middle of the front row of the scrum who tries to hook the ball. **2** *sl.* a prostitute. **3** a person or thing that hooks.

■ **2** see PROSTITUTE *n.* 1a.

hooker[2] /hŏŏkkər/ *n.* **1** a small Dutch or Irish fishing-vessel. **2** *derog.* any ship. [Du. *hoeker* f. *hoek* HOOK]

Hooke's law /hŏŏks/ *n.* the law that the strain in a solid is proportional to the applied stress within the elastic limit of that solid. [R. *Hooke*, Engl. scientist d. 1703]

hookey /hŏŏkki/ *n.* (also **hooky**) *US* □ **blind hookey** a gambling guessing-game at cards. **play hookey** *sl.* play truant. [19th c.: orig. unkn.]

hookworm /hŏŏkwurm/ *n.* **1** any of various nematode worms, with hooklike mouthparts for attachment and feeding, infesting humans and animals. **2** a disease caused by one of these, often resulting in severe anaemia.

hooligan /hōōligən/ *n.* a young ruffian, esp. a member of a gang. □□ **hooliganism** *n.* [19th c.: orig. unkn.]

■ see THUG.

hoon / hōōn/ *n.* & *v. Austral. sl.* ● *n.* a lout or idiot. ● *v.intr.* behave like a hoon. [orig. unkn.]

hoop[1] /hōōp/ *n.* & *v.* ● *n.* **1** a circular band of metal, wood, etc., esp. for binding the staves of casks etc. or for forming part of a framework. **2 a** a ring bowled along by a child. **b** a large ring usu. with paper stretched over it for circus performers to jump through. **3** an arch of iron etc. through which the balls are hit in croquet. **4** *hist.* **a** a circle of flexible material for expanding a woman's petticoat or skirt. **b** (in full **hoop petticoat**) a petticoat expanded with this. **5 a** a band in contrasting colour on a jockey's blouse, sleeves, or cap. **b** *Austral. colloq.* a jockey. ● *v.tr.* **1** bind with a hoop or hoops. **2** encircle with or as with a hoop. □ **be put** (or **go**) **through the hoop** (or **hoops**) undergo an ordeal. **hoop-iron** iron in long thin strips for binding casks etc. **hoop-la 1** *Brit.* a game in which rings are thrown in an attempt to encircle one of various prizes. **2** *sl.* commotion. **3** *sl.* pretentious nonsense. [OE *hōp* f. WG]

■ *n.* **1, 2** see RING[1] *n.* 2. ● *v.* **2** see CIRCLE *v.* 2.

hoop[2] var. of WHOOP.

hoopoe /hōōpōō/ *n.* a salmon-pink bird, *Upupa epops*, with black and white wings and tail, a large erectile crest, and a long decurved bill. [alt. of ME *hoop* f. OF *huppe* f. L *upupa*, imit. of its cry]

hooray /hooráy/ *int.* **1** = HURRAH. **2** *Austral.* & *NZ* goodbye. □ **Hooray Henry** /hóoray/ *Brit. sl.* a rich ineffectual young man, esp. one who is fashionable, extroverted, and conventional. [var. of HURRAH]

hooroo / hoorōō/ *int.* & *n.* (also **hurroo**) *Austral. colloq.* = HURRAH. [alt. of HOORAY, HURRAH]

hoosegow /hóōsgow/ *n. US sl.* a prison. [Amer. Sp. *juzgao*, Sp. *juzgado* tribunal f. L *judicatum* neut. past part. of *judicare* JUDGE]
■ see PRISON *n.* 1.

hoot /hōōt/ *n.* & *v.* ● *n.* **1** an owl's cry. **2** the sound made by a motor horn or a steam whistle. **3** a shout expressing scorn or disapproval; an inarticulate shout. **4** *colloq.* **a** laughter. **b** a cause of this. **5** (also **two hoots**) *sl.* anything at all (*don't care a hoot*; *don't give a hoot*; *doesn't matter two hoots*). ● *v.* **1** *intr.* **a** (of an owl) utter its cry. **b** (of a motor horn or steam whistle) make a hoot. **c** (often foll. by *at*) make loud sounds, esp. of scorn or disapproval or *colloq.* merriment (*hooted with laughter*). **2** *tr.* **a** assail with scornful shouts. **b** (often foll. by *out*, *away*) drive away by hooting. **3** *tr.* sound (a motor horn or steam whistle). [ME *hūten* (v.), perh. imit.]
■ *n.* **1** see SQUAWK *n.* 1. **3** see JEER *n.* **4 a** see LAUGH *n.* 1. **5** see DAMN *n.* 2. ● *v.* **1 c** see LAUGH *v.* 1. **2** see SQUAWK *v.*

hootch var. of HOOCH.

hootenanny /hōōt'nanni/ *n.* (*pl.* **-ies**) *US colloq.* an informal gathering with folk music. [orig. dial., = 'gadget']

hooter /hōōtər/ *n.* **1** *Brit.* a siren or steam whistle, esp. as a signal for work to begin or cease. **2** *Brit.* the horn of a motor vehicle. **3** *sl.* a nose. **4** a person or animal that hoots.

hoots /hōōts/ *int. Sc.* & *N.Engl.* expressing dissatisfaction or impatience. [natural exclam.: cf. Sw. *hut* begone, Welsh *hwt* away, Ir. *ut* out, all in similar sense]

Hoover /hōōvər/ *n.* & *v.* ● *n. propr.* a vacuum cleaner (properly one made by the Hoover company). ● *v.* (**hoover**) **1** *tr.* (also *absol.*) clean (a carpet etc.) with a vacuum cleaner. **2** (foll. by *up*) **a** *tr.* suck up with or as with a vacuum cleaner (*hoovered up the crumbs*). **b** *absol.* clean a room etc. with a vacuum cleaner (*decided to hoover up before they arrived*). [W. H. *Hoover*, Amer. manufacturer d. 1932]
■ *v.* see CLEAN *v.* 1.

hooves *pl.* of HOOF.

hop[1] /hop/ *v.* & *n.* ● *v.* (**hopped, hopping**) **1** *intr.* (of a bird, frog, etc.) spring with two or all feet at once. **2** *intr.* (of a person) jump on one foot. **3** *tr.* cross (a ditch etc.) by hopping. **4** *intr. colloq.* **a** make a quick trip. **b** make a quick change of position or location. **5** *tr. colloq.* **a** jump into (a vehicle). **b** obtain (a ride) in this way. **6** *tr.* (usu. as **hopping** *n.*) (esp. of aircraft) pass quickly from one (place of a specified type) to another (*cloud-hopping*; *hedge-hopping*). ● *n.* **1** a hopping movement. **2** *colloq.* an informal dance. **3** a short flight in an aircraft; the distance travelled by air without landing; a stage of a flight or journey. □ **hop in** (or **out**) *colloq.* get into (or out of) a car etc. **hop it** *Brit. sl.* go away. **hopping mad** *colloq.* very angry. **hop, skip** (or **step**), **and jump** = *triple jump*. **hop the twig** (or **stick**) *sl.* **1** depart suddenly. **2** die. **on the hop** *colloq.* **1** unprepared (*caught on the hop*). **2** bustling about. [OE *hoppian*]
■ *v.* **1** jump, leap, bound, spring, vault. **4 a** pop, nip, run, take a (short) trip, travel, come, go. ● *n.* **1** jump, leap, bound, spring, vault. **2** *colloq.* disco, bop; see also DANCE *n.* **3** (short) trip *or* flight *or* journey. □ **hop in** jump in, get in, climb in. **hop it** see RUN *v.* 2. **hopping mad** see FURIOUS 1, 2. **hop the twig 1** see RUN *v.* 2. **2** see DIE[1] 1. **on the hop 1** in the act, unready; see also UNPREPARED.

hop[2] /hop/ *n.* & *v.* ● *n.* **1** a climbing plant, *Humulus lupulus*, cultivated for the cones borne by the female. **2** (in *pl.*) **a** the ripe cones of this, used to give a bitter flavour to beer. **b** *Austral.* & *NZ colloq.* beer. **3** *US sl.* opium or any other narcotic. ● *v.* (**hopped, hopping**) **1** *tr.* flavour with hops. **2** *intr.* produce or pick hops. **3** *tr. US sl.* (foll. by *up*) stimulate with a drug. (esp. as **hopped up**). □ **hop-bind** (or **-bine**) the climbing stem of the hop. **hop-sack** (or **-sacking**) **1 a** a coarse material made from hemp etc. **b** sacking for hops made from this. **2** a coarse clothing fabric of a loose plain weave. [ME *hoppe* f. MLG, MDu. *hoppe*]

hope /hōp/ *n.* & *v.* ● *n.* **1** (in *sing.* or *pl.*; often foll. by *of*, *that*) expectation and desire combined, e.g. for a certain thing to occur (*hope of getting the job*). **2 a** a person, thing, or circumstance that gives cause for hope. **b** ground of hope, promise. **3** what is hoped for. **4** *archaic* a feeling of trust. ● *v.* **1** *intr.* (often foll. by *for*) feel hope. **2** *tr.* expect and desire. **3** *tr.* feel fairly confident. □ **hope against hope** cling to a mere possibility. **hope chest** *US* = *bottom drawer*. **not a** (or **some**) **hope!** *colloq.* no chance at all. □□ **hoper** *n.* [OE *hopa*]
■ *n.* **1, 3** desire, wish, expectation; ambition, dream; yearning, hankering, craving, longing, fancy; see also AMBITION 2. **2 b** prospect, promise, expectation, expectancy, confidence, anticipation, security, faith, conviction, belief, trust. ● *v.* **1, 2** expect, wait, trust; anticipate, contemplate, foresee; (*hope for*) wish, want, desire, look for, seek. **3** (*hope to*) count *or* rely on *or* upon, expect *or* intend to; see also TRUST *v.* 1. □ **not a hope** see *not an earthly* (EARTHLY).

hopeful /hōpfōōl/ *adj.* & *n.* ● *adj.* **1** feeling hope. **2** causing or inspiring hope. **3** likely to succeed, promising. ● *n.* (in full **young hopeful**) **1** a person likely to succeed. **2** *iron.* a person likely to be disappointed. □□ **hopefulness** *n.*
■ *adj.* **1** wishful, desirous, anxious, expectant; sanguine, confident, assured, buoyant, bullish; see also *optimistic* (OPTIMISM). **2, 3** promising, bright, rosy, cheering, reassuring, heartening, encouraging, auspicious, propitious, inspiriting, positive.

hopefully /hōpfōōli/ *adv.* **1** in a hopeful manner. **2** *disp.* (qualifying a whole sentence) it is to be hoped (*hopefully, the car will be ready by then*).
■ **1** expectantly, optimistically, sanguinely, confidently. **2** with (any) luck, if things go well, all being well, it is hoped.

hopeless /hōpliss/ *adj.* **1** feeling no hope. **2** admitting no hope (*a hopeless case*). **3** inadequate, incompetent (*am hopeless at tennis*). **4** without hope of success; futile. □□ **hopelessly** *adv.* **hopelessness** *n.*
■ **1** despairing, despondent, forlorn, disconsolate, inconsolable, depressed, dejected, melancholy, downcast, gloomy, miserable, discouraged, wretched, sorrowful, sad, unhappy. **2** desperate, beyond hope *or* saving, irreparable, beyond repair, irremediable, lost, irretrievable. **3** bad, poor, incompetent, inadequate, inept, unqualified, unfit, unskilful, deficient, feeble, ineffectual, *esp. Brit.* rubbishy, *colloq.* useless, *sl.* dud. **4** futile, vain, unavailing, impossible, impracticable, unworkable, pointless, worthless, useless, *archaic* bootless.

hophead /hóp-hed/ *n. sl.* **1** *US* a drug addict. **2** *Austral.* & *NZ* a drunkard.
■ **1** see ADDICT *n.* 1. **2** see ALCOHOLIC *n.*

hoplite /hóplīt/ *n.* a heavily-armed foot-soldier of ancient Greece. [Gk *hoplitēs* f. *hoplon* weapon]

hopper[1] /hóppər/ *n.* **1** a person who hops. **2** a hopping arthropod, esp. a flea or cheese-maggot or young locust. **3 a** a container tapering downward (orig. having a hopping motion) through which grain passes into a mill. **b** a similar contrivance in various machines. **4 a** a barge carrying away mud etc. from a dredging-machine and discharging it. **b** a railway truck able to discharge coal etc. through its floor.

hopper[2] /hóppər/ *n.* a hop-picker.

hopple /hópp'l/ *v.* & *n.* ● *v.tr.* fasten together the legs of (a horse etc.) to prevent it from straying etc. ● *n.* an apparatus for this. [prob. LG: cf. HOBBLE and early Flem. *hoppelen* = MDu. *hobelen* jump, dance]

hopscotch /hópskoch/ *n.* a children's game of hopping over squares or oblongs marked on the ground to retrieve a flat stone etc. [HOP[1] + SCOTCH[1]]

horary /hórəri/ *adj. archaic* **1** of the hours. **2** occurring every hour, hourly. [med.L *horarius* f. L *hora* HOUR]

horde /hord/ *n.* **1 a** usu. *derog.* a large group, a gang. **b** a moving swarm or pack (of insects, wolves, etc.). **2** a troop of Tartar or other nomads. [Pol. *horda* f. Turki *ordī*, *ordū* camp: cf. URDU]

horehound /hórhownd/ *n.* (also **hoarhound**) **1 a** a herbaceous plant, *Marrubium vulgare*, with a white cottony covering on its stem and leaves. **b** its bitter aromatic juice used against coughs etc. **2** a herbaceous plant, *Ballota nigra*, with an unpleasant aroma. [OE *hāre hūne* f. *hār* HOAR + *hūne* a plant]

horizon /hərī́z'n/ *n.* **1 a** the line at which the earth and sky appear to meet. **b** (in full **apparent** or **sensible** or **visible horizon**) the line at which the earth and sky would appear to meet but for irregularities and obstructions; a circle where the earth's surface touches a cone whose vertex is at the observer's eye. **c** (in full **celestial** or **rational** or **true horizon**) a great circle of the celestial sphere, the plane of which passes through the centre of the earth and is parallel to that of the apparent horizon of a place. **2** limit of mental perception, experience, interest, etc. **3** a geological stratum or set of strata, or layer of soil, with particular characteristics. **4** *Archaeol.* the level at which a particular set of remains is found. □ **on the horizon** (of an event) just imminent or becoming apparent. [ME f. OF *orizon(te)* f. LL *horizon -ontis* f. Gk *horizōn* (*kuklos*) limiting (circle)]

■ **2** view, purview, range, scope, vista, compass, perspective, ken, field of vision, limit(s). □ **on the horizon** see *in the pipeline* (PIPELINE).

horizontal /hórrizónt'l/ *adj.* & *n.* ● *adj.* **1 a** parallel to the plane of the horizon, at right angles to the vertical (*horizontal plane*). **b** (of machinery etc.) having its parts working in a horizontal direction. **2 a** combining firms engaged in the same stage of production (*horizontal integration*). **b** involving social groups of equal status etc. **3** of or at the horizon. ● *n.* a horizontal line, plane, etc. □□ **horizontality** /-tálliti/ *n.* **horizontally** *adv.* **horizontalness** *n.* [F *horizontal* or mod.L *horizontalis* (as HORIZON)]

■ *adj.* **1 a** level, flat, plane; prone, supine, prostrate.

hormone /hórmōn/ *n.* **1** *Biochem.* a regulatory substance produced in an organism and transported in tissue fluids such as blood or sap to stimulate cells or tissues into action. **2** a synthetic substance with a similar effect. □□ **hormonal** /-mṓn'l/ *adj.* [Gk *hormōn* part. of *hormaō* impel]

horn /horn/ *n.* & *v.* ● *n.* **1 a** a hard permanent outgrowth, often curved and pointed, on the head of cattle, rhinoceroses, giraffes, and other esp. hoofed mammals, found singly, in pairs, or one in front of another. **b** the structure of a horn, consisting of a core of bone encased in keratinized skin. **2** each of two deciduous branched appendages on the head of (esp. male) deer. **3** a hornlike projection on the head of other animals, e.g. a snail's tentacle, the crest of a horned owl, etc. **4** the substance of which horns are composed. **5** anything resembling or compared to a horn in shape. **6** *Mus.* **a** = *French horn.* **b** a wind instrument played by lip vibration, orig. made of horn, now usu. of brass. **c** a horn player. **7** an instrument sounding a warning or other signal (*car horn*; *foghorn*). **8** a receptacle or instrument made of horn, e.g. a drinking-vessel or powder-flask etc. **9** a horn-shaped projection. **10** the extremity of the moon or other crescent. **11 a** an arm or branch of a river, bay, etc. **b** (**the Horn**) Cape Horn. **12** a pyramidal peak formed by glacial action. **13** *coarse sl.* an erect penis. **14** the hornlike emblem of a cuckold. ● *v.tr.* **1** (esp. as **horned** *adj.*) provide with horns. **2** gore with the horns. □ **horn in** *sl.* **1** (usu. foll. by *on*) intrude. **2** interfere. **horn of plenty** a cornucopia. **horn-rimmed** (esp. of spectacles) having rims made of horn or a substance resembling it. **on the horns of a dilemma** faced with a decision involving equally unfavourable alternatives. □□ **hornist** *n.* (in sense 6 of *n.*). **hornless** *adj.* **hornlike** *adj.* [OE f. Gmc, rel. to L *cornu*]

■ *n.* **7** see ALARM *n.* 2a. ● *v.* **2** see GORE².

hornbeam /hórnbeem/ *n.* any tree of the genus *Carpinus*, with a smooth bark and a hard tough wood.

hornbill /hórnbil/ *n.* any bird of the family Bucerotidae, with a hornlike excrescence on its large red or yellow curved bill.

hornblende /hórnblend/ *n.* a dark-brown, black, or green mineral occurring in many igneous and metamorphic rocks, and composed of calcium, magnesium, and iron silicates. [G (as HORN, BLENDE)]

hornbook /hórnbŏŏk/ *n. hist.* a leaf of paper containing the alphabet, the Lord's Prayer, etc., mounted on a wooden tablet with a handle, and protected by a thin plate of horn.

horned /hornd/ *adj.* having a horn. □ **horned owl** an owl, *Bubo virginianus*, with hornlike feathers over the ears. **horned toad 1** an American lizard, *Phrynosoma cornutum*, covered with spiny scales. **2** any SE Asian toad of the family Pelobatidae, with horn-shaped extensions over the eyes.

hornet /hórnit/ *n.* a large wasp, *Vespa crabro*, with a brown and yellow striped body, and capable of inflicting a serious sting. □ **stir up a hornets' nest** provoke or cause trouble or opposition. [prob. f. MLG, MDu. *horn(e)te*, corresp. to OE *hyrnet*, perh. rel. to HORN]

hornpipe /hórnpīp/ *n.* **1** a lively dance, usu. by one person (esp. associated with sailors). **2** the music for this. [name of an obs. wind instrument partly of horn: ME, f. HORN + PIPE]

hornstone /hórnstōn/ *n.* a brittle siliceous rock.

hornswoggle /hórnswogg'l/ *v.tr. sl.* cheat, hoax. [19th c.: orig. unkn.]

hornwort /hórnwurt/ *n.* any aquatic rootless plant of the genus *Ceratophyllum*, with forked leaves.

horny /hórni/ *adj.* (**hornier, horniest**) **1** of or like horn. **2** hard like horn, callous (*horny-handed*). **3** *sl.* sexually excited. □□ **horniness** *n.*

■ **3** see *lustful* (LUST).

horologe /hórrəloj/ *n. archaic* a timepiece. [ME f. OF *orloge* f. L *horologium* f. Gk *hōrologion* f. *hōra* time + *-logos* -telling]

horology /hərólləji/ *n.* the art of measuring time or making clocks, watches, etc.; the study of this. □□ **horologer** *n.* **horologic** /hórrəlójik/ *adj.* **horological** /hórrəlójik'l/ *adj.* **horologist** *n.* [Gk *hōra* time + -LOGY]

horoscope /hórrəskōp/ *n. Astrol.* **1** a forecast of a person's future based on a diagram showing the relative positions of the stars and planets at that person's birth. **2** such a diagram (*cast a horoscope*). **3** observation of the sky and planets at a particular moment, esp. at a person's birth. □□ **horoscopic** /-skóppik/ *adj.* **horoscopical** /-skóppik'l/ *adj.* **horoscopy** /həróskəpi/ *n.* [F f. L *horoscopus* f. Gk *hōroskopos* f. *hōra* time + *skopos* observer]

horrendous /hərέndəss/ *adj.* horrifying; awful. □□ **horrendously** *adv.* **horrendousness** *n.* [L *horrendus* gerundive of *horrēre*: see HORRID]

■ see HORRIBLE 1.

horrent /hórrənt/ *adj. poet.* **1** bristling. **2** shuddering. [L *horrēre*: see HORRID]

horrible /hórrib'l/ *adj.* **1** causing or likely to cause horror; hideous, shocking. **2** *colloq.* unpleasant, excessive (*horrible weather*; *horrible noise*). □□ **horribleness** *n.* **horribly** *adv.* [ME f. OF *(h)orrible* f. L *horribilis* f. *horrēre*: see HORRID]

■ **1** awful, horrendous, hideous, horrid, horrifying, horrific, terrible, terrifying, dreadful, abominable, abhorrent, appalling, frightening, frightful, ghastly, grim, grisly, ghoulish, gruesome, loathsome, repulsive, revolting, disgusting, sickening, shocking, atrocious, nauseating, nauseous, harrowing, blood-curdling, unspeakable, monstrous, contemptible, despicable. **2** unpleasant, disagreeable, nasty, atrocious, objectionable, obnoxious, offensive, *colloq.* awful, detestable, horrid, terrible, dreadful, abominable, beastly, ghastly, frightful, shocking, accursed, infernal; see also REVOLTING.

horrid /hórrid/ *adj.* **1** horrible, revolting. **2** *colloq.* unpleasant, disagreeable (*horrid weather*; *horrid children*). **3** *poet.* rough, bristling. □□ **horridly** *adv.* **horridness** *n.* [L *horridus* f. *horrēre* bristle, shudder]

■ **1, 2** see HORRIBLE.

horrific /hərίffik/ *adj.* horrifying. □□ **horrifically** *adv.* [F *horrifique* or L *horrificus* f. *horrēre*: see HORRID]

■ see HORRIBLE 1.

horrify /hórrifī/ *v.tr.* (**-ies, -ied**) arouse horror in; shock, scandalize. □□ **horrification** /-fikáysh'n/ *n.* **horrifiedly**

/-fīdli/ *adv.* **horrifying** *adj.* **horrifyingly** *adv.* [L *horrificare* (as HORRIFIC)]
■ startle, upset, outrage, dismay, appal, distress, scandalize; see also SHOCK[1] *v.* 1.

horripilation /hórripiláysh'n/ *n. literary* = *goose-flesh.* [LL *horripilatio* f. L *horrēre* to bristle + *pilus* hair]

horror /hórrər/ *n.* & *adj.* ● *n.* **1** a painful feeling of loathing and fear. **2 a** (often foll. by *of*) intense dislike. **b** (often foll. by *at*) *colloq.* intense dismay. **3 a** a person or thing causing horror. **b** *colloq.* a bad or mischievous person etc. **4** (in *pl.*; prec. by *the*) a fit of horror, depression, or nervousness, esp. as in delirium tremens. **5** a terrified and revolted shuddering. **6** (in *pl.*) an exclamation of dismay. ● *attrib. adj.* (of literature, films, etc.) designed to attract by arousing pleasurable feelings of horror. □ **Chamber of Horrors** a place full of horrors (orig. a room of criminals etc. in Madame Tussaud's waxworks). **horror-struck** (or **-stricken**) horrified, shocked. [ME f. OF (*h*)*orrour* f. L *horror -oris* (as HORRID)]
■ *n.* **1** fear, distress, dread, fright, alarm, upset, perturbation, panic, terror, trepidation, anxiety, *angst*, apprehension, uneasiness, queasiness, nervousness. **2 a** repugnance, dread, hatred, revulsion, detestation, abhorrence, distaste, dislike, aversion, antipathy, hostility, animosity, animus, rancour, odium. **3 b** see ROGUE *n.* 1, RASCAL. □ **horror-struck** (or **-stricken**) see *scared* (SCARE *v.* 2).

hors concours /ór kONkóor/ *adj.* **1** unrivalled, unequalled. **2** (of an exhibit or exhibitor) not competing for a prize. [F, lit. 'outside competition']

hors de combat /ór də kÓNbaa/ *adj.* out of the fight, disabled. [F]

hors-d'œuvre /ordőrvrə, -dörv/ *n.* an appetizer served at the beginning of a meal or (occasionally) during a meal. [F, lit. 'outside the work']
■ appetizer, antipasto, smorgasbord, starter.

horse /horss/ *n.* & *v.* ● *n.* **1 a** a solid-hoofed plant-eating quadruped, *Equus caballus*, with flowing mane and tail, used for riding and to carry and pull loads. **b** an adult male horse; a stallion or gelding. **c** any other four-legged mammal of the genus *Equus*, including asses and zebras. **d** (*collect.*; as *sing.*) cavalry. **e** a representation of a horse. **2** a vaulting-block. **3** a supporting frame esp. with legs (*clothes-horse*). **4** *sl.* heroin. **5** *colloq.* a unit of horsepower. **6** *Naut.* any of various ropes and bars. **7** *Mining* an obstruction in a vein. ● *v.* **1** *intr.* (foll. by *around*) fool about. **2** *tr.* provide (a person or vehicle) with a horse or horses. **3** *intr.* mount or go on horseback. □ **from the horse's mouth** (of information etc.) from the person directly concerned or another authoritative source. **horse-and-buggy** *US* old-fashioned, bygone. **horse-block** a small platform of stone or wood for mounting a horse. **horse-brass** see BRASS. **horse-breaker** one who breaks in horses. **horse chestnut 1** any large ornamental tree of the genus *Aesculus*, with upright conical clusters of white or pink or red flowers. **2** the dark brown fruit of this (like an edible chestnut, but with a coarse bitter taste). **horse-cloth** a cloth used to cover a horse, or as part of its trappings. **horse-coper** a horse-dealer. **horse-doctor** a veterinary surgeon attending horses. **horse-drawn** (of a vehicle) pulled by a horse or horses. **Horse Guards 1** (in the UK) the cavalry brigade of the household troops. **2** the headquarters of such cavalry, esp. a building in Whitehall. **horse latitudes** a belt of calms in each hemisphere between the trade winds and the westerlies. **horse-mackerel** any large fish of the mackerel type, e.g. the scad or the tunny. **horse-mushroom** a large edible mushroom, *Agaricus arvensis*. **horse opera** *US sl.* a western film. **horse-pistol** a pistol for use by a horseman. **horse-pond** a pond for watering and washing horses, proverbial as a place for ducking obnoxious persons. **horse-race** a race between horses with riders. **horse-racing** the sport of conducting horse-races. **horse sense** *colloq.* plain common sense. **horses for courses** the matching of tasks and talents. **horse's neck** *sl.* a drink of flavoured ginger ale usu. with spirits. **horse-soldier** a soldier mounted on a horse. **horse-trading 1** *US* dealing in horses. **2** shrewd bargaining. **to horse!** (as a command) mount your horses. □□ **horseless** *adj.* **horselike** *adj.* [OE *hors* f. Gmc]

horseback /hórsbak/ *n.* the back of a horse, esp. as sat on in riding. □ **on horseback** mounted on a horse.

horsebean /hórsbeen/ *n.* a broad bean used as fodder.

horsebox /hórsboks/ *n. Brit.* a closed vehicle for transporting a horse or horses.

horseflesh /hórsflesh/ *n.* **1** the flesh of a horse, esp. as food. **2** horses collectively.

horsefly /hórsflī/ *n.* (*pl.* **-flies**) any of various biting dipterous insects of the family Tabanidae troublesome esp. to horses.

horsehair /hórss-hair/ *n.* hair from the mane or tail of a horse, used for padding etc.

horseleech /hórsleech/ *n.* **1** a large kind of leech feeding by swallowing not sucking. **2** an insatiable person (cf. Prov. 30:15).

horseless /hórsliss/ *adj.* without a horse. □ **horseless carriage** *archaic* a motor car.

horseman /hórsmən/ *n.* (*pl.* **-men**) **1** a rider on horseback. **2** a skilled rider.

horsemanship /hórsmənship/ *n.* the art of riding on horseback; skill in doing this.
■ equestrianism, manège; seat.

horseplay /hórsplay/ *n.* boisterous play.
■ see PLAY *n.* 1.

horsepower /hórspowr/ *n.* (*pl.* same) **1** an imperial unit of power equal to 550 foot-pounds per second (about 750 watts). ¶ Abbr.: **hp**. **2** the power of an engine etc. measured in terms of this.

horseradish /hórsraddish/ *n.* **1** a cruciferous plant, *Armoracia rusticana*, with long lobed leaves. **2** the pungent root of this scraped or grated as a condiment, often made into a sauce.

horseshoe /hórss-shōō/ *n.* **1** an iron shoe for a horse shaped like the outline of the hard part of the hoof. **2** a thing of this shape; an object shaped like C or U (e.g. a magnet, a table, a Spanish or Islamic arch). □ **horseshoe crab** a large marine arthropod, *Xiphosura polyphemus*, with a horseshoe-shaped shell and a long tail-spine: also called *king-crab*.

horsetail /hórstayl/ *n.* **1** the tail of a horse (formerly used in Turkey as a standard, or as an ensign denoting the rank of a pasha). **2** any cryptogamous plant of the genus *Equisetum*, like a horse's tail, with a hollow jointed stem and scale-like leaves. **3** = *pony-tail*.

horsewhip /hórswip/ *n.* & *v.* ● *n.* a whip for driving horses. ● *v.tr.* (**-whipped, -whipping**) beat with a horsewhip.
■ *n.* see WHIP *n.* ● *v.* see WHIP *v.* 1.

horsewoman /hórswŏŏmmən/ *n.* (*pl.* **-women**) **1** a woman who rides on horseback. **2** a skilled woman rider.

horst /horst/ *n. Geol.* a raised elongated block of land bounded by faults on both sides. [G, = heap]

horsy /hórsi/ *adj.* (also **horsey**) (**horsier, horsiest**) **1** of or like a horse. **2** concerned with or devoted to horses or horse-racing. **3** affectedly using the dress and language of a groom or jockey. □□ **horsily** *adv.* **horsiness** *n.*

hortative /hórtətiv/ *adj.* (also **hortatory** /hórtətəri/) tending or serving to exhort. □□ **hortation** /hortáysh'n/ *n.* [L *hortativus* f. *hortari* exhort]

hortensia /horténsiə/ *n.* a kind of hydrangea, *Hydrangea macrophylla*, with large rounded infertile flower heads. [mod.L f. *Hortense* Lepaute, 18th-c. Frenchwoman]

horticulture /hórtikulchər/ *n.* the art of garden cultivation. □□ **horticultural** /-kúlchərəl/ *adj.* **horticulturist** /-kúlchərist/ *n.* [L *hortus* garden, after AGRICULTURE]

hortus siccus /hórtəss sikkəss/ *n.* **1** an arranged collection of dried plants. **2** a collection of uninteresting facts etc. [L, = dry garden]

Hos. *abbr.* Hosea (Old Testament).

hosanna /hōzánnə/ *n.* & *int.* a shout of adoration (Matt. 21: 9, 15, etc.). [ME f. LL f. Gk *hōsanna* f. Heb. *hôšaʽnā* for *hôšîʽa-nnâ* save now!]

hose /hōz/ *n.* & *v.* ● *n.* **1** (also **hose-pipe**) a flexible tube conveying water for watering plants etc., putting out fires, etc. **2 a** (*collect.*; as *pl.*) stockings and socks (esp. in trade use). **b** *hist.* breeches (*doublet and hose*). ● *v.tr.* **1** (often foll. by *down*) water or spray or drench with a hose. **2** provide with hose. □ **half-hose** socks. [OE f. Gmc]
■ *n.* **1** see PIPE *n.* 1. ● *v.* **1** see WATER *v.* 1.

hosier /hṓziər, hṓzhər/ *n.* a dealer in hosiery.

hosiery /hṓziəri, hṓzhəri/ *n.* **1** stockings and socks. **2** *Brit.* knitted or woven underwear.

hospice /hóspiss/ *n.* **1** *Brit.* a home for people who are ill (esp. terminally) or destitute. **2** a lodging for travellers, esp. one kept by a religious order. [F f. L *hospitium* (as HOST[2])]
■ **1** see HOME *n.* 4. **2** see MONASTERY.

hospitable /hóspitəb'l, hospít-/ *adj.* **1** giving or disposed to give welcome and entertainment to strangers or guests. **2** disposed to welcome something readily, receptive. □□ **hospitably** *adv.* [F f. *hospiter* f. med.L *hospitare* entertain (as HOST[2])]
■ **1** welcoming, courteous, genial, friendly, agreeable, amicable, cordial, warm, congenial, generous. **2** open-minded, receptive, amenable, approachable, tolerant.

hospital /hóspit'l/ *n.* **1** an institution providing medical and surgical treatment and nursing care for ill or injured people. **2** *hist.* **a** a hospice. **b** an establishment of the Knights Hospitallers. **3** *Law* a charitable institution (also in proper names, e.g. *Christ's Hospital*). □ **hospital corners** a way of tucking in sheets, used by nurses. **hospital fever** a kind of typhus formerly prevalent in crowded hospitals. **hospital ship** a ship to receive sick and wounded seamen, or to take sick and wounded soldiers home. **hospital train** a train taking wounded soldiers from a battlefield. [ME f. OF f. med.L *hospitale* neut. of L *hospitalis* (adj.) (as HOST[2])]
■ **1** medical centre, health centre, infirmary, dispensary, sanatorium, *US* sanitarium.

hospitaler *US* var. of HOSPITALLER.

hospitalism /hóspitəliz'm/ *n.* the adverse effects of a prolonged stay in hospital.

hospitality /hóspitálliti/ *n.* the friendly and generous reception and entertainment of guests or strangers. [ME f. OF *hospitalité* f. L *hospitalitas -tatis* (as HOSPITAL)]
■ friendliness, amicability, cordiality, warmth, congeniality, sociability, generosity.

hospitalize /hóspitəlīz/ *v.tr.* (also **-ise**) send or admit (a patient) to hospital. □□ **hospitalization** /-záysh'n/ *n.*

hospitaller /hóspitələr/ *n.* (*US* **hospitaler**) **1** a member of a charitable religious order. **2** a chaplain (in some London hospitals). [ME f. OF *hospitalier* f. med.L *hospitalarius* (as HOSPITAL)]

host[1] /hōst/ *n.* **1** (usu. foll. by *of*) a large number of people or things. **2** *archaic* an army. **3** (in full **heavenly host**) *Bibl.* **a** the sun, moon, and stars. **b** the angels. □ **host** (or **hosts**) **of heaven** = sense 3 of *n.* **is a host in himself** can do as much as several ordinary people. **Lord** (or **Lord God**) **of hosts** God as Lord over earthly or heavenly armies. [ME f. OF f. L *hostis* stranger, enemy, in med.L 'army']
■ **1, 2** army, swarm, crowd, horde, multitude, throng, mob, pack, herd, troop, legion, drove.

host[2] /hōst/ *n.* & *v.* ● *n.* **1** a person who receives or entertains another as a guest. **2** the landlord of an inn (*mine host*). **3** *Biol.* an animal or plant having a parasite or commensal. **4** an animal or person that has received a transplanted organ etc. **5** the compère of a show, esp. of a television or radio programme. ● *v.tr.* act as host to (a person) or at (an event). [ME f. OF *oste* f. L *hospes -pitis* host, guest]
■ *n.* **2** innkeeper, hotelier, hotel-keeper, landlord, landlady, manager, manageress, proprietor, *Brit.* publican. **5** master of ceremonies, MC, presenter, *Brit.* compère, *colloq.* emcee, announcer. ● *v.* entertain, act the host to, play host to; have, hold.

host[3] /hōst/ *n.* the bread consecrated in the Eucharist. [ME f. OF *(h)oiste* f. L *hostia* victim]

hosta /hóstə/ *n.* any perennial garden plant of the genus *Hosta* (formerly *Funkia*) with green or variegated ornamental leaves and loose clusters of tubular mauve or white flowers. [mod.L, f. N. T. *Host*, Austrian physician d. 1834]

hostage /hóstij/ *n.* **1** a person seized or held as security for the fulfilment of a condition. **2** a pledge or security. □ **a hostage to fortune** an acquisition, commitment, etc., regarded as endangered by unforeseen circumstances. □□ **hostageship** *n.* [ME f. OF *(h)ostage* ult. f. LL *obsidatus* hostageship f. L *obses obsidis* hostage]
■ **1** see CAPTIVE *n.* **2** security, surety, gage; see also PLEDGE *n.* 2.

hostel /hóst'l/ *n.* **1** *Brit.* **a** a house of residence or lodging for students, nurses, etc. **b** a place providing temporary accommodation for the homeless etc. **2** = *youth hostel.* **3** *archaic* an inn. [ME f. OF *(h)ostel* f. med.L (as HOSPITAL)]

hostelling /hóstəling/ *n.* (*US* **hosteling**) the practice of staying in youth hostels, esp. while travelling. □□ **hosteller** *n.*

hostelry /hóstəlri/ *n.* (*pl.* **-ies**) *archaic* or *literary* an inn. [ME f. OF *(h)ostelerie* f. *(h)ostelier* innkeeper (as HOSTEL)]
■ see PUB 1.

hostess /hṓstiss/ *n.* **1** a woman who receives or entertains a guest. **2** a woman employed to welcome and entertain customers at a nightclub etc. **3** a stewardess on an aircraft, train, etc. (*air hostess*). [ME f. OF *(h)ostesse* (as HOST[2])]

hostile /hóstīl/ *adj.* **1** of an enemy. **2** (often foll. by *to*) unfriendly, opposed. □ **hostile witness** *Law* a witness who appears hostile to the party calling him or her and therefore untrustworthy. □□ **hostilely** *adv.* [F *hostile* or L *hostilis* (as HOST[1])]
■ **1** enemy, warring, combative, opposing, militant, aggressive, fighting. **2** opposed, antagonistic, contrary, adverse; averse, loath; unfriendly, inimical, unsympathetic, inhospitable, unfavourable, unwelcoming; see also COLD *adj.* 4.

hostility /hostílliti/ *n.* (*pl.* **-ies**) **1** being hostile, enmity. **2** a state of warfare. **3** (in *pl.*) acts of warfare. **4** opposition (in thought etc.). [F *hostilité* or LL *hostilitas* (as HOSTILE)]
■ **1** antagonism, enmity, antipathy, animus, ill will, malevolence, malice, aversion, unfriendliness, hatred; see also ANIMOSITY. **3** (*hostilities*) war, warfare, fighting, combat, action, bloodshed. **4** see OPPOSITION 1–3.

hostler /óslər/ *n.* **1** = OSTLER. **2** *US* a person in charge of vehicles or machines, esp. railway engines, when they are not in use. [ME f. *hosteler* (as OSTLER)]

hot /hot/ *adj.*, *v.*, & *adv.* ● *adj.* (**hotter, hottest**) **1 a** having a relatively or noticeably high temperature. **b** (of food or drink) prepared by heating and served without cooling. **2** producing the sensation of heat (*hot fever*; *hot flush*). **3** (of pepper, spices, etc.) pungent. **4** (of a person) feeling heat. **5 a** ardent, passionate, excited. **b** (often foll. by *for*, *on*) eager, keen (*in hot pursuit*). **c** angry or upset. **d** lustful. **e** exciting. **6 a** (of news etc.) fresh, recent. **b** *Brit. colloq.* (of Treasury bills) newly issued. **7** *Hunting* (of the scent) fresh and strong, indicating that the quarry has passed recently. **8 a** (of a player) very skilful. **b** (of a competitor in a race or other sporting event) strongly fancied to win (*a hot favourite*). **c** (of a hit, return, etc., in ball games) difficult for an opponent to deal with. **d** *colloq.* currently popular or in demand. **9** (of music, esp. jazz) strongly rhythmical and emotional. **10 a** difficult or awkward to deal with. **b** *sl.* (of goods) stolen, esp. easily identifiable and hence difficult to dispose of. **c** *sl.* (of a person) wanted by the police. **11 a** live, at a high voltage. **b** *sl.* radioactive. **12** *colloq.* (of information) unusually reliable (*hot tip*). **13** (of a colour, shade, etc.) suggestive of heat; intense, bright. ● *v.* (**hotted, hotting**) (usu. foll. by *up*) *Brit. colloq.* **1** *tr.* & *intr.* make or become hot. **2** *tr.* & *intr.* make or become active, lively, exciting, or dangerous. ● *adv.* **1** angrily, severely (*give it* *him hot*). **2** eagerly. □ **go hot and cold** feel alternately hot and cold owing to fear etc. **have the hots for** *sl.* be sexually attracted to. **hot air** *sl.* empty, boastful, or excited talk. **hot-air balloon** a balloon (see BALLOON *n.* 2) consisting of a bag in which air is heated by burners located below it, causing it to rise. **hot blast** a blast of heated air forced into a furnace. **hot-blooded** ardent, passionate. **hot cathode** a cathode heated to emit electrons. **hot cross bun** see BUN. **hot dog** *n.* a hot sausage sandwiched in a soft roll. ● *int. US sl.* expressing approval. **hot flush** see FLUSH[1]. **hot gospeller** see GOSPELLER. **hot line** a direct exclusive line of communication, esp. for emergencies. **hot metal** *Printing* using type made from molten metal. **hot money** capital transferred at frequent intervals. **hot potato** *colloq.* a controversial or awkward matter or situation. **hot-press** *n.* a press of glazed boards and hot metal plates for smoothing paper or cloth or making plywood. ● *v.tr.* press (paper etc.) in this. **hot rod** a motor vehicle modified to have extra power and speed. **hot seat** *sl.* **1** a position of difficult responsibility. **2** the electric chair. **hot-short** (of metal) brittle in its hot state (cf. COLD-SHORT). **hot spot 1** a small region that is relatively hot. **2** a lively or dangerous place. **hot spring** a spring of naturally hot water. **hot stuff** *colloq.* **1** a formidably capable person. **2** an important person or thing. **3** a sexually attractive person. **4** a spirited, strong-willed, or passionate person. **5** a book, film, etc. with a strongly erotic content. **hot-tempered** impulsively angry. **hot under the collar** angry, resentful, or embarrassed. **hot war** an open war, with active hostilities. **hot water** *colloq.* difficulty, trouble, or disgrace (*be in hot water*; *get into hot water*). **hot-water bottle** (*US* **bag**) a container, usu. made of rubber, filled with hot water, esp. to warm a bed. **hot well 1** = *hot spring*. **2** a reservoir in a condensing steam engine. **hot-wire** operated by the expansion of heated wire. **like hot cakes** see CAKE. **make it** (or **things**) **hot for a person** persecute a person. **not so hot** *colloq.* only mediocre. □□ **hotly** *adv.* **hotness** *n.* **hottish** *adj.* [OE *hāt* f. Gmc: cf. HEAT]

■ *adj.* **1** fiery, white-hot, red-hot, piping hot, burning, blistering, roasting, torrid, sultry, flaming, tropical, *colloq.* scorching, sizzling, boiling, baking, scalding, steaming, simmering, sweltering. **3** spicy, peppery, sharp, piquant, pungent. **5 a** intense, fervent, zealous, ardent, enthusiastic, passionate, fervid, feverish, vehement, excited, fiery, fierce, animated, earnest, violent. **b** eager, keen, avid, anxious, burning. **c** see ANGRY 1. **d** lustful, lecherous, libidinous, lickerish, oversexed, sex-crazed, sex-mad, *formal* concupiscent; sexy, sensual, aroused, randy, *sl.* horny. **e** see EXCITING. **6 a** recent, fresh, new, latest, brand-new. **8 a** see SKILFUL. **d** popular, sought-after, commercial, saleable, marketable. **10 a** dangerous, precarious, risky, sensitive, delicate, unstable, touchy, unpredictable. **11 a** electrified, live, charged, powered. **12** see RELIABLE. **13** intense, vivid, striking, bright, brilliant, dazzling, loud. ● *v.* **1** heat, warm up, heat up, reheat, *US* warm over, *Brit. colloq.* hot up. **2** (*hot up*) intensify, liven up, get going; build up, heighten, increase; *colloq.* swing. □ **have the hots for** see DESIRE *v.* 1. **hot air** blather, bunkum, verbiage, talk, bluff, bluster, wind, pretentiousness, pomposity, bombast, grandiloquence, magniloquence, flatulence, flatulency, rodomontade, claptrap, *sl.* bosh, gas, guff; see also DRIVEL *n.* **hot-blooded** see PASSIONATE **hot dog** (*int.*) see BRILLIANT *adj.* 4. **hot stuff 1** see GENIUS 1b. **3** see BEAUTY 3. **hot-tempered** see IRRITABLE 1. **hot under the collar** see ANGRY 1. **hot water** see DIFFICULTY 2b. **make it** (or **things**) **hot for a person** *colloq.* give a person hell; see also PERSECUTE 2, PUNISH 1. **not so hot** see MEDIOCRE 2. □□ **hotly** intensively, energetically, doggedly, persistently, zealously, fervently, fervidly, ardently, warmly, enthusiastically.

hotbed /hótbed/ *n.* **1** a bed of earth heated by fermenting manure. **2** (foll. by *of*) an environment promoting the growth of something, esp. something unwelcome (*hotbed of vice*).

■ **2** breeding ground, fertile source, hothouse.

hotchpotch /hóchpoch/ *n.* (also (esp. in sense 3) **hotchpot** /-pot/) **1** a confused mixture, a jumble. **2** a dish of many mixed ingredients, esp. a mutton broth or stew with vegetables. **3** *Law* the reunion and blending of properties for the purpose of securing equal division (esp. of the property of an intestate parent). [ME f. AF & OF *hochepot* f. OF *hocher* shake + POT[1]: *-potch* by assim.]

■ **1** hodgepodge, miscellany, mixture, gallimaufry, jumble, farrago, *mélange*, mishmash, medley, hash, conglomeration, mixed bag *or* bunch, olio, olla podrida, pot-pourri, rag-bag, welter, *colloq.* omnium gatherum. **2** olio, olla podrida; see also STEW[1] *n.* 1.

hotel /hōtél/ *n.* **1** an establishment providing accommodation and meals for payment. **2** *Austral.* & *NZ* a public house. [F *hôtel*, later form of HOSTEL]

■ **1** inn; motel, motor hotel, bed and breakfast, *auberge*, *gasthaus*, *pension*, b & b, guest-house, *archaic or literary* hostelry, *Austral. colloq.* pub. **2** see PUB 1.

hotelier /hōtélliər/ *n.* a hotel-keeper. [F *hôtelier* f. OF *hostelier*: see HOSTELRY]

■ see PROPRIETOR 2.

hotfoot /hótfŏŏt/ *adv.*, *v.*, & *adj.* ● *adv.* in eager haste. ● *v.tr.* hurry eagerly (esp. *hotfoot it*). ● *adj.* acting quickly.

■ *v.* see HURRY *v.* 1.

hothead /hót-hed/ *n.* an impetuous person.

hotheaded /hót-héddid/ *adj.* impetuous, excitable. □□ **hotheadedly** *adv.* **hotheadedness** *n.*

■ impetuous, excitable, volatile, rash, hasty, wild, foolhardy, reckless, precipitate, thoughtless, heedless, madcap.

hothouse /hót-howss/ *n.* & *adj.* ● *n.* **1** a heated building, usu. largely of glass, for rearing plants out of season or in a climate colder than is natural for them. **2** an environment that encourages the rapid growth or development of something. ● *adj.* (*attrib.*) characteristic of something reared in a hothouse; sheltered, sensitive.

■ *n.* **1** hotbed, greenhouse, glasshouse, conservatory. **2** see HOTBED 2. ● *adj.* dainty, delicate, sensitive, fragile, frail, pampered, overprotected, sheltered, shielded.

hotplate /hótplayt/ *n.* a heated metal plate etc. (or a set of these) for cooking food or keeping it hot.

hotpot /hótpot/ *n.* a casserole of meat and vegetables, usu. with a layer of potato on top.

hotshot /hótshot/ *n.* & *adj.* esp. *US colloq.* ● *n.* an important or exceptionally able person. ● *adj.* (*attrib.*) important, able, expert, suddenly prominent.

■ *n.* see BIGWIG.

hotspur /hótspur/ *n.* a rash person. [sobriquet of Sir H. Percy, d. 1403]

Hottentot /hótt'ntot/ *n.* & *adj.* ● *n.* **1** a member of a stocky Negroid people of SW Africa. **2** their language. ● *adj.* of this people. [Afrik., perh. = stammerer, with ref. to their mode of pronunc.]

hottie /hótti/ *n.* (also **hotty**) (*pl.* **-ies**) *colloq.* a hot-water bottle.

Houdini /hoodeéni/ *n.* **1** an ingenious escape. **2** a person skilled at escaping. [H. *Houdini*, professional name of E. Weiss, American escapologist d. 1926]

hough /hok/ *n.* & *v. Brit.* ● *n.* **1** = HOCK[1]. **2** a cut of beef etc. from this and the leg above it. ● *v.tr.* hamstring. □□ **hougher** *n.* [ME *ho(u)gh* = OE *hōh* (heel) in *hōhsinu* hamstring]

hoummos var. of HUMMUS.

hound /hownd/ *n.* & *v.* ● *n.* **1 a** a dog used for hunting, esp. one able to track by scent. **b** (**the hounds**) *Brit.* a pack of foxhounds. **2** *colloq.* a despicable man. **3** a runner who follows a trail in hare and hounds. **4** a person keen in pursuit of something (usu. in *comb.*: *news-hound*). ● *v.tr.* **1** harass or pursue relentlessly. **2** chase or pursue with a hound. **3** (foll. by *at*) set (a dog or person) on (a quarry). **4**

urge on or nag (a person). □ **hound's tongue** *Bot.* a tall plant, *Cynoglossum officinale*, with tongue-shaped leaves. **hound's-tooth** a check pattern with notched corners suggestive of a canine tooth. **ride to hounds** go fox-hunting on horseback. □□ **hounder** *n.* **houndish** *adj.* [OE *hund* f. Gmc]

■ *n.* **2** see WRETCH 2. ● *v.* **1** persecute, pursue, chase, annoy, pester, harry, badger, *colloq.* hassle, *Austral. colloq.* heavy; see also HARASS 1. **4** see URGE *v.* 2, NAG[1] *v.* 1, 3a, b.

hour /owr/ *n.* **1** a twenty-fourth part of a day and night, 60 minutes. **2** a time of day, a point in time (*a late hour; what is the hour?*). **3** (in *pl.* with preceding numerals in form 18.00, 20.30, etc.) this number of hours and minutes past midnight on the 24-hour clock (*will assemble at 20.00 hours*). **4 a** a period set aside for some purpose (*lunch hour; keep regular hours*). **b** (in *pl.*) a fixed period of time for work, use of a building, etc. (*office hours; opening hours*). **5** a short indefinite period of time (*an idle hour*). **6** the present time (*question of the hour*). **7** a time for action etc. (*the hour has come*). **8** the distance traversed in one hour by a means of transport stated or implied (*we are an hour from London*). **9** *RC Ch.* **a** prayers to be said at one of seven fixed times of day (*book of hours*). **b** any of these times. **10** (prec. by *the*) each time o'clock of a whole number of hours (*buses leave on the hour; on the half hour; at quarter past the hour*). **11** *Astron.* 15° of longitude or right ascension. □ **after hours** after closing-time. **hour-hand** the hand on a clock or watch which shows the hour. **hour-long** *adj.* lasting for one hour. ● *adv.* for one hour. **till all hours** till very late. [ME *ure* etc. f. AF *ure*, OF *ore, eure* f. L *hora* f. Gk *hōra* season, hour]

■ **2** see MOMENT 3.

hourglass /ówrglaass/ *n.* a reversible device with two connected glass bulbs containing sand that takes an hour to pass from the upper to the lower bulb.

houri /hoóri/ *n.* a beautiful young woman, esp. in the Muslim Paradise. [F f. Pers. *ḥūrī* f. Arab. *ḥūr* pl. of *ḥawra'* gazelle-like (in the eyes)]

hourly /ówrli/ *adj.* & *adv.* ● *adj.* **1** done or occurring every hour. **2** frequent, continual. **3** reckoned hour by hour (*hourly wage*). ● *adv.* **1** every hour. **2** frequently, continually.

house *n.* & *v.* ● *n.* /howss/ (*pl.* /hówziz/) **1 a** a building for human habitation. **b** (*attrib.*) (of an animal) kept in, frequenting, or infesting houses (*house-cat; housefly*). **2** a building for a special purpose (*opera-house; summer-house*). **3** a building for keeping animals or goods (*hen-house*). **4 a** a religious community. **b** the buildings occupied by it. **5 a** a body of pupils living in the same building at a boarding-school. **b** such a building. **c** a division of a day-school for games, competitions, etc. **6 a** a college of a university. **b** (**the House**) Christ Church, Oxford. **7** a family, esp. a royal family; a dynasty (*House of York*). **8 a** a firm or institution. **b** its place of business. **c** (**the House**) *Brit. colloq.* the Stock Exchange. **9 a** a legislative or deliberative assembly. **b** the building where it meets. **c** (**the House**) (in the UK) the House of Commons or Lords; (in the US) the House of Representatives. **10 a** an audience in a theatre, cinema, etc. **b** a performance in a theatre or cinema (*second house starts at 9 o'clock*). **c** a theatre. **11** *Astrol.* a twelfth part of the heavens. **12** (*attrib.*) living in a hospital as a member of staff (*house officer; house physician; house surgeon*). **13 a** a place of public refreshment, a restaurant or inn (*coffee-house; public house*). **b** (*attrib.*) (of wine) selected by the management of a restaurant, hotel, etc. to be offered at a special price. **14** *US* a brothel. **15** *Sc.* a dwelling that is one of several in a building. **16** *Brit. sl.* = HOUSEY-HOUSEY. **17** an animal's den, shell, etc. **18** (**the House**) *Brit. hist. euphem.* the workhouse. ● *v.tr.* /howz/ **1** provide (a person, a population, etc.) with a house or houses or other accommodation. **2** store (goods etc.). **3 a** serve as accommodation for, contain. **b** enclose or encase (a part or fitting). **4** fix in a socket, mortise, etc. □ **as safe as houses** thoroughly or completely safe. **house-agent** *Brit.* an agent for the sale and letting of houses. **house and home** (as an emphatic) home. **house arrest** detention in one's own house etc., not in prison. **house-broken** = *house-trained.* **house church 1** a charismatic church independent of traditional denominations. **2** a group meeting in a house as part of the activities of a church. **house-dog** a dog kept to guard a house. **house-father** a man in charge of a house, esp. of a home for children. **house-flag** a flag indicating to what firm a ship belongs. **house guest** a guest staying for some days in a private house. **house-hunting** seeking a house to live in. **house-husband** a husband who carries out the household duties traditionally carried out by a housewife. **house lights** the lights in the auditorium of a theatre. **house magazine** a magazine published by a firm and dealing mainly with its own activities. **house-martin** a black and white swallow-like bird, *Delichon urbica*, which builds a mud nest on house walls etc. **house-mother** a woman in charge of a house, esp. of a home for children. **house music** a style of pop music typically using drum machines and synthesized bass lines with sparse repetitive vocals and a fast beat. **house of cards 1** an insecure scheme etc. **2** a structure built (usu. by a child) out of playing cards. **House of Commons** (in the UK) the elected chamber of Parliament. **house of God** a church, a place of worship. **house of ill fame** *archaic* a brothel. **House of Keys** (in the Isle of Man) the elected chamber of Tynwald. **House of Lords 1** (in the UK) the chamber of Parliament composed of peers and bishops. **2** a committee of specially qualified members of this appointed as the ultimate judicial appeal court. **House of Representatives** the lower house of the US Congress and other legislatures. **house-parent** a house-mother or house-father. **house party** a group of guests staying at a country house etc. **house-plant** a plant grown indoors. **house-proud** attentive to, or unduly preoccupied with, the care and appearance of the home. **Houses of Parliament 1** the Houses of Lords and Commons regarded together. **2** the buildings where they meet. **house sparrow** a common brown and grey sparrow, *Passer domesticus*, which nests in the eaves and roofs of houses. **house style** a particular printer's or publisher's etc. preferred way of presentation. **house-to-house** performed at or carried to each house in turn. **house-trained** *Brit.* **1** (of animals) trained to be clean in the house. **2** *colloq.* well-mannered. **house-warming** a party celebrating a move to a new home. **keep house** provide for or manage a household. **keep** (or **make**) **a House** secure the presence of enough members for a quorum in the House of Commons. **keep open house** provide general hospitality. **keep to the house** (or **keep the house**) stay indoors. **like a house on fire 1** vigorously, fast. **2** successfully, excellently. **on the house** at the management's expense, free. **play house** play at being a family in its home. **put** (or **set**) **one's house in order** make necessary reforms. **set up house** begin to live in a separate dwelling. □□ **houseful** *n.* (*pl.* **-fuls**). **houseless** *adj.* [OE *hūs, hūsian*, f. Gmc]

■ *n.* **1 a** residence, home, abode, homestead, domicile, lodging(s), *formal* dwelling(-place), *Austral. sl.* kipsie; building, edifice, structure. **7** family, line, lineage, dynasty, clan. **8 a** establishment, institution, firm, concern, company, business, organization, enterprise, undertaking, *colloq.* outfit. **9 a** legislature, legislative body, congress, parliament, assembly, council, diet. **10 b** see PERFORMANCE 2. **c** auditorium, theatre, concert-hall. **14** bawdy-house, brothel, whore-house, bagnio, *US* bordello, sporting house, *archaic* house of ill repute *or* fame, stews, *sl.* crib, drum, *Brit. sl.* kip, kip-house, knocking-shop. **17** den, lair, burrow, hole, nest, set; shell. ● *v.* **1** shelter, accommodate, domicile, lodge, quarter, put up, board, harbour, *Mil.* billet. **2** see STORE *v.* 1. **3 a** contain, accommodate, quarter. **b** see ENCLOSE 1, 6. □ **house of God** church, chapel, place of worship. **house of ill fame** see HOUSE *n.* 14 above. **house-proud** homey, domestic, domesticated, home-loving; see TIDY *adj.* 2. **house-to-house** door-to-door. **house-trained 1** see DOMESTIC *adj.* 3.

2 see COURTEOUS. **like a house on fire 1** see FAST[1] *adv.* 1. **2** see WELL[1] *adv.* 9. **on the house** free, gratis, for nothing, without charge, at no charge, as a gift. **put one's house in order** see REFORM *v.* 1.

houseboat /hówsbōt/ *n.* a boat fitted up for living in.

housebound /hówsbownd/ *adj.* unable to leave one's house through illness etc.

houseboy /hówsboy/ *n.* a boy or man as a servant in a house.
■ see SERVANT.

housebreaker /hówsbraykər/ *n.* **1** a person guilty of housebreaking. **2** *Brit.* a person who is employed to demolish houses.
■ **1** see BURGLAR.

housebreaking /hówsbrayking/ *n.* the act of breaking into a building, esp. in daytime, to commit a crime. ¶ In 1968 replaced as a statutory crime in English law by *burglary*.

housecarl /hówskaarl/ *n.* (also **housecarle**) *hist.* a member of the bodyguard of a Danish or English king or noble. [OE *húscarl* f. ON *húskarl* f. *hús* HOUSE + *karl* man: cf. CARL]

housecoat /hówskōt/ *n.* a woman's garment for informal wear in the house, usu. a long dresslike coat.
■ see ROBE *n.* 2.

housecraft /hówskraaft/ *n.* *Brit.* skill in household management.

housefly /hówsflī/ *n.* any fly of the family Muscidae, esp. *Musca domestica*, breeding in decaying organic matter and often entering houses.

household /hówss-hōld/ *n.* **1** the occupants of a house regarded as a unit. **2** a house and its affairs. **3** (prec. by *the*) (in the UK) the royal household. □ **household gods 1** gods presiding over a household, esp. the lares and penates. **2** the essentials of home life. **household troops** (in the UK) troops nominally employed to guard the sovereign. **household word** (or **name**) **1** a familiar name or saying. **2** a familiar person or thing.
■ **1** family, ménage. **3** see TRAIN *n.* 4.

householder /hówss-hōldər/ *n.* **1** a person who owns or rents a house. **2** the head of a household.
■ **1** see LANDLORD 1, OCCUPANT.

housekeep /hówskeep/ *v.intr.* (*past* and *past part.* **-kept**) *colloq.* keep house.

housekeeper /hówskeepər/ *n.* **1** a person, esp. a woman, employed to manage a household. **2** a person in charge of a house, office, etc.
■ **1** see SERVANT 1.

housekeeping /hówskeeping/ *n.* **1** the management of household affairs. **2** money allowed for this. **3** operations of maintenance, record-keeping, etc., in an organization.

houseleek /hówsleek/ *n.* a plant, *Sempervivum tectorum*, with pink flowers, growing on walls and roofs.

housemaid /hówsmayd/ *n.* a female servant in a house, esp. in charge of reception rooms and bedrooms. □ **housemaid's knee** inflammation of the kneecap, often due to excessive kneeling.

houseman /hówsmən/ *n.* (*pl.* **-men**) **1** *Brit.* a resident doctor at a hospital etc. **2** = HOUSEBOY.

housemaster /hówsmaastər/ *n.* (*fem.* **housemistress** /-mistriss/) the teacher in charge of a house at a boarding-school.

houseroom /hówsrŏŏm, -rōōm/ *n.* space or accommodation in one's house. □ **not give houseroom to** not have in any circumstances.

housetop /hówstop/ *n.* the roof of a house. □ **proclaim** (or **shout** etc.) **from the housetops** announce publicly.

housewife /hówswīf/ *n.* (*pl.* **-wives**) **1** a woman (usu. married) managing a household. **2** /húzzif/ a case for needles, thread, etc. □□ **housewifely** *adj.* **housewifeliness** *n.* [ME *hus(e)wif* f. HOUSE + WIFE]

housewifery /hówswifri/ *n.* **1** housekeeping. **2** skill in this, housecraft.

housework /hówswurk/ *n.* regular work done in housekeeping, e.g. cleaning and cooking.

housey-housey /hówsihówsi, hówzihówzi/ *n.* (also **housie-housie**) *Brit. sl.* a gambling form of lotto.

housing[1] /hówzing/ *n.* **1 a** dwelling-houses collectively. **b** the provision of these. **2** shelter, lodging. **3** a rigid casing, esp. for moving or sensitive parts of a machine. **4** the hole or niche cut in one piece of wood to receive some part of another in order to join them. □ **housing estate** a residential area planned as a unit.
■ **1, 2** homes, houses, lodging(s), quarters, accommodation, habitation, *US* accommodations, *formal* dwellings, dwelling-places; shelter, protection. **3** case, casing, cover, covering, enclosure, container, box, shield.

housing[2] /hówzing/ *n.* a cloth covering put on a horse for protection or ornament. [ME = covering, f. obs. *house* f. OF *houce* f. med.L *hultia* f. Gmc]

hove *past* of HEAVE.

hovel /hóvv'l/ *n.* **1** a small miserable dwelling. **2** a conical building enclosing a kiln. **3** an open shed or outhouse. [ME: orig. unkn.]
■ **1** shack, shanty, hut, crib; pigsty, *US* pigpen, *colloq.* dump. **3** hut, outhouse; see also SHED[1].

hover /hóvvər/ *v.* & *n.* ● *v.intr.* **1** (of a bird, helicopter, etc.) remain in one place in the air. **2** (often foll. by *about*, *round*) wait close at hand, linger. **3** remain undecided. ● *n.* **1** hovering. **2** a state of suspense. □ **hover-fly** (*pl.* **-flies**) any fly of the family Syrphidae which hovers with rapidly beating wings. □□ **hoverer** *n.* [ME f. obs. *hove* hover, linger]
■ *v.* **1** float, hang, poise, be *or* hang suspended, hang in the air. **2** linger, loiter, wait, hang about *or* around. **3** see HESITATE 1.

hovercraft /hóvvərkraaft/ *n.* (*pl.* same) a vehicle or craft that travels over land or water on a cushion of air provided by a downward blast.

hoverport /hóvvərport/ *n.* a terminal for hovercraft.

hovertrain /hóvvərtrayn/ *n.* a train that travels on a cushion of air like a hovercraft.

how[1] /how/ *adv.*, *conj.*, & *n.* ● *interrog. adv.* **1** by what means, in what way (*how do you do it?*; *tell me how you do it*; *how could you behave so disgracefully?*; *but how to bridge the gap?*). **2** in what condition, esp. of health (*how is the patient?*; *how do things stand?*). **3 a** to what extent (*how far is it?*; *how would you like to take my place?*; *how we laughed!*). **b** to what extent good or well, what . . . like (*how was the film?*; *how did they play?*). ● *rel. adv.* in whatever way, as (*do it how you can*). ● *conj. colloq.* that (*told us how he'd been in India*). ● *n.* the way a thing is done (*the how and why of it*). □ **and how!** *sl.* very much so (chiefly used ironically or intensively). **here's how!** I drink to your good health. **how about 1** would you like (*how about a game of chess?*). **2** what is to be done about. **3** what is the news about. **how are you? 1** what is your state of health? **2** = *how do you do?* **how come?** see COME. **how do?** an informal greeting on being introduced to a stranger. **how do you do?** a formal greeting. **how-do-you-do** (or **how-d'ye-do**) *n.* (*pl.* **-dos**) an awkward situation. **how many** what number. **how much 1** what amount (*how much do I owe you?*; *did not know how much to take*). **2** what price (*how much is it?*). **3** (as *interrog.*) *joc.* what? ('*She is a hedonist.*' '*A how much?*'). **how now?** *archaic* what is the meaning of this? **how so?** how can you show that that is so? **how's that? 1** what is your opinion or explanation of that? **2** *Cricket* (said to an umpire) is the batsman out or not? [OE *hū* f. WG]

how[2] /how/ *int.* a greeting used by N. American Indians. [perh. f. Sioux *háo*, Omaha *hau*]

howbeit /hówbeé-it/ *adv. archaic* nevertheless.

howdah /hówdə/ *n.* a seat for two or more, usu. with a canopy, for riding on the back of an elephant or camel. [Urdu *hawda* f. Arab. *hawdaj* litter]

howdy /hówdi/ *int. US* = *how do you do?* [corrupt.]

however /hówévvər/ *adv.* **1 a** in whatever way (*do it however you want*). **b** to whatever extent, no matter how (*must go however inconvenient*). **2** nevertheless. **3** *colloq.* (as an emphatic) in what way, by what means (*however did that happen?*).
■ **1 a** no matter how, in whatever way *or* manner, to whatever manner *or* extent *or* degree, howsoever, in any way *or* manner *or* respect, anyhow, how. **b** no matter how, regardless (of) how, notwithstanding how. **2** nevertheless, nonetheless, despite that, in spite of that, still, though, yet, even so, be that as it may, at any rate, anyway, anyhow, at all events, in any event, in any case, *Sc.*, *Austral.*, & *NZ* but. **3** how, in what way *or* manner, by what means, *colloq.* how on earth, how in the world.

howitzer /hówitsər/ *n.* a short gun for high-angle firing of shells at low velocities. [Du. *houwitser* f. G *Haubitze* f. Czech *houfnice* catapult]

howl /howl/ *n.* & *v.* ● *n.* **1** a long loud doleful cry uttered by a dog, wolf, etc. **2** a prolonged wailing noise, e.g. as made by a strong wind. **3** a loud cry of pain or rage. **4** a yell of derision or merriment. **5** *Electronics* a howling noise in a loudspeaker due to electrical or acoustic feedback. ● *v.* **1** *intr.* make a howl. **2** *intr.* weep loudly. **3** *tr.* utter (words) with a howl. □ **howl down** prevent (a speaker) from being heard by howls of derision. [ME *houle* (v.), prob. imit.: cf. OWL]
■ *n.* **1** yowl, ululation, wail, yelp, cry. **3** cry, shout, yell, bellow, scream, roar, *US colloq.* holler. ● *v.* **1** yowl, cry, wail, ululate, bay; shout, yell, bellow, scream, roar, *US colloq.* holler. **2** see CRY *v.* 2a.

howler /hówlər/ *n.* **1** *colloq.* a glaring mistake. **2** a S. American monkey of the genus *Alouatta*. **3** a person or animal that howls.
■ **1** blunder, mistake, error, gaffe, *faux pas*, *colloq.* slip-up, *sl.* bloomer, boner, clanger, bish, goof, screw-up, boo-boo, floater, *Brit. sl.* boob, cock-up, *US sl.* clinker.

howling /hówling/ *adj.* **1** that howls. **2** *sl.* extreme (*a howling shame*). **3** *archaic* dreary (*howling wilderness*). □ **howling dervish** see DERVISH.

howsoever /hówsō-évvər/ *adv.* (also *poet.* **howsoe'er** /-sō-áir/) **1** in whatsoever way. **2** to whatsoever extent.
■ **1** see HOWEVER 1a.

hoy[1] /hoy/ *int.* & *n.* ● *int.* used to call attention, drive animals, or *Naut.* hail or call aloft. ● *n. Austral.* a game of chance resembling bingo, using playing cards. [ME: natural cry]

hoy[2] /hoy/ *n. hist.* a small vessel, usu. rigged as a sloop, carrying passengers and goods esp. for short distances. [MDu. *hoei*, *hoede*, of unkn. orig.]

hoy[3] /hoy/ *v.tr. Austral. sl.* throw. [Brit. dial.: orig. unkn.]
■ see THROW *v.* 1, 2.

hoya /hóyə/ *n.* any climbing shrub of the genus *Hoya*, with pink, white, or yellow waxy flowers. [mod.L f. T. *Hoy*, Engl. gardener d. 1821]

hoyden /hóyd'n/ *n.* a boisterous girl. □□ **hoydenish** *adj.* [orig. = rude fellow, prob. f. MDu. *heiden* (= HEATHEN)]

Hoyle /hoyl/ *n.* □ **according to Hoyle** *adv.* correctly, exactly. ● *adj.* correct, exact. [E. *Hoyle*, Engl. writer on card-games d. 1769]

h.p. *abbr.* **1** horsepower. **2** hire purchase. **3** high pressure.

HQ *abbr.* headquarters.

HR *abbr. US* House of Representatives.

hr. *abbr.* hour.

HRH *abbr.* Her or His Royal Highness.

hrs. *abbr.* hours.

HSH *abbr.* Her or His Serene Highness.

HT *abbr.* high tension.

hub /hub/ *n.* **1** the central part of a wheel, rotating on or with the axle, and from which the spokes radiate. **2** a central point of interest, activity, etc. □ **hub-cap** a cover for the hub of a vehicle's wheel. [16th c.: perh. = HOB[1]]
■ **2** centre, focus, focal point, pivot, heart, core, nucleus, navel.

hubble-bubble /húbb'lbúbb'l/ *n.* **1** a rudimentary form of hookah. **2** a bubbling sound. **3** confused talk. [redupl. of BUBBLE]
■ **1** see PIPE *n.* 2a.

hubbub /húbbub/ *n.* **1** a confused din, esp. from a crowd of people. **2** a disturbance or riot. [perh. of Ir. orig.: cf. Gael. *ubub* int. of contempt, Ir. *abú*, used in battle-cries]
■ **1** see NOISE *n.* **2** see DISTURBANCE 2.

hubby /húbbi/ *n.* (*pl.* **-ies**) *colloq.* a husband. [abbr.]
■ see HUSBAND *n.*

hubris /hyŏŏbriss/ *n.* **1** arrogant pride or presumption. **2** (in Greek tragedy) excessive pride towards or defiance of the gods, leading to nemesis. □□ **hubristic** /-brístik/ *adj.* [Gk]
■ **1** see PRIDE *n.* 2.

huckaback /húkkəbak/ *n.* a stout linen or cotton fabric with a rough surface, used for towelling. [17th c.: orig. unkn.]

huckleberry /húkk'lbəri/ *n.* (*pl.* **-ies**) **1** any low-growing N. American shrub of the genus *Gaylussacia*. **2** the blue or black soft fruit of this plant. [prob. alt. of *hurtleberry*, WHORTLEBERRY]

huckster /húkstər/ *n.* & *v.* ● *n.* **1** a mercenary person. **2** *US* a publicity agent, esp. for broadcast material. **3** a pedlar or hawker. ● *v.* **1** *intr.* bargain, haggle. **2** *tr.* carry on a petty traffic in. **3** *tr.* adulterate. [ME prob. f. LG: cf. dial. *huck* to bargain, HAWKER[1]]
■ *n.* **3** see PEDLAR. ● *v.* **1** see BARGAIN *v.* **2** see PEDDLE.

huddle /húdd'l/ *v.* & *n.* ● *v.* **1** *tr.* & *intr.* (often foll. by *up*) crowd together; nestle closely. **2** *intr.* & *refl.* (often foll. by *up*) coil one's body into a small space. **3** *tr. Brit.* heap together in a muddle. ● *n.* **1** a confused or crowded mass of people or things. **2** *colloq.* a close or secret conference (esp. in **go into a huddle**). **3** confusion, bustle. [16th c.: perh. f. LG and ult. rel. to HIDE[3]]
■ *v.* **1** cluster, gather, crowd *or* press together, throng *or* flock together, nestle, squeeze together. **3** see LUMP[1] *v.* ● *n.* **1** cluster, group, bunch, clump, pack, herd, crowd, throng, mass. **2** meeting, conference, discussion, consultation, confabulation, *colloq.* confab. **3** see CONFUSION 2.

hue /hyoo/ *n.* **1 a** a colour or tint. **b** a variety or shade of colour caused by the admixture of another. **2** the attribute of a colour by virtue of which it is discernible as red, green, etc. □□ **-hued** *adj.* **hueless** *adj.* [OE *hīew*, *hēw* form, beauty f. Gmc: cf. ON *hȳ* down on plants]
■ **1** colour, tint, shade, tinge, tone, cast, tincture.

hue and cry /hyoo/ *n.* **1** a loud clamour or outcry. **2** *hist.* **a** a loud cry raised for the pursuit of a wrongdoer. **b** a proclamation for the capture of a criminal. [AF *hu e cri* f. OF *hu* outcry (f. *huer* shout) + *e* and + *cri* cry]
■ **1** see RACKET[2] 1a.

huff /huf/ *v.* & *n.* ● *v.* **1** *intr.* give out loud puffs of air, steam, etc. **2** *intr.* bluster loudly or threateningly (*huffing and puffing*). **3** *intr.* & *tr.* take or cause to take offence. **4** *tr. Draughts* remove (an opponent's man that could have made a capture) from the board as a forfeit (orig. after blowing on the piece). ● *n.* a fit of petty annoyance. □ **in a huff** annoyed and offended. □□ **huffish** *adj.* [imit. of the sound of blowing]
■ *v.* **1** see PUFF *v.* 4. **2** puff, bluster, storm about; see also RAGE *v.* ● *n.* see TANTRUM. □ **in a huff** piqued, irritated, annoyed, offended, in high dudgeon, in a pet, hot under the collar, furious, *colloq.* (all) het up, peeved, in a stink; see also ANGRY 1.

huffy /húffi/ *adj.* (**huffier, huffiest**) **1** apt to take offence. **2** offended. □□ **huffily** *adv.* **huffiness** *n.*
■ see IRRITABLE 1.

hug /hug/ *v.* & *n.* ● *v.tr.* (**hugged, hugging**) **1** squeeze tightly in one's arms, esp. with affection. **2** (of a bear) squeeze (a person) between its forelegs. **3** keep close to (the shore, kerb, etc.). **4** cherish or cling to (prejudices etc.). **5** *refl.* congratulate or be pleased with (oneself). ● *n.* **1** a strong clasp with the arms. **2** a squeezing grip in wrestling.

□□ **huggable** *adj.* [16th c.: prob. f. Scand.: cf. ON *hugga* console]
■ *v.* **1** clasp, squeeze, cuddle; see also EMBRACE *v.* 1. **3** follow closely, cling to, stay *or* keep near *or* close to. ● *n.* **1** embrace, clasp, squeeze, *colloq.* clinch. **2** grip, clinch.

huge /hyōōj/ *adj.* **1** extremely large; enormous. **2** (of immaterial things) very great (*a huge success*). □□ **hugeness** *n.* [ME *huge* f. OF *ahuge, ahoge*, of unkn. orig.]
■ **1** large, great, enormous, gigantic, giant, immense, massive, gargantuan, mammoth, colossal, monumental, titanic, elephantine, leviathan, vast, *colloq.* jumbo, terrific, *sl.* whopping. **2** tremendous, prodigious, stupendous, colossal, immense, enormous, great, massive, *colloq.* terrific.

hugely /hyōōjli/ *adv.* **1** enormously (*hugely successful*). **2** very much (*enjoyed it hugely*).
■ **1** see HIGHLY 1. **2** see VERY *adv.*

hugger-mugger /húggərmúggər/ *adj., adv., n.,* & *v.* ● *adj.* & *adv.* **1** in secret. **2** confused; in confusion. ● *n.* **1** secrecy. **2** confusion. ● *v.intr.* proceed in a secret or muddled fashion. [prob. rel. to ME *hoder* huddle, *mokere* conceal: cf. 15th-c. *hoder moder*, 16th-c. *hucker mucker* in the same sense]
■ *adj.* & *adv.* **1** see FURTIVE 1. **2** see *chaotic* (CHAOS). ● *n.* **2** see CHAOS 1a.

Hughie / hyōō-ee/ *n. Austral.* & *NZ sl.* the imaginary being responsible for the weather (esp. *send her down, Hughie!*). [dimin. of male forename *Hugh* + -IE]

Huguenot /hyōōgənō, -not/ *n. hist.* a French Protestant. [F, assim. of *eiguenot* (f. Du. *eedgenot* f. Swiss G *Eidgenoss* confederate) to the name of a Geneva burgomaster *Hugues*]

huh /hə/ *int.* expressing disgust, surprise, etc. [imit.]

hula /hōōlə/ *n.* (also **hula-hula**) a Polynesian dance performed by women, with flowing movements of the arms. □ **hula hoop** a large hoop for spinning round the body with hula-like movements. **hula skirt** a long grass skirt. [Hawaiian]

hulk /hulk/ *n.* **1 a** the body of a dismantled ship, used as a store vessel etc. **b** (in *pl.*) *hist.* this used as a prison. **2** an unwieldy vessel. **3** *colloq.* a large clumsy-looking person or thing. [OE *hulc* & MLG, MDu. *hulk*: cf. Gk *holkas* cargo ship]
■ **1 a** shipwreck, wreck, shell, skeleton. **3** oaf, lout, lubber, lump, *colloq.* galoot, *sl.* clod, *Austral. sl.* hoon, *US sl.* klutz.

hulking /húlking/ *adj. colloq.* bulky; large and clumsy.
■ clumsy, awkward, ungainly, ungraceful, inelegant, lubberly, oafish, loutish; unwieldy, cumbersome, bulky; see also MASSIVE 1–3.

hull[1] /hul/ *n.* & *v.* ● *n.* the body or frame of a ship, airship, flying boat, etc. ● *v.tr.* pierce the hull of (a ship) with gunshot etc. [ME, perh. rel. to HOLD[2]]
■ *n.* framework, skeleton, frame, structure, body. ● *v.* pierce, hole, puncture, bore into, penetrate.

hull[2] /hul/ *n.* & *v.* ● *n.* **1** the outer covering of a fruit, esp. the pod of peas and beans, the husk of grain, or the green calyx of a strawberry. **2** a covering. ● *v.tr.* remove the hulls from (fruit etc.). [OE *hulu* ult. f. *helan* cover: cf. HELE]
■ *n.* shell, pod, case, husk, skin, peel, rind, *US* shuck; covering, casing. ● *v.* shell, peel, skin, husk, *US* shuck.

hullabaloo /húlləbəlōō/ *n.* (*pl.* **hullabaloos**) an uproar or clamour. [18th c.: redupl. of *hallo, hullo*, etc.]
■ see UPROAR.

hullo var. of HELLO.

hum[1] /hum/ *v.* & *n.* ● *v.* (**hummed, humming**) **1** *intr.* make a low steady continuous sound like that of a bee. **2** *tr.* (also *absol.*) sing (a wordless tune) with closed lips. **3** *intr.* utter a slight inarticulate sound. **4** *intr. colloq.* be in an active state (*really made things hum*). **5** *intr. Brit. colloq.* smell unpleasantly. ● *n.* **1** a humming sound. **2** an unwanted low-frequency noise caused by variation of electric current, usu. the alternating frequency of the mains, in an amplifier etc. **3** *Brit. colloq.* a bad smell. □ **hum and haw** (or **ha**) hesitate, esp. in speaking. □□ **hummable** *adj.* **hummer** *n.* [ME, imit.]
■ *v.* **1** buzz, drone, murmur, whirr, purr, vibrate. **4** bustle, stir, be active, move, happen. **5** smell, stink, reek, *Brit. colloq.* pong. ● *n.* **1** buzz, drone, murmur, murmuring, whirr, purr, vibration.

hum[2] /həm/ *int.* expressing hesitation or dissent. [imit.]

human /hyōōmən/ *adj.* & *n.* ● *adj.* **1** of or belonging to the genus *Homo*. **2** consisting of human beings (*the human race*). **3** of or characteristic of mankind as opposed to God or animals or machines, esp. susceptible to the weaknesses of mankind (*is only human*). **4** showing (esp. the better) qualities of man (*proved to be very human*). ● *n.* a human being. □ **human being** any man or woman or child of the species *Homo sapiens*. **human chain** a line of people formed for passing things along, e.g. buckets of water to the site of a fire. **human engineering 1** the management of industrial labour, esp. as regards man–machine relationships. **2** the study of this. **human equation** a bias or prejudice. **human interest** (in a newspaper story etc.) reference to personal experience and emotions etc. **human nature** the general characteristics and feelings of mankind. **human relations** relations with or between people or individuals. **human rights** rights held to be justifiably belonging to any person. **human shield** a person or persons placed in the line of fire in order to discourage attack. □□ **humanness** *n.* [ME *humain(e)* f. OF f. L *humanus* f. *homo* human being]
■ *adj.* **1–3** mortal, anthropoid, hominoid, manlike, defenceless, weak, vulnerable, fallible. **4** kind, kindly, kind-hearted, considerate, charitable, compassionate, merciful, benign, benignant, tender, gentle, forgiving, lenient, benevolent, beneficent, generous, magnanimous, humanitarian, understanding, accommodating, sympathetic, good-natured, humane, sensitive. ● *n.* human being, person, individual, being, mortal, soul. □ **human being** see HUMAN *n.* above.

humane /hyoomáyn/ *adj.* **1** benevolent, compassionate. **2** inflicting the minimum of pain. **3** (of a branch of learning) tending to civilize or confer refinement. □ **humane killer** an instrument for the painless slaughter of animals. □□ **humanely** *adv.* **humaneness** *n.* [var. of HUMAN, differentiated in sense in the 18th c.]
■ **1** see BENEVOLENT 1.

humanism /hyōōməniz'm/ *n.* **1** an outlook or system of thought concerned with human rather than divine or supernatural matters. **2** a belief or outlook emphasizing common human needs and seeking solely rational ways of solving human problems, and concerned with mankind as responsible and progressive intellectual beings. **3** (often **Humanism**) literary culture, esp. that of the Renaissance humanists.

humanist /hyōōmənist/ *n.* **1** an adherent of humanism. **2** a humanitarian. **3** a student (esp. in the 14th–16th c.) of Roman and Greek literature and antiquities. □□ **humanistic** /-nístik/ *adj.* **humanistically** /-nístikəli/ *adv.* [F *humaniste* f. It. *umanista* (as HUMAN)]

humanitarian /hyoománnitáiriən/ *n.* & *adj.* ● *n.* **1** a person who seeks to promote human welfare. **2** a person who advocates or practises humane action; a philanthropist. ● *adj.* relating to or holding the views of humanitarians. □□ **humanitarianism** *n.*
■ *n.* Good Samaritan, philanthropist, philanthrope, benefactor, benefactress, altruist, do-gooder. ● *adj.* see HUMAN *adj.* 4.

humanity /hyoománniti/ *n.* (*pl.* **-ies**) **1 a** the human race. **b** human beings collectively. **c** the fact or condition of being human. **2** humaneness, benevolence. **3** (in *pl.*) human attributes. **4** (in *pl.*) learning or literature concerned with human culture, esp. the study of Latin and Greek literature and philosophy. [ME f. OF *humanité* f. L *humanitas -tatis* (as HUMAN)]
■ **1 a, b** human race, human beings, people, society, humankind, *Homo sapiens*, man, mankind. **c** humanness, human nature, manhood. **2** humaneness, kindness, kindliness, kind-heartedness, consideration, charitableness,

open-heartedness, warm-heartedness, good will, benevolence, compassion, mercifulness, mercy, benignity, tenderness, warmth, beneficence, generosity, unselfishness, magnanimity, understanding, tact, tactfulness, sympathy, sensitivity. **4** (*the humanities*) see ART[1] 6.

humanize /hyóomənīz/ *v.tr.* (also **-ise**) **1** make human; give a human character to. **2** make humane. ▫▫ **humanization** /-záysh'n/ *n.* [F *humaniser* (as HUMAN)]
▪ **1** personify, personalize.

humankind /hyóomənkīnd/ *n.* human beings collectively.

humanly /hyóomənli/ *adv.* **1** by human means (*I will do it if it is humanly possible*). **2** in a human manner. **3** from a human point of view. **4** with human feelings.

humble /húmb'l/ *adj.* & *v.* ● *adj.* **1 a** having or showing a low estimate of one's own importance. **b** offered with or affected by such an estimate (*if you want my humble opinion*). **2** of low social or political rank (*humble origins*). **3** (of a thing) of modest pretensions, dimensions, etc. ● *v.tr.* **1** make humble; bring low; abase. **2** lower the rank or status of. ▫ **eat humble pie** make a humble apology; accept humiliation. ▫▫ **humbleness** *n.* **humbly** *adv.* [ME *umble*, *humble* f. OF *umble* f. L *humilis* lowly f. *humus* ground: *humble pie* f. UMBLES]
▪ *adj.* **1 a** modest, reserved, self-effacing, unassuming, unpresuming, retiring; submissive, meek, servile, obsequious, deferential, mild, respectful, subservient. **2** lowly, low, inferior, mean, ignoble, ordinary, plebeian, common, simple, obscure, unimportant, undistinguished, insignificant; low-born. **3** unpretentious, unostentatious, unprepossessing, small; see also MODEST 5. ● *v.* **1** chasten, bring *or* pull down, subdue, abase, demean, lower, reduce, make a person eat humble pie, shame, humiliate, crush, break, mortify, chagrin, take a person down a peg *or* notch, put a person in his *or* her place, *colloq.* put down. **2** debase, degrade, demote, downgrade; see also REDUCE 6.

humble-bee /húmb'lbee/ *n.* = BUMBLE-BEE. [ME prob. f. MLG *hummelbē*, MDu. *hommel*, OHG *humbal*]

humbug /húmbug/ *n.* & *v.* ● *n.* **1** deceptive or false talk or behaviour. **2** an impostor. **3** *Brit.* a hard boiled sweet usu. flavoured with peppermint. ● *v.* (**humbugged, humbugging**) **1** *intr.* be or behave like an impostor. **2** *tr.* deceive, hoax. ▫▫ **humbuggery** *n.* [18th c.: orig. unkn.]
▪ *n.* **1** see CANT[1] *n.* 1. **2** see IMPOSTOR 1. ● *v.* **2** see DUPE *v.*

humdinger /húmdíngər/ *n. sl.* an excellent or remarkable person or thing. [20th c.: orig. unkn.]

humdrum /húmdrum/ *adj.* & *n.* ● *adj.* **1** commonplace, dull. **2** monotonous. ● *n.* **1** commonplaceness, dullness. **2** a monotonous routine etc. [16th c.: prob. f. HUM[1] by redupl.]
▪ *adj.* dull, boring, tedious, tiresome, wearisome, monotonous, unvaried, unvarying, routine, undiversified, unchanging, repetitious, uneventful, unexciting, uninteresting, prosaic, mundane, ordinary, commonplace, banal, dry, insipid, jejune.

humectant /hyooméktənt/ *adj.* & *n.* ● *adj.* retaining or preserving moisture. ● *n.* a substance, esp. a food additive, used to reduce loss of moisture. [L *(h)umectant-* part. stem of *(h)umectare* moisten f. *umēre* be moist]

humeral /hyóomərəl/ *adj.* **1** of the humerus or shoulder. **2** worn on the shoulder. [F *huméral* & LL *humeralis* (as HUMERUS)]

humerus /hyóomərəss/ *n.* (*pl.* **humeri** /-rī/) **1** the bone of the upper arm in man. **2** the corresponding bone in other vertebrates. [L, = shoulder]

humic /hyóomik/ *adj.* of or consisting of humus.

humid /hyóomid/ *adj.* (of the air or climate) warm and damp. ▫▫ **humidly** *adv.* [F *humide* or L *humidus* f. *umēre* be moist]
▪ damp, moist, muggy, clammy, sticky, steamy, sultry, wet.

humidifier /hyoomíddifīər/ *n.* a device for keeping the atmosphere moist in a room etc.

humidify /hyoomíddifī/ *v.tr.* (**-ies, -ied**) make (air etc.) humid or damp. ▫▫ **humidification** /-fikáysh'n/ *n.*

humidity /hyoomíddti/ *n.* (*pl.* **-ies**) **1** a humid state. **2** moisture. **3** the degree of moisture esp. in the atmosphere. ▫ **relative humidity** the proportion of moisture to the value for saturation at the same temperature. [ME f. OF *humidité* or L *humiditas* (as HUMID)]
▪ see DAMP *n.* 1.

humidor /hyóomidor/ *n.* a room or container for keeping cigars or tobacco moist. [HUMID after *cuspidor*]

humify /hyóomifī/ *v.tr.* & *intr.* (**-ies, -ied**) make or be made into humus. ▫▫ **humification** /-fikáysh'n/ *n.*

humiliate /hyoomílliayt/ *v.tr.* make humble; injure the dignity or self-respect of. ▫▫ **humiliating** *adj.* **humiliatingly** *adv.* **humiliation** /-áysh'n/ *n.* **humiliator** *n.* [LL *humiliare* (as HUMBLE)]
▪ disgrace, shame, discredit, abase, pull down, take down, put to shame, embarrass, humble, lower, demean, *colloq.* put down, flatten, score points off, show up; see also HUMBLE *v.* 1. ▫▫ **humiliation** disgrace, shame, mortification, dishonour, ignominy, indignity, discredit, loss of face, obloquy, abasement, detraction, degradation, derogation, belittlement, disparagement, embarrassment.

humility /hyoomílliti/ *n.* **1** humbleness, meekness. **2** a humble condition. [ME f. OF *humilité* f. L *humilitas -tatis* (as HUMBLE)]
▪ **1** humbleness, modesty, meekness, self-effacement, shyness, diffidence, timidity, timorousness, bashfulness, mildness, unpretentiousness, submissiveness, servility, self-abasement. **2** modesty, lowliness, simplicity, ordinariness, plainness.

hummingbird /húmmingburd/ *n.* any small nectar-feeding tropical bird of the family Trochilidae that makes a humming sound by the vibration of its wings when it hovers.

humming-top /húmmingtop/ *n.* a child's top which hums as it spins.

hummock /húmmək/ *n.* **1** a hillock or knoll. **2** *US* a piece of rising ground, esp. in a marsh. **3** a hump or ridge in an ice-field. ▫▫ **hummocky** *adj.* [16th c.: orig. unkn.]
▪ see MOUND[1] *n.* 3.

hummus /hóomməss/ *n.* (also **hoummos**) a thick sauce or spread made from ground chick-peas and sesame oil flavoured with lemon and garlic. [Turk. *humus* mashed chick-peas]

humongous /hyoomúnggəss/ *adj.* (also **humungous**) *sl.* extremely large or massive. [20th c.: orig. uncert.]

humor *US* var. of HUMOUR.

humoral /hyóomərəl/ *adj.* **1** *hist.* of the four bodily humours. **2** *Med.* relating to body fluids, esp. as distinct from cells. [F *humoral* or med.L *humoralis* (as HUMOUR)]

humoresque /hyóomərésk/ *n.* a short lively piece of music. [G *Humoreske* f. *Humor* HUMOUR]

humorist /hyóomərist/ *n.* **1** a facetious person. **2** a humorous talker, actor, or writer. ▫▫ **humoristic** /-rístik/ *adj.*
▪ **2** see COMEDIAN.

humorous /hyóomərəss/ *adj.* **1** showing humour or a sense of humour. **2** facetious, comic. ▫▫ **humorously** *adv.* **humorousness** *n.*
▪ **1** amusing, witty, droll, whimsical, waggish, jocular, jocose, playful. **2** funny, comical, facetious, laughable, risible, farcical, side-splitting, hilarious, uproarious, *colloq.* hysterical, killing.

humour /hyóomər/ *n.* & *v.* (*US* **humor**) ● *n.* **1 a** the condition of being amusing or comic (less intellectual and more sympathetic than wit). **b** the expression of humour in literature, speech, etc. **2** (in full **sense of humour**) the ability to perceive or express humour or take a joke. **3** a mood or state of mind (*bad humour*). **4** an inclination or whim (*in the humour for fighting*). **5** (in full **cardinal humour**) *hist.* each of the four chief fluids of the body (blood, phlegm, choler, melancholy), thought to determine a person's physical and mental qualities. ● *v.tr.* **1** gratify or indulge (a person or taste etc.). **2** adapt oneself to; make concessions to. ▫ **out of humour** displeased. ▫▫

-humoured *adj.* **humourless** *adj.* **humourlessly** *adv.* **humourlessness** *n.* [ME f. AF *umour*, *humour*, OF *umor*, *humor* f. L *humor* moisture (as HUMID)]

■ *n.* **1 a** funniness, comedy, facetiousness, drollery; jocoseness, jocosity, jocularity, waggishness. **b** comedy, farce, jokes, jests, *colloq.* wisecracks, gags. **3** mood, frame *or* state of mind, temper, spirits, disposition, inclination, attitude. ● *v.* **1** soothe, gratify, placate, please, mollify, indulge, appease, pamper, cosset, coddle, mollycoddle, jolly, baby, spoil. □ **out of humour** in a (bad) mood, displeased; see also MOODY *adj.*

humous /hyóóməss/ *adj.* like or consisting of humus.

hump /hump/ *n.* & *v.* ● *n.* **1** a rounded protuberance on the back of a camel etc., or as an abnormality on a person's back. **2** a rounded raised mass of earth etc. **3** a mound over which railway vehicles are pushed so as to run by gravity to the required place in a marshalling yard. **4** a critical point in an undertaking, ordeal, etc. **5** (prec. by *the*) *Brit. sl.* a fit of depression or vexation (*it gives me the hump*). **6** *coarse sl.* an act of sexual intercourse; a sexual partner. ● *v.tr.* **1 a** (often foll. by *about*) *colloq.* lift or carry (heavy objects etc.) with difficulty. **b** esp. *Austral.* hoist up, shoulder (one's pack etc.). **2** make hump-shaped. **3** annoy, depress. **4** *coarse sl.* have sexual intercourse with. ¶ In sense 4 usually considered a taboo word. □ **hump bridge** = *humpback bridge*. **live on one's hump** *colloq.* be self-sufficient. **over the hump** over the worst; well begun. □□ **humped** *adj.* **humpless** *adj.* [17th c.: perh. rel. to LG *humpel* hump, LG *humpe*, Du. *homp* lump, hunk (of bread)]

■ *n.* **1** bulge, lump, bump, protuberance, protrusion, projection, knob, node, hunch, enlargement, swelling, growth, excrescence, tumescence. **2** mound, hummock, hillock. **4** crisis, critical time *or* moment *or* point, turning-point, *colloq.* crunch. ● *v.* **1 a** drag, lug, haul, carry, heave, *colloq.* schlep(p). **2** hunch, arch, curve, crook, bend. **3** see ANNOY 1, DEPRESS 2.

humpback /húmpbak/ *n.* **1 a** a deformed back with a hump. **b** a person having this. **2** a baleen whale, *Megaptera novaeangliae*, with a dorsal fin forming a hump. □ **humpback bridge** *Brit.* a small bridge with a steep ascent and descent. □□ **humpbacked** *adj.*

humph /həmf/ *int.* & *n.* an inarticulate sound expressing doubt or dissatisfaction. [imit.]

humpty-dumpty /húmptidúmpti/ *n.* (*pl.* **-ies**) **1** a short dumpy person. **2** a person or thing that once overthrown cannot be restored. [the nursery rhyme *Humpty-Dumpty*, perh. ult. f. HUMPY[1], DUMPY]

humpy[1] /húmpi/ *adj.* (**humpier**, **humpiest**) **1** having a hump or humps. **2** humplike.

humpy[2] /húmpi/ *n.* (*pl.* **-ies**) *Austral.* a primitive hut. [Aboriginal *oompi*, infl. by HUMP]

humus /hyóóməss/ *n.* the organic constituent of soil, usu. formed by the decomposition of plants and leaves by soil bacteria. □□ **humusify** *v.tr.* & *intr.* (**-ies, -ied**). [L, = soil]

■ see SOIL[1] 1.

Hun /hun/ *n.* **1** a member of a warlike Asiatic nomadic people who invaded and ravaged Europe in the 4th–5th c. **2** *offens.* a German (esp. in military contexts). **3** an uncivilized devastator; a vandal. □□ **Hunnish** *adj.* [OE *Hūne* pl. f. LL *Hunni* f. Gk *Hounnoi* f. Turki *Hun-yü*]

hunch /hunch/ *v.* & *n.* ● *v.* **1** *tr.* bend or arch into a hump. **2** *tr.* thrust out or up to form a hump. **3** *intr.* (usu. foll. by *up*) *US* sit with the body hunched. ● *n.* **1** *colloq.* an intuitive feeling or conjecture. **2** *US colloq.* a hint. **3** a hump. **4** a thick piece. [16th c.: orig. unkn.]

■ *v.* **1** see HUMP *v.* 2. ● *n.* **1** intuition, feeling, impression, suspicion, premonition, presentiment, idea. **2** see HINT *n.* 1. **3** see HUMP *n.* 1. **4** hunk, chunk; see also SLAB *n.*

hunchback /húnchbak/ *n.* = HUMPBACK. □□ **hunchbacked** *adj.*

hundred /húndrəd/ *n.* & *adj.* ● *n.* (*pl.* **hundreds** or (in sense 1) **hundred**) (in *sing.*, prec. by *a* or *one*) **1** the product of ten and ten. **2** a symbol for this (100, c, C). **3** a set of a hundred things. **4** (in *sing.* or *pl.*) *colloq.* a large number. **5** (in *pl.*) the years of a specified century (*the seventeen hundreds*). **6** *Brit. hist.* a subdivision of a county or shire, having its own court. ● *adj.* **1** that amount to a hundred. **2** used to express whole hours in the 24-hour system (*thirteen hundred hours*). □ **a** (or **one**) **hundred per cent** *adv.* entirely, completely. ● *adj.* **1** entire, complete. **2** (usu. with *neg.*) fully recovered. **hundreds and thousands** tiny coloured sweets used chiefly for decorating cakes etc. □□ **hundredfold** *adj.* & *adv.* **hundredth** *adj.* & *n.* [OE f. Gmc]

■ *n.* **4** (*hundreds*) see SCORE *n.* 3.

hundredweight /húndrədwayt/ *n.* (*pl.* same or **-weights**) **1** (in full **long hundredweight**) *Brit.* a unit of weight equal to 112 lb. avoirdupois (about 50.8 kg). **2** (in full **metric hundredweight**) a unit of weight equal to 50 kg. **3** (in full **short hundredweight**) *US* a unit of weight equal to 100 lb. (about 45.4 kg).

hung *past* and *past part.* of HANG.

Hungarian /hunggáiriən/ *n.* & *adj.* ● *n.* **1 a** a native or national of Hungary in E. Europe. **b** a person of Hungarian descent. **2** the Finno-Ugric language of Hungary. ● *adj.* of or relating to Hungary or its people or language. [med.L *Hungaria* f. *Hungari* Magyar nation]

hunger /húnggər/ *n.* & *v.* ● *n.* **1** a feeling of pain or discomfort, or (in extremes) an exhausted condition, caused by lack of food. **2** (often foll. by *for*, *after*) a strong desire. ● *v.intr.* **1** (often foll. by *for*, *after*) have a craving or strong desire. **2** feel hunger. □ **hunger march** a march undertaken by a body of unemployed etc. to call attention to their condition. **hunger marcher** a person who goes on a hunger march. **hunger strike** the refusal of food as a form of protest, esp. by prisoners. **hunger striker** a person who takes part in a hunger strike. [OE *hungor*, *hyngran* f. Gmc]

■ *n.* **1** hungriness, emptiness, ravenousness, *archaic* famine. **2** yearning, desire, craving, itch, thirst, longing, hankering, *colloq.* yen. ● *v.* **1** (*hunger for* or *after*) long for, crave, yearn for, desire, thirst for, want, hanker after, *colloq.* have a yen for. **2** have an empty stomach, feel starving.

hungry /húnggri/ *adj.* (**hungrier**, **hungriest**) **1** feeling or showing hunger; needing food. **2** inducing hunger (*a hungry air*). **3 a** eager, greedy, craving. **b** *Austral.* mean, stingy. **4** (of soil) poor, barren. □□ **hungrily** *adv.* **hungriness** *n.* [OE *hungrig* (as HUNGER)]

■ **1** famished, ravenous, hollow, sharp-set, *archaic or joc.* esurient, *colloq.* peckish, empty, starving, starved. **3 a** craving, eager, avid, greedy, keen, dying, yearning, desirous, longing, hungering, thirsting, thirsty, hankering, voracious, covetous. **b** see MEAN[2] 1. **4** see BARREN *adj.* 1b.

hunk /hungk/ *n.* **1 a** a large piece cut off (*a hunk of bread*). **b** a thick or clumsy piece. **2** *colloq.* **a** a very large person. **b** esp. *US* a sexually attractive man. □□ **hunky** *adj.* (**hunkier**, **hunkiest**). [19th c.: prob. f. Flem. *hunke*]

hunkers /húngkərz/ *n.pl.* the haunches. [orig. Sc., f. *hunker* crouch, squat]

hunky-dory /húngkidóri/ *adj.* esp. *US colloq.* excellent. [19th c.: orig. unkn.]

hunt /hunt/ *v.* & *n.* ● *v.* **1** *tr.* (also *absol.*) **a** pursue and kill (wild animals, esp. foxes, or game), esp. on horseback and with hounds, for sport or food. **b** (of an animal) chase (its prey). **2** *intr.* (foll. by *after*, *for*) seek, search (*hunting for a pen*). **3** *intr.* **a** oscillate. **b** (of an engine etc.) run alternately too fast and too slow. **4** *tr.* (foll. by *away* etc.) drive off by pursuit. **5** *tr.* scour (a district) in pursuit of game. **6** *tr.* (as **hunted** *adj.*) (of a look etc.) expressing alarm or terror as of one being hunted. **7** *tr.* (foll. by *down*, *up*) move the place of (a bell) in ringing the changes. ● *n.* **1** the practice of hunting or an instance of this. **2 a** an association of people engaged in hunting with hounds. **b** an area where hunting takes place. **3** an oscillating motion. □ **hunt down** pursue and capture. **hunt out** find by searching; track down. [OE *huntian*, weak grade of *hentan* seize]

■ *v.* **1** chase, pursue, dog, hound, stalk, trail, track (down); shoot. **2** (*hunt for* or *after*) seek (out), search for, go in search of *or* for, look (high and low) for, quest for, go in quest of; (*hunt through*) see SEARCH *v.* 1, 3. **4** drive off *or* away; see also SHOO *v.* **5** see SCOUR². **6** (**hunted**) see *scared* (SCARE *v.* 2). ● *n.* **1** chase, pursuit, tracking, stalking, hunting, pursuance; search, quest. □ **hunt down** see *track down* (TRACK¹). **hunt out** see *track down* (TRACK¹).

huntaway /húntəway/ *n. Austral.* & *NZ* a dog trained to drive sheep forward.

hunter /húntər/ *n.* **1 a** (*fem.* **huntress**) a person or animal that hunts. **b** a horse used in hunting. **2** a person who seeks something. **3** a watch with a hinged cover protecting the glass. □ **hunter's moon** the next full moon after the harvest moon.

■ **1 a** huntsman, stalker, tracker, Nimrod. **2** seeker, searcher, quester.

hunting /húnting/ *n.* the practice of pursuing and killing wild animals, esp. for sport. □ **hunting-crop** see CROP *n.* 3. **hunting-ground 1** a place suitable for hunting. **2** a source of information or object of exploitation likely to be fruitful. **hunting horn** a straight horn used in hunting. **hunting pink** see PINK¹. [OE *huntung* (as HUNT)]

Huntington's chorea /húntingtənz/ *n. Med.* see CHOREA. [G. *Huntington*, Amer. neurologist, d. 1916]

huntsman /húntsmən/ *n.* (*pl.* **-men**) **1** a hunter. **2** a hunt official in charge of hounds.

hurdle /húrd'l/ *n.* & *v.* ● *n.* **1** *Athletics* **a** each of a series of light frames to be cleared by athletes in a race. **b** (in *pl.*) a hurdle-race. **2** an obstacle or difficulty. **3** a portable rectangular frame strengthened with withes or wooden bars, used as a temporary fence etc. **4** *hist.* a frame on which traitors were dragged to execution. ● *v.* **1** *Athletics* **a** *intr.* run in a hurdle-race. **b** *tr.* clear (a hurdle). **2** *tr.* fence off etc. with hurdles. **3** *tr.* overcome (a difficulty). [OE *hyrdel* f. Gmc]

■ *n.* **2** barrier, obstacle, impediment, hindrance, obstruction, bar, handicap, restraint, snag, (stumbling) block, difficulty, complication, problem. ● *v.* **1 b** clear, leap (over), vault (over), jump (over), bound over, spring over. **3** overcome, surmount, get over; see also SOLVE.

hurdler /húrdlər/ *n.* **1** *Athletics* a person who runs in hurdle-races. **2** a person who makes hurdles.

hurdy-gurdy /húrdigúrdi/ *n.* (*pl.* **-ies**) **1** a musical instrument with a droning sound, played by turning a handle, esp. one with a rosined wheel turned by the right hand to sound the drone-strings, and keys played by the left hand. **2** *colloq.* a barrel-organ. [prob. imit.]

hurl /hurl/ *v.* & *n.* ● *v.* **1** *tr.* throw with great force. **2** *tr.* utter (abuse etc.) vehemently. **3** *intr.* play hurling. ● *n.* **1** a forceful throw. **2** the act of hurling. [ME, prob. imit., but corresp. in form and partly in sense with LG *hurreln*]

■ *v.* **1** throw, toss, shy, sling, fling, pitch, cast, fire, propel, launch, let fly, *colloq.* chuck, heave, *Austral. sl.* hog. ● *n.* **1** see THROW *n.* 1.

Hurler's syndrome /húrlərz/ *n. Med.* a defect in metabolism resulting in mental retardation, a protruding abdomen, and deformities of the bones, including an abnormally large head. Also called GARGOYLISM. [G. *Hurler*, Ger. paediatrician]

hurling /húrling/ *n.* (also **hurley** /húrli/) **1** an Irish game somewhat resembling hockey, played with broad sticks. **2** a stick used in this.

hurly-burly /húrlibúrli/ *n.* boisterous activity; commotion. [redupl. f. HURL]

■ see DISTURBANCE 2.

hurrah /hoorāa/ *int.*, *n.*, & *v.* (also **hurray** /hooráy/) ● *int.* & *n.* an exclamation of joy or approval. ● *v.intr.* cry or shout 'hurrah' or 'hurray'. [alt. of earlier *huzza*, perh. orig. a sailor's cry when hauling]

■ *int.* & *n.* see CHEER *n.* 1. ● *v.* see CHEER *v.* 2.

hurricane /húrrikən, -kayn/ *n.* **1** a storm with a violent wind, esp. a W. Indian cyclone. **2** *Meteorol.* a wind of 65 knots (75 m.p.h.) or more, force 12 on the Beaufort scale. **3** a violent commotion. □ **hurricane-bird** a frigate-bird. **hurricane-deck** a light upper deck on a ship etc. **hurricane-lamp** an oil-lamp designed to resist a high wind. [Sp. *huracan* & Port. *furacão* of Carib orig.]

■ **1, 2** cyclone, tornado, typhoon, whirlwind, twister, storm, gale. **3** see STIR¹ *n.* 2.

hurry /húrri/ *n.* & *v.* ● *n.* (*pl.* **-ies**) **1 a** great haste. **b** (with *neg.* or *interrog.*) a need for haste (*there is no hurry*; *what's the hurry?*). **2** (often foll. by *for*, or *to* + infin.) eagerness to get a thing done quickly. ● *v.* (**-ies**, **-ied**) **1** *intr.* move or act with great or undue haste. **2** *tr.* (often foll. by *away*, *along*) cause to move or proceed in this way. **3** *tr.* (as **hurried** *adj.*) hasty; done rapidly owing to lack of time. □ **hurry along** (or **up**) make or cause to make haste. **in a hurry 1** hurrying, rushed; in a rushed manner. **2** *colloq.* easily or readily (*you will not beat that in a hurry*; *shall not ask again in a hurry*). □□ **hurriedly** *adv.* **hurriedness** *n.* [16th c.: imit.]

■ *n.* **1 a** rush, hustle, (hustle and) bustle. **b** haste, pressure; see also *urgency* (URGENT). **2** see *eagerness* (EAGER). ● *v.* **1** rush, hasten, make haste, hotfoot (it), *colloq.* get cracking, get a move on, skedaddle, step on it, step on the gas, leg it, *US colloq.* hightail (it), *US sl.* get a wiggle on; speed, race, dash, hustle, scurry, fly, run, shoot, scuttle, go hell for leather, *colloq.* tear, scoot; speed up, accelerate. **2** push, press, drive; urge, egg on, spur (on). **3** (**hurried**) hasty, feverish, frantic, hectic, breakneck, frenetic, impetuous, rushed, precipitate, swift, quick, speedy; brief, short; superficial, cursory, offhand, perfunctory, slapdash. □ **hurry along** (or **up**) see HURRY *v.* 1, 2 above. **in a hurry 2** easily, readily, quickly.

hurry-scurry /húrriskúrri/ *n.*, *adj.*, & *adv.* ● *n.* disorderly haste. ● *adj.* & *adv.* in confusion. [jingling redupl. of HURRY]

hurst /hurst/ *n.* **1** a hillock. **2** a sandbank in the sea or a river. **3** a wood or wooded eminence. [OE *hyrst*, rel. to OS, OHG *hurst*, *horst*]

hurt /hurt/ *v*, *n.*, & *adj.* ● *v.* (*past* and *past part.* **hurt**) **1** *tr.* (also *absol.*) cause pain or injury to. **2** *tr.* cause mental pain or distress to (a person, feelings, etc.). **3** *intr.* suffer pain or harm (*my arm hurts*). **4** *tr.* cause damage to, be detrimental to. ● *n.* **1** bodily or material injury. **2** harm, wrong. **3** mental pain or distress. ● *adj.* expressing emotional pain; distressed, aggrieved. □□ **hurtless** *adj.* [ME f. OF *hurter*, *hurt* ult. perh. f. Gmc]

■ *v.* **1** harm, injure, wound. **2** distress, grieve, affect, afflict, depress, upset, disappoint, pain, cut to the quick, affront, offend. **3** ache, throb, pound, be sore *or* painful, sting, twinge; smart, burn. **4** damage, impair, mar, spoil, vitiate, ruin. ● *n.* **1** wound, damage; see also INJURY 1. **2** harm, injury, damage, wrong; see also GRIEVANCE. **3** pain, distress, discomfort, suffering, torment, torture, agony; anguish, misery, sadness, depression, *archaic or literary* woe, *literary* dolour. ● *adj.* injured, wronged, pained, rueful, grieved, unhappy, distressed, aggrieved, sad, wretched, woebegone, sorrowful, mournful.

hurtful /húrtfŏŏl/ *adj.* causing (esp. mental) hurt; causing damage or harm. □□ **hurtfully** *adv.* **hurtfulness** *n.*

■ nasty, cruel, cutting, malicious, mean, unkind, wounding, spiteful; harmful, injurious, detrimental, pernicious, disadvantageous, damaging, deleterious, destructive, noxious, baneful, mischievous, *literary* noisome.

hurtle /húrt'l/ *v.* **1** *intr.* & *tr.* move or hurl rapidly or with a clattering sound. **2** *intr.* come with a crash. [HURT in obs. sense 'strike forcibly']

■ **1** rush (headlong), plunge; tear, shoot, race, speed.

husband /húzbənd/ *n.* & *v.* ● *n.* a married man esp. in relation to his wife. ● *v.tr.* manage thriftily; use (resources) economically. □□ **husbander** *n.* **husbandhood** *n.* **husbandless** *adj.* **husbandlike** *adj.* **husbandly** *adj.* **husbandship** *n.* [OE *hūsbonda* house-dweller f. ON *húsbóndi* (as HOUSE, *bóndi* one who has a household)]

■ *n.* spouse, partner, *colloq.* mate, old man, hubby; groom, bridegroom. ● *v.* budget, economize on, manage.

husbandry /húzbəndri/ *n.* **1** farming. **2 a** management of resources. **b** careful management.
■ **1** see *farming* (FARM). **2** see ECONOMY 2a.

hush /hush/ *v.*, *int.*, & *n.* ● *v.* **1** *tr.* & *intr.* (often as **hushed** *adj.*) make or become silent, quiet, or muted. **2** *tr.* calm (disturbance, disquiet, etc.); soothe, allay. ● *int.* calling for silence. ● *n.* an expectant stillness or silence. □ **hush money** money paid to prevent the disclosure of a discreditable matter. **hush puppy** *US* quickly fried maize bread. **hush up** suppress public mention of (an affair). [back-form. f. obs. *husht* int., = quiet!, taken as a past part.]
■ *v.* **1** shush, silence, still, quiet, *Brit.* quieten; (**hushed**) muted, soft, quiet, *Mus.* piano. **2** soothe, allay, calm, quiet, mollify, pacify, placate, tranquillize, *Brit.* quieten. ● *int.* shush, quiet, be *or* keep quiet, hold your tongue *or* peace, *colloq.* shut up, clam up, button up, *esp. Sc.* & *Ir. dial.* whisht, *sl.* shut your face *or* trap *or* head *or* mouth, *esp. Brit. sl.* shut your gob, put a sock in it, *Brit. sl.* belt up, *esp. US sl.* button your lip. ● *n.* silence, quiet, stillness, peace, tranquillity. □ **hush up** suppress, repress, cover up, hide, conceal, keep quiet.

hushaby /húshəbī/ *int.* (also **hushabye**) used to lull a child.

hush-hush /húshhúsh/ *adj. colloq.* (esp. of an official plan or enterprise etc.) highly secret or confidential.
■ see SECRET *adj.* 3.

husk /husk/ *n.* & *v.* ● *n.* **1** the dry outer covering of some fruits or seeds, esp. of a nut or *US* maize. **2** the worthless outside part of a thing. ● *v.tr.* remove a husk or husks from. [ME, prob. f. LG *hūske* sheath, dimin. of *hūs* HOUSE]
■ *n.* **1** see SKIN *n.* 4. ● *v.* see SHELL *v.* 1.

husky[1] /húski/ *adj.* (**huskier, huskiest**) **1** (of a person or voice) dry in the throat; hoarse. **2** of or full of husks. **3** dry as a husk. **4** tough, strong, hefty. □□ **huskily** *adv.* **huskiness** *n.*
■ **1** hoarse, gruff, rasping, rough, raucous. **4** brawny, strapping, sturdy, burly, well-built, robust, hefty, rugged, powerful, strong, thickset, muscular, tough, beefy.

husky[2] /húski/ *n.* (*pl.* **-ies**) **1** a dog of a powerful breed used in the Arctic for pulling sledges. **2** this breed. [perh. contr. f. ESKIMO]

huss /huss/ *n.* dogfish as food. [ME *husk*, of unkn. orig.]

hussar /hoozaár/ *n.* **1** a soldier of a light cavalry regiment. **2** a Hungarian light horseman of the 15th c. [Magyar *huszár* f. OSerb. *husar* f. It. *corsaro* CORSAIR]

Hussite /hússīt/ *n. hist.* a member or follower of the movement begun by John *Huss*, Bohemian religious and nationalist reformer d. 1415. □□ **Hussitism** *n.*

hussy /hússi/ *n.* (*pl.* **-ies**) *derog.* an impudent or immoral girl or woman. [phonetic reduction of HOUSEWIFE (the orig. sense)]
■ see SLUT.

hustings /hústingz/ *n.* **1** parliamentary election proceedings. **2** *Brit. hist.* a platform from which (before 1872) candidates for Parliament were nominated and addressed electors. [late OE *husting* f. ON *hústhing* house of assembly]

hustle /húss'l/ *v.* & *n.* ● *v.* **1** *tr.* push roughly; jostle. **2** *tr.* **a** (foll. by *into*, *out of*, etc.) force, coerce, or deal with hurriedly or unceremoniously (*hustled them out of the room*). **b** (foll. by *into*) coerce hurriedly (*was hustled into agreeing*). **3** *intr.* push one's way; hurry, bustle. **4** *tr. sl.* **a** obtain by forceful action. **b** swindle. **5** *intr. sl.* engage in prostitution. ● *n.* **1 a** an act or instance of hustling. **b** forceful or strenuous activity. **2** *colloq.* a fraud or swindle. [MDu. *husselen* shake, toss, frequent. of *hutsen*, orig. imit.]
■ *v.* **1** shove, push, jostle, elbow, thrust, force. **2 a** (*hustle into* or *out of*, etc.) force *or* coerce *or* drive into *or* out of *or* through, push *or* shove into *or* out of *or* through, eject from, hasten into *or* out of *or* through, press through, expedite through, *sl.* bounce out of. **b** coerce, force, press, *colloq.* bounce. **3** rush, push, hurry, hasten, run, sprint, dash, scuttle, scurry, bustle. **4 b** see SWINDLE *v.* **5** walk the streets, *Brit. sl.* be *or* go on the game. ● *n.* **1 a** pushing, jostling, buffeting, jarring, elbowing, shoving, nudging. **b** action, activity, stir, movement. **2** see SWINDLE *n.* 1, 3.

hustler /húslər/ *n. sl.* **1** an active, enterprising, or unscrupulous individual. **2** a prostitute.
■ **2** see PROSTITUTE *n.* 1a.

hut /hut/ *n.* & *v.* ● *n.* **1** a small simple or crude house or shelter. **2** *Mil.* a temporary wooden etc. house for troops. ● *v.* (**hutted, hutting**) **1** *tr.* provide with huts. **2** *tr. Mil.* place (troops etc.) in huts. **3** *intr.* lodge in a hut. □□ **hutlike** *adj.* [F *hutte* f. MHG *hütte*]
■ *n.* **1** cabin, shack, shanty, *Austral.* gunyah, *poet.* cot.

hutch /huch/ *n.* **1** a box or cage, usu. with a wire mesh front, for keeping small pet animals. **2** *derog.* a small house. [ME, = coffer, f. OF *huche* f. med.L *hutica*, of unkn. orig.]
■ **1** see CAGE *n.*

hutment /hútmənt/ *n. Mil.* an encampment of huts.

HWM *abbr.* high-water mark.

hwyl /hŏŏ-il/ *n.* an emotional quality inspiring impassioned eloquence. [Welsh]

Hy. *abbr.* Henry.

hyacinth /hī́əsinth/ *n.* **1** any bulbous plant of the genus *Hyacinthus* with racemes of usu. purplish-blue, pink, or white bell-shaped fragrant flowers. **2** = *grape hyacinth*. **3** the purplish-blue colour of the hyacinth flower. **4** an orange variety of zircon used as a precious stone. **5** *poet.* hair or locks like the hyacinth flower (as a Homeric epithet of doubtful sense). □ **wild** (or **wood**) **hyacinth** = BLUEBELL 1. □□ **hyacinthine** /-síntheen/ *adj.* [F *hyacinthe* f. L *hyacinthus* f. Gk *huakinthos*, flower and gem, also the name of a youth loved by Apollo]

Hyades /hī́ədeez/ *n.pl.* a group of stars in Taurus near the Pleiades, whose heliacal rising was once thought to foretell rain. [ME f. Gk *Huades* (by popular etym. f. *huō* rain, but perh. f. *hus* pig)]

hyaena var. of HYENA.

hyalin /hī́əlin/ *n.* a clear glassy substance produced as a result of the degeneration of certain body tissues. [Gk *hualos* glass + -IN]

hyaline /hī́əlin, -līn, -leen/ *adj.* & *n.* ● *adj.* glasslike, vitreous, transparent. ● *n. literary* a smooth sea, clear sky, etc. □ **hyaline cartilage** *n.* a common type of cartilage. [L *hyalinus* f. Gk *hualinos* f. *hualos* glass]

hyalite /hī́əlīt/ *n.* a colourless variety of opal. [Gk *hualos* glass]

hyaloid /hī́əloyd/ *adj. Anat.* glassy. □ **hyaloid membrane** a thin transparent membrane enveloping the vitreous humour of the eye. [F *hyaloïde* f. LL *hyaloides* f. Gk *hualoeidēs* (as HYALITE)]

hybrid /hī́brid/ *n.* & *adj.* ● *n.* **1** *Biol.* the offspring of two plants or animals of different species or varieties. **2** often *offens.* a person of mixed racial or cultural origin. **3** a thing composed of incongruous elements, e.g. a word with parts taken from different languages. ● *adj.* **1** bred as a hybrid from different species or varieties. **2** *Biol.* heterogeneous. **3** of mixed character; derived from incongruous elements or unlike sources. □ **hybrid vigour** heterosis. □□ **hybridism** *n.* **hybridity** /-bríddiiti/ *n.* [L *hybrida*, (*h*)*ibrida* offspring of a tame sow and wild boar, child of a freeman and slave, etc.]
■ *n.* **1** cross-breed, cross, mongrel. **2** Creole, mestizo, *derog.* mongrel, *offens.* half-breed, *often offens.* half-caste. **3** mixture, composite, combination, compound, blend, amalgam, amalgamation, mix, union, conjunction, grouping. ● *adj.* **3** see DIVERSE.

hybridize /hī́bridīz/ *v.* (also **-ise**) **1** *tr.* subject (a species etc.) to cross-breeding. **2** *intr.* **a** produce hybrids. **b** (of an animal or plant) interbreed. □□ **hybridizable** *adj.* **hybridization** /-záysh'n/ *n.*

hydatid /hī́dətid/ *n. Med.* **1** a cyst containing watery fluid (esp. one formed by, and containing, a tapeworm larva). **2** a tapeworm larva. □□ **hydatidiform** /-tíddiform/ *adj.* [mod.L *hydatis* f. Gk *hudatis -idos* watery vesicle f. *hudōr hudatos* water]

hydra /hī́drə/ *n.* **1** a freshwater polyp of the genus *Hydra* with tubular body and tentacles around the mouth. **2** any water-snake. **3** something which is hard to destroy. [ME f. L f. Gk *hudra* water-snake, esp. a fabulous one with many heads that grew again when cut off]

hydrangea /hīdráynjə/ *n.* any shrub of the genus *Hydrangea* with large white, pink, or blue flowers. [mod.L f. Gk *hudōr* water + *aggos* vessel (from the cup-shape of its seed-capsule)]

hydrant /hī́drənt/ *n.* a pipe (esp. in a street) with a nozzle to which a hose can be attached for drawing water from the main. [irreg. f. HYDRO- + -ANT]
■ stand pipe, fire-plug.

hydrate /hī́drayt/ *n.* & *v.* ● *n. Chem.* a compound of water combined with another compound or with an element. ● *v.tr.* **1 a** combine chemically with water. **b** (as **hydrated** *adj.*) chemically bonded to water. **2** cause to absorb water. □□ **hydratable** *adj.* **hydration** /-dráysh'n/ *n.* **hydrator** *n.* [F f. Gk *hudōr* water]

hydraulic /hīdráwlik, -dróllik/ *adj.* **1** (of water, oil, etc.) conveyed through pipes or channels usu. by pressure. **2** (of a mechanism etc.) operated by liquid moving in this manner (*hydraulic brakes*; *hydraulic lift*). **3** of or concerned with hydraulics (*hydraulic engineer*). **4** hardening under water (*hydraulic cement*). □ **hydraulic press** a device in which the force applied to a fluid creates a pressure which when transmitted to a larger volume of fluid gives rise to a greater force. **hydraulic ram** an automatic pump in which the kinetic energy of a descending column of water raises some of the water above its original level. □□ **hydraulically** *adv.* **hydraulicity** /-líssiti/ *n.* [L *hydraulicus* f. Gk *hudraulikos* f. *hudōr* water + *aulos* pipe]

hydraulics /hīdráwliks, -drólliks/ *n.pl.* (usu. treated as *sing.*) the science of the conveyance of liquids through pipes etc. esp. as motive power.

hydrazine /hī́drəzeen/ *n. Chem.* a colourless alkaline liquid which is a powerful reducing agent and is used as a rocket propellant. ¶ Chem. formula: N_2H_4. [HYDROGEN + AZO- + -INE[4]]

hydride /hī́drīd/ *n. Chem.* a binary compound of hydrogen with an element, esp. with a metal.

hydriodic acid /hī́driόddik, hī́drī-/ *n. Chem.* a solution of the colourless gas hydrogen iodide in water. ¶ Chem. formula: HI. [HYDROGEN + IODINE]

hydro /hī́drō/ *n.* (*pl.* **-os**) *colloq.* **1** a hotel or clinic etc. orig. providing hydropathic treatment. **2** a hydroelectric power plant. [abbr.]

hydro- /hī́drō/ *comb. form* (also **hydr-** before a vowel) **1** having to do with water (*hydroelectric*). **2** *Med.* affected with an accumulation of serous fluid (*hydrocele*). **3** *Chem.* combined with hydrogen (*hydrochloric*). [Gk *hudro-* f. *hudōr* water]

hydrobromic acid /hī́drōbrṓmik/ *n. Chem.* a solution of the colourless gas hydrogen bromide in water. ¶ Chem. formula: HBr.

hydrocarbon /hī́drōkaárb'n/ *n. Chem.* a compound of hydrogen and carbon.

hydrocele /hī́drəseel/ *n. Med.* the accumulation of serous fluid in a body sac.

hydrocephalus /hī́drəséffələss/ *n. Med.* an abnormal amount of fluid within the brain, esp. in young children, which makes the head enlarge and can cause mental deficiency. □□ **hydrocephalic** /-sifállik/ *adj.*

hydrochloric acid /hī́drəklórik, -klórrik/ *n. Chem.* a solution of the colourless gas hydrogen chloride in water. ¶ Chem. formula: HCl.

hydrochloride /hī́drəklórīd/ *n. Chem.* a compound of an organic base with hydrochloric acid.

hydrocortisone /hī́drəkórtizōn/ *n. Biochem.* a steroid hormone produced by the adrenal cortex, used medicinally to treat inflammation and rheumatism.

hydrocyanic acid /hī́drəsīánnik/ *n. Chem.* a highly poisonous volatile liquid with a characteristic odour of bitter almonds. ¶ Chem. formula: HCN. Also called *prussic acid.*

hydrodynamics /hī́drōdīnámmiks/ *n.* the science of forces acting on or exerted by fluids (esp. liquids). □□ **hydrodynamic** *adj.* **hydrodynamical** *adj.* **hydrodynamicist** /-misist/ *n.* [mod.L *hydrodynamicus* (as HYDRO-, DYNAMIC)]

hydroelectric /hī́drō-iléktrik/ *adj.* **1** generating electricity by utilization of water-power. **2** (of electricity) generated in this way. □□ **hydroelectricity** /-trissiti/ *n.*

hydrofluoric acid /hī́drōflóorik/ *n. Chem.* a solution of the colourless liquid hydrogen fluoride in water. ¶ Chem. formula: HF.

hydrofoil /hī́drəfoyl/ *n.* **1** a boat equipped with a device consisting of planes for lifting its hull out of the water to increase its speed. **2** this device. [HYDRO-, after AEROFOIL]

hydrogen /hī́drəjən/ *n. Chem.* a colourless gaseous element, without taste or odour, the lightest of the elements and occurring in water and all organic compounds. ¶ Symb.: **H.** □ **hydrogen bomb** an immensely powerful bomb utilizing the explosive fusion of hydrogen nuclei: also called H-BOMB. **hydrogen bond** a weak electrostatic interaction between an electronegative atom and a hydrogen atom bonded to a different electronegative atom. **hydrogen peroxide** a colourless viscous unstable liquid with strong oxidizing properties. ¶ Chem. formula: H_2O_2. **hydrogen sulphide** a colourless poisonous gas with a disagreeable smell, formed by rotting animal matter. ¶ Chem. formula: H_2S. □□ **hydrogenous** /-drójinəss/ *adj.* [F *hydrogène* (as HYDRO-, -GEN)]

hydrogenase /hīdrójinayz, -nayss/ *n. Biochem.* any enzyme which catalyses the oxidation of hydrogen and the reduction of protons.

hydrogenate /hīdrójinayt, hī́drəjənayt/ *v.tr.* charge with or cause to combine with hydrogen. □□ **hydrogenation** /-náysh'n/ *n.*

hydrography /hīdrógrəfi/ *n.* the science of surveying and charting seas, lakes, rivers, etc. □□ **hydrographer** *n.* **hydrographic** /hī́drəgráffik/ *adj.* **hydrographical** /hī́drəgráffik'l/ *adj.* **hydrographically** /hī́drəgráffikəli/ *adv.*

hydroid /hī́droyd/ *adj.* & *n. Zool.* any usu. polypoid hydrozoan of the order Hydroida, including hydra.

hydrolase /hī́drōlayz, -layss/ *n. Biochem.* any enzyme which catalyses the hydrolysis of a substrate.

hydrology /hīdrólləji/ *n.* the science of the properties of the earth's water, esp. of its movement in relation to land. □□ **hydrologic** /hī́drəlójik/ *adj.* **hydrological** /hī́drəlójik'l/ *adj.* **hydrologically** /hī́drəlójikəli/ *adv.* **hydrologist** *n.*

hydrolyse /hī́drəlīz/ *v.tr.* & *intr.* (*US* **hydrolyze**) subject to or undergo the chemical action of water.

hydrolysis /hīdróllisiss/ *n.* the chemical reaction of a substance with water, usu. resulting in decomposition. □□ **hydrolytic** /hī́drəlíttik/ *adj.*

hydromagnetic /hī́drəmagnéttik/ *adj.* involving hydrodynamics and magnetism; magnetohydrodynamic.

hydromania /hī́drəmáyniə/ *n.* a craving for water.

hydromechanics /hī́drōmikánniks/ *n.* the mechanics of liquids; hydrodynamics.

hydrometer /hīdrómmitər/ *n.* an instrument for measuring the density of liquids. □□ **hydrometric** /hī́drəmétrik/ *adj.* **hydrometry** *n.*

hydronium ion /hīdrṓniəm/ *n. Chem.* = HYDROXONIUM ION. [contr.]

hydropathy /hīdróppəthi/ *n.* the (medically unorthodox) treatment of disease by external and internal application of water. □□ **hydropathic** /hī́drəpáthik/ *adj.* **hydropathist** *n.* [HYDRO-, after HOMOEOPATHY etc.]

hydrophil /hī́drəfil/ *adj.* (also **hydrophile** /-fīl/) = HYDROPHILIC. [as HYDROPHILIC]

hydrophilic /hī́drəfillik/ *adj.* **1** having an affinity for water. **2** wettable by water. [HYDRO- + Gk *philos* loving]

hydrophobia /hī́drəfṓbiə/ *n.* **1** a morbid aversion to water, esp. as a symptom of rabies in man. **2** rabies, esp. in man. [LL f. Gk *hudrophobia* (as HYDRO-, -PHOBIA)]

hydrophobic /hī́drəfṓbik/ *adj.* **1** of or suffering from hydrophobia. **2 a** lacking an affinity for water. **b** not readily wettable.

hydrophone /hī́drəfōn/ *n.* an instrument for the detection of sound-waves in water.

hydrophyte /hī́drəfīt/ *n.* an aquatic plant, or a plant which needs much moisture.

hydroplane /hī́drəplayn/ *n.* & *v.* ● *n.* **1** a light fast motor boat designed to skim over the surface of water. **2** a finlike attachment which enables a submarine to rise and fall in water. ● *v.intr.* **1** (of a boat) skim over the surface of water with its hull lifted. **2** = AQUAPLANE *v.* 2.

hydroponics /hīdrəpónniks/ *n.* the process of growing plants in sand, gravel, or liquid, without soil and with added nutrients. ▫▫ **hydroponic** *adj.* **hydroponically** *adv.* [HYDRO- + Gk *ponos* labour]

hydroquinone /hī́drəkwinnōn/ *n.* a substance formed by the reduction of quinone, used as a photographic developer.

hydrosphere /hī́drəsfeer/ *n.* the waters of the earth's surface.

hydrostatic /hī́drəstáttik/ *adj.* of the equilibrium of liquids and the pressure exerted by liquid at rest. ▫ **hydrostatic press** = *hydraulic press.* ▫▫ **hydrostatical** *adj.* **hydrostatically** *adv.* [prob. f. Gk *hudrostatēs* hydrostatic balance (as HYDRO-, STATIC)]

hydrostatics /hī́drəstáttiks/ *n.pl.* (usu. treated as *sing.*) the branch of mechanics concerned with the hydrostatic properties of liquids.

hydrotherapy /hī́drəthérrəpi/ *n.* the use of water in the treatment of disorders, usu. exercises in swimming pools for arthritic or partially paralysed patients. ▫▫ **hydrotherapist** *n.* **hydrotherapic** *adj.*

hydrothermal /hī́drəthérm'l/ *adj.* of the action of heated water on the earth's crust. ▫▫ **hydrothermally** *adv.*

hydrothorax /hī́drəthóraks/ *n.* the condition of having fluid in the pleural cavity.

hydrotropism /hīdrótrəpiz'm/ *adj.* a tendency of plant roots etc. to turn to or from moisture.

hydrous /hī́drəss/ *adj. Chem.* & *Mineral.* containing water. [Gk *hudōr hudro-* water]

hydroxide /hīdróksīd/ *n. Chem.* a metallic compound containing oxygen and hydrogen either in the form of the hydroxide ion (OH^-) or the hydroxyl group (–OH).

hydroxonium ion /hī́droksṓniəm/ *n. Chem.* the hydrated hydrogen ion, H_3O^+. [HYDRO- + OXY-^{2} + *-onium*]

hydroxy- /hīdróksi/ *comb. form Chem.* having a hydroxide ion (or ions) or a hydroxyl group (or groups) (*hydroxybenzoic acid*). [HYDROGEN + OXYGEN]

hydroxyl /hīdróksil/ *n. Chem.* the univalent group containing hydrogen and oxygen, as -OH. [HYDROGEN + OXYGEN + -YL]

hydrozoan /hī́drəzṓən/ *n.* & *adj.* ● *n.* any aquatic coelenterate of the class *Hydrozoa* of mainly marine polyp or medusoid forms, including hydra and Portuguese man-of-war. [mod.L *Hydrozoa* (as HYDRA, Gk *zōion* animal)]

hyena /hī-éénə/ *n.* (also **hyaena**) any flesh-eating mammal of the order Hyaenidae, with hind limbs shorter than forelimbs. ▫ **laughing hyena** *n.* a hyena, *Crocuta crocuta*, whose howl is compared to a fiendish laugh. [ME f. OF *hyene* & L *hyaena* f. Gk *huaina* fem. of *hus* pig]

hygiene /hī́jeen/ *n.* **1 a** a study, or set of principles, of maintaining health. **b** conditions or practices conducive to maintaining health. **2** sanitary science. [F *hygiène* f. mod.L *hygieina* f. Gk *hugieinē* (*tekhnē*) (art) of health f. *hugiēs* healthy]

hygienic /hījéénik/ *adj.* conducive to hygiene; clean and sanitary. ▫▫ **hygienically** *adv.*

■ clean, sanitary; sterile, disinfected, germ-free, aseptic.

hygienics /hījééniks/ *n.pl.* (usu. treated as *sing.*) = HYGIENE 1a.

hygienist /hījeenist/ *n.* a specialist in the promotion and practice of cleanliness for the preservation of health.

hygro- /hī́grō/ *comb. form* moisture. [Gk *hugro-* f. *hugros* wet, moist]

hygrology /hīgrólləji/ *n.* the study of the humidity of the atmosphere etc.

hygrometer /hīgrómmitər/ *n.* an instrument for measuring the humidity of the air or a gas. ▫▫ **hygrometric** /hī́grəmétrik/ *adj.* **hygrometry** *n.*

hygrophilous /hīgróffiləss/ *adj.* (of a plant) growing in a moist environment.

hygrophyte /hī́grəfīt/ *n.* = HYDROPHYTE.

hygroscope /hī́grəskōp/ *n.* an instrument which indicates but does not measure the humidity of the air.

hygroscopic /hī́grəskóppik/ *adj.* **1** of the hygroscope. **2** (of a substance) tending to absorb moisture from the air. ▫▫ **hygroscopically** *adv.*

hying *pres. part.* of HIE.

hylic /hī́lik/ *adj.* of matter; material. [LL *hylicus* f. Gk *hulikos* f. *hulē* matter]

hylo- /hī́lō/ *comb. form* matter. [Gk *hulo-* f. *hulē* matter]

hylomorphism /hī́ləmórfiz'm/ *n.* the theory that physical objects are composed of matter and form. [HYLO- + Gk *morphē* form]

hylozoism /hī́ləzṓ-iz'm/ *n.* the doctrine that all matter has life. [HYLO- + Gk *zōē* life]

hymen /hī́men/ *n. Anat.* a membrane which partially closes the opening of the vagina and is usu. broken at the first occurrence of sexual intercourse. ▫▫ **hymenal** *adj.* [LL f. Gk *humēn* membrane]

hymeneal /hī́minééəl/ *adj. literary* of or concerning marriage. [*Hymen* (L f. Gk *Humēn*) Greek and Roman god of marriage]

■ see NUPTIAL *adj.*

hymenium /hīméeniəm/ *n.* (*pl.* **hymenia** /-niə/) the spore-bearing surface of certain fungi. [mod.L f. Gk *humenion* dimin. of *humēn* membrane]

hymenopteran /hī́mənóptərən/ *n.* any insect of the order *Hymenoptera* having four transparent wings, including bees, wasps, and ants. ▫▫ **hymenopterous** *adj.* [mod.L *hymenoptera* f. Gk *humenopteros* membrane-winged (as HYMENIUM, *pteron* wing)]

hymn /him/ *n.* & *v.* ● *n.* **1** a song of praise, esp. to God in Christian worship, usu. a metrical composition sung in a religious service. **2** a song of praise in honour of a god or other exalted being or thing. ● *v.* **1** *tr.* praise or celebrate in hymns. **2** *intr.* sing hymns. ▫ **hymn-book** a book of hymns. ▫▫ **hymnic** /hímnik/ *adj.* [ME *ymne* etc. f. OF *ymne* f. L *hymnus* f. Gk *humnos*]

■ *n.* see SONG.

hymnal /hímn'l/ *n.* & *adj.* ● *n.* a hymn-book. ● *adj.* of hymns. [ME f. med.L *hymnale* (as HYMN)]

hymnary /hímnəri/ *n.* (*pl.* **-ies**) a hymn-book.

hymnody /hímnədi/ *n.* (*pl.* **-ies**) **1 a** the singing of hymns. **b** the composition of hymns. **2** hymns collectively. ▫▫ **hymnodist** *n.* [med.L *hymnodia* f. Gk *humnōidia* f. *humnos* hymn: cf. PSALMODY]

hymnographer /himnógrəfər/ *n.* a writer of hymns. ▫▫ **hymnography** *n.* [Gk *humnographos* f. *humnos* hymn]

hymnology /himnólləji/ *n.* (*pl.* **-ies**) **1** the composition or study of hymns. **2** hymns collectively. ▫▫ **hymnologist** *n.*

hyoid /hī́oyd/ *n.* & *adj. Anat.* ● *n.* (in full **hyoid bone**) a U-shaped bone in the neck which supports the tongue. ● *adj.* of or relating to this. [F *hyoïde* f. mod.L *hyoïdes* f. Gk *huoeidēs* shaped like the letter upsilon (*hu*)]

hyoscine /hī́əseen/ *n.* a poisonous alkaloid found in plants of the nightshade family, esp. of the genus *Scopolia*, and used as an antiemetic in motion sickness and a preoperative medication for examination of the eye. Also called SCOPOLAMINE. [f. HYOSCYAMINE]

hyoscyamine /hīəsīəmeen/ *n.* a poisonous alkaloid obtained from henbane, having similar properties to hyoscine. [mod.L *hyoscyamus* f. Gk *huoskuamos* henbane f. *hus huos* pig + *kuamos* bean]

hypaesthesia /hīpiss-théeziə/ *n.* (*US* **hypesthesia**) a diminished capacity for sensation, esp. of the skin. ▫▫ **hypaesthetic** /-théttik/ *adj.* [mod.L (as HYPO-, Gk *-aisthēsia* f. *aisthanomai* perceive)]

hypaethral /hīpéethrəl/ *adj.* (also **hypethral**) **1** open to the sky; roofless. **2** open-air. [L *hypaethrus* f. Gk *hupaithros* (as HYPO-, *aithēr* air)]

hypallage /hīpálləji/ *n. Rhet.* the transposition of the natural relations of two elements in a proposition (e.g. *Melissa shook her doubtful curls*). [LL f. Gk *hupallagē* (as HYPO-, *allassō* exchange)]

hype[1] /hīp/ *n.* & *v. sl.* ● *n.* **1** extravagant or intensive publicity promotion. **2** cheating; a trick. ● *v.tr.* **1** promote (a product) with extravagant publicity. **2** cheat, trick. [20th c.: orig. unkn.]

■ *n.* **1** see ADVERTISEMENT 2. ● *v.* **1** see PROMOTE 3.

hype[2] /hīp/ *n. sl.* **1** a drug addict. **2** a hypodermic needle or injection. ▫ **hyped up** stimulated by or as if by a hypodermic injection. [abbr. of HYPODERMIC]

■ **1** see ADDICT *n.* 1.

hyper- /hīpər/ *prefix* meaning: **1** over, beyond, above (*hyperphysical*). **2** exceeding (*hypersonic*). **3** excessively; above normal (*hyperbole*; *hypersensitive*). [Gk *huper* over, beyond]

hyperactive /hīpəráktiv/ *adj.* (of a person, esp. a child) abnormally active. ▫▫ **hyperactivity** /-tívviti/ *n.*

■ see ACTIVE *adj.* 1a.

hyperaemia /hīpəréemiə/ *n.* (*US* **hyperemia**) an excessive quantity of blood in the vessels supplying an organ or other part of the body. ▫▫ **hyperaemic** *adj.* [mod.L (as HYPER-, -AEMIA)]

hyperaesthesia /hīpəreess-théeziə/ *n.* (*US* **hyperesthesia**) an excessive physical sensibility, esp. of the skin. ▫▫ **hyperaesthetic** /-théttik/ *adj.* [mod.L (as HYPER-, Gk *-aisthēsia* f. *aisthanomai* perceive)]

hyperbaric /hīpərbárrik/ *adj.* (of a gas) at a pressure greater than normal. [HYPER- + Gk *barus* heavy]

hyperbaton /hīpérbəton/ *n. Rhet.* the inversion of the normal order of words, esp. for the sake of emphasis (e.g. *this I must see*). [L f. Gk *huperbaton* (as HYPER-, *bainō* go)]

hyperbola /hīpérbələ/ *n.* (*pl.* **hyperbolas** or **hyperbolae** /-lee/) *Geom.* the plane curve of two equal branches, produced when a cone is cut by a plane that makes a larger angle with the base than the side of the cone (cf. ELLIPSE). [mod.L f. Gk *huperbolē* excess (as HYPER-, *ballō* to throw)]

hyperbole /hīpérbəli/ *n. Rhet.* an exaggerated statement not meant to be taken literally. ▫▫ **hyperbolical** /hīpərbóllik'l/ *adj.* **hyperbolically** /hīpərbóllikəli/ *adv.* **hyperbolism** *n.* [L (as HYPERBOLA)]

■ see *exaggeration* (EXAGGERATE).

hyperbolic /hīpərbóllik/ *adj. Geom.* of or relating to a hyperbola. ▫ **hyperbolic function** a function related to a rectangular hyperbola, e.g. a hyperbolic cosine.

hyperboloid /hīpérbəloyd/ *n. Geom.* a solid or surface having plane sections that are hyperbolas, ellipses, or circles. ▫▫ **hyperboloidal** *adj.*

hyperborean /hīpəboreéən, -bórian/ *n.* & *adj.* ● *n.* **1** an inhabitant of the extreme north of the earth. **2** (**Hyperborean**) (in Greek mythology) a member of a race worshipping Apollo and living in a land of sunshine and plenty beyond the north wind. ● *adj.* of the extreme north of the earth. [LL *hyperboreanus* f. L *hyperboreus* f. Gk *huperboreos* (as HYPER-, *Boreas* god of the north wind)]

hyperconscious /hīpərkónshəss/ *adj.* (foll. by *of*) acutely or excessively aware.

hypercritical /hīpərkríttik'l/ *adj.* excessively critical, esp. of small faults. ▫▫ **hypercritically** *adv.*

■ see OVERCRITICAL.

hyperemia *US* var. of HYPERAEMIA.

hyperesthesia *US* var. of HYPERAESTHESIA.

hyperfocal distance /hīpərfōk'l/ *n.* the distance on which a camera lens can be focused to bring the maximum range of object-distances into focus.

hypergamy /hīpérgəmi/ *n.* marriage to a person of equal or superior caste or class. [HYPER- + Gk *gamos* marriage]

hyperglycaemia /hīpərglīseémiə/ *n.* (*US* **hyperglycemia**) an excess of glucose in the bloodstream, often associated with diabetes mellitus. ▫▫ **hyperglycaemic** *adj.* [HYPER- + GLYCO- + -AEMIA]

hypergolic /hīpərgóllik/ *adj.* (of a rocket propellant) igniting spontaneously on contact with an oxidant etc. [G *Hypergol* (perh. as HYPO-, ERG[1], -OL)]

hypericum /hīpérrikəm/ *n.* any shrub of the genus *Hypericum* with five-petalled yellow flowers. Also called ST JOHN'S WORT. [L f. Gk *hupereikon* (as HYPER-, *ereikē* heath)]

hypermarket /hīpərmaarkit/ *n. Brit.* a very large self-service store with a wide range of goods and extensive car-parking facilities, usu. outside a town. [transl. F *hypermarché* (as HYPER-, MARKET)]

hypermetropia /hīpərmitrōpiə/ *n.* the condition of having long sight. ▫▫ **hypermetropic** /-tróppik/ *adj.* [mod.L f. HYPER- + Gk *metron* measure, *ōps* eye]

■ long-sightedness, presbyopia, *esp. US* far-sightedness.

hyperon /hīpəron/ *n. Physics* an unstable elementary particle which is classified as a baryon apart from the neutron or proton. [HYPER- + -ON]

hyperopia /hīpərōpiə/ *n.* = HYPERMETROPIA. ▫▫ **hyperopic** /-róppik/ *adj.* [mod.L f. HYPER- + Gk *ōps* eye]

hyperphysical /hīpərfízzik'l/ *adj.* supernatural. ▫▫ **hyperphysically** *adv.*

hyperplasia /hīpərpláyziə/ *n.* the enlargement of an organ or tissue from the increased production of cells. [HYPER- + Gk *plasis* formation]

hypersensitive /hīpərsénsitiv/ *adj.* abnormally or excessively sensitive. ▫▫ **hypersensitiveness** *n.* **hypersensitivity** /-tívviti/ *n.*

■ see SENSITIVE *adj.* 2.

hypersonic /hīpərsónnik/ *adj.* **1** relating to speeds of more than five times the speed of sound (Mach 5). **2** relating to sound-frequencies above about a thousand million hertz. ▫▫ **hypersonically** *adv.* [HYPER-, after SUPERSONIC, ULTRASONIC]

hypersthene /hīpərss-theen/ *n.* a rock-forming mineral, magnesium iron silicate, of greenish colour. [F *hypersthène* (as HYPER-, Gk *sthenos* strength, from its being harder than hornblende]

hypertension /hīpərténsh'n/ *n.* **1** abnormally high blood pressure. **2** a state of great emotional tension. ▫▫ **hypertensive** /-ténsiv/ *adj.*

hyperthermia /hīpərthérmiə/ *n. Med.* the condition of having a body-temperature greatly above normal. ▫▫ **hyperthermic** *adj.* [HYPER- + Gk *thermē* heat]

hyperthyroidism /hīpərthīroydiz'm/ *n. Med.* overactivity of the thyroid gland, resulting in rapid heartbeat and an increased rate of metabolism. ▫▫ **hyperthyroid** *n.* & *adj.* **hyperthyroidic** *adj.*

hypertonic /hīpərtónnik/ *adj.* **1** (of muscles) having high tension. **2** (of a solution) having a greater osmotic pressure than another solution. ▫▫ **hypertonia** /-tōniə/ *n.* (in sense 1). **hypertonicity** /-tənissiti/ *n.*

hypertrophy /hīpértrəfi/ *n.* the enlargement of an organ or tissue from the increase in size of its cells. ▫▫ **hypertrophic** /hīpərtróffik/ *adj.* **hypertrophied** *adj.* [mod.L *hypertrophia* (as HYPER-, Gk *-trophia* nourishment)]

hyperventilation /hīpərvéntiláysh'n/ *n.* breathing at an abnormally rapid rate, resulting in an increased loss of carbon dioxide.

hypethral var. of HYPAETHRAL.

hypha /hīfə/ *n.* (*pl.* **hyphae** /-fee/) a filament in the mycelium of a fungus. ▫▫ **hyphal** *adj.* [mod.L f. Gk *huphē* web]

hyphen /hī́f'n/ *n.* & *v.* ● *n.* the sign (-) used to join words semantically or syntactically (as in *fruit-tree*, *pick-me-up*, *rock-forming*), to indicate the division of a word at the end of a line, or to indicate a missing or implied element (as in *man- and womankind*). ● *v.tr.* **1** write (a compound word) with a hyphen. **2** join (words) with a hyphen. [LL f. Gk *huphen* together f. *hupo* under + *hen* one]

hyphenate /hī́fənayt/ *v.tr.* = HYPHEN *v.* □□ **hyphenation** /-náysh'n/ *n.*

hypno- /hípnō/ *comb. form* sleep, hypnosis. [Gk *hupnos* sleep]

hypnogenesis /hípnōjénnisiss/ *n.* the induction of a hypnotic state.

hypnology /hipnólləji/ *n.* the science of the phenomena of sleep. □□ **hypnologist** *n.*

hypnopaedia /hípnōpeédiə/ *n.* learning by hearing while asleep.

hypnosis /hipnṓsiss/ *n.* **1** a state like sleep in which the subject acts only on external suggestion. **2** artificially produced sleep. [mod.L f. Gk *hupnos* sleep + -OSIS]

hypnotherapy /hípnōthérrəpi/ *n.* the treatment of disease by hypnosis.

hypnotic /hipnóttik/ *adj.* & *n.* ● *adj.* **1** of or producing hypnosis. **2** (of a drug) soporific. ● *n.* **1** a thing, esp. a drug, that produces sleep. **2** a person under or open to the influence of hypnotism. □□ **hypnotically** *adv.* [F *hypnotique* f. LL *hypnoticus* f. Gk *hupnōtikos* f. *hupnoō* put to sleep]

■ *adj.* **1** see *enchanting* (ENCHANT). **2** see NARCOTIC *adj.* ● *n.* **1** see NARCOTIC *n.*

hypnotism /hípnətiz'm/ *n.* the study or practice of hypnosis. □□ **hypnotist** *n.*

hypnotize /hípnətīz/ *v.tr.* (also **-ise**) **1** produce hypnosis in. **2** fascinate; capture the mind of (a person). □□ **hypnotizable** *adj.* **hypnotizer** *n.*

■ **2** fascinate, mesmerize, entrance, cast a spell over *or* on, captivate, enchant, charm, spellbind, bewitch.

hypo[1] /hī́pō/ *n. Photog.* the chemical sodium thiosulphate (incorrectly called hyposulphite) used as a photographic fixer. [abbr.]

hypo[2] /hī́pō/ *n.* (*pl.* **-os**) *colloq.* = HYPODERMIC *n.* [abbr.]

hypo- /hī́pō/ *prefix* (usu. **hyp-** before a vowel or *h*) **1** under (*hypodermic*). **2** below normal (*hypoxia*). **3** slightly (*hypomania*). **4** *Chem.* containing an element combined in low valence (*hypochlorous*). [Gk f. *hupo* under]

hypoblast /hī́pəblast/ *n. Biol.* = ENDODERM. [mod.L *hypoblastus* (as HYPO-, -BLAST)]

hypocaust /hī́pəkawst/ *n.* a hollow space under the floor in ancient Roman houses, into which hot air was sent for heating a room or bath. [L *hypocaustum* f. Gk *hupokauston* place heated from below (as HYPO-, *kaiō*, *kau-* burn)]

hypochondria /hī́pəkóndriə/ *n.* **1** abnormal anxiety about one's health. **2** morbid depression without real cause. [LL f. Gk *hupokhondria* soft parts of the body below the ribs, where melancholy was thought to arise (as HYPO-, *khondros* sternal cartilage)]

■ see VAPOUR *n.* 4.

hypochondriac /hī́pəkóndriak/ *n.* & *adj.* ● *n.* a person suffering from hypochondria. ● *adj.* (also **hypochondriacal** /-drī́ək'l/) of or affected by hypochondria. [F *hypocondriaque* f. Gk *hupokhondriakos* (as HYPOCHONDRIA)]

hypocoristic /hī́pəkorístik/ *adj. Gram.* of the nature of a pet name. [Gk *hupokoristikos* f. *hupokorizomai* call by pet names]

hypocotyl /hī́pəkóttil/ *n. Bot.* the part of the stem of an embryo plant beneath the stalks of the seed leaves or cotyledons and directly above the root.

hypocrisy /hipókrisi/ *n.* (*pl.* **-ies**) **1** the assumption or postulation of moral standards to which one's own behaviour does not conform; dissimulation, pretence. **2** an instance of this. [ME f. OF *ypocrisie* f. eccl.L *hypocrisis* f. Gk *hupokrisis* acting of a part, pretence (as HYPO-, *krinō* decide, judge)]

■ **1** deceit, deceitfulness, duplicity, double-dealing, deception, play-acting, falseness, fakery, falsity, Pharisaism, insincerity, sanctimony, sanctimoniousness, *colloq.* phoniness; dissumulation, pretence. **2** see DECEIT 2.

hypocrite /híppəkrit/ *n.* a person given to hypocrisy. □□ **hypocritical** /-kríttik'l/ *adj.* **hypocritically** /-kríttikəli/ *adv.* [ME f. OF *ypocrite* f. eccl.L f. Gk *hupokritēs* actor (as HYPOCRISY)]

■ deceiver, double-dealer, faker, pretender, Pharisee, whited sepulchre, *sl.* creeping Jesus. □□ **hypocritical** deceiving, dissembling, two-faced, dishonest; see also INSINCERE.

hypocycloid /hī́pəsī́kloyd/ *n. Math.* the curve traced by a point on the circumference of a circle rolling on the interior of another circle. □□ **hypocycloidal** /-klóyd'l/ *adj.*

hypodermic /hī́pədérmik/ *adj.* & *n.* ● *adj. Med.* **1** of or relating to the area beneath the skin. **2 a** (of a drug etc. or its application) injected beneath the skin. **b** (of a needle, syringe, etc.) used to do this. ● *n.* a hypodermic injection or syringe. □□ **hypodermically** *adv.* [HYPO- + Gk *derma* skin]

hypogastrium /hī́pəgástriəm/ *n.* (*pl.* **hypogastria** /-striə/) the part of the central abdomen which is situated below the region of the stomach. □□ **hypogastric** *adj.* [mod.L f. Gk *hupogastrion* (as HYPO-, *gastēr* belly)]

hypogean /hī́pəjeéən/ *adj.* (also **hypogeal** /-jeéəl/) **1** (existing or growing) underground. **2** (of seed germination) with the seed leaves remaining below the ground. [LL *hypogeus* f. Gk *hupogeios* (as HYPO-, *gē* earth)]

hypogene /hī́pəjeen/ *adj. Geol.* produced under the surface of the earth. [HYPO- + Gk *gen-* produce]

hypogeum /hī́pəjeéəm/ *n.* (*pl.* **hypogea** /-jeéə/) an underground chamber. [L f. Gk *hupogeion* neut. of *hupogeios*: see HYPOGEAL]

hypoglycaemia /hī́pōglīseémiə/ *n.* (*US* **hypoglycemia**) a deficiency of glucose in the bloodstream. □□ **hypoglycaemic** *adj.* [HYPO- + GLYCO- + -AEMIA]

hypoid /hī́poyd/ *n.* a gear with the pinion offset from the centre-line of the wheel, to connect non-intersecting shafts. [perh. f. HYPERBOLOID]

hypolimnion /hī́pəlímniən/ *n.* (*pl.* **hypolimnia** /-niə/) the lower layer of water in stratified lakes. [HYPO- + Gk *limnion* dimin. of *limnē* lake]

hypomania /hī́pəmáyniə/ *n.* a minor form of mania. □□ **hypomanic** /-mánnik/ *adj.* [mod.L f. G *Hypomanie* (as HYPO-, MANIA)]

hyponasty /hī́pənasti/ *n. Bot.* the tendency in plant-organs for growth to be more rapid on the under-side. □□ **hyponastic** /-nástik/ *adj.* [HYPO- + Gk *nastos* pressed]

hypophysis /hīpóffisiss/ *n.* (*pl.* **hypophyses** /-seez/) *Anat.* = *pituitary gland.* □□ **hypophyseal** /hī́pəfízziəl/ *adj.* (also **-physial**). [mod.L f. Gk *hupophusis* offshoot (as HYPO-, *phusis* growth)]

hypostasis /hīpóstəsiss/ *n.* (*pl.* **hypostases** /-seez/) **1** *Med.* an accumulation of fluid or blood in the lower parts of the body or organs under the influence of gravity, in cases of poor circulation. **2** *Metaphysics* an underlying substance, as opposed to attributes or to that which is unsubstantial. **3** *Theol.* **a** the person of Christ, combining human and divine natures. **b** each of the three persons of the Trinity. □□ **hypostasize** *v.tr.* (also **-ise**) (in senses 1, 2). [eccl.L f. Gk *hupostasis* (as HYPO-, STASIS standing, state)]

hypostatic /hī́pəstáttik/ *adj.* (also **hypostatical**) *Theol.* relating to the three persons of the Trinity. □ **hypostatic union** the divine and human natures in Christ.

hypostyle /hī́pəstīl/ *adj. Archit.* having a roof supported by pillars. [Gk *hupostulos* (as HYPO-, STYLE)]

hypotaxis /hī́pətáksiss/ *n. Gram.* the subordination of one clause to another. □□ **hypotactic** /-táktik/ *adj.* [Gk *hupotaxis* (as HYPO-, *taxis* arrangement)]

hypotension /hī́pəténsh'n/ *n.* abnormally low blood pressure. □□ **hypotensive** *adj.*

hypotenuse /hīpóttənyōōz/ *n.* the side opposite the right angle of a right-angled triangle. [L *hypotenusa* f. Gk *hupoteinousa* (*grammē*) subtending (line) fem. part. of *hupoteinō* (as HYPO-, *teinō* stretch)]

hypothalamus /hīpəthálləməss/ *n.* (*pl.* **-mi** /-mī/) *Anat.* the region of the brain which controls body-temperature, thirst, hunger, etc. □□ **hypothalamic** *adj.* [mod.L formed as HYPO-, THALAMUS]

hypothec /hīpóthik/ *n.* (in Roman and Scottish law) a right established by law over property belonging to a debtor. □□ **hypothecary** /hīpóthikəri/ *adj.* [F *hypothèque* f. LL *hypotheca* f. Gk *hupothēkē* deposit (as HYPO-, *tithēmi* place)]

hypothecate /hīpóthikayt/ *v.tr.* **1** pledge, mortgage. **2** hypothesize. □□ **hypothecation** /-káysh'n/ *n.* **hypothecator** *n.* [med.L *hypothecare* (as HYPOTHEC)]
■ see PAWN² *v.*

hypothermia /hīpōthérmiə/ *n. Med.* the condition of having an abnormally low body-temperature. [HYPO- + Gk *thermē* heat]

hypothesis /hīpóthisiss/ *n.* (*pl.* **hypotheses** /-seez/) **1** a proposition made as a basis for reasoning, without the assumption of its truth. **2** a supposition made as a starting-point for further investigation from known facts (cf. THEORY). **3** a groundless assumption. [LL f. Gk *hupothesis* foundation (as HYPO-, THESIS)]
■ **1** postulate, premise, proposition, *Logic* premiss. **2** assumption, theory; see also SUPPOSITION 1, 2. **3** see PRESUMPTION 2.

hypothesize /hīpóthisīz/ *v.* (also **-ise**) **1** *intr.* frame a hypothesis. **2** *tr.* assume as a hypothesis. □□ **hypothesist** /-sist/ *n.* **hypothesizer** *n.*
■ see SPECULATE 1, 2.

hypothetical /hīpəthéttik'l/ *adj.* **1** of or based on or serving as a hypothesis. **2** supposed but not necessarily real or true. □□ **hypothetically** *adv.*
■ assumed, supposed, presumed, hypothesized, suppositional, suppositious; conjectural, conjectured, surmised, imagined, imaginary, speculative, theoretical.

hypothyroidism /hīpōthīroydiz'm/ *n. Med.* subnormal activity of the thyroid gland, resulting in cretinism in children, and mental and physical slowing in adults. □□ **hypothyroid** *n.* & *adj.* **hypothyroidic** /-róydik/ *adj.*

hypoventilation /hīpōvéntiláysh'n/ *n.* breathing at an abnormally slow rate, resulting in an increased amount of carbon dioxide in the blood.

hypoxaemia /hīpokseémiə/ *n.* (*US* **hypoxemia**) *Med.* an abnormally low concentration of oxygen in the blood. [mod.L (as HYPO-, OXYGEN, -AEMIA)]

hypoxia /hīpóksiə/ *n. Med.* a deficiency of oxygen reaching the tissues. □□ **hypoxic** *adj.* [HYPO- + OX- + -IA¹]

hypso- /hípsō/ *comb. form* height. [Gk *hupsos* height]

hypsography /hipsógrəfi/ *n.* a description or mapping of the contours of the earth's surface. □□ **hypsographic** /-səgráffik/ *adj.* **hypsographical** /-səgráffik'l/ *adj.*

hypsometer /hipsómmitər/ *n.* **1** a device for calibrating thermometers at the boiling point of water. **2** this instrument when used to estimate height above sea level. □□ **hypsometric** /-səmétrik/ *adj.*

hyrax /hīraks/ *n.* any small mammal of the order *Hyracoidea*, including rock-rabbit and dassie. [mod.L f. Gk *hurax* shrew-mouse]

hyson /hīs'n/ *n.* a kind of green China tea. [Chin. *xichun*, lit. 'bright spring']

hyssop /híssəp/ *n.* **1** any small bushy aromatic herb of the genus *Hyssopus*, esp. *H. officinalis*, formerly used medicinally. **2** *Bibl.* **a** a plant whose twigs were used for sprinkling in Jewish rites. **b** a bunch of this used in purification. [OE (*h*)*ysope* (reinforced in ME by OF *ysope*) f. L *hyssopus* f. Gk *hyssōpos*, of Semitic orig.]

hysterectomy /hístəréktəmi/ *n.* (*pl.* **-ies**) the surgical removal of the womb. □□ **hysterectomize** *v.tr.* (also **-ise**). [Gk *hustera* womb + -ECTOMY]

hysteresis /hístəreéssiss/ *n. Physics* the lagging behind of an effect when its cause varies in amount etc., esp. of magnetic induction behind the magnetizing force. [Gk *husterēsis* f. *hustereō* be behind f. *husteros* coming after]

hysteria /histeériə/ *n.* **1** a wild uncontrollable emotion or excitement. **2** a functional disturbance of the nervous system, of psychoneurotic origin. [mod.L (as HYSTERIC)]
■ **2** see MANIA 1.

hysteric /histérrik/ *n.* & *adj.* ● *n.* **1** (in *pl.*) **a** a fit of hysteria. **b** *colloq.* overwhelming mirth or laughter (*we were in hysterics*). **2** a hysterical person. ● *adj.* = HYSTERICAL. [L f. Gk *husterikos* of the womb (*hustera*), hysteria being thought to occur more frequently in women than in men and to be associated with the womb]

hysterical /histérrik'l/ *adj.* **1** of or affected with hysteria. **2** morbidly or uncontrolledly emotional. **3** *colloq.* extremely funny or amusing. □□ **hysterically** *adv.*
■ **1** see MAD *adj.* 1. **2** irrational, distracted, rabid, frantic, frenzied, wild, berserk, uncontrolled, uncontrollable, unrestrained, unrestrainable; beside oneself. **3** hilarious, side-splitting, uproarious, farcical, comic(al), funny.

hysteron proteron /hístəron próttəron/ *n. Rhet.* a figure of speech in which what should come last is put first; an inversion of the natural order (e.g. *I die! I faint! I fail!*). [LL f. Gk *husteron proteron* the latter (put in place of) the former]

Hz *abbr.* hertz.

Ii

I[1] /ī/ *n.* (also **i**) (*pl.* **Is** or **I's**) **1** the ninth letter of the alphabet. **2** (as a Roman numeral) 1. □ **I-beam** a girder of I-shaped section.

I[2] /ī/ *pron.* & *n.* ● *pron.* (*obj.* **me**; *poss.* **my, mine**; *pl.* **we**) used by a speaker or writer to refer to himself or herself. ● *n.* (**the I**) *Metaphysics* the ego; the subject or object of self-consciousness. [OE f. Gmc]

I[3] *symb. Chem.* the element iodine.

I[4] *abbr.* (also **I.**) **1** Island(s). **2** Isle(s).

-i[1] /i, ī/ *suffix* forming the plural of nouns from Latin in *-us* or from Italian in *-e* or *-o* (*foci*; *dilettanti*; *timpani*). ¶ Plural in *-s* or *-es* is often also possible.

-i[2] /i/ *suffix* forming adjectives from names of countries or regions in the Near or Middle East (*Israeli*; *Pakistani*). [adj. suffix in Semitic and Indo-Iranian languages]

-i- a connecting vowel esp. forming words in *-ana*, *-ferous*, *-fic*, *-form*, *-fy*, *-gerous*, *-vorous* (cf. -O-). [from or after F f. L]

IA *abbr. US* Iowa (in official postal use).

Ia. *abbr.* Iowa.

-ia[1] /iə/ *suffix* **1** forming abstract nouns (*mania*; *utopia*), often in *Med.* (*anaemia*; *pneumonia*). **2** *Bot.* forming names of classes and genera (*dahlia*; *fuchsia*). **3** forming names of countries (*Australia*; *India*). [from or after L & Gk]

-ia[2] /iə/ *suffix* forming plural nouns or the plural of nouns: **1** from Greek in *-ion* or Latin in *-ium* (*paraphernalia*; *regalia*; *amnia*; *labia*). **2** *Zool.* the names of groups (*Mammalia*).

IAA *abbr.* indoleacetic acid.

IAEA *abbr.* International Atomic Energy Agency.

-ial /iəl/ *suffix* forming adjectives (*celestial*; *dictatorial*; *trivial*). [from or after F *-iel* or L *-ialis*: cf. -AL]

iamb /íamb/ *n.* an iambus. [Anglicized f. IAMBUS]

iambic /īámbik/ *adj.* & *n.* *Prosody* ● *adj.* of or using iambuses. ● *n.* (usu. in *pl.*) iambic verse. [F *iambique* f. LL *iambicus* f. Gk *iambikos* (as IAMBUS)]

iambus /īámbəss/ *n.* (*pl.* **iambuses** or **-bi** /-bī/) *Prosody* a foot consisting of one short (or unstressed) followed by one long (or stressed) syllable. [L f. Gk *iambos* iambus, lampoon, f. *iaptō* assail in words, from its use by Gk satirists]

-ian /iən/ *suffix* var. of -AN. [from or after F *-ien* or L *-ianus*]

-iasis /īəsiss/ *suffix* the usual form of -ASIS.

IATA /ee-aátə/ *abbr.* International Air Transport Association.

iatrogenic /īátrəjénnik/ *adj.* (of a disease etc.) caused by medical examination or treatment. [Gk *iatros* physician + -GENIC]

ib. var. of IBID.

IBA *abbr.* (in the UK) Independent Broadcasting Authority.

Iberian /ībeériən/ *adj.* & *n.* ● *adj.* of ancient Iberia, the peninsula now comprising Spain and Portugal; of Spain and Portugal. ● *n.* **1** a native of ancient Iberia. **2** any of the languages of ancient Iberia. [L *Iberia* f. Gk *Ibēres* Spaniards]

Ibero- /ibáirō/ *comb. form* Iberian; Iberian and (*Ibero-American*).

ibex /íbeks/ *n.* (*pl.* **ibexes**) a wild goat, *Capra ibex*, esp. of mountainous areas of Europe, N. Africa, and Asia, with a chin beard and thick curved ridged horns. [L]

ibid. *abbr.* (also **ib.**) in the same book or passage etc. [L *ibidem* in the same place]

-ibility /ibílliti/ *suffix* forming nouns from, or corresponding to, adjectives in *-ible* (*possibility*; *credibility*). [F *-ibilité* or L *-ibilitas*]

ibis /íbiss/ *n.* (*pl.* **ibises**) any wading bird of the family Threskiornithidae with a curved bill, long neck, and long legs, and nesting in colonies. □ **sacred ibis** an ibis, *Threskiornis aethiopicus*, native to Africa and Madagascar, venerated by the ancient Egyptians. [ME f. L f. Gk]

-ible /ib'l/ *suffix* forming adjectives meaning 'that may or may be' (see -ABLE) (*terrible*; *forcible*; *possible*). [F *-ible* or L *-ibilis*]

-ibly /ibli/ *suffix* forming adverbs corresponding to adjectives in *-ible*.

IBM *abbr.* International Business Machines.

Ibo /eébō/ *n.* (also **Igbo**) (*pl.* same or **-os**) **1** a member of a Black people of SE Nigeria. **2** the language of this people. [native name]

IBRD *abbr.* International Bank for Reconstruction and Development (also known as the *World Bank*).

IC *abbr.* integrated circuit.

i/c *abbr.* **1** in charge. **2** in command. **3** internal combustion.

-ic /ik/ *suffix* **1** forming adjectives (*Arabic*; *classic*; *public*) and nouns (*critic*; *epic*; *mechanic*; *music*). **2** *Chem.* in higher valence or degree of oxidation (*ferric*; *sulphuric*) (see also -OUS). **3** denoting a particular form or instance of a noun in *-ics* (*aesthetic*; *tactic*). [from or after F *-ique* or L *-icus* or Gk *-ikos*: cf. -ATIC, -ETIC, -FIC, -OTIC]

-ical /ik'l/ *suffix* **1** forming adjectives corresponding to nouns or adjectives, usu. in *-ic* (*classical*; *comical*; *farcical*; *musical*). **2** forming adjectives corresponding to nouns in *-y* (*pathological*).

-ically /ikəli/ *suffix* forming adverbs corresponding to adjectives in *-ic* or *-ical* (*comically*; *musically*; *tragically*).

ICAO *abbr.* International Civil Aviation Organization.

ICBM *abbr.* intercontinental ballistic missile.

ICE *abbr.* **1** (in the UK) Institution of Civil Engineers. **2** internal-combustion engine.

ice /īss/ *n.* & *v.* ● *n.* **1 a** frozen water, a brittle transparent crystalline solid. **b** a sheet of this on the surface of water (*fell through the ice*). **2** *Brit.* a portion of ice-cream or water-ice (*would you like an ice?*). **3** *sl.* diamonds. **4** *Austral.* an unemotional or cold-blooded person. ● *v.* **1** *tr.* mix with or cool in ice (*iced drinks*). **2** *tr.* & *intr.* (often foll. by *over*, *up*) **a** cover or become covered with ice. **b** freeze. **3** *tr.* cover (a cake etc.) with icing. **4** *US sl.* kill. □ **ice age** a glacial period, esp. in the Pleistocene epoch. **ice-axe** a tool used by mountain-climbers for cutting footholds. **ice-bag** an ice-filled rubber bag for medical use. **ice-blue** a very pale blue. **ice-boat 1** a boat mounted on runners for travelling on ice. **2** a boat used for breaking ice on a river etc. **ice-bound** confined by ice. **ice-breaker 1** = *ice-boat* 2. **2** something that serves to relieve inhibitions, start a conversation, etc. **ice bucket** a bucket-like container with chunks of ice, used to keep a bottle of wine chilled. **ice-cap** a permanent covering of ice e.g. in polar regions. **ice-cold** as cold as ice. **ice-cream** a sweet creamy frozen food, usu.

flavoured. **ice-cube** a small block of ice made in a refrigerator. **ice-fall** a steep part of a glacier like a frozen waterfall. **ice-field** an expanse of ice, esp. in polar regions. **ice-fish** a capelin. **ice floe** = FLOE. **ice hockey** a form of hockey played on ice with a puck. **ice house** a building often partly or wholly underground for storing ice. **ice** (or **iced**) **lolly** *Brit.* a piece of flavoured ice, often with chocolate or ice-cream, on a stick. **ice-pack 1** = *pack ice.* **2** a quantity of ice applied to the body for medical etc. purposes. **ice-pick** a needle-like implement with a handle for splitting up small pieces of ice. **ice-plant** a plant, *Mesembryanthemum crystallinum*, with leaves covered with crystals or vesicles looking like ice specks. **ice-rink** = RINK 1. **ice-skate** *n.* a skate consisting of a boot with a blade beneath, for skating on ice. ● *v.intr.* skate on ice. **ice-skater** a person who skates on ice. **ice station** a meteorological research centre in polar regions. **on ice 1** (of an entertainment, sport, etc.) performed by skaters. **2** *colloq.* held in reserve; awaiting further attention. **on thin ice** in a risky situation. [OE *īs* f. Gmc]

■ *v.* **1** cool, chill, refrigerate. **2** see FREEZE *v.* 1. □ **ice-cold** see COLD *adj.* 1, 4. **on ice 2** see ABEYANCE.

-ice /iss/ *suffix* forming (esp. abstract) nouns (*avarice*; *justice*; *service*) (cf. -ISE[2]).

iceberg /ísberg/ *n.* **1** a large floating mass of ice detached from a glacier or ice-sheet and carried out to sea. **2** an unemotional or cold-blooded person. □ **iceberg lettuce** any of various crisp lettuces with a freely blanching head. **the tip of the iceberg** a small perceptible part of something (esp. a difficulty) the greater part of which is hidden. [prob. f. Du. *ijsberg* f. *ijs* ice + *berg* hill]

iceblink /ísblingk/ *n.* a luminous appearance on the horizon, caused by a reflection from ice.

iceblock /ísblok/ *n. Austral.* & *NZ* = *ice lolly*.

icebox /ísboks/ *n.* **1** a compartment in a refrigerator for making and storing ice. **2** *US* a refrigerator.

Icelander /íslǝndǝr/ *n.* **1** a native or national of Iceland, an island in the N. Atlantic. **2** a person of Icelandic descent.

Icelandic /íslándik/ *adj.* & *n.* ● *adj.* of or relating to Iceland. ● *n.* the language of Iceland.

Iceland lichen /íslǝnd/ *n.* (also **Iceland moss**) a mountain and moorland lichen, *Cetraria islandica*, with edible branching fronds.

Iceland poppy /íslǝnd/ *n.* an Arctic poppy, *Papaver nudicaule*, with red or yellow flowers.

Iceland spar /íslǝnd/ *n.* a transparent variety of calcite with the optical property of strong double refraction.

iceman /ísmǝn/ *n.* (*pl.* **-men**) esp. *US* **1** a man skilled in crossing ice. **2** a man who sells or delivers ice.

I.Chem.E. *abbr.* (in the UK) Institution of Chemical Engineers.

I Ching /ee chíng/ *n.* an ancient Chinese manual of divination based on symbolic trigrams and hexagrams. [Chin. *yijing* book of changes]

ichneumon /iknyóomǝn/ *n.* **1** (in full **ichneumon wasp**) any small hymenopterous insect of the family Ichneumonidae, depositing eggs in or on the larva of another insect as food for its own larva. **2** a mongoose of N. Africa, *Herpestes ichneumon*, noted for destroying crocodile eggs. [L f. Gk *ikhneumōn* spider-hunting wasp f. *ikhneuō* trace f. *ikhnos* footstep]

ichnography /iknógrǝfi/ *n.* (*pl.* **-ies**) **1** the ground-plan of a building, map of a region, etc. **2** a drawing of this. [F *ichnographie* or L *ichnographia* f. Gk *ikhnographia* f. *ikhnos* track: see -GRAPHY]

ichor /íkor/ *n.* **1** (in Greek mythology) fluid flowing like blood in the veins of the gods. **2** *poet.* bloodlike fluid. **3** *hist.* a watery fetid discharge from a wound etc. □□ **ichorous** /íkǝrǝss/ *adj.* [Gk *ikhōr*]

■ **1, 2** see FLUID *n.* 1. **3** see DISCHARGE *n.* 5.

ichthyo- /íkthiō/ *comb. form* fish. [Gk *ikhthus* fish]

ichthyoid /íkthioyd/ *adj.* & *n.* ● *adj.* fishlike. ● *n.* any fishlike vertebrate.

ichthyolite /íkthiǝlīt/ *n.* a fossil fish.

ichthyology /íkthiólǝji/ *n.* the study of fishes. □□ **ichthyological** /-thiǝlójik'l/ *adj.* **ichthyologist** *n.*

ichthyophagous /íkthióffǝgǝss/ *adj.* fish-eating. □□ **ichthyophagy** /-óffǝji/ *n.*

ichthyosaurus /ikthiǝsáwrǝss/ *n.* (also **ichthyosaur** /íkthiǝsawr/) any extinct marine reptile of the order Ichthyosauria, with long head, tapering body, four flippers, and usu. a large tail. [ICHTHYO- + Gk *sauros* lizard]

ichthyosis /íkthiṓsiss/ *n.* a skin disease which causes the epidermis to become dry and horny like fish scales. □□ **ichthyotic** /-thióttik/ *adj.* [Gk *ikhthus* fish + -OSIS]

ICI *abbr.* Imperial Chemical Industries.

-ician /ísh'n/ *suffix* forming nouns denoting persons skilled in or concerned with subjects having nouns (usu.) in *-ic* or *-ics* (*magician*; *politician*). [from or after F *-icien* (as -IC, -IAN)]

icicle /ísik'l/ *n.* a hanging tapering piece of ice, formed by the freezing of dripping water. [ME f. ICE + *ickle* (now dial.) icicle]

icing /ísing/ *n.* **1** a coating of sugar etc. on a cake or biscuit. **2** the formation of ice on a ship or aircraft. □ **icing on the cake** an attractive though inessential addition or enhancement. **icing sugar** *Brit.* finely powdered sugar for making icing for cakes etc.

■ **1** glaze, coating, *US* frosting. □ **icing on the cake** bonus, (fringe) benefit, added attraction, extra, reward, perquisite, *Brit. colloq.* perk.

-icist /isist/ *suffix* = -ICIAN (*classicist*). [-IC + -IST]

-icity /íssiti/ *suffix* forming abstract nouns esp. from adjectives in *-ic* (*authenticity*; *publicity*). [-IC + -ITY]

-ick /ik/ *suffix archaic* var. of -IC.

icky /íkki/ *adj.* (also **ikky**) *colloq.* **1** sweet, sticky, sickly. **2** (as a general term of disapproval) nasty, repulsive. [20th c.: orig. unkn.]

■ **1** see SWEET *adj.* 1. **2** see REVOLTING.

-icle /ik'l/ *suffix* forming (orig. diminutive) nouns (*article*; *particle*). [formed as -CULE]

icon /íkon/ *n.* (also **ikon**) **1** a devotional painting or carving, usu. on wood, of Christ or another holy figure, esp. in the Eastern Church. **2** an image or statue. **3** *Computing* a symbol or graphic representation on a VDU screen of a program, option, or window, esp. one of several for selection. **4** *Linguistics* a sign which has a characteristic in common with the thing it signifies. [L f. Gk *eikōn* image]

■ **2** see IMAGE *n.* 1.

iconic /īkónnik/ *adj.* **1** of or having the nature of an image or portrait. **2** (of a statue) following a conventional type. **3** *Linguistics* that is an icon. □□ **iconicity** /íkǝníssiti/ *n.* (esp. in sense 3). [L *iconicus* f. Gk *eikonikos* (as ICON)]

icono- /īkónnō/ *comb. form* an image or likeness. [Gk *eikōn*]

iconoclasm /īkónnǝklaz'm/ *n.* **1** the breaking of images. **2** the assailing of cherished beliefs. [ICONOCLAST after *enthusiasm* etc.]

iconoclast /īkónnǝklast/ *n.* **1** a person who attacks cherished beliefs. **2** a person who destroys images used in religious worship, esp. *hist.* during the 8th–9th c. in the Churches of the East, or as a Puritan of the 16th–17th c. □□ **iconoclastic** /-klástik/ *adj.* **iconoclastically** /-klástikǝli/ *adv.* [med.L *iconoclastes* f. eccl.Gk *eikonoklastēs* (as ICONO-, *klaō* break)]

■ **1** see NONCONFORMIST.

iconography /íkǝnógrǝfi/ *n.* (*pl.* **-ies**) **1** the illustration of a subject by drawings or figures. **2 a** the study of portraits, esp. of an individual. **b** the study of artistic images or symbols. **3** a treatise on pictures or statuary. **4** a book whose essence is pictures. □□ **iconographer** *n.* **iconographic** /-nǝgráffik/ *adj.* **iconographical** /-nǝgráffik'l/ *adj.* **iconographically** /-nǝgráffikǝli/ *adv.* [Gk *eikonographia* sketch (as ICONO- + -GRAPHY)]

iconolatry /íkǝnóllǝtri/ *n.* the worship of images. □□ **iconolater** *n.* [eccl.Gk *eikonolatreia* (as ICONO-, -LATRY)]

iconology /íkǝnóllǝji/ *n.* **1** an artistic theory developed from iconography (see ICONOGRAPHY 2b). **2** symbolism.

iconostasis /ĭkənóstəsiss, ĭkónəstássiss/ *n.* (*pl.* **iconostases** /-seez/) (in the Eastern Church) a screen bearing icons and separating the sanctuary from the nave. [mod.Gk *eikonostasis* (as ICONO-, STASIS)]

icosahedron /ĭkəsəheedrən, -hédrən/ *n.* a solid figure with twenty faces. ▫▫ **icosahedral** *adj.* [LL *icosahedrum* f. Gk *eikosaedron* f. *eikosi* twenty + -HEDRON]

-ics /iks/ *suffix* (treated as *sing.* or *pl.*) forming nouns denoting arts or sciences or branches of study or action (*athletics*; *politics*) (cf. -IC 3). [from or after F pl. *-iques* or L pl. *-ica* or Gk pl. *-ika*]

icterus /iktərəss/ *n. Med.* = JAUNDICE. ▫▫ **icteric** /iktérrik/ *adj.* [L f. Gk *ikteros*]

ictus /iktəss/ *n.* (*pl.* same or **ictuses**) **1** *Prosody* rhythmical or metrical stress. **2** *Med.* a stroke or seizure; a fit. [L, = blow f. *icere* strike]
▪ **1** see STRESS *n.* 3b, c. **2** see SEIZURE 2.

icy /ísi/ *adj.* (**icier, iciest**) **1** very cold. **2** covered with or abounding in ice. **3** (of a tone or manner) unfriendly, hostile (*an icy stare*). ▫▫ **icily** *adv.* **iciness** *n.*
▪ **1** ice-cold, frigid, glacial, freezing, frozen, gelid, hyperborean, wintry, bitter, raw, cold, chilling, chilly, *colloq.* perishing, arctic, nippy, polar, Siberian, *literary* chill. **2** frozen (over), glacial, ice-bound; glazed, glassy, slippery. **3** cold, cool, chilly, frigid, distant, aloof, remote, formal, reserved, unemotional, callous, forbidding, unfriendly, hostile, stony, flinty, steely, *literary* chill. ▫▫ **icily** coldly, frostily, forbiddingly, stonily, unemotionally. **iciness** coldness, frost, slipperiness; frigidity, stiffness, formality, aloofness, hostility.

ID *abbr.* **1** esp. *US* identification, identity (*ID card*). **2** *US* Idaho (in official postal use).
▪ **1** see IDENTIFICATION 2, 3.

I'd /īd/ *contr.* **1** I had. **2** I should; I would.

id /id/ *n. Psychol.* the inherited instinctive impulses of the individual as part of the unconscious. [L, = that, transl. G *es*]

id. *abbr.* = IDEM.

i.d. *abbr.* inner diameter.

-id[1] /id/ *suffix* forming adjectives (*arid*; *rapid*). [F *-ide* f. L *-idus*]

-id[2] /id/ *suffix* forming nouns: **1** general (*pyramid*). **2** *Biol.* of structural constituents (*plastid*). **3** *Bot.* of a plant belonging to a family with a name in *-aceae* (*orchid*). [from or after F *-ide* f. L *-is -idis* f. Gk *-is -ida* or *-idos*]

-id[3] /id/ *suffix* forming nouns denoting: **1** *Zool.* an animal belonging to a family with a name in *-idae* or a class with a name in *-ida* (*canid*; *arachnid*). **2** a member of a person's family (*Seleucid* from Seleucus). **3** *Astron.* **a** a meteor in a group radiating from a specified constellation (*Leonid* from Leo). **b** a star of a class like one in a specified constellation (*cepheid*). [from or after L *-ides*, pl. *-idae* or *-ida*]

-id[4] /id/ *suffix* esp. *US* var. of -IDE.

IDA *abbr.* International Development Association.

ide /īd/ *n.* a freshwater fish, *Leuciscus idus*, used as food. Also called ORFE. [mod.L *idus* f. Sw. *id*]

-ide /īd/ *suffix* (also esp. *US* **-id**) *Chem.* forming nouns denoting: **1** binary compounds of an element (the suffix *-ide* being added to the abbreviated name of the more electronegative element etc.) (*sodium chloride*; *lead sulphide*; *calcium carbide*). **2** various other compounds (*amide*; *anhydride*; *peptide*; *saccharide*). **3** elements of a series in the periodic table (*actinide*; *lanthanide*). [orig. in OXIDE]

idea /īdeeə/ *n.* **1** a conception or plan formed by mental effort (*have you any ideas?*; *had the idea of writing a book*). **2 a** a mental impression or notion; a concept. **b** a vague belief or fancy (*had an idea you were married*; *had no idea where you were*). **c** an opinion; an outlook or point of view (*had some funny ideas about marriage*). **3** an intention, purpose, or essential feature (*the idea is to make money*). **4** an archetype or pattern as distinguished from its realization in individual cases. **5** *Philos.* **a** (in Platonism) an eternally existing pattern of which individual things in any class are imperfect copies. **b** a concept of pure reason which transcends experience. ▫ **get** (or **have**) **ideas** *colloq.* be ambitious, rebellious, etc. **have no idea** *colloq.* **1** not know at all. **2** be completely incompetent. **not one's idea of** *colloq.* not what one regards as (*not my idea of a pleasant evening*). **put ideas into a person's head** suggest ambitions etc. he or she would not otherwise have had. **that's an idea** *colloq.* that proposal etc. is worth considering. **the very idea!** *colloq.* an exclamation of disapproval or disagreement. ▫▫ **idea'd** *adj.* **ideaed** *adj.* **idealess** *adj.* [Gk *idea* form, pattern f. stem *id-* see]
▪ **1** concept, conception, construct, thought, notion, plan, design, scheme, suggestion, recommendation. **2 a, b** notion, impression, picture, (mental) image, concept, conception, fantasy, dream; belief, fancy, perception, understanding, awareness, apprehension, inkling, suspicion, hint, hunch, suggestion, clue, intimation, guess, estimate, estimation. **c** belief, opinion, hypothesis, theory, sentiment, feeling, teaching(s), doctrine, tenet, principle, philosophy, (point of) view, viewpoint, outlook, notion, conviction, position, stance. **3** intention, aim, goal, purpose, objective, object, end, point, essence, reason, *raison d'être*, motive. **4** see IDEAL *n.* 2a.

ideal /īdeeəl/ *adj.* & *n.* ● *adj.* **1 a** answering to one's highest conception. **b** perfect or supremely excellent. **2 a** existing only in idea. **b** visionary. **3** embodying an idea. **4** relating to or consisting of ideas; dependent on the mind. ● *n.* **1** a perfect type, or a conception of this. **2 a** an actual thing as a standard for imitation. **b** (often in *pl.*) a moral principle or standard of behaviour. ▫ **ideal gas** a hypothetical gas consisting of molecules occupying negligible space and without attraction for each other, thereby obeying simple laws. ▫▫ **ideally** *adv.* [ME f. F *idéal* f. LL *idealis* (as IDEA)]
▪ *adj.* **1** perfect, faultless, excellent, supreme, best, choice, consummate, complete, exemplary, model, idyllic; see also PERFECT *adj.* 2a. **2** conceptual, imagined, imaginary, unreal, abstract, notional, theoretical, illusory, fictitious, fanciful, fancied, Utopian, idealistic, romantic, mythical, mythic, chimeric(al), visionary, fantastic. ● *n.* **1** acme, epitome, paragon, nonpareil, (standard of) perfection, optimum, quintessence, ideality. **2 a** model, standard, criterion, paradigm, exemplar, example, pattern, idea. **b** cause; (*ideals*) principles, morals, morality, (code of) ethics, standards; see also IDEOLOGY. ▫▫ **ideally** under *or* in the best of circumstances, at best, in a perfect world, all things being equal *or* considered, if all goes well; theoretically, in theory, in principle; perfectly.

idealism /īdeeəliz'm/ *n.* **1** the practice of forming or following after ideals, esp. unrealistically (cf. REALISM). **2** the representation of things in ideal or idealized form. **3** imaginative treatment. **4** *Philos.* any of various systems of thought in which the objects of knowledge are held to be in some way dependent on the activity of mind (cf. REALISM). ▫▫ **idealist** *n.* **idealistic** /-lístik/ *adj.* **idealistically** /-lístikəli/ *adv.* [F *idéalisme* or G *Idealismus* (as IDEAL)]
▪ **1** Utopianism, quixotism, quixotry, romanticism, dreaming. ▫▫ **idealist** idealizer, romantic, optimist, dreamer; see also VISIONARY *n.* **idealistic** romantic, Utopian, optimistic, quixotic, impractical, unrealistic, romanticized, visionary, *colloq.* starry-eyed. **idealistically** unrealistically, impractically; romantically, optimistically, quixotically.

ideality /īdiálliti/ *n.* (*pl.* **-ies**) **1** the quality of being ideal. **2** an ideal thing.

idealize /īdeeəlīz/ *v.tr.* (also **-ise**) **1** regard or represent (a thing or person) in ideal form or character. **2** exalt in thought to ideal perfection or excellence. ▫▫ **idealization** /-záysh'n/ *n.* **idealizer** *n.*
▪ exalt, elevate, glorify, worship, ennoble, deify, apotheosize, put on a pedestal, romanticize. ▫▫ **idealization** see PERFECTION 3. **idealizer** see VISIONARY *n.*

ideate /ídiayt/ *v. Psychol.* **1** *tr.* imagine, conceive. **2** *intr.* form ideas. ▫▫ **ideation** /-áysh'n/ *n.* **ideational** /-áyshən'l/ *adj.* **ideationally** /-áyshənəli/ *adv.* [med.L *ideare* form an idea (as IDEA)]

idée fixe /éeday féeks/ *n.* (*pl.* ***idées fixes*** *pronunc.* same) an idea that dominates the mind; an obsession. [F, lit. 'fixed idea']
■ see OBSESSION.

idée reçue /éeday rəsyóo/ *n.* (*pl.* ***idées reçues*** *pronunc.* same) a generally accepted notion or opinion. [F]
■ see OPINION 1, 3.

idem /íddem/ *adv.* & *n.* ● *adv.* in the same author. ● *n.* the same word or author. [ME f. L]

identical /īdéntik'l/ *adj.* **1** (often foll. by *with*) (of different things) agreeing in every detail. **2** (of one thing viewed at different times) one and the same. **3** (of twins) developed from a single fertilized ovum, therefore of the same sex and usu. very similar in appearance. **4** *Logic* & *Math.* expressing an identity. ▫▫ **identically** *adv.* **identicalness** *n.* [med.L *identicus* (as IDENTITY)]
■ **1** twin, duplicate, matching, corresponding, indistinguishable, interchangeable, equal, equivalent; the same, similar, like, alike, comparable, homogeneous, uniform; (*identical with*) the same as, interchangeable *or* of a piece *or* uniform with, equal *or* equivalent to. **2** (very) same, selfsame, one and the same. ▫▫ **identically** see ALIKE *adv.*

identification /īdéntifikáysh'n/ *n.* **1 a** the act or an instance of identifying; recognition, pinpointing. **b** association of oneself with the feelings, situation, characteristics, etc. of another person or group of people. **2** a means of identifying a person. **3** (*attrib.*) serving to identify (esp. the bearer) (*identification card*). ▫ **identification parade** an assembly of persons from whom a suspect is to be identified.
■ **1 a** classification, classifying, cataloguing, categorization, categorizing, pigeon-holing, recognition, distinguishing, indication, perception, detection, selection, naming, labelling, pinpointing, designation, characterization, denomination; authentication, verification, establishment, certification, substantiation, corroboration. **b** empathy, sympathy, involvement, rapport, relationship, connection, association, affiliation. **2** identity card, passport, driving-licence, badge, credentials, papers *esp. US* ID, ID card. **3** (*attrib.*) identity, *esp. US* ID. ▫ **identification parade** identity parade, line-up.

identifier /īdéntifīər/ *n.* **1** a person or thing that identifies. **2** *Computing* a sequence of characters used to identify or refer to a set of data.
■ **1** see LABEL *n.* 1.

identify /īdéntifī/ *v.* (**-ies, -ied**) **1** *tr.* establish the identity of; recognize. **2** *tr.* establish or select by consideration or analysis of the circumstances (*identify the best method of solving the problem*). **3** *tr.* (foll. by *with*) associate (a person or oneself) inseparably or very closely (with a party, policy, etc.). **4** *tr.* (often foll. by *with*) treat (a thing) as identical. **5** *intr.* (foll. by *with*) **a** regard oneself as sharing characteristics of (another person). **b** associate oneself. ▫▫ **identifiable** *adj.* [med.L *identificare* (as IDENTITY)]
■ **1, 2** recognize, classify, categorize, catalogue, pigeon-hole, sort (out), specify, establish, pinpoint, home *or* zero in on, name, label, tag, place, mark, single out, point out, find, locate, isolate, work out, discover, decide on, select, choose, diagnose, *colloq.* put one's finger on. **3** associate, connect, link, equate. **4** equate, parallel, couple, connect, associate, relate. **5** (*identify with*) empathize with, sympathize with, relate to, appreciate, understand, *sl.* dig. ▫▫ **identifiable** see *discernible* (DISCERN).

Identikit /īdéntikit/ *n.* (often *attrib.*) *propr.* a reconstructed picture of a person (esp. one sought by the police) assembled from transparent strips showing typical facial features according to witnesses' descriptions. [IDENTITY + KIT[1]]

identity /īdéntiti/ *n.* (*pl.* **-ies**) **1 a** the quality or condition of being a specified person or thing. **b** individuality, personality (*felt he had lost his identity*). **2** identification or the result of it (*a case of mistaken identity*; *identity card*). **3** the state of being the same in substance, nature, qualities, etc.; absolute sameness (*no identity of interests between them*). **4** *Algebra* **a** the equality of two expressions for all values of the quantities expressed by letters. **b** an equation expressing this, e.g. $(x + 1)^2 = x^2 + 2x + 1$. **5** *Math.* **a** (in full **identity element**) an element in a set, left unchanged by any operation to it. **b** a transformation that leaves an object unchanged. ▫ **identity crisis** a temporary period during which an individual experiences a feeling of loss or breakdown of identity. **identity parade** = *identification parade.* [LL *identitas* f. L *idem* same]
■ **1** personality, individuality, distinctiveness, uniqueness, particularity, singularity, selfhood. **2** see IDENTIFICATION 1a. **3** sameness, oneness, unity, equality; indistinguishability, correspondence, interchangeability, agreement, accord, congruence. ▫ **identity parade** identification parade, line-up.

ideogram /íddiəgram/ *n.* a character symbolizing the idea of a thing without indicating the sequence of sounds in its name (e.g. a numeral, and many Chinese characters). [Gk *idea* form + -GRAM]
■ see SIGN *n.* 2.

ideograph /íddiəgraaf/ *n.* = IDEOGRAM. ▫▫ **ideographic** /-gráffik/ *adj.* **ideography** /íddiógrəfi/ *n.* [Gk *idea* form + -GRAPH]

ideologue /ídiəlog/ *n.* **1** a theorist; a visionary. **2** an adherent of an ideology. [F *idéologue* f. Gk *idea* (see IDEA) + -LOGUE]

ideology /īdiólləji/ *n.* (*pl.* **-ies**) **1** the system of ideas at the basis of an economic or political theory (*Marxist ideology*). **2** the manner of thinking characteristic of a class or individual (*bourgeois ideology*). **3** visionary speculation. **4** *archaic* the science of ideas. ▫▫ **ideological** /īdiəlójik'l/ *adj.* **ideologically** /īdiəlójikəli/ *adv.* **ideologist** *n.* [F *idéologie* (as IDEOLOGUE)]
■ **1, 2** belief(s), convictions, tenets, credo, philosophy, principles, canons, creed, dogma, teachings, doctrine; see also IDEAL *n.* 2b.

ides /īdz/ *n.pl.* the eighth day after the nones in the ancient Roman calendar (the 15th day of March, May, July, October, the 13th of other months). [ME f. OF f. L *idus* (pl.), perh. f. Etruscan]

idiocy /íddiəsi/ *n.* (*pl.* **-ies**) **1** utter foolishness; idiotic behaviour or an idiotic action. **2** extreme mental imbecility. [ME f. IDIOT, prob. after *lunacy*]
■ **1** see *stupidity* (STUPID).

idiolect /íddiəlekt/ *n.* the form of language used by an individual person. [Gk *idios* own + *-lect* in DIALECT]
■ see LANGUAGE 2, 3a, b.

idiom /íddiəm/ *n.* **1** a group of words established by usage and having a meaning not deducible from those of the individual words (as in *over the moon, see the light*). **2** a form of expression peculiar to a language, person, or group of people. **3 a** the language of a people or country. **b** the specific character of this. **4** a characteristic mode of expression in music, art, etc. [F *idiome* or LL *idioma* f. Gk *idiōma -matos* private property f. *idios* own, private]
■ **1** expression, (set) phrase, phrasing, locution, cliché, collocation, saying. **2, 3** idiolect, phraseology, vernacular, dialect, argot, patois, jargon, cant, parlance, form *or* mode of expression; language, tongue, speech, *colloq.* lingo.

idiomatic /íddiəmáttik/ *adj.* **1** relating to or conforming to idiom. **2** characteristic of a particular language. ▫▫ **idiomatically** *adv.* [Gk *idiōmatikos* peculiar (as IDIOM)]

idiopathy /íddióppəthi/ *n. Med.* any disease or condition of unknown cause or that arises spontaneously. ▫▫ **idiopathic** /íddiəpáthik/ *adj.* [mod.L *idiopathia* f. Gk *idiopatheia* f. *idios* own + -PATHY]

idiosyncrasy /íddiōsíngkrəsi/ *n.* (*pl.* **-ies**) **1** a mental constitution, view or feeling, or mode of behaviour, peculiar to a person. **2** anything highly individualized or eccentric. **3** a mode of expression peculiar to an author. **4** *Med.* a physical constitution peculiar to a person. ▫▫ **idiosyncratic** /-kráttik/ *adj.* **idiosyncratically** /-kráttikəli/ *adv.* [Gk *idiosugkrasia* f. *idios* own + *sun* together + *krasis* mixture]

■ **1** see CHARACTERISTIC *n.* **2** see *eccentricity* (ECCENTRIC). ▫▫ **idiosyncratic** see CHARACTERISTIC *adj.*, ECCENTRIC *adj.*

idiot /iddiət/ *n.* **1** *colloq.* a stupid person; an utter fool. **2** a person deficient in mind and permanently incapable of rational conduct. ▫ **idiot board** (or **card**) *colloq.* a board displaying a television script to a speaker as an aid to memory. **idiot box** *colloq.* a television set. ▫▫ **idiotic** /iddióttik/ *adj.* **idiotically** /iddióttikəli/ *adv.* [ME f. OF f. L *idiota* ignorant person f. Gk *idiōtēs* private person, layman, ignorant person f. *idios* own, private]

■ **1** see FOOL[1] *n.* 1. ▫▫ **idiotic** see STUPID *adj.* 1, 5; 2. **idiotically** see MADLY 1.

idle /ī́d'l/ *adj.* & *v.* ● *adj.* (**idler, idlest**) **1** lazy, indolent. **2** not in use; not working; unemployed. **3** (of time etc.) unoccupied. **4** having no special basis or purpose (*idle rumour*; *idle curiosity*). **5** useless. **6** (of an action, thought, or word) ineffective, worthless, vain. ● *v.* **1 a** *intr.* (of an engine) run slowly without doing any work. **b** *tr.* cause (an engine) to idle. **2** *intr.* be idle. **3** *tr.* (foll. by *away*) pass (time etc.) in idleness. ▫ **idle wheel** an intermediate wheel between two geared wheels, esp. to allow them to rotate in the same direction. ▫▫ **idleness** *n.* **idly** *adv.* [OE *īdel* empty, useless]

■ *adj.* **1** lazy, indolent, listless, lethargic, slothful, languid, shiftless, lackadaisical, fainéant. **2** unused, not in use, inactive, unoccupied, non-operative, not working, stationary; unemployed, out of work, redundant, jobless, workless, unwaged, at leisure, at liberty, between assignments, *Brit. euphem.* resting. **3** unoccupied, free, empty, vacant, unfilled, unused. **4** aimless, purposeless; baseless, groundless; offhand. **5, 6** useless, worthless, otiose, pointless, insignificant, meaningless, senseless, unimportant, trivial, trifling, nugatory, shallow, frivolous, superficial, *colloq.* piffling; ineffective, vain, unavailing, futile, unproductive, fruitless, unfruitful, abortive, *archaic* bootless. ● *v.* **1 a** tick over. **2** laze (about), loiter, kill *or* mark time, loaf, loll, lounge, take it easy, mess around *or* about, fool around *or* about, potter *or US* putter about *or* around, *Brit. colloq.* muck around *or* about, *sl.* goof off *or* around, *US sl.* lallygag. **3** (*idle away*) waste, fritter away, while away, kill, pass, spend, squander. ▫▫ **idleness** inactivity, inaction, unemployment, leisure; laziness, lethargy, torpor, indolence, sluggishness, sloth, slothfulness, shiftlessness, inertia, lassitude, *flânerie*, *dolce far niente*. **idly** lazily, listlessly, indolently, unproductively, purposelessly, worthlessly, pointlessly, meaninglessly, senselessly; unconsciously, unthinkingly, mechanically, indifferently, offhandedly, aimlessly, thoughtlessly, obliviously.

idler /ī́dlər/ *n.* **1** a habitually lazy person. **2** = *idle wheel.*

■ **1** layabout, loafer, lounger, slacker, shirker, skiver, drone, fainéant, clock-watcher, sluggard, dawdler, laggard, lazybones, ne'er-do-well, *US* gold brick, *archaic* slugabed, *colloq.* lounge lizard, slob, *sl.* slouch, *Austral. sl.* warb, *US sl.* couch potato.

Ido /éedō/ *n.* an artificial universal language based on Esperanto. [Ido, = offspring]

idol /ī́d'l/ *n.* **1** an image of a deity etc. used as an object of worship. **2** *Bibl.* a false god. **3** a person or thing that is the object of excessive or supreme adulation (*cinema idol*). **4** *archaic* a phantom. [ME f. OF *idole* f. L *idolum* f. Gk *eidōlon* phantom f. *eidos* form]

■ **1** (graven) image, icon, effigy, symbol, fetish, totem, *NZ* tiki. **3** god, hero *or* heroine, star, superstar, celebrity, pin-up, luminary, favourite, pet, darling, *colloq.* sacred cow.

idolater /īdóllətər/ *n.* (*fem.* **idolatress** /-triss/) **1** a worshipper of idols. **2** (often foll. by *of*) a devoted admirer. ▫▫ **idolatrous** *adj.* [ME *idolatrer* f. OF or f. *idolatry* or f. OF *idolâtre*, ult. f. Gk *eidōlolatrēs* (as IDOL, -LATER)]

■ **1** see PAGAN *n.* ▫▫ **idolatrous** see HEATHEN *adj.*

idolatry /īdóllətri/ *n.* **1** the worship of idols. **2** great adulation. [OF *idolatrie* (as IDOLATER)]

■ see WORSHIP *n.*

idolize /ī́dəlīz/ *v.* (also **-ise**) **1** *tr.* venerate or love extremely or excessively. **2** *tr.* make an idol of. **3** *intr.* practise idolatry. ▫▫ **idolization** /-záysh'n/ *n.* **idolizer** *n.*

■ **1, 2** venerate, deify, worship, apotheosize, adore, revere, reverence, exalt, glorify, put on a pedestal, lionize, adulate, honour, admire, look up to. ▫▫ **idolization** see *veneration* (VENERATE). **idolizer** worshipper, admirer, adulator, adorer; devotee, aficionado, fan, *sl.* groupie.

idyll /iddil/ *n.* (also **idyl**) **1** a short description in verse or prose of a picturesque scene or incident, esp. in rustic life. **2** an episode suitable for such treatment, usu. a love-story. ▫▫ **idyllist** *n.* **idyllize** *v.tr.* (also **-ise**). [L *idyllium* f. Gk *eidullion*, dimin. of *eidos* form]

■ **1** pastoral, eclogue.

idyllic /idíllik/ *adj.* **1** blissfully peaceful and happy. **2** of or like an idyll. ▫▫ **idyllically** *adv.*

■ **1** blissful, heavenly, paradisal, paradisical, paradisaical, paradisiacal, heavenly, Arcadian; halcyon, blessed, perfect, ideal, idealized; pastoral, rustic, bucolic, unspoilt *or* unspoiled, peaceful, pacific. ▫▫ **idyllically** blissfully; blessedly, perfectly, ideally; pastorally, rustically, bucolically, peacefully, pacifically.

i.e. *abbr.* that is to say. [L *id est*]

■ see NAMELY.

-ie /i/ *suffix* **1** var. of -Y[2] (*dearie*; *nightie*). **2** *archaic* var. of -Y[1], -Y[3] (*litanie*; *prettie*). [earlier form of -Y]

IEE *abbr.* (in the UK) Institution of Electrical Engineers.

-ier /iər/ *suffix* forming personal nouns denoting an occupation or interest: **1** with stress on the preceding element (*grazier*). **2** with stress on the suffix (*cashier*; *brigadier*). [sense 1 ME of various orig.; sense 2 F *-ier* f. L *-arius*]

IF *abbr.* intermediate frequency.

if /if/ *conj.* & *n.* ● *conj.* **1** introducing a conditional clause: **a** on the condition or supposition that; in the event that (*if he comes I will tell him*; *if you are tired we will rest*). **b** (with past tense) implying that the condition is not fulfilled (*if I were you*; *if I knew I would say*). **2** even though (*I'll finish it, if it takes me all day*). **3** whenever (*if I am not sure I ask*). **4** whether (*see if you can find it*). **5 a** expressing wish or surprise (*if I could just try!*; *if it isn't my old hat!*). **b** expressing a request (*if you wouldn't mind opening the door?*). **6** with implied reservation, = and perhaps not (*very rarely if at all*). **7** (with reduction of the protasis to its significant word) if there is or it is etc. (*took little if any*). **8** despite being (*a useful if cumbersome device*). ● *n.* a condition or supposition (*too many ifs about it*). ▫ **if only 1** even if for no other reason than (*I'll come if only to see her*). **2** (often *ellipt.*) an expression of regret (*if only I had thought of it*; *if only I could swim!*). **if so** if that is the case. [OE *gif*]

■ *conj.* **1** see SUPPOSE 5.

IFC *abbr.* International Finance Corporation.

iff /if/ *conj. Logic* & *Math.* = if and only if. [arbitrary extension of *if*]

iffy /iffi/ *adj.* (**iffier, iffiest**) *colloq.* uncertain, doubtful.

■ see DOUBTFUL 2.

Igbo var. of IBO.

igloo /igloo/ *n.* an Eskimo dome-shaped dwelling, esp. one built of snow. [Eskimo, = house]

igneous /igniəss/ *adj.* **1** of fire; fiery. **2** *Geol.* (esp. of rocks) produced by volcanic or magmatic action. [L *igneus* f. *ignis* fire]

ignis fatuus /igniss fátyooəss/ *n.* (*pl.* **ignes fatui** /igneez fátyoo-i/) a will-o'-the-wisp. [mod.L, = foolish fire, because of its erratic movement]

■ see ILLUSION 4.

ignite /ignīt/ *v.* **1** *tr.* set fire to; cause to burn. **2** *intr.* catch fire. **3** *tr. Chem.* heat to the point of combustion or chemical change. **4** *tr.* provoke or excite (feelings etc.). □□ **ignitable** *adj.* **ignitability** /-təbílliti/ *n.* **ignitible** *adj.* **ignitibility** /-tibílliti/ *n.* [L *ignire ignit-* f. *ignis* fire]
■ **1** see FIRE *v.* 5a. **2** kindle, catch fire, burst into flame. **4** see EXCITE 1a, b.

igniter /ignītər/ *n.* **1** a device for igniting a fuel mixture in an engine. **2** a device for causing an electric arc.

ignition /igníshʼn/ *n.* **1** a mechanism for, or the action of, starting the combustion of mixture in the cylinder of an internal-combustion engine. **2** the act or an instance of igniting or being ignited. □ **ignition key** a key to operate the ignition of a motor vehicle. [F *ignition* or med.L *ignitio* (as IGNITE)]

ignitron /ignītrən/ *n. Electr.* a mercury-arc rectifier able to carry large currents. [IGNITE + -TRON]

ignoble /ignṓbʼl/ *adj.* (**ignobler, ignoblest**) **1** dishonourable, mean, base. **2** of low birth, position, or reputation. □□ **ignobility** /-nəbílliti/ *n.* **ignobly** *adv.* [F *ignoble* or L *ignobilis* (as IN-[1], *nobilis* noble)]
■ **1** see BASE[2] 1. **2** see HUMBLE *adj.* 2. □□ **ignobility** see VULGARITY.

ignominious /ignəmínniəss/ *adj.* **1** causing or deserving ignominy. **2** humiliating. □□ **ignominiously** *adv.* **ignominiousness** *n.* [ME f. F *ignominieux* or L *ignominiosus*]
■ **1** see INFAMOUS 1.

ignominy /ignəmini/ *n.* **1** dishonour, infamy. **2** *archaic* infamous conduct. [F *ignominie* or L *ignominia* (as IN-[1], *nomen* name)]
■ **1** see *infamy* (INFAMOUS).

ignoramus /ignəráyməss/ *n.* (*pl.* **ignoramuses**) an ignorant person. [L, = we do not know: in legal use (formerly of a grand jury rejecting a bill) we take no notice of it; mod. sense perh. from a character in Ruggle's *Ignoramus* (1615) exposing lawyers' ignorance]

ignorance /ignərənss/ *n.* (often foll. by *of*) lack of knowledge (about a thing). [ME f. OF f. L *ignorantia* (as IGNORANT)]
■ unawareness, obliviousness, unfamiliarity, unconsciousness, benightedness, *literary* nescience; inexperience, greenness, innocence, simplicity, naïvety.

ignorant /ignərənt/ *adj.* **1 a** lacking knowledge or experience. **b** (foll. by *of, in*) uninformed (about a fact or subject). **2** *colloq.* ill-mannered, uncouth. □□ **ignorantly** *adv.* [ME f. OF f. L *ignorare ignorant-* (as IGNORE)]
■ **1 a** unknowing, unaware, unenlightened, unconscious, unwitting, benighted, in the dark, oblivious, *literary* nescient; uneducated, unschooled, uninitiated, uninformed, inexperienced, green, naïve, fresh, innocent, unsophisticated, unread, unlearned, unlettered, unversed, untaught, illiterate. **b** (*ignorant of*) unaware of, unconscious of, uninformed about, unfamiliar with, unacquainted with, unschooled in, unversed in, untutored in, inexperienced in *or* with, unconversant with, unenlightened about, in the dark about *or* as to, oblivious to *or* of, innocent of. **2** ill-mannered, uncouth, rude, discourteous, unchivalrous, impolite, uncivil, boorish, gauche, ill-bred, bad-mannered.

ignore /ignór/ *v.tr.* **1** refuse to take notice of or accept. **2** intentionally disregard. □□ **ignorer** *n.* [F *ignorer* or L *ignorare* not know, ignore (as IN-[1], *gno-* know)]
■ **1** reject, snub, brush aside, cut, cold-shoulder, give the cold shoulder, send to Coventry, turn one's back on, *colloq.* give the go-by, turn up one's nose at, *US colloq.* freeze out. **2** disregard, overlook, pass over *or* by, skip, omit, leave out, neglect; turn a blind eye to, turn a deaf ear to, be blind to, turn one's back on, wink at, brush off *or* aside.

iguana /igwaánə/ *n.* any of various large lizards of the family Iguanidae native to America, the W. Indies, and the Pacific islands, having a dorsal crest and throat appendages. [Sp. f. Carib *iwana*]

iguanodon /igwaánədon/ *n.* a large extinct plant-eating dinosaur of the genus *Iguanodon*, with forelimbs smaller than hind limbs. [IGUANA (from its resemblance to this), after *mastodon* etc.]

i.h.p. *abbr.* indicated horsepower.

IHS *abbr.* Jesus. [ME f. LL, repr. Gk *IHΣ* = *Iēs(ous)* Jesus: often taken as an abbr. of various Latin words]

ikebana /íkkibaánə/ *n.* the art of Japanese flower arrangement, with formal display according to strict rules. [Jap., = living flowers]

ikky var. of ICKY.

ikon var. of ICON.

IL *abbr. US* Illinois (in official postal use).

il- /il/ *prefix* assim. form of IN-[1], IN-[2] before *l*.

-il /il/ *suffix* (also **-ile** /īl/) forming adjectives or nouns denoting relation (*civil; utensil*) or capability (*agile; sessile*). [OF f. L *-ilis*]

ilang-ilang var. of YLANG-YLANG.

ILEA /illiə/ *abbr.* Inner London Education Authority.

ilea *pl.* of ILEUM.

ileostomy /illióstəmi/ *n.* (*pl.* **-ies**) a surgical operation in which the ileum is brought through the abdominal wall to create an artificial opening for the evacuation of the intestinal contents. [ILEUM + Gk *stoma* mouth]

ileum /illiəm/ *n.* (*pl.* **ilea** /illiə/) *Anat.* the third and last portion of the small intestine. □□ **ileac** *adj.* [var. of ILIUM]

ileus /illiəss/ *n. Med.* any painful obstruction of the intestine, esp. of the ileum. [L f. Gk *(e)ileos* colic]

ilex /īleks/ *n.* **1** any tree or shrub of the genus *Ilex*, esp. the common holly. **2** the holm-oak. [ME f. L]

ilia *pl.* of ILIUM.

iliac /illiak/ *adj.* of the lower body or ilium (*iliac artery*). [LL *iliacus* (as ILIUM)]

ilium /illiəm/ *n.* (*pl.* **ilia** /illiə/) **1** the bone forming the upper part of each half of the human pelvis. **2** the corresponding bone in animals. [ME f. L]

ilk /ilk/ *n.* **1** *colloq. disp.* a family, class, or set (*not of the same ilk as you*). ¶ Usu. *derog.* and therefore best avoided. **2** (in **of that ilk**) *Sc.* of the same (name) (*Guthrie of that ilk* = of Guthrie). [OE *ilca* same]
■ **1** see TYPE *n.* 1.

Ill. *abbr.* Illinois.

I'll /īl/ *contr.* I shall; I will.

ill /il/ *adj., adv., & n.* ● *adj.* **1** (usu. *predic.*; often foll. by *with*) out of health; sick (*is ill; was taken ill with pneumonia; mentally ill people*). **2** (of health) unsound, disordered. **3** wretched, unfavourable (*ill fortune; ill luck*). **4** harmful (*ill effects*). **5** hostile, unkind (*ill feeling*). **6** *archaic* morally bad. **7** faulty, unskilful (*ill taste; ill management*). **8** (of manners or conduct) improper. ● *adv.* **1** badly, wrongly (*ill-matched*). **2 a** imperfectly (*ill-provided*). **b** scarcely (*can ill afford to do it*). **3** unfavourably (*it would have gone ill with them*). ● *n.* **1** injury, harm. **2** evil; the opposite of good. □ **do an ill turn to** harm (a person or a person's interests). **ill-advised 1** (of a person) foolish or imprudent. **2** (of a plan etc.) not well formed or considered. **ill-advisedly** /-ədvīzidli/ in a foolish or badly considered manner. **ill-affected** (foll. by *towards*) not well disposed. **ill-assorted** not well matched. **ill at ease** embarrassed, uneasy. **ill-behaved** see BEHAVE. **ill blood** bad feeling; animosity. **ill-bred** badly brought up; rude. **ill breeding** bad manners. **ill-considered** = *ill-advised*. **ill-defined** not clearly defined. **ill-disposed 1** (often foll. by *towards*) unfavourably disposed. **2** disposed to evil; malevolent. **ill-equipped** (often foll. by *to* + infin.) not adequately equipped or qualified. **ill fame** see FAME. **ill-fated** destined to or bringing bad fortune. **ill-favoured** (*US* **-favored**) unattractive, displeasing, objectionable. **ill feeling** bad feeling; animosity. **ill-founded** (of an idea etc.) not well founded; baseless. **ill-gotten** gained by wicked or unlawful means. **ill humour** moroseness, irritability. **ill-humoured** bad-tempered. **ill-judged** unwise; badly considered. **ill-mannered** having bad manners; rude. **ill nature** churlishness, unkindness. **ill-natured** churlish, unkind. **ill-naturedly** churlishly. **ill-omened** attended by bad omens. **ill-starred** unlucky; destined to failure. **ill success** partial or complete failure. **ill temper** moroseness. **ill-tempered** morose, irritable. **ill-timed** done or occurring at an inappropriate time. **ill-treat** (or **-use**) treat badly; abuse. **ill-treatment** (or **ill use**) abuse; bad treatment. **ill will** bad feeling; animosity. **an ill wind** an unfavourable or untoward circumstance (with ref. to the proverb *it's an ill wind that blows nobody good*). **speak ill of** say something unfavourable about. [ME f. ON *illr*, of unkn. orig.]

■ *adj.* **1** sick, unwell, not well, unhealthy, ailing, indisposed, infirm, poorly, bad, in bad health, in a bad way, the worse for wear, diseased, afflicted, out of sorts, off colour, weak, sickly, invalid(ed), valetudinarian, nauseous, *colloq.* seedy, under the weather, *Austral. colloq.* not too clever, *Brit. colloq.* a bit off, ropy. **2** bad, unsound, poor, mediocre, weak, frail, delicate, unstable, disordered. **3** bad, adverse, unfavourable, unpropitious, untoward, unpromising, inauspicious, unlucky, unfortunate, miserable, wretched, disastrous; disturbing, ominous, sinister, unwholesome. **4** harmful, hurtful, injurious, detrimental, damaging, noxious, pernicious, deleterious, dangerous, destructive, bad, baleful, unfavourable, adverse, *literary* nocuous, *poet.* baneful; disastrous, catastrophic, ruinous, cataclysmic. **5** hostile, unfriendly, antagonistic, belligerent, malevolent, malicious, unkind, harsh, cruel. **6** bad, wicked, sinful, evil, iniquitous, nefarious, immoral, depraved, degenerate, vicious, vile, corrupt, wrong. **7** bad, poor, deficient, faulty; inadequate, unskilful, incompetent, inexpert, inept. **8** improper, unseemly, unsuitable, inappropriate. ● *adv.* **1** wrongly, badly, incorrectly, mistakenly, falsely, erroneously, inaccurately, imprecisely; wrongfully, awkwardly, improperly, unfairly, unjustly, unsatisfactorily, poorly, harshly, unkindly, maliciously, malevolently. **2 a** badly, imperfectly, insufficiently, unsatisfactorily, poorly, incompletely, patchily, faultily, defectively. **b** scarcely, hardly, barely, only just, not really; by no means, in no way. **3** badly, adversely, disastrously, unfavourably. ● *n.* **1** harm, damage, injury, hurt, mischief, trouble, misfortune, misery, affliction, pain, distress, woefulness, discomfort, unpleasantness, disaster, catastrophe, cataclysm, calamity, adversity, suffering, ruin, destruction, *archaic or literary* woe. **2** wrong, injustice, inequity, evil, sin, transgression, abuse. □ **do an ill turn to** see HARM *v.* **ill-advised 1** foolish, imprudent, foolhardy, unwise, reckless, rash, hasty, impetuous, incautious, short-sighted, improvident, ignorant, ill-informed, uninformed. **2** ill-considered, ill-judged, injudicious, misguided, unwise, imprudent, inadvisable, inappropriate, impolitic, wrong-headed, thoughtless, indiscreet, inexpedient. **ill-advisedly** foolishly, imprudently, unwisely, injudiciously, misguidedly, impetuously, rashly, recklessly, hastily, heedlessly, thoughtlessly, mindlessly. **ill-affected** (*ill-affected towards*) ill-disposed towards, antipathetic to, unsympathetic towards, opposed to, resistant to, against, anti. **ill-assorted** ill-matched, mismated, mismatched, incompatible, incongruous. **ill at ease** uncomfortable, embarrassed, uneasy, edgy, on edge, fidgety, nervous, anxious, disturbed, distressed, troubled, awkward, unsure, uncertain. **ill blood** see *ill will* below. **ill-bred** see *ill-mannered* below. **ill breeding** see INCIVILITY. **ill-considered** see *ill-advised* 2 above. **ill-defined** see INDEFINITE 1. **ill-disposed 1** see *ill-affected* above. **2** see EVIL *adj.* 1. **ill-equipped** see UNQUALIFIED 1. **ill-fated** see INAUSPICIOUS 1. **ill feeling** see *ill will* below. **ill-founded** groundless, baseless, without foundation, unsupported, unsubstantiated, empty, unjustified, unproven, uncorroborated, unsound, erroneous, invalid. **ill-gotten** see UNLAWFUL. **ill humour** ill temper, irritability, irascibility, crossness, grumpiness, moodiness, sulkiness, gloominess, sullenness, moroseness, peevishness, churlishness, surliness, petulance, huffiness; volatility. **ill-humoured** see IRRITABLE 1. **ill-judged** see *ill-advised* 2 above. **ill-mannered** rude, discourteous, impolite, ill-bred, uncouth, boorish, uncivil, disrespectful, uncourtly, ungallant, ungracious, indecorous, ungentlemanly, unladylike, impudent, insolent, insulting, impertinent, brazen. **ill nature** see *ill humour* above. **ill-natured** see SURLY. **ill-naturedly** churlishly, irritably, bad-temperedly, surlily, meanly, crustily, sourly, peevishly, querulously, testily, grumpily, sulkily, rudely, uncivilly, acidly, caustically, *colloq.* grouchily. **ill-omened** see INAUSPICIOUS. **ill-starred** see INAUSPICIOUS 1. **ill temper** see *ill humour* above. **ill-tempered** see IRRITABLE 1. **ill-timed** see INOPPORTUNE. **ill-treat** (or **-use**) mistreat, maltreat, abuse, persecute, wrong, harm, hurt, injure, beat up, batter, knock about *or* around, *colloq.* manhandle; misuse, mishandle. **ill-treatment** (or **ill use**) see ABUSE *n.* 4. **ill will** bad *or* ill feeling, resentment, bad *or* ill blood, dislike, animosity, hatred, hate, loathing, abhorrence, detestation, malevolence, malice, hostility, enmity, animus, antipathy, aversion, rancour, acrimony, spite, venom, vitriol, acerbity. **an ill wind** misfortune, adversity, mishap, calamity, catastrophe, disaster, tragedy, blow, shock, reverse, stroke of bad luck. **speak ill of** see VILIFY.

illation /iláysh'n/ *n.* **1** a deduction or conclusion. **2** a thing deduced. [L *illatio* f. *illatus* past part. of *inferre* INFER]

illative /iláytiv, íllətiv/ *adj.* **1 a** (of a word) stating or introducing an inference. **b** inferential. **2** *Gram.* (of a case) denoting motion into. □□ **illatively** *adv.* [L *illativus* (as ILLATION)]

illegal /ileeg'l/ *adj.* **1** not legal. **2** contrary to law. □□ **illegality** /-gálliti/ *n.* (*pl.* **-ies**). **illegally** *adv.* [F *illégal* or med.L *illegalis* (as IN-[1], LEGAL)]

■ **1** unlawful, unofficial, unsanctioned, unlicensed, unauthorized, unconstitutional, *attrib.* wildcat. **2** unlawful, illegitimate, criminal, felonious, illicit, outlawed, prohibited, banned, interdicted, forbidden, proscribed, wrong(ful), *verboten*, actionable, *Austral.* & *NZ sl.* sly; see also CROOKED 2, LAWLESS 2. □□ **illegality** unlawfulness, illegitimacy, criminality, illicitness. **illegally** unlawfully, criminally, illegitimately, feloniously, illicitly, wrongfully.

illegible /iléjib'l/ *adj.* not legible. □□ **illegibility** /-bílliti/ *n.* **illegibly** *adv.*

■ unreadable, unintelligible, indecipherable, indistinct, unclear; scrawled, scrawly, scribbled, scribbly.

illegitimate *adj.*, *n.*, & *v.* ● *adj.* /illijíttimət/ **1** (of a child) born of parents not married to each other. **2** not authorized by law; unlawful. **3** improper. **4** wrongly inferred. **5** physiologically abnormal. ● *n.* /illijíttimət/ a person whose position is illegitimate, esp. by birth. ● *v.tr.* /illijíttimayt/ declare or pronounce illegitimate. □□ **illegitimacy** *n.* **illegitimately** *adv.* [LL *illegitimus*, after LEGITIMATE]

■ *adj.* **1** bastard, natural, fatherless, unfathered, adulterine, misbegotten, born out of wedlock, born on the wrong side of the blanket. **2** see ILLEGAL. **3** irregular, improper, incorrect, non-standard, invalid, unauthorized, spurious. **5** see ABNORMAL. ● *n.* bastard, love-child, natural child.

illiberal /ilíbbərəl/ *adj.* **1** intolerant, narrow-minded. **2** without liberal culture. **3** not generous; stingy. **4** vulgar, sordid. □□ **illiberality** /-rálliti/ *n.* (*pl.* **-ies**). **illiberally** *adv.* [F *illibéral* f. L *illiberalis* mean, sordid (as IN-[1], LIBERAL)]

■ **1** see INTOLERANT. **3** see SELFISH. □□ **illiberality** see *intolerance* (INTOLERANT).

illicit /ilíssit/ *adj.* **1** unlawful, forbidden (*illicit dealings*). **2** secret, furtive (*an illicit cigarette*). □□ **illicitly** *adv.* **illicitness** *n.*

■ **1** see ILLEGAL 2. **2** underhand, underhanded, secret, furtive, clandestine, back-door, sneaky, sly, shady, *Austral.* & *NZ sl.* sly. □□ **illicitly** see *illegally* (ILLEGAL), *secretly* (SECRET).

illimitable /ilímmitəb'l/ *adj.* limitless. □□ **illimitability** /-bílliti/ *n.* **illimitableness** *n.* **illimitably** *adv.* [LL *illimitatus* f. L *limitatus* (as IN-[1], L *limitatus* past part. of *limitare* LIMIT)]
▪ see LIMITLESS.

illiquid /ilíkwid/ *adj.* (of assets) not easily converted into cash. □□ **illiquidity** /-kwídditi/ *n.*

illiterate /ilíttərət/ *adj.* & *n.* ● *adj.* **1** unable to read. **2** uneducated. ● *n.* an illiterate person. □□ **illiteracy** *n.* **illiterately** *adv.* **illiterateness** *n.* [L *illitteratus* (as IN-[1], *litteratus* LITERATE)]
▪ *adj.* **1** unlettered. **2** uneducated, unschooled, untaught, benighted, ignorant, unenlightened. ● *n.* non-reader; lowbrow, ignoramus. □□ **illiteracy, illiterateness** ignorance, unawareness, inexperience, lack of education.

illness /ílniss/ *n.* **1** a disease, ailment, or malady. **2** the state of being ill.
▪ **1** disease, sickness, disorder, infection, affliction, ailment, malady, complaint, condition, trouble, infirmity, disability, indisposition, affection, *sl.* bug; malaise, queasiness, nausea. **2** ill health, bad health, valetudinarianism, indisposition, sickness, infirmity, disability.

illogical /ilójik'l/ *adj.* devoid of or contrary to logic. □□ **illogicality** /-kálliti/ *n.* (*pl.* **-ies**). **illogically** *adv.*
▪ see UNREASONABLE 2. □□ **illogicality** see ABSURDITY 1, 2.

illude /ilóod, ilyóod/ *v.tr. literary* trick or deceive. [ME, = mock, f. L *illudere* (as ILLUSION)]

illume /ilóom, ilyóom/ *v.tr. poet.* light up; make bright. [shortening of ILLUMINE]

illuminant /ilóominənt, ilyóo-/ *n.* & *adj.* ● *n.* a means of illumination. ● *adj.* serving to illuminate. □□ **illuminance** *n.* [L *illuminant-* part. stem of *illuminare* ILLUMINATE]

illuminate /ilóominayt, ilyóo-/ *v.tr.* **1** light up; make bright. **2** decorate (buildings etc.) with lights as a sign of festivity. **3** decorate (an initial letter, a manuscript, etc.) with gold, silver, or brilliant colours. **4** help to explain (a subject etc.). **5** enlighten spiritually or intellectually. **6** shed lustre on. □□ **illuminating** *adj.* **illuminatingly** *adv.* **illumination** /-náysh'n/ *n.* **illuminative** /-naytiv, -nətiv/ *adj.* **illuminator** *n.* [L *illuminare* (as IN-[2], *lumen luminis* light)]
▪ **1** light (up), brighten, lighten, make bright *or* light, throw *or* cast light on *or* upon, inflame, *literary* illumine, *poet.* illume. **2** emblazon, deck out, light up, decorate, bedeck, make resplendent. **3** decorate, adorn, embellish, enrich, ornament, emblazon, rubricate, illustrate, highlight. **4** clarify, throw *or* cast *or* shed light on *or* upon, elucidate, explain, explicate, make plain, reveal, illustrate, *rhet. or poet.* enlighten. **5** see ENLIGHTEN 1a, 3b. **6** add lustre to, shed lustre on, enhance, enrich, highlight. □□ **illumination** lighting, light, brightness, radiance, luminosity, incandescence, fluorescence, phosphorescence; enlightenment, insight, revelation, edification, instruction, awareness, understanding, clarification, information, learning. **illuminator** illustrator, rubricator, decorator, embellisher, enhancer; clarifier, explainer, explicator, elucidator.

illuminati /ilóominaáti, ilyóo-/ *n.pl.* **1** persons claiming to possess special knowledge or enlightenment. **2** (**Illuminati**) *hist.* any of various intellectual movements or societies of illuminati. □□ **illuminism** /ilóominiz'm, ilyóo-/ *n.* **illuminist** /ilóominist, ilyóo-/ *n.* [pl. of L *illuminatus* or It. *illuminato* past part. (as ILLUMINATE)]

illumine /ilóomin, ilyóo-/ *v.tr. literary* **1** light up; make bright. **2** enlighten spiritually. [ME f. OF *illuminer* f. L (as ILLUMINATE)]

illusion /ilóozh'n, ilyóo-/ *n.* **1** deception, delusion. **2** a misapprehension of the true state of affairs. **3 a** the faulty perception of an external object. **b** an instance of this. **4** a figment of the imagination. **5** = *optical illusion.* □ **be under the illusion** (foll. by *that* + clause) believe mistakenly. □□ **illusional** *adj.* [ME f. F f. L *illusio -onis* f. *illudere* mock (as IN-[2], *ludere lus-* play)]
▪ **1** deception, deceiving, deceit, trick, trickery, *archaic* sleight (of hand); delusion, deluding, fancy. **2** misconception, misapprehension, misunderstanding, misjudgement, misbelief, fallacy, error, miscalculation, mistake, mistaken *or* false impression. **3** hallucination, delusion, misconstruction, mistake, error. **4** fantasy, hallucination, phantasm, phantom, chimera, phantasmagoria, mirage, day-dream, aberration, vision, spectre, figment of the imagination, will-o'-the-wisp, ignis fatuus. **5** mirage, trick of the light, *trompe-l'oeil.* □ **be under the illusion** labour under the illusion *or* misapprehension, fancy, be convinced, convince oneself, believe, take it. □□ **illusional** see ILLUSORY.

illusionist /ilóozhənist, ilyóo-/ *n.* a person who produces illusions; a conjuror. □□ **illusionism** *n.* **illusionistic** /-nístik/ *adj.*

illusive /ilóossiv, ilyóo-/ *adj.* = ILLUSORY. [med.L *illusivus* (as ILLUSION)]

illusory /ilóossəri, ilyóo-/ *adj.* **1** deceptive (esp. as regards value or content). **2** having the character of an illusion. □□ **illusorily** *adv.* **illusoriness** *n.* [eccl.L *illusorius* (as ILLUSION)]
▪ deceptive, misleading, illusive, delusive, illusional, beguiling, tricky, specious, seeming, apparent; hallucinatory, fanciful, fancied, imaginary, imagined, fictional, unreal, untrue, fallacious, false. □□ **illusorily** deceptively, delusively, misleadingly, beguilingly, speciously, seemingly, apparently; see also *imaginarily* (IMAGINARY).

illustrate /íllәstrayt/ *v.tr.* **1 a** provide (a book, newspaper, etc.) with pictures. **b** elucidate (a description etc.) by drawings or pictures. **2** serve as an example of. **3** explain or make clear, esp. by examples. [L *illustrare* (as IN-[2], *lustrare* light up)]
▪ **1 b** see ILLUMINATE 4. **2** exemplify, typify, represent, epitomize, instance, instantiate, embody, personify. **3** explain, explicate, elucidate, clarify, make plain; illuminate, shed *or* throw *or* cast light on *or* upon.

illustration /íllәstráysh'n/ *n.* **1** a drawing or picture illustrating a book, magazine article, etc. **2** an example serving to elucidate. **3** the act or an instance of illustrating. □□ **illustrational** *adj.* [ME f. OF f. L *illustratio -onis* (as ILLUSTRATE)]
▪ **1** picture, (line) drawing, painting, sketch, diagram, image, figure, cartoon, artwork, design, graphic, *Computing* icon; engraving, etching, cut, woodcut, linocut, photogravure, duotone, half-tone, print, plate; vignette, frontispiece. **2** example, case (in point), instance, exemplification; sample, specimen, exemplar. **3** depiction, representation, illumination; explanation, clarification, explication, elucidation.

illustrative /íllәstrәtiv/ *adj.* (often foll. by *of*) serving as an explanation or example. □□ **illustratively** *adv.*
▪ see EXEMPLARY 3.

illustrator /íllәstraytәr/ *n.* a person who makes illustrations, esp. for magazines, books, advertising copy, etc.

illustrious /ilússtriәss/ *adj.* distinguished, renowned. □□ **illustriously** *adv.* **illustriousness** *n.* [L *illustris* (as ILLUSTRATE)]
▪ distinguished, famous, noted, renowned, famed, eminent, well-known, prominent, important, notable, respected, esteemed, great, venerable, honoured, acclaimed, celebrated, star, *colloq.* legendary.

Illyrian /ilírriәn/ *adj.* & *n.* ● *adj.* **1** of or relating to Illyria on the Balkan coast of the Adriatic (corresponding to parts of modern Albania and the former Yugoslavia). **2** of the language-group represented by modern Albanian. ● *n.* **1** a native of Illyria; a person of Illyrian descent. **2 a** the language of Illyria. **b** the language-group represented by modern Albanian.

illywhacker /ílliwakkәr/ *n. Austral. sl.* a professional trickster. [20th c.: orig. unkn.]

■ see *swindler* (SWINDLE).

ilmenite /ílmənīt/ *n.* a black ore of titanium. [*Ilmen* mountains in the Urals]

ILO *abbr.* International Labour Organization.

ILR *abbr.* Independent Local Radio.

-ily /ili/ *suffix* forming adverbs corresponding to adjectives in -*y* (see -Y[1], -LY[2]).

I'm /īm/ *contr.* I am.

im- /im/ *prefix* assim. form of IN-[1], IN-[2] before *b*, *m*, *p*.

image /ímmij/ *n.* & *v.* ● *n.* **1** a representation of the external form of an object, e.g. a statue (esp. of a saint etc. as an object of veneration). **2** the character or reputation of a person or thing as generally perceived. **3** an optical appearance or counterpart produced by light or other radiation from an object reflected in a mirror, refracted through a lens, etc. **4** semblance, likeness (*God created man in His own image*). **5** a person or thing that closely resembles another (*is the image of his father*). **6** a typical example. **7** a simile or metaphor. **8 a** a mental representation. **b** an idea or conception. **9** *Math.* a set formed by mapping from another set. ● *v.tr.* **1** make an image of; portray. **2** reflect, mirror. **3** describe or imagine vividly. **4** typify. ▫▫ **imageable** *adj.* **imageless** *adj.* [ME f. OF f. L *imago -ginis*, rel. to IMITATE]

■ *n.* **1** representation, picture, sculpture, statue, effigy, figure, portrait, icon; idol, graven image, fetish, totem, *NZ* tiki. **2** character, reputation, (public) face, persona, appearance, profile, aspect. **3** reflection, impression, picture, simulacrum. **4** likeness, semblance, appearance, aspect, guise; form, shape, mould, cast. **5** double, twin, duplicate, copy, counterpart, facsimile, replica, analogue, mirror image, enantiomorph, *doppelgänger*, clone, simulacrum, (dead) ringer, *colloq.* spitting image; chip off the old block. **6** example, epitome, model, type, archetype, paradigm; embodiment, incarnation, personification, materialization. **7** figure (of speech), trope, metaphor, simile, *literary* conceit; word-painting, word-picture. **8** impression, concept, conception, perception, thought, idea, notion, vision, (mental) picture, *Psychol.* imago. ● *v.* **1** see PORTRAY 1, 2. **2** see REFLECT 1a. **3** picture, depict, portray, visualize, envisage, envision, conceive of, dream up, imagine, see in one's mind's eye. **4** see TYPIFY.

imagery /ímmijəri/ *n.* **1** figurative illustration, esp. as used by an author for particular effects. **2** images collectively. **3** statuary, carving. **4** mental images collectively. [ME f. OF *imagerie* (as IMAGE)]

■ **1** figurativeness, word-painting, symbolism; metaphor(s), simile(s), conceit(s), figures (of speech). **2** artwork, graphics, design, illustration, representation; pictures, visuals, paintings, drawings, illustrations, sketches, figures, diagrams, cartoons. **4** (visual) perception, visualization; ideas, (mental) images, (mental) pictures, impressions, concepts, conceptions, notions, fancies, thoughts.

imaginable /imájinəb'l/ *adj.* that can be imagined (*the greatest difficulty imaginable*). ▫▫ **imaginably** *adv.* [ME f. LL *imaginabilis* (as IMAGINE)]

■ see *thinkable* (THINK).

imaginal /imájin'l/ *adj.* **1** of an image or images. **2** *Zool.* of an imago. [L *imago imagin-*: see IMAGE]

imaginary /imájinəri/ *adj.* **1** existing only in the imagination. **2** *Math.* being the square root of a negative quantity, and plotted graphically in a direction usu. perpendicular to the axis of real quantities (see REAL[1]). ▫▫ **imaginarily** *adv.* [ME f. L *imaginarius* (as IMAGE)]

■ **1** fictitious, fictive, fanciful, fancied, imagined, made-up, unreal, *colloq.* pretend; untrue, non-existent, false, fallacious, notional, abstract, illusory, illusive, chimerical, visionary, mythical, mythic, fabulous, fantastic, legendary, mythological. ▫▫ **imaginarily** fictitiously, fancifully, unreally, illusorily, fallaciously, falsely.

imagination /imájináysh'n/ *n.* **1** a mental faculty forming images or concepts of external objects not present to the senses. **2** the ability of the mind to be creative or resourceful. **3** the process of imagining. [ME f. OF f. L *imaginatio -onis* (as IMAGINE)]

■ **1** fantasy, mind's eye, fancy. **2** imaginativeness, creativity, creativeness, creative power(s), inventiveness, invention, innovation, innovativeness, ingenuity, insight, inspiration, vision; resourcefulness, lateral thinking, originality, unorthodoxy, individuality, nonconformity. **3** visualization, conception, vision.

imaginative /imájinətiv/ *adj.* **1** having or showing in a high degree the faculty of imagination. **2** given to using the imagination. ▫▫ **imaginatively** *adv.* **imaginativeness** *n.* [ME f. OF *imaginatif -ive* f. med.L *imaginativus* (as IMAGINE)]

■ **1** creative, original, ingenious, inventive, innovative, inspired, inspiring, insightful, inspirational, enterprising, clever, resourceful. **2** romantic, dreamy, dreaming, fanciful, poetic, poetical, visionary, whimsical. ▫▫ **imaginatively** creatively, originally, ingeniously, inventively, innovatively, enterprisingly, resourcefully; fancifully, fantastically, dreamily, poetically, romantically, whimsically, fictionally. **imaginativeness** see IMAGINATION 2.

imagine /imájin/ *v.tr.* **1 a** form a mental image or concept of. **b** picture to oneself (something non-existent or not present to the senses). **2** (often foll. by *to* + infin.) think or conceive (*imagined them to be soldiers*). **3** guess (*cannot imagine what they are doing*). **4** (often foll. by *that* + clause) suppose; be of the opinion (*I imagine you will need help*). **5** (in *imper.*) as an exclamation of surprise (*just imagine!*). ▫▫ **imaginer** *n.* [ME f. OF *imaginer* f. L *imaginari* (as IMAGE)]

■ **1** picture, envisage, envision, contemplate, ponder, meditate (on), visualize, see (in one's mind's eye), think of, conceive of; think up, conceptualize, create, concoct, devise, invent, dream up, *colloq.* cook up. **2** think, understand, conceive, suppose, believe, assume, suspect, judge, consider, reckon, *formal* deem. **3** guess, conjecture, estimate, hypothesize, speculate, theorize. **4** suppose, expect, believe, think, be of the opinion, opine, consider, gather, surmise, fancy, guess, suspect, reckon, assume, presume, take it, infer, take it for granted *or* as given.

imagines *pl.* of IMAGO.

imaginings /imájiningz/ *n.pl.* fancies, fantasies.

imagism /immijiz'm/ *n.* a movement in early 20th-c. poetry which sought clarity of expression through the use of precise images. ▫▫ **imagist** *n.* **imagistic** /-jístik/ *adj.*

imago /imáygō/ *n.* (*pl.* **-os** or **imagines** /imájineez/) **1** the final and fully developed stage of an insect after all metamorphoses, e.g. a butterfly or beetle. **2** *Psychol.* an idealized mental picture of oneself or others, esp. a parent. [mod.L sense of *imago* IMAGE]

imam /imaám/ *n.* **1** a leader of prayers in a mosque. **2** a title of various Muslim leaders, esp. of one succeeding Muhammad as leader of Islam. ▫▫ **imamate** /-mayt/ *n.* [Arab. *'imām* leader f. *'amma* precede]

imbalance /imbállənss/ *n.* **1** lack of balance. **2** disproportion.

■ **2** see DISPROPORTION.

imbecile /ímbiseel/ *n.* & *adj.* ● *n.* **1** a person of abnormally weak intellect, esp. an adult with a mental age of about five. **2** *colloq.* a stupid person. ● *adj.* mentally weak; stupid, idiotic. ▫▫ **imbecilely** *adv.* **imbecilic** /-síllik/ *adj.* **imbecility** /-sílliti/ *n.* (*pl.* **-ies**). [F *imbécil(l)e* f. L *imbecillus* (as IN-[1], *baculum* stick) orig. in sense 'without supporting staff']

■ *n.* **2** see FOOL[1] *n.* 1. ● *adj.* see STUPID *adj.* 1, 5. ▫▫ **imbecilic** see STUPID *adj.* 1, 5. **imbecility** see *stupidity* (STUPID).

imbed var. of EMBED.

imbibe /imbīb/ *v.tr.* **1** (also *absol.*) drink (esp. alcoholic liquor). **2 a** absorb or assimilate (ideas etc.). **b** absorb (moisture etc.). **3** inhale (air etc.). □□ **imbiber** *n.* **imbibition** /imbibish'n/ *n.* [ME f. L *imbibere* (as IN-[2], *bibere* drink)]

■ **1** see DRINK *v.* 1.

imbricate *v.* & *adj.* ● *v.tr.* & *intr.* /imbrikayt/ arrange (leaves, the scales of a fish, etc.), or be arranged, so as to overlap like roof-tiles. ● *adj.* /imbrikət/ having scales etc. arranged in this way. □□ **imbrication** /-káysh'n/ *n.* [L *imbricare imbricat-* cover with rain-tiles f. *imbrex -icis* rain-tile f. *imber* shower]

■ *v.* see OVERLAP *v.* 1, 2. □□ **imbrication** see OVERLAP *n.*

imbroglio /imbrṓliō/ *n.* (*pl.* **-os**) **1** a confused or complicated situation. **2** a confused heap. [It. *imbrogliare* confuse (as EMBROIL)]

■ **1** see PREDICAMENT.

imbrue /imbrōō/ *v.tr.* (foll. by *in*, *with*) *literary* stain (one's hand, sword, etc.). [OF *embruer* bedabble (as IN-[2], *breu* ult. f. Gmc, rel. to BROTH)]

imbue /imbyōō/ *v.tr.* (**imbues, imbued, imbuing**) (often foll. by *with*) **1** inspire or permeate (with feelings, opinions, or qualities). **2** saturate. **3** dye. [orig. as past part., f. F *imbu* or L *imbutus* f. *imbuere* moisten]

■ **1** see PERMEATE. **2** see SATURATE 1, 6.

I.Mech.E. *abbr.* (in the UK) Institution of Mechanical Engineers.

IMF *abbr.* International Monetary Fund.

imide /immīd/ *n. Chem.* an organic compound containing the group (-CO.NH.CO.-) formed by replacing two of the hydrogen atoms in ammonia by carbonyl groups. [orig. F: arbitrary alt. of AMIDE]

I.Min.E. *abbr.* (in the UK) Institution of Mining Engineers.

imine /immeen/ *n. Chem.* a compound containing the group (-NH-) formed by replacing two of the hydrogen atoms in ammonia by other groups. [G *Imin* arbitrary alt. of *Amin* AMINE]

imitate /immitayt/ *v.tr.* **1** follow the example of; copy the action(s) of. **2** mimic. **3** make a copy of; reproduce. **4** be (consciously or not) like. □□ **imitable** *adj.* **imitator** *n.* [L *imitari imitat-*, rel. to *imago* IMAGE]

■ **1** emulate, copy, match, parallel, echo, mirror, reflect, pattern oneself on *or* after, model oneself on *or* after; take after, follow *or* tread in a person's footsteps, take a leaf out of a person's book. **2** mimic, copy, affect, ape, parrot, monkey, emulate, simulate, impersonate, do an impression of; parody, satirize, burlesque, caricature, travesty, mock, *colloq.* spoof, take off, *Brit. colloq.* send up. **3** copy, reproduce, duplicate, replicate, clone; counterfeit, fake, forge, simulate. **4** be like, mirror, reflect, match, take after, resemble, compare with, go with, accord with, coordinate with, correspond with. □□ **imitable** copiable, easy to copy, easily copied, reproducible, duplicable, replicable, forgeable; easy to impersonate, open to parody, mockable; matchable, comparable. **imitator** emulator, copier, simulator; forger, counterfeiter, faker; see also MIMIC *n.*

imitation /immitáysh'n/ *n.* & *adj.* ● *n.* **1** the act or an instance of imitating or being imitated. **2** a copy. **3** *Mus.* the repetition of a phrase etc., usu. at a different pitch, in another part or voice. ● *adj.* made in imitation of something genuine; counterfeit, fake (*imitation leather*). [F *imitation* or L *imitatio* (as IMITATE)]

■ *n.* **1** reproduction, duplication, replication, simulation, mimicry, apery, emulation, impersonation, impression; parody, satirization, burlesque, caricature, mockery, travesty, *colloq.* take-off, *Brit. colloq.* send-up. **2** copy, replica, replication, reproduction, simulation, dummy, facsimile, duplicate, duplication, simulacrum; fake, forgery, counterfeit. ● *adj.* counterfeit, fake, synthetic, artificial, simulated, reproduction, factitious, man-made, sham, ersatz, mock, bogus, *colloq.* phoney.

imitative /immitətiv/ *adj.* **1** (often foll. by *of*) imitating; following a model or example. **2** counterfeit. **3** of a word: **a** that reproduces a natural sound (e.g. *fizz*). **b** whose sound is thought to correspond to the appearance etc. of the object or action described (e.g. *blob*). □ **imitative arts** painting and sculpture. □□ **imitatively** *adv.* **imitativeness** *n.* [LL *imitativus* (as IMITATE)]

■ **2** see COUNTERFEIT *adj.* 2.

immaculate /imákyoolət/ *adj.* **1** pure, spotless; perfectly clean or neat and tidy. **2** perfectly or extremely well executed (*an immaculate performance*). **3** free from fault; innocent. **4** *Biol.* not spotted. □ **Immaculate Conception** *RC Ch.* the doctrine that God preserved the Virgin Mary from the taint of original sin from the moment she was conceived. □□ **immaculacy** *n.* **immaculately** *adv.* **immaculateness** *n.* [ME f. L *immaculatus* (as IN-[1], *maculatus* f. *macula* spot)]

■ **1** spotless, stainless, unblemished, pure, clean, untarnished, unsullied, unsoiled, untainted, unblemished, pristine, snow-white, spick and span, tidy, neat, dapper, spruce; smart, trim, well-groomed. **2** faultless, flawless, perfect, errorless, unerring, impeccable; definitive, authoritative, infallible, irreproachable, consummate; exemplary; accurate, correct. **3** pure, faultless, innocent, blameless, sinless, impeccable, irreproachable, guileless, virtuous; virginal, virgin, intact, chaste, maidenly, vestal; pristine, undefiled, untainted, uncorrupted, unspoiled, unblemished, stainless, unadulterated.

immanent /immənənt/ *adj.* **1** (often foll. by *in*) indwelling, inherent. **2** (of the supreme being) permanently pervading the universe (opp. TRANSCENDENT). □□ **immanence** *n.* **immanency** *n.* **immanentism** *n.* **immanentist** *n.* [LL *immanēre* (as IN-[2], *manēre* remain)]

■ **1** see INHERENT 1.

immaterial /imməteeriəl/ *adj.* **1** of no essential consequence; unimportant. **2** not material; incorporeal. □□ **immateriality** /-riálliti/ *n.* **immaterialize** *v.tr.* (also **-ise**). **immaterially** *adv.* [ME f. LL *immaterialis* (as IN-[1], MATERIAL)]

■ **1** unimportant, inconsequential, insignificant, nugatory, trivial, trifling, petty, paltry, negligible, minor, slight, flimsy, light, unessential, inessential, non-essential, of little account *or* value, *colloq.* footling, piffling, piddling. **2** airy, incorporeal, disembodied, discarnate, ethereal, ephemeral, evanescent, insubstantial, unsubstantial, impalpable, intangible; metaphysical, spiritual, transcendental, unearthly, supernatural, extramundane, other-worldly.

immaterialism /imməteeriəliz'm/ *n.* the doctrine that matter has no objective existence. □□ **immaterialist** *n.*

immature /imməty**oo**r/ *adj.* **1** not mature or fully developed. **2** lacking emotional or intellectual development. **3** unripe. □□ **immaturely** *adv.* **immaturity** *n.* [L *immaturus* (as IN-[1], MATURE)]

■ **1** undeveloped, pubescent, youthful, young, juvenile, teenage, teenaged; rudimentary, half-grown, unformed, unfledged, fledgling, budding, embryonic; unfinished, incomplete, imperfect, untried, maturing, raw, crude. **2** babyish, childish, childlike, puerile, juvenile, green, callow, unsophisticated, naïve, inexperienced, (still) wet behind the ears, jejune, innocent, guileless, unfledged, fresh, tender. **3** unripe, unripened, undeveloped, green; unready, early, too early, unseasonable. □□ **immaturity** see YOUTH 1, INEXPERIENCE.

immeasurable /imézhərəb'l/ *adj.* not measurable; immense. □□ **immeasurability** /-bílliti/ *n.* **immeasurableness** *n.* **immeasurably** *adv.*

■ measureless, limitless, illimitable, indeterminable, boundless, unbounded, unlimited, inestimable, unfathomable, infinite, endless, never-ending, interminable, innumerable, unmeasurable, uncountable, incalculable, uncounted, untold, numberless; vast, immense, huge, great, enormous, giant, gigantic, massive, tremendous, colossal, titanic; see also GREAT 1a.

immediate /imeédiət/ *adj.* **1** occurring or done at once or without delay (*an immediate reply*). **2** nearest, next; not separated by others (*the immediate vicinity*; *the immediate* *future*; *my immediate neighbour*). **3** most pressing or urgent; of current concern (*our immediate concern was to get him to hospital*). **4** (of a relation or action) having direct effect; without an intervening medium or agency (*the immediate cause of death*). **5** (of knowledge, reactions, etc.) intuitive, gained or exhibited without reasoning. □□ **immediacy** *n.* **immediateness** *n.* [ME f. F *immédiat* or LL *immediatus* (as IN-¹, MEDIATE)]

■ **1** instantaneous, instant, prompt, swift, rapid, speedy, quick, express; unhesitating, spontaneous, abrupt, sudden. **2** nearest, next, closest, adjacent, proximate, near, nearby, close, imminent. **3** pressing, urgent, instant, critical, compelling, vital, important, serious; existing, present, current, actual. **4** direct, proximate. **5** intuitive, direct, basic, spontaneous, instinctive, visceral, emotional, irrational, unreasoned, unthinking, unhesitating, involuntary, mechanical, automatic, reflex, knee-jerk, gut.

immediately /imeédiətli/ *adv.* & *conj.* ● *adv.* **1** without pause or delay. **2** without intermediary. ● *conj.* as soon as.

■ *adv.* **1** at once, without delay, instantly, instantaneously, promptly, right away, now, right now, here and now, this (very) instant, this second, this minute, forthwith, directly, straight away, unhesitatingly, without hesitation, then and there, there and then, on the spot, without more ado, post-haste, *tout de suite*, in a wink, in a twinkle, in the twinkling of an eye, in two shakes of a lamb's *or* dog's tail, *US* in short order; *archaic or joc.* instanter, *colloq.* p.d.q., before you can say Jack Robinson *or* knife, pronto, in a jiffy, lickety-split. **2** direct(ly); closely, intimately; at first hand, from the horse's mouth. ● *conj.* as soon as, the (very) moment *or* second *or* instant *or* minute (that), once, when, *colloq.* directly.

immedicable /iméddikəb'l/ *adj.* that cannot be healed or cured. □□ **immedicably** *adv.* [L *immedicabilis* (as IN-¹, MEDICABLE)]

immemorial /immimóriəl/ *adj.* **1** ancient beyond memory or record. **2** very old. □□ **immemorially** *adv.* [med.L *immemorialis* (as IN-¹, MEMORIAL)]

immense /iménss/ *adj.* **1** immeasurably large or great; huge. **2** very great; considerable (*made an immense difference*). **3** *colloq.* very good. □□ **immenseness** *n.* **immensity** *n.* [ME f. F f. L *immensus* immeasurable (as IN-¹, *mensus* past part. of *metiri* measure)]

■ **1** enormous, extensive, vast, huge, massive, voluminous, tremendous, staggering, stupendous, mammoth, monstrous, gargantuan, colossal, gigantic, giant, titanic, Cyclopean, elephantine, *colloq.* jumbo, *sl.* humongous; see also GREAT 1a. **2** see CONSIDERABLE 1, 2. **3** see FANTASTIC 1.

immensely /iménsli/ *adv.* **1** very much (*enjoyed myself immensely*). **2** to an immense degree.

■ **1** see HIGHLY 1.

immerse /iméss/ *v.tr.* **1 a** (often foll. by *in*) dip, plunge. **b** cause (a person) to be completely under water. **2** (often *refl.* or in *passive*; often foll. by *in*) absorb or involve deeply. **3** (often foll. by *in*) bury, embed. [L *immergere* (as IN-², *mergere mers-* dip)]

■ **1** plunge, sink, submerge, dip, dunk, duck, douse, souse, steep, imbue, soak, bathe, drown, flood, swamp. **2** absorb, involve, engross, engage, occupy, plunge, sink, submerge, bury; (*immersed*) preoccupied, wrapped up, engrossed, involved, absorbed. **3** bury, embed, enclose, envelop, cover (up *or* over).

immersion /imérsh'n/ *n.* **1** the act or an instance of immersing; the process of being immersed. **2** baptism by immersing the whole person in water. **3** mental absorption. **4** *Astron.* the disappearance of a celestial body behind another or in its shadow. □ **immersion heater** an electric heater designed for direct immersion in a liquid to be heated, esp. as a fixture in a hot-water tank. [ME f. LL *immersio* (as IMMERSE)]

■ **1** see PLUNGE *n.*

immigrant /immigrənt/ *n.* & *adj.* ● *n.* a person who immigrates. ● *adj.* **1** immigrating. **2** of or concerning immigrants.

■ *n.* newcomer, incomer, migrant, settler, arrival, *US colloq.* wetback; alien, foreigner, non-native, outlander, outsider. ● *adj.* **1** incoming, immigratory, migrant. **2** (ethnic-)minority, alien, foreign, non-native.

immigrate /immigrayt/ *v.* **1** *intr.* come as a permanent resident to a country other than one's native land. **2** *tr.* bring in (a person) as an immigrant. □□ **immigration** /-gráysh'n/ *n.* **immigratory** *adj.* [L *immigrare* (as IN-², MIGRATE)]

■ **1** see MIGRATE.

imminent /imminənt/ *adj.* **1** (of an event, esp. danger) impending; about to happen. **2** *archaic* overhanging. □□ **imminence** *n.* **imminently** *adv.* [L *imminēre imminent-* overhang, project]

■ **1** impending, looming, threatening, menacing, at hand, immediate, close *or* near at hand, forthcoming, coming, approaching, nearing, drawing near *or* close *or* nigh, in the offing, on the horizon, in the wind, *esp. US* upcoming, *archaic or dial.* nigh. □□ **imminence** forthcomingness, nearness, closeness, immediacy, immediateness; threat, menace. **imminently** threateningly, menacingly; see also SOON *adv.* 1.

immiscible /imíssib'l/ *adj.* (often foll. by *with*) that cannot be mixed. □□ **immiscibility** /-bílliti/ *n.* **immiscibly** *adv.* [LL *immiscibilis* (as IN-¹, MISCIBLE)]

immitigable /imíttigəb'l/ *adj.* that cannot be mitigated. □□ **immitigably** *adv.* [LL *immitigabilis* (as IN-¹, MITIGATE)]

immittance /imítt'nss/ *n. Electr.* admittance or impedance (when not distinguished). [*im*pedance + ad*mittance*]

immixture /imíks-chər/ *n.* **1** the process of mixing up. **2** (often foll. by *in*) being involved.

immobile /imṓbīl/ *adj.* **1** not moving. **2** not able to move or be moved. □□ **immobility** /-bílliti/ *n.* [ME f. OF f. L *immobilis* (as IN-¹, MOBILE)]

■ **1** see STATIC *adj.* **2** see *fixed* (FIX *v.* 20a). □□ **immobility** see *inactivity* (INACTIVE).

immobilize /imṓbilīz/ *v.tr.* (also **-ise**) **1** make or keep immobile. **2** make (a vehicle or troops) incapable of being moved. **3** keep (a limb or patient) restricted in movement for healing purposes. **4** restrict the free movement of. **5** withdraw (coins) from circulation to support banknotes. □□ **immobilization** /-záysh'n/ *n.* **immobilizer** *n.* [F *immobiliser* (as IMMOBILE)]

■ **1** see FREEZE *v.* 6a, ARREST *v.* 2. **2** see INCAPACITATE 1.

immoderate /imóddərət/ *adj.* excessive; lacking moderation. □□ **immoderately** *adv.* **immoderateness** *n.* **immoderation** /-ráysh'n/ *n.* [ME f. L *immoderatus* (as IN-¹, MODERATE)]

■ excessive, extreme, exorbitant, unreasonable, inordinate, extravagant, profligate, intemperate, outrageous, preposterous, exaggerated, overblown, unrestrained, undue, *colloq.* over-the-top. □□ **immoderately** see OVERLY. **immoderateness**, **immoderation** see EXCESS *n.* 4a.

immodest /imóddist/ *adj.* **1** lacking modesty; forward, impudent. **2** lacking due decency. □□ **immodestly** *adv.* **immodesty** *n.* [F *immodeste* or L *immodestus* (as IN-¹, MODEST)]

■ **1** brazen, forward, bold, impudent, impertinent, brash, arrogant, insolent, presumptuous, disrespectful, brassy, as bold as brass, cheeky, *colloq.* fresh. **2** indecent, shameless, shameful, indecorous, undignified, indelicate, improper, wanton, loose, unrestrained, provocative, flaunting, promiscuous, brassy, obscene, lewd, smutty, dirty, lascivious, bawdy, coarse. □□ **immodesty** see PRESUMPTION 1, IMPROPRIETY 1.

immolate /imməlayt/ *v.tr.* **1** kill or offer as a sacrifice. **2** *literary* sacrifice (a valued thing). □□ **immolation** /-láysh'n/ *n.* **immolator** *n.* [L *immolare* sprinkle with sacrificial meal (as IN-², *mola* MEAL²)]

■ **1** see SACRIFICE *v.* 3. **2** see SACRIFICE *v.* 1. □□ **immolation** see SACRIFICE *n.* 1a, 2a.

immoral /imórrəl/ *adj.* **1** not conforming to accepted standards of morality (cf. AMORAL). **2** morally wrong (esp. in sexual matters). **3** depraved, dissolute. □□ **immorality** /ímmərálliti/ *n.* (*pl.* **-ies**). **immorally** *adv.*

■ **1** unacceptable, unethical, unprincipled, reprobate, disgraceful, reprehensible, taboo, indecent, disreputable, indecorous, indelicate. **2** corrupt, bad, wicked, evil, iniquitous, sinful, impure, unprincipled, abandoned, base, wrong, vile, depraved, dissolute, degenerate, reprobate, unregenerate, nefarious, flagitious, villainous, treacherous, unscrupulous, dishonest. **3** depraved, dissolute, unprincipled, debauched, indecent, immodest, wanton, libertine, loose, promiscuous, lecherous, lustful, libidinous, carnal, salacious, lubricious, licentious, lascivious, lewd, obscene, pornographic, dirty, perverted, smutty, filthy, *formal* concupiscent. □□ **immorality** unacceptability, amorality, unprincipledness, reprobation, reprehensibility; see also VICE[1] 1, 2. **immorally** see BADLY 1, FAST[1] *adv.* 5.

immortal /imórt'l/ *adj.* & *n.* ● *adj.* **1 a** living for ever; not mortal. **b** divine. **2** unfading, incorruptible. **3** likely or worthy to be famous for all time. ● *n.* **1 a** an immortal being. **b** (in *pl.*) the gods of antiquity. **2** a person (esp. an author) of enduring fame. **3** (**Immortal**) a member of the French Academy. □□ **immortality** /immortálliti/ *n.* **immortalize** *v.tr.* (also **-ise**). **immortalization** /-līzáysh'n/ *n.* **immortally** *adv.* [ME f. L *immortalis* (as IN-[1], MORTAL)]

■ *adj.* **1 a** undying, eternal, deathless, everlasting, imperishable, never-ending, endless, ceaseless, perpetual, timeless, constant, permanent, indestructible, *rhet.* sempiternal. **b** divine, godlike, deiform; heavenly, celestial, supernal, unearthly, extramundane; spiritual, superhuman, supernatural, transcendent. **2** unfading, perpetual, lasting, constant, imperishable, indestructible, incorruptible, indissoluble, enduring, abiding, perennial, evergreen; stable, steady, immutable, durable, unfaltering, unwavering. **3** famous, glorious, renowned, legendary, celebrated, lauded, honoured; timeless, classic. ● *n.* **1 a** god, goddess, deity, divinity; demigod, demiurge; spirit, numen, angel. **b** (*immortals*) gods, Olympians, *collect.* pantheon; *Rom. Hist.* lares, penates. **2** legend, great, genius, phenomenon, luminary, giant. □□ **immortality** deathlessness, everlastingness, imperishability, endlessness, ceaselessness, perpetuity, timelessness, constancy, permanence, indestructibility, incorruptibility, indissolubility, immutability, durability; divinity, deity, heavenliness, unearthliness, spirituality, transcendence; see also GLORY *n.* 1. **immortalize** make immortal, apotheosize, deify, canonize; exalt, glorify, celebrate, honour, beatify, ennoble, extol. **immortalization** apotheosis, deification, canonization; exaltation, glorification, beatification, extolment. **immortally** eternally, deathlessly, everlastingly, imperishably, endlessly, ceaselessly, perpetually, constantly, permanently, indestructibly, unfadingly, enduringly, unwaveringly; divinely, celestially, supernally, superhumanly, transcendently; timelessly, famously, gloriously, classically.

immortelle /ímmortél/ *n.* a composite flower of papery texture retaining its shape and colour after being dried, esp. a helichrysum. [F, fem. of *immortel* IMMORTAL]

immovable /imoóvəb'l/ *adj.* & *n.* (also **immoveable**) ● *adj.* **1** that cannot be moved. **2** steadfast, unyielding. **3** emotionless. **4** not subject to change (*immovable law*). **5** motionless. **6** *Law* (of property) consisting of land, houses, etc. ● *n.* (in *pl.*) *Law* immovable property. □ **immovable feast** a religious feast-day that occurs on the same date each year. □□ **immovability** /-bílliti/ *n.* **immovableness** *n.* **immovably** *adv.*

■ *adj.* **1** unmovable, fixed, fast, rooted, planted, grounded, anchored, moored, set, riveted, frozen, rigid, stiff, immobile, motionless, stationary, static, stable. **2** steadfast, staunch, unshakeable, unswerving, firm, determined, rigid, unyielding, unbending, unwavering, resolute, unflinching, dogged, stubborn, inflexible, obdurate, adamant, adamantine, stony. **3** emotionless, unemotional, unmoved, unfeeling, impassive, unresponsive, unsympathetic, inexorable, hard-hearted, cold, hard as nails, steely, stony, cold-hearted. **4** unchangeable, immutable, unalterable, changeless, unchanging, invariable, unvarying, incommutable, irreversible, irrevocable, inexorable, inflexible. **5** motionless, unmoving, stationary, static, still, stock-still, at a standstill; jammed, wedged, stuck (fast), solid (as a rock), fixed, tight, stiff.

immune /imyoón/ *adj.* **1 a** (often foll. by *against, from, to*) protected against an infection owing to the presence of specific antibodies, or through inoculation or inherited or acquired resistance. **b** relating to immunity (*immune mechanism*). **2** (foll. by *from, to*) free or exempt from or not subject to (some undesirable factor or circumstance). □ **immune response** the reaction of the body to the introduction into it of an antigen. [ME f. L *immunis* exempt from public service or charge (as IN-[1], *munis* ready for service): sense 1 f. F *immun*]

■ **1 a** inoculated, vaccinated, immunized; resistant, protected, shielded. **2** (*immune to* or *from*) free from, exempt from, safe from, protected from *or* against, proof against, insusceptible *or* unsusceptible to, impervious to, untouched by, unaffected by, unconcerned by; not liable to, excused from, absolved from.

immunity /imyoóniti/ *n.* (*pl.* **-ies**) **1** *Med.* the ability of an organism to resist infection, by means of the presence of circulating antibodies and white blood cells. **2** freedom or exemption from an obligation, penalty, or unfavourable circumstance. [ME f. L *immunitas* (as IMMUNE): sense 1 f. F *immunité*]

■ **1** resistance, insusceptibility, unsusceptibility, protection, safety. **2** freedom, exemption, non-liability, invulnerability, protection, safety, excuse, release, exclusion, privilege, indemnity, amnesty, exoneration, absolution.

immunize /ímyoonīz/ *v.tr.* (also **-ise**) make immune, esp. to infection, usu. by inoculation. □□ **immunization** /-záysh'n/ *n.* **immunizer** *n.*

immuno- /ímyoonō/ *comb. form* immunity to infection.

immunoassay /ímyoonō-ássay/ *n. Biochem.* the determination of the presence or quantity of a substance, esp. a protein, through its properties as an antigen or antibody.

immunochemistry /ímyoonōkémmistri/ *n.* the chemistry of immune systems, esp. in mammalian tissues.

immunodeficiency /ímyoonōdifishənsi/ *n.* a reduction in a person's normal immune defences.

immunogenic /ímyoonōjénnik/ *adj. Biochem.* of, relating to, or possessing the ability to elicit an immune response.

immunoglobulin /ímyoonōglóbyoolin/ *n. Biochem.* any of a group of structurally related proteins which function as antibodies.

immunology /ímyoonólləji/ *n.* the scientific study of immunity. □□ **immunologic** /-nəlójik/ *adj.* **immunological** /-nəlójik'l/ *adj.* **immunologically** /-nəlójikəli/ *adv.* **immunologist** *n.*

immunosuppressed /ímyoonōsəprést/ *adj.* (of an individual) rendered partially or completely unable to react immunologically.

immunosuppression /ímyoonōsəprésh'n/ *n. Biochem.* the partial or complete suppression of the immune response of an individual, esp. to maintain the survival of an organ after a transplant operation. □□ **immunosuppressant** *n.*

immunosuppressive /ímyoonōsəpréssiv/ *adj.* & *n.* ● *adj.* partially or completely suppressing the immune response of an individual. ● *n.* an immunosuppressive drug.

immunotherapy /ímyoonōthérrəpi/ *n. Med.* the prevention or treatment of disease with substances that stimulate the immune response.

immure /imyóor/ *v.tr.* **1** enclose within walls; imprison. **2** *refl.* shut oneself away. ◻◻ **immurement** *n.* [F *emmurer* or med.L *immurare* (as IN-², *murus* wall)]
■ **1** see ENCLOSE 1, 6.

immutable /imyóotəb'l/ *adj.* **1** unchangeable. **2** not subject to variation in different cases. ◻◻ **immutability** /-bílliti/ *n.* **immutably** *adv.* [ME f. L *immutabilis* (as IN-¹, MUTABLE)]
■ **2** see CHANGELESS. ◻◻ **immutability** see FINALITY.

imp /imp/ *n.* & *v.* ● *n.* **1** a mischievous child. **2** a small mischievous devil or sprite. ● *v.tr.* **1** add feathers to (the wing of a falcon) to restore or improve its flight. **2** *archaic* enlarge; add by grafting. [OE *impa, impe* young shoot, scion, *impian* graft: ult. f. Gk *emphutos* implanted, past part. of *emphuō*]
■ *n.* **1** urchin, gamin, gamine, mischief-maker, (little) devil, (little) horror, (young *or* little) monkey, puck, brat, *US* hellion, *archaic* jackanapes, *colloq.* scamp, *Brit. colloq.* pickle, *often joc.* rascal, *joc.* rogue. **2** devil, demon, sprite, elf, gnome, pixie, leprechaun, puck, brownie, fairy, troll, kobold, *literary* fay; evil spirit, hobgoblin, goblin, hob, bogey, gremlin, *archaic* bugbear.

impact *n.* & *v.* ● *n.* /ímpakt/ **1** (often foll. by *on, against*) the action of one body coming forcibly into contact with another. **2** an effect or influence, esp. when strong. ● *v.* /impákt/ **1** *tr.* (often foll. by *in, into*) press or fix firmly. **2** *tr.* (as **impacted** *adj.*) **a** (of a tooth) wedged between another tooth and the jaw. **b** (of a fractured bone) with the parts crushed together. **c** (of faeces) lodged in the intestine. **3** *intr.* **a** (foll. by *against, on*) come forcibly into contact with a (larger) body or surface. **b** (foll. by *on*) have a pronounced effect. ◻◻ **impaction** /impáksh'n/ *n.* [L *impact-* part. stem of *impingere* IMPINGE]
■ *n.* **1** collision, contact, percussion, crash, smash, bump, bang, thump, slam, smack, blow, *colloq.* whack. **2** effect, impression, influence, import, meaning, bearing, force, thrust, weight, burden, brunt, repercussions, result(s), consequence(s). ● *v.* **1** compress, press in, force in, push in, wedge in, ram in *or* down. **2 a** (**impacted**) wedged, wedged in, compressed, forced in, rammed in *or* down. **3b** (*impact on*) affect, influence, modify, alter, change. ◻◻ **impaction** see PRESSURE *n.* 1a, b.

impair /impáir/ *v.tr.* damage or weaken. ◻◻ **impairment** *n.* [ME *empeire* f. OF *empeirier* (as IN-², LL *pejorare* f. L *pejor* worse)]
■ damage, cripple, harm, hurt, injure, spoil, mar, ruin, wreck; weaken, lessen, debilitate, enfeeble, enervate, attenuate. ◻◻ **impairment** damage, harm, injury, marring; weakening, enfeeblement, debilitation, undermining, worsening, deterioration; reduction, decrease, diminution.

impala /impaálə, -pállə/ *n.* (*pl.* same) a small antelope, *Aepyceros melampus*, of S. and E. Africa, capable of long high jumps. [Zulu]

impale /impáyl/ *v.tr.* **1** (foll. by *on, upon, with*) transfix or pierce with a sharp instrument. **2** *Heraldry* combine (two coats of arms) by placing them side by side on one shield separated by a vertical line down the middle. ◻◻ **impalement** *n.* [F *empaler* or med.L *impalare* (as IN-², *palus* stake)]
■ **1** transfix, spear, skewer, spit, spike, stick, run through; stab, pierce, perforate, puncture, prick. ◻◻ **impalement** transfixion; see also PUNCTURE *n.* 1.

impalpable /impálpəb'l/ *adj.* **1** not easily grasped by the mind; intangible. **2** imperceptible to the touch. **3** (of powder) very fine; not containing grains that can be felt. ◻◻ **impalpability** /-bílliti/ *n.* **impalpably** *adv.* [F *impalpable* or LL *impalpabilis* (as IN-¹, PALPABLE)]
■ **1** see INTANGIBLE *adj.* 2. **2** see INSUBSTANTIAL 1.

impanel var. of EMPANEL.

impark /impaárk/ *v.tr.* **1** enclose (animals) in a park. **2** enclose (land) for a park. [ME f. AF *enparker*, OF *emparquer* (as IN-², *parc* PARK)]

impart /impaárt/ *v.tr.* (often foll. by *to*) **1** communicate (news etc.). **2** give a share of (a thing). ◻◻ **impartable** *adj.* **impartation** /ímpaartáysh'n/ *n.* **impartment** *n.* [ME f. OF *impartir* f. L *impartire* (as IN-², *pars* part)]
■ **1** communicate, tell, relate, report, convey, transmit, pass on; reveal, divulge, disclose, confide; mention, intimate, hint, suggest. **2** give, donate, bestow, convey, confer, transfer, grant, cede, afford, award.

impartial /impaársh'l/ *adj.* treating all sides in a dispute etc. equally; unprejudiced, fair. ◻◻ **impartiality** /-shiálliti/ *n.* **impartially** *adv.*
■ equitable, even-handed, neutral, unbiased, objective, uncoloured, unprejudiced, fair, fair-minded, just, true, honest; disinterested, dispassionate, detached, uninvolved. ◻◻ **impartiality** see *objectivity* (OBJECTIVE). **impartially** see FAIRLY 1.

impassable /impaássəb'l/ *adj.* that cannot be traversed. ◻◻ **impassability** /-bílliti/ *n.* **impassableness** *n.* **impassably** *adv.*
■ see DENSE 1, INACCESSIBLE 1.

impasse /ámpass, ím-/ *n.* a position from which progress is impossible; deadlock. [F (as IN-¹, *passer* PASS¹)]
■ deadlock, dead end, stalemate, nonplus, cul-de-sac, blind alley, *US* stand-off, *colloq.* catch-22; corner, dilemma, predicament, double bind, *colloq.* fix, hole; block, blockage, standstill.

impassible /impássib'l/ *adj.* **1** impassive. **2** incapable of feeling or emotion. **3** incapable of suffering injury. **4** *Theol.* not subject to suffering. ◻◻ **impassibility** /-bílliti/ *n.* **impassibleness** *n.* **impassibly** *adv.* [ME f. OF f. eccl.L *impassibilis* (as IN-¹, PASSIBLE)]

impassion /impásh'n/ *v.tr.* fill with passion; arouse emotionally. [It. *impassionare* (as IN-², PASSION)]
■ see INSPIRE 1, 2.

impassioned /impásh'nd/ *adj.* deeply felt; ardent (*an impassioned plea*).
■ passionate, soulful, vehement, heartfelt, earnest, sincere, honest, wholehearted, full-hearted, profound, deep; ardent, intense, animated, fiery, inflamed, glowing, heated, warm, spirited, vigorous, inspired, emotional, stirring, rousing, aroused, fervent, fervid, feverish, fevered, zealous, eager, enthusiastic.

impassive /impássiv/ *adj.* **1 a** deficient in or incapable of feeling emotion. **b** undisturbed by passion; serene. **2** without sensation. **3** not subject to suffering. ◻◻ **impassively** *adv.* **impassiveness** *n.* **impassivity** /-sívviti/ *n.*
■ **1 a** unfeeling, emotionless, unemotional, stolid, callous, stony, impassible, hard-hearted, cold-hearted, cold-blooded, cold, uncaring, unsympathetic, heartless. **b** dispassionate, passionless, unemotional, emotionless, cold, objective, indifferent, detached, nonchalant, insouciant, unconcerned, remote, aloof, reserved, apathetic, cool; serene, calm, unruffled, undisturbed, unmoved, composed, controlled, contained, stoic(al); imperturbable, unimpressionable, phlegmatic, stolid. **2** insensible, insensate, insentient, unfeeling, unconscious, lifeless, dead, inanimate, wooden, mechanical; numb, benumbed, anaesthetized, paralysed, torpid. **3** anaesthetized, numb, benumbed, deadened, frozen, dulled, *Theol.* impassible. ◻◻ **impassiveness, impassivity** see INDIFFERENCE 1.

impasto /impástō/ *n. Art* **1** the process of laying on paint thickly. **2** this technique of painting. [It. *impastare* (as IN-², *pastare* paste)]

impatiens /impáyshi-enz/ *n.* any plant of the genus *Impatiens*, including busy Lizzie and touch-me-not. [mod.L f. IMPATIENT]

impatient /impáysh'nt/ *adj.* **1 a** (often foll. by *at, with*) lacking patience or tolerance. **b** (of an action) showing a lack of patience. **2** (often foll. by *for*, or *to* + infin.) restlessly eager. **3** (foll. by *of*) intolerant. ◻◻ **impatience** *n.* **impatiently** *adv.* [ME f. OF f. L *impatiens* (as IN-¹, PATIENT)]
■ **1 a** curt, short, abrupt, waspish, brusque, snappish, intolerant, *colloq.* uptight; irritable, irascible, testy, quick-tempered, short-tempered, hot-tempered,

querulous, peevish. **b** hasty, precipitate, abrupt, rash, impetuous, unconsidered, cursory, hurried, rushed, headlong. **2** restless, uneasy, nervous, fidgety, agitated, restive, unquiet, fretful, agog, chafing, expectant, *poet.* athirst; (*impatient to*) eager to, anxious to, keen to, itching to, dying to, longing to, yearning to. **3** (*impatient of*) intolerant of, prejudiced against, biased against, unforgiving of, disapproving of. □□ **impatience** curtness, shortness, abruptness, waspishness, brusqueness, snappishness, intolerance; irritability, irascibility, testiness, temper, querulousness, peevishness; haste, hastiness, rashness, impetuosity, precipitateness, cursoriness, hurriedness; restlessness, uneasiness, nervousness, restiveness, fretfulness, expectancy; anxiousness, anxiety, keenness, longing, yearning, desire; prejudice, bias, unforgivingness, disapproval. **impatiently** curtly, shortly, abruptly, waspishly, brusquely, snappishly, intolerantly, irritably, irascibly, testily, querulously, peevishly; hastily, rashly, impetuously, precipitately, cursorily, hurriedly, headlong, in a rush; unforgivingly, disapprovingly; keenly.

impeach /impeéch/ *v.tr.* **1** *Brit.* charge with a crime against the State, esp. treason. **2** *US* charge (the holder of a public office) with misconduct. **3** call in question, disparage (a person's integrity etc.). □□ **impeachable** *adj.* **impeachment** *n.* [ME f. OF *empecher* impede f. LL *impedicare* entangle (as IN-[2], *pedica* fetter f. *pes pedis* foot)]

■ **1, 2** accuse, charge, arraign, indict, incriminate, implicate, inculpate, blame, censure. **3** challenge, call into *or* in question, question, attack, assail, denounce, inveigh against, declaim against, disparage, discredit, impugn, deprecate, belittle, asperse, cast aspersions on, deplore, slander, malign, vilify. □□ **impeachable** chargeable, arraignable, indictable, censurable; questionable, challengeable, assailable, discreditable, impugnable, deplorable. **impeachment** see ACCUSATION, CHALLENGE *n.* 3.

impeccable /impékkəb'l/ *adj.* **1** (of behaviour, performance, etc.) faultless, exemplary. **2** not liable to sin. □□ **impeccability** /-bílliti/ *n.* **impeccably** *adv.* [L *impeccabilis* (as IN-[1], *peccare* sin)]

■ **1** faultless, flawless, perfect, errorless, unerring, exemplary, ideal, consummate, correct, *Brit. colloq.* spot on; proper, spotless, immaculate, unblemished, pure, unimpeachable, blameless. **2** blameless, sinless, pure, immaculate, irreproachable; innocent, chaste, virginal, virtuous, decent, proper.

impecunious /impikyoóniəss/ *adj.* having little or no money. □□ **impecuniosity** /-nióssiti/ *n.* **impecuniousness** *n.* [IN-[1] + obs. *pecunious* having money f. L *pecuniosus* f. *pecunia* money f. *pecu* cattle]

■ see POOR 1. □□ **impecuniosity, impecuniousness** see POVERTY 1.

impedance /impeéd'nss/ *n.* **1** *Electr.* the total effective resistance of an electric circuit etc. to alternating current, arising from ohmic resistance and reactance. **2** an analogous mechanical property. [IMPEDE + -ANCE]

impede /impeéd/ *v.tr.* retard by obstructing; hinder. [L *impedire* shackle the feet of (as IN-[2], *pes* foot)]

■ obstruct, bar, block, thwart, check, hinder, baulk, inhibit, hamper, handicap, encumber, shackle, stymie, check, curb, brake, restrain, retard, slow (down), hold up, delay, foil, confound, frustrate, spike, stop, *archaic or literary* stay.

impediment /impéddimənt/ *n.* **1** a hindrance or obstruction. **2** a defect in speech, e.g. a lisp or stammer. □□ **impedimental** /-ménťl/ *adj.* [ME f. L *impedimentum* (as IMPEDE)]

■ **1** hindrance, obstacle, inhibition, obstruction, bar, barrier, block, check, curb, restraint, encumbrance, restriction, stricture, hitch, snag, bottleneck, hold-up, delay.

impedimenta /impéddiméntə/ *n.pl.* **1** encumbrances. **2** travelling equipment, esp. of an army. [L, pl. of *impedimentum*: see IMPEDIMENT]

■ **2** see PARAPHERNALIA.

impel /impél/ *v.tr.* (**impelled, impelling**) **1** drive, force, or urge into action. **2** drive forward; propel. □□ **impellent** *adj.* & *n.* **impeller** *n.* [ME f. L *impellere* (as IN-[2], *pellere puls-* drive)]

■ **1** see FORCE[1] *v.* 1. **2** see PROPEL 1.

impend /impénd/ *v.intr.* **1** be about to happen. **2** (often foll. by *over*) **a** (of a danger) be threatening. **b** hang; be suspended. □□ **impending** *adj.* [L *impendēre* (as IN-[2], *pendēre* hang)]

■ **1** be imminent, be close *or* near (at hand), be forthcoming, be about to happen, approach, brew, be in view, be in prospect, be in store, be in the offing, be on the horizon, be in the air, be on the cards. **2 a** threaten, loom, menace, lour. **b** hang, overhang, dangle, be suspended, *archaic poet.* depend. □□ **impending** imminent, approaching, close *or* near (at hand), forthcoming, to come, in view, in prospect, in store, in the offing, on the horizon, in the air, on the cards; menacing.

impenetrable /impénnitrəb'l/ *adj.* **1** that cannot be penetrated. **2** inscrutable, unfathomable. **3** inaccessible to ideas, influences, etc. **4** *Physics* (of matter) having the property such that a body is incapable of occupying the same place as another body at the same time. □□ **impenetrability** /-bílliti/ *n.* **impenetrableness** *n.* **impenetrably** *adv.* [ME f. F *impénétrable* f. L *impenetrabilis* (as IN-[1], PENETRATE)]

■ **1** see DENSE 1, *resistant* (RESIST). **2** see INCOMPREHENSIBLE. □□ **impenetrability, impenetrableness** see PERPLEXITY 3.

impenitent /impénnit'nt/ *adj.* not repentant or penitent. □□ **impenitence** *n.* **impenitency** *n.* **impenitently** *adv.* [eccl.L *impaenitens* (as IN-[1], PENITENT)]

■ see UNREPENTANT.

imperative /impérrətiv/ *adj.* & *n.* ● *adj.* **1** urgent. **2** obligatory. **3** commanding, peremptory. **4** *Gram.* (of a mood) expressing a command (e.g. *come here!*). ● *n.* **1** *Gram.* the imperative mood. **2** a command. □□ **imperatival** /impérrətīv'l/ *adj.* **imperatively** *adv.* **imperativeness** *n.* [LL *imperativus* f. *imperare* command (as IN-[2], *parare* make ready)]

■ *adj.* **1** urgent, pressing, exigent; important, compelling, serious, high-priority, vital, essential, *colloq. disp.* crucial. **2** obligatory, mandatory, compulsory, necessary, indispensable, essential, vital, *colloq. disp.* crucial; required, demanded, *de rigueur*. **3** imperious, commanding, magisterial, lordly, high-handed, autocratic, dictatorial, tyrannical, despotic, authoritarian, arbitrary, prescriptive, dogmatic; peremptory, overbearing, domineering, *colloq.* bossy. ● *n.* **2** see COMMAND *n.* 1. □□ **imperativeness** imperiousness, lordliness, authoritarianism, high-handedness, peremptoriness, prescriptiveness, *colloq.* bossiness; see also *urgency* (URGENT), NECESSITY 2, 3.

imperator /impəraátor/ *n. Rom.Hist.* commander (a title conferred under the Republic on a victorious general and under the Empire on the emperor). □□ **imperatorial** /impərətóriəl/ *adj.* [L (as IMPERATIVE)]

imperceptible /impərséptib'l/ *adj.* **1** that cannot be perceived. **2** very slight, gradual, or subtle. □□ **imperceptibility** /-bílliti/ *n.* **imperceptibly** *adv.* [F *imperceptible* or med.L *imperceptibilis* (as IN-[1], PERCEPTIBLE)]

■ **1** indiscernible, unnoticeable, invisible, inaudible, indistinguishable, undetectable, inappreciable; ill-defined, obscure, unclear, vague, shadowy, faint, muted, muffled. **2** inconsiderable, insignificant, unnoticeable, insensible, slight, subtle, gradual; minute, tiny, minuscule, infinitesimal, microscopic.

impercipient /impərsíppiənt/ *adj.* lacking in perception. □□ **impercipience** *n.*

imperfect /impérfikt/ *adj.* & *n.* ● *adj.* **1** not fully formed or done; faulty, incomplete. **2** *Gram.* (of a tense) denoting a (usu. past) action in progress but not completed at the time in question (e.g. *they were singing*). **3** *Mus.* (of a cadence) ending on the dominant chord. ● *n.* the imperfect tense. □ **imperfect rhyme** *Prosody* a rhyme that only partly satisfies the usual criteria (e.g. *love* and *move*). □□ **imperfectly** *adv.* [ME *imparfit* etc. f. OF *imparfait* f. L *imperfectus* (as IN-[1], PERFECT)]
■ *adj.* **1** incomplete, unfinished, unformed, undeveloped, immature, unready, crude, rudimentary, raw; deficient, wanting, patchy, defective, flawed, faulty, not working, out of order, inoperative, unserviceable. □□ **imperfectly** see *sketchily* (SKETCHY), WRONG *adv.*

imperfection /impərféksh'n/ *n.* **1** incompleteness. **2 a** faultiness. **b** a fault or blemish. [ME f. OF *imperfection* or LL *imperfectio* (as IMPERFECT)]
■ **1** incompleteness, patchiness, rudimentariness; insufficiency, inadequacy, deficiency, shortfall. **2** faultiness, fault, fallibility, failing, error, deficiency, defect, flaw, blemish, shortcoming, foible, weak spot, frailty, infirmity, weakness, Achilles heel.

imperfective /impərféktiv/ *adj.* & *n.* *Gram.* ● *adj.* (of a verb aspect etc.) expressing an action without reference to its completion (opp. PERFECTIVE). ● *n.* an imperfective aspect or form of a verb.

imperforate /impérfərət/ *adj.* **1** not perforated. **2** *Anat.* lacking the normal opening. **3** (of a postage stamp) lacking perforations.

imperial /impeériəl/ *adj.* & *n.* ● *adj.* **1** of or characteristic of an empire or comparable sovereign State. **2 a** of or characteristic of an emperor. **b** supreme in authority. **c** majestic, august. **d** magnificent. **3** (of non-metric weights and measures) used or formerly used by statute in the UK (*imperial gallon*). ● *n.* a former size of paper, 762 x 559 mm (30 x 22 inches). □□ **imperially** *adv.* [ME f. OF f. L *imperialis* f. *imperium* command, authority]
■ *adj.* **1** sovereign, crown, monarchal, monarchic, monarchical, royal, dynastic. **2 a** imperatorial, royal, regal, sovereign, majestic, kingly, kinglike, queenly, queenlike, princely, princelike, aristocratic. **b** supreme, absolute, commanding, pre-eminent, predominant, paramount, ruling, dominant, authoritative. **c** majestic, stately, dignified, exalted, grand, imposing, august, venerable, impressive. **d** magnificent, splendid, grand, superb, excellent, awe-inspiring; sumptuous, luxurious, gorgeous, lavish, rich, fine. **3** UK, British; non-metric, pre-decimal; avoirdupois. □□ **imperially** magnificently, splendidly, grandly, superbly, excellently, sumptuously, luxuriously, gorgeously, lavishly, richly, fabulously; imposingly, impressively, majestically, royally, regally.

imperialism /impeériəliz'm/ *n.* **1** an imperial rule or system. **2** usu. *derog.* a policy of acquiring dependent territories or extending a country's influence through trade, diplomacy, etc. □□ **imperialistic** /-lístik/ *adj.* **imperialistically** /-lístikəli/ *adv.* **imperialize** *v.tr.* (also **-ise**).

imperialist /impeériəlist/ *n.* & *adj.* ● *n.* usu. *derog.* an advocate or agent of imperial rule or of imperialism. ● *adj.* of or relating to imperialism or imperialists.

imperil /impérril/ *v.tr.* (**imperilled, imperilling**; *US* **imperiled, imperiling**) bring or put into danger.
■ see ENDANGER.

imperious /impeériəss/ *adj.* **1** overbearing, domineering. **2** urgent, imperative. □□ **imperiously** *adv.* **imperiousness** *n.* [L *imperiosus* f. *imperium* command, authority]
■ **1** see *domineering* (DOMINEER).

imperishable /impérrishəb'l/ *adj.* that cannot perish. □□ **imperishability** /-bílliti/ *n.* **imperishableness** *n.* **imperishably** *adv.*
■ see IMMORTAL *adj.* 2, PERMANENT.

imperium /impeériəm, -pérriəm/ *n.* absolute power or authority. [L, = command, authority]

impermanent /impérmənənt/ *adj.* not permanent; transient. □□ **impermanence** *n.* **impermanency** *n.* **impermanently** *adv.*
■ see TRANSIENT *adj.*

impermeable /impérmiəb'l/ *adj.* **1** that cannot be penetrated. **2** *Physics* that does not permit the passage of fluids. □□ **impermeability** /-bílliti/ *n.* [F *imperméable* or LL *impermeabilis* (as IN-[1], PERMEABLE)]
■ **1** impenetrable, impassable, impervious, inaccessible; closed, sealed, vitrified, hermetic, airtight, watertight, waterproof, damp-proof. □□ **impermeability** impenetrability, impassability, imperviousness, inaccessibility.

impermissible /impərmíssib'l/ *adj.* not allowable. □□ **impermissibility** /-bílliti/ *n.*

impersonal /impérsən'l/ *adj.* **1** having no personality. **2** having no personal feeling or reference. **3** *Gram.* **a** (of a verb) used only with a formal subject (usu. *it*) and expressing an action not attributable to a definite subject (e.g. *it is snowing*). **b** (of a pronoun) = INDEFINITE. □□ **impersonality** /-nálliti/ *n.* **impersonally** *adv.* [LL *impersonalis* (as IN-[1], PERSONAL)]
■ **1** mechanical, machine-like, wooden, rigid, stiff, starchy, stilted, stuffy, prim, formal, cold, unfriendly, cool, unemotional, matter-of-fact, detached, objective. **2** disinterested, dispassionate, detached, aloof, neutral, objective, fair, equitable, unprejudiced, unbiased.

impersonate /impérsənayt/ *v.tr.* **1** pretend to be (another person) for the purpose of entertainment or fraud. **2** act (a character). □□ **impersonation** /-náysh'n/ *n.* **impersonator** *n.* [IN-[2] + L *persona* PERSON]
■ **2** see ACT *v.* 5a. □□ **impersonation** see IMPRESSION 3. **impersonator** see MIMIC *n.*

impertinent /impértinənt/ *adj.* **1** rude or insolent; lacking proper respect. **2** out of place; absurd. **3** esp. *Law* irrelevant, intrusive. □□ **impertinence** *n.* **impertinently** *adv.* [ME f. OF or LL *impertinens* (as IN-[1], PERTINENT)]
■ **1** presumptuous, impudent, insolent, disrespectful, discourteous, uncivil, impolite, rude, cheeky, saucy, pert, brassy, brazen, brash, immodest, forward, audacious, bold, *US* nervy, *colloq.* fresh, lippy; see also TACTLESS. **2** absurd, incongruous, preposterous, illogical, irrational, nonsensical, laughable, silly. **3** see IRRELEVANT. □□ **impertinence** presumption, presumptuousness, impudence, insolence, disrespect, discourtesy, incivility, impoliteness, rudeness, cheek, sauciness, pertness, brassiness, brazenness, effrontery, nerve, brashness, immodesty, forwardness, audacity, boldness, *colloq.* brass, *sl.* chutzpah, gall; absurdity, incongruousness, illogicality, irrationality, outlandishness, silliness; see also *irrelevance* (IRRELEVANT).

imperturbable /impərtúrbəb'l/ *adj.* not excitable; calm. □□ **imperturbability** /-bílliti/ *n.* **imperturbableness** *n.* **imperturbably** *adv.* [ME f. LL *imperturbabilis* (as IN-[1], PERTURB)]
■ see CALM *adj.* 2. □□ **imperturbability** see SELF-CONTROL.

impervious /impérviəss/ *adj.* (usu. foll. by *to*) **1** not responsive to an argument etc. **2** not affording passage to a fluid. □□ **imperviously** *adv.* **imperviousness** *n.* [L *impervius* (as IN-[1], PERVIOUS)]
■ **1** see UNAFFECTED 1. **2** impermeable, watertight, waterproof. □□ **imperviousness** see TOLERANCE 4.

impetigo /impitígō/ *n.* a contagious bacterial skin infection forming pustules and yellow crusty sores. □□ **impetiginous** /impitíjinəss/ *adj.* [ME f. L *impetigo -ginis* f. *impetere* assail]

impetuous /impétyooəss/ *adj.* **1** acting or done rashly or with sudden energy. **2** moving forcefully or rapidly. □□ **impetuosity** /-tyoo-óssiti/ *n.* **impetuously** *adv.* **impetuousness** *n.* [ME f. OF *impetueux* f. LL *impetuosus* (as IMPETUS)]
■ **1** sudden, hasty, abrupt, quick, precipitate, spontaneous, unpremeditated, impulsive, unplanned, unreflective, unthinking, unreasoned, rash, spur-of-the-moment,

offhand, reckless, headlong. □□ **impetuosity, impetuousness** see HASTE *n.* 2. **impetuously** see *hastily* (HASTY).

impetus /ímpitəss/ *n.* **1** the force or energy with which a body moves. **2** a driving force or impulse. [L, = assault, force, f. *impetere* assail (as IN-², *petere* seek)]
■ **1** force, energy, momentum; propulsion, impulsion, motion. **2** impulse, drive, thrust, driving force, stimulus, push, goad, stimulation, incentive, motivation, encouragement, inducement, inspiration, spark; see also SPUR *n.* 2.

impi /ímpi/ *n.* (*pl.* **impis**) *S.Afr.* **1** a band of armed men. **2** *hist.* an African tribal army or regiment. [Zulu, = regiment, armed band]

impiety /impī́əti/ *n.* (*pl.* **-ies**) **1** a lack of piety or reverence. **2** an act etc. showing this. [ME f. OF *impieté* or L *impietas* (as IN-¹, PIETY)]
■ see SACRILEGE.

impinge /impínj/ *v.tr.* (usu. foll. by *on*, *upon*) **1** make an impact; have an effect. **2** encroach. □□ **impingement** *n.* **impinger** *n.* [L *impingere* drive (a thing) at (as IN-², *pangere* fix, drive)]
■ **2** see INFRINGE 2.

impious /ímpiəss/ *adj.* **1** not pious. **2** wicked, profane. □□ **impiously** *adv.* **impiousness** *n.* [L *impius* (as IN-¹, PIOUS)]
■ **1** irreligious, irreverent, unholy, ungodly, godless; sacrilegious, blasphemous. **2** profane, unholy, godless, wicked, sinful, evil, iniquitous, satanic, diabolic, diabolical, perverted, reprobate; see also IMMORAL 2. □□ **impiousness** ungodliness, unholiness, godlessness, irreligion, profanity, sacrilege, blasphemy; see also SIN¹ *n.* 1.

impish /ímpish/ *adj.* of or like an imp; mischievous. □□ **impishly** *adv.* **impishness** *n.*
■ see MISCHIEVOUS 1, 2. □□ **impishness** see MISCHIEF 1–3.

implacable /implákkəb'l/ *adj.* that cannot be appeased; inexorable. □□ **implacability** /-bílliti/ *n.* **implacably** *adv.* [ME f. F *implacable* or L *implacabilis* (as IN-¹, PLACABLE)]
■ unappeasable, irreconcilable, unforgiving, intractable, uncompromising, inflexible, inexorable, unyielding, unrelenting, relentless, hard, rigid, unsympathetic, ruthless, cruel, pitiless, merciless; see also MORTAL *adj.* 5.

implant *v.* & *n.* ● *v.tr.* /impláant/ **1** (often foll. by *in*) insert or fix. **2** (often foll. by *in*) instil (a principle, idea, etc.) in a person's mind. **3** plant. **4** *Med.* **a** insert (tissue etc.) in a living body. **b** (in *passive*) (of a fertilized ovum) become attached to the wall of the womb. ● *n.* /ímplaant/ **1** a thing implanted. **2** a thing implanted in the body, e.g. a piece of tissue or a capsule containing material for radium therapy. □□ **implantation** /-táysh'n/ *n.* [F *implanter* or LL *implantare* engraft (as IN-², PLANT)]
■ *v.* **1** insert, inlay, embed, fix, fasten, introduce, put, place, graft, engraft. **2** instil, introduce, sow, plant, insinuate, inject; inoculate, indoctrinate, inculcate, engrain, impress, imprint. **3** plant, transplant, root, embed, inlay, graft, engraft. ● *n.* insert, inlay, fixture; graft, scion, transplant. □□ **implantation** insertion, introduction; insinuation, injection, inoculation, indoctrination, inculcation, impression; transplantation.

implausible /impláwzib'l/ *adj.* not plausible. □□ **implausibility** /-bílliti/ *n.* **implausibly** *adv.*
■ improbable, unplausible, unlikely, doubtful, dubious, questionable, debatable, equivocal, unbelievable, incredible, farcical, far-fetched, unconvincing, unreasonable, suspect, suspicious, *sl.* fishy.

implead /impléed/ *v.tr.* *Law* **1** prosecute or take proceedings against (a person). **2** involve (a person etc.) in a suit. [ME f. AF *empleder*, OF *empleidier* (as EN-¹, PLEAD)]

implement *n.* & *v.* ● *n.* /ímplimənt/ **1** a tool, instrument, or utensil. **2** (in *pl.*) equipment; articles of furniture, dress, etc. **3** *Law* performance of an obligation. ● *v.tr.* /ímpliment/ **1 a** put (a decision, plan, etc.) into effect. **b** fulfil (an undertaking). **2** complete (a contract etc.). **3** fill up; supplement. □□ **implementation** /implimentáysh'n/ *n.* [ME f. med.L *implementa* (pl.) f. *implēre* employ (as IN-², L *plēre plet-* fill)]
■ *n.* **1** utensil, tool, instrument, apparatus, device, appliance, contrivance, mechanism, (piece of) equipment, gadget, *derog.* or *joc.* contraption. **2** (*implements*) equipment, machinery, gadgetry, paraphernalia, gear, tackle, kit, set. ● *v.* **1, 2** carry out, execute, accomplish, perform, complete, achieve, (put into) effect, bring about, cause, fulfil, realize. **3** supplement, add to, augment, increase; see also FILL *v.* 1. □□ **implementation** see EXECUTION 2, *fulfilment* (FULFIL).

implicate *v.* & *n.* ● *v.tr.* /ímplikayt/ **1** (often foll. by *in*) show (a person) to be concerned or involved (in a charge, crime, etc.). **2** (in *passive*; often foll. by *in*) be affected or involved. **3** lead to as a consequence or inference. ● *n.* /ímplikət/ a thing implied. □□ **implicative** /implíkkətiv/ *adj.* **implicatively** /implíkkətivli/ *adv.* [L *implicatus* past part. of *implicare* (as IN-², *plicare*, *plicat-* or *plicit-* fold)]
■ *v.* **1** incriminate, inculpate, connect, involve, embroil, associate, *sl.* frame; inform on, *colloq.* rat on, *sl.* squeal on, *Austral. sl.* dob, *Brit. sl.* grass (on), *US sl.* finger. **2** (*be implicated*) be involved, be included, be connected, be associated, be embroiled, be ensnared, be entrapped, be enmeshed, be entangled. **3** imply, entail, mean, necessitate; suggest, hint at, intimate. ● *n.* see IMPLICATION. □□ **implicative** incriminatory, inculpative, inculpatory; see also CIRCUMSTANTIAL 2.

implication /ìmplikáysh'n/ *n.* **1** what is involved in or implied by something else. **2** the act of implicating or implying. □ **by implication** by what is implied or suggested rather than by formal expression. [ME f. L *implicatio* (as IMPLICATE)]
■ consequence, import, purport, meaning, inference, substance, essence, sense, significance, drift, pith, denotation, connotation, conclusion, implicate; incrimination, inculpation, association, involvement, entanglement; entailment, suggestion, intimation, hint, insinuation, innuendo. □ **by implication** see *implicitly* (IMPLICIT).

implicit /implíssit/ *adj.* **1** implied though not plainly expressed. **2** (often foll. by *in*) virtually contained. **3** absolute, unquestioning, unreserved (*implicit obedience*). **4** *Math.* (of a function) not expressed directly in terms of independent variables. □□ **implicitly** *adv.* **implicitness** *n.* [F *implicite* or L *implicitus* (as IMPLICATE)]
■ **1** implied, indirect, inferrable, understood, unspoken, undeclared, tacit, inferential, latent. **2** inherent, intrinsic, underlying, basic, integral, built-in. **3** absolute, unquestioning, unquestioned, unqualified, total, whole, complete, sheer, outright, out-and-out, all-out, categorical, unmitigated, unalloyed, undiluted, unlimited, unconditional, unreserved, utter, perfect, full, wholehearted. □□ **implicitly** indirectly, by implication, impliedly, tacitly, inferentially, latently; inherently, intrinsically, integrally; absolutely, unquestioningly, totally, wholly, completely, unmitigatedly, unconditionally, unreservedly, categorically, utterly, fully, wholeheartedly.

implode /implṓd/ *v.intr.* & *tr.* burst or cause to burst inwards. □□ **implosion** /-plṓzh'n/ *n.* **implosive** /-plṓsiv, -plṓziv/ *adj.* [IN-² + L *-plodere*, after EXPLODE]

implore /implór/ *v.tr.* **1** (often foll. by *to* + infin.) entreat (a person). **2** beg earnestly for. □□ **imploring** *adj.* **imploringly** *adv.* [F *implorer* or L *implorare* invoke with tears (as IN-², *plorare* weep)]
■ see BEG 2.

imply /implī́/ *v.tr.* (**-ies, -ied**) **1** (often foll. by *that* + clause) strongly suggest the truth or existence of (a thing not expressly asserted). **2** insinuate, hint (*what are you implying?*). **3** signify. □□ **implied** *adj.* **impliedly** *adv.* [ME f. OF *emplier* f. L *implicare* (as IMPLICATE)]

■ **1** entail, point to, indicate, suggest, implicate, mean, necessitate; *disp.* infer. **2** hint (at), intimate, insinuate, suggest, *disp.* infer; allude to, refer to. **3** signify, signal, indicate, mean, express, denote, connote, betoken; involve, entail, evidence, necessitate, assume, presume. □□ **implied** see IMPLICIT 1. **impliedly** see *implicitly* (IMPLICIT).

impolder /impṓldər/ *v.tr.* (also **empolder**) *Brit.* **1** make a polder of. **2** reclaim from the sea. [Du. *inpolderen* (as IN-², POLDER)]

impolite /ímpəlīt/ *adj.* (**impolitest**) ill-mannered, uncivil, rude. □□ **impolitely** *adv.* **impoliteness** *n.* [L *impolitus* (as IN-¹, POLITE)]
■ ill-mannered, uncivil, rude, discourteous, disrespectful, impudent, insolent, boorish, crude, indecorous, indelicate, unrefined, ill-bred, vulgar, coarse, ungracious, ungentlemanly, unladylike, unchivalrous, impertinent, pert, saucy, brassy, cheeky, *colloq.* fresh, lippy. □□ **impoliteness** see DISRESPECT.

impolitic /impóllitik/ *adj.* **1** inexpedient, unwise. **2** not politic. □□ **impoliticly** *adv.*
■ **1** see FOOLISH. **2** see TACTLESS.

imponderable /impóndərəb'l/ *adj.* & *n.* ● *adj.* **1** that cannot be estimated or assessed in any definite way. **2** very light. **3** *Physics* having no weight. ● *n.* (usu. in *pl.*) something difficult or impossible to assess. □□ **imponderability** /-bílliti/ *n.* **imponderably** *adv.*
■ *adj.* **1** immeasurable, inestimable, inconceivable, unthinkable, incomprehensible; subtle, tenuous, rarefied, abstract. **2** light (as a feather), unsubstantial, insubstantial, tenuous, weightless; airy, ethereal. ● *n.* see INTANGIBLE.

import *v.* & *n.* ● *v.tr.* /impórt, ím-/ **1** bring in (esp. foreign goods or services) to a country. **2** (often foll. by *that* + clause) **a** imply, indicate, signify. **b** express, make known. ● *n.* /import/ **1** the process of importing. **2 a** an imported article or service. **b** (in *pl.*) an amount imported (*imports exceeded £50m.*). **3** what is implied; meaning. **4** importance. □□ **importable** /impórtəb'l/ *adj.* **importation** /importáysh'n/ *n.* **importer** /impórtər/ *n.* (all in sense 1 of *v.*). [ME f. L *importare* bring in, in med.L = imply, be of consequence (as IN-², *portare* carry)]
■ *v.* **1** bring *or* carry in, bring into the country, convey (in), introduce; buy from abroad, source from abroad; smuggle (in), run. **2** imply, mean, indicate, convey, denote, betoken, signify, signal, express, show, make known, state, communicate, put *or* get across. ● *n.* **1** importation, introduction. **2 b** (*imports*) foreign goods, imported goods *or* articles, foreigners. **3** meaning, sense, denotation, signification, gist, drift, thrust, intention, implication, implicate, purport, connotation, suggestion, intimation. **4** importance, significance, weight, consequence, moment, substance. □□ **importation** see IMPORT *n.* 1 above. **importer** introducer, buyer, dealer; smuggler.

importance /impórt'nss/ *n.* **1** the state of being important. **2** weight, significance. **3** personal consequence; dignity. [F f. med.L *importantia* (as IMPORT)]
■ **1** momentousness, weightiness, gravity, seriousness, effect, authority, status, greatness, prominence, pre-eminence, precedence, consequence; pretentiousness, pomposity, grandness. **2** significance, consequence, import, value, worth, weight, account, concern, moment, substance, matter. **3** eminence, distinction, esteem, standing, status, station, position, rank, dignity, prominence, pre-eminence, grandeur, prestige, power, influence, note, worth; self-importance, arrogance, pomposity.

important /impórt'nt/ *adj.* **1** (often foll. by *to*) of great effect or consequence; momentous. **2** (of a person) having high rank or status, or great authority. **3** pretentious, pompous. **4** (*absol.* in parenthetic construction) what is a more important point or matter (*they are willing and, more important, able*). ¶ Use of *importantly* here is *disp.* □□ **importantly** *adv.* (see note above). [F f. med.L (as IMPORT)]
■ **1** significant, consequential, critical, all-important, urgent, portentous, weighty, grave, serious, pressing, substantial, momentous, world-shaking, material, signal, *colloq. disp.* crucial, *disp.* vital. **2** leading, prominent, notable, noted, noteworthy, worthy, eminent, distinguished, respected, high-ranking, top-level, high-level, superior, outstanding, foremost, conspicuous; impressive, influential, well-connected, powerful, formidable, mighty. **3** pretentious, pompous, consequential, grand, arrogant; see also *self-important* (SELF-IMPORTANCE).

importunate /impórtyoonət/ *adj.* **1** making persistent or pressing requests. **2** (of affairs) urgent. □□ **importunately** *adv.* **importunity** /importyóōniti/ *n.* [L *importunus* inconvenient (as IN-¹, *portunus* f. *portus* harbour)]
■ **1** see INSISTENT 1. □□ **importunity** see *urgency* (URGENT).

importune /impórtyōōn, -tyóōn/ *v.tr.* **1** solicit (a person) pressingly. **2** solicit for an immoral purpose. [F *importuner* or med.L *importunari* (as IMPORTUNATE)]
■ **1** see SOLICIT 1, 2. **2** see SOLICIT 3.

impose /impṓz/ *v.* **1** *tr.* (often foll. by *on*, *upon*) require (a tax, duty, charge, or obligation) to be paid or undertaken (by a person etc.). **2** *tr.* enforce compliance with. **3** *intr.* & *refl.* (foll. by *on*, *upon*, or *absol.*) demand the attention or commitment of (a person); take advantage of (*I do not want to impose on you any longer*; *I did not want to impose*). **4** *tr.* (often foll. by *on*, *upon*) palm (a thing) off on (a person). **5** *tr. Printing* lay (pages of type) in the proper order ready for printing. **6** *intr.* (foll. by *on*, *upon*) exert influence by an impressive character or appearance. **7** *intr.* (often foll. by *on*, *upon*) practise deception. **8** *tr. archaic* (foll. by *upon*) place (a thing). [ME f. F *imposer* f. L *imponere imposit-* inflict, deceive (as IN-², *ponere* put)]
■ **1, 2** enjoin, prescribe, dictate, enforce, demand, require, saddle a person with, burden a person with; administer, set, place, put, lay, *often joc.* inflict; (*impose a tax*) exact *or* levy *or* raise a tax. **3** (*impose on* or *upon*) take advantage of, exploit, force *or* foist oneself (up)on, presume (up)on, put upon, put a person out, *often joc.* inflict oneself (up)on; intrude (up)on, inconvenience, interrupt, trouble, bother, disturb, discommode, take up a person's time, *colloq.* hassle. **4** thrust, force, foist, palm off, fob off, *often joc.* inflict. **6** (*impose on* or *upon*) impress, make an impression on, have *or* exert an influence on, influence, persuade, convince. **7** see DISSIMULATE.

imposing /impṓzing/ *adj.* impressive, formidable, esp. in appearance. □□ **imposingly** *adv.* **imposingness** *n.*
■ see IMPRESSIVE 1.

imposition /ìmpəzísh'n/ *n.* **1** the act or an instance of imposing; the process of being imposed. **2** an unfair or resented demand or burden. **3** a tax or duty. **4** *Brit.* work set as a punishment at school. [ME f. OF *imposition* or L *impositio* f. *imponere*: see IMPOSE]
■ **1** enjoinment, prescription, dictation, infliction, enforcement, requirement, demand; administration, application, introduction. **2** demand, burden, onus, weight, trial, hardship, cross, affliction, oppression; intrusion, inconvenience, disturbance, bother, nuisance, *colloq.* hassle. **3** taxation, exaction, tax, duty, levy, tithe, charge.

impossibility /impóssibílliti/ *n.* (*pl.* **-ies**) **1** the fact or condition of being impossible. **2** an impossible thing or circumstance. [F *impossibilité* or L *impossibilitas* (as IMPOSSIBLE)]

impossible /impóssib'l/ *adj.* **1** not possible; that cannot be done, occur, or exist (*it is impossible to alter them*; *such a thing is impossible*). **2** (loosely) not easy; not convenient; not easily believable. **3** *colloq.* (of a person or thing) outrageous, intolerable. □□ **impossibly** *adv.* [ME f. OF *impossible* or L *impossibilis* (as IN-¹, POSSIBLE)]

■ **1** unrealizable, unattainable, impracticable, Heath Robinson, unworkable, infeasible, unfeasible, unresolvable, unsolvable, out of the question, *esp. US* impractical; self-contradictory, paradoxical, illogical, unreasonable, inconsistent, inconceivable, fantastic, unimaginable, unthinkable, absurd, nonsensical, ludicrous, preposterous, crazy. **2** difficult, problematic, problematical, awkward, inconvenient, inopportune, inexpedient, disruptive, troublesome, bothersome; unbelievable, implausible, unconvincing, far-fetched, improbable, unlikely, doubtful, dubious, questionable, debatable. **3** intolerable, unbearable, insupportable, unsupportable, unendurable, insufferable, unacceptable, unmanageable, impracticable; outrageous, absurd, preposterous, ridiculous, outlandish, crazy, weird, *outré*. □□ **impossibly** paradoxically, illogically, unreasonably, inconsistently, inconceivably, unimaginably, unthinkably, absurdly, nonsensically, ludicrously, preposterously, crazily; unattainably, unachievably, impracticably, unworkably; difficultly, problematically, awkwardly, inconveniently, inopportunely, inexpediently, disruptively, troublesomely; unbelievably, implausibly, unconvincingly, improbably, doubtfully, dubiously, questionably, debatably; intolerably, unbearably, insupportably, unsupportably, unendurably, insufferably, unacceptably, outrageously, ridiculously, outlandishly, weirdly.

impost[1] /impōst/ *n.* **1** a tax, duty, or tribute. **2** a weight carried by a horse in a handicap race. [F f. med.L *impost-* part. stem of L *imponere*: see IMPOSE]
■ **1** see TAX *n.* 1.

impost[2] /impōst/ *n.* the upper course of a pillar, carrying an arch. [F *imposte* or It. *imposta* fem. past part. of *imporre* f. L *imponere*: see IMPOSE]

impostor /impóstər/ *n.* (also **imposter**) **1** a person who assumes a false character or pretends to be someone else. **2** a swindler. □□ **impostorous** *adj.* **impostrous** *adj.* [F *imposteur* f. LL *impostor* (as IMPOST[1])]
■ **1** impersonator, personator, humbug, fraud, phoney, *Austral.* bunyip. **2** swindler, deceiver, trickster, cheat, fraud, confidence man, mountebank, charlatan, hypocrite, humbug, flimflammer, *US* four-flusher, *colloq.* shark, *sl.* con man, *Austral. sl.* illywhacker.

imposture /impóss-chər/ *n.* the act or an instance of fraudulent deception. [F f. LL *impostura* (as IMPOST[1])]
■ see DECEIT.

impotent /impət'nt/ *adj.* **1 a** powerless; lacking all strength. **b** helpless. **c** ineffective. **2 a** (esp. of a male) unable, esp. for a prolonged period, to achieve a sexual erection or orgasm. **b** *colloq.* unable to procreate; infertile. □□ **impotence** *n.* **impotency** *n.* **impotently** *adv.* [ME f. OF f. L *impotens* (as IN-[1], POTENT[1])]
■ **1 a, b** weak, powerless, impuissant, enervated, enfeebled, spent, wasted, decrepit, debilitated, exhausted, worn out, effete, *colloq.* all in, *Brit. sl.* knackered; helpless, palsied, frail, feeble. **c** inadequate, ineffective, ineffectual, inept, incompetent, useless. **2 b** sterile, barren, infertile. □□ **impotence, impotency** weakness, powerlessness, impuissance, enervation, enfeeblement, wasting, decrepitude, debilitation, exhaustion, effeteness; helplessness, frailty, feebleness, inadequacy, inefficacy, ineffectualness, ineffectiveness, ineptness, incompetence; sterility, infertility.

impound /impównd/ *v.tr.* **1** confiscate. **2** take possession of. **3** shut up (animals) in a pound. **4** shut up (a person or thing) as in a pound. **5** (of a dam etc.) collect or confine (water). □□ **impoundable** *adj.* **impounder** *n.* **impoundment** *n.*
■ **1, 2** see CONFISCATE. **3, 4** see PEN[2] *v.*

impoverish /impóvvərish/ *v.tr.* (often as **impoverished** *adj.*) **1** make poor. **2** exhaust the strength or natural fertility of. □□ **impoverishment** *n.* [ME f. OF *empoverir* (as EN-[1], *povre* POOR)]
■ **1** see RUIN *v.* 1a; (**impoverished**) destitute, poor, poverty-stricken, penurious, beggared, needy, necessitous, impecunious, in desperate *or* dire straits, straitened, in distress, badly off, bankrupt, insolvent, ruined, (financially) embarrassed, *colloq.* (dead *or* flat) broke, pinched, up against it, on one's uppers, short, strapped (for cash), *Brit. sl.* skint, stony-broke. **2** see WEAKEN 1; (**impoverished**) stripped, barren, desolate, wasted, empty, depleted, denuded, drained, exhausted. □□ **impoverishment** see LOSS 3.

impracticable /impráktikəb'l/ *adj.* **1** impossible in practice. **2** (of a road etc.) impassable. **3** (of a person or thing) unmanageable. □□ **impracticability** /-bílliti/ *n.* **impracticableness** *n.* **impracticably** *adv.*
■ **1** see IMPOSSIBLE 1. **2** impassable, impenetrable, inaccessible, closed, shut, blocked, barred, obstructed, clogged (up), jammed. **3** see IMPOSSIBLE 3.

impractical /impráktik'l/ *adj.* **1** not practical. **2** esp. *US* not practicable. □□ **impracticality** /-kálliti/ *n.* **impractically** *adv.*
■ **1** theoretical, idealistic, abstract, speculative, academic, doctrinaire, unrealistic, unpractical; unworldly, other-worldly, visionary, romantic, quixotic, *colloq.* starry-eyed, airy-fairy, *sl.* crackpot; ineffective, ineffectual, useless, hopeless, vain. **2** see IMPOSSIBLE. □□ **impracticality** idealism, speculativeness, unworldliness, romanticism, quixotism, quixotry, ineffectuality, ineffectualness, ineffectiveness, uselessness; see also *madness* (MAD).

imprecate /imprikayt/ *v.tr.* (often foll. by *upon*) invoke, call down (evil). □□ **imprecatory** *adj.* [L *imprecari* (as IN-[2], *precari* pray)]
■ see SWEAR *v.* 4.

imprecation /ímprikáysh'n/ *n.* **1** a spoken curse; a malediction. **2** imprecating.
■ **1** see CURSE *n.* 1.

imprecise /imprisíss/ *adj.* not precise. □□ **imprecisely** *adv.* **impreciseness** *n.* **imprecision** /-sízh'n/ *n.*
■ inexact, inaccurate, inexplicit, indefinite, ill-defined, indistinct, vague, hazy, cloudy, blurred, fuzzy, woolly, ambiguous; incorrect, wrong, erroneous, wide of the mark, out, untrue, improper, mistaken, fallacious, false. □□ **impreciseness, imprecision** inexactitude, inexactness, inaccuracy, inexplicitness, indefiniteness, indistinctness, vagueness, haziness, cloudiness, fuzziness, woolliness, ambiguity; incorrectness, wrongness, erroneousness, error, mistakenness, mistake, fallaciousness, fallacy, falseness, falsehood.

impregnable[1] /imprégnəb'l/ *adj.* **1** (of a fortified position) that cannot be taken by force. **2** resistant to attack or criticism. □□ **impregnability** /-bílliti/ *n.* **impregnably** *adv.* [ME f. OF *imprenable* (as IN-[1], *prendre* take)]
■ impenetrable, unassailable, well-fortified, thick-skinned, watertight, resistant, tenable; inviolable, invulnerable, invincible, unconquerable, unbeatable, insuperable, indomitable, immune, safe, secure; strong, stout, sturdy, staunch, solid, stable. □□ **impregnability** impenetrability, unassailability, unassailableness, resistance, tenability; inviolability, invulnerability, invincibility, unconquerableness, indomitability, indomitableness, immunity, safety, security.

impregnable[2] /imprégnəb'l/ *adj.* that can be impregnated.

impregnate *v.* & *adj.* ● *v.tr.* /impregnayt/ **1** (often foll. by *with*) fill or saturate. **2** (often foll. by *with*) imbue, fill (with feelings, moral qualities, etc.). **3 a** make (a female) pregnant. **b** *Biol.* fertilize (a female reproductive cell or ovum). ● *adj.* /imprégnət/ **1** pregnant. **2** (often foll. by *with*) permeated. □□ **impregnation** /impregnáysh'n/ *n.* [LL *impregnare impregnat-* (as IN-[2], *pregnare* be pregnant)]
■ *v.* **1, 2** saturate, drench, soak, steep, permeate, penetrate, pervade, fill, suffuse, infuse, imbue. **3** fertilize, inseminate, fecundate, make pregnant, *archaic* get with child, get in an interesting *or* delicate condition, *colloq.* get in trouble *or* in the family way, *Brit. sl.* put *or* get in

the (pudding) club, *US sl.* knock up. ● *adj.* **1** see PREGNANT 1. ▫▫ **impregnation** saturation, permeation, permeance, penetration, pervasion, suffusion, infusion; fertilization, insemination, fecundation.

impresario /imprisaáriō/ *n.* (*pl.* **-os**) an organizer of public entertainments, esp. the manager of an operatic, theatrical, or concert company. [It. f. *impresa* undertaking]

imprescriptible /impriskríptib'l/ *adj. Law* (of rights) that cannot be taken away by prescription or lapse of time. [med.L *imprescriptibilis* (as IN-[1], PRESCRIBE)]
■ see INALIENABLE.

impress[1] *v.* & *n.* ● *v.tr.* /imprέss/ **1** (often foll. by *with*) **a** affect or influence deeply. **b** evoke a favourable opinion or reaction from (a person) (*was most impressed with your efforts*). **2** (often foll. by *on*) emphasize (an idea etc.) (*must impress on you the need to be prompt*). **3** (often foll. by *on*) **a** imprint or stamp. **b** apply (a mark etc.) with pressure. **4** make a mark or design on (a thing) with a stamp, seal, etc. **5** *Electr.* apply (voltage etc.) from outside. ● *n.* /ímpress/ **1** the act or an instance of impressing. **2** a mark made by a seal, stamp, etc. **3** a characteristic mark or quality. **4** = IMPRESSION 1. ▫▫ **impressible** /imprέssib'l/ *adj.* [ME f. OF *empresser* (as EN-[1], PRESS[1])]
■ *v.* **1 a** affect, touch, move, reach, stir, strike, sway, influence, persuade, convince, *sl.* grab. **b** (*impressed with*) struck by *or* with, taken with, *sl.* grabbed by. **2** stress, emphasize, underline, bring home, draw a person's attention to. **3, 4** stamp, mark, imprint, print, engrave, emboss. ● *n.* **1** see IMPRESSION 4. **2** see STAMP *n.* 2, 4. **3** see STAMP *n.* 6a. ▫▫ **impressible** see IMPRESSIONABLE.

impress[2] /imprέss/ *v.tr. hist.* **1** force (men) to serve in the army or navy. **2** seize (goods etc.) for public service. ▫▫ **impressment** *n.* [IN-[2] + PRESS[2]]

impression /impréshʼn/ *n.* **1** an effect produced (esp. on the mind or feelings). **2** a notion or belief (esp. a vague or mistaken one) (*my impression is they are afraid*). **3** an imitation of a person or sound, esp. done to entertain. **4 a** the impressing of a mark. **b** a mark impressed. **5** an unaltered reprint from standing type or plates (esp. as distinct from *edition*). **6 a** the number of copies of a book, newspaper, etc., issued at one time. **b** the printing of these. **7** a print taken from a wood engraving. **8** *Dentistry* a negative copy of the teeth or mouth made by pressing them into a soft substance. ▫▫ **impressional** *adj.* [ME f. OF f. L *impressio -onis* f. *imprimere impress-* (as IN-[2], PRESS[1])]
■ **1** sensation, feeling, sense, perception, awareness, consciousness; impact, effect, influence. **2** notion, belief, conception, idea, fancy, feeling, suspicion, hunch. **3** impersonation, imitation, parody, satire, *colloq.* take-off, *Brit. colloq.* send-up. **4** stamp, impress, brand, mark; dent, indentation, depression, hollow. **5** printing, reprinting, reprint; copy. **6** issue, print, run, print run.

impressionable /impréshənəb'l/ *adj.* easily influenced; susceptible to impressions. ▫▫ **impressionability** /-bílliti/ *n.* **impressionably** *adv.* [F *impressionnable* f. *impressionner* (as IMPRESSION)]
■ suggestible, susceptible, susceptive, persuadable, persuasible, convincible, receptive, responsive, impressible; soft, pliable, malleable, mouldable.

impressionism /impréshəniz'm/ *n.* **1** a style or movement in art concerned with expression of feeling by visual impression, esp. from the effect of light on objects. **2** a style of music or writing that seeks to describe a feeling or experience rather than achieve accurate depiction or systematic structure. ▫▫ **impressionist** *n.* [F *impressionnisme* (after *Impression: Soleil levant*, title of a painting by Monet, 1872)]

impressionistic /impréshənístik/ *adj.* **1** in the style of impressionism. **2** subjective, unsystematic. ▫▫ **impressionistically** *adv.*

impressive /imprέssiv/ *adj.* **1** impressing the mind or senses, esp. so as to cause approval or admiration. **2** (of language, a scene, etc.) tending to excite deep feeling. ▫▫ **impressively** *adv.* **impressiveness** *n.*
■ **1** imposing, formidable, awesome, awe-inspiring, portentous, redoubtable, powerful, striking; grand, august, dignified, stately, majestic, magnificent. **2** evocative, moving, affecting, stimulating, exciting, stirring, powerful, provocative, arousing, emotional. ▫▫ **impressively** imposingly, formidably, awesomely, awe-inspiringly, redoubtably, powerfully, commandingly, augustly, grandly, majestically, magnificently; evocatively, movingly, affectingly, stimulatingly, excitingly, stirringly, provocatively, arousingly, emotionally. **impressiveness** imposingness, formidableness, awesomeness, power, dignity, stateliness, augustness, grandness, grandeur, majesty, magnificence; evocativeness, excitingness, provocativeness, emotion.

imprest /imprest/ *n.* money advanced to a person for use in State business. [orig. *in prest* f. OF *prest* loan, advance pay: see PRESS[2]]

imprimatur /ímprimáytər, -maátər, -toor/ *n.* **1** *RC Ch.* an official licence to print (an ecclesiastical or religious book etc.). **2** official approval. [L, = let it be printed]
■ **2** see APPROVAL.

imprimatura /impreématóorə/ *n.* (in painting) a coloured transparent glaze as a primer. [It. *imprimitura* f. *imprimere* IMPRESS[1]]

imprint *v.* & *n.* ● *v.tr.* /imprínt/ **1** (often foll. by *on*) impress or establish firmly, esp. on the mind. **2 a** (often foll. by *on*) make a stamp or impression of (a figure etc.) on a thing. **b** make an impression on (a thing) with a stamp etc. ● *n.* /ímprint/ **1** an impression or stamp. **2** the printer's or publisher's name and other details printed in a book. [ME f. OF *empreinter empreint* f. L *imprimere*: see IMPRESSION]
■ *v.* **2** see STAMP *v.* 2. ● *n.* **1** see IMPRESSION 4.

imprinting /imprínting/ *n.* **1** in senses of IMPRINT *v.* **2** *Zool.* the development in a young animal of a pattern of recognition and trust for its own species.

imprison /imprízz'n/ *v.tr.* **1** put into prison. **2** confine; shut up. ▫▫ **imprisonment** *n.* [ME f. OF *emprisoner* (as EN-[1], PRISON)]
■ **1** incarcerate, detain, remand, jail, lock up *or* away, intern, shut up, put behind bars, put away, put inside, put in *or* throw into irons, *Brit.* send down, *US* send up, *poet.* prison, *sl.* jug, lag. **2** confine, shut in *or* up, block in *or* up, box in *or* up, hem in, circumscribe, immure, intern, impound, cloister, constrain, restrain, restrict, coop (up), cabin, mew (up), cage, encage, chain, fetter, trammel, *Brit.* gate. ▫▫ **imprisonment** incarceration, detention, remand, internment, custody, *archaic* durance, *hist.* penal servitude, *sl.* time, bird, *Brit. sl.* porridge, *US sl.* bum rap; confinement, circumscription, immurement, impoundment, constraint, restraint, restriction.

improbable /impróbbəb'l/ *adj.* **1** not likely to be true or to happen. **2** difficult to believe. ▫▫ **improbability** /-bílliti/ *n.* **improbably** *adv.* [F *improbable* or L *improbabilis* (as IN-[1], PROBABLE)]
■ **1** unlikely, doubtful, dubious, in doubt, questionable, debatable, unrealistic, unimaginable, unthinkable, inconceivable, impossible. **2** see IMPLAUSIBLE.

improbity /imprṓbiti/ *n.* (*pl.* **-ies**) **1** wickedness; lack of moral integrity. **2** dishonesty. **3** a wicked or dishonest act. [L *improbitas* (as IN-[1], PROBITY)]

impromptu /imprómptyoo/ *adj.*, *adv.*, & *n.* ● *adj.* & *adv.* extempore, unrehearsed. ● *n.* **1** an extempore performance or speech. **2** a short piece of usu. solo instrumental music, often songlike. [F f. L *in promptu* in readiness: see PROMPT]
■ *adj.* & *adv.* see EXTEMPORANEOUS *adj.*

improper /imprόppər/ *adj.* **1 a** unseemly; indecent. **b** not in accordance with accepted rules of behaviour. **2** inaccurate, wrong. **3** not properly so called. ▫ **improper fraction** a fraction in which the numerator is greater than or equal to the denominator. ▫▫ **improperly** *adv.* [F *impropre* or L *improprius* (as IN-[1], PROPER)]

■ **1 a** unseemly, unbecoming, untoward; indecent, indecorous, unladylike, ungentlemanly, indelicate, immodest, impolite, injudicious, indiscreet, tactless, rude, suggestive, risqué, blue, *US* off colour. **b** impolite, unacceptable, unsuitable, inappropriate, unfitting, unbefitting, incongruous, infelicitous, inapplicable, inapt, inapposite, malapropos, out of keeping, out of place, uncalled-for. **2** wrong, mistaken, erroneous, false, incorrect, inaccurate, inexact, imprecise, amiss, faulty, untrue; irregular, abnormal. **3** wrongly-named, miscalled, misnamed, so-called, nominal, spurious.

impropriate /imprṓpriayt/ *v.tr. Brit.* **1** annex (an ecclesiastical benefice) to a corporation or person as property. **2** place (tithes or ecclesiastical property) in lay hands. ▫▫ **impropriation** /-áysh'n/ *n.* [AL *impropriare* (as IN-², *proprius* own)]

impropriator /imprṓpriaytər/ *n. Brit.* a person to whom a benefice is impropriated.

impropriety /imprəprī́əti/ *n.* (*pl.* **-ies**) **1** lack of propriety; indecency. **2** an instance of improper conduct etc. **3** incorrectness. **4** unfitness. [F *impropriété* or L *improprietas* (as IN-¹, *proprius* proper)]

■ **1** unseemliness, untowardness, indecorousness, indecorum, bad *or* poor taste, indelicacy, immodesty, impudicity, suggestiveness, indecency, immorality, sinfulness, wickedness, lewdness, lasciviousness. **2** gaffe, gaucherie, *faux pas*, slip, blunder, mistake, error. **3** incorrectness, erroneousness, falsity, falseness, inaccuracy, inaccurateness, inexactitude, inexactness, imprecision, impreciseness, irregularity, abnormality. **4** unfitness, unsuitableness, unsuitability, inappropriateness, inaptness, inaptitude, unaptness, inapplicability, infelicity, infelicitousness, incongruity, incongruousness, incompatibility, inopportuneness.

improvable /imprṓōvəb'l/ *adj.* **1** that can be improved. **2** suitable for cultivation. ▫▫ **improvability** /-bílliti/ *n.*

improve /imprṓōv/ *v.* **1 a** *tr. & intr.* make or become better. **b** *intr.* (foll. by *on*, *upon*) produce something better than. **2** *absol.* (as **improving** *adj.*) giving moral benefit (*improving literature*). [orig. *emprowe*, *improwe* f. AF *emprower* f. OF *emprou* f. *prou* profit, infl. by PROVE]

■ **1 a** better, upgrade, enhance, polish (up), refine, elaborate, add to, lift, develop, extend, increase, advance, heighten, intensify, perfect, *literary* meliorate, *formal* ameliorate; amend, repair, mend, put *or* set right, reform, recast, revise, revamp, refurbish, recondition, overhaul, renovate, modernize, update, remodel, retouch, touch up, give a new lease of (*or US* on) life; redress, rectify, correct, emend, alter, edit; get better, pick up, look up, take a turn for the better, *Brit. colloq.* be on the up and up; recover, recuperate, revive, convalesce, rally, make progress, progress, come on, be on the upgrade, thrive, prosper, gain strength *or* ground, turn over a new leaf. **b** (*improve on* or *upon*) better, surpass, beat, exceed, excel, efface, eclipse, cap, *colloq.* best. **2** (**improving**) edifying, instructive, uplifting, regenerative, beneficial, salutary, healthy; heart-warming.

improvement /imprṓōvmənt/ *n.* **1** the act or an instance of improving or being improved. **2** something that improves, esp. an addition or alteration that adds to value. **3** something that has been improved. [ME f. AF *emprowement* (as IMPROVE)]

■ **1, 2** betterment, enhancement, refinement, elaboration, development, extension, addition, increase, intensification, lift, *formal* amelioration; amendment, repair, reform, revision, revamp, refurbishment, overhaul, renovation, modernization, update, touch-up; rectification, correction, emendation, alteration; recovery, recuperation, convalescence, rally, progress. **3** advance, progression, change (for the better), breakthrough, upgrade.

improver /imprṓōvər/ *n.* **1** a person who improves. **2** *Brit.* a person who works for low wages while acquiring skill and experience in a trade.

improvident /imprόvvid'nt/ *adj.* **1** lacking foresight or care for the future. **2** not frugal; thriftless. **3** heedless, incautious. ▫▫ **improvidence** *n.* **improvidently** *adv.*

■ **1, 3** imprudent, injudicious, indiscreet, incautious, unwary, short-sighted, myopic, *esp. US* near-sighted; rash, impetuous, hasty, impulsive, reckless, heedless, careless, unthinking, unmindful, headlong. **2** thriftless, unthrifty, spendthrift, uneconomical, wasteful, profligate, prodigal, extravagant, lavish, profuse, penny wise and pound foolish. ▫▫ **improvidence** see *imprudence* (IMPRUDENT), EXTRAVAGANCE 1.

improvise /imprəvīz/ *v.tr.* (also *absol.*) **1** compose or perform (music, verse, etc.) extempore. **2** provide or construct (a thing) extempore. ▫▫ **improvisation** /-záysh'n/ *n.* **improvisational** /-záyshən'l/ *adj.* **improvisatorial** /-zətóriəl/ *adj.* **improvisatory** /-záytəri/ *adj.* **improviser** *n.* [F *improviser* or It. *improvvisare* f. *improvviso* extempore, f. L *improvisus* past part. (as IN-¹, PROVIDE)]

■ **1** ad lib, extemporize, vamp, scat, play (it) by ear, *colloq.* jam. **2** invent, concoct, devise, contrive, make up, throw together. ▫▫ **improvisation** ad lib, extemporization, impromptu, happening, vamp, scat, *colloq.* jam (session); invention, concoction, device, contrivance; makeshift, lash-up, stopgap. **improvisational, improvisatorial, improvisatory** ad lib, extempore, extemporaneous, impromptu, unrehearsed, unprepared, *colloq.* off the cuff; made-up, thrown together, makeshift, stopgap, drumhead.

imprudent /imprṓōd'nt/ *adj.* rash, indiscreet. ▫▫ **imprudence** *n.* **imprudently** *adv.* [ME f. L *imprudens* (as IN-¹, PRUDENT)]

■ rash, hasty, reckless, heedless, precipitate, unthinking, impulsive, incautious, inconsiderate, impetuous, improvident, indiscreet, injudicious, irresponsible, ill-judged, ill-considered, ill-advised, unadvised, inadvisable, unwise, impolitic, inexpedient, careless, foolish, foolhardy, inane, silly, perverse, wrong, wrong-headed, hare-brained, mad, *colloq.* crazy, insane, *esp. Brit. colloq.* daft. ▫▫ **imprudence** indiscretion, injudiciousness, incautiousness, unguardedness, unwariness, improvidence, rashness, recklessness, audacity, boldness, temerity, impulsiveness, hastiness, haste, impetuousness, impetuosity, thoughtlessness, insensitivity, tactlessness, heedlessness, carelessness, naïvety, foolishness, foolhardiness, folly.

impudent /impyood'nt/ *adj.* **1** insolently disrespectful; impertinent. **2** shamelessly presumptuous. **3** unblushing. ▫▫ **impudence** *n.* **impudently** *adv.* [ME f. L *impudens* (as IN-¹, *pudēre* be ashamed)]

■ **1, 2** insolent, disrespectful, contemptuous, insulting, contumelious, ill-mannered, uncivil, discourteous, rude, impolite, impertinent, pert, saucy, brassy, cheeky, cocky, cocksure, *US* nervy, *colloq.* fresh, lippy; arrogant, presumptuous, audacious, bold, brazen, brash, forward, immodest, *colloq.* pushy. **3** unblushing, unabashed, unashamed, shameless, immodest; blatant, flagrant, barefaced. ▫▫ **impudence** insolence, disrespect, contempt, contumely, incivility, discourtesy, rudeness, impoliteness, impertinence, pertness, sauciness, brass, effrontery, cheek, cockiness, *colloq.* nerve, sauce, *sl.* chutzpah, gall; arrogance, presumption, presumptuousness, audacity, boldness, brazenness, brashness, forwardness, barefacedness, immodesty, shamelessness, *colloq.* pushiness; *US* back talk, *colloq.* lip, mouth, *Austral. & NZ colloq.* hide, *Brit. colloq.* backchat.

impudicity /impyoodíssiti/ *n.* shamelessness, immodesty. [F *impudicité* f. L *impudicus* (as IMPUDENT)]

impugn /impyṓōn/ *v.tr.* challenge or call in question (a statement, action, etc.). ▫▫ **impugnable** *adj.* **impugnment** *n.* [ME f. L *impugnare* assail (as IN-², *pugnare* fight)]

■ see CHALLENGE *v.* 2.

impuissant /impyŏŏ-is'nt/ *adj.* impotent, weak. □□ **impuissance** *n.* [F (as IN-[1], PUISSANT)]
■ see FEEBLE 1, 2.

impulse /impulss/ *n.* **1** the act or an instance of impelling; a push. **2** an impetus. **3** *Physics* **a** an indefinitely large force acting for a very short time but producing a finite change of momentum (e.g. the blow of a hammer). **b** the change of momentum produced by this or any force. **4** a wave of excitation in a nerve. **5** mental incitement. **6** a sudden desire or tendency to act without reflection (*did it on impulse*). □ **impulse buying** the unpremeditated buying of goods as a result of a whim or impulse. [L *impulsus* (as IMPEL)]
■ **1** see PUSH *n.* 1. **2** see IMPETUS 2. **5** see *incitation, incitement* (INCITE). **6** see FANCY *n.* 2.

impulsion /impúlsh'n/ *n.* **1** the act or an instance of impelling. **2** a mental impulse. **3** impetus. [ME f. OF f. L *impulsio -onis* (as IMPEL)]

impulsive /impúlsiv/ *adj.* **1** (of a person or conduct etc.) apt to be affected or determined by sudden impulse. **2** tending to impel. **3** *Physics* acting as an impulse. □□ **impulsively** *adv.* **impulsiveness** *n.* [ME f. F *impulsif -ive* or LL *impulsivus* (as IMPULSION)]
■ **1** impetuous, spontaneous, spur-of-the-moment, snap, instinctive, involuntary, unthinking, unpremeditated, unplanned, unreasoned, unconsidered, extemporaneous, *Mus.* capriccioso; unpredictable, irregular, capricious; quick, sudden, immediate, precipitate, abrupt, hasty, rash, headlong, reckless, devil-may-care, madcap, wild, foolhardy. □□ **impulsively** impetuously, instinctively, spontaneously, unpredictably, capriciously; see also *hastily* (HASTY). **impulsiveness** impetuousness, impetuosity, spontaneity, unthinkingness; unpredictableness, unpredictability, capriciousness, caprice; see also HASTE *n.* 2.

impunity /impyŏŏniti/ *n.* exemption from punishment or from the injurious consequences of an action. □ **with impunity** without having to suffer the normal injurious consequences (of an action). [L *impunitas* f. *impunis* (as IN-[1], *poena* penalty)]
■ see *exemption* (EXEMPT).

impure /impyŏŏr/ *adj.* **1** mixed with foreign matter; adulterated. **2 a** dirty. **b** ceremonially unclean. **3** unchaste. **4** (of a colour) mixed with another colour. □□ **impurely** *adv.* **impureness** *n.* [ME f. L *impurus* (as IN-[1], *purus* pure)]
■ **1** mixed, admixed, alloyed, base, debased, adulterated, *US* cut. **2 a** see DIRTY *adj.* 1. **b** unclean, unhallowed, forbidden, disallowed, *Judaism* trefa, not kosher. **3** unchaste, immoral, sinful, wicked, evil, vile, unvirtuous, unvirginal, corrupted, defiled, debased, vitiated, degenerate, depraved, loose, wanton, lustful, promiscuous, libidinous, dissolute, licentious, obscene, prurient, dirty, filthy, lubricious, salacious, lascivious, lewd, lecherous. □□ **impureness** see IMPURITY 1.

impurity /impyŏŏriti/ *n.* (*pl.* **-ies**) **1** the quality or condition of being impure. **2** an impure thing or constituent. [F *impurité* or L *impuritas* (as IMPURE)]
■ **1** impureness, baseness, adulteration, pollution, contamination, defilement; uncleanness, dirtiness, foulness, filthiness, muckiness, griminess, squalidness, sordidness, *colloq.* crumminess, *Brit. sl.* grottiness; unchasteness, unchastity, immorality, sinfulness, wickedness, evil, vileness, corruption, degeneration, depravity, looseness, wantonness, lust, lustfulness, promiscuity, promiscuousness, libidinousness, dissoluteness, licentiousness, obscenity, prurience, lubricity, salaciousness, lasciviousness, lewdness, lecherousness. **2** adulterant, admixture, contaminant, pollutant, foreign matter *or* body; see also DIRT *n.* 1.

impute /impyŏŏt/ *v.tr.* (foll. by *to*) **1** regard (esp. something undesirable) as being done or caused or possessed by. **2** *Theol.* ascribe (righteousness, guilt, etc.) to (a person) by virtue of a similar quality in another. □□ **imputable** *adj.* **imputation** /-táysh'n/ *n.* **imputative** /-tətiv/ *adj.* [ME f. OF *imputer* f. L *imputare* enter in the account (as IN-[2], *putare* reckon)]
■ **1** (*impute to*) ascribe to, blame on, assign to, attribute to, put *or* set down to, lay on, lay at the door of. □□ **imputable** assignable, attributable, ascribable. **imputation** ascription, attribution, blame.

imshi /imshi/ *int. Austral. colloq.* be off! [colloq. (Egyptian) Arabic]

I.Mun.E. *abbr.* (in the UK) Institution of Municipal Engineers.

IN *abbr. US* Indiana (in official postal use).

In *symb. Chem.* the element indium.

in /in/ *prep., adv., & adj.* ● *prep.* **1** expressing inclusion or position within limits of space, time, circumstance, etc. (*in England; in bed; in the rain*). **2** during the time of (*in the night; in 1989*). **3** within the time of (*will be back in two hours*). **4 a** with respect to (*blind in one eye; good in parts*). **b** as a kind of (*the latest thing in luxury*). **5** as a proportionate part of (*one in three failed; a gradient of one in six*). **6** with the form or arrangement of (*packed in tens; falling in folds*). **7** as a member of (*in the army*). **8** concerned with (*is in politics*). **9** as or regarding the content of (*there is something in what you say*). **10** within the ability of (*does he have it in him?*). **11** having the condition of; affected by (*in bad health; in danger*). **12** having as a purpose (*in search of; in reply to*). **13** by means of or using as material (*drawn in pencil; modelled in bronze*). **14 a** using as the language of expression (*written in French*). **b** (of music) having as its key (*symphony in C*). **15** (of a word) having as a beginning or ending (*words in un-*). **16** wearing as dress (*in blue; in a suit*). **17** with the identity of (*found a friend in Mary*). **18** (of an animal) pregnant with (*in calf*). **19** into (with a verb of motion or change: *put it in the box; cut it in two*). **20** introducing an indirect object after a verb (*believe in; engage in; share in*). **21** forming adverbial phrases (*in any case; in reality; in short*). ● *adv.* expressing position within limits, or motion to such a position: **1** into a room, house, etc. (*come in*). **2** at home, in one's office, etc. (*is not in*). **3** so as to be enclosed or confined (*locked in*). **4** in a publication (*is the advertisement in?*). **5** in or to the inward side (*rub it in*). **6 a** in fashion, season, or office (*long skirts are in; strawberries are not yet in*). **b** elected (*the Democrat got in*). **7** exerting favourable action or influence (*their luck was in*). **8** *Cricket* (of a player or side) batting. **9** (of transport) at the platform etc. (*the train is in*). **10** (of a season, harvest, order, etc.) having arrived or been received. **11** *Brit.* (of a fire) continuing to burn. **12** denoting effective action (*join in*). **13** (of the tide) at the highest point. **14** (in *comb.*) *colloq.* denoting prolonged or concerted action, esp. by large numbers (*sit-in; teach-in*). ● *adj.* **1** internal; living in; inside (*in-patient*). **2** fashionable, esoteric (*the in thing to do*). **3** confined to or shared by a group of people (*in-joke*). □ **in all** see ALL. **in at** present at; contributing to (*in at the kill*). **in between** see BETWEEN *adv.* **in-between** *attrib.adj. colloq.* intermediate (*at an in-between stage*). **in for 1** about to undergo (esp. something unpleasant). **2** competing in or for. **3** involved in; committed to. **in on** sharing in; privy to (a secret etc.). **ins and outs** (often foll. by *of*) all the details (of a procedure etc.). **in so far as** see FAR. **in that** because; in so far as. **in with** on good terms with. [OE *in, inn*, orig. as adv. with verbs of motion]
■ *prep.* **16** see WEAR[1] *v.* 1. ● *adv.* **6 a** see FASHIONABLE. □ **in-between** see INTERMEDIATE *adj.* **in on** see PRIVY *adj.* 1. **ins and outs** see ROPE *n.* 3a. **in with** on good terms with, *en rapport* with, tuned in to.

in. *abbr.* inch(es).

in-[1] /in/ *prefix* (also **il-**, **im-**, **ir-**) added to: **1** adjectives, meaning 'not' (*inedible; insane*). **2** nouns, meaning 'without, lacking' (*inaction*). [L]

in-[2] /in/ *prefix* (also **il-** before *l*, **im-** before *b, m, p*, **ir-** before *r*) in, on, into, towards, within (*induce; influx; insight; intrude*). [IN, or from or after L *in* IN *prep.*]

-in /in/ *suffix Chem.* forming names of: **1** neutral substances (*gelatin*). **2** antibiotics (*penicillin*). [-INE[4]]

-ina /éenə/ *suffix* denoting: **1** feminine names and titles (*Georgina*; *tsarina*). **2** names of musical instruments (*concertina*). **3** names of zoological classification categories (*globigerina*). [It. or Sp. or L]

inability /innəbílliti/ *n.* **1** the state of being unable. **2** a lack of power or means.
■ incapacity, incapability, disability, incompetence, impotence, powerlessness, helplessness, *Med.* insufficiency.

in absentia /in abséntiə/ *adv.* in (his, her, or their) absence. [L]

inaccessible /innaksséssib'l/ *adj.* **1** not accessible; that cannot be reached. **2** (of a person) not open to advances or influence; unapproachable. ▫▫ **inaccessibility** /-bílliti/ *n.* **inaccessibleness** *n.* **inaccessibly** *adv.* [ME f. F *inaccessible* or LL *inaccessibilis* (as IN-[1], ACCESSIBLE)]
■ **1** unreachable, unapproachable, impenetrable, impassable, out of the way, beyond reach, out of reach, off the beaten track, remote, secluded, sequestered, rock-bound, *colloq.* unget-at-able, uncome-at-able; exclusive, restricted, select. **2** unreachable, unobtainable, unavailable; see also UNAPPROACHABLE 2. ▫▫ **inaccessibility, inaccessibleness** unreachableness, unapproachability, unapproachableness, impenetrability, impassability, impassableness, remoteness, seclusion, sequestration; exclusivity, exclusiveness, restrictedness, selectness; unavailability, distance, aloofness, reserve, standoffishness, unfriendliness, coolness, coldness, frigidity.

inaccurate /inákyoorət/ *adj.* not accurate. ▫▫ **inaccuracy** *n.* (*pl.* **-ies**). **inaccurately** *adv.*
■ inexact, imprecise, incorrect, erroneous, mistaken, wrong, false, untrue, fallacious, faulty, flawed, imperfect, improper, amiss, awry, out, off target, not on target, wide of the mark, *colloq.* off beam; careless, loose, sloppy, scrappy, scratchy, slapdash, slipshod, casual. ▫▫ **inaccuracy** carelessness, looseness, sloppiness, scrappiness, scratchiness, casualness; see also *impreciseness* (IMPRECISE), ERROR 1.

inaction /inákshʼn/ *n.* **1** lack of action. **2** sluggishness, inertness.
■ **1** see *inactivity* (INACTIVE). **2** see *idleness* (IDLE).

inactivate /ináktivayt/ *v.tr.* make inactive or inoperative. ▫▫ **inactivation** /-váyshʼn/ *n.*
■ see INCAPACITATE 1.

inactive /ináktiv/ *adj.* **1** not active or inclined to act. **2** passive. **3** indolent. ▫▫ **inactively** *adv.* **inactivity** /-tívviti/ *n.*
■ **1, 2** passive, unmoving, inert, motionless, immobile, immobilized, still, stationary, stagnant, static, lifeless, inanimate, dormant, abeyant, in abeyance, resting, supine; idle, non-functioning, inoperative, unoccupied, unemployed, jobless, out of work, out of a job; see also QUIET *adj.* 1. **3** indolent, lazy, idle, slothful, shiftless, fainéant, sluggish, listless, torpid, lethargic, lackadaisical, languid. ▫▫ **inactivity** inaction, passiveness, passivity, motionlessness, immobility, stillness, stasis, stagnancy, inertia, inertness, lifelessness, inanimation; dormancy, hibernation, *Zool.* aestivation; idleness, unemployment, joblessness; indolence, laziness, sloth, shiftlessness, sluggishness, listlessness, torpor, torpidity, lethargy, languidness; see also QUIET *n.* 1.

inadequate /ináddikwət/ *adj.* (often foll. by *to*) **1** not adequate; insufficient. **2** (of a person) incompetent; unable to deal with a situation. ▫▫ **inadequacy** *n.* (*pl.* **-ies**). **inadequately** *adv.*
■ **1** unsatisfactory, unacceptable, no good, not good enough, imperfect, incomplete, deficient, deprived, defective, flawed, faulty, bad, poor, pathetic, meagre, faint, slender, slight, scanty, sparse, skimpy, incommensurate; insufficient, not enough, too little, scarce, (in) short (supply). **2** incompetent, incapable, unqualified, inapt, unapt, impotent, powerless, useless, hopeless, inept, helpless, terrible, *sl. offens.* spastic. ▫▫ **inadequacy** unsatisfactoriness, unacceptableness, imperfection, incompleteness, deficiency, defectiveness, flaw, fault, faultiness, poorness, poverty, meagreness, faintness, scantiness, sparseness, skimpiness, insufficiency, scarcity; see also *incompetence* (INCOMPETENT).

inadmissible /innədmíssib'l/ *adj.* that cannot be admitted or allowed. ▫▫ **inadmissibility** /-bílliti/ *n.* **inadmissibly** *adv.*
■ impermissible, unallowable, disallowed, unacceptable, intolerable, unendurable, exceptionable, objectionable, inapplicable, inappropriate, unsuitable, improper, illegitimate, invalid, incorrect, wrong, forbidden, prohibited.

inadvertent /innədvért'nt/ *adj.* **1** (of an action) unintentional. **2 a** not properly attentive. **b** negligent. ▫▫ **inadvertence** *n.* **inadvertency** *n.* **inadvertently** *adv.* [IN-[1] + obs. *advertent* attentive (as ADVERT[2])]
■ **1** unintentional, unintended, unpremeditated, unthinking, unwitting, unconscious, unplanned, unstudied, undesigned, uncalculated, *colloq.* off the cuff; accidental, chance. **2** inattentive, unobservant, unwary, unaware, unmindful, unheeding, unheedful, heedless, preoccupied, distracted, oblivious, negligent, forgetful, careless; see also ABSENT-MINDED. ▫▫ **inadvertence, inadvertency** unthinkingness, unwittingness, inattentiveness, unwariness, unawareness, unmindfulness, heedlessness, preoccupation, distraction, obliviousness, negligence, forgetfulness, carelessness; see also *absent-mindedness* (ABSENT-MINDED). **inadvertently** see *by accident* (ACCIDENT), *absent-mindedly* (ABSENT-MINDED).

inadvisable /innədvī́zəb'l/ *adj.* not advisable. ▫▫ **inadvisability** /-bílliti/ *n.* [ADVISABLE]
■ see *ill-advised* 2 (ILL).

inalienable /ináyliənəb'l/ *adj.* that cannot be transferred to another; not alienable. ▫▫ **inalienability** /-bílliti/ *n.* **inalienably** *adv.*
■ untransferable, non-transferable, non-negotiable; inviolable, sacrosanct, unchallengeable, absolute, inherent, *Law* unalienable, imprescriptible, entailed, *literary* indefeasible.

inalterable /ináwltərəb'l, inóltər-/ *adj.* not alterable; that cannot be changed. ▫▫ **inalterability** /-bílliti/ *n.* **inalterably** *adv.* [med.L *inalterabilis* (as IN-[1], *alterabilis* alterable)]

inamorato /inámməraáatō/ *n.* (*pl.* **-os**; *fem.* **inamorata** /-tə/) a lover. [It., past part. of *inamorare* enamour (as IN-[2], *amore* f. L *amor* love)]

inane /ináyn/ *adj.* **1** silly, senseless. **2** empty, void. ▫▫ **inanely** *adv.* **inaneness** *n.* **inanity** /-ánniti/ *n.* (*pl.* **-ies**). [L *inanis* empty, vain]
■ **1** silly, asinine, vacuous, absurd, fatuous, empty-headed, foolish, witless, pointless, senseless, nonsensical, unreasonable, preposterous, ludicrous, ridiculous, laughable, risible, mad, lunatic, stupid, idiotic, *colloq.* dopey, crazy, moronic, imbecilic, cretinous, dotty, *esp. Brit. colloq.* daft, *esp. US colloq.* dumb, *sl.* goofy, screwy, cracked, nutty, nuts, daffy, batty, dippy, wacky, cuckoo, kooky, loony, bonkers, *Brit. sl.* barmy, crackers. **2** empty, void, vacant, unfilled, hollow, vacuous.

inanimate /inánnimət/ *adj.* **1** not animate; not endowed with (esp. animal) life. **2** lifeless; showing no sign of life. **3** spiritless, dull. ▫ **inanimate nature** everything other than the animal world. ▫▫ **inanimately** *adv.* **inanimation** /-máyshʼn/ *n.* [LL *inanimatus* (as IN-[1], ANIMATE)]
■ **1** lifeless, insentient, dead, defunct; inorganic, non-organic, mineral. **2** lifeless, exanimate, inert, inactive, motionless, immobile, unmoving, still. **3** spiritless, soulless, lifeless, cold, dead; flat, flaccid, dull, vapid, sluggish, slow, listless, torpid, inactive.

inanition /innənísh'n/ *n.* emptiness, esp. exhaustion from lack of nourishment. [ME f. LL *inanitio* f. L *inanire* make empty (as INANE)]

inappellable /innəpélləb'l/ *adj.* that cannot be appealed against. [obs.F *inappelable* (as IN-[1], *appeler* APPEAL)]

inapplicable /ináplikəb'l, innəplík-/ *adj.* (often foll. by *to*) not applicable; unsuitable. ▫▫ **inapplicability** /-bílliti/ *n.* **inapplicably** *adv.*

▪ irrelevant, unrelated, unconnected, extraneous, beside the point, wide of *or* beside *or* off the mark, malapropos, impertinent; inappropriate, unsuitable, unsuited, inapt, inapposite.

inapposite /ináppəzit/ *adj.* not apposite; out of place. ▫▫ **inappositely** *adv.* **inappositeness** *n.*

▪ see INAPPROPRIATE.

inappreciable /ínnəpréeshəb'l/ *adj.* **1** imperceptible; not worth reckoning. **2** that cannot be appreciated. ▫▫ **inappreciably** *adv.*

▪ **1** see IMPERCEPTIBLE 2.

inappreciation /innəpreeshiáysh'n/ *n.* failure to appreciate. ▫▫ **inappreciative** /-préeshətiv/ *adj.*

inappropriate /innəprṓpriət/ *adj.* not appropriate. ▫▫ **inappropriately** *adv.* **inappropriateness** *n.*

▪ unsuitable, unsuited, unfitting, unbefitting, inapt, inapposite, out of keeping, incongruous, infelicitous, inopportune, untimely, irrelevant, inapplicable, malapropos, extraneous.

inapt /inápt/ *adj.* **1** not apt or suitable. **2** unskilful. ▫▫ **inaptitude** *n.* **inaptly** *adv.* **inaptness** *n.*

▪ **1** see INAPPROPRIATE. ▫▫ **inaptitude, inaptness** see IMPROPRIETY 4.

inarch /inaárch/ *v.tr.* graft (a plant) by connecting a growing branch without separation from the parent stock. [IN-[2] + ARCH[1] *v.*]

inarguable /inaárgyooəb'l/ *adj.* that cannot be argued about or disputed. ▫▫ **inarguably** *adv.*

inarticulate /ínnaartíkyoolət/ *adj.* **1** unable to speak distinctly or express oneself clearly. **2** (of speech) not articulate; indistinctly pronounced. **3** dumb. **4** esp. *Anat.* not jointed. ▫▫ **inarticulately** *adv.* **inarticulateness** *n.* [LL *inarticulatus* (as IN-[1], ARTICULATE)]

▪ **1** unclear, incomprehensible, unintelligible, incoherent, confused, muddled, mixed-up, jumbled, wild, irrational, illogical, disjointed, discursive, rambling, unconnected, digressive. **2** mumbled, muttered, murmurous, indistinct, unclear, unintelligible, muffled, blurred, garbled, scrambled, faltering, halting, jerky. **3** dumb, mute, voiceless, silent; speechless, tongue-tied, dumbstruck, dumbfounded, lost *or* at a loss for words, *sl.* gobsmacked.

inartistic /ínnaartístik/ *adj.* **1** not following the principles of art. **2** lacking skill or talent in art; not appreciating art. ▫▫ **inartistically** *adv.*

▪ **1** see RUDE 3. **2** see UNGRACEFUL. ▫▫ **inartistically** see BADLY 1.

inasmuch /ínnəzmúch/ *adv.* (foll. by *as*) **1** since, because. **2** to the extent that. [ME, orig. *in as much*]

▪ **1** (*inasmuch as*) see BECAUSE.

inattentive /ínnəténtiv/ *adj.* **1** not paying due attention; heedless. **2** neglecting to show courtesy. ▫▫ **inattention** *n.* **inattentively** *adv.* **inattentiveness** *n.*

▪ heedless, careless, unthinking, unmindful, incautious, unwary, unguarded, inadvertent, unobservant; detached, distracted, *distrait*, absent-minded, oblivious, abstracted, in a brown study, (with one's head) in the clouds, in a world of one's own, unconcerned, apathetic, uncaring, neglectful, negligent, slack, remiss. ▫▫ **inattention, inattentiveness** incaution, unthinkingness, unmindfulness, unwariness, unguardedness, inadvertence, inadvertency; see also NEGLIGENCE, *absent-mindedness* (ABSENT-MINDED).

inaudible /ináwdib'l/ *adj.* that cannot be heard. ▫▫ **inaudibility** /-bílliti/ *n.* **inaudibly** *adv.*

▪ unheard, out of earshot, imperceptible, indistinct; low, faint, muted, quiet, soft, muffled, stifled, whispered. ▫▫ **inaudibility** quietness, faintness, softness.

inaugural /ináwgyoorəl/ *adj.* & *n.* ● *adj.* **1** of inauguration. **2** (of a lecture etc.) given by a person being inaugurated. ● *n.* an inaugural speech etc. [F f. *inaugurer* (as INAUGURATE)]

▪ *adj.* see INTRODUCTORY.

inaugurate /ináwgyoorayt/ *v.tr.* **1** admit (a person) formally to office. **2** initiate the public use of (a building etc.). **3** begin, introduce. **4** enter with ceremony upon (an undertaking etc.). ▫▫ **inauguration** /-ráysh'n/ *n.* **inaugurator** *n.* **inauguratory** *adj.* [L *inaugurare* (as IN-[2], *augurare* take omens: see AUGUR)]

▪ **1** install, induct, invest, instate, crown, enthrone, frock, ordain, chair. **2** open, declare open, establish, launch, unveil, take the wraps off. **3, 4** initiate, begin, start, originate, set up, launch, institute, introduce, usher in, enter upon, get under way, get going, get started, set rolling, *colloq.* get off the ground, *formal* commence. ▫▫ **inauguration** installation, induction, investiture, instatement, coronation, enthronement, ordainment, ordination; establishment, launch, initiation, institution, introduction, *colloq.* kick-off.

inauspicious /innawspíshəss/ *adj.* **1** ill-omened, unpropitious. **2** unlucky. ▫▫ **inauspiciously** *adv.* **inauspiciousness** *n.*

▪ **1** ill-omened, ill-starred, ill-fated, doomed, fateful, unpropitious, unpromising, unfavourable, unlucky, unfortunate, unhappy; sinister, ominous, menacing, dark, gloomy, black, threatening. **2** see UNFORTUNATE *adj.* 1.

inboard /inbord/ *adv.* & *adj.* ● *adv.* within the sides of or towards the centre of a ship, aircraft, or vehicle. ● *adj.* situated inboard.

inborn /inbórn/ *adj.* existing from birth; implanted by nature.

▪ innate, congenital, inherent, inherited, hereditary, inbred, natural, native, constitutional, deep-seated, deep-rooted, ingrained, instinctive, instinctual, connate.

inbreathe /inbréeth/ *v.tr.* **1** breathe in or absorb. **2** inspire (a person).

inbred /inbréd/ *adj.* **1** inborn. **2** produced by inbreeding.

▪ see INBORN.

inbreeding /inbréeding/ *n.* breeding from closely related animals or persons. ▫▫ **inbreed** *v.tr.* & *intr.* (*past* and *past part.* **inbred**).

inbuilt /inbilt/ *adj.* incorporated as part of a structure.

Inc. *abbr. US* Incorporated.

Inca /íngkə/ *n.* a member of an American Indian people in Peru before the Spanish conquest. ▫▫ **Incaic** /ingkáyik/ *adj.* **Incan** *adj.* [Quechua, = lord, royal person]

incalculable /inkálkyooləb'l/ *adj.* **1** too great for calculation. **2** that cannot be reckoned beforehand. **3** (of a person, character, etc.) uncertain. ▫▫ **incalculability** /-bílliti/ *n.* **incalculably** *adv.*

▪ **1** see IMMEASURABLE.

in camera see CAMERA.

incandesce /ínkandéss/ *v.intr.* & *tr.* glow or cause to glow with heat. [back-form. f. INCANDESCENT]

▪ see GLOW *v.* 1.

incandescent /ínkandéss'nt/ *adj.* **1** glowing with heat. **2** shining brightly. **3** (of an electric or other light) produced by a glowing white-hot filament. ▫▫ **incandescence** *n.* **incandescently** *adv.* [F f. L *incandescere* (as IN-[2], *candescere* inceptive of *candēre* be white)]

▪ **1, 2** glowing, aglow, fervent, red-hot, white-hot, radiant, *poet.* fervid; alight, ablaze, aflame, ardent, flaming, burning, fiery, on fire. ▫▫ **incandescence** glow, fervour, fervency, red heat, white heat, *poet.* fervidity; fire, blaze, flame, fieriness, ardency; see also *radiance* (RADIANT).

incantation /ínkantáysh'n/ *n.* **1 a** a magical formula. **b** the use of this. **2** a spell or charm. ▫▫ **incantational** *adj.* **incantatory** *adj.* [ME f. OF f. LL *incantatio -onis* f. *incantare* chant, bewitch (as IN-[2], *cantare* sing)]

▪ **1a, 2** see SPELL[2] 1.

incapable /inkáypəb'l/ *adj.* **1** (often foll. by *of*) **a** not capable. **b** lacking the required quality or characteristic (favourable or adverse) (*incapable of hurting anyone*). **2** not capable of rational conduct or of managing one's own affairs (*drunk and incapable*). ▫▫ **incapability** /-bílliti/ *n.* **incapably** *adv.* [F *incapable* or LL *incapabilis* (as IN-[1], *capabilis* CAPABLE)]

■ **1** (*incapable of*) **a** unable to, powerless to, incompetent to, unfit to, not equipped to, unqualified to, impotent to, unequal to, not up to. **b** unable to, not equipped to, not the type to, insusceptible to, resistant to, impervious to, ill-disposed to, disinclined to, not open to. **2** incapacitated, disabled, *hors de combat*, inoperative, immobilized, helpless, impuissant, paralysed, paralytic.

incapacitate /inkəpássitayt/ *v.tr.* **1** render incapable or unfit. **2** disqualify. ▫▫ **incapacitant** *n.* **incapacitation** /-táysh'n/ *n.*

■ **1** immobilize, inactivate, deactivate, put out of action *or* commission; indispose, disable, cripple, paralyse, lame, wound, maim, impair, weaken, enfeeble, enervate, exhaust, devitalize. **2** see DISQUALIFY.

incapacity /inkəpássiti/ *n.* (*pl.* **-ies**) **1** inability; lack of the necessary power or resources. **2** legal disqualification. **3** an instance of incapacity. [F *incapacité* or LL *incapacitas* (as IN-[1], CAPACITY)]

■ **1** see INABILITY.

incarcerate /inkaársərayt/ *v.tr.* imprison or confine. ▫▫ **incarceration** /-ráysh'n/ *n.* **incarcerator** *n.* [med.L *incarcerare* (as IN-[2], L *carcer* prison)]

■ see IMPRISON. ▫▫ **incarceration** see *imprisonment* (IMPRISON).

incarnadine /inkaárnədīn/ *adj.* & *v. poet.* ● *adj.* flesh-coloured or crimson. ● *v.tr.* dye this colour. [F *incarnadin -ine* f. It. *incarnadino* (for *-tino*) f. *incarnato* INCARNATE *adj.*]

incarnate *adj.* & *v.* ● *adj.* /inkaárnət/ **1** (of a person, spirit, quality, etc.) embodied in flesh, esp. in human form (*is the devil incarnate*). **2** represented in a recognizable or typical form (*folly incarnate*). ● *v.tr.* /inkaarnayt, -kaárnayt/ **1** embody in flesh. **2** put (an idea etc.) into concrete form; realize. **3** (of a person etc.) be the living embodiment of (a quality). [ME f. eccl.L *incarnare incarnat-* make flesh (as IN-[2], L *caro carnis* flesh)]

■ *adj.* **1** see PHYSICAL *adj.* 1. **2** see PHYSICAL *adj.* 2. ● *v.* **1** embody, flesh. **2** see EMBODY 1, 3. **3** see PERSONIFY 3.

incarnation /inkaarnáysh'n/ *n.* **1 a** embodiment in (esp. human) flesh. **b** (**the Incarnation**) *Theol.* the embodiment of God the Son in human flesh as Jesus Christ. **2** (often foll. by *of*) a living type (of a quality etc.). **3** *Med.* the process of forming new flesh. [ME f. OF f. eccl.L *incarnatio -onis* (as INCARNATE)]

■ **1, 2** see *embodiment* (EMBODY).

incase var. of ENCASE.

incautious /inkáwshəss/ *adj.* heedless, rash. ▫▫ **incaution** *n.* **incautiously** *adv.* **incautiousness** *n.*

■ see RASH[1]. ▫▫ **incautiously** see *hastily* (HASTY).

incendiary /inséndiəri/ *adj.* & *n.* ● *adj.* **1** (of a substance or device, esp. a bomb) designed to cause fires. **2 a** of or relating to the malicious setting on fire of property. **b** guilty of this. **3** tending to stir up strife; inflammatory. ● *n.* (*pl.* **-ies**) **1** an incendiary bomb or device. **2** an incendiary person. ▫▫ **incendiarism** *n.* [ME f. L *incendiarius* f. *incendium* conflagration f. *incendere incens-* set fire to]

■ *adj.* **3** see INFLAMMATORY 1. ● *n.* **2** see AGITATOR 1.

incense[1] /insenss/ *n.* & *v.* ● *n.* **1** a gum or spice producing a sweet smell when burned. **2** the smoke of this, esp. in religious ceremonial. ● *v.tr.* **1** treat or perfume (a person or thing) with incense. **2** burn incense to (a deity etc.). **3** suffuse with fragrance. ▫▫ **incensation** /-sáysh'n/ *n.* [ME f. OF *encens*, *encenser* f. eccl.L *incensum* a thing burnt, incense: see INCENDIARY]

incense[2] /insénss/ *v.tr.* (often foll. by *at*, *with*, *against*) enrage; make angry. [ME f. OF *incenser* (as INCENDIARY)]

■ see ENRAGE.

incensory /insensəri/ *n.* (*pl.* **-ies**) = CENSER. [med.L *incensorium* (as INCENSE[1])]

incentive /inséntiv/ *n.* & *adj.* ● *n.* **1** (often foll. by *to*) a motive or incitement, esp. to action. **2** a payment or concession to stimulate greater output by workers. ● *adj.* serving to motivate or incite. [ME f. L *incentivus* setting the tune f. *incinere incent-* sing to (as IN-[2], *canere* sing)]

■ *n.* **1** incitement, encouragement, promotion, motivation, enticement, lure, inducement, carrot, fillip, stimulus, goad, prod, provocation, spur, *sl.* come-on; motive, impetus, impulse, mainspring. **2** payment, bonus, reward, extra, perquisite, *Brit. colloq.* perk. ● *adj.* motivational, promotional.

incept /insépt/ *v.* **1** *tr. Biol.* (of an organism) take in (food etc.). **2** *intr. Brit. hist.* take a master's or doctor's degree at a university. ▫▫ **inceptor** *n.* (in sense 2). [L *incipere incept-* begin (as IN-[2], *capere* take)]

inception /insépsh'n/ *n.* a beginning. [ME f. OF *inception* or L *inceptio* (as INCEPT)]

■ see BEGINNING 1, 2.

inceptive /inséptiv/ *adj.* & *n.* ● *adj.* **1 a** beginning. **b** initial. **2** *Gram.* (of a verb) that denotes the beginning of an action. ● *n.* an inceptive verb. [LL *inceptivus* (as INCEPT)]

incertitude /insértityōōd/ *n.* uncertainty, doubt. [F *incertitude* or LL *incertitudo* (as IN-[1], CERTITUDE)]

incessant /inséss'nt/ *adj.* unceasing, continual, repeated. ▫▫ **incessancy** *n.* **incessantly** *adv.* **incessantness** *n.* [F *incessant* or LL *incessans* (as IN-[1], *cessans* pres. part. of L *cessare* CEASE)]

■ see CONTINUAL. ▫▫ **incessantly** see *endlessly* (ENDLESS).

incest /insest/ *n.* sexual intercourse between persons regarded as too closely related to marry each other. [ME f. L *incestus* (as IN-[1], *castus* CHASTE)]

incestuous /inséstyooəss/ *adj.* **1** involving or guilty of incest. **2** (of human relations generally) excessively restricted or resistant to wider influence. ▫▫ **incestuously** *adv.* **incestuousness** *n.* [LL *incestuosus* (as INCEST)]

inch[1] /inch/ *n.* & *v.* ● *n.* **1** a unit of linear measure equal to one-twelfth of a foot (2.54 cm). **2 a** (as a unit of rainfall) a quantity that would cover a horizontal surface to a depth of 1 inch. **b** (of atmospheric or other pressure) an amount that balances the weight of a column of mercury 1 inch high. **3** (as a unit of map-scale) so many inches representing 1 mile on the ground (*a 4-inch map*). **4** a small amount (usu. with *neg.*: *would not yield an inch*). ● *v.tr.* & *intr.* move gradually in a specified way (*inched forward*). ▫ **every inch 1** entirely (*looked every inch a queen*). **2** the whole distance or area (*combed every inch of the garden*). **give a person an inch and he** or **she will take a mile** (or orig. **an ell**) a person once conceded to will demand much. **inch by inch** gradually; bit by bit. **within an inch of** almost to the point of. [OE *ynce* f. L *uncia* twelfth part: cf. OUNCE[1]]

■ *v.* crawl, creep, edge, work one's way; see also EASE *v.* 5b. ▫ **inch by inch** see *by degrees* (DEGREE).

inch[2] /inch/ *n.* esp. *Sc.* a small island (esp. in place-names). [ME f. Gael. *innis*]

inchmeal /inchmeel/ *adv.* by inches; little by little; gradually. [f. INCH[1] + MEAL[1]]

■ see *gradually* (GRADUAL).

inchoate /inkṓ-ayt/ *adj.* & *v.* ● *adj.* **1** just begun. **2** undeveloped, rudimentary, unformed. ● *v.tr.* begin; originate. ▫▫ **inchoately** *adv.* **inchoateness** *n.* **inchoation** /-áysh'n/ *n.* **inchoative** /-kṓətiv/ *adj.* [L *inchoatus* past part. of *inchoare* (as IN-[2], *choare* begin)]

■ *adj.* see UNDEVELOPED.

inchworm /inchwurm/ *n.* = *measuring-worm* (see MEASURE).

incidence /insid'nss/ *n.* **1** (often foll. by *of*) the fact, manner, or rate, of occurrence or action. **2** the range, scope, or extent of influence of a thing. **3** *Physics* the falling of a line, or of a thing moving in a line, upon a surface. **4** the act or an instance of coming into contact with a thing. ▫ **angle of incidence** the angle which an incident line, ray, etc., makes with the perpendicular to the surface at the point of

incidence. [ME f. OF *incidence* or med.L *incidentia* (as INCIDENT)]
■ **1** frequency, rate, degree, extent, occurrence, prevalence; quantity, amount, number. **2** see RANGE *n.* 1a–c.

incident /ínsid'nt/ *n.* & *adj.* ● *n.* **1 a** an event or occurrence. **b** a minor or detached event attracting general attention or noteworthy in some way. **2** a hostile clash, esp. of troops of countries at war (*a frontier incident*). **3** a distinct piece of action in a play or a poem. **4** *Law* a privilege, burden, etc., attaching to an obligation or right. ● *adj.* **1 a** (often foll. by *to*) apt or liable to happen; naturally attaching or dependent. **b** (foll. by *to*) *Law* attaching to. **2** (often foll. by *on, upon*) (of light etc.) falling or striking. [ME f. F *incident* or L *incidere* (as IN-², *cadere* fall)]
■ *n.* **1 a** event, occurrence, occasion, happening, proceeding, circumstance, fact, case, experience. **b** event, occasion, happening, function, scene, episode, to-do, *colloq.* affair, do. **2** clash, confrontation, disturbance, commotion, fracas, skirmish, fight, unpleasantness, upset, quarrel, scene, affair, dispute, altercation, argument, disagreement, *colloq.* dust-up, set-to, ding-dong, scrap. ● *adj.* **1** (*incident to*) appurtenant to, pertinent to, pertaining to, attaching to, incidental to, liable to happen to, usual for, typical of; dependent on.

incidental /ínsidént'l/ *adj.* **1** (often foll. by *to*) **a** having a minor role in relation to a more important thing, event, etc. **b** not essential. **c** casual, happening by chance. **2** (foll. by *to*) liable to happen. **3** (foll. by *on, upon*) following as a subordinate event. □ **incidental music** music used as a background to the action of a film, broadcast, etc.
■ **1 a** secondary, subordinate, subsidiary, ancillary, auxiliary, supplementary, supplemental, peripheral, minor, inferior, lesser. **b** non-essential, unessential, inessential, unnecessary, dispensable, expendable, peripheral, extraneous, accidental; unimportant, inconsequential, trivial, lightweight, insignificant, negligible, petty, trifling, paltry. **c** casual, chance, fortuitous, aleatory, random, haphazard, serendipitous, unpredictable, accidental, coincidental, adventitious, unplanned, unlooked-for, *colloq.* fluky. **2** (*incidental to*) see INCIDENT *adj.* □ **incidental music** score, soundtrack; see also *background music*.

incidentally /ínsidéntəli/ *adv.* **1** by the way; as an unconnected remark. **2** in an incidental way.
■ **1** by the way, by the by, apropos, parenthetically, in passing, *en passant*. **2** secondarily, subordinately, subsidiarily, supplementarily, supplementally, peripherally, extraneously, unnecessarily; coincidentally, casually, as luck would have it, accidentally, by chance, *archaic or poet.* perchance.

incinerate /insínnərayt/ *v.tr.* **1** consume (a body etc.) by fire. **2** reduce to ashes. □□ **incineration** /-ráysh'n/ *n.* [med.L *incinerare* (as IN-², *cinis -eris* ashes)]
■ see BURN¹ *v.* 1.

incinerator /insínnəraytər/ *n.* a furnace or apparatus for burning esp. refuse to ashes.

incipient /insíppiənt/ *adj.* **1** beginning. **2** in an initial stage. □□ **incipience** *n.* **incipiency** *n.* **incipiently** *adv.* [L *incipere incipient-* (as INCEPT)]
■ see INITIAL *adj.*

incise /insı̄z/ *v.tr.* **1** make a cut in. **2** engrave. [F *inciser* f. L *incidere incis-* (as IN-², *caedere* cut)]
■ **2** see CARVE 1, 2.

incision /insízh'n/ *n.* **1** a cut; a division produced by cutting; a notch. **2** the act of cutting into a thing. [ME f. OF *incision* or LL *incisio* (as INCISE)]
■ **1** cut, slit, gash, slash, cleft, notch, score, nick, snick, scratch, scarification, *archaic* scotch.

incisive /insı̄siv/ *adj.* **1** mentally sharp; acute. **2** clear and effective. **3** cutting, penetrating. □□ **incisively** *adv.* **incisiveness** *n.* [med.L *incisivus* (as INCISE)]
■ **1** sharp, keen, acute, razor-sharp, piercing, perspicacious, perceptive, percipient, intelligent, clever, canny, shrewd, astute, smart, quick, alert, aware, *colloq.* on the ball. **2** clear, concise, succinct, terse, laconic, pithy, to the point, effective; aphoristic, epigrammatic, crisp, brisk, direct, plain, straightforward. **3** cutting, biting, mordant, trenchant, critical, caustic, sarcastic, ironic, cynical, sardonic, penetrating; pungent, acrid, stinging, corrosive, acerbic, acid, sharp, tart, bitter, acrimonious.

incisor /insı̄zər/ *n.* a cutting-tooth, esp. at the front of the mouth. [med.L, = cutter (as INCISE)]

incite /insı̄t/ *v.tr.* (often foll. by *to*) urge or stir up. □□ **incitation** /-táysh'n/ *n.* **incitement** *n.* **inciter** *n.* [ME f. F *inciter* f. L *incitare* (as IN-², *citare* rouse)]
■ urge, exhort, encourage, prompt, move, drive, push, egg on, excite, rally, rouse, arouse, wake, waken, awaken, instigate, stir, bestir, stir *or* whip *or* work up, agitate, stimulate, entice, goad, spur, prod, provoke, inspire, inflame, fire, *archaic* prick; foment. □□ **incitation, incitement** exhortation, encouragement, motivation, instigation, persuasion, drive, push, excitement, arousal, agitation, stimulus, stimulation, enticement, persuasion, spur, provocation, inspiration, inflammation; fomentation; rabble-rousing; see also INCENTIVE *n.* 1. **inciter** see *arouser* (AROUSE), *rabble-rouser* (RABBLE¹).

incivility /ínsivílliti/ *n.* (*pl.* **-ies**) **1** rudeness, discourtesy. **2** a rude or discourteous act. [F *incivilité* or LL *incivilitas* (as IN-¹, CIVILITY)]
■ **1** rudeness, boorishness, coarseness, discourtesy, discourteousness, disrespect, unmannerliness, indecorum, indecorousness, impoliteness, tactlessness, ungentlemanliness, bad breeding, ill breeding, bad manners, misbehaviour; see also *impertinence* (IMPERTINENT). **2** see MISSTEP 2.

inclement /inklémmənt/ *adj.* (of the weather or climate) severe, esp. cold or stormy. □□ **inclemency** *n.* (*pl.* **-ies**). **inclemently** *adv.* [F *inclément* or L *inclemens* (as IN-¹, CLEMENT)]
■ extreme, intemperate, severe, adverse, harsh, rigorous, rough, violent; stormy, rainy, squally, blustery, raw, tempestuous; see also BAD *adj.* 2a. □□ **inclemency** see *severity* (SEVERE).

inclination /inklináysh'n/ *n.* **1** (often foll. by *to*) a disposition or propensity. **2** (often foll. by *for*) a liking or affection. **3** a leaning, slope, or slant. **4** the difference of direction of two lines or planes, esp. as measured by the angle between them. **5** the dip of a magnetic needle. [ME f. OF *inclination* or L *inclinatio* (as INCLINE)]
■ **1** disposition, predisposition, tendency, bent, bias, leaning, preference, turn, cast, proclivity, propensity, attitude, proneness, susceptibility, predilection, partiality, desire, *literary* velleity; see also WISH *n.* **2** affection, fondness, love, liking, penchant, weakness, soft spot, taste, fancy. **3** slope, slant, angle, bend, leaning, tilt, nod; see also INCLINE *n.*

incline *v.* & *n.* ● *v.* /inklı̄n/ **1** *tr.* (usu. in *passive*; often foll. by *to, for,* or *to* + infin.) **a** make (a person, feelings, etc.) willing or favourably disposed (*am inclined to think so*; *does not incline me to agree*). **b** give a specified tendency to (a thing) (*the door is inclined to bang*). **2** *intr.* **a** be disposed (*I incline to think so*). **b** (often foll. by *to, towards*) tend. **3** *intr.* & *tr.* lean or turn away from a given direction, esp. the vertical. **4** *tr.* bend (the head, body, or oneself) forward or downward. ● *n.* /ínklīn/ **1** a slope. **2** an inclined plane. □ **inclined plane** a sloping plane (esp. as a means of reducing the force needed to raise a load). **incline one's ear** (often foll. by *to*) listen favourably. □□ **incliner** *n.* [ME *encline* f. OF *encliner* f. L *inclinare* (as IN-², *clinare* bend)]
■ *v.* **1** make, lead, get, persuade, convince, influence, dispose, predispose, prejudice, bias; (*inclined*) see WILLING *adj.*, LIKELY *adj.* 1. **2** be disposed *or* predisposed, have a mind, show favour *or* preference, be biased *or* prejudiced, gravitate; tend, be prone, be liable *or* likely *or* apt. **3, 4** lean, bend, bow, nod, stoop, slant, tilt, angle, bank, slope, tip, arch; (*inclined*) see OBLIQUE *adj.* 1. ● *n.* slope, pitch, grade, gradient, slant, ramp, hill,

dip, descent, declivity, rise, ascent, acclivity. □ **incline one's ear** lend an ear, give a fair hearing; give one's full *or* undivided attention, pay attention; (*incline one's ear to*) heed.

inclinometer /ínklinómmitər/ *n.* **1** an instrument for measuring the angle between the direction of the earth's magnetic field and the horizontal. **2** an instrument for measuring the inclination of an aircraft or ship to the horizontal. **3** an instrument for measuring a slope. [L *inclinare* INCLINE *v.* + -METER]

inclose var. of ENCLOSE.

inclosure var. of ENCLOSURE.

include /inklóod/ *v.tr.* **1** comprise or reckon in as part of a whole; place in a class or category. **2** (as **including** *prep.*) if we include (*six members, including the chairman*). **3** treat or regard as so included. **4** (as **included** *adj.*) shut in; enclosed. □ **include out** *colloq.* or *joc.* specifically exclude. □□ **includable** *adj.* **includible** *adj.* **inclusion** /-klóozh'n/ *n.* [ME f. L *includere inclus-* (as IN-[2], *claudere* shut)]

■ **1** incorporate, embody, comprise, embrace, cover, encompass, number, take in, admit, subsume, comprehend, contain; classify, categorize, group, file, list, catalogue, tabulate, register; see also SELECT *v.* **2** (**including**) see INCLUSIVE 1. **3** count, number, allow for, take into account, involve. **4** (**included**) enclosed, contained, wrapped, enveloped, packaged, inserted, encompassed, lodged. □ **include out** see EXCLUDE 3. □□ **inclusion** incorporation, involvement, subsumption, embracement; admission, categorization, selection, choice; enclosure, packaging, insertion, encompassment.

inclusive /inklóossiv/ *adj.* **1** (often foll. by *of*) including, comprising. **2** with the inclusion of the extreme limits stated (*pages 7 to 26 inclusive*). **3** including all the normal services etc. (*a hotel offering inclusive terms*). □ **inclusive language** language that is deliberately non-sexist, esp. avoiding the use of masculine pronouns to cover both men and women. □□ **inclusively** *adv.* **inclusiveness** *n.* [med.L *inclusivus* (as INCLUDE)]

■ **1** (*inclusive of*) including, embracing, comprising, taking in, covering, incorporating, embodying. **3** comprehensive, all-in, catch-all, overall, full, thorough, across the board, all-in-one, all-encompassing, umbrella, blanket; general, wide, broad, deep, extensive.

incog /inkóg/ *adj., adv., & n. colloq.* = INCOGNITO. [abbr.]

incognito /ínkogneétō/ *adj., adv., & n.* ● *adj. & adv.* with one's name or identity kept secret (*was travelling incognito*). ● *n.* (*pl.* **-os**) **1** a person who is incognito. **2** the pretended identity or anonymous character of such a person. [It., = unknown, f. L *incognitus* (as IN-[1], *cognitus* past part. of *cognoscere* know)]

■ *adj. & adv.* in disguise, in camouflage, under cover, under a false *or* assumed name, in plain clothes, *colloq.* incog; disguised, unidentified, unrecognized, camouflaged, masked; anonymous(ly), covert(ly), secret(ly), clandestine(ly); (*adj.*) plain-clothes, unrecognizable, mysterious; (*adv.*) on the sly, *colloq.* on the q.t. ● *n.* **1** mystery man *or* woman, masquerader, *colloq.* incog. **2** false *or* assumed identity *or* name, alias, pseudonym, *nom de guerre*; disguise, masquerade, camouflage, mask, cover, smokescreen; act, charade, sham, pretence.

incognizant /inkógniz'nt/ *adj.* (foll. by *of*) unaware; not knowing. □□ **incognizance** *n.*

■ see UNAWARE *adj.* 1.

incoherent /ínkōheerənt/ *adj.* **1** (of a person) unable to speak intelligibly. **2** (of speech etc.) lacking logic or consistency. **3** *Physics* (of waves) having no definite or stable phase relationship. □□ **incoherence** *n.* **incoherency** *n.* (*pl.* **-ies**). **incoherently** *adv.*

■ **1** inarticulate, unintelligible, incomprehensible, delirious, raving, confused, rambling, obscure. **2** illogical, irrational, wild, unstructured, disconnected, disjointed, loose, unconnected, uncoordinated, disorganized, disordered, confused, garbled, mixed up, jumbled, muddled, scrambled; rambling, discursive, digressive, raggle-taggle.

incombustible /inkəmbústib'l/ *adj.* that cannot be burnt or consumed by fire. □□ **incombustibility** /-bílliti/ *n.* [ME f. med.L *incombustibilis* (as IN-[1], COMBUSTIBLE)]

■ non-flammable, not inflammable, non-flam, fireproof, fire-resistant, fire-retardant, asbestine; flame-proof, heat-resistant, heatproof, ovenproof.

income /inkum/ *n.* the money or other assets received, esp. periodically or in a year, from one's business, lands, work, investments, etc. □ **income group** a section of the population determined by income. **income tax** a tax levied on income. [ME (orig. = arrival), prob. f. ON *innkoma*: in later use f. *come in*]

■ earnings, revenue(s), receipts, return(s), proceeds, turnover, incomings, takings, *esp. US* take; see also PROFIT *n.* 2. □ **income tax** see TAX *n.* 1.

incomer /ínkummər/ *n.* **1** a person who comes in. **2** a person who arrives to settle in a place; an immigrant. **3** an intruder. **4** a successor.

-incomer /inkummər/ *comb. form* earning a specified kind or level of income (*middle-incomer*).

incoming /inkumming/ *adj. & n.* ● *adj.* **1** coming in (*the incoming tide; incoming telephone calls*). **2** succeeding another person or persons (*the incoming tenant*). **3** immigrant. **4** (of profit) accruing. ● *n.* **1** (usu. in *pl.*) revenue, income. **2** the act of arriving or entering.

■ *n.* **1** see INCOME. **2** see ARRIVAL 1.

incommensurable /inkəménshərəb'l, -ménsyərəb'l/ *adj.* (often foll. by *with*) **1** not comparable in respect of magnitude. **2** incapable of being measured. **3** *Math.* (of a magnitude or magnitudes) having no common factor, integral or fractional. **4** *Math.* irrational. □□ **incommensurability** /-bílliti/ *n.* **incommensurably** *adv.* [LL *incommensurabilis* (as IN-[1], COMMENSURABLE)]

incommensurate /inkəménshərət, -ménsyərət/ *adj.* **1** (often foll. by *with, to*) out of proportion; inadequate. **2** = INCOMMENSURABLE. □□ **incommensurately** *adv.* **incommensurateness** *n.*

■ **1** see DISPROPORTIONATE.

incommode /inkəmṓd/ *v.tr.* **1** hinder, inconvenience. **2** trouble, annoy. [F *incommoder* or L *incommodare* (as IN-[1], *commodus* convenient)]

■ **1** see INCONVENIENCE *v.*

incommodious /inkəmṓdiəss/ *adj.* not affording good accommodation; uncomfortable. □□ **incommodiously** *adv.* **incommodiousness** *n.*

■ see *cramped* (CRAMP *v.* 4).

incommunicable /inkəmyóónikəb'l/ *adj.* **1** that cannot be communicated or shared. **2** that cannot be uttered or told. **3** that does not communicate; uncommunicative. □□ **incommunicability** /-bílliti/ *n.* **incommunicableness** *n.* **incommunicably** *adv.* [LL *incommunicabilis* (as IN-[1], COMMUNICABLE)]

incommunicado /ínkəmyoonikaádō/ *adj.* **1** without or deprived of the means of communication with others. **2** (of a prisoner) in solitary confinement. [Sp. *incomunicado* past part. of *incomunicar* deprive of communication]

incommunicative /ínkəmyóónikətiv/ *adj.* not communicative; taciturn. □□ **incommunicatively** *adv.* **incommunicativeness** *n.*

incommutable /inkəmyóótəb'l/ *adj.* **1** not changeable. **2** not commutable. □□ **incommutably** *adv.* [ME f. L *incommutabilis* (as IN-[1], COMMUTABLE)]

incomparable /inkómpərəb'l/ *adj.* **1** without an equal; matchless. **2** (often foll. by *with, to*) not to be compared. □□ **incomparability** /-bílliti/ *n.* **incomparableness** *n.* **incomparably** *adv.* [ME f. OF f. L *incomparabilis* (as IN-[1], COMPARABLE)]

■ **1** beyond compare, without equal, unequalled, matchless, peerless, unparalleled, unrivalled, *hors concours*, nonpareil, transcendent, perfect, surpassing, supreme, superior, superlative, unsurpassed, unsurpassable.

incompatible /inkəmpáttib'l/ *adj.* **1** opposed in character; discordant. **2** (often foll. by *with*) inconsistent. **3** (of persons) unable to live, work, etc., together in harmony. **4** (of drugs) not suitable for taking at the same time. **5** (of equipment, machinery, etc.) not capable of being used in combination. □□ **incompatibility** /-bílliti/ *n.* **incompatibleness** *n.* **incompatibly** *adv.* [med.L *incompatibilis* (as IN-¹, COMPATIBLE)]

■ **1, 3** mismatched, unsuited, discordant, clashing, jarring, inconsistent, contradictory, conflicting, repugnant, uncongenial, inconsonant, irreconcilable, incongruous, out of keeping; antithetical, antithetic, opposed, opposite, contrary, antipathetic, antagonistic, hostile. **2** see UNLIKE *adj.* 1. □□ **incompatibility, incompatibleness** mismatch, discord, discordance, discordancy, inconsistency, contradictoriness, conflict, repugnance, uncongeniality, irreconcilability, incongruousness; disagreement, dissent, opposition, disaccord, dissimilarity, difference.

incompetent /inkómpit'nt/ *adj.* & *n.* ● *adj.* **1** (often foll. by *to* + infin.) not qualified or able to perform a particular task or function (*an incompetent builder*). **2** showing a lack of skill (*an incompetent performance*). **3** *Med.* (esp. of a valve or sphincter) not able to perform its function. ● *n.* an incompetent person. □□ **incompetence** *n.* **incompetency** *n.* **incompetently** *adv.* [F *incompétent* or LL *incompetens* (as IN-¹, COMPETENT)]

■ *adj.* **1** unqualified, inexpert, unfit, unable, incapable, *esp. US sl.* out to lunch; inadequate, insufficient, not good enough, deficient; unapt, inapt, unsuitable. **2** unskilled, unskilful, inept, maladroit, inexpert, awkward, clumsy, bungling, gauche, *colloq.* cack-handed; useless, hopeless, *colloq.* terrible, past it; inadequate, insufficient, ineffective, ineffectual, inefficient. ● *n.* bungler, botcher, bodger, blunderer, flounderer, bumbler, oaf, *colloq.* galoot, *US colloq.* lummox, *sl.* duffer, slouch, *Brit. sl.* buffer. □□ **incompetence, incompetency** inability, incapability, incapacity, inexpertness, inadequacy, insufficiency, deficiency, inaptitude, inaptness, unaptness, unsuitability, unsuitableness; lack of skill, ineptitude, ineptness, maladroitness, awkwardness, clumsiness, gaucheness, *colloq.* cack-handedness; uselessness, hopelessness, inadequacy, insufficiency, inefficiency, ineffectiveness, ineffectuality, ineffectualness.

incomplete /inkəmpleet/ *adj.* not complete. □□ **incompletely** *adv.* **incompleteness** *n.* [ME f. LL *incompletus* (as IN-¹, COMPLETE)]

■ unfinished, imperfect, undone, unaccomplished, unformed, undeveloped, deficient, defective, partial, sketchy, crude, rudimentary, rough, fragmentary, patchy. □□ **incompleteness** see IMPERFECTION 1.

incomprehensible /inkómprihénsib'l/ *adj.* (often foll. by *to*) that cannot be understood. □□ **incomprehensibility** /-bílliti/ *n.* **incomprehensibleness** *n.* **incomprehensibly** *adv.* [ME f. L *incomprehensibilis* (as IN-¹, COMPREHENSIBLE)]

■ unintelligible, incoherent, inarticulate, unreadable, illegible, indecipherable, undecipherable, unfathomable, impenetrable, inscrutable; abstruse, arcane, recondite, cryptic, obscure, opaque, dark, occult, *colloq.* weird; enigmatic, mysterious, unaccountable, mystifying, puzzling, perplexing, baffling, deep, over a person's head; *attrib.* gibberish, *colloq.* (all) Greek to a person, gobbledegook *or* gobbledygook, *Brit. colloq.* double Dutch.

incomprehension /inkómprihénsh'n/ *n.* failure to understand.

incompressible /inkəmpréssib'l/ *adj.* that cannot be compressed. □□ **incompressibility** /-bílliti/ *n.*

inconceivable /inkənseévəb'l/ *adj.* **1** that cannot be imagined. **2** *colloq.* very remarkable. □□ **inconceivability** /-bílliti/ *n.* **inconceivableness** *n.* **inconceivably** *adv.*

■ **1** unimaginable, unthinkable, impossible, unrealistic, improbable; overwhelming, staggering, *colloq.* mind-boggling. **2** see MIRACULOUS 1, 3.

inconclusive /inkənkloóssiv/ *adj.* (of an argument, evidence, or action) not decisive or convincing. □□ **inconclusively** *adv.* **inconclusiveness** *n.*

■ indecisive, indefinite, unsettled, unestablished, undemonstrated, unproved, unproven, undecided, undetermined, moot, (still) open, indeterminate, unresolved, pending, in limbo, in the air; doubtful, vague, ambiguous, unfocused.

incondensable /inkəndénsəb'l/ *adj.* that cannot be condensed, esp. that cannot be reduced to a liquid or solid condition.

incongruous /inkónggrooəss/ *adj.* **1** out of place; absurd. **2** (often foll. by *with*) disagreeing; out of keeping. □□ **incongruity** /-groó-iti/ *n.* (*pl.* **-ies**). **incongruously** *adv.* **incongruousness** *n.* [L *incongruus* (as IN-¹, CONGRUOUS)]

■ inharmonious, disharmonious, disagreeing, out of place, out of keeping, discordant, dissonant, unapt, inappropriate, unsuitable, unbecoming, unseemly, unsuited, unfitting, unfit, improper, malapropos, not meet; out of step, out of line, inconsistent, discrepant, disparate, different, contrary; contradictory, paradoxical, nonsensical, illogical, absurd, ridiculous, preposterous, ludicrous.

inconsecutive /inkənsékyootiv/ *adj.* lacking sequence; inconsequent. □□ **inconsecutively** *adv.* **inconsecutiveness** *n.*

inconsequent /inkónsikwənt/ *adj.* **1** not following naturally; irrelevant. **2** lacking logical sequence. **3** disconnected. □□ **inconsequence** *n.* **inconsequently** *adv.* [L *inconsequens* (as IN-¹, CONSEQUENT)]

inconsequential /inkónsikwénsh'l, inkon-/ *adj.* **1** unimportant. **2** = INCONSEQUENT. □□ **inconsequentiality** /-shiálliti/ *n.* (*pl.* **-ies**). **inconsequentially** *adv.* **inconsequentialness** *n.*

■ **1** unimportant, insignificant, trivial, trifling, nugatory, inconsiderable, inappreciable, negligible, minor, little, small, paltry, petty, minuscule, immaterial, slight, lightweight, worthless, expendable, no-account, of no account, derisory, *colloq.* piddling, piffling, small-time. **2** see IRRELEVANT.

inconsiderable /inkənsiddərəb'l/ *adj.* **1** of small size, value, etc. **2** not worth considering. □□ **inconsiderableness** *n.* **inconsiderably** *adv.* [obs. F *inconsidérable* or LL *inconsiderabilis* (as IN-¹, CONSIDERABLE)]

■ see INSIGNIFICANT 1.

inconsiderate /inkənsiddərət/ *adj.* **1** (of a person or action) thoughtless, rash. **2** lacking in regard for the feelings of others. □□ **inconsiderately** *adv.* **inconsiderateness** *n.* **inconsideration** /-ráysh'n/ *n.* [L *inconsideratus* (as IN-¹, CONSIDERATE)]

■ **1** see IMPRUDENT. **2** thoughtless, unthoughtful, unconcerned, uncaring, selfish, callous, heartless, unsympathetic, insensitive, undiplomatic, tactless, rude, impolite.

inconsistent /inkənsistənt/ *adj.* **1** acting at variance with one's own principles or former conduct. **2** (often foll. by *with*) not in keeping; discordant, incompatible. **3** (of a single thing) incompatible or discordant; having self-contradictory parts. □□ **inconsistency** *n.* (*pl.* **-ies**). **inconsistently** *adv.*

■ **1, 3** inconstant, irregular, changeable, variable, capricious, fickle, erratic, uneven, unstable, unsteady, unpredictable, unreliable, undependable; self-contradictory, paradoxical, incoherent, illogical, irrational, absurd, preposterous. **2** see INCONGRUOUS, STEP *n.* 9.

inconsolable /inkənsóləb'l/ *adj.* (of a person, grief, etc.) that cannot be consoled or comforted. □□ **inconsolability** /-bílliti/ *n.* **inconsolableness** *n.* **inconsolably** *adv.* [F *inconsolable* or L *inconsolabilis* (as IN-¹, *consolabilis* f. *consolari* CONSOLE¹)]

■ unconsolable, disconsolate, broken-hearted, heartbroken, desolated, desolate, forlorn, despairing, miserable, woebegone, wretched, heartsick, grief-stricken.

inconsonant /inkónsənənt/ *adj.* (often foll. by *with, to*) not harmonious; not compatible. ▫▫ **inconsonance** *n.* **inconsonantly** *adv.*

inconspicuous /inkənspíkyooəss/ *adj.* **1** not conspicuous; not easily noticed. **2** *Bot.* (of flowers) small, pale, or green. ▫▫ **inconspicuously** *adv.* **inconspicuousness** *n.* [L *inconspicuus* (as IN-[1], CONSPICUOUS)]

■ **1** unnoticeable, unobtrusive, unostentatious, insignificant, indistinguishable, undistinguished, indefinite, faint; unseen, unnoticed, in the background, behind the scenes, backstage, out of *or* away from the public eye, out of the limelight *or* spotlight; modest, unassuming, discreet, sober, quiet, low-key, low-profile.

inconstant /inkónstənt/ *adj.* **1** (of a person) fickle, changeable. **2** frequently changing; variable, irregular. ▫▫ **inconstancy** *n.* (*pl.* **-ies**). **inconstantly** *adv.* [ME f. OF f. L *inconstans -antis* (as IN-[1], CONSTANT)]

■ fickle, capricious, changeable, mercurial, volatile, flighty, moody, fitful, vacillating, fluctuating, wavering, irresolute, unsteady, unsteadfast, unreliable, undependable, erratic, irregular, unstable, unsettled, variable, *literary* mutable; see also INCONSISTENT 1, 3. ▫▫ **inconstancy** changeableness, changeability, irregularity, variability, unsteadiness, unsteadfastness, *literary* mutability; fickleness, capriciousness, caprice, volatility, mercuriality, unreliability, flightiness, moodiness; faithlessness, unfaithfulness.

incontestable /inkəntéstəb'l/ *adj.* that cannot be disputed. ▫▫ **incontestability** /-bílliti/ *n.* **incontestably** *adv.* [F *incontestable* or med.L *incontestabilis* (as IN-[1], *contestabilis* f. L *contestari* CONTEST)]

■ see INCONTROVERTIBLE. ▫▫ **incontestably** see *undoubtedly* (UNDOUBTED).

incontinent /inkóntinənt/ *adj.* **1** unable to control movements of the bowels or bladder or both. **2** lacking self-restraint (esp. in regard to sexual desire). **3** (foll. by *of*) unable to control. ▫▫ **incontinence** *n.* **incontinently** *adv.* [ME f. OF or L *incontinens* (as IN-[1], CONTINENT[2])]

■ **1** wet, *Med.* enuretic. **2** unrestrained, unconstrained, unrestricted, uncontrolled, uncontrollable, ungoverned, ungovernable, unbridled, uncurbed; lecherous, libidinous, lascivious, promiscuous, libertine, lustful, lewd, debauched, wanton, dissolute, loose, lubricious, salacious, profligate, obscene, dirty, filthy. ▫▫ **incontinence** bedwetting, *Med.* enuresis; unrestrainedness, unrestrictedness, uncontrollableness, ungovernability; lechery, libidinousness, lasciviousness, lustfulness, lewdness, debauchery, wantonness, dissoluteness, salaciousness, profligacy, obscenity.

incontrovertible /ínkontrəvértib'l/ *adj.* indisputable, indubitable. ▫▫ **incontrovertibility** /-bílliti/ *n.* **incontrovertibly** *adv.*

■ uncontrovertible, indisputable, indubitable, undeniable, incontestable, unquestionable, irrefutable, sure, certain, definite, definitive, final, established, absolute, positive, *Austral.* & *NZ* fair. ▫▫ **incontrovertibility** see FINALITY. **incontrovertibly** see *undoubtedly* (UNDOUBTED).

inconvenience /inkənveéniənss/ *n.* & *v.* ● *n.* **1** lack of suitability to personal requirements or ease. **2** a cause or instance of this. ● *v.tr.* cause inconvenience to. [ME f. OF f. LL *inconvenientia* (as INCONVENIENT)]

■ *n.* **1** troublesomeness, cumbersomeness, unwieldiness, burdensomeness, onerousness, disadvantageousness, awkwardness, inexpediency, inopportuneness, inappropriateness, untimeliness. **2** trouble, nuisance, bother, annoyance, irritation, awkwardness, burden, difficulty, hindrance, impediment, disturbance, disruption, discomfort, upset, disadvantage, drawback, *Sc.* fash, *colloq.* hassle, pain (in the neck), *esp. US sl.* pain in the butt. ● *v.* discommode, incommode, trouble, disturb, disrupt, upset, put out, bother, annoy, irritate, irk, *colloq.* hassle.

inconvenient /inkənveéniənt/ *adj.* **1** unfavourable to ease or comfort; not convenient. **2** awkward, troublesome. ▫▫ **inconveniently** *adv.* [ME f. OF f. L *inconveniens -entis* (as IN-[1], CONVENIENT)]

■ disadvantageous, troublesome, bothersome, annoying, irritating, irksome, unsettling, disturbing, upsetting, disrupting; cumbersome, unwieldy, burdensome, onerous, awkward; inappropriate, inexpedient, inopportune, untimely, ill-timed.

inconvertible /ínkənvértib'l/ *adj.* **1** not convertible. **2** (esp. of currency) not convertible into another form on demand. ▫▫ **inconvertibility** /-bílliti/ *n.* **inconvertibly** *adv.* [F *inconvertible* or LL *inconvertibilis* (as IN-[1], CONVERTIBLE)]

incoordination /ínkō̆-ordináysh'n/ *n.* lack of coordination, esp. of muscular action.

incorporate *v.* & *adj.* ● *v.* /inkórpərayt/ **1** *tr.* (often foll. by *in, with*) unite; form into one body or whole. **2** *intr.* become incorporated. **3** *tr.* combine (ingredients) into one substance. **4** *tr.* admit as a member of a company etc. **5** *tr.* **a** constitute as a legal corporation. **b** (as **incorporated** *adj.*) forming a legal corporation. ● *adj.* /inkórpərət/ **1** (of a company etc.) formed into a legal corporation. **2** embodied. ▫▫ **incorporation** /-ráysh'n/ *n.* **incorporator** *n.* [ME f. LL *incorporare* (as IN-[2], L *corpus -oris* body)]

■ *v.* **1, 3** unite, unify, integrate, associate, amalgamate, combine, consolidate; assimilate, merge, mix, blend, fuse. **2** unite, integrate, amalgamate, combine, coalesce, assimilate, associate, merge, fuse, blend. **4** see INCLUDE 1. ▫▫ **incorporation** union, unification, integration, association, amalgamation, combination, combine, consolidation, assimilation, merger, mixture, blend, fusion, coalescence; see also *inclusion* (INCLUDE).

incorporeal /inkorpóriəl/ *adj.* **1** not composed of matter. **2** of immaterial beings. **3** *Law* having no physical existence. ▫▫ **incorporeality** /-riálliti/ *n.* **incorporeally** *adv.* **incorporeity** /-pəreé-iti/ *n.* [L *incorporeus* (as INCORPORATE)]

■ **1, 2** see IMMATERIAL 2.

incorrect /inkərékt/ *adj.* **1** not in accordance with fact; wrong. **2** (of style etc.) improper, faulty. ▫▫ **incorrectly** *adv.* **incorrectness** *n.* [ME f. OF or L *incorrectus* (as IN-[1], CORRECT)]

■ **1** wrong, mistaken, inaccurate, untrue, imprecise, inexact, erroneous, mistaken, out, off, false, fallacious, wide of the mark, *colloq.* off beam. **2** see IMPROPER 2.

incorrigible /inkórrijib'l/ *adj.* **1** (of a person or habit) incurably bad or depraved. **2** not readily improved. ▫▫ **incorrigibility** /-bílliti/ *n.* **incorrigibleness** *n.* **incorrigibly** *adv.* [ME f. OF *incorrigible* or L *incorrigibilis* (as IN-[1], CORRIGIBLE)]

■ **1** evil, bad, immoral, wicked, vicious, vile, sinful, depraved, corrupt, villainous, criminal; naughty, mischievous, ill-behaved. **2** inveterate, engrained, ingrained, hardened, habitual, incurable, unchangeable, dyed in the wool, out and out, unalterable, intractable, stubborn, obdurate, *colloq. disp.* chronic.

incorruptible /inkərúptib'l/ *adj.* **1** that cannot be corrupted, esp. by bribery. **2** that cannot decay; everlasting. ▫▫ **incorruptibility** /-bílliti/ *n.* **incorruptibly** *adv.* [ME f. OF *incorruptible* or eccl.L *incorruptibilis* (as IN-[1], CORRUPT)]

■ **1** moral, noble, upright, righteous, pure, upstanding, honourable, good, virtuous, honest, straightforward, straight, unimpeachable, Rhadamanthine; see also TRUSTWORTHY. **2** everlasting, lasting, enduring; see also IMMORTAL *adj.* 2. ▫▫ **incorruptibility** see INTEGRITY 1.

increase *v.* & *n.* ● *v.* /inkreéss/ **1** *tr.* & *intr.* make or become greater in size, amount, etc., or more numerous. **2** *intr.* advance (in quality, attainment, etc.). **3** *tr.* intensify (a quality). ● *n.* /inkreess/ **1** the act or process of becoming greater or more numerous; growth, enlargement. **2** (of people, animals, or plants) growth in numbers; multiplication. **3** the amount or extent of an increase. ▫ **on the increase** increasing, esp. in frequency. ▫▫ **increasable**

adj. **increaser** *n.* **increasingly** *adv.* [ME f. OF *encreiss-* stem of *encreistre* f. L *increscere* (as IN-², *crescere* grow)]

■ *v.* **1** (*tr.* & *intr.*) multiply, propagate, breed; augment, build up, enlarge, amplify, expand, extend, develop, broaden, widen, lengthen, heighten; escalate, accelerate, speed up; inflate, dilate, distend, swell; (*tr.*) add to, maximize, raise, lift, step up, *sl.* crank up; (*intr.*) grow, jump, soar, shoot up, rocket, explode, snowball, wax, flourish, proliferate, spread, *literary* burgeon. **2** appreciate, improve, get better, advance, progress, make progress, move (on *or* ahead *or* forward), climb. **3** intensify, enhance, sharpen, strengthen, reinforce, emphasize, point up, highlight; aggrandize, magnify, jazz up, *sl.* beef up. ● *n.* **1, 2** multiplication, propagation, proliferation, explosion; augmentation, increment, addition, enlargement, expansion, extension, development, amplification; acceleration, escalation, growth, jump, rise, spread, distension, inflation, dilation; appreciation, improvement, advance, progress; magnification, aggrandizement. **3** increment, gain, rise, growth, jump, lift, addition, advance, improvement, appreciation, *colloq.* boost. □ **on the increase** on the rise, on the way up, on the upgrade, increasing, growing, proliferating, escalating. □□ **increasingly** progressively, more and more, cumulatively; constantly, ever, still.

incredible /inkréddib'l/ *adj.* **1** that cannot be believed. **2** *colloq.* hard to believe; amazing. □□ **incredibility** /-bílliti/ *n.* **incredibleness** *n.* **incredibly** *adv.* [ME f. L *incredibilis* (as IN-¹, CREDIBLE)]

■ **1, 2** unbelievable, beyond belief, inconceivable, unimaginable, unthinkable; impossible, absurd, preposterous, ridiculous, far-fetched, unrealistic, fictitious, fabulous, legendary, mythical, mythic, implausible, improbable, unlikely, doubtful, dubious, questionable, suspect, suspicious, *colloq.* funny, *sl.* fishy, *US* & *Austral. sl.* unreal; see also *amazing* (AMAZE).

incredulous /inkrédyooləss/ *adj.* (often foll. by *of*) unwilling to believe. □□ **incredulity** /inkridyŏŏliti/ *n.* **incredulously** *adv.* **incredulousness** *n.* [L *incredulus* (as IN-¹, CREDULOUS)]

■ disbelieving, unbelieving, mistrustful, distrustful, dubious, doubtful, sceptical, suspicious, interrogatory, questioning; cynical. □□ **incredulity, incredulousness** see DISTRUST *n.*

increment /ínkrimənt/ *n.* **1 a** an increase or addition, esp. one of a series on a fixed scale. **b** the amount of this. **2** *Math.* a small amount by which a variable quantity increases. □□ **incremental** /-mént'l/ *adj.* [ME f. L *incrementum* f. *increscere* INCREASE]

■ **1 a** see INCREASE *n.* 1, 2. **b** see INCREASE *n.* 3.

incriminate /inkrímminayt/ *v.tr.* **1** tend to prove the guilt of (*incriminating evidence*). **2** involve in an accusation. **3** charge with a crime. □□ **incrimination** /-náysh'n/ *n.* **incriminatory** *adj.* [LL *incriminare* (as IN-², L *crimen* offence)]

■ **1** inculpate, point to, blame. **2** involve, embroil, enmesh, entangle, associate, connect, *sl.* frame. **3** accuse, charge, indict, arraign, impeach, inculpate, denounce, put in the dock. □□ **incrimination** see IMPLICATION, ACCUSATION.

incrust var. of ENCRUST.

incrustation /inkrustáysh'n/ *n.* **1** the process of encrusting or state of being encrusted. **2** a crust or hard coating, esp. of fine material. **3** a concretion or deposit on a surface. **4** a facing of marble etc. on a building. [F *incrustation* or LL *incrustatio* (as ENCRUST)]

■ **2** see SKIN *n.* 4. **3** see DEPOSIT *n.* 3.

incubate /íngkyoobayt/ *v.* **1** *tr.* sit on or artificially heat (eggs) in order to bring forth young birds etc. **2** *tr.* cause the development of (bacteria etc.) by creating suitable conditions. **3** *intr.* sit on eggs; brood. [L *incubare* (as IN-², *cubare cubit-* or *cubat-* lie)]

■ **1, 3** hatch, sit on; brood. **2** breed, grow, raise, develop, nurse, nurture.

incubation /íngkyoobáysh'n/ *n.* **1 a** the act of incubating. **b** brooding. **2** *Med.* **a** a phase through which the germs causing a disease pass before the development of the first symptoms. **b** the period of this. □□ **incubational** *adj.* **incubative** /íngkyoobaytiv/ *adj.* **incubatory** /íngkyoobaytəri/ *adj.* [L *incubatio* (as INCUBATE)]

incubator /íngkyoobaytər/ *n.* **1** an apparatus used to provide a suitable temperature and environment for a premature baby or one of low birth-weight. **2** an apparatus used to hatch eggs or grow micro-organisms.

incubus /íngkyoobəss/ *n.* (*pl.* **incubuses** or **incubi** /-bī/) **1** an evil spirit supposed to descend on sleeping persons. **2** a nightmare. **3** a person or thing that oppresses like a nightmare. [ME f. LL, = L *incubo* nightmare (as INCUBATE)]

incudes *pl.* of INCUS.

inculcate /ínkulkayt/ *v.tr.* (often foll. by *upon, in*) urge or impress (a fact, habit, or idea) persistently. □□ **inculcation** /-káysh'n/ *n.* **inculcator** *n.* [L *inculcare* (as IN-², *calcare* tread f. *calx calcis* heel)]

■ see DIN *v.* □□ **inculcation** see DISCIPLINE *n.* 2a.

inculpate /ínkulpayt/ *v.tr.* **1** involve in a charge. **2** accuse, blame. □□ **inculpation** /-páysh'n/ *n.* **inculpative** /inkúlpətiv/ *adj.* **inculpatory** /inkúlpətəri/ *adj.* [LL *inculpare* (as IN-², *culpare* blame f. *culpa* fault)]

■ **1** see INCRIMINATE 2, 3. **2** see INCRIMINATE 3.

incumbency /inkúmbənsi/ *n.* (*pl.* **-ies**) the office, tenure, or sphere of an incumbent.

■ place, position, office; see also TENURE 1, 2.

incumbent /inkúmb'nt/ *adj.* & *n.* ● *adj.* **1** (foll. by *on, upon*) resting as a duty (*it is incumbent on you to warn them*). **2** (often foll. by *on*) lying, pressing. **3** in occupation or having the tenure of a post or position. ● *n.* the holder of an office or post, esp. an ecclesiastical benefice. [ME f. AL *incumbens* pres. part. of L *incumbere* lie upon (as IN-², *cubare* lie)]

■ *adj.* **1** obligatory, necessary, required, requisite, mandatory, compulsory, binding; (*incumbent on*) expected of. **2** recumbent, prone, prostrate, supine; pressing. **3** in office, sitting, reigning, presiding; current. ● *n.* holder, office-holder, occupant; official, functionary, officer.

incunable /inkyŏŏnəb'l/ *n.* = INCUNABULUM 1. [F, formed as INCUNABULUM]

incunabulum /inkyoonábyooləm/ *n.* (*pl.* **incunabula** /-lə/) **1** a book printed at an early date, esp. before 1501. **2** (in *pl.*) the early stages of the development of a thing. [L *incunabula* swaddling-clothes, cradle (as IN-², *cunae* cradle)]

incur /inkúr/ *v.tr.* (**incurred, incurring**) suffer, experience, or become subject to (something unpleasant) as a result of one's own behaviour etc. (*incurred huge debts*). □□ **incurrable** *adj.* [ME f. L *incurrere incurs-* (as IN-², *currere* run)]

■ suffer, experience, undergo, face, sustain, meet (with), come in for; bring upon *or* on (oneself), draw, attract, arouse, provoke, invite, expose (oneself) to, lay (oneself) open to.

incurable /inkyóorəb'l/ *adj.* & *n.* ● *adj.* that cannot be cured. ● *n.* a person who cannot be cured. □□ **incurability** /-bílliti/ *n.* **incurableness** *n.* **incurably** *adv.* [ME f. OF *incurable* or LL *incurabilis* (as IN-¹, CURABLE)]

■ *adj.* irremediable, immedicable, inoperable, irreparable, irredeemable, irreversible; fatal, terminal, hopeless; see also INCORRIGIBLE 2. ● *n.* terminal, *sl.* goner.

incurious /inkyóoriəss/ *adj.* **1** lacking curiosity. **2** heedless, careless. □□ **incuriosity** /-ióssiti/ *n.* **incuriously** *adv.* **incuriousness** *n.* [L *incuriosus* (as IN-¹, CURIOUS)]

incursion /inkúrsh'n/ *n.* an invasion or attack, esp. when sudden or brief. □□ **incursive** /-kúrsiv/ *adj.* [ME f. L *incursio* (as INCUR)]

■ see ATTACK *n.* 1.

incurve /inkúrv/ *v.tr.* **1** bend into a curve. **2** (as **incurved** *adj.*) curved inwards. □□ **incurvation** /-váysh'n/ *n.* [L *incurvare* (as IN-², CURVE)]

incus /íngkəss/ *n.* (*pl.* **incudes** /-kyŏŏdeez/) the small anvil-shaped bone in the middle ear, in contact with the malleus and stapes. [L, = anvil]

incuse /inkyōōz/ *n.*, *v.*, & *adj.* ● *n.* an impression hammered or stamped on a coin. ● *v.tr.* **1** mark (a coin) with a figure by stamping. **2** impress (a figure) on a coin by stamping. ● *adj.* hammered or stamped on a coin. [L *incusus* past part. of *incudere* (as IN-², *cudere* forge)]

Ind. *abbr.* **1** Independent. **2 a** India. **b** Indian. **3** Indiana.

indaba /indaábə/ *n. S.Afr.* **1** a conference between or with members of S. African native tribes. **2** *colloq.* one's problem or concern. [Zulu, = business]

indebted /indéttid/ *adj.* (usu. foll. by *to*) **1** owing gratitude or obligation. **2** owing money. □□ **indebtedness** *n.* [ME f. OF *endetté* past part. of *endetter* involve in debt (as EN-¹, *detter* f. *dette* DEBT)]

■ **1** obliged, beholden, bound, in a person's debt; liable, responsible, accountable; grateful, thankful, appreciative. **2** in debt, embarrassed, encumbered, overdrawn, in the red, *esp. US colloq.* in hock; insolvent, bankrupt. □□ **indebtedness** see DEBT.

indecent /indeéss'nt/ *adj.* **1** offending against recognized standards of decency. **2** unbecoming; highly unsuitable (*with indecent haste*). □ **indecent assault** a sexual attack not involving rape. **indecent exposure** the intentional act of publicly and indecently exposing one's body, esp. the genitals. □□ **indecency** *n.* (*pl.* **-ies**). **indecently** *adv.* [F *indécent* or L *indecens* (as IN-¹, DECENT)]

■ **1** shameless, shameful, offensive, outrageous, repellent, repulsive, distasteful, ill-mannered, rude, suggestive, coarse, risqué, vulgar, blue, obscene, gross, rank, prurient, dirty, foul, filthy, pornographic, scatological, salacious, lascivious, licentious, lewd, lubricious, smutty, vile, degenerate, debauched, *Gk Hist.* ithyphallic, *colloq.* near the knuckle, *euphem.* adult. **2** unseemly, indecorous, indelicate, immodest, improper, unbecoming, unsuitable, unfit, inappropriate; in bad taste. □ **indecent assault** molestation, violation, sexual assault. □□ **indecency** shamelessness, shamefulness, offensiveness, outrageousness, repellence, repellency, repulsiveness, distastefulness, rudeness, suggestiveness, coarseness, vulgarity, obscenity, grossness, rankness, prurience, dirtiness, foulness, filthiness, pornography, salaciousness, lasciviousness, licentiousness, lewdness, lubricity, smuttiness, vileness, degeneracy; see also IMPROPRIETY 1.

indecipherable /indisífərəb'l/ *adj.* that cannot be deciphered.

■ see ILLEGIBLE.

indecision /indisízh'n/ *n.* lack of decision; hesitation. [F *indécision* (as IN-¹, DECISION)]

■ indecisiveness, irresolution, irresoluteness, uncertainty, incertitude, doubt, ambivalence, tentativeness, hesitation, hesitance, hesitancy, tremulousness, vacillation, fluctuation, shilly-shally, *colloq.* dither.

indecisive /indisísiv/ *adj.* **1** not decisive. **2** undecided, hesitating. □□ **indecisively** *adv.* **indecisiveness** *n.*

■ **1** indefinite, indeterminate, undecided, undetermined, inconclusive, (still) open, unresolved, unsettled, moot, doubtful, vague, ambiguous. **2** undecided, irresolute, uncertain, in two minds, ambivalent, doubtful, dubious, tentative, hesitant, tremulous, shilly-shally, wishy-washy, *colloq.* dithery, all of a dither.

indeclinable /índiklínəb'l/ *adj. Gram.* **1** that cannot be declined. **2** having no inflections. [ME f. F *indéclinable* f. L *indeclinabilis* (as IN-¹, DECLINE)]

indecorous /indékərəss/ *adj.* **1** improper. **2** in bad taste. □□ **indecorously** *adv.* **indecorousness** *n.* [L *indecorus* (as IN-¹, *decorus* seemly)]

■ **1** see IMPROPER 1a. **2** see IMPROPER 1b. □□ **indecorously** see FAST¹ *adv.* 5. **indecorousness** see IMPROPRIETY 1.

indecorum /indikórəm/ *n.* **1** lack of decorum. **2** improper behaviour. [L, neut. of *indecorus*: see INDECOROUS]

■ **1** see INCIVILITY. **2** see IMPROPRIETY 1.

indeed /indeéd/ *adv.* & *int.* ● *adv.* **1** in truth; really; yes, that is so (*they are, indeed, a remarkable family*). **2** expressing emphasis or intensification (*I shall be very glad indeed; indeed it is; very, indeed inordinately, proud of it*). **3** admittedly (*there are indeed exceptions*). **4** in point of fact (*if indeed such a thing is possible*). **5** expressing an approving or ironic echo (*who is this Mr Smith? — who is he indeed?*). ● *int.* expressing irony, contempt, incredulity, etc.

■ *adv.* **1** truly, truthfully, really, in reality, in fact, actually, *archaic* verily, yea, *archaic or joc.* forsooth, *literary* in truth; seriously, (all) joking aside *or* apart, on *or* upon my word, on *or* upon my honour, *colloq.* honour bright; exactly, precisely; yes, (that's) right, that's true, that is so, assuredly, *Brit.* rather, *US* check, *colloq.* I'll say. **2** certainly, surely, to be sure, assuredly, doubtless, doubtlessly, undoubtedly, without doubt, no doubt, undeniably, definitely, positively, absolutely, by all means, *archaic* certes; not to say, nay, to say the least. **3** admittedly, undeniably, granted, (it is) true; of course, no doubt, certainly, naturally. **4** in (point of) fact, as a matter of fact, in reality, to be realistic. ● *int.* is that so *or* a fact?, really, *colloq.* you don't say (so), uh-huh, *sl.* no kidding; gracious, mercy, fancy (that), imagine, (upon) my word, by Jove, (well) I'm blessed, well I (do) declare, my (sainted) aunt, (my) goodness, (good) Lord, good heavens, *Brit.* I say, *colloq.* my stars, well I'm *or* I'll be damned, *Brit. sl.* crikey, (cor) blimey, gorblimey; really?, bah, phooey, (stuff and) nonsense, rubbish, rot, fudge, *archaic* go to, *colloq.* come off it, get away, go on, garn, tell me another, pull the other one, tell that to the (horse) marines, oh yeah?, *iron.* pigs might fly, *Brit. sl.* cor, coo.

indefatigable /índifáttigəb'l/ *adj.* (of a person, quality, etc.) that cannot be tired out; unwearying, unremitting. □□ **indefatigability** /-bílliti/ *n.* **indefatigably** *adv.* [obs. F *indéfatigable* or L *indefatigabilis* (as IN-¹, *defatigare* wear out)]

■ see TIRELESS. □□ **indefatigably** see HARD *adv.* 1.

indefeasible /indifeézib'l/ *adj. literary* (esp. of a claim, rights, etc.) that cannot be lost. □□ **indefeasibility** /-bílliti/ *n.* **indefeasibly** *adv.*

■ see INALIENABLE.

indefectible /índiféktib'l/ *adj.* **1** unfailing; not liable to defect or decay. **2** faultless. [IN-¹ + *defectible* f. LL *defectibilis* (as DEFECT)]

indefensible /índifénsib'l/ *adj.* that cannot be defended or justified. □□ **indefensibility** /-bílliti/ *n.* **indefensibly** *adv.*

■ see INEXCUSABLE.

indefinable /indifínəb'l/ *adj.* that cannot be defined or exactly described. □□ **indefinably** *adv.*

■ see INEXPRESSIBLE.

indefinite /indéffinit/ *adj.* **1** vague, undefined. **2** unlimited. **3** *Gram.* not determining the person, thing, time, etc., referred to. □ **indefinite article** see ARTICLE. **indefinite integral** see INTEGRAL. **indefinite pronoun** *Gram.* a pronoun indicating a person, amount, etc., without being definite or particular, e.g. *any, some, anyone*. □□ **indefiniteness** *n.* [L *indefinitus* (as IN-¹, DEFINITE)]

■ **1** vague, uncertain, unsure, ambiguous, equivocal, doubtful, dubious, questionable, demurrable, debatable, moot, in doubt, open to question; inexplicit, non-specific, unspecified, general, undefined, unsettled, indeterminate, imprecise, inexact; ill-defined, blurred, blurry, hazy, indistinct, obscure, dim, fuzzy, unrecognizable, indistinguishable; see also INDECISIVE 1. **2** unlimited, unrestricted, unbounded, indeterminate; unknown, uncounted, untold, undefined; uncountable, undefinable, indefinable, indeterminable, immeasurable, incalculable, limitless, boundless, endless, infinite.

indefinitely /indéffinitli/ *adv.* **1** for an unlimited time (*was postponed indefinitely*). **2** in an indefinite manner.

■ **2** see *at random* (RANDOM), *vaguely* (VAGUE).

indehiscent /indihiss'nt/ *adj. Bot.* (of fruit) not splitting open when ripe. □□ **indehiscence** *n.*

indelible /indéllib'l/ *adj.* **1** that cannot be rubbed out or (in abstract senses) removed. **2** (of ink etc.) that makes indelible marks. □□ **indelibility** /-bílliti/ *n.* **indelibly** *adv.* [F *indélébile* or L *indelebilis* (as IN-¹, *delebilis* f. *delēre* efface)]

■ **1** ineradicable, ineffaceable, inexpungible; everlasting, permanent, enduring, abiding, lasting, constant, durable, fixed, ingrained, engrained, persistent; imperishable, indestructible, immortal, undying, eternal.

indelicate /indéllikət/ *adj.* **1** coarse, unrefined. **2** tactless. **3** tending to indecency. ◻◻ **indelicacy** *n.* (*pl.* **-ies**). **indelicately** *adv.*

■ **1** coarse, rough, crude, rough-hewn, unrefined, vulgar, common, gross; rude, boorish, loutish, uncivilized, uncouth, ill-mannered, offensive, impolite, discourteous, uncivil, unmannerly, ungentlemanly, unladylike, immodest, indecorous, unseemly, in poor *or* bad taste, tasteless, inelegant, ill-bred. **2** tactless, undiplomatic, gauche, clumsy, insensitive, unfeeling; crude, gruff, bluff, blunt, brusque, abrupt, surly, abrasive, churlish, rude, close to *or* near the bone. **3** see INDECENT 1.

indemnify /indémnifi/ *v.tr.* (**-ies, -ied**) **1** (often foll. by *from, against*) protect or secure (a person) in respect of harm, a loss, etc. **2** (often foll. by *for*) secure (a person) against legal responsibility for actions. **3** (often foll. by *for*) compensate (a person) for a loss, expenses, etc. ◻◻ **indemnification** /-fikáysh'n/ *n.* **indemnifier** *n.* [L *indemnis* unhurt (as IN-[1], *damnum* loss, damage)]

■ **3** see COMPENSATE 1. ◻◻ **indemnification** see INSURANCE 1, RESTITUTION 2.

indemnity /indémniti/ *n.* (*pl.* **-ies**) **1 a** compensation for loss incurred. **b** a sum paid for this, esp. a sum exacted by a victor in war etc. as one condition of peace. **2** security against loss. **3** legal exemption from penalties etc. incurred. [ME f. F *indemnité* or LL *indemnitas -tatis* (as INDEMNIFY)]

■ **1** compensation, consideration, restitution, reparation(s), redress, quid pro quo; atonement, expiation, satisfaction; indemnification, guarantee fund; recompense, repayment, reimbursement, remuneration, return. **2** security, protection, safety, insurance, assurance, guarantee, underwriting, warranty, endorsement, certification. **3** see *exemption* (EXEMPT).

indemonstrable /indémənstrəb'l, índimón-/ *adj.* that cannot be proved (esp. of primary or axiomatic truths).

indene /indeen/ *n. Chem.* a colourless flammable liquid hydrocarbon obtained from coal tar and used in making synthetic resins. [INDOLE + -ENE]

indent[1] *v.* & *n.* ● *v.* /indént/ **1** *tr.* start (a line of print or writing) further from the margin than other lines, e.g. to mark a new paragraph. **2** *tr.* **a** divide (a document drawn up in duplicate) into its two copies with a zigzag line dividing them and ensuring identification. **b** draw up (usu. a legal document) in exact duplicate. **3** *Brit.* **a** *intr.* (often foll. by *on, upon* a person, *for* a thing) make a requisition (orig. a written order with a duplicate). **b** *tr.* order (goods) by requisition. **4** *tr.* make toothlike notches in. **5** *tr.* form deep recesses in (a coastline etc.). ● *n.* /indent/ **1** *Brit.* **a** an order (esp. from abroad) for goods. **b** an official requisition for stores. **2** an indented line. **3** indentation. **4** an indenture. ◻◻ **indenter** *n.* **indentor** *n.* [ME f. AF *endenter* f. AL *indentare* (as IN-[2], L *dens dentis* tooth)]

■ *n.* **3** see INDENTATION 2.

indent[2] /indént/ *v.tr.* **1** make a dent in. **2** impress (a mark etc.). [ME f. IN-[2] + DENT]

indentation /indentáysh'n/ *n.* **1** the act or an instance of indenting; the process of being indented. **2** a cut or notch. **3** a zigzag. **4** a deep recess in a coastline etc.

■ **1** see also ORDER *n.* 2. **2** notch, nick, snick, groove, joggle, gouge, cut, score, slash, *archaic* scotch; dent, depression, impression, cranny, hollow, dimple, pit, kick; serration, dentil, crenel, crenation, crenature; *Anat.* hilum, recess. **3** zigzag; scalloping, herring-bone, stagger.

indention /indénsh'n/ *n.* **1** the indenting of a line in printing or writing. **2** = INDENTATION.

indenture /indénchər/ *n.* & *v.* ● *n.* **1** an indented document (see INDENT[1] *v.* 2). **2** (usu. in *pl.*) a sealed agreement or contract. **3** a formal list, certificate, etc. ● *v.tr. hist.* bind (a person) by indentures, esp. as an apprentice. ◻◻ **indentureship** *n.* [ME (orig. Sc.) f. AF *endenture* (as INDENT[1])]

■ *n.* **2** see DEED *n.* 4. ● *v.* see APPRENTICE *v.*

independence /indipéndənss/ *n.* **1** (often foll. by *of, from*) the state of being independent. **2** independent income. ◻ **Independence Day** a day celebrating the anniversary of national independence, esp. 4 July in the US.

■ **1** freedom, liberty, *laissez-aller*, independency, autonomy, self-rule, home rule, self-determination, self-government, autarchy, sovereignty; confidence, self-confidence, self-sufficiency, self-reliance, self-dependence, self-assurance.

independency /indipéndənsi/ *n.* (*pl.* **-ies**) **1** an independent State. **2** = INDEPENDENCE.

independent /indipéndənt/ *adj.* & *n.* ● *adj.* **1 a** (often foll. by *of*) not depending on authority or control. **b** self-governing. **2 a** not depending on another person for one's opinion or livelihood. **b** (of income or resources) making it unnecessary to earn one's living. **3** unwilling to be under an obligation to others. **4** *Polit.* not belonging to or supported by a party. **5** not depending on something else for its validity, efficiency, value, etc. (*independent proof*). **6** (of broadcasting, a school, etc.) not supported by public funds. **7** (**Independent**) *hist.* Congregational. ● *n.* **1** a person who is politically independent. **2** (**Independent**) *hist.* a Congregationalist. ◻◻ **independently** *adv.*

■ *adj.* **1 a** unregulated, uncontrolled; unrestrained, unrestricted, unfettered, untrammelled, unbound, unbridled, unconstrained, *dégagé(e)*, *Law sui juris*; substantive, self-existent, free-standing, standalone. **b** self-governing, self-governed, self-determining, self-determined, autonomous, autarchic, autarchical, autocephalous, sovereign, plenipotentiary, *hist.* allodial; freelance. **2a, 3** self-reliant, self-contained, self-sufficient, autonomous, sufficient, *Biol.* free-living; self-willed, self-assured, (self-)confident, freethinking, bold, individualistic, bohemian, unconventional, unorthodox. **4** non-party, unaffiliated, non-partisan, non-aligned, unaligned; disinterested, neutral, impartial, unprejudiced, unbiased. **5** objective, external, outside, neutral, equitable, disinterested, dispassionate, unbiased, impartial; detached, uninvolved, separate, unconnected, unrelated, distinct. **6** non-governmental, self-financing, private, voluntary. ● *n.* **1** individual, nonconformist, maverick, loner. ◻◻ **independently** freely, unrestrictedly, without restriction, without let or hindrance; voluntarily, of one's own accord, of one's own volition *or* free will, off one's own bat, in one's own name, on one's own responsibility, autonomously, autarchically; substantively, absolutely; self-reliantly, self-sufficiently, self-assuredly, (self-)confidently, boldly; externally, objectively, disinterestedly, impartially; separately, singly, individually, one by one, one at a time, severally, unconnectedly, unrelatedly, distinctly, apart; alone, on one's *or* its own, by oneself *or* itself, single-handed(ly), solo, under one's *or* its own steam; personally, privately.

in-depth see DEPTH.

indescribable /indiskrī́bəb'l/ *adj.* **1** too unusual or extreme to be described. **2** vague, indefinite. ◻◻ **indescribability** /-bílliti/ *n.* **indescribably** *adv.*

■ **1** see INEXPRESSIBLE. **2** see NONDESCRIPT *adj.*

indestructible /indistrúktib'l/ *adj.* that cannot be destroyed. ◻◻ **indestructibility** /-bílliti/ *n.* **indestructibly** *adv.*

■ everlasting, eternal, endless, undying, immortal, deathless, imperishable, indelible, ineradicable, inexpungible, ineffaceable; unchangeable, immutable, unalterable, permanent, fixed, unchanging, changeless, constant, perennial; unbreakable, non-breakable, shatter-proof; see also DURABLE.

indeterminable /inditérminəb'l/ *adj.* **1** that cannot be ascertained. **2** (of a dispute etc.) that cannot be settled. ◻◻ **indeterminably** *adv.* [ME f. LL *indeterminabilis* (as IN-[1], L *determinare* DETERMINE)]

■ **1** see INDEFINITE 1.

indeterminate /inditérminət/ *adj.* **1** not fixed in extent, character, etc. **2** left doubtful; vague. **3** *Math.* (of a quantity) not limited to a fixed value by the value of another quantity. **4** (of a judicial sentence) such that the convicted person's conduct determines the date of release. □ **indeterminate vowel** the obscure vowel /ə/ heard in '*a* moment *ago*'; a schwa. □□ **indeterminacy** *n.* **indeterminately** *adv.* **indeterminateness** *n.* [ME f. LL *indeterminatus* (as IN-[1], DETERMINATE)]

■ **1** see INDEFINITE. **2** see VAGUE 1.

indetermination /inditérmináysh'n/ *n.* **1** lack of determination. **2** the state of being indeterminate.

indeterminism /inditérminiz'm/ *n.* the belief that human action is not wholly determined by motives. □□ **indeterminist** *n.* **indeterministic** /-nístik/ *adj.*

index /índeks/ *n.* & *v.* ● *n.* (*pl.* **indexes** or esp. in technical use **indices** /índiseez/) **1** an alphabetical list of names, subjects, etc., with references, usu. at the end of a book. **2** = *card index.* **3** (in full **index number**) a number showing the variation of prices or wages as compared with a chosen base period (*retail price index*; *Dow-Jones index*). **4** *Math.* **a** the exponent of a number. **b** the power to which it is raised. **5 a** a pointer, esp. on an instrument, showing a quantity, a position on a scale, etc. **b** an indicator of a trend, direction, tendency, etc. **c** (usu. foll. by *of*) a sign, token, or indication of something. **6** *Physics* a number expressing a physical property etc. in terms of a standard (*refractive index*). **7** *Computing* a set of items each of which specifies one of the records of a file and contains information about its address. **8** (**Index**) *RC Ch. hist.* a list of books forbidden to Roman Catholics to read. **9** *Printing* a symbol shaped like a pointing hand, used to draw attention to a note etc. ● *v.tr.* **1** provide (a book etc.) with an index. **2** enter in an index. **3** relate (wages etc.) to the value of a price index. □ **index finger** the forefinger. **index-linked** related to the value of a retail price index. □□ **indexation** /-sáysh'n/ *n.* **indexer** *n.* **indexible** /índeks-, indéks-/ *adj.* **indexical** /indéks-/ *adj.* **indexless** *adj.* [ME f. L *index indicis* forefinger, informer, sign: sense 8 f. L *Index librorum prohibitorum* list of prohibited books]

■ *n.* **1** table of contents, directory, catalogue, register, inventory, itemization, list, listing, guide, key, ABC; gazetteer, dictionary, lexicon, vocabulary, concordance, thesaurus. **3** ratio, quotient, factor, measure, formula, figure. **5** pointer, indicator, needle, gnomon, guide, marker, *Computing* cursor; mark, sign, token, hint, clue. □ **index finger** forefinger, first finger.

India ink /índiə/ *n. US* = *Indian ink.* [*India* in Asia: see INDIAN]

Indiaman /índiəmən/ *n.* (*pl.* **-men**) *Naut. hist.* a ship engaged in trade with India or the East Indies.

Indian /índiən/ *n.* & *adj.* ● *n.* **1 a** a native or national of India. **b** a person of Indian descent. **2** (in full **American Indian**) a member of the aboriginal peoples of America or their descendants. **3** any of the languages of the aboriginal peoples of America. ● *adj.* **1** of or relating to India, or to the subcontinent comprising India, Pakistan, and Bangladesh. **2** of or relating to the aboriginal peoples of America. □ **Indian clubs** a pair of bottle-shaped clubs swung to exercise the arms in gymnastics. **Indian corn** maize. **Indian elephant** the elephant, *Elephas maximus*, of India, which is smaller than the African elephant. **Indian file** = *single file*. **Indian hemp** see HEMP 1. **Indian ink** *Brit.* **1** a black pigment made orig. in China and Japan. **2** a dark ink made from this, used esp. in drawing and technical graphics. **Indian Ocean** the ocean between Africa to the west, and Australia to the east. **Indian rope-trick** the supposed Indian feat of climbing an upright unsupported length of rope. **Indian summer 1** a period of unusually dry warm weather sometimes occurring in late autumn. **2** a late period of life characterized by comparative calm. [ME f. *India* ult. f. Gk *Indos* the River Indus f. Pers. *Hind*: cf. HINDU]

India paper /índiə/ *n.* **1** a soft absorbent kind of paper orig. imported from China, used for proofs of engravings. **2** a very thin tough opaque printing-paper.

indiarubber /índiərúbbər/ *n.* = RUBBER[1] 2.

Indic /índik/ *adj.* & *n.* ● *adj.* of the group of Indo-European languages comprising Sanskrit and its modern descendants. ● *n.* this language-group. [L *Indicus* f. Gk *Indikos* INDIAN]

indicate /índikayt/ *v.tr.* (often foll. by *that* + clause) **1** point out; make known; show. **2** be a sign or symptom of; express the presence of. **3** (often in *passive*) suggest; call for; require or show to be necessary (*stronger measures are indicated*). **4** admit to or state briefly (*indicated his disapproval*). **5** (of a gauge etc.) give as a reading. [L *indicare* (as IN-[2], *dicare* make known)]

■ **1, 4** point out, designate, point to *or* at, mark, specify, identify, pinpoint, particularize, single out, call *or* direct attention to, show, display, exhibit, signal; manifest, demonstrate, make clear, make known; admit to, disclose, register, express, mention, state, say, tell. **2** signify, betoken, denote, manifest, imply, suggest, betoken, bespeak, reveal, evince, evidence. **3** call for, require, demand, need, recommend; suggest, hint (at), imply, intimate. **5** read, register, show, display, record.

indication /índikáysh'n/ *n.* **1 a** the act or an instance of indicating. **b** something that suggests or indicates; a sign or symptom. **2** something indicated or suggested; esp. in *Med.*, a remedy or treatment that is suggested by the symptoms. **3** a reading given by a gauge or instrument. [F f. L *indicatio* (as INDICATE)]

■ **1 a** designation, specification, identification, particularization; show, display, exhibition, signal, manifestation, demonstration; admission, disclosure, registration, expression, mention, statement. **b** sign, signal, symptom, manifestation, token, *Computing* prompt; suggestion, hint, intimation, inkling, clue, implication; omen, portent, forewarning, warning, augury, foreshadowing, foretoken; (*indications*) evidence, data, indicia. **3** reading, read-out, level, score; measure, degree.

indicative /indíkkətiv/ *adj.* & *n.* ● *adj.* **1** (foll. by *of*) suggestive; serving as an indication. **2** *Gram.* (of a mood) denoting simple statement of a fact. ● *n. Gram.* **1** the indicative mood. **2** a verb in this mood. □□ **indicatively** *adv.* [ME f. F *indicatif -ive* f. LL *indicativus* (as INDICATE)]

■ *adj.* **1** suggestive, symptomatic, indicatory, significative, denotative, indexical, indicial; characteristic, typical.

indicator /índikaytər/ *n.* **1** a person or thing that indicates. **2** a device indicating the condition of a machine etc. **3** a recording instrument attached to an apparatus etc. **4** a board in a railway station etc. giving current information. **5** a device (esp. a flashing light) on a vehicle to show that it is about to change direction. **6** a substance which changes colour at a given stage in a chemical reaction. **7** *Physics* & *Med.* a radioactive tracer.

■ **1** pointer, designator, marker, specifier, identifier, signaller; displayer; needle, gnomon, index, guide, *Computing* cursor. **2, 3** instrument, gauge, pressure gauge, meter, monitor, recorder, counter, log; flight-recorder, black box; dial, display, panel, instrument panel, read-out, LCD, LED. **4** board, indicator board, screen; notice-board, *US* bulletin-board. **5** flasher, blinker, *colloq.* winker, *Brit. hist.* trafficator. **6** litmus (paper); *Chem.* phenolphthalein, fluorescein.

indicatory /indíkkətəri, -tri/ *adj.* = INDICATIVE *adj.* 1.

indices *pl.* of INDEX.

indicia /indíshə/ *n.pl.* **1** distinguishing or identificatory marks. **2** signs, indications. [pl. of L *indicium* (as INDEX)]

indicial /indísh'l/ *adj.* **1** of the nature or form of an index. **2** of the nature of indicia; indicative.

indict /indít/ *v.tr.* accuse (a person) formally by legal process. □□ **indictee** /-teé/ *n.* **indicter** *n.* [ME f. AF *enditer* indict f. OF *enditier* declare f. Rmc *indictare* (unrecorded: as IN-[2], DICTATE)]

■ accuse, charge, arraign, impeach, incriminate, inculpate, prosecute, take to court, put in the dock, summon, summons; denounce, blame. ▫▫ **indictee** (the) accused, defendant, respondent; co-respondent. **indicter** see *accuser* (ACCUSE).

indictable /indī́təb'l/ *adj.* **1** (of an offence) rendering the person who commits it liable to be charged with a crime. **2** (of a person) so liable.

indictment /indī́tmənt/ *n.* **1** the act of indicting. **2 a** a formal accusation. **b** a legal process in which this is made. **c** a document containing a charge. **3** something that serves to condemn or censure. [ME f. AF *enditement* (as INDICT)]

■ **1, 2a, c** see ACCUSATION.

indie /indi/ *n.* & *adj. colloq.* ● *n.* an independent record or film company. ● *adj.* (of a pop group or record label) independent, not belonging to one of the major companies.

Indies /indiz/ *n.pl.* (prec. by *the*) *archaic* India and adjacent regions (see also *East Indies*, *West Indies*). [pl. of obs. *Indy* India]

indifference /indifrənss/ *n.* **1** lack of interest or attention. **2** unimportance (*a matter of indifference*). **3** neutrality. [L *indifferentia* (as INDIFFERENT)]

■ **1** unconcern, apathy, carelessness, pococurantism, listlessness, *disp.* disinterest; coolness, nonchalance, insouciance, aloofness, detachment, coldness, phlegm, stolidity, callousness, insensibility, impassiveness, impassivity; disregard, see also *absent-mindedness* (ABSENT-MINDED). **2** unimportance, insignificance, irrelevance, unconcern, inconsequence, inconsequentiality, triviality. **3** dispassion, disinterest, disinterestedness, impartiality, neutrality, objectivity, fairness, equitableness, even-handedness.

indifferent /indifrənt/ *adj.* **1** neither good nor bad; average, mediocre. **2 a** not especially good. **b** fairly bad. **3** (often prec. by *very*) decidedly inferior. **4** (foll. by *to*) having no partiality for or against; having no interest in or sympathy for. **5** chemically, magnetically, etc., neutral. ▫▫ **indifferently** *adv.* [ME f. OF *indifferent* or L *indifferens* (as IN-[1], DIFFERENT)]

■ **1** average, mediocre, fair (to middling), middling, *comme ci, comme ça*, neutral, ordinary, commonplace, everyday, *colloq.* common or garden; uninspired, undistinguished, colourless, bland; insipid, wishy-washy, dull, flat. **2 a** tolerable, passable, acceptable, satisfactory, all right, not bad, *colloq.* OK. **b** second-rate, so so, lightweight, mediocre, lukewarm, poor, inferior, shoddy, substandard, unsatisfactory, not too good, *colloq.* not so hot, *sl.* naff, *NZ sl.* half-pie; see also BAD *adj.* 1. **3** see BAD *adj.* 1. **4** impartial, neutral, even-handed, objective, fair, fair-minded, equitable, unbiased, unprejudiced, uncoloured, non-partisan, disinterested, dispassionate, impassive, aloof, detached, distant, removed; unconcerned, apathetic, uninterested, listless, uncaring, cool, nonchalant, insouciant, blasé, lukewarm, Laodicean, lackadaisical; unsympathetic, insensitive, unfeeling, unemotional, inconsiderate, callous, cold, phlegmatic, stolid.

indifferentism /indifrəntiz'm/ *n.* an attitude of indifference, esp. in religious matters. ▫▫ **indifferentist** *n.*

indigenize /indíjinīz/ *v.tr.* (also **-ise**) **1** make indigenous; subject to native influence. **2** subject to increased use of indigenous people in government etc. ▫▫ **indigenization** /-záysh'n/ *n.*

indigenous /indíjinəss/ *adj.* **1 a** (esp. of flora or fauna) originating naturally in a region. **b** (of people) born in a region. **2** (foll. by *to*) belonging naturally to a place. ▫▫ **indigenously** *adv.* **indigenousness** *n.* [L *indigena* f. *indi-* = IN-[2] + *gen-* be born]

■ native, local, endemic; aboriginal, autochthonous, autochthonal, autochthonic.

indigent /indijənt/ *adj.* needy, poor. ▫▫ **indigence** *n.* [ME f. OF f. LL *indigēre* f. *indi-* = IN-[2] + *egēre* need]

■ see POOR 1. ▫▫ **indigence** see POVERTY 1.

indigested /indījéstid/ *adj.* **1** shapeless. **2** ill-considered. **3** not digested.

indigestible /indijéstib'l/ *adj.* **1** difficult or impossible to digest. **2** too complex or awkward to read or comprehend easily. ▫▫ **indigestibility** /-bílliti/ *n.* **indigestibly** *adv.* [F *indigestible* or LL *indigestibilis* (as IN-[1], DIGEST)]

indigestion /indijéss-chən/ *n.* **1** difficulty in digesting food. **2** pain or discomfort caused by this. ▫▫ **indigestive** *adj.* [ME f. OF *indigestion* or LL *indigestio* (as IN-[1], DIGESTION)]

■ dyspepsia, waterbrash, brash, acidity, heartburn, acidosis, *Med.* pyrosis; stomach-ache, upset stomach, stomach upset, *colloq.* bellyache, tummy-ache, collywobbles; wind, flatulence.

indignant /indígnənt/ *adj.* feeling or showing scornful anger or a sense of injured innocence. ▫▫ **indignantly** *adv.* [L *indignari indignant-* regard as unworthy (as IN-[1], *dignus* worthy)]

■ disgruntled, vexed, huffish, in a huff, in a pet, sore, displeased, resentful, up in arms, hot under the collar, cross; piqued, irritated, irked, slighted, annoyed, exasperated, *colloq.* peeved, uptight, riled, miffed, *US sl.* pissed, ticked off; see also ANGRY 1.

indignation /indignáysh'n/ *n.* scornful anger at supposed unjust or unfair conduct or treatment. [ME f. OF *indignation* or L *indignatio* (as INDIGNANT)]

■ vexation, irritation, annoyance, exasperation, displeasure, resentment, pique, umbrage; anger, fury, rage, *literary* ire, wrath, *poet. or archaic* choler; see also ANGER *n.*

indignity /indígniti/ *n.* (*pl.* **-ies**) **1** unworthy treatment. **2** a slight or insult. **3** the humiliating quality of something (*the indignity of my position*). [F *indignité* or L *indignitas* (as INDIGNANT)]

■ **1, 2** injustice, mistreatment; dishonour, embarrassment, disrespect, discourtesy, *colloq.* kick in the teeth; reproach, contumely, obloquy, offence, injury, abuse, outrage, affront, slap in the face, insult, slight, snub, *colloq.* put-down. **3** abjectness, wretchedness, miserableness, pitifulness.

indigo /indigō/ *n.* (*pl.* **-os**) **1 a** a natural blue dye obtained from the indigo plant. **b** a synthetic form of this dye. **2** any plant of the genus *Indigofera*. **3** (in full **indigo blue**) a colour between blue and violet in the spectrum. ▫▫ **indigotic** /-góttik/ *adj.* [16th-c. *indico* (f. Sp.), *indigo* (f. Port.) f. L *indicum* f. Gk *indikon* INDIAN (dye)]

indirect /indīrékt/ *adj.* **1** not going straight to the point. **2** (of a route etc.) not straight. **3** not directly sought or aimed at (*an indirect result*). **4** (of lighting) from a concealed source and diffusely reflected. ▫ **indirect object** *Gram.* a person or thing affected by a verbal action but not primarily acted on (e.g. *him* in *give him the book*). **indirect question** *Gram.* a question in reported speech (e.g. *they asked who I was*). **indirect speech** (or **oration**) = *reported speech* (see REPORT). **indirect tax** a tax levied on goods and services and not on income or profits. ▫▫ **indirectly** *adv.* **indirectness** *n.* [ME f. OF *indirect* or med.L *indirectus* (as IN-[1], DIRECT)]

■ **1, 2** oblique, circuitous, devious, tortuous, twisty, sinuous, winding, rambling, roundabout, erratic, crooked, zigzag, zigzagged; circumlocutory, circumlocutional, circumlocutionary, periphrastic, discursive, digressive, excursive. **3** secondary, ancillary, collateral, incidental, side, subordinate, subsidiary, accessory, additional, accidental, adventitious. ▫ **indirect speech, indirect oration** reported speech, oblique oration *or* speech.

indiscernible /indisérnib'l/ *adj.* that cannot be discerned or distinguished from another. ▫▫ **indiscernibility** /-bílliti/ *n.* **indiscernibly** *adv.*

■ see FAINT *adj.* 1, INDISTINGUISHABLE.

indiscipline /indíssiplin/ *n.* lack of discipline.

indiscreet /indiskréet/ *adj.* **1** not discreet; revealing secrets. **2** injudicious, unwary. ▫▫ **indiscreetly** *adv.* **indiscreetness** *n.* [ME f. LL *indiscretus* (as IN-[1], DISCREET)]

■ **1** garrulous, loquacious, talkative, gossipy, chattery, prating, *colloq.* gabby; untrustworthy, unreliable, undependable, irresponsible, feckless. **2** imprudent, injudicious, incautious, unguarded, unwary, improvident, impolitic, ill-advised, ill-judged, ill-considered, rash, reckless, audacious, bold, impulsive, hasty, impetuous, *literary* temerarious; thoughtless, insensitive, undiplomatic, tactless, heedless, careless, unthinking, mindless, unwise, naïve, foolish, foolhardy.

indiscrete /indiskréet/ *adj.* not divided into distinct parts. [L *indiscretus* (as IN-[1], DISCRETE)]

indiscretion /indiskrésh'n/ *n.* **1** lack of discretion; indiscreet conduct. **2** an indiscreet action, remark, etc. [ME f. OF *indiscretion* or LL *indiscretio* (as IN-[1], DISCRETION)]
■ **1** garrulousness, loquaciousness, talkativeness; see also *imprudence* (IMPRUDENT). **2** gaffe, *faux pas*, misstep, blunder, error, mistake, slip, lapse, solecism, *US* bull, *colloq.* (bad) break, slip-up, howler, *sl.* booboo, boner, bish, bloomer, clanger, floater, *Brit. sl.* boob.

indiscriminate /indiskrímminət/ *adj.* **1** making no distinctions. **2** confused, promiscuous. □□ **indiscriminately** *adv.* **indiscriminateness** *n.* **indiscrimination** /-náysh'n/ *n.* **indiscriminative** *adj.* [IN-[1] + *discriminate* (adj.) f. L *discriminatus* past part. (as DISCRIMINATE)]
■ **1** undiscriminating, indiscriminative, unselective, uncritical, arbitrary, random. **2** confused, haphazard, chaotic, erratic, random, disorganized, unorganized, jumbled, scrambled, mixed-up, promiscuous, uncoordinated, higgledy-piggledy; casual, unmethodical, unsystematic.

indispensable /indispénsəb'l/ *adj.* **1** (often foll. by *to*, *for*) that cannot be dispensed with; necessary. **2** (of a law, duty, etc.) that is not to be set aside. □□ **indispensability** /-bílliti/ *n.* **indispensableness** *n.* **indispensably** *adv.* [med.L *indispensabilis* (as IN-[1], DISPENSABLE)]
■ **1** necessary, obligatory, compulsory, mandatory, imperative, needful, requisite, essential, of the essence, vital, life-and-death, key, important, urgent, compelling, *colloq. disp.* crucial. **2** unavoidable, inescapable, ineluctable, overriding, incontestable, undeniable, inexorable.

indispose /indispṓz/ *v.tr.* **1** (often foll. by *for*, or *to* + infin.) make unfit or unable. **2** (often foll. by *towards*, *from*, or *to* + infin.) make averse.
■ **1** see INCAPACITATE 1.

indisposed /indispṓzd/ *adj.* **1** slightly unwell. **2** averse or unwilling.
■ **1** see ILL *adj.* 1. **2** averse, disinclined, loath, unwilling, reluctant, hesitant.

indisposition /indispəzísh'n/ *n.* **1** ill health, a slight or temporary ailment. **2** disinclination. **3** aversion. [F *indisposition* or IN-[1] + DISPOSITION]
■ **1** see ILLNESS.

indisputable /indispyṓotəb'l/ *adj.* **1** that cannot be disputed. **2** unquestionable. □□ **indisputability** /-bílliti/ *n.* **indisputableness** *n.* **indisputably** *adv.* [LL *indisputabilis* (as IN-[1], DISPUTABLE)]
■ see INCONTROVERTIBLE.

indissolubilist /indisólyoobilist/ *n.* & *adj.* ● *n.* a person who believes that the Church should not remarry divorcees. ● *adj.* of or holding this belief.

indissoluble /indisólyoob'l/ *adj.* **1** that cannot be dissolved or decomposed. **2** lasting, stable (*an indissoluble bond*). □□ **indissolubility** /-bílliti/ *n.* **indissolubly** *adv.* [L *indissolubilis* (as IN-[1], DISSOLUBLE)]
■ □□ **indissolubly** see *inextricably* (INEXTRICABLE).

indistinct /indistíngkt/ *adj.* **1** not distinct. **2** confused, obscure. □□ **indistinctly** *adv.* **indistinctness** *n.* [ME f. L *indistinctus* (as IN-[1], DISTINCT)]
■ **1** uncertain, unsure, undecided, undetermined, indefinite, ambivalent, doubtful, vague; indistinguishable, undistinguishable, inseparable, undifferentiated. **2** confused, unclear, indeterminate, indefinite, ill-defined; blurred, blurry, fuzzy, hazy, foggy, misty, muddy, murky, dim, shadowy, bleary, obscure, vague; faint, imperceptible, indiscernible, indistinguishable; muffled, murmurous, garbled, scrambled, unintelligible, inarticulate, incomprehensible, illegible.

indistinctive /indistíngktiv/ *adj.* not having distinctive features. □□ **indistinctively** *adv.* **indistinctiveness** *n.*

indistinguishable /indistínggwishəb'l/ *adj.* (often foll. by *from*) not distinguishable. □□ **indistinguishableness** *n.* **indistinguishably** *adv.*
■ undistinguishable, inseparable, undifferentiated, indistinct; identical, (the) same, alike, similar, (two) of a kind; see also INDISTINCT 2.

indite /indī́t/ *v.tr. formal* or *joc.* **1** put (a speech etc.) into words. **2** write (a letter etc.). [ME f. OF *enditier*: see INDICT]
■ see WRITE 7.

indium /índiəm/ *n. Chem.* a soft silvery-white metallic element occurring naturally in zinc blende etc., used for electroplating and in semiconductors. ¶ Symb.: **In.** [L *indicum* indigo with ref. to its characteristic spectral lines]

indivertible /indivértib'l/ *adj.* that cannot be turned aside. □□ **indivertibly** *adv.*

individual /individyooəl/ *adj.* & *n.* ● *adj.* **1** single. **2** particular, special; not general. **3** having a distinct character. **4** characteristic of a particular person. **5** designed for use by one person. ● *n.* **1** a single member of a class. **2** a single human being as distinct from a family or group. **3** *colloq.* a person (*a most unpleasant individual*). [ME, = indivisible, f. med.L *individualis* (as IN-[1], *dividuus* f. *dividere* DIVIDE)]
■ *adj.* **1** single, sole, solitary, only, lone, one, alone; lonely, lonesome. **2, 3** particular, singular, specific, separate, distinct, discrete; special, peculiar, distinctive, different, unusual, odd, extraordinary, original, unique. **4** characteristic, typical, distinctive, idiosyncratic, peculiar; personal, own, *archaic* proper. **5** single, one-man; personal, custom-built, custom-made, made to measure, made to order. ● *n.* **2** person, human (being), (living) soul, mortal, man, woman, child. **3** one, customer; *colloq.* character, party, sort; see also FELLOW 1.

individualism /individyooəliz'm/ *n.* **1** the habit or principle of being independent and self-reliant. **2** a social theory favouring the free action of individuals. **3** self-centred feeling or conduct; egoism. □□ **individualist** *n.* **individualistic** /-lístik/ *adj.* **individualistically** /-lístikəli/ *adv.*
■ □□ **individualist** independent, freethinker, nonconformist, maverick, loner, lone wolf; *Philos.* solipsist. **individualistic** see INDEPENDENT *adj.* 2, 3.

individuality /individyoo-álliti/ *n.* (*pl.* **-ies**) **1** individual character, esp. when strongly marked. **2** (in *pl.*) individual tastes etc. **3** separate existence.
■ **1** see *eccentricity* (ECCENTRIC). **2** (*individualities*) see DIVERSITY.

individualize /individyooəlīz/ *v.tr.* (also **-ise**) **1** give an individual character to. **2** specify. □□ **individualization** /-záysh'n/ *n.*
■ **1** see DISTINGUISH 2. **2** see SPECIFY.

individually /individyooəli/ *adv.* **1** personally; in an individual capacity. **2** in a distinctive manner. **3** one by one; not collectively.
■ **1** see PERSONALLY 5, ALONE 1b. **3** one at a time, singly, one by one, separately, severally, apart.

individuate /individyoo-ayt/ *v.tr.* individualize; form into an individual. □□ **individuation** /-áysh'n/ *n.* [med.L *individuare* (as INDIVIDUAL)]

indivisible /indivízzib'l/ *adj.* **1** not divisible. **2** not distributable among a number. □□ **indivisibility** /-bílliti/ *n.* **indivisibly** *adv.* [ME f. LL *indivisibilis* (as IN-[1], DIVISIBLE)]

Indo- /índō/ *comb. form* Indian; Indian and. [L *Indus* f. Gk *Indos*]

Indo-Aryan /índō-áiriən/ *n.* & *adj.* ● *n.* **1** a member of any of the Aryan peoples of India. **2** the Indic group of languages. ● *adj.* of or relating to the Indo-Aryans or Indo-Aryan.

Indo-Chinese /indōchīnéez/ *adj.* & *n.* ● *adj.* of or relating to Indo-China in SE Asia. ● *n.* a native of Indo-China; a person of Indo-Chinese descent.

indocile /indṓsīl/ *adj.* not docile. ◻◻ **indocility** /-dəsílliti/ *n.* [F *indocile* or L *indocilis* (as IN-[1], DOCILE)]

indoctrinate /indóktrinayt/ *v.tr.* **1** teach (a person or group) systematically or for a long period to accept (esp. partisan or tendentious) ideas uncritically. **2** teach, instruct. ◻◻ **indoctrination** /-náysh'n/ *n.* **indoctrinator** *n.* [IN-[2] + DOCTRINE + -ATE[3]]

■ train, teach, instruct, school, discipline, drill; brainwash, propagandize.

Indo-European /indō-yoórəpéeən/ *adj.* & *n.* ● *adj.* **1** of or relating to the family of languages spoken over the greater part of Europe and Asia as far as N. India. **2** of or relating to the hypothetical parent language of this family. ● *n.* **1** the Indo-European family of languages. **2** the hypothetical parent language of all languages belonging to this family. **3** (usu. in *pl.*) a speaker of an Indo-European language.

Indo-Iranian /índō-iráyniən/ *adj.* & *n.* ● *adj.* of or relating to the subfamily of Indo-European languages spoken chiefly in N. India and Iran. ● *n.* this subfamily.

indole /indōl/ *n. Chem.* an organic compound with a characteristic odour formed on the reduction of indigo. [INDIGO + L *oleum* oil]

indoleacetic acid /índōləséetik/ *n. Biochem.* any of the several isomeric acetic acid derivatives of indole, esp. one found as a natural growth hormone in plants. ¶ Abbr.: **IAA**. [INDOLE + ACETIC]

indolent /indələnt/ *adj.* **1** lazy; wishing to avoid activity or exertion. **2** *Med.* causing no pain (*an indolent tumour*). ◻◻ **indolence** *n.* **indolently** *adv.* [LL *indolens* (as IN-[1], *dolēre* suffer pain)]

■ **1** lazy, slothful, sluggish, idle, lethargic, shiftless, languorous, languid, torpid, inert, inactive, stagnant, fainéant, listless. ◻◻ **indolence** laziness, slothfulness, sloth, sluggishness, idleness, lethargy, shiftlessness, languor, languidness, lassitude, listlessness, torpor, torpidity, inertia, inaction, inactivity, *dolce far niente*.

Indology /indólləji/ *n.* the study of Indian history, literature, etc. ◻◻ **Indologist** *n.*

indomitable /indómmitəb'l/ *adj.* **1** that cannot be subdued; unyielding. **2** stubbornly persistent. ◻◻ **indomitability** /-bílliti/ *n.* **indomitableness** *n.* **indomitably** *adv.* [LL *indomitabilis* (as IN-[1], L *domitare* tame)]

■ **1** unconquerable, unbeatable, irrepressible, unstoppable, invincible, unyielding, unswerving, unwavering, unflinching. **2** resolute, resolved, determined, stubborn, steadfast, staunch, persistent, indefatigable, untiring, tireless, unflagging, undaunted, dauntless, fearless, unafraid, intrepid, brave, courageous, plucky, mettlesome.

Indonesian /indənéezyən, -néezh'n, -néesh'n/ *n.* & *adj.* ● *n.* **1 a** a native or national of Indonesia in SE Asia. **b** a person of Indonesian descent. **2** a member of the chief pre-Malay population of the E. Indies. **3** a language of the group spoken in the E. Indies, esp. the official language of the Indonesian Republic (see also BAHASA INDONESIA). ● *adj.* of or relating to Indonesia or its people or language. [*Indonesia* f. INDIES after *Polynesia*]

indoor /indor/ *adj.* situated, carried on, or used within a building or under cover (*indoor aerial*; *indoor games*). [earlier *within-door*: cf. INDOORS]

indoors /indórz/ *adv.* into or within a building. [earlier *within doors*]

indorse var. of ENDORSE.

indraught /índraaft/ *n.* (*US* **indraft**) **1** the drawing in of something. **2** an inward flow or current.

indrawn /indráwn/ *adj.* **1** (of breath etc.) drawn in. **2** aloof.

indri /indri/ *n.* (*pl.* **indris**) a large lemur, *Indri indri*, of Madagascar. [Malagasy *indry* behold, mistaken for its name]

indubitable /indyoóbitəb'l/ *adj.* that cannot be doubted. ◻◻ **indubitably** *adv.* [F *indubitable* or L *indubitabilis* (as IN-[1], *dubitare* to doubt)]

■ see CERTAIN *adj.* 1b. ◻◻ **indubitably** see *undoubtedly* (UNDOUBTED).

induce /indyoóss/ *v.tr.* **1** (often foll. by *to* + infin.) prevail on; persuade. **2** bring about; give rise to. **3** *Med.* bring on (labour) artificially, esp. by use of drugs. **4** *Electr.* produce (a current) by induction. **5** *Physics* cause (radioactivity) by bombardment. **6** infer; derive as a deduction. ◻◻ **inducer** *n.* **inducible** *adj.* [ME f. L *inducere induct-* (as IN-[2], *ducere* lead)]

■ **1** lead, persuade, influence, prevail on *or* upon, sway, move, convince, get, talk into, prompt, incite, instigate, actuate, motivate, impel, encourage, inspire, stimulate, nudge, push, press, urge, prod, goad, spur, egg on, coax, cajole, lure, entice, inveigle, seduce. **2** cause, bring about *or* on, produce, give rise to, engender, create, generate, lead to; effect, occasion, set in motion.

inducement /indyoósmənt/ *n.* **1** (often foll. by *to*) an attraction that leads one on. **2** a thing that induces.

■ **1** attraction, lure, incentive, stimulus, enticement, bait, encouragement, incitement, provocation, spur. **2** lure, bait, carrot, spur, *sl.* come-on; see also INCENTIVE *n.* 2.

induct /indúkt/ *v.tr.* (often foll. by *to*, *into*) **1** introduce formally into possession of a benefice. **2** install into a room, office, etc. **3** introduce, initiate. **4** *US* enlist (a person) for military service. ◻◻ **inductee** /induktée/ *n.* [ME (as INDUCE)]

■ **1** install, inaugurate, invest, instate, establish, swear in; ordain. **2** install, move in, establish. **3** introduce, initiate, inaugurate, originate. **4** call up, enlist, conscript, enrol, recruit, register, *US* draft.

inductance /indúktənss/ *n. Electr.* the property of an electric circuit that causes an electromotive force to be generated by a change in the current flowing.

induction /indúksh'n/ *n.* **1** the act or an instance of inducting or inducing. **2** *Med.* the process of bringing on (esp. labour) by artificial means. **3** *Logic* **a** the inference of a general law from particular instances (cf. DEDUCTION). **b** *Math.* a means of proving a theorem by showing that if it is true of any particular case it is true of the next case in a series, and then showing that it is indeed true in one particular case. **c** (foll. by *of*) the production of (facts) to prove a general statement. **4** (often *attrib.*) a formal introduction to a new job, position, etc. (*attended an induction course*). **5** *Electr.* **a** the production of an electric or magnetic state by the proximity (without contact) of an electrified or magnetized body. **b** the production of an electric current in a conductor by a change of magnetic field. **6** the drawing of a fuel mixture into the cylinders of an internal-combustion engine. **7** *US* enlistment for military service. ◻ **induction-coil** a coil for generating intermittent high voltage from a direct current. **induction heating** heating by an induced electric current. [ME f. OF *induction* or L *inductio* (as INDUCE)]

■ **1** see *initiation* (INITIATE), INSTALLATION 1.

inductive /indúktiv/ *adj.* **1** (of reasoning etc.) of or based on induction. **2** of electric or magnetic induction. ◻◻ **inductively** *adv.* **inductiveness** *n.* [LL *inductivus* (as INDUCE)]

■ **1** see LOGICAL 1–3.

inductor /indúktər/ *n.* **1** *Electr.* a component (in a circuit) which possesses inductance. **2** a person who inducts a member of the clergy. [L (as INDUCE)]

indue var. of ENDUE.

indulge /indúlj/ *v.* **1** *intr.* (often foll. by *in*) take pleasure freely. **2** *tr.* yield freely to (a desire etc.). **3** *tr.* gratify the wishes of; favour (*indulged them with money*). **4** *intr. colloq.* take alcoholic liquor. ◻◻ **indulger** *n.* [L *indulgēre indult-* give free rein to]

■ **1** wallow, luxuriate, be (self-)indulgent; gormandize, feast, carouse, banquet; (*indulge in*) yield to, succumb to, treat oneself to. **2** yield to, give in to, allow, gratify. **3** gratify, humour, oblige, minister to, cater to, pander to, treat; favour, pamper, baby, pet, cosset, mollycoddle, coddle, mother, spoil. **4** see DRINK *v.* 2.

indulgence /indúljənss/ *n.* **1 a** the act of indulging. **b** the state of being indulgent. **2** something indulged in. **3** *RC Ch.* the remission of temporal punishment in purgatory, still due for sins after absolution. **4** a privilege granted. □ **Declaration of Indulgence** the proclamation of religious liberties, esp. under Charles II in 1672 and James II in 1687. [ME f. OF f. L *indulgentia* (as INDULGENT)]

■ **1 a** self-indulgence, self-gratification; allowance, acceptance, forgiveness, remission, pardon. **b** self-indulgence, luxury, extravagance, profligacy, dissipation, self-satisfaction; tolerance, sufferance, understanding, patience, good will, forbearance, kindness, mercy, forgiveness. **2** treat, luxury, extravagance; fling.

indulgent /indúljənt/ *adj.* **1** ready or too ready to overlook faults etc. **2** indulging or tending to indulge. □□ **indulgently** *adv.* [F *indulgent* or L *indulgere indulgent-* (as INDULGE)]

■ tolerant, permissive, patient, understanding, forbearing, lenient, easygoing, relaxed, liberal, lax, soft, kind, kindly, well-disposed, agreeable.

indumentum /indyooméntəm/ *n.* (*pl.* **indumenta** /-tə/) *Bot.* the covering of hairs on part of a plant, esp. when dense. [L, = garment]

induna /indóonə/ *n.* **1** *S.Afr.* a tribal councillor or headman. **2 a** an African foreman. **b** a person in authority. [Nguni *inDuna* captain, councillor]

indurate /indyoorayt/ *v.* **1** *tr.* & *intr.* make or become hard. **2** *tr.* make callous or unfeeling. **3** *intr.* become inveterate. □□ **induration** /-ráysh'n/ *n.* **indurative** *adj.* [L *indurare* (as IN-[2], *durus* hard)]

indusium /indyóoziəm/ *n.* (*pl.* **indusia** /-ziə/) **1** a membranous shield covering the fruit-cluster of a fern. **2** a collection of hairs enclosing the stigma of some flowers. **3** the case of a larva. □□ **indusial** *adj.* [L, = tunic, f. *induere* put on (a garment)]

industrial /indústriəl/ *adj.* & *n.* ● *adj.* **1** of or relating to industry or industries. **2** designed or suitable for industrial use (*industrial alcohol*). **3** characterized by highly developed industries (*the industrial nations*). ● *n.* (in *pl.*) shares in industrial companies. □ **industrial action** *Brit.* any action, esp. a strike or work to rule, taken by employees as a protest. **industrial archaeology** the study of machines, factories, bridges, etc., formerly used in industry. **industrial estate** *Brit.* an area of land developed for the siting of industrial enterprises. **industrial relations** the relations between management and workers in industries. **the Industrial Revolution** the rapid development of a nation's industry (esp. in Britain in the late 18th and early 19th c.). □□ **industrially** *adv.* [INDUSTRY + -AL: in 19th c. partly f. F *industriel*]

■ *adj.* **1** see TECHNICAL 1.

industrialism /indústriəliz'm/ *n.* a social or economic system in which manufacturing industries are prevalent.

industrialist /indústriəlist/ *n.* a person engaged in the management of industry.

■ see *manufacturer* (MANUFACTURE).

industrialize /indústriəlīz/ *v.* (also **-ise**) **1** *tr.* introduce industries to (a country or region etc.). **2** *intr.* become industrialized. □□ **industrialization** /-záysh'n/ *n.*

industrious /indústriəss/ *adj.* diligent, hard-working. □□ **industriously** *adv.* **industriousness** *n.* [F *industrieux* or LL *industriosus* (as INDUSTRY)]

■ hard-working, diligent, sedulous, assiduous, Stakhanovist, workaholic; conscientious, earnest, painstaking; persistent, pertinacious, dogged, tenacious, untiring, tireless, indefatigable, unflagging; busy, energetic, vigorous, active, dynamic, enterprising, *colloq.* bustling. □□ **industriousness** see INDUSTRY 2, 3.

industry /indəstri/ *n.* (*pl.* **-ies**) **1 a** a branch of trade or manufacture. **b** trade and manufacture collectively (*incentives to industry*). **2** concerted or copious activity (*the building was a hive of industry*). **3 a** diligence. **b** *colloq.* the diligent study of a particular topic (*the Shakespeare industry*). **4** habitual employment in useful work. [ME, = skill, f. F *industrie* or L *industria* diligence]

■ **1** business, enterprise, commerce, trade, line, (line of) work; manufacture, production, fabrication. **2** busyness, industriousness, activity, (hustle and) bustle, dynamism, energy, vigour; work, labour, toil. **3** industriousness, diligence, assiduity, assiduousness, sedulity, sedulousness, Stakhanovism; conscientiousness, earnestness, painstakingness, application; persistence, persistency, perseverance, doggedness, determination, tenacity, tenaciousness, tirelessness, indefatigability; energy, vigour, exertion, effort, determination.

indwell /indwél/ *v.* (*past* and *past part.* **indwelt**) *literary* **1** *intr.* (often foll. by *in*) be permanently present as a spirit, principle, etc. **2** *tr.* inhabit spiritually. □□ **indweller** *n.*

■ □□ **indweller** see OCCUPANT 1.

-ine[1] /īn, in/ *suffix* forming adjectives, meaning 'belonging to, of the nature of' (*Alpine*; *asinine*). [from or after F *-in -ine*, or f. L *-inus*]

-ine[2] /īn/ *suffix* forming adjectives esp. from names of minerals, plants, etc. (*crystalline*). [L *-inus* from or after Gk *-inos*]

-ine[3] /in, een/ *suffix* forming feminine nouns (*heroine*; *margravine*). [F f. L *-ina* f. Gk *-inē*, or f. G *-in*]

-ine[4] *suffix* **1** /in/ forming (esp. abstract) nouns (*discipline*; *medicine*). **2** /een, in/ *Chem.* forming nouns denoting derived substances, esp. alkaloids, halogens, amines, and amino acids. [F f. L *-ina* (fem.) = -INE[1]]

inebriate *v.*, *adj.*, & *n.* ● *v.tr.* /ineébriayt/ **1** make drunk; intoxicate. **2** excite. ● *adj.* /ineébriət/ drunken. ● *n.* /ineébriət/ a drunken person, esp. a habitual drunkard. □□ **inebriation** /-áysh'n/ *n.* **inebriety** /-brī́əti/ *n.* [ME f. L *inebriatus* past part. of *inebriare* (as IN-[2], *ebrius* drunk)]

■ *v.* **1** see INTOXICATE 1. **2** see INTOXICATE 2. □□ **inebriety** see *drunkenness* (DRUNKEN).

inedible /inéddib'l/ *adj.* not edible, esp. not suitable for eating (cf. UNEATABLE). □□ **inedibility** /-bílliti/ *n.*

■ see UNPALATABLE.

inedited /inédditid/ *adj.* **1** not published. **2** published without editorial alterations or additions.

ineducable /inédyookəb'l/ *adj.* incapable of being educated, esp. through mental retardation. □□ **ineducability** /-bílliti/ *n.*

ineffable /inéffəb'l/ *adj.* **1** unutterable; too great for description in words. **2** that must not be uttered. □□ **ineffability** /-bílliti/ *n.* **ineffably** *adv.* [ME f. OF *ineffable* or L *ineffabilis* (as IN-[1], *effari* speak out, utter)]

■ **1** unutterable, inexpressible, indefinable, undefinable, indescribable, incommunicable, unspeakable, beyond description, beyond words. **2** unmentionable, taboo.

ineffaceable /innifáysəb'l/ *adj.* that cannot be effaced. □□ **ineffaceability** /-bílliti/ *n.* **ineffaceably** *adv.*

■ see INDELIBLE.

ineffective /innifékiv/ *adj.* **1** not producing any effect or the desired effect. **2** (of a person) inefficient; not achieving results. **3** lacking artistic effect. □□ **ineffectively** *adv.* **ineffectiveness** *n.*

■ **1** ineffectual, inefficacious, unsuccessful, unavailing; unproductive, unfruitful, fruitless, barren, vain, idle, futile, pointless, useless, *archaic* bootless; insufficient, inadequate; inoperative. **2** inefficient, incompetent, incapable, ineffectual; unskilled, unskilful, inexpert, inept; idle, otiose, redundant, shiftless.

ineffectual /innifékt yooəl, -fékchooəl/ *adj.* **1 a** without effect. **b** not producing the desired or expected effect. **2** (of a person) lacking the ability to achieve results (*an ineffectual leader*). □□ **ineffectuality** /-féktyoo-álliti, -fékchoo-álliti/ *n.* **ineffectually** *adv.* **ineffectualness** *n.* [ME f. med.L *ineffectualis* (as IN-[1], EFFECTUAL)]

■ **1** see INEFFECTIVE 1. **2** incapable, incompetent, impotent, powerless, inefficient, inadequate, insufficient; weak, feeble, tame, lame; see also INEFFECTIVE 2.

inefficacious /innefikáyshəss/ *adj.* (of a remedy etc.) not producing the desired effect. □□ **inefficaciously** *adv.* **inefficaciousness** *n.* **inefficacy** /inéffikəsi/ *n.*
■ see INEFFECTIVE 1.

inefficient /innifish'nt/ *adj.* **1** not efficient. **2** (of a person) not fully capable; not well qualified. □□ **inefficiency** *n.* **inefficiently** *adv.*
■ **1** uneconomical, uneconomic, wasteful, extravagant; unproductive, unprofitable, unfruitful, fruitless, ineffectual, inefficacious, ineffective; unprofessional, amateurish, disorganized, sloppy, lax, loose, slipshod. **2** ineffective, ineffectual, incompetent, incapable, unqualified, inexpert, unskilled, unskilful, inept, unfit. □□ **inefficiency** wastefulness, extravagance, unproductiveness, unprofitableness, unfruitfulness, fruitlessness; amateurishness, disorganization, sloppiness, laxity, laxness, looseness. **inefficiently** uneconomically, wastefully, extravagantly; unproductively, unprofitably, unfruitfully, fruitlessly; unprofessionally, amateurishly, sloppily, laxly, loosely.

inelastic /innilástik/ *adj.* **1** not elastic. **2** unadaptable, inflexible, unyielding. □□ **inelastically** *adv.* **inelasticity** /-lastíssiti/ *n.*
■ **1** see INFLEXIBLE 1. **2** see INFLEXIBLE 2.

inelegant /inélligənt/ *adj.* **1** ungraceful. **2 a** unrefined. **b** (of a style) unpolished. □□ **inelegance** *n.* **inelegantly** *adv.* [F *inélégant* f. L *inelegans* (as IN-[1], ELEGANT)]
■ **1** see UNGRACEFUL. **2** see UNREFINED. □□ **inelegance** see *ineptitude* (INEPT).

ineligible /inéllijib'l/ *adj.* **1** not eligible. **2** undesirable. □□ **ineligibility** /-bílliti/ *n.* **ineligibly** *adv.*
■ unqualified, disqualified; unacceptable, unsuitable, unfit, inappropriate, improper.

ineluctable /innilúktəb'l/ *adj.* **1** against which it is useless to struggle. **2** that cannot be escaped from. □□ **ineluctability** /-bílliti/ *n.* **ineluctably** *adv.* [L *ineluctabilis* (as IN-[1], *eluctari* struggle out)]
■ **2** see INEVITABLE 1. □□ **ineluctably** see NECESSARILY.

inept /inépt/ *adj.* **1** unskilful. **2** absurd, silly. **3** out of place. □□ **ineptitude** *n.* **ineptly** *adv.* **ineptness** *n.* [L *ineptus* (as IN-[1], APT)]
■ **1** unskilful, unskilled, inapt, inexpert, amateurish, inefficient, incompetent, maladroit, clumsy, awkward, bungling, bumbling, gauche, unhandy, ungainly, *colloq.* cack-handed, *esp. US sl.* out to lunch. **2** absurd, ridiculous, silly, preposterous, nonsensical, outlandish. **3** out of place, out of keeping, inappropriate, inexpedient, unsuitable, inapt, improper, outlandish. □□ **ineptitude, ineptness** unskilfulness, inaptitude, inaptness, inexpertness, amateurishness, inefficiency, incompetence, maladroitness, clumsiness, awkwardness, unhandiness, ungainliness, gaucherie, *colloq.* cack-handedness; absurdity, ridiculousness, silliness, preposterousness, outlandishness; inappropriateness, inexpediency, unsuitability, unsuitableness.

inequable /inékwəb'l/ *adj.* **1** not fairly distributed. **2** not uniform. [L *inaequabilis* uneven (as IN-[1], EQUABLE)]

inequality /innikwólliti/ *n.* (*pl.* **-ies**) **1 a** lack of equality in any respect. **b** an instance of this. **2** the state of being variable. **3** (of a surface) irregularity. **4** *Math.* a formula affirming that two expressions are not equal. [ME f. OF *inequalité* or L *inaequalitas* (as IN-[1], EQUALITY)]
■ **1** disparity, difference, discrepancy, incongruence, incongruity, inconsistency, dissimilarity, imbalance; inequity, unfairness, injustice, partiality, bias, prejudice. **2** see *dissimilarity* (DISSIMILAR). **3** irregularity, unevenness, bumpiness, lumpiness, coarseness, roughness, jaggedness, cragginess.

inequitable /inékwitəb'l/ *adj.* unfair, unjust. □□ **inequitably** *adv.*
■ see UNREASONABLE 1.

inequity /inékwiti/ *n.* (*pl.* **-ies**) unfairness, bias.
■ see INEQUALITY 1.

ineradicable /inniráddikəb'l/ *adj.* that cannot be rooted out. □□ **ineradicably** *adv.*
■ see INDELIBLE.

inerrant /inérrənt/ *adj.* not liable to err. □□ **inerrancy** *n.* [L *inerrans* (as IN-[1], ERR)]

inert /inért/ *adj.* **1** without inherent power of action, motion, or resistance. **2** without active chemical or other properties. **3** sluggish, slow. □ **inert gas** = *noble gas.* □□ **inertly** *adv.* **inertness** *n.* [L *iners inert-* (as IN-[1], *ars* ART[1])]
■ **1** motionless, immobile, static, stationary, still, inanimate, dead, lifeless, nerveless, passive, quiet, quiescent. **2** inactive, unreactive, unresponsive, passive, neutral. **3** sluggish, slow, torpid, dull, inactive, leaden, slack, passive, supine, dormant, listless, languid, languorous, idle, indolent, lazy, slothful, *archaic* otiose. □□ **inertness** see INERTIA.

inertia /inérshə, -shiə/ *n.* **1** *Physics* a property of matter by which it continues in its existing state of rest or uniform motion in a straight line, unless that state is changed by an external force. **2** inertness, sloth. □ **inertia reel** a reel device which allows a vehicle seat-belt to unwind freely but which locks under force of impact or rapid deceleration. **inertia selling** the sending of unsolicited goods in the hope of making a sale. □□ **inertial** *adj.* **inertialess** *adj.* [L (as INERT)]
■ **2** inertness, immobility, motionlessness, stasis, stationariness, stillness, inanimation, deadness, lifelessness, nervelessness, passivity, quiescence, quiescency, dormancy, inactivity, unresponsiveness; neutrality; apathy, sluggishness, slowness, torpor, torpidity, dullness, idleness, indolence, laziness, lassitude, listlessness, languor, slothfulness, sloth.

inescapable /inniskáypəb'l/ *adj.* that cannot be escaped or avoided. □□ **inescapability** /-bílliti/ *n.* **inescapably** *adv.*
■ see UNAVOIDABLE. □□ **inescapably** see NECESSARILY.

-iness /iniss/ *suffix* forming nouns corresponding to adjectives in *-y* (see -Y[1], -LY[2]).

inessential /innisénsh'l/ *adj.* & *n.* ● *adj.* **1** not necessary. **2** dispensable. ● *n.* an inessential thing.
■ *adj.* **1** see UNNECESSARY *adj.* 1. **2** see DISPENSABLE.

inestimable /inéstiməb'l/ *adj.* too great, intense, precious, etc., to be estimated. □□ **inestimably** *adv.* [ME f. OF f. L *inaestimabilis* (as IN-[1], ESTIMABLE)]
■ priceless, invaluable, valuable above *or* beyond *or* without price, precious, costly, valuable; incalculable, uncountable, innumerable, countless, untold, numberless; immeasurable, measureless, unfathomable, limitless, illimitable, boundless, unbounded, infinite, endless, never-ending, interminable, vast, immense, huge, great, enormous, giant, gigantic, massive, colossal, titanic, prodigious, *colloq.* tremendous.

inevitable /inévvitəb'l/ *adj.* **1 a** unavoidable; sure to happen. **b** that is bound to occur or appear. **2** *colloq.* that is tiresomely familiar. **3** (of character-drawing, the development of a plot, etc.) so true to nature etc. as to preclude alternative treatment or solution; convincing. □□ **inevitability** /-bílliti/ *n.* **inevitableness** *n.* **inevitably** *adv.* [L *inevitabilis* (as IN-[1], *evitare* avoid)]
■ **1** unavoidable, inescapable, ineluctable, inexorable, incontestable, irrevocable, unchangeable, destined, fated, ordained, decreed; assured, guaranteed, certain, sure, automatic. **2** familiar, usual, common, commonplace, everyday, frequent, traditional, customary, habitual, routine, typical. **3** see REALISTIC 1.

inexact /innigzákt/ *adj.* not exact. □□ **inexactitude** *n.* **inexactly** *adv.* **inexactness** *n.*
■ inaccurate, erroneous, incorrect, wrong, false, faulty, fallacious, mistaken, wide of the mark, out; imprecise, vague, indefinite, ill-defined, ambiguous, fuzzy, woolly, blurry, hazy, cloudy, muddled; approximate, rough, loose, estimated.

inexcusable /innikskyóozəb'l/ *adj.* (of a person, action, etc.) that cannot be excused or justified. □□ **inexcusably** *adv.* [ME f. L *inexcusabilis* (as IN-[1], EXCUSE)]

■ unpardonable, unforgivable, irremissible, inexpiable; reprehensible, blameworthy, censurable, reproachable, reprovable, condemnable; unjustifiable, unjustified, indefensible, unwarrantable.

inexhaustible /innigzáwstib'l/ *adj.* **1** that cannot be exhausted or used up. **2** that cannot be worn out. □□ **inexhaustibility** /-bílliti/ *n.* **inexhaustibly** *adv.*

■ **1** limitless, boundless, unlimited, unbounded, unrestricted, endless, infinite, never-ending; renewable. **2** untiring, tireless, indefatigable, unflagging, unfailing, unfaltering, unwearying, unwearied.

inexorable /inéksərəb'l/ *adj.* **1** relentless. **2** (of a person or attribute) that cannot be persuaded by request or entreaty. □□ **inexorability** /-bílliti/ *n.* **inexorably** *adv.* [F *inexorable* or L *inexorabilis* (as IN-[1], *exorare* entreat)]

■ **1** see RELENTLESS 1. **2** see OBSTINATE. □□ **inexorability** see NECESSITY 1. **inexorably** see NECESSARILY.

inexpedient /innikspéediənt/ *adj.* not expedient. □□ **inexpediency** *n.*

■ see *ill-advised* 2 (ILL).

inexpensive /innikspénsiv/ *adj.* **1** not expensive, cheap. **2** offering good value for the price. □□ **inexpensively** *adv.* **inexpensiveness** *n.*

■ cheap, economical, low-cost, cut-price, cut-rate, economy, budget, reasonable, *colloq.* dirt cheap, *sl.* cheapo.

inexperience /innikspéeriənss/ *n.* lack of experience, or of the resulting knowledge or skill. □□ **inexperienced** *adj.* [F *inexpérience* f. LL *inexperientia* (as IN-[1], EXPERIENCE)]

■ immaturity, innocence, callowness, naïvety, greenness, rawness, unsophistication, unsophisticatedness, unworldliness, amateurishness, inexpertness. □□ **inexperienced** untrained, unschooled, uninformed, uninitiated, unpractised, untried, unseasoned, unskilled, unskilful, amateurish, inexpert; immature, callow, unsophisticated, unworldly, innocent, naïve, green, fresh, raw, coltish, unfledged, new, young, (still) wet behind the ears.

inexpert /inékspert/ *adj.* unskilful; lacking expertise. □□ **inexpertly** *adv.* **inexpertness** *n.* [OF f. L *inexpertus* (as IN-[1], EXPERT)]

■ see INEPT 1. □□ **inexpertly** see POORLY *adv.*

inexpiable /inékspiəb'l/ *adj.* (of an act or feeling) that cannot be expiated or appeased. □□ **inexpiably** *adv.* [L *inexpiabilis* (as IN-[1], EXPIATE)]

■ see INEXCUSABLE.

inexplicable /innikspliíkkəb'l, inéks-/ *adj.* that cannot be explained or accounted for. □□ **inexplicability** /-bílliti/ *n.* **inexplicably** *adv.* [F *inexplicable* or L *inexplicabilis* that cannot be unfolded (as IN-[1], EXPLICABLE)]

■ unexplainable, unaccountable, unintelligible, incomprehensible, unexplained, insoluble, inscrutable; enigmatic, cryptic, puzzling, mystifying, mysterious, perplexing, baffling, bewildering; phenomenal, miraculous, supernatural, preternatural, magical, occult, arcane, psychic, uncanny.

inexplicit /innikspllíssit/ *adj.* not definitely or clearly expressed. □□ **inexplicitly** *adv.* **inexplicitness** *n.*

■ see INDEFINITE 1.

inexpressible /innikspréssib'l/ *adj.* that cannot be expressed in words. □□ **inexpressibly** *adv.*

■ unutterable, ineffable, indefinable, undefinable, indescribable, incommunicable, unspeakable, beyond description, beyond words.

inexpressive /innikspréssiv/ *adj.* not expressive. □□ **inexpressively** *adv.* **inexpressiveness** *n.*

inexpungible /innikspúnjib'l/ *adj.* that cannot be expunged or obliterated.

■ see INDELIBLE.

in extenso /in eksténsō/ *adv.* in full; at length. [L]

inextinguishable /innikstínggwishəb'l/ *adj.* **1** not quenchable; indestructible. **2** (of laughter etc.) irrepressible.

■ **1** unquenchable; indestructible, imperishable, inexpungible, ineffaceable, ineradicable, permanent, enduring, undying, eternal, everlasting. **2** see IRREPRESSIBLE.

in extremis /in ekstréemiss/ *adj.* **1** at the point of death. **2** in great difficulties. [L]

■ **1** see DYING.

inextricable /inékstrikəb'l, innikstrík-/ *adj.* **1** (of a circumstance) that cannot be escaped from. **2** (of a knot, problem, etc.) that cannot be unravelled or solved. **3** intricately confused. □□ **inextricability** /-bílliti/ *n.* **inextricably** *adv.* [ME f. L *inextricabilis* (as IN-[1], EXTRICATE)]

■ **1** mazy, labyrinthine, Daedalian, jungly; tricky, thorny, difficult, awkward, tough; impossible, paradoxical, *attrib.* catch-22. **2, 3** intricate, complex, complicated, involved, convoluted, convolutional, involute, involuted, confused, knotty, tangled, tangly; insoluble, unresolvable, insurmountable, unanswerable, impossible, difficult, tough, hard; perplexing, baffling, bewildering. □□ **inextricably** inescapably, ineluctably, unavoidably, irretrievably, inseparably, inevitably, necessarily; intricately; totally, completely.

infallible /infállib'l/ *adj.* **1** incapable of error. **2** (of a method, test, proof, etc.) unfailing; sure to succeed. **3** *RC Ch.* (of the Pope) unable to err in pronouncing dogma as doctrinally defined. □□ **infallibility** /-bílliti/ *n.* **infallibly** *adv.* [ME f. F *infaillible* or LL *infallibilis* (as IN-[1], FALLIBLE)]

■ **1, 2** impeccable, perfect, incontestable, undisputable, unquestionable, incontrovertible, irrefutable, indubitable, undeniable; unerring, faultless, flawless, errorless, error-free; unfailing, dependable, reliable, trustworthy, guaranteed, assured, sure, certain, secure, sound, foolproof, *archaic or joc.* trusty, *colloq.* sure-fire.

infamous /infəməss/ *adj.* **1** notoriously bad; having a bad reputation. **2** abominable. **3** (in ancient law) deprived of all or some rights of a citizen on account of serious crime. □□ **infamously** *adv.* **infamy** /infəmi/ *n.* (*pl.* **-ies**). [ME f. med.L *infamosus* f. L *infamis* (as IN-[1], FAME)]

■ **1** notorious, disreputable, of ill fame *or* repute, discreditable, dishonourable, ignominious, scandalous. **2** bad, awful, wicked, evil, iniquitous, villainous, heinous, vile, abominable, execrable, abhorrent, opprobrious, misbegotten, despicable, loathsome, detestable, odious, foul, base, low, scurvy, seamy, rotten, atrocious, flagitious, revolting, monstrous, egregious, outrageous, shameful, disgraceful. □□ **infamy** notoriety, ill repute, ill fame, disrepute, shame, ignominy, obloquy, disgrace, dishonour, stigma, discredit; wickedness, evil, iniquity, villainy, heinousness, vileness, abomination, outrage, abhorrence, opprobrium, loathsomeness, hatefulness, odiousness, odium, atrocity, repulsiveness, monstrosity, egregiousness, shame, shamefulness, disgrace, disgracefulness.

infancy /infənsi/ *n.* (*pl.* **-ies**) **1** early childhood; babyhood. **2** an early state in the development of an idea, undertaking, etc. **3** *Law* the state of being a minor. [L *infantia* (as INFANT)]

■ **1** babyhood, early childhood *or* days *or* years; childhood, boyhood, girlhood, pupillage, juvenescence; cradle. **2** inception, incipience, incipiency, early *or* initial stage(s); beginning(s), start, outset, *formal* commencement; birth, nascency, emergence, dawn, cradle. **3** minority.

infant /inf'nt/ *n.* **1 a** a child during the earliest period of its life. **b** *Brit.* a schoolchild below the age of seven years. **2** (esp. *attrib.*) a thing in an early stage of its development. **3** *Law* a minor; a person under 18. □ **infant mortality** death before the age of one. [ME f. OF *enfant* f. L *infans* unable to speak (as IN-[1], *fans fantis* pres. part. of *fari* speak)]

■ **1 a** see CHILD 1b. **b** see CHILD 1a. **3** see MINOR *n.*

infanta /infántə/ *n. hist.* a daughter of the ruling monarch of Spain or Portugal (usu. the eldest daughter who is not heir to the throne). [Sp. & Port., fem. of INFANTE]

infante /infánti/ *n. hist.* the second son of the ruling monarch of Spain or Portugal. [Sp. & Port. f. L (as INFANT)]

infanticide /infántisīd/ *n.* **1** the killing of an infant soon after birth. **2** the practice of killing newborn infants. **3** a person who kills an infant. □□ **infanticidal** /-sīd'l/ *adj.* [F f. LL *infanticidium, -cida* (as INFANT)]
■ **1, 2** see MURDER *n.* 1.

infantile /infəntīl/ *adj.* **1 a** like or characteristic of a child. **b** childish, immature (*infantile humour*). **2** in its infancy. □ **infantile paralysis** poliomyelitis. □□ **infantility** /-tílliti/ *n.* (*pl.* **-ies**). [F *infantile* or L *infantilis* (as INFANT)]
■ **1** childish, childlike, babyish, puerile, juvenile, pre-pubescent, pubescent, youthful, young, immature, unfledged, (still) wet behind the ears, green, tender. **2** incipient, inceptive, nascent, emergent, budding; embryonic, rudimentary, undeveloped, unformed, fledgling.

infantilism /infántiliz'm/ *n.* **1** childish behaviour. **2** *Psychol.* the persistence of infantile characteristics or behaviour in adult life.

infantry /infəntri/ *n.* (*pl.* **-ies**) a body of soldiers who march and fight on foot; foot-soldiers collectively. [F *infanterie* f. It. *infanteria* f. *infante* youth, infantryman (as INFANT)]

infantryman /infəntrimən/ *n.* (*pl.* **-men**) a soldier of an infantry regiment.
■ see SOLDIER *n.*

infarct /infaarkt/ *n. Med.* a small localized area of dead tissue caused by an inadequate blood supply. □□ **infarction** /infaárksh'n/ *n.* [mod.L *infarctus* (as IN-[2], L *farcire farct-* stuff)]

infatuate /infátyoo-ayt/ *v.tr.* **1** inspire with intense usu. transitory fondness or admiration. **2** affect with extreme folly. □□ **infatuation** /-áysh'n/ *n.* [L *infatuare* (as IN-[2], *fatuus* foolish)]
■ **1** see CAPTIVATE. □□ **infatuation** see PASSION 1, 3a, 4a.

infatuated /infátyoo-aytid/ *adj.* (often foll. by *with*) affected by an intense fondness or admiration.
■ fascinated, spellbound, besotted, possessed, obsessed, *US sl.* hipped; taken, beguiled, enchanted, bewitched, charmed, enraptured, hypnotized, mesmerized, captivated, enamoured, *archaic or literary* smitten; (*infatuated with*) fond of, mad about *or* on, *colloq.* crazy about, struck on, stuck on, soft on, dotty about *or* on, *esp. Brit. colloq.* daft about, *Brit. colloq.* soppy on, potty about, *sl.* gone on.

infauna /infawnə/ *n.* any animals which live just below the surface of the seabed. [Da. *ifauna* (as IN-[2], FAUNA)]

infeasible /inféezib'l/ *adj.* not feasible; that cannot easily be done. □□ **infeasibility** /-bílliti/ *n.*
■ see IMPOSSIBLE 1, 2.

infect /inf ékt/ *v.tr.* **1** contaminate (air, water, etc.) with harmful organisms or noxious matter. **2** affect (a person) with disease etc. **3** instil bad feeling or opinion into (a person). □□ **infector** *n.* [ME f. L *inficere infect-* taint (as IN-[2], *facere* make)]
■ **1** see CONTAMINATE. **2** see ATTACK *v.* 4.

infection /inféksh'n/ *n.* **1 a** the process of infecting or state of being infected. **b** an instance of this; an infectious disease. **2** communication of disease, esp. by the agency of air or water etc. **3 a** moral contamination. **b** the diffusive influence of example, sympathy, etc. [ME f. OF *infection* or LL *infectio* (as INFECT)]
■ **1 b** see DISEASE 1, 3.

infectious /infékshəss/ *adj.* **1** infecting with disease. **2** (of a disease) liable to be transmitted by air, water, etc. **3** (of emotions etc.) apt to spread; quickly affecting others. □□ **infectiously** *adv.* **infectiousness** *n.*
■ **1** infective, corruptive, malignant, virulent; poisonous, toxic, *archaic* miasmic, miasmal, miasmatic. **2, 3** contagious, catching, taking, communicable, transmissible, transmittable.

infective /inféktiv/ *adj.* **1** capable of infecting with disease. **2** infectious. □□ **infectiveness** *n.* [L *infectivus* (as INFECT)]

infelicitous /ínfilíssitəss/ *adj.* not felicitous; unfortunate. □□ **infelicitously** *adv.*
■ see INAPPROPRIATE.

infelicity /ínfilíssiti/ *n.* (*pl.* **-ies**) **1 a** inaptness of expression etc. **b** an instance of this. **2 a** unhappiness. **b** a misfortune. [ME f. L *infelicitas* (as IN-[1], FELICITY)]
■ **1 a** see IMPROPRIETY 1. **b** see IMPROPRIETY 2. **2 b** see MISFORTUNE 2.

infer /infér/ *v.tr.* (**inferred, inferring**) (often foll. by *that* + clause) **1** deduce or conclude from facts and reasoning. **2** *disp.* imply, suggest. □□ **inferable** *adj.* (also **inferrable**). [L *inferre* (as IN-[2], *ferre* bring)]
■ **1** deduce, derive, conclude, draw the (*or* a) conclusion, take it; surmise, understand, gather. **2** see IMPLY 1.

inference /infərənss/ *n.* **1** the act or an instance of inferring. **2** *Logic* **a** the forming of a conclusion from premisses. **b** a thing inferred. □□ **inferential** /-rénsh'l/ *adj.* **inferentially** /-rénshəli/ *adv.* [med.L *inferentia* (as INFER)]
■ deduction, conclusion, implication, implicate, derivation; understanding, surmise; *Law* presumption.

inferior /inféeriər/ *adj.* & *n.* ● *adj.* **1** (often foll. by *to*) **a** lower; in a lower position. **b** of lower rank, quality, etc. **2** poor in quality. **3** (of a planet) having an orbit within the earth's. **4** *Bot.* situated below an ovary or calyx. **5** (of figures or letters) written or printed below the line. ● *n.* **1** a person inferior to another, esp. in rank. **2** an inferior letter or figure. □□ **inferiorly** *adv.* [ME f. L, compar. of *inferus* that is below]
■ *adj.* **1** lower, lesser, junior, minor, smaller, *archaic* nether; second, subordinate, secondary, ancillary, auxiliary, subsidiary, subaltern, petty, *US* downscale. **2** second-rate, second-class, third-class, poor man's; poor, mean, bad, mediocre, common, coarse, (very) indifferent, low-grade, low-quality, low-class, cheap, cheapjack, cheap and nasty, trashy, tawdry, gimcrack, *Brit.* rubbishy, tinpot, *colloq.* crummy, lousy, tatty, measly, manky, *sl.* naff, ragtime, cheesy; imperfect, inadequate, defective, faulty, flawed, substandard, shoddy, slipshod. **5** subscript. ● *n.* **1** subordinate, junior, satellite, doormat, *derog.* underling; menial, lackey, *colloq.* dogsbody, stooge, *esp. US sl.* gofer. **2** subscript, *Math.* suffix.

inferiority /inféeriórriti/ *n.* the state of being inferior. □ **inferiority complex** an unrealistic feeling of general inadequacy caused by actual or supposed inferiority in one sphere, sometimes marked by aggressive behaviour in compensation.
■ juniority, subordination, secondariness, subsidiarity, pettiness; poverty, poorness, meanness, mediocrity, commonness, coarseness, cheapness, trashiness, tawdriness, *colloq.* crumminess, lousiness, tattiness, measliness, *sl.* cheesiness; imperfection, inadequacy, defectiveness, faultiness, shoddiness.

infernal /inférn'l/ *adj.* **1 a** of hell or the underworld. **b** hellish, fiendish. **2** *colloq.* detestable, tiresome. □□ **infernally** *adv.* [ME f. OF f. LL *infernalis* f. L *infernus* situated below]
■ **1** hellish, hell-like, Hadean, Stygian, Plutonian, Tartarean, chthonic, chthonian; fiendish, fiendlike, devilish, diabolic, diabolical, demonic, demoniac, demoniacal, satanic, Mephistophelean; damnable, execrable, abominable, malicious, malevolent, wicked, evil, iniquitous, flagitious, *colloq.* damned, *literary* maleficent. **2** see TIRESOME 2.

inferno /infernō/ *n.* (*pl.* **-os**) **1** a raging fire. **2** a scene of horror or distress. **3** hell, esp. with ref. to Dante's *Divine Comedy*. [It. f. LL *infernus* (as INFERNAL)]
■ **1** blaze, fire, conflagration, holocaust. **3** see HELL 1.

infertile /infértīl/ *adj.* not fertile. □□ **infertility** /-tílliti/ *n.* [F *infertile* or LL *infertilis* (as IN-[1], FERTILE)]
■ unproductive, non-productive, sterile, barren, unfruitful, fruitless, *Bot.* acarpous.

infest /infést/ *v.tr.* (of harmful persons or things, esp. vermin or disease) overrun (a place) in large numbers. □□

infestation /-stáysh'n/ *n.* [ME f. F *infester* or L *infestare* assail f. *infestus* hostile]
■ overrun, invade, plague, beset, take over; swarm over, overspread, pervade, permeate, penetrate, infiltrate, flood, inundate; parasitize.

infidel /infid'l/ *n.* & *adj.* ● *n.* **1** a person who does not believe in religion or in a particular religion; an unbeliever. **2** usu. *hist.* an adherent of a religion other than Christianity, esp. a Muslim. ● *adj.* **1** that is an infidel. **2** of unbelievers. [ME f. F *infidèle* or L *infidelis* (as IN-[1], *fidelis* faithful)]
■ *n.* **1** unbeliever, heathen, heretic, pagan, agnostic, atheist, nullifidian, irreligionist, sceptic, disbeliever, freethinker. ● *adj.* unbelieving, heathen, heretic, pagan, agnostic, atheistic, atheistical, sceptic, sceptical, freethinking, *archaic* ethnic; Gentile.

infidelity /infidélliti/ *n.* (*pl.* **-ies**) **1 a** disloyalty or unfaithfulness, esp. to a husband or wife. **b** an instance of this. **2** disbelief in Christianity or another religion. [ME f. F *infidélité* or L *infidelitas* (as INFIDEL)]
■ **1 a** unfaithfulness, adultery, faithlessness, disloyalty, deceit, deception, betrayal, *colloq.* two-timing; duplicity, double-dealing, perfidy, treachery, falseness. **b** adultery, cuckoldry, (love) affair, *affaire*, liaison, amour, entanglement, romance, fling, *sl.* bit on the side. **2** disbelief, unbelief, unbelievingness, heathenism, heresy, paganism, agnosticism, atheism, irreligionism, apostasy, scepticism, freethinking.

infield /infeeld/ *n.* **1** *Cricket* **a** the part of the ground near the wicket. **b** the fielders stationed there. **2** *Baseball* **a** the area between the four bases. **b** the four fielders stationed on its boundaries. **3** farm land around or near a homestead. **4 a** arable land. **b** land regularly manured and cropped. ▫▫ **infielder** *n.* (in sense 2).

infighting /infiting/ *n.* **1** hidden conflict or competitiveness within an organization. **2** boxing at closer quarters than arm's length. ▫▫ **infighter** *n.*
■ **1** see FACTION[1] 2.

infill /infil/ *n.* & *v.* ● *n.* **1** material used to fill a hole, gap, etc. **2** the placing of buildings to occupy the space between existing ones. ● *v.tr.* fill in (a cavity etc.).

infilling /infilling/ *n.* = INFILL *n.*

infiltrate /infiltrayt/ *v.* **1** *tr.* **a** gain entrance or access to surreptitiously and by degrees (as spies etc.). **b** cause to do this. **2** *tr.* permeate by filtration. **3** *tr.* (often foll. by *into*, *through*) introduce (fluid) by filtration. ▫▫ **infiltration** /-tráysh'n/ *n.* **infiltrator** *n.* [IN-[2] + FILTRATE]
■ **1 a** see ENTER 2. **2** see PERMEATE. ▫▫ **infiltration** see INVASION 1. **infiltrator** see INTRUDER.

infinite /infinit/ *adj.* & *n.* ● *adj.* **1** boundless, endless. **2** very great. **3** (usu. with *pl.*) innumerable; very many (*infinite resources*). **4** *Math.* **a** greater than any assignable quantity or countable number. **b** (of a series) that may be continued indefinitely. **5** *Gram.* (of a verb part) not limited by person or number, e.g. infinitive, gerund, and participle. ● *n.* **1** (**the Infinite**) God. **2** (**the infinite**) infinite space. ▫▫ **infinitely** *adv.* **infiniteness** *n.* [ME f. L *infinitus* (as IN-[1], FINITE)]
■ *adj.* **1–3** boundless, unbounded, limitless, unlimited, illimitable, interminable, endless, never-ending, perpetual, undying, everlasting, eternal, unending, without end, inexhaustible, bottomless, unfathomable, indeterminable, indeterminate, inestimable, immeasurable, measureless, incalculable, innumerable, numberless, uncountable, countless, uncounted, untold, multitudinous, vast, immense, astronomical, enormous, huge, great, gigantic, giant, massive, colossal, titanic, prodigious, *colloq.* tremendous. ● *n.* **1** (**the Infinite**) see GOD *n.* 2. **2** (**the infinite**) see UNIVERSE 1a.

infinitesimal /infinitéssim'l/ *adj.* & *n.* ● *adj.* infinitely or very small. ● *n.* an infinitesimal amount. ▫ **infinitesimal calculus** the differential and integral calculuses regarded as one subject. ▫▫ **infinitesimally** *adv.* [mod.L *infinitesimus* f. INFINITE: cf. CENTESIMAL]
■ *adj.* see MINUTE[2] 1.

infinitive /infinnitiv/ *n.* & *adj.* ● *n.* a form of a verb expressing the verbal notion without reference to a particular subject, tense, etc. (e.g. *see* in *we came to see*, *let him see*). ● *adj.* having this form. ▫▫ **infinitival** /-tīv'l/ *adj.* **infinitivally** /-tīvəli/ *adv.* [L *infinitivus* (as IN-[1], *finitivus* definite f. *finire finit-* define)]

infinitude /infinnityood/ *n.* **1** the state of being infinite; boundlessness. **2** (often foll. by *of*) a boundless number or extent. [L *infinitus*: see INFINITE, -TUDE]

infinity /infinniti/ *n.* (*pl.* **-ies**) **1** the state of being infinite. **2** an infinite number or extent. **3** infinite distance. **4** *Math.* infinite quantity. ¶ Symb.: ∞ [ME f. OF *infinité* or L *infinitas* (as INFINITE)]
■ **1** see ETERNITY 1, 3. **2** see LOT *n.* 1. **3** see ETERNITY 1, 3.

infirm /infúrm/ *adj.* **1** physically weak, esp. through age. **2** (of a person, mind, judgement, etc.) weak, irresolute. ▫▫ **infirmity** *n.* (*pl.* **-ies**). **infirmly** *adv.* [ME f. L *infirmus* (as IN-[1], FIRM[1])]
■ **1** weak, frail, decrepit, enfeebled, feeble, debilitated, weakened, fragile, withered, worn-out, *archaic* stricken in years; doddering, unstable, unsteady, unsound, shaky, wobbly; see also ILL *adj.* 1. **2** weak, irresolute, hesitant, undecided, uncertain, unsettled, indefinite, unresolved, undetermined, in two minds, ambivalent, inconstant. ▫▫ **infirmity** weakness, feebleness, enfeeblement, frailness, frailty, debility, decrepitude, fragility; instability, unstableness, unsteadiness, unsoundness, shakiness, wobbliness, sickliness; irresoluteness, irresolution, hesitancy, indecision, uncertainty, indefiniteness, unresolvedness, ambivalence, inconstancy, vacillation; illness, affliction, ailment, malady, indisposition, complaint, disorder, defect, disability.

infirmary /infúrməri/ *n.* (*pl.* **-ies**) **1** a hospital. **2** a place for those who are ill in a monastery, school, etc. [med.L *infirmaria* (as INFIRM)]
■ **1** hospital, health centre, polyclinic, clinic, sanatorium, nursing home, lazaret, lazaretto, *hist.* pest-house. **2** sickbay, first-aid post *or* station, *Brit.* sanatorium, san, surgery, *US* sanitarium; dispensary.

infix *v.* & *n.* ● *v.tr.* /infiks/ **1** (often foll. by *in*) **a** fix (a thing in another). **b** impress (a fact etc. in the mind). **2** *Gram.* insert (a formative element) into the body of a word. ● *n.* /infiks/ *Gram.* a formative element inserted in a word. ▫▫ **infixation** /-sáysh'n/ *n.* [L *infigere infix-* (as IN-[2], FIX): (n.) after *prefix*, *suffix*]

in flagrante delicto /in fləgránti dilíktō/ *adv.* in the very act of committing an offence. [L, = in blazing crime]

inflame /infláym/ *v.* **1** *tr.* & *intr.* (often foll. by *with*, *by*) provoke or become provoked to strong feeling, esp. anger. **2** *Med.* **a** *intr.* become hot, reddened, and sore. **b** *tr.* (esp. as **inflamed** *adj.*) cause inflammation or fever in (a body etc.); make hot. **3** *tr.* aggravate. **4** *intr.* & *tr.* catch or set on fire. **5** *tr.* light up with or as if with flames. ▫▫ **inflamer** *n.* [ME f. OF *enflammer* f. L *inflammare* (as IN-[2], *flamma* flame)]
■ **1** provoke, incense, anger, enrage, madden, infuriate, impassion, whip *or* lash up, work up, exasperate, *colloq.* rile; arouse, rouse, incite, touch off, ignite, excite, foment, agitate, stir (up), fire (up), heat, *literary* enkindle; stimulate, animate, move, motivate, urge, prod, goad, spur (on), rally. **2 a** burn, redden, chafe, itch, smart, sting. **b** irritate, make sore, nettle; (**inflamed**) irritated, sore, angry, chafing, chafed, red, swollen, heated, hot, fevered, feverish, infected, septic. **3** aggravate, exacerbate, intensify, deepen, heighten, increase, augment, fan, fuel. **4** ignite, combust, light, set fire to, set on fire, set alight, set ablaze, kindle, *US sl.* torch; catch fire, burst into flame(s), blaze up, flare, flash. **5** see ILLUMINATE 1.

inflammable /inflámməb'l/ *adj.* & *n.* ● *adj.* **1** easily set on fire; flammable. **2** easily excited. ● *n.* (usu. in *pl.*) an inflammable substance. ▫▫ **inflammability** /-billiti/ *n.*

inflammableness *n.* **inflammably** *adv.* [INFLAME after F *inflammable*]
■ *adj.* combustible, flammable, ignitable, explosive, fiery. **2** excitable, combustible, explosive, irascible, choleric, short-tempered, quick-tempered, irritable, nervous, edgy, high(ly)-strung, volatile, hotheaded, *Brit. sl.* waxy.

inflammation /infləmáysh'n/ *n.* **1** the act or an instance of inflaming. **2** *Med.* a localized physical condition with heat, swelling, redness, and usu. pain, esp. as a reaction to injury or infection. [L *inflammatio* (as INFLAME)]
■ **1** provocation, enragement, infuriation; arousal, incitement, excitement, fomentation, agitation, stimulation, animation; aggravation, exacerbation, intensification; ignition, combustion. **2** irritation, redness, soreness, tenderness, swelling, eruption, rash, hives, prickly heat, *Med.* exanthema.

inflammatory /inflámmətəri, -tri/ *adj.* **1** (esp. of speeches, leaflets, etc.) tending to cause anger etc. **2** of or tending to inflammation of the body.
■ **1** excitatory, provocative, maddening, infuriating, exasperating, irritating, rabble-rousing, seditious. **2** irritating, irritative, irritant, caustic.

inflatable /infláytəb'l/ *adj.* & *n.* ● *adj.* that can be inflated. ● *n.* an inflatable plastic or rubber object.
■ *adj.* see EXPANSIVE 1.

inflate /infláyt/ *v.tr.* **1** distend (a balloon etc.) with air. **2** (usu. foll. by *with*; usu. in *passive*) puff up (a person with pride etc.). **3 a** (often *absol.*) bring about inflation (of the currency). **b** raise (prices) artificially. **4** (as **inflated** *adj.*) (esp. of language, sentiments, etc.) bombastic. □□ **inflatedly** *adv.* **inflatedness** *n.* **inflater** *n.* **inflator** *n.* [L *inflare inflat-* (as IN-², *flare* blow)]
■ **1** blow up, pump up, distend, expand, enlarge, swell. **2** puff up *or* out, swell; balloon, dilate, distend, expand, enlarge. **4** (**inflated**) grandiloquent, bombastic, tumid, orotund, high-flown, pompous, pretentious, extravagant, magniloquent; exaggerated, conceited, overblown, grandiose, puffed up, overstated.

inflation /infláysh'n/ *n.* **1 a** the act or condition of inflating or being inflated. **b** an instance of this. **2** *Econ.* **a** a general increase in prices and fall in the purchasing value of money. **b** an increase in available currency regarded as causing this. □□ **inflationary** *adj.* **inflationism** *n.* **inflationist** *n.* & *adj.* [ME f. L *inflatio* (as INFLATE)]
■ **1** see *exaggeration* (EXAGGERATE), EXPANSION 1. **2 a** see INCREASE *n.* 1, 2.

inflect /inflékt/ *v.* **1** *tr.* change the pitch of (the voice, a musical note, etc.). **2** *Gram.* **a** *tr.* change the form of (a word) to express tense, gender, number, mood, etc. **b** *intr.* (of a word, language, etc.) undergo such change. **3** *tr.* bend inwards; curve. □□ **inflective** *adj.* [ME f. L *inflectere inflex-* (as IN-², *flectere* bend)]

inflection /infléksh'n/ *n.* (also **inflexion**) **1 a** the act or condition of inflecting or being inflected. **b** an instance of this. **2** *Gram.* **a** the process or practice of inflecting words. **b** an inflected form of a word. **c** a suffix etc. used to inflect, e.g. *-ed*. **3** a modulation of the voice. **4** *Geom.* a change of curvature from convex to concave at a particular point on a curve. □□ **inflectional** *adj.* **inflectionally** *adv.* **inflectionless** *adj.* [F *inflection* or L *inflexio* (as INFLECT)]
■ **1** see INTONATION 1.

inflexible /infléksib'l/ *adj.* **1** unbendable. **2** stiff; immovable; obstinate (*old and inflexible in his attitudes*). **3** unchangeable; inexorable. □□ **inflexibility** /-billiti/ *n.* **inflexibly** *adv.* [L *inflexibilis* (as IN-¹, FLEXIBLE)]
■ **1** unbendable, unbending, stiff, rigid, inelastic, hard, steely, unmalleable, unyielding, solid. **2** stiff, unbending, rigid, firm, unyielding, stiff-necked, steely, stony, uncompromising, rigorous, severe, Rhadamanthine; adamant, determined, fixed, resolute, resolved, unshakeable, immovable; obdurate, obstinate, stubborn, pigheaded, mulish. **3** unchangeable, intractable, immutable, unadaptable, unaccommodating, uncompliant, invariable, unvaried, unvarying, hard and fast; inexorable, ineluctable, inescapable, unavoidable, definite, certain, sure, firm.

inflict /inflíkt/ *v.tr.* (usu. foll. by *on*, *upon*) **1** administer, deal (a stroke, wound, defeat, etc.). **2** (also *refl.*) often *joc.* impose (suffering, a penalty, oneself, one's company, etc.) on (*shall not inflict myself on you any longer*). □□ **inflictable** *adj.* **inflicter** *n.* **inflictor** *n.* [L *infligere inflict-* (as IN-², *fligere* strike)]
■ **1** administer, deal, serve, impose, apply, visit, levy, wreak, cause, force.

infliction /inflíksh'n/ *n.* **1** the act or an instance of inflicting. **2** something inflicted, esp. a troublesome or boring experience. [LL *inflictio* (as INFLICT)]
■ **1** see IMPOSITION 1. **2** see IMPOSITION 2.

inflight /inflīt/ *attrib.adj.* occurring or provided during an aircraft flight.

inflorescence /inflərέss'nss/ *n.* **1** *Bot.* **a** the complete flower-head of a plant including stems, stalks, bracts, and flowers. **b** the arrangement of this. **2** the process of flowering. [mod.L *inflorescentia* f. LL *inflorescere* (as IN-², FLORESCENCE)]

inflow /inflō/ *n.* **1** a flowing in. **2** something that flows in. □□ **inflowing** *n.* & *adj.*

influence /infloōənss/ *n.* & *v.* ● *n.* **1 a** (usu. foll. by *on*, *upon*) the effect a person or thing has on another. **b** (usu. foll. by *over*, *with*) moral ascendancy or power. **c** a thing or person exercising such power (*is a good influence on them*). **2** *Astrol.* an ethereal fluid supposedly flowing from the stars and affecting character and destiny. **3** *Electr. archaic* = INDUCTION. ● *v.tr.* exert influence on; have an effect on. □ **under the influence** *colloq.* affected by alcoholic drink. □□ **influenceable** *adj.* **influencer** *n.* [ME f. OF *influence* or med.L *influentia* inflow f. L *influere* flow in (as IN-², *fluere* flow)]
■ *n.* **1** effect, impact, bearing, impression; power, force, potency, pressure, weight, leverage, pull, *colloq.* clout; hold, sway, control, mastery, authority, ascendancy; agent. ● *v.* affect, act *or* play *or* work on; sway, change, transform, modify, alter; move, drive, impel, force, urge; bias, persuade, motivate, induce, incline; impress (upon), bring pressure to bear on *or* upon, manipulate, pressurize, pressure. □ **under the influence** see DRUNK *adj.* 1.

influent /infloōənt/ *adj.* & *n.* ● *adj.* flowing in. ● *n.* a tributary stream. [ME f. L (as INFLUENCE)]

influential /infloo-énsh'l/ *adj.* having a great influence or power (*influential in the financial world*). □□ **influentially** *adv.* [med.L *influentia* INFLUENCE]
■ powerful, weighty, strong, forceful, impressive; authoritative, important, substantial, significant, telling; dominant, leading, predominant; effective, effectual, efficacious; instrumental; persuasive.

influenza /infloo-énzə/ *n.* a highly contagious virus infection causing fever, severe aching, and catarrh, often occurring in epidemics. □□ **influenzal** *adj.* [It. f. med.L *influentia* INFLUENCE]

influx /influks/ *n.* **1** a continual stream of people or things (*an influx of complaints*). **2** (usu. foll. by *into*) a flowing in, esp. of a stream etc. [F *influx* or LL *influxus* (as IN-², FLUX)]

info /infō/ *n. colloq.* information. [abbr.]

infold var. of ENFOLD.

inform /infórm/ *v.* **1** *tr.* (usu. foll. by *of*, *about*, *on*, or *that*, *how* + clause) tell (*informed them of their rights*; *informed us that the train was late*). **2** *intr.* (usu. foll. by *against*, *on*) make an accusation. **3** *tr.* (usu. foll. by *with*) *literary* inspire or imbue (a person, heart, or thing) with a feeling, principle, quality, etc. **4** *tr.* impart its quality to; permeate. □□ **informant** *n.* [ME f. OF *enfo(u)rmer* f. L *informare* give shape to, fashion, describe (as IN-², *forma* form)]
■ **1** tell, notify, apprise, enlighten, advise, brief, acquaint, tip off, report to, communicate to, *colloq.* fill in, put a person wise, *Brit. sl.* gen up. **2** turn informer, name names, *colloq.* scream, *sl.* sing, squeak, squeal, *Brit. school*

sl. sneak; (*inform against* or *on*) accuse, incriminate, inculpate, implicate, identify, betray, denounce, *archaic* delate, peach, *colloq.* tell on, rat on, blow the whistle on, peach on *or* against, split on, *sl.* snitch on, put the finger on, *Austral. sl.* dob in, pool, shelf, *Austral.* & *NZ sl.* put a person's pot on, *Brit. sl.* grass on, shop, *US sl.* finger, fink on. **4** see PERMEATE. ▫▫ **informant** see INFORMER.

informal /infórm'l/ *adj.* **1** without ceremony or formality (*just an informal chat*). **2** (of language, clothing, etc.) everyday; normal. ▫ **informal vote** *NZ* & *Austral.* an invalid vote or voting paper. ▫▫ **informality** /-málliti/ *n.* (*pl.* **-ies**). **informally** *adv.*

■ unceremonious, unstructured, unstilted, unaffected, unpretentious, unstuffy, casual, natural, free, free and easy, relaxed, unofficial, *Diplomacy* officious, *colloq.* unbuttoned; colloquial, vernacular; familiar, ordinary, simple, everyday, folksy, *colloq.* common or garden. ▫▫ **informality** see EASE *n.* 2b, c.

informatics /infərmáttiks/ *n.pl.* (usu. treated as *sing.*) the science of processing data for storage and retrieval; information science. [transl. Russ. *informatika* (as INFORMATION, -ICS)]

information /infərmáysh'n/ *n.* **1 a** something told; knowledge. **b** (usu. foll. by *on*, *about*) items of knowledge; news (*the latest information on the crisis*). **2** *Law* (usu. foll. by *against*) a charge or complaint lodged with a court or magistrate. **3 a** the act of informing or telling. **b** an instance of this. ▫ **information retrieval** the tracing of information stored in books, computers, etc. **information science** the study of the processes for storing and retrieving information. **information theory** *Math.* the quantitative study of the transmission of information by signals etc. ▫▫ **informational** *adj.* **informationally** *adv.* [ME f. OF f. L *informatio -onis* (as INFORM)]

■ **1** knowledge, news, data, report(s), communication, facts, details, message(s) *literary* tidings; word, advice, intelligence, *colloq.* info, low-down, *sl.* dope, *Austral. sl.* drum, *Brit. sl.* gen, *US sl.* poop. **2** see CHARGE *n.* 2. **3** notification, advice, enlightenment, briefing, report, communication.

informative /infórmətiv/ *adj.* (also **informatory** /infórmətəri, -tri/) giving information; instructive. ▫▫ **informatively** *adv.* **informativeness** *n.* [med.L *informativus* (as INFORM)]

■ communicative, instructive, educational, edifying, revealing, illuminating, enlightening; clarificatory, explanatory, elucidatory, helpful; forthcoming.

informed /infórmd/ *adj.* **1** knowing the facts; instructed (*his answers show that he is badly informed*). **2** educated; intelligent. ▫▫ **informedly** /also infórmidli/ *adv.* **informedness** /also infórmidniss/ *n.*

■ **1** knowledgeable, aware, in touch, *au fait*, *au courant*, up to date, posted, in the picture, *colloq.* in the know, filled in; conversant (with), acquainted (with), (well-)versed (in), well up (on *or* in), cognizant (of). **2** (well-)educated, erudite, learned, well-read, cultured, cultivated, knowledgeable; intelligent, wise, smart, bright, clever, brainy, *US sl.* savvy.

informer /infórmər/ *n.* **1** a person who informs against another. **2** a person who informs or advises.

■ **1** informant, tell-tale, taleteller, stool-pigeon, *US* tattle-tale, *colloq.* supergrass, weasel, *hist.* beagle, *sl.* snitch, finger, squealer, nose, shopper, *Austral. sl.* fizgig, shelf, *Brit. sl.* grass, nark, *Brit. school sl.* sneak, *esp. US sl.* ratfink, *US sl.* fink, stoolie, *US* & *Austral. sl.* dog; traitor, betrayer, fifth-columnist, spy, rat, *colloq.* mole. **2** informant, source, reporter, correspondent, communicator; consultant, adviser, counsel, counsellor, guide, mentor.

infra /infrə/ *adv.* below, further on (in a book or writing). [L, = below]

■ see BELOW *adv.* 1.

infra- /infrə/ *comb. form* **1** below (opp. SUPRA-). **2** *Anat.* below or under a part of the body. [from or after L *infra* below, beneath]

infraction /infráksh'n/ *n.* esp. *Law* a violation or infringement. ▫▫ **infract** *v.tr.* **infractor** *n.* [L *infractio* (as INFRINGE)]

■ see *infringement* (INFRINGE).

infra dig /infrə díg/ *predic.adj. colloq.* beneath one's dignity; unbecoming. [abbr. of L *infra dignitatem*]

■ see BASE[2] 2.

infrangible /infránjib'l/ *adj.* **1** unbreakable. **2** inviolable. ▫▫ **infrangibility** /-bílliti/ *n.* **infrangibleness** *n.* **infrangibly** *adv.* [obs.F *infrangible* or med.L *infrangibilis* (as IN-[1], FRANGIBLE)]

infrared /infrəréd/ *adj.* **1** having a wavelength just greater than the red end of the visible light spectrum but less than that of radio waves. **2** of or using such radiation.

infrasonic /infrəsónnik/ *adj.* of or relating to sound waves with a frequency below the lower limit of human audibility. ▫▫ **infrasonically** *adv.*

infrasound /infrəsownd/ *n.* sound waves with frequencies below the lower limit of human audibility.

infrastructure /infrəstrukchər/ *n.* **1 a** the basic structural foundations of a society or enterprise; a substructure or foundation. **b** roads, bridges, sewers, etc., regarded as a country's economic foundation. **2** permanent installations as a basis for military etc. operations. [F (as INFRA-, STRUCTURE)]

■ **1 a** see BASIS 1, 2.

infrequent /infréekwənt/ *adj.* not frequent. ▫▫ **infrequency** *n.* **infrequently** *adv.* [L *infrequens* (as IN-[1], FREQUENT)]

■ occasional, rare, seldom; uncommon, unusual, unwonted, exceptional, stray; irregular, sporadic, intermittent. ▫▫ **infrequently** occasionally, rarely, seldom, once in a blue moon, exceptionally; between times, sometimes, at times; irregularly, sporadically, intermittently, (every) now and then, (every) now and again, every so often, from time to time, (every) once in a while.

infringe /infrínj/ *v.* **1** *tr.* **a** act contrary to; violate (a law, an oath, etc.). **b** act in defiance of (another's rights etc.). **2** *intr.* (usu. foll. by *on*, *upon*) encroach; trespass. ▫▫ **infringement** *n.* **infringer** *n.* [L *infringere infract-* (as IN-[2], *frangere* break)]

■ **1** violate, contravene, break, disobey, transgress, overstep; flout, disregard, ignore, defy, challenge, thumb one's nose at, *sl.* cock a snook at. **2** (*infringe on* or *upon*) encroach on *or* upon, impinge on *or* upon, intrude on *or* upon, obtrude on *or* upon, trespass on *or* upon, break in on, butt in on, barge in on, interrupt, invade, *sl.* horn in on. ▫▫ **infringement** violation, breach, contravention, infraction, disobedience, non-compliance, transgression; encroachment, impingement, intrusion, obtrusion, interruption, invasion, *Law* trespass.

infula /infyoolə/ *n.* (*pl.* **infulae** /-lee/) *Eccl.* either of the two ribbons on a bishop's mitre. [L, = woollen fillet worn by priest etc.]

infundibular /infundíbyoolər/ *adj.* funnel-shaped. [L *infundibulum* funnel f. *infundere* pour in (as IN-[2], *fundere* pour)]

infuriate *v.* & *adj.* ● *v.tr.* /infyŏŏriayt/ fill with fury; enrage. ● *adj.* /infyŏŏriət/ *literary* excited to fury; frantic. ▫▫ **infuriating** *adj.* **infuriatingly** /infyŏŏriaytingli/ *adv.* **infuriation** /-áysh'n/ *n.* [med.L *infuriare infuriat-* (as IN-[2], L *furia* FURY)]

■ *v.* enrage, anger, madden, incense, make a person's blood boil, inflame, work *or* stir *or* fire up, arouse, provoke, vex, pique, gall, annoy, irritate, bother, chafe, fret, agitate, irk, nettle, goad, exasperate, exacerbate, make a person's hackles rise, get *or* put a person's back up, get on a person's nerves, *colloq.* needle, miff, peeve, rile, wind up, get under a person's skin, make a person see red, get a person's dander up, get a person's goat, get across, *sl.* bug, *Brit. sl.* brown off, cheese off, *US sl.* burn up.

infuse /infyŏŏz/ *v.* **1** *tr.* (usu. foll. by *with*) imbue; pervade (*anger infused with resentment*). **2** *tr.* steep (herbs, tea, etc.)

in liquid to extract the content. **3** *tr.* (usu. foll. by *into*) instil (grace, spirit, life, etc.). **4** *intr.* undergo infusion (*let it infuse for five minutes*). **5** *tr.* (usu. foll. by *into*) pour (a thing). □□ **infusable** *adj.* **infuser** *n.* **infusive** /-fyŏŏssiv/ *adj.* [ME f. L *infundere infus-* (as IN-[2], *fundere* pour)]
■ **1** see SUFFUSE. **2, 4** brew, soak, sleep. **3** see INSTIL 1.

infusible /infyŏŏzib'l/ *adj.* not able to be fused or melted. □□ **infusibility** /-billiti/ *n.*

infusion /infyŏŏzh'n/ *n.* **1** a liquid obtained by infusing. **2** an infused element; an admixture. **3** *Med.* a slow injection of a substance into a vein or tissue. **4 a** the act of infusing. **b** an instance of this. [ME f. F *infusion* or L *infusio* (as INFUSE)]
■ **1** see SOLUTION 2b.

infusorial earth /ínfyoozóriəl, -sóriəl/ *n.* = KIESELGUHR. [mod.L *infusoria*, formerly a class of protozoa found in decaying animal or vegetable matter (as INFUSE)]

-ing[1] /ing/ *suffix* forming gerunds and nouns from verbs (or occas. from nouns), denoting: **1 a** the verbal action or its result (*asking*; *carving*; *fighting*; *learning*). **b** the verbal action as described or classified in some way (*tough going*). **2** material used for or associated with a process etc. (*piping*; *washing*). **3** an occupation or event (*banking*; *wedding*). **4** a set or arrangement of (*colouring*; *feathering*). [OE *-ung*, *-ing* f. Gmc]

-ing[2] /ing/ *suffix* **1** forming the present participle of verbs (*asking*; *fighting*), often as adjectives (*charming*; *strapping*). **2** forming adjectives from nouns (*hulking*) and verbs (*balding*). [ME alt. of OE *-ende*, later *-inde*]

-ing[3] /ing/ *suffix* forming nouns meaning 'one belonging to' or 'one having the quality of', surviving esp. in names of coins and fractional parts (*farthing*; *gelding*; *riding*). [OE f. Gmc]

ingather /ín-gáthər/ *v.tr.* gather in; assemble.

ingathering /in-gáthəring/ *n.* the act or an instance of gathering in, esp. of a harvest.

ingeminate /injémminayt/ *v.tr. literary* repeat; reiterate. □ **ingeminate peace** constantly urge peace. [L *ingeminare ingeminat-* (as IN-[2], GEMINATE)]

ingenious /injéeniəss/ *adj.* **1** clever at inventing, constructing, organizing, etc.; skilful; resourceful. **2** (of a machine, theory, etc.) cleverly contrived. □□ **ingeniously** *adv.* **ingeniousness** *n.* [ME, = talented, f. F *ingénieux* or L *ingeniosus* f. *ingenium* cleverness: cf. ENGINE]
■ clever, skilful, skilled, adept, adroit, dexterous, deft, slick, handy, inventive, *US sl.* crackerjack; resourceful, creative, imaginative, original; gifted, talented, brilliant, bright, smart; acute, astute, sharp, shrewd, cunning, crafty, canny; neat, *colloq.* cute.

ingénue /ánzhaynyŏŏ/ *n.* **1** an innocent or unsophisticated young woman. **2** *Theatr.* **a** such a part in a play. **b** the actress who plays this part. [F, fem. of *ingénu* INGENUOUS]
■ **1** see INNOCENT *n.*

ingenuity /injinyŏŏ-iti/ *n.* skill in devising or contriving; ingeniousness. [L *ingenuitas* ingenuousness (as INGENUOUS): Engl. meaning by confusion of INGENIOUS with INGENUOUS]
■ ingeniousness, cleverness, skill, craft, art, artfulness, adeptness, aptness, dexterity, dexterousness, adroitness, deftness, handiness, inventiveness; resourcefulness, creativity, creativeness, imagination, imaginativeness, originality; giftedness, brilliance, brightness, smartness, acuteness, sharpness, canniness, shrewdness, cunning; genius, talent, flair, gift, knack, ability, capability, proficiency, prowess, facility, faculty.

ingenuous /injényooəss/ *adj.* **1** innocent; artless. **2** open; frank. □□ **ingenuously** *adv.* **ingenuousness** *n.* [L *ingenuus* free-born, frank (as IN-[2], root of *gignere* beget)]
■ **1** naïve, simple, innocent, unsophisticated, natural, childlike, suggestible, trusting, unsuspecting, gullible, credulous, green; artless, guileless, sincere, genuine, undeceitful, truthful, above-board, *colloq.* on the level; straight, plain, uncomplicated, unaffected. **2** frank, candid, open, transparent, straightforward, plain; forthright, direct, four-square, outspoken, blunt, bluff, honest; free, uninhibited, unabashed, unreserved; trustworthy, honourable, (fair and) square, fair, just.

ingest /injést/ *v.tr.* **1** take in (food etc.); eat. **2** absorb (facts, knowledge, etc.). □□ **ingestion** /injéss-chən/ *n.* **ingestive** *adj.* [L *ingerere ingest-* (as IN-[2], *gerere* carry)]
■ **1** see SWALLOW[1] *v.* 1.

inglenook /ingg'lnŏŏk/ *n.* a space within the opening on either side of a large fireplace. [dial. (orig. Sc.) *ingle* fire burning on a hearth, perh. f. Gael. *aingeal* fire, light + NOOK]

inglorious /in-glóriəss/ *adj.* **1** shameful; ignominious. **2** not famous. □□ **ingloriously** *adv.* **ingloriousness** *n.*
■ **1** see SHAMEFUL. **2** see OBSCURE *adj.* 6. □□ **ingloriousness** see OBSCURITY 1.

-ingly /ingli/ *suffix* forming adverbs esp. denoting manner of action or nature or condition (*dotingly*; *charmingly*; *slantingly*).

ingoing /in-gōing/ *adj.* **1** going in; entering. **2** penetrating; thorough.

ingot /inggot, -gət/ *n.* a usu. oblong piece of cast metal, esp. of gold, silver, or steel. [ME: perh. f. IN[1] + *goten* past part. of OE *geotan* cast]

ingraft var. of ENGRAFT.

ingrain *adj.* & *v.* ● *adj.* /ín-grayn/ **1** inherent; ingrained. **2** (of textiles) dyed in the fibre, before being woven. ● *v.tr.* /ín-gráyn/cause (a dye) to sink deeply into the texture of a fabric; cause to become embedded. □ **ingrain carpet** a reversible carpet, with different colours interwoven.

ingrained /in-gráynd/ *attrib. adj.* ingrate **1** deeply rooted; inveterate. **2** thorough. **3** (of dirt etc.) deeply embedded. □□ **ingrainedly** /-gráynidli/ *adv.* [var. of *engrained*: see ENGRAIN]
■ **1** engrained, deep-rooted, established, fixed, deep-seated, fundamental, basic, essential, inherent, inborn, innate, inbred, inherited, hereditary; inveterate, habitual, hardened, incurable, incorrigible, unchangeable, unalterable, dyed in the wool, out and out. **2** see THOROUGH 3. **3** engrained, embedded, ground-in; indelible, ineradicable, ineffaceable, inexpungible, stubborn.

ingrate /in-grayt/ *n.* & *adj. formal* or *literary* ● *n.* an ungrateful person. ● *adj.* ungrateful. [ME f. L *ingratus* (as IN-[1], *gratus* grateful)]

ingratiate /in-gráyshiayt/ *v.refl.* (usu. foll. by *with*) bring oneself into favour. □□ **ingratiating** *adj.* **ingratiatingly** *adv.* **ingratiation** /-áysh'n/ *n.* [L *in gratiam* into favour]
■ (*ingratiate oneself with*) flatter, adulate, cultivate, curry favour with, dance attendance on, fawn on *or* upon, grovel to, cringe to, toady to, bow and scrape to, kowtow to, *US* shine up to, *colloq.* crawl to, creep to, suck up to, smarm, sweet-talk, *Brit. colloq.* chat up, *US colloq.* cosy up to. □□ **ingratiating** flattering, adulatory, fawning, grovelling, toadyish, servile, obsequious, sycophantic, wheedling, unctuous, oily, buttery, slimy, sugary, saccharine, *colloq.* creepy, smarmy, bootlicking, sweet-talking.

ingratitude /in-gráttityōōd/ *n.* a lack of due gratitude. [ME f. OF *ingratitude* or LL *ingratitudo* (as INGRATE)]
■ unthankfulness, ungratefulness, thanklessness; snakiness.

ingravescent /in-grəvéss'nt/ *adj. Med.* (of a disease etc.) growing worse. □□ **ingravescence** *n.* [L *ingravescere* (as IN-[2], *gravescere* grow heavy f. *gravis* heavy)]

ingredient /in-gréediənt/ *n.* a component part or element in a recipe, mixture, or combination. [ME f. L *ingredi ingress-* enter (as IN-[2], *gradi* step)]
■ constituent, element, part, component, factor, admixture; (*ingredients*) contents, makings.

ingress /in-gress/ *n.* **1 a** the act or right of going in or entering. **b** an entrance. **2** *Astron.* the start of an eclipse or transit. □□ **ingression** /in-grésh'n/ *n.* [ME f. L *ingressus* (as INGREDIENT)]

■ **1** see ENTRANCE[1] 1, 4; 3.

in-group /in-groop/ *n.* a small exclusive group of people with a common interest.

ingrowing /in-gróing/ *adj.* growing inwards, esp. (of a toenail) growing into the flesh. □□ **ingrown** *adj.* **ingrowth** *n.*

inguinal /íngwinəl/ *adj.* of the groin. □□ **inguinally** *adv.* [L *inguinalis* f. *inguen -inis* groin]

ingulf var. of ENGULF.

ingurgitate /in-gúrjitayt/ *v.tr.* **1** swallow greedily. **2** engulf. □□ **ingurgitation** /-táysh'n/ *n.* [L *ingurgitare ingurgitat-* (as IN-², *gurges gurgitis* whirlpool)]

inhabit /inhábbit/ *v.tr.* (**inhabited, inhabiting**) (of a person or animal) dwell in; occupy (a region, town, house, etc.). □□ **inhabitability** /-təbílliti/ *n.* **inhabitable** *adj.* **inhabitant** *n.* **inhabitation** /-táysh'n/ *n.* [ME *inhabite, enhabite* f. OF *enhabiter* or L *inhabitare* (as IN-², *habitare* dwell): see HABIT]

■ reside in, live in, be domiciled in, occupy, tenant, *archaic* abide in, *literary* dwell in; populate, people; colonize. □□ **inhabitant** resident, householder, tenant, inmate, occupant, *Brit.* occupier; citizen, native, national, local, *literary* dweller, *poet.* denizen.

inhabitancy /inhábbitənsi/ *n.* (also **inhabitance** /-t'nss/) residence as an inhabitant, esp. during a specified period so as to acquire rights etc.

inhalant /inháylənt/ *n.* a medicinal preparation for inhaling.

inhale /inháyl/ *v.tr.* (often *absol.*) breathe in (air, gas, tobacco-smoke, etc.). □□ **inhalation** /-həláysh'n/ *n.* [L *inhalare* breathe in (as IN-², *halare* breathe)]

■ breathe in, inspire, inbreathe, draw (in), suck in, take a breath of; sniff (up), *sl.* snort.

inhaler /inháylər/ *n.* a portable device used for relieving esp. asthma by inhaling.

inharmonic /inhaarmónnik/ *adj.* esp. *Mus.* not harmonic.

inharmonious /ínhaarmóniəss/ *adj.* esp. *Mus.* not harmonious. □□ **inharmoniously** *adv.*

■ see *mismatched* (MISMATCH *v.*).

inhere /inheér/ *v.intr.* (often foll. by *in*) **1** exist essentially or permanently in (*goodness inheres in that child*). **2** (of rights etc.) be vested in (a person etc.). [L *inhaerēre inhaes-* (as IN-², *haerēre* to stick)]

inherent /inheérənt, inhérrənt/ *adj.* (often foll. by *in*) **1** existing in something, esp. as a permanent or characteristic attribute. **2** vested in (a person etc.) as a right or privilege. □□ **inherence** *n.* **inherently** *adv.* [L *inhaerēre inhaerent-* (as INHERE)]

■ **1** innate, connate, inborn, congenital, inherited, hereditary, inbred, natural, native, constitutional, ingrained, engrained, in one's blood, bred in the bone; essential, intrinsic, implicit, basic, fundamental, elementary, radical, structural, organic, integral, built-in; indwelling, immanent. **2** fundamental, basic, essential, elementary; inalienable, inviolable, sacrosanct, unchallengeable, absolute, *Law* unalienable, imprescriptible, entailed, *literary* indefeasible.

inherit /inhérrit/ *v.* (**inherited, inheriting**) **1** *tr.* receive (property, rank, title, etc.) by legal descent or succession. **2** *tr.* derive (a quality or characteristic) genetically from one's ancestors. **3** *absol.* succeed as an heir (*a younger son rarely inherits*). □□ **inheritor** *n.* (*fem.* **inheritress** or **inheritrix**). [ME f. OF *enheriter* f. LL *inhereditare* (as IN-², L *heres heredis* heir)]

■ **1** come into, succeed to, fall *or* be *or* become heir to, be bequeathed, be left, be willed. **3** succeed, take over, become heir, receive an inheritance. □□ **inheritor** *etc.* see HEIR.

inheritable /inhérritəb'l/ *adj.* **1** capable of being inherited. **2** capable of inheriting. □□ **inheritability** /-bílliti/ *n.* [ME f. AF (as INHERIT)]

■ **1** see HEREDITARY 1.

inheritance /inhérrit'nss/ *n.* **1** something that is inherited. **2 a** the act of inheriting. **b** an instance of this. □ **inheritance tax** a tax levied on property etc. acquired by gift or inheritance. ¶ Introduced in the UK in 1986 to replace *Capital Transfer Tax*. [ME f. AF *inheritaunce* f. OF *enheriter*: see INHERIT]

■ **1** patrimony, heritage, legacy, bequest, birthright. **2** endowment, succession, bequeathal.

inhesion /inheézh'n/ *n. formal* the act or fact of inhering. [LL *inhaesio* (as INHERE)]

inhibit /inhíbbit/ *v.tr.* (**inhibited, inhibiting**) **1** hinder, restrain, or prevent (an action or progress). **2** (as **inhibited** *adj.*) subject to inhibition. **3 a** (usu. foll. by *from* + verbal noun) forbid or prohibit (a person etc.). **b** (esp. in ecclesiastical law) forbid (an ecclesiastic) to exercise clerical functions. □□ **inhibitive** *adj.* **inhibitor** *n.* **inhibitory** *adj.* [L *inhibēre* (as IN-², *habēre* hold)]

■ **1** hinder, hamper, restrain, impede, obstruct, interfere with, check, prevent, stop, discourage, deter, repress, suppress, frustrate, hold back, bridle, shackle, muzzle, cramp, curb, control. **2** (**inhibited**) pent up, repressed, restrained, suppressed, bottled up; shy, reticent, reserved, self-conscious, abashed, embarrassed, defensive, on the defensive, *colloq.* uptight, *sl.* hung up. **3** (*inhibit from*) forbid to, prohibit from, interdict from, bar from, ban from, keep from, stop, restrain from, discourage from, deter from.

inhibition /inhibísh'n/ *n.* **1** *Psychol.* a restraint on the direct expression of an instinct. **2** *colloq.* an emotional resistance to a thought, an action, etc. (*has inhibitions about singing in public*). **3** *Law* an order forbidding alteration to property rights. **4 a** the act of inhibiting. **b** the process of being inhibited. [ME f. OF *inhibition* or L *inhibitio* (as INHIBIT)]

■ **1, 2** bar, barrier, defence mechanism, blockage, psychological block, mental block, check, curb, stricture, restraint, constraint, impediment, hindrance, interference, *sl.* hang-up; self-consciousness, defensiveness, shyness, reticence, embarrassment. **4** prohibition, interdiction, bar, ban, proscription; prevention, repression, suppression.

inhomogeneous /inhómməjeéniəss, inhómə-/ *adj.* not homogeneous. □□ **inhomogeneity** /-jineé-iti/ *n.*

inhospitable /inhospíttəb'l, inhóspi-/ *adj.* **1** not hospitable. **2** (of a region, coast, etc.) not affording shelter etc. □□ **inhospitableness** *n.* **inhospitably** *adv.* [obs. F (as IN-¹, HOSPITABLE)]

■ **1** unwelcoming, unreceptive, uninviting, unsociable, unsocial, aloof, cold, icy, cool, standoffish, unfriendly, inimical, antisocial, hostile, intolerant, xenophobic. **2** uninviting, bleak, grim, harsh, barren, bare, cheerless, forbidding, hostile; unfavourable, unpromising, unpropitious, inauspicious; uninhabitable.

inhospitality /inhóspitálliti/ *n.* the act or process of being inhospitable. [L *inhospitalitas* (as IN-¹, HOSPITALITY)]

in-house *adj.* & *adv.* ● *adj.* /inhówss/ done or existing within an institution, company, etc. (*an in-house project*). ● *adv.* /inhówss/ internally, without outside assistance.

inhuman /inhyoomən/ *adj.* **1** (of a person, conduct, etc.) brutal; unfeeling; barbarous. **2** not of a human type. □□ **inhumanly** *adv.* [L *inhumanus* (as IN-¹, HUMAN)]

■ **1** brutal, savage, barbaric, barbarous, beastly, bestial, ferocious, bloodthirsty, murderous; vicious, merciless, cruel, pitiless, ruthless, heartless, cold-blooded, stony-hearted, hard-hearted, unfeeling, unkind, unkindly, callous, insensitive, unsympathetic, severe, inhumane. **2** non-human, animal, bestial, brutal, brutish; devilish, fiendish, diabolic, diabolical, demonic, demoniac.

inhumane /inhyoomáyn/ *adj.* not humane. □□ **inhumanely** *adv.* [L *inhumanus* (see INHUMAN) & f. IN-¹ + HUMANE, orig. = INHUMAN]

■ see MERCILESS.

inhumanity /inhyoománniti/ *n.* (*pl.* **-ies**) **1** brutality; barbarousness; callousness. **2** an inhumane act.

■ **1** see BARBARITY 1.

inhume /inhyóom/ *v.tr. literary* bury. □□ **inhumation** /-máysh'n/ *n.* [L *inhumare* (as IN-[2], *humus* ground)]

■ bury, inter, lay to rest. □□ **inhumation** see FUNERAL *n.*

inimical /inímmik'l/ *adj.* (usu. foll. by *to*) **1** hostile. **2** harmful. □□ **inimically** *adv.* [LL *inimicalis* f. L *inimicus* (as IN-[1], *amicus* friend)]

■ **1** see HOSTILE 2. **2** see DETRIMENTAL.

inimitable /inímmitəb'l/ *adj.* impossible to imitate. □□ **inimitability** /-bílliti/ *n.* **inimitableness** *n.* **inimitably** *adv.* [F *inimitable* or L *inimitabilis* (as IN-[1], *imitabilis* imitable)]

■ see UNPARALLELED. □□ **inimitability** see SUPERIORITY. **inimitably** see PERFECTLY 3.

iniquity /iníkwiti/ *n.* (*pl.* **-ies**) **1** wickedness; unrighteousness. **2** a gross injustice. □□ **iniquitous** *adj.* **iniquitously** *adv.* **iniquitousness** *n.* [ME f. OF *iniquité* f. L *iniquitas -tatis* f. *iniquus* (as IN-[1], *aequus* just)]

■ **1** see SIN[1] 1. **2** see SCANDAL 1b.

initial /inísh'l/ *adj.*, *n.*, & *v.* ● *adj.* of, existing, or occurring at the beginning (*initial stage*; *initial expenses*). ● *n.* **1** = *initial letter.* **2** (usu. in *pl.*) the first letter or letters of the words of a (esp. a person's) name or names. ● *v.tr.* (**initialled, initialling**; *US* **initialed, initialing**) mark or sign with one's initials. □ **initial letter** (or **consonant**) a letter or consonant at the beginning of a word. **initial teaching alphabet** a 44-letter phonetic alphabet used to help those beginning to read and write English. □□ **initially** *adv.* [L *initialis* f. *initium* beginning f. *inire init-* go in]

■ *adj.* first, prime, primary, original; aboriginal, autochthonal, autochthonic, autochthonous; incipient, nascent, inaugural; opening, starting, introductory, prefatory. ● *n.* **2** (*initials*) monogram. ● *v.* sign, endorse. □□ **initially** see *in the first instance* (INSTANCE).

initialism /iníshəliz'm/ *n.* a group of initial letters used as an abbreviation for a name or expression, each letter being pronounced separately (e.g. *BBC*) (cf. ACRONYM).

■ see ABBREVIATION.

initialize /iníshəlīz/ *v.tr.* (also **-ise**) (often foll. by *to*) *Computing* set to the value or put in the condition appropriate to the start of an operation. □□ **initialization** /-záysh'n/ *n.*

initiate *v.*, *n.*, & *adj.* ● *v.tr.* /iníshiayt/ **1** begin; set going; originate. **2 a** (usu. foll. by *into*) admit (a person) into a society, an office, a secret, etc., esp. with a ritual. **b** (usu. foll. by *in*, *into*) instruct (a person) in science, art, etc. ● *n.* /iníshiət/ a person who has been newly initiated. ● *adj.* /iníshiət/ (of a person) newly initiated (*an initiate member*). □□ **initiation** /-áysh'n/ *n.* **initiator** *n.* **initiatory** /iníshiətəri, iníshətəri/ *adj.* [L *initiare* f. *initium*: see INITIAL]

■ *v.* **1** begin, start, originate, pioneer, introduce, instigate, install, institute, set up, inaugurate, open, found, establish, set in motion, get under way, launch, float, get *or* set going, *colloq.* kick off, *formal* commence; create, generate, sow, cause, give rise to, spark (off), trigger, set off, touch off, actuate, activate. **2 a** admit, accept, introduce, induct, swear in, enrol, install; familiarize, break in, blood. **b** teach, instruct, train, tutor, drill, coach, school, ground, educate, guide, prepare. ● *n.* novice, beginner, apprentice, recruit, acolyte, neophyte, tiro, newcomer, new boy, new girl, greenhorn, tenderfoot, fledgling, learner, freshman, *US* cub, punk, *Austral. colloq.* jackaroo, *Brit. colloq.* fresher, *sl.* rookie; noviciate, catechumen. ● *adj.* new, novice, apprentice, fledgling, *sl.* rookie. □□ **initiation** beginning, start, inception, origination, initiative, introduction, instigation, installation, institution, inauguration, opening, foundation, establishment, launch, flotation, début, *colloq.* kick-off, *formal* commencement; creation, generation, actuation, activation; admittance, acceptance, introduction, induction, enrolment, investiture, ordination; education, teaching, instruction, training, preparation, schooling, grounding.

initiative /iníshətiv, iníshiətiv/ *n.* & *adj.* ● *n.* **1** the ability to initiate things; enterprise (*I'm afraid he lacks all initiative*). **2** a first step; origination (*a peace initiative*). **3** the power or right to begin something. **4** *Polit.* (esp. in Switzerland and some US States) the right of citizens outside the legislature to originate legislation. ● *adj.* beginning; originating. □ **have the initiative** esp. *Mil.* be able to control the enemy's movements. **on one's own initiative** without being prompted by others. **take the initiative** (usu. foll. by *in* + verbal noun) be the first to take action. [F (as INITIATE)]

■ **1** leadership, enterprise, resourcefulness, self-motivation, aggressiveness, drive, push, dynamism, energy, vigour, dash, go, zip, snap, *colloq.* gumption, get-up-and-go, vim, pep, zing. **2** (first) move, (first) step, lead, opening move *or* gambit, *démarche*; see also *initiation* (INITIATE). □ **have the initiative** call the shots *or* tune, be in control, be in command, have the upper hand, pull the strings, be in the driver's seat, be in charge, be in the saddle, rule the roost, be at the wheel. **on one's own initiative** unprompted, unaided, off one's own bat, independently, in one's own name, on one's own responsibility; see also VOLUNTARILY. **take the initiative** be the first, take the first step(s), make the first move, start *or* set the ball rolling, break the ice; see also *have the initiative* above.

inject /injékt/ *v.tr.* **1** *Med.* **a** (usu. foll. by *into*) drive or force (a solution, medicine, etc.) by or as if by a syringe. **b** (usu. foll. by *with*) fill (a cavity etc.) by injecting. **c** administer medicine etc. to (a person) by injection. **2** place or insert (an object, a quality, etc.) into something (*may I inject a note of realism?*). □□ **injectable** *adj.* & *n.* **injector** *n.* [L *injicere* (as IN-[2], *jacere* throw)]

■ **1** drive *or* force *or* shoot in, insert, introduce, intromit, transfuse; *sl.* fix, shoot (up), mainline, pop; inoculate, syringe. **2** introduce, insert, instil, bring in, interject, throw in.

injection /injéksh'n/ *n.* **1 a** the act of injecting. **b** an instance of this. **2** a liquid or solution (to be) injected (*prepare a morphine injection*). □ **injection moulding** the shaping of rubber or plastic articles by injecting heated material into a mould. [F *injection* or L *injectio* (as INJECT)]

■ shot, inoculation, vaccination.

injudicious /injoodíshəss/ *adj.* unwise; ill-judged. □□ **injudiciously** *adv.* **injudiciousness** *n.*

■ see *ill-advised* 2 (ILL). □□ **injudiciousness** see *imprudence* (IMPRUDENT).

Injun /injən/ *n. colloq. US* or *dial.* an American Indian. [corrupt.]

injunction /injúnksh'n/ *n.* **1** an authoritative warning or order. **2** *Law* a judicial order restraining a person from an act or compelling redress to an injured party. □□ **injunctive** *adj.* [LL *injunctio* f. L *injungere* ENJOIN]

■ **1** prohibition, interdict, interdiction, restriction, restraint, order, mandate, directive, command, direction, instruction, ruling, dictate, diktat, ukase, exhortation; warning, admonition.

injure /injər/ *v.tr.* **1** do physical harm or damage to; hurt (*was injured in a road accident*). **2** harm or impair (*illness might injure her chances*). **3** do wrong to. □□ **injurer** *n.* [back-form. f. INJURY]

■ **1** harm, hurt, damage, wreck, maim, cripple, break, fracture; assault, molest, beat up; wound, spill a person's blood, cut, lacerate, gash, scrape, scratch, scar, disfigure; bruise, contuse, strain, pull, wrench, rip, tear, rack, wear, gall, chafe; burn, scorch, *poet.* scathe. **2** impair, harm, damage, ruin, cripple, mar, spoil, disable; vitiate, tarnish, weaken, undermine, shake, prejudice. **3** wrong, offend, abuse, insult, malign, vilify, calumniate, asperse, libel, slander, defame, smear, discredit, dishonour, outrage, affront, humiliate, slight, *sl.* do a person dirt; hurt, wound, mistreat, misuse, ill-treat, maltreat, oppress, persecute, *Law* damnify.

injured /injərd/ *adj.* **1** harmed or hurt (*the injured passengers*). **2** offended; wronged (*in an injured tone*).

injurious /injoŏriəss/ *adj.* **1** hurtful. **2** (of language) insulting; libellous. **3** wrongful. □□ **injuriously** *adv.* **injuriousness** *n.* [ME f. F *injurieux* or L *injuriosus* (as INJURY)]
■ **1** hurtful, malicious, nasty, spiteful, harsh, unpleasant, mischievous, *literary* maleficent; damaging, deleterious, detrimental, unfavourable, adverse, ruinous, bad; harmful, pernicious, noxious, toxic, poisonous, destructive, malignant, dangerous, insalubrious, unhealthy. **2** abusive, offensive, insulting, scathing, scornful, derogatory, deprecatory, contemptuous, catty, abrasive, barbed; slanderous, libellous, defamatory, calumnious, calumniatory, scurrilous, scandalous, malicious. **3** wrongful, unfair, unjust, underhand(ed), improper, dirty; iniquitous, nefarious, wicked, evil, sinful, unlawful, bad, wrong.

injury /ínjəri/ *n.* (*pl.* **-ies**) **1 a** physical harm or damage. **b** an instance of this (*suffered head injuries*). **2** esp. *Law* **a** wrongful action or treatment. **b** an instance of this. **3** damage to one's good name etc. □ **injury time** *Brit. Football* extra playing-time allowed by a referee to compensate for time lost in dealing with injuries. [ME f. AF *injurie* f. L *injuria* a wrong (as IN-[1], *jus juris* right)]
■ **1** damage, hurt, harm, impairment, disablement, disfigurement, wreckage, mayhem; break, breakage, fracture, laceration, wound, cut, gash, scrape, scratch, scarring, scar; bruise, contusion, strain, pull, wrench, tear, rip. **2** wrong, abuse, maltreatment, mistreatment, ill-treatment, ill use; injustice, unjustness, wrongdoing, misdeed, outrage, offence, affront, insult, mischief, malice, ill, ill turn, disservice. **3** damage, insult, abuse, calumny, slander, libel, defamation, slur, smear, blot, aspersion.

injustice /injústiss/ *n.* **1** a lack of fairness or justice. **2** an unjust act. □ **do a person an injustice** judge a person unfairly. [ME f. OF f. L *injustitia* (as IN-[1], JUSTICE)]
■ **1** unfairness, unjustness, wrong, inequity, inequality, iniquity, invidiousness, oppression, wrongfulness, unrighteousness; favouritism, discrimination, bias, partiality, partisanship, prejudice, bigotry, one-sidedness. **2** wrong, injury, outrage, abuse, ill turn, bad turn, disservice. □ **do a person an injustice** wrong a person, get a person wrong, misjudge a person, misread a person, underestimate a person, undervalue a person.

ink /ingk/ *n.* & *v.* ● *n.* **1 a** a coloured fluid used for writing with a pen, marking with a rubber stamp, etc. **b** a thick paste used in printing, duplicating, in ball-point pens, etc. **2** *Zool.* a black liquid ejected by a cuttlefish, octopus, etc. to confuse a predator. ● *v.tr.* **1** (usu. foll. by *in*, *over*, etc.) mark with ink. **2** cover (type etc.) with ink before printing. **3** apply ink to. **4** (as **inked** *adj.*) *Austral. sl.* drunk. □ **ink-blot test** = RORSCHACH TEST. **ink-cap** any fungus of the genus *Coprinus*. **ink-horn** *hist.* a small portable horn container for ink. **ink out** obliterate with ink. **ink-pad** an ink-soaked pad, usu. in a box, used for inking a rubber stamp etc. **ink-well** a pot for ink usu. housed in a hole in a desk. □□ **inker** *n.* [ME *enke*, *inke* f. OF *enque* f. LL *encau(s)tum* f. Gk *egkauston* purple ink used by Roman emperors for signature (as EN-[2], CAUSTIC)]
■ *v.* **4** (**inked**) see DRUNK *adj.* 1.

inkling /ingkling/ *n.* (often foll. by *of*) a slight knowledge or suspicion; a hint. [ME *inkle* utter in an undertone, of unkn. orig.]
■ suspicion, clue, (the faintest *or* foggiest) idea, (the faintest) notion, glimmering; hint, intimation, indication, suggestion, tip, tip-off, whisper.

inkstand /ingkstand/ *n.* a stand for one or more ink bottles, often incorporating a pen tray etc.

inky /ingki/ *adj.* (**inkier**, **inkiest**) of, as black as, or stained with ink. □□ **inkiness** *n.*

inlaid *past* and *past part.* of INLAY.

inland *adj.*, *n.*, & *adv.* ● *adj.* /inlənd, inland/ **1** situated in the interior of a country. **2** esp. *Brit.* carried on within the limits of a country; domestic (*inland trade*). ● *n.* /inlənd, inland/ the parts of a country remote from the sea or frontiers; the interior. ● *adv.* /inlánd/ in or towards the interior of a country. □ **inland duty** a tax payable on inland trade. **inland revenue** *Brit.* revenue consisting of taxes and inland duties. **Inland Revenue** (in the UK) the government department responsible for assessing and collecting such taxes. □□ **inlander** *n.* **inlandish** *adj.*
■ *n.* **1** see INTERIOR *n.* 2.

in-law /inlaw/ *n.* (often in *pl.*) a relative by marriage.
■ see RELATION 2.

inlay *v.* & *n.* ● *v.tr.* /inláy/ (*past* and *past part.* **inlaid** /inláyd/) **1 a** (usu. foll. by *in*) embed (a thing in another) so that the surfaces are even. **b** (usu. foll. by *with*) ornament (a thing with inlaid work). **2** (as **inlaid** *adj.*) (of a piece of furniture etc.) ornamented by inlaying. **3** insert (a page, an illustration, etc.) in a space cut in a larger thicker page. ● *n.* /inlay/ **1** inlaid work. **2** material inlaid. **3** a filling shaped to fit a tooth-cavity. □□ **inlayer** *n.* [IN-[2] + LAY[1]]
■ *v.* **1 a** see IMPLANT *v.* 1.

inlet /inlet, -lit/ *n.* **1** a small arm of the sea, a lake, or a river. **2** a piece inserted, esp. in dressmaking etc. **3** a way of entry. [ME f. IN + LET[1] *v.*]
■ **1** see CREEK 1. **3** see ENTRY 3a.

inlier /inlīər/ *n. Geol.* a structure or area of older rocks completely surrounded by newer rocks. [IN, after *outlier*]

in-line /inlīn/ *adj.* **1** having parts arranged in a line. **2** constituting an integral part of a continuous sequence of operations or machines.

in loco parentis /in lōkō pəréntiss/ *adv.* in the place or position of a parent (used of a teacher etc. responsible for children). [L]

inly /inli/ *adv. poet.* **1** inwardly; in the heart. **2** intimately; thoroughly. [OE *innlīce* (as IN, -LY[2])]

inlying /inlī-ing/ *adj.* situated within, or near a centre.

inmate /inmayt/ *n.* (usu. foll. by *of*) **1** an occupant of a hospital, prison, institution, etc. **2** an occupant of a house etc., esp. one of several. [prob. orig. INN + MATE[1], assoc. with IN]
■ **1** prisoner, convict, captive, internee, detainee, jailbird, *sl.* con, (old) lag, *US sl.* yardbird; patient, case. **2** inhabitant, occupant, resident, tenant; sharer.

in medias res /in meédiass ráyz/ *adv.* **1** into the midst of things. **2** into the middle of a story, without preamble. [L]

in memoriam /in mimóriam/ *prep.* & *n.* ● *prep.* in memory of (a dead person). ● *n.* a written article or notice etc. in memory of a dead person; an obituary. [L]

inmost /inmōst, -məst/ *adj.* **1** most inward. **2** most intimate; deepest. [OE *innemest* (as IN, -MOST)]

inn /in/ *n.* **1** a public house providing alcoholic liquor for consumption on the premises, and sometimes accommodation etc. **2** *hist.* a house providing accommodation, esp. for travellers. □ **Inn of Court** *Brit. Law* **1** each of the four legal societies having the exclusive right of admitting people to the English bar. **2** any of the sets of buildings in London belonging to these societies. **3** a similar society in Ireland. **Inns of Chancery** *Brit. hist.* buildings in London formerly used as hostels for law students. [OE *inn* (as IN)]
■ **1** see PUB 1. **2** see HOTEL 1.

innards /innərdz/ *n.pl. colloq.* **1** entrails. **2** works (of an engine etc.). [dial. etc. pronunc. of *inwards*: see INWARD *n.*]
■ **1** see GUT *n.* 1, 2. **2** see WORK *n.* 8.

innate /ináyt, innayt/ *adj.* **1** inborn; natural. **2** *Philos.* originating in the mind. □□ **innately** *adv.* **innateness** *n.* [ME f. L *innatus* (as IN-[2], *natus* past part. of *nasci* be born)]
■ **1** see INBORN. □□ **innately** see NATURALLY 1.

inner /innər/ *adj.* & *n.* ● *adj.* (usu. *attrib.*) **1** further in; inside; interior (*the inner compartment*). **2** (of thoughts, feelings, etc.) deeper; more secret. ● *n. Archery* **1** a division of the target next to the bull's-eye. **2** a shot that strikes this. □ **inner bar** *Brit. Law* Queen's or King's Counsel collectively. **inner city** the central most densely populated area of a city (also (with hyphen) *attrib.*: *inner-city housing*). **inner-directed** *Psychol.* governed by standards formed in childhood. **inner man** (or **woman** or **person**) **1** the soul or mind. **2** *joc.* the stomach. **inner planet** an inferior planet (see INFERIOR *adj.* 3). **inner space 1** the region between the earth and outer space, or below the surface of the sea. **2** the part of the mind not normally accessible to consciousness. **inner-spring** *US* = *interior-sprung*. **Inner Temple** one of the two Inns of Court on the site of the Temple in London (cf. *Middle Temple*). **inner tube** a separate inflatable tube inside the cover of a pneumatic tyre. □□ **innerly** *adv.* **innermost** *adj.* **innerness** *n.* [OE *innera* (adj.), compar. of IN]

■ *adj.* **1** see INTERIOR *adj.* 1. **2** see INTERIOR *adj.* 5. □ **inner man** (or **woman** or **person**) **1** see SUBCONSCIOUS *n.* □□ **innermost** see SUBCONSCIOUS *adj.*

innervate /innərvayt, inér-/ *v.tr.* supply (an organ etc.) with nerves. □□ **innervation** /-váysh'n/ *n.* [IN-[2] + L *nervus* nerve + -ATE[3]]

inning /inning/ *n. US* an innings at baseball etc. [*in* (v.) go in (f. IN)]

innings /inningz/ *n.* (*pl.* same or *colloq.* **inningses**) **1** esp. *Cricket* **a** the part of a game during which a side is in or batting. **b** the play of or score achieved by a player during a turn at batting. **2** a period during which a government, party, cause, etc. is in office or effective. **3 a** a period during which a person can achieve something. **b** *colloq.* a person's life span (*had a good innings and died at 94*).

innkeeper /inkeepər/ *n.* a person who keeps an inn.

■ see LANDLORD 2.

innocent /innəs'nt/ *adj.* & *n.* ● *adj.* **1** free from moral wrong; sinless. **2** (usu. foll. by *of*) not guilty (of a crime etc.). **3 a** simple; guileless; naïve. **b** pretending to be guileless. **4** harmless. **5** (foll. by *of*) *colloq.* without, lacking (*appeared, innocent of shoes*). ● *n.* **1** an innocent person, esp. a young child. **2** (in *pl.*) the young children killed by Herod after the birth of Jesus (Matt. 2:16). □ **Innocents'** (or **Holy Innocents'**) **Day** the day, 28 Dec., commemorating the massacre of the innocents. □□ **innocence** *n.* **innocency** *n.* **innocently** *adv.* [ME f. OF *innocent* or L *innocens innocent-* (as IN-[1], *nocēre* hurt)]

■ *adj.* **1** virtuous, moral, righteous, good, pure, chaste, virgin(al), undefiled, untainted, unstained, unsullied, pristine, sinless, uncorrupted, immaculate, spotless, unblemished, unpolluted, *colloq.* white. **2** not guilty, guiltless, blameless, (in the) clear, unimpeachable, above suspicion, above reproach, honest, faultless. **3 a** simple, unsuspecting, unsuspicious, ingenuous, trusting, trustful, gullible, credulous, dewy-eyed, *archaic* silly; guileless, artless, unaffected, unsophisticated, unworldly, naïve, green, inexperienced, callow, childlike. **b** demure, coy, meek, *Brit.* twee. **4** harmless, well-intentioned, safe, tame, innocuous, innoxious, inoffensive, unoffending, unobjectionable; platonic. **5** see DESTITUTE 2. ● *n.* **1** infant, babe, child, cherub; *ingénue*, dove, virgin; simpleton, *colloq.* muggins, *sl.* mug, sucker, soft *or* easy touch.

innocuous /inókyooəss/ *adj.* **1** not injurious; harmless. **2** inoffensive. □□ **innocuity** /innəkyóō-iti/ *n.* **innocuously** *adv.* **innocuousness** *n.* [L *innocuus* (as IN-[1], *nocuus* formed as INNOCENT)]

■ **1** see HARMLESS 1. **2** see INOFFENSIVE. □□ **innocuousness** see PURITY 2.

innominate /inómminət/ *adj.* unnamed. □ **innominate bone** *n. Anat.* the bone formed from the fusion of the ilium, ischium, and pubis; the hip-bone. [LL *innominatus* (as IN-[1], NOMINATE)]

■ see NAMELESS 1, 3, 5.

innovate /innəvayt/ *v.intr.* **1** bring in new methods, ideas, etc. **2** (often foll. by *in*) make changes. □□ **innovation** /-váysh'n/ *n.* **innovational** /-váyshən'l/ *adj.* **innovator** *n.* **innovative** *adj.* **innovativeness** *n.* **innovatory** /-vaytəri/ *adj.* [L *innovare* make new, alter (as IN-[2], *novus* new)]

■ **1** break new ground, pioneer, blaze a trail. **2** make changes, make alterations, modernize, remodel, revamp. □□ **innovation** originality, inventiveness, creativity, imagination, imaginativeness; novelty, invention; modernization, alteration, change. **innovative** see ORIGINAL *adj.* 2.

innoxious /inókshəss/ *adj.* harmless. □□ **innoxiously** *adv.* **innoxiousness** *n.* [L *innoxius* (as IN-[1], NOXIOUS)]

innuendo /inyoo-éndō/ *n.* & *v.* ● *n.* (*pl.* **-oes** or **-os**) **1** an allusive or oblique remark or hint, usu. disparaging. **2** a remark with a double meaning, usu. suggestive. ● *v.intr.* (**-oes**, **-oed**) make innuendoes. [L, = by nodding at, by pointing to: ablat. gerund of *innuere* nod at (as IN-[2], *nuere* nod)]

■ *n.* **1** allusion, insinuation, imputation, slur, suggestion, hint, intimation, implication, overtone. **2** *double entendre*; equivoque, pun, play on words, paronomasia, quibble. ● *v.* be suggestive; pun, equivocate, quibble.

Innuit var. of INUIT.

innumerable /inyóōmərəb'l/ *adj.* too many to be counted. □□ **innumerability** /-bílliti/ *n.* **innumerably** *adv.* [ME f. L *innumerabilis* (as IN-[1], NUMERABLE)]

■ see MANY *adj.*

innumerate /inyóōmərət/ *adj.* having no knowledge of or feeling for mathematical operations; not numerate. □□ **innumeracy** /-rəsi/ *n.* [IN-[1], NUMERATE]

innutrition /inyootrísh'n/ *n.* lack of nutrition. □□ **innutritious** *adj.*

inobservance /innəbzérv'nss/ *n.* **1** inattention. **2** (usu. foll. by *of*) non-observance (of a law etc.). [F *inobservance* or L *inobservantia* (as IN-[1], OBSERVANCE)]

inoculate /inókyoolayt/ *v.tr.* **1 a** treat (a person or animal) with a small quantity of the agent of a disease, in the form of vaccine or serum, usu. by injection, to promote immunity against the disease. **b** implant (a disease) by means of vaccine. **2** instil (a person) with ideas or opinions. □□ **inoculable** *adj.* **inoculation** /-láysh'n/ *n.* **inoculative** /-lətiv/ *adj.* **inoculator** *n.* [orig. in sense 'insert (a bud) into a plant': L *inoculare inoculat-* engraft (as IN-[2], *oculus* eye, bud)]

■ **1** see INJECT 1. □□ **inoculation** shot, vaccination, injection; see IMMUNITY 1.

inoculum /inókyooləm/ *n.* (*pl.* **inocula** /-lə/) any substance used for inoculation. [mod.L (as INOCULATE)]

■ see PREVENTIVE *n.*

inodorous /inṓdərəss/ *adj.* having no smell; odourless.

in-off /innof/ *n. Billiards* the act of pocketing a ball by bouncing it off another ball.

inoffensive /innəfénsiv/ *adj.* not objectionable; harmless. □□ **inoffensively** *adv.* **inoffensiveness** *n.*

■ harmless, unobjectionable, innocuous, innoxious, unoffending; neutral, safe, tame; mild, bland, retiring; platonic.

inoperable /inóppərəb'l/ *adj.* **1** *Surgery* that cannot suitably be operated on (*inoperable cancer*). **2** that cannot be operated; inoperative. □□ **inoperability** /-bílliti/ *n.* **inoperably** *adv.* [F *inopérable* (as IN-[1], OPERABLE)]

■ **1** see INCURABLE *adj.* **2** see DUFF[2] 2.

inoperative /inóppərətiv/ *adj.* not working or taking effect.

■ see *out of order* 1 (ORDER).

inopportune /inóppərtyōōn/ *adj.* not appropriate, esp. as regards time; unseasonable. □□ **inopportunely** *adv.* **inopportuneness** *n.* [L *inopportunus* (as IN-[1], OPPORTUNE)]

■ inappropriate, malapropos, inconvenient, inexpedient, unsuited, unsuitable, out of place, unseemly, untoward, unpropitious, unfavourable, inauspicious, ill-chosen, unfortunate; ill-timed, untimely, unseasonable; premature, hasty, too early.

inordinate /inórdinət/ *adj.* **1** immoderate; excessive. **2** intemperate. **3** disorderly. □□ **inordinately** *adv.* [ME f. L *inordinatus* (as IN-[1], *ordinatus* past part. of *ordinare* ORDAIN)]

■ **1, 2** immoderate, unrestrained, unbridled, untamed, intemperate, violent; extreme, excessive, exorbitant, disproportionate, out of all proportion, extravagant, overdone, overblown; outrageous, preposterous, unconscionable, unreasonable, unwarrantable, unjustifiable, undue, uncalled-for, unwarranted. **3** see DISORDERLY 1.

inorganic /innorgánnik/ *adj.* **1** *Chem.* (of a compound) not organic, usu. of mineral origin (opp. ORGANIC). **2** without organized physical structure. **3** not arising by natural growth; extraneous. **4** *Philol.* not explainable by normal etymology. □ **inorganic chemistry** the chemistry of inorganic compounds. □□ **inorganically** *adv.*
■ **1** see INANIMATE 1.

inosculate /inóskyoolayt/ *v.intr.* & *tr.* **1** join by running together. **2** join closely. □□ **inosculation** /-láysh'n/ *n.* [IN-[2] + L *osculare* provide with a mouth f. *osculum* dimin. of *os* mouth]

in-patient /inpaysh'nt/ *n.* a patient who lives in hospital while under treatment.

in propria persona /in própriə persónə/ *adv.* in his or her own person. [L]

input /inpŏŏt/ *n.* & *v.* ● *n.* **1** what is put in or taken in, or operated on by any process or system. **2** *Electronics* **a** a place where, or a device through which, energy, information, etc., enters a system (*a tape recorder with inputs for microphone and radio*). **b** energy supplied to a device or system; an electrical signal. **3** the information fed into a computer. **4** the action or process of putting in or feeding in. **5** a contribution of information etc. ● *v.tr.* (**inputting;** *past* and *past part.* **input** or **inputted**) (often foll. by *into*) **1** put in. **2** *Computing* supply (data, programs, etc., to a computer, program, etc.). □ **input-** (or **input/**) **output** *Computing* etc. of, relating to, or for input and output. □□ **inputter** *n.*

inquest /inkwest, ing-/ *n.* **1** *Law* **a** an inquiry by a coroner's court into the cause of a death. **b** a judicial inquiry to ascertain the facts relating to an incident etc. **c** a coroner's jury. **2** *colloq.* a discussion analysing the outcome of a game, an election, etc. [ME f. OF *enqueste* (as ENQUIRE)]
■ **1** see INQUIRY 1.

inquietude /inkwī-ityood, ing-/ *n.* uneasiness of mind or body. [ME f. OF *inquietude* or LL *inquietudo* f. L *inquietus* (as IN-[1], *quietus* quiet)]

inquiline /inkwilīn, ing-/ *n.* an animal living in the home of another; a commensal. □□ **inquilinous** /-līnəss/ *adj.* [L *inquilinus* sojourner (as IN-[2], *colere* dwell)]

inquire /inkwīr, ing-/ *v.* **1** *intr.* seek information formally; make a formal investigation. **2** *intr.* & *tr.* = ENQUIRE. □□ **inquirer** *n.* [var. of ENQUIRE]
■ **1** ask questions, make enquiries *or* inquiries; (*inquire into*) investigate, research, explore, probe, look into, examine, study, explore, survey, inspect, scrutinize. **2** ask, query, question, enquire; request, demand, seek; ask about *or* after.

inquiry /inkwīri, ing-/ *n.* (*pl.* **-ies**) **1** an investigation, esp. an official one. **2** = ENQUIRY. □ **inquiry agent** *Brit.* a private detective.
■ **1** enquiry, investigation, probe, examination, research, search, inspection, study, exploration, survey, scrutiny, inquest, interrogation, cross-examination, inquisition, grilling. **2** enquiry, question, query, interrogation; request, demand. □ **inquiry agent** private detective, *US* operative, *colloq.* private eye, eye, sleuth, sleuth-hound, snoop, snooper, tec, *sl.* (private) dick, gumshoe, *US sl.* peeper, shamus.

inquisition /inkwizish'n, ing-/ *n.* **1** usu. *derog.* an intensive search or investigation. **2** a judicial or official inquiry. **3** (**the Inquisition**) *RC Ch. hist.* an ecclesiastical tribunal for the suppression of heresy, esp. in Spain, operating through torture and execution. □□ **inquisitional** *adj.* [ME f. OF f. L *inquisitio -onis* examination (as INQUIRE)]
■ **1** see INVESTIGATION. **2** see INQUIRY 1.

inquisitive /inkwízzitiv, ing-/ *adj.* **1** unduly curious; prying. **2** seeking knowledge; inquiring. □□ **inquisitively** *adv.* **inquisitiveness** *n.* [ME f. OF *inquisitif -ive* f. LL *inquisitivus* (as INQUISITION)]
■ **1** prying, curious, *colloq.* nosy, snoopy; intrusive, meddlesome, busy. **2** inquiring, curious, interested, investigative. □□ **inquisitiveness** see INTEREST *n.* 1a.

inquisitor /inkwízzitər, ing-/ *n.* **1** an official investigator. **2** *hist.* an officer of the Inquisition. □ **Grand Inquisitor** the director of the court of Inquisition in some countries. **Inquisitor-General** the head of the Spanish Inquisition. [F *inquisiteur* f. L *inquisitor -oris* (as INQUIRE)]

inquisitorial /inkwízzitóriəl, ing-/ *adj.* **1** of or like an inquisitor. **2** offensively prying. **3** *Law* (of a trial etc.) in which the judge has a prosecuting role (opp. ACCUSATORIAL). □□ **inquisitorially** *adv.* [med.L *inquisitorius* (as INQUISITOR)]

inquorate /inkwórayt, ing-/ *adj.* not constituting a quorum.

in re /in reé, ráy/ *prep.* = RE[1]. [L, = in the matter of]

INRI *abbr.* Jesus of Nazareth, King of the Jews. [L *Iesus Nazarenus Rex Iudaeorum*]

inroad /inrōd/ *n.* **1** (often in *pl.*) **a** (usu. foll. by *on, into*) an encroachment; a using up of resources etc. (*makes inroads on my time*). **b** (often foll. by *in, into*) progress, an advance (*making inroads into a difficult market*). **2** a hostile attack; a raid. [IN + ROAD[1] in sense 'riding']
■ **1 a** invasion, incursion, intrusion, encroachment. **b** advance, progress, breakthrough. **2** raid, attack, foray; penetration.

inrush /inrush/ *n.* a rushing in; an influx. □□ **inrushing** *adj.* & *n.*

ins. *abbr.* **1** inches. **2** insurance.

insalubrious /insəlóobriəss, -lyóobriəss/ *adj.* (of a climate or place) unhealthy. □□ **insalubrity** *n.* [L *insalubris* (as IN-[1], SALUBRIOUS)]
■ see UNHEALTHY 2a, b.

insane /insáyn/ *adj.* **1** not of sound mind; mad. **2** *colloq.* extremely foolish; irrational. □□ **insanely** *adv.* **insaneness** *n.* **insanity** /-sánniti/ *n.* (*pl.* **-ies**). [L *insanus* (as IN-[1], *sanus* healthy)]
■ **1** psychotic, neurotic, schizophrenic, schizoid, psychoneurotic, *Psychol.* manic-depressive; mad, demented, out of one's mind *or* wits, manic, maniacal, lunatic, crazed, flighty, mad as a hatter *or* March hare, *colloq.* crack-brained, crazy, certifiable, mental, schizo, round the bend, up the wall, not all there, out to lunch, *esp. Brit. colloq.* daft, *sl.* cracked, screwy, loopy, loony, dippy, wacky, nutty (as a fruitcake), nuts, bats, batty, cuckoo, kooky, loco, gaga, up the creek *or* pole, off one's rocker *or* chump *or* head *or* nut, out of one's head *or* skull, off-the-wall, bonkers, *Austral. sl.* dilly, *Brit. sl.* barmy, potty, crackers, round the twist, *US sl.* wacko, flaky; (*be insane*) have bats in the belfry, *colloq.* have a screw loose; (*go insane*) take leave of one's senses, *sl.* lose one's marbles, go bananas, go ape, flip one's lid. **2** foolish, silly, fatuous, asinine, inane, stupid, brainless, senseless, witless, feeble-minded, empty-headed, simple, *colloq.* crazy, idiotic, imbecilic, moronic, dumb, halfwitted, pinheaded, addle-brained, scatterbrained, *esp. Brit. colloq.* gormless, daft, *sl.* nutty, screwy, loopy, loony, dippy, nuts, bats, batty, bonkers, *Austral. sl.* dilly, *Brit. sl.* barmy, potty, crackers, *US sl.* nerdy; mad, wild, reckless, hare-brained, irresponsible, irrational, absurd, ridiculous, preposterous, ludicrous, nonsensical. □□ **insanity** madness, dementedness, lunacy, mental illness *or* disorder, dementia (praecox), psychosis, schizophrenia, (mental) derangement, mania, psychoneurosis, neurosis, *colloq.* craziness, *esp. Brit. colloq.* daftness, *sl.* screwiness, looniness, wackiness, nuttiness, battiness, *Brit. sl.* barminess, pottiness, *US sl.* flakiness; folly, foolishness, silliness, fatuity, asininity, stupidity, senselessness, witlessness, feeble-mindedness, pinheadedness, *colloq.* idiocy, imbecility, dumbness, halfwittedness, *esp. Brit. colloq.* gormlessness; absurdity, nonsense, nonsensicality, ridiculousness, preposterousness, ludicrousness, irrationality, irresponsibility, wildness, recklessness.

insanitary /insánnitəri, -tri/ *adj.* not sanitary; dirty or germ-carrying.
■ see SORDID 1.

insatiable /insáyshəb'l/ *adj.* **1** unable to be satisfied. **2** (usu. foll. by *of*) extremely greedy. □□ **insatiability** /-bílliti/ *n.* **insatiably** *adv.* [ME f. OF *insaciable* or L *insatiabilis* (as IN-[1], SATIATE)]
■ **1** see UNQUENCHABLE. **2** see GREEDY 1. □□ **insatiability** see GREED.

insatiate /insáyshiət/ *adj.* never satisfied. [L *insatiatus* (as IN-[1], SATIATE)]

inscape /ínskayp/ *n. literary* the unique inner quality or essence of an object etc. as shown in a work of art, esp. a poem. [perh. f. IN-[2] + -SCAPE]

inscribe /inskrī́b/ *v.tr.* **1 a** (usu. foll. by *in*, *on*) write or carve (words etc.) on stone, metal, paper, a book, etc. **b** (usu. foll. by *with*) mark (a sheet, tablet, etc.) with characters. **2** (usu. foll. by *to*) write an informal dedication (to a person) in or on (a book etc.). **3** enter the name of (a person) on a list or in a book. **4** *Geom.* draw (a figure) within another so that some or all points of it lie on the boundary of the other (cf. CIRCUMSCRIBE). **5** (esp. as **inscribed** *adj.*) *Brit.* issue (stock etc.) in the form of shares with registered holders. □□ **inscribable** *adj.* **inscriber** *n.* [L *inscribere inscript-* (as IN-[2], *scribere* write)]
■ **1 a** see WRITE 2–4. **2** dedicate, address, assign. **3** see ENTER 3.

inscription /inskrípsh'n/ *n.* **1** words inscribed, esp. on a monument, coin, stone, or in a book etc. **2 a** the act of inscribing, esp. the informal dedication of a book etc. **b** an instance of this. □□ **inscriptional** *adj.* **inscriptive** *adj.* [ME f. L *inscriptio* (as INSCRIBE)]
■ **1** dedication, address, message.

inscrutable /inskróotəb'l/ *adj.* wholly mysterious, impenetrable. □□ **inscrutability** /-bílliti/ *n.* **inscrutableness** *n.* **inscrutably** *adv.* [ME f. eccl.L *inscrutabilis* (as IN-[1], *scrutari* search: see SCRUTINY)]
■ see MYSTERIOUS. □□ **inscrutability** see MYSTERY[1] 2.

insect /ínsekt/ *n.* **1 a** any arthropod of the class Insecta, having a head, thorax, abdomen, two antennae, three pairs of thoracic legs, and usu. one or two pairs of thoracic wings. **b** (loosely) any other small segmented invertebrate animal. **2** an insignificant or contemptible person or creature. □□ **insectile** /-séktīl/ *adj.* [L *insectum* (*animal*) notched (animal) f. *insecare insect-* (as IN-[2], *secare* cut)]
■ **1** see BUG *n.* 1.

insectarium /insektáiriəm/ *n.* (also **insectary** /inséktəri/) (*pl.* **insectariums** or **insectaries**) a place for keeping insects.

insecticide /inséktisīd/ *n.* a substance used for killing insects. □□ **insecticidal** /-sīd'l/ *adj.*

insectivore /inséktivor/ *n.* **1** any mammal of the order Insectivora feeding on insects etc., e.g. a hedgehog or mole. **2** any plant which captures and absorbs insects. □□ **insectivorous** /-tívvərəss/ *adj.* [F f. mod.L *insectivorus* (as INSECT, -VORE: see -VOROUS)]

insecure /ínsikyóor/ *adj.* **1** (of a person or state of mind) uncertain; lacking confidence. **2 a** unsafe; not firm or fixed. **b** (of ice, ground, etc.) liable to give way. **c** lacking security, unprotected. □□ **insecurely** *adv.* **insecurity** /-kyóoriti/ *n.*
■ **1** uncertain, unsure, irresolute, hesitant, undecided, unsettled; unsound, unreliable, untrustworthy; diffident, nervous, nervy, shaky, jumpy, jittery, unnerved, uncomfortable, disconcerted, apprehensive, anxious, worried. **2 a, b** unsafe, dangerous, perilous, precarious; unsound, weak, flimsy, unsubstantial, insubstantial, infirm, weak, frail; rickety, rocky, shaky, wobbly, unstable, unsteady, unreliable, untrustworthy, treacherous. **c** unprotected, vulnerable, unguarded, defenceless, undefended, exposed, open.

inselberg /ins'lberg, ínz-/ *n.* an isolated hill or mountain rising abruptly from its surroundings. [G, = island mountain]

inseminate /insémminayt/ *v.tr.* **1** introduce semen into (a female) by natural or artificial means. **2** sow (seed etc.). □□ **insemination** /-náysh'n/ *n.* **inseminator** *n.* [L *inseminare* (as IN-[2], SEMEN)]
■ **1** see FERTILIZE 2.

insensate /insénsayt/ *adj.* **1** without physical sensation; unconscious. **2** without sensibility; unfeeling. **3** stupid. □□ **insensately** *adv.* [eccl.L *insensatus* (as IN-[1], *sensatus* f. *sensus* SENSE)]
■ **1** see SENSELESS 1, 4. **2** see *thick-skinned* (THICK).

insensibility /insénsibílliti/ *n.* **1** unconsciousness. **2** a lack of mental feeling or emotion; hardness. **3** (often foll. by *to*) indifference. [F *insensibilité* or LL *insensibilitas* (as INSENSIBLE)]
■ **1** see OBLIVION. **3** see INDIFFERENCE 1.

insensible /insénsib'l/ *adj.* **1 a** without one's mental faculties; unconscious. **b** (of the extremities etc.) numb; without feeling. **2** (usu. foll. by *of*, *to*) unaware; indifferent (*insensible of her needs*). **3** without emotion; callous. **4** too small or gradual to be perceived; inappreciable. □□ **insensibly** *adv.* [ME f. OF *insensible* or L *insensibilis* (as IN-[1], SENSIBLE)]
■ **1** insensate, insentient, lifeless, inanimate, dead; unconscious, senseless, *colloq.* out, dead to the world; numb, benumbed, anaesthetized, frozen, paralysed, torpid, unfeeling. **2** (*insensible of* or *to*) unaware *or* unmindful of, oblivious to, blind *or* deaf to, heedless *or* unconscious of, unaffected *or* untouched *or* unmoved by; indifferent *or* insensitive *or* impervious to. **3** unfeeling, emotionless, unemotional, impassive, passionless, dispassionate, cold, clinical, objective, detached, unconcerned, nonchalant, insouciant, indifferent, apathetic; callous, cold-hearted, hard-hearted, steely, stony, heartless, uncaring, unsympathetic. **4** see IMPERCEPTIBLE 2.

insensitive /insénsitiv/ *adj.* (often foll. by *to*) **1** unfeeling; boorish; crass. **2** not sensitive to physical stimuli. □□ **insensitively** *adv.* **insensitiveness** *n.* **insensitivity** /-tívviti/ *n.*
■ **1** see THOUGHTLESS 1. □□ **insensitivity** see *imprudence* (IMPRUDENT).

insentient /insénsh'nt/ *adj.* not sentient; inanimate. □□ **insentience** *n.*
■ see INSENSIBLE 1.

inseparable /inséppərəb'l/ *adj.* & *n.* ● *adj.* **1** (esp. of friends) unable or unwilling to be separated. **2** *Gram.* (of a prefix, or a verb in respect of it) unable to be used as a separate word, e.g.: *dis-*, *mis-*, *un-*. ● *n.* (usu. in *pl.*) an inseparable person or thing, esp. a friend. □□ **inseparability** /-bílliti/ *n.* **inseparably** *adv.* [ME f. L *inseparabilis* (as IN-[1], SEPARABLE)]
■ *adj.* **1** see CLOSE[1] *adj.* 2a, b, ONE *adj.* 5. □□ **inseparably** see *inextricably* (INEXTRICABLE).

insert *v.* & *n.* ● *v.tr.* /insért/ **1** (usu. foll. by *in*, *into*, *between*, etc.) place, fit, or thrust (a thing) into another. **2** (usu. foll. by *in*, *into*) introduce (a letter, word, article, advertisement, etc.) into a newspaper etc. **3** (as **inserted** *adj.*) *Anat.* etc. (of a muscle etc.) attached (at a specific point). ● *n.* /ínsert/ something inserted, e.g. a loose page in a magazine, a piece of cloth in a garment, a shot in a cinema film. □□ **insertable** *adj.* **inserter** *n.* [L *inserere* (as IN-[2], *serere sert-* join)]
■ *v.* **1** inset, inlay, place *or* put *or* stick in, feed, load, intromit, introduce; interpolate, interject, interpose, throw in. ● *n.* inset, inlay; interpolation, interjection; insertion, addition, addendum, supplement, advertisement, broadside, brochure, handbill, circular, *US* flyer, *colloq.* ad, *Brit. colloq.* advert.

insertion /insérsh'n/ *n.* **1** the act or an instance of inserting. **2** an amendment etc. inserted in writing or printing. **3** each appearance of an advertisement in a newspaper etc. **4** an ornamental section of needlework inserted into plain material (*lace insertions*). **5** the manner or place of attachment of a muscle, an organ, etc. **6** the placing of a spacecraft in an orbit. [LL *insertio* (as INSERT)]

■ **2** see INSERT *n.*

in-service /inserviss/ *adj.* (of training) intended for those actively engaged in the profession or activity concerned.

inset *n.* & *v.* ● *n.* /inset/ **1 a** an extra page or pages inserted in a folded sheet or in a book; an insert. **b** a small map, photograph, etc., inserted within the border of a larger one. **2** a piece let into a dress etc. ● *v.tr.* /insét/ (**insetting**; *past* and *past part.* **inset** or **insetted**) **1** put in as an inset. **2** decorate with an inset. ▫▫ **insetter** *n.*

inshallah /inshállə/ *int.* if Allah wills it. [Arab. *in šā' Allah*]

inshore /inshór/ *adv.* & *adj.* at sea but close to the shore. ▫ **inshore of** nearer to shore than.

inside *n., adj., adv.,* & *prep.* ● *n.* /insīd/ **1 a** the inner side or surface of a thing. **b** the inner part; the interior. **2 a** (of a path) the side next to the wall or away from the road. **b** (of a double-decker bus) the lower section. **3** (usu. in *pl.*) *colloq.* **a** the stomach and bowels (*something wrong with my insides*). **b** the operative part of a machine etc. **4** *colloq.* a position affording inside information (*knows someone on the inside*). ● *adj.* /insīd/ **1** situated on or in, or derived from, the inside; (of information etc.) available only to those on the inside. **2** *Football* & *Hockey* nearer to the centre of the field (*inside forward*; *inside left*; *inside right*). ● *adv.* /insīd/ **1** on, in, or to the inside. **2** *sl.* in prison. ● *prep.* /insīd/ **1** on the inner side of; within (*inside the house*). **2** in less than (*inside an hour*). ▫ **inside country** *Austral.* settled areas near the coast. **inside information** information not accessible to outsiders. **inside job** *colloq.* a crime committed by a person living or working on the premises burgled etc. **inside of** *colloq.* **1** in less than (a week etc.). **2** *Brit.* the middle part of. **inside out** with the inner surface turned outwards. **inside story** = *inside information.* **inside track 1** the track which is shorter, because of the curve. **2** a position of advantage. **know a thing inside out** know a thing thoroughly. **turn inside out 1** turn the inner surface of outwards. **2** *colloq.* ransack; cause confusion in. [IN + SIDE]

■ *n.* **1** inner side, inner surface; lining, backing, reverse; interior, centre, middle, core, heart. **3** (*insides*) **a** bowels, entrails, viscera, gut(s), stomach, *colloq.* innards; *colloq.* works, doings. **b** see WORK *n.* 8. ● *adj.* **1** internal, interior; indoor; private, secret, confidential, clandestine, privileged, exclusive, *archaic* privy. **2** central, *attrib.* centre. ● *adv.* **1** indoors; on *or* to the inside; centrally, at heart, fundamentally, basically, at bottom, by nature, deep down. **2** in prison *or* jail, behind bars, *colloq.* doing time, *esp. US colloq.* in hock, *sl.* in clink *or* jug *or* stir, in the can *or* cooler *or* nick *or* slammer, *Brit. sl.* banged up, in the choky, doing bird, *US sl.* in hoosegow, in the slam. ● *prep.* within, *colloq.* inside of; in under, in less than. ▫ **inside of 1** see INSIDE *prep.* above. **2** see INSIDE *n.* 1 above. **inside out** outside in, wrong side out, reversed. **know a thing inside out** know a thing like the back of one's hand, know a thing backwards. **turn inside out 1** reverse, invert, *Physiol.* evert, *Med.* & *Physiol.* evaginate. **2** see MESS *v.* 1.

insider /insīdər/ *n.* **1** a person who is within a society, organization, etc. (cf. OUTSIDER). **2** a person privy to a secret, esp. when using it to gain advantage. ▫ **insider dealing** *Stock Exch.* the illegal practice of trading to one's own advantage through having access to confidential information.

insidious /insíddiəss/ *adj.* **1** proceeding or progressing inconspicuously but harmfully (*an insidious disease*). **2** treacherous; crafty. ▫▫ **insidiously** *adv.* **insidiousness** *n.* [L *insidiosus* cunning f. *insidiae* ambush (as IN-[2], *sedēre* sit)]

■ **2** see SINISTER 2. ▫▫ **insidiously** see *behind a person's back* (BEHIND). **insidiousness** see PERFIDY.

insight /insīt/ *n.* (usu. foll. by *into*) **1** the capacity of understanding hidden truths etc., esp. of character or situations. **2** an instance of this. ▫▫ **insightful** *adj.* **insightfully** *adv.* [ME, = 'discernment', prob. of Scand. & LG orig. (as IN-[2], SIGHT)]

■ perception, percipience, sensitivity, perspicacity, perceptiveness, perspicaciousness, discernment, acuteness, acuity, acumen, sharpness, shrewdness, understanding, judgement, judiciousness, comprehension, vision, *sl.* savvy.

insignia /insígniə/ *n.* (treated as *sing.* or *pl.*; usu. foll. by *of*) **1** badges (*wore his insignia of office*). **2** distinguishing marks. [L, pl. of *insigne* neut. of *insignis* distinguished (as IN-[2], *signis* f. *signum* SIGN)]

■ **1** see SYMBOL *n.*

insignificant /insignífikənt/ *adj.* **1** unimportant; trifling. **2** (of a person) undistinguished. **3** meaningless. ▫▫ **insignificance** *n.* **insignificancy** *n.* **insignificantly** *adv.*

■ **1** unimportant, paltry, trifling, petty, trivial, nugatory, of no account, minor, inconsequential, insubstantial, unsubstantial, negligible, inconsiderable, niggling, puny, small, *Brit.* twopenny-halfpenny, tinpot, *US* dinky, picayune, *colloq.* small-time, piddling, *Brit. sl.* potty; expendable, unessential, non-essential. **2** undistinguished, unexceptional, unremarkable, inconspicuous, unobtrusive, unnoticeable, low-key; ordinary, run-of-the-mill, mediocre, everyday, humble, simple; obscure, unheard-of, little-known, unknown, unsung. **3** meaningless, senseless, pointless, irrelevant, purposeless, vain, empty, vacuous, hollow; absurd, nonsensical, ridiculous, preposterous, fatuous.

insincere /insinseer/ *adj.* not sincere; not candid. ▫▫ **insincerely** *adv.* **insincerity** /-sérriti/ *n.* (*pl.* **-ies**). [L *insincerus* (as IN-[1], SINCERE)]

■ dishonest, deceitful, untruthful, false, lying, mendacious, deceptive, underhand, underhanded, *colloq.* crooked, phoney; disingenuous, affected, synthetic, artificial, pseudo, hollow, empty, hypocritical; duplicitous, two-faced, double-faced, double-dealing, treacherous, faithless, perfidious; machiavellian, sly, cunning, crafty, slick, glib, foxy, vulpine, wily, artful, evasive, tricky, *colloq.* shifty; unctuous, slimy, slippery. ▫▫ **insincerity** see AFFECTATION 1, CANT[1] *n.* 1.

insinuate /insínyoo-ayt/ *v.tr.* **1** (often foll. by *that* + clause) convey indirectly or obliquely; hint (*insinuated that she was lying*). **2** (often *refl.*; usu. foll. by *into*) **a** introduce (oneself, a person, etc.) into favour, office, etc., by subtle manipulation. **b** introduce (a thing, an idea, oneself, etc.) subtly or deviously into a place (*insinuated himself into the Royal Box*). ▫▫ **insinuation** /-áysh'n/ *n.* **insinuative** *adj.* **insinuator** *n.* **insinuatory** /-sínyooətəri, -tri/ *adj.* [L *insinuare insinuat-* (as IN-[2], *sinuare* to curve)]

■ **1** suggest, hint, intimate, imply, whisper, indicate. **2 a, b** (*insinuate oneself*) worm *or* work (one's way), insert oneself, manoeuvre oneself *or* one's way, infiltrate. **b** inject, infuse, instil, introduce, slip. ▫▫ **insinuation** see IMPLICATION, INNUENDO *n.* 1.

insipid /insíppid/ *adj.* **1** lacking vigour or interest; dull. **2** lacking flavour; tasteless. ▫▫ **insipidity** /-píddit/ *n.* **insipidly** *adv.* **insipidness** *n.* [F *insipide* or LL *insipidus* (as IN-[1], *sapidus* SAPID)]

■ **1** see TEDIOUS. **2** see TASTELESS 1. ▫▫ **insipidity, insipidness** see TEDIUM.

insist /insíst/ *v.tr.* (usu. foll. by *that* + clause; also *absol.*) maintain or demand positively and assertively (*insisted that he was innocent*; *give me the bag! I insist!*). ▫ **insist on** demand or maintain (*I insist on being present*; *insists on his suitability*). ▫▫ **insister** *n.* **insistingly** *adv.* [L *insistere* stand on, persist (as IN-[2], *sistere* stand)]

■ demand, require; importune, urge, exhort; argue, remonstrate, expostulate; swear, asseverate, declare, assert, avow, emphasize, underline, stress, *formal* aver; maintain, persist. ▫ **insist on** demand, exact, stipulate, order, command; make a point of, stand on; maintain, assert, swear to, declare.

insistent /insístənt/ *adj.* **1** (often foll. by *on*) insisting; demanding positively or continually (*is insistent on taking me with him*). **2** obtruding itself on the attention (*the insistent*

rattle of the window frame). □□ **insistence** *n.* **insistency** *n.* **insistently** *adv.*
▪ **1** emphatic, firm, explicit, affirmative, positive, peremptory; assertive, importunate, urgent; dogged, persistent, tenacious, resolute, determined, uncompromising, unfaltering, unwavering, unrelenting, stubborn, obstinate, unyielding. **2** obtrusive, intrusive; importunate, persistent, nagging, unrelenting; clamorous, loud, noisy.

in situ /in sityōō/ *adv.* **1** in its place. **2** in its original place. [L]

insobriety /insəbrī́-iti/ *n.* intemperance, esp. in drinking.
▪ see *drunkenness* (DRUNKEN).

insofar /insōfaár/ *adv.* = *in so far* (see FAR).

insolation /insōláysh'n/ *n.* exposure to the sun's rays, esp. for bleaching. [L *insolatio* f. *insolare* (as IN-², *solare* f. *sol* sun)]

insole /insōl/ *n.* **1** a removable sole worn in a boot or shoe for warmth etc. **2** the fixed inner sole of a boot or shoe.

insolent /insələnt/ *adj.* offensively contemptuous or arrogant; insulting. □□ **insolence** *n.* **insolently** *adv.* [ME, = 'arrogant', f. L *insolens* (as IN-¹, *solens* pres. part. of *solēre* be accustomed)]
▪ disrespectful, contemptuous, contumelious, insulting, rude, uncivil, offensive, insubordinate; arrogant, brazen, brassy, brash, bold, presumptuous, impertinent, impudent, pert, saucy, cheeky, cocky, cocksure, *US* nervy, *colloq.* pushy, fresh, lippy. □□ **insolence** see BRASS *n.* 8, *impudence* (IMPUDENT).

insoluble /insólyoob'l/ *adj.* **1** incapable of being solved. **2** incapable of being dissolved. □□ **insolubility** /-bílliti/ *n.* **insolubilize** /-bilīz/ *v.tr.* (also **-ise**). **insolubleness** *n.* **insolubly** *adv.* [ME f. OF *insoluble* or L *insolubilis* (as IN-¹, SOLUBLE)]
▪ **1** see MYSTERIOUS.

insolvable /insólvəb'l/ *adj.* = INSOLUBLE.

insolvent /insólv'nt/ *adj.* & *n.* ● *adj.* **1** unable to pay one's debts. **2** relating to insolvency (*insolvent laws*). ● *n.* a debtor. □□ **insolvency** *n.*
▪ **1** bankrupt, in receivership, ruined, failed, collapsed, gone to the wall, wound up, embarrassed, *Austral.* unfinancial, *colloq.* (gone) bust, broke, on the rocks. □□ **insolvency** see FAILURE 6, POVERTY 1.

insomnia /insómniə/ *n.* habitual sleeplessness; inability to sleep. □□ **insomniac** /-niak/ *n.* & *adj.* [L f. *insomnis* sleepless (as IN-¹, *somnus* sleep)]
▪ □□ **insomniac** (*adj.*) see SLEEPLESS.

insomuch /insōmúch/ *adv.* **1** (foll. by *that* + clause) to such an extent. **2** (foll. by *as*) inasmuch. [ME, orig. *in so much*]
▪ see CONSIDERING 1.

insouciant /insóōssiənt, ANSŌŌSSYON/ *adj.* carefree; unconcerned. □□ **insouciance** *n.* **insouciantly** *adv.* [F (as IN-¹, *souciant* pres. part. of *soucier* care)]
▪ see CAREFREE. □□ **insouciance** see INDIFFERENCE 1. **insouciantly** see GAILY 1.

inspan /inspán/ *v.* (**inspanned, inspanning**) *S.Afr.* **1** *tr.* (also *absol.*) **a** yoke (oxen etc.) in a team to a vehicle. **b** harness an animal or animals to (a wagon). **2** *tr.* harness (people or resources) into service. [Du. *inspannen* stretch (as IN-², SPAN²)]

inspect /inspékt/ *v.tr.* **1** look closely at or into. **2** examine (a document etc.) officially. □□ **inspection** *n.* [L *inspicere inspect-* (as IN-², *specere* look at), or its frequent. *inspectare*]
▪ examine, look at *or* into *or* over *or* round, see over, view, survey; observe, study, watch, eye; scrutinize, peruse, probe, pore over, audit, check (through), read through, go over, run one's eye over, scan; investigate, check up on, check out, run the rule over, *colloq.* have a look-see, *Brit. sl.* suss out. □□ **inspection** see EXAMINATION 1, 2.

inspector /inspéktər/ *n.* **1** a person who inspects. **2** an official employed to supervise a service, a machine, etc., and make reports. **3** *Brit.* a police officer below a superintendent and above a sergeant in rank. □ **inspector general** a chief inspector. **inspector of taxes** (in the UK) an official of the Inland Revenue responsible for collecting taxes. □□ **inspectorate** /-tərət/ *n.* **inspectorial** /-tóriəl/ *adj.* **inspectorship** *n.* [L (as INSPECT)]

inspiration /inspiráysh'n/ *n.* **1 a** a supposed creative force or influence on poets, artists, musicians, etc., stimulating the production of works of art. **b** a person, principle, faith, etc. stimulating artistic or moral fervour and creativity. **c** a similar divine influence supposed to have led to the writing of Scripture etc. **2** a sudden brilliant, creative, or timely idea. **3** a drawing in of breath; inhalation. □□ **inspirational** *adj.* **inspirationism** *n.* **inspirationist** *n.* [ME f. OF f. LL *inspiratio -onis* (as INSPIRE)]
▪ **1 a** genius, oracle, afflatus, (the) Muse(s), duende, life-force, fire, spark, *poet.* Hippocrene; stimulus, stimulation, encouragement, impetus, lift, fillip; spirit, passion, ardour, zeal, enthusiasm, energy, vigour, sparkle, imagination. **b** luminary, lamp, lodestar, rudder, guide, guiding light *or* star; watchword. **2** revelation, vision, stroke of genius, flash, spark, *colloq.* brainwave, *US colloq.* brainstorm. **3** inhalation, sniff, gasp, pull, draw.

inspirator /inspiraytər/ *n.* an apparatus for drawing in air or vapour. [LL (as INSPIRE)]

inspire /inspī́r/ *v.tr.* **1** stimulate or arouse (a person) to esp. creative activity, esp. by supposed divine or supernatural agency (*your faith inspired him*; *inspired by God*). **2 a** (usu. foll. by *with*) animate (a person) with a feeling. **b** (usu. foll. by *into*) instil (a feeling) into a person etc. **c** (usu. foll. by *in*) create (a feeling) in a person. **3** prompt; give rise to (*the poem was inspired by the autumn*). **4** (as **inspired** *adj.*) **a** (of a work of art etc.) as if prompted by or emanating from a supernatural source; characterized by inspiration (*an inspired speech*). **b** (of a guess) intuitive but accurate. **5** (also *absol.*) breathe in (air etc.); inhale. □□ **inspiratory** /inspī́rətəri, -tri/ *adj.* **inspiredly** /-ridli/ *adv.* **inspirer** *n.* **inspiring** *adj.* **inspiringly** *adv.* [ME f. OF *inspirer* f. L *inspirare* breathe in (as IN-², *spirare* breathe)]
▪ **1, 2** stimulate, move, arouse, rouse, stir, wake, awaken; uplift, buoy (up), buttress, encourage, rally, strengthen, support, reinforce, fortify, confirm, affirm, *colloq.* boost; inspirit, invigorate, energize, enliven, vitalize, animate, vivify, galvanize, carry away, excite, quicken, fire (up), provoke, *literary* enkindle. **3** activate, actuate, instigate, prompt, cause, create, trigger, set off, spark (off), provoke, excite, *literary* enkindle. **4** (**inspired**) creative, original, insightful, visionary, intuitive; ingenious, inventive, innovative, brilliant. **5** see INHALE.

inspirit /inspírrit/ *v.tr.* (**inspirited, inspiriting**) **1** put life into; animate. **2** (usu. foll. by *to*, or *to* + infin.) encourage (a person). □□ **inspiriting** *adj.* **inspiritingly** *adv.*
▪ **1** see ANIMATE *v.* **2** see ANIMATE *v.* 3, 4, ENCOURAGE 1. □□ **inspiriting** see REFRESHING, ROUSING.

inspissate /inspíssayt/ *v.tr. literary* thicken; condense. □□ **inspissation** /-sáysh'n/ *n.* [LL *inspissare inspissat-* (as IN-², L *spissus* thick)]
▪ see THICKEN.

inspissator /inspisaytər/ *n.* an apparatus for thickening serum etc. by heat.

inst. *abbr.* **1** = INSTANT *adj.* 4 (*the 6th inst.*). **2** institute. **3** institution.

instability /instəbílliti/ *n.* (*pl.* **-ies**) **1** a lack of stability. **2** *Psychol.* unpredictability in behaviour etc. **3** an instance of instability. [ME f. F *instabilité* f. L *instabilitas -tatis* f. *instabilis* (as IN-¹, STABLE¹)]
▪ **1, 3** see *fluctuation* (FLUCTUATE).

install /instáwl/ *v.tr.* (also **instal**) (**installed, installing**) **1** place (equipment, machinery, etc.) in position ready for use. **2** place (a person) in an office or rank with ceremony (*installed in the office of chancellor*). **3** establish (oneself, a person, etc.) in a place, condition, etc. (*installed herself at the head of the table*). □□ **installant** *adj.* & *n.* **installer** *n.* [med.L *installare* (as IN-², *stallare* f. *stallum* STALL¹)]

■ **1** fit, set up, mount, site, fix *or* set (in place); connect (up), *Electr.* wire up. **2** invest, instate, enthrone, chair, inaugurate, induct, swear in, establish, institute, initiate. **3** place, put, position, settle, seat, sit, ensconce, establish.

installation /instəláysh'n/ *n.* **1 a** the act or an instance of installing. **b** the process or an instance of being installed. **2** a piece of apparatus, a machine, etc. installed or the place where it is installed. [med.L *installatio* (as INSTALL)]

■ **1** investiture, instatement, enthronement, inauguration, induction, swearing-in, initiation, establishment, institution, ordination, coronation; placement, emplacement, settlement; installing, fitting, setting up, mounting, siting, fixing, building in; connection, plumbing in, wiring up. **2** fitting, fitment, machine, machinery, apparatus, equipment, gear; plant, factory, depot, station, warehouse, establishment.

instalment /instáwlmənt/ *n.* (*US* **installment**) **1** a sum of money due as one of several usu. equal payments for something, spread over an agreed period of time. **2** any of several parts, esp. of a television or radio serial or a magazine story, published or shown in sequence at intervals. □ **instalment plan** payment by instalments, esp. hire purchase. [alt. f. obs. *estallment* f. AF *estalement* f. *estaler* fix: prob. assoc. with INSTALLATION]

■ **2** episode, part, chapter.

instance /ínstənss/ *n.* & *v.* ● *n.* **1** an example or illustration of (*just another instance of his lack of determination*). **2** a particular case (*that's not true in this instance*). **3** *Law* a legal suit. ● *v.tr.* cite (a fact, case, etc.) as an instance. □ **at the instance of** at the request or suggestion of. **court of first instance** *Law* a court of primary jurisdiction. **for instance** as an example. **in the first** (or **second** etc.) **instance** in the first (or second etc.) place; at the first (or second etc.) stage of a proceeding. [ME f. OF f. L *instantia* (as INSTANT)]

■ *n.* **1** case (in point), example, exemplar, exemplification, illustration. **2** case, situation, event, occasion, occurrence, (set of) circumstance(s). ● *v.* adduce, quote, cite, allude to. □ **at the instance of** at the request of, at the suggestion of, *literary* at the behest of; (as) per, in accordance with. **for instance** for example, e.g., like, (such) as, say, as an example, by way of illustration. **in the first instance** in the first place, for a start, *colloq.* for a kick-off; at the beginning *or* start, initially, originally, at first.

instancy /ínstənsi/ *n.* **1** urgency. **2** pressing nature. [L *instantia*: see INSTANCE]

instant /ínstənt/ *adj.* & *n.* ● *adj.* **1** occurring immediately (*gives an instant result*). **2 a** (of food etc.) ready for immediate use, with little or no preparation. **b** prepared hastily and with little effort (*I have no instant solution*). **3** urgent; pressing. **4** *Commerce* of the current month (*the 6th instant*). **5** *archaic* of the present moment. ● *n.* **1** a precise moment of time, esp. the present (*come here this instant*; *went that instant*; *told you the instant I heard*). **2** a short space of time (*was there in an instant*; *not an instant too soon*). □ **instant replay** the immediate repetition of part of a filmed sports event, often in slow motion. [ME f. F f. L *instare instant-* be present, press upon (as IN-², *stare* stand)]

■ *adj.* **1** instantaneous, immediate, direct, unhesitating, ready, spontaneous, unconsidered, on the spot, overnight; abrupt, precipitate, sudden, swift, speedy, quick. **2a** ready, ready-made, ready-to-serve, precooked, freeze-dried, *attrib.* convenience; ready-to-wear, off-the-peg; ready-mixed. **3** urgent, pressing, compelling, critical, imperative, exigent; crying. ● *n.* **1** moment, second, point (in time), minute; flash, twinkle, twinkling (of an eye), trice, *colloq.* jiffy, mo, sec, *Brit. colloq.* tick. □ **instant replay** (action *or* slow-motion) replay, playback, rerun.

instantaneous /instəntáyniəss/ *adj.* **1** occurring or done in an instant or instantly. **2** *Physics* existing at a particular instant. □□ **instantaneity** /instəntənée-iti/ *n.* **instantaneously** *adv.* **instantaneousness** *n.* [med.L *instantaneus* f. L *instans* (as INSTANT) after eccl.L *momentaneus*]

■ **1** instant, immediate, direct, unhesitating, spontaneous, prompt, ready, on the spot, overnight; abrupt, precipitate, sudden, swift, speedy, quick; unconsidered. □□ **instantaneously** instantly, immediately, at once, (right) now, right *or* straight away, directly, forthwith, this (very) minute *or* second *or* instant *or* moment, here and now, then and there, there and then, on the spot, without more ado, without delay *or* hesitation, unhesitatingly, spontaneously, *tout de suite*, promptly, post-haste, in a wink *or* trice *or* twinkle, in the twinkling of an eye, in two shakes of a lamb's *or* dog's tail, *US* momentarily, in short order, *archaic or joc.* instanter, *colloq.* pronto, in a jiffy, lickety-split, p.d.q., before you can say Jack Robinson *or* knife. **instantaneousness** see *rapidity* (RAPID).

instanter /instántər/ *adv. archaic* or *joc.* immediately; at once. [L f. *instans* (as INSTANT)]

■ see IMMEDIATELY *adv.* 1.

instantiate /instánshiayt/ *v.tr.* represent by an instance. □□ **instantiation** /-áysh'n/ *n.* [L *instantia*: see INSTANCE]

instantly /ínstəntli/ *adv.* **1** immediately; at once. **2** *archaic* urgently; pressingly.

■ **1** see IMMEDIATELY *adv.* 1.

instar /ínstaar/ *n.* a stage in the life of an insect etc. between two periods of moulting. [L, = form]

instate /instáyt/ *v.tr.* (often foll. by *in*) install; establish. [IN-² + STATE]

■ see INSTALL 2.

in statu pupillari /in státyoo pyoopilaári/ *adj.* **1** under guardianship, esp. as a pupil. **2** in a junior position at university; not having a master's degree. [L]

instauration /instawráysh'n/ *n. formal* **1** restoration; renewal. **2** an act of instauration. □□ **instaurator** /ínstawraytər/ *n.* [L *instauratio* f. *instaurare* (as IN-²: cf. RESTORE)]

instead /instéd/ *adv.* **1** (foll. by *of*) as a substitute or alternative to; in place of (*instead of this one*; *stayed instead of going*). **2** as an alternative (*took me instead*) (cf. STEAD). [ME, f. IN + STEAD]

■ **1** (*instead of*) in place of, in lieu of, in a person's *or* a thing's place *or* stead, as an alternative to, as a substitute to *or* for; rather than, in preference to; as opposed to, as contrasted with. **2** as an alternative, rather; by contrast.

instep /ínstep/ *n.* **1** the inner arch of the foot between the toes and the ankle. **2** the part of a shoe etc. fitting over or under this. **3** a thing shaped like an instep. [16th c.: ult. formed as IN-² + STEP, but immed. orig. uncert.]

instigate /ínstigayt/ *v.tr.* **1** bring about by incitement or persuasion; provoke (*who instigated the inquiry?*). **2** (usu. foll. by *to*) urge on, incite (a person etc.) to esp. an evil act. □□ **instigation** /-gáysh'n/ *n.* **instigative** /-gətiv/ *adj.* **instigator** *n.* [L *instigare instigat-*]

■ **1** see PROVOKE 2. **2** see INDUCE 1. □□ **instigation** see *incitement* (INCITE). **instigator** see TROUBLEMAKER.

instil /instíl/ *v.tr.* (*US* **instill**) (**instilled, instilling**) (often foll. by *into*) **1** introduce (a feeling, idea, etc.) into a person's mind etc. gradually. **2** put (a liquid) into something in drops. □□ **instillation** /-láysh'n/ *n.* **instiller** *n.* **instilment** *n.* [L *instillare* (as IN-², *stillare* drop): cf. DISTIL]

■ **1** infuse, insinuate, ingrain, engrain, implant, sow; inspire, inculcate, din. **2** drip, dribble, trickle, sprinkle.

instinct *n.* & *adj.* ● *n.* /ínstingkt/ **1 a** an innate, usu. fixed, pattern of behaviour in most animals in response to certain stimuli. **b** a similar propensity in human beings to act without conscious intention; innate impulsion. **2** (usu. foll. by *for*) unconscious skill; intuition. ● *predic.adj.* /instíngkt/ (foll. by *with*) imbued, filled (with life, beauty, force, etc.). □□ **instinctual** /-stíngktyooəl/ *adj.* **instinctually** /-stíngktyooəli/ *adv.* [ME, = 'impulse', f. L *instinctus* f. *instinguere* incite (as IN-², *stinguere stinct-* prick)]

■ *n.* **1** impulsion, drive, (unconditional) reflex, *Biol.* tropism; nature, character, tendency, proclivity, inclination, propensity, predisposition; subconscious, unconscious, *Psychol.* id. **2** skill, bent, talent, flair, faculty, capacity, aptitude, facility, knack; feel, feeling, empathy, (sixth) sense, sensitivity, understanding, insight, awareness, grasp. ● *predic.adj.* (*instinct with*) replete with, full of; pregnant with, rich in *or* with, alive with. □□ **instinctual** see INSTINCTIVE.

instinctive /instíngktiv/ *adj.* **1** relating to or prompted by instinct. **2** apparently unconscious or automatic (*an instinctive reaction*). □□ **instinctively** *adv.*
■ **1** instinctual, natural, unconditioned; innate, native, inborn, inbred, inherent, intrinsic, congenital, constitutional, essential, fundamental, elementary, structural, organic. **2** unconscious, subconscious, automatic, mechanical, knee-jerk, spontaneous, immediate, involuntary, irrational, intuitional, intuitive; reflex, visceral, *attrib.* gut.

institute /instityōōt/ *n.* & *v.* ● *n.* **1 a** a society or organization for the promotion of science, education, etc. **b** a building used by an institute. **2** *Law* (usu. in *pl.*) a digest of the elements of a legal subject (*Institutes of Justinian*). **3** a principle of instruction. **4** *US* a brief course of instruction for teachers etc. ● *v.tr.* **1** establish; found. **2 a** initiate (an inquiry etc.). **b** begin (proceedings) in a court. **3** (usu. foll. by *to*, *into*) appoint (a person) as a cleric in a church etc. [ME f. L *institutum* design, precept, neut. past part. of *instituere* establish, arrange, teach (as IN-[2], *statuere* set up)]
■ *n.* **1** establishment, institution, foundation, society, company, organization, association, league, alliance, guild; school, college, academy, university, seminary; hospital, clinic, medical *or* health centre; sanatorium, (nursing) home, asylum, *US* sanitarium. **3** see PRINCIPLE *n.* 1. ● *v.* **1** establish, found, create, form, set up, inaugurate, launch, organize. **2** initiate, start, begin, set up, inaugurate, originate, pioneer, introduce, launch, usher in, instigate, set in motion, get going, get under way, *formal* commence. **3** install, induct, appoint, ordain, frock.

institution /instityōōsh'n/ *n.* **1** the act or an instance of instituting. **2 a** a society or organization founded esp. for charitable, religious, educational, or social purposes. **b** a building used by an institution. **3** an established law, practice, or custom. **4** *colloq.* (of a person, a custom, etc.) a familiar object. **5** the establishment of a cleric etc. in a church. [ME f. OF f. L *institutio -onis* (as INSTITUTE)]
■ **1** establishment, formation, creation, foundation, inauguration, launch, organization; initiation, start, beginning, origination, introduction, instigation, *formal* commencement. **2** see INSTITUTE *n.* 1. **3** custom, tradition, habit, practice, usage, routine, order (of the day), code (of practice), convention, principle, rule, regulation, law; doctrine, dogma, (received) wisdom. **4** fixture, regular, *habitué*, *colloq.* part of the furniture. **5** installation, induction, appointment, ordination, *archaic* sacring.

institutional /instityōōshən'l/ *adj.* **1** of or like an institution. **2** typical of institutions, esp. in being regimented or unimaginative (*the food was dreadfully institutional*). **3** (of religion) expressed or organized through institutions (churches etc.). **4** *US* (of advertising) intended to create prestige rather than immediate sales. □□ **institutionalism** *n.* **institutionally** *adv.*

institutionalize /instityōōshənəlīz/ *v.tr.* (also **-ise**) **1** (as **institutionalized** *adj.*) (of a prisoner, a long-term patient, etc.) made apathetic and dependent after a long period in an institution. **2** place or keep (a person) in an institution. **3** convert into an institution; make institutional. □□ **institutionalization** /-záysh'n/ *n.*
■ **2** see *put away* 3 (PUT[1]).

Inst.P. *abbr.* (in the UK) Institute of Physics.

instruct /instrúkt/ *v.tr.* **1** (often foll. by *in*) teach (a person) a subject etc. (*instructed her in French*). **2** (usu. foll. by *to* + infin.) direct; command (*instructed him to fill in the hole*). **3** (often foll. by *of*, or *that* etc. + clause) inform (a person) of a fact etc. **4** *Brit.* **a** (of a client or solicitor) give information to (a solicitor or counsel). **b** authorize (a solicitor or counsel) to act for one. [ME f. L *instruere instruct-* build, teach (as IN-[2], *struere* pile up)]
■ **1** teach, tutor, give lessons *or* classes; educate, school, train, drill, coach, prime, ground; guide, inform, prepare, edify, enlighten; indoctrinate, imbue. **2** direct, enjoin, counsel, advise, recommend, require, charge, tell, order, command, *archaic or literary* bid; give instructions, summon. **3** see INFORM *v.* 1. **4** authorize, appoint, *Brit. Law* brief.

instruction /instrúksh'n/ *n.* **1** (often in *pl.*) a direction; an order (*gave him his instructions*). **2** teaching; education (*took a course of instruction*). **3** *Law* (in *pl.*) directions to a solicitor or counsel. **4** *Computing* a direction in a computer program defining and effecting an operation. □□ **instructional** *adj.* [ME f. OF f. LL *instructio -onis* (as INSTRUCT)]
■ **1** direction, directive, bidding, enjoinment, injunction, advice, guidance, counsel, precept, recommendation, guideline, brief, prescription, requirement, order, command, dictate. **2** teaching, tuition, tutelage, education, schooling, training, coaching, grounding, *Mil.* drill; lesson(s), class(es), apprenticeship; guidance, information, preparation, edification, enlightenment; indoctrination, inculcation.

instructive /instrúktiv/ *adj.* tending to instruct; conveying a lesson; enlightening (*found the experience instructive*). □□ **instructively** *adv.* **instructiveness** *n.*
■ didactic, prescriptive, educational, instructional; informative, informational, informatory, edifying, enlightening, illuminating, elucidatory, elucidative, explanatory, revealing, helpful.

instructor /instrúktər/ *n.* (*fem.* **instructress** /-strúktriss/) **1** a person who instructs; a teacher, demonstrator, etc. **2** *US* a university teacher ranking below professor. □□ **instructorship** *n.*
■ **1** educator, preceptor, teacher, tutor, trainer, coach, demonstrator; professor, lecturer, don, schoolteacher, schoolmaster, schoolmistress, master, mistress, governess, *archaic* doctor, *archaic or derog.* pedagogue; mentor, adviser, guide, counsellor.

instrument /instrəmənt/ *n.* & *v.* ● *n.* **1** a tool or implement, esp. for delicate or scientific work. **2** (in full **musical instrument**) a device for producing musical sounds by vibration, wind, percussion, etc. **3 a** a thing used in performing an action (*the meeting was an instrument in his success*). **b** a person made use of (*is merely their instrument*). **4** a measuring-device, esp. in an aeroplane, serving to determine its position in darkness etc. **5** a formal, esp. legal, document. ● *v.tr.* **1** arrange (music) for instruments. **2** equip with instruments (for measuring, recording, controlling, etc.). □ **instrument board** (or **panel**) a surface, esp. in a car or aeroplane, containing the dials etc. of measuring-devices. [ME f. OF *instrument* or L *instrumentum* (as INSTRUCT)]
■ *n.* **1** implement, tool, device, apparatus, utensil, appliance, contrivance, mechanism, gadget, doodah, *Brit.* gubbins, *colloq.* widget, whatsit, *US colloq.* hickey, *derog. or joc.* contraption, *sl.* jigger, gismo; what-d'you-call-it, what's-its (*or* -his)-name, *colloq.* thingumabob, thingumajig, thingummy, thingy, whatnot. **3 a** agency, means, instrumentality, way, mechanism, *colloq.* wherewithal; factor, agent, (prime) mover, catalyst. **b** pawn, puppet, tool, cat's-paw, dummy; factotum, hack, drudge, *colloq.* stooge, dogsbody, *esp. US sl.* gofer. **4** gauge, meter, dial, indicator, monitor, (flight-)recorder, log, black box. **5** contract, (legal) document, (written) agreement, pact, compact, paper, certificate. ● *v.* **1** score, arrange, orchestrate. **2** equip, fit out, kit out, rig out.
□ **instrument board** (or **panel**) instrumentation, dash, dashboard, panel, control panel; display.

instrumental /instrəmént'l/ *adj.* & *n.* ● *adj.* **1** (usu. foll. by *to*, *in*, or *in* + verbal noun) serving as an instrument or means (*was instrumental in finding the money*). **2** (of music) performed on instruments, without singing (cf. VOCAL). **3** of, or arising from, an instrument (*instrumental error*). **4** *Gram.* of or in the instrumental. ● *n.* **1** a piece of music performed by instruments, not by the voice. **2** *Gram.* the case of nouns and pronouns (and words in grammatical agreement with them) indicating a means or instrument. □□ **instrumentalist** /-méntəlist/ *n.* **instrumentality** /-tálliti/ *n.* **instrumentally** *adv.* [ME f. F f. med.L *instrumentalis* (as INSTRUMENT)]

■ *adj.* **1** of service, influential, contributory, agential, subservient; catalytic, helpful, useful, conducive, effective, efficacious, beneficial, valuable, advantageous; significant, important.

instrumentation /instrəmentáysh'n/ *n.* **1 a** the arrangement or composition of music for a particular group of musical instruments. **b** the instruments used in any one piece of music. **2 a** the design, provision, or use of instruments in industry, science, etc. **b** such instruments collectively. [F f. *instrumenter* (as INSTRUMENT)]

■ **1 a** see ARRANGEMENT 5.

insubordinate /insəbórdinət/ *adj.* disobedient; rebellious. □□ **insubordinately** *adv.* **insubordination** /-náysh'n/ *n.*

■ disobedient, recalcitrant, defiant, contumacious, uncooperative, fractious, *Brit.* unbiddable; rebellious, refractory, mutinous, seditious, insurgent, insurrectional, insurrectionary, revolutionary; perverse, contrary, cross-grained, awkward, obstinate, stubborn, pigheaded, intractable, naughty, unruly, obstreperous, *Brit. colloq.* stroppy, *sl.* Bolshie. □□ **insubordination** see REBELLION.

insubstantial /insəbstánsh'l, -staánsh'l/ *adj.* **1** lacking solidity or substance. **2** not real. □□ **insubstantiality** /-shiálliti/ *n.* **insubstantially** *adv.* [LL *insubstantialis* (as IN-[1], SUBSTANTIAL)]

■ **1** unsubstantial, flimsy, frail, weak, feeble, fragile, tenuous, meagre, slight, paltry, puny, shaky, tinny, rickety, ramshackle, jerry-built, cardboard, *attrib.* pasteboard, *colloq. usu. derog.* itsy-bitsy; thin, light, fine, gossamer, wispy, fluffy, diaphanous, threadbare; airy, aeriform, frothy, *colloq.* airy-fairy. **2** unsubstantial, unreal, false, empty, illusory, illusive, imaginary, fanciful, fantastic, visionary, dreamlike, hallucinatory, chimerical, phantom, phantasmal, phantasmic; immaterial, intangible, impalpable, incorporeal, bodiless, spiritual, ethereal, airy.

insufferable /insúffərəb'l/ *adj.* **1** intolerable. **2** unbearably arrogant or conceited etc. □□ **insufferableness** *n.* **insufferably** *adv.*

■ **1** intolerable, unbearable, insupportable, unsupportable, unendurable; unacceptable, *colloq.* too much, *Brit. colloq.* a bit thick. **2** arrogant, conceited, objectionable, unpleasant, obnoxious, awful, dreadful, unspeakable, *colloq.* impossible, ghastly.

insufficiency /insəfishənsi/ *n.* **1** the condition of being insufficient. **2** *Med.* the inability of an organ to perform its normal function (*renal insufficiency*). [ME f. LL *insufficientia* (as INSUFFICIENT)]

■ **1** see LACK *n.*

insufficient /insəfish'nt/ *adj.* not sufficient; inadequate. □□ **insufficiently** *adv.* [ME f. OF f. LL *insufficiens* (as IN-[1], SUFFICIENT)]

■ deficient, skimpy, scanty, scant, scarce, meagre, thin, too little, not enough, inadequate; unsatisfactory, disappointing, unacceptable, no good, not good enough.

insufflate /insəflayt/ *v.tr.* **1** *Med.* **a** blow or breathe (air, gas, powder, etc.) into a cavity of the body etc. **b** treat (the nose etc.) in this way. **2** *Theol.* blow or breathe on (a person) to symbolize spiritual influence. □□ **insufflation** /-fláysh'n/ *n.* [LL *insufflare insufflat-* (as IN-[2], *sufflare* blow upon)]

insufflator /insəflaytər/ *n.* **1** a device for blowing powder on to a surface in order to make fingerprints visible. **2** an instrument for insufflating.

insular /insyoolər/ *adj.* **1 a** of or like an island. **b** separated or remote, like an island. **2** ignorant of or indifferent to cultures, peoples, etc., outside one's own experience; narrow-minded. **3** of a British variant of Latin handwriting current in the Middle Ages. **4** (of climate) equable. □□ **insularism** *n.* **insularity** /-lárriti/ *n.* **insularly** *adv.* [LL *insularis* (as INSULATE)]

■ **2** see PROVINCIAL *adj.* 2. □□ **insularity** see PROVINCIALISM 1.

insulate /insyoolayt/ *v.tr.* **1** prevent the passage of electricity, heat, or sound from (a thing, room, etc.) by interposing non-conductors. **2** detach (a person or thing) from its surroundings; isolate. **3** *archaic* make (land) into an island. □ **insulating tape** an adhesive tape used to cover exposed electrical wires etc. □□ **insulation** /-láysh'n/ *n.* [L *insula* island + -ATE[3]]

■ **1** protect, shield, isolate; wrap, lag, cover. **2** detach, separate, isolate, segregate, set *or* keep apart, sequester, quarantine; shelter, cushion.

insulator /insyoolaytər/ *n.* **1** a thing or substance used for insulation against electricity, heat, or sound. **2** an insulating device to support telegraph wires etc. **3** a device preventing contact between electrical conductors.

insulin /insyoolin/ *n. Biochem.* a hormone produced in the pancreas by the islets of Langerhans, regulating the amount of glucose in the blood and the lack of which causes diabetes. [L *insula* island + -IN]

insult *v.* & *n.* ● *v.tr.* /insúlt/ **1** speak to or treat with scornful abuse or indignity. **2** offend the self-respect or modesty of. ● *n.* /insult/ **1** an insulting remark or action. **2** *colloq.* something so worthless or contemptible as to be offensive. **3** *Med.* **a** an agent causing damage to the body. **b** such damage. □□ **insulter** *n.* **insultingly** *adv.* [F *insulte* or L *insultare* (as IN-[2], *saltare* frequent. of *salire salt-* leap)]

■ *v.* **1** abuse, malign, revile, calumniate, call a person names, slander, libel, defame, vilify, bespatter, dishonour, be rude to, *colloq.* put down, *sl.* slag (off), *esp. US sl.* dump on; snub, cut (dead), spurn, shun, ignore, give the cold shoulder (to). **2** offend, give offence, affront, outrage, scandalize, injure, hurt, slight, pique, displease, chagrin, hurt a person's feelings, tread on a person's toes, humiliate, *colloq.* miff, put a person's nose out of joint. ● *n.* **1** offence, affront, indignity, discourtesy, rudeness, dishonour, outrage; vilification, calumniation, abuse, slander, calumny, libel, defamation, slur, *sl.* verbal; slight, snub, cut, rebuff, slap in the face, *colloq.* put-down.

insuperable /insóópərəb'l, insyóó-/ *adj.* **1** (of a barrier) impossible to surmount. **2** (of a difficulty etc.) impossible to overcome. □□ **insuperability** /-bílliti/ *n.* **insuperably** *adv.* [ME f. OF *insuperable* or L *insuperabilis* (as IN-[1], SUPERABLE)]

■ **1** see INVINCIBLE.

insupportable /insəpórtəb'l/ *adj.* **1** unable to be endured. **2** unjustifiable. □□ **insupportableness** *n.* **insupportably** *adv.* [F (as IN-[1], SUPPORT)]

■ **1** see INSUFFERABLE 1. **2** see UNTENABLE.

insurance /inshóórənss/ *n.* **1** the act or an instance of insuring. **2 a** a sum paid for this; a premium. **b** a sum paid out as compensation for theft, damage, loss, etc. **3** = *insurance policy*. **4** a measure taken to provide for a possible contingency (*take an umbrella as insurance*). □ **insurance agent** *Brit.* a person employed to collect premiums door to door. **insurance company** *Brit.* a company engaged in the business of insurance. **insurance policy** *Brit.* **1** a contract of insurance. **2** a document detailing such a policy and constituting a contract. **insurance stamp** *Brit. hist.* a stamp certifying the payment of a sum, usu. paid weekly, for National Insurance. [earlier *ensurance* f. OF *enseürance* (as ENSURE)]

■ **1** assurance, indemnity, indemnification, guarantee, guaranty, warranty, bond, security, protection, cover. **2 a** premium; price, fee, charge; outlay, expenditure. **b** compensation, damages, reparation, reimbursement, recompense, redress. **4** precaution, provision, safety measure, safeguard, cover.

insure /inshóor/ *v.tr.* **1** (often foll. by *against*; also *absol.*) secure the payment of a sum of money in the event of loss or damage to (property, life, a person, etc.) by regular payments or premiums (*insured the house for £100,000; we have insured against flood damage*) (cf. ASSURANCE). **2** (of the owner of a property, an insurance company, etc.) secure the payment of (a sum of money) in this way. **3** (usu. foll. by *against*) provide for (a possible contingency) (*insured themselves against the rain by taking umbrellas*). **4** *US* = ENSURE. □□ **insurable** *adj.* **insurability** /-shóorəbílliti/ *n.* [ME, var. of ENSURE]
■ **1** see COVER *v.* 7. **2** see UNDERWRITE 1.

insured /inshóord/ *adj.* & *n.* ● *adj.* covered by insurance. ● *n.* (usu. prec. by *the*) a person etc. covered by insurance.

insurer /inshóorər/ *n.* **1** a person or company offering insurance policies for premiums; an underwriter. **2** a person who takes out insurance.

insurgent /insúrjənt/ *adj.* & *n.* ● *adj.* **1** rising in active revolt. **2** (of the sea etc.) rushing in. ● *n.* a rebel; a revolutionary. □□ **insurgence** *n.* **insurgency** *n.* (*pl.* **-ies**). [F f. L *insurgere insurrect-* (as IN-[2], *surgere* rise)]
■ *adj.* **1** see REBELLIOUS 1. ● *n.* see REBEL. □□ **insurgence, insurgency** see REBELLION.

insurmountable /ínsərmówntəb'l/ *adj.* unable to be surmounted or overcome. □□ **insurmountably** *adv.*
■ see INEXTRICABLE 2, 3.

insurrection /ínsəréksh'n/ *n.* a rising in open resistance to established authority; a rebellion. □□ **insurrectionary** *adj.* **insurrectionist** *n.* [ME f. OF f. LL *insurrectio -onis* (as INSURGENT)]
■ see REBELLION. □□ **insurrectionary** see REBELLIOUS 1. **insurrectionist** see REBEL.

insusceptible /insəséptib'l/ *adj.* (usu. foll. by *of*, *to*) not susceptible (of treatment, to an influence, etc.). □□ **insusceptibility** /-bílliti/ *n.*
■ see IMMUNE 1a. □□ **insusceptibility** see IMMUNITY 1.

in-swinger /inswingər/ *n.* **1** *Cricket* a ball bowled with a swing towards the batsman. **2** *Football* a pass or kick that sends the ball curving towards the goal.

int. *abbr.* **1** interior. **2** internal. **3** international.

intact /intákt/ *adj.* **1** entire; unimpaired. **2** untouched. □□ **intactness** *n.* [ME f. L *intactus* (as IN-[1], *tactus* past part. of *tangere* touch)]
■ **1** whole, entire, complete, integral, solid, (all) in one piece, undivided, uncut, together, unabridged; unimpaired, perfect, flawless, sound, unbroken, undiminished. **2** untouched, inviolate, unblemished, unscathed, uninjured, unharmed, undamaged, unsullied, undefiled, untainted; maiden, virgin.

intagliated /intálliaytid/ *adj.* decorated with surface carving. [It. *intagliato* past part. of *intagliare* cut into]

intaglio /intálliō, -taáliō/ *n.* & *v.* ● *n.* (*pl.* **-os**) **1** a gem with an incised design (cf. CAMEO). **2** an engraved design. **3** a carving, esp. incised, in hard material. **4** a process of printing from an engraved design. ● *v.tr.* (**-oes, -oed**) **1** engrave (material) with a sunk pattern or design. **2** engrave (such a design). [It. (as INTAGLIATED)]

intake /íntayk/ *n.* **1 a** the action of taking in. **b** an instance of this. **2** a number or the amount taken in or received. **3** a place where water is taken into a channel or pipe from a river, or fuel or air enters an engine etc. **4** an airway into a mine. **5** *N.Engl.* land reclaimed from a moor etc.
■ **2** see DIET[1] *n.* 1.

intangible /intánjib'l/ *adj.* & *n.* ● *adj.* **1** unable to be touched; not solid. **2** unable to be grasped mentally. ● *n.* something that cannot be precisely measured or assessed. □□ **intangibility** /-bílliti/ *n.* **intangibly** *adv.* [F *intangible* or med.L *intangibilis* (as IN-[1], TANGIBLE)]
■ *adj.* **1** untouchable, impalpable, abstract, unsubstantial, insubstantial, immaterial, ethereal, spiritual, vaporous, airy, misty, incorporeal, bodiless, weightless. **2** incomprehensible, inconceivable, unintelligible, unfathomable, imponderable, inestimable, impenetrable; subtle, rarefied, vague, obscure, dim, imprecise, indefinite, shadowy, fleeting, elusive, evanescent. ● *n.* imponderable; abstract; abstraction.

intarsia /intaársiə/ *n.* the craft of using wood inlays, esp. as practised in 15th-c. Italy. [It. *intarsio*]

integer /íntijər/ *n.* **1** a whole number. **2** a thing complete in itself. [L (adj.) = untouched, whole: see ENTIRE]
■ **1** see NUMBER *n.* 1.

integral *adj.* & *n.* ● *adj.* /íntigrəl, *disp.* intégrəl/ **1 a** of a whole or necessary to the completeness of a whole. **b** forming a whole (*integral design*). **c** whole, complete. **2** *Math.* **a** of or denoted by an integer. **b** involving only integers, esp. as coefficients of a function. ● *n.* /íntigrəl/ *Math.* **1** a quantity of which a given function is the derivative, either containing an indeterminate additive constant (**indefinite integral**), or calculated as the difference between its values at specified limits (**definite integral**). **2** a function satisfying a given differential equation. □ **integral calculus** mathematics concerned with finding integrals, their properties and application, etc. (cf. *differential calculus*). □□ **integrality** /-grálliti/ *n.* **integrally** *adv.* [LL *integralis* (as INTEGER)]
■ *adj.* **1 a** essential, necessary, indispensable; basic, elementary, elemental, fundamental, intrinsic, inherent, organic, built-in. **b, c** whole, complete, entire, intact, (all) in one piece; in-line.

integrand /íntigrand/ *n.* *Math.* a function that is to be integrated. [L *integrandus* gerundive of *integrare*: see INTEGRATE]

integrant /íntigrənt/ *adj.* (of parts) making up a whole; component. [F *intégrant* f. *intégrer* (as INTEGRATE)]

integrate *v.* & *adj.* ● *v.* /íntigrayt/ **1** *tr.* **a** combine (parts) into a whole. **b** complete (an imperfect thing) by the addition of parts. **2** *tr.* & *intr.* bring or come into equal participation in or membership of society, a school, etc. **3** *tr.* desegregate, esp. racially (a school etc.). **4** *tr.* *Math.* **a** find the integral of. **b** (as **integrated** *adj.*) indicating the mean value or total sum of (temperature, an area, etc.). ● *adj.* /íntigrət/ **1** made up of parts. **2** whole; complete. □ **integrated circuit** *Electronics* a small chip etc. of material replacing several separate components in a conventional electrical circuit. □□ **integrable** /íntigrəb'l/ *adj.* **integrability** /íntigrəbílliti/ *n.* **integrative** /íntigrətiv/ *adj.* [L *integrare integrat-* make whole (as INTEGER)]
■ *v.* **1–3** unite, unify, bring *or* put together, assemble, pool, coordinate; merge, blend, mix, mingle, compound, combine, coalesce, *literary* commingle; amalgamate, consolidate, embody, incorporate, desegregate; fuse, bind, bond, join, connect, knit, link, mesh.

integration /íntigráysh'n/ *n.* **1** the act or an instance of integrating. **2** the intermixing of persons previously segregated. **3** *Psychol.* the combination of the diverse elements of perception etc. in a personality. □□ **integrationist** *n.* [L *integratio* (as INTEGRATE)]
■ **1** see *amalgamation* (AMALGAMATE).

integrator /íntigraytər/ *n.* **1** an instrument for indicating or registering the total amount or mean value of some physical quality, as area, temperature, etc. **2** a person or thing that integrates.

integrity /intégriti/ *n.* **1** moral uprightness; honesty. **2** wholeness; soundness. [ME f. F *intégrité* or L *integritas* (as INTEGER)]
■ **1** rectitude, uprightness, righteousness, decency, honour, principle, morality, goodness, virtue, incorruptibility; probity, purity, honesty, veracity, trustworthiness. **2** wholeness, entirety, totality, completeness, unity, oneness, togetherness; soundness, coherence, consistency, validity.

integument /intégyoomənt/ *n.* a natural outer covering, as a skin, husk, rind, etc. □□ **integumental** /- mént'l/ *adj.* **integumentary** /-méntəri/ *adj.* [L *integumentum* f. *integere* (as IN-[2], *tegere* cover)]

■ see SKIN *n.* 4.

intellect /intilekt/ *n.* **1 a** the faculty of reasoning, knowing, and thinking, as distinct from feeling. **b** the understanding or mental powers (of a particular person etc.) (*his intellect is not great*). **2 a** a clever or knowledgeable person. **b** the intelligentsia regarded collectively (*the combined intellect of four universities*). [ME f. OF *intellect* or L *intellectus* understanding (as INTELLIGENT)]

■ **1** rationality, reason, reasoning, understanding, insight, acumen, penetration, perspicacity, perception, percipience, discernment, judgement; intelligence, mind, brainpower, brain(s), braininess, wit(s), head, *archaic* headpiece, *colloq.* nous, grey matter, *sl.* savvy, loaf. **2** see INTELLECTUAL *n.*

intellection /intiléksh'n/ *n.* the action or process of understanding (opp. IMAGINATION). □□ **intellective** *adj.* [ME f. med.L *intellectio* (as INTELLIGENT)]

intellectual /intiléktyooəl/ *adj.* & *n.* ● *adj.* **1** of or appealing to the intellect. **2** possessing a high level of understanding or intelligence; cultured. **3** requiring, or given to the exercise of, the intellect. ● *n.* a person possessing a highly developed intellect. □□ **intellectuality** /-léktyoo-álliti/ *n.* **intellectualize** /-léktyooəlīz/ *v.tr.* & *intr.* (also **-ise**). **intellectually** *adv.* [ME f. L *intellectualis* (as INTELLECT)]

■ *adj.* **1** mental, cerebral, rational; abstract, noetic, academic, speculative, theoretical. **2** intelligent, insightful, analytical, perspicacious, percipient, clever, brainy, bright, smart, sharp, *US sl.* savvy; thoughtful, academic, bookish, scholarly, donnish, scholastic, *derog.* Bloomsbury; cultured, erudite, learned, (well-)educated, *colloq.* highbrow. **3** profound, abstract, thought-provoking, *colloq.* highbrow; deep, unfathomable, abstruse, intricate, knotty, involved, tricky, difficult, hard. ● *n.* thinker, intellect, mastermind, genius, *colloq.* egghead, highbrow, brain, know-all, *esp. Brit. colloq.* boffin, *derog.* bluestocking; scholar, academician, professor, savant, sage, guru, polymath, pundit, authority.

intellectualism /intiléktyooəliz'm/ *n.* **1** the exercise, esp. when excessive, of the intellect at the expense of the emotions. **2** *Philos.* the theory that knowledge is wholly or mainly derived from pure reason. □□ **intellectualist** *n.*

intelligence /intéllijənss/ *n.* **1 a** the intellect; the understanding. **b** (of a person or an animal) quickness of understanding; wisdom. **2 a** the collection of information, esp. of military or political value. **b** people employed in this. **c** information; news. **3** an intelligent or rational being. □ **intelligence department** a usu. government department engaged in collecting esp. secret information. **intelligence quotient** a number denoting the ratio of a person's intelligence to the normal or average. **intelligence test** a test designed to measure intelligence rather than acquired knowledge. □□ **intelligential** /-jénsh'l/ *adj.* [ME f. OF f. L *intelligentia* (as INTELLIGENT)]

■ **1 a** see INTELLECT 1. **b** cleverness, astuteness, brightness, smartness, sharpness, keenness, acuteness, acuity, incisiveness, quickness, alertness, quick-wittedness, shrewdness, wit, brainpower, IQ; (common) sense, mother *or* native wit, *colloq.* nous; wisdom, sagacity, sageness, acumen, insight, perspicacity, perception, percipience, perspicaciousness, understanding, discernment, judgement, acumen, penetration, *literary* sapience. **2 a** espionage, spying. **b** secret service, *Brit.* MI5, MI6, *US* CIA; resident(s), residency. **c** see INFORMATION 1.

intelligent /intéllijənt/ *adj.* **1** having or showing intelligence, esp. of a high level. **2** quick of mind; clever. **3 a** (of a device or machine) able to vary its behaviour in response to varying situations and requirements and past experience. **b** (esp. of a computer terminal) having its own data-processing capability; incorporating a microprocessor (opp. DUMB). □□ **intelligently** *adv.* [L *intelligere intellect-* understand (as INTER-, *legere* gather, pick out, read)]

■ **1** rational, cerebral, intellectual, analytical, logical, insightful, discerning, understanding, aware, receptive. **2** bright, brilliant, smart, clever, astute, quick, quick-witted, keen, sharp, sharp-witted, alert, shrewd, knowing, canny, perspicacious, perceptive, percipient, apt, gifted, brainy, *archaic* apprehensive; wise, sage, sagacious, discerning, judicious, sensible, informed, educated, enlightened, knowledgeable, *literary* sapient, *US sl.* savvy.

intelligentsia /intéllijéntsiə/ *n.* **1** the class of intellectuals regarded as possessing culture and political initiative. **2** people doing intellectual work; intellectuals. [Russ. f. Pol. *inteligencja* f. L *intelligentia* (as INTELLIGENT)]

■ intellectuals, literati, illuminati, brains (*US*) brain trust; see also INTELLECTUAL *n.*

intelligible /intéllijib'l/ *adj.* **1** (often foll. by *to*) able to be understood; comprehensible. **2** *Philos.* able to be understood only by the intellect, not by the senses. □□ **intelligibility** /-bílliti/ *n.* **intelligibly** *adv.* [L *intelligibilis* (as INTELLIGENT)]

■ **1** understandable, comprehensible, perspicuous, apprehensible, coherent, articulate, rational, logical, clear, plain, lucid, distinct, unambiguous; accountable, fathomable, decipherable, decodable, legible, readable, audible; (*be intelligible*) make sense, fall into place, hang together, *colloq.* add up, figure, click.

Intelpost /intelpōst/ *n.* the international electronic transmission of messages and graphics by fax, telex, etc. [*Int*ernational *El*ectronic *Post*]

Intelsat /intelsat/ *n.* an international organization of countries operating a system of commercial communication satellites. [*Int*ernational *Tel*ecommunications *Sat*ellite Consortium]

intemperate /intémpərət/ *adj.* **1** (of a person, conduct, or speech) immoderate; unbridled; violent (*used intemperate language*). **2 a** given to excessive indulgence in alcohol. **b** excessively indulgent in one's appetites. □□ **intemperance** *n.* **intemperately** *adv.* **intemperateness** *n.* [ME f. L *intemperatus* (as IN-[1], TEMPERATE)]

■ **1** see IMMODERATE. **2 b** see SELF-INDULGENT. □□ **intemperance** see EXCESS *n.* 4a. **intemperately** see FAST[1] *adj.* 9. **intemperateness** see *prodigality* (PRODIGAL).

intend /inténd/ *v.tr.* **1** have as one's purpose; propose (*we intend to go; we intend going; we intend that it shall be done*). **2** (usu. foll. by *for, as*) design or destine (a person or a thing) (*I intend him to go; I intend it as a warning*). **3** mean (*what does he intend by that?*). **4** (in *passive*; foll. by *for*) **a** be meant for a person to have or use etc. (*they are intended for the children*). **b** be meant to represent (*the picture is intended for you*). **5** (as **intending** *adj.*) who intends to be (*an intending visitor*). [ME *entende, intende* f. OF *entendre, intendre* f. L *intendere intent-* or *intens-* strain, direct, purpose (as IN-[2], *tendere* stretch, tend)]

■ **1, 2** have (it) in mind *or* in view, be going, plan, set out, aim, purpose, design, mean, contemplate, think, propose, *colloq.* plan on; resolve, determine, destine, will. **3** mean, signify, indicate, express, imply, suggest, intimate, drive at, get at, refer to, denote, allude to, hint (at). **4a** (*intended for*) for, meant for, designed for, destined for, supposed to be for, with a person *or* a thing in mind. **5** (**intending**) prospective, aspirant, aspiring, *often derog.* would-be.

intendant /inténdənt/ *n.* **1** (esp. as a title of foreign officials) a superintendent or manager of a department of public business etc. **2** the administrator of an opera house or theatre. □□ **intendancy** *n.* [F f. L *intendere* (as INTEND)]

intended /inténdid/ *adj.* & *n.* ● *adj.* **1** done on purpose; intentional. **2** designed, meant. ● *n. colloq.* the person one intends to marry; one's fiancé or fiancée (*is this your intended?*). □□ **intendedly** *adv.*

■ *adj.* **1** see INTENTIONAL. **2** see *destined* (DESTINE). ● *n.* see FIANCÉ.

intense /inténss/ *adj.* (**intenser, intensest**) **1** (of a quality etc.) existing in a high degree; violent; forceful (*intense* *cold*). **2** (of a person) feeling, or apt to feel, strong emotion (*very intense about her music*). **3** (of a feeling or action etc.) extreme (*intense joy*; *intense thought*). ▫▫ **intensely** *adv.* **intenseness** *n.* [ME f. OF *intens* or L *intensus* (as INTEND)]

▪ **1, 3** extreme, excessive, immoderate, intemperate, overpowering, acute, serious, severe, sharp, deep, profound, high, great, heavy, deadly, *colloq.* terrific, *Brit. colloq.* chronic; strong, fierce, harsh, violent, towering, consuming, powerful, forceful, concentrated, exquisite, hard, vehement, furious, frantic, fervent, fervid, heated, ardent, burning, torrid, unmitigated, *colloq.* flaming, *iron.* glorious; glaring, bright, full, vivid, acid. **2** emotional, passionate, impassioned, vehement, ardent, fervent, fervid, effusive, demonstrative, sentimental, *literary* perfervid; hysterical, over-emotional, obsessive, *colloq.* manic, neurotic, *sl.* nutty, nuts; temperamental, high(ly)-strung, tense, touchy, sensitive, testy, *colloq.* uptight. ▫▫ **intenseness** see INTENSITY 1.

intensifier /inténsifīər/ *n.* **1** a person or thing that intensifies. **2** *Gram.* = INTENSIVE *n.*

intensify /inténsifī/ *v.* (**-ies**, **-ied**) **1** *tr.* & *intr.* make or become intense or more intense. **2** *tr. Photog.* increase the opacity of (a negative). ▫▫ **intensification** /-fikáysh'n/ *n.*

▪ **1** strengthen, reinforce, deepen; increase, inflate, magnify, enlarge, amplify, augment; extend, develop, build (up), *colloq.* boost; enhance, heighten, sharpen, whet, concentrate, focus, emphasize, point up, highlight; quicken, speed up, accelerate, escalate, step up, rev up, tone up, *sl.* crank up; heat (up), warm up, *Brit. colloq.* hot up; double, redouble, multiply, proliferate; enliven, brighten, jazz up; exacerbate, aggravate, inflame, worsen, add to, stir up, fire up, excite, fan, fuel, *colloq.* blow up.

intension /inténsh'n/ *n.* **1** *Logic* the internal content of a concept. **2** *formal* the intensity, or high degree, of a quality. **3** *formal* the strenuous exertion of the mind or will. ▫▫ **intensional** *adj.* **intensionally** *adv.* [L *intensio* (as INTEND)]

intensity /inténsiti/ *n.* (*pl.* **-ies**) **1** the quality or an instance of being intense. **2** esp. *Physics* the measurable amount of some quality, e.g. force, brightness, a magnetic field, etc.

▪ **1** intenseness, extremeness, extremity, acuteness, seriousness, severity, sharpness, depth, profoundness, profundity, height, greatness, heaviness, strength, fierceness, ferocity, harshness, violence, power, force, forcefulness, vehemence, fervency, fervour, ardour, ardency, torridity; emotion, emotionality, passion, passionateness, devotion. **2** concentration, strength, force, power, potency, energy; brightness, vividness, brilliance, brilliancy, richness.

intensive /inténsiv/ *adj.* & *n.* ● *adj.* **1** thorough, vigorous; directed to a single point, area, or subject (*intensive study*; *intensive bombardment*). **2** of or relating to intensity as opp. to extent; producing intensity. **3** serving to increase production in relation to costs (*intensive farming methods*). **4** (usu. in *comb.*) *Econ.* making much use of (*a labour-intensive industry*). **5** *Gram.* (of an adjective, adverb, etc.) expressing intensity; giving force, as *really* in *my feet are really cold.* ● *n. Gram.* an intensive adjective, adverb, etc. ▫ **intensive care** medical treatment with constant monitoring etc. of a dangerously ill patient (also (with hyphen) *attrib.*: *intensive-care unit*). ▫▫ **intensively** *adv.* **intensiveness** *n.* [F *intensif -ive* or med.L *intensivus* (as INTEND)]

▪ *adj.* **1** thorough, thoroughgoing, concentrated, exhaustive, in-depth; vigorous, energetic, dynamic, all-out; rigorous, painstaking, meticulous, assiduous, detailed.

intent /intént/ *n.* & *adj.* ● *n.* (usu. without article) intention; a purpose (*with intent to defraud*; *my intent to reach the top*; *with evil intent*). ● *adj.* **1** (usu. foll. by *on*) **a** resolved; bent; determined (*was intent on succeeding*). **b** attentively occupied (*intent on his books*). **2** (esp. of a look) earnest; eager; meaningful. ▫ **to all intents and purposes** practically; virtually. ▫▫ **intently** *adv.* **intentness** *n.* [ME *entent* f. OF f. L *intentus* (as INTEND)]

▪ *n.* see INTENTION 1. ● *adj.* **1 a** bent, set, resolved, determined, committed, decided, resolute, firm; keen, eager, zealous, avid, enthusiastic. **b** rapt, engrossed, absorbed, involved, wrapped up, deep. **2** earnest, sincere, serious, studious, thoughtful, solemn, grave, intense, steady, resolute, determined; diligent, eager, keen, zealous, conscientious, assiduous, industrious, hard-working, enthusiastic; meaningful, significant, expressive. ▫ **to all intents and purposes** virtually, practically, for all practical purposes, effectively, in effect, in all but name, more or less, (almost) as good as, pretty well, almost, as near as dammit, *colloq.* just about. ▫▫ **intently** avidly, eagerly, keenly, zealously, enthusiastically; closely, intensely, hard, searchingly, studiously, attentively, concentratedly, fixedly, raptly, steadily, steadfastly, diligently, conscientiously, assiduously, industriously; unflinchingly, continuously, doggedly, unremittingly, resolvedly, determinedly, resolutely, firmly; earnestly, sincerely, seriously, thoughtfully, solemnly, gravely.

intention /inténsh'n/ *n.* **1** (often foll. by *to* + infin., or *of* + verbal noun) a thing intended; an aim or purpose (*it was not his intention to interfere*; *have no intention of staying*). **2** the act of intending (*done without intention*). **3** *colloq.* (usu. in *pl.*) a person's, esp. a man's, designs in respect to marriage (*are his intentions strictly honourable?*). **4** *Logic* a conception. ▫ **first intention** *Med.* the healing of a wound by natural contact of the parts. **first intentions** *Logic* one's primary conceptions of things (e.g. a tree, an oak). **intention tremor** *Med.* a trembling of a part of a body when commencing a movement. **second intention** *Med.* the healing of a wound by granulation. **second intentions** *Logic* one's secondary conceptions (e.g. difference, identity, species). **special** (or **particular**) **intention** *RC Ch.* a special aim or purpose for which a mass is celebrated, prayers are said, etc. ▫▫ **intentioned** *adj.* (usu. in *comb.*). [ME *entencion* f. OF f. L *intentio* stretching, purpose (as INTEND)]

▪ **1** aim, purpose, intent, motive, design, goal, end, point, object, objective, target, ambition, aspiration. **2** premeditation, contemplation, resolution, determination; meaning, signification, indication, implication, intimation, suggestion, allusion.

intentional /inténshən'l/ *adj.* done on purpose. ▫▫ **intentionality** /-nálliti/ *n.* **intentionally** *adv.* [F *intentionnel* or med.L *intentionalis* (as INTENTION)]

▪ intended, deliberate, wilful, purposeful, voluntary, conscious; calculated, planned, premeditated, preconceived, meant. ▫▫ **intentionally** deliberately, on purpose, purposely, wilfully, consciously, wittingly, calculatedly, calculatingly, knowingly, pointedly, of one's (own) free will, on one's own, with one's eyes (wide) open.

inter /intér/ *v.tr.* (**interred**, **interring**) deposit (a corpse etc.) in the earth, a tomb, etc.; bury. [ME f. OF *enterrer* f. Rmc (as IN-^{2}, L *terra* earth)]

▪ bury, lay to rest, *literary* inhume.

inter. *abbr.* intermediate.

inter- /intər/ *comb. form* **1** between, among (*intercontinental*). **2** mutually, reciprocally (*interbreed*). [OF *entre-* or L *inter* between, among]

interact /intərákt/ *v.intr.* act reciprocally; act on each other. ▫▫ **interactant** *adj.* & *n.*

▪ see COOPERATE.

interaction /intəráksh'n/ *n.* **1** reciprocal action or influence. **2** *Physics* the action of atomic and subatomic particles on each other.

▪ **1** see COOPERATION, INTERCOURSE 1.

interactive /intəráktiv/ *adj.* **1** reciprocally active; acting upon or influencing each other. **2** (of a computer or other electronic device) allowing a two-way flow of information between it and a user, responding to the user's input. ▫▫ **interactively** *adv.* [INTERACT, after *active*]

■ **1** see MUTUAL 1, 3.

inter alia /intər áyliə, álliə/ *adv.* among other things. [L]

inter-allied /intərállīd/ *adj.* relating to two or more allies (in war etc.).

interarticular /intəraartíkyoolər/ *adj.* between the contiguous surfaces of a joint.

interatomic /intərətómmik/ *adj.* between atoms.

interbank /intərbangk/ *adj.* agreed, arranged, or operating between banks (*interbank loan*).

interbed /intərbéd/ *v.tr.* (**-bedded**, **-bedding**) embed (one thing) among others.

interblend /intərblénd/ *v.* **1** *tr.* (usu. foll. by *with*) mingle (things) together. **2** *intr.* blend with each other.

interbreed /intərbreéd/ *v.* (*past* and *past part.* **-bred** /-bréd/) **1** *intr.* & *tr.* breed or cause to breed with members of a different race or species to produce a hybrid. **2** *tr.* breed within one family etc. in order to produce desired characteristics (cf. CROSS-BREED).

intercalary /intérkələri, -kálləri/ *adj.* **1 a** (of a day or a month) inserted in the calendar to harmonize it with the solar year, e.g. 29 Feb. in leap years. **b** (of a year) having such an addition. **2** interpolated; intervening. [L *intercalari(u)s* (as INTERCALATE)]

intercalate /intérkəlayt/ *v.tr.* **1** (also *absol.*) insert (an intercalary day etc.). **2** interpose (anything out of the ordinary course). **3** (as **intercalated** *adj.*) (of strata etc.) interposed. □□ **intercalation** /-láysh'n/ *n.* [L *intercalare intercalat-* (as INTER-, *calare* proclaim)]

■ **1, 2** see INSERT *v.*

intercede /intərseéd/ *v.intr.* (usu. foll. by *with*) interpose or intervene on behalf of another; plead (*they interceded with the king for his life*). □□ **interceder** *n.* [F *intercéder* or L *intercedere intercess-* intervene (as INTER-, *cedere* go)]

■ see INTERVENE. □□ **interceder** see *go-between* (GO[1]).

intercellular /intərsélyoolər/ *adj. Biol.* located or occurring between cells.

intercensal /intərséns'l/ *adj.* between two censuses.

intercept *v.* & *n.* ● *v.tr.* /intərsépt/ **1** seize, catch, or stop (a person, message, vehicle, ball, etc.) going from one place to another. **2** (usu. foll. by *from*) cut off (light etc.). **3** check or stop (motion etc.). **4** *Math.* mark off (a space) between two points etc. ● *n.* /intərsept/ *Math.* the part of a line between two points of intersection with usu. the coordinate axes or other lines. □□ **interception** /-sépsh'n/ *n.* **interceptive** /-séptiv/ *adj.* [L *intercipere intercept-* (as INTER-, *capere* take)]

■ *v.* **1–3** stop, halt, interrupt, arrest, trap, cut off, head off, thwart, ambush, waylay; check, block, bar, obstruct, dam, keep *or* hold back, prevent, hinder, impede, restrain, suppress; seize, catch, snatch, grab, take possession of, take a person prisoner, capture; take *or* carry away, appropriate, commandeer; deflect, re-route. □□ **interception** see PREVENTION.

interceptor /intərséptər/ *n.* **1** an aircraft used to intercept enemy raiders. **2** a person or thing that intercepts.

intercession /intərsésh'n/ *n.* **1** the act of interceding, esp. by prayer. **2** an instance of this. **3** a prayer. □□ **intercessional** *adj.* **intercessor** *n.* **intercessorial** /-sesóriəl/ *adj.* **intercessory** *adj.* [F *intercession* or L *intercessio* (as INTERCEDE)]

interchange *v.* & *n.* ● *v.tr.* /intərcháynj/ **1** (of two people) exchange (things) with each other. **2** put each of (two things) in the other's place; alternate. ● *n.* /intərchaynj/ **1** (often foll. by *of*) a reciprocal exchange between two people etc. **2** alternation (*the interchange of woods and fields*). **3** a road junction designed so that traffic streams do not intersect. □□ **interchangeable** *adj.* **interchangeability** /-cháynjəbilliti/ *n.* **interchangeableness** *n.* **interchangeably** *adv.* [ME f. OF *entrechangier* (as INTER-, CHANGE)]

■ *v.* **1** see EXCHANGE *v.* **2** see ALTERNATE *v.* 3. ● *n.* **1** see EXCHANGE *n.* 1. **2** see ALTERNATION. **3** see JUNCTION 2. □□ **interchangeable** see COORDINATE *adj.* 1; SYNONYMOUS 1.

inter-city /intərsítti/ *adj.* existing or travelling between cities.

inter-class /intərklaáss/ *adj.* existing or conducted between different social classes.

intercollegiate /intərkəleéjət/ *adj.* existing or conducted between colleges or universities.

intercolonial /intərkəlṓniəl/ *adj.* existing or conducted between colonies.

intercom /intərkom/ *n. colloq.* a system of intercommunication by radio or telephone between or within offices, aircraft, etc. [abbr.]

intercommunicate /intərkəmyṓōnikayt/ *v.intr.* **1** communicate reciprocally. **2** (of rooms etc.) have free passage into each other; have a connecting door. □□ **intercommunication** /-káysh'n/ *n.* **intercommunicative** /-kətiv/ *adj.*

intercommunion /intərkəmyṓōniən/ *n.* **1** mutual communion. **2** a mutual action or relationship, esp. between Christian denominations.

intercommunity /intərkəmyṓōniti/ *n.* **1** the quality of being common to various groups etc. **2** having things in common.

interconnect /intərkənékt/ *v.tr.* & *intr.* connect with each other. □□ **interconnection** /-néksh'n/ *n.*

■ □□ **interconnection** see RELATION 1a, c.

intercontinental /intərkóntinént'l/ *adj.* connecting or travelling between continents. □□ **intercontinentally** *adv.*

■ see INTERNATIONAL 1, 2.

interconvert /intərkənvért/ *v.tr.* & *intr.* convert into each other. □□ **interconversion** *n.* **interconvertible** *adj.*

intercooling /intərkṓōling/ *n.* the cooling of gas between successive compressions, esp. in a car or truck engine. □□ **intercool** *v.tr.* **intercooler** *n.*

intercorrelate /intərkórrəlayt/ *v.tr.* & *intr.* correlate with one another. □□ **intercorrelation** /-láysh'n/ *n.*

intercostal /intərkóst'l/ *adj.* between the ribs (of the body or a ship). □□ **intercostally** *adv.*

intercounty /intərkównti/ *adj.* existing or conducted between counties.

intercourse /intərkorss/ *n.* **1** communication or dealings between individuals, nations, etc. **2** = *sexual intercourse.* **3** communion between human beings and God. [ME f. OF *entrecours* exchange, commerce, f. L *intercursus* (as INTER-, *currere curs-* run)]

■ **1** communication, dealings, interaction, contact; relations, relationship; commerce, traffic, trade, business, exchange.

intercrop /intərkróp/ *v.tr.* (also *absol.*) (**-cropped**, **-cropping**) raise (a crop) among plants of a different kind, usu. in the space between rows. □□ **intercropping** *n.*

intercross /intərkróss/ *v.* **1** *tr.* & *intr.* lay or lie across each other. **2 a** *intr.* (of animals) breed with each other. **b** *tr.* cause to do this.

intercrural /intərkrṓōrəl/ *adj.* between the legs.

intercurrent /intərkúrrənt/ *adj.* **1** (of a time or event) intervening. **2** *Med.* **a** (of a disease) occurring during the progress of another. **b** recurring at intervals. □□ **intercurrence** *n.* [L *intercurrere intercurrent-* (as INTERCOURSE)]

intercut /intərkút/ *v.tr.* (**-cutting**; *past* and *past part.* **-cut**) *Cinematog.* alternate (shots) with contrasting shots by cutting.

interdenominational /intərdinómminàyshən'l/ *adj.* concerning more than one (religious) denomination. □□ **interdenominationally** *adv.*

interdepartmental /intərdeépaartmént'l/ *adj.* concerning more than one department. □□ **interdepartmentally** *adv.*

interdepend /intərdipénd/ *v.intr.* depend on each other. □□ **interdependence** *n.* **interdependency** *n.* **interdependent** *adj.*

■ □□ **interdependence** see RELATION 1c. **interdependent** see RELATED 2.

interdict *n.* & *v.* ● *n.* /intərdikt/ **1** an authoritative prohibition. **2** *RC Ch.* a sentence debarring a person, or esp. a place, from ecclesiastical functions and privileges. **3** *Sc. Law* an injunction. ● *v.tr.* /intərdíkt/ **1** prohibit (an action). **2** forbid the use of. **3** (usu. foll. by *from* + verbal noun) restrain (a person). **4** (usu. foll. by *to*) forbid (a thing) to a person. ▫▫ **interdiction** /-díksh'n/ *n.* **interdictory** /-díktəri/ *adj.* [ME f. OF *entredit* f. L *interdictum* past part. of *interdicere* interpose, forbid by decree (as INTER-, *dicere* say)]

■ *n.* **1** see PROHIBITION. ● *v.* **1** see PROHIBIT 1. **4** see FORBID 2. ▫▫ **interdiction** see PROHIBITION.

interdigital /intərdíjit'l/ *adj.* between the fingers or toes. ▫▫ **interdigitally** *adv.*

interdigitate /intərdíjitayt/ *v.intr.* interlock like clasped fingers. [INTER- + L *digitus* finger + -ATE³]

interdisciplinary /intərdíssiplinnəri/ *adj.* of or between more than one branch of learning.

interest /íntrəst, -trist/ *n.* & *v.* ● *n.* **1 a** a feeling of curiosity or concern (*have no interest in fishing*). **b** a quality exciting curiosity or holding the attention (*this magazine lacks interest*). **c** the power of an issue, action, etc. to hold the attention; noteworthiness, importance (*findings of no particular interest*). **2** a subject, hobby, etc., in which one is concerned (*his interests are gardening and sport*). **3** advantage or profit, esp. when financial (*it is in your interest to go*; *look after your own interests*). **4** money paid for the use of money lent, or for not requiring the repayment of a debt. **5** (usu. foll. by *in*) **a** a financial stake (in an undertaking etc.). **b** a legal concern, title, or right (in property). **6 a** a party or group having a common interest (*the brewing interest*). **b** a principle in which a party or group is concerned. **7** the selfish pursuit of one's own welfare, self-interest. ● *v.tr.* **1** excite the curiosity or attention of (*your story interests me greatly*). **2** (usu. foll. by *in*) cause (a person) to take a personal interest or share (*can I interest you in a holiday abroad?*). **3** (as **interested** *adj.*) having a private interest; not impartial or disinterested (*an interested party*). ▫ **at interest** (of money borrowed) on the condition that interest is payable. **declare an** (or **one's**) **interest** make known one's financial etc. interests in an undertaking before it is discussed. **in the interest** (or **interests**) **of** as something that is advantageous to. **lose interest** become bored or boring. **with interest** with increased force etc. (*returned the blow with interest*). ▫▫ **interestedly** *adv.* **interestedness** *n.* [ME, earlier *interesse* f. AF f. med.L, alt. app. after OF *interest*, both f. L *interest*, 3rd sing. pres. of *interesse* matter, make a difference (as INTER-, *esse* be)]

■ *n.* **1 a** curiosity, concern, inquisitiveness, fascination, attention, attentiveness, enthusiasm, eagerness, keenness, avidity, zeal, excitement, passion, taste, relish. **b** appeal, excitement, attraction, attractiveness, allure, allurement, fascination. **c** noteworthiness, significance, importance, weight, moment, matter, note, import, concern, consequence. **2** hobby, pastime, recreation, diversion, avocation, pursuit, relaxation, amusement, entertainment, *sl.* bag; occupation, business. **3** profit, advantage, gain, benefit, good, use, avail, worth, value. **4** charge, fee, price, cost; percentage, rate, level, *US sl.* vigorish. **5 a** stake, participation, involvement, investment, share, portion, piece, cut, percentage, *sl.* (piece of the) action. **b** title, entitlement, right, claim, concern, stake. **6a** industry, business, concern, field; fraternity, party, lobby, side, lot. **7** self-interest, egoism, egotism, egocentrism, selfishness. ● *v.* **1** engage, absorb, engross, fascinate, intrigue; distract, divert, amuse, entertain, attract, draw, catch, capture, captivate, hold, occupy; excite, incite, provoke, arouse, affect, quicken, infect, animate, kindle, fire. **2** influence, induce, persuade, talk a person into, move, tempt, dispose, incline, prevail (up)on; enrol, enlist, involve, concern. **3** (**interested**) concerned, involved, partial, biased, prejudiced, partisan. ▫ **in the interest** (*or* **interests**) **of** for the benefit of, for the sake of; to a person *or* a thing's advantage; on *or* *US* in behalf of (*or* on *or* *US* in a person's behalf), in support of. **lose interest** become *or* get bored *or* tired, become *or* get fed up *or* impatient *or* sick and tired, *Brit. sl.* become *or* get browned off *or* pissed off; become boring, go flat, lose one's sparkle, peter out, trail off, tail off, *colloq.* go downhill. **with interest** *sl.* in spades, *Brit. sl.* with knobs on.

interesting /íntrəsting, -tristing/ *adj.* causing curiosity; holding the attention. ▫ **in an interesting condition** *archaic* pregnant. ▫▫ **interestingly** *adv.* **interestingness** *n.*

■ fascinating, intriguing, attractive, tempting, inviting; provocative, stimulating, exciting, entertaining, eventful, *colloq.* juicy; absorbing, thought-provoking, engaging, gripping, riveting, engrossing, compelling, spellbinding, enchanting, captivating.

interface /íntərfayss/ *n.* & *v.* ● *n.* **1** esp. *Physics* a surface forming a common boundary between two regions. **2** a point where interaction occurs between two systems, processes, subjects, etc. (*the interface between psychology and education*). **3** esp. *Computing* an apparatus for connecting two pieces of equipment so that they can be operated jointly. ● *v.tr.* & *intr.* (often foll. by *with*) connect with (another piece of equipment etc.) by an interface.

■ *n.* **1** see SURFACE *n.* 2.

interfacial /intərfáysh'l/ *adj.* **1** included between two faces of a crystal or other solid. **2** of or forming an interface. ▫▫ **interfacially** *adv.* (esp. in sense 2).

interfacing /íntərfaysing/ *n.* a stiffish material, esp. buckram, between two layers of fabric in collars etc.

interfemoral /intərfémmərəl/ *adj.* between the thighs.

interfere /intərfeer/ *v.intr.* **1** (usu. foll. by *with*) **a** (of a person) meddle; obstruct a process etc. **b** (of a thing) be a hindrance; get in the way. **2** (usu. foll. by *in*) take part or intervene, esp. without invitation or necessity. **3** (foll. by *with*) *euphem.* molest or assault sexually. **4** *Physics* (of light or other waves) combine so as to cause interference. **5** (of a horse) knock one leg against another. ▫▫ **interferer** *n.* **interfering** *adj.* **interferingly** *adv.* [OF *s'entreferir* strike each other (as INTER-, *ferir* f. L *ferire* strike)]

■ **1** (*interfere with*) meddle with, hinder, get in the way of, impede, hamper, block, obstruct, inhibit, encumber, slow (down), hold back, retard, handicap, trammel, set back; disrupt, disturb, mess up, frustrate, subvert, sabotage; tinker with, fiddle with, monkey with, mess (about) with, *Brit. colloq.* muck about (*or* around) with. **2** intrude, interrupt, butt in, barge in, break in, intervene, intercede, interpose, put *or* stick one's oar in, thrust oneself *or* one's nose in, *sl.* horn in; pry, meddle, *colloq.* snoop, kibitz, poke one's nose in, *Austral. sl.* poke one's bib in. **3** (*interfere with*) see MOLEST 2. ▫▫ **interfering** see INTRUSIVE.

interference /intərfeerənss/ *n.* **1** (usu. foll. by *with*) **a** the act of interfering. **b** an instance of this. **2** the fading or disturbance of received radio signals by the interference of waves from different sources, or esp. by atmospherics or unwanted signals. **3** *Physics* the combination of two or more wave motions to form a resultant wave in which the displacement is reinforced or cancelled. ▫▫ **interferential** /-fərénsh'l/ *adj.*

■ **1** hindrance, obstruction, inhibition, encumbrance; disruption, disturbance, subversion; intrusion, interruption, intervention, intercession, interposition; impediment, block; meddlesomeness. **2** disturbance, static, noise, atmospherics, snow, ghosting, crosstalk, *Electronics* hiss, *Telephony* babble.

interferometer /intərfərómmitər/ *n.* an instrument for measuring wavelengths etc. by means of interference phenomena. ▫▫ **interferometric** /-férrəmétrik/ *adj.* **interferometrically** /-férrəmétrikəli/ *adv.* **interferometry** *n.*

interferon /intərfeeron/ *n. Biochem.* any of various proteins that can inhibit the development of a virus in a cell etc. [INTERFERE + -ON]

interfibrillar /intərfíbrilər/ *adj.* between fibrils.

interfile /intərfíl/ *v.tr.* **1** file (two sequences) together. **2** file (one or more items) into an existing sequence.

■ see FILE[1] *v.* 1.

interflow *v.* & *n.* ● *v.intr.* /íntərflṓ/ flow into each other. ● *n.* /íntərflō/ the process or result of this.

interfluent /intərflóoənt/ *adj.* flowing into each other. [L *interfluere interfluent-* (as INTER-, *fluere* flow)]

interfuse /íntərfyóoz/ *v.* **1** *tr.* **a** (usu. foll. by *with*) mix (a thing) with; intersperse. **b** blend (things) together. **2** *intr.* (of two things) blend with each other. □□ **interfusion** /-fyóozh'n/ *n.* [L *interfundere interfus-* (as INTER-, *fundere* pour)]

intergalactic /intərgəláktik/ *adj.* of or situated between two or more galaxies. □□ **intergalactically** *adv.*

interglacial /intərgláysh'l, -gláysiəl/ *adj.* between glacial periods.

intergovernmental /intərgúvvərnmént'l/ *adj.* concerning or conducted between two or more governments. □□ **intergovernmentally** *adv.*

intergradation /intərgrədáysh'n/ *n.* the process of merging together by gradual change of the constituents.

intergrade *v.* & *n.* ● *v.intr.* /intərgráyd/ pass into another form by intervening grades. ● *n.* /íntərgrayd/ such a grade.

intergrowth /íntərgrōth/ *n.* the growing of things into each other.

interim /íntərim/ *n.*, *adj.*, & *adv.* ● *n.* the intervening time (*in the interim he had died*). ● *adj.* intervening; provisional, temporary. ● *adv. archaic* meanwhile. □ **interim dividend** a dividend declared on the basis of less than a full year's results. [L, as INTER- + adv. suffix *-im*]

■ *n.* meanwhile, meantime, interval. ● *adj.* see PROVISIONAL *adj.* ● *adv.* see MEANWHILE *adv.*

interior /intéeriər/ *adj.* & *n.* ● *adj.* **1** inner (opp. EXTERIOR). **2** remote from the coast or frontier; inland. **3** internal; domestic (opp. FOREIGN). **4** (usu. foll. by *to*) situated further in or within. **5** existing in the mind or soul; inward. **6** drawn, photographed, etc. within a building. **7** coming from inside. ● *n.* **1** the interior part; the inside. **2** the interior part of a country or region. **3 a** the home affairs of a country. **b** a department dealing with these (*Minister of the Interior*). **4** a representation of the inside of a building or a room (*Dutch interior*). **5** the inner nature; the soul. □ **interior angle** the angle between adjacent sides of a rectilinear figure. **interior decoration** (or **design**) the decoration or design of the interior of a building, a room, etc. **interior monologue** a form of writing expressing a character's inner thoughts. **interior-sprung** (of a mattress etc.) with internal springs. □□ **interiorize** *v.tr.* (also **-ise**). **interiorly** *adv.* [L, compar. f. *inter* among]

■ *adj.* **1** inside, internal, inner, inward. **2** inland, upland, up-country, high, midland, land-locked. **3** internal, domestic, national, civil, home, local, indigenous. **4** inner, inside, further in. **5** inner, innermost, inmost, inward, private, intimate, personal, individual; mental, intellectual, cerebral; secret, hidden, veiled, covert. **6** indoor, internal, inside; cross-sectional, cutaway. ● *n.* **1** inside; centre, middle, heart, core, depths. **2** centre, middle, heart; inland, heartland, upland, hinterland. **3** home affairs, internal affairs, domestic affairs. **5** see SOUL 1, 2.

interject /intərjékt/ *v.tr.* **1** utter (words) abruptly or parenthetically. **2** interrupt with. □□ **interjectory** *adj.* [L *interjicere* (as INTER-, *jacere* throw)]

■ **2** see INTERPOSE 1.

interjection /intərjéksh'n/ *n.* an exclamation, esp. as a part of speech (e.g. *ah!*, *dear me!*). □□ **interjectional** *adj.* [ME f. OF f. L *interjectio -onis* (as INTERJECT)]

■ exclamation, ejaculation, cry, utterance; interpolation, interruption.

interknit /intərnít/ *v.tr.* & *intr.* (**-knitting**; *past* and *past part.* **-knitted** or **-knit**) knit together; intertwine.

interlace /intərláyss/ *v.* **1** *tr.* bind intricately together; interweave. **2** *tr.* mingle, intersperse. **3** *intr.* cross each other intricately. □□ **interlacement** *n.* [ME f. OF *entrelacier* (as INTER-, LACE *v.*)]

■ **1, 3** see WEAVE[1] *v.* 1b.

interlanguage /íntərlanggwij/ *n.* a language or use of language having features of two others, often a pidgin or dialect form.

interlap /intərláp/ *v.intr.* (**-lapped, -lapping**) overlap.

interlard /intərlaárd/ *v.tr.* (usu. foll. by *with*) mix (writing or speech) with unusual words or phrases. [F *entrelarder* (as INTER-, LARD *v.*)]

interleaf /íntərleef/ *n.* (*pl.* **-leaves**) an extra (usu. blank) leaf between the leaves of a book.

interleave /intərléev/ *v.tr.* insert (usu. blank) leaves between the leaves of (a book etc.).

interleukin /íntərlóokin/ *n. Biochem.* any of several glycoproteins produced by leucocytes for regulating immune responses. [INTER- + LEUCOCYTE]

interlibrary /íntərlībrəri/ *adj.* between libraries (esp. *interlibrary loan*).

interline[1] /intərlín/ *v.tr.* **1** insert words between the lines of (a document etc.). **2** insert (words) in this way. □□ **interlineation** /-línniáysh'n/ *n.* [ME f. med.L *interlineare* (as INTER-, LINE[1])]

interline[2] /íntərlín/ *v.tr.* put an extra lining between the ordinary lining and the fabric of (a garment).

■ line, face, cover.

interlinear /íntərlínniər/ *adj.* written or printed between the lines of a text. [ME f. med.L *interlinearis* (as INTER-, LINEAR)]

interlining /íntərlīning/ *n.* material used to interline a garment.

interlink /intərlíngk/ *v.tr.* & *intr.* link or be linked together.

interlobular /íntərlóbyoolər/ *adj.* situated between lobes.

interlock /intərlók/ *v.*, *adj.*, & *n.* ● *v.* **1** *intr.* engage with each other by overlapping or by the fitting together of projections and recesses. **2** *tr.* (usu. in *passive*) lock or clasp within each other. ● *adj.* (of a fabric) knitted with closely interlocking stitches. ● *n.* a device or mechanism for connecting or coordinating the function of different components. □□ **interlocker** *n.*

■ *v.* **2** see MESH *v.* 1.

interlocutor /intərlókyootər/ *n.* (*fem.* **interlocutrix** /-triks/) a person who takes part in a dialogue or conversation. □□ **interlocution** /-ləkyóosh'n/ *n.* [mod.L f. L *interloqui interlocut-* interrupt in speaking (as INTER-, *loqui* speak)]

interlocutory /intərlókyootəri/ *adj.* **1** of dialogue or conversation. **2** *Law* (of a decree etc.) given provisionally in a legal action. [med.L *interlocutorius* (as INTERLOCUTOR)]

interloper /íntərlōpər/ *n.* **1** an intruder. **2** a person who interferes in others' affairs, esp. for profit. □□ **interlope** *v.intr.* [INTER- + *loper* as in *landloper* vagabond f. MDu. *landlooper*]

■ **1** see INTRUDER. □□ **interlope** see MEDDLE.

interlude /íntərlood, -lyood/ *n.* **1 a** a pause between the acts of a play. **b** something performed or done during this pause. **2 a** an intervening time, space, or event that contrasts with what goes before or after. **b** a temporary amusement or entertaining episode. **3** a piece of music played between other pieces, the verses of a hymn, etc. [ME, = a light dramatic item between the acts of a morality play, f. med.L *interludium* (as INTER-, *ludus* play)]

■ **1, 2** interval, intermission, pause, stop, stoppage, interruption, break, hiatus, lacuna, gap, halt, wait; breathing-space, rest, spell, lull, respite, *colloq.* let-up; parenthesis, entr'acte, divertissement, diversion, intermezzo, distraction; change. **3** symphony, *Mus.* verset, ritornello.

intermarriage /intərmárrij/ *n.* **1** marriage between people of different races, castes, families, etc. **2** (loosely) marriage between near relations.

intermarry /íntərmárri/ *v.intr.* (**-ies, -ied**) (foll. by *with*) (of races, castes, families, etc.) become connected by marriage.

intermediary /intərméediəri/ *n.* & *adj.* ● *n.* (*pl.* **-ies**) an intermediate person or thing, esp. a mediator. ● *adj.*

acting as mediator; intermediate. [F *intermédiaire* f. It. *intermediario* f. L *intermedius* (as INTERMEDIATE)]

■ *n.* go-between, middleman, entrepreneur, mediator, intermediate, intermediator, broker, agent, factor, deputy, representative, messenger, third party; peacemaker, arbitrator, negotiator, arbiter, referee, umpire, judge. ● *adj.* mediatory, entrepreneurial; see also INTERMEDIATE *adj.*

intermediate *adj.*, *n.*, & *v.* ● *adj.* /ìntərméediət/ coming between two things in time, place, order, character, etc. ● *n.* /ìntərméediət/ **1** an intermediate thing. **2** a chemical compound formed by one reaction and then used in another, esp. during synthesis. ● *v.intr.* /ìntərméediayt/ (foll. by *between*) act as intermediary; mediate. □ **intermediate frequency** the frequency to which a radio signal is converted during heterodyne reception. □□ **intermediacy** /-diəsi/ *n.* **intermediately** *adv.* **intermediateness** *n.* **intermediation** /-diáysh'n/ *n.* **intermediator** /-diaytər/ *n.* [med.L *intermediatus* (as INTER-, *medius* middle)]

■ *adj.* middle, medial, midway, halfway, transitional, intermediary, inter., inter-, meso-, mid-, *Law* mesne, *colloq.* in-between. ● *n.* **1** compromise, middle course *or* way, halfway house, *literary via media.* ● *v.* mediate, arbitrate, referee, umpire.

interment /intérmənt/ *n.* the burial of a corpse, esp. with ceremony.

■ see BURIAL 1.

intermesh /ìntərmésh/ *v.tr.* & *intr.* make or become meshed together.

intermezzo /ìntərmétsō/ *n.* (*pl.* **intermezzi** /-si/ or **-os**) **1 a** a short connecting instrumental movement in an opera or other musical work. **b** a similar piece performed independently. **c** a short piece for a solo instrument. **2** a short light dramatic or other performance inserted between the acts of a play. [It. f. L *intermedium* interval (as INTERMEDIATE)]

interminable /intérminəb'l/ *adj.* **1** endless. **2** tediously long or habitual. **3** with no prospect of an end. □□ **interminableness** *n.* **interminably** *adv.* [ME f. OF *interminable* or LL *interminabilis* (as IN-[1], TERMINATE)]

■ **1, 3** see ENDLESS 2. **2** see LENGTHY 2. □□ **interminably** see NON-STOP *adv.*

intermingle /ìntərmíngg'l/ *v.tr.* & *intr.* (often foll. by *with*) mix together; mingle.

■ see MIX *v.* 1, 3, 4a.

intermission /ìntərmísh'n/ *n.* **1** a pause or cessation. **2** an interval between parts of a play, film, concert, etc. **3** a period of inactivity. [F *intermission* or L *intermissio* (as INTERMIT)]

■ **1, 3** pause, stop, stoppage, cessation, halt, break, interruption, hiatus, lacuna, interval, gap, wait; breathing-space, rest, spell, lull, respite, *colloq.* let-up. **2** interval, interlude, parenthesis, entr'acte.

intermit /ìntərmít/ *v.* (**intermitted, intermitting**) **1** *intr.* esp. *Med.* stop or cease activity briefly (e.g. of a fever, or a pulse). **2** *tr.* suspend; discontinue for a time. [L *intermittere intermiss-* (as INTER-, *mittere* let go)]

■ **2** suspend, interrupt, put in *or* into abeyance, shelve, stop *or* break off *or* discontinue temporarily.

intermittent /ìntərmítt'nt/ *adj.* occurring at intervals; not continuous or steady. □□ **intermittence** /-mít'nss/ *n.* **intermittency** /-míttənsi/ *n.* **intermittently** *adv.* [L *intermittere intermittent-* (as INTERMIT)]

■ sporadic, occasional, irregular, random, spasmodic, fitful, broken, on-off, stop-go; discontinuous, unsteady, variable, changeable, inconstant; periodic, cyclic(al), rhythmic(al), seasonal.

intermix /ìntərmíks/ *v.tr.* & *intr.* mix together. □□ **intermixable** *adj.* **intermixture** *n.* [back-form. f. *intermixed, intermixt* f. L *intermixtus* past part. of *intermiscēre* mix together (as INTER-, *miscēre* mix)]

■ see MINGLE.

intermolecular /ìntərməlékyoolər/ *adj.* between molecules.

intern *n.* & *v.* ● *n.* /íntern/ (also **interne**) *US* a recent graduate or advanced student living in a hospital and acting as an assistant physician or surgeon. ● *v.* **1** *tr.* /intérn/ confine; oblige (a prisoner, alien, etc.) to reside within prescribed limits. **2** *intr.* /íntern/ *US* serve as an intern. □□ **internment** *n.* **internship** *n.* [F *interne* f. L *internus* internal]

■ *v.* **1** see IMPRISON. □□ **internment** see CAPTIVITY.

internal /intérn'l/ *adj.* & *n.* ● *adj.* **1** of or situated in the inside or invisible part. **2** relating or applied to the inside of the body (*internal injuries*). **3** of a nation's domestic affairs. **4** (of a student) attending a university etc. as well as taking its examinations. **5** used or applying within an organization. **6 a** of the inner nature of a thing; intrinsic. **b** of the mind or soul. ● *n.* (in *pl.*) intrinsic qualities. □ **internal-combustion engine** an engine with its motive power generated by the explosion of gases or vapour with air in a cylinder. **internal energy** the energy in a system arising from the relative positions and interactions of its parts. **internal evidence** evidence derived from the contents of the thing discussed. **internal exile** see EXILE *n.* 1. **internal rhyme** a rhyme involving a word in the middle of a line and another at the end of the line or in the middle of the next. □□ **internality** /-nálliti/ *n.* **internalize** *v.tr.* (also **-ise**). **internalization** /-līzáysh'n/ *n.* **internally** *adv.* [mod.L *internalis* (as INTERN)]

■ *adj.* **1, 2** inside, interior, inward, inner; covert, hidden, secret, veiled, unseen, invisible. **3** domestic, interior, national, civil, home, local, indigenous. **5** in-house, intramural. **6** see INTRINSIC.

internat. *abbr.* international.

international /ìntərnáshən'l/ *adj.* & *n.* ● *adj.* **1** existing, involving, or carried on between two or more nations. **2** agreed on or used by all or many nations (*international date-line; international driving licence*). ● *n.* **1 a** a contest, esp. in sport, between teams representing different countries. **b** a member of such a team. **2 a** (**International**) any of four associations founded (1864–1936) to promote socialist or communist action. **b** a member of any of these. □ **international law** a body of rules established by custom or treaty and agreed as binding by nations in their relations with one another. **international system of units** a system of physical units based on the metre, kilogram, second, ampere, kelvin, candela, and mole, with prefixes to indicate multiplication or division by a power of ten. **international unit** a standard quantity of a vitamin etc. □□ **internationality** /-nálliti/ *n.* **internationally** *adv.*

■ *adj.* worldwide, world, global, universal, intercontinental, multinational, cosmopolitan; supranational, general, extensive; ecumenical; foreign.

Internationale /ìntərnáshyənaàl/ *n.* **1** (prec. by *the*) an (orig. French) revolutionary song adopted by socialists. **2** = INTERNATIONAL *n.* 2a. [F, fem. of *international* (adj.) f. INTERNATIONAL]

internationalism /ìntərnáshənəliz'm/ *n.* **1** the advocacy of a community of interests among nations. **2** (**Internationalism**) the principles of any of the Internationals. □□ **internationalist** *n.*

internationalize /ìntərnáshənəlīz/ *v.tr.* (also **-ise**) **1** make international. **2** bring under the protection or control of two or more nations. □□ **internationalization** /-záysh'n/ *n.*

interne *US* var. of INTERN *n.*

internecine /ìntərneéssīn/ *adj.* mutually destructive. [orig. = deadly, f. L *internecinus* f. *internecio* massacre f. *internecare* slaughter (as INTER-, *necare* kill)]

internee /ínterneé/ *n.* a person interned.

■ see PRISONER.

internist /intérnist/ *n. Med.* **1** a specialist in internal diseases. **2** *US* a general practitioner.

internode /íntərnōd/ *n.* **1** *Bot.* a part of a stem between two of the knobs from which leaves arise. **2** *Anat.* a slender part between two joints, esp. the bone of a finger or toe.

internuclear /ìntərnyōōkliər/ *adj.* between nuclei.

internuncial /intərnúnsh'l/ *adj.* (of nerves) communicating between different parts of the system. [*internuncio* ambassador f. It. *internunzio*]

interoceanic /intərṓshiánnik/ *adj.* between or connecting two oceans.

interoceptive /íntərōséptiv/ *adj. Biol.* relating to stimuli produced within an organism, esp. in the viscera. [irreg. f. L *internus* interior + RECEPTIVE]

interosculate /íntəróskyoolayt/ *v.intr.* = INOSCULATE.

interosseous /íntəróssiəss/ *adj.* between bones.

interparietal /intərpərī́ət'l/ *adj.* between the right and left parietal bones of the skull. □□ **interparietally** *adv.*

interpellate /intérpelayt/ *v.tr.* (in European parliaments) interrupt the order of the day by demanding an explanation from (the Minister concerned). □□ **interpellation** /-láysh'n/ *n.* **interpellator** *n.* [L *interpellare interpellat-* (as INTER-, *pellere* drive)]

interpenetrate /intərpénnitrayt/ *v.* **1** *intr.* (of two things) penetrate each other. **2** *tr.* pervade; penetrate thoroughly. □□ **interpenetration** /-tráysh'n/ *n.* **interpenetrative** /-trətiv/ *adj.*

interpersonal /intərpérsən'l/ *adj.* (of relations) occurring between persons, esp. reciprocally. □□ **interpersonally** *adv.*

interplait /intərplát/ *v.tr.* & *intr.* plait together.

interplanetary /íntərplánnitəri, -tri/ *adj.* **1** between planets. **2** relating to travel between planets.

interplay /intərplay/ *n.* **1** reciprocal action. **2** the operation of two things on each other.

interplead /intərpleéd/ *v.* **1** *intr.* litigate with each other to settle a point concerning a third party. **2** *tr.* cause to do this. □□ **interpleader** *n.* [ME f. AF *enterpleder* (as INTER-, PLEAD)]

Interpol /intərpol/ *n.* International Criminal Police Organization. [abbr.]

interpolate /intérpəlayt/ *v.tr.* **1 a** insert (words) in a book etc., esp. to give false impressions as to its date etc. **b** make such insertions in (a book etc.). **2** interject (a remark) in a conversation. **3** estimate (values) from known ones in the same range. □□ **interpolation** /-láysh'n/ *n.* **interpolative** /-lətiv/ *adj.* **interpolator** *n.* [L *interpolare* furbish up (as INTER-, *polire* POLISH[1])]

■ **1** see INSERT *v.* **2** see INTERPOSE 2. □□ **interpolation** see INSERT *n.*, INTERJECTION.

interpose /intərpṓz/ *v.* **1** *tr.* (often foll. by *between*) place or insert (a thing) between others. **2** *tr.* say (words) as an interruption. **3** *tr.* exercise or advance (a veto or objection) so as to interfere. **4** *intr.* (foll. by *between*) intervene (between parties). [F *interposer* f. L *interponere* put (as INTER-, POSE[1])]

■ **1** see INSERT *v.* **2** interject, interpolate, put *or* throw in. **4** see INTERFERE 2.

interposition /intərpəzísh'n/ *n.* **1** the act of interposing. **2** a thing interposed. **3** an interference. [ME f. OF *interposition* or L *interpositio* (as INTER-, POSITION)]

■ see INTERFERENCE 1.

interpret /intérprit/ *v.* (**interpreted, interpreting**) **1** *tr.* explain the meaning of (foreign or abstruse words, a dream, etc.). **2** *tr.* make out or bring out the meaning of (creative work). **3** *intr.* act as an interpreter, esp. of foreign languages. **4** *tr.* explain or understand (behaviour etc.) in a specified manner (*interpreted his gesture as mocking*). □□ **interpretable** *adj.* **interpretability** /-təbílliti/ *n.* **interpretation** /-táysh'n/ *n.* **interpretational** /-táyshən'l/ *adj.* **interpretative** /-tətiv/ *adj.* **interpretive** *adj.* **interpretively** *adv.* [ME f. OF *interpreter* or L *interpretari* explain, translate f. *interpres -pretis* explainer]

■ **1, 2** explain, explicate, clarify, elucidate, illuminate, throw *or* shed light on; define, spell out, simplify, paraphrase; decipher, decode, translate, gloss, make sense (out) of, figure *or* work out, unravel. **3** translate; lip-read. **4** explain, understand, construe, take (to mean), read, see, analyse, diagnose. □□ **interpretation** explanation, explication, exegesis, clarification, elucidation, illumination, exposition, definition, simplification, paraphrase; performance, rendering, rendition, twist, treatment, approach; decipherment, translation, gloss; understanding, construal, reading, analysis, diagnosis.

interpreter /intérpritər/ *n.* a person who interprets, esp. one who translates speech orally. [ME f. AF *interpretour*, OF *interpreteur* f. LL *interpretator -oris* (as INTERPRET)]

interprovincial /intərprəvínsh'l/ *adj.* situated or carried on between provinces.

interracial /intəráysh'l/ *adj.* existing between or affecting different races. □□ **interracially** *adv.*

interregnum /intərégnəm/ *n.* (*pl.* **interregnums** or **interregna** /-nə/) **1** an interval when the normal government is suspended, esp. between successive reigns or regimes. **2** an interval or pause. [L (as INTER-, *regnum* reign)]

■ see INTERVAL 1.

interrelate /íntəriláyt/ *v.tr.* relate (two or more things) to each other. □□ **interrelation** *n.* **interrelationship** *n.*

interrogate /intérrəgayt/ *v.tr.* ask questions of (a person) esp. closely, thoroughly, or formally. □□ **interrogator** *n.* [ME f. L *interrogare interrogat-* ask (as INTER-, *rogare* ask)]

■ see QUESTION 1, 2.

interrogation /intérrəgáysh'n/ *n.* **1** the act or an instance of interrogating; the process of being interrogated. **2** a question or enquiry. □ **interrogation point** (or **mark** etc.) = *question mark*. □□ **interrogational** *adj.* [ME f. F *interrogation* or L *interrogatio* (as INTERROGATE)]

■ questioning, examination, cross-examination, investigation, third degree, grilling; inquiry, enquiry, query, inquest, probe, *usu. derog.* inquisition.

interrogative /intəróggətiv/ *adj.* & *n.* ● *adj.* **1 a** of or like a question; used in questions. **b** *Gram.* (of an adjective or pronoun) asking a question (e.g. *who?*, *which?*). **2** having the form or force of a question. **3** suggesting enquiry (*an interrogative tone*). ● *n.* an interrogative word (e.g. *what?*, *why?*). □□ **interrogatively** *adv.* [LL *interrogativus* (as INTERROGATE)]

interrogatory /intəróggətəri, -tri/ *adj.* & *n.* ● *adj.* questioning; of or suggesting enquiry (*an interrogatory eyebrow*). ● *n.* (*pl.* **-ies**) a formal set of questions, esp. *Law* one formally put to an accused person etc. [LL *interrogatorius* (as INTERROGATE)]

interrupt /intərúpt/ *v.tr.* **1** act so as to break the continuous progress of (an action, speech, a person speaking, etc.). **2** obstruct (a person's view etc.). **3** break or suspend the continuity of. □□ **interruptible** *adj.* **interruption** /-rúpsh'n/ *n.* **interruptive** *adj.* **interruptory** *adj.* [ME f. L *interrumpere interrupt-* (as INTER-, *rumpere* break)]

■ **1** break in on, intrude into, butt in on, barge in on, *sl.* horn in on; heckle, snap up, take up; punctuate; disturb, disrupt, derange; hold up, halt, cut off *or* short; (*absol.*) break in, strike in, cut in, *colloq.* chip in. **2** block, cut off, obstruct, impede, hinder, hamper, interfere with. **3** discontinue, suspend, break off, adjourn, leave off, cut short; halt, stop, end, arrest, terminate, cease, pause. □□ **interruption** intrusion, disturbance, interference, intervention, disruption, derangement; stoppage, hold-up, halt, delay, check; obstruction, blockage, impediment, hindrance; break, adjournment, respite, rest, lull, stop, pause, intermission, interlude; gap, interval, lacuna, hiatus, space, *Prosody* caesura, *colloq.* let-up; suspension, cessation, termination, cut, *literary* surcease.

interrupter /íntərúptər/ *n.* (also **interruptor**) **1** a person or thing that interrupts. **2** a device for interrupting, esp. an electric circuit.

intersect /intərsékt/ *v.* **1** *tr.* divide (a thing) by passing or lying across it. **2** *intr.* (of lines, roads, etc.) cross or cut each other. [L *intersecare intersect-* (as INTER-, *secare* cut)]

■ **1** see CROSS *v.* 1. **2** see CROSS *v.* 2a.

intersection /intərséksh'n/ *n.* **1** the act of intersecting. **2** a place where two roads intersect. **3** a point or line common

to lines or planes that intersect. ▫▫ **intersectional** *adj.* [L *intersectio* (as INTERSECT)]
■ **1** see MEETING 1. **2** see JUNCTION 2.

interseptal /intərséptəl/ *adj.* between septa or partitions.

intersex /íntərseks/ *n.* **1** the abnormal condition of being intermediate between male and female. **2** an individual in this condition.

intersexual /intərséksyooəl, -sékshooəl/ *adj.* **1** existing between the sexes. **2** of intersex. ▫▫ **intersexuality** /-séksyoo-álliti, -sékshoo-álliti/ *n.* **intersexually** *adv.*

interspace *n.* & *v.* ● *n.* /íntərspayss/ an interval of space or time. ● *v.tr.* /intərspáyss/ put interspaces between.
■ *n.* see INTERVAL 1.

interspecific /intərspəsíffik/ *adj.* formed from different species.

intersperse /intərspérss/ *v.tr.* **1** (often foll. by *between*, *among*) scatter; place here and there. **2** (foll. by *with*) diversify (a thing or things with others so scattered). ▫▫ **interspersion** *n.* [L *interspergere interspers-* (as INTER-, *spargere* scatter)]
■ **2** see PUNCTUATE.

interspinal /intərspī́n'l/ *adj.* (also **interspinous** /-spī́nəss/) between spines or spinous processes.

interstate *adj.* & *n.* *US* ● *adj.* /intərstáyt/ existing or carried on between States, esp. of the US. ● *n.* /íntərstayt/ a motorway, esp. crossing a State boundary.

interstellar /intərstéllər/ *adj.* occurring or situated between stars.

interstice /intérstiss/ *n.* **1** an intervening space. **2** a chink or crevice. [L *interstitium* (as INTER-, *sistere stit-* stand)]
■ **1** see INTERVAL 1.

interstitial /intərstísh'l/ *adj.* of, forming, or occupying interstices. ▫▫ **interstitially** *adv.*

intertextuality /intərtékstyoo-álliti/ *n.* the relationship between esp. literary texts.

intertidal /intərtī́d'l/ *adj.* of or relating to the area which is covered at high tide and uncovered at low tide.

intertribal /intərtrī́b'l/ *adj.* existing or occurring between different tribes.

intertrigo /intərtrī́gō/ *n.* (*pl.* **-os**) *Med.* inflammation from the rubbing of one area of skin on another. [L f. *interterere intertrit-* (as INTER-, *terere* rub)]

intertwine /intərtwī́n/ *v.* **1** *tr.* (often foll. by *with*) entwine (together). **2** *intr.* become entwined. ▫▫ **intertwinement** *n.*
■ see ENTWINE 1, 3.

intertwist /intərtwíst/ *v.tr.* twist together.
■ see TANGLE[1] *v.* 1.

interval /íntərv'l/ *n.* **1** an intervening time or space. **2** *Brit.* a pause or break, esp. between the parts of a theatrical or musical performance. **3** the difference in pitch between two sounds. **4** the distance between persons or things in respect of qualities. ▫ **at intervals** here and there; now and then. ▫▫ **intervallic** /-vállik/ *adj.* [ME ult. f. L *intervallum* space between ramparts, interval (as INTER-, *vallum* rampart)]
■ **1** meanwhile, meantime, interim, interregnum; interspace, interstice, space, gap, blank, opening, lacuna, hiatus, window, daylight, clearance; pause, time, spell, period, span, time-lag, lapse, wait, delay. **2** intermission, interlude, entr'acte, parenthesis, break, pause; recess, rest (period), half-time, respite. ▫ **at intervals** here and there, (round) about, (all) around *or* round; (every) now and again, (every) now and then, periodically, (every) once in a while, occasionally, on occasion, off and on, on and off, intermittently, (every) so often, from time to time, sporadically.

intervene /intərvéen/ *v.intr.* (often foll. by *between*, *in*) **1** occur in time between events. **2** interfere; come between so as to prevent or modify the result or course of events. **3** be situated between things. **4** come in as an extraneous factor or thing. **5** *Law* interpose in a lawsuit as a third party. ▫▫ **intervener** *n.* **intervenient** *adj.* **intervenor** *n.* [L *intervenire* (as INTER-, *venire* come)]
■ **2** interfere, meddle, intrude, strike in, put *or* stick one's oar in, *colloq.* poke one's nose in; interrupt, break in, barge in, butt in, strike in, *sl.* horn in; step in, intercede, mediate.

intervention /intərvénsh'n/ *n.* **1** the act or an instance of intervening. **2** interference, esp. by a State in another's affairs. **3** mediation. [ME f. F *intervention* or L *interventio* (as INTERVENE)]
■ **1, 2** see INTERFERENCE 1. **3** see AGENCY 2b.

interventionist /intərvénshənist/ *n.* a person who favours intervention.

intervertebral /intərvértibrəl/ *adj.* between vertebrae.

interview /íntərvyōō/ *n.* & *v.* ● *n.* **1** an oral examination of an applicant for employment, a college place, etc. **2** a conversation between a reporter etc. and a person of public interest, used as a basis of a broadcast or publication. **3** a meeting of persons face to face, esp. for consultation. ● *v.tr.* **1** hold an interview with. **2** question to discover the opinions or experience of (a person). ▫▫ **interviewee** /-vyōō-ée/ *n.* **interviewer** *n.* [F *entrevue* f. *s'entrevoir* see each other (as INTER-, *voir* f. L *vidēre* see: see VIEW)]
■ *n.* **1** examination, evaluation, appraisal, vetting, assessment, grilling; viva voce, *colloq.* oral; *Brit. colloq.* viva. **2** conversation, discussion, talk, chat, tête-à-tête; press conference, audience. **3** meeting, conference, discussion, consultation, colloquy, dialogue. ● *v.* **1** examine, appraise, evaluate, assess. **2** question, interrogate, sound out, quiz, pump, grill, viva voce, *US* check out, *colloq.* vet, *Brit. colloq.* viva; talk *or* chat with *or* to. ▫▫ **interviewee** see CANDIDATE 1, 3.

interwar /intərwáwr/ *adj.* existing in the period between two wars, esp. the two world wars.

interweave /intərwéev/ *v.tr.* (*past* **-wove** /-wṓv/; *past part.* **-woven** /-wṓv'n/) **1** (often foll. by *with*) weave together. **2** blend intimately.
■ **1** see WEAVE[1] *v.* 1b.

interwind /intərwī́nd/ *v.tr.* & *intr.* (*past* and *past part.* **-wound** /-wównd/) wind together.

interwork /intərwúrk/ *v.* **1** *intr.* work together or interactively. **2** *tr.* interweave.

intestate /intéstət/ *adj.* & *n.* ● *adj.* (of a person) not having made a will before death. ● *n.* a person who has died intestate. ▫▫ **intestacy** /-téstəsi/ *n.* [ME f. L *intestatus* (as IN-[1], *testari testat-* make a will f. *testis* witness)]

intestine /intéstin/ *n.* (in *sing.* or *pl.*) the lower part of the alimentary canal from the end of the stomach to the anus. ▫ **large intestine** the caecum, colon, and rectum collectively. **small intestine** the duodenum, jejunum, and ileum collectively. ▫▫ **intestinal** /also intestī́n'l/ *adj.* [L *intestinum* f. *intestinus* internal]
■ see BOWEL 1.

inthrall *US* var. of ENTHRAL.

intifada /intifáadə/ *n.* a movement of Palestinian uprising in the Israeli-occupied West Bank and Gaza Strip, beginning in 1987. [Arab., = uprising]

intimacy /íntiməsi/ *n.* (*pl.* **-ies**) **1** the state of being intimate. **2** an intimate act, esp. sexual intercourse. **3** an intimate remark; an endearment.
■ **1** see FRIENDSHIP 1. **2** see SEX *n.* 5.

intimate[1] /íntimət/ *adj.* & *n.* ● *adj.* **1** closely acquainted; familiar, close (*an intimate friend*; *an intimate relationship*). **2** private and personal (*intimate thoughts*). **3** (usu. foll. by *with*) having sexual relations. **4** (of knowledge) detailed, thorough. **5** (of a relationship between things) close. **6** (of mixing etc.) thorough. **7** essential, intrinsic. **8** (of a place etc.) friendly; promoting close personal relationships. ● *n.* a very close friend. ▫▫ **intimately** *adv.* [L *intimus* inmost]
■ *adj.* **1** close, attached, inseparable, devoted, friendly, *colloq.* pally, chummy, thick; near, personal, familiar, bosom, boon, special, particular, dear, cherished. **2** private, personal, interior, secret, confidential, hidden, *archaic* privy; interesting; spicy, *colloq.* juicy. **4, 6** detailed, deep, profound, extensive, comprehensive, full,

complete, total, thorough, exhaustive, meticulous, painstaking. **5** close, near, tight. **7** essential, intrinsic, inherent, fundamental, basic, elemental, elementary, organic, natural. **8** friendly, congenial, convivial, clubby, easy, relaxed, casual, informal, *colloq.* laid-back; cosy, snug, homely, comfortable, warm, welcoming, tête-à-tête, *gemütlich*, *colloq.* comfy. ● *n.* (best) friend, (boon) companion, second self, confidant, crony, familiar, partner, boyfriend, girlfriend, *alter ego*, *fidus Achates*, comrade, mate, soul mate, brother, sister, *colloq.* sidekick, chum, pal, *Austral.* & *NZ colloq.* cobber, *Brit. colloq.* oppo, *esp. US colloq.* buddy, *amigo*, *joc.* (old) retainer, *sl.* mucker, *rhyming sl.* china (plate).

intimate[2] /íntimayt/ *v.tr.* **1** (often foll. by *that* + clause) state or make known. **2** imply, hint. ▫▫ **intimater** *n.* **intimation** /-máysh'n/ *n.* [LL *intimare* announce f. L *intimus* inmost]

■ **1** state, make (it) known, announce, say, assert, asseverate, declare, affirm, mention, impart, *formal* aver; maintain, claim, allege. **2** hint, imply, suggest, insinuate; indicate, give a person to understand; warn, caution, tip a person off. ▫▫ **intimation** see HINT *n.* 1.

intimidate /intímmidayt/ *v.tr.* frighten or overawe, esp. to subdue or influence. ▫▫ **intimidation** /-dáysh'n/ *n.* **intimidator** *n.* [med.L *intimidare* (as IN-[2], *timidare* f. *timidus* TIMID)]

■ frighten, terrify, petrify, scare, alarm, ruffle, unnerve, daunt, cow, dismay, awe, overawe, *archaic* concuss; terrorize, tyrannize, bully, menace, threaten, pressure, pressurize, railroad, browbeat, hector, *US* haze, *colloq.* faze, psych (out), bulldoze, lean on, push around, put the screws on, *sl.* put the frighteners on. ▫▫ **intimidation** see TERROR 1, THREAT 1.

intinction /intíngksh'n/ *n. Eccl.* the dipping of the Eucharistic bread in the wine so that the communicant receives both together. [LL *intinctio* f. L *intingere intinct-* (as IN-[2], TINGE)]

intitule /intítyōōl/ *v.tr. Brit.* entitle (an Act of Parliament etc.). [OF *intituler* f. LL *intitulare* (as IN-[2], *titulare* f. *titulus* title)]

into /íntoo, íntə/ *prep.* **1** expressing motion or direction to a point on or within (*walked into a tree*; *ran into the house*). **2** expressing direction of attention or concern (*will look into it*). **3** expressing a change of state (*turned into a dragon*; *separated into groups*; *forced into cooperation*). **4** *colloq.* interested in; knowledgeable about (*is really into art*). [OE *intō* (as IN, TO)]

intolerable /intóllərəb'l/ *adj.* that cannot be endured. ▫▫ **intolerableness** *n.* **intolerably** *adv.* [ME f. OF *intolerable* or L *intolerabilis* (as IN-[1], TOLERABLE)]

■ see UNBEARABLE.

intolerant /intóllərənt/ *adj.* not tolerant, esp. of views, beliefs, or behaviour differing from one's own. ▫▫ **intolerance** *n.* **intolerantly** *adv.* [L *intolerans* (as IN-[1], TOLERANT)]

■ impatient, unforgiving, uncompromising, inflexible; (self-)opinionated, narrow-minded, blinkered, illiberal, dogmatic; biased, prejudiced, bigoted. ▫▫ **intolerance** impatience, unforgivingness, uncompromisingness, inflexibility; opinionatedness, self-opinion, narrow-mindedness, illiberality, dogmatism; bias, prejudice, bigotry.

intonate /íntənayt/ *v.tr.* intone. [med.L *intonare*: see INTONE]

intonation /íntənáysh'n/ *n.* **1** modulation of the voice; accent. **2** the act of intoning. **3** accuracy of pitch in playing or singing (*has good intonation*). **4** the opening phrase of a plainsong melody. ▫▫ **intonational** *adj.* [med.L *intonatio* (as INTONE)]

■ **1** accent, accentuation, (tonal) inflection, cadence, prosody, tone (of voice), tonicity, tonality, modulation, pitch. **2** chanting; articulation, pronunciation, phonation, vocalization, utterance. **3** (perfect *or* absolute) pitch.

intone /intṓn/ *v.tr.* **1** recite (prayers etc.) with prolonged sounds, esp. in a monotone. **2** utter with a particular tone. ▫▫ **intoner** *n.* [med.L *intonare* (as IN-[2], L *tonus* TONE)]

■ chant, sing, cantillate.

in toto /in tṓtō/ *adv.* completely. [L]

■ see ENTIRELY 1.

intoxicant /intóksikənt/ *adj.* & *n.* ● *adj.* intoxicating. ● *n.* an intoxicating substance.

■ *n.* see LIQUOR *n.* 1.

intoxicate /intóksikayt/ *v.tr.* **1** make drunk. **2** excite or elate beyond self-control. ▫▫ **intoxication** /-káysh'n/ *n.* [med.L *intoxicare* (as IN-[2], *toxicare* poison f. L *toxicum*): see TOXIC]

■ **1** inebriate, stupefy, befuddle, *sl.* zonk; fluster, mellow. **2** excite, arouse, overwhelm, elate, exhilarate, delight, enchant, transport, carry away, entrance, enrapture, captivate, ravish, thrill, galvanize, electrify, make one's head spin, take one's breath away, *colloq.* get, freak (out), bowl over, turn on, *sl.* send, zonk. ▫▫ **intoxication** see *drunkenness* (DRUNKEN).

intoxicating /intóksikayting/ *adj.* **1** liable to cause intoxication; alcoholic. **2** exhilarating, exciting. ▫▫ **intoxicatingly** *adv.*

■ **1** alcoholic, spirituous, inebriant; potent. **2** exhilarating, invigorating, thrilling, exciting, heady, potent, stimulating, electrifying, entrancing, fascinating.

intra- /íntrə/ *prefix* forming adjectives usu. from adjectives, meaning 'on the inside, within' (*intramural*). [L *intra* inside]

intracellular /íntrəsélyoolər/ *adj. Biol.* located or occurring within a cell or cells.

intracranial /íntrəkráyniəl/ *adj.* within the skull. ▫▫ **intracranially** *adv.*

intractable /intráktəb'l/ *adj.* **1** hard to control or deal with. **2** difficult, stubborn. ▫▫ **intractability** /-bílliti/ *n.* **intractableness** *n.* **intractably** *adv.* [L *intractabilis* (as IN-[1], TRACTABLE)]

■ see STUBBORN. ▫▫ **intractability** see *obstinacy* (OBSTINATE).

intrados /intráydoss/ *n.* the lower or inner curve of an arch. [F (as INTRA-, *dos* back f. L *dorsum*)]

intramolecular /íntrəməlékyoolər/ *adj.* within a molecule.

intramural /íntrəmyóorəl/ *adj.* **1** situated or done within walls. **2** forming part of normal university or college studies. ▫▫ **intramurally** *adv.*

intramuscular /íntrəmúskyoolər/ *adj.* in or into a muscle or muscles.

intransigent /intránsijənt, intránz-/ *adj.* & *n.* ● *adj.* uncompromising, stubborn. ● *n.* an intransigent person. ▫▫ **intransigence** /-jənss/ *n.* **intransigency** /-jənsi/ *n.* **intransigently** *adv.* [F *intransigeant* f. Sp. *los intransigentes* extreme republicans in Cortes, ult. formed as IN-[1] + L *transigere transigent-* come to an understanding (as TRANS-, *agere* act)]

■ *adj.* see STUBBORN. ▫▫ **intransigence** see *obstinacy* (OBSTINATE).

intransitive /intránzitiv, intraánz-/ *adj.* (of a verb or sense of a verb) that does not take or require a direct object (whether expressed or implied), e.g. *look* in *look at the sky* (opp. TRANSITIVE). ▫▫ **intransitively** *adv.* **intransitivity** /-tívviti/ *n.* [LL *intransitivus* (as IN-[1], TRANSITIVE)]

intra-uterine /íntrəyóotərīn, -rin/ *adj.* within the womb.

intravenous /íntrəvéenəss/ *adj.* in or into a vein or veins. ▫▫ **intravenously** *adv.* [INTRA- + L *vena* vein]

in-tray /íntray/ *n.* a tray for incoming documents, letters, etc.

intrepid /intréppid/ *adj.* fearless; very brave. ▫▫ **intrepidity** /-tripídditi/ *n.* **intrepidly** *adv.* [F *intrépide* or L *intrepidus* (as IN-[1], *trepidus* alarmed)]

■ fearless, unafraid, dauntless, undaunted, unshrinking; courageous, brave, valiant, valorous, heroic, lion-hearted, martial, manly, manful, *archaic or joc.* doughty, *colloq.* spunky, gutsy; bold, daring, audacious, spirited, plucky, game, gallant, dashing, adventurous, venturesome, daredevil; steadfast, resolute, indomitable,

stout, tough, hardy, gritty, stalwart, stout-hearted.
□□ **intrepidity** see ASSURANCE 5a, BRAVERY.

intricate /íntrikət/ *adj.* very complicated; perplexingly detailed or obscure. □□ **intricacy** /-kəsi/ *n.* (*pl.* **-ies**). **intricately** *adv.* [ME f. L *intricare intricat-* (as IN-[2], *tricare* f. *tricae* tricks)]
■ complicated, complex, involved, convoluted, convolutional, involute, involuted, tangled, tangly, knotty, tortuous, sinuous, labyrinthine; elaborate, Byzantine, fancy, ornate, rococo, flowery, busy, detailed; obscure, perplexing, puzzling, mystifying, enigmatic.
□□ **intricacy** see SUBTLETY 1.

intrigant /íntrigənt/ *n.* (*fem.* **intrigante**) an intriguer. [F *intriguant* f. *intriguer*: see INTRIGUE]

intrigue *v.* & *n.* ● *v.* /intréeg/ (**intrigues, intrigued, intriguing**) **1** *intr.* (foll. by *with*) **a** carry on an underhand plot. **b** use secret influence. **2** *tr.* arouse the curiosity of; fascinate. ● *n.* /intréeg, ín-/ **1** an underhand plot or plotting. **2** *archaic* a secret love affair. □□ **intriguer** /intréegər/ *n.* **intriguing** /intréeging/*adj.* (esp. in sense 2 of *v.*). **intriguingly** *adv.* [F *intrigue* (n.), *intriguer* (v.) f. It. *intrigo*, *intrigare* f. L (as INTRICATE)]
■ *v.* **1** conspire, plot, machinate, scheme, collude, connive, manoeuvre. **2** interest, engross, absorb, engage; fascinate, beguile, captivate, enthral, allure, attract, charm. ● *n.* **1** conspiracy, plot, scheme, machination, collusion, cabal, manoeuvre, stratagem; connivance, trickery, chicanery, double-dealing, skulduggery, subterfuge. **2** see AFFAIR 3. □□ **intriguing** see INTERESTING.

intrinsic /intrínzik/ *adj.* inherent, essential; belonging naturally (*intrinsic value*). □□ **intrinsically** *adv.* [ME, = interior, f. F *intrinsèque* f. LL *intrinsecus* f. L *intrinsecus* (adv.) inwardly]
■ inherent, essential, implicit, basic, fundamental, elemental, natural, native, innate, connate, proper, peculiar, inborn, inbred, congenital, inherited, hereditary, constitutional, organic, structural, underlying, built-in, integral, ingrained, engrained, instinctive, in one's blood; immanent, indwelling, internal.

intro /íntrō/ *n.* (*pl.* **-os**) *colloq.* an introduction. [abbr.]

intro- /íntrō/ *comb. form* into (*introgression*). [L *intro* to the inside]

introduce /intrədyóoss/ *v.tr.* **1** (foll. by *to*) make (a person or oneself) known by name to another, esp. formally. **2** announce or present to an audience. **3** bring (a custom, idea, etc.) into use. **4** bring (a piece of legislation) before a legislative assembly. **5** (foll. by *to*) draw the attention or extend the understanding of (a person) to a subject. **6** insert; place in. **7** bring in; usher in; bring forward. **8** begin; occur just before the start of. □□ **introducer** *n.* **introducible** *adj.* [ME f. L *introducere introduct-* (as INTRO-, *ducere* lead)]
■ **1** (*introduce to*) acquaint with, present to, make known to. **2** present, give, offer; announce. **3** inaugurate, initiate, instigate, originate, pioneer, set *or* get going, get under way, bring in, set in motion; establish, institute, set up, put in, install, implant, induct. **4** put forward, propose, table, move, present. **5** (*introduce to*) acquaint with, familiarize with, inform of *or* about, tell about, make aware of, draw *or* direct a person's attention to, open a person's eyes to; notify of, apprise of, advise of *or* about. **6** see INSERT *v.* **7** bring in *or* forward *or* up, advance, present, raise, broach, mention, moot; drag in, foist in, lug in, trot out. **8** begin, start, open, get going *or* started, put into operation *or* motion, *colloq.* get off the ground, kick off, *formal* commence; precede, come *or* go before; preface, prelude, prologue.

introduction /intrədúksh'n/ *n.* **1** the act or an instance of introducing; the process of being introduced. **2** a formal presentation of one person to another. **3** an explanatory section at the beginning of a book etc. **4** a preliminary section in a piece of music, often thematically different from the main section. **5** an introductory treatise on a subject. **6** a thing introduced. [ME f. OF *introduction* or L *introductio* (as INTRODUCE)]
■ **1** see INSTITUTION 1. **2** presentation, *Austral.* & *NZ sl.* knock-down. **3, 5** see PREAMBLE.

introductory /intrədúktəri, -tri/ *adj.* serving as an introduction; preliminary. [LL *introductorius* (as INTRODUCTION)]
■ opening, initial, inaugural, initiatory; prefatory, prodromal, prodromic, preambular, preludial, preliminary, precursory, preparatory; first, primary, basic, fundamental, elementary, rudimentary.

introit /íntroyt/ *n.* a psalm or antiphon sung or said while the priest approaches the altar for the Eucharist. [ME f. OF f. L *introitus* f. *introire introit-* enter (as INTRO-, *ire* go)]

introjection /intrəjéksh'n/ *n.* the unconscious incorporation of external ideas into one's mind. [INTRO- after *projection*]

intromit /intrəmít/ *v.tr.* (**intromitted, intromitting**) **1** *archaic* (foll. by *into*) let in, admit. **2** insert. □□ **intromission** /-mísh'n/ *n.* **intromittent** *adj.* [L *intromittere intromiss-* introduce (as INTRO-, *mittere* send)]
■ **2** see INJECT 1.

introspection /intrəspéksh'n/ *n.* the examination or observation of one's own mental and emotional processes etc. □□ **introspective** *adj.* **introspectively** *adv.* **introspectiveness** *n.* [L *introspicere introspect-* look inwards (as INTRO-, *specere* look)]
■ □□ **introspective** see THOUGHTFUL 1.

introvert *n.*, *adj.*, & *v.* ● *n.* /íntrəvert/ **1** *Psychol.* a person predominantly concerned with his or her own thoughts and feelings rather than with external things. **2** a shy inwardly thoughtful person. ● *adj.* /íntrəvert/ (also **introverted** /-tid/) typical or characteristic of an introvert. ● *v.tr.* /intrəvért/ **1** *Psychol.* direct (one's thoughts or mind) inwards. **2** *Zool.* withdraw (an organ etc.) within its own tube or base, like the finger of a glove. □□ **introversion** /-vérsh'n/ *n.* **introversive** /-vérsiv/ *adj.* **introverted** *adj.* **introvertive** /-vértiv/ *adj.* [INTRO- + *vert* as in INVERT]
■ *adj.* (**introverted**) see SHY 1.

intrude /intróod/ *v.* (foll. by *on, upon, into*) **1** *intr.* come uninvited or unwanted; force oneself abruptly on others. **2** *tr.* thrust or force (something unwelcome) on a person. □□ **intrudingly** *adv.* [L *intrudere intrus-* (as IN-[2], *trudere* thrust)]
■ **1** encroach, impinge, obtrude, trespass, infringe, invade; interfere, meddle, put *or* stick one's oar in, *colloq.* poke one's nose in; intervene, step in; (*intrude on* or *into*) break in on, interrupt, butt in on, barge in on, push in on, *colloq.* muscle in on, *sl.* horn in on. **2** see THRUST *v.* 2.

intruder /intróodər/ *n.* a person who intrudes, esp. into a building with criminal intent.
■ housebreaker, (cat) burglar, thief, robber, night-hawk, *sl.* cracksman, *US sl.* yegg; incomer, interloper, encroacher, impinger, obtruder, trespasser, infringer, invader; gatecrasher, unwelcome visitor, cuckoo in the nest, squatter; interferer, meddler, busybody, *colloq.* snoop, snooper, kibitzer, *Brit. colloq.* Nosy Parker.

intrusion /intróozh'n/ *n.* **1** the act or an instance of intruding. **2** an unwanted interruption etc. **3** *Geol.* an influx of molten rock between or through strata etc. but not reaching the surface. **4** the occupation of a vacant estate etc. to which one has no claim. **5** *Phonet.* the addition of a sound between words or syllables to facilitate pronunciation, e.g. the *r* in *saw a film* (/sáwrəfilm/). [ME f. OF *intrusion* or med.L *intrusio* (as INTRUDE)]
■ **1** see IMPOSITION 2. **2** see *interruption* (INTERRUPT).

intrusive /intróossiv/ *adj.* **1** that intrudes or tends to intrude. **2** characterized by intrusion. □□ **intrusively** *adv.* **intrusiveness** *n.*
■ interfering, interruptive, interruptory, intervenient, obtrusive, invasive; meddlesome, prying, inquisitive, busy, officious, *colloq.* nosy, snoopy; importunate, forward, presumptuous, *colloq.* pushy; uninvited, undesirable, unwelcome, uncalled-for, unwanted, unsought.

intrust var. of ENTRUST.

intubate /intyoobayt/ *v.tr. Med.* insert a tube into the trachea for ventilation, usu. during anaesthesia. ▫▫ **intubation** /-báysh'n/ *n.* [IN-² + L *tuba* tube]

intuit /intyóo-it/ *v.* **1** *tr.* know by intuition. **2** *intr.* receive knowledge by direct perception. ▫▫ **intuitable** *adj.* [L *intueri intuit-* consider (as IN-², *tueri* look)]

■ see SENSE *v.*

intuition /intyoo-ísh'n/ *n.* **1** immediate apprehension by the mind without reasoning. **2** immediate apprehension by a sense. **3** immediate insight. ▫▫ **intuitional** *adj.* [LL *intuitio* (as INTUIT)]

■ instinct, insight, inspiration, sixth sense, (extrasensory) perception, sensitivity, percipience, perceptiveness, perspicacity; presentiment, premonition, foreboding, hunch, sense, impression, notion, inkling, funny feeling, sneaking suspicion, *Buddhism* satori.

intuitionism /íntyoo-ishəniz'm/ *n.* (also **intuitionalism**) *Philos.* the belief that primary truths and principles (esp. of ethics and metaphysics) are known directly by intuition. ▫▫ **intuitionist** *n.*

intuitive /intyóo-itiv/ *adj.* **1** of, characterized by, or possessing intuition. **2** perceived by intuition. ▫▫ **intuitively** *adv.* **intuitiveness** *n.* [med.L *intuitivus* (as INTUIT)]

■ see INSTINCTIVE 2.

intuitivism /intyóo-itiviz'm/ *n.* the doctrine that ethical principles can be established by intuition. ▫▫ **intuitivist** *n.*

intumesce /intyoomés/ *v.intr.* swell up. ▫▫ **intumescence** *n.* **intumescent** *adj.* [L *intumescere* (as IN-², *tumescere* incept. of *tumēre* swell)]

■ ▫▫ **intumescence** see GROWTH 4.

intussusception /íntəssəsépsh'n/ *n.* **1** *Med.* the inversion of one portion of the intestine within another. **2** *Bot.* the deposition of new cellulose particles in a cell wall, to increase the surface area of the cell. [F *intussusception* or mod.L *intussusceptio* f. L *intus* within + *susceptio* f. *suscipere* take up]

intwine var. of ENTWINE.

Inuit /inyoo-it, innoo-it/ *n.* (also **Innuit**) (*pl.* same or **Inuits**) a N. American Eskimo. [Eskimo *inuit* people]

inundate /innəndayt/ *v.tr.* (often foll. by *with*) **1** flood. **2** overwhelm (*inundated with enquiries*). ▫▫ **inundation** /-dáysh'n/ *n.* [L *inundare* flow (as IN-², *unda* wave)]

■ **1** see FLOOD *v.* 1. **2** see GLUT *v.* 2, 3. ▫▫ **inundation** see FLOOD *n.* 1.

inure /inyóor/ *v.* **1** *tr.* (often in *passive*; foll. by *to*) accustom (a person) to something esp. unpleasant. **2** *intr. Law* come into operation; take effect. ▫▫ **inurement** *n.* [ME f. AF *eneurer* f. phr. *en eure* (both unrecorded) in use or practice, f. *en* in + OF *e(u)vre* work f. L *opera*]

■ **1** see CONDITION *v.* 2.

in utero /in yóotərō/ *adv.* in the womb; before birth. [L]

in vacuo /in vákyoo-ō/ *adv.* in a vacuum. [L]

invade /inváyd/ *v.tr.* (often *absol.*) **1** enter (a country etc.) under arms to control or subdue it. **2** swarm into. **3** (of a disease) attack (a body etc.). **4** encroach upon (a person's rights, esp. privacy). ▫▫ **invader** *n.* [L *invadere invas-* (as IN-², *vadere* go)]

■ **1** see OCCUPY 4. **2** see INFEST. **3** see ATTACK *v.* 4. **4** see ENCROACH 1. ▫▫ **invader** see INTRUDER.

invaginate /invájinayt/ *v.tr.* **1** put in a sheath. **2** turn (a tube) inside out. ▫▫ **invagination** /-náysh'n/ *n.* [IN-² + L *vagina* sheath]

invalid[1] *n.* & *v.* ● *n.* /invəleed, -lid/ **1** a person enfeebled or disabled by illness or injury. **2** (*attrib.*) **a** of or for invalids (*invalid car; invalid diet*). **b** being an invalid (*caring for her invalid mother*). ● *v.* /invəleed/ (**invalided, invaliding**) **1** *tr.* (often foll. by *out* etc.) remove from active service (one who has become an invalid). **2** *tr.* (usu. in *passive*) disable (a person) by illness. **3** *intr.* become an invalid. ▫▫ **invalidism** *n.* [L *invalidus* weak, infirm (as IN-¹, VALID)]

■ *n.* **1** valetudinarian, convalescent, patient, casualty, sufferer, cripple. **2 a** disabled. **b** disabled, handicapped, incapacitated, crippled, weakened, debilitated, lame; game, *archaic* halt; see also ILL *adj.* 1. ● *v.* **2** disable, incapacitate, indispose, immobilize, hospitalize, put out of action, lay up, cripple, paralyse, lame, wound, maim, weaken, enfeeble. **3** take to one's bed, keep one's bed, be(come) confined to a wheelchair, become housebound.

invalid[2] /invállid/ *adj.* not valid, esp. having no legal force. ▫▫ **invalidly** *adv.* [L *invalidus* (as INVALID[1])]

■ (null and) void, null (and void), worthless, lapsed; false, spurious, bad, ineffective, *sl.* dud; illegitimate, illegal, unauthorized, irregular, non-standard, improper, foul; untrue, erroneous, unsound, untenable, incorrect, wrong, faulty, imperfect, impaired.

invalidate /invállidayt/ *v.tr.* **1** make (esp. an argument etc.) invalid. **2** remove the validity or force of (a treaty, contract, etc.). ▫▫ **invalidation** /-dáysh'n/ *n.* [med.L *invalidare invalidat-* (as IN-¹, *validus* VALID)]

■ **1** see DISPROVE. **2** see REVOKE *v.* ▫▫ **invalidation** see REPEAL *n.*

invalidity /invəlídditi/ *n.* **1** lack of validity. **2** bodily infirmity. [F *invalidité* or med.L *invaliditas* (as INVALID[1])]

invaluable /inválуooəb'l/ *adj.* above valuation; inestimable. ▫▫ **invaluableness** *n.* **invaluably** *adv.*

■ priceless, inestimable, above *or* beyond *or* without price, precious, costly, valuable, expensive, dear; irreplaceable, unique.

Invar /invaar/ *n. propr.* an iron-nickel alloy with a negligible coefficient of expansion, used in the manufacture of clocks and scientific instruments. [abbr. of INVARIABLE]

invariable /inváiriəb'l/ *adj.* **1** unchangeable. **2** always the same. **3** *Math.* constant, fixed. ▫▫ **invariability** /-bílliti/ *n.* **invariableness** *n.* **invariably** *adv.* [F *invariable* or LL *invariabilis* (as IN-¹, VARIABLE)]

■ **1** immutable, unchangeable, unalterable, unmodifiable, hard and fast; incommutable, irreversible, irrevocable, inexorable, inflexible. **2** unchanging, changeless, unvarying, invariant, constant, static, steady, stable, flat, level, even, regular, uniform; unfailing, unwavering, certain; permanent, fixed, enduring, abiding, eternal, perpetual; unaltered, unchanged, unvaried, unmodified; fast, set, rigid.

invariant /inváiriənt/ *adj.* & *n.* ● *adj.* invariable. ● *n. Math.* a function which remains unchanged when a specified transformation is applied. ▫▫ **invariance** *n.*

■ *adj.* see INVARIABLE 2.

invasion /inváyzh'n/ *n.* **1** the act of invading or process of being invaded. **2** an entry of a hostile army into a country. ▫▫ **invasive** /-váysiv/ *adj.* [F *invasion* or LL *invasio* (as INVADE)]

■ **1** occupation, incursion, intrusion, infiltration, encroachment, infringement, transgression, violation. **2** occupation, incursion, raid, foray, inroad, attack, assault, onslaught, aggression, offensive, drive, push, advance, storming, blitzkrieg. ▫▫ **invasive** see INTRUSIVE.

invective /invéktiv/ *n.* **1 a** strongly attacking words. **b** the use of these. **2** abusive rhetoric. [ME f. OF f. LL *invectivus* attacking (as INVEIGH)]

■ see ABUSE *n.* 2.

inveigh /inváy/ *v.intr.* (foll. by *against*) speak or write with strong hostility. [L *invehi* go into, assail (as IN-², *vehi* passive of *vehere vect-* carry)]

■ (*inveigh against*) see ATTACK *v.* 3.

inveigle /inváyg'l, -véeg'l/ *v.tr.* (foll. by *into*, or *to* + infin.) entice; persuade by guile. ▫▫ **inveiglement** *n.* [earlier *enve(u)gle* f. AF *envegler*, OF *aveugler* to blind f. *aveugle* blind prob. f. Rmc *ab oculis* (unrecorded) without eyes]

■ see ENTICE. ▫▫ **inveiglement** see *cajolery* (CAJOLE).

invent /invént/ *v.tr.* **1** create by thought, devise; originate (a new method, an instrument, etc.). **2** concoct (a false story etc.). ▫▫ **inventable** *adj.* [ME, = discover, f. L *invenire invent-* find, contrive (as IN-², *venire vent-* come)]

■ **1** create, devise, contrive, think up, dream up, hatch, conceive, concoct, make up, imagine, formulate, improvise, design, mastermind; originate, generate, father, pioneer, innovate; coin, mint; strike, hit upon, discover. **2** fabricate, make up, concoct, trump up, manufacture, forge, *archaic* feign, *colloq.* cook up.

invention /invénsh'n/ *n.* **1** the process of inventing. **2** a thing invented; a contrivance, esp. one for which a patent is granted. **3** a fictitious story. **4** inventiveness. **5** *Mus.* a short piece for keyboard, developing a simple idea. [ME f. L *inventio* (as INVENT)]
■ **1** creation, conception, contrivance, concoction, formulation, improvisation, innovation, design, origination, generation; discovery; fabrication, manufacture. **2** creation, contrivance, concoction, design, discovery, device, gadget, innovation, *colloq.* gimmick, *derog. or joc.* contraption, *sl.* gismo. **3** fiction, fabrication, figment, fantasy, tale, fable, fib, cock-and-bull story, fairy story *or* tale, *colloq.* story, yarn, tall story *or* tale; falsehood, lie, untruth, white lie, half-truth, *sl.* whopper, *rhyming sl.* porky (pie); fake, sham, pretence, prevarication. **4** inventiveness, originality, creativeness, creativity, ingenuity, inspiration, ingeniousness, imagination, imaginativeness, resourcefulness, innovation; giftedness, cleverness, brilliance.

inventive /invéntiv/ *adj.* **1** able or inclined to invent; original in devising. **2** showing ingenuity of devising. □□ **inventively** *adv.* **inventiveness** *n.* [ME f. F *inventif -ive* or med.L *inventivus* (as INVENT)]
■ see ORIGINAL 2. □□ **inventiveness** see ORIGINALITY 1, 2, INVENTION 4.

inventor /invéntər/ *n.* (*fem.* **inventress** /-triss/) a person who invents, esp. as an occupation.
■ see CREATOR 1.

inventory /invəntəri, -tri/ *n.* & *v.* ● *n.* (*pl.* **-ies**) **1** a complete list of goods in stock, house contents, etc. **2** the goods listed in this. **3** *US* the total of a firm's commercial assets. ● *v.tr.* (**-ies, -ied**) **1** make an inventory of. **2** enter (goods) in an inventory. [ME f. med.L *inventorium* f. LL *inventarium* (as INVENT)]
■ *n.* **1** see LIST[1] *n.*

inverse /inverss, -vérss/ *adj.* & *n.* ● *adj.* inverted in position, order, or relation. ● *n.* **1** the state of being inverted. **2** (often foll. by *of*) a thing that is the opposite or reverse of another. **3** *Math.* an element which, when combined with a given element in an operation, produces the identity element for that operation. □ **inverse proportion** (or **ratio**) a relation between two quantities such that one increases in proportion as the other decreases. **inverse square law** a law by which the intensity of an effect, such as gravitational force, illumination, etc., changes in inverse proportion to the square of the distance from the source. □□ **inversely** *adv.* [L *inversus* past part. of *invertere*: see INVERT]
■ *adj.* see REVERSE *adj.*

inversion /invérsh'n/ *n.* **1** the act of turning upside down or inside out. **2** the reversal of a normal order, position, or relation. **3** the reversal of the order of words, for rhetorical effect. **4** the reversal of the normal variation of air temperature with altitude. **5** the process or result of inverting. **6** the reversal of direction of rotation of a plane of polarized light. **7** homosexuality. □□ **inversive** /-vérsiv/ *adj.* [L *inversio* (as INVERT)]

invert *v.* & *n.* ● *v.tr.* /invért/ **1** turn upside down. **2** reverse the position, order, or relation of. **3** *Mus.* change the relative position of the notes of (a chord or interval) by placing the lowest note higher, usu. by an octave. **4** subject to inversion. ● *n.* /invert/ **1** a homosexual. **2** an inverted arch, as at the bottom of a sewer. □ **inverted comma** = *quotation mark.* **inverted snob** a person who likes or takes pride in what a snob might be expected to disapprove of. **invert sugar** a mixture of dextrose and laevulose. □□ **inverter** /invértər/ *n.* **invertible** /invértib'l/ *adj.* **invertibility** /-bílliti/ *n.* [L *invertere invers-* (as IN-[2], *vertere* turn)]
■ *v.* **1, 2** see REVERSE *v.* 1.

invertebrate /invértibrət, -brayt/ *adj.* & *n.* ● *adj.* **1** (of an animal) not having a backbone. **2** lacking firmness of character. ● *n.* an invertebrate animal. [mod.L *invertebrata* (pl.) (as IN-[1], VERTEBRA)]
■ *adj.* **1** spineless. **2** see SPINELESS 2.

invest /invést/ *v.* **1** *tr.* (often foll. by *in*) apply or use (money), esp. for profit. **2** *intr.* (foll. by *in*) **a** put money for profit (into stocks etc.). **b** *colloq.* buy (*invested in a new car*). **3** *tr.* **a** (foll. by *with*) provide *or* endue (a person with qualities, insignia, or rank). **b** (foll. by *in*) attribute or entrust (qualities or feelings to a person). **4** *tr.* cover as a garment. **5** *tr.* lay siege to. □□ **investable** *adj.* **investible** *adj.* **investor** *n.* [ME f. F *investir* or L *investire investit-* (as IN-[2], *vestire* clothe f. *vestis* clothing): sense 1 f. It. *investire*]
■ **1** allot, put in *or* up, contribute, devote, supply, provide, sink, lay out, spend; venture, risk, stake, gamble, hazard, chance. **2 a** speculate, *Brit. colloq.* punt; (*invest in*) buy into, buy shares in, buy *or* take a stake in, back, finance, underwrite, *US colloq.* stake. **b** (*invest in*) buy, purchase, *colloq.* splash *or* lash out on. **3 a** provide, endue, endow, furnish, supply; instate, install, inaugurate, induct, initiate, ordain. **b** entrust, attribute, assign, trust. **4** see COVER *v.* 3a. **5** besiege, lay siege to, beleaguer.
□□ **investor** see *backer* (BACK).

investigate /invéstigayt/ *v.* **1** *tr.* **a** inquire into; examine; study carefully. **b** make an official inquiry into. **2** *intr.* make a systematic inquiry or search. □□ **investigator** *n.* **investigatory** /-gətəri, -gətri/ *adj.* [L *investigare investigat-* (as IN-[2], *vestigare* track)]
■ **1** enquire into, inquire into, make inquiries into, check (up) on, probe, delve into, explore, look into, research, consider, study, analyse, examine, scrutinize, inspect, survey, look at, check, search, sift (through), winnow, go through *or* over (with a fine-tooth comb), check through, *US* check out; follow up, pursue.

investigation /invéstigáysh'n/ *n.* **1** the process or an instance of investigating. **2** a formal examination or study.
■ enquiry, inquiry, check, probe, exploration, research, consideration, sounding, study, analysis, examination, scrutiny, inspection, survey, review, look, search, poke, rummage; inquest, *usu. derog.* inquisition, *colloq.* post-mortem.

investigative /invéstigətiv/ *adj.* seeking or serving to investigate, esp. (of journalism) inquiring intensively into controversial issues.
■ see INQUISITIVE 2.

investiture /invéstityoor/ *n.* **1** the formal investing of a person with honours or rank, esp. a ceremony at which a sovereign confers honours. **2** (often foll. by *with*) the act of enduing (with attributes). [ME f. med.L *investitura* (as INVEST)]
■ **1** see *initiation* (INITIATE).

investment /invéstmənt/ *n.* **1** the act or process of investing. **2** money invested. **3** property etc. in which money is invested. **4** the act of besieging; a blockade. □ **investment trust** a trust that buys and sells shares in selected companies to make a profit for its members.
■ **2** see STAKE[2] *n.* 2. **3** see STOCK *n.* 5.

inveterate /invéttərət/ *adj.* **1** (of a person) confirmed in an (esp. undesirable) habit etc. (*an inveterate gambler*). **2 a** (of a habit etc.) long-established. **b** (of an activity, esp. an undesirable one) habitual. □□ **inveteracy** /-rəsi/ *n.* **inveterately** *adv.* [ME f. L *inveterare inveterat-* make old (as IN-[2], *vetus veteris* old)]
■ **1** see INCORRIGIBLE 2. **2 b** see INGRAINED 1.
□□ **inveterately** see *usually* (USUAL).

invidious /invíddiəss/ *adj.* (of an action, conduct, attitude, etc.) likely to excite resentment or indignation against the person responsible, esp. by real or seeming injustice (*an invidious position; an invidious task*). □□ **invidiously** *adv.* **invidiousness** *n.* [L *invidiosus* f. *invidia* ENVY]

invigilate /invíjilayt/ *v.intr. Brit.* supervise candidates at an examination. □□ **invigilation** /-láysh'n/ *n.* **invigilator** *n.*

[orig. = keep watch, f. L *invigilare invigilat-* (as IN-[2], *vigilare* watch f. *vigil* watchful)]
■ ▫▫ **invigilator** see MONITOR *n.* 1.

invigorate /inviggərayt/ *v.tr.* give vigour or strength to. ▫▫ **invigorating** *adj.* **invigoratingly** *adv.* **invigoration** /-ráysh'n/ *n.* **invigorative** /-rətiv/ *adj.* **invigorator** *n.* [IN-[2] + med.L *vigorare vigorat-* make strong]
■ fortify, strengthen, reinforce, bolster (up), brace, encourage, hearten, inspirit, animate, energize, enliven, vitalize, vivify, quicken, stimulate, perk up, tone up, *colloq.* boost, pep up; exhilarate, refresh, revive, restore, rejuvenate. ▫▫ **invigorating** bracing, stimulating, exhilarating, tonic, restorative, refreshing, encouraging, rousing, heartening. **invigoration** see REFRESHMENT 1.

invincible /invínsib'l/ *adj.* unconquerable; that cannot be defeated. ▫▫ **invincibility** /-bílliti/ *n.* **invincibleness** *n.* **invincibly** *adv.* [ME f. OF f. L *invincibilis* (as IN-[1], VINCIBLE)]
■ unconquerable, unbeatable, indomitable, insuperable, unstoppable; invulnerable, indestructible, unassailable, impregnable, impenetrable.

inviolable /invī́ələb'l/ *adj.* not to be violated or profaned. ▫▫ **inviolability** /-bílliti/ *n.* **inviolably** *adv.* [F *inviolable* or L *inviolabilis* (as IN-[1], VIOLATE)]
■ see SACRED 2b.

inviolate /invī́ələt/ *adj.* not violated or profaned. ▫▫ **inviolacy** /-ləsi/ *n.* **inviolately** *adv.* **inviolateness** *n.* [ME f. L *inviolatus* (as IN-[1], *violare, violat-* treat violently)]
■ see SACRED 2b.

invisible /invízzib'l/ *adj.* **1** not visible to the eye, either characteristically or because hidden. **2** too small to be seen or noticed. **3** artfully concealed (*invisible mending*). ▫ **invisible exports** (or **imports** etc.) items, esp. services, involving payment between countries but not constituting tangible commodities. ▫▫ **invisibility** /-bílliti/ *n.* **invisibleness** *n.* **invisibly** *adv.* [ME f. OF *invisible* or L *invisibilis* (as IN-[1], VISIBLE)]
■ **1, 2** unseeable, imperceptible, undetectable, indiscernible, unnoticeable, indistinguishable, *poet.* sightless; latent, hidden, blind, unseen, backstage, out of sight; microscopic, infinitesimal, minuscule. **3** veiled, covert, secret, masked, hidden, disguised, camouflaged; subtle, faint.

invitation /invitáysh'n/ *n.* **1 a** the process of inviting or fact of being invited, esp. to a social occasion. **b** the spoken or written form in which a person is invited. **2** the action or an act of enticing; attraction, allurement.
■ **1** summons, request, call, bidding, challenge, *colloq.* invite. **2** attraction, inducement, allure, allurement, enticement, temptation, magnetism, bait, lure, draw, pull.

invite *v.* & *n.* ● *v.* /invī́t/ **1** *tr.* (often foll. by *to*, or *to* + infin.) ask (a person) courteously to come, or to do something (*were invited to lunch*; *invited them to reply*). **2** *tr.* make a formal courteous request for (*invited comments*). **3** *tr.* tend to call forth unintentionally (something unwanted). **4 a** *tr.* attract. **b** *intr.* be attractive. ● *n.* /invīt/ *colloq.* an invitation. ▫▫ **invitee** /-tée/ *n.* **inviter** *n.* [F *inviter* or L *invitare*]
■ *v.* **1** ask, summon, *archaic or literary* bid. **2** see BID *v.* 2b. **3** see INCUR. **4** see TEMPT 2. ● *n.* see INVITATION 1.

inviting /invī́ting/ *adj.* **1** attractive. **2** enticing, tempting. ▫▫ **invitingly** *adv.* **invitingness** *n.*
■ attractive, appealing, catching, taking, fetching, winsome, captivating, fascinating, intriguing, engaging; enticing, tempting, alluring, luring, seductive, beguiling, bewitching, entrancing, tantalizing, irresistible.

in vitro /in véetrō/ *adv. Biol.* (of processes or reactions) taking place in a test-tube or other laboratory environment (opp. IN VIVO). [L, = in glass]

in vivo /in véevō/ *adv. Biol.* (of processes) taking place in a living organism. [L, = in a living thing]

invocation /invəkáysh'n/ *n.* **1** the act or an instance of invoking, esp. in prayer. **2** an appeal to a supernatural being or beings, e.g. the Muses, for psychological or spiritual inspiration. **3** *Eccl.* the words 'In the name of the Father' etc. used as the preface to a sermon etc. ▫▫ **invocatory** /invókkətəri, -tri/ *adj.* [ME f. OF f. L *invocatio -onis* (as INVOKE)]
■ intercession, petition, prayer, supplication, entreaty, obsecration, litany, *archaic* orison; puja.

invoice /invoyss/ *n.* & *v.* ● *n.* a list of goods shipped or sent, or services rendered, with prices and charges; a bill. ● *v.tr.* **1** make an invoice of (goods and services). **2** send an invoice to (a person). [earlier *invoyes* pl. of *invoy* = ENVOY[2]]
■ *n.* see BILL[1] *n.* 1. ● *v.* bill, charge, debit.

invoke /invṓk/ *v.tr.* **1** call on (a deity etc.) in prayer or as a witness. **2** appeal to (the law, a person's authority, etc.). **3** summon (a spirit) by charms. **4** ask earnestly for (vengeance, help, etc.). ▫▫ **invocable** *adj.* **invoker** *n.* [F *invoquer* f. L *invocare* (as IN-[2], *vocare* call)]
■ **1, 2, 4** see APPEAL *v.* 1.

involucre /invəlo͞okər, -lyo͞okər/ *n.* **1** a covering or envelope. **2** *Anat.* a membranous envelope. **3** *Bot.* a whorl of bracts surrounding an inflorescence. ▫▫ **involucral** /-lo͞okrəl, -lyo͞okrəl/ *adj.* [F *involucre* or L *involucrum* (as INVOLVE)]

involuntary /invóllәntəri, -tri/ *adj.* **1** done without the exercise of the will; unintentional. **2** (of a limb, muscle, or movement) not under the control of the will. ▫▫ **involuntarily** *adv.* **involuntariness** *n.* [LL *involuntarius* (as IN-[1], VOLUNTARY)]
■ unconscious, unthinking, unpremeditated, unintentional, unwitting; impulsive, instinctive, instinctual, natural, automatic, mechanical, spontaneous, reflex, convulsionary, knee-jerk, conditioned, uncontrollable.

involute /invəlo͞ot, -lyo͞ot/ *adj.* & *n.* ● *adj.* **1** involved, intricate. **2** curled spirally. **3** *Bot.* rolled inwards at the edges. ● *n. Geom.* the locus of a point fixed on a straight line that rolls without sliding on a curve and is in the plane of that curve (cf. EVOLUTE). [L *involutus* past part. of *involvere*: see INVOLVE]

involuted /invəlo͞otid, -lyo͞otid/ *adj.* **1** complicated, abstruse. **2** = INVOLUTE *adj.* 2.
■ **1** see INTRICATE.

involution /invəlo͞osh'n, -lyo͞osh'n/ *n.* **1** the process of involving. **2** an entanglement. **3** intricacy. **4** curling inwards. **5** a part that curls upwards. **6** *Math.* the raising of a quantity to any power. **7** *Physiol.* the reduction in size of an organ in old age, or when its purpose has been fulfilled (esp. the uterus after childbirth). ▫▫ **involutional** *adj.* [L *involutio* (as INVOLVE)]

involve /invólv/ *v.tr.* **1** (often foll. by *in*) cause (a person or thing) to participate, or share the experience or effect (in a situation, activity, etc.). **2** imply, entail, make necessary. **3** (foll. by *in*) implicate (a person in a charge, crime, etc.). **4** include or affect in its operations. **5** (as **involved** *adj.*) **a** (often foll. by *in*) concerned or interested. **b** complicated in thought or form. [ME f. L *involvere involut-* (as IN-[2], *volvere* roll)]
■ **1** include, bring *or* take in, engage, engross, occupy, interest, absorb, immerse, employ. **2** imply, entail, necessitate, require, presuppose, assume; mean, suggest, indicate, implicate, betoken, point to, signify, evidence. **3** implicate, incriminate, inculpate; concern, connect, associate, draw in, mix up, catch up, entangle, enmesh, ensnare, embroil. **4** concern, affect, touch, relate to, bear on *or* upon, have a bearing on *or* upon, be relevant *or* germane to, apply to, influence, be of importance *or* interest to, have something to do with, regard; include, subsume, contain, comprise, cover, embrace, incorporate, encompass, embody, comprehend; number among, count in. **5** (**involved**) **a** concerned, included, implicated, affected; interested, engaged, absorbed, busy; partial, biased, prejudiced, partisan. **b** complicated, complex, intricate, convoluted, convolutional, involute, involuted, tangled, tangly, knotty, tortuous, sinuous, elaborate, Byzantine, labyrinthine.

involvement /invólvmənt/ *n.* **1** (often foll. by *in, with*) the act or an instance of involving; the process of being involved.

2 financial embarrassment. **3** a complicated affair or concern.
■ **1** see TIE *n.* 3. **3** complication, complexity, intricacy, convolution; see also PREDICAMENT.

invulnerable /invúlnərəb'l/ *adj.* that cannot be wounded or hurt, physically or mentally. □□ **invulnerability** /-bílliti/ *n.* **invulnerably** *adv.* [L *invulnerabilis* (as IN-[1], VULNERABLE)]
■ see INVINCIBLE. □□ **invulnerability** see IMMUNITY 2.

inward /inwərd/ *adj.* & *adv.* ● *adj.* **1** directed toward the inside; going in. **2** situated within. **3** mental, spiritual. ● *adv.* (also **inwards**) **1** (of motion or position) towards the inside. **2** in the mind or soul. [OE *innanweard* (as IN, -WARD)]
■ *adj.* **1, 2** interior, inside, internal, inner.

inwardly /inwərdli/ *adv.* **1** on the inside. **2** in the mind or soul. **3** (of speaking) not aloud; inaudibly. [OE *inweardlīce* (as INWARD)]

inwardness /inwərdniss/ *n.* **1** inner nature; essence. **2** the condition of being inward. **3** spirituality.

inwards var. of INWARD *adv.*

inweave /inweév/ *v.tr.* (also **enweave**) (*past* **-wove** /-wṓv/; *past part.* **-woven** /-wṓv'n/) **1** weave (two or more things) together. **2** intermingle.

inwrap var. of ENWRAP.

inwreathe var. of ENWREATHE.

inwrought /inráwt/ *adj.* **1 a** (often foll. by *with*) (of a fabric) decorated (with a pattern). **b** (often foll. by *in, on*) (of a pattern) wrought (in or on a fabric). **2** closely blended.

inyala /inyaálə/ *n.* (also **nyala** /nyaálə/) (*pl.* same) a large antelope, *Tragelaphus angasi*, native to S. Africa, with curved horns having a single complete turn. [Zulu]

IOC *abbr.* International Olympic Committee.

iodic /īóddik/ *adj. Chem.* containing iodine in chemical combination (*iodic acid*). □□ **iodate** /ī́ədayt/ *n.*

iodide /ī́ədīd/ *n. Chem.* any compound of iodine with another element or group.

iodinate /īóddinayt, ī́ədin-/ *v.tr.* treat or combine with iodine. □□ **iodination** /-náysh'n/ *n.*

iodine /ī́ədeen, -in/ *n.* **1** *Chem.* a non-metallic element of the halogen group, forming black crystals and a violet vapour, used in medicine and photography, and important as an essential element for living organisms. ¶ Symb.: **I**. **2** a solution of this in alcohol used as a mild antiseptic. [F *iode* f. Gk *iōdēs* violet-like f. *ion* violet + -INE[4]]

iodism /ī́ədiz'm/ *n. Med.* a condition caused by an overdose of iodides.

iodize /ī́ədīz/ *v.tr.* (also **-ise**) treat or impregnate with iodine. □□ **iodization** /-záysh'n/ *n.*

iodo- /ī-ṓdō/ *comb. form* (usu. **iod-** before a vowel) *Chem.* iodine.

iodoform /ī-ṓdəform, -óddəform/ *n.* a pale yellow volatile sweet-smelling solid compound of iodine with antiseptic properties. ¶ Chem. formula: CHI_3. [IODINE after *chloroform*]

IOM *abbr.* Isle of Man.

ion /ī́ən/ *n.* an atom or group of atoms that has lost one or more electrons (= CATION), or gained one or more electrons (= ANION). □ **ion exchange** the exchange of ions of the same charge between a usu. aqueous solution and a solid, used in water-softening etc. **ion exchanger** a substance or equipment for this process. [Gk, neut. pres. part. of *eimi* go]

-ion *suffix* (usu. as **-sion**, **-tion**, **-xion**; see -ATION, -ITION, -UTION.) forming nouns denoting: **1** verbal action (*excision*). **2** an instance of this (*a suggestion*). **3** a resulting state or product (*vexation*; *concoction*). [from or after F *-ion* or L *-io -ionis*]

Ionian /ī-ṓniən/ *n.* & *adj.* ● *n.* a native or inhabitant of ancient Ionia in W. Asia Minor. ● *adj.* of or relating to Ionia or the Ionians. □ **Ionian mode** *Mus.* the mode represented by the natural diatonic scale C–C. [L *Ionius* f. Gk *Iōnios*]

Ionic /īónnik/ *adj.* & *n.* ● *adj.* **1** of the order of Greek architecture characterized by a column with scroll-shapes on either side of the capital. **2** of the ancient Greek dialect used in Ionia. ● *n.* the Ionic dialect. [L *Ionicus* f. Gk *Iōnikos*]

ionic /īónnik/ *adj.* of, relating to, or using ions. □□ **ionically** *adv.*

ionization /ī́ənīzáysh'n/ *n.* (also **-isation**) the process of producing ions as a result of solvation, heat, radiation, etc. □ **ionization chamber** an instrument for detecting ionizing radiation.

ionize /ī́ənīz/ *v.tr.* & *intr.* (also **-ise**) convert or be converted into an ion or ions. □ **ionizing radiation** a radiation of sufficient energy to cause ionization in the medium through which it passes. □□ **ionizable** *adj.*

ionizer /ī́ənīzər/ *n.* any thing which produces ionization, esp. a device used to improve the quality of the air in a room etc.

ionosphere /īónnəsfeer/ *n.* an ionized region of the atmosphere above the stratosphere, extending to about 1,000 km above the earth's surface and able to reflect radio waves for long-distance transmission round the earth (cf. TROPOSPHERE). □□ **ionospheric** /-sférrik/ *adj.*

-ior[1] /iər/ *suffix* forming adjectives of comparison (*senior*; *ulterior*). [L]

-ior[2] var. of -IOUR.

iota /ī-ṓtə/ *n.* **1** the ninth letter of the Greek alphabet (*Ι*, *ι*). **2** (usu. with *neg.*) the smallest possible amount. [Gk *iōta*]
■ **2** see BIT[1] 1.

IOU /ī-ō-yṓō/ *n.* a signed document acknowledging a debt. [= I owe you]

-iour /iər/ *suffix* (also **-ior**) forming nouns (*saviour*; *warrior*). [-I- (as a stem element) + -OUR[2], -OR[1]]

-ious /-iəss, -əss/ *suffix* forming adjectives meaning 'characterized by, full of', often corresponding to nouns in *-ion* (*cautious*; *curious*; *spacious*). [from or after F *-ieux* f. L *-iosus*]

IOW *abbr.* Isle of Wight.

IPA *abbr.* International Phonetic Alphabet (or Association).

IPCS *abbr.* (in the UK) Institution of Professional Civil Servants.

ipecac /íppikak/ *n. colloq.* ipecacuanha. [abbr.]

ipecacuanha /íppikákyoo-aánə/ *n.* the root of a S. American shrub, *Cephaelis ipecacuanha*, used as an emetic and purgative. [Port. f. Tupi-Guarani *ipekaaguéne* emetic creeper]

ipomoea /ípəmeéə/ *n.* any twining plant of the genus *Ipomoea*, having trumpet-shaped flowers, e.g. the sweet potato and morning glory. [mod.L f. Gk *ips ipos* worm + *homoios* like]

ips *abbr.* (also **i.p.s.**) inches per second.

ipse dixit /ípsi díksit/ *n.* a dogmatic statement resting merely on the speaker's authority. [L, he himself said it (orig. of Pythagoras)]

ipsilateral /ípsiláttərəl/ *adj.* belonging to or occurring on the same side of the body. [irreg. f. L *ipse* self + LATERAL]

ipsissima verba /ipsíssimə vérbə/ *n.pl.* the precise words. [L]

ipso facto /ípsō fáktō/ *adv.* **1** by that very fact or act. **2** thereby. [L]

IQ *abbr.* intelligence quotient.
■ see MENTALITY 2.

-ique *archaic* var. of -IC.

IR *abbr.* infrared.

Ir *symb. Chem.* the element iridium.

ir- /ir/ *prefix* assim. form of IN-[1], IN-[2] before *r*.

IRA *abbr.* Irish Republican Army.

irade /iraádi/ *n. hist.* a written decree of the Sultan of Turkey. [Turk. f. Arab. *'irāda* will]

Iranian /iráyniən/ *adj.* & *n.* ● *adj.* **1** of or relating to Iran (formerly Persia) in the Middle East. **2** of the Indo-European group of languages including Persian, Pashto, Avestan, and Kurdish. ● *n.* **1** a native or national of Iran. **2** a person of Iranian descent.

Iraqi /iraáki/ *adj.* & *n.* ● *adj.* of or relating to Iraq in the Middle East. ● *n.* (*pl.* **Iraqis**) **1 a** a native or national of Iraq. **b** a person of Iraqi descent. **2** the form of Arabic spoken in Iraq.

irascible /irássib'l/ *adj.* irritable; hot-tempered. □□ **irascibility** /-bílliti/ *n.* **irascibly** *adv.* [ME f. F f. LL *irascibilis* f. L *irasci* grow angry f. *ira* anger]
■ see IRRITABLE 1. □□ **irascibility** see TEMPER *n.* 3.

irate /īráyt/ *adj.* angry, enraged. □□ **irately** *adv.* **irateness** *n.* [L *iratus* f. *ira* anger]
■ see ANGRY 1.

IRBM *abbr.* intermediate-range ballistic missile.

ire /īr/ *n. literary* anger. □□ **ireful** *adj.* [ME f. OF f. L *ira*]
■ see ANGER *n.* □□ **ireful** see ANGRY 1.

irenic /īreénik/ *adj.* (also **irenical, eirenic**) *literary* aiming or aimed at peace. [Gk *eirēnikos*: see EIRENICON]

irenicon var. of EIRENICON.

iridaceous /irridáyshəss/ *adj. Bot.* of or relating to the family Iridaceae of plants growing from bulbs, corms, or rhizomes, e.g. iris, crocus, and gladiolus. [mod.L *iridaceus* (as IRIS)]

iridescent /írridéss'nt/ *adj.* **1** showing rainbow-like luminous or gleaming colours. **2** changing colour with position. □□ **iridescence** *n.* **iridescently** *adv.* [L IRIS + -ESCENT]
■ see OPALESCENT.

iridium /iríddiəm/ *n. Chem.* a hard white metallic element of the transition series used esp. in alloys. ¶ Symb.: **Ir**. [mod.L f. L IRIS + -IUM]

iris /īriss/ *n.* **1** the flat circular coloured membrane behind the cornea of the eye, with a circular opening (pupil) in the centre. **2** any herbaceous plant of the genus *Iris*, usu. with tuberous roots, sword-shaped leaves, and showy flowers. **3** (in full **iris diaphragm**) an adjustable diaphragm of thin overlapping plates for regulating the size of a central hole esp. for the admission of light to a lens. [ME f. L *iris iridis* f. Gk *iris iridos* rainbow, iris]

Irish /īrish/ *adj.* & *n.* ● *adj.* of or relating to Ireland; of or like its people. ● *n.* **1** the Celtic language of Ireland. **2** (prec. by *the*; treated as *pl.*) the people of Ireland. □ **Irish bull** = BULL[3]. **Irish coffee** coffee mixed with Irish whiskey and served with cream on top. **Irish moss** dried carrageen. **Irish Sea** the sea between England and Wales and Ireland. **Irish stew** a stew of mutton, potato, and onion. **Irish terrier** a rough-haired light reddish-brown breed of terrier. [ME f. OE *Iras* the Irish]

Irishman /īrishmən/ *n.* (*pl.* **-men**) a man who is Irish by birth or descent.

Irishwoman /īrishwŏŏmmən/ *n.* (*pl.* **-women**) a woman who is Irish by birth or descent.

iritis /īrītiss/ *n.* inflammation of the iris.

irk /urk/ *v.tr.* (usu. *impers.*; often foll. by *that* + clause) irritate, bore, annoy. [ME: orig. unkn.]
■ irritate, anger, enrage, madden, infuriate, incense, make a person's blood boil, annoy, pique, vex, exasperate, chafe, nettle, gall, grate on, jar on, hump, put out, get *or* put a person's back up, get on a person's nerves, *Brit.* get a person's blood up, *colloq.* get, get across, rile, needle, miff, peeve, wind up, make a person see red, get a person's goat, *Brit. colloq.* get on a person's wick, *disp.* aggravate, *sl.* bug, get up a person's nose, *Brit. sl.* brown off, cheese off, nark, *US sl.* burn up; bother, worry, nag, pester, provoke, bait, goad, torment, play up, fret, rub up the wrong way, *US* ride, *colloq.* hassle, get under a person's skin; bore, make a person fed up, get a person down.

irksome /úrksəm/ *adj.* tedious, annoying, tiresome. □□ **irksomely** *adv.* **irksomeness** *n.* [ME, = tired etc., f. IRK + -SOME[1]]
■ irritating, maddening, infuriating, annoying, vexing, vexatious, exasperating, galling, grating, bothersome, pestilential, *colloq.* pestilent, *US colloq.* pesky, *disp.* aggravating, *Austral. sl.* on the nose; troublesome, burdensome, tiresome, trying, tedious, boring, wearisome, uninteresting; *colloq.* accursed, confounded, blasted, damned, damnable, *US colloq.* darned.

IRO *abbr.* **1** (in the UK) Inland Revenue Office. **2** International Refugee Organization.

iroko /irṓkō/ *n.* (*pl.* **-os**) **1** either of two African trees *Chlorophora excelsa* or *C. regia*. **2** the light-coloured hard wood from these trees. [Ibo]

iron /īrn/ *n.*, *adj.*, & *v.* ● *n.* **1** *Chem.* a silver-white ductile metallic element occurring naturally as haematite, magnetite, etc., much used for tools and implements, and an essential element in all living organisms. ¶ Symb.: **Fe**. **2** this as a type of unyieldingness or a symbol of firmness (*man of iron*; *will of iron*). **3** a tool or implement made of iron (*branding iron*; *curling iron*). **4** a household, now usu. electrical, implement with a flat base which is heated to smooth clothes etc. **5** a golf club with an iron or steel sloping face used for lofting the ball. **6** (usu. in *pl.*) a fetter (*clapped in irons*). **7** (usu. in *pl.*) a stirrup. **8** (often in *pl.*) an iron support for a malformed leg. **9** a preparation of iron as a tonic or dietary supplement (*iron tablets*). ● *adj.* **1** made of iron. **2** very robust. **3** unyielding, merciless (*iron determination*). ● *v.tr.* **1** smooth (clothes etc.) with an iron. **2** furnish or cover with iron. **3** shackle with irons. □ **in irons** handcuffed, chained, etc. **Iron Age** *Archaeol.* the period following the Bronze Age when iron replaced bronze in the making of implements and weapons. **iron-bark** any of various eucalyptus trees with a thick solid bark and hard dense timber. **iron-bound 1** bound with iron. **2** rigorous; hard and fast. **3** (of a coast) rock-bound. **Iron Cross** the highest German military decoration for bravery. **Iron Curtain** *hist.* a notional barrier to the passage of people and information between the former Soviet bloc and the West. **iron hand** firmness or inflexibility (cf. *velvet glove*). **iron in the fire** an undertaking, opportunity, or commitment (usu. in *pl.*: *too many irons in the fire*). **ironing-board** a flat surface usu. on legs and of adjustable height on which clothes etc. are ironed. **iron lung** a rigid case fitted over a patient's body, used for administering prolonged artificial respiration by means of mechanical pumps. **iron maiden** *hist.* an instrument of torture consisting of a coffin-shaped box lined with iron spikes. **iron-mould** (*US* **-mold**) a spot caused by iron-rust or an ink-stain, esp. on fabric. **iron-on** able to be fixed to the surface of a fabric etc. by ironing. **iron out** remove or smooth over (difficulties etc.). **iron pyrites** see PYRITES. **iron ration** a small emergency supply of food. □□ **ironer** *n.* **ironing** *n.* (in sense 1 of *v.*). **ironless** *adj.* **iron-like** *adj.* [OE *īren*, *īsern* f. Gmc, prob. f. Celt.]
■ *n.* **6** (*irons*) see MANACLE *n.* 1. ● *adj.* **3** see GRIM 2. ● *v.* **1** see PRESS[1] *v.* 2a. □ **iron hand** see *oppressor* (OPPRESS).

ironclad *adj.* & *n.* ● *adj.* /īrnklád/ **1** clad or protected with iron. **2** impregnable; rigorous. ● *n.* /īrnklad/ *hist.* an early name for a 19th-c. warship built of iron or protected by iron plates.

ironic /īrónnik/ *adj.* (also **ironical**) **1** using or displaying irony. **2** in the nature of irony. □□ **ironically** *adv.* [F *ironique* or LL *ironicus* f. Gk *eirōnikos* dissembling (as IRONY[1])]
■ see SATIRICAL. □□ **ironically** see *with one's tongue in one's cheek* (TONGUE).

ironist /īrənist/ *n.* a person who uses irony. □□ **ironize** *v.intr.* (also **-ise**). [Gk *eirōn* dissembler + -IST]

ironmaster /īrnmaastər/ *n.* a manufacturer of iron.

ironmonger /īrnmunggər/ *n. Brit.* a dealer in hardware etc. □□ **ironmongery** *n.* (*pl.* **-ies**).

Ironsides /īrnsīdz/ *n.* a man of great bravery, esp. (as *pl.*) Cromwell's troopers in the English Civil War.

ironstone /īrnstōn/ *n.* **1** any rock containing a substantial proportion of an iron compound. **2** a kind of hard white opaque stoneware.

ironware /īrnwair/ *n.* articles made of iron, esp. domestic implements.

ironwork /īrnwurk/ *n.* **1** things made of iron. **2** work in iron.

ironworks /írnwurks/ *n.* (as *sing.* or *pl.*) a place where iron is smelted or iron goods are made.

irony[1] /írəni/ *n.* (*pl.* **-ies**) **1** an expression of meaning, often humorous or sarcastic, by the use of language of a different or opposite tendency. **2** an ill-timed or perverse arrival of an event or circumstance that is in itself desirable. **3** the use of language with one meaning for a privileged audience and another for those addressed or concerned. [L *ironia* f. Gk *eirōneia* simulated ignorance f. *eirōn* dissembler]

■ **1** see SATIRE 1.

irony[2] /í-ərni/ *adj.* of or like iron.

Iroquoian /irrəkwóyən/ *n.* & *adj.* ● *n.* **1** a language family of eastern N. America, including Cherokee and Mohawk. **2** a member of the Iroquois Indians. ● *adj.* of or relating to the Iroquois or the Iroquoian language family or one of its members.

Iroquois /irrəkwoy/ *n.* & *adj.* ● *n.* (*pl.* same) **1 a** an American Indian confederacy of five peoples formerly inhabiting New York State. **b** a member of any of these peoples. **2** any of the languages of these peoples. ● *adj.* of or relating to the Iroquois or their languages. [F f. Algonquian]

irradiant /iráydiənt/ *adj. literary* shining brightly. ▫▫ **irradiance** *n.*

irradiate /iráydiayt/ *v.tr.* **1** subject to (any form of) radiation. **2** shine upon; light up. **3** throw light on (a subject). ▫▫ **irradiative** /-diətiv/ *adj.* [L *irradiare irradiat-* (as IN-[2], *radiare* f. *radius* RAY[1])]

irradiation /iráydiáysh'n/ *n.* **1** the process of irradiating. **2** shining, illumination. **3** the apparent extension of the edges of an illuminated object seen against a dark background. [F *irradiation* or LL *irradiatio* (as IRRADIATE)]

irrational /iráshən'l/ *adj.* **1** illogical; unreasonable. **2** not endowed with reason. **3** *Math.* (of a root etc.) not rational; not commensurate with the natural numbers (e.g. a non-terminating decimal). ▫▫ **irrationality** /-nálliti/ *n.* **irrationalize** *v.tr.* (also **-ise**). **irrationally** *adv.* [L *irrationalis* (as IN-[1], RATIONAL)]

■ **1, 2** see UNREASONABLE 2. ▫▫ **irrationality** see ABSURDITY 1, 2. **irrationally** see MADLY 1.

irreclaimable /irrikláyməb'l/ *adj.* that cannot be reclaimed or reformed. ▫▫ **irreclaimably** *adv.*

■ see IRRETRIEVABLE.

irreconcilable /irékkənsīləb'l/ *adj.* & *n.* ● *adj.* **1** implacably hostile. **2** (of ideas etc.) incompatible. ● *n.* **1** an uncompromising opponent of a political measure etc. **2** (usu. in *pl.*) any of two or more items, ideas, etc., that cannot be made to agree. ▫▫ **irreconcilability** /-bílliti/ *n.* **irreconcilableness** *n.* **irreconcilably** *adv.*

■ *adj.* **1** see IMPLACABLE. **2** see INCOMPATIBLE 1, 3.

irrecoverable /irrikúvvərəb'l/ *adj.* that cannot be recovered or remedied. ▫▫ **irrecoverably** *adv.*

■ see IRRETRIEVABLE.

irrecusable /írrikyóōzəb'l/ *adj.* that must be accepted. [F *irrécusable* or LL *irrecusabilis* (as IN-[1], *recusare* refuse)]

irredeemable /irridéeməb'l/ *adj.* **1** that cannot be redeemed. **2** hopeless, absolute. **3 a** (of a government annuity) not terminable by repayment. **b** (of paper currency) for which the issuing authority does not undertake ever to pay coin. ▫▫ **irredeemability** /-bílliti/ *n.* **irredeemably** *adv.*

■ **1, 2** see INCURABLE *adj.*

irredentist /írridéntist/ *n.* a person, esp. in 19th-c. Italy, advocating the restoration to his or her country of any territory formerly belonging to it. ▫▫ **irredentism** *n.* [It. *irredentista* f. (*Italia*) *irredenta* unredeemed (Italy)]

irreducible /irridyóōssib'l/ *adj.* **1** that cannot be reduced or simplified. **2** (often foll. by *to*) that cannot be brought to a desired condition. ▫▫ **irreducibility** /-bílliti/ *n.* **irreducibly** *adv.*

irrefragable /iréfrəgəb'l/ *adj.* **1** (of a statement, argument, or person) unanswerable, indisputable. **2** (of rules etc.) inviolable. ▫▫ **irrefragably** *adv.* [LL *irrefragabilis* (as IN-[1], *refragari* oppose)]

irrefrangible /irrifránjib'l/ *adj.* **1** inviolable. **2** *Optics* incapable of being refracted.

irrefutable /iréfyootəb'l, írrifyóōt-/ *adj.* that cannot be refuted. ▫▫ **irrefutability** /-bílliti/ *n.* **irrefutably** *adv.* [LL *irrefutabilis* (as IN-[1], REFUTE)]

■ see INCONTROVERTIBLE. ▫▫ **irrefutability** see FINALITY. **irrefutably** see *undoubtedly* (UNDOUBTED).

irregardless /írrigaárdliss/ *adj.* & *adv. US dial.* or *joc.* = REGARDLESS. [prob. blend of IRRESPECTIVE and REGARDLESS]

irregular /irégyoolər/ *adj.* & *n.* ● *adj.* **1** not regular; unsymmetrical, uneven; varying in form. **2** (of a surface) uneven. **3** contrary to a rule, moral principle, or custom; abnormal. **4** uneven in duration, order, etc. **5** (of troops) not belonging to the regular army. **6** *Gram.* (of a verb, noun, etc.) not inflected according to the usual rules. **7** disorderly. **8** (of a flower) having unequal petals etc. ● *n.* (in *pl.*) irregular troops. ▫▫ **irregularity** /-lárriti/ *n.* (*pl.* **-ies**). **irregularly** *adv.* [ME f. OF *irreguler* f. LL *irregularis* (as IN-[1], REGULAR)]

■ *adj.* **1, 2** unequal, inequable, unsymmetrical, asymmetric(al), free-form, lopsided, skew, eccentric, deformed, bent, deviant; sprawling, ragged, rough-and-tumble; patchy, blotchy, scraggly, spotty, mottled, variegated, *colloq.* splodgy, wiggly; uneven, bumpy, bulgy, lumpy, coarse, rough, pitted, jagged, craggy, rocky, rugged, broken, crazy. **3** illegitimate, improper, incorrect, non-standard, invalid, unauthorized, spurious; abnormal, peculiar, unusual, uncommon, odd, strange, unconventional, divergent, exceptional, unnatural, untypical, extraordinary, singular, weird, eccentric, bizarre, quirky, wayward, anomalous, aberrant, queer, freakish, deformed, deviant, offbeat, *colloq.* oddball, kinky, way-out. **4** sporadic, aperiodic, episodic, random, erratic, haphazard, fitful, spasmodic, broken, uneven, abrupt, discontinuous, on-and-off, stop-and-go, stop-go, occasional; inconstant, unstable, changeable, variable, undependable, unpredictable, unreliable, mercurial, volatile, flighty, fickle, capricious; casual, *colloq.* promiscuous, *literary* mutable. **7** see DISORDERLY 1. ▫▫ **irregularity** inequality, unevenness, bumpiness, lumpiness, coarseness, roughness, jaggedness, cragginess; anomaly, mistake, oversight; see also BUMP *n.* 2.

irrelative /irélləṭiv/ *adj.* **1** (often foll. by *to*) unconnected, unrelated. **2** having no relations; absolute. **3** irrelevant. ▫▫ **irrelatively** *adv.*

irrelevant /irélliv'nt/ *adj.* (often foll. by *to*) not relevant; not applicable (to a matter in hand). ▫▫ **irrelevance** *n.* **irrelevancy** *n.* **irrelevantly** *adv.*

■ inappropriate, inapplicable, beside *or* off the point, beside *or* off *or* wide of the mark, out of the picture, not the question, neither here nor there, inapposite, malapropos, out of place, inapt, unapt, inconsequent, inconsequential, irrelative, intrusive, *esp. Law* impertinent; unrelated, unconnected, extraneous, extrinsic, peripheral, tangential, gratuitous. ▫▫ **irrelevance, irrelevancy** impertinence, intrusiveness, inapplicability, inappropriateness, unrelatedness, gratuitousness.

irreligion /írrilíjən/ *n.* disregard of or hostility to religion. ▫▫ **irreligionist** *n.* [F *irréligion* or L *irreligio* (as IN-[1], RELIGION)]

irreligious /írrilíjəss/ *adj.* **1** indifferent or hostile to religion. **2** lacking a religion. ▫▫ **irreligiously** *adv.* **irreligiousness** *n.*

■ **1** see IRREVERENT. **2** see HEATHEN 2.

irremediable /irriméediəb'l/ *adj.* that cannot be remedied. ▫▫ **irremediably** *adv.* [L *irremediabilis* (as IN-[1], REMEDY)]

■ see HOPELESS 2.

irremissible /irrimíssib'l/ *adj.* **1** unpardonable. **2** unalterably obligatory. ▫▫ **irremissibly** *adv.* [ME f. OF *irremissible* or eccl.L *irremissibilis* (as IN-[1], REMISSIBLE)]

irremovable /irrimóovəb'l/ *adj.* that cannot be removed, esp. from office. □□ **irremovability** /-bílliti/ *n.* **irremovably** *adv.*

irreparable /iréppərəb'l, *disp.* irripárrəb'l/ *adj.* (of an injury, loss, etc.) that cannot be rectified or made good. □□ **irreparability** /-bílliti/ *n.* **irreparableness** *n.* **irreparably** *adv.* [ME f. OF f. L *irreparabilis* (as IN-[1], REPARABLE)]
■ see HOPELESS 2.

irreplaceable /irripláysəb'l/ *adj.* **1** that cannot be replaced. **2** of which the loss cannot be made good. □□ **irreplaceably** *adv.*
■ **2** see INVALUABLE.

irrepressible /irripréssib'l/ *adj.* that cannot be repressed or restrained. □□ **irrepressibility** /-bílliti/ *n.* **irrepressibleness** *n.* **irrepressibly** *adv.*
■ unrestrainable, inextinguishable, uncontainable, uncontrollable, unmanageable, ungovernable, unstoppable, indomitable, irresistible; incorrigible, headstrong, wayward; ebullient, buoyant, effervescent, bubbly, exuberant, boisterous.

irreproachable /irripróchəb'l/ *adj.* faultless, blameless. □□ **irreproachability** /-bílliti/ *n.* **irreproachableness** *n.* **irreproachably** *adv.* [F *irréprochable* (as IN-[1], REPROACH)]
■ blameless, unimpeachable, beyond reproach, innocent, above suspicion; faultless, impeccable, spotless, unblemished, flawless, perfect, exemplary, ideal; honest, pure, sinless, decent.

irresistible /irrizístib'l/ *adj.* **1** too strong or convincing to be resisted. **2** delightful; alluring. □□ **irresistibility** /-bílliti/ *n.* **irresistibleness** *n.* **irresistibly** *adv.* [med.L *irresistibilis* (as IN-[1], RESIST)]
■ **1** unstoppable, unconquerable, indomitable, inexorable, relentless, unavoidable, ineluctable, inescapable, overpowering, overwhelming, overriding, forceful, magnetic; irrepressible, uncontrollable, ungovernable, uncontainable, unmanageable; compulsive. **2** attractive, appealing, alluring, luring, enticing, seductive, inviting, tempting, tantalizing; charming, delightful, captivating, enchanting, ravishing, fascinating.

irresolute /irézzəloot, -lyoot/ *adj.* **1** hesitant, undecided. **2** lacking in resoluteness. □□ **irresolutely** *adv.* **irresoluteness** *n.* **irresolution** /-lóosh'n, -lyóosh'n/ *n.*
■ **1** hesitant, undecided, undetermined, unresolved, indecisive, uncertain, unsure, in two minds, wavering, ambivalent, doubtful, dubious, vague, tentative, tremulous, dithery, shilly-shally, wishy-washy, half-hearted. **2** unsteadfast, unstable, inconstant, erratic, fickle, changeable, capricious, flighty, moody, fitful; weak, infirm, spineless, faint-hearted, half-baked, feeble, feckless, *Brit. colloq.* wet.

irresolvable /irrizólvəb'l/ *adj.* **1** that cannot be resolved into its components. **2** (of a problem) that cannot be solved.

irrespective /irrispéktiv/ *adj.* (foll. by *of*) not taking into account; regardless of. □□ **irrespectively** *adv.*
■ (*irrespective of*) regardless of, notwithstanding, despite, in spite of, without regard to, independent of, no matter; apart from, ignoring, discounting, disregarding, excluding, exclusive of.

irresponsible /irrispónsib'l/ *adj.* **1** acting or done without due sense of responsibility. **2** not responsible for one's conduct. □□ **irresponsibility** /-bílliti/ *n.* **irresponsibly** *adv.*
■ **1** careless, reckless, feckless, devil-may-care; rash, unthinking, thoughtless, unconsidered, ill-considered, heedless, headlong, hasty, wild, hotheaded; unreliable, undependable, untrustworthy. **2** unaccountable, not responsible *or* answerable. □□ **irresponsibility** see *stupidity* (STUPID).

irresponsive /irrispónsiv/ *adj.* (often foll. by *to*) not responsive. □□ **irresponsively** *adv.* **irresponsiveness** *n.*

irretrievable /irritréevəb'l/ *adj.* that cannot be retrieved or restored. □□ **irretrievability** /-bílliti/ *n.* **irretrievably** *adv.*
■ irrecoverable, irreclaimable, irreparable, beyond repair, incurable, irremediable, irredeemable, irreversible, irrevocable; hopeless, desperate, lost, gone.

irreverent /irévvərənt/ *adj.* lacking reverence. □□ **irreverence** *n.* **irreverential** /-rénsh'l/ *adj.* **irreverently** *adv.* [L *irreverens* (as IN-[1], REVERENT)]
■ blasphemous, impious, profane, sacrilegious, unholy, ungodly, godless, irreligious; disrespectful, contemptuous, insulting, insolent, rude, discourteous, uncivil, offensive, derisive, impudent, impertinent, saucy, cheeky, pert, *US* nervy, *colloq.* fresh, lippy.

irreversible /irrivérsib'l/ *adj.* not reversible or alterable. □□ **irreversibility** /-bílliti/ *n.* **irreversibly** *adv.*
■ irrevocable, unchangeable, unalterable, immutable, permanent, fixed, final, flat; irredeemable, irreparable, irretrievable; decided, unquestionable, indisputable, settled.

irrevocable /irévvəkəb'l, *disp.* irrivókəb'l/ *adj.* **1** unalterable. **2** gone beyond recall. □□ **irrevocability** /-bílliti/ *n.* **irrevocably** *adv.* [ME f. L *irrevocabilis* (as IN-[1], REVOKE)]
■ **1** irreversible, unchangeable, unalterable, inalterable, immutable, fixed, final, flat; permanent, everlasting; irredeemable, irreparable; settled, decided, unquestionable, indisputable. **2** irrecoverable, irretrievable, irreclaimable, lost, gone, beyond recall; desperate, hopeless.

irrigate /írrigayt/ *v.tr.* **1 a** water (land) by means of channels. **b** (of a stream etc.) supply (land) with water. **2** *Med.* supply (a wound etc.) with a constant flow of liquid. **3** refresh as with moisture. □□ **irrigable** *adj.* **irrigation** /-gáysh'n/ *n.* **irrigative** *adj.* **irrigator** *n.* [L *irrigare* (as IN-[2], *rigare* moisten)]
■ **1** see WATER *v.* 1.

irritable /íritəb'l/ *adj.* **1** easily annoyed or angered. **2** (of an organ etc.) very sensitive to contact. **3** *Biol.* responding actively to physical stimulus. □□ **irritability** /-bílliti/ *n.* **irritably** *adv.* [L *irritabilis* (as IRRITATE)]
■ **1** irascible, testy, tetchy, touchy, over-sensitive, prickly, huffy, waspish, snuffy, short-tempered, quick-tempered, hot-tempered, *colloq.* snappy, snappish, ratty, *Brit. sl.* waxy; peevish, cross, fiery, fractious, crabbed, crabby, crusty, bad-tempered, ill-tempered, ill-humoured, cantankerous, curmudgeonly, quarrelsome, querulous, grumpy, crotchety, *esp. US* cranky, *colloq.* grouchy, grumpish, *Austral. & NZ colloq.* crook, *Brit. colloq.* like a bear with a sore head, *US colloq.* peckish, *sl.* narky, *Austral. sl.* snaky, lemony; impatient, petulant, intolerant, nervous, edgy, on edge, out of sorts. **2** sensitive, delicate, tender; hypersensitive. □□ **irritability** see *impatience* (IMPATIENT).

irritant /írit'nt/ *adj. & n.* ● *adj.* causing irritation. ● *n.* an irritant substance. □□ **irritancy** *n.*

irritate /írritayt/ *v.tr.* **1** excite to anger; annoy. **2** stimulate discomfort or pain in (a part of the body). **3** *Biol.* stimulate (an organ) to action. □□ **irritatedly** *adv.* **irritating** *adj.* **irritatingly** *adv.* **irritation** /-táysh'n/ *n.* **irritative** *adj.* **irritator** *n.* [L *irritare irritat-*]
■ **1** anger, enrage, infuriate, madden, incense, make a person's blood boil; irk, annoy, pique, vex, exasperate, chafe, nettle, gall, grate on, jar on, hump, put out, get *or* put a person's back up, get on a person's nerves, make a person's hackles rise, *Brit.* get a person's blood up, *colloq.* get, get across, rile, needle, miff, peeve, make a person see red, get a person's goat, *Brit. colloq.* get on a person's wick, *disp.* aggravate, *sl.* bug, get up a person's nose, *Brit. sl.* brown off, cheese off, nark, *US sl.* burn up; bother, worry, nag, trouble, pester, provoke, bait, goad, torment, wind up, play up, fret, rub up the wrong way, *US* ride, *colloq.* hassle, get under a person's skin, get on a person's nerves, get in a person's hair, drive a person up the wall. **2** hurt, pain, sting, burn, nettle, chafe, inflame, redden. □□ **irritating** see IRKSOME. **irritation** see ANNOYANCE 1, BOTHER *n.* 1, INFLAMMATION 2.

irrupt /irúpt/ *v.intr.* (foll. by *into*) enter forcibly or violently. □□ **irruption** /irúpsh'n/ *n.* [L *irrumpere irrupt-* (as IN-², *rumpere* break)]

Is. *abbr.* **1 a** Island(s). **b** Isle(s). **2** (also **Isa.**) Isaiah (Old Testament).

is *3rd sing. present* of BE.

isagogic /ísəgójik/ *adj.* introductory. [L *isagogicus* f. Gk *eisagōgikos* f. *eisagōgē* introduction f. *eis* into + *agōgē* leading f. *agō* lead]

isagogics /ísəgójiks/ *n.* an introductory study, esp. of the literary and external history of the Bible.

isatin /ísətin/ *n. Chem.* a red crystalline derivative of indole used in the manufacture of dyes. [L *isatis* woad f. Gk]

ISBN *abbr.* international standard book number.

ischaemia /iskéemiə/ *n.* (*US* **ischemia**) *Med.* a reduction of the blood supply to part of the body. □□ **ischaemic** *adj.* [mod.L f. Gk *iskhaimos* f. *iskhō* keep back]

ischium /ískiəm/ *n.* (*pl.* **ischia** /-kiə/) the curved bone forming the base of each half of the pelvis. □□ **ischial** *adj.* [L f. Gk *iskhion* hip-joint: cf. SCIATIC]

-ise¹ *suffix* var. of -IZE. ¶ See the note at *-ize*.

-ise² /īz, eez/ *suffix* forming nouns of quality, state, or function (*exercise*; *expertise*; *franchise*; *merchandise*). [from or after F or OF *-ise* f. L *-itia* etc.]

-ise³ *suffix* var. of -ISH².

isentropic /ísentróppik/ *adj.* having equal entropy. [ISO- + ENTROPY]

-ish¹ /ish/ *suffix* forming adjectives: **1** from nouns, meaning: **a** having the qualities or characteristics of (*boyish*). **b** of the nationality of (*Danish*). **2** from adjectives, meaning 'somewhat' (*thickish*). **3** *colloq.* denoting an approximate age or time of day (*fortyish*; *six-thirtyish*). [OE *-isc*]

-ish² /ish/ *suffix* (also **-ise** /īz/) forming verbs (*vanish*; *advertise*). [from or after F *-iss-* (in extended stems of verbs in *-ir*) f. L *-isc-* incept. suffix]

isinglass /ízingglaass/ *n.* **1** a kind of gelatin obtained from fish, esp. sturgeon, and used in making jellies, glue, etc. **2** mica. [corrupt. of obs. Du. *huisenblas* sturgeon's bladder, assim. to GLASS]

Islam /ízlaam, -lam, -láam/ *n.* **1** the religion of the Muslims, a monotheistic faith regarded as revealed through Muhammad as the Prophet of Allah. **2** the Muslim world. □□ **Islamic** /izlámmik/ *adj.* **Islamism** *n.* **Islamist** *n.* **Islamize** *v.tr.* (also **-ise**). **Islamization** /-mīzáysh'n/ *n.* [Arab. *islām* submission (to God) f. *aslama* resign oneself]

island /īlənd/ *n.* **1** a piece of land surrounded by water. **2** anything compared to an island, esp. in being surrounded in some way. **3** = *traffic island*. **4 a** a detached or isolated thing. **b** *Physiol.* a detached portion of tissue or group of cells (cf. ISLET). **5** *Naut.* a ship's superstructure, bridge, etc. [OE *īgland* f. *īg* island + LAND: first syll. infl. by ISLE]
■ **1** islet, cay, key, atoll, *Brit.* ait, holm, *esp. Sc.* inch, *Sc.* skerry, *poet.* isle.

islander /īləndər/ *n.* a native or inhabitant of an island.

isle /īl/ *n. poet.* (and in place-names) an island or peninsula, esp. a small one. [ME *ile* f. OF *ile* f. L *insula*: later ME & OF *isle* after L]

islet /īlit/ *n.* **1** a small island. **2** *Anat.* a portion of tissue structurally distinct from surrounding tissues. **3** an isolated place. □ **islets of Langerhans** *Physiol.* groups of pancreatic cells secreting insulin and glucagon. [OF, dimin. of *isle* ISLE]

ism /ízz'm/ *n. colloq.* usu. *derog.* any distinctive but unspecified doctrine or practice of a kind with a name in *-ism*.
■ see SECT 2.

-ism /ízz'm/ *suffix* forming nouns, esp. denoting: **1** an action or its result (*baptism*; *organism*). **2** a system, principle, or ideological movement (*Conservatism*; *jingoism*; *feminism*). **3** a state or quality (*heroism*; *barbarism*). **4** a basis of prejudice or discrimination (*racism*; *sexism*). **5** a peculiarity in language (*Americanism*). **6** a pathological condition (*alcoholism*; *Parkinsonism*). [from or after F *-isme* f. L *-ismus* f. Gk *-ismos* or *-isma* f. *-izō* -IZE]

Ismaili /izmīli/ *n.* (*pl.* **Ismailis**) a member of a Muslim Shiite sect that arose in the 8th c. [*Ismail* a son of the patriarch Ibrāhim (= Abraham)]

isn't /ízz'nt/ *contr.* is not.

ISO *abbr.* **1** (in the UK) Imperial Service Order. **2** International Organization for Standardization.

iso- /ísō/ *comb. form* **1** equal (*isometric*). **2** *Chem.* isomeric, esp. of a hydrocarbon with a branched chain of carbon atoms (*isobutane*). [Gk *isos* equal]

isobar /ísōbaar/ *n.* **1** a line on a map connecting positions having the same atmospheric pressure at a given time or on average over a given period. **2** a curve for a physical system at constant pressure. **3** one of two or more isotopes of different elements, with the same atomic weight. □□ **isobaric** /-bárrik/ *adj.* [Gk *isobarēs* of equal weight (as ISO-, *baros* weight)]

isocheim /ísōkīm/ *n.* a line on a map connecting places having the same average temperature in winter. [ISO- + Gk *kheima* winter weather]

isochromatic /ísōkrōmáttik/ *adj.* of the same colour.

isochronous /īsókrənəss/ *adj.* **1** occurring at the same time. **2** occupying equal time. □□ **isochronously** *adv.* [ISO- + Gk *khronos* time]

isoclinal /ísōklīn'l/ *adj.* (also **isoclinic** /-klínnik/) **1** *Geol.* (of a fold) in which the two limbs are parallel. **2** corresponding to equal values of magnetic dip. [ISO- + CLINE]

isoclinic var. of ISOCLINAL.

isodynamic /ísōdīnámmik/ *adj.* corresponding to equal values of (magnetic) force.

isoenzyme /íso-enzīm/ *n. Biochem.* one of two or more enzymes with identical function but different structure.

isogeotherm /ísōjée-ōtherm/ *n.* a line or surface connecting points in the interior of the earth having the same temperature. □□ **isogeothermal** /-thérm'l/ *adj.*

isogloss /ísōgloss/ *n.* a line on a map marking an area having a distinct linguistic feature.

isogonic /ísōgónnik/ *adj.* corresponding to equal values of magnetic declination.

isohel /ísōhel/ *n.* a line on a map connecting places having the same duration of sunshine. [ISO- + Gk *hēlios* sun]

isohyet /ísōhī-it/ *n.* a line on a map connecting places having the same amount of rainfall in a given period. [ISO- + Gk *huetos* rain]

isolate /ísəlayt/ *v.tr.* **1 a** place apart or alone, cut off from society. **b** place (a patient thought to be contagious or infectious) in quarantine. **2 a** identify and separate for attention (*isolated the problem*). **b** *Chem.* separate (a substance) from a mixture. **3** insulate (electrical apparatus). □□ **isolable** /ísələb'l/ *adj.* **isolatable** *adj.* **isolator** *n.* [orig. in past part., f. F *isolé* f. It. *isolato* f. LL *insulatus* f. L *insula* island]
■ **1** separate, detach, insulate, segregate, set *or* keep apart, sequester, seclude, cloister, cut off, maroon, exclude, shut out; shun, cut, ostracize, send to Coventry, avoid, ignore, snub, cold-shoulder, boycott; quarantine; shelter, cushion. **2** see IDENTIFY 1, 2.

isolated /ísəlaytid/ *adj.* **1** lonely; cut off from society or contact; remote (*feeling isolated*; *an isolated farmhouse*). **2** untypical, unique (*an isolated example*).
■ **1** lonesome, lonely, solitary, forlorn; alone, separate, secluded, remote, sequestered, cut off, out of the way, cloistered, sheltered, unfrequented, lone, uninhabited; unconnected, detached; hermitic, eremitic(al), anchoretic, anchoritic, troglodytic(al), monastic, monkish, reclusive, withdrawn. **2** unique, single, solitary, singular; untypical, exceptional, particular, special, individual, *colloq.* one-off.

isolating /ísəlayting/ *adj.* (of a language) having each element as an independent word without inflections.

isolation /ísəláysh'n/ *n.* the act or an instance of isolating; the state of being isolated or separated. □ **in isolation** considered singly and not relatively. **isolation hospital**

(or **ward** etc.) a hospital, ward, etc., for patients with contagious or infectious diseases.
■ see SECLUSION 1.

isolationism /īsəláyshəniz'm/ *n.* the policy of holding aloof from the affairs of other countries or groups esp. in politics. ▫▫ **isolationist** *n.*

isoleucine /īsōlo͞osseen/ *n. Biochem.* an amino acid that is a constituent of proteins and an essential nutrient. [G *Isoleucin* (see ISO-, LEUCINE)]

isomer /īsəmər/ *n.* **1** *Chem.* one of two or more compounds with the same molecular formula but a different arrangement of atoms and different properties. **2** *Physics* one of two or more atomic nuclei that have the same atomic number and the same mass number but different energy states. ▫▫ **isomeric** /-mérrik/ *adj.* **isomerism** /īsómməriz'm/ *n.* **isomerize** /īsómmərīz/ *v.* (also **-ise**). [G f. Gk *isomerēs* sharing equally (as ISO-, *meros* share)]

isomerous /īsómmərəss/ *adj. Bot.* (of a flower) having the same number of petals in each whorl. [Gk *isomerēs*: see ISOMER]

isometric /īsōmétrik/ *adj.* **1** of equal measure. **2** *Physiol.* (of muscle action) developing tension while the muscle is prevented from contracting. **3** (of a drawing etc.) with the plane of projection at equal angles to the three principal axes of the object shown. **4** *Math.* (of a transformation) without change of shape or size. ▫▫ **isometrically** *adv.* **isometry** /īsómmitri/ *n.* (in sense 4). [Gk *isometria* equality of measure (as ISO-, -METRY)]

isometrics /īsōmétriks/ *n.pl.* a system of physical exercises in which muscles are caused to act against each other or against a fixed object.
■ see EXERCISE *n.* 3.

isomorph /īsōmorf/ *n.* an isomorphic substance or organism. [ISO- + Gk *morphē* form]

isomorphic /īsōmórfik/ *adj.* (also **isomorphous** /-fəss/) **1** exactly corresponding in form and relations. **2** *Crystallog.* having the same form. ▫▫ **isomorphism** *n.*

-ison /is'n/ *suffix* forming nouns, = -ATION (*comparison*; *garrison*; *jettison*; *venison*). [OF *-aison* etc. f. L *-atio* etc.: see -ATION]

isophote /īsōfōt/ *n.* a line (imaginary or in a diagram) of equal brightness or illumination. [ISO- + Gk *phōs phōtos* light]

isopleth /īsōpleth/ *n.* a line on a map connecting places having equal incidence of a meteorological feature. [ISO- + Gk *plēthos* fullness]

isopod /īsōpod/ *n.* any crustacean of the order *Isopoda*, including woodlice and slaters, often parasitic and having a flattened body with seven pairs of legs. [F *isopode* f. mod.L *Isopoda* (as ISO-, Gk *pous podos* foot)]

isosceles /īsóssileez/ *adj.* (of a triangle) having two sides equal. [LL f. Gk *isoskelēs* (as ISO-, *skelos* leg)]

isoseismal /īsōsīzm'l/ *adj.* & *n.* (also **isoseismic** /-mik/) ● *adj.* having equal strength of earthquake shock. ● *n.* a line on a map connecting places having an equal strength of earthquake shock.

isostasy /īsóstəsi/ *n. Geol.* the general state of equilibrium of the earth's crust, with the rise and fall of land relative to sea. ▫▫ **isostatic** /īsōstáttik/ *adj.* [ISO- + Gk *stasis* station]

isothere /īsōtheer/ *n.* a line on a map connecting places having the same average temperature in the summer. [ISO- + Gk *theros* summer]

isotherm /īsōtherm/ *n.* **1** a line on a map connecting places having the same temperature at a given time or on average over a given period. **2** a curve for changes in a physical system at a constant temperature. ▫▫ **isothermal** /-thérm'l/ *adj.* **isothermally** /-thérməli/ *adv.* [F *isotherme* (as ISO-, Gk *thermē* heat)]

isotonic /īsōtónnik/ *adj.* **1** having the same osmotic pressure. **2** *Physiol.* (of muscle action) taking place with normal contraction. ▫▫ **isotonically** *adv.* **isotonicity** /-təníssiti/ *n.* [Gk *isotonos* (as ISO-, TONE)]

isotope /īsətōp/ *n. Chem.* one of two or more forms of an element differing from each other in relative atomic mass, and in nuclear but not chemical properties. ▫▫ **isotopic** /-tóppik/ *adj.* **isotopically** /-tóppikəli/ *adv.* **isotopy** /īsóttəpi/ *n.* [ISO- + Gk *topos* place (i.e. in the periodic table of elements)]

isotropic /īsōtróppik/ *adj.* having the same physical properties in all directions (opp. ANISOTROPIC). ▫▫ **isotropically** *adv.* **isotropy** /īsótrəpi/ *n.* [ISO- + Gk *tropos* turn]

I-spy /ī-spī/ *n.* a game in which players try to identify something observed by one of them and identified by its initial letter.

Israeli /izráyli/ *adj.* & *n.* ● *adj.* of or relating to the modern State of Israel in the Middle East. ● *n.* **1** a native or national of Israel. **2** a person of Israeli descent. [*Israel*, a later name of Jacob, ult. f. Heb. *yisrā'ēl* he that strives with God (Gen. 32:28) + -I²]

Israelite /izriəlīt, -rəlīt/ *n. hist.* a native of ancient Israel; a Jew.

ISSN *abbr.* international standard serial number.

issuant /ishooənt, íssyoo-/ *adj. Heraldry* (esp. of a beast with only the upper part shown) rising from the bottom or top of a bearing.

issue /ísho͞o, íssyo͞o/ *n.* & *v.* ● *n.* **1 a** a giving out or circulation of shares, notes, stamps, etc. **b** a quantity of coins, supplies, copies of a newspaper or book etc., circulated or put on sale at one time. **c** an item or amount given out or distributed. **d** each of a regular series of a magazine etc. (*the May issue*). **2 a** an outgoing, an outflow. **b** a way out, an outlet esp. the place of the emergence of a stream etc. **3** a point in question; an important subject of debate or litigation. **4** a result; an outcome; a decision. **5** *Law* children, progeny (*without male issue*). **6** *archaic* a discharge of blood etc. ● *v.* (**issues**, **issued**, **issuing**) **1** *intr.* (often foll. by *out*, *forth*) *literary* go or come out. **2** *tr.* **a** send forth; publish; put into circulation. **b** supply, esp. officially or authoritatively (foll. by *to*, *with*: *issued passports to them*; *issued them with passports*; *issued orders to the staff*). **3** *intr.* **a** (often foll. by *from*) be derived or result. **b** (foll. by *in*) end, result. **4** *intr.* (foll. by *from*) emerge from a condition. ▫ **at issue 1** under discussion; in dispute. **2** at variance. **issue of fact** (or **law**) a dispute at law when the significance of a fact or facts is denied or when the application of the law is contested. **join** (or **take**) **issue** identify an issue for argument (foll. by *with*, *on*). **make an issue of** make a fuss about; turn into a subject of contention. ▫▫ **issuable** *adj.* **issuance** *n.* **issueless** *adj.* **issuer** *n.* [ME f. OF ult. f. L *exitus* past part. of *exire* EXIT]
■ *n.* **1 a** output, circulation, production, publication, distribution, flotation, issuance, dissemination, promulgation. **b** printing, run, edition. **c** dividend, bonus, yield, payment. **d** copy, number, version, edition, instalment. **2** outflow, outgoing, flux, efflux, effluxion, emanation, debouchment, issuance, emergence, emanation, discharge, outlet, vent, spout, egress, exit. **3** point (in question), topic, subject, talking-point, matter, question, affair, business; problem, difficulty, crux, controversy, dispute, trouble, *colloq.* thing. **4** result, event, outcome, upshot, progeny, effect, consequence, end-product, *sl.* pay-off; conclusion, decision, judgement, finding, ruling, verdict. **5** children, sons, daughters, descendants, heirs, offspring, progeny, scions; young, litter, brood, *archaic* seed. **6** see DISCHARGE *n.* 5. ● *v.* **1** go out *or* forth, come out *or* forth, emerge, emanate, flow out, discharge, pour, stream, escape, exit, *archaic* sally (forth). **2 a** send out *or* forth, put *or* give out, set out *or* forth, make known, make public, publicize, circulate, distribute, hand out, release, deliver, broadcast, disseminate; publish, announce, proclaim, promulgate; *Brit.* inscribe (*shares*). **b** supply, provide, furnish; equip, outfit, rig (out *or* up), fit (out *or* up). **3 a** arise, derive, result, originate, spring, stem, emerge, flow, proceed, emanate, come. **b** end (up), finish, result, conclude, culminate. **4** emerge, come out, appear,

surface; come to life, hatch, peep out. □ **at issue** under discussion, in question, at stake, on the agenda, moot; the point, alive; in contention, in dispute. **join** (or **take**) **issue** disagree, argue, quarrel, contend; (*take issue with*) dispute, question, take exception to, query, challenge, contest, oppose, deny. **make an issue of** kick up *or* make a fuss about, complain about, grumble *or* moan about, *colloq.* gripe *or* grouch *or* whinge *or* bitch about, kick up *or* make a stink about, *sl.* beef about.

-ist /ist/ *suffix* forming personal nouns (and in some senses related adjectives) denoting: **1** an adherent of a system etc. in *-ism*: see -ISM 2 (*Marxist*; *fatalist*). **2 a** a member of a profession (*pathologist*). **b** a person concerned with something (*tobacconist*). **3** a person who uses a thing (*violinist*; *balloonist*; *motorist*). **4** a person who does something expressed by a verb in *-ize* (*plagiarist*). **5** a person who subscribes to a prejudice or practises discrimination (*racist*; *sexist*). [OF *-iste*, L *-ista* f. Gk *-istēs*]

isthmian /ísmiən, ísth-/ *adj.* of or relating to an isthmus, esp. (**Isthmian**) to the Isthmus of Corinth in southern Greece.

isthmus /ísməss, ísth-/ *n.* **1** a narrow piece of land connecting two larger bodies of land. **2** *Anat.* a narrow part connecting two larger parts. [L f. Gk *isthmos*]

istle /ístli/ *n.* a fibre used for cord, nets, etc., obtained from agave. [Mex. *ixtli*]

IT *abbr.* information technology.

It. *abbr.* Italian.

it[1] /it/ *pron.* (*poss.* **its**; *pl.* **they**) **1** the thing (or occas. the animal or child) previously named or in question (*took a stone and threw it*). **2** the person in question (*Who is it? It is I; is it a boy or a girl?*). **3** as the subject of an impersonal verb (*it is raining*; *it is winter*; *it is Tuesday*; *it is two miles to Bath*). **4** as a substitute for a deferred subject or object (*it is intolerable, this delay*; *it is silly to talk like that*; *I take it that you agree*). **5** as a substitute for a vague object (*brazen it out*; *run for it!*). **6** as the antecedent to a relative word (*it was an owl I heard*). **7** exactly what is needed (*absolutely it*). **8** the extreme limit of achievement. **9** *colloq.* sexual intercourse; sex appeal. **10** (in children's games) a player who has to perform a required feat, esp. to catch the others. □ **that's it** *colloq.* that is: **1** what is required. **2** the difficulty. **3** the end, enough. **this is it** *colloq.* **1** the expected event is at hand. **2** this is the difficulty. [OE *hit* neut. of HE]

it[2] /it/ *n. colloq.* Italian vermouth (*gin and it*). [abbr.]

i.t.a. *abbr.* (also **ITA**) initial teaching alphabet.

ital. *abbr.* italic (type).

Italian /itályən/ *n.* & *adj.* ● *n.* **1 a** a native or national of Italy. **b** a person of Italian descent. **2** the Romance language used in Italy and parts of Switzerland. ● *adj.* of or relating to Italy or its people or language. □ **Italian vermouth** a sweet kind of vermouth. [ME f. It. *Italiano* f. *Italia* Italy]

Italianate /itályənayt/ *adj.* of Italian style or appearance. [It. *Italianato*]

italic /itállik/ *adj.* & *n.* ● *adj.* **1 a** *Printing* of the sloping kind of letters now used esp. for emphasis or distinction and in foreign words. **b** (of handwriting) compact and pointed like early Italian handwriting. **2** (**Italic**) of ancient Italy. ● *n.* **1** a letter in italic type. **2** this type. [L *italicus* f. Gk *italikos* Italian (because introduced by Aldo Manuzio of Venice)]

italicize /itállisīz/ *v.tr.* (also **-ise**) print in italics. □□ **italicization** /-záysh'n/ *n.*

Italiot /itálliət/ *n.* & *adj.* ● *n.* an inhabitant of the Greek colonies in ancient Italy. ● *adj.* of or relating to the Italiots. [Gk *Italiōtēs* f. *Italia* Italy]

Italo- /ittəlō/ *comb. form* Italian; Italian and.

itch /ich/ *n.* & *v.* ● *n.* **1** an irritation in the skin. **2** an impatient desire; a hankering. **3** (prec. by *the*) (in general use) scabies. ● *v.intr.* **1** feel an irritation in the skin, causing a desire to scratch it. **2** (usu. foll. by *to* + infin.) (of a person) feel a desire to do something (*am itching to tell you the news*). □ **itching palm** avarice. **itch-mite** a parasitic arthropod, *Sarcoptes scabiei*, which burrows under the skin causing scabies. [OE *gycce*, *gyccan* f. WG]

■ *n.* **1** itchiness, irritation, tickle, tingle, prickle. **2** desire, craving, hankering, hunger, thirst, yearning, longing, urge, impulse, compulsion, *colloq.* yen. ● *v.* **1** tickle; tingle, prickle. **2** desire, crave, hanker, hunger, thirst, yearn, pine, long, die, have an urge; wish, want, need.

itchy /íchi/ *adj.* (**itchier**, **itchiest**) having or causing an itch. □ **have itchy feet** *colloq.* **1** be restless. **2** have a strong urge to travel. □□ **itchiness** *n.*

■ see PRICKLY 3, RESTLESS 2, 3. □□ **itchiness** see PRICKLE *n.* 3.

it'd /ittəd/ *contr. colloq.* **1** it had. **2** it would.

-ite[1] /īt/ *suffix* forming nouns meaning 'a person or thing connected with': **1** in names of persons: **a** as natives of a country (*Israelite*). **b** often *derog.* as followers of a movement etc. (*pre-Raphaelite*; *Trotskyite*). **2** in names of things: **a** fossil organisms (*ammonite*). **b** minerals (*graphite*). **c** constituent parts of a body or organ (*somite*). **d** explosives (*dynamite*). **e** commercial products (*ebonite*; *vulcanite*). **f** salts of acids having names in *-ous* (*nitrite*; *sulphite*). [from or after F *-ite* f. L *-ita* f. Gk *-itēs*]

-ite[2] /īt, it/ *suffix* **1** forming adjectives (*erudite*; *favourite*). **2** forming nouns (*appetite*). **3** forming verbs (*expedite*; *unite*). [from or after L *-itus* past part. of verbs in *-ēre*, *-ere*, and *-ire*]

item /ītəm/ *n.* & *adv.* ● *n.* **1 a** any of a number of enumerated or listed things. **b** an entry in an account. **2** an article, esp. one for sale (*household items*). **3** a separate or distinct piece of news, information, etc. ● *adv. archaic* (introducing the mention of each item) likewise, also. [orig. as adv.: L, = in like manner, also]

■ *n.* **1, 2** thing, article, object; entry, point, detail, particular, subject, matter, element, component, ingredient, unit. **3** piece, article, feature, fact, story, filler; mention, notice, note.

itemize /ītəmīz/ *v.tr.* (also **-ise**) state or list item by item. □□ **itemization** /-záysh'n/ *n.* **itemizer** *n.*

■ enumerate, list, particularize, detail, specify, document, schedule, inventory, catalogue, take stock of; reel off, recite, rattle off; check off, tick off, run through, number, count, record.

iterate /íttərayt/ *v.tr.* repeat; state repeatedly. □□ **iteration** /-ráysh'n/ *n.* [L *iterare iterat-* f. *iterum* again]

■ see REITERATE. □□ **iteration** see ECHO *n.* 1.

iterative /íttərətiv/ *adj. Gram.* = FREQUENTATIVE. □□ **iteratively** *adv.*

ithyphallic /ithifállik/ *adj. Gk Hist.* **1 a** of the phallus carried in Bacchic festivals. **b** (of a statue etc.) having an erect penis. **2** lewd, licentious. **3** (of a poem or metre) used for Bacchic hymns. [LL *ithyphallicus* f. Gk *ithuphallikos* f. *ithus* straight, *phallos* PHALLUS]

■ **2** see INDECENT 1.

-itic /íttik/ *suffix* forming adjectives and nouns corresponding to nouns in *-ite*, *-itis*, etc. (*Semitic*; *arthritic*; *syphilitic*). [from or after F *-itique* f. L *-iticus* f. Gk *-itikos*: see -IC]

itinerant /ītínnərənt, i-/ *adj.* & *n.* ● *adj.* travelling from place to place. ● *n.* an itinerant person; a tramp. □ **itinerant judge** (or **minister** etc.) a judge, minister, etc. travelling within a circuit. □□ **itineracy** *n.* **itinerancy** *n.* [LL *itinerari* travel f. L *iter itiner-* journey]

■ *adj.* see MIGRANT *adj.* ● *n.* see MIGRANT *n.*

itinerary /ītínnərəri, i-/ *n.* & *adj.* ● *n.* (*pl.* **-ies**) **1** a detailed route. **2** a record of travel. **3** a guidebook. ● *adj.* of roads or travelling. [LL *itinerarius* (adj.), *-um* (n.) f. L *iter*: see ITINERANT]

■ **1** see ROUTE.

itinerate /ītínnərayt, i-/ *v.intr.* travel from place to place or (of a minister etc.) within a circuit. □□ **itineration** /-ráysh'n/ *n.* [LL *itinerari*: see ITINERANT]

-ition /ish'n/ *suffix* forming nouns, = -ATION (*admonition*; *perdition*; *position*). [from or after F *-ition* or L *-itio -itionis*]

-itious[1] /ishəss/ *suffix* forming adjectives corresponding to nouns in *-ition* (*ambitious*; *suppositious*). [L *-itio* etc. + -OUS]

-itious[2] /ishəss/ *suffix* forming adjectives meaning 'related to, having the nature of' (*adventitious*; *supposititious*). [L *-icius* + -OUS, commonly written with *t* in med.L manuscripts]

-itis /ītiss/ *suffix* forming nouns, esp.: **1** names of inflammatory diseases (*appendicitis*; *bronchitis*). **2** *colloq.* in extended uses with ref. to conditions compared to diseases (*electionitis*). [Gk *-itis*, forming fem. of adjectives in *-itēs* (with *nosos* 'disease' implied)]

-itive /itiv/ *suffix* forming adjectives, = -ATIVE (*positive*; *transitive*). [from or after F *-itif -itive* or L *-itivus* f. participial stems in *-it-*: see -IVE]

it'll /itt'l/ *contr. colloq.* it will; it shall.

ITN *abbr.* (in the UK) Independent Television News.

ITO *abbr.* International Trade Organization.

-itor /itər/ *suffix* forming agent nouns, usu. from Latin words (sometimes via French) (*creditor*). See also -OR[1].

-itory /itəri, itri/ *suffix* forming adjectives meaning 'relating to or involving (a verbal action)' (*inhibitory*). See also -ORY[2]. [L *-itorius*]

-itous /itəss/ *suffix* forming adjectives corresponding to nouns in *-ity* (*calamitous*; *felicitous*). [from or after F *-iteux* f. L *-itosus*]

its /its/ *poss.pron.* of it; of itself (*can see its advantages*).

it's /its/ *contr.* **1** it is. **2** it has.

itself /itsélf/ *pron.* emphatic and refl. form of IT[1]. □ **by itself** apart from its surroundings, automatically, spontaneously. **in itself** viewed in its essential qualities (*not in itself a bad thing*). [OE f. IT[1] + SELF, but often treated as ITS + SELF (cf. *its own self*)]

itsy-bitsy /itsibítsi/ *adj.* (also **itty-bitty** /ittibítti/) *colloq.* usu. *derog.* tiny, insubstantial, slight. [redupl. of LITTLE, infl. by BIT[1]]

■ see TINY.

ITU *abbr.* International Telecommunication Union.

ITV *abbr.* (in the UK) Independent Television.

-ity /iti/ *suffix* forming nouns denoting: **1** quality or condition (*authority*; *humility*; *purity*). **2** an instance or degree of this (*a monstrosity*; *humidity*). [from or after F *-ité* f. L *-itas -itatis*]

IU *abbr.* international unit.

IUD *abbr.* **1** intra-uterine (contraceptive) device. **2** intra-uterine death (of the foetus before birth).

-ium /iəm/ *suffix* forming nouns denoting esp.: **1** (also **-um**) names of metallic elements (*uranium*; *tantalum*). **2** a region of the body (*pericardium*; *hypogastrium*). **3** a biological structure (*mycelium*; *prothallium*). [from or after L *-ium* f. Gk *-ion*]

IUPAC /yoōpak/ *abbr.* International Union of Pure and Applied Chemistry.

IV *abbr.* intravenous.

I've /īv/ *contr.* I have.

-ive /iv/ *suffix* forming adjectives meaning 'tending to, having the nature of', and corresponding nouns (*suggestive*; *corrosive*; *palliative*; *coercive*; *talkative*). □□ **-ively** *suffix* forming adverbs. **-iveness** *suffix* forming nouns. [from or after F *-if -ive* f. L *-ivus*]

IVF *abbr. in vitro* fertilization.

ivied /īvid/ *adj.* overgrown with ivy.

ivory /īvəri/ *n.* (*pl.* **-ies**) **1** a hard creamy-white substance composing the main part of the tusks of an elephant, hippopotamus, walrus, and narwhal. **2** the colour of this. **3** (usu. in *pl.*) **a** an article made of ivory. **b** *sl.* anything made of or resembling ivory, esp. a piano key or a tooth. □ **fossil ivory** ivory from the tusks of a mammoth. **ivory black** black pigment from calcined ivory or bone. **ivory-nut** the seed of a corozo palm, *Phytelephas macrocarpa*, used as a source of vegetable ivory for carving: also called *corozo-nut*. **ivory tower** a state of seclusion or separation from the ordinary world and the harsh realities of life. **vegetable ivory** a hard white material obtained from the endosperm of the ivory-nut. □□ **ivoried** *adj.* [ME f. OF *yvoire* ult. f. L *ebur eboris*]

ivy /īvi/ *n.* (*pl.* **-ies**) **1** a climbing evergreen shrub, *Hedera helix*, with usu. dark-green shining five-angled leaves. **2** any of various other climbing plants including ground ivy and poison ivy. □ **Ivy League** a group of universities in the eastern US. [OE *īfig*]

IWW *abbr.* Industrial Workers of the World.

ixia /iksiə/ *n.* any iridaceous plant of the genus *Ixia* of S. Africa, with large showy flowers. [L f. Gk, a kind of thistle]

izard /izzaard/ *n.* a chamois. [F *isard*, of unkn. orig.]

-ize /īz/ *suffix* (also **-ise**) forming verbs, meaning: **1** make or become such (*Americanize*; *pulverize*; *realize*). **2** treat in such a way (*monopolize*; *pasteurize*). **3 a** follow a special practice (*economize*). **b** have a specified feeling (*sympathize*). **4** affect with, provide with, or subject to (*oxidize*; *hospitalize*). ¶ The form *-ize* has been in use in English since the 16th c.; it is widely used in American English, but is not an Americanism. The alternative spelling *-ise* (reflecting a French influence) is in common use, esp. in British English, and is obligatory in certain cases: (*a*) where it forms part of a larger word-element, such as *-mise* (= sending) in *compromise*, and *-prise* (= taking) in *surprise*; and (*b*) in verbs corresponding to nouns with *-i-* in the stem, such as *advertise* and *televise*. □□ **-ization** /īzáysh'n/ *suffix* forming nouns. **-izer** *suffix* forming agent nouns. [from or after F *-iser* f. LL *-izare* f. Gk *-izō*]

Jj

J[1] /jay/ *n.* (also **j**) (*pl.* **Js** or **J's**) **1** the tenth letter of the alphabet. **2** (as a Roman numeral) = *i* in a final position (*ij*; *vj*).

J[2] *abbr.* (also **J.**) **1** joule(s). **2** Judge. **3** Justice.

jab /jab/ *v.* & *n.* ● *v.tr.* (**jabbed, jabbing**) **1 a** poke roughly. **b** stab. **2** (foll. by *into*) thrust (a thing) hard or abruptly. ● *n.* **1** an abrupt blow with one's fist or a pointed implement. **2** *colloq.* a hypodermic injection, esp. a vaccination. [orig. Sc. var. of JOB[2]]
■ *v.* **1 a** poke, dig, punch, job; nudge, elbow. **b** stab, stick; spear, lance, skewer, spike, spit, prick. **2** thrust, push, shove, lunge, drive, jam, ram, poke. ● *n.* **1** poke, dig, thrust, job, stab, shove, lunge, ram; punch, hit, cuff, thump, rap, blow, clout, *US* slug, *colloq.* whack, thwack, sock, bop, *esp. US colloq.* bust, *sl.* wallop, biff, conk. **2** injection, inoculation, vaccination, *colloq.* shot, *sl.* bang, *esp. US sl.* hit.

jabber /jábbər/ *v.* & *n.* ● *v.* **1** *intr.* chatter volubly and incoherently. **2** *tr.* utter (words) fast and indistinctly. ● *n.* meaningless jabbering; a gabble. [imit.]
■ *v.* **1** chatter, blather, babble, burble, gibber, gabble, drivel, prate, prattle, tattle, rattle (on), gush, cackle, *colloq. or dial.* yammer, yatter (on), *colloq.* natter, gas, jaw, yap, witter, *esp. Brit. colloq.* waffle, rabbit (on *or* away), *sl. derog.* yack. **2** gabble, babble; prate, prattle, tattle. ● *n.* jabbering, chatter, blather, babble, gibber, burble, gabble, prate, prating, prattle, rattle, cackle, *colloq. or dial.* yammer, natter, *colloq.* jaw, yap, *esp. Brit. colloq.* waffle, *sl. derog.* yack; gibberish, twaddle, nonsense, drivel, rubbish, jargon, gobbledegook, balderdash, claptrap, bunkum, wind, *colloq.* hogwash, tripe, malarkey, piffle, flapdoodle, *Brit. colloq.* double Dutch, *sl.* eyewash, hooey, bosh, boloney, hot air, gas, (tommy-)rot, *Brit. sl.* codswallop.

jabberwocky /jábbərwokki/ *n.* (*pl.* **-ies**) a piece of nonsensical writing or speech, esp. for comic effect. [title of a poem in Lewis Carroll's *Through the Looking-Glass* (1871)]
■ see NONSENSE.

jabiru /jábbiroo/ *n.* **1** a large stork, *Jabiru mycteria*, of Central and S. America. **2** a black-necked stork, *Xenorhyncus asiaticus*, of Asia and Australia. [Tupi-Guarani *jabirú*]

jaborandi /jábbərándi/ *n.* (*pl.* **jaborandis**) **1** any shrub of the genus *Pilocarpus*, of S. America. **2** the dried leaflets of this, having diuretic and diaphoretic properties. [Tupi-Guarani *jaburandi*]

jabot /zhábbō/ *n.* an ornamental frill or ruffle of lace etc. on the front of a shirt or blouse. [F, orig. = crop of a bird]

jacana /jákkənə, jáss-/ *n.* any of various small tropical wading birds of the family Jacanidae, with elongated toes and hind-claws which enable them to walk on floating leaves etc. [Port. *jaçanã* f. Tupi-Guarani *jasaná*]

jacaranda /jákkərándə/ *n.* **1** any tropical American tree of the genus *Jacaranda*, with trumpet-shaped blue flowers. **2** any tropical American tree of the genus *Dalbergia*, with hard scented wood. [Tupi-Guarani *jacarandá*]

jacinth /jássinth, jáy-/ *n.* a reddish-orange variety of zircon used as a gem. [ME *iacynt* etc. f. OF *iacinte* or med.L *jacint(h)us* f. L *hyacinthus* HYACINTH]

jack[1] /jak/ *n.* & *v.* ● *n.* **1** a device for lifting heavy objects, esp. the axle of a vehicle off the ground while changing a wheel etc. **2** a court-card with a picture of a man, esp. a soldier, page, or knave, etc. **3** a ship's flag, esp. one flown from the bow and showing nationality. **4** a device using a single plug to connect an electrical circuit. **5** a small white ball in bowls, at which the players aim. **6 a** = JACKSTONE. **b** (in *pl.*) a game of jackstones. **7** (**Jack**) the familiar form of *John* esp. typifying the common man or the male of a species (*I'm all right, Jack*). **8** the figure of a man striking the bell on a clock. **9** *sl.* a detective; a policeman. **10** *US sl.* money. **11** = LUMBERJACK. **12** = STEEPLEJACK. **13** a device for turning a spit. **14** any of various marine perchlike fish of the family Carangidae, including the amberjack. **15** a device for plucking the string of a harpsichord etc., one being operated by each key. ● *v.tr.* **1** (usu. foll. by *up*) raise with or as with a jack (in sense 1). **2** (usu. foll. by *up*) *colloq.* raise e.g. prices. **3** (foll. by *off*) **a** go away, depart. **b** *coarse sl.* masturbate. □ **before you can say Jack Robinson** *colloq.* very quickly or suddenly. **every man jack** each and every person. **Jack Frost** frost personified. **jack in** (or **up**) *sl.* abandon (an attempt etc.). **jack-in-the-box** a toy figure that springs out of a box when it is opened. **jack-in-office** a self-important minor official. **jack of all trades** a person who can do many different kinds of work. **jack-o'-lantern** **1** a will-o'-the wisp. **2** a lantern made esp. from a pumpkin with holes for facial features. **jack plane** a medium-sized plane for use in rough joinery. **jack plug** a plug for use with a jack (see sense 4 of *n.*). **Jack tar** a sailor. **Jack-the-lad** *colloq.* a brash, self-assured young man. **on one's jack** (or **Jack Jones**) *sl.* alone; on one's own. [ME *Iakke*, a pet-name for *John*, erron. assoc. with F *Jacques* James]
■ *n.* **3** see FLAG[1] *n.* 1a. ● *v.* **2** see RAISE *v.* 3. **3 a** see LEAVE[1] *v.* 1b, 3, 4. □ **jack in** (or **up**) see ABANDON *v.* 1. **Jack-the-lad** see LAD 3. **on one's jack** (or **Jack Jones**) see ALONE 1a, b.

jack[2] /jak/ *n.* **1** = BLACKJACK[3]. **2** *hist.* a sleeveless padded tunic worn by foot-soldiers. [ME f. OF *jaque*, of uncert. orig.]

jackal /jákk'l/ *n.* **1** any of various wild doglike mammals of the genus *Canis*, esp. *C. aureus*, found in Africa and S. Asia, usu. hunting or scavenging for food in packs. **2** *colloq.* **a** a person who does preliminary drudgery for another. **b** a person who assists another's immoral behaviour. [Turk. *çakal* f. Pers. *šagāl*]
■ **2 a** see *yes-man*.

jackanapes /jákkənayps/ *n. archaic* **1** a pert or insolent fellow. **2** a mischievous child. **3** a tame monkey. [earliest as *Jack Napes* (1450): supposed to refer to the Duke of Suffolk, whose badge was an ape's clog and chain]

jackaroo /jákkəroo/ *n.* (also **jackeroo**) *Austral. colloq.* a novice on a sheep-station or cattle-station. [JACK[1] + KANGAROO]

jackass /jákkass/ *n.* **1** a male ass. **2** a stupid person.
■ **2** see FOOL[1] *n.* 1.

jackboot /jákboot/ *n.* **1** a large boot reaching above the knee. **2** this as a symbol of fascism or military oppression. □□ **jackbooted** *adj.*

jackdaw /jákdaw/ *n.* a small grey-headed crow, *Corvus monedula*, often frequenting rooftops and nesting in tall buildings, and noted for its inquisitiveness (cf. DAW).

jackeroo var. of JACKAROO.

jacket /jákkit/ *n.* & *v.* ● *n.* **1 a** a sleeved short outer garment. **b** a thing worn esp. round the torso for protection or support (*life-jacket*). **2** a casing or covering, e.g. as insulation round a boiler. **3** = *dust-jacket*. **4** the skin of a potato, esp. when baked whole. **5** an animal's coat. ● *v.tr.* (**jacketed, jacketing**) cover with a jacket. □ **jacket potato** a baked potato served with the skin on. [ME f. OF *ja(c)quet* dimin. of *jaque* JACK[2]]

■ **1 a** see COAT *n.* 1. **2** see WRAPPER 1, 2.

jackfish /jákfish/ *n.* (*pl.* same) = PIKE[1].

jackfruit /jákfro͞ot/ *n.* **1** an East Indian tree, *Artocarpus heterophyllus*, bearing fruit resembling breadfruit. **2** this fruit. [Port. *jaca* f. Malayalam *chakka* + FRUIT]

jackhammer /ják-hammər/ *n.* *US* a pneumatic hammer or drill.

jackknife /jáknīf/ *n.* & *v.* ● *n.* (*pl.* **-knives**) **1** a large clasp-knife. **2** a dive in which the body is first bent at the waist and then straightened. ● *v.intr.* (**-knifed, -knifing**) (of an articulated vehicle) fold against itself in an accidental skidding movement.

■ **1** see KNIFE *n.* 1b.

jackpot /jákpot/ *n.* a large prize or amount of winnings, esp. accumulated in a game or lottery etc. □ **hit the jackpot** *colloq.* **1** win a large prize. **2** have remarkable luck or success. [JACK[1] *n.* 2 + POT[1]: orig. in a form of poker with two jacks as minimum to open the pool]

■ see WINDFALL.

jackrabbit /jákrabbit/ *n.* *US* any of various large prairie hares of the genus *Lepus* with very long ears and hind legs.

Jack Russell /jak rúss'l/ *n.* **1** a terrier of a breed with short legs. **2** this breed.

jacksnipe /jáksnīp/ *n.* a small snipe, *Lymnocryptes minimus*.

jackstaff /jákstaaf/ *n.* *Naut.* **1** a staff at the bow of a ship for a jack. **2** a staff carrying the flag that is to show above the masthead.

■ see POLE[1] *n.*

jackstone /jákstōn/ *n.* **1** a small piece of metal etc. used with others in tossing-games. Also called JACK[1]. **2** (in *pl.*) **a** a game with a ball and jackstones. **b** the game of jacks.

jackstraw /jákstraw/ *n.* a spillikin.

Jacky = JACKY JACKY.

Jacky Jacky /jákki jákki/ *n.* *Austral. sl. offens.* **1** a nickname for an Aborigine. **2** the typical Aborigine.

Jacobean /jákkəbeéən/ *adj.* & *n.* ● *adj.* **1** of or relating to the reign of James I of England. **2** (of furniture) in the style prevalent then, esp. of the colour of dark oak. ● *n.* a Jacobean person. [mod.L *Jacobaeus* f. eccl.L *Jacobus* James f. Gk *Iakōbos* Jacob]

Jacobin /jákkəbin/ *n.* **1 a** *hist.* a member of a radical democratic club established in Paris in 1789 in the old convent of the Jacobins (see sense 2). **b** any extreme radical. **2** *archaic* a Dominican friar. **3** (**jacobin**) a pigeon with reversed feathers on the back of its neck like a cowl. □□ **Jacobinic** /-bínnik/ *adj.* **Jacobinical** /-bínnik'l/ *adj.* **Jacobinism** *n.* [orig. in sense 2 by assoc. with the Rue St Jacques in Paris: ME f. F f. med.L *Jacobinus* f. eccl.L *Jacobus*]

Jacobite /jákkəbīt/ *n.* *hist.* a supporter of James II of England after his removal from the throne in 1688, or of the Stuarts. □□ **Jacobitical** /-bíttik'l/ *adj.* **Jacobitism** *n.* [L *Jacobus* James: see JACOBEAN]

Jacob's ladder /jáykəbz/ *n.* **1** a plant, *Polemonium caeruleum*, with corymbs of blue or white flowers, and leaves suggesting a ladder. **2** a rope-ladder with wooden rungs. [f. Jacob's dream of a ladder reaching to heaven, as described in Gen. 28:12]

Jacob's staff /jáykəbz/ *n.* **1** a surveyor's iron-shod rod used instead of a tripod. **2** an instrument for measuring distances and heights. [f. the staffs used by Jacob, as described in Gen. 30:37–43]

jaconet /jákkənit/ *n.* a cotton cloth like cambric, esp. a dyed waterproof kind for poulticing etc. [Urdu *jagannāthi* f. *Jagannath* (now Puri) in India, its place of origin: see JUGGERNAUT]

Jacquard /jákkaard/ *n.* **1** an apparatus with perforated cards, fitted to a loom to facilitate the weaving of figured fabrics. **2** (in full **Jacquard loom**) a loom fitted with this. **3** a fabric or article made with this, with an intricate variegated pattern. [J. M. *Jacquard*, Fr. inventor d. 1834]

jactitation /jáktitáysh'n/ *n.* **1** *Med.* **a** the restless tossing of the body in illness. **b** the twitching of a limb or muscle. **2** *archaic* the offence of falsely claiming to be a person's wife or husband. [med.L *jactitatio* false declaration f. L *jactitare* boast, frequent. of *jactare* throw: sense 1 f. earlier *jactation*]

Jacuzzi /jəko͞ozi/ *n.* (*pl.* **Jacuzzis**) *propr.* a large bath with underwater jets of water to massage the body. [name of the inventor and manufacturers]

jade[1] /jayd/ *n.* **1** a hard usu. green stone composed of silicates of calcium and magnesium, or of sodium and aluminium, used for ornaments and implements. **2** the green colour of jade. [F: *le jade* for *l'ejade* f. Sp. *piedra de ijada* stone of the flank, i.e. stone for colic (which it was believed to cure)]

jade[2] /jayd/ *n.* **1** an inferior or worn-out horse. **2** *derog.* a disreputable woman. [ME: orig. unkn.]

■ **1** nag, hack, *sl.* screw, dog. **2** trollop, slattern, drab, lady of easy virtue, whore, hussy, scarlet woman, slag, *colloq.* floozie, *derog.* slut, *sl.* tart, moll, *US sl.* broad.

jaded /jáydid/ *adj.* tired or worn out; surfeited. □□ **jadedly** *adv.* **jadedness** *n.*

■ exhausted, weary, tired (out), dead tired, dog-tired, spent, raddled, toil-worn, broken down, decrepit, effete, *colloq.* fagged (out), done (in), dead beat, *US colloq.* bushed, pooped, *sl.* knackered, *Brit. sl.* clapped out; blasé, fed up, *sl.* brassed off, *Brit. sl.* browned off, cheesed (off); hackneyed, trite; sated, satiated, cloyed, surfeited, glutted, gorged, sick (and tired), slaked; dull, bored.

jadeite /jáydīt/ *n.* a green, blue, or white sodium aluminium silicate form of jade.

j'adoube /zhaado͞ob/ *int.* *Chess* a declaration by a player intending to adjust the placing of a piece without making a move with it. [F, = I adjust]

jaeger /yáygər/ *n.* (also **yager**) *US* = SKUA. [G *Jäger* hunter f. *jagen* to hunt]

Jaffa /jáffə/ *n.* a large oval thick-skinned variety of orange. [*Jaffa* in Israel, near where it was first grown]

jag[1] /jag/ *n.* & *v.* ● *n.* a sharp projection of rock etc. ● *v.tr.* (**jagged, jagging**) **1** cut or tear unevenly. **2** make indentations in. □□ **jagger** *n.* [ME, prob. imit.]

jag[2] /jag/ *n. sl.* **1** a drinking-bout; a spree. **2** a period of indulgence in an activity, emotion, etc. [orig. 16th c., = load for one horse: orig. unkn.]

■ **1** (drinking-)bout, carouse, carousal, orgy, bacchanal, soak, *Sc.* skite, *archaic* wassail, *colloq.* souse, *Brit. colloq.* pub-crawl, *sl.* binge, booze-up, drunk, bender, *Brit. sl.* blind; frolic, romp, rollick, fling, debauch, *colloq.* lark, spree, *sl.* razzle-dazzle. **2** fit, spell, burst, stint, bout.

jagged /jággid/ *adj.* **1** with an unevenly cut or torn edge. **2** deeply indented; with sharp points. □□ **jaggedly** *adv.* **jaggedness** *n.*

■ **1** jaggy, rough, uneven, ragged, coarse; chipped; craggy, irregular. **2** jaggy, indented, serrated, crenellated, sawtooth(ed), toothed, spiky, notched, notchy, zigzag, *Bot.* & *Zool.* dentate, *Zool.* denticulate.

jaggy /jággi/ *adj.* (**jaggier, jaggiest**) **1** = JAGGED. **2** (also **jaggie**) *Sc.* prickly.

jaguar /jágyooər/ *n.* a large flesh-eating spotted feline, *Panthera onca*, of Central and S. America. [Tupi-Guarani *jaguara*]

jaguarundi /jágwərúndi/ *n.* (*pl.* **jaguarundis**) a long-tailed slender feline, *Felis yaguarondi*, of Central and S. America. [Tupi-Guarani]

jai alai /hī́ əlī́/ *n.* a game like pelota played with large curved wicker baskets. [Sp. f. Basque *jai* festival + *alai* merry]

jail /jayl/ *n.* & *v.* (also **gaol**) ● *n.* **1** a place to which persons are committed by a court for detention. **2** confinement in a jail. ● *v.tr.* put in jail. □ **jail-bait** *sl.* a girl under the age of consent. [ME *gayole* f. OF *jaiole, jeole* & ONF *gaole* f. Rmc dimin. of L *cavea* CAGE]

■ *n.* **1** prison, coop, pen, labour camp, prison camp, lock-up, bagnio, *US* calaboose, penitentiary, brig, *archaic* bridewell, *dial.* fleet, *hist.* bastille, gatehouse, roundhouse, Stalag, *sl.* slammer, big house, can, bird, clink, cooler, jug, stir, slammer, *Brit. sl.* choky, glasshouse, nick, quod, *US sl.* hoosegow, pen, pokey, slam; reform school, *Brit.* detention centre, youth custody centre, *Brit. hist.* Borstal, *US* & *hist.* reformatory. **2** imprisonment, incarceration, internment, detention, detainer, confinement, custody, committal, remand, limbo, hard labour, *archaic* durance, *colloq.* time, *hist.* penal servitude, *Brit. sl.* porridge, hard, *rhyming sl.* bird. ● *v.* imprison, incarcerate, detain, remand, lock up *or* away, intern, shut up, put behind bars, put away, put inside, put in *or* throw into irons, *Brit.* send down, *US* send up, *poet.* prison, *sl.* lag, *Brit. sl.* bang up.

jailbird /jáylburd/ *n.* (also **gaolbird**) a prisoner or habitual criminal.

■ see PRISONER.

jailbreak /jáylbrayk/ *n.* (also **gaolbreak**) an escape from jail.

■ see ESCAPE *n.* 1.

jailer /jáylər/ *n.* (also **gaoler**) a person in charge of a jail or of the prisoners in it.

■ governor, *US* warden; prison officer, *Brit.* warder, wardress, *US* guard, *archaic* turnkey, *sl.* screw.

Jain /jīn/ *n.* & *adj.* ● *n.* an adherent of a non-Brahminical Indian religion. ● *adj.* of or relating to this religion. □□ **Jainism** *n.* **Jainist** *n.* [Hindi f. Skr. *jainas* saint, victor f. *jīna* victorious]

jake /jayk/ *adj. Austral.* & *NZ sl.* all right; satisfactory. [20th c.: orig. uncert.]

■ see OK[1] *adj.*

jalap /jálləp/ *n.* a purgative drug obtained esp. from the tuberous roots of a Mexican climbing plant, *Exogonium purga*. [F f. Sp. *jalapa* f. *Jalapa, Xalapa*, city in Mexico, f. Aztec *Xalapan* sand by the water]

jalopy /jəlóppi/ *n.* (*pl.* **-ies**) *colloq.* a dilapidated old motor vehicle. [20th c.: orig. unkn.]

■ see RATTLETRAP.

jalousie /zhálloozee/ *n.* a blind or shutter made of a row of angled slats to keep out rain etc. and control the influx of light. [F (as JEALOUSY)]

Jam. *abbr.* **1** Jamaica. **2** James (New Testament).

jam[1] /jam/ *v.* & *n.* ● *v.tr.* & *intr.* (**jammed, jamming**) **1 a** *tr.* (usu. foll. by *into*) squeeze or wedge into a space. **b** *intr.* become wedged. **2 a** *tr.* cause (machinery or a component) to become wedged or immovable so that it cannot work. **b** *intr.* become jammed in this way. **3** *tr.* push or cram together in a compact mass. **4** *intr.* (foll. by *in, on to*) push or crowd (*they jammed on to the bus*). **5** *tr.* **a** block (a passage, road, etc.) by crowding or obstructing. **b** (foll. by *in*) obstruct the exit of (*we were jammed in*). **6** *tr.* (usu. foll. by *on*) apply (brakes etc.) forcefully or abruptly. **7** *tr.* make (a radio transmission) unintelligible by causing interference. **8** *intr. colloq.* (in jazz etc.) extemporize with other musicians. ● *n.* **1** a squeeze or crush. **2** a crowded mass (*traffic jam*). **3** *colloq.* an awkward situation or predicament. **4** a stoppage (of a machine etc.) due to jamming. **5** (in full **jam session**) *colloq.* improvised playing by a group of jazz musicians. □ **jam-packed** *colloq.* full to capacity. □□ **jammer** *n.* [imit.]

■ *v.* **1, 3, 4** cram, force, push, thrust, wedge, stuff, press, ram, squash, squeeze, shove, crush, pack, crowd, pile; crunch, scrunch, crumple, compact. **2** lock, seize, freeze; immobilize. **5** block, obstruct, congest, fill up, snarl up, foul (up), tangle up, clog, plug, stop up, barricade, hem in, shut in *or* off. **6** (*jam on*) slam on, ram on; apply, activate, actuate. **8** see IMPROVISE 1. ● *n.* **1** crush, squeeze, squash, press. **2** mass, crowd, pack, swarm, horde, throng, mob, multitude; obstruction, blockage, congestion, bottleneck, *Brit.* tailback, *colloq.* snarl-up. **3** trouble, difficulty, predicament, crisis, emergency, plight, imbroglio, quandary, mess, *colloq.* bind, fix, hole, pickle, hot water, spot, scrape, *disp.* dilemma. **4** stoppage, blockage, seizure. **5** see *improvisation* (IMPROVISE). □ **jam-packed** full (up), replete, brim-full, packed (out), bursting at the seams, chock-a-block, chock-full, solid.

jam[2] /jam/ *n.* & *v.* ● *n.* **1** a conserve of fruit and sugar boiled to a thick consistency. **2** *Brit. colloq.* something easy or pleasant (*money for jam*). ● *v.tr.* (**jammed, jamming**) **1** spread jam on. **2** make (fruit etc.) into jam. □ **jam tomorrow** a pleasant thing often promised but usu. never forthcoming. [perh. = JAM[1]]

jamb /jam/ *n. Archit.* a side post or surface of a doorway, window, or fireplace. [ME f. OF *jambe* ult. f. LL *gamba* hoof]

jambalaya /jámbəlī́ə/ *n.* a dish of rice with shrimps, chicken, etc. [Louisiana F f. mod. Prov. *jambalaia*]

jamberoo /jámbəro͞o/ *n. Austral.* a spree. [alt. of JAMBOREE]

■ see JAMBOREE.

jamboree /jámbərée/ *n.* **1** a celebration or merrymaking. **2** a large rally of Scouts. [19th c.: orig. unkn.]

■ **1** party, gathering, celebration, fête, fair, festival, carnival, frolic, revelry, revel, jubilee, cakes and ale, gaiety, high jinks, jollity, festivity, fun, *Austral.* Mardi Gras, jamberoo, *colloq.* get-together, jolly, spree, shindig, do, rave(-up), *Austral. colloq.* shivoo, jollo, *Brit. colloq.* beanfeast, knees-up, *sl.* bash, ball, *Austral. sl.* ding, *Brit. sl.* beano, *US sl.* wingding.

jamjar /jámjaar/ *n.* a glass jar for containing jam.

jammy /jámmi/ *adj.* (**jammier, jammiest**) **1** covered with jam. **2** *Brit. colloq.* **a** lucky. **b** profitable.

Jan. *abbr.* January.

jane /jayn/ *n. sl.* a woman (*a plain jane*). [the name *Jane*]

jangle /jángg'l/ *v.* & *n.* ● *v.* **1** *intr.* & *tr.* make, or cause (a bell etc.) to make, a harsh metallic sound. **2** *tr.* irritate (the nerves etc.) by discordant sound or speech etc. ● *n.* a harsh metallic sound. [ME f. OF *jangler*, of uncert. orig.]

■ *v.* **1** ring, jingle, tinkle, chime; clang, clank, clatter, rattle, clash, crash. **2** see JAR[2] *v.* 1, 2. ● *n.* ring, jingle, tinkle, tintinnabulation, chime; clang, clank, clatter, rattle, clash, crash, clangour.

Janglish /jángglish/ *n.* = JAPLISH. [*Japanese* + E*nglish*]

janissary var. of JANIZARY.

janitor /jánnitər/ *n.* **1** a doorkeeper. **2** a caretaker of a building. □□ **janitorial** /-tóriəl/ *adj.* [L f. *janua* door]

■ **1** see PORTER[2].

janizary /jánnizəri/ *n.* (also **janissary** /-səri/) (*pl.* **-ies**) **1** *hist.* a member of the Turkish infantry forming the Sultan's guard in the 14th–19th c. **2** a devoted follower or supporter. [ult. f. Turk. *yeniçeri* f. *yeni* new + *çeri* troops]

jankers /jángkərz/ *n. Mil. sl.* punishment for defaulters. [20th c.: orig. unkn.]

January /jányoori/ *n.* (*pl.* **-ies**) the first month of the year. [ME f. AF *Jenever* f. L *Januarius* (*mensis*) (month) of Janus the guardian god of doors and beginnings]

Jap /jap/ *n.* & *adj. colloq.* often *offens.* = JAPANESE. [abbr.]

japan /jəpán/ *n.* & *v.* ● *n.* **1** a hard usu. black varnish, esp. of a kind brought orig. from Japan. **2** work in a Japanese style. ● *v.tr.* (**japanned, japanning**) **1** varnish with japan. **2** make black and glossy as with japan. [*Japan* in E. Asia]

Japanese /jáppənéez/ *n.* & *adj.* ● *n.* (*pl.* same) **1 a** a native or national of Japan. **b** a person of Japanese descent. **2** the language of Japan. ● *adj.* of or relating to Japan, its people, or its language. □ **Japanese cedar** = CRYPTOMERIA. **Japanese print** a colour print from woodblocks. **Japanese quince** = JAPONICA.

jape /jayp/ *n.* & *v.* ● *n.* a practical joke. ● *v.intr.* play a joke. □□ **japery** *n.* [ME: orig. uncert.]
■ *n.* see TRICK *n.* 5.

Japlish /jáplish/ *n.* a blend of Japanese and English, used in Japan. [*Japanese* + Eng*lish*]

japonica /jəpónnikə/ *n.* any flowering shrub of the genus *Chaenomeles*, esp. *C. speciosa*, with round white, green, or yellow edible fruits and bright red flowers. Also called *Japanese quince*. [mod.L, fem. of *japonicus* Japanese]

jar[1] /jaar/ *n.* **1 a** a container of glass, earthenware, plastic, etc., usu. cylindrical. **b** the contents of this. **2** *Brit. colloq.* a glass of beer. □□ **jarful** *n.* (*pl.* **-fuls**). [F *jarre* f. Arab. *jarra*]
■ **1** receptacle, vessel, container, crock, urn, pot, vase, jug, pitcher, ewer, flagon, carafe, amphora, bottle, jamjar, glass, *Archaeol.* pithos, *archaic* cruse. **2** glass, *colloq.* pint, half, *Austral. colloq.* stubby, *Austral. sl.* tinny, middy, tube; beer, ale, *Brit. sl.* wallop.

jar[2] /jaar/ *v.* & *n.* ● *v.* (**jarred, jarring**) **1** *intr.* (often foll. by *on*) (of sound, words, manner, etc.) sound discordant or grating (on the nerves etc.). **2 a** *tr.* (foll. by *against*, *on*) strike or cause to strike with vibration or a grating sound. **b** *intr.* (of a body affected) vibrate gratingly. **3** *tr.* send a shock through (a part of the body) (*the fall jarred his neck*). **4** *intr.* (often foll. by *with*) (of an opinion, fact, etc.) be at variance; be in conflict or in dispute. ● *n.* **1** a jarring sound or sensation. **2** a physical shock or jolt. **3** lack of harmony; disagreement. [16th c.: prob. imit.]
■ *v.* **1, 2** grate, jangle; stridulate, vibrate, rattle, clatter; rasp, scratch, scrape, grind, screech. **3** shock, jolt, jounce, jerk, bump, bounce, bang, knock, shake (up), jog, joggle, rock, disturb, agitate, *esp. Brit.* judder.
4 disagree, conflict, clash, discord, be at odds *or* variance. ● *n.* **1** discord, discordance, discordancy, cacophony, dissonance, clash, squall, jangle, crash, clatter, clang, clank. **2** jolt, lurch, bump, jerk, bounce, knock, start, shock, surprise. **3** disharmony, disagreement, discord, discordance, discordancy, disaccord, difference, dissent, conflict, dispute, argument, strife, contention, quarrel, feud, squabble, argument, altercation, dissension, clash.

jar[3] /jaar/ *n.* □ **on the jar** ajar. [late form of obs. *char* turn: see AJAR[1], CHAR[2]]

jardinière /zhaardinyáir/ *n.* **1** an ornamental pot or stand for the display of growing plants. **2** a dish of mixed vegetables. [F]

jargon[1] /jaargən/ *n.* **1** words or expressions used by a particular group or profession (*medical jargon*). **2** barbarous or debased language. **3** gibberish. □□ **jargonic** /-gónnik/ *adj.* **jargonistic** /-nístik/ *adj.* **jargonize** *v.tr.* & *intr.* (also **-ise**). [ME f. OF: orig. unkn.]
■ **1, 2** cant, argot, idiom, vernacular, terminology, slang, parlance, patter, *colloq.* lingo; patois, dialect, speech, talk; pidgin, *hist.* lingua franca. **3** gibberish, twaddle, nonsense, drivel, rubbish, gobbledegook, balderdash, claptrap, bunkum, wind, *colloq.* hogwash, tripe, malarkey, piffle, flapdoodle, *Brit. colloq.* double Dutch, *sl.* eyewash, hooey, bosh, boloney, hot air, gas, (tommy-)rot, *Brit. sl.* codswallop; jabber, jabbering, chatter, blather, babble, gibber, burble, gabble, prate, prating, prattle, rattle, cackle, abracadabra, *colloq.* jaw, yap, gab, natter, *colloq. or dial.* yammer, yatter, *esp. Brit. colloq.* waffle, *sl. derog.* yack.

jargon[2] /jaargən/ *n.* (also **jargoon** /jaargoon/) a translucent, colourless, or smoky variety of zircon. [F f. It. *giargone*, prob. ult. formed as ZIRCON]

jargonelle /jaargənél/ *n.* an early-ripening variety of pear. [F, dimin. of JARGON[2]]

jarl /yaarl/ *n. hist.* a Norse or Danish chief. [ON, orig. = man of noble birth, rel. to EARL]

jarrah /járrə/ *n.* **1** the Australian mahogany gum-tree, *Eucalyptus marginata*. **2** the durable timber of this. [Aboriginal *djarryl*]

Jas. *abbr.* James (also in New Testament).

jasmine /jázmin/ *n.* (also **jasmin, jessamin** /jéssəmin/, **jessamine** /jéssəmin/) any of various ornamental shrubs of the genus *Jasminum* usu. with white or yellow flowers. □ **jasmine tea** a tea perfumed with dried jasmine blossom. [F *jasmin, jessemin* f. Arab. *yās(a)mīn* f. Pers. *yāsamīn*]

jaspé /jáspay/ *adj.* like jasper; randomly coloured (esp. of cotton fabric). [F, past part. of *jasper* marble f. *jaspe* JASPER]

jasper /jáspər/ *n.* an opaque variety of quartz, usu. red, yellow, or brown in colour. [ME f. OF *jasp(r)e* f. L *iaspis* f. Gk, of oriental orig.]

Jat /jaat/ *n.* a member of an Indo-Aryan people widely distributed in NW India. [Hindi *jāṭ*]

jato /jáytō/ *n.* (*pl.* **-os**) *Aeron.* **1** jet-assisted take-off. **2** an auxiliary power unit providing extra thrust at take-off. [abbr.]

jaundice /jáwndiss/ *n.* & *v.* ● *n.* **1** *Med.* a condition with yellowing of the skin or whites of the eyes, often caused by obstruction of the bile duct or by liver disease. **2** disordered (esp. mental) vision. **3** envy. ● *v.tr.* **1** affect with jaundice. **2** (esp. as **jaundiced** *adj.*) affect (a person) with envy, resentment, or jealousy. [ME *iaunes* f. OF *jaunice* yellowness f. *jaune* yellow]
■ *n.* **2, 3** envy, jealousy, resentment, resentfulness, bitterness, spleen, spite. ● *v.* **2** see PREJUDICE *v.* 1; (**jaundiced**) envious, jealous, resentful, splenetic, yellow, bitter, disenchanted; cynical, spiteful, hostile, unfriendly, critical, disapproving; biased, prejudiced.

jaunt /jawnt/ *n.* & *v.* ● *n.* a short excursion for enjoyment. ● *v.intr.* take a jaunt. □ **jaunting car** a light two-wheeled horse-drawn vehicle formerly used in Ireland. [16th c.: orig. unkn.]
■ *n.* see EXCURSION 1.

jaunty /jáwnti/ *adj.* (**jauntier, jauntiest**) **1** cheerful and self-confident. **2** sprightly. □□ **jauntily** *adv.* **jauntiness** *n.* [earlier *jentee* f. F *gentil* GENTLE]
■ cheerful, buoyant, high-spirited, jovial, jolly, merry, gay, cheery, *colloq.* chirpy, *esp. US colloq.* chipper; self-confident, perky, frisky, lively, sprightly, brisk, vivacious, spry; dashing, rakish, debonair, dapper, *colloq.* natty, sporty.

Java Man /jaavə/ *n.* a prehistoric type of man whose remains were found in Java. [*Java* in Indonesia]

Javan /jaav'n/ *n.* & *adj.* = JAVANESE.

Javanese /jaavəneez/ *n.* & *adj.* ● *n.* (*pl.* same) **1 a** a native of Java in Indonesia. **b** a person of Javanese descent. **2** the language of Java. ● *adj.* of or relating to Java, its people, or its language.

Java sparrow /jaavə/ *n.* a finch, *Padda oryzivora*.

javelin /jávvəlin, jávlin/ *n.* **1** a light spear thrown in a competitive sport or as a weapon. **2** the athletic event or sport of throwing the javelin. [F *javeline*, *javelot* f. Gallo-Roman *gabalottus*]
■ **1** see LANCE *n.* 1.

jaw /jaw/ *n.* & *v.* ● *n.* **1 a** each of the upper and lower bony structures in vertebrates forming the framework of the mouth and containing the teeth. **b** the parts of certain invertebrates used for the ingestion of food. **2 a** (in *pl.*) the mouth with its bones and teeth. **b** the narrow mouth of a valley, channel, etc. **c** the gripping parts of a tool or machine. **d** gripping-power (*jaws of death*). **3** *colloq.* **a** talkativeness; tedious talk (*hold your jaw*). **b** a sermonizing talk; a lecture. ● *v. colloq.* **1** *intr.* speak esp. at tedious length. **2** *tr.* **a** persuade by talking. **b** admonish or lecture. □ **jaw-breaker** *colloq.* a word that is very long or hard to pronounce. [ME f. OF *joe* cheek, jaw, of uncert. orig.]
■ *n.* **2 a** (*jaws*) see MOUTH *n.* 1. ● *v.* **1** see PRATTLE *v.*

jawbone /jáwbōn/ *n.* **1** each of the two bones forming the lower jaw in most mammals. **2** these two combined into one in other mammals.

jay /jay/ *n.* **1 a** a noisy chattering European bird, *Garrulus glandarius*, with vivid pinkish-brown, blue, black, and white plumage. **b** any other bird of the subfamily Garrulinae. **2 a** person who chatters impertinently. [ME f. OF f. LL *gaius*, *gaia*, perh. f. L praenomen *Gaius*: cf. *jackdaw*, *robin*]

jaywalk /jáywawk/ *v.intr.* cross or walk in the street or road without regard for traffic. □□ **jaywalker** *n.*

jazz /jaz/ *n.* & *v.* ● *n.* **1** music of African-American origin characterized by improvisation, syncopation, and usu. a regular or forceful rhythm. **2** *sl.* pretentious talk or behaviour, nonsensical stuff (*all that jazz*). ● *v.intr.* play or dance to jazz. □ **jazz up** brighten or enliven. □□ **jazzer** *n.* [20th c.: orig. uncert.]

jazzman /jázman/ *n.* (*pl.* **-men**) a jazz-player.

jazzy /jázzi/ *adj.* (**jazzier, jazziest**) **1** of or like jazz. **2** vivid, unrestrained, showy. □□ **jazzily** *adv.* **jazziness** *n.*

■ **2** see LOUD *adj.* 2.

JCB /jáyseebée/ *n. propr.* a type of mechanical excavator with a shovel at the front and a digging arm at the rear. [*J. C. B*amford, the makers]

JCL *abbr.* *Computing* job-control language.

JCR *abbr.* *Brit.* Junior Common (or Combination) Room.

jealous /jélləss/ *adj.* **1** (often foll. by *of*) fiercely protective (of rights etc.). **2** afraid, suspicious, or resentful of rivalry in love or affection. **3** (often foll. by *of*) envious or resentful (of a person or a person's advantages etc.). **4** (of God) intolerant of disloyalty. **5** (of inquiry, supervision, etc.) vigilant. □□ **jealously** *adv.* [ME f. OF *gelos* f. med.L *zelosus* ZEALOUS]

■ **1** protective, possessive, defensive. **2** distrustful, mistrustful, suspicious, resentful; anxious, afraid, insecure. **3** envious, resentful, bitter, jaundiced; green (with envy), green-eyed, covetous. **4** intolerant, impatient, uncompromising; demanding, tough, insistent. **5** vigilant, watchful, alert, sharp, observant, careful, wary, guarded, on one's guard. □□ **jealously** protectively, possessively, defensively; distrustfully, mistrustfully, suspiciously, resentfully, bitterly, anxiously; enviously, covetously; intolerantly, impatiently, uncompromisingly; vigilantly, watchfully, observantly, carefully, guardedly, warily.

jealousy /jélləsi/ *n.* (*pl.* **-ies**) **1** a jealous state or feeling. **2** an instance of this. [ME f. OF *gelosie* (as JEALOUS)]

■ **1** see ENVY *n.*

jean /jeen/ *n.* twilled cotton cloth. [ME, attrib. use of *Jene* f. OF *Janne* f. med.L *Janua* Genoa]

jeans /jeenz/ *n.pl.* trousers made of jean or (more usually) denim, for informal wear.

Jeep /jeep/ *n. propr.* a small sturdy esp. military motor vehicle with four-wheel drive. [orig. US, f. *GP* = *g*eneral *p*urposes, infl. by 'Eugene the Jeep', an animal in a comic strip]

jeepers /jéepərz/ *int.* *US sl.* expressing surprise etc. [corrupt. of *Jesus*]

jeer /jeer/ *v.* & *n.* ● *v.* **1** *intr.* (usu. foll. by *at*) scoff derisively. **2** *tr.* scoff at; deride. ● *n.* a scoff or taunt. □□ **jeeringly** *adv.* [16th c.: orig. unkn.]

■ *v.* **1** scoff, mock, laugh, fleer, flout, sneer, gibe, tease, heckle, boo, catcall, *Brit.* barrack; (*jeer at*) scoff at, mock (at), laugh at, fleer at, flout (at), ridicule, deride, make fun *or* sport of, poke fun at, have a fling at, twit, chaff, rag, tease, taunt, gibe at, gird at, sneer at, boo, heckle, catcall, *Brit.* barrack, *Austral.* & *NZ* chiack, *archaic* smoke, *colloq.* have a shy at, rib, *sl.* ballyrag, *Austral.* & *NZ sl.* sling off at. **2** scoff at, mock (at), laugh at, fleer at, flout (at), ridicule, deride, make fun *or* sport of, poke fun at, have a fling at, twit, chaff, rag, tease, taunt, gibe at, gird at, sneer at, boo, heckle, catcall, *Brit.* barrack, *Austral.* & *NZ* chiack, *archaic* smoke, *colloq.* have a shy at, rib, *sl.* ballyrag, *Austral.* & *NZ sl.* sling off at. ● *n.* scoff, taunt, gibe, fleer, flout, sneer, gird, boo, hoot, catcall, *colloq.* raspberry.

Jeez /jeez/ *int.* *sl.* a mild expression of surprise, discovery, etc. (cf. GEE[1]). [abbr. of JESUS]

jehad var. of JIHAD.

Jehovah /jəhṓvə/ *n.* the Hebrew name of God in the Old Testament. □ **Jehovah's Witness** a member of a millenarian Christian sect rejecting the supremacy of the State and religious institutions over personal conscience, faith, etc. [med.L *Iehoua(h)* f. Heb. *YHVH* (with the vowels of *adonai* 'my lord' included: see YAHWEH]

■ see LORD *n.* 4.

Jehovist /jəhṓvist/ *n.* = YAHWIST.

jejune /jijṓōn/ *adj.* **1** intellectually unsatisfying; shallow. **2** puerile. **3** (of ideas, writings, etc.) meagre, scanty; dry and uninteresting. **4** (of the land) barren, poor. □□ **jejunely** *adv.* **jejuneness** *n.* [orig. = fasting, f. L *jejunus*]

■ **1** see BANAL. **2** see IMMATURE 2. **3** see PROSAIC 2.

jejunum /jijṓōnəm/ *n.* *Anat.* the part of the small intestine between the duodenum and ileum. [L, neut. of *jejunus* fasting]

Jekyll and Hyde /jékkil ənd hīd/ *n.* a person alternately displaying opposing good and evil personalities. [R. L. Stevenson's story *The Strange Case of Dr Jekyll and Mr Hyde*]

jell /jel/ *v.intr.* *colloq.* **1 a** set as a jelly. **b** (of ideas etc.) take a definite form. **2** (of two different things) cohere. [back-form. f. JELLY]

■ **1** set, congeal, solidify, harden, coagulate, thicken, stiffen, gelatinize; form, take form *or* shape, crystallize, materialize, come together, hang together, make sense, *colloq.* add up. **2** cohere, hang together, bond, connect, bind, marry, fuse, combine, unite.

jellaba var. of DJELLABA.

jellify /jéllifī/ *v.tr.* & *intr.* (**-ies, -ied**) turn into jelly; make or become like jelly. □□ **jellification** /-fikáysh'n/ *n.*

jelly /jélli/ *n.* & *v.* ● *n.* (*pl.* **-ies**) **1 a** a soft stiffish semi-transparent preparation of boiled sugar and fruit-juice or milk etc., often cooled in a mould and eaten as a dessert. **b** a similar preparation of fruit-juice etc. for use as a jam or a condiment (*redcurrant jelly*). **c** a similar preparation derived from meat, bones, etc., and gelatin (*marrowbone jelly*). **2** any substance of a similar consistency. **3** *Brit. sl.* gelignite (cf. GELLY). ● *v.* (**-ies, -ied**) **1** *intr.* & *tr.* set or cause to set as a jelly, congeal. **2** *tr.* set (food) in a jelly (*jellied eels*). □ **jelly baby** *Brit.* a jelly-like sweet in the stylized shape of a baby. **jelly bag** a bag for straining juice for jelly. **jelly bean** a jelly-like sweet in the shape of a bean. □□ **jelly-like** *adj.* [ME f. OF *gelee* frost, jelly, f. Rmc *gelata* f. L *gelare* freeze f. *gelu* frost]

■ *n.* **1 b** see PRESERVE *n.* 1.

jellyfish /jéllifish/ *n.* (*pl.* usu. **same**) **1** a marine coelenterate of the class Scyphozoa having an umbrella-shaped jelly-like body and stinging tentacles. **2** *colloq.* a feeble person.

■ **2** see WEAKLING.

jemmy /jémmi/ *n.* & *v.* (*US* **jimmi** /jimmi/) ● *n.* (*pl.* **-ies** or **jimmis**) a burglar's short crowbar, usu. made in sections. ● *v.tr.* (**-ies, -ied**) force open with a jemmy. [pet-form of the name *James*]

■ *v.* see FORCE[1] *v.* 2.

je ne sais quoi /zhə nə say kwaá/ *n.* an indefinable something. [F, = I do not know what]

jennet /jénnit/ *n.* a small Spanish horse. [F *genet* f. Sp. *jinete* light horseman f. Arab. *zenāta* Berber tribe famous as horsemen]

jenny /jénni/ *n.* (*pl.* **-ies**) **1** *hist.* = *spinning-jenny*. **2** a female donkey or ass. **3** a locomotive crane. □ **jenny-wren** a popular name for a female wren. [pet-form of the name *Janet*]

jeopardize /jéppərdīz/ *v.tr.* (also **-ise**) endanger; put into jeopardy.

■ endanger, imperil, threaten, menace, expose; risk, hazard, venture, stake, gamble.

jeopardy /jéppərdi/ *n.* **1** danger, esp. of severe harm or loss. **2** *Law* danger resulting from being on trial for a criminal

offence. [ME *iuparti* f. OF *ieu parti* divided (i.e. even) game, f. L *jocus* game + *partitus* past part. of *partire* divide f. *pars partis* part]
■ **1** danger, peril; threat, menace, exposure, liability, vulnerability; risk, hazard, chance, uncertainty.

Jer. *abbr.* Jeremiah (Old Testament).

jerbil var. of GERBIL.

jerboa /jerbṓə/ *n.* any small desert rodent of the family Dipodidae with long hind legs and the ability to make large jumps. [mod.L f. Arab. *yarbū'* flesh of loins, jerboa]

jeremiad /jérrimī́ad/ *n.* a doleful complaint or lamentation; a list of woes. [F *jérémiade* f. *Jérémie* Jeremiah f. eccl.L *Jeremias*, with ref. to the Lamentations of Jeremiah in the Old Testament]
■ see LAMENT *n.* 1.

Jeremiah /jérrimī́ə/ *n.* a dismal prophet, a denouncer of the times. [with ref. to *Jeremiah* (as JEREMIAD)]

jerk[1] /jerk/ *n.* & *v.* ● *n.* **1** a sharp sudden pull, twist, twitch, start, etc. **2** a spasmodic muscular twitch. **3** (in *pl.*) *Brit. colloq.* exercises (*physical jerks*). **4** *sl.* a fool; a stupid or contemptible person. ● *v.* **1** *intr.* move with a jerk. **2** *tr.* pull, thrust, twist, etc., with a jerk. **3** *tr.* throw with a suddenly arrested motion. **4** *tr. Weight-lifting* raise (a weight) from shoulder-level to above the head. □ **jerk off** *coarse sl.* masturbate. ¶ Usually considered a taboo use. □□ **jerker** *n.* [16th c.: perh. imit.]
■ *n.* **1, 2** pull, wrench, tug, twist, tweak, *colloq.* yank; lurch, jolt, bump; start, jump, twitch, spasm, shudder. **3** (*jerks*) see EXERCISE *n.* 3. **4** fool, *sl.* creep, *Brit. sl.* pillock, prat, git, *US sl.* nerd, dweeb; see also DOLT. ● *v.* **1** lurch, jolt, jump, start, jig, jiggle, wriggle, twitch, shudder, recoil, *colloq.* wiggle. **2** wrench, pull, tug, whip, shove, thrust, push, jostle, nudge, twist, tweak, snatch, pluck, *Austral.* & *NZ* snig, *colloq.* yank. **3** pitch, throw, propel, launch, cast, *colloq.* chuck.

jerk[2] /jerk/ *v.tr.* cure (beef) by cutting it in long slices and drying it in the sun. [Amer. Sp. *charquear* f. *charqui* f. Quechua *echarqui* dried flesh]

jerkin /jérkin/ *n.* **1** a sleeveless jacket. **2** *hist.* a man's close-fitting jacket, often of leather. [16th c.: orig. unkn.]

jerky /jérki/ *adj.* (**jerkier, jerkiest**) **1** having sudden abrupt movements. **2** spasmodic. □□ **jerkily** *adv.* **jerkiness** *n.*
■ **1** see BUMPY 2. **2** see SPASMODIC 1.

jeroboam /jérrəbṓəm/ *n.* a wine bottle of 4–12 times the ordinary size. [*Jeroboam* king of Israel (1 Kings 11:28, 14: 16)]

Jerry /jérri/ *n.* (*pl.* **-ies**) *Brit. sl.* **1** a German (esp. in military contexts). **2** the Germans collectively. [prob. alt. of *German*]

jerry[1] /jérri/ *n.* (*pl.* **-ies**) *Brit. sl.* a chamber-pot.

jerry[2] /jérri/ *v.intr. Austral. sl.* understand, realize. [20th c.: orig. unkn.]
■ see UNDERSTAND 7.

jerry-builder /jérribildər/ *n.* a builder of unsubstantial houses with poor-quality materials. □□ **jerry-building** *n.* **jerry-built** *adj.*
■ □□ **jerry-built** see RAMSHACKLE.

jerrycan /jérrikan/ *n.* (also **jerrican**) a kind of (orig. German) petrol- or water-can. [JERRY + CAN[2]]

jerrymander var. of GERRYMANDER.

jersey /jérzi/ *n.* (*pl.* **-eys**) **1 a** a knitted usu. woollen pullover or similar garment. **b** a plain-knitted (orig. woollen) fabric. **2** (**Jersey**) a light brown dairy cow from Jersey. [*Jersey*, largest of the Channel Islands]

Jerusalem artichoke /jərṓōssələm/ *n.* **1** a species of sunflower, *Helianthus tuberosus*, with edible underground tubers. **2** this tuber used as a vegetable. [corrupt. of It. *girasole* sunflower]

jess /jess/ *n.* & *v.* ● *n.* a short strap of leather, silk, etc., put round the leg of a hawk in falconry. ● *v.tr.* put jesses on (a hawk etc.). [ME *ges* f. OF *ges, get* ult. f. L *jactus* a throw f. *jacere jact-* to throw]

jessamin (also **jessamine**) var. of JASMINE.

jest /jest/ *n.* & *v.* ● *n.* **1 a** a joke. **b** fun. **2 a** raillery, banter. **b** an object of derision (*a standing jest*). ● *v.intr.* **1** joke; make jests. **2** fool about; play or act triflingly. □ **in jest** in fun. □□ **jestful** *adj.* [orig. = exploit, f. OF *geste* f. L *gesta* neut. pl. past part. of *gerere* do]
■ *n.* **1 a** see JOKE *n.* 1. **b** see SPORT *n.* 3. **2 a** see BANTER *n.* ● *v.* see JOKE *v.* 1. □ **in jest** see *in fun* (FUN).

jester /jéstər/ *n.* a professional joker or 'fool' at a medieval court etc., traditionally wearing a cap and bells and carrying a 'sceptre'.
■ see FOOL[1] *n.* 2.

Jesuit /jézyoo-it/ *n.* a member of the Society of Jesus, a Roman Catholic order founded by St Ignatius Loyola and others in 1534. [F *jésuite* or mod.L *Jesuita* f. *Jesus*: see JESUS]

Jesuitical /jézyoo-ittik'l/ *adj.* **1** of or concerning the Jesuits. **2** often *offens.* dissembling or equivocating, in the manner once associated with Jesuits. □□ **Jesuitically** *adv.*
■ **2** see EVASIVE 1, 3, 4.

Jesus /jeézəss/ *int. colloq.*, *offens.* an exclamation of surprise, dismay, etc. [name of the founder of the Christian religion d. *c.* AD 30]
■ see GOD *int.*

jet[1] /jet/ *n.* & *v.* ● *n.* **1** a stream of water, steam, gas, flame, etc. shot out esp. from a small opening. **2** a spout or nozzle for emitting water etc. in this way. **3 a** a jet engine. **b** an aircraft powered by one or more jet engines. ● *v.* (**jetted, jetting**) **1** *intr.* spurt out in jets. **2** *tr.* & *intr. colloq.* send or travel by jet plane. □ **jet engine** an engine using jet propulsion for forward thrust, esp. of an aircraft. **jet lag** extreme tiredness and other bodily effects felt after a long flight involving marked differences of local time. **jet-propelled 1** having jet propulsion. **2** (of a person etc.) very fast. **jet propulsion** propulsion by the backward ejection of a high-speed jet of gas etc. **jet set** *colloq.* wealthy people frequently travelling by air, esp. for pleasure. **jet-setter** *colloq.* a member of the jet set. **jet stream 1** a narrow current of very strong winds encircling the globe several miles above the earth. **2** the stream from a jet engine. [earlier as verb (in sense 1): F *jeter* throw ult. f. L *jactare* frequent. of *jacere jact-* throw]
■ *n.* **1** see GUSH *n.* 1. **3 b** see PLANE[1] *n.* 3. ● *v.* **1** see GUSH *v.* 1. □ **jet-setter** see TRAVELLER 1.

jet[2] /jet/ *n.* **1 a** a hard black variety of lignite capable of being carved and highly polished. **b** (*attrib.*) made of this. **2** (in full **jet-black**) a deep glossy black colour. [ME f. AF *geet*, OF *jaiet* f. L *gagates* f. Gk *gagatēs* f. *Gagai* in Asia Minor]

jeté /zhetáy/ *n. Ballet* a spring or leap with one leg forward and the other stretched backwards. [F, past part. of *jeter* throw: see JET[1]]

jetsam /jétsəm/ *n.* discarded material washed ashore, esp. that thrown overboard to lighten a ship etc. (cf. FLOTSAM). [contr. of JETTISON]

jettison /jéttis'n, -z'n/ *v.* & *n.* ● *v.tr.* **1 a** throw (esp. heavy material) overboard to lighten a ship, hot-air balloon, etc. **b** drop (goods) from an aircraft. **2** abandon; get rid of (something no longer wanted). ● *n.* the act of jettisoning. [ME f. AF *getteson*, OF *getaison* f. L *jactatio -onis* f. *jactare* throw: see JET[1]]
■ **2** see *throw away* 1.

jetton /jétt'n/ *n.* a counter with a stamped or engraved design esp. for insertion like a coin to operate a machine etc. [F *jeton* f. *jeter* throw, add up accounts: see JET[1]]

jetty /jétti/ *n.* (*pl.* **-ies**) **1** a pier or breakwater constructed to protect or defend a harbour, coast, etc. **2** a landing-pier. [ME f. OF *jetee*, fem. past part. of *jeter* throw: see JET[1]]
■ see PIER 1a.

jeu d'esprit /zhṓ despreé/ *n.* (*pl.* ***jeux d'esprit*** *pronunc.* same) a witty or humorous (usu. literary) trifle. [F, = game of the spirit]

jeunesse dorée /zhṓness dóray/ *n.* = *gilded youth* (see GILD[1]). [F]

Jew /jōō/ *n.* & *v.* ● *n.* **1** a person of Hebrew descent or whose religion is Judaism. **2** *sl. offens.* (as a stereotype) a person considered to be parsimonious or to drive a hard bargain in trading. ¶ The stereotype, which is now deeply offensive, arose from historical associations of Jews as moneylenders in medieval England. ● *v.tr.* (**jew**) *sl. offens.* get a financial advantage over. □ **jew's harp** a small lyre-shaped musical instrument held between the teeth and struck with the finger. [ME f. OF *giu* f. L *judaeus* f. Gk *ioudaios* ult. f. Heb. *y^ehûdî* f. *y^ehûdâh* Judah]

jewel /jōōəl/ *n.* & *v.* ● *n.* **1 a** a precious stone. **b** this as used for its hardness as a bearing in watchmaking. **2** a personal ornament containing a jewel or jewels. **3** a precious person or thing. ● *v.tr.* (**jewelled, jewelling**; *US* **jeweled, jeweling**) **1** (esp. as **jewelled** *adj.*) adorn or set with jewels. **2** (in watchmaking) set with jewels. □ **jewel-fish** a scarlet and green tropical cichlid fish, *Hemichromis bimaculatus*. □□ **jewelly** *adj.* [ME f. AF *juel, jeuel*, OF *joel*, of uncert. orig.]

■ *n.* **1a** gem, gemstone, brilliant, *bijou*, *colloq.* sparkler, *sl.* rock, shiner. **3** treasure, gem, pearl; marvel, find, godsend; prize, boon, blessing; masterpiece. ● *v.* **1** adorn, ornament, bedeck, gild, enrich, embellish.

jeweller /jōōələr/ *n.* (*US* **jeweler**) a maker of or dealer in jewels or jewellery. □ **jeweller's rouge** finely ground rouge for polishing. [ME f. AF *jueler*, OF *juelier* (as JEWEL)]

jewellery /jōōəlri/ *n.* (also **jewelry** /jōōəlri/) jewels or other ornamental objects, esp. for personal adornment, regarded collectively. [ME f. OF *juelerie* and f. JEWEL, JEWELLER]

■ gems, precious stones, jewels, ornaments, adornments, finery, *bijouterie*, treasures, regalia.

Jewess /jōō-ess/ *n.* a female Jew.

jewfish /jōōfish/ *n.* **1** a grouper, *Epinephelus itajara*, of N. American, Atlantic, and Pacific coasts. **2** any of various large Australian fish used as food, esp. the mulloway.

Jewish /jōō-ish/ *adj.* **1** of or relating to Jews. **2** of Judaism. □□ **Jewishly** *adv.* **Jewishness** *n.*

Jewry /jōori/ *n.* (*pl.* **-ies**) **1** Jews collectively. **2** *hist.* a Jews' quarter in a town etc. [ME f. AF *juerie*, OF *juierie* (as JEW)]

Jezebel /jézzəbel/ *n.* a shameless or immoral woman. [*Jezebel*, wife of Ahab in the Old Testament (1 Kings 16, 19, 21)]

■ see WANTON *n.*

jib[1] /jib/ *n.* & *v.* ● *n.* **1** a triangular staysail from the outer end of the jib-boom to the top of the foremast or from the bowsprit to the masthead. **2** the projecting arm of a crane. ● *v.tr.* & *intr.* (**jibbed, jibbing**) (of a sail etc.) pull or swing round from one side of the ship to the other; gybe. □ **jib-boom** a spar run out from the end of the bowsprit. [17th c.: orig. unkn.]

jib[2] /jib/ *v.intr.* (**jibbed, jibbing**) **1 a** (of an animal, esp. a horse) stop and refuse to go on; move backwards or sideways instead of going on. **b** (of a person) refuse to continue. **2** (foll. by *at*) show aversion to (a person or course of action). □□ **jibber** *n.* [19th c.: orig. unkn.]

■ **1** see HESITATE 2.

jibba /jíbbə/ *n.* (also **jibbah**) a long coat worn by Muslim men. [Egypt. var. of Arab. *jubba*]

jibe[1] var. of GIBE.

jibe[2] *US* var. of GYBE.

jibe[3] /jīb/ *v.intr.* (usu. foll. by *with*) *US colloq.* agree; be in accord. [19th c.: orig. unkn.]

■ see AGREE 3a.

jiff /jif/ *n.* (also **jiffy**, *pl.* **-ies**) *colloq.* a short time; a moment (*in a jiffy*; *half a jiff*). [18th c.: orig. unkn.]

■ see MOMENT 1, 2.

Jiffy bag /jiffi/ *n. propr.* a type of padded envelope for postal use.

jig /jig/ *n.* & *v.* ● *n.* **1 a** a lively dance with leaping movements. **b** the music for this, usu. in triple time. **2** a device that holds a piece of work and guides the tools operating on it. ● *v.* (**jigged, jigging**) **1** *intr.* dance a jig. **2** *tr.* & *intr.* move quickly and jerkily up and down. **3** *tr.* work on or equip with a jig or jigs. □ **jig about** fidget. [16th c.: orig. unkn.]

■ *v.* **2** see JERK[1] *v.* 1.

jigger[1] /jíggər/ *n.* **1** *Naut.* **a** a small tackle consisting of a double and single block with a rope. **b** a small sail at the stern. **c** a small smack having this. **2** *sl.* a gadget. **3** *Golf* an iron club with a narrow face. **4** *Billiards colloq.* a cue-rest. **5 a** a measure of spirits etc. **b** a small glass holding this. **6** a person or thing that jigs.

■ **1 a** see SPAR[1]. **2** see CONTRAPTION. **5** see DRINK *n.* 2b.

jigger[2] /jíggər/ *n.* **1** = CHIGOE. **2** *US* = CHIGGER 2. [corrupt.]

jiggered /jíggərd/ *adj. colloq.* (as a mild oath) confounded (*I'll be jiggered*). [euphem.]

jiggery-pokery /jíggəripṓkəri/ *n. Brit. colloq.* deceitful or dishonest dealing, trickery. [cf. Sc. *joukery-pawkery* f. *jouk* dodge, skulk]

■ see TRICKERY.

jiggle /jígg'l/ *v.* (often foll. by *about* etc.) **1** *tr.* shake lightly; rock jerkily. **2** *intr.* fidget. □□ **jiggly** *adj.* [JIG or JOGGLE[1]]

■ **1** jog, joggle, jig, shake, agitate, wriggle, jerk, wag, *colloq.* waggle, wiggle. **2** see FIDGET *v.* 1.

jigsaw /jigsaw/ *n.* **1 a** (in full **jigsaw puzzle**) a puzzle consisting of a picture on board or wood etc. cut into irregular interlocking pieces to be reassembled. **b** a mental puzzle resolvable by assembling various pieces of information. **2** a machine saw with a fine blade enabling it to cut curved lines in a sheet of wood, metal, etc.

jihad /jihád, -haad/ *n.* (also **jehad**) a holy war undertaken by Muslims against unbelievers. [Arab. *jihād*]

■ see CRUSADE *n.* 1b.

jill var. of GILL[4].

jilt /jilt/ *v.* & *n.* ● *v.tr.* abruptly reject or abandon (a lover etc.). ● *n.* a person (esp. a woman) who jilts a lover. [17th c.: orig. unkn.]

■ *v.* throw over, reject, abandon, discard, desert, break (up) with, walk *or* run out on, cast off *or* aside, finish with, leave in the lurch, forsake, dismiss, brush off, give a person the brush-off, *colloq.* drop, dump, chuck, give a person the elbow *or* push, *sl.* ditch.

Jim Crow /jim krṓ/ *n. US* **1** the practice of segregating Blacks. **2** *offens.* a Black. **3** an implement for straightening iron bars or bending rails by screw pressure. □□ **Jim Crowism** *n.* (in sense 1). [nickname]

■ □□ **Jim Crowism** see SEGREGATION 1.

jim-jams /jímjamz/ *n.pl.* **1** *sl.* = *delirium tremens*. **2** *colloq.* a fit of depression or nervousness. [fanciful redupl.]

■ **2** see NERVE *n.* 3b.

jimmi *US* var. of JEMMY.

jimmygrant /jímmigrànt/ *n. Austral. rhyming sl.* an immigrant.

Jimmy Woodser /jímmi wŏŏdzər/ *n. Austral.* **1** a person who drinks alone. **2** a drink taken on one's own. [Jimmy *Wood*, name of a character in the poem of that name by Barcroft Boake]

jimson /jíms'n/ *n.* (in full **jimson weed**) *US* a highly poisonous tall weed, *Datura stramonium*, with large trumpet-shaped flowers. [*Jamestown* in Virginia]

jingle /jíngg'l/ *n.* & *v.* ● *n.* **1** a mixed noise as of bells or light metal objects being shaken together. **2 a** a repetition of the same sound in words, esp. as an aid to memory or to attract attention. **b** a short verse of this kind used in advertising etc. ● *v.* **1** *intr.* & *tr.* make or cause to make a jingling sound. **2** *intr.* (of writing) be full of alliterations, rhymes, etc. □□ **jingly** *adj.* (**jinglier, jingliest**). [ME: imit.]

■ *n.* **1** tinkle, ring, tintinnabulation, clink, chink, chime, jangle. **2 a** tautophony, alliteration, assonance, *Rhet.* anaphora. **b** tune, ditty, song, rhyme, verse, poem, lyric, doggerel; slogan, *sl.* buzz-word. ● *v.* **1** tinkle, ring, clink, chink, chime, jangle.

jingo /jínggō/ *n.* (*pl.* **-oes**) a supporter of policy favouring war; a blustering patriot. □ **by jingo!** a mild oath. □□ **jingoism** *n.* **jingoist** *n.* **jingoistic** /-gō-ístik/ *adj.* [17th c.:

orig. a conjuror's word: polit. sense from use of *by jingo* in a popular song, then applied to patriots]
■ jingoist, militarist, warmonger, *Polit.* hawk; patriot, nationalist, loyalist, chauvinist, flag-waver. □ **by jingo!** see INDEED *int.* □□ **jingoism** militarism, warmongering, belligerence, bellicosity, *Polit.* hawkishness; patriotism, nationalism, loyalism, chauvinism, flag-waving, *sl.* flag-wagging. **jingoist** see JINGO above. **jingoistic** militaristic, warmongering, belligerent, bellicose, warlike, *Polit.* hawkish; patriotic, nationalist, nationalistic, chauvinistic.

jink /jingk/ *v.* & *n.* ● *v.* **1** *intr.* move elusively; dodge. **2** *tr.* elude by dodging. ● *n.* an act of dodging or eluding. [orig. Sc.: prob. imit. of nimble motion]

jinker /jingkər/ *n.* & *v. Austral.* ● *n.* **1** a wheeled conveyance for moving heavy logs. **2** a light, two-wheeled cart. ● *v.tr.* convey by jinker. [Sc. *janker* long pole on wheels used for carrying logs]

jinnee /jineé/ *n.* (also **jinn, djinn** /jin/) (*pl.* **jinn** or **djinn**) (in Muslim mythology) an intelligent being lower than the angels, able to appear in human and animal forms, and having power over people. [Arab. *jinnī*, pl. *jinn*: cf. GENIE]

jinx /jingks/ *n.* & *v. colloq.* ● *n.* a person or thing that seems to cause bad luck. ● *v.tr.* (often in *passive*) subject (a person) to an unlucky force. [perh. var. of *jynx* wryneck, charm]
■ *n.* (evil) spell, curse, (unlucky) charm, evil eye, voodoo, bogey, Jonah, *esp. US* hoodoo, *US* hex, *Austral. colloq.* mazz, *sl.* kiss of death. ● *v.* curse, bewitch, cast a spell on, voodoo, overlook, damn, doom, condemn, sabotage, *Austral.* point the bone at, *esp. US* hoodoo, *US* hex, *sl.* give a person *or* thing the kiss of death.

jitter /jíttər/ *n.* & *v. colloq.* ● *n.* (**the jitters**) extreme nervousness. ● *v.intr.* be nervous; act nervously. □□ **jittery** *adj.* **jitteriness** *n.* [20th c.: orig. unkn.]
■ *n.* (*the jitters*) nervousness, jitteriness, tension, anxiety, anxiousness, fretfulness, restlessness, uneasiness, skittishness, apprehension, the shakes, DT, (the) fidgets, nerves, the horrors, *colloq.* the creeps, the jim-jams, the jumps, twitch, cold feet, the willies, *sl.* the heebie-jeebies, *Brit. sl.* the needle; stage fright, *US* buck fever. □□ **jittery** see NERVOUS 1–3, 5. **jitteriness** see JITTER *n.* above.

jitterbug /jíttərbug/ *n.* & *v.* ● *n.* **1** a nervous person. **2** *hist.* **a** a fast popular dance. **b** a person fond of dancing this. ● *v.intr.* (**-bugged, -bugging**) dance the jitterbug.

jiu-jitsu var. of JU-JITSU.

jive /jīv/ *n.* & *v.* ● *n.* **1** a jerky lively style of dance esp. popular in the 1950s. **2** music for this. **3** *US sl.* talk, conversation, esp. when misleading or pretentious. ● *v.intr.* **1** dance the jive. **2** play jive music. □□ **jiver** *n.* [20th c.: orig. uncert.]

jizz /jiz/ *n.* the characteristic impression given by an animal or plant. [20th c.: orig. unkn.]

Jnr. *abbr.* Junior.

jo /jō/ *n.* (*pl.* **joes**) *Sc.* a sweetheart or beloved. [var. of JOY]

job[1] /job/ *n.* & *v.* ● *n.* **1** a piece of work, esp. one done for hire or profit. **2** a paid position of employment. **3** *colloq.* anything one has to do. **4** *colloq.* a difficult task (*had a job to find them*). **5** a product of work, esp. if well done. **6** *Computing* an item of work regarded separately. **7** *sl.* a crime, esp. a robbery. **8** a transaction in which private advantage prevails over duty or public interest. **9** a state of affairs or set of circumstances (*is a bad job*). ● *v.* (**jobbed, jobbing**) **1 a** *intr.* do jobs; do piece-work. **b** *tr.* (usu. foll. by *out*) let or deal with for profit; subcontract. **2 a** *intr.* deal in stocks. **b** *tr.* buy and sell (stocks or goods) as a middleman. **3 a** *intr.* turn a position of trust to private advantage. **b** *tr.* deal corruptly with (a matter). **4** *tr. US sl.* swindle. □ **job-control language** *Computing* a language enabling the user to determine the tasks to be undertaken by the operating system. **job-hunt** *colloq.* seek employment. **job lot** a miscellaneous group of articles, esp. bought together. **jobs for the boys** *colloq.* profitable situations etc. to reward one's supporters. **job-sharing** an arrangement by which a full-time job is done jointly by several part-time employees who share the remuneration. **just the job** *colloq.* exactly what is wanted. **make a job** (or **good job**) **of** do thoroughly or successfully. **on the job** *colloq.* **1** at work; in the course of doing a piece of work. **2** engaged in sexual intercourse. **out of a job** unemployed. [16th c.: orig. unkn.]
■ *n.* **1, 3** task, assignment, chore, (piece of) work, project, undertaking, charge; business, affair, matter, activity, operation. **2** employment, position, post, occupation, appointment, situation, vocation, calling, living, livelihood, *colloq.* berth, *Austral. sl.* grip; career, profession, *métier*, trade, craft, field, area, province, line; responsibility, concern, function, duty, role, mission. **4** problem, difficulty, hardship, hard time, strain, problem, obstacle; nuisance, bother, toil, grind, drudgery, hard work, *colloq.* headache, pain (in the neck), hassle, *esp. US sl.* pain in the butt. **5** (end) result, (end-)product, outcome, effect. **7** crime, felony; robbery, burglary, hold-up, *colloq.* stick-up, *sl.* caper. **8** scheme, enterprise, racket, game, *colloq.* lark; swindle, dodge, trick, ruse, confidence trick *or US* game, fraud, rig, *colloq.* rip-off, *sl.* caper, con, gyp, *US sl.* scam. **9** see SITUATION 2. ● *v.* **1 a** work; freelance, *colloq.* temp. **b** (*job out*) let out, assign, apportion, allot, share out, contract, hire, employ, subcontract, farm out, consign, commission. **2** trade, deal, do business. **3** take advantage, cheat, *colloq.* cook the books; exploit, misemploy, misapply, misappropriate, misuse, manipulate, manoeuvre, rig, *colloq.* set up. **4** see SWINDLE *v.* □ **just the job** the very thing, *Austral.* just the glassy, *colloq.* (just) what the doctor ordered. **out of a job** see UNEMPLOYED 1.

job[2] /job/ *v.* & *n.* ● *v.* (**jobbed, jobbing**) **1** *tr.* prod; stab slightly. **2** *intr.* (foll. by *at*) thrust. ● *n.* a prod or thrust; a jerk at a horse's bit. [ME, app. imit.: cf. JAB]

jobber /jóbbər/ *n.* **1** *Brit.* a principal or wholesaler dealing on the Stock Exchange. ¶ Up to Oct. 1986 permitted to deal only with brokers, not directly with the public. From Oct. 1986 the name has ceased to be in official use (see BROKER 2). **2** *US* **a** a wholesaler. **b** *derog.* a broker (see BROKER 2). **3** a person who jobs. [JOB[1]]
■ **2 a** see DEALER.

jobbery /jóbbəri/ *n.* corrupt dealing.
■ see GRAFT[2] *n.* 1.

jobbing /jóbbing/ *adj.* working on separate or occasional jobs (esp. of a computer, gardener, or printer).

jobcentre /jóbsentər/ *n. Brit.* any of several government offices displaying information about available jobs.

jobless /jóbliss/ *adj.* without a job; unemployed. □□ **joblessness** *n.*
■ see UNEMPLOYED 1.

Job's comforter /jōbz/ *n.* a person who under the guise of comforting aggravates distress. [the patriarch *Job* in the Old Testament (Job 16:2)]
■ see MISERY 3.

jobsheet /jóbsheet/ *n.* a sheet for recording details of jobs done.

Job's tears /jōbz/ *n.pl.* the seeds of a grass, *Coix lacryma-jobi*, used as beads. [the patriarch *Job* in the Old Testament]

jobwork /jóbwurk/ *n.* work done and paid for by the job.

Jock /jok/ *n. sl.* a Scotsman. [Sc. form of the name *Jack* (see JACK[1])]

jock[1] /jok/ *n. colloq.* a jockey. [abbr.]

jock[2] /jok/ *n. US sl.* = JOCKSTRAP 2. [abbr.]

jockey /jókki/ *n.* & *v.* ● *n.* (*pl.* **-eys**) a rider in horse-races, esp. a professional one. ● *v.* (**-eys, -eyed**) **1** *tr.* **a** trick or cheat (a person). **b** outwit. **2** *tr.* (foll. by *away, out, in*, etc.) draw (a person) by trickery. **3** *intr.* cheat. □ **jockey cap** a cap with a long peak, as worn by jockeys. **jockey for position** try to gain an advantageous position esp. by skilful manoeuvring or unfair action. □□ **jockeydom** *n.* **jockeyship** *n.* [dimin. of JOCK]
■ *v.* **1, 2** see BEGUILE 3.

jockstrap /jókstrap/ *n.* **1** a support or protection for the male genitals, worn esp. by sportsmen. **2** *US sl.* an athletic (rather than intellectual) young man. [sl. *jock* genitals + STRAP]

jocose /jəkṓss/ *adj.* **1** playful in style. **2** fond of joking, jocular. □□ **jocosely** *adv.* **jocoseness** *n.* **jocosity** /-kóssiti/ *n.* (*pl.* **-ies**). [L *jocosus* f. *jocus* jest]
■ see HUMOROUS 1. □□ **jocoseness, jocosity** see HUMOUR *n.* 1a.

jocular /jókyoolər/ *adj.* **1** merry; fond of joking. **2** of the nature of a joke; humorous. □□ **jocularity** /-lárriti/ *n.* (*pl.* **-ies**). **jocularly** *adv.* [L *jocularis* f. *joculus* dimin. of *jocus* jest]
■ see HUMOROUS 1. □□ **jocularity** see HUMOUR *n.* 1. **jocularly** see *with one's tongue in one's cheek* (TONGUE).

jocund /jókkənd/ *adj. literary* merry, cheerful, sprightly. □□ **jocundity** /jəkúnditi/ *n.* (*pl.* **-ies**). **jocundly** *adv.* [ME f. OF f. L *jocundus, jucundus* f. *juvare* delight]
■ see JOYFUL. □□ **jocundity** see JOY *n.* 1.

jodhpurs /jódpərz/ *n.pl.* long breeches for riding etc., close-fitting from the knee to the ankle. [*Jodhpur* in India]

Joe Bloggs /jō blógz/ *n. Brit. colloq.* a hypothetical average man.
■ see PEOPLE *n.* 2.

Joe Blow /jō blṓ/ *n. US colloq.* = JOE BLOGGS.

joey /jṓ-i/ *n.* (*pl.* **-eys**) *Austral.* **1** a young kangaroo. **2** a young animal. [Aboriginal *joè*]

jog /jog/ *v.* & *n.* ● *v.* (**jogged, jogging**) **1** *intr.* run at a slow pace, esp. as physical exercise. **2** *intr.* (of a horse) move at a jogtrot. **3** *intr.* (often foll. by *on, along*) proceed laboriously; trudge. **4** *intr.* go on one's way. **5** *intr.* proceed; get through the time (*we must jog on somehow*). **6** *intr.* move up and down with an unsteady motion. **7** *tr.* nudge (a person), esp. to arouse attention. **8** *tr.* shake with a push or jerk. **9** *tr.* stimulate (a person's or one's own memory). ● *n.* **1** a shake, push, or nudge. **2** a slow walk or trot. [ME: app. imit.]
■ *v.* **1** run, trot, lope. **3** plod, labour, toil, slog, drag, trudge, tramp, crawl, creep, inch, shuffle. **4, 5** go on, continue, carry on, advance, proceed, push *or* press on. **6, 8** bounce, shake, jolt, joggle, jiggle, jounce, jerk, jar, pitch. **7** nudge, prod, push; poke, bump, shove, elbow. **9** stimulate, arouse, stir, prompt, activate; refresh. ● *n.* **1** shake, push, nudge, prod, poke, shove, jolt, jerk, joggle. **2** jogtrot, trot, run, dogtrot; walk, stroll, amble, ramble, saunter, tramp, trudge.

jogger /jóggər/ *n.* a person who jogs, esp. one who runs for physical exercise.
■ see RUNNER 1.

joggle[1] /jógg'l/ *v.* & *n.* ● *v.tr.* & *intr.* shake or move by or as if by repeated jerks. ● *n.* **1** a slight shake. **2** the act or action of joggling. [frequent. of JOG]
■ *v.* see SHAKE *v.* 1, 2, 5. ● *n.* see SHAKE *n.* 1.

joggle[2] /jógg'l/ *n.* & *v.* ● *n.* **1** a joint of two pieces of stone or timber, contrived to prevent their sliding on one another. **2** a notch in one of the two pieces, a projection in the other, or a small piece let in between the two, for this purpose. ● *v.tr.* join with a joggle. [perh. f. *jog* = JAG[1]]

jogtrot /jógtrot/ *n.* **1** a slow regular trot. **2** a monotonous progression.

john /jon/ *n. US sl.* a lavatory. [the name *John*]

John Bull /jon bŏŏl/ *n.* a personification of England or the typical Englishman. [the name of a character repr. the English nation in J. Arbuthnot's satire *Law is a Bottomless Pit* (1712)]

John Dory /jon dóri/ *n.* (*pl.* **-ies**) a European marine fish, *Zeus faber*, with a laterally flattened body and a black spot on each side.

John Hop /jon hóp/ *n. Austral. sl.* a police officer. [rhyming sl. for *cop*]

johnny /jónni/ *n.* (*pl.* **-ies**) *Brit. colloq.* a fellow; a man. □ **johnny-come-lately** *colloq.* a recently arrived person. [familiar form of the name *John*]

Johnsonian /jonsṓniən/ *adj.* **1** of or relating to Samuel Johnson, English man of letters and lexicographer (d. 1784). **2** typical of his style of writing.

joie de vivre /zhwaá də veévrə/ *n.* a feeling of healthy and exuberant enjoyment of life. [F, = joy of living]
■ see JOY *n.* 1.

join /joyn/ *v.* & *n.* ● *v.* **1** *tr.* (often foll. by *to, together*) put together; fasten, unite (one thing or person to another or several together). **2** *tr.* connect (points) by a line etc. **3** *tr.* become a member of (an association, society, organization, etc.). **4** *tr.* take one's place with or in (a company, group, procession, etc.). **5** *tr.* **a** come into the company of (a person). **b** (foll. by *in*) take part with (others) in an activity etc. (*joined me in condemnation of the outrage*). **c** (foll. by *for*) share the company of for a specified occasion (*may I join you for lunch?*). **6** *intr.* (often foll. by *with, to*) come together; be united. **7** *intr.* (often foll. by *in*) take part with others in an activity etc. **8** *tr.* be or become connected or continuous with (*the Inn joins the Danube at Passau*). ● *n.* a point, line, or surface at which two or more things are joined. □ **join battle** begin fighting. **join forces** combine efforts. **join hands 1 a** clasp each other's hands. **b** clasp one's hands together. **2** combine in an action or enterprise. **join up 1** enlist for military service. **2** (often foll. by *with*) unite, connect. □□ **joinable** *adj.* [ME f. OF *joindre* (stem *joign-*) f. L *jungere junct-* join: cf. YOKE]
■ *v.* **1, 2** unite, unify, connect (up), conjoin, combine, add, couple, twin, marry, wed, mate, link, yoke; merge, fuse, knit, weld, solder, glue, stick, cement, tack; attach, fasten, nail, tie, tag on, knot, scarf, seam, sew (up), splice, bridge. **3, 4** enter, enlist in, enrol in, sign (up) with; ally *or* associate oneself with, fall in with, team up with, throw in one's lot with, attach oneself to. **5** go *or* come *or* be with, accompany, tag on *or* along with, team up with, *colloq.* string along with. **6** unite, combine, merge, mingle, integrate, amalgamate, coalesce; collaborate, cooperate, team up, join forces, club together. **7** (*join in*) participate, take part, share, get *or* become involved, climb *or* jump on the bandwagon. **8** meet, touch, abut (on), adjoin, converge with, coincide with, connect with, merge with, unite with, join up with, combine with, integrate with; reach, arrive at, hit. ● *n.* see JOINT *n.* 1. □ **join forces** see JOIN *v.* 6 above. **join up 1** see ENLIST 1. **2** see JOIN *v.* 8 above.

joinder /jóyndər/ *n. Law* the act of bringing together. [AF f. OF *joindre* to join]

joiner /jóynər/ *n.* **1** a person who makes furniture and light woodwork. **2** *colloq.* a person who readily joins societies etc. □□ **joinery** *n.* (in sense 1). [ME f. AF *joignour*, OF *joigneor* (as JOIN)]

joint /joynt/ *n., adj.,* & *v.* ● *n.* **1 a** a place at which two things are joined together. **b** a point at which, or a contrivance by which, two parts of an artificial structure are joined. **2** a structure in an animal body by which two bones are fitted together. **3 a** any of the parts into which an animal carcass is divided for food. **b** any of the parts of which a body is made up. **4** *sl.* a place of meeting for drinking etc. **5** *sl.* a marijuana cigarette. **6** the part of a stem from which a leaf or branch grows. **7** a piece of flexible material forming the hinge of a book-cover. **8** *Geol.* a fissure in a mass of rock. ● *adj.* **1** held or done by, or belonging to, two or more persons etc. in conjunction (*a joint mortgage; joint action*). **2** sharing with another in some action, state, etc. (*joint author; joint favourite*). ● *v.tr.* **1** connect by joints. **2** divide (a body or member) at a joint or into joints. **3** fill up the joints of (masonry etc.) with mortar etc.; trim the surface of (a mortar joint). **4** prepare (a board etc.) for being joined to another by planing its edge. □ **joint account** a bank account held by more than one person, each of whom has the right to deposit and withdraw funds. **joint and several** (of a bond etc.) signed by more than one person, of whom each is liable for the whole sum. **joint stock** capital held jointly; a common fund. **joint-stock company** one formed on the basis of a joint stock. **out of**

joint 1 (of a bone) dislocated. **2** out of order. □□ **jointless** *adj.* **jointly** *adv.* [ME f. OF, past part. of *joindre* JOIN]
■ *n.* **1** join, juncture, connection, junction, intersection, commissure, linkage, articulation; link, weld, knot, splice, seam, gusset, bond, suture; bracket, brace, hinge. **4** bar, (night)club, drinking-den, *colloq.* dive, honky-tonk, *sl.* clip-joint, watering-hole, *US hist. sl.* speakeasy. **5** *sl.* reefer, spliff. ● *adj.* **1, 2** shared, common, communal, collective, combined, cooperative, collaborative; mutual, reciprocal. ● *v.* **1** articulate, hinge; link, couple, connect.

jointer /jóyntər/ *n.* **1 a** a plane for jointing. **b** a tool for jointing or pointing masonry. **2** a worker employed in jointing wires, pipes, etc.

jointress /jóyntriss/ *n.* a widow who holds a jointure. [obs. *jointer* joint possessor]

jointure /jóynchər/ *n.* & *v.* ● *n.* an estate settled on a wife for the period during which she survives her husband. ● *v.tr.* provide (a wife) with a jointure. [ME f. OF f. L *junctura* (as JOIN)]

joist /joyst/ *n.* each of a series of parallel supporting beams of timber, steel, etc., used in floors, ceilings, etc. □□ **joisted** *adj.* [ME f. OF *giste* ult. f. L *jacēre* lie]

jojoba /hōhṓbə/ *n.* a plant, *Simmondsia chinensis*, with seeds yielding an oily extract used in cosmetics etc. [Mex. Sp.]

joke /jōk/ *n.* & *v.* ● *n.* **1 a** a thing said or done to excite laughter. **b** a witticism or jest. **2** a ridiculous thing, person, or circumstance. ● *v.* **1** *intr.* make jokes. **2** *tr.* poke fun at; banter. □ **no joke** *colloq.* a serious matter. □□ **jokingly** *adv.* **joky** *adj.* (also **jokey**). **jokily** *adv.* **jokiness** *n.* [17th c. (*joque*), orig. sl.: perh. f. L *jocus* jest]
■ *n.* **1** quip, gag, jest, waggery, witticism, *colloq.* crack, funny, wisecrack, one-liner, *sl.* josh; pun, wordplay, *bon mot*, *double entendre*; story, anecdote, shaggy-dog story, *colloq.* chestnut, old one; lark, frolic, laugh, *colloq.* giggle, scream; prank, jape, practical joke, trick, booby trap, hoax, *Austral.* goak, *colloq.* put-on. **2** farce, mockery, absurdity, nonsense, travesty, charade, caricature, *colloq.* laugh; laughing-stock, figure of fun, fool, ass, standing joke, *colloq.* goat. ● *v.* **1** jest, banter, tease, fool (about *or* around), *colloq.* kid, *sl.* josh, *Brit. sl.* rot; quip, pun, *colloq.* wisecrack; frolic, skylark. **2** see BANTER *v.* 1. □□ **jokingly** see *with one's tongue in one's cheek* (TONGUE).

joker /jṓkər/ *n.* **1** a person who jokes. **2** *sl.* a fellow; a man. **3** a playing-card usu. with a figure of a jester, used in some games esp. as a wild card. **4** *US* a clause unobtrusively inserted in a bill or document and affecting its operation in a way not immediately apparent. **5** an unexpected factor or resource. □ **the joker in the pack** an unpredictable factor or participant.
■ **1** comic, (stand-up) comedian *or* comedienne, jokesmith, funny man, gag man, gagster, humorist, wag, wit, punster, buffoon, *farceur*, *colloq.* card, kidder; clown, mountebank, merry andrew, *Theatr.* pierrot, *archaic* droll, *hist.* zany; jester, fool; trickster, prankster, practical joker. **2** see FELLOW 1. **4** fine *or* small print, catch, hitch, trap, twist, snag, pitfall. **5** unknown quantity, surprise package, the joker in the pack; trump (card). □ **the joker in the pack** see JOKER 5 above.

jokesmith /jṓksmith/ *n.* a skilled user or inventor of jokes.
■ see JOKER 1.

jolie laide /zhóllee láyd/ *n.* (*pl.* ***jolies laides*** *pronunc.* same) = BELLE LAIDE. [F f. *jolie* pretty + *laide* ugly]

jollify /jóllifī/ *v.tr.* & *intr.* (**-ies, -ied**) make or be merry, esp. in drinking. □□ **jollification** /-fikáysh'n/ *n.*
■ □□ **jollification** see FESTIVITY 1.

jollity /jólliti/ *n.* (*pl.* **-ies**) **1** merrymaking; festiveness. **2** (in *pl.*) festivities. [ME f. OF *jolivеté* (as JOLLY[1])]
■ see FESTIVITY 1.

jollo /jóllō/ *n.* *Austral. colloq.* a spree; a party.
■ see PARTY *n.* 1.

jolly[1] /jólli/ *adj.*, *adv.*, *v.*, & *n.* ● *adj.* (**jollier, jolliest**) **1** cheerful and good-humoured; merry. **2** festive, jovial. **3** slightly drunk. **4** *colloq.* (of a person or thing) very pleasant, delightful (often *iron.*: *a jolly shame*). ● *adv. colloq.* very (*they were jolly unlucky*). ● *v.tr.* (**-ies, -ied**) **1** (usu. foll. by *along*) *colloq.* coax or humour (a person) in a friendly way. **2** chaff, banter. ● *n.* (*pl.* **-ies**) *colloq.* a party or celebration; an outing. □ **Jolly Roger** a pirates' black flag, usu. with the skull and crossbones. □□ **jollily** *adv.* **jolliness** *n.* [ME f. OF *jolif* gay, pretty, perh. f. ON *jól* YULE]
■ *adj.* **1, 2** merry, cheerful, cheery, good-humoured, happy, joyful, joyous, gleeful, gay, sunny; convivial, jovial, festive, jubilant, exuberant, vivacious, lively, high-spirited, *colloq.* chirpy; playful, frolicsome, frisky, sportive, jocose, jocular, light-hearted, buoyant, carefree, mirthful, *literary* jocund. **3** tipsy, *colloq.* woozy, elevated, happy, *Brit. colloq.* merry, tiddly, *Brit. sl.* squiffy; see also DRUNK *adj.* 1. ● *adv.* see VERY *adv.* ● *v.* **1** (*jolly along*) coax, humour, appease, cajole, wheedle, urge (on). **2** see BANTER *v.* 1. ● *n.* outing, jaunt, junket, trip; see also PARTY *n.* 1.

jolly[2] /jólli/ *n.* (*pl.* **-ies**) (in full **jolly boat**) a clinker-built ship's boat smaller than a cutter. [18th c.: orig. unkn.: perh. rel. to YAWL]
■ see TENDER[3].

jolt /jōlt, jolt/ *v.* & *n.* ● *v.* **1** *tr.* disturb or shake from the normal position (esp. in a moving vehicle) with a jerk. **2** *tr.* give a mental shock to; perturb. **3** *intr.* (of a vehicle) move along with jerks, as on a rough road. ● *n.* **1** such a jerk. **2** a surprise or shock. □□ **jolty** *adj.* (**joltier, joltiest**). [16th c.: orig. unkn.]
■ *v.* **1** jar, jerk, jounce, bump, bang, knock, nudge, jog, joggle, shake, rock, bounce, rattle, disturb, agitate, *colloq.* yank. **2** shock, shake (up), disturb, perturb, rattle, agitate, unnerve, unsettle, disconcert; astonish, astound, amaze, surprise, startle, stun, dumbfound, stupefy, stagger, electrify, strike dumb, daze. **3** lurch, jerk, stagger, shudder, rock, rattle, *esp. Brit.* judder. ● *n.* **1** lurch, jerk, stagger, shudder, *esp. Brit.* judder; jar, jounce, bump, bang, knock, nudge, jog, joggle, shake, jump, bounce. **2** shock, surprise, blow, start, bolt from the blue, bombshell.

Jon. *abbr.* **1** Jonah (Old Testament). **2** Jonathan.

Jonah /jṓnə/ *n.* a person who seems to bring bad luck. [*Jonah* in the Old Testament]
■ see JINX *n.*

jongleur /zhonglṓr/ *n. hist.* an itinerant minstrel. [F, var. of *jougleur* JUGGLER]
■ see MINSTREL.

jonquil /jóngkwil/ *n.* a bulbous plant, *Narcissus jonquilla*, with clusters of small fragrant yellow flowers. [mod.L *jonquilla* or F *jonquille* f. Sp. *junquillo* dimin. of *junco*: see JUNCO]

Jordanian /jordáyniən/ *adj.* & *n.* ● *adj.* of or relating to the kingdom of Jordan in the Middle East. ● *n.* **1** a native or national of Jordan. **2** a person of Jordanian descent. [*Jordan*, river flowing into the Dead Sea]

jorum /jórəm/ *n.* **1** a large drinking-bowl. **2** its contents, esp. punch. [perh. f. *Joram* (2 Sam. 8:10)]

Jos. *abbr.* Joseph.

Josh. *abbr.* Joshua (Old Testament).

josh /josh/ *n.* & *v. sl.* ● *n.* a good-natured or teasing joke. ● *v.* **1** *tr.* tease or banter. **2** *intr.* indulge in ridicule. □□ **josher** *n.* [19th c.: orig. unkn.]
■ *v.* **1** see TEASE *v.*

joss[1] /joss/ *n.* a Chinese idol. □ **joss-house** a Chinese temple. **joss-stick** a stick of fragrant tinder mixed with clay, burnt as incense. [perh. ult. f. Port. *deos* f. L *deus* god]

joss[2] /joss/ *n. Austral.* a person of influence and importance. [Brit. dial.]
■ see DIGNITARY.

josser /jóssər/ *n. Brit. sl.* **1** a fool. **2** a fellow. [JOSS + -ER[1]: cf. Austral. sense 'clergyman']

jostle /jóss'l/ *v.* & *n.* ● *v.* **1** *tr.* push against; elbow. **2** *tr.* (often foll. by *away*, *from*, etc.) push (a person) abruptly or

roughly. **3** *intr.* (foll. by *against*) knock or push, esp. in a crowd. **4** *intr.* (foll. by *with*) struggle; have a rough exchange. ● *n.* **1** the act or an instance of jostling. **2** a collision. [ME: earlier *justle* f. JOUST + -LE[4]]
▪ *v.* **1–3** see PUSH *v.* 7. **4** see STRUGGLE *v.* 3.

jot /jot/ *v.* & *n.* ● *v.tr.* (**jotted, jotting**) (usu. foll. by *down*) write briefly or hastily. ● *n.* (usu. with *neg.* expressed or implied) a very small amount (*not one jot*). [earlier as noun: L f. Gk *iōta*: see IOTA]
▪ *v.* (*jot down*) make a note of, write *or* note (down), put *or* set *or* take down, scribble (down), scrawl, pen, record. ● *n.* bit, scrap, grain, speck, mite, iota, whit, rap, hoot, particle, tittle, *colloq.* smidgen, *US colloq.* tad, *sl.* two hoots; (*not a jot*) not in the slightest, not at all, no whit, never *or* not a whit.

jotter /jóttər/ *n.* a small pad or notebook for making notes etc.
▪ see PAD[1] *n.* 2.

jotting /jótting/ *n.* (usu. in *pl.*) a note; something jotted down.
▪ see NOTE *n.* 1.

joule /jo͞ol/ *n.* the SI unit of work or energy equal to the work done by a force of one newton when its point of application moves one metre in the direction of action of the force, equivalent to a watt-second. ¶ Symb.: **J.** [J. P. *Joule*, Engl. physicist d. 1889]

jounce /jownss/ *v.tr.* & *intr.* bump, bounce, jolt. [ME: orig. unkn.]
▪ see JOLT *v.* 1.

journal /júrn'l/ *n.* **1** a newspaper or periodical. **2** a daily record of events. **3** *Naut.* a logbook. **4** a book in which business transactions are entered, with a statement of the accounts to which each is to be debited and credited. **5** the part of a shaft or axle that rests on bearings. **6** (**the Journals**) *Parl.* a record of daily proceedings. [ME f. OF *jurnal* f. LL *diurnalis* DIURNAL]
▪ **1** newspaper, paper, organ, periodical, magazine, gazette, newsletter, review, tabloid, broadsheet, news-sheet, pictorial, *colloq.* daily, *derog.* rag; weekly, fortnightly, monthly, quarterly. **2** diary, chronicle, record, log(book), yearbook, annal(s); almanac, calendar. **4** daybook, ledger.

journalese /júrnəleéz/ *n.* a hackneyed style of language characteristic of some newspaper writing.

journalism /júrnəliz'm/ *n.* the business or practice of writing and producing newspapers.

journalist /júrnəlist/ *n.* a person employed to report for or edit a newspaper, journal, or newscast. ▫▫ **journalistic** /-lístik/ *adj.* **journalistically** /-lístikəli/ *adv.*
▪ reporter, newspaperman, pressman, newsman, (gossip) columnist, publicist, (special) correspondent, commentator, news-hound, hack, news-gatherer, legman, *Austral.* roundsman, *US* wireman, staffer, *colloq.* stringer, *Austral. colloq.* journo, *US colloq.* scribe; (*journalists*) the press, *Brit.* Fleet Street, the lobby, *joc.* the fourth estate; paparazzo; editor, sub-editor, copy-editor, City editor, *US* city editor; newscaster, newsreader, broadcaster.

journalize /júrnəlīz/ *v.tr.* (also **-ise**) record in a private journal.

journey /júrni/ *n.* & *v.* ● *n.* (*pl.* **-eys**) **1** an act of going from one place to another, esp. at a long distance. **2** the distance travelled in a specified time (*a day's journey*). **3** the travelling of a vehicle along a route at a stated time. ● *v.intr.* (**-eys, -eyed**) make a journey. ▫▫ **journeyer** *n.* [ME f. OF *jornee* day, day's work or travel, ult. f. L *diurnus* daily]
▪ *n.* voyage, expedition, odyssey, trek; trip, excursion, tour, outing, junket, jaunt, errand, *archaic or joc.* peregrination; cruise, flight, drive, ride, run, crossing, passage, hop, lap, circuit; walk, meander, ramble, tramp, stroll, march, *colloq. or dial.* traipse; pilgrimage, mission; course, route, career, way, transit, traverse, transition, progress, advance, travel. ● *v.* travel, tour, voyage, go (abroad *or* overseas), make *or* take a trip, make one's way, make a pilgrimage, trek, rove, range, wander, roam, cruise, gad (about), *archaic or joc.* peregrinate, *colloq.* gallivant, *literary or archaic* wend one's way.
▫▫ **journeyer** see TRAVELLER 1.

journeyman /júrnimən/ *n.* (*pl.* **-men**) **1** a qualified mechanic or artisan who works for another. **2** *derog.* **a** a reliable but not outstanding worker. **b** a mere hireling. [JOURNEY in obs. sense 'day's work' + MAN]
▪ **1** see TRADESMAN.

journo /júrnō/ *n.* (*pl/* **-os**) *Austral. colloq.* a journalist. [shortened form of JOURNALIST + -O]

joust /jowst/ *n.* & *v. hist.* ● *n.* a combat between two knights on horseback with lances. ● *v.intr.* engage in a joust. ▫▫ **jouster** *n.* [ME f. OF *juster* bring together ult. f. L *juxta* near]
▪ *n.* see TOURNAMENT 3. ● *v.* see FIGHT *v.* 1a.

Jove /jōv/ *n.* (in Roman mythology) Jupiter. ▫ **by Jove!** an exclamation of surprise or approval. [ME f. L *Jovis* genit. of OL *Jovis* used as genit. of JUPITER]

jovial /jōviəl/ *adj.* **1** merry. **2** convivial. **3** hearty and good-humoured. ▫▫ **joviality** /-viálliti/ *n.* **jovially** *adv.* [F f. LL *jovialis* of Jupiter (as JOVE), with ref. to the supposed influence of the planet Jupiter on those born under it]
▪ see MERRY 1. ▫▫ **joviality** see MERRIMENT.

Jovian /jōviən/ *adj.* **1** (in Roman mythology) of or like Jupiter. **2** of the planet Jupiter.

jowar /jow-waár/ *n.* = DURRA. [Hindi *jawār*]

jowl[1] /jowl/ *n.* **1** the jaw or jawbone. **2** the cheek (*cheek by jowl*). ▫▫ **-jowled** *adj.* (in *comb.*). [ME *chavel* jaw f. OE *ceafl*]

jowl[2] /jowl/ *n.* **1** the external loose skin on the throat or neck when prominent. **2** the dewlap of oxen, wattle of a bird, etc. ▫▫ **jowly** *adj.* [ME *cholle* neck f. OE *ceole*]

joy /joy/ *n.* & *v.* ● *n.* **1** (often foll. by *at, in*) a vivid emotion of pleasure; extreme gladness. **2** a thing that causes joy. **3** *Brit. colloq.* satisfaction, success (*got no joy*). ● *v.* esp. *poet.* **1** *intr.* rejoice. **2** *tr.* gladden. ▫ **joy-bells** bells rung on festive occasions. **wish a person joy of** *iron.* be gladly rid of (what that person has to deal with). ▫▫ **joyless** *adj.* **joylessly** *adv.* [ME f. OF *joie* ult. f. L *gaudium* f. *gaudēre* rejoice]
▪ *n.* **1** delight, elation, exaltation, ecstasy, exhilaration, exultation, rapture; bliss, heaven, paradise; gladness, felicity, happiness, contentment, pleasure, gratification, satisfaction, enjoyment; gaiety, fun, cheerfulness, sparkle, sunshine, radiance, cheer, glee, buoyancy, joviality, jollity, joyfulness, joyousness, jubilation, jubilee, merriment, light-heartedness, *joie de vivre*, *literary* jocundity. **2** delight, pleasure, treat; blessing, treasure, boon, godsend, gem, meat and drink. **3** see SUCCESS 1. ● *v.* **1** see REJOICE 1. **2** see GLADDEN.
▫▫ **joyless** sad, unhappy, miserable, depressed, dejected, mournful, downhearted, downcast, cast down, despondent, dispirited, melancholy, heavy-hearted, cheerless, doleful, grief-stricken, crestfallen, wretched, disconsolate, inconsolable, morose, heartsick, sorrowful, woeful, woebegone; gloomy, depressing, dispiriting, disheartening, dreary, lugubrious, cheerless, dismal, bleak, inhospitable, desolate, grim, austere, severe.

Joycean /jóysiən/ *adj.* & *n.* ● *adj.* of or characteristic of James Joyce, Irish poet and novelist (d. 1941) or his writings. ● *n.* a specialist in or admirer of Joyce's works.

joyful /jóyfo͝ol/ *adj.* full of, showing, or causing joy. ▫▫ **joyfully** *adv.* **joyfulness** *n.*
▪ cheerful, happy, buoyant, gleeful, merry, jovial, jolly, joyous, jubilant, gay, light-hearted, sunny, *literary* jocund, *poet.* blithe, blithesome; glad, pleased, delighted, happy, elated, ecstatic, exhilarated, exultant, overjoyed, jubilant, rapt, rapturous, in seventh heaven, over the moon, *colloq.* on cloud nine *or* seven, tickled (pink *or* to death).

joyous /jóyəss/ *adj.* (of an occasion, circumstance, etc.) characterized by pleasure or joy; joyful. ▫▫ **joyously** *adv.* **joyousness** *n.*
▪ see JOYFUL. ▫▫ **joyously** see *happily* (HAPPY). **joyousness** see JOY *n.* 1.

joyride /jóyrīd/ *n.* & *v. colloq.* ● *n.* a ride for pleasure in a motor car, esp. without the owner's permission. ● *v.intr.* (*past* **-rode** /-rōd/; *past part.* **-ridden** /-ridd'n/) go for a joyride. □□ **joyrider** *n.*

joystick /jóystik/ *n.* **1** *colloq.* the control column of an aircraft. **2** a lever that can be moved in several directions to control the movement of an image on a VDU screen.

JP *abbr.* Justice of the Peace.

Jr. *abbr.* Junior.

jt. *abbr.* joint.

jube /jo͞ob/ *n. Austral.* & *NZ* = JUJUBE 2. [abbr.]

jubilant /jo͞obilənt/ *adj.* exultant, rejoicing, joyful. □□ **jubilance** *n.* **jubilantly** *adv.* [L *jubilare jubilant-* shout for joy]

■ see JOYFUL. □□ **jubilantly** see GAILY 1.

jubilate /jo͞obilayt/ *v.intr.* exult; be joyful. □□ **jubilation** /-láysh'n/ *n.* [L *jubilare* (as JUBILANT)]

■ □□ **jubilation** see JOY *n.* 1.

jubilee /jo͞obilee/ *n.* **1** a time or season of rejoicing. **2** an anniversary, esp. the 25th or 50th. **3** *Jewish Hist.* a year of emancipation and restoration, kept every 50 years. **4** *RC Ch.* a period of remission from the penal consequences of sin, granted under certain conditions for a year usu. at intervals of 25 years. **5** exultant joy. [ME f. OF *jubilé* f. LL *jubilaeus* (*annus*) (year) of jubilee ult. f. Heb. *yōḇēl*, orig. = ram, ram's-horn trumpet]

■ **1** see JAMBOREE.

Jud. *abbr.* Judith (Apocrypha).

Judaeo- /joodée-ō/ *comb. form* (*US* **Judeo-**) Jewish; Jewish and. [L *judaeus* Jewish]

Judaic /joodáyik/ *adj.* of or characteristic of the Jews or Judaism. [L *Judaicus* f. Gk *Ioudaïkos* f. *Ioudaios* JEW]

Judaism /jo͞odayiz'm/ *n.* **1** the religion of the Jews, with a belief in one God and a basis in Mosaic and rabbinical teachings. **2** the Jews collectively. □□ **Judaist** *n.* [ME f. LL *Judaismus* f. Gk *Ioudaïsmos* (as JUDAIC)]

Judaize /jo͞odayīz/ *v.* (also **-ise**) **1** *intr.* follow Jewish customs or rites. **2** *tr.* **a** make Jewish. **b** convert to Judaism. □□ **Judaization** /-záysh'n/ *n.* [LL *judaizare* f. Gk *ioudaïzō* (as JUDAIC)]

Judas /jo͞odəss/ *n.* **1** a person who betrays a friend. **2** (**judas**) a peep-hole in a door. □ **Judas-tree** a Mediterranean tree, *Cercis siliquastrum*, with purple flowers usu. appearing before the leaves. [*Judas* Iscariot who betrayed Christ (Luke 22)]

■ **1** see TRAITOR.

judder /júddər/ *v.* & *n.* esp. *Brit.* ● *v.intr.* **1** (esp. of a mechanism) vibrate noisily or violently. **2** (of a singer's voice) oscillate in intensity. ● *n.* an instance of juddering. [imit.: cf. SHUDDER]

■ *v.* **1** see JOLT *v.* 3. **2** see VIBRATE 3. ● *n.* see JOLT *n.* 1.

Judeo- *US* var. of JUDAEO-.

Judg. *abbr.* Judges (Old Testament).

judge /juj/ *n.* & *v.* ● *n.* **1** a public officer appointed to hear and try causes in a court of justice. **2** a person appointed to decide a dispute or contest. **3 a** a person who decides a question. **b** a person regarded in terms of capacity to decide on the merits of a thing or question (*am no judge of that*; *a good judge of art*). **4** *Jewish Hist.* a leader having temporary authority in Israel in the period between Joshua and the Kings. ● *v.* **1** *tr.* **a** try (a cause) in a court of justice. **b** pronounce sentence on (a person). **2** *tr.* form an opinion about; estimate, appraise. **3** *tr.* act as a judge of (a dispute or contest). **4** *tr.* (often foll. by *to* + infin. or *that* + clause) conclude, consider, or suppose. **5** *intr.* **a** form a judgement. **b** act as judge. □ **Judge Advocate General** an officer in supreme control of the courts martial in the armed forces. **Judges' Rules** *Brit.* rules regarding the admissibility of an accused's statements as evidence. □□ **judgelike** *adj.* **judgeship** *n.* [ME f. OF *juge* (n.), *juger* (v.) f. L *judex judicis* f. *jus* law + *-dicus* speaking]

■ *n.* **1** justice, magistrate, jurist, the bench, official (principal), seneschal, deemster, alcalde, *Brit.* jurat, Common Serjeant, *Brit.* & *hist.* recorder, reeve, *Sc.* sheriff-depute, *US* surrogate, burgess, squire, *esp. hist.* bailie, *Brit. sl.* beak. **2** arbitrator, arbiter, umpire, referee, adjudicator, mediator, moderator, assessor, examiner, appraiser, evaluator. **3 b** connoisseur, expert, authority, specialist, pundit, *arbiter elegantiarum*; reviewer, critic. ● *v.* **1 a** try, hear, sit on, adjudicate, adjudge, decide; weigh. **b** sentence, pronounce *or* pass sentence on, pass judgement on. **2** reckon, estimate, figure, gauge, measure, weigh (up), size up, assess, evaluate, appraise, value, count, rate, rank; decide, determine. **3** adjudicate, adjudge, arbitrate, referee, umpire, mediate, moderate. **4** regard, hold, believe, perceive, suppose, consider, think, *formal* deem; find, conclude, infer, decide, determine. **5 a** make up one's mind, decide, take *or* reach *or* come to a conclusion *or* decision. **b** adjudicate, arbitrate, referee, umpire, mediate, moderate, officiate.

judgement /újmənt/ *n.* (also **judgment**) **1** the critical faculty; discernment (*an error of judgement*). **2** good sense. **3** an opinion or estimate (*in my judgement*). **4** the sentence of a court of justice; a decision by a judge. **5** often *joc.* a misfortune viewed as a deserved recompense (*it is a judgement on you for getting up late*). **6** criticism. □ **against one's better judgement** contrary to what one really feels to be advisable. **judgement by default** see DEFAULT. **Judgement Day** the day on which the Last Judgement is believed to take place. **judgement-seat** a judge's seat; a tribunal. **the Last Judgement** (in some beliefs) the judgement of mankind expected to take place at the end of the world. [ME f. OF *jugement* (as JUDGE)]

■ **1, 2** discretion, discernment, discrimination, judiciousness, prudence, wisdom, sagacity, perspicacity, perception, percipience, acumen, acuity, insight, reason, reasoning, logic, intellect, mentality, understanding; intelligence, level-headedness, (good) sense, common sense, (mother *or* native) wit, *colloq.* nous, gumption, horse sense, *sl.* loaf. **3** opinion, (point of) view, belief, (way of) thinking, conviction, feeling, sentiment, idea, notion, impression, conception, perception; estimate, evaluation, estimation, appraisal, analysis, assessment; criticism, critique, review. **4** decision, sentence, ruling, finding, adjudication, verdict, pronouncement, conclusion, determination, decree. **5** punishment, penalty, sentence, (just) deserts. **6** criticism, censure, disapproval, reproof, condemnation. □ **against one's better judgement** reluctantly, unwillingly, grudgingly. **Judgement Day** doomsday, doom; the Last Judgement. **the Last Judgement** see *Judgement Day* above.

judgemental /jujméntʼl/ *adj.* (also **judgmental**) **1** of or concerning or by way of judgement. **2** condemning, critical. □□ **judgementally** *adv.*

■ **2** see CRITICAL 1.

judicature /jo͞odikəchər, -dikkəchər/ *n.* **1** the administration of justice. **2** a judge's office or term of office. **3** judges collectively. **4** a court of justice. [med.L *judicatura* f. L *judicare* to judge]

judicial /joodísh'l/ *adj.* **1** of, done by, or proper to a court of law. **2** having the function of judgement (*a judicial assembly*). **3** of or proper to a judge. **4** expressing a judgement; critical. **5** impartial. **6** regarded as a divine judgement. □ **judicial factor** *Sc.* an official receiver. **judicial separation** the separation of man and wife by decision of a court. □□ **judicially** *adv.* [ME f. L *judicialis* f. *judicium* judgement f. *judex* JUDGE]

■ **1, 2** legal, judiciary, juridical, forensic; official. **3** judgelike, magisterial. **4** critical, judgemental; censorious, disparaging, deprecatory, deprecative, condemnatory. **5** impartial, equitable, even-handed, neutral, unbiased, objective, uncoloured, unprejudiced, fair, fair-minded, just, true, honest, disinterested, dispassionate, detached, uninvolved.

judiciary /joodíshəri/ *n.* (*pl.* **-ies**) the judges of a State collectively. [L *judiciarius* (as JUDICIAL)]

judicious /joodíshəss/ *adj.* **1** sensible, prudent. **2** sound in discernment and judgement. □□ **judiciously** *adv.* **judiciousness** *n.* [F *judicieux* f. L *judicium* (as JUDICIAL)]
■ sensible, reasonable, logical, sane, prudent, careful, sound, sober, cautious, considered, (well-)advised, circumspect, provident, politic, diplomatic, discreet; wise, sage, sagacious, insightful, clear-sighted, intelligent, perceptive, percipient, perspicacious, discerning, canny, shrewd, astute, *literary* sapient.

judo /jóōdō/ *n.* a sport of unarmed combat derived from ju-jitsu. □□ **judoist** *n.* [Jap. f. *jū* gentle + *dō* way]

Judy /jóōdi/ *n.* (*pl.* **-ies**) **1** see PUNCH[4]. **2** (also **judy**) *sl.* a woman. [pet-form of the name *Judith*]

jug /jug/ *n.* & *v.* ● *n.* **1 a** a deep vessel for holding liquids, with a handle and often with a spout or lip shaped for pouring. **b** the contents of this; a jugful. **2** *US* a large jar with a narrow mouth. **3** *sl.* prison. **4** (in *pl.*) *US coarse sl.* a woman's breasts. ● *v.tr.* (**jugged, jugging**) **1** (usu. as **jugged** *adj.*) stew or boil (a hare or rabbit) in a covered vessel. **2** *sl.* imprison. □□ **jugful** *n.* (*pl.* **-fuls**). [perh. f. *Jug*, pet-form of the name *Joan* etc.]
■ *n.* **1, 2** pitcher, ewer, jar, boat, toby jug, *US* creamer, *archaic* greybeard; urn, carafe, bottle, flask, decanter. **3** see PRISON *n.* 1. ● *v.* **1** stew, boil, simmer, steam, braise, casserole. **2** see IMPRISON 1.

Jugendstil /yóōgənt-shteel/ *n.* the German name for *art nouveau*. [G f. *Jugend* youth + *Stil* style]

juggernaut /júggərnawt/ *n.* **1** esp. *Brit.* a large heavy motor vehicle, esp. an articulated lorry. **2** a huge or overwhelming force or object. **3** (**Juggernaut**) an institution or notion to which persons blindly sacrifice themselves or others. [Hindi *Jagannath* f. Skr. *Jagannātha* = lord of the world: name of an idol of Krishna in Hindu mythol., carried in procession on a huge cart under which devotees are said to have formerly thrown themselves]

juggins /júgginz/ *n.* *Brit. sl.* a simpleton. [perh. f. proper name *Juggins* (as JUG): cf. MUGGINS]

juggle /júgg'l/ *v.* & *n.* ● *v.* **1 a** *intr.* (often foll. by *with*) perform feats of dexterity, esp. by tossing objects in the air and catching them, keeping several in the air at the same time. **b** *tr.* perform such feats with. **2** *tr.* continue to deal with (several activities) at once, esp. with ingenuity. **3** *intr.* (foll. by *with*) & *tr.* **a** deceive or cheat. **b** misrepresent (facts). **c** rearrange adroitly. ● *n.* **1** a piece of juggling. **2** a fraud. [ME, back-form. f. JUGGLER or f. OF *jogler*, *jugler* f. L *joculari* jest f. *joculus* dimin. of *jocus* jest]
■ *v.* **3 a** see DECEIVE 1. **b** misrepresent, misstate, distort, falsify, alter, manipulate, massage, tamper with, rig, *colloq.* fix, doctor, cook, *sl.* fiddle. **c** rearrange, reposition, reset, redo, reshuffle; shuffle, change, alter, modify, shift, switch, transpose. ● *n.* **1** prestidigitation, legerdemain; dexterity, wizardry, sleight of hand. **2** fraud, deception, deceit, trickery, swindle, legerdemain, sophistry, humbug, flimflam, hocus-pocus, hoax, trick, dodge, *colloq.* rip-off, *Brit. colloq.* jiggery-pokery, *sl.* funny business, gyp, *US sl.* scam.

juggler /júglər/ *n.* **1 a** a person who juggles. **b** a conjuror. **2** a trickster or impostor. □□ **jugglery** *n.* [ME f. OF *jouglere -eor* f. L *joculator -oris* (as JUGGLE)]
■ □□ **jugglery** see HOCUS-POCUS *n.* 3.

Jugoslav var. of YUGOSLAV.

jugular /júgyoolər/ *adj.* & *n.* ● *adj.* **1** of the neck or throat. **2** (of fish) having ventral fins in front of the pectoral fins. ● *n.* = *jugular vein*. □ **jugular vein** any of several large veins of the neck which carry blood from the head. [LL *jugularis* f. L *jugulum* collar-bone, throat, dimin. of *jugum* YOKE]

jugulate /júgyoolayt/ *v.tr.* **1** kill by cutting the throat. **2** arrest the course of (a disease etc.) by a powerful remedy. [L *jugulare* f. *jugulum* (as JUGULAR)]

juice /jōoss/ *n.* **1** the liquid part of vegetables or fruits. **2** the fluid part of an animal body or substance, esp. a secretion (*gastric juice*). **3** the essence or spirit of anything. **4** *colloq.* petrol or electricity as a source of power. **5** *US sl.* alcoholic liquor. □□ **juiceless** *adj.* [ME f. OF *jus* f. L *jus* broth, juice]
■ **1** sap, liquid, fluid; crush. **3** see ESSENCE 1. **4** *Brit.* petrol, *US* gasoline, *US colloq.* gas; electricity, current, power.

juicer /jóōssər/ *n.* *US sl.* an alcoholic.

juicy /jóōssi/ *adj.* (**juicier, juiciest**) **1** full of juice; succulent. **2** *colloq.* substantial or interesting; racy, scandalous. **3** *colloq.* profitable. □□ **juicily** *adv.* **juiciness** *n.*
■ **1** succulent, lush, ripe, mellow, luscious. **2** substantial, significant, considerable, consequential; interesting, intriguing, fascinating, stirring, thrilling, exciting, entertaining, eventful, sensational, lurid, colourful, vivid, provocative, stimulating, suggestive, scandalous, racy, spicy, risqué. **3** see PROFITABLE 1.

ju-jitsu /joojítsōō/ *n.* (also **jiu-jitsu, ju-jutsu**) a Japanese system of unarmed combat and physical training. [Jap. *jūjutsu* f. *jū* gentle + *jutsu* skill]

ju-ju /jóōjōō/ *n.* **1** a charm or fetish of some W. African peoples. **2** a supernatural power attributed to this. [perh. f. F *joujou* toy]
■ **1** see TALISMAN.

jujube /jóōjōōb/ *n.* **1 a** any plant of the genus *Zizyphus* bearing edible acidic berry-like fruits. **b** this fruit. **2** a lozenge of gelatin etc. flavoured with or imitating this. [F *jujube* or med.L *jujuba* ult. f. Gk *zizuphon*]

ju-jutsu var. of JU-JITSU.

jukebox /jóōkboks/ *n.* a machine that automatically plays a selected musical recording when a coin is inserted. [Gullah *juke* disorderly + BOX[1]]

Jul. *abbr.* July.

julep /jóōlep/ *n.* **1 a** a sweet drink, esp. as a vehicle for medicine. **b** a medicated drink as a mild stimulant etc. **2** *US* iced and flavoured spirits and water (*mint julep*). [ME f. OF f. Arab. *julāb* f. Pers. *gulāb* f. *gul* rose + *āb* water]

Julian /jóōliən/ *adj.* of or associated with Julius Caesar. □ **Julian calendar** a calendar introduced by Julius Caesar, in which the year consisted of 365 days, every fourth year having 366 (cf. GREGORIAN CALENDAR). [L *Julianus* f. *Julius*]

julienne /jóōli-én/ *n.* & *adj.* ● *n.* foodstuff, esp. vegetables, cut into short thin strips. ● *adj.* cut into thin strips. [F f. the name *Jules* or *Julien*]

Juliet cap /jóōliət/ *n.* a small network ornamental cap worn by brides etc. [the heroine of Shakesp. *Romeo & Juliet*]

July /joolī́/ *n.* (*pl.* **Julys**) the seventh month of the year. [ME f. AF *julie* f. L *Julius* (*mensis* month), named after Julius Caesar]

jumble /júmb'l/ *v.* & *n.* ● *v.* **1** *tr.* (often foll. by *up*) confuse; mix up. **2** *intr.* move about in disorder. ● *n.* **1** a confused state or heap; a muddle. **2** *Brit.* articles collected for a jumble sale. □ **jumble sale** *Brit.* a sale of miscellaneous usu. second-hand articles, esp. for charity. □□ **jumbly** *adj.* [prob. imit.]
■ *v.* **1** confuse, disorder, mix (up), confound, muddle, shuffle, disarrange, disorganize, upset, mess (up), scramble, garble, tangle, entangle, snarl (up). **2** see MILL[1] *v.* 4. ● *n.* **1** muddle, tangle, mess, clutter, mêlée, imbroglio; disorder, confusion, disarray, chaos; gallimaufry, hash, hotchpotch, hodgepodge, mishmash, assortment, medley, miscellany, mixture, patchwork. **2** rummage, lumber, junk; bric-à-brac, bits and pieces *or* bobs. □ **jumble sale** bazaar, car-boot sale, *Brit.* bring-and-buy sale, *US* rummage sale, garage sale.

jumbo /júmbō/ *n.* & *adj.* *colloq.* ● *n.* (*pl.* **-os**) **1** a large animal (esp. an elephant), person, or thing. **2** (in full **jumbo jet**) a large airliner with capacity for several hundred passengers. ¶ Usu. applied specifically to the Boeing 747. ● *adj.* **1** very large of its kind. **2** extra large (*jumbo packet*). [19th c. (orig. of a person): orig. unkn.: popularized as the name of a zoo elephant sold in 1882]
■ *n.* **1** giant, monster, colossus, behemoth, leviathan, *colloq.*

hulk, *sl.* whopper. ● *adj.* huge, immense, gigantic, enormous, vast, massive, monstrous, gargantuan, colossal, mammoth, giant, titanic, elephantine, Cyclopean; oversize, extra size, outsize, king-size, queen-size, economy(-size); large, big, *colloq.* thumping, hulking; *sl.* whopping, humongous; see also BIG *adj.* 1a.

jumbuck /júmbuk/ *n. Austral. colloq.* a sheep. [Aboriginal]

jump /jump/ *v.* & *n.* ● *v.* **1** *intr.* move off the ground or other surface (usu. upward, at least initially) by sudden muscular effort in the legs. **2** *intr.* (often foll. by *up*, *from*, *in*, *out*, etc.) move suddenly or hastily in a specified way (*we jumped into the car*). **3** *intr.* give a sudden bodily movement from shock or excitement etc. **4** *intr.* undergo a rapid change, esp. an advance in status. **5** *intr.* (often foll. by *about*) change or move rapidly from one idea or subject to another. **6 a** *intr.* rise or increase suddenly (*prices jumped*). **b** *tr.* cause to do this. **7** *tr.* **a** pass over (an obstacle, barrier, etc.) by jumping. **b** move or pass over (an intervening thing) to a point beyond. **8** *tr.* skip or pass over (a passage in a book etc.). **9** *tr.* cause (a thing, or an animal, esp. a horse) to jump. **10** *intr.* (foll. by *to*, *at*) reach a conclusion hastily. **11** *tr.* (of a train) leave (the rails) owing to a fault. **12** *tr.* ignore and pass (a red traffic-light etc.). **13** *tr.* get on or off (a train etc.) quickly, esp. illegally or dangerously. **14** *tr.* pounce on or attack (a person) unexpectedly. **15** *tr.* take summary possession of (a claim allegedly abandoned or forfeit by the former occupant). ● *n.* **1** the act or an instance of jumping. **2 a** a sudden bodily movement caused by shock or excitement. **b** (**the jumps**) *colloq.* extreme nervousness or anxiety. **3** an abrupt rise in amount, price, value, status, etc. **4** an obstacle to be jumped, esp. by a horse. **5 a** a sudden transition. **b** a gap in a series, logical sequence, etc. □ **get** (or **have**) **the jump on** *colloq.* get (or have) an advantage over (a person) by prompt action. **jump at** accept eagerly. **jump bail** see BAIL[1]. **jump down a person's throat** *colloq.* reprimand or contradict a person fiercely. **jumped-up** *colloq.* upstart; presumptuously arrogant. **jump the gun** see GUN. **jumping-off place** (or **point** etc.) the place or point of starting. **jump-jet** a jet aircraft that can take off and land vertically. **jump-lead** a cable for conveying current from the battery of a motor vehicle to boost (or recharge) another. **jump-off** a deciding round in a showjumping competition. **jump on** *colloq.* attack or criticize severely and without warning. **jump out of one's skin** *colloq.* be extremely startled. **jump the queue 1** push forward out of one's turn. **2** take unfair precedence over others. **jump-rope** *US* a skipping-rope. **jump seat** *US* a folding extra seat in a motor vehicle. **jump ship** (of a seaman) desert. **jump-start** *v.tr.* start (a motor vehicle) by pushing it or with jump-leads. ● *n.* the action of jump-starting. **jump suit** a one-piece garment for the whole body, of a kind orig. worn by paratroopers. **jump to it** *colloq.* act promptly and energetically. **one jump ahead** one stage further on than a rival etc. **on the jump** *colloq.* on the move; in a hurry. □□ **jumpable** *adj.* [16th c.: prob. imit.]

■ *v.* **1, 2** leap, bound, spring, hop, skip, dive, pounce; hurdle, vault; caper, gambol, prance, *sl.* cavort. **3** start, jerk, lurch, jolt, lunge, wince, flinch, recoil, shy, twitch, shudder. **4, 6** advance, increase, progress, improve, move (on *or* ahead *or* forward *or* up); climb, rise, gain, surge, soar, rocket, shoot up, escalate. **5** leap, skip, hop, pass, move, shift, switch, change. **7** hurdle, vault, clear, leap, hop, leap-frog. **8, 12** skip (over *or* past), omit, pass over *or* by, bypass, go past, avoid, leave out, ignore, disregard, overlook, gloss over. **10** leap, rush, hasten. **14** see ATTACK *v.* 1. ● *n.* **1** leap, bound, spring, hop, skip, dive, pounce; hurdle, vault, caper, gambol, prance. **2 a** start, lurch, jolt, jerk, shy, spasm, twitch, recoil, wince, flinch, shudder. **b** (**the jumps**) nervousness, tension, anxiety, anxiousness, fretfulness, restlessness, uneasiness, skittishness, apprehension, the shakes, DT, (the) fidgets, nerves, the horrors, *colloq.* the jim-jams, the jitters, twitch, cold feet, *sl.* the heebie-jeebies, *Brit. sl.* the needle; stage fright, *US* buck fever. **3** rise, increase, appreciation, advance, gain, surge, lift, escalation, upsurge, increment, elevation, leap, *US* hike, *colloq.* boost. **4** obstacle, hurdle, fence, barricade, rail, obstruction; (*Showjumping*) gate, wall, ditch, water, oxer. **5** switch, shift, transition, change; break, gap, interval, hiatus, lacuna, space, hole, breach, rift, interruption, *Prosody* caesura. □ **get** (or **have**) **the jump on** get *or* have the advantage over, get *or* have the upper hand over. **jump at** snatch, seize (on), grab (at), leap at, pounce on, grasp, accept, *colloq.* swoop up. **jump down a person's throat** contradict, oppose, take issue with, *archaic or literary* gainsay, *colloq.* bite a person's head off; reprimand, rebuke, upbraid, castigate, give a person a tongue-lashing, give a person a rap on *or* over the knuckles, *colloq.* give a person a telling-off *or* dressing-down, give a person a slap on the wrist. **jumped-up** upstart, parvenu; see also ARROGANT. **jump on** attack, berate, flay, launch into, have a go at, come down on (like a ton of bricks), crack down on, *colloq.* lay into, set about. **jump to it** look sharp, get on with it, *colloq.* get cracking, look lively, crack on, *sl.* get *or* pull one's finger out, get weaving.

jumper[1] /júmpər/ *n.* **1** a knitted pullover. **2** a loose outer jacket of canvas etc. worn by sailors. **3** *US* a pinafore dress. [prob. f. (17th-c., now dial.) *jump* short coat perh. f. F *jupe* f. Arab. *jubba*]

jumper[2] /júmpər/ *n.* **1** a person or animal that jumps. **2** *Electr.* a short wire used to make or break a circuit. **3** a rope made fast to keep a yard, mast, etc., from jumping. **4** a heavy chisel-ended iron bar for drilling blast-holes.

jumping bean /júmping/ *n.* the seed of a Mexican plant that jumps with the movement of the larva inside.

jumping jack /júmping/ *n.* **1** a small firework producing repeated explosions. **2** a toy figure of a man, with movable limbs.

jumpy /júmpi/ *adj.* (**jumpier**, **jumpiest**) **1** nervous; easily startled. **2** making sudden movements, esp. of nervous excitement. □□ **jumpily** *adv.* **jumpiness** *n.*

■ **1** nervous, tense, agitated, anxious, fretful, uneasy, edgy, on edge, fidgety, ill at ease, restless, restive, panicky, overwrought, keyed up, nervy, squirrelly, flustered, agitated, rattled, *colloq.* jittery, het up, uptight, neurotic; highly-strung, sensitive, temperamental, excitable, skittish, *colloq.* windy, *Austral. sl.* toey, *US sl.* spooky. **2** twitchy, jerky, tremulous, fluttery, *colloq.* all of a tremble, jittery.

Jun. *abbr.* **1** June. **2** Junior.

junco /júngkō/ *n.* (*pl.* **-os** or **-oes**) any small American finch of the genus *Junco*. [Sp. f. L *juncus* rush plant]

junction /júngksh'n/ *n.* **1** a point at which two or more things are joined. **2** a place where two or more railway lines or roads meet, unite, or cross. **3** the act or an instance of joining. **4** *Electronics* a region of transition in a semi-conductor between regions where conduction is mainly by electrons and regions where it is mainly by holes. □ **junction box** a box containing a junction of electric cables etc. [L *junctio* (as JOIN)]

■ **1** join, union, juncture, connection, contact, commissure, abutment, articulation; link, linkage, weld, knot, splice, seam, gusset, bond, suture; bracket, brace, hinge. **2** intersection, crossing, union, conjunction, meeting, meeting-point, confluence, convergence, corner; crossroad(s), interchange, turn-off; *Brit.* point(s). **3** union, unification, connection, convergence, conjunction, juncture, combination, addition, coupling, twinning, marriage, merger, fusion, alliance, integration, amalgamation, coalition.

juncture /júngkchər/ *n.* **1** a critical convergence of events; a critical point of time (*at this juncture*). **2** a place where things join. **3** an act of joining. [ME f. L *junctura* (as JOIN)]

■ **1** pass, hump, situation, *colloq.* crunch; point, time, moment (in time), stage, period. **2** see JUNCTION 1. **3** see JUNCTION 3.

June /jo͞on/ *n.* the sixth month of the year. [ME f. OF *juin* f. L *Junius* var. of *Junonius* sacred to Juno]

Jungian /yo͝ongiən/ *adj.* & *n.* ● *adj.* of the Swiss psychologist Carl Jung (d. 1961) or his system of analytical psychology. ● *n.* a supporter of Jung or of his system.

jungle /júngg'l/ *n.* **1 a** land overgrown with underwood or tangled vegetation, esp. in the tropics. **b** an area of such land. **2** a wild tangled mass. **3** a place of bewildering complexity or confusion, or of a struggle for survival (*blackboard jungle*). □ **jungle fever** a severe form of malaria. **law of the jungle** a state of ruthless competition. □□ **jungled** *adj.* **jungly** *adj.* [Hindi *jangal* f. Skr. *jangala* desert, forest]
■ **1** rain forest. **2** see TANGLE[1] *n.* 2.

junior /jo͞oniər/ *adj.* & *n.* ● *adj.* **1** less advanced in age. **2** (foll. by *to*) inferior in age, standing, or position. **3** the younger (esp. appended to a name for distinction from an older person of the same name). **4** of less or least standing; of the lower or lowest position (*junior partner*). **5** *Brit.* (of a school) having pupils in a younger age-range, usu. 7–11. **6** *US* of the year before the final year at university, high school, etc. ● *n.* **1** a junior person. **2** one's inferior in length of service etc. **3** a junior student. **4** a barrister who is not a QC. **5** *US colloq.* a young male child, esp. in relation to his family. □ **junior college** *US* a college offering a two-year course esp. in preparation for completion at senior college. **junior common** (or **combination**) **room** *Brit.* **1** a room for social use by the junior members of a college. **2** the junior members collectively. **junior lightweight** see LIGHTWEIGHT. **junior middleweight** see MIDDLEWEIGHT. □□ **juniority** /-niórriti/ *n.* [L, compar. of *juvenis* young]
■ *adj.* **2** (*junior to*) younger than; lower than, inferior to, subordinate to, secondary to, beneath, under, behind. **3** (the) younger, *Brit.* minor. **4** lower, lesser, minor, smaller, secondary, subordinate, inferior; lowest, least. **5** (*junior school*) primary school, elementary school, *Brit.* first school, middle school, preparatory *or* prep school, *US* grammar school, grade school. ● *n.* **1, 2** subordinate, inferior, *derog.* underling; minor, youth, youngster, juvenile, child, boy, girl, baby, *archaic or colloq.* young thing, *colloq.* young'un, *sl.* sprog. □□ **juniority** see INFERIORITY.

juniper /jo͞onipər/ *n.* any evergreen shrub or tree of the genus *Juniperus*, esp. *J. communis* with prickly leaves and dark purple berry-like cones. □ **oil of juniper** oil from juniper cones used in medicine and in flavouring gin etc. [ME f. L *juniperus*]

junk[1] /jungk/ *n.* & *v.* ● *n.* **1** discarded articles; rubbish. **2** anything regarded as of little value. **3** *sl.* a narcotic drug, esp. heroin. **4** old cables or ropes cut up for oakum etc. **5** *Brit.* a lump or chunk. **6** *Naut.* hard salt meat. **7** a lump of fibrous tissue in the sperm whale's head, containing spermaceti. ● *v.tr.* discard as junk. □ **junk bond** *Stock Exch.* a bond bearing high interest but deemed to be a risky investment. **junk food** food with low nutritional value. **junk mail** unsolicited advertising matter sent by post. **junk shop** a shop selling cheap second-hand goods or antiques. [ME: orig. unkn.]
■ *n.* **1, 2** rubbish, waste, refuse, litter, scrap, garbage, debris, detritus, dross, (the) dreg(s), lees, leavings, reject(s), flotsam and jetsam, *US* trash, *esp. US sl.* dreck; lumber, rummage, paraphernalia, stuff, odds and ends, waifs and strays, *colloq.* truck; see also NONSENSE. **3** heroin, *sl.* smack, dynamite, H, horse, speedball, sugar. ● *v.* discard, dispose of, dispense with, dump, get rid of, throw out *or* away, toss (out *or* aside *or* away), scrap, cast (aside), jettison, *colloq.* chuck (out *or* away), bin, get shot of, *sl.* ditch, *Brit. sl.* bung (out *or* away).

junk[2] /jungk/ *n.* a flat-bottomed sailing vessel used in the China seas, with a prominent stem and lugsails. [obs. F *juncque*, Port. *junco*, or Du. *jonk*, f. Jav. *djong*]

junker /yo͝ongkər/ *n. hist.* **1** a young German nobleman. **2** a member of an exclusive (Prussian) aristocratic party. □□ **junkerdom** *n.* [G, earlier *Junkher* f. OHG (as YOUNG, HERR)]

junket /júngkit/ *n.* & *v.* ● *n.* **1** a dish of sweetened and flavoured curds, often served with fruit or cream. **2** a feast. **3** a pleasure outing. **4** *US* an official's tour at public expense. ● *v.intr.* (**junketed, junketing**) feast, picnic. □□ **junketing** *n.* [ME *jonket* f. OF *jonquette* rush-basket (used to carry junket) f. *jonc* rush f. L *juncus*]
■ **3** see OUTING.

junkie /júngki/ *n. sl.* a drug addict.
■ see ADDICT *n.* 1.

Junr. *abbr.* Junior.

junta /júntə/ *n.* **1 a** a political or military clique or faction taking power after a revolution or *coup d'état*. **b** a secretive group; a cabal. **2** a deliberative or administrative council in Spain or Portugal. [Sp. & Port. f. L *juncta*, fem. past part. (as JOIN)]
■ **1** clique, faction, camarilla, cabal, mafia; coterie, gang, band, set, ring, party, group.

Jupiter /jo͞opitər/ *n.* the largest planet of the solar system, orbiting about the sun between Mars and Saturn. [ME f. L *Jupiter* king of the gods f. OL *Jovis pater*]

jural /jo͝orəl/ *adj.* **1** of law. **2** of rights and obligations. [L *jus juris* law, right]

Jurassic /joorássik/ *adj.* & *n. Geol.* ● *adj.* of or relating to the second period of the Mesozoic era with evidence of many large dinosaurs, the first birds (including Archaeopteryx), and mammals. ¶ Cf. Appendix VII. ● *n.* this era or system. [F *jurassique* f. *Jura* (Mountains): cf. *Triassic*]

jurat[1] /jo͝orat/ *n. Brit.* **1** a municipal officer (esp. of the Cinque Ports) holding a position similar to that of an alderman. **2** an honorary judge or magistrate in the Channel Islands. [ME f. med.L *juratus* past part. of L *jurare* swear]

jurat[2] /jo͝orat/ *n.* a statement of the circumstances in which an affidavit was made. [L *juratum* neut. past part. (as JURAT[1])]

juridical /jooríddik'l/ *adj.* **1** of judicial proceedings. **2** relating to the law. □□ **juridically** *adv.* [L *juridicus* f. *jus juris* law + *-dicus* saying f. *dicere* say]
■ see JUDICIAL 1, 2.

jurisconsult /jo͝oriskənsúlt/ *n.* a person learned in law; a jurist. [L *jurisconsultus* f. *jus juris* law + *consultus* skilled: see CONSULT]

jurisdiction /jo͝orisdíksh'n/ *n.* **1** (often foll. by *over*, *of*) the administration of justice. **2 a** legal or other authority. **b** the extent of this; the territory it extends over. □□ **jurisdictional** *adj.* [ME *jurisdiccioun* f. OF *jurediction*, *juridiction*, L *jurisdictio* f. *jus juris* law + *dictio* DICTION]
■ **1** authority, supervision, superintendence. **2** authority, power, prerogative, dominion, sovereignty, say, control, rule, ascendancy, hegemony, influence; province, district, area, territory, compass, realm, range, orbit, sphere (of influence), reach, clutches; shrievalty, *Law* bailiwick, *hist.* leet, *Brit. hist.* soke.

jurisprudence /jo͝orispro͞od'nss/ *n.* **1** the science or philosophy of law. **2** skill in law. □□ **jurisprudent** *adj.* & *n.* **jurisprudential** /-dénsh'l/ *adj.* [LL *jurisprudentia* f. L *jus juris* law + *prudentia* knowledge: see PRUDENT]

jurist /jo͝orist/ *n.* **1** an expert in law. **2** a legal writer. **3** *US* a lawyer. □□ **juristic** /-rístik/ *adj.* **juristical** /-rístik'l/ *adj.* [F *juriste* or med.L *jurista* f. *jus juris* law]
■ **3** see LAWYER.

juror /jo͝orər/ *n.* **1** a member of a jury. **2** a person who takes an oath (cf. NONJUROR). [ME f. AF *jurour*, OF *jureor* f. L *jurator -oris* f. *jurare jurat-* swear]

jury /jo͝ori/ *n.* (*pl.* **-ies**) **1** a body of usu. twelve persons sworn to render a verdict on the basis of evidence submitted to them in a court of justice. **2** a body of persons selected to award prizes in a competition. □ **jury-box** the enclosure for the jury in a lawcourt. [ME f. AF & OF *juree* oath, inquiry, f. *jurata* fem. past part. of L *jurare* swear]

juryman /jŏŏrimən/ *n.* (*pl.* **-men**) a member of a jury.

jury-rigged /jŏŏririgd/ *adj. Naut.* having temporary make-shift rigging. [perh. ult. f. OF *ajurie* aid]

jurywoman /jŏŏriwŏŏmmən/ *n.* (*pl.* **-women**) a woman member of a jury.

jussive /jússiv/ *adj. Gram.* expressing a command. [L *jubēre juss-* command]

just /just/ *adj.* & *adv.* ● *adj.* **1** acting or done in accordance with what is morally right or fair. **2** (of treatment etc.) deserved (*a just reward*). **3** (of feelings, opinions, etc.) well-grounded (*just resentment*). **4** right in amount etc.; proper. ● *adv.* **1** exactly (*just what I need*). **2** exactly or nearly at this or that moment; a little time ago (*I have just seen them*). **3** *colloq.* simply, merely (*we were just good friends*; *it just doesn't make sense*). **4** barely; no more than (*I just managed it*; *just a minute*). **5** *colloq.* positively (*it is just splendid*). **6** quite (*not just yet*; *it is just as well that I checked*). **7** *colloq.* really, indeed (*won't I just tell him!*). **8** in questions, seeking precise information (*just how did you manage?*). □ **just about** *colloq.* almost exactly; almost completely. **just in case 1** lest. **2** as a precaution. **just now 1** at this moment. **2** a little time ago. **just so 1** exactly arranged (*they like everything just so*). **2** it is exactly as you say. □□ **justly** *adv.* **justness** *n.* [ME f. OF *juste* f. L *justus* f. *jus* right]

■ *adj.* **1** fair, equitable, impartial, reasonable, fair-minded, even-handed, neutral, objective, non-partisan, unbiased, unprejudiced, indifferent, disinterested, dispassionate; upright, righteous, right-minded, honourable, honest, ethical, moral, principled, conscientious, scrupulous, straight, square, decent, good, correct, upstanding, virtuous, lawful, legitimate. **2** well-deserved, well-earned, due, rightful, merited; condign. **3** well-grounded, justified, justifiable, well-founded, legitimate, valid, reasonable, rightful. **4** fitting, befitting, fit, proper, appropriate, due, right, rightful, suitable, correct. ● *adv.* **1, 6** exactly, precisely, completely, perfectly, totally, utterly, wholly, fully, entirely, thoroughly, altogether, in every respect, in all respects, perfectly, expressly, explicitly, unreservedly, quite, *Brit. colloq.* down to the ground, bang on. **2** only *or* just now, (just) a moment ago, (very) recently; lately, latterly. **3, 4** only, merely, simply, solely, nothing but, at best, at most, no more than; only just, barely, hardly, scarcely, narrowly, by a hair's breadth, by the skin of one's teeth. **5, 7** positively, absolutely, emphatically, altogether, categorically, definitely, utterly, thoroughly, entirely; certainly, unquestionably, undeniably, assuredly, undoubtedly, unmistakably, indubitably; really, truly, indeed. **8** exactly, accurately, specifically. □ **just about** nearly, almost, virtually, practically, for all practical purposes, as good as, all but, more or less, approximately, *archaic or rhet.* wellnigh, *colloq.* pretty much *or* nearly *or* well; not quite. **just in case 1** lest, for fear that. **just now 1** see NOW *adv.* 1, 4. **2** see JUST *adv.* 2 above. **just so 1** neat, tidy, systematic, perfect, exact, accurate. **2** that's right, that's it, quite so, even so, exactly, precisely, *colloq.* absolutely, *Brit. colloq.* bang on.

justice /jústiss/ *n.* **1** just conduct. **2** fairness. **3** the exercise of authority in the maintenance of right. **4** judicial proceedings (*was duly brought to justice*; *the Court of Justice*). **5 a** a magistrate. **b** a judge, esp. (in England) of the Supreme Court of Judicature. □ **do justice to** treat fairly or appropriately; show due appreciation of. **do oneself justice** perform in a manner worthy of one's abilities. **in justice to** out of fairness to. **Justice of the Peace** an unpaid lay magistrate appointed to preserve the peace in a county, town, etc., hear minor cases, grant licences, etc. **Mr** (or **Mrs**) **Justice** *Brit.* a form of address or reference to a Supreme Court Judge. **with justice** reasonably. □□ **justiceship** *n.* (in sense 5). [ME f. OF f. L *justitia* (as JUST)]

■ **1–3** uprightness, righteousness, honourableness, honesty, ethicality, morality, probity, principle, conscientiousness, scrupulousness, scruple(s), straightness, squareness, decency, goodness, correctness, virtue; sportsmanship, fair play; lawfulness, rightfulness, legitimacy; fairness, justness, equity, equality, equitableness, impartiality, fair-mindedness, even-handedness, neutrality, objectivity, objectiveness, indifference, disinterest, dispassionateness; law, right. **4** court (of justice), lawcourt, courtroom, court of law, tribunal; bar, bench. **5** see JUDGE *n.* 1.

justiciable /justishəb'l/ *adj.* liable to legal consideration. [OF f. *justicier* bring to trial f. med.L *justitiare* (as JUSTICE)]

justiciary /justíshyəri/ *n.* & *adj.* ● *n.* (*pl.* **-ies**) an administrator of justice. ● *adj.* of the administration of justice. [med.L *justitiarius* f. L *justitia*: see JUSTICE]

justifiable /jústifīəb'l/ *adj.* that can be justified or defended. □ **justifiable homicide** killing regarded as lawful and without criminal guilt, esp. the execution of a death sentence. □□ **justifiability** /-bílliti/ *n.* **justifiableness** *n.* **justifiably** *adv.* [F f. *justifier*: see JUSTIFY]

■ see LEGITIMATE *adj.* □□ **justifiably** see TRULY 5.

justify /jústifī/ *v.tr.* (**-ies, -ied**) **1** show the justice or rightness of (a person, act, etc.). **2** demonstrate the correctness of (an assertion etc.). **3** adduce adequate grounds for (conduct, a claim, etc.). **4 a** (esp. in *passive*) (of circumstances) be such as to justify. **b** vindicate. **5** (as **justified** *adj.*) just, right (*am justified in assuming*). **6** *Theol.* declare (a person) righteous. **7** *Printing* adjust (a line of type) to fill a space evenly. □□ **justification** /-fikáysh'n/ *n.* **justificatory** /-fikaytəri/ *adj.* **justifier** *n.* [ME f. F *justifier* f. LL *justificare* do justice to f. L *justus* JUST]

■ **1, 2, 4** vindicate, legitimate, legitimatize, legitimize, legalize, rationalize, substantiate, defend, support, uphold, sustain, validate, warrant, confirm, explain, rationalize, account for. **3** excuse, explain, apologize for, condone. **5** (**justified**) see RIGHT *adj.* 1. □□ **justification** see ARGUMENT 2, BASIS 1, 2.

jut /jut/ *v.* & *n.* ● *v.intr.* (**jutted, jutting**) (often foll. by *out*, *forth*) protrude, project. ● *n.* a projection; a protruding point. [var. of JET[1]]

■ *v.* project, protrude, stick out, extend, overhang, beetle.

Jute /jōōt/ *n.* a member of a Low-German tribe that settled in Britain in the 5th–6th c. □□ **Jutish** *adj.* [repr. med.L *Jutae, Juti*, in OE *Eotas, Iotas* = Icel. *Iótar* people of Jutland in Denmark]

jute /jōōt/ *n.* **1** a rough fibre made from the bark of E. Indian plants of the genus *Corchorus*, used for making twine and rope, and woven into sacking, mats, etc. **2** either of two plants *Corchorus capsularis* or *C. olitorius* yielding this fibre. [Bengali *jhōṭo* f. Skr. *jūṭa* = *jaṭā* braid of hair]

juvenescence /jōōvinéss'nss/ *n.* **1** youth. **2** the transition from infancy to youth. □□ **juvenescent** *adj.* [L *juvenescere* reach the age of youth f. *juvenis* young]

■ see CHILDHOOD.

juvenile /jōōvənīl/ *adj.* & *n.* ● *adj.* **1 a** young, youthful. **b** of or for young persons. **2** suited to or characteristic of youth. **3** often *derog.* immature (*behaving in a very juvenile way*). ● *n.* **1** a young person. **2** *Commerce* a book intended for young people. **3** an actor playing the part of a youthful person. □ **juvenile court** a court for the trial of children under 17. **juvenile delinquency** offences committed by a person or persons below the age of legal responsibility. **juvenile delinquent** such an offender. □□ **juvenilely** *adv.* **juvenility** /-nílliti/ *n.* [L *juvenilis* f. *juvenis* young]

■ *adj.* **1 a** young, youthful, adolescent, prepubescent, pubescent, under age, minor, teenage(d); boyish, girlish, childlike. **1b, 2** young person's *or* people's, adolescent, junior, teenage, infant, children's. **3** immature, adolescent, childish, infantile, babyish, puerile, unsophisticated, green, callow, naïve, inexperienced, (still) wet behind the ears, jejune, innocent, guileless, unfledged, raw, tender. ● *n.* **1** youth, boy, girl, child, adolescent, minor, teenager, youngster, schoolboy, schoolgirl, schoolchild, infant, toddler, stripling, whippersnapper, lad, *Ir.* spalpeen, *Sc.* & *N.Engl. or poet.*

lass, *archaic* younker, *colloq.* young'un, teeny-bopper, weeny-bopper, kid, *sl.* sprog.

juvenilia /jŏŏvənílliə/ *n.pl.* works produced by an author or artist in youth. [L, neut. pl. of *juvenilis* (as JUVENILE)]

juxtapose /júkstəpṓz/ *v.tr.* **1** place (things) side by side. **2** (foll. by *to*, *with*) place (a thing) beside another. □□ **juxtaposition** /-pəzísh'n/ *n.* **juxtapositional** /-pəzíshən'l/ *adj.* [F *juxtaposer* f. L *juxta* next: see POSE[1]]

Kk

K[1] /kay/ *n.* (also **k**) (*pl.* **Ks** or **K's**) the eleventh letter of the alphabet.

K[2] *abbr.* (also **K.**) **1** kelvin(s). **2** King, King's. **3** Köchel (catalogue of Mozart's works). **4** (also **k**) (prec. by a numeral) **a** *Computing* a unit of 1,024 (i.e. 2^{10}) bytes or bits, or loosely 1,000. **b** 1,000. [sense 4 as abbr. of KILO-]

K[3] *symb. Chem.* the element potassium.

k *abbr.* **1** kilo-. **2** knot(s).

Kaaba /kaàəbə/ *n.* (also **Caaba**) a sacred building at Mecca, the Muslim Holy of Holies containing the sacred black stone. [Arab. *Ka'ba*]

kabbala var. of CABBALA.

kabuki /kəbo͝oki/ *n.* a form of popular traditional Japanese drama with highly stylized song, acted by males only. [Jap. f. *ka* song + *bu* dance + *ki* art]

kachina /kəcheénə/ *n.* **1** an American Indian ancestral spirit. **2** (in full **kachina dancer**) a person who represents a kachina in ceremonial dances. □ **kachina doll** a wooden doll representing a kachina. [Hopi, = supernatural]

Kaddish /káddish/ *n. Judaism* **1** a Jewish mourner's prayer. **2** a doxology in the synagogue service. [Aram. *ḳaddîš* holy]

kadi var. of CADI.

Kaffir /káffər/ *n.* **1 a** a member of the Xhosa-speaking peoples of S. Africa. **b** the language of these peoples. **2** *S.Afr. offens.* any Black African. [Arab. *kāfir* infidel f. *kafara* not believe]

kaffiyeh var. of KEFFIYEH.

Kafir /káffər/ *n.* a native of the Hindu Kush mountains of NE Afghanistan. [formed as KAFFIR]

Kafkaesque /káfkəésk/ *adj.* (of a situation, atmosphere, etc.) impenetrably oppressive, nightmarish, in a manner characteristic of the fictional world of Franz Kafka, German-speaking novelist (d. 1924).
■ see *nightmarish* (NIGHTMARE).

kaftan var. of CAFTAN.

kai /kī/ *n. NZ colloq.* food. [Maori]

kail var. of KALE.

kailyard var. of KALEYARD.

kaiser /kīzər/ *n. hist.* an emperor, esp. the German Emperor, the Emperor of Austria, or the head of the Holy Roman Empire. □□ **kaisership** *n.* [in mod. Eng. f. G *Kaiser* and Du. *keizer*; in ME f. OE *cāsere* f. Gmc adoption (through Gk *kaisar*) of L *Caesar*: see CAESAR]

kaka /kaàkaa/ *n.* (*pl.* **kakas**) a large New Zealand parrot, *Nestor meridionalis*, with olive-brown plumage. [Maori]

kakapo /kaàkəpō/ *n.* (*pl.* **-os**) an owl-like flightless New Zealand parrot, *Strigops habroptilus*. [Maori, = night kaka]

kakemono /kákkimṓnō/ *n.* (*pl.* **-os**) a vertical Japanese wall-picture, usu. painted or inscribed on paper or silk and mounted on rollers. [Jap. f. *kake-* hang + *mono* thing]

kala-azar /kaàlə-əzaàr/ *n.* a tropical disease caused by the parasitic protozoan *Leishmania donovani*, which is transmitted to man by sandflies. [Assamese f. *kālā* black + *āzār* disease]

kale /kayl/ *n.* (also **kail**) **1** a variety of cabbage, esp. one with wrinkled leaves and no compact head. Also called *curly kale*. **2** *US sl.* money. [ME, northern form of COLE]
■ **2** see MONEY 1.

kaleidoscope /kəlī́dəskōp/ *n.* **1** a tube containing mirrors and pieces of coloured glass or paper, whose reflections produce changing patterns when the tube is rotated. **2** a constantly changing group of bright or interesting objects. □□ **kaleidoscopic** /-skóppik/ *adj.* **kaleidoscopical** /-skóppik'l/ *adj.* [Gk *kalos* beautiful + *eidos* form + -SCOPE]
■ □□ **kaleidoscopic** see GAY *adj.* 3, PROTEAN 1.

kalends var. of CALENDS.

kaleyard /káyl-yaard/ *n.* (also **kailyard**) *Sc.* a kitchen garden. □ **kaleyard school** a group of 19th-c. fiction writers including J. M. Barrie, who described local town life in Scotland in a romantic vein and with much use of the vernacular. [KALE + YARD[2]]

kali /kálli, káyli/ *n.* a glasswort, *Salsola kali*, with fleshy jointed stems, having a high soda content. [Arab. *ḳalī* ALKALI]

kalmia /kálmiə/ *n.* a N. American evergreen shrub of the genus *Kalmia*, esp. *K. latifolia*, with showy pink flowers. [mod.L f. P. *Kalm*, Sw. botanist d. 1779]

Kalmuck /kálmuk/ *adj.* & *n.* ● *adj.* of or relating to a people living on the north-western shores of the Caspian Sea. ● *n.* **1** a member of this people. **2** the language of this people. [Russ. *kalmyk*]

kalong /kaàlong/ *n.* any of various fruit-eating bats of the family Pteropodidae, esp. *Pteropus edulis*; a flying fox. [Malay]

kalpa /kálpə/ *n. Hinduism* & *Buddhism* the period between the beginning and the end of the world considered as the day of Brahma (4,320 million human years). [Skr.]

Kama /kaàmə/ *n.* the Hindu god of love. □ **Kama Sutra** /sṓotrə/ an ancient Sanskrit treatise on the art of erotic love. [Skr.]

kame /kaym/ *n.* a short ridge of sand and gravel deposited from the water of a melted glacier. [Sc. form of COMB]

kamikaze /kámmikaàzi/ *n.* & *adj.* ● *n. hist.* **1** a Japanese aircraft loaded with explosives and deliberately crashed by its pilot on its target. **2** the pilot of such an aircraft. ● *adj.* **1** of or relating to a kamikaze. **2** reckless, dangerous, potentially self-destructive. [Jap. f. *kami* divinity + *kaze* wind]

kampong /kámpong/ *n.* a Malayan enclosure or village. [Malay: cf. COMPOUND[2]]

Kampuchean /kámpoocheéən/ *n.* & *adj.* = CAMBODIAN. [*Kampuchea*, native name for Cambodia]

Kan. *abbr.* Kansas.

kana /kaànə/ *n.* any of various Japanese syllabaries. [Jap.]

kanaka /kənákkə, -naàkə/ *n.* a South Sea Islander, esp. (formerly) one employed in forced labour in Australia. [Hawaiian, = man]

Kanarese /kánnəreéz/ *n.* (*pl.* same) **1** a member of a Dravidian people living in western India. **2** the language of this people. [*Kanara* in India]

kanga /kánggə/ *n. Austral.* **1** = KANGAROO. **2** *rhyming sl.* on *screw* a prison warder. [abbr.]

kangaroo /kánggəro͞o/ *n.* a plant-eating marsupial of the genus *Macropus*, native to Australia and New Guinea, with a long tail and strongly developed hind quarters enabling it to travel by jumping. □ **kangaroo closure** *Brit. Parl.* a closure involving the chairperson of a committee selecting some amendments for discussion and excluding others. **kangaroo court** an improperly constituted or illegal court held by strikers etc. **kangaroo mouse** any small rodent of the genus *Microdipodops*, native to N. America, with long hind legs for hopping. **kangaroo paw** any plant of the genus *Angiozanthos*, with green and red woolly flowers. **kangaroo-rat** any burrowing rodent of the genus *Dipodomys*, having elongated hind feet. **kangaroo vine** an evergreen climbing plant, *Cissus antarctica*, with tooth-edged leaves. [Aboriginal name]

kanji /kánji/ *n.* Japanese writing using Chinese characters. [Jap. f. *kan* Chinese + *ji* character]

Kannada /kánnədə/ *n.* the Kanarese language. [Kanarese *kannaḍa*]

kanoon /kənóon/ *n.* an instrument like a zither, with fifty to sixty strings. [Pers. or Arab. *ḳānūn*]

Kans. *abbr.* Kansas.

KANU /kaánoo/ *abbr.* Kenya African National Union.

kaolin /káyəlin/ *n.* a fine soft white clay produced by the decomposition of other clays or feldspar, used esp. for making porcelain and in medicines. Also called *china clay.* □□ **kaolinic** /-línnik/ *adj.* **kaolinize** *v.tr.* (also **-ise**). [F f. Chin. *gaoling* the name of a mountain f. *gao* high + *ling* hill]

kaon /káyon/ *n. Physics* a meson having a mass several times that of a pion. [*ka* repr. the letter *K* (as symbol for the particle) + -ON]

kapellmeister /kəpélmīstər/ *n.* (*pl.* same) the conductor of an orchestra, opera, choir, etc., esp. in German contexts. [G f. *Kapelle* court orchestra f. It. *cappella* CHAPEL + *Meister* master]

kapok /káypok/ *n.* a fine fibrous cotton-like substance found surrounding the seeds of a tropical tree, *Ceiba pentandra*, used for stuffing cushions, soft toys, etc. [ult. f. Malay *kāpoq*]

kappa /káppə/ *n.* the tenth letter of the Greek alphabet (*K*, *κ*). [Gk]

kaput /kapóot/ *predic.adj. sl.* broken, ruined; done for. [G *kaputt*]

■ see BROKEN 1.

karabiner /kárrəbeénər/ *n.* a coupling link with safety closure, used by mountaineers. [G, lit. 'carbine']

karakul /kárrəkool/ *n.* (also **caracul**) **1** a variety of Asian sheep with a dark curled fleece when young. **2** fur made from or resembling this. Also called *Persian lamb.* [Russ.]

karaoke /kárriōki/ *n.* a form of entertainment in which people sing popular songs as soloists against a pre-recorded backing. □ **karaoke bar** (or **club**) a bar or club with this form of entertainment. [Jap., = empty orchestra]

karat *US* var. of CARAT 2.

karate /kəraáti/ *n.* a Japanese system of unarmed combat using the hands and feet as weapons. [Jap. f. *kara* empty + *te* hand]

karma /kaármə/ *n. Buddhism* & *Hinduism* **1** the sum of a person's actions in previous states of existence, viewed as deciding his or her fate in future existences. **2** destiny. □□ **karmic** *adj.* [Skr., = action, fate]

■ **2** see DESTINY 2.

Karoo /kəróo/ *n.* (also **Karroo**) an elevated semi-desert plateau in S. Africa. [Afrik. f. Hottentot *karo* dry]

karri /kárri/ *n.* (*pl.* **karris**) **1** a tall W. Australian tree, *Eucalyptus diversicolor*, with a hard red wood. **2** the timber from this. [Aboriginal]

Karroo var. of KAROO.

karst /kaarst/ *n.* a limestone region with underground drainage and many cavities and passages caused by the dissolution of the rock. [the *Karst*, a limestone region in the north-west of the former Yugoslavia]

karyo- /kárriō/ *comb. form Biol.* denoting the nucleus of a cell. [Gk *karuon* kernel]

karyokinesis /kárriōkineéssiss/ *n. Biol.* the division of a cell nucleus during mitosis. [KARYO- + Gk *kinēsis* movement f. *kineō* move]

karyotype /kárriətīp/ *n.* the number and structure of the chromosomes in the nucleus of a cell.

kasbah /kázbaa/ *n.* (also **casbah**) **1** the citadel of a N. African city. **2** an Arab quarter near this. [F *casbah* f. Arab. *kas(a)ba* citadel]

katabatic /káttəbáttik/ *adj. Meteorol.* (of wind) caused by air flowing downwards (cf. ANABATIC). [Gk *katabatikos* f. *katabainō* go down]

katabolism var. of CATABOLISM.

katakana /káttəkaánə/ *n.* an angular form of Japanese kana. [Jap., = side kana]

kathode var. of CATHODE.

katydid /káytidid/ *n.* any of various green grasshoppers of the family Tettigoniidae, native to the US. [imit. of the sound it makes]

kauri /kówri/ *n.* (*pl.* **kauris**) a coniferous New Zealand tree, *Agathis australis*, which produces valuable timber and a resin. □ **kauri-gum** this resin. [Maori]

kava /kaávə/ *n.* **1** a Polynesian shrub, *Piper methysticum.* **2** an intoxicating drink made from the crushed roots of this. [Polynesian]

kawa-kawa /kaáwəkaawə/ *n.* a New Zealand shrub, *Macropiper excelsum*, with aromatic leaves. [Maori]

kayak /kīak/ *n.* **1** an Eskimo one-man canoe consisting of a light wooden frame covered with sealskins. **2** a small covered canoe resembling this. [Eskimo]

kayo /kayṓ/ *v.* & *n. colloq.* ● *v.tr.* (**-oes, -oed**) knock out; stun by a blow. ● *n.* (*pl.* **-os**) a knockout. [repr. pronunc. of *KO*]

■ *v.* see *knock out* 1. ● *n.* knockout, *coup de grâce*, *colloq.* K.O.

kazoo /kəzóo/ *n.* a toy musical instrument into which the player sings or hums. [19th c., app. with ref. to the sound produced]

KB *abbr.* (in the UK) King's Bench.

KBE *abbr.* (in the UK) Knight Commander of the Order of the British Empire.

KC *abbr.* **1** King's College. **2** King's Counsel.

kc *abbr.* kilocycle(s).

KCB *abbr.* (in the UK) Knight Commander of the Order of the Bath.

KCMG *abbr.* (in the UK) Knight Commander of the Order of St Michael and St George.

kc/s *abbr.* kilocycles per second.

KCVO *abbr.* (in the UK) Knight Commander of the Royal Victorian Order.

KE *abbr.* kinetic energy.

kea /keéə, káyə/ *n.* a parrot, *Nestor notabilis*, of New Zealand, with brownish-green and red plumage. [Maori, imit.]

kebab /kibáb/ *n.* (usu. in *pl.*) small pieces of meat, vegetables, etc., packed closely and cooked on a skewer. [Urdu f. Arab. *kabāb*]

kedge /kej/ *v.* & *n.* ● *v.* **1** *tr.* move (a ship) by means of a hawser attached to a small anchor. **2** *intr.* (of a ship) move in this way. ● *n.* (in full **kedge-anchor**) a small anchor for this purpose. [perh. a specific use of obs. *cagge*, dial. *cadge* bind, tie]

kedgeree /kéjəri, -reé/ *n.* **1** an Indian dish of rice, split pulse, onions, eggs, etc. **2** a European dish of fish, rice, hard-boiled eggs, etc. [Hindi *khichṛī*, Skr. *k'rsara* dish of rice and sesame]

keek /keek/ *v.* & *n. Sc.* ● *v.intr.* peep. ● *n.* a peep. [ME *kike*: cf. MDu., MLG *kīken*]

■ *v.* see PEEP¹ *v.* ● *n.* see PEEP¹ *n.*

keel¹ /keel/ *n.* & *v.* ● *n.* **1** the lengthwise timber or steel structure along the base of a ship, airship, or some aircraft, on which the framework of the whole is built up. **2** *poet.* a ship. **3** a ridge along the breastbone of many birds; a carina. **4** *Bot.* a prow-shaped pair of petals in a corolla etc. ● *v.* **1**

(often foll. by *over*) **a** *intr.* turn over or fall down. **b** *tr.* cause to do this. **2** *tr.* & *intr.* turn keel upwards. ▫▫ **keelless** *adj.* [ME *kele* f. ON *kjölr* f. Gmc]

■ *v.* **1** see FALL *v.* 2a. **2** see CAPSIZE.

keel[2] /keel/ *n. Brit. hist.* **1** a flat-bottomed vessel, esp. of the kind formerly used on the River Tyne etc. for loading coal-ships. **2** an amount carried by such a vessel. [ME *kele* f. MLG *kēl*, MDu. *kiel* ship, boat, f. Gmc]

keelhaul /kéelhawl/ *v.tr.* **1** *hist.* drag (a person) through the water under the keel of a ship as a punishment. **2** scold or rebuke severely.

■ **2** see CASTIGATE.

keelson /kéels'n/ *n.* (also **kelson** /kéls'n/) a line of timber fastening a ship's floor-timbers to its keel. [ME *kelswayn*, perh. f. LG *kielswīn* f. *kiel* KEEL[1] + (prob.) *swīn* SWINE used as the name of a timber]

keen[1] /keen/ *adj.* **1** (of a person, desire, or interest) eager, ardent (*a keen sportsman; keen to be involved*). **2** (foll. by *on*) much attracted by; fond of or enthusiastic about. **3 a** (of the senses) sharp; highly sensitive. **b** (of memory etc.) clear, vivid. **4** (of a person) intellectually acute; (of a remark etc.) quick, sharp, biting. **5 a** having a sharp edge or point. **b** (of an edge etc.) sharp. **6** (of a sound, light, etc.) penetrating, vivid, strong. **7** (of a wind, frost, etc.) piercingly cold. **8** (of a pain etc.) acute, bitter. **9** *Brit.* (of a price) competitive. **10** *colloq.* excellent. ▫▫ **keenly** *adv.* **keenness** *n.* [OE *cēne* f. Gmc]

■ **1** enthusiastic, avid, zealous, devoted, ardent, fervent, fervid, earnest, impassioned, passionate, enthused, intense, active, agog; eager, itching, bursting, raring, anxious. **2** (*keen on*) fond of, enthusiastic about, enamoured of, devoted to, interested in, intent on, *colloq.* sweet on, *Austral.* & *NZ colloq.* shook on. **3 a** sharp, acute, sensitive, penetrating, discriminating, fine, discerning, perceptive. **b** vivid, clear, detailed, specific, unmistaken, unmistakable, distinct. **4** intelligent, sharp, acute, perceptive, perspicacious, percipient, sensitive, discerning, astute, smart, bright, discriminating, discriminative, quick(-witted), shrewd, clever, canny, cunning, crafty, wise; trenchant, incisive, cutting, rapier-like, pointed, mordant, acid, vitriolic, acerbic, astringent, biting, acrid, acrimonious, stinging, scorching, caustic, searing, withering, virulent, pungent, sarcastic, sardonic. **5** sharp, sharpened, honed, pointed, incisive, razor-sharp, razor-like, rapier-like, knife-edged. **7** piercing, penetrating, bitter, chilling, biting. **8** painful, bitter, acute, throbbing, searing, burning, fierce, grievous, severe, distressing, distressful, excruciating, strong, deep, profound, intense, extreme, poignant, heartfelt. ▫▫ **keenness** see ENTHUSIASM 1, INTELLIGENCE 1b.

keen[2] /keen/ *n.* & *v.* ● *n.* an Irish funeral song accompanied with wailing. ● *v.* **1** *intr.* utter the keen. **2** *tr.* bewail (a person) in this way. **3** *tr.* utter in a wailing tone. ▫▫ **keener** *n.* [Ir. *caoine* f. *caoinim* wail]

■ *n.* dirge, elegy, keening, knell, lament, lamentation, requiem, monody, threnody, epicedium, *Sc.* & *Ir.* coronach. ● *v.* **1** see MOAN 1, 3. **2** weep for, lament, mourn, grieve for, sorrow for, bewail, bemoan.

keep /keep/ *v.* & *n.* ● *v.* (*past* and *past part.* **kept** /kept/) **1** *tr.* have continuous charge of; retain possession of; save or hold on to. **2** *tr.* (foll. by *for*) retain or reserve for a future occasion or time (*will keep it for tomorrow*). **3** *tr.* & *intr.* retain or remain in a specified condition, position, course, etc. (*keep cool; keep off the grass; keep them happy*). **4** *tr.* put or store in a regular place (*knives are kept in this drawer*). **5** *tr.* (foll. by *from*) cause to avoid or abstain from something (*will keep you from going too fast*). **6** *tr.* detain; cause to be late (*what kept you?*). **7** *tr.* **a** observe or pay due regard to (a law, custom, etc.) (*keep one's word*). **b** honour or fulfil (a commitment, undertaking, etc.). **c** respect the commitment implied by (a secret etc.). **d** act fittingly on the occasion of (*keep the sabbath*). **8** *tr.* own and look after (animals) for amusement or profit (*keeps bees*). **9** *tr.* **a** provide for the sustenance of (a person, family, etc.). **b** (foll. by *in*) maintain (a person) with a supply of. **10** *tr.* manage (a shop, business, etc.). **11 a** *tr.* maintain (accounts, a diary, etc.) by making the requisite entries. **b** *tr.* maintain (a house) in proper order. **12** *tr.* have (a commodity) regularly on sale (*do you keep buttons?*). **13** *tr.* **a** confine or detain (a person, animal, etc.). **b** guard or protect (a person or place, a goal in football, etc.). **14** *tr.* preserve in being; continue to have (*keep order*). **15** *intr.* (foll. by verbal noun) continue or do repeatedly or habitually (*why do you keep saying that?*). **16** *tr.* continue to follow (a way or course). **17** *intr.* **a** (esp. of perishable commodities) remain in good condition. **b** (of news or information etc.) admit of being withheld for a time. **18** *tr.* remain in (one's bed, room, house, etc.). **19** *tr.* retain one's place in (a seat or saddle, one's ground, etc.) against opposition or difficulty. **20** *tr.* maintain (a person) in return for sexual favours (*a kept woman*). ● *n.* **1** maintenance or the essentials for this (esp. food) (*hardly earn your keep*). **2** charge or control (*is in your keep*). **3** *hist.* a tower or stronghold. ▫ **for keeps** *colloq.* (esp. of something received or won) permanently, indefinitely. **how are you keeping?** how are you? **keep at** persist or cause to persist with. **keep away** (often foll. by *from*) **1** avoid being near. **2** prevent from being near. **keep back 1** remain or keep at a distance. **2** retard the progress of. **3** conceal; decline to disclose. **4** retain, withhold (*kept back £50*). **keep one's balance 1** remain stable; avoid falling. **2** retain one's composure. **keep down 1** hold in subjection. **2** keep low in amount. **3** lie low; stay hidden. **4** manage not to vomit (food eaten). **keep one's feet** manage not to fall. **keep-fit** regular exercises to promote personal fitness and health. **keep one's hair on** see HAIR. **keep one's hand in** see HAND. **keep in 1** confine or restrain (one's feelings etc.). **2** remain or confine indoors. **3** keep (a fire) burning. **keep in mind** take into account having remembered. **keep in with** remain on good terms with. **keep off 1** stay or cause to stay away from. **2** ward off; avert. **3** abstain from. **4** avoid (a subject) (*let's keep off religion*). **keep on 1** continue to do something; do continually (*kept on laughing*). **2** continue to use or employ. **3** (foll. by *at*) pester or harass. **keep out 1** keep or remain outside. **2** exclude. **keep state 1** maintain one's dignity. **2** be difficult of access. **keep to 1** adhere to (a course, schedule, etc.). **2** observe (a promise). **3** confine oneself to. **keep to oneself 1** avoid contact with others. **2** refuse to disclose or share. **keep together** remain or keep in harmony. **keep track of** see TRACK[1]. **keep under** hold in subjection. **keep up 1** maintain (progress etc.). **2** prevent (prices, one's spirits, etc.) from sinking. **3** keep in repair, in an efficient or proper state, etc. **4** carry on (a correspondence etc.). **5** prevent (a person) from going to bed, esp. when late. **6** (often foll. by *with*) manage not to fall behind. **keep up with the Joneses** strive to compete socially with one's neighbours. **keep one's word** see WORD. **kept woman** a woman maintained or supported in return for sexual favours. ▫▫ **keepable** *adj.* [OE *cēpan*, of unkn. orig.]

■ *v.* **1** retain, hold, hang *or* hold on to, preserve, conserve, have, save, maintain, control; accumulate, save (up), amass, hoard (up), husband, put *or* stow away; take care *or* charge of, mind, tend, care for, take care of, look after, guard, keep an eye on, watch over, protect, safeguard, have custody of, be responsible for. **3** stay, remain. **4** store, stow, maintain, preserve. **5** prevent, keep *or* hold back, restrain, (hold in) check, restrict, prohibit, forbid, inhibit, block, curb, deter, discourage. **6** detain, delay, slow up, hold (up), hold *or* set back. **7 a** keep to, abide by, follow, obey, mind, adhere to, stick to, attend to, pay attention to, heed, regard, observe, respect, acknowledge, defer to, accede to, agree to. **b** honour, fulfil, follow, carry out, conform to, keep faith with, respect. **c** harbour, maintain, safeguard, conceal, keep dark, keep hidden, hush up, bury; withhold, not breathe a word about, keep under wraps. **d** celebrate, observe, solemnize, honour, memorialize, commemorate. **8** raise, rear, look after. **9 a** maintain, feed, nourish, nurture, foster, provide for, support, sustain, provision, victual, board. **b** supply *or* stock *or* furnish with. **10** manage, run, have, maintain, supervise, superintend, be responsible for. **12** stock, have in stock, carry, store, trade in, deal in. **13** confine, detain; imprison, incarcerate, jail *or Brit also* gaol; defend, guard, protect, cover, safeguard, shield. **15** keep on, go on, continue, carry on, persist in, persevere in. **16** keep to, maintain, follow, stick to. **17** last, keep fresh, stay *or* remain fresh, be preserved, survive. **18** stay in, remain in. **20** support, finance, provide for, subsidize, maintain. ● *n.* **1** upkeep, maintenance, support, room and board, subsistence, food, sustenance, living. **2** charge, control, care, custody, protection, keeping, safekeeping. **3** tower, stronghold, fortress, donjon, *archaic* dungeon. □ **for keeps** permanently, once and for all, for good, for ever, indefinitely. **keep at** persist in, persevere in, stick at, follow to a conclusion, peg away at, *colloq.* plug away at; (*keep at it*) hold out, keep going *or* trying, be steadfast, see it through, peg along, stay the distance *or* course; be determined, be firm, be unwavering, be resolute, *colloq.* hang on, stick it out, *US colloq.* hang in. **keep away 1** (*keep away from*) see AVOID 1. **keep back 2** see *hold back* (HOLD[2]), SUPPRESS 2. **3, 4** see WITHHOLD 1. **keep down 1, 2** see SUPPRESS 2, TYRANNIZE. **3** see HIDE[1] *v.* 2. **keep in 1** keep *or* hold back, repress, suppress, stifle, smother, muzzle, bottle up, withhold, conceal, hide, shroud, mask, camouflage. **2** confine, shut in *or* up, coop up, fence in, detain. **keep in mind** see *bear in mind* (BEAR[1]). **keep off 1, 3, 4** see AVOID 1. **2** see *hold off*. **keep on 1** keep, continue, carry on, persist in, persevere in. **3** pester, harass, *colloq.* go on at. **keep to 1, 2** see KEEP *v.* 7 above.

keeper /keépər/ *n.* **1** a person who keeps or looks after something or someone. **2** a custodian of a museum, art gallery, forest, etc. **3 a** = GAMEKEEPER. **b** a person in charge of animals in a zoo. **4 a** = *wicket-keeper*. **b** = GOALKEEPER. **5** a fruit etc. that remains in good condition. **6** a bar of soft iron across the poles of a horseshoe magnet to maintain its strength. **7 a** a plain ring to preserve a hole in a pierced ear lobe; a sleeper. **b** a ring worn to guard against the loss of a more valuable one.
■ **1, 2** custodian, guardian, guard, warden, caretaker; warder, nurse, attendant, *sl.* minder.

keeping /keéping/ *n.* **1** custody, charge (*in safe keeping*). **2** agreement, harmony (esp. *in* or *out of keeping*).
■ **1** see CARE 4a. **2** see STEP 9a.

keepsake /keépsayk/ *n.* a thing kept for the sake of or in remembrance of the giver.
■ memento, souvenir, token, reminder, remembrance, relic.

keeshond /káyss-hond/ *n.* **1** a dog of a Dutch breed with long thick hair like a large Pomeranian. **2** this breed. [Du.]

kef /kef/ *n.* (also **kif** /kif/) **1** a drowsy state induced by marijuana etc. **2** the enjoyment of idleness. **3** a substance smoked to produce kef. [Arab. *kayf* enjoyment, well-being]

keffiyeh /kefeéyay/ *n.* (also **kaffiyeh**) a Bedouin Arab's kerchief worn as a head-dress. [Arab. *keffiya*, *kūfiyya*, perh. f. LL *cofea* COIF]

keg /keg/ *n.* a small barrel, usu. of less than 10 gallons or (in the US) 30 gallons. □ **keg beer** beer supplied from a sealed metal container. [ME *cag* f. ON *kaggi*, of unkn. orig.]
■ cask, barrel, butt, hogshead, tun, *hist.* puncheon.

keister /keéstər, kīstər/ *n. US sl.* **1** the buttocks. **2** a suitcase, satchel, handbag, etc. [orig. unkn.]
■ **1** see BUTTOCK. **2** see BAG *n.* 2a.

keloid /keéloyd/ *n.* fibrous tissue formed at the site of a scar or injury. [Gk *khēlē* claw + -OID]

kelp /kelp/ *n.* **1** any of several large broad-fronded brown seaweeds esp. of the genus *Laminaria*, suitable for use as manure. **2** the calcined ashes of seaweed formerly used in glass-making and soap manufacture because of their high content of sodium, potassium, and magnesium salts. [ME *cülp(e)*, of unkn. orig.]

kelpie /kélpi/ *n. Sc.* **1** a water-spirit, usu. in the form of a horse, reputed to delight in the drowning of travellers etc. **2** an Australian sheepdog orig. bred from a Scottish collie. [18th c.: orig. unkn.]

kelson var. of KEELSON.

Kelt var. of CELT.

kelt /kelt/ *n.* a salmon or sea trout after spawning. [ME: orig. unkn.]

kelter var. of KILTER.

kelvin /kélvin/ *n.* the SI unit of thermodynamic temperature, equal in magnitude to the degree celsius. ¶ Abbr.: **K.** □ **Kelvin scale** a scale of temperature with absolute zero as zero. [Lord *Kelvin*, Brit. physicist d. 1907]

kemp /kemp/ *n.* coarse hair in wool. □□ **kempy** *adj.* [ME f. ON *kampr* beard, whisker]

kempt /kempt/ *adj.* combed; neatly kept. [past part. of (now dial.) *kemb* COMB *v.* f. OE *cemban* f. Gmc]
■ (*well-kempt*) see TRIM *adj.* 1.

ken /ken/ *n.* & *v.* ● *n.* range of sight or knowledge (*it's beyond my ken*). ● *v.tr.* (**kenning**; *past* and *past part.* **kenned** or **kent**) *Sc.* & *N.Engl.* **1** recognize at sight. **2** know. [OE *cennan* f. Gmc]
■ *n.* see HORIZON. ● *v.* **1** see KNOW 3. **2** see KNOW 1.

kendo /kéndō/ *n.* a Japanese form of fencing with two-handed bamboo swords. [Jap., = sword-way]

kennel /kénn'l/ *n.* & *v.* ● *n.* **1** a small shelter for a dog. **2** (in *pl.*) a breeding or boarding establishment for dogs. **3** a mean dwelling. ● *v.* (**kennelled, kennelling**; *US* **kenneled, kenneling**) **1** *tr.* put into or keep in a kennel. **2** *intr.* live in or go to a kennel. [ME f. OF *chenil* f. med.L *canile* (unrecorded) f. L *canis* dog]

kenning /kénning/ *n.* a compound expression in Old English and Old Norse poetry, e.g. *oar-steed* = ship. [ME, = 'teaching' etc. f. KEN]

kenosis /kinṓsiss/ *n. Theol.* the renunciation of the divine nature, at least in part, by Christ in the Incarnation. □□ **kenotic** /-nóttik/ *adj.* [Gk. *kenōsis* f. *kenoō* to empty f. *kenos* empty]

kenspeckle /kénspekk'l/ *adj. Sc.* conspicuous. [*kenspeck* of Scand. orig.: rel. to KEN]

kent *past* and *past part.* of KEN.

Kentish /kéntish/ *adj.* of Kent in England. □ **Kentish fire** *Brit.* a prolonged volley of rhythmic applause or a demonstration of dissent. [OE *Centisc* f. *Cent* f. L *Cantium*]

kentledge /kéntlij/ *n. Naut.* pig-iron etc. used as permanent ballast. [F *quintelage* ballast, with assim. to *kentle* obs. var. of QUINTAL]

Kenyan /kényən, keén-/ *adj.* & *n.* ● *adj.* of or relating to Kenya in E. Africa. ● *n.* **a** a native or national of Kenya. **b** a person of Kenyan descent.

kepi /képpi, káypi/ *n.* (*pl.* **kepis**) a French military cap with a horizontal peak. [F *képi* f. Swiss G *Käppi* dimin. of *kappe* cap]

Kepler's laws /képlərz/ *n.pl.* three theorems describing orbital motion. □□ **Keplerian** /-leériən/ *adj.* [J. *Kepler* Ger. astronomer d. 1630]

kept *past* and *past part.* of KEEP.

keratin /kérrətin/ *n.* a fibrous protein which occurs in hair, feathers, hooves, claws, horns, etc. [Gk *keras keratos* horn + -IN]

keratinize /kérrətinīz/ *v.tr.* & *intr.* (also **-ise**) cover or become covered with a deposit of keratin. □□ **keratinization** /-záysh'n/ *n.*

keratose /kérrətōss/ *adj.* (of sponge) composed of a horny substance. [Gk *keras keratos* horn + -OSE[1]]

kerb /kerb/ *n. Brit.* a stone edging to a pavement or raised path. □ **kerb-crawler** a person who indulges in kerb-crawling. **kerb-crawling** the practice of driving slowly along the edge of a road, soliciting or harassing esp. female passers-by. **kerb drill** precautions, esp. looking to right and left, before crossing a road. [var. of CURB]

kerbstone /kérbstōn/ *n.* each of a series of stones forming a kerb.

kerchief /kércheef, -chif/ *n.* **1** a cloth used to cover the head. **2** *poet.* a handkerchief. ▫▫ **kerchiefed** *adj.* [ME *curchef* f. AF *courchef*, OF *couvrechief* f. *couvrir* COVER + CHIEF head]

kerf /kerf/ *n.* **1** a slit made by cutting, esp. with a saw. **2** the cut end of a felled tree. [OE *cyrf* f. Gmc (as CARVE)]

kerfuffle /kərfúff'l/ *n.* esp. *Brit. colloq.* a fuss or commotion. [Sc. *curfuffle* f. *fuffle* to disorder: imit.]
■ see FUSS *n.* 1, 2a.

kermes /kérmiz/ *n.* **1** the female of a bug, *Kermes ilicis*, with a berry-like appearance. **2** (in full **kermes oak**) an evergreen oak, *Quercus coccifera*, of S. Europe and N. Africa, on which this insect feeds. **3** a red dye made from the dried bodies of these insects. **4** (in full **kermes mineral**) a bright red hydrous trisulphide of antimony. [F *kermès* f. Arab. & Pers. *ḳirmiz*: rel. to CRIMSON]

kermis /kérmiss/ *n.* **1** a periodical country fair, esp. in the Netherlands. **2** *US* a charity bazaar. [Du., orig. = mass on the anniversary of the dedication of a church, when yearly fair was held: f. *kerk* formed as CHURCH + *mis*, *misse* MASS[2]]
■ see FAIR[2] 2.

kern[1] /kern/ *n. Printing* the part of a metal type projecting beyond its body or shank. ▫▫ **kerned** *adj.* [perh. f. F *carne* corner f. OF *charne* f. L *cardo cardinis* hinge]

kern[2] /kern/ *n.* (also **kerne**) **1** *hist.* a light-armed Irish foot-soldier. **2** a peasant; a boor. [ME f. Ir. *ceithern*]

kernel /kérn'l/ *n.* **1** a central, softer, usu. edible part within a hard shell of a nut, fruit stone, seed, etc. **2** the whole seed of a cereal. **3** the nucleus or essential part of anything. [OE *cyrnel*, dimin. of CORN[1]]
■ **1, 2** grain, seed, pip, stone; nut, *US* (nut-)meat. **3** centre, core, nucleus, heart, essence, quintessence, substance, gist, pith, nub, crux, quiddity.

kero /kérrō/ *n. Austral.* = KEROSENE. [abbr.]

kerosine /kérrəseen/ *n.* (also **kerosene**) esp. *US* a fuel oil suitable for use in jet engines and domestic heating boilers; paraffin oil. [Gk *kēros* wax + -ENE]

Kerry /kérri/ *n.* (*pl.* **-ies**) **1** an animal of a breed of small black dairy cattle. **2** this breed. [*Kerry* in Ireland]

Kerry blue /kérri/ *n.* **1** a terrier of a breed with a silky blue-grey coat. **2** this breed.

kersey /kérzi/ *n.* (*pl.* **-eys**) **1** a kind of coarse narrow cloth woven from long wool, usu. ribbed. **2** a variety of this. [ME, prob. f. *Kersey* in Suffolk]

kerseymere /kérzimeer/ *n.* a twilled fine woollen cloth. [alt. of *cassimere*, var. of CASHMERE, assim. to KERSEY]

keskidee var. of KISKADEE.

kestrel /késtrəl/ *n.* any small falcon, esp. *Falco tinnunculus*, which hovers whilst searching for its prey. [ME *castrell*, perh. f. F dial. *casserelle*, F *créc(er)elle*, perh. imit. of its cry]

ketch /kech/ *n.* a two-masted fore-and-aft rigged sailing-boat with a mizen-mast stepped forward of the rudder and smaller than its foremast. [ME *catche*, prob. f. CATCH]

ketchup /kéchup/ *n.* (also **catchup** /káchup/) a spicy sauce made from tomatoes, mushrooms, vinegar, etc., used as a condiment. [Chin. dial. *kōechiap* pickled-fish brine]

ketone /keétōn/ *n.* any of a class of organic compounds in which two hydrocarbon groups are linked by a carbonyl group, e.g. propanone (acetone). ▫ **ketone body** *Biochem.* any of several ketones produced in the body during the metabolism of fats. ▫▫ **ketonic** /kitónnik/ *adj.* [G *Keton* alt. of *Aketon* ACETONE]

ketonuria /keétōnyóoriə/ *n.* the excretion of abnormally large amounts of ketone bodies in the urine.

ketosis /kitṓsiss/ *n.* a condition characterized by raised levels of ketone bodies in the body, associated with fat metabolism and diabetes. ▫▫ **ketotic** /-tóttik/ *adj.*

kettle /kétt'l/ *n.* a vessel, usu. of metal with a lid, spout, and handle, for boiling water in. ▫ **kettle hole** a depression in the ground in a glaciated area. **a pretty** (or **fine**) **kettle of fish** an awkward state of affairs. ▫▫ **kettleful** *n.* (*pl.* **-fuls**). [ME f. ON *ketill* ult. f. L *catillus* dimin. of *catinus* deep food-vessel]
■ ▫ **a pretty** (or **fine**) **kettle of fish** see MESS *n.* 2.

kettledrum /kétt'ldrum/ *n.* a large drum shaped like a bowl with a membrane adjustable for tension (and so pitch) stretched across. ▫▫ **kettledrummer** *n.*

keV *abbr.* kilo-electronvolt.

Kevlar /kévlər/ *n. propr.* a synthetic fibre of high tensile strength used esp. as a reinforcing agent in the manufacture of rubber products, e.g. tyres.

kewpie /kyóopi/ *n.* a small chubby doll with wings and a curl or topknot. [CUPID + -IE]

key[1] /kee/ *n.*, *adj.*, & *v.* ● *n.* (*pl.* **keys**) **1** an instrument, usu. of metal, for moving the bolt of a lock forwards or backwards to lock or unlock. **2** a similar implement for operating a switch in the form of a lock. **3** an instrument for grasping screws, pegs, nuts, etc., esp. one for winding a clock etc. **4** a lever depressed by the finger in playing the organ, piano, flute, concertina, etc. **5** (often in *pl.*) each of several buttons for operating a typewriter, word processor, or computer terminal, etc. **6** what gives or precludes the opportunity for or access to something. **7** a place that by its position gives control of a sea, territory, etc. **8 a** a solution or explanation. **b** a word or system for solving a cipher or code. **c** an explanatory list of symbols used in a map, table, etc. **d** a book of solutions to mathematical problems etc. **e** a literal translation of a book written in a foreign language. **f** the first move in a chess-problem solution. **9** *Mus.* a system of notes definitely related to each other, based on a particular note, and predominating in a piece of music; tone or pitch (*a study in the key of C major*). **10** a tone or style of thought or expression. **11** a piece of wood or metal inserted between others to secure them. **12** the part of a first coat of wall plaster that passes between the laths and so secures the rest. **13** the roughness of a surface, helping the adhesion of plaster etc. **14** the samara of a sycamore etc. **15** a mechanical device for making or breaking an electric circuit, e.g. in telegraphy. ● *adj.* essential; of vital importance (*the key element in the problem*). ● *v.tr.* (**keys, keyed**) **1** (foll. by *in*, *on*, etc.) fasten with a pin, wedge, bolt, etc. **2** (often foll. by *in*) enter (data) by means of a keyboard. **3** roughen (a surface) to help the adhesion of plaster etc. **4** (foll. by *to*) align or link (one thing to another). **5** regulate the pitch of the strings of (a violin etc.). **6** word (an advertisement in a particular periodical) so that answers to it can be identified (usu. by varying the form of address given). ▫ **key industry** an industry essential to the carrying on of others, e.g. coal-mining, dyeing. **key map** a map in bare outline, to simplify the use of a full map. **key money** *Brit.* a payment demanded from an incoming tenant for the provision of a key to the premises. **key-ring** a ring for keeping keys on. **key signature** *Mus.* any of several combinations of sharps or flats after the clef at the beginning of each staff indicating the key of a composition. **key up** (often foll. by *to*, or *to* + infin.) make (a person) nervous or tense; excite. ▫▫ **keyer** *n.* **keyless** *adj.* [OE *cǣg*, of unkn. orig.]
■ *n.* **1** latchkey, skeleton key, passkey, opener. **4** (*keys*) ivories. **5** button. **8 a** clue, cue, guide, solution, answer, indication, indicator, explanation, description, explication, clarification, translation. **b** keyword, password. **c** legend, code, table. **9** scale, mode, tonality, pitch, tone, timbre, level, frequency. **10** mood, tenor, tone, pitch, humour, style, vein, character. ● *adj.* important, essential, vital, necessary, crucial, critical, main, pivotal, fundamental, principal, chief, major, leading, criterial, central. ● *v.* **2** type, input, keyboard. ▫ **key up** see EXCITE *v.* 2. ▫▫ **keyer** keyboarder, typist.

key[2] /kee/ *n.* a low-lying island or reef, esp. in the W. Indies (cf. CAY). [Sp. *cayo* shoal, reef, infl. by QUAY]

keyboard /keébord/ *n.* & *v.* ● *n.* **1** a set of keys on a typewriter, computer, piano, etc.; the keys of a computer terminal regarded as a person's place of work. **2** an electronic musical instrument with keys arranged as on a piano. ● *v.tr.*

& *intr.* enter (data) by means of a keyboard; work at a keyboard. □□ **keyboarder** *n.*
■ *n.* **1** ivories, keys; see also TERMINAL *n.* 5. **2** synthesizer, electric *or* electronic piano, electric *or* electronic organ.
● *v.* key (in), type, typewrite, input; transcribe.

keyhole /kéehōl/ *n.* a hole by which a key is put into a lock. □ **keyhole surgery** minimally invasive surgery carried out through a very small incision.

Keynesian /káynziən/ *adj.* & *n.* ● *adj.* of or relating to the economic theories of J. M. Keynes (d. 1946), esp. regarding State control of the economy through money and taxation. ● *n.* an adherent of these theories. □□ **Keynesianism** *n.*

keynote /kéenōt/ *n.* **1** a prevailing tone or idea (*the keynote of the whole occasion*). **2** (*attrib.*) intended to set the prevailing tone at a meeting or conference (*keynote address*). **3** *Mus.* the note on which a key is based.
■ **1** see THEME 1.

keypad /kéepad/ *n.* a miniature keyboard or set of buttons for operating a portable electronic device, telephone, etc.

keypunch /kéepunch/ *n.* & *v.* ● *n.* a device for transferring data by means of punched holes or notches on a series of cards or paper tape. ● *v.tr.* transfer (data) by means of a keypunch. □□ **keypuncher** *n.*

keystone /kéestōn/ *n.* **1** the central principle of a system, policy, etc., on which all the rest depends. **2** a central stone at the summit of an arch locking the whole together.
■ crux, linchpin, basis, principle, foundation, base, bedrock, cornerstone.

keystroke /kéestrōk/ *n.* a single depression of a key on a keyboard, esp. as a measure of work.

keyway /kéeway/ *n.* a slot for receiving a machined key.

keyword /kéewurd/ *n.* **1** the key to a cipher etc. **2 a** a word of great significance. **b** a significant word used in indexing.
■ see KEY[1] 8.

KG *abbr.* (in the UK) Knight of the Order of the Garter.

kg *abbr.* kilogram(s).

KGB /káyjeebée/ *n.* the State security police of the former USSR from 1954. [Russ., abbr. of *Komitet gosudarstvennoĭ bezopasnosti* committee of State security]

Kgs. *abbr.* Kings (Old Testament).

khaddar /káddər/ *n.* Indian homespun cloth. [Hindi]

khaki /kaáki/ *adj.* & *n.* ● *adj.* dust-coloured; dull brownish-yellow. ● *n.* (*pl.* **khakis**) **1** khaki fabric of twilled cotton or wool, used esp. in military dress. **2** the dull brownish-yellow colour of this. [Urdu *ḵākī* dust-coloured f. *ḵāk* dust]

khalasi /kəlássi/ *n.* (*pl.* **khalasis**) a native Indian servant or labourer, esp. one employed as a seaman. [Hind.]

khamsin /kámsin/ *n.* (also **hamsin** /hám-/) an oppressive hot south or south-east wind occurring in Egypt for about 50 days in March, April, and May. [Arab. *ḵamsīn* f. *ḵamsūn* fifty]
■ see STORM *n.* 1.

khan[1] /kaan, kan/ *n.* **1** a title given to rulers and officials in Central Asia, Afghanistan, etc. **2** *hist.* **a** the supreme ruler of the Turkish, Tartar, and Mongol tribes. **b** the emperor of China in the Middle Ages. □□ **khanate** *n.* [Turki *ḵān* lord]

khan[2] /kaan, kan/ *n.* a caravanserai. [Arab. *ḵān* inn]

Khedive /kidéev/ *n. hist.* the title of the viceroy of Egypt under Turkish rule 1867–1914. □□ **Khedival** *adj.* **Khedivial** *adj.* [F *khédive*, ult. f. Pers. *ḵadīv* prince]

Khmer /kmair/ *n.* & *adj.* ● *n.* **1** a native of the ancient Khmer kingdom in SE Asia, or of modern Cambodia. **2** the language of this people. ● *adj.* of the Khmers or their language. [native name]

kHz *abbr.* kilohertz.

kiang /kiáng/ *n.* a wild Tibetan ass, *Equus hemionus kiang*, with a thick furry coat. [Tibetan *kyang*]

kibble[1] /kibb'l/ *v.tr.* grind coarsely. [18th c.: orig. unkn.]
■ see GRIND *v.* 1a.

kibble[2] /kíbb'l/ *n. Brit.* an iron hoisting-bucket used in mines. [G *Kübel* (cf. OE *cyfel*) f. med.L *cupellus*, corn-measure, dimin. of *cuppa* cup]

kibbutz /kibŏŏts/ *n.* (*pl.* **kibbutzim** /-bŏŏtseém/) a communal esp. farming settlement in Israel. [mod.Heb. *ḳibbūṣ* gathering]

kibbutznik /kibŏŏtsnik/ *n.* a member of a kibbutz. [Yiddish (as KIBBUTZ)]

kibe /kīb/ *n.* an ulcerated chilblain, esp. on the heel. [ME, prob. f. Welsh *cibi*]

kibitka /kibítkə/ *n.* **1** a type of Russian hooded sledge. **2 a** a Tartar's circular tent, covered with felt. **b** a Tartar household. [Russ. f. Tartar *kibitz*]

kibitz /kíbbits/ *v.intr. colloq.* act as a kibitzer. [Yiddish f. G *kiebitzen* (as KIBITZER)]
■ see MEDDLE.

kibitzer /kíbbitsər, kibítsər/ *n. colloq.* **1** an onlooker at cards etc., esp. one who offers unwanted advice. **2** a busybody, a meddler. [Yiddish *kibitser* f. G *Kiebitz* lapwing, busybody]
■ **2** see BUSYBODY 1.

kiblah /kíblə/ *n.* (also **qibla**) **1** the direction of the Kaaba (the sacred building at Mecca), to which Muslims turn at prayer. **2** = MIHRAB. [Arab. *ḳibla* that which is opposite]

kibosh /kī́bosh/ *n.* (also **kybosh**) *sl.* nonsense. □ **put the kibosh on** put an end to; finally dispose of. [19th c.: orig. unkn.]
■ see DRIVEL *n.* □ **put the kibosh on** see VETO *v.*

kick[1] /kik/ *v.* & *n.* ● *v.* **1** *tr.* strike or propel forcibly with the foot or hoof etc. **2** *intr.* (usu. foll. by *at*, *against*) **a** strike out with the foot. **b** express annoyance at or dislike of (treatment, a proposal etc.); rebel against. **3** *tr. sl.* give up (a habit). **4** *tr.* (often foll. by *out* etc.) expel or dismiss forcibly. **5** *refl.* be annoyed with oneself (*I'll kick myself if I'm wrong*). **6** *tr. Football* score (a goal) by a kick. **7** *intr. Cricket* (of a ball) rise sharply from the pitch. ● *n.* **1 a** a blow with the foot or hoof etc. **b** the delivery of such a blow. **2** *colloq.* **a** a sharp stimulant effect, esp. of alcohol (*has some kick in it*; *a cocktail with a kick in it*). **b** (often in *pl.*) a pleasurable thrill (*did it just for kicks*; *got a kick out of flying*). **3** strength, resilience (*have no kick left*). **4** *colloq.* a specified temporary interest or enthusiasm (*on a jogging kick*). **5** the recoil of a gun when discharged. **6** *Brit. Football colloq.* a player of specified kicking ability (*is a good kick*). □ **kick about** (or **around**) *colloq.* **1 a** drift idly from place to place. **b** be unused or unwanted. **2 a** treat roughly or scornfully. **b** discuss (an idea) unsystematically. **kick against the pricks** see PRICK. **kick the bucket** *sl.* die. **kick-down** a device for changing gear in a motor vehicle by full depression of the accelerator. **kick one's heels** see HEEL. **kick in 1** knock down (a door etc.) by kicking. **2** esp. *US sl.* contribute (esp. money); pay one's share. **kick in the pants** (or **teeth**) *colloq.* a humiliating punishment or set-back. **kick off 1 a** *Football* begin or resume a match. **b** *colloq.* begin. **2** remove (shoes etc.) by kicking. **kick-off 1** *Football* the start or resumption of a match. **2** (in **for a kick-off**) *colloq.* for a start (*that's wrong for a kick-off*). **kick over the traces** see TRACE[2]. **kick-pleat** a pleat in a narrow skirt to allow freedom of movement. **kick-turn** a standing turn in skiing. **kick up** (or **kick up a fuss, dust**, etc.) create a disturbance; object or register strong disapproval. **kick up one's heels** frolic. **kick a person upstairs** shelve a person by giving him or her promotion or a title. □□ **kickable** *adj.* **kicker** *n.* [ME *kike*, of unkn. orig.]
■ *v.* **1** punt, foot, *colloq.* boot; strike, hit, shoot, pass.
2 b see PROTEST 1. **3** see DISCONTINUE. **4** see *turn out* 1.
● *n.* **1** punt, hit, drop-kick, strike, shot, pass, *colloq.* boot.
2 see THRILL *n.* 1. **3** see PUNCH[1] *n.* 3. **4** see FIXATION.
5 recoil, backlash, rebound. □ **kick about** (or **around**)
1 a see *knock about* 2. **b** lie about *or* around, knock about *or* around, hang about *or* around. **2 a** see *knock about* 1.
b discuss, debate, talk over. **kick the bucket** see DIE[1] 1.
kick in 1 knock down, smash in, throw down, demolish, destroy, wreck. **2** see PAY[1] *v.* 5. **kick off 1** see START 1, 2.
kick up fuss, make a fuss; see also COMPLAIN 1.

kick[2] /kik/ *n.* an indentation in the bottom of a glass bottle. [19th c.: orig. unkn.]

kickback /kíkbak/ *n. colloq.* **1** the force of a recoil. **2** payment for collaboration, esp. collaboration for profit.
■ **1** see BACKLASH 2. **2** share, cut, compensation, remuneration, recompense, commission, percentage, reward; bribe, hush money, protection (money), *esp. US* payola, *colloq.* graft, *esp. US colloq.* plugola, *Brit. sl.* backhander; *sl.* boodle, pay-off.
kickshaw /kíkshaw/ *n.* **1** *archaic*, usu. *derog.* a fancy dish in cookery. **2** something elegant but insubstantial; a toy or trinket. [F *quelque chose* something]
■ **2** see GEWGAW, TOY *n.* 2.
kicksorter /kíksortər/ *n. colloq.* a device for analysing electrical pulses according to amplitude.
kickstand /kíkstand/ *n.* a rod attached to a bicycle or motor cycle and kicked into a vertical position to support the vehicle when stationary.
kick-start /kíkstaart/ *n.* & *v.* ● *n.* (also **kick-starter**) **1** a device to start the engine of a motor cycle etc. by the downward thrust of a pedal. **2** a boost or push to start or restart a process etc. ● *v.tr.* **1** start (a motor cycle etc.) in this way. **2** start or restart (a process etc.) by providing some initial impetus.
■ *n.* **2** see BOOST *n.* ● *v.* **2** see BOOST *v.* 1a.
kid[1] /kid/ *n.* & *v.* ● *n.* **1** a young goat. **2** the leather made from its skin. **3** *colloq.* a child or young person. ● *v.intr.* (**kidded, kidding**) (of a goat) give birth. □ **handle with kid gloves** handle in a gentle, delicate, or gingerly manner. **kid brother** (or **sister**) *sl.* a younger brother or sister. **kid-glove** (*attrib.*) dainty or delicate. **kids' stuff** *sl.* something very simple. [ME *kide* f. ON *kith* f. Gmc]
■ *n.* **3** see CHILD 1a. □ **kid's stuff** see BREEZE[1] *n.* 5.
kid[2] /kid/ *v.* (**kidded, kidding**) *colloq.* **1** *tr.* & *also refl.* deceive, trick (*don't kid yourself*; *kidded his mother that he was ill*). **2** *tr.* & *intr.* tease (*only kidding*). □ **no kidding** (or **kid**) *sl.* that is the truth. □□ **kidder** *n.* **kiddingly** *adv.* [perh. f. KID[1]]
■ **1** see FOOL *v.* 2. **2** see TAUNT *v.* □ **no kidding** see INDEED *int.* □□ **kidder** see JOKER 1.
kid[3] /kid/ *n. hist.* a small wooden tub, esp. a sailor's mess tub for grog or rations. [perh. var. of KIT[1]]
Kidderminster carpet /kíddərminstər/ *n.* a carpet made of two cloths of different colours woven together so that the carpet is reversible. [*Kidderminster* in S. England]
kiddie /kíddi/ *n.* (also **kiddy**) (*pl.* **-ies**) *sl.* = KID[1] *n.* 3.
kiddle /kídd'l/ *n.* **1** a barrier in a river with an opening fitted with nets etc. to catch fish. **2** an arrangement of fishing-nets hung on stakes along the seashore. [ME f. AF *kidel*, OF *quidel, guidel*]
kiddo /kíddō/ *n.* (*pl.* **-os**) *sl.* = KID[1] *n.* 3.
kiddy var. of KIDDIE.
kidnap /kídnap/ *v.tr.* (**kidnapped, kidnapping**; *US* **kidnaped, kidnaping**) **1** carry off (a person etc.) by illegal force or fraud esp. to obtain a ransom. **2** steal (a child). □□ **kidnapper** *n.* [back-form. f. *kidnapper* f. KID[1] + *nap* = NAB]
■ abduct, capture, seize, carry off, hold as hostage, hold for ransom, snatch, make off with, take away. □□ **kidnapper** abductor, hostage-taker, *colloq.* baby-snatcher
kidney /kídni/ *n.* (*pl.* **-eys**) **1** either of a pair of organs in the abdominal cavity of mammals, birds, and reptiles, which remove nitrogenous wastes from the blood and excrete urine. **2** the kidney of a sheep, ox, or pig as food. **3** temperament, nature, kind (*a man of that kidney*; *of the right kidney*). □ **kidney bean 1** a dwarf French bean. **2** a scarlet runner bean. **kidney dish** a kidney-shaped dish, esp. one used in surgery. **kidney machine** = *artificial kidney*. **kidney-shaped** shaped like a kidney, with one side concave and the other convex. **kidney vetch** a herbaceous plant, *Anthyllis vulneraria*: also called *lady's finger*. [ME *kidnei*, pl. *kidneiren*, app. partly f. *ei* EGG[1]]
■ **3** see NATURE 3, 5, CHARACTER *n.* 1.
kidskin /kídskin/ *n.* = KID[1] *n.* 2.
kiekie /kéekee/ *n.* a New Zealand climbing plant with edible bracts, and leaves which are used for basket-making etc. [Maori]

kieselguhr /kéez'lgoor/ *n.* diatomaceous earth forming deposits in lakes and ponds and used as a filter, filler, insulator, etc., in various manufacturing processes. [G f. *Kiesel* gravel + dial. *Guhr* earthy deposit]
kif var. of KEF.
kike /kīk/ *n.* esp. *US sl. offens.* a Jew. [20th c.: orig. uncert.]
Kikuyu /kikóoyōō/ *n.* & *adj.* ● *n.* (*pl.* same or **Kikuyus**) **1** a member of an agricultural Negro people, the largest Bantu-speaking group in Kenya. **2** the language of this people. ● *adj.* of or relating to this people or their language. [native name]
kilderkin /kíldərkin/ *n.* **1** a cask for liquids etc., holding 16 or 18 gallons. **2** this measure. [ME, alt. of *kinderkin* f. MDu. *kinde(r)kin, kinneken*, dimin. of *kintal* QUINTAL]
kill[1] /kil/ *v.* & *n.* ● *v.tr.* **1 a** deprive of life or vitality; put to death; cause the death of. **b** (*absol.*) cause or bring about death (*must kill to survive*). **2** destroy; put an end to (feelings etc.) (*overwork killed my enthusiasm*). **3** *refl.* (often foll. by pres. part.) *colloq.* **a** overexert oneself (*don't kill yourself lifting them all at once*). **b** laugh heartily. **4** *colloq.* overwhelm (a person) with amusement, delight, etc. (*the things he says really kill me*). **5** switch off (a spotlight, engine, etc.). **6** *colloq.* delete (a line, paragraph, etc.) from a computer file. **7** *colloq.* cause pain or discomfort to (*my feet are killing me*). **8** pass (time, or a specified amount of it) usu. while waiting for a specific event (*had an hour to kill before the interview*). **9** defeat (a bill in Parliament). **10** *colloq.* consume the entire contents of (a bottle of wine etc.). **11 a** *Tennis* etc. hit (the ball) so skilfully that it cannot be returned. **b** stop (the ball) dead. **12** neutralize or render ineffective (taste, sound, colour, etc.) (*thick carpet killed the sound of footsteps*). ● *n.* **1** an act of killing (esp. an animal). **2** an animal or animals killed, esp. by a sportsman. **3** *colloq.* the destruction or disablement of an enemy aircraft, submarine, etc. □ **dressed to kill** dressed showily, alluringly, or impressively. **in at the kill** present at or benefiting from the successful conclusion of an enterprise. **kill off 1** get rid of or destroy completely (esp. a number of persons or things). **2** (of an author) bring about the death of (a fictional character). **kill or cure** (usu. *attrib.*) (of a remedy etc.) drastic, extreme. **kill two birds with one stone** achieve two aims at once. **kill with kindness** spoil (a person) with overindulgence. [ME *cülle, kille*, perh. ult. rel. to QUELL]
■ *v.* **1 a** execute, murder, assassinate, put to death, cause the death of, liquidate, dispatch, take a person's life, put an end to, kill off, exterminate, put a person out of his *or* her misery, snuff out, extinguish, obliterate, eradicate, destroy, annihilate, ruin, waste, devastate, ravage, massacre, slaughter, decimate, butcher, *literary or joc.* slay; (*of animals*) put down, put to sleep; *colloq.* do away with, finish (off); *sl.* do in, bump *or* knock off, *esp. US sl.* hit, rub out, *US sl.* ice. **2** destroy, put an end to, quash, suppress, stifle, crush, stamp out, extinguish, check, get rid of, eradicate, wipe out, eliminate, expunge, clear away, sweep away, remove, weed out, root out, defeat, veto, cancel, *colloq.* do away with. **3 a** exhaust, tire (out), fatigue, weary, fag (out); overexert, strain, tax, overtire, overwork, *Brit. sl.* knacker. **b** (*kill oneself*) laugh oneself silly, split one's sides, roll on the floor, roll in the aisles, shake with laughter, be in fits, *colloq.* be in hysterics, have hysterics, be in stitches, crack up. **4** see AMUSE 1. **5** see *turn off* 1. **6** delete, erase, expunge, remove, cut out, strike out, withdraw. **7** hurt, pain, torment, torture. **8** consume, use up, spend, while away, occupy, fill, pass, idle away, take up, waste, fritter (away), squander. **10** see DEVOUR 1, SWALLOW *v.* 1. **12** muffle, neutralize, deaden, damp, silence, nullify, dull, absorb, smother, stifle, suppress, still. ● *n.* **1** death, killing, end, finish, deathblow, *coup de grâce;* termination, denouement, dispatch, conclusion. **2** game, prey; quarry; bag.
kill[2] /kil/ *n. US dial.* a stream, creek, or tributary river.
killdeer /kíldeer/ *n.* a large American plover, *Charadrius vociferus*, with a plaintive song. [imit.]

killer /kíllər/ *n.* **1 a** a person, animal, or thing that kills. **b** a murderer. **2** *colloq.* **a** an impressive, formidable, or excellent thing (*this one is quite difficult, but the next one is a real killer*). **b** a hilarious joke. **c** a decisive blow (*his brilliant header proved to be the killer*). □ **killer instinct 1** an innate tendency to kill. **2** a ruthless streak. **killer whale** a voracious cetacean, *Orcinus orca*, with a white belly and prominent dorsal fin.
■ **1** murderer, assassin, slayer, cutthroat, butcher, exterminator, Bluebeard, ripper, *colloq.* hatchet man, *sl.* hit man. **2 a** wonder, marvel, prodigy, paragon, portent, *Austral.* the glassy, *colloq.* beauty, dandy, pippin, blinder, bobby-dazzler, ripsnorter, *Austral. colloq.* trimmer, *sl.* corker, humdinger, daisy, lulu, the bee's knees, the cat's whiskers *or* pyjamas, *Austral.* & *NZ sl.* bottler, beaut, *esp. US sl.* dilly; *colloq.* toughie, facer, hard *or* tough nut to crack.

killick /kíllik/ *n.* **1** a heavy stone used by small craft as an anchor. **2** a small anchor. **3** *Brit. Naut. sl.* a leading seaman. [17th c.: orig. unkn.]

killifish /kíllifish/ *n.* **1** any small fresh- or brackish-water fish of the family Cyprinodontidae, many of which are brightly coloured. **2** a brightly-coloured tropical aquarium fish, *Pterolebias peruensis*. [perh. f. KILL[2] + FISH[1]]

killing /kílling/ *n.* & *adj.* ● *n.* **1 a** the causing of death. **b** an instance of this. **2** a great (esp. financial) success (*make a killing*). ● *adj. colloq.* **1** overwhelmingly funny. **2** exhausting; very strenuous. □ **killing-bottle** a bottle containing poisonous vapour to kill insects collected as specimens. □□ **killingly** *adv.*
■ *n.* **1** murder, carnage, butchery, execution, slaughter, bloodshed, death, massacre, genocide, liquidation, mass murder *or* destruction, decimation, extermination, annihilation, blood bath, manslaughter; slaying, homicide, fatality. **2** coup, bonanza, success, windfall, stroke of luck, stroke of good fortune, gain, profit, *colloq.* hit, *Austral. colloq.* purple patch, *Austral.* & *NZ sl.* spin. ● *adj.* **1** see UPROARIOUS 2. **2** devastating, ruinous, destructive, punishing, exhausting, debilitating, fatiguing, wearying, draining, tiring, enervating, difficult, hard, taxing, arduous, strenuous.

killjoy /kíljoy/ *n.* a person who throws gloom over or prevents other people's enjoyment.
■ spoilsport, damper, dampener, malcontent, pessimist, cynic, prophet of doom, Cassandra, *colloq.* grouch, grump, wet blanket, sourpuss, misery (guts), *esp. US sl.* party pooper.

kiln /kiln/ *n.* a furnace or oven for burning, baking, or drying, esp. for calcining lime or firing pottery etc. [OE *cylene* f. L *culina* kitchen]

kiln-dry /kíldrī/ *v.tr.* (**-ies, -ied**) dry in a kiln.

kilo /kéelō/ *n.* (*pl.* **-os**) **1** a kilogram. **2** a kilometre. [F: abbr.]

kilo- /kíllō/ *comb. form* denoting a factor of 1,000 (esp. in metric units). ¶ Abbr.: **k**, or **K** in *Computing*. [F f. Gk *khilioi* thousand]

kilobyte /kílləbīt/ *n. Computing* 1,024 (i.e. 2^{10}) bytes as a measure of memory size.

kilocalorie /kílləkalləri/ *n.* = CALORIE 2.

kilocycle /kílləsīk'l/ *n.* a former measure of frequency, equivalent to 1 kilohertz. ¶ Abbr.: **kc**.

kilogram /kílləgram/ *n.* (also **-gramme**) the SI unit of mass, equivalent to the international standard kept at Sèvres near Paris (approx. 2.205 lb.). ¶ Abbr.: **kg**. [F *kilogramme* (as KILO, GRAM[1])]

kilohertz /kílləherts/ *n.* a measure of frequency equivalent to 1,000 cycles per second. ¶ Abbr.: **kHz**.

kilojoule /kílləjōōl/ *n.* 1,000 joules, esp. as a measure of the energy value of foods. ¶ Abbr.: **kJ**.

kilolitre /kílləleetər/ *n.* (*US* **-liter**) 1,000 litres (equivalent to 220 imperial gallons). ¶ Abbr.: **kl**.

kilometre /kílləmeetər, *disp.* kilómmitər/ *n.* (*US* **kilometer**) a metric unit of measurement equal to 1,000 metres (approx. 0.62 miles). ¶ Abbr.: **km**. □□ **kilometric** /kíləmétrik/ *adj.* [F *kilomètre* (as KILO-, METRE[1])]

kiloton /kíllətun/ *n.* (also **kilotonne**) a unit of explosive power equivalent to 1,000 tons of TNT.

kilovolt /kílləvōlt/ *n.* 1,000 volts. ¶ Abbr.: **kV**.

kilowatt /kílləwot/ *n.* 1,000 watts. ¶ Abbr.: **kW**.

kilowatt-hour /kílləwot-ówr/ *n.* a measure of electrical energy equivalent to a power consumption of 1,000 watts for one hour. ¶ Abbr.: **kWh**.

kilt /kilt/ *n.* & *v.* ● *n.* **1** a skirtlike garment, usu. of pleated tartan cloth and reaching to the knees, as traditionally worn by Highland men. **2** a similar garment worn by women and children. ● *v.tr.* **1** tuck up (skirts) round the body. **2** (esp. as **kilted** *adj.*) gather in vertical pleats. □□ **kilted** *adj.* [orig. as verb: ME, of Scand. orig.]

kilter /kíltər/ *n.* (also **kelter** /kél-/) good working order (esp. *out of kilter*). [17th c.: orig. unkn.]
■ (*out of kilter*) see BROKEN 1.

kiltie /kílti/ *n.* a wearer of a kilt, esp. a kilted Highland soldier.

kimberlite /kímbərlīt/ *n. Mineral.* a rare igneous blue-tinged rock sometimes containing diamonds, found in South Africa and Siberia. Also called *blue ground* (see BLUE[1]). [*Kimberley* in S. Africa]

kimono /kimṓnō/ *n.* (*pl.* **-os**) **1** a long loose Japanese robe worn with a sash. **2** a European dressing-gown modelled on this. □□ **kimonoed** *adj.* [Jap.]
■ see WRAPPER 4.

kin /kin/ *n.* & *adj.* ● *n.* one's relatives or family. ● *predic.adj.* (of a person) related (*we are kin*; *he is kin to me*) (see also AKIN). □ **kith and kin** see KITH. **near of kin** closely related by blood, or in character. **next of kin** see NEXT. □□ **kinless** *adj.* [OE *cynn* f. Gmc]
■ *n.* family, relatives, relations, folks, kindred, kinsfolk, kith and kin, kinsmen, kinswomen, stock, clan, people, blood relations, blood relatives, *US* kinfolk. ● *adj.* related, akin (to), kindred, consanguineous, cognate, agnate.

-kin /kin/ *suffix* forming diminutive nouns (*catkin*; *manikin*). [from or after MDu. *-kijn*, *-ken*, OHG *-chin*]

kina /kéenə/ *n.* the monetary unit of Papua New Guinea. [Papuan]

kinaesthesia /kínnəss-théeziə/ *n.* (*US* **kinesthesia**) a sense of awareness of the position and movement of the voluntary muscles of the body. □□ **kinaesthetic** /-théttik/ *adj.* [Gk *kineō* move + *aisthēsis* sensation]

kincob /kínkob/ *n.* a rich Indian fabric embroidered with gold or silver. [Urdu f. Pers. *kamkāb* f. *kamkā* damask]

kind[1] /kīnd/ *n.* **1 a** a race or species (*human kind*). **b** a natural group of animals, plants, etc. (*the wolf kind*). **2** class, type, sort, variety (*what kind of job are you looking for?*). ¶ In sense 2, *these* (or *those*) *kind* is often encountered when followed by a plural, as in *I don't like these kind of things*, but *this kind* and *these kinds* are usually preferred. **3** each of the elements of the Eucharist (*communion under* (or *in*) *both kinds*). **4** the manner or fashion natural to a person etc. (*act after their kind*; *true to kind*). □ **kind of** *colloq.* to some extent (*felt kind of sorry*; *I kind of expected it*). **a kind of** used to imply looseness, vagueness, exaggeration, etc., in the term used (*a kind of Jane Austen of our times*; *I suppose he's a kind of doctor*). **in kind 1** in the same form, likewise (*was insulted and replied in kind*). **2** (of payment) in goods or labour as opposed to money (*received their wages in kind*). **3** in character or quality (*differ in degree but not in kind*). **law of kind** *archaic* nature in general; the natural order. **nothing of the kind 1** not at all like the thing in question. **2** (expressing denial) not at all. **of its kind** within the limitations of its own class (*good of its kind*). **of a kind 1** *derog.* scarcely deserving the name (*a choir of a kind*). **2** similar in some important respect (*they're two of a kind*). **one's own kind** those with whom one has much in common. **something of the kind** something like the thing in question. [OE *cynd(e)*, *gecynd(e)* f. Gmc]

■ **1** race, species, genus, breed, type, group, order. **2** sort, type, variety, category, kidney, style, genre, species, set, class, cast, mould; brand, make, stamp. **4** nature, character, manner, description, persuasion. □ **kind of** see LITTLE *adv.* 3. **in kind 1** see LIKEWISE *adv.* 2. **of a kind 1** of sorts. **2** birds of a feather, *US* of a *or* the same stripe, *colloq. disp.* of the same ilk.

kind[2] /kīnd/ *adj.* **1** of a friendly, generous, benevolent, or gentle nature. **2** (usu. foll. by *to*) showing friendliness, affection, or consideration. **3 a** affectionate. **b** *archaic* loving. [OE *gecynde* (as KIND[1]): orig. = 'natural, native']

■ **1–3a** friendly, kindly, nice, congenial, affable, approachable, amiable, obliging, accommodating, amicable, well-disposed, courteous, good, good-natured, benevolent, well-meaning, well-wishing, thoughtful, well-intentioned, generous, big-hearted, humanitarian, charitable, philanthropic, gentle, understanding, sympathetic, considerate, lenient, tolerant, indulgent, compassionate, kind-hearted, gracious, warm, warm-hearted, cordial, tender-hearted, affectionate.

kinda /kīndə/ *colloq.* = *kind of*. [corrupt.]

kinder /kíndər/ *n. Austral.* = KINDERGARTEN. [abbr.]

kindergarten /kíndərgaart'n/ *n.* an establishment for pre-school learning. [G, = children's garden]

■ nursery school, playgroup.

kind-hearted /kīndhaartid/ *adj.* of a kind disposition. □□ **kind-heartedly** *adv.* **kind-heartedness** *n.*

■ see KIND[2]. □□ **kind-heartedly** see KINDLY[1] 1. **kind-heartedness** see KINDNESS 1.

kindle /kínd'l/ *v.* **1** *tr.* light or set on fire (a flame, fire, substance, etc.). **2** *intr.* catch fire, burst into flame. **3** *tr.* arouse or inspire (*kindle enthusiasm for the project*; *kindle jealousy in a rival*). **4** *intr.* (usu. foll. by *to*) respond, react (to a person, an action, etc.) (*kindle to his courage*). **5** *intr.* become animated, glow with passion etc. (*her imagination kindled*). **6** *tr.* & *intr.* make or become bright (*kindle the embers to a glow*). □□ **kindler** *n.* [ME f. ON *kynda*, kindle: cf. ON *kindill* candle, torch]

■ **1** ignite, light, set alight, set fire to, set afire. **2** catch fire, burst into flame. **3** inflame, fire, foment, incite, instigate, provoke, prompt, goad, spur, whip up, stir (up), work up, excite, agitate, shake up, jolt, arouse, rouse, (a)waken, inspire, inspirit, stimulate, animate, enliven, energize, galvanize *archaic* prick.

kindling /kíndling/ *n.* small sticks etc. for lighting fires.

kindly[1] /kīndli/ *adv.* **1** in a kind manner (*spoke to the child kindly*). **2** often *iron.* used in a polite request or demand (*kindly acknowledge this letter*; *kindly leave me alone*). □ **look kindly upon** regard sympathetically. **take a thing kindly** like or be pleased by it. **take kindly to** be pleased by or endeared to (a person or thing). **thank kindly** thank very much. [OE *gecyndelīce* (as KIND[2])]

■ **1** cordially, graciously, obligingly, amiably, amicably, kind-heartedly, politely, genially, courteously, thoughtfully, considerately, hospitably, agreeably, pleasantly. **2** please, be so kind as to, be good enough to.

kindly[2] /kīndli/ *adj.* (**kindlier**, **kindliest**) **1** kind, kind-hearted. **2** (of climate etc.) pleasant, genial. **3** *archaic* native-born (*a kindly Scot*). □□ **kindlily** *adv.* **kindliness** *n.* [OE *gecyndelic* (as KIND[1])]

■ **1** see KIND[2]. □□ **kindliness** see KINDNESS 1.

kindness /kīndniss/ *n.* **1** the state or quality of being kind. **2** a kind act.

■ **1** friendliness, kind-heartedness, warm-heartedness, graciousness, goodness, good-naturedness, good-heartedness, goodwill, benevolence, benignity, humaneness, humanity, decency, tenderness, gentleness, kindliness, charity, charitableness, generosity, philanthropy, beneficence, compassion, sympathy, understanding, thoughtfulness, consideration, cordiality, hospitality, warmth, geniality, indulgence, tolerance, patience. **2** favour, good deed *or* turn, service, act of kindness *or* generosity; obligation.

kindred /kíndrid/ *n.* & *adj.* ● *n.* **1** one's relations, referred to collectively. **2** a relationship by blood. **3** a resemblance or affinity in character. ● *adj.* **1** related by blood or marriage. **2** allied or similar in character (*other kindred symptoms*). □ **kindred spirit** a person whose character and outlook have much in common with one's own. [ME f. KIN + *-red* f. OE *rǣden* condition]

■ *n.* **1** see KIN *n.* ● *adj.* **1** related, consanguineous, cognate, agnate. **2** close, associated, related, united, allied, analogous, like, similar, matching, parallel, common, related; akin.

kine /kīn/ *archaic pl.* of COW[1].

kinematics /kinnimáttiks, kī-/ *n.pl.* (usu. treated as *sing.*) the branch of mechanics concerned with the motion of objects without reference to the forces which cause the motion. □□ **kinematic** *adj.* **kinematically** *adv.* [Gk *kinēma -matos* motion f. *kineō* move + -ICS]

kinematograph var. of CINEMATOGRAPH.

kinesics /kineéssiks/ *n.pl.* (usu. treated as *sing.*) **1** the study of body movements and gestures which contribute to communication. **2** these movements; body language. [Gk *kinēsis* motion (as KINETIC)]

kinesiology /kineéssiólləji/ *n.* the study of the mechanics of body movements.

kinesthesia *US* var. of KINAESTHESIA.

kinetic /kinéttik, kī-/ *adj.* of or due to motion. □ **kinetic art** a form of art that depends on movement for its effect. **kinetic energy** the energy of motion. **kinetic theory** a theory which explains the physical properties of matter in terms of the motions of its constituent particles. □□ **kinetically** *adv.* [Gk *kinētikos* f. *kineō* move]

■ see MOTIVE *adj.*

kinetics /kinéttiks, kī-/ *n.pl.* **1** = DYNAMICS 1a. **2** (usu. treated as *sing.*) the branch of physical chemistry concerned with measuring and studying the rates of chemical reactions.

kinetin /kīnitin/ *n. Biochem.* a synthetic kinin used to stimulate cell division in plants. [as KINETIC + -IN]

kinfolk *US* var. of KINSFOLK.

king /king/ *n.* & *v.* ● *n.* **1** (as a title usu. **King**) a male sovereign, esp. the hereditary ruler of an independent State. **2** a person or thing pre-eminent in a specified field or class (*railway king*). **3** a large (or the largest) kind of plant, animal, etc. (*king penguin*). **4** *Chess* the piece on each side which the opposing side has to checkmate to win. **5** a piece in draughts with extra capacity of moving, made by crowning an ordinary piece that has reached the opponent's baseline. **6** a court-card bearing a representation of a king and usu. ranking next below an ace. **7** (**the King**) (in the UK) the national anthem when there is a male sovereign. **8** (**Kings** or **Books of Kings**) two Old Testament books dealing with history, esp. of the kingdom of Judah. ● *v.tr.* make (a person) king. □ **King Charles spaniel** a spaniel of a small black and tan breed. **king cobra** a large and venomous hooded Indian snake, *Ophiophagus hannah*. **king-crab 1** = *horseshoe crab*. **2** *US* any of various large edible spider crabs. **king-fish** any of various large fish, esp. the opah or mulloway. **king it 1** play or act the king. **2** (usu. foll. by *over*) govern, control. **King James Bible** (or **Version**) = *Authorized Version* (see AUTHORIZE). **King of Arms** *Heraldry* (in the UK) a chief herald (at the College of Arms: Garter, Clarenceux, and Norroy and Ulster; in Scotland: Lyon). **king of beasts** the lion. **king of birds** the eagle. **King of the Castle** a children's game consisting of trying to displace a rival from a mound. **King of Kings 1** God. **2** the title assumed by many eastern kings. **king-post** an upright post from the tie-beam of a roof to the apex of a truss. **King's Bench** see BENCH. **king's bishop, knight,** etc. *Chess* (of pieces which exist in pairs) the piece starting on the king's side of the board. **King's bounty** see BOUNTY. **King's colour** see COLOUR. **King's Counsel** see COUNSEL. **King's English** see ENGLISH. **King's evidence** see EVIDENCE. **king's evil** *hist.* scrofula, formerly held to be curable by the royal touch. **King's Guide** see GUIDE. **King's highway** see HIGHWAY. **king-size** (or **-sized**) larger than normal; very large. **King's Messenger** see MESSENGER. **king's pawn** *Chess* the pawn in front of the king at the beginning of a game. **King's Proctor** see PROCTOR. **king's ransom** a fortune. **King's Scout** see SCOUT[1]. **King's speech** see SPEECH. ◻◻ **kinghood** *n.* **kingless** *adj.* **kinglike** *adj.* **kingly** *adj.* **kingliness** *n.* **kingship** *n.* [OE *cyning*, *cyng* f. Gmc]

▪ *n.* **1** prince, crowned head, majesty, sovereign, monarch, ruler, regent, *colloq.* royal. **2** see BIGWIG. ◻ **King of Kings 1** see SAVIOUR 2. **king-size** see BIG *adj.* 1a. **king's ransom** see MINT[2] *n.* 2. ◻◻ **kinglike, kingly** see ROYAL 5. **kingship** see *sovereignty* (SOVEREIGN).

kingbird /kíngburd/ *n.* any flycatcher of the genus *Tyrannus*, with olive-grey plumage and long pointed wings.

kingbolt /kíngbōlt/ *n.* = KINGPIN.

kingcraft /kíng-kraaft/ *n. archaic* the skilful exercise of kingship.

kingcup /kíng-kup/ *n. Brit.* a marsh marigold.

kingdom /kíngdəm/ *n.* **1** an organized community headed by a king. **2** the territory subject to a king. **3 a** the spiritual reign attributed to God (*Thy kingdom come*). **b** the sphere of this (*kingdom of heaven*). **4** a domain belonging to a person, animal, etc. **5** a province of nature (*the vegetable kingdom*). **6** a specified mental or emotional province (*kingdom of the heart*; *kingdom of fantasy*). **7** *Biol.* the highest category in taxonomic classification. ◻ **come into** (or **to**) **one's kingdom** achieve recognition or supremacy. **kingdom come** *colloq.* eternity; the next world. **till kingdom come** *colloq.* for ever. ◻◻ **kingdomed** *adj.* [OE *cyningdōm* (as KING)]

▪ **1** empire, sovereignty, principality, monarchy, *formal esp. Law* realm. **2** see DOMINION 2. **4** field, area, domain, province, sphere (of influence), orbit, ambit, territory, home ground, *colloq.* patch, *joc.* bailiwick, *sl.* turf. ◻ **till kingdom come** for ever, eternally, everlastingly, in perpetuity, till doomsday, *colloq.* till the cows come home.

kingfisher /kíngfishər/ *n.* any bird of the family Alcedinidae esp. *Alcedo atthis* with a long sharp beak and brightly coloured plumage, which dives for fish in rivers etc.

kinglet /kínglit/ *n.* **1** a petty king. **2** *US* any of various small birds of the family Regulidae, esp. the goldcrest.

kingmaker /kíngmaykər/ *n.* a person who makes kings, leaders, etc., through the exercise of political influence, orig. with ref. to the Earl of Warwick in the reign of Henry VI of England.

kingpin /kíngpin/ *n.* **1 a** a main or large bolt in a central position. **b** a vertical bolt used as a pivot. **2** an essential person or thing, esp. in a complex system; the most important person in an organization.

▪ **1** see PIVOT *n.* 1. **2** see BIGWIG, LEADER 1.

kinin /kī́nin/ *n.* **1** any of a group of polypeptides present in the blood after tissue damage. **2** any of a group of compounds which promote cell division and inhibit ageing in plants. [Gk *kineō* move + -IN]

kink /kingk/ *n.* & *v.* ● *n.* **1 a** a short backward twist in wire or tubing etc. such as may cause an obstruction. **b** a tight wave in human or animal hair. **2** a mental twist or quirk. ● *v.intr.* & *tr.* form or cause to form a kink. [MLG *kinke* (v.) prob. f. Du. *kinken*]

▪ *n.* **1** twist, crimp, tangle, knot, wrinkle, curl, coil, curlicue, crinkle. **2** crotchet, quirk, whim, caprice, fancy, vagary, eccentricity, idiosyncrasy, peculiarity; difficulty, complication, flaw, hitch, snag, defect, imperfection, distortion, deformity.

kinkajou /kíngkəjōō/ *n.* a Central and S. American nocturnal fruit-eating mammal, *Potos flavus*, with a prehensile tail and living in trees. [F *quincajou* f. N.Amer. Ind.: cf. Algonquian *kwingwaage* wolverine]

kinky /kíngki/ *adj.* (**kinkier, kinkiest**) **1** *colloq.* **a** given to or involving abnormal sexual behaviour. **b** (of clothing etc.) bizarre in a sexually provocative way. **2** strange, eccentric. **3** having kinks or twists. ◻◻ **kinkily** *adv.* **kinkiness** *n.* [KINK + -Y[1]]

▪ **1 a** perverted, unnatural, deviant, degenerate, warped, abnormal, depraved. **b** suggestive, sexy. **2** outlandish, peculiar, odd, queer, quirky, bizarre, crotchety, eccentric, strange, peculiar, idiosyncratic, different, offbeat, unorthodox, capricious, irregular, erratic, unconventional, unique, freakish, weird, fantastic, whimsical. **3** crisp, frizzy, frizzed, frizzled, curly, crimped, wiry; knotted, tangled, twisted. ◻◻ **kinkiness** see PERVERSION 3b, ODDITY 3.

kino /keénō/ *n.* (*pl.* **-os**) a catechu-like gum produced by various trees and used in medicine and tanning as an astringent. [W. Afr.]

-kins /kinz/ *suffix* = -KIN, often with suggestions of endearment (*babykins*).

kinsfolk /kínzfōk/ *n.pl.* (*US* **kinfolk**) one's relations by blood.

▪ see KIN *n.*

kinship /kínship/ *n.* **1** blood relationship. **2** the sharing of characteristics or origins.

▪ **1** consanguinity, (blood) relationship, (family) ties, (common) descent, lineage, flesh and blood. **2** affinity; connection, correspondence, closeness, concordance, parallelism, relationship, similarity, association, agreement, alliance.

kinsman /kínzmən/ *n.* (*pl.* **-men**; *fem.* **kinswoman**, *pl.* **-women**) **1** a blood relation or *disp.* a relation by marriage. **2** a member of one's own tribe or people.

▪ **1** see RELATION 2.

kiosk /keé-osk/ *n.* **1** a light open-fronted booth or cubicle from which food, newspapers, tickets, etc. are sold. **2** a telephone box. **3** *Austral.* a building in which refreshments are served in a park, zoo, etc. **4** a light open pavilion in Turkey and Iran. [F *kiosque* f. Turk. *kiūshk* pavilion f. Pers. *guš*]

▪ **1** booth, stall, stand, cubicle, shop. **2** call-box, telephone booth, telephone cubicle, *Brit.* telephone box. **3** see STALL[1] *n.* 1.

kip[1] /kip/ *n.* & *v. Brit. sl.* ● *n.* **1** a sleep or nap. **2** a bed or cheap lodging-house. **3** (also **kip-house** or **-shop**) a brothel. ● *v.intr.* (**kipped, kipping**) **1** sleep, take a nap. **2** (foll. by *down*) lie or settle down to sleep. [cf. Da. *kippe* mean hut]

▪ *n.* **1** see SLEEP *n.* 2. **2** see PIT[1] *n.* 8. **3** see BROTHEL. ● *v.* **1** see DOZE *v.*

kip[2] /kip/ *n.* the hide of a young or small animal as used for leather. [ME: orig. unkn.]

kip[3] /kip/ *n.* (*pl.* same or **kips**) the basic monetary unit of Laos. [Thai]

kip[4] /kip/ *n. Austral. sl.* a small piece of wood from which coins are spun in the game of two-up. [perh. f. E dial.: cf. *keper* a flat piece of wood preventing a horse from eating the corn, or Ir. dial. *kippeen* f. Ir. *cipín* a little stick]

kipper /kíppər/ *n.* & *v.* ● *n.* **1** a kippered fish, esp. herring. **2** a male salmon in the spawning season. ● *v.tr.* cure (a herring etc.) by splitting open, salting, and drying in the open air or smoke. [ME: orig. uncert.]

▪ *v.* see PRESERVE *v.* 4a.

kipsie /kípsi/ *n.* (also **kipsy**) (*pl.* **-ies**) *Austral. sl.* a house, home, lean-to, or shelter. [perh. f. KIP[1]]

kir /kur/ *n.* a drink made from dry white wine and crème de cassis. [Canon Felix *Kir* d. 1968, said to have invented the recipe]

kirby-grip /kúrbigrip/ *n.* (also **Kirbigrip** *propr.*) a type of sprung hairgrip. [*Kirby*, part of orig. manufacturer's name]

Kirghiz /keergíz, kúrgiz/ *n.* & *adj.* ● *n.* (*pl.* same) **1** a member of a Mongol people living in central Asia between the Volga and the Irtysh rivers. **2** the language of this people. ● *adj.* of or relating to this people or their language. [Kirghiz]

kirk /kurk/ *n. Sc.* & *N.Engl.* **1** a church. **2** (**the Kirk** or **the Kirk of Scotland**) the Church of Scotland as distinct from the Church of England or from the Episcopal Church in Scotland. ◻ **Kirk-session 1** the lowest court in the Church of Scotland. **2** *hist.* the lowest court in other Presbyterian Churches, composed of ministers and elders. [ME f. ON *kirkja* f. OE *cir(i)ce* CHURCH]

kirkman /kúrkmən/ *n.* (*pl.* **-men**) *Sc.* & *N.Engl.* a member of the Church of Scotland.

kirsch /keersh/ *n.* (also **kirschwasser** /keérshvussər/) a brandy distilled from the fermented juice of cherries. [G *Kirsche* cherry, *Wasser* water]

kirtle /kúrt'l/ *n. archaic* **1** a woman's gown or outer petticoat. **2** a man's tunic or coat. [OE *cyrtel* f. Gmc, ult. perh. f. L *curtus* short]

kiskadee /kískədeé/ *n.* (also **keskidee** /késkideé/) a tyrant flycatcher, *Pitangus sulphuratus*, of Central and S. America, with brown and yellow plumage. [imit. of its cry]

kismet /kízmet/ *n.* destiny, fate. [Turk. f. Arab. *ķisma(t)* f. *ķasama* divide]
■ see DESTINY 2.

kiss /kiss/ *v.* & *n.* ● *v.* **1** *tr.* touch with the lips, esp. as a sign of love, affection, greeting, or reverence. **2** *tr.* express (greeting or farewell) in this way. **3** *absol.* (of two persons) touch each others' lips in this way. **4** *tr.* (also *absol.*) (of a snooker ball etc. in motion) lightly touch (another ball). ● *n.* **1** a touch with the lips in kissing. **2** the slight impact when one snooker ball etc. lightly touches another. **3** a small sweetmeat or piece of confectionery. □ **kiss and tell** recount one's sexual exploits. **kiss a person's arse** *coarse sl.* act obsequiously towards a person. **kiss away** remove (tears etc.) by kissing. **kiss-curl** a small curl of hair on the forehead, at the nape, or in front of the ear. **kiss the dust** submit abjectly; be overthrown. **kiss goodbye to** *colloq.* accept the loss of. **kiss the ground** prostrate oneself as a token of homage. **kissing cousin** (or **kin** or **kind**) a distant relative (given a formal kiss on occasional meetings). **kissing-gate** *Brit.* a gate hung in a V- or U-shaped enclosure, to let one person through at a time. **kiss of death** an apparently friendly act which causes ruin. **kiss off** *sl.* **1** dismiss, get rid of. **2** go away, die. **kiss of life** mouth-to-mouth resuscitation. **kiss of peace** *Eccl.* a ceremonial kiss, esp. during the Eucharist, as a sign of unity. **kiss the rod** accept chastisement submissively. □□ **kissable** *adj.* [OE *cyssan* f. Gmc]
■ *v.* **1** peck (on the cheek), give a kiss to, plant a kiss on, caress, smother with kisses, *archaic or US colloq.* buss, *colloq.* neck, *joc.* osculate. **3** *archaic* spoon, *colloq.* smooch, neck, canoodle, *joc.* osculate, *Brit. sl.* snog. **4** touch, brush, graze. ● *n.* **1** peck, caress, smack, X, *archaic or US colloq.* buss, *joc.* osculation, *sl.* smacker; *colloq.* smooch, *Brit. sl.* snog. □ **kiss goodbye to** say farewell to, give up, relinquish, abandon, forsake, desert, renounce, repudiate, forget (about), dismiss, disregard, ignore, *archaic or literary* bid adieu to. **kiss of death** see JINX *n.* **kiss off 2** see *beat it.*

kisser /kíssər/ *n.* **1** a person who kisses. **2** (orig. *Boxing*) *sl.* the mouth; the face.
■ **2** see MOUTH *n.* 1.

kissogram /kíssəgram/ *n.* (also **Kissagram** *propr.*) a novelty telegram or greetings message delivered with a kiss.

kissy /kíssi/ *adj. colloq.* given to kissing (*not the kissy type*).

kist var. of CIST[1].

Kiswahili /kiswaaheéli/ *n.* one of the six languages preferred for use in Africa by the Organization for African Unity. [Swahili *ki-* prefix for an abstract or inanimate object]

kit[1] /kit/ *n.* & *v.* ● *n.* **1** a set of articles, equipment, or clothing needed for a specific purpose (*first-aid kit*; *bicycle-repair kit*). **2** the clothing etc. needed for any activity, esp. sport (*football kit*). **3** a set of all the parts needed to assemble an item, e.g. a piece of furniture, a model, etc. **4** *Brit.* a wooden tub. ● *v.tr.* (**kitted, kitting**) (often foll. by *out, up*) equip with the appropriate clothing or tools. □ **the whole kit and caboodle** see CABOODLE. [ME f. MDu. *kitte* wooden vessel, of unkn. orig.]
■ *n.* **1** apparatus, gear, equipment, rig, outfit, set, paraphernalia, effects, appurtenances, accoutrements, tackle, trappings, supplies; instruments, tools, utensils, implements. **2** see COSTUME *n.* ● *v.* see CLOTHE 1.

kit[2] /kit/ *n.* **1** a kitten. **2** a young fox, badger, etc. [abbr.]

kit[3] /kit/ *n. hist.* a small fiddle esp. as used by a dancing-master. [perh. f. L *cithara*; see CITTERN]

kitbag /kitbag/ *n.* a large, usu. cylindrical bag used for carrying a soldier's, traveller's, or sportsman's equipment.
■ see PACK[1] *n.* 1.

kit-cat /kítkat/ *n.* (in full **kit-cat portrait**) a portrait of less than half length, but including one hand; usu. 36 x 28 in. [named after a series of portraits of the members of the *Kit-Cat* Club, an early 18th-c. Whig society]

kitchen /kíchin/ *n.* **1** the room or area where food is prepared and cooked. **2** (*attrib.*) of or belonging to the kitchen (*kitchen knife*; *kitchen table*). **3** *sl.* the percussion section of an orchestra. □ **everything but the kitchen sink** everything imaginable. **kitchen cabinet** a group of unofficial advisers thought to be unduly influential. **kitchen garden** a garden where vegetables and sometimes fruit or herbs are grown. **kitchen midden** a prehistoric refuse-heap which marks an ancient settlement, chiefly containing bones, seashells, etc. **kitchen-sink** (in art forms) depicting extreme realism, esp. drabness or sordidness (*kitchen-sink school of painting*; *kitchen-sink drama*). **kitchen tea** *Austral.* & *NZ* a party held before a wedding to which female guests bring items of kitchen equipment as presents. [OE *cycene* f. L *coquere* cook]
■ **1** kitchenette, cookhouse, scullery; *Naut.* galley, caboose. □ **everything but the kitchen sink** see WORK *n.* 10. **kitchen garden** see ALLOTMENT 1.

Kitchener bun /kíchinər/ *n. Austral.* a cream-filled bun coated with cinnamon and sugar. [1st Earl *Kitchener* d. 1916]

kitchenette /kíchinét/ *n.* a small kitchen or part of a room fitted as a kitchen.

kitchenware /kíchinwair/ *n.* the utensils used in the kitchen.

kite /kīt/ *n.* & *v.* ● *n.* **1** a toy consisting of a light framework with thin material stretched over it, flown in the wind at the end of a long string. **2** any of various soaring birds of prey esp. of the genus *Milvus* with long wings and usu. a forked tail. **3** *Brit. sl.* an aeroplane. **4** *sl.* a fraudulent cheque, bill, or receipt. **5** *Geom.* a quadrilateral figure symmetrical about one diagonal. **6** *sl.* a letter or note, esp. one that is illicit or surreptitious. **7** (in *pl.*) the highest sail of a ship, set only in a light wind. **8** *archaic* a dishonest person, a sharper. ● *v.* **1** *intr.* soar like a kite. **2** *tr.* (also *absol.*) originate or pass (fraudulent cheques, bills, or receipts). **3** *tr.* (also *absol.*) raise (money by dishonest means) (*kite a loan*). □ **kite balloon** a sausage-shaped captive balloon for military observations. **kite-flying** fraudulent practice. [OE *cӯta*, of unkn. orig.]

Kitemark /kītmaark/ *n.* (in the UK) the official kite-shaped mark on goods approved by the British Standards Institution.

kith /kith/ *n.* □ **kith and kin** friends and relations. [OE *cӯthth* f. Gmc]
■ □ **kith and kin** see KIN *n.*

kitsch /kich/ *n.* (often *attrib.*) garish, pretentious, or sentimental art, usu. vulgar and worthless (*kitsch plastic models of the royal family*). □□ **kitschy** *adj.* (**kitschier, kitschiest**). **kitschiness** *n.* [G]
■ □□ **kitschy** tasteless, tawdry, garish, gaudy, coarse, crude, vulgar, unstylish, pretentious, sentimental, worthless.

kitten /kitt'n/ *n.* & *v.* ● *n.* **1** a young cat. **2** a young ferret etc. ● *v.intr.* & *tr.* (of a cat etc.) give birth or give birth to. □ **have kittens** *Brit. colloq.* be extremely upset, anxious, or nervous. [ME *kito(u)n*, *ketoun* f. OF *chitoun*, *chetoun* dimin. of *chat* CAT]

kittenish /kíttənish/ *adj.* **1** like a young cat; playful and lively. **2** flirtatious. □□ **kittenishly** *adv.* **kittenishness** *n.* [KITTEN]
■ **1** playful, lively, sportive, (high-)spirited, frisky, sprightly. **2** coy, seductive, flirtatious, coquettish.

kittiwake /kíttiwayk/ *n.* either of two small gulls, *Rissa tridactyla* and *R. brevirostris*, nesting on sea cliffs. [imit. of its cry]

kittle /kítt'l/ *adj.* (also **kittle-cattle** /kítt'lkatt'l/) **1** (of a person) capricious, rash, or erratic in behaviour. **2** difficult to deal with. [ME (now Sc. & dial.) *kittle* tickle, prob. f. ON *kitla*]

kitty[1] /kítti/ *n.* (*pl.* **-ies**) **1** a fund of money for communal use. **2** the pool in some card-games. **3** the jack in bowls. [19th c.: orig. unkn.]

■ **1** fund, reserve, pool, purse, bank, collection. **2** pool, pot, jackpot, stakes.

kitty[2] /kítti/ *n.* (*pl.* **-ies**) a pet-name or a child's name for a kitten or cat.

kiwi /kéewee/ *n.* (*pl.* **kiwis**) **1** a flightless New Zealand bird of the genus *Apteryx* with hairlike feathers and a long bill. Also called APTERYX. **2** (**Kiwi**) *colloq.* a New Zealander, esp. a soldier or member of a national sports team. □ **kiwi fruit** (or **berry**) the fruit of a climbing plant, *Actinidia chinensis*, having a thin hairy skin, green flesh, and black seeds: also called *Chinese gooseberry*. [Maori]

kJ *abbr.* kilojoule(s).

KKK *abbr. US* Ku Klux Klan.

kl *abbr.* kilolitre(s).

Klaxon /kláks'n/ *n. propr.* a horn or warning hooter, orig. on a motor vehicle. [name of the manufacturing company]

Kleenex /kléeneks/ *n.* (*pl.* same or **Kleenexes**) orig. *US propr.* an absorbent disposable paper tissue, used esp. as a handkerchief.

Klein bottle /klīn/ *n. Math.* a closed surface with only one side, formed by passing the neck of a tube through the side of the tube to join the hole in the base. [F. *Klein*, Ger. mathematician d. 1925]

klepht /kleft/ *n.* **1** a member of the original body of Greeks who refused to submit to the Turks in the 15th c. **2** any of their descendants. **3** a brigand or bandit. [mod. Gk *klephtēs* f. Gk *kleptēs* thief]

kleptomania /kléptōmáyniə/ *n.* a recurrent urge to steal, usu. without regard for need or profit. □□ **kleptomaniac** /-niak/ *n.* & *adj.* [Gk *kleptēs* thief + -MANIA]

■ □□ **kleptomaniac** (*n.*) see THIEF.

klieg /kleeg/ *n.* (also **klieg light**) a powerful lamp in a film studio etc. [A. T. & J. H. *Kliegl*, Amer. inventors d. 1927, 1959]

klipspringer /klípspringər/ *n.* a S. African dwarf antelope, *Oreotragus oreotragus*, which can bound up and down rocky slopes. [Afrik. f. *klip* rock + *springer* jumper]

Klondike /klóndīk/ *n.* a source of valuable material. [*Klondike* in Yukon, Canada, where gold was found in 1896]

kloof /kloof/ *n.* a steep-sided ravine or valley in S. Africa. [Du., = cleft]

kludge /kluj/ *n.* orig. *US sl.* **1** an ill-assorted collection of poorly matching parts. **2** *Computing* a machine, system, or program that has been badly put together.

klutz /kluts/ *n. US sl.* **a** a clumsy awkward person. **b** a fool. □□ **klutzy** *adj.* [Yiddish f. G *Klotz* wooden block]

klystron /klīstron/ *n.* an electron tube that generates or amplifies microwaves by velocity modulation. [Gk *kluzō klus-* wash over]

km *abbr.* kilometre(s).

K-meson /kaymézzon, -méezon/ *n.* = KAON. [K (see KAON) + MESON]

kn. *abbr. Naut.* knot(s).

knack /nak/ *n.* **1** an acquired or intuitive faculty of doing a thing adroitly. **2** a trick or habit of action or speech etc. (*has a knack of offending people*). **3** *archaic* an ingenious device (see KNICK-KNACK). [ME, prob. identical with *knack* sharp blow or sound f. LG, ult. imit.]

■ **1** genius, intuition, talent, gift, facility, faculty, skill, aptitude, bent; ability, flair, dexterity, capacity, adroitness, proficiency, expertise, skilfulness. **2** habit, trick, art, technique.

knacker /nákkər/ *n.* & *v. Brit.* ● *n.* **1** a buyer of useless horses for slaughter. **2** a buyer of old houses, ships, etc. for the materials. ● *v.tr. sl.* **1** kill. **2** (esp. as **knackered** *adj.*) exhaust, wear out. [19th c.: orig. unkn.]

■ *v.* **2** see TIRE[1] 1; (**knackered**) see TIRED 1.

knackery /nákkəri/ *n.* (*pl.* **-ies**) a knacker's yard or business.

knag /nag/ *n.* **1** a knot in wood; the base of a branch. **2** a short dead branch. **3** a peg for hanging things on. □□ **knaggy** *adj.* [ME, perh. f. LG *Knagge*]

knap[1] /nap/ *n.* chiefly *dial.* the crest of a hill or of rising ground. [OE *cnæp(p)*, perh. rel. to ON *knappr* knob]

knap[2] /nap/ *v.tr.* (**knapped, knapping**) **1** break (stones for roads or building, flints, or *Austral.* ore) with a hammer. **2** *archaic* knock, rap, snap asunder. □□ **knapper** *n.* [ME, imit.]

knapsack /nápsak/ *n.* a soldier's or hiker's bag with shoulder-straps, carried on the back, and usu. made of canvas or weatherproof material. [MLG, prob. f. *knappen* bite + SACK[1]]

■ see PACK[1] *n.* 1.

knapweed /nápweed/ *n.* any of various plants of the genus *Centaurea*, having thistle-like purple flowers. [ME, orig. *knopweed* f. KNOP + WEED]

knar /naar/ *n.* a knot or protuberance in a tree trunk, root, etc. [ME *knarre*, rel. to MLG, M.Du., MHG *knorre* knobbed protuberance]

knave /nayv/ *n.* **1** a rogue, a scoundrel. **2** = JACK[1] *n.* 2. □□ **knavery** *n.* (*pl.* **-ies**). **knavish** *adj.* **knavishly** *adv.* **knavishness** *n.* [OE *cnafa* boy, servant, f. WG]

■ **1** see ROGUE *n.* 1. □□ **knavery, knavishness** see DEVILRY. **knavish** see DISHONEST.

knawel /náwəl/ *n.* any low-growing plant of the genus *Scleranthus*. [G *Knauel*]

knead /need/ *v.tr.* **1 a** work (a yeast mixture, clay, etc.) into dough, paste, etc. by pummelling. **b** make (bread, pottery, etc.) in this way. **2** blend or weld together (*kneaded them into a unified group*). **3** massage (muscles etc.) as if kneading. □□ **kneadable** *adj.* **kneader** *n.* [OE *cnedan* f. Gmc]

■ **1 a** pummel, punch, pound, knock, thump, work, manipulate. **b** see MOULD[1] *v.* 1, 2. **3** massage, rub (down), manipulate.

knee /nee/ *n.* & *v.* ● *n.* **1 a** (often *attrib.*) the joint between the thigh and the lower leg in humans. **b** the corresponding joint in other animals. **c** the area around this. **d** the upper surface of the thigh of a sitting person; the lap (*held her on his knee*). **2** the part of a garment covering the knee. **3** anything resembling a knee in shape or position, esp. a piece of wood or iron bent at an angle, a sharp turn in a graph, etc. ● *v.tr.* (**knees, kneed, kneeing**) **1** touch or strike with the knee (*kneed the ball past him*; *kneed him in the groin*). **2** *colloq.* cause (trousers) to bulge at the knee. □ **bend** (or **bow**) **the knee** kneel, esp. in submission. **bring a person to his** or **her knees** reduce a person to submission. **knee-bend** the action of bending the knee, esp. as a physical exercise in which the body is raised and lowered without the use of the hands. **knee-breeches** close-fitting trousers reaching to or just below the knee. **knee-deep 1** (usu. foll. by *in*) **a** immersed up to the knees. **b** deeply involved. **2** so deep as to reach the knees. **knee-high** so high as to reach the knees. **knee-hole** a space for the knees, esp. under a desk. **knee-jerk 1** a sudden involuntary kick caused by a blow on the tendon just below the knee. **2** (*attrib.*) predictable, automatic, stereotyped. **knee-joint 1** = senses 1a, b of *n.* **2** a joint made of two pieces hinged together. **knee-length** reaching the knees. **knee-pan** the kneecap. **knees-up** *Brit. colloq.* a lively party or gathering. **on** (or **on one's**) **bended knee** (or **knees**) kneeling, esp. in supplication, submission, or worship. [OE *cnēo(w)*]

■ □ **knee-breeches** see SHORTS 1. **knee-deep 1 b** (*knee deep in*) see AMONG 1. **knee-jerk 2** see AUTOMATIC *adj.* 2a. **knees-up** see JAMBOREE.

kneecap /néekap/ *n.* & *v.* ● *n.* **1** the convex bone in front of the knee-joint. **2** a protective covering for the knee. ● *v.tr.* (**-capped, -capping**) *colloq.* shoot (a person) in the knee or leg as a punishment, esp. for betraying a terrorist group. □□ **kneecapping** *n.*

kneel /neel/ *v.intr.* (*past* and *past part.* **knelt** /nelt/ or esp. *US* **kneeled**) fall or rest on the knees or a knee. [OE *cnēowlian* (as KNEE)]
■ bend the knee, bow the knee, get down on one's knees, genuflect, crouch, bow, stoop.

kneeler /néelər/ *n.* **1** a hassock or cushion used for kneeling, esp. in church. **2** a person who kneels.

knell /nel/ *n.* & *v.* ● *n.* **1** the sound of a bell, esp. when rung solemnly for a death or funeral. **2** an announcement, event, etc., regarded as a solemn warning of disaster. ● *v.* **1** *intr.* **a** (of a bell) ring solemnly, esp. for a death or funeral. **b** make a doleful or ominous sound. **2** *tr.* proclaim by or as by a knell (*knelled the death of all their hopes*). □ **ring the knell of** announce or herald the end of. [OE *cnyll*, *cnyllan*: perh. infl. by *bell*]
■ *n.* **1** see TOLL² *n.* **2** see WARNING 2. ● *v.* **1** see RING² *v.* 1.

knelt *past* and *past part.* of KNEEL.

Knesset /knéssit/ *n.* the parliament of modern Israel. [Heb., lit. gathering]

knew *past* of KNOW.

knickerbocker /níkkərbokkər/ *n.* **1** (in *pl.*) loose-fitting breeches gathered at the knee or calf. **2** (**Knickerbocker**) **a** a New Yorker. **b** a descendant of the original Dutch settlers in New York. □ **Knickerbocker Glory** ice-cream served with other ingredients in a tall glass. [Diedrich *Knickerbocker*, pretended author of W. Irving's *History of New York* (1809)]

knickers /níkkərz/ *n.pl.* **1** *Brit.* a woman's or girl's undergarment covering the body from the waist or hips to the top of the thighs and having leg-holes or separate legs. **2** esp. *US* **a** knickerbockers. **b** a boy's short trousers. **3** (as *int.*) *Brit. sl.* an expression of contempt. [abbr. of KNICKERBOCKER]
■ **1** see PANTS 1. **2** see TROUSERS 1.

knick-knack /níknak/ *n.* **1** a useless and usu. worthless ornament; a trinket. **2** a small, dainty article of furniture, dress, etc. □□ **knick-knackery** *n.* **knick-knackish** *adj.* [redupl. of *knack* in obs. sense 'trinket']
■ **1** see GEWGAW. **2** see ORNAMENT *n.* 1, 2.

knife /nīf/ *n.* & *v.* ● *n.* (*pl.* **knives** /nīvz/) **1 a** a metal blade used as a cutting tool with usu. one long sharp edge fixed rigidly in a handle or hinged (cf. PENKNIFE). **b** a similar tool used as a weapon. **2** a cutting-blade forming part of a machine. **3** (as **the knife**) a surgical operation or operations. ● *v.tr.* **1** cut or stab with a knife. **2** *sl.* bring about the defeat of (a person) by underhand means. □ **at knife-point** threatened with a knife or an ultimatum etc. **before you can say knife** *colloq.* very quickly or suddenly. **get one's knife into** treat maliciously or vindictively, persecute. **knife-board** a board on which knives are cleaned. **knife-edge 1** the edge of a knife. **2** a position of extreme danger or uncertainty. **3** a steel wedge on which a pendulum etc. oscillates. **4** = ARÊTE. **knife-grinder 1** a travelling sharpener of knives etc. **2** a person who grinds knives etc. during their manufacture. **knife-machine** a machine for cleaning knives. **knife-pleat** a narrow flat pleat on a skirt etc., usu. overlapping another. **knife-rest** a metal or glass support for a carving-knife or -fork at table. **knife-throwing** a circus etc. act in which knives are thrown at targets. **that one could cut with a knife** *colloq.* (of an accent, atmosphere, etc.) very obvious, oppressive, etc. □□ **knifelike** *adj.* **knifer** *n.* [OE *cnīf* f. ON *knífr* f. Gmc]
■ *n.* **1 a** blade, cutting edge, cutter; penknife, pocket knife. **b** sword, rapier, sabre, dagger, stiletto, cutlass, bayonet, switch-blade, flick-knife, jackknife, *hist.* skean, *literary* poniard, *poet.* brand. ● *v.* **1** stab, pierce, slash, cut, slit, wound. □ **before you can say knife** see *swiftly* (SWIFT).

knight /nīt/ *n.* & *v.* ● *n.* **1** a man awarded a non-hereditary title (*Sir*) by a sovereign in recognition of merit or service. **2** *hist.* **a** a man, usu. noble, raised esp. by a sovereign to honourable military rank after service as a page and squire. **b** a military follower or attendant, esp. of a lady as her champion in a war or tournament. **3** a man devoted to the service of a woman, cause, etc. **4** *Chess* a piece usu. shaped like a horse's head. **5 a** *Rom.Hist.* a member of the class of *equites*, orig. the cavalry of the Roman army. **b** *Gk Hist.* a citizen of the second class in Athens. **6** (in full **knight of the shire**) *hist.* a gentleman representing a shire or county in parliament. ● *v.tr.* confer a knighthood on. □ **knight bachelor** (*pl.* **knights bachelor**) a knight not belonging to a special order. **knight commander** see COMMANDER. **knight errant 1** a medieval knight wandering in search of chivalrous adventures. **2** a man of a chivalrous or quixotic nature. **knight-errantry** the practice or conduct of a knight errant. **Knight Hospitaller** (*pl.* **Knights Hospitaller**) a member of an order of monks with a military history, founded at Jerusalem *c.*1050. **knight in shining armour** a chivalrous rescuer or helper, esp. of a woman. **knight marshal** *hist.* an officer of the royal household with judicial functions. **knight of the road** *colloq.* **1** a highwayman. **2** a commercial traveller. **3** a tramp. **4** a lorry driver or taxi driver. **knight-service** *hist.* the tenure of land by military service. **Knight Templar** (*pl.* **Knights Templar**) a member of a religious and military order for the protection of pilgrims to the Holy Land, suppressed in 1312. □□ **knighthood** *n.* **knightlike** *adj.* **knightly** *adj.* & *adv. poet.* **knightliness** *n.* [OE *cniht* boy, youth, hero f. WG]
■ *n.* **3** see PROTECTOR. □ **knight errant 2** see SAVIOUR *n.* 1. **knight-errantry** see CHIVALRY 2. **knight of the road 3** see DRIFTER.

knightage /nītij/ *n.* **1** knights collectively. **2** a list and account of knights.

knish /knish/ *n.* a dumpling of flaky dough filled with cheese etc. and baked or fried. [Yiddish f. Russ.]

knit /nit/ *v.* & *n.* ● *v.* (**knitting**; *past* and *past part.* **knitted** or (esp. in senses 2–4) **knit**) **1** *tr.* (also *absol.*) **a** make (a garment, blanket, etc.) by interlocking loops of esp. wool with knitting-needles. **b** make (a garment etc.) with a knitting machine. **c** make (a plain stitch) in knitting (*knit one, purl one*). **2 a** *tr.* contract (the forehead) in vertical wrinkles. **b** *intr.* (of the forehead) contract; frown. **3** *tr.* & *intr.* (often foll. by *together*) make or become close or compact esp. by common interests etc. (*a close-knit group*). **4** *intr.* (often foll. by *together*) (of parts of a broken bone) become joined; heal. ● *n.* knitted material or a knitted garment. □ **knit up 1** make or repair by knitting. **2** conclude, finish, or end. □□ **knitter** *n.* [OE *cnyttan* f. WG: cf. KNOT¹]
■ *v.* **2** furrow, contract, wrinkle, knot, crease; frown. **3** join *or* fasten *or* weave (together), interweave, interlace, interconnect, intertwine, link, bind, unite, tie (up *or* together), integrate, consolidate, combine, compact. **4** grow (together), heal, mend, join.

knitting /nítting/ *n.* **1** a garment etc. in the process of being knitted. **2 a** the act of knitting. **b** an instance of this. □ **knitting-machine** a machine used for mechanically knitting garments etc. **knitting-needle** a thin pointed rod of steel, wood, plastic, etc., used esp. in pairs for knitting.

knitwear /nítwair/ *n.* knitted garments.

knives *pl.* of KNIFE.

knob /nob/ *n.* & *v.* ● *n.* **1 a** a rounded protuberance, esp. at the end or on the surface of a thing. **b** a handle of a door, drawer, etc., shaped like a knob. **c** a knob-shaped attachment for pulling, turning, etc. (*press the knob under the desk*). **2** a small, usu. round, piece (of butter, coal, sugar, etc.). ● *v.* (**knobbed, knobbing**) **1** *tr.* provide with knobs. **2** *intr.* (usu. foll. by *out*) bulge. □ **with knobs on** *Brit. sl.* that and more (used as a retort to an insult, in emphatic agreement, etc.) (*and the same to you with knobs on*). □□ **knobby** *adj.* **knoblike** *adj.* [ME f. MLG *knobbe* knot, knob, bud: cf. KNOP, NOB², NUB]
■ *n.* **1 a** boss, stud, protuberance, projection, protrusion, swelling, bump, node, knobble, knop. **b** handle. **c** button, control, switch, dial. **2** nub, lump, pat; piece. □□ **knobby** see BUMPY 1.

knobble /nóbb'l/ *n.* a small knob. □□ **knobbly** *adj.* [ME, dimin. of KNOB: cf. Du. & LG *knobbel*]

■ □□ **knobbly** see BUMPY 1.

knobkerrie /nóbkerri/ *n.* a short stick with a knobbed head used as a weapon esp. by S. African tribes. [after Afrik. *knopkierie*]

knobstick /nóbstik/ *n.* **1** = KNOBKERRIE. **2** *archaic* = BLACKLEG.

knock /nok/ *v.* & *n.* ● *v.* **1 a** *tr.* strike (a hard surface) with an audible sharp blow (*knocked the table three times*). **b** *intr.* strike, esp. a door to gain admittance (*can you hear someone knocking?*; *knocked at the door*). **2** *tr.* make (a hole, a dent, etc.) by knocking (*knock a hole in the fence*). **3** *tr.* (usu. foll. by *in*, *out*, *off*, etc.) drive (a thing, a person, etc.) by striking (*knocked the ball into the hole*; *knocked those ideas out of his head*; *knocked her hand away*). **4** *tr. sl.* criticize. **5** *intr.* **a** (of a motor or other engine) make a thumping or rattling noise esp. as the result of a loose bearing. **b** = PINK[3]. **6** *tr. Brit. sl.* make a strong impression on, astonish. **7** *tr. Brit. coarse sl. offens.* = *knock off* 7. ● *n.* **1** an act of knocking. **2** a sharp rap, esp. at a door. **3** an audible sharp blow. **4** the sound of knocking in esp. a motor engine. **5** *Cricket colloq.* an innings. □ **knock about** (or **around**) **1** strike repeatedly; treat roughly (*knocked her about*). **2** lead a wandering adventurous life; wander aimlessly. **3** be present without design or volition (*there's a cup knocking about somewhere*). **4** (usu. foll. by *with*) be associated socially (*knocks about with his brother*). **knock against 1** collide with. **2** come across casually. **knock back 1** *Brit. sl.* eat or drink, esp. quickly. **2** *Brit. sl.* disconcert. **3** *colloq.* refuse, rebuff. **knock-back** *n. colloq.* a refusal, a rebuff. **knock the bottom out of** see BOTTOM. **knock down 1** strike (esp. a person) to the ground with a blow. **2** demolish. **3** (usu. foll. by *to*) (at an auction) dispose of (an article) to a bidder by a knock with a hammer (*knocked the Picasso down to him for a million*). **4** *colloq.* lower the price of (an article). **5** take (machinery, furniture, etc.) to pieces for transportation. **6** *US sl.* steal. **7** *Austral.* & *NZ sl.* spend (a pay cheque etc.) freely. **knock-down** *attrib.adj.* **1** (of a blow, misfortune, argument, etc.) overwhelming. **2** *Brit.* (of a price) very low. **3** (of a price at auction) reserve. **4** (of furniture etc.) easily dismantled and reassembled. ● *n. Austral.* & *NZ sl.* an introduction (to a person). **knock for knock agreement** an agreement between insurance companies by which each pays its own policyholder regardless of liability. **knock one's head against** come into collision with (unfavourable facts or conditions). **knocking-shop** *Brit. sl.* a brothel. **knock into a cocked hat** see COCK[1]. **knock into the middle of next week** *colloq.* send (a person) flying, esp. with a blow. **knock into shape** see SHAPE. **knock-kneed** having knock knees. **knock knees** an abnormal condition with the legs curved inwards at the knee. **knock off 1** strike off with a blow. **2** *colloq.* **a** finish work (*knocked off at 5.30*). **b** finish (work) (*knocked off work early*). **3** *colloq.* dispatch (business). **4** *colloq.* rapidly produce (a work of art, verses, etc.). **5** (often foll. by *from*) deduct (a sum) from a price, bill, etc. **6** *sl.* steal. **7** *Brit. coarse sl. offens.* have sexual intercourse with (a woman). **8** *sl.* kill. **knock on** *Rugby Football* drive (a ball) with the hand or arm towards the opponents' goal-line. **knock-on** *n.* an act of knocking on. **knock-on effect** a secondary, indirect, or cumulative effect. **knock on the head 1** stun or kill (a person) by a blow on the head. **2** *colloq.* put an end to (a scheme etc.). **knock on** (or **knock**) **wood** *US* = *touch wood.* **knock out 1** make (a person) unconscious by a blow on the head. **2** knock down (a boxer) for a count of 10, thereby winning the contest. **3** defeat, esp. in a knockout competition. **4** *sl.* astonish. **5** (*refl.*) *colloq.* exhaust (*knocked themselves out swimming*). **6** *colloq.* make or write (a plan etc.) hastily. **7** empty (a tobacco-pipe) by tapping. **8** *Austral.*, *NZ*, & *US sl.* earn. **knock sideways** *colloq.* disconcert; astonish. **knock spots off** defeat easily. **knock together** put together or assemble hastily or roughly. **knock under** submit. **knock up 1** make or arrange hastily. **2** drive upwards with a blow. **3 a** become exhausted or ill. **b** exhaust or make ill. **4** *Brit.* arouse (a person) by a knock at the door. **5** *Cricket* score (runs) rapidly. **6** esp. *US sl.* make pregnant. **7** practise a ball game before formal play begins. **knock-up** *n.* a practice at tennis etc. **take a** (or **the**) **knock** be hard hit financially or emotionally. [ME f. OE *cnocian*: prob. imit.]

■ *v.* **1** strike, hit, rap, thump, bang, bash, hammer, tap, *archaic or literary* smite, *colloq.* whack, thwack; see also BEAT *v.* 1, 2a. **4** criticize, deprecate, carp at, cavil at, disparage, run down, *colloq.* slag (off), put down, pan, rubbish, *Brit. colloq.* slate. **6** see *knock out* 4 below. ● *n.* **1, 2** rap, tap, thump, banging, pounding, hammering. **3** blow, punch, jab, smack, right, left, cuff, clout, *colloq.* thwack, whack, bop, *sl.* biff, conk. □ **knock about** (or **around**) **1** beat (up), maltreat, mistreat, maul, batter, abuse, hit, strike, *colloq.* manhandle. **2** wander, roam, ramble, rove, travel, gad about. **4** associate, consort, socialize, fraternize, keep company, *sl.* hang out. **knock back 1** see GULP *v.* 1. **2** see *put off* 4. **3** see REBUFF *v.* **knock-back** see REFUSAL 1. **knock down 1** strike down, fell, floor, cut down. **2** raze, demolish, destroy, level, wreck, lay in ruins, throw down, pull down, tear down. **4** see REDUCE 7. **5** dismantle, pull down, pull *or* take to pieces, take apart, take down. **6** see *knock off* 6 below. **7** squander, waste, fritter away, spend, use up, exhaust, *sl.* blow. **knock off 2 a** stop work(ing), quit, go home, clock off *or* out, lock up, close down. **b** stop, finish, cease, terminate, quit. **3** dispatch, make quick *or* short work of, complete, finish, bring to an end, polish off. **4** see *knock up* 1 below. **5** see DEDUCT. **6** steal, pilfer, thieve, rob, *colloq.* lift, *sl.* pinch, *Brit. sl.* nick, *US sl.* knock down. **8** see KILL[1] *v.* 1. **knock out 1, 2** knock *or* render unconscious, floor, prostrate, trounce, whip, *colloq.* flatten, K.O., kayo. **3** see ELIMINATE 3. **4** overwhelm, overcome, daze, stagger, astound, astonish, bewilder, stun, *colloq.* bowl over, knock for six, *sl.* blow a person's mind. **knock together** see *knock up* 1 below. **knock up 1** knock off *or* together, put together, throw together, whip up, improvise. **4** arouse, (a)waken, wake up. **6** impregnate, make pregnant, *archaic* get with child.

knockabout /nókkəbowt/ *adj.* & *n.* ● *attrib.adj.* **1** (of comedy) boisterous; slapstick. **2** (of clothes) suitable for rough use. **3** *Austral.* of a farm or station handyman. ● *n.* **1** *Austral.* a farm or station handyman. **2** a knockabout performer or performance.

■ *adj.* **1** see BOISTEROUS 1. ● *n. Austral.* & *NZ* rouseabout, *Austral. sl.* blue tongue.

knocker /nókkər/ *n.* **1** a metal or wooden instrument hinged to a door for knocking to call attention. **2** a person or thing that knocks. **3** (in *pl.*) *coarse sl.* a woman's breasts. **4** a person who buys or sells door to door. □ **knocker-up** *Brit. hist.* a person employed to rouse early workers by knocking at their doors or windows. **on the knocker 1 a** (buying or selling) from door to door. **b** (obtained) on credit. **2** *Austral.* & *NZ colloq.* promptly. **up to the knocker** *Brit. sl.* in good condition; to perfection.

■ □ **on the knocker 2** see *on the dot* (DOT).

knockout /nókkowt/ *n.* **1** the act of making unconscious by a blow. **2** *Boxing* etc. a blow that knocks an opponent out. **3** a competition in which the loser in each round is eliminated (also *attrib.*: *a knockout round*). **4** *colloq.* an outstanding or irresistible person or thing. □ **knockout drops** a drug added to a drink to cause unconsciousness.

■ **2** *coup de grâce*, *colloq.* K.O., kayo. **4** success, sensation, triumph, wonder, *colloq.* hit, winner, smash, smash hit, stunner. □ **knockout drops** see SEDATIVE *n.*

knoll[1] /nōl/ *n.* a small hill or mound. [OE *cnoll* hilltop, rel. to MDu., MHG *knolle* clod, ON *knollr* hilltop]

■ hillock, hummock, mound, barrow, hill, elevation, rise.

knoll[2] /nōl/ *v.* & *n. archaic* ● *v.* **1** *tr.* & *intr.* = KNELL. **2** *tr.* summon by the sound of a bell. ● *n.* = KNELL. [ME, var. of KNELL: perh. imit.]

knop /nop/ *n.* **1** a knob, esp. ornamental. **2** an ornamental loop or tuft in yarn. **3** *archaic* a flower-bud. [ME f. MLG, MDu. *knoppe*]

■ **1** see KNOB *n.* 1a.

knopkierie /knópkeeri/ *n. S.Afr.* = KNOBKERRIE. [Afrik.]

knot[1] /not/ *n.* & *v.* ● *n.* **1 a** an intertwining of a rope, string, tress of hair, etc., with another, itself, or something else to join or fasten together. **b** a set method of tying a knot (*a reef knot*). **c** a ribbon etc. tied as an ornament and worn on a dress etc. **d** a tangle in hair, knitting, etc. **2 a** a unit of a ship's or aircraft's speed equivalent to one nautical mile per hour (see *nautical mile*). **b** a division marked by knots on a log-line, as a measure of speed. **c** *colloq.* a nautical mile. **3** (usu. foll. by *of*) a group or cluster (*a small knot of journalists at the gate*). **4** something forming or maintaining a union; a bond or tie, esp. of wedlock. **5** a hard lump of tissue in an animal or human body. **6 a** a knob or protuberance in a stem, branch, or root. **b** a hard mass formed in a tree trunk at the intersection with a branch. **c** a round cross-grained piece in timber where a branch has been cut through. **d** a node on the stem of a plant. **7** a difficulty; a problem. **8** a central point in a problem or the plot of a story etc. **9** (in full **porter's knot**) *Brit. hist.* a double shoulder-pad and forehead-loop used for carrying loads. ● *v.* (**knotted, knotting**) **1** *tr.* tie (a string etc.) in a knot. **2** *tr.* entangle. **3** *tr.* knit (the brows). **4** *tr.* unite closely or intricately (*knotted together in intrigue*). **5 a** *intr.* make knots for fringing. **b** *tr.* make (a fringe) with knots. □ **at a rate of knots** *colloq.* very fast. **get knotted!** *sl.* an expression of disbelief, annoyance, etc. **knot-garden** an intricately designed formal garden. **knot-hole** a hole in a piece of timber where a knot has fallen out (sense 6). **tie in knots** *colloq.* baffle or confuse completely. □□ **knotless** *adj.* **knotter** *n.* **knotting** *n.* (esp. in sense 5 of *v.*). [OE *cnotta* f. WG]

■ *n.* **1 a** tie, bond, twist. **d** snarl, tangle. **3** collection, assemblage, group, aggregation, congregation, crowd, cluster, bunch, gathering, company, gang, crowd, throng, *archaic* band. **6 a** knob, protuberance, knar, knur, excrescence. **d** node, nodule. ● *v.* **1** fasten, tie, bind, secure, lash, tether, affix, fix, attach. **2** see ENTANGLE 1, 2. **3** see KNIT *v.* 2. **4** unite, join, connect, link, bond. □ **tie in knots** see BEMUSE.

knot[2] /not/ *n.* a small sandpiper, *Calidris canutus*. [ME: orig. unkn.]

knotgrass /nótgraass/ *n.* **1** a common weed, *Polygonum aviculare*, with creeping stems and small pink flowers. **2** = POLYGONUM. Also called KNOTWEED.

knotty /nótti/ *adj.* (**knottier, knottiest**) **1** full of knots. **2** hard to explain; puzzling (*a knotty problem*). □□ **knottily** *adv.* **knottiness** *n.*

■ **1** see GNARLED. **2** see *perplexing* (PERPLEX), DIFFICULT 1b.

knotweed /nótweed/ *n.* = POLYGONUM.

knotwork /nótwurk/ *n.* ornamental work representing or consisting of intertwined cords.

knout /nowt, no͞ot/ *n.* & *v.* ● *n. hist.* a scourge used in imperial Russia, often causing death. ● *v.tr.* flog with a knout. [F f. Russ. *knut* f. Icel. *knútr*, rel. to KNOT[1]]

■ *n.* see LASH *n.* 2.

know /nō/ *v.* & *n.* ● *v.* (*past* **knew** /nyo͞o/; *past part.* **known** /nōn/) **1** *tr.* (often foll. by *that, how, what*, etc.) **a** have in the mind; have learnt; be able to recall (*knows a lot about cars*; *knows what to do*). **b** (also *absol.*) be aware of (a fact) (*he knows I am waiting*; *I think he knows*). **c** have a good command of (a subject or language) (*knew German*; *knows his tables*). **2** *tr.* be acquainted or friendly with (a person or thing). **3** *tr.* **a** recognize; identify (*I knew him at once*; *knew him for an American*). **b** (foll. by *to* + infin.) be aware of (a person or thing) as being or doing what is specified (*knew them to be rogues*). **c** (foll. by *from*) be able to distinguish (one from another) (*did not know him from Adam*). **4** *tr.* be subject to (*her joy knew no bounds*). **5** *tr.* have personal experience of (fear etc.). **6** *tr.* (as **known** *adj.*) **a** publicly acknowledged (*a known thief*; *a known fact*). **b** *Math.* (of a quantity etc.) having a value that can be stated. **7** *intr.* have understanding or knowledge. **8** *tr. archaic* have sexual intercourse with. ● *n.* (in phr. **in the know**) *colloq.* well-informed; having special knowledge. □ **all one knows** (or **knows how**) **1** all one can (*did all he knew to stop it*). **2** *adv.* to the utmost of one's power (*tried all she knew*). **before one knows where one is** with baffling speed. **be not to know 1** have no way of learning (*wasn't to know they'd arrive late*). **2** be not to be told (*she's not to know about the party*). **don't I know it!** *colloq.* an expression of rueful assent. **don't you know** *colloq.* or *joc.* an expression used for emphasis (*such a bore, don't you know*). **for all** (or **aught**) **I know** so far as my knowledge extends. **have been known to** be known to have done (*they have been known to not turn up*). **I knew it!** I was sure that this would happen. **I know what** I have a new idea, suggestion, etc. **know about** have information about. **know-all** *colloq.* a person who seems to know everything. **know best** be or claim to be better informed etc. than others. **know better than** (foll. by *that*, or *to* + infin.) be wise, well-informed, or well-mannered enough to avoid (specified behaviour etc.). **know by name 1** have heard the name of. **2** be able to give the name of. **know by sight** recognize the appearance (only) of. **know how** know the way to do something. **know-how** *n.* **1** practical knowledge; technique, expertise. **2** natural skill or invention. **know-it-all** = *know-all*. **know-nothing 1** an ignorant person. **2** an agnostic. **know of** be aware of; have heard of (*not that I know of*). **know one's own mind** be decisive, not vacillate. **know the ropes** (or **one's stuff**) be fully knowledgeable or experienced. **know a thing or two** be experienced or shrewd. **know what's what** have adequate knowledge of the world, life, etc. **know who's who** be aware of who or what each person is. **not if I know it** only against my will. **not know that ...** *colloq.* be fairly sure that ... not (*I don't know that I want to go*). **not know what hit one** be suddenly injured, killed, disconcerted, etc. **not want to know** refuse to take any notice of. **what do you know** (or **know about that**)? *colloq.* an expression of surprise. **you know** *colloq.* **1** an expression implying something generally known or known to the hearer (*you know, the pub on the corner*). **2** an expression used as a gap-filler in conversation. **you know something** (or **what**)? I am going to tell you something. **you-know-what** (or **-who**) a thing or person unspecified but understood. **you never know** nothing in the future is certain. □□ **knowable** *adj.* **knower** *n.* [OE *(ge)cnāwan*, rel. to CAN[1], KEN]

■ *v.* **1 a** understand, comprehend, be familiar with, grasp, be acquainted with, be versed in, be skilled in, have at one's fingertips. **b** be aware of, be conscious of, be cognizant of, be informed of, be advised of, have knowledge of. **2** be acquainted with, be familiar with, be friendly with, be a friend of. **3 a** recognize, identify, place, recall, remember, recollect. **c** distinguish, separate, differentiate, discriminate. **5** see EXPERIENCE *v.* 2. **6** (**known**) **a** see *well-known*. ● *n.* (**in the know**) see *well-informed*. □ **know-all** see *wise guy*. **know-how** (*n.*) see TECHNIQUE 1. **know one's own mind** be decided, be resolved, be firm, be resolute, be decisive, be sure, be certain, be positive, be (self-)assured, be (self-)confident, be in touch with oneself.

knowing /nōing/ *n.* & *adj.* ● *n.* the state of being aware or informed of any thing. ● *adj.* **1** usu. *derog.* cunning; sly. **2** showing knowledge; shrewd. □ **there is no knowing** no one can tell. □□ **knowingness** *n.*

■ *n.* see KNOWLEDGE 1. ● *adj.* **1** conspiratorial, conspiratory, secret, private; significant, meaningful, eloquent, expressive; shrewd, canny, artful, sly, leery, wily, crafty, cunning. **2** wise, clever, shrewd, (well-)informed, knowledgeable, aware, expert, qualified, astute, perceptive, intelligent, sagacious.

knowingly /nōingli/ *adv.* **1** consciously; intentionally (*had never knowingly injured him*). **2** in a knowing manner (*smiled knowingly*).

■ **1** see *deliberately* (DELIBERATE).

knowledge /nóllij/ *n.* **1 a** (usu. foll. by *of*) awareness or familiarity gained by experience (of a person, fact, or thing) (*have no knowledge of their character*). **b** a person's range of information (*is not within his knowledge*). **c** specific information; facts or intelligence about something (*received knowledge of their imminent departure*). **2 a** (usu. foll. by *of*) a theoretical or practical understanding of a subject, language, etc. (*has a good knowledge of Greek*). **b** the sum of what is known (*every branch of knowledge*). **c** learning, scholarship. **3** *Philos.* true, justified belief; certain understanding, as opp. to opinion. **4** = *carnal knowledge.* □ **come to one's knowledge** become known to one. **to my knowledge 1** so far as I know. **2** as I know for certain. [ME *knaulege*, with earlier *knawlechen* (v.) formed as KNOW + OE *-lǣcan* f. *lāc* as in WEDLOCK]

■ **1 a** knowing, familiarity, awareness, apprehension, cognition, grasp, understanding, discernment, consciousness, conception, insight. **b** ken, perception. **c** facts, information, data, intelligence. **2 a** acquaintance, acquaintanceship, familiarity, understanding, appreciation, conversance, expertise, experience, adeptness, proficiency. **c** schooling, education, scholarship, instruction, learning, erudition.

knowledgeable /nóllijəb'l/ *adj.* (also **knowledgable**) well-informed; intelligent. □□ **knowledgeability** /-billiti/ *n.* **knowledgeableness** *n.* **knowledgeably** *adv.*

■ aware, *au fait*, *au courant*, up to date, (well-)informed, (well-)acquainted, cognizant, familiar, enlightened, expert, knowing, *colloq.* in the know; well-educated, erudite, learned, cultured, well-read, intelligent, sophisticated, (worldly-)wise, sage, sagacious.

known *past part.* of KNOW.

Knt. *abbr.* Knight.

knuckle /núkk'l/ *n.* & *v.* ● *n.* **1** the bone at a finger-joint, esp. that adjoining the hand. **2 a** a projection of the carpal or tarsal joint of a quadruped. **b** a joint of meat consisting of this with the adjoining parts, esp. of bacon or pork. ● *v.tr.* strike, press, or rub with the knuckles. □ **go the knuckle** *Austral. sl.* fight, punch. **knuckle-bone 1** bone forming a knuckle. **2** the bone of a sheep or other animal corresponding to or resembling a knuckle. **3** a knuckle of meat. **knuckle-bones 1** animal knuckle-bones used in the game of jacks. **2** the game of jacks. **knuckle down** (often foll. by *to*) **1** apply oneself seriously (to a task etc.). **2** give in; submit. **knuckle sandwich** *sl.* a punch in the mouth. **knuckle under** give in; submit. **rap on** (or **over**) **the knuckles** see RAP[1]. □□ **knuckly** *adj.* [ME *knokel* f. MLG, MDu. *knökel*, dimin. of *knoke* bone]

■ □ **knuckle down 1** see APPLY 5; see (*knuckle down to*) *buckle* (*down*) *to*. **2** see SUBMIT 1a, BUCKLE *v.* 2. **knuckle under** see SUBMIT 1a, BUCKLE *v.* 2. **rap on** (or **over**) **the knuckles** see CASTIGATE.

knuckleduster /núkk'ldustər/ *n.* a metal guard worn over the knuckles in fighting, esp. to increase the effect of the blows.

knucklehead /núkk'lhed/ *n. colloq.* a slow-witted or stupid person.

knur /nur/ *n.* (also **knurr**) **1** a hard excrescence on the trunk of a tree. **2** a hard concretion. [ME *knorre*, var. of KNAR]

knurl /nurl/ *n.* a small projecting knob, ridge, etc. □□ **knurled** /nurld/ *adj.* [KNUR]

KO *abbr.* **1** knockout. **2** kick-off.

■ **1** knockout, *coup de grâce*, *colloq.* kayo.

koa /kṓə/ *n.* **1** a Hawaiian tree, *Acacia koa*, which produces dark red wood. **2** this wood. [Hawaiian]

koala /kō-áalə/ *n.* an Australian bearlike marsupial, *Phascolarctos cinereus*, having thick grey fur and feeding on eucalyptus leaves. ¶ The fuller form *koala bear* is now considered incorrect. [Aboriginal *kūl(l)a*]

koan /kṓ-an/ *n.* a riddle used in Zen Buddhism to demonstrate the inadequacy of logical reasoning. [Jap., = public matter (for thought)]

kobold /kṓbold/ *n.* (in Germanic mythology): **1** a familiar spirit; a brownie. **2** an underground spirit in mines etc. [G]

■ **1** see IMP *n.* 2.

Köchel number /kṓkh'l/ *n. Mus.* a number given to each of Mozart's compositions in the complete catalogue of his works compiled by Köchel and his successors. [L. von *Köchel*, Austrian scientist d. 1877]

KO'd /kayṓd/ *adj.* knocked out. [abbr.]

Kodiak /kṓdiak/ *n.* (in full **Kodiak bear**) a large Alaskan brown bear, *Ursus arctos middendorffi*. [*Kodiak* Island, Alaska]

koel /kṓəl/ *n.* a dark-coloured cuckoo, *Eudynamys scolopacea*. [Hindi *kōīl* f. Skr. *kokila*]

kohl /kōl/ *n.* a black powder, usu. antimony sulphide or lead sulphide, used as eye make-up esp. in Eastern countries. [Arab. *kuḥl*]

kohlrabi /kōlraábi/ *n.* (*pl.* **kohlrabies**) a variety of cabbage with an edible turnip-like swollen stem. [G f. It. *cavoli rape* (pl.) f. med.L *caulorapa* (as COLE, RAPE[2])]

koine /kóyni/ *n.* **1** the common language of the Greeks from the close of the classical period to the Byzantine era. **2** a common language shared by various peoples; a lingua franca. [Gk *koinē* (*dialektos*) common (language)]

kola var. of COLA.

kolinsky /kəlínski/ *n.* (*pl.* **-ies**) **1** the Siberian mink, *Mustela sibirica*, having a brown coat in winter. **2** the fur of this. [Russ. *kolinskiĭ* f. *Kola* in NW Russia]

kolkhoz /kólkoz, kulk-háwz/ *n.* a collective farm in the former USSR. [Russ. f. *kollektivnoe khozyaĭstvo* collective farm]

komitadji (also **komitaji**) var. of COMITADJI.

komodo dragon /kəmṓdō/ *n.* (also **komodo lizard**) a large monitor lizard, *Varanus komodoensis*, native to the E. Indies. [*Komodo* Island in Indonesia]

Komsomol /kómsəmol/ *n. hist.* **1** an organization for Communist youth in the former Soviet Union. **2** a member of this. [Russ. f. *Kommunisticheskiĭ soyuz molodezhi* Communist League of Youth]

koodoo var. of KUDU.

kook /ko͞ok/ *n.* & *adj. US sl.* ● *n.* a crazy or eccentric person. ● *adj.* crazy; eccentric. [20th c.: prob. f. CUCKOO]

■ *n.* see WEIRDO.

kookaburra /ko͝okkəburrə/ *n.* any Australian kingfisher of the genus *Dacelo*, esp. *D. novaeguineae*, which makes a strange laughing cry. Also called *laughing jackass*. [Aboriginal]

kooky /ko͞oki/ *adj.* (**kookier**, **kookiest**) *sl.* crazy or eccentric. □□ **kookily** *adv.* **kookiness** *n.*

■ see MAD *adj.* 1.

kop /kop/ *n.* **1** *S.Afr.* a prominent hill or peak. **2** (**Kop**) *Football* a high bank of terracing for standing spectators, esp. supporting the home side. [Afrik. f. Du., = head: cf. COP[2]]

kopek (also **kopeck**) var. of COPECK.

kopi /kṓpi/ *n. Austral.* powdered gypsum. [Aboriginal]

koppie /kóppi/ *n.* (also **kopje**) *S.Afr.* a small hill. [Afrik. *koppie*, Du. *kopje*, dimin. of *kop* head]

koradji /kəráji/ *n.* (*pl.* **koradjis**) *Austral.* an Aboriginal medicine man. [Aboriginal]

Koran /koraán, kə-/ *n.* (also **Qur'an** /kə-/) the Islamic sacred book, believed to be the word of God as dictated to Muhammad and written down in Arabic. □□ **Koranic** /-ránnik, -raánik/ *adj.* [Arab. *ḳur'ān* recitation f. *ḳara'a* read]

■ see SCRIPTURE 2a.

Korean /kəreéən/ *n.* & *adj.* ● *n.* **1** a native or national of N. or S. Korea in SE Asia. **2** the language of Korea. ● *adj.* of or relating to Korea or its people or language.

korfball /kórfbawl/ *n.* a game like basketball played by two teams consisting of 6 men and 6 women each. [Du. *korfbal* f. *korf* basket + *bal* ball]

kosher /kṓshər, kósh-/ *adj.* & *n.* ● *adj.* **1** (of food or premises in which food is sold, cooked, or eaten) fulfilling the requirements of Jewish law. **2** *colloq.* correct; genuine; legitimate. ● *n.* **1** kosher food. **2** a kosher shop. [Heb. *kāšēr* proper]

■ *adj.* **2** see AUTHENTIC, PERMISSIBLE.

koto /kṓtō/ *n.* (*pl.* **-os**) a Japanese musical instrument with 13 long esp. silk strings. [Jap.]

kotow var. of KOWTOW.

koumiss /ko͞omiss/ *n.* (also **kumiss, kumis**) a fermented liquor prepared from esp. mare's milk, used by Asian nomads and medicinally. [Tartar *kumiz*]

kourbash /ko͝orbash/ *n.* (also **kurbash**) a whip, esp. of hippopotamus hide, used as an instrument of punishment in Turkey and Egypt. [Arab. *kurbāj* f. Turk. *kırbāç* whip]

kowhai /kṓ-wī/ *n.* any of several trees or shrubs of the genus *Sophora*, esp. *S. microphylla* native to New Zealand, with pendant clusters of yellow flowers. [Maori]

kowtow /kowtów/ *n.* & *v.* (also **kotow** /kōtów/) ● *n. hist.* the Chinese custom of kneeling and touching the ground with the forehead in worship or submission. ● *v.intr.* **1** *hist.* perform the kowtow. **2** (usu. foll. by *to*) act obsequiously. [Chin. *ketou* f. *ke* knock + *tou* head]

▪ *v.* **2** genuflect, salaam, prostrate oneself, bow (down), pay court, (bow and) scrape, cringe, fawn, grovel, toady, pander, truckle; (*kowtow to*) dance attendance on, play up to, lick a person's boots, *US* shine up, *colloq.* butter up, suck up to.

KP *n. US Mil. colloq.* **1** enlisted men detailed to help the cooks. **2** kitchen duty. [abbr. of *kitchen police*]

k.p.h. *abbr.* kilometres per hour.

Kr *symb. Chem.* the element krypton.

kraal /kraal/ *n. S.Afr.* **1** a village of huts enclosed by a fence. **2** an enclosure for cattle or sheep. [Afrik. f. Port. *curral*, of Hottentot orig.]

kraft /kraaft/ *n.* (in full **kraft paper**) a kind of strong smooth brown wrapping paper. [G f. Sw., = strength]

krait /krīt/ *n.* any venomous snake of the genus *Bungarus* of E. Asia. [Hindi *karait*]

kraken /kraákən/ *n.* a large mythical sea-monster said to appear off the coast of Norway. [Norw.]

krans /kraanss/ *n. S.Afr.* a precipitous or overhanging wall of rocks. [Afrik. f. Du. *krans* coronet]

Kraut /krowt/ *n. sl. offens.* a German. [shortening of SAUERKRAUT]

kremlin /krémlin/ *n.* **1** a citadel within a Russian town. **2** (**the Kremlin**) **a** the citadel in Moscow. **b** the Russian or former USSR Government housed within it. [F, f. Russ. *Kreml'*, of Tartar orig.]

kriegspiel /kreégshpeel/ *n.* **1** a war-game in which blocks representing armies etc. are moved about on maps. **2** a form of chess with an umpire, in which each player has only limited information about the opponent's moves. [G f. *Krieg* war + *Spiel* game]

▪ **1** exercise, war-game, training; manoeuvres.

krill /kril/ *n.* tiny planktonic crustaceans found in the seas around the Antarctic and eaten by baleen whales. [Norw. *kril* tiny fish]

krimmer /krímmər/ *n.* a grey or black fur obtained from the wool of young Crimean lambs. [G f. *Krim* Crimea]

kris /kreess/ *n.* (also **crease, creese**) a Malay or Indonesian dagger with a wavy blade. [ult. f. Malay *k(i)rīs*]

▪ see DAGGER.

Krishnaism /kríshnəiz'm/ *n. Hinduism* the worship of Krishna as an incarnation of Vishnu.

kromesky /krəméski/ *n.* (*pl.* **-ies**) a croquette of minced meat or fish, rolled in bacon and fried. [app. f. Pol. *kromeczka* small slice]

krona /krṓnə/ *n.* **1** (*pl.* **kronor** /krṓnər/) the chief monetary unit of Sweden. **2** (*pl.* **kronur** /krṓnər/) the chief monetary unit of Iceland. [Sw. & Icel., = CROWN]

krone /krṓnə/ *n.* (*pl.* **kroner** /krṓnər/) the chief monetary unit of Denmark and of Norway. [Da. & Norw., = CROWN]

Kroo var. of KRU.

Kru /kro͞o/ *n.* & *adj.* (also **Kroo**) ● *n.* (*pl.* same) a member of a Black seafaring people on the coast of Liberia. ● *adj.* of or concerning the Kru. [W. Afr.]

krugerrand /kro͞ogərand, -raant/ *n.* a S. African gold coin depicting President Kruger. [S. J. P. *Kruger*, S. Afr. statesman d. 1904, + RAND[1]]

krummhorn /krúmhorn/ *n.* (also **crumhorn**) a medieval wind instrument with a double reed and a curved end. [G f. *krumm* crooked + *Horn* HORN]

krypton /krípton/ *n. Chem.* an inert gaseous element of the noble gas group, forming a small portion of the earth's atmosphere and used in fluorescent lamps etc. ¶ Symb.: **Kr**. [Gk *krupton* hidden, neut. adj. f. *kruptō* hide]

KS *abbr.* **1** *US* Kansas (in official postal use). **2** *Brit.* King's Scholar.

Kshatriya /kshátriə, kshaá-/ *n.* a member of the second of the four great Hindu castes, the military caste. [Skr. f. *kshatra* rule]

K. St. J. *abbr.* Knight of the Order of St John.

KT *abbr.* **1** Knight Templar. **2** (in the UK) Knight of the Order of the Thistle.

Kt. *abbr.* Knight.

kt. *abbr.* knot.

Ku *symb. Chem.* the element kurchatovium.

kudos /kyo͞odoss/ *n. colloq.* glory; renown. [Gk]

▪ praise, acclaim, glory, fame, renown, prestige, honour, plaudit(s), applause, admiration, acclamation, accolade, *formal* laudation.

kudu /ko͞odo͞o/ *n.* (also **koodoo**) either of two African antelopes, *Tragelaphus strepsiceros* or *T. imberbis*, with white stripes and corkscrew-shaped ridged horns. [Xhosa-Kaffir *iqudu*]

kudzu /kúdzo͞o/ *n.* (in full **kudzu vine**) a quick-growing climbing plant, *Pueraria thunbergiana*, with reddish-purple flowers. [Jap. *kuzu*]

Kufic /kyo͞ofik/ *n.* & *adj.* (also **Cufic**) ● *n.* an early angular form of the Arabic alphabet found chiefly in decorative inscriptions. ● *adj.* of or in this type of script. [*Cufa*, a city S. of Baghdad in Iraq]

Ku Klux Klan /ko͞o kluks klán, kyo͞o-/ *n.* a secret society of White people in the southern States of the US, orig. formed after the Civil War and dedicated to persecuting and terrorizing Blacks. ▫▫ **Ku Klux Klansman** *n.* (*pl.* **-men**). [perh. f. Gk *kuklos* circle + CLAN]

kukri /ko͝okri/ *n.* (*pl.* **kukris**) a curved knife broadening towards the point, used by Gurkhas. [Hindi *kukrī*]

kulak /ko͞olak/ *n. hist.* a peasant working for personal profit in Soviet Russia. [Russ., = fist, tight-fisted person]

kulan /ko͞olən/ *n.* a wild ass of SW Asia, closely related to the kiang. [Tartar]

kultur /ko͝oltoór/ *n.* esp. *derog.* German civilization and culture, seen as racist, authoritarian, and militaristic. [G f. L *cultura* CULTURE]

kulturkampf /ko͝oltoórkampf/ *n. hist.* the conflict in 19th-c. Germany between the civil and ecclesiastical authorities esp. as regards the control of schools. [G (as KULTUR, *Kampf* struggle)]

kumara /ko͞omərə/ *n. NZ* a sweet potato. [Maori]

kumis (also **kumiss**) var. of KOUMISS.

kümmel /ko͝omm'l/ *n.* a sweet liqueur flavoured with caraway and cumin seeds. [G (as CUMIN)]

kumquat /kúmkwot/ *n.* (also **cumquat**) **1** an orange-like fruit with a sweet rind and acid pulp, used in preserves. **2** any shrub or small tree of the genus *Fortunella* yielding this. [Cantonese var. of Chin. *kin kü* golden orange]

kung fu /ko͝ong fo͞o, kung/ *n.* the Chinese form of karate. [Chin. *gongfu* f. *gong* merit + *fu* master]

kurbash var. of KOURBASH.

kurchatovium /kúrchətṓviəm/ *n. Chem.* = RUTHERFORDIUM. ¶ Symb.: **Ku**. [I. V. *Kurchatov*, Russ. physicist d. 1960]

Kurd /kurd/ *n.* a member of a mainly pastoral Aryan Islamic people living in Kurdistan (contiguous areas of Iraq, Iran, and Turkey). [Kurdish]

kurdaitcha /kərdíchə/ *n. Austral.* **1** the tribal use of a bone in spells intended to cause sickness or death. **2** a man empowered to point the bone at a victim. [Aboriginal]

Kurdish /kúrdish/ *adj.* & *n.* ● *adj.* of or relating to the Kurds or their language. ● *n.* the Iranian language of the Kurds.

kurrajong /kúrrəjong/ *n.* (also **currajong**) an Australian tree, *Brachychiton populneum*, which produces a tough bast fibre. [Aboriginal]

kursaal /ko͝orzaal/ *n.* **1** a building for the use of visitors at a health resort, esp. at a German spa. **2** a casino. [G f. *Kur* CURE + *Saal* room]

kurta /kúrtə/ *n.* (also **kurtha**) a loose shirt or tunic worn by esp. Hindu men and women. [Hind.]

kurtosis /kurtṓsiss/ *n. Statistics* the sharpness of the peak of a frequency-distribution curve. [mod.L f. Gk *kurtōsis* bulging f. *kurtos* convex]

kV *abbr.* kilovolt(s).

kvass /kvaass/ *n.* a fermented beverage, low in alcohol, made from rye-flour or bread with malt in the former Soviet Union. [Russ. *kvas*]

kvetch /kvech/ *n.* & *v. US sl.* ● *n.* an objectionable person, esp. one who complains a great deal. ● *v.* complain, whine. □□ **kvetcher** *n.*

kW *abbr.* kilowatt(s).

KWAC /kwak/ *n. Computing* etc. keyword and context. [abbr.]

kwacha /kwaáchə/ *n.* the chief monetary unit of Zambia. [native word, = dawn]

kwashiorkor /kwóshiórkor/ *n.* a form of malnutrition caused by a protein deficiency of diet, esp. in young children in the tropics. [native name in Ghana]

kWh *abbr.* kilowatt-hour(s).

KWIC /kwik/ *n. Computing* etc. keyword in context. [abbr.]

KWOC /kwok/ *n. Computing* etc. keyword out of context. [abbr.]

KY *abbr. US* Kentucky (in official postal use).

Ky. *abbr.* Kentucky.

kyanite /kíənīt/ *n.* a blue crystalline mineral of aluminium silicate. □□ **kyanitic** /-níttik/ *adj.* [Gk *kuanos* dark blue]

kyanize /kíənīz/ *v.tr.* (also **-ise**) treat (wood) with a solution of corrosive sublimate to prevent decay. [J. H. *Kyan*, Ir. inventor d. 1850]

kybosh var. of KIBOSH.

kyle /kīl/ *n.* (in Scotland) a narrow channel between islands or between an island and the mainland. [Gael. *caol* strait]

kylie /kīli/ *n. W. Austral.* a boomerang. [Aboriginal]

kylin /keélin/ *n.* a mythical composite animal figured on Chinese and Japanese ceramics. [Chin. *qilin* f. *qi* male + *lin* female]

kyloe /kīlō/ *n. Brit.* **1** an animal of a breed of small usu. black long-horned highland cattle. **2** this breed. [*Kyloe* in Northumberland]

kymograph /kīməgraaf/ *n.* an instrument for recording variations in pressure, e.g. in sound waves or in blood within blood-vessels. □□ **kymographic** /-gráffik/ *adj.* [Gk *kuma* wave + -GRAPH]

kyphosis /kīfṓsiss/ *n. Med.* excessive outward curvature of the spine, causing hunching of the back (opp. LORDOSIS). □□ **kyphotic** /-fóttik/ *adj.* [mod.L f. Gk *kuphōsis* f. *kuphos* bent]

Kyrie /keériay/ (in full **Kyrie eleison** /iláyizon, -son, ayláy-/) *n.* **1 a** a short repeated invocation used in the RC and Greek Orthodox Churches, esp. at the beginning of the Mass. **b** a response sometimes used in the Anglican Communion Service. **2** a musical setting of the Kyrie. [ME f. med.L f. Gk *Kurie eleēson* Lord, have mercy]

L

L[1] /el/ *n.* (also **l**) (*pl.* **Ls** or **L's**) **1** the twelfth letter of the alphabet. **2** (as a Roman numeral) 50. **3** a thing shaped like an L, esp. a joint connecting two pipes at right angles.

L[2] *abbr.* (also **L.**) **1** Lake. **2** *Brit.* learner driver (cf. L-PLATE). **3** Liberal. **4** Licentiate. **5** *Biol.* Linnaeus. **6** Lire.

l *abbr.* (also **l.**) **1** left. **2** line. **3** litre(s). **4** length. **5** *archaic* pound(s) (money).

£ *abbr.* (preceding a numeral) pound or pounds (of money). [L *libra*]

LA *abbr.* **1** Library Association. **2** Los Angeles. **3** *US* Louisiana (in official postal use).

La *symb. Chem.* the element lanthanum.

La. *abbr.* Louisiana.

la var. of LAH.

laager /la͞agər/ *n.* & *v.* ● *n.* **1** esp. *S.Afr.* a camp or encampment, esp. formed by a circle of wagons. **2** *Mil.* a park for armoured vehicles. ● *v.* **1** *tr.* **a** form (vehicles) into a laager. **b** encamp (people) in a laager. **2** *intr.* encamp. [Afrik. f. Du. *leger*: see LEAGUER[2]]

Lab. *abbr.* **1** Labour. **2** Labrador.

lab /lab/ *n. colloq.* a laboratory. [abbr.]

labarum /lábbərəm/ *n.* **1** a symbolic banner. **2** Constantine the Great's imperial standard, with Christian symbols added to Roman military symbols. [LL: orig. unkn.]
▪ **1** see STANDARD *n.* 4.

labdanum var. of LADANUM.

labefaction /lábbifáksh'n/ *n. literary* a shaking, weakening, or downfall. [L *labefacere* weaken f. *labi* fall + *facere* make]

label /láyb'l/ *n.* & *v.* ● *n.* **1** a usu. small piece of paper, card, linen, metal, etc., for attaching to an object and giving its name, information about it, instructions for use, etc. **2** esp. *derog.* a short classifying phrase or name applied to a person, a work of art, etc. **3 a** a small fabric label sewn into a garment bearing the maker's name. **b** the logo, title, or trademark of esp. a fashion or recording company (*brought it out under his own label*). **c** the piece of paper in the centre of a gramophone record describing its contents etc. **4** an adhesive stamp on a parcel etc. **5** a word placed before, after, or in the course of a dictionary definition etc. to specify its subject, register, nationality, etc. **6** *Archit.* a dripstone. **7** *Heraldry* the mark of an eldest son, consisting of a superimposed horizontal bar with usu. three downward projections. ● *v.tr.* (**labelled, labelling**) **1** attach a label to. **2** (usu. foll. by *as*) assign to a category (*labelled them as irresponsible*). **3 a** replace (an atom) by an atom of a usu. radioactive isotope as a means of identification. **b** replace an atom in (a molecule) or atoms in the molecules of (a substance). **4** (as **labelled** *adj.*) made identifiable by the replacement of atoms. ▫▫ **labeller** *n.* [ME f. OF, = ribbon, prob. f. Gmc (as LAP[1])]
▪ *n.* **1** ticket, sticker, stamp, imprint, hallmark, earmark, mark, marker, (price) tag, tally, name-tag, name-tape, name-plate, identification, identifier, *Brit.* docket, *esp. US* ID; book-plate, ex-libris; care-label; bar-code. **2** name, denomination, designation, category, classification, characterization, description, term, tag, epithet; sobriquet, nickname, *colloq.* handle, *formal* appellation, *sl.* moniker. **3** trade mark, trade name, brand, logo, mark, device, design, *Brit. archaic* chop. ● *v.* **1** ticket, tag, stamp, imprint, hallmark, earmark, brand, mark, docket, identify. **2** name, denominate, designate, call, term, dub, brand, classify, categorize, pigeon-hole, class, characterize, describe, portray, identify.

labia *pl.* of LABIUM.

labial /láybiəl/ *adj.* & *n.* ● *adj.* **1 a** of the lips. **b** *Zool.* of, like, or serving as a lip, a liplike part, or a labium. **2** *Dentistry* designating the surface of a tooth adjacent to the lips. **3** *Phonet.* (of a sound) requiring partial or complete closure of the lips (e.g. *p, b, f, v, m, w*; and vowels in which lips are rounded, e.g. *oo* in moon). ● *n. Phonet.* a labial sound. ▫ **labial pipe** *Mus.* an organ-pipe having lips; a flue-pipe. ▫▫ **labialism** *n.* **labialize** *v.tr.* (also **-ise**). **labially** *adv.* [med.L *labialis* f. L *labia* lips]

labiate /láybiət/ *n.* & *adj.* ● *n.* any plant of the family Labiatae, including mint and rosemary, having square stems and a corolla or calyx divided into two parts suggesting lips. ● *adj.* **1** *Bot.* of or relating to the Labiatae. **2** *Bot.* & *Zool.* like a lip or labium. [mod.L *labiatus* (as LABIUM)]

labile /láybīl, -bil/ *adj. Chem.* (of a compound) unstable; liable to displacement or change esp. if an atom or group is easily replaced by other atoms or groups. ▫▫ **lability** /ləbílliti/ *n.* [ME f. LL *labilis* f. *labi* to fall]
▪ see CHANGEABLE 1.

labio- /láybiō/ *comb. form* of the lips. [as LABIUM]

labiodental /láybiōdént'l/ *adj.* (of a sound) made with the lips and teeth, e.g. *f* and *v*.

labiovelar /láybiōveélər/ *adj.* (of a sound) made with the lips and soft palate, e.g. *w*.

labium /láybiəm/ *n.* (*pl.* **labia** /-biə/) **1** (usu. in *pl.*) *Anat.* each of the two pairs of skin folds that enclose the vulva. **2** the lower lip in the mouth-parts of an insect or crustacean. **3** a lip, esp. the lower one of a labiate plant's corolla. ▫ **labia majora** /məjórə/ the larger outer pair of labia (in sense 1). **labia minora** /minórə/ the smaller inner pair of labia (in sense 1). [L, = lip]

labor etc. *US* & *Austral.* var. of LABOUR etc.

laboratory /ləbórrətəri, -tri/ *n.* (*pl.* **-ies**) a room or building fitted out for scientific experiments, research, teaching, or the manufacture of drugs and chemicals. [med.L *laboratorium* f. L *laborare* LABOUR]

laborious /ləbóriəss/ *adj.* **1** needing hard work or toil (*a laborious task*). **2** (esp. of literary style) showing signs of toil; pedestrian; not fluent. ▫▫ **laboriously** *adv.* **laboriousness** *n.* [ME f. OF *laborieus* f. L *laboriosus* (as LABOUR)]
▪ **1** arduous, strenuous, toilsome, difficult, tough, hard, stiff, Herculean, burdensome, onerous, ponderous, back-breaking, gruelling, painful, exhausting, taxing, tiring, fatiguing, wearying, wearisome, uphill. **2** laboured, strained, forced, artificial, ponderous, stilted, pedestrian, stiff, unnatural, wooden; deliberate, affected, studied.

labour /láybər/ *n.* & *v.* (*US, Austral.* **labor**) ● *n.* **1 a** physical or mental work; exertion; toil. **b** such work considered as supplying the needs of a community. **2 a** workers, esp. manual, considered as a class or political force (*a dispute between capital and labour*). **b** (**Labour**) the Labour Party. **3** the process of childbirth, esp. the period from the start of uterine contractions to delivery (*has been in labour for three hours*). **4** a particular task, esp. of a difficult nature. ● *v.* **1** *intr.* work hard; exert oneself. **2** *intr.* (usu. foll. by *for*, or *to* + infin.) strive for a purpose (*laboured to fulfil his promise*). **3** *tr.* **a** treat at excessive length; elaborate needlessly (*I will not labour the point*). **b** (as **laboured** *adj.*) done with great effort; not spontaneous or fluent. **4** *intr.* (often foll. by *under*) suffer under (a disadvantage or delusion) (*laboured under universal disapproval*). **5** *intr.* proceed with trouble or difficulty (*laboured slowly up the hill*). **6** *intr.* (of a ship) roll or pitch heavily. **7** *tr. archaic* or *poet.* till (the ground). □ **labour camp** a prison camp enforcing a regime of hard labour. **Labour Day** May 1 (or in the US and Canada the first Monday in September), celebrated in honour of working people. **Labour Exchange** *Brit. colloq.* or *hist.* an employment exchange; a jobcentre. **labour force** the body of workers employed, esp. at a single plant. **labouring man** a labourer. **labour-intensive** (of a form of work) needing a large work force. **labour in vain** make a fruitless effort. **labour-market** the supply of labour with reference to the demand on it. **labour of Hercules** a task needing enormous strength or effort. **labour of love** a task done for pleasure, not reward. **Labour Party 1** a British political party formed to represent the interests of ordinary working people. **2** any similar political party in other countries. **labour-saving** (of an appliance etc.) designed to reduce or eliminate work. **labour union** *US* a trade union. **lost labour** fruitless effort. [ME f. OF *labo(u)r*, *labourer* f. L *labor*, *-oris*, *laborare*]

■ *n.* **1** toil, (hard) work, exertion, effort, industry, slog, strain, drudgery, donkey-work, pains, trouble, slavery, *colloq.* sweat, grind, elbow-grease, *Brit. colloq.* fag, *literary* travail, *sl.* (hard) graft, *Austral. sl.* yakka. **2 a** workers, workforce, employees, labourers, workmen, workpeople, working people, (labour) force, (the) factory floor, (the) shop floor, men, help; wage-earners, (the) working class. **b** (*Labour*) see *Labour Party* below. **3** childbirth, *accouchement*, confinement, *archaic* childbed, *formal* parturition, *literary* travail; labour pains, contractions, throes; delivery. **4** task, job, chore, undertaking, mission, assignment, stint, trial. ● *v.* **1, 2** work, toil, exert oneself, sweat, slave (away), peg away, slog (away), beaver (away), grind (away), drudge, strain, strive, struggle, *Brit. colloq.* swot, *literary* travail. **3 a** belabour, dwell on, overdo, overemphasize, harp on, overstress, (over)strain, stretch, force, press, push. **b** (**laboured**) strained, forced, difficult, hard, laborious, heavy; overdone, excessive, overwrought, ornate, elaborate, overworked, over-embellished, contrived, affected, artificial, unnatural. **4** (*labour under*) suffer under, endure, struggle with *or* under, bear, undergo, live *or* go through, submit to, be disadvantaged by. **5** work (one's way), struggle, grind, slog, plough, lumber, plod, trudge, tramp, make one's way. **6** see PITCH[1] *v.* 6. □ **labour camp** prison camp, concentration camp, *hist.* Stalag. **labour force** see LABOUR *n.* 2a above. **Labour Party** the left, left-wingers, socialists.

labourer /láybərər/ *n.* (*US* **laborer**) **1** a person doing unskilled, usu. manual, work for wages. **2** a person who labours. [ME f. OF *laboureur* (as LABOUR)]

■ **1** worker, workman, working man, labouring man, artisan, hand, blue-collar worker, manual worker, slave, drudge, coolie, khalasi, hodman, roustabout, *hist.* serf, *Austral.* & *NZ* rouseabout, *Brit.* navvy; peasant, peon, fellah, *hist.* muzhik, kulak, *Brit.* Hodge, *Sc.* & *hist.* cottar.

Labourite /láybərīt/ *n.* (also *US* **Laborite**) a member or follower of the Labour Party.

labra *pl.* of LABRUM.

Labrador /lábrədor/ *n.* (in full **Labrador dog** or **retriever**) **1** a retriever of a breed with a black or golden coat often used as a gun dog or as a guide for a blind person. **2** this breed. [*Labrador* in Canada]

labret /lábrit/ *n.* a piece of shell, bone, etc., inserted in the lip as an ornament. [LABRUM]

labrum /láybrəm/ *n.* (*pl.* **labra** /-brə/) the upper lip in the mouth-parts of an insect. [L, = lip: rel. to LABIUM]

laburnum /ləbúrnəm/ *n.* any small tree of the genus *Laburnum* with racemes of golden flowers yielding poisonous seeds. Also called *golden chain*. [L]

labyrinth /lábbərinth/ *n.* **1** a complicated irregular network of passages or paths etc.; a maze. **2** an intricate or tangled arrangement. **3** *Anat.* the complex arrangement of bony and membranous canals and chambers of the inner ear which constitute the organs of hearing and balance. □ **labyrinth fish** = GOURAMI. □□ **labyrinthian** /-rínthiən/ *adj.* **labyrinthine** /-rínthīn/ *adj.* [F *labyrinthe* or L *labyrinthus* f. Gk *laburinthos*]

■ **1** maze; complex, network, web, criss-cross, plexus, warren. **2** tangle, jungle, snarl, knot; see also TANGLE[1] *n.* □□ **labyrinthian, labyrinthine** maze-like, mazy, tortuous, convoluted, intricate, involute, complicated, complex, Byzantine, tangled, knotty; confusing, perplexing, puzzling, enigmatic, baffling.

LAC *abbr.* Leading Aircraftman.

lac[1] /lak/ *n.* a resinous substance secreted as a protective covering by the lac insect, and used to make varnish and shellac. □ **lac insect** an Asian scale insect, *Laccifer lacca*, living in trees. [ult. f. Hind. *lākh* f. Prakrit *lakkha* f. Skr. *lākṣā*]

lac[2] var. of LAKH.

laccolith /lákkəlith/ *n. Geol.* a lens-shaped intrusion of igneous rock which thrusts the overlying strata into a dome. [Gk *lakkos* reservoir + -LITH]

lace /layss/ *n.* & *v.* ● *n.* **1** a fine open fabric, esp. of cotton or silk, made by weaving thread in patterns and used esp. to trim blouses, underwear, etc. **2** a cord or leather strip passed through eyelets or hooks on opposite sides of a shoe, corsets, etc., pulled tight and fastened. **3** braid used for trimming esp. dress uniform (*gold lace*). ● *v.* **1** *tr.* (usu. foll. by *up*) **a** fasten or tighten (a shoe, corsets, etc.) with a lace or laces. **b** compress the waist of (a person) with a laced corset. **2** *tr.* flavour or fortify (coffee, beer, etc.) with a dash of spirits. **3** *tr.* (usu. foll. by *with*) **a** streak (a sky etc.) with colour (*cheek laced with blood*). **b** interlace or embroider (fabric) with thread etc. **4** *tr.* & (foll. by *into*) *intr. colloq.* lash, beat, defeat. **5** *tr.* (often foll. by *through*) pass (a shoelace etc.) through. **6** *tr.* trim with lace. □ **lace-glass** Venetian glass with lacelike designs. **lace-pillow** a cushion placed on the lap and providing support in lacemaking. **lace-up** ● *n.* a shoe fastened with a lace. ● *attrib.adj.* (of a shoe etc.) fastened by a lace or laces. [ME f. OF *laz*, *las*, *lacier* ult. f. L *laqueus* noose]

■ *n.* **1** openwork, filigree, tracery, net, netting, bobbinet, mesh, web; needle-point, needle-lace, point-lace, filet, bobbin-lace, pillow-lace, crochet, tatting, macramé. **2** shoelace, shoestring, bootlace, cord, string, thong, tie, lacing. **3** braid, edging, trimming, braiding, *passementerie*, ricrac, soutache, fringe, ruff, ruffle, lacing, *archaic* purfling, *hist.* tucker, *colloq.* scrambled egg. ● *v.* **1** fasten, tighten, tie (up), do up, secure, knot, truss. **2** fortify, strengthen, flavour, season, spice (up), enliven, liven up, *colloq.* spike. **3 a** streak, stripe, striate, line, mark, smear, daub. **b** interlace, embroider, thread, weave, interweave. **4** (*lace into*) see BEAT *v.* 1,3a. **5** thread, string, weave; loop. **6** trim, decorate, embellish, garnish, elaborate, adorn, ornament.

lacemaker /láysmaykər/ *n.* a person who makes lace, esp. professionally. □□ **lacemaking** *n.*

lacerate /lássərayt/ *v.tr.* **1** mangle or tear (esp. flesh or tissue). **2** distress or cause pain to (the feelings, the heart, etc.). □□ **lacerable** *adj.* **laceration** /-ráysh'n/ *n.* [L *lacerare* f. *lacer* torn]

▪ **1** mangle, tear, rip, gash, cut, hack, slash, claw, wound, *archaic or rhet.* rend. **2** see HURT *v.* 2. ▫▫ **laceration** see INJURY 1, TEAR[1] *n.* 1.

lacertian /ləsértiən/ *n.* & *adj.* (also **lacertilian** /lássərtílliən/, **lacertine** /lássərtīn/) ● *n.* any reptile of the suborder Lacertilia, including lizards. ● *adj.* of or relating to the Lacertilia; lizard-like, saurian. [L *lacerta* lizard]

lacewing /láyswing/ *n.* a neuropterous insect.

lacewood /láyswood/ *n.* the timber of the plane tree.

laches /láchiz, láy-/ *n. Law* delay in performing a legal duty, asserting a right, claiming a privilege, etc. [ME f. AF *laches(se)*, OF *laschesse* f. *lasche* ult. f. L *laxus* loose]

lachryma Christi /lákrimə krísti/ *n.* any of various wines from the slopes of Mt. Vesuvius. [L, = Christ's tear]

lachrymal /lákrim'l/ *adj.* & *n.* (also **lacrimal, lacrymal**) ● *adj.* **1** *literary* of or for tears. **2** (usu. as **lacrimal**) *Anat.* concerned in the secretion of tears (*lacrimal canal*; *lacrimal duct*). ● *n.* **1** = *lachrymal vase.* **2** (in *pl.*) (usu. as **lacrimals**) the lacrimal organs. ▫ **lachrymal vase** *hist.* a phial holding the tears of mourners at a funeral. [ME f. med.L *lachrymalis* f. L *lacrima* tear]

lachrymation /lákrimáysh'n/ *n.* (also **lacrimation, lacrymation**) *formal* the flow of tears. [L *lacrimatio* f. *lacrimare* weep (as LACHRYMAL)]

lachrymator /lákrimaytər/ *n.* an agent irritating the eyes, causing tears.

lachrymatory /lákrimətəri/ *adj.* & *n.* ● *adj. formal* of or causing tears. ● *n.* (*pl.* **-ies**) a name applied to phials of a kind found in ancient Roman tombs and thought to be lachrymal vases.

lachrymose /lákrimōss/ *adj. formal* given to weeping; tearful. ▫▫ **lachrymosely** *adv.* [L *lacrimosus* f. *lacrima* tear]
▪ see TEARFUL 1.

lacing /láysing/ *n.* **1** lace trimming, esp. on a uniform. **2** a laced fastening on a shoe or corsets. **3** *colloq.* a beating. **4** a dash of spirits in a beverage. ▫ **lacing course** a strengthening course built into an arch or wall.
▪ **2** see LACE *n.* 2.

laciniate /ləsinniət/ *adj.* (also **laciniated** /-niaytid/) *Bot.* & *Zool.* divided into deep narrow irregular segments; fringed. ▫▫ **laciniation** /-niáysh'n/ *n.* [L *lacinia* flap of a garment]

lack /lak/ *n.* & *v.* ● *n.* (usu. foll. by *of*) an absence, want, or deficiency (*a lack of talent*; *felt the lack of warmth*). ● *v.tr.* be without or deficient in (*lacks courage*). ▫ **for lack of** owing to the absence of (*went hungry for lack of money*). **lack for** lack. [ME *lac*, *lacen*, corresp. to MDu., MLG *lak* deficiency, MDu. *laken* to lack]
▪ *n.* absence, want, deficiency, need, dearth, famine, scarcity, shortage, paucity, poverty, insufficiency, deficit, inadequacy, defect. ● *v.* want (for), be deficient in, be *or* fall short of, be without, be *or* stand in want *or* need of; need, require.

lackadaisical /lákkədáyzik'l/ *adj.* **1** unenthusiastic; listless; idle. **2** feebly sentimental and affected. ▫▫ **lackadaisically** *adv.* **lackadaisicalness** *n.* [archaic *lackaday*, *-daisy* (int.): see ALACK]
▪ **1** unenthusiastic, dull, apathetic, insouciant, uncaring, careless, casual, unconcerned, indifferent, blasé, cold, cool, lukewarm, tepid, half-hearted, Laodicean, phlegmatic, unemotional, unexcitable, impassive, uninterested, unimpressed, uninspired, unmoved, unresponsive; listless, lethargic, languorous, languid, lazy, sluggish, lifeless, spiritless, weak, weary; idle, indolent, shiftless, inactive, torpid, slothful, fainéant. **2** see AFFECTED 3.

lacker var. of LACQUER.

lackey /lákki/ *n.* & *v.* (also **lacquey**) ● *n.* (*pl.* **-eys**) **1** *derog.* **a** a servile political follower. **b** an obsequious parasitical person. **2 a** a (usu. liveried) footman or manservant. **b** a servant. ● *v.tr.* (**-eys, -eyed**) *archaic* behave servilely to; dance attendance on. ▫ **lackey moth** a moth, *Malacosoma neustria*, developing from a brightly striped caterpillar. [F *laquais*, obs. *alaquais* f. Cat. *alacay* = Sp. ALCALDE]
▪ **2** see SERVANT 1.

lacking /lákking/ *adj.* **1** absent or deficient (*money was lacking*; *is lacking in determination*). **2** *colloq.* deficient in intellect; mentally subnormal.
▪ **1** see DEFICIENT 1.

lackland /lákland/ *n.* & *adj.* ● *n.* **1** a person having no land. **2** (**Lackland**) a nickname for King John of England. ● *adj.* having no land.

lacklustre /láklustər/ *adj.* (*US* **lackluster**) **1** lacking in vitality, force, or conviction. **2** (of the eye) dull.
▪ **1** drab, dull, lifeless, colourless, lustreless, dingy, dismal, dreary; unexciting, boring, tedious, uninteresting; prosaic, unimaginative, flat, one-dimensional, two-dimensional, insipid, vapid, bland, wishy-washy; undistinguished, indifferent, mediocre, *sl.* naff; half-hearted, unenthusiastic; flimsy, feeble, weak, puny, pale, poor, lame, unconvincing. **2** see DULL *adj.* 4b.

Laconian /ləkṓniən/ *n.* & *adj.* ● *n.* an inhabitant or the dialect of ancient Laconia. ● *adj.* of the Laconian dialect or people; Spartan. [L *Laconia* Sparta f. Gk *Lakōn* Spartan]

laconic /ləkónnik/ *adj.* **1** (of a style of speech or writing) brief; concise; terse. **2** (of a person) laconic in speech etc. ▫▫ **laconically** *adv.* **laconicism** /-nisiz'm/ *n.* [L f. Gk *Lakōnikos* f. *Lakōn* Spartan, the Spartans being known for their terse speech]
▪ see CONCISE. ▫▫ **laconicism** see BREVITY.

laconism /lákkəniz'm/ *n.* **1** brevity of speech. **2** a short pithy saying. [Gk *lakōnismos* f. *lakōnizō* behave like a Spartan: see LACONIC]

lacquer /lákkər/ *n.* & *v.* (also **lacker**) ● *n.* **1** a sometimes coloured liquid made of shellac dissolved in alcohol, or of synthetic substances, that dries to form a hard protective coating for wood, brass, etc. **2** a chemical substance sprayed on hair to keep it in place. **3** the sap of the lacquer-tree used to varnish wood etc. ● *v.tr.* coat with lacquer. ▫ **lacquer-tree** an E. Asian tree, *Rhus verniciflua*, the sap of which is used as a hard-wearing varnish for wood. ▫▫ **lacquerer** *n.* [obs. F *lacre* sealing-wax, f. unexpl. var. of Port. *laca* LAC[1]]
▪ *n.* **1** see GLAZE *n.* 1. ● *v.* see GLAZE *v.* 6.

lacquey var. of LACKEY.

lacrimal var. of LACHRYMAL.

lacrimation var. of LACHRYMATION.

lacrosse /ləkróss/ *n.* a game like hockey, but with a ball driven by, caught, and carried in a crosse. [F f. *la* the + CROSSE]

lacrymal var. of LACHRYMAL.

lacrymation var. of LACHRYMATION.

lactase /láktayz, -tayss/ *n. Biochem.* any of a group of enzymes which catalyse the hydrolysis of lactose to glucose and galactose. [F f. *lactose* LACTOSE]

lactate[1] /laktáyt/ *v.intr.* (of mammals) secrete milk. [as LACTATION]

lactate[2] /láktayt/ *n. Chem.* any salt or ester of lactic acid.

lactation /laktáysh'n/ *n.* **1** the secretion of milk by the mammary glands. **2** the suckling of young. [L *lactare* suckle f. *lac lactis* milk]

lacteal /láktiəl/ *adj.* & *n.* ● *adj.* **1** of milk. **2** conveying chyle or other milky fluid. ● *n.* (in *pl.*) the lymphatic vessels of the small intestine which absorb digested fats. [L *lacteus* f. *lac lactis* milk]

lactescence /laktéss'nss/ *n.* **1** a milky form or appearance. **2** a milky juice. [L *lactescere* f. *lactēre* be milky (as LACTIC)]

lactescent /laktéss'nt/ *adj.* **1** milky. **2** yielding a milky juice.

lactic /láktik/ *adj. Chem.* of, relating to, or obtained from milk. ▫ **lactic acid** a clear odourless syrupy carboxylic acid formed in sour milk, and produced in the muscle tissues during strenuous exercise. [L *lac lactis* milk]

lactiferous /laktíffərəss/ *adj.* yielding milk or milky fluid. [LL *lactifer* (as LACTIC)]

lacto- /láktō/ *comb. form* milk. [L *lac lactis* milk]

lactobacillus /láktōbəsílləss/ *n.* (*pl.* **-bacilli** /-lī/) *Biol.* any Gram-positive rod-shaped bacterium of the genus *Lactobacillus*, producing lactic acid from the fermentation of carbohydrates.

lactometer /laktómmitər/ *n.* an instrument for testing the density of milk.

lactone /láktōn/ *n. Chem.* any of a class of cyclic esters formed by the elimination of water from a hydroxy-carboxylic acid. [G *Lacton*]

lactoprotein /láktōprṓteen/ *n.* the albuminous constituent of milk.

lactose /láktōss, -tōz/ *n. Chem.* a sugar that occurs in milk, and is less sweet than sucrose. [as LACTO-]

lacuna /ləkyóōnə/ *n.* (*pl.* **lacunae** /-nee/ or **lacunas**) **1** a hiatus, blank, or gap. **2** a missing portion or empty page, esp. in an ancient MS, book, etc. **3** *Anat.* a cavity or depression, esp. in bone. □□ **lacunal** *adj.* **lacunar** *adj.* **lacunary** *adj.* **lacunose** *adj.* [L, = pool, f. *lacus* LAKE[1]]

■ **1** see GAP *n.* 1.

lacustrine /ləkústrīn/ *adj. formal* or *Biol.* **1** of or relating to lakes. **2** living or growing in or beside a lake. [L *lacus* LAKE[1], after *palustris* marshy]

LACW *abbr.* Leading Aircraftwoman.

lacy /láysi/ *adj.* (**lacier, laciest**) of or resembling lace fabric. □□ **lacily** *adv.* **laciness** *n.*

lad /lad/ *n.* **1 a** a boy or youth. **b** a young son. **2** (esp. in *pl.*) *colloq.* a man; a fellow, esp. a workmate, drinking companion, etc. (*he's one of the lads*). **3** *colloq.* a high-spirited fellow; a rogue (*he's a bit of a lad*). **4** *Brit.* a stable-worker (regardless of age). □ **lad's love** = SOUTHERNWOOD. [ME *ladde*, of unkn. orig.]

■ **1** youth, boy, son, child, adolescent, minor, teenager, juvenile, young man, youngster, schoolboy, schoolchild, infant, toddler, stripling, whippersnapper, *Austral.* & *dial.* tacker, *Ir.* spalpeen, *archaic* younker, *archaic or colloq.* young thing, *colloq.* kid, young'un, fellow, shaver, laddie, *Austral. colloq.* ankle-biter, *joc.* little man, *sl.* sprog; (street) urchin, gamin, guttersnipe. **2** man, fellow, boy, *colloq.* guy, chap, *Brit. sl.* bloke; (*lads*) team, set, group, band, *colloq.* mob, bunch, gang, crowd, *derog.* pack. **3** rake, *colloq.* card, Jack-the-lad, *colloq. usu. archaic* blade; *colloq.* lager lout, *offens.* young turk, *Brit. sl.* wide boy; knave, scoundrel, picaroon, scallywag, *archaic or joc.* rapscallion, *colloq.* crook, scamp, *often joc.* rascal, *usu. joc.* villain.

ladanum /láddənəm/ *n.* (also **labdanum** /lábdənəm/) a gum resin from plants of the genus *Cistus*, used in perfumery etc. [L f. Gk *ladanon* f. *lēdon* mastic]

ladder /láddər/ *n.* & *v.* ● *n.* **1** a set of horizontal bars of wood or metal fixed between two uprights and used for climbing up or down. **2** *Brit.* a vertical strip of unravelled fabric in a stocking etc. resembling a ladder. **3 a** a hierarchical structure. **b** such a structure as a means of advancement, promotion, etc. ● *v. Brit.* **1** *intr.* (of a stocking etc.) develop a ladder. **2** *tr.* cause a ladder in (a stocking etc.). □ **ladder-back** an upright chair with a back resembling a ladder. **ladder-stitch** transverse bars in embroidery. **ladder tournament** a sporting contest with each participant listed and entitled to a higher place by defeating the one above. [OE *hlǣd(d)er*, ult. f. Gmc: cf. LEAN[1]]

laddie /láddi/ *n. colloq.* a young boy or lad.

lade /layd/ *v.* (*past part.* **laden** /láyd'n/) **1** *tr.* **a** put cargo on board (a ship). **b** ship (goods) as cargo. **2** *intr.* (of a ship) take on cargo. **3** *tr.* (as **laden** *adj.*) (usu. foll. by *with*) **a** (of a vehicle, donkey, person, tree, table, etc.) heavily loaded. **b** (of the conscience, spirit, etc.) painfully burdened with sin, sorrow, etc. [OE *hladan*]

■ **1a, 2** see LOAD *v.* 1, 2. **3 a** (**laden**) see LOADED 1.

la-di-da /laadidaa/ *adj.* & *n. colloq.* ● *adj.* pretentious or snobbish, esp. in manner or speech. ● *n.* **1** a la-di-da person. **2** la-di-da speech or manners. [imit. of an affected manner of speech]

■ *adj.* see SUPERCILIOUS.

ladies *pl.* of LADY.

ladify var. of LADYFY.

Ladin /ladéen/ *n.* the Rhaeto-Romanic dialect of the Engadine in Switzerland. [Romansh, f. L *latinus* LATIN]

lading /láyding/ *n.* **1** a cargo. **2** the act or process of lading.

Ladino /ladéenō/ *n.* (*pl.* **-os**) **1** the Spanish dialect of the Sephardic Jews. **2** a mestizo or Spanish-speaking white person in Central America. [Sp., orig. = Latin, f. L (as LADIN)]

ladle /láyd'l/ *n.* & *v.* ● *n.* **1** a large long-handled spoon with a cup-shaped bowl used for serving esp. soups and gravy. **2** a vessel for transporting molten metal in a foundry. ● *v.tr.* (often foll. by *out*) transfer (liquid) from one receptacle to another. □ **ladle out** distribute, esp. lavishly. □□ **ladleful** *n.* (*pl.* **-fuls**). **ladler** *n.* [OE *hlædel* f. *hladan* LADE]

■ *n.* **1** see SCOOP *n.* 1. ● *v.* see SCOOP *v.* 1.

lady /láydi/ *n.* (*pl.* **-ies**) **1 a** a woman regarded as being of superior social status or as having the refined manners associated with this (cf. GENTLEMAN). **b** (**Lady**) a title used by peeresses, female relatives of peers, the wives and widows of knights, etc. **2** (often *attrib.*) a woman; a female person or animal (*ask that lady over there*; *lady butcher*; *lady dog*). **3** *colloq.* **a** a wife. **b** a man's girlfriend. **4** a ruling woman (*lady of the house*; *lady of the manor*). **5** (in *pl.* as a form of address) a female audience or the female part of an audience. **6** *hist.* a woman to whom a man, esp. a knight, is chivalrously devoted; a mistress. □ **find the lady** = *three-card trick.* **the Ladies** (or **Ladies'**) *Brit.* a women's public lavatory. **ladies' chain** a figure in a quadrille etc. **ladies' fingers** = OKRA (cf. *lady's finger*). **Ladies' Gallery** a public gallery in the House of Commons, reserved for women. **ladies'** (or **lady's**) **man** a man fond of female company; a seducer. **ladies' night** a function at a men's club etc. to which women are invited. **ladies' room** a women's lavatory in a hotel, office, etc. **Lady altar** the altar in a Lady chapel. **Lady Bountiful** a patronizingly generous lady of the manor etc. (a character in Farquhar's *The Beaux' Stratagem*). **Lady chapel** a chapel in a large church or cathedral, usu. to the E. of the high altar, dedicated to the Virgin Mary. **Lady Day** the Feast of the Annunciation, 25 Mar. **lady-fern** a slender fern, *Athyrium filix-femina.* **lady-in-waiting** a lady attending a queen or princess. **lady-killer** a practised and habitual seducer. **lady-love** a man's sweetheart. **Lady Mayoress** the wife of a Lord Mayor. **Lady Muck** *sl. derog.* a socially pretentious woman. **lady of the bedchamber** = *lady-in-waiting.* **lady of the night** a prostitute. **lady of easy virtue** a sexually promiscuous woman; a prostitute. **lady's bedstraw** a yellow-flowered herbaceous plant, *Galium verum.* **lady's companion** a roll containing cottons etc. **lady's finger 1** = *kidney vetch.* **2** = LADYFINGER (cf. *ladies' fingers*). **lady's maid** a lady's personal maidservant. **lady's mantle** any rosaceous plant of the genus *Alchemilla* with yellowish-green clustered flowers. **lady-smock** = *cuckoo flower* 1. **lady's slipper** any orchidaceous plant of the genus *Cypripedium*, with a usu. yellow slipper-shaped lip on its flowers. **lady's tresses** any white-flowered orchid of the genus *Spiranthes.* **Lady Superior** the head of a convent or nunnery in certain orders. **my lady** a form of address used chiefly by servants etc. to holders of the title 'Lady'. **my lady wife** *joc.* my wife. **old lady** *colloq.* **1** a mother. **2** a wife or mistress. **Our Lady** the Virgin Mary. □□ **ladyhood** *n.* [OE *hlǣfdige* f. *hlāf* LOAF[1] + (unrecorded) *dig-* knead, rel. to DOUGH): in *Lady Day* etc. f. OE genit. *hlǣfdigan* (Our) Lady's]

■ **1** see NOBLE *n.* 1. **2** see WOMAN 1. **3** see WOMAN 3. □ **the Ladies** see TOILET 1. **ladies' man** see *charmer* (CHARM). **ladies' room** see TOILET 1. **lady-in-waiting** see WOMAN 9. **lady-killer** see *charmer* (CHARM). **lady-love** see WOMAN 3. **lady's maid** see SERVANT 1.

ladybird /láydiburd/ *n.* a coleopterous insect of the family Coccinellidae, with wing-covers usu. of a reddish-brown colour with black spots.

ladybug /láydibug/ *n. US* = LADYBIRD.

ladyfinger /láydifinggər/ *n. US* a finger-shaped sponge cake.

ladyfy /láydifī/ *v.tr.* (also **ladify**) (**-ies, -ied**) **1** make a lady of. **2** call (a person) 'lady'. **3** (as **ladyfied** *adj.*) having the manner of a fine lady.

ladylike /láydilīk/ *adj.* **1 a** with the modesty, manners, etc., of a lady. **b** befitting a lady. **2** (of a man) effeminate.
■ **1** refined, cultured, polished, elegant, gracious, genteel, nice, courteous, polite, courtly, mannerly, well-mannered, well-bred, dignified, respectable, proper, correct, decorous, seemly, *joc.* couth; well-born, high-born, aristocratic, patrician, noble, blue-blooded, top-drawer, upper-class, county, *colloq.* posh, *esp. Brit. colloq.* U, *Brit. sl.* Sloaney. **2** effeminate, unmanly, unmasculine, emasculate, precious, epicene, milky, womanly, girlish, feminine, namby-pamby, niminy-piminy, miminy-piminy, *archaic* feminal, *colloq.* camp, sissy, *usu. derog.* womanish, *sl.* limp-wristed, nancy, *Brit. sl.* poncey, *Brit. sl. derog.* poofy.

ladyship /láydiship/ *n. archaic* being a lady. □ **her** (or **your** or **their**) **ladyship** (or **ladyships**) **1** a respectful form of reference or address to a Lady or Ladies. **2** *iron.* a form of reference or address to a woman thought to be giving herself airs.

laevo- /leévō/ *comb. form* (also **levo-**) on or to the left. [L *laevus* left]

laevorotatory /leévō-rṓtətəri/ *adj.* (*US* **levorotatory**) *Chem.* having the property of rotating the plane of a polarized light ray to the left (anticlockwise facing the oncoming radiation).

laevulose /leévyoolōss, -lōz/ *n.* (*US* **levulose**) = FRUCTOSE. [LAEVO- + -ULE + -OSE[2]]

lag[1] /lag/ *v.* & *n.* ● *v.intr.* (**lagged, lagging**) **1** (often foll. by *behind*) fall behind; not keep pace. **2** *US Billiards* make the preliminary strokes that decide which player shall begin. ● *n.* **1** a delay. **2** *Physics* **a** retardation in a current or movement. **b** the amount of this. □ **lag of tide** the interval by which a tide falls behind mean time at the 1st and 3rd quarters of the moon (cf. PRIMING[2]). □□ **lagger** *n.* [orig. = hindmost person, hang back: perh. f. a fanciful distortion of LAST[1] in a children's game (*fog, seg, lag,* = 1st, 2nd, last, in dial.)]
■ *v.* **1** fall behind, straggle, trail, hang back, linger, be in arrears, tail off *or* away, dawdle, dally, *colloq.* dilly-dally. ● *n.* **1** delay, interval, gap, hiatus, interruption, interlude, stop, stoppage, wait, suspension, lull, deferment, deferral, postponement, hold-up. □□ **lagger** see LAGGARD *n.*

lag[2] /lag/ *v.* & *n.* ● *v.tr.* (**lagged, lagging**) enclose or cover in lagging. ● *n.* **1** the non-heat-conducting cover of a boiler etc.; lagging. **2** a piece of this. [prob. f. Scand.: cf. ON *lǫgg* barrel-rim, rel. to LAY[1]]

lag[3] /lag/ *n.* & *v. sl.* ● *n.* (esp. as **old lag**) a habitual convict. ● *v.tr.* (**lagged, lagging**) **1** send to prison. **2** apprehend; arrest. [19th c.: orig. unkn.]

lagan /lággən/ *n.* goods or wreckage lying on the bed of the sea, sometimes with a marking buoy etc. for later retrieval. [OF, perh. of Scand. orig., f. root of LIE[1], LAY[1]]

lager /laágər/ *n.* a kind of beer, effervescent and light in colour and body. □ **lager lout** *colloq.* a youth who behaves badly as a result of excessive drinking. [G *Lagerbier* beer brewed for keeping f. *Lager* store]
■ □ **lager lout** see ROWDY *n.*

lagerphone /laágərfōn/ *n. Austral.* an improvised musical instrument employing beer bottle tops.

laggard /lággərd/ *n.* & *adj.* ● *n.* a dawdler; a person who lags behind. ● *adj.* dawdling; slow. □□ **laggardly** *adj.* & *adv.* **laggardness** *n.* [LAG[1]]
■ *n.* dawdler, straggler, loiterer, slouch, sluggard, loafer, snail, plodder, *Brit.* slowcoach, *US* slowpoke. ● *adj.* see SLOW *adj.* 1. □□ **laggardness** see *sluggishness* (SLUGGISH).

lagging /lágging/ *n.* material providing heat insulation for a boiler, pipes, etc. [LAG[2]]

lagomorph /lággəmorf/ *n. Zool.* any mammal of the order Lagomorpha, including hares and rabbits. [Gk *lagōs* hare + *morphē* form]

lagoon /ləgōōn/ *n.* **1** a stretch of salt water separated from the sea by a low sandbank, coral reef, etc. **2** the enclosed water of an atoll. **3** *US, Austral.,* & *NZ* a small freshwater lake near a larger lake or river. **4** an artificial pool for the treatment of effluent or to accommodate an overspill from surface drains during heavy rain. [F *lagune* or It. & Sp. *laguna* f. L *lacuna*: see LACUNA]

lah /laa/ *n.* (also **la**) *Mus.* **1** (in tonic sol-fa) the sixth note of a major scale. **2** the note A in the fixed-doh system. [ME f. L *labii*: see GAMUT]

lahar /laáhaar/ *n.* a mud-flow composed mainly of volcanic debris. [Jav.]

laic /láyik/ *adj.* & *n.* ● *adj.* non-clerical; lay; secular; temporal. ● *n. formal* a lay person; a non-cleric. □□ **laical** *adj.* **laically** *adv.* [LL f. Gk *laïkos* f. *laos* people]
■ *adj.* see SECULAR *adj.* 1.

laicity /layíssiti/ *n.* the status or influence of the laity.

laicize /láyisīz/ *v.tr.* (also **-ise**) **1** make (an office etc.) tenable by lay people. **2** subject (a school or institution) to the control of lay people. **3** secularize. □□ **laicization** /-záysh'n/ *n.*

laid *past* and *past part.* of LAY[1].

lain *past part.* of LIE[1].

lair[1] /lair/ *n.* & *v.* ● *n.* **1 a** a wild animal's resting-place. **b** a person's hiding-place; a den (*tracked him to his lair*). **2** a place where domestic animals lie down. **3** *Brit.* a shed or enclosure for cattle on the way to market. ● *v.* **1** *intr.* go to or rest in a lair. **2** *tr.* place (an animal) in a lair. □□ **lairage** *n.* [OE *leger* f. Gmc: cf. LIE[1]]
■ *n.* **1 a** den, burrow, hole, nest, tunnel, cave, hollow, covert. **b** hideaway, hiding-place, snuggery, den, nest, refuge, cover, retreat, *colloq.* hide-out, hidey-hole, sanctum.

lair[2] /lair/ *n.* & *v. Austral. sl.* ● *n.* a youth or man who dresses flashily and shows off. ● *v.intr.* (often foll. by *up*) behave or dress like a lair. □□ **lairy** *adj.* [*lair* back-form. f. *lairy*; *lairy* alt. f. LEERY]

laird /laird/ *n. Sc.* a landed proprietor. □□ **lairdship** *n.* [Sc. form of LORD]

laissez-aller /léssayálay/ *n.* (also ***laisser-aller***) unconstrained freedom; an absence of constraint. [F, = let go]
■ see LAISSEZ-FAIRE.

laissez-faire /léssayfáir/ *n.* (also ***laisser-faire***) the theory or practice of governmental abstention from interference in the workings of the market etc. [F, = let act]
■ free enterprise, free market economics, non-intervention, non-interference, deregulation, free trade; freedom, individualism, *laissez-aller.*

laissez-passer /léssaypássay/ *n.* (also ***laisser-passer***) a document allowing the holder to pass; a permit. [F, = let pass]

laity /láyiti/ *n.* (usu. prec. by *the*; usu. treated as *pl.*) **1** lay people, as distinct from the clergy. **2** non-professionals. [ME f. LAY[2] + -ITY]

lake[1] /layk/ *n.* a large body of water surrounded by land. □ **the Great Lakes** the Lakes Superior, Huron, Michigan, Erie, and Ontario, along the boundary of the US and Canada. **Lake District** (or **the Lakes**) the region of the English lakes in Cumbria. **lake-dweller** a prehistoric inhabitant of lake-dwellings. **lake-dwellings** prehistoric huts built on piles driven into the bed or shore of a lake. **Lake Poets** Coleridge, Southey, and Wordsworth, who lived in and were inspired by the Lake District. □□ **lakeless** *adj.* **lakelet** *n.* [ME f. OF *lac* f. L *lacus* basin, pool, lake]
■ see POOL[1] *n.* 1.

lake[2] /layk/ *n.* **1** a reddish colouring orig. made from lac (*crimson lake*). **2** a complex formed by the action of dye and mordants applied to fabric to fix colour. **3** any insoluble product of a soluble dye and mordant. [var. of LAC[1]]

Lakeland /láyklənd/ *n.* = *Lake District.* □ **Lakeland terrier** **1** a terrier of a small stocky breed originating in the Lake District. **2** this breed.

lakeside /láyksīd/ *attrib.adj.* beside a lake.

lakh /lak, laak/ *n.* (also **lac**) *Ind.* (usu. foll. by *of*) a hundred thousand (rupees etc.). [Hind. *lākh* f. Skr. *lakṣa*]

Lallan /lállən/ *n.* & *adj. Sc.* ● *n.* (now usu. **Lallans**) a Lowland Scots dialect, esp. as a literary language. ● *adj.* of or concerning the Lowlands of Scotland. [var. of LOWLAND]

lallation /laláysh'n/ *n.* **1** the pronunciation of *r* as *l.* **2** imperfect speech, esp. that of young children. [L *lallare lallat-* sing a lullaby]

lallygag /lálligag/ *v.intr.* (**lallygagged, lallygagging**) *US sl.* **1** loiter. **2** cuddle amorously. [20th c.: orig. unkn.]
■ **1** see LOAF[2] *v.* 1.

Lam. *abbr.* Lamentations (Old Testament).

lam[1] /lam/ *v.* (**lammed, lamming**) *sl.* **1** *tr.* thrash; hit. **2** *intr.* (foll. by *into*) hit (a person etc.) hard with a stick etc. [perh. f. Scand.: cf. ON *lemja* beat so as to LAME]

lam[2] /lam/ *n.* □ **on the lam** *US sl.* in flight, esp. from the police. [20th c.: orig. unkn.]

lama /laámə/ *n.* a Tibetan or Mongolian Buddhist monk. □□ **Lamaism** *n.* **Lamaist** *n.* & *adj.* [Tibetan *blama* (with silent *b*)]

Lamarckism /ləmaárkiz'm/ *n.* the theory of evolution devised by Lamarck, French botanist and zoologist (d. 1829), based on the inheritance of acquired characteristics. □□ **Lamarckian** *n.* & *adj.*

lamasery /laáməsəri, ləmaássəri/ *n.* (*pl.* **-ies**) a monastery of lamas. [F *lamaserie* irreg. f. *lama* LAMA]
■ see MONASTERY.

lamb /lam/ *n.* & *v.* ● *n.* **1** a young sheep. **2** the flesh of a lamb as food. **3** a mild or gentle person, esp. a young child. ● *v.* **1 a** *tr.* (in *passive*) (of a lamb) be born. **b** *intr.* (of a ewe) give birth to lambs. **2** *tr.* tend (lambing ewes). □ **The Lamb** (or **The Lamb of God**) a name for Christ (see John 1:29) (cf. AGNUS DEI). **lamb's fry** lamb's testicles or other offal as food. **lamb's lettuce** a plant, *Valerianella locusta*, used in salad. **lamb's-tails** catkins from the hazel tree. **like a lamb** meekly, obediently. □□ **lamber** *n.* **lambhood** *n.* **lambkin** *n.* **lamblike** *adj.* [OE *lamb* f. Gmc]
■ □□ **lamblike** see PASSIVE 2.

lambada / lambaádə/ *n.* a fast erotic Brazilian dance in which couples dance with their hips touching each other.

lambaste /lambáyst/ *v.tr.* (also **lambast** /-bást/) *colloq.* **1** thrash; beat. **2** criticize severely. [LAM[1] + BASTE[3]]
■ **1** thrash, give a person a thrashing *or* beating, trounce, whip, scourge, flog, lash, strap, welt, leather, horsewhip, cane, birch, *colloq.* thwack, whack, give a person a hiding, *esp. US colloq.* whale, *sl.* belt, paste, tan a person's hide; beat, bludgeon, drub, maul, pummel, batter, bash, baste, belabour, cudgel, club, clout, thump, *sl.* clobber, whop, wallop, duff up, rough up, paste, fill in, give a person a going-over. **2** censure, rebuke, berate, scold, rate, upbraid, chastise, reprimand, admonish, reprove, belabour, reproach, reprehend, revile, attack, abuse, rail at, harangue, excoriate, castigate, keelhaul, flay, rap a person's knuckles, slap a person's wrist, take to task, call down, haul *or* call over the coals, *archaic or literary* chide, *colloq.* dress down, give a person a dressing-down, carpet, put a person on the carpet, tell off, tick off, lay into, bawl out, *US colloq.* chew out, *literary* objurgate, *sl.* ballyrag, *Austral.* & *NZ sl.* go off at, *Brit. sl.* have a go at, slag off.

lambda /lámdə/ *n.* **1** the eleventh letter of the Greek alphabet (Λ, λ). **2** (as λ) the symbol for wavelength. [ME f. Gk *la(m)bda*]

lambent /lámb'nt/ *adj.* **1** (of a flame or a light) playing on a surface with a soft radiance but without burning. **2** (of the eyes, sky, etc.) softly radiant. **3** (of wit etc.) lightly brilliant. □□ **lambency** *n.* **lambently** *adv.* [L *lambere lambent-* lick]
■ **1** see BRIGHT *adj.* 1. □□ **lambency** see GLOW *n.* 1. **lambently** see BRIGHT *adv.*

lambert /lámbərt/ *n.* a former unit of luminance, equal to the emission or reflection of one lumen per square centimetre. [J. H. *Lambert*, Ger. physicist d. 1777]

lambrequin /lámbrikin, lámbər-/ *n.* **1** *US* a short piece of drapery hung over the top of a door or a window or draped on a mantelpiece. **2** *Heraldry* = MANTLING. [F f. Du. (unrecorded) *lamperkin*, dimin. of *lamper* veil]
■ **1** see DRAPERY 2.

lambskin /lámskin/ *n.* a prepared skin from a lamb with the wool on or as leather.

lambswool /lámzwŏŏl/ *n.* (also **lamb's-wool**) soft fine wool from a young sheep used in knitted garments etc.

lame /laym/ *adj.* & *v.* ● *adj.* **1** disabled, esp. in the foot or leg; limping; unable to walk normally (*lame in his right leg*). **2 a** (of an argument, story, excuse, etc.) unconvincing; unsatisfactory; weak. **b** (of verse etc.) halting. ● *v.tr.* **1** make lame; disable. **2** harm permanently. □ **lame-brain** *US colloq.* a stupid person. **lame duck 1** a disabled or weak person. **2** a defaulter on the Stock Exchange. **3** a firm etc. in financial difficulties. **4** *US* an official (esp. the President) in the final period of office, after the election of a successor. □□ **lamely** *adv.* **lameness** *n.* **lamish** *adj.* [OE *lama* f. Gmc]
■ *adj.* **1** disabled, handicapped, limping, game, *Vet.* spavined, *archaic* halt, *Brit. sl.* gammy. **2 a** unconvincing, unpersuasive, feeble, puny, weak, flimsy, thin, lacklustre, half-hearted, half-baked, pale, poor, ineffective, unsatisfactory, unacceptable, inadequate, insufficient, disappointing. **b** halting, awkward, hesitant, uneven, stiff, stilted, stumbling. ● *v.* cripple, hamstring, disable, handicap, incapacitate, lay up, invalid; maim, damage, hurt, injure, impair, ruin, wreck, mar, spoil, mutilate, *colloq.* crock (up). □ **lame-brain** see FOOL[1] *n.* 1.

lamé /laámay/ *n.* & *adj.* ● *n.* a fabric with gold or silver threads interwoven. ● *adj.* (of fabric, a dress, etc.) having such threads. [F]

lamella /ləméllə/ *n.* (*pl.* **lamellae** /-lee/) **1** a thin layer, membrane, scale, or platelike tissue or part, esp. in bone tissue. **2** *Bot.* a membranous fold in a chloroplast. □□ **lamellar** *adj.* **lamellate** /lámməlayt/ *adj.* **lamelliform** *adj.* **lamellose** /-lōss/ *adj.* [L, dimin. of *lamina*: see LAMINA]
■ **1** see SCALE[1] *n.* 1. □□ **lamellar, lamellate** see SCALY.

lamellibranch /ləméllibrangk/ *n.* any aquatic mollusc having a shell formed of two pieces or valves, e.g. a mussel or oyster. Also called BIVALVE. [LAMELLA + Gk *bragkhia* gills]

lamellicorn /ləméllikorn/ *n.* & *adj.* ● *n.* any beetle of the family Lamellicornia, having lamelliform antennae, including the stag beetle, cockchafer, dung-beetle, etc. ● *adj.* having lamelliform antennae. [mod.L *lamellicornis* f. L *lamella* (see LAMELLA) + *cornu* horn]

lament /ləmént/ *n.* & *v.* ● *n.* **1** a passionate expression of grief. **2** a song or poem of mourning or sorrow. ● *v.tr.* (also *absol.*) **1** express or feel grief for or about; regret (*lamented the loss of his ticket*). **2** (as **lamented** *adj.*) a conventional expression referring to a recently dead person (*your late lamented father*). □ **lament for** (or **over**) mourn or regret. □□ **lamenter** *n.* **lamentingly** *adv.* [L *lamentum*]
■ *n.* **1** lamentation, moan, wail, ululation, whine, jeremiad, *colloq. or dial.* yammer, *literary or archaic* plaint; grief, sorrow, mourning, wake, *poet.* dole. **2** lamentation, keen, dirge, elegy, Requiem, monody, threnody, epicedium, *Sc.* & *Ir.* coronach. ● *v.* **1** mourn, bemoan, bewail, wail, ululate, weep (over), grieve (for *or* over), keen (over), sorrow (for *or* over), sigh (for *or* over), *archaic or poet.* plain; regret, rue, deplore, deprecate, complain (of *or* about).

lamentable /lámməntəb'l, *disp.* ləmént-/ *adj.* **1** (of an event, fate, condition, character, etc.) deplorable; regrettable. **2** *archaic* mournful. □□ **lamentably** *adv.* [ME f. OF *lamentable* or L *lamentabilis* (as LAMENT)]

■ **1** deplorable, wretched, piteous, miserable, regrettable, pitiful, forlorn, pitiable, pathetic, unfortunate, tragic, sad, sorrowful, terrible, awful, intolerable. **2** see MOURNFUL 1.

lamentation /lámməntáysh'n/ *n.* **1** the act or an instance of lamenting. **2** a lament. □ **Lamentations of Jeremiah** an Old Testament book concerning the destruction of Jerusalem in the 6th c. BC. [ME f. OF *lamentation* or L *lamentatio* (as LAMENT)]
■ see LAMENT *n.*

lamina /lámminə/ *n.* (*pl.* **laminae** /-nee/) a thin plate or scale, e.g. of bone, stratified rock, or vegetable tissue. □□ **laminose** *adj.* [L]
■ see SCALE[1] *n.* 1.

laminar /lámminər/ *adj.* **1** consisting of laminae. **2** *Physics* (of a flow) taking place along constant streamlines, not turbulent.
■ **1** see SCALY.

laminate *v.*, *n.*, & *adj.* ● *v.* /lámminayt/ **1** *tr.* beat or roll (metal) into thin plates. **2** *tr.* overlay with metal plates, a plastic layer, etc. **3** *tr.* manufacture by placing layer on layer. **4** *tr.* & *intr.* split or be split into layers or leaves. ● *n.* /lámminət/ a laminated structure or material, esp. of layers fixed together to form rigid or flexible material. ● *adj.* /lámminət/ in the form of lamina or laminae. □□ **lamination** /-náysh'n/ *n.* **laminator** *n.* [LAMINA + -ATE[2], -ATE[3]]
■ *v.* **2** see PLATE *v.* 1.

lamington /lámmingtən/ *n. Austral.* & *NZ* a square of sponge cake coated in chocolate icing and desiccated coconut. [C.W. Ballie, Baron *Lamington*, Governor of Qld., d. 1940]

Lammas /lámməss/ *n.* (in full **Lammas Day**) the first day of August, formerly observed as harvest festival. [OE *hlāfmæsse* (as LOAF[1], MASS[2])]

lammergeyer /lámmərgīər/ *n.* a large vulture, *Gypaetus barbatus*, with a very large wingspan (often of 3 m) and dark beardlike feathers on either side of its beak. [G *Lämmergeier* f. *Lämmer* lambs + *Geier* vulture]

lamp /lamp/ *n.* & *v.* ● *n.* **1** a device for producing a steady light, esp.: **a** an electric bulb, and usu. its holder and shade or cover (*bedside lamp*; *bicycle lamp*). **b** an oil-lamp. **c** a usu. glass holder for a candle. **d** a gas-jet and mantle. **2** a source of spiritual or intellectual inspiration. **3** *poet.* the sun, the moon, or a star. **4** a device producing esp. ultraviolet or infrared radiation as a treatment for various complaints. ● *v.* **1** *intr. poet.* shine. **2** *tr.* supply with lamps; illuminate. **3** *tr. US sl.* look at. □ **lamp-chimney** a glass cylinder enclosing and making a draught for an oil-lamp flame. **lamp-holder** a device for supporting a lamp, esp. an electric one. **lamp standard** = LAMPPOST. □□ **lampless** *adj.* [ME f. OF *lampe* f. LL *lampada* f. accus. of L *lampas* torch f. Gk]
■ *n.* **1** see LIGHT[1] *n.* 4a.

lampblack /lámpblak/ *n.* a pigment made from soot.

lamplight /lámplīt/ *n.* light given by a lamp or lamps.
■ see LIGHT[1] *n.* 2.

lamplighter /lámplītər/ *n. hist.* **1** a person who lights street lamps. **2** *US* a spill for lighting lamps. □ **like a lamplighter** with great speed.

lampoon /lampoōn/ *n.* & *v.* ● *n.* a satirical attack on a person etc. ● *v.tr.* satirize. □□ **lampooner** *n.* **lampoonery** *n.* **lampoonist** *n.* [F *lampon*, conjectured to be f. *lampons* let us drink f. *lamper* gulp down f. *laper* LAP[3]]
■ *n.* burlesque, caricature, satire, satirization, parody, pasquinade, squib, mockery, *colloq.* take-off, *Brit. colloq.* send-up. ● *v.* satirize, burlesque, caricature, parody, *archaic* squib, *colloq.* take off, *Brit. colloq.* send up, *sl.* take the mickey (out of); mock, ridicule, scoff at, laugh at, deride, guy, poke fun at, run down, have a go at.

lamppost /lámp-pōst/ *n.* a tall post supporting a street-light.

lamprey /lámpri/ *n.* (*pl.* **-eys**) any eel-like aquatic vertebrate of the family Petromyzonidae, without scales, paired fins, or jaws, but having a sucker mouth with horny teeth and a rough tongue. [ME f. OF *lampreie* f. med.L *lampreda*: cf. LL *lampetra* perh. f. L *lambere* lick + *petra* stone]

lampshade /lámpshayd/ *n.* a translucent cover for a lamp used to soften or direct its light.
■ see SHADE *n.* 7, 8.

Lancastrian /langkástriən/ *n.* & *adj.* ● *n.* **1** a native of Lancashire or Lancaster in NW England. **2** *hist.* a follower of the House of Lancaster or of the Red Rose party supporting it in the Wars of the Roses (cf. YORKIST). ● *adj.* of or concerning Lancashire or Lancaster, or the House of Lancaster.

lance /laanss/ *n.* & *v.* ● *n.* **1 a** a long weapon with a wooden shaft and a pointed steel head, used by a horseman in charging. **b** a similar weapon used for spearing a fish, killing a harpooned whale, etc. **2** a metal pipe supplying oxygen to burn metal. **3** = LANCER. ● *v.tr.* **1** *Surgery* prick or cut open with a lancet. **2** pierce with a lance. **3** *poet.* fling; launch. □ **break a lance** (usu. foll. by *for*, *with*) argue. **lance-bombardier** a rank in the Royal Artillery corresponding to lance-corporal in the infantry. **lance-corporal** the lowest rank of NCO in the Army. **lance-jack** *Brit. sl.* a lance-corporal or lance-bombardier. **lance-sergeant** a corporal acting as sergeant. **lance-snake** = FER DE LANCE. [ME f. OF *lancier* f. L *lancea*: *lance-corporal* on analogy of obs. *lancepesade* lowest grade of NCO ult. f. It. *lancia spezzata* broken lance]
■ *n.* **1** spear, pike, javelin, shaft, assegai, *literary* steel; gaff, gig, leister. ● *v.* **1** prick, cut (open), pierce, puncture, incise, slit. **2** pierce, impale, transfix, spear, run through, skewer, spit, spike, stick, stab, penetrate.

lancelet /laánslit/ *n.* any small non-vertebrate fishlike chordate of the family Branchiostomidae, that burrows in sand. [LANCE *n.* + -LET, with ref. to its thin form]

lanceolate /laánsiələt/ *adj.* shaped like a lance-head, tapering to each end. [LL *lanceolatus* f. *lanceola* dimin. of *lancea* lance]

lancer /laánsər/ *n.* **1** *hist.* a soldier of a cavalry regiment armed with lances. **2** (in *pl.*) **a** a quadrille for 8 or 16 pairs. **b** the music for this. [F *lancier* (as LANCE)]

lancet /laánsit/ *n.* a small broad two-edged surgical knife with a sharp point. □ **lancet arch** (or **light** or **window**) a narrow arch or window with a pointed head. □□ **lanceted** *adj.* [ME f. OF *lancette* (as LANCE)]

lancewood /laánswŏŏd/ *n.* a tough elastic wood from a W. Indian tree *Oxandra lanceolata*, used for carriage-shafts, fishing-rods, etc.

Lancs. *abbr.* Lancashire.

Land /lunt/ *n.* (*pl.* **Länder** /léndər/) a province of Germany or Austria. [G (as LAND)]

land /land/ *n.* & *v.* ● *n.* **1** the solid part of the earth's surface (opp. SEA, WATER, AIR). **2 a** an expanse of country; ground; soil. **b** such land in relation to its use, quality, etc., or (often prec. by *the*) as a basis for agriculture (*building land*; *this is good land*; *works on the land*). **3** a country, nation, or State (*land of hope and glory*). **4 a** landed property. **b** (in *pl.*) estates. **5** the space between the rifling-grooves in a gun. **6** *Sc.* a building containing several dwellings. **7** *S.Afr.* ground fenced off for tillage. **8** a strip of plough or pasture land parted from others by drain-furrows. ● *v.* **1 a** *tr.* & *intr.* set or go ashore. **b** *intr.* (often foll. by *at*) disembark (*landed at the harbour*). **2** *tr.* bring (an aircraft, its passengers, etc.) to the ground or the surface of water. **3** *intr.* (of an aircraft, bird, parachutist, etc.) alight on the ground or water. **4** *tr.* bring (a fish) to land. **5** *tr.* & *intr.* (also *refl.*; often foll. by *up*) *colloq.* bring to, reach, or find oneself in a certain situation, place, or state (*landed himself in jail*; *landed up in France*; *landed her in trouble*; *landed up penniless*). **6** *tr. colloq.* **a** deal (a person etc.) a blow etc. (*landed him one in the eye*). **b** (foll. by *with*) present (a person) with (a problem, job, etc.). **7** *tr.* set down (a person, cargo, etc.) from a vehicle, ship, etc. **8** *tr. colloq.* win or obtain (a prize, job, etc.) esp. against strong competition. □ **how the land lies** what is the state of affairs. **in the land of the living** *joc.* still alive. **land-agency 1** the stewardship of an estate. **2**

an agency for the sale etc. of estates. **land-agent 1** the steward of an estate. **2** an agent for the sale of estates. **land-bank** a bank issuing banknotes on the securities of landed property. **land breeze** a breeze blowing towards the sea from the land, esp. at night. **land-bridge** a neck of land joining two large land masses. **land-crab** a crab, *Cardisoma guanhumi*, that lives in burrows inland and migrates in large numbers to the sea to breed. **land force** (or **forces**) armies, not naval or air forces. **land-form** a natural feature of the earth's surface. **land-girl** *Brit.* a woman doing farm work, esp. in wartime. **land-grabber** an illegal seizer of land, esp. a person who took the land of an evicted Irish tenant. **land-law** (usu. in *pl.*) the law of landed property. **land-line** a means of telecommunication over land. **land-locked** almost or entirely enclosed by land. **land mass** a large area of land. **land-mine 1** an explosive mine laid in or on the ground. **2** a parachute mine. **land of cakes** Scotland. **land office** *US* an office recording dealings in public land. **land-office business** *US* enormous trade. **land of Nod** sleep (with pun on the phr. in Gen. 4:16). **land on one's feet** attain a good position, job, etc., by luck. **Land's End** the westernmost point of Cornwall and of England. **land-tax** *hist.* a tax assessed on landed property. **land-tie** a rod, beam, or piece of masonry securing or supporting a wall etc. by connecting it with the ground. **land-wind** a wind blowing seaward from the land. **land yacht** a vehicle with wheels and sails for recreational use on a beach etc. □□ **lander** *n.* **landless** *adj.* **landward** *adj.* & *adv.* **landwards** *adv.* [OE f. Gmc]

■ *n.* **1** earth, (solid) ground, dry land, terra firma. **2 a** dirt, earth, soil, ground, turf, sod, loam. **b** plot, patch, tract, parcel (of land), allotment, property, area, *US* lot. **3** country, nation, state, territory, domain, fatherland, motherland, homeland, native land, *formal esp. Law* realm. **4** property, ground(s), landed property, *Law* immovables, real property *or* estate; acreage, estate(s), *Law* realty. ● *v.* **1, 3** arrive, alight, light, touch *or* come *or* go down, splash down, settle (on *or* upon), come to rest; berth, dock, disembark, debark, go ashore, dismount, *esp. US* deplane. **2** bring *or* take down, *colloq.* ditch. **4** catch, hook, net, take, capture. **5** (*tr.*) get, bring, lead; (*intr.*) arrive, come, go, find oneself, appear, turn up, end up, finish up, *colloq.* show *or* roll up, blow in, fetch up. **6** deal, give, administer, dispense; present, leave, provide, supply, furnish, *literary* mete out. **7** set *or* put down, unload, offload, disembark, debark; discharge, empty, dump. **8** get, secure, obtain, acquire, procure, pick up, get hold of; win, gain, earn, receive, come into, *colloq.* pull down. □ **land on one's feet** strike lucky, strike oil, *colloq.* strike it rich, hit the jackpot, *Brit. colloq.* turn up trumps.

landau /lándaw/ *n.* a four-wheeled enclosed carriage with a removable front cover and a back cover that can be raised and lowered. [*Landau* near Karlsruhe in Germany, where it was first made]

landaulet /lándawlét/ *n.* **1** a small landau. **2** *hist.* a car with a folding hood over the rear seats.

landed /lándid/ *adj.* **1** owning land (*landed gentry*). **2** consisting of, including, or relating to land (*landed property*).

Länder *pl.* of LAND.

landfall /lándfawl/ *n.* the approach to land, esp. for the first time on a sea or air journey.

landfill /lándfil/ *n.* **1** waste material etc. used to landscape or reclaim areas of ground. **2** the process of disposing of rubbish in this way. □ **landfill site** a place where rubbish is disposed of by burying it in the ground.

landgrave /lándgrayv/ *n.* (*fem.* **landgravine** /-grəveen/) *hist.* **1** a count having jurisdiction over a territory. **2** the title of certain German princes. □□ **landgraviate** /-gráyviət/ *n.* [MLG *landgrave*, MHG *lantgrāve* (as LAND, G *Graf* COUNT²)]

landholder /lándhōldər/ *n.* the proprietor or, esp., the tenant of land.

■ see PROPRIETOR 1.

landing /lánding/ *n.* **1 a** the act or process of coming to land. **b** an instance of this. **c** (also **landing-place**) a place where ships etc. land. **2 a** a platform between two flights of stairs, or at the top or bottom of a flight. **b** a passage leading to upstairs rooms. □ **landing-craft** any of several types of craft esp. designed for putting troops and equipment ashore. **landing-gear** the undercarriage of an aircraft. **landing-net** a net for landing a large fish which has been hooked. **landing-stage** a platform, often floating, on which goods and passengers are disembarked. **landing-strip** an airstrip.

■ **1 a, b** touchdown, splashdown; belly-landing, crash landing, forced landing, pancake landing, three-point landing, *sl.* greaser; disembarkation, debarkation, arrival. **c** landing-place, landing-stage, dock, pier, jetty, wharf, quay, slipway.

landlady /lándlaydi/ *n.* (*pl.* **-ies**) **1** a woman who lets land, a building, part of a building, etc., to a tenant. **2** a woman who keeps a public house, boarding-house, or lodgings.

■ **1** see LANDLORD 1. **2** proprietress, manageress, hostess, publican, innkeeper, hotelier, restaurateur, lady of the house, mistress.

ländler /léndlər/ *n.* **1** an Austrian dance in triple time, a precursor of the waltz. **2** the music for a ländler. [G f. *Landl* Upper Austria]

landloper /lándlōpər/ *n.* esp. *Sc.* a vagabond. [MDu. *landlooper* (as LAND, *loopen* run, formed as LEAP)]

landlord /lándlord/ *n.* **1** a man who lets land, a building, part of a building, etc., to a tenant. **2** a man who keeps a public house, boarding-house, or lodgings.

■ **1** (property) owner, lessor, landowner, householder, landholder, freeholder. **2** host, publican, proprietor, innkeeper, hotelier, manager, restaurateur, *archaic* mine host.

landlubber /lándlubbər/ *n.* a person unfamiliar with the sea or sailing.

landmark /lándmaark/ *n.* **1 a** a conspicuous object in a district etc. **b** an object marking the boundary of an estate, country, etc. **2** an event, change, etc. marking a stage or turning-point in history etc. **3** *attrib.* serving as a landmark; signifying an important change, development, etc.

■ **1** feature, oriflamme, monument; cairn, obelisk, *Archit.* terminus, *Gk Antiq.* herm. **2** turning-point, watershed, divide, milestone. **3** (*attrib.*) critical, crucial, pivotal, seminal, important, historic, significant, ground-breaking, precedent-setting, momentous, notable, noteworthy, major.

landocracy /landókrəsi/ *n.* (*pl.* **-ies**) *joc.* the landed class. □□ **landocrat** /lándəkrat/ *n.*

landowner /lándōnər/ *n.* an owner of land. □□ **landowning** *adj.* & *n.*

■ see PROPRIETOR 1.

landrail /lándrayl/ *n.* = CORNCRAKE.

landscape /lándskayp, láns-/ *n.* & *v.* ● *n.* **1** natural or imaginary scenery, as seen in a broad view. **2** (often *attrib.*) a picture representing this; the genre of landscape painting. **3** (in graphic design etc.) a format in which the width of an illustration etc. is greater than the height (cf. PORTRAIT). ● *v.tr.* (also *absol.*) improve (a piece of land) by landscape gardening. □ **landscape gardener** (or **architect**) a person who plans the layout of landscapes, esp. extensive grounds. **landscape gardening** (or **architecture**) the laying out of esp. extensive grounds to resemble natural scenery. **landscape-marble** marble with treelike markings. **landscape-painter** an artist who paints landscapes. □□ **landscapist** *n.* [MDu. *landscap* (as LAND, -SHIP)]

■ *n.* **1** prospect, view, scene, aspect, vista, panorama; countryside, scenery, terrain, *paysage*.

landslide /lándslīd/ *n.* **1** the sliding down of a mass of land from a mountain, cliff, etc. **2** an overwhelming majority for one side in an election.

■ **1** landslip, earth-slip, avalanche, mud-slide.

landslip /lándslip/ *n.* = LANDSLIDE 1.

landsman /lándzmən/ *n.* (*pl.* **-men**) a non-sailor.

lane /layn/ *n.* **1** a narrow, often rural, road, street, or path. **2** a division of a road for a stream of traffic (*three-lane highway*). **3** a strip of track or water for a runner, rower, or swimmer in a race. **4** a path or course prescribed for or regularly followed by a ship, aircraft, etc. (*ocean lane*). **5** a gangway between crowds of people, objects, etc. □ **it's a long lane that has no turning** change is inevitable. [OE: orig. unkn.]

■ **1** see ROAD[1] 1, WALK *n.* 3a.

langlauf /lánglowf/ *n.* cross-country skiing; a cross-country skiing race. [G, = long run]

langouste /lonGgoost, lónggoost/ *n.* a crawfish or spiny lobster. [F]

langoustine /lónggoostéen, lónggoosteen/ *n.* = NORWAY LOBSTER. [F]

lang syne /lang sín/ *adv.* & *n.* *Sc.* ● *adv.* in the distant past. ● *n.* the old days (cf. AULD LANG SYNE). [= long since]

language /lánggwij/ *n.* **1** the method of human communication, either spoken or written, consisting of the use of words in an agreed way. **2** the language of a particular community or country etc. (*speaks several languages*). **3 a** the faculty of speech. **b** a style or the faculty of expression; the use of words, etc. (*his language was poetic; hasn't the language to express it*). **c** (also **bad language**) coarse, crude, or abusive speech (*didn't like his language*). **4** a system of symbols and rules for writing computer programs or algorithms. **5** any method of expression (*the language of mime; sign language*). **6** a professional or specialized vocabulary. **7** literary style. □ **language laboratory** a room equipped with tape recorders etc. for learning a foreign language. **language of flowers** a set of symbolic meanings attached to different flowers. **speak the same language** have a similar outlook, manner of expression, etc. [ME f. OF *langage* ult. f. L *lingua* tongue]

■ **1, 5** communication, intercourse, interaction; words, speech, diction, articulation, expression, talk. **2** tongue, dialect, idiolect, patois, idiom, parlance, argot, slang, vocabulary, terminology, vernacular, *colloq.* lingo. **3 a, b** speech, utterance, articulation; expression, diction, style, phraseology, phrasing, turn of phrase; vocabulary, wording; enunciation, pronunciation, accent; facility, fluency, *colloq.* gift of the gab. **c** (**bad language**) see ABUSE *n.* 2. **6** jargon, cant, argot, idiom, slang, parlance, patter, idiolect, *colloq.* lingo; vocabulary, terminology. **7** see STYLE *n.* 2, 3. □ **speak the same language** see eye to eye, see things the same way, be two of a kind, be soul mates, be of one *or* the same mind, *colloq.* be on the same wavelength.

langue de chat /lóng də shaá/ *n.* a very thin finger-shaped crisp biscuit or piece of chocolate. [F, = cat's tongue]

langue d'oc /long dók/ *n.* the form of medieval French spoken south of the Loire, the basis of modern Provençal. [OF *langue* language f. L *lingua* tongue + *de* of + *oc* (f. L *hoc*) the form for *yes*]

langue d'oïl /lonG dóy/ *n.* medieval French as spoken north of the Loire, the basis of modern French. [as LANGUE D'OC + *oïl* (f. L *hoc ille*) the form for *yes*]

languid /lánggwid/ *adj.* **1** lacking vigour; idle; inert; apathetic. **2** (of ideas etc.) lacking force; uninteresting. **3** (of trade etc.) slow-moving; sluggish. **4** faint; weak. □□ **languidly** *adv.* **languidness** *n.* [F *languide* or L *languidus* (as LANGUISH)]

■ **1** see IDLE *adj.* 1. **3** see LAZY 3. **4** see FEEBLE 1. □□ **languidness** see LETHARGY 1.

languish /lánggwish/ *v.intr.* **1** be or grow feeble; lose or lack vitality. **2** put on a sentimentally tender or languid look. □ **languish for** droop or pine for. **languish under** suffer under (esp. depression, confinement, etc.). □□ **languisher** *n.* **languishingly** *adv.* **languishment** *n.* [ME f. OF *languir*, ult. f. L *languēre*, rel. to LAX]

■ **1** see ROT *v.* 2b.

languor /lánggər/ *n.* **1** lack of energy or alertness; inertia; idleness; dullness. **2** faintness; fatigue. **3** a soft or tender mood or effect. **4** an oppressive stillness (of the air etc.). □□ **languorous** *adj.* **languorously** *adv.* [ME f. OF f. L *languor -oris* (as LANGUISH)]

■ **1** see INERTIA 2. **2** see FATIGUE *n.* 1. □□ **languorous** see INERT 3.

langur /lunggóor/ *n.* any of various Asian long-tailed monkeys esp. of the genus *Presbytis*. [Hindi]

laniary /lánniəri/ *adj.* & *n.* ● *adj.* (of a tooth) adapted for tearing; canine. ● *n.* (*pl.* **-ies**) a laniary tooth. [L *laniarius* f. *lanius* butcher f. *laniare* to tear]

laniferous /ləníffərəss/ *adj.* (also **lanigerous** /ləníjərəss/) wool-bearing. [L *lanifer*, *-ger* f. *lana* wool]

■ see WOOLLY *adj.* 1.

lank /langk/ *adj.* **1** (of hair, grass, etc.) long, limp, and straight. **2** thin and tall. **3** shrunken; spare. □□ **lankly** *adv.* **lankness** *n.* [OE *hlanc* f. Gmc: cf. FLANK, LINK[1]]

lanky /lángki/ *adj.* (**lankier**, **lankiest**) (of limbs, a person, etc.) ungracefully thin and long or tall. □□ **lankily** *adv.* **lankiness** *n.*

■ spindly, gangling, gangly, rangy, lank; thin, lean, gaunt, skinny, twiggy, scraggy, bony.

lanner /lánnər/ *n.* a S. European falcon, *Falco biarmicus*, esp. the female. [ME f. OF *lanier* perh. f. OF *lanier* cowardly, orig. = weaver f. L *lanarius* wool-merchant f. *lana* wool]

lanneret /lánnərit/ *n.* a male lanner, smaller than the female. [ME f. OF *laneret* (as LANNER)]

lanolin /lánnəlin/ *n.* a fat found naturally on sheep's wool and used purified for cosmetics etc. [G f. L *lana* wool + *oleum* oil]

lansquenet /lánskənət/ *n.* **1** a card-game of German origin. **2** a German mercenary soldier in the 16th–17th c. [F f. G *Landsknecht* (as LAND, *Knecht* soldier f. OHG *kneht*: see KNIGHT)]

lantana /lantáynə/ *n.* any evergreen shrub of the genus *Lantana*, with usu. yellow or orange flowers. [mod.L]

lantern /lántərn/ *n.* **1 a** a lamp with a transparent usu. glass case protecting a candle flame etc. **b** a similar electric etc. lamp. **c** its case. **2 a** a raised structure on a dome, room, etc., glazed to admit light. **b** a similar structure for ventilation etc. **3** the light-chamber of a lighthouse. **4** = *magic lantern*. □ **lantern fish** any marine fish of the family Myctophidae, having small light organs on the head and body. **lantern-fly** (*pl.* **-flies**) any tropical homopterous insect of the family Fulgoridae, formerly thought to be luminous. **lantern-jawed** having lantern jaws. **lantern jaws** long thin jaws and chin, giving a hollow look to the face. **lantern-slide** a slide for projection by a magic lantern etc. (see SLIDE *n.* 5b). **lantern-wheel** a lantern-shaped gearwheel; a trundle. [ME f. OF *lanterne* f. L *lanterna* f. Gk *lamptēr* torch, lamp]

■ **1a, b** see LIGHT[1] *n.* 4a.

lanthanide /lánthənīd/ *n.* *Chem.* an element of the lanthanide series. □ **lanthanide series** a series of 15 metallic elements from lanthanum to lutetium in the periodic table, having similar chemical properties: also called *rare earths* (see RARE[1]). [G *Lanthanid* (as LANTHANUM)]

lanthanum /lánthənəm/ *n.* *Chem.* a silvery metallic element of the lanthanide series which occurs naturally and is used in the manufacture of alloys. ¶ Symb.: **La**. [Gk *lanthanō* escape notice, from having remained undetected in cerium oxide]

lanugo /lənyóogō/ *n.* fine soft hair, esp. that which covers the body and limbs of a human foetus. [L, = down f. *lana* wool]

lanyard /lányərd, -yaard/ *n.* **1** a cord hanging round the neck or looped round the shoulder, esp. of a Scout or sailor etc., to which a knife, a whistle, etc., may be attached. **2** *Naut.* a short rope or line used for securing, tightening, etc. **3** a cord attached to a breech mechanism for firing a gun. [ME f. OF *laniere*, *lasniere*: assim. to YARD[1]]

Laodicean /láyōdiseéən/ *adj.* & *n.* ● *adj.* lukewarm or half-hearted, esp. in religion or politics. ● *n.* such a person. [L *Laodicea* in Asia Minor (with ref. to the early Christians there: see Rev. 3:16)]
■ *adj.* see LUKEWARM 2.

Laotian /lówshiən, laa-ṓshiən/ *n.* & *adj.* ● *n.* **1 a** a native or national of Laos in SE Asia. **b** a person of Laotian descent. **2** the language of Laos. ● *adj.* of or relating to Laos or its people or language.

lap[1] /lap/ *n.* **1 a** the front of the body from the waist to the knees of a sitting person (*sat on her lap; caught it in his lap*). **b** the clothing, esp. a skirt, covering the lap. **c** the front of a skirt held up to catch or contain something. **2** a hollow among hills. **3** a hanging flap on a garment, a saddle, etc. □ **in** (or **on**) **a person's lap** as a person's responsibility. **in the lap of the gods** (of an event etc.) open to chance; beyond human control. **in the lap of luxury** in extremely luxurious surroundings. **lap-dog** a small pet dog. **lap robe** *US* a travelling-rug. □□ **lapful** *n.* (*pl.* **-fuls**). [OE *læppa* fold, flap]

lap[2] /lap/ *n.* & *v.* ● *n.* **1 a** one circuit of a racetrack etc. **b** a section of a journey etc. (*finally we were on the last lap*). **2 a** an amount of overlapping. **b** an overlapping or projecting part. **3 a** a layer or sheet (of cotton etc. being made) wound on a roller. **b** a single turn of rope, silk, thread, etc., round a drum or reel. **4** a rotating disk for polishing a gem or metal. ● *v.* (**lapped**, **lapping**) **1** *tr.* lead or overtake (a competitor in a race) by one or more laps. **2** *tr.* (often foll. by *about, round*) coil, fold, or wrap (a garment etc.) round esp. a person. **3** *tr.* (usu. foll. by *in*) enfold or swathe (a person) in wraps etc. **4** *tr.* (as **lapped** *adj.*) (usu. foll. by *in*) protectively encircled; enfolded caressingly. **5** *tr.* surround (a person) with an influence etc. **6** *intr.* (usu. foll. by *over*) project; overlap. **7** *tr.* cause to overlap. **8** *tr.* polish (a gem etc.) with a lap. □ **half-lap** = *lap joint.* **lap joint** the joining of rails, shafts, etc., by halving the thickness of each at the joint and fitting them together. **lap of honour** a ceremonial circuit of a football pitch, a track, etc., by a winner or winners. **lap-strake** *n.* a clinker-built boat. ● *adj.* clinker-built. **lap-weld** *v.tr.* weld with overlapping edges. ● *n.* such a weld. [ME, prob. f. LAP[1]]
■ *n.* **1 a** circuit, orbit, round, circle, tour, trip, revolution. **b** see LEG *n.* 7. **2 b** flap, projection, overlap. ● *v.* **3** see SWATHE *v.* **6, 7** see OVERLAP *v.* 1, 2, PROJECT *v.* 2.

lap[3] /lap/ *v.* & *n.* ● *v.* (**lapped**, **lapping**) **1** *tr.* **a** (also *absol.*) (usu. of an animal) drink (liquid) with the tongue. **b** (usu. foll. by *up, down*) consume (liquid) greedily. **c** (usu. foll. by *up*) consume (gossip, praise, etc.) greedily. **2 a** *tr.* (of water) move or beat upon (a shore) with a rippling sound as of lapping. **b** *intr.* (of waves etc.) move in ripples; make a lapping sound. ● *n.* **1 a** the process or an act of lapping. **b** the amount of liquid taken up. **2** the sound of wavelets on a beach. **3** liquid food for dogs. **4** *sl.* **a** a weak beverage. **b** any liquor. [OE *lapian* f. Gmc]
■ *v.* **1 a, b** lick up, drink, slurp; gulp (down), swallow, swill, guzzle, toss off, *colloq.* swig, *literary* quaff, *Brit. sl.* knock back; consume, soak (up). **c** (*lap up*) enjoy, bask in; accept, believe, credit, swallow (whole), *colloq.* fall for, *sl.* buy. **2 b** wash, splash, ripple, plash, break, roll, purl. ● *n.* **1** lick, slurp, gulp, swill, *colloq.* swig. **2** wash, splash, ripple, plash.

laparoscope /láppərəskōp/ *n. Surgery* a fibre optic instrument inserted through the abdominal wall to give a view of the organs in the abdomen. □□ **laparoscopy** /-róskəpi/ *n.* (*pl.* **-ies**). [Gk *lapara* flank + -SCOPE]

laparotomy /láppəróttəmi/ *n.* (*pl.* **-ies**) a surgical incision into the abdominal cavity for exploration or diagnosis. [Gk *lapara* flank + -TOMY]

lapel /ləpél/ *n.* the part of a coat, jacket, etc., folded back against the front round the neck opening. □□ **lapelled** *adj.* [LAP[1] + -EL]

lapicide /láppisīd/ *n.* a person who cuts or engraves on stone. [L *lapicida* irreg. f. *lapis -idis* stone: see -CIDE]

lapidary /láppidəri/ *adj.* & *n.* ● *adj.* **1** concerned with stone or stones. **2** engraved upon stone. **3** (of writing style) dignified and concise, suitable for inscriptions. ● *n.* (*pl.* **-ies**) a cutter, polisher, or engraver of gems. [ME f. L *lapidarius* f. *lapis -idis* stone]

lapilli /ləpíllī/ *n.pl.* stone fragments ejected from volcanoes. [It. f. L, pl. dimin. of *lapis* stone]

lapis lazuli /láppiss lázyooli, -lī/ *n.* **1** a blue mineral containing sodium aluminium silicate and sulphur, used as a gemstone. **2** a bright blue pigment formerly made from this. **3** its colour. [ME f. L *lapis* stone + med.L *lazuli* genit. of *lazulum* f. Pers. (as AZURE)]

Laplander /láplandər/ *n.* **1** a native or national of Lapland. **2** a person of this descent. [*Lapland* f. Sw. *Lappland* (as LAPP, LAND)]

Lapp /lap/ *n.* & *adj.* ● *n.* **1** a member of a nomadic Mongol people of N. Scandinavia. **2** the language of this people. ● *adj.* of or relating to the Lapps or their language. [Sw. *Lapp*, perh. orig. a term of contempt: cf. MHG *lappe* simpleton]

lappet /láppit/ *n.* **1** a small flap or fold of a garment etc. **2** a hanging or loose piece of flesh, such as a lobe or wattle. □□ **lappeted** *adj.* [LAP[1] + -ET[1]]
■ **1** see FLAP *n.* 1.

Lappish /láppish/ *adj.* & *n.* ● *adj.* = LAPP *adj.* ● *n.* the Lapp language.

lapse /laps/ *n.* & *v.* ● *n.* **1** a slight error; a slip of memory etc. **2** a weak or careless decline into an inferior state. **3** (foll. by *of*) an interval or passage of time (*after a lapse of three years*). **4** *Law* the termination of a right or privilege through disuse or failure to follow appropriate procedures. ● *v.intr.* **1** fail to maintain a position or standard. **2** (foll. by *into*) fall back into an inferior or previous state. **3** (of a right or privilege etc.) become invalid because it is not used or claimed or renewed. **4** (as **lapsed** *adj.*) (of a person or thing) that has lapsed. □ **lapse rate** *Meteorol.* the rate at which the temperature falls with increasing altitude. □□ **lapser** *n.* [L *lapsus* f. *labi laps-* glide, slip, fall]
■ *n.* **1** slip, error, mistake, fault, oversight, omission, peccadillo, *lapsus linguae or calami*; stumble, blunder, botch, gaffe, solecism, *colloq.* slip-up, *esp. US colloq.* blooper, flub, *sl.* fluff, goof, booboo, clanger, bloomer, *Brit. sl.* boob. **2** decline, lowering, deterioration, degeneration, diminution, drop, fall, slump, descent. **3** gap, break, interval, intermission, interruption, pause, lull, lacuna, hiatus, space, time-lag, period; wait, delay. ● *v.* **1, 2** relapse, slip (back), revert, fall (back *or* off), drop (off), diminish; sink, slump, decline, subside, deteriorate, degenerate; stumble, trip up. **3** run out, be up, be discontinued, become void, expire, terminate, end, come to an end, finish, cease, stop, peter out, die, *esp. Law* determine. **4** (**lapsed**) invalid, (null and) void, worthless; fallen, failed.

lapstone /lápstōn/ *n.* a shoemaker's stone held in the lap and used to beat leather on.

lapsus calami /lápsəss kálləmī/ *n.* (*pl.* same) a slip of the pen. [L: see LAPSE]

lapsus linguae /lápsəss línggwī/ *n.* a slip of the tongue. [L: see LAPSE]
■ see TRIP *n.* 2.

laptop /láptop/ *n.* (often *attrib.*) a microcomputer that is portable and suitable for use while travelling.

lapwing /lápwing/ *n.* a plover, *Vanellus vanellus*, with black and white plumage, crested head, and a shrill cry. [OE *hlēapewince* f. *hlēapan* LEAP + WINK: assim. to LAP[1], WING]

larboard /laárbərd/ *n.* & *adj. Naut. archaic* = PORT[3]. [ME *lade-, ladde-, lathe-* (perh. = LADE + BOARD): later assim. to *starboard*]

larceny /laárs'ni/ *n.* (*pl.* **-ies**) the theft of personal property. ¶ In 1968 replaced as a statutory crime in English law by *theft.* □□ **larcener** *n.* **larcenist** *n.* **larcenous** *adj.* [OF *larcin* f. L *latrocinium* f. *latro* robber, mercenary f. Gk *latreus*]
■ see THEFT 1. □□ **larcenous** see LAWLESS 2.

larch /laarch/ *n.* **1** a deciduous coniferous tree of the genus *Larix*, with bright foliage and producing tough timber. **2**

(in full **larchwood**) its wood. [MHG *larche* ult. f. L *larix -icis*]

lard /laard/ *n.* & *v.* ● *n.* the internal fat of the abdomen of pigs, esp. when rendered and clarified for use in cooking and pharmacy. ● *v.tr.* **1** insert strips of fat or bacon in (meat etc.) before cooking. **2** (foll. by *with*) embellish (talk or writing) with foreign or technical terms. [ME f. OF *lard* bacon f. L *lardum, laridum*, rel. to Gk *larinos* fat]

larder /laárdər/ *n.* **1** a room or cupboard for storing food. **2** a wild animal's store of food, esp. for winter. [ME f. OF *lardier* f. med.L *lardarium* (as LARD)]

lardon /laárd'n/ *n.* (also **lardoon** /-dóon/) a strip of fat bacon used to lard meat. [ME f. F *lardon* (as LARD)]

lardy /laárdi/ *adj.* like or with lard. □ **lardy-cake** *Brit.* a cake made with lard, currants, etc.

■ see GREASY 1.

lares /laáreez/ *n.pl. Rom.Hist.* the household gods. □ **lares and penates** the home. [L]

large /laarj/ *adj.* & *n.* ● *adj.* **1** of considerable or relatively great size or extent. **2** of the larger kind (*the large intestine*). **3** of wide range; comprehensive. **4** pursuing an activity on a large scale (*large farmer*). ● *n.* (**at large**) **1** at liberty. **2** as a body or whole (*popular with the people at large*). **3** (of a narration etc.) at full length and with all details. **4** without a specific target (*scatters insults at large*). **5** *US* representing a whole area and not merely a part of it (*congressman at large*). □ **in large** on a large scale. **large as life** see LIFE. **large-minded** liberal; not narrow-minded. **larger than life** see LIFE. **large-scale** made or occurring on a large scale or in large amounts. □□ **largeness** *n.* **largish** *adj.* [ME f. OF f. fem. of L *largus* copious]

■ *adj.* **1, 2** big, great, wide, broad, beamy, long, tall, high, capacious, roomy, spacious, voluminous, king-size, extensive, sizeable, substantial, considerable, ample, biggish, man-size(d); bigger, greater, major, main, principal; bulky, hefty, stout, thickset, chunky, stocky, heavy-set, brawny, husky, sturdy, muscular, strapping, beefy, burly, solid, weighty, heavy, ponderous, mighty, *colloq.* hulking, hunky, whacking, thumping, *sl.* whopping; corpulent, fat, obese, rotund, portly, plump, adipose, overweight, gross, outsize, oversize(d); see also IMMENSE 1. **3** wide, wide-ranging, extensive, comprehensive, far-reaching, sweeping, widespread, broad, expansive, exhaustive, thorough, in-depth, all-out. **4** large-scale, grand, macro-, major, *attrib.* mass; epic, heroic, Homeric. ● *n.* (**at large**) **1** see FREE *adj.* 3b. **2** as a whole, collectively, in the aggregate, in the lump, in a body, altogether, over all, overall. **3** see *at length* 1 (LENGTH). **4** see *at random* (RANDOM). □ **large-scale** see LARGE *adj.* 4 above.

largely /laárjli/ *adv.* to a great extent; principally (*is largely due to laziness*).

■ to a great extent, in great part, in great measure, mostly, chiefly, mainly, principally, by and large; as a rule, generally, in general, in the main, on the whole, pretty much, essentially, at bottom, basically, in essence, fundamentally.

largesse /laarzhéss/ *n.* (also **largess**) **1** money or gifts freely given, esp. on an occasion of rejoicing, by a person in high position. **2** generosity, beneficence. [ME f. OF *largesse* ult. f. L *largus* copious]

■ **1** gifts, presents, grants, bonuses, endowments, favour(s), contributions, donations, hand-outs, gratuities, bounty, *hist.* alms. **2** generosity, beneficence, munificence, bounty, liberality, open-handedness, lavishness, benevolence, *poet.* bounteousness; philanthropy, charity, support, subvention, aid, help, subsidy.

larghetto /laargéttō/ *adv., adj.,* & *n. Mus.* ● *adv.* & *adj.* in a fairly slow tempo. ● *n.* (*pl.* **-os**) a larghetto passage or movement. [It., dimin. of LARGO]

largo /laárgō/ *adv., adj.,* & *n. Mus.* ● *adv.* & *adj.* in a slow tempo and dignified in style. ● *n.* (*pl.* **-os**) a largo passage or movement. [It., = broad]

lariat /lárriət/ *n.* **1** a lasso. **2** a tethering-rope, esp. used by cowboys. [Sp. *la reata* f. *reatar* tie again (as RE-, L *aptare* adjust f. *aptus* APT, fit)]

■ **1** see LASSO *n.*

lark[1] /laark/ *n.* **1** any small bird of the family Alaudidae with brown plumage, elongated hind claws and tuneful song, esp. the skylark. **2** any of various similar birds such as the meadow lark. [OE *lāferce, læwerce*, of unkn. orig.]

lark[2] /laark/ *n.* & *v. colloq.* ● *n.* **1** a frolic or spree; an amusing incident; a joke. **2** *Brit.* a type of activity, affair, etc. (*fed up with this digging lark*). ● *v.intr.* (foll. by *about*) play tricks; frolic. □□ **larky** *adj.* **larkiness** *n.* [19th c.: orig. uncert.]

■ *n.* **1** frolic, escapade, adventure, caper, fling, romp, rollick, revel, antic, laugh, *colloq.* spree, giggle, scream, *sl.* razzle-dazzle; joke, gag, jape, game, trick, prank, horseplay, shenanigan(s), mischief, practical joke, booby-trap, hoax, *Austral.* goak, *colloq.* put-on. **2** procedure, rigmarole, nonsense, *derog.* business, *colloq.* palaver, performance, *Brit. sl.* carry-on. ● *v.* **1** (*lark about*) jape, fool (about *or* around), mess about *or* around, *colloq.* kid, *Brit. colloq.* muck about *or* around; frolic, caper, romp, revel, rollick, play (about *or* around), sport, gambol, skylark, *sl.* cavort.

larkspur /laárkspur/ *n.* any of various plants of the genus *Consolida*, with a spur-shaped calyx.

larn /laarn/ *v. colloq.* or *joc.* **1** *intr.* = LEARN. **2** *tr.* teach (*that'll larn you*). [dial. form of LEARN]

larrikin /lárrikin/ *n. Austral.* a hooligan. [also Engl. dial.: perh. f. the name *Larry* (pet-form of *Lawrence*) + -KIN]

■ see THUG 1.

larrup /lárrəp/ *v.tr.* (**larruped, larruping**) *colloq.* thrash. [dial.: perh. f. LATHER]

Larry /lárri/ *n.* □ **as happy as Larry** *colloq.* extremely happy. [20th c.: orig. uncert.: cf. LARRIKIN]

larva /laárvə/ *n.* (*pl.* **larvae** /-vee/) **1** the stage of development of an insect between egg and pupa, e.g. a caterpillar. **2** an immature form of other animals that undergo some metamorphosis, e.g. a tadpole. □□ **larval** *adj.* **larvicide** /laárvisīd/ *n.* [L, = ghost, mask]

laryngeal /lərínjiəl/ *adj.* **1** of or relating to the larynx. **2** *Phonet.* (of a sound) made in the larynx.

laryngitis /lárrinjītiss/ *n.* inflammation of the larynx. □□ **laryngitic** /-jíttik/ *adj.*

laryngoscope /lərínggəskōp/ *n.* an instrument for examining the larynx, or for inserting a tube through it.

laryngotomy /lárringgóttəmi/ *n.* (*pl.* **-ies**) a surgical incision of the larynx, esp. to provide an air passage when breathing is obstructed.

larynx /lárringks/ *n.* (*pl.* **larynges** /lərínjeez/) the hollow muscular organ forming an air passage to the lungs and holding the vocal cords in humans and other mammals. [mod.L f. Gk *larugx -ggos*]

lasagne /ləsányə, -saányə/ *n.* pasta in the form of sheets or wide ribbons, esp. as cooked and served with minced meat and cheese sauce. [It., pl. of *lasagna* f. L *lasanum* cooking-pot]

Lascar /láskər/ *n.* an E. Indian seaman. [ult. f. Urdu & Pers. *laškar* army]

lascivious /ləsívviəss/ *adj.* **1** lustful. **2** inciting to or evoking lust. □□ **lasciviously** *adv.* **lasciviousness** *n.* [ME f. LL *lasciviosus* f. L *lascivia* lustfulness f. *lascivus* sportive, wanton]

■ **1** lustful, randy, lecherous, sexy, licentious, lewd, dirty, prurient, salacious, libidinous, erotic, sensual, lubricious, promiscuous, depraved, dissolute, ruttish, goatish, wanton, debauched, hot, *formal* concupiscent, *sl.* horny. **2** pornographic, obscene, blue, indecent, gross, coarse, vile, offensive, ribald, bawdy, suggestive, lurid, salacious, risqué, sexy, smutty, dirty, filthy, *euphem.* adult, *sl.* horny.

lase /layz/ *v.intr.* **1** function as or in a laser. **2** (of a substance) undergo the physical processes employed in a laser. [back-form. f. LASER]

laser /láyzər/ *n.* a device that generates an intense beam of coherent monochromatic radiation in the infrared, visible, or ultraviolet region of the electromagnetic spectrum, by stimulated emission of photons from an excited source. [*l*ight *a*mplification by *s*timulated *e*mission of *r*adiation: cf. MASER]

laserdisc /láyzərdisk/ *n.* = DISC 4b.

laservision /láyzərvizh'n/ *n.* a system for the reproduction of video signals recorded on a disc with a laser. [LASER + VISION, after TELEVISION]

lash /lash/ *v.* & *n.* ● *v.* **1** *intr.* make a sudden whiplike movement with a limb or flexible instrument. **2** *tr.* beat with a whip, rope, etc. **3** *intr.* pour or rush with great force. **4** *intr.* (foll. by *at*, *against*) strike violently. **5** *tr.* castigate in words. **6** *tr.* urge on as with a lash. **7** *tr.* (foll. by *down*, *together*, etc.) fasten with a cord, rope, etc. **8** *tr.* (of rain, wind, etc.) beat forcefully upon. ● *n.* **1 a** a sharp blow made by a whip, rope, etc. **b** (prec. by *the*) punishment by beating with a whip etc. **2** the flexible end of a whip. **3** (usu. in *pl.*) an eyelash. □ **lash out 1** (often foll. by *at*) speak or hit out angrily. **2** spend money extravagantly, be lavish. **lash-up** a makeshift or improvised structure or arrangement. □□ **lasher** *n.* **lashingly** *adv.* (esp. in senses 4–5 of *v.*). **lashless** *adj.* [ME: prob. imit.]

■ *v.* **1, 2** whip, flail, thrash, thresh; (*tr.*) flog, beat, switch, scourge, horsewhip, strap, leather, flick, crack, *colloq.* thwack, lambaste, whack, give a person a (good) hiding *or* thrashing *or* drubbing *or* belting, *esp. US colloq.* whale, *sl.* belt, tan a person's hide. **3** pour, rush, gush, flow, flood, stream, spurt, spew, cascade, rain, teem, bucket, pelt. **4, 8** crash, beat, thrash, pound, dash, hit, strike, batter, pelt, *colloq.* thwack, whack. **5** see LAMBASTE 2. **6** see URGE *v.* 1. **7** fasten, tie, bind, attach, secure, rope, fix, strap, make fast. ● *n.* **1 a** stroke, blow, strike, clout, hit, smack, thump, crack, lick, *archaic* stripe, *colloq.* whack, thwack, *sl.* belt; slash, cut. **b** (*the lash*) whipping, flogging, flagellation. **2** whip, scourge, thong, quirt, bull-whip, horsewhip, kourbash, rawhide, sjambok, *esp. Austral.* pizzle, *Bibl.* scorpion, *hist.* rope's end, cat-o'-nine-tails, cat, knout. □ **lash out 1** (*lash out at*) hit out at, attack, tear into, *colloq.* lay into; berate, have a go at, rap, abuse, revile, inveigh against, flay, belabour, *colloq.* lambaste, jump on. **2** spend, expend, pay out, *colloq.* shell out, splash out; see also LAVISH *v.*

lashing /láshing/ *n.* **1** a beating. **2** cord used for lashing.

■ **1** see WHIPPING 1.

lashings /láshingz/ *n.pl. Brit. colloq.* (foll. by *of*) plenty; an abundance.

■ see ABUNDANCE 1.

lass /lass/ *n.* esp. *Sc.* & *N.Engl.* or *poet.* a girl or young woman. [ME *lasce* ult. f. ON *laskwa* unmarried (fem.)]

■ girl, young woman, young lady, woman, schoolgirl, miss, mademoiselle, Fräulein, *Ir.* colleen, *archaic* demoiselle, *archaic or literary* damsel, *archaic or poet.* maiden, maid, *poet.* nymph, *colloq.* lassie, filly, popsy, floozie, nymphet, *joc.* wench, *joc. or derog.* baggage, chit, gill, *sl.* chick, gal, petticoat, *Austral.* & *NZ sl.* sheila, brush, *Brit. sl.* bird, *US sl.* frail, dame, broad, *sl. derog.* piece, heifer; gamine, tomboy, minx, sylph, rosebud, *colloq.* peach, sex kitten, puss, *Brit. colloq.* dolly-bird, madam, *sl.* baby, cutie, doll, *US sl.* babe, fox; see also YOUTH *n.* 4.

Lassa fever /lássə/ *n.* an acute and often fatal febrile viral disease of tropical Africa. [*Lassa* in Nigeria, where first reported]

lassie /lássi/ *n. colloq.* = LASS.

lassitude /lássityōōd/ *n.* **1** languor, weariness. **2** disinclination to exert or interest oneself. [F *lassitude* or L *lassitudo* f. *lassus* tired]

■ see LETHARGY 1.

lasso /lasōō, lássō/ *n.* & *v.* ● *n.* (*pl.* **-os** or **-oes**) a rope with a noose at one end, used esp. in N. America for catching cattle etc. ● *v.tr.* (**-oes, -oed**) catch with a lasso. □□ **lassoer** *n.* [Sp. *lazo* LACE]

■ *n.* lariat, noose, *US* rope. ● *v.* noose, snare, rope.

last[1] /laast/ *adj.*, *adv.*, & *n.* ● *adj.* **1** after all others; coming at or belonging to the end. **2 a** most recent; next before a specified time (*last Christmas*; *last week*). **b** preceding; previous in a sequence (*got on at the last station*). **3** only remaining (*the last biscuit*; *our last chance*). **4** (prec. by *the*) least likely or suitable (*the last person I'd want*; *the last thing I'd have expected*). **5** the lowest in rank (*the last place*). ● *adv.* **1** after all others (esp. in *comb.*: *last-mentioned*). **2** on the last occasion before the present (*when did you last see him?*). **3** (esp. in enumerating) lastly. ● *n.* **1** a person or thing that is last, last-mentioned, most recent, etc. **2** (prec. by *the*) the last mention or sight etc. (*shall never hear the last of it*). **3** the last performance of certain acts (*breathed his last*). **4** (prec. by *the*) **a** the end or last moment. **b** death. □ **at last** (or **long last**) in the end; after much delay. **last agony** the pangs of death. **last ditch** a place of final desperate defence (often (with hyphen) *attrib.*). **Last Judgement** see JUDGEMENT. **last minute** (or **moment**) the time just before an important event (often (with hyphen) *attrib.*). **last name** surname. **last post** see POST[3]. **last rites** sacred rites for a person about to die. **the last straw** a slight addition to a burden or difficulty that makes it finally unbearable. **the Last Supper** that of Christ and his disciples on the eve of the Crucifixion, as recorded in the New Testament. **last thing** *adv.* very late, esp. as a final act before going to bed. **the last word 1** a final or definitive statement (*always has the last word*; *is the last word on this subject*). **2** (often foll. by *in*) the latest fashion. **on one's last legs** see LEG. **pay one's last respects** see RESPECT. **to** (or **till**) **the last** till the end; esp. till death. [OE *latost* superl.: see LATE]

■ *adj.* **1, 5** final, concluding, terminal, ultimate, extreme; hindmost, rearmost, aftermost, eventual; definitive, conclusive, decisive; bottom, lowest, worst. **2** latest, newest, most recent *or* up to date; precedent, preceding, previous, prior, former, foregoing, antecedent, earlier. **3** final, ultimate; residual, leftover, surviving, remaining, outstanding; see also ONLY *adj.* ● *adv.* **3** finally, lastly, in fine, in conclusion. ● *n.* **2** end, finish. **4 a** see END *n.* 3. **b** see DEATH *n.* 1. □ **at last** finally, eventually, ultimately, at length. **last ditch** (*attrib.*) final, extreme, desperate. **the last word 2** all the rage, the latest, state of the art, *dernier cri*.

last[2] /laast/ *v.intr.* **1** remain unexhausted or adequate or alive for a specified or considerable time; suffice (*enough food to last us a week*; *the battery lasts and lasts*). **2** continue for a specified time (*the journey lasts an hour*). □ **last out** remain adequate or in existence for the whole of a period previously stated or implied. [OE *lǣstan* f. Gmc]

■ continue, go on, keep on, carry on; survive, live, persist, remain, stay, hold out, last out, go the distance, stand up, wear, endure, withstand, resist, *archaic* abide, *colloq.* stick it out; keep, stay fresh; suffice, serve, do.

last[3] /laast/ *n.* a shoemaker's model for shaping or repairing a shoe or boot. □ **stick to one's last** not meddle with what one does not understand. [OE *lǣste* last, *lǣst* boot, *lāst* footprint f. Gmc]

■ mould, matrix, form, model, pattern.

lasting /laásting/ *adj.* **1** continuing, permanent. **2** durable. □□ **lastingly** *adv.* **lastingness** *n.*

■ permanent, constant, perpetual, imperishable, indestructible, incorruptible, indissoluble, long, everlasting, undying, unfading, perennial, evergreen, eternal, enduring, abiding, durable, persistent, continuing, long-lasting, long-lived, long-running, long-term, steady, steadfast, lifelong.

lastly /laástli/ *adv.* finally; in the last place.

■ see *finally* (FINAL).

lat. *abbr.* latitude.

latch /lach/ *n.* & *v.* ● *n.* **1** a bar with a catch and lever used as a fastening for a gate etc. **2** a spring-lock preventing a door from being opened from the outside without a key after being shut. ● *v.tr.* & *intr.* fasten or be fastened with a

latch. □ **latch on** (often foll. by *to*) *colloq.* **1** attach oneself (to). **2** understand. **on the latch** fastened by the latch only, not locked. [prob. f. (now dial.) *latch* (v.) seize f. OE *læccan* f. Gmc]
■ *n.* **2** see LOCK[1] *n.* 1. ● *v.* see LOCK[1] *v.* 1. □ **latch on 2** see UNDERSTAND 1, 2.

latchkey /láchkee/ *n.* (*pl.* **-eys**) a key of an outer door. □ **latchkey child** a child who is alone at home after school until a parent returns from work.
■ see KEY[1] *n.* 1.

late /layt/ *adj.* & *adv.* ● *adj.* **1** after the due or usual time; occurring or done after the proper time (*late for dinner*; *a late milk delivery*). **2 a** far on in the day or night or in a specified time or period. **b** far on in development. **3** flowering or ripening towards the end of the season (*late strawberries*). **4** (prec. by *the* or *my*, *his*, etc.) no longer alive or having the specified status (*my late husband*; *the late president*). **5** of recent date (*the late storms*). **6** (as **latest**, prec. by *the*) fashionable, up to date. ● *adv.* **1** after the due or usual time (*arrived late*). **2** far on in time (*this happened later on*). **3** at or till a late hour. **4** at a late stage of development. **5** formerly but not now (*late of the Scillies*). □ **at the latest** as the latest time envisaged (*will have done it by six at the latest*). **late in the day** *colloq.* at a late stage in the proceedings, esp. too late to be useful. **late Latin** Latin of about AD 200–600. **the latest 1** the most recent news etc. (*have you heard the latest?*). **2** the current fashion. □□ **lateness** *n.* [OE *læt* (adj.), *late* (adv.) f. Gmc]
■ *adj.* **1** tardy, delayed, overdue, belated, behind time, latish, behindhand, in arrears, dilatory, unpunctual, *US* past due. **4** dead, departed, lamented, *formal* deceased; former, past, ex-, one-time, erstwhile, sometime, *ci-devant*, *archaic* whilom. **5** recent, latest, last. **6** (**the latest**) fashionable, current, modern, stylish, à la mode, up to the minute, up to date, in vogue, voguish, in, all the rage, *colloq.* with it, flash, swinging, *colloq. often derog.* trendy, *sl.* groovy, hip. ● *adv.* **1** tardily, unpunctually, belatedly, latish. **5** formerly, previously, once, at one time, sometime, *ci-devant*, *archaic* erstwhile, erst, whilom, *formal* heretofore; recently, lately, of late, latterly; hitherto. □ **the latest 2** see VOGUE 1.

latecomer /láytkummər/ *n.* a person who arrives late.

lateen /ləteén/ *adj.* (of a ship) rigged with a lateen sail. □ **lateen sail** a triangular sail on a long yard at an angle of 45° to the mast. [F (*voile*) *latine* Latin (sail), because common in the Mediterranean]

lately /láytli/ *adv.* not long ago; recently; in recent times. [OE *lætlīce* (as LATE, -LY[2])]
■ recently, (of) late, latterly; just; hitherto.

La Tène /laa tén/ *adj.* of or relating to the second Iron-Age culture of central and W. Europe. [*La Tène* in Switzerland, where remains of it were first identified]

latent /láyt'nt/ *adj.* **1** concealed, dormant. **2** existing but not developed or manifest. □ **latent heat** *Physics* the heat required to convert a solid into a liquid or vapour, or a liquid into a vapour, without change of temperature. **latent image** *Photog.* an image not yet made visible by developing. □□ **latency** *n.* **latently** *adv.* [L *latēre latent-* be hidden]
■ **1** see DORMANT 2b. **2** see POTENTIAL *adj.*

-later /lətər/ *comb. form* denoting a person who worships a particular thing or person (*idolater*). [Gk: see LATRIA]

lateral /láttərəl/ *adj.* & *n.* ● *adj.* **1** of, at, towards, or from the side or sides. **2** descended from a brother or sister of a person in direct line. ● *n.* a side part etc., esp. a lateral shoot or branch. □ **lateral line** *Zool.* a visible line along the side of a fish consisting of a series of sense organs acting as vibration receptors. **lateral thinking** a method of solving problems indirectly or by apparently illogical methods. □□ **laterally** *adv.* [L *lateralis* f. *latus lateris* side]
■ □□ **laterally** see SIDEWAYS *adv.*

laterite /láttərīt/ *n.* a red or yellow ferruginous clay, friable and hardening in air, used for making roads in the tropics. □□ **lateritic** /-ríttik/ *adj.* [L *later* brick + -ITE[1]]

latex /láyteks/ *n.* (*pl.* **latexes** or **latices** /-tiseez/) **1** a milky fluid of mixed composition found in various plants and trees, esp. the rubber tree, and used for commercial purposes. **2** a synthetic product resembling this. [L, = liquid]

lath /laath/ *n.* & *v.* ● *n.* (*pl.* **laths** /laaths, laathz/) a thin flat strip of wood, esp. each of a series forming a framework or support for plaster etc. ● *v.tr.* attach laths to (a wall or ceiling). □ **lath and plaster** a common material for interior walls and ceilings etc. [OE *lætt*]

lathe /layth/ *n.* a machine for shaping wood, metal, etc., by means of a rotating drive which turns the piece being worked on against changeable cutting tools. [prob. rel. to ODa. *lad* structure, frame, f. ON *hlath*, rel. to *hlatha* LADE]

lather /laáthər, láthər/ *n.* & *v.* ● *n.* **1** a froth produced by agitating soap etc. and water. **2** frothy sweat, esp. of a horse. **3** a state of agitation. ● *v.* **1** *intr.* (of soap etc.) form a lather. **2** *tr.* cover with lather. **3** *intr.* (of a horse etc.) develop or become covered with lather. **4** *tr. colloq.* thrash. □□ **lathery** *adj.* [OE *lēathor* (n.), *lēthran* (v.)]
■ *n.* **1** froth, foam, spume, suds, bubbles. **3** fuss, flutter, panic, bother, *colloq.* dither, tizzy, state, flap, stew, sweat, *literary* pother. ● *v.* **1** soap (up), suds; foam, froth, spume; whip (up). **2** soap, suds. **3** sweat (up), foam, froth. **4** see BEAT *v.* 1.

lathi /laáti/ *n.* (*pl.* **lathis**) (in India) a long heavy iron-bound bamboo stick used as a weapon, esp. by police. [Hindi *lāṭhī*]

latices *pl.* of LATEX.

Latin /láttin/ *n.* & *adj.* ● *n.* **1** the Italic language of ancient Rome and its empire, originating in Latium. **2** *Rom.Hist.* an inhabitant of ancient Latium in Central Italy. ● *adj.* **1** of or in Latin. **2** of the countries or peoples (e.g. France and Spain) using languages developed from Latin. **3** *Rom.Hist.* of or relating to ancient Latium or its inhabitants. **4** of the Roman Catholic Church. □ **Latin America** the parts of Central and S. America where Spanish or Portuguese is the main language. **Latin American** *n.* a native of Latin America. ● *adj.* of or relating to Latin America. **Latin Church** the Western Church. □□ **Latinism** *n.* **Latinist** *n.* [ME f. OF *Latin* or L *Latinus* f. *Latium*]
■ *adj.* **3** see CLASSICAL 1a.

Latinate /láttinayt/ *adj.* having the character of Latin.

Latinize /láttinīz/ *v.* (also **-ise**) **1** *tr.* give a Latin or Latinate form to. **2** *tr.* translate into Latin. **3** *tr.* make conformable to the ideas, customs, etc., of the ancient Romans, Latin peoples, or Latin Church. **4** *intr.* use Latin forms, idioms, etc. □□ **Latinization** /-záysh'n/ *n.* **Latinizer** *n.* [LL *latinizare* (as LATIN)]

latish /láytish/ *adj.* & *adv.* fairly late.

latitude /láttityōōd/ *n.* **1** *Geog.* **a** the angular distance on a meridian north or south of the equator, expressed in degrees and minutes. **b** (usu. in *pl.*) regions or climes, esp. with reference to temperature (*warm latitudes*). **2** freedom from narrowness; liberality of interpretation. **3** tolerated variety of action or opinion (*was allowed much latitude*). **4** *Astron.* the angular distance of a celestial body or point from the ecliptic. □ **high latitudes** regions near the poles. **low latitudes** regions near the equator. □□ **latitudinal** /-tyōōdin'l/ *adj.* **latitudinally** /-tyōōdinəli/ *adv.* [ME, = breadth, f. L *latitudo -dinis* f. *latus* broad]
■ **2, 3** see LEEWAY.

latitudinarian /láttityōōdináiriən/ *adj.* & *n.* ● *adj.* allowing latitude esp. in religion; showing no preference among varying creeds and forms of worship. ● *n.* a person with a latitudinarian attitude. □□ **latitudinarianism** *n.* [L *latitudo -dinis* breadth + -ARIAN]
■ *adj.* see TOLERANT 1. ● *n.* see LIBERAL *n.* 1.

latria /látriə/ *n.* *Theol.* supreme worship allowed to God alone. [LL f. Gk *latreia* worship f. *latreuō* serve]

latrine /ləteén/ *n.* a communal lavatory, esp. in a camp, barracks, etc. [F f. L *latrina*, shortening of *lavatrina* f. *lavare* wash]

■ see TOILET *n.* 1.

-latry /lətri/ *comb. form* denoting worship (*idolatry*). [Gk *latreia*: see LATRIA]

latten /látt'n/ *n.* an alloy of copper and zinc, often rolled into sheets, and formerly used for monumental brasses and church articles. [ME *latoun* f. OF *laton, leiton*]

latter /láttər/ *adj.* **1 a** denoting the second-mentioned of two, or *disp.* the last-mentioned of three or more. **b** (prec. by *the*; usu. *absol.*) the second- or last-mentioned person or thing. **2** nearer to the end (*the latter part of the year*). **3** recent. **4** belonging to the end of a period, of the world, etc. □ **latter-day** modern, newfangled. **Latter-day Saints** the Mormons' name for themselves. [OE *lætra*, compar. of *læt* LATE]

■ □ **latter-day** see MODERN.

latterly /láttərli/ *adv.* **1** in the latter part of life or of a period. **2** recently.

■ **2** see LATELY.

lattice /láttiss/ *n.* **1 a** a structure of crossed laths or bars with spaces between, used as a screen, fence, etc. **b** (in full **lattice-work**) laths arranged in lattice formation. **2** *Crystallog.* a regular periodic arrangement of atoms, ions, or molecules in a crystalline solid. □ **lattice frame** (or **girder**) a girder or truss made of top and bottom members connected by struts usu. crossing diagonally. **lattice window** a window with small panes set in diagonally crossing strips of lead. □□ **latticed** *adj.* **latticing** *n.* [ME f. OF *lattis* f. *latte* lath f. WG]

■ **1** see MESH *n.* 1, 2, 3a.

Latvian /látviən/ *n.* & *adj.* ● *n.* **1 a** a native of Latvia, a Baltic republic. **b** a person of Latvian descent. **2** the language of Latvia. ● *adj.* of or relating to Latvia or its people or language.

laud /lawd/ *v.* & *n.* ● *v.tr.* praise or extol, esp. in hymns. ● *n.* **1** *literary* praise; a hymn of praise. **2** (in *pl.*) the traditional morning prayer of the Roman Catholic Church. [ME: (n.) f. OF *laude*, (v.) f. L *laudare*, f. L *laus laudis* praise]

■ *v.* praise, extol, acclaim, exalt, eulogize, panegyrize, hymn, celebrate, sing the praises of, honour, glorify, applaud; build up, cry up, write up, promote, advance, puff, recommend, commend, *colloq.* boost, crack up.

laudable /láwdəb'l/ *adj.* commendable, praiseworthy. □□ **laudability** /-bílliti/ *n.* **laudably** *adv.* [ME f. L *laudabilis* (as LAUD)]

■ praiseworthy, commendable, meritorious, creditable, admirable, estimable, worthy, good; outstanding, excellent, exemplary, noteworthy, notable.

laudanum /láwdnəm, lód-/ *n.* a solution containing morphine and prepared from opium, formerly used as a narcotic painkiller. [mod.L, the name given by Paracelsus to a costly medicament, later applied to preparations containing opium: perh. var. of LADANUM]

laudation /lawdáysh'n/ *n. formal* praise. [L *laudatio -onis* (as LAUD)]

■ see TRIBUTE 1.

laudatory /láwdətəri, -tri/ *adj.* (also **laudative** /-tiv/) expressing praise.

■ laudative, praiseful, eulogistic, panegyrical, encomiastic, complimentary, flattering; favourable, glowing, good.

laugh /laaf/ *v.* & *n.* ● *v.* **1** *intr.* make the spontaneous sounds and movements usual in expressing lively amusement, scorn, derision, etc. **2** *tr.* express by laughing. **3** *tr.* bring (a person) into a certain state by laughing (*laughed them into agreeing*). **4** *intr.* (foll. by *at*) ridicule, make fun of (*laughed at us for going*). **5** *intr.* (**be laughing**) *colloq.* be in a fortunate or successful position. **6** *intr.* esp. *poet.* make sounds reminiscent of laughing. ● *n.* **1** the sound or act or manner of laughing. **2** *colloq.* a comical or ridiculous person or thing. □ **have the last laugh** be ultimately the winner. **laugh in a person's face** show open scorn for a person. **laugh off** get rid of (embarrassment or humiliation) with a jest. **laugh on the other side of one's face** change from enjoyment or amusement to displeasure, shame, apprehension, etc. **laugh out of court** deprive of a hearing by ridicule. **laugh up one's sleeve** be secretly or inwardly amused. □□ **laugher** *n.* [OE *hlæhhan, hliehhan* f. Gmc]

■ *v.* **1** titter, giggle, tee-hee, chuckle, chortle, guffaw, split one's sides, scream, shriek (with laughter), go into hysterics, roar (with laughter), *colloq.* crack up, kill oneself, roll about, *literary* cachinnate; snigger, snicker, fleer; bray, neigh, cackle, hoot, *sl.* crease up. **4** (*laugh at*) deride, ridicule, mock (at), jeer (at), poke fun at, guy, make fun *or* sport of, make merry over, make a fool *or* monkey *or* ass of, scoff at, sneer at, chaff, twit, tease, pull a person's leg, taunt, rag, have a fling *or* go at, run down, heckle, catcall, *Brit.* barrack, *archaic* smoke, *colloq.* have a shy at, rib, *sl.* ballyrag, take the mickey out of, *Austral.* & *NZ sl.* sling off at, *coarse sl.* take the piss out of; see also LAMPOON *v.* **5** (*be laughing*) be in clover, be well off, be made, ride high, *colloq.* have it made, *Brit. colloq.* turn up trumps, be on a winner, be on a winning ticket. ● *n.* **1** titter, giggle, tee-hee, chuckle, chortle, snigger, snicker, cackle, guffaw, roar, scream, shriek, *literary* cachinnation. **2** joke, frolic, *colloq.* lark, giggle, hoot, scream, riot; prank, jape, practical joke, trick; farce, mockery, absurdity, nonsense, travesty, charade, caricature; laughing-stock, figure of fun, fool, ass, standing joke, *colloq.* goat. □ **have the last laugh** have the last word; come out on top, come off best, come off the winner. **laugh in a person's face** see SCORN *v.* 1 **laugh off** brush aside, shrug off, pooh-pooh; spurn, dismiss, reject, disregard, ignore, belittle, minimize.

laughable /laáfəb'l/ *adj.* ludicrous; highly amusing. □□ **laughably** *adv.*

■ see LUDICROUS.

laughing /laáfing/ *n.* & *adj.* ● *n.* laughter. ● *adj.* in senses of LAUGH *v.* □ **laughing-gas** nitrous oxide as an anaesthetic, formerly used without oxygen and causing an exhilarating effect when inhaled. **laughing hyena** see HYENA. **laughing jackass** = KOOKABURRA. **laughing-stock** a person or thing open to general ridicule. **no laughing matter** something serious. □□ **laughingly** *adv.*

■ □ **laughing-stock** fool, exhibition, spectacle.

laughter /laáftər/ *n.* the act or sound of laughing. [OE *hleahtor* f. Gmc]

■ see LAUGH *n.* 1.

launce /laanss, lanss/ *n.* a sand eel. [perh. f. LANCE: cf. *garfish*]

launch[1] /lawnch/ *v.* & *n.* ● *v.* **1** *tr.* set (a vessel) afloat. **2** *tr.* hurl or send forth (a weapon, rocket, etc.). **3** *tr.* start or set in motion (an enterprise, a person on a course of action, etc.). **4** *tr.* formally introduce (a new product) with publicity etc. **5** *intr.* (often foll. by *out, into*, etc.) **a** make a start, esp. on an ambitious enterprise. **b** burst into strong language etc. ● *n.* the act or an instance of launching. □ **launch** (or **launching**) **pad** a platform with a supporting structure, from which rockets are launched. [ME f. AF *launcher*, ONF *lancher*, OF *lancier* LANCE *v.*]

■ *v.* **1, 3, 4** float; set in motion, get under way, get going, get started; initiate, begin, start (off), originate, pioneer, spearhead, inaugurate, institute, introduce, usher in, embark upon, enter upon, *colloq.* kick off, *formal* commence; establish, organize, set up, mount, found, open. **2** shoot, fire, discharge, propel, project, hurl, throw, toss, sling, pitch, fling, heave, catapult, send (off *or* up), dispatch, let go (with), deliver, release, *poet.* lance. **5 a** start, set out *or* off, begin, get under way, go. **b** burst, break, erupt, explode. ● *n.* flotation; initiation, start, beginning, début, origin, origination, conception, inauguration, institution, introduction, presentation, *colloq.* kick-off, *formal* commencement; establishment, organization, foundation, opening; firing, (moon)shot, take-off, discharge, propulsion, dispatch, delivery.

launch[2] /lawnch/ *n.* **1** a large motor boat, used esp. for pleasure. **2** a man-of-war's largest boat. [Sp. *lancha* pinnace perh. f. Malay *lancharan* f. *lanchār* swift]

■ **1** boat, skiff, tender, motor boat, runabout, gig, dinghy.

launcher /láwnchər/ *n.* a structure or device to hold a rocket during launching.

launder /láwndər/ *v.* & *n.* ● *v.tr.* **1** wash and iron (clothes, linen, etc.). **2** *colloq.* transfer (funds) to conceal a dubious or illegal origin. ● *n.* a channel for conveying liquids, esp. molten metal. □□ **launderer** *n.* [ME *launder* (n.) washer of linen, contr. of *lavander* f. OF *lavandier* ult. f. L *lavanda* things to be washed, neut. pl. gerundive of *lavare* wash]
■ *v.* **1** wash, clean, scrub, cleanse, rinse, soap, *literary* lave; starch; iron, press, smooth. **2** legitimize, legitimatize, legalize.

launderette /lawndrét/ *n.* (also **laundrette**) an establishment with coin-operated washing-machines and driers for public use.

laundress /láwndriss/ *n.* a woman who launders clothes, linen, etc., esp. professionally.

laundry /láwndri/ *n.* (*pl.* **-ies**) **1** an establishment for washing clothes or linen. **2** clothes or linen for laundering or newly laundered. [contr. f. *lavendry* (f. OF *lavanderie*) after LAUNDER]

laureate /lórriət, lóriət/ *adj.* & *n.* ● *adj.* **1** wreathed with laurel as a mark of honour. **2** consisting of laurel; laurel-like. ● *n.* **1** a person who is honoured for outstanding creative or intellectual achievement (*Nobel laureate*). **2** = *Poet Laureate.* □□ **laureateship** *n.* [L *laureatus* f. *laurea* laurel-wreath f. *laurus* laurel]

laurel /lórrəl/ *n.* & *v.* ● *n.* **1** = BAY². **2 a** (in *sing.* or *pl.*) the foliage of the bay-tree used as an emblem of victory or distinction in poetry usu. formed into a wreath or crown. **b** (in *pl.*) honour or distinction. **3** any plant with dark-green glossy leaves like a bay-tree, e.g. cherry-laurel, mountain laurel, spurge laurel. ● *v.tr.* (**laurelled, laurelling**; *US* **laureled, laureling**) wreathe with laurel. □ **look to one's laurels** beware of losing one's pre-eminence. **rest on one's laurels** be satisfied with what one has done and not seek further success. [ME *lorer* f. OF *lorier* f. Prov. *laurier* f. *laur* f. L *laurus*]
■ *n.* **2 b** (*laurels*) honour(s), distinction(s), fame, awards, trophy, trophies, tributes, rewards; acclaim, acclamation, glory, renown, esteem, admiration, approbation, accolade(s), regard, respect, prestige, celebrity, popularity, reputation, *colloq.* kudos. □ **rest on one's laurels** be *or* get complacent *or* self-satisfied *or* smug *or* overconfident; sit back, relax, take it easy, ease up *or* off.

laurustinus /lórrəstī́nəss/ *n.* an evergreen winter-flowering shrub, *Viburnum tinus*, with dense glossy green leaves and white or pink flowers. [mod.L f. L *laurus* laurel + *tinus* wild laurel]

lav /lav/ *n. Brit. colloq.* lavatory. [abbr.]

lava /laávə/ *n.* **1** the molten matter which flows from a volcano. **2** the solid substance which it forms on cooling. [It. f. *lavare* wash f. L]

lavabo /ləvaábō/ *n.* (*pl.* **-os**) **1** *RC Ch.* **a** the ritual washing of the celebrant's hands at the offertory of the Mass. **b** a towel or basin used for this. **2** a monastery washing-trough. **3** a wash-basin. [L, = I will wash, first word of Psalm 26:6]
■ **1b, 2, 3** see SINK *n.* 1.

lavage /lávvij/ *n. Med.* the washing-out of a body cavity, such as the colon or stomach, with water or a medicated solution. [F f. *laver* wash: see LAVE]

lavation /ləváysh'n/ *n. formal* washing. [L *lavatio* f. *lavare* wash]

lavatorial /lávvətóriəl/ *adj.* (esp. of humour) relating to lavatories and their use.

lavatory /lávvətəri, -tri/ *n.* (*pl.* **-ies**) **1** a large receptacle for urine and faeces, usu. with running water and a flush mechanism as a means of disposal. **2** a room or compartment containing one or more of these. □ **lavatory paper** = *toilet paper.* [ME, = washing vessel, f. LL *lavatorium* f. L *lavare lavat-* wash]
■ bowl, *Brit.* pan; toilet, water-closet, WC, earth closet, ladies' room, men's (room), powder-room, latrine, *Naut.* head(s), *Brit.* (public) convenience, the Ladies, *US* bathroom, rest room, washroom, (little) boys' *or* girls' room, outhouse, *US or archaic* privy, *colloq.* throne, thunder-box, *Brit. colloq.* loo, lav, the Gents, *Brit. euphem.* cloakroom, *US euphem.* comfort station, *Brit. propr.* Elsan, *Austral. sl.* dyke, toot, *Brit. sl.* bog, *US sl.* can, john. □ **lavatory paper** toilet paper *or* roll, *Brit. colloq.* bumf, *Brit. sl.* bog paper *or* roll.

lave /layv/ *v.tr. literary* **1** wash, bathe. **2** (of water) wash against; flow along. [ME f. OF *laver* f. L *lavare* wash, perh. coalescing with OE *lafian*]
■ **1** see WASH *v.* 1, 3.

lavender /lávvindər/ *n.* & *v.* ● *n.* **1 a** any small evergreen shrub of the genus *Lavandula*, with narrow leaves and blue, purple, or pink aromatic flowers. **b** its flowers and stalks dried and used to scent linen, clothes, etc. **2** a pale blue colour with a trace of red. ● *v.tr.* put lavender among (linen etc.). □ **lavender-water** a perfume made from distilled lavender, alcohol, and ambergris. [ME f. AF *lavendre*, ult. f. med.L *lavandula*]

laver¹ /láyvər, laávər/ *n.* any of various edible seaweeds, esp. *Porphyra umbilicalis*, having sheetlike fronds. □ **laver bread** a Welsh dish of laver which is boiled, dipped in oatmeal, and fried. [L]

laver² /láyvər/ *n.* **1** *Bibl.* a large brass vessel for Jewish priests' ritual ablutions. **2** *archaic* a washing or fountain basin; a font. [ME *lavo(u)r* f. OF *laveo(i)r* f. LL (as LAVATORY)]

lavish /lávvish/ *adj.* & *v.* ● *adj.* **1** giving or producing in large quantities; profuse. **2** generous, unstinting. **3** excessive, over-abundant. ● *v.tr.* (often foll. by *on*) bestow or spend (money, effort, praise, etc.) abundantly. □□ **lavishly** *adv.* **lavishness** *n.* [ME f. obs. *lavish*, *lavas* (n.) profusion f. OF *lavasse* deluge of rain f. *laver* wash]
■ *adj.* **1** profuse, abundant, plentiful, ample, copious, prolific, liberal, effusive, *disp.* fulsome, *poet.* plenteous; lush, luxuriant, luxurious, opulent, plush, sumptuous, rich, handsome, princely, generous. **2** generous, liberal, open-handed, free-handed, bountiful, munificent, unstinting, unsparing, unselfish, effusive, free, *poet.* bounteous; kind, beneficent, charitable, big-hearted, great-hearted, magnanimous, sporting, *Brit.* decent, *archaic* gentle. **3** excessive, immoderate, inordinate, uncurbed, unrestrained, intemperate, disproportionate, extravagant, exorbitant, exaggerated, undue, extreme, unreasonable, outrageous; wasteful, profligate, wanton, prodigal, improvident, overgenerous; over-abundant, superabundant, overfull, bursting at the seams, superfluous, *colloq.* over-the-top. ● *v.* spend, expend, disburse, pay, lash out, *colloq.* splash out, splurge; squander, waste, throw away, fritter (away), drivel away, dissipate; shower, rain, pour, heap, bestow, *sl.* dish out, blow.

law /law/ *n.* **1 a** a rule enacted or customary in a community and recognized as enjoining or prohibiting certain actions and enforced by the imposition of penalties. **b** a body of such rules (*the law of the land*; *forbidden under Scots law*). **2** the controlling influence of laws; a state of respect for laws (*law and order*). **3** laws collectively as a social system or subject of study (*was reading law*). **4** (with defining word) any of the specific branches or applications of law (*commercial law*; *law of contract*). **5** binding force or effect (*their word is law*). **6** (prec. by *the*) **a** the legal profession. **b** *colloq.* the police. **7** the statute and common law (opp. EQUITY). **8** (in *pl.*) jurisprudence. **9 a** the judicial remedy; litigation. **b** the lawcourts as providing this (*go to law*). **10** a rule of action or procedure, e.g. in a game, social context, form of art, etc. **11** a regularity in natural occurrences, esp. as formulated or propounded in particular instances (*the laws of nature*; *the law of gravity*; *Parkinson's law*). **12 a** divine commandments as expressed in the Bible or other sources. **b** (**Law of Moses**) the precepts of the Pentateuch. □ **at** (or

in) **law** according to the laws. **be a law unto oneself** do what one feels is right; disregard custom. **go to law** take legal action; make use of the lawcourts. **law-abiding** obedient to the laws. **law-abidingness** obedience to the laws. **law agent** (in Scotland) a solicitor. **law centre** *Brit.* an independent publicly-funded advisory service on legal matters. **Law Lord** a member of the House of Lords qualified to perform its legal work. **law of diminishing returns** see DIMINISH. **law of nature** = *natural law.* **laws of war** the limitations on belligerents' action recognized by civilized nations. **law term** a period appointed for the sitting of lawcourts. **lay down the law** be dogmatic or authoritarian. **take the law into one's own hands** redress a grievance by one's own means, esp. by force. [OE *lagu* f. ON *lag* something 'laid down' or fixed, rel. to LAY[1]]

■ **1 a** rule, regulation, ordinance, statute, act, enactment, measure, edict, decree, order, directive, injunction, command, commandment, precept, canon, mandate, ukase, *Brit.* by-law, *hist.* constitution. **b** constitution, rules (and regulations), book (of words), code, charter. **2** justice, right, equity, fairness, order, law and order; lawfulness, rightfulness, legitimacy, legality. **5** (*predic.*) final, conclusive, indisputable, binding, incontrovertible, definitive; irrevocable, immutable, unchangeable, unalterable, irreversible. **6 b** see POLICE *n.* 1, 2. **9** remedy, redress, reparation; litigation, suit (at law), lawsuit, (legal) action, case; (the) court(s), lawcourt, court of law, courtroom, tribunal, bench, bar. **10** rule, regulation, principle, direction, guide, guideline. **11** principle, proposition, theory, theorem, axiom; postulate, hypothesis; deduction, conclusion, inference, corollary, lemma, formula. □ **law-abiding** obedient, respectful, dutiful, decent, proper, upright, respectable, honest, virtuous, unimpeachable, peaceable, principled, disciplined, well-behaved, orderly, civilized, solid, *literary* duteous. **lay down the law** dictate, command, order, direct, give orders.

lawbreaker /láwbraykər/ *n.* a person who breaks the law. □□ **lawbreaking** *n.* & *adj.*

■ see *offender* (OFFEND).

lawcourt /láwkort/ *n.* a court of law.

■ see BAR[1] *n.* 5d.

lawful /láwfŏŏl/ *adj.* conforming with, permitted by, or recognized by law; not illegal or (of a child) illegitimate. □□ **lawfully** *adv.* **lawfulness** *n.*

■ legal, licit, legitimate, constitutional, just, rightful, *de jure*, valid, proper; permissible, allowable, justifiable, authorized.

lawgiver /láwgivvər/ *n.* a person who lays down laws.

lawless /láwliss/ *adj.* **1** having no laws or enforcement of them. **2** disregarding laws. **3** unbridled, uncontrolled. □□ **lawlessly** *adv.* **lawlessness** *n.*

■ **1** anarchic, anarchical, anarchistic, chaotic, disorderly, unruly, unregulated. **2** unlawful, criminal, felonious, illegal, illicit, larcenous, *colloq.* crooked, *sl.* bent; dishonest, corrupt, venal; villainous, nefarious, wicked, sinful, flagitious, iniquitous, treacherous. **3** unbridled, uncontrolled, unconstrained, unrestrained, unchecked, undisciplined, wild, unruly, rogue, boisterous, riotous, rampant, out of hand *or* control.

lawmaker /láwmaykər/ *n.* a legislator.

■ see POLITICIAN 1.

lawman /láwman/ *n.* (*pl.* **-men**) *US* a law-enforcement officer, esp. a sheriff or policeman.

■ see OFFICER *n.* 2.

lawn[1] /lawn/ *n.* a piece of grass kept mown and smooth in a garden, park, etc. □ **lawn tennis** the usual form of tennis, played with a soft ball on outdoor grass or a hard court. [ME *laund* glade f. OF *launde* f. OCelt., rel. to LAND]

■ grass, green, turf, sod, *archaic or literary* greensward, *literary* sward.

lawn[2] /lawn/ *n.* a fine linen or cotton fabric used for clothes. □□ **lawny** *adj.* [ME, prob. f. *Laon* in France]

lawnmower /láwnmōər/ *n.* a machine for cutting the grass on a lawn.

lawrencium /lərénsiəm/ *n. Chem.* an artificially made transuranic radioactive metallic element. ¶ Symb.: **Lw**. [E. O. *Lawrence*, Amer. physicist d. 1958]

lawsuit /láwsōōt, -syōōt/ *n.* the process or an instance of making a claim in a lawcourt.

■ see CASE[1] 5a.

lawyer /lóyər, láwyər/ *n.* a member of the legal profession, esp. a solicitor. □□ **lawyerly** *adj.* [ME *law(i)er* f. LAW]

■ counsel, advocate, barrister(-at-law), member of the Bar, legal practitioner, Commissioner for Oaths, *Brit.* Queen's Counsel, QC, bencher, *Brit.* recorder, solicitor, *US* attorney(-at-law), jurist, counselor(-at-law), squire, *colloq.* mouthpiece; pettifogger, *esp. US colloq.* shyster.

lax /laks/ *adj.* **1** lacking care, concern, or firmness. **2** loose, relaxed; not compact. **3** *Phonet.* pronounced with the vocal muscles relaxed. □□ **laxity** *n.* **laxly** *adv.* **laxness** *n.* [ME, = loose, f. L *laxus*: rel. to SLACK[1]]

■ **1** careless, uncaring, devil-may-care, thoughtless, unthinking, negligent, neglectful, remiss, inattentive, unobservant, cursory, lackadaisical, perfunctory, loose, slipshod, slack, casual, untidy, hit-or-miss, loose, scrappy, scratchy, sloppy; imprecise, inexact, inaccurate, indefinite, non-specific, vague, shapeless, amorphous, general; permissive, weak, indulgent, lenient, easygoing, liberal, soft, relaxed, happy-go-lucky, nonchalant, carefree, insouciant, *colloq.* laid-back. **2** loose, relaxed, open; supple, loose-limbed, flexible, slack, limp, soft.

laxative /láksətiv/ *adj.* & *n.* ● *adj.* tending to stimulate or facilitate evacuation of the bowels. ● *n.* a laxative medicine. [ME f. OF *laxatif -ive* or LL *laxativus* f. L *laxare* loosen (as LAX)]

■ *adj.* see PURGATIVE *adj.* 2. ● *n.* see PURGATIVE *n.* 2.

lay[1] /lay/ *v.* & *n.* ● *v.* (*past* and *past part.* **laid** /layd/) **1** *tr.* place on a surface, esp. horizontally or in the proper or specified place. **2** *tr.* put or bring into a certain or the required position or state (*lay a carpet*). **3** *intr. dial.* or *erron.* lie. ¶ This use, incorrect in standard English, is probably partly encouraged by confusion with *lay* as the past of *lie*, as in *the dog lay on the floor* which is correct; *the dog is laying on the floor* is not correct. **4** *tr.* make by laying (*lay the foundations*). **5** *tr.* (often *absol.*) (of a hen bird) produce (an egg). **6** *tr.* **a** cause to subside or lie flat. **b** deal with to remove (a ghost, fear, etc.). **7** *tr.* place or present for consideration (a case, proposal, etc.). **8** *tr.* set down as a basis or starting-point. **9** *tr.* (usu. foll. by *on*) attribute or impute (blame etc.). **10** *tr.* locate (a scene etc.) in a certain place. **11** *tr.* prepare or make ready (a plan or a trap). **12** *tr.* prepare (a table) for a meal. **13** *tr.* place or arrange the material for (a fire). **14** *tr.* put down as a wager; stake. **15** *tr.* (foll. by *with*) coat or strew (a surface). **16** *tr. sl. offens.* have sexual intercourse with (esp. a woman). ● *n.* **1** the way, position, or direction in which something lies. **2** *sl. offens.* a partner (esp. female) in sexual intercourse. **3** the direction or amount of twist in rope-strands. □ **in lay** (of a hen) laying eggs regularly. **laid-back** *colloq.* relaxed, unbothered, easygoing. **laid paper** paper with the surface marked in fine ribs. **laid up** confined to bed or the house. **lay about one 1** hit out on all sides. **2** criticize indiscriminately. **lay aside 1** put to one side. **2** cease to practise or consider. **3** save (money etc.) for future needs. **lay at the door of** see DOOR. **lay back** cause to slope back from the vertical. **lay bare** expose, reveal. **lay a charge** make an accusation. **lay claim to** claim as one's own. **lay down 1** put on the ground. **2** relinquish; give up (an office). **3** formulate or insist on (a rule or principle). **4** pay or wager (money). **5** begin to construct (a ship or railway). **6** store (wine) in a cellar. **7** set down on paper. **8** sacrifice (one's life). **9** convert (land) into pasture. **10** record (esp. popular music). **lay down the law** see LAW. **lay one's hands on** obtain, acquire, locate. **lay hands on 1** seize or attack. **2** place one's hands on or over, esp. in confirmation, ordination, or spiritual healing. **lay hold of** seize or grasp. **lay**

in provide oneself with a stock of. **lay into** *colloq.* punish or scold heavily. **lay it on thick** (or **with a trowel**) *colloq.* flatter or exaggerate grossly. **lay low** overthrow, kill, or humble. **lay off 1** discharge (workers) temporarily because of a shortage of work. **2** *colloq.* desist. **lay-off** *n.* **1** a temporary discharge of workers. **2** a period when this is in force. **lay on 1** provide (a facility, amenity, etc.). **2** impose (a penalty, obligation, etc.). **3** inflict (blows). **4** spread on (paint etc.). **lay on the table** see TABLE. **lay open 1** break the skin of. **2** (foll. by *to*) expose (to criticism etc.). **lay out 1** spread out. **2** expose to view. **3** prepare (a corpse) for burial. **4** *colloq.* knock unconscious. **5** dispose (grounds etc.) according to a plan. **6** expend (money). **7** *refl.* (foll. by *to* + infin.) take pains (to do something) (*laid themselves out to help*). **lay store by** see STORE. **lay to rest** bury in a grave. **lay up 1** store, save. **2** put (a ship etc.) out of service. **lay waste** see WASTE. [OE *lecgan* f. Gmc]

■ *v.* **1** place, put (down), set (down), lay down, position, deposit. **2** put down, fit. **3** see LIE[1] *v.* 1. **6 a** flatten, flat, pat (down), press, roll, planish, smooth, tamp. **b** (*lay to rest*) exorcize; destroy, drive out, get rid of, expel, eject, oust, remove; see also SUPPRESS *v.* 1. **7** see PRESENT[2] *v.* 1. **9** attribute, impute, ascribe, assign, direct, lodge, refer, aim, pin. **10** see LOCATE 2, 4. **11** see PREPARE 1. **12, 13** set, arrange, prepare; spread. **14** stake, bet, wager, gamble, hazard, risk, venture, chance, put up *or* down, lay down. **15** see COAT *v.* 1. **16** copulate with, couple with, have (sexual) intercourse with, sleep with, go to bed with, make love to, possess, take, have one's (wicked) way with, *Law* have carnal knowledge of, *archaic* lie with, know, *archaic or joc.* fornicate with, *colloq.* bed, have sex with, go all the way with, *sl.* make, make it with. ● *n.* **1** see POSITION *n.* 1, 2. □ **laid-back** see *relaxed* (RELAX *v.* 5). **laid up** see SICK[1] *adj.* 2. **lay about one 1** hit out, lash out, strike out. **lay aside 2** see *put aside* 2. **3** see *put by*. **lay bare** see EXPOSE 5. **lay claim to** see CLAIM *v.* 1a. **lay down 1** see LAY[1] *v.* 1 above. **2** see RELINQUISH 1, 2. **3** formulate, set down, put down; insist on, stand on, exact. **4** see LAY[1] *v.* 14 above. **6** see STORE *v.* 2. **7** put *or* set down, put in writing, commit to writing *or* paper. **8** see SACRIFICE *v.* 3. **lay one's hands on** see OBTAIN 1. **lay hold of** seize, grasp, grab, snatch, catch *or* get hold of, get, *sl.* nab. **lay in** see *stock up* 2. **lay it on thick** see EXAGGERATE 1, FLATTER 1. **lay low** see *put down* 1, 2 (PUT[1]). **lay off 1** suspend; dismiss, discharge, release, let go, axe, boot (out), *colloq.* sack, kick out. **2** see CEASE *v.* **lay on 1** see PROVIDE 1, 2a. **2** see IMPOSE 1, 2. **3** see INFLICT 1. **4** see SPREAD *v.* 1b. **lay open 2** see EXPOSE 3. **lay out 1** see SPREAD *v.* 1a. **2** see EXPOSE 7. **4** see *knock out* 1. **5** see DISPOSE 2. **6** see SPEND 1. **lay up 1** see STORE *v.* 2.

lay[2] /lay/ *adj.* **1 a** non-clerical. **b** not ordained into the clergy. **2 a** not professionally qualified, esp. in law or medicine. **b** of or done by such persons. □ **lay brother** (or **sister**) a person who has taken the vows of a religious order but is not ordained and is employed in ancillary or manual work. **lay reader** a lay person licensed to conduct some religious services. [ME f. OF *lai* f. eccl.L *laicus* f. Gk *laïkos* LAIC]

■ **1** laic, non-clerical, non-ecclesiastical, civil; secular, profane, temporal, worldly. **2** amateur, non-professional, unprofessional, non-specialist, popular.

lay[3] /lay/ *n.* **1** a short lyric or narrative poem meant to be sung. **2** a song. [ME f. OF *lai*, Prov. *lais*, of unkn. orig.]

■ lyric, ballad, *hist.* ode; see also SONG 1.

lay[4] *past* of LIE[1].

layabout /láyəbowt/ *n.* a habitual loafer or idler.

■ see IDLER 1.

lay-by /láybī/ *n.* (*pl.* **lay-bys**) **1** *Brit.* an area at the side of an open road where vehicles may stop. **2** a similar arrangement on a canal or railway. **3** *Austral.* & *NZ* a system of paying a deposit to secure an article for later purchase.

layer /láyər/ *n.* & *v.* ● *n.* **1** a thickness of matter, esp. one of several, covering a surface. **2** a person or thing that lays. **3** a hen that lays eggs. **4** a shoot fastened down to take root while attached to the parent plant. ● *v.tr.* **1 a** arrange in layers. **b** cut (hair) in layers. **2** propagate (a plant) as a layer. □ **layer-out** a person who prepares a corpse for burial. □□ **layered** *adj.* [ME f. LAY[1] + -ER[1]]

■ *n.* **1** see FILM *n.* 1. ● *v.* **1 a** see SPREAD *v.* 1b, 4a.

layette /layét/ *n.* a set of clothing, toilet articles, and bedclothes for a newborn child. [F, dimin. of OF *laie* drawer f. MDu. *laege*]

lay figure *n.* **1** a dummy or jointed figure of a human body used by artists for arranging drapery on etc. **2** an unrealistic character in a novel etc. **3** a person lacking in individuality. [*lay* f. obs. *layman* f. Du. *leeman* f. obs. *led* joint]

layman /láymən/ *n.* (*pl.* **-men**; *fem.* **laywoman**, *pl.* **-women**) **1** any non-ordained member of a Church. **2** a person without professional or specialized knowledge in a particular subject.

layout /láyowt/ *n.* **1** the disposing or arrangement of a site, ground, etc. **2** the way in which plans, printed matter, etc., are arranged or set out. **3** something arranged or set out in a particular way. **4** the make-up of a book, newspaper, etc.

layover /láyōvər/ *n.* a period of rest or waiting before a further stage in a journey etc.; a stopover.

layshaft /láyshaaft/ *n.* a second or intermediate transmission shaft in a machine.

lazar /lázzər/ *n.* *archaic* a poor and diseased person, esp. a leper. [ME f. med.L *lazarus* f. the name in Luke 16:20]

lazaret /lázzərét/ *n.* (also **lazaretto** /-réttō/) (*pl.* **lazarets** or **lazarettos**) **1** a hospital for diseased people, esp. lepers. **2** a building or ship for quarantine. **3** the after part of a ship's hold, used for stores. [(F *lazaret*) f. It. *lazzaretto* f. *lazzaro* LAZAR]

laze /layz/ *v.* & *n.* ● *v.* **1** *intr.* spend time lazily or idly. **2** *tr.* (often foll. by *away*) pass (time) in this way. ● *n.* a spell of lazing. [back-form. f. LAZY]

lazuli /lázyooli, -lī/ *n.* = LAPIS LAZULI. [abbr.]

lazy /láyzi/ *adj.* (**lazier, laziest**) **1** disinclined to work, doing little work. **2** of or inducing idleness. **3** (of a river etc.) slow-moving. □□ **lazily** *adv.* **laziness** *n.* [earlier *laysie, lasie, laesy*, perh. f. LG: cf. LG *lasich* idle]

■ **1** indolent, slothful, sluggish, idle, lethargic, shiftless, languorous, languid, torpid, inert, inactive, fainéant, listless, drowsy, dull, slack, lax, *archaic* otiose. **2** easy, easygoing, relaxed, nonchalant, happy-go-lucky, devil-may-care, carefree, dreamy, *colloq.* laid-back. **3** slow, slow-moving, languid, languorous, sluggish, torpid, stagnant, sullen, tortoise-like, snail-like.

lazybones /láyzibōnz/ *n.* (*pl.* same) *colloq.* a lazy person.

■ see IDLER 1.

lb. *abbr.* a pound or pounds (weight). [L *libra*]

l.b. *abbr.* *Cricket* leg-bye(s), leg-byed.

LBC *abbr.* London Broadcasting Company.

L/Bdr *abbr.* Lance-Bombardier.

l.b.w. *abbr.* *Cricket* leg before wicket.

l.c. *abbr.* **1** in the passage etc. cited. **2** lower case. **3** letter of credit. [sense 1 f. L *loco citato*]

LCC *abbr.* *hist.* London County Council.

LCD *abbr.* **1** liquid crystal display. **2** lowest (or least) common denominator.

LCM *abbr.* lowest (or least) common multiple.

L/Cpl *abbr.* Lance-Corporal.

LD *abbr.* lethal dose, usu. with a following numeral indicating the percentage of a group of animals killed by such a dose (LD_{50}).

Ld. *abbr.* Lord.

Ldg. *abbr.* Leading (Seaman etc.).

LDS *abbr.* Licentiate in Dental Surgery.

-le[1] /'l/ *suffix* forming nouns, esp.: **1** names of appliances or instruments (*handle*; *thimble*). **2** names of animals and plants (*beetle*; *thistle*). ¶ The suffix has ceased to be syllabic in *fowl*, *snail*, *stile*. [ult. from or repr. OE *-el* etc. f. Gmc, with many IE cognates]

-le[2] /'l/ *suffix* (also **-el**) forming nouns with (or orig. with) diminutive sense, or = -AL (*angle*; *castle*; *mantle*; *syllable*;

novel; *tunnel*). [ME *-el*, *-elle* f. OF ult. f. L forms *-ellus*, *-ella*, etc.]

-le[3] /'l/ *suffix* forming adjectives, often with (or orig. with) the sense 'apt or liable to' (*brittle*; *fickle*; *little*; *nimble*). [ME f. OE *-el* etc. f. Gmc, corresp. to L *-ulus*]

-le[4] /'l/ *suffix* forming verbs, esp. expressing repeated action or movement or having diminutive sense (*bubble*; *crumple*; *wriggle*). ¶ Examples from OE are *handle*, *nestle*, *startle*, *twinkle*. [OE *-lian* f. Gmc]

LEA *abbr.* (in the UK) Local Education Authority.

lea /lee/ *n. poet.* a piece of meadow or pasture or arable land. [OE *lēa(h)* f. Gmc]

■ see MEADOW.

leach /leech/ *v.* **1** *tr.* make (a liquid) percolate through some material. **2** *tr.* subject (bark, ore, ash, or soil) to the action of percolating fluid. **3** *tr.* & *intr.* (foll. by *away*, *out*) remove (soluble matter) or be removed in this way. □□ **leacher** *n.* [prob. repr. OE *leccan* to water, f. WG]

■ **1, 3** see PERCOLATE 1.

lead[1] /leed/ *v.*, *n.*, & *adj.* ● *v.* (*past* and *past part.* **led** /led/) **1** *tr.* cause to go with one, esp. by guiding or showing the way or by going in front and taking a person's hand or an animal's halter etc. **2** *tr.* **a** direct the actions or opinions of. **b** (often foll. by *to*, or *to* + infin.) guide by persuasion or example or argument (*what led you to that conclusion?*; *was led to think you may be right*). **3** *tr.* (also *absol.*) provide access to; bring to a certain position or destination (*this door leads you into a small room*; *the road leads to Lincoln*; *the path leads uphill*). **4** *tr.* pass or go through (a life etc. of a specified kind) (*led a miserable existence*). **5** *tr.* **a** have the first place in (*lead the dance*; *leads the world in sugar production*). **b** (*absol.*) go first; be ahead in a race or game. **c** (*absol.*) be pre-eminent in some field. **6** *tr.* be in charge of (*leads a team of researchers*). **7** *tr.* **a** direct by example. **b** set (a fashion). **c** be the principal player of (a group of musicians). **8** *tr.* (also *absol.*) begin a round of play at cards by playing (a card) or a card of (a particular suit). **9** *intr.* (foll. by *to*) have as an end or outcome; result in (*what does all this lead to?*). **10** *intr.* (foll. by *with*) *Boxing* make an attack (with a particular blow). **11 a** *intr.* (foll. by *with*) (of a newspaper) use a particular item as the main story (*led with the Stock Market crash*). **b** *tr.* (of a story) be the main feature of (a newspaper or part of it) (*the royal wedding will lead the front page*). **12** *tr.* (foll. by *through*) make (a liquid, strip of material, etc.) pass through a pulley, channel, etc. ● *n.* **1** guidance given by going in front; example. **2 a** a leading place; the leadership (*is in the lead*; *take the lead*). **b** the amount by which a competitor is ahead of the others (*a lead of ten yards*). **3** a clue, esp. an early indication of the resolution of a problem (*is the first real lead in the case*). **4** a strap or cord for leading a dog etc. **5** a conductor (usu. a wire) conveying electric current from a source to an appliance. **6 a** the chief part in a play etc. **b** the person playing this. **7** (in full **lead story**) the item of news given the greatest prominence in a newspaper or magazine. **8 a** the act or right of playing first in a game or round of cards. **b** the card led. **9** the distance advanced by a screw in one turn. **10 a** an artificial watercourse, esp. one leading to a mill. **b** a channel of water in an ice-field. ● *attrib.adj.* leading, principal, first. □ **lead astray** see ASTRAY. **lead by the nose** cajole (a person) into compliance. **lead a person a dance** see DANCE. **lead-in 1** an introduction, opening, etc. **2** a wire leading in from outside, esp. from an aerial to a receiver or transmitter. **lead off 1** begin; make a start. **2** *colloq.* lose one's temper. **lead-off** *n.* an action beginning a process. **lead on 1** entice into going further than was intended. **2** mislead or deceive. **lead time** the time between the initiation and completion of a production process. **lead up the garden path** *colloq.* mislead. **lead up to 1** form an introduction to, precede; prepare for. **2** direct one's talk gradually or cautiously to a particular topic etc. **lead the way** see WAY. □□ **leadable** *adj.* [OE *lǣdan* f. Gmc]

■ *v.* **1** conduct, take, convey, move, walk, steer, pilot, guide, show (the way), escort, accompany, usher, shepherd. **2** bring, guide, take, direct, move, induce, cause, influence, prompt, incline, persuade, dispose, convince. **3** go, run, communicate with, connect with; bring, take, carry, convey. **4** pass, spend, go through, experience, live through; suffer, bear, endure, undergo. **5** be *or* go first, be top, be in the lead; take the lead, be *or* move *or* go *or* forge ahead, take up *or* make the running; excel, dominate, shine, be pre-eminent; surpass, exceed, precede, outstrip, distance, outrun, outpace, overshadow, outdo, beat. **6, 7a** be in charge of, run, head (up), direct, supervise, manage, be responsible for, superintend, oversee, govern, command, control, administer, preside, chair, spearhead; captain, skipper. **9** (*lead to*) result in, create, engender, cause, bring on *or* about, produce, give rise to, be conducive to, contribute to. ● *n.* **1** direction, guidance, leadership, precedent, example, model, exemplar, pattern, standard. **2** front, vanguard, van, pole position, first place; supremacy, priority, primacy, pre-eminence; advantage, edge, advance, margin, gap, distance. **3** tip, clue, indication, pointer, hint, suggestion, cue, intimation; evidence, information, advice, tip-off. **4** leash, tether, restraint, cord, rope, chain; strap, curb, halter, rein, leading-strings *or* -reins. **5** wire, cable, cord, *Brit.* flex. **6** protagonist, principal, hero, heroine, leading role, leading lady *or* man, star; prima donna, diva; prima ballerina. ● *attrib. adj.* leading, foremost, first; main, chief, principal, premier, paramount. □ **lead-in 1** introduction, opening, overture, preamble, preface, prelude, prolegomenon, prologue, *colloq.* intro. **lead off 1** see BEGIN 1, 5. **lead on 1** lure, allure, entice, seduce, beguile, inveigle, tempt, draw on, suck in, *colloq.* sweet-talk, soft-soap. **2** see MISLEAD. **lead up the garden path** see MISLEAD. **lead up to 1** precede, introduce, usher in; prepare *or* pave *or* clear (the way) for, do the groundwork *or* spadework for. **2** approach, broach, bring up, present, introduce, work up *or* round to, get (up) to.

lead[2] /led/ *n.* & *v.* ● *n.* **1** *Chem.* a heavy bluish-grey soft ductile metallic element occurring naturally in galena and used in building and the manufacture of alloys. ¶ Symb.: **Pb**. **2 a** graphite. **b** a thin length of this for use in a pencil. **3** a lump of lead used in sounding water. **4** (in *pl.*) *Brit.* **a** strips of lead covering a roof. **b** a piece of lead-covered roof. **5** (in *pl.*) *Brit.* lead frames holding the glass of a lattice or stained-glass window. **6** *Printing* a blank space between lines of print (orig. with ref. to the metal strip used to give this space). **7** (*attrib.*) made of lead. ● *v.tr.* **1** cover, weight, or frame (a roof or window panes) with lead. **2** *Printing* separate lines of (printed matter) with leads. **3** add a lead compound to (petrol etc.). □ **lead acetate** a white crystalline compound of lead that dissolves in water to form a sweet-tasting solution. **lead balloon** a failure, an unsuccessful venture **lead-free** (of petrol) without added tetraethyl lead. **lead pencil** a pencil of graphite enclosed in wood. **lead-poisoning** acute or chronic poisoning by absorption of lead into the body. **lead shot** = SHOT[1] 3b. **lead tetraethyl** = TETRAETHYL LEAD. **lead wool** a fibrous form of lead, used for jointing water pipes. □□ **leadless** *adj.* [OE *lēad* f. WG]

leaden /lédd'n/ *adj.* **1** of or like lead. **2** heavy, slow, burdensome (*leaden limbs*). **3** inert, depressing (*leaden rule*). **4** lead-coloured (*leaden skies*). □ **leaden seal** a stamped piece of lead holding the ends of a wire used as a fastening. □□ **leadenly** *adv.* **leadenness** *n.* [OE *lēaden* (as LEAD[2])]

■ **2** heavy, weighty, massive, dense, ponderous, slow, sluggish, slow-moving, onerous, burdensome, oppressive. **3** inert, lifeless, inanimate, sluggish, listless, inactive, lethargic, languid, languorous, torpid, spiritless, stagnant, static, stationary, dense, heavy, dull, numbing, depressing, oppressive. **4** grey, ashen, smoky, livid, dull, drab, dingy, murky, gloomy, dark, sombre, glowering,

lowering, dreary, dismal, oppressive, sullen; cloudy, overcast, sunless.

leader /leédər/ *n.* **1 a** a person or thing that leads. **b** a person followed by others. **2 a** the principal player in a music group or of the first violins in an orchestra. **b** *US* a conductor of an orchestra. **3** *Brit.* = *leading article.* **4** a short strip of non-functioning material at each end of a reel of film or recording tape for connection to the spool. **5** (in full **Leader of the House**) *Brit.* a member of the government officially responsible for initiating business in Parliament. **6** a shoot of a plant at the apex of a stem or of the main branch. **7** (in *pl.*) *Printing* a series of dots or dashes across the page to guide the eye, esp. in tabulated material. **8** the horse placed at the front in a team or pair. ▫▫ **leaderless** *adj.* **leadership** *n.* [OE *lǣdere* (as LEAD[1])]

▪ **1** chief, head, director, chairman, chairwoman, chairperson, chair, principal, manager, executive, supremo, kingpin, *colloq.* boss, number one, *Brit. colloq.* gaffer, *sl.* (big) cheese, *US sl.* (head) honcho, Mr Big; king, queen, sovereign, monarch, ruler, governor, president, premier, head of state, prime minister; commander(-in-chief), commandant, admiral, warlord, chieftain, caudillo, Duce, führer, *hist.* pendragon; initiator, pioneer, organizer, brain(s), fugleman, father, apostle, pillar; aga, ayatollah, imam, sharif, sheikh, maharishi, rabbi, Roshi, *hist.* Mahdi, *esp. hist.* caliph; conductor, pilot, guide, escort; figurehead, flagship, standard-bearer, leading light, protagonist, pace-setter, trend-setter; tribune *US* sachem, *hist.* demagogue; akela, Brown Owl, Guider, sixer; captain, skipper. **2** conductor, director, bandmaster, bandleader; *esp. US* concert-master. **3** see *leading article* (LEADING[1]). ▫▫ **leadership** direction, guidance, lead, leading, command, regulation, control, management, executive, supervision, superintendence, running, administration, organization, operation, influence, initiative; governorship, directorship, chairmanship, headship; rule, sway, monarchy, government, presidency, premiership, regime, reign, sovereignty, hegemony; apostolate.

leading[1] /leéding/ *adj.* & *n.* ● *adj.* chief; most important. ● *n.* guidance, leadership. ▫ **leading aircraftman** the rank above aircraftman in the RAF. **leading article** a newspaper article giving the editorial opinion. **leading counsel** the senior barrister of two or more in a case. **leading edge 1** the foremost edge of an aerofoil, esp. a wing or propeller blade. **2** *Electronics* the part of a pulse in which the amplitude increases (opp. *trailing edge*). **3** *colloq.* the forefront of development, esp. in technology. **leading lady** the actress playing the principal part. **leading light** a prominent and influential person. **leading man** the actor playing the principal part. **leading note** *Mus.* = SUBTONIC. **leading question** a question that prompts the answer wanted. **leading seaman** the rank next below NCO in the Royal Navy. **leading-strings** (or **-reins**) **1** strings for guiding children learning to walk. **2** oppressive supervision or control. **leading tone** *US Mus.* = *leading note.*

▪ *adj.* chief, principal, main, prime, cardinal, capital, foremost, head, premier, top, front, key, star, supreme, first, greatest, best, paramount, primary, pre-eminent, predominant, dominant, major, central, essential, *US* banner; important, outstanding, prominent, influential, great, grand; peerless, matchless, unequalled, unrivalled, unsurpassed. ● *n.* see *leadership* (LEADER). ▫ **leading article** editorial, lead (story), *Brit.* leader. **leading lady, leading man** see LEAD[1] *n.* 6. **leading light** see STAR *n.* 8a.

leading[2] /lédding/ *n. Printing* = LEAD[2] *n.* 6.

leadwort /lédwurt/ *n.* = PLUMBAGO 2.

leaf /leef/ *n.* & *v.* ● *n.* (*pl.* **leaves** /leevz/) **1 a** each of several flattened usu. green structures of a plant, usu. on the side of a stem or branch and the main organ of photosynthesis. **b** other similar plant structures, e.g. bracts, sepals, and petals (*floral leaf*). **2 a** foliage regarded collectively. **b** the state of having leaves out (*a tree in leaf*). **3** the leaves of tobacco or tea. **4** a single thickness of paper, esp. in a book with each side forming a page. **5** a very thin sheet of metal, esp. gold or silver. **6 a** the hinged part or flap of a door, shutter, table, etc. **b** an extra section inserted to extend a table. ● *v.* **1** *intr.* put forth leaves. **2** *tr.* (foll. by *through*) turn over the pages of (a book etc.). ▫ **leaf-green** the colour of green leaves. **leaf insect** any insect of the family Phylliidae, having a flattened body leaflike in appearance. **leaf-miner** any of various larvae burrowing in leaves, esp. moth caterpillars of the family Gracillariidae. **leaf-monkey** a langur. **leaf-mould** soil consisting chiefly of decayed leaves. **leaf spring** a spring made of strips of metal. **leaf-stalk** a petiole. ▫▫ **leafage** *n.* **leafed** *adj.* (also in *comb.*). **leafless** *adj.* **leaflessness** *n.* **leaflike** *adj.* [OE *lēaf* f. Gmc]

▪ *n.* **1** see BLADE 3. **4** see SHEET[1] *n.* 6. ● *v.* **2** see THUMB *v.* 2. ▫ **leaf-stalk** see STALK[1] 2. ▫▫ **leafless** see BARE *adj.* 2a.

leafhopper /leéfhoppər/ *n.* any homopterous insect of the family Cicadellidae, which sucks the sap of plants and often causes damage and spreads disease.

leaflet /leéflit/ *n.* & *v.* ● *n.* **1** a young leaf. **2** *Bot.* any division of a compound leaf. **3** a sheet of (usu. printed) paper (sometimes folded but not stitched) giving information, esp. for free distribution. ● *v.tr.* (**leafleted, leafleting**) distribute leaflets to.

▪ *n.* **3** pamphlet, folder, brochure, booklet, handbill, bill, circular, hand-out, *US* flyer; advertisement, *Brit. colloq.* advert; (*leaflets*) documentation, junk mail, *colloq.* literature, *Brit. colloq. usu. derog.* bumf.

leafy /leéfi/ *adj.* (**leafier, leafiest**) **1** having many leaves; (of a place) rich in foliage, verdant. **2** resembling a leaf. ▫▫ **leafiness** *n.*

▪ **1** foliate; green, verdant, lush; tree-lined, woody, *literary* bosky; shady, shadowy.

league[1] /leeg/ *n.* & *v.* ● *n.* **1** a collection of people, countries, groups, etc., combining for a particular purpose, esp. mutual protection or cooperation. **2** an agreement to combine in this way. **3** a group of sports clubs which compete over a period for a championship. **4** a class of contestants. ● *v.intr.* (**leagues, leagued, leaguing**) (often foll. by *together*) join in a league. ▫ **in league** allied, conspiring. **league football** *Austral.* Rugby League or Australian Rules football played in leagues. **league table 1** a listing of competitors as a league, showing their ranking according to performance. **2** any list of ranking order. [F *ligue* or It. *liga*, var. of *lega* f. *legare* bind f. L *ligare*]

▪ *n.* **1, 3** confederation, federation, union, association, coalition, alliance, combination, confederacy, organization; guild, society, institute, body, fraternity, band, fellowship, club, party; cabal, gang, group, ring, circle, syndicate, pool. **2** pact, bond, covenant, contract, agreement, arrangement, treaty. **4** class, grade, rank, level; division, category, group, classification. ● *v.* ally, unite, combine, associate, affiliate, confederate, collaborate, band together, join (forces), team up, get together, *colloq.* gang up; conspire, collude, plot, connive, scheme. ▫ **in league** allied, united, in alliance, in collusion, *sl.* in cahoots; conspiring.

league[2] /leeg/ *n. archaic* a varying measure of travelling-distance by land, usu. about three miles. [ME, ult. f. LL *leuga, leuca*, of Gaulish orig.]

leaguer[1] /leégər/ *n.* esp. *US* a member of a league.

leaguer[2] /leégər/ *n.* & *v.* = LAAGER. [Du. *leger* camp, rel. to LAIR[1]]

leak /leek/ *n.* & *v.* ● *n.* **1 a** a hole in a vessel, pipe, or container etc. caused by wear or damage, through which matter, esp. liquid or gas, passes accidentally in or out. **b** the matter passing in or out through this. **c** the act or an instance of leaking. **2 a** a similar escape of electrical charge. **b** the charge that escapes. **3** the intentional disclosure of secret information. ● *v.* **1 a** *intr.* (of liquid, gas, etc.) pass in or out through a leak. **b** *tr.* lose or admit (liquid, gas, etc.) through a leak. **2** *tr.* intentionally disclose (secret information). **3** *intr.* (often foll. by *out*) (of a secret, secret information) become known. □ **have** (or **take**) **a leak** *sl.* urinate. □□ **leaker** *n.* [ME prob. f. LG]

■ *n.* **1 a** hole, fissure, crack, chink, crevice, aperture, opening, puncture, perforation, cut, break, breach, rip, split, gash, rent, tear, gap, flaw. **b, c** leakage, discharge, trickle, escape, seepage, spillage, ooze, secretion, exudation, flow, outflow, effluence, efflux, emanation, *archaic* issue. **3** disclosure, revelation, leakage, exposure, divulgence, divulgement, divulgation, publication, release. ● *v.* **1 a** come *or* go *or* get out, escape, issue, emerge, spill (out), trickle (out), drip (out), dribble (out), seep (out), ooze (out), exude, pour *or* stream *or* flow out, extravasate. **b** discharge, spill, drip, ooze, exude, secrete, stream, pour, dribble, extravasate. **2** disclose, divulge, reveal, bring to light, impart, betray, tell, report, publish, release, give *or* let out, make known *or* public; let slip, blab, *colloq.* spill the beans about. **3** (*leak out*) transpire, come *or* get out, escape, emerge, trickle out, come to light, become known. □ **have a leak** see URINATE.

leakage /leékij/ *n.* **1** the action or result of leaking. **2** what leaks in or out. **3** an intentional disclosure of secret information.

■ **1, 2** see LEAK *n.* 1b, c. **3** see LEAK *n.* 3.

leaky /leéki/ *adj.* (**leakier, leakiest**) **1** having a leak or leaks. **2** given to letting out secrets. □□ **leakiness** *n.*

leal /leel/ *adj. Sc.* loyal, honest. [ME f. AF *leal*, OF *leel*, *loial* (as LOYAL)]

lean[1] /leen/ *v.* & *n.* ● *v.* (*past* and *past part.* **leaned** /leend, lent/ or **leant** /lent/) **1** *intr.* & *tr.* (often foll. by *across*, *back*, *over*, etc.) be or place in a sloping position; incline from the perpendicular. **2** *intr.* & *tr.* (foll. by *against*, *on*, *upon*) rest or cause to rest for support against etc. **3** *intr.* (foll. by *on*, *upon*) rely on; derive support from. **4** *intr.* (foll. by *to*, *towards*) be inclined or partial to; have a tendency towards. ● *n.* a deviation from the perpendicular; an inclination (*has a decided lean to the right*). □ **lean on** *colloq.* put pressure on (a person) to act in a certain way. **lean over backwards** see BACKWARDS. **lean-to** (*pl.* **-tos**) a building with its roof leaning against a larger building or a wall. [OE *hleonian*, *hlinian* f. Gmc]

■ *v.* **1** slope, incline, slant, tilt, bend, tip. **2** (*tr.*) rest, prop, set, put, lay, place, position; (*intr.*) lie, rest, repose, recline, be propped *or* supported *or* sustained. **3** (*lean on*) rely on, depend on, count on, bank on, pin one's faith *or* hopes on; believe *or* trust in, have confidence in, be sure *or* certain of. **4** (*lean to* or *towards*) favour, gravitate towards, tend towards, be disposed towards, prefer, show *or* have a preference for, incline towards, be inclined *or* partial to, be *or* lean on the side of, be biased towards, have a tendency to *or* towards, be in favour of. ● *n.* inclination, slant, tilt, tip, slope, pitch, rake, cant, camber, ramp, angle, deviation. □ **lean on** pressure, pressurize, put pressure on, bring pressure to bear on; intimidate, squeeze, railroad, browbeat, threaten, menace, *colloq.* bulldoze, heavy, put the screws on, *sl.* put the frighteners on. **lean-to** see SHED[1] 1.

lean[2] /leen/ *adj.* & *n.* ● *adj.* **1** (of a person or animal) thin; having no superfluous fat. **2** (of meat) containing little fat. **3 a** meagre; of poor quality (*lean crop*). **b** not nourishing (*lean diet*). **4** unremunerative. ● *n.* the lean part of meat. □ **lean years** years of scarcity. □□ **leanly** *adv.* **leanness** *n.* [OE *hlǣne* f. Gmc]

■ *adj.* **1** thin, slim, slender, spare, skinny, bony, meagre, skeletal, scraggy, scrawny, emaciated, wasted, gaunt, haggard, pinched, raw-boned, weasel-faced, hollow-cheeked, rangy, wiry, lanky, spindly, lank, angular, gangling, gangly, twiggy, reedy; undernourished, underfed, underweight, anorexic, anorectic, *colloq.* nothing but *or* all skin and bone(s). **3 a** meagre, poor, scanty, scant, skimpy, inadequate, deficient, insufficient, sparse; unfruitful, unproductive, barren, infertile, bare, arid. **4** unremunerative, unfruitful, unprofitable, fruitless; hard, bad, tough, difficult; impoverished, poverty-stricken, penurious.

leaning /leéning/ *n.* a tendency or partiality.

■ tendency, partiality, bent, inclination, bias, prejudice, predilection, liking, taste, preference, penchant, disposition, propensity, predisposition, proclivity, affinity, sympathy.

leap /leep/ *v.* & *n.* ● *v.* (*past* and *past part.* **leaped** /leept, lept/ or **leapt** /lept/) **1** *intr.* jump or spring forcefully. **2** *tr.* jump across. **3** *intr.* (of prices etc.) increase dramatically. **4** *intr.* hurry, rush; proceed without pausing for thought (*leapt to the wrong conclusion*; *leapt to their defence*). ● *n.* a forceful jump. □ **by leaps and bounds** with startlingly rapid progress. **leap at 1** rush towards, pounce upon. **2** accept eagerly. **leap in the dark** a daring step or enterprise whose consequences are unpredictable. **leap to the eye** be immediately apparent. **leap year** a year, occurring once in four, with 366 days (including 29th Feb. as an intercalary day). □□ **leaper** *n.* [OE *hlȳp*, *hlēapan* f. Gmc: *leap year* prob. refers to the fact that feast-days after Feb. in such a year fall two days later (instead of the normal one day later) than in the previous year]

■ *v.* **1** jump, spring, bound, hop, skip; gambol, caper, prance, curvet, *sl.* cavort. **2** jump, hurdle, vault, clear, leap-frog, hop (over), negotiate. **3** jump, increase, climb, rise, surge, soar, rocket, shoot up, escalate. **4** jump, rush, hurry, hasten. ● *n.* jump, spring, bound, vault, hurdle, hop, skip; climb, rise, surge, upsurge, escalation, lift, *colloq.* boost, *US* hike. □ **by leaps and bounds** rapidly, quickly, swiftly, speedily, fast, at a gallop, *colloq.* at a rate of knots, like a dose of salts, like greased lightning, like a bat out of hell, *Brit. colloq.* like a bomb, *literary* apace, *Brit. sl.* like the clappers. **leap at 2** jump at, accept, be eager for, take; seize (on), grab (at), pounce on, grasp, *colloq.* swoop up(on).

leap-frog /leépfrog/ *n.* & *v.* ● *n.* a game in which players in turn vault with parted legs over another who is bending down. ● *v.* (**-frogged, -frogging**) **1** *intr.* (foll. by *over*) perform such a vault. **2** *tr.* vault over in this way. **3** *tr.* & *intr.* (of two or more people, vehicles, etc.) overtake alternately.

learn /lern/ *v.* (*past* and *past part.* **learned** /lernt, lernd/ or **learnt** /lernt/) **1** *tr.* gain knowledge of or skill in by study, experience, or being taught. **2** *tr.* (foll. by *to* + infin.) acquire or develop a particular ability (*learn to swim*). **3** *tr.* commit to memory (*will try to learn your names*). **4** *intr.* (foll. by *of*) be informed about. **5** *tr.* (foll. by *that*, *how*, etc. + clause) become aware of by information or from observation. **6** *intr.* receive instruction; acquire knowledge or skill. **7** *tr. archaic* or *sl.* teach. □ **learn one's lesson** see LESSON. □□ **learnable** *adj.* **learnability** /lérnəbílliti/ *n.* [OE *leornian* f. Gmc: cf. LORE[1]]

■ **1, 2** be taught; be instructed in, have *or* take lessons in; master, study, get to know, get to grips with, get the hang of, *archaic* con. **3** memorize, commit to memory, learn by heart *or* rote; remember, retain, keep in mind. **4** (*learn of*) find out (about), discover, uncover, unearth, determine, identify, ascertain; hear of *or* about, gather, pick up, chance *or* hit upon, come across. **5** find out, discover, gather, hear, see, understand, grasp, comprehend, discern, perceive, realize, recognize, *colloq.* twig; conclude, infer, deduce. **6** study, train, practise, revise. **7** see TEACH 1.

learned /lérnid/ *adj.* **1** having much knowledge acquired by study. **2** showing or requiring learning (*a learned work*). **3** studied or pursued by learned persons. **4** concerned with the interests of learned persons; scholarly (*a learned journal*). **5** *Brit.* as a courteous description of a lawyer in certain formal contexts (*my learned friend*). □□ **learnedly** *adv.* **learnedness** *n.* [ME f. LEARN in the sense 'teach']

■ **1** knowledgeable, (well-)informed, erudite, (well-)educated, lettered, well-read, literate, cultured; scholarly, academic, intellectual, scholastic, *colloq.* highbrow; expert, authoritative, *au fait*, *au courant*, *colloq.* in the know; experienced, skilled, practised, accomplished, (well-)versed, (well-)trained, (well-)grounded. **2–4** scholarly, academic, intellectual, cerebral, *colloq.* highbrow; abstract, theoretical, abstruse, formal, profound, deep, philosophical; educational, academical, collegiate; pedantic, scholastic, donnish, professorial, bookish, literary.

learner /lérnər/ *n.* **1** a person who is learning a subject or skill. **2** (in full **learner driver**) a person who is learning to drive a motor vehicle and has not yet passed a driving test.
■ **1** student, pupil, trainee, apprentice; beginner, novice, tiro, initiate, neophyte, acolyte, newcomer, recruit, greenhorn, tenderfoot, *US* punk, cub, *Austral. colloq.* jackaroo, *sl.* rookie.

learning /lérning/ *n.* knowledge acquired by study. [OE *leornung* (as LEARN)]
■ knowledge, lore, wisdom, erudition; schooling, education, instruction, scholarship, illumination; information, facts, data, intelligence; culture.

lease /leess/ *n.* & *v.* ● *n.* an agreement by which the owner of a building or land allows another to use it for a specified time, usu. in return for payment. ● *v.tr.* grant or take on lease. □ **a new lease of** (*US* **on**) **life** a substantially improved prospect of living, or of use after repair. □□ **leasable** *adj.* **leaser** *n.* [ME f. AF *les*, OF *lais*, *leis* f. *lesser*, *laissier* leave f. L *laxare* make loose (*laxus*)]
■ *n.* rental, hire, charter, *Brit.* let, *Sc.* feu; sublease, sublet, underlet; agreement, contract, arrangement, settlement, deal. ● *v.* rent (out), let (out), hire (out), charter, *Law* demise; sublet, sublease.

leaseback /le͞esbak/ *n.* the leasing of a property back to the vendor.

leasehold /le͞ess-hōld/ *n.* & *adj.* ● *n.* **1** the holding of property by lease. **2** property held by lease. ● *adj.* held by lease. □□ **leaseholder** *n.*
■ □□ **leaseholder** see TENANT *n.* 1.

leash /leesh/ *n.* & *v.* ● *n.* a thong for holding a dog; a dog's lead. ● *v.tr.* **1** put a leash on. **2** restrain. □ **straining at the leash** eager to begin. [ME f. OF *lesse*, *laisse* f. specific use of *laisser* let run on a slack lead: see LEASE]
■ *n.* see LEAD[1] *n.* 4. ● *v.* see TETHER *v.*

least /leest/ *adj.*, *n.*, & *adv.* ● *adj.* **1** smallest, slightest, most insignificant. **2** (prec. by *the*; esp. with *neg.*) any at all (*it does not make the least difference*). **3** (of a species or variety) very small (*least tern*). ● *n.* the least amount. ● *adv.* in the least degree. □ **at least 1** at all events; anyway; even if there is doubt about a more extended statement. **2** (also **at the least**) not less than. **in the least** (or **the least**) (usu. with *neg.*) in the smallest degree; at all (*not in the least offended*). **least common denominator, multiple** see DENOMINATOR, MULTIPLE. **to say the least** (or **the least of it**) used to imply the moderation of a statement (*that is doubtful to say the least*). [OE *lǣst*, *lǣsest* f. Gmc]
■ *adj.* **1** see MINIMUM *adj.* **3** see LITTLE *adj.* 7. ● *n.* see MINIMUM *n.*

leastways /le͞estwayz/ *adv.* (also **leastwise** /-wīz/) *dial.* or at least, or rather.

leat /leet/ *n. Brit.* an open watercourse conducting water to a mill etc. [OE *-gelǣt* (as Y- + root of LET[1])]

leather /lét͟hər/ *n.* & *v.* ● *n.* **1 a** material made from the skin of an animal by tanning or a similar process. **b** (*attrib.*) made of leather. **2** a piece of leather for polishing with. **3** the leather part or parts of something. **4** *sl.* a cricket-ball or football. **5** (in *pl.*) leather clothes, esp. leggings, breeches, or clothes for wearing on a motor cycle. **6** a thong (*stirrup-leather*). ● *v.tr.* **1** cover with leather. **2** polish or wipe with a leather. **3** beat, thrash (orig. with a leather thong). □ **leather-jacket 1** *Brit.* a crane-fly grub with a tough skin. **2** any of various tough-skinned marine fish of the family Monacanthidae. **leather-neck** *Naut. sl.* a soldier or (esp. *US*) a marine (with reference to the leather stock formerly worn by them). [OE *lether* f. Gmc]
■ *n.* **1** see HIDE[2] *n.* 1. ● *v.* **3** see BEAT *v.* 1.

leatherback /lét͟hərbak/ *n.* a large marine turtle, *Dermochelys coriacea*, having a thick leathery carapace.

leathercloth /lét͟hərkloth/ *n.* strong fabric coated to resemble leather.

leatherette /lét͟hərét/ *n.* imitation leather.

leathern /lét͟hərn/ *n. archaic* made of leather.

leathery /lét͟həri/ *adj.* **1** like leather. **2** (esp. of meat etc.) tough. □□ **leatheriness** *n.*
■ **2** see TOUGH *adj.* 1.

leave[1] /leev/ *v.* & *n.* ● *v.* (*past* and *past part.* **left** /left/) **1 a** *tr.* go away from; cease to remain in or on (*left him quite well an hour ago*; *leave the track*; *leave here*). **b** *intr.* (often foll. by *for*) depart (*we leave tomorrow*; *has just left for London*). **2** *tr.* cause to or let remain; depart without taking (*has left his gloves*; *left a slimy trail*; *left a bad impression*; *six from seven leaves one*). **3** *tr.* (also *absol.*) cease to reside at or attend or belong to or work for (*has left the school*; *I am leaving for another firm*). **4** *tr.* abandon, forsake, desert. **5** *tr.* have remaining after one's death (*leaves a wife and two children*). **6** *tr.* bequeath. **7** *tr.* (foll. by *to* + infin.) allow (a person or thing) to do something without interference or assistance (*leave the future to take care of itself*). **8** *tr.* (foll. by *to*) commit or refer to another person (*leave that to me*; *nothing was left to chance*). **9** *tr.* **a** abstain from consuming or dealing with. **b** (in *passive*; often foll. by *over*) remain over. **10** *tr.* **a** deposit or entrust (a thing) to be attended to, collected, delivered, etc., in one's absence (*left a message with his secretary*). **b** depute (a person) to perform a function in one's absence. **11** *tr.* allow to remain or cause to be in a specified state or position (*left the door open*; *the performance left them unmoved*; *left nothing that was necessary undone*). **12** *tr.* pass (an object) so that it is in a specified relative direction (*leave the church on the left*). ● *n.* the position in which a player leaves the balls in billiards, croquet, etc. □ **be left with 1** retain (a feeling etc.). **2** be burdened with (a responsibility etc.). **be well left** be well provided for by a legacy etc. **get left** *colloq.* be deserted or worsted. **have left** have remaining (*has no friends left*). **leave alone 1** refrain from disturbing, not interfere with. **2** not have dealings with. **leave be** *colloq.* refrain from disturbing, not interfere with. **leave behind 1** go away without. **2** leave as a consequence or a visible sign of passage. **3** pass. **leave a person cold** (or **cool**) not impress or excite a person. **leave go** *colloq.* relax one's hold. **leave hold of** cease holding. **leave it at that** *colloq.* abstain from comment or further action. **leave much** (or **a lot** etc.) **to be desired** be highly unsatisfactory. **leave off 1** come to or make an end. **2** discontinue (*leave off work*; *leave off talking*). **3** not wear. **leave out** omit, not include. **leave over** *Brit.* leave to be considered, settled, or used later. **leave a person to himself** or **herself 1** not attempt to control a person. **2** leave a person solitary. **left at the post** beaten from the start of a race. **left for dead** abandoned as being beyond rescue. **left luggage** *Brit.* luggage deposited for later retrieval, esp. at a railway station. □□ **leaver** *n.* [OE *lǣfan* f. Gmc]
■ *v.* **1b, 3, 4** depart, go *or* move (away *or* off), get *or* be away *or* off, be gone, be on one's way, go one's way, (make an) exit, get going, set off, check out, take off, *colloq.* fly, be off, push off, clear off, disappear, vanish, skedaddle, scram, up sticks, *Brit. colloq.* flit, *sl.* shove off, slope off, buzz off, beat it, split, *Austral. sl.* go through, *Brit. sl.* do a bunk, hop it, *US sl.* vamoose; say goodbye, take one's leave, *archaic or literary* bid farewell *or* adieu; retire, (beat a) retreat, withdraw, decamp, pull out; quit, get *or* go *or* jump out of, disembark from, evacuate; desert, abandon, forsake; break (up) with, jilt, walk *or* run out on, throw over, cast off *or* aside, turn one's back on, leave in the lurch, discard, drop, *colloq.* dump, *sl.* ditch. **2** leave behind; forget, go without, mislay, lose. **6** see BEQUEATH 1, 2. **7** allow, let, permit, authorize, *archaic* suffer. **8** entrust, commit, consign, refer, assign, delegate, hand over, deliver, give. **9 a** abstain *or* refrain

from, avoid, shun, keep *or* stay off *or* away from, keep *or* steer clear of, leave alone, *literary* eschew. **b** (*left over*) remaining, over; extra, spare, excess, unwanted.
10 a deposit, entrust, consign, lodge, place, put, keep, store, stow, *colloq.* stash (away). □ **be left with 1** retain, keep, hold on to, preserve, *colloq.* hang on to. **2** be burdened *or* saddled *or* lumbered with. **leave alone 1** lay off, leave be, leave in peace. **2** see LEAVE[1] *v.* 9a above. **leave be** see *leave alone* 1 above. **leave behind 1, 2** see LEAVE[1] *v.* 2 above. **leave off 1, 2** see END *v.* 1. **leave out** see OMIT 1.

leave[2] /leev/ *n.* **1** (often foll. by *to* + infin.) permission. **2 a** (in full **leave of absence**) permission to be absent from duty. **b** the period for which this lasts. □ **by** (or **with**) **your leave** often *iron.* an expression of apology for taking a liberty or making an unwelcome statement. **on leave** legitimately absent from duty. **take one's leave** bid farewell. **take one's leave of** bid farewell to. **take leave of one's senses** see SENSE. **take leave to** venture or presume to. [OE *lēaf* f. WG: cf. LIEF, LOVE]
■ **1** permission, authority, authorization, licence, consent, assent, agreement, acquiescence, sufferance, approval, blessing, sanction, dispensation, go-ahead, thumbs up, *colloq.* green light. **2** furlough, time off, holiday, vacation, sabbatical; R and R, free time; sick-leave. □ **take one's leave** see LEAVE[1] *v.* 1b, 3, 4.

leaved /leevd/ *adj.* **1** having leaves. **2** (in *comb.*) having a leaf or leaves of a specified kind or number (*four-leaved clover*).

leaven /lévv'n/ *n.* & *v.* ● *n.* **1** a substance added to dough to make it ferment and rise, esp. yeast, or fermenting dough reserved for the purpose. **2 a** a pervasive transforming influence (cf. Matt. 13:33). **b** (foll. by *of*) a tinge or admixture of a specified quality. ● *v.tr.* **1** ferment (dough) with leaven. **2 a** permeate and transform. **b** (foll. by *with*) modify with a tempering element. □ **the old leaven** traces of the unregenerate state (cf. 1 Cor. 5:6-8). [ME f. OF *levain* f. Gallo-Roman spec. use of L *levamen* relief f. *levare* lift]
■ *v.* **1** see FERMENT *v.* 1.

leaves *pl.* of LEAF.

leavings /leévingz/ *n.pl.* things left over, esp. as worthless.
■ see LEFTOVER *n.*

Lebanese /lébbəneéz/ *adj.* & *n.* ● *adj.* of or relating to Lebanon in the Middle East. ● *n.* (*pl.* same) **1** a native or national of Lebanon. **2** a person of Lebanese descent.

Lebensraum /láybənzrowm/ *n.* the territory which a State or nation believes is needed for its natural development. [G, = living-space (orig. with reference to Germany, esp. in the 1930s)]

lech /lech/ *v.* & *n. colloq.* ● *v.intr.* feel lecherous; behave lustfully. ● *n.* **1** a strong desire, esp. sexual. **2** a lecher. [back-form. f. LECHER: (n.) perh. f. *letch* longing]

lecher /léchər/ *n.* a lecherous man; a debauchee. [ME f. OF *lecheor* etc. f. *lechier* live in debauchery or gluttony f. Frank., rel. to LICK]
■ see LIBERTINE *n.* 1.

lecherous /léchərəss/ *adj.* lustful, having strong or excessive sexual desire. □□ **lecherously** *adv.* **lecherousness** *n.* [ME f. OF *lecheros* etc. f. *lecheur* LECHER]
■ lustful, randy, lascivious, sexy, licentious, lewd, dirty, filthy, prurient, salacious, libidinous, erotic, sensual, lubricious, promiscuous, depraved, dissolute, ruttish, goatish, goaty, hot, fast, wanton, *formal* concupiscent, *sl.* horny.

lechery /léchəri/ *n.* unrestrained indulgence of sexual desire. [ME f. OF *lecherie* f. *lecheur* LECHER]
■ see DESIRE *n.* 2.

lecithin /léssithin/ *n.* **1** any of a group of phospholipids found naturally in animals, egg-yolk, and some higher plants. **2** a preparation of this used to emulsify foods etc. [Gk *lekithos* egg-yolk + -IN]

lectern /léktərn/ *n.* **1** a stand for holding a book in a church or chapel, esp. for a bible from which lessons are to be read. **2** a similar stand for a lecturer etc. [ME *lettorne* f. OF *let(t)run*, med.L *lectrum* f. *legere lect-* read]

lection /léksh'n/ *n.* a reading of a text found in a particular copy or edition. [L *lectio* reading (as LECTERN)]

lectionary /lékshənəri/ *n.* (*pl.* **-ies**) **1** a list of portions of Scripture appointed to be read at divine service. **2** a book containing such portions. [ME f. med.L *lectionarium* (as LECTION)]

lector /léktor/ *n.* **1** a reader, esp. of lessons in a church service. **2** (*fem.* **lectrice** /lektreéss/) a lecturer or reader, esp. one employed in a foreign university to give instruction in his or her native language. [L f. *legere lect-* read]

lecture /lékchər/ *n.* & *v.* ● *n.* **1** a discourse giving information about a subject to a class or other audience. **2** a long serious speech esp. as a scolding or reprimand. ● *v.* **1** *intr.* (often foll. by *on*) deliver a lecture or lectures. **2** *tr.* talk seriously or reprovingly to (a person). **3** *tr.* instruct or entertain (a class or other audience) by a lecture. [ME f. OF *lecture* or med.L *lectura* f. L (as LECTOR)]
■ *n.* **1** speech, address, talk, presentation, demonstration, paper, dissertation, disquisition, lesson, instruction, declamation, harangue, screed, *literary* discourse, *sl.* spiel; seminar, workshop. **2** speech, sermon, scolding, tongue-lashing, upbraiding, castigation, reproof, reprimand, rebuke, reproach, remonstration, rap on *or* over the knuckles, *colloq.* talking-to, dressing-down, telling-off, ticking off, wigging, *US colloq.* chewing-out; curtain lecture; harangue, diatribe, philippic; censure, criticism. ● *v.* **1** make *or* deliver *or* give a speech *or* address *or* talk *or* presentation, give a paper, speak, talk, discourse, *colloq.* go on, *sl.* spiel; sermonize, hold forth, moralize, pontificate, preach, declaim, *esp. joc. or derog.* orate. **2** reprove, reprimand, rebuke, reproach, scold, upbraid, berate, rate, castigate, harangue, remonstrate with, give a person a tongue-lashing *or* dressing-down, give a person a rap on *or* over the knuckles, have a go at, *archaic or literary* chide, *colloq.* wig, carpet, tell off, tick off, give a person a telling-off *or* ticking-off *or* talking-to, lambaste, *US colloq.* chew out, *esp. Austral. sl.* earbash; admonish, warn, caution, counsel, advise. **3** see INSTRUCT 1.

lecturer /lékchərər/ *n.* a person who lectures, esp. as a teacher in higher education.
■ see TEACHER.

lectureship /lékchərship/ *n.* the office of lecturer. ¶ The form *lecturership*, which is strictly more regular, is in official use at Oxford University and elsewhere, but is not widely current.

lecythus /léssithəss/ *n.* (*pl.* **lecythi** /-thī/) *Gk Antiq.* a thin narrow-necked vase or flask. [Gk *lēkuthos*]

LED *abbr.* light-emitting diode.

led *past* and *past part.* of LEAD[1].

lederhosen /láydərhōz'n/ *n.pl.* leather shorts as worn by men in Bavaria etc. [G, = leather trousers]

ledge /lej/ *n.* **1** a narrow horizontal surface projecting from a wall etc. **2** a shelflike projection on the side of a rock or mountain. **3** a ridge of rocks, esp. below water. **4** *Mining* a stratum of metal-bearing rock. □□ **ledged** *adj.* **ledgy** *adj.* [perh. f. ME *legge* LAY[1]]
■ **1** shelf, ridge, projection, overhang, sill, step; mantelpiece, windowsill.

ledger /léjər/ *n.* **1** a tall narrow book in which a firm's accounts are kept, esp. one which is the principal book of a set and contains debtor-and-creditor accounts. **2** a flat gravestone. **3** a horizontal timber in scaffolding, parallel to the face of the building. □ **ledger line** *Mus.* = LEGER LINE. **ledger-tackle** a kind of fishing tackle in which a lead weight keeps the bait on the bottom. [ME f. senses of Du. *ligger* and *legger* (f. *liggen* LIE[1], *leggen* LAY[1]) & pronunc. of ME *ligge, legge*]
■ **1** see JOURNAL 4.

lee /lee/ *n.* **1** shelter given by a neighbouring object (*under the lee of*). **2** (in full **lee side**) the sheltered side, the side away from the wind (opp. *weather side*). □ **lee-board** a plank frame fixed to the side of a flat-bottomed vessel and let down into the water to diminish leeway. **lee shore** the shore to leeward of a ship. [OE *hlēo* f. Gmc]

leech[1] /leech/ *n.* **1** any freshwater or terrestrial annelid worm of the class *Hirudinea* with suckers at both ends, esp. *Hirudo medicinalis*, a bloodsucking parasite of vertebrates formerly much used medically. **2** a person who extorts profit from or sponges on others. □ **like a leech** persistently or clingingly present. [OE *lǣce*, assim. to LEECH[2]]

■ **2** see BLOODSUCKER 2.

leech[2] /leech/ *n. archaic* or *joc.* a physician; a healer. [OE *lǣce* f. Gmc]

leech[3] /leech/ *n.* **1** a perpendicular or sloping side of a square sail. **2** the side of a fore-and-aft sail away from the mast or stay. [ME, perh. rel. to ON *lik*, a nautical term of uncert. meaning]

leechcraft /leéchkraaft/ *n. archaic* the art of healing. [OE *lǣcecræft* (as LEECH[2], CRAFT)]

leek /leek/ *n.* **1** an alliaceous plant, *Allium porrum*, with flat overlapping leaves forming an elongated cylindrical bulb, used as food. **2** this as a Welsh national emblem. [OE *lēac* f. Gmc]

leer[1] /leer/ *v.* & *n.* ● *v.intr.* look slyly or lasciviously or maliciously. ● *n.* a leering look. □□ **leeringly** *adv.* [perh. f. obs. *leer* cheek f. OE *hlēor*, as though 'to glance over one's cheek']

■ *v.* (*leer at*) ogle, eye (up), make eyes at, give a person the (glad) eye. ● *n.* ogle, *colloq.* the (glad) eye, the once-over.

leer[2] var. of LEHR.

leery /leéri/ *adj.* (**leerier**, **leeriest**) *sl.* **1** knowing, sly. **2** (foll. by *of*) wary. □□ **leeriness** *n.* [perh. f. obs. *leer* looking askance f. LEER[1] + -Y[1]]

■ **1** knowing, sly, cunning, crafty, artful, clever, sharp, canny, wily, guileful, shrewd, devious, disingenuous, tricky, furtive, *colloq.* shifty. **2** wary, suspicious, sceptical, dubious, doubtful, distrustful, cautious, chary, careful, *colloq.* cagey.

lees /leez/ *n.pl.* **1** the sediment of wine etc. (*drink to the lees*). **2** dregs, refuse. [pl. of ME *lie* f. OF *lie* f. med.L *lia* f. Gaulish]

■ **1** see SEDIMENT 1. **2** see RUBBISH *n.* 2.

leet[1] /leet/ *n. hist.* **1** (in full **Court leet**) a yearly or half-yearly court of record that lords of certain manors might hold. **2** its jurisdiction or district. [ME f. AF *lete* (= AL *leta*), of unkn. orig.]

leet[2] /leet/ *n. Sc.* a selected list of candidates for some office. □ **short leet** = *short list*. [ME *lite* etc., prob. f. AF & OF *lit(t)e*, var. of *liste* LIST[1]]

leeward /leéwərd, *Naut.* lóoərd/ *adj.*, *adv.*, & *n.* ● *adj.* & *adv.* on or towards the side sheltered from the wind (opp. WINDWARD). ● *n.* the leeward region, side, or direction (*to leeward*; *on the leeward of*).

leewardly /leéwərdli, lóoərdli/ *adj.* (of a ship) apt to drift to leeward.

leeway /leéway/ *n.* **1** the sideways drift of a ship to leeward of the desired course. **2 a** allowable deviation or freedom of action. **b** *US* margin of safety. □ **make up leeway** struggle out of a bad position, recover lost time, etc.

■ **2** latitude, scope, freedom, range, play, (elbow-)room, (breathing-)space; safety factor, margin of error.

left[1] /left/ *adj.*, *adv.*, & *n.* (opp. RIGHT). ● *adj.* **1** on or towards the side of the human body which corresponds to the position of west if one regards oneself as facing north. **2** on or towards the part of an object which is analogous to a person's left side or (with opposite sense) which is nearer to an observer's left hand. **3** (also **Left**) *Polit.* of the Left. ● *adv.* on or to the left side. ● *n.* **1** the left-hand part or region or direction. **2** *Boxing* **a** the left hand. **b** a blow with this. **3 a** (often **Left**) *Polit.* a group or section favouring radical socialism (orig. the more radical section of a continental legislature, seated on the president's left); such radicals collectively. **b** the more advanced or innovative section of any group. **4** the side of a stage which is to the left of a person facing the audience. **5** (esp. in marching) the left foot. **6** the left wing of an army. □ **have two left feet** be clumsy. **left and right** = *right and left*. **left bank** the bank of a river on the left facing downstream. **left bower** see BOWER[3]. **left field** *Baseball* the part of the outfield to the left of the batter as he or she faces the pitcher. **left hand 1** the hand of the left side. **2** (usu. prec. by *at*, *on*, *to*) the region or direction on the left side of a person. **left-hand** *adj.* **1** on or towards the left side of a person or thing (*left-hand drive*). **2** done with the left hand (*left-hand blow*). **3 a** (of rope) twisted counter-clockwise. **b** (of a screw) = LEFT-HANDED. **left turn** a turn that brings one's front to face as one's left side did before. **left wing 1** the radical or socialist section of a political party. **2** the left side of a football etc. team on the field. **3** the left side of an army. **left-wing** *adj.* socialist, radical. **left-winger** a person on the left wing. **marry with the left hand** marry morganatically (see LEFT-HANDED). □□ **leftish** *adj.* [ME *lüft*, *lift*, *left*, f. OE, orig. sense 'weak, worthless']

■ *adj.* **1, 2** left-hand, sinistral, *Naut. archaic* larboard, *Heraldry* & *archaic* sinister. **3** left-wing, socialist(ic), Labour, *Polit.* leftist, *colloq.* red, *esp. derog.* pink, *sl.* Bolshie; progressive, progressivist, radical, liberal, democratic; communist(ic), Bolshevik, Marxist(-Leninist). ● *n.* **1, 4** left hand, port, *Naut. archaic* larboard; stage left. **3** left wing, left-wingers, socialists, Labour, *Polit.* leftists, *colloq.* lefties, reds, *sl.* Bolshies; progressives, progressivists, radicals, liberals, democrats; communists. □ **have two left feet** be clumsy *or* awkward *or* gauche *or* ungainly. **left hand 2** see LEFT[1] *n.* 1, 4 above. **left-hand 1** see LEFT[1] *adj.* 1, 2 above. **left wing 1** see LEFT[1] *n.* 3 above. **left-wing** see LEFT[1] *adj.* 3 above. **left-winger** socialist, Bolshevik, Bolshevist, *Polit.* leftist, *colloq.* red, *sl.* Bolshie; progressive, radical, liberal, democrat; communist.

left[2] *past* and *past part.* of LEAVE[1].

left-handed /léft-hándid/ *adj.* **1** using the left hand by preference as more serviceable than the right. **2** (of a tool etc.) made to be used with the left hand. **3** (of a blow) struck with the left hand. **4 a** turning to the left; towards the left. **b** (of a racecourse) turning anticlockwise. **c** (of a screw) advanced by turning to the left (anticlockwise). **5** awkward, clumsy. **6 a** (of a compliment) ambiguous. **b** of doubtful sincerity or validity. **7** (of a marriage) morganatic (from a German custom by which the bridegroom gave the bride his left hand in such marriages). □□ **left-handedly** *adv.* **left-handedness** *n.*

■ **1** sinistral, *colloq.* southpaw, cack-handed. **4** left-hand; anticlockwise, *US* counter-clockwise. **5** see AWKWARD 2. **6** ambiguous, backhanded, equivocal, questionable, dubious, doubtful; insincere, hollow, empty, false.

left-hander /léft-hándər/ *n.* **1** a left-handed person. **2** a left-handed blow.

leftie var. of LEFTY.

leftism /léftiz'm/ *n. Polit.* the principles or policy of the left. □□ **leftist** *n.* & *adj.*

■ □□ **leftist** (*n.*) see PROGRESSIVE *n.* (*adj.*) see LEFT[1] *adj.* 3.

leftmost /léftmōst/ *adj.* furthest to the left.

leftover /léftōvər/ *adj.* & *n.* ● *adj.* remaining over; not used up or disposed of. ● *n.* (in *pl.*) items (esp. of food) remaining after the rest has been used.

■ *adj.* remaining, residual, extra, superfluous, excess, unused, uneaten. ● *n.* (*leftovers*) remains, remainders, remnants, scraps, leavings, crumbs, rejects, dregs, lees; rest, residue, residuum, balance; surplus, excess, superfluity, overage, odds and ends, waifs and strays, flotsam and jetsam, *colloq.* truck; debris, refuse, waste, rubbish, dross, junk.

leftward /léftwərd/ *adv.* & *adj.* ● *adv.* (also **leftwards** /-wərdz/) towards the left. ● *adj.* going towards or facing the left.

lefty /léfti/ *n.* (also **leftie**) (*pl.* **-ies**) *colloq.* **1** *Polit.* a left-winger. **2** a left-handed person.

leg /leg/ *n.* & *v.* ● *n.* **1 a** each of the limbs on which a person or animal walks and stands. **b** the part of this from the hip to the ankle. **2** a leg of an animal or bird as food. **3** an artificial leg (*wooden leg*). **4** a part of a garment covering a leg or part of a leg. **5 a** a support of a chair, table, bed, etc. **b** a long thin support or prop, esp. a pole. **6** *Cricket* the half of the field (as divided lengthways through the pitch) in which the striker's feet are placed (opp. OFF). **7 a** a section of a journey. **b** a section of a relay race. **c** a stage in a competition. **d** one of two or more games constituting a round. **8** one branch of a forked object. **9** *Naut.* a run made on a single tack. **10** *archaic* an obeisance made by drawing back one leg and bending it while keeping the front leg straight. ● *v.tr.* (**legged, legging**) propel (a boat) through a canal tunnel by pushing with one's legs against the tunnel sides. □ **feel** (or **find**) **one's legs** become able to stand or walk. **give a person a leg up** help a person to mount a horse etc. or get over an obstacle or difficulty. **have the legs of** be able to go further than. **have no legs** *colloq.* (of a golf ball etc.) have not enough momentum to reach the desired point. **keep one's legs** not fall. **leg before wicket** *Cricket* (of a batsman) out because of illegally obstructing the ball with a part of the body other than the hand. **leg break** *Cricket* **1** a ball which deviates from the leg side after bouncing. **2** such deviation. **leg-bye** see BYE[1]. **leg-cutter** *Cricket* a fast leg break. **leg-iron** a shackle or fetter for the leg. **leg it** *colloq.* walk or run fast. **leg-of-mutton sail** a triangular mainsail. **leg-of-mutton sleeve** a sleeve which is full and loose on the upper arm but close-fitting on the forearm. **leg-pull** *colloq.* a hoax. **leg-rest** a support for a seated invalid's leg. **leg-room** space for the legs of a seated person. **leg-show** a theatrical performance by scantily-dressed women. **leg slip** *Cricket* a fielder stationed for a ball glancing off the bat to the leg side behind the wicket. **leg spin** *Cricket* a type of spin which causes the ball to deviate from the leg side after bouncing. **leg stump** *Cricket* the stump on the leg side. **leg theory** *Cricket* bowling to leg with fielders massed on that side. **leg trap** *Cricket* a group of fielders near the wicket on the leg side. **leg warmer** either of a pair of tubular knitted garments covering the leg from ankle to thigh. **not have a leg to stand on** be unable to support one's argument by facts or sound reasons. **on one's last legs** near death or the end of one's usefulness etc. **on one's legs 1** (also **on one's hind legs**) standing esp. to make a speech. **2** well enough to walk about. **take to one's legs** run away. □□ **legged** /legd, léggid/ *adj.* (also in *comb.*). **legger** *n.* [ME f. ON *leggr* f. Gmc]

■ *n.* **1, 3** shank; calf, thigh, ham; limb, member, *Zool.* appendage; prosthesis, peg-leg; (*legs*) *colloq.* pins, *joc.* stumps. **2** shank, ham, gammon, gigot, haunch, drumstick, hock, *Brit.* hough; joint. **4** trouser(s), legging(s), stocking(s), hose. **5** cabriole, spindle; support, brace, prop, upright, standard, column, pillar, post. **7** section, part, stage, segment, portion, stretch, lap. **8** branch, fork, prong. □ **give a person a leg up** help a person (up), give a person a (helping) hand, lend a person a hand, aid, assist, support; push, *colloq.* boost. **leg it** see RUN *v.* 1, 3. **leg-pull** see HOAX *n.* **on one's last legs** decrepit, moribund, worn-out, spent, wasted, debilitated, exhausted, shattered, the worse for wear, *archaic* stricken in years, *colloq.* all in, *sl.* knackered, *Brit. sl.* clapped out; weak, frail, enfeebled, feeble, infirm; run-down, falling apart *or* to pieces, broken-down, dilapidated, rickety, ramshackle, tumbledown.

legacy /léggəsi/ *n.* (*pl.* **-ies**) **1** a gift left in a will. **2** something handed down by a predecessor (*legacy of corruption*). □ **legacy-hunter** a person who pays court to another to secure a legacy. [ME f. OF *legacie* legateship f. med.L *legatia* f. L *legare* bequeath]

■ **1** see BEQUEST 2.

legal /léeg'l/ *adj.* **1** of or based on law; concerned with law; falling within the province of law. **2** appointed or required by law. **3** permitted by law, lawful. **4** recognized by law, as distinct from equity. **5** *Theol.* **a** of the Mosaic law. **b** of salvation by works rather than by faith. □ **legal aid** payment from public funds allowed, in cases of need, to help pay for legal advice or proceedings. **legal fiction** an assertion accepted as true (though probably fictitious) to achieve a useful purpose, esp. in legal matters. **legal holiday** *US* a public holiday established by law. **legal proceedings** see PROCEEDING. **legal separation** see SEPARATION. **legal tender** currency that cannot legally be refused in payment of a debt (usu. up to a limited amount for coins not made of gold). □□ **legally** *adv.* [F *légal* or L *legalis* f. *lex legis* law: cf. LEAL, LOYAL]

■ **1** judicial, juridical, jurisprudent, jurisprudential, forensic. **2** constitutional, statutory, statutable. **3** lawful, legitimate, licit, acceptable, permissible, permitted, admissible, authorized, constitutional, *de jure*, right, proper, correct, valid, *colloq.* legit, kosher. □ **legal tender** see MONEY 1.

legalese /léegəléez/ *n. colloq.* the technical language of legal documents.

legalism /léegəliz'm/ *n.* **1** excessive adherence to law or formula. **2** *Theol.* adherence to the Law rather than to the Gospel, the doctrine of justification by works. □□ **legalist** *n.* **legalistic** /-lístik/ *adj.* **legalistically** /-lístikəli/ *adv.*

■ **1** strictness, rigidity, fastidiousness, niceness, literalness, literality, pedantry, pettiness, pettifoggery, narrow-mindedness, hair-splitting, cavilling, quibbling, *colloq.* nit-picking; litigiousness, disputatiousness, contentiousness. □□ **legalistic** literal, strict, rigid; fastidious, nice, pedantic, niggling, petty, pettifogging, narrow-minded, hair-splitting, cavilling, quibbling, *colloq.* nit-picking, *often offens.* Jesuitical; disputatious, contentious, litigious.

legality /ligálliti, leegál-/ *n.* (*pl.* **-ies**) **1** lawfulness. **2** legalism. **3** (in *pl.*) obligations imposed by law. [F *légalité* or med.L *legalitas* (as LEGAL)]

legalize /léegəlīz/ *v.tr.* (also **-ise**) **1** make lawful. **2** bring into harmony with the law. □□ **legalization** /-záysh'n/ *n.*

■ see LEGITIMATE *v.* 1. □□ **legalization** see SANCTION *n.* 2.

legate /léggət/ *n.* **1** a member of the clergy representing the Pope. **2** *Rom.Hist.* **a** a deputy of a general. **b** a governor or deputy governor of a province. **3** *archaic* an ambassador or delegate. □ **legate a latere** /aa láttəray/ a papal legate of the highest class, with full powers. □□ **legateship** *n.* **legatine** /-tin/ *adj.* [OE f. OF *legat* f. L *legatus* past part. of *legare* depute, delegate]

legatee /léggətée/ *n.* the recipient of a legacy. [as LEGATOR + -EE]

legation /ligáysh'n/ *n.* **1** a body of deputies. **2 a** the office and staff of a diplomatic minister (esp. when not having ambassadorial rank). **b** the official residence of a diplomatic minister. **3** a legateship. **4** the sending of a legate or deputy. [ME f. OF *legation* or L *legatio* (as LEGATE)]

■ **1** see MISSION 3.

legato /ligaátō/ *adv.*, *adj.*, & *n. Mus.* ● *adv.* & *adj.* in a smooth flowing manner, without breaks between notes (cf. STACCATO, TENUTO). ● *n.* (*pl.* **-os**) **1** a legato passage. **2** legato playing. [It., = bound, past part. of *legare* f. L *ligare* bind]

legator /ligáytər/ *n.* the giver of a legacy. [archaic *legate* bequeath f. L *legare* (as LEGACY)]

legend /léjənd/ *n.* **1 a** a traditional story sometimes popularly regarded as historical but unauthenticated; a myth. **b** such stories collectively. **c** a popular but unfounded belief. **d** *colloq.* a subject of such beliefs (*became a legend in his own lifetime*). **2 a** an inscription, esp. on a coin or medal. **b** *Printing* a caption. **c** wording on a map etc. explaining the symbols used. **3** *hist.* **a** the story of a saint's life. **b** a collection of lives of saints or similar stories. □□ **legendry** *n.* [ME (in sense 3) f. OF *legende* f. med.L *legenda* what is to be read, neut. pl. gerundive of L *legere* read]

■ **1 a–c** myth, folklore, fable, romance, tradition, fiction; story, (folk-)tale, epic, saga, Edda, Haggadah. **d** immortal, hero, great, genius, phenomenon, wonder, luminary, giant, god, goddess, deity, divinity, demigod, demiurge; star, celebrity, idol, superstar, name, classic. **2** inscription, motto, slogan, title, caption, wording; key, code, table.

legendary /léjəndəri/ *adj.* **1** of or connected with legends. **2** described in a legend. **3** *colloq.* remarkable enough to be a subject of legend. **4** based on a legend. ▫▫ **legendarily** *adv.* [med.L *legendarius* (as LEGEND)]
▪ **1, 2, 4** mythic, mythical, folkloric, folkloristic, traditional, romantic, epic, heroic, fabled, *literary* storied; fabulous, fictional, fictitious, story-book, fairy-tale, unreal, imaginary, fanciful. **3** phenomenal, remarkable, extraordinary, wonderful, marvellous, exceptional, notable, noteworthy, eminent, prominent, great, classic, immortal, superhuman; illustrious, famous, fabled, celebrated, noted, famed, well-known, renowned, acclaimed.

legerdemain /léjərdəmáyn/ *n.* **1** sleight of hand; conjuring or juggling. **2** trickery, sophistry. [ME f. F *léger de main* light of hand, dexterous]
▪ **1** see JUGGLE *n.* 1. **2** see TRICKERY.

leger line /léjər/ *n. Mus.* a short line added for notes above or below the range of a staff. [var. of LEDGER]

legging /légging/ *n.* (usu. in *pl.*) a stout protective outer covering for the leg from the knee to the ankle.

leggy /léggi/ *adj.* (**leggier, leggiest**) **1 a** long-legged. **b** (of a woman) having attractively long legs. **2** long-stemmed. ▫▫ **legginess** *n.*
▪ **1 a** see TALL *adj.* 1.

leghorn /léggorn, ligórn/ *n.* **1 a** fine plaited straw. **b** a hat of this. **2** (**Leghorn**) **a** a bird of a small hardy breed of domestic fowl. **b** this breed. [*Leghorn* (Livorno) in Italy, from where the straw and fowls were imported]

legible /léjib'l/ *adj.* (of handwriting, print, etc.) clear enough to read; readable. ▫▫ **legibility** /-bílliti/ *n.* **legibly** *adv.* [ME f. LL *legibilis* f. *legere* read]
▪ clear, plain, distinct, unambiguous; readable, decipherable, understandable, intelligible, decodable.

legion /leéjən/ *n.* & *adj.* ● *n.* **1** a division of 3,000–6,000 men, including a complement of cavalry, in the ancient Roman army. **2** a large organized body. **3** a vast host, multitude, or number. ● *predic.adj.* great in number (*his good works have been legion*). ▫ **American Legion** (in the US) an association of ex-servicemen formed in 1919. **foreign legion** a body of foreign volunteers in a modern, esp. French, army. **Legion of Honour** a French order of distinction founded in 1802. **Royal British Legion** (in the UK) an association of ex-servicemen (and now women) formed in 1921. [ME f. OF f. L *legio -onis* f. *legere* choose]
▪ **3** see HOST[1].

legionary /leéjənəri/ *adj.* & *n.* ● *adj.* of a legion or legions. ● *n.* (*pl.* **-ies**) a member of a legion. [L *legionarius* (as LEGION)]

legioned /leéjənd/ *adj. poet.* arrayed in legions.

legionella /leéjənéllə/ *n.* the bacterium *Legionella pneumophila*, which causes legionnaires' disease.

legionnaire /leéjənáir/ *n.* **1** a member of a foreign legion. **2** a member of the American Legion or the Royal British Legion. ▫ **legionnaires' disease** a form of bacterial pneumonia first identified after an outbreak at an American Legion meeting in 1976 (cf. LEGIONELLA). [F *légionnaire* (as LEGION)]

legislate /léjislayt/ *v.intr.* **1** make laws. **2** (foll. by *for*) make provision by law. [back-form. f. LEGISLATION]

legislation /léjisláysh'n/ *n.* **1** the process of making laws. **2** laws collectively. [LL *legis latio* f. *lex legis* law + *latio* proposing f. *lat-* past part. stem of *ferre* bring]
▪ **1** see PASSAGE[1] 7. **2** see MEASURE *n.* 9.

legislative /léjislətiv/ *adj.* of or empowered to make legislation. ▫▫ **legislatively** *adv.*

legislator /léjislaytər/ *n.* **1** a member of a legislative body. **2** a lawgiver. [L (as LEGISLATION)]
▪ **1** see POLITICIAN 1.

legislature /léjislaychər, -ləchər/ *n.* the legislative body of a State.
▪ see PARLIAMENT 2.

legit /lijít/ *adj.* & *n. colloq.* ● *adj.* legitimate. ● *n.* **1** legitimate drama. **2** an actor in legitimate drama. [abbr.]
▪ *adj.* see PERMISSIBLE.

legitimate *adj.* & *v.* ● *adj.* /lijíttimət/ **1 a** (of a child) born of parents lawfully married to each other. **b** (of a parent, birth, descent, etc.) with, of, through, etc., a legitimate child. **2** lawful, proper, regular, conforming to the standard type. **3** logically admissible. **4 a** (of a sovereign's title) based on strict hereditary right. **b** (of a sovereign) having a legitimate title. **5** constituting or relating to serious drama as distinct from musical comedy, revue, etc. ● *v.tr.* /lijíttimayt/ **1** make legitimate by decree, enactment, or proof. **2** justify, serve as a justification for. ▫▫ **legitimacy** /-məsi/ *n.* **legitimately** /-mətli/ *adv.* **legitimation** /-máysh'n/ *n.* [med.L *legitimare* f. L *legitimus* lawful f. *lex legis* law]
▪ *adj.* **1, 2** lawful, licit, legal, proper; constitutional, *de jure*, statutory, statutable, permissible, allowable, justifiable, authorized, rightful; regular, standard, correct, conventional, established, orthodox, official; authentic, genuine, bona fide, real. **3** logical, justifiable, reasonable, rational, valid, sound, right, correct, proper. ● *v.* **1** legitimize, legitimatize, legalize, authorize, sanction, permit, allow, license. **2** justify, warrant, vindicate, validate, rationalize, account for, explain; substantiate, defend, uphold, confirm, certify; *colloq.* launder.

legitimatize /lijíttimətīz/ *v.tr.* (also **-ise**) legitimize. ▫▫ **legitimatization** /-záysh'n/ *n.*
▪ see AUTHORIZE 1. ▫▫ **legitimatization** see SANCTION 2.

legitimism /lijíttimiz'm/ *n.* adherence to a sovereign or pretender whose claim is based on direct descent (esp. in French and Spanish history). ▫▫ **legitimist** *n.* & *adj.* [F *légitimisme* f. *légitime* LEGITIMATE]

legitimize /lijíttimīz/ *v.tr.* (also **-ise**) **1** make legitimate. **2** serve as a justification for. ▫▫ **legitimization** /-záysh'n/ *n.*
▪ **1** see AUTHORIZE 1. **2** see JUSTIFY 1, 2, 4. ▫▫ **legitimization** see SANCTION 2.

legless /légliss/ *adj.* **1** having no legs. **2** *sl.* drunk, esp. too drunk to stand.

legman /légman/ *n.* (*pl.* **-men**) a person employed to go about gathering news or running errands etc.
▪ see JOURNALIST.

Lego /léggō/ *n. propr.* a construction toy consisting of interlocking plastic building blocks. [Da. *leg godt* play well f. *lege* to play]

legume /légyoom/ *n.* **1** the seed pod of a leguminous plant. **2** any seed, pod, or other edible part of a leguminous plant used as food. [F *légume* f. L *legumen -minis* f. *legere* pick, because pickable by hand]

leguminous /ligyoominəss/ *adj.* of or like the family Leguminosae, including peas and beans, having seeds in pods and usu. root nodules able to fix nitrogen. [mod.L *leguminosus* (as LEGUME)]

legwork /légwurk/ *n.* work which involves a lot of walking, travelling, or physical activity.

lehr /leer/ *n.* (also **leer**) a furnace used for the annealing of glass. [17th c.: orig. unkn.]

lei[1] /láyee, lay/ *n.* a Polynesian garland of flowers. [Hawaiian]

lei[2] *pl.* of LEU.

Leibnizian /lībnítsiən/ *adj.* & *n.* ● *adj.* of or relating to the philosophy of G. W. Leibniz, German philosopher (d. 1716), esp. regarding matter as a multitude of monads and assuming a pre-established harmony between spirit and matter. ● *n.* a follower of this philosophy.

Leicester /léstər/ *n.* a kind of mild firm cheese, usu. orange-coloured and orig. made in Leicestershire.

Leics. *abbr.* Leicestershire.

leishmaniasis /leéshmənī́əsiss/ *n.* any of several diseases caused by parasitic protozoans of the genus *Leishmania* transmitted by the bite of sandflies. [W. B. *Leishman*, Brit. physician d. 1926]

leister /léestər/ *n.* & *v.* ● *n.* a pronged salmon-spear. ● *v.tr.* pierce with a leister. [ON *ljóstr* f. *ljósta* to strike]

leisure /lézhər/ *n.* **1** free time; time at one's own disposal. **2** enjoyment of free time. **3** (usu. foll. by *for*, or *to* + infin.) opportunity afforded by free time. □ **at leisure 1** not occupied. **2** in an unhurried manner. **at one's leisure** when one has time. □□ **leisureless** *adj.* [ME f. AF *leisour*, OF *leisir* ult. f. L *licēre* be allowed]

■ **1** spare *or* free time, time off; holiday, vacation, break, leave, furlough; respite, relief, rest, breathing-space. **2** recreation, fun, entertainment, amusement, enjoyment, diversion, R and R; ease, (peace and) quiet, relaxation, tranquillity, repose. **3** see OPPORTUNITY 1, 2. □ **at leisure 1** see IDLE *adj.* 2. **2** unhurriedly, calmly, steadily, deliberately; casually, easily, freely, in one's own time, at one's leisure, at one's convenience. **at one's leisure** see *at leisure* 2 above.

leisured /lézhərd/ *adj.* having ample leisure.

■ leisurely, comfortable, easy, undemanding, restful, carefree.

leisurely /lézhərli/ *adj.* & *adv.* ● *adj.* having leisure; acting or done at leisure; unhurried, relaxed. ● *adv.* without hurry. □□ **leisureliness** *n.*

■ *adj.* see UNHURRIED. ● *adv.* see SLOW *adv.* 1.

leisurewear /lézhərwair/ *n.* informal clothes, especially tracksuits and other sportswear.

leitmotif /lītmōteef/ *n.* (also **leitmotiv**) a recurrent theme associated throughout a musical, literary, etc. composition with a particular person, idea, or situation. [G *Leitmotiv* (as LEAD[1], MOTIVE)]

■ see MOTIF 1.

lek[1] /lek/ *n.* the chief monetary unit of Albania. [Albanian]

lek[2] /lek/ *n.* a patch of ground used by groups of certain birds during the breeding season as a setting for the males' display and their meeting with the females. [perh. f. Sw. *leka* to play]

LEM *abbr.* lunar excursion module.

leman /lémmən/ *n.* (*pl.* **lemans**) *archaic* **1** a lover or sweetheart. **2** an illicit lover, esp. a mistress. [ME *leofman* (as LIEF, MAN)]

■ see LOVE *n.* 4, 5.

lemma /lémmə/ *n.* **1** an assumed or demonstrated proposition used in an argument or proof. **2 a** a heading indicating the subject or argument of a literary composition, a dictionary entry, etc. **b** (*pl.* **lemmata** /-mətə/) a heading indicating the subject or argument of an annotation. **3** a motto appended to a picture etc. [L f. Gk *lēmma -matos* thing assumed, f. the root of *lambanō* take]

lemme /lémmi/ *colloq.* let me. [corrupt.]

lemming /lémming/ *n.* any small arctic rodent of the genus *Lemmus*, esp. *L. lemmus* of Norway which is reputed to rush headlong into the sea and drown during migration. [Norw.]

lemon /lémmən/ *n.* **1 a** a pale-yellow thick-skinned oval citrus fruit with acidic juice. **b** a tree of the species *Citrus limon* which produces this fruit. **2** a pale-yellow colour. **3** *colloq.* a person or thing regarded as feeble or unsatisfactory or disappointing. □ **lemon balm** a bushy plant, *Melissa officinalis*, with leaves smelling and tasting of lemon. **lemon curd** (or **cheese**) a conserve made from lemons, butter, eggs, and sugar, with the consistency of cream cheese. **lemon drop** a boiled sweet flavoured with lemon. **lemon geranium** a lemon-scented pelargonium, *Pelargonium crispum*. **lemon grass** any fragrant tropical grass of the genus *Cymbopogon*, yielding an oil smelling of lemon. **lemon squash** *Brit.* a soft drink made from lemons and other ingredients, often sold in concentrated form. **lemon-squeezer** a device for extracting the juice from a lemon. **lemon thyme** a herb, *Thymus citriodorus*, with lemon-scented leaves used for flavouring. **lemon verbena** (or **plant**) a shrub, *Lippia citriodora*, with lemon-scented leaves. [ME f. OF *limon* f. Arab. *līma*: cf. LIME[2]]

■ **3** see FAILURE 2.

lemonade /lémmənáyd/ *n.* **1** an effervescent or still drink made from lemon juice. **2** a synthetic substitute for this.

■ see POP[1] *n.* 2.

lemon sole *n.* a flat-fish, *Microstomus kitt*, of the plaice family. [F *limande*]

lemony /lémməni/ *adj.* **1** tasting or smelling of lemons. **2** *Austral.* & *NZ sl.* irritable.

■ **1** see SOUR *adj.* 1. **2** see IRRITABLE 1.

lemur /léemər/ *n.* any arboreal primate of the family Lemuridae native to Madagascar, with a pointed snout and long tail. [mod.L f. L *lemures* (pl.) spirits of the dead, from its spectre-like face]

lend /lend/ *v.tr.* (*past* and *past part.* **lent** /lent/) **1** (usu. foll. by *to*) grant (to a person) the use of (a thing) on the understanding that it or its equivalent shall be returned. **2** allow the use of (money) at interest. **3** bestow or contribute (something temporary) (*lend assistance*; *lends a certain charm*). □ **lend an ear** (or **one's ears**) listen. **lend a hand** = *give a hand* (see HAND). **lending library** a library from which books may be temporarily taken away with or *Brit.* without direct payment. **lend itself to** (of a thing) be suitable for. **Lend-Lease** *hist.* an arrangement made in 1941 whereby the US supplied equipment etc. to the UK and its allies, orig. as a loan in return for the use of British-owned military bases. **lend oneself to** accommodate oneself to (a policy or purpose). □□ **lendable** *adj.* **lender** *n.* **lending** *n.* [ME, earlier *lēne(n)* f. OE *lǣnan* f. *lǣn* LOAN[1]]

■ **1, 2** loan, advance, put out, *Brit. colloq.* sub; rent (out), lease (out), let (out), charter (out). **3** bestow, contribute, impart, furnish, provide, give, confer, add. □ **lend an ear** see LISTEN 1, 2. **lend itself to** be suitable *or* appropriate to *or* for, be applicable *or* adaptable to.

length /length, *disp.* lengkth/ *n.* **1** measurement or extent from end to end; the greater of two or the greatest of three dimensions of a body. **2** extent in, of, or with regard to, time (*a stay of some length*; *the length of a speech*). **3** the distance a thing extends (*at arm's length*; *ships a cable's length apart*). **4** the length of a horse, boat, etc., as a measure of the lead in a race. **5** a long stretch or extent (*a length of hair*). **6** a degree of thoroughness in action (*went to great lengths*; *prepared to go to any length*). **7** a piece of material of a certain length (*a length of cloth*). **8** *Prosody* the quantity of a vowel or syllable. **9** *Cricket* **a** the distance from the batsman at which the ball pitches (*the bowler keeps a good length*). **b** the proper amount of this. **10** the extent of a garment in a vertical direction when worn. **11** the full extent of one's body. □ **at length 1** (also **at full** or **great** etc. **length**) in detail, without curtailment. **2** after a long time, at last. [OE *lengthu* f. Gmc (as LONG[1])]

■ **1, 3, 5** span, reach, extent, distance, stretch; measure, size, magnitude, dimension. **2** time, duration, stretch, term, period, while, span, interval. **6** trouble, inconvenience, bother, nuisance; (*lengths*) pains. □ **at length 1** in detail, in depth, comprehensively, thoroughly, completely, exhaustively, extensively, at large. **2** at last, finally, in the end, ultimately, eventually.

lengthen /léngthən, léngkthən/ *v.* **1** *tr.* & *intr.* make or become longer. **2** *tr.* make (a vowel) long. □□ **lengthener** *n.*

■ **1** extend, elongate, stretch, expand, pad out; drag out, draw out, prolong, protract, continue; grow, enlarge, amplify; let down.

lengthman /léngthmən/ *n.* (*pl.* **-men**) *Brit.* a person employed to maintain a section of railway or road.

lengthways /léngthwayz, léngkth-/ *adv.* in a direction parallel with a thing's length.

lengthwise /léngthwīz, léngkth-/ *adv.* & *adj.* ● *adv.* lengthways. ● *adj.* lying or moving lengthways.

lengthy /léngthi, léngkthi/ *adj.* (**lengthier**, **lengthiest**) **1** of unusual length. **2** (of speech, writing, style, a speaker, etc.) tedious, prolix. □□ **lengthily** *adv.* **lengthiness** *n.*

■ **1** long, extensive, extended, elongated, *Bot.* & *Zool.* elongate. **2** tedious, boring, dull, uninteresting, wearying, wearisome, tiresome, laborious, endless, unending, interminable; prolix, over-long, protracted, long-drawn(-out), long-winded, wordy, verbose, rambling, pleonastic.

lenient /leéniənt/ *adj.* **1** merciful, tolerant, not disposed to severity. **2** (of punishment etc.) mild. **3** *archaic* emollient. □□ **lenience** *n.* **leniency** *n.* **leniently** *adv.* [L *lenire lenit-* soothe f. *lenis* gentle]
■ **1, 2** merciful, compassionate, forgiving, clement, forbearing, indulgent, charitable, humane, tolerant, magnanimous, generous, patient, understanding, tender-hearted, kind-hearted; liberal, latitudinarian, permissive, easygoing, easy, moderate; soft, mild, gentle, kind, tender.

Leninism /lénniniz'm/ *n.* Marxism as interpreted and applied by Lenin. □□ **Leninist** *n.* & *adj.* **Leninite** *n.* & *adj.* [V. I. *Lenin* (name assumed by V. I. Ulyanov), Russian statesman d. 1924]

lenition /leenísh'n/ *n.* (in Celtic languages) the process or result of articulating a consonant softly. [L *lenis* soft, after G *Lenierung*]

lenitive /lénnitiv/ *adj.* & *n.* ● *adj. Med.* soothing. ● *n.* **1** *Med.* a soothing drug or appliance. **2** a palliative. [ME f. med.L *lenitivus* (as LENIENT)]
■ *adj.* see *soothing* (SOOTHE). ● *n.* see TRANQUILLIZER.

lenity /lénniti/ *n.* (*pl.* **-ies**) *literary* **1** mercifulness, gentleness. **2** an act of mercy. [F *lénité* or L *lenitas* f. *lenis* gentle]
■ **1** see HUMANITY 2.

leno /leénō/ *n.* (*pl.* **-os**) an open-work fabric with the warp threads twisted in pairs before weaving. [F *linon* f. *lin* flax f. L *linum*]

lens /lenz/ *n.* **1** a piece of a transparent substance with one or (usu.) both sides curved for concentrating or dispersing light-rays esp. in optical instruments. **2** a combination of lenses used in photography. **3** *Anat.* = *crystalline lens.* **4** *Physics* a device for focusing or otherwise modifying the direction of movement of light, sound, electrons, etc. □□ **lensed** *adj.* **lensless** *adj.* [L *lens lentis* lentil (from the similarity of shape)]
■ **1** see GLASS *n.* 2i.

Lent /lent/ *n.* **1** *Eccl.* the period from Ash Wednesday to Holy Saturday, of which the 40 weekdays are devoted to fasting and penitence in commemoration of Christ's fasting in the wilderness. **2** (in *pl.*) the boat races held at Cambridge in the Lent term. □ **Lent lily** *Brit.* a daffodil, esp. a wild one. **Lent term** *Brit.* the term at a university etc. in which Lent falls. [ME f. LENTEN]

lent *past* and *past part.* of LEND.

-lent /lənt/ *suffix* forming adjectives (*pestilent*; *violent*) (cf. -ULENT). [L *-lentus* -ful]

Lenten /léntən/ *adj.* of, in, or appropriate to, Lent. □ **Lenten fare** food without meat. [orig. as noun, = spring, f. OE *lencten* f. Gmc, rel. to LONG[1], perh. with ref. to lengthening of the day in spring: now regarded as adj. f. LENT + -EN[2]]

lenticel /léntisel/ *n. Bot.* any of the raised pores in the stems of woody plants that allow gas exchange between the atmosphere and the internal tissues. [mod.L *lenticella* dimin. of L *lens*: see LENS]

lenticular /lentíkyoolər/ *adj.* **1** shaped like a lentil or a biconvex lens. **2** of the lens of the eye. [L *lenticularis* (as LENTIL)]

lentil /léntil/ *n.* **1** a leguminous plant, *Lens culinaris*, yielding edible biconvex seeds. **2** this seed, esp. used as food with the husk removed. [ME f. OF *lentille* f. L *lenticula* (as LENS)]

lento /léntō/ *adj.* & *adv. Mus.* ● *adj.* slow. ● *adv.* slowly. [It.]

lentoid /léntoyd/ *adj.* = LENTICULAR 1. [L *lens* (see LENS) + -OID]

Leo /leé-ō/ *n.* (*pl.* **-os**) **1** a constellation, traditionally regarded as contained in the figure of a lion. **2 a** the fifth sign of the zodiac (the Lion). **b** a person born when the sun is in this sign. [OE f. L, = LION]

Leonid /leéənid/ *n.* any of the meteors that seem to radiate from the direction of the constellation Leo. [L *leo* (see LEO) *leonis* + -ID[3]]

Leonine /leéənīn/ *adj.* & *n.* ● *adj.* of Pope Leo; made or invented by Pope Leo. ● *n.* (in *pl.*) leonine verse. □ **Leonine City** the part of Rome round the Vatican fortified by Pope Leo IV. **leonine verse 1** medieval Latin verse in hexameter or elegiac metre with internal rhyme. **2** English verse with internal rhyme. [the name *Leo* (as LEONINE)]

leonine /leéənīn/ *adj.* **1** like a lion. **2** of or relating to lions. [ME f. OF *leonin -ine* or L *leoninus* f. *leo leonis* lion]

leopard /léppərd/ *n.* (*fem.* **leopardess** /-diss/) **1** a large African or Asian feline, *Panthera pardus*, with either a black-spotted yellowish-fawn or all black coat. Also called PANTHER. **2** *Heraldry* a lion passant guardant as in the arms of England. **3** (*attrib.*) spotted like a leopard (*leopard moth*). □ **leopard's bane** any plant of the genus *Doronicum*, with large yellow daisy-like flowers. [ME f. OF f. LL f. late Gk *leopardos* (as LION, PARD)]

leotard /leéətaard/ *n.* a close-fitting one-piece garment worn by ballet-dancers, acrobats, etc. [J. *Léotard*, French trapeze artist d. 1870]

leper /léppər/ *n.* **1** a person suffering from leprosy. **2** a person shunned on moral grounds. [ME, prob. attrib. use of *leper* leprosy f. OF *lepre* f. L *lepra* f. Gk, fem. of *lepros* scaly f. *lepos* scale]
■ **2** see UNDESIRABLE *n.*

lepidopterous /léppidóptərəss/ *adj.* of the order Lepidoptera of insects, with four scale-covered wings often brightly coloured, including butterflies and moths. □□ **lepidopteran** *adj.* & *n.* **lepidopterist** *n.* [Gk *lepis -idos* scale + *pteron* wing]

leporine /léppərīn/ *adj.* of or like hares. [L *leporinus* f. *lepus -oris* hare]

leprechaun /léprəkawn/ *n.* a small mischievous sprite in Irish folklore. [OIr. *luchorpán* f. *lu* small + *corp* body]
■ see IMP *n.* 2.

leprosy /léprəsi/ *n.* **1** a contagious bacterial disease that affects the skin, mucous membranes, and nerves, causing disfigurement. Also called HANSEN'S DISEASE. **2** moral corruption or contagion. [LEPROUS + -Y[3]]

leprous /léprəss/ *adj.* **1** suffering from leprosy. **2** like or relating to leprosy. [ME f. OF f. LL *leprosus* f. *lepra*: see LEPER]

lepta *pl.* of LEPTON[1].

lepto- /léptō/ *comb. form* small, narrow. [Gk *leptos* fine, small, thin, delicate]

leptocephalic /léptəsifállik/ *adj.* (also **leptocephalous** /-séffələss/) narrow-skulled.

leptodactyl /léptōdáktil/ *adj.* & *n.* ● *adj.* having long slender toes. ● *n.* a bird having these.

lepton[1] /léptən/ *n.* (*pl.* **lepta** /-tə/) a Greek coin worth one-hundredth of a drachma. [Gk *lepton* (*nomisma* coin) neut. of *leptos* small]

lepton[2] /lépton/ *n.* (*pl.* **leptons**) *Physics* any of a class of elementary particles which do not undergo strong interaction, e.g. an electron, muon, or neutrino. [LEPTO- + -ON]

leptospirosis /léptəspirṓsiss/ *n.* an infectious disease caused by bacteria of the genus *Leptospira*, that occurs in rodents, dogs, and other mammals, and can be transmitted to man. [LEPTO- + SPIRO-[1] + -OSIS]

leptotene /léptəteen/ *n. Biol.* the first stage of the prophase of meiosis in which each chromosome is apparent as two fine chromatids. [LEPTO- + Gk *tainia* band]

lesbian /lézbiən/ *n.* & *adj.* ● *n.* a homosexual woman. ● *adj.* **1** of homosexuality in women. **2** (**Lesbian**) of Lesbos. □□ **lesbianism** *n.* [L *Lesbius* f. Gk *Lesbios* f. *Lesbos*, island in the Aegean Sea, home of Sappho (see SAPPHIC)]

lese-majesty /leez májisti/ *n.* (also **lèse-majesté** /layz mázhestay/) **1** treason. **2** an insult to a sovereign or ruler. **3** presumptuous conduct. [F *lèse-majesté* f. L *laesa majestas* injured sovereignty f. *laedere laes-* injure + *majestas* MAJESTY]

lesion /leézh'n/ *n.* **1** damage. **2** injury. **3** *Med.* a morbid change in the functioning or texture of an organ etc. [ME f. OF f. L *laesio -onis* f. *laedere laes-* injure]

▪ **2** see WOUND[1] *n.* 1.

less /less/ *adj.*, *adv.*, *n.*, & *prep.* ● *adj.* **1** smaller in extent, degree, duration, number, etc. (*of less importance*; *in a less degree*). **2** of smaller quantity, not so much (opp. MORE) (*find less difficulty*; *eat less meat*). **3** *disp.* fewer (*eat less biscuits*). **4** of lower rank etc. (*no less a person than*; *James the Less*). ● *adv.* to a smaller extent, in a lower degree. ● *n.* a smaller amount or quantity or number (*cannot take less*; *for less than £10*; *is little less than disgraceful*). ● *prep.* minus (*made £1,000 less tax*). □ **in less than no time** *joc.* very quickly or soon. **much** (or **still**) **less** with even greater force of denial (*do not suspect him of negligence, much less of dishonesty*). [OE *lǣssa* (adj.), *lǣs* (adv.), f. Gmc]

-less /liss/ *suffix* forming adjectives and adverbs: **1** from nouns, meaning 'not having, without, free from' (*doubtless*; *powerless*). **2** from verbs, meaning 'not affected by or doing the action of the verb' (*fathomless*; *tireless*). □□ **-lessly** *suffix* forming adverbs. **-lessness** *suffix* forming nouns. [OE *-lēas* f. *lēas* devoid of]

lessee /lesseé/ *n.* (often foll. by *of*) a person who holds a property by lease. □□ **lesseeship** *n.* [ME f. AF past part., OF *lessé* (as LEASE)]

▪ see TENANT *n.* 1.

lessen /léss'n/ *v.tr.* & *intr.* make or become less, diminish.

▪ see DIMINISH 1.

lesser /léssər/ *adj.* (usu. *attrib.*) not so great as the other or the rest (*the lesser evil*; *the lesser celandine*). [double compar., f. LESS + -ER[3]]

▪ see INFERIOR *adj.* 1.

lesson /léss'n/ *n.* & *v.* ● *n.* **1 a** an amount of teaching given at one time. **b** the time assigned to this. **2** (in *pl.*; foll. by *in*) systematic instruction (*gives lessons in dancing*; *took lessons in French*). **3** a thing learnt or to be learnt by a pupil; an assignment. **4 a** an occurrence, example, rebuke, or punishment, that serves or should serve to warn or encourage (*let that be a lesson to you*). **b** a thing inculcated by experience or study. **5** a passage from the Bible read aloud during a church service, esp. either of two readings at morning and evening prayer in the Church of England. ● *v.tr. archaic* **1** instruct. **2** admonish, rebuke. □ **learn one's lesson** profit from or bear in mind a particular (usu. unpleasant) experience. **teach a person a lesson** punish a person, esp. as a deterrent. [ME f. OF *leçon* f. L *lectio -onis*: see LECTION]

▪ **1 a** class, session, period. **2** (*lessons*) instruction, teaching, tutoring, schooling, classes, coaching, tutelage, tuition; course (of study); practice, drilling. **3** exercise, drill, reading, lecture, recitation; assignment, homework, task. **4** example, exemplar, model, guide, maxim, paragon; deterrent, discouragement; warning, admonition; message, moral, homily, precept; punishment, chastisement, chastening, castigation, scolding, chiding, rebuke, reprimand, reproof, *colloq.* talking-to. **5** reading, scripture passage, text, Epistle, lection, pericope.

lessor /lesór/ *n.* a person who lets a property by lease. [AF f. *lesser*: see LEASE]

▪ see LANDLORD 1.

lest /lest/ *conj.* **1** in order that not, for fear that (*lest we forget*). **2** that (*afraid lest we should be late*). [OE *thȳ lǣs the* whereby less that, later *the lǣste*, ME *lest(e)*]

▪ see *in case* 2 (CASE[1]).

let[1] /let/ *v.* & *n.* ● *v.* (**letting**; *past* and *past part.* **let**) **1** *tr.* **a** allow to, not prevent or forbid (*we let them go*). **b** cause to (*let me know*; *let it be known*). **2** *tr.* (foll. by *into*) **a** allow to enter. **b** make acquainted with (a secret etc.). **c** inlay in. **3** *tr. Brit.* grant the use of (rooms, land, etc.) for rent or hire (*was let to the new tenant for a year*). **4** *tr.* allow or cause (liquid or air) to escape (*let blood*). **5** *tr.* award (a contract for work). **6** *aux.* supplying the first and third persons of the imperative in exhortations (*let us pray*), commands (*let it be done at once*; *let there be light*), assumptions (*let AB be equal to CD*), and permission or challenge (*let him do his worst*). ● *n. Brit.* the act or an instance of letting a house, room, etc. (*a long let*). □ **let alone 1** not to mention, far less or more (*hasn't got a television, let alone a video*). **2** = *let be*. **let be** not interfere with, attend to, or do. **let down 1** lower. **2** fail to support or satisfy, disappoint. **3** lengthen (a garment). **4** deflate (a tyre). **let-down** *n.* a disappointment. **let down gently** avoid humiliating abruptly. **let drop** (or **fall**) **1** drop (esp. a word or hint) intentionally or by accident. **2** (foll. by *on*, *upon*, *to*) *Geom.* draw (a perpendicular) from an outside point to a line. **let fly 1** (often foll. by *at*) attack physically or verbally. **2** discharge (a missile). **let go 1** release, set at liberty. **2 a** (often foll. by *of*) lose or relinquish one's hold. **b** lose hold of. **3** cease to think or talk about. **let oneself go 1** give way to enthusiasm, impulse, etc. **2** cease to take trouble, neglect one's appearance or habits. **let in 1** allow to enter (*let the dog in*; *let in a flood of light*; *this would let in all sorts of evils*). **2** (usu. foll. by *for*) involve (a person, often oneself) in loss or difficulty. **3** (foll. by *on*) allow (a person) to share privileges, information, etc. **4** inlay (a thing) in another. **let oneself in** enter a building by means of a latchkey. **let loose** release or unchain (a dog, fury, a maniac, etc.). **let me see** see SEE[1]. **let off 1 a** fire (a gun). **b** explode (a bomb or firework). **2** allow or cause (steam, liquid, etc.) to escape. **3** allow to alight from a vehicle etc. **4 a** not punish or compel. **b** (foll. by *with*) punish lightly. **5** *Brit.* let (part of a house etc.). **6** *Brit. colloq.* break wind. **let-off** *n.* being allowed to escape something. **let off steam** see STEAM. **let on** *colloq.* **1** reveal a secret. **2** pretend (*let on that he had succeeded*). **let out 1** allow to go out, esp. through a doorway. **2** release from restraint. **3** (often foll. by *that* + clause) reveal (a secret etc.). **4** make (a garment) looser esp. by adjustment at a seam. **5** put out to rent esp. to several tenants, or to contract. **6** exculpate. **7** give vent or expression to; emit (a sound etc.) **let-out** *n. colloq.* an opportunity to escape. **let rip** see RIP[1]. **let slip** see SLIP[1]. **let through** allow to pass. **let up** *colloq.* **1** become less intense or severe. **2** relax one's efforts. **let-up** *n. colloq.* **1** a reduction in intensity. **2** a relaxation of effort. **to let** available for rent. [OE *lǣtan* f. Gmc, rel. to LATE]

▪ *v.* **1 a** allow (to), permit (to), sanction (to), give permission *or* leave (to), authorize (to), license (to), *archaic* suffer (to). **b** arrange for, enable *or* cause (to). **2** (*let into*) **a** admit to, allow into, take into, receive into. **b** acquaint with, make acquainted with, inform *or* notify *or* apprise *or* advise of, brief about, put a person in the picture about, update about, bring up to date about, *colloq.* fill in on. **3** rent (out), hire (out), lease (out), charter (out), sublet (out). **5** contract (out), subcontract (out), farm (out), delegate. □ **let down 1** lower, move *or* bring *or* put down, drop. **2** fail, frustrate; disappoint, disenchant, dissatisfy, disillusion. **let-down** see DISAPPOINTMENT 1. **let fly 1** see *lash out* 1. **2** see *let off* 1 below. **let go 1** see *let out* 1, 2 below. **2** (*let go of*) leave (hold of), release, drop, give up, unloose, loose, loosen, relax one's grip on; abandon, relinquish, surrender, lose. **3** drop, give up, abandon, ignore, disregard, pay no heed *or* attention to. **let loose** see RELEASE *v.* 1. **let off 1** discharge, fire, let fly; detonate, explode, set off. **2** release, discharge; give vent to. **4 a** pardon, forgive, excuse, release, discharge, exempt (from), excuse *or* relieve from, spare (from), let go, exonerate, absolve, clear, acquit, vindicate, *colloq.* let off the hook, *formal* exculpate. **let on 1** talk, tell, blab, give the game *or* show away, let the cat out of the bag, *colloq.* spill the beans, blow the whistle, *sl.* squeal, *Brit. sl.* blow the gaff. **2** (*let on that*) pretend that, make as if, (put on an) act as if. **let out 1, 2** (let) loose, unloose, liberate, set at liberty, (set) free, release, let go, discharge, emancipate, *hist.* manumit. **3** reveal, divulge, disclose, confess, admit, give away, tell, leak; release, advertise, announce, publicize. **5** rent (out), hire (out), lease (out), charter (out), sublet (out). **7** give vent *or* expression to, express; give out, emit, produce. **let up 1** decrease, abate, ease (up), slacken (off), diminish, lessen, subside, moderate; soften, ebb, fade, weaken, peter out, run out of steam, die away *or* down. **2** take a break, have a rest, slow down, *esp. US* take time out, *colloq.* take *or* have a breather. **let-up** abatement, slackening, weakening, lessening; stop, cessation, break, intermission, suspension, *esp. US* time out, remission, moderation, lull, respite, pause, breathing-space, time off, *colloq.* breather, *literary* surcease.

let[2] /let/ *n.* & *v.* ● *n.* **1** (in lawn tennis, squash, etc.) an obstruction of a ball or a player in certain ways, requiring the ball to be served again. **2** (*archaic* except in **without let or hindrance**) obstruction, hindrance. ● *v.tr.* (**letting**; *past* and *past part.* **letted** or **let**) *archaic* hinder, obstruct. [OE *lettan* f. Gmc, rel. to LATE]

■ **2** impediment, obstacle, encumbrance, hurdle, block, stumbling-block.

-let /lit, lət/ *suffix* forming nouns, usu. diminutives (*flatlet; leaflet*) or denoting articles of ornament or dress (*anklet*). [orig. corresp. (in *bracelet, crosslet,* etc.) to F *-ette* added to nouns in *-el*]

lethal /leéthəl/ *adj.* causing or sufficient to cause death. □ **lethal chamber** a chamber in which animals may be killed painlessly with gas. **lethal dose** the amount of a toxic compound or drug that causes death in humans or animals. □□ **lethality** /lithálliti/ *n.* **lethally** *adv.* [L *let(h)alis* f. *letum* death]

■ deadly, fatal, mortal, terminal, deathly, murderous, life-threatening.

lethargy /léthərji/ *n.* **1** lack of energy or vitality; a torpid, inert, or apathetic state. **2** *Med.* morbid drowsiness or prolonged and unnatural sleep. □□ **lethargic** /lithaárjik/ *adj.* **lethargically** /lithaárjikəli/ *adv.* [ME f. OF *litargie* f. LL *lethargia* f. Gk *lēthargia* f. *lēthargos* forgetful f. *lēth-, lanthanomai* forget]

■ **1** sluggishness, sloth, dullness, heaviness, laziness, indolence, phlegm, idleness, languidness, languor, lassitude, listlessness, *dolce far niente*, inactivity, inertia, torpor, stupor, *literary* hebetude; unconcern, indifference, apathy. **2** weariness, tiredness, fatigue, weakness, exhaustion, drowsiness, sleepiness, somnolence, lassitude, debility. □□ **lethargic** sluggish, slow, dull, heavy, lazy, indolent, phlegmatic, slothful, idle, languid, languorous, listless, fainéant, inactive, torpid, stuporous, comatose; indifferent, apathetic, weary, tired, fatigued, enervated, weak, exhausted, drowsy, sleepy, somnolent, *colloq.* fagged (out), *Brit. sl.* knackered.

Lethe /leéthee/ *n.* **1** (in Greek mythology) a river in Hades producing forgetfulness of the past. **2** such forgetfulness. □□ **Lethean** /leetheéən/ *adj.* [L, use of Gk *lēthē* forgetfulness (as LETHARGY)]

■ □□ **Lethean** see OBLIVIOUS.

let's /lets/ *contr.* let us (*let's go now*).

Lett /let/ *n. archaic* = LATVIAN *n.* 1. [G *Lette* f. Latvian *Latvi*]

letter /léttər/ *n.* & *v.* ● *n.* **1 a** a character representing one or more of the simple or compound sounds used in speech, any of the alphabetic symbols. **b** (in *pl.*) *colloq.* the initials of a degree etc. after the holder's name. **c** *US* a school or college initial as a mark of proficiency in games etc. **2 a** a written, typed, or printed communication, usu. sent by post or messenger. **b** (in *pl.*) an addressed legal or formal document for any of various purposes. **3** the precise terms of a statement, the strict verbal interpretation (opp. SPIRIT *n.* 6) (*according to the letter of the law*). **4** (in *pl.*) **a** literature. **b** acquaintance with books, erudition. **c** authorship (*the profession of letters*). **5** *Printing* **a** types collectively. **b** a fount of type. ● *v.tr.* **1 a** inscribe letters on. **b** impress a title etc. on (a book-cover). **2** classify with letters. □ **letter-bomb** a terrorist explosive device in the form of a postal packet. **letter-box** esp. *Brit.* a box or slot into which letters are posted or delivered. **letter-card** a folded card with a gummed edge for posting as a letter. **letter-heading** = LETTERHEAD. **letter of comfort** an assurance about a debt, short of a legal guarantee, given to a bank by a third party. **letter of credence** see CREDENCE. **letter of credit** see CREDIT. **letter-perfect** *Theatr.* knowing one's part perfectly. **letter-quality** of the quality of printing suitable for a business letter; producing print of this quality. **letters missive** see MISSIVE. **letters of administration** authority to administer the estate of an intestate. **letters of marque** see MARQUE[2]. **letters patent** see PATENT. **letter-writer 1** a person who writes letters. **2** a book giving guidance on writing letters. **man of letters** a scholar or author. **to the letter** with adherence to every detail. □□ **letterer** *n.* **letterless** *adj.* [ME f. OF *lettre* f. L *litera, littera* letter of alphabet, (in pl.) epistle, literature]

■ *n.* **1 a** character, symbol, sign, grapheme. **b** (*letters*) initials. **2 a** communication, note, line, message, dispatch, *formal or joc.* epistle, *joc.* missive; postcard, card, memorandum; (*letters*) correspondence, mail, post. **4** (*letters*) literature, (creative) writing, fiction; the humanities, belles-lettres, the classics; culture, the world of letters, learning, scholarship. **5** fount(s), face(s), type; typeface. ● *v.* **1 a** inscribe, mark, initial. □ **letter-box** postbox, pillar-box, *US* mailbox, drop. **to the letter** precisely, literally, exactly, accurately, strictly, unerringly, scrupulously, faithfully, *sic*, letter for letter, *literatim*, word for word, verbatim, closely, *formal* thus.

lettered /léttərd/ *adj.* well-read or educated.

■ literate, literary, (well-)educated, well-read, erudite, scholarly, learned, well-informed, academic, (well-)schooled, enlightened, knowledgeable, (well-)versed, accomplished, refined, cultured, cultivated.

letterhead /léttərhed/ *n.* **1** a printed heading on stationery. **2** stationery with this.

lettering /léttəring/ *n.* **1** the process of inscribing letters. **2** letters inscribed.

letterpress /léttərpress/ *n.* **1 a** the contents of an illustrated book other than the illustrations. **b** printed matter relating to illustrations. **2** printing from raised type, not from lithography or other planographic processes.

Lettic /léttik/ *adj.* & *n. archaic* ● *adj.* **1** = LATVIAN *adj.* **2** of or relating to the Baltic branch of languages. ● *n.* = LATVIAN *n.* 2.

Lettish /léttish/ *adj.* & *n. archaic* = LATVIAN *adj., n.* 2.

lettuce /léttiss/ *n.* **1** a composite plant, *Lactuca sativa*, with crisp edible leaves used in salads. **2** any of various plants resembling this. [ME *letus(e)*, rel. to OF *laituë* f. L *lactuca* f. *lac lactis* milk, with ref. to its milky juice]

leu /láyoo/ *n.* (*pl.* **lei** /lay/) the basic monetary unit of Romania. [Romanian, = lion]

leucine /lóosseen/ *n. Biochem.* an amino acid present in protein and essential in the diet of vertebrates. [F f. Gk *leukos* white + -IN]

leuco- /lookō/ *comb. form* white. [Gk *leukos* white]

leucocyte /lookəsīt/ *n.* (also **leukocyte**) **1** a white blood cell. **2** any blood cell that contains a nucleus. □□ **leucocytic** /-sittik/ *adj.*

leucoma /lookómə/ *n.* a white opacity in the cornea of the eye.

leucorrhoea /lookəreéə/ *n.* a whitish or yellowish discharge of mucus from the vagina.

leucotomy /lookóttəmi/ *n.* (*pl.* **-ies**) the surgical lesions of white nerve fibres within the brain, formerly used in psychosurgery.

leukaemia /lookeémiə/ *n.* (*US* **leukemia**) *Med.* any of a group of malignant diseases in which the bone-marrow and other blood-forming organs produce increased numbers of leucocytes. □□ **leukaemic** *adj.* [mod.L f. G *Leukämie* f. Gk *leukos* white + *haima* blood]

leukocyte var. of LEUCOCYTE.

Lev. *abbr.* Leviticus (Old Testament).

Levant /livánt/ *n.* (prec. by *the*) the eastern part of the Mediterranean with its islands and neighbouring countries.

□ **Levant morocco** high-grade large-grained morocco leather. [F, pres. part. of *lever* rise, used as noun = point of sunrise, east]

levant /livánt/ *v.intr. Brit.* abscond or bolt, esp. with betting or gaming losses unpaid. [perh. f. LEVANT]

■ see FLEE 1.

levanter[1] /livántər/ *n.* **1** a strong easterly Mediterranean wind. **2** (**Levanter**) a native or inhabitant of the Levant in the eastern Mediterranean.

levanter[2] /livántər/ *n.* a person who levants.

Levantine /livántīn, lévvən-/ *adj.* & *n.* ● *adj.* of or trading to the Levant. ● *n.* a native or inhabitant of the Levant.

levator /liváytər/ *n.* a muscle that lifts the structure into which it is inserted. [L, = one who lifts f. *levare* raise]

levee[1] /lévvi/ *n.* **1** *archaic* or *US* an assembly of visitors or guests, esp. at a formal reception. **2** *hist.* (in the UK) an assembly held by the sovereign or sovereign's representative at which men only were received. **3** *hist.* a reception of visitors on rising from bed. [F *levé* var. of *lever* rising f. *lever* to rise: see LEVY]

■ **1, 2** see PARTY[1] *n.* 1.

levee[2] /lévvi, livée/ *n. US* **1** an embankment against river floods. **2** a natural embankment built up by a river. **3** a landing-place, a quay. [F *levée* fem. past part. of *lever* raise: see LEVY]

level /lévv'l/ *n.*, *adj.*, & *v.* ● *n.* **1** a horizontal line or plane. **2** a height or value reached, a position on a real or imaginary scale (*eye level*; *sugar level in the blood*; *danger level*). **3** a social, moral, or intellectual standard. **4** a plane of rank or authority (*discussions at Cabinet level*). **5 a** an instrument giving a line parallel to the plane of the horizon for testing whether things are horizontal. **b** *Surveying* an instrument for giving a horizontal line of sight. **6** a more or less level surface. **7** a flat tract of land. **8** a floor or storey in a building, ship, etc. ● *adj.* **1** having a flat and even surface; not bumpy. **2** horizontal; perpendicular to the plumb-line. **3** (often foll. by *with*) **a** on the same horizontal plane as something else. **b** having equality with something else. **c** (of a spoonful etc.) with the contents flat with the brim. **4** even, uniform, equable, or well-balanced in quality, style, temper, judgement, etc. **5** (of a race) having the leading competitors close together. ● *v.* (**levelled, levelling**; *US* **leveled, leveling**) **1** *tr.* make level, even, or uniform. **2** *tr.* (often foll. by *to* (or *with*) *the ground, in the dust*) raze or demolish. **3** *tr.* (also *absol.*) aim (a missile or gun). **4** *tr.* (also *absol.*; foll. by *at, against*) direct (an accusation, criticism, or satire). **5** *tr.* abolish (distinctions). **6** *intr.* (usu. foll. by *with*) *sl.* be frank or honest. **7** *tr.* place on the same level. **8** *tr.* (also *absol.*) *Surveying* ascertain differences in the height of (land). □ **do one's level best** *colloq.* do one's utmost; make all possible efforts. **find one's level 1** reach the right social, intellectual, etc. place in relation to others. **2** (of a liquid) reach the same height in receptacles or regions which communicate with each other. **level crossing** *Brit.* a crossing of a railway and a road, or two railways, at the same level. **level down** bring down to a standard. **levelling-screw** a screw for adjusting parts of a machine etc. to an exact level. **level off** make or become level or smooth. **level out** make or become level, remove differences from. **level pegging** *Brit.* equality of scores or achievements. **level up** bring up to a standard. **on the level** *colloq.* *adv.* honestly, without deception. ● *adj.* honest, truthful. **on a level with 1** in the same horizontal plane as. **2** equal with. □□ **levelly** *adv.* **levelness** *n.* [ME f. OF *livel* ult. f. L *libella* dimin. of *libra* scales, balance]

■ *n.* **1** plane, horizontal. **2** position, grade; extent, measure, amount, quantity, size, magnitude; situation, stratum, tier, echelon, step, station, point, stage; elevation, height, altitude, depth. **3** class, position, status, standing, rank; plane; standard(s), (degree of) competence; see also TOUCHSTONE 2. **4** see RANK[1] *n.* 1a. **8** floor, storey, tier, deck. ● *adj.* **1** even, smooth, plane, uniform, flat, flush, straight; uninterrupted, unbroken, unvarying, continuous, true. **2** horizontal, flat; prone, supine. **3 a** parallel, even, flush. **b** the same, equal, equivalent, on a par, consistent. **4** even, uniform, consistent, invariable, unvarying, unalterable, unchanging, unfluctuating; (well-)balanced, unruffled, imperturbable, constant, steady; equable, even-tempered, composed, calm, poised, placid, self-possessed, level-headed. **5** even, tied, equal, neck and neck, fifty-fifty, *Brit.* level pegging, *US* nip and tuck, *colloq.* even Stephen(s). ● *v.* **1** level off *or* out, plateau (out), even (out *or* up), smooth (out), flatten (out), iron (out). **2** raze, demolish, destroy, lay waste, devastate, knock down, tear down, pull down, flatten, wreck, bulldoze. **3** aim, point, direct, train, focus, turn; (*absol.*) take aim, draw a bead, zero in. **4** (*level at*) aim at, focus on, direct to, address to, turn on. **6** (*level with*) be *or* play fair with, be straight *or* open *or* straightforward *or* frank *or* honest with, tell the truth to, *colloq.* be up front with. □ **level off, level out** see LEVEL *v.* 1 above. **level pegging** draw, tie, dead heat, stalemate, deadlock; see also LEVEL *adj.* 5 above. **on the level** (*adv.*) straight (out), openly, candidly, fairly, freely, publicly, frankly, directly, sincerely, honestly, straightforwardly, plainly, *colloq.* upfront, *esp. US colloq.* on the up and up. (*adj.*) straight, straightforward, honest, direct, sincere, candid, frank, square, open, unbiased, fair, above-board, *colloq.* upfront, *esp. US colloq.* on the up and up.

level-headed /lévv'lhéddid/ *adj.* mentally well-balanced, cool, sensible. □□ **level-headedly** *adv.* **level-headedness** *n.*

■ sensible, (well-)balanced, sane, reasonable, rational, commonsensical, level, unruffled, undisturbed, unperturbed, imperturbable, equable, even-tempered, composed, calm, collected, tranquil, serene, poised, cool, relaxed, self-possessed, *colloq.* unflappable.

leveller /lévvələr/ *n.* (*US* **leveler**) **1** a person who advocates the abolition of social distinctions. **2** (**Leveller**) *hist.* an extreme radical dissenter in 17th-c. England. **3** a person or thing that levels.

lever /leévər/ *n.* & *v.* ● *n.* **1** a bar resting on a pivot, used to help lift a heavy or firmly fixed object. **2** *Mech.* a simple machine consisting of a rigid bar pivoted about a fulcrum (fixed point) which can be acted upon by a force (effort) in order to move a load. **3** a projecting handle moved to operate a mechanism. **4** a means of exerting moral pressure. ● *v.* **1** *intr.* use a lever. **2** *tr.* (often foll. by *away, out, up,* etc.) lift, move, or act on with a lever. □ **lever escapement** a mechanism connecting the escape wheel and the balance wheel using two levers. **lever watch** a watch with a lever escapement. [ME f. OF *levier, leveor* f. *lever* raise: see LEVY]

■ *n.* **3** see CONTROL *n.* 5. ● *v.* **2** see LIFT *v.* 1.

leverage /leévərij/ *n.* **1** the action of a lever; a way of applying a lever. **2** the power of a lever; the mechanical advantage gained by use of a lever. **3** a means of accomplishing a purpose; power, influence. **4** a set or system of levers. **5** *US Commerce* gearing. □ **leveraged buyout** esp. *US* the buyout of a company by its management using outside capital.

■ **1, 2** see PURCHASE *n.* 4a. **3** see INFLUENCE *n.* 1.

leveret /lévvərit/ *n.* a young hare, esp. one in its first year. [ME f. AF, dimin. of *levre*, OF *lievre* f. L *lepus leporis* hare]

leviable see LEVY.

leviathan /livī́əthən/ *n.* **1** *Bibl.* a sea-monster. **2** anything very large or powerful, esp. a ship. **3** an autocratic monarch or State (in allusion to a book by Hobbes, 1651). [ME f. LL f. Heb. *liwyāṯān*]

■ **2** see JUMBO *n.*

levigate /lévvigayt/ *v.tr.* **1** reduce to a fine smooth powder. **2** make a smooth paste of. □□ **levigation** /-gáysh'n/ *n.* [L *levigare levigat-* f. *levis* smooth]

■ **1** see POWDER *v.* 2. **2** see PULP *v.* 1.

levin /lévvin/ *n. archaic* **1** lightning. **2** a flash of lightning. [ME *leven(e)*, prob. f. ON]

levirate /leévirət, lév-/ *n.* a custom of the ancient Jews and some other peoples by which a man is obliged to marry his brother's widow. ▫▫ **leviratic** /-ráttik/ *adj.* **leviratical** /-ráttik'l/ *adj.* [L *levir* brother-in-law + -ATE[1]]

Levis /leévīz/ *n.pl. propr.* a type of (orig. blue) denim jeans or overalls reinforced with rivets. [*Levi* Strauss, orig. US manufacturer in 1860s]

levitate /lévvitayt/ *v.* **1** *intr.* rise and float in the air (esp. with reference to spiritualism). **2** *tr.* cause to do this. ▫▫ **levitation** /-táysh'n/ *n.* **levitator** *n.* [L *levis* light, after GRAVITATE]

Levite /leévīt/ *n.* a member of the tribe of Levi, esp. of that part of it which provided assistants to the priests in the worship in the Jewish temple. [ME f. LL *levita* f. Gk *leuitēs* f. *Leui* f. Heb. *lēwî* Levi]

Levitical /livíttik'l/ *adj.* **1** of the Levites or the tribe of Levi. **2** of the Levites' ritual. **3** of Leviticus. [LL *leviticus* f. Gk *leuitikos* (as LEVITE)]

levity /lévviti/ *n.* **1** lack of serious thought, frivolity, unbecoming jocularity. **2** inconstancy. **3** undignified behaviour. **4** *archaic* lightness of weight. [L *levitas* f. *levis* light]
▪ **1** light-heartedness, lightness, frivolity, frivolousness, flippancy, trivialization, triviality, trifling, facetiousness, silliness, hilarity. **2** fickleness, inconstancy, inconsistency, changeableness, unreliability, unreliableness, undependability, flightiness. **3** silliness, foolery, foolishness, tomfoolery, folly; antics. **4** lightness, unsubstantiality, thinness, weightlessness.

levo- *US* var. of LAEVO-.

levodopa /leévədṓpə/ *n.* laevorotatory dopa.

levulose *US* var. of LAEVULOSE.

levy /lévvi/ *v.* & *n.* ● *v.tr.* (**-ies, -ied**) **1 a** impose (a rate or toll). **b** raise (contributions or taxes). **c** (also *absol.*) raise (a sum of money) by legal execution or process (*the debt was levied on the debtor's goods*). **d** seize (goods) in this way. **e** extort (*levy blackmail*). **2** enlist or enrol (troops etc.). **3** (usu. foll. by *upon, against*) wage, proceed to make (war). ● *n.* (*pl.* **-ies**) **1 a** the collecting of a contribution, tax, etc., or of property to satisfy a legal judgement. **b** a contribution, tax, etc., levied. **2 a** the act or an instance of enrolling troops etc. **b** (in *pl.*) men enrolled. **c** a body of men enrolled. **d** the number of men enrolled. ▫▫ **leviable** *adj.* [ME f. OF *levee* fem. past part. of *lever* f. L *levare* raise f. *levis* light]
▪ *v.* **1 a, b** impose, charge, exact, demand; raise. **2** see MOBILIZE *v.* 1a. **3** see INFLICT. ● *n.* **1 b** see TAX *n.* 1.

lewd /lyōōd/ *adj.* **1** lascivious. **2** indecent, obscene. ▫▫ **lewdly** *adv.* **lewdness** *n.* [OE *lǣwede* LAY[2], of unkn. orig.]
▪ **1** lascivious, lustful, randy, lecherous, sexy, licentious, dirty, prurient, salacious, libidinous, erotic, sensual, lubricious, promiscuous, depraved, dissolute, ruttish, goatish, wanton, debauched, hot, *formal* concupiscent, *sl.* horny. **2** indecent, obscene, smutty, crude, coarse, foul, dirty, filthy, rude, pornographic, gross, bawdy, ribald, scurrilous, raw, blue, sexy, risqué, offensive, suggestive, (sexually) explicit, *euphem.* adult.

lewis /lōō-iss/ *n.* an iron contrivance for gripping heavy blocks of stone or concrete for lifting. [18th c.: orig. unkn.]

Lewis gun /lōō-iss/ *n.* a light machine-gun with a magazine, air cooling, and operation by gas from its own firing. [I. N. *Lewis*, Amer. soldier d. 1931, its inventor]

lewisite /lōō-isīt/ *n.* an irritant gas that produces blisters, developed for use in chemical warfare. [W. L. *Lewis*, Amer. chemist d. 1943 + -ITE[1]]

lex domicilii /léks domisílli-ī/ *n. Law* the law of the country in which a person is domiciled. [L]

lexeme /lékseem/ *n. Linguistics* a basic lexical unit of a language comprising one or several words, the elements of which do not separately convey the meaning of the whole. [LEXICON + -EME]

lex fori /leks fórī/ *n. Law* the law of the country in which an action is brought. [L]

lexical /léksik'l/ *adj.* **1** of the words of a language. **2** of or as of a lexicon. ▫▫ **lexically** *adv.* [Gk *lexikos*, *lexikon*: see LEXICON]
▪ **1** see LITERAL *adj.* 1.

lexicography /léksikógrəfi/ *n.* the compiling of dictionaries. ▫▫ **lexicographer** *n.* **lexicographic** /-kəgráffik/ *adj.* **lexicographical** /-kəgráffik'l/ *adj.* **lexicographically** /-kəgráffikəli/ *adv.*

lexicology /léksikóllәji/ *n.* the study of the form, history, and meaning of words. ▫▫ **lexicological** /-kəlójik'l/ *adj.* **lexicologically** /-kəlójikəli/ *adv.* **lexicologist** *n.*

lexicon /léksikən/ *n.* **1** a dictionary, esp. of Greek, Hebrew, Syriac, or Arabic. **2** the vocabulary of a person, language, branch of knowledge, etc. [mod.L f. Gk *lexikon* (*biblion* book), neut. of *lexikos* f. *lexis* word f. *legō* speak]
▪ **1** see DICTIONARY 1.

lexigraphy /leksígrəfi/ *n.* a system of writing in which each character represents a word. [Gk *lexis* (see LEXICON) + -GRAPHY]

lexis /léksiss/ *n.* **1** words, vocabulary. **2** the total stock of words in a language. [Gk: see LEXICON]

lex loci /leks lṓsī/ *n. Law* the law of the country in which a transaction is performed, a tort is committed, or a property is situated. [L]

lex talionis /léks taliṓniss/ *n.* the law of retaliation, whereby a punishment resembles the offence committed, in kind and degree. [L]

ley[1] /lay/ *n.* a field temporarily under grass. ▫ **ley farming** alternate growing of crops and grass. [ME (orig. adj.), perh. f. OE, rel. to LAY[1], LIE[1]]

ley[2] /lee, lay/ *n.* the supposed straight line of a prehistoric track, usu. between hilltops. [var. of LEA]

Leyden jar /líd'n/ *n.* an early form of capacitor consisting of a glass jar with layers of metal foil on the outside and inside. [*Leyden* (now *Leiden*) in Holland, where it was invented (1745)]

LF *abbr.* low frequency.

LH *abbr. Biochem.* luteinizing hormone.

l.h. *abbr.* left hand.

LI *abbr.* **1** Light Infantry. **2** *US* Long Island.

Li *symb. Chem.* the element lithium.

liability /līəbílliti/ *n.* (*pl.* **-ies**) **1** the state of being liable. **2** a person or thing that is troublesome as an unwelcome responsibility; a handicap. **3** what a person is liable for, esp. (in *pl.*) debts or pecuniary obligations.
▪ **1** answerability, responsibility, accountability, accountableness; exposure, susceptibility, vulnerability. **2** burden, handicap, disadvantage, drawback, hindrance, impediment, encumbrance, millstone, cross (to bear), snag, hitch, difficulty, barrier, obstacle, obstruction, fly in the ointment, *Brit. colloq.* spanner in the works, *offens.* nigger in the woodpile. **3** (*liabilities*) obligations, debts, indebtedness, arrears, debits, dues.

liable /līəb'l/ *predic.adj.* **1** legally bound. **2** (foll. by *to*) subject to (a tax or penalty). **3** (foll. by *to* + infin.) under an obligation. **4** (foll. by *to*) exposed or open to (something undesirable). **5** *disp.* (foll. by *to* + infin.) apt, likely (*it is liable to rain*). **6** (foll. by *for*) answerable. [ME perh. f. AF f. OF *lier* f. L *ligare* bind]
▪ **1** (legally *or* statutorily) bound, responsible. **3** obliged, under an obligation, obligated, (duty-)bound, due, beholden. **4** exposed, susceptible, vulnerable, open, subject, given, predisposed, tending. **5** prone, apt, inclined, disposed, expected, due, likely, of a mind. **6** responsible, accountable, blameable, answerable, chargeable.

liaise /liáyz/ *v.intr.* (foll. by *with, between*) *colloq.* establish cooperation, act as a link. [back-form. f. LIAISON]

liaison /liáyzon/ *n.* **1** communication or cooperation, esp. between military forces or units. **2** an illicit sexual relationship. **3** the binding or thickening agent of a sauce. **4** the sounding of an ordinarily silent final consonant before a word beginning with a vowel (or a mute *h* in French). ▫ **liaison officer** an officer acting as a link between allied forces or units of the same force. [F f. *lier* bind f. L *ligare*]

■ **1** connection, communication, contact, link(age), cooperation, relationship, relations, tie(s). **2** (love) affair, amour, relationship, *affair* (*de cœur*), romance, entanglement, flirtation, fling, *archaic* intrigue, *Brit. sl.* carry-on, bit on the side.

liana /liaánə/ *n.* (also **liane** /-aán/) any of several climbing and twining plants of tropical forests. [F *liane, lierne* clematis, of uncert. orig.]

liar /lī́ər/ *n.* a person who tells a lie or lies, esp. habitually. □ **liar dice** a game with poker dice in which the result of a throw may be announced falsely. [OE *lēogere* (as LIE², -AR⁴)]

■ fibber, fibster, fabricator, prevaricator, perjurer, falsifier, teller of tales, romancer, fabulist, false witness, *colloq.* storyteller.

lias /lī́əss/ *n.* **1** (**Lias**) *Geol.* the lower strata of the Jurassic system of rocks, consisting of shales and limestones rich in fossils. **2** a blue limestone rock found in SW England. □□ **liassic** /līássik/ *adj.* (in sense 1). [ME f. OF *liois* hard limestone, prob. f. Gmc]

Lib. *abbr.* Liberal.

lib /lib/ *n. colloq.* liberation (*women's lib*). [abbr.]

libation /lībáysh'n, li-/ *n.* **1 a** the pouring out of a drink-offering to a god. **b** such a drink-offering. **2** *joc.* a drink. [ME f. L *libatio* f. *libare* pour as offering]

libber /líbbər/ *n. colloq.* an advocate of women's liberation.

libel /lī́b'l/ *n.* & *v.* ● *n.* **1** *Law* **a** a published false statement damaging to a person's reputation (cf. SLANDER). **b** the act of publishing this. **2 a** a false and defamatory written statement. **b** (foll. by *on*) a thing that brings discredit by misrepresentation etc. (*the portrait is a libel on him*; *the book is a libel on human nature*). **3 a** (in civil and ecclesiastical law) the plaintiff's written declaration. **b** *Sc. Law* a statement of the grounds of a charge. **4** (in full **public libel**) *Law* the publication of a libel that also involves the criminal law. ● *v.tr.* (**libelled, libelling**; *US* **libeled, libeling**) **1** defame by libellous statements. **2** accuse falsely and maliciously. **3** *Law* publish a libel against. **4** (in ecclesiastical law) bring a suit against. □ **criminal libel** *Law* a deliberate defamatory statement in a permanent form. □□ **libeller** *n.* [ME f. OF f. L *libellus* dimin. of *liber* book]

■ *n.* **2 a** defamation, vilification, denigration, slander, calumny, detraction, obloquy, misrepresentation, prevarication; aspersion, lie, untruth, false insinuation, falsehood, imputation, allegation, *archaic or US* slur. **b** slur, smear, blot, stain, smirch. ● *v.* **1, 2** defame, vilify, denigrate, denounce, deprecate, decry, depreciate, belittle, disparage, disgrace, dishonour, shame, humiliate, mortify, abuse, *formal* derogate; slander, calumniate, lie about, misrepresent, asperse, cast aspersions on, give a bad name to, speak ill of, slur, smear, malign, stain, blacken, discredit, besmirch, stigmatize, traduce, *US* bad-mouth.

libellous /lī́bələss/ *adj.* containing or constituting a libel. □□ **libellously** *adv.*

■ see *slanderous* (SLANDER).

liber /lī́bər/ *n.* bast. [L, = bark]

liberal /líbbərəl, líbrəl/ *adj.* & *n.* ● *adj.* **1** given freely; ample, abundant. **2** (often foll. by *of*) giving freely, generous, not sparing. **3** open-minded, not prejudiced. **4** not strict or rigorous; (of interpretation) not literal. **5** for general broadening of the mind, not professional or technical (*liberal studies*). **6 a** favouring individual liberty, free trade, and moderate political and social reform. **b** (**Liberal**) of or characteristic of Liberals or a Liberal Party. **7** *Theol.* regarding many traditional beliefs as dispensable, invalidated by modern thought, or liable to change (*liberal Protestant*; *liberal Judaism*). ● *n.* **1** a person of liberal views. **2** (**Liberal**) a supporter or member of a Liberal Party. □ **liberal arts 1** *US* the arts as distinct from science and technology. **2** *hist.* the medieval trivium and quadrivium. **Liberal Democrat** (in the UK) a member of a party (formerly the *Social and Liberal Democrats*) formed from the Liberal Party and members of the Social Democratic Party. **Liberal Party** a political party advocating liberal policies. ¶ In the UK the name was discontinued in official use in 1988, when the party regrouped with others to form the Social and Liberal Democrats (see *Liberal Democrat*). □□ **liberalism** *n.* **liberalist** *n.* **liberalistic** /-lístik/ *adj.* **liberally** *adv.* **liberalness** *n.* [ME, orig. = befitting a free man, f. OF f. L *liberalis* f. *liber* free (man)]

■ *adj.* **1** lavish, handsome, ample, abundant, plentiful, profuse, copious, luxuriant, prolific, *poet.* bounteous. **2** bountiful, free, generous, open-hearted, open, open-handed, giving, charitable, philanthropic, munificent, magnanimous, big, big-hearted, unstinting, ungrudging, unselfish, unsparing, *poet.* bounteous. **3** fair, broad-minded, open-minded, large-minded, unprejudiced, unbigoted, unjaundiced, unbiased, tolerant, relaxed, permissive, lax; unopinionated, disinterested, impartial, dispassionate. **4** free, flexible, wide, lenient, loose, broad, open, non-restrictive; casual, imprecise, inexact. **6** progressive, progressivist, libertine, freethinking, libertarian, reformist, humanistic, left (of centre), latitudinarian, non-partisan, unaligned, non-aligned, individualistic, independent, *S.Afr. verligte.* ● *n.* **1** progressive, libertarian, reformer, progressivist, latitudinarian, independent, freethinker, leftist, left-winger, *S.Afr. verligte.*

liberality /líbbərálliti/ *n.* **1** free giving, munificence. **2** freedom from prejudice, breadth of mind. [ME f. OF *liberalite* or L *liberalitas* (as LIBERAL)]

■ **1** see LARGESSE 2.

liberalize /líbbərəlīz/ *v.tr.* & *intr.* (also **-ise**) make or become more liberal or less strict. □□ **liberalization** /-záysh'n/ *n.* **liberalizer** *n.*

■ broaden, widen, extend, expand, stretch, enlarge; loosen, ease, slacken, relax, modify, change, moderate, soften.

liberate /líbbərayt/ *v.tr.* **1** (often foll. by *from*) set at liberty, set free. **2** free (a country etc.) from an oppressor or an enemy occupation. **3** (often as **liberated** *adj.*) free (a person) from rigid social conventions, esp. in sexual behaviour. **4** *sl.* steal. **5** *Chem.* release (esp. a gas) from a state of combination. □□ **liberator** *n.* [L *liberare liberat-* f. *liber* free]

■ **1** (set) free, release, set at liberty, (let) loose, let go *or* out *or* off, deliver, rescue, unfetter, unshackle, emancipate, enfranchise, *hist.* manumit, *literary* disenthral. **2** deliver, free, emancipate. **3** (**liberated**) emancipated, reformed; uninhibited, free, new. **4** steal, pilfer, filch, appropriate, *colloq.* lift, *formal or joc.* purloin, *Brit. sl.* nick; see also TAKE *v.* 14a.

liberation /líbbəráysh'n/ *n.* the act or an instance of liberating; the state of being liberated. □ **liberation theology** a theory which interprets liberation from social, political, and economic oppression as an anticipation of ultimate salvation. □□ **liberationist** *n.* [ME f. L *liberatio* f. *liberare*: see LIBERATE]

■ freeing, deliverance, emancipation, enfranchisement, affranchisement, rescue, release; freedom, liberty.

libertarian /líbbərtáiriən/ *n.* & *adj.* ● *n.* **1** an advocate of liberty. **2** a believer in free will (opp. NECESSITARIAN). ● *adj.* believing in free will. □□ **libertarianism** *n.*

■ *n.* **1** see LIBERAL *n.* 1.

libertine /líbbərteen, -tin, -tīn/ *n.* & *adj.* ● *n.* **1** a dissolute or licentious person. **2** a free thinker on religion. **3** a person who follows his or her own inclinations. ● *adj.* **1** licentious, dissolute. **2** freethinking. **3** following one's own inclinations. □□ **libertinage** *n.* **libertinism** *n.* [L *libertinus* freedman f. *libertus* made free f. *liber* free]

■ *n.* **1** lecher, reprobate, profligate, rake, roué, debaucher, debauchee, dissipator, playboy, *US* sport, *literary* wanton; womanizer, seducer, adulterer, philanderer, Don Juan, Lothario, Casanova, Romeo, lady-killer, *archaic or joc.* fornicator, *colloq.* stud, *sl.* wolf. **2** freethinker, liberal, libertarian, latitudinarian. **3** liberal, independent, individualist. ● *adj.* **1** licentious, lecherous, reprobate, profligate, rakish, philandering, dissolute, immoral, degenerate, depraved, debauched, decadent, dirty, filthy, amoral, wanton, lewd, lascivious, prurient, lubricious, salacious, libidinous; see also LEWD 1. **2, 3** see LIBERAL *adj.* 6.

liberty /líbbərti/ *n.* (*pl.* **-ies**) **1 a** freedom from captivity, imprisonment, slavery, or despotic control. **b** a personification of this. **2 a** the right or power to do as one pleases. **b** (foll. by *to* + infin.) right, power, opportunity, permission. **c** *Philos.* freedom from control by fate or necessity. **3 a** (usu. in *pl.*) a right, privilege, or immunity, enjoyed by prescription or grant. **b** (in *sing.* or *pl.*) *hist.* an area having such privileges etc., esp. a district controlled by a city though outside its boundary or an area outside a prison where some prisoners might reside. **4** setting aside of rules or convention. □ **at liberty 1** free, not imprisoned (*set at liberty*). **2** (foll. by *to* + infin.) entitled, permitted. **3** available, disengaged. **Liberty Bell** (in the US) a bell in Philadelphia rung at the adoption of the Declaration of Independence. **liberty boat** *Brit. Naut.* a boat carrying liberty men. **liberty bodice** a close-fitting under-bodice. **liberty hall** a place where one may do as one likes. **liberty horse** a horse performing in a circus without a rider. **liberty man** *Brit. Naut.* a sailor with leave to go ashore. **liberty of the subject** the rights of a subject under constitutional rule. **Liberty ship** *hist.* a prefabricated US-built freighter of the war of 1939-45. **take liberties 1** (often foll. by *with*) behave in an unduly familiar manner. **2** (foll. by *with*) deal freely or superficially with rules or facts. **take the liberty** (foll. by *to* + infin., or *of* + verbal noun) presume, venture. [ME f. OF *liberté* f. L *libertas -tatis* f. *liber* free]

■ **1** freedom, independence, self-determination, autonomy, self-rule, self-government, sovereignty; emancipation, liberation. **2** freedom, licence, leave, power, authority, prerogative, *carte blanche*; choice, option, alternative; latitude, elbow-room, margin, scope; free will. **3 a** freedom, franchise, privilege, prerogative; (*liberties*) (civil *or* human) rights. □ **at liberty 1** free, uninhibited, unfettered, unconstrained, unrestricted, unrestrained; see also FREE *adj.* 3. **2** free, permitted, allowed, given leave *or* permission, authorized, entitled, given the go-ahead, *colloq.* given the green light. **3** ready, disposed, on hand, available, disengaged. **take liberties 1** be unrestrained *or* overfamiliar *or* forward *or* aggressive *or* impudent *or* impertinent *or* audacious *or* improper; display *or* exercise boldness *or* impropriety *or* presumption *or* presumptuousness *or* indecorum *or* unseemliness *or* arrogance. **take the liberty** presume, venture, be presumptuous *or* bold *or* uninhibited, make (so) bold, go so far, have the audacity *or* effrontery, *colloq.* have the nerve.

libidinous /libíddinəss/ *adj.* lustful. □□ **libidinously** *adv.* **libidinousness** *n.* [ME f. L *libidinosus* f. *libido -dinis* lust]
■ see *lustful* (LUST). □□ **libidinousness** see LUST *n.* 1, 3.

libido /libeédō, libī́dō/ *n.* (*pl.* **-os**) *Psychol.* psychic drive or energy, esp. that associated with sexual desire. □□ **libidinal** /libíddin'l/ *adj.* **libidinally** *adv.* [L: see LIBIDINOUS]
■ see LUST *n.* 3.

Lib-Lab /líbláb/ *adj. Brit. hist.* Liberal and Labour. [abbr.]

Libra /leébrə, lib-, lī́b-/ *n.* **1** a constellation, traditionally regarded as contained in the figure of scales. **2 a** the seventh sign of the zodiac (the Balance or Scales). **b** a person born when the sun is in this sign. □□ **Libran** *n.* & *adj.* [ME f. L, orig. = pound weight]

librarian /lībráiriən/ *n.* a person in charge of, or an assistant in, a library. □□ **librarianship** *n.* [L *librarius*: see LIBRARY]

library /lī́brəri/ *n.* (*pl.* **-ies**) **1 a** a collection of books etc. for use by the public or by members of a group. **b** a person's collection of books. **2** a room or building containing a collection of books (for reading or reference rather than for sale). **3 a** a similar collection of films, records, computer routines, etc. **b** the place where these are kept. **4** a series of books issued by a publisher in similar bindings etc., usu. as a set. **5** a public institution charged with the care of a collection of books, films, etc. □ **library edition** a strongly bound edition. **library school** a college or a department in a university or polytechnic teaching librarianship. **library science** the study of librarianship. [ME f. OF *librairie* f. L *libraria* (*taberna* shop), fem. of *librarius* bookseller's, of books, f. *liber libri* book]
■ **2** see STUDY *n.* 3.

libration /lībráysh'n/ *n.* an apparent oscillation of a heavenly body, esp. the moon, by which the parts near the edge of the disc are alternately in view and out of view. [L *libratio* f. *librare* f. *libra* balance]
■ see SWING *n.* 1, 2.

libretto /librétto/ *n.* (*pl.* **libretti** /-ti/ or **-os**) the text of an opera or other long musical vocal work. □□ **librettist** *n.* [It., dimin. of *libro* book f. L *liber libri*]
■ see LYRIC *n.* 3.

Librium /líbriəm/ *n. propr.* a white crystalline drug used as a tranquillizer.

Libyan /líbbiən, líbyən/ *adj.* & *n.* ● *adj.* **1** of or relating to modern Libya in N. Africa. **2** of ancient N. Africa west of Egypt. **3** of or relating to the Berber group of languages. ● *n.* **1 a** a native or national of modern Libya. **b** a person of Libyan descent. **2** an ancient language of the Berber group.

lice *pl.* of LOUSE.

licence /lī́s'nss/ *n.* (*US* **license**) **1** a permit from an authority to own or use something (esp. a dog, gun, television set, or vehicle), do something (esp. marry, print something, preach, or drive on a public road), or carry on a trade (esp. in alcoholic liquor). **2** leave, permission (*have I your licence to remove the fence?*). **3 a** liberty of action, esp. when excessive; disregard of law or propriety, abuse of freedom. **b** licentiousness. **4** a writer's or artist's irregularity in grammar, metre, perspective, etc., or deviation from fact, esp. for effect (*poetic licence*). **5** a university certificate of competence in a faculty. □ **license plate** *US* the number plate of a licensed vehicle. [ME f. OF f. L *licentia* f. *licēre* be lawful: *-se* by confusion with LICENSE]
■ **1** permit, pass, certificate, credential(s), paper(s), document(s), warrant, warranty, certification, authorization, dispensation. **2** leave, permission, authorization, authority, entitlement, dispensation, empowerment, right, sanction, *carte blanche*, freedom, latitude, free choice, liberty, privilege; charter, franchise. **3** lack of control *or* restraint, laxness, laxity, looseness; libertinism, libertinage, profligateness, profligacy, excessiveness, immoderation, immoderateness, wantonness, debauchery, dissoluteness, dissipation. **4** disregard, deviation, departure, nonconformity, non-compliance, divergence, independence, individuality.

license /lī́s'nss/ *v.tr.* (also **licence**) **1** grant a licence to (a person). **2** authorize the use of (premises) for a certain purpose, esp. the sale and consumption of alcoholic liquor. **3** authorize the publication of (a book etc.) or the performance of (a play). **4** *archaic* allow. □ **licensed victualler** see VICTUALLER. □□ **licensable** *adj.* **licenser** *n.* **licensor** *n.* [ME f. LICENCE: *-se* on analogy of the verbs PRACTISE, PROPHESY, perh. after ADVISE, where the sound differs from the corresp. noun]
■ **1** entitle, grant rights to, allow, permit, enable, empower. **3** authorize, allow, permit, certify, sanction, approve.

licensee /lī́sənseé/ *n.* the holder of a licence, esp. to sell alcoholic liquor.

licentiate /līsénshiət, -shət/ *n.* **1** a holder of a certificate of competence to practise a certain profession, or of a university licence. **2** a licensed preacher not yet having an appointment, esp. in a Presbyterian church. [ME f. med.L *licentiatus* past part. of *licentiare* f. L *licentia*: see LICENCE]

licentious /līsénshəss/ *adj.* **1** immoral in sexual relations. **2** *archaic* disregarding accepted rules or conventions. □□ **licentiously** *adv.* **licentiousness** *n.* [L *licentiosus* f. *licentia*: see LICENCE]
■ **1** see IMMORAL 3. □□ **licentiousness** see *indecency* (INDECENT).

lichee var. of LYCHEE.

lichen /líkən, líchən/ *n.* **1** any plant organism of the group Lichenes, composed of a fungus and an alga in symbiotic association, usu. of green, grey, or yellow tint and growing on and colouring rocks, tree-trunks, roofs, walls, etc. **2** any of several types of skin disease in which small round hard lesions occur close together. ▫▫ **lichened** *adj.* (in sense 1). **lichenology** /-nólləji/ *n.* (in sense 1). **lichenous** *adj:* (in sense 2). [L f. Gk *leikhēn*]

lich-gate /líchgayt/ *n.* (also **lych-gate**) a roofed gateway to a churchyard where a coffin awaits the clergyman's arrival. [ME f. OE *līc* corpse f. Gmc + GATE[1]]

licit /líssit/ *adj.* not forbidden; lawful. ▫▫ **licitly** *adv.* [L *licitus* past part. of *licēre* be lawful]

▪ see LEGAL 3.

lick /lik/ *v.* & *n.* ● *v.tr.* & *intr.* **1** *tr.* pass the tongue over, esp. to taste, moisten, or (of animals) clean. **2** *tr.* bring into a specified condition or position by licking (*licked it all up*; *licked it clean*). **3 a** *tr.* (of a flame, waves, etc.) touch; play lightly over. **b** *intr.* move gently or caressingly. **4** *tr. colloq.* **a** defeat, excel. **b** surpass the comprehension of (*has got me licked*). **5** *tr. colloq.* thrash. ● *n.* **1** an act of licking with the tongue. **2** = *salt-lick*. **3** *colloq.* a fast pace (*at a lick*; *at full lick*). **4** *colloq.* **a** a small amount, quick treatment with (foll. by *of*: *a lick of paint*). **b** a quick wash. **5** a smart blow with a stick etc. ▫ **a lick and a promise** *colloq.* a hasty performance of a task, esp. of washing oneself. **lick a person's boots** (or **shoes**) toady; be servile. **lick into shape** see SHAPE. **lick one's lips** (or **chops**) **1** look forward with relish. **2** show one's satisfaction. **lick one's wounds** be in retirement after defeat. ▫▫ **licker** *n.* (also in *comb.*). [OE *liccian* f. WG]

▪ *v.* **4** see OVERCOME 1. ▫ **lick a person's boots** see TRUCKLE *v.* **lick one's lips 2** see SAVOUR *v.* 1.

lickerish /líkkərish/ *adj.* (also **liquorish**) **1** lecherous. **2 a** fond of fine food. **b** greedy, longing. [ME *lickerous* f. OF *lecheros*: see LECHER]

▪ **1** see LECHEROUS.

lickety-split /líkkətisplít/ *adv. colloq.* at full speed; headlong. [prob. f. LICK (cf. *at full lick*) + SPLIT]

▪ see *quickly* (QUICK).

licking /líkking/ *n. colloq.* **1** a thrashing. **2** a defeat.

lickspittle /líkspitt'l/ *n.* a toady.

▪ see *yes-man*.

licorice var. of LIQUORICE.

lictor /líktor/ *n.* (usu. in *pl.*) *Rom.Hist.* an officer attending the consul or other magistrate, bearing the fasces, and executing sentence on offenders. [ME f. L, perh. rel. to *ligare* bind]

lid /lid/ *n.* **1** a hinged or removable cover, esp. for the top of a container. **2** = EYELID. **3** the operculum of a shell or a plant. **4** *sl.* a hat. ▫ **put the lid** (or **tin lid**) **on** *Brit. colloq.* **1** be the culmination of. **2** put a stop to. **take the lid off** *colloq.* expose (a scandal etc.). ▫▫ **lidded** *adj.* (also in *comb.*). **lidless** *adj.* [OE *hlid* f. Gmc]

▪ **1** see COVER *n.* 1a.

lido /leédō, lī-/ *n.* (*pl.* **-os**) a public open-air swimming-pool or bathing-beach. [It. f. *Lido*, the name of a bathing-beach near Venice, f. L *litus* shore]

▪ see BEACH *n.*

lie[1] /lī/ *v.* & *n.* ● *v.intr.* (**lying** /lī-ing/; *past* **lay** /lay/; *past part.* **lain** /layn/) **1** be in or assume a horizontal position on a supporting surface; be at rest on something. **2** (of a thing) rest flat on a surface (*snow lay on the ground*). **3** (of abstract things) remain undisturbed or undiscussed etc. (*let matters lie*). **4 a** be kept or remain or be in a specified, esp. concealed, state or place (*lie hidden*; *lie in wait*; *malice lay behind those words*; *they lay dying*; *the books lay unread*; *the money is lying in the bank*). **b** (of abstract things) exist, reside; be in a certain position or relation (foll. by *in*, *with*, etc.: *the answer lies in education*; *my sympathies lie with the family*). **5 a** be situated or stationed (*the village lay to the east*; *the ships are lying off the coast*). **b** (of a road, route, etc.) lead (*the road lies over mountains*). **c** be spread out to view (*the desert lay before us*). **6** (of the dead) be buried in a grave. **7** (foll. by *with*) *archaic* have sexual intercourse. **8** *Law* be admissible or sustainable (*the objection will not lie*). **9** (of a game-bird) not rise. ● *n.* **1 a** the way or direction or position in which a thing lies. **b** *Golf* the position of a golf ball when about to be struck. **2** the place of cover of an animal or a bird. ▫ **as far as in me lies** to the best of my power. **let lie** not raise (a controversial matter etc.) for discussion etc. **lie about** (or **around**) be left carelessly out of place. **lie ahead** be going to happen; be in store. **lie back** recline so as to rest. **lie down** assume a lying position; have a short rest. **lie-down** *n.* a short rest. **lie down under** accept (an insult etc.) without protest. **lie heavy** cause discomfort or anxiety. **lie in 1** remain in bed in the morning. **2** *archaic* be brought to bed in childbirth. **lie-in** *n.* a prolonged stay in bed in the morning. **lie in state** (of a deceased great personage) be laid in a public place of honour before burial. **lie low 1** keep quiet or unseen. **2** be discreet about one's intentions. **lie off** *Naut.* stand some distance from shore or from another ship. **the lie of the land** the current state of affairs. **lie over** be deferred. **lie to** *Naut.* come almost to a stop facing the wind. **lie up** (of a ship) go into dock or be out of commission. **lie with** (often foll. by *to* + infin.) be the responsibility of (a person) (*it lies with you to answer*). **take lying down** (usu. with *neg.*) accept (defeat, rebuke, etc.) without resistance or protest etc. [OE *licgan* f. Gmc]

▪ *v.* **1** lie down, recline, stretch out, prostrate oneself, be prostrate *or* recumbent *or* prone *or* supine; rest, repose, lean, be supported. **2** rest, be level *or* flat. **3** rest, drop, cease, lapse. **4 b** exist, be, rest, remain, belong, reside. **5** be found, be, exist, be located *or* positioned *or* situated *or* placed *or* stationed. ▫ **lie ahead** see IMPEND 1. **lie back** see RECLINE 1. **lie down** prostrate oneself; have a rest *or* lie-down, take to one's bed; see also LIE[1] *v.* 1 above, REST[1] *v.* 1, 2. **lie-down** see REST[1] *n.* 1. **lie low 1** hide, remain concealed, stay in hiding, go into hiding, keep out of sight, go to ground, *sl.* lie doggo. **the lie of the land** state of affairs, condition, situation; atmosphere, mood, spirit, temper, character.

lie[2] /lī/ *n.* & *v.* ● *n.* **1** an intentionally false statement (*tell a lie*; *pack of lies*). **2** imposture; false belief (*live a lie*). ● *v.intr.* & *tr.* (**lies, lied, lying** /lī-ing/) **1** *intr.* **a** tell a lie or lies (*they lied to me*). **b** (of a thing) be deceptive (*the camera cannot lie*). **2** *tr.* (usu. *refl.*; foll. by *into*, *out of*) get (oneself) into or out of a situation by lying (*lied themselves into trouble*; *lied my way out of danger*). ▫ **give the lie to** serve to show the falsity of (a supposition etc.). **lie-detector** an instrument for determining whether a person is telling the truth by testing for physiological changes considered to be symptomatic of lying. [OE *lyge lēogan* f. Gmc]

▪ *n.* **1** falsehood, untruth, falsification, misrepresentation, false statement, fiction, invention, prevarication, fib, fabrication, stretching of the truth, half-truth, disinformation, exaggeration, overstatement, cock-and-bull story, fairy story *or* tale, *colloq.* (tall) story, (tall) tale, *sl.* whopper, porky (pie). ● *v.* **1 a** tell a lie, tell tales, prevaricate, fabricate *or* misrepresent *or* twist the evidence, invent stories, commit perjury, perjure *or* forswear oneself, exaggerate, fib. **b** deceive, misinform, misrepresent *or* distort *or* falsify *or* pervert the evidence. ▫ **give the lie to** see EXPLODE *v.* 4. **lie-detector** polygraph.

Liebfraumilch /leébfrowmilk/ *n.* a light white wine from the Rhine region. [G f. *Liebfrau* the Virgin Mary, the patroness of the convent where it was first made + *Milch* milk]

lied /leed, leet/ *n.* (*pl.* **lieder** /leédər/) a type of German song, esp. of the Romantic period, usu. for solo voice with piano accompaniment. [G]

lief /leef/ *adv. archaic* gladly, willingly. (usu. **had lief, would lief**) [orig. as adj. f. OE *lēof* dear, pleasant, f. Gmc, rel. to LEAVE[2], LOVE]

▪ see SOON 4.

liege /leej/ *adj.* & *n.* usu. *hist.* ● *adj.* (of a superior) entitled to receive or (of a vassal) bound to give feudal service or allegiance. ● *n.* **1** (in full **liege lord**) a feudal superior or sovereign. **2** (usu. in *pl.*) a vassal or subject. [ME f. OF *lige, liege* f. med.L *laeticus*, prob. f. Gmc]

liegeman /leéjman/ *n.* (*pl.* **-men**) *hist.* a sworn vassal; a faithful follower.
■ see SUBJECT *n.* 4.

lien /leéən/ *n. Law* a right over another's property to protect a debt charged on that property. [F f. OF *loien* f. L *ligamen* bond f. *ligare* bind]

lierne /li-érn/ *n. Archit.* (in vaulting) a short rib connecting the bosses and intersections of the principal ribs. [ME f. F: see LIANA]

lieu /lyōō/ *n.* □ **in lieu 1** instead. **2** (foll. by *of*) in the place of. [ME f. F f. L *locus* place]
■ □ **in lieu 2** (*in lieu of*) see *in place of* (PLACE).

Lieut. *abbr.* Lieutenant.

lieutenant /lefténnənt/ *n.* **1** a deputy or substitute acting for a superior. **2 a** an army officer next in rank below captain. **b** a naval officer next in rank below lieutenant commander. **3** *US* a police officer next in rank below captain. □ **lieutenant colonel** (or **commander** or **general**) officers ranking next below colonel, commander, or general. **lieutenant-governor** the acting or deputy governor of a State, province, etc., under a governor or Governor-General. **Lieutenant of the Tower** the acting commandant of the Tower of London. □□ **lieutenancy** *n.* (*pl.* **-ies**). [ME f. OF (as LIEU, TENANT)]
■ **1** see AIDE, DEPUTY.

life /līf/ *n.* (*pl.* **lives** /līvz/) **1** the condition which distinguishes active animals and plants from inorganic matter, including the capacity for growth, functional activity, and continual change preceding death. **2 a** living things and their activity (*insect life; is there life on Mars?*). **b** human presence or activity (*no sign of life*). **3 a** the period during which life lasts, or the period from birth to the present time or from the present time to death (*have done it all my life; will regret it all my life; life membership*). **b** the duration of a thing's existence or of its ability to function; validity, efficacy, etc. (*the battery has a life of two years*). **4 a** a person's state of existence as a living individual (*sacrificed their lives; took many lives*). **b** a living person (*many lives were lost*). **5 a** an individual's occupation, actions, or fortunes; the manner of one's existence (*that would make life easy; start a new life*). **b** a particular aspect of this (*love-life; private life*). **6** the active part of existence; the business and pleasures of the world (*travel is the best way to see life*). **7** man's earthly or supposed future existence. **8 a** energy, liveliness, animation (*full of life; put some life into it!*). **b** an animating influence (*was the life of the party*). **c** (of an inanimate object) power, force; ability to perform its intended function. **9** the living, esp. nude, form or model (*taken from the life*). **10** a written account of a person's life; a biography. **11** *colloq.* a sentence of imprisonment for life (*they were all serving life*). **12** a chance; a fresh start (*cats have nine lives; gave the player three lives*). □ **come to life 1** emerge from unconsciousness or inactivity; begin operating. **2** (of an inanimate object) assume an imaginary animation. **for dear** (or **one's**) **life** as if or in order to escape death; as a matter of extreme urgency (*hanging on for dear life; run for your life*). **for life** for the rest of one's life. **for the life of** (foll. by pers. pron.) even if (one's) life depended on it (*cannot for the life of me remember*). **give one's life 1** (foll. by *for*) die; sacrifice oneself. **2** (foll. by *to*) dedicate oneself. **large as life** *colloq.* in person, esp. prominently (*stood there large as life*). **larger than life 1** exaggerated. **2** (of a person) having an exuberant personality. **life-and-death** vitally important; desperate (*a life-and-death struggle*). **life cycle** the series of changes in the life of an organism including reproduction. **life expectancy** the average period that a person at a specified age may expect to live. **life-force** inspiration or a driving force or influence. **life-form** an organism. **life-giving** that sustains life or uplifts and revitalizes. **Life Guards** (in the UK) a regiment of the royal household cavalry. **life history** the story of a person's life, esp. told at tedious length. **life insurance** insurance for a sum to be paid on the death of the insured person. **life-jacket** a buoyant or inflatable jacket for keeping a person afloat in water. **life peer** *Brit.* a peer whose title lapses on death. **life-preserver 1** a short stick with a heavily loaded end. **2** a life-jacket etc. **life-raft** an inflatable or timber etc. raft for use in an emergency instead of a boat. **life-saver** *colloq.* **1** a thing that saves one from serious difficulty. **2** *Austral.* & *NZ* = LIFEGUARD. **life sciences** biology and related subjects. **life sentence 1** a sentence of imprisonment for life. **2** an illness or commitment etc. perceived as a continuing threat to one's freedom. **life-size** (or **-sized**) of the same size as the person or thing represented. **life-support** *adj.* (of equipment) allowing vital functions to continue in an adverse environment or during severe disablement. **life-support machine** *Med.* a ventilator or respirator. **life's-work** a task etc. pursued throughout one's lifetime. **lose one's life** be killed. **a matter of life and death** a matter of vital importance. **not on your life** *colloq.* most certainly not. **save a person's life 1** prevent a person's death. **2** save a person from serious difficulty. **take one's life in one's hands** take a crucial personal risk. **to the life** true to the original. [OE *līf* f. Gmc]
■ **1** existence, being; sentience, animateness, animation, viability. **2** existence; animal life, plant life; human existence *or* life, people. **3** existence, lifetime, lifespan, time, duration, days; validity, efficacy, force, period of use. **4 b** person, mortal, being, human (being), individual, soul. **5** existence, living, way of life, walk of life, lifestyle; province, sphere, field, line, career, business; obsession, preoccupation, passion, fixation, compulsion, *colloq.* thing, *sl.* bag. **8** energy, liveliness, animation, vitality, sprightliness, vivacity, sparkle, dazzle, dash, vigour, verve, zest, flavour, pungency, freshness, effervescence, brio, flair, vim, exuberance, enthusiasm, *colloq.* pep, zing, get-up-and-go; soul, spirit, spark of life, vital spark, moving spirit, life-force, *élan*; lifeblood, dynamic force; power, force, bounce, resilience, elasticity. **10** biography, autobiography, memoir(s), (life) story, diary, journal. □ **come to life 1** see EMERGE 1, BEGIN 2, 4. **give one's life 1** (*give one's life for*) lay down one's life for, sacrifice oneself for *or* to; see also DIE[1] 1. **2** (*give one's life to*) dedicate oneself to, give oneself to, commit oneself to, devote oneself *or* one's life to, spend oneself for *or* on. **large as life** see *in person* (PERSON). **larger than life 1** see TALL 4. **2** see EXUBERANT 1. **life-and-death** see VITAL 2. **life's-work** see VOCATION 2. **lose one's life** see DIE[1] 1. **a matter of life and death** see NECESSITY 2, 3.

lifebelt /līfbelt/ *n.* a belt of buoyant or inflatable material for keeping a person afloat in water.

lifeblood /līfblud/ *n.* **1** the blood, as being necessary to life. **2** the vital factor or influence.
■ **2** see LIFE 8.

lifeboat /līfbōt/ *n.* **1** a specially constructed boat launched from land to rescue those in distress at sea. **2** a ship's small boat for use in emergency.

lifebuoy /līfboy/ *n.* a buoyant support (usu. a ring) for keeping a person afloat in water.

lifeguard /līfgaard/ *n.* an expert swimmer employed to rescue bathers from drowning.

lifeless /līfliss/ *adj.* **1** lacking life; no longer living. **2** unconscious. **3** lacking movement or vitality. □□ **lifelessly** *adv.* **lifelessness** *n.* [OE *līflēas* (as LIFE, -LESS)]
■ **1** dead, departed, demised, cold, stiff, dead as a doornail, *formal* deceased; inanimate, inorganic; barren, desert, desolate, bare, sterile, bleak, empty, uninhabited, unoccupied, dreary, waste. **2** unconscious, insensate, in a faint, inert, unmoving, corpse-like, dead, insensible, immobile, inanimate, out for the count, *colloq.* (out) cold, dead to the world, *literary* in a swoon. **3** inactive, passive, dull, boring, tiresome, heavy, lacklustre, torpid, tedious, flat, stale, uninteresting, colourless, uninspiring, vapid, wooden; spiritless, lethargic, enervated, exhausted.

lifelike /lī́flīk/ *adj.* closely resembling the person or thing represented. □□ **lifelikeness** *n.*
■ authentic, realistic, natural, naturalistic, true to life, real, faithful, animated, lively, graphic, vivid.

lifeline /lī́flīn/ *n.* **1 a** a rope etc. used for life-saving, e.g. that attached to a lifebuoy. **b** a diver's signalling line. **2** a sole means of communication or transport. **3** a fold in the palm of the hand, regarded as significant in palmistry. **4** an emergency telephone counselling service.

lifelong /lī́flong/ *adj.* lasting a lifetime.
■ see LASTING.

lifer /lī́fər/ *n. sl.* a person serving a life sentence.

lifestyle /lī́fstīl/ *n.* the particular way of life of a person or group.
■ see CULTURE *n.* 2.

lifetime /lī́ftīm/ *n.* **1** the duration of a person's life. **2** the duration of a thing or its usefulness. **3** *colloq.* an exceptionally long time. □ **of a lifetime** such as does not occur more than once in a person's life (*the chance of a lifetime*; *the journey of a lifetime*).
■ **1, 2** see LIFE 3.

lift /lift/ *v.* & *n.* ● *v.* **1** *tr.* (often foll. by *up*, *off*, *out*, etc.) raise or remove to a higher position. **2** *intr.* go up; be raised; yield to an upward force (*the window will not lift*). **3** *tr.* give an upward direction to (the eyes or face). **4** *tr.* **a** elevate to a higher plane of thought or feeling (*the news lifted their spirits*). **b** make less heavy or dull; add interest to (something esp. artistic). **c** enhance, improve (*lifted their game after half-time*). **5** *intr.* (of a cloud, fog, etc.) rise, disperse. **6** *tr.* remove (a barrier or restriction). **7** *tr.* transport (supplies, troops, etc.) by air. **8** *tr. colloq.* **a** steal. **b** plagiarize (a passage of writing etc.). **9** *Phonet.* **a** *tr.* make louder; raise the pitch of. **b** *intr.* (of the voice) rise. **10** *tr.* dig up (esp. potatoes etc. at harvest). **11** *intr.* (of a floor) swell upwards, bulge. **12** *tr.* hold or have on high (*the church lifts its spire*). **13** *tr.* hit (a cricket-ball) into the air. **14** *tr.* (usu. in *passive*) perform cosmetic surgery on (esp. the face or breasts) to reduce sagging. ● *n.* **1** the act of lifting or process of being lifted. **2** a free ride in another person's vehicle (*gave them a lift*). **3 a** *Brit.* a platform or compartment housed in a shaft for raising and lowering persons or things to different floors of a building or different levels of a mine etc. **b** a similar apparatus for carrying persons up or down a mountain etc. (see *ski-lift*). **4 a** transport by air (see AIRLIFT *n.*). **b** a quantity of goods transported by air. **5** the upward pressure which air exerts on an aerofoil to counteract the force of gravity. **6** a supporting or elevating influence; a feeling of elation. **7** a layer of leather in the heel of a boot or shoe, esp. to correct shortening of a leg or increase height. **8 a** a rise in the level of the ground. **b** the extent to which water rises in a canal lock. □ **lift down** pick up and bring to a lower position. **lift a finger** (or **hand** etc.) (in *neg.*) make the slightest effort (*didn't lift a finger to help*). **lift off** (of a spacecraft or rocket) rise from the launching pad. **lift-off** *n.* the vertical take-off of a spacecraft or rocket. **lift up one's head** hold one's head high with pride. **lift up one's voice** sing out. □□ **liftable** *adj.* **lifter** *n.* [ME f. ON *lypta* f. Gmc]
■ *v.* **1** raise, elevate; hoist (up), heave (up), pull up, lever, put *or* pick up. **2** see RISE *v.* 1. **3** raise, elevate, tilt (upwards). **4 a** raise, elevate, dignify, ennoble, uplift, upgrade, promote, advance, exalt, *colloq.* boost. **b** enliven, liven up, brighten, lighten, (re)vitalize, enhance, improve, jazz up, *colloq.* pep up. **c** enhance, improve, raise, make better, *formal* ameliorate. **5** rise, disperse, disappear, dissipate, disintegrate, vanish, break up, float away. **6** remove, raise, discontinue, end, terminate, stop, cease, put an end to, put a stop to; take away, get rid of, shift, transfer, withdraw, cancel, rescind, void, annul. **7** airlift. **8 a** steal, appropriate, pilfer, pocket, thieve, take, *formal or joc.* purloin, *sl.* pinch, liberate, *Brit. sl.* nick, *rhyming sl.* half-inch. **b** copy, imitate, plagiarize, appropriate, steal, pirate, *formal or joc.* purloin; abstract, borrow, *colloq.* crib, *sl.* pinch. **9 a** amplify, louden, make louder, increase; raise. **b** rise, go up. ● *n.* **1** raising, elevation, rise, increase, improvement; hoist, push, shove, heave, uplift. **2** ride, *colloq.* hitch. **3 a** *US* elevator. **4** airlift. **6** encouragement, stimulus, uplift, inducement, inspiration, hope, reassurance, cheering up, *colloq.* shot in the arm, boost. **8** incline, inclination, elevation, climb, rise, slope. □ **lift a finger** (or **hand**) make any attempt *or* effort, make a move, do one's part, do anything, contribute. **lift off** see *take off* 6. **lift-off** see *take-off* 1.

ligament /líggəmənt/ *n.* **1** *Anat.* **a** a short band of tough flexible fibrous connective tissue linking bones together. **b** any membranous fold keeping an organ in position. **2** *archaic* a bond of union. □□ **ligamental** /-mént'l/ *adj.* **ligamentary** /-méntəri/ *adj.* **ligamentous** /-méntəss/ *adj.* [ME f. L *ligamentum* bond f. *ligare* bind]
■ **1** sinew, tendon, *Anat.* vinculum, *Physiol.* bridle.

ligand /líggənd/ *n. Chem.* an ion or molecule attached to a metal atom by covalent bonding in which both electrons are supplied by one atom. [L *ligandus* gerundive of *ligare* bind]

ligate /ligáyt/ *v.tr. Surgery* tie up (a bleeding artery etc.). □□ **ligation** *n.* [L *ligare ligat-*]

ligature /líggəchər/ *n.* & *v.* ● *n.* **1** a tie or bandage, esp. in surgery for a bleeding artery etc. **2** *Mus.* a slur; a tie. **3** *Printing* two or more letters joined, e.g. *æ*. **4** a bond; a thing that unites. **5** the act of tying or binding. ● *v.tr.* bind or connect with a ligature. [ME f. LL *ligatura* f. L *ligare ligat-* tie, bind]
■ **1** see TIE *n.* 1. **2** see TIE *n.* 7.

liger /lī́gər/ *n.* the offspring of a lion and a tigress (cf. TIGON). [portmanteau word f. LION + TIGER]

light[1] /līt/ *n.*, *v.*, & *adj.* ● *n.* **1** the natural agent (electromagnetic radiation of wavelength between about 390 and 740 nm) that stimulates sight and makes things visible. **2** the medium or condition of the space in which this is present. **3** an appearance of brightness (*saw a distant light*). **4 a** a source of light, e.g. the sun, or a lamp, fire, etc. **b** (in *pl.*) illuminations. **5** (often in *pl.*) a traffic-light (*went through a red light*; *stop at the lights*). **6 a** the amount or quality of illumination in a place (*bad light stopped play*). **b** one's fair or usual share of this (*you are standing in my light*). **7 a** a flame or spark serving to ignite (*struck a light*). **b** a device producing this (*have you got a light?*). **8** the aspect in which a thing is regarded or considered (*appeared in a new light*). **9 a** mental illumination; elucidation, enlightenment. **b** hope, happiness; a happy outcome. **c** spiritual illumination by divine truth. **10** vivacity, enthusiasm, or inspiration visible in a person's face, esp. in the eyes. **11** (in *pl.*) a person's mental powers or ability (*according to one's lights*). **12** an eminent person (*a leading light*). **13 a** the bright part of a thing; a highlight. **b** the bright parts of a picture etc. esp. suggesting illumination (*light and shade*). **14 a** a window or opening in a wall to let light in. **b** the perpendicular division of a mullioned window. **c** a pane of glass esp. in the side or roof of a greenhouse. **15** (in a crossword etc.) each of the items filling a space and to be deduced from the clues. **16** *Law* the light falling on windows, the obstruction of which by a neighbour is illegal. ● *v.* (*past* **lit** /lit/; *past part.* **lit** or (*attrib.*) **lighted**) **1** *tr.* & *intr.* set burning or begin to burn; ignite. **2** *tr.* provide with light or lighting. **3** *tr.* show (a person) the way or surroundings with a light. **4** *intr.* (usu. foll. by *up*) (of the face or eyes) brighten with animation. ● *adj.* **1** well provided with light; not dark. **2** (of a colour) pale (*light blue*; *a light-blue ribbon*). □ **bring** (or **come**) **to light** reveal or be revealed. **festival of lights 1** = HANUKKAH. **2** = DIWALI. **in a good** (or **bad**) **light** giving a favourable (or unfavourable) impression. **in** (the) **light of** having regard to; drawing information from. **light-bulb** a glass bulb containing an inert gas and a metal filament, providing light when an electric current is passed through. **lighting-up time** the time during or after which vehicles on the road must show the prescribed lights. **light meter** an instrument for measuring the intensity of the light, esp.

to show the correct photographic exposure. **light of day 1** daylight, sunlight. **2** general notice; public attention. **light of one's life** usu. *joc.* a much-loved person. **light-pen** (or **-gun**) **1** a penlike or gunlike photosensitive device held to the screen of a computer terminal for passing information on to it. **2** a light-emitting device used for reading bar-codes. **light show** a display of changing coloured lights for entertainment. **light up 1** *colloq.* begin to smoke a cigarette etc. **2** switch on lights or lighting; illuminate a scene. **light-year 1** *Astron.* the distance light travels in one year, nearly 6 million million miles. **2** (in *pl.*) *colloq.* a long distance or great amount. **lit up** *colloq.* drunk. **out like a light** deeply asleep or unconscious. **throw** (or **shed**) **light on** help to explain. □□ **lightish** *adj.* **lightless** *adj.* **lightness** *n.* [OE *lēoht, līht, līhtan* f. Gmc]

■ *n.* **2** illumination, brightness, brilliance, radiance, luminosity; daylight, lamplight, candlelight, firelight, gaslight, torchlight, starlight, moonlight, sunshine, sun, sunlight. **3** beam, ray, shaft of light, brilliance, brightness, radiance, radiation, luminescence, glare, gleam, glow, reflection, luminosity, shine, shining, sparkle, scintillation, incandescence, phosphorescence, fluorescence. **4 a** lamp, light-bulb, bulb, torch, illuminant, beacon, lantern, candle, sun, star, flame, blaze, flare, headlight, headlamp, street-light, street lamp, *US* flashlight. **b** (*lights*) illuminations, light show, *son et lumière*. **5** (*lights*) traffic light(s), traffic signal(s), signals, stop light(s). **7** match, lighter, spill, taper, fire, flame, ignition. **8** see ASPECT 1b. **9 a** elucidaton, enlightenment, illumination, clarification, edification, insight, awareness, understanding, simplification, explanation. **b** see HOPE *n.* 2, *happiness* (HAPPY). ● *v.* **1** turn on, switch on, put on; set alight, set *or* put a match to, kindle, touch off, set fire to, set burning, fire; ignite; come on. **2** illuminate, light up, cast light on *or* upon, lighten, brighten, *literary* illumine, *poet.* illume. **3** direct, guide, escort, pilot. **4** (*light up*) lighten, brighten, cheer up, liven up, perk up. ● *adj.* **1** (well-)illuminated, bright, alight, (well-)lit, (well-)lighted, shining, luminous, brilliant, beaming, incandescent, phosphorescent, fluorescent, sunny, *literary* effulgent. **2** pale, light-hued, pastel, faded, subdued, washed-out. □ **bring** (or **come**) **to light** reveal, unearth, find, uncover, unveil, discover, expose, disclose, make known; be revealed, be unearthed, be uncovered, be unveiled, be discovered, be exposed, be disclosed, appear, come out, turn up, transpire, develop, evolve, emerge. **in** (**the**) **light of** having regard to, considering, in view of, in consideration of, taking into account, keeping *or* bearing in mind, paying attention to. **light show** see LIGHT[1] *n.* 4b above. **out like a light** see UNCONSCIOUS *adj.* **throw** (or **shed**) **light on** explain, elucidate, simplify, clarify, clear up.

light[2] /līt/ *adj., adv.,* & *v.* ● *adj.* **1** of little weight; not heavy; easy to lift. **2 a** relatively low in weight, amount, density, intensity, etc. (*light arms; light traffic; light metal; light rain; a light breeze*). **b** deficient in weight (*light coin*). **c** (of an isotope etc.) having not more than the usual mass. **3 a** carrying or suitable for small loads (*light aircraft; light railway*). **b** (of a ship) unladen. **c** carrying only light arms, armaments, etc. (*light brigade; light infantry*). **d** (of a locomotive) with no train attached. **4 a** (of food, a meal, etc.) small in amount; easy to digest (*had a light lunch*). **b** (of drink) not heavy on the stomach or strongly alcoholic. **5 a** (of entertainment, music, etc.) intended for amusement, rather than edification; not profound. **b** frivolous, thoughtless, trivial (*a light remark*). **6** (of sleep or a sleeper) easily disturbed. **7** easily borne or done (*light duties*). **8** nimble; quick-moving (*a light step; light of foot; a light rhythm*). **9** (of a building etc.) graceful, elegant, delicate. **10** (of type) not heavy or bold. **11 a** free from sorrow; cheerful (*a light heart*). **b** giddy (*light in the head*). **12** (of soil) not dense; porous. **13** (of pastry, sponge, etc.) fluffy and well-aerated during cooking and with the fat fully absorbed. **14** (of a woman) unchaste or wanton; fickle. ● *adv.* **1** in a light manner (*tread light; sleep light*). **2** with a minimum load or minimum luggage (*travel light*). ● *v.intr.* (*past* and *past part.* **lit** /lit/ or **lighted**) **1** (foll. by *on, upon*) come upon or find by chance. **2** *archaic* **a** alight, descend. **b** (foll. by *on*) land on (shore etc.). □ **lighter-than-air** (of an aircraft) weighing less than the air it displaces. **light-fingered** given to stealing. **light flyweight** see FLYWEIGHT. **light-footed** nimble. **light-footedly** nimbly. **light-headed** giddy, frivolous, delirious. **light-headedly** in a light-headed manner. **light-headedness** being light-headed. **light-hearted 1** cheerful. **2** (unduly) casual, thoughtless. **light-heartedly** in a light-hearted manner. **light-heartedness** being light-hearted. **light heavyweight** see HEAVYWEIGHT. **light industry** the manufacture of small or light articles. **light into** *colloq.* attack. **light middleweight** see MIDDLEWEIGHT. **light out** *colloq.* depart. **light touch** delicate or tactful treatment. **light welterweight** see WELTERWEIGHT. **make light of** treat as unimportant. **make light work of** do a thing quickly and easily. □□ **lightish** *adj.* **lightness** *n.* [OE *lēoht, līht, līhtan* f. Gmc, the verbal sense from the idea of relieving a horse etc. of weight]

■ *adj.* **1** lightweight, portable, transportable, manageable. **2 a** faint, gentle, mild, slight, delicate, insignificant. **b** lightweight, underweight, deficient, skinny, slight, gaunt; see also LEAN[2] *adj.* 1. **4 a** small, simple, digestible, modest, moderate. **5 a** amusing, entertaining, witty, diverting, pleasing, pleasurable, humorous; lightweight, middle-of-the-road. **b** frivolous, thoughtless, trivial; see also INCONSEQUENTIAL 1. **7** easy, not burdensome, endurable, bearable, tolerable, supportable, undemanding, effortless, untaxing, moderate, manageable, *colloq.* cushy. **8** nimble, quick-moving, agile, active, swift, spry, lithe, sprightly, lightsome, buoyant, light-footed, limber, lissom, deft, quick, *colloq.* nippy. **11 a** cheerful, happy, gay, sunny, merry, light-hearted, happy-go-lucky, free and easy, untroubled, insouciant, easygoing, joyful, glad, optimistic, jovial, jolly, *poet.* blithe. **b** see DIZZY *adj.* 1a. ● *v.* **1** (*light on* or *upon*) chance *or* happen *or* stumble *or* hit (up)on, come across, encounter, find, meet up with, *colloq.* spot. □ **light-fingered** thieving; cunning, crafty, slick, furtive, dishonest, crooked. **light-footed** see LIGHT[2] *adj.* 8 above. **light-headed** see DIZZY *adj.* 1. **light-hearted** see LIGHT[2] *adj.* 11a above. **light into** assail, assault, pounce *or* fall on *or* upon, beat, belabour, *colloq.* lambaste; abuse, give a tongue-lashing to, harangue, upbraid, scold, berate, *colloq.* lace into; see also ATTACK *v.* 1, 3. **make light of** dismiss, write off, shrug off, gloss over, blink at, brush aside; trivialize; ridicule; see also DISREGARD *v.* 2, *play down*.

lighten[1] /lít'n/ *v.* **1 a** *tr.* & *intr.* make or become lighter in weight. **b** *tr.* reduce the weight or load of. **2** *tr.* bring relief to (the heart, mind, etc.). **3** *tr.* mitigate (a penalty).

■ **2** relieve, cheer (up), brighten, gladden, perk up, uplift, buoy up, hearten, comfort, reassure, restore. **3** see MITIGATE, TEMPER *v.* 2.

lighten[2] /lít'n/ *v.* **1 a** *tr.* shed light on. **b** *tr.* & *intr.* make or grow lighter or brighter. **2** *intr.* **a** shine brightly; flash. **b** emit lightning (*it is lightening*).

■ **1** illuminate, shed *or* cast light upon, brighten, light up, *literary* illumine, *poet.* illume.

lightening /lít'ning/ *n.* a drop in the level of the womb during the last weeks of pregnancy.

lighter[1] /lítər/ *n.* a device for lighting cigarettes etc.

■ see LIGHT[1] *n.* 7.

lighter[2] /lítər/ *n.* a boat, usu. flat-bottomed, for transferring goods from a ship to a wharf or another ship. [ME f. MDu. *lichter* (as LIGHT[2] in the sense 'unload')]

lighterage /lítərij/ *n.* **1** the transference of cargo by means of a lighter. **2** a charge made for this.

lighterman /lítərmən/ *n.* (*pl.* **-men**) a person who works on a lighter.

lighthouse /lít-howss/ *n.* a tower or other structure containing a beacon light to warn or guide ships at sea.

■ see BEACON 1a, 2.

lighting /līting/ *n.* **1** equipment in a room or street etc. for producing light. **2** the arrangement or effect of lights.
■ **2** see *illumination* (ILLUMINATE).

lightly /lītli/ *adv.* in a light (esp. frivolous or unserious) manner. □ **get off lightly** escape with little or no punishment. **take lightly** not be serious about (a thing).

lightning /lītning/ *n.* & *adj.* ● *n.* a flash of bright light produced by an electric discharge between clouds or between clouds and the ground. ● *attrib.adj.* very quick (*with lightning speed*). □ **lightning-conductor** (or **-rod**) a metal rod or wire fixed to an exposed part of a building or to a mast to divert lightning into the earth or sea. **lightning strike** a strike by workers at short notice, esp. without official union backing. [ME, differentiated from *lightening*, verbal noun f. LIGHTEN[2]]
■ *n.* see BOLT[1] *n.* 3. ● *attrib.adj.* see RAPID *adj.* 1, 2.

lightproof /lītpro͞of/ *adj.* able to resist the harmful effects of (esp. excessive) light.

lights /līts/ *n.pl.* the lungs of sheep, pigs, bullocks, etc., used as a food esp. for pets. [ME, noun use of LIGHT[2]: cf. LUNG]

lightship /lītship/ *n.* a moored or anchored ship with a beacon light.

lightsome /lītsəm/ *adj.* gracefully light; nimble; merry. □□ **lightsomely** *adv.* **lightsomeness** *n.*
■ see LIGHT[2] *adj.* 8.

lightweight /lītwayt/ *adj.* & *n.* ● *adj.* **1** (of a person, animal, garment, etc.) of below average weight. **2** of little importance or influence. ● *n.* **1** a lightweight person, animal, or thing. **2 a** a weight in certain sports intermediate between featherweight and welterweight, in the amateur boxing scale 57–60 kg but differing for professionals, wrestlers, and weightlifters. **b** a sportsman of this weight. □ **junior lightweight 1** a weight in professional boxing of 57.1–59 kg. **2** a professional boxer of this weight.
■ *adj.* **1** see LIGHT[2] *adj.* 1. **2** see INCONSEQUENTIAL 1. ● *n.* **1** see WEAKLING *n.*

lightwood /lītwo͝od/ *n.* **1** a tree with a light wood. **2** *US* wood or a tree with wood that burns with a bright flame.

ligneous /ligniəss/ *adj.* **1** (of a plant) woody (opp. HERBACEOUS). **2** of the nature of wood. [L *ligneus* (as LIGNI-)]
■ see WOODEN 1.

ligni- /ligni/ *comb. form* wood. [L *lignum* wood]

lignify /lignifī/ *v.tr.* & *intr.* (**-ies, -ied**) *Bot.* make or become woody by the deposition of lignin.

lignin /lignin/ *n. Bot.* a complex organic polymer deposited in the cell-walls of many plants making them rigid and woody. [as LIGNI- + -IN]

lignite /lignīt/ *n.* a soft brown coal showing traces of plant structure, intermediate between bituminous coal and peat. □□ **lignitic** /-nittik/ *adj.* [F (as LIGNI-, -ITE[1])]

lignocaine /lignəkayn/ *n. Pharm.* a local anaesthetic for the gums, mucous membranes, or skin, usu. given by injection. [*ligno-* (as LIGNI-) for XYLO- + COCA + -INE[4]]

lignum vitae /lignəm vīti, veetī/ *n.* = GUAIACUM 2a. [L, = wood of life]

ligroin /ligrō-in/ *n. Chem.* a volatile hydrocarbon mixture obtained from petroleum and used as a solvent. [20th c.: orig. unkn.]

ligulate /ligyoolət/ *adj. Bot.* having strap-shaped florets. [formed as LIGULE + -ATE[2]]

ligule /ligyo͞ol/ *n. Bot.* a narrow projection from the top of a leaf-sheath of a grass. [L *ligula* strap, spoon f. *lingere* lick]

ligustrum /ligústrəm/ *n.* = PRIVET. [L]

likable var. of LIKEABLE.

like[1] /līk/ *adj., prep., adv., conj.,* & *n.* ● *adj.* (often governing a noun as if a transitive participle such as *resembling*) (**more like, most like**) **1 a** having some or all of the qualities of another or each other or an original; alike (*in like manner*; *as like as two peas*; *is very like her brother*). **b** resembling in some way, such as; in the same class as (*good writers like Dickens*). **c** (usu. in pairs correlatively) as one is so will the other be (*like mother, like daughter*). **2** characteristic of (*it is not like them to be late*). **3** in a suitable state or mood for (doing or having something) (*felt like working*; *felt like a cup of tea*). ● *prep.* in the manner of; to the same degree as (*drink like a fish*; *sell like hot cakes*; *acted like an idiot*). ● *adv.* **1** *archaic* likely (*they will come, like enough*). **2** *archaic* in the same manner (foll. by *as*: *sang like as a nightingale*). **3** *sl.* so to speak (*did a quick getaway, like*; *as I said, like, I'm no Shakespeare*). ● *conj. colloq. disp.* **1** as (*cannot do it like you do*). **2** as if (*ate like they were starving*). ● *n.* **1** a counterpart; an equal; a similar person or thing (*shall not see its like again*; *compare like with like*). **2** (prec. by *the*) a thing or things of the same kind (*will never do the like again*). □ **and the like** and similar things; et cetera (*music, painting, and the like*). **be nothing like** (usu. with compl.) be in no way similar or comparable or adequate. **like anything** see ANYTHING. **like** (or **as like**) **as not** *colloq.* probably. **like-minded** having the same tastes, opinions, etc. **like-mindedly** in accordance with the same tastes etc. **like-mindedness** being like-minded. **like so** *colloq.* like this; in this manner. **the likes of** *colloq.* a person such as. **more like it** *colloq.* nearer what is required. [ME *līc, līk*, shortened form of OE *gelīc* ALIKE]
■ *adj.*. **1 a** similar (to), akin (to), allied (to), parallel (to *or* with), comparable (to *or* with), equivalent (to), equal (to), identical (to), cognate (with), analogous (to), correspondent (to), close (to), homologous (to *or* with), of a piece (with), (much) the same (as), along the same lines (as), not unlike, *archaic* corresponding (to). **b** resembling, in the same class as, comparable to *or* with; such as, for example, e.g., for instance. **2** typical of, in character of *or* with, indicative of, representative of, illustrative of. **3** in the mood for *or* to, disposed to, inclined to, willing to, eager for *or* to, anxious to. ● *prep.* similar to, identical to *or* with, in the same way as, in *or* after the manner of, similarly to, after the fashion of, along the same lines as. ● *adv.* **1** see LIKELY *adv.* **2** so to speak, as it were, in a way, somehow, in some way or another. ● *conj.* **1** as, just as, in the same way as. **2** as if, as though. ● *n.* **1** match, equal, peer, fellow, counterpart, twin, equivalent. **2** (*the like*) the same kind *or* sort *or* ilk *or* type *or* kidney *or* breed *or* mould *or* cast *or* strain of thing, a similar kind *or* sort *or* ilk *or* type *or* kidney *or* breed *or* mould *or* cast *or* strain of thing. □ **and the like** see *and all the rest* (REST[2]). **like as not** see LIKELY *adv.* **like-minded** see UNITED *adj.* 3. **like-mindedness** see UNITY 2. **like so** see THUS 1.

like[2] /līk/ *v.* & *n.* ● *v.tr.* **1 a** find agreeable or enjoyable or satisfactory (*like reading*; *like the sea*; *like to dance*). **b** be fond of (a person). **2 a** choose to have; prefer (*like my coffee black*; *do not like such things discussed*). **b** wish for or be inclined to (*would like a cup of tea*; *should like to come*). **3** (usu. in *interrog.*; prec. by *how*) feel about; regard (*how would you like it if it happened to you?*). ● *n.* (in *pl.*) the things one likes or prefers. □ **I like that!** *iron.* as an exclamation expressing affront. **like it or not** *colloq.* whether it is acceptable or not. [OE *līcian* f. Gmc]
■ *v.* **1** be fond of, approve of, appreciate, be partial to, have a fondness for, have a liking for, have a weakness for, take to, delight in, take pleasure in, derive *or* get pleasure from, find agreeable *or* congenial, be *or* feel attracted to, be *or* feel favourably impressed by, relish, love, adore, adulate, *colloq.* fancy, take a shine to, get a kick out of, *sl.* dig, get off on, groove on, get a charge out of, get a buzz from, *US sl.* get a bang from *or* out of. **2** prefer, choose, go for, want, feel inclined to have, have (half) a mind to have, rather *or* sooner have, wish, desire. ● *n.* (*likes*) preference(s), favourite(s), *colloq.* thing, cup of tea, *sl.* bag; see also WEAKNESS 4.

-like /līk/ *comb. form* forming adjectives from nouns, meaning 'similar to, characteristic of' (*doglike*; *shell-like*; *tortoise-like*). ¶ In formations intended as nonce-words, or not generally current, the hyphen should be used. It may be omitted when the first element is of one syllable, but nouns in *-l* always require it.

likeable /líkəb'l/ *adj.* (also **likable**) pleasant; easy to like. □□ **likeableness** *n.* **likeably** /-bli/ *adv.*
■ genial, amiable, congenial, *simpatico*, agreeable, pleasing, attractive, appealing, nice, friendly, winning, charming, engaging, good-natured, winsome.

likelihood /líklihood/ *n.* probability; the quality or fact of being likely. □ **in all likelihood** very probably.
■ strong *or* distinct possibility, good chance, good prospect; probability, likeliness.

likely /líkli/ *adj.* & *adv.* ● *adj.* **1** probable; such as well might happen or be true (*it is not likely that they will come; the most likely place is London; a likely story*). **2** (foll. by *to* + infin.) to be reasonably expected (*he is not likely to come now*). **3** promising; apparently suitable (*this is a likely spot; three likely lads*). ● *adv.* probably (*is very likely true*). □ **as likely as not** probably. **not likely!** *colloq.* certainly not, I refuse. □□ **likeliness** *n.* [ME f. ON *líkligr* (as LIKE[1], -LY[1])]
■ *adj.* **1** probable, expected, conceivable, reasonable, credible, believable, plausible, tenable. **2** disposed, apt, inclined, odds-on, expected, on the cards, *disp.* liable. **3** fitting, suitable, probable, seemly, right, proper, qualified, acceptable, appropriate, apposite, promising, applicable, relevant, *archaic* meet. ● *adv.* probably, no doubt, in all probability, *archaic* like enough, *colloq.* (as) like as not. □ **as likely as not** see LIKELY *adv.* above.

liken /líkən/ *v.tr.* (foll. by *to*) point out the resemblance of (a person or thing to another). [ME f. LIKE[1] + -EN[1]]
■ compare, equate, match, juxtapose, associate, correlate.

likeness /líkniss/ *n.* **1** (foll. by *between, to*) resemblance. **2** (foll. by *of*) a semblance or guise (*in the likeness of a ghost*). **3** a portrait or representation (*is a good likeness*). [OE *gelīknes* (as LIKE[1], -NESS)]
■ **1** similarity, resemblance, correspondence, analogy, agreement, similitude, closeness, sameness, parallelism. **2** appearance, semblance, guise, figure, image, look, outward form, shape, style, air, cast, *literary* mien. **3** copy, replica, facsimile, duplicate, reproduction, double, look-alike, clone, spitting image, model, painting, picture, portrait, portrayal, sketch, delineation, drawing, print, photograph, sculpture, statue, statuette, image, simulacrum, icon.

likewise /líkwīz/ *adv.* **1** also, moreover, too. **2** similarly (*do likewise*). [for *in like wise*]
■ **1** also, moreover, too, as well, furthermore, further, besides, in addition, additionally, to boot. **2** the same, in like manner, in the same manner *or* way, similarly.

liking /líking/ *n.* **1** what one likes; one's taste (*is it to your liking?*). **2** (foll. by *for*) regard or fondness; taste or fancy (*had a liking for toffee*). [OE *līcung* (as LIKE[2], -ING[1])]
■ **1** taste, fancy, preference, *formal* pleasure. **2** affinity, affection, love, partiality, bias, preference, bent, predilection, predisposition, favour, fondness, inclination, propensity, appreciation, regard, taste, penchant; eye, relish, appetite, soft spot, weakness, fancy.

lilac /lílək/ *n.* & *adj.* ● *n.* **1** any shrub or small tree of the genus *Syringa*, esp. *S. vulgaris* with fragrant pale pinkish-violet or white blossoms. **2** a pale pinkish-violet colour. ● *adj.* of this colour. [obs. F f. Sp. f. Arab. *līlāk* f. Pers. *līlak*, var. of *nīlak* bluish f. *nīl* blue]

liliaceous /lílliáyshəss/ *adj.* **1** of or relating to the family Liliaceae of plants with elongated leaves growing from a corm, bulb, or rhizome, e.g. tulip, lily, or onion. **2** lily-like. [LL *liliaceus* f. L *lilium* lily]

lilliputian /líllipyóosh'n/ *n.* & *adj.* ● *n.* a diminutive person or thing. ● *adj.* diminutive. [*Lilliput* in Swift's *Gulliver's Travels*]
■ *adj.* see DIMINUTIVE *adj.* 1.

Lilo /lílō/ *n.* (*pl.* **-os**) *propr.* a type of inflatable mattress. [f. *lie low*]

lilt /lilt/ *n.* & *v.* ● *n.* **1 a** a light springing rhythm or gait. **b** a song or tune marked by this. **2** (of the voice) a characteristic cadence or inflection; a pleasant accent. ● *v.intr.* (esp. as **lilting** *adj.*) move or speak etc. with a lilt (*a lilting step; a lilting melody*). [ME *lilte, lülte*, of unkn. orig.]
■ *n.* **1 a** see RHYTHM 1, 2. ● *v.* (**lilting**) see MUSICAL *adj.* 2.

lily /lílli/ *n.* (*pl.* **-ies**) **1 a** any bulbous plant of the genus *Lilium* with large trumpet-shaped often spotted flowers on a tall slender stem, e.g. the madonna lily and tiger lily. **b** any of several other plants of the family Liliaceae with similar flowers, e.g. the African lily. **c** the water lily. **2** a person or thing of special whiteness or purity. **3** a heraldic fleur-de-lis. **4** (*attrib.*) **a** delicately white (*a lily hand*). **b** pallid. □ **lily-livered** cowardly. **lily of the valley** any liliaceous plant of the genus *Convallaria*, with oval leaves in pairs and racemes of white bell-shaped fragrant flowers. **lily-pad** a floating leaf of a water lily. **lily-white 1** as white as a lily. **2** faultless. □□ **lilied** *adj.* [OE *lilie* f. L *lilium* prob. f. Gk *leirion*]
■ □ **lily-livered** see COWARDLY *adj.* 1. **lily-white 1** see WHITE *adj.* 1. **2** see UNTARNISHED.

lima bean /léemə/ *n.* **1** a tropical American bean plant, *Phaseolus limensis*, having large flat white edible seeds. **2** the seed of this plant. [*Lima* in Peru]

limb[1] /lim/ *n.* **1** any of the projecting parts of a person's or animal's body used for contact or movement. **2** a large branch of a tree. **3** a branch of a cross. **4** a spur of a mountain. **5** a clause of a sentence. □ **out on a limb 1** isolated, stranded. **2** at a disadvantage. **tear limb from limb** violently dismember. **with life and limb** (esp. escape) without grave injury. □□ **limbed** *adj.* (also in *comb.*). **limbless** *adj.* [OE *lim* f. Gmc]
■ **1** see LEG *n.* 1, 3. **2** see BRANCH *n.* 1.

limb[2] /lim/ *n.* **1** *Astron.* **a** a specified edge of the sun, moon, etc. (*eastern limb; lower limb*). **b** the graduated edge of a quadrant etc. **2** *Bot.* the broad part of a petal, sepal, or leaf. [F *limbe* or L *limbus* hem, border]

limber[1] /límbər/ *adj.* & *v.* ● *adj.* **1** lithe, agile, nimble. **2** flexible. ● *v.* (usu. foll. by *up*) **1** *tr.* make (oneself or a part of the body etc.) supple. **2** *intr.* warm up in preparation for athletic etc. activity. □□ **limberness** *n.* [16th c.: orig. uncert.]
■ *adj.* **1** see NIMBLE 1. **2** see FLEXIBLE 1. ● *v.* see EXERCISE *v.* 3a. □□ **limberness** see *flexibility* (FLEXIBLE).

limber[2] /límbər/ *n.* & *v.* ● *n.* the detachable front part of a gun-carriage, consisting of two wheels, axle, pole, and ammunition-box. ● *v.* **1** *tr.* attach a limber to (a gun etc.). **2** *intr.* fasten together the two parts of a gun-carriage. [ME *limo(u)r*, app. rel. to med.L *limonarius* f. *limo -onis* shaft]

limbo[1] /límbō/ *n.* (*pl.* **-os**) **1** (in some Christian beliefs) the supposed abode of the souls of unbaptized infants, and of the just who died before Christ. **2** an intermediate state or condition of awaiting a decision etc. **3** prison, confinement. **4** a state of neglect or oblivion. [ME f. med.L phr. *in limbo*, f. *limbus*: see LIMB[2]]
■ **2, 4** (*in limbo*) up in the air, consigned to oblivion, in abeyance, suspended, hanging (fire), neither here nor there, on hold, treading water, holding one's breath, on the shelf, on the back burner; see also OBSCURITY 1. **3** imprisonment, prison, confinement, incarceration, internment, detention, captivity.

limbo[2] /límbō/ *n.* (*pl.* **-os**) a W. Indian dance in which the dancer bends backwards to pass under a horizontal bar which is progressively lowered to a position just above the ground. [a W. Indian word, perh. = LIMBER[1]]

Limburger /límburgər/ *n.* a soft white cheese with a characteristic strong smell, orig. made in Limburg. [Du. f. *Limburg* in Belgium]

lime[1] /līm/ *n.* & *v.* ● *n.* **1** (in full **quicklime**) a white caustic alkaline substance (calcium oxide) obtained by heating limestone and used for making mortar or as a fertilizer or bleach etc. **2** = BIRDLIME. ● *v.tr.* **1** treat (wood, skins, land, etc.) with lime. **2** *archaic* catch (a bird etc.) with birdlime. □ **lime water** an aqueous solution of calcium hydroxide used esp. to detect the presence of carbon dioxide. □□ **limeless** *adj.* **limy** *adj.* (**limier, limiest**). [OE *līm* f. Gmc, rel. to LOAM]

lime[2] /līm/ *n.* **1 a** a round citrus fruit like a lemon but greener, smaller, and more acid. **b** the tree, *Citrus aurantifolia*, bearing this. **2** (in full **lime-juice**) the juice of limes as a drink and formerly esp. as a cure for scurvy. **3** (in full **lime-green**) a pale green colour like a lime. [F f. mod.Prov. *limo*, Sp. *lima* f. Arab. *līma*: cf. LEMON]

lime[3] /līm/ *n.* **1** (in full **lime-tree**) any ornamental tree of the genus *Tilia*, esp. *T. europaea* with heart-shaped leaves and fragrant yellow blossom. Also called LINDEN. **2** the wood of this. [alt. of *line* = OE *lind* = LINDEN]

limekiln /lī́mkiln/ *n.* a kiln for heating limestone to produce quicklime.

limelight /lī́mlīt/ *n.* **1** an intense white light obtained by heating a cylinder of lime in an oxyhydrogen flame, used formerly in theatres. **2** (prec. by *the*) the full glare of publicity; the focus of attention.
■ **2** see SPOTLIGHT *n.* 3.

limepit /lī́mpit/ *n.* a pit containing lime for steeping hides to remove hair.

limerick /límmərik/ *n.* a humorous or comic form of five-line stanza with a rhyme-scheme *aabba*. [said to be from the chorus 'will you come up to Limerick?' sung between improvised verses at a gathering: f. *Limerick* in Ireland]

limestone /lī́mstōn/ *n. Geol.* a sedimentary rock composed mainly of calcium carbonate, used as building material and in the making of cement.

limewash /lī́mwosh/ *n.* a mixture of lime and water for coating walls.

Limey /lī́mi/ *n.* (*pl.* **-eys**) *US sl. offens.* a British person (orig. a sailor) or ship. [LIME[2], because of the former enforced consumption of lime-juice in the British Navy]

limit /límmit/ *n.* & *v.* ● *n.* **1** a point, line, or level beyond which something does not or may not extend or pass. **2** (often in *pl.*) the boundary of an area. **3** the greatest or smallest amount permissible or possible (*upper limit*; *lower limit*). **4** *Math.* a quantity which a function or sum of a series can be made to approach as closely as desired. ● *v.tr.* (**limited, limiting**) **1** set or serve as a limit to. **2** (foll. by *to*) restrict. □ **be the limit** *colloq.* be intolerable or extremely irritating. **off limits** *US* out of bounds. **within limits** moderately; with some degree of freedom. **without limit** with no restriction. □□ **limitable** *adj.* **limitative** /-tətiv/ *adj.* **limiter** *n.* [ME f. L *limes limitis* boundary, frontier]
■ *n.* **1, 2** extent, end, limitation, check, curb, restriction, restraint; border, edge, boundary, bound(s), (boundary *or* border *or* partition) line, frontier, perimeter, periphery, fringe, verge, margin; area, ambit, territory, confines, zone, region, quarter, district, precinct(s). ● *v.* **1** check, curb, bridle, restrict, restrain, hold in check. **2** restrict, confine, delimit, narrow, focus, guide, channel; set, define, determine, fix. □ **be the limit** be the end, be the last straw, be the straw that broke the camel's back, be all (that) one can take, be (more than) enough, be too much, *colloq.* be it. **off limits** see TABOO *adj.* **within limits** see *moderately* (MODERATE).

limitary /límmitəri/ *adj.* **1** subject to restriction. **2** of, on, or serving as a limit.

limitation /límmitáysh'n/ *n.* **1** the act or an instance of limiting; the process of being limited. **2** a condition of limited ability (often in *pl.*: *know one's limitations*). **3** a limiting rule or circumstance (often in *pl.*: *has its limitations*). **4** a legally specified period beyond which an action cannot be brought, or a property right is not to continue. [ME f. L *limitatio* (as LIMIT)]
■ **1** see CHECK[1] *n.* 2c. **3** see QUALIFICATION 3a.

limited /límmitid/ *adj.* **1** confined within limits. **2** not great in scope or talents (*has limited experience*). **3 a** few, scanty, restricted (*limited accommodation*). **b** restricted to a few examples (*limited edition*). □ **limited** (or **limited liability**) **company** a company whose owners are legally responsible only to a limited amount for its debts. **limited liability** *Brit.* the status of being legally responsible only to a limited amount for debts of a trading company. □□ **limitedly** *adv.* **limitedness** *n.*
■ **1** confined, circumscribed, restricted, fixed, predetermined, determinate, finite, checked, curbed, constrained. **2, 3a** narrow, restrictive, restricted, meagre, sparing; small, little, few, scanty, reduced, minimal; unimaginative, unperceptive, slow-witted, dull, thick, slow, stupid.

limitless /límmitliss/ *adj.* **1** extending or going on indefinitely (*a limitless expanse*). **2** unlimited (*limitless generosity*). □□ **limitlessly** *adv.* **limitlessness** *n.*
■ unlimited, unrestricted, unrestrained, unconfined, unbounded, boundless, uncircumscribed, extensive, vast, immense, enormous, illimitable; endless, interminable, never-ending, inexhaustible, unceasing, incessant, undefined, immeasurable, innumerable, numberless, incalculable, countless, unending, perpetual, everlasting, eternal, *literary* myriad.

limn /lim/ *v.tr.* **1** *archaic* paint (esp. a miniature portrait). **2** *hist.* illuminate (manuscripts). □□ **limner** *n.* [obs. *lumine* illuminate f. OF *luminer* f. L *luminare*: see LUMEN]
■ **1** see PAINT *v.* 2.

limnology /limnólləji/ *n.* the study of the physical phenomena of lakes and other fresh waters. □□ **limnological** /-nəlójik'l/ *adj.* **limnologist** *n.* [Gk *limnē* lake + -LOGY]

limo /límmō/ *n.* (*pl.* **-os**) *US colloq.* a limousine. [abbr.]

limousine /límmoozeén/ *n.* a large luxurious motor car, often with a partition behind the driver. [F, orig. a caped cloak worn in the former French province of *Limousin*]

limp[1] /limp/ *v.* & *n.* ● *v.intr.* **1** walk lamely. **2** (of a damaged ship, aircraft, etc.) proceed with difficulty. **3** (of verse) be defective. ● *n.* a lame walk. □□ **limper** *n.* **limpingly** *adv.* [rel. to obs. *limphalt* lame, OE *lemp-healt*]
■ *v.* **1** hobble, stagger, totter, dodder, falter. ● *n.* hobble, stagger, totter; hobbling, staggering, tottering, doddering, faltering, *Med.* claudication.

limp[2] /limp/ *adj.* **1** not stiff or firm; easily bent. **2** without energy or will. **3** (of a book) having a soft cover. □ **limp-wristed** *sl.* homosexual or effeminate; weak, feeble. □□ **limply** *adv.* **limpness** *n.* [18th c.: orig. unkn.: perh. rel. to LIMP[1] in the sense 'hanging loose']
■ **1** slack, soft, drooping, floppy, loose, lax, flexible, pliable; relaxed, flaccid, flabby. **2** exhausted, tired, fatigued, worn out, spent, enervated, wasted, debilitated, frail; weak, feeble; half-hearted, lukewarm, spineless, namby-pamby, wishy-washy, *colloq.* gutless.

limpet /límpit/ *n.* **1** any of various marine gastropod molluscs, esp. the common limpet *Patella vulgata*, with a shallow conical shell and a broad muscular foot that sticks tightly to rocks. **2** a clinging person. □ **limpet mine** a mine designed to be attached to a ship's hull and set to explode after a certain time. [OE *lempedu* f. med.L *lampreda* limpet, LAMPREY]

limpid /límpid/ *adj.* **1** (of water, eyes, etc.) clear, transparent. **2** (of writing) clear and easily comprehended. □□ **limpidity** /-pídditi/ *n.* **limpidly** *adv.* **limpidness** *n.* [F *limpide* or L *limpidus*, perh. rel. to LYMPH]
■ **1** see CLEAR *adj.* 3a. □□ **limpidity** see CLARITY.

linage /lī́nij/ *n.* **1** the number of lines in printed or written matter. **2** payment by the line.

linchpin /línchpin/ *n.* **1** a pin passed through an axle-end to keep a wheel in position. **2** a person or thing vital to an enterprise, organization, etc. [ME *linch* f. OE *lynis* + PIN]
■ **2** see MAINSTAY 1.

Lincoln green /língkən/ *n.* a bright green cloth of a kind orig. made at Lincoln in E. England.

Lincs. *abbr.* Lincolnshire.

linctus /língktəss/ *n.* a syrupy medicine, esp. a soothing cough mixture. [L f. *lingere* lick]

lindane /líndayn/ *n. Chem.* a colourless crystalline chlorinated derivative of cyclohexane used as an insecticide. [T. van der *Linden*, Du. chemist b. 1884]

linden /líndən/ *n.* a lime-tree. [(orig. adj.) f. OE *lind* lime-tree: cf. LIME[3]]

line[1] /līn/ *n.* & *v.* ● *n.* **1** a continuous mark or band made on a surface (*drew a line*). **2** use of lines in art, esp. draughtsmanship or engraving (*boldness of line*). **3** a thing resembling such a mark, esp. a furrow or wrinkle. **4** *Mus.* **a** each of (usu. five) horizontal marks forming a stave in musical notation. **b** a sequence of notes or tones forming an instrumental or vocal melody. **5 a** a straight or curved continuous extent of length without breadth. **b** the track of a moving point. **6 a** a contour or outline, esp. as a feature of design (*admired the sculpture's clean lines; this year's line is full at the back; the ship's lines*). **b** a facial feature (*the cruel line of his mouth*). **7 a** (on a map or graph) a curve connecting all points having a specified common property. **b** (**the Line**) the Equator. **8 a** a limit or boundary. **b** a mark limiting the area of play, the starting or finishing point in a race, etc. **c** the boundary between a credit and a debit in an account. **9 a** a row of persons or things. **b** a direction as indicated by them (*line of march*). **c** *US* a queue. **10 a** a row of printed or written words. **b** a portion of verse written in one line. **11** (in *pl.*) **a** a piece of poetry. **b** the words of an actor's part. **c** a specified amount of text etc. to be written out as a school punishment. **12** a short letter or note (*drop me a line*). **13** (in *pl.*) = *marriage lines*. **14** a length of cord, rope, wire, etc., usu. serving a specified purpose, esp. a fishing-line or clothes-line. **15 a** a wire or cable for a telephone or telegraph. **b** a connection by means of this (*am trying to get a line*). **16 a** a single track of a railway. **b** one branch or route of a railway system, or the whole system under one management. **17 a** a regular succession of buses, ships, aircraft, etc., plying between certain places. **b** a company conducting this (*shipping line*). **18** a connected series of persons following one another in time (esp. several generations of a family); stock, succession (*a long line of craftsmen; next in line to the throne*). **19 a** a course or manner of procedure, conduct, thought, etc. (*did it along these lines; don't take that line with me*). **b** policy (*the party line*). **c** conformity (*bring them into line*). **20** a direction, course, or channel (*lines of communication*). **21** a department of activity; a province; a branch of business (*not in my line*). **22** a class of commercial goods (*a new line in hats*). **23** *colloq.* a false or exaggerated account or story; a dishonest approach (*gave me a line about missing the bus*). **24 a** a connected series of military fieldworks, defences, etc. (*behind enemy lines*). **b** an arrangement of soldiers or ships side by side; a line of battle (*ship of the line*). **c** (prec. by *the*) regular army regiments (not auxiliary forces or Guards). **25** each of the very narrow horizontal sections forming a television picture. **26** a narrow range of the spectrum that is noticeably brighter or darker than the adjacent parts. **27** the level of the base of most letters in printing and writing. **28** (as a measure) one twelfth of an inch. ● *v.* **1** *tr.* mark with lines. **2** *tr.* cover with lines (*a face lined with pain*). **3** *tr.* & *intr.* position or stand at intervals along (*crowds lined the route*). □ **all along the line** at every point. **bring into line** make conform. **come into line** conform. **end of the line** the point at which further effort is unproductive or one can go no further. **get a line on** *colloq.* learn something about. **in line for** likely to receive. **in the line of** in the course of (esp. duty). **in** (or **out of**) **line with** in (or not in) alignment or accordance with. **lay** (or **put**) **it on the line** speak frankly. **line-drawing** a drawing in which images are produced from variations of lines. **line of fire** the expected path of gunfire, a missile, etc. **line of force** *Physics* an imaginary line which represents the strength and direction of a magnetic, gravitational, or electric field at any point. **line of march** the route taken in marching. **line of vision** the straight line along which an observer looks. **line-out** (in Rugby Football) parallel lines of opposing forwards at right angles to the touchline for the throwing in of the ball. **line printer** a machine that prints output from a computer a line at a time rather than character by character. **line up 1** arrange or be arranged in a line or lines. **2** have ready; organize (*had a job lined up*). **line-up** *n.* **1** a line of people for inspection. **2** an arrangement of persons in a team or nations etc. in an alliance. **on the line 1** at risk (*put my reputation on the line*). **2** speaking on the telephone. **3** (of a picture in an exhibition) hung with its centre about level with the spectator's eye. **out of line 1** not in alignment; discordant. **2** inappropriate; (of behaviour etc.) improper. **step out of line** behave inappropriately. [ME *line*, *ligne* f. OF *ligne* ult. f. L *linea* f. *linum* flax, & f. OE *līne* rope, series]

■ *n.* **1** stroke, score; rule, underline, underscore; diagonal, slash, virgule, solidus, oblique, *hist.* shilling-mark. **3** wrinkle, crease, crinkle, furrow, crow's-foot. **6** outline, contour, silhouette, profile. **8a** border, borderline, limit, boundary, frontier, edge; demarcation line; threshold. **9a** row, strip, belt, band, train, column, rank, file; *Brit. colloq.* crocodile. **c** row, *esp. Brit.* queue; *Brit.* tailback. **11b** (*lines*) part, role, script, words. **12** note, card, postcard, letter, *US* postal card. **14** cord, string, wire, rope, cable, *Naut.* hawser. **16b** railway, *esp. US* railroad. **17b** company, firm; see also BUSINESS 8. **18** succession, series; ancestry, descent, stock, lineage, family, parentage, extraction, genealogy, clan, tribe; tradition. **19a** course, direction, path, way, route, road, track, procedure, tack, policy, game, strategy, tactic(s), approach, plan. **b** (party) policy, strategy, approach, plan; see also PLATFORM 6. **c** conformity, harmony, agreement, accord, keeping, consistency; obedience. **21** department, province, field, area, activity, forte, speciality, specialization, *esp. US* specialty; branch of business, profession, (line of) work, job, *colloq.* racket. **22** stock, brand, make, type, kind, variety. **23** story, (sales) pitch, *sl.* spiel. **24b** formation; vanguard, *Mil.* front (line). ● *v.* **1** rule, inscribe, score, underline, underscore; contour, hatch, cross-hatch. **2** furrow, wrinkle, crease. **3** edge, border, fringe. □ **get a line on** see LEARN 4, 5, UNDERSTAND 1, 2. **in line for** likely to receive, ready for, up for, being considered for, under consideration for, a candidate for, in the running for, *Brit.* short-listed for, on the short list for. **in** (or **out of**) **line with** (*in line with*) in alignment with, aligned with, true to, plumb *or* flush with; in agreement *or* accord *or* accordance *or* conformity *or* step *or* harmony with, harmonious with; (*out of line with*) out of alignment with, not aligned with, misaligned with, out of true *or* balance with; out of step with, inconsistent with, discrepant *or* disparate *or* different from, contrary to. **line up 1** align, array, straighten, order; form a line, get in line, form ranks *or* columns, *esp. Brit.* queue (up), *US* stand on line. **2** organize, prepare, ready, assemble, set up, put *or* set in place, develop, formulate, arrange (for), coordinate; secure, get (hold of), obtain, contract for; uncover, dig up, acquire, engage, hire, sign (up), contract with, employ.

line[2] /līn/ *v.tr.* **1 a** cover the inside surface of (a garment, box, etc.) with a layer of usu. different material. **b** serve as a lining for. **2** cover as if with a lining (*shelves lined with books*). **3** *colloq.* fill, esp. plentifully. □ **line one's pocket** (or **purse**) make money, usu. by corrupt means. [ME f. obs. *line* flax, with ref. to the use of linen for linings]

■ **1** interline, cover, face. **2, 3** fill, pack, pad, cram, crowd. □ **line one's pocket** make money, accept bribes, *colloq.* graft, be on the make.

lineage /línni-ij/ *n.* lineal descent; ancestry, pedigree. [ME f. OF *linage*, *lignage* f. Rmc f. L *linea* LINE[1]]

■ extraction, ancestry, family tree, pedigree, descent, stock, line, bloodline, parentage, genealogy; forebears, forefathers, family, people, clan, tribe; descendants, succession, progeny, offspring.

lineal /línniəl/ *adj.* **1** in the direct line of descent or ancestry. **2** linear; of or in lines. □□ **lineally** *adv.* [ME f. OF f. LL *linealis* (as LINE[1])]

■ **1** see DIRECT *adj.* 4.

lineament /línniəmənt/ *n.* (usu. in *pl.*) a distinctive feature or characteristic, esp. of the face. [ME f. L *lineamentum* f. *lineare* make straight f. *linea* LINE[1]]

■ see TRAIT.

linear /línniər/ *adj.* **1 a** of or in lines; in lines rather than masses (*linear development*). **b** of length (*linear extent*). **2**

long and narrow and of uniform breadth. **3** involving one dimension only. □ **linear accelerator** *Physics* an accelerator in which particles travel in straight lines, not in closed orbits. **Linear B** a form of Bronze Age writing found in Crete and parts of Greece and recording a form of Mycenaean Greek: an earlier undeciphered form (**Linear A**) also exists. **linear equation** an equation between two variables that gives a straight line when plotted on a graph. **linear motor** a motor producing straight-line (not rotary) motion by means of a magnetic field. □□ **linearity** /-niárriti/ *n.* **linearize** *v.tr.* (also **-ise**). **linearly** *adv.* [L *linearis* f. *linea* LINE[1]]

■ **1a, 3** see STRAIGHT *adj.* 1.

lineation /línniáysh'n/ *n.* **1** a marking with or drawing of lines. **2** a division into lines. [ME f. L *lineatio* f. *lineare* make straight]

lineman /línmən/ *n.* (*pl.* **-men**) **1 a** a person who repairs and maintains telephone or electrical etc. lines. **b** a person who tests the safety of railway lines. **2** *US Football* a player in the line formed before a scrimmage.

linen /línnin/ *n.* & *adj.* ● *n.* **1 a** cloth woven from flax. **b** a particular kind of this. **2** (*collect.*) articles made or orig. made of linen, calico, etc., as sheets, cloths, etc. ● *adj.* made of linen or flax (*linen cloth*). □ **linen basket** a basket for soiled clothes. **wash one's dirty linen in public** be indiscreet about one's domestic quarrels etc. [OE *līnen* f. WG, rel. to obs. *line* flax]

■ **1** *archaic* flax. **2** *archaic* napery; bedclothes, bedlinen(s), sheets and pillowcases; table linen(s), tablecloths and napkins; towels and flannels.

linenfold /línninfōld/ *n.* (often *attrib.*) a carved or moulded ornament representing a fold or scroll of linen (*linenfold panelling*).

liner[1] /línər/ *n.* a ship or aircraft etc. carrying passengers on a regular line. □ **liner train** a fast goods train with detachable containers on permanently coupled wagons.

■ ship, boat, vessel; aircraft, airliner, jet, *esp. Brit.* aeroplane.

liner[2] /línər/ *n.* a removable lining.

-liner /línər/ *comb. form* (prec. by a numeral, usu. *one* or *two*) *colloq.* a spoken passage of a specified number of lines in a play etc. (*a one-liner*).

linesman /línzmən/ *n.* (*pl.* **-men**) **1** (in games played on a pitch or court) an umpire's or referee's assistant who decides whether a ball falls within the playing area or not. **2** *Brit.* = LINEMAN 1.

ling[1] /ling/ *n.* a long slender marine fish, *Molva molva*, of N. Europe, used as food. [ME *leng(e)*, prob. f. MDu, rel. to LONG[1]]

ling[2] /ling/ *n.* any of various heathers, esp. *Calluna vulgaris.* □□ **lingy** *adj.* [ME f. ON *lyng*]

-ling[1] /ling/ *suffix* **1** denoting a person or thing: **a** connected with (*hireling*; *sapling*). **b** having the property of being (*weakling*; *underling*) or undergoing (*starveling*). **2** denoting a diminutive (*duckling*), often derogatory (*lordling*). [OE (as -LE[1] + -ING[3]): sense 2 f. ON]

-ling[2] /ling/ *suffix* forming adverbs and adjectives (*darkling*; *grovelling*) (cf. -LONG). [OE f. Gmc]

linga /línggə/ *n.* (also **lingam** /línggam/) a phallus, esp. as the Hindu symbol of Siva. [Skr. *lingam*, lit. 'mark']

linger /línggər/ *v.intr.* **1 a** be slow or reluctant to depart. **b** stay about. **c** (foll. by *over*, *on*, etc.) dally (*lingered over dinner*; *lingered on what they said*). **2** (esp. of an illness) be protracted. **3** (foll. by *on*) (of a dying person or custom) be slow in dying; drag on feebly. □□ **lingerer** *n.* **lingering** *adj.* **lingeringly** *adv.* [ME *lenger*, frequent. of *leng* f. OE *lengan* f. Gmc, rel. to LENGTHEN]

■ **1** stay (behind), remain, loiter, delay, hang about *or* around, *archaic or literary* tarry, *colloq.* hang on, stick around; pause, idle, dally, dawdle, shilly-shally, *colloq.* dilly-dally; procrastinate, dither, temporize. **2** persist, endure, continue, drag on, be protracted. □□ **lingering** long, (long-)drawn-out, persistent, protracted, slow; remaining.

lingerie /lánzhəri/ *n.* women's underwear and nightclothes. [F f. *linge* linen]

■ see UNDERCLOTHES.

lingo /línggō/ *n.* (*pl.* **-os** or **-oes**) *colloq.* **1** a foreign language. **2** the vocabulary of a special subject or group of people. [prob. f. Port. *lingoa* f. L *lingua* tongue]

■ **1** language, tongue, speech; dialect, vernacular, patois, idiom, pidgin, Creole. **2** jargon, argot, slang, cant, parlance, idiom, language; vocabulary, terminology; gobbledegook, gibberish, mumbo-jumbo.

lingua franca /linggwə frángkə/ *n.* (*pl.* **lingua francas**) **1** a language adopted as a common language between speakers whose native languages are different. **2** a system for mutual understanding. **3** *hist.* a mixture of Italian with French, Greek, Arabic, and Spanish, used in the Levant. [It., = Frankish tongue]

■ **1, 2** see LANGUAGE *n.* 6.

lingual /línggwəl/ *adj.* **1** of or formed by the tongue. **2** of speech or languages. □□ **lingualize** *v.tr.* (also **-ise**). **lingually** *adv.* [med.L *lingualis* f. L *lingua* tongue, language]

linguiform /línggwiform/ *adj. Bot., Zool.,* & *Anat.* tongue-shaped. [L *lingua* tongue + -FORM]

linguist /línggwist/ *n.* a person skilled in languages or linguistics. [L *lingua* language]

linguistic /linggwístik/ *adj.* of or relating to language or the study of languages. □□ **linguistically** *adv.*

linguistics /linggwístiks/ *n.* the scientific study of language and its structure. □□ **linguistician** /-stísh'n/ *n.* [F *linguistique* or G *Linguistik* (as LINGUIST)]

linguodental /línggwōdént'l/ *adj.* (of a sound) made with the tongue and teeth. [L *lingua* tongue + DENTAL]

liniment /línnimənt/ *n.* an embrocation, usu. made with oil. [LL *linimentum* f. L *linire* smear]

■ see LOTION.

lining /líning/ *n.* **1** a layer of material used to line a surface etc. **2** an inside layer or surface etc. (*stomach lining*).

■ **2** see INSIDE *n.* 1.

link[1] /lingk/ *n.* & *v.* ● *n.* **1** one loop or ring of a chain etc. **2 a** a connecting part, esp. a thing or person that unites or provides continuity; one in a series. **b** a state or means of connection. **3** a means of contact by radio or telephone between two points. **4** a means of travel or transport between two places. **5** = *cuff-link* (see CUFF[1]). **6** a measure equal to one-hundredth of a surveying chain (7.92 inches). ● *v.* **1** *tr.* (foll. by *together*, *to*, *with*) connect or join (two things or one to another). **2** *tr.* clasp or intertwine (hands or arms). **3** *intr.* (foll. by *on*, *to*, *in to*) be joined; attach oneself to (a system, company, etc.). □ **link up** (foll. by *with*) connect or combine. **link-up** *n.* an act or result of linking up. [ME f. ON f. Gmc]

■ *n.* **2 a** tie, bond, coupling, connector, vinculum; element, constituent, component. **b** linkage, connection, tie-in, relation, relationship, association, affiliation, interdependence. **5** cuff-link, stud. ● *v.* **1** connect, couple, join, fasten (together), unite; concatenate; tie (up *or* in *or* together), associate, relate, identify. **2** intertwine, clasp.

link[2] /lingk/ *n. hist.* a torch of pitch and tow for lighting the way in dark streets. [16th c.: perh. f. med.L *li(n)chinus* wick f. Gk *lukhnos* light]

linkage /língkij/ *n.* **1** a connection. **2** a system of links; a linking or link.

■ **1** see CONNECTION *n.* 1. **2** see JOINT *n.* 1.

linkman /língkman/ *n.* (*pl.* **-men**) **1** a person providing continuity in a broadcast programme. **2** a player between the forwards and half-backs or strikers and backs in football etc.

links /lingks/ *n.pl.* **1** (treated as *sing.* or *pl.*) a golf-course, esp. one having undulating ground, coarse grass, etc. **2** *Sc. dial.* level or undulating sandy ground near a seashore, with turf and coarse grass. [pl. of *link* 'rising ground' f. OE *hlinc*]

linn /lin/ *n. Sc.* **1 a** a waterfall. **b** a pool below this. **2** a precipice; a ravine. [Gael. *linne*]
■ **1 a** see WATERFALL. **2** see RAVINE.

Linnaean /linéeən, lináyən/ *adj.* & *n.* ● *adj.* of or relating to the Swedish naturalist Linnaeus (Linné, d. 1778) or his system of binary nomenclature in the classification of plants and animals. ● *n.* a follower of Linnaeus. ¶ Spelt *Linnean* in *Linnean Society*.

linnet /línnit/ *n.* a finch, *Acanthis cannabina*, with brown and grey plumage. [OF *linette* f. *lin* flax (the bird feeding on flax-seeds)]

lino /líːnō/ *n.* (*pl.* **-os**) linoleum. [abbr.]

linocut /líːnōkut/ *n.* **1** a design or form carved in relief on a block of linoleum. **2** a print made from this. □□ **linocutting** *n.*
■ **2** see ILLUSTRATION 1.

linoleum /linṓliəm/ *n.* a material consisting of a canvas backing thickly coated with a preparation of linseed oil and powdered cork etc., used esp. as a floor-covering. □□ **linoleumed** *adj.* [L *linum* flax + *oleum* oil]

Linotype /líːnōtīp/ *n. Printing propr.* a composing-machine producing lines of words as single strips of metal, used esp. for newspapers. [= *line o' type*]

linsang /línsang/ *n.* any of various civet-like cats, esp. of the genus *Poiana* of Africa. [Jav.]

linseed /línseed/ *n.* the seed of flax. □ **linseed cake** pressed linseed used as cattle-food. **linseed meal** ground linseed. **linseed oil** oil extracted from linseed and used in paint and varnish. [OE *līnsǣd* f. *līn* flax + *sǣd* seed]

linsey-woolsey /línziwŏŏlzi/ *n.* a fabric of coarse wool woven on a cotton warp. [ME f. *linsey* coarse linen, prob. f. *Lindsey* in Suffolk + WOOL, with jingling ending]

linstock /línstok/ *n. hist.* a match-holder used to fire cannon. [earlier *lintstock* f. Du. *lontstok* f. *lont* match + *stok* stick, with assim. to LINT]

lint /lint/ *n.* **1** a fabric, orig. of linen, with a raised nap on one side, used for dressing wounds. **2** fluff. **3** *Sc.* flax. □□ **linty** *adj.* [ME *lyn(n)et*, perh. f. OF *linette* linseed f. *lin* flax]
■ **2** see FLUFF *n.* 1. □□ **linty** see FUZZY 1a.

lintel /lint'l/ *n. Archit.* a horizontal supporting piece of timber, stone, etc., across the top of a door or window. □□ **lintelled** *adj.* (*US* **linteled**). [ME f. OF *lintel* threshold f. Rmc *limitale* (unrecorded), infl. by LL *liminare* f. L *limen* threshold]

linter /líntər/ *n. US* **1** a machine for removing the short fibres from cotton seeds after ginning. **2** (in *pl.*) these fibres. [LINT + -ER[1]]

liny /líːni/ *adj.* (**linier, liniest**) marked with lines; wrinkled.

lion /líːən/ *n.* **1** (*fem.* **lioness** /-niss/) a large feline, *Panthera leo*, of Africa and S. Asia, with a tawny coat and, in the male, a flowing shaggy mane. **2** (**the Lion**) the zodiacal sign or constellation Leo. **3** a brave or celebrated person. **4** the lion as a national emblem of Great Britain or as a representation in heraldry. □ **lion-heart** a courageous person (esp. as a sobriquet of Richard I of England). **lion-hearted** brave and generous. **the lion's share** the largest or best part. □□ **lionhood** *n.* **lion-like** *adj.* [ME f. AF *liun* f. L *leo -onis* f. Gk *leōn leontos*]
■ **3** see DIGNITARY. □ **lion-hearted** see INTREPID. **the lion's share** see MAJORITY 1.

lionize /líːənīz/ *v.tr.* (also **-ise**) treat as a celebrity. □□ **lionization** /-záysh'n/ *n.* **lionizer** *n.*
■ see GLORIFY 3.

lip /lip/ *n.* & *v.* ● *n.* **1 a** either of the two fleshy parts forming the edges of the mouth-opening. **b** a thing resembling these. **c** = LABIUM. **2** the edge of a cup, vessel, etc., esp. the part shaped for pouring from. **3** *colloq.* impudent talk (*that's enough of your lip!*). ● *v.tr.* (**lipped, lipping**) **1 a** touch with the lips; apply the lips to. **b** touch lightly. **2** *Golf* **a** hit a ball just to the edge of (a hole). **b** (of a ball) reach the edge of (a hole) but fail to drop in. □ **bite one's lip** repress an emotion; stifle laughter, a retort, etc. **curl one's lip** express scorn. **hang on a person's lips** listen attentively to a person. **lick one's lips** see LICK. **lip-read** (*past* and *past part.* **-read** /-red/) (esp. of a deaf person) understand (speech) entirely from observing a speaker's lip-movements. **lip-reader** a person who lip-reads. **lip-service** an insincere expression of support etc. **pass a person's lips** be eaten, drunk, spoken, etc. **smack one's lips** part the lips noisily in relish or anticipation, esp. of food. □□ **lipless** *adj.* **liplike** *adj.* **lipped** *adj.* (also in *comb.*). [OE *lippa* f. Gmc]
■ **2** see RIM *n.* 1. **3** see *impudence* (IMPUDENT). □ **lip-service** see CANT[1] *n.* 1.

lipase /lípayz, -payss/ *n. Biochem.* an enzyme that catalyses the decomposition of fats. [Gk *lipos* fat + -ASE]

lipid /líppid/ *n. Chem.* any of a group of organic compounds that are insoluble in water but soluble in organic solvents, including fatty acids, oils, waxes, and steroids. [F *lipide* (as LIPASE)]

lipidosis /lippidṓsiss/ *n.* (also **lipoidosis** /lippoy-/) (*pl.* **-doses** /-seez/) any disorder of lipid metabolism in the body tissues.

Lipizzaner var. of LIPPIZANER.

lipography /lipógrəfi/ *n.* the omission of letters or words in writing. [Gk *lip-* stem of *leipō* omit + -GRAPHY]

lipoid /líppoyd/ *adj.* resembling fat.

lipoprotein /lípōprṓteen/ *n. Biochem.* any of a group of proteins that are combined with fats or other lipids. [Gk *lipos* fat + PROTEIN]

liposome /lípōsōm/ *n. Biochem.* a minute artificial spherical sac usu. of a phospholipid membrane enclosing an aqueous core. [G. *Liposom*: see LIPID]

liposuction /lípōsuksh'n/ *n.* a technique in cosmetic surgery for removing excess fat from under the skin by suction. [Gk *lipos* fat + SUCTION]

Lippizaner /lippitsaánər/ *n.* (also **Lipizzaner**) **1** a horse of a fine white breed used esp. in displays of dressage. **2** this breed. [G f. *Lippiza* in Slovenia]

lippy /líppi/ *adj.* (**lippier, lippiest**) *colloq.* **1** insolent, impertinent. **2** talkative.

lipsalve /lípsalv/ *n.* **1** a preparation, usu. in stick form, to prevent or relieve sore lips. **2** flattery.

lipstick /lípstik/ *n.* a small stick of cosmetic for colouring the lips.

liquate /likwáyt/ *v.tr.* separate or purify (metals) by liquefying. □□ **liquation** /-kwáysh'n/ *n.* [L *liquare* melt, rel. to LIQUOR]

liquefy /líkwifī/ *v.tr.* & *intr.* (also **liquify**) (**-ies, -ied**) *Chem.* make or become liquid. □□ **liquefacient** /-fáysh'nt/ *adj.* & *n.* **liquefaction** /-fáksh'n/ *n.* **liquefactive** /-fáktiv/ *adj.* **liquefiable** *adj.* **liquefier** *n.* [F *liquéfier* f. L *liquefacere* f. *liquēre* be liquid]
■ see DISSOLVE *v.* 1.

liquescent /likwéss'nt/ *adj.* becoming or apt to become liquid. [L *liquescere* (as LIQUEFY)]

liqueur /likyóor/ *n.* any of several strong sweet alcoholic spirits, variously flavoured, usu. drunk after a meal. [F, = LIQUOR]

liquid /líkwid/ *adj.* & *n.* ● *adj.* **1** having a consistency like that of water or oil, flowing freely but of constant volume. **2** having the qualities of water in appearance; translucent (*liquid blue; a liquid lustre*). **3** (of a gas, e.g. air, hydrogen) reduced to a liquid state by intense cold. **4** (of sounds) clear and pure; harmonious, fluent. **5** (of assets) easily converted into cash; also, having ready cash or liquid assets. **6** not fixed; fluid (*liquid opinions*). ● *n.* **1** a liquid substance. **2** *Phonet.* the sound of *l* or *r*. □ **liquid crystal** a turbid liquid with some order in its molecular arrangement. **liquid crystal display** a form of visual display in electronic devices, in which the reflectivity of a matrix of liquid crystals changes as a signal is applied. **liquid measure** a unit for measuring the volume of liquids. **liquid paraffin** *Pharm.* a colourless odourless oily liquid obtained from

petroleum and used as a laxative. ◻◻ **liquidly** *adv.* **liquidness** *n.* [ME f. L *liquidus* f. *liquēre* be liquid]
■ *adj.* **1, 3** fluid, liquefied; melted, runny, watery, aqueous; molten. **2** clear, transparent, translucent, limpid, pellucid; watery, aqueous. **4** clear, pure, distinct, clarion, bell-like; fluent, flowing, smooth, polished, harmonious, melodious, sweet(-sounding). **5** convertible, realizable, disposable; solvent, *colloq.* flush. **6** see FLUID *adj.* 2. ● *n.* **1** fluid, liquor, juice, sap, solution.

liquidambar /líkwidámbər/ *n.* **1** any tree of the genus *Liquidambar* yielding a resinous gum. **2** this gum. [mod.L app. f. L *liquidus* (see LIQUID) + med.L *ambar* amber]

liquidate /líkwidayt/ *v.* **1 a** *tr.* wind up the affairs of (a company or firm) by ascertaining liabilities and apportioning assets. **b** *intr.* (of a company) be liquidated. **2** *tr.* clear or pay off (a debt). **3** *tr.* put an end to or get rid of (esp. by violent means). [med.L *liquidare* make clear (as LIQUID)]
■ **1** see *wind up* 5 (WIND²). **2** see PAY¹ *v.* 2. **3** see KILL¹ *v.* 1.

liquidation /líkwidáysh'n/ *n.* the process of liquidating a company etc. ◻ **go into liquidation** (of a company etc.) be wound up and have its assets apportioned.

liquidator /líkwidaytər/ *n.* a person called in to wind up the affairs of a company etc.

liquidity /likwídditi/ *n.* (*pl.* **-ies**) **1** the state of being liquid. **2 a** availability of liquid assets. **b** (in *pl.*) liquid assets. [F *liquidité* or med.L *liquiditas* (as LIQUID)]

liquidize /líkwidīz/ *v.tr.* (also **-ise**) reduce (esp. food) to a liquid or puréed state.

liquidizer /líkwidīzər/ *n.* a machine for liquidizing.

liquify var. of LIQUEFY.

liquor /líkkər/ *n.* & *v.* ● *n.* **1** an alcoholic (esp. distilled) drink. **2** water used in brewing. **3** other liquid, esp. that produced in cooking. **4** *Pharm.* a solution of a specified drug in water. ● *v.tr.* **1** dress (leather) with grease or oil. **2** steep (malt etc.) in water. [ME f. OF *lic(o)ur* f. L *liquor -oris* (as LIQUID)]
■ *n.* **1** spirit(s), alcohol, (strong) drink, intoxicant(s), *colloq.* booze, fire-water, *Austral.* & *NZ colloq.* grog, *US colloq.* hooch, *sl.* hard stuff, gut-rot, rot-gut, moonshine, *esp. US sl.* lush, *US sl.* red-eye. **3** liquid, fluid, extract, stock, broth, infusion; distillate, concentrate.

liquorice /líkkəriss, -rish/ *n.* (also **licorice**) **1** a black root extract used as a sweet and in medicine. **2** the leguminous plant *Glycyrrhiza glabra* from which it is obtained. [ME f. AF *lycorys*, OF *licoresse* f. LL *liquiritia* f. Gk *glukurrhiza* f. *glukus* sweet + *rhiza* root]

liquorish /líkkərish/ *adj.* **1** = LICKERISH. **2** fond of or indicating a fondness for liquor. ◻◻ **liquorishly** *adv.* **liquorishness** *n.* [var. of LICKERISH, misapplied]

lira /léerə/ *n.* (*pl.* **lire** /léere, léeri/) **1** the chief monetary unit of Italy. **2** the chief monetary unit of Turkey. [It. f. Prov. *liura* f. L *libra* pound (weight etc.)]

lisle /līl/ *n.* (in full **lisle thread**) a fine smooth cotton thread for stockings etc. [*Lisle*, former spelling of *Lille* in France, where orig. made]

lisp /lisp/ *n.* & *v.* ● *n.* **1** a speech defect in which *s* is pronounced like *th* in *thick* and *z* is pronounced like *th* in *this*. **2** a rippling of waters; a rustling of leaves. ● *v.intr.* & *tr.* speak or utter with a lisp. ◻◻ **lisper** *n.* **lispingly** *adv.* [OE *wlispian* (recorded in *āwlyspian*) f. *wlisp* (adj.) lisping, of uncert. orig.]

lissom /líssəm/ *adj.* (also **lissome**) lithe, supple, agile. ◻◻ **lissomly** *adv.* **lissomness** *n.* [ult. f. LITHE + -SOME¹]
■ see SUPPLE *adj.* 1.

list¹ /list/ *n.* & *v.* ● *n.* **1** a number of connected items, names, etc., written or printed together usu. consecutively to form a record or aid to memory (*shopping list*). **2** (in *pl.*) **a** palisades enclosing an area for a tournament. **b** the scene of a contest. **3** *Brit.* **a** a selvage or edge of cloth, usu. of different material from the main body. **b** such edges used as a material. ● *v.* **1** *tr.* **a** make a list of. **b** enumerate; name one by one as if in a list. **2** *tr.* enter in a list. **3** *tr.* (as **listed** *adj.*) **a** (of securities) approved for dealings on the Stock Exchange. **b** (of a building in the UK) officially designated as being of historical importance and having protection from demolition or major alterations. **4** *tr.* & *intr. archaic* enlist. ◻ **enter the lists** issue or accept a challenge. **list price** the price of something as shown in a published list. ◻◻ **listable** *adj.* [OE *liste* border, strip f. Gmc]
■ *n.* **1** listing, itemization, inventory, index, catalogue, *catalogue raisonné*, programme, schedule, register, roll, record, file, directory, roster, *esp. Brit.* rota, *US* slate. ● *v.* **1 a** itemize, inventory, index, catalogue, schedule, record. **b** enumerate, name, cite, quote, recount, recite, reel off, rattle off, itemize. **2** register, enter, enrol, inventory, log, book, note, record, catalogue.

list² /list/ *v.* & *n.* ● *v.intr.* (of a ship etc.) lean over to one side, esp. owing to a leak or shifting cargo (cf. HEEL²). ● *n.* the process or an instance of listing. [17th c.: orig. unkn.]
■ *v.* lean (over), tilt, slant, heel, lurch, tip, careen, cant, incline, slope. ● *n.* lean, tilt, slant, heel, lurch, tip, cant, slope, inclination, careenage, camber.

listen /líss'n/ *v.intr.* **1 a** make an effort to hear something. **b** attentively hear a person speaking. **2** (foll. by *to*) **a** give attention with the ear (*listened to my story*). **b** take notice of; respond to advice or a request or to the person expressing it. **3** (also **listen out**) (often foll. by *for*) seek to hear or be aware of by waiting alertly. ◻ **listen in 1** eavesdrop; tap a private conversation, esp. one by telephone. **2** use a radio receiving set. **listening-post 1 a** a point near an enemy's lines for detecting movements by sound. **b** a station for intercepting electronic communications. **2** a place for the gathering of information from reports etc. [OE *hlysnan* f. WG]
■ **1, 2** pay attention, attend, take *or* pay heed, lend an ear, be all ears, prick up one's ears, keep one's ears open, *archaic* hark, *archaic or literary* hearken, *colloq.* tune in; (*listen to*) heed, take notice of, mind, hang upon; obey, follow, respect, accept. **3** (*listen (out) for*) wait for, await; look out for, watch out for, keep one's ears open for. ◻ **listen in 1** eavesdrop, apply a tap, spy, pry, *colloq.* snoop.

listenable /líss'nəb'l/ *adj.* easy or pleasant to listen to. ◻◻ **listenability** /-bílliti/ *n.*

listener /líss'nər/ *n.* **1** a person who listens. **2** a person receiving broadcast radio programmes.

lister /lístər/ *n. US* a plough with a double mould-board. [*list* prepare land for a crop + -ER¹]

listeria /listéeriə/ *n.* any motile rodlike bacterium of the genus *Listeria*, esp. *L. monocytogenes* infecting humans and animals eating contaminated food. [mod.L f. J. *Lister*, Engl. surgeon d. 1912]

listing /lísting/ *n.* **1** a list or catalogue (see LIST¹ 1). **2** the drawing up of a list. **3** *Brit.* selvage (see LIST¹ *n.* 3).
■ **1** see LIST¹ *n.* 1.

listless /lístliss/ *adj.* lacking energy or enthusiasm; disinclined for exertion. ◻◻ **listlessly** *adv.* **listlessness** *n.* [ME f. obs. *list* inclination + -LESS]
■ sluggish, lethargic, languid, languorous, torpid, leaden, inanimate, lifeless, spiritless, weak, spent, weary, tired, exhausted, drained, enervated, *colloq.* fagged (out), knocked out, done in, all in, *esp. Brit. colloq.* whacked, *US colloq.* bushed, pooped, *sl.* wiped out; shiftless, indolent, idle; unenthusiastic, indifferent, apathetic, lackadaisical, lukewarm, tepid, cool.

lit *past* and *past part.* of LIGHT¹, LIGHT².

litany /líttəni/ *n.* (*pl.* **-ies**) **1 a** a series of petitions for use in church services or processions, usu. recited by the clergy and responded to in a recurring formula by the people. **b** (**the Litany**) that contained in the Book of Common Prayer. **2** a tedious recital (*a litany of woes*). [ME f. OF *letanie* f. eccl.L *litania* f. Gk *litaneia* prayer f. *litē* supplication]
■ **1** petition, prayer, invocation, supplication, entreaty, obsecration. **2** recitation, recital, enumeration, listing, list, catalogue, inventory.

litchi var. of LYCHEE.

-lite /līt/ *suffix* forming names of minerals (*rhyolite*; *zeolite*). [F f. Gk *lithos* stone]

liter *US* var. of LITRE.

literacy /líttərəsi/ *n.* the ability to read and write. [LITERATE + -ACY after *illiteracy*]

literae humaniores /líttərī hōōmánniórez/ *n. Brit.* the name of the school of classics and philosophy at Oxford University. [L, = the more humane studies]

literal /líttərəl/ *adj.* & *n.* ● *adj.* **1** taking words in their usual or primary sense without metaphor or allegory (*literal interpretation*). **2** following the letter, text, or exact or original words (*literal translation; a literal transcript*). **3** (in full **literal-minded**) (of a person) prosaic; matter-of-fact. **4 a** not exaggerated (*the literal truth*). **b** so called without exaggeration (*a literal extermination*). **5** *colloq. disp.* so called with some exaggeration or using metaphor (*a literal avalanche of mail*). **6** of, in, or expressed by a letter or the letters of the alphabet. **7** *Algebra* not numerical. ● *n. Printing* a misprint of a letter. □□ **literality** /-rálliti/ *n.* **literalize** *v.tr.* (also **-ise**). **literally** *adv.* **literalness** *n.* [ME f. OF *literal* or LL *litteralis* f. L *littera* (as LETTER)]

■ *adj.* **1** denotative, dictionary, lexical; see also LITERAL *adj.* 4 below. **2** verbatim, word for word; exact, precise, faithful, strict. **3** prosaic, colourless, dull, banal, unimaginative, pedestrian, humdrum, boring, tedious; down-to-earth, matter-of-fact. **4** basic, essential, pure, simple, simplistic, real, objective, true, actual, genuine, bona fide; unvarnished, unadulterated, unexaggerated, unembellished. □□ **literally** word for word, verbatim, *literatim*; faithfully, strictly, exactly, precisely, closely, rigorously; *sic, formal* thus; at one's word; actually, really, genuinely, truly; prosaically, colourlessly, dully, unimaginatively, boringly, tediously.

literalism /líttərəliz'm/ *n.* insistence on a literal interpretation; adherence to the letter. □□ **literalist** *n.* **literalistic** /-lístik/ *adj.*

literary /líttərəri/ *adj.* **1** of, constituting, or occupied with books or literature or written composition, esp. of the kind valued for quality of form. **2** well informed about literature. **3** (of a word or idiom) used chiefly in literary works or other formal writing. □ **literary executor** see EXECUTOR. **literary history** the history of the treatment of a subject in literature. □□ **literarily** *adv.* **literariness** *n.* [L *litterarius* (as LETTER)]

■ **1** artistic, belletristic, poetic, dramatic. **2** well-read, lettered, bookish, bibliophilic; erudite, cultured, cultivated, refined, learned, knowledgeable, (well-)informed, (well-)educated, scholarly, *colloq.* highbrow. **3** poetic, dramatic; formal, written.

literate /líttərət/ *adj.* & *n.* ● *adj.* able to read and write. ● *n.* a literate person. □□ **literately** *adv.* [ME f. L *litteratus* (as LETTER)]

■ *adj.* see LEARNED 1.

literati /líttəraátee/ *n.pl.* **1** men of letters. **2** the learned class. [L, pl. of *literatus* (as LETTER)]

■ see INTELLIGENTSIA.

literatim /líttəraátim/ *adv.* letter for letter; textually, literally. [med.L]

literation /líttəráysh'n/ *n.* the representation of sounds etc. by a letter or group of letters. [L *litera* LETTER]

literature /líttərəchər, lítrə-/ *n.* **1** written works, esp. those whose value lies in beauty of language or in emotional effect. **2** the realm of letters. **3** the writings of a country or period. **4** literary production. **5** *colloq.* printed matter, leaflets, etc. **6** the material in print on a particular subject (*there is a considerable literature on geraniums*). [ME, = literary culture, f. L *litteratura* (as LITERATE)]

■ **1, 3** (creative) writings, books, publications, work(s), texts, composition(s); poetry, drama, fiction, essays, novels. **2** (creative) writing, fiction; letters, belles-lettres, the world of letters, the arts, the humanities, the classics; culture, learning, scholarship. **4** output, creation, *œuvre*, production. **5** documentation, paperwork, document(s), paper(s); brochure(s), pamphlet(s), leaflet(s), booklet(s), manuals, hand-out(s), publicity, blurb, prospectus(es), handbill(s), leaflet(s), circular(s), *Brit. colloq. usu. derog.* bumf; information, facts, data, details, instructions, specifications. **6** books, texts, work(s), publications; information, detail(s), data.

-lith /lith/ *suffix* denoting types of stone (*laccolith; monolith*). [Gk *lithos* stone]

litharge /lítharj/ *n.* a usu. red crystalline form of lead monoxide. [ME f. OF *litarge* f. L *lithargyrus* f. Gk *litharguros* f. *lithos* stone + *arguros* silver]

lithe /līth/ *adj.* flexible, supple. □□ **lithely** *adv.* **litheness** *n.* **lithesome** *adj.* [OE *līthe* f. Gmc]

■ see SUPPLE *adj.* 1.

lithia /líthiə/ *n.* lithium oxide. □ **lithia water** water containing lithium salts and used against gout. [mod.L, alt. of earlier *lithion* f. Gk neut. of *litheios* f. *lithos* stone, after *soda* etc.]

lithic /líthik/ *adj.* **1** of, like, or made of stone. **2** *Med.* of a calculus. [Gk *lithikos* (as LITHIA)]

lithium /líthiəm/ *n. Chem.* a soft silver-white metallic element, the lightest metal, used in alloys and in batteries. ¶ Symb.: **Li**. [LITHIA + -IUM]

litho /līthō/ *n.* & *v. colloq.* ● *n.* = LITHOGRAPHY. ● *v.tr.* (**-oes, -oed**) produce by lithography. [abbr.]

litho- /líthō, līthō/ *comb. form* stone. [Gk *lithos* stone]

lithograph /líthəgraaf, līthə-/ *n.* & *v.* ● *n.* a lithographic print. ● *v.tr.* **1** print by lithography. **2** write or engrave on stone. [back-form. f. LITHOGRAPHY]

■ *n.* see ENGRAVING.

lithography /lithógrəfi/ *n.* a process of obtaining prints from a stone or metal surface so treated that what is to be printed can be inked but the remaining area rejects ink. □□ **lithographer** *n.* **lithographic** /líthəgráffik/ *adj.* **lithographically** /líthəgráffikəli/ *adv.* [G *Lithographie* (as LITHO-, -GRAPHY)]

lithology /lithólləji/ *n.* the science of the nature and composition of rocks. □□ **lithological** /líthəlójik'l/ *adj.*

lithophyte /líthəfīt/ *n. Bot.* a plant that grows on stone.

lithopone /líthəpōn/ *n.* a white pigment of zinc sulphide, barium sulphate, and zinc oxide. [LITHO- + Gk *ponos* work]

lithosphere /líthəsfeer/ *n.* **1** the layer including the earth's crust and upper mantle. **2** solid earth (opp. HYDROSPHERE, ATMOSPHERE). □□ **lithospheric** /-sférrik/ *adj.*

lithotomy /lithóttəmi/ *n.* (*pl.* **-ies**) the surgical removal of a stone from the urinary tract, esp. the bladder. □□ **lithotomist** *n.* **lithotomize** *v.tr.* (also **-ise**). [LL f. Gk *lithotomia* (as LITHO-, -TOMY)]

lithotripsy /líthətripsi/ *n.* (*pl.* **-ies**) a treatment using ultrasound to shatter a stone in the bladder into small particles that can be passed through the urethra. □□ **lithotripter** *n.* **lithotriptic** *adj.* [LITHO- + Gk *tripsis* rubbing f. *tribo* rub]

Lithuanian /líthyoo-áyniən, líthoo-/ *n.* & *adj.* ● *n.* **1 a** a native of Lithuania, a Baltic republic. **b** a person of Lithuanian descent. **2** the language of Lithuania. ● *adj.* of or relating to Lithuania or its people or language.

litigant /líttigənt/ *n.* & *adj.* ● *n.* a party to a lawsuit. ● *adj.* engaged in a lawsuit. [F (as LITIGATE)]

■ *n.* litigator, party; plaintiff, appellant, suitor, petitioner, suer, defendant, accused.

litigate /líttigayt/ *v.* **1** *intr.* go to law; be a party to a lawsuit. **2** *tr.* contest (a point) in a lawsuit. □□ **litigable** /líttigəb'l/ *adj.* **litigation** /-gáysh'n/ *n.* **litigator** *n.* [L *litigare litigat-* f. *lis litis* lawsuit]

■ **1** go to law *or* court, take (legal) action. **2** see CONTEST *v.* 1. □□ **litigation** lawsuit, suit (at law), case, (legal) action; (legal) remedy, redress, reparation. **litigator** see LITIGANT *n.*

litigious /litíjəss/ *adj.* **1** given to litigation; unreasonably fond of going to law. **2** disputable in a lawcourt; offering matter for a lawsuit. **3** of lawsuits. □□ **litigiously** *adv.* **litigiousness** *n.* [ME f. OF *litigieux* or L *litigiosus* f. *litigium* litigation: see LITIGATE]

litmus /lítməss/ *n.* a dye obtained from lichens that is red under acid conditions and blue under alkaline conditions. □ **litmus paper** a paper stained with litmus to be used as a test for acids or alkalis. **litmus test 1** a test for acids and alkalis using litmus paper. **2** a simple test to establish true character. [ME f. ONorw. *litmosi* f. ON *litr* dye + *mosi* moss]

litotes /lītōteez/ *n.* ironical understatement, esp. the expressing of an affirmative by the negative of its contrary (e.g. *I shan't be sorry* for *I shall be glad*). [LL f. Gk *litotēs* f. *litos* plain, meagre]

litre /léetər/ *n.* (*US* **liter**) a metric unit of capacity, formerly defined as the volume of one kilogram of water under standard conditions, now equal to 1 cubic decimetre (about 1.75 pints). □□ **litreage** /léetərij/ *n.* [F f. *litron*, an obs. measure of capacity, f. med.L f. Gk *litra* a Sicilian monetary unit]

Litt.D. *abbr.* Doctor of Letters. [L *Litterarum Doctor*]

litter /líttər/ *n.* & *v.* ● *n.* **1 a** refuse, esp. paper, discarded in an open or public place. **b** odds and ends lying about. **c** (*attrib.*) for disposing of litter (*litter-bin*). **2** a state of untidiness, disorderly accumulation of papers etc. **3** the young animals brought forth at a birth. **4** a vehicle containing a couch shut in by curtains and carried on men's shoulders or by beasts of burden. **5** a framework with a couch for transporting the sick and wounded. **6 a** straw, rushes, etc., as bedding, esp. for animals. **b** straw and dung in a farmyard. ● *v.tr.* **1** make (a place) untidy with litter. **2** scatter untidily and leave lying about. **3** give birth to (whelps etc.). **4** (often foll. by *down*) **a** provide (a horse etc.) with litter as bedding. **b** spread litter or straw on (a floor) or in (a stable). □ **litter-lout** = LITTERBUG. □□ **littery** *adj.* (in senses 1, 2 of *n.*). [ME f. AF *litere*, OF *litiere* f. med.L *lectaria* f. L *lectus* bed]

■ *n.* **1** rubbish, refuse, waste, garbage, *US* trash; debris, detritus, scrap, dross, junk. **2** see MESS *n.* 1. **3** brood, offspring, young, progeny, *Law* issue; farrow. **4, 5** sedan chair, palanquin, *hist.* chair; stretcher. **6 a** bed, bedding, straw. ● *v.* **1** clutter (up), mess (up), muck up. **2** strew, scatter, spread, toss, throw.

littérateur /líttəraatőr/ *n.* a literary person. [F]

■ see WRITER 2.

litterbug /líttərbug/ *n.* a person who carelessly leaves litter in a public place.

little /lítt'l/ *adj.*, *n.*, & *adv.* ● *adj.* (**littler**, **littlest**; **less** /less/ or **lesser** /léssər/; **least** /leest/) **1** small in size, amount, degree, etc.; not great or big: often used to convey affectionate or emotional overtones, or condescension, not implied by *small* (*a friendly little chap*; *a silly little fool*; *a nice little car*). **2 a** short in stature (*a little man*). **b** of short distance or duration (*will go a little way with you*; *wait a little while*). **3** (prec. by *a*) a certain though small amount of (*give me a little butter*). **4** trivial; relatively unimportant (*exaggerates every little difficulty*). **5** not much; inconsiderable (*gained little advantage from it*). **6** operating on a small scale (*the little shopkeeper*). **7** as a distinctive epithet: **a** of a smaller or the smallest size etc. (*little finger*). **b** that is the smaller or smallest of the name (*little auk*; *little grebe*). **8** young or younger (*a little boy*; *my little sister*). **9** as of a child, evoking tenderness, condescension, amusement, etc. (*we know their little ways*). **10** mean, paltry, contemptible (*you little sneak*). ● *n.* **1** not much; only a small amount (*got very little out of it*; *did what little I could*). **2** (usu. prec. by *a*) **a** a certain but no great amount (*knows a little of everything*; *every little helps*). **b** a short time or distance (*after a little*). ● *adv.* (**less**, **least**) **1** to a small extent only (*little-known authors*; *is little more than speculation*). **2** not at all; hardly (*they little thought*). **3** (prec. by *a*) somewhat (*is a little deaf*). □ **in little** on a small scale. **the Little Bear** see BEAR[2]. **little by little** by degrees; gradually. **little end** the smaller end of a connecting-rod, attached to the piston. **little finger** the smallest finger, at the outer end of the hand. **little man** esp. *joc.* (as a form of address) a boy. **little ones** young children or animals. **little or nothing** hardly anything. **the little people** fairies. **Little Russian** *hist.* *n.* a Ukrainian. ● *adj.* Ukrainian. **little slam** *Bridge* the winning of 12 tricks. **the little woman** *colloq.* often *derog.* one's wife. **no little** considerable, a good deal of (*took no little trouble over it*). **not a little** *n.* much; a great deal. ● *adv.* extremely (*not a little concerned*). □□ **littleness** *n.* [OE *lȳtel* f. Gmc]

■ *adj.* **1, 2a** small, short, slight, diminutive, compact, petite, bijou, *esp. Sc. or colloq.* wee; miniature, baby, toy, dwarf, pygmy, midget; undersized, puny; microscopic, minuscule, infinitesimal, mini-, micro-, *colloq.* teeny, teeny-weeny, teensy, teensy-weensy, *colloq. usu. derog.* itsy-bitsy. **2b** short, brief, fractional, infinitesimal. **3** (*a little*) some, a (little) bit of; a piece of, a spot of, a scrap of, a drop of, a dab of, a taste of, a trace of, a touch of, a suspicion of, a hint of. **4** trivial, trifling, small, minor, petty, paltry, slight, *colloq.* piddling, piffling; insignificant, inconsiderable, unimportant, inconsequential, negligible. **5** not much, hardly any, scant, meagre, thin, poor, minimal, slender, inconsiderable, negligible. **6** small, small-scale, small-time; modest, unpretentious, humble, simple, plain, ordinary. **7** smaller, little, lesser, minor; smallest, littlest, least. **8** young, youthful, baby, small; younger, junior. **9** childlike, childish, innocent; silly, funny; dear, lovable, darling. **10** contemptible, wretched, despicable, loathsome, vile, scurvy, low, mean, paltry, cheap, petty, *US* picayune, *Brit. colloq.* twopenny(-halfpenny), *US colloq.* two-bit. ● *n.* **1** not much, hardly *or* scarcely anything; a pittance, *colloq.* peanuts, chicken-feed. **2 a** bit, piece, spot, scrap, drop, dab, taste, trace, touch, suspicion, hint, *colloq.* smidgen, *US colloq.* tad. **b** while, time, period, stretch. ● *adv.* **1, 2** scarcely, hardly, barely; not much; rarely, seldom; never, not at all, by no means, noway, nowise. **3** (*a little*) somewhat, slightly, a (little) bit, rather, quite, moderately, fairly, pretty, *colloq.* sort of, kind of, kinda. □ **little by little** see *gradually* (GRADUAL). **little man** see BOY *n.* 1, 2. **little ones** see YOUNG *n.* **no little** see CONSIDERABLE 2. **not a little** (*n.*) see LOT *n.* 1. (*adv.*) see *extremely* (EXTREME).

littoral /líttərəl/ *adj.* & *n.* ● *adj.* of or on the shore of the sea, a lake, etc. ● *n.* a region lying along a shore. [L *littoralis* f. *litus litoris* shore]

■ *n.* see COAST *n.* 1a.

liturgical /litúrjik'l/ *adj.* of or related to liturgies or public worship. □□ **liturgically** *adv.* **liturgist** /líttərjist/ *n.* [med.L f. Gk *leitourgikos* (as LITURGY)]

■ see SOLEMN 2.

liturgy /líttərji/ *n.* (*pl.* **-ies**) **1 a** a form of public worship. **b** a set of formularies for this. **c** public worship in accordance with a prescribed form. **2** (**the Liturgy**) the Book of Common Prayer. **3** the Communion office of the Orthodox Church. **4** *Gk Antiq.* a public office or duty performed voluntarily by a rich Athenian. [F *liturgie* or LL *liturgia* f. Gk *leitourgia* public worship f. *leitourgos* minister f. *leit-* public + *ergon* work]

■ **1 b** see FORMULA 3a.

livable var. of LIVEABLE.

live[1] /liv/ *v.* **1** *intr.* have (esp. animal) life; be or remain alive. **2** *intr.* (foll. by *on*) subsist or feed (*lives on fruit*). **3** *intr.* (foll. by *on*, *off*) depend for subsistence (*lives off the family*; *lives on income from investments*). **4** *intr.* (foll. by *on*, *by*) sustain one's position or repute (*live on their reputation*; *lives by his wits*). **5** *tr.* **a** (with compl.) spend, pass, experience (*lived a happy life*). **b** express in one's life (*was living a lie*). **6** *intr.* conduct oneself in a specified way (*live quietly*). **7** *intr.* arrange one's habits, expenditure, feeding, etc. (*live modestly*). **8** *intr.* make or have one's abode. **9** *intr.* (foll. by *in*) spend the daytime (*the room does not seem to be lived in*). **10** *intr.* (of a person or thing) survive. **11** *intr.* (of a ship) escape destruction. **12** *intr.* enjoy life intensely or to the full (*you haven't lived till you've drunk champagne*). □ **live and let live** condone others' failings so as to be similarly tolerated. **live down** (usu. with *neg.*) cause (past guilt, embarrassment, etc.) to be forgotten by different conduct over a period of time (*you'll never live that down!*). **live in** *Brit.* (of a domestic employee) reside on the premises of one's work. **live-in** *attrib.adj.* (of a sexual partner) cohabiting. **live it up** *colloq.* live gaily and extravagantly. **live out 1** survive (a danger, difficulty, etc.). **2** (of a domestic employee) reside away from one's place of work. **live through** survive; remain alive at the end of. **live to** survive and reach (*lived to a great age*). **live to oneself** live in isolation. **live together** (esp. of a man and woman not married to each other) share a home and have a sexual relationship. **live up to** honour or fulfil; put into practice (principles etc.). **live with 1** share a home with. **2** tolerate; find congenial. **long live . . .!** an exclamation of loyalty (to a person etc. specified). [OE *libban*, *lifian*, f. Gmc]

■ **1–4** exist, be alive, breathe, draw breath, function; survive, thrive, subsist, stay alive, keep oneself alive, sustain oneself, keep going, persist, last, persevere, endure; (*live on*) feed on, eat, use, consume; depend on. **5 a** spend, pass, experience, lead, have, go through. **8, 9** reside, be, settle; remain, stay, sojourn, lodge, put up, room, *archaic* abide, *archaic or dial.* bide, *literary* dwell; (*live in*) occupy, inhabit, tenant, populate. **10, 11** survive, pull *or* come through; emerge, walk away; go on, continue. □ **live it up** see *enjoy oneself*. **live through** see WEATHER *v.* **live to** see REACH *v.* 5. **live up to** see FULFIL 1, 2.

live[2] /līv/ *adj.* **1** (*attrib.*) that is alive; living. **2** (of a broadcast) heard or seen at the time of its performance, not from a recording. **3** full of power, energy, or importance; not obsolete or exhausted (*disarmament is still a live issue*). **4** expending or still able to expend energy in various forms, esp.: **a** (of coals) glowing, burning. **b** (of a shell) unexploded. **c** (of a match) unkindled. **d** (of a wire etc.) connected to a source of electrical power. **5** (of rock) not detached, seeming to form part of the earth's frame. **6** (of a wheel or axle etc. in machinery) moving or imparting motion. □ **live bait** small fish used to entice prey. **live load** the weight of persons or goods in a building or vehicle. **live oak** an American evergreen tree, *Quercus virginiana*. **live wire** an energetic and forceful person. [aphetic form of ALIVE]

■ **1** living, alive, breathing, animate, existent, *archaic* quick, *joc.* in the land of the living, among the living; viable. **3** energetic, lively, spirited, vigorous, active, dynamic, busy; current, contemporary; contemporaneous. **4 a** burning, glowing, aglow, ablaze, aflame, alight, afire, on fire, in flames, flaming, red-hot, white-hot. **b** unexploded, explosive; loaded, charged, primed. **c** unkindled, unstruck, unused. **d** alive, charged, electrified. □ **live wire** fire-ball, tiger, demon, *colloq.* dynamo, ripsnorter.

liveable /lívvəb'l/ *adj.* (also **livable**) **1** (of a house, room, climate, etc.) fit to live in. **2** (of a life) worth living. **3** (of a person) companionable; easy to live with. □□ **liveability** /-bílliti/ *n.* **liveableness** *n.*

■ **1** see HABITABLE.

livelihood /lívlihŏŏd/ *n.* a means of living; sustenance. [OE *līflād* f. *līf* LIFE + *lād* course (see LOAD): assim. to obs. *livelihood* liveliness]

■ see SUSTENANCE 2.

livelong[1] /lívlong/ *adj. poet.* or *rhet.* in its entire length or apparently so (*the livelong day*). [ME *lefe longe* (as LIEF, LONG[1]): assim. to LIVE[1]]

livelong[2] /lívlong/ *n.* an orpine. [LIVE[1] + LONG[1]]

lively /līvli/ *adj.* (**livelier, liveliest**) **1** full of life; vigorous, energetic. **2** brisk (*a lively pace*). **3** vigorous, stimulating (*a lively discussion*). **4** vivacious, jolly, sociable. **5** *joc.* exciting, dangerous, difficult (*the press is making things lively for them*). **6** (of a colour) bright and vivid. **7** lifelike, realistic (*a lively description*). **8** (of a boat etc.) rising lightly to the waves. □□ **livelily** *adv.* **liveliness** *n.* [OE *līflīc* (as LIFE, -LY[1])]

■ **1** vital, animate, alive; spry, vivacious, frisky, sprightly, jaunty, pert, perky, cheery, bouncy, effervescent, bubbly, exuberant, volatile, skittish, kittenish, *US* peart, *colloq.* peppy, breezy, chirpy, full of beans; vigorous, energetic, active, dynamic, lusty, spirited, animated, eager, dashing, *colloq.* zappy, zippy; racy; busy, bustling; see also AGILE. **2** brisk, crisp, smart, bourré, keen, busy, spanking, sprightly, *colloq.* snappy; quick, fast, rapid, swift. **3** vigorous, stimulating, exciting, stirring; scintillating, sparkling; see also BOISTEROUS 1. **4** vivacious, jolly, jovial, sociable, convivial, festive, exuberant, hearty, high-spirited, *colloq.* swinging. **5** dangerous, precarious, risky, exciting, hot; difficult, tricky, awkward. **6** bright, brilliant, vivid, intense, bold, strong, loud, fluorescent; colourful, cheerful. **7** see LIFELIKE.

liven /līv'n/ *v.tr.* & *intr.* (often foll. by *up*) *colloq.* brighten, cheer.

■ enliven, brighten (up), cheer (up), perk up; hearten, stimulate, *colloq.* pep up.

liver[1] /lívvər/ *n.* **1 a** a large lobed glandular organ in the abdomen of vertebrates, functioning in many metabolic processes including the regulation of toxic materials in the blood, secreting bile, etc. **b** a similar organ in other animals. **2** the flesh of an animal's liver as food. **3** (in full **liver-colour**) a dark reddish-brown. □ **liver chestnut** see CHESTNUT. **liver fluke** either of two types of fluke, esp. *Fasciola hepatica*, the adults of which live within the liver tissues of vertebrates, and the larvae within snails. **liver of sulphur** a liver-coloured mixture of potassium sulphides etc., used as a lotion in skin disease. **liver salts** *Brit.* salts to cure dyspepsia or biliousness. **liver sausage** a sausage containing cooked liver etc. □□ **liverless** *adj.* [OE *lifer* f. Gmc]

liver[2] /lívvər/ *n.* a person who lives in a specified way (*a clean liver*).

liverish /lívvərish/ *adj.* **1** suffering from a disorder of the liver. **2** peevish, glum. □□ **liverishly** *adv.* **liverishness** *n.*

Liverpudlian /lívvərpúdliən/ *n.* & *adj.* ● *n.* a native of Liverpool in NW England. ● *adj.* of or relating to Liverpool. [joc. f. *Liverpool* + PUDDLE]

liverwort /lívvərwurt/ *n.* any small leafy or thalloid bryophyte of the class Hepaticae, of which some have liver-shaped parts.

livery[1] /lívvəri/ *n.* (*pl.* **-ies**) **1 a** distinctive clothing worn by a member of a City Company or by a servant. **b** membership of a City livery company. **2** a distinctive guise or marking or outward appearance (*birds in their winter livery*). **3** a distinctive colour scheme in which the vehicles, aircraft, etc., of a particular company or line are painted. **4** *US* a place where horses can be hired. **5** *hist.* a provision of food or clothing for retainers etc. **6** *Law* **a** the legal delivery of property. **b** a writ allowing this. □ **at livery** (of a horse) kept for the owner and fed and groomed for a fixed charge. **livery company** *Brit.* one of the London City Companies that formerly had a distinctive costume. **livery stable** a stable where horses are kept at livery or let out for hire. □□ **liveried** *adj.* (esp. in senses 1, 2). [ME f. AF *liveré*, OF *livrée*, fem. past part. of *livrer* DELIVER]

■ **1 a** see UNIFORM *n.*

livery[2] /lívvəri/ *adj.* **1** of the consistency or colour of liver. **2** *Brit.* (of soil) tenacious. **3** *colloq.* liverish.

liveryman /lívvərimən/ *n.* (*pl.* **-men**) **1** *Brit.* a member of a livery company. **2** a keeper of or attendant in a livery stable.

lives *pl.* of LIFE.

livestock /līvstok/ *n.* (usu. treated as *pl.*) animals, esp. on a farm, regarded as an asset.

■ see STOCK *n.* 4.

livid /lívvid/ *adj.* **1** *colloq.* furiously angry. **2 a** of a bluish leaden colour. **b** discoloured as by a bruise. □□ **lividity** /livídditi/ *n.* **lividly** *adv.* **lividness** *n.* [F *livide* or L *lividus* f. *livēre* be bluish]

■ **1** see ANGRY 1. **2** see GREY 1.

living /lívving/ *n.* & *adj.* ● *n.* **1** a livelihood or means of maintenance (*made my living as a journalist; what does she do for a living?*). **2** *Brit. Eccl.* a position as a vicar or rector with an income or property. ● *adj.* **1** contemporary; now existent (*the greatest living poet*). **2** (of a likeness or image of a person) exact. **3** (of a language) still in vernacular use. **4** (of water) perennially flowing. **5** (of rock etc.) = LIVE² 5. □ **living death** a state of hopeless misery. **living-room** a room for general day use. **living will** a written statement of a person's desire not to be kept alive by artificial means in the event of terminal illness or accident. **within living memory** within the memory of people still living.

■ *n.* **1** see SUSTENANCE 2. ● *adj.* **1** see ALIVE 1. □ **living-room** see PARLOUR.

lixiviate /liksívviayt/ *v.tr.* separate (a substance) into soluble and insoluble constituents by the percolation of liquid. □□ **lixiviation** /-áysh'n/ *n.* [L *lixivius* made into lye f. *lix* lye]

lizard /lízzərd/ *n.* any reptile of the suborder Lacertilia, having usu. a long body and tail, four legs, movable eyelids, and a rough or scaly hide. [ME f. OF *lesard(e)* f. L *lacertus*]

LJ *abbr.* (*pl.* **L JJ**) (in the UK) Lord Justice.

LL *abbr.* Lord Lieutenant.

ll. *abbr.* lines.

'll *v.* (usu. after pronouns) shall, will (*I'll; that'll*). [abbr.]

llama /laáamə/ *n.* **1** a S. American ruminant, *Lama glama*, kept as a beast of burden and for its soft woolly fleece. **2** the wool from this animal, or cloth made from it. [Sp., prob. f. Quechua]

llanero /lyaanáirō/ *n.* (*pl.* **-os**) an inhabitant of the llanos. [Sp.]

llano /laánō, lyaá-/ *n.* (*pl.* **-os**) a treeless grassy plain or steppe, esp. in S. America. [Sp. f. L *planum* plain]

■ see PLAIN¹ *n.* 1.

LL B *abbr.* Bachelor of Laws. [L *legum baccalaureus*]

LL D *abbr.* Doctor of Laws. [L *legum doctor*]

LL M *abbr.* Master of Laws. [L *legum magister*]

Lloyd's /loydz/ *n.* an incorporated society of underwriters in London. □ **Lloyd's List** a daily publication devoted to shipping news. **Lloyd's Register 1** an annual alphabetical list of ships assigned to various classes. **2** a society that produces this. [after the orig. meeting in a coffee-house established in 1688 by Edward *Lloyd*]

LM *abbr.* **1** long metre. **2** lunar module.

lm *abbr.* lumen(s).

ln *abbr.* natural logarithm. [mod.L *logarithmus naturalis*]

lo /lō/ *int. archaic* calling attention to an amazing sight. □ **lo and behold** *joc.* a formula introducing a surprising or unexpected fact. [OE *lā* int. of surprise etc., & ME *lō* = *lōke* LOOK]

loach /lōch/ *n.* any small edible freshwater fish of the family Cobitidae. [ME f. OF *loche*, of unkn. orig.]

load /lōd/ *n.* & *v.* ● *n.* **1 a** what is carried or is to be carried; a burden. **b** an amount usu. or actually carried (often in *comb.*: *a busload of tourists; a lorry-load of bricks*). **2** a unit of measure or weight of certain substances. **3** a burden or commitment of work, responsibility, care, grief, etc. **4** (in *pl.*; often foll. by *of*) *colloq.* plenty; a lot. **5 a** *Electr.* the amount of power supplied by a generating system at any given time. **b** *Electronics* an impedance or circuit that receives or develops the output of a transistor or other device. **6** the weight or force borne by the supporting part of a structure. **7** a material object or force acting as a weight or clog. **8** the resistance of machinery to motive power. ● *v.* **1** *tr.* **a** put a load on or aboard (a person, vehicle, ship, etc.). **b** place (a load or cargo) aboard a ship, on a vehicle, etc. **2** *intr.* (often foll. by *up*) (of a ship, vehicle, or person) take a load aboard, pick up a load. **3** *tr.* (often foll. by *with*) **a** add weight to; be a weight or burden upon. **b** oppress (*a stomach loaded with food*). **4** *tr.* strain the bearing-capacity of (*a table loaded with food*). **5** *tr.* (also **load up**) (foll. by *with*) **a** supply overwhelmingly (*loaded us with work*). **b** assail overwhelmingly (*loaded us with abuse*). **6** *tr.* charge (a firearm) with ammunition. **7** *tr.* insert (the required operating medium) in a device, e.g. film in a camera, magnetic tape in a tape recorder, a program into a computer, etc. **8** *tr.* add an extra charge to (an insurance premium) in the case of a poorer risk. **9** *tr.* **a** weight with lead. **b** give a bias to (dice, a roulette wheel, etc.) with weights. □ **get a load of** *sl.* listen attentively to; notice. **load-displacement** (or **-draught**) the displacement of a ship when laden. **load line** a Plimsoll line. [OE *lād* way, journey, conveyance, f. Gmc: rel. to LEAD¹, LODE]

■ *n.* **1** cargo, consignment, shipment, quantity; see also LOAD *n.* 2, 6, 7 below. **2, 6, 7** weight, charge, encumbrance, burden; impediment, *archaic* clog. **3** burden, pressure, strain, stress, commitment, imposition, responsibility, encumbrance, millstone, cross, albatross; care, anxiety, worry, trouble, hardship, trial. **4** (*loads*) see LOT *n.* 1. ● *v.* **1** lade, charge, freight; fill, pack, stuff, cram, jam; stack, pile, heap, stow, install. **3–5** burden, weight, encumber, saddle, lumber; overload, overwhelm, oppress, crush, tax, strain; see also LOAD *v.* 1 above. **6** charge, arm, prime. □ **get a load of** listen to, pay attention to, lend an ear to, hear, take note of, notice, look at, watch, observe, examine, study, view, inspect, *colloq.* check out.

loaded /lṓdid/ *adj.* **1** bearing or carrying a load. **2** *sl.* **a** wealthy. **b** drunk. **c** *US* drugged. **3** (of dice etc.) weighted or given a bias. **4** (of a question or statement) charged with some hidden or improper implication.

■ **1** laden, charged, full, filled (up); packed, stuffed, crammed, cram-full, chock-a-block, chock-full; burdened, weighted (down), overloaded; (*of a gun*) primed, armed, ready. **2 a** see WEALTHY. **b** see DRUNK *adj.* 1. **c** drugged, intoxicated, stupefied, euphoric, *colloq.* turned on, tripping, on a trip, *sl.* stoned, spaced (out), (far) gone. **3** weighted, biased; crooked. **4** tricky, trick, insidious, devious; charged, pregnant; improper, misleading, disingenuous; biased, prejudiced, prejudicial.

loader /lṓdər/ *n.* **1** a loading-machine. **2** (in *comb.*) a gun, machine, lorry, etc., loaded in a specified way (*breech-loader*). **3** an attendant who loads guns at a shoot. □□ **-loading** *adj.* (in *comb.*) (in sense 2).

loading /lṓding/ *n.* **1** *Electr.* the maximum current or power taken by an appliance. **2** an increase in an insurance premium due to a factor increasing the risk involved (see LOAD *v.* 8). **3** *Austral.* an increment added to a basic wage for special skills etc.

loadstar var. of LODESTAR.

loadstone var. of LODESTONE.

loaf¹ /lōf/ *n.* (*pl.* **loaves** /lōvz/) **1** a portion of baked bread, usu. of a standard size or shape. **2** a quantity of other food formed into a particular shape (*sugar loaf; meat loaf*). **3** *sl.* the head, esp. as a source of common sense (*use your loaf*). □ **loaf sugar** a sugar loaf as a whole or cut into lumps. [OE *hlāf* f. Gmc]

■ **1** bun, (bridge) roll, baguette, pitta, twist, *esp. Austral.* & *NZ* damper, *Brit.* bap, cob, bloomer, *Ind.* chapatti, poppadam, *NZ* barracouta, *Sc.* & *N.Engl.* bannock, *US* bagel, pone, *sl.* dodger. **2** brick, cake, roll, block, chunk, hunk, slab, lump, cube, square. **3** head, *colloq.* noddle, *sl.* noggin, nut, *US sl.* bean; brain(s), (common) sense, *archaic* headpiece, *colloq.* nous, gumption, grey matter, *sl.* common.

loaf² /lōf/ *v.* & *n.* ● *v.* **1** *intr.* (often foll. by *about, around*) spend time idly; hang about. **2** *tr.* (foll. by *away*) waste (time) idly (*loafed away the morning*). **3** *intr.* saunter. ● *n.* an act or spell of loafing. [prob. a back-form. f. LOAFER]

■ *v.* **1** idle, lounge (about *or* around), hang about *or* around, loiter, loll, laze (about *or* around), mess about *or* around, potter (about *or* around), kill time, take it easy, *sl.* goof off *or* around, *Austral.* & *NZ sl.* bludge, *Brit. sl.* skive, *Brit. sl. esp. Mil.* scrimshank, *US sl.* bum (about *or* around), lallygag. **2** (*loaf away*) waste, fritter away, idle away, while away, kill; pass, spend. **3** see SAUNTER *v.*

loafer /lṓfər/ *n.* **1** an idle person. **2** (**Loafer**) *propr.* a leather shoe shaped like a moccasin with a flat heel. [perh. f. G *Landläufer* vagabond]
■ **1** idler, layabout, lounger, slacker, shirker, *flâneur*, drone, fainéant, sluggard, ne'er-do-well, good-for-nothing, wastrel, *archaic* slugabed, *colloq.* lazybones, lounge lizard, waster, *Austral. & NZ sl.* bludger, *Brit. sl.* skiver, *Brit. sl. esp. Mil.* scrimshanker, *US sl.* bum, bummer, gold brick.

loam /lōm/ *n.* **1** a fertile soil of clay and sand containing decayed vegetable matter. **2** a paste of clay and water with sand, chopped straw, etc., used in making bricks, plastering, etc. ▫▫ **loamy** *adj.* **loaminess** *n.* [OE *lām* f. WG, rel. to LIME[1]]
■ **1** see SOIL[1] 1.

loan[1] /lōn/ *n.* & *v.* ● *n.* **1** something lent, esp. a sum of money to be returned normally with interest. **2** the act of lending or state of being lent. **3** funds acquired by the State, esp. from individuals, and regarded as a debt. **4** a word, custom, etc., adopted by one people from another. ● *v.tr.* lend (esp. money). ▫ **loan shark** *colloq.* a person who lends money at exorbitant rates of interest. **loan-translation** an expression adopted by one language from another in a more or less literally translated form. **on loan** acquired or given as a loan. ▫▫ **loanable** *adj.* **loanee** /lōnée/ *n.* **loaner** *n.* [ME *lan* f. ON *lán* f. Gmc: cf. LEND]
■ *n.* **1, 2** advance, allowance, credit, accommodation, *Brit. colloq.* sub; hire, rental, lease, charter; mortgage; imprest. ● *v.* lend, advance, allow, credit, put out, *Brit. colloq.* sub; rent (out), hire (out), lease (out), charter (out).

loan[2] /lōn/ *n.* (also **loaning** /lṓning/) *Sc.* **1** a lane. **2** an open place where cows are milked. [ME var. of LANE]

loanholder /lṓnhōldər/ *n.* **1** a person holding securities for a loan. **2** a mortgagee.

loanword /lṓnwurd/ *n.* a word adopted, usu. with little modification, from a foreign language.

loath /lōth/ *predic.adj.* (also **loth**) (usu. foll. by *to* + infin.) disinclined, reluctant, unwilling (*was loath to admit it*). ▫ **nothing loath** *adj.* quite willing. [OE *lāth* f. Gmc]
■ disinclined, reluctant, unwilling, indisposed, ill-disposed, resistant, averse, opposed.

loathe /lōth/ *v.tr.* regard with disgust; abominate, detest. ▫▫ **loather** *n.* **loathing** *n.* [OE *lāthian* f. Gmc, rel. to LOATH]
■ detest, hate, dislike, abhor, abominate, execrate; regard *or* view with horror *or* repugnance *or* disgust, despise, shudder at, shrink *or* recoil from, have no use for, *literary* contemn. ▫▫ **loathing** detestation, hatred, abhorrence, abomination, execration; horror, repugnance, revulsion, disgust, distaste, aversion, antipathy, phobia.

loathsome /lṓthsəm/ *adj.* arousing hatred or disgust; offensive, repulsive. ▫▫ **loathsomely** *adv.* **loathsomeness** *n.* [ME f. *loath* disgust f. LOATHE]
■ detestable, abhorrent, odious, hateful, execrable, abominable, despicable, damnable, contemptible; obnoxious, offensive, horrible, disgusting, abhorrent, hideous, repellent, repulsive, repugnant, nauseating, sickening, revolting, nasty, ghastly, gruesome, *literary* noisome; vile, foul, rank.

loaves *pl.* of LOAF[1].

lob /lob/ *v.* & *n.* ● *v.tr.* (**lobbed, lobbing**) **1** hit or throw (a ball or missile etc.) slowly or in a high arc. **2** send (an opponent) a lobbed ball. ● *n.* **1 a** a ball struck in a high arc. **b** a stroke producing this result. **2** *Cricket* a slow underarm ball. [earlier as noun, prob. f. LG or Du.]
■ *v.* **1** loft, toss; pitch, shy, heave, fling, hurl, throw, launch, cast, propel, bowl, *colloq.* chuck, sling. ● *n.* **1 b** loft, toss; pitch, shy, heave, fling, throw; hit, shot, *colloq.* swipe.

lobar /lṓbər/ *adj.* **1** of the lungs (*lobar pneumonia*). **2** of, relating to, or affecting a lobe.

lobate /lṓbayt/ *adj. Biol.* having a lobe or lobes. ▫▫ **lobation** /-báysh'n/ *n.*

lobby /lóbbi/ *n.* & *v.* ● *n.* (*pl.* **-ies**) **1** a porch, ante-room, entrance-hall, or corridor. **2 a** (in the House of Commons) a large hall used esp. for interviews between MPs and members of the public. **b** (also **division lobby**) each of two corridors to which MPs retire to vote. **3 a** a body of persons seeking to influence legislators on behalf of a particular interest (*the anti-abortion lobby*). **b** an organized attempt by members of the public to influence legislators (*a lobby of MPs*). **4** (prec. by *the*) (in the UK) a group of journalists who receive unattributable briefings from the government (*lobby correspondent*). ● *v.* (**-ies, -ied**) **1** *tr.* solicit the support of (an influential person). **2** *tr.* (of members of the public) seek to influence (the members of a legislature). **3** *intr.* frequent a parliamentary lobby. **4** *tr.* (foll. by *through*) get (a bill etc.) through a legislature, by interviews etc. in the lobby. ▫▫ **lobbyer** *n.* **lobbyism** *n.* **lobbyist** *n.* [med.L *lobia, lobium* LODGE]
■ *n.* **1** porch, ante-room, foyer, (entrance-)hall, vestibule, entry; reception (room), waiting-room; corridor, hall, hallway, passage; *Archit.* tambour. **3** pressure group, *Brit.* ginger group; faction, party, fraternity, group, interest; crusade. ● *v.* **1, 2** petition, appeal to, call on *or* upon, solicit, importune, push, press, pressure, pressurize, urge; persuade, influence, sway.

lobe /lōb/ *n.* **1** a roundish and flattish projecting or pendulous part, often each of two or more such parts divided by a fissure (*lobes of the brain*). **2** = *ear lobe* (see EAR[1]). ▫▫ **lobed** *adj.* **lobeless** *adj.* [LL f. Gk *lobos* lobe, pod]

lobectomy /ləbéktəmi/ *n.* (*pl.* **-ies**) *Surgery* the excision of a lobe of an organ such as the thyroid gland, lung, etc.

lobelia /ləbéeliə/ *n.* any plant of the genus *Lobelia*, with blue, scarlet, white, or purple flowers having a deeply cleft corolla. [M. de *Lobel*, Flemish botanist in England d. 1616]

lobotomy /ləbóttəmi/ *n.* (*pl.* **-ies**) *Surgery* = LEUCOTOMY. [LOBE + -TOMY]

lobscouse /lóbskowss/ *n.* a sailor's dish of meat stewed with vegetables and ship's biscuit. [18th c.: orig. unkn.: cf. Du. *lapskous*, Da., Norw., G *Lapskaus*]

lobster /lóbstər/ *n.* & *v.* ● *n.* **1** any large marine crustacean of the family Nephropidae, with stalked eyes and two pincer-like claws as the first pair of ten limbs. **2** its flesh as food. ● *v.intr.* catch lobsters. ▫ **lobster-pot** a basket in which lobsters are trapped. **lobster thermidor** /thérmidor/ a mixture of lobster meat, mushrooms, cream, egg yolks, and sherry, cooked in a lobster shell. [OE *lopustre*, corrupt. of L *locusta* crustacean, locust: *thermidor* f. the name of the 11th month of the Fr. revolutionary calendar]

lobule /lóbyool/ *n.* a small lobe. ▫▫ **lobular** *adj.* **lobulate** /-lət/ *adj.* [LOBE]

lobworm /lóbwurm/ *n.* **1** a large earthworm used as fishing-bait. **2** = LUGWORM. [LOB in obs. sense 'pendulous object']

local /lṓk'l/ *adj.* & *n.* ● *adj.* **1** belonging to or existing in a particular place or places. **2** peculiar to or only encountered in a particular place or places. **3** of or belonging to the neighbourhood (*the local doctor*). **4** of or affecting a part and not the whole, esp. of the body (*local pain; a local anaesthetic*). **5** in regard to place. ● *n.* a local person or thing, esp.: **1** an inhabitant of a particular place regarded with reference to that place. **2** a local train, bus, etc. **3** (often prec. by *the*) *Brit. colloq.* a local public house. **4** a local anaesthetic. **5** *US* a local branch of a trade union. ▫ **local authority** *Brit.* an administrative body in local government. **local Derby** see DERBY. **local government** a system of administration of a county, district, parish, etc., by the elected representatives of those who live there. **local option** (or **veto**) esp. *US* a system whereby the inhabitants of a district may prohibit the sale of alcoholic liquor there. **local preacher** a Methodist lay person authorized to conduct services in a particular circuit. **local time 1** time measured from the sun's transit over the meridian of a place. **2** the time as reckoned in a particular place, esp. with reference to an event recorded there. **local train** a train stopping at all the stations on its route. ▫▫ **locally** *adv.* **localness** *n.* [ME f. OF f. LL *localis* f. L *locus* place]

▪ *adj.* **1–3** indigenous, native, endemic; topical; regional, territorial, provincial, district, state, county, departmental, divisional, municipal, city, urban, town, village, neighbourhood; neighbouring, nearby. **4** localized, peculiar, particular, specific; restricted, limited. ● *n.* **1** resident, native, national, (fellow) citizen, townsman, townswoman, *poet.* denizen.

locale /lōkaal/ *n.* a scene or locality, esp. with reference to an event or occurrence taking place there. [F *local* (n.) (as LOCAL), respelt to indicate stress: cf. MORALE]

▪ scene, site, setting, locality, neighbourhood, vicinity, environment, district, quarter; situation, location, spot, place, venue.

localism /lṓkəliz'm/ *n.* **1** preference for what is local. **2** a local idiom, custom, etc. **3 a** attachment to a place. **b** a limitation of ideas etc. resulting from this.

▪ **2** see PROVINCIALISM 2.

locality /lōkálliti/ *n.* (*pl.* **-ies**) **1** a district or neighbourhood. **2** the site or scene of something, esp. in relation to its surroundings. **3** the position of a thing; the place where it is. [F *localité* or LL *localitas* (as LOCAL)]

▪ **1** see NEIGHBOURHOOD 1. **2, 3** see SPOT *n.* 2a, b.

localize /lṓkəlīz/ *v.tr.* (also **-ise**) **1** restrict or assign to a particular place. **2** invest with the characteristics of a particular place. **3** attach to districts; decentralize. ▫▫ **localizable** *adj.* **localization** /-záysh'n/ *n.*

locate /lōkáyt/ *v.* **1** *tr.* discover the exact place or position of (*locate the enemy's camp*). **2** *tr.* establish or install in a place or in its proper place. **3** *tr.* state the locality of. **4** *tr.* (in *passive*) be situated. **5** *intr.* (often foll. by *in*) *US* take up residence or business (in a place). ▫▫ **locatable** *adj.* **locator** *n.* [L *locare locat-* f. *locus* place]

▪ **1, 3** discover, detect, find out, identify, determine, ascertain, pinpoint, track down, uncover, unearth, sniff *or* smoke *or* search out, lay *or* put *or* one's hands on, point to, *colloq.* put one's finger on, *Brit. sl.* suss out; find, come across, chance *or* hit upon, turn up. **2, 4** establish, place, put, position, situate, site, set (up), fix, install, mount, lay, station, perch, settle, base. **5** see SETTLE¹ 1, 2a, b.

location /lōkáysh'n/ *n.* **1** a particular place; the place or position in which a person or thing is. **2** the act of locating or process of being located. **3** an actual place or natural setting featured in a film or broadcast, as distinct from a simulation in a studio (*filmed entirely on location*). **4** *S.Afr.* an area where Blacks are obliged to live, usu. on the outskirts of a town or city. [L *locatio* (as LOCATE)]

▪ **1** place, position, spot, situation, site, scene, setting, locale, station, address, venue. **2** placement, establishment, orientation, situation, installation, mounting, settlement; discovery, detection, identification.

locative /lókkətiv/ *n.* & *adj. Gram.* ● *n.* the case of nouns, pronouns, and adjectives, expressing location. ● *adj.* of or in the locative. [formed as LOCATE + -IVE, after *vocative*]

loc. cit. *abbr.* in the passage already cited. [L *loco citato*]

loch /lok, lokh/ *n. Sc.* **1** a lake. **2** an arm of the sea, esp. when narrow or partially land-locked. [ME f. Gael.]

▪ **2** see GULF *n.* 1.

lochia /lókkiə, lṓ-/ *n.* a discharge from the uterus after childbirth. ▫▫ **lochial** *adj.* [mod.L f. Gk *lokhia* neut. pl. of *lokhios* of childbirth]

loci *pl.* of LOCUS.

loci classici *pl.* of LOCUS CLASSICUS.

lock¹ /lok/ *n.* & *v.* ● *n.* **1** a mechanism for fastening a door, lid, etc., with a bolt that requires a key of a particular shape, or a combination of movements (see *combination lock*), to work it. **2** a confined section of a canal or river where the level can be changed for raising and lowering boats between adjacent sections by the use of gates and sluices. **3 a** the turning of the front wheels of a vehicle to change its direction of motion. **b** (in full **full lock**) the maximum extent of this. **4** an interlocked or jammed state. **5** *Wrestling* a hold that keeps an opponent's limb fixed. **6** (in full **lock forward**) *Rugby Football* a player in the second row of a scrum. **7** an appliance to keep a wheel from revolving or slewing. **8** a mechanism for exploding the charge of a gun. **9** = *airlock* 2. ● *v.* **1 a** *tr.* fasten with a lock. **b** *tr.* (foll. by *up*) shut and secure (esp. a building) by locking. **c** *intr.* (of a door, window, box, etc.) have the means of being locked. **2** *tr.* (foll. by *up, in, into*) enclose (a person or thing) by locking or as if by locking. **3** *tr.* (often foll. by *up, away*) store or allocate inaccessibly (*capital locked up in land*). **4** *tr.* (foll. by *in*) hold fast (in sleep or enchantment etc.). **5** *tr.* (usu. in *passive*) (of land, hills, etc.) enclose. **6** *tr.* & *intr.* make or become rigidly fixed or immovable. **7** *intr.* & *tr.* become or cause to become jammed or caught. **8** *tr.* (often in *passive*; foll. by *in*) entangle in an embrace or struggle. **9** *tr.* provide (a canal etc.) with locks. **10** *tr.* (foll. by *up, down*) convey (a boat) through a lock. **11** *intr.* go through a lock on a canal etc. ▫ **lock-keeper** a keeper of a lock on a river or canal. **lock-knit** knitted with an interlocking stitch. **lock-nut** *Mech.* a nut screwed down on another to keep it tight. **lock on to** locate or cause to locate by radar etc. and then track. **lock out 1** keep (a person) out by locking the door. **2** (of an employer) submit (employees) to a lockout. **lock step** marching with each person as close as possible to the one in front. **lock stitch** a stitch made by a sewing-machine by firmly locking together two threads or stitches. **lock, stock, and barrel** *n.* the whole of a thing. ● *adv.* completely. **under lock and key** securely locked up. ▫▫ **lockable** *adj.* **lockless** *adj.* [OE *loc* f. Gmc]

▪ *n.* **1** padlock, deadlock, hasp, bolt, latch, bar, hook, clasp, catch, fastening; keyhole, mortise, selvage, tumbler. ● *v.* **1a, b** padlock, bolt, secure, fasten, seal, bar, latch; shut, close. **2** shut up *or* in *or* away, enclose, put away, put *or* keep under lock and key; imprison, jail, incarcerate, detain, remand, put *or* keep behind bars, put in *or* throw into irons, *poet.* prison, *sl.* put inside. **3** sink, put away, tie up, commit; invest. **4, 8** hold (fast), retain, secure, imprison, enchain; clasp, grip, seize, pin, engage, clutch, clench, entangle, entwine, enfold. **5** see ENCLOSE 1, 6. **6** jam, stick, seize (up), freeze, solidify; immobilize, fix. **7** catch, snag, lodge; see also LOCK¹ *v.* 6 above. ▫ **lock on to** locate, pinpoint, identify, fix; track, follow, pursue, keep track of, *colloq.* keep tabs *or* a tab on. **lock out 1** exclude, shut out, close out, keep out, bar, debar. **lock, stock, and barrel** (*adv.*) see *completely* (COMPLETE).

lock² /lok/ *n.* **1 a** a portion of hair that coils or hangs together. **b** (in *pl.*) the hair of the head. **2** a tuft of wool or cotton. ▫▫ **-locked** *adj.* (in *comb.*). [OE *locc* f. Gmc]

▪ **1 a** tress, curl, ringlet, coil, strand; forelock, cow-lick, lovelock, kiss-curl. **b** (*locks*) hair, tresses, *colloq.* mane. **2** tuft, aigrette, floccus, flock; tag, *Austral.* & *NZ* dag.

lockage /lókkij/ *n.* **1** the amount of rise and fall effected by canal locks. **2** a toll for the use of a lock. **3** the construction or use of locks. **4** locks collectively; the aggregate of locks constructed.

locker /lókkər/ *n.* **1** a small lockable cupboard or compartment, esp. each of several for public use. **2** *Naut.* a chest or compartment for clothes, stores, ammunition, etc. **3** a person or thing that locks. ▫ **locker-room** a room containing lockers (in sense 1), esp. in a pavilion or sports centre.

▪ **1** see COMPARTMENT *n.* 1. **2** see TRUNK 4.

locket /lókkit/ *n.* **1** a small ornamental case holding a portrait, lock of hair, etc., and usu. hung from the neck. **2** a metal plate or band on a scabbard. [OF *locquet* dimin. of *loc* latch, lock, f. WG (as LOCK¹)]

▪ **1** see PENDANT.

lockfast /lókfaast/ *adj. Sc.* secured with a lock.

lockjaw /lókjaw/ *n.* = TRISMUS. ¶ Not in technical use.

lockout /lókkowt/ *n.* the exclusion of employees by their employer from their place of work until certain terms are agreed to.
■ see EXCLUSION.

locksman /lóksmən/ *n.* (*pl.* **-men**) a lock-keeper.

locksmith /lóksmith/ *n.* a maker and mender of locks.

lock-up /lókkup/ *n.* & *adj.* ● *n.* **1** a house or room for the temporary detention of prisoners. **2** *Brit.* non-residential premises etc. that can be locked up, esp. a small shop or storehouse. **3 a** the locking up of premises for the night. **b** the time of doing this. **4 a** the unrealizable state of invested capital. **b** an amount of capital locked up. ● *attrib.adj. Brit.* that can be locked up (*lock-up shop*).
■ **1** see PRISON *n.* 1.

loco[1] /lṓkō/ *n.* (*pl.* **-os**) *colloq.* a locomotive engine. [abbr.]

loco[2] /lṓkō/ *adj.* & *n.* ● *adj. sl.* crazy. ● *n.* (*pl.* **-oes** or **-os**) (in full **loco-weed**) a poisonous leguminous plant of the US causing brain disease in cattle eating it. [Sp., = insane]
■ *adj.* see CRAZY 1.

locomotion /lṓkəmṓsh'n/ *n.* **1** motion or the power of motion from one place to another. **2** travel; a means of travelling, esp. an artificial one. [L *loco* ablat. of *locus* place + *motio* MOTION]

locomotive /lṓkəmṓtiv/ *n.* & *adj.* ● *n.* (in full **locomotive engine**) an engine powered by steam, diesel fuel, or electricity, used for pulling trains. ● *adj.* **1** of or relating to or effecting locomotion (*locomotive power*). **2** having the power of or given to locomotion; not stationary.

locomotor /lṓkəmṓtər/ *adj.* of or relating to locomotion. [LOCOMOTION + MOTOR]

loculus /lókyooləss/ *n.* (*pl.* **loculi** /-lī/) *Zool.*, *Anat.*, & *Bot.* each of a number of small separate cavities. □□ **locular** *adj.* [L, dimin. of *locus*: see LOCUS]

locum /lṓkəm/ *n. colloq.* = LOCUM TENENS. [abbr.]

locum tenens /lṓkəm téenenz, tén-/ *n.* (*pl.* **locum tenentes** /tinénteez/) a deputy acting esp. for a cleric or doctor. □□ **locum tenency** /ténnənsi/ *n.* [med.L, one holding a place: see LOCUS, TENANT]
■ see SUBSTITUTE *n.* 1a.

locus /lṓkəss, lók-/ *n.* (*pl.* **loci** /lṓsī, -kī, -kee/) **1** a position or point, esp. in a text, treatise, etc. **2** *Math.* a curve etc. formed by all the points satisfying a particular equation of the relation between coordinates, or by a point, line, or surface moving according to mathematically defined conditions. **3** *Biol.* the position of a gene, mutation, etc. on a chromosome. [L, = place]
■ **1** see PLACE *n.* 1a, b.

locus classicus /lṓkəss klássikəss, lók-/ *n.* (*pl.* ***loci classici*** /lṓsī klássisī, lókkee klássikee/) the best known or most authoritative passage on a subject. [L]

locus standi /lṓkəss stándī, lók-/ *n.* a recognized or identifiable (esp. legal) status.

locust /lṓkəst/ *n.* **1** any of various African and Asian grasshoppers of the family Acrididae, migrating in swarms and destroying vegetation. **2** *US* a cicada. **3** (in full **locust bean**) a carob. **4** (in full **locust tree**) **a** a carob tree. **b** = ACACIA 2. **c** = KOWHAI. □ **locust-bird** (or **-eater**) any of various birds feeding on locusts. [ME f. OF *locuste* f. L *locusta* lobster, locust]

locution /ləkyṓosh'n/ *n.* **1** a word or phrase, esp. considered in regard to style or idiom. **2** style of speech. [ME f. OF *locution* or L *locutio* f. *loqui locut-* speak]
■ **1** see PHRASE *n.* 1.

lode /lōd/ *n.* a vein of metal ore. [var. of LOAD]
■ see VEIN *n.* 5.

loden /lṓd'n/ *n.* **1** a thick waterproof woollen cloth. **2** the dark green colour in which this is often made. [G]

lodestar /lṓdstaar/ *n.* (also **loadstar**) **1** a star that a ship etc. is steered by, esp. the pole star. **2 a** a guiding principle. **b** an object of pursuit. [LODE in obs. sense 'way, journey' + STAR]
■ **1** see GUIDE *n.* 7. **2** see GUIDE *n.* 5.

lodestone /lṓdstōn/ *n.* (also **loadstone**) **1** magnetic oxide of iron, magnetite. **2 a** a piece of this used as a magnet. **b** a thing that attracts.

lodge /loj/ *n.* & *v.* ● *n.* **1** a small house at the gates of a park or in the grounds of a large house, occupied by a gatekeeper, gardener, etc. **2** any large house or hotel, esp. in a resort. **3** a house occupied in the hunting or shooting season. **4 a** a porter's room or quarters at the gate of a college or other large building. **b** the residence of a head of a college, esp. at Cambridge. **5** the members or the meeting-place of a branch of a society such as the Freemasons. **6** a local branch of a trade union. **7** a beaver's or otter's lair. **8** a N. American Indian's tent or wigwam. ● *v.* **1** *tr.* deposit in court or with an official a formal statement of (complaint or information). **2** *tr.* deposit (money etc.) for security. **3** *tr.* bring forward (an objection etc.). **4** *tr.* (foll. by *in*, *with*) place (power etc.) in a person or group. **5** *tr.* & *intr.* make or become fixed or caught without further movement (*the bullet lodged in his brain*; *the tide lodges mud in the cavities*). **6** *tr.* **a** provide with sleeping quarters. **b** receive as a guest or inmate. **c** establish as a resident in a house or room or rooms. **7** *intr.* reside or live, esp. as a guest paying for accommodation. **8** *tr.* serve as a habitation for; contain. **9** *tr.* (in *passive*; foll. by *in*) be contained in. **10 a** *tr.* (of wind or rain) flatten (crops). **b** *intr.* (of crops) be flattened in this way. [ME *loge* f. OF *loge* arbour, hut, f. med.L *laubia*, *lobia* (see LOBBY) f. Gmc]
■ *n.* **1** gatehouse, cottage, toll-house. **2** house, grange, villa; hotel. **3** house, cottage, chalet, cabin, *Brit.* shooting-box. **4 a** gatehouse, lodgings, quarters. **5, 6** branch, chapter, order, fellowship, wing, group, *Printing* chapel, *US* local. ● *v.* **1** deposit, set *or* put *or* lay down, leave, consign, entrust, place, put; see also LODGE *v.* 3 below. **2** lay *or* put away, set aside, store, keep, save, bank, pay in, *colloq.* stash (away); see also LODGE *v.* 1 above. **3** bring (forward), make, put, lay, submit, set forth *or* out, register, enter, record, file. **4** see PLACE *v.* 1. **5** wedge, catch, become *or* get fixed, embed *or* become embedded; see also STICK[2] 6. **6** accommodate, board, put up, quarter, house, *Mil.* billet; shelter, harbour, take in. **7** reside, live, stay, stop, put up, *US* room, *archaic* abide, *literary* dwell. **8** see HOUSE *v.* 1, CONTAIN 1. **9** see INCLUDE 4.

lodgement /lójmənt/ *n.* **1** the act of lodging or process of being lodged. **2** the depositing or a deposit of money. **3** an accumulation of matter intercepted in fall or transit. [F *logement* (as LODGE)]

lodger /lójər/ *n.* a person receiving accommodation in another's house for payment.
■ see GUEST *n.* 2.

lodging /lójing/ *n.* **1** temporary accommodation (*a lodging for the night*). **2** (in *pl.*) a room or rooms (other than in a hotel) rented for lodging in. **3** a dwelling-place. **4** (in *pl.*) the residence of a head of a college at Oxford. □ **lodging-house** a house in which lodgings are let.
■ **1** see ACCOMMODATION 1. **2** (*lodgings*) accommodation, rooms, quarters, *Mil.* billet, *US* accommodations, *Brit. colloq.* diggings, digs. **3** see HOUSE *n.* 1.

lodicule /lóddikyōōl/ *n. Bot.* a small green or white scale below the ovary of a grass flower. [L *lodicula* dimin. of *lodix* coverlet]

loess /lṓ-iss, löss/ *n.* a deposit of fine light-coloured wind-blown dust found esp. in the basins of large rivers and very fertile when irrigated. □□ **loessial** /lō-éssiəl, lṓssiəl/ *adj.* [G *Löss* f. Swiss G *lösch* loose f. *lösen* loosen]

loft /loft/ *n.* & *v.* ● *n.* **1** the space under the roof of a house, above the ceiling of the top floor; an attic. **2** a room over a stable, esp. for hay and straw. **3** a gallery in a church or hall (*organ-loft*). **4** *US* an upstairs room. **5** a pigeon-house. **6** *Golf* **a** a backward slope in a club-head. **b** a lofting stroke. ● *v.tr.* **1 a** send (a ball etc.) high up. **b** clear (an obstacle) in this way. **2** (esp. as **lofted** *adj.*) give a loft to (a golf club). [OE f. ON *lopt* air, sky, upper room, f. Gmc (as LIFT)]

■ *n.* **6 b** see LOB *n.* 1b. ● *v.* **1 a** see LOB *v.* 1.

lofter /lóftər/ *n.* a golf club for lofting the ball.

lofty /lófti/ *adj.* (**loftier, loftiest**) **1** *literary* (of things) of imposing height, towering, soaring (*lofty heights*). **2** consciously haughty, aloof, or dignified (*lofty contempt*). **3** exalted or noble; sublime (*lofty ideals*). □□ **loftily** *adv.* **loftiness** *n.* [ME f. LOFT as in *aloft*]
■ **1** tall, high, elevated, towering, soaring. **2** haughty, aloof, grand, grandiose, dignified, arrogant, disdainful, condescending, contemptuous, scornful, supercilious, contumelious, patronizing, superior, overweening, pompous, snobbish, *colloq.* high and mighty, snotty, snooty, uppity, *esp. Brit. colloq.* uppish, *esp. Brit. sl.* toffee-nosed, *literary* vainglorious. **3** exalted, noble, majestic, imposing, grand, magnificent, regal, imperial, thoroughbred, aristocratic, magisterial, august, stately, venerable, distinguished, dignified, elevated, eminent, celebrated, honoured, honourable, respected, renowned, famous, prominent, illustrious, notable, leading, pre-eminent, sublime, immortal. □□ **loftiness** see *arrogance* (ARROGANT), NOBILITY 1.

log[1] /log/ *n.* & *v.* ● *n.* **1** an unhewn piece of a felled tree, or a similar rough mass of wood, esp. cut for firewood. **2 a** a float attached to a line wound on a reel for gauging the speed of a ship. **b** any other apparatus for the same purpose. **3** a record of events occurring during and affecting the voyage of a ship or aircraft (including the rate of a ship's progress shown by a log: see sense 2). **4** any systematic record of things done, experienced, etc. **5** = LOGBOOK. ● *v.tr.* (**logged, logging**) **1 a** enter (the distance made or other details) in a ship's logbook. **b** enter details about (a person or event) in a logbook. **c** (of a ship) achieve (a certain distance). **2 a** enter (information) in a regular record. **b** attain (a cumulative total of time etc. recorded in this way) (*logged 50 hours on the computer*). **3** cut into logs. □ **like a log 1** in a helpless or stunned state (*fell like a log under the left hook*). **2** without stirring (*slept like a log*). **log cabin** a hut built of logs. **log in** = *log on*. **log-jam 1** a crowded mass of logs in a river. **2** a deadlock. **log-line** a line to which a ship's log (see sense 2 a. of *n.*) is attached. **log on** (or **off**) go through the procedures to begin (or conclude) use of a computer system. [ME: orig. unkn.]
■ *n.* **3–5** see RECORD *n.* 1. ● *v.* **1a, b, 2a** see RECORD *v.* 1.

log[2] /log/ *n.* a logarithm (esp. prefixed to a number or algebraic symbol whose logarithm is to be indicated). □ **log table** (usu. in *pl.*) a table of logarithms. [abbr.]

-log *US* var. of -LOGUE.

logan /lṓgən/ *n.* (in full **logan-stone**) a poised heavy stone rocking at a touch. [= *logging* f. dial. *log* to rock + STONE]

loganberry /lṓgənbəri/ *n.* (*pl.* **-ies**) **1** a hybrid, *Rubus loganobaccus*, between a blackberry and a raspberry with dull red acid fruits. **2** the fruit of this plant. [J. H. *Logan*, Amer. horticulturalist d. 1928 + BERRY]

logarithm /lóggəri<u>th</u>əm/ *n.* **1** one of a series of arithmetic exponents tabulated to simplify computation by making it possible to use addition and subtraction instead of multiplication and division. **2** the power to which a fixed number or base (see BASE[1] 7) must be raised to produce a given number (*the logarithm of 1000 to base 10 is 3*). ¶ Abbr.: **log.** □ **common logarithm** a logarithm to the base 10. **natural** (or **Napierian**) **logarithm** a logarithm to the base *e* (2.71828. . . .). ¶ Abbr.: **ln** or **log$_e$**. □□ **logarithmic** /-rí<u>th</u>mik/ *adj.* **logarithmically** /-rí<u>th</u>mikəli/ *adv.* [mod.L *logarithmus* f. Gk *logos* reckoning, ratio + *arithmos* number]

logbook /lógbŏŏk/ *n.* **1** a book containing a detailed record or log. **2** *Brit.* a document recording the registration details of a motor vehicle. ¶ Now officially called *vehicle registration document*.
■ **1** see JOURNAL 2.

log$_e$ /logeé/ *abbr.* natural logarithm.

loge /lōzh/ *n.* a private box or enclosure in a theatre. [F]

-loger /ləjər/ *comb. form* forming nouns, = -LOGIST. [after *astrologer*]

logger /lóggər/ *n. US* a lumberjack.

loggerhead /lóggərhed/ *n.* **1** an iron instrument with a ball at the end heated for melting pitch etc. **2** any of various large-headed animals, esp. a turtle (*Caretta caretta*) or shrike (*Lanius ludovicianus*). **3** *archaic* a blockhead or fool. □ **at loggerheads** (often foll. by *with*) disagreeing or disputing. [prob. f. dial. *logger* block of wood for hobbling a horse + HEAD]
■ □ **at loggerheads** see *at odds* (ODDS).

loggia /lṓjə, lójə/ *n.* **1** an open-sided gallery or arcade. **2** an open-sided extension of a house. [It., = LODGE]

logging /lógging/ *n.* the work of cutting and preparing forest timber.

logia *pl.* of LOGION.

logic /lójik/ *n.* **1 a** the science of reasoning, proof, thinking, or inference. **b** a particular scheme of or treatise on this. **2 a** a chain of reasoning (*I don't follow your logic*). **b** the correct or incorrect use of reasoning (*your logic is flawed*). **c** ability in reasoning (*argues with great learning and logic*). **d** arguments (*is not governed by logic*). **3 a** the inexorable force or compulsion of a thing (*the logic of events*). **b** the necessary consequence of (an argument, decision, etc.). **4 a** a system or set of principles underlying the arrangements of elements in a computer or electronic device so as to perform a specified task. **b** logical operations collectively. □□ **logician** /ləjísh'n/ *n.* [ME f. OF *logique* f. LL *logica* f. Gk *logikē* (*tekhnē*) (art) of reason: see LOGOS]
■ **1, 2** reasoning, thinking, argument, rationale, *literary* ratiocination; deduction, inference; philosophy, *Philos.* dialectics; reasonableness, rationality, intelligence, sense, judgement, judiciousness.

-logic /lójik/ *comb. form* (also **-logical**) forming adjectives corresponding esp. to nouns in *-logy* (*pathological*; *theological*). [from or after Gk *-logikos*: see -IC, -ICAL]

logical /lójik'l/ *adj.* **1** of logic or formal argument. **2** not contravening the laws of thought, correctly reasoned. **3** deducible or defensible on the ground of consistency; reasonably to be believed or done. **4** capable of correct reasoning. □ **logical atomism** *Philos.* the theory that all propositions can be analysed into simple independent elements. **logical necessity** the compulsion to believe that of which the opposite is inconceivable. **logical positivism** (or **empiricism**) a form of positivism in which symbolic logic is used and linguistic problems of meaning are emphasized. □□ **logicality** /-kálliti/ *n.* **logically** *adv.* [med.L *logicalis* f. LL *logica* (as LOGIC)]
■ **1** syllogistic, inferential, deductive, inductive. **2, 3** valid, sound, legitimate, justifiable, deducible, defensible, tenable, reasonable, rational, consistent, coherent; correct, right, indisputable, irrefutable, incontrovertible, incontestable, unquestionable, undeniable; plausible, credible, believable; sensible, intelligent, well-thought-out, practical. **4** see INTELLIGENT 1.

logion /lṓgiən/ *n.* (*pl.* **logia** /-giə/) a saying attributed to Christ, esp. one not recorded in the canonical Gospels. [Gk, = oracle f. *logos* word]

-logist /ləjist/ *comb. form* forming nouns denoting a person skilled or involved in a branch of study etc. with a name in *-logy* (*archaeologist*; *etymologist*).

logistics /ləjístiks/ *n.pl.* **1** the organization of moving, lodging, and supplying troops and equipment. **2** the detailed organization and implementation of a plan or operation. □□ **logistic** *adj.* **logistical** *adj.* **logistically** *adv.* [F *logistique* f. *loger* lodge]

logo /lṓgō, lóggō/ *n.* (*pl.* **-os**) *colloq.* = LOGOTYPE 2. [abbr.]

logogram /lóggəgram/ *n.* a sign or character representing a word, esp. in shorthand. [Gk *logos* word + -GRAM]

logomachy /ləgómməki/ *n.* (*pl.* **-ies**) *literary* a dispute about words; controversy turning on merely verbal points. [Gk *logomakhia* f. *logos* word + *makhia* fighting]

logorrhoea /lóggəreéə/ *n.* (*US* **logorrhea**) an excessive flow of words esp. in mental illness. □□ **logorrhoeic** *adj.* [Gk *logos* word + *rhoia* flow]

Logos /lóggoss/ *n.* the Word of God, or Second Person of the Trinity. [Gk, = word, reason]

logotype /lóggətīp/ *n.* **1** *Printing* a single piece of type that prints a word or group of separate letters. **2 a** an emblem or device used as the badge of an organization in display material. **b** *Printing* a single piece of type that prints this. [Gk *logos* word + TYPE]
■ **2 a** see EMBLEM 1, 3.

logrolling /lógrōling/ *n.* *US* **1** *colloq.* the practice of exchanging favours, esp. (in politics) of exchanging votes to mutual benefit. **2** a sport in which two contestants stand on a floating log and try to knock each other off. □□ **logroll** *v.intr.* & *tr.* **logroller** *n.* [polit. sense f. phr. *you roll my log and I'll roll yours*]

-logue /log/ *comb. form* (*US* **-log**) **1** forming nouns denoting talk (*dialogue*) or compilation (*catalogue*). **2** = -LOGIST (*ideologue*). [from or after F *-logue* f. Gk *-logos, -logon*]

logwood /lógwŏŏd/ *n.* **1** a W. Indian tree, *Haematoxylon campechianum*. **2** the wood of this, producing a substance used in dyeing.

-logy /ləji/ *comb. form* forming nouns denoting: **1** (usu. as **-ology**) a subject of study or interest (*archaeology*; *zoology*). **2** a characteristic of speech or language (*tautology*). **3** discourse (*trilogy*). [F *-logie* or med.L *-logia* f. Gk (as LOGOS)]

loin /loyn/ *n.* **1** (in *pl.*) the part of the body on both sides of the spine between the false ribs and the hip-bones. **2** a joint of meat that includes the loin vertebrae. [ME f. OF *loigne* ult. f. L *lumbus*]
■ **1** (*loins*) flanks, sides.

loincloth /lóynkloth/ *n.* a cloth worn round the loins, esp. as a sole garment.

loiter /lóytər/ *v.* **1** *intr.* hang about; linger idly. **2** *intr.* travel indolently and with long pauses. **3** *tr.* (foll. by *away*) pass (time etc.) in loitering. □ **loiter with intent** hang about in order to commit a felony. □□ **loiterer** *n.* [ME f. MDu. *loteren* wag about]
■ **1, 2** see *hang about* 1. □□ **loiterer** see LAGGARD *n.*

loll /lol/ *v.* **1** *intr.* stand, sit, or recline in a lazy attitude. **2** *intr.* (foll. by *out*) (of the tongue) hang out. **3** *tr.* (foll. by *out*) hang (one's tongue) out. **4** *tr.* let (one's head or limbs) rest lazily on something. □□ **loller** *n.* [ME: prob. imit.]
■ **1** see LOUNGE *v.* **4** see SLOUCH *v.* 1.

Lollard /lóllərd/ *n.* any of the followers of the 14th-c. religious reformer John Wyclif. □□ **Lollardism** *n.* [MDu. *lollaerd* f. *lollen* mumble]

lollipop /lóllipop/ *n.* a large usu. flat rounded boiled sweet on a small stick. □ **lollipop man** (or **lady** or **woman**) *Brit. colloq.* an official using a circular sign on a stick to stop traffic for children to cross the road, esp. near a school. [perh. f. dial. *lolly* tongue + POP[1]]

lollop /lólləp/ *v.intr.* (**lolloped, lolloping**) *colloq.* **1** flop about. **2** move or proceed in a lounging or ungainly way. [prob. f. LOLL, assoc. with TROLLOP]

lolly /lólli/ *n.* (*pl.* **-ies**) **1** *colloq.* **a** a lollipop. **b** *Austral.* a sweet. **c** *Brit.* = *ice lolly*. **2** *Brit. sl.* money. [abbr. of LOLLIPOP]
■ **2** see MONEY 1.

Lombard /lómbaard/ *n.* & *adj.* ● *n.* **1** a member of a Germanic people who conquered Italy in the 6th c. **2** a native of Lombardy in N. Italy. **3** the dialect of Lombardy. ● *adj.* of or relating to the Lombards or Lombardy. □□ **Lombardic** /-baárdik/ *adj.* [ME f. OF *lombard* or MDu. *lombaerd*, f. It. *lombardo* f. med.L *Longobardus* f. L *Langobardus* f. Gmc]

Lombardy poplar /lómbərdi/ *n.* a variety of poplar with an especially tall slender form.

loment /lṓmənt/ *n.* *Bot.* a kind of pod that breaks up when mature into one-seeded joints. □□ **lomentaceous** /-táyshəss/ *adj.* [L *lomentum* bean-meal (orig. cosmetic) f. *lavare* wash]

London clay /lúndən/ *n.* a geological formation in the lower division of Eocene in SE England. [*London*, capital of the UK]

Londoner /lúndənər/ *n.* a native or inhabitant of London.

London plane /lúndən/ *n.* a hybrid plane-tree resistant to smoke and therefore often planted in streets.

London pride /lúndən/ *n.* a pink-flowered saxifrage, *Saxifraga urbium*.

lone /lōn/ *attrib.adj.* **1** (of a person) solitary; without a companion or supporter. **2** (of a place) unfrequented, uninhabited, lonely. **3** *literary* feeling or causing to feel lonely. □ **lone hand 1** a hand played or a player playing against the rest at quadrille and euchre. **2** a person or action without allies. **lone wolf** a person who prefers to act alone. [ME, f. ALONE]
■ **1, 3** see LONELY 1. **2** see ISOLATED 1. □ **lone wolf** see *individualist* (INDIVIDUALISM).

lonely /lṓnli/ *adj.* (**lonelier, loneliest**) **1** solitary, companionless, isolated. **2** (of a place) unfrequented. **3** sad because without friends or company. □ **lonely heart** a lonely person (in sense 3). □□ **loneliness** *n.*
■ **1** solitary, sole, lone, one, single, solo, alone, unaccompanied, companionless, lonesome; isolated, separate, cut off, detached. **2** unfrequented, uninhabited, deserted, desolate, sequestered, remote, out of the way, cut off, secluded, isolated. **3** see FORLORN 1.
□□ **loneliness** lonesomeness, aloneness, solitude, desolation, isolation, seclusion.

loner /lṓnər/ *n.* a person or animal that prefers not to associate with others.
■ see *individualist* (INDIVIDUALISM).

lonesome /lṓnsəm/ *adj.* **1** solitary, lonely. **2** feeling lonely or forlorn. **3** causing such a feeling. □ **by** (or **on**) **one's lonesome** all alone. □□ **lonesomely** *adv.* **lonesomeness** *n.*
■ **1** see LONELY 1. **2** see FORLORN 1. □ **by** (or **on**) **one's lonesome** see ALONE 1a.

long[1] /long/ *adj.*, *n.*, & *adv.* ● *adj.* (**longer** /lónggər/; **longest** /lónggist/) **1** measuring much from end to end in space or time; not soon traversed or finished (*a long line*; *a long journey*; *a long time ago*). **2** (following a measurement) in length or duration (*2 metres long*; *the vacation is two months long*). **3** relatively great in extent or duration (*a long meeting*). **4 a** consisting of a large number of items (*a long list*). **b** seemingly more than the stated amount; tedious, lengthy (*ten long miles*; *tired after a long day*). **5** of elongated shape. **6 a** lasting or reaching far back or forward in time (*a long friendship*). **b** (of a person's memory) retaining things for a long time. **7** far-reaching; acting at a distance; involving a great interval or difference. **8** *Phonet.* & *Prosody* of a vowel or syllable: **a** having the greater of the two recognized durations. **b** stressed. **c** (of a vowel in English) having the pronunciation shown in the name of the letter (as in *pile* and *cute* which have a long *i* and *u*, as distinct from *pill* and *cut*) (cf. SHORT *adj.* 6). **9** (of odds or a chance) reflecting or representing a low level of probability. **10** *Stock Exch.* **a** (of stocks) bought in large quantities in advance, with the expectation of a rise in price. **b** (of a broker etc.) buying etc. on this basis. **11** (of a bill of exchange) maturing at a distant date. **12** (of a cold drink) large and refreshing. **13** *colloq.* (of a person) tall. **14** (foll. by *on*) *colloq.* well supplied with. ● *n.* **1** a long interval or period (*shall not be away for long*; *it will not take long*). **2** *Phonet.* **a** a long syllable or vowel. **b** a mark indicating that a vowel is long. **3 a** long-dated stock. **b** a person who buys this. ● *adv.* (**longer** /lónggər/; **longest** /lónggist/) **1** by or for a long time (*long before*; *long ago*; *long live the king!*). **2** (following nouns of duration) throughout a specified time (*all day long*). **3** (in *compar.*; with *neg.*) after an implied point of time (*shall not wait any longer*). □ **as** (or **so**) **long as 1** during the whole time that. **2** provided that; only if. **at long last** see LAST[1]. **before long** fairly soon (*shall see you before long*). **be long** (often foll. by *pres. part.* or *in* + verbal noun) take a long time; be slow (*was long finding it out*; *the chance was long in coming*; *I shan't be long*).

by a long chalk see CHALK. **in the long run 1** over a long period. **2** eventually; finally. **long ago** in the distant past. **long-ago** *adj*. that is in the distant past. **the long and the short of it 1** all that can or need be said. **2** the eventual outcome. **long-case clock** a grandfather clock. **long-chain** (of a molecule) containing a chain of many carbon atoms. **long-dated** (of securities) not due for early payment or redemption. **long-day** (of a plant) needing a long daily period of light to cause flowering. **long-distance 1** (of a telephone call, public transport, etc.) between distant places. **2** (of a weather forecast) long-range. **long division** division of numbers with details of the calculations written down. **long dozen** thirteen. **long-drawn** (or **-drawn-out**) prolonged, esp. unduly. **long face** a dismal or disappointed expression. **long-faced** with a long face. **long field** *Cricket* **1** = *long off*. **2** = *long on*. **3** the part of the field behind the bowler. **long figure** (or **price**) a heavy cost. **long haul 1** the transport of goods or passengers over a long distance. **2** a prolonged effort or task. **long-headed** shrewd, far-seeing, sagacious. **long-headedness** being long-headed. **long hop** a short-pitched easily hit ball in cricket. **long hundredweight** see HUNDREDWEIGHT. **long in the tooth** rather old (orig. of horses, from the recession of the gums with age). **long johns** *colloq*. underpants with full-length legs. **long jump** an athletic contest of jumping as far as possible along the ground in one leap. **long leg** *Cricket* **1** a fielder far behind the batsman on the leg side. **2** this position. **long-legged** speedy. **long-life** (of consumable goods) treated to preserve freshness. **long-lived** having a long life; durable. **long measure** a measure of length (metres, miles, etc.). **long metre** *Mus*. **1** a hymn stanza of four lines with eight syllables each. **2** a quatrain of iambic tetrameters with alternate lines rhyming. **long off** (or **on**) *Cricket* **1** a fielder far behind the bowler and towards the off (or on) side. **2** this position. **long-player** a long-playing record. **long-playing** (of a gramophone record) playing for about 20–30 minutes on each side. **long-range 1** (of a missile etc.) having a long range. **2** of or relating to a period of time far into the future. **long-running** continuing for a long time. **long ship** *hist*. a long narrow warship with many rowers, used esp. by the Vikings. **long shot 1** a wild guess or venture. **2** a bet at long odds. **3** *Cinematog*. a shot including objects at a distance. **long sight** the ability to see clearly only what is comparatively distant. **long-sleeved** with sleeves reaching to the wrist. **long-standing** that has long existed; not recent. **long-suffering** bearing provocation patiently. **long-sufferingly** in a long-suffering manner. **long suit 1** many cards of one suit in a hand (esp. more than 3 or 4 in a hand of 13). **2** a thing at which one excels. **long-term** occurring in or relating to a long period of time (*long-term plans*). **long-time** that has been such for a long time. **long ton** see TON[1]. **long tongue** loquacity. **long vacation** *Brit*. the summer vacation of lawcourts and universities. **long waist** a low or deep waist of a dress or body. **long wave** a radio wave of frequency less than 300 kHz. **not by a long shot** by no means. □□ **longish** *adj*. [OE *long*, *lang*]

■ *adj*. **1, 3–5, 7** lengthy, great, big, extensive, considerable; extended, elongated, *Bot*. & *Zool*. elongate; prolonged, sustained, protracted, long-drawn-out, prolix, long-winded; endless, interminable, unending; numerous, innumerable; time-consuming; far-reaching, long-distance. **6 a** see LASTING. **b** retentive, tenacious, good, photographic. **13** see TALL *adj*. 1. □ **as** (or **so**) **long as 1** while, all the time (that). **2** provided (that), on condition that, (only) if. **before long** see SOON 1. **in the long run 2** see *finally* (FINAL). **not by a long shot** no way, in *or* under no circumstances, by no (manner of) means, on no account, never, *Brit*. not by a long chalk.

long[2] /long/ *v.intr*. (foll. by *for* or *to* + infin.) have a strong wish or desire for. [OE *langian* seem long to]

■ wish, crave, want, yearn, desire, hunger, fancy, covet, dream, hanker, *esp. Sc*. weary, *colloq*. yen; eat one's heart out.

long. *abbr*. longitude.

-long /long/ *comb. form* forming adjectives and adverbs: **1** for the duration of (*lifelong*). **2** = -LING[2] (*headlong*).

longboard /lóngbord/ *n*. *US* a type of surfboard.

longboat /lóngbōt/ *n*. a sailing ship's largest boat.

longbow /lóngbō/ *n*. a bow drawn by hand and shooting a long feathered arrow.

longe var. of LUNGE[2].

longeron /lónjərən/ *n*. a longitudinal member of a plane's fuselage. [F, = girder]

longevity /lonjévviti/ *n*. long life. [LL *longaevitas* f. L *longus* long + *aevum* age]

longhair /lónghair/ *n*. a person characterized by the associations of long hair, esp. a hippie or intellectual.

■ see HIPPIE, SCHOLAR 1.

longhand /lónghand/ *n*. ordinary handwriting (as opposed to shorthand or typing or printing).

■ see WRITING 2.

longhorn /lónghorn/ *n*. **1** one of a breed of cattle with long horns. **2** any beetle of the family Cerambycidae with long antennae.

longhouse /lónghowss/ *n*. a tribal communal dwelling, esp. in N. America and the Far East.

longicorn /lónjikorn/ *n*. a longhorn beetle. [mod.L *longicornis* f. L *longus* long + *cornu* horn]

longing /lónging/ *n*. & *adj*. ● *n*. a feeling of intense desire. ● *adj*. having or showing this feeling. □□ **longingly** *adv*.

■ *n*. craving, wish, yearning, hunger, fancy, desire, hankering, *colloq*. yen. ● *adj*. see DESIROUS 2.

longitude /lónggityōōd, lónj-/ *n*. **1** *Geog*. the angular distance east or west from a standard meridian such as Greenwich to the meridian of any place. ¶ Symb.: λ. **2** *Astron*. the angular distance of a celestial body north or south of the ecliptic measured along a great circle through the body and the poles of the ecliptic. [ME f. L *longitudo -dinis* f. *longus* long]

longitudinal /lónggityóodin'l, lónj-/ *adj*. **1** of or in length. **2** running lengthwise. **3** of longitude. □ **longitudinal wave** a wave vibrating in the direction of propagation. □□ **longitudinally** *adv*.

longshore /lóngshor/ *adj*. **1** existing on or frequenting the shore. **2** directed along the shore. [*along shore*]

longshoreman /lóngshormən/ *n*. (*pl*. **-men**) *US* a docker.

long-sighted /lóngsītid/ *adj*. **1** having long sight. **2** having imagination or foresight. □□ **long-sightedly** *adv*. **long-sightedness** *n*.

■ **1** see FAR-SIGHTED 2. **2** see FAR-SIGHTED 1. □□ **long-sightedness** see FORESIGHT 1.

longstop /lóngstop/ *n*. **1** *Cricket* **a** a position directly behind the wicket-keeper. **b** a fielder in this position. **2** a last resort.

longueur /longgőr/ *n*. **1** a tedious passage in a book etc. **2** a tedious stretch of time. [F, = length]

longways /lóngwayz/ *adv*. (also **longwise** /lóngwīz/) = LENGTHWAYS.

long-winded /lóngwíndid/ *adj*. **1** (of speech or writing) tediously lengthy. **2** able to run a long distance without rest. □□ **long-windedly** *adv*. **long-windedness** *n*.

■ **1** see TEDIOUS. □□ **long-windedness** see TEDIUM, TAUTOLOGY.

lonicera /lənissərə/ *n*. **1** a dense evergreen shrub, *Lonicera nitidum*, much used as hedging. **2** = HONEYSUCKLE. [A. *Lonicerus*, Ger. botanist d. 1586]

loo[1] /lōō/ *n*. *Brit*. *colloq*. a lavatory. [20th c.: orig. uncert.]

■ see LAVATORY.

loo[2] /lōō/ *n*. **1** a round card-game with penalties paid to the pool. **2** this penalty. □ **loo table** a kind of circular table. [abbr. of obs. *lanterloo* f. F *lanturlu*, refrain of a song]

loof var. of LUFF.

loofah /lóofə/ *n*. (also **luffa** /lúffə/) **1** a climbing gourdlike plant, *Luffa cylindrica*, native to Asia, producing edible marrow-like fruits. **2** the dried fibrous vascular system of this fruit used as a sponge. [Egypt. Arab. *lūfa*, the plant]

look /lŏŏk/ *v.*, *n.*, & *int.* ● *v.* **1 a** *intr.* (often foll. by *at*) use one's sight; turn one's eyes in some direction. **b** *tr.* turn one's eyes on; contemplate or examine (*looked me in the eyes*). **2** *intr.* **a** make a visual or mental search (*I'll look in the morning*). **b** (foll. by *at*) consider, examine (*we must look at the facts*). **3** *intr.* (foll. by *for*) **a** search for. **b** hope or be on the watch for. **c** expect. **4** *intr.* inquire (*when one looks deeper*). **5** *intr.* have a specified appearance; seem (*look a fool*; *look foolish*). **6** *intr.* (foll. by *to*) **a** consider; take care of; be careful about (*look to the future*). **b** rely on (a person or thing) (*you can look to me for support*). **c** expect. **7** *intr.* (foll. by *into*) investigate or examine. **8** *tr.* (foll. by *what*, *where*, etc. + clause) ascertain or observe by sight (*look where we are*). **9** *intr.* (of a thing) face or be turned, or have or afford an outlook, in a specified direction. **10** *tr.* express, threaten, or show (an emotion etc.) by one's looks. **11** *intr.* (foll. by *that* + clause) take care; make sure. **12** *intr.* (foll. by *to* + infin.) expect (*am looking to finish this today*). ● *n.* **1** an act of looking; the directing of the eyes to look at a thing or person; a glance (*a scornful look*). **2** (in *sing.* or *pl.*) the appearance of a face; a person's expression or personal aspect. **3** the (esp. characteristic) appearance of a thing (*the place has a European look*). ● *int.* (also **look here!**) calling attention, expressing a protest, etc. □ **look after 1** attend to; take care of. **2** follow with the eye. **3** seek for. **look one's age** appear to be as old as one really is. **look-alike** a person or thing closely resembling another (*a Prince Charles look-alike*). **look alive** (or **lively**) *colloq.* be brisk and alert. **look as if** suggest by appearance the belief that (*it looks as if he's gone*). **look back 1** (foll. by *on*, *upon*, *to*) turn one's thoughts to (something past). **2** (usu. with *neg.*) cease to progress (*since then we have never looked back*). **3** *Brit.* make a further visit later. **look before you leap** avoid precipitate action. **look daggers** see DAGGER. **look down on** (or **upon** or **look down one's nose at**) regard with contempt or a feeling of superiority. **look for trouble** see TROUBLE. **look forward to** await (an expected event) eagerly or with specified feelings. **look in** make a short visit or call. **look-in** *n. colloq.* **1** an informal call or visit. **2** a chance of participation or success (*never gets a look-in*). **look a person in the eye** (or **eyes** or **face**) look directly and unashamedly at him or her. **look like 1** have the appearance of. **2** *Brit.* seem to be (*they look like winning*). **3** threaten or promise (*it looks like rain*). **4** indicate the presence of (*it looks like woodworm*). **look on 1** (often foll. by *as*) regard (*looks on you as a friend*; *looked on them with disfavour*). **2** be a spectator; avoid participation. **look oneself** appear in good health (esp. after illness etc.). **look out 1** direct one's sight or put one's head out of a window etc. **2** (often foll. by *for*) be vigilant or prepared. **3** (foll. by *on*, *over*, etc.) have or afford a specified outlook. **4** search for and produce (*shall look one out for you*). **look over 1** inspect or survey (*looked over the house*). **2** examine (a document etc.) esp. cursorily (*shall look it over*). **look round 1** look in every or another direction. **2** examine the objects of interest in a place (*you must come and look round sometime*). **3** examine the possibilities etc. with a view to deciding on a course of action. **look-see** *colloq.* a survey or inspection. **look sharp** act promptly; make haste (orig. = keep strict watch). **look small** see SMALL. **look through 1** examine the contents of, esp. cursorily. **2** penetrate (a pretence or pretender) with insight. **3** ignore by pretending not to see (*I waved, but you just looked through me*). **look up 1** search for (esp. information in a book). **2** *colloq.* go to visit (a person) (*had intended to look them up*). **3** raise one's eyes (*looked up when I went in*). **4** improve, esp. in price, prosperity, or well-being (*things are looking up all round*). **look a person up and down** scrutinize a person keenly or contemptuously. **look up to** respect or venerate. **not like the look of** find alarming or suspicious. □□ **-looking** *adj.* (in *comb.*). [OE *lōcian* f. WG]

■ *v.* **1a, 2b** (*look at*) observe, regard, view, scan, stare at; survey, inspect, scrutinize, study, examine, consider, contemplate, pay attention to, look over, attend, notice; watch, witness, see, *literary* behold, *US sl.* eyeball. **2a, 3a** search, take *or* have a look, hunt, seek. **3b, c** (*look for*) expect, hope for, aim at, *disp.* anticipate; seek, demand, require. **4, 7** inquire; examine, study, investigate, inspect, delve, dig, probe, scrutinize, explore, search, research, check. **5** seem (to be), appear (to be). **6** (*look to*) **a** consider, attend to, pay attention to, mind, heed, take care of, see to, deal with. **b, c** count on, reckon on, rely on, bank on; aim to. **8** see, observe, check, find out, ascertain, work out. **9** face, point, be turned; turn. **10** show, display, exhibit, express; threaten. ● *n.* **1** gaze, glance, glare, stare, *Austral.* gink, *Austral. sl.* geek, *Austral.* & *NZ sl.* squiz, *rhyming sl.* butcher's. **2, 3** appearance, aspect, bearing, manner, air, demeanour; expression, countenance, face, *literary* mien. ● *int.* (**look here!**) hey, oi, listen to me. □ **look after 1** care for, take care of, be responsible for, attend (to), mind, watch (over), serve, wait on, nurse, protect, guard. **look-alike** twin, double, exact *or* perfect likeness *or* match, clone, *doppelgänger*, (dead) ringer, *colloq.* spitting image, (very) spit. **look down on** disdain, despise, scorn, disparage, spurn, sneer at, *colloq.* turn up one's nose at, *formal* derogate, *literary* contemn, misprize. **look forward to** anticipate, await, wait for; expect, count *or* rely on *or* upon. **look out 2** be careful, be alert, be vigilant, be prepared, be on the qui vive, be watchful, watch out, beware, pay attention, be on (one's) guard. **3** (*look out on* or *over*) have a view over, front on, overlook, give (out) on to. **look over 1** inspect, survey, examine. **2** look at, examine, scan, study, check (out *or* over), *US sl.* eyeball. **look up 1** seek, search for, look for, hunt for, try to find, track *or* run down. **2** visit, call on, look *or* drop in on, get in touch with. **4** improve, get better, pick up, show improvement, progress, gain, make headway *or* progress. **look up to** admire, regard highly, respect, esteem, honour, revere, worship, idolize, venerate.

looker /lŏŏkkər/ *n.* **1** a person having a specified appearance (*a good-looker*). **2** *colloq.* an attractive woman. □ **looker-on** a person who is a mere spectator.

■ **2** see BEAUTY 3. □□ **looker-on** see SPECTATOR.

looking-glass /lŏŏkking-glaass/ *n.* a mirror for looking at oneself.

■ see MIRROR *n.* 1.

lookout /lŏŏkkowt/ *n.* **1** a watch or looking out (*on the lookout for bargains*). **2 a** a post of observation. **b** a person or party or boat stationed to keep watch. **3** a view over a landscape. **4** a prospect of luck (*it's a bad lookout for them*). **5** *colloq.* a person's own concern.

■ **1** alert, qui vive; guard, watch. **2 b** guard, sentry, sentinel, watchman. **5** responsibility, worry, concern, problem, difficulty, *colloq.* headache.

loom[1] /lōōm/ *n.* an apparatus for weaving yarn or thread into fabric. [ME *lōme* f. OE *gelōma* tool]

loom[2] /lōōm/ *v.* & *n.* ● *v.intr.* (often foll. by *up*) **1** come into sight dimly, esp. as a vague and often magnified or threatening shape. **2** (of an event or prospect) be ominously close. ● *n.* a vague often exaggerated first appearance of land at sea etc. [prob. f. LG or Du.: cf. E Fris. *lōmen* move slowly, MHG *lüemen* be weary]

■ *v.* **1** appear, emerge, take shape *or* form, materialize, surface, arise. **2** menace, impend, threaten, hang, hover.

loon /lōōn/ *n.* **1** *US* any aquatic diving bird of the family Gaviidae, with a long slender body and a sharp bill; a diver. **2** *colloq.* a crazy person (cf. LOONY). [alt. f. *loom* f. ON *lómr*]

■ **2** see FOOL[1] *n.* 1.

loony /lōōni/ *n.* & *adj. sl.* ● *n.* (*pl.* **-ies**) a mad or silly person; a lunatic. ● *adj.* (**loonier, looniest**) crazy, silly. □ **loony-bin** *sl.* a mental home or hospital. □□ **looniness** *n.* [abbr. of LUNATIC]

■ *n.* see MADMAN. ● *adj.* see CRAZY 1.

loop /lōōp/ *n.* & *v.* ● *n.* **1 a** a figure produced by a curve, or a doubled thread etc., that crosses itself. **b** anything forming this figure. **2** a similarly shaped attachment or ornament formed of cord or thread etc. and fastened at the crossing. **3**

a ring or curved piece of material as a handle etc. **4** a contraceptive coil. **5** (in full **loop-line**) a railway or telegraph line that diverges from a main line and joins it again. **6** a manoeuvre in which an aeroplane describes a vertical loop. **7** *Skating* a manoeuvre describing a curve that crosses itself, made on a single edge. **8** *Electr.* a complete circuit for a current. **9** an endless strip of tape or film allowing continuous repetition. **10** *Computing* a programmed sequence of instructions that is repeated until or while a particular condition is satisfied. ● *v.* **1** *tr.* form (thread etc.) into a loop or loops. **2** *tr.* enclose with or as with a loop. **3** *tr.* (often foll. by *up, back, together*) fasten or join with a loop or loops. **4** *intr.* **a** form a loop. **b** move in looplike patterns. **5** *intr.* (also **loop the loop**) *Aeron.* perform an aerobatic loop. [ME: orig. unkn.]

■ *n.* **1–3** hoop, noose, ring, circle, bow, eye, eyelet, coil, whorl. ● *v.* **1–4** twist, coil, wind, circle, curl, turn, ring, *Naut.* bend.

looper /lōōpər/ *n.* **1** a caterpillar of the geometer moth which progresses by arching itself into loops. **2** a device for making loops.

loophole /lōōp-hōl/ *n.* & *v.* ● *n.* **1** a means of evading a rule etc. without infringing the letter of it. **2** a narrow vertical slit in a wall for shooting or looking through or to admit light or air. ● *v.tr.* make loopholes in (a wall etc.). [ME *loop* in the same sense + HOLE]

■ *n.* **1** outlet, way out, escape, get-out, *colloq.* dodge, let-out; subterfuge, pretext, evasion, quibble.

loopy /lōōpi/ *adj.* (**loopier, loopiest**) **1** *sl.* crazy. **2** having many loops.

■ **1** see MAD *adj.* 1.

loose /lōōss/ *adj., n.,* & *v.* ● *adj.* **1 a** not or no longer held by bonds or restraint. **b** (of an animal) not confined or tethered etc. **2** detached or detachable from its place (*has come loose*). **3** not held together or contained or fixed. **4** not specially fastened or packaged (*loose papers; had her hair loose*). **5** hanging partly free (*a loose end*). **6** slack, relaxed; not tense or tight. **7** not compact or dense (*loose soil*). **8** (of language, concepts, etc.) inexact; conveying only the general sense. **9** (preceding an agent noun) doing the expressed action in a loose or careless manner (*a loose thinker*). **10** morally lax; dissolute (*loose living*). **11** (of the tongue) likely to speak indiscreetly. **12** (of the bowels) tending to diarrhoea. **13** *Sport* **a** (of a ball) in play but not in any player's possession. **b** (of play etc.) with the players not close together. **14** *Cricket* **a** (of bowling) inaccurately pitched. **b** (of fielding) careless or bungling. **15** (in *comb.*) loosely (*loose-flowing; loose-fitting*). ● *n.* **1** a state of freedom or unrestrainedness. **2** loose play in football (*in the loose*). **3** free expression. ● *v.tr.* **1** release; set free; free from constraint. **2** untie or undo (something that constrains). **3** detach from moorings. **4** relax (*loosed my hold on it*). **5** discharge (a bullet or arrow etc.). □ **at a loose end** (*US* **at loose ends**) (of a person) unoccupied, esp. temporarily. **loose box** a compartment for a horse, in a stable or vehicle, in which it can move about. **loose change** money as coins in the pocket etc. for casual use. **loose cover** *Brit.* a removable cover for a chair or sofa etc. **loose-leaf** *adj.* (of a notebook, manual, etc.) with each leaf separate and removable. ● *n.* a loose-leaf notebook etc. **loose-limbed** having supple limbs. **loose order** an arrangement of soldiers etc. with wide intervals. **on the loose 1** escaped from captivity. **2** having a free enjoyable time. **play fast and loose** ignore one's obligations, be unreliable, trifle. □□ **loosely** *adv.* **looseness** *n.* **loosish** *adj.* [ME *lōs* f. ON *lauss* f. Gmc]

■ *adj.* **1** unconfined, untied, unfettered, released, freed, unshackled, unchained; free, at liberty, at large, on the loose, untrammelled; (*break loose*) see ESCAPE *v.* 1. **2** unattached, unconnected, disconnected, detached, free, unsecured, unfastened; movable, detachable. **3–5** untied, unbound, unsecured, unfastened, unpackaged, free; (*of clothing*) baggy, slack, flowing; (*of hair*) down; strewn *or* spread *or* tossed *or* thrown about *or* around, scattered (about *or* around), dispersed. **6** slack, relaxed, lax, limp, soft, floppy. **8, 9** general, broad, rough, free, vague, rambling, disconnected, unstructured, unconnected, discontinuous, non-specific, unspecific, indefinite, imprecise, inexact, inaccurate; offhand, casual, untidy, slapdash, negligent, careless, sloppy, lax. **10** wanton, dissolute, lax, debauched, immoral, promiscuous, abandoned, fast, libertine, profligate, licentious, lewd, perverted, corrupt. ● *v.* **1** let go, (set) free, release, let *or* set *or* turn loose; liberate, deliver. **2–4** untie, undo, unfasten, let go, disengage, relax, release, ease, loosen, slacken; cast off. **5** let go, let fly, fire, discharge, shoot, unleash, release, deliver, emit, give out. □ **at a loose end** unoccupied, unemployed, purposeless, aimless, adrift, drifting, *colloq.* betwixt and between.

loosen /lōōss'n/ *v.* **1** *tr.* & *intr.* make or become less tight or compact or firm. **2** *tr.* make (a regime etc.) less severe. **3** *tr.* release (the bowels) from constipation. **4** *tr.* relieve (a cough) from dryness. □ **loosen a person's tongue** make a person talk freely. **loosen up** = *limber up* (see LIMBER[1]). □□ **loosener** *n.*

■ **1** loose, ease, release, undo, unfasten, unhook, unbutton, unlace, untie, unbind, unbuckle; unscrew; soften, weaken; detach, separate.

loosestrife /lōōss-strīf/ *n.* **1** any marsh plant of the genus *Lysimachia*, esp. the golden or yellow loosestrife, *L. vulgaris*. **2** any plant of the genus *Lythrum*, esp. the purple loosestrife *L. salicaria*, with racemes of star-shaped purple flowers. [LOOSE + STRIFE, taking the Gk name *lusimakhion* (f. *Lusimakhos*, its discoverer) as if directly f. *luō* undo + *makhē* battle]

loot /lōōt/ *n.* & *v.* ● *n.* **1** goods taken from an enemy; spoil. **2** booty; illicit gains made by an official. **3** *sl.* money. ● *v.tr.* **1** rob (premises) or steal (goods) left unprotected, esp. after riots or other violent events. **2** plunder or sack (a city, building, etc.). **3** carry off as booty. □□ **looter** *n.* [Hindi *lūṭ*]

■ *n.* **1, 2** booty, spoils, plunder, prize, haul, *sl.* swag, boodle. ● *v.* plunder, sack, ransack, rob, pillage, raid, ravage, maraud, *literary* despoil; see also STEAL *v.* 1.

lop[1] /lop/ *v.* & *n.* ● *v.* (**lopped, lopping**) **1** *tr.* **a** (often foll. by *off, away*) cut or remove (a part or parts) from a whole, esp. branches from a tree. **b** remove branches from (a tree). **2** *tr.* (often foll. by *off, away*) remove (items) as superfluous. **3** *intr.* (foll. by *at*) make lopping strokes on (a tree etc.). ● *n.* parts lopped off, esp. branches and twigs of trees. □ **lop and top** (or **crop**) the trimmings of a tree. □□ **lopper** *n.* [ME f. OE *loppian* (unrecorded): cf. obs. *lip* to prune]

■ *v.* **1, 2** chop (off), trim, top, head, crop, prune, dock, clip, snip (off), shear (off), cut (off), pare, shorten, hack (off), amputate.

lop[2] /lop/ *v.* (**lopped, lopping**) **1** *intr.* & *tr.* hang limply. **2** *intr.* (foll. by *about*) slouch, dawdle; hang about. **3** *intr.* move with short bounds. **4** *tr.* (of an animal) let (the ears) hang. □ **lop-ears** drooping ears. **lop-eared** (of an animal) having drooping ears. □□ **loppy** *adj.* [rel. to LOB]

lope /lōp/ *v.* & *n.* ● *v.intr.* (esp. of animals) run with a long bounding stride. ● *n.* a long bounding stride. [ME, var. of Sc. *loup* f. ON *hlaupa* LEAP]

■ *v.* see RUN *v.* 1, 3.

lopho- /lōfō, lóffō/ *comb. form Zool.* crested. [Gk *lophos* crest]

lophobranch /lōfəbrangk, lóf-/ *adj.* (of a fish) having the gills arranged in tufts. [LOPHO- + BRANCHIA]

lophodont /lōfədont, lóf-/ *n.* & *adj.* ● *adj.* having transverse ridges on the grinding surface of molar teeth. ● *n.* an animal with these teeth. [LOPHO- + Gk *odous odont-* tooth]

lophophore /lōfəfor, lóf-/ *n.* a tentacled disc at the mouth of bryozoans and brachiopods.

lopolith /lóppōlith/ *n. Geol.* a large saucer-shaped intrusion of igneous rock. [Gk *lopas* basin + -LITH]

lopsided /lópsīdid/ *adj.* with one side lower or smaller than the other; unevenly balanced. □□ **lopsidedly** *adv.* **lopsidedness** *n.* [LOP[2] + SIDE]

■ uneven, askew, one-sided, awry, unsymmetrical, asymmetric(al), unequal, crooked, irregular, *colloq.* cock-eyed; unbalanced, biased, disproportionate, unfair, warped, twisted.

loquacious /lokwáyshəss/ *adj.* **1** talkative. **2** (of birds or water) chattering, babbling. □□ **loquaciously** *adv.* **loquaciousness** *n.* **loquacity** /-kwássiti/ *n.* [L *loquax -acis* f. *loqui* talk]

■ **1** see TALKATIVE.

loquat /lṓkwot/ *n.* **1** a rosaceous tree, *Eriobotrya japonica*, bearing small yellow egg-shaped fruits. **2** this fruit. [Chin. dial. *luh kwat* rush orange]

loquitur /lókwitər/ *v.intr.* (he or she) speaks (with the speaker's name following, as a stage direction or to inform the reader). [L]

lor /lor/ *int. Brit. sl.* an exclamation of surprise or dismay. [abbr. of LORD]

loran /lórən/ *n.* a system of long-distance navigation in which position is determined from the intervals between signal pulses received from widely spaced radio transmitters. [*lo*ng-*ra*nge *n*avigation]

lord /lord/ *n.*, *int.*, & *v.* ● *n.* **1** a master or ruler. **2** *hist.* a feudal superior, esp. of a manor. **3** a peer of the realm or a person entitled to the title *Lord*, esp. a marquess, earl, viscount, or baron. **4** (**Lord**) (often prec. by *the*) a name for God or Christ. **5** (**Lord**) **a** prefixed as the designation of a marquess, earl, viscount, or baron. **b** prefixed to the Christian name of the younger son of a duke or marquess. **c** (**the Lords**) = *House of Lords*. **6** *Astrol.* the ruling planet (of a sign, house, or chart). ● *int.* (**Lord**) expressing surprise, dismay, etc. ● *v.tr.* confer the title of Lord upon. □ **live like a lord** live sumptuously. **Lord Advocate** the principal law-officer of the Crown in Scotland. **Lord Bishop** the ceremonious title of any bishop. **Lord Chamberlain** see CHAMBERLAIN. **Lord** (or **Lord High**) **Chancellor** (in the UK) the highest officer of the Crown, presiding in the House of Lords etc. **Lord Chief Justice** (in the UK) the president of the Queen's Bench Division. **lord it over** domineer. **Lord Lieutenant 1** (in the UK) the chief executive authority and head of magistrates in each county. **2** *hist.* the viceroy of Ireland. **Lord Mayor** the title of the mayor in London and some other large cities. **Lord Ordinary** see ORDINARY *n.* 5. **lord over** (usu. in *passive*) domineer, rule over. **Lord President of the Council** (in the UK) the cabinet minister presiding at the Privy Council. **Lord Privy Seal** (in the UK) a senior cabinet minister without official duties. **Lord Provost** the head of a municipal corporation or borough in certain Scottish cities. **lords and ladies** wild arum. **Lords Commissioners** the members of a board performing the duties of a high State office put in commission. **Lord's Day** Sunday. **Lords of Session** the judges of the Scottish Court of Session. **Lord's Prayer** the Our Father, the prayer taught by Christ to his disciples. **Lords spiritual** the bishops in the House of Lords. **Lord's Supper** the Eucharist. **Lords temporal** the members of the House of Lords other than the bishops. **Our Lord** a name for Christ. **Sea Lord** a naval member of the Admiralty Board. □□ **lordless** *adj.* **lordlike** *adj.* [OE *hlāford* f. *hlāfweard* = bread-keeper (as LOAF[1], WARD)]

■ *n.* **1** master, monarch, ruler, sovereign. **3** noble, nobleman, peer, aristocrat; marquess, earl, count, viscount, baron. **4** (**Lord** or **the Lord**) God, the Almighty, Our Lord, the Creator, the Supreme Being, Christ, Jesus, Jehovah. ● *int.* see GOD *int.* □ **lord it over** domineer, pull rank on, *colloq.* boss (about *or* around).

lordling /lórdling/ *n.* usu. *derog.* a minor lord.

lordly /lórdli/ *adj.* (**lordlier**, **lordliest**) **1** haughty, imperious. **2** suitable for a lord. □□ **lordliness** *n.* [OE *hlāfordlic* (as LORD)]

■ **1** see *snobbish* (SNOB). **2** see NOBLE *adj.* 1. □□ **lordliness** see *snobbery* (SNOB).

lordosis /lordṓsiss/ *n. Med.* inward curvature of the spine (opp. KYPHOSIS). □□ **lordotic** /-dóttik/ *adj.* [mod.L f. Gk *lordōsis* f. *lordos* bent backwards]

lordship /lórdship/ *n.* **1** (usu. **Lordship**) a title used in addressing or referring to a man with the rank of Lord or a judge or a bishop (*Your Lordship*; *His Lordship*). **2** (foll. by *of*, *over*) dominion, rule, or ownership. **3** the condition of being a lord. [OE *hlāfordscipe* (as LORD, -SHIP)]

Lordy /lórdi/ *int.* = LORD *int.*

lore[1] /lor/ *n.* a body of traditions and knowledge on a subject or held by a particular group (*herbal lore*; *gypsy lore*). [OE *lār* f. Gmc, rel. to LEARN]

■ folklore, beliefs, culture, tradition(s), mythology, myths, *literary* mythi; teaching(s), doctrine, wisdom; knowledge, learning, erudition.

lore[2] /lor/ *n. Zool.* a straplike surface between the eye and upper mandible in birds, or between the eye and nostril in snakes. [L *lorum* strap]

lorgnette /lornyét/ *n.* (in *sing.* or *pl.*) a pair of eyeglasses or opera-glasses held by a long handle. [F f. *lorgner* to squint]

loricate /lórrikət/ *adj.* & *n. Zool.* ● *adj.* having a defensive armour of bone, plates, scales, etc. ● *n.* an animal with this. [L *loricatus* f. *lorica* breastplate f. *lorum* strap]

lorikeet /lórrikeet/ *n.* any of various small brightly coloured parrots of the subfamily Loriinae, including the rainbow lorikeet. [dimin. of LORY, after *parakeet*]

loris /lóriss/ *n.* (*pl.* same) either of two small tailless nocturnal primates, *Loris tardigradus* of S. India (**slender loris**), and *Nycticebus coucang* of the E. Indies (**slow loris**). [F perh. f. obs. Du. *loeris* clown]

lorn /lorn/ *adj. literary* desolate, forlorn, abandoned. [past part. of obs. *leese* f. OE *-lēosan* lose]

lorry /lórri/ *n. Brit.* (*pl.* **-ies**) **1** a large strong motor vehicle for transporting goods etc. **2** a long flat low wagon. **3** a truck used on railways and tramways. [19th c.: orig. uncert.]

lory /lóri/ *n.* (*pl.* **-ies**) any of various brightly-coloured Australasian parrots of the subfamily Loriinae. [Malay *lūrī*]

lose /lo͞oz/ *v.* (*past* and *past part.* **lost** /lost/) **1** *tr.* be deprived of or cease to have, esp. by negligence or misadventure. **2** *tr.* **a** be deprived of (a person, esp. a close relative) by death. **b** suffer the loss of (a baby) in childbirth. **3** *tr.* become unable to find; fail to keep in sight or follow or mentally grasp (*lose one's way*). **4** *tr.* let or have pass from one's control or reach (*lose one's chance*; *lose one's bearings*). **5** *tr.* be defeated in (a game, race, lawsuit, battle, etc.). **6** *tr.* evade; get rid of (*lost our pursuers*). **7** *tr.* fail to obtain, catch, or perceive (*lose a train*; *lose a word*). **8** *tr.* forfeit (a stake, deposit, right to a thing, etc.). **9** *tr.* spend (time, efforts, etc.) to no purpose (*lost no time in raising the alarm*). **10** *intr.* **a** suffer loss or detriment; incur a disadvantage. **b** be worse off, esp. financially. **11** *tr.* cause (a person) the loss of (*will lose you your job*). **12** *intr.* & *tr.* (of a timepiece) become slow; become slow by (a specified amount of time). **13** *tr.* (in *passive*) **a** disappear, perish; be dead (*was lost in the war*). **b** fall, sin; be damned (*souls lost to drunkenness and greed*). **14** (as **lost** *adj.*) **a** gone, stray, mislaid; forgotten (*lost valuables*; *a lost art*). **b** dead, destroyed (*lost comrades*). **c** damned, fallen (*lost souls in hell*). □ **be lost** (or **lose oneself**) **in** be engrossed in. **be lost on** be wasted on, or not noticed or appreciated by. **be lost to** be no longer affected by or accessible to (*is lost to pity*; *is lost to the world*). **be lost without** have great difficulty if deprived of (*am lost without my diary*). **get lost** *sl.* (usu. in *imper.*) go away. **lose one's balance 1** fail to remain stable; fall. **2** fail to retain one's composure. **lose one's cool** *colloq.* lose one's composure. **lose face** be humiliated; lose one's credibility. **lose ground** see GROUND[1]. **lose one's head** see HEAD. **lose heart** be discouraged. **lose one's heart** see HEART. **lose one's nerve** become timid or irresolute. **lose out** (often foll. by *on*) *colloq.* be unsuccessful; not get a fair chance or advantage (in). **lose sleep over a thing** lie awake worrying about a thing. **lose one's temper** become angry. **lose time** allow time to pass with something unachieved etc. **lose touch** see TOUCH. **lose track of** see TRACK[1]. **lose the** (or **one's**) **way** become lost; fail to reach one's destination. **losing battle** a contest or effort in which failure seems certain. **lost cause 1** an enterprise etc. with no chance of success. **2** a person one can no longer hope to influence. **lost generation 1** a generation with many of its men killed in war, esp. that of 1914–18. **2** an emotionally and culturally

unstable generation coming to maturity, esp. in 1915–25. □□ **losable** *adj.* [OE *losian* perish, destroy f. *los* loss]
■ **1–3** mislay, misplace, displace, part with; suffer the loss of, be deprived of. **4, 5, 8, 10** give up, forfeit; yield, capitulate, admit defeat, succumb, be defeated *or* conquered, suffer defeat, be beaten *or* overcome *or* worsted *or* bested, *colloq.* lose out. **6** elude, evade, escape, slip, throw *or* shake off, give a person the slip, get rid of. **7** miss. **9** waste, let slip, squander, dissipate, fritter *or* trifle away; consume, use (up), expend, spend. **13 a** (*be lost*) see DISAPPEAR, DIE[1] 1. **b** see SIN[1] *v.* 1. **14** (**lost**) **a** gone, departed, vanished, stray(ed); missing, mislaid, misplaced, irrecoverable; wasted, misspent, gone by the board, squandered, spent, *colloq.* out of the window, down the drain; forgotten, past, bygone, extinct, obsolete, buried. **b** dead, departed, fallen, late; destroyed, demolished, devastated, ruined, wrecked, irreparable, unsalvageable, irreclaimable, irremediable. **c** damned, cursed, accursed, abandoned, corrupt, fallen, wanton, unchaste, dissolute; hopeless, irredeemable. □ **get lost** see *beat it.* **lose one's balance 1** see SLIP[1] *v.* 1. **lose one's cool** see EXPLODE 2. **lose one's nerve** see PANIC[1] *v.* **lose out** see LOSE 4, 5, 8, 10 above. **lose one's temper** see EXPLODE 2. **lost cause** see DISASTER 2, FAILURE 2.

loser /lóozər/ *n.* **1** a person or thing that loses or has lost (esp. a contest or game) (*is a poor loser*; *the loser pays*). **2** *colloq.* a person who regularly fails.
■ **2** also-ran, failure, lead balloon, *colloq.* wash-out, non-starter, lemon, schlemiel, sad sack, *sl.* flop, dud, no-hoper, *US sl.* schnook.

loss /loss/ *n.* **1** the act or an instance of losing; the state of being lost. **2** a person, thing, or amount lost. **3** the detriment or disadvantage resulting from losing (*that is no great loss*). □ **at a loss** (sold etc.) for less than was paid for it. **be at a loss** be puzzled or uncertain. **be at a loss for words** not know what to say. **loss adjuster** an insurance agent who assesses the amount of compensation arising from a loss. **loss-leader** an item sold at a loss to attract customers. [ME *los, loss* prob. back-form. f. *lost*, past part. of LOSE]
■ **1** deprivation, bereavement, privation, denial, sacrifice, forfeiture, disappearance; defeat, set-back, disadvantage, disappointment, failure, downfall, collapse, breakdown, ruin; drubbing, trouncing. **2** diminution, erosion, reduction, impoverishment, depletion, shrinkage, waste, wastage; debit, liability; casualty, death. **3** disadvantage, detriment, harm, impairment, injury, damage. □ **be at a loss** be confused *or* baffled *or* perplexed *or* puzzled *or* mystified *or* bewildered *or* confounded *or* adrift *or* helpless *or* disorient(at)ed *or* (all) at sea.

lost *past* and *past part.* of LOSE.

lot /lot/ *n.* & *v.* ● *n.* **1** *colloq.* (prec. by *a* or in *pl.*) **a** a large number or amount (*a lot of people*; *lots of chocolate*). **b** *colloq.* much (*a lot warmer*; *smiles a lot*; *is lots better*). **2 a** each of a set of objects used in making a chance selection. **b** this method of deciding (*chosen by lot*). **3** a share, or the responsibility resulting from it. **4** a person's destiny, fortune, or condition. **5** esp. *US* a plot; an allotment of land (*parking lot*). **6** an article or set of articles for sale at an auction etc. **7** a number or quantity of associated persons or things. ● *v.tr.* (**lotted, lotting**) divide into lots. □ **bad lot** a person of bad character. **cast** (or **draw**) **lots** decide by means of lots. **throw in one's lot with** decide to share the fortunes of. **the** (or **the whole**) **lot** the whole number or quantity. **a whole lot** *colloq.* very much (*is a whole lot better*). [OE *hlot* portion, choice f. Gmc]
■ *n.* **1** (*a lot* or *lots*) a good *or* great deal, plenty, reams, a mass *or* masses, mountains *or* a mountain, *colloq.* oodles, zillions, loads, tons *or* a ton, stacks *or* a stack, piles *or* a pile, heaps *or* a heap, pots *or* a pot, *US colloq.* scads; (*a lot of*) many, numerous, innumerable, countless, *literary* myriad; not a little. **2 b** lottery, raffle; drawing lots *or* straws. **3** share, portion, division, interest, part, allotment, assignment, apportionment, ration, allowance. **4** luck, fortune, destiny, fate, karma, plight, doom, end. **7** collection, batch, consignment, assortment, group, portion, set, quantity, grouping. □ **the** (or **the whole**) **lot** everything, *sl.* the whole caboodle.

loth var. of LOATH.

Lothario /ləthaáriō, -tháiriō/ *n.* (*pl.* **-os**) a rake or libertine. [a character in Rowe's *Fair Penitent* (1703)]
■ see LIBERTINE *n.* 1.

lotion /lṓsh'n/ *n.* a medicinal or cosmetic liquid preparation applied externally. [ME f. OF *lotion* or L *lotio* f. *lavare lot-* wash]
■ cream, liniment, balm, salve, ointment, embrocation, unguent, pomade.

lottery /lóttəri/ *n.* (*pl.* **-ies**) **1** a means of raising money by selling numbered tickets and giving prizes to the holders of numbers drawn at random. **2** an enterprise, process, etc., whose success is governed by chance (*life is a lottery*). [prob. f. Du. *loterij* (as LOT)]
■ **1** raffle, sweepstake, draw, pool, *Brit.* tombola.

lotto /lóttō/ *n.* a game of chance like bingo, but with numbers drawn instead of called. [It.]

lotus /lṓtəss/ *n.* **1** (in Greek mythology) a legendary plant inducing luxurious languor when eaten. **2 a** any water lily of the genus *Nelumbo*, esp. *N. nucifera* of India, with large pink flowers. **b** this flower used symbolically in Hinduism and Buddhism. **3** an Egyptian water lily, *Nymphaea lotus*, with white flowers. **4** any plant of the genus *Lotus*, e.g. bird's foot trefoil. □ **lotus-eater** a person given to indolent enjoyment. **lotus-land** a place of indolent enjoyment. **lotus position** a cross-legged position of meditation with the feet resting on the thighs. [L f. Gk *lōtos*, of Semitic orig.]

louche /loōsh/ *adj.* disreputable, shifty. [F, = squinting]
■ see DISREPUTABLE 1.

loud /lowd/ *adj.* & *adv.* ● *adj.* **1 a** strongly audible, esp. noisily or oppressively so. **b** able or liable to produce loud sounds (*a loud engine*). **c** clamorous, insistent (*loud complaints*). **2** (of colours, design, etc.) gaudy, obtrusive. **3** (of behaviour) aggressive and noisy. ● *adv.* in a loud manner. □ **loud hailer** an electronic device for amplifying the sound of the voice so that it can be heard at a distance. **loud-mouth** *colloq.* a loud-mouthed person. **loud-mouthed** *colloq.* noisily self-assertive; vociferous. **out loud 1** aloud. **2** loudly (*laughed out loud*). □□ **louden** *v.tr.* & *intr.* **loudish** *adj.* **loudly** *adv.* **loudness** *n.* [OE *hlūd* f. WG]
■ *adj.* **1** deafening, ear-splitting, ear-piercing, booming, blaring, stentorian, thunderous, sonorous, noisy, piercing, *Mus.* fortissimo; clamorous, insistent. **2** tawdry, garish, flashy, gaudy, tasteless, extravagant, showy, ostentatious, jazzy, *colloq.* splashy, *sl.* snazzy. **3** loud-mouthed, brash, vociferous, raucous; see also ROWDY *adj.*

loudspeaker /lowdspeékər/ *n.* an apparatus that converts electrical impulses into sound, esp. music and voice.

lough /lok, lokh/ *n. Ir.* = LOCH. [Ir. *loch* LOCH, assim. to the related obs. ME form *lough*]

louis /loō-i/ *n.* (*pl.* same /loō-iz/) *hist.* (in full **louis d'or** /dor/) a former French gold coin worth about 20 francs. [*Louis*, the name of kings of France]

lounge /lownj/ *v.* & *n.* ● *v.intr.* **1** recline comfortably and casually; loll. **2** stand or move about idly. ● *n.* **1** a place for lounging, esp.: **a** a public room (e.g. in a hotel). **b** a place in an airport etc. with seats for waiting passengers. **c** a sitting-room in a house. **2** a spell of lounging. □ **lounge bar** *Brit.* a more comfortable room for drinking in a public house. **lounge lizard** *colloq.* an idler in fashionable society. **lounge suit** *Brit.* a man's formal suit for ordinary day wear. [perh. f. obs. *lungis* lout]
■ *v.* idle, loaf, laze, loll, languish. ● *n.* **1 a, b** lobby, foyer, waiting-room, reception (room). **c** sitting-room, living-room, front room, parlour, salon. □ **lounge bar** saloon (bar), cocktail bar, *Brit.* snug.

lounger /lównjər/ *n.* **1** a person who lounges. **2** a piece of furniture for relaxing on. **3** a casual garment for wearing when relaxing.

loupe /lōōp/ *n.* a small magnifying glass used by jewellers etc. [F]

lour /lowr/ *v.* & *n.* (also **lower**) ● *v.intr.* **1** frown; look sullen. **2** (of the sky etc.) look dark and threatening. ● *n.* **1** a scowl. **2** a gloomy look (of the sky etc.). □□ **louringly** *adv.* **loury** *adj.* [ME *loure*, of unkn. orig.]
■ *v.* **1** frown, scowl, glower; sulk, pout, mope. **2** darken; threaten, menace, loom.

louse /lowss/ *n.* & *v.* ● *n.* **1** (*pl.* **lice** /līss/) **a** a parasitic insect, *Pediculus humanus*, infesting the human hair and skin and transmitting various diseases. **b** any insect of the order Anoplura or Mallophaga parasitic on mammals, birds, fish, or plants. **2** *sl.* (*pl.* **louses**) a contemptible or unpleasant person. ● *v.tr.* remove lice from. □ **louse up** *sl.* make a mess of. [OE *lūs*, pl. *lȳs*]
■ **2** see WRETCH 2. □ **louse up** see BOTCH *v.* 1.

lousewort /lówswurt/ *n.* any plant of the genus *Pedicularis* with purple-pink flowers found in marshes and wet places.

lousy /lówzi/ *adj.* (**lousier, lousiest**) **1** infested with lice. **2** *colloq.* very bad; disgusting (also as a term of general disparagement). **3** *colloq.* (often foll. by *with*) well supplied, teeming (with). □□ **lousily** *adv.* **lousiness** *n.*
■ **1** pedicular, pediculous. **2** awful, terrible, mean, contemptible, low, base, hateful, detestable, despicable, vile, wretched, miserable, scurvy, dirty, vicious, *sl.* rotten; bad, poor, inferior; low-quality, shoddy, shabby, miserable, second-rate. **3** (*lousy with*) alive with, awash with, overflowing with, overloaded with, swarming with, teeming with, crawling with, knee-deep in.

lout /lowt/ *n.* a rough, crude, or ill-mannered person (usu. a man). □□ **loutish** *adj.* **loutishly** *adv.* **loutishness** *n.* [perh. f. archaic *lout* to bow]
■ see ROWDY *n.* □□ **loutish** see ROUGH *adj.* 4a.

louvre /lōōvər/ *n.* (also **louver**) **1** each of a set of overlapping slats designed to admit air and some light and exclude rain. **2** a domed structure on a roof with side openings for ventilation etc. □ **louvre-boards** the slats or boards making up a louvre. □□ **louvred** *adj.* [ME f. OF *lover*, *lovier* skylight, prob. f. Gmc]

lovable /lúvvəb'l/ *adj.* (also **loveable**) inspiring or deserving love or affection. □□ **lovability** /-bílliti/ *n.* **lovableness** *n.* **lovably** *adv.*
■ adorable, darling, dear, cherished, likeable, attractive, engaging, fetching, taking, alluring, endearing, appealing, winsome, sweet, tender, cuddly, affectionate, charming, enchanting, *US* cunning, *esp. US colloq.* cute, *literary* lovesome.

lovage /lúvvij/ *n.* **1** a S. European herb, *Levisticum officinale*, used for flavouring etc. **2** a white-flowered umbelliferous plant, *Ligusticum scoticum*. [ME *loveache* alt. f. OF *levesche* f. LL *levisticum* f. L *ligusticum* neut. of *ligusticus* Ligurian]

lovat /lúvvət/ *n.* (also *attrib.*) a muted green colour found esp. in tweed and woollen garments. [*Lovat* in Scotland]

love /luv/ *n.* & *v.* ● *n.* **1** an intense feeling of deep affection or fondness for a person or thing; great liking. **2** sexual passion. **3** sexual relations. **4 a** a beloved one; a sweetheart (often as a form of address). **b** *Brit. colloq.* a form of address regardless of affection. **5** *colloq.* a person of whom one is fond. **6** affectionate greetings (*give him my love*). **7** (often **Love**) a representation of Cupid. **8** (in some games) no score; nil. ● *v.tr.* **1** (also *absol.*) feel love or deep fondness for. **2** delight in; admire; greatly cherish. **3** *colloq.* like very much (*loves books*). **4** (foll. by verbal noun, or *to* + infin.) be inclined, esp. as a habit; greatly enjoy; find pleasure in (*children love dressing up*; *loves to find fault*). □ **fall in love** (often foll. by *with*) develop a great (esp. sexual) love (for). **for love** for pleasure not profit. **for the love of** for the sake of. **in love** (often foll. by *with*) deeply enamoured (of). **love affair** a romantic or sexual relationship between two people in love; a passion for something. **love-apple** *archaic* a tomato. **love-bird** any of various African and Madagascan parrots, esp. *Agapornis personata*. **love-child** an illegitimate child. **love-feast 1** a meal affirming brotherly love among early Christians. **2** a religious service of Methodists, etc., imitating this. **love game** a game in which the loser makes no score. **love-hate relationship** an intensely emotional relationship in which one or each party has ambivalent feelings of love and hate for the other. **love-in-a-mist** a blue-flowered garden plant, *Nigella damascena*, with many delicate green bracts. **love-letter** a letter expressing feelings of sexual love. **love-lies-bleeding** a garden plant, *Amaranthus caudatus*, with drooping spikes of purple-red blooms. **love-match** a marriage made for love's sake. **love-nest** a place of intimate lovemaking. **love-seat** an armchair or small sofa for two. **make love** (often foll. by *to*) **1** have sexual intercourse (with). **2** *archaic* pay amorous attention (to). **not for love or money** *colloq.* not in any circumstances. **out of love** no longer in love. □□ **loveworthy** *adj.* [OE *lufu* f. Gmc]
■ *n.* **1** warmth, affection, attachment, fondness, tenderness, devotion, attraction, friendship, amity, regard, admiration, fancy, adoration, adulation; liking, delight, enjoyment, pleasure, fondness, predilection, bent, leaning, proclivity, inclination, disposition, weakness, partiality, preference, taste, relish; sympathy, concern, charity, care, solicitude, affinity, rapport, harmony, brotherhood, sisterhood, fellow-feeling. **2** ardour, passion, lust, fervour, rapture, infatuation. **4a, 5** darling, beloved, sweetheart, sweet, dear(est), *esp. US* honey, *colloq.* lovey, sweetie(-pie), *usu. joc.* light of one's life; lover, true-love, mate, *archaic* paramour; intended, betrothed; girlfriend, inamorata, lady-love, young lady, fiancée; boyfriend, beau, inamorato, suitor, young man, fiancé, *archaic* leman, *poet.* swain. ● *v.* **1** cherish, admire, adore, be in love with, lose one's heart to, worship, idolize, dote on, treasure, be infatuated with, think the world of, adulate, hold dear, like, be mad about, *colloq.* be crazy *or* nuts *or* wild about, have a crush on, *sl.* be hung up on. **2–4** cherish, delight in, take pleasure in, derive pleasure *or* enjoyment from, relish, be partial to, have a passion *or* preference *or* taste for, be attracted to, be captivated by, be fond of, like, enjoy, appreciate, value, be mad about, *colloq.* get a kick out of, be crazy *or* nuts *or* wild about, *sl.* go a bundle on, *US sl.* get a bang from *or* out of. □ **love affair** amour, liaison, affair, *affaire (de cœur)*, romance, relationship, *archaic* intrigue; passion, mania. **love-letter** *often joc.* billet-doux. **make love** embrace, cuddle, caress, fondle, *colloq.* neck, pet, canoodle; romance; have sexual intercourse, *colloq.* have sex; take, *archaic* know.

loveable var. of LOVABLE.

lovebite /lúvbīt/ *n.* a red mark on the neck, caused by biting during lovemaking.

loveless /lúvliss/ *adj.* without love; unloving or unloved or both. □□ **lovelessly** *adv.* **lovelessness** *n.*

lovelock /lúvlok/ *n.* a curl or lock of hair worn on the temple or forehead.

lovelorn /lúvlorn/ *adj.* pining from unrequited love.

lovely /lúvli/ *adj.* & *n.* ● *adj.* (**lovelier, loveliest**) **1** exquisitely beautiful. **2** *colloq.* pleasing, delightful. ● *n.* (*pl.* **-ies**) *colloq.* a pretty woman. □ **lovely and** *colloq.* delightfully (*lovely and warm*). □□ **lovelily** *adv.* **loveliness** *n.* [OE *luflic* (as LOVE)]
■ *adj.* **1** good-looking, pretty, handsome, attractive, comely, fair, fetching, engaging, captivating, alluring, enticing, bewitching, ravishing, gorgeous, exquisite, beautiful, *literary* pulchritudinous, lovesome, *poet.* beauteous. **2** satisfying, satisfactory, agreeable, enjoyable, gratifying, nice, pleasing, pleasant, pleasurable, engaging, delightful.

lovemaking /lúvmayking/ *n.* **1** amorous sexual activity, esp. sexual intercourse. **2** *archaic* courtship.
■ **1** see SEX 5.

lover /lúvvər/ *n.* **1** a person in love with another. **2** a person with whom another is having sexual relations. **3** (in *pl.*) a

couple in love or having sexual relations. **4** a person who likes or enjoys something specified (*a music lover*; *a lover of words*). □□ **loverless** *adj.*
■ **1** see LOVE *n.* 4a, 5. **4** see ENTHUSIAST.

lovesick /lúvsik/ *adj.* languishing with romantic love. □□ **lovesickness** *n.*

lovesome /lúvsəm/ *adj. literary* lovely, lovable.

lovey /lúvvi/ *n.* (*pl.* **-eys**) *colloq.* love, sweetheart (esp. as a form of address).

lovey-dovey /lúvvidúvvi/ *adj. colloq.* fondly affectionate, esp. unduly sentimental.

loving /lúvving/ *adj.* & *n.* ● *adj.* feeling or showing love; affectionate. ● *n.* affection; active love. □ **loving-cup** a two-handled drinking-cup passed round at banquets. **loving-kindness** tenderness and consideration. □□ **lovingly** *adv.* **lovingness** *n.* [OE *lufiende* (as LOVE)]
■ *adj.* see AFFECTIONATE. □□ **lovingly** see *fondly* (FOND).

low[1] /lō/ *adj.*, *n.*, & *adv.* ● *adj.* **1** of less than average height; not high or tall or reaching far up (*a low wall*). **2 a** situated close to ground or sea level etc.; not elevated in position (*low altitude*). **b** (of the sun) near the horizon. **c** (of latitude) near the equator. **3** of or in humble rank or position (*of low birth*). **4** of small or less than normal amount or extent or intensity (*low price*; *low temperature*; *low in calories*). **5** small or reduced in quantity (*stocks are low*). **6** coming below the normal level (*a dress with a low neck*). **7 a** dejected; lacking vigour (*feeling low*; *in low spirits*). **b** poorly nourished; indicative of poor nutrition. **8** (of a sound) not shrill or loud or high-pitched. **9** not exalted or sublime; commonplace. **10** unfavourable (*a low opinion*). **11** abject, mean, vulgar (*low cunning*; *low slang*). **12** (in *compar.*) situated on less high land or to the south. **13** (of a geographical period) earlier. ● *n.* **1** a low or the lowest level or number (*the dollar has reached a new low*). **2** an area of low pressure. ● *adv.* **1** in or to a low position or state. **2** in a low tone (*speak low*). **3** (of a sound) at or to a low pitch. □ **low-born** of humble birth. **Low Church** the section of the Church of England giving a low place to ritual, priestly authority, and the sacraments. **low-class** of low quality or social class. **low comedy** that in which the subject and the treatment border on farce. **Low Countries** the Netherlands, Belgium, and Luxembourg. **low-cut** (of a dress etc.) made with a low neckline. **low-down** *adj.* abject, mean, dishonourable. ● *n. colloq.* (usu. foll. by *on*) the relevant information (about). **lowest common denominator, multiple** see DENOMINATOR, MULTIPLE. **low frequency** (in radio) 30–300 kilohertz. **low gear** see GEAR. **Low German** see GERMAN. **low-grade** of low quality or strength. **low-key** lacking intensity or prominence; restrained. **Low Latin** medieval and later forms of Latin. **low-level** *Computing* (of a programming language) close in form to machine language. **low-loader** a lorry with a low floor and no sides, for heavy loads. **low-lying** at low altitude (above sea level etc.). **low mass** see MASS[2]. **low-pitched 1** (of a sound) low. **2** (of a roof) having only a slight slope. **low pressure 1** little demand for activity or exertion. **2** an atmospheric condition with pressure below average. **low profile** avoidance of attention or publicity. **low-profile** *adj.* **1** having a low profile. **2** (of a motor-vehicle tyre) having a greater width than usual in relation to height. **low relief** see RELIEF 6a. **low-rise** (of a building) having few storeys. **low season** the period of fewest visitors at a resort etc. **low-spirited** dejected, dispirited. **low-spiritedness** dejection, depression. **low spirits** dejection, depression. **Low Sunday** the Sunday after Easter. **low tide** the time or level of the tide at its ebb. **low water** the tide at its lowest. **low-water mark 1** the level reached at low water. **2** a minimum recorded level or value etc. **Low Week** the week beginning with Low Sunday. □□ **lowish** *adj.* **lowness** *n.* [ME *lāh* f. ON *lágr* f. Gmc]
■ *adj.* **1** short, squat, little, small, stubby, stumpy, stunted. **2 a** low-lying. **3** humble, poor, low-born, lowly, base, base-born, inferior, plebeian, proletarian, ignoble. **4** small, reduced. **5** inadequate, insufficient, deficient, down, short, sparse, scanty, scant, limited. **7** weak, frail, feeble, debilitated, enervated, sickly, unhealthy, infirm, shaky, decrepit, ill, sick; ineffectual, ineffective; miserable, dismal, wretched, abysmal, sorry, abject, destitute; unhappy, depressed, dejected, sad, gloomy, melancholy, low-spirited, dispirited, despondent, disconsolate, blue, downcast, down, glum, morose, crestfallen, broken-hearted, heartbroken, tearful, sorrowful, mournful, heavy-hearted, *formal* lachrymose. **8** quiet, hushed, soft, subdued, gentle, muted, low-pitched, muffled, stifled, indistinct, whispered, murmured, murmurous. **9** inferior, second-rate, poor, bad, low-grade, not up to par, worthless, shoddy, shabby, mediocre, substandard; commonplace. **10** unfavourable, critical, adverse. **11** base, vile, abject, contemptible, despicable, mean, menial, servile, ignoble, degraded, foul, dastardly, depraved, nasty, sordid; coarse, unrefined, indelicate, risqué, indecent, unseemly, vulgar, crude, common, rude, gross, offensive, smutty, dirty. □ **low-born** see LOW[1] *adj.* 3 above. **low-cut** revealing, *décolleté*. **low-down** (*n.*) information, intelligence, data, facts, inside story *or* information, *colloq.* info, *sl.* dope. **low-pitched 1** see LOW[1] *adj.* 8 above. **low-spirited** see LOW[1] *adj.* 7 above.

low[2] /lō/ *n.* & *v.* ● *n.* a sound made by cattle; a moo. ● *v.intr.* utter this sound. [OE *hlōwan* f. Gmc]
■ *v.* moo, bellow.

lowboy /lṓboy/ *n. US* a low chest or table with drawers and short legs.
■ see CABINET 1a.

lowbrow /lṓbrow/ *adj.* & *n.* ● *adj.* not highly intellectual or cultured. ● *n.* a lowbrow person. □□ **lowbrowed** *adj.*
■ *adj.* see PHILISTINE *adj.* ● *n.* see PHILISTINE *n.*

lower[1] /lṓər/ *adj.* & *adv.* ● *adj.* (*compar.* of LOW[1]). **1** less high in position or status. **2** situated below another part (*lower lip*; *lower atmosphere*). **3 a** situated on less high land (*Lower Egypt*). **b** situated to the South (*Lower California*). **4** (of a mammal, plant, etc.) evolved to a relatively small degree (e.g. a platypus or fungus). ● *adv.* in or to a lower position, status, etc. □ **lower case** see CASE[2]. **lower class** working-class people and their families. **lower-class** *adj.* of the lower class. **lower deck 1** the deck of a ship situated immediately over the hold. **2** the petty officers and men of a ship collectively. **Lower House** the larger and usu. elected body in a legislature, esp. in Britain, the House of Commons. **lower regions** (or **world**) hell; the realm of the dead. □□ **lowermost** *adj.*
■ *adj.* **1** further down, under, *archaic* nether; see also INFERIOR *adj.* 1. **2, 3a** under, *archaic* nether; bottom, inferior. **3 b** southern, southerly, southernmost, south. **4** see PRIMITIVE *adj.* 7, 8. ● *adv.* see DOWNWARD *adv.* □ **lower-class** see PLEBEIAN *adj.* 1. **lower regions** see HELL 1.

lower[2] /lṓər/ *v.* **1** *tr.* let or haul down. **2** *tr.* & *intr.* make or become lower. **3** *tr.* reduce the height or pitch or elevation of (*lower your voice*; *lower one's eyes*). **4** *tr.* degrade. **5** *tr.* & *intr.* diminish.
■ **1** let *or* move *or* bring *or* put *or* haul down, drop. **2, 5** drop, reduce, decrease, mark down, discount, lessen, diminish, downgrade, cut, slash, lop, take down, crop, trim. **3** turn down, quiet, moderate, modulate, soften, tone down, *Brit.* quieten. **4** abase, debase, degrade, discredit, shame, disgrace, demean, belittle, humble, humiliate; (*lower oneself*) see CONDESCEND 1.

lower[3] var. of LOUR.

lowland /lṓlənd/ *n.* & *adj.* ● *n.* **1** (usu. in *pl.*) low-lying country. **2** (**Lowland**) (usu. in *pl.*) the region of Scotland lying south and east of the Highlands. ● *adj.* of or in lowland or the Scottish Lowlands. □□ **lowlander** *n.* (also **Lowlander**).
■ *n.* **1** see FLAT[1] *n.* 2.

lowlight /lṓlīt/ *n.* **1** a monotonous or dull period; a feature of little prominence (*one of the lowlights of the evening*). **2** (usu. in *pl.*) a dark tint in the hair produced by dyeing. [after HIGHLIGHT]

lowly /lṓli/ *adj.* (**lowlier, lowliest**) **1** humble in feeling, behaviour, or status. **2** modest, unpretentious. **3** (of an organism) evolved to only a slight degree. ▫▫ **lowlily** *adv.* **lowliness** *n.*
■ **1** see HUMBLE *adj.* 2. **2** see MODEST 5. **3** see PRIMITIVE *adj.* 7, 8.

low-minded /lṓmíndid/ *adj.* vulgar or ignoble in mind or character. ▫▫ **low-mindedness** *n.*

lox[1] /loks/ *n.* liquid oxygen. [abbr.]

lox[2] /loks/ *n. US* smoked salmon. [Yiddish *laks*]

loyal /lóyəl/ *adj.* **1** (often foll. by *to*) true or faithful (to duty, love, or obligation). **2** steadfast in allegiance; devoted to the legitimate sovereign or government of one's country. **3** showing loyalty. ▫ **loyal toast** a toast to the sovereign. ▫▫ **loyally** *adv.* [F f. OF *loial* etc. f. L *legalis* LEGAL]
■ faithful, true, dependable, devoted, trustworthy, steady, steadfast, staunch, trusted, reliable, stable, unswerving, unwavering, dedicated, constant, *archaic* trusty; patriotic.

loyalist /lóyəlist/ *n.* **1** a person who remains loyal to the legitimate sovereign etc., esp. in the face of rebellion or usurpation. **2** (**Loyalist**) a supporter of Parliamentary union between Great Britain and Northern Ireland. ▫▫ **loyalism** *n.*

loyalty /lóyəlti/ *n.* (*pl.* **-ies**) **1** the state of being loyal. **2** (often in *pl.*) a feeling or application of loyalty.
■ faithfulness, fidelity, dependability, devotedness, devotion, allegiance, patriotism, trustworthiness, steadfastness, staunchness, firmness, reliability, stability, dedication, constancy.

lozenge /lózzinj/ *n.* **1** a rhombus or diamond figure. **2** a small sweet or medicinal tablet, orig. lozenge-shaped, for dissolving in the mouth. **3** a lozenge-shaped pane in a window. **4** *Heraldry* a lozenge-shaped device. **5** the lozenge-shaped facet of a cut gem. ▫▫ **lozenged** *adj.* (in sense 4). **lozengy** *adj.* [ME f. OF *losenge*, ult. of Gaulish or Iberian orig.]
■ **2** see TABLET 1a.

LP *abbr.* **1** long-playing (gramophone record). **2** low pressure.
■ **1** see RECORD *n.* 3a.

LPG *abbr.* liquefied petroleum gas.

L-plate /él-playt/ *n. Brit.* a sign bearing the letter L, attached to the front and rear of a motor vehicle to indicate that it is being driven by a learner.

LPO *abbr.* London Philharmonic Orchestra.

LSD *abbr.* lysergic acid diethylamide.

l.s.d. /éllesdeé/ *n.* (also **£.s.d.**) *Brit.* **1** pounds, shillings, and pence (in former British currency). **2** money, riches. [L *librae, solidi, denarii*]

LSE *abbr.* London School of Economics.

LSO *abbr.* London Symphony Orchestra.

Lt. *abbr.* **1** Lieutenant. **2** light.

LTA *abbr.* Lawn Tennis Association.

Ltd. *abbr.* Limited.

Lu *symb. Chem.* the element lutetium.

lubber /lúbbər/ *n.* a big clumsy fellow; a lout. ▫ **lubber line** *Naut.* a line marked on a compass, showing the ship's forward direction. ▫▫ **lubberlike** *adj.* **lubberly** *adj.* & *adv.* [ME, perh. f. OF *lobeor* swindler, parasite f. *lober* deceive]
■ ▫▫ **lubberly** (*adj.*) see CLUMSY 1.

lubra /lóóbrə/ *n. Austral.* sometimes *derog.* an Aboriginal woman. [F *loubra* f. Tasmanian]

lubricant /lóóbrikənt/ *n.* & *adj.* ● *n.* a substance used to reduce friction. ● *adj.* lubricating.
■ *n.* see OIL *n.*

lubricate /lóóbrikayt/ *v.tr.* **1** reduce friction in (machinery etc.) by applying oil or grease etc. **2** make slippery or smooth with oil or grease. ▫▫ **lubrication** /-káysh'n/ *n.* **lubricative** /-kətiv/ *adj.* **lubricator** *n.* [L *lubricare lubricat-* f. *lubricus* slippery]
■ oil, grease.

lubricious /loobríshəss/ *adj.* (also **lubricous** /lóóbrikəss/) **1** slippery, smooth, oily. **2** lewd, prurient, evasive. ▫▫ **lubricity** *n.* [L *lubricus* slippery]
■ **2** see LEWD. ▫▫ **lubricity** see *indecency* (INDECENT).

Lucan /lóókən/ *adj.* of or relating to St Luke. [eccl.L *Lucas* f. Gk *Loukas* Luke]

luce /looss/ *n.* a pike (fish), esp. when full-grown. [ME f. OF *lus, luis* f. LL *lucius*]

lucent /lóóss'nt/ *adj. literary* **1** shining, luminous. **2** translucent. ▫▫ **lucency** *n.* **lucently** *adv.* [L *lucēre* shine (as LUX)]

lucerne /loosérn/ *n.* (also **lucern**) *Brit.* = ALFALFA. [F *luzerne* f. mod. Prov. *luzerno* glow-worm, with ref. to its shiny seeds]

lucid /lóóssid/ *adj.* **1** expressing or expressed clearly; easy to understand. **2** of or denoting intervals of sanity between periods of insanity or dementia. **3** *Bot.* with a smooth shining surface. **4** *poet.* bright. ▫▫ **lucidity** /-síddity/ *n.* **lucidly** *adv.* **lucidness** *n.* [L *lucidus* (perh. through F *lucide* or It. *lucido*) f. *lucēre* shine (as LUX)]
■ **1** see CLEAR *adj.* 6b. **2** see RIGHT *adj.* 5, SANE 1. **4** see VIVID 1. ▫▫ **lucidity** see CLARITY.

Lucifer /lóóssifər/ *n.* **1** Satan. **2** *poet.* the morning star (the planet Venus). **3** (**lucifer**) *archaic* a friction match. [OE f. L, = light-bringing, morning-star (as LUX, *-fer* f. *ferre* bring)]
■ **1** see DEVIL *n.* 1, 2.

luck /luk/ *n.* **1** chance regarded as the bringer of good or bad fortune. **2** circumstances of life (beneficial or not) brought by this. **3** good fortune; success due to chance (*in luck*; *out of luck*). ▫ **for luck** to bring good fortune. **good luck 1** good fortune. **2** an omen of this. **hard luck** worse fortune than one deserves. **no such luck** *colloq.* unfortunately not. **try one's luck** make a venture. **with luck** if all goes well. **worse luck** *colloq.* unfortunately. [ME f. LG *luk* f. MLG *geluke*]
■ **1, 2** fortune, chance; destiny, fate, accident, fortuity, *US* happenstance, *Austral. colloq.* mozzle; fluke. **3** good fortune, good luck, serendipity; stroke of luck, *colloq.* break; success.

luckily /lúkkili/ *adv.* **1** (qualifying a whole sentence or clause) fortunately (*luckily there was enough food*). **2** in a lucky or fortunate manner.
■ fortunately, mercifully, happily; opportunely, propitiously, well.

luckless /lúkliss/ *adj.* having no luck; unfortunate. ▫▫ **lucklessly** *adv.* **lucklessness** *n.*
■ see UNFORTUNATE *adj.* 1.

lucky /lúkki/ *adj.* (**luckier, luckiest**) **1** having or resulting from good luck, esp. as distinct from skill or design or merit. **2** bringing good luck (*a lucky mascot*). **3** fortunate, appropriate (*a lucky guess*). ▫ **lucky dip** *Brit.* a tub containing different articles concealed in wrapping or bran etc., and chosen at random by participants. ▫▫ **luckiness** *n.*
■ **1** fortunate; favoured, charmed, blessed; *Austral. sl.* tinny. **2** providential, propitious, favourable, auspicious, advantageous. **3** fortunate, timely, opportune, convenient, fortuitous, appropriate, happy.

lucrative /lóókrətiv/ *adj.* profitable, yielding financial gain. ▫▫ **lucratively** *adv.* **lucrativeness** *n.* [ME f. L *lucrativus* f. *lucrari* to gain]
■ see PROFITABLE 1.

lucre /lóókər/ *n. derog.* financial profit or gain. ▫ **filthy lucre** see FILTHY. [ME f. F *lucre* or L *lucrum*]
■ see PROFIT *n.* 2.

lucubrate /lóókyoobrayt/ *v.intr. literary* **1** write or study, esp. by night. **2** express one's meditations in writing. ▫▫ **lucubrator** *n.* [L *lucubrare lucubrat-* work by lamplight (as LUX)]
■ **1** see STUDY *v.* 2.

lucubration /lóókyoobráysh'n/ *n. literary* **1** nocturnal study or meditation. **2** (usu. in *pl.*) literary writings, esp. of a pedantic or elaborate character. [L *lucubratio* (as LUCUBRATE)]

Lucullan /lookúllən/ *adj.* profusely luxurious. [L. Licinius *Lucullus*, Roman general of 1st c. BC famous for his lavish banquets]

lud /lud/ *n. Brit.* □ **m'lud** (or **my lud**) a form of address to a judge in a court of law. [corrupt. of LORD]

Luddite /lúddīt/ *n.* & *adj.* ● *n.* **1** *hist.* a member of any of the bands of English artisans who rioted against mechanization and destroyed machinery (1811–16). **2** a person opposed to increased industrialization or new technology. ● *adj.* of the Luddites or their beliefs. □□ **Luddism** *n.* **Ludditism** *n.* [perh. f. Ned *Lud*, who destroyed machinery *c.* 1779]

ludicrous /lo͞odikrəss/ *adj.* absurd or ridiculous; laughable. □□ **ludicrously** *adv.* **ludicrousness** *n.* [L *ludicrus* prob. f. *ludicrum* stage play]
■ ridiculous, laughable, absurd, farcical, nonsensical, preposterous, incongruous, asinine, foolish, silly, zany, crazy, comical, risible; funny, facetious, droll, waggish, jocular, witty, jocose.

ludo /lo͞odō/ *n. Brit.* a simple board game in which counters are moved round according to the throw of dice. [L, = I play]

lues /lo͞o-eez/ *n.* (in full **lues venerea** /vineéria/) syphilis. □□ **luetic** /loo-éttik/ *adj.* [L]

luff /luf/ *n.* & *v.* (also **loof** /lo͞of/) *Naut.* ● *n.* **1** the edge of the fore-and-aft sail next to the mast or stay. **2** *Brit.* the broadest part of the ship's bow where the sides begin to curve in. ● *v.tr.* (also *absol.*) **1** steer (a ship) nearer the wind. **2** turn (the helm) so as to achieve this. **3** obstruct (an opponent in yacht-racing) by sailing closer to the wind. **4** raise or lower (the jib of a crane or derrick). [ME *lo(o)f* f. OF *lof*, prob. f. LG]

luffa var. of LOOFAH.

Luftwaffe /lo͞oftvaffə/ *n. hist.* the German Air Force. [G f. *Luft* air + *Waffe* weapon]

lug[1] /lug/ *v.* & *n.* ● *v.* (**lugged, lugging**) **1** *tr.* **a** drag or tug (a heavy object) with effort or violence. **b** (usu. foll. by *round, about*) carry (something heavy) around with one. **2** *tr.* (usu. foll. by *in, into*) introduce (a subject etc.) irrelevantly. **3** *tr.* (usu. foll. by *along, to*) force (a person) to join in an activity. **4** *intr.* (usu. foll. by *at*) pull hard. ● *n.* **1** a hard or rough pull. **2** (in *pl.*) *US* affectation (*put on lugs*). [ME, prob. f. Scand.: cf. Sw. *lugga* pull a person's hair f. *lugg* forelock]
■ *v.* **1, 4** drag, tug, tow, haul, heave, pull; carry, transport, *colloq.* schlep, *esp. US colloq.* tote.

lug[2] /lug/ *n.* **1** *Sc.* or *colloq.* an ear. **2** a projection on an object by which it may be carried, fixed in place, etc. **3** esp. *US sl.* a lout; a sponger; a stupid person. [prob. of Scand. orig.: cf. LUG[1]]

lug[3] /lug/ *n.* = LUGWORM. [17th c.: orig. unkn.]

lug[4] /lug/ *n.* = LUGSAIL. [abbr.]

luge /lo͞ozh/ *n.* & *v.* ● *n.* a light toboggan for one or two people, ridden in the sitting position. ● *v.intr.* ride on a luge. [Swiss F]

Luger /lo͞ogər/ *n.* a type of German automatic pistol. [G. *Luger*, German firearms expert d. 1922]

luggage /lúggij/ *n.* suitcases, bags, etc. to hold a traveller's belongings. □ **luggage-van** *Brit.* a railway carriage for travellers' luggage. [LUG[1] + -AGE]
■ baggage, bags, suitcases, gear, impedimenta, paraphernalia, things, belongings.

lugger /lúggər/ *n.* a small ship carrying two or three masts with a lugsail on each. [LUGSAIL + -ER[1]]

lughole /lúg-hōl, lúggōl/ *n. sl.* the ear orifice. [LUG[2] + HOLE]

lugsail /lúgsayl, -s'l/ *n. Naut.* a quadrilateral sail which is bent on and hoisted from a yard. [prob. f. LUG[2]]

lugubrious /loogo͞obriəss/ *adj.* doleful, mournful, dismal. □□ **lugubriously** *adv.* **lugubriousness** *n.* [L *lugubris* f. *lugēre* mourn]
■ see DISMAL 1, 2. □□ **lugubriously** see *sadly* (SAD). **lugubriousness** see MELANCHOLY *n.*

lugworm /lúgwurm/ *n.* any polychaete worm of the genus *Arenicola*, living in muddy sand and leaving characteristic worm-casts on lower shores, and often used as bait by fishermen. [LUG[3]]

lukewarm /lo͞okwáwrm/ *adj.* **1** moderately warm; tepid. **2** unenthusiastic, indifferent. □□ **lukewarmly** *adv.* **lukewarmness** *n.* [ME f. (now dial.) *luke*, *lew* f. OE]
■ **1** tepid, cool, (at) room temperature, warm; *chambré.* **2** cool, indifferent, half-hearted, chilly, phlegmatic, unresponsive, unenthusiastic, unexcited, nonchalant, lackadaisical, apathetic, noncommittal, insouciant, Laodicean, unmoved, *colloq.* laid-back, unenthused.

lull /lul/ *v.* & *n.* ● *v.* **1** *tr.* soothe or send to sleep gently. **2** *tr.* (usu. foll. by *into*) deceive (a person) into confidence (*lulled into a false sense of security*). **3** *tr.* allay (suspicions etc.) usu. by deception. **4** *intr.* (of noise, a storm, etc.) abate or fall quiet. ● *n.* a temporary quiet period in a storm or in any activity. [ME, imit. of sounds used to quieten a child]
■ *v.* **1** soothe, calm, quiet, hush, pacify, mollify, tranquillize, *Brit.* quieten. ● *n.* pause, respite, interlude, intermission, interval, break, hiatus, interruption, stop, halt, lapse, delay, *Prosody* caesura, *colloq.* let-up; quiet, quiescence, hush, calm, calmness, stillness, silence, peace, peacefulness, tranquillity.

lullaby /lúlləbī/ *n.* & *v.* ● *n.* (*pl.* **-ies**) **1** a soothing song to send a child to sleep. **2** the music for this. ● *v.tr.* (**-ies, -ied**) sing to sleep. [as LULL + *-by* as in BYE-BYE[2]]

lulu /lo͞olo͞o/ *n. sl.* a remarkable or excellent person or thing. [19th c., perh. f. *Lulu*, pet form of *Louise*]
■ see KILLER 2a.

lumbago /lumbáygō/ *n.* rheumatic pain in the muscles of the lower back. [L f. *lumbus* loin]

lumbar /lúmbər/ *adj. Anat.* relating to the loin, esp. the lower back area. □ **lumbar puncture** the withdrawal of spinal fluid from the lower back with a hollow needle, usu. for diagnosis. [med.L *lumbaris* f. L *lumbus* loin]

lumber[1] /lúmbər/ *v.intr.* (usu. foll. by *along, past, by*, etc.) move in a slow clumsy noisy way. □□ **lumbering** *adj.* [ME *lomere*, perh. imit.]

lumber[2] /lúmbər/ *n.* & *v.* ● *n.* **1** disused articles of furniture etc. inconveniently taking up space. **2** useless or cumbersome objects. **3** *US* partly prepared timber. ● *v.* **1** *tr.* **a** (usu. foll. by *with*) leave (a person etc.) with something unwanted or unpleasant (*always lumbering me with the cleaning*). **b** (as **lumbered** *adj.*) in an unwanted or inconvenient situation (*afraid of being lumbered*). **2** *tr.* (usu. foll. by *together*) heap or group together carelessly. **3** *tr.* (usu. foll. by *up*) obstruct. **4** *intr.* cut and prepare forest timber for transport. □ **lumber-jacket** a jacket, usu. of warm checked material, of the kind worn by lumberjacks. **lumber-room** a room where disused or cumbrous things are kept. □□ **lumberer** *n.* (in sense 4 of *v.*). **lumbering** *n.* (in sense 4 of *v.*). [perh. f. LUMBER[1]: later assoc. with obs. *lumber* pawnbroker's shop]
■ *n.* **1, 2** odds and ends, junk, clutter, jumble, rejects, white elephants. **3** timber, wood, beams, planks, boards. ● *v.* **1** encumber, burden, load, overload, saddle, impose upon, land.

lumberjack /lúmbərjak/ *n.* (also **lumberman** *pl.* **-men**) esp. *US* one who fells, prepares, or conveys lumber.

lumbersome /lúmbərsəm/ *adj.* unwieldy, awkward.

lumbrical muscle /lúmbrik'l/ *n.* any of the muscles flexing the fingers or toes. [mod.L *lumbricalis* f. L *lumbricus* earthworm, with ref. to its shape]

lumen /lo͞omen/ *n.* **1** *Physics* the SI unit of luminous flux, equal to the amount of light emitted per second in a unit solid angle of one steradian from a uniform source of one candela. ¶ Abbr.: **lm.** **2** *Anat.* (*pl.* **lumina** /-minə/) a cavity within a tube, cell, etc. □□ **luminal** /lo͞omin'l/ *adj.* [L *lumen luminis* a light, an opening]

Luminal /lo͞omin'l/ *n. propr.* phenobarbitone. [as LUMEN + *-al* as in *veronal*]

luminance /lo͞ominənss/ *n. Physics* the intensity of light emitted from a surface per unit area in a given direction. [L *luminare* illuminate (as LUMEN)]

luminary /lo͞ominəri/ *n.* (*pl.* **-ies**) **1** *literary* a natural light-giving body, esp. the sun or moon. **2** a person as a

source of intellectual light or moral inspiration. **3** a prominent member of a group or gathering (*a host of show-business luminaries*). [ME f. OF *luminarie* or LL *luminarium* f. L LUMEN]
▪ **2** see INSPIRATION 1b. **3** see CELEBRITY 1.

luminescence /lo͞ominéss'nss/ *n.* the emission of light by a substance other than as a result of incandescence. ▫▫ **luminescent** *adj.* [as LUMEN + -ESCENCE (see -ESCENT)]
▪ see LIGHT[1] *n.* 3. ▫▫ **luminescent** see LUMINOUS 2, 4.

luminiferous /lo͞ominíffərəss/ *adj.* producing or transmitting light.

luminous /lo͞ominəss/ *adj.* **1** full of or shedding light; radiant, bright, shining. **2** phosphorescent, visible in darkness (*luminous paint*). **3** (esp. of a writer or a writer's work) throwing light on a subject. **4** of visible radiation (*luminous intensity*). ▫▫ **luminosity** /-nóssiti/ *n.* **luminously** *adj.* **luminousness** *n.* [ME f. OF *lumineux* or L *luminosus*]
▪ **1** shiny, shining, bright, brilliant, lighted (up), lit (up), illuminated, radiant, alight, resplendent, lustrous, gleaming, shimmering, glistening, sparkling, dazzling, *literary* refulgent, effulgent. **2, 4** glowing, aglow, luminescent, incandescent, phosphorescent, fluorescent. **3** illuminating, illuminative; clear, lucid, perspicuous, percipient, perspicacious, penetrating, discerning, perceptive, clear-eyed, clear-headed, keen, acute, sharp, explicit, incisive.

lumme /lúmmi/ *int. Brit. sl.* an expression of surprise or interest. [= (*Lord*) *love me*]

lummox /lúmməks/ *n. US colloq.* a clumsy or stupid person. [19th c. in US & dial.: orig. unkn.]
▪ see CLOD 2.

lump[1] /lump/ *n.* & *v.* ● *n.* **1** a compact shapeless or unshapely mass. **2** *sl.* a quantity or heap. **3** a tumour, swelling, or bruise. **4** a heavy, dull, or ungainly person. **5** (prec. by *the*) *Brit.* casual workers in the building and other trades. ● *v.* **1** *tr.* (usu. foll. by *together*, *with*, *in with*, *under*, etc.) mass together or group indiscriminately. **2** *tr.* carry or throw carelessly (*lumping crates round the yard*). **3** *intr.* become lumpy. **4** *intr.* (usu. foll. by *along*) proceed heavily or awkwardly. **5** *intr.* (usu. foll. by *down*) sit down heavily. ▫ **in the lump** taking things as a whole; in a general manner. **lump in the throat** a feeling of pressure there, caused by emotion. **lump sugar** sugar shaped into lumps or cubes. **lump sum 1** a sum covering a number of items. **2** money paid down at once (opp. INSTALMENT). ▫▫ **lumper** *n.* (in sense 2 of v.). [ME, perh. of Scand. orig.]
▪ *n.* **1, 2** piece, gobbet, clod, chunk, clot, wad, clump, hunk, nugget; cube, wedge, cake; mass, heap, pile, quantity. **3** bump, growth, protuberance, protrusion, prominence, bulge, excrescence, tumour, swelling, tumescence, nodule, knob; wen, cyst, boil, carbuncle, blister, wart, corn, bruise. **4** see CLOD 2. ● *v.* **1** (*lump together*) combine, join, consolidate, collect, bunch, group, unite, mass, aggregate, blend, mix, throw *or* put together.

lump[2] /lump/ *v.tr. colloq.* endure or suffer (a situation) ungraciously. ▫ **like it or lump it** put up with something whether one likes it or not. [imit.: cf. *dump*, *grump*, etc.]
▪ tolerate, suffer, put up with, bear, stand, endure, allow, *literary* brook.

lumpectomy /lumpéktəmi/ *n.* (*pl.* **-ies**) the surgical removal of a usu. cancerous lump from the breast.

lumpenproletariat /lúmpənprōlitáiriət/ *n.* (esp. in Marxist terminology) the unorganized and unpolitical lower orders of society, not interested in revolutionary advancement. ▫▫ **lumpen** *adj.* [G f. *Lumpen* rag, rogue: see PROLETARIAT]
▪ ▫▫ **lumpen** see RUSTIC *adj.* 2.

lumpfish /lúmpfish/ *n.* (*pl.* **-fishes** or **-fish**) a spiny-finned fish, *Cyclopterus lumpus*, of the N. Atlantic with modified pelvic fins for clinging to objects. [MLG *lumpen*, MDu. *lumpe* (perh. = LUMP[1]) + FISH[1]]

lumpish /lúmpish/ *adj.* **1** heavy and clumsy. **2** stupid, lethargic. ▫▫ **lumpishly** *adv.* **lumpishness** *n.*
▪ **1** see AWKWARD 2. **2** see STUPID *adj.* 1, 5.
▫▫ **lumpishness** see *stupidity* (STUPID).

lumpsucker /lúmpsukkər/ *n.* = LUMPFISH.

lumpy /lúmpi/ *adj.* (**lumpier, lumpiest**) **1** full of or covered with lumps. **2** (of water) cut up by the wind into small waves. ▫▫ **lumpily** *adv.* **lumpiness** *n.*
▪ **1** chunky, bumpy, uneven, granular, grainy.

lunacy /lo͞onəsi/ *n.* (*pl.* **-ies**) **1** insanity (orig. of the intermittent kind attributed to changes of the moon); the state of being a lunatic. **2** *Law* such mental unsoundness as interferes with civil rights or transactions. **3** great folly or eccentricity; a foolish act.
▪ **1, 2** madness, insanity, dementia, craziness, derangement, psychosis, mania; *Law* diminished responsibility. **3** folly, foolishness, bad *or* poor judgement, illogicality, senselessness, ridiculousness, irrationality, foolhardiness, stupidity; eccentricity.

luna moth /lo͞onə/ *n.* a N. American moth, *Actias luna*, with crescent-shaped spots on its pale green wings. [L *luna*, = moon (from its markings)]

lunar /lo͞onər/ *adj.* **1** of, relating to, or determined by the moon. **2** concerned with travel to the moon and related research. **3** (of light, glory, etc.) pale, feeble. **4** crescent-shaped, lunate. **5** of or containing silver (from alchemists' use of *luna* (= moon) for 'silver'). ▫ **lunar caustic** silver nitrate, esp. in stick form. **lunar cycle** = METONIC CYCLE. **lunar distance** the angular distance of the moon from the sun, a planet, or a star, used in finding longitude at sea. **lunar module** a small craft used for travelling between the moon's surface and a spacecraft in orbit around the moon. **lunar month 1** the period of the moon's revolution, esp. the interval between new moons of about $29^1/_2$ days. **2** (in general use) a period of four weeks. **lunar nodes** the points at which the moon's orbit cuts the ecliptic. **lunar observation** the finding of longitude by lunar distance. **lunar orbit 1** the orbit of the moon round the earth. **2** an orbit round the moon. **lunar year** a period of 12 lunar months. [L *lunaris* f. *luna* moon]

lunate /lo͞onayt/ *adj.* & *n.* ● *adj.* crescent-shaped. ● *n.* a crescent-shaped prehistoric implement etc. ▫ **lunate bone** a crescent-shaped bone in the wrist. [L *lunatus* f. *luna* moon]

lunatic /lo͞onətik/ *n.* & *adj.* ● *n.* **1** an insane person. **2** someone foolish or eccentric. ● *adj.* mad, foolish. ▫ **lunatic asylum** *hist.* a mental home or hospital. **lunatic fringe** an extreme or eccentric minority group. [ME f. OF *lunatique* f. LL *lunaticus* f. L *luna* moon]
▪ *n.* see MADMAN. ● *adj.* see MAD *adj.* 1.

lunation /loonáysh'n/ *n.* the interval between new moons, about $29^1/_2$ days. [ME f. med.L *lunatio* (as LUNATIC)]

lunch /lunch/ *n.* & *v.* ● *n.* **1** the meal eaten in the middle of the day. **2** a light meal eaten at any time. ● *v.* **1** *intr.* eat one's lunch. **2** *tr.* provide lunch for. ▫ **lunch-box** a container for a packed meal. **lunch-hour** (or **-time**) a break from work, when lunch is eaten. **out to lunch** esp. *US sl.* unaware; incompetent. ▫▫ **luncher** *n.* [LUNCHEON]
▪ *n.* see MEAL[1].

luncheon /lúnchən/ *n. formal* lunch. ▫ **luncheon meat** a usu. tinned block of ground meat ready to cut and eat. **luncheon voucher** *Brit.* a voucher or ticket issued to employees and exchangeable for food at many restaurants and shops. [17th c.: orig. unkn.]
▪ see MEAL[1].

luncheonette /lúnchənét/ *n.* orig. *US* a small restaurant or snack bar serving light lunches.

lune /lo͞on/ *n. Geom.* a crescent-shaped figure formed on a sphere or plane by two arcs intersecting at two points. [F f. L *luna* moon]

lunette /loonét/ *n.* **1** an arched aperture in a domed ceiling to admit light. **2** a crescent-shaped or semicircular space or alcove which contains a painting, statue, etc. **3** a watch-glass of flattened shape. **4** a ring through which a hook is placed to attach a vehicle to the vehicle towing it. **5** a temporary

fortification with two faces forming a salient angle, and two flanks. **6** *RC Ch.* a holder for the consecrated host in a monstrance. [F, dimin. of *lune* (see LUNE)]
■ **1, 2** see CRESCENT *n.* 2.

lung /lung/ *n.* either of the pair of respiratory organs which bring air into contact with the blood in humans and many other vertebrates. □ **lung-power** the power of one's voice. □□ **lunged** *adj.* **lungful** *n.* (*pl.* **-fuls**). **lungless** *adj.* [OE *lungen* f. Gmc, rel. to LIGHT²]

lunge¹ /lunj/ *n.* & *v.* ● *n.* **1** a sudden movement forward. **2** a thrust with a sword etc., esp. the basic attacking move in fencing. **3** a movement forward by bending the front leg at the knee while keeping the back leg straight. ● *v.* **1** *intr.* make a lunge. **2** *intr.* (usu. foll. by *at*, *out*) deliver a blow from the shoulder in boxing. **3** *tr.* drive (a weapon etc.) violently in some direction. [earlier *allonge* f. F *allonger* lengthen f. *à* to + *long* LONG¹]
■ *n.* **1** dive, plunge, rush, leap, jump, spring, pounce. **2** thrust, jab, strike. ● *v.* **1** dive, plunge, charge, pounce, dash, bound, jump. **2, 3** thrust, stab, jab; cut, strike, hit.

lunge² /lunj, lyŏŏnj/ *n.* & *v.* (also **longe**)/lonj/ ● *n.* **1** a long rope on which a horse is held and made to move in a circle round its trainer. **2** a circular exercise-ground for training horses. ● *v.tr.* exercise (a horse) with or in a lunge. [F *longe*, *allonge* (as LUNGE¹)]

lungfish /lúngfish/ *n.* any freshwater fish of the order Dipnoi, having gills and a modified swim bladder used as lungs, and able to aestivate to survive drought.

lungi /lŏŏnggee/ *n.* (*pl.* **lungis**) a length of cotton cloth, usu. worn as a loincloth in India, or as a skirt in Burma where it is the national dress for both sexes. [Urdu]

lungwort /lúngwurt/ *n.* **1** any herbaceous plant of the genus *Pulmonaria*, esp. *P. officinalis* with white-spotted leaves likened to a diseased lung. **2** a lichen, *Lobaria pulmonaria*, used as a remedy for lung disease.

lunisolar /lŏŏnisṓlər/ *adj.* of or concerning the sun and moon. □ **lunisolar period** a period of 532 years between the repetitions of both solar and lunar cycles. **lunisolar year** a year with divisions regulated by changes of the moon and an average length made to agree with the solar year. [L *luna* moon + *sol* sun]

lunula /lŏŏnyoolə/ *n.* (*pl.* **lunulae** /-lee/) **1** a crescent-shaped mark, esp. the white area at the base of the fingernail. **2** a crescent-shaped Bronze-Age ornament. [L, dimin. of *luna* moon]

lupin /lŏŏpin/ *n.* (also **lupine** /-pin/) **1** any plant of the genus *Lupinus*, with long tapering spikes of blue, purple, pink, white, or yellow flowers. **2** (in *pl.*) seeds of the lupin. [ME f. L *lupinus*]

lupine /lŏŏpīn/ *adj.* of or like a wolf or wolves. [L *lupinus* f. *lupus* wolf]
■ see RAPACIOUS.

lupus /lŏŏpəss/ *n.* any of various ulcerous skin diseases, esp. tuberculosis of the skin. □ **lupus vulgaris** /vulgáariss/ tuberculosis with dark red patches on the skin, usu. due to direct inoculation of the tuberculosis bacillus into the skin. □□ **lupoid** *adj.* **lupous** *adj.* [L, = wolf]

lur /loor/ *n.* (also **lure** /lyoor/) a bronze S-shaped trumpet of prehistoric times, still used in Scandinavia to call cattle. [Da. & Norw.]

lurch¹ /lurch/ *n.* & *v.* ● *n.* a stagger, a sudden unsteady movement or leaning. ● *v.intr.* stagger, move suddenly and unsteadily. [orig. Naut., *lee-lurch* alt. of *lee-latch* drifting to leeward]
■ *n.* stagger, sway, pitch; list, tilt, toss. ● *v.* stagger, sway, stumble, reel; roll, tilt, veer, pitch, list, heel, wallow.

lurch² /lurch/ *n.* □ **leave in the lurch** desert (a friend etc.) in difficulties. [orig. = a severe defeat in a game, f. F *lourche* (also the game itself, like backgammon)]
■ □ **leave in the lurch** desert, abandon, forsake; drop, jilt.

lurcher /lúrchər/ *n.* **1** *Brit.* a cross-bred dog, usu. a retriever, collie, or sheepdog crossed with a greyhound, used esp. for hunting and by poachers. **2** *archaic* a petty thief, swindler, or spy. [f. obs. *lurch* (v.) var. of LURK]
■ **1** see MONGREL *n.* **2** see BURGLAR *n.*

lure¹ /lyoor, loor/ *v.* & *n.* ● *v.tr.* **1** (usu. foll. by *away*, *into*) entice (a person, an animal, etc.) usu. with some form of bait. **2** attract back again or recall (a person, animal, etc.) with the promise of a reward. ● *n.* **1** a thing used to entice. **2** (usu. foll. by *of*) the attractive or compelling qualities (of a pursuit etc.). **3** a falconer's apparatus for recalling a hawk, consisting of a bunch of feathers attached to a thong, within which the hawk finds food while being trained. □□ **luring** *adj.* **luringly** *adv.* [ME f. OE *luere* f. Gmc]
■ *v.* tempt, attract, induce, coax, inveigle, seduce, draw in, entice, lead on, decoy, charm, persuade, allure, catch. ● *n.* **1** bait, decoy, attraction, temptation, inducement, magnet, siren song, charm, carrot, *sl.* come-on.

lure² var. of LUR.

Lurex /lyŏŏreks, lŏŏr-/ *n. propr.* **1** a type of yarn which incorporates a glittering metallic thread. **2** fabric made from this yarn.

lurid /lyŏŏrid, lŏŏr-/ *adj.* **1** vivid or glowing in colour (*lurid orange*). **2** of an unnatural glare (*lurid nocturnal brilliance*). **3** sensational, horrifying, or terrible (*lurid details*). **4** showy, gaudy (*paperbacks with lurid covers*). **5** ghastly, wan (*lurid complexion*). **6** *Bot.* of a dingy yellowish brown. □ **cast a lurid light on** explain or reveal (facts or character) in a horrific, sensational, or shocking way. □□ **luridly** *adv.* **luridness** *n.* [L *luridus* f. *luror* wan or yellow colour]
■ **1, 2** glaring, fiery, flaming, burning, aglow, glowing, glowering; fluorescent, loud, vivid, garish. **3** sensational, vivid, shocking, startling, graphic, melodramatic; ghastly, horrid, horrifying, horrendous, gory, grisly, gruesome, macabre, revolting, disgusting, appalling, frightful, terrible, awful. **4** showy, gaudy; loud, cheap, garish. **5** pale, ghastly, ashen, sallow, wan, pallid, baleful.

lurk /lurk/ *v.* & *n.* ● *v.intr.* **1** linger furtively or unobtrusively. **2 a** lie in ambush. **b** (usu. foll. by *in*, *under*, *about*, etc.) hide, esp. for sinister purposes. **3** (as **lurking** *adj.*) latent, semi-conscious (*a lurking suspicion*). ● *n. Austral. colloq.* a dodge, racket, or scheme; a method of profitable business. □□ **lurker** *n.* [ME perh. f. LOUR with frequent. *-k* as in TALK]
■ *v.* **1, 2** linger, loiter; skulk, slink, prowl, steal, sneak, hide, (lie in) wait, lie low. **3** (**lurking**) see *sneaking* (SNEAK *v.* 4). ● *n.* see RACKET² 2.

luscious /lúshəss/ *adj.* **1 a** richly sweet in taste or smell. **b** *colloq.* delicious. **2** (of literary style, music, etc.) over-rich in sound, imagery, or voluptuous suggestion. **3** voluptuously attractive. □□ **lusciously** *adv.* **lusciousness** *n.* [ME perh. alt. of obs. *licious* f. DELICIOUS]
■ **1** delicious, mouth-watering, tasty, toothsome, savoury, appetizing, rich, sweet, epicurean, ambrosial, palatable, pleasant, *literary* delectable; succulent, juicy, *colloq.* scrumptious, yummy, scrummy.

lush¹ /lush/ *adj.* **1** (of vegetation, esp. grass) luxuriant and succulent. **2** luxurious. □□ **lushly** *adv.* **lushness** *n.* [ME, perh. var. of obs. *lash* soft, f. OF *lasche* lax (see LACHES): assoc. with LUSCIOUS]
■ **1** luxuriant, thick, lavish, flourishing, verdant, green, dense, overgrown, exuberant; juicy, succulent, fresh, moist, ripe. **2** palatial, extravagant, elaborate, luxurious, opulent, sumptuous, *colloq.* ritzy, plush, plushy.

lush² /lush/ *n.* & *v.* esp. *US sl.* ● *n.* **1** alcohol, liquor. **2** an alcoholic, a drunkard. ● *v.* **1** *tr.* & *intr.* drink (alcohol). **2** *tr.* ply with alcohol. [18th c.: perh. joc. use of LUSH¹]

lust /lust/ *n.* & *v.* ● *n.* **1** strong sexual desire. **2 a** (usu. foll. by *for*, *of*) a passionate desire for (*a lust for power*). **b** (usu. foll. by *of*) a passionate enjoyment of (*the lust of battle*). **3** (usu. in *pl.*) a sensuous appetite regarded as sinful (*the lusts of the flesh*). ● *v.intr.* (usu. foll. by *after*, *for*) have a strong or excessive (esp. sexual) desire. □□ **lustful** *adj.* **lustfully** *adv.* **lustfulness** *n.* [OE f. Gmc]

■ *n.* **1, 3** passion, desire, sensuality, libido, libidinousness, sexuality, lustfulness, sexual appetite, *formal* concupiscence, *sl.* horniness. **2** desire, drive, energy, voracity, avidity, avidness, ambition, ravenousness. ● *v.* (*lust after*) desire, crave, hunger *or* thirst *or* hanker for *or* after, ache for. □□ **lustful** libidinous, carnal, licentious, lewd, prurient, lascivious, salacious, randy, *formal* concupiscent, *sl.* horny.

luster *US* var. of LUSTRE[1].

lustra *pl.* of LUSTRUM.

lustral /lústrəl/ *adj.* relating to or used in ceremonial purification. [L *lustralis* (as LUSTRUM)]

lustrate /lústrayt/ *v.tr.* purify by expiatory sacrifice, ceremonial washing, or other such rite. □□ **lustration** /-stráysh'n/ *n.* [L *lustrare* (as LUSTRUM)]

■ see PURIFY.

lustre[1] /lústər/ *n.* & *v.* (*US* **luster**) ● *n.* **1** gloss, brilliance, or sheen. **2** a shining or reflective surface. **3 a** a thin metallic coating giving an iridescent glaze to ceramics. **b** = LUSTREWARE. **4** a radiance or attractiveness; splendour, glory, distinction (of achievements etc.) (*add lustre to*; *shed lustre on*). **5 a** a prismatic glass pendant on a chandelier etc. **b** a cut-glass chandelier or candelabra. **6 a** *Brit.* a thin dress-material with a cotton warp, woollen weft, and a glossy surface. **b** any fabric with a sheen or gloss. ● *v.tr.* put lustre on (pottery, a cloth, etc.). □□ **lustreless** *adj.* (*US* **lusterless**). **lustrous** *adj.* **lustrously** *adv.* **lustrousness** *n.* [F f. It. *lustro* f. *lustrare* f. L *lustrare* illuminate]

■ *n.* **1** sheen, gleam, glow, gloss, luminosity, luminousness, radiance, brilliance, iridescence. **4** radiance, attractiveness; glory, splendour, renown, brilliance, honour, distinction, fame, illustriousness. □□ **lustrous** glossy, shiny, shined, polished, burnished.

lustre[2] /lústər/ *n.* (*US* **luster**) = LUSTRUM. [ME, Anglicized f. LUSTRUM]

lustreware /lústərwair/ *n.* (*US* **lusterware**) ceramics with an iridescent glaze. [LUSTRE[1]]

lustrum /lústrəm/ *n.* (*pl.* **lustra** /lústrə/ or **lustrums**) a period of five years. [L, an orig. purificatory sacrifice after a quinquennial census]

lusty /lústi/ *adj.* (**lustier, lustiest**) **1** healthy and strong. **2** vigorous or lively. □□ **lustily** *adv.* **lustiness** *n.* [ME f. LUST + -Y[1]]

■ vigorous, healthy, strong, energetic, robust, hale and hearty, lively, husky, powerful; buxom, substantial.

lusus /lóōssəss/ *n.* (in full ***lusus naturae*** /nətyoóree, -toórī/) a freak of nature. [L]

■ see MONSTER 3, 4.

lutanist var. of LUTENIST.

lute[1] /lōōt, lyōōt/ *n.* a guitar-like instrument with a long neck and a pear-shaped body, much used in the 14th–17th c. [ME f. F *lut*, *leüt*, prob. f. Prov. *laüt* f. Arab. *al-'ūd*]

lute[2] /lōōt, lyōōt/ *n.* & *v.* ● *n.* **1** clay or cement used to stop a hole, make a joint airtight, coat a crucible, protect a graft, etc. **2** a rubber seal for a jar etc. ● *v.tr.* apply lute to. [ME f. OF *lut* f. L *lutum* mud, clay]

lutecium var. of LUTETIUM.

lutein /lóōti-in/ *n. Chem.* a pigment of a deep yellow colour found in egg-yolk etc. [L *luteum* yolk of egg, neut. of *luteus* yellow]

luteinizing hormone /lóōtənīzing/ *n. Biochem.* a hormone secreted by the anterior pituitary gland that in females stimulates ovulation and in males stimulates the synthesis of androgen. ¶ Abbr.: **LH.** [LUTEIN]

lutenist /lóōtənist, lyóō-/ *n.* (also **lutanist**) a lute-player. [med.L *lutanista* f. *lutana* LUTE[1]]

luteo- /lóōtiō/ *comb. form* orange-coloured. [as LUTEOUS + -O-]

luteofulvous /lóōtiōfúlvəss/ *adj.* orange-tawny.

luteous /lóōtiəss/ *adj.* of a deep orange yellow or greenish yellow. [L *luteus* f. *lutum* WELD[2]]

lutestring /lóōtstring, lyóōt-/ *n. archaic* a glossy silk fabric. [app. f. *lustring* f. F *lustrine* or It. *lustrino* f. *lustro* LUSTRE[1]]

lutetium /looteéshəm/ *n.* (also **lutecium**) *Chem.* a silvery metallic element of the lanthanide series. ¶ Symb.: **Lu.** [F *lutécium* f. L *Lutetia* the ancient name of Paris]

Lutheran /lóōthərən/ *n.* & *adj.* ● *n.* **1** a follower of Martin Luther, Ger. religious reformer d. 1546. **2** a member of the Church which accepts the Augsburg confession of 1530, with justification by faith alone as a cardinal doctrine. ● *adj.* of or characterized by the theology of Martin Luther. □□ **Lutheranism** *n.* **Lutheranize** *v.tr.* & *intr.* (also **-ise**).

Lutine bell /lóōteen/ *n.* a bell kept at Lloyd's in London and rung whenever there is an important announcement to be made to the underwriters. [HMS *Lutine*, which sank in 1799, whose bell it was]

luting /lóōting, lyóō-/ *n.* = LUTE[2] *n.*

lutz /lōōts/ *n.* a jump in ice-skating in which the skater takes off from the outside back edge of one skate and lands, after a complete rotation in the air, on the outside back edge of the opposite skate. [prob. f. Gustave *Lussi* b. 1898, who invented it]

lux /luks/ *n.* (*pl.* same) *Physics* the SI unit of illumination, equivalent to one lumen per square metre. ¶ Abbr.: **lx.** [L *lux lucis* light]

luxe /lōōks, luks/ *n.* luxury (cf. DE LUXE). [F f. L *luxus*]

Luxembourger /lúksəmburgər/ *n.* **1** a native or national of Luxembourg. **2** a person of Luxembourg descent.

luxuriant /lugzyoóriənt, luksyoór-, lugzhoór-/ *adj.* **1** (of vegetation etc.) lush, profuse in growth. **2** prolific, exuberant, rank (*luxuriant imagination*). **3** (of literary or artistic style) florid, richly ornate. □□ **luxuriance** *n.* **luxuriantly** *adv.* [L *luxuriare* grow rank f. *luxuria* LUXURY]

■ **1** abundant, profuse, copious, lush, rich, *poet.* bounteous; overflowing, full, luxurious. **2** lavish, full, rank, prolific, thriving, rife, exuberant, lush, abounding, abundant, superabundant, dense, fruitful, teeming, *poet.* plenteous. **3** ornate, elaborate, decorated, fancy, rococo, baroque, flowery, frilly, florid, overdone, flamboyant, showy, ostentatious, gaudy, garish, flashy.

luxuriate /lugzyoóriayt, luksyoór-, lugzhoór-/ *v.intr.* **1** (foll. by *in*) take self-indulgent delight in, enjoy in a luxurious manner. **2** take one's ease, relax in comfort.

■ **1** (*luxuriate in*) wallow in, swim in, bask in, indulge in, delight in, relish, revel in, savour, enjoy, appreciate, like, love. **2** take one's ease, live in luxury *or* comfort, be *or* live in the lap of luxury, take it easy, enjoy oneself, live off *or* on the fat of the land, have the time of one's life, *colloq.* live the life of Riley, *sl.* have a ball.

luxurious /lugzyoóriəss, luksyoór-, lugzhoór-/ *adj.* **1** supplied with luxuries. **2** extremely comfortable. **3** fond of luxury, self-indulgent, voluptuous. □□ **luxuriously** *adv.* **luxuriousness** *n.* [ME f. OF *luxurios* f. L *luxuriosus* (as LUXURY)]

■ **1** opulent, sumptuous, grand, extravagant, lavish, magnificent, splendid, voluptuous, de luxe, high-class, fancy, swanky, plush, *colloq.* ritzy, plushy, posh, *esp. US colloq.* swank; epicurean, gourmet. **3** self-indulgent, voluptuous, voluptuary, sybaritic, hedonistic, pampered.

luxury /lúkshəri/ *n.* (*pl.* **-ies**) **1** choice or costly surroundings, possessions, food, etc.; luxuriousness (*a life of luxury*). **2** something desirable for comfort or enjoyment, but not indispensable. **3** (*attrib.*) providing great comfort, expensive (*a luxury flat*; *a luxury holiday*). [ME f. OF *luxurie*, *luxure* f. L *luxuria* f. *luxus* abundance]

■ **1** opulence, splendour, sumptuousness, grandeur, luxe, extravagance, magnificence, richness; luxuriousness, indulgence, self-indulgence, hedonism, sybaritism, voluptuousness. **2** frill, extravagance, extra, indulgence, treat. **3** (*attrib.*) see OPULENT 1, EXPENSIVE 1.

LV *abbr. Brit.* luncheon voucher.

Lw *symb. Chem.* the element lawrencium.

LWM *abbr.* low-water mark.

lx *abbr.* lux.

LXX *abbr.* Septuagint.

-ly[1] /li/ *suffix* forming adjectives esp. from nouns, meaning: **1** having the qualities of (*princely*; *manly*). **2** recurring at intervals of (*daily*; *hourly*). [from or after OE *-lic* f. Gmc, rel. to LIKE[1]]

-ly[2] /li/ *suffix* forming adverbs from adjectives, denoting esp. manner or degree (*boldly*; *happily*; *miserably*; *deservedly*; *amusingly*). [from or after OE *-līce* f. Gmc (as -LY[1])]

lycanthrope /líkənthrōp/ *n.* **1** a werewolf. **2** an insane person who believes that he or she is an animal, esp. a wolf. [mod.L *lycanthropus* f. Gk (as LYCANTHROPY)]

lycanthropy /līkánthrəpi/ *n.* **1** the mythical transformation of a person into a wolf (see also WEREWOLF). **2** a form of madness involving the delusion of being a wolf, with changed appetites, voice, etc. [mod.L *lycanthropia* f. Gk *lukanthrōpia* f. *lukos* wolf + *anthrōpos* man]

lycée /léessay/ *n.* (*pl.* **lycées**) a State secondary school in France. [F f. L (as LYCEUM)]

Lyceum /līséeəm/ *n.* **1 a** the garden at Athens in which Aristotle taught philosophy. **b** Aristotelian philosophy and its followers. **2** (**lyceum**) *US hist.* a literary institution, lecture-hall, or teaching-place. [L f. Gk *Lukeion* neut. of *Lukeios* epithet of Apollo (from whose neighbouring temple the Lyceum was named)]

lychee /líchee/ *n.* (also **litchi, lichee**) **1** a sweet fleshy fruit with a thin spiny skin. **2** the tree, *Nephelium litchi*, orig. from China, bearing this. [Chin. *lizhi*]

lych-gate var. of LICH-GATE.

lychnis /líkniss/ *n.* any herbaceous plant of the genus *Lychnis*, including ragged robin. [L f. Gk *lukhnis* a red flower f. *lukhnos* lamp]

lycopod /líkəpod/ *n.* any of various club-mosses, esp. of the genus *Lycopodium*. [Anglicized form of LYCOPODIUM]

lycopodium /līkəpṓdiəm/ *n.* **1** = LYCOPOD. **2** a fine powder of spores from this, used as an absorbent in surgery, and in making fireworks etc. [mod.L f. Gk *lukos* wolf + *pous podos* foot]

Lycra /líkrə/ *n. propr.* an elastic polyurethane fibre or fabric used esp. for close-fitting sports clothing.

Lydian /líddiən/ *adj.* & *n.* ● *n.* **1** a native or inhabitant of ancient Lydia in W. Asia Minor. **2** the language of this people. ● *adj.* of or relating to the people of Lydia or their language. □ **Lydian mode** *Mus.* the mode represented by the natural diatonic scale F–F. [L *Lydius* f. Gk *Ludios* of Lydia]

lye /lī/ *n.* **1** water that has been made alkaline by lixiviation of vegetable ashes. **2** any strong alkaline solution, esp. of potassium hydroxide used for washing or cleansing. [OE *lēag* f. Gmc: cf. LATHER]

lying[1] /lí-ing/ *pres. part.* of LIE[1]. ● *n.* a place to lie (*a dry lying*).

lying[2] /lí-ing/ *pres. part.* of LIE[2]. ● *adj.* deceitful, false. □□ **lyingly** *adv.*

■ untruthful, false, mendacious, hypocritical, dishonest, deceitful, deceptive, duplicitous, treacherous, perfidious.

lyke-wake /líkwayk/ *n. Brit.* a night-watch over a dead body. [perh. f. ON: cf. LICH(-GATE), WAKE[1]]

lymph /limf/ *n.* **1** *Physiol.* a colourless fluid containing white blood cells, drained from the tissues and conveyed through the body in the lymphatic system. **2** this fluid used as a vaccine. **3** exudation from a sore etc. **4** *poet.* pure water. □ **lymph gland** (or **node**) a small mass of tissue in the lymphatic system where lymph is purified and lymphocytes are formed. □□ **lymphoid** *adj.* **lymphous** *adj.* [F *lymphe* or L *lympha*, *limpa* water]

lymphatic /limfáttik/ *adj.* & *n.* ● *adj.* **1** of or secreting or conveying lymph (*lymphatic gland*). **2** (of a person) pale, flabby, or sluggish. ● *n.* a veinlike vessel conveying lymph. □ **lymphatic system** a network of vessels conveying lymph. [orig. = frenzied, f. L *lymphaticus* mad f. Gk *numpholēptos* seized by nymphs: now assoc. with LYMPH (on the analogy of *spermatic* etc.)]

■ *adj.* **2** see SUPINE *adj.* 3.

lymphocyte /límfəsīt/ *n.* a form of leucocyte occurring in the blood, in lymph, etc. □□ **lymphocytic** /-síttik/ *adj.*

lymphoma /limfṓmə/ *n.* (*pl.* **lymphomata** /-mətə/) any malignant tumour of the lymph nodes, excluding leukaemia.

lyncean /linséeən/ *adj.* lynx-eyed, keen-sighted. [L *lynceus* f. Gk *lugkeios* f. *lugx* LYNX]

lynch /linch/ *v.tr.* (of a body of people) put (a person) to death for an alleged offence without a legal trial. □ **lynch law** the procedure of a self-constituted illegal court that punishes or executes. **lynch mob** a group of people intent on lynching someone. □□ **lyncher** *n.* **lynching** *n.* [*Lynch's law*, after Capt. W. *Lynch* of Virginia *c.*1780]

■ see HANG *v.* 7a.

lynchet /línchit/ *n.* (in the UK) a ridge or ledge formed by ancient ploughing on a slope. [*linch* f. OE *hlinc*: cf. LINKS]

lynchpin var. of LINCHPIN.

lynx /lingks/ *n.* **1** a medium-sized feline, *Felis lynx*, with short tail, spotted fur, and tufted ear-tips. **2** its fur. □ **lynx-eyed** keen-sighted. □□ **lynxlike** *adj.* [ME f. L f. Gk *lugx*]

■ □ **lynx-eyed** see *sharp-eyed*.

Lyon /líən/ *n.* (in full **Lord Lyon** or **Lyon King of Arms**) the chief herald of Scotland. □ **Lyon Court** the court over which he presides. [archaic form. of LION: named f. the lion on the royal shield]

lyophilic /līəfíllik/ *adj.* (of a colloid) readily dispersed by a solvent. [Gk *luō* loosen, dissolve + Gk *philos* loving]

lyophilize /līóffilīz/ *v.tr.* (also **-ise**) freeze-dry.

lyophobic /līəfṓbik/ *adj.* (of a colloid) not lyophilic. [Gk *luō* loosen, dissolve + -PHOBIC (see -PHOBIA)]

lyrate /lírət/ *adj. Biol.* lyre-shaped.

lyre /līr/ *n. Gk Antiq.* an ancient stringed instrument like a small U-shaped harp, played usu. with a plectrum and accompanying the voice. □ **lyre-bird** any Australian bird of the family Menuridae, the male of which has a lyre-shaped tail display. **lyre-flower** a bleeding heart. [ME f. OF *lire* f. L *lyra* f. Gk *lura*]

lyric /lírrik/ *adj.* & *n.* ● *adj.* **1** (of poetry) expressing the writer's emotions, usu. briefly and in stanzas or recognized forms. **2** (of a poet) writing in this manner. **3** of or for the lyre. **4** meant to be sung, fit to be expressed in song, songlike (*lyric drama*; *lyric opera*). ● *n.* **1** a lyric poem or verse. **2** (in *pl.*) lyric verses. **3** (usu. in *pl.*) the words of a song. [F *lyrique* or L *lyricus* f. Gk *lurikos* (as LYRE)]

■ *adj.* **1, 2** personal, subjective, individual; sentimental, rhapsodic, lyrical. **4** melodic, song-like, musical, melodious, lyrical; sweet, dulcet, graceful, silvery, lilting, mellifluous, mellow, light. ● *n.* **3** (*lyrics*) libretto, words.

lyrical /lírrik'l/ *adj.* **1** = LYRIC *adj.* 1, 2. **2** resembling, couched in, or using language appropriate to, lyric poetry. **3** *colloq.* highly enthusiastic (*wax lyrical about*). □□ **lyrically** *adv.* **lyricalness** *n.*

■ **2** see LYRIC *adj.* 1, 2. **3** enthusiastic, ecstatic, encomiastic, rapturous, rhapsodic, effusive, impassioned, emotional, ebullient, exuberant, panegyrical, eulogistic.

lyricism /lírrisiz'm/ *n.* **1** the character or quality of being lyric or lyrical. **2** a lyrical expression. **3** high-flown sentiments.

lyricist /lírrisist/ *n.* a person who writes the words to a song.

lyrist *n.* **1** /līrist/ a person who plays the lyre. **2** /lírrist/ a lyric poet. [L *lyrista* f. Gk *luristēs* f. *lura* lyre]

■ **2** see POET.

lyse /līss/ *v.tr.* & *intr. Biol.* bring about or undergo lysis. [back-form. f. LYSIS]

lysergic acid /līsérjik/ *n.* a crystalline acid extracted from ergot or prepared synthetically. □ **lysergic acid diethylamide** /dī-éthiləmīd/ a powerful hallucinogenic drug. ¶ Abbr.: **LSD**. [hydro*lys*is + *erg*ot + -IC]

lysin /lísin/ *n. Biol.* a protein in the blood able to cause lysis. [G *Lysine*]

lysine /líseen/ *n. Biochem.* an amino acid present in protein and essential in the diet of vertebrates. [G *Lysin*, ult. f. LYSIS]

lysis /lísiss/ *n.* (*pl.* **lyses** /-seez/) *Biol.* the disintegration of a cell. [L f. Gk *lusis* loosening f. *luō* loosen]

-lysis /lisiss/ *comb. form* forming nouns denoting disintegration or decomposition (*electrolysis*; *haemolysis*).

Lysol /līsol/ *n. propr.* a mixture of cresols and soft soap, used as a disinfectant. [LYSIS + -OL[2]]

lysosome /līsəsōm/ *n. Biol.* a cytoplasmic organelle in eukaryotic cells containing degradative enzymes enclosed in a membrane. [LYSIS + -SOME[3]]

lysozyme /līsəzīm/ *n. Biochem.* an enzyme found in tears and egg-white which catalyses the destruction of cell walls of certain bacteria. [LYSIS + ENZYME]

lytic /littik/ *adj.* of, relating to, or causing lysis.

-lytic /littik/ *comb. form* forming adjectives corresponding to nouns in *-lysis*. [Gk *lutikos* (as LYSIS)]

Mm

M[1] /em/ *n.* (*pl.* **Ms** or **M's**) **1** the thirteenth letter of the alphabet. **2** (as a Roman numeral) 1,000.

M[2] *abbr.* (also **M.**) **1** Master. **2** (in titles) Member of. **3** *Monsieur*. **4** (in the UK in road designations) motorway. **5** mega-. **6** *Chem.* molar.

m *abbr.* (also **m.**) **1 a** masculine. **b** male. **2** married. **3** *Cricket* maiden (over). **4** mile(s). **5** metre(s). **6** million(s). **7** minute(s). **8** *Currency* mark(s). **9** mare. **10** milli-.

m' *adj.* = MY (*m'lud*).

'm *n. colloq.* madam (in *yes'm* etc.).

MA *abbr.* **1** Master of Arts. **2** *US* Massachusetts (in official postal use).

ma /maa/ *n. colloq.* mother. [abbr. of MAMMA[1]]

ma'am /mam, maam, məm/ *n.* madam (used esp. in addressing royalty). [contr.]

Mac /mak/ *n. colloq.* **1** a Scotsman. **2** *US* man (esp. as a form of address). [*Mac-* as a patronymic prefix in many Scottish and Irish surnames]

mac /mak/ *n.* (also **mack**) *Brit. colloq.* mackintosh. [abbr.]

macabre /məkaábər/ *adj.* grim, gruesome. [ME f. OF *macabré* perh. f. *Macabé* a Maccabee, with ref. to a miracle play showing the slaughter of the Maccabees]

▪ grim, ghastly, grisly, gory, gruesome, grotesque, ghoulish, fiendish, eerie, fearsome, frightful, frightening, terrifying, terrible, dreadful, dire; deathly, deadly, deathlike, ghostly, cadaverous.

macadam /məkáddəm/ *n.* **1** material for road-making with successive layers of compacted broken stone. **2** = TARMACADAM. ▫▫ **macadamize** *v.tr.* (also **-ise**). [J. L. *McAdam*, Brit. surveyor d. 1836, who advocated using this material]

macadamia /mákkədáymiə/ *n.* any Australian evergreen tree of the genus *Macadamia*, esp. *M. ternifolia*, bearing edible nutlike seeds. [J. *Macadam*, Austral. chemist d. 1865]

macaque /məkák/ *n.* any monkey of the genus *Macaca*, including the rhesus monkey and Barbary ape, having prominent cheek pouches and usu. a long tail. [F f. Port. *macaco* f. Fiot *makaku* some monkeys f. *kaku* monkey]

macaroni /mákkərṓni/ *n.* **1** a tubular variety of pasta. **2** (*pl.* **macaronies**) *hist.* an 18th-c. British dandy affecting Continental fashions. [It. *maccaroni* f. late Gk *makaria* food made from barley]

macaronic /mákkərónnik/ *n.* & *adj.* ● *n.* (in *pl.*) burlesque verses containing Latin (or other foreign) words and vernacular words with Latin etc. terminations. ● *adj.* (of verse) of this kind. [mod.L *macaronicus* f. obs. It. *macaronico*, joc. formed as MACARONI]

macaroon /mákkərṓōn/ *n.* a small light cake or biscuit made with white of egg, sugar, and ground almonds or coconut. [F *macaron* f. It. (as MACARONI)]

Macassar /məkássər/ *n.* (in full **Macassar oil**) a kind of oil formerly used as a dressing for the hair. [*Macassar*, now in Indonesia, from where its ingredients were said to come]

macaw /məkáw/ *n.* any long-tailed brightly coloured parrot of the genus *Ara* or *Anodorhynchus*, native to S. and Central America. [Port. *macao*, of unkn. orig.]

Macc. *abbr.* Maccabees (Apocrypha).

Maccabees /mákkəbeez/ *n.pl.* (in full **Books of the Maccabees**) four books of Jewish history and theology, of which the first and second are in the Apocrypha. ▫▫ **Maccabean** /-bee̍ən/ *adj.* [the name of a Jewish family that led a revolt *c.*170 BC under Judas *Maccabaeus*]

McCarthyism /məkaárthi-iz'm/ *n.* (esp. in the US) the policy of hunting out suspected or known Communists and removing them esp. from government departments. [J. R. *McCarthy*, US senator d. 1957]

McCoy /məkóy/ *n. colloq.* ▫ **the** (or **the real**) **McCoy** the real thing; the genuine article. [19th c.: orig. uncert.]

mace[1] /mayss/ *n.* **1** a staff of office, esp. the symbol of the Speaker's authority in the House of Commons. **2** *hist.* a heavy club usu. having a metal head and spikes. **3** a stick used in the game of bagatelle. **4** = *mace-bearer*. ▫ **mace-bearer** an official who carries a mace on ceremonial occasions. [ME f. OF *mace*, *masse* f. Rmc *mattea* (unrecorded) club]

mace[2] /mayss/ *n.* the dried outer covering of the nutmeg, used as a spice. [ME *macis* (taken as pl.) f. OF *macis* f. L *macir* a red spicy bark]

macédoine /mássidwaan/ *n.* mixed vegetables or fruit, esp. cut up small or in jelly. [F, = Macedonia, with ref. to the mixture of peoples there]

macer /máysər/ *n.* a mace-bearer, esp. *Sc.* an official keeping order in a lawcourt. [ME f. OF *massier* f. *masse*: see MACE[1]]

macerate /mássərayt/ *v.* **1** *tr.* & *intr.* make or become soft by soaking. **2** *intr.* waste away by fasting. ▫▫ **maceration** /-ráysh'n/ *n.* **macerator** *n.* [L *macerare macerat-*]

Mach /maak, mak/ *n.* (in full **Mach number**) the ratio of the speed of a body to the speed of sound in the surrounding medium. ▫ **Mach one** (or **two** etc.) the speed (or twice the speed) of sound. [E. *Mach*, Austrian physicist d. 1916]

machete /məchétti, məshétti/ *n.* (also **matchet** /máchit/) a broad heavy knife used in Central America and the W. Indies as an implement and weapon. [Sp. f. *macho* hammer f. LL *marcus*]

machiavellian /mákkiəvélliən/ *adj.* elaborately cunning; scheming, unscrupulous. ▫▫ **machiavellianism** *n.* [N. dei *Machiavelli*, Florentine statesman and political writer d. 1527, who advocated resort to morally questionable methods in the interests of the State]

▪ deceitful, cunning, shrewd, crafty, wily, foxy, scheming, tricky, perfidious, nefarious, treacherous, sneaky, unscrupulous.

machicolate /məchíkkəlayt/ *v.tr.* (usu. as **machicolated** *adj.*) furnish (a parapet etc.) with openings between supporting corbels for dropping stones etc. on attackers. ▫▫ **machicolation** /-láysh'n/ *n.* [OF *machicoler*, ult. f. Prov. *machacol* f. *macar* crush + *col* neck]

machinable /məshee̍nəb'l/ *adj.* capable of being cut by machine tools. ▫▫ **machinability** /-bílliti/ *n.*

machinate /mákkinayt, másh-/ *v.intr.* lay plots; intrigue. ▫▫ **machination** /-náysh'n/ *n.* **machinator** *n.* [L *machinari* contrive (as MACHINE)]

▪ conspire, plot, scheme, collude, connive, intrigue, manoeuvre, design. ▫▫ **machination** plot, scheme, intrigue, manoeuvre, design, stratagem, ruse, trick, trickery, artifice, dirty trick(s), wile, *colloq.* ploy; tactic(s), move, gambit.

machine /məsheén/ *n.* & *v.* ● *n.* **1** an apparatus using or applying mechanical power, having several parts each with a definite function and together performing certain kinds of work. **2** a particular kind of machine, esp. a vehicle, a piece of electrical or electronic apparatus, etc. **3** an instrument that transmits a force or directs its application. **4** the controlling system of an organization etc. (*the party machine*). **5** a person who acts mechanically and with apparent lack of emotion. ● *v.tr.* make or operate on with a machine (esp. in sewing or manufacturing). □ **machine code** (or **language**) a computer language that a particular computer can respond to directly. **machine-readable** in a form that a computer can process. **machine tool** a mechanically operated tool for working on metal, wood, or plastics. **machine-tooled 1** shaped by a machine tool. **2** (of artistic presentation etc.) precise, slick, esp. excessively so. [F f. L *machina* f. Gk *makhana* Doric form of *mēkhanē* f. *mēkhos* contrivance]

■ *n.* **1, 3** mechanism, device, apparatus, contrivance, appliance, instrument, implement, tool, utensil, gadget, *derog. or joc.* contraption, *sl.* gismo. **2** engine, motor, prime mover, vehicle; car, motor car, *US* automobile, *US colloq.* auto. **4** organization, system; ring, gang, cabal, clique, party, faction. ● *v.* shape, make, manufacture; sew (up).

machine-gun /məsheéngun/ *n.* & *v.* ● *n.* an automatic gun giving continuous fire. ● *v.tr.* (**-gunned, -gunning**) shoot at with a machine-gun. □□ **machine-gunner** *n.*

machinery /məsheénəri/ *n.* (*pl.* **-ies**) **1** machines collectively. **2** the components of a machine; a mechanism. **3** (foll. by *of*) an organized system. **4** (foll. by *for*) the means devised or available (*the machinery for decision-making*).

■ **1** see APPARATUS. **2** see WORK *n.* 8.

machinist /məsheénist/ *n.* **1** a person who operates a machine, esp. a sewing-machine or a machine tool. **2** a person who makes machinery.

■ **1** see OPERATIVE *n.* 1.

machismo /məchízmō, -kízmō/ *n.* exaggeratedly assertive manliness; a show of masculinity. [Sp. f. *macho* MALE f. L *masculus*]

■ manliness, virility, masculinity, *colloq.* grit, guts.

Machmeter /maákmeetər, mák-/ *n.* an instrument indicating air speed in the form of a Mach number.

macho /máchō/ *adj.* & *n.* ● *adj.* showily manly or virile. ● *n.* (*pl.* **-os**) **1** a macho man. **2** = MACHISMO. [MACHISMO]

■ *adj.* manly, masculine, virile; proud, arrogant.

machtpolitik /maákhtpoliteek/ *n.* power politics. [G]

macintosh var. of MACKINTOSH.

mack var. of MAC.

mackerel /mákrəl/ *n.* (*pl.* same or **mackerels**) a N. Atlantic marine fish, *Scomber scombrus*, with a greenish-blue body, used for food. □ **mackerel shark** a porbeagle. **mackerel sky** a sky dappled with rows of small white fleecy clouds, like the pattern on a mackerel's back. [ME f. AF *makerel*, OF *maquerel*]

mackintosh /mákkintosh/ *n.* (also **macintosh**) **1** *Brit.* a waterproof coat or cloak. **2** cloth waterproofed with rubber. [C. *Macintosh*, Sc. inventor d. 1843, who orig. patented the cloth]

mackle /mákk'l/ *n.* a blurred impression in printing. [F *macule* f. L *macula* blemish: see MACULA]

macle /mákk'l/ *n.* **1** a twin crystal. **2** a dark spot in a mineral. [F f. L (as MACKLE)]

McNaughten rules /mək-náwt'n/ *n.pl.* (also **M'Naghten rules**) *Brit.* rules governing the decision as to the criminal responsibility of an insane person. [*McNaughten* or *McNaughtan*, name of a 19th-c. accused person]

macramé /məkraámi/ *n.* **1** the art of knotting cord or string in patterns to make decorative articles. **2** articles made in this way. [Turk. *makrama* bedspread f. Arab. *mikrama*]

macro /mákrō/ *n.* (also **macro-instruction**) *Computing* a series of abbreviated instructions expanded automatically when required.

macro- /mákrō/ *comb. form* **1** long. **2** large, large-scale. [Gk *makro-* f. *makros* long, large]

macrobiotic /mákrōbīóttik/ *adj.* & *n.* ● *adj.* relating to or following a diet intended to prolong life, comprising pure vegetable foods, brown rice, etc. ● *n.* (in *pl.*; treated as *sing.*) the use or theory of such a dietary system.

macrocarpa /mákrōkaárpə/ *n.* an evergreen tree, *Cupressus macrocarpa*, often cultivated for hedges or wind-breaks. [mod.L f. Gk MACRO- + *karpos* fruit]

macrocephalic /mákrōsifállik/ *adj.* (also **macrocephalous** /-séffələss/) having a long or large head. □□ **macrocephaly** /-séffəli/ *n.*

macrocosm /mákrōkoz'm/ *n.* **1** the universe. **2** the whole of a complex structure. □□ **macrocosmic** /-kózmik/ *adj.* **macrocosmically** /-kózmikəli/ *adv.*

■ **1** see UNIVERSE 1a.

macroeconomics /mákrō-eékənómmiks/ *n.* the study of large-scale or general economic factors, e.g. national productivity. □□ **macroeconomic** *adj.*

macromolecule /mákrōmóllikyōōl/ *n. Chem.* a molecule containing a very large number of atoms. □□ **macromolecular** /-məlékyoolər/ *adj.*

macron /mákron/ *n.* a written or printed mark (¯) over a long or stressed vowel. [Gk *makron* neut. of *makros* large]

macrophage /mákrōfayj/ *n.* a large phagocytic white blood cell usu. occurring at points of infection.

macrophotography /mákrōfətógrəfi/ *n.* photography producing photographs larger than life.

macropod /mákrōpod/ *n.* any plant-eating mammal of the family Macropodidae native to Australia and New Guinea, including kangaroos and wallabies. [MACRO- + Gk *pous podos* foot]

macroscopic /mákrōskóppik/ *adj.* **1** visible to the naked eye. **2** regarded in terms of large units. □□ **macroscopically** *adv.*

macula /mákyoolə/ *n.* (*pl.* **maculae** /-lee/) **1** a dark spot, esp. a permanent one, in the skin. **2** (in full **macula lutea** /lōōtiə/) the region of greatest visual acuity in the retina. □□ **macular** *adj.* **maculation** /-láysh'n/ *n.* [L, = spot, mesh]

mad /mad/ *adj.* & *v.* ● *adj.* (**madder, maddest**) **1** insane; having a disordered mind. **2** (of a person, conduct, or an idea) wildly foolish. **3** (often foll. by *about*, *on*) wildly excited or infatuated (*mad about football*; *is chess-mad*). **4** *colloq.* angry. **5** (of an animal) rabid. **6** wildly light-hearted. ● *v.* (**madded, madding**) **1** *tr. US* make angry. **2** *intr. archaic* be mad; act madly (*the madding crowd*). □ **as mad as a hatter** see HATTER. **like mad** *colloq.* with great energy, intensity, or enthusiasm. **mad cow disease** *colloq.* = BSE. **mad keen** *colloq.* extremely eager. □□ **madness** *n.* [OE *gemǣded* part. form f. *gemād* mad]

■ *adj.* **1** psychotic, neurotic, schizophrenic, schizoid, psychoneurotic, *Psychol.* manic-depressive; insane, deranged, certifiable, crazed, demented, lunatic, unhinged, delirious, out of one's mind *or* wits, manic, maniacal, (mentally) unbalanced, mentally ill, of unsound mind, *non compos* (*mentis*); (*often derog.*) crack-brained, flighty, touched, twisted, mad as a hatter *or* March hare, *colloq.* crazy, mental, dotty, not all there, out to lunch, round the bend, *esp. Brit. colloq.* daft, *sl.* out of one's head, screwy, cuckoo, kooky, gaga, cracked, off-the-wall, nutty (as a fruit cake), nuts, loony, goofy, dippy, loopy, loco, wacky, batty, bats, off one's rocker *or* chump *or* head, bananas, bonkers, *Austral. sl.* dilly, *Brit. sl.* potty, round the twist, barmy, balmy, crackers, *US sl.* wacko, flaky. **2** foolish, silly, childish, immature, puerile, wild, nonsensical, foolhardy, madcap, heedless, senseless, absurd, imprudent, unwise, indiscreet, rash, ill-advised, ill-considered, hare-brained, reckless, extravagant, irrational, fatuous. **3** crazy, infatuated, ardent, enthusiastic, eager, avid, zealous, passionate, fervent, fervid, keen, fanatical, wild, *colloq.* crazy, dotty, *sl.* nuts, nutty, *Brit. sl.* potty. **4** furious, angry, infuriated, incensed, enraged, irate, fuming, berserk, irritated, provoked, exasperated, *archaic* wrathful, wroth. **5** wild, ferocious; rabid. □ **like mad** madly, feverishly, in a frenzy, frenziedly, desperately, excitedly, violently, wildly, hysterically, furiously, *colloq.* like crazy; enthusiastically, fervently, ardently. □□ **madness** insanity, lunacy, mania, dementia, psychosis, mental illness; lunacy, folly, foolishness, nonsense, senselessness, ridiculousness, pointlessness, illogicality, illogicalness, impracticality, preposterousness, futility, *colloq.* craziness.

madam /máddəm/ *n.* **1** a polite or respectful form of address or mode of reference to a woman. **2** *Brit. colloq.* a conceited or precocious girl or young woman. **3** a woman brothel-keeper. [ME f. OF *ma dame* my lady]
■ **2** miss, young lady. **3** see PROCURER.

Madame /mədaám, máddəm/ *n.* **1** (*pl.* **Mesdames** /maydaám, -dám/) a title or form of address used of or to a French-speaking woman, corresponding to Mrs or madam. **2** (**madame**) = MADAM 1. [F (as MADAM)]

madcap /mádkap/ *adj.* & *n.* ● *adj.* **1** wildly impulsive. **2** undertaken without forethought. ● *n.* a wildly impulsive person.
■ *adj.* see IMPULSIVE.

madden /mádd'n/ *v.* **1** *tr.* & *intr.* make or become mad. **2** *tr.* irritate intensely. □□ **maddening** *adj.* **maddeningly** *adv.*
■ **2** infuriate, anger, enrage, incense, provoke, inflame, work *or* stir *or* fire up, arouse, vex, pique, gall, annoy, irritate, bother, irk, nettle, exasperate, goad, bait, badger, torment, plague, bedevil, make a person's blood boil, make a person's hackles rise, get *or* put a person's back up, drive a person mad, *Brit.* get a person's blood up, get on a person's nerves, *colloq.* drive a person crazy *or* up the wall *or* round the bend, rile, needle, miff, peeve, get across, wind up, get under a person's skin, make a person see red, get a person's dander up, get a person's goat, *sl.* bug, *Brit. sl.* drive a person round the twist, brown off, cheese off, *US sl.* burn up, tick off.

madder /máddər/ *n.* **1** a herbaceous plant, *Rubia tinctorum*, with yellowish flowers. **2** a red dye obtained from the root of the madder, or its synthetic substitute. [OE *mædere*]

made /mayd/ **1** *past* and *past part.* of MAKE. **2** *adj.* (usu. in *comb.*) **a** (of a person or thing) built or formed (*well-made*; *strongly-made*). **b** successful (*a self-made man*). □ **have it made** *colloq.* be sure of success. **made for** ideally suited to. **made of** consisting of. **made of money** *colloq.* very rich.

Madeira /mədeérə/ *n.* **1** a fortified white wine from the island of Madeira off the coast of N. Africa. **2** (in full **Madeira cake**) a kind of rich sponge cake.

madeleine /máddəlayn/ *n.* a small fancy sponge cake. [F]

Mademoiselle /máddəmwəzél/ *n.* (*pl.* **Mesdemoiselles**) /máydmwə-/ **1** a title or form of address used of or to an unmarried French-speaking woman, corresponding to Miss or madam. **2** (**mademoiselle**) **a** a young Frenchwoman. **b** a French governess. [F f. *ma* my + *demoiselle* DAMSEL]
■ **1, 2a** see MISS[2].

madhouse /mádhowss/ *n.* **1** *archaic* or *colloq.* a mental home or hospital. **2** *colloq.* a scene of extreme confusion or uproar.
■ **1** see BEDLAM 2. **2** see BEDLAM 1.

madly /mádli/ *adv.* **1** in a mad manner. **2** *colloq.* **a** passionately. **b** extremely.
■ **1** insanely, hysterically, dementedly, wildly, distractedly, frenziedly; foolishly, stupidly, inanely, ridiculously, ludicrously, idiotically, absurdly, irrationally, senselessly, *colloq.* crazily. **2 a** passionately, ardently, fervently, furiously, fervidly, wildly, ferociously, fiercely, energetically, desperately, like mad, vehemently, feverishly, excitedly, fanatically, violently, impetuously. **b** excessively, extremely, desperately, intensely, wildly, exceedingly.

madman /mádmən/ *n.* (*pl.* **-men**) a man who is mad.
■ lunatic, psychopath, psychotic, maniac, *colloq.* psycho, *sl.* crackpot, loony, nut, nutcase, fruit cake, *Brit. sl.* nutter, *US sl.* screwball, kook.

Madonna /mədónnə/ *n. Eccl.* **1** (prec. by *the*) a name for the Virgin Mary. **2** (usu. **madonna**) a picture or statue of the Madonna. □ **madonna lily** the white *Lilium candidum*, as shown in many pictures of the Madonna. [It. f. *ma* = *mia* my + *donna* lady f. L *domina*]

madras /mədráss/ *n.* a strong cotton fabric with coloured or white stripes, checks, etc. [*Madras* in India]

madrepore /mádripor/ *n.* **1** any perforated coral of the genus *Madrepora*. **2** the animal producing this. □□ **madreporic** /-pórrik/ *adj.* [F *madrépore* or mod.L *madrepora* f. It. *madrepora* f. *madre* mother + *poro* PORE[1]]

madrigal /mádrig'l/ *n.* **1** a usu. 16th-c. or 17th-c. part-song for several voices, usu. arranged in elaborate counterpoint and without instrumental accompaniment. **2** a short love poem. □□ **madrigalian** /-gáyliən/ *adj.* **madrigalesque** /-gəlésk/ *adj.* **madrigalist** *n.* [It. *madrigale* f. med.L *matricalis* mother (church), formed as MATRIX]

madwoman /mádwoŏmmən/ *n.* (*pl.* **-women**) a woman who is mad.
■ see MANIAC *n.* 1.

Maecenas /mīseénəss/ *n.* a generous patron of literature or art. [Gaius *Maecenas*, Roman statesman d. 8 BC, the patron of Horace and Virgil]

maelstrom /máylstrəm/ *n.* **1** a great whirlpool. **2** a state of confusion. [early mod. Du. f. *malen* grind, whirl + *stroom* STREAM]
■ **1** see WHIRLPOOL. **2** see CHAOS 1a.

maenad /meénad/ *n.* **1** a bacchante. **2** a frenzied woman. □□ **maenadic** /-náddik/ *adj.* [L *Maenas Maenad-* f. Gk *Mainas -ados* f. *mainomai* rave]

maestoso /mīstṓzō/ *adj.*, *adv.*, & *n. Mus.* ● *adj.* & *adv.* to be performed majestically. ● *n.* (*pl.* **-os**) a piece of music to be performed in this way. [It.]

maestro /mī́strō/ *n.* (*pl.* **maestri** /-stri/ or **-os**) (often as a respectful form of address) **1** a distinguished musician, esp. a conductor or performer. **2** a great performer in any sphere, esp. artistic. [It., = master]
■ see VIRTUOSO 1a.

Mae West /may wést/ *n. sl.* an inflatable life-jacket. [the name of an American film actress d. 1980, noted for her large bust]

Mafia /máffiə, maá-/ *n.* **1** an organized international body of criminals, orig. in Sicily, now also in Italy and the US. **2** (**mafia**) a group regarded as exerting a hidden sinister influence. [It. dial. (Sicilian), = bragging]
■ **1** see UNDERWORLD 1.

Mafioso /máffiṓsō, maá-/ *n.* (*pl.* **Mafiosi** /-si/) a member of the Mafia. [It. (as MAFIA)]
■ see GANGSTER.

mag[1] /mag/ *n. colloq.* a magazine (periodical). [abbr.]

mag[2] /mag/ *v.* & *n.* esp. *Austral.* ● *v.intr.* chatter or talk incessantly. ● *n.* a chatterbox. [f. MAGPIE]

mag. *abbr.* **1** magnesium. **2** magneto. **3** magnetic.

magazine /mággəzeén/ *n.* **1** a periodical publication containing articles, stories, etc., usu. with photographs, illustrations, etc. **2** a chamber for holding a supply of cartridges to be fed automatically to the breech of a gun. **3** a similar device feeding a camera, slide projector, etc. **4** a store for arms, ammunition, and provisions for use in war. **5** a store for explosives. [F *magasin* f. It. *magazzino* f. Arab. *makẖāzin* pl. of *makẖzan* storehouse f. *kẖazana* store up]
■ **1** periodical, publication; see also JOURNAL 1. **4** arsenal, ammunition *or* munitions dump, armoury.

magdalen /mágdəlin/ *n.* **1** a reformed prostitute. **2** a home for reformed prostitutes. [Mary *Magdalene* of Magdala in Galilee (Luke 8:2), identified (prob. wrongly) with the sinner of Luke 7:37: f. eccl.L *Magdalena* f. Gk *Magdalēnē*]

Magdalenian /mágdəleéniən/ *adj.* & *n. Archaeol.* ● *adj.* of the latest palaeolithic period in Europe, characterized by horn and bone tools. ● *n.* the culture of this period. [F *Magdalénien* of La *Madeleine*, Dordogne, France, where remains were found]

mage /mayj/ *n. archaic* **1** a magician. **2** a wise and learned person. [ME, Anglicized f. MAGUS]

Magellanic cloud /májilánnik/ *n.* each of two galaxies visible in the southern sky. [F. *Magellan*, Port. explorer d. 1521]

magenta /məjéntə/ *n.* & *adj.* ● *n.* **1** a brilliant mauvish-crimson shade. **2** an aniline dye of this colour; fuchsine. ● *adj.* of or coloured with magenta. [*Magenta* in N. Italy, site of a battle (1859) fought shortly before the dye was discovered]

maggot /mággət/ *n.* **1** a larva, esp. of the cheese-fly or bluebottle. **2** a whimsical fancy. ▫▫ **maggoty** *adj.* [ME perh. alt. f. *maddock*, earlier *mathek* f. ON *mathkr*: cf. MAWKISH]

magi *pl.* of MAGUS.

magian /máyjiən/ *adj.* & *n.* ● *adj.* of the magi or Magi. ● *n.* **1** a magus or Magus. **2** a magician. ▫▫ **magianism** *n.* [L *magus*: see MAGUS]

magic /májik/ *n., adj.,* & *v.* ● *n.* **1 a** the supposed art of influencing the course of events by the occult control of nature or of the spirits. **b** witchcraft. **2** conjuring tricks. **3** an inexplicable or remarkable influence producing surprising results. **4** an enchanting quality or phenomenon. ● *adj.* **1** of or resulting from magic. **2** producing surprising results. **3** *colloq.* wonderful, exciting. ● *v.tr.* (**magicked, magicking**) change or create by magic, or apparently so. ▫ **like magic** very effectively or rapidly. **magic away** cause to disappear as if by magic. **magic carpet** a mythical carpet able to transport a person on it to any desired place. **magic eye 1** a photoelectric device used in equipment for detection, measurement, etc. **2** a small cathode-ray tube used to indicate the correct tuning of a radio receiver. **magic lantern** a simple form of image-projector using slides. **magic mushroom** a mushroom producing psilocybin. **magic square** a square divided into smaller squares each containing a number such that the sums of all vertical, horizontal, or diagonal rows are equal. [ME f. OF *magique* f. L *magicus* adj., LL *magica* n., f. Gk *magikos* (as MAGUS)]

■ *n.* **1** witchcraft, sorcery, wizardry, black magic, necromancy, the black art, voodoo, devilry, diabolism, occultism, theurgy, white magic. **2** legerdemain, conjuring, prestidigitation, sleight of hand, illusion, hocus-pocus, trickery. **4** enchantment, allure, allurement, charm, bewitchment, spell, witchery, witchcraft, wizardry, glamour, fascination, magnetism. ● *adj.* **1** magical, miraculous, necromantic, occult, mystic, shamanistic, theurgical. **2** magical, miraculous, marvellous, amazing, surprising, awe-inspiring. **3** see MARVELLOUS, EXCITING. ▫ **like magic** see FAST *adj.* 1, *like a charm* (CHARM).

magical /májik'l/ *adj.* **1** of or relating to magic. **2** resembling magic; produced as if by magic. **3** wonderful, enchanting. ▫▫ **magically** *adv.*

■ **1** see MAGIC *adj.* 1. **2** miraculous. **3** magic, wonderful, enchanting, entrancing, bewitching, fascinating, spellbinding, charming, magnetic; see also MARVELLOUS.

magician /məjísh'n/ *n.* **1** a person skilled in or practising magic. **2** a conjuror. **3** a person with exceptional skill. [ME f. OF *magicien* f. LL *magica* (as MAGIC)]

■ **1** wizard, sorcerer, sorceress, magus, necromancer, enchanter, enchantress, Houdini, Circe, witch, *archaic* warlock; thaumaturge, theurgist. **2** conjuror, illusionist, *formal* prestidigitator. **3** virtuoso, wizard, genius, marvel, miracle-worker, thaumaturge, *colloq.* whiz.

magilp var. of MEGILP.

Maginot line /mázhinō/ *n.* **1** a line of fortifications along the NE border of France begun in 1929, overrun in 1940. **2** a line of defence on which one relies blindly. [A. *Maginot*, Fr. minister of war d. 1932]

magisterial /májistéeriəl/ *adj.* **1** imperious. **2** invested with authority. **3** of or conducted by a magistrate. **4** (of a work, opinion, etc.) highly authoritative. ▫▫ **magisterially** *adv.* [med.L *magisterialis* f. LL *magisterius* f. L *magister* MASTER]

■ **1** see *overbearing* (OVERBEAR 1a), POMPOUS 1.

magisterium /májistéeriəm/ *n. RC Ch.* the official teaching of a bishop or pope. [L, = the office of a master (as MAGISTERIAL)]

magistracy /májistrəsi/ *n.* (*pl.* **-ies**) **1** the office or authority of a magistrate. **2** magistrates collectively.

magistral /məjístrəl/ *adj.* **1** of a master or masters. **2** *Pharm.* (of a remedy etc.) devised and made up for a particular case (cf. OFFICINAL). [F *magistral* or L *magistralis* f. *magister* MASTER]

magistrate /májistrət, -strayt/ *n.* **1** a civil officer administering the law. **2** an official conducting a court for minor cases and preliminary hearings (*magistrates' court*). ▫▫ **magistrateship** *n.* **magistrature** /-strətyoor/ *n.* [ME f. L *magistratus* (as MAGISTRAL)]

■ see JUDGE *n.* 1.

Maglemosian /mággəlmṓziən/ *n.* & *adj.* ● *n.* a N. European mesolithic culture, characterized by bone and stone implements. ● *adj.* of or relating to this culture. [*Maglemose* in Denmark, where articles from it were found]

maglev /máglev/ *n.* (usu. *attrib.*) magnetic levitation, a system in which trains glide above the track in a magnetic field. [abbr.]

magma /mágmə/ *n.* (*pl.* **magmata** /-mətə/ or **magmas**) **1** fluid or semifluid material from which igneous rock is formed by cooling. **2** a crude pasty mixture of mineral or organic matter. ▫▫ **magmatic** /-máttik/ *adj.* [ME, = a solid residue f. L f. Gk *magma -atos* f. the root of *massō* knead]

Magna Carta /mágnə kaártə/ *n.* (also **Magna Charta**) **1** a charter of liberty and political rights obtained from King John of England in 1215. **2** any similar document of rights. [med.L, = great charter]

magnanimous /magnánniməss/ *adj.* nobly generous; not petty in feelings or conduct. ▫▫ **magnanimity** /mágnənímmiti/ *n.* **magnanimously** *adv.* [L *magnanimus* f. *magnus* great + *animus* soul]

■ see GENEROUS 2. ▫▫ **magnanimity** see HUMANITY 2.

magnate /mágnayt, -nit/ *n.* a wealthy and influential person, esp. in business (*shipping magnate; financial magnate*). [ME f. LL *magnas -atis* f. L *magnus* great]

■ see TYCOON.

magnesia /magnéezhə, -shə, -zyə/ *n.* **1** *Chem.* magnesium oxide. **2** (in general use) hydrated magnesium carbonate, a white powder used as an antacid and laxative. ▫▫ **magnesian** *adj.* [ME f. med.L f. Gk *Magnēsia* (*lithos*) (stone) of Magnesia in Asia Minor, orig. referring to loadstone]

magnesite /mágnisīt/ *n.* a white or grey mineral form of magnesium carbonate.

magnesium /magnéeziəm/ *n. Chem.* a silvery metallic element occurring naturally in magnesite and dolomite, used for making light alloys and important as an essential element in living organisms. ¶ Symb.: **Mg.** ▫ **magnesium flare** (or **light**) a blinding white light produced by burning magnesium wire.

magnet /mágnit/ *n.* **1** a piece of iron, steel, alloy, ore, etc., usu. in the form of a bar or horseshoe, having properties of attracting or repelling iron. **2** a lodestone. **3** a person or thing that attracts. [ME f. L *magnes magnetis* f. Gk *magnēs* = *Magnēs -ētos* (*lithos*) (stone) of Magnesia: cf. MAGNESIA]

■ **3** see LURE[1] *n.*

magnetic /magnéttik/ *adj.* **1 a** having the properties of a magnet. **b** producing, produced by, or acting by magnetism. **2** capable of being attracted by or acquiring the properties of a magnet. **3** very attractive or alluring (*a magnetic personality*). ▫ **magnetic compass** = COMPASS 1. **magnetic disk** see DISC. **magnetic equator** an imaginary line, near the equator, on which a magnetic needle has no dip. **magnetic field** a region of variable force around magnets, magnetic materials, or current-carrying conductors. **magnetic inclination** = DIP *n.* 8. **magnetic mine** a submarine mine detonated by the proximity of a magnetized body such as that of a ship. **magnetic moment** the property of a magnet that interacts with an applied field to give a mechanical moment. **magnetic needle** a piece of magnetized steel used as an indicator on the dial of a compass and in magnetic and electrical apparatus, esp. in telegraphy. **magnetic north** the point indicated by the north end of a compass needle. **magnetic pole 1** each of the points near the extremities of the axis of rotation of the earth or another body where a magnetic needle dips vertically. **2** each of the regions of an artificial or natural magnet, from which the magnetic forces appear to originate. **magnetic storm** a disturbance of the earth's magnetic field caused by charged particles from the sun etc. **magnetic tape** a tape coated with magnetic material for recording sound or pictures or for the storage of information. □□ **magnetically** *adv.* [LL *magneticus* (as MAGNET)]

■ **3** attractive, attracting, engaging, captivating, enthralling, seductive, alluring, entrancing, bewitching, beguiling, arresting, spellbinding, irresistible, charismatic, winning, winsome, inviting.

magnetism /mágnitiz'm/ *n.* **1 a** magnetic phenomena and their study. **b** the property of producing these phenomena. **2** attraction; personal charm. [mod.L *magnetismus* (as MAGNET)]

■ **2** attraction, appeal, allure, magic, lure, attractiveness, charm, pull, seductiveness, irresistibility, draw, charisma, sex appeal.

magnetite /mágnitīt/ *n.* magnetic iron oxide. [G *Magnetit* (as MAGNET)]

magnetize /mágnitīz/ *v.tr.* (also **-ise**) **1** give magnetic properties to. **2** make into a magnet. **3** attract as or like a magnet. □□ **magnetizable** *adj.* **magnetization** /-záysh'n/ *n.* **magnetizer** *n.*

magneto /magneétō/ *n.* (*pl.* **-os**) an electric generator using permanent magnets and producing high voltage, esp. for the ignition of an internal-combustion engine. [abbr. of MAGNETO-ELECTRIC]

magneto- /magneétō/ *comb. form* indicating a magnet or magnetism. [Gk *magnēs*: see MAGNET]

magneto-electric /magneétō-iléktrik/ *adj.* (of an electric generator) using permanent magnets. □□ **magneto-electricity** /-trissiti/ *n.*

magnetograph /magneétəgraaf/ *n.* an instrument for recording measurements of magnetic quantities.

magnetometer /mágnitómmitər/ *n.* an instrument measuring magnetic forces, esp. the earth's magnetism. □□ **magnetometry** *n.*

magnetomotive /magneétōmṓtiv/ *adj.* (of a force) being the sum of the magnetizing forces along a circuit.

magneton /mágniton/ *n.* a unit of magnetic moment in atomic and nuclear physics. [F *magnéton* (as MAGNETIC)]

magnetosphere /magneétəsfeer/ *n.* the region surrounding a planet, star, etc. in which its magnetic field is effective.

magnetron /mágnitron/ *n.* an electron tube for amplifying or generating microwaves, with the flow of electrons controlled by an external magnetic field. [MAGNET + -TRON]

magnificat /magnífiikat/ *n.* **1** a song of praise. **2** (**Magnificat**) the hymn of the Virgin Mary (Luke 1:46–55) used as a canticle. [f. the opening words *magnificat anima mea Dominum* my soul magnifies the Lord]

magnification /mágnifikáysh'n/ *n.* **1** the act or an instance of magnifying; the process of being magnified. **2** the amount or degree of magnification. **3** the apparent enlargement of an object by a lens.

■ **1** enlargement, amplification; build-up, strengthening, enhancement, aggrandizement, raising, elevation, increase, expansion, heightening, glorification, ennoblement. **2** enlargement, amplification.

magnificent /magnífis'nt/ *adj.* **1** splendid, stately. **2** sumptuously or lavishly constructed or adorned. **3** *colloq.* fine, excellent. □□ **magnificence** *n.* **magnificently** *adv.* [F *magnificent* or L *magnificus* f. *magnus* great]

■ **1** glorious, grand, impressive, imposing, awe-inspiring, brilliant, commanding, august, noble, majestic, regal, splendid, stately, distinguished, elegant, great, exalted, sublime, outstanding. **2** sumptuous, lavish, resplendent, opulent, rich, luxurious. **3** see SUPERB.

magnifico /magnífikō/ *n.* (*pl.* **-oes**) a magnate or grandee. [It., = MAGNIFICENT: orig. with ref. to Venice]

magnify /mágnifī/ *v.tr.* (**-ies, -ied**) **1** make (a thing) appear larger than it is, as with a lens. **2** exaggerate. **3** intensify. **4** *archaic* extol, glorify. □ **magnifying glass** a lens used to produce an enlarged image. □□ **magnifiable** *adj.* **magnifier** *n.* [ME f. OF *magnifier* or L *magnificare* (as MAGNIFICENT)]

■ **1** enlarge, expand, amplify, inflate, increase, augment. **2** exaggerate, overstate, *colloq.* blow up. **3** intensify, heighten, build up, dramatize, *colloq.* boost; aggravate, worsen, exacerbate. **4** see GLORIFY 3.

magniloquent /magníllәkwәnt/ *adj.* **1** grand or grandiose in speech. **2** boastful. □□ **magniloquence** *n.* **magniloquently** *adv.* [L *magniloquus* f. *magnus* great + *-loquus* -speaking]

■ **1** see RHETORICAL 1a, 2, 3. **2** see BOASTFUL.

□□ **magniloquence** see RHETORIC 2a.

magnitude /mágnityood/ *n.* **1** largeness. **2** size. **3** importance. **4 a** the degree of brightness of a star (see also *absolute magnitude*, *apparent magnitude*). **b** a class of stars arranged according to this (*of the third magnitude*). □ **of the first magnitude** very important. [ME f. L *magnitudo* f. *magnus* great]

■ **1, 2** greatness, size, extent, bigness, immensity, enormousness, dimension(s). **3** significance, consequence, note; see also IMPORTANCE 1, 2.

magnolia /magnṓliә/ *n.* **1** any tree or shrub of the genus *Magnolia*, cultivated for its dark-green foliage and large waxlike flowers in spring. **2** a pale creamy-pink colour. [mod.L f. P. *Magnol*, Fr. botanist d. 1715]

magnox /mágnoks/ *n.* any of various magnesium-based alloys used to enclose uranium fuel elements in a nuclear reactor. [*mag*nesium *no ox*idation]

magnum /mágnәm/ *n.* (*pl.* **magnums**) **1** a wine bottle of about twice the standard size. **2 a** a cartridge or shell that is especially powerful or large. **b** (often *attrib.*) a cartridge or gun adapted so as to be more powerful than its calibre suggests. [L, neut. of *magnus* great]

magnum opus /mágnәm ṓpәss/ *n.* **1** a great and usu. large work of art, literature, etc. **2** the most important work of an artist, writer, etc. [L, = great work: see OPUS]

■ see MASTERPIECE.

magpie /mágpī/ *n.* **1** a European and American crow, *Pica pica*, with a long pointed tail and black and white plumage. **2** any of various birds with plumage like a magpie, esp. *Gymnorhina tibicen* of Australia. **3** an idle chatterer. **4** a person who collects things indiscriminately. **5 a** the division of a circular target next to the outer one. **b** a rifle shot which strikes this. [*Mag*, abbr. of *Margaret* + PIE^2]

magsman /mágzmәn/ *n.* *Austral. sl.* **1** a confidence man. **2** a storyteller, a raconteur.

maguey /mágway/ *n.* an agave plant, esp. one yielding pulque. [Sp. f. Haitian]

magus /máygәss/ *n.* (*pl.* **magi** /máyjī/) **1** a member of a priestly caste of ancient Persia. **2** a sorcerer. **3** (**the** (**three**) **Magi**) the 'wise men' from the East who brought gifts to the infant Christ (Matt. 2:1). [ME f. L f. Gk *magos* f. OPers. *magus*]

Magyar /mágyaar/ *n.* & *adj.* ● *n.* **1** a member of a Ural-Altaic people now predominant in Hungary. **2** the language of this people. ● *adj.* of or relating to this people or language. [native name]

maharaja /maáhәraájә/ *n.* (also **maharajah**) *hist.* a title of some Indian princes. [Hindi *mahārājā* f. *mahā* great + RAJA]

maharanee /maáhәraáni/ *n.* (also **maharani**) *hist.* a maharaja's wife or widow. [Hindi *mahārānī* f. *mahā* great + RANEE]

maharishi /maáhərishi/ *n.* a great Hindu sage or spiritual leader. [Hindi f. *mahā* great + RISHI]

mahatma /məhátmə/ *n.* **1 a** (in India etc.) a person regarded with reverence. **b** a sage. **2** each of a class of persons in India and Tibet supposed by some to have preternatural powers. [Skr. *mahātman* f. *mahā* great + *ātman* soul]

Mahayana /maáhəyaánə/ *n.* a school of Buddhism practised in China, Japan, and Tibet. [Skr. f. *mahā* great + *yāna* vehicle]

Mahdi /maádi/ *n.* (*pl.* **Mahdis**) **1** a spiritual and temporal messiah expected by Muslims. **2** esp. *hist.* a leader claiming to be this Messiah. ▫▫ **Mahdism** *n.* **Mahdist** *n.* [Arab. *mahdīy* he who is guided right, past part. of *hadā* guide]

mah-jong /maajóng/ *n.* (also **mah-jongg**) a Chinese game for four resembling rummy and played with 136 or 144 pieces called tiles. [Chin. dial. *ma-tsiang*, lit. sparrows]

mahlstick var. of MAULSTICK.

mahogany /məhóggəni/ *n.* (*pl.* **-ies**) **1 a** a reddish-brown wood used for furniture. **b** the colour of this. **2** any tropical tree of the genus *Swietenia*, esp. *S. mahagoni*, yielding this wood. [17th c.: orig. unkn.]

mahonia /məhṓniə/ *n.* any evergreen shrub of the genus *Mahonia*, with yellow bell-shaped or globular flowers. [F *mahonne*, Sp. *mahona*, It. *maona*, Turk. *māwuna*]

mahout /məhówt/ *n.* (in India etc.) an elephant-driver or -keeper. [Hindi *mahāut* f. Skr. *mahāmātra* high official, lit. 'great in measure']

Mahratta var. of MARATHA.

Mahratti var. of MARATHI.

mahseer /maásseer/ *n.* either of two freshwater Indian fish, *Barbus putitora* or *B. tor*, used as food. [Hindi *mahāsir*]

maid /mayd/ *n.* **1** a female domestic servant. **2** *archaic* or *poet.* a girl or young woman. ▫ **maid of honour 1** an unmarried lady attending a queen or princess. **2** a kind of small custard tart. **3** esp. *US* a principal bridesmaid. ▫▫ **maidish** *adj.* [ME, abbr. of MAIDEN]

■ **1** housemaid, maidservant, domestic, chambermaid, lady's maid, charwoman, *Brit.* daily. **2** girl, young woman, young lady, schoolgirl, miss, mademoiselle, signorina, Fräulein, *Ir.* colleen, *esp. Sc. & N.Engl. or poet.* lass, *archaic* demoiselle, *archaic or literary* damsel, *archaic or poet.* maiden, *colloq.* nymphet, lassie, filly, *joc.* wench, *poet.* nymph. ▫ **maid of honour** **1** lady-in-waiting, *archaic or hist.* woman.

maidan /mīdaán/ *n. Anglo-Ind.* **1** an open space in or near a town. **2** a parade-ground. [Urdu f. Arab. *maydān*]

maiden /máyd'n/ *n.* **1 a** *archaic* or *poet.* a girl; a young unmarried woman. **b** (*attrib.*) unmarried (*maiden aunt*). **2** *Cricket* = *maiden over.* **3** (*attrib.*) (of a female animal) unmated. **4** (often *attrib.*) **a** a horse that has never won a race. **b** a race open only to such horses. **5** (*attrib.*) being or involving the first attempt or occurrence (*maiden speech*; *maiden voyage*). ▫ **maiden name** a wife's surname before marriage. **maiden over** *Cricket* an over in which no runs are scored off the bat. ▫▫ **maidenhood** *n.* **maidenish** *adj.* **maidenlike** *adj.* **maidenly** *adj.* [OE *mægden*, dimin. f. *mægeth* f. Gmc]

■ **1** see MAID 2. **2** see UNMARRIED. **5** inaugural, first, initial, *US colloq.* shakedown.

maidenhair /máyd'nhair/ *n.* (in full **maidenhair fern**) a fern of the genus *Adiantum*, esp. *A. capillus-veneris*, with fine hairlike stalks and delicate fronds. ▫ **maidenhair tree** =GINKGO.

maidenhead /máyd'nhed/ *n.* **1** virginity. **2** the hymen.

maidservant /máydserv'nt/ *n.* a female domestic servant.

■ see SERVANT.

maieutic /may-ṓōtik/ *adj.* (of the Socratic mode of enquiry) serving to bring a person's latent ideas into clear consciousness. [Gk *maieutikos* f. *maieuomai* act as a midwife f. *maia* midwife]

maigre /máygər/ *adj. RC Ch.* **1** (of a day) on which abstinence from meat is ordered. **2** (of food) suitable for eating on maigre days. [F, lit. lean: cf. MEAGRE]

mail[1] /mayl/ *n.* & *v.* ● *n.* **1 a** letters and parcels etc. conveyed by post. **b** the postal system. **c** one complete delivery or collection of mail. **d** one delivery of letters to one place, esp. to a business on one occasion. **2** a vehicle carrying mail. **3** *hist.* a bag of letters for conveyance by post. ● *v.tr.* esp. *US* send (a letter etc.) by post. ▫ **mail-boat** a boat carrying mail. **mail carrier** *US* a postman or postwoman. **mail cart** *Brit. hist.* **1** a cart for carrying mail by road. **2** a light vehicle for carrying children. **mail coach** a railway coach or *hist.* stagecoach used for carrying mail. **mail drop** *US* a receptacle for mail. **mailing list** a list of people to whom advertising matter, information, etc., is to be posted. **mail order** an order for goods sent by post. **mail-order firm** a firm doing business by post. **mail train** a train carrying mail. [ME f. OF *male* wallet f. WG]

■ *n.* **1 a** correspondence, letters (and parcels), *Brit.* post. **b** postal system *or* service, Post Office, *Brit.* post. **c** delivery, collection, *Brit.* post. **d** delivery, *Brit.* post. ● *v.* post, send, dispatch.

mail[2] /mayl/ *n.* & *v.* ● *n.* **1** armour made of rings, chains, or plates, joined together flexibly. **2** the protective shell, scales, etc., of an animal. ● *v.tr.* clothe with or as if with mail. ▫ **coat of mail** a jacket covered with mail or composed of mail. **mailed fist** physical force. ▫▫ **mailed** *adj.* [ME f. OF *maille* f. L *macula* spot, mesh]

mailable /máyləb'l/ *adj.* acceptable for conveyance by post.

mailbag /máylbag/ *n.* a large sack or bag for carrying mail.

mailbox /máylboks/ *n. US* a letter-box.

maillot /mayṓ/ *n.* **1** tights for dancing, gymnastics, etc. **2** a woman's one-piece bathing-suit. **3** a jersey. [F]

mailman /máylmən/ *n.* (*pl.* **-men**) *US* a postman.

mailshot /máylshot/ *n.* a dispatch of mail, esp. advertising and promotional material, to a large number of addresses.

maim /maym/ *v.tr.* **1** cripple, disable, mutilate. **2** harm, impair (*emotionally maimed by neglect*). [ME *maime* etc. f. OF *mahaignier* etc., of unkn. orig.]

■ **1** cripple, disable, mutilate, lame, incapacitate, wound, wing, hamstring, put out of action *or* commission **2** harm, impair, injure, damage.

main[1] /mayn/ *adj.* & *n.* ● *adj.* **1** chief in size, importance, extent, etc.; principal (*the main part*; *the main point*). **2** exerted to the full (*by main force*). ● *n.* **1** a principal channel, duct, etc., for water, sewage, etc. (*water main*). **2** (usu. in *pl.*; prec. by *the*) **a** the central distribution network for electricity, gas, water, etc. **b** a domestic electricity supply as distinct from batteries. **3** *archaic* or *poet.* **a** the ocean or oceans (*the Spanish Main*). **b** the mainland. ▫ **in the main** for the most part. **main brace** *Naut.* the brace attached to the main yard. **the main chance** one's own interests. **main course 1** the chief course of a meal. **2** *Naut.* the mainsail. **main deck** *Naut.* **1** the deck below the spar-deck in a man-of-war. **2** the upper deck between the poop and the forecastle in a merchantman. **main line 1** a chief railway line. **2** *sl.* a principal vein, esp. as a site for a drug injection (cf. MAINLINE). **3** *US* a chief road or street. **main stem** *US colloq.* = *main street.* **main street** the principal street of a town. **Main Street** *US* materialistic philosophy (after Sinclair Lewis's novel, 1920). **main yard** *Naut.* the yard on which the mainsail is extended. **with might and main** with all one's force. [ME, partly f. ON *megenn*, *megn* (adj.), partly f. OE *mægen-* f. Gmc: (n.) orig. = physical force]

■ *adj.* **1** chief, primary, prime, (most) important, principal, cardinal, paramount, first, foremost, leading, pre-eminent, predominant, predominating, dominant, ranking, major; outstanding; largest, biggest, greatest, strongest; necessary, essential, basic, particular, fundamental, critical, crucial, vital. **2** sheer, brute, utter, pure, out-and-out, absolute. ● *n.* **1** pipe, duct, channel, line, pipeline, conduit, water *or* gas main. **2** power (supply), grid. ▫ **in the main** see MAINLY. **main street** *Brit.* high street.

main[2] /mayn/ *n.* **1** (in the game of hazard) a number (5, 6, 7, 8, or 9) called by a player before dice are thrown. **2** a match between fighting-cocks. [16th c.: prob. orig. *main chance*: see MAIN[1]]

mainframe /máynfraym/ *n.* **1** the central processing unit and primary memory of a computer. **2** (often *attrib.*) a large computer system.

mainland /máynlənd/ *n.* **1** a large continuous extent of land, excluding neighbouring islands etc. **2** (**Mainland**) the largest island in Orkney and in Shetland. ▫▫ **mainlander** *n.*

mainline /máynlīn/ *v. sl.* **1** *intr.* take drugs intravenously. **2** *tr.* inject (drugs) intravenously. ▫▫ **mainliner** *n.*

mainly /máynli/ *adv.* for the most part; chiefly.
■ in the main, chiefly, principally, predominantly, generally, above all, on the whole, in general, mostly, most of all, effectively, essentially, at bottom, first and foremost, for the most part, largely, by and large, primarily, as a rule, usually, all in all, on balance, for all practical purposes.

mainmast /máynmaast/ *n. Naut.* the principal mast of a ship.

mainplane /máynplayn/ *n.* the principal supporting surface of an aircraft (cf. TAILPLANE).

mainsail /máynsayl, -s'l/ *n. Naut.* **1** (in a square-rigged vessel) the lowest sail on the mainmast. **2** (in a fore-and-aft rigged vessel) a sail set on the after part of the mainmast.

mainspring /máynspring/ *n.* **1** the principal spring of a mechanical watch, clock, etc. **2** a chief motive power; an incentive.

mainstay /máynstay/ *n.* **1** a chief support (*has been his mainstay since his trouble*). **2** *Naut.* a stay from the maintop to the foot of the foremast.
■ **1** (sheet) anchor, bulwark, buttress, support.

mainstream /máynstreem/ *n.* **1** (often *attrib.*) the prevailing trend in opinion, fashion, etc. **2** a type of jazz based on the 1930s swing style and consisting esp. of solo improvisation on chord sequences. **3** the principal current of a river.
■ **1** see CURRENT *n.* 3. **3** see CURRENT *n.* 1.

maintain /mayntáyn/ *v.tr.* **1** cause to continue; keep up, preserve (a state of affairs, an activity, etc.) (*maintained friendly relations*). **2** (often foll. by *in*; often *refl.*) support (life, a condition, etc.) by work, nourishment, expenditure, etc. (*maintained him in comfort*; *maintained themselves by fishing*). **3** (often foll. by *that* + clause) assert (an opinion, statement, etc.) as true (*maintained that she was the best*; *his story was true, he maintained*). **4** preserve or provide for the preservation of (a building, machine, road, etc.) in good repair. **5** give aid to (a cause, party, etc.). **6** provide means for (a garrison etc. to be equipped). ▫ **maintained school** *Brit.* a school supported from public funds. ▫▫ **maintainable** *adj.* **maintainability** /-nəbílliti/ *n.* [ME f. OF *maintenir* ult. f. L *manu tenēre* hold in the hand]
■ **1, 2** continue, preserve, persevere in, keep going, persist in, keep (up), carry on, retain, perpetuate, prolong, sustain, uphold; nurture, support. **3** hold, state, say, declare, claim, assert, allege, testify, contend, avow, announce, proclaim, profess, insist (on), affirm, *formal* aver. **4** look after, take care of, care for, preserve, keep up, service, keep in repair *or* service. **5** see SUPPORT *v.* 13.

maintainer /mayntáynər/ *n.* **1** a person or thing that maintains. **2** (also **maintainor**) *Law hist.* a person guilty of maintenance (see MAINTENANCE 3).

maintenance /máyntənənss/ *n.* **1** the process of maintaining or being maintained. **2 a** the provision of the means to support life, esp. by work etc. **b** (also **separate maintenance**) a husband's or wife's provision for a spouse after separation or divorce; alimony. **3** *Law hist.* the offence of aiding a party in litigation without lawful cause. [ME f. OF f. *maintenir*: see MAINTAIN]
■ **1** upkeep, care, servicing, preservation, conservation, support, *formal* sustentation; continuation, continuance, perpetuation, prolongation. **2 a** upkeep, livelihood, subsistence, support, allowance, living, sustenance, stipend, subvention, contribution, keep.

maintop /máyntop/ *n. Naut.* a platform above the head of the lower mainmast.

maintopmast /mayntópməst/ *n. Naut.* a mast above the head of the lower mainmast.

maiolica /məyóllikə/ *n.* a white tin-glazed earthenware decorated with metallic colours, orig. popular in the Mediterranean area during the Renaissance (see also MAJOLICA). [It. f. former name of Majorca]

maisonette /máyzənét/ *n.* (also **maisonnette**) **1** a part of a house, block of flats, etc., forming separate living accommodation, usu. on two floors and having a separate entrance. **2** a small house. [F *maisonnette* dimin. of *maison* house]

maître d'hôtel /métrə dōtél, máyt-/ *n.* **1** the manager, head steward, etc., of a hotel. **2** a head waiter. [F, = master of (the) house]
■ **2** see WAITER.

maize /mayz/ *n.* **1** a cereal plant, *Zea mays*, native to N. America, yielding large grains set in rows on a cob. **2** the cobs or grains of this (see CORN[1]). [F *maïs* or Sp. *maiz*, of Carib orig.]

Maj. *abbr.* Major.

majestic /məjéstik/ *adj.* showing majesty; stately and dignified; grand, imposing. ▫▫ **majestically** *adv.*
■ dignified, grand, imperial, regal, royal, kingly, queenly, princely, noble, lordly, lofty, elevated, exalted, glorious, magnificent, monumental, impressive, striking, imposing, awesome, splendid, marvellous.

majesty /májisti/ *n.* (*pl.* **-ies**) **1** impressive stateliness, dignity, or authority, esp. of bearing, language, the law, etc. **2 a** royal power. **b** (**Majesty**) part of several titles given to a sovereign or a sovereign's wife or widow or used in addressing them (*Your Majesty*; *Her Majesty the Queen Mother*). **3** a picture of God or Christ enthroned within an aureole. ▫ **Her** (or **His**) **Majesty's** part of the title of several State institutions (*Her Majesty's Stationery Office*). [ME f. OF *majesté* f. L *majestas -tatis* (as MAJOR)]
■ **1** authority, stateliness; see also DIGNITY 1. **2 b** Royal Highness, *archaic* Sire.

Majlis /májliss/ *n. Polit.* the parliament of various N. African or Middle Eastern countries, esp. Iran. [Pers., = assembly]

majolica /məyóllikə, məjól-/ *n.* (also **maiolica**) **1** a 19th-c. trade name for earthenware with coloured decoration on an opaque white glaze. **2** = MAIOLICA. [alt. f. MAIOLICA]

major /máyjər/ *adj.*, *n.*, & *v.* ● *adj.* **1** important, large, serious, significant (*a major road*; *a major war*; *the major consideration must be their health*). **2** (of an operation) serious or life-threatening. **3** *Mus.* **a** (of a scale) having intervals of a semitone between the third and fourth, and seventh and eighth degrees. **b** (of an interval) greater by a semitone than a minor interval (*major third*). **c** (of a key) based on a major scale, tending to produce a bright or joyful effect (*D major*). **4** of full age. **5** *Brit.* (appended to a surname, esp. in public schools) the elder of two brothers or the first to enter the school (*Smith major*). **6** *Logic* **a** (of a term) occurring in the predicate or conclusion of a syllogism. **b** (of a premiss) containing a major term. ● *n.* **1** *Mil.* **a** an army officer next below lieutenant-colonel and above captain. **b** an officer in charge of a section of band instruments (*drum major*; *pipe major*). **2** a person of full age. **3** *US* **a** a student's special subject or course. **b** a student specializing in a specified subject (*a philosophy major*). **4** *Logic* a major term or premiss. ● *v.intr.* (foll. by *in*) *US* study or qualify in as a special subject (*majored in theology*). ▫ **major axis** the axis of a conic, passing through its foci. **major-general** an officer next below a lieutenant-general. **major league** *US* a league of major importance in baseball etc. **major part** (often foll. by *of*) the majority. **major piece** *Chess* a rook or queen. **major planet** Jupiter, Saturn, Uranus, or Neptune. **major prophet** Isaiah, Jeremiah, Ezekiel, or Daniel. **major suit** *Bridge* spades or hearts. ▫▫ **majorship** *n.* [ME f. L, compar. of *magnus* great]
■ *adj.* **1** vital, important, critical, crucial, principal, foremost, paramount, primary, prime, main, big, large, biggest, pre-eminent, notable, noteworthy, significant,

outstanding, dominant, dominating; serious, grave; larger, greater, bigger, chief. **4** see MATURE *adj.* 1. ● *n.* **2** adult, grown-up. **3 a** specialization. **b** specialist. ● *v.* read, specialize. □ **major part** bulk, greater part; see also MAJORITY 1.

major-domo /máyjərdṓmō/ *n.* (*pl.* **-os**) **1** the chief official of an Italian or Spanish princely household. **2** a house-steward; a butler. [orig. *mayordome* f. Sp. *mayordomo*, It. *maggiordomo* f. med.L *major domus* highest official of the household (as MAJOR, DOME)]
■ **2** see SERVANT.

majorette /máyjərét/ *n.* = *drum majorette.* [abbr.]

majority /məjórriti/ *n.* (*pl.* **-ies**) **1** (usu. foll. by *of*) the greater number or part. ¶ Strictly used only with countable nouns, e.g. *a majority of people*, and not with mass nouns, e.g. *a majority of the work.* **2** *Polit.* **a** the number by which the votes cast for one party, candidate, etc. exceed those of the next in rank (*won by a majority of 151*). **b** a party etc. receiving the greater number of votes. **3** full legal age (*attained his majority*). **4** the rank of major. □ **the great majority 1** much the greater number. **2** *euphem.* the dead (*has joined the great majority*). **in the majority** esp. *Polit.* belonging to or constituting a majority party etc. **majority rule** the principle that the greater number should exercise greater power. **majority verdict** a verdict given by more than half of the jury, but not unanimous. [F *majorité* f. med.L *majoritas -tatis* (as MAJOR)]
■ **1** bulk, preponderance, mass, better *or* best part, lion's share. **3** adulthood, maturity, seniority, womanhood, manhood. □ **the great majority 1** the vast majority, (by far the) most people.

majuscule /májəskyōōl/ *n.* & *adj.* ● *n. Palaeog.* **1** a large letter, whether capital or uncial. **2** large lettering. ● *adj.* of, written in, or concerning majuscules. □□ **majuscular** /məjúskyoolər/ *adj.* [F f. L *majuscula* (*littera* letter), dimin. of MAJOR]

make /mayk/ *v.* & *n.* ● *v.* (*past* and *past part.* **made** /mayd/) **1** *tr.* construct; create; form from parts or other substances (*made a table; made it out of cardboard; made him a sweater*). **2** *tr.* (foll. by *to* + infin.) cause or compel (a person etc.) to do something (*make him repeat it; was made to confess*). **3** *tr.* **a** cause to exist; create; bring about (*made a noise; made an enemy*). **b** cause to become or seem (*made an exhibition of myself; made him angry*). **c** appoint; designate (*made him a Cardinal*). **4** *tr.* compose; prepare; draw up (*made her will; made a film about Japan*). **5** *tr.* constitute; amount to (*makes a difference; 2 and 2 make 4; this makes the tenth time*). **6** *tr.* **a** undertake or agree to (an aim or purpose) (*made a promise; make an effort*). **b** execute or perform (a bodily movement, a speech, etc.) (*made a face; made a bow*). **7** *tr.* gain, acquire, procure (money, a profit, etc.) (*made £20,000 on the deal*). **8** *tr.* prepare (tea, coffee, a dish, etc.) for consumption (*made egg and chips*). **9** *tr.* **a** arrange bedclothes tidily on (a bed) ready for use. **b** arrange and light materials for (a fire). **10** *intr.* **a** proceed (*made towards the river*). **b** (foll. by *to* + infin.) begin an action (*he made to go*). **11** *tr. colloq.* **a** arrive at (a place) or in time for (a train etc.) (*made the border before dark; made the six o'clock train*). **b** manage to attend; manage to attend on (a certain day) or at (a certain time) (*couldn't make the meeting last week; can make any day except Friday*). **c** achieve a place in (*made the first eleven; made the six o'clock news*). **d** *US* achieve the rank of (*made colonel in three years*). **12** *tr.* establish or enact (a distinction, rule, law, etc.). **13** *tr.* consider to be; estimate as (*what do you make the time?; do you make that a 1 or a 7?*). **14** *tr.* secure the success or advancement of (*his mother made him; it made my day*). **15** *tr.* accomplish (a distance, speed, score, etc.) (*made 60 m.p.h. on the motorway*). **16** *tr.* **a** become by development or training (*made a great leader*). **b** serve as (*a log makes a useful seat*). **17** *tr.* (usu. foll. by *out*) represent as; cause to appear as (*makes him out a liar*). **18** *tr.* form in the mind; feel (*I make no judgement*). **19** *tr.* (foll. by *it* + compl.) **a** determine, establish, or choose (*let's make it Tuesday; made it my business to know*). **b** bring to (a chosen value etc.) (*decided to make it a dozen*). **20** *tr. sl.* have sexual relations with. **21** *tr. Cards* **a** win (a trick). **b** play (a card) to advantage. **c** win the number of tricks that fulfils (a contract). **d** shuffle (a pack of cards) for dealing. **22** *tr. Cricket* score (runs). **23** *tr. Electr.* complete or close (a circuit) (opp. BREAK[1]). **24** *intr.* (of the tide) begin to flow or ebb. ● *n.* **1** (esp. of a product) a type, origin, brand, etc. of manufacture (*different make of car; our own make*). **2** a kind of mental, moral, or physical structure or composition. **3** an act of shuffling cards. **4** *Electr.* **a** the making of contact. **b** the position in which this is made. □ **be made for** be ideally suited to. **be made of** consist of (*cake made of marzipan*). **have it made** *colloq.* be sure of success. **made dish** a dish prepared from several separate foods. **made man** a man who has attained success. **made of money** *colloq.* very rich. **made road** a properly surfaced road of tarmac, concrete, etc. **made to measure** (of a suit etc.) made to a specific customer's measurements. **made to order** see ORDER. **make after** *archaic* pursue. **make against** be unfavourable to. **make as if** (or **though**) (foll. by *to* + infin. or conditional) act as if the specified circumstances applied (*made as if to leave; made as if he would hit me; made as if I had not noticed*). **make away** (or **off**) depart hastily. **make away with 1** get rid of; kill. **2** squander. **3** = *make off with.* **make-believe** (or **-belief**) **1** pretence. **2** pretended. **make believe** pretend. **make conversation** talk politely. **make a day** (or **night** etc.) **of it** devote a whole day (or night etc.) to an activity. **make do 1** manage with the limited or inadequate means available. **2** (foll. by *with*) manage with (something) as an inferior substitute. **make an entrance** see ENTRANCE[1]. **make an example of** punish as a warning to others. **make a fool of** see FOOL[1]. **make for 1** tend to result in (happiness etc.). **2** proceed towards (a place). **3** assault; attack. **4** confirm (an opinion). **make friends** (often foll. by *with*) become friendly. **make fun of** see FUN. **make good** see GOOD. **make a habit of** see HABIT. **make a hash of** see HASH[1]. **make hay** see HAY[1]. **make head or tail of** see HEAD. **make headway** advance, progress. **make a House** *Polit.* secure the presence of enough members for a quorum or support in the House of Commons. **make it 1** *colloq.* succeed in reaching, esp. in time. **2** *colloq.* be successful. **3** (usu. foll. by *with*) *sl.* have sexual intercourse (with). **make it up 1** be reconciled, esp. after a quarrel. **2** fill in a deficit. **make it up to** remedy negligence, an injury, etc. to (a person). **make light of** see LIGHT[2]. **make love** see LOVE. **make a meal of** see MEAL[1]. **make merry** see MERRY. **make money** acquire wealth or an income. **make the most of** see MOST. **make much** (or **little** or **the best**) **of 1** derive much (or little etc.) advantage from. **2** give much (or little etc.) attention, importance, etc., to. **make a name for oneself** see NAME. **make no bones about** see BONE. **make nothing of 1** do without hesitation. **2** treat as a trifle. **3** be unable to understand, use, or deal with. **make of 1** construct from. **2** conclude to be the meaning or character of (*can you make anything of it?*). **make off** = *make away.* **make off** (or **away**) **with** carry away; steal. **make oneself scarce** see SCARCE. **make or break** (or **mar**) cause the success or ruin of. **make out 1 a** distinguish by sight or hearing. **b** decipher (handwriting etc.). **2** understand (*can't make him out*). **3** assert; pretend (*made out he liked it*). **4** *colloq.* make progress; fare (*how did you make out?*). **5** (usu. foll. by *to, in favour of*) draw up; write out (*made out a cheque to her*). **6** prove or try to prove (*how do you make that out?*). **7** (often foll. by *with*) esp. *US colloq.* **a** engage in sexual play or petting. **b** form a sexual relationship. **make over 1** transfer the possession of (a thing) to a person. **2** refashion (a garment etc.). **make a point of** see POINT. **make sail** *Naut.* **1** spread a sail or sails. **2** start a voyage. **make shift** see SHIFT. **make so bold as to** see BOLD. **make time 1** (usu. foll. by *for* or *to* + infin.) find an occasion when time is available. **2** (usu. foll. by *with*) esp. *US sl.* make sexual advances (to a person). **make-up 1** cosmetics for the face etc., either generally or to create an actor's appearance or disguise. **2** the appearance of the face etc. when cosmetics have been applied (*his make-up was not convincing*). **3** *Printing* the making up of a type. **4** *Printing* the type made up. **5** a person's character, temperament, etc. **6** the composition or constitution of a thing. **make up 1** serve or act to overcome (a deficiency). **2** complete (an amount, a party, etc.). **3** compensate. **4** be reconciled. **5** put together; compound; prepare (*made up the medicine*). **6** sew (parts of a garment etc.) together. **7** get (a sum of money, a company, etc.) together. **8** concoct (a story). **9** (of parts) compose (a whole). **10 a** apply cosmetics. **b** apply cosmetics to. **11** settle (a dispute). **12** prepare (a bed) for use with fresh sheets etc. **13** *Printing* arrange (type) in pages. **14** compile (a list, an account, a document, etc.). **15** arrange (a marriage etc.). **make up one's mind** decide, resolve. **make up to** curry favour with; court. **make water 1** urinate. **2** (of a ship) take in water. **make way 1** (often foll. by *for*) allow room for others to proceed. **2** achieve progress. **make one's way** proceed. **make with** *US colloq.* supply; perform; proceed with (*made with the feet and left in a hurry*). **on the make** *colloq.* **1** intent on gain. **2** looking for sexual partners. **self-made man** etc. a man etc. who has succeeded by his own efforts. □□ **makable** *adj.* [OE *macian* f. WG: rel. to MATCH[1]]

■ *v.* **1** build, assemble, construct, erect, put together, set up, fashion, form, mould, shape, frame, create, originate, fabricate, manufacture, produce, put out, forge, contrive, devise. **2** cause, compel, force, impel, coerce, provoke, urge, exhort, press, pressure, pressurize, require, command, order, induce, persuade, prevail (up)on, insist (up)on, oblige. **3** bring about, occasion, cause, give rise to; produce, create, generate; appoint, name, select, choose, elect, vote (in as), designate, authorize, commission, delegate, depute, deputize, assign, sanction, approve, affirm, certify, confirm. **4** make out *or* up, draw (up), create, write, sign, frame. **5** amount to, constitute, represent, add up to, total, come to. **6 a** see UNDERTAKE 1. **b** deliver, present; see also EXECUTE 2. **7** earn, reap, garner, take in, get, procure, gather, clear, realize, gross, net, pocket, acquire, obtain, receive, *Austral.*, *NZ*, & *US sl.* knock out; win, gain, *colloq.* pull down; return, fetch. **8** prepare, cook, *US colloq.* fix. **9 a** prepare, arrange, rearrange, tidy (up), neaten (up). **b** lay, prepare, arrange. **10 a** (*make for*) head for *or* towards, aim for, steer (a course) for, proceed towards, be bound for. **11 a** reach, arrive at, attain, get (to), win, achieve, accomplish. **c** achieve, get on *or* in. **12** enact, pass, frame, establish, institute; set up, organize. **13** judge, think, calculate, estimate, reckon, gauge, suppose. **15** reach, accomplish, make; do, go *or* travel *or* move at; score, get (to), achieve, earn. **16 a** become, change *or* turn *or* grow into, prove *or* come to be, turn out to be, perform as. **b** serve as, be suitable for *or* as. **17** present as, depict as, characterize as, describe as, delineate as, show as, define as, portray as, paint as; declare. **20** seduce, *sl.* make it with; see also LAY[1] *v.* 16. **22** score, get, earn, secure. ● *n.* **1** kind, brand, style, sort, type, mark, marque. **2** see *make-up* 5 below. □ **have it made** see LAUGH *v.* 5. **made of money** see *in the money* (MONEY). **make after** see PURSUE 1. **make as if** (or **though**) pretend, feign, act as if *or* as though, affect, make a show *or* pretence of, give the impression of, make out, make believe. **make away** *or* **off** run away *or* off, flee, fly, abscond, take to one's heels, decamp, beat a (hasty) retreat, (make a) run for it, take off, *colloq.* clear out, skedaddle, skip (out *or* off), make tracks, scram, *US colloq.* hightail (it), *sl.* beat it, skip it, cut and run, take a powder, *US sl.* vamoose. **make away with 1** see KILL *v.* 1a. **2** see WASTE *v.* 1. **make-believe** (or **belief**) **1** see PRETENCE 1. **2** see FICTITIOUS 2. **make believe** pretend, fancy, play-act, dream, fantasize, imagine, act as if. **make conversation** make polite conversation, make small talk; see also CHAT[1] *v.* **make do 1, 2** get by *or* along, cope, scrape by *or* along, manage, muddle through, survive. **make for 1** promote, contribute to, be conducive to, favour, facilitate; see also LEAD[1] *v.* 9. **2** see MAKE *v.* 10a above. **3** assault, attack, set upon, charge, rush (at), pounce upon, fall upon *or* on, go for, lunge at, storm, assail. **make headway** advance, progress, make progress *or* way, move forward, go, gain (ground), get *or* go ahead, proceed, get going. **make it 1** arrive, get there, show up, appear, turn up. **2** succeed, prosper, triumph, win, make good, *colloq.* make the grade. **3** (*make it with*) see LAY[1] *v.* 16. **make it up 1** see *make up* 4 below. **make much of 2** emphasize, stress; see also MAXIMIZE. **make nothing of 1** think nothing of, make no bones about, not hesitate to. **2** play down, downplay; see also *make light of* (LIGHT[2]). **3** not make head or tail of, not understand. **make of 2** infer *or* deduce *or* derive *or* conclude *or* draw *or* surmise *or* understand *or* gather. **make off** see *make away* above. **make off with** steal, rob, filch, pilfer, walk away *or* off with, *colloq.* borrow, liberate, *formal or joc.* purloin, *sl.* pinch, hook, rip off, lift, swipe. **make out 1** see, discern, detect, discover, distinguish, *literary* descry, espy. **2** understand, fathom, comprehend, figure out, perceive, follow, grasp, see, decipher, read. **3** suggest, imply, hint, insinuate, indicate, intimate; pretend, make to appear, make as if *or* as though, make believe. **4** see FARE *v.* 1. **5** complete, fill in, fill up, *US* fill out; draw (up), write (out). **6** see PROVE 1. **make over 1** transfer, hand over, sign over, convey, assign, turn over. **2** do over, remodel, refashion, redecorate, alter. **make sail 2** set sail, put (out) to sea. **make time 2** (*make time with*) see *chat up*. **make-up 1** cosmetics, *maquillage*, greasepaint, *colloq.* warpaint. **5** temperament, constitution, character, cast, disposition, personality, make. **6** constitution, arrangement, construction, composition, format, configuration, build, form. **make up 1** redress, overcome. **2** complete, fill out, finish (out), flesh out. **3** compensate, redress, make good, atone, make amends. **4** be reconciled, make peace, come to terms, bury the hatchet. **5** put together, construct, build; compound; prepare. **8** hatch, invent, concoct, devise, create, construct, dream up, originate, coin, compose, *colloq.* cook up. **9** compose, form, constitute, *disp.* comprise. **11** see SETTLE[1] 5–7, 8b. **12** see MAKE *v.* 9a above. **14** see COMPILE 1. **make up one's mind** see DECIDE 1. **make up to** see INGRATIATE. **make water 1** see URINATE. **2** leak, take *or* let in water. **make way 1** move aside, clear the way, allow to pass, make room *or* space. **2** see *get on* 1. **make one's way** see PROCEED 1. **on the make 1** aggressive, assertive, go-ahead, enterprising, vigorous, energetic, *colloq.* pushy. **2** *sl.* cruising.

makeover /máykōvər/ *n.* a complete transformation or remodelling.

maker /máykər/ *n.* **1** (often in *comb.*) a person or thing that makes. **2** (**our, the,** etc. **Maker**) God. **3** *archaic* a poet.
■ **1** see CREATOR 1. **2** (**our** or **the Maker**) see CREATOR 2.

makeshift /máykshift/ *adj.* & *n.* ● *adj.* temporary; serving for the time being (*a makeshift arrangement*). ● *n.* a temporary substitute or device.
■ *adj.* temporary, *ad interim*, stopgap, expedient, emergency, improvised, ad hoc, tentative, stand-by. ● *n.* expedient, improvisation, substitute; see also STOPGAP.

makeweight /máykwayt/ *n.* **1** a small quantity or thing added to make up the full weight. **2** an unimportant extra person. **3** an unimportant point added to make an argument seem stronger.

making /máyking/ *n.* **1** in senses of MAKE *v.* **2** (in *pl.*) **a** earnings; profit. **b** (foll. by *of*) essential qualities or ingredients (*has the makings of a general*; *we have the makings of a meal*). **c** *US* & *Austral. colloq.* paper and tobacco for rolling a cigarette. □ **be the making of** ensure the success or favourable development of. **in the making** in the course of being made or formed. [OE *macung* (as MAKE)]
■ **2 b** see INGREDIENT.

mako[1] /máakō/ *n.* (*pl.* **-os**) a blue shark, *Isurus oxyrinchus*. [Maori]

mako[2] /máakkō/ *n.* (*pl.* **-os**) a small New Zealand tree, *Aristotelia serrata*, with clusters of dark-red berries and large racemes of pink flowers. Also called WINEBERRY. [Maori]

Mal. *abbr.* Malachi (Old Testament).

mal- /mal/ *comb. form* **1 a** bad, badly (*malpractice*; *maltreat*). **b** faulty, faultily (*malfunction*). **2** not (*maladroit*). [F *mal* badly f. L *male*]

malabsorption /málləbsórpsh'n/ *n.* imperfect absorption of food material by the small intestine.

malacca /məlákkə/ *n.* (in full **malacca cane**) a rich-brown cane from the stem of the palm-tree *Calamus scipionum*, used for walking-sticks etc. [*Malacca* in Malaysia]

malachite /mállәkīt/ *n.* a bright-green mineral of hydrous copper carbonate, taking a high polish and used for ornament. [OF *melochite* f. L *molochites* f. Gk *molokhitis* f. *molokhē* = *malakhē* mallow]

malaco- /málləkō/ *comb. form* soft. [Gk *malakos* soft]

malacology /málləkólləji/ *n.* the study of molluscs.

malacostracan /mállәkóstrәkәn/ *n.* & *adj.* ● *n.* any crustacean of the class Malacostraca, including crabs, shrimps, lobsters, and krill. ● *adj.* of or relating to this class. [MALACO- + Gk *ostrakon* shell]

maladaptive /mállədáptiv/ *adj.* (of an individual, species, etc.) failing to adjust adequately to the environment, and undergoing emotional, behavioural, physical, or mental repercussions. ▫▫ **maladaptation** /málladdaptáysh'n/ *n.*

maladjusted /mállәjústid/ *adj.* **1** not correctly adjusted. **2** (of a person) unable to adapt to or cope with the demands of a social environment. ▫▫ **maladjustment** *n.*

■ **2** see *disturbed* (DISTURB 4).

maladminister /mállədmínnistər/ *v.tr.* manage or administer inefficiently, badly, or dishonestly. ▫▫ **maladministration** /-stráysh'n/ *n.*

maladroit /mállədróyt/ *adj.* clumsy; bungling. ▫▫ **maladroitly** *adv.* **maladroitness** *n.* [F (as MAL-, ADROIT)]

■ see CLUMSY 1. ▫▫ **maladroitly** see ROUGHLY 1. **maladroitness** see *ineptitude* (INEPT).

malady /mállədi/ *n.* (*pl.* **-ies**) **1** an ailment; a disease. **2** a morbid or depraved condition; something requiring a remedy. [ME f. OF *maladie* f. *malade* sick ult. f. L *male* ill + *habitus* past part. of *habēre* have]

■ **1** see DISEASE.

mala fide /máylə fídi/ *adj.* & *adv.* ● *adj.* acting or done in bad faith. ● *adv.* in bad faith. [L]

Malaga /mállәgә/ *n.* a sweet fortified wine from Málaga in S. Spain.

Malagasy /mállәgássi/ *adj.* & *n.* ● *adj.* of or relating to Madagascar, an island in the Indian Ocean. ● *n.* the language of Madagascar. [orig. *Malegass*, *Madegass* f. *Madagascar*]

malagueña /mállәgényә/ *n.* **1** a Spanish dance resembling the fandango. **2** a piece of music for or in the style of a fandango. [Sp. (as MALAGA)]

malaise /məláyz/ *n.* **1** a non-specific bodily discomfort not associated with the development of a disease. **2** a feeling of uneasiness. [F f. OF *mal* bad + *aise* EASE]

■ **1** see AILMENT. **2** see DISCONTENT *n.*

malamute /mállәmyōōt/ *n.* (also **malemute**) an Eskimo dog. [name of an Alaskan Eskimo tribe]

malanders var. of MALLENDERS.

malapert /mállәpert/ *adj.* & *n. archaic* ● *adj.* impudent; saucy. ● *n.* an impudent or saucy person. [ME f. OF (as MAL-, *apert* = *espert* EXPERT)]

malapropism /mállәproppiz'm/ *n.* (also **malaprop** /mállәprop/) the use of a word in mistake for one sounding similar, to comic effect, e.g. *allegory* for *alligator*. [Mrs *Malaprop* (f. MALAPROPOS) in Sheridan's *The Rivals* (1775)]

malapropos /mallaprəpṓ/ *adv.*, *adj.*, & *n.* ● *adv.* inopportunely; inappropriately. ● *adj.* inopportune; inappropriate. ● *n.* something inappropriately said, done, etc. [F *mal à propos* f. *mal* ill: see APROPOS]

■ *adj.* see INAPPROPRIATE.

malar /máylər/ *adj.* & *n.* ● *adj.* of the cheek. ● *n.* a bone of the cheek. [mod.L *malaris* f. L *mala* jaw]

malaria /məláiriə/ *n.* **1** an intermittent and remittent fever caused by a protozoan parasite of the genus *Plasmodium*, introduced by the bite of a mosquito. **2** *archaic* an unwholesome atmosphere caused by the exhalations of marshes, to which this fever was formerly attributed. ▫▫ **malarial** *adj.* **malarian** *adj.* **malarious** *adj.* [It. *mal'aria* bad air]

malarkey /məlaárki/ *n. colloq.* humbug; nonsense. [20th c.: orig. unkn.]

■ see NONSENSE.

malathion /mállәthī́әn/ *n.* an insecticide containing phosphorus, with low toxicity to plants. [diethyl *male*ate + *thio*-acid + -ON]

Malay /məláy/ *n.* & *adj.* ● *n.* **1 a** a member of a people predominating in Malaysia and Indonesia. **b** a person of Malay descent. **2** the language of this people, the official language of Malaysia. ● *adj.* of or relating to this people or language. ▫▫ **Malayan** *n.* & *adj.* [Malay *malāyu*]

Malayalam /mállәyaálәm/ *n.* the Dravidian language of the State of Kerala in S. India. [native]

Malayo- /məláyō/ *comb. form* Malayan and (*Malayo-Chinese*). [MALAY]

malcontent /málkәntent/ *n.* & *adj.* ● *n.* a discontented person; a rebel. ● *adj.* discontented or rebellious. [F (as MAL-, CONTENT[1])]

■ *n.* see TROUBLEMAKER. ● *adj.* see DISGRUNTLED.

mal de mer /mál də máir/ *n.* seasickness. [F, = sickness of (the) sea]

male /mayl/ *adj.* & *n.* ● *adj.* **1** of the sex that can beget offspring by fertilization or insemination (*male child*; *male dog*). **2** of men or male animals, plants, etc.; masculine (*the male sex*; *a male-voice choir*). **3 a** (of plants or their parts) containing only fertilizing organs. **b** (of plants) thought of as male because of colour, shape, etc. **4** (of parts of machinery etc.) designed to enter or fill the corresponding female part (*a male screw*). ● *n.* a male person or animal. ▫ **male chauvinist** (**pig**) a man who is prejudiced against women or regards women as inferior. **male fern** a common lowland fern, *Dryopteris filixmas*. **male menopause** a crisis of potency, confidence, etc., supposed to afflict men in middle life. ▫▫ **maleness** *n.* [ME f. OF *ma(s)le*, f. L *masculus* f. *mas* a male]

■ *adj.* **2** masculine, man's; virile, manful, macho; see also MANLY 1. ● *n.* see MAN *n.* 1. ▫ **male chauvinist** sexist, misogynist, chauvinist, woman-hater, *colloq.* MCP.

malediction /mállidíksh'n/ *n.* **1** a curse. **2** the utterance of a curse. ▫▫ **maledictive** *adj.* **maledictory** *adj.* [ME f. L *maledictio* f. *maledicere* speak evil of f. *male* ill + *dicere dict-* speak]

■ see CURSE *n.* 1.

malefactor /mállifaktər/ *n.* a criminal; an evil-doer. ▫▫ **malefaction** /-fáksh'n/ *n.* [ME f. L f. *malefacere malefact-* f. *male* ill + *facere* do]

■ see CRIMINAL *n.* ▫▫ **malefaction** see OFFENCE 1.

malefic /məléffik/ *adj. literary* (of magical arts etc.) harmful; baleful. [L *maleficus* f. *male* ill]

maleficent /məléffis'nt/ *adj. literary* **1** (often foll. by *to*) hurtful. **2** criminal. ▫▫ **maleficence** *n.* [*maleficence* formed as MALEFIC after *malevolence*]

maleic acid /məláyik/ *n.* a colourless crystalline organic acid used in making synthetic resins. [F *maléique* (as MALIC ACID)]

malemute var. of MALAMUTE.

malevolent /məlévvələnt/ *adj.* wishing evil to others. ▫▫ **malevolence** *n.* **malevolently** *adv.* [OF *malivolent* or f. L *malevolens* f. *male* ill + *volens* willing, part. of *velle*]

■ see EVIL *adj.* 1. ▫▫ **malevolence** see HOSTILITY 1.

malfeasance /malfeéz'nss/ *n. Law* evil-doing. ▫▫ **malfeasant** *n.* & *adj.* [AF *malfaisance* f. OF *malfaisant* (as MAL-, *faisant* part. of *faire* do f. L *facere*): cf. MISFEASANCE]

malformation /málformáysh'n/ *n.* faulty formation. ▫▫ **malformed** /-fórmd/ *adj.*

■ see ABNORMALITY 2. ▫▫ **malformed** see DEFORMED.

malfunction /málfúngksh'n/ *n.* & *v.* ● *n.* a failure to function in a normal or satisfactory manner. ● *v.intr.* fail to function normally or satisfactorily.

■ *n.* see TROUBLE *n.* 4. ● *v.* see *go wrong* 2 (WRONG).

mali /maáli/ *n.* (*pl.* **malis**) *Ind.* a member of the gardener caste; a gardener. [Hindi]

malic acid /mállik/ *n.* an organic acid found in unripe apples and other fruits. [F *malique* f. L *malum* apple]

malice /mälliss/ *n.* **1 a** the intention to do evil. **b** a desire to tease, esp. cruelly. **2** *Law* wrongful intention, esp. as increasing the guilt of certain offences. ▫ **malice aforethought** (or **prepense**) *Law* the intention to commit a crime, esp. murder. [ME f. OF f. L *malitia* f. *malus* bad]

■ **1** see HOSTILITY 1.

malicious /məlíshəss/ *adj.* characterized by malice; intending or intended to do harm. ▫▫ **maliciously** *adv.* **maliciousness** *n.* [OF *malicius* f. L *malitiosus* (as MALICE)]

■ see VICIOUS 1, 3. ▫▫ **maliciousness** see VENOM 2.

malign /məlín/ *adj.* & *v.* ● *adj.* **1** (of a thing) injurious. **2** (of a disease) malignant. **3** malevolent. ● *v.tr.* speak ill of; slander. ▫▫ **maligner** *n.* **malignity** /məlígniti/ *n.* (*pl.* **-ies**). **malignly** *adv.* [ME f. OF *malin maligne*, *malignier* f. LL *malignare* contrive maliciously f. L *malignus* f. *malus* bad: cf. BENIGN]

■ *adj.* **1, 3** see EVIL *adj.* 2. ● *v.* see SLANDER *v.* ▫▫ **malignity** see VENOM 2.

malignant /məlígnənt/ *adj.* **1 a** (of a disease) very virulent or infectious (*malignant cholera*). **b** (of a tumour) tending to invade normal tissue and recur after removal; cancerous. **2** harmful; feeling or showing intense ill will. ▫ **malignant pustule** a form of anthrax. ▫▫ **malignancy** *n.* (*pl.* **-ies**). **malignantly** *adv.* [LL *malignare* (as MALIGN)]

■ **1** virulent, infectious, pernicious, harmful, injurious, life-threatening, invasive, cancerous. **2** harmful, injurious, malign, malevolent, evil, malicious, pernicious, vicious, spiteful, bitter, hateful, venomous; cankered.

malinger /məlínggər/ *v.intr.* exaggerate or feign illness in order to escape duty, work, etc. ▫▫ **malingerer** *n.* [back-form. f. *malingerer* app. f. F *malingre*, perh. formed as MAL- + *haingre* weak]

■ ▫▫ **malingerer** see TRUANT *n.*

mall /mal, mawl/ *n.* **1** a sheltered walk or promenade. **2** an enclosed shopping precinct. **3** *hist.* **a** = PALL-MALL. **b** an alley used for this. [var. of MAUL: applied to *The Mall* in London (orig. a pall-mall alley)]

■ **1, 2** see PARADE *n.* 4.

mallard /mállaard/ *n.* (*pl.* same or **mallards**) **1** a wild duck or drake, *Anas platyrhynchos*, of the northern hemisphere. **2** the flesh of the mallard. [ME f. OF prob. f. *maslart* (unrecorded, as MALE)]

malleable /mállìəb'l/ *adj.* **1** (of metal etc.) able to be hammered or pressed permanently out of shape without breaking or cracking. **2** adaptable; pliable, flexible. ▫▫ **malleability** /-bílliti/ *n.* **malleably** *adv.* [ME f. OF f. med.L *malleabilis* f. L *malleare* to hammer f. *malleus* hammer]

■ **1** see PLASTIC 1a. **2** see ADAPTABLE 1. ▫▫ **malleability** see *flexibility* (FLEXIBLE).

mallee /málli/ *n. Austral.* **1** any of several types of eucalyptus, esp. *Eucalyptus dumosa*, that flourish in arid areas. **2** a scrub formed by mallee. ▫ **mallee-bird** (or **-fowl** or **-hen**) a megapode, *Leipoa ocellata*, resembling a turkey. [Aboriginal]

mallei *pl.* of MALLEUS.

mallemuck var. of MOLLYMAWK.

mallenders /mállǝndǝrz/ *n.pl.* (also **malanders**) a dry scabby eruption behind a horse's knee. [ME f. OF *malandre* (sing.) f. L *malandria* (pl.) neck-pustules]

malleolus /məleéələss/ *n.* (*pl.* **malleoli** /-lī/) *Anat.* a bone with the shape of a hammer-head, esp. each of those forming a projection on either side of the ankle. [L, dimin. of *malleus* hammer]

mallet /mállit/ *n.* **1** a hammer, usu. of wood. **2** a long-handled wooden hammer for striking a croquet or polo ball. [ME f. OF *maillet* f. *mailler* to hammer f. *mail* hammer f. L *malleus*]

malleus /mállìəss/ *n.* (*pl.* **mallei** /-li-ī/) *Anat.* a small bone in the middle ear transmitting the vibrations of the tympanum to the incus. [L, = hammer]

mallow /mállō/ *n.* **1** any plant of the genus *Malva*, esp. *M. sylvestris*, with hairy stems and leaves and pink or purple flowers. **2** any of several other plants of the family Malvaceae, including marsh mallow and tree mallow. [OE *meal(u)we* f. L *malva*]

malm /maam/ *n.* **1** a soft chalky rock. **2** a loamy soil produced by the disintegration of this rock. **3** a fine-quality brick made originally from malm, marl, or a similar chalky clay. [OE *mealm-* (in compounds) f. Gmc]

malmsey /maámzi/ *n.* a strong sweet wine orig. from Greece, now chiefly from Madeira. [ME f. MDu., MLG *malmesie*, *-eye*, f. *Monemvasia* in S. Greece: cf. MALVOISIE]

malnourished /málnúrrisht/ *adj.* suffering from malnutrition.

malnourishment /málnúrrishmənt/ *n.* = MALNUTRITION.

malnutrition /málnyootrísh'n/ *n.* a dietary condition resulting from the absence of some foods or essential elements necessary for health; insufficient nutrition.

malodorous /malṓdərəss/ *adj.* evil-smelling.

■ see SMELLY.

Malpighian layer /malpíggiən/ *n.* a layer of proliferating cells in the epidermis. [M. *Malpighi*, It. physician d. 1694]

malpractice /malpráktiss/ *n.* **1** improper or negligent professional treatment, esp. by a medical practitioner. **2 a** criminal wrongdoing; misconduct. **b** an instance of this.

malt /mawlt, molt/ *n.* & *v.* ● *n.* **1** barley or other grain that is steeped, germinated, and dried, esp. for brewing or distilling and vinegar-making. **2** *colloq.* malt whisky; malt liquor. ● *v.* **1** *tr.* convert (grain) into malt. **2** *intr.* (of seeds) become malt when germination is checked by drought. ▫ **malted milk 1** a hot drink made from dried milk and a malt preparation. **2** the powdered mixture from which this is made. **malt-house** a building used for preparing and storing malt. **malt liquor** alcoholic liquor made from malt by fermentation, not distillation, e.g. beer, stout. **malt whisky** whisky made from malted barley. [OE *m(e)alt* f. Gmc, rel. to MELT]

Maltese /máwlteéz, mól-/ *n.* & *adj.* ● *n.* **1** (*pl.* same) **a** a native or national of Malta, an island in the W. Mediterranean. **b** a person of Maltese descent. **2** the language of Malta. ● *adj.* of or relating to Malta or its people or language. ▫ **Maltese cross** a cross with arms of equal length broadening from the centre, often indented at the ends. **Maltese dog** (or **terrier**) a small breed of spaniel or terrier.

maltha /málthə/ *n.* a cement made of pitch and wax or other ingredients. [L f. Gk]

Malthusian /malthyṓōziən/ *adj.* & *n.* ● *adj.* of or relating to T. R. Malthus, English clergyman and economist (d. 1834) or his theories, esp. that sexual restraint should be exercised as a means of preventing an increase of the population beyond its means of subsistence. ● *n.* a follower of Malthus. ▫▫ **Malthusianism** *n.*

malting /máwlting, mól-/ *n.* **1** the process or an instance of brewing or distilling with malt. **2** = *malt-house*.

maltose /máwltōz, mól-/ *n. Chem.* a sugar produced by the hydrolysis of starch under the action of the enzymes in malt, saliva, etc. [F (as MALT)]

maltreat /máltreét/ *v.tr.* ill-treat. ▫▫ **maltreater** *n.* **maltreatment** *n.* [F *maltraiter* (as MAL-, TREAT)]

■ see *ill-treat*. ▫▫ **maltreatment** see ABUSE *n.* 4.

maltster /máwltstər, mól-/ *n.* a person who makes malt.

malty /máwlti, mól-/ *adj.* (**maltier, maltiest**) of, containing, or resembling malt. ▫▫ **maltiness** *n.*

malvaceous /malváyshəss/ *adj. Bot.* of or relating to the genus *Malva* or the family Malvaceae, which includes mallow. [L *malvaceus* f. *malva* MALLOW]

malversation /málvərsáysh'n/ *n. formal* **1** corrupt behaviour in a position of trust. **2** (often foll. by *of*) corrupt administration (of public money etc.). [F f. *malverser* f. L *male* badly + *versari* behave]

malvoisie /málvwəzée/ *n.* = MALMSEY. [ME f. OF *malvesie* f. F form of *Monemvasia*: see MALMSEY]

mam /mam/ *n. colloq.* mother. [formed as MAMA]

mama /mámmə, məmaá/ *n. colloq.* (esp. as a child's term) = MAMMA.

mamba /mámbə/ *n.* any venomous African snake of the genus *Dendroaspis*, esp. the green mamba (*D. angusticeps*) or black mamba (*D. polylepis*). [Zulu *imamba*]

mambo /mámbō/ *n.* & *v.* ● *n.* (*pl.* **-os**) **1** a Latin American dance like the rumba. **2** the music for this. ● *v.intr.* (**-oes, -oed**) perform the mambo. [Amer. Sp. prob. f. Haitian]

mamelon /mámmələn/ *n.* a small rounded hillock. [F, = nipple f. *mamelle* breast f. L MAMILLA]

Mameluke /mámməlōōk/ *n. hist.* a member of the military class (orig. Caucasian slaves) that ruled Egypt 1254–1811. [F *mameluk*, ult. f. Arab. *mamlūk* slave f. *malaka* possess]

mamilla /məmíllə/ *n.* (*US* **mammilla**) (*pl.* **mamillae** /-lee/) **1** the nipple of a woman's breast. **2** a nipple-shaped organ etc. ▫▫ **mamillary** /mámmiləri/ *adj.* **mamillate** /mámmilayt/ *adj.* [L, dimin. of MAMMA²]

mamma¹ /mámmə/ *n.* (also **momma** /mómmə/) *colloq.* (esp. as a child's term) mother. [imit. of child's *ma, ma*]
■ see MOTHER *n.* 1.

mamma² /mámmə/ *n.* (*pl.* **mammae** /-mee/) **1** a milk-secreting organ of female mammals. **2** a corresponding non-secretory structure in male mammals. ▫▫ **mammiform** *adj.* [OE f. L]

mammal /mámm'l/ *n.* any vertebrate of the class Mammalia, usu. a warm-blooded quadruped with hair or fur, the females of which possess milk-secreting mammae for the nourishment of the young, and including human beings, dogs, rabbits, whales, etc. ▫▫ **mammalian** /-máyliən/ *adj.* & *n.* **mammalogy** /-málləji/ *n.* [mod.L *mammalia* neut. pl. of L *mammalis* (as MAMMA²)]

mammaliferous /mámməlíffərəss/ *adj. Geol.* containing mammalian remains.

mammary /mámməri/ *adj.* of the human female breasts or milk-secreting organs of other mammals. ▫ **mammary gland** the milk-producing gland of female mammals. [MAMMA² + -ARY¹]

mammee /mamée/ *n.* a tropical American tree, *Mammea americana*, with large red-rinded yellow-pulped fruit. [Sp. *mamei* f. Haitian]

mammilla *US* var. of MAMILLA.

mammography /mamógrəfi/ *n. Med.* an X-ray technique of diagnosing and locating abnormalities (esp. tumours) of the breasts. [MAMMA² + -GRAPHY]

Mammon /mámmən/ *n.* **1** wealth regarded as a god or as an evil influence. **2** the worldly rich. ▫▫ **Mammonish** *adj.* **Mammonism** *n.* **Mammonist** *n.* **Mammonite** *n.* [ME f. LL *Mam(m)ona* f. Gk *mamōnas* f. Aram. *māmōn* riches: see Matt. 6:24, Luke 16:9–13]

mammoth /mámməth/ *n.* & *adj.* ● *n.* any large extinct elephant of the genus *Mammuthus*, with a hairy coat and curved tusks. ● *adj.* huge. [Russ. *mamo(n)t*]
■ *adj.* see HUGE 1.

mammy /mámmi/ *n.* (*pl.* **-ies**) **1** a child's word for mother. **2** *US* a Black nursemaid or nanny in charge of White children. [formed as MAMMA¹]

Man. *abbr.* Manitoba.

man /man/ *n.* & *v.* ● *n.* (*pl.* **men** /men/) **1** an adult human male, esp. as distinct from a woman or boy. **2 a** a human being; a person (*no man is perfect*). **b** human beings in general; the human race (*man is mortal*). **3** a person showing characteristics associated with males (*she's more of a man than he is*). **4 a** a worker; an employee (*the manager spoke to the men*). **b** a manservant or valet. **c** *hist.* a vassal. **5 a** (usu. in *pl.*) soldiers, sailors, etc., esp. non-officers (*was in command of 200 men*). **b** an individual, usu. male, person (*fought to the last man*). **c** (usu. prec. by *the*, or *poss. pron.*) a person regarded as suitable or appropriate in some way; a person fulfilling requirements (*I'm your man*; *not the man for the job*). **6 a** a husband (*man and wife*). **b** *colloq.* a boyfriend or lover. **7 a** a human being of a specified historical period or character (*Renaissance man*). **b** a type of prehistoric man named after the place where the remains were found (*Peking man*; *Piltdown man*). **8** any one of a set of pieces used in playing chess, draughts, etc. **9** (as second element in *comb.*) a man of a specified nationality, profession, skill, etc. (*Dutchman*; *clergyman*; *horseman*; *gentleman*). **10 a** an expression of impatience etc. used in addressing a male (*nonsense, man!*). **b** *colloq.* a general mode of address among hippies etc. (*blew my mind, man!*). **11** (prec. by *a*) a person; one (*what can a man do?*). **12** a person pursued; an opponent etc. (*the police have so far not caught their man*). **13** (**the Man**) *US sl.* **a** the police. **b** *Black sl.* White people. **14** (in *comb.*) a ship of a specified type (*merchantman*; *Indiaman*). ● *v.tr.* (**manned, manning**) **1** supply (a ship, fort, factory, etc.) with a person or people for work or defence etc. **2** work or service or defend (a specified piece of equipment, a fortification, etc.) (*man the pumps*). **3** *Naut.* place men at (a part of a ship). **4** fill (a post or office). **5** (usu. *refl.*) fortify the spirits or courage of (*manned herself for the task*). ▫ **as one man** in unison; in agreement. **be a man** be courageous; not show fear. **be one's own man 1** be free to act; be independent. **2** be in full possession of one's faculties etc. **man about town** a fashionable man of leisure. **man and boy** from childhood. **man-at-arms** (*pl.* **men-at-arms**) *archaic* a soldier, esp. when heavily armed and mounted. **man Friday** see FRIDAY. **man-hour** (or **-day** etc.) an hour (or day etc.) regarded in terms of the amount of work that could be done by one person within this period. **man in the moon** the semblance of a face seen on the surface of a full moon. **man in** (*US* **on**) **the street** an ordinary average person, as distinct from an expert. **man-made** (esp. of a textile fibre) made by man, artificial, synthetic. **man of God 1** a clergyman. **2** a male saint. **man of honour** a man whose word can be trusted. **man of the house** the male head of a household. **man of letters** a scholar; an author. **man of the moment** a man of importance at a particular time. **man of straw 1** an insubstantial person; an imaginary person set up as an opponent. **2** a stuffed effigy. **3** a person undertaking a financial commitment without adequate means. **4** a sham argument set up to be defeated. **man-of-war** an armed ship, esp. of a specified country. **man of the world** see WORLD. **man-size** (or **-sized**) **1** of the size of a man; very large. **2** big enough for a man. **man to man** with candour; honestly. **men's** (or **men's room**) a usu. public lavatory for men. **my** (or **my good**) **man** a patronizing mode of address to a man. **separate** (or **sort out**) **the men from the boys** *colloq.* find those who are truly virile, competent, etc. **to a man** all without exception. ▫▫ **manless** *adj.* [OE *man(n)*, pl. *menn*, *mannian*, f. Gmc]
■ *n.* **1** gentleman, male, *colloq.* guy, fellow, chap, *sl.* geezer, *Brit. sl.* bloke, *sl. often derog.* gink. **2 a** person, human being, mortal. **b** people, human beings, mankind, mortals, *Homo sapiens*, humanity, humankind, the human race. **4 a** see WORKER. **b** valet, manservant, servant, *joc.* retainer; houseboy, houseman. **c** see SLAVE *n.* 1. **5 b** see INDIVIDUAL *n.* 2, 3. **6 a** see HUSBAND *n.* **b** see LOVE *n.* 4a, 5. **11** see ONE *pron.* 1, 2. **12** see QUARRY². **13 a** (**the Man**) see POLICE *n.* ● *v.* **1** staff; crew. **5** see FORTIFY 2. ▫ **as one man** in unison, as one, together, in agreement, harmonious, in harmony. **man about town** see SWELL *n.* 4, TRENDY *n.* **man-at-arms** see SOLDIER *n.* **man in** (*US* **on**) **the street** layman, laywoman. **man of God 1** see CLERGYMAN. **man of the house** patriarch, paterfamilias, father. **man of letters** see SCHOLAR 1, AUTHOR *n.* 1. **man of straw 1** lightweight, *colloq.* pushover; see also WET *n.* 3. **man-size** (or **-sized**) **1** see

LARGE *adj.* 1, 2. **man to man** see HONESTLY 1. **men's** (or **men's room**) see LAVATORY.

mana /maánə/ *n.* **1** power; authority; prestige. **2** supernatural or magical power. [Maori]

manacle /mánnək'l/ *n.* & *v.* • *n.* (usu. in *pl.*) **1** a fetter or shackle for the hand; a handcuff. **2** a restraint. • *v.tr.* fetter with manacles. [ME f. OF *manicle* handcuff f. L *manicula* dimin. of *manus* hand]

▪ *n.* **1** (*manacles*) shackles, fetters, handcuffs, chains, irons, *colloq.* cuffs, *sl.* bracelets, *Brit. sl.* darbies; see also RESTRAINT 6. **2** see RESTRAINT 2. • *v.* shackle, fetter, handcuff, restrain, put *or* throw *or* clap in irons, chain (up).

manage /mánnij/ *v.* & *n.* • *v.* **1** *tr.* organize; regulate; be in charge of (a business, household, team, a person's career, etc.). **2** *tr.* (often foll. by *to* + infin.) succeed in achieving; contrive (*managed to arrive on time*; *managed a smile*; *managed to ruin the day*). **3** *intr.* **a** (often foll. by *with*) succeed in one's aim, esp. against heavy odds (*managed with one assistant*). **b** meet one's needs with limited resources etc. (*just about manages on a pension*). **4** *tr.* gain influence with or maintain control over (a person etc.) (*cannot manage their teenage son*). **5** *tr.* (also *absol.*; often prec. by *can*, *be able to*) **a** cope with; make use of (*couldn't manage another bite*; *can you manage by yourself?*). **b** be free to attend on (a certain day) or at (a certain time) (*can you manage Thursday?*). **6** *tr.* handle or wield (a tool, weapon, etc.). **7** *tr.* take or have charge or control of (an animal or animals, esp. cattle). • *n. archaic* **1 a** the training of a horse. **b** the trained movements of a horse. **2** a riding-school (cf. MANÈGE). [It. *maneggiare*, *maneggio* ult. f. L *manus* hand]

▪ *v.* **1** handle, administer, run, supervise, look after, watch over, direct, head, oversee, superintend, preside over, be in charge (of), take care of, control, organize; rule (over), govern, regulate. **2, 3, 5a** succeed, contrive; function, make do, make it, shift (for oneself), get along *or* by *or* on, make out, muddle through, survive, cope. **4** handle, cope *or* deal with, control, govern, manipulate. **6** see WIELD 1.

manageable /mánnijəb'l/ *adj.* able to be easily managed, controlled, or accomplished etc. ▫▫ **manageability** /-bílliti/ *n.* **manageableness** *n.* **manageably** *adv.*

▪ controllable; tractable, compliant, amenable, docile, tameable, tame, trainable, teachable, manipulable, submissive.

management /mánnijmənt/ *n.* **1** the process or an instance of managing or being managed. **2 a** the professional administration of business concerns, public undertakings, etc. **b** the people engaged in this. **c** (prec. by *the*) a governing body; a board of directors or the people in charge of running a business, regarded collectively. **3** (usu. foll. by *of*) *Med.* the technique of treating a disease etc. **4** trickery; deceit.

▪ **1** managing, control, supervision, manipulation, handling, direction, directing, directorship, administration, government, conduct, governance, operation, running, superintendence, command, guidance, stewardship. **2 b, c** administration, executive(s), bosses, directors, board (of directors), directorate, *colloq.* (top) brass. **4** see TRICKERY.

manager /mánnijər/ *n.* **1** a person controlling or administering a business or part of a business. **2** a person controlling the affairs, training, etc. of a person or team in sports, entertainment, etc. **3** *Brit. Parl.* a member of either House of Parliament appointed with others for some duty in which both Houses are concerned. **4** a person regarded in terms of skill in household or financial or other management (*a good manager*). ▫▫ **managerial** /mánnijeériəl/ *adj.* **managerially** /-jeériəli/ *adv.* **managership** *n.*

▪ **1** supervisor, superintendent, director, executive, head, proprietor, overseer, foreman, forewoman, administrator, chief, manageress, *US* straw boss, *colloq.* boss. **2** impresario, administrator; see also DIRECTOR 2.

manageress /mánnijərés/ *n.* a woman manager, esp. of a shop, hotel, theatre, etc.

managing /mánnijing/ *adj.* **1** (in *comb.*) having executive control or authority (*managing director*). **2** (*attrib.*) fond of controlling affairs etc. **3** *archaic* economical.

manakin /mánnəkin/ *n.* any small bird of the family Pipridae of Central and S. America, the males of which are often brightly coloured. [var. of MANIKIN]

mañana /manyaánə/ *adv.* & *n.* • *adv.* in the indefinite future (esp. to indicate procrastination). • *n.* an indefinite future time. [Sp., = tomorrow]

manatee /mánnəteé/ *n.* any large aquatic plant-eating mammal of the genus *Trichechus*, with paddle-like forelimbs, no hind limbs, and a powerful tail. [Sp. *manati* f. Carib *manattouï*]

manchineel /mánchineél/ *n.* a W. Indian tree, *Hippomane mancinella*, with a poisonous and caustic milky sap and acrid apple-like fruit. [F *mancenille* f. Sp. *manzanilla* dimin. of *manzana* apple]

Manchu /manchoō/ *n.* & *adj.* • *n.* **1** a member of a people in China, descended from a Tartar people, who formed the last imperial dynasty (1644-1912). **2** the language of the Manchus, now spoken in part of NE China. • *adj.* of or relating to the Manchu people or their language. [Manchu, =pure]

manciple /mánsip'l/ *n.* an officer who buys provisions for a college, an Inn of Court, etc. [ME f. AF & OF f. L *mancipium* purchase f. *manceps* buyer f. *manus* hand + *capere* take]

Mancunian /mangkyoōniən/ *n.* & *adj.* • *n.* a native of Manchester in NW England. • *adj.* of or relating to Manchester. [L *Mancunium* Manchester]

-mancy /mansi/ *comb. form* forming nouns meaning 'divination by' (*geomancy*; *necromancy*). ▫▫ **-mantic** *comb. form* forming adjectives. [OF *-mancie* f. LL *-mantia* f. Gk *manteia* divination]

Mandaean /mandeéən/ *n.* & *adj.* • *n.* **1** a member of a Gnostic sect surviving in Iraq and claiming descent from John the Baptist. **2** the language of this sect. • *adj.* of or concerning the Mandaeans or their language. [Aram. *mandaïia* Gnostics f. *manda* knowledge]

mandala /mándələ/ *n.* **1** a symbolic circular figure representing the universe in various religions. **2** *Psychol.* such a symbol in a dream, representing the dreamer's search for completeness and self-unity. [Skr. *máṇḍala* disc]

mandamus /mandáyməss/ *n. Law* a judicial writ issued as a command to an inferior court, or ordering a person to perform a public or statutory duty. [L, = we command]

mandarin[1] /mándərin/ *n.* **1** (**Mandarin**) the most widely spoken form of Chinese and the official language of China. **2** *hist.* a Chinese official in any of nine grades of the pre-Communist civil service. **3 a** a party leader; a bureaucrat. **b** a powerful member of the establishment. **4 a** a nodding Chinese figure, usu. of porcelain. **b** porcelain etc. decorated with Chinese figures in mandarin dress. ▫ **mandarin collar** a small close-fitting upright collar. **mandarin duck** a small Chinese duck, *Aix galericulata*, noted for its bright plumage. **mandarin sleeve** a wide loose sleeve. ▫▫ **mandarinate** *n.* [Port. *mandarim* f. Malay f. Hindi *mantrī* f. Skr. *mantrin* counsellor]

▪ **3** see MOGUL.

mandarin[2] /mándərin/ *n.* (also **mandarine** /-reen/) (in full **mandarin orange**) **1** a small flattish deep-coloured orange with a loose skin. **2** the tree, *Citrus reticulata*, yielding this. Also called TANGERINE. [F *mandarine* (perh. as MANDARIN[1], with ref. to the official's yellow robes)]

mandatary /mándətəri, -tri/ *n.* (*pl.* **-ies**) esp. *hist.* a person or State receiving a mandate. [LL *mandatarius* (as MANDATE)]

mandate /mándayt/ *n.* & *v.* • *n.* **1** an official command or instruction by an authority. **2** support for a policy or course of action, regarded by a victorious party, candidate, etc., as derived from the wishes of the people in an election. **3** a commission to act for another. **4** *Law* a commission by which a party is entrusted to perform a service, often gratuitously and with indemnity against loss by that party.

5 *hist.* a commission from the League of Nations to a member State to administer a territory. **6** a papal decree or decision. ● *v.tr.* **1** instruct (a delegate) to act or vote in a certain way. **2** (usu. foll. by *to*) *hist.* commit (a territory etc.) to a mandatary. ▫▫ **mandator** *n.* [L *mandatum*, neut. past part. of *mandare* command f. *manus* hand + *dare* give: sense 2 of n. after F *mandat*]

■ *n.* **1** see COMMAND *n.* 1. **2** see APPROVAL. **6** see DECREE *n.* 1. ● *v.* **1** see DECREE *v.* **2** see REQUISITION *v.*

mandatory /mándətəri, -tri/ *adj.* & *n.* ● *adj.* **1** of or conveying a command. **2** compulsory. ● *n.* (*pl.* **-ies**) = MANDATARY. ▫▫ **mandatorily** *adv.* [LL *mandatorius* f. L (as MANDATE)]

■ *adj.* **2** compulsory, obligatory, requisite, required, essential, demanded, necessary, needed.

mandible /mándib'l/ *n.* **1** the jaw, esp. the lower jaw in mammals and fishes. **2** the upper or lower part of a bird's beak. **3** either half of the crushing organ in an arthropod's mouth-parts. ▫▫ **mandibular** /-díbyoolər/ *adj.* **mandibulate** /-díbyoolət/ *adj.* [ME f. OF *mandible* or LL *mandibula* f. *mandere* chew]

mandolin /mándəlín/ *n.* (also **mandoline**) a musical instrument resembling a lute, having paired metal strings plucked with a plectrum. ▫▫ **mandolinist** *n.* [F *mandoline* f. It. *mandolino* dimin. of MANDOLA]

mandorla /mandórlə/ *n.* = VESICA 2. [It., = almond]

mandragora /mandrággərə/ *n. hist.* the mandrake, esp. as a type of narcotic (Shakesp. *Othello* III. iii. 334). [OE f. med.L f. L f. Gk *mandragoras*]

mandrake /mándrayk/ *n.* a poisonous plant, *Mandragora officinarum*, with white or purple flowers and large yellow fruit, having emetic and narcotic properties and possessing a root once thought to resemble the human form and to shriek when plucked. [ME *mandrag(g)e*, prob. f. MDu. *mandrag(r)e* f. med.L (as MANDRAGORA): assoc. with MAN + *drake* dragon (cf. DRAKE[1])]

mandrel /mándrəl/ *n.* **1 a** a shaft in a lathe to which work is fixed while being turned. **b** a cylindrical rod round which metal or other material is forged or shaped. **2** *Brit.* a miner's pick. [16th c.: orig. unkn.]

mandrill /mándril/ *n.* a large W. African baboon, *Papio sphinx*, the adult of which has a brilliantly coloured face and blue-coloured buttocks. [prob. f. MAN + DRILL[3]]

manducate /mándyookayt/ *v.tr. literary* chew; eat. ▫▫ **manducation** /-káysh'n/ *n.* **manducatory** /-kətəri, -kaytəri/ *adj.* [L *manducare manducat-* chew f. *manduco* guzzler f. *mandere* chew]

mane /mayn/ *n.* **1** long hair growing in a line on the neck of a horse, lion, etc. **2** *colloq.* a person's long hair. ▫▫ **maned** *adj.* (also in *comb.*). **maneless** *adj.* [OE *manu* f. Gmc]

manège /manáyzh/ *n.* (also **manege**) **1** a riding-school. **2** the movements of a trained horse. **3** horsemanship. [F *manège* f. It. (as MANAGE)]

manes /maánayz, máyneez/ *n.pl.* **1** the deified souls of dead ancestors. **2** (as *sing.*) the revered ghost of a dead person. [ME f. L]

maneuver *US* var. of MANOEUVRE.

manful /mánfōōl/ *adj.* brave; resolute. ▫▫ **manfully** *adv.* **manfulness** *n.*

■ see INTREPID. ▫▫ **manfulness** see SPIRIT *n.* 5c.

mangabey /mánggəbay/ *n.* any small long-tailed W. African monkey of the genus *Cercocebus*. [*Mangabey*, a region of Madagascar]

manganese /mánggəneez/ *n.* **1** *Chem.* a grey brittle metallic transition element used with steel to make alloys. ¶ Symb.: **Mn**. **2** (in full **manganese oxide**) the black mineral oxide of this used in the manufacture of glass. ▫▫ **manganic** /-gánnik/ *adj.* **manganous** /mánggənəss/ *adj.* [F *manganèse* f. It. *manganese*, alt. f. MAGNESIA]

mange /maynj/ *n.* a skin disease in hairy and woolly animals, caused by an arachnid parasite and occasionally communicated to man. [ME *mangie*, *maniewe* f. OF *manjue*, *mangeue* itch f. *mangier manju-* eat f. L *manducare* chew]

mangel /mángg'l/ *n.* (also **mangold** /mángg'ld/) (in full **mangel-wurzel, mangold-wurzel** /-wurz'l/) a large kind of beet, *Beta vulgaris*, used as cattle food. [G *Mangoldwurzel* f. *Mangold* beet + *Wurzel* root]

manger /máynjər/ *n.* a long open box or trough in a stable etc., for horses or cattle to eat from. [ME f. OF *mangeoire*, *mangeure* ult. f. L (as MANDUCATE)]

mange-tout /mónzhtōō/ *n.* the sugar-pea. [F, = eat-all]

mangle[1] /mángg'l/ *n.* & *v.* esp. *Brit. hist.* ● *n.* a machine having two or more cylinders usu. turned by a handle, between which wet clothes etc. are squeezed and pressed. ● *v.tr.* press (clothes etc.) in a mangle. [Du. *mangel(stok)* f. *mangelen* to mangle, ult. f. Gk *magganon* + *stok* staff, STOCK]

mangle[2] /mángg'l/ *v.tr.* **1** hack, cut about, or mutilate by blows etc. **2** spoil (a quotation, text, etc.) by misquoting, mispronouncing, etc. **3** cut roughly so as to disfigure. ▫▫ **mangler** *n.* [AF *ma(ha)ngler*, app. frequent. of *mahaignier* MAIM]

■ **1** hack, cut, lacerate, chop (up), crush, damage, cripple, maim, destroy, mutilate, butcher, deform, disfigure, spoil, mar, ruin, wreck. **2** butcher, mutilate, spoil, mar, ruin, wreck. **3** hack, cut, lacerate, chop (up), disfigure, spoil, mar, ruin, wreck.

mango /mánggō/ *n.* (*pl.* **-oes** or **-os**) **1** a fleshy yellowish-red fruit, eaten ripe or used green for pickles etc. **2** the Indian evergreen tree, *Mangifera indica*, bearing this. [Port. *manga* f. Malay *mangā* f. Tamil *mānkāy* f. *mān* mango-tree + *kāy* fruit]

mangold (also **mangold-wurzel**) var. of MANGEL.

mangonel /mánggən'l/ *n. Mil. hist.* a military engine for throwing stones etc. [ME f. OF *mangonel(le)*, f. med.L *manganellus* dimin. of LL *manganum* f. Gk *magganon*]

mangosteen /mánggəsteen/ *n.* **1** a white juicy-pulped fruit with a thick reddish-brown rind. **2** the E. Indian tree, *Garcinia mangostana*, bearing this. [Malay *manggustan*]

mangrove /mánggrōv/ *n.* any tropical tree or shrub of the genus *Rhizophora*, growing in shore-mud with many tangled roots above ground. [17th c.: orig. uncert.: assim. to GROVE]

mangy /máynji/ *adj.* (**mangier, mangiest**) **1** (esp. of a domestic animal) having mange. **2** squalid; shabby. ▫▫ **mangily** *adv.* **manginess** *n.*

■ **1** scabious, scabby. **2** scruffy, dirty, sleazy, sorry, squalid, slovenly, unkempt, slummy, dingy, seedy, poor, shabby, mean, low, bedraggled, raggedy, ragged, moth-eaten, the worse for wear, *Austral. sl.* warby.

manhandle /mánhánd'l/ *v.tr.* **1** move (heavy objects) by human effort. **2** *colloq.* handle (a person) roughly.

■ **2** hustle, jostle, tousle, molest, shove, maul, *esp. Brit.* frogmarch, *colloq.* paw, *sl.* bounce, *US sl.* roust.

manhattan /manhátt'n/ *n.* a cocktail made of vermouth, whisky, etc. [*Manhattan*, borough of New York City]

manhole /mánhōl/ *n.* a covered opening in a floor, pavement, sewer, etc. for workmen to gain access.

manhood /mánhōōd/ *n.* **1** the state of being a man rather than a child or woman. **2 a** manliness; courage. **b** a man's sexual potency. **3** the men of a country etc. **4** the state of being human.

■ **2 a** masculinity, manliness, manfulness, virility, machismo, courage, bravery, pluck, boldness, determination, resolution, fortitude, spirit, *colloq.* guts, grit. **4** see HUMANITY 1c.

manhunt /mánhunt/ *n.* an organized search for a person, esp. a criminal.

mania /máyniə/ *n.* **1** *Psychol.* mental illness marked by periods of great excitement and violence. **2** (often foll. by *for*) excessive enthusiasm; an obsession (*has a mania for jogging*). [ME f. LL f. Gk, = madness f. *mainomai* be mad, rel. to MIND]

■ **1** madness, lunacy, insanity, dementia, dementedness, derangement, hysteria, mental illness *or* disorder, *colloq.* craziness. **2** rage, craze, passion, fad; obsession, compulsion, urge, fascination, preoccupation, yearning, craving, desire, *cacoethes*, *colloq.* yen.

-mania /máyniə/ *comb. form* **1** *Psychol.* denoting a special type of mental abnormality or obsession (*megalomania*; *nymphomania*). **2** denoting extreme enthusiasm or admiration (*bibliomania*; *Anglomania*).

maniac /máyniak/ *n.* & *adj.* ● *n.* **1** *colloq.* a person exhibiting extreme symptoms of wild behaviour etc.; a madman. **2** *colloq.* an obsessive enthusiast. **3** *Psychol. archaic* a person suffering from mania. ● *adj.* of or behaving like a maniac. ▫▫ **maniacal** /mənīək'l/ *adj.* **maniacally** /mənīəkəli/ *adv.* [LL *maniacus* f. late Gk *maniakos* (as MANIA)]

■ *n.* **1** madman, madwoman, lunatic, psychopath, psychotic, *sl.* crackpot, nut, nutcase, loony, *Brit. sl.* nutter, *US sl.* kook. **2** fanatic, fan, enthusiast, zealot, nympholept, *colloq.* freak, *sl.* fiend, nut. ● *adj.* see *maniacal* below. ▫▫ **maniacal** manic, maniac, insane, lunatic, mad, demented, deranged, mentally ill, *non compos* (*mentis*), psychotic; hysterical, berserk, wild, *colloq.* crazy, *sl.* loony.

-maniac /máyniak/ *comb. form* forming adjectives and nouns meaning 'affected with -mania' or 'a person affected with -mania' (*nymphomaniac*).

manic /mánnik/ *adj.* of or affected by mania. ▫ **manic-depressive** *Psychol. adj.* affected by or relating to a mental disorder with alternating periods of elation and depression. ● *n.* a person having such a disorder. ▫▫ **manically** *adv.*

■ see MAD *adj.* 1.

Manichee /mánniki/ *n.* **1** an adherent of a religious system of the 3rd–5th c., representing Satan in a state of everlasting conflict with God. **2** *Philos.* a dualist (see DUALISM). ▫▫ **Manichean** /-kéeən/ *adj.* & *n.* (also **Manichaean**). **Manicheism** /-kée-iz'm/ *n.* (also **Manichaeism**). [LL *Manichaeus* f. late Gk *Manikhaios*, f. *Manes* or *Manichaeus* Persian founder of the sect]

manicure /mánnikyoor/ *n.* & *v.* ● *n.* **1** a usu. professional cosmetic treatment of the hands and fingernails. **2** = MANICURIST. ● *v.tr.* apply a manicure to (the hands or a person). [F f. L *manus* hand + *cura* care]

manicurist /mánnikyoorist/ *n.* a person who manicures hands and fingernails professionally.

manifest[1] /mánnifest/ *adj.* & *v.* ● *adj.* clear or obvious to the eye or mind (*his distress was manifest*). ● *v.* **1** *tr.* display or show (a quality, feeling, etc.) by one's acts etc. **2** *tr.* show plainly to the eye or mind. **3** *tr.* be evidence of; prove. **4** *refl.* (of a thing) reveal itself. **5** *intr.* (of a ghost) appear. ▫▫ **manifestation** /-stáysh'n/ *n.* **manifestative** /-féstətiv/ *adj.* **manifestly** *adv.* [ME f. OF *manifeste* (adj.), *manifester* (v.) or L *manifestus*, *manifestare* f. *manus* hand + *festus* (unrecorded) struck]

■ *adj.* apparent, clear, evident, obvious, plain, patent, blatant, conspicuous, unmistakable, discernible, recognizable, comprehensible, distinct, palpable, definite, explicit, unambiguous, unquestionable, indubitable, indisputable. ● *v.* **1, 2** show, demonstrate, exhibit, evince, reveal, disclose, display, betray; express, declare. **3** corroborate, substantiate, attest; see also PROVE 1. **4** reveal *or* show *or* exhibit itself. **5** materialize. ▫▫ **manifestation** display, exhibition, demonstration, show, disclosure, appearance, exposure, presentation, sign, indication, mark, expression, example, instance; declaration, avowal, publication, announcement; materialization. **manifestly** evidently, clearly, obviously, plainly, apparently, patently, unmistakably, palpably, unquestionably, indubitably, undoubtedly, indisputably.

manifest[2] /mánnifest/ *n.* & *v.* ● *n.* **1** a cargo-list for the use of customs officers. **2** a list of passengers in an aircraft or of trucks etc. in a goods train. ● *v.tr.* record (names, cargo, etc.) in a manifest. [It. *manifesto*: see MANIFESTO]

manifesto /mánnifésto/ *n.* (*pl.* **-os**) a public declaration of policy and aims esp. issued before an election by a political party, candidate, government, etc. [It. f. *manifestare* f. L (as MANIFEST[1])]

■ declaration, platform, programme.

manifold /mánnifōld/ *adj.* & *n.* ● *adj. literary* **1** many and various (*manifold vexations*). **2** having various forms, parts, applications, etc. **3** performing several functions at once. ● *n.* **1** a thing with many different forms, parts, applications, etc. **2** *Mech.* a pipe or chamber branching into several openings. ▫▫ **manifoldly** *adv.* **manifoldness** *n.* [OE *manigfeald* (as MANY, -FOLD)]

■ *adj.* **1, 2** diverse, diversified, multifarious, varied, various, assorted, multiplex, miscellaneous, sundry, many-sided, *archaic or literary* divers. ● *n.* **1** composite, amalgam; see also BLEND *n.*

manikin /mánnikin/ *n.* (also **mannikin**) **1** a little man; a dwarf. **2** an artist's lay figure. **3** an anatomical model of the body. **4** (usu. **mannikin**) any small finchlike bird of the genus *Lonchura*, native to Africa and Australasia. [Du. *manneken*, dimin. of *man* MAN]

■ dwarf, midget, homunculus.

Manila /mənillə/ *n.* (also **Manilla**) **1** a cigar or cheroot made in Manila. **2** (in full **Manila hemp**) the strong fibre of a Philippine tree, *Musa textilis*, used for rope etc. **3** (also **manila**) a strong brown paper made from Manila hemp or other material and used for wrapping paper, envelopes, etc. [*Manila* in the Philippines]

manilla /mənillə/ *n.* a metal bracelet used by African tribes as a medium of exchange. [Sp., prob. dimin. of *mano* hand f. L *manus*]

manille /mənil/ *n.* the second best trump or honour in ombre or quadrille. [F f. Sp. *malilla* dimin. of *mala* bad f. L *malus*]

manioc /mánniok/ *n.* **1** cassava. **2** the flour made from it. [Tupi *mandioca*]

maniple /mánnip'l/ *n.* **1** *Rom.Hist.* a subdivision of a legion, containing 120 or 60 men. **2** a Eucharistic vestment consisting of a strip hanging from the left arm. [OF *maniple* or L *manipulus* handful, troop f. *manus* hand]

manipulate /mənipyoolayt/ *v.tr.* **1** handle, treat, or use, esp. skilfully (a tool, question, material, etc.). **2** manage (a person, situation, etc.) to one's own advantage, esp. unfairly or unscrupulously. **3** manually examine and treat (a part of the body). **4** *Computing* alter, edit, or move (text, data, etc.). **5** stimulate (the genitals). ▫▫ **manipulable** /-ləb'l/ *adj.* **manipulability** /-ləbilliti/ *n.* **manipulatable** *adj.* **manipulation** /-láysh'n/ *n.* **manipulator** *n.* **manipulatory** /-lətəri/ *adj.* [back-form. f. *manipulation* f. F *manipulation* f. mod.L *manipulatio* (as MANIPLE), after F *manipuler*]

■ **1** handle, control, operate, direct, work, use, treat, employ. **2** manage, handle, control, manoeuvre, orchestrate, choreograph, influence, use, exploit, play on, utilize; massage, rig, falsify, juggle, tamper with, doctor, *colloq.* cook, *sl.* fiddle. **5** see HANDLE *v.* 1.

manipulative /mənipyoolətiv/ *adj.* **1** characterized by unscrupulous exploitation of a situation, person, etc., for one's own ends. **2** of or concerning manipulation. ▫▫ **manipulatively** *adv.* **manipulativeness** *n.*

■ **1** see CALCULATING.

Manit. *abbr.* Manitoba.

manitou /mánnitoo/ *n.* *Amer. Ind.* **1** a good or evil spirit as an object of reverence. **2** something regarded as having supernatural power. [Algonquian *manito*, *-tu* he has surpassed]

mankind *n.* **1** /mankīnd/ the human species. **2** /mánkīnd/ male people, as distinct from female.

■ **1** see HUMANITY 1a, b.

manky /mángki/ *adj.* (**mankier**, **mankiest**) *colloq.* **1** bad, inferior, defective. **2** dirty. [obs. *mank* mutilated, defective]

■ **1** see INFERIOR *adj.* 2. **2** see DIRTY *adj.* 1.

manlike /mánlīk/ *adj.* **1** having the qualities of a man. **2** (of a woman) mannish. **3** (of an animal, shape, etc.) resembling a human being.

■ **1** see MANLY 1.

manly /mánli/ *adj.* (**manlier**, **manliest**) **1** having qualities regarded as admirable in a man, such as courage, frankness, etc. **2** (of a woman) mannish. **3** (of things, qualities, etc.) befitting a man. ▫▫ **manliness** *n.*

▪ **1** manful, virile, courageous, bold, brave, intrepid, valorous, valiant, dauntless, fearless, plucky, daring, venturesome, stout-hearted, resolute, stable, steadfast, unflinching, unwavering, unshrinking, chivalrous, gallant, noble, heroic; masculine, male, macho, red-blooded. **2** masculine, *usu. derog.* mannish, *sl.* butch.

manna /mánnə/ *n.* **1** the substance miraculously supplied as food to the Israelites in the wilderness (Exod. 16). **2** an unexpected benefit (esp. *manna from heaven*). **3** spiritual nourishment, esp. the Eucharist. **4** the sweet dried juice from the manna-ash and other plants, used as a mild laxative. ▫ **manna-ash** an ash tree native to S. Europe, *Fraxinus ornus.* [OE f. LL f. Gk f. Aram. *mannā* f. Heb. *mān*, explained as = *mān hū?* what is it?, but prob. = Arab. *mann* exudation of common tamarisk (*Tamarix gallica*)]

manned /mand/ *adj.* (of an aircraft, spacecraft, etc.) having a human crew. [past part. of MAN]

mannequin /mánnikin/ *n.* **1** a model employed by a dressmaker etc. to show clothes to customers. **2** a window dummy. [F, = MANIKIN]

▪ **2** dummy, model, figure.

manner /mánnər/ *n.* **1** a way a thing is done or happens (*always dresses in that manner*). **2** (in *pl.*) **a** social behaviour (*it is bad manners to stare*). **b** polite or well-bred behaviour (*he has no manners*). **c** modes of life; conditions of society. **3** a person's outward bearing, way of speaking, etc. (*has an imperious manner*). **4 a** a style in literature, art, etc. (*in the manner of Rembrandt*). **b** = MANNERISM 2a. **5** *archaic* a kind or sort (*what manner of man is he?*). ▫ **all manner of** many different kinds of. **comedy of manners** satirical portrayal of social behaviour, esp. of the upper classes. **in a manner of speaking** in some sense; to some extent; so to speak. **manner of means** see MEANS. **to the manner born 1** *colloq.* naturally at ease in a specified job, situation, etc. **2** destined by birth to follow a custom or way of life (Shakesp. *Hamlet* I. iv. 17). ▫▫ **mannerless** *adj.* (in sense 2b of *n.*). [ME f. AF *manere*, OF *maniere* ult. f. L *manuarius* of the hand (*manus*)]

▪ **1** way, mode, style, technique, procedure, method, fashion; means, approach. **2** (*manners*) etiquette, decorum, (good) form, politeness, protocol, *politesse*, *colloq.* the done thing; civility, ceremony, social code, social graces, formalities, niceties, proprieties, *convenances*. **3** air, behaviour, demeanour, bearing, deportment, conduct, attitude, aspect, *literary* comportment, mien. **5** see KIND[1] 2. ▫ **all manner of** all kinds of. **in a manner of speaking** so to speak, figuratively *or* metaphorically speaking; see also *partially* (PARTIAL).

mannered /mánnərd/ *adj.* **1** (in *comb.*) behaving in a specified way (*ill-mannered; well-mannered*). **2** (of a style, artist, writer, etc.) showing idiosyncratic mannerisms. **3** (of a person) eccentrically affected in behaviour.

▪ **1** (*comb.*) -behaved. **2, 3** artificial, contrived, stilted, stiff, affected, insincere, pompous, pretentious, posed, unnatural, pseudo, *colloq.* phoney.

mannerism /mánnəriz'm/ *n.* **1** a habitual gesture or way of speaking etc.; an idiosyncrasy. **2 a** excessive addiction to a distinctive style in art or literature. **b** a stylistic trick. **3** a style of Italian art preceding the Baroque, characterized by lengthened figures. ▫▫ **mannerist** *n.* **manneristic** /-rístik/ *adj.* **manneristical** /-rístik'l/ *adj.* **manneristically** /-rístikəli/ *adv.* [MANNER]

▪ **1** quirk, peculiarity, idiosyncrasy, trait, characteristic, habit.

mannerly /mánnərli/ *adj.* & *adv.* ● *adj.* well-mannered; polite. ● *adv.* politely. ▫▫ **mannerliness** *n.*

▪ *adj.* see POLITE 1. ▫▫ **mannerliness** see PROPRIETY 2.

mannikin var. of MANIKIN.

mannish /mánnish/ *adj.* **1** usu. *derog.* (of a woman) masculine in appearance or manner. **2** characteristic of a man. ▫▫ **mannishly** *adv.* **mannishness** *n.* [OE *mennisc* f. (and assim. to) MAN]

manoeuvre /mənōōvər/ *n.* & *v.* (*US* **maneuver**) ● *n.* **1** a planned and controlled movement or series of moves. **2** (in *pl.*) a large-scale exercise of troops, warships, etc. **3 a** an often deceptive planned or controlled action designed to gain an objective. **b** a skilful plan. ● *v.* **1** *intr.* & *tr.* perform or cause to perform a manoeuvre (*manoeuvred the car into the space*). **2** *intr.* & *tr.* perform or cause (troops etc.) to perform military manoeuvres. **3 a** *tr.* (usu. foll. by *into, out, away*) force, drive, or manipulate (a person, thing, etc.) by scheming or adroitness. **b** *intr.* use artifice. ▫▫ **manoeuvrable** *adj.* **manoeuvrability** /-vrəbilliti/ *n.* **manoeuvrer** *n.* [F *manœuvre*, *manœuvrer* f. med.L *manuoperare* f. L *manus* hand + *operari* to work]

▪ *n.* **1, 3** move, stratagem, tactic, trick, gambit, subterfuge, ruse, dodge, artifice, device, wile, *démarche*, strategy, plan, plot, scheme, intrigue, machination, *colloq.* ploy. **2** (*manoeuvres*) exercise(s), war-game(s). ● *v.* **1** manipulate, run, drive, guide, navigate, steer. **3** manipulate, contrive, plot, scheme, machinate, intrigue, trick, devise, engineer, finesse, manage, *colloq.* finagle, wangle.

manometer /mənómmitər/ *n.* a pressure gauge for gases and liquids. ▫▫ **manometric** /mánnəmétrik/ *adj.* [F *manomètre* f. Gk *manos* thin]

ma non troppo see TROPPO[1].

manor /mánnər/ *n.* **1** (also **manor-house**) **a** a large country house with lands. **b** the house of the lord of the manor. **2** *Brit.* **a** a unit of land consisting of a lord's demesne and lands rented to tenants etc. **b** *hist.* a feudal lordship over lands. **3** *Brit. colloq.* the district covered by a police station. ▫▫ **manorial** /mənóriəl/ *adj.* [ME f. AF *maner*, OF *maneir*, f. L *manēre* remain]

▪ **1a, 2a** see ESTATE 1. **1 b** see PALACE 2.

manpower /mánpowr/ *n.* **1** the power generated by a man working. **2** the number of people available for work, service, etc.

manqué /móngkay/ *adj.* (placed after noun) that might have been but is not; unfulfilled (*a comic actor manqué*). [F, past part. of *manquer* lack]

mansard /mánsaard/ *n.* a roof which has four sloping sides, each of which becomes steeper halfway down. [F *mansarde* f. F. *Mansart*, Fr. architect d. 1666]

manse /manss/ *n.* the house of a minister, esp. a Scottish Presbyterian. ▫ **son** (or **daughter**) **of the manse** the child of a Presbyterian etc. minister. [ME f. med.L *mansus, -sa, -sum*, house f. *manēre mans-* remain]

manservant /mánserv'nt/ *n.* (*pl.* **menservants**) a male servant.

▪ see SERVANT.

-manship /mənship/ *suffix* forming nouns denoting skill in a subject or activity (*craftsmanship; gamesmanship*).

mansion /mánsh'n/ *n.* **1** a large house. **2** (usu. in *pl.*) *Brit.* a large building divided into flats. ▫ **mansion-house** *Brit.* the house of a lord mayor or a landed proprietor. **the Mansion House** the official residence of the Lord Mayor of London. [ME f. OF f. L *mansio -onis* a staying (as MANSE)]

▪ **1** see PALACE.

manslaughter /mánslawtər/ *n.* **1** the killing of a human being. **2** *Law* the unlawful killing of a human being without malice aforethought.

▪ see KILLING *n.* 1.

mansuetude /mánswityōōd/ *n. archaic* meekness, docility, gentleness. [ME f. OF *mansuetude* or L *mansuetudo* f. *mansuetus* gentle, tame f. *manus* hand + *suetus* accustomed]

manta /mántə/ *n.* any large ray of the family Mobulidae, esp. *Manta birostris*, having winglike pectoral fins and a whiplike tail. [Amer. Sp., = large blanket]

mantel /mánt'l/ *n.* **1** = MANTELPIECE 1. **2** = MANTELSHELF. [var. of MANTLE]

mantelet /mántəlit/ *n.* (also **mantlet** /mántlit/) **1** *hist.* a woman's short loose sleeveless mantle. **2** a bulletproof screen for gunners. [ME f. OF, dimin. of *mantel* MANTLE]

mantelpiece /mánt'lpeess/ *n.* **1** a structure of wood, marble, etc. above and around a fireplace. **2** = MANTELSHELF.
mantelshelf /mánt'lshelf/ *n.* a shelf above a fireplace.
mantic /mántik/ *adj. formal* of or concerning divination or prophecy. [Gk *mantikos* f. *mantis* prophet]
mantid /mántid/ *n.* = MANTIS.
mantilla /mantíllə/ *n.* a lace scarf worn by Spanish women over the hair and shoulders. [Sp., dimin. of *manta* MANTLE]
mantis /mántiss/ *n.* (*pl.* same or **mantises**) any insect of the family Mantidae, feeding on other insects etc. □ **praying mantis** a mantis, *Mantis religiosa*, that holds its forelegs in a position suggestive of hands folded in prayer, while waiting to pounce on its prey. [Gk, = prophet]
mantissa /mantíssə/ *n.* the part of a logarithm after the decimal point. [L, = makeweight]
mantle /mánt'l/ *n.* & *v.* ● *n.* **1** a loose sleeveless cloak, esp. of a woman. **2** a covering (*a mantle of snow*). **3** responsibility or authority, esp. as passing from one person to another (see 2 Kings 2:13). **4** a fragile lacelike tube fixed round a gas-jet to give an incandescent light. **5** an outer fold of skin enclosing a mollusc's viscera. **6** a bird's back, scapulars, and wing-coverts, esp. if of a distinctive colour. **7** the region between the crust and the core of the earth. ● *v.* **1** *tr.* clothe in or as if in a mantle; cover, conceal, envelop. **2** *intr.* **a** (of the blood) suffuse the cheeks. **b** (of the face) glow with a blush. **3** *intr.* (of a liquid) become covered with a coating or scum. [ME f. OF f. L *mantellum* cloak]
▪ *n.* **1** cloak, cape, wrap, shawl, *hist.* pelisse. **2** covering, cover, sheet, veil, blanket, screen, cloak, shroud, pall, canopy, curtain. **3** responsibility, charge, burden, duty; power, right; see also AUSPICE 1. ● *v.* **1** cover, clothe, envelop, surround, encircle, shroud, veil, screen, obscure, cloak, conceal, hide, mask, wrap, disguise. **2 b** see GLOW *v.* 2.
mantlet var. of MANTELET.
mantling /mántling/ *n. Heraldry* **1** ornamental drapery etc. behind and around a shield. **2** a representation of this. [MANTLE + ING[1]]
mantra /mántrə/ *n.* **1** a word or sound repeated to aid concentration in meditation, orig. in Hinduism and Buddhism. **2** a Vedic hymn. [Skr., = instrument of thought f. *man* think]
▪ **1** see CHANT *n.*
mantrap /mántrap/ *n.* a trap for catching poachers, trespassers, etc.
mantua /mántyooə/ *n. hist.* a woman's loose gown of the 17th–18th c. [corrupt. of *manteau* (F, as MANTLE) after *Mantua* in Italy]
manual /mányooəl/ *adj.* & *n.* ● *adj.* **1** of or done with the hands (*manual labour*). **2** (of a machine etc.) worked by hand, not automatically. ● *n.* **1 a** a book of instructions, esp. for operating a machine or learning a subject; a handbook (*a computer manual*). **b** any small book. **2** an organ keyboard played with the hands not the feet. **3** *Mil.* an exercise in handling a rifle etc. **4** *hist.* a book of the forms to be used by priests in the administration of the Sacraments. □ **manual alphabet** sign language. □□ **manually** *adv.* [ME f. OF *manuel*, f. (and later assim. to) L *manualis* f. *manus* hand]
▪ *adj.* **1** hand, blue-collar. **2** hand-operated. ● *n.* **1** handbook, companion, vade-mecum, *formal* enchiridion; directions, instructions, guide.
manufactory /mányoofáktəri/ *n.* (*pl.* **-ies**) *archaic* = FACTORY. [MANUFACTURE, after *factory*]
manufacture /mányoofákchər/ *n.* & *v.* ● *n.* **1 a** the making of articles esp. in a factory etc. **b** a branch of an industry (*woollen manufacture*). **2** esp. *derog.* the merely mechanical production of literature, art, etc. ● *v.tr.* **1** make (articles), esp. on an industrial scale. **2** invent or fabricate (evidence, a story, etc.). **3** esp. *derog.* make or produce (literature, art, etc.) in a mechanical way. □□ **manufacturable** *adj.* **manufacturability** /-chərəbílliti/ *n.* **manufacturer** *n.* [F f. It. *manifattura* & L *manufactum* made by hand]
▪ *n.* **1** making, (mass) production, construction, building, assembly, fabrication, turning *or* putting out, putting together. ● *v.* **1** make, (mass-)produce, construct, build, assemble, fabricate, put together, turn out, create, originate. **2** concoct, create, contrive, invent, make up, fabricate, think up, *colloq.* cook up. **3** churn out, *colloq.* knock off. □□ **manufacturer** maker, producer, processor, industrialist; fabricator.
manuka /manōōkə, maánəkə/ *n. Austral.* & *NZ* a small tree, *Leptospermum scoparium*, with aromatic leaves and hard timber. [Maori]
manumit /mányoomít/ *v.tr.* (**manumitted, manumitting**) *hist.* set (a slave) free. □□ **manumission** /-mísh'n/ *n.* [ME f. L *manumittere manumiss-* f. *manus* hand + *emittere* send forth]
manure /mənyóor/ *n.* & *v.* ● *n.* **1** animal dung, esp. of horses, used for fertilizing land. **2** any compost or artificial fertilizer. ● *v.tr.* (also *absol.*) apply manure to (land etc.). □□ **manurial** *adj.* [ME f. AF *mainoverer* = OF *manouvrer* MANOEUVRE]
▪ *n.* **1** see DUNG *n.* ● *v.* see FERTILIZE *v.* 1.
manuscript /mányooskript/ *n.* & *adj.* ● *n.* **1** a book, document, etc. written by hand. **2** an author's handwritten or typed text, submitted for publication. **3** handwritten form (*produced in manuscript*). ● *adj.* written by hand. [med.L *manuscriptus* f. *manu* by hand + *scriptus* past part. of *scribere* write]
▪ *adj.* handwritten, holograph.
Manx /mangks/ *adj.* & *n.* ● *adj.* of or relating to the Isle of Man. ● *n.* **1** the now extinct Celtic language formerly spoken in the Isle of Man. **2** (prec. by *the*; treated as *pl.*) the Manx people. □ **Manx cat** a tailless cat. [ON f. OIr. *Manu* Isle of Man]
Manxman /mángksmən/ *n.* (*pl.* **-men**; *fem.* **Manxwoman**, *pl.* **-women**) a native of the Isle of Man.
many /ménni/ *adj.* & *n.* ● *adj.* (**more** /mor/; **most** /mōst/) great in number; numerous (*many times*; *many people*; *many a person*; *his reasons were many*). ● *n.* (as *pl.*) **1** a large number (*many like skiing*; *many went*). **2** (prec. by *the*) the multitude of esp. working people. □ **as many** the same number of (*six mistakes in as many lines*). **as many again** the same number additionally (*sixty here and as many again there*). **be too** (or **one too**) **many for** outwit, baffle. **a good** (or **great**) **many** a large number. **many-sided** having many sides, aspects, interests, capabilities, etc. **many-sidedness** *n.* the fact or state of being many-sided. **many's the time** often (*many's the time we saw it*). **many a time** many times. [OE *manig*, ult. f. Gmc]
▪ *adj.* numerous, multitudinous, profuse, innumerable, numberless, uncountable, *literary* myriad. ● *n.* **1** a good *or* great deal, hordes *or* a horde, crowds *or* a crowd, swarms *or* a swarm, throngs *or* a throng, masses *or* a mass, mountains *or* a mountain, a profusion, multitudes *or* a multitude, a good *or* great many, an abundance, plenty, shoals *or* a shoal, flocks *or* a flock, droves *or* a drove, torrents *or* a torrent, floods *or* a flood, numbers *or* a number, scores, *or* a score, *colloq.* lots *or* a lot, hundreds *or* a hundred, oodles, zillions, loads *or* a load, stacks *or* a stack, piles *or* a pile, heaps *or* a heap, pots *or* a pot, tons *or* a ton, *US colloq.* scads. **2** (*the many*) see *the great unwashed* (UNWASHED). □ **be too** (or **one too**) **many for** outwit, *colloq.* outsmart; see also PERPLEX 1. **a good** (or **great**) **many** see MANY *n.* 1 above. **many-sided** see MANIFOLD *adj.*, VERSATILE 1. **many-sidedness** see VARIETY 1, *versatility* (VERSATILE). **many's the time, many a time** see OFTEN.
manzanilla /mánzəníllə/ *n.* a pale very dry Spanish sherry. [Sp., lit. 'camomile']
manzanita /mánzəneétə/ *n.* any of several evergreen shrubs of the genus *Arctostaphylos*, esp. *A. manzanita*, native to California. [Sp., dimin. of *manzana* apple]
Maoism /mówiz'm/ *n.* the Communist doctrines of Mao Zedong (d. 1976), Chinese statesman. □□ **Maoist** *n.* & *adj.*

Maori /mówri/ *n.* & *adj.* ● *n.* (*pl.* same or **Maoris**) **1** a member of the Polynesian aboriginal people of New Zealand. **2** the language of the Maori. ● *adj.* of or concerning the Maori or their language. [native name]

map /map/ *n.* & *v.* ● *n.* **1 a** a usu. flat representation of the earth's surface, or part of it, showing physical features, cities, etc. (cf. GLOBE). **b** a diagrammatic representation of a route etc. (*drew a map of the journey*). **2** a two-dimensional representation of the stars, the heavens, etc., or of the surface of a planet, the moon, etc. **3** a diagram showing the arrangement or components of a thing. **4** *sl.* the face. ● *v.tr.* (**mapped, mapping**) **1** represent (a country etc.) on a map. **2** *Math.* associate each element of (a set) with one element of another set. □ **map out** arrange in detail; plan (a course of conduct etc.). **off the map** *colloq.* **1** of no account; obsolete. **2** very distant. **on the map** *colloq.* prominent, important. **wipe off the map** *colloq.* obliterate. □□ **mapless** *adj.* **mappable** *adj.* **mapper** *n.* [L *mappa* napkin: in med.L *mappa* (*mundi*) map (of the world)]
■ *n.* **1–3** see CHART *n.* ● *v.* **1** see CHART *v.*

maple /máyp'l/ *n.* **1** any tree or shrub of the genus *Acer* grown for shade, ornament, wood, or its sugar. **2** the wood of the maple. □ **maple-leaf** the leaf of the maple, used as an emblem of Canada. **maple sugar** a sugar produced by evaporating the sap of the sugar maple etc. **maple syrup** a syrup produced from the sap of the sugar maple etc. [ME *mapul* etc. f. OE *mapeltrēow, mapulder*]

maquette /məkét/ *n.* **1** a sculptor's small preliminary model in wax, clay, etc. **2** a preliminary sketch. [F f. It. *machietta* dimin. of *macchia* spot]

maquillage /mákkeeyaazh/ *n.* **1** make-up; cosmetics. **2** the application of make-up. [F f. *maquiller* make up f. OF *masquiller* stain]
■ **1** see *make-up* 1.

Maquis /makée/ *n.* **1** the French resistance movement during the German occupation (1940–45). **2** a member of this. [F, = brushwood, f. Corsican It. *macchia* thicket]
■ **1** see UNDERGROUND *n.* 2.

Mar. *abbr.* March.

mar /maar/ *v.tr.* (**marred, marring**) **1** ruin. **2** impair the perfection of; spoil; disfigure. [OE *merran* hinder]
■ **1** damage, wreck, ruin, impair, harm, hurt. **2** impair, damage, mutilate, deface, blight, blot, spoil, scar, disfigure, taint, stain, tarnish.

marabou /márrəboo/ *n.* (also **marabout**) **1** a large W. African stork, *Leptoptilos crumeniferus*. **2** a tuft of down from the wing or tail of the marabou used as a trimming for hats etc. [F f. Arab. *murābiṭ* holy man (see MARABOUT), the stork being regarded as holy]

marabout /márrəboot/ *n.* **1** a Muslim hermit or monk, esp. in N. Africa. **2** a shrine marking a marabout's burial-place. [F f. Port. *marabuto* f. Arab. *murābiṭ* holy man f. *ribāṭ* frontier station, where he acquired merit by combat against the infidel]

maraca /mərákkə/ *n.* a hollow clublike gourd or gourd-shaped container filled with beans etc. and usu. shaken in pairs as a percussion instrument in Latin American music. [Port. *maracá*, prob. f. Tupi]

maraschino /márrəskéenō/ *n.* (*pl.* **-os**) a strong sweet liqueur made from a small black Dalmatian cherry. □ **maraschino cherry** a cherry preserved in maraschino and used to decorate cocktails etc. [It. f. *marasca* small black cherry, for *amarasca* f. *amaro* bitter f. L *amarus*]

marasmus /mərázməss/ *n.* a wasting away of the body. □□ **marasmic** *adj.* [mod.L f. Gk *marasmos* f. *marainō* wither]

Maratha /məraatə, -rattə/ *n.* (also **Mahratta**) a member of a warrior people native to the modern Indian State of Maharashtra. [Hindi *Marhaṭṭa* f. Skr. *Māhārāshṭra* great kingdom]

Marathi /məraati, -rátti/ *n.* (also **Mahratti**) the language of the Marathas. [MARATHA]

marathon /márrəthən/ *n.* **1** a long-distance running race, usu. of 26 miles 385 yards (42.195 km). **2** a long-lasting or difficult task, operation, etc. (often *attrib.*: *a marathon shopping expedition*). □□ **marathoner** *n.* [*Marathon* in Greece, scene of a victory over the Persians in 490 BC: a messenger was said to have run to Athens with the news, but the account has no authority]

maraud /məráwd/ *v.* **1** *intr.* **a** make a plundering raid. **b** pilfer systematically; plunder. **2** *tr.* plunder (a place). □□ **marauder** *n.* [F *marauder* f. *maraud* rogue]
■ see PLUNDER *v.* 2. □□ **marauder** see THIEF.

marble /maarb'l/ *n.* & *v.* ● *n.* **1** limestone in a metamorphic crystalline (or granular) state, and capable of taking a polish, used in sculpture and architecture. **2** (often *attrib.*) **a** anything made of marble (*a marble clock*). **b** anything resembling marble in hardness, coldness, durability, etc. (*her features were marble*). **3 a** a small ball of marble, glass, clay, etc., used as a toy. **b** (in *pl.*; treated as *sing.*) a game using these. **4** (in *pl.*) *sl.* one's mental faculties (*he's lost his marbles*). **5** (in *pl.*) a collection of sculptures (*Elgin Marbles*). ● *v.tr.* **1** (esp. as **marbled** *adj.*) stain or colour (paper, the edges of a book, soap, etc.) to look like variegated marble. **2** (as **marbled** *adj.*) (of meat) streaked with alternating layers of lean and fat. □ **marble cake** a cake with a mottled appearance, made of light and dark sponge. □□ **marbly** *adj.* [ME f. OF *marbre*, *marble*, f. L *marmor* f. Gk *marmaros* shining stone]
■ *v.* **1** (**marbled**) see *mottled* (MOTTLE).

marbling /maarbling/ *n.* **1** colouring or marking like marble. **2** streaks of fat in lean meat.

marc /maark/ *n.* **1** the refuse of pressed grapes etc. **2** a brandy made from this. [F f. *marcher* tread, MARCH[1]]

Marcan /maarkən/ *adj.* of or relating to St Mark. [L *Marcus* Mark]

marcasite /maarkəsīt/ *n.* **1** a yellowish crystalline iron sulphide mineral. **2** these bronze-yellow crystals used in jewellery. [ME f. med.L *marcasita*, f. Arab. *marḳašīṭā* f. Pers.]

marcato /maarkaatō/ *adv.* & *adj.* *Mus.* played with emphasis. [It., = marked]

marcel /maarsél/ *n.* & *v.* ● *n.* (in full **marcel wave**) a deep wave in the hair. ● *v.tr.* (**marcelled, marcelling**) wave (hair) with a deep wave. [*Marcel* Grateau, Paris hairdresser d. 1936, who invented the method]

marcescent /maarséss'nt/ *adj.* (of part of a plant) withering but not falling. □□ **marcescence** *n.* [L *marcescere* incept. of *marcēre* wither]

March /maarch/ *n.* the third month of the year. □ **March hare** a hare in the breeding season, characterized by excessive leaping, strange behaviour, etc. (*mad as a March hare*). [ME f. OF *march(e)*, dial. var. of *marz*, *mars*, f. L *Martius* (*mensis*) (month) of Mars]

march[1] /maarch/ *v.* & *n.* ● *v.* **1** *intr.* (usu. foll. by *away*, *off*, *out*, etc.) walk in a military manner with a regular measured tread. **2** *tr.* (often foll. by *away*, *on*, *off*, etc.) cause to march or walk (*marched the army to Moscow*; *marched him out of the room*). **3** *intr.* **a** walk or proceed steadily, esp. across country. **b** (of events etc.) continue unrelentingly (*time marches on*). **4** *intr.* take part in a protest march. ● *n.* **1 a** the act or an instance of marching. **b** the uniform step of troops etc. (*a slow march*). **2** a long difficult walk. **3** a procession as a protest or demonstration. **4** (usu. foll. by *of*) progress or continuity (*the march of events*). **5 a** a piece of music composed to accompany a march. **b** a composition of similar character and form. □ **marching order** *Mil.* equipment or a formation for marching. **marching orders** **1** *Mil.* the direction for troops to depart for war etc. **2** a dismissal (*gave him his marching orders*). **march on 1** advance towards (a military objective). **2** proceed. **march past** *n.* the marching of troops past a saluting-point at a review. ● *v.intr.* (of troops) carry out a march past. **on the march 1** marching. **2** in steady progress. □□ **marcher** *n.* [F *marche* (n.), *marcher* (v.), f. LL *marcus* hammer]
■ *v.* **1** parade, step, stride, strut, tread, pace, walk. **2** see *pack off*. **3 a** see WALK *v.* 1, 2. **4** see DEMONSTRATE 4. ● *n.* **1 a** parade, procession, cortège, walk. **2** walk, trek, slog,

hike; see also TRAMP *n.* 3. **3** see DEMONSTRATION 2. **4** see PROGRESS *n.* 2. □ **marching orders 2** see *dismissal* (DISMISS). **march on 2** see PROCEED 1.

march[2] /maarch/ *n.* & *v.* ● *n. hist.* **1** (usu. in *pl.*) a boundary, a frontier (esp. of the borderland between England and Scotland or Wales). **2** a tract of often disputed land between two countries. ● *v.intr.* (foll. by *upon, with*) (of a country, an estate, etc.) have a common frontier with, border on. [ME f. OF *marche, marchir* ult. f. Gmc: cf. MARK[1]]

marcher /maárchər/ *n.* an inhabitant of a march or border district.

marchioness /maárshənéss/ *n.* **1** the wife or widow of a marquess. **2** a woman holding the rank of marquess in her own right (cf. MARQUISE). [med.L *marchionissa* f. *marchio -onis* captain of the marches (as MARCH[2])]
■ see PEER[2] *n.* 1.

marchpane /maárchpayn/ *archaic* var. of MARZIPAN.

Mardi Gras /maárdi graá/ *n.* **1 a** Shrove Tuesday in some Catholic countries. **b** merrymaking on this day. **2** the last day of a carnival etc. **3** *Austral.* a carnival or fair at any time. [F, = fat Tuesday]

mardy /maárdi/ *adj. dial.* sulky, whining, spoilt. [dial. *mard* spoilt, alt. of *marred* f. MAR]

mare[1] /mair/ *n.* **1** the female of any equine animal, esp. the horse. **2** *sl. derog.* a woman. □ **mare's nest** an illusory discovery. **mare's tail 1** a tall slender marsh plant, *Hippuris vulgaris*. **2** (in *pl.*) long straight streaks of cirrus cloud. [ME f. OE *mearh* horse f. Gmc: cf. MARSHAL]

mare[2] /maáray/ *n.* (*pl.* **maria** /maáriə/ or **mares**) **1** (in full **mare clausum** /klówsōōm/) *Law* the sea under the jurisdiction of a particular country. **2** (in full **mare liberum** /leébərōōm/) *Law* the sea open to all nations. **3 a** any of a number of large dark flat areas on the surface of the moon, once thought to be seas. **b** a similar area on Mars. [L, = sea]

maremma /mərémmə/ *n.* (*pl.* **maremme** /-mi/) low marshy unhealthy land near a seashore. [It. f. L *maritima* (as MARITIME)]

margarine /maárjəreén, maárgə-/ *n.* a butter-substitute made from vegetable oils or animal fats with milk etc. [F, misapplication of a chem. term, f. *margarique* f. Gk *margaron* pearl]
■ spread, *US* oleomargarine.

margay /maárgay/ *n.* a small wild S. American cat, *Felis wiedii*. [F f. Tupi *mbaracaïa*]

marge[1] /maarj/ *n. Brit. colloq.* margarine. [abbr.]

marge[2] /maarj/ *n. poet.* a margin or edge. [F f. L *margo* (as MARGIN)]

margin /maárjin/ *n.* & *v.* ● *n.* **1** the edge or border of a surface. **2 a** the blank border on each side of the print on a page etc. **b** a line ruled esp. on exercise paper, marking off a margin. **3** an amount (of time, money, etc.) by which a thing exceeds, falls short, etc. (*won by a narrow margin; a margin of profit*). **4** the lower limit of possibility, success, etc. (*his effort fell below the margin*). **5** *Austral.* an increment to a basic wage, paid for skill. **6** a sum deposited with a stockbroker to cover the risk of loss on a transaction on account. ● *v.tr.* (**margined, margining**) provide with a margin or marginal notes. □ **margin of error** a usu. small difference allowed for miscalculation, change of circumstances, etc. **margin release** a device on a typewriter allowing a word to be typed beyond the margin normally set. [ME f. L *margo -ginis*]
■ *n.* **1** edge, border, perimeter, periphery; rim, lip, side, brink, verge. **3** majority, amount, gap, difference, shortfall, deficit, surplus, excess, profit. **4** limit(s), bound(s), boundary (line), border, frontier, line. **5** increment, increase, addition, bonus.

marginal /maárjin'l/ *adj.* **1 a** of or written in a margin. **b** having marginal notes. **2 a** of or at the edge; not central. **b** not significant or decisive (*the work is of merely marginal interest*). **3** *Brit.* (of a parliamentary seat or constituency) having a small majority at risk in an election. **4** close to the limit, esp. of profitability. **5** (of the sea) adjacent to the shore of a State. **6** (of land) difficult to cultivate; unprofitable. **7** barely adequate; unprovided for. □ **marginal cost** the cost added by making one extra copy etc. □□ **marginality** /-nálliti/ *n.* **marginally** *adv.* [med.L *marginalis* (as MARGIN)]
■ **2 b** borderline, minimal, small, slight, negligible, insignificant, tiny, infinitesimal; disputable, questionable, doubtful, dubious. **6** see UNPROFITABLE, BARREN *adj.* 1b.

marginalia /maárjináyliə/ *n.pl.* marginal notes. [med.L, neut. pl. of *marginalis*]
■ see NOTE *n.* 2, 5.

marginalize /maárjinəlīz/ *v.tr.* (also **-ise**) make or treat as insignificant. □□ **marginalization** /-záysh'n/ *n.*

marginate *v.* & *adj.* ● *v.tr.* /maárjinayt/ **1** = MARGINALIZE. **2** provide with a margin or border. ● *adj.* /maárjinət/ *Biol.* having a distinct margin or border. □□ **margination** /-náysh'n/ *n.*

margrave /maárgrayv/ *n. hist.* the hereditary title of some princes of the Holy Roman Empire (orig. of a military governor of a border province). □□ **margravate** /maárgrəvət/ *n.* [MDu. *markgrave* border count (as MARK[1], *grave* COUNT[2] f. OLG *grēve*)]

margravine /maárgrəveen/ *n. hist.* the wife of a margrave. [Du. *markgravin* (as MARGRAVE)]

marguerite /maárgəreét/ *n.* an ox-eye daisy. [F f. L *margarita* f. Gk *margaritēs* f. *margaron* pearl]

maria *pl.* of MARE[2].

mariage de convenance /márriaázh də kóNvənóNss/ *n.* = *marriage of convenience*. [F]

Marian /máiriən/ *adj. RC Ch.* of or relating to the Virgin Mary (*Marian vespers*). [L *Maria* Mary]

marigold /márrigōld/ *n.* any plant of the genus *Calendula* or *Tagetes*, with golden or bright yellow flowers. [ME f. *Mary* (prob. the Virgin) + dial. *gold*, OE *golde*, prob. rel. to GOLD]

marijuana /márrihwaánə/ *n.* (also **marihuana**) **1** the dried leaves, flowering tops, and stems of the hemp, used as an intoxicating or hallucinogenic drug usu. smoked in cigarettes. **2** the plant yielding these (cf. HEMP). [Amer. Sp.]

marimba /mərímbə/ *n.* **1** a xylophone played by natives of Africa and Central America. **2** a modern orchestral instrument derived from this. [Congo]

marina /məreénə/ *n.* a specially designed harbour with moorings for pleasure-yachts etc. [It. & Sp. fem. adj. f. *marino* f. L (as MARINE)]

marinade /márrináyd/ *n.* & *v.* ● *n.* **1** a mixture of wine, vinegar, oil, spices, etc., in which meat, fish, etc., is soaked before cooking. **2** meat, fish, etc., soaked in this liquid. ● *v.tr.* soak (meat, fish, etc.) in a marinade. [F f. Sp. *marinada* f. *marinar* pickle in brine f. *marino* (as MARINE)]
■ *v.* see SOAK *v.* 1.

marinate /márrinayt/ *v.tr.* = MARINADE. □□ **marination** /-náysh'n/ *n.* [It. *marinare* or F *mariner* (as MARINE)]

marine /məreén/ *adj.* & *n.* ● *adj.* **1** of, found in, or produced by the sea. **2 a** of or relating to shipping or naval matters (*marine insurance*). **b** for use at sea. ● *n.* **1** a country's shipping, fleet, or navy (*mercantile marine; merchant marine*). **2** a member of a body of troops trained to serve on land or sea. **3** a picture of a scene at sea. □ **marine stores** new or old ships' material etc. sold as merchandise. **marine trumpet** a large single-stringed viol with a trumpet-like tone. **tell that to the marines** (or **horse marines**) *colloq.* an expression of disbelief. [ME f. OF *marin marine* f. L *marinus* f. *mare* sea]
■ *adj.* **1** maritime, sea, oceanic, aquatic, salt-water, pelagic, thalassic. **2** maritime, nautical, naval, seafaring, seagoing, ocean-going, sea. ● *n.* **1** shipping, fleet, navy, flotilla, naval force, armada. □ **tell that to the marines** (or **horse marines**) see *go on!* (GO[1]).

mariner /márrinər/ *n.* a seaman. ☐ **mariner's compass** a compass showing magnetic or true north and the bearings from it. [ME f. AF *mariner*, OF *marinier* f. med.L *marinarius* f. L (as MARINE)]
■ see SAILOR.

Mariolatry /máiriólllətri/ *n. derog.* idolatrous worship of the Virgin Mary. [L *Maria* Mary + -LATRY, after *idolatry*]

marionette /márriənét/ *n.* a puppet worked by strings. [F *marionnette* f. *Marion* dimin. of *Marie* Mary]

Marist /maárist/ *n.* a member of the Roman Catholic Society of Mary. [F *Mariste* f. *Marie* Mary]

marital /márrit'l/ *adj.* **1** of marriage or the relations between husband and wife. **2** of or relating to a husband. ☐☐ **maritally** *adv.* [L *maritalis* f. *maritus* husband]
■ **1** see NUPTIAL *adj.*

maritime /márritīm/ *adj.* **1** connected with the sea or seafaring (*maritime insurance*). **2** living or found near the sea. [L *maritimus* f. *mare* sea]
■ **1** see MARINE 2. **2** see MARINE 1.

marjoram /maárjərəm/ *n.* either of two aromatic herbs, *Origanum vulgare* (**wild marjoram**) or *Majorana hortensis* (**sweet marjoram**), the fresh or dried leaves of which are used as a flavouring in cookery. [ME & OF *majorane* f. med.L *majorana*, of unkn. orig.]

mark¹ /maark/ *n.* & *v.* ● *n.* **1** a trace, sign, stain, scar, etc., on a surface, face, page, etc. **2** (esp. in *comb.*) **a** a written or printed symbol (*exclamation mark*; *question mark*). **b** a numerical or alphabetical award denoting excellence, conduct, proficiency, etc. (*got a good mark for effort*; *gave him a black mark*; *gained 46 marks out of 50*). **3** (usu. foll. by *of*) a sign or indication of quality, character, feeling, etc. (*took off his hat as a mark of respect*). **4 a** a sign, seal, etc., used for distinction or identification. **b** a cross etc. made in place of a signature by an illiterate person. **5 a** a target, object, goal, etc. (*missed the mark with his first play*). **b** a standard for attainment (*his work falls below the mark*). **6** a line etc. indicating a position; a marker. **7** (usu. **Mark**) (followed by a numeral) a particular design, model, etc., of a car, aircraft, etc. (*this is the Mark 2 model*). **8** a runner's starting-point in a race. **9** *Naut.* a piece of material etc. used to indicate a position on a sounding-line. **10 a** *Rugby Football* a heel-mark on the ground made by a player who has caught the ball direct from a kick, knock-on, or throw-forward by an opponent. **b** *Austral. Rules* the catching before it reaches the ground of a ball kicked at least ten metres; the spot from which the subsequent kick is taken. **11** *sl.* the intended victim of a swindler etc. **12** *Boxing* the pit of the stomach. **13** *hist.* a tract of land held in common by a Teutonic or medieval German village community. ● *v.tr.* **1 a** make a mark on (a thing or person), esp. by writing, cutting, scraping, etc. **b** put a distinguishing or identifying mark, initials, name, etc., on (clothes etc.) (*marked the tree with their initials*). **2 a** allot marks to; correct (a student's work etc.). **b** record (the points gained in games etc.). **3** attach a price to (goods etc.) (*marked the doll at 50p*). **4** (often foll. by *by*) show or manifest (displeasure etc.) (*marked his anger by leaving early*). **5** notice or observe (*she marked his agitation*). **6 a** characterize or be a feature of (*the day was marked by storms*). **b** acknowledge, recognize, celebrate (*marked the occasion with a toast*). **7** name or indicate (a place on a map, the length of a syllable, etc.) by a sign or mark. **8** characterize (a person or a thing) as (*marked them as weak*). **9 a** *Brit.* keep close to so as to prevent the free movement of (an opponent in sport). **b** *Austral. Rules* catch (the ball). **10** (as **marked** *adj.*) having natural marks (*is marked with silver spots*). **11** (of a graduated instrument) show, register (so many degrees etc.). **12** *US* & *Austral.* castrate (a lamb). ☐ **one's mark** *colloq.* **1** what one prefers. **2** an opponent, object, etc., of one's own size, calibre, etc. (*the little one's more my mark*). **beside** (or **off** or **wide of**) **the mark 1** not to the point; irrelevant. **2** not accurate. **make one's mark** attain distinction. **mark down 1** mark (goods etc.) at a lower price. **2** make a written note of. **3** choose (a person) as one's victim. **mark-down** *n.* a reduction in price. **mark off** (often foll. by *from*) separate (one thing from another) by a boundary etc. (*marked off the subjects for discussion*). **mark of mouth** a depression in a horse's incisor indicating age. **mark out 1** plan (a course of action etc.). **2** destine (*marked out for success*). **3** trace out boundaries, a course, etc. **mark time 1** *Mil.* march on the spot, without moving forward. **2** act routinely; go through the motions. **3** await an opportunity to advance. **mark up 1** mark (goods etc.) at a higher price. **2** mark or correct (text etc.) for typesetting or alteration. **mark-up** *n.* **1** the amount added to the cost price of goods to cover overhead charges, profit, etc. **2** the corrections made in marking up text. **mark you** please note (*without obligation, mark you*). **off the mark 1** having made a start. **2** = *beside the mark*. **of mark** noteworthy. **on the mark** ready to start. **on your mark** (or **marks**) (as an instruction) get ready to start (esp. a race). **up to the mark** reaching the usual or normal standard, esp. of health. [OE *me(a)rc* (n.), *mearcian* (v.), f. Gmc]
■ *n.* **1** spot, stain, scar, blemish, smear, smudge, trace, impression, dent, nick, scratch, pock(-mark), streak, line, sign, *colloq.* splodge, splotch. **2a, 3, 4a** sign, symbol, emblem, device, hallmark, seal, earmark, fingerprint, badge, characteristic, token, brand, stamp, label, identification, indication; feature, attribute, trait, quality, property. **2 b** rating, grade, grading, score. **5 a** target, goal, objective, aim, purpose, end, object. **b** standard, criterion, norm, yardstick, level, measure; margin. **6** marker, indicator, guide, signpost, landmark. ● *v.* **1 a** spot, stain, blemish, smear, smudge, streak, dent, trace, pock-mark, nick, scratch, cut, chip, pit, bruise. **2** correct; grade, evaluate, assess, appraise. **3** label; price. **4** signify, indicate, show, manifest, express. **5** pay attention to, attend (to), pay heed to, note, notice, take notice of, heed, watch, see, look at, observe. **6a, 8** brand, stamp, identify, characterize, distinguish. **6 b** acknowledge, observe, salute, honour, note; see also CELEBRATE *v.* 1. **7** signify, indicate, show, manifest, express, designate, identify, specify, tick, label, *US* check. **10** (**marked**) see SPOTTY 1. ☐ **beside** (or **off** or **wide of**) **the mark 1** see IRRELEVANT. **2** see INACCURATE. **make one's mark** succeed, get ahead, triumph, distinguish oneself, attain distinction, bring honour upon oneself, acquit oneself well, have an effect, *colloq.* make it big, make the grade. **mark down 1** reduce, devalue, discount. **2** write (down), record, register, make a note of, note (down). **mark off** see SEPARATE *v.* 6a. **mark out 1** see DESIGN *v.* 1. **2** see DESTINE. **mark time 2** act routinely *or* mechanically *or* perfunctorily, go through the motions. **3** see WAIT *v.* 1a. **mark up 1** increase, *esp. US* hike, *colloq.* up. **mark you** mind, note, I might add. **of mark** see NOTEWORTHY.

mark² /maark/ *n.* **1 a** = DEUTSCHMARK. **b** *hist.* = OSTMARK. **2** *hist.* **a** a denomination of weight for gold and silver. **b** English money of account. [OE *marc*, prob. rel. to med.L *marca*, *marcus*]

marked /maarkt/ *adj.* **1** having a visible mark. **2** clearly noticeable; evident (*a marked difference*). **3** (of playing-cards) having distinctive marks on their backs to assist cheating. ☐ **marked man 1** a person whose conduct is watched with suspicion or hostility. **2** a person destined to succeed. ☐☐ **markedly** /-kidli/ *adv.* **markedness** /-kidniss/ *n.* [OE (past part. of MARK¹)]
■ **1** see SPOTTY 1. **2** noticeable, conspicuous, decided, pronounced, considerable, remarkable, significant, signal, unmistakable, prominent, obvious, patent, evident, apparent.

marker /maárkər/ *n.* **1** a stone, post, etc., used to mark a position, place reached, etc. **2** a person or thing that marks. **3** a felt-tipped pen with a broad tip. **4** a person who records a score, esp. in billiards. **5** a flare etc. used to direct a pilot to a target. **6** a bookmark. **7** *US sl.* a promissory note; an IOU.

market /maárkit/ *n.* & *v.* ● *n.* **1 a** the gathering of people for the purchase and sale of provisions, livestock, etc., esp. with a number of different vendors. **b** the time of this. **2** an open space or covered building used for this. **3** (often foll. by *for*) a demand for a commodity or service (*goods find a ready market*). **4** a place or group providing such a demand. **5** conditions as regards, or opportunity for, buying or selling. **6** the rate of purchase and sale, market value (*the market fell*). **7** (prec. by *the*) the trade in a specified commodity (*the corn market*). **8** (**the Market**) *Brit.* the European Economic Community. ● *v.* (**marketed, marketing**) **1** *tr.* sell. **2** *tr.* offer for sale. **3** *intr.* buy or sell goods in a market. □ **be in the market for** wish to buy. **be on** (or **come into**) **the market** be offered for sale. **make a market** *Stock Exch.* induce active dealing in a stock or shares. **market cross** a structure erected in a market-place, orig. a stone cross, later an arcaded building. **market-day** a day on which a market is regularly held, usu. weekly. **market garden** a place where vegetables and fruit are grown for the market etc. **market gardener** a person who owns or is employed in a market garden. **market maker** *Brit.* a member of the Stock Exchange granted certain privileges and trading to prescribed regulations. **market-place 1** an open space where a market is held in a town. **2** the scene of actual dealings. **market price** the price in current dealings. **market research** the study of consumers' needs and preferences. **market town** *Brit.* a town where a market is held. **market value** value as a saleable thing (opp. *book value*). **put on the market** offer for sale. □□ **marketer** *n.* **marketing** *n.* [ME ult. f. L *mercatus* f. *mercari* buy: see MERCHANT]

■ *n.* **1 a** market-place, exchange. **2** shop, store, bazaar, supermarket, superstore, hypermarket. **3, 4** demand, call, trade; outlet; clientele. **7** see TRADE *n.* 1a, b. ● *v.* **1, 2** sell, merchandise, retail, vend, peddle, hawk, make available, furnish. □ **be on** (or **come into**) **the market** be on *or* for *or* up for sale, be on offer, *US* be on the block. **put on the market** put on *or* up for sale, offer for sale, *US* put on the block.

marketable /maárkitəb'l/ *adj.* able or fit to be sold. □□ **marketability** /-bílliti/ *n.*

marketeer /maárkiteér/ *n.* **1** a supporter of the EEC and British membership of it. **2** a marketer.

markhor /maárkor/ *n.* a large spiral-horned wild goat, *Capra falconeri*, of N. India. [Pers. *mār-kẖwār* f. *mār* serpent + *kẖwār* -eating]

marking /maárking/ *n.* (usu. in *pl.*) **1** an identification mark, esp. a symbol on an aircraft. **2** the colouring of an animal's fur, feathers, skin, etc. □ **marking-ink** indelible ink for marking linen etc.

marksman /maárksmən/ *n.* (*pl.* **-men**) a person skilled in shooting, esp. with a pistol or rifle. □□ **marksmanship** *n.*

■ see SHOT[1] *n.* 6.

marl[1] /maarl/ *n.* & *v.* ● *n.* soil consisting of clay and lime, with fertilizing properties. ● *v.tr.* apply marl to (the ground). □□ **marly** *adj.* [ME f. OF *marle* f. med.L *margila* f. L *marga*]

marl[2] /maarl/ *n.* **1** a mottled yarn of differently coloured threads. **2** the fabric made from this. [shortening of *marbled*: see MARBLE]

marlin /maárlin/ *n.* *US* any of various large long-nosed marine fish of the family *Istophoridae*, esp. the blue marlin *Makaira nigricans*. [MARLINSPIKE, with ref. to its pointed snout]

marline /maárlin/ *n.* *Naut.* a thin line of two strands. □ **marline-spike** = MARLINSPIKE. [ME f. Du. *marlijn* f. *marren* bind + *lijn* LINE[1]]

marlinspike /maárlinspīk/ *n.* *Naut.* a pointed iron tool used to separate strands of rope or wire. [orig. app. *marling-spike* f. *marl* fasten with marline (f. Du. *marlen* frequent. of MDu. *marren* bind) + -ING[1] + SPIKE[1]]

marlite /maárlīt/ *n.* a kind of marl that is not reduced to powder by the action of the air.

marmalade /maármәlayd/ *n.* a preserve of citrus fruit, usu. bitter oranges, made like jam. □ **marmalade cat** a cat with orange fur. [F *marmelade* f. Port. *marmelada* quince jam f. *marmelo* quince f. L *melimelum* f. Gk *melimēlon* f. *meli* honey + *mēlon* apple]

■ see PRESERVE *n.* 1.

Marmite /maármīt/ *n.* **1** *Brit. propr.* a preparation made from yeast extract and vegetable extract, used in sandwiches and for flavouring. **2** (**marmite**) /also maarmeét/ an earthenware cooking vessel. [F, = cooking-pot]

marmoreal /maarmóriəl/ *adj.* *poet.* of or like marble. □□ **marmoreally** *adv.* [L *marmoreus* (as MARBLE)]

marmoset /maármәzet/ *n.* any of several small tropical American monkeys of the family Callitricidae, having a long bushy tail. [OF *marmouset* grotesque image, of unkn. orig.]

marmot /maármət/ *n.* any burrowing rodent of the genus *Marmota*, with a heavy-set body and short bushy tail. [F *marmotte* prob. f. Romansh *murmont* f. L *murem* (nominative *mus*) *montis* mountain mouse]

marocain /márrəkayn/ *n.* a dress-fabric of ribbed crêpe. [F, = Moroccan f. *Maroc* Morocco]

Maronite /márrənīt/ *n.* a member of a sect of Syrian Christians dwelling chiefly in Lebanon. [med.L *Maronita* f. *Maro* the 5th-c. Syrian founder]

maroon[1] /mərŏŏn/ *adj.* & *n.* ● *adj.* brownish-crimson. ● *n.* **1** this colour. **2** an explosive device giving a loud report. [F *marron* chestnut f. It. *marrone* f. med.Gk *maraon*]

maroon[2] /mərŏŏn/ *v.* & *n.* ● *v.tr.* **1** leave (a person) isolated in a desolate place (esp. an island). **2** (of a person or a natural phenomenon) cause (a person) to be unable to leave a place. ● *n.* **1** a person descended from a group of fugitive slaves in the remoter parts of Surinam and the W. Indies. **2** a marooned person. [F *marron* f. Sp. *cimarrón* wild f. *cima* peak]

■ *v.* abandon, cast away, desert, strand, forsake; isolate, seclude, cut off. ● *n.* **2** castaway.

marque[1] /maark/ *n.* a make of motor car, as distinct from a specific model (*the Jaguar marque*). [F, = MARK[1]]

marque[2] /maark/ *n.* *hist.* □ **letters of marque** (or **marque and reprisal**) **1** a licence to fit out an armed vessel and employ it in the capture of an enemy's merchant shipping. **2** (in *sing.*) a ship carrying such a licence. [ME f. F f. Prov. *marca* f. *marcar* seize as a pledge]

marquee /maarkeé/ *n.* **1** a large tent used for social or commercial functions. **2** *US* a canopy over the entrance to a large building. [MARQUISE, taken as pl. & assim. to -EE]

marquess /maárkwiss/ *n.* a British nobleman ranking between a duke and an earl (cf. MARQUIS). □□ **marquessate** /-kwisət/ *n.* [var. of MARQUIS]

marquetry /maárkitri/ *n.* (also **marqueterie**) inlaid work in wood, ivory, etc. [F *marqueterie* f. *marqueter* variegate f. MARQUE[1]]

marquis /maárkwiss/ *n.* a foreign nobleman ranking between a duke and a count (cf. MARQUESS). □□ **marquisate** /-kwisət/ *n.* [ME f. OF *marchis* f. Rmc (as MARCH[2], -ESE)]

marquise /maarkeéz/ *n.* **1 a** the wife or widow of a marquis. **b** a woman holding the rank of marquis in her own right (cf. MARCHIONESS). **2** a finger-ring set with an oval pointed cluster of gems. **3** *archaic* = MARQUEE. [F, fem. of MARQUIS]

marquisette /maárkizét/ *n.* a fine light cotton, rayon, or silk fabric for net curtains etc. [F, dimin. of MARQUISE]

marram /márrəm/ *n.* a shore grass, *Ammophila arenaria*, that binds sand with its tough rhizomes. [ON *marálmr* f. *marr* sea + *hálmr* HAULM]

marriage /márrij/ *n.* **1** the legal union of a man and a woman in order to live together and often to have children. **2** an act or ceremony establishing this union. **3** one particular union of this kind (*by a previous marriage*). **4** an intimate union (*the marriage of true minds*). **5** *Cards* the union of a king and queen of the same suit. □ **by marriage** as a result of a marriage (*related by marriage*). **in marriage** as husband or wife (*give in marriage*; *take in marriage*). **marriage bureau**

an establishment arranging introductions between persons wishing to marry. **marriage certificate** a certificate certifying the completion of a marriage ceremony. **marriage guidance** counselling of couples who have problems in married life. **marriage licence** a licence to marry. **marriage lines** *Brit.* a marriage certificate. **marriage of convenience** a marriage concluded to achieve some practical purpose, esp. financial or political. **marriage settlement** an arrangement securing property between spouses. [ME f. OF *mariage* f. *marier* MARRY[1]]

■ **1** matrimony, wedlock. **2** nuptials, wedding. **4** association, alliance, connection, coupling, union, merger, amalgamation, integration.

marriageable /márrijəb'l/ *adj.* **1** fit for marriage, esp. old or rich enough to marry. **2** (of age) fit for marriage. □□ **marriageability** /-bílliti/ *n.*

married /márrid/ *adj.* & *n.* ● *adj.* **1** united in marriage. **2** of or relating to marriage (*married name*; *married life*). ● *n.* (usu. in *pl.*) a married person (*young marrieds*).

■ *adj.* **1** see ATTACHED 2. **2** see *matrimonial* (MATRIMONY).

marron glacé /márron glaássay/ *n.* (*pl.* **marrons glacés** *pronunc.* same) a chestnut preserved in and coated with sugar. [F, = iced chestnut: cf. GLACÉ]

marrow /márrō/ *n.* **1** (in full **vegetable marrow**) **a** a large usu. white-fleshed edible gourd used as food. **b** the plant, *Cucurbita pepo*, yielding this. **2** a soft fatty substance in the cavities of bones, often taken as typifying vitality. **3** the essential part. □ **to the marrow** right through. □□ **marrowless** *adj.* **marrowy** *adj.* [OE *mearg*, *mærg* f. Gmc]

■ **3** see ESSENCE 1.

marrowbone /márrōbōn/ *n.* a bone containing edible marrow.

marrowfat /márrōfat/ *n.* a kind of large pea.

marry[1] /márri/ *v.* (**-ies, -ied**) **1** *tr.* **a** take as one's wife or husband in marriage. **b** (often foll. by *to*) (of a priest etc.) join (persons) in marriage. **c** (of a parent or guardian) give (a son, daughter, etc.) in marriage. **2** *intr.* **a** enter into marriage. **b** (foll. by *into*) become a member of (a family) by marriage. **3** *tr.* **a** unite intimately. **b** correlate (things) as a pair. **c** *Naut.* splice (rope-ends) together without increasing their girth. □ **marry off** find a wife or husband for. [ME f. OF *marier* f. L *maritare* f. *maritus* husband]

■ **1 a** get married to, lead down the aisle *or* to the altar, *archaic* espouse, have *or* take to wife, *colloq.* get hitched *or* spliced to, *usu. formal or literary* wed. **b** join in wedlock *or* (holy) matrimony, *usu. formal or literary* wed. **c** give away, marry off, *archaic* espouse. **2 a** get married, become man and wife, *colloq.* get hitched *or* spliced, tie the knot, *usu. formal or literary* wed. **3 a** fit (together), unite, unify, bond, weld, fuse, put together, couple, join, link; ally, amalgamate, combine. **b** match (up).

marry[2] /márri/ *int. archaic* expressing surprise, asseveration, indignation, etc. [ME, = (the Virgin) *Mary*]

marrying /márri-ing/ *adj.* likely or inclined to marry (*not a marrying man*).

Mars /maarz/ *n.* a reddish planet, fourth in order of distance from the sun and next beyond the earth. [L *Mars Martis* the Roman god of war]

Marsala /maarsaálə/ *n.* a dark sweet fortified dessert wine. [*Marsala* in Sicily, where orig. made]

Marseillaise /maársayáyz, maársəláyz/ *n.* the national anthem of France, first sung in Paris by Marseilles patriots. [F, fem. adj. f. *Marseille* Marseilles]

marsh /maarsh/ *n.* **1** low land flooded in wet weather and usu. watery at all times. **2** (*attrib.*) of or inhabiting marshland. □ **marsh fever** malaria. **marsh gas** methane. **marsh-harrier** a European harrier, *Circus aeruginosus* (see HARRIER[3]). **marsh mallow** a shrubby herbaceous plant, *Althaea officinalis*, the roots of which were formerly used to make marshmallow. **marsh marigold** a golden-flowered ranunculaceous plant, *Caltha palustris*, growing in moist meadows etc.: also called KINGCUP. **marsh tit** a grey tit, *Parus palustris*, inhabiting marshland. **marsh trefoil** the buckbean. □□ **marshy** *adj.* (**marshier, marshiest**). **marshiness** *n.* [OE *mer(i)sc* f. WG]

■ **1** swamp, bog, fen, slough, quag, mire, quagmire.

marshal /maársh'l/ *n.* & *v.* ● *n.* **1** (**Marshal**) **a** a high-ranking officer in the armed forces (*Air Marshal*; *Field Marshal*; *Marshal of France*). **b** a high-ranking officer of state (*Earl Marshal*). **2** an officer arranging ceremonies, controlling procedure at races, etc. **3** *US* the head of a police or fire department. **4** (in full **judge's marshal**) *Brit.* an official accompanying a judge on circuit, with secretarial and social duties. ● *v.* (**marshalled, marshalling**; *US* **marshaled, marshaling**) **1** *tr.* arrange (soldiers, facts, one's thoughts, etc.) in due order. **2** *tr.* (often foll. by *into*, *to*) conduct (a person) ceremoniously. **3** *tr. Heraldry* combine (coats of arms). **4** *intr.* take up positions in due arrangement. □ **marshalling yard** a railway yard in which goods trains etc. are assembled. **Marshal of the Royal Air Force** an officer of the highest rank in the Royal Air Force. □□ **marshaller** *n.* **marshalship** *n.* [ME f. OF *mareschal* f. LL *mariscalcus* f. Gmc, lit. 'horse-servant']

■ *v.* **1** see MUSTER *v.*

marshland /maárshlənd/ *n.* land consisting of marshes.

■ see SWAMP *n.*

marshmallow /maarshmállō/ *n.* a soft sweet made of sugar, albumen, gelatin, etc.

marsupial /maarsóopiəl/ *n.* & *adj.* ● *n.* any mammal of the order Marsupialia, characterized by being born incompletely developed and usu. carried and suckled in a pouch on the mother's belly. ● *adj.* **1** of or belonging to this order. **2** of or like a pouch (*marsupial muscle*). [mod.L *marsupialis* f. L *marsupium* f. Gk *marsupion* pouch, dimin. of *marsipos* purse]

mart /maart/ *n.* **1** a trade centre. **2** an auction-room. **3 a** a market. **b** a market-place. [ME f. obs. Du. *mart*, var. of *markt* MARKET]

martagon /maártəgən/ *n.* a lily, *Lilium martagon*, with small purple turban-like flowers. [F f. Turk. *martagān* a form of turban]

Martello /maartéllō/ *n.* (*pl.* **-os**) (also **Martello tower**) a small circular fort, usu. on the coast to prevent a hostile landing. [alt. f. Cape *Mortella* in Corsica, where such a tower proved difficult to capture in 1794]

marten /maártin/ *n.* any weasel-like carnivore of the genus *Martes*, having valuable fur. [ME f. MDu. *martren* f. OF (*peau*) *martrine* marten (fur) f. *martre* f. WG]

martensite /maártinzīt/ *n.* the chief constituent of hardened steel. [A. *Martens*, German metallurgist d. 1914 + -ITE[1]]

martial /maársh'l/ *adj.* **1** of or appropriate to warfare. **2** warlike, brave; fond of fighting. □ **martial arts** fighting sports such as judo and karate. **martial law** military government, involving the suspension of ordinary law. □□ **martially** *adv.* [ME f. OF *martial* or L *martialis* of the Roman god Mars: see MARS]

■ **1** military, soldierly, naval, fighting, service. **2** warlike, belligerent, bellicose, pugnacious, militant; courageous, brave, valorous, valiant, stalwart, staunch, stout-hearted.

Martian /maársh'n/ *adj.* & *n.* ● *adj.* of the planet Mars. ● *n.* a hypothetical inhabitant of Mars. [ME f. OF *martien* or L *Martianus* f. *Mars*: see MARS]

martin /maártin/ *n.* any of several swallows of the family Hirundinidae, esp. the house-martin and sand-martin. [prob. f. St *Martin*: see MARTINMAS]

martinet /maártinét/ *n.* a strict (esp. military or naval) disciplinarian. □□ **martinettish** *adj.* (also **martinetish**). [J. *Martinet*, 17th-c. French drill-master]

■ see DISCIPLINARIAN.

martingale /maártinggayl/ *n.* **1** a strap, or set of straps, fastened at one end to the noseband of a horse and at the other end to the girth, to prevent rearing etc. **2** *Naut.* a rope for holding down the jib-boom. **3** a gambling system of continually doubling the stakes in the hope of an eventual win that must yield a net profit. [F, of uncert. orig.]

Martini /maarte̍eni/ *n.* **1** *propr.* a type of vermouth. **2** a cocktail made of gin and French vermouth, and sometimes orange bitters etc. [*Martini* & Rossi, Italian firm selling vermouth]

Martinmas /ma̍artinməss/ *n.* St Martin's day, 11 Nov. [ME f. St *Martin*, bishop of Tours in the 4th c., + MASS²]

martlet /ma̍artlit/ *n.* **1** *Heraldry* an imaginary footless bird borne as a charge. **2** *archaic* **a** a swift. **b** a house-martin. [F *martelet* alt. f. *martinet* dimin. f. MARTIN]

martyr /ma̍artər/ *n.* & *v.* ● *n.* **1 a** a person who is put to death for refusing to renounce a faith or belief. **b** a person who suffers for adhering to a principle, cause, etc. **2** (foll. by *to*) a constant sufferer from (an ailment). ● *v.tr.* **1** put to death as a martyr. **2** torment. □ **make a martyr of oneself** accept or pretend to accept unnecessary discomfort etc. [OE *martir* f. eccl.L *martyr* f. Gk *martur*, *martus* -*uros* witness]
■ *n.* **1** see VICTIM 1, 2. ● *v.* see PERSECUTE 1.

martyrdom /ma̍artərdəm/ *n.* **1** the sufferings and death of a martyr. **2** torment. [OE *martyrdōm* (as MARTYR, -DOM)]
■ **1** see PASSION 5a.

martyrize /ma̍artərīz/ *v.tr.* & *refl.* (also **-ise**) make a martyr of. □□ **martyrization** /-zāysh'n/ *n.*

martyrology /ma̍artəro̍lləji/ *n.* (*pl.* **-ies**) **1** a list or register of martyrs. **2** the history of martyrs. □□ **martyrological** /-rəlójik'l/ *adj.* **martyrologist** *n.* [med.L *martyrologium* f. eccl.Gk *marturologion* (as MARTYR, *logos* account)]

martyry /ma̍artəri/ *n.* (*pl.* **-ies**) a shrine or church erected in honour of a martyr. [ME f. med.L *martyrium* f. Gk *marturion* martyrdom (as MARTYR)]

marvel /ma̍arv'l/ *n.* & *v.* ● *n.* **1** a wonderful thing. **2** (often foll. by *of*) a wonderful example (*a marvel of engineering; she's a marvel of patience*). ● *v.intr.* (**marvelled, marvelling**; *US* **marveled, marveling**) *literary* **1** (foll. by *at*, or *that* + clause) feel surprise or wonder. **2** (foll. by *how*, *why*, etc. + clause) wonder. □ **marvel of Peru** a showy garden plant, *Mirabilis jalapa*, with flowers opening in the afternoon. □□ **marveller** *n.* [ME f. OF *merveille*, *merveiller* f. LL *mirabilia* neut. pl. of L *mirabilis* f. *mirari* wonder at: see MIRACLE]
■ *n.* **1** miracle, phenomenon; see also WONDER *n.* 2. **2** wonder, miracle, model, paragon. ● *v.* **1** wonder, be awed *or* amazed *or* agog *or* astonished, gape. **2** see WONDER *v.* 3.

marvellous /ma̍arvələss/ *adj.* (*US* **marvelous**) **1** astonishing. **2** excellent. **3** extremely improbable. □□ **marvellously** *adv.* **marvellousness** *n.* [ME f. OF *merveillos* f. *merveille*: see MARVEL]
■ **1, 3** wonderful, astonishing, amazing, astounding, surprising, remarkable, extraordinary, phenomenal, miraculous, unbelievable, incredible, breathtaking, mind-boggling. **2** glorious, splendid, superb, excellent, spectacular, sensational, unparalleled, far-out, *colloq.* terrific, great, fantastic, fabulous, out of this world, smashing, super, wild, *Brit. colloq.* spot *or* bang on, *sl.* crazy, groovy, wicked.

Marxism /ma̍arksiz'm/ *n.* the political and economic theories of Karl Marx, German political philosopher (d. 1883), predicting the overthrow of capitalism and the eventual attainment of a classless society with the State controlling the means of production. □ **Marxism-Leninism** Marxism as developed by Lenin. □□ **Marxist** *n.* & *adj.* **Marxist-Leninist** *n.* & *adj.*

marzipan /ma̍arzipan/ *n.* & *v.* ● *n.* **1** a paste of ground almonds, sugar, etc., made up into small cakes etc., or used to coat large cakes. **2** a piece of marzipan. ● *v.tr.* (**marzipanned, marzipanning**) cover with or as with marzipan. [G f. It. *marzapane*]

Masai /ma̍assī/ *n.* & *adj.* ● *n.* (*pl.* same or **Masais**) **1 a** a pastoral people of mainly Hamitic stock living in Kenya and Tanzania. **b** a member of this people. **2** the Nilotic language of the Masai. ● *adj.* of or relating to the Masai or their language. [Bantu]

mascara /maska̍arə/ *n.* a cosmetic for darkening the eyelashes. [It. *mascara*, *maschera* MASK]

mascle /másk'l/ *n.* *Heraldry* a lozenge voided, with a central lozenge-shaped aperture. [ME f. AF f. AL *ma(s)cula* f. L MACULA]

mascon /máskon/ *n.* *Astron.* a concentration of dense matter below the moon's surface, producing a gravitational pull. [*mass concentration*]

mascot /máskot/ *n.* a person, animal, or thing that is supposed to bring good luck. [F *mascotte* f. mod. Prov. *mascotto* fem. dimin. of *masco* witch]

masculine /máskyoolin/ *adj.* & *n.* ● *adj.* **1** of or characteristic of men. **2** manly, vigorous. **3** (of a woman) having qualities considered appropriate to a man. **4** *Gram.* of or denoting the gender proper to men's names. ● *n.* *Gram.* the masculine gender; a masculine word. □□ **masculinely** *adv.* **masculineness** *n.* **masculinity** /-línniti/ *n.* [ME f. OF *masculin* -*ine* f. L *masculinus* (as MALE)]
■ *adj.* **2** see MANLY 1. **3** see MANLY 2.

maser /máyzər/ *n.* a device using the stimulated emission of radiation by excited atoms to amplify or generate coherent monochromatic electromagnetic radiation in the microwave range (cf. LASER). [*m*icrowave *a*mplification by the *s*timulated *e*mission of *r*adiation]

mash /mash/ *n.* & *v.* ● *n.* **1** a soft mixture. **2** a mixture of boiled grain, bran, etc., given warm to horses etc. **3** *Brit. colloq.* mashed potatoes (*sausage and mash*). **4** a mixture of malt and hot water used to form wort for brewing. **5** a soft pulp made by crushing, mixing with water, etc. ● *v.tr.* **1** reduce (potatoes etc.) to a uniform mass by crushing. **2** crush or pound to a pulp. **3** mix (malt) with hot water to form wort. □□ **masher** *n.* [OE *māsc* f. WG, perh. rel. to MIX]
■ *n.* **1, 5** see PULP *n.* 2. ● *v.* **1, 2** see CRUSH *v.* 1.

mashie /máshi/ *n.* *Golf* an iron formerly used for lofting or for medium distances. [perh. f. F *massue* club]

mask /maask/ *n.* & *v.* ● *n.* **1** a covering for all or part of the face: **a** worn as a disguise, or to appear grotesque and amuse or terrify. **b** made of wire, gauze, etc., and worn for protection (e.g. by a fencer) or by a surgeon to prevent infection of a patient. **c** worn to conceal the face at balls etc. and usu. made of velvet or silk. **2** a respirator used to filter inhaled air or to supply gas for inhalation. **3** a likeness of a person's face, esp. one made by taking a mould from the face (*death-mask*). **4** a disguise or pretence (*throw off the mask*). **5** a hollow model of a human head worn by ancient Greek and Roman actors. **6** *Photog.* a screen used to exclude part of an image. **7** the face or head of an animal, esp. a fox. **8** = *face-pack*. **9** *archaic* a masked person. ● *v.tr.* **1** cover (the face etc.) with a mask. **2** disguise or conceal (a taste, one's feelings, etc.). **3** protect from a process. **4** *Mil.* **a** conceal (a battery etc.) from the enemy's view. **b** hinder (an army etc.) from action by observing with adequate force. **c** hinder (a friendly force) by standing in its line of fire. □ **masking tape** adhesive tape used in painting to cover areas on which paint is not wanted. □□ **masker** *n.* [F *masque* f. It. *maschera* f. Arab. *masḵara* buffoon f. *saḵira* to ridicule]
■ *n.* **1 c** domino. **4** disguise, guise, camouflage, show, semblance, pretence, cover, cover-up, false colours, concealment, cloak, façade, veil. ● *v.* **1** see VEIL *v.* **2** disguise, camouflage, cover (up), conceal, hide, obscure, veil, screen, shroud.

masked /maaskt/ *adj.* wearing or disguised with a mask. □ **masked ball** a ball at which masks are worn.
■ see INCOGNITO *adj.* & *adv.* □ **masked ball** masquerade, fancy dress ball.

maskinonge /máskinonj, -nónji/ *n.* a large N. American pike, *Esox masquinongy*, esp. in the Great Lakes. [ult. f. Ojibwa, = great fish]

masochism /mássəkiz'm/ *n.* **1** a form of (esp. sexual) perversion characterized by gratification derived from one's own pain or humiliation (cf. SADISM). **2** *colloq.* the enjoyment of what appears to be painful or tiresome. □□ **masochist** *n.* **masochistic** /-kístik/ *adj.* **masochistically** /-kístikəli/

adv. [L. von Sacher-*Masoch*, Austrian novelist d. 1895, who described cases of it]

mason /máys'n/ *n.* & *v.* ● *n.* **1** a person who builds with stone. **2** (**Mason**) a Freemason. ● *v.tr.* build or strengthen with masonry. □ **mason's mark** a device carved on stone by the mason who dressed it. [ME f. OF *masson, maçonner*, ONF *machun*, prob. ult. f. Gmc]

Mason–Dixon line /máys'ndíks'n/ *n.* (in the US) the boundary between Maryland and Pennsylvania, taken as the northern limit of the slave-owning States before the abolition of slavery. [C. *Mason* & J. *Dixon*, 18th-c. English astronomers who surveyed it]

Masonic /məsónnik/ *adj.* of or relating to Freemasons.

masonry /máysənri/ *n.* **1 a** the work of a mason. **b** stonework. **2** (**Masonry**) Freemasonry. [ME f. OF *maçonerie* (as MASON)]

Masorah /mássərə/ *n.* (also **Massorah**) a body of traditional information and comment on the text of the Hebrew Bible. [Heb. *māsōreṯ*, perh. = bond]

Masorete /mássəreet/ *n.* (also **Massorete**) a Jewish scholar contributing to the Masorah. □□ **Masoretic** /-réttik/ *adj.* [F *Massoret* & mod.L *Massoreta*, orig. a misuse of Heb. (see MASORAH), assim. to -ETE]

masque /maask/ *n.* **1** a dramatic and musical entertainment esp. of the 16th and 17th c., orig. of pantomime, later with metrical dialogue. **2** a dramatic composition for this. □□ **masquer** *n.* [var. of MASK]

masquerade /maáskəráyd, más-/ *n.* & *v.* ● *n.* **1** a false show or pretence. **2** a masked ball. ● *v.intr.* (often foll. by *as*) appear in disguise, assume a false appearance. □□ **masquerader** *n.* [F *mascarade* f. Sp. *mascarada* f. *máscara* mask]

■ *n.* **1** disguise, deception, pose, pretence, dissimulation, bluff, subterfuge, fakery, imposture, play-acting, act, (false) front, cover-up, camouflage, *colloq.* put-on. ● *v.* (*masquerade as*) pretend to be, pass oneself off as, impersonate, simulate, pose as.

Mass. *abbr.* Massachusetts.

mass[1] /mass/ *n.*, *v.*, & *adj.* ● *n.* **1** a coherent body of matter of indefinite shape. **2** a dense aggregation of objects (*a mass of fibres*). **3** (in *sing.* or *pl.*; foll. by *of*) a large number or amount. **4** (usu. foll. by *of*) an unbroken expanse (of colour etc.). **5** (prec. by *a*; foll. by *of*) covered or abounding in (*was a mass of cuts and bruises*). **6** a main portion (of a painting etc.) as perceived by the eye. **7** (prec. by *the*) **a** the majority. **b** (in *pl.*) the ordinary people. **8** *Physics* the quantity of matter a body contains. **9** (*attrib.*) relating to, done by, or affecting large numbers of people or things; large-scale (*mass audience*; *mass action*; *mass murder*). ● *v.tr.* & *intr.* **1** assemble into a mass or as one body (*massed bands*). **2** *Mil.* (with ref. to troops) concentrate or be concentrated. □ **centre of mass** a point representing the mean position of matter in a body or system. **in the mass** in the aggregate. **law of mass action** the principle that the rate of a chemical reaction is proportional to the masses of the reacting substances. **mass defect** the difference between the mass of an isotope and its mass number. **mass energy** a body's ability to do work according to its mass. **mass media** = MEDIA[1] 2. **mass noun** *Gram.* a noun that is not countable and cannot be used with the indefinite article or in the plural (e.g. *bread*). **mass number** the total number of protons and neutrons in a nucleus. **mass observation** *Brit.* the study and recording of the social habits and opinions of ordinary people. **mass-produce** produce by mass production. **mass production** the production of large quantities of a standardized article by a standardized mechanical process. **mass spectrograph** an apparatus separating isotopes, molecules, and molecular fragments according to mass by their passage in ionic form through electric and magnetic fields. **mass spectrometer** a device similar to a mass spectrograph but employing electrical detection. **mass spectrum** the distribution of ions shown by the use of a mass spectrograph or mass spectrometer. □□ **massless** *adj.* [ME f. OF *masse, masser* f. L *massa* f. Gk *maza* barley-cake: perh. rel. to *massō* knead]

■ *n.* **1, 2** pile, heap, mountain, load, stack, mound, bunch, bundle, lot, batch, quantity, hoard, store, collection, accumulation, aggregation, conglomeration, agglomeration, congeries, assortment, miscellany, assemblage; block, concretion, chunk, lump, hunk, nugget. **3** abundance, quantity, profusion, multitude, horde, host, mob, crowd, throng, drove, herd, swarm, legion, score, number, *colloq.* bunch, ton, mountain, barrel, pile, load, bags, oodles, lots, oceans, *US colloq.* scads, slew. **4** sea, pool, flood, sheet; see also EXPANSE. **5** (*be a mass of*) see ABOUND 2. **6, 7a** majority, best *or* better *or* greater part, bulk, body, preponderance, lion's share. **7 b** (*the masses*) the common people, the plebeians, (the) *hoi polloi*, the lower class(es), *colloq. usu. derog.* the plebs, *derog.* the (common) herd, *esp. derog.* the proletariat. ● *v.* amass, pile *or* heap up, gather, aggregate, accumulate, collect, assemble, congregate, group, cluster, concentrate; meet, get *or* come together, forgather, throng, convene, flock together; rally, marshal, muster, mobilize.

mass[2] /mass, maass/ *n.* (often **Mass**) **1** the Eucharist, esp. in the Roman Catholic Church. **2** a celebration of this. **3** the liturgy used in the mass. **4** a musical setting of parts of this. □ **high mass** mass with incense, music, and usu. the assistance of a deacon and subdeacon. **low mass** mass with no music and a minimum of ceremony. [OE *mæsse* f. eccl.L *missa* f. L *mittere miss-* dismiss, perh. f. the concluding dismissal *Ite, missa est* Go, it is the dismissal]

massacre /mássəkər/ *n.* & *v.* ● *n.* **1** a general slaughter (of persons, occasionally of animals). **2** an utter defeat or destruction. ● *v.tr.* **1** make a massacre of. **2** murder (esp. a large number of people) cruelly or violently. [OF, of unkn. orig.]

■ *n.* **1** slaughter, carnage, annihilation, blood bath, killing, execution, extermination, butchery, (mass) murder, slaying, liquidation, pogrom, holocaust, genocide. **2** see DEFEAT *n.*, DESTRUCTION 1. ● *v.* **1** see DEFEAT *v.* 1, *wipe out* 1a. **2** slaughter, annihilate, kill, execute, exterminate, butcher, murder, liquidate, destroy, eliminate, obliterate, eradicate, put to the sword, mow down, *disp.* decimate, *literary or joc.* slay, *sl.* bump off.

massage /mássaazh, -saaj/ *n.* & *v.* ● *n.* **1** the rubbing, kneading, etc., of muscles and joints of the body with the hands, to stimulate their action, cure strains, etc. **2** an instance of this. ● *v.tr.* **1** apply massage to. **2** manipulate (statistics) to give an acceptable result. □ **massage parlour 1** an establishment providing massage. **2** *euphem.* a brothel. □□ **massager** *n.* [F f. *masser* treat with massage, perh. f. Port. *amassar* knead, f. *massa* dough: see MASS[1]]

■ *n.* rub, rubbing, rub-down, manipulation, kneading. ● *v.* **1** rub (down), manipulate, knead. **2** manipulate, doctor, falsify, *sl.* fiddle. □ **massage parlour 2** see BROTHEL.

massasauga /mássəsáwgə/ *n.* a small N. American rattlesnake, *Sistrurus catenatus.* [irreg. f. *Mississagi* River, Ontario]

massé /mássay/ *n. Billiards* a stroke made with the cue held nearly vertical. [F, past part. of *masser* make such a stroke (as MACE[1])]

masseter /maseétər/ *n.* either of two chewing-muscles which run from the temporal bone to the lower jaw. [Gk *masētēr* f. *masaomai* chew]

masseur /masőr/ *n.* (*fem.* **masseuse** /masőz/) a person who provides massage professionally. [F f. *masser*: see MASSAGE]

massicot /mássikət/ *n.* yellow lead monoxide, used as a pigment. [F, perh. rel. to It. *marzacotto* unguent prob. f. Arab. *mashaḳūnyā*]

massif /másseef, maseéf/ *n.* a compact group of mountain heights. [F *massif* used as noun: see MASSIVE]

massive /mássiv/ *adj.* **1** large and heavy or solid. **2** (of the features, head, etc.) relatively large; of solid build. **3** exceptionally large (*took a massive overdose*). **4** substantial, impressive (*a massive reputation*). **5** *Mineral.* not visibly crystalline. **6** *Geol.* without structural divisions. □□ **massively** *adv.* **massiveness** *n.* [ME f. F *massif -ive* f. OF *massiz* ult. f. L *massa* MASS¹]

■ **1–3** big, large, oversized, huge, bulky, enormous, immense, gigantic, towering, mammoth, colossal, titanic, vast, tremendous, prodigious, mountainous, gargantuan, Cyclopean, elephantine, monster, monstrous, mighty, weighty, ponderous, strapping, *colloq.* jumbo, whacking, hulking, *sl.* walloping, whopping, humongous, *Brit. sl.* ginormous. **4** see IMPRESSIVE 1.

Massorah var. of MASORAH.

Massorete var. of MASORETE.

mast¹ /maast/ *n.* & *v.* ● *n.* **1** a long upright post of timber, iron, etc., set up on a ship's keel, esp. to support sails. **2** a post or lattice-work upright for supporting a radio or television aerial. **3** a flag-pole (*half-mast*). **4** (in full **mooring-mast**) a strong steel tower to the top of which an airship can be moored. ● *v.tr.* furnish (a ship) with masts. □ **before the mast** serving as an ordinary seaman (quartered in the forecastle). □□ **masted** *adj.* (also in *comb.*). **master** *n.* (also in *comb.*). [OE *mæst* f. WG]

■ *n.* **1–3** see POLE¹ *n.* 1.

mast² /maast/ *n.* the fruit of the beech, oak, chestnut, and other forest-trees, esp. as food for pigs. [OE *mæst* f. WG, prob. rel. to MEAT]

mastaba /mástəbə/ *n.* **1** *Archaeol.* an ancient Egyptian tomb with sloping sides and a flat roof. **2** a bench, usu. of stone, attached to a house in Islamic countries. [Arab. *maṣṭabah*]

mastectomy /mastéktəmi/ *n.* (*pl.* **-ies**) *Surgery* the amputation of a breast. [Gk *mastos* breast + -ECTOMY]

master /maástər/ *n.*, *adj.*, & *v.* ● *n.* **1 a** a person having control of persons or things. **b** an employer. **c** a male head of a household (*master of the house*). **d** the owner of a dog, horse, etc. **e** the owner of a slave. **f** *Naut.* the captain of a merchant ship. **g** *Hunting* the person in control of a pack of hounds etc. **2** a male teacher or tutor, esp. a schoolmaster. **3 a** the head of a college, school, etc. **b** the presiding officer of a livery company, Masonic lodge, etc. **4** a person who has or gets the upper hand (*we shall see which of us is master*). **5** a person skilled in a particular trade and able to teach others (often *attrib.*: *master carpenter*). **6** a holder of a university degree orig. giving authority to teach in the university (*Master of Arts*; *Master of Science*). **7 a** a revered teacher in philosophy etc. **b** (**the Master**) Christ. **8** a great artist. **9** *Chess* etc. a player of proved ability at international level. **10** an original version (e.g. of a film or gramophone record) from which a series of copies can be made. **11** (**Master**) **a** a title prefixed to the name of a boy not old enough to be called *Mr* (*Master T. Jones*; *Master Tom*). **b** *archaic* a title for a man of high rank, learning, etc. **12** (in England and Wales) an official of the Supreme Court. **13** a machine or device directly controlling another (cf. SLAVE). **14** (**Master**) a courtesy title of the eldest son of a Scottish viscount or baron (*the Master of Falkland*). ● *adj.* **1** commanding, superior (*a master spirit*). **2** main, principal (*master bedroom*). **3** controlling others (*master plan*). ● *v.tr.* **1** overcome, defeat. **2** reduce to subjection. **3** acquire complete knowledge of (a subject) or facility in using (an instrument etc.). **4** rule as a master. □ **be master of 1** have at one's disposal. **2** know how to control. **be one's own master** be independent or free to do as one wishes. **make oneself master of** acquire a thorough knowledge of or facility in using. **Master Aircrew** an RAF rank equivalent to warrant-officer. **master-at-arms** (*pl.* **masters-at-arms**) the chief police officer on a man-of-war or a merchant ship. **master-class** a class given by a person of distinguished skill, esp. in music. **master-hand 1** a person having commanding power or great skill. **2** the action of such a person. **master-key** a key that opens several locks, each of which also has its own key. **master mariner 1** the captain of a merchant ship. **2** a seaman certified competent to be captain. **master mason 1** a skilled mason, or one in business on his or her own account. **2** a fully qualified Freemason, who has passed the third degree. **Master of Ceremonies** see CEREMONY. **Master of the Rolls** (in England and Wales) a judge who presides over the Court of Appeal and was formerly in charge of the Public Record Office. **master-stroke** an outstandingly skilful act of policy etc. **master-switch** a switch controlling the supply of electricity etc. to an entire system. **master touch** a masterly manner of dealing with something. **master-work** a masterpiece. □□ **masterdom** *n.* **masterhood** *n.* **masterless** *adj.* [OE *mægester* (later also f. OF *maistre*) f. L *magister*, prob. rel. to *magis* more]

■ *n.* **1** owner, head, chief, leader, chieftain, commander, lord, governor, director, controller, employer, manager, overseer, supervisor, superintendent, taskmaster, slave-driver, principal, sovereign, monarch, ruler, kingpin, skipper, Pooh-Bah, *US* high muck-a-muck, *colloq.* boss, bigwig, top dog, *Brit. colloq.* gaffer, *sl.* (big) cheese, *US sl.* big wheel, Mr Big, honcho. **2** teacher, tutor, schoolmaster, instructor, guide, leader, guru, swami. **3 a** see HEAD *n.* 6a. **4** chief, leader, *colloq.* boss. **5** expert, authority, craftsman, adept, maestro, mastermind, past master, old hand, virtuoso, genius, ace, wizard, *esp. Brit. colloq.* dab hand, *US colloq.* maven, *US sl.* crackerjack. **7 b** (**the Master**) Christ, Jesus; see also LORD *n.* 4. ● *adj.* **1** commanding, superior, controlling. **2** biggest, principal, chief; see also MAIN¹ *adj.* 1. **3** commanding, superior, controlling, prime, basic, chief, overall. ● *v.* **1, 2** control, overcome, repress, suppress, subdue, subjugate, bridle, check, quell, get the better of, defeat, conquer. **3** learn, grasp, become expert in, know a thing inside out, know, understand. **4** see CONTROL *v.* 1, 2. □ **be master of 2** see CONTROL *v.* 3. **be one's own master** be one's own man, *colloq.* do one's own thing. **master-hand 1** see EXPERT *n.* **master-work** see MASTERPIECE.

masterful /maástərfōōl/ *adj.* **1** imperious, domineering. **2** masterly. ¶ Normally used of a person, whereas *masterly* is used of achievements, abilities, etc. □□ **masterfully** *adv.* **masterfulness** *n.*

■ **1** authoritarian, dictatorial, tyrannical, despotic, arbitrary, domineering, imperious, overbearing, arrogant, dominating, autocratic, high-handed, magisterial, overweening, self-willed. **2** masterly, adept, expert, excellent, superior, superb, adroit, exquisite, superlative, supreme, consummate, accomplished, peerless, matchless, first-rate, proficient, dexterous, deft, skilful, skilled, *colloq.* crack.

masterly /maástərli/ *adj.* worthy of a master; very skilful (*a masterly piece of work*). □□ **masterliness** *n.*

■ see SKILFUL. □□ **masterliness** see FACILITY 1, 2.

mastermind /maástərmīnd/ *n.* & *v.* ● *n.* **1 a** a person with an outstanding intellect. **b** such an intellect. **2** the person directing an intricate operation. ● *v.tr.* plan and direct (a scheme or enterprise).

■ *n.* genius, mind, intellect, brain; planner, contriver, conceiver, creator, architect. ● *v.* plan, devise, conceive, think up, engineer, design, generate, create, manage, direct, organize, develop, work up *or* out.

masterpiece /maástərpeess/ *n.* **1** an outstanding piece of artistry or workmanship. **2** a person's best work.

■ **1** master-work, *magnum opus*, *tour de force*, jewel, work of art, *pièce de résistance*. **2** *chef-d'œuvre*, master-work, *magnum opus*, *tour de force*, jewel, *pièce de résistance*.

mastership /maástərship/ *n.* **1** the position or function of a master, esp. a schoolmaster. **2** dominion, control.

mastersinger /maástərsingər/ *n.* = MEISTERSINGER.

mastery /maástəri/ *n.* **1** dominion, sway. **2** masterly skill. **3** (often foll. by *of*) comprehensive knowledge or use of a subject or instrument. **4** (prec. by *the*) the upper hand. [ME f. OF *maistrie* (as MASTER)]

■ **1, 4** see SWAY *n.* 1. **2** see SKILL. **3** see COMMAND *n.* 2.

masthead /maást-hed/ *n.* & *v.* ● *n.* **1** the highest part of a ship's mast, esp. that of a lower mast as a place of observation or punishment. **2** the title of a newspaper etc. at the head of the front or editorial page. • *v.tr.* **1** send (a sailor) to the masthead. **2** raise (a sail) to its position on the mast.

mastic /mástik/ *n.* **1** a gum or resin exuded from the bark of the mastic tree, used in making varnish. **2** (in full **mastic tree**) the evergreen tree, *Pistacia lentiscus*, yielding this. **3** a waterproof filler and sealant used in building. **4** a liquor flavoured with mastic gum. [ME f. OF f. LL *mastichum* f. L *mastiche* f. Gk *mastikhē*, perh. f. *mastikhaō* (see MASTICATE) with ref. to its use as chewing-gum]

masticate /mástikayt/ *v.tr.* grind or chew (food) with one's teeth. □□ **mastication** /-káysh'n/ *n.* **masticator** *n.* **masticatory** *adj.* [LL *masticare masticat-* f. Gk *mastikhaō* gnash the teeth]

■ see CHEW *v.*

mastiff /mástif, maás-/ *n.* **1** a dog of a large strong breed with drooping ears and pendulous lips. **2** this breed of dog. [ME ult. f. OF *mastin* ult. f. L *mansuetus* tame; see MANSUETUDE]

mastitis /mastítiss/ *n.* an inflammation of the mammary gland (the breast or udder). [Gk *mastos* breast + -ITIS]

mastodon /mástədon/ *n.* a large extinct mammal of the genus *Mammut*, resembling the elephant but having nipple-shaped tubercles on the crowns of its molar teeth. □□ **mastodontic** /-dóntik/ *adj.* [mod.L f. Gk *mastos* breast + *odous odontos* tooth]

mastoid /mástoyd/ *adj.* & *n.* • *adj.* shaped like a woman's breast. • *n.* **1** = *mastoid process.* **2** *colloq.* mastoiditis. □ **mastoid process** a conical prominence on the temporal bone behind the ear, to which muscles are attached. [F *mastoïde* or mod.L *mastoides* f. Gk *mastoeidēs* f. *mastos* breast]

mastoiditis /mástoydítiss/ *n.* inflammation of the mastoid process.

masturbate /mástərbayt/ *v.intr.* & *tr.* arouse oneself sexually or cause (another person) to be aroused by manual stimulation of the genitals. □□ **masturbation** /-báysh'n/ *n.* **masturbator** *n.* **masturbatory** *adj.* [L *masturbari masturbat-*]

■ □□ **masturbation** onanism, self-gratification, *Psychol.* auto-erotism, *archaic* self-abuse.

mat[1] /mat/ *n.* & *v.* • *n.* **1** a piece of coarse material for wiping shoes on, esp. a doormat. **2** a piece of cork, rubber, plastic, etc., to protect a surface from the heat or moisture of an object placed on it. **3** a piece of resilient material for landing on in gymnastics, wrestling, etc. **4** a piece of coarse fabric of plaited rushes, straw, etc., for lying on, packing furniture, etc. **5** a small rug. • *v.* (**matted, matting**) **1 a** *tr.* (esp. as **matted** *adj.*) entangle in a thick mass (*matted hair*). **b** *intr.* become matted. **2** *tr.* cover or furnish with mats. □ **on the mat** *sl.* being reprimanded (orig. in the army, on the orderly-room mat before the commanding officer). [OE *m(e)att(e)* f. WG f. LL *matta*]

mat[2] var. of MATT.

mat[3] /mat/ *n.* = MATRIX 1. [abbr.]

matador /máttədor/ *n.* **1** a bullfighter whose task is to kill the bull. **2** a principal card in ombre, quadrille, etc. **3** a domino game in which the piece played must make a total of seven. [Sp. f. *matar* kill f. Pers. *māt* dead]

Mata Hari /maátaa haári/ *n.* a beautiful and seductive female spy. [name taken by M. G. Zelle, d. 1917, f. Malay *mata* eye + *hari* day]

match[1] /mach/ *n.* & *v.* • *n.* **1** a contest or game of skill etc. in which persons or teams compete against each other. **2 a** a person able to contend with another as an equal (*meet one's match; be more than a match for*). **b** a person equal to another in some quality (*we shall never see his match*). **c** a person or thing exactly like or corresponding to another. **3** a marriage. **4** a person viewed in regard to his or her eligibility for marriage, esp. as to rank or fortune (*an excellent match*). • *v.* **1 a** *tr.* be equal to or harmonious with; correspond to in some essential respect (*the curtains match the wallpaper*). **b** *intr.* (often foll. by *with*) correspond; harmonize (*his socks do not match; does the ribbon match with your hat?*). **c** (as **matching** *adj.*) having correspondence in some essential respect (*matching curtains*). **2** *tr.* (foll. by *against, with*) place (a person etc.) in conflict, contest, or competition with (another). **3** *tr.* find material etc. that matches (another) (*can you match this silk?*). **4** *tr.* find a person or thing suitable for another (*matching unemployed workers with vacant posts*). **5** *tr.* prove to be a match for. **6** *tr. Electronics* produce or have an adjustment of (circuits) such that maximum power is transmitted between them. **7** *tr.* (usu. foll. by *with*) *archaic* join (a person) with another in marriage. □ **make a match** bring about a marriage. **match play** *Golf* play in which the score is reckoned by counting the holes won by each side (cf. *stroke play*). **match point 1** *Tennis* etc. **a** the state of a game when one side needs only one more point to win the match. **b** this point. **2** *Bridge* a unit of scoring in matches and tournaments. **to match** corresponding in some essential respect with what has been mentioned (*yellow dress with gloves to match*). **well-matched** fit to contend with each other, live together, etc., on equal terms. □□ **matchable** *adj.* [OE *gemæcca* mate, companion, f. Gmc]

■ *n.* **1** contest, competition, game, meet, tourney, tournament, bout, duel, trial. **2 a, b** equal, equivalent, like, peer, fellow, mate. **c** parallel, replica, copy, double, twin, look-alike, facsimile, counterpart. **3** marriage, betrothal, alliance, combination, compact, contract, partnership, union, affiliation. **4** catch, prospect, candidate. • *v.* **1 a, b** fit, suit; accord, agree, harmonize, go (together), coordinate, blend, correspond. **c** (**matching**) corresponding, comparable, equivalent, complementary; see also IDENTICAL 1. **2** (*match against* or *with*) pit *or* set *or* put against, play off against. **4** match up, join, marry, unite, link, combine, put together, pair up *or* off, conjoin. **5** equal, be equivalent to, resemble, compare with, measure up to, compete with, vie with, rival. **7** marry, join in wedlock *or* (holy) matrimony, *usu. formal or literary* wed. □ **well-matched** well-suited, compatible.

match[2] /mach/ *n.* **1** a short thin piece of wood, wax, etc., tipped with a composition that can be ignited by friction. **2** a piece of wick, cord, etc., designed to burn at a uniform rate, for firing a cannon etc. [ME f. OF *mesche, meiche*, perh. f. L *myxa* lamp-nozzle]

matchboard /máchbord/ *n.* a board with a tongue cut along one edge and a groove along another, so as to fit with similar boards.

matchbox /máchboks/ *n.* a box for holding matches.

matchet var. of MACHETE.

matchless /máchliss/ *adj.* without an equal, incomparable. □□ **matchlessly** *adv.*

■ unique, original, peerless, unequalled, without equal, *hors concours*, inimitable, unmatched, incomparable, unparalleled, beyond compare.

matchlock /máchlok/ *n. hist.* **1** an old type of gun with a lock in which a match was placed for igniting the powder. **2** such a lock.

matchmaker /máchmaykər/ *n.* a person fond of scheming to bring about marriages. □□ **matchmaking** *n.*

matchstick /máchstik/ *n.* the stem of a match.

matchwood /máchwŏŏd/ *n.* **1** wood suitable for matches. **2** minute splinters. □ **make matchwood of** smash utterly.

mate[1] /mayt/ *n.* & *v.* • *n.* **1** a friend or fellow worker. **2** *colloq.* a general form of address, esp. to another man. **3 a** each of a pair, esp. of birds. **b** *colloq.* a partner in marriage. **c** (in *comb.*) a fellow member or joint occupant of (*team-mate; room-mate*). **4** *Naut.* an officer on a merchant ship subordinate to the master. **5** an assistant to a skilled worker (*plumber's mate*). • *v.* (often foll. by *with*) **1 a** *tr.* bring (animals or birds) together for breeding. **b** *intr.* (of animals or birds) come together for breeding. **2 a** *tr.* join (persons) in marriage. **b** *intr.* (of persons) be joined in marriage. **3** *intr. Mech.* fit well. □□ **mateless** *adj.* [ME f. MLG *mate* f. *gemate* messmate f. WG, rel. to MEAT]

■ *n.* **1** companion, associate, colleague, fellow worker, co-worker, comrade, crony, ally, friend, *alter ego*, second self, *US* cohort, *colloq.* chum, pal, *esp. US colloq.* buddy, *sl.* mucker. **3 a** fellow, twin, counterpart. **b** spouse, partner, helpmate, consort, husband, wife, *colloq.* better half, hubby, old man *or* lady *or* woman, *rhyming sl.* trouble and strife, china. **5** see ASSISTANT. ● *v.* **1 a** pair (up), match (up), marry, join, unite, couple, link (up), *usu. formal or literary* wed. **b** breed, couple, copulate, pair (up). **2 a** marry, join in wedlock *or* (holy) matrimony, *usu. formal or literary* wed. **3** mesh, engage, dovetail, match (up), fit (together), synchronize, join.

mate[2] /mayt/ *n.* & *v.tr. Chess* = CHECKMATE. □ **fool's mate** a series of moves in which the first player is mated at the second player's second move. **scholar's mate** a series of moves in which the second player is mated at the first player's fourth move. [ME f. F *mat(er)*: see CHECKMATE]

maté /máttay/ *n.* **1** an infusion of the leaves of a S. American shrub, *Ilex paraguayensis*. **2** this shrub, or its leaves. **3** a vessel in which these leaves are infused. [Sp. *mate* f. Quechua *mati*]

matelot /mátlō/ *n.* (also **matlow, matlo**) *Brit. sl.* a sailor. [F *matelot*]

matelote /máttəlōt/ *n.* a dish of fish etc. with a sauce of wine and onions. [F (as MATELOT)]

mater /máytər/ *n. Brit. sl.* mother. ¶ Now only in jocular or affected use. [L]

materfamilias /máytərfəmílliass/ *n.* the woman head of a family or household (cf. PATERFAMILIAS). [L f. *mater* mother + *familia* FAMILY]

material /mətéeriəl/ *n.* & *adj.* ● *n.* **1** the matter from which a thing is made. **2** cloth, fabric. **3** (in *pl.*) things needed for an activity (*building materials*; *cleaning materials*; *writing materials*). **4** a person or thing of a specified kind or suitable for a purpose (*officer material*). **5** (in *sing.* or *pl.*) information etc. to be used in writing a book etc. (*experimental material*; *materials for a biography*). **6** (in *sing.* or *pl.*, often foll. by *of*) the elements or constituent parts of a substance. ● *adj.* **1** of matter; corporeal. **2** concerned with bodily comfort etc. (*material well-being*). **3** (of conduct, points of view, etc.) not spiritual. **4** (often foll. by *to*) important, essential, relevant (*at the material time*). **5** concerned with the matter, not the form, of reasoning. □□ **materiality** /-riálliti/ *n.* [ME f. OF *materiel*, *-al*, f. LL *materialis* f. L (as MATTER)]

■ *n.* **1** substance, fabric; matter, stuff. **2** cloth, fabric, textile, stuff. **3** (*materials*) constituents, elements, components. **5** information, data, facts, statistics, figures, documents, documentation, papers, notes, resources. **6** see ELEMENT 1. ● *adj.* **1** physical, tangible, concrete, solid, real, substantial, palpable, corporeal, bodily, *archaic* substantive. **2** bodily, physical, corporal. **3** worldly, earthly, mundane, temporal, secular, lay, materialistic. **4** consequential, important, significant, essential, relevant.

materialism /mətéeriəliz'm/ *n.* **1** a tendency to prefer material possessions and physical comfort to spiritual values. **2** *Philos.* **a** the opinion that nothing exists but matter and its movements and modifications. **b** the doctrine that consciousness and will are wholly due to material agency. **3** *Art* a tendency to lay stress on the material aspect of objects. □□ **materialist** *n.* **materialistic** /-lístik/ *adj.* **materialistically** /-lístikəli/ *adv.*

■ □□ **materialistic** greedy, acquisitive, selfish, commercial, sybaritic, *colloq. usu. derog.* yuppie.

materialize /mətéeriəlīz/ *v.* (also **-ise**) **1** *intr.* become actual fact. **2 a** *tr.* cause (a spirit) to appear in bodily form. **b** *intr.* (of a spirit) appear in this way. **3** *intr. colloq.* appear or be present when expected. **4** *tr.* represent or express in material form. **5** *tr.* make materialistic. □□ **materialization** /-záysh'n/ *n.*

■ **1** happen, come to pass, take place, occur, become manifest *or* real, be realized, be actualized. **3** appear, turn up; take shape *or* form, form, emerge.

materially /mətéeriəli/ *adv.* **1** substantially, considerably. **2** in respect of matter.

■ **1** substantially, palpably, significantly, seriously, essentially, basically, considerably, greatly, much.

materia medica /mateéeriə méddikə/ *n.* **1** the remedial substances used in the practice of medicine. **2** the study of the origin and properties of these substances. [mod.L, transl. Gk *hulē iatrikē* healing material]

matériel /mətéeri-él/ *n.* available means, esp. materials and equipment in warfare (opp. PERSONNEL). [F (as MATERIAL)]

maternal /mətérn'l/ *adj.* **1** of or like a mother. **2** motherly. **3** related through the mother (*maternal uncle*). **4** of the mother in pregnancy and childbirth. □□ **maternalism** *n.* **maternalistic** /-lístik/ *adj.* **maternally** *adv.* [ME f. OF *maternel* or L *maternus* f. *mater* mother]

■ **1, 2** motherly, warm, nurturing, caring, understanding, affectionate, tender, kind, kindly, devoted, fond, doting; maternalistic; matriarchal.

maternity /mətérniti/ *n.* **1** motherhood. **2** motherliness. **3** (*attrib.*) **a** for women during and just after childbirth (*maternity hospital*; *maternity leave*). **b** suitable for a pregnant woman (*maternity dress*; *maternity wear*). [F *maternité* f. med.L *maternitas -tatis* f. L *maternus* f. *mater* mother]

■ **1** motherhood, parenthood.

mateship /máytship/ *n. Austral.* companionship, fellowship.

■ see COMPANIONSHIP.

matey /máyti/ *adj.* & *n.* (also **maty**) ● *adj.* (**matier, matiest**) (often foll. by *with*) sociable; familiar and friendly. ● *n. Brit.* (*pl.* **-eys**) *colloq.* (usu. as a form of address) mate, companion. □□ **mateyness** *n.* (also **matiness**). **matily** *adv.*

■ *adj.* see FRIENDLY *adj.* 2.

math /math/ *n. US colloq.* mathematics (cf. MATHS). [abbr.]

mathematical /máthimáttik'l/ *adj.* **1** of or relating to mathematics. **2** (of a proof etc.) rigorously precise. □ **mathematical induction** = INDUCTION 3b. **mathematical tables** tables of logarithms and trigonometric values etc. □□ **mathematically** *adv.* [F *mathématique* or L *mathematicus* f. Gk *mathēmatikos* f. *mathēma -matos* science f. *manthanō* learn]

■ **1** arithmetical. **2** precise, exact, rigorous.

mathematics /máthimáttiks/ *n.pl.* **1** (also treated as *sing.*) the abstract science of number, quantity, and space studied in its own right (**pure mathematics**), or as applied to other disciplines such as physics, engineering, etc. (**applied mathematics**). **2** (as *pl.*) the use of mathematics in calculation etc. □□ **mathematician** /-mətish'n/ *n.* [prob. f. F *mathématiques* pl. f. L *mathematica* f. Gk *mathēmatika*: see MATHEMATICAL]

maths /maths/ *n. Brit. colloq.* mathematics (cf. MATH). [abbr.]

Matilda /mətíldə/ *n. Austral. sl.* a bushman's bundle; a swag. □ **waltz** (or **walk**) **Matilda** carry a swag. [the name *Matilda*]

matinée /máttinay/ *n.* (*US* **matinee**) an afternoon performance in the theatre, cinema, etc. □ **matinée coat** (or **jacket**) a baby's short coat. **matinée idol** a handsome actor admired chiefly by women. [F, = what occupies a morning f. *matin* morning (as MATINS)]

matins /máttinz/ *n.* (also **mattins**) (as *sing* or *pl.*) **1 a** a service of morning prayer in the Church of England. **b** the office of one of the canonical hours of prayer, properly a night office, but also recited with lauds at daybreak or on the previous evening. **2** (also **matin**) *poet.* the morning song of birds. [ME f. OF *matines* f. eccl.L *matutinas*, accus. fem. pl. adj. f. L *matutinus* of the morning f. *Matuta* dawn-goddess]

matlo (also **matlow**) var. of MATELOT.

matrass /mátrəss/ *n. hist.* a long-necked glass vessel with a round or oval body, used for distilling etc. [F *matras*, of uncert. orig.]

matriarch /máytriaark/ *n.* a woman who is the head of a family or tribe. □□ **matriarchal** /-aárk'l/ *adj.* [L *mater* mother, on the false analogy of PATRIARCH]

▪ see MOTHER *n.* 1.

matriarchy /máytriaarki/ *n.* (*pl.* **-ies**) a form of social organization in which the mother is the head of the family and descent is reckoned through the female line.

matric /mətrík/ *n. Brit. colloq.* matriculation. [abbr.]

matrices *pl.* of MATRIX.

matricide /máytrisīd/ *n.* **1** the killing of one's mother. **2** a person who does this. ▫▫ **matricidal** *adj.* [L *matricida*, *matricidium* f. *mater matris* mother]

matriculate /mətríkyoolayt/ *v.* **1** *intr.* be enrolled at a college or university. **2** *tr.* admit (a student) to membership of a college or university. ▫▫ **matriculatory** *adj.* [med.L *matriculare matriculat-* enrol f. LL *matricula* register, dimin. of L MATRIX]

matriculation /mətríkyooláysh'n/ *n.* **1** the act or an instance of matriculating. **2** an examination to qualify for this.

matrilineal /mátrilínniəl/ *adj.* of or based on kinship with the mother or the female line. ▫▫ **matrilineally** *adv.* [L *mater matris* mother + LINEAL]

matrilocal /mátrilṓk'l/ *adj.* of or denoting a custom in marriage where the husband goes to live with the wife's community. [L *mater matris* mother + LOCAL]

matrimony /mátriməni/ *n.* (*pl.* **-ies**) **1** the rite of marriage. **2** the state of being married. **3 a** a card-game. **b** the combination of king and queen of trumps in some card-games. ▫▫ **matrimonial** /-mṓniəl/ *adj.* **matrimonially** /-mṓniəli/ *adv.* [ME f. AF *matrimonie*, OF *matremoi(g)ne* f. L *matrimonium* f. *mater matris* mother]

▪ **1** marriage (service), wedding service. **2** marriage, wedlock. ▫▫ **matrimonial** marital, marriage, wedding, conjugal, nuptial; married, wedded, connubial.

matrix /máytriks/ *n.* (*pl.* **matrices** /-triseez/ or **matrixes**) **1** a mould in which a thing is cast or shaped, such as a gramophone record, printing type, etc. **2 a** an environment or substance in which a thing is developed. **b** a womb. **3** a mass of fine-grained rock in which gems, fossils, etc., are embedded. **4** *Math.* a rectangular array of elements in rows and columns that is treated as a single element. **5** *Biol.* the substance between cells or in which structures are embedded. **6** *Computing* a gridlike array of interconnected circuit elements. ▫ **matrix printer** = *dot matrix printer* (see DOT[1]). [L, = breeding-female, womb, register f. *mater matris* mother]

▪ **1** see MOULD[1] *n.* 1, 5.

matron /máytrən/ *n.* **1** a married woman, esp. a dignified and sober one. **2** a woman managing the domestic arrangements of a school etc. **3** *Brit.* a woman in charge of the nursing in a hospital. ¶ Now usu. called *senior nursing officer*. ▫ **matron of honour** a married woman attending the bride at a wedding. ▫▫ **matronhood** *n.* [ME f. OF *matrone* f. L *matrona* f. *mater matris* mother]

matronly /máytrənli/ *adj.* like or characteristic of a matron, esp. in respect of staidness or portliness.

Matt. *abbr.* Matthew (esp. in the New Testament).

matt /mat/ *adj.*, *n.*, & *v.* (also **mat**) ● *adj.* (of a colour, surface, etc.) dull, without lustre. ● *n.* **1** a border of dull gold round a framed picture. **2** (in full **matt paint**) paint formulated to give a dull flat finish (cf. GLOSS[1]). **3** the appearance of unburnished gold. ● *v.tr.* (**matted, matting**) **1** make (gilding etc.) dull. **2** frost (glass). [F *mat*, *mater*, identical with *mat* MATE[2]]

▪ *adj.* see FLAT[1] *adj.* 8a.

matte[1] /mat/ *n.* an impure product of the smelting of sulphide ores, esp. those of copper or nickel. [F]

matte[2] /mat/ *n. Cinematog.* a mask to obscure part of an image and allow another image to be superimposed, giving a combined effect. [F]

matter /máttər/ *n.* & *v.* ● *n.* **1 a** physical substance in general, as distinct from mind and spirit. **b** that which has mass and occupies space. **2** a particular substance (*colouring matter*). **3** (prec. by *the*; often foll. by *with*) the thing that is amiss (*what is the matter?*; *there is something the matter with him*). **4** material for thought or expression. **5 a** the substance of a book, speech, etc., as distinct from its manner or form. **b** *Logic* the particular content of a proposition, as distinct from its form. **6** a thing or things of a specified kind (*printed matter*; *reading matter*). **7** an affair or situation being considered, esp. in a specified way (*a serious matter*; *a matter for concern*; *the matter of your overdraft*). **8** *Physiol.* **a** any substance in or discharged from the body (*faecal matter*; *grey matter*). **b** pus. **9** (foll. by *of*, *for*) what is or may be a good reason for (complaint, regret, etc.). **10** *Printing* the body of a printed work, as type or as printed sheets. ● *v.intr.* **1** (often foll. by *to*) be of importance; have significance (*it does not matter to me when it happened*). **2** secrete or discharge pus. ▫ **as a matter of fact** in reality (esp. to correct a falsehood or misunderstanding). **for that matter** (or **for the matter of that**) **1** as far as that is concerned. **2** and indeed also. **in the matter of** as regards. **a matter of 1** approximately (*for a matter of 40 years*). **2** a thing that relates to, depends on, or is determined by (*a matter of habit*; *only a matter of time before they agree*). **a matter of course** see COURSE. **a matter of fact 1** what belongs to the sphere of fact as distinct from opinion etc. **2** *Law* the part of a judicial inquiry concerned with the truth of alleged facts (see also MATTER-OF-FACT). **a matter of form** a mere routine. **a matter of law** *Law* the part of a judicial inquiry concerned with the interpretation of the law. **a matter of record** see RECORD. **no matter 1** (foll. by *when*, *how*, etc.) regardless of (*will do it no matter what the consequences*). **2** it is of no importance. **what is the matter with** surely there is no objection to. **what matter?** that need not worry us. [ME f. AF *mater(i)e*, OF *matiere* f. L *materia* timber, substance, subject of discourse]

▪ *n.* **1, 2** material, substance, stuff. **3** problem, difficulty, trouble; complication, worry. **4, 5** content, essentials, pith, theme, argument, purport, implication; signification, meaning, import. **7** situation, issue, question, affair, business, subject, topic, condition, thing, fact, concern; occurrence, episode, incident, event, occasion, proceeding. **8** see DISCHARGE *n.* 5. ● *v.* **1** be important *or* of importance, count, be of consequence, make a difference. ▫ **as a matter of fact** see *in fact* 1 (FACT). **in the matter of** see CONCERNING. **a matter of 1** see *approximately* (APPROXIMATE). **2** see QUESTION *n.* 3, 5. **a matter of fact 1** reality, actuality, certainty, truth. **a matter of form** see FORMALITY 1. **what matter?** *colloq.* so what?, so?

matter-of-fact /máttərəfákt/ *adj.* (see also MATTER). **1** unimaginative, prosaic. **2** unemotional. ▫▫ **matter-of-factly** *adv.* **matter-of-factness** *n.*

▪ **1** straightforward, direct, forthright, factual, unvarnished, unembellished, unadorned; sober, unimaginative, unartistic, prosaic, unpoetic, dry, dull, boring, tiresome, flat, mundane, lifeless, featureless, colourless. **2** see DISINTERESTED 1, HONEST *adj.* 2.

matting /mátting/ *n.* **1** fabric of hemp, bast, grass, etc., for mats (*coconut matting*). **2** in senses of MAT[1] *v.*

mattins var. of MATINS.

mattock /máttək/ *n.* an agricultural tool shaped like a pickaxe, with an adze and a chisel edge as the ends of the head. [OE *mattuc*, of unkn. orig.]

mattoid /máttoyd/ *n.* a person of erratic mind, a mixture of genius and fool. [It. *mattoide* f. *matto* insane]

mattress /mátriss/ *n.* a fabric case stuffed with soft, firm, or springy material, or a similar case filled with air or water, used on or as a bed. [ME f. OF *materas* f. It. *materasso* f. Arab. *almaṭrah* the place, the cushion f. *ṭaraḥa* throw]

maturate /mátyoorayt/ *v.intr. Med.* (of a boil etc.) come to maturation. [L *maturatus* (as MATURE *v.*)]

maturation /mátyooráysh'n/ *n.* **1 a** the act or an instance of maturing; the state of being matured. **b** the ripening of fruit. **2** *Med.* **a** the formation of purulent matter. **b** the causing of this. ▫▫ **maturative** /mətyóorətiv/ *adj.* [ME f. F *maturation* or med.L *maturatio* f. L (as MATURE *v.*)]

■ **1 a** see DEVELOPMENT 1.

mature /mətyŏŏr/ *adj.* & *v.* ● *adj.* (**maturer, maturest**) **1** with fully developed powers of body and mind, adult. **2** complete in natural development, ripe. **3** (of thought, intentions, etc.) duly careful and adequate. **4** (of a bill etc.) due for payment. ● *v.* **1 a** *tr.* & *intr.* develop fully. **b** *tr.* & *intr.* ripen. **c** *intr.* come to maturity. **2** *tr.* perfect (a plan etc.). **3** *intr.* (of a bill etc.) become due for payment. □ **mature student** an adult student who is older than most students. □□ **maturely** *adv.* **matureness** *n.* **maturity** *n.* [ME f. L *maturus* timely, early]

■ *adj.* **1** adult, grown (up), full-grown, fully grown, of age, full-fledged, fully fledged, developed, experienced, knowledgeable, sophisticated. **2** ripe, ready, ripened, mellow, aged, seasoned. **3** see MEASURED 2. ● *v.* **1 a, c** age, develop; grow up, come of age, *Med.* maturate. **b** mellow, age, season, come to maturity; ripen, bring to maturity. **2** develop, perfect, refine, polish, bring to fruition. □□ **maturity** adulthood, majority; ripeness, readiness, mellowness; perfection, completion, fullness, consummation.

matutinal /mátyootī́n'l, mətyŏŏtin'l/ *adj.* **1** of or occurring in the morning. **2** early. [LL *matutinalis* f. L *matutinus*: see MATINS]

maty var. of MATEY.

matzo /maátsō/ *n.* (*pl.* **-os** or **matzoth** /-sōt/) **1** a wafer of unleavened bread for the Passover. **2** such bread collectively. [Yiddish f. Heb. *maṣṣāh*]

maud /mawd/ *n.* **1** a Scots shepherd's grey striped plaid. **2** a travelling-rug like this. [18th c.: orig. unkn.]

maudlin /máwdlin/ *adj.* & *n.* ● *adj.* weakly or tearfully sentimental, esp. in a tearful and effusive stage of drunkenness. ● *n.* weak or mawkish sentiment. [ME f. OF *Madeleine* f. eccl.L *Magdalena* MAGDALEN, with ref. to pictures of Mary Magdalen weeping]

■ *adj.* sentimental, (over-)emotional, mawkish, tearful, weepy, mushy, romantic, *colloq.* soupy, slushy, *Brit. colloq.* soppy, *formal* lachrymose.

maul /mawl/ *v.* & *n.* ● *v.tr.* **1** beat and bruise. **2** handle roughly or carelessly. **3** damage by criticism. ● *n.* **1** *Rugby Football* a loose scrum with the ball off the ground. **2** a brawl. **3** a special heavy hammer, commonly of wood, esp. for driving piles. □□ **mauler** *n.* [ME f. OF *mail* f. L *malleus* hammer]

■ *v.* **1** see *knock about*. ● *n.* **2** see BRAWL *n.*

maulstick /máwlstik/ *n.* (also **mahlstick**) a light stick with a padded leather ball at one end, held by a painter in one hand to support the other hand. [Du. *maalstok* f. *malen* to paint + *stok* stick]

maunder /máwndər/ *v.intr.* **1** talk in a dreamy or rambling manner. **2** move or act listlessly or idly. [perh. f. obs. *maunder* beggar, to beg]

Maundy /máwndi/ *n.* (in the UK) the distribution of money on the Thursday before Easter (see below). □ **Maundy money** specially minted silver coins distributed by the British sovereign on Maundy Thursday. **Maundy Thursday** the Thursday before Easter. [ME f. OF *mandé* f. L *mandatum* MANDATE, commandment (see John 13:34)]

mausoleum /máwsəleéəm/ *n.* a large and grand tomb. [L f. Gk *Mausōleion* f. *Mausōlos* Mausolus king of Caria (4th c. BC), to whose tomb the name was orig. applied]

■ see TOMB 3.

mauve /mōv/ *adj.* & *n.* ● *adj.* pale purple. ● *n.* **1** this colour. **2** a bright but delicate pale purple dye from coal-tar aniline. □□ **mauvish** *adj.* [F, lit. = mallow, f. L *malva*]

maven /máyv'n/ *n.* *US colloq.* an expert or connoisseur. [Heb. *mēḇīn*]

maverick /mávvərik/ *n.* **1** *US* an unbranded calf or yearling. **2** an unorthodox or independent-minded person. [S. A. *Maverick*, Texas engineer and rancher d. 1870, who did not brand his cattle]

■ **2** see *individualist* (INDIVIDUALISM).

mavis /máyviss/ *n. poet.* or *dial.* a song thrush. [ME f. OF *mauvis*, of uncert. orig.]

maw /maw/ *n.* **1 a** the stomach of an animal. **b** the jaws or throat of a voracious animal. **2** *colloq.* the stomach of a greedy person. [OE *maga* f. Gmc]

mawkish /máwkish/ *adj.* **1** sentimental in a feeble or sickly way. **2** having a faint sickly flavour. □□ **mawkishly** *adv.* **mawkishness** *n.* [obs. *mawk* maggot f. ON *mathkr* f. Gmc]

■ **1** see SENTIMENTAL.

max. *abbr.* maximum. □ **to the max** *US sl.* to the utmost, to the fullest extent.

maxi /máksi/ *n.* (*pl.* **maxis**) *colloq.* a maxi-coat, -skirt, etc. [abbr.]

maxi- /máksi/ *comb. form* very large or long (*maxi-coat*). [abbr. of MAXIMUM: cf. MINI-]

maxilla /maksíllə/ *n.* (*pl.* **maxillae** /-lee/) **1** the jaw or jawbone, esp. the upper jaw in most vertebrates. **2** the mouth-part of many arthropods used in chewing. □□ **maxillary** *adj.* [L, = jaw]

maxim /máksim/ *n.* a general truth or rule of conduct expressed in a sentence. [ME f. F *maxime* or med.L *maxima* (*propositio*), fem. adj. (as MAXIMUM)]

■ saying, proverb, axiom, aphorism, adage, byword, saw, apophthegm, epigram, motto, slogan; cliché, truism.

maxima *pl.* of MAXIMUM.

maximal /máksim'l/ *adj.* being or relating to a maximum; the greatest possible in size, duration, etc. □□ **maximally** *adv.*

maximalist /máksiməlist/ *n.* a person who rejects compromise and expects a full response to (esp. political) demands. [MAXIMAL, after Russ. *maksimalist*]

maximize /máksimīz/ *v.tr.* (also **-ise**) increase or enhance to the utmost. □□ **maximization** /-záysh'n/ *n.* **maximizer** *n.* [L *maximus*: see MAXIMUM]

■ increase, broaden, improve, magnify, augment, add to, expand, build up, enlarge; enhance, embroider, embellish, elaborate; inflate, overplay, overdo, overstate, exaggerate, oversell, make much of, overstress.

maximum /máksiməm/ *n.* & *adj.* ● *n.* (*pl.* **maxima** /-mə/) the highest possible or attainable amount. ● *adj.* that is a maximum. [mod.L, neut. of L *maximus*, superl. of *magnus* great]

■ *n.* utmost, uttermost, greatest, most, highest, extreme, extremity, limit, peak, pinnacle, crest, top, summit, zenith, apex, acme, apogee, climax. ● *adj.* maximal, greatest, most, utmost, uttermost, superlative, supreme, paramount, extreme, highest, top, topmost, climactic, crowning.

maxwell /mákswel/ *n.* a unit of magnetic flux in the c.g.s. system, equal to that induced through one square centimetre by a perpendicular magnetic field of one gauss. [J. C. *Maxwell*, Brit. physicist d. 1879]

May /may/ *n.* **1** the fifth month of the year. **2** (**may**) the hawthorn or its blossom. **3** *poet.* bloom, prime. □ **may-apple** an American herbaceous plant, *Podophyllum peltatum*, bearing a yellow egg-shaped fruit in May. **May-bug** a cockchafer. **May Day** 1 May esp. as a festival with dancing, or as an international holiday in honour of workers. **May queen** a girl chosen to preside over celebrations on May Day. **Queen of the May** = *May queen.* [ME f. OF *mai* f. L *Maius* (*mensis*) (month) of the goddess *Maia*]

may /may/ *v.aux.* (*3rd sing. present* **may**; *past* **might** /mīt/) **1** (often foll. by *well* for emphasis) expressing possibility (*it may be true*; *I may have been wrong*; *you may well lose your way*). **2** expressing permission (*you may not go*; *may I come in?*). ¶ Both *can* and *may* are used to express permission; in more formal contexts *may* is usual since *can* also denotes capability (*can I move?* = am I physically able to move?; *may I move* = am I allowed to move?). **3** expressing a wish (*may he live to regret it*). **4** expressing uncertainty or irony in questions (*who may you be?*; *who are you, may I ask?*). **5** in purpose clauses and after *wish*, *fear*, etc. (*take such measures as may avert disaster*; *hope he may succeed*). □ **be that as it may** (or **that is as may be**) that may or may not be so (implying that there are other factors) (*be that as* *it may, I still want to go*). [OE *mæg* f. Gmc, rel. to MAIN[1], MIGHT[2]]

Maya /maáyə/ *n.* **1** (*pl.* same or **Mayas**) a member of an ancient Indian people of Central America. **2** the language of this people. □□ **Mayan** *adj.* & *n.* [native name]

maya /maáyə/ *n. Hinduism* a marvel or illusion, esp. in the phenomenal universe. [Skr. *māyā*]

maybe /máybee/ *adv.* perhaps, possibly. [ME f. *it may be*]
■ see PERHAPS.

mayday /máyday/ *n.* an international radio distress-signal used esp. by ships and aircraft. [repr. pronunc. of F *m'aidez* help me]

mayest /máyist/ *archaic* = MAYST.

mayflower /máyflowr/ *n.* any of various flowers that bloom in May, esp. the trailing arbutus, *Epigaea repens*.

mayfly /máyflī/ *n.* (*pl.* **-flies**) **1** any insect of the order Ephemeroptera, living briefly in spring in the adult stage. **2** an imitation mayfly used by anglers.

mayhap /máyháp/ *adv. archaic* perhaps, possibly. [ME f. *it may hap*]
■ see PERHAPS.

mayhem /máyhem/ *n.* **1** violent or damaging action. **2** rowdy confusion, chaos. **3** *hist.* the crime of maiming a person so as to render him or her partly or wholly defenceless. [AF *mahem*, OF *mayhem* (as MAIM)]
■ **1** violence, havoc, destruction, devastation. **2** commotion, confusion, disorder, chaos.

maying /máying/ *n.* & *adj.* participation in May Day festivities. [ME f. MAY]

mayn't /máyənt/ *contr.* may not.

mayonnaise /máyənáyz/ *n.* **1** a thick creamy dressing made of egg-yolks, oil, vinegar, etc. **2** a (usu. specified) dish dressed with this (*chicken mayonnaise*). [F, perh. f. *mahonnais* -*aise* of Port *Mahon* on Minorca]

mayor /mair/ *n.* **1** the head of the municipal corporation of a city or borough. **2** (in England, Wales, and N. Ireland) the head of a district council with the status of a borough. □□ **mayoral** *adj.* **mayorship** *n.* [ME f. OF *maire* f. L (as MAJOR)]

mayoralty /máirəlti/ *n.* (*pl.* **-ies**) **1** the office of mayor. **2** a mayor's period of office. [ME f. OF *mairalté* (as MAYOR)]

mayoress /máiriss/ *n.* **1** a woman holding the office of mayor. **2** the wife of a mayor. **3** a woman fulfilling the ceremonial duties of a mayor's wife.

maypole /máypōl/ *n.* a pole painted and decked with flowers and ribbons, for dancing round on May Day.

mayst /mayst/ *archaic 2nd sing. present* of MAY.

mayweed /máyweed/ *n.* the stinking camomile, *Anthemis cotula*. [earlier *maidwede* f. obs. *maithe(n)* f. OE *magothe*, *mægtha* + WEED]

mazard /mázzərd/ *n.* (also **mazzard**) **1** the wild sweet cherry, *Prunus avium*, of Europe. **2** *archaic* a head or face. [alt. of MAZER]

mazarine /mázzəreén/ *n.* & *adj.* a rich deep blue. [17th c., perh. f. the name of Cardinal *Mazarin*, French statesman d. 1661, or Duchesse de *Mazarin*, French noblewoman d. 1699]

maze /mayz/ *n.* & *v.* ● *n.* **1** a network of paths and hedges designed as a puzzle for those who try to penetrate it. **2** a complex network of paths or passages; a labyrinth. **3** confusion, a confused mass, etc. ● *v.tr.* (esp. as **mazed** *adj.*) bewilder, confuse. □□ **mazy** *adj.* (**mazier, maziest**). [ME, orig. as *mased* (adj.): rel. to AMAZE]
■ *n.* **2** labyrinth, complex, network, warren. **3** see TANGLE[1] *n.* ● *v.* (**mazed**) see *confused* (CONFUSE 4b).

mazer /máyzər/ *n. hist.* a hardwood drinking-bowl, usu. silver-mounted. [ME f. OF *masere* f. Gmc]

mazurka /məzúrkə/ *n.* **1** a usu. lively Polish dance in triple time. **2** the music for this. [F *mazurka* or G *Masurka*, f. Pol. *mazurka* woman of the province *Mazovia*]

mazzard var. of MAZARD.

MB *abbr.* **1** Bachelor of Medicine. **2** *Computing* megabyte. [sense 1 f. L *Medicinae Baccalaureus*]

MBA *abbr.* Master of Business Administration.

MBE *abbr.* Member of the Order of the British Empire.

MC *abbr.* **1** Master of Ceremonies. **2** (in the UK) Military Cross. **3** (in the US) Member of Congress. **4** music cassette (of pre-recorded audiotape).
■ **1** see HOST[2] *n.* 5.

Mc *abbr.* megacycle(s).

MCC *abbr.* Marylebone Cricket Club.

McCarthyism, McCoy see at MACC-.

M.Ch. *abbr.* (also **M.Chir.**) Master of Surgery. [L *Magister Chirurgiae*]

mCi *abbr.* millicurie(s).

McNaughten see at MACN-.

M.Com. *abbr.* Master of Commerce.

MCP *abbr. colloq.* male chauvinist pig.

MCR *abbr. Brit.* Middle Common Room.

Mc/s *abbr.* megacycles per second.

MD *abbr.* **1** Doctor of Medicine. **2** Managing Director. **3** *US* Maryland (in official postal use). **4** mentally deficient. [sense 1 f. L *Medicinae Doctor*]
■ **1** see DOCTOR *n.* 1a. **2** see HEAD *n.* 6a.

Md *symb. Chem.* the element mendelevium.

Md. *abbr.* Maryland.

MDMA *abbr.* methylenedioxymethamphetamine, an amphetamine-based drug that causes euphoric and hallucinatory effects, originally produced as an appetite suppressant (see ECSTASY 3).

MDT *abbr. US* Mountain Daylight Time.

ME *abbr.* **1** *US* Maine (in official postal use). **2** myalgic encephalomyelitis, an obscure disease with symptoms like those of influenza and prolonged periods of tiredness and depression.

Me. *abbr.* **1** Maine. **2** *Maître* (title of a French advocate).

me[1] /mee, mi/ *pron.* **1** *objective case* of I[2] (*he saw me*). **2** *colloq.* = I[2] (*it's me all right; is taller than me*). **3** *US colloq.* myself, to or for myself (*I got me a gun*). **4** *colloq.* used in exclamations (*ah me!; dear me!; silly me!*). □ **me and mine** me and my relatives. [OE *me*, *mē* accus. & dative of I[2] f. Gmc]

me[2] /mee/ *n.* (also **mi**) *Mus.* **1** (in tonic sol-fa) the third note of a major scale. **2** the note E in the fixed-doh system. [ME f. L *mira*: see GAMUT]

mea culpa /mé-ee kúlpə, máyə kŏŏlpə/ *n.* & *int.* ● *n.* an acknowledgement of one's fault or error. ● *int.* expressing such an acknowledgement. [L, = by my fault]

mead[1] /meed/ *n.* an alcoholic drink of fermented honey and water. [OE *me(o)du* f. Gmc]

mead[2] /meed/ *n. poet.* or *archaic* = MEADOW. [OE *mǣd* f. Gmc, rel. to MOW[1]]

meadow /méddō/ *n.* **1** a piece of grassland, esp. one used for hay. **2** a piece of low well-watered ground, esp. near a river. □ **meadow brown** a common brown butterfly, *Maniola jurtina*. **meadow-grass** a perennial creeping grass, *Poa pratensis*. **meadow lark** *US* any songbird of the genus *Sturnella*, esp. the yellow-breasted *S. magna* of N. America. **meadow pipit** a common pipit, *Anthus pratensis*, native to Europe, Asia, and Africa. **meadow rue** any ranunculaceous plant of the genus *Thalictrum*, esp. *T. flavum* with small yellow flowers. **meadow saffron** a perennial plant, *Colchicum autumnale*, abundant in meadows, with lilac flowers: also called *autumn crocus*. □□ **meadowy** *adj.* [OE *mǣdwe*, oblique case of *mǣd*: see MEAD[2]]
■ **1** field, pasture, *poet.* lea, *poet. or archaic* mead.

meadowsweet /méddōsweet/ *n.* **1** a rosaceous plant, *Filipendula ulmaria*, common in meadows and damp places, with creamy-white fragrant flowers. **2** any of several rosaceous plants of the genus *Spiraea*, native to N. America.

meagre /méegər/ *adj.* (*US* **meager**) **1** lacking in amount or quality (*a meagre salary*). **2** (of literary composition, ideas, etc.) lacking fullness, unsatisfying. **3** (of a person or animal) lean, thin. □□ **meagrely** *adv.* **meagreness** *n.* [ME f. AF *megre*, OF *maigre* f. L *macer*]

■ **1** scanty, poor, paltry, inadequate, skimpy, scrimpy, sparse, insufficient, bare, puny, trifling, niggardly, exiguous, *colloq.* piddling, measly, *Brit. colloq.* pathetic. **2** spare, simplified, oversimplified, bare, inadequate, deficient, undetailed, unsatisfying. **3** spare, skinny, scrawny, bony, emaciated, gaunt, thin, lean, bare-boned, (half-)starved, underfed, undernourished.

meal[1] /meel/ *n.* **1** an occasion when food is eaten. **2** the food eaten on one occasion. □ **make a meal of 1** treat (a task etc.) too laboriously or fussily. **2** consume as a meal. **meals on wheels** *Brit.* a service by which meals are delivered to old people, invalids, etc. **meal-ticket 1** a ticket entitling one to a meal, esp. at a specified place with reduced cost. **2** a person or thing that is a source of food or income. [OE *mǣl* mark, fixed time, meal f. Gmc]

■ spread, collation, *formal* repast, *literary* refection; dinner, supper, breakfast, lunch, tea, brunch, *formal* luncheon; food, victuals, nourishment. □ **make a meal of 1** overdo, overplay, carry to extremes, carry too far, do to excess.

meal[2] /meel/ *n.* **1** the edible part of any grain or pulse (usu. other than wheat) ground to powder. **2** *Sc.* oatmeal. **3** *US* maize flour. **4** any powdery substance made by grinding. □ **meal-beetle** an insect, *Tenebrio molitor*, infesting granaries etc. **meal-worm** the larva of the meal-beetle. [OE *melu* f. Gmc]

mealie /méeli/ *n.* (also **mielie**) *S.Afr.* **1** (usu. in *pl.*) maize. **2** a corn-cob. [Afrik. *mielie* f. Port. *milho* maize, millet f. L *milium*]

mealtime /méeltīm/ *n.* any of the usual times of eating.

mealy /méeli/ *adj.* (**mealier, mealiest**) **1 a** of or like meal; soft and powdery. **b** containing meal. **2** (of a complexion) pale. **3** (of a horse) spotty. **4** (in full **mealy-mouthed**) not outspoken; ingratiating; afraid to use plain expressions. □ **mealy bug** any insect of the genus *Pseudococcus*, infesting vines etc., whose body is covered with white powder. □□ **mealiness** *n.*

■ **2** see PALE[1] *adj.* 1. **3** see SPOTTY 1. **4** mincing, reticent, reluctant, hesitant, equivocal, ambiguous, indirect, euphemistic, roundabout, vague, circumlocutory, periphrastic; see also OBSEQUIOUS.

mean[1] /meen/ *v.tr.* (*past* and *past part.* **meant** /ment/) **1 a** (often foll. by *to* + infin.) have as one's purpose or intention; have in mind (*they really mean mischief*; *I didn't mean to break it*). **b** (foll. by *by*) have as a motive in explanation (*what do you mean by that?*). **2** (often in *passive*) design or destine for a purpose (*mean it to be used*; *mean it for a stopgap*; *is meant to be a gift*). **3** intend to convey or indicate or refer to (a particular thing or notion) (*I mean we cannot go*; *I mean Richmond in Surrey*). **4** entail, involve (*it means catching the early train*). **5** (often foll. by *that* + clause) portend, signify (*this means trouble*; *your refusal means that we must look elsewhere*). **6** (of a word) have as its explanation in the same language or its equivalent in another language. **7** (foll. by *to*) be of some specified importance to (a person), esp. as a source of benefit or object of affection etc. (*that means a lot to me*). □ **mean business** be in earnest. **mean it** not be joking or exaggerating. **mean to say** really admit (usu. in *interrog.*: *do you mean to say you have lost it?*). **mean well** (often foll. by *to, towards, by*) have good intentions. [OE *mænan* f. WG, rel. to MIND]

■ **1, 2** intend, design, purpose, plan, aim, have in mind, contemplate, have in view; want, wish, expect, hope. **4, 6** denote, signify, connote, indicate, designate, represent, betoken, signal; imply, entail, involve. **5** portend, foretell, foreshadow, promise, presage, augur, herald; show, signify.

mean[2] /meen/ *adj.* **1** niggardly; not generous or liberal. **2** (of an action) ignoble, small-minded. **3** (of a person's capacity, understanding, etc.) inferior, poor. **4** (of housing) not imposing in appearance; shabby. **5 a** malicious, ill-tempered. **b** *US* vicious or aggressive in behaviour. **6** *colloq.* skilful, formidable (*is a mean fighter*). **7** *colloq.* ashamed (*feel mean*). □ **no mean** a very good (*that is no mean achievement*). **mean White** = *poor White*. □□ **meanly** *adv.* **meanness** *n.* [OE *mǣne, gemǣne* f. Gmc]

■ **1** stingy, miserly, tight, close, near, parsimonious, penurious, stinting, niggardly, penny-pinching, tight-fisted, close-fisted, uncharitable, ungenerous, *Austral.* hungry, *Brit. colloq.* mingy. **2** ignoble, small-minded, low, base, abject; meanspirited, small, petty, near. **3** inferior, poor, low. **4** inferior, poor, lowly, abject, modest, humble, run-down, sorry, miserable, scruffy, seedy, shabby, squalid, mangy, wretched, sordid, dismal, dreary. **5** unkind, malicious, cruel, unaccommodating, disobliging; cantankerous, churlish, nasty, hostile, ill-tempered, bad-tempered, sour, unpleasant. **6** formidable, excellent, wonderful, marvellous, great, exceptional, effective, skilful, skilled, *esp. US sl.* bad. **7** see ASHAMED 1.

mean[3] /meen/ *n.* & *adj.* ● *n.* **1** a condition, quality, virtue, or course of action equally removed from two opposite (usu. unsatisfactory) extremes. **2** *Math.* **a** the term or one of the terms midway between the first and last terms of an arithmetical or geometrical etc. progression (*2 and 8 have the arithmetic mean 5 and the geometric mean 4*). **b** the quotient of the sum of several quantities and their number, the average. ● *adj.* **1** (of a quantity) equally far from two extremes. **2** calculated as a mean. □ **mean free path** the average distance travelled by a gas molecule etc. between collisions. **mean sea level** the sea level halfway between the mean levels of high and low water. **mean sun** an imaginary sun moving in the celestial equator at the mean rate of the real sun, used in calculating solar time. **mean time** the time based on the movement of the mean sun. [ME f. AF *meen* f. OF *meien, moien* f. L *medianus* MEDIAN]

■ *n.* average, middle, norm, (happy) medium; balance. ● *adj.* middle, centre, intermediate, medial, medium, median, average, middling.

meander /miándər/ *v.* & *n.* ● *v.intr.* **1** wander at random. **2** (of a stream) wind about. ● *n.* **1 a** a curve in a winding river etc. **b** a crooked or winding path or passage. **2** a circuitous journey. **3** an ornamental pattern of lines winding in and out; a fret. [L *maeander* f. Gk *Maiandros*, the name of a winding river in Phrygia]

■ *v.* wander, ramble, zigzag, snake, wind, twist, turn; stroll, amble, rove, *colloq.* swan around *or* about, *sl.* mosey. ● *n.* **1** turn, turning, twist, curve, loop, bend, coil, zigzag, convolution; oxbow; tortuosity, flexuosity, anfractuosity.

meandrine /miándrin/ *adj.* full of windings (esp. of corals of the genus *Meandrina*, with a surface like a human brain). [MEANDER + -INE[1]]

meanie /méeni/ *n.* (also **meany**) (*pl.* **-ies**) *colloq.* a mean, niggardly, or small-minded person.

meaning /méening/ *n.* & *adj.* ● *n.* **1** what is meant by a word, action, idea, etc. **2** significance. **3** importance. ● *adj.* expressive, significant (*a meaning glance*). □□ **meaningly** *adv.*

■ *n.* **1, 2** sense, import, content, signification, denotation, message, substance, gist; purport, implication, drift, spirit, connotation, significance, intention; interpretation, explanation. **3** see IMPORTANCE 2. ● *adj.* see EXPRESSIVE 1.

meaningful /méeningfōōl/ *adj.* **1** full of meaning; significant. **2** *Logic* able to be interpreted. □□ **meaningfully** *adv.* **meaningfulness** *n.*

■ **1** significant, important, consequential, serious, sober, deep, substantial, pithy, telling, weighty, valid, relevant, *archaic* substantive; suggestive, pregnant, tell-tale, revealing, pointed, sententious, expressive, eloquent.

meaningless /méeningliss/ *adj.* having no meaning or significance. □□ **meaninglessly** *adv.* **meaninglessness** *n.*

■ empty, hollow, vacuous, insubstantial, unsubstantial, absurd, silly, foolish, fatuous, asinine, ridiculous, preposterous, nonsensical; trivial, nugatory, trifling, puny, paltry, worthless, not worth anything *or* a straw *or* a rap, valueless, inconsequential, unimportant, of no moment, vain, pointless, senseless, purposeless, undirected, irrelevant, insignificant.

means /meenz/ *n.pl.* **1** (often treated as *sing.*) that by which a result is brought about (*a means of quick travel*). **2 a** money resources (*live beyond one's means*). **b** wealth (*a man of means*). □ **by all means** (or **all manner of means**) **1** certainly. **2** in every possible way. **3** at any cost. **by means of** by the agency or instrumentality of (a thing or action). **by no means** (or **no manner of means**) not at all; certainly not. **means test** an official inquiry to establish need before financial assistance from public funds is given. [pl. of MEAN³]

▪ **1** instrument, agency, method, process, technique, mode, manner, way(s), approach, course, procedure, avenue, medium, vehicle. **2** resources, funds, money, cash, wealth, capital, finances, backing, support, *colloq.* wherewithal. □ **by all means** (or **all manner of means**) **1** absolutely, definitely, certainly, surely, assuredly, of course, positively. **3** in any event, at all events, no matter what, without fail, at any cost, at all costs, in any case. **by means of** by dint of, via, through, by way of, with the help *or* aid of, employing, using, utilizing. **by no means** (or **no manner of means**) in no way, not at all, definitely *or* absolutely *or* certainly not, on no account, not conceivably, not in one's wildest dreams, not by any stretch of the imagination, *colloq.* no way.

meant *past* and *past part.* of MEAN¹.

meantime /meéntīm/ *adv.* & *n.* ● *adv.* = MEANWHILE. ¶ Less usual than *meanwhile.* ● *n.* the intervening period (esp. *in the meantime*). [MEAN³ + TIME]

▪ *adv.* see MEANWHILE *adv.* ● *n.* see MEANWHILE *n.*

meanwhile /meénwīl/ *adv.* & *n.* ● *adv.* **1** in the intervening period of time. **2** at the same time. ● *n.* the intervening period (esp. *in the meanwhile*). [MEAN³ + WHILE]

▪ *adv.* in the meanwhile, meantime, in the meantime, in the interim, *archaic* interim; for the moment, temporarily, for now, for the time being, *ad interim.* ● *n.* interim, meantime, interval.

meany var. of MEANIE.

measles /meéz'lz/ *n.pl.* (also treated as *sing.*) **1 a** an acute infectious viral disease marked by red spots on the skin. **b** the spots of measles. **2** a tapeworm disease of pigs. [ME *masele(s)* prob. f. MLG *masele*, MDu. *masel* pustule (cf. Du. *mazelen* measles), OHG *masala*: change of form prob. due to assim. to ME *meser* leper]

measly /meézli/ *adj.* (**measlier, measliest**) **1** *colloq.* inferior, contemptible, worthless. **2** *colloq. derog.* ridiculously small in size, amount, or value. **3** of or affected with measles. **4** (of pork) infested with tapeworms. [MEASLES + -Y¹]

▪ **1** inferior, contemptible, worthless; see also WRETCHED 2. **2** sparse, scanty, meagre, paltry, pathetic, skimpy, puny, miserly, niggardly, miserable, beggarly, stingy, *Brit. colloq.* mingy.

measurable /mézhərəb'l/ *adj.* that can be measured. □ **within a measurable distance of** getting near (something undesirable). □□ **measurability** /-bílliti/ *n.* **measurably** *adv.* [ME f. OF *mesurable* f. LL *mensurabilis* f. L *mensurare* (as MEASURE)]

measure /mézhər/ *n.* & *v.* ● *n.* **1** a size or quantity found by measuring. **2** a system of measuring (*liquid measure; linear measure*). **3** a rod or tape etc. for measuring. **4** a vessel of standard capacity for transferring or determining fixed quantities of liquids etc. (*a pint measure*). **5 a** the degree, extent, or amount of a thing. **b** (foll. by *of*) some degree of (*there was a measure of wit in her remark*). **6** a unit of capacity, e.g. a bushel (*20 measures of wheat*). **7** a factor by which a person or thing is reckoned or evaluated (*their success is a measure of their determination*). **8** (usu. in *pl.*) suitable action to achieve some end (*took measures to ensure a good profit*). **9** a legislative enactment. **10** a quantity contained in another an exact number of times. **11** a prescribed extent or quantity. **12** *Printing* the width of a page or column of type. **13 a** poetical rhythm; metre. **b** a metrical group of a dactyl or two iambuses, trochees, spondees, etc. **14** *US Mus.* a bar or the time-content of a bar. **15** *archaic* a dance. **16** a mineral stratum (*coal measures*). ● *v.* **1** *tr.* ascertain the extent or quantity of (a thing) by comparison with a fixed unit or with an object of known size. **2** *intr.* be of a specified size (*it measures six inches*). **3** *tr.* ascertain the size and proportion of (a person) for clothes. **4** *tr.* estimate (a quality, person's character, etc.) by some standard or rule. **5** *tr.* (often foll. by *off*) mark (a line etc. of a given length). **6** *tr.* (foll. by *out*) deal or distribute (a thing) in measured quantities. **7** *tr.* (foll. by *with, against*) bring (oneself or one's strength etc.) into competition with. **8** *tr. poet.* traverse (a distance). □ **beyond measure** excessively. **for good measure** as something beyond the minimum; as a finishing touch. **in a** (or **some**) **measure** partly. **made to measure** see MAKE. **measure up 1 a** determine the size etc. of by measurement. **b** take comprehensive measurements. **2** (often foll. by *to*) have the necessary qualifications (for). **measuring-jug** (or **-cup**) a jug or cup marked to measure its contents. **measuring-tape** a tape marked to measure length. **measuring-worm** the caterpillar of the geometer moth. [ME f. OF *mesure* f. L *mensura* f. *metiri mens-* measure]

▪ *n.* **1** amount, quantity, magnitude, amplitude, size, bulk, mass, extent, reach, dimension(s), measurement(s), scope, proportions, range, spread; capacity, volume; width, length, breadth, height; weight. **2, 3** scale, gauge, yardstick, rule, ruler, tape-measure; system, standard, criterion, method; barometer. **4** measuring-jug *or* -cup. **5, 6** quota, allotment, ration, share, amount, degree, extent, proportion, quantity, allowance; portion, part, unit. **7** assessment, evaluation, valuation, appraisal, value, gauge, rank, rating, measurement, stamp, estimation. **8** (*measures*) step(s), action, course (of action); plan(s), method, means, avenue, tactic(s), way, direction, approach, technique, procedure(s). **9** bill, resolution, legislation, act, statute, law; plan, proposal. **13, 14** beat, rhythm, cadence, metre, time; bar. ● *v.* **1** rank, rate, gauge, meter, weigh, calculate, reckon, compute, calibrate, determine, ascertain, figure out *or* up, assess, appraise, estimate, evaluate, judge, value; survey, find out. **4** see JUDGE *v.* 2. **5** measure off, mark off *or* out, limit, delimit, fix, pace off *or* out. **6** (*measure out*) dole out, ration (out), parcel out, apportion, allot, share out, assign, allocate, *literary* mete out; give out, deal out, distribute, issue, pass out, hand out, dispense, disperse, spread around *or* about. **8** see TRAVERSE *v.* 1. □ **beyond measure** see *unduly* (UNDUE). **for good measure** to boot, as well, in addition, additionally, as a dividend, into the bargain, besides, as *or* for a bonus, moreover, furthermore. **in a** (or **some**) **measure** see *partially* (PARTIAL). **measure up 1** see MEASURE *v.* 1 above. **2** qualify (for), be suitable (for); (*measure up to*) meet, equal, fulfil, match, reach, attain, be equal to, be fit *or* fitted for, be up to. **measuring-jug** (or **-cup**) measure.

measured /mézhərd/ *adj.* **1** rhythmical; regular in movement (*a measured tread*). **2** (of language) carefully considered. □□ **measuredly** *adv.*

▪ **1** rhythmic(al), regular, regulated, steady, uniform, even, monotonous. **2** careful, cautious, prudent, calculated, studied, considered, deliberate, systematic, sober, intentional, planned, regulated, premeditated, well-thought-out, reasoned.

measureless /mézhərliss/ *adj.* not measurable; infinite. □□ **measurelessly** *adv.*

measurement /mézhərmənt/ *n.* **1** the act or an instance of measuring. **2** an amount determined by measuring. **3** (in *pl.*) detailed dimensions.

▪ **1** ascertainment, determination, assessment, estimation, appraisal, evaluation, valuation, judgement, calculation, computation, mensuration, commensuration, metage.

2 dimension, extent, size, amount, measure, magnitude, amplitude; length, breadth, height, width, depth; area; volume, capacity; weight, tonnage; (elapsed) time, period; (square *or* cubic) footage, (square) yardage, mileage, acreage.

meat /meet/ *n.* **1** the flesh of animals (esp. mammals) as food. **2** (foll. by *of*) the essence or chief part of. **3** *US* the edible part of fruits, nuts, eggs, shellfish, etc. **4** *archaic* **a** food of any kind. **b** a meal. □ **meat and drink** a source of great pleasure. **meat-axe** a butcher's cleaver. **meat-fly** (*pl.* **-flies**) a fly that breeds in meat. **meat loaf** minced or chopped meat moulded into the shape of a loaf and baked. **meat safe** a cupboard for storing meat, usu. of wire gauze etc. □□ **meatless** *adj.* [OE *mete* food f. Gmc]

■ **1** flesh. **2** pith, core, heart, marrow, kernel, essence, gist, substance, basics, essentials, crux. **3** flesh, pulp, marrow, kernel, soft part. **4** food, nourishment, sustenance, victuals, nutriment, provisions, edibles, eatables, *colloq.* eats, grub, *formal* viands, *formal or joc.* comestibles, *joc.* provender, *sl.* chow. □ **meat and drink** see JOY *n.* 2.

meatball /méetbawl/ *n.* minced meat compressed into a small round ball.

meatus /miáytəss/ *n.* (*pl.* same or **meatuses**) *Anat.* a channel or passage in the body or its opening. [L, = passage f. *meare* flow, run]

meaty /méeti/ *adj.* (**meatier**, **meatiest**) **1** full of meat; fleshy. **2** of or like meat. **3** full of substance. □□ **meatily** *adv.* **meatiness** *n.*

Mecca /mékkə/ *n.* **1** a place one aspires to visit. **2** the birthplace of a faith, policy, pursuit, etc. [*Mecca* in Arabia, birthplace of Muhammad and chief place of Muslim pilgrimage]

mechanic /mikánnik/ *n.* a skilled worker, esp. one who makes or uses or repairs machinery. [ME (orig. as adj.) f. OF *mecanique* or L *mechanicus* f. Gk *mēkhanikos* (as MACHINE)]

■ engineer, technician, repairman.

mechanical /mikánnik'l/ *adj.* **1** of or relating to machines or mechanisms. **2** working or produced by machinery. **3** (of a person or action) like a machine; automatic; lacking originality. **4 a** (of an agency, principle, etc.) belonging to mechanics. **b** (of a theory etc.) explaining phenomena by the assumption of mechanical action. **5** of or relating to mechanics as a science. □ **mechanical advantage** the ratio of exerted to applied force in a machine. **mechanical drawing** a scale drawing of machinery etc. done with precision instruments. **mechanical engineer** a person skilled in the branch of engineering dealing with the design, construction, and repair of machines. **mechanical equivalent of heat** the conversion factor between heat energy and mechanical energy. □□ **mechanicalism** *n.* (in sense 4). **mechanically** *adv.* **mechanicalness** *n.* [ME f. L *mechanicus* (as MECHANIC)]

■ **2** automatic, automated, machine-driven, robotic; machine-made. **3** automatic, reflex, involuntary, instinctive, routine, habitual, unconscious, perfunctory, machine-like, robot-like.

mechanician /mékkənísh'n/ *n.* a person skilled in constructing machinery.

mechanics /mikánniks/ *n.pl.* (usu. treated as *sing.*) **1** the branch of applied mathematics dealing with motion and tendencies to motion. **2** the science of machinery. **3** the method of construction or routine operation of a thing.

mechanism /mékkəniz'm/ *n.* **1** the structure or adaptation of parts of a machine. **2** a system of mutually adapted parts working together in or as in a machine. **3** the mode of operation of a process. **4** *Art* mechanical execution; technique. **5** *Philos.* the doctrine that all natural phenomena, including life, allow mechanical explanation by physics and chemistry. [mod.L *mechanismus* f. Gk (as MACHINE)]

■ **1** machinery, workings, works, structure, system, organization, arrangement. **2** movement, action, moving parts, gears; device, apparatus. **3** way, means, method, procedure, approach, technique, medium, process, agency. **5** materialism, mechanicalism.

mechanist /mékkənist/ *n.* **1** a mechanician. **2** an expert in mechanics. **3** *Philos.* a person who holds the doctrine of mechanism. □□ **mechanistic** /-nístik/ *adj.* **mechanistically** /-nístikəli/ *adv.*

mechanize /mékkənīz/ *v.tr.* (also **-ise**) **1** give a mechanical character to. **2** introduce machines in. **3** *Mil.* equip with tanks, armoured cars, etc. (orig. as a substitute for horse-drawn vehicles and cavalry). □□ **mechanization** /-záysh'n/ *n.* **mechanizer** *n.*

mechano- /mékkənō/ *comb. form* mechanical. [Gk *mēkhano-* f. *mēkhanē* machine]

mechanoreceptor /mékkənō-riséptər/ *n. Biol.* a sensory receptor that responds to mechanical stimuli such as touch or sound.

mechatronics /mékkətrónniks/ *n.* the science of the combination of electronics and mechanics in developing new manufacturing techniques. [*mechan*ics + elec*tronics*]

Mechlin /méklin/ *n.* (in full **Mechlin lace**) lace made at Mechlin (now Mechelen or Malines) in Belgium.

M.Econ. *abbr.* Master of Economics.

meconium /mikṓniəm/ *n. Med.* a dark substance forming the first faeces of a newborn infant. [L, lit. poppy-juice, f. Gk *mēkōnion* f. *mēkōn* poppy]

M.Ed. *abbr.* Master of Education.

Med /med/ *n. colloq.* the Mediterranean Sea. [abbr.]

med. *abbr.* medium.

medal /médd'l/ *n.* a piece of metal, usu. in the form of a disc, struck or cast with an inscription or device to commemorate an event etc., or awarded as a distinction to a soldier, scholar, athlete, etc., for services rendered, for proficiency, etc. □ **medal play** *Golf* = *stroke play*. □□ **medalled** *adj.* **medallic** /midállik/ *adj.* [F *médaille* f. It. *medaglia* ult. f. L *metallum* METAL]

■ see DECORATION 3.

medallion /midályən/ *n.* **1** a large medal. **2** a thing shaped like this, e.g. a decorative panel or tablet, portrait, etc. [F *médaillon* f. It. *medaglione* augment. of *medaglia* (as MEDAL)]

■ **1** see PENDANT 1, 2. **2** see PLAQUE.

medallist /méddəlist/ *n.* (*US* **medalist**) **1** a recipient of a (specified) medal (*gold medallist*). **2** an engraver or designer of medals.

meddle /médd'l/ *v.intr.* (often foll. by *with*, *in*) interfere in or busy oneself unduly with others' concerns. □□ **meddler** *n.* [ME f. OF *medler*, var. of *mesler* ult. f. L *miscēre* mix]

■ interfere, intrude, butt in, thrust one's nose in, pry, intervene, interlope, tamper, *colloq.* snoop, poke one's nose in, kibitz, *Austral. sl.* poke one's bib in.

meddlesome /médd'lsəm/ *adj.* fond of meddling; interfering. □□ **meddlesomely** *adv.* **meddlesomeness** *n.*

■ see NOSY *adj.* □□ **meddlesomeness** interference, interruption, intrusiveness, obtrusiveness, invasiveness, prying, inquisitiveness, officiousness, presumptuousness, *colloq.* nosiness, snooping.

Mede /meed/ *n. hist.* a member of an Indo-European people which established an empire in Media in Persia (modern Iran) in the 7th c. BC. □□ **Median** *adj.* [ME f. L *Medi* (pl.) f. Gk *Mēdoi*]

media[1] /méediə/ *n.pl.* **1** *pl.* of MEDIUM. **2** (usu. prec. by *the*) the main means of mass communication (esp. newspapers and broadcasting) regarded collectively. ¶ Use as a mass noun with a singular verb is common (e.g. *the media is on our side*), but is generally disfavoured (cf. AGENDA, DATA). □ **media event** an event primarily intended to attract publicity.

media[2] /méediə/ *n.* (*pl.* **mediae** /-di-ee/) **1** *Phonet.* a voiced stop, e.g. *g*, *b*, *d*. **2** *Anat.* a middle layer of the wall of an artery or other vessel. [L, fem. of *medius* middle]

mediaeval var. of MEDIEVAL.

medial /méediəl/ *adj.* **1** situated in the middle. **2** of average size. □□ **medially** *adv.* [LL *medialis* f. L *medius* middle]

■ **1** see MIDDLE *adj.* 1, 2. **2** see MEDIUM *adj.*

median /meédiən/ *adj.* & *n.* ● *adj.* situated in the middle. ● *n.* **1** *Anat.* a median artery, vein, nerve, etc. **2** *Geom.* a straight line drawn from any vertex of a triangle to the middle of the opposite side. **3** *Math.* the middle value of a series of values arranged in order of size. □□ **medianly** *adv.* [F *médiane* or L *medianus* (as MEDIAL)]

■ *adj.* see CENTRAL 1.

mediant /meédiənt/ *n. Mus.* the third note of a diatonic scale of any key. [F *médiante* f. It. *mediante* part. of obs. *mediare* come between, f. L (as MEDIATE)]

mediastinum /meédiəsteénəm/ *n.* (*pl.* **mediastina** /-nə/) *Anat.* a membranous middle septum, esp. between the lungs. □□ **mediastinal** *adj.* [mod.L f. med.L *mediastinus* medial, after L *mediastinus* drudge f. *medius* middle]

mediate *v.* & *adj.* ● *v.* /meédiayt/ **1** *intr.* (often foll. by *between*) intervene (between parties in a dispute) to produce agreement or reconciliation. **2** *tr.* be the medium for bringing about (a result) or for conveying (a gift etc.). **3** *tr.* form a connecting link between. ● *adj.* /meédiət/ **1** connected not directly but through some other person or thing. **2** involving an intermediate agency. □□ **mediately** /-ətli/ *adv.* **mediation** /-áysh'n/ *n.* **mediator** /meédiaytər/ *n.* **mediatory** /meédiətəri/ *adj.* [LL *mediare mediat-* f. L *medius* middle]

■ *v.* **1** arbitrate, referee, umpire, moderate, liaise, intercede, *archaic* conciliate; see also NEGOTIATE 1, 2. **3** see CONNECT 1a, b. □□ **mediator** arbitrator, arbiter, referee, umpire, judge, negotiator, intermediary, go-between, middleman, moderator, liaison, intercessor, interceder, conciliator, appeaser, peacemaker.

medic[1] /méddik/ *n. colloq.* a medical practitioner or student. [L *medicus* physician f. *medēri* heal]

medic[2] var. of MEDICK.

medicable /méddikəb'l/ *adj.* admitting of remedial treatment. [L *medicabilis* (as MEDICATE)]

Medicaid /méddikayd/ *n.* (in the US) a Federal system of health insurance for those requiring financial assistance. [MEDICAL + AID]

medical /méddik'l/ *adj.* & *n.* ● *adj.* **1** of or relating to the science of medicine in general. **2** of or relating to conditions requiring medical and not surgical treatment (*medical ward*). ● *n. colloq.* a medical examination. □ **medical certificate** a certificate of fitness or unfitness to work etc. **medical examination** an examination to determine a person's physical fitness. **medical jurisprudence** the law relating to medicine. **medical officer** *Brit.* a person in charge of the health services of a local authority or other organization. **medical practitioner** a physician or surgeon. □□ **medically** *adv.* [F *médical* or med.L *medicalis* f. L *medicus*: see MEDIC[1]]

■ □ **medical practitioner** see DOCTOR *n.* 1a.

medicament /midíkkəmənt, méddikə-/ *n.* a substance used for medical treatment. [F *médicament* or L *medicamentum* (as MEDICATE)]

■ see MEDICINE 2.

Medicare /méddikair/ *n.* (in the US) a Federal system of health insurance for persons over 65 years of age. [MEDICAL + CARE]

medicate /méddikayt/ *v.tr.* **1** treat medically. **2** impregnate with a medicinal substance. □□ **medicative** /méddikətiv/ *adj.* [L *medicari medicat-* administer remedies to f. *medicus*: see MEDIC[1]]

■ **1** see TREAT *v.* 3.

medication /méddikáysh'n/ *n.* **1** a substance used for medical treatment. **2** treatment using drugs.

■ **1** see MEDICINE 2.

Medicean /medeéchiən/ *adj.* of the Medici family, rulers of Florence in the 15th c. [mod.L *Mediceus* f. It. *Medici*]

medicinal /midíssin'l/ *adj.* & *n.* ● *adj.* (of a substance) having healing properties. ● *n.* a medicinal substance. □□ **medicinally** *adv.* [ME f. OF f. L *medicinalis* (as MEDICINE)]

■ *adj.* healing, remedial, therapeutic(al), curative, restorative, sanative, analeptic, *Med.* roborant. ● *n.* see MEDICINE 2.

medicine /médsin, méddi-/ *n.* **1** the science or practice of the diagnosis, treatment, and prevention of disease, esp. as distinct from surgical methods. **2** any drug or preparation used for the treatment or prevention of disease, esp. one taken by mouth. **3** a spell, charm, or fetish which is thought to cure afflictions. □ **a dose** (or **taste**) **of one's own medicine** treatment such as one is accustomed to giving others. **medicine ball** a stuffed leather ball thrown and caught for exercise. **medicine chest** a box containing medicines etc. **medicine man** a person believed to have magical powers of healing, esp. among N. American Indians. **take one's medicine** submit to something disagreeable. [ME f. OF *medecine* f. L *medicina* f. *medicus*: see MEDIC[1]]

■ **1** *esp. archaic* physic. **2** medication, medicament, remedy, drug, pharmaceutical, prescription, *esp. archaic* physic; nostrum, panacea, cure-all. □ **medicine man** healer, witch-doctor, shaman. **take one's medicine** face the music; see also *bite the bullet*.

medick /meédik/ *n.* (also **medic**) any leguminous plant of the genus *Medicago*, esp. alfalfa. [ME f. L *medica* f. Gk *Mēdikē poa* Median grass]

medico /méddikō/ *n.* (*pl.* **-os**) *colloq.* a medical practitioner or student. [It. f. L (as MEDIC[1])]

medico- /méddikō/ *comb. form* medical; medical and (*medico-legal*). [L *medicus* (as MEDIC[1])]

medieval /méddi-eév'l/ *adj.* (also **mediaeval**) **1** of, or in the style of, the Middle Ages. **2** *colloq.* old-fashioned, archaic. □ **medieval history** the history of the 5th–15th c. **medieval Latin** Latin of about AD 600–1500. □□ **medievalism** *n.* **medievalist** *n.* **medievalize** *v.tr.* & *intr.* (also **-ise**). **medievally** *adv.* [mod.L *medium aevum* f. L *medius* middle + *aevum* age]

■ **2** see ANTIQUATED.

mediocre /meédiṓkər/ *adj.* **1** of middling quality, neither good nor bad. **2** second-rate. [F *médiocre* or f. L *mediocris* of middle height or degree f. *medius* middle + *ocris* rugged mountain]

■ **1** middling, indifferent, ordinary, commonplace, average, medium, everyday, run-of-the-mill, pedestrian, undistinguished, uninspired, unimaginative, unexceptional, tolerable, fair (to middling), not (that *or* too) good, not bad, so so, *colloq.* common or garden. **2** second-rate, third-rate, inferior, poor, *colloq.* nothing to write home about, no great shakes.

mediocrity /meédiókriti/ *n.* (*pl.* **-ies**) **1** the state of being mediocre. **2** a mediocre person or thing.

■ **1** see INFERIORITY.

meditate /mééditayt/ *v.* **1** *intr.* **a** exercise the mind in (esp. religious) contemplation. **b** (usu. foll. by *on*, *upon*) focus on a subject in this manner. **2** *tr.* plan mentally; design. □□ **meditation** /-táysh'n/ *n.* **meditator** *n.* [L *meditari* contemplate]

■ **1** reflect, think, ponder, study, ruminate, cogitate, contemplate, cerebrate, be lost in thought, be in a brown study, *literary* muse. **2** consider, contemplate, mull over, reflect on *or* upon, ponder on *or* over, chew over, plan, scheme, devise, design, conceive, frame, think up, have in mind.

meditative /mædditətiv/ *adj.* **1** inclined to meditate. **2** indicative of meditation. □□ **meditatively** *adv.* **meditativeness** *n.*

■ **1** thoughtful, pensive, contemplative, reflective, studious, cogitative, abstracted, rapt, engrossed, lost *or* deep in thought, ruminative, brooding.

Mediterranean /mædditəráyniən/ *n.* & *adj.* ● *n.* **1** a large landlocked sea bordered by S. Europe, SW Asia, and N. Africa. **2** a native of a country bordering on the Mediterranean. ● *adj.* **1** of or characteristic of the Mediterranean or its surrounding region (*Mediterranean climate*; *Mediterranean cookery*). **2** (of a person) dark-complexioned and not tall. [L *mediterraneus* inland f. *medius* middle + *terra* land]

medium /méediəm/ *n.* & *adj.* ● *n.* (*pl.* **media** or **mediums**) **1** the middle quality, degree, etc. between extremes (*find a happy medium*). **2** the means by which something is communicated (*the medium of sound*; *the medium of television*). **3** the intervening substance through which impressions are conveyed to the senses etc. (*light passing from one medium into another*). **4** *Biol.* the physical environment or conditions of growth, storage, or transport of a living organism (*the shape of a fish is ideal for its fluid medium*; *growing mould on the surface of a medium*). **5** an agency or means of doing something (*the medium through which money is raised*). **6** the material or form used by an artist, composer, etc. (*language as an artistic medium*). **7** the liquid (e.g. oil or gel) with which pigments are mixed for use in painting. **8** (*pl.* **mediums**) a person claiming to be in contact with the spirits of the dead and to communicate between the dead and the living. ● *adj.* **1** between two qualities, degrees, etc. **2** average; moderate (*of medium height*). □ **medium bowler** *Cricket* a bowler who bowls at a medium pace. **medium dry** (of sherry, wine, etc.) having a flavour intermediate between dry and sweet. **medium frequency** a radio frequency between 300 kHz and 3 MHz. **medium of circulation** something that serves as an instrument of commercial transactions, e.g. coin. **medium-range** (of an aircraft, missile, etc.) able to travel a medium distance. **medium wave** a radio wave of medium frequency. □□ **mediumism** *n.* (in sense 8 of *n.*). **mediumistic** /-místik/ *adj.* (in sense 8 of *n.*). **mediumship** *n.* (in sense 8 of *n.*). [L, = middle, neut. of *medius*]

■ *n.* **1** average, middle, mid-point, compromise, centre, mean, norm. **2, 5, 6** means, method, mode, approach, instrument, device, mechanism, intermediation, technique, contrivance, agency, expedient, way, course, route, road, avenue, channel, conveyance, vehicle. **3** atmosphere, environment, ambience, milieu. **4** see ENVIRONMENT 1, 2. **8** see PSYCHIC *n.* ● *adj.* average, middle, mid, medial, median, normal, standard, usual, everyday, ordinary.

medlar /médlər/ *n.* **1** a rosaceous tree, *Mespilus germanica*, bearing small brown apple-like fruits. **2** the fruit of this tree which is eaten when decayed. [ME f. OF *medler* f. L *mespila* f. Gk *mespilē*, *-on*]

medley /médli/ *n.*, *adj.*, & *v.* ● *n.* (*pl.* **-eys**) **1** a varied mixture; a miscellany. **2** a collection of musical items from one work or various sources arranged as a continuous whole. ● *adj. archaic* mixed; motley. ● *v.tr.* (**-eys**, **-eyed**) *archaic* make a medley of; intermix. □ **medley relay** a relay race between teams in which each member runs a different distance, swims a different stroke, etc. [ME f. OF *medlee* var. of *meslee* f. Rmc (as MEDDLE)]

■ *n.* **1** mixture, assortment, combination, miscellany, *mélange*, collection, conglomeration, agglomeration, hotchpotch, olio, blend, gallimaufry, pastiche, pot-pourri, salmagundi, olla podrida, mishmash, mixed bag, jumble, mess, farrago, stew, goulash, *colloq.* omnium gatherum. ● *adj.* see MIXED. ● *v.* see MIX *v.* 1, 3, 4a.

Medoc /maydók, méddok/ *n.* a fine red claret from the Médoc region of SW France.

medulla /midúllə/ *n.* **1** the inner region of certain organs or tissues usu. when it is distinguishable from the outer region or cortex, as in hair or a kidney. **2** the myelin layer of certain nerve fibres. **3** the soft internal tissue of plants. □ **medulla oblongata** /óblonggaátə/ the continuation of the spinal cord within the skull, forming the lowest part of the brain stem. □□ **medullary** *adj.* [L, = pith, marrow, prob. rel. to *medius* middle]

medusa /midyōōssə/ *n.* (*pl.* **medusae** /-see/ or **medusas**) **1** a jellyfish. **2** a free-swimming form of any coelenterate, having tentacles round the edge of a usu. umbrella-shaped jelly-like body, e.g. a jellyfish. □□ **medusan** *adj.* [L f. Gk *Medousa*, name of a Gorgon with snakes instead of hair]

meed /meed/ *n. literary* or *archaic* **1** reward. **2** merited portion (of praise etc.). [OE *mēd* f. WG, rel. to Goth. *mizdō*, Gk *misthos* reward]

meek /meek/ *adj.* **1** humble and submissive; suffering injury etc. tamely. **2** piously gentle in nature. □□ **meekly** *adv.* **meekness** *n.* [ME *me(o)c* f. ON *mjúkr* soft, gentle]

■ modest, humble, submissive, unassuming, unambitious, unpretentious, mild, bland, patient, deferential, shy, retiring, lowly, tame, timid, weak, docile, compliant, yielding, acquiescent, unaggressive, non-militant, tractable, manageable, subdued, repressed, spiritless, suppressed, broken, *colloq.* wimpish.

meerkat /méerkat/ *n.* the suricate. [Du., = sea-cat]

meerschaum /méershəm/ *n.* **1** a soft white form of hydrated magnesium silicate, chiefly found in Turkey, which resembles clay. **2** a tobacco-pipe with the bowl made from this. [G, = sea-foam f. *Meer* sea + *Schaum* foam, transl. Pers. *kef-i-daryā*, with ref. to its frothiness]

meet[1] /meet/ *v.* & *n.* ● *v.* (*past* and *past part.* **met** /met/) **1 a** *tr.* encounter (a person or persons) by accident or design; come face to face with. **b** *intr.* (of two or more people) come into each other's company by accident or design (*decided to meet on the bridge*). **2** *tr.* go to a place to be present at the arrival of (a person, train, etc.). **3 a** *tr.* (of a moving object, line, feature of landscape, etc.) come together or into contact with (*where the road meets the flyover*). **b** *intr.* come together or into contact (*where the sea and the sky meet*). **4 a** *tr.* make the acquaintance of (*delighted to meet you*). **b** *intr.* (of two or more people) make each other's acquaintance. **5** *intr.* & *tr.* come together or come into contact with for the purposes of conference, business, worship, etc. (*the committee meets every week*; *the union met management yesterday*). **6** *tr.* **a** (of a person or a group) deal with or answer (a demand, objection, etc.) (*met the original proposal with hostility*). **b** satisfy or conform with (proposals, deadlines, a person, etc.) (*agreed to meet the new terms*; *did my best to meet them on that point*). **7** *tr.* pay (a bill etc.); provide the funds required by (a cheque etc.) (*meet the cost of the move*). **8** *tr.* & (foll. by *with*) *intr.* experience, encounter, or receive (success, disaster, a difficulty, etc.) (*met their death*; *met with many problems*). **9** *tr.* oppose in battle, contest, or confrontation. **10** *intr.* (of clothes, curtains, etc.) join or fasten correctly (*my jacket won't meet*). ● *n.* **1** the assembly of riders and hounds for a hunt. **2** the assembly of competitors for various sporting activities, esp. athletics. □ **make ends meet** see END. **meet the case** be adequate. **meet the eye** (or **the ear**) be visible (or audible). **meet a person's eye** check if another person is watching and look into his or her eyes in return. **meet a person half way** make a compromise, respond in a friendly way to the advances of another person. **meet up** *colloq.* happen to meet. **meet with 1** see sense 8 of *v.* **2** receive (a reaction) (*met with the committee's approval*). **3** esp. *US* = sense 1a of *v.* **more in it than meets the eye** hidden qualities or complications. □□ **meeter** *n.* [OE *mētan* f. Gmc: cf. MOOT]

■ *v.* **1** encounter, come across, chance on *or* upon, happen on *or* upon, stumble on *or* into, see, run across *or* into, *esp. US* meet with, *colloq.* bump into; rendezvous (with), get together (with). **3** link up, join, come together, unite, touch, intersect. **4** make the acquaintance of, be introduced to. **5** convene, assemble, gather, get together, collect, forgather, congregate. **6** answer, deal with, handle, satisfy, fulfil, take care of, dispose of, heed, observe, carry out. **7** pay, settle, defray, liquidate. **8** encounter, be met by, experience; undergo, endure, suffer, have, go through. **9** see FIGHT *v.* 1a. ● *n.* competition, contest, meeting, match, tourney, tournament, rally. □ **meet the case** see SUFFICE 1. **meet with 2** see RECEIVE 4.

meet[2] /meet/ *adj. archaic* suitable, fit, proper. □□ **meetly** *adv.* **meetness** *n.* [ME *(i)mete* repr. OE *gemǣte* f. Gmc, rel. to METE[1]]

■ fitting, appropriate, proper, fit, congruous; see also SUITABLE.

meeting /méeting/ *n.* **1** in senses of MEET[1]. **2** an assembly of people, esp. the members of a society, committee, etc., for discussion or entertainment. **3** = *race meeting*. **4** an assembly (esp. of Quakers) for worship. **5** the persons assembled (*address the meeting*). □ **meeting-house** a place of worship, esp. of Quakers etc.

▪ **1** appointment, engagement, rendezvous, encounter, assignation, *archaic* tryst; convergence, converging, confluence, joining, union, junction, conjunction, intersection. **2, 5** assembly, convention, conference, gathering, congress, conclave, session, congregation, convocation, *US* caucus, *colloq.* get-together. **3** see MEET[1] *n.*

mega /méggə/ *adj.* & *adv. sl.* ● *adj.* **1** excellent. **2** enormous. ● *adv.* extremely. [Gk f. as MEGA-]

mega- /méggə/ *comb. form* **1** large. **2** denoting a factor of one million (10^6) in the metric system of measurement. ¶ Abbr.: **M.** [Gk f. *megas* great]

megabuck /méggəbuk/ *n. US colloq.* a million dollars.

megabyte /méggəbīt/ *n. Computing* 1,048,576 (i.e. 2^{20}) bytes as a measure of data capacity, or loosely 1,000,000. ¶ Abbr.: **MB**.

megadeath /méggədeth/ *n.* the death of one million people (esp. as a unit in estimating the casualties of war).

megahertz /méggəherts/ *n.* one million hertz, esp. as a measure of frequency of radio transmissions. ¶ Abbr.: **MHz**.

megalith /méggəlith/ *n. Archaeol.* a large stone, esp. one placed upright as a monument or part of one. [MEGA- + Gk *lithos* stone]

megalithic /méggəlíthik/ *adj. Archaeol.* made of or marked by the use of large stones.

megalo- /méggəlō/ *comb. form* great (*megalomania*). [Gk f. *megas megal-* great]

megalomania /méggələmáyniə/ *n.* **1** a mental disorder producing delusions of grandeur. **2** a passion for grandiose schemes. □□ **megalomaniac** *adj.* & *n.* **megalomaniacal** /-mənī́ək'l/ *adj.* **megalomanic** /-mánnik/ *adj.*

megalopolis /méggəlóppəliss/ *n.* **1** a great city or its way of life. **2** an urban complex consisting of a city and its environs. □□ **megalopolitan** /-ləpóllit'n/ *adj.* & *n.* [MEGA- + Gk *polis* city]

megalosaurus /méggələsáwrəss/ *n.* a large flesh-eating dinosaur of the genus *Megalosaurus*, with stout hind legs and small forelimbs. [MEGALO- + Gk *sauros* lizard]

megaphone /méggəfōn/ *n.* a large funnel-shaped device for amplifying the sound of the voice.

megapode /méggəpōd/ *n.* (also **megapod** /-pod/) any bird of the family Megapodidae, native to Australasia, that builds a mound of debris for the incubation of its eggs, e.g. a mallee fowl. [mod.L *Megapodius* (genus-name) formed as MEGA- + Gk *pous podos* foot]

megaron /méggəron/ *n.* the central hall of a large Mycenaean house. [Gk, = hall]

megaspore /méggəspor/ *n.* the larger of the two kinds of spores produced by some ferns (cf. MICROSPORE).

megastar /méggəstaar/ *n.* a very famous person, esp. in the world of entertainment.

megaton /méggətun/ *n.* (also **megatonne**) a unit of explosive power equal to one million tons of TNT.

megavolt /méggəvōlt/ *n.* one million volts, esp. as a unit of electromotive force. ¶ Abbr.: **MV**.

megawatt /méggəwot/ *n.* one million watts, esp. as a measure of electrical power as generated by power stations. ¶ Abbr.: **MW**.

Megger /méggər/ *n. Electr. propr.* an instrument for measuring electrical insulation resistance. [cf. MEGOHM]

megilp /məgílp/ *n.* (also **magilp**) a mixture of mastic resin and linseed oil, added to oil paints, much used in the 19th c. [18th c.: orig. unkn.]

megohm /méggōm/ *n. Electr.* one million ohms. [MEGA- + OHM]

megrim[1] /méegrim/ *n.* **1** *archaic* migraine. **2** a whim, a fancy. **3** (in *pl.*) **a** depression; low spirits. **b** staggers, vertigo in horses etc. [ME *mygrane* f. OF MIGRAINE]

megrim[2] /mégrim/ *n.* any deep-water flat-fish of the family *Lepidorhombus*, esp. *L. whiffiagonis*. Also called *sail-fluke*. [19th c.: orig. unkn.]

meiosis /mīṓsiss/ *n.* **1** *Biol.* a type of cell division that results in daughter cells with half the chromosome number of the parent cell (cf. MITOSIS). **2** = LITOTES. □□ **meiotic** /mīóttik/ *adj.* **meiotically** /mīóttikəli/ *adv.* [mod.L f. Gk *meiōsis* f. *meioō* lessen f. *meiōn* less]

Meissen /mī́s'n/ *n.* a hard-paste porcelain made since 1710. [*Meissen* near Dresden in Germany]

Meistersinger /mī́stərsingər/ *n.* (*pl.* same) a member of one of the 14th–16th-c. German guilds for lyric poets and musicians. [G f. *Meister* MASTER + *Singer* SINGER (see SING)]

melamine /mélləmeen/ *n.* **1** a white crystalline compound that can be copolymerized with methanal to give thermosetting resins. **2** (in full **melamine resin**) a plastic made from melamine and used esp. for laminated coatings. [*melam* (arbitrary) + AMINE]

melancholia /méllənkṓliə/ *n.* a mental illness marked by depression and ill-founded fears. [LL: see MELANCHOLY]

melancholy /méllənkəli/ *n.* & *adj.* ● *n.* (*pl.* **-ies**) **1** a pensive sadness. **2 a** mental depression. **b** a habitual or constitutional tendency to this. **3** *hist.* one of the four humours; black bile (see HUMOUR *n.* 5). ● *adj.* (of a person) sad, gloomy; (of a thing) saddening, depressing; (of words, a tune, etc.) expressing sadness. □□ **melancholic** /-kóllik/ *adj.* **melancholically** /-kóllikəli/ *adv.* [ME f. OF *melancolie* f. LL *melancholia* f. Gk *melagkholia* f. *melas melanos* black + *kholē* bile]

▪ *n.* **1, 2** sadness, sorrow, misery, gloom, unhappiness, the blues, moroseness, melancholia, depression, dejection, dejectedness, despondence, despondency, downheartedness, glumness, gloominess, woefulness, lugubriousness, disconsolateness, dispiritedness, cheerlessness, mournfulness, sorrowfulness, miserableness, anguish, *archaic or literary* woe, *literary* dolour. ● *adj.* sad, morose, depressed, unhappy, dejected, despondent, blue, downhearted, glum, gloomy, woeful, woebegone, lugubrious, disconsolate, downcast, dispirited, low-spirited, cheerless, crestfallen, chap-fallen, forlorn, heartbroken, mournful, sorrowful, miserable, dismal, low, *colloq.* down in the mouth, (down) in the dumps; saddening, depressing.

Melanesian /méllənéeziən, -zh'n/ *n.* & *adj.* ● *n.* **1** a member of the dominant Negroid people of Melanesia, an island group in the W. Pacific. **2** the language of this people. ● *adj.* of or relating to this people or their language. [*Melanesia* f. Gk *melas* black + *nēsos* island]

mélange /maylóNzh/ *n.* a mixture, a medley. [F f. *mêler* mix (as MEDDLE)]

▪ see MIXTURE 2.

melanin /méllənin/ *n.* a dark-brown to black pigment occurring in the hair, skin, and iris of the eye, that is responsible for tanning of the skin when exposed to sunlight. [Gk *melas melanos* black + -IN]

melanism /mélləniz'm/ *n.* an unusual darkening of body tissues caused by excessive production of melanin.

melanoma /méllənṓmə/ *n.* a malignant tumour of melanin-forming cells, usu. in the skin. [MELANIN + -OMA]

▪ see TUMOUR.

melanosis /méllənṓsiss/ *n.* **1** = MELANISM. **2** a disorder in the body's production of melanin. □□ **melanotic** /-nóttik/ *adj.* [mod.L f. Gk (as MELANIN)]

Melba /mélbə/ *n.* □ **do a Melba** *Austral. sl.* **1** return from retirement. **2** make several farewell appearances. **Melba sauce** a sauce made from puréed raspberries thickened with icing sugar. **Melba toast** very thin crisp toast. **peach Melba** a dish of ice-cream and peaches with liqueur or sauce. [Dame Nellie *Melba*, Austral. operatic soprano d. 1931]

meld[1] /meld/ *v.* & *n.* ● *v.tr.* (also *absol.*) (in rummy, canasta, etc.) lay down or declare (one's cards) in order to score points. ● *n.* a completed set or run of cards in any of these games. [G *melden* announce]

meld² /meld/ *v.tr.* & *intr.* orig. *US* merge, blend, combine. [perh. f. MELT + WELD¹]

■ see BLEND *v.*

mêlée /méllay/ *n.* (*US* **melee**) **1** a confused fight, skirmish, or scuffle. **2** a muddle. [F (as MEDLEY)]

■ **1** see SKIRMISH *n.* 1. **2** see JUMBLE *n.* 1.

melic /méllik/ *adj.* (of a poem, esp. a Gk lyric) meant to be sung. [L *melicus* f. Gk *melikos* f. *melos* song]

meliorate /meéliərayt/ *v.tr.* & *intr. literary* improve (cf. AMELIORATE). ▫▫ **melioration** /-ráysh'n/ *n.* **meliorative** /-rətiv/ *adj.* [LL *meliorare* (as MELIORISM)]

■ see IMPROVE 1a. ▫▫ **melioration** see REFORM *n.*

meliorism /meéliəriz'm/ *n.* a doctrine that the world may be made better by human effort. ▫▫ **meliorist** *n.* [L *melior* better + -ISM]

melisma /milízmə/ *n.* (*pl.* **melismata** /-mətə/ or **melismas**) *Mus.* a group of notes sung to one syllable of text. ▫▫ **melismatic** /-máttik/ *adj.* [Gk]

melliferous /miliffərəss/ *adj.* yielding or producing honey. [L *mellifer* f. *mel* honey]

mellifluous /milífloоəss/ *adj.* (of a voice or words) pleasing, musical, flowing. ▫▫ **mellifluence** *n.* **mellifluent** *adj.* **mellifluously** *adv.* **mellifluousness** *n.* [ME f. OF *melliflue* or LL *mellifluus* f. *mel* honey + *fluere* flow]

■ see TUNEFUL.

mellow /méllō/ *adj.* & *v.* ● *adj.* **1** (of sound, colour, light) soft and rich, free from harshness. **2** (of character) softened or matured by age or experience. **3** genial, jovial. **4** partly intoxicated. **5** (of fruit) soft, sweet, and juicy. **6** (of wine) well-matured, smooth. **7** (of earth) rich, loamy. ● *v.tr.* & *intr.* make or become mellow. ▫ **mellow out** *US sl.* relax. ▫▫ **mellowly** *adv.* **mellowness** *n.* [ME, perh. f. attrib. use of OE *melu*, *melw-* MEAL²]

■ *adj.* **1** soft, softened, subtle, muted, pastel; musical, melodious, full, pure, rich, sweet, dulcet, mellifluous, euphonious, mature, deep. **2, 3** easygoing, genial, gentle, good-natured, easy, cordial, friendly, warm, amiable, agreeable, pleasant, cheerful, happy, jovial; see also MATURE *adj.* 1. **4** see DRUNK *adj.* 1. **5** soft, juicy, luscious, delicious, rich, sweet, flavourful, full-flavoured, ready, ripe, mature, ripened, aged. **6** see SMOOTH *adj.* 8b. **7** see RICH 5. ● *v.* mature, ripen, age, season, sweeten, develop, soften.

melodeon /milṓdiən/ *n.* (also **melodion**) **1** a small organ popular in the 19th c., similar to the harmonium. **2** a small German accordion, played esp. by folk musicians. [MELODY + HARMONIUM with Graecized ending]

melodic /milóddik/ *adj.* **1** of or relating to melody. **2** having or producing melody. ▫ **melodic minor** a scale with the sixth and seventh degrees raised when ascending and lowered when descending. ▫▫ **melodically** *adv.* [F *mélodique* f. LL *melodicus* f. Gk *melōidikos* (as MELODY)]

■ see TUNEFUL.

melodious /milṓdiəss/ *adj.* **1** of, producing, or having melody. **2** sweet-sounding. ▫▫ **melodiously** *adv.* **melodiousness** *n.* [ME f. OF *melodieus* (as MELODY)]

■ **1** see TUNEFUL. **2** sweet(-sounding), dulcet, tuneful, euphonious, harmonious, melodic, lyrical, musical, mellifluous, mellifluent, silvery, golden.

melodist /méllədist/ *n.* **1** a composer of melodies. **2** a singer.

melodize /méllədīz/ *v.* (also **-ise**) **1** *intr.* make a melody or melodies; make sweet music. **2** *tr.* make melodious. ▫▫ **melodizer** *n.*

melodrama /mélladraamə/ *n.* **1** a sensational dramatic piece with crude appeals to the emotions and usu. a happy ending. **2** the genre of drama of this type. **3** language, behaviour, or an occurrence suggestive of this. **4** *hist.* a play with songs interspersed and with orchestral music accompanying the action. ▫▫ **melodramatic** /-drəmáttik/ *adj.* **melodramatically** /-drəmáttikəli/ *adv.* **melodramatist** /-drámmətist/ *n.* **melodramatize** /-drámmətīz/ *v.tr.* (also **-ise**). [earlier *melodrame* f. F *mélodrame* f. Gk *melos* music + F *drame* DRAMA]

■ **2** fantasy, Gothic horror. **3** see DRAMA 4. ▫▫ **melodramatic** sensational, sensationalistic, dramatic, stagy, theatrical, (over-)sentimental, (over-)sentimentalized, histrionic, overdrawn, overworked, overwrought, overdone, exaggerated, *colloq.* blood-and-thunder, hammy, *esp. US colloq.* schmaltzy, *US sl.* hokey.

melodramatics /mélladramáttiks/ *n.pl.* melodramatic behaviour, action, or writing.

melody /méllədi/ *n.* (*pl.* **-ies**) **1** an arrangement of single notes in a musically expressive succession. **2** the principal part in harmonized music. **3** a musical arrangement of words. **4** sweet music, tunefulness. [ME f. OF *melodie* f. LL *melodia* f. Gk *melōidia* f. *melos* song]

■ **1–3** song, tune, air, strain, measure, theme, refrain. **4** tunefulness, melodiousness, euphony, harmony, musicality, sweetness.

melon /méllən/ *n.* **1** the sweet fruit of various gourds. **2** the gourd producing this (*honeydew melon*; *water melon*). ▫ **cut the melon 1** decide a question. **2** share abundant profits among a number of people. [ME f. OF f. LL *melo -onis* abbr. of L *melopepo* f. Gk *mēlopepōn* f. *mēlon* apple + *pepōn* gourd f. *pepōn* ripe]

melt /melt/ *v.* & *n.* ● *v.* **1** *intr.* become liquefied by heat. **2** *tr.* change to a liquid condition by heat. **3** *tr.* (as **molten** *adj.*) (usu. of materials that require a great deal of heat to melt them) liquefied by heat (*molten lava*; *molten lead*). **4 a** *intr.* & *tr.* dissolve. **b** *intr.* (of food) be easily dissolved in the mouth. **5** *intr.* **a** (of a person, feelings, the heart, etc.) be softened as a result of pity, love, etc. **b** dissolve into tears. **6** *tr.* soften (a person, feelings, the heart, etc.) (*a look to melt a heart of stone*). **7** *intr.* (usu. foll. by *into*) change or merge imperceptibly into another form or state (*night melted into dawn*). **8** *intr.* (often foll. by *away*) (of a person) leave or disappear unobtrusively (*melted into the background*; *melted away into the crowd*). **9** *intr.* (usu. as **melting** *adj.*) (of sound) be soft and liquid (*melting chords*). **10** *intr. colloq.* (of a person) suffer extreme heat (*I'm melting in this thick jumper*). ● *n.* **1** liquid metal etc. **2** an amount melted at any one time. **3** the process or an instance of melting. ▫ **melt away** disappear or make disappear by liquefaction. **melt down 1** melt (esp. metal articles) in order to reuse the raw material. **2** become liquid and lose structure (cf. MELTDOWN). **melting-point** the temperature at which any given solid will melt. **melting-pot 1** a pot in which metals etc. are melted and mixed. **2** a place where races, theories, etc. are mixed, or an imaginary pool where ideas are mixed together. **melt water** water formed by the melting of snow and ice, esp. from a glacier. ▫▫ **meltable** *adj.* & *n.* **melter** *n.* **meltingly** *adv.* [OE *meltan*, *mieltan* f. Gmc, rel. to MALT]

■ *v.* **1, 2, 4** soften, thaw, liquefy, fuse, dissolve; liquidize; deliquesce. **5, 6** soften, thaw; mollify, assuage, touch, move, disarm, mellow. **7** blend, fade, merge, change, disappear, dissolve, shrink. **8** disappear, dissolve, vanish, evaporate, go away, fade, pass, shrink. **10** swelter, stifle, suffocate, burn, *colloq.* roast, bake, boil. ● *n.* **3** see THAW *n.* ▫ **melt away** see DISAPPEAR 1. **melt down** see MELT *v.* 1, 2, 4 above.

meltdown /méltdown/ *n.* **1** the melting of (and consequent damage to) a structure, esp. the overheated core of a nuclear reactor. **2** a disastrous event, esp. a rapid fall in share prices.

melton /méltən/ *n.* cloth with a close-cut nap, used for overcoats etc. [*Melton Mowbray* in central England]

member /mémbər/ *n.* **1** a person belonging to a society, team, etc. **2** (**Member**) a person formally elected to take part in the proceedings of certain organizations (*Member of Parliament*; *Member of Congress*). **3** (also *attrib.*) a part or branch of a political body (*member State*; *a member of the EEC*). **4** a constituent portion of a complex structure. **5** a part of a sentence, equation, group of figures, mathematical set, etc. **6 a** any part or organ of the body, esp. a limb. **b** = PENIS. **7** used in the title awarded to a person admitted to

(usu. the lowest grade of) certain honours (*Member of the British Empire*). ▫▫ **membered** *adj.* (also in *comb.*). **memberless** *adj.* [ME f. OF *membre* f. L *membrum* limb]
■ **1, 3** associate, fellow. **4** see ELEMENT 1.

membership /mémbərship/ *n.* **1** being a member. **2** the number of members. **3** the body of members.
■ **1** see BELONGING 2. **2, 3** see FACULTY 4.

membrane /mémbrayn/ *n.* **1** any pliable sheetlike structure acting as a boundary, lining, or partition in an organism. **2** a thin pliable sheet or skin of various kinds. ▫▫ **membranaceous** /-brənáyshəss/ *adj.* **membraneous** /-bráyniəss/ *adj.* **membranous** /-brənəss/ *adj.* [L *membrana* skin of body, parchment (as MEMBER)]
■ see SHEET[1] *n.* 2a, 3.

membrum virile /mémbrəm virīli/ *n. archaic* the penis. [L, = male member]

memento /miméntō/ *n.* (*pl.* **-oes** or **-os**) an object kept as a reminder or a souvenir of a person or an event. [L, imper. of *meminisse* remember]
■ souvenir, keepsake, remembrance, reminder, relic, trophy, token; (*mementoes*) memorabilia.

memento mori /miméntō mórī, -rī/ *n.* a warning or reminder of death (e.g. a skull). [L, = remember you must die]

memo /mémmō/ *n.* (*pl.* **-os**) *colloq.* memorandum. [abbr.]
■ see MEMORANDUM.

memoir /mémwaar/ *n.* **1** a historical account or biography written from personal knowledge or special sources. **2** (in *pl.*) an autobiography or a written account of one's memory of certain events or people. **3 a** an essay on a learned subject specially studied by the writer. **b** (in *pl.*) the proceedings or transactions of a learned society (*Memoirs of the American Mathematical Society*). ▫▫ **memoirist** *n.* [F *mémoire* (masc.), special use of *mémoire* (fem.) MEMORY]
■ **1** account, report, reportage, narrative, journal, record, biography, life; annals, history, chronology. **2** (*memoirs*) autobiography, reminiscences, recollections, memories, diary, confessions, life story. **3 a** see ESSAY *n.* 1.

memorabilia /mémmərəbílliə/ *n.pl.* **1** souvenirs of memorable events. **2** *archaic* memorable or noteworthy things. [L, neut. pl. (as MEMORABLE)]
■ **1** souvenirs, remembrances, reminders, relics, trophies, tokens.

memorable /mémmərəb'l/ *adj.* **1** worth remembering, not to be forgotten. **2** easily remembered. ▫▫ **memorability** /-bílliti/ *n.* **memorableness** *n.* **memorably** *adv.* [ME f. F *mémorable* or L *memorabilis* f. *memorare* bring to mind f. *memor* mindful]
■ unforgettable, catchy; noteworthy, notable, remarkable, significant, important, momentous, eventful, historic, illustrious, celebrated, worthy, great.

memorandum /mémmərándəm/ *n.* (*pl.* **memoranda** /-də/ or **memorandums**) **1** a note or record made for future use. **2** an informal written message, esp. in business, diplomacy, etc. **3** *Law* a document recording the terms of a contract or other legal details. [ME f. L neut. sing. gerundive of *memorare*: see MEMORABLE]
■ **1, 2** note, record, minute, reminder, message, *esp. Brit.* chit, *colloq.* memo.

memorial /mimóriəl/ *n.* & *adj.* ● *n.* **1** an object, institution, or custom established in memory of a person or event (*the Albert Memorial*). **2** (often in *pl.*) *hist.* a statement of facts as the basis of a petition etc.; a record; an informal diplomatic paper. ● *adj.* intending to commemorate a person or thing (*memorial service*). ▫ **Memorial Day** *US* a day on which those who died on active service are remembered, usu. the last Monday in May. ▫▫ **memorialist** *n.* [ME f. OF *memorial* or L *memorialis* (as MEMORY)]
■ *n.* **1** monument, marker, plaque, cenotaph, statue; remembrance, reminder. **2** see RECORD *n.* 1. ● *adj.* commemorative, remembrance.

memorialize /mimóriəlīz/ *v.tr.* (also **-ise**) **1** commemorate. **2** address a memorial to (a person or body).
■ **1** honour, commemorate, pay homage *or* respect *or* tribute to, remember, celebrate, mark.

memoria technica /mimóriə téknikə/ *n.* a system or contrivance used to assist the memory. [mod.L, = artificial memory]

memorize /mémmərīz/ *v.tr.* (also **-ise**) commit to memory. ▫▫ **memorizable** *adj.* **memorization** /-záysh'n/ *n.* **memorizer** *n.*
■ learn by heart *or* rote, commit to memory, learn word for word; retain, remember.

memory /mémməri/ *n.* (*pl.* **-ies**) **1** the faculty by which things are recalled to or kept in the mind. **2 a** this faculty in an individual (*my memory is beginning to fail*). **b** one's store of things remembered (*buried deep in my memory*). **3** a recollection or remembrance (*the memory of better times*). **4** the storage capacity of a computer or other electronic machinery. **5** the remembrance of a person or thing (*his mother's memory haunted him*). **6 a** the reputation of a dead person (*his memory lives on*). **b** in formulaic phrases used of a dead sovereign etc. (*of blessed memory*). **7** the length of time over which the memory or memories of any given person or group extends (*within living memory*; *within the memory of anyone still working here*). **8** the act of remembering (*a deed worthy of memory*). ▫ **commit to memory** learn (a thing) so as to be able to recall it. **from memory** without verification in books etc. **in memory of** to keep alive the remembrance of. **memory bank** (or **board**) the memory device of a computer etc. **memory lane** (usu. prec. by *down, along*) an imaginary and sentimental journey into the past. **memory mapping** *Computing* the allocation of peripheral devices to appear located within the main memory of a computer. [ME f. OF *memorie*, *memoire* f. L *memoria* f. *memor* mindful, remembering, rel. to MOURN]
■ **1, 2a** recall, recollection, retention. **3, 5** recollection, remembrance; reminiscence, thought. **4** memory bank *or* board. **6 a** see NAME *n.* 4. **8** remembrance, recollection. ▫ **commit to memory** see LEARN 3.

memsahib /mémsaa-ib, -saab/ *n. Anglo-Ind. hist.* a European married woman in India, as spoken of or to by Indians. [MA'AM + SAHIB]

men *pl.* of MAN.

menace /ménniss/ *n.* & *v.* ● *n.* **1** a threat. **2** a dangerous or obnoxious thing or person. **3** *joc.* a pest, a nuisance. ● *v.tr.* & *intr.* threaten, esp. in a malignant or hostile manner. ▫▫ **menacer** *n.* **menacing** *adj.* **menacingly** *adv.* [ME ult. f. L *minax -acis* threatening f. *minari* threaten]
■ *n.* **1** threat, danger, peril, hazard, risk; intimidation, scare, warning, commination. **2** threat, danger, peril. **3** see PEST 1. ● *v.* threaten, intimidate, daunt, terrorize, terrify, cow, bully, frighten, scare, alarm. ▫▫ **menacing** threatening, ominous, minatory, baleful, black, dark, glowering, frightening, imtimidating, louring.

ménage /maynaázh/ *n.* the members of a household. [OF *manaige* ult. f. L (as MANSION)]
■ see FAMILY 1.

ménage à trois /maynaázh aa trwaá/ *n.* an arrangement in which three people live together, usu. a married couple and the lover of one of them. [F, = household of three (as MÉNAGE)]

menagerie /minájəri/ *n.* **1** a collection of wild animals in captivity for exhibition etc. **2** the place where these are housed. [F *ménagerie* (as MÉNAGE)]
■ zoo, zoological garden, (safari) park.

menaquinone /ménnəkwínnōn/ *n.* one of the K vitamins, produced by bacteria found in the large intestine, essential for the blood-clotting process. Also called *vitamin* K_2. [chem. deriv. of *methyl-naphthoquinone*]

menarche /menaárki/ *n.* the onset of first menstruation. [mod.L formed as MENO- + Gk *arkhē* beginning]

mend /mend/ *v.* & *n.* ● *v.* **1** *tr.* restore to a sound condition; repair (a broken article, a damaged road, torn clothes, etc.). **2** *intr.* regain health. **3** *tr.* improve (*mend matters*). **4** *tr.* add fuel to (a fire). ● *n.* a darn or repair in material etc. (*a mend* *in my shirt*). □ **mend one's fences** make peace with a person. **mend one's manners** improve one's behaviour. **mend or end** improve or abolish. **mend one's pace** go faster; alter one's pace to another's. **mend one's ways** reform, improve one's habits. **on the mend** improving in health or condition. □□ **mendable** *adj.* **mender** *n.* [ME f. AF *mender* f. *amender* AMEND]

▪ *v.* **1** repair, fix, patch (up), rectify, correct, remedy, restore. **2** heal, improve, recover, convalesce, recuperate, rehabilitate, get better. **3** correct, improve, better, reform, revise, rectify, set *or* put right, emend, *formal* ameliorate. **4** stoke, feed, fuel. ● *n.* repair, patch, darn. □ **mend one's fences** see *make up* 4. **mend one's pace** see *speed up*. **mend one's ways** reform, turn over a new leaf, go straight. **on the mend** recovering, recuperating, convalescing, convalescent, improving.

mendacious /mendáyshəss/ *adj.* lying, untruthful. □□ **mendaciously** *adv.* **mendaciousness** *n.* **mendacity** /-dássiti/ *n.* (*pl.* **-ies**). [L *mendax -dacis* perh. f. *mendum* fault]

▪ see LYING[2]. □□ **mendaciousness, mendacity** see *falsity* (FALSE).

mendelevium /méndəleéviəm/ *n. Chem.* an artificially made transuranic radioactive metallic element. ¶ Symb.: **Md**. [D. I. *Mendeleev*, Russ. chemist d. 1907]

Mendelism /méndəliz'm/ *n.* the theory of heredity based on the recurrence of certain inherited characteristics transmitted by genes. □□ **Mendelian** /-deéliən/ *adj.* & *n.* [G. J. *Mendel*, Austrian botanist d. 1884 + -ISM]

mendicant /méndikənt/ *adj.* & *n.* ● *adj.* **1** begging. **2** (of a friar) living solely on alms. ● *n.* **1** a beggar. **2** a mendicant friar. □□ **mendicancy** *n.* **mendicity** /-díssiti/ *n.* [L *mendicare* beg f. *mendicus* beggar f. *mendum* fault]

▪ *n.* **1** see BEGGAR *n.* 1, 2.

mending /ménding/ *n.* **1** the action of a person who mends. **2** things, esp. clothes, to be mended.

menfolk /ménfōk/ *n.pl.* **1** men in general. **2** the men of one's family.

menhaden /menháyd'n/ *n.* any large herring-like fish of the genus *Brevoortia*, of the E. coast of N. America, yielding valuable oil and used for manure. [Algonquian: cf. Narragansett *munnawhatteaûg*]

menhir /ménheer/ *n. Archaeol.* a tall upright usu. prehistoric monumental stone. [Breton *men* stone + *hir* long]

menial /meéniəl/ *adj.* & *n.* ● *adj.* **1** (esp. of unskilled domestic work) degrading, servile. **2** usu. *derog.* (of a servant) domestic. ● *n.* **1** a menial servant. **2** a servile person. □□ **menially** *adv.* [ME f. OF *meinee* household]

▪ *adj.* lowly, servile, humble, subservient, base, low, mean, slavish, demeaning, degrading, ignoble; routine, unskilled, domestic. ● *n.* **1** lackey, serf, drudge, slave, underling, *Brit.* fag, *colloq.* dogsbody, *Brit. colloq. derog.* skivvy, *usu. derog.* flunkey, *derog.* minion, *esp. US sl.* gofer. **2** toady, sycophant, lickspittle, *colloq.* bootlicker, yes-man.

meningitis /ménninjītiss/ *n.* an inflammation of the meninges due to infection by viruses or bacteria. □□ **meningitic** /-jíttik/ *adj.*

meninx /meéningks/ *n.* (*pl.* **meninges** /minínjeez/) (usu. in *pl.*) any of the three membranes that line the skull and vertebral canal and enclose the brain and spinal cord (dura mater, arachnoid, pia mater). □□ **meningeal** /minínjiəl/ *adj.* [mod.L f. Gk *mēnigx -iggos* membrane]

meniscus /minískəss/ *n.* (*pl.* **menisci** /-níssī/) **1** *Physics* the curved upper surface of a liquid in a tube. **2** a lens that is convex on one side and concave on the other. **3** *Math.* a crescent-shaped figure. □□ **meniscoid** *adj.* [mod.L f. Gk *mēniskos* crescent, dimin. of *mēnē* moon]

Mennonite /ménnənīt/ *n.* a member of a Protestant sect originating in Friesland in the 16th c., emphasizing adult baptism and rejecting Church organization, military service, and public office. [*Menno* Simons, its founder, d. 1561]

meno- /ménnō/ *comb. form* menstruation. [Gk *mēn mēnos* month]

menology /minólləji/ *n.* (*pl.* **-ies**) a calendar, esp. that of the Greek Church, with biographies of the saints. [mod.L *menologium* f. eccl.Gk *mēnologion* f. *mēn* month + *logos* account]

menopause /ménnəpawz/ *n.* **1** the ceasing of menstruation. **2** the period in a woman's life (usu. between 45 and 50) when this occurs (see also *male menopause*). □□ **menopausal** /-páwz'l/ *adj.* [mod.L *menopausis* (as MENO-, PAUSE)]

menorah /minórə/ *n.* a seven-armed candelabrum used in Jewish worship, esp. as a symbol of Judaism. [Heb., = candlestick]

menorrhagia /ménnəráyjiə/ *n.* abnormally heavy bleeding at menstruation. [MENO- + stem of Gk *rhēgnumi* burst]

menorrhoea /ménnəreéə/ *n.* ordinary flow of blood at menstruation. [MENO- + Gk *rhoia* f. *rheō* flow]

menses /ménseez/ *n.pl.* **1** blood and other materials discharged from the uterus at menstruation. **2** the time of menstruation. [L, pl. of *mensis* month]

Menshevik /ménshəvik/ *n. hist.* a member of the non-Leninist wing of the Russian Social Democratic Workers' Party (cf. BOLSHEVIK). [Russ. *Men'shevik* a member of the minority (*men'she* less)]

mens rea /menz reéə/ *n.* criminal intent; the knowledge of wrongdoing. [L, = guilty mind]

menstrual /ménstrooəl/ *adj.* of or relating to the menses or menstruation. □ **menstrual cycle** the process of ovulation and menstruation in female primates. [ME f. L *menstrualis* f. *mensis* month]

menstruate /ménstroo-ayt/ *v.intr.* undergo menstruation. [LL *menstruare menstruat-* (as MENSTRUAL)]

menstruation /ménstroo-áysh'n/ *n.* the process of discharging blood and other materials from the uterus in sexually mature non-pregnant women at intervals of about one lunar month until the menopause.

menstruous /ménstrooəss/ *adj.* **1** of or relating to the menses. **2** menstruating. [ME f. OF *menstrueus* or LL *menstruosus* (as MENSTRUAL)]

menstruum /ménstrooəm/ *n.* (*pl.* **menstrua** /-strooə/) a solvent. [ME f. L, neut. of *menstruus* monthly f. *mensis* month f. the alchemical parallel between transmutation into gold and the supposed action of menses on the ovum]

mensurable /ménsyoorəb'l/ *adj.* **1** measurable, having fixed limits. **2** *Mus.* = MENSURAL 2. [F *mensurable* or LL *mensurabilis* f. *mensurare* to measure f. L *mensura* MEASURE]

mensural /ménsyoorəl/ *adj.* **1** of or involving measure. **2** *Mus.* of or involving a fixed rhythm or notes of definite duration (cf. PLAINSONG). [L *mensuralis* f. *mensura* MEASURE]

mensuration /ménsyooráysh'n/ *n.* **1** measuring. **2** *Math.* the measuring of geometric magnitudes such as the lengths of lines, areas of surfaces, and volumes of solids. [LL *mensuratio* (as MENSURABLE)]

menswear /ménzwair/ *n.* clothes for men.

-ment /mənt/ *suffix* **1** forming nouns expressing the means or result of the action of a verb (*abridgement*; *embankment*). **2** forming nouns from adjectives (*merriment*; *oddment*). [from or after F f. L *-mentum*]

mental /mént'l/ *adj.* & *n.* ● *adj.* **1** of or in the mind. **2** done by the mind. **3** *colloq.* **a** insane. **b** crazy, wild, eccentric (*is mental about pop music*). ● *n. colloq.* a mental patient. □ **mental age** the degree of a person's mental development expressed as an age at which the same degree is attained by an average person. **mental arithmetic** arithmetic performed in the mind. **mental asylum** (or **home** or **hospital** or **institution**) an establishment for the care of mental patients. **mental cruelty** the infliction of suffering on another's mind, esp. *Law* as grounds for divorce. **mental defective** esp. *US* a person with impaired mental abilities. **mental deficiency** imperfect mental development leading to abnormally low intelligence. **mental illness** a disorder of the mind. **mental nurse** a nurse dealing with mentally ill patients. **mental patient** a sufferer from mental illness.

mental reservation a qualification tacitly added in making a statement etc. □□ **mentally** *adv.* [ME f. OF *mental* or LL *mentalis* f. L *mens -ntis* mind]

■ *adj.* **1, 2** intellectual, cognitive, cerebral, comprehensive, perceptual, rational, conceptual, theoretical, noetic, abstract. **3a** lunatic, mad, psychotic, demented, mentally ill, unstable, unbalanced, deranged, disturbed; (*often derog.*) *colloq.* crazy, certifiable, dotty, *esp. Brit. colloq.* daft, *sl.* off one's rocker, nutty, batty, loony, screwy, bonkers, nuts, bananas, loco, *Austral. sl.* not the full quid, *Brit. sl.* barmy, crackers.

mentalism /méntəliz'm/ *n.* **1** *Philos.* the theory that physical and psychological phenomena are ultimately only explicable in terms of a creative and interpretative mind. **2** *Psychol.* the primitive tendency to personify in spirit form the forces of nature, or endow inert objects with the quality of 'soul'. □□ **mentalist** *n.* **mentalistic** /-lístik/ *adj.*

mentality /mentálliti/ *n.* (*pl.* **-ies**) **1** mental character or disposition. **2** kind or degree of intelligence. **3** what is in or of the mind.

■ **1** inclination, attitude, bent, mind-set, disposition, character, frame of mind, temperament, outlook, view. **2** intelligence, brain, capacity, intellect, wit, sense, judgement, acuity, acumen, IQ, rationality, understanding, mental age. **3** intellectualism, intellectuality, rationality, rationalism, rationalization.

mentation /mentáysh'n/ *n.* **1** mental action. **2** state of mind. [L *mens -ntis* mind]

menthol /ménthol/ *n.* a mint-tasting organic alcohol found in oil of peppermint etc., used as a flavouring and to relieve local pain. [G f. L *mentha* MINT[1]]

mentholated /ménthəlaytid/ *adj.* treated with or containing menthol.

mention /ménsh'n/ *v.* & *n.* ● *v.tr.* **1** refer to briefly. **2** specify by name. **3** reveal or disclose (*do not mention this to anyone*). **4** (in dispatches) award (a person) a minor honour for meritorious, usu. gallant, military service. ● *n.* **1** a reference, esp. by name, to a person or thing. **2** (in dispatches) a military honour awarded for outstanding conduct. □ **don't mention it** said in polite dismissal of an apology or thanks. **make mention** (or **no mention**) **of** refer (or not refer) to. **not to mention** introducing a fact or thing of secondary or (as a rhetorical device) of primary importance. □□ **mentionable** *adj.* [OF f. L *mentio -onis* f. the root of *mens* mind]

■ *v.* **1, 2** speak *or* write about, refer to, allude to, touch on *or* upon, make mention of, talk of, bring up *or* in, introduce, broach, call *or* direct attention to, note, name, cite, acknowledge; point out, indicate, make known, adduce, report, quote. **3** divulge, reveal, intimate, disclose, impart, suggest, hint at, imply, insinuate. ● *n.* **1** reference, referral, allusion, note, citation, mentioning; announcement, remark. **2** citation; recognition, tribute, acknowledgement, praise. □ **don't mention it** (it was a) pleasure; see also *no sweat* (SWEAT). **make mention of** see REFER 7, 8. **make no mention of** see OMIT 1.

mentor /méntor/ *n.* an experienced and trusted adviser. [F f. L f. Gk *Mentōr* adviser of the young Telemachus in Homer's *Odyssey* and Fénelon's *Télémaque*]

■ see ADVISER.

menu /ményoo/ *n.* **1 a** a list of dishes available in a restaurant etc. **b** a list of items to be served at a meal. **2** *Computing* a list of options showing the commands or facilities available. □ **menu-driven** (of a program or computer) used by making selections from menus. [F, = detailed list, f. L *minutus* MINUTE[2]]

meow var. of MIAOW.

MEP *abbr.* Member of the European Parliament.

mepacrine /méppəkrin/ *n.* *Brit.* quinacrine. [*methyl* + *pa*ludism (malaria) + *acridine*]

Mephistopheles /méffistóffileez/ *n.* **1** an evil spirit to whom Faust, in the German legend, sold his soul. **2** a fiendish person. □□ **Mephistophelean** /-léeən/ *adj.* **Mephistophelian** /-féeliən/ *adj.* [G (16th c.), of unkn. orig.]

■ □□ **Mephistophelian** see SATANIC.

mephitis /mifítiss/ *n.* **1** a noxious emanation, esp. from the earth. **2** a foul-smelling or poisonous stench. □□ **mephitic** /-fíttik/ *adj.* [L]

■ see STENCH. □□ **mephitic** see STINKING *adj.* 1.

-mer /mər/ *comb. form* denoting a substance of a specified class, esp. a polymer (*dimer*; *isomer*; *tautomer*). [Gk *meros* part, share]

meranti /məránti/ *n.* a white, red, or yellow hardwood timber from any of various Malayan trees of the genus *Shorea*. [Malay]

mercantile /mérkəntīl/ *adj.* **1** of trade, trading. **2** commercial. **3** mercenary, fond of bargaining. □ **mercantile marine** shipping employed in commerce not war. [F f. It. f. *mercante* MERCHANT]

■ **1, 2** commercial, business, trade, trading, marketing, market. **3** see MERCENARY *adj.*

mercantilism /mérkəntiliz'm/ *n.* an old economic theory that money is the only form of wealth. □□ **mercantilist** *n.*

mercaptan /merkáptən/ *n.* = THIOL. [mod.L *mercurium captans* capturing mercury]

Mercator projection /merkáytər/ *n.* (also **Mercator's projection**) a projection of a map of the world on to a cylinder so that all the parallels of latitude have the same length as the equator, first published in 1569 and used esp. for marine charts and certain climatological maps. [G. *Mercator* (Latinized f. Kremer), Flemish-born geographer d. 1594]

mercenary /mérsinəri, -sinri/ *adj.* & *n.* ● *adj.* primarily concerned with money or other reward (*mercenary motives*). ● *n.* (*pl.* **-ies**) a hired soldier in foreign service. □□ **mercenariness** *n.* [ME f. L *mercenarius* f. *merces -edis* reward]

■ *adj.* money-grabbing, grasping, greedy, acquisitive, covetous, predatory, avaricious, money-grubbing. ● *n.* soldier of fortune, *usu. derog.* hireling.

mercer /mérsər/ *n.* *Brit.* a dealer in textile fabrics, esp. silk and other costly materials. □□ **mercery** *n.* (*pl.* **-ies**). [ME f. AF *mercer*, OF *mercier* ult. f. L *merx mercis* goods]

mercerize /mérsərīz/ *v.tr.* (also **-ise**) treat (cotton fabric or thread) under tension with caustic alkali to give greater strength and impart lustre. [J. *Mercer*, alleged inventor of the process d. 1866]

merchandise /mérchəndīz/ *n.* & *v.* ● *n.* goods for sale. ● *v.* **1** *intr.* trade, traffic. **2** *tr.* trade or traffic in. **3** *tr.* **a** put on the market, promote the sale of (goods etc.). **b** advertise, publicize (an idea or person). □□ **merchandisable** *adj.* **merchandiser** *n.* [ME f. OF *marchandise* f. *marchand*: see MERCHANT]

■ *n.* goods, commodities, products, stock, staples, produce. ● *v.* **1, 2** trade, deal, traffic, distribute, retail, (buy and) sell. **3** promote, advertise, publicize, market.

merchant /mérchənt/ *n.* **1** a wholesale trader, esp. with foreign countries. **2** esp. *US* & *Sc.* a retail trader. **3** *colloq.* usu. *derog.* a person showing a partiality for a specified activity or practice (*speed merchant*). □ **merchant bank** esp. *Brit.* a bank dealing in commercial loans and finance. **merchant banker** a member of a merchant bank. **merchant marine** *US* = *merchant navy*. **merchant navy** a nation's commercial shipping. **merchant prince** a wealthy merchant. **merchant ship** = MERCHANTMAN . [ME f. OF *marchand*, *marchant* ult. f. L *mercari* trade f. *merx mercis* merchandise]

■ **1** distributor, wholesaler, broker, agent, factor, forwarder; businessman, businesswoman, merchant prince, tycoon, magnate, baron, *US* jobber, *colloq.* mogul. **2** dealer, retailer, seller, shopkeeper, store owner, trader, tradesman, tradeswoman, vendor. **3** see FREAK *n.* 3b.

merchantable /mérchəntəb'l/ *adj.* saleable, marketable. [ME f. *merchant* (v.) f. OF *marchander* f. *marchand*: see MERCHANT]

merchantman /mérchəntmən/ *n.* (*pl.* **-men**) a ship conveying merchandise.

merciful /mérsifŏŏl/ *adj.* having or showing or feeling mercy. □□ **mercifulness** *n.*
■ compassionate, sympathetic, forgiving, kind, kindly, clement, kind-hearted, forbearing, sparing, lenient, tender, humane, mild, tender-hearted, soft-hearted, gracious, generous, magnanimous, benignant, beneficent, charitable, considerate, indulgent, *often iron.* big.

mercifully /mérsifŏŏli/ *adv.* **1** in a merciful manner. **2** (qualifying a whole sentence) fortunately (*mercifully, the sun came out*).
■ **2** see *happily* (HAPPY).

merciless /mérsiliss/ *adj.* **1** pitiless. **2** showing no mercy. □□ **mercilessly** *adv.* **mercilessness** *n.*
■ cruel, pitiless, ruthless, heartless, unmerciful, inhumane, inhuman, brutal, savage, barbarous, barbaric, barbarian, crude, rude, rough, harsh, tough, callous, hard, hard-hearted, tyrannical, stony-hearted, cold, severe, unsparing, unsympathetic, unforgiving, malevolent, uncharitable, unmoved, unbending, inflexible, relentless, unrelenting, inexorable.

mercurial /merkyŏŏriəl/ *adj.* & *n.* ● *adj.* **1** (of a person) sprightly, ready-witted, volatile. **2** of or containing mercury. **3** (**Mercurial**) of the planet Mercury. ● *n.* a drug containing mercury. □□ **mercurialism** *n.* **mercuriality** /-riálliti/ *n.* **mercurially** *adv.* [ME f. OF *mercuriel* or L *mercurialis* (as MERCURY)]
■ *adj.* **1** see VOLATILE *adj.* 2. □□ **mercuriality** see *inconstancy* (INCONSTANT).

mercury /mérkyoori/ *n.* **1** *Chem.* a silvery-white heavy liquid metallic element occurring naturally in cinnabar and used in barometers, thermometers, and amalgams; quicksilver. ¶ Symb.: **Hg.** **2** (**Mercury**) the planet nearest to the sun. **3** any plant of the genus *Mercurialis*, esp. *M. perenne*. □ **mercury vapour lamp** a lamp in which light is produced by an electric discharge through mercury vapour. □□ **mercuric** /-kyŏŏrik/ *adj.* **mercurous** *adj.* [ME f. L *Mercurius* messenger of the gods and god of traders f. *merx mercis* merchandise]

mercy /mérsi/ *n.* & *int.* ● *n.* (*pl.* **-ies**) **1** compassion or forbearance shown to enemies or offenders in one's power. **2** the quality of compassion. **3** an act of mercy. **4** (*attrib.*) administered or performed out of mercy or pity for a suffering person (*mercy killing*). **5** something to be thankful for (*small mercies*). ● *int.* expressing surprise or fear. □ **at the mercy of 1** wholly in the power of. **2** liable to danger or harm from. **have mercy on** (or **upon**) show mercy to. **mercy flight** the transporting by air of an injured or sick person from a remote area to a hospital. [ME f. OF *merci* f. L *merces -edis* reward, in LL pity, thanks]
■ *n.* **1, 2** compassion, forbearance, pity, quarter, tolerance, sympathy, favour, forgiveness, kindness, kindliness, leniency, tenderness, humanity, humaneness, liberality, kind-heartedness, tender-heartedness, soft-heartedness, graciousness, generosity, magnanimity, benignity, beneficence, charity, thoughtfulness, consideration, indulgence. **3** errand of mercy, kindness, favour. **4** see MERCIFUL. **5** see LUCK 3. ● *int.* see BOY *int.* □ **at the mercy of 1** in the power of, under a person's thumb. **have mercy on** (or **upon**) see SPARE *v.* 2a.

mere[1] /meer/ *attrib.adj.* (**merest**) that is solely or no more or better than what is specified (*a mere boy; no mere theory*). □ **mere right** *Law* a right in theory. □□ **merely** *adv.* [ME f. AF *meer*, OF *mier* f. L *merus* unmixed]
■ bare, basic, sheer, simple, very; least, nothing but. □□ **merely** only, simply, solely, purely, no more than; barely, scarcely.

mere[2] /meer/ *n. archaic* or *poet.* a lake or pond. [OE f. Gmc]

mere[3] /mérri/ *n.* a Maori war-club, esp. one made of greenstone. [Maori]

meretricious /mérritríshəss/ *adj.* **1** (of decorations, literary style, etc.) showily but falsely attractive. **2** of or befitting a prostitute. □□ **meretriciously** *adv.* **meretriciousness** *n.* [L *meretricius* f. *meretrix -tricis* prostitute f. *merēri* be hired]

merganser /mergánsər/ *n.* any of various diving fish-eating northern ducks of the genus *Mergus*, with a long narrow serrated hooked bill. Also called SAWBILL. [mod.L f. L *mergus* diver f. *mergere* dive + *anser* goose]

merge /merj/ *v.* **1** *tr.* & *intr.* (often foll. by *with*) **a** combine or be combined. **b** join or blend gradually. **2** *intr.* & *tr.* (foll. by *in*) lose or cause to lose character and identity in (something else). **3** *tr.* (foll. by *in*) embody (a title or estate) in (a larger one). □□ **mergence** *n.* [L *mergere mers-* dip, plunge, partly through legal AF *merger*]
■ **1** combine, coalesce, unite, join, amalgamate, consolidate, blend, mix, mingle, fuse, conflate, *literary* commingle; pool.

merger /mérjər/ *n.* **1** the combining of two commercial companies etc. into one. **2** a merging, esp. of one estate in another. **3** *Law* the absorbing of a minor offence in a greater one. [AF (as MERGE)]
■ **1, 2** combination, coalescence, union, amalgamation, consolidation, coalition, merging, pooling, blending, mixing, mingling, fusing, fusion, *literary* commingling.

meridian /məriddiən/ *n.* & *adj.* ● *n.* **1** a circle passing through the celestial poles and zenith of any place on the earth's surface. **2 a** a circle of constant longitude, passing through a given place and the terrestrial poles. **b** the corresponding line on a map. **3** *archaic* the point at which a sun or star attains its highest altitude. **4** prime; full splendour. ● *adj.* **1** of noon. **2** of the period of greatest splendour, vigour, etc. [ME f. OF *meridien* or L *meridianus* (adj.) f. *meridies* midday f. *medius* middle + *dies* day]

meridional /məriddiən'l/ *adj.* & *n.* ● *adj.* **1** of or in the south (esp. of Europe). **2** of or relating to a meridian. ● *n.* an inhabitant of the south (esp. of France). [ME f. OF f. LL *meridionalis* irreg. f. L *meridies*: see MERIDIAN]

meringue /məráng/ *n.* **1** a confection of sugar, the white of eggs, etc., baked crisp. **2** a small cake or shell of this, usu. decorated or filled with whipped cream etc. [F, of unkn. orig.]

merino /məréenō/ *n.* (*pl.* **-os**) **1** (in full **merino sheep**) a variety of sheep with long fine wool. **2** a soft woollen or wool-and-cotton material like cashmere, orig. of merino wool. **3** a fine woollen yarn. [Sp., of uncert. orig.]

meristem /mérristem/ *n. Bot.* a plant tissue consisting of actively dividing cells forming new tissue. □□ **meristematic** /-stəmáttik/ *adj.* [Gk *meristos* divisible f. *merizō* divide f. *meros* part, after *xylem*]

merit /mérrit/ *n.* & *v.* ● *n.* **1** the quality of deserving well. **2** excellence, worth. **3** (usu. in *pl.*) **a** a thing that entitles one to reward or gratitude. **b** esp. *Law* intrinsic rights and wrongs (*the merits of a case*). **4** *Theol.* good deeds as entitling to a future reward. ● *v.tr.* (**merited, meriting**) deserve or be worthy of (reward, punishment, consideration, etc.). □ **make a merit of** regard or represent (one's own conduct) as praiseworthy. **on its merits** with regard only to its intrinsic worth. **Order of Merit** *Brit.* an order founded in 1902, for distinguished achievement. [ME f. OF *merite* f. L *meritum* price, value, = past part. of *merēri* earn, deserve]
■ *n.* **1, 2** worth, worthiness, value, excellence, quality, virtue, good, goodness. **3** (*merits*) **a** assets, advantage(s). **b** rights and wrongs. ● *v.* earn, deserve, warrant, rate, have a right *or* claim to, be entitled to, be qualified for, be worthy of. □ **make a merit of** sing the praises of, praise; see GLORIFY 3.

meritocracy /mérritókrəsi/ *n.* (*pl.* **-ies**) **1** government by persons selected competitively according to merit. **2** a group of persons selected in this way. **3** a society governed by meritocracy.

meritorious /mérritóriəss/ *adj.* **1** (of a person or act) having merit; deserving reward, praise, or gratitude. **2** deserving commendation for thoroughness etc. □□ **meritoriously** *adv.* **meritoriousness** *n.* [ME f. L *meritorius* f. *merēri merit-* earn]
■ honourable, laudable, praiseworthy, commendable, creditable, admirable, estimable, excellent, exemplary, outstanding.

merle /merl/ *n. Sc.* or *archaic* a blackbird. [ME f. F f. L *merula*]

merlin /mérlin/ *n.* a small European or N. American falcon, *Falco columbarius*, that hunts small birds. [ME f. AF *merilun* f. OF *esmerillon* augment. f. *esmeril* f. Frank.]

merlon /mérlon/ *n.* the solid part of an embattled parapet between two embrasures. [F f. It. *merlone* f. *merlo* battlement]

mermaid /mérmayd/ *n.* an imaginary half-human sea creature, with the head and trunk of a woman and the tail of a fish. [ME f. MERE[2] in obs. sense 'sea' + MAID]

merman /mérman/ *n.* (*pl.* **-men**) the male equivalent of a mermaid.

mero- /mérrō/ *comb. form* partly, partial. [Gk *meros* part]

-merous /mərəss/ *comb. form* esp. *Bot.* having so many parts (*dimerous*; *5-merous*). [Gk (as MERO-)]

Merovingian /mérrōvínjiən/ *adj.* & *n.* ● *adj.* of or relating to the Frankish dynasty founded by Clovis and reigning in Gaul and Germany *c.*500–750. ● *n.* a member of this dynasty. [F *mérovingien* f. med.L *Merovingi* f. L *Meroveus* name of the reputed founder]

merriment /mérrimənt/ *n.* **1** exuberant enjoyment; being merry. **2** mirth, fun.

■ jollity, joviality, merrymaking, revelry, gaiety, high *or* good spirits, mirth, mirthfulness, joyfulness, felicity, jubilation, festivity, exhilaration, buoyancy, exuberance, cheer, cheerfulness, glee, fun, hilarity, enjoyment, happiness.

merry /mérri/ *adj.* (**merrier, merriest**) **1 a** joyous. **b** full of laughter or gaiety. **2** *Brit. colloq.* slightly drunk. □ **make merry 1** be festive; enjoy oneself. **2** (foll. by *over*) make fun of. **merry andrew** a mountebank's assistant; a clown or buffoon. **merry thought** esp. *Brit.* the wishbone of a bird. **play merry hell with** see HELL. □□ **merrily** *adv.* **merriness** *n.* [OE *myrige* f. Gmc]

■ **1** cheerful, happy, gay, cheery, jolly, jovial, in high *or* good spirits, mirthful, joyful, joyous, hilarious, jubilant, gamesome, festive, exuberant, vivacious, convivial, buoyant, gleeful, carefree, light-hearted, delighted, *poet.* blithe. **2** see DRUNK *adj.* 1. □ **make merry 1** celebrate, carouse, frolic; see also REVEL *v.* 1. **2** see TEASE *v.* **merry andrew** see CLOWN *n.* 1.

merry-go-round /mérrigōrownd/ *n.* **1** a revolving machine with wooden horses or cars for riding on at a fair etc. **2** a cycle of bustling activities.

■ **1** roundabout, whirligig, *US* carousel.

merrymaking /mérrimayking/ *n.* festivity, fun. □□ **merrymaker** *n.*

■ see FUN *n.* 3.

mesa /máysə/ *n. US* an isolated flat-topped hill with steep sides, found in landscapes with horizontal strata. [Sp., lit. table, f. L *mensa*]

mésalliance /mayzálliɔnss/ *n.* a marriage with a person of a lower social position. [F (as MIS-[2], ALLIANCE)]

mescal /méskal/ *n.* **1 a** maguey. **b** liquor obtained from this. **2** a peyote cactus. □ **mescal buttons** disc-shaped dried tops from the peyote cactus, eaten or chewed as an intoxicant. [Sp. *mezcal* f. Nahuatl *mexcalli*]

mescaline /méskəleen/ *n.* (also **mescalin** /-lin/) a hallucinogenic alkaloid present in mescal buttons.

Mesdames *pl.* of MADAME.

Mesdemoiselles *pl.* of MADEMOISELLE.

mesembryanthemum /mizémbriánthiməm/ *n.* any of various succulent plants of the genus *Mesembryanthemum* of S. Africa, having daisy-like flowers in a wide range of bright colours that fully open in sunlight. [mod.L f. Gk *mesembria* noon + *anthemon* flower]

mesencephalon /méssenséffəlon/ *n.* the part of the brain developing from the middle of the primitive or embryonic brain. Also called MIDBRAIN. [Gk *mesos* middle + *encephalon* brain: see ENCEPHALIC]

mesentery /méssəntəri/ *n.* (*pl.* **-ies**) a double layer of peritoneum attaching the stomach, small intestine, pancreas, spleen, and other abdominal organs to the posterior wall of the abdomen. □□ **mesenteric** /-térrik/ *adj.* **mesenteritis** /-rītiss/ *n.* [med.L *mesenterium* f. Gk *mesenterion* (as MESO-, *enteron* intestine)]

mesh /mesh/ *n.* & *v.* ● *n.* **1** a network fabric or structure. **2** each of the open spaces or interstices between the strands of a net or sieve etc. **3** (in *pl.*) **a** a network. **b** a snare. **4** (in *pl.*) *Physiol.* an interlaced structure. ● *v.* **1** *intr.* (often foll. by *with*) (of the teeth of a wheel) be engaged (with others). **2** *intr.* be harmonious. **3** *tr.* catch in or as in a net. □ **in mesh** (of the teeth of wheels) engaged. [earlier *meish* etc. f. MDu. *maesche* f. Gmc]

■ *n.* **1–3a** mesh-work, network, netting, net, web, webbing, lattice, lattice-work, screen, screening, interlacing, lace-work, grid, grate, grating, trellis, trellis-work, decussation, reticulation, reticle, reticulum, graticule, plexus, *Anat.* rete; interstice. **3 b** (*meshes*) grip, clutch(es), grasp, web, trap, snare, entanglement, tangle. ● *v.* **1** engage, fit (together), dovetail, knit, enmesh, match, interlock. **2** see JELL 2. **3** catch, entangle, enmesh, grab, trap, entrap, snare, ensnare; involve, implicate.

mesial /meéziəl/ *adj. Anat.* of, in, or directed towards the middle line of a body. □□ **mesially** *adv.* [irreg. f. Gk *mesos* middle]

mesmerism /mézməriz'm/ *n.* **1** *Psychol.* **a** a hypnotic state produced in a person by another's influence over the will and nervous system. **b** a doctrine concerning this. **c** an influence producing this. **2** fascination. □□ **mesmeric** /mezmérrik/ *adj.* **mesmerically** /-mérrikəli/ *adv.* **mesmerist** *n.* [F. A. *Mesmer*, Austrian physician d. 1815]

■ **2** see SPELL[2] 2.

mesmerize /mézmərīz/ *v.tr.* (also **-ise**) **1** *Psychol.* hypnotize; exercise mesmerism on. **2** fascinate, spellbind. □□ **mesmerization** /-záysh'n/ *n.* **mesmerizer** *n.* **mesmerizingly** *adv.*

■ **2** see FASCINATE 1.

mesne /meen/ *adj. Law* intermediate. □ **mesne lord** *hist.* a lord holding an estate from a superior feudal lord. **mesne process** proceedings in a suit intervening between a primary and final process. **mesne profits** profits received from an estate by a tenant between two dates. [ME f. law F, var. of AF *meen*, MEAN[3]: cf. DEMESNE]

meso- /méssō, méz-/ *comb. form* middle, intermediate. [Gk *mesos* middle]

mesoblast /méssōblast/ *n. Biol.* the middle germ-layer of an embryo.

mesoderm /méssōderm/ *n. Biol.* = MESOBLAST. [MESO- + Gk *derma* skin]

mesolithic /mézzōlíthik/ *adj. Archaeol.* of or concerning the Stone Age between the palaeolithic and neolithic periods. [MESO- + Gk *lithos* stone]

mesomorph /méssōmorf/ *n.* a person with a compact and muscular build of body (cf. ECTOMORPH, ENDOMORPH). □□ **mesomorphic** /-mórfik/ *adj.* [MESO- + Gk *morphē* form]

■ □□ **mesomorphic** see MUSCULAR.

meson /mézzon, meézon/ *n. Physics* any of a class of elementary particles believed to participate in the forces that hold nucleons together in the atomic nucleus. □□ **mesic** /mézzik, meéz-/ *adj.* **mesonic** /mizónnik/ *adj.* [earlier *mesotron*: cf. MESO-, -ON]

mesophyll /méssōfil/ *n.* the inner tissue of a leaf. [MESO- + Gk *phullon* leaf]

mesophyte /méssōfīt/ *n.* a plant needing only a moderate amount of water.

mesosphere /méssōsfeer/ *n.* the region of the atmosphere extending from the top of the stratosphere to an altitude of about 50 miles.

Mesozoic /méssōzṓ-ik/ *adj.* & *n. Geol.* ● *adj.* of or relating to an era of geological time marked by the development of dinosaurs, and with evidence of the first mammals, birds, and flowering plants. ¶ Cf. Appendix VII. ● *n.* this era (cf. CENOZOIC, PALAEOZOIC). [MESO- + Gk *zōion* animal]

mesquite /méskeet/ *n.* (also **mesquit**) any N. American leguminous tree of the genus *Prosopis*, esp. *P. juliflora.* □ **mesquite bean** a pod from the mesquite, used as fodder. [Mex. Sp. *mezquite*]

mess /mess/ *n.* & *v.* ● *n.* **1** a dirty or untidy state of things (*the room is a mess*). **2** a state of confusion, embarrassment, or trouble. **3** something causing a mess, e.g. spilt liquid etc. **4** a domestic animal's excreta. **5 a** a company of persons who take meals together, esp. in the armed forces. **b** a place where such meals or recreation take place communally. **c** a meal taken there. **6** *derog.* a disagreeable concoction or medley. **7** a liquid or mixed food for hounds etc. **8** a portion of liquid or pulpy food. ● *v.* **1** *tr.* (often foll. by *up*) **a** make a mess of; dirty. **b** muddle; make into a state of confusion. **2** *intr.* (foll. by *with*) interfere with. **3** *intr.* take one's meals. **4** *intr. colloq.* defecate. □ **make a mess of** bungle (an undertaking). **mess about** (or **around**) **1** act desultorily. **2** *colloq.* make things awkward for; cause arbitrary inconvenience to (a person). **mess-hall** a military dining area. **mess-jacket** a short close-fitting coat worn at the mess. **mess kit** a soldier's cooking and eating utensils. **mess of pottage** a material comfort etc. for which something higher is sacrificed (Gen. 25:29–34). **mess tin** a small container as part of a mess kit. [ME f. OF *mes* portion of food f. LL *missus* course at dinner, past part. of *mittere* send]

■ *n.* **1** chaos, disorder, disarray, disorganization, muddle, disarrangement, clutter, hotchpotch, litter, tangle, jumble, confusion, mishmash, *colloq.* shambles; untidiness. **2** predicament, difficulty, plight, trouble, quandary, imbroglio, foul-up, pretty kettle of fish, *colloq.* stew, fix, hot water, pickle, jam, can of worms, *disp.* dilemma, *sl.* screw-up, snafu. **5 b** mess-hall, canteen, refectory. **6** concoction, mixture, medley, miscellany, hash, hotchpotch, gallimaufry, farrago, olio, olla podrida. ● *v.* **1** dirty, clutter up, make untidy, turn upside down, pull to pieces, upset, muddle, disarrange, disarray, dishevel, tousle, *US colloq.* muss (up); ruin, destroy, wreck, bungle, botch, foul up, *colloq.* make a hash *or* shambles of, *Brit. colloq.* muck up. **2** (*mess with*) interfere in *or* with, intervene in, meddle with *or* in, intrude in, butt in *or* into, tinker with, tamper with, get involved in *or* with. **3** see EAT 1b. **4** see DEFECATE. □ **make a mess of** see BOTCH *v.* 1. **mess about** (or **around**) **1** fool *or* play (about *or* around), poke *or* fiddle about *or* around, potter (about *or* around), *Brit. colloq.* muck about *or* around; dally, waste time, dawdle, loiter, *US sl.* lallygag. **2** cause trouble, cause complications for, create difficulties for, *Brit. colloq.* muck about *or* around. **mess-hall** mess, canteen, refectory.

message /méssij/ *n.* & *v.* ● *n.* **1** an oral or written communication sent by one person to another. **2 a** an inspired or significant communication from a prophet, writer, or preacher. **b** the central import or meaning of an artistic work etc. **3** a mission or errand. **4** (in *pl.*) *Sc.* & *N.Engl.* things bought; shopping. ● *v.tr.* **1** send as a message. **2** transmit (a plan etc.) by signalling etc. □ **get the message** *colloq.* understand what is meant. **message stick** *Austral.* a stick carved with significant marks, carried as identification by Aboriginal messengers. [ME f. OF ult. f. L *mittere miss-* send]

■ *n.* **1** communication, bulletin, report, communiqué, news, dispatch, information, word, intelligence, *literary* tidings; note, letter, memorandum, *joc.* missive. **2 b** idea, point, import, meaning, essence, implication. **3** see MISSION 1a.

Messeigneurs *pl.* of MONSEIGNEUR.

messenger /méssinjər/ *n.* **1** a person who carries a message. **2** a person employed to carry messages. □ **King's** (or **Queen's**) **Messenger** a courier in the diplomatic service. **messenger RNA** a form of RNA carrying genetic information from DNA to a ribosome. ¶ Abbr.: **mRNA**. [ME & OF *messager* (as MESSAGE): *-n-* as in *harbinger*, *passenger*, etc.]

■ envoy, emissary, nuncio, intermediary, go-between, *archaic* legate; page, errand-boy, errand-girl, courier, runner, dispatch-rider, *esp. US sl.* gofer; herald, harbinger.

Messiah /misī́ə/ *n.* **1** a liberator or would-be liberator of an oppressed people or country. **2 a** the promised deliverer of the Jews. **b** (usu. prec. by *the*) Christ regarded as this. □□ **Messiahship** *n.* [ME f. OF *Messie* ult. f. Heb. *māšîaḥ* anointed]

■ **1** deliverer, liberator, emancipator, saviour, redeemer, rescuer.

Messianic /méssiánnik/ *adj.* **1** of the Messiah. **2** inspired by hope or belief in a Messiah. □□ **Messianism** /misī́əniz'm/ *n.* [F *messianique* (as MESSIAH) after *rabbinique* rabbinical]

Messieurs *pl.* of MONSIEUR.

messmate /mésmayt/ *n.* a person with whom one regularly takes meals, esp. in the armed forces.

Messrs /méssərz/ *pl.* of MR. [abbr. of MESSIEURS]

messuage /méswij/ *n. Law* a dwelling-house with outbuildings and land assigned to its use. [ME f. AF: perh. an alternative form of *mesnage* dwelling]

messy /méssi/ *adj.* (**messier**, **messiest**) **1** untidy or dirty. **2** causing or accompanied by a mess. **3** difficult to deal with; full of awkward complications. □□ **messily** *adv.* **messiness** *n.*

■ **1, 2** see UNTIDY.

mestizo /mesteézō/ *n.* (*pl.* **-os**; *fem.* **mestiza** /-zə/, *pl.* **-as**) a Spaniard or Portuguese of mixed race, esp. the offspring of a Spaniard and an American Indian. [Sp. ult. f. L *mixtus* past part. of *miscēre* mix]

met[1] *past* and *past part.* of MEET[1].

met[2] /met/ *adj. colloq.* **1** meteorological. **2** metropolitan. **3** (**the Met**) **a** (in full **the Met Office**) (in the UK) the Meteorological Office. **b** the Metropolitan Police in London. **c** the Metropolitan Opera House in New York. [abbr.]

meta- /méttə/ *comb. form* (usu. **met-** before a vowel or *h*) **1** denoting change of position or condition (*metabolism*). **2** denoting position: **a** behind. **b** after or beyond (*metaphysics*; *metacarpus*). **c** of a higher or second-order kind (*metalanguage*). **3** *Chem.* **a** relating to two carbon atoms separated by one other in a benzene ring. **b** relating to a compound formed by dehydration (*metaphosphate*). [Gk *meta-*, *met-*, *meth-* f. *meta* with, after]

metabolism /mitábbəliz'm/ *n.* all the chemical processes that occur within a living organism, resulting in energy production (**destructive metabolism**) and growth (**constructive metabolism**). □□ **metabolic** /méttəbóllik/ *adj.* **metabolically** /méttəbóllikəli/ *adv.* [Gk *metabolē* change (as META-, *bolē* f. *ballō* throw)]

metabolite /mitábbəlīt/ *n. Physiol.* a substance formed in or necessary for metabolism.

metabolize /mitábbəlīz/ *v.tr.* & *intr.* (also **-ise**) process or be processed by metabolism. □□ **metabolizable** *adj.*

metacarpus /méttəkaárpəss/ *n.* (*pl.* **metacarpi** /-pī/) **1** the set of five bones of the hand that connects the wrist to the fingers. **2** this part of the hand. □□ **metacarpal** *adj.* [mod.L f. Gk *metakarpon* (as META-, CARPUS)]

metacentre /méttəsentər/ *n.* (*US* **metacenter**) the point of intersection between a line (vertical in equilibrium) through the centre of gravity of a floating body and a vertical line through the centre of pressure after a slight angular displacement, which must be above the centre of gravity to ensure stability. □□ **metacentric** /-séntrik/ *adj.* [F *métacentre* (as META-, CENTRE)]

metage /meétij/ *n.* **1** the official measuring of a load of coal etc. **2** the duty paid for this. [METE[1] + -AGE]

metagenesis /méttəjénnisiss/ *n.* the alternation of generations between sexual and asexual reproduction. □□ **metagenetic** /-jinéttik/ *adj.* [mod.L (as META-, GENESIS)]

metal /métt'l/ *n.*, *adj.*, & *v.* ● *n.* **1 a** any of a class of chemical elements such as gold, silver, iron, and tin, usu. lustrous ductile solids and good conductors of heat and electricity and forming basic oxides. **b** an alloy of any of these. **2** material used for making glass, in a molten state. **3** *Heraldry* gold or silver as tincture. **4** (in *pl.*) the rails of a railway line. **5** = *road-metal* (see ROAD[1]). ● *adj.* made of metal. ● *v.tr.* (**metalled, metalling**; *US* **metaled, metaling**) **1** provide or fit with metal. **2** *Brit.* make or mend (a road) with road-metal. □ **metal detector** an electronic device giving a signal when it locates metal. **metal fatigue** fatigue (see FATIGUE *n.* 2) in metal. [ME f. OF *metal* or L *metallum* f. Gk *metallon* mine]

metalanguage /méttəlanggwij/ *n.* **1** a form of language used to discuss a language. **2** a system of propositions about propositions.

metallic /mitállik/ *adj.* **1** of, consisting of, or characteristic of metal or metals. **2** sounding sharp and ringing, like struck metal. **3** having the sheen or lustre of metals. □□ **metallically** *adv.* [L *metallicus* f. Gk *metallikos* (as METAL)]
■ **2** see TINNY *adj.* 3b.

metalliferous /méttəlíffərəss/ *adj.* bearing or producing metal. [L *metallifer* (as METAL, -FEROUS)]

metallize /méttəlīz/ *v.tr.* (also **-ise**; *US* **metalize**) **1** render metallic. **2** coat with a thin layer of metal. □□ **metallization** /-záysh'n/ *n.*

metallography /méttəlógrəfi/ *n.* the descriptive science of the structure and properties of metals. □□ **metallographic** /mitálləgráffik/ *adj.* **metallographical** /mitálləgráffik'l/ *adj.* **metallographically** /mitálləgráffikəli/ *adv.*

metalloid /méttəloyd/ *adj.* & *n.* ● *adj.* having the form or appearance of a metal. ● *n.* any element intermediate in properties between metals and non-metals, e.g. boron, silicon, and germanium.

metallurgy /mitállərji, méttəlurji/ *n.* the science concerned with the production, purification, and properties of metals and their application. □□ **metallurgic** /méttəlúrjik/ *adj.* **metallurgical** /méttəlúrjik'l/ *adj.* **metallurgically** /méttəlúrjikəli/ *adv.* **metallurgist** *n.* [Gk *metallon* metal + *-ourgia* working]

metalwork /métt'lwurk/ *n.* **1** the art of working in metal. **2** metal objects collectively. □□ **metalworker** *n.*

metamere /méttəmeer/ *n. Zool.* each of several similar segments, that contain the same internal structures, of an animal body. [META- + Gk *meros* part]

metameric /méttəmérrik/ *adj.* **1** *Chem.* having the same proportional composition and molecular weight, but different functional groups and chemical properties. **2** *Zool.* of or relating to metameres. □□ **metamer** /méttəmər/ *n.* **metamerism** /metámməriz'm/ *n.*

metamorphic /méttəmórfik/ *adj.* **1** of or marked by metamorphosis. **2** *Geol.* (of rock) that has undergone transformation by natural agencies such as heat and pressure. □□ **metamorphism** *n.* [META- + Gk *morphē* form]

metamorphose /méttəmórfōz/ *v.tr.* **1** change in form. **2** (foll. by *to, into*) **a** turn (into a new form). **b** change the nature of. [F *métamorphoser* f. *métamorphose* METAMORPHOSIS]
■ see CHANGE *v.* 1.

metamorphosis /méttəmórfəsiss, -morfṓsiss/ *n.* (*pl.* **metamorphoses** /-seez/) **1** a change of form (by natural or supernatural means). **2** a changed form. **3** a change of character, conditions, etc. **4** *Zool.* the transformation between an immature form and an adult form, e.g. from a pupa to an insect, or from a tadpole to a frog. [L f. Gk *metamorphōsis* f. *metamorphoō* transform (as META-, *morphoō* f. *morphē* form)]
■ **1, 3, 4** see CHANGE *n.* 1.

metaphase /méttəfayz/ *n. Biol.* the stage of meiotic or mitotic cell division when the chromosomes become attached to the spindle fibres.

metaphor /méttəfor/ *n.* **1** the application of a name or descriptive term or phrase to an object or action to which it is imaginatively but not literally applicable (e.g. *a glaring error*). **2** an instance of this. □□ **metaphoric** /-fórrik/ *adj.* **metaphorical** /-fórrik'l/ *adj.* **metaphorically** /-fórrikəli/ *adv.* [F *métaphore* or L *metaphora* f. Gk *metaphora* f. *metapherō* transfer]
■ figure (of speech), analogy, analogue, image, trope, symbol; simile; symbolism, imagery. □□ **metaphoric, metaphorical** non-literal, analogical, analogous, figurative, symbolic, tropological.

metaphrase /méttəfrayz/ *n.* & *v.* ● *n.* literal translation. ● *v.tr.* put into other words. □□ **metaphrastic** /-frástik/ *adj.* [mod.L *metaphrasis* f. Gk *metaphrasis* f. *metaphrazō* translate]
■ *v.* see PARAPHRASE *v.*

metaphysic /méttəfizzik/ *n.* a system of metaphysics.

metaphysical /méttəfizzik'l/ *adj.* & *n.* ● *adj.* **1** of or relating to metaphysics. **2** based on abstract general reasoning. **3** excessively subtle or theoretical. **4** incorporeal; supernatural. **5** visionary. **6** (of poetry, esp. in the 17th c. in England) characterized by subtlety of thought and complex imagery. ● *n.* (**the Metaphysicals**) the metaphysical poets. □□ **metaphysically** *adv.*
■ *adj.* **2** see ABSTRACT *adj.* 1a. **3** see SUBTLE 1, THEORETICAL. **4** see SUPERNATURAL *adj.*

metaphysics /méttəfizziks/ *n.pl.* (usu. treated as *sing.*) **1** the theoretical philosophy of being and knowing. **2** the philosophy of mind. **3** *colloq.* abstract or subtle talk; mere theory. □□ **metaphysician** /-zísh'n/ *n.* **metaphysicize** /-fizzisīz/ *v.intr.* [ME *metaphysic* f. OF *metaphysique* f. med.L *metaphysica* ult. f. Gk *ta meta ta phusika* the things after the Physics, from the sequence of Aristotle's works]
■ **1, 2** see PHILOSOPHY 1.

metaplasia /méttəpláyziə/ *n. Physiol.* an abnormal change in the nature of a tissue. □□ **metaplastic** /-plástik/ *adj.* [mod.L f. G *Metaplase* f. Gk *metaplasis* (as META-, *plasis* f. *plassō* to mould)]

metapsychology /méttəsīkólləji/ *n.* the study of the nature and functions of the mind beyond what can be studied experimentally. □□ **metapsychological** /-kəlójik'l/ *adj.*

metastable /méttəstáyb'l/ *adj.* **1** (of a state of equilibrium) stable only under small disturbances. **2** passing to another state so slowly as to seem stable. □□ **metastability** /-stəbílliti/ *n.*

metastasis /metástəsiss/ *n.* (*pl.* **metastases** /-seez/) *Physiol.* **1** the transference of a bodily function, disease, etc., from one part or organ to another. **2** the transformation of chemical compounds into others in the process of assimilation by an organism. □□ **metastasize** *v.intr.* (also **-ise**). **metastatic** /méttəstáttik/ *adj.* [LL f. Gk f. *methistēmi* change]
■ **2** see TRANSITION. □□ **metastasize** see SPREAD *v.* 2.

metatarsus /méttətáarsəss/ *n.* (*pl.* **metatarsi** /-sī/) **1** the part of the foot between the ankle and the toes. **2** the set of bones in this. □□ **metatarsal** *adj.* [mod.L (as META-, TARSUS)]

metathesis /mitáthisiss/ *n.* (*pl.* **metatheses** /-seez/) **1** *Gram.* the transposition of sounds or letters in a word. **2** *Chem.* the interchange of atoms or groups of atoms between two molecules. **3** an instance of either of these. □□ **metathetic** /méttəthéttik/ *adj.* **metathetical** /méttəthéttik'l/ *adj.* [LL f. Gk *metatithēmi* transpose]

metazoan /méttəzṓən/ *n.* & *adj. Zool.* ● *n.* any animal of the subkingdom Metazoa, having multicellular and differentiated tissues. ● *adj.* of or relating to the Metazoans. [*Metazoa* f. Gk META- + *zōia* pl. of *zōion* animal]

mete[1] /meet/ *v.tr.* **1** (usu. foll. by *out*) *literary* apportion or allot (a punishment or reward). **2** *poet.* or *Bibl.* measure. □ **mete-wand** (or **-yard**) a standard of estimation. [OE *metan* f. Gmc., rel. to MEET[1]]
■ **1** (*mete out*) deal (out), apportion, distribute, dole (out), allot, assign, allocate, parcel out, share (out), ration (out), measure out, dispense, hand out, give out, pass out, *sl.* dish out. **2** see MEASURE *v.* 1.

mete[2] /meet/ *n.* a boundary or boundary stone. [ME f. OF f. L *meta* boundary, goal]

metempsychosis /méttempsīkṓsiss/ *n.* (*pl.* **-psychoses** /-seez/) **1** the supposed transmigration of the soul of a human being or animal at death into a new body of the same or a different species. **2** an instance of this. □□ **metempsychosist** *n.* [LL f. Gk *metempsukhōsis* (as META-, EN-², *psukhē* soul)]

■ transmigration, reincarnation, rebirth.

meteor /meétiər/ *n.* **1** a small body of matter from outer space that becomes incandescent as a result of friction with the earth's atmosphere. **2** a streak of light emanating from a meteor. □ **meteor shower** a group of meteors appearing to come from one point in the sky. [ME f. mod.L *meteorum* f. Gk *meteōron* neut. of *meteōros* lofty, (as META-, *aeirō* raise)]

meteoric /meétiórrik/ *adj.* **1 a** of or relating to the atmosphere. **b** dependent on atmospheric conditions. **2** of meteors. **3** rapid like a meteor; dazzling, transient (*meteoric rise to fame*). □ **meteoric stone** a meteorite. □□ **meteorically** *adv.*

■ **3** brief, short-lived, temporary, transitory, transient, ephemeral, evanescent, impermanent, fleeting, momentary, swift, overnight; brilliant, dazzling, flashing, spectacular, sensational.

meteorite /meétiərīt/ *n.* a fallen meteor, or fragment of natural rock or metal, that reaches the earth's surface from outer space. □□ **meteoritic** /-ríttik/ *adj.*

meteorograph /meétiərəgraaf/ *n.* an apparatus that records several meteorological phenomena at the same time. [F *météorographe* (as METEOR, -GRAPH)]

meteoroid /meétiəroyd/ *n.* any small body moving in the solar system that becomes visible as it passes through the earth's atmosphere as a meteor. □□ **meteoroidal** /-róyd'l/ *adj.*

meteorology /meétiərólləji/ *n.* **1** the study of the processes and phenomena of the atmosphere, esp. as a means of forecasting the weather. **2** the atmospheric character of a region. □□ **meteorological** /-rəlójik'l/ *adj.* **meteorologically** /-rəlójikəli/ *adv.* **meteorologist** *n.* [Gk *meteōrologia* (as METEOR)]

meter¹ /meétər/ *n.* & *v.* ● *n.* **1** a person or thing that measures, esp. an instrument for recording a quantity of gas, electricity, etc. supplied, present, or needed. **2** = *parking-meter* (see PARK). ● *v.tr.* measure by means of a meter. [ME f. METE¹ + -ER¹]

■ *n.* **1** see INDICATOR 2, 3. ● *v.* see MEASURE *v.* 1.

meter² *US* var. of METRE¹.

meter³ *US* var. of METRE².

-meter /mitər, meetər/ *comb. form* **1** forming nouns denoting measuring instruments (*barometer*). **2** *Prosody* forming nouns denoting lines of poetry with a specified number of measures (*pentameter*).

methadone /méthədōn/ *n.* a potent narcotic analgesic drug used to relieve severe pain, as a linctus to suppress coughs, and as a substitute for morphine or heroin. [6-di*meth*yl*a*mino-4,4-*d*iphenyl-3-heptan*one*]

methamphetamine /méthamféttəmin, -meen/ *n.* an amphetamine derivative with quicker and longer action, used as a stimulant. [METHYL + AMPHETAMINE]

methanal /méthənal/ *n. Chem.* = FORMALDEHYDE. [METHANE + ALDEHYDE]

methane /méthayn, meé-/ *n. Chem.* a colourless odourless inflammable gaseous hydrocarbon, the simplest in the alkane series, and the main constituent of natural gas. ¶ Chem. formula: CH_4. [METHYL + -ANE²]

methanoic acid /méthənṓ-ik/ *n. Chem.* = FORMIC ACID. [METHANE + -IC]

methanol /méthənol/ *n. Chem.* a colourless volatile inflammable liquid, used as a solvent. ¶ Chem. formula: CH_3OH. Also called *methyl alcohol*. [METHANE + ALCOHOL]

methinks /mithíngks/ *v.intr.* (*past* **methought** /mitháwt/) *archaic* it seems to me. [OE *mē thyncth* f. *mē* dative of ME¹ + *thyncth* 3rd sing. of *thyncan* seem, THINK]

methionine /methī́əneen/ *n. Biochem.* an amino acid containing sulphur and an important constituent of proteins. [METHYL + Gk *theion* sulphur]

metho /méthō/ *n.* (*pl.* **-os**) *Austral. sl.* **1** methylated spirit. **2** a person addicted to drinking methylated spirit. [abbr.]

method /méthəd/ *n.* **1** a special form of procedure esp. in any branch of mental activity. **2** orderliness; regular habits. **3** the orderly arrangement of ideas. **4** a scheme of classification. **5** *Theatr.* a technique of acting based on the actor's thorough emotional identification with the character. □ **method in one's madness** sense in what appears to be foolish or strange behaviour. [F *méthode* or L *methodus* f. Gk *methodos* pursuit of knowledge (as META-, *hodos* way)]

■ **1** way, means, procedure, approach, route, avenue, road, mode, manner, technique, process, routine, *modus operandi*; plan, scheme, programme, program, course, practice, pattern, system, heuristic, *Math.* algorithm; methodology. **2, 3** arrangement, order, system, structure, organization, design, pattern, orderliness, neatness, regularity, discipline. **4** see SCHEME *n.* 1a, SYSTEM 4a.

methodical /mithóddik'l/ *adj.* (also **methodic**) characterized by method or order. □□ **methodically** *adv.* [LL *methodicus* f. Gk *methodikos* (as METHOD)]

■ organized, ordered, systematic, structured, businesslike, orderly, neat, tidy, regular, routine, balanced, disciplined, painstaking, meticulous, deliberate; plodding, laboured.

Methodist /méthədist/ *n.* **1** a member of any of several Protestant religious bodies (now united) originating in the 18th-c. evangelistic movement of Charles and John Wesley and George Whitefield. **2** (**methodist**) a person who follows or advocates a particular method or system of procedure. □□ **Methodism** *n.* **Methodistic** /-dístik/ *adj.* **Methodistical** /-dístik'l/ *adj.* [mod.L *methodista* (as METHOD): sense 1 prob. from following a specified 'method' of devotional study]

methodize /méthədīz/ *v.tr.* (also **-ise**) **1** reduce to order. **2** arrange in an orderly manner. □□ **methodizer** *n.*

methodology /méthədólləji/ *n.* (*pl.* **-ies**) **1** the science of method. **2** a body of methods used in a particular branch of activity. □□ **methodological** /-dəlójik'l/ *adj.* **methodologically** /-dəlójikəli/ *adv.* **methodologist** *n.* [mod.L *methodologia* or F *méthodologie* (as METHOD)]

■ **2** see SYSTEM 4a.

methought *past* of METHINKS.

meths /meths/ *n. Brit. colloq.* methylated spirit. [abbr.]

Methuselah /mithyoo͞zələ/ *n.* **1** a very old person or thing. **2** (**methuselah**) a wine bottle of about eight times the standard size. [ME: the name of a patriarch said to have lived 969 years (Gen. 5:27)]

methyl /méthil, meéthīl/ *n. Chem.* the univalent hydrocarbon radical CH_3, present in many organic compounds. □ **methyl alcohol** = METHANOL. **methyl benzene** = TOLUENE. □□ **methylic** /mithíllik/ *adj.* [G *Methyl* or F *méthyle*, back-form. f. G *Methylen*, F *méthylène*: see METHYLENE]

methylate /méthilayt/ *v.tr.* **1** mix or impregnate with methanol. **2** introduce a methyl group into (a molecule or compound). □ **methylated spirit** (or **spirits**) alcohol impregnated with methanol to make it unfit for drinking and exempt from duty. □□ **methylation** /-láysh'n/ *n.*

methylene /méthileen/ *n. Chem.* the highly reactive divalent group of atoms CH_2. [F *méthylène* f. Gk *methu* wine + *hulē* wood + -ENE]

metic /méttik/ *n. Gk Antiq.* an alien living in a Greek city with some privileges of citizenship. [irreg. f. Gk *metoikos* (as META-, *oikos* dwelling)]

meticulous /mətíkyooləss/ *adj.* **1** giving great or excessive attention to details. **2** very careful and precise. □□ **meticulously** *adv.* **meticulousness** *n.* [L *meticulosus* f. *metus* fear]

■ careful, precise, accurate, exact, fastidious, scrupulous, thorough, particular, painstaking, punctilious, fussy, finicky, demanding, strict, critical, exacting, perfectionist, *colloq.* pernickety.

métier /métyay/ *n.* **1** one's trade, profession, or department of activity. **2** one's forte. [F ult. f. L *ministerium* service]

■ **1** see TRADE *n.* 2.

metis /mayteéss/ *n.* (*pl.* **metis**; *fem.* **metisse**, *pl.* **metisses**) a person of mixed race, esp. the offspring of a White person and an American Indian in Canada. [F *métis*, OF *mestis* f. Rmc, rel. to MESTIZO]

metol /méttol/ *n.* a white soluble powder used as a photographic developer. [G, arbitrary name]

Metonic cycle /mitónnik/ *n.* a period of 19 years (235 lunar months) covering all the changes of the moon's position relative to the sun and the earth. [Gk *Metōn*, Athenian astronomer of the 5th c. BC]

metonym /méttənim/ *n.* a word used in metonymy. [back-form. f. METONYMY, after *synonym*]

metonymy /mitónnimi/ *n.* the substitution of the name of an attribute or adjunct for that of the thing meant (e.g. *Crown* for *king*, *the turf* for *horse-racing*). ▫▫ **metonymic** /méttənímmik/ *adj.* **metonymical** /méttənímmik'l/ *adj.* [LL *metonymia* f. Gk *metōnumia* (as META-, *onoma*, *onuma* name)]

metope /méttōp/ *n. Archit.* a square space between triglyphs in a Doric frieze. [L *metopa* f. Gk *metopē* (as META-, *opē* hole for a beam-end)]

metre[1] /meétər/ *n.* (*US* **meter**) a metric unit and the base SI unit of linear measure, equal to about 39.4 inches, and reckoned as the length of the path travelled by light in a vacuum during 1/299,792,458 of a second. ▫ **metre-kilogram-second** denoting a system of measure using the metre, kilogram, and second as the basic units of length, mass, and time. ¶ Abbr.: **mks.** ▫▫ **metreage** /meétərij/ *n.* [F *mètre* f. Gk *metron* measure]

metre[2] /meétər/ *n.* (*US* **meter**) **1 a** any form of poetic rhythm, determined by the number and length of feet in a line. **b** a metrical group or measure. **2** the basic pulse and rhythm of a piece of music. [OF *metre* f. L *metrum* f. Gk *metron* MEASURE]

▪ see RHYTHM 1, 2.

metric /métrik/ *adj.* of or based on the metre. ▫ **metric system** the decimal measuring system with the metre, litre, and gram (or kilogram) as units of length, volume, and mass (see also SI). **metric ton** (or **tonne**) 1,000 kilograms (2205 lb.). [F *métrique* (as METRE[1])]

-metric /métrik/ *comb. form* (also **-metrical** /-k'l/) forming adjectives corresponding to nouns in *-meter* and *-metry* (*thermometric*; *geometric*). ▫▫ **-metrically** *comb. form* forming adverbs. [from or after F *-métrique* f. L (as METRICAL)]

metrical /métrik'l/ *adj.* **1** of, relating to, or composed in metre (*metrical psalms*). **2** of or involving measurement (*metrical geometry*). ▫▫ **metrically** *adv.* [ME f. L *metricus* f. Gk *metrikos* (as METRE[2])]

▪ **1** see POETIC 1b.

metricate /métrikayt/ *v.intr.* & *tr.* change or adapt to a metric system of measurement. ▫▫ **metrication** /-káysh'n/ *n.* **metricize** /-trisīz/ *v.tr.* (also **-ise**).

metritis /mitrítiss/ *n.* inflammation of the womb. [Gk *mētra* womb + -ITIS]

metro /métrō/ *n.* (*pl.* **-os**) an underground railway system in a city, esp. Paris. [F *métro*, abbr. of *métropolitain* METROPOLITAN]

▪ see UNDERGROUND *n.* 1.

metrology /mitrólləji/ *n.* the scientific study of measurement. ▫▫ **metrologic** /métrəlójik/ *adj.* **metrological** /métrəlójik'l/ *adj.* [Gk *metron* measure + -LOGY]

metronome /métrənōm/ *n. Mus.* an instrument marking time at a selected rate by giving a regular tick. ▫▫ **metronomic** /-nómmik/ *adj.* [Gk *metron* measure + *nomos* law]

metronymic /métrənímmik/ *adj.* & *n.* ● *adj.* (of a name) derived from the name of a mother or female ancestor. ● *n.* a metronymic name. [Gk *mētēr mētros* mother, after *patronymic*]

metropolis /mitróppəliss/ *n.* **1** the chief city of a country; a capital city. **2** a metropolitan bishop's see. **3** a centre of activity. [LL f. Gk *mētropolis* parent State f. *mētēr mētros* mother + *polis* city]

▪ **1** capital, (capital) city, megalopolis, municipality. **3** see HUB.

metropolitan /métrəpóllit'n/ *adj.* & *n.* ● *adj.* **1** of or relating to a metropolis, esp. as distinct from its environs (*metropolitan New York*). **2** belonging to, forming or forming part of, a mother country as distinct from its colonies etc. (*metropolitan France*). **3** of an ecclesiastical metropolis. ● *n.* **1** (in full **metropolitan bishop**) a bishop having authority over the bishops of a province, in the Western Church equivalent to archbishop, in the Orthodox Church ranking above archbishop and below patriarch. **2** an inhabitant of a metropolis. ▫ **metropolitan county** *hist.* (in England) each of six units of local government centred on a large urban area (in existence 1974–86). **metropolitan magistrate** *Brit.* a paid professional magistrate in London (cf. *stipendiary magistrate*). ▫▫ **metropolitanate** *n.* (in sense 1 of *n.*). **metropolitanism** *n.* [ME f. LL *metropolitanus* f. Gk *mētropolitēs* (as METROPOLIS)]

▪ *adj.* **1** see MUNICIPAL.

metrorrhagia /meétrō-ráyjiə/ *n.* abnormal bleeding from the womb. [mod.L f. Gk *mētra* womb + *-rrhage* as HAEMORRHAGE]

-metry /mitri/ *comb. form* forming nouns denoting procedures and systems corresponding to instruments in *-meter* (*calorimetry*; *thermometry*). [after *geometry* etc. f. Gk *-metria* f. *-metrēs* measurer]

mettle /mětt'l/ *n.* **1** the quality of a person's disposition or temperament (*a chance to show your mettle*). **2** natural ardour. **3** spirit, courage. ▫ **on one's mettle** incited to do one's best. ▫▫ **mettled** *adj.* (also in *comb.*). **mettlesome** *adj.* [var. of METAL *n.*]

▪ **1** see DISPOSITION 1b. **2, 3** see SPIRIT *n.* 5c.
▫▫ **mettlesome** see SPIRITED.

meu /myōō/ *n.* (also **mew**) = BALDMONEY. [irreg. f. L *meum* f. Gk *mēon*]

meunière /mőnyáir/ *adj.* (esp. of fish) cooked or served in lightly browned butter with lemon juice and parsley (*sole meunière*). [F (*à la*) *meunière* (in the manner of) a miller's wife]

MeV *abbr.* mega-electronvolt(s).

mew[1] /myōō/ *v.* & *n.* ● *v.intr.* (of a cat, gull, etc.) utter its characteristic cry. ● *n.* this sound, esp. of a cat. [ME: imit.]

mew[2] /myōō/ *n.* a gull, esp. the common gull, *Larus canus*. [OE *mǣw* f. Gmc]

mew[3] /myōō/ *n.* & *v.* ● *n.* a cage for hawks, esp. while moulting. ● *v.tr.* **1** put (a hawk) in a cage. **2** (often foll. by *up*) shut up; confine. [ME f. OF *mue* f. *muer* moult f. L *mutare* change]

mew[4] var. of MEU.

mewl /myōōl/ *v.intr.* (also **mule**) **1** cry feebly; whimper. **2** mew like a cat. [imit.: cf. MIAUL]

▪ **1** see CRY *v.* 2a.

mews /myōōz/ *n. Brit.* a set of stabling round an open yard or along a lane, now often converted into dwellings. [pl. (now used as sing.) of MEW[3], orig. of the royal stables on the site of hawks' mews at Charing Cross]

Mexican /méksikən/ *n.* & *adj.* ● *n.* **1 a** a native or national of Mexico, a country in Southern N. America. **b** a person of Mexican descent. **2** a language spoken in Mexico, esp. Nahuatl. ● *adj.* **1** of or relating to Mexico or its people. **2** of Mexican descent. [Sp. *mexicano*]

mezereon /mizeériən/ *n.* a small European and Asian shrub, *Daphne mezereum*, with fragrant purplish red flowers and red berries. [med.L f. Arab. *māzaryūn*]

mezuzah /mezōōzə/ *n.* (*pl.* **mezuzoth** /-zōth/) a parchment inscribed with religious texts and attached in a case to the doorpost of a Jewish house as a sign of faith. [Heb. *mᵉzûzāh* doorpost]

mezzanine /métsəneen, mézzə-/ *n.* **1** a low storey between two others (usu. between the ground and first floors). **2** *Brit. Theatr.* **a** a floor or space beneath the stage. **b** *US* a dress circle. [F f. It. *mezzanino* dimin. of *mezzano* middle f. L *medianus* MEDIAN]

mezza voce /métsə vṓchay/ *adv. Mus.* with less than the full strength of the voice or sound. [It., = half voice]

mezzo /métsō/ *adv.* & *n. Mus.* ● *adv.* half, moderately. ● *n.* (in full **mezzo-soprano**) (*pl.* **-os**) **1 a** a female singing-voice between soprano and contralto. **b** a singer with this voice. **2** a part written for mezzo-soprano. □ **mezzo forte** fairly loud. **mezzo piano** fairly soft. [It., f. L *medius* middle]

mezzo-relievo /métsō-rileévō/ *n.* (also **mezzo-rilievo** /métsō-rilyáyvō/) (*pl.* **-os**) a raised surface in the form of half-relief, in which the figures project half their true proportions. [It. *mezzo-rilievo* = half-relief]

mezzotint /métsōtint/ *n.* & *v.* ● *n.* **1** a method of printing or engraving in which the surface of a plate is roughened by scraping so that it produces tones and half-tones. **2** a print produced by this process. ● *v.tr.* engrave in mezzotint. □□ **mezzotinter** *n.* [It. *mezzotinto* f. *mezzo* half + *tinto* tint]

MF *abbr.* medium frequency.

mf *abbr.* mezzo forte.

MFH *abbr. Brit.* Master of Foxhounds.

MG *abbr.* **1** machine-gun. **2** Morris Garages (as a make of car).

Mg *symb. Chem.* the element magnesium.

mg *abbr.* milligram(s).

Mgr. *abbr.* **1** Manager. **2** *Monseigneur*. **3** Monsignor.

mho /mō/ *n.* (*pl.* **-os**) *Electr.* the reciprocal of an ohm, a former unit of conductance. [OHM reversed]

MHR *abbr.* (in the US and Australia) Member of the House of Representatives.

MHz *abbr.* megahertz.

MI *abbr.* **1** *US* Michigan (in official postal use). **2** *Brit. hist.* Military Intelligence.

M.I.5 *abbr.* (in the UK) the department of Military Intelligence concerned with State security. ¶ Not in official use.

M.I.6 *abbr.* (in the UK) the department of Military Intelligence concerned with espionage. ¶ Not in official use.

mi var. of ME².

mi. *abbr. US* mile(s).

miaow /miaá-oo/ *n.* & *v.* (also **meow**) ● *n.* the characteristic cry of a cat. ● *v.intr.* make this cry. [imit.]
■ *n.* meow, mew; caterwaul. ● *v.* meow, mew, miaul; caterwaul.

miasma /miázmə, mī-/ *n.* (*pl.* **miasmata** /-mətə/ or **miasmas**) *archaic* an infectious or noxious vapour. □□ **miasmal** *adj.* **miasmatic** /-máttik/ *adj.* **miasmic** *adj.* **miasmically** *adv.* [Gk, = defilement, f. *miainō* pollute]
■ see VAPOUR *n.* 1. □□ **miasmal, miasmatic, miasmic** see SMELLY.

miaul /miáwl/ *v.intr.* cry like a cat; mew. [F *miauler*: imit.]

Mic. *abbr.* Micah (Old Testament).

mica /mī́kə/ *n.* any of a group of silicate minerals with a layered structure, esp. muscovite. □ **mica-schist** (or **slate**) a fissile rock containing quartz and mica. □□ **micaceous** /-káyshəss/ *adj.* [L, = crumb]

mice *pl.* of MOUSE.

micelle /misél, mī-/ *n. Chem.* an aggregate of molecules in a colloidal solution, as occurs e.g. when soap dissolves in water. [mod.L *micella* dimin. of L *mica* crumb]

Mich. *abbr.* **1** Michaelmas. **2** Michigan.

Michaelmas /míkk'lməss/ *n.* the feast of St Michael, 29 September. □ **Michaelmas daisy** an autumn-flowering aster. **Michaelmas term** *Brit.* (in some universities) the autumn term. [OE *sancte Micheles mæsse* Saint Michael's mass: see MASS²]

mick /mik/ *n. sl. offens.* **1** an Irishman. **2** a Roman Catholic. [pet-form of the name *Michael*]

mickery /míkkəri/ *n. Austral.* (also **mickerie**) a water-hole or excavated well, esp. in a dry river-bed. [Aborig. *migri*]

mickey /míkki/ *n.* (also **micky**) □ **take the mickey** (often foll. by *out of*) *sl.* tease, mock, ridicule. [20th c.: orig. uncert.]

Mickey Finn /míkki fín/ *n. sl.* **1** a strong alcoholic drink, esp. adulterated with a narcotic or laxative. **2** the adulterant itself. [20th c.: orig. uncert.]

mickle /míkk'l/ *adj.* & *n.* (also **muckle** /múkk'l/) *archaic* or *Sc.* ● *adj.* much, great. ● *n.* a large amount. □ **many a little makes a mickle** (orig. *erron.* **many a mickle makes a muckle**) many small amounts accumulate to make a large amount. [ME f. ON *mikell* f. Gmc]

micky var. of MICKEY.

micro /mī́krō/ *n.* (*pl.* **-os**) *colloq.* **1** = MICROCOMPUTER. **2** = MICROPROCESSOR.

micro- /mī́krō/ *comb. form* **1** small (*microchip*). **2** denoting a factor of one millionth (10^{-6}) (*microgram*). ¶ Symb.: μ. [Gk *mikro-* f. *mikros* small]
■ **1** mini-.

microanalysis /mī́krōənállisiss/ *n.* the quantitative analysis of chemical compounds using a sample of a few milligrams.

microbe /mī́krōb/ *n.* a minute living being; a micro-organism (esp. bacteria causing disease and fermentation). □□ **microbial** /-krṓbiəl/ *adj.* **microbic** /-krṓbik/ *adj.* [F f. Gk *mikros* small + *bios* life]
■ micro-organism, germ, bacterium, *sl.* bug.

microbiology /mī́krōbīólləji/ *n.* the scientific study of micro-organisms, e.g. bacteria, viruses, and fungi. □□ **microbiological** /-bīəlójik'l/ *adj.* **microbiologically** /-bīəlójikəli/ *adv.* **microbiologist** *n.*

microburst /mī́krōburst/ *n.* a particularly violent wind shear, esp. during a thunderstorm.

microcephaly /mī́krōséffəli/ *n.* an abnormal smallness of the head in relation to the rest of the body. □□ **microcephalic** /-sifállik/ *adj.* & *n.* **microcephalous** /-séffələss/ *adj.*

microchip /mī́krōchip/ *n.* a small piece of semiconductor (usu. silicon) used to carry electronic circuits.

microcircuit /mī́krōsurkit/ *n.* an integrated circuit on a microchip. □□ **microcircuitry** *n.*

microclimate /mī́krōklīmit/ *n.* the climate of a small local area, e.g. inside a greenhouse. □□ **microclimatic** /-máttik/ *adj.* **microclimatically** /-máttikəli/ *adv.*

microcode /mī́krōkōd/ *n.* **1** = MICROINSTRUCTION. **2** = MICROPROGRAM.

microcomputer /mī́krōkəmpyōōtər/ *n.* a small computer that contains a microprocessor as its central processor.

microcopy /mī́krōkoppi/ *n.* & *v.* ● *n.* (*pl.* **-ies**) a copy of printed matter that has been reduced by microphotography. ● *v.tr.* (**-ies, -ied**) make a microcopy of.

microcosm /mī́krəkoz'm/ *n.* **1** (often foll. by *of*) a miniature representation. **2** mankind viewed as the epitome of the universe. **3** any community or complex unity viewed in this way. □□ **microcosmic** /-kózmik/ *adj.* **microcosmically** /-kózmikəli/ *adv.* [ME f. F *microcosme* or med.L *microcosmus* f. Gk *mikros kosmos* little world]

microdot /mī́krōdot/ *n.* a microphotograph of a document etc. reduced to the size of a dot.

micro-economics /mī́krō-eékənómmiks/ *n.* the branch of economics dealing with individual commodities, producers, etc.

micro-electronics /mī́krō-illektrónniks/ *n.* the design, manufacture, and use of microchips and microcircuits.

microfiche /mī́krōfeesh/ *n.* (*pl.* same or **microfiches**) a flat rectangular piece of film bearing microphotographs of the pages of a printed text or document.

microfilm /mī́krōfilm/ *n.* & *v.* ● *n.* a length of film bearing microphotographs of documents etc. ● *v.tr.* photograph (a document etc.) on microfilm.

microfloppy /mī́krōfloppi/ *n.* (*pl.* **-ies**) (in full **microfloppy disk**) *Computing* a floppy disk with a diameter of less than $5^1/_4$ inches (usu. $3^1/_2$ inches).

microform /mī́krōform/ *n.* microphotographic reproduction on film or paper of a manuscript etc.

microgram /mī́krōgram/ *n.* one-millionth of a gram.

micrograph /mī́krōgraaf/ *n.* a photograph taken by means of a microscope.

microgroove /mī́krōgrōōv/ *n.* a very narrow groove on a long-playing gramophone record.

microinstruction /mī́krō-instrúksh'n/ *n.* a machine-code instruction that effects a basic operation in a computer system.

microlight /mī́krōlīt/ *n.* a kind of motorized hang-glider.

microlith /mī́krōlith/ *n. Archaeol.* a minute worked flint usu. as part of a composite tool. ▫▫ **microlithic** /-líthik/ *adj.*

micromesh /mī́krōmesh/ *n.* (often *attrib.*) material, esp. nylon, consisting of a very fine mesh.

micrometer /mīkrómmitər/ *n.* a gauge for accurately measuring small distances, thicknesses, etc. ▫▫ **micrometry** *n.*

micrometre /mī́krōmeetər/ *n.* one-millionth of a metre.

microminiaturization /mī́krōmínnichərīzáysh'n/ *n.* (also **-isation**) the manufacture of very small electronic devices by using integrated circuits.

micron /mī́kron/ *n.* one-millionth of a metre. [Gk *mikron* neut. of *mikros* small: cf. MICRO-]

Micronesian /mī́krəneezh'n/ *adj.* & *n.* ● *adj.* of or relating to Micronesia, an island-group in the W. Pacific. ● *n.* a native of Micronesia. [*Micronesia*, formed as MICRO- + Gk *nēsos* island]

micro-organism /mī́krō-órgəniz'm/ *n.* any of various microscopic organisms, including algae, bacteria, fungi, protozoa, and viruses.
■ see MICROBE.

microphone /mī́krəfōn/ *n.* an instrument for converting sound waves into electrical energy variations which may be reconverted into sound after transmission by wire or radio or after recording. ▫▫ **microphonic** /-fónnik/ *adj.*
■ bug, transmitter, *colloq.* mike.

microphotograph /mī́krōfṓtəgraaf/ *n.* a photograph reduced to a very small size.

microphyte /mī́krōfīt/ *n.* a microscopic plant.

microprocessor /mī́krōprṓsessər/ *n.* an integrated circuit that contains all the functions of a central processing unit of a computer.

microprogram /mī́krōprṓgram/ *n.* a microinstruction program that controls the functions of a central processing unit of a computer.

micropyle /mī́krōpīl/ *n. Bot.* a small opening in the surface of an ovule, through which pollen passes. [MICRO- + Gk *pulē* gate]

microscope /mī́krəskōp/ *n.* an instrument magnifying small objects by means of a lens or lenses so as to reveal details invisible to the naked eye. [mod.L *microscopium* (as MICRO-, -SCOPE)]

microscopic /mī́krəskóppik/ *adj.* **1** so small as to be visible only with a microscope. **2** extremely small. **3** regarded in terms of small units. **4** of the microscope. ▫▫ **microscopical** *adj.* (in sense 4). **microscopically** *adv.*
■ **1, 2** see TINY.

microscopy /mīkróskəpi/ *n.* the use of the microscope. ▫▫ **microscopist** *n.*

microsecond /mī́krōsekkənd/ *n.* one-millionth of a second.

Microsoft /mī́krōsoft/ *n. propr.* an operating system for microcomputers. [the name of the developing company]

microsome /mī́krōsōm/ *n. Biol.* a small particle of organelle fragments obtained by centrifugation of homogenized cells. [MICRO- + -SOME[3]]

microspore /mī́krōspor/ *n.* the smaller of the two kinds of spore produced by some ferns.

microstructure /mī́krōstrukchər/ *n.* (in a metal or other material) the arrangement of crystals etc. which can be made visible and examined with a microscope.

microsurgery /mī́krōsurjəri/ *n.* intricate surgery performed using microscopes, enabling the tissue to be operated on with miniaturized precision instruments. ▫▫ **microsurgical** /-súrjik'l/ *adj.*

microswitch /mī́krōswich/ *n.* a switch that can be operated rapidly by a small movement.

microtome /mī́krōtōm/ *n.* an instrument for cutting extremely thin sections of material for examination under a microscope. [MICRO- + -TOME]

microtone /mī́krōtōn/ *n. Mus.* an interval smaller than a semitone.

microtubule /mī́krōtyōōbyōōl/ *n. Biol.* a minute protein filament occurring in cytoplasm and involved in forming the spindles during cell division etc.

microwave /mī́krōwayv/ *n.* & *v.* ● *n.* **1** an electromagnetic wave with a wavelength in the range 0.001–0.3m. **2** (in full **microwave oven**) an oven that uses microwaves to cook or heat food quickly. ● *v.tr.* (**-ving**) cook in a microwave oven.

micrurgy /mī́krurji/ *n.* the manipulation of individual cells etc. under a microscope. [MICRO- + Gk *-ourgia* work]

micturition /míktyoorísh'n/ *n. formal* or *Med.* urination. [L *micturire micturit-*, desiderative f. *mingere mict-* urinate]

mid[1] /mid/ *attrib.adj.* **1** (usu. in *comb.*) that is the middle of (*in mid-air; from mid-June to mid-July*). **2** that is in the middle; medium, half. **3** *Phonet.* (of a vowel) pronounced with the tongue neither high nor low. [OE *midd* (recorded only in oblique cases), rel. to L *medius*, Gk *mesos*]
■ **1, 2** see MIDDLE *adj.* 1, 2.

mid[2] /mid/ *prep. poet.* = AMID. [abbr. f. AMID]

Midas touch /mī́dəss/ *n.* the ability to turn one's activities to financial advantage. [*Midas*, king of Phrygia, whose touch was said to turn all things to gold]

midbrain /mídbrayn/ *n.* the part of the brain developing from the middle of the primitive or embryonic brain.

midday /míd-dáy/ *n.* the middle of the day; noon. [OE *middæg* (as MID[1], DAY)]
■ noon, noontide, twelve noon, 1200 hours, high noon.

midden /mídd'n/ *n.* **1** a dunghill. **2** a refuse heap near a dwelling. **3** = *kitchen midden.* [ME *myddyng*, of Scand. orig.: cf. Da. *mødding* muck heap]

middle /mídd'l/ *adj.*, *n.*, & *v.* ● *attrib.adj.* **1** at an equal distance from the extremities of a thing. **2** (of a member of a group) so placed as to have the same number of members on each side. **3** intermediate in rank, quality, etc. **4** average (*of middle height*). **5** (of a language) of the period between the old and modern forms. **6** *Gram.* designating the voice of (esp. Greek) verbs that expresses reciprocal or reflexive action. ● *n.* **1** (often foll. by *of*) the middle point or position or part. **2** a person's waist. **3** *Gram.* the middle form or voice of a verb. **4** = *middle term.* ● *v.tr.* **1** place in the middle. **2** *Football* return (the ball) from the wing to the midfield. **3** *Cricket* strike (the ball) with the middle of the bat. **4** *Naut.* fold in the middle. ▫ **in the middle of** (often foll. by *verbal noun*) in the process of; during. **middle age** the period between youth and old age, about 45 to 60. **middle-aged** in middle age. **the Middle Ages** the period of European history from the fall of the Roman Empire in the West (5th c.) to the fall of Constantinople (1453), or more narrowly from *c.*1000 to 1453. **middle-age** (or **-aged**) **spread** the increased bodily girth often associated with middle age. **Middle America 1** Mexico and Central America. **2** the middle class in the US, esp. as a conservative political force. **middle C** *Mus.* the C near the middle of the piano keyboard, the note between the treble and bass staves, at about 260 Hz. **middle class** the class of society between the upper and the lower, including professional and business workers and their families. **middle-class** *adj.* of the middle class. **middle common room** *Brit.* a common room for the use of graduate members of a college who are not Fellows. **middle course** a compromise between two extremes. **middle distance 1** (in a painted or actual landscape) the part between the foreground and the background. **2** *Athletics* a race distance of esp. 400 or 800 metres. **middle ear** the cavity of the central part of the ear behind the drum. **the Middle East** the area covered by countries from Egypt to Iran inclusive. **Middle Eastern** of or in the Middle East. **Middle English** the English language from *c.*1150 to 1500. **middle finger** the finger next to the forefinger. **middle game** the central phase of a chess game, when strategies are developed. **middle name 1** a person's name placed after the first name and before the surname. **2** a person's most characteristic quality (*sobriety is my middle* *name*). **middle-of-the-road** (of a person, course of action, etc.) moderate; avoiding extremes. **middle passage** the sea journey between W. Africa and the W. Indies (with ref. to the slave trade). **middle school** *Brit.* a school for children from about 9 to 13 years old. **middle-sized** of medium size. **Middle Temple** one of the two Inns of Court on the site of the Temple in London (cf. *Inner Temple*). **middle term** *Logic* the term common to both premisses of a syllogism. **middle watch** the watch from midnight to 4 a.m. **middle way 1** = *middle course*. **2** the eightfold path of Buddhism between indulgence and asceticism. **Middle West** (in the US) the region adjoining the northern Mississippi. [OE *middel* f. Gmc]

■ *adj.* **1, 2** central, centre, medial, median, *Anat.* mesial; midway, mid, halfway; inner, inside. **3** see INTERMEDIATE *adj.* **4** normal, mean; see also AVERAGE *adj.* 1a. ● *n.* **1** centre, mid-point, midst, halfway point; heart, bull's-eye. **2** midriff, waist, stomach. □ **in the middle of** halfway *or* midway through, in the midst of; during. **middle class** (petty *or* petite) bourgeoisie; *US* Middle America. **middle-class** see BOURGEOIS *adj.* 1a. **middle name 2** see HALLMARK *n.* 2. **middle-of-the-road** see MODERATE *adj.* 1. **middle-sized** average, medium-sized; see also MEDIUM *adj.*

middlebrow /mídd'lbrow/ *adj.* & *n. colloq.* ● *adj.* claiming to be or regarded as only moderately intellectual. ● *n.* a middlebrow person.

middleman /mídd'lman/ *n.* (*pl.* **-men**) **1** any of the traders who handle a commodity between its producer and its consumer. **2** an intermediary.

■ see INTERMEDIARY *n.*

middleweight /mídd'lwayt/ *n.* **1** a weight in certain sports intermediate between welterweight and light heavyweight, in the amateur boxing scale 71-5 kg but differing for professionals, wrestlers, and weightlifters. **2** a sportsman of this weight. □ **junior middleweight 1** a weight in professional boxing of 66.7-69.8 kg. **2** a professional boxer of this weight. **light middleweight 1** a weight in amateur boxing of 67-71 kg. **2** an amateur boxer of this weight.

middling /mídling/ *adj.*, *n.*, & *adv.* ● *adj.* **1 a** moderately good (esp. *fair to middling*). **b** second-rate. **2** (of goods) of the second of three grades. ● *n.* (in *pl.*) middling goods, esp. flour of medium fineness. ● *adv.* **1** fairly or moderately (*middling good*). **2** *colloq.* fairly well (esp. in health). □□ **middlingly** *adv.* [ME, of Sc. orig.: prob. f. MID[1] + -LING[2]]

■ *adj.* **1** see MODERATE *adj.* 2, 4.

Middx. *abbr.* Middlesex.

middy[1] /míddi/ *n.* (*pl.* **-ies**) **1** *colloq.* a midshipman. **2** (in full **middy blouse**) a woman's or child's loose blouse with a collar like that worn by sailors.

middy[2] /míddi/ *n.* (*pl.* **-ies**) *Austral. sl.* a measure of beer of varying size. [20th c.: orig. unkn.]

Mideast /míddeést/ *n. US* = *Middle East.*

midfield /mídfeéld/ *n. Football* the central part of the pitch, away from the goals. □□ **midfielder** *n.*

midge /mij/ *n.* **1** *colloq.* **a** a gnatlike insect. **b** a small person. **2 a** any dipterous non-biting insect of the family *Chironomidae*. **b** any similar insect of the family *Ceratopogonidae* with piercing mouthparts for sucking blood or eating smaller insects. [OE *mycg(e)* f. Gmc]

midget /míjit/ *n.* **1** an extremely small person or thing. **2** (*attrib.*) very small. [MIDGE + -ET[1]]

■ **2** (*attrib.*) see SMALL *adj.* 1.

midgut /mídgút/ *n.* the middle part of the alimentary canal, including the small intestine.

MIDI /míddi/ *n.* a system for using combinations of electronic equipment, esp. audio and computer equipment. [acronym of *musical instrument digital interface*]

midi /míddi/ *n.* (*pl.* **midis**) a garment of medium length, usu. reaching to mid-calf. [MID[1] after MINI]

midibus /míddibuss/ *n.* a bus seating up to about 25 passengers.

midinette /míddinét/ *n.* a Parisian shop-girl, esp. a milliner's assistant. [F f. *midi* midday + *dînette* light dinner]

midiron /míddīrn/ *n. Golf* an iron giving medium lift.

midland /mídlənd/ *n.* & *adj.* ● *n.* **1** (**the Midlands**) the inland counties of central England. **2** the middle part of a country. ● *adj.* **1** of or in the midland or Midlands. **2** Mediterranean. □□ **midlander** *n.*

mid-life /mídlīf/ *n.* middle age. □ **mid-life crisis** an emotional crisis of self-confidence that can occur in early middle age.

midline /mídlīn/ *n.* a median line, or plane of bilateral symmetry.

midmost /mídmōst/ *adj.* & *adv.* in the very middle.

midnight /mídnīt/ *n.* **1** the middle of the night; 12 o'clock at night. **2** intense darkness. □ **midnight blue** a very dark blue. **midnight sun** the sun visible at midnight during the summer in polar regions. [OE *midniht* (as MID[1], NIGHT)]

mid-off /míddóf/ *n. Cricket* the position of the fielder near the bowler on the off side.

mid-on /míddón/ *n. Cricket* the position of the fielder near the bowler on the on side.

Midrash /mídrash/ *n.* (*pl.* **Midrashim** /-shím/) an ancient commentary on part of the Hebrew scriptures. [Bibl. Heb. *midrāš* commentary]

midrib /mídrib/ *n.* the central rib of a leaf.

midriff /mídrif/ *n.* **1 a** the region of the front of the body between the thorax and abdomen. **b** the diaphragm. **2** a garment or part of a garment covering the abdomen. [OE *midhrif* (as MID[1], *hrif* belly)]

■ **1a** see MIDDLE *n.* 2.

midship /mídship/ *n.* the middle part of a ship or boat.

midshipman /mídshipmən/ *n.* (*pl.* **-men**) **1** *Brit.* a naval officer of rank between naval cadet and sub-lieutenant. **2** *US* a naval cadet.

midships /mídships/ *adv.* = AMIDSHIPS.

midst /midst/ *prep.* & *n.* ● *prep. poet.* amidst. ● *n.* middle (now only in phrases as below). □ **in the midst of** among; in the middle of. **in our** (or **your** or **their**) **midst** among us (or you or them). [ME *middest*, *middes* f. *in middes*, *in middan* (as IN, MID[1])]

■ □ **in the midst of** in the middle of, halfway *or* midway through; during; see also AMONG 1.

midsummer /mídsúmmər/ *n.* the period of or near the summer solstice, about 21 June. □ **Midsummer** (or **Midsummer's**) **Day** 24 June. **midsummer madness** extreme folly. [OE *midsumor* (as MID[1], SUMMER[1])]

midtown /mídtown/ *n. US* the central part of a city between the downtown and uptown areas.

midway /mídwáy/ *adv.* in or towards the middle of the distance between two points.

Midwest /mídwést/ *n.* = *Middle West.*

midwicket /mídwíkkit/ *n. Cricket* the position of a fielder on the leg side opposite the middle of the pitch.

midwife /mídwīf/ *n.* (*pl.* **-wives** /-wīvz/) a person (usu. a woman) trained to assist women in childbirth. □□ **midwifery** /-wifri/ *n.* [ME, prob. f. obs. prep. *mid* with + WIFE woman, in the sense of 'one who is with the mother']

midwinter /mídwíntər/ *n.* the period of or near the winter solstice, about 22 Dec. [OE (as MID[1], WINTER)]

mielie var. of MEALIE.

mien /meen/ *n. literary* a person's look or bearing, as showing character or mood. [prob. f. obs. *demean* f. DEMEAN[2], assim. to F *mine* expression]

■ see LOOK *n.* 2, 3.

miff /mif/ *v.* & *n. colloq.* ● *v.tr.* (usu. in *passive*) put out of humour; offend. ● *n.* **1** a petty quarrel. **2** a huff. [perh. imit.: cf. G *muff*, exclam. of disgust]

■ *v.* see OFFEND 1, 2.

might[1] /mīt/ *past* of MAY, used esp.: **1** in reported speech, expressing possibility (*said he might come*) or permission (*asked if I might leave*) (cf. MAY 1,2). **2** (foll. by perfect infin.) expressing a possibility based on a condition not fulfilled (*if you'd looked you might have found it*; *but for the* *radio we might not have known*). **3** (foll. by present infin. or perfect infin.) expressing complaint that an obligation or expectation is not or has not been fulfilled (*he might offer to help; they might have asked; you might have known they wouldn't come*). **4** expressing a request (*you might call in at the butcher's*). **5** *colloq.* **a** = MAY 1 (*it might be true*). **b** (in tentative questions) = MAY 2 (*might I have the pleasure of this dance?*). **c** = MAY 4 (*who might you be?*). □ **might as well** expressing that it is probably at least as desirable to do a thing as not to do it (*finished the work and decided they might as well go to lunch; won't win but might as well try*). **might-have-been** *colloq.* **1** a past possibility that no longer applies. **2** a person who could have been more eminent.

might[2] /mīt/ *n.* **1** great bodily or mental strength. **2** power to enforce one's will (usu. in contrast with *right*). □ **with all one's might** to the utmost of one's power. **with might and main** see MAIN[1]. [OE *miht, mieht* f. Gmc, rel. to MAY]
▪ **1** strength, power, energy, force, muscle, mightiness, potency, *archaic* puissance. **2** influence, authority, weight, sway, dominion, ascendancy, superiority, capability, capacity, power, effectiveness, *colloq.* clout.

mightn't /mī́t'nt/ *contr.* might not.

mighty /mī́ti/ *adj.* & *adv.* ● *adj.* (**mightier, mightiest**) **1** powerful or strong, in body, mind, or influence. **2** massive, bulky. **3** *colloq.* great, considerable. ● *adv. colloq.* very (*a mighty difficult task*). □□ **mightily** *adv.* **mightiness** *n.* [OE *mihtig* (as MIGHT[2])]
▪ *adj.* **1** powerful, strong, potent, influential, dominant, predominant, ascendant, weighty, authoritarian, autocratic, indomitable; muscular, robust, strapping, sturdy, brawny, burly, well-built, able-bodied, hardy, hunky, hefty, *archaic or joc.* doughty. **2** big, large, huge, grand, great, enormous, gigantic, tremendous, towering, monumental, prodigious, massive, bulky. **3** see CONSIDERABLE 1, 2. ● *adv.* see VERY *adv.*

mignonette /minyənét/ *n.* **1 a** any of various plants of the genus *Reseda*, esp. *R. odorata*, with fragrant grey-green flowers. **b** the colour of these. **2** a light fine narrow pillow-lace. [F *mignonnette* dimin. of *mignon* small]

migraine /méegrayn, mī́-/ *n.* a recurrent throbbing headache that usually affects one side of the head, often accompanied by nausea and disturbance of vision. □□ **migrainous** *adj.* [F f. LL *hemicrania* f. Gk *hēmikrania* (as HEMI-, CRANIUM): orig. of a headache confined to one side of the head]

migrant /mī́grənt/ *adj.* & *n.* ● *adj.* that migrates. ● *n.* a migrant person or animal, esp. a bird.
▪ *adj.* transient, migratory, itinerant, peripatetic, nomadic, gypsy, vagrant. ● *n.* wanderer, rover, drifter, gypsy, nomad, itinerant, transient, migrator, wayfarer, bird of passage, traveller, vagrant, *archaic or joc.* peregrinator, *US colloq.* wetback, *sl.* didicoi.

migrate /mīgráyt/ *v.intr.* **1** (of people) move from one place of abode to another, esp. in a different country. **2** (of a bird or fish) change its area of habitation with the seasons. **3** move under natural forces. □□ **migration** /-gráysh'n/ *n.* **migrational** /-gráyshən'l/ *adj.* **migrator** *n.* **migratory** *adj.* [L *migrare migrat-*]
▪ go, move, travel, settle, resettle, relocate, move house; emigrate, immigrate; wander, roam, voyage, rove, drift, range.

mihrab /méeraab/ *n.* a niche or slab in a mosque, used to show the direction of Mecca. [Arab. *miḥrāb* praying-place]

mikado /mikaádō/ *n.* (*pl.* **-os**) *hist.* the emperor of Japan. [Jap. f. *mi* august + *kado* door]

Mike /mīk/ *n. sl.* □ **for the love of Mike** an exclamation of entreaty or dismay. [abbr. of the name *Michael*]

mike[1] /mīk/ *n. colloq.* a microphone. [abbr.]

mike[2] /mīk/ *v.* & *n. Brit. sl.* ● *v.intr.* shirk work; idle. ● *n.* an act of shirking. [19th c.: orig. unkn.]

mil /mil/ *n.* one-thousandth of an inch, as a unit of measure for the diameter of wire etc. [L *millesimum* thousandth f. *mille* thousand]

milady /miláydi/ *n.* (*pl.* **-ies**) **1** an English noblewoman or great lady. **2** a form used in speaking of or to such a person. [F f. E *my lady*: cf. MILORD]

milage var. of MILEAGE.

Milanese /míllənéez/ *adj.* & *n.* ● *adj.* of or relating to Milan in N. Italy. ● *n.* (*pl.* same) a native of Milan. □ **Milanese silk** a finely woven silk or rayon.

milch /milch/ *adj.* (of a domestic mammal) giving or kept for milk. □ **milch cow** a source of easy profit, esp. a person. [ME *m(i)elche* repr. OE *mielce* (unrecorded) f. Gmc: see MILK]

mild /mīld/ *adj.* **1** (esp. of a person) gentle and conciliatory. **2** (of a rule, punishment, illness, feeling, etc.) moderate; not severe. **3** (of the weather, esp. in winter) moderately warm. **4 a** (of food, tobacco, etc.) not sharp or strong in taste etc. **b** *Brit.* (of beer) not strongly flavoured with hops (cf. BITTER). **5** (of medicine) operating gently. **6** tame, feeble; lacking energy or vivacity. □ **mild steel** steel containing a small percentage of carbon, strong and tough but not readily tempered. □□ **milden** *v.tr.* & *intr.* **mildish** *adj.* **mildness** *n.* [OE *milde* f. Gmc]
▪ **1** placid, peaceful, calm, tranquil, tolerant, mellow, inoffensive, gentle, serene, good-natured, affable, amiable, kind, kindly, equable, easygoing, temperate, non-violent, conciliatory, indulgent, merciful, forgiving, compassionate, lenient, forbearing, peaceable, pacific, passive, submissive, yielding, tractable, meek, unassuming, modest, quiet, subdued. **2** see LENIENT. **3** clement, balmy, warm, fair, pleasant, temperate, placid, moderate. **5** soothing, demulcent, emollient, gentle, calming, *Med.* lenitive. **6** see TAME *adj.* 3.

mildew /míldyoo/ *n.* & *v.* ● *n.* **1** a destructive growth of minute fungi on plants. **2** a similar growth on paper, leather, etc. exposed to damp. ● *v.tr.* & *intr.* taint or be tainted with mildew. □□ **mildewy** *adj.* [OE *mildēaw* f. Gmc]
▪ *n.* see MOULD[2]. ● *v.* see SPOIL *v.* 3a. □□ **mildewy** see MOULDY 1.

mildly /mī́ldli/ *adv.* in a mild fashion. □ **to put it mildly** as an understatement (implying the reality is more extreme).
▪ see *quietly* (QUIET).

mile /mīl/ *n.* **1** (also **statute mile**) a unit of linear measure equal to 1,760 yards (approx. 1.609 kilometres). **2** *hist.* a Roman measure of 1,000 paces (approx. 1,620 yards). **3** (in *pl.*) *colloq.* a great distance or amount (*miles better; beat them by miles*). **4** a race extending over a mile. [OE *mīl* ult. f. L *mil(l)ia* pl. of *mille* thousand (see sense 2)]

mileage /mī́lij/ *n.* (also **milage**) **1 a** a number of miles travelled, used, etc. **b** the number of miles travelled by a vehicle per unit of fuel. **2** travelling expenses (per mile). **3** *colloq.* benefit, profit, advantage.
▪ **1 a** see DISTANCE *n.* 2.

milepost /mī́lpōst/ *n.* a post one mile from the finishing-post of a race etc.

miler /mī́lər/ *n. colloq.* a person or horse qualified or trained specially to run a mile.

milestone /mī́lstōn/ *n.* **1** a stone set up beside a road to mark a distance in miles. **2** a significant event or stage in a life, history, project, etc.
▪ **2** see LANDMARK 2.

milfoil /mílfoyl/ *n.* the common yarrow, *Achillea millefolium*, with small white flowers and finely divided leaves. [ME f. OF f. L *millefolium* f. *mille* thousand + *folium* leaf, after Gk *muriophullon*]

miliary /mílliəri/ *adj.* **1** like a millet-seed in size or form. **2** (of a disease) having as a symptom a rash with lesions resembling millet-seed. [L *miliarius* f. *milium* millet]

milieu /milyő, méelyö/ *n.* (*pl.* **milieux** or **milieus** /-lyőz/) one's environment or social surroundings. [F f. *mi* MID[1] + *lieu* place]
▪ environment, climate, surroundings, environs, background, neighbourhood, *US* precincts; ambience, sphere, setting, atmosphere, medium, element.

militant /míllit'nt/ *adj.* & *n.* ● *adj.* **1** combative; aggressively active esp. in support of a (usu. political) cause. **2** engaged in warfare. ● *n.* **1** a militant person, esp. a political activist. **2** a person engaged in warfare. □□ **militancy** *n.* **militantly** *adv.* [ME f. OF f. L (as MILITATE)]
■ *adj.* **1** aggressive, combative, pugnacious, belligerent, hostile, contentious, antagonistic, offensive, truculent, fierce, ferocious, warlike, bellicose, martial, jingoistic, hawkish. **2** warring, fighting, combatant, embattled; at war, up in arms. ● *n.* **1** activist, fighter, campaigner. **2** aggressor, combatant, belligerent, warrior, soldier.

militarism /míllitəriz'm/ *n.* **1** the spirit or tendencies of a professional soldier. **2** undue prevalence of the military spirit or ideals. □□ **militaristic** /-rístik/ *adj.* **militaristically** /-rístikəli/ *adv.* [F *militarisme* (as MILITARY)]
■ □□ **militaristic** see WARLIKE 1.

militarist /míllitərist/ *n.* **1** a person dominated by militaristic ideas. **2** a student of military science.

militarize /míllitərīz/ *v.tr.* (also **-ise**) **1** equip with military resources. **2** make military or warlike. **3** imbue with militarism. □□ **militarization** /-záysh'n/ *n.*

military /míllitəri, tri/ *adj.* & *n.* ● *adj.* of, relating to, or characteristic of soldiers or armed forces. ● *n.* (as *sing.* or *pl.*; prec. by *the*) members of the armed forces, as distinct from civilians and the police. □ **military honours** marks of respect paid by troops at the burial of a soldier, to royalty, etc. **military police** a corps responsible for police and disciplinary duties in the army. **military policeman** a member of the military police. □□ **militarily** *adv.* **militariness** *n.* [F *militaire* or L *militaris* f. *miles militis* soldier]
■ *adj.* martial, soldierly, army, fighting, service. ● *n.* (*the military*) (armed) services *or* forces, army, air force, soldiery.

militate /míllitayt/ *v.intr.* (usu. foll. by *against*) (of facts or evidence) have force or effect (*what you say militates against our opinion*). ¶ Often confused with *mitigate*. [L *militare militat-* f. *miles militis* soldier]
■ (*militate against*) work *or* go *or* operate against, foil, counter, countervail (against), cancel (out); resist, oppose.

militia /milíshə/ *n.* a military force, esp. one raised from the civil population and supplementing a regular army in an emergency. [L, = military service f. *miles militis* soldier]

militiaman /milíshəmən/ *n.* (*pl.* **-men**) a member of a militia.

milk /milk/ *n.* & *v.* ● *n.* **1** an opaque white fluid secreted by female mammals for the nourishment of their young. **2** the milk of cows, goats, or sheep as food. **3** the milklike juice of plants, e.g. in the coconut. **4** a milklike preparation of herbs, drugs, etc. ● *v.tr.* **1** draw milk from (a cow, ewe, goat, etc.). **2 a** exploit (a person) esp. financially. **b** get all possible advantage from (a situation). **3** extract sap, venom, etc. from. **4** *sl.* tap (telegraph or telephone wires etc.). □ **cry over spilt milk** lament an irremediable loss or error. **in milk** secreting milk. **milk and honey** abundant means of prosperity. **milk and water** a feeble or insipid or mawkish discourse or sentiment. **milk bar** a snack bar selling milk drinks and other refreshments. **milk chocolate** chocolate for eating, made with milk. **milk float** *Brit.* a small usu. electric vehicle used in delivering milk. **milk-leg** a painful swelling, esp. of the legs, after childbirth. **milk-loaf** a loaf of bread made with milk. **milk of human kindness** kindness regarded as natural to humanity. **Milk of Magnesia** *Brit. propr.* a white suspension of magnesium hydroxide usu. in water as an antacid or laxative. **milk of sulphur** the amorphous powder of sulphur formed by precipitation. **milk-powder** milk dehydrated by evaporation. **milk pudding** a pudding of rice, sago, tapioca, etc., baked with milk in a dish. **milk round 1** a fixed route on which milk is delivered regularly. **2** a regular trip or tour involving calls at several places. **milk run** a routine expedition or service journey. **milk shake** a drink of milk, flavouring, etc., mixed by shaking or whisking. **milk sugar** lactose. **milk tooth** a temporary tooth in young mammals. **milk-vetch** any leguminous yellow-flowered plant of the genus *Astragalus*. **milk-white** white like milk. □□ **milker** *n.* [OE *milc, milcian* f. Gmc]
■ *n.* **3** latex; see also JUICE 1. **4** see SOLUTION 2b. ● *v.* **2** exploit, bleed, drain, take advantage of. □ **milk and honey** prosperity, riches, wealth, opulence. **milk-round 2** round(s), circuit.

milkmaid /mílkmayd/ *n.* a girl or woman who milks cows or works in a dairy.

milkman /mílkmən/ *n.* (*pl.* **-men**) a person who sells or delivers milk.

milksop /mílksop/ *n.* a spiritless man or youth.
■ coward, weakling, namby-pamby, mollycoddle, cry-baby, nancy (boy), *colloq.* sissy, *Brit. colloq.* chinless wonder, wet, mummy's boy, *colloq. derog.* pansy, *poet. or archaic* caitiff, *Austral.* & *NZ sl. derog.* sook.

milkweed /mílkweed/ *n.* any of various wild plants with milky juice.

milkwort /mílkwurt/ *n.* any plant of the genus *Polygala*, formerly supposed to increase women's milk.

milky /mílki/ *adj.* (**milkier, milkiest**) **1** of, like, or mixed with milk. **2** (of a gem or liquid) cloudy; not clear. **3** effeminate; weakly amiable. □ **Milky Way** a faintly luminous band of light emitted by countless stars encircling the heavens; the Galaxy. □□ **milkiness** *n.*
■ **2** see FILMY 2. **3** see EFFEMINATE.

mill[1] /mil/ *n.* & *v.* ● *n.* **1 a** a building fitted with a mechanical apparatus for grinding corn. **b** such an apparatus. **2** an apparatus for grinding any solid substance to powder or pulp (*pepper-mill*). **3 a** a building fitted with machinery for manufacturing processes etc. (*cotton-mill*). **b** such machinery. **4 a** a boxing-match. **b** a fist fight. ● *v.* **1** *tr.* grind (corn), produce (flour), or hull (seeds) in a mill. **2** *tr.* produce regular ribbed markings on the edge of (a coin). **3** *tr.* cut or shape (metal) with a rotating tool. **4** *intr.* (often foll. by *about, around*) (of people or animals) move in an aimless manner, esp. in a confused mass. **5** *tr.* thicken (cloth etc.) by fulling. **6** *tr.* beat (chocolate etc.) to froth. **7** *tr. sl.* beat, strike, fight. □ **go** (or **put**) **through the mill** undergo (or cause to undergo) intensive work or training etc. **mill-dam** a dam put across a stream to make it usable by a mill. **mill-hand** a worker in a mill or factory. **mill-race** a current of water that drives a mill-wheel. **mill-wheel** a wheel used to drive a water-mill. □□ **millable** *adj.* [OE *mylen* ult. f. LL *molinum* f. L *mola* grindstone, mill f. *molere* grind]
■ *n.* **1b, 2** grinder, quern, crusher, roller. **3 a** plant, factory, works, workshop, shop, foundry. **4** see BOUT 2a. ● *v.* **1** grind, crush, hull, comminute, powder, pulverize, granulate, pound, triturate, crunch, *archaic* bray. **4** (*mill about* or *around*) crowd, throng, swarm. **7** see BEAT *v.* 1, FIGHT *v.* 1a.

mill[2] /mil/ *n. US* one-thousandth of a dollar as money of account. [L *millesimum* thousandth: cf. CENT]

millboard /mílbord/ *n.* stout pasteboard for bookbinding etc.

millefeuille /meelfő-i/ *n.* a rich confection of puff pastry split and filled with jam, cream, etc. [F, = thousand-leaf]

millenarian /míllináiriən/ *adj.* & *n.* ● *adj.* **1** of or related to the millennium. **2** believing in the millennium. ● *n.* a person who believes in the millennium. [as MILLENARY]
■ *adj.* chiliastic, millenary, millenialist. ● *n.* chiliast, millenary, millenialist.

millenary /milénnəri/ *n.* & *adj.* ● *n.* (*pl.* **-ies**) **1** a period of 1,000 years. **2** the festival of the 1,000th anniversary of a person or thing. **3** a person who believes in the millennium. ● *adj.* of or relating to a millenary. [LL *millenarius* consisting of a thousand f. *milleni* distrib. of *mille* thousand]

millennium /miléniəm/ *n.* (*pl.* **millenniums** or **millennia** /-niə/) **1** a period of 1,000 years, esp. that of Christ's prophesied reign in person on earth (Rev. 20:1–5). **2** a period of good government, great happiness, and prosperity.

□□ **millennial** *adj.* **millennialist** *n.* & *adj.* [mod.L f. L *mille* thousand after BIENNIUM]

millepede var. of MILLIPEDE.

millepore /míllipor/ *n.* a reef-building coral of the order Milleporina, with polyps protruding through pores in the calcareous exoskeleton. [F *millépore* or mod.L *millepora* f. L *mille* thousand + *porus* PORE[1]]

miller /míllər/ *n.* **1** the proprietor or tenant of a corn-mill. **2** a person who works or owns a mill. □ **miller's thumb** a small spiny freshwater fish, *Cottus gobio*: also called BULLHEAD. [ME *mylnere*, prob. f. MLG, MDu. *molner*, *mulner*, OS *mulineri* f. LL *molinarius* f. *molina* MILL[1], assim. to MILL[1]]

millesimal /miléssim'l/ *adj.* & *n.* ● *adj.* **1** thousandth. **2** of or belonging to a thousandth. **3** of or dealing with thousandths. ● *n.* a thousandth part. □□ **millesimally** *adv.* [L *millesimus* f. *mille* thousand]

millet /míllit/ *n.* **1** any of various cereal plants, esp. *Panicum miliaceum*, bearing a large crop of small nutritious seeds. **2** the seed of this. □ **millet-grass** a tall woodland grass, *Milium effusum*. [ME f. F, dimin. of *mil* f. L *milium*]

milli- /mílli/ *comb. form* a thousand, esp. denoting a factor of one thousandth. ¶ Abbr.: **m.** [L *mille* thousand]

milliammeter /mílliámmitər/ *n.* an instrument for measuring electrical current in milliamperes.

milliampere /mílliámpair/ *n.* one thousandth of an ampere, a measure for small electrical currents.

milliard /mílyərd, -yaard/ *n. Brit.* one thousand million. ¶ Now largely superseded by *billion*. [F f. *mille* thousand]

millibar /míllibaar/ *n.* one-thousandth of a bar, the cgs unit of atmospheric pressure equivalent to 100 pascals.

milligram /mílligram/ *n.* one-thousandth of a gram.

millilitre /millileetər/ *n.* one-thousandth of a litre (0.002 pint).

millimetre /millimeetər/ *n.* one-thousandth of a metre (0.039 in.).

milliner /míllinər/ *n.* a person who makes or sells women's hats. □□ **millinery** *n.* [orig. = vendor of goods from *Milan*]

million /mílyən/ *n.* & *adj.* ● *n.* (*pl.* same or (in sense 2) **millions**) (in *sing.* prec. by *a* or *one*) **1** a thousand thousand. **2** (in *pl.*) *colloq.* a very large number (*millions of years*). **3** (prec. by *the*) the bulk of the population. **4 a** *Brit.* a million pounds. **b** *US* a million dollars. ● *adj.* that amount to a million. □ **gone a million** *Austral. sl.* completely defeated. □□ **millionfold** *adj.* & *adv.* **millionth** *adj.* & *n.* [ME f. OF, prob. f. It. *millione* f. *mille* thousand + *-one* augment. suffix]

■ *n.* **2** (*millions*) see SCORE *n.* 3.

millionaire /mílyənáir/ *n.* (*fem.* **millionairess** /-riss/) **1** a person whose assets are worth at least one million pounds, dollars, etc. **2** a person of great wealth. [F *millionnaire* (as MILLION)]

■ see TYCOON.

millipede /míllipeed/ *n.* (also **millepede**) any arthropod of the class Diplopoda, having a long segmented body with two pairs of legs on each segment. [L *millepeda* wood-louse f. *mille* thousand + *pes pedis* foot]

millisecond /míllisekkənd/ *n.* one-thousandth of a second.

millpond /mílpond/ *n.* a pool of water retained by a mill-dam for the operation of a mill. □ **like a millpond** (of a stretch of water) very calm.

Mills bomb /milz/ *n.* an oval hand-grenade. [invented by Sir W. *Mills* d. 1932]

millstone /mílstōn/ *n.* **1** each of two circular stones used for grinding corn. **2** a heavy burden or responsibility (cf. Matt. 18:6).

■ **2** see BURDEN *n.* 1, 2.

millwright /mílrīt/ *n.* a person who designs or builds mills.

milometer /mīlómmitər/ *n.* an instrument for measuring the number of miles travelled by a vehicle.

milord /milórd/ *n. hist.* an Englishman travelling in Europe in aristocratic style. [F f. E *my lord*: cf. MILADY]

milt /milt/ *n.* **1** the spleen in mammals. **2** an analogous organ in other vertebrates. **3** a sperm-filled reproductive gland of a male fish. [OE *milt(e)* f. Gmc, perh. rel. to MELT]

milter /míltər/ *n.* a male fish in spawning-time.

mimbar /mímbaar/ *n.* (also **minbar** /mín-/) a stepped platform for preaching in a mosque. [Arab. *minbar*]

mime /mīm/ *n.* & *v.* ● *n.* **1** the theatrical technique of suggesting action, character, etc. by gesture and expression without using words. **2** a theatrical performance using this technique. **3** *Gk* & *Rom. Antiq.* a simple farcical drama including mimicry. **4** (also **mime artist**) a practitioner of mime. ● *v.* **1** *tr.* (also *absol.*) convey (an idea or emotion) by gesture without words. **2** *intr.* (often foll. by *to*) (of singers etc.) mouth the words of a song etc. along with a soundtrack (*mime to a record*). □□ **mimer** *n.* [L *mimus* f. Gk *mimos*]

mimeograph /mímmiəgraaf/ *n.* & *v.* ● *n.* **1** (often *attrib.*) a duplicating machine which produces copies from a stencil. **2** a copy produced in this way. ● *v.tr.* reproduce (text or diagrams) by this process. [irreg. f. Gk *mimeomai* imitate: see -GRAPH]

mimesis /mimeéssiss, mī-/ *n. Biol.* a close external resemblance of an animal to another that is distasteful or harmful to predators of the first. [Gk *mimēsis* imitation]

mimetic /miméttik/ *adj.* **1** relating to or habitually practising imitation or mimicry. **2** *Biol.* of or exhibiting mimesis. □□ **mimetically** *adv.* [Gk *mimētikos* imitation (as MIMESIS)]

■ **1** see MIMIC *adj.*

mimic /mímmik/ *v.*, *n.*, & *adj.* ● *v.tr.* (**mimicked, mimicking**) **1** imitate (a person, gesture, etc.) esp. to entertain or ridicule. **2** copy minutely or servilely. **3** (of a thing) resemble closely. ● *n.* a person skilled in imitation. ● *adj.* having an aptitude for mimicry; imitating; imitative of a thing, esp. for amusement. □□ **mimicker** *n.* [L *mimicus* f. Gk *mimikos* (as MIME)]

■ *v.* **1** mock, ridicule, satirize, caricature, parody, make fun of, lampoon, impersonate, *colloq.* take off; imitate, ape, copy, simulate. **2** reproduce, duplicate, copy; see also IMITATE 3. **3** mirror, echo; see also RESEMBLE. ● *n.* impersonator, imitator, impressionist, caricaturist, parodist; *colloq.* copycat. ● *adj.* imitative, mimetic; imitation, mock, simulated, sham, make-believe, pretend(ed).

mimicry /mímmikri/ *n.* (*pl.* **-ies**) **1** the act or art of mimicking. **2** a thing that mimics another. **3** *Zool.* mimesis.

■ **1** see IMITATION *n.* 1.

miminy-piminy /mímminipímmini/ *adj.* overrefined, finical (cf. NIMINY-PIMINY & NAMBY-PAMBY). [imit.]

mimosa /mimṓzə/ *n.* **1** any leguminous shrub of the genus *Mimosa*, esp. *M. pudica*, having globular usu. yellow flowers and sensitive leaflets which droop when touched. **2** any of various acacia plants with showy yellow flowers. [mod.L, app. f. L (as MIME, from being as sensitive as animals) + *-osa* fem. suffix]

mimulus /mímyooləss/ *n.* any flowering plant of the genus *Mimulus*, including musk and the monkey flower. [mod.L, app. dimin. of L (as MIME, perh. with ref. to its masklike flowers)]

Min /min/ *n.* any of the Chinese languages or dialects spoken in the Fukien province in SE China. [Chin.]

Min. *abbr.* **1** Minister. **2** Ministry.

min. *abbr.* **1** minute(s). **2** minimum. **3** minim (fluid measure).

mina var. of MYNA.

minaret /mínnərét/ *n.* a slender turret connected with a mosque and having a balcony from which the muezzin calls at hours of prayer. □□ **minareted** *adj.* [F *minaret* or Sp. *minarete* f. Turk. *minare* f. Arab. *manār(a)* lighthouse, minaret f. *nār* fire, light]

■ see TOWER *n.* 1a.

minatory /mínnətəri/ *adj.* threatening, menacing. [LL *minatorius* f. *minari minat-* threaten]

■ see *threatening* (THREATEN).

minbar var. of MIMBAR.

mince /minss/ *v.* & *n.* ● *v.* **1** *tr.* cut up or grind (esp. meat) into very small pieces. **2** *tr.* (usu. with *neg.*) restrain (one's

words etc.) within the bounds of politeness. **3** *intr.* (usu. as **mincing** *adj.*) speak or walk with an affected delicacy. ● *n.* esp. *Brit.* minced meat. □ **mince matters** (usu. with *neg.*) use polite expressions etc. **mince pie** a usu. small round pie containing mincemeat. □□ **mincer** *n.* **mincingly** *adv.* (in sense 3 of *v.*). [ME f. OF *mincier* ult. f. L (as MINUTIA)]
■ *v.* **1** see *cut up* 1, GRIND *v.* 1a. **3** (**mincing**) effeminate, dainty, delicate, niminy-piminy, foppish, dandyish, affected, precious, chichi, *Brit. usu. derog.* twee.

mincemeat /mínsmeet/ *n.* a mixture of currants, raisins, sugar, apples, candied peel, spices, and often suet. □ **make mincemeat of** utterly defeat (a person, argument, etc.).

mind /mīnd/ *n.* & *v.* ● *n.* **1 a** the seat of consciousness, thought, volition, and feeling. **b** attention, concentration (*my mind keeps wandering*). **2** the intellect; intellectual powers; aptitude. **3** remembrance, memory (*it went out of my mind; I can't call it to mind*). **4** one's opinion (*we're of the same mind*). **5** a way of thinking or feeling (*shocking to the Victorian mind*). **6** the focus of one's thoughts or desires (*put one's mind to it*). **7** the state of normal mental functioning (*lose one's mind; in one's right mind*). **8** a person as embodying mental faculties (*a great mind*). ● *v.tr.* **1** (usu. with *neg.* or *interrog.*) object to (*do you mind if I smoke?; I don't mind your being late*). **2 a** remember; take care to (*mind you come on time*). **b** (often foll. by *out*) take care; be careful. **3** have charge of temporarily (*mind the house while I'm away*). **4** apply oneself to, concern oneself with (business, affairs, etc.) (*I try to mind my own business*). **5** give heed to; notice (*mind the step; don't mind the expense; mind how you go*). **6** *US* & *Ir.* be obedient to (*mind what your mother says*). □ **be in two minds** be undecided. **be of a mind** (often foll. by *to* + infin.) be prepared or disposed. **cast one's mind back** think back; recall an earlier time. **come into a person's mind** be remembered. **come to mind** (of a thought, idea, etc.) suggest itself. **don't mind me** *iron.* do as you please. **do you mind!** *iron.* an expression of annoyance. **give a person a piece of one's mind** scold or reproach a person. **have a good** (or **great** or **half a**) **mind to** (often as a threat, usu. unfulfilled) feel tempted to (*I've a good mind to report you*). **have** (**it**) **in mind** intend. **have a mind of one's own** be capable of independent opinion. **have on one's mind** be troubled by the thought of. **in one's mind's eye** in one's imagination or mental view. **mind-bending** *colloq.* (esp. of a psychedelic drug) influencing or altering one's state of mind. **mind-blowing** *sl.* **1** confusing, shattering. **2** (esp. of drugs etc.) inducing hallucinations. **mind-boggling** *colloq.* overwhelming, startling. **mind out for** guard against, avoid. **mind over matter** the power of the mind asserted over the physical universe. **mind one's Ps & Qs** be careful in one's behaviour. **mind-read** discern the thoughts of (another person). **mind-reader** a person capable of mind-reading. **mind-set** habits of mind formed by earlier events. **mind the shop** have charge of affairs temporarily. **mind you** an expression used to qualify a previous statement (*I found it quite quickly; mind you, it wasn't easy*). **mind your back** (or **backs**) *colloq.* an expression to indicate that a person wants to get past. **never mind 1** an expression used to comfort or console. **2** (also **never you mind**) an expression used to evade a question. **3** disregard (*never mind the cost*). **open** (or **close**) **one's mind to** be receptive (or unreceptive) to (changes, new ideas, etc.). **out of one's mind** crazy. **put a person in mind of** remind a person of. **put** (or **set**) **a person's mind at rest** reassure a person. **put a person or thing out of one's mind** deliberately forget. **read a person's mind** discern a person's thoughts. **to my mind** in my opinion. [ME *mynd* f. OE *gemynd* f. Gmc]
■ *n.* **1b, 6** consciousness, awareness; attention, thoughts, concentration, attentiveness; see also PERCEPTION, SENSITIVITY. **2** intelligence, intellect, wit(s), mentality, brain, brains, brainpower, sense, sagacity, wisdom, perception, percipience, reason, astuteness, insight, shrewdness, sapience, *colloq.* grey matter; aptitude, head, perception, capacity. **3** memory, recollection; remembrance. **4** opinion, sentiment, attitude, (point of) view, feeling, judgement, belief, viewpoint, standpoint, position. **5** intention, disposition, temper, temperament, humour, fancy, tendency, bent, inclination, bias, persuasion, mentality. **7** see SANITY 1. **8** intellect, intellectual, sage, genius, thinker, *colloq.* brain. ● *v.* **1** object to, resent, take offence at, be offended by, dislike, be troubled *or* annoyed by, care about, disapprove of, be bothered *or* affronted by. **2 a** remember to, not forget to, take care to, make sure to, be sure to. **b** (*mind out*) watch out, look out, take care, be careful. **3** watch over, take care of, care for, look after, sit with, babysit, guard, keep an eye on *or* out for, have *or* take charge of, attend to. **4** see *address oneself to* 2, *mind one's own business* (BUSINESS). **5, 6** heed, give heed to, attend to, pay attention to, obey, listen to, make *or* take note of, mark, note, notice; watch, be careful of, take care with, be cautious of, be concerned about *or* over. □ **be in two minds** vacillate, waver, shilly-shally, dither, be uncertain *or* unsure, be undecided *or* ambivalent, hesitate, *Brit.* haver, *colloq.* dilly-dally. **cast one's mind back** see REMINISCE. **come to mind** see OCCUR 3. **do you mind!** see MIND *v.* 2b above. **give a person a piece of one's mind** castigate, scold, rebuke, reprimand, rail at, reprove, reproach, chastise, upbraid, berate, read a person the Riot Act, haul *or* call over the coals, *colloq.* tell off, dress down, bawl out, give a person hell, *US colloq.* chew out. **have** (**it**) **in mind** see INTEND 1, 2. **have on one's mind** be preoccupied by, be troubled *or* plagued by the thought of. **mind-bending** mind-altering, *sl.* mind-blowing; psychedelic, hallucinogenic. **mind-blowing 1** see OVERWHELMING. **2** see *mind-bending* above. **mind-boggling** see OVERWHELMING. **mind out for** see WATCH *v.* 3, AVOID 1. **mind-read** read a person's mind. **mind you** see THOUGH *adv.* **never mind 2** see *mind one's own business* (BUSINESS). **3** ignore, disregard, forget, pay no attention to, do not think twice about, do not give a second thought to, erase *or* obliterate *or* cancel from the mind. **out of one's mind** see CRAZY 1. **put a person in mind of** remind of, cause to remember. **put** (or **set**) **a person's mind at rest** see REASSURE. **put a thing out of one's mind** see FORGET 4. **read a person's mind** mind-read. **to my mind** as I see it, in my opinion *or* judgement *or* view, in my book, for my money, if you ask me, from my point of view, to my way of thinking, personally.

minded /mīndid/ *adj.* **1** (in *comb.*) **a** inclined to think in some specified way (*mathematically minded; fair-minded*). **b** having a specified kind of mind (*high-minded*). **c** interested in or enthusiastic about a specified thing (*car-minded*). **2** (usu. foll. by *to* + infin.) disposed or inclined (to an action).

minder /mīndər/ *n.* **1 a** a person whose job it is to attend to a person or thing. **b** (in *comb.*) (*child-minder; machine-minder*). **2** *sl.* **a** a bodyguard, esp. a person employed to protect a criminal. **b** a thief's assistant.
■ **1** child-minder, babysitter, sitter, nanny, nurse, governess. **2 a** bodyguard, protector; see also ESCORT *n.* 1.

mindful /mīndfool/ *adj.* (often foll. by *of*) taking heed or care; being conscious. □□ **mindfully** *adv.* **mindfulness** *n.*
■ aware, alert, attentive, alive, conscious, heedful, careful, conscientious, watchful, vigilant, on the qui vive, on the lookout, circumspect, cautious.

mindless /mīndliss/ *adj.* **1** lacking intelligence; stupid. **2** not requiring thought or skill (*totally mindless work*). **3** (usu. foll. by *of*) heedless of (advice etc.). □□ **mindlessly** *adv.* **mindlessness** *n.*
■ **1** stupid, asinine, obtuse, idiotic, thoughtless, witless, senseless, brainless, feeble-minded, fatuous, *colloq.* thick, thickheaded, moronic, imbecilic, *esp. Brit. colloq.* gormless. **2** perfunctory, unthinking; see also MECHANICAL 3. **3** heedless, unaware; see also INATTENTIVE.

mine[1] /mīn/ *poss.pron.* **1** the one or ones belonging to or associated with me (*it is mine; mine are over there*). **2** (*attrib.*

before a vowel) *archaic* = MY (*mine eyes have seen*; *mine host*). □ **of mine** of or belonging to me (*a friend of mine*). [OE *mīn* f. Gmc]

mine[2] /mīn/ *n.* & *v.* ● *n.* **1** an excavation in the earth for extracting metal, coal, salt, etc. **2** an abundant source (of information etc.). **3** a receptacle filled with explosive and placed in the ground or in the water for destroying enemy personnel, ships, etc. **4 a** a subterranean gallery in which explosive is placed to blow up fortifications. **b** *hist.* a subterranean passage under the wall of a besieged fortress. ● *v.tr.* **1** obtain (metal, coal, etc.) from a mine. **2** (also *absol.*, often foll. by *for*) dig in (the earth etc.) for ore etc. **3 a** dig or burrow in (usu. the earth). **b** delve into (an abundant source) for information etc. **c** make (a hole, passage, etc.) underground. **4** lay explosive mines under or in. **5** = UNDERMINE. □ **mine-detector** an instrument for detecting the presence of mines. □□ **mining** *n.* [ME f. OF *mine*, *miner*, perh. f. Celt.]

■ *n.* **1** pit, excavation; colliery, coalfield. **2** source, quarry, store, storehouse, supply, deposit, depository, repository, reserve, hoard, reservoir, well-spring; fund, mint, gold-mine, treasury. ● *v.* **1, 2** excavate, dig, quarry, extract, scoop out *or* up, remove, unearth; derive, extract, draw. **3 a, c** dig *or* burrow in; gouge (out), scoop (out), hollow out. **b** ransack, search, rake through, scour, scan, read, survey, look through, probe.

minefield /mīnfeeld/ *n.* **1** an area planted with explosive mines. **2** a subject or situation presenting unseen hazards.

minelayer /mīnlayər/ *n.* a ship or aircraft for laying mines.

miner /mīnər/ *n.* **1** a person who works in a mine. **2** any burrowing insect or grub. □ **miner's right** *Austral.* a licence to dig for gold etc. on private or public land. [ME f. OF *minëor*, *minour* (as MINE[2])]

mineral /minnərəl/ *n.* & *adj.* ● *n.* **1** any of the species into which inorganic substances are classified. **2** a substance obtained by mining. **3** (often in *pl.*) *Brit.* an artificial mineral water or other effervescent drink. ● *adj.* **1** of or containing a mineral or minerals. **2** obtained by mining. □ **mineral oil** petroleum or one of its distillation products. **mineral water 1** water found in nature with some dissolved salts present. **2** an artificial imitation of this, esp. soda water. **3** any effervescent non-alcoholic drink. **mineral wax** a fossil resin, esp. ozocerite. **mineral wool** a wool-like substance made from inorganic material, used for packing etc. [ME f. OF *mineral* or med.L *mineralis* f. *minera* ore f. OF *miniere* mine]

mineralize /minnərəlīz/ *v.* (also **-ise**) **1** *v.tr.* & *intr.* change wholly or partly into a mineral. **2** *v.tr.* impregnate (water etc.) with a mineral substance.

mineralogy /minnərálləji/ *n.* the scientific study of minerals. □□ **mineralogical** /-rəlójik'l/ *adj.* **mineralogist** *n.*

minestrone /minnistrṓni/ *n.* a soup containing vegetables and pasta, beans, or rice. [It.]

minesweeper /mīnsweepər/ *n.* a ship for clearing away floating and submarine mines.

minever var. of MINIVER.

mineworker /mīnwurkər/ *n.* a person who works in a mine, esp. a coalmine.

Ming /ming/ *n.* **1** the dynasty ruling China 1368-1644. **2** Chinese porcelain made during the rule of this dynasty. [Chin.]

mingle /mingg'l/ *v.* **1** *tr.* & *intr.* mix, blend. **2** *intr.* (often foll. by *with*) (of a person) move about, associate. □ **mingle their** etc. **tears** *literary* weep together. □□ **mingler** *n.* [ME *mengel* f. obs. *meng* f. OE *mengan*, rel. to AMONG]

■ **1** mix, blend, intermingle, intermix, combine, amalgamate, merge, compound, marry, join, unite, *literary* commingle. **2** mix, socialize, associate, fraternize, hobnob, consort, spend time, hang about *or* around, rub shoulders, *colloq.* pal up, *sl.* hang out; (*mingle with*) join, circulate among, move *or* go about among.

mingy /minji/ *adj.* (**mingier**, **mingiest**) *Brit. colloq.* mean, stingy. □□ **mingily** *adv.* [perh. f. MEAN[2] and STINGY]

■ see MEAN[2] 1.

mini /minni/ *n.* (*pl.* **minis**) **1** *colloq.* a miniskirt, minidress, etc. **2** (**Mini**) *propr.* a make of small car. [abbr.]

mini- /minni/ *comb. form* miniature; very small or minor of its kind (*minibus*; *mini-budget*). [abbr. of MINIATURE]

■ micro-.

miniature /minnichər/ *adj.*, *n.*, & *v.* ● *adj.* **1** much smaller than normal. **2** represented on a small scale. ● *n.* **1** any object reduced in size. **2** a small-scale minutely finished portrait. **3** this branch of painting (*portrait in miniature*). **4** a picture or decorated letters in an illuminated manuscript. ● *v.tr.* represent on a smaller scale. □ **in miniature** on a small scale. **miniature camera** a camera producing small negatives. □□ **miniaturist** *n.* (in senses 2 and 3 of n.). [It. *miniatura* f. med.L *miniatura* f. L *miniare* rubricate, illuminate f. L *minium* red lead, vermilion]

■ *adj.* small, small-scale, little, tiny, diminutive, minute, minimal, minuscule, mini-, microscopic, midget, dwarf, baby, pygmy, pocket, Lilliputian, *esp. Sc.* or *colloq.* wee.

miniaturize /minnichərīz/ *v.tr.* (also **-ise**) produce in a smaller version; make small. □□ **miniaturization** /-záysh'n/ *n.*

minibus /minnibuss/ *n.* a small bus for about twelve passengers.

minicab /minnikab/ *n.* *Brit.* a car used as a taxi, but not licensed to ply for hire.

minicomputer /minnikəmpyōōtər/ *n.* a computer of medium power, more than a microcomputer but less than a mainframe.

minikin /minnikin/ *adj.* & *n.* ● *adj.* **1** diminutive. **2** affected, mincing. ● *n.* a diminutive creature. [obs. Du. *minneken* f. *minne* love + *-ken*, *-kijn* -KIN]

minim /minnim/ *n.* **1** *Mus.* a note having the time value of two crotchets or half a semibreve and represented by a hollow ring with a stem. Also called *half-note*. **2** one-sixtieth of a fluid drachm, about a drop. **3** an object or portion of the smallest size or importance. **4** a single down-stroke of the pen. [ME f. L *minimus* smallest]

minima *pl.* of MINIMUM.

minimal /minnim'l/ *adj.* **1** very minute or slight. **2** being or related to a minimum. **3** the least possible in size, duration, etc. **4** *Art* etc. characterized by the use of simple or primary forms or structures etc., often geometric or massive (*huge minimal forms in a few colours*). □□ **minimalism** *n.* (in sense 4). **minimally** *adv.* (in senses 1–3). [L *minimus* smallest]

■ **1** see MINUTE[2] 1. **2, 3** least, smallest, minutest, littlest, tiniest, slightest; minimum, nominal, token.

minimalist /minniməlist/ *n.* **1** (also *attrib.*) a person advocating small or moderate reform in politics (opp. MAXIMALIST). **2** = MENSHEVIK. **3** a person who advocates or practises minimal art. □□ **minimalism** *n.*

minimax /minnimaks/ *n.* **1** *Math.* the lowest of a set of maximum values. **2** (usu. *attrib.*) **a** a strategy that minimizes the greatest risk to a participant in a game etc. **b** the theory that in a game with two players, a player's smallest possible maximum loss is equal to the same player's greatest possible minimum gain. [MINIMUM + MAXIMUM]

minimize /minnimīz/ *v.* (also **-ise**) **1** *tr.* reduce to, or estimate at, the smallest possible amount or degree. **2** *tr.* estimate or represent at less than the true value or importance. **3** *intr.* attain a minimum value. □□ **minimization** /-záysh'n/ *n.* **minimizer** *n.*

■ **1** reduce, shrink, lessen, diminish, prune, abbreviate, pare (down), cut (down), curtail, abridge, shorten, decrease. **2** belittle, de-emphasize, downplay, play down, make little *or* light of, disparage, decry, deprecate, depreciate, devalue, undervalue, underrate, underestimate, talk down, *literary* misprize.

minimum /minniməm/ *n.* & *adj.* (*pl.* **minima** /-mə/) ● *n.* the least possible or attainable amount (*reduced to a minimum*). ● *adj.* that is a minimum. □ **minimum lending rate** the announced minimum percentage at which a central bank will discount bills (cf. *base rate* (see BASE[1])).

¶ Abolished in the UK in 1981. **minimum wage** the lowest wage permitted by law or special agreement. [L, neut. of *minimus* least]
▪ *n.* (rock) bottom, base, floor, lower limit. ● *adj.* minimal, minutest, littlest, least, slightest, lowest, rock-bottom.

minion /mínyən/ *n. derog.* **1** a servile agent; a slave. **2** a favourite servant, animal, etc. **3** a favourite of a sovereign etc. [F *mignon*, OF *mignot*, of Gaulish orig.]
▪ **1** see FLUNKEY 1.

minipill /mínnipil/ *n.* a contraceptive pill containing progestogen only (not oestrogen).

miniseries /mínniseeriz/ *n.* a short series of television programmes on a common theme.

miniskirt /mínniskurt/ *n.* a very short skirt.

minister /mínnistər/ *n.* & *v.* ● *n.* **1** a head of a government department. **2** (in full **minister of religion**) a member of the clergy, esp. in the Presbyterian and Nonconformist Churches. **3** a diplomatic agent, usu. ranking below an ambassador. **4** (usu. foll. by *of*) a person employed in the execution of (a purpose, will, etc.) (*a minister of justice*). **5** (in full **minister general**) the superior of some religious orders. ● *v.* **1** *intr.* (usu. foll. by *to*) render aid or service (to a person, cause, etc.). **2** *tr.* (usu. foll. by *with*) *archaic* furnish, supply, etc. □ **ministering angel** a kind-hearted person, esp. a woman, who nurses or comforts others (with ref. to Mark 1:13). **Minister of the Crown** *Brit. Parl.* a member of the Cabinet. **Minister of State** a government minister, in the UK usu. regarded as holding a rank below that of Head of Department. **Minister without Portfolio** a government minister who has Cabinet status, but is not in charge of a specific Department of State. □□ **ministrable** *adj.* [ME f. OF *ministre* f. L *minister* servant f. *minus* less]
▪ *n.* **1, 3** envoy, delegate, diplomat, ambassador, emissary, (minister) plenipotentiary, envoy extraordinary, consul, agent, chargé d'affaires, *archaic* legate; *Brit.* Cabinet Minister. **2** cleric, clergyman, clergywoman, ecclesiastic, pastor, reverend, churchman, divine, parson, preacher, man of the cloth, evangelist, curate, *curé*, chaplain, padre, *sl.* sky pilot, *orig. Naut. sl.* holy Joe. **4** see OFFICER 1, 3, 4. ● *v.* **1** (*minister to*) attend (to *or* on *or* upon), wait on, care for, look after, see to, accommodate; serve, supply, aid, help, assist, support. **2** see SUPPLY[1] *v.* 1, 2. □ **ministering angel** angel, saint, comforter; see also NURSE *n.*

ministerial /mínnisteériəl/ *adj.* **1** of a minister of religion or a minister's office. **2** instrumental or subsidiary in achieving a purpose (*ministerial in bringing about a settlement*). **3 a** of a government minister. **b** siding with the Ministry against the Opposition. □□ **ministerialist** *n.* (in sense 3b). **ministerially** *adv.* [F *ministériel* or LL *ministerialis* f. L (as MINISTRY)]
▪ **1** see CLERICAL 1.

ministration /mínnistráysh'n/ *n.* **1** (usu. in *pl.*) aid or service (*the kind ministrations of his neighbours*). **2** ministering, esp. in religious matters. **3** (usu. foll. by *of*) the supplying (of help, justice, etc.). □□ **ministrant** /mínnistrənt/ *adj.* & *n.* **ministrative** /mínnistrətiv/ *adj.* [ME f. OF *ministration* or L *ministratio* (as MINISTER)]

ministry /mínnistri/ *n.* (*pl.* **-ies**) **1 a** a government department headed by a minister. **b** the building which it occupies (*the Ministry of Defence*). **2 a** (prec. by *the*) the vocation or profession of a religious minister (*called to the ministry*). **b** the office of a religious minister, priest, etc. **c** the period of tenure of this. **3** (prec. by *the*) the body of ministers of a government or of a religion. **4** a period of government under one Prime Minister. **5** ministering, ministration. [ME f. L *ministerium* (as MINISTER)]
▪ **1** office, bureau, agency; see also DEPARTMENT 1a. **2, 3** (*the ministry*) priesthood, the church, the pulpit, the cloth, holy orders; clergy, clergymen, clergywomen; see also CABINET 2. **4** term (of office); see also ADMINISTRATION 2, 3.

miniver /mínnivər/ *n.* (also **minever**) plain white fur used in ceremonial costume. [ME f. AF *menuver*, OF *menu vair* (as MENU, VAIR)]

mink /mingk/ *n.* **1** either of two small semi-aquatic stoatlike animals of the genus *Mustela*, *M. vison* of N. America and *M. intreola* of Europe. **2** the thick brown fur of these. **3** a coat made of this. [cf. Sw. *mänk*, *menk*]

minke /míngkə/ *n.* a small baleen whale, *Balaenoptera acutorostrata*, with a pointed snout. [prob. f. *Meincke*, the name of a Norw. whaler]

Minn. *abbr.* Minnesota.

minnesinger /mínnisingər/ *n.* a German lyric poet and singer of the 12th–14th c. [G, = love-singer]

minnow /mínnō/ *n.* any of various small freshwater fish of the carp family, esp. *Phoxinus phoxinus*. [late ME *menow*, perh. repr. OE *mynwe* (unrecorded), *myne*: infl. by ME *menuse*, *menise* f. OF *menuise*, ult. rel. to MINUTIA]

Minoan /minṓən/ *adj.* & *n. Archaeol.* ● *adj.* of or relating to the Bronze Age civilization centred on Crete (*c.*3000–1100 BC). ● *n.* **1** an inhabitant of Minoan Crete or the Minoan world. **2** the language or scripts associated with the Minoans. [named after the legendary Cretan king *Minos* (Gk *Minōs*), to whom the palace excavated at Knossos was attributed]

minor /mī́nər/ *adj.*, *n.*, & *v.* ● *adj.* **1** lesser or comparatively small in size or importance (*minor poet*; *minor operation*). **2** *Mus.* **a** (of a scale) having intervals of a semitone between the second and third, fifth and sixth, and seventh and eighth degrees. **b** (of an interval) less by a semitone than a major interval. **c** (of a key) based on a minor scale, tending to produce a melancholy effect. **3** *Brit.* (in schools) indicating the younger of two children from the same family or the second to enter the school (usu. put after the name). **4** *Logic* **a** (of a term) occurring as the subject of the conclusion of a categorical syllogism. **b** (of a premiss) containing the minor term in a categorical syllogism. ● *n.* **1** a person under the legal age limit or majority (*no unaccompanied minors*). **2** *Mus.* a minor key etc. **3** *US* a student's subsidiary subject or course (cf. MAJOR). **4** *Logic* a minor term or premiss. ● *v.intr.* (foll. by *in*) *US* (of a student) undertake study in (a subject) as a subsidiary to a main subject. □ **in a minor key** (of novels, events, people's lives, etc.) understated, uneventful. **minor axis** *Geom.* (of a conic) the axis perpendicular to the major axis. **minor canon** a cleric who is not a member of the chapter, who assists in daily cathedral services. **minor league** *US* (in baseball, football, etc.) a league of professional clubs other than the major leagues. **minor orders** see ORDER. **minor piece** *Chess* a bishop or a knight. **minor planet** an asteroid. **minor prophet** any of the prophets from Hosea to Malachi, whose surviving writings are not lengthy. **minor suit** *Bridge* diamonds or clubs. [L, = smaller, less, rel. to *minuere* lessen]
▪ *adj.* **1** lesser, smaller, secondary, subordinate, subsidiary; insignificant, obscure, inconsequential, unimportant, trifling, trivial, negligible, inconsiderable, slight, petty, paltry, small, two a penny, *US* minor league, picayune, *colloq.* small-time, one-horse, *US colloq.* two-bit. ● *n.* **1** child, youngster, youth, stripling, teenager, adolescent, schoolboy, schoolgirl, boy, girl, lad, infant, ward, *esp. Sc. & N.Engl. or poet.* lass, *colloq.* laddie, lassie.

minority /mīnórriti/ *n.* (*pl.* **-ies**) **1** (often foll. by *of*) a smaller number or part, esp. within a political party or structure. **2** the number of votes cast for this (*a minority of two*). **3** the state of having less than half the votes or of being supported by less than half of the body of opinion (*in the minority*). **4** a relatively small group of people differing from others in the society of which they are a part in race, religion, language, political persuasion, etc. **5** (*attrib.*) relating to or done by the minority (*minority interests*). **6 a** the state of being under full legal age. **b** the period of this. [F *minorité* or med.L *minoritas* f. L *minor*: see MINOR]
▪ **6** see CHILDHOOD.

Minotaur /mī́nətawr/ *n.* (in Greek mythology) a man with a bull's head, kept in a Cretan labyrinth and fed with human flesh. [ME f. OF f. L *Minotaurus* f. Gk *Minōtauros* f. *Minōs*, legendary king of Crete (see MINOAN) + *tauros* bull]

minster /mínstər/ *n.* **1** a large or important church (*York Minster*). **2** the church of a monastery. [OE *mynster* f. eccl.L *monasterium* f. Gk *monastērion* MONASTERY]

minstrel /mínstrəl/ *n.* **1** a medieval singer or musician, esp. singing or reciting poetry. **2** *hist.* a person who entertained patrons with singing, buffoonery, etc. **3** (usu. in *pl.*) a member of a band of public entertainers with blackened faces etc., performing songs and music ostensibly of Negro origin. [ME f. OF *menestral* entertainer, servant, f. Prov. *menest(ai)ral* officer, employee, musician, f. LL *ministerialis* official, officer: see MINISTERIAL]

▪ **1, 2** troubadour, balladeer, *hist.* skald, minnesinger, bard, *jongleur*.

minstrelsy /mínstrəlsi/ *n.* (*pl.* **-ies**) **1** the minstrel's art. **2** a body of minstrels. **3** minstrel poetry. [ME f. OF *menestralsie* (as MINSTREL)]

mint[1] /mint/ *n.* **1** any aromatic plant of the genus *Mentha.* **2** a peppermint sweet or lozenge. □ **mint julep** *US* a sweet iced alcoholic drink of bourbon flavoured with mint. **mint sauce** chopped mint in vinegar and sugar, usu. eaten with lamb. □□ **minty** *adj.* (**mintier, mintiest**). [OE *minte* ult. f. L *ment(h)a* f. Gk *minthē*]

mint[2] /mint/ *n.* & *v.* ● *n.* **1** a place where money is coined, usu. under State authority. **2** a vast sum of money (*making a mint*). **3** a source of invention etc. (*a mint of ideas*). ● *v.tr.* **1** make (coin) by stamping metal. **2** invent, coin (a word, phrase, etc.). □ **in mint condition** (or **state**) freshly minted; (of books etc.) as new. **mint-mark** a mark on a coin to indicate the mint at which it was struck. **mint-master** the superintendent of coinage at a mint. **mint par** (in full **mint parity**) **1** the ratio between the gold equivalents of currency in two countries. **2** their rate of exchange based on this. □□ **mintage** *n.* [OE *mynet* f. WG f. L *moneta* MONEY]

▪ *n.* **2** (small) fortune, king's ransom, millions, billions, wad(s), *colloq.* pile, heap(s), packet, pot(s), loads, *sl.* bundle, *Brit. sl.* bomb, *US sl.* big bucks. **3** see MINE[2] *n.* 2. ● *v.* **1** stamp, coin, produce. **2** see COIN *v.* 3.

minuend /mínyoo-end/ *n. Math.* a quantity or number from which another is to be subtracted. [L *minuendus* gerundive of *minuere* diminish]

minuet /mínyoo-ét/ *n.* & *v.* ● *n.* **1** a slow stately dance for two in triple time. **2** *Mus.* the music for this, or music in the same rhythm and style, often as a movement in a suite, sonata, or symphony. ● *v.intr.* (**minueted, minueting**) dance a minuet. [F *menuet*, orig. adj. = fine, delicate, dimin. of *menu*: see MENU]

minus /mīnəss/ *prep., adj.,* & *n.* ● *prep.* **1** with the subtraction of (*7 minus 4 equals 3*). ¶ Symb.: –. **2** (of temperature) below zero (*minus 2°*). **3** *colloq.* lacking; deprived of (*returned minus their dog*). ● *adj.* **1** *Math.* negative. **2** *Electronics* having a negative charge. ● *n.* **1** = *minus sign.* **2** *Math.* a negative quantity. **3** a disadvantage. □ **minus sign** the symbol –, indicating subtraction or a negative value. [L, neut. of *minor* less]

minuscule /mínnəskyōōl/ *n.* & *adj.* ● *n.* **1** *Palaeog.* a kind of cursive script developed in the 7th c. **2** a lower-case letter. ● *adj.* **1** lower-case. **2** *colloq.* extremely small or unimportant. □□ **minuscular** /minúskyoolər/ *adj.* [F f. L *minuscula* (*littera* letter) dimin. of *minor*: see MINOR]

▪ *adj.* **2** see MINUTE[2] 1.

minute[1] /mínnit/ *n.* & *v.* ● *n.* **1** the sixtieth part of an hour. **2** a distance covered in one minute (*twenty minutes from the station*). **3 a** a moment; an instant; a point of time (*expecting her any minute*; *the train leaves in a minute*). **b** (prec. by *the*) *colloq.* the present time (*what are you doing at the minute?*). **c** (foll. by *clause*) as soon as (*call me the minute you get back*). **4** the sixtieth part of an angular degree. **5** (in *pl.*) a brief summary of the proceedings at a meeting. **6** an official memorandum authorizing or recommending a course of action. ● *v.tr.* **1** record (proceedings) in the minutes. **2** send the minutes to (a person). □ **just** (or **wait**) **a minute** **1** a request to wait for a short time. **2** as a prelude to a query or objection. **minute-gun** a gun fired at intervals of a minute at funerals etc. **minute-hand** the hand on a watch or clock which indicates minutes. **minute steak** a thin slice of steak to be cooked quickly. **up to the minute** completely up to date. [ME f. OF f. LL *minuta* (n.), f. fem. of *minutus* MINUTE[2]: senses 1 & 4 of noun f. med.L *pars minuta prima* first minute part (cf. SECOND[2]): senses 5 & 6 perh. f. med.L *minuta scriptura* draft in small writing]

▪ *n.* **3 a** instant, (split) second, flash, moment, trice, *colloq.* sec, jiff, tick, mo, *Brit. colloq.* two ticks. **b** (*at the minute*) at present, at the present moment *or* time, now, at the moment, this moment. **5** (*minutes*) log, record, journal, transcript, notes, summary, résumé, proceedings, transactions. **6** see MEMORANDUM. ● *v.* **1** record, transcribe, take down, write down, make a note of, document, log. □ **just** (or **wait**) **a minute** wait (a moment *or* second), hold on, *colloq.* hang on. **up to the minute** latest, newest, modern, up to date, fashionable, smart, all the rage, in vogue, stylish, in fashion, à la mode, in, *colloq.* with it, *colloq. often derog.* trendy, *sl.* hip.

minute[2] /mīnyōōt/ *adj.* (**minutest**) **1** very small. **2** trifling, petty. **3** (of an inquiry, inquirer, etc.) accurate, detailed, precise. □□ **minutely** *adv.* **minuteness** *n.* [ME f. L *minutus* past part. of *minuere* lessen]

▪ **1** small, little, tiny, minuscule, minimal, miniature, infinitesimal, microscopic, diminutive, mini-, baby, Lilliputian, *esp. Sc. or colloq.* wee, *archaic* piccaninny, *colloq.* pint-sized, teeny, teeny-weeny, *colloq. usu. derog.* itsy-bitsy. **2** unimportant, petty, insignificant, slight, mere, trifling, trivial, minor, small, little, *US* picayune, *colloq.* piffling, piddling. **3** see PRECISE 2.

Minuteman /mínnitman/ *n.* (*pl.* **-men**) *US* **1** a political watchdog or activist. **2** a type of three-stage intercontinental ballistic missile. **3** *hist.* an American militiaman of the revolutionary period (ready to march at a minute's notice).

minutia /mīnyōōshiə, mi-/ *n.* (*pl.* **-iae** /-shi-ee/) (usu. in *pl.*) a precise, trivial, or minor detail. [L, = smallness, in pl. trifles f. *minutus*: see MINUTE[2]]

▪ see REFINEMENT 6.

minx /mingks/ *n.* a pert, sly, or playful girl. □□ **minxish** *adj.* **minxishly** *adv.* [16th c.: orig. unkn.]

▪ see FLIRT *n.*

Miocene /míəseen/ *adj.* & *n. Geol.* ● *adj.* of or relating to the fourth epoch of the Tertiary period with evidence for the diversification of primates, including early apes. ¶ Cf. Appendix VII. ● *n.* this epoch or system. [irreg. f. Gk *meiōn* less + *kainos* new]

miosis /mīṓsiss/ *n.* (also **myosis**) excessive constriction of the pupil of the eye. □□ **miotic** /mīóttik/ *adj.* [Gk *muō* shut the eyes + -OSIS]

mirabelle /mírrəbél/ *n.* **1 a** a European variety of plum-tree, *Prunus insititia*, bearing small round yellow fruit. **b** a fruit from this tree. **2** a liqueur distilled from this fruit. [F]

miracle /mírrək'l/ *n.* **1** an extraordinary event attributed to some supernatural agency. **2 a** any remarkable occurrence. **b** a remarkable development in some specified area (*an economic miracle*; *the German miracle*). **3** (usu. foll. by *of*) a remarkable or outstanding specimen (*the plan was a miracle of ingenuity*). □ **miracle drug** a drug which represents a breakthrough in medical science. **miracle play** a medieval play based on the Bible or the lives of the saints. [ME f. OF f. L *miraculum* object of wonder f. *mirari* wonder f. *mirus* wonderful]

▪ see WONDER *n.* 2. □ **miracle drug** see ELIXIR 1c.

miraculous /mirákyooləss/ *adj.* **1** of the nature of a miracle. **2** supernatural. **3** remarkable, surprising. □□ **miraculously** *adv.* **miraculousness** *n.* [F *miraculeux* or med.L *miraculosus* f. L (as MIRACLE)]

▪ **1, 3** marvellous, wonderful, incredible, unbelievable, inexplicable, unexplainable, extraordinary, spectacular, amazing, astounding, astonishing, mind-boggling, surprising, remarkable, phenomenal, fantastic, fabulous, far-out, *colloq.* out of this world, *poet.* wondrous, *sl.* crazy. **2** magical, preternatural, superhuman; see also SUPERNATURAL *adj.*

mirador /mírrədór/ *n.* a turret or tower etc. attached to a building, and commanding an excellent view. [Sp. f. *mirar* to look]

mirage /mírraazh/ *n.* **1** an optical illusion caused by atmospheric conditions, esp. the appearance of a sheet of water in a desert or on a hot road from the reflection of light. **2** an illusory thing. [F f. *se mirer* be reflected, f. L *mirare* look at]

■ see ILLUSION 3.

MIRAS /mī́rass/ *abbr.* (also **Miras**) mortgage interest relief at source.

mire /mīr/ *n.* & *v.* ● *n.* **1** a stretch of swampy or boggy ground. **2** mud, dirt. ● *v.* **1** *tr.* & *intr.* plunge or sink in a mire. **2** *tr.* involve in difficulties. □ **in the mire** in difficulties. [ME f. ON *mýrr* f. Gmc, rel. to MOSS]

■ *n.* **1** swamp, bog, fen, marsh, quag, quagmire, slough, *literary* morass. **2** mud, ooze, muck, slime, dirt. ● *v.* **2** bog down, entangle, tangle, enmesh, mesh, involve, ensnare, trap. □ **in the mire** see *in trouble* 1 (TROUBLE).

mirepoix /meerpwaá/ *n.* sautéd chopped vegetables, used in sauces etc. [F, f. Duc de *Mirepoix*, Fr. general d. 1757]

mirk var. of MURK.

mirky var. of MURKY.

mirror /mírrər/ *n.* & *v.* ● *n.* **1** a polished surface, usu. of amalgam-coated glass or metal, which reflects an image; a looking-glass. **2** anything regarded as giving an accurate reflection or description of something else. ● *v.tr.* reflect as in a mirror. □ **mirror carp** a breed of carp with large shiny scales. **mirror finish** a reflective surface. **mirror image** an identical image, but with the structure reversed, as in a mirror. **mirror symmetry** symmetry as of an object and its reflection. **mirror writing** backwards writing, like ordinary writing reflected in a mirror. [ME f. OF *mirour* ult. f. L *mirare* look at]

■ *n.* **1** looking-glass, glass, speculum, reflector. **2** reflection, reproduction, picture, representation, replication, image, *colloq.* spitting image. ● *v.* reflect, reproduce, represent, depict, repeat, echo, send back. □ **mirror image** enantiomorph.

mirth /murth/ *n.* merriment, laughter. □□ **mirthful** *adj.* **mirthfully** *adv.* **mirthfulness** *n.* **mirthless** *adj.* **mirthlessly** *adv.* **mirthlessness** *n.* [OE *myrgth* (as MERRY)]

■ merriment, merrymaking, jollity, gaiety, fun, laughter, amusement, frolic, joviality, joyousness, revelry, rejoicing, glee, high spirits, mirthfulness, hilarity, buoyancy, *literary* jocundity.

MIRV *abbr.* multiple independently-targeted re-entry vehicle (a type of missile).

mis-[1] /miss/ *prefix* added to verbs and verbal derivatives: meaning 'amiss', 'badly', 'wrongly', 'unfavourably' (*mislead; misshapen; mistrust*). [OE f. Gmc]

mis-[2] /miss/ *prefix* occurring in a few words adopted from French meaning 'badly', 'wrongly', 'amiss', 'ill-', or having a negative force (*misadventure; mischief*). [OF *mes-* ult. f. L *minus* (see MINUS): assim. to MIS-[1]]

misaddress /míssədréss/ *v.tr.* **1** address (a letter etc.) wrongly. **2** address (a person) wrongly, esp. impertinently.

■ **1** see MISDIRECT.

misadventure /míssədvénchər/ *n.* **1** *Law* an accident without concomitant crime or negligence (*death by misadventure*). **2** bad luck. **3** a misfortune. [ME f. OF *mesaventure* f. *mesavenir* turn out badly (as MIS-[2], ADVENT: cf. ADVENTURE)]

■ **1** see ACCIDENT 2. **2, 3** see MISFORTUNE 2.

misalign /míssəlī́n/ *v.tr.* give the wrong alignment to. □□ **misalignment** *n.*

misalliance /míssəlī́ənss/ *n.* an unsuitable alliance, esp. an unsuitable marriage. □□ **misally** *v.tr.* (**-ies, -ied**). [MIS-[1] + ALLIANCE, after MÉSALLIANCE]

■ *mésalliance*, mismarriage, mismatch, bad match.

misanthrope /mízzənthrōp, míss-/ *n.* (also **misanthropist** /mizánthrəpist/) **1** a person who hates mankind. **2** a person who avoids human society. □□ **misanthropic** /-thróppik/ *adj.* **misanthropical** /-thróppik'l/ *adj.* **misanthropically** /-thróppikəli/ *adv.* **misanthropy** /mizánthrəpi/ *n.* **misanthropize** /mizánthrəpīz/ *v.intr.* (also **-ise**). [F f. Gk *misanthrōpos* f. *misos* hatred + *anthrōpos* man]

■ **2** loner, hermit, recluse, anchorite, lone wolf. □□ **misanthropic** antisocial, unsocial, unsociable, unfriendly.

misapply /míssəplī́/ *v.tr.* (**-ies, -ied**) apply (esp. funds) wrongly. □□ **misapplication** /míssaplikáysh'n/ *n.*

■ see MISUSE *v.* 1. □□ **misapplication** see MISUSE *n.*

misapprehend /míssaprihénd/ *v.tr.* misunderstand (words, a person). □□ **misapprehension** /-hénsh'n/ *n.* **misapprehensive** *adj.*

■ see MISUNDERSTAND.

misappropriate /míssəprṓpriayt/ *v.tr.* apply (usu. another's money) to one's own use, or to a wrong use. □□ **misappropriation** /-áysh'n/ *n.*

■ embezzle, steal, filch, pilfer, pocket, peculate; *formal* defalcate; misapply, misuse, pervert, misemploy.

misbegotten /mísbigótt'n/ *adj.* **1** illegitimate, bastard. **2** contemptible, disreputable.

■ **1** see ILLEGITIMATE *adj.* 1. **2** see CONTEMPTIBLE.

misbehave /mísbiháyv/ *v.intr.* & *refl.* (of a person or machine) behave badly. □□ **misbehaver** *n.* **misbehaviour** *n.*

■ behave badly *or* improperly, be bad *or* naughty *or* mischievous *or* disobedient, cause trouble, play up, *colloq.* carry on, act up, raise hell, raise Cain. □□ **misbehaviour** naughtiness, badness, misconduct, misdemeanour(s), disorderliness, disobedience, delinquency, disorderly conduct, rowdyism.

misbelief /mísbileéf/ *n.* **1** wrong or unorthodox religious belief. **2** a false opinion or notion.

■ **2** see DELUSION.

misc. *abbr.* miscellaneous.

miscalculate /mískálkyoolayt/ *v.tr.* (also *absol.*) calculate (amounts, results, etc.) wrongly. □□ **miscalculation** /-láysh'n/ *n.*

■ misjudge, miscount, misread; underestimate, undervalue, underrate; overestimate, overvalue, overrate. □□ **miscalculation** see ERROR 1.

miscall /mískáwl/ *v.tr.* **1** call by a wrong or inappropriate name. **2** *archaic* or *dial.* call (a person) names.

miscarriage /miskárrij/ *n.* **1** a spontaneous abortion, esp. before the 28th week of pregnancy. **2** *Brit.* the failure (of a plan, letter, etc.) to reach completion or its destination. □ **miscarriage of justice** any failure of the judicial system to attain the ends of justice. [MISCARRY, after CARRIAGE]

■ **1** *colloq.* miss. **2** failure, abortion, collapse, breakdown, failing, non-fulfilment; defeat, frustration.

miscarry /mískárri/ *v.intr.* (**-ies, -ied**) **1** (of a woman) have a miscarriage. **2** *Brit.* (of a letter etc.) fail to reach its destination. **3** (of a business, plan, etc.) fail, be unsuccessful.

■ **3** abort; fail, fall through, break down, go wrong, founder, come to nothing *or* naught, go awry, come to grief, go amiss, misfire, go up *or* end up in smoke, *US colloq.* go belly up.

miscast /mískaást/ *v.tr.* (*past* and *past part.* **-cast**) allot an unsuitable part to (an actor).

miscegenation /míssijináysh'n/ *n.* the interbreeding of races, esp. of Whites and non-Whites. [irreg. f. L *miscēre* mix + *genus* race]

miscellanea /míssəláyniə/ *n.pl.* **1** a literary miscellany. **2** a collection of miscellaneous items. [L neut. pl. (as MISCELLANEOUS)]

■ **2** see SUNDRY *n.*

miscellaneous /míssəláyniəss/ *adj.* **1** of mixed composition or character. **2** (foll. by pl. noun) of various kinds. **3** (of a person) many-sided. □□ **miscellaneously** *adv.* **miscellaneousness** *n.* [L *miscellaneus* f. *miscellus* mixed f. *miscēre* mix]

■ **1, 2** varied, heterogeneous, diverse, mixed, diversified, motley, sundry, assorted, various, varying, multifarious, multiform, multiplex, *archaic or literary* divers, *literary* manifold.

miscellany /misélləni/ *n.* (*pl.* **-ies**) **1** a mixture, a medley. **2** a book containing a collection of stories etc., or various literary compositions. □□ **miscellanist** *n.* [F *miscellanées* (fem. pl.) or L MISCELLANEA]

■ **1** mixture, assortment, variety, medley, diversity, mixed bag, job lot, rag-bag, *mélange*, pot-pourri, gallimaufry, motley, hotchpotch, salmagundi, olio, olla podrida, hash, jumble, *colloq.* omnium gatherum, *derog.* mess.

mischance /mischaánss/ *n.* **1** bad luck. **2** an instance of this. [ME f. OF *mesch(e)ance* f. *mescheoir* (as MIS-[2], CHANCE)]

■ see MISFORTUNE 2.

mischief /míschif/ *n.* **1** conduct which is troublesome, but not malicious, esp. in children. **2** pranks, scrapes (*get into mischief*; *keep out of mischief*). **3** playful malice, archness, satire (*eyes full of mischief*). **4** harm or injury caused by a person or thing. **5** a person or thing responsible for harm or annoyance (*that loose connection is the mischief*). **6** (prec. by *the*) the annoying part or aspect (*the mischief of it is that* etc.). □ **do a person a mischief** wound or kill a person. **get up to** (or **make**) **mischief** create discord. **mischief-maker** one who encourages discord, esp. by gossip etc. [ME f. OF *meschief* f. *meschever* (as MIS-[2], *chever* come to an end f. *chef* head: see CHIEF)]

■ **1–3** misbehaviour, naughtiness, impishness, roguishness, devilry, mischievousness, playfulness, devilment, pranks, scrapes, *colloq.* monkey business, shenanigan(s), monkey tricks, *US colloq.* monkeyshines, *often joc.* rascality. **4** harm, injury, damage, detriment, trouble, hurt, wrong, difficulty, disruption, destruction, misfortune, evil. **5, 6** trouble, worry, bother, *colloq.* pain; see also NUISANCE. □ **get up to** (or **make**) **mischief** cause *or* make trouble, stir (up), play up, put *or* set the cat among the pigeons, stir up a hornets' nest, *colloq.* start something, make waves.

mischievous /míschivəss/ *adj.* **1** (of a person) disposed to mischief. **2** (of conduct) playfully malicious. **3** (of a thing) having harmful effects. □□ **mischievously** *adv.* **mischievousness** *n.* [ME f. AF *meschevous* f. OF *meschever*: see MISCHIEF]

■ **1, 2** naughty, impish, roguish, devilish, elfish, puckish, pucklike, *colloq.* scampish, *often joc.* rascally. **3** harmful, injurious, hurtful, damaging, pernicious, detrimental, destructive, deleterious, dangerous, spiteful, malicious, vicious, malign, baleful, baneful, noxious, wicked, evil, bad.

misch metal /mish/ *n.* an alloy of lanthanide metals, usu. added to iron to improve its malleability. [G *mischen* mix + *Metall* metal]

miscible /míssib'l/ *adj.* (often foll. by *with*) capable of being mixed. □□ **miscibility** /-bílliti/ *n.* [med.L *miscibilis* f. L *miscēre* mix]

misconceive /mískənseev/ *v.* **1** *intr.* (often foll. by *of*) have a wrong idea or conception. **2** *tr.* (as **misconceived** *adj.*) badly planned, organized, etc. **3** *tr.* misunderstand (a word, person, etc.). □□ **misconceiver** *n.* **misconception** /-sépsh'n/ *n.*

■ **1, 3** misunderstand, misconstrue, misjudge, miscalculate, mistake, misapprehend, misinterpret, misread; get *or* have the wrong idea, get (hold of) the wrong end of the stick. **2** (**misconceived**) badly planned, ill-organized, ill-judged, ill thought out. □□ **misconception** false *or* wrong notion *or* idea, misunderstanding, misconstruction, misjudgement, miscalculation, misapprehension, mistaken belief, error, mistake, delusion.

misconduct *n.* & *v.* ● *n.* /miskóndukt/ **1** improper or unprofessional behaviour. **2** bad management. ● *v.* /miskəndúkt/ **1** *refl.* misbehave. **2** *tr.* mismanage.

■ *n.* **1** see *misbehaviour* (MISBEHAVE). ● *v.* **2** see MISHANDLE 1.

misconstrue /mískənstróo/ *v.tr.* (**-construes, -construed, -construing**) **1** interpret (a word, action, etc.) wrongly. **2** mistake the meaning of (a person). □□ **misconstruction** /-strúksh'n/ *n.*

■ see MISINTERPRET. □□ **misconstruction** see MISUNDERSTANDING 1.

miscopy /miskóppi/ *v.tr.* (**-ies, -ied**) copy (text etc.) incorrectly.

miscount /miskównt/ *v.* & *n.* ● *v.tr.* (also *absol.*) count wrongly. ● *n.* a wrong count.

■ *v.* see MISCALCULATE.

miscreant /mískriənt/ *n.* & *adj.* ● *n.* **1** a vile wretch, a villain. **2** *archaic* a heretic. ● *adj.* **1** depraved, villainous. **2** *archaic* heretical. [ME f. OF *mescreant* (as MIS-[2], *creant* part. of *croire* f. L *credere* believe)]

■ *n.* **1** villain, criminal, wrongdoer, felon, malefactor, rogue, reprobate, scoundrel, knave, scallywag, blackguard, wretch, hooligan, ruffian, hoodlum, thug, *Austral.* larrikin, *archaic or joc.* varlet, rapscallion, *colloq.* scamp, crook, baddy, *often joc.* rascal, *poet. or archaic* caitiff, *US sl.* hood, mug. ● *adj.* **1** villainous, criminal, felonious, corrupt, malevolent, evil, wicked, depraved, base, nefarious, iniquitous, vicious, unprincipled, wretched, reprobate, scoundrelly, mischievous, *often joc.* rascally, *literary* malefic.

miscue /miskyóo/ *n.* & *v.* ● *n.* (in snooker etc.) the failure to strike the ball properly with the cue. ● *v.intr.* (**-cues, -cued, -cueing** or **-cuing**) make a miscue.

misdate /misdáyt/ *v.tr.* date (an event, a letter, etc.) wrongly.

misdeal /misdéel/ *v.* & *n.* ● *v.tr.* (also *absol.*) (*past* and *past part.* **-dealt** /-délt/) make a mistake in dealing (cards). ● *n.* **1** a mistake in dealing cards. **2** a misdealt hand.

misdeed /misdéed/ *n.* an evil deed, a wrongdoing; a crime. [OE *misdǣd* (as MIS-[1], DEED)]

■ offence, crime, felony, wrongdoing, misdoing, transgression, misdemeanour, fault, misconduct, sin, trespass, wrong, peccadillo.

misdemeanant /mísdiméenənt/ *n.* a person convicted of a misdemeanour or guilty of misconduct. [archaic *misdemean* misbehave]

misdemeanour /mísdiméenər/ *n.* (*US* **misdemeanor**) **1** an offence, a misdeed. **2** *Law* an indictable offence, (in the UK formerly) less heinous than a felony.

■ see OFFENCE 1.

misdiagnose /misdíəgnóz/ *v.tr.* diagnose incorrectly. □□ **misdiagnosis** /-nósiss/ *n.*

misdial /misdíəl/ *v.tr.* (also *absol.*) (**-dialled, -dialling**; *US* **-dialed, -dialing**) dial (a telephone number etc.) incorrectly.

misdirect /mísdīrékt, -dirékt/ *v.tr.* **1** direct (a person, letter, blow, etc.) wrongly. **2** (of a judge) instruct (the jury) wrongly. □□ **misdirection** *n.*

■ misguide, misadvise; misaddress; see also MISINFORM.

misdoing /misdóoing/ *n.* a misdeed.

misdoubt /misdówt/ *v.tr.* **1** have doubts or misgivings about the truth or existence of. **2** be suspicious about; suspect that.

miseducation /míssedyookáysh'n/ *n.* wrong or faulty education. □□ **miseducate** /-édyookayt/ *v.tr.*

mise en scène /méez ON sén/ *n.* **1** *Theatr.* the scenery and properties of a play. **2** the setting or surroundings of an event. [F]

■ **1** see SET[2] 18. **2** see SETTING.

misemploy /míssimplóy/ *v.tr.* employ or use wrongly or improperly. □□ **misemployment** *n.*

■ see MISUSE *v.* 1.

miser /mízər/ *n.* **1** a person who hoards wealth and lives miserably. **2** an avaricious person. [L, = wretched]

■ skinflint, hoarder, niggard, penny-pincher, pinchpenny, cheese-parer, Scrooge, *colloq.* money-grubber, *esp. US colloq.* cheapskate.

miserable /mízzərəb'l/ *adj.* **1** wretchedly unhappy or uncomfortable (*felt miserable*). **2** unworthy, inadequate (*a miserable hovel*); contemptible. **3** causing wretchedness or discomfort (*miserable weather*). **4** *Sc.*, *Austral.*, & *NZ* stingy, mean. □□ **miserableness** *n.* **miserably** *adv.* [ME f. F *misérable* f. L *miserabilis* pitiable f. *miserari* to pity f. *miser* wretched]

■ **1** wretched, unhappy, depressed, woeful, woebegone, sad, dejected, forlorn, disconsolate, despondent, heartbroken, sorrowful, broken-hearted, mournful, abject, desolate, desperate, despairing, downhearted, melancholy, glum, low-spirited, dispirited, gloomy, dismal, tearful, upset, cut up, *colloq.* down, *formal* lachrymose. **2** inadequate, unworthy, poor, sorry, pitiful, pathetic, lamentable, squalid, wretched, shabby, mean, contemptible. **3** unpleasant, inclement, untoward, bad, unfavourable, awful, terrible, adverse, *colloq.* lousy, *sl.* rotten. **4** see MEAN[2] 1.

misère /mizáir/ *n. Cards* (in solo whist etc.) a declaration undertaking to win no tricks. [F, = poverty, MISERY]

miserere /mízzəráiri, -réeri/ *n.* **1** a cry for mercy. **2** = MISERICORD 1. [ME f. L, imper. of *miserēri* have mercy (as MISER); first word of Ps. 51 in Latin]

misericord /mizérrikord/ *n.* **1** a shelving projection on the under side of a hinged seat in a choir stall serving (when the seat is turned up) to help support a person standing. **2** an apartment in a monastery in which some relaxations of discipline are permitted. **3** a dagger for dealing the death stroke. [ME f. OF *misericorde* f. L *misericordia* f. *misericors* compassionate f. stem of *miserēri* pity + *cor cordis* heart]

miserly /mī́zərli/ *adj.* like a miser, niggardly. □□ **miserliness** *n.* [MISER]

■ stingy, niggardly, penny-pinching, parsimonious, mean, cheese-paring, tight-fisted, close, close-fisted, mercenary, avaricious, greedy, covetous, penurious, *Austral.* hungry, *colloq.* money-grubbing, tight, *Brit. colloq.* mingy.

misery /mízzəri/ *n.* (*pl.* **-ies**) **1** a wretched state of mind, or of outward circumstances. **2** a thing causing this. **3** *colloq.* a constantly depressed or discontented person. **4** = MISÈRE. □ **put out of its** etc. **misery 1** release (a person, animal, etc.) from suffering or suspense. **2** kill (an animal in pain). [ME f. OF *misere* or L *miseria* (as MISER)]

■ **1** unhappiness, distress, discomfort, wretchedness, sadness, melancholy, sorrow, heartache, grief, anguish, depression, despair, desperation, desolation, despondency, gloom, *archaic or literary* woe, *literary* dolour; squalor, poverty, destitution, privation, indigence, penury, sordidness. **2** hardship, suffering, calamity, disaster, curse, misfortune, ordeal, trouble, catastrophe, trial, tribulation, adversity, burden, affliction, *archaic or literary* woe. **3** spoilsport, damper, killjoy, Job's comforter, malcontent, pessimist, cynic, prophet of doom, Cassandra, *colloq.* wet blanket, grouch, grump, sourpuss, *US sl.* party pooper. □ **put out of its** etc. **misery 1** release, relieve, free, deliver, rescue, save, spare. **2** see *put down* 7 (PUT[1]).

misfeasance /misféez'nss/ *n. Law* a transgression, esp. the wrongful exercise of lawful authority. [ME f. OF *mesfaisance* f. *mesfaire* misdo (as MIS-[2], *faire* do f. L *facere*): cf. MALFEASANCE]

misfield /misféeld/ *v.* & *n.* ● *v.tr.* (also *absol.*) (in cricket, baseball, etc.) field (the ball) badly. ● *n.* an instance of this.

misfire /misfī́r/ *v.* & *n.* ● *v.intr.* **1** (of a gun, motor engine, etc.) fail to go off or start or function regularly. **2** (of an action etc.) fail to have the intended effect. ● *n.* a failure of function or intention.

■ *v.* **2** fail, abort, miscarry, go wrong, fizzle out, fall through, *colloq.* go phut, *sl.* flop, come a cropper. ● *n.* miscarriage, failure, malfunction, *sl.* dud, flop.

misfit /mísfit/ *n.* **1** a person unsuited to a particular kind of environment, occupation, etc. **2** a garment etc. that does not fit. □ **misfit stream** *Geog.* a stream not corresponding in size to its valley.

■ **1** eccentric, individual, nonconformist, maverick, round (*or* square) peg in a square (*or* round) hole.

misfortune /misfórchoon, -fórtyoon/ *n.* **1** bad luck. **2** an instance of this.

■ **1** bad luck, ill luck, ill fortune, hard luck, infelicity, adversity. **2** accident, misadventure, mishap, calamity, catastrophe, mischance, disaster, contretemps, tragedy, blow, shock, loss; reverse, stroke of bad luck.

misgive /misgív/ *v.tr.* (*past* **-gave** /-gáyv/; *past part.* **-given** /-gívv'n/) (often foll. by *about*, *that*) (of a person's mind, heart, etc.) fill (a person) with suspicion or foreboding.

misgiving /mísgivving/ *n.* (usu. in *pl.*) a feeling of mistrust or apprehension.

■ apprehension, mistrust, worry, concern, anxiety, qualm, scruple, disquiet, hesitation, doubt, question, uncertainty, suspicion, unease, uneasiness, discomfort; dread, premonition, foreboding, (funny) feeling.

misgovern /mísgúvvərn/ *v.tr.* govern (a State etc.) badly. □□ **misgovernment** *n.*

misguide /mísgī́d/ *v.tr.* **1** (as **misguided** *adj.*) mistaken in thought or action. **2** mislead, misdirect. □□ **misguidance** *n.* **misguidedly** *adv.* **misguidedness** *n.*

■ **1** (**misguided**) mistaken, wrong, misdirected, foolish, unreasoning, erroneous, misled, misplaced, imprudent, unwise, impolitic, ill-advised, ill-judged, beside *or* off *or* wide of the mark. **2** see MISLEAD.

mishandle /míss-hánd'l/ *v.tr.* **1** deal with incorrectly or ineffectively. **2** handle (a person or thing) roughly or rudely; ill-treat.

■ **1** mismanage, bungle, botch, misconduct, mess up, muddle, muff, make a mess of, *colloq.* make a hash of, *sl.* screw up, *Brit. sl.* cock up. **2** abuse, mistreat, maltreat, ill-treat, brutalize, maul, molest, injure, hurt, harm, knock about *or* around, *colloq.* manhandle.

mishap /míss-hap/ *n.* an unlucky accident.

■ see MISFORTUNE 2.

mishear /míss-héer/ *v.tr.* (*past* and *past part.* **-heard** /-hérd/) hear incorrectly or imperfectly.

mishit *v.* & *n.* ● *v.tr.* /míss-hít/ (**-hitting**; *past* and *past part.* **-hit**) hit (a ball etc.) faultily. ● *n.* /míss-hit/ a faulty or bad hit.

mishmash /míshmash/ *n.* a confused mixture. [ME, reduplication of MASH]

■ mess, medley, hash, gallimaufry, farrago, pot-pourri, jumble, pastiche, mixture, salmagundi, hotchpotch, *mélange*, olio, olla podrida, *colloq.* omnium gatherum.

Mishnah /míshnə/ *n.* a collection of precepts forming the basis of the Talmud, and embodying Jewish oral law. □□ **Mishnaic** /-náyik/ *adj.* [Heb. *mišnāh* (teaching by) repetition]

misidentify /míssīdéntifī/ *v.tr.* (**-ies**, **-ied**) identify erroneously. □□ **misidentification** /-fikáysh'n/ *n.*

■ (*misidentify as*) see MISTAKE *v.* 2.

misinform /míssinfórm/ *v.tr.* give wrong information to, mislead. □□ **misinformation** /-fərmáysh'n/ *n.*

■ misguide, mislead, misadvise, misdirect, delude, deceive, dupe, fool, gull, lead astray, put *or* throw off the scent, *colloq.* slip *or* put one over on, pull a fast one on, *sl.* con, *US sl.* give a bum steer to. □□ **misinformation** disinformation; (*piece of misinformation*) red herring, false trail, false scent.

misinterpret /míssintérprit/ *v.tr.* (**-interpreted**, **-interpreting**) **1** interpret wrongly. **2** draw a wrong inference from. □□ **misinterpretation** /-táysh'n/ *n.* **misinterpreter** *n.*

■ misunderstand, misconstrue, misconceive, misread, misjudge, misapprehend, mistake.

misjudge /mísjúj/ *v.tr.* (also *absol.*) **1** judge wrongly. **2** have a wrong opinion of. □□ **misjudgement** *n.* (also **misjudgment**).

■ see MISTAKE *v.* 1.

miskey /miskée/ *v.tr.* (**-keys**, **-keyed**) key (data) wrongly.

miskick *v.* & *n.* ● *v.tr.* /mískík/ (also *absol.*) kick (a ball etc.) badly or wrongly. ● *n.* /mískik/ an instance of this.

mislay /mísláy/ *v.tr.* (*past* and *past part.* **-laid** /-láyd/) **1** unintentionally put (a thing) where it cannot readily be found. **2** *euphem.* lose.
▪ misplace, lose.

mislead /misleéd/ *v.tr.* (*past* and *past part.* **-led** /-léd/) **1** cause (a person) to go wrong, in conduct, belief, etc. **2** lead astray or in the wrong direction. ▫▫ **misleader** *n.*
▪ misinform, lead astray, misguide, misdirect, put *or* throw off the scent, pull the wool over a person's eyes, fool, outwit, bluff, hoodwink, trick, humbug, deceive, dupe, gull, flimflam, take in, *archaic* wilder, *colloq.* bamboozle, lead up the garden path, slip *or* put one over on, *literary* cozen, *sl.* con, take, *US sl.* give a bum steer to.

misleading /mísleéding/ *adj.* causing to err or go astray; imprecise, confusing. ▫▫ **misleadingly** *adv.* **misleadingness** *n.*
▪ see FALSE *adj.* 2b.

mislike /míslík/ *v.tr.* & *n. archaic* dislike. [OE *mislīcian* (as MIS-[1], LIKE[2])]

mismanage /mismánnij/ *v.tr.* manage badly or wrongly. ▫▫ **mismanagement** *n.*
▪ see MISHANDLE 1.

mismarriage /mísmárrij/ *n.* an unsuitable marriage or alliance. [MIS-[1] + MARRIAGE]

mismatch *v.* & *n.* ● *v.tr.* /mísmách/ (usu. as **mismatched** *adj.*) match unsuitably or incorrectly, esp. in marriage. ● *n.* /mismach/ a bad match.
▪ *v.* (**mismatched**) mismated, ill-matched, incompatible, unfit, inappropriate, unsuited, unsuitable, incongruous, disparate, uncongenial, inconsistent, inharmonious, discordant. ● *n.* see MISALLIANCE.

mismated /mísmáytid/ *adj.* **1** (of people) not suited to each other, esp. in marriage. **2** (of objects) not matching.

mismeasure /misméz͟hər/ *v.tr.* measure or estimate incorrectly. ▫▫ **mismeasurement** *n.*

misname /misnáym/ *v.tr.* = MISCALL.

misnomer /misnṓmər/ *n.* **1** a name or term used wrongly. **2** the wrong use of a name or term. [ME f. AF f. OF *mesnom(m)er* (as MIS-[2], *nommer* name f. L *nominare* formed as NOMINATE)]

misogamy /misóggəmi/ *n.* the hatred of marriage. ▫▫ **misogamist** *n.* [Gk *misos* hatred + *gamos* marriage]

misogyny /misójini/ *n.* the hatred of women. ▫▫ **misogynist** *n.* **misogynous** *adj.* [Gk *misos* hatred + *gunē* woman]

mispickel /míspik'l/ *n. Mineral.* arsenical pyrites. [G]

misplace /mispláyss/ *v.tr.* **1** put in the wrong place. **2** bestow (affections, confidence, etc.) on an inappropriate object. **3** time (words, actions, etc.) badly. ▫▫ **misplacement** *n.*
▪ **1** see LOSE 1–3.

misplay /mispláy/ *v.* & *n.* ● *v.tr.* play (a ball, card, etc.) in a wrong or ineffective manner. ● *n.* an instance of this.

misprint *n.* & *v.* ● *n.* /mísprint/ a mistake in printing. ● *v.tr.* /misprínt/ print wrongly.
▪ *n.* error, mistake, erratum, typographical error, printer's *or* printing error, *Printing* literal, *colloq.* typo.

misprision[1] /misprí͟zh'n/ *n. Law* **1** (in full **misprision of a felony** or **of treason**) the deliberate concealment of one's knowledge of a crime, treason, etc. **2** a wrong action or omission. [ME f. AF *mesprisioun* f. OF *mesprison* error f. *mesprendre* to mistake (as MIS-[2], *prendre* take)]

misprision[2] /misprí͟zh'n/ *n.* **1** a misreading, misunderstanding, etc. **2** (usu. foll. by *of*) a failure to appreciate the value of a thing. **3** *archaic* contempt. [MISPRIZE after MISPRISION[1]]

misprize /mispríz/ *v.tr. literary* despise, scorn; fail to appreciate. [ME f. OF *mesprisier* (as MIS-[1], PRIZE[1])]

mispronounce /mísprənównss/ *v.tr.* pronounce (a word etc.) wrongly. ▫▫ **mispronunciation** /-nunsiáysh'n/ *n.*

misquote /miskwṓt/ *v.tr.* quote wrongly. ▫▫ **misquotation** /-táysh'n/ *n.*
▪ see TWIST *v.* 5. ▫▫ **misquotation** see MISSTATEMENT.

misread /misreéd/ *v.tr.* (*past* and *past part.* **-read** /-réd/) read or interpret (text, a situation, etc.) wrongly.
▪ see MISINTERPRET.

misremember /mísrimémbər/ *v.tr.* remember imperfectly or incorrectly.

misreport /mísripórt/ *v.* & *n.* ● *v.tr.* give a false or incorrect report of. ● *n.* a false or incorrect report.
▪ *v.* see GARBLE 2. ● *n.* see MISSTATEMENT.

misrepresent /mísreprizént/ *v.tr.* represent wrongly; give a false or misleading account or idea of. ▫▫ **misrepresentation** /-táysh'n/ *n.* **misrepresentative** *adj.*
▪ distort, twist, pervert, garble, misstate, mangle; falsify, belie, disguise, colour.

misrule /mísrṓol/ *n.* & *v.* ● *n.* bad government; disorder. ● *v.tr.* govern badly.

Miss. *abbr.* Mississippi.

miss[1] /miss/ *v.* & *n.* ● *v.* **1** *tr.* (also *absol.*) fail to hit, reach, find, catch, etc. (an object or goal). **2** *tr.* fail to catch (a bus, train, etc.). **3** *tr.* fail to experience, see, or attend (an occurrence or event). **4** *tr.* fail to meet (a person); fail to keep (an appointment). **5** *tr.* fail to seize (an opportunity etc.) (*I missed my chance*). **6** *tr.* fail to hear or understand (*I'm sorry, I missed what you said*). **7** *tr.* **a** regret the loss or absence of (a person or thing) (*did you miss me while I was away?*). **b** notice the loss or absence of (an object) (*bound to miss the key if it isn't there*). **8** *tr.* avoid (*go early to miss the traffic*). **9** *tr.* = *miss out* 1. **10** *intr.* (of an engine etc.) fail, misfire. ● *n.* **1** a failure to hit, reach, attain, connect, etc. **2** *colloq.* = MISCARRIAGE 1. ▫ **be missing** see MISSING *adj.* **give (a thing) a miss** avoid, leave alone (*gave the party a miss*). **miss the boat** (or **bus**) lose an opportunity. **miss fire** (of a gun) fail to go off or hit the mark (cf. MISFIRE). **a miss is as good as a mile** the fact of failure or escape is not affected by the narrowness of the margin. **miss out 1** omit, leave out (*missed out my name from the list*). **2** (usu. foll. by *on*) *colloq.* fail to get or experience (*always misses out on the good times*). **not miss much** be alert. **not miss a trick** never fail to seize an opportunity, advantage, etc. ▫▫ **missable** *adj.* [OE *missan* f. Gmc]
▪ *v.* **3** absent oneself from, be absent from; see also CUT *v.* 12. **6** misunderstand, misinterpret, misconstrue, misapprehend, mistake. **7** long for, yearn for, pine for, want, need, wish for. **8** see AVOID 1. ▫ **give (a thing) a miss** see AVOID 1. **miss out 1** omit, leave out, pass up, pass over, overlook, disregard, ignore. **2** (*miss out on*) let slip (by), let pass, miss.

miss[2] /miss/ *n.* **1** a girl or unmarried woman. **2** (**Miss**) **a** the title of an unmarried woman or girl, or of a married woman retaining her maiden name for professional purposes. **b** the title of a beauty queen (*Miss World*). **3** usu. *derog.* or *joc.* a girl, esp. a schoolgirl, with implications of silliness etc. **4** the title used to address a female schoolteacher, shop assistant, etc. ▫▫ **missish** *adj.* (in sense 3). [abbr. of MISTRESS]
▪ **1, 3** girl, (young) lady, (young) woman, bachelor girl, mademoiselle, Fräulein, signorina, *Ir.* colleen, *esp. Sc.* & *N.Engl. or poet.* lass, *archaic* demoiselle, *archaic or literary* damsel, *archaic or poet.* maid, maiden, *colloq.* lassie, filly, popsy, nymphet, floozy, *joc.* wench, *poet.* nymph, *sl.* gal, chick, petticoat, *Austral.* & *NZ sl.* sheila, brush, *Brit. sl.* bird; schoolgirl, teenager, *esp. US* coed, *colloq.* teeny-bopper, weeny-bopper; spinster, *derog.* old maid.

missal /miss'l/ *n. RC Ch.* **1** a book containing the texts used in the service of the Mass throughout the year. **2** a book of prayers, esp. an illuminated one. [ME f. med.L *missale* neut. of eccl.L *missalis* of the mass f. *missa* MASS[2]]

missel-thrush var. of MISTLE-THRUSH.

misshape /miss-sháyp/ *v.tr.* give a bad shape or form to; distort.
▪ see DISTORT 1a.

misshapen /miss-sháyp'n/ *adj.* ill-shaped, deformed, distorted. ▫▫ **misshapenly** *adv.* **misshapenness** *n.*

■ ill-shaped, distorted, twisted, contorted, crooked, deformed, crippled, malformed, grotesque, awry, warped, gnarled, ill-made, monstrous.

missile /míssīl/ *n.* **1** an object or weapon suitable for throwing at a target or for discharge from a machine. **2** a weapon, esp. a nuclear weapon, directed by remote control or automatically. □□ **missilery** /-sīlri/ *n.* [L *missilis* f. *mittere miss-* send]
■ projectile, brickbat

missing /míssing/ *adj.* **1** not in its place; lost. **2** (of a person) not yet traced or confirmed as alive but not known to be dead. **3** not present. □ **missing link 1** a thing lacking to complete a series. **2** a hypothetical intermediate type, esp. between humans and apes.
■ **3** see ABSENT *adj.* 1.

mission /mísh'n/ *n.* **1 a** a particular task or goal assigned to a person or group. **b** a journey undertaken as part of this. **c** a person's vocation (*mission in life*). **2** a military or scientific operation or expedition for a particular purpose. **3** a body of persons sent, esp. to a foreign country, to conduct negotiations etc. **4 a** a body sent to propagate a religious faith. **b** a field of missionary activity. **c** a missionary post or organization. **d** a place of worship attached to a mission. **5** a particular course or period of preaching, services, etc., undertaken by a parish or community. [F *mission* or L *missio* f. *mittere miss-* send]
■ **1 a** task, duty, function, purpose, job, office, work, assignment, errand, charge, business, commission, undertaking, aim, goal, objective. **c** calling, occupation, vocation, trade, line (of work), profession, *métier*. **2** see EXPEDITION 1. **3** delegation, legation, deputation, commission, committee, group.

missionary /míshənəri, -shənri/ *adj.* & *n.* ● *adj.* of, concerned with, or characteristic of, religious missions. ● *n.* (*pl.* **-ies**) a person doing missionary work. □ **missionary position** *colloq.* a position for sexual intercourse with the woman lying on her back and the man lying on top and facing her. [mod.L *missionarius* f. L (as MISSION)]
■ *n.* evangelist, preacher, proselytizer.

missioner /míshənər/ *n.* **1** a missionary. **2** a person in charge of a religious mission.

missis /míssiz/ *n.* (also **missus** /-səz/) *sl.* or *joc.* **1** a form of address to a woman. **2** a wife. □ **the missis** my or your wife. [corrupt. of MISTRESS: cf. MRS]

missive /míssiv/ *n.* **1** *joc.* a letter, esp. a long and serious one. **2** an official letter. □ **letter** (or **letters**) **missive** a letter from a sovereign to a dean and chapter nominating a person to be elected bishop. [ME f. med.L *missivus* f. L (as MISSION)]
■ letter, communication, message, dispatch, *formal or joc.* epistle.

misspell /míss-spél/ *v.tr.* (*past* and *past part.* **-spelt** or **-spelled**) spell wrongly.

misspelling /míss-spélling/ *n.* a wrong spelling.

misspend /míss-spénd/ *v.tr.* (*past* and *past part.* **-spent** /-spént/) (esp. as **misspent** *adj.*) spend amiss or wastefully.
■ see WASTE *v.* 1; (**misspent**) wasted, squandered, idle, dissipated, thrown away, profitless, prodigal.

misstate /míss-stáyt/ *v.tr.* state wrongly or inaccurately.
■ see TWIST *v.* 5.

misstatement /míss-stáytmənt/ *n.* a wrong or inaccurate statement.
■ falsification, misreport, misquotation, distortion, misrepresentation, misconstruction, misinterpretation, perversion, lie, falsehood, untruth, fabrication; error, inaccuracy.

misstep /míss-stép/ *n.* **1** a wrong step or action. **2** a *faux pas*.
■ **1** false step, blunder, mistake, error, bad *or* wrong *or* false move, trip, stumble, slip. **2** indiscretion, mistake, lapse, *faux pas*, oversight, error, gaffe, *colloq.* slip-up, howler, *esp. US colloq.* blooper, flub, *sl.* bloomer, goof, booboo, clanger, *Brit. sl.* boob.

missus var. of MISSIS.

missy /míssi/ *n.* (*pl.* **-ies**) an affectionate or derogatory form of address to a young girl.

mist /mist/ *n.* & *v.* ● *n.* **1 a** water vapour near the ground in minute droplets limiting visibility. **b** condensed vapour settling on a surface and obscuring glass etc. **2** dimness or blurring of the sight caused by tears etc. **3** a cloud of particles resembling mist. ● *v.tr.* & *intr.* (usu. foll. by *up*, *over*) cover or become covered with mist or as with mist. □□ **mistful** *adj.* **mistlike** *adj.* [OE f. Gmc]
■ *n.* **1, 3** fog, haze, smog, cloud, vapour; drizzle, mizzle, *literary* brume. ● *v.* (*mist up* or *over*) cloud (up *or* over), fog, dim, blur, film, steam up; becloud, befog.

mistake /mistáyk/ *n.* & *v.* ● *n.* **1** an incorrect idea or opinion; a thing incorrectly done or thought. **2** an error of judgement. ● *v.tr.* (*past* **mistook** /-stŏŏk/; *past part.* **mistaken** /-stáykən/) **1** misunderstand the meaning or intention of (a person, a statement, etc.). **2** (foll. by *for*) wrongly take or identify (*mistook me for you*). **3** choose wrongly (*mistake one's vocation*). □ **and** (or **make**) **no mistake** *colloq.* undoubtedly. **by mistake** accidentally; in error. **there is no mistaking** one is sure to recognize (a person or thing). □□ **mistakable** *adj.* **mistakably** *adv.* [ME f. ON *mistaka* (as MIS-[1], TAKE)]
■ *n.* misconception, misapprehension, miscalculation, misjudgement; error, fault, slip, erratum; bad move, false step, misstep, gaffe, blunder, botch, fumble, *faux pas*, indiscretion, *colloq.* slip-up, howler, *esp. US colloq.* blooper, flub, *sl.* booboo, bloomer, goof, clanger, *Brit. sl.* boob. ● *v.* **1** misunderstand, misinterpret, misjudge, misconstrue, take the wrong way, get wrong, misread, misapprehend. **2** (*mistake for*) mix up with, confuse with, take for, misidentify as. □ **by mistake** see *by accident* (ACCIDENT).

mistaken /mistáykən/ *adj.* **1** wrong in opinion or judgement. **2** based on or resulting from this (*mistaken loyalty*; *mistaken identity*). □□ **mistakenly** *adv.* **mistakenness** *n.*
■ wrong, erroneous, fallacious, false, inaccurate, incorrect, amiss, misinformed, faulty, in error, off, out, wide of the mark, in the wrong, barking up the wrong tree, on the wrong track, *colloq.* off beam; flawed, warped, distorted, twisted, misguided, *colloq.* cock-eyed.

misteach /míss-teéch/ *v.tr.* (*past* and *past part.* **-taught** /-táwt/) teach wrongly or incorrectly.

mister /místər/ *n.* **1** a man without a title of nobility etc. (*a mere mister*). **2** *sl.* or *joc.* a form of address to a man. [weakened form of MASTER in unstressed use before a name: cf. MR]

mistigris /místigriss/ *n.* *Cards* **1** a blank card used as a wild card in a form of draw poker. **2** this game. [F *mistigri* jack of clubs]

mistime /míss-tī́m/ *v.tr.* say or do at the wrong time. [OE *mistīmian* (as MIS-[1], TIME)]

mistitle /míss-tī́t'l/ *v.tr.* give the wrong title or name to.

mistle thrush /míss'l/ *n.* (also **missel thrush**) a large thrush, *Turdus viscivorus*, with a spotted breast, that feeds on mistletoe berries. [OE *mistel* basil, mistletoe, of unkn. orig.]

mistletoe /míss'ltō/ *n.* **1** a parasitic plant, *Viscum album*, growing on apple and other trees and bearing white glutinous berries in winter. **2** a similar plant, *Phoradendron flavescens*, native to N. America. [OE *misteltān* (as MISTLE (THRUSH), *tān* twig)]

mistook *past* of MISTAKE.

mistral /místraál/ *n.* a cold northerly wind that blows down the Rhône valley and S. France into the Mediterranean. [F & Prov. f. L (as MAGISTRAL)]

mistranslate /míss-tranzláyt, míss-traanz-/ *v.tr.* translate incorrectly. □□ **mistranslation** *n.*
■ see TWIST *v.* 5.

mistreat /míss-treét/ *v.tr.* treat badly. □□ **mistreatment** *n.*
■ abuse, maltreat, ill-use, ill-treat, misuse, *colloq.* manhandle; damage, harm, hurt, injure; molest, maul, brutalize, *sl.* rough up. □□ **mistreatment** abuse,

maltreatment, ill use, ill-treatment, misuse, *colloq.* manhandling; molestation, brutalization, *sl.* roughing-up.

mistress /místriss/ *n.* **1** a female head of a household. **2 a** a woman in authority over others. **b** the female owner of a pet. **3** a woman with power to control etc. (often foll. by *of*: *mistress of the situation*). **4** *Brit.* **a** a female teacher (*music mistress*). **b** a female head of a college etc. **5 a** a woman (other than his wife) with whom a married man has a (usu. prolonged) sexual relationship. **b** *archaic* or *poet.* a woman loved and courted by a man. **6** *archaic* or *dial.* (as a title) = MRS. □ **Mistress of the Robes** a lady in charge of the Queen's wardrobe. [ME f. OF *maistresse* f. *maistre* MASTER]
■ **4** schoolmistress, instructress, governess, teacher; headmistress. **5** lover, girlfriend, kept woman, the other woman, concubine, inamorata, *archaic or derog.* paramour, *literary* doxy, *sl. derog.* fancy woman.

mistrial /míss-trī́əl/ *n.* **1** a trial rendered invalid through some error in the proceedings. **2** *US* a trial in which the jury cannot agree on a verdict.

mistrust /míss-trúst/ *v.* & *n.* ● *v.tr.* **1** be suspicious of. **2** feel no confidence in (a person, oneself, one's powers, etc.). ● *n.* **1** suspicion. **2** lack of confidence.
■ *v.* suspect, distrust, be suspicious of, doubt, misdoubt, be *or* feel wary *or* doubtful of *or* about, have (one's) doubts about, question, have reservations about, *sl.* be leery of. ● *n.* suspicion, distrust, doubt, scepticism, wariness, reservation, chariness, misgiving(s), uncertainty, unsureness, apprehension, apprehensiveness, caution, *sl.* leeriness.

mistrustful /míss-trústfŏŏl/ *adj.* **1** (foll. by *of*) suspicious. **2** lacking confidence or trust. □□ **mistrustfully** *adv.* **mistrustfulness** *n.*
■ **1** see SUSPICIOUS 1, 2.

misty /místi/ *adj.* (**mistier, mistiest**) **1** of or covered with mist. **2** indistinct or dim in outline. **3** obscure, vague (*a misty idea*). □□ **mistily** *adv.* **mistiness** *n.* [OE *mistig* (as MIST)]
■ cloudy, foggy, hazy; fuzzy, dim, blurred, blurry; unclear, indistinct, vague, dark, murky, opaque, shadowy, obscure.

mistype /míss-tī́p/ *v.tr.* type wrongly. [MIS-[1] + TYPE]

misunderstand /míssundərstánd/ *v.tr.* (*past* and *past part.* **-understood** /-stŏŏd/) **1** fail to understand correctly. **2** (usu. as **misunderstood** *adj.*) misinterpret the words or actions of (a person).
■ misconceive, misconstrue, misinterpret, misapprehend, get wrong, get the wrong idea about, get (hold of) the wrong end of the stick about, misread, misjudge, miscalculate, miss the point of.

misunderstanding /míssundərstánding/ *n.* **1** a failure to understand correctly. **2** a slight disagreement or quarrel.
■ **1** misconception, misconstruction, misinterpretation, misapprehension, misreading, misjudgement, miscalculation, wrong idea, wrong *or* false impression. **2** disagreement, discord, dispute, argument, difference, dissension, controversy, quarrel, rift, falling out.

misusage /míssyŏŏssij/ *n.* **1** wrong or improper usage. **2** ill-treatment.

misuse *v.* & *n.* ● *v.tr.* /míssyŏŏz/ **1** use wrongly; apply to the wrong purpose. **2** ill-treat. ● *n.* /míssyŏŏss/ wrong or improper use or application. □□ **misuser** *n.*
■ *v.* **1** abuse, misapply, misemploy, misappropriate; pervert. **2** see MISTREAT. ● *n.* misapplication, misusage, misappropriation, misemployment; perversion; corruption, solecism, malapropism, barbarism, catachresis, ungrammaticality, infelicity; see also *mistreatment* (MISTREAT).

MIT *abbr.* Massachusetts Institute of Technology.

mite[1] /mīt/ *n.* any small arachnid of the order Acari, having four pairs of legs when adult. □□ **mity** *adj.* [OE *mīte* f. Gmc]

mite[2] /mīt/ *n.* & *adv.* ● *n.* **1** *hist.* a Flemish copper coin of small value. **2** any small monetary unit. **3** a small object or person, esp. a child. **4** a modest contribution; the best one can do (*offered my mite of comfort*). ● *adv.* (usu. prec. by *a*) *colloq.* somewhat (*is a mite shy*). [ME f. MLG, MDu. *mīte* f. Gmc: prob. the same as MITE[1]]
■ *n.* **3** see PARTICLE 2.

miter *US* var. of MITRE.

Mithraism /míthrayiz'm/ *n.* the cult of the ancient Persian god Mithras associated with the sun. □□ **Mithraic** /-thráyik/ *adj.* **Mithraist** *n.* [L *Mithras* f. Gk *Mithras* f. OPers. *Mithra* f. Skr. *Mitra*]

mithridatize /mithríddətīz/ *v.tr.* (also **-ise**) render proof against a poison by administering gradually increasing doses of it. □□ **mithridatic** /-dáttik/ *adj.* **mithridatism** /-dətiz'm/ *n.* [f. *mithridate* a supposed universal antidote attributed to *Mithridates* VI, king of Pontus d. 63 BC]

mitigate /míttigayt/ *v.tr.* make milder or less intense or severe; moderate (*your offer certainly mitigated their hostility*). ¶ Often confused with *militate*. □ **mitigating circumstances** *Law* circumstances permitting greater leniency. □□ **mitigable** *adj.* **mitigation** /-gáysh'n/ *n.* **mitigator** *n.* **mitigatory** *adj.* [ME f. L *mitigare mitigat-* f. *mitis* mild]
■ moderate, temper, reduce, abate, lessen, decrease, relieve, ease, relax, alleviate, remit, assuage, allay, slacken, tone down, lighten, appease, palliate, mollify, calm, tranquillize, soothe, placate, still, soften, dull, blunt, take the edge off, quiet, *Brit.* quieten.

mitochondrion /mī́təkóndriən/ *n.* (*pl.* **mitochondria** /-driə/) *Biol.* an organelle found in most eukaryotic cells, containing enzymes for respiration and energy production. [mod.L f. Gk *mitos* thread + *khondrion* dimin. of *khondros* granule]

mitosis /mitṓsiss, mī-/ *n.* *Biol.* a type of cell division that results in two daughter cells each having the same number and kind of chromosomes as the parent nucleus (cf. MEIOSIS). □□ **mitotic** /-tóttik/ *adj.* [mod.L f. Gk *mitos* thread]

mitral /mī́trəl/ *adj.* of or like a mitre. □ **mitral valve** a two-cusped valve between the left atrium and the left ventricle of the heart. [mod.L *mitralis* f. L *mitra* girdle]

mitre /mī́tər/ *n.* & *v.* (*US* **miter**) ● *n.* **1** a tall deeply-cleft head-dress worn by bishops and abbots, esp. as a symbol of office. **2** the joint of two pieces of wood or other material at an angle of 90°, such that the line of junction bisects this angle. **3** a diagonal join of two pieces of fabric that meet at a corner, made by folding. ● *v.* **1** *tr.* bestow the mitre on. **2** *tr.* & *intr.* join with a mitre. □ **mitre-block** (or **board** or **box**) a guide for a saw in cutting mitre-joints. **mitre-wheels** a pair of bevelled cog-wheels with teeth set at 45° and axes at right angles. □□ **mitred** *adj.* [ME f. OF f. L *mitra* f. Gk *mitra* girdle, turban]

mitt /mit/ *n.* **1** = MITTEN 1. **2** a glove leaving the fingers and thumb-tip exposed. **3** *sl.* a hand or fist. **4** a baseball glove for catching the ball. [abbr. of MITTEN]
■ **3** see HAND *n.* 1a.

mitten /mítt'n/ *n.* **1** a glove with two sections, one for the thumb and the other for all four fingers. **2** *sl.* (in *pl.*) boxing gloves. □□ **mittened** *adj.* [ME f. OF *mitaine* ult. f. L *medietas* half: see MOIETY]

mittimus /míttiməss/ *n.* a warrant committing a person to prison. [ME f. L, = we send]

mitzvah /mítsvaa/ *n.* (*pl.* **mitzvoth** /-vot/) in Judaism: **1** a precept or commandment. **2** a good deed done from religious duty. [Heb. *miṣwāh* commandment]

mix /miks/ *v.* & *n.* ● *v.* **1** *tr.* combine or put together (two or more substances or things) so that the constituents of each are diffused among those of the other(s). **2** *tr.* prepare (a compound, cocktail, etc.) by combining the ingredients. **3** *tr.* combine an activity etc. with another simultaneously (*mix business and pleasure*). **4** *intr.* **a** join, be mixed, or combine, esp. readily (*oil and water will not mix*). **b** be compatible. **c** be sociable (*must learn to mix*). **5** *intr.* **a** (foll.

by *with*) (of a person) be harmonious or sociable with; have regular dealings with. **b** (foll. by *in*) participate in. **6** *tr.* drink different kinds of (alcoholic liquor) in close succession. ● *n.* **1 a** the act or an instance of mixing; a mixture. **b** the proportion of materials etc. in a mixture. **2** *colloq.* a group of persons of different types (*social mix*). **3** the ingredients prepared commercially for making a cake etc. or for a process such as making concrete. **4** the merging of film pictures or sound. □ **be mixed up in** (or **with**) be involved in or with (esp. something undesirable). **mix in** be harmonious or sociable. **mix it** *colloq.* start fighting. **mix up 1** mix thoroughly. **2** confuse; mistake the identity of. **mix-up** *n.* a confusion, misunderstanding, or mistake. □□ **mixable** *adj.* [back-form. f. MIXED (taken as past part.)]

■ *v.* **1, 3** combine, blend, merge, unite, alloy, mingle, intermingle, amalgamate, join, *literary* commingle; incorporate, put together, stir, mix up. **2** see PREPARE 2. **4 a** combine, blend, merge, unite, mingle, intermingle, amalgamate, coalesce, join, incorporate, *literary* commingle. **b** be compatible, go together. **4c, 5** socialize, be sociable, mix in; fraternize, consort, hobnob, go round *or* around *or* about, keep company, associate, *colloq.* hang about *or* around, *sl.* hang out. ● *n.* **1 a** see MIXTURE. □ **be mixed up in** *or* **with** be involved in, be implicated in, be included in, be connected with, be drawn *or* dragged into. **mix in** see MIX *v.* 4c, 5 above. **mix up 1** see MIX *v.* 1, 3 above. **2** confuse, confound, bewilder, muddle, perplex, puzzle, fluster, upset, addle, disturb, *US joc.* discombobulate; snarl, ensnarl, tangle, entangle, scramble, jumble; mistake, misidentify, get the wrong way round; interchange, exchange, swap (over *or* around). **mix-up** confusion, misunderstanding, mess, muddle, hotchpotch, tangle, jumble, botch, mistake, mishmash, foul-up, *sl.* screw-up, snafu, *Brit. sl.* cock-up.

mixed /mikst/ *adj.* **1** of diverse qualities or elements. **2** containing persons from various backgrounds etc. **3** for or involving persons of both sexes (*a mixed school*; *mixed bathing*). □ **mixed bag** (or **bunch**) a diverse assortment of things or persons. **mixed blessing** a thing having advantages and disadvantages. **mixed crystal** one formed from more than one substance. **mixed doubles** *Tennis* a doubles game with a man and a woman as partners on each side. **mixed economy** an economic system combining private and State enterprise. **mixed farming** farming of both crops and livestock. **mixed feelings** a mixture of pleasure and dismay about something. **mixed grill** a dish of various grilled meats and vegetables etc. **mixed marriage** a marriage between persons of different races or religions. **mixed metaphor** a combination of inconsistent metaphors (e.g. *this tower of strength will forge ahead*). **mixed number** an integer and a proper fraction. **mixed-up** *colloq.* mentally or emotionally confused; socially ill-adjusted. □□ **mixedness** /míksidniss/ *n.* [ME *mixt* f. OF *mixte* f. L *mixtus* past part. of *miscēre* mix]

■ **1** diverse, diversified, assorted, heterogeneous, sundry, miscellaneous, varied, various, multiform, *archaic* medley, *archaic or literary* divers; (*of ancestry etc.*) hybrid, half-bred, mongrel, interbred, cross-bred, *often offens.* half-caste; (*of feelings etc.*) confused, muddled, conflicting, contradictory, opposing, clashing, opposite. □ **mixed bag** or **bunch** see MEDLEY *n.* **mixed-up** see *confused* (CONFUSE 4).

mixer /míksər/ *n.* **1** a device for mixing foods etc. or for processing other materials. **2** a person who manages socially in a specified way (*a good mixer*). **3** a (usu. soft) drink to be mixed with another. **4** *Broadcasting* & *Cinematog.* **a** a device for merging input signals to produce a combined output in the form of sound or pictures. **b** a person who operates this. □ **mixer tap** a tap through which mixed hot and cold water is drawn by means of separate controls.

mixture /míks-chər/ *n.* **1** the process of mixing or being mixed. **2** the result of mixing; something mixed; a combination. **3** *Chem.* the product of the random distribution of one substance through another without any chemical reaction taking place between the components, as distinct from a chemical compound. **4** ingredients mixed together to produce a substance, esp. a medicine (*cough mixture*). **5** a person regarded as a combination of qualities and attributes. **6** gas or vaporized petrol or oil mixed with air, forming an explosive charge in an internal-combustion engine. □ **the mixture as before** the same treatment repeated. [ME f. F *mixture* or L *mixtura* (as MIXED)]

■ **1** mixing, amalgamation, combination, blend, association, synthesis, interweaving, merger, fusion. **2** assortment, amalgam, amalgamation, medley, compound, alloy, combination, composite, blend, jumble, mix, miscellany, *mélange*, mess, mishmash, hotchpotch, gallimaufry, farrago, olio, olla podrida, hash, pot-pourri, salmagundi, *colloq.* omnium gatherum.

mizen /mízz'n/ *n.* (also **mizzen**) *Naut.* (in full **mizen-sail**) the lowest fore-and-aft sail of a fully rigged ship's mizen-mast. □ **mizen-mast** the mast next aft of the mainmast. **mizen yard** that on which the mizen is extended. [ME f. F *misaine* f. It. *mezzana* mizen-sail, fem. of *mezzano* middle: see MEZZANINE]

mizzle[1] /mízz'l/ *n.* & *v.intr.* drizzle. □□ **mizzly** *adj.* [ME, prob. f. LG *miseln*: cf. MDu. *miezelen*]

■ *n.* see MIST *n.* ● *v.* see RAIN *v.* 1.

mizzle[2] /mízz'l/ *v.intr. Brit. sl.* run away; decamp. [18th c.: orig. unkn.]

■ see ESCAPE *v.* 1.

Mk. *abbr.* **1** the German mark. **2** Mark (esp. in the New Testament).

mks *abbr.* metre-kilogram-second.

Mkt. *abbr.* Market.

ml *abbr.* **1** millilitre(s). **2** mile(s).

MLA *abbr.* **1** Member of the Legislative Assembly. **2** Modern Language Association (of America).

MLC *abbr.* Member of the Legislative Council.

MLD *abbr.* minimum lethal dose.

MLF *abbr.* multilateral nuclear force.

M.Litt. *abbr.* Master of Letters. [L *Magister Litterarum*]

Mlle *abbr.* (*pl.* **Mlles**) *Mademoiselle.*

MLR *abbr.* minimum lending rate.

MM *abbr.* **1** *Messieurs.* **2** (in the UK) Military Medal. **3** Maelzel's metronome.

mm *abbr.* millimetre(s).

Mme *abbr.* (*pl.* **Mmes**) *Madame.*

m.m.f. *abbr.* magnetomotive force.

M.Mus. *abbr.* Master of Music.

MN *abbr.* **1** *Brit.* Merchant Navy. **2** *US* Minnesota (in official postal use).

Mn *symb. Chem.* the element manganese.

M'Naghten rules var. of McNAUGHTEN RULES (see at MACN-).

mnemonic /nimónnik/ *adj.* & *n.* ● *adj.* of or designed to aid the memory. ● *n.* a mnemonic device. □□ **mnemonically** *adv.* **mnemonist** /neémənist/ *n.* [med.L *mnemonicus* f. Gk *mnēmonikos* f. *mnēmōn* mindful]

mnemonics /nimónniks/ *n.pl.* (usu. treated as *sing.*) **1** the art of improving memory. **2** a system for this.

MO *abbr.* **1** Medical Officer. **2** money order. **3** *US* Missouri (in official postal use).

Mo *symb. Chem.* the element molybdenum.

Mo. *abbr.* Missouri.

mo[1] /mō/ *n.* (*pl.* **mos**) *colloq.* a moment (*wait a mo*). [abbr.]

■ see MOMENT 1, 2.

mo[2] /mō/ *n. Austral.* & *NZ colloq.* (*pl.* **-os**) = MOUSTACHE. [abbr.]

mo. *abbr. US* month.

m.o. *abbr. modus operandi.*

moa /mṓə/ *n.* (*pl.* **moas**) any extinct flightless New Zealand bird of the family Dinornithidae, resembling the ostrich. [Maori]

moan /mōn/ *n.* & *v.* ● *n.* **1** a long murmur expressing physical or mental suffering. **2** a low plaintive sound of wind etc. **3** a complaint; a grievance. ● *v.* **1** *intr.* make a moan or moans. **2** *intr. colloq.* complain or grumble. **3** *tr.* **a** utter with moans. **b** lament. ▫▫ **moaner** *n.* **moanful** *adj.* **moaningly** *adv.* [ME f. OE *mān* (unrecorded) f. Gmc]

■ *n.* **1, 2** lament, lamentation, groan, wail, ululation, sigh, sob, cry; sough, soughing. **3** complaint, grievance, grumble, *colloq.* grouse, gripe, whinge, *sl.* beef. ● *v.* **1, 3** sigh, cry, wail, sob, snivel, bawl, keen; mourn, lament, bemoan, weep, sorrow, grieve, mewl, ululate, *literary* pule. **2** complain, lament, groan, wail, grumble, whine, whimper, *colloq.* bitch, grouse, gripe, whinge, *sl.* beef.

moat /mōt/ *n.* & *v.* ● *n.* a deep defensive ditch round a castle, town, etc., usu. filled with water. ● *v.tr.* surround with or as with a moat. [ME *mot(e)* f. OF *mote, motte* mound]

■ *n.* see CHANNEL[1] *n.* 5a, 6.

mob /mob/ *n.* & *v.* ● *n.* **1** a disorderly crowd; a rabble. **2** (prec. by *the*) usu. *derog.* the populace. **3** *colloq.* a gang; an associated group of persons. **4** *Austral.* a flock or herd. ● *v.tr.* & *intr.* (**mobbed, mobbing**) **1** *tr.* **a** crowd round in order to attack or admire. **b** (of a mob) attack. **c** *US* crowd into (a building). **2** *intr.* assemble in a mob. ▫ **mob law** (or **rule**) law or rule imposed and enforced by a mob. ▫▫ **mobber** *n.* & *adj.* [abbr. of *mobile*, short for L *mobile vulgus* excitable crowd: see MOBILE]

■ *n.* **1** rabble, horde, host, legion, press, throng, crowd, pack, herd, swarm, crush, jam, multitude, mass, body, assemblage, collection, group, *colloq.* gaggle. **2** (*the mob*) the rabble, the riff-raff, the proletariat, the populace, the (general) public, the masses, the rank and file, the *hoi polloi*, the *canaille*, the lower class, *colloq.* the great unwashed. **3** see GANG[1] *n.* ● *v.* **1 a** crowd (round *or* around), jostle, throng, surround, beset, clamour over, swoop down on *or* upon. **b** see ATTACK *v.* 1. **2** see UNITE 2.

mob-cap /móbkap/ *n. hist.* a woman's large indoor cap covering all the hair, worn in the 18th and early 19th c. [obs. (18th-c.) *mob*, orig. = slut + CAP]

mobile /mṓbīl/ *adj.* & *n.* ● *adj.* **1** movable; not fixed; free or able to move or flow easily. **2** (of the face etc.) readily changing its expression. **3** (of a shop, library, etc.) accommodated in a vehicle so as to serve various places. **4** (of a person) able to change his or her social status. ● *n.* a decorative structure that may be hung so as to turn freely. ▫ **mobile home** a large caravan permanently parked and used as a residence. **mobile sculpture** a sculpture having moving parts. ▫▫ **mobility** /məbílliti/ *n.* [ME f. F f. L *mobilis* f. *movēre* move]

■ *adj.* **1, 3** movable, non-stationary, unfixed, *Zool.* & *Bot.* motile; portable, transportable; motorized, travelling; ambulatory, *Med.* ambulant; agile, versatile, nimble, quick, alert, active, responsive. **2** expressive, sensitive, animated, plastic, flexible. ▫▫ **mobility** see MOTION *n.* 1.

mobilize /mṓbilīz/ *v.* (also **-ise**) **1 a** *tr.* organize for service or action (esp. troops in time of war). **b** *intr.* be organized in this way. **2** *tr.* render movable; bring into circulation. ▫▫ **mobilizable** *adj.* **mobilization** /-záysh'n/ *n.* **mobilizer** *n.* [F *mobiliser* (as MOBILE)]

■ **1 a** assemble, marshal, conscript, enrol, enlist, organize, muster, levy, rally, activate, call up, prepare, ready, *US* draft.

Möbius strip /mṓbiəss/ *n. Math.* a one-sided surface formed by joining the ends of a rectangle after twisting one end through 180°. [A. F. *Möbius*, Ger. mathematician d. 1868]

mobocracy /mobókrəsi/ *n.* (*pl.* **-ies**) *colloq.* **1** rule by a mob. **2** a ruling mob.

mobster /móbstər/ *n. sl.* a gangster.

■ see GANGSTER.

moccasin /mókkəsin/ *n.* **1** a type of soft leather slipper or shoe with combined sole and heel, as orig. worn by N. American Indians. **2** (in full **water moccasin**) *US* a poisonous American snake of the genus *Agkistrodon piscivorus*. [Amer. Ind. *mockasin, makisin*]

mocha /mókkə/ *n.* **1** a coffee of fine quality. **2** a beverage or flavouring made with this, often with chocolate added. **3** a soft kind of sheepskin. [*Mocha*, a port on the Red Sea, from where the coffee first came]

mock /mok/ *v.*, *adj.*, & *n.* ● *v.* **1 a** *tr.* ridicule; scoff at. **b** *intr.* (foll. by *at*) act with scorn or contempt for. **2** *tr.* mimic contemptuously. **3** *tr.* jeer, defy, or delude contemptuously. ● *attrib.adj.* sham, imitation (esp. without intention to deceive); pretended (*a mock battle*; *mock cream*). ● *n.* **1** a thing deserving scorn. **2** (in *pl.*) *colloq.* mock examinations. ▫ **make mock** (or **a mock**) **of** ridicule. **mock-heroic** *adj.* (of a literary style) burlesquing a heroic style. ● *n.* such a style. **mock moon** paraselene. **mock orange** a white-flowered heavy-scented shrub, *Philadelphus coronarius*. **mock sun** parhelion. **mock turtle soup** soup made from a calf's head etc. to resemble turtle soup. **mock-up** an experimental model or replica of a proposed structure etc. ▫▫ **mockable** *adj.* **mockingly** *adv.* [ME *mokke, mocque* f. OF *mo(c)quer* deride f. Rmc]

■ *v.* **1, 3** deride, ridicule, make fun of, tease, taunt, tantalize, jeer (at), gibe (at), thumb one's nose at, chaff, laugh at, poke fun at, make sport of, guy, scorn, abuse, delude, scoff at, sneer at, fleer at, disdain, disparage, decry, defy, flout, *colloq.* rib, kid, *sl.* take the mickey out of, cock a snook at, rag, *Austral.* & *NZ sl.* sling off at. **2** ape, mimic, imitate, caricature, lampoon, satirize, parody, burlesque, travesty, copy, *colloq.* spoof, take off, *Brit. colloq.* send up. ● *adj.* substitute, artificial, simulated, fake, synthetic, imitation, false, ersatz, sham, feigned, *colloq.* phoney, pseudo; pretended, make-believe, *colloq.* pretend.

mocker[1] /mókkər/ *n.* a person who mocks. ▫ **put the mockers on** *sl.* **1** bring bad luck to. **2** put a stop to.

mocker[2] /mókkər/ *n. Austral.* & *NZ sl.* clothing, dress. [orig. unkn.]

mockery /mókkəri/ *n.* (*pl.* **-ies**) **1 a** derision, ridicule. **b** a subject or occasion of this. **2** (often foll. by *of*) a counterfeit or absurdly inadequate representation. **3** a ludicrously or insultingly futile action etc. [ME f. OF *moquerie* (as MOCK)]

■ **1a** ridicule, derision, disdain, taunting, disparagement, abuse, scorn, contempt, contumely, decrial, belittlement. **1b, 2** caricature, parody, burlesque, travesty, farce, *colloq.* spoof, take-off, *Brit. colloq.* send-up. **3** absurdity; see also JOKE *n.* 2.

mockingbird /mókkingburd/ *n.* a bird that mimics the notes of other birds, esp. the American songbird *Mimus polyglottos*.

MOD *abbr.* (in the UK) Ministry of Defence.

mod[1] /mod/ *adj.* & *n. colloq.* ● *adj.* modern, esp. in style of dress. ● *n. Brit.* a young person (esp. in the 1960s) of a group aiming at sophistication and smart modern dress. ▫ **mod cons** modern conveniences. [abbr.]

■ *adj.* see MODERN *adj.*

mod[2] /mod/ *prep. Math.* = MODULO. [abbr.]

mod[3] /mod/ *n.* a Highland Gaelic meeting for music and poetry. [Gael. *mōd*]

modal /mṓd'l/ *adj.* **1** of or relating to mode or form as opposed to substance. **2** *Gram.* **a** of or denoting the mood of a verb. **b** (of an auxiliary verb, e.g. *would*) used to express the mood of another verb. **c** (of a particle) denoting manner. **3** *Statistics* of or relating to a mode; occurring most frequently in a sample or population. **4** *Mus.* denoting a style of music using a particular mode. **5** *Logic* (of a proposition) in which the predicate is affirmed of the subject with some qualification, or which involves the affirmation of possibility, impossibility, necessity, or contingency. ▫▫ **modally** *adv.* [med.L *modalis* f. L (as MODE)]

modality /mədálliti/ *n.* (*pl.* **-ies**) **1** the state of being modal. **2** (in *sing.* or *pl.*) a prescribed method of procedure. [med.L *modalitas* (as MODAL)]

mode /mōd/ *n.* **1** a way or manner in which a thing is done; a method of procedure. **2** a prevailing fashion or custom. **3** *Computing* a way of operating or using a system (*print mode*). **4** *Statistics* the value that occurs most frequently in a given set of data. **5** *Mus.* **a** each of the scale systems that result when the white notes of the piano are played consecutively over an octave (*Lydian mode*). **b** each of the two main modern scale systems, the major and minor (*minor mode*). **6** *Logic* **a** the character of a modal proposition. **b** = MOOD[2]. **7** *Physics* any of the distinct kinds or patterns of vibration of an oscillating system. **8** *US Gram.* = MOOD[2]. [F *mode* and L *modus* measure]

■ **1** way, manner, method, approach, form, course, fashion, procedure, technique, system, *modus operandi*, m.o., methodology, standard operating procedure, *archaic* wise. **2** fashion, style, look, vogue; trend, rage, craze, fad. **3** status, condition, state, configuration, set-up.

model /módd'l/ *n.* & *v.* ● *n.* **1** a representation in three dimensions of an existing person or thing or of a proposed structure, esp. on a smaller scale (often *attrib.*: *a model train*). **2** a simplified (often mathematical) description of a system etc., to assist calculations and predictions. **3** a figure in clay, wax, etc., to be reproduced in another material. **4** a particular design or style of a structure or commodity, esp. of a car. **5 a** an exemplary person or thing (*a model of self-discipline*). **b** (*attrib.*) ideal, exemplary (*a model student*). **6** a person employed to pose for an artist or photographer or to display clothes etc. by wearing them. **7** a garment etc. by a well-known designer, or a copy of this. ● *v.* (**modelled, modelling**; *US* **modeled, modeling**) **1** *tr.* **a** fashion or shape (a figure) in clay, wax, etc. **b** (foll. by *after*, *on*, etc.) form (a thing in imitation of). **2 a** *intr.* act or pose as a model. **b** *tr.* (of a person acting as a model) display (a garment). **3** *tr.* devise a (usu. mathematical) model of (a phenomenon, system, etc.). **4** *tr.* *Painting* cause to appear three-dimensional. □□ **modeller** *n.* [F *modelle* f. It. *modello* ult. f. L *modulus*: see MODULUS]

■ *n.* **1, 3** representation, replica, mock-up, maquette, scale model, working model, miniature, dummy, mannequin; image, likeness, facsimile, copy, imitation. **4** design, kind, type, style, version; variety, sort, form, fashion; brand, mark. **5 a** original, archetype, prototype, pattern, paragon, ideal, exemplar, example, standard, epitome, acme, perfection, *beau idéal*, cream, *crème de la crème*, *ne plus ultra*, nonpareil, nonsuch. **b** ideal, exemplary, perfect, archetypal, unequalled, consummate, inimitable. **6** subject, sitter, poser. ● *v.* **1 a** fashion, mould, shape, form, sculpt, carve (out); make, fabricate, produce. **b** (*model after* or *on*) imitate, copy, pattern on *or* after, emulate, follow. **2** pose, sit; display, show (off), exhibit; wear, sport.

modem /mṓdem/ *n.* a combined device for modulation and demodulation, e.g. between a computer and a telephone line. [*mo*dulator + *dem*odulator]

moderate *adj.*, *n.*, & *v.* ● *adj.* /móddərət/ **1** avoiding extremes; temperate in conduct or expression. **2** fairly or tolerably large or good. **3** (of the wind) of medium strength. **4** (of prices) fairly low. ● *n.* /móddərət/ a person who holds moderate views, esp. in politics. ● *v.* /móddərayt/ **1** *tr.* & *intr.* make or become less violent, intense, rigorous, etc. **2** *tr.* (also *absol.*) act as a moderator of or to. **3** *tr.* *Physics* retard (neutrons) with a moderator. □□ **moderately** /-rətli/ *adv.* **moderateness** /-rətniss/ *n.* **moderatism** /móddərətiz'm/ *n.* [ME f. L *moderatus* past part. of *moderare* reduce, control: rel. to MODEST]

■ *adj.* **1** temperate, calm, reasonable, cool, judicious, rational, balanced, unexcessive, modest, sober, sensible, commonsensical, controlled, deliberate, steady; centre, middle-of-the-road, mainstream, non-radical, non-reactionary. **2, 4** fair, middling, average, ordinary, medium, middle, modest, mediocre, unexceptional, fair to middling; lowish. ● *n.* non-radical, non-reactionary, *Polit. often derog.* centrist, *Brit. Polit. colloq.* wet. ● *v.* **1** abate, calm, mollify, soothe, ease, relax, alleviate, mitigate, soften, dull, blunt, cushion, relieve, reduce, lessen, remit, slacken, diminish, decrease, defuse, temper, *colloq.* let up. **2** mediate, arbitrate, referee, judge, chair, supervise, preside (over), coordinate, run, regulate, manage, direct. □□ **moderately** somewhat, rather, quite, fairly, comparatively, slightly, passably, more or less, *colloq.* pretty; to some extent, within reason, to a certain extent, to a degree, to some degree, in some measure, *colloq.* sort of, kind of; in moderation, within limits, temperately.

moderation /móddəráysh'n/ *n.* **1** the process or an instance of moderating. **2** the quality of being moderate. **3** *Physics* the retardation of neutrons by a moderator (see MODERATOR 5). **4** (in *pl.*) (**Moderations**) the first public examination in some faculties for the Oxford BA degree. □ **in moderation** in a moderate manner or degree. [ME f. OF f. L *moderatio -onis* (as MODERATE)]

■ **1** see RELAXATION 3, 4. **2** see TEMPERANCE 1.

moderato /móddəraatō/ *adj.*, *adv.*, & *n.* *Mus.* ● *adj.* & *adv.* performed at a moderate pace. ● *n.* (*pl.* **-os**) a piece of music to be performed in this way. [It. (as MODERATE)]

moderator /móddəraytər/ *n.* **1** an arbitrator or mediator. **2** a presiding officer. **3** *Eccl.* a Presbyterian minister presiding over an ecclesiastical body. **4** an examiner for Moderations. **5** *Physics* a substance used in a nuclear reactor to retard neutrons. □□ **moderatorship** *n.* [ME f. L (as MODERATE)]

■ **1** mediator, arbiter, arbitrator, judge, referee, umpire. **2** chair, chairperson, chairman, chairwoman, presiding officer, president, coordinator, leader; anchorman, anchor; master of ceremonies, MC, toastmaster, *Brit.* compère, *colloq.* emcee.

modern /móddərn/ *adj.* & *n.* ● *adj.* **1** of the present and recent times. **2** in current fashion; not antiquated. ● *n.* (usu. in *pl.*) a person living in modern times. □ **modern English** English from about 1500 onwards. **modern history** history from the end of the Middle Ages to the present day. □□ **modernity** /-dérniti/ *n.* **modernly** *adv.* **modernness** *n.* [F *moderne* or LL *modernus* f. L *modo* just now]

■ *adj.* up to date, current, contemporary, today's, new, fresh, novel, brand-new, up to the minute, present-day, latest, new-fashioned, *derog.* newfangled; à la mode, modish, in vogue, fashionable, in fashion, stylish, in style, chic, in, *colloq.* hot, with it, mod, *colloq. often derog.* trendy, *sl.* hip, hep.

modernism /móddərniz'm/ *n.* **1 a** modern ideas or methods. **b** the tendency of religious belief to harmonize with modern ideas. **2** a modern term or expression. □□ **modernist** *n.* **modernistic** /-nístik/ *adj.* **modernistically** /-nístikəli/ *adv.*

■ □□ **modernistic** see *streamlined* (STREAMLINE *v.* 3b).

modernize /móddərnīz/ *v.* (also **-ise**) **1** *tr.* make modern; adapt to modern needs or habits. **2** *intr.* adopt modern ways or views. □□ **modernization** /-záysh'n/ *n.* **modernizer** *n.*

■ **1** renovate, streamline, redo, redecorate, refurbish, refurnish, update, rejuvenate, refresh, revamp, redesign, remodel, refashion, remake, *colloq.* do over; develop. □□ **modernization** see IMPROVEMENT, DEVELOPMENT 1.

modest /móddist/ *adj.* **1** having or expressing a humble or moderate estimate of one's own merits or achievements. **2** diffident, bashful, retiring. **3** decorous in manner and conduct. **4** moderate or restrained in amount, extent, severity, etc.; not excessive or exaggerated (*a modest sum*). **5** (of a thing) unpretentious in appearance etc. □□ **modestly** *adv.* [F *modeste* f. L *modestus* keeping due measure]

■ **1, 2** unassuming, unpresuming, humble, unpretentious, unobtrusive, reserved, retiring, diffident, shy, bashful, demure, coy, self-effacing, self-conscious, reticent, reluctant, timid, meek, timorous. **3** see DECOROUS. **4** moderate, limited, understated, unexaggerated, reasonable, sensible, constrained, restricted, restrained. **5** humble, simple, plain, ordinary, unpretentious, homely, lowly, unexceptional, unostentatious; bare, spartan; inconspicuous, unobtrusive.

modesty /móddisti/ *n.* the quality of being modest.

■ see HUMILITY, PURITY 2.

modicum /móddikəm/ *n.* (foll. by *of*) a small quantity. [L, = short distance or time, neut. of *modicus* moderate f. *modus* measure] bit, trifle, jot, (jot or) tittle, atom, scintilla, spark, particle, iota, speck, grain, whit, scrap, shred, snippet, sliver, fragment, splinter, morsel, crumb, ounce, dram, drop, dash, spot, touch, tinge, hint, suggestion, *colloq.* smidgen, *US colloq.* tad.

modification /móddifikáysh'n/ *n.* **1** the act or an instance of modifying or being modified. **2** a change made. [F or f. L *modificatio* (as MODIFY)]
▪ see ADAPTATION.

modifier /móddifīər/ *n.* **1** a person or thing that modifies. **2** *Gram.* a word, esp. an adjective or noun used attributively, that qualifies the sense of another word (e.g. *good* and *family* in *a good family house*).

modify /móddifī/ *v.tr.* (**-ies, -ied**) **1** make less severe or extreme; tone down (*modify one's demands*). **2** make partial changes in; make different. **3** *Gram.* qualify or expand the sense of (a word etc.). **4** *Phonet.* change (a vowel) by umlaut. **5** *Chem.* change or replace all the substituent radicals of a polymer, thereby changing its physical properties such as solubility etc. (*modified starch*). ▫▫ **modifiable** *adj.* **modificatory** /-fikáytəri/ *adj.* [ME f. OF *modifier* f. L *modificare* (as MODE)]
▪ **1** reduce, decrease, diminish, lessen, moderate, temper, soften, lower, abate, tone down, modulate; qualify, limit, restrict. **2** adjust, adapt, change, transform, alter, revise, amend, redo, remake, remould, reshape, reconstruct, reform, revamp, refashion, remodel, rework, reword, reorient(ate), reorganize.

modillion /mədílyən/ *n. Archit.* a projecting bracket under the corona of a cornice in the Corinthian and other orders. [F *modillon* f. It. *modiglione* ult. f. L *mutulus* mutule]

modish /mṓdish/ *adj.* fashionable. ▫▫ **modishly** *adv.* **modishness** *n.*
▪ see FASHIONABLE. ▫▫ **modishness** see CHIC *n.*

modiste /mōdéest/ *n.* a milliner; a dressmaker. [F (as MODE)]
▪ see DRESSMAKER.

Mods /modz/ *n.pl. colloq.* Moderations (see MODERATION 4). [abbr.]

modular /módyoolər/ *adj.* of or consisting of modules or moduli. ▫▫ **modularity** /-lárriti/ *n.* [mod.L *modularis* f. L *modulus*: see MODULUS]

modulate /módyoolayt/ *v.* **1** *tr.* **a** regulate or adjust. **b** moderate. **2** *tr.* adjust or vary the tone or pitch of (the speaking voice). **3** *tr.* alter the amplitude or frequency of (a wave) by a wave of a lower frequency to convey a signal. **4** *intr.* & *tr. Mus.* (often foll. by *from, to*) change or cause to change from one key to another. ▫▫ **modulation** /-láysh'n/ *n.* **modulator** *n.* [L *modulari modulat-* to measure f. *modus* measure]
▪ **1, 2** adjust, regulate, set, tune, balance, temper, moderate, modify, vary; lower, tune *or* tone down, turn down, soften.

module /módyool/ *n.* **1** a standardized part or independent unit used in construction, esp. of furniture, a building, or an electronic system. **2** an independent self-contained unit of a spacecraft (*lunar module*). **3** a unit or period of training or education. **4** **a** a standard or unit of measurement. **b** *Archit.* a unit of length for expressing proportions, e.g. the semidiameter of a column at the base. [F *module* or L *modulus*: see MODULUS]

modulo /módyoolō/ *prep.* & *adj. Math.* using, or with respect to, a modulus (see MODULUS 2). [L, ablat. of MODULUS]

modulus /módyooləss/ *n.* (*pl.* **moduli** /-lī/) *Math.* **1** **a** the magnitude of a real number without regard to its sign. **b** the positive square root of the sum of the squares of the real and imaginary parts of a complex number. **2** a constant factor or ratio. **3** (in number theory) a number used as a divisor for considering numbers in sets giving the same remainder when divided by it. **4** a constant indicating the relation between a physical effect and the force producing it. [L, = measure, dimin. of *modus*]

modus operandi /mṓdəss óppərándi/ *n.* (*pl.* ***modi operandi*** /mṓdi/) **1** the particular way in which a person performs a task or action. **2** the way a thing operates. [L, = way of operating: see MODE]
▪ see WAY *n.* 4a.

modus vivendi /mṓdəss vivéndi/ *n.* (*pl.* ***modi vivendi*** /mṓdi/) **1** a way of living or coping. **2** **a** an arrangement whereby those in dispute can carry on pending a settlement. **b** an arrangement between people who agree to differ. [L, = way of living: see MODE]

mofette /məfét/ *n.* **1** a fumarole. **2** an exhalation of vapour from this. [F *mofette* or Neapolitan It. *mofetta*]

mog /mog/ *n.* (also **moggie** /móggi/) *Brit. sl.* a cat. [20th c.: of dial. orig.]

Mogadon /móggədon/ *n. propr.* the drug nitrazepam, used to treat insomnia.

mogul /mṓg'l/ *n.* **1** *colloq.* an important or influential person. **2** (**Mogul**) *hist.* **a** = MUGHAL. **b** (often **the Great Mogul**) any of the emperors of Delhi in the 16th–19th c. [Pers. *muġul*: see MUGHAL]
▪ **1** magnate, tycoon, baron, mandarin, nabob, VIP, *colloq.* big shot *or* noise, bigwig, *esp. US colloq.* hotshot, *sl.* big gun, big cheese, big Chief *or* Daddy, *US sl.* (big) wheel, Mr Big.

MOH *abbr.* Medical Officer of Health.

mohair /mṓhair/ *n.* **1** the hair of the angora goat. **2** a yarn or fabric from this, either pure or mixed with wool or cotton. [ult. f. Arab. *mukayyar*, lit. choice, select]

Mohammedan var. of MUHAMMADAN.

Mohawk /mṓhawk/ *n.* **1** **a** a member of a tribe of N. American Indians. **b** the language of this tribe. **2** *Skating* a step from either edge of the skate to the same edge on the other foot in the opposite direction. [native name]

Mohican /mōhéekən/ *n.* & *adj.* ● *n.* a member of a N. American Indian people of Connecticut. ● *adj.* **1** of or relating to this people. **2** (of a hairstyle) resembling that of the Mohicans, with the head shaved except for a strip of hair from the middle of the forehead to the back of the neck, often worn in long spikes. [native name]

moho /mṓhō/ *n.* (*pl.* **-os**) *Geol.* a boundary of discontinuity separating the earth's crust and mantle. [A. *Mohorovičić*, Yugoslav seismologist d. 1936]

moidore /móydor/ *n. hist.* a Portuguese gold coin, current in England in the 18th c. [Port. *moeda d'ouro* money of gold]

moiety /móyəti/ *n.* (*pl.* **-ies**) *Law* or *literary* **1** a half. **2** each of the two parts into which a thing is divided. [ME f. OF *moité, moitié* f. L *medietas -tatis* middle f. *medius* (adj.) middle]

moil /moyl/ *v.* & *n. archaic* ● *v.intr.* drudge (esp. *toil and moil*). ● *n.* drudgery. [ME f. OF *moillier* moisten, paddle in mud, ult. f. L *mollis* soft]

moire /mwaar/ *n.* (in full **moire antique**) watered fabric, orig. mohair, now usu. silk. [F (earlier *mouaire*) f. MOHAIR]

moiré /mwáaray/ *adj.* & *n.* ● *adj.* **1** (of silk) watered. **2** (of metal) having a patterned appearance like watered silk. ● *n.* **1** this patterned appearance. **2** = MOIRE. [F, past part. of *moirer* (as MOIRE)]

moist /moyst/ *adj.* **1** **a** slightly wet; damp. **b** (of the season etc.) rainy. **2** (of a disease) marked by a discharge of matter etc. **3** (of the eyes) wet with tears. ▫▫ **moistly** *adv.* **moistness** *n.* [ME f. OF *moiste*, ult. from or rel. to L *mucidus* (see MUCUS) and *musteus* fresh (see MUST²)]
▪ **1** **a** damp, wet, wettish, dampish, dewy, dank, humid, soggy, moisture-laden, clammy, muggy, steamy, misty, foggy. **b** damp, wet, rainy, drizzly. **3** tearful, teary, misty, wet.

moisten /móys'n/ *v.tr.* & *intr.* make or become moist.
▪ see WATER *v.* 1.

moisture /móyss-chər/ *n.* water or other liquid diffused in a small quantity as vapour, or within a solid, or condensed on a surface. ▫▫ **moistureless** *adj.* [ME f. OF *moistour* (as MOIST)]
▪ see WET *n.* 1.

moisturize /móyss-chərīz/ *v.tr.* (also **-ise**) make less dry (esp. the skin by use of a cosmetic). ▫▫ **moisturizer** *n.*

moke /mōk/ *n. sl.* **1** *Brit.* a donkey. **2** *Austral.* a very poor horse. [19th c.: orig. unkn.]

moksa /móksə/ *n. Hinduism* etc. release from the cycle of rebirth. [Skr. *mokṣa*]

mol /mōl/ *abbr.* = MOLE[4].

molal /mṓləl/ *adj. Chem.* (of a solution) containing one mole of solute per kilogram of solvent. □□ **molality** /məlálliti/ *n.* [MOLE[4] + -AL]

molar[1] /mṓlər/ *adj.* & *n.* ● *adj.* (usu. of a mammal's back teeth) serving to grind. ● *n.* a molar tooth. [L *molaris* f. *mola* millstone]

molar[2] /mṓlər/ *adj.* **1** of or relating to mass. **2** acting on or by means of large masses or units. [L *moles* mass]

molar[3] /mṓlər/ *adj. Chem.* **1** of a mass of substance usu. per mole (*molar latent heat*). **2** (of a solution) containing one mole of solute per litre of solvent. □□ **molarity** /məlárriti/ *n.* [MOLE[4] + -AR[1]]

molasses /məlássiz/ *n.pl.* (treated as *sing.*) **1** uncrystallized syrup extracted from raw sugar during refining. **2** *US* treacle. [Port. *melaço* f. LL *mellaceum* MUST[2] f. *mel* honey]

mold *US* var. of MOULD[1], MOULD[2], MOULD[3].

molder *US* var. of MOULDER.

molding *US* var. of MOULDING.

moldy *US* var. of MOULDY.

mole[1] /mōl/ *n.* **1** any small burrowing insect-eating mammal of the family Talpidae, esp. *Talpa europaea*, with dark velvety fur and very small eyes. **2** *colloq.* **a** a spy established deep within an organization and usu. dormant for a long period while attaining a position of trust. **b** a betrayer of confidential information. [ME *molle*, prob. f. MDu. *moll(e)*, *mol*, MLG *mol*, *mul*]
■ **2 a** see SPY *n.*

mole[2] /mōl/ *n.* a small often slightly raised dark blemish on the skin caused by a high concentration of melanin. [OE *māl* f. Gmc]

mole[3] /mōl/ *n.* **1** a massive structure serving as a pier, breakwater, or causeway. **2** an artificial harbour. [F *môle* f. L *moles* mass]

mole[4] /mōl/ *n. Chem.* the SI unit of amount of substance equal to the quantity containing as many elementary units as there are atoms in 0.012 kg of carbon-12. [G *Mol* f. *Molekül* MOLECULE]

mole[5] /mōl/ *n. Med.* an abnormal mass of tissue in the uterus. [F *môle* f. L *mola* millstone]

molecular /məlékyoolər/ *adj.* of, relating to, or consisting of molecules. □ **molecular biology** the study of the structure and function of large molecules associated with living organisms. **molecular sieve** a crystalline substance with pores of molecular dimensions which permit the entry of certain molecules but are impervious to others. **molecular weight** = *relative molecular mass*. □□ **molecularity** /-lárriti/ *n.* **molecularly** *adv.*

molecule /móllikyōōl/ *n.* **1** *Chem.* the smallest fundamental unit (usu. a group of atoms) of a chemical compound that can take part in a chemical reaction. **2** (in general use) a small particle. [F *molécule* f. mod.L *molecula* dimin. of L *moles* mass]
■ **2** see PARTICLE 2.

molehill /mṓlhil/ *n.* a small mound thrown up by a mole in burrowing. □ **make a mountain out of a molehill** exaggerate the importance of a minor difficulty.
■ □ **make a mountain out of a molehill** make heavy weather of a thing, make a meal of a thing.

moleskin /mṓlskin/ *n.* **1** the skin of a mole used as fur. **2 a** a kind of cotton fustian with its surface shaved before dyeing. **b** (in *pl.*) clothes, esp. trousers, made of this.

molest /məlést/ *v.tr.* **1** annoy or pester (a person) in a hostile or injurious way. **2** attack or interfere with (a person), esp. sexually. □□ **molestation** /móllestáysh'n, mṓl-/ *n.* **molester** *n.* [OF *molester* or L *molestare* annoy f. *molestus* troublesome]
■ **1** annoy, irritate, vex, disturb, pester, badger, provoke, nettle, tease, harass, harry, worry, hector, irk, bother, gall, chafe, torment, beleaguer, *US* roil, *colloq.* needle, plague. **2** accost, meddle with, interfere with, abuse, attack, assault, ill-treat, harm, maltreat, *colloq.* manhandle, paw, *sl.* grope; rape, ravish, violate.

moline /məlīn/ *adj. Heraldry* (of a cross) having each extremity broadened and curved back. [prob. f. AF *moliné* f. *molin* MILL[1], because of the resemblance to the iron support of a millstone]

moll /mol/ *n. sl.* **1** a gangster's female companion. **2** a prostitute. [pet-form of the name *Mary*]
■ **2** see PROSTITUTE *n.* 1a.

mollify /móllifī/ *v.tr.* (**-ies, -ied**) **1** appease, pacify. **2** reduce the severity of; soften. □□ **mollification** /-fikáysh'n/ *n.* **mollifier** *n.* [ME f. F *mollifier* or L *mollificare* f. *mollis* soft]
■ **1** see CALM *v.* **2** see MODERATE *v.* 1.

mollusc /mólləsk/ *n.* (*US* **mollusk**) any invertebrate of the phylum Mollusca, with a soft body and usu. a hard shell, including limpets, snails, cuttlefish, oysters, mussels, etc. □□ **molluscan** /məlúskən/ *adj.* **molluscoid** /məlúskoyd/ *adj.* **molluscous** /məlúskəss/ *adj.* [mod.L *mollusca* neut. pl. of L *molluscus* f. *mollis* soft]

mollycoddle /móllikodd'l/ *v.* & *n.* ● *v.tr.* coddle, pamper. ● *n.* an effeminate man or boy; a milksop. [formed as MOLL + CODDLE]
■ *v.* see PAMPER. ● *n.* see MILKSOP.

mollymawk /móllimawk/ *n.* (also **mallemuck** /mállimuk/) any of various small kinds of albatross or similar birds. [Du. *mallemok* f. *mal* foolish + *mok* gull]

Moloch /mṓlok/ *n.* **1 a** a Canaanite idol to whom children were sacrificed. **b** a tyrannical object of sacrifices. **2** (**moloch**) the spiny slow-moving grotesque Australian reptile, *Moloch horridus*. [LL f. Gk *Molokh* f. Heb. *mōleḵ*]

Molotov cocktail /móllətof/ *n.* a crude incendiary device usu. consisting of a bottle filled with inflammable liquid. [V. M. *Molotov*, Russian statesman d. 1986]

molt *US* var. of MOULT.

molten /mṓltən/ *adj.* melted, esp. made liquid by heat. [past part. of MELT]
■ see LIQUID *adj.* 1, 3.

molto /móltō/ *adv. Mus.* very (*molto sostenuto*; *allegro molto*). [It. f. L *multus* much]

moly /mṓli/ *n.* (*pl.* **-ies**) **1** an alliaceous plant, *Allium moly*, with small yellow flowers. **2** a mythical herb with white flowers and black roots, endowed with magic properties. [L f. Gk *mōlu*]

molybdenite /məlíbdinīt/ *n.* molybdenum disulphide as an ore.

molybdenum /məlíbdinəm/ *n. Chem.* a silver-white brittle metallic transition element occurring naturally in molybdenite and used in steel to give strength and resistance to corrosion. ¶ Symb.: **Mo**. [mod.L, earlier *molybdena*, orig. = molybdenite, lead ore: L *molybdena* f. Gk *molubdaina* plummet f. *molubdos* lead]

mom /mom/ *n. US colloq.* mother. [abbr. of MOMMA]

moment /mṓmənt/ *n.* **1** a very brief portion of time; an instant. **2** a short period of time (*wait a moment*) (see also MINUTE[1]). **3** an exact or particular point of time (*at last the moment arrived*; *I came the moment you called*). **4** importance (*of no great moment*). **5** *Physics* & *Mech.* etc. **a** the turning effect produced by a force acting at a distance on an object. **b** this effect expressed as the product of the force and the distance from its line of action to a point. □ **at the moment** at this time; now. **in a moment 1** very soon. **2** instantly. **man** (or **woman** etc.) **of the moment** the one of importance at the time in question. **moment of inertia** *Physics* the quantity by which the angular acceleration of a body must be multiplied to give corresponding torque. **moment of truth** a time of crisis or test (orig. the final sword-thrust in a bullfight). **not for a** (or **one**) **moment** never; not at all. **this moment** immediately; at once (*come here this moment*). [ME f. OF f. L *momentum*: see MOMENTUM]

■ **1, 2** instant, second, minute, flash, half a second, two seconds, *colloq.* jiff, jiffy, mo, tick. **3** instant, time, second, minute; point (in time), juncture, stage. **4** importance, weight, consequence, significance, import, gravity, seriousness, prominence, concern, note, interest, consideration. □ **at the moment** see NOW *adv.* 1, 4. **in a moment** see SOON 1. **this moment** see IMMEDIATELY *adv.* 1.

momenta *pl.* of MOMENTUM.

momentarily /mṓməntərili, -térrili, -trili/ *adv.* **1** for a moment. **2** *US* **a** at any moment. **b** instantly.

■ **1** see *briefly* (BRIEF). **2 a** see SOON 1. **b** see *instantaneously* (INSTANTANEOUS).

momentary /mṓməntəri, -tri/ *adj.* **1** lasting only a moment. **2** short-lived; transitory. □□ **momentariness** *n.* [L *momentarius* (as MOMENT)]

■ fleeting, temporary, ephemeral, evanescent, impermanent, fugitive, passing, transitory, brief, short-lived, quick, short.

momently /mṓməntli/ *adv. literary* **1** from moment to moment. **2** every moment. **3** for a moment.

momentous /məméntəss/ *adj.* having great importance. □□ **momentously** *adv.* **momentousness** *n.*

■ important, weighty, consequential, significant, grave, serious, decisive, crucial, critical, vital, pivotal, portentous.

momentum /məméntəm/ *n.* (*pl.* **momenta** /-tə/) **1** *Physics* the quantity of motion of a moving body, measured as a product of its mass and velocity. **2** the impetus gained by movement. **3** strength or continuity derived from an initial effort. [L f. *movimentum* f. *movēre* move]

■ energy, force, drive, strength, impetus, power, impulse, thrust, push.

momma /mómmə/ *n.* var. of MAMMA[1].

mommy /mómmi/ *n.* (*pl.* **-ies**) esp. *US* = MUMMY[1].

Mon. *abbr.* Monday.

monad /mónnad, mṓ-/ *n.* **1** the number one; a unit. **2** *Philos.* any ultimate unit of being (e.g. a soul, an atom, a person, God). **3** *Biol.* a simple organism, e.g. one assumed as the first in the genealogy of living beings. □□ **monadic** /mənáddik/ *adj.* **monadism** *n.* (in sense 2). [F *monade* or LL *monas monad-* f. Gk *monas -ados* unit f. *monos* alone]

monadelphous /mónnədélfəss/ *adj. Bot.* **1** (of stamens) having filaments united into one bundle. **2** (of a plant) with such stamens. [Gk *monos* one + *adelphos* brother]

monadnock /mənádnok/ *n.* a steep-sided isolated hill resistant to erosion and rising above a plain. [Mount *Monadnock* in New Hampshire, US]

monandry /mənándri/ *n.* **1** the custom of having only one husband at a time. **2** *Bot.* the state of having a single stamen. □□ **monandrous** *adj.* [MONO- after *polyandry*]

monarch /mónnərk/ *n.* **1** a sovereign with the title of king, queen, emperor, empress, or the equivalent. **2** a supreme ruler. **3** a powerful or pre-eminent person. **4** a large orange and black butterfly, *Danaus plexippus.* □□ **monarchal** /mənaárk'l/ *adj.* **monarchic** /mənaárkik/ *adj.* **monarchical** /mənaárkik'l/ *adj.* **monarchically** /mənaárkikəli/ *adv.* [ME f. F *monarque* or LL *monarcha* f. Gk *monarkhēs*, *-os*, f. *monos* alone + *arkhō* to rule]

■ **1, 2** ruler, sovereign, potentate, crowned head; queen, king. **3** ruler, sovereign, chief, lord, master, owner, tsar, supremo, *colloq.* boss.

monarchism /mónnərkiz'm/ *n.* the advocacy of or the principles of monarchy. □□ **monarchist** *n.* [F *monarchisme* (as MONARCHY)]

monarchy /mónnərki/ *n.* (*pl.* **-ies**) **1** a form of government with a monarch at the head. **2** a State with this. □□ **monarchial** /monaárkiəl/ *adj.* [ME f. OF *monarchie* f. LL *monarchia* f. Gk *monarkhia* the rule of one (as MONARCH)]

■ **1** monocracy, autocracy, royalism, monarchism. **2** kingdom, empire, domain, principality, *formal esp. Law* realm.

monastery /mónnəstəri, -stri/ *n.* (*pl.* **-ies**) the residence of a religious community, esp. of monks living in seclusion. [ME f. eccl.L *monasterium* f. eccl.Gk *monastērion* f. *monazō* live alone f. *monos* alone]

■ abbey, cloister, priory, friary, *Buddhism* vihara, lamasery, *Ind.* ashram.

monastic /mənástik/ *adj.* & *n.* ● *adj.* **1** of or relating to monasteries or the religious communities living in them. **2** resembling these or their way of life; solitary and celibate. ● *n.* a monk or other follower of a monastic rule. □□ **monastically** *adv.* **monasticism** /-tisiz'm/ *n.* **monasticize** /-tisīz/ *v.tr.* (also **-ise**). [F *monastique* or LL *monasticus* f. Gk *monastikos* (as MONASTERY)]

■ *adj.* **2** see ISOLATED 1. ● *n.* see MONK. □□ **monastically** see *severely* (SEVERE).

monatomic /mónnətómmik/ *adj. Chem.* **1** (esp. of a molecule) consisting of one atom. **2** having one replaceable atom or radical.

monaural /mónnáwrəl/ *adj.* **1** = MONOPHONIC. **2** of or involving one ear. □□ **monaurally** *adv.* [MONO- + AURAL[1]]

monazite /mónnəzīt/ *n.* a phosphate mineral containing rare-earth elements and thorium. [G *Monazit* f. Gk *monazō* live alone (because of its rarity)]

mondaine /mondén/ *adj.* & *n.* ● *adj.* **1** of the fashionable world. **2** worldly. ● *n.* a worldly or fashionable woman. [F, fem. of *mondain*: see MUNDANE]

Monday /múnday, -di/ *n.* & *adv.* ● *n.* the second day of the week, following Sunday. ● *adv. colloq.* **1** on Monday. **2** (**Mondays**) on Mondays; each Monday. [OE *mōnandæg* day of the moon, transl. LL *lunae dies*]

Monel /mṓn'l/ *n.* (in full **Monel metal**) *propr.* a nickel-copper alloy with high tensile strength and resisting corrosion. [A. *Monell*, US businessman d. 1921]

monetarism /múnnitəriz'm/ *n.* the theory or practice of controlling the supply of money as the chief method of stabilizing the economy.

monetarist /múnnitərist/ *n.* & *adj.* ● *n.* an advocate of monetarism. ● *adj.* in accordance with the principles of monetarism.

monetary /múnnitəri, -tri/ *adj.* **1** of the currency in use. **2** of or consisting of money. □□ **monetarily** *adv.* [F *monétaire* or LL *monetarius* f. L (as MONEY)]

■ **2** pecuniary, fiscal, financial, capital, cash, money; numismatic.

monetize /múnnitīz/ *v.tr.* (also **-ise**) **1** give a fixed value as currency. **2** put (a metal) into circulation as money. □□ **monetization** /-záysh'n/ *n.* [F *monétiser* f. L (as MONEY)]

money /múnni/ *n.* **1 a** a current medium of exchange in the form of coins and banknotes. **b** a particular form of this (*silver money*). **2** (*pl.* **-eys** or **-ies**) (in *pl.*) sums of money. **3 a** wealth; property viewed as convertible into money. **b** wealth as giving power or influence (*money speaks*). **c** a rich person or family (*has married into money*). **4 a** money as a resource (*time is money*). **b** profit, remuneration (*in it for the money*). □ **for my money** in my opinion or judgement; for my preference (*is too aggressive for my money*). **have money to burn** see BURN[1]. **in the money** *colloq.* having or winning a lot of money. **money box** a box for saving money dropped through a slit. **money-changer** a person whose business it is to change money, esp. at an official rate. **money for jam** (or **old rope**) *colloq.* profit for little or no trouble. **money-grubber** *colloq.* a person greedily intent on amassing money. **money-grubbing** *n.* this practice. ● *adj.* given to this. **money market** *Stock Exch.* trade in short-term stocks, loans, etc. **money of account** see ACCOUNT. **money order** an order for payment of a specified sum, issued by a bank or Post Office. **money spider** a small household spider supposed to bring financial luck. **money-spinner** a thing that brings in a profit. **money's-worth** good value for one's money. **put money into** invest in. □□ **moneyless**

adj. [ME f. OF *moneie* f. L *moneta* mint, money, orig. a title of Juno, in whose temple at Rome money was minted]
■ **1** currency, legal tender, medium of exchange, specie, (hard) cash, ready money, banknotes, paper money, coin(s), (small) change, *Brit.* notes, *esp. Sc.* silver, *US* bills, greenbacks, *US* & *Austral.* roll, *colloq.* shekels, *US colloq.* folding money, *derog. or joc.* pelf, *joc.* filthy lucre, *sl.* dosh, loot, dough, bread, spondulicks, boodle, oof, scratch, stuff, readies, the ready, moolah, green, *Brit. sl.* lolly, rhino, brass, *US sl.* kale, bucks. **3** resources, wealth, fortune, funds, finance(s), capital, affluence, means, (liquid) assets, riches, *colloq.* wherewithal, *sl.* bundle. **4 b** gain, remuneration, (net) profit, take, *colloq.* percentage, rake-off; see also PAY[1] *n.* □ **for my money** in my opinion *or* view *or* judgement, to my mind, as I see it; for my liking *or* preference. **in the money** rich, wealthy, affluent, moneyed, well off, well-to-do, prosperous, in clover, *colloq.* flush, in *or* on Easy Street, well-heeled, rolling in it, rolling in money *or* dough, filthy rich, *sl.* loaded, stinking rich. **money-grubber** see MISER. **money-grubbing** see MISERLY. **money-spinner** bonanza, gold-mine, Golconda, golden goose, *sl.* (nice little) earner; milk and honey. **put money into** see INVEST 2a.

moneybags /múnnibagz/ *n.pl.* (treated as *sing.*) *colloq.* usu. *derog.* a wealthy person.

moneyed /múnnid/ *adj.* **1** having much money; wealthy. **2** consisting of money (*moneyed assistance*).
■ **1** see WEALTHY.

moneylender /múnnilendər/ *n.* a person who lends money, esp. as a business, at interest. □□ **moneylending** *n.* & *adj.*

moneymaker /múnnimaykər/ *n.* **1** a person who earns much money. **2** a thing, idea, etc., that produces much money. □□ **moneymaking** *n.* & *adj.*
■ □□ **moneymaking** (*adj.*) see SUCCESSFUL.

moneywort /múnniwurt/ *n.* a trailing evergreen plant, *Lysimachia nummularia*, with round glossy leaves and yellow flowers.

monger /múnggər/ *n.* (usu. in *comb.*) **1** a dealer or trader (*fishmonger*; *ironmonger*). **2** usu. *derog.* a person who promotes or deals in something specified (*warmonger*; *scaremonger*). [OE *mangere* f. *mangian* to traffic f. Gmc, ult. f. L *mango* dealer]
■ **1** see SELLER.

Mongol /móngg'l/ *adj.* & *n.* ● *adj.* **1** of or relating to the Asian people now inhabiting Mongolia in Central Asia. **2** resembling this people, esp. in appearance. **3** (**mongol**) often *offens.* suffering from Down's syndrome. ● *n.* **1** a Mongolian. **2** (**mongol**) often *offens.* a person suffering from Down's syndrome. [native name: perh. f. *mong* brave]

Mongolian /monggṓliən/ *n.* & *adj.* ● *n.* a native or inhabitant of Mongolia; the language of Mongolia. ● *adj.* of or relating to Mongolia or its people or language.

mongolism /mónggəliz'm/ *n.* = DOWN'S SYNDROME. ¶ The term *Down's syndrome* is now much preferred in medical circles. [MONGOL + -ISM, because its physical characteristics were thought to be reminiscent of Mongolians]

Mongoloid /mónggəloyd/ *adj.* & *n.* ● *adj.* **1** characteristic of the Mongolians, esp. in having a broad flat yellowish face. **2** (**mongoloid**) often *offens.* having the characteristic symptoms of Down's syndrome. ● *n.* a Mongoloid or mongoloid person.

mongoose /mónggōōss/ *n.* (*pl.* **mongooses**) any of various small flesh-eating civet-like mammals of the family Viverridae, esp. of the genus *Herpestes*. [Marathi *mangūs*]

mongrel /múnggrəl, móng-/ *n.* & *adj.* ● *n.* **1** a dog of no definable type or breed. **2** any other animal or plant resulting from the crossing of different breeds or types. **3** *derog.* a person of mixed race. ● *adj.* of mixed origin, nature, or character. □□ **mongrelism** *n.* **mongrelize** *v.tr.* (also **-ise**). **mongrelization** /-līzáysh'n/ *n.* **mongrelly** *adj.* [earlier *meng-*, *mang-* f. Gmc: prob. rel. to MINGLE]
■ *n.* **1** cross-breed, mixed breed, half-breed, *Biol.* hybrid, *Brit.* lurcher, *derog.* mutt, *esp. US sl.* pooch.

'mongst *poet.* var. of AMONGST. [see AMONG]

monial /mṓniəl/ *n.* a mullion. [ME f. OF *moinel* middle f. *moien* MEAN[3]]

monicker var. of MONIKER.

monies see MONEY 2.

moniker /mónnikər/ *n.* (also **monicker**, **monniker**) *sl.* a name. [19th c.: orig. unkn.]

moniliform /mənílliform/ *adj.* with a form suggesting a string of beads. [F *moniliforme* or mod.L *moniliformis* f. L *monile* necklace]

monism /mónniz'm, mṓn-/ *n.* **1** any theory denying the duality of matter and mind. **2** the doctrine that only one ultimate principle or being exists. □□ **monist** *n.* **monistic** /-nístik/ *adj.* [mod.L *monismus* f. Gk *monos* single]

monition /mənísh'n/ *n.* **1** (foll. by *of*) *literary* a warning (of danger). **2** *Eccl.* a formal notice from a bishop or ecclesiastical court admonishing a person not to commit an offence. [ME f. OF f. L *monitio -onis* (as MONITOR)]
■ **1** see CAUTION *n.* 2.

monitor /mónnitər/ *n.* & *v.* ● *n.* **1** any of various persons or devices for checking or warning about a situation, operation, etc. **2** a school pupil with disciplinary or other special duties. **3 a** a television receiver used in a studio to select or verify the picture being broadcast. **b** = *visual display unit*. **4** a person who listens to and reports on foreign broadcasts etc. **5** a detector of radioactive contamination. **6** *Zool.* any tropical lizard of the genus *Varanus*, supposed to give warning of the approach of crocodiles. **7** a heavily armed shallow-draught warship. ● *v.tr.* **1** act as a monitor of. **2** maintain regular surveillance over. **3** regulate the strength of (a recorded or transmitted signal). □□ **monitorial** /-tóriəl/ *adj.* **monitorship** *n.* [L f. *monēre monit-* warn]
■ *n.* **1** watchdog, supervisor, sentinel, guard, guardian, custodian; *Brit.* invigilator, *US* proctor. **2** *esp. Brit.* prefect, *Brit.* praepostor. ● *v.* **1, 2** watch, oversee, observe, check (out *or* up on), audit, supervise, superintend, scan, examine, study, follow, keep an eye on, survey, keep track of, track, trace, record, vet, *colloq.* keep tabs on.

monitory /mónnitəri, -tri/ *adj.* & *n.* ● *adj. literary* giving or serving as a warning. ● *n.* (*pl.* **-ies**) *Eccl.* a letter of admonition from the pope or a bishop. [L *monitorius* (as MONITION)]
■ *adj.* see EXEMPLARY 2a.

monk /mungk/ *n.* a member of a religious community of men living under certain vows esp. of poverty, chastity, and obedience. □□ **monkish** *adj.* [OE *munuc* ult. f. Gk *monakhos* solitary f. *monos* alone]
■ brother, religious, coenobite, monastic, friar.

monkey /múngki/ *n.* & *v.* ● *n.* (*pl.* **-eys**) **1** any of various New World and Old World primates esp. of the families Cebidae (including capuchins), Callitrichidae (including marmosets and tamarins), and Cercopithecidae (including baboons and apes). **2** a mischievous person, esp. a child (*young monkey*). **3** *sl.* **a** *Brit.* £500. **b** *US* $500. **4** (in full **monkey engine**) a machine hammer for pile-driving etc. ● *v.* (**-eys, -eyed**) **1** *tr.* mimic or mock. **2** *intr.* (often foll. by *with*) tamper or play mischievous tricks. **3** *intr.* (foll. by *around*, *about*) fool around. □ **have a monkey on one's back** *sl.* be a drug addict. **make a monkey of** humiliate by making appear ridiculous. **monkey bread** the baobab tree or its fruit. **monkey business** *colloq.* mischief. **monkey flower** a mimulus, esp. *Mimulus cardinalis*, with bright yellow flowers. **monkey-jacket** a short close-fitting jacket worn by sailors etc. or at a mess. **monkey-nut** a peanut. **monkey-puzzle** a coniferous tree, *Araucaria araucaria*, native to Chile, with downward-pointing branches and small close-set leaves. **monkey-suit** *colloq.* evening dress. **monkey tricks** *colloq.* mischief. **monkey wrench** a wrench with an adjustable jaw. □□ **monkeyish** *adj.* [16th c.: orig. unkn. (perh. LG)]

■ *n.* **1** simian, ape, primate. **2** imp, devil, mischief-maker, *archaic or joc.* rapscallion, *colloq.* scamp, *often joc.* rascal. ● *v.* **1** mimic, imitate, impersonate, copy, ape, duplicate; see also MOCK *v.* 2. **2, 3** fool around, play, fiddle, meddle, interfere, mess (about *or* around), tinker, tamper, *Brit. colloq.* muck about *or* around. □ **make a monkey of** make a fool *or* laughing-stock of; see also PARODY *v.* **monkey business, monkey tricks** see MISCHIEF 1–3.

monkeyshine /múngkishīn/ *n.* (usu. in *pl.*) *US colloq.* = *monkey tricks.*

monkfish /múnkfish/ *n.* **1** an angler-fish, esp. *Lophius piscatorius*, often used as food. **2** a large cartilaginous fish, *Squatina squatina*, with a flattened body and large pectoral fins. Also called *angel-shark.*

monkshood /múngks-hōōd/ *n. Bot.* a poisonous garden plant *Aconitum napellus*, with hood-shaped blue or purple flowers.

monniker var. of MONIKER.

mono /mónnō/ *adj.* & *n. colloq.* ● *adj.* monophonic. ● *n.* (*pl.* **-os**) a monophonic record, reproduction, etc. [abbr.]

mono- /mónnō/ *comb. form* (usu. **mon-** before a vowel) **1** one, alone, single. **2** *Chem.* (forming names of compounds) containing one atom or group of a specified kind. [Gk f. *monos* alone]

monoacid /mónnō-ássid/ *adj. Chem.* (of a base) having one replaceable hydroxide ion.

monobasic /mónnōbáysik/ *adj. Chem.* (of an acid) having one replaceable hydrogen atom.

monocarpic /mónnōkaárpik/ *adj.* (also **monocarpous** /-kaárpəss/) *Bot.* bearing fruit only once. [MONO- + Gk *karpos* fruit]

monocausal /mónnōkáwz'l/ *adj.* in terms of a sole cause.

monocephalous /mónnōséffələss/ *adj. Bot.* having only one head.

monochord /mónnəkord/ *n. Mus.* an instrument with a single string and a movable bridge, used esp. to determine intervals. [ME f. OF *monocorde* f. LL *monochordon* f. Gk *monokhordon* (as MONO-, CHORD[1])]

monochromatic /mónnəkrəmáttik/ *adj.* **1** *Physics* (of light or other radiation) of a single wavelength or frequency. **2** containing only one colour. □□ **monochromatically** *adv.*

monochromatism /mónnōkrṓmətiz'm/ *n.* complete colour-blindness in which all colours appear as shades of one colour.

monochrome /mónnəkrōm/ *n.* & *adj.* ● *n.* a photograph or picture done in one colour or different tones of this, or in black and white only. ● *adj.* having or using only one colour or in black and white only. □□ **monochromic** /-krṓmik/ *adj.* [ult. f. Gk *monokhrōmatos* (as MONO-, *khrōmatos* f. *khrōma* colour)]

monocle /mónnək'l/ *n.* a single eyeglass. □□ **monocled** *adj.* [F, orig. adj. f. LL *monoculus* one-eyed (as MONO-, *oculus* eye)]

monocline /mónnōklīn/ *n. Geol.* a bend in rock strata that are otherwise uniformly dipping or horizontal. □□ **monoclinal** /-klīn'l/ *adj.* [MONO- + Gk *klinō* lean, dip]

monoclinic /mónnōklínnik/ *adj.* (of a crystal) having one axial intersection oblique. [MONO- + Gk *klinō* lean, slope]

monoclonal /mónnōklṓn'l/ *adj.* forming a single clone; derived from a single individual or cell. □ **monoclonal antibodies** antibodies produced artificially by a single clone and consisting of identical antibody molecules.

monocoque /mónnəkok/ *n. Aeron.* an aircraft or vehicle structure in which the chassis is integral with the body. [F (as MONO-, *coque* shell)]

monocot /mónnōkot/ *n.* = MONOCOTYLEDON. [abbr.]

monocotyledon /mónnəkóttileéd'n/ *n. Bot.* any flowering plant with a single cotyledon. □□ **monocotyledonous** *adj.*

monocracy /mənókrəsi/ *n.* (*pl.* **-ies**) government by one person only. □□ **monocratic** /mónnəkráttik/ *adj.*

■ see DESPOTISM.

monocular /mənókyoolər/ *adj.* with or for one eye. □□ **monocularly** *adj.* [LL *monoculus* having one eye]

monoculture /mónnōkulchər/ *n.* the cultivation of a single crop.

monocycle /mónnəsīk'l/ *n.* = UNICYCLE.

monocyte /mónnəsīt/ *n. Biol.* a large type of leucocyte.

monodactylous /mónnədáktiləss/ *adj.* having one finger, toe, or claw.

monodrama /mónnōdraamə/ *n.* a dramatic piece for one performer.

monody /mónnədi/ *n.* (*pl.* **-ies**) **1** an ode sung by a single actor in a Greek tragedy. **2** a poem lamenting a person's death. **3** *Mus.* a composition with only one melodic line. □□ **monodic** /mənóddik/ *adj.* **monodist** *n.* [LL *monodia* f. Gk *monōidia* f. *monōidos* singing alone (as MONO-, ODE)]

■ **2** see LAMENT *n.* 2.

monoecious /məneéshəss/ *adj.* **1** *Bot.* with unisexual male and female organs on the same plant. **2** *Zool.* hermaphrodite. [mod.L *Monoecia* the class of such plants (Linnaeus) f. Gk *monos* single + *oikos* house]

monofilament /mónnōfilləmənt/ *n.* **1** a single strand of man-made fibre. **2** a type of fishing line using this.

monogamy /mənóggəmi/ *n.* **1** the practice or state of being married to one person at a time. **2** *Zool.* the habit of having only one mate at a time. □□ **monogamist** *n.* **monogamous** *adj.* **monogamously** *adv.* [F *monogamie* f. eccl.L f. Gk *monogamia* (as MONO-, *gamos* marriage)]

monogenesis /mónnōjénnisiss/ *n.* (also **monogeny** /mənójini/) **1** the theory of the development of all beings from a single cell. **2** the theory that mankind descended from one pair of ancestors. □□ **monogenetic** /-jinéttik/ *adj.*

monoglot /mónnəglot/ *adj.* & *n.* ● *adj.* using only one language. ● *n.* a monoglot person.

monogram /mónnəgram/ *n.* two or more letters, esp. a person's initials, interwoven as a device. □□ **monogrammatic** /-grəmáttik/ *adj.* **monogrammed** *adj.* [F *monogramme* f. LL *monogramma* f. Gk (as MONO-, -GRAM)]

■ see SIGN *n.* 2.

monograph /mónnəgraaf/ *n.* & *v.* ● *n.* a separate treatise on a single subject or an aspect of it. ● *v.tr.* write a monograph on. □□ **monographer** /mənógrəfər/ *n.* **monographist** /mənógrəfist/ *n.* **monographic** /mónnəgráffik/ *adj.* [earlier *monography* f. mod.L *monographia* f. *monographus* writer on a single genus or species (as MONO-, -GRAPH, -GRAPHY)]

■ *n.* treatise, dissertation, disquisition, essay, paper.

monogynous /mənójinəss/ *adj. Bot.* having only one pistil.

monogyny /mənójini/ *n.* the custom of having only one wife at a time.

monohull /mónnōhul/ *n.* a boat with a single hull.

monohybrid /mónnōhībrid/ *n.* a hybrid with respect to only one allele.

monohydric /mónnōhīdrik/ *adj. Chem.* containing one hydroxyl group.

monokini /mónnōkeéni/ *n.* a woman's one-piece beach-garment equivalent to the lower half of a bikini. [MONO- + BIKINI, by false assoc. with BI-]

monolayer /mónnōlayər/ *n. Chem.* a layer only one molecule in thickness.

monolingual /mónnōlínggwəl/ *adj.* speaking or using only one language.

monolith /mónnəlith/ *n.* **1** a single block of stone, esp. shaped into a pillar or monument. **2** a person or thing like a monolith in being massive, immovable, or solidly uniform. **3** a large block of concrete. □□ **monolithic** /-líthik/ *adj.* [F *monolithe* f. Gk *monolithos* (as MONO-, *lithos* stone)]

■ □□ **monolithic** massive, huge, enormous, monumental, imposing, colossal, gigantic, giant; featureless, uniform, undifferentiated, characterless; rigid, impenetrable, invulnerable, unbending, inflexible, solid, stolid, intractable, immovable.

monologue /mónnəlog/ *n.* **1 a** a scene in a drama in which a person speaks alone. **b** a dramatic composition for one performer. **2** a long speech by one person in a conversation etc. □□ **monologic** /-lójik/ *adj.* **monological** /-lójik'l/ *adj.*

monologist /mənólləjist/ *n.* (also **-loguist**). **monologize** /mənólləjīz/ *v.intr.* (also **-ise**). [F f. Gk *monologos* speaking alone (as MONO-, -LOGUE)]
■ see SPEECH 2.

monomania /mónnəmáyniə/ *n.* obsession of the mind by one idea or interest. □□ **monomaniac** *n.* & *adj.* **monomaniacal** /-mənīək'l/ *adj.* [F *monomanie* (as MONO-, -MANIA)]
■ see *fanaticism* (FANATIC). □□ **monomaniac** (*n.*) see CRANK².

monomark /mónnōmaark/ *n. Brit.* a combination of letters, with or without figures, registered as an identification mark for goods, articles, addresses, etc.

monomer /mónnəmər/ *n. Chem.* **1** a unit in a dimer, trimer, or polymer. **2** a molecule or compound that can be polymerized. □□ **monomeric** /-mérrik/ *adj.*

monomial /mənṓmiəl/ *adj.* & *n. Math.* ● *adj.* (of an algebraic expression) consisting of one term. ● *n.* a monomial expression. [MONO- after *binomial*]

monomolecular /mónnōməlékyoolər/ *adj. Chem.* (of a layer) only one molecule in thickness.

monomorphic /mónnəmórfik/ *adj.* (also **monomorphous** /-mórfəss/) *Biochem.* not changing form during development. □□ **monomorphism** *n.*

mononucleosis /mónnōnyōōkliṓsiss/ *n.* an abnormally high proportion of monocytes in the blood, esp. = *glandular fever*. [MONO- + NUCLEO- + -OSIS]

monopetalous /mónnəpéttələss/ *adj. Bot.* having the corolla in one piece, or the petals united into a tube.

monophonic /mónnəfónnik/ *adj.* **1** (of sound-reproduction) using only one channel of transmission (cf. STEREOPHONIC). **2** *Mus.* homophonic. □□ **monophonically** *adv.* [MONO- + Gk *phōnē* sound]

monophthong /mónnəf-thong/ *n. Phonet.* a single vowel sound. □□ **monophthongal** /-thóngg'l/ *adj.* [Gk *monophthoggos* (as MONO-, *phthoggos* sound)]

Monophysite /mənóffizīt, mónnō-/ *n.* a person who holds that there is only one nature (partly divine, partly and subordinately human) in the person of Christ. [eccl.L *monophysita* f. eccl.Gk *monophusitēs* (as MONO-, *phusis* nature)]

monoplane /mónnōplayn/ *n.* an aeroplane with one set of wings (cf. BIPLANE).

monopolist /mənóppəlist/ *n.* a person who has or advocates a monopoly. □□ **monopolistic** /-lístik/ *adj.*

monopolize /mənóppəlīz/ *v.tr.* (also **-ise**) **1** obtain exclusive possession or control of (a trade or commodity etc.). **2** dominate or prevent others from sharing in (a conversation, person's attention, etc.). □□ **monopolization** /-záysh'n/ *n.* **monopolizer** *n.*
■ corner, control, dominate, *colloq.* hog.

monopoly /mənóppəli/ *n.* (*pl.* **-ies**) **1 a** the exclusive possession or control of the trade in a commodity or service. **b** this conferred as a privilege by the State. **2 a** a commodity or service that is subject to a monopoly. **b** a company etc. that possesses a monopoly. **3** (foll. by *of*, *US on*) exclusive possession, control, or exercise. [L *monopolium* f. Gk *monopōlion* (as MONO-, *pōleō* sell)]
■ **3** exclusive *or* supreme control.

monorail /mónnō-rayl/ *n.* a railway in which the track consists of a single rail, usu. elevated with the train units suspended from it.

monosaccharide /mónnōsákkərīd/ *n. Chem.* a sugar that cannot be hydrolysed to give a simpler sugar, e.g. glucose.

monosodium glutamate /mónnōsṓdiəm glṓōtəmayt/ *n. Chem.* a sodium salt of glutamic acid used to flavour food (cf. GLUTAMATE).

monospermous /mónnəspérməss/ *adj. Bot.* having one seed. [MONO- + Gk *sperma* seed]

monostichous /mənóstikəss/ *adj. Bot.* & *Zool.* arranged in or consisting of one layer or row. [MONO- + Gk *stikhos* row]

monosyllabic /mónnəsilábbik/ *adj.* **1** (of a word) having one syllable. **2** (of a person or statement) using or expressed in monosyllables. □□ **monosyllabically** *adv.*

monosyllable /mónnəsilləb'l/ *n.* a word of one syllable. □ **in monosyllables** in simple direct words.

monotheism /mónnəthee-iz'm/ *n.* the doctrine that there is only one God. □□ **monotheist** *n.* **monotheistic** /-ístik/ *adj.* **monotheistically** /-ístikəli/ *adv.* [MONO- + Gk *theos* god]

monotint /mónnōtint/ *n.* = MONOCHROME.

monotone /mónnətōn/ *n.* & *adj.* ● *n.* **1** a sound or utterance continuing or repeated on one note without change of pitch. **2** sameness of style in writing. ● *adj.* without change of pitch. [mod.L *monotonus* f. late Gk *monotonos* (as MONO-, TONE)]

monotonic /mónnətónnik/ *adj.* **1** uttered in a monotone. **2** *Math.* (of a function or quantity) varying in such a way that it either never decreases or never increases. □□ **monotonically** *adv.*

monotonous /mənóttənəss/ *adj.* **1** lacking in variety; tedious through sameness. **2** (of a sound or utterance) without variation in tone or pitch. □□ **monotonize** *v.tr.* (also **-ise**). **monotonously** *adv.* **monotonousness** *n.*
■ boring, tedious, dull, tiresome, humdrum, sleep-inducing, soporific, wearisome, wearying, tiring, repetitious, prosaic, banal, dry, dry as dust, uninteresting, dreary, colourless, unexciting, run-of-the-mill, ordinary, commonplace, routine, uneventful, everyday, mechanical; unvaried, unvarying, unchanging.

monotony /mənóttəni/ *n.* **1** the state of being monotonous. **2** dull or tedious routine.
■ **1** see TEDIUM.

monotreme /mónnətreem/ *n.* any mammal of the order Monotremata, native to Australia and New Guinea, including the duckbill and spiny anteater, laying large yolky eggs through a common opening for urine, faeces, etc. [MONO- + Gk *trēma -matos* hole]

monotype /mónnətīp/ *n.* **1** (**Monotype**) *Printing propr.* a typesetting machine that casts and sets up types in individual characters. **2** an impression on paper made from an inked design painted on glass or metal.

monotypic /mónnətíppik/ *adj.* having only one type or representative.

monovalent /mónnəváylənt/ *adj. Chem.* having a valency of one; univalent. □□ **monovalence** *n.* **monovalency** *n.*

monoxide /mənóksīd/ *n. Chem.* an oxide containing one oxygen atom (*carbon monoxide*). [MONO- + OXIDE]

Monroe doctrine /munrṓ/ *n.* the US policy of objecting to intervention by European powers in the affairs of Latin America. [J. *Monroe*, US President d. 1831, who formulated it]

Monseigneur /mónsenyṓr/ *n.* (*pl.* ***Messeigneurs*** /méssenyṓr/) a title given to an eminent French person, esp. a prince, cardinal, archbishop, or bishop. [F f. *mon* my + *seigneur* lord]

Monsieur /məsyṓr/ *n.* (*pl.* **Messieurs** /mesyṓr/) **1** the title or form of address used of or to a French-speaking man, corresponding to Mr or sir. **2** a Frenchman. [F f. *mon* my + *sieur* lord]

Monsignor /monseényər, -nyór/ *n.* (*pl.* **Monsignori** /-nyóri/) the title of various Roman Catholic prelates, officers of the papal court, etc. [It., after MONSEIGNEUR: see SIGNOR]

monsoon /monsṓōn/ *n.* **1** a wind in S. Asia, esp. in the Indian Ocean, blowing from the south west in summer (**wet monsoon**) and the north east in winter (**dry monsoon**). **2** a rainy season accompanying a wet monsoon. **3** any other wind with periodic alternations. □□ **monsoonal** *adj.* [obs. Du. *monssoen* f. Port. *monção* f. Arab. *mawsim* fixed season f. *wasama* to mark]

■ **3** see STORM *n.* 1.

mons pubis /monz pyōōbiss/ *n.* a rounded mass of fatty tissue lying over the joint of a man's pubic bones. [L, = mount of the pubes]

monster /mónstər/ *n.* **1** an imaginary creature, usu. large and frightening, compounded of incongruous elements. **2** an inhumanly cruel or wicked person. **3** a misshapen animal or plant. **4** a large hideous animal or thing (e.g. a building). **5** (*attrib.*) huge; extremely large of its kind. [ME f. OF *monstre* f. L *monstrum* portent, monster f. *monēre* warn]

■ **1** beast, fiend, ogre, giant, dragon, brute, demon, troll, bogeyman. **2** see DEVIL *n.* 3a. **3, 4** mutant, mutation, freak, deformity, *lusus* (*naturae*); monstrosity, eyesore, horror. **5** see HUGE 1, GIGANTIC.

monstera /monstéerə/ *n.* any climbing plant of the genus *Monstera*, including Swiss cheese plant. [mod.L, perh. f. L *monstrum* monster (from the odd appearance of its leaves)]

monstrance /mónstrənss/ *n. RC Ch.* a vessel in which the Host is exposed for veneration. [ME, = demonstration, f. med.L *monstrantia* f. L *monstrare* show]

monstrosity /monstróssiti/ *n.* (*pl.* **-ies**) **1** a huge or outrageous thing. **2** monstrousness. **3** = MONSTER 3. [LL *monstrositas* (as MONSTROUS)]

■ **1** see MONSTER 3, 4. **2** monstrousness, heinousness, horribleness, horridness, hideousness, awfulness, nightmarishness, dreadfulness, frightfulness, horror, hellishness, ghoulishness, fiendishness, barbarity.

monstrous /mónstrəss/ *adj.* **1** like a monster; abnormally formed. **2** huge. **3 a** outrageously wrong or absurd. **b** atrocious. ▫▫ **monstrously** *adv.* **monstrousness** *n.* [ME f. OF *monstreux* or L *monstrosus* (as MONSTER)]

■ **1** awful, horrible, horrid, horrific, horrendous, horrifying, hideous, ugly, nightmarish, dreadful, grisly, gruesome, disgusting, nauseous, nauseating, repulsive, repellent, revolting, frightful, grotesque, hellish, ghoulish, freakish, fiendish. **2** gigantic, giant, huge, vast, enormous, colossal, monster, gargantuan, immense, tremendous, titanic, prodigious, massive, towering, elephantine, mammoth, *colloq.* jumbo. **3** outrageous, shocking, scandalous, atrocious, appalling, wicked, villainous, evil, ugly, vile, insensitive, cruel, base, debased, shameful, shameless, infamous, barbaric, barbarous, savage, inhuman, brutish, beastly, disgraceful, nefarious, egregious, heinous, foul, flagitious, loathsome, depraved; merciless, ruthless, brutal, vicious.

mons Veneris /monz vénnəriss/ *n.* a rounded mass of fatty tissue on a woman's abdomen above the vulva. [L, = mount of Venus]

Mont. *abbr.* Montana.

montage /montaazh/ *n.* **1 a** a process of selecting, editing, and piecing together separate sections of cinema or television film to form a continuous whole. **b** a sequence of such film as a section of a longer film. **2 a** the technique of producing a new composite whole from fragments of pictures, words, music, etc. **b** a composition produced in this way. [F f. *monter* MOUNT[1]]

montane /móntayn/ *adj.* of or inhabiting mountainous country. [L *montanus* (as MOUNT[2], -ANE[1])]

montbretia /monbréeshə/ *n.* a hybrid plant of the genus *Crocosmia*, with bright orange-yellow trumpet-shaped flowers. [mod.L f. A. F. E. Coquebert de *Montbret*, Fr. botanist d. 1801]

monte /mónti/ *n. Cards* **1** a Spanish game of chance, played with 45 cards. **2** (in full **three-card monte**) a game of Mexican origin played with three cards, similar to three-card trick. [Sp., = mountain, heap of cards]

Monte Carlo method /mónti kaárlō/ *n. Statistics* a method of using the random sampling of numbers in order to estimate the solution to a numerical problem. [*Monte Carlo* in Monaco, famous for its gambling casino]

Montessori /móntisóri/ *n.* (usu. *attrib.*) a system of education (esp. of young children) that seeks to develop natural interests and activities rather than use formal teaching methods. [Maria *Montessori*, It. educationist d. 1952, who initiated it]

month /munth/ *n.* **1** (in full **calendar month**) **a** each of usu. twelve periods into which a year is divided. **b** a period of time between the same dates in successive calendar months. **2** a period of 28 days or of four weeks. **3** = *lunar month*. ▫ **month of Sundays** a very long period. [OE *mōnath* f. Gmc, rel. to MOON]

monthly /múnthli/ *adj.*, *adv.*, & *n.* ● *adj.* done, produced, or occurring once a month. ● *adv.* once a month; from month to month. ● *n.* (*pl.* **-ies**) **1** a monthly periodical. **2** (in *pl.*) *colloq.* a menstrual period.

■ *n.* **1** see PERIODICAL *n.*

monticule /móntikyōōl/ *n.* **1** a small hill. **2** a small mound caused by a volcanic eruption. [F f. LL *monticulus* dimin. of *mons* MOUNT[2]]

monument /mónyoomənt/ *n.* **1** anything enduring that serves to commemorate or make celebrated, esp. a structure or building. **2** a stone or other structure placed over a grave or in a church etc. in memory of the dead. **3** an ancient building or site etc. that has survived or been preserved. **4** (foll. by *of*, *to*) a typical or outstanding example (*a monument of indiscretion*). **5** a written record. [ME f. F f. L *monumentum* f. *monēre* remind]

■ **1–3** marker, cairn, memorial, tablet, shrine; sepulchre, gravestone, tombstone, headstone, tomb, mausoleum, cenotaph. **4** model, archetype, pattern, paragon, nonpareil, perfect specimen, example, exemplar. **5** see RECORD *n.* 1.

monumental /mónyoomént'l/ *adj.* **1 a** extremely great; stupendous (*a monumental achievement*). **b** (of a literary work) massive and permanent. **2** of or serving as a monument. **3** *colloq.* (as an intensifier) very great; calamitous (*a monumental blunder*). ▫ **monumental mason** a maker of tombstones etc. ▫▫ **monumentality** /-tálliti/ *n.* **monumentally** *adv.*

■ **1 a** staggering, awe-inspiring, outstanding, prominent, stupendous, vast, awesome, epoch-making, historic, history-making, memorable, lasting, permanent, unforgettable, significant, notable, noteworthy, impressive, marvellous, prodigious, wonderful, spectacular, magnificent, grand, striking, glorious, enduring, classic, *poet.* wondrous. **b** massive, huge, gigantic, enormous, prodigious, colossal, immense, vast, tremendous. **2** commemorative, memorial. **3** egregious, catastrophic, calamitous, huge, enormous, abject, unforgivable, unbelievable, monstrous, *colloq.* awful, terrible, *sl.* whopping.

monumentalize /mónyooméntəlīz/ *v.tr.* (also **-ise**) record or commemorate by or as by a monument.

-mony /məni/ *suffix* forming nouns esp. denoting an abstract state or quality (*acrimony*; *testimony*). [L *-monia*, *-monium*, rel. to -MENT]

moo /mōō/ *v.* & *n.* ● *v.intr.* (**moos, mooed**) make the characteristic vocal sound of cattle; = LOW[2]. ● *n.* (*pl.* **moos**) this sound. ▫ **moo-cow** a childish name for a cow. [imit.]

mooch /mōōch/ *v. colloq.* **1** *intr.* loiter or saunter desultorily. **2** *tr.* esp. *US* **a** steal. **b** beg. ▫▫ **moocher** *n.* [ME, prob. f. OF *muchier* hide, skulk]

■ **1** see WANDER *v.* 1. **2 b** see BEG 1b, c.

mood[1] /mōōd/ *n.* **1** a state of mind or feeling. **2** (in *pl.*) fits of melancholy or bad temper. **3** (*attrib.*) inducing a particular mood (*mood music*). ▫ **in the** (or **no**) **mood** (foll. by *for*, or *to* + infin.) inclined (or disinclined) (*was in no mood to agree*). [OE *mōd* mind, thought, f. Gmc]

■ **1** humour, attitude, inclination, disposition, nature, temper, frame of mind, spirit, atmosphere, sense, feeling. **2** (*moods*) see TEMPER *n.* 2b. ▫ **in the mood** ready, willing, eager, keen, (well-)disposed, inclined, minded. **in no mood** unwilling, disinclined, not happy *or* willing *or* keen.

mood[2] /mōōd/ *n.* **1** *Gram.* **a** a form or set of forms of a verb serving to indicate whether it is to express fact, command, wish, etc. (*subjunctive mood*). **b** the distinction of meaning expressed by different moods. **2** *Logic* any of the classes into which each of the figures of a valid categorical syllogism is subdivided. [var. of MODE, assoc. with MOOD[1]]

moody /mo͞odi/ *adj.* & *n.* ● *adj.* (**moodier, moodiest**) given to changes of mood; gloomy, sullen. ● *n. colloq.* a bad mood; a tantrum. □□ **moodily** *adv.* **moodiness** *n.* [OE *mōdig* brave (as MOOD[1])]

▪ *adj.* fickle, volatile, capricious, mercurial, unstable, fitful, flighty, unsteady, changeable, erratic, inconstant, undependable, unreliable, unpredictable, *Sc.* kittle; testy, crotchety, short-tempered, abrupt, short, curt, impatient, crabby, crusty, huffy, huffish, crabbed, cantankerous, curmudgeonly, ill-humoured, ill-tempered, cranky, petulant, waspish, temperamental, snappish, snappy, irritable, peevish, touchy; sullen, gloomy, glum, moping, mopy, mopish, sulky, sulking, morose, brooding, broody, dour, cheerless, dismal, lugubrious, saturnine. ● *n.* see TEMPER *n.* 2b.

Moog /mo͞og/ *n.* (in full **Moog synthesizer**) *propr.* an electronic instrument with a keyboard, for producing a wide variety of musical sounds: see SYNTHESIZER. [R. A. *Moog*, Amer. engineer b. 1934, who invented it]

moolah /mo͞olə/ *n. sl.* money. [20th c.: orig. unkn.]

moolvi /mo͞olvi/ *n.* (also **moolvie**) **1** a Muslim doctor of the law. **2** a learned person or teacher (esp. as a term of respect among Muslims in India). [Urdu *mulvī* f. Arab. *mawlawīy* judicial: cf. MULLAH]

moon /mo͞on/ *n.* & *v.* ● *n.* **1 a** the natural satellite of the earth, orbiting it monthly, illuminated by the sun and reflecting some light to the earth. **b** this regarded in terms of its waxing and waning in a particular month (*new moon*). **c** the moon when visible (*there is no moon tonight*). **2** a satellite of any planet. **3** (prec. by *the*) something desirable but unattainable (*promised them the moon*). **4** *poet.* a month. ● *v.* **1** *intr.* (often foll. by *about, around*, etc.) move or look listlessly. **2** *tr.* (foll. by *away*) spend (time) in a listless manner. **3** *intr.* (foll. by *over*) act aimlessly or inattentively from infatuation for (a person). □ **moon boot** a thickly-padded boot designed for low temperatures. **moon-faced** having a round face. **over the moon** extremely happy or delighted. □□ **moonless** *adj.* [OE *mōna* f. Gmc, rel. to MONTH]

▪ □ **over the moon** see OVERJOYED.

moonbeam /mo͞onbeem/ *n.* a ray of moonlight.

mooncalf /mo͞onkaaf/ *n.* a born fool.

▪ see FOOL[1] *n.* 1.

moonfish /mo͞onfish/ *n.* = OPAH.

Moonie /mo͞oni/ *n. sl.* a member of the Unification Church. [Sun Myung *Moon*, its founder]

moonlight /mo͞onlīt/ *n.* & *v.* ● *n.* **1** the light of the moon. **2** (*attrib.*) lighted by the moon. ● *v.intr.* (**-lighted**) *colloq.* have two paid occupations, esp. one by day and one by night. □ **moonlight flit** a hurried departure by night, esp. to avoid paying a debt. □□ **moonlighter** *n.*

▪ **1** see LIGHT[1] *n.* 2.

moonlit /mo͞onlit/ *adj.* lighted by the moon.

moonquake /mo͞onkwayk/ *n.* a tremor of the moon's surface.

moonrise /mo͞onrīz/ *n.* **1** the rising of the moon. **2** the time of this.

moonscape /mo͞onskayp/ *n.* **1** the surface or landscape of the moon. **2** an area resembling this; a wasteland.

moonset /mo͞onset/ *n.* **1** the setting of the moon. **2** the time of this.

moonshee /mo͞onshee/ *n.* (also **munshi**) a secretary or language-teacher in India. [Urdu *munshī* f. Arab. *munšī* writer]

moonshine /mo͞onshīn/ *n.* **1** foolish or unrealistic talk or ideas. **2** *sl.* illicitly distilled or smuggled alcoholic liquor. **3** moonlight.

▪ **1** (stuff and) nonsense, rubbish, humbug, drivel, twaddle, balderdash, blather, claptrap, garbage, *colloq.* taradiddle, hogwash, malarkey, piffle, tripe, tosh, line, razzmatazz, *sl.* hot air, bosh, gas, eyewash, bunk, guff, bilge, (tommy-)rot, bull, hooey, *esp. US sl.* hokum, jive. **2** *Ir.* poteen, *US colloq.* hooch. **3** moonlight, moonbeams.

moonshiner /mo͞onshīnər/ *n. US sl.* an illicit distiller or smuggler of alcoholic liquor.

moonshot /mo͞onshot/ *n.* the launching of a spacecraft to the moon.

moonstone /mo͞onstōn/ *n.* feldspar of pearly appearance.

moonstruck /mo͞onstruk/ *adj.* mentally deranged.

moony /mo͞oni/ *adj.* (**moonier, mooniest**) **1** listless; stupidly dreamy. **2** of or like the moon.

Moor /moor, mor/ *n.* a member of a Muslim people of mixed Berber and Arab descent, inhabiting NW Africa. [ME f. OF *More* f. L *Maurus* f. Gk *Mauros* inhabitant of Mauretania, a region of N. Africa]

moor[1] /moor, mor/ *n.* **1** a tract of open uncultivated upland, esp. when covered with heather. **2** a tract of ground preserved for shooting. **3** *US* a fen. □□ **moorish** *adj.* **moory** *adj.* [OE *mōr* waste land, marsh, mountain, f. Gmc]

▪ **1** heath, moorland, wasteland, *N.Engl.* fell. **3** fen, marsh.

moor[2] /moor, mor/ *v.* **1** *tr.* make fast (a boat, buoy, etc.) by attaching a cable etc. to a fixed object. **2** *intr.* (of a boat) be moored. □□ **moorage** *n.* [ME *more*, prob. f. LG or MLG *mōren*]

▪ secure, tie up, make fast, dock, berth, anchor; fix.

moorcock /moorkok, mór-/ *n.* a male moorfowl.

moorfowl /moorfowl, mór-/ *n.* a red grouse.

moorhen /moorhen, mór-/ *n.* **1** a small aquatic bird, *Gallinula chloropus*, with long legs and a short red-yellow bill. **2** a female moorfowl.

mooring /mooring, mór-/ *n.* **1 a** a fixed object to which a boat, buoy, etc., is moored. **b** (often in *pl.*) a place where a boat etc. is moored. **2** (in *pl.*) a set of permanent anchors and chains laid down for ships to be moored to.

▪ **1a, 2** anchor, sheet anchor.

Moorish /moorish, mór-/ *adj.* of or relating to the Moors. □ **Moorish idol** a brightly-coloured Pacific fish of the genus *Zanclus*.

moorland /moorlənd, mór-/ *n.* an extensive area of moor.

▪ see PLAIN[1] *n.*

moose /mo͞oss/ *n.* (*pl.* same) a N. American deer; an elk. [Narragansett *moos*]

moot /mo͞ot/ *adj.*, *v.*, & *n.* ● *adj.* (orig. the noun used *attrib.*) **1** debatable, undecided (*a moot point*). **2** *US Law* having no practical significance. ● *v.tr.* raise (a question) for discussion. ● *n.* **1** *hist.* an assembly. **2** *Law* a discussion of a hypothetical case as an academic exercise. [OE *mōt*, and *mōtian* converse, f. Gmc, rel. to MEET[1]]

▪ *adj.* **1** debatable, arguable, undecided, undetermined, controversial, doubtful, disputable, open to debate, at issue, indefinite, problematic(al), questionable, open (to question *or* to discussion), contestable, unsettled, unresolved, (up) in the air, unconcluded. ● *v.* raise, bring up *or* forward, introduce, broach, put forward, proffer, posit, propound, advance, submit, suggest.

mop[1] /mop/ *n.* & *v.* ● *n.* **1** a wad or bundle of cotton or synthetic material fastened to the end of a stick, for cleaning floors etc. **2** a similarly-shaped large or small implement for various purposes. **3** anything resembling a mop, esp. a thick mass of hair. **4** an act of mopping or being mopped (*gave it a mop*). ● *v.tr.* (**mopped, mopping**) **1** wipe or clean with or as with a mop. **2 a** wipe tears or sweat etc. from (one's face or brow etc.). **b** wipe away (tears etc.). □ **mop up 1** wipe up with or as with a mop. **2** *colloq.* absorb (profits etc.). **3** dispatch; make an end of. **4** *Mil.* **a** complete the occupation of (a district etc.) by capturing or killing enemy troops left there. **b** capture or kill (stragglers). □□ **moppy** *adj.* [ME *mappe*, perh. ult. rel. to L *mappa* napkin]

▪ *n.* **4** see WIPE *n.* ● *v.* see WIPE *v.* 1.

mop[2] /mop/ *n. Brit. hist.* an autumn fair or gathering at which farm-hands and servants were formerly hired. [perh. = *mop-fair*, at which a mop was carried by a maidservant seeking employment]

mope /mōp/ *v.* & *n.* ● *v.intr.* be gloomily depressed or listless; behave sulkily. ● *n.* **1** a person who mopes. **2** (**the mopes**) low spirits. ▫▫ **moper** *n.* **mopish** *adj.* **mopy** *adj.* (**mopier, mopiest**). **mopily** *adv.* **mopiness** *n.* [16th c.: prob. rel. to *mope, mopp(e)* fool]
■ *v.* see SULK *v.* ▫▫ **mopy** see MOODY *adj.*

moped /mṓped/ *n.* a motorized bicycle with an engine capacity below 50 cc. [Sw. (as MOTOR, PEDAL[1])]

mophead /móp-hed/ *n.* a person with thick matted hair.

mopoke /mṓpōk/ *n.* (also **morepork** /máwpawk/) **1** a boobook. **2** an Australian nocturnal insect-eating bird, *Podargus strigoides.* Also called FROGMOUTH. [imit. of the bird's cry]

moppet /móppit/ *n. colloq.* (esp. as a term of endearment) a baby or small child. [obs. *moppe* baby, doll]

moquette /mokét/ *n.* a thick pile or looped material used for carpets and upholstery. [F, perh. f. obs. It. *mocaiardo* mohair]

mor /mor/ *n.* humus formed under acid conditions. [Da.]

moraine /məráyn/ *n.* an area covered by rocks and debris carried down and deposited by a glacier. ▫▫ **morainal** *adj.* **morainic** *adj.* [F f. It. dial. *morena* f. F dial. *mor(re)* snout f. Rmc]

moral /mórrəl/ *adj.* & *n.* ● *adj.* **1 a** concerned with goodness or badness of human character or behaviour, or with the distinction between right and wrong. **b** concerned with accepted rules and standards of human behaviour. **2 a** conforming to accepted standards of general conduct. **b** capable of moral action (*man is a moral agent*). **3** (of rights or duties etc.) founded on moral law. **4 a** concerned with morals or ethics (*moral philosophy*). **b** (of a literary work etc.) dealing with moral conduct. **5** concerned with or leading to a psychological effect associated with confidence in a right action (*moral courage; moral support; moral victory*). ● *n.* **1 a** a moral lesson (esp. at the end) of a fable, story, event, etc. **b** a moral maxim or principle. **2** (in *pl.*) moral behaviour, e.g. in sexual conduct. ▫ **moral certainty** probability so great as to allow no reasonable doubt. **moral law** the conditions to be satisfied by any right course of action. **moral majority** the majority of people, regarded as favouring firm moral standards (orig. *Moral Majority*, name of a right-wing US movement). **moral philosophy** the branch of philosophy concerned with ethics. **moral pressure** persuasion by appealing to a person's moral sense. **Moral Re-Armament 1** = OXFORD GROUP. **2** the beliefs of this organization, esp. as applied to international relations. **moral science** systematic knowledge as applied to morals. **moral sense** the ability to distinguish right and wrong. ▫▫ **morally** *adv.* [ME f. L *moralis* f. *mos moris* custom, pl. *mores* morals]
■ *adj.* **1, 4** ethical; moralizing, moralistic, deontic, prescriptive. **2** ethical, right, good, pure, honest, proper, upright, honourable, decent, respectable, high-minded, virtuous, upstanding, righteous, principled, scrupulous, incorruptible, noble, just. ● *n.* **1** lesson, homily, teaching, point, message; aphorism, maxim, precept, apophthegm, adage, saw, proverb, motto, slogan. **2** (*morals*) behaviour, conduct, mores, beliefs, habits, customs, practices, principles, scruples, ethics, ideals, standards; probity, morality, rectitude, integrity.

morale /məraál/ *n.* the mental attitude or bearing of a person or group, esp. as regards confidence, discipline, etc. [F *moral* respelt to preserve the pronunciation]
■ dedication, spirit(s), unity, *esprit de corps*; disposition, attitude, confidence, self-confidence, self-esteem.

moralism /mórrəliz'm/ *n.* **1** a natural system of morality. **2** religion regarded as moral practice.

moralist /mórrəlist/ *n.* **1** a person who practises or teaches morality. **2** a person who follows a natural system of ethics. ▫▫ **moralistic** /-lístik/ *adj.* **moralistically** /-lístikəli/ *adv.*
■ see PURITAN *n.*

morality /mərálliti/ *n.* (*pl.* **-ies**) **1** the degree of conformity of an idea, practice, etc., to moral principles. **2** right moral conduct. **3** a lesson in morals. **4** the science of morals. **5** a particular system of morals (*commercial morality*). **6** (in *pl.*) moral principles; points of ethics. **7** (in full **morality play**) *hist.* a kind of drama with personified abstract qualities as the main characters and inculcating a moral lesson, popular in the 16th c. [ME f. OF *moralité* or LL *moralitas* f. L (as MORAL)]
■ **1, 2, 6** ethics, morals, principle(s), mores, standards, ideals; honesty, right, rightness, righteousness, rectitude, integrity, propriety, justice, fair play, fairness, decency, probity, uprightness. **5** behaviour, conduct, habit(s), custom(s), mores, attitude; see also ETIQUETTE.

moralize /mórrəlīz/ *v.* (also **-ise**) **1** *intr.* (often foll. by *on*) indulge in moral reflection or talk. **2** *tr.* interpret morally; point the moral of. **3** *tr.* make moral or more moral. ▫▫ **moralization** /-záysh'n/ *n.* **moralizer** *n.* **moralizingly** *adv.* [F *moraliser* or med.L *moralizare* f. L (as MORAL)]
■ **1** see PREACH 2.

morass /mərás/ *n.* **1** an entanglement; a disordered situation, esp. one impeding progress. **2** *literary* a bog or marsh. [Du. *moeras* (assim. to *moer* MOOR[1]) f. MDu. *marasch* f. OF *marais* marsh f. med.L *mariscus*]
■ **1** entanglement, confusion, muddle, mess, quagmire, tangle. **2** bog, marsh, swamp, fen, quag, mire, quagmire, slough, marshland, quicksand, *Sc.* & *N.Engl.* moss.

moratorium /mórrətóriəm/ *n.* (*pl.* **moratoriums** or **moratoria** /-riə/) **1** (often foll. by *on*) a temporary prohibition or suspension (of an activity). **2 a** a legal authorization to debtors to postpone payment. **b** the period of this postponement. [mod.L, neut. of LL *moratorius* delaying f. L *morari morat-* to delay f. *mora* delay]
■ **1** halt, prohibition, freeze, suspension, stay, postponement, delay, waiting-period, respite, hiatus.

Moravian /mərάyviən/ *n.* & *adj.* ● *n.* **1** a native of Moravia, now part of the Czech Republic. **2** a member of a Protestant sect founded in Saxony by emigrants from Moravia, holding views derived from the Hussites and accepting the Bible as the only source of faith. ● *adj.* of, relating to, or characteristic of Moravia or its people.

moray /moráy/ *n.* any tropical eel-like fish of the family Muraenidae, esp. *Muraena helena* found in Mediterranean waters. [Port. *moreia* f. L f. Gk *muraina*]

morbid /mórbid/ *adj.* **1 a** (of the mind, ideas, etc.) unwholesome, sickly; macabre. **b** given to morbid feelings. **2** *colloq.* melancholy. **3** *Med.* of the nature of or indicative of disease. ▫ **morbid anatomy** the anatomy of diseased organs, tissues, etc. ▫▫ **morbidity** /-bídditi/ *n.* **morbidly** *adv.* **morbidness** *n.* [L *morbidus* f. *morbus* disease]
■ **1 a** unhealthy, unwholesome, disordered, unsound, sick, sickly; grim, ghoulish, macabre, monstrous, ghastly, grotesque, grisly, gruesome. **2** gloomy, lugubrious, glum, morose, sombre, blue, sad, despondent, depressed, dejected, downcast; see also MELANCHOLY *adj.*

morbific /morbíffik/ *adj.* causing disease. [F *morbifique* or mod.L *morbificus* f. L *morbus* disease]

morbilli /morbílli/ *n.pl.* **1** measles. **2** the spots characteristic of measles. [L, pl. of *morbillus* pustule f. *morbus* disease]

mordant /mórd'nt/ *adj.* & *n.* ● *adj.* **1** (of sarcasm etc.) caustic, biting. **2** pungent, smarting. **3** corrosive or cleansing. **4** (of a substance) serving to fix colouring-matter or gold leaf on another substance. ● *n.* a mordant substance (in senses 3, 4 of *adj.*). ▫▫ **mordancy** *n.* **mordantly** *adv.* [ME f. F, part. of *mordre* bite f. L *mordēre*]
■ **1** see BITING 2.

mordent /mórd'nt/ *n. Mus.* **1** an ornament consisting of one rapid alternation of a written note with the note immediately below it. **2** a pralltriller. [G f. It. *mordente* part. of *mordēre* bite]

more /mor/ *adj., n.,* & *adv.* ● *adj.* **1** existing in a greater or additional quantity, amount, or degree (*more problems than last time; bring some more water*). **2** greater in degree (*more's the pity; the more fool you*). ● *n.* a greater quantity, number, or amount (*more than three people; more to it than meets the eye*). ● *adv.* **1** in a greater degree (*do it more carefully*). **2** to

a greater extent (*people like to walk more these days*). **3** forming the comparative of adjectives and adverbs, esp. those of more than one syllable (*more absurd*; *more easily*). **4** again (*once more*; *never more*). **5** moreover. □ **more and more** in an increasing degree. **more like it** see LIKE[1]. **more of** to a greater extent (*more of a poet than a musician*). **more or less 1** in a greater or less degree. **2** approximately; as an estimate. **more so** of the same kind to a greater degree. [OE *māra* f. Gmc]
■ □ **more or less 1** see SOMEWHAT *adv*. **2** see *approximately* (APPROXIMATE).

moreen /moreen/ *n*. a strong ribbed woollen or cotton material for curtains etc. [perh. fanciful f. MOIRE]

moreish /mórish/ *adj*. (also **morish**) *colloq*. pleasant to eat, causing a desire for more.

morel[1] /mərél/ *n*. an edible fungus, *Morchella esculenta*, with ridged mushroom caps. [F *morille* f. Du. *morilje*]

morel[2] /mərél/ *n*. nightshade. [ME f. OF *morele* fem. of *morel* dark brown ult. f. L *Maurus* MOOR]

morello /mərélō/ *n*. (*pl*. **-os**) a sour kind of dark cherry. [It. *morello* blackish f. med.L *morellus* f. L (as MOREL[1])]

moreover /mórṓvər/ *adv*. (introducing or accompanying a new statement) further, besides.
■ furthermore, further, besides, not only that, more than that, what is more; to boot, into the bargain, in addition, additionally, as well, also, too, *archaic* withal.

morepork var. of MOPOKE.

mores /mórayz, -reez/ *n.pl*. customs or conventions regarded as essential to or characteristic of a community. [L, pl. of *mos* custom]
■ see CULTURE *n*. 2.

Moresco var. of MORISCO.

Moresque /morésk/ *adj*. (of art or architecture) Moorish in style or design. [F f. It. *moresco* f. *Moro* MOOR]

morganatic /mórgənáttik/ *adj*. **1** (of a marriage) between a person of high rank and another of lower rank, the spouse and children having no claim to the possessions or title of the person of higher rank. **2** (of a wife) married in this way. □□ **morganatically** *adv*. [F *morganatique* or G *morganatisch* f. med.L *matrimonium ad morganaticam* 'marriage with a morning gift', the husband's gift to the wife after consummation being his only obligation in such a marriage]

morgue /morg/ *n*. **1** a mortuary. **2** (in a newspaper office) a room or file of miscellaneous information, esp. for future obituaries. [F, orig. the name of a Paris mortuary]

moribund /mórribund/ *adj*. **1** at the point of death. **2** lacking vitality. **3** on the decline, stagnant. □□ **moribundity** /-búnditi/ *n*. [L *moribundus* f. *mori* die]
■ **1** dying, *in extremis*, at death's door, failing, fading, with one foot in the grave, half-dead, breathing one's last, expiring, on one's last legs, on one's deathbed, on the way out. **2** see LIFELESS 1, 3. **3** declining, obsolescent, weak, waning, on the wane *or* decline, dying out; stagnating, stagnant.

Morisco /məriskō/ *n*. & *adj*. (also **Moresco** /-réskō/) ● *n*. (*pl*. **-os** or **-oes**) **1** a Moor, esp. in Spain. **2** a morris dance. ● *adj*. Moorish. [Sp. f. *Moro* MOOR]

morish var. of MOREISH.

Mormon /mórmən/ *n*. a member of the Church of Jesus Christ of Latter-Day Saints, a millenary religion founded in 1830 by Joseph Smith on the basis of revelations in the Book of Mormon. □□ **Mormonism** *n*.

morn /morn/ *n*. *poet*. morning. [OE *morgen* f. Gmc]

mornay /mórnay/ *n*. a cheese-flavoured white sauce. [20th c.: orig. uncert.]

morning /mórning/ *n*. & *int*. ● *n*. **1** the early part of the day, esp. from sunrise to noon (*this morning*; *during the morning*; *morning coffee*). **2** this time spent in a particular way (*had a busy morning*). **3** sunrise, daybreak. **4** a time compared with the morning, esp. the early part of one's life etc. ● *int*. = *good morning* (see GOOD *adj*. 14). □ **in the morning 1** during or in the course of the morning. **2** *colloq*. tomorrow. **morning after** *colloq*. a hangover. **morning-after pill** a contraceptive pill effective when taken some hours after intercourse. **morning coat** a coat with tails, and with the front cut away below the waist. **morning dress** a man's morning coat and striped trousers. **morning glory** any of various twining plants of the genus *Ipomoea*, with trumpet-shaped flowers. **morning-room** a sitting-room for the morning. **morning sickness** nausea felt in the morning in pregnancy. **morning star** a planet or bright star, usu. Venus, seen in the east before sunrise. **morning watch** *Naut*. the 4–8 a.m. watch. [ME *mor(we)ning* f. *morwen* MORN + -ING[1] after *evening*]
■ *n*. **1, 2** a.m., *Naut. or Law or archaic* forenoon, *poet*. morn. **3** dawn, daybreak, sunrise, cock crow, *esp. US* sun-up.

Moro /mórō/ *n*. (*pl*. **-os**) a Muslim living in the Philippines. [Sp., = MOOR]

Moroccan /mərókkən/ *n*. & *adj*. ● *n*. **1** a native or national of Morocco in N. Africa. **2** a person of Moroccan descent. ● *adj*. of or relating to Morocco.

morocco /mərókkō/ *n*. (*pl*. **-os**) **1** a fine flexible leather made (orig. in Morocco) from goatskins tanned with sumac, used esp. in bookbinding and shoemaking. **2** an imitation of this in grained calf etc.

moron /móron/ *n*. **1** *colloq*. a very stupid or foolish person. **2** an adult with a mental age of about 8–12. □□ **moronic** /mərónnik/ *adj*. **moronically** /mərónnikəli/ *adv*. **moronism** *n*. [Gk *mōron*, neut. of *mōros* foolish]
■ **1** see FOOL[1] *n*. 1.

morose /mərṓss/ *adj*. sullen and ill-tempered. □□ **morosely** *adv*. **moroseness** *n*. [L *morosus* peevish etc. f. *mos moris* manner]
■ see SULLEN *adj*. 1.

morph /morf/ *n*. = ALLOMORPH. [back-form.]

morpheme /mórfeem/ *n*. *Linguistics* **1** a morphological element considered in respect of its functional relations in a linguistic system. **2** a meaningful morphological unit of a language that cannot be further divided (e.g. *in*, *come*, *-ing*, forming *incoming*). □□ **morphemic** /-féemik/ *adj*. **morphemically** /-féemikəli/ *adv*. [F *morphème* f. Gk *morphē* form, after PHONEME]

morphemics /morféemiks/ *n.pl*. (usu. treated as *sing*.) *Linguistics* the study of word structure.

morphia /mórfiə/ *n*. (in general use) = MORPHINE.

morphine /mórfeen/ *n*. an analgesic and narcotic drug obtained from opium and used medicinally to relieve pain. □□ **morphinism** /-finiz'm/ *n*. [G *Morphin* & mod.L *morphia* f. *Morpheus* god of sleep]

morphing /mórfing/ *n*. a computer graphics technique used in film-making, whereby an image is apparently transformed into another by a smooth progression; the act or process of changing one image into another using this technique. [shortened f. METAMORPHOSIS + -ING[1]]

morphogenesis /mórfəjénnisiss/ *n*. *Biol*. the development of form in organisms. □□ **morphogenetic** /-jinéttik/ *adj*. **morphogenic** *adj*. [mod.L f. Gk *morphē* form + GENESIS]

morphology /morfólləji/ *n*. the study of the forms of things, esp.: **1** *Biol*. the study of the forms of organisms. **2** *Philol*. **a** the study of the forms of words. **b** the system of forms in a language. □□ **morphological** /mórfəlójik'l/ *adj*. **morphologically** /-fəlójikəli/ *adv*. **morphologist** *n*. [Gk *morphē* form + -LOGY]

Morris chair /mórriss/ *n*. a type of plain easy chair with an adjustable back. [William *Morris*, Engl. poet and craftsman d. 1896]

morris dance /mórriss/ *n*. a traditional English dance by groups of people in fancy costume, usu. as characters in legend, with ribbons and bells. □□ **morris dancer** *n*. **morris dancing** *n*. [*morys*, var. of MOORISH]

morrow /mórrō/ *n*. (usu. prec. by *the*) *literary* **1** the following day. **2** the time following an event. [ME *morwe*, *moru* (as MORN)]

Morse /morss/ *n*. & *v*. ● *n*. (in full **Morse code**) an alphabet or code in which letters are represented by combinations of long and short light or sound signals. ● *v.tr.* & *intr.* signal by Morse code. [S. F. B. *Morse*, Amer. electrician d. 1872, who devised it]

morsel /mórs'l/ *n.* a mouthful; a small piece (esp. of food). [ME f. OF, dimin. of *mors* a bite f. *mordēre mors-* to bite]
■ mouthful, bite, gobbet, spoonful, taste, sample, nibble, bit, drop, dollop, soupçon; crumb, fragment, scrap, sliver, splinter, shard, shred, particle, atom, speck, whit, fraction, grain, granule, pinch, piece, *colloq.* smidgen, *US* & *Austral. colloq.* skerrick.

mort /mort/ *n. Hunting* a note sounded when the quarry is killed. [ME f. OF f. L *mors mortis* death]

mortadella /mórtədéllə/ *n.* (*pl.* **mortadelle** /-délle/) a large spiced pork sausage. [It. dimin., irreg. f. L *murtatum* seasoned with myrtle berries]

mortal /mórt'l/ *adj.* & *n.* ● *adj.* **1 a** (of a living being, esp. a human) subject to death. **b** (of material or earthly existence) temporal, ephemeral. **2** (often foll. by *to*) causing death; fatal. **3** (of a battle) fought to the death. **4** associated with death (*mortal agony*). **5** (of an enemy) implacable. **6** (of pain, fear, an affront, etc.) intense, very serious. **7** *colloq.* **a** very great (*in a mortal hurry*). **b** long and tedious (*for two mortal hours*). **8** *colloq.* conceivable, imaginable (*every mortal thing*; *of no mortal use*). ● *n.* **1** a mortal being, esp. a human. **2** *joc.* a person described in some specified way (*a thirsty mortal*). □ **mortal sin** *Theol.* a grave sin that is regarded as depriving the soul of divine grace. □□ **mortally** *adv.* [ME f. OF *mortal*, *mortel* or L *mortalis* f. *mors mortis* death]
■ *adj.* **1** human; physical, bodily, corporeal, corporal, fleshly, earthly, worldly, perishable; transitory, temporal, transient, ephemeral. **2** deadly, fatal, lethal, terminal. **5** relentless, implacable, unrelenting, bitter, deadly, unappeasable. **6** abject, extreme, awful, great, enormous, intense, terrible, inordinate, dire, serious. ● *n.* human (being), man, woman, person, soul, individual, creature.

mortality /mortálliti/ *n.* (*pl.* **-ies**) **1** the state of being subject to death. **2** loss of life on a large scale. **3 a** the number of deaths in a given period etc. **b** (in full **mortality rate**) a death rate. [ME f. OF *mortalité* f. L *mortalitas -tatis* (as MORTAL)]

mortar /mórtər/ *n.* & *v.* ● *n.* **1** a mixture of lime with cement, sand, and water, used in building to bond bricks or stones. **2** a short large-bore cannon for firing shells at high angles. **3** a contrivance for firing a lifeline or firework. **4** a vessel made of hard material, in which ingredients are pounded with a pestle. ● *v.tr.* **1** plaster or join with mortar. **2** attack or bombard with mortar shells. □□ **mortarless** *adj.* (in sense 1). **mortary** *adj.* (in sense 1). [ME f. AF *morter*, OF *mortier* f. L *mortarium*: partly from LG]
■ *n.* **1** see CEMENT *n.*

mortarboard /mórtərbord/ *n.* **1** an academic cap with a stiff flat square top. **2** a flat board with a handle on the under-surface, for holding mortar in bricklaying etc.

mortgage /mórgij/ *n.* & *v.* ● *n.* **1 a** a conveyance of property by a debtor to a creditor as security for a debt (esp. one incurred by the purchase of the property), on the condition that it shall be returned on payment of the debt within a certain period. **b** a deed effecting this. **2 a** a debt secured by a mortgage. **b** a loan resulting in such a debt. ● *v.tr.* **1** convey (a property) by mortgage. **2** (often foll. by *to*) pledge (oneself, one's powers, etc.). □ **mortgage rate** the rate of interest charged by a mortgagee. □□ **mortgageable** *adj.* [ME f. OF, = dead pledge f. *mort* f. L *mortuus* dead + *gage* GAGE[1]]
■ *n.* **2** see LOAN[1] *n.* ● *v.* see PAWN[2] *v.*

mortgagee /mórgijeé/ *n.* the creditor in a mortgage, usu. a bank or building society.

mortgager /mórgijər/ *n.* (also **mortgagor** /-jór/) the debtor in a mortgage.

mortice var. of MORTISE.

mortician /mortísh'n/ *n. US* an undertaker; a manager of funerals. [L *mors mortis* death + -ICIAN]
■ see UNDERTAKER.

mortify /mórtifī/ *v.* (**-ies, -ied**) **1** *tr.* **a** cause (a person) to feel shamed or humiliated. **b** wound (a person's feelings). **2** *tr.* bring (the body, the flesh, the passions, etc.) into subjection by self-denial or discipline. **3** *intr.* (of flesh) be affected by gangrene or necrosis. □□ **mortification** /-fikáysh'n/ *n.* **mortifying** *adj.* **mortifyingly** *adv.* [ME f. OF *mortifier* f. eccl.L *mortificare* kill, subdue f. *mors mortis* death]
■ **1** humiliate, shame, humble, embarrass, abash, chagrin, rebuff, crush, wound, discomfit, deflate, bring down, degrade, chasten, subdue, suppress, make a person eat humble pie, *colloq.* put down. **2** punish, castigate, discipline, control, subdue, subjugate. **3** gangrene, fester, putrefy, rot, decompose, decay, *Med.* & *Physiol.* necrose.

mortise /mórtiss/ *n.* & *v.* (also **mortice**) ● *n.* a hole in a framework designed to receive the end of another part, esp. a tenon. ● *v.tr.* **1** join securely, esp. by mortise and tenon. **2** cut a mortise in. □ **mortise lock** a lock recessed into a mortise in the frame of a door or window etc. [ME f. OF *mortoise* f. Arab. *murtazz* fixed in]

mortmain /mórtmayn/ *n. Law* **1** the status of lands or tenements held inalienably by an ecclesiastical or other corporation. **2** the land or tenements themselves. [ME f. AF, OF *mortemain* f. med.L *mortua manus* dead hand, prob. in allusion to impersonal ownership]

mortuary /mórtyoori/ *n.* & *adj.* ● *n.* (*pl.* **-ies**) a room or building in which dead bodies may be kept until burial or cremation. ● *adj.* of or concerning death or burial. [ME f. AF *mortuarie* f. med.L *mortuarium* f. L *mortuarius* f. *mortuus* dead]

morula /móroolə/ *n.* (*pl.* **morulae** /-lee/) a fully segmented ovum from which a blastula is formed. [mod.L, dimin. of L *morum* mulberry]

morwong /mórwong/ *n.* any of various fish of the family Cheilodactylidae, native to Australasia, used as food. [Aboriginal]

Mosaic /mōzáyik/ *adj.* of or associated with Moses (in the Hebrew Bible). □ **Mosaic Law** the laws attributed to Moses and listed in the Pentateuch. [F *mosaïque* or mod.L *Mosaicus* f. *Moses* f. Heb. *Mōšeh*]

mosaic /mōzáyik/ *n.* & *v.* ● *n.* **1 a** a picture or pattern produced by an arrangement of small variously coloured pieces of glass or stone etc. **b** work of this kind as an art form. **2** a diversified thing. **3** an arrangement of photosensitive elements in a television camera. **4** *Biol.* a chimera. **5** (in full **mosaic disease**) a virus disease causing leaf-mottling in plants, esp. tobacco, maize, and sugar cane. **6** (*attrib.*) **a** of or like a mosaic. **b** diversified. ● *v.tr.* (**mosaicked, mosaicking**) **1** adorn with mosaics. **2** combine into or as into a mosaic. □ **mosaic gold 1** tin disulphide. **2** an alloy of copper and zinc used in cheap jewellery etc. □□ **mosaicist** /-záyisist/ *n.* [ME f. F *mosaïque* f. It. *mosaico* f. med.L *mosaicus*, *musaicus* f. Gk *mous(e)ion* mosaic work f. *mousa* MUSE[1]]

mosasaurus /mṓsəsáwrəss/ *n.* any large extinct marine reptile of the genus *Mosasaurus*, with a long slender body and flipper-like limbs. [mod.L f. *Mosa* river Meuse (near which it was first discovered) + Gk *sauros* lizard]

moschatel /móskətél/ *n.* a small plant, *Adoxa moschatellina*, with pale-green flowers and a musky smell. [F *moscatelle* f. It. *moscatella* f. *moscato* musk]

moselle /mōzél/ *n.* a light medium-dry white wine produced in the valley of the river Moselle in Germany.

mosey /mṓzi/ *v.intr.* (**-eys, -eyed**) (often foll. by *along*) *sl.* walk in a leisurely or aimless manner. [19th c.: orig. unkn.]
■ see STROLL *v.*

moshav /mōsháav/ *n.* (*pl.* **moshavim**) a cooperative association of Israeli smallholders. [Heb. *mōšāḇ*, lit. 'dwelling']

Moslem var. of MUSLIM.

mosque /mosk/ *n.* a Muslim place of worship. [F *mosquée* f. It. *moschea* f. Arab. *masjid*]

■ see TEMPLE[1].

mosquito /moskéétō/ *n.* (*pl.* **-oes**) any of various slender biting insects, esp. of the genus *Culex*, *Anopheles*, or *Aedes*, the female of which punctures the skin of humans and other animals with a long proboscis to suck their blood and transmits diseases such as filariasis and malaria. □ **mosquito-boat** *US* a motor torpedo-boat. **mosquito-net** a net to keep off mosquitoes. [Sp. & Port., dimin. of *mosca* f. L *musca* fly]

moss /moss/ *n.* & *v.* ● *n.* **1** any small cryptogamous plant of the class Musci, growing in dense clusters on the surface of the ground, in bogs, on trees, stones, etc. **2** *Sc.* & *N.Engl.* a bog, esp. a peatbog. ● *v.tr.* cover with moss. □ **moss agate** agate with mosslike dendritic markings. **moss-grown** overgrown with moss. **moss-hag** *Sc.* broken ground from which peat has been taken. **moss-stitch** alternate plain and purl in knitting. □□ **mosslike** *adj.* [OE *mos* bog, moss f. Gmc]

■ *n.* **2** see SWAMP *n.*

mossie /mózzi/ *n.* esp. *Austral. sl.* = MOSQUITO.

mosso /móssō/ *adv.* *Mus.* with animation or speed. [It., past part. of *muovere* move]

mosstrooper /móstrōōpər/ *n.* a freebooter of the Scottish Border in the 17th c.

mossy /móssi/ *adj.* (**mossier, mossiest**) **1** covered in or resembling moss. **2** *US sl.* antiquated, old-fashioned. □□ **mossiness** *n.*

most /mōst/ *adj.*, *n.*, & *adv.* ● *adj.* **1** existing in the greatest quantity or degree (*you have made most mistakes*; *see who can make the most noise*). **2** the majority of; nearly all of (*most people think so*). ● *n.* **1** the greatest quantity or number (*this is the most I can do*). **2** (**the most**) *sl.* the best of all. **3** the majority (*most of them are missing*). ● *adv.* **1** in the highest degree (*this is most interesting*; *what most annoys me*). **2** forming the superlative of adjectives and adverbs, esp. those of more than one syllable (*most certain*; *most easily*). **3** *US colloq.* almost. □ **at most** no more or better than (*this is at most a makeshift*). **at the most 1** as the greatest amount. **2** not more than. **for the most part 1** as regards the greater part. **2** usually. **make the most of 1** employ to the best advantage. **2** represent at its best or worst. **Most Honourable** a title given to marquises and to members of the Privy Council and the Order of the Bath. **Most Reverend** a title given to archbishops and to Roman Catholic bishops. [OE *māst* f. Gmc]

■ □ **at most** see JUST *adv.* 3, 4. **for the most part 2** see *usually* (USUAL).

-most /mōst/ *suffix* forming superlative adjectives and adverbs from prepositions and other words indicating relative position (*foremost*; *uttermost*). [OE *-mest* f. Gmc]

mostly /mōstli/ *adv.* **1** as regards the greater part. **2** usually.

■ **2** see *usually* (USUAL).

MOT *abbr.* **1** (in the UK) Ministry of Transport. **2** (in full **MOT test**) a compulsory annual test of motor vehicles of more than a specified age.

mot /mō/ *n.* (*pl.* ***mots*** *pronunc.* same) a witty saying. □ ***mot juste*** /zhōōst/ (*pl.* ***mots justes*** *pronunc.* same) the most appropriate expression. [F, = word, ult. f. L *muttum* uttered sound f. *muttire* murmur]

■ see EPIGRAM 3.

mote /mōt/ *n.* a speck of dust. [OE *mot*, corresp. to Du. *mot* dust, sawdust, of unkn. orig.]

■ see SPECK *n.* 2.

motel /mōtél/ *n.* a roadside hotel providing accommodation for motorists and parking for their vehicles. [portmanteau word f. MOTOR + HOTEL]

■ see HOTEL 1.

motet /mōtét/ *n.* *Mus.* a short sacred choral composition. [ME f. OF, dimin. of *mot*: see MOT]

moth /moth/ *n.* **1** any usu. nocturnal insect of the order Lepidoptera excluding butterflies, having a stout body and without clubbed antennae. **2** any small lepidopterous insect of the family Tineidae breeding in cloth etc., on which its larva feeds. □ **moth-eaten 1** damaged or destroyed by moths. **2** antiquated, time-worn. [OE *moththe*]

■ □□ **moth-eaten 2** see *time-worn*.

mothball /móthbawl/ *n.* & *v.* ● *n.* a ball of naphthalene etc. placed in stored clothes to keep away moths. ● *v.tr.* **1** place in mothballs. **2** leave unused. □ **in mothballs** stored unused for a considerable time.

■ *v.* **2** see TABLE *v.* 2.

mother /múthər/ *n.* & *v.* ● *n.* **1 a** a woman in relation to a child or children to whom she has given birth. **b** (in full **adoptive mother**) a woman who has continuous care of a child, esp. by adoption. **2** any female animal in relation to its offspring. **3** a quality or condition etc. that gives rise to another (*necessity is the mother of invention*). **4** (in full **Mother Superior**) the head of a female religious community. **5** *archaic* (esp. as a form of address) an elderly woman. **6** (*attrib.*) **a** designating an institution etc. regarded as having maternal authority (*Mother Church*; *mother earth*). **b** designating the main ship, spacecraft, etc., in a convoy or mission (*the mother craft*). ● *v.tr.* **1** give birth to; be the mother of. **2** protect as a mother. **3** give rise to; be the source of. **4** acknowledge or profess oneself the mother of. □ **Mother Carey's chicken** = *storm petrel* 1. **mother country** a country in relation to its colonies. **mother-figure** an older woman who is regarded as a source of nurture, support, etc. **Mother Goose rhyme** *US* a nursery rhyme. **mother-in-law** (*pl.* **mothers-in-law**) the mother of one's husband or wife. **mother-in-law's tongue** a plant, *Sansevieria trifasciata*, with long erect pointed leaves. **mother-lode** *Mining* the main vein of a system. **mother-naked** stark naked. **mother-of-pearl** a smooth iridescent substance forming the inner layer of the shell of some molluscs. **Mother's Day 1** *Brit.* = MOTHERING SUNDAY. **2** *US* an equivalent day on the second Sunday in May. **mother's ruin** *colloq.* gin. **mother's son** *colloq.* a man (*every mother's son of you*). **mother tongue 1** one's native language. **2** a language from which others have evolved. **mother wit** native wit; common sense. □□ **motherless** *adj.* **motherlessness** *n.* **motherlike** *adj.* & *adv.* [OE *mōdor* f. Gmc]

■ *n.* **1** parent, materfamilias, matriarch, mammy, *colloq.* ma, mam, mama, mamma, old lady, old woman, *Brit. colloq.* mummy, mum, *US colloq.* mom, mommy, *Brit. sl.* mater; nourisher, nurturer, nurse. **2** dam. **3** origin, genesis; see also SOURCE *n.* 1, 2. ● *v.* **1** give birth to, have, deliver, bear, bring forth *or* into the world, *US colloq.* birth, *derog.* whelp. **2** nurture, nourish, nurse, care for, look after, protect, shelter, watch over, take care of; pamper, baby, coddle, spoil, indulge, fuss over, overprotect. **3** see CAUSE *v.* 1.

mothercraft /múthərkraaft/ *n.* skill in or knowledge of looking after children as a mother.

motherhood /múthərhōōd/ *n.* **1** the condition or fact of being a mother. **2** (*attrib.*) *US* & *Austral.* (of an issue, report, etc.) protective, withholding the worst aspects.

Mothering Sunday /múthəring/ *n.* *Brit.* the fourth Sunday in Lent, traditionally a day for honouring mothers with gifts.

motherland /múthərland/ *n.* one's native country.

■ see COUNTRY 3.

motherly /múthərli/ *adj.* **1** like or characteristic of a mother in affection, care, etc. **2** of or relating to a mother. □□ **motherliness** *n.* [OE *mōdorlic* (as MOTHER)]

■ see MATERNAL 1, 2.

mothproof /móthprōōf/ *adj.* & *v.* ● *adj.* (of clothes) treated so as to repel moths. ● *v.tr.* treat (clothes) in this way.

mothy /móthi/ *adj.* (**mothier, mothiest**) infested with moths.

motif /mōtéef/ *n.* **1** a distinctive feature or dominant idea in artistic or literary composition. **2** *Mus.* = FIGURE *n.* 10. **3** an ornament of lace etc. sewn separately on a garment. **4** an ornament on a vehicle identifying the maker, model, etc. [F (as MOTIVE)]

■ **1** theme, idea, topic, subject, concept, leitmotif; pattern, figure, refrain, device, element, convention.

motile /mṓtīl/ *adj. Zool.* & *Bot.* capable of motion. ▫▫ **motility** /-tílliti/ *n.* [L *motus* motion (as MOVE)]

motion /mṓsh'n/ *n.* & *v.* ● *n.* **1** the act or process of moving or of changing position. **2** a particular manner of moving the body in walking etc. **3** a change of posture. **4** a gesture. **5** a formal proposal put to a committee, legislature, etc. **6** *Law* an application for a rule or order of court. **7 a** an evacuation of the bowels. **b** (in *sing.* or *pl.*) faeces. **8** a piece of moving mechanism. ● *v.* (often foll. by *to* + infin.) **1** *tr.* direct (a person) by a sign or gesture. **2** *intr.* (often foll. by *to* a person) make a gesture directing (*motioned to me to leave*). ▫ **go through the motions 1** make a pretence; do something perfunctorily or superficially. **2** simulate an action by gestures. **in motion** moving; not at rest. **motion picture** (often (with hyphen) *attrib.*) a film (see FILM *n.* 3) with the illusion of movement. **put** (or **set**) **in motion** set going or working. ▫▫ **motional** *adj.* **motionless** *adj.* [ME f. OF f. L *motio -onis* (as MOVE)]

■ *n.* **1** movement, moving, change, shift, shifting, action, going, travelling, travel, progress, passage, transit; activity, commotion, stir, agitation, turmoil, turbulence. **2** gait, bearing, carriage, tread, walk, step, pace. **4** gesture, gesticulation, signal, sign. **5** proposal, suggestion, proposition, recommendation, offering, submission. ● *v.* gesture, beckon, signal, wave; gesticulate, sign. ▫ **go through the motions 1** see PRETEND *v.* 2b. ▫▫ **motionless** see STILL[1] *adj.* 1.

motivate /mṓtivayt/ *v.tr.* **1** supply a motive to; be the motive of. **2** cause (a person) to act in a particular way. **3** stimulate the interest of (a person in an activity). ▫▫ **motivation** /-váysh'n/ *n.* **motivational** /-váyshən'l/ *adj.* **motivationally** /-váyshənəli/ *adv.*

■ prompt, activate, move, inspire, incite, induce, actuate, stimulate, provoke, influence, encourage, occasion, bring about, cause; excite, egg (on), urge, prod, spur, galvanize, goad, rouse, arouse, stir (up), wheedle, coax, persuade, cajole, tempt, push, impel, drive, instigate. ▫▫ **motivation** inducement, incentive, stimulus, motivating force, stimulation, incitement, influence, cause, reason, motive, rationale, ground(s); attraction, lure, enticement, goad, spur, urge, prod.

motive /mṓtiv/ *n.*, *adj.*, & *v.* ● *n.* **1** a factor or circumstance that induces a person to act in a particular way. **2** = MOTIF. ● *adj.* **1** tending to initiate movement. **2** concerned with movement. ● *v.tr.* = MOTIVATE. ▫ **motive power** a moving or impelling power, esp. a source of energy used to drive machinery. ▫▫ **motiveless** *adj.* **motivelessly** *adv.* **motivelessness** *n.* **motivity** /-tívviti/ *n.* [ME f. OF *motif* (adj. & n.) f. LL *motivus* (adj.) (as MOVE)]

■ *n.* **1** motivating force, stimulus, inducement, incentive, motivation; cause, reason, justification, rationale, ground(s), explanation. ● *adj.* **1** driving, impelling, propelling, propulsive, kinetic, activating, operative, moving.

motley /mótli/ *adj.* & *n.* ● *adj.* (**motlier**, **motliest**) **1** diversified in colour. **2** of varied character (*a motley crew*). ● *n.* **1** an incongruous mixture. **2** *hist.* the particoloured costume of a jester. ▫ **wear motley** play the fool. [ME *mottelay*, perh. ult. rel. to MOTE]

■ *adj.* **1** see *variegated* (VARIEGATE). **2** see MISCELLANEOUS. ● *n.* **1** see MISCELLANY.

moto-cross /mṓtōkross/ *n.* cross-country racing on motor cycles. [MOTOR + CROSS-]

moto perpetuo /mṓtō pərpétyoo-ō/ *n. Mus.* a usu. fast-moving instrumental composition consisting mainly of notes of equal value. [It., = perpetual motion]

motor /mṓtər/ *n.* & *v.* ● *n.* **1** a thing that imparts motion. **2** a machine (esp. one using electricity or internal combustion) supplying motive power for a vehicle etc. or for some other device with moving parts. **3** *Brit.* = *motor car.* **4** (*attrib.*) **a** giving, imparting, or producing motion. **b** driven by a motor (*motor-mower*). **c** of or for motor vehicles. **d** *Anat.* relating to muscular movement or the nerves activating it. ● *v.intr.* & *tr. Brit.* go or convey in a motor vehicle. ▫ **motor area** the part of the frontal lobe of the brain associated with the initiation of muscular action. **motor bicycle** a motor cycle or moped. **motor bike** *colloq.* = *motor cycle.* **motor boat** a motor-driven boat. **motor car** *Brit.* see CAR 1. **motor cycle** a two-wheeled motor-driven road vehicle without pedal propulsion. **motor cyclist** a rider of a motor cycle. **motor mouth** *US sl.* a person who talks incessantly and trivially. **motor nerve** a nerve carrying impulses from the brain or spinal cord to a muscle. **motor scooter** see SCOOTER. **motor vehicle** a road vehicle powered by an internal-combustion engine. ▫▫ **motorial** /mōtóriəl/ *adj.* (in sense 4a of *n.*). **motory** *adj.* (in sense 4a of *n.*). [L, = mover (as MOVE)]

■ *n.* **1** see ENGINE. ● *v.* see DRIVE *v.* 3b. ▫ **motor boat** see BOAT *n.*

motorable /mṓtərəb'l/ *adj.* (of a road) that can be used by motor vehicles.

motorcade /mṓtərkayd/ *n.* a procession of motor vehicles. [MOTOR, after *cavalcade*]

■ see PROCESSION 1.

motorist /mṓtərist/ *n.* the driver of a motor car.

motorize /mṓtərīz/ *v.tr.* (also **-ise**) **1** equip (troops etc.) with motor transport. **2** provide with a motor for propulsion etc. ▫▫ **motorization** /-záysh'n/ *n.*

motorman /mṓtərman/ *n.* (*pl.* **-men**) the driver of an underground train, tram, etc.

motorway /mṓtərway/ *n. Brit.* a main road with separate carriageways and limited access, specially constructed and controlled for fast motor traffic.

■ autobahn, autopista, autoroute, autostrada, *US* interstate, expressway, turnpike.

Motown /mṓtown/ *n.* music with rhythm and blues elements, associated with Detroit. [shortening of *Motor Town*, a name for Detroit]

motte /mot/ *n.* a mound forming the site of a castle, camp, etc. [ME f. OF *mote* (as MOAT)]

mottle /mótt'l/ *v.* & *n.* ● *v.tr.* (esp. as **mottled** *adj.*) mark with spots or smears of colour. ● *n.* **1** an irregular arrangement of spots or patches of colour. **2** any of these spots or patches. [prob. back-form. f. MOTLEY]

■ *v.* see DAPPLE *v.*; (**mottled**) dappled, brindled, marbled, streaked, splotchy, blotched, blotchy, freckled, spotted, spotty, patchy, speckled, flecked, sprinkled, spattered, splashed, streaky, stippled, pied, piebald, *colloq.* splodgy; multicoloured, variegated, particoloured.

motto /móttō/ *n.* (*pl.* **-oes**) **1** a maxim adopted as a rule of conduct. **2** a phrase or sentence accompanying a coat of arms or crest. **3** a sentence inscribed on some object and expressing an appropriate sentiment. **4** verses etc. in a paper cracker. **5** a quotation prefixed to a book or chapter. **6** *Mus.* a recurrent phrase having some symbolical significance. [It. (as MOT)]

■ **1, 3, 5** maxim, proverb, saying, adage, saw, aphorism, apophthegm, gnome, slogan; catchword, battle-cry, byword, guide, moral, principle, rule, precept.

moue /mōō/ *n.* = POUT[1] *n.* [F]

moufflon /mṓōflon/ *n.* (also **mouflon**) a wild mountain sheep, *Ovis musimon*, of S. Europe. [F *mouflon* f. It. *muflone* f. Rmc]

mouillé /mṓō-yay/ *adj. Phonet.* (of a consonant) palatalized. [F, = wetted]

moujik var. of MUZHIK.

mould[1] /mōld/ *n.* & *v.* (*US* **mold**) ● *n.* **1** a hollow container into which molten metal etc. is poured or soft material is pressed to harden into a required shape. **2 a** a metal or earthenware vessel used to give shape to puddings etc. **b** a pudding etc. made in this way. **3** a form or shape, esp. of an animal body. **4** *Archit.* a moulding or group of mouldings. **5** a frame or template for producing mouldings. **6** character or disposition (*in heroic mould*). ● *v.tr.* **1** make (an object) in a required shape or from certain ingredients (*was moulded* *out of clay*). **2** give a shape to. **3** influence the formation or development of (*consultation helps to mould policies*). **4** (esp. of clothing) fit closely to (*the gloves moulded his hands*). □□ **mouldable** *adj.* **moulder** *n.* [ME *mold(e)*, app. f. OF *modle* f. L *modulus*: see MODULUS]

■ *n.* **1, 5** form, cast, matrix, die; template, pattern, frame. **3** form, shape, pattern, format, structure, build, construction, design, arrangement, organization, configuration, kind, brand, make, line, type, stamp, cut. **6** character, nature, disposition, stamp, type, kind, kidney, sort, *colloq. disp.* ilk. ● *v.* **1, 2** shape, form, make, work, fashion, configure, sculpture, sculpt, model, knead, construct; carve, cut; forge, cast, stamp, die-cast. **3** influence, shape, form, affect, make, control, direct, guide, lead.

mould[2] /mōld/ *n.* (*US* **mold**) a woolly or furry growth of minute fungi occurring esp. in moist warm conditions. [ME prob. f. obs. *mould* adj.; past part. of *moul* grow mouldy f. ON *mygla*]

■ mildew, fungus, must, mustiness; blight, smut.

mould[3] /mōld/ *n.* (*US* **mold**) **1** loose earth. **2** the upper soil of cultivated land, esp. when rich in organic matter. □ **mould-board** the board in a plough that turns over the furrow-slice. [OE *molde* f. Gmc., rel. to MEAL[2]]

■ soil, earth, dirt, loam, topsoil, humus.

moulder /mṓldər/ *v.intr.* (*US* **molder**) **1** decay to dust. **2** (foll. by *away*) rot or crumble. **3** deteriorate. [perh. f. MOULD[3], but cf. Norw. dial. *muldra* crumble]

■ **1, 2** see DECAY *v.* 1a.

moulding /mṓlding/ *n.* (*US* **molding**) **1 a** an ornamentally shaped outline as an architectural feature, esp. in a cornice. **b** a strip of material in wood or stone etc. for use as moulding. **2** similar material in wood or plastic etc. used for other decorative purposes, e.g. in picture-framing.

■ see BORDER *n.* 3.

mouldy /mṓldi/ *adj.* (*US* **moldy**) (**-ier, -iest**) **1** covered with mould. **2** stale; out of date. **3** *colloq.* (as a general term of disparagement) dull, miserable, boring. □□ **mouldiness** *n.*

■ **1** musty, mildewy, mildewed, mouldering, blighted, smutty; decayed, decaying, carious, spoilt, rotten, rotting, putrid, putrescent, putrefying, rancid, rank, decomposed, decomposing. **2** aged, ancient, out-dated, old-fashioned, antediluvian, unused, stale. **3** see DULL *adj.* 2.

moulin /mōōlaN/ *n.* a nearly vertical shaft in a glacier, formed by surface water percolating through a crack in the ice. [F, lit. = mill]

moult /mōlt/ *v.* & *n.* (*US* **molt**) ● *v.* **1** *intr.* shed feathers, hair, a shell, etc., in the process of renewing plumage, a coat, etc. **2** *tr.* (of an animal) shed (feathers, hair, etc.). ● *n.* the act or an instance of moulting (*is in moult once a year*). □□ **moulter** *n.* [ME *moute* f. OE *mutian* (unrecorded) f. L *mutare* change: *-l-* after *fault* etc.]

■ *v.* see SHED[2].

mound[1] /mownd/ *n.* & *v.* ● *n.* **1** a raised mass of earth, stones, or other compacted material. **2** a heap or pile. **3** a hillock. ● *v.tr.* **1** heap up in a mound or mounds. **2** enclose with mounds. [16th c. (orig. = hedge or fence): orig. unkn.]

■ *n.* **1, 2** heap, pile, stack; tumulus, (kitchen) midden, *Archaeol.* tell, barrow. **3** hillock, rise, hummock, hill, hump, bank, elevation, knoll, swell, dune, slope, tor, *US* butte. ● *v.* **1** see PILE[1] *v.* 1.

mound[2] /mownd/ *n. Heraldry* a ball of gold etc. representing the earth, and usu. surmounting a crown. [ME f. OF *monde* f. L *mundus* world]

mount[1] /mownt/ *v.* & *n.* ● *v.* **1** *tr.* ascend or climb (a hill, stairs, etc.). **2** *tr.* **a** get up on (an animal, esp. a horse) to ride it. **b** set (a person) on horseback. **c** provide (a person) with a horse. **d** (as **mounted** *adj.*) serving on horseback (*mounted police*). **3** *tr.* go up or climb on to (a raised surface). **4** *intr.* **a** move upwards. **b** (often foll. by *up*) increase, accumulate. **c** (of a feeling) become stronger or more intense (*excitement was mounting*). **d** (of the blood) rise into the cheeks. **5** *tr.* (esp. of a male animal) get on to (a female) to copulate. **6** *tr.* (often foll. by *on*) place (an object) on an elevated support. **7** *tr.* **a** set in or attach to a backing, setting, or other support. **b** attach (a picture etc.) to a mount or frame. **c** fix (an object for viewing) on a microscope slide. **8** *tr.* **a** arrange (a play, exhibition, etc.) or present for public view or display. **b** take action to initiate (a programme, campaign, etc.). **9** *tr.* prepare (specimens) for preservation. **10** *tr.* **a** bring into readiness for operation. **b** raise (guns) into position on a fixed mounting. **11** *intr.* rise to a higher level of rank, power, etc. ● *n.* **1** a backing, setting, or other support on which a picture etc. is set for display. **2** the margin surrounding a picture or photograph. **3 a** a horse available for riding. **b** an opportunity to ride a horse, esp. as a jockey. **4** = *stamp-hinge* (see HINGE). □ **mount guard** (often foll. by *over*) perform the duty of guarding; take up sentry duty. □□ **mountable** *adj.* **mounter** *n.* [ME f. OF *munter*, *monter* ult. f. L (as MOUNT[2])]

■ *v.* **1** climb (up), go up, ascend, scale, clamber up, make one's way up. **2a, 3** climb *or* get *or* clamber (up) on (to); bestride, straddle, bestraddle. **4 a** rise (up), ascend, soar, fly (up), rocket (upwards), *esp. archaic* & *poet.* arise. **b, c** increase, wax, rise, escalate, intensify, swell, expand, grow; multiply, pile up, build up, accumulate. **6–8, 10** display, exhibit, put on display *or* exhibit *or* exhibition, present, install; stage, prepare, ready, put on, put in place, set up; arrange, coordinate, compose, organize, set in motion, launch; frame, set off, back. ● *n.* **1, 2** backing, setting, support, mounting, background, set, arrangement, backdrop, scene. **3 a** horse, *archaic* palfrey, *archaic or poet.* steed, *poet.* charger. **b** ride.

mount[2] /mownt/ *n. archaic* (except before a name): mountain, hill (*Mount Everest*; *Mount of Olives*). [ME f. OE *munt* & OF *mont* f. L *mons montis* mountain]

■ see MOUNTAIN 1.

mountain /mówntin/ *n.* **1** a large natural elevation of the earth's surface rising abruptly from the surrounding level; a large or high and steep hill. **2** a large heap or pile; a huge quantity (*a mountain of work*). **3** a large surplus stock of a commodity (*butter mountain*). □ **make a mountain out of a molehill** see MOLEHILL. **mountain ash 1** a tree, *Sorbus aucuparia*, with delicate pinnate leaves and scarlet berries: also called ROWAN. **2** any of several Australian eucalypts. **mountain bike** a bicycle with a light sturdy frame, broad deep-treaded tyres, and multiple gears, originally designed for riding on mountainous terrain. **mountain chain** a connected series of mountains. **mountain goat** a white goatlike animal, *Oreamnos americanus*, of the Rocky Mountains etc. **mountain laurel** a N. American shrub, *Kalmia latifolia*. **mountain lion** a puma. **mountain panther** = OUNCE[2]. **mountain range** a line of mountains connected by high ground. **mountain sickness** a sickness caused by the rarefaction of the air at great heights. **Mountain Time** *US* the standard time of parts of Canada and the US in or near the Rocky Mountains. **move mountains 1** achieve spectacular results. **2** make every possible effort. □□ **mountainy** *adj.* [ME f. OF *montaigne* ult. f. L (as MOUNT[2])]

■ **1** height, elevation, eminence, prominence, peak, alp, tor, summit, *N.Engl.* fell, *Sc.* ben, *S. Afr.* berg, *archaic* mount. **2, 3** heap, pile, stack, mound, accumulation, abundance, mass, *colloq.* ton(s), heaps, piles, stacks; surplus, surfeit, plethora, excess, oversupply, glut. □ **move mountains 1** work *or* perform miracles *or* a miracle, work *or* do wonders, achieve the impossible, do the unheard of. **2** pull all the stops out, bend over backwards, do one's utmost *or* best, make every effort.

mountaineer /mówntinéer/ *n.* & *v.* ● *n.* **1** a person skilled in mountain-climbing. **2** a person living in an area of high mountains. ● *v.intr.* climb mountains as a sport. □□ **mountaineering** *n.*

mountainous /mówntinəss/ *adj.* **1** (of a region) having many mountains. **2** huge.

■ **1** craggy, alpine, hilly, *Austral.* rangy. **2** huge, towering, high, steep, enormous, immense, formidable, mighty, monumental, prodigious, staggering; see also GIGANTIC.

mountainside /mówntinsīd/ *n.* the slope of a mountain below the summit.

mountebank /mówntibangk/ *n.* **1** a swindler; a charlatan. **2** a clown. **3** *hist.* an itinerant quack appealing to an audience from a platform. ▫▫ **mountebankery** *n.* [It. *montambanco* = *monta in banco* climb on bench: see MOUNT[1], BENCH]
■ **1** see *swindler* (SWINDLE). **2** see JOKER 1.

Mountie /mównti/ *n. colloq.* a member of the Royal Canadian Mounted Police.

mounting /mównting/ *n.* **1** = MOUNT[1] *n.* 1. **2** in senses of MOUNT[1] *v.* ▫ **mounting-block** a block of stone placed to help a rider mount a horse.

mourn /morn/ *v.* **1** *tr.* & (foll. by *for*) *intr.* feel or show deep sorrow or regret for (a dead person, a lost thing, a past event, etc.). **2** *intr.* show conventional signs of grief for a period after a person's death. [OE *murnan*]
■ grieve, lament, sorrow, bemoan, bewail, keen, weep; regret, rue.

mourner /mórnər/ *n.* **1** a person who mourns, esp. at a funeral. **2** a person hired to attend a funeral.

mournful /mórnfŏŏl/ *adj.* **1** doleful, sad, sorrowing. **2** expressing or suggestive of mourning. ▫▫ **mournfully** *adv.* **mournfulness** *n.*
■ sad, sorrowful, sorrowing, dismal, melancholy, blue, afflicted, doleful, grief-stricken, rueful, forlorn, woebegone, sombre, lugubrious, funereal, joyless, dispirited, cheerless, unhappy, downhearted, heavy-hearted, disconsolate, heartbroken, inconsolable, despondent, desolate, despairing, heartsick, overcome, prostrate, *literary or joc.* dolorous; grievous, distressing, upsetting, tragic, saddening, disheartening, depressing, lamentable.

mourning /mórning/ *n.* **1** the expression of deep sorrow, esp. for a dead person, by the wearing of solemn dress. **2** the clothes worn in mourning. ▫ **in mourning** assuming the signs of mourning, esp. in dress. **mourning-band** a band of black crape etc. round a person's sleeve or hat as a token of mourning. **mourning dove** an American dove with a plaintive note, *Zenaida macroura*. **mourning-paper** notepaper with a black edge. **mourning-ring** a ring worn as a memorial of a deceased person.
■ **1** grief, lament, grieving, lamentation, sorrowing, keening, weeping, wailing; anguish, sorrow, misery, sadness, woefulness, melancholy, heartache, despondency, despair, desolation, *archaic or literary* woe. **2** black, sackcloth (and ashes), *archaic* (widow's) weeds.

mousaka var. of MOUSSAKA.

mouse /mowss/ *n.* & *v.* ● *n.* (*pl.* **mice** /mīss/) **1 a** any of various small rodents of the family Muridae, esp. of the genus *Mus*. **b** any of several similar rodents such as a small shrew or vole. **2** a timid or feeble person. **3** *Computing* a small hand-held device which controls the cursor on a VDU screen. **4** *sl.* a black eye. ● *v.intr.* /also mowz/ **1** (esp. of a cat, owl, etc.) hunt for or catch mice. **2** (foll. by *about*) search industriously; prowl about as if searching. ▫ **mouse-coloured 1** dark-grey with a yellow tinge. **2** nondescript light brown. **mouse deer** a chevrotain. **mouse hare** a pika. ▫▫ **mouselike** *adj.* & *adv.* **mouser** *n.* [OE *mūs*, pl. *mȳs* f. Gmc]
■ *n.* **2** see COWARD *n.* ● *v.* **2** see PROWL *v.*
▫ **mouse-coloured 2** mousy, dun, grey, greyish-brown, brownish-grey, brownish, brown, dull-coloured, drab.

mousetrap /mówstrap/ *n.* **1** a sprung trap with bait for catching and usu. killing mice. **2** (often *attrib.*) cheese of poor quality.

moussaka /moosaákə/ *n.* (also **mousaka**) a Greek dish of minced meat, aubergine, etc. with a cheese sauce. [mod. Gk or Turk.]

mousse /mŏŏss/ *n.* **1 a** a dessert of whipped cream, eggs, etc., usu. flavoured with fruit or chocolate. **b** a meat or fish purée made with whipped cream etc. **2** a preparation applied to the hair enabling it to be styled more easily. **3** a mixture of oil and sea-water which forms a froth on the surface of the water after an oil-spill. [F, = moss, froth]

mousseline /mŏŏsleén/ *n.* **1** a muslin-like fabric of silk etc. **2** a sauce of seasoned or sweet eggs and cream. [F: see MUSLIN]

moustache /məstaásh/ *n.* (*US* **mustache**) **1** hair left to grow on a man's upper lip. **2** a similar growth round the mouth of some animals. ▫ **moustache cup** a cup with a partial cover to protect the moustache when drinking. ▫▫ **moustached** *adj.* [F f. It. *mostaccio* f. Gk *mustax -akos*]

Mousterian /mŏŏsteériən/ *adj. Archaeol.* of or relating to the flint workings of the middle palaeolithic epoch, dated to *c.*70,000–30,000 BC, and attributed to Neanderthal peoples. [F *moustérien* f. *Le Moustier* in SW France, where remains were found]

mousy /mówsi/ *adj.* (**mousier, mousiest**) **1** of or like a mouse. **2** (of a person) shy or timid; ineffectual. **3** = *mouse-coloured*. ▫▫ **mousily** *adv.* **mousiness** *n.*
■ **2** timid, cowering, timorous, shy, self-effacing, diffident, ineffectual.

mouth *n.* & *v.* ● *n.* /mowth/ (*pl.* **mouths** /mowt͟hz/) **1 a** an external opening in the head, through which most animals admit food and emit communicative sounds. **b** (in humans and some animals) the cavity behind it containing the means of biting and chewing and the vocal organs. **2 a** the opening of a container such as a bag or sack. **b** the opening of a cave, volcano, etc. **c** the open end of a woodwind or brass instrument. **d** the muzzle of a gun. **3** the place where a river enters the sea. **4** *colloq.* **a** talkativeness. **b** impudent talk; cheek. **5** an individual regarded as needing sustenance (*an extra mouth to feed*). **6** a horse's readiness to feel and obey the pressure of the bit. **7** an expression of displeasure; a grimace ● *v.* /mowt͟h/ **1** *tr.* & *intr.* utter or speak solemnly or with affectations; rant, declaim (*mouthing platitudes*). **2** *tr.* utter very distinctly. **3** *intr.* **a** move the lips silently. **b** grimace. **4** *tr.* take (food) in the mouth. **5** *tr.* touch with the mouth. **6** *tr.* train the mouth of (a horse). ▫ **give mouth** (of a dog) bark, bay. **keep one's mouth shut** *colloq.* not reveal a secret. **mouth-organ** = HARMONICA. **mouth-to-mouth** (of resuscitation) in which a person breathes into a subject's lungs through the mouth. **mouth-watering 1** (of food etc.) having a delicious smell or appearance. **2** tempting, alluring. **put words into a person's mouth** represent a person as having said something in a particular way. **take the words out of a person's mouth** say what another was about to say. ▫▫ **mouthed** /mowt͟hd/ *adj.* (also in *comb.*). **mouther** /mówt͟hər/ *n.* **mouthless** /mówthliss/ *adj.* [OE *mūth* f. Gmc]
■ *n.* **1** lips, jaws, orifice, *sl.* trap, kisser, chops, mush, bazoo, *esp. Brit. sl.* gob, *US sl.* yap; muzzle, maw; *Zool.* stoma. **2 a, b** opening, aperture, doorway, door, gateway, gate, access, entrance, entry, entry-way, way in; exit, way out; passage, passageway, orifice, vent. **3** outfall, debouchment, embouchure, outlet. **4** talkativeness, garrulousness, loquaciousness; bragging, boasting, braggadocio, bombast, rodomontade, fustian, claptrap, *sl.* hot air, gas; disrespect, impudence, insolence, sauciness, rudeness, impertinence, pertness, boldness, audacity, presumptuousness, brashness, flippancy, cheek, *colloq.* lip, sauce, freshness, *Brit. colloq.* backchat, *US colloq.* sass, back talk. **7** grimace, pout, *moue*, face. ● *v.* **1, 2** utter, say, speak, pronounce, announce, enunciate, articulate, voice, sound, express, vocalize; rant, declaim, *esp. joc. or derog.* orate. ▫ **keep one's mouth shut** play one's cards close to one's chest, give nothing away, not give the game away, keep quiet, say nothing, keep to oneself, tell no one, play dumb, not tell a soul, *colloq.* keep it under one's hat.

mouthful /mówthfŏŏl/ *n.* (*pl.* **-fuls**) **1** a quantity, esp. of food, that fills the mouth. **2** a small quantity. **3** a long or complicated word or phrase. **4** *US colloq.* something important said.
■ **1** morsel, bite, spoonful, lump, chunk, hunk. **2** see MODICUM. **3** tongue-twister.

mouthpiece /mówthpeess/ *n.* **1 a** the part of a musical instrument placed between or against the lips. **b** the part of a telephone for speaking into. **c** the part of a tobacco-pipe placed between the lips. **2 a** a person who speaks for another or others. **b** *colloq.* a lawyer. **3** a part attached as an outlet.

■ **1 a** embouchure. **b** handset, receiver. **2 a** spokesman, spokeswoman, spokesperson, agent, representative, intermediator, mediator, delegate. **b** attorney, *esp. US colloq.* shyster; see also LAWYER.

mouthwash /mówthwosh/ *n.* **1** a liquid antiseptic etc. for rinsing the mouth or gargling. **2** *colloq.* nonsense.

■ **1** see WASH *n.* 7, 10. **2** see DRIVEL *n.*

mouthy /mówthi/ *adj.* (**mouthier**, **mouthiest**) **1** ranting, railing. **2** bombastic.

movable /mōōvəb'l/ *adj.* & *n.* (also **moveable**) ● *adj.* **1** that can be moved. **2** *Law* (of property) of the nature of a chattel, as distinct from land or buildings. **3** (of a feast or festival) variable in date from year to year. ● *n.* **1** an article of furniture that may be removed from a house, as distinct from a fixture. **2** (in *pl.*) personal property. □ **movable-doh** *Mus.* applied to a system of sight-singing in which doh is the keynote of any major scale (cf. *fixed-doh*). □□ **movability** /-billiti/ *n.* **movableness** *n.* **movably** *adv.* [ME f. OF (as MOVE)]

■ *adj.* **1** portable, transportable, transferable. **3** floating, variable, changeable, unfixed.

move /mōōv/ *v.* & *n.* ● *v.* **1** *intr.* & *tr.* change one's position or posture, or cause to do this. **2** *tr.* & *intr.* put or keep in motion; rouse, stir. **3 a** *intr.* make a move in a board-game. **b** *tr.* change the position of (a piece) in a board-game. **4** *intr.* (often foll. by *about*, *away*, etc.) go or pass from place to place. **5** *intr.* take action, esp. promptly (*moved to reduce unemployment*). **6** *intr.* make progress (*the project is moving fast*). **7** *intr.* **a** change one's place of residence. **b** (of a business etc.) change to new premises (also *tr.*: *move house*; *move offices*). **8** *intr.* (foll. by *in*) live or be socially active in (a specified place or group etc.) (*moves in the best circles*). **9** *tr.* affect (a person) with (usu. tender or sympathetic) emotion. **10** *tr.* **a** (foll. by *in*) stimulate (laughter, anger, etc., in a person). **b** (foll. by *to*) provoke (a person to laughter etc.). **11** *tr.* (foll. by *to*, or *to* + infin.) prompt or incline (a person to a feeling or action). **12 a** *tr.* cause (the bowels) to be evacuated. **b** *intr.* (of the bowels) be evacuated. **13** *tr.* (often foll. by *that* + clause) propose in a meeting, deliberative assembly, etc. **14** *intr.* (foll. by *for*) make a formal request or application. **15** *intr.* (of merchandise) be sold. ● *n.* **1** the act or an instance of moving. **2** a change of house, business premises, etc. **3** a step taken to secure some action or effect; an initiative. **4 a** the changing of the position of a piece in a board-game. **b** a player's turn to do this. □ **get a move on** *colloq.* **1** hurry up. **2** make a start. **make a move** take action. **move along** (or **on**) change to a new position, esp. to avoid crowding, getting in the way, etc. **move heaven and earth** see HEAVEN. **move in 1** take possession of a new house. **2** get into a position of influence, interference, etc. **3** get into a position of readiness or proximity (for an offensive action etc.). **move mountains** see MOUNTAIN. **move out 1** leave one's home; change one's place of residence. **2** leave a position, job, etc. **move over** (or **up**) adjust one's position to make room for another. **on the move 1** progressing. **2** moving about. [ME f. AF *mover*, OF *moveir* f. L *movēre mot-*]

■ *v.* **1, 4** shift, stir, budge, make a move, go, set off, start off; proceed, advance, progress, make headway, pass, travel, voyage, migrate, transfer; see also LEAVE[1] *v.* 1b, 3, 4. **2, 10, 11** arouse, rouse, provoke, actuate, lead, prompt, spur, motivate, influence, impel, inspire, incline, make, excite, stir (up), stimulate; prod, remind. **5** make a move, take action, take the initiative, begin *or* start to act, proceed, do something. **6** see PROGRESS *v.* 1. **7** move house, move out, move away, relocate, decamp, pull (up) stakes, leave, depart, change residence, emigrate, go *or* make *or* take off, transfer, *colloq.* up sticks, *formal* remove, *sl.* split. **8** circulate, mix, mingle, go round *or* around, move round *or* around, socialize, fraternize, keep company, hobnob, associate, *colloq.* hang around *or* about, *sl.* hang out. **9** affect, touch, stir (up), shake (up), agitate, hit (hard), upset, strike, disturb, ruffle, disquiet, have an effect on, make an impression on, *archaic or literary* smite; stir, agitate. **13, 14** propose, put forward *or* forth, forward, advance, submit, suggest, advocate, propound, request. ● *n.* **1, 2** gesture, gesticulation, action, motion, movement, stirring; change, change-over, relocation, transfer, shift, removal. **3** step, initiative; manoeuvre, device, trick, caper, dodge, stratagem, artifice, ruse, action, act, deed, gambit, *colloq.* ploy. **4 b** turn, time, opportunity, chance, *colloq.* shot, go. □ **get a move on 1** hurry (up), hasten, make haste, rush, run, *colloq.* step on it *or* on the gas. **2** begin, start, make a start, get started, get going, get moving, get under way, stir *or* bestir oneself, *colloq.* get cracking, get *or* set *or* start the ball rolling, get the show on the road, *formal* commence. **make a move** see MOVE *v.* 5 above. **move in 2** step in, intercede, intervene, become involved; see also INTRUDE 1. **move over** (or **up**) see SHIFT *v.* 1. **on the move 1** proceeding, progressing, advancing, moving ahead, succeeding, *colloq.* on the go. **2** travelling, in transit, on the way, on one's way, on the road, moving, *colloq.* on the go.

moveable var. of MOVABLE.

movement /mōōvmənt/ *n.* **1** the act or an instance of moving or being moved. **2 a** the moving parts of a mechanism (esp. a clock or watch). **b** a particular group of these. **3 a** a body of persons with a common object (*the peace movement*). **b** a campaign undertaken by such a body. **4** (usu. in *pl.*) a person's activities and whereabouts, esp. at a particular time. **5** *Mus.* a principal division of a longer musical work, self-sufficient in terms of key, tempo, structure, etc. **6** the progressive development of a poem, story, etc. **7** motion of the bowels. **8 a** an activity in a market for some commodity. **b** a rise or fall in price. **9** a mental impulse. **10** a development of position by a military force or unit. **11** a prevailing tendency in the course of events or conditions; trend. [ME f. OF f. med.L *movimentum* (as MOVE)]

■ **1** move, motion, relocation, repositioning, moving, migration, shift, transfer, flow, displacement; manoeuvre, manoeuvring; action, activity, stir, stirring; gesture, gesticulation, flicker, sign, signal. **2** mechanism, works, workings, moving parts, machinery, action, gears, *colloq.* innards. **3** front, faction, party, group, wing, lobby; campaign, crusade, drive. **6** development, unfolding, progression, progress, momentum, advancement. **8** change, advance, activity, action, shift, decline, increase, decrease, rise, fall; progress, development. **11** drift, trend, tendency, course, swing.

mover /mōōvər/ *n.* **1** a person or thing that moves. **2** a person who moves a proposition. **3** *US* a remover of furniture. **4** the author of a fruitful idea.

■ **2, 4** see INSTRUMENT *n.* 3a.

movie /mōōvi/ *n.* esp. *US colloq.* **1** a motion-picture film. **2** (in full **movie-house**) a cinema.

■ motion picture, film, moving picture, *Brit. colloq.* flick, *esp. US colloq.* talkie; cinema.

moving /mōōving/ *adj.* **1** that moves or causes to move. **2** affecting with emotion. □ **moving pavement** a structure like a conveyor belt for pedestrians. **moving picture** a continuous picture of events obtained by projecting a sequence of photographs taken at very short intervals. **moving staircase** an escalator. □□ **movingly** *adv.* (in sense 2).

■ **1** active, mobile, unfixed, travelling, going, operating, working, in motion, on the move. **2** touching, poignant, emotive, affecting, pathetic, heart-rending, emotional, telling, effective, impressive, striking, compelling; stirring, exciting, thrilling, inspiring, inspirational, persuasive.

mow[1] /mō/ *v.tr.* (*past part.* **mowed** or **mown**) **1** cut down (grass, hay, etc.) with a scythe or machine. **2** cut down the produce of (a field) or the grass etc. of (a lawn) by mowing. □ **mow down** kill or destroy randomly or in great numbers.

□□ **mowable** *adj.* **mower** *n.* [OE *māwan* f. Gmc, rel. to MEAD[2]]
■ cut (down), scythe, trim, shear. □ **mow down** annihilate, kill, massacre, butcher, slaughter, exterminate, liquidate, eradicate, wipe out, cut down, cut to pieces, destroy, *disp.* decimate.

mow[2] /mō/ *n. US* or *dial.* **1** a stack of hay, corn, etc. **2** a place in a barn where hay etc. is heaped. [OE *mūga*]

moxa /móksə/ *n.* a downy substance from the dried leaves of *Artemisia moxa* etc., burnt on the skin in oriental medicine as a counterirritant. [Jap. *mogusa* f. *moe kusa* burning herb]

moxie /móksi/ *n. US sl.* energy, courage, daring. [trade name of a drink]

mozz /moz/ *n. Austral. colloq.* a jinx, a malign influence (esp. *put the mozz on*). [abbr. of MOZZLE]

mozzarella /mótsərélla/ *n.* an Italian curd cheese orig. of buffalo milk. [It.]

mozzle /mózz'l/ *n. Austral. colloq.* luck, fortune. [Heb. *mazzā*]

MP *abbr.* **1** Member of Parliament. **2 a** military police. **b** military policeman.
■ **1** see POLITICIAN.

mp *abbr.* mezzo piano.

m.p. *abbr.* melting-point.

m.p.g. *abbr.* miles per gallon.

m.p.h. *abbr.* miles per hour.
■ see VELOCITY 3.

M.Phil. *abbr.* Master of Philosophy.

MR *abbr.* Master of the Rolls.

Mr /místər/ *n.* (*pl.* **Messrs**) **1** the title of a man without a higher title (*Mr Jones*). **2** a title prefixed to a designation of office etc. (*Mr President*; *Mr Speaker*). □ **Mr Big** *US sl.* the head of an organization; any important person. **Mr Right** *joc.* a woman's destined husband. [abbr. of MISTER]

MRA *abbr.* Moral Re-Armament.

MRBM *abbr.* medium-range ballistic missile.

MRC *abbr.* (in the UK) Medical Research Council.

MRCA *abbr.* multi-role combat aircraft.

mRNA *abbr. Biol.* messenger RNA.

MRPhS *abbr.* Member of the Royal Pharmaceutical Society.

Mrs /míssiz/ *n.* (*pl.* same or **Mesdames**) the title of a married woman without a higher title (*Mrs Jones*). [abbr. of MISTRESS: cf. MISSIS]

MS *abbr.* **1** manuscript. **2** Master of Science. **3** Master of Surgery. **4** *US* Mississippi (in official postal use). **5** *US* motor ship. **6** multiple sclerosis.

Ms /miz, məz/ *n.* the title of a woman without a higher title, used regardless of marital status. [combination of MRS, MISS[2]]

MSC *abbr.* (in the UK) Manpower Services Commission.

M.Sc. *abbr.* Master of Science.

MS-DOS /émmesdóss/ *abbr. Computing* Microsoft disk operating system.

MSF *abbr.* (in the UK) Manufacturing, Science, and Finance (Union).

Msgr. *abbr. US* **1** *Monseigneur*. **2** Monsignor.

MSS /eméssiz/ *abbr.* manuscripts.

MST *abbr.* (in Canada and the US) Mountain Standard Time.

MT *abbr.* **1** mechanical transport. **2** *US* Montana (in official postal use).

Mt. *abbr.* Mount.

MTB *abbr.* motor torpedo-boat.

M.Tech. *abbr.* Master of Technology.

mu /myōō/ *n.* **1** the twelfth Greek letter (*M*, *μ*). **2** (*μ*, as a symbol) = MICRO- 2. □ **mu-meson** = MUON. [Gk]

much /much/ *adj.*, *n.*, & *adv.* ● *adj.* **1** existing or occurring in a great quantity (*much trouble*; *not much rain*; *too much noise*). **2** (prec. by *as*, *how*, *that*, etc.) with relative rather than distinctive sense (*I don't know how much money you want*). ● *n.* **1** a great quantity (*much of that is true*). **2** (prec. by *as*, *how*, *that*, etc.) with relative rather than distinctive sense (*we do not need that much*). **3** (usu. in *neg.*) a noteworthy or outstanding example (*not much to look at*; *not much of a party*). ● *adv.* **1 a** in a great degree (*much to my surprise*; *is much the same*). **b** (qualifying a verb or past participle) greatly (*they much regret the mistake*; *I was much annoyed*). ¶ *Much* implies a strong verbal element in the participle, whereas *very* implies a strong adjectival element: compare the second example above with *I was very annoyed*. **c** qualifying a comparative or superlative adjective (*much better*; *much the most likely*). **2** for a large part of one's time (*is much away from home*). □ **as much** the extent or quantity just specified; the idea just mentioned (*I thought as much*; *as much as that?*). **a bit much** *colloq.* somewhat excessive or immoderate. **make much of** see MAKE. **much as** even though (*cannot come, much as I would like to*). **much less** see LESS. **much obliged** see OBLIGE. **not much** *colloq.* **1** *iron.* very much. **2** certainly not. **not much in it** see IN. **too much** *colloq.* an intolerable situation etc. (*that really is too much*). **too much for 1** more than a match for. **2** beyond what is endurable by. □□ **muchly** *adv. joc.* [ME f. *muchel* MICKLE: for loss of *el* cf. BAD, WENCH]
■ *n.* **1** see LOT *n.* 1. ● *adv.* **2** see OFTEN.

muchness /múchniss/ *n.* greatness in quantity or degree. □ **much of a muchness** very nearly the same or alike.

mucilage /myōōssilij/ *n.* **1** a viscous substance obtained from plant seeds etc. by maceration. **2** *US* a solution of gum. □□ **mucilaginous** /-lájinəss/ *adj.* [ME f. F f. LL *mucilago -ginis* musty juice (MUCUS)]

muck /muk/ *n.* & *v.* ● *n.* **1** farmyard manure. **2** *colloq.* dirt or filth; anything disgusting. **3** *colloq.* an untidy state; a mess. ● *v.tr.* **1** (usu. foll. by *up*) *Brit. colloq.* bungle (a job). **2** (foll. by *out*) remove muck from. **3** make dirty or untidy. **4** manure with muck. □ **make a muck of** *colloq.* bungle. **muck about** (or **around**) *Brit. colloq.* **1** potter or fool about. **2** (foll. by *with*) fool or interfere with. **muck in** *Brit.* (often foll. by *with*) share tasks etc. equally. **muck sweat** *Brit. colloq.* a profuse sweat. [ME *muk* prob. f. Scand.: cf. ON *myki* dung, rel. to MEEK]
■ *n.* **1, 2** ordure, manure, dung, excrement, faeces, droppings, guano; dirt, filth, bilge, slime, sludge, ooze, scum, sewage, mire, mud, feculence, *Brit. colloq.* gunge, *sl.* gunk, *esp. US sl.* grunge. **3** see MESS *n.* 1. ● *v.* **1** (*muck up*) muff (up), spoil, make a mess of, botch, mess up, bungle, *colloq.* make a muck of, foul up, *sl.* screw up, *Brit. sl.* cock up. □ **make a muck of** see MUCK *v.* above. **muck about 1** potter *or* fool about *or* around, waste time, idle, loiter, mess around *or* about. **2** (*muck about with*) see INTERFERE 1.

mucker /múkkər/ *n. sl.* **1** a friend or companion. **2** *US* a rough or coarse person. **3** *Brit.* a heavy fall. □□ **muckerish** *adj.* (in senses 1 and 2). [prob. f. *muck in*: see MUCK]

muckle var. of MICKLE.

muckrake /múkrayk/ *v.intr.* search out and reveal scandal, esp. among famous people. □□ **muckraker** *n.* **muckraking** *n.*

mucky /múkki/ *adj.* (**muckier**, **muckiest**) **1** covered with muck. **2** dirty. □□ **muckiness** *n.*
■ see DIRTY *adj.* 1.

muco- /myōōkō/ *comb. form Biochem.* mucus, mucous.

mucopolysaccharide /myōōkōpóllisákkərīd/ *n. Biochem.* any of a group of polysaccharides whose molecules contain sugar residues and are often found as components of connective tissue.

mucosa /myookṓsə/ *n.* (*pl.* **mucosae** /-see/) a mucous membrane. [mod.L, fem. of *mucosus*: see MUCOUS]

mucous /myōōkəss/ *adj.* of or covered with mucus. □ **mucous membrane** a mucus-secreting epithelial tissue lining many body cavities and tubular organs. □□ **mucosity** /-kóssiti/ *n.* [L *mucosus* (as MUCUS)]
■ see SLIMY 1, 2.

mucro /myōōkrō/ *n.* (*pl.* **mucrones** /-krṓneez/) *Bot.* & *Zool.* a sharp-pointed part or organ. □□ **mucronate** /-krənət/ *adj.* [L *mucro -onis* sharp point]

mucus /myo͞okəss/ *n.* **1** a slimy substance secreted by a mucous membrane. **2** a gummy substance found in all plants. **3** a slimy substance exuded by some animals, esp. fishes. [L]

mud /mud/ *n.* **1** wet soft earthy matter. **2** hard ground from the drying of an area of this. **3** what is worthless or polluting. □ **as clear as mud** *colloq.* not at all clear. **fling** (or **sling** or **throw**) **mud** speak disparagingly or slanderously. **here's mud in your eye!** *colloq.* a drinking-toast. **mud-bath 1** a bath in the mud of mineral springs, esp. to relieve rheumatism etc. **2** a muddy scene or occasion. **mud-brick** a brick made from baked mud. **mud-flat** a stretch of muddy land left uncovered at low tide. **mud pack** a cosmetic paste applied thickly to the face. **mud pie** mud made into a pie shape by a child. **mud puppy** *US* a large nocturnal salamander, *Necturus maculosus*, of eastern USA. **mud skipper** any of various gobies of the family Periophthalmidae, able to leave the water and leap on the mud. **mud-slinger** *colloq.* one given to making abusive or disparaging remarks. **mud-slinging** *colloq.* abuse, disparagement. **mud volcano** a volcano discharging mud. **one's name is mud** one is unpopular or in disgrace. [ME *mode*, *mudde*, prob. f. MLG *mudde*, MHG *mot* bog]

■ **1** muck, ooze, slime, mire, clay, sludge, silt, dirt. □ **fling** (or **sling** or **throw**) **mud** see DISPARAGE *v.* **mud-slinger** see GOSSIP *n.* 3. **mud-slinging** see ABUSE *n.* 2.

muddle /múdd'l/ *v.* & *n.* ● *v.* **1** *tr.* (often foll. by *up*, *together*) bring into disorder. **2** *tr.* bewilder, confuse. **3** *tr.* mismanage (an affair). **4** *tr. US* crush and mix (the ingredients for a drink). **5** *intr.* (often foll. by *with*) busy oneself in a confused and ineffective way. ● *n.* **1** disorder. **2** a muddled condition. □ **make a muddle of 1** bring into disorder. **2** bungle. **muddle along** (or **on**) progress in a haphazard way. **muddle-headed** stupid, confused. **muddle-headedness** stupidity; a confused state. **muddle through** succeed by perseverance rather than skill or efficiency. **muddle up** confuse (two or more things). □□ **muddler** *n.* **muddlingly** *adv.* [perh. f. MDu. *moddelen*, frequent. of *modden* dabble in mud (as MUD)]

■ *v.* **1, 3** confuse, mix up, jumble, scramble, entangle, tangle, mess up, disorder, muddle up, disarrange, disorganize; bungle, botch, mismanage, muff. **2** bewilder, confuse, confound, mystify, baffle, mix up, disorient(ate), befuddle, perplex, bemuse, puzzle, befog. ● *n.* mess, confusion, mix-up, jumble, tangle, disorder, hotchpotch, mishmash, *colloq.* stew, *sl.* screw-up, snafu, *Brit. sl.* cock-up. □ **muddle along** (or **on**) see MANAGE *v.* 2, 3, 5a. **muddle-headed** see STUPID *adj.* 1, 5, *confused* (CONFUSE 4). **muddle-headedness** see *stupidity* (STUPID). **muddle through** manage, cope, make it, scrape by *or* through *or* along, contrive, make do, get by *or* along. **muddle up** see MUDDLE *v.* 1, 3 above.

muddy /múddi/ *adj.* & *v.* ● *adj.* (**muddier, muddiest**) **1** like mud. **2** covered in or full of mud. **3** (of liquid) turbid. **4** mentally confused. **5** obscure. **6** (of light) dull. **7** (of colour) impure. ● *v.tr.* (**-ies, -ied**) make muddy. □□ **muddily** *adv.* **muddiness** *n.*

■ *adj.* **2** fouled, muddied, mud-spattered, dirty, grubby, grimy, soiled, mud-caked, slimy, mucky, miry, *poet.* befouled; oozy, squelchy, squishy, squashy, boggy, fenny, marshy, swampy, feculent. **4, 5** confused, muddled, addled, mixed-up; unclear, vague, obscure, dull, dim, fuzzy. **6, 7** drab, dull, subdued, blurred, dingy, matt, washed out, flat; murky, impure. ● *v.* dirty, soil, begrime, smirch, besmirch, spatter, bespatter; obscure, dull, dim, confuse, mix up, befog, cloud.

mudfish /múdfish/ *n.* any fish that burrows in mud, esp. the bowfin.

mudflap /múdflap/ *n.* a flap hanging behind the wheel of a vehicle, to catch mud and stones etc. thrown up from the road.

mudguard /múdgaard/ *n.* a curved strip or cover over a wheel of a bicycle or motor cycle to reduce the amount of mud etc. thrown up from the road.

mudlark /múdlaark/ *n.* **1** *hist.* a destitute child searching in river mud for objects of value. **2** *hist.* a street urchin.

■ **2** see GUTTERSNIPE.

mudstone /múdstōn/ *n.* a dark clay rock.

muesli /mo͞ozli, myo͞o-/ *n.* a breakfast food of crushed cereals, dried fruits, nuts, etc., eaten with milk. [Swiss G]

muezzin /moo-ézzin/ *n.* a Muslim crier who proclaims the hours of prayer usu. from a minaret. [Arab. *mu'addin* part. of *'addana* proclaim]

muff[1] /muf/ *n.* a fur or other covering, usu. in the form of a tube with an opening at each end for the hands to be inserted for warmth. [Du. *mof*, MDu. *moffel*, *muffel* f. med.L *muff(u)la*, of unkn. orig.]

muff[2] /muf/ *v.* & *n.* ● *v.tr.* **1** bungle; deal clumsily with. **2** fail to catch or receive (a ball etc.). **3** blunder in (a theatrical part etc.). ● *n.* **1** a person who is awkward or stupid, orig. in some athletic sport. **2** a failure, esp. to catch a ball at cricket etc. □□ **muffish** *adj.* [19th c.: orig. unkn.]

■ *v.* **1** see BOTCH *v.* 1.

muffin /múffin/ *n.* **1** *Brit.* a light flat round spongy cake, eaten toasted and buttered. **2** *US* a similar round cake made from batter or dough. □ **muffin-man** *Brit.* (formerly) a seller of muffins in the street. [18th c.: orig. unkn.]

muffle[1] /múff'l/ *v.* & *n.* ● *v.tr.* **1** (often foll. by *up*) wrap or cover for warmth. **2** cover or wrap up (a source of sound) to reduce its loudness. **3** (usu. as **muffled** *adj.*) stifle (an utterance, e.g. a curse). **4** prevent from speaking. ● *n.* **1** a receptacle in a furnace where substances may be heated without contact with combustion products. **2** a similar chamber in a kiln for baking painted pottery. [ME: (n.) f. OF *moufle* thick glove; (v.) perh. f. OF *enmoufler* f. *moufle*]

■ *v.* **1** wrap, swathe, swaddle, cloak, envelop, cover (up), enfold, shroud, conceal, protect, *literary* enshroud. **2–4** deaden, silence, suppress, stifle, subdue, damp (down), dampen, mute, hush, quiet(en), tone down, still.

muffle[2] /múff'l/ *n.* the thick part of the upper lip and nose of ruminants and rodents. [F *mufle*, of unkn. orig.]

muffler /múflər/ *n.* **1** a wrap or scarf worn for warmth. **2** any of various devices used to deaden sound in musical instruments. **3** *US* the silencer of a motor vehicle.

■ **1** scarf, shawl, wrap, stole, boa.

mufti[1] /múfti/ *n.* a Muslim legal expert empowered to give rulings on religious matters. [Arab. *muftī*, part. of *'aftā* decide a point of law]

mufti[2] /múfti/ *n.* plain clothes worn by a person who also wears (esp. military) uniform (*in mufti*). [19th c.: perh. f. MUFTI[1]]

mug[1] /mug/ *n.* & *v.* ● *n.* **1 a** a drinking-vessel, usu. cylindrical and with a handle and used without a saucer. **b** its contents. **2** *sl.* the face or mouth of a person. **3** *Brit. sl.* **a** a simpleton. **b** a gullible person. **4** *US sl.* a hoodlum or thug. ● *v.* (**mugged, mugging**) **1** *tr.* rob (a person) with violence esp. in a public place. **2** *tr.* fight; thrash. **3** *tr.* strangle. **4** *intr. sl.* make faces, esp. before an audience, a camera, etc. □ **a mug's game** *Brit. colloq.* a foolish or unprofitable activity. **mug shot** *sl.* a photograph of a face, esp. for official purposes. □□ **mugger** *n.* (esp. in sense 1 of *v.*). **mugful** *n.* (*pl.* **-fuls**). **mugging** *n.* (in sense 1 of *v.*). [prob. f. Scand.: sense 2 of *n.* prob. f. the representation of faces on mugs, and sense 3 prob. from this]

■ *n.* **1** jug, tankard, stein, toby jug, pot, beaker, cup, jar, flagon, *archaic* stoup. **2** face, features, countenance, mouth, *Brit. colloq.* phiz, phizog, *literary* visage, *sl.* kisser, mush, *Brit. sl.* clock, dial, *US sl.* pan. **3** fool, simpleton, dupe, gull, innocent, *colloq.* chump, soft *or* easy touch, *Brit. colloq.* muggins, *sl.* sucker, duffer, *Austral. sl.* dill. **4** see THUG. ● *v.* **1** set upon, rob, assault; see also ATTACK *v.* 1. **2** see BEAT *v.* 1. **3** strangle, garrotte, throttle; stifle, suffocate, smother, choke, asphyxiate. **4** make *or* pull a face, grimace.

mug[2] /mug/ *v.tr.* (**mugged, mugging**) *Brit.* (usu. foll. by *up*) *sl.* learn (a subject) by concentrated study. [19th c.: orig. unkn.]

▪ (*mug up*) study, get up, *Brit. colloq.* swot (up), bone up, *literary* lucubrate.

mugger[1] see MUG[1].

mugger[2] /múggər/ *n.* a broad-nosed Indian crocodile, *Crocodylus palustris*, venerated by many Hindus. [Hindi *magar*]

muggins /múgginz/ *n.* (*pl.* same or **mugginses**) **1** *colloq.* **a** a simpleton. **b** a person who is easily outwitted (often with allusion to oneself: *so muggins had to pay*). **2** a card-game like snap. [perh. the surname *Muggins*, with allusion to MUG[1]]
▪ **1** see DOLT.

muggy /múggi/ *adj.* (**muggier, muggiest**) (of the weather, a day, etc.) oppressively damp and warm; humid. ▫▫ **mugginess** *n.* [dial. *mug* mist, drizzle f. ON *mugga*]
▪ humid, damp, sticky, sultry, oppressive, steamy, close, stuffy; moist, soggy.

Mughal /mo͞ogaal/ *n.* **1** a Mongolian. **2** (*attrib.*) denoting the Muslim dynasty in India in the 16th–19th c. (cf. MOGUL 2b). [Pers. *muġūl* MONGOL]

mugwort /múgwurt/ *n.* any of various plants of the genus *Artemisia*, esp. *A. vulgaris*, with silver-grey aromatic foliage. [OE *mucgwyrt* (as MIDGE, WORT)]

mugwump /múgwump/ *n. US* **1** a great man; a boss. **2** a person who holds aloof, esp. from party politics. [Algonquian *mugquomp* great chief]

Muhammadan /məhámmad'n/ *n.* & *adj.* (also **Mohammedan**) = MUSLIM. ¶ A term not used or favoured by Muslims, and often regarded as *offens.* ▫▫ **Muhammadanism** *n.* [*Muhammad*, Arabian prophet d. 632]

mujahidin /mo͞ojaahidēen/ *n.pl.* (also **mujahedin, -deen**) guerrilla fighters in Islamic countries, esp. supporting Muslim fundamentalism. [Pers. & Arab. *mujāhidīn* pl. of *mujāhid* one who fights a JIHAD]

mulatto /myoolátto͞/ *n.* & *adj.* ● *n.* (*pl.* **-os** or **-oes**) a person of mixed White and Black parentage. ● *adj.* of the colour of mulattos; tawny. [Sp. *mulato* young mule, *mulatto*, irreg. f. *mulo* MULE[1]]

mulberry /múlbəri/ *n.* (*pl.* **-ies**) **1** any deciduous tree of the genus *Morus*, grown originally for feeding silkworms, and now for its fruit and ornamental qualities. **2** its dark-red or white berry. **3** a dark-red or purple colour. [ME *mol-*, *mool-*, *mulberry*, dissim. f. *murberie* f. OE *mōrberie*, f. L *morum*: see BERRY]

mulch /mulch, mulsh/ *n.* & *v.* ● *n.* a mixture of wet straw, leaves, etc., spread around or over a plant to enrich or insulate the soil. ● *v.tr.* treat with mulch. [prob. use as noun of *mulsh* soft: cf. dial. *melsh* mild f. OE *melsc*]
▪ *v.* see FERTILIZE 1.

mulct /mulkt/ *v.* & *n.* ● *v.tr.* **1** extract money from by fine or taxation. **2 a** (often foll. by *of*) deprive by fraudulent means; swindle. **b** obtain by swindling. ● *n.* a fine. [earlier *mult(e)* f. L *multa*, *mulcta*: (v.) through F *mulcter* & L *mulctare*]
▪ *v.* **1** see FINE[2] *v.* **2** see SWINDLE *v.* ● *n.* see FINE[2] *n.*

mule[1] /myo͞ol/ *n.* **1** the offspring (usu. sterile) of a male donkey and a female horse, or (in general use) of a female donkey and a male horse (cf. HINNY[1]), used as a beast of burden. **2** a stupid or obstinate person. **3** (often *attrib.*) a hybrid and usu. sterile plant or animal (*mule canary*). **4** (in full **spinning mule**) a kind of spinning-machine producing yarn on spindles. [ME f. OF *mul(e)* f. L *mulus mula*]

mule[2] /myo͞ol/ *n.* a light shoe or slipper without a back. [F]

mule[3] var. of MEWL.

muleteer /myo͞olitēer/ *n.* a mule-driver. [F *muletier* f. *mulet* dimin. of OF *mul* MULE[1]]

mulga /múlgə/ *n. Austral.* **1** a small spreading tree, *Acacia aneura*. **2** the wood of this tree. **3** scrub or bush. **4** *colloq.* the outback. [Aboriginal]

muliebrity /myo͞oli-ébriti/ *n. literary* **1** womanhood. **2** the normal characteristics of a woman. **3** softness, effeminacy. [LL *muliebritas* f. L *mulier* woman]

mulish /myo͞olish/ *adj.* **1** like a mule. **2** stubborn. ▫▫ **mulishly** *adv.* **mulishness** *n.*
▪ **2** see STUBBORN.

mull[1] /mul/ *v.tr.* & *intr.* (often foll. by *over*) ponder or consider. [perh. f. *mull* grind to powder, ME *mul* dust f. MDu.]
▪ (*mull over*) ponder, consider, study, think over *or* about, cogitate (on *or* over *or* about), evaluate, turn over, weigh (up), deliberate (on *or* over), reflect on, review, examine, contemplate, meditate (on), chew over, ruminate (on *or* over), *archaic* con (over), *literary* muse on.

mull[2] /mul/ *v.tr.* warm (wine or beer) with added sugar, spices, etc. [17th c.: orig. unkn.]

mull[3] /mul/ *n. Sc.* a promontory. [ME: cf. Gael. *maol*, Icel. *múli*]

mull[4] /mul/ *n.* humus formed under non-acid conditions. [G f. Da. *muld*]

mull[5] /mul/ *n.* a thin soft plain muslin. [abbr. of *mulmull* f. Hindi *malmal*]

mullah /múllə/ *n.* a Muslim learned in Islamic theology and sacred law. [Pers., Turk., Urdu *mullā* f. Arab. *mawlā*]

mullein /múllin/ *n.* any herbaceous plant of the genus *Verbascum*, with woolly leaves and yellow flowers. [ME f. OF *moleine* f. Gaulish]

muller /múllər/ *n.* a stone or other heavy weight used for grinding material on a slab. [ME, perh. f. AF *moldre* grind]

mullet /múllit/ *n.* any fish of the family Mullidae (**red mullet**) or Mugilidae (**grey mullet**), usu. with a thick body and a large blunt-nosed head, commonly used as food. [ME f. OF *mulet* dimin. of L *mullus* red mullet f. Gk *mollos*]

mulligatawny /mùlligətáwni/ *n.* a highly seasoned soup orig. from India. [Tamil *milagutannir* pepper-water]

mullion /múlyən/ *n.* (also **munnion** /mún-/) a vertical bar dividing the lights in a window (cf. TRANSOM). ▫▫ **mullioned** *adj.* [prob. an altered form of MONIAL]

mullock /múllək/ *n.* **1** *Austral.* or *dial.* refuse, rubbish. **2** *Austral.* **a** rock containing no gold. **b** refuse from which gold has been extracted. **3** *Austral.* ridicule. [ME dimin. of *mul* dust, rubbish, f. MDu.]
▪ **1** see REFUSE[2]. **3** see RIDICULE *n.*

mulloway /múlləway/ *n. Austral.* a large marine fish, *Sciaena antarctica*, used as food. [19th c.: orig. unkn.]

multangular /multánggyoolər/ *adj.* having many angles. [med.L *multangularis* (as MULTI-, ANGULAR)]

multi- /múlti/ *comb. form* many; more than one. [L f. *multus* much, many]

multi-access /múltiáksess/ *n.* (often *attrib.*) the simultaneous connection to a computer of a number of terminals.

multiaxial /múltiáksiəl/ *adj.* of or involving several axes.

multicellular /múltisélyoolər/ *adj. Biol.* having many cells.

multichannel /múltichánn'l/ *adj.* employing or possessing many communication or television channels.

multicolour /múltikúllər/ *adj.* (also **multicoloured**) of many colours.
▪ see *variegated* (VARIEGATE 1, 3).

multicultural /múltikúlchərəl/ *adj.* of or relating to or constituting several cultural or ethnic groups within a society. ▫▫ **multiculturalism** *n.* **multiculturally** *adv.*

multidimensional /múltidīménshən'l, -di-/ *adj.* of or involving more than three dimensions. ▫▫ **multidimensionality** /-nálliti/ *n.* **multidimensionally** *adv.*

multidirectional /múltidīrékshən'l, -di-/ *adj.* of, involving, or operating in several directions.

multifaceted /múltifássitid/ *adj.* having several facets.
▪ see SOPHISTICATED 2.

multifarious /múltifáiriəss/ *adj.* **1** (foll. by pl. noun) many and various. **2** having great variety. ▫▫ **multifariously** *adv.* **multifariousness** *n.* [L *multifarius*]
▪ see VARIOUS 2.

multifid /múltifid/ *adj. Bot.* & *Zool.* divided into many parts. [L *multifidus* (as MULTI-, *fid-* stem of *findere* cleave)]

multifoil /múltifoyl/ *n. Archit.* an ornament consisting of more than five foils.

multiform /múltiform/ *n.* (usu. *attrib.*) **1** having many forms. **2** of many kinds. □□ **multiformity** /-fórmiti/ *n.*

■ see DIVERS.

multifunctional /múltifúngkshən'l/ *adj.* having or fulfilling several functions.

multigrade /múltigrayd/ *n.* (usu. *attrib.*) an engine oil etc. meeting the requirements of several standard grades.

multilateral /múltiláttərəl/ *adj.* **1 a** (of an agreement, treaty, conference, etc.) in which three or more parties participate. **b** performed by more than one party (*multilateral disarmament*). **2** having many sides. □□ **multilaterally** *adv.*

multilingual /múltilínggwəl/ *adj.* in or using several languages. □□ **multilingually** *adv.*

multimillion /múltimílyən/ *attrib.adj.* costing or involving several million (pounds, dollars, etc.) (*multimillion dollar fraud*).

multimillionaire /múltimílyənáir/ *n.* a person with a fortune of several millions.

multinational /múltináshən'l/ *adj.* & *n.* ● *adj.* **1** (of a business organization) operating in several countries. **2** relating to or including several nationalities or ethnic groups. ● *n.* a multinational company. □□ **multinationally** *adv.*

multinomial /múltinṓmiəl/ *adj.* & *n. Math.* = POLYNOMIAL. [MULTI-, after *binomial*]

multiparous /multíppərəss/ *adj.* **1** bringing forth many young at a birth. **2** having borne more than one child. [MULTI- + -PAROUS]

multipartite /múltipaártīt/ *adj.* divided into many parts.

multiphase /múltifayz/ *n. Electr.* = POLYPHASE.

multiple /múltip'l/ *adj.* & *n.* ● *adj.* **1** having several or many parts, elements, or individual components. **2** (foll. by pl. noun) many and various. **3** *Bot.* (of fruit) collective. ● *n.* **1** a number that may be divided by another a certain number of times without a remainder (*56 is a multiple of 7*). **2** a multiple shop or store. □ **least** (or **lowest**) **common multiple** the least quantity that is a multiple of two or more given quantities. **multiple-choice** (of a question in an examination) accompanied by several possible answers from which the correct one has to be chosen. **multiple personality** *Psychol.* the apparent existence of two or more distinct personalities in one individual. **multiple sclerosis** see SCLEROSIS. **multiple shop** (or **store**) *Brit.* a shop or store with branches in several places. **multiple standard** see STANDARD. **multiple star** several stars so close as to seem one, esp. when forming a connected system. □□ **multiply** *adv.* [F f. LL *multiplus* f. L (as MULTIPLEX)]

multiplex /múltipleks/ *adj.* & *v.* ● *adj.* **1** manifold; of many elements. **2** involving simultaneous transmission of several messages along a single channel of communication. ● *v.tr.* incorporate into a multiplex signal or system. □□ **multiplexer** *n.* (also **multiplexor**). [L (as MULTI-, *-plex* *-plicis* -fold)]

■ *adj.* **1** see MANIFOLD *adj.*

multipliable /múltiplīəb'l/ *adj.* that can be multiplied.

multiplicable /múltiplíkkəb'l/ *adj.* = MULTIPLIABLE. [OF *multiplicable* or med.L *multiplicabilis* f. L (as MULTIPLY)]

multiplicand /múltiplikánd/ *n.* a quantity to be multiplied by a multiplier. [med.L *multiplicandus* gerundive of L *multiplicare* (as MULTIPLY)]

multiplication /múltiplikáysh'n/ *n.* **1** the arithmetical process of multiplying. **2** the act or an instance of multiplying. □ **multiplication sign** the sign (x) to indicate that one quantity is to be multiplied by another, as in 2 x 3 = 6. **multiplication table** a list of multiples of a particular number, usu. from 1 to 12. □□ **multiplicative** /-plíkkətiv/ *adj.* [ME f. OF *multiplication* or L *multiplicatio* (as MULTIPLY)]

■ **2** see INCREASE *n.* 1, 2.

multiplicity /múltiplíssiti/ *n.* (*pl.* **-ies**) **1** manifold variety. **2** (foll. by *of*) a great number. [LL *multiplicitas* (as MULTIPLEX)]

■ **1** see VARIETY 2.

multiplier /múltiplīər/ *n.* **1** a quantity by which a given number is multiplied. **2** *Econ.* a factor by which an increment of income exceeds the resulting increment of saving or investment. **3** *Electr.* an instrument for increasing by repetition the intensity of a current, force, etc.

multiply /múltiplī/ *v.* (**-ies**, **-ied**) **1** *tr.* (also *absol.*) obtain from (a number) another that is a specified number of times its value (*multiply 6 by 4 and you get 24*). **2** *intr.* increase in number esp. by procreation. **3** *tr.* produce a large number of (instances etc.). **4** *tr.* **a** breed (animals). **b** propagate (plants). [ME f. OF *multiplier* f. L *multiplicare* (as MULTIPLEX)]

■ **2** see INCREASE *v.* 1.

multipolar /múltipṓlər/ *adj.* having many poles (see POLE[2]).

multiprocessing /múltiprṓsessing/ *n. Computing* processing by a number of processors sharing a common memory and common peripherals.

multiprogramming /múltiprṓgramming/ *n. Computing* the execution of two or more independent programs concurrently.

multi-purpose /múltipúrpəss/ *n.* (*attrib.*) having several purposes.

■ see VERSATILE 2.

multiracial /múltiráysh'l/ *adj.* relating to or made up of many human races. □□ **multiracially** *adv.*

multi-role /múltirṓl/ *n.* (*attrib.*) having several roles or functions.

multi-stage /múltistayj/ *n.* (*attrib.*) (of a rocket etc.) having several stages of operation.

multi-storey /múltistóri/ *n.* (*attrib.*) (of a building) having several (esp. similarly designed) storeys.

■ see TALL *adj.* 3.

multitude /múltityo͞od/ *n.* **1** (often foll. by *of*) a great number. **2** a large gathering of people; a crowd. **3** (**the multitude**) the common people. **4** the state of being numerous. [ME f. OF f. L *multitudo -dinis* f. *multus* many]

■ **1** see MANY *n.* 1. **2** see CROWD *n.* 1. **3** see PEOPLE *n.* 2.

multitudinous /múltityo͞odinəss/ *adj.* **1** very numerous. **2** consisting of many individuals or elements. **3** (of an ocean etc.) vast. □□ **multitudinously** *adv.* **multitudinousness** *n.* [L (as MULTITUDE)]

■ **1, 2** see MANY *adj.*

multi-user /múltiyo͞ozər/ *n.* (*attrib.*) (of a computer system) having a number of simultaneous users (cf. MULTI-ACCESS).

multivalent /múltiváylənt/ *adj. Chem.* **1** having a valency of more than two. **2** having a variable valency. □□ **multivalency** *n.*

multivalve /múltivalv/ *n.* (*attrib.*) (of a shell etc.) having several valves.

multiversity /múltivérsiti/ *n.* (*pl.* **-ies**) a large university with many different departments. [MULTI- + UNIVERSITY]

multivocal /multívvək'l/ *adj.* having many meanings.

multi-way /múltiway/ *n.* (*attrib.*) having several paths of communication etc.

mum[1] /mum/ *n. Brit. colloq.* mother. [abbr. of MUMMY[1]]

mum[2] /mum/ *adj. colloq.* silent (*keep mum*). □ **mum's the word** say nothing. [ME: imit. of closed lips]

■ silent, mute, close-mouthed, quiet, tight-lipped. □ **mum's the word** don't tell a soul, keep quiet, keep it to yourself, say nothing, tell no-one, play dumb, *colloq.* keep it under one's hat, *esp. US sl.* button one's lip.

mum[3] /mum/ *v.intr.* (**mummed**, **mumming**) act in a traditional masked mime. [cf. MUM[2] and MLG *mummen*]

mumble /múmb'l/ *v.* & *n.* ● *v.* **1** *intr.* & *tr.* speak or utter indistinctly. **2** *tr.* bite or chew with or as with toothless gums. ● *n.* an indistinct utterance. □□ **mumbler** *n.* **mumblingly** *adv.* [ME *momele*, as MUM[2]: cf. LG *mummelen*]

■ *v.* **1** murmur, mutter, slur, swallow one's words.

mumbo-jumbo /múmbōjúmbō/ *n.* (*pl.* **-jumbos**) **1** meaningless or ignorant ritual. **2** language or action intended to mystify or confuse. **3** an object of senseless veneration. [*Mumbo Jumbo*, a supposed African idol]

▪ **1** spell, incantation, chant, formula, charm, abracadabra, rite, ritual, rigmarole, conjuration, magic. **2** gibberish, nonsense, rubbish, hocus-pocus, gobbledegook, drivel, humbug, bunkum, jargon, double-talk, mystique, rigmarole, jabberwocky, blather, moonshine, claptrap, *colloq.* hogwash, malarkey, piffle, tosh, *sl.* eyewash, poppycock, rot, tommy-rot, bilge, bosh, bull, hooey, bunk.

mummer /múmmər/ *n.* **1** an actor in a traditional masked mime. **2** *archaic* or *derog.* an actor in the theatre. [ME f. OF *momeur* f. *momer* MUM[3]]

mummery /múmməri/ *n.* (*pl.* **-ies**) **1** ridiculous (esp. religious) ceremonial. **2** a performance by mummers. [OF *momerie* (as MUMMER)]

mummify /múmmifī/ *v.tr.* (**-ies**, **-ied**) **1** embalm and preserve (a body) in the form of a mummy (see MUMMY[2]). **2** (usu. as **mummified** *adj.*) shrivel or dry up (tissues etc.). □□ **mummification** /-fikáysh'n/ *n.*

mummy[1] /múmmi/ *n.* (*pl.* **-ies**) *Brit. colloq.* mother. □ **mummy's boy** a boy or man who is excessively influenced by or attached to his mother. [imit. of a child's pronunc.: cf. MAMMA[1]]
▪ see MOTHER *n.* 1.

mummy[2] /múmmi/ *n.* (*pl.* **-ies**) **1** a body of a human being or animal embalmed for burial, esp. in ancient Egypt. **2** a dried-up body. **3** a pulpy mass (*beat it to a mummy*). **4** a rich brown pigment. [F *momie* f. med.L *mumia* f. Arab. *mūmiyā* f. Pers. *mūm* wax]

mumps /mumps/ *n.pl.* **1** (treated as *sing.*) a contagious and infectious viral disease with swelling of the parotid salivary glands in the face. **2** a fit of sulks. □□ **mumpish** *adj.* (in sense 2). [archaic *mump* be sullen]

munch /munch/ *v.tr.* eat steadily with a marked action of the jaws. [ME, imit.: cf. CRUNCH]
▪ chew, crunch, masticate, champ, chomp, scrunch.

mundane /múndáyn/ *adj.* **1** dull, routine. **2** of this world; worldly. □□ **mundanely** *adv.* **mundaneness** *n.* **mundanity** /-dánniti/ *n.* (*pl.* **-ies**). [ME f. OF *mondain* f. LL *mundanus* f. L *mundus* world]
▪ **1** see HUMDRUM *adj.* **2** see WORLDLY 1.

mung /mung/ *n.* (in full **mung bean**) a leguminous plant, *Phaseolus aureus*, native to India and used as food. [Hindi *mūng*]

mungo /múnggō/ *n.* (*pl.* **-os**) the short fibres recovered from heavily felted material. [19th c.: orig. uncert.]

municipal /myoonissip'l/ *adj.* of or concerning a municipality or its self-government. □□ **municipalize** *v.tr.* (also **-ise**). **municipalization** /-līzáysh'n/ *n.* **municipally** *adv.* [L *municipalis* f. *municipium* free city f. *municeps -cipis* citizen with privileges f. *munia* civic offices + *capere* take]
▪ civic, civil, metropolitan, urban, city, town, borough, parish, council.

municipality /myoonissipálliti/ *n.* (*pl.* **-ies**) **1** a town or district having local government. **2** the governing body of this area. [F *municipalité* f. *municipal* (as MUNICIPAL)]
▪ **1** city, metropolis, town, borough, district, *Brit. hist.* or *Austral.* & *NZ* township.

munificent /myoonniffis'nt/ *adj.* (of a giver or a gift) splendidly generous, bountiful. □□ **munificence** *n.* **munificently** *adv.* [L *munificent-*, var. stem of *munificus* f. *munus* gift]
▪ see GENEROUS 1.

muniment /myoonimənt/ *n.* (usu. in *pl.*) **1** a document kept as evidence of rights or privileges etc. **2** an archive. [ME f. OF f. L *munimentum* defence, in med.L title-deed f. *munire munit-* fortify]

munition /myoonish'n/ *n.* & *v.* ● *n.* (usu. in *pl.*) military weapons, ammunition, equipment, and stores. ● *v.tr.* supply with munitions. [F f. L *munitio -onis* fortification (as MUNIMENT)]
▪ *n.* (*munitions*) see HARDWARE 2.

munitioner /myoonishənər/ *n.* a person who makes or supplies munitions.

munnion var. of MULLION.

munshi var. of MOONSHEE.

munt /moont/ *n. S.Afr. sl. offens.* a Black African. [Bantu *umuntu* person]

muntjac /múntjak/ *n.* (also **muntjak**) any small deer of the genus *Muntiacus* native to SE Asia, the male having tusks and small antlers. [Sundanese *minchek*]

Muntz metal /munts/ *n.* an alloy (60% copper, 40% zinc) used for sheathing ships etc. [G. F. *Muntz*, Engl. manufacturer d. 1857]

muon /myoo-on/ *n. Physics* an unstable elementary particle like an electron, but with a much greater mass. [μ (MU), as the symbol for it]

murage /myoorij/ *n. hist.* a tax levied for building or repairing the walls of a town. [ME f. OF, in med.L *muragium* f. OF *mur* f. L *murus* wall]

mural /myoorəl/ *n.* & *adj.* ● *n.* a painting executed directly on a wall. ● *adj.* **1** of or like a wall. **2** on a wall. □ **mural crown** *Rom. Antiq.* a crown or garland given to the soldier who was first to scale the wall of a besieged town. □□ **muralist** *n.* [F f. L *muralis* f. *murus* wall]

murder /múrdər/ *n.* & *v.* ● *n.* **1** the unlawful premeditated killing of a human being by another (cf. MANSLAUGHTER). **2** *colloq.* an unpleasant, troublesome, or dangerous state of affairs (*it was murder here on Saturday*). ● *v.tr.* **1** kill (a human being) unlawfully, esp. wickedly or inhumanly. **2** *Law* kill (a human being) with a premeditated motive. **3** *colloq.* utterly defeat or spoil by a bad performance, mispronunciation etc. (*murdered the soliloquy in the second act*). □ **cry blue murder** *sl.* make an extravagant outcry. **get away with murder** *colloq.* do whatever one wishes and escape punishment. **murder will out** murder cannot remain undetected. □□ **murderer** *n.* **murderess** *n.* [OE *morthor* & OF *murdre* f. Gmc]
▪ *n.* **1** homicide, killing, slaying, assassination; slaughter, butchery, genocide, massacre, liquidation, extermination, eradication, *disp.* decimation; bloodshed, carnage; regicide, patricide, matricide, parricide, fratricide, uxoricide, infanticide. **2** see HELL 2. ● *v.* **1** kill, assassinate, put to death, destroy, butcher, massacre, liquidate, exterminate, eradicate, annihilate, extinguish, slaughter, lay low, eliminate, take out, snuff out, *colloq.* polish off, *literary or joc.* slay, *sl.* wipe out, bump off, knock off, do in, *esp. US sl.* rub out, *US sl.* waste, ice. **3** spoil, ruin, mar, destroy, wreck, kill, mangle, butcher, mutilate. □□ **murderer, murderess** killer, assassin, homicide, cutthroat, executioner, butcher, *literary or joc.* slayer, *sl.* hit man.

murderous /múrdərəss/ *adj.* **1** (of a person, weapon, action, etc.) capable of, intending, or involving murder or great harm. **2** *colloq.* extremely troublesome, unpleasant, or dangerous. □□ **murderously** *adv.* **murderousness** *n.*
▪ **1** fatal, lethal, deadly, deathly, mortal; destructive, devastating, sanguinary, bloody, brutal, savage, bloodthirsty, barbarous, cruel, inhuman, *poet. or rhet.* fell. **2** strenuous, stressful, difficult, arduous, exhausting, harrowing, rigorous, intolerable, unbearable, *colloq.* hellish, killing.

mure /myoor/ *v.tr. archaic* **1** immure. **2** (foll. by *up*) wall up or shut up in an enclosed space. [ME f. OF *murer* f. *mur*: see MURAGE]

murex /myooreks/ *n.* (*pl.* **murices** /-riseez/ or **murexes**) any gastropod mollusc of the genus *Murex*, yielding a purple dye. [L]

murine /myoorin/ *adj.* of or like a mouse or mice. [L *murinus* f. *mus muris* mouse]

murk /murk/ *n.* & *adj.* (also **mirk**) ● *n.* **1** darkness, poor visibility. **2** air obscured by fog etc. ● *adj. archaic* (of night, day, place, etc.) = MURKY. [prob. f. Scand.: cf. ON *myrkr*]
▪ *n.* **1** see GLOOM *n.* 1.

murky /múrki/ *adj.* (also **mirky**) (**-ier**, **-iest**) **1** dark, gloomy. **2** (of darkness) thick, dirty. **3** suspiciously obscure (*murky past*). □□ **murkily** *adv.* **murkiness** *n.*

■ **1, 2** dark, gloomy, threatening, dim, clouded, cloudy, overcast, grey, dismal, dreary, bleak, sombre, grim, funereal, shady, shadowy; thick, dirty. **3** see SHADY 3.

murmur /múrmər/ *n.* & *v.* ● *n.* **1** a subdued continuous sound, as made by waves, a brook, etc. **2** a softly spoken or nearly inarticulate utterance. **3** *Med.* a recurring sound heard in the auscultation of the heart and usu. indicating abnormality. **4** a subdued expression of discontent. ● *v.* **1** *intr.* make a subdued continuous sound. **2** *tr.* utter (words) in a low voice. **3** *intr.* (usu. foll. by *at*, *against*) complain in low tones, grumble. ▫▫ **murmurer** *n.* **murmuringly** *adv.* **murmurous** *adj.* [ME f. OF *murmurer* f. L *murmurare*: cf. Gk *mormurō* (of water) roar, Skr. *marmaras* noisy]
■ *n.* **1** undercurrent, undertone, background noise *or* sound, rumble, mumble, drone, buzz, murmuring, hum, *literary* susurration, susurrus. **2** see WHISPER *n.* 1. **4** mutter, complaint, grumble, *colloq.* grouse; see also MOAN *n.* 3. ● *v.* **1, 2** mumble, mutter; whisper, drone, buzz, hum. **3** complain, grumble, mutter, moan, *colloq.* grouse, grouch, gripe, *Brit. colloq.* chunter.

murphy /múrfi/ *n.* (*pl.* **-ies**) *sl.* a potato. [Ir. surname]

Murphy's Law /múrfiz/ *n. joc.* any of various maxims about the perverseness of things.

murrain /múrrin/ *n.* **1** an infectious disease of cattle, carried by parasites. **2** *archaic* a plague, esp. the potato blight during the Irish famine in the mid-19th c. [ME f. AF *moryn*, OF *morine* f. *morir* f. L *mori* die]

murrey /múrri/ *n.* & *adj.* *archaic* ● *n.* the colour of a mulberry; a deep red or purple. ● *adj.* of this colour. [ME f. OF *moré* f. med.L *moratus* f. *morum* mulberry]

murther /múrthər/ *archaic* var. of MURDER.

Mus.B. *abbr.* (also **Mus. Bac.**) Bachelor of Music. [L *Musicae Baccalaureus*]

muscadel var. of MUSCATEL.

Muscadet /múskəday/ *n.* **1** a white wine from the Loire region of France. **2** a variety of grape from which the wine is made. [*Muscadet* variety of grape]

muscadine /múskədin, -dīn/ *n.* a variety of grape with a musk flavour, used chiefly in wine-making. [perh. Engl. form f. Prov. MUSCAT]

muscarine /múskərin/ *n.* a poisonous alkaloid from the fungus *Amanita muscaria*. [L *muscarius* f. *musca* fly]

muscat /múskət/ *n.* **1** a sweet fortified white wine made from muscadines. **2** a muscadine. [F f. Prov. *muscat muscade* (adj.) f. *musc* MUSK]

muscatel /múskətél/ *n.* (also **muscadel** /-dél/) **1** = MUSCAT. **2** a raisin from a muscadine grape. [ME f. OF f. Prov. dimin. of *muscat*: see MUSCAT]

muscle /múss'l/ *n.* & *v.* ● *n.* **1** a fibrous tissue with the ability to contract, producing movement in or maintaining the position of an animal body. **2** the part of an animal body that is composed of muscles. **3** physical power or strength. ● *v.intr.* (usu. foll. by *in*) *colloq.* force oneself on others; intrude by forceful means. ▫ **muscle-bound** with muscles stiff and inelastic through excessive exercise or training. **muscle-man** a man with highly developed muscles, esp. one employed as an intimidator. **not move a muscle** be completely motionless. ▫▫ **muscled** *adj.* (usu. in *comb.*). **muscleless** *adj.* **muscly** *adj.* [F f. L *musculus* dimin. of *mus* mouse, from the fancied mouselike form of some muscles]
■ *n.* **3** see STRENGTH 1.

muscology /muskólləji/ *n.* the study of mosses. ▫▫ **muscologist** *n.* [mod.L *muscologia* f. L *muscus* moss]

muscovado /múskəvaádō/ *n.* (*pl.* **-os**) an unrefined sugar made from the juice of sugar cane by evaporation and draining off the molasses. [Sp. *mascabado* (sugar) of the lowest quality]

Muscovite /múskəvīt/ *n.* & *adj.* ● *n.* **1** a native or citizen of Moscow. **2** *archaic* a Russian. ● *adj.* **1** of or relating to Moscow. **2** *archaic* of or relating to Russia. [mod.L *Muscovita* f. *Muscovia* = MUSCOVY]

muscovite /múskəvīt/ *n.* a silver-grey form of mica with a sheetlike crystalline structure that is used in the manufacture of electrical equipment etc. [obs. MUSCOVY *glass* (in the same sense) + -ITE[1]]

Muscovy /múskəvi/ *n.* *archaic* Russia. ▫ **Muscovy duck** a tropical American duck, *Cairina moschata*, having a small crest and red markings on its head. [obs. F *Muscovie* f. mod.L *Moscovia* f. Russ. *Moskva* Moscow]

muscular /múskyoolər/ *adj.* **1** of or affecting the muscles. **2** having well-developed muscles. ▫ **muscular Christianity** a Christian life of cheerful physical activity as described in the writings of Charles Kingsley. **muscular dystrophy** see DYSTROPHY. **muscular rheumatism** = MYALGIA. **muscular stomach** see STOMACH. ▫▫ **muscularity** /-lárriti/ *n.* **muscularly** *adv.* [earlier *musculous* (as MUSCLE)]
■ **2** sinewy, brawny, burly, powerful, well-built, strapping, rugged, husky, robust, athletic, sturdy, well-muscled, broad-shouldered, *colloq.* hunky.

musculature /múskyooləchər/ *n.* the muscular system of a body or organ. [F f. L (as MUSCLE)]

Mus.D. *abbr.* (also **Mus. Doc.**) Doctor of Music. [L *Musicae Doctor*]

muse[1] /myōōz/ *n.* **1** (as **the Muses**) (in Greek and Roman mythology) nine goddesses, the daughters of Zeus and Mnemosyne, who inspire poetry, music, drama, etc. **2** (usu. prec. by *the*) **a** a poet's inspiring goddess. **b** a poet's genius. [ME f. OF *muse* or L *musa* f. Gk *mousa*]

muse[2] /myōōz/ *v.* & *n.* ● *v.* *literary* **1** *intr.* **a** (usu. foll. by *on*, *upon*) ponder, reflect. **b** (usu. foll. by *on*) gaze meditatively (on a scene etc.). **2** *tr.* say meditatively. ● *n.* *archaic* a fit of abstraction. [ME f. OF *muser* to waste time f. Rmc perh. f. med.L *musum* muzzle]
■ *v.* **1 a** cogitate, meditate, reflect, contemplate, ruminate, think, consider, deliberate, mull, brood, ponder; be absorbed (in thought), be in a brown study, dream, day-dream, be in a trance *or* reverie; (*muse on*) weigh, evaluate, study, chew over, revolve.

musette /myoozét/ *n.* **1 a** a kind of small bagpipe with bellows, common in the French court in the 17th–18th c. **b** a tune imitating the sound of this. **2** a small oboe-like double-reed instrument in 19th-c. France. **3** a popular dance in the courts of Louis XIV and XV. **4** *US* a small knapsack. [ME f. OF, dimin. of *muse* bagpipe]

museum /myoozéeəm/ *n.* a building used for storing and exhibiting objects of historical, scientific, or cultural interest. ▫ **museum piece 1** a specimen of art etc. fit for a museum. **2** *derog.* an old-fashioned or quaint person or object. ▫▫ **museology** /myōōziólləji/ *n.* [L f. Gk *mouseion* seat of the Muses: see MUSE[1]]

mush[1] /mush/ *n.* **1** soft pulp. **2** feeble sentimentality. **3** *US* maize porridge. **4** *sl.* the mouth; the face. ▫▫ **mushy** *adj.* (**mushier, mushiest**). **mushily** *adv.* **mushiness** *n.* [app. var. of MASH]
■ **1** see PULP *n.* 2. **2** see *sentimentality* (SENTIMENTAL). **4** see FACE *n.* 1, MOUTH *n.* 1. ▫▫ **mushy** soft, pulpy, doughy, spongy, sloppy, slushy, *colloq.* squishy, squidgy, squashy, *sl.* gooey; mawkish, maudlin, sentimental, romantic, saccharine, sugary, syrupy, *colloq.* corny, *Brit. colloq.* wet, *esp. US colloq.* schmaltzy. **mushiness** see *sentimentality* (SENTIMENTAL).

mush[2] /mush/ *v.* & *n.* *US* ● *v.intr.* **1** (in *imper.*) used as a command to dogs pulling a sledge to urge them forward. **2** go on a journey across snow with a dog-sledge. ● *n.* a journey across snow with a dog-sledge. [prob. corrupt. f. F *marchons* imper. of *marcher* advance]

mushroom /múshrōōm, -rōōm/ *n.* & *v.* ● *n.* **1** the usu. edible spore-producing body of various fungi, esp. *Agaricus campestris*, with a stem and domed cap, proverbial for its rapid growth. **2** the pinkish-brown colour of this. **3** any item resembling a mushroom in shape (*darning mushroom*). **4** (usu. *attrib.*) something that appears or develops suddenly or is ephemeral; an upstart. ● *v.intr.* **1** appear or develop rapidly. **2** expand and flatten like a mushroom cap. **3** gather mushrooms. ▫ **mushroom cloud** a cloud suggesting the shape of a mushroom, esp. from a nuclear explosion. **mushroom growth 1** a sudden development or expansion. **2** anything undergoing this. ▫▫ **mushroomy** *adj.* [ME f. OF *mousseron* f. LL *mussirio -onis*]

■ *v.* **1** see PROLIFERATE. **2** see SWELL *v.* 1.

music /myóozik/ *n.* **1** the art of combining vocal or instrumental sounds (or both) to produce beauty of form, harmony, and expression of emotion. **2** the sounds so produced. **3** musical compositions. **4** the written or printed score of a musical composition. **5** certain pleasant sounds, e.g. birdsong, the sound of a stream, etc. ▫ **music box** *US* = *musical box.* **music centre** equipment combining radio, record-player, tape recorder, etc. **music drama** Wagnerian-type opera without formal arias etc. and governed by dramatic considerations. **music-hall** *Brit.* **1** variety entertainment, popular *c.*1850–1914, consisting of singing, dancing, and novelty acts. **2** a theatre where this took place. **music of the spheres** see SPHERE. **music-paper** paper printed with staves for writing music. **music stand** a rest or frame on which sheet music or a score is supported. **music stool** a stool for a pianist, usu. with adjustable height. **music theatre** in late 20th-c. music, the combination of elements from music and drama in new forms distinct from traditional opera, esp. as designed for small groups of performers. **music to one's ears** something very pleasant to hear. [ME f. OF *musique* f. L *musica* f. Gk *mousikē* (*tekhnē* art) of the Muses (*mousa* Muse: see MUSE[1])]

■ **2** see STRAIN[1] *n.* 4. **4** see SCORE *n.* 5a.

musical /myóozik'l/ *adj.* & *n.* ● *adj.* **1** of or relating to music. **2** (of sounds, a voice, etc.) melodious, harmonious. **3** fond of or skilled in music (*the musical one of the family*). **4** set to or accompanied by music. ● *n.* a musical film or comedy. ▫ **musical box** *Brit.* a mechanical instrument playing a tune by causing a toothed cylinder to strike a comblike metal plate within a box. **musical bumps** a game similar to musical chairs, with players sitting on the floor and the one left standing eliminated. **musical chairs 1** a party game in which the players compete in successive rounds for a decreasing number of chairs. **2** a series of changes or political manoeuvring etc. after the manner of the game. **musical comedy** a light dramatic entertainment of songs, dialogue, and dancing, connected by a slender plot. **musical film** a film in which music is an important feature. **musical glasses** an instrument in which notes are produced by rubbing graduated glass bowls or tubes. **musical saw** a bent saw played with a violin bow. ▫▫ **musicality** /-kálliti/ *n.* **musicalize** *v.tr.* (also **-ise**). **musically** *adv.* **musicalness** *n.* [ME f. OF f. med.L *musicalis* f. L *musica*: see MUSIC]

■ *adj.* **2** tuneful, melodic, harmonious, lilting, lyrical, melodious, mellifluous, dulcet, sweet, euphonious, sonorous.

musicale /myóozikaál/ *n. US* a musical party. [F fem. adj. (as MUSICAL)]

musician /myoozish'n/ *n.* a person who plays a musical instrument, esp. professionally, or is otherwise musically gifted. ▫▫ **musicianly** *adj.* **musicianship** *n.* [ME f. OF *musicien* f. *musique* (as MUSIC, -ICIAN)]

■ see PLAYER 2.

musicology /myóozikólləji/ *n.* the study of music other than that directed to proficiency in performance or composition. ▫▫ **musicologist** *n.* **musicological** /-kəlójik'l/ *adj.* [F *musicologie* or MUSIC + -LOGY]

musique concrète /myoozeék konkrét/ *n.* = *concrete music.* [F]

musk /musk/ *n.* **1** a strong-smelling reddish-brown substance produced by a gland in the male musk deer and used as an ingredient in perfumes. **2** the plant, *Mimulus moschatus*, with pale-green ovate leaves and yellow flowers (orig. with a smell of musk which is no longer perceptible in modern varieties). ▫ **musk deer** any small Asian deer of the genus *Moschus*, having no antlers and in the male having long protruding canine teeth. **musk duck** the Australian duck *Biziura lobata*, having a musky smell. **musk melon** the common yellow or green melon, *Cucumis melo*, usu. with a raised network of markings on the skin. **musk ox** a large goat-antelope, *Ovibos moschatus*, native to N. America, with a thick shaggy coat and small curved horns. **musk-rose** a rambling rose, *Rosa moschata*, with large white flowers smelling of musk. **musk thistle** a nodding thistle, *Carduus nutans*, whose flowers have a musky fragrance. **musk-tree** (or **-wood**) an Australian tree, *Olearia argyrophylla*, with a musky smell. ▫▫ **musky** *adj.* (**muskier, muskiest**). **muskiness** *n.* [ME f. LL *muscus* f. Pers. *mušk*, perh. f. Skr. *muṣka* scrotum (from the shape of the musk deer's gland)]

muskeg /múskeg/ *n.* a level swamp or bog in Canada. [Cree]

muskellunge /múskəlunj/ *n.* = MASKINONGE. [Algonquian]

musket /múskit/ *n. hist.* an infantryman's (esp. smooth-bored) light gun, often supported on the shoulder. ▫ **musket-shot 1** a shot fired from a musket. **2** the range of this shot. [F *mousquet* f. It. *moschetto* crossbow bolt f. *mosca* fly]

musketeer /múskiteer/ *n. hist.* a soldier armed with a musket.

musketry /múskitri/ *n.* **1** muskets, or soldiers armed with muskets, referred to collectively. **2** the knowledge of handling muskets.

muskrat /múskrat/ *n.* **1** a large aquatic rodent, *Ondatra zibethica*, native to N. America, having a musky smell. Also called MUSQUASH. **2** the fur of this.

Muslim /móozlim, múz-/ *n.* & *adj.* (also **Moslem** /mózləm/) ● *n.* a follower of the Islamic religion. ● *adj.* of or relating to the Muslims or their religion. [Arab. *muslim*, part. of *aslama*: see ISLAM]

muslin /múzlin/ *n.* **1** a fine delicately woven cotton fabric. **2** *US* a cotton cloth in plain weave. ▫▫ **muslined** *adj.* [F *mousseline* f. It. *mussolina* f. *Mussolo* Mosul in Iraq, where it was made]

musmon /múzmən/ *n. Zool.* = MOUFFLON. [L *musimo* f. Gk *mousmōn*]

muso /myóozō/ *n.* (*pl.* **-os**) *sl.* a musician, esp. a professional. [abbr.]

musquash /múskwosh/ *n.* = MUSKRAT. [Algonquian]

muss /muss/ *v.* & *n. US colloq.* ● *v.tr.* (often foll. by *up*) disarrange; throw into disorder. ● *n.* a state of confusion; untidiness, mess. ▫▫ **mussy** *adj.* [app. var. of MESS]

■ *v.* see MESS *v.* 1. ▫▫ **mussy** see UNTIDY.

mussel /múss'l/ *n.* **1** any bivalve mollusc of the genus *Mytilus*, living in sea water and often used for food. **2** any similar freshwater mollusc of the genus *Margaritifer* or *Anodonta*, forming pearls. [ME f. OE *mus(c)le* & MLG *mussel*, ult. rel. to L *musculus* (as MUSCLE)]

Mussulman /múss'lmən/ *n.* & *adj. archaic* ● *n.* (*pl.* **-mans** or **-men**) a Muslim. ● *adj.* of or concerning Muslims. [Pers. *musulmān* orig. adj. f. *muslim* (as MUSLIM)]

must[1] /must/ *v.* & *n.* ● *v.aux.* (*3rd sing. present* **must**; *past* **had to** or in indirect speech **must**) (foll. by infin., or *absol.*) **1 a** be obliged to (*you must go to school*; *must we leave now?*; *said he must go*; *I must away*). ¶ The negative (i.e. lack of obligation) is expressed by *not have to* or *need not*; *must not* denotes positive forbidding, as in *you must not smoke.* **b** in ironic questions (*must you slam the door?*). **2** be certain to (*we must win in the end*; *you must be her sister*; *he must be mad*; *they must have left by now*; *seemed as if the roof must blow off*). **3** ought to (*we must see what can be done*; *it must be said that*). **4** expressing insistence (*I must ask you to leave*). **5** (foll. by *not* + infin.) **a** not be permitted to, be forbidden to (*you must not smoke*). **b** ought not; need not (*you mustn't think he's angry*; *you must not worry*). **c** expressing insistence that something should not be done (*they must not be told*). **6** (as past or historic present) expressing the perversity of destiny (*what must I do but break my leg*). ● *n. colloq.* a thing that cannot or should not be overlooked or missed (*if you go to London St Paul's is a must*). ▫ **I must say** often *iron.* I cannot refrain from saying (*I must say he made a*

good attempt; a fine way to behave, I must say). **must needs** see NEEDS. [OE *mōste* past of *mōt* may]
■ *v.* **1, 3, 4** ought to, should, have to, need to, be obliged to, be required to, be *or* feel compelled *or* forced to. ● *n.* necessity, requisite, requirement, obligation, *sine qua non*, essential.

must[2] /must/ *n.* grape-juice before fermentation is complete. [OE f. L *mustum* neut. of *mustus* new]

must[3] /must/ *n.* mustiness, mould. [back-form. f. MUSTY]

must[4] /must/ *adj.* & *n.* (also **musth**) ● *adj.* (of a male elephant or camel) in a state of frenzy. ● *n.* this state. [Urdu f. Pers. *mast* intoxicated]

mustache *US* var. of MOUSTACHE.

mustachio /məstaashiō/ *n.* (*pl.* **-os**) (often in *pl.*) *archaic* a moustache. □□ **mustachioed** *adj.* [Sp. *mostacho* & It. *mostaccio* (as MOUSTACHE)]

mustang /mústang/ *n.* a small wild horse native to Mexico and California. □ **mustang grape** a grape from the wild vine *Vitis candicans*, of the southern US, used for making wine. [Sp. *mestengo* f. *mesta* company of graziers, & Sp. *mostrenco*]

mustard /mústərd/ *n.* **1 a** any of various plants of the genus *Brassica* with slender pods and yellow flowers, esp. *B. nigra*. **b** any of various plants of the genus *Sinapis*, esp. *S. alba*, eaten at the seedling stage, often with cress. **2** the seeds of these which are crushed, made into a paste, and used as a spicy condiment. **3** the brownish-yellow colour of this condiment. **4** *sl.* a thing which adds piquancy or zest. □ **mustard gas** a colourless oily liquid, whose vapour is a powerful irritant and vesicant. **mustard plaster** a poultice made with mustard. **mustard seed 1** the seed of the mustard plant. **2** a small thing capable of great development (Matt. 13:31). [ME f. OF *mo(u)starde*: orig. the condiment as prepared with MUST[2]]

muster /mústər/ *v.* & *n.* ● *v.* **1** *tr.* collect (orig. soldiers) for inspection, to check numbers, etc. **2** *tr.* & *intr.* collect, gather together. **3** *tr. Austral.* round up (livestock). ● *n.* **1** the assembly of persons for inspection. **2** an assembly, a collection. **3** *Austral.* a rounding up of livestock. **4** *Austral. sl.* the number of people attending (a meeting, etc.) (*had a good muster*). □ **muster-book** a book for registering military personnel. **muster in** *US* enrol (recruits). **muster out** *US* discharge (soldiers etc.). **muster-roll** an official list of officers and men in a regiment or ship's company. **muster up** collect or summon (courage, strength, etc.). **pass muster** be accepted as adequate. □□ **musterer** *n.* (in sense 3 of n. & v.). [ME f. OF *mo(u)stre* ult. f. L *monstrare* show]
■ *v.* **1, 2** call together, assemble, convene, collect, mobilize, rally, round up, gather, marshal; muster up, summon (up), *formal* convoke; come together. ● *n.* **1, 2** rally, assembly, assemblage, convocation, meet, meeting, convention, congress, round-up, gathering, congregation, aggregation, turnout. □ **pass muster** come *or* be up to scratch, measure up, be acceptable *or* adequate, be good enough, *colloq.* make the grade, come *or* be up to snuff.

musth var. of MUST[4].

mustn't /múss'nt/ *contr.* must not.

musty /músti/ *adj.* (**mustier**, **mustiest**) **1** mouldy. **2** of a mouldy or stale smell or taste. **3** stale, antiquated (*musty old books*). □□ **mustily** *adv.* **mustiness** *n.* [perh. alt. f. *moisty* (MOIST) by assoc. with MUST[2]]
■ **1, 2** mouldy, damp, mildewed, mildewy, rancid, spoilt, decayed, rotten, putrid, fetid, fusty, stale. **3** stale, old-fashioned, antiquated, ancient, out of date, bygone, *passé*, obsolete, archaic, *colloq.* antediluvian; tired, hoary, worn out, trite, clichéd, *colloq.* old hat.

mutable /myóotəb'l/ *adj. literary* **1** liable to change. **2** fickle. □□ **mutability** /-bílliti/ *n.* [L *mutabilis* f. *mutare* change]
■ **1** see CHANGEABLE 1. **2** see FICKLE.

mutagen /myóotəjən/ *n.* an agent promoting mutation, e.g. radiation. □□ **mutagenic** /-jénnik/ *adj.* **mutagenesis** /-jénnisiss/ *n.* [MUTATION + -GEN]

mutant /myóot'nt/ *adj.* & *n.* ● *adj.* resulting from mutation. ● *n.* a mutant form. [L *mutant-* part. f. *mutare* change]

mutate /myootáyt/ *v.intr.* & *tr.* undergo or cause to undergo mutation. [back-form. f. MUTATION]
■ see TRANSFORM *v.*

mutation /myootáysh'n/ *n.* **1** the process or an instance of change or alteration. **2** a genetic change which, when transmitted to offspring, gives rise to heritable variations. **3** a mutant. **4 a** an umlaut. **b** (in a Celtic language) a change of a consonant etc. determined by a preceding word. □□ **mutational** *adj.* **mutationally** *adv.* [ME f. L *mutatio* f. *mutare* change]
■ **1** change, alteration, modification, transformation, metamorphosis, transmutation, transfiguration, evolution, variation. **3** deformity, monstrosity, freak, mutant; anomaly, departure.

mutatis mutandis /mootaatiss mootándiss, myoo-/ *adv.* (in comparing cases) making the necessary alterations. [L]

mutch /much/ *n. dial.* a woman's or child's linen cap. [ME f. MDu. *mutse* MHG *mütze* f. med.L *almucia* AMICE[2]]

mute /myoot/ *adj.*, *n.*, & *v.* ● *adj.* **1** silent, refraining from or temporarily bereft of speech. **2** not emitting articulate sound. **3** (of a person or animal) dumb. **4** not expressed in speech (*mute protest*). **5 a** (of a letter) not pronounced. **b** (of a consonant) plosive. **6** (of hounds) not giving tongue. ● *n.* **1** a dumb person (*a deaf mute*). **2** *Mus.* **a** a clamp for damping the resonance of the strings of a violin etc. **b** a pad or cone for damping the sound of a wind instrument. **3** an unsounded consonant. **4** an actor whose part is in a dumb show. **5** a dumb servant in oriental countries. **6** a hired mourner. ● *v.tr.* **1** deaden, muffle, or soften the sound of (a thing, esp. a musical instrument). **2 a** tone down, make less intense. **b** (as **muted** *adj.*) (of colours etc.) subdued (*a muted green*). □ **mute button** a device on a telephone etc. to temporarily prevent the caller from hearing what is being said at the receiver's end. **mute swan** the common white swan. □□ **mutely** *adv.* **muteness** *n.* [ME f. OF *muet*, dimin. of *mu* f. L *mutus*, assim. to L]
■ *adj.* **1–3** silent, dumb, speechless, voiceless, wordless, tight-lipped, taciturn, tacit, reserved, quiet, *colloq.* mum. **4** unspoken, unsaid, silent; see also TACIT. ● *v.* **1, 2a** deaden, silence, muffle, stifle, dampen, damp (down), subdue, soften, suppress, quiet, hush, restrain, soft-pedal, turn down, tone down, quieten (down).

mutilate /myóotilayt/ *v.tr.* **1 a** deprive (a person or animal) of a limb or organ. **b** destroy the use of (a limb or organ). **2** render (a book etc.) imperfect by excision or some act of destruction. □□ **mutilation** /-láysh'n/ *n.* **mutilative** /-lətiv/ *adj.* **mutilator** *n.* [L *mutilare* f. *mutilus* maimed]
■ **1** maim, disfigure, mangle, cripple, lame, butcher, disable; dismember, hack *or* cut *or* tear *or* rip to pieces. **2** deface, vandalize, spoil, mar, ruin, damage, destroy; bowdlerize, censor.

mutineer /myóotinéer/ *n.* a person who mutinies. [F *mutinier* f. *mutin* rebellious f. *muete* movement ult. f. L *movēre* move]
■ see REBEL *n.*

mutinous /myóotinəss/ *adj.* rebellious; tending to mutiny. □□ **mutinously** *adv.* [obs. *mutine* rebellion f. F *mutin*: see MUTINEER]
■ rebellious, revolutionary, subversive, seditious, insurgent, insurrectionary; recalcitrant, refractory, contumacious, obstinate, defiant, insubordinate, disobedient, unruly, unmanageable, ungovernable, uncontrollable.

mutiny /myóotini/ *n.* & *v.* ● *n.* (*pl.* **-ies**) an open revolt against constituted authority, esp. by soldiers or sailors against their officers. ● *v.intr.* (**-ies**, **-ied**) (often foll. by *against*) revolt; engage in mutiny. [obs. *mutine* (as MUTINOUS)]
■ *n.* revolt, rebellion, revolution, insurgency, insurgence, insurrection, uprising. ● *v.* rebel, rise up, revolt; disobey, subvert, agitate.

mutism /myóotiz'm/ *n.* muteness; silence; dumbness. [F *mutisme* f. L (as MUTE)]

muton /myóoton/ *n. Biol.* the smallest element of genetic material capable of giving rise to a mutant individual.

mutt /mut/ *n.* **1** *sl.* an ignorant, stupid, or blundering person. **2** *derog.* a dog. [abbr. of *mutton-head*]
■ **2** see MONGREL *n.*

mutter /múttər/ *v.* & *n.* ● *v.* **1** *intr.* speak low in a barely audible manner. **2** *intr.* (often foll. by *against*, *at*) murmur or grumble about. **3** *tr.* utter (words etc.) in a low tone. **4** *tr.* say in secret. ● *n.* **1** muttered words or sounds. **2** muttering. □□ **mutterer** *n.* **mutteringly** *adv.* [ME, rel. to MUTE]
■ *v.* **1, 3** mumble, murmur, grunt; see also WHISPER *v.* 1. **2** grumble, complain, moan, *colloq.* grouch, grouse, gripe, *Brit. colloq.* chunter.

mutton /mútt'n/ *n.* **1** the flesh of sheep used for food. **2** *joc.* a sheep. □ **mutton-bird** *Austral.* **1** any bird of the genus *Puffinus*, esp. the short-tailed shearwater, *P. tenuirostris*. **2** any of various petrels. **mutton chop 1** a piece of mutton, usu. the rib and half vertebra to which it is attached. **2** (in full **mutton chop whisker**) a side whisker shaped like this. **mutton dressed as lamb** *colloq.* a usu. middle-aged or elderly woman dressed or made up to appear younger. **mutton-head** *colloq.* a dull, stupid person. **mutton-headed** *colloq.* dull, stupid. □□ **muttony** *adj.* [ME f. OF *moton* f. med.L *multo -onis* prob. f. Gaulish]

mutual /myóochooəl, -tyooəl/ *adj.* **1** (of feelings, actions, etc.) experienced or done by each of two or more parties with reference to the other or others (*mutual affection*). **2** *colloq. disp.* common to two or more persons (*a mutual friend*; *a mutual interest*). **3** standing in (a specified) relation to each other (*mutual well-wishers*; *mutual beneficiaries*). □ **mutual fund** *US* a unit trust. **mutual inductance** the property of an electric circuit that causes an electromotive force to be generated in it by change in the current flowing through a magnetically linked circuit. **mutual induction** the production of an electromotive force between adjacent circuits that are magnetically linked. **mutual insurance** insurance in which some or all of the profits are divided among the policyholders. □□ **mutuality** /-choo-álliti, -tyoo-álliti/ *n.* **mutually** *adv.* [ME f. OF *mutuel* f. L *mutuus* mutual, borrowed, rel. to *mutare* change]
■ **1, 3** reciprocal, reciprocated; interactive, complementary. **2** communal, joint, shared; see also COMMON *adj.* 2.

mutualism /myóochooəliz'm, myóotyoo-/ *n.* **1** the doctrine that mutual dependence is necessary to social well-being. **2** mutually beneficial symbiosis. □□ **mutualist** *n.* & *adj.* **mutualistic** /-lístik/ *adj.* **mutualistically** /-lístikəli/ *adv.*

mutuel /myóotyooəl/ *n.* esp. *US* a totalizator; a *pari-mutuel*. [abbr. of PARI-MUTUEL]

mutule /myóotyool/ *n. Archit.* a block derived from the ends of wooden beams projecting under a Doric cornice. [F f. L *mutulus*]

muu-muu /móomoo/ *n.* a woman's loose brightly-coloured dress. [Hawaiian]

Muzak /myóozak/ *n.* **1** *propr.* a system of music transmission for playing in public places. **2** (**muzak**) recorded light background music. [alt. f. MUSIC]

muzhik /móozhik/ *n.* (also **moujik**) *hist.* a Russian peasant. [Russ. *muzhik*]
■ see PEASANT.

muzzle /múzz'l/ *n.* & *v.* ● *n.* **1** the projecting part of an animal's face, including the nose and mouth. **2** a guard, usu. made of straps or wire, fitted over an animal's nose and mouth to stop it biting or feeding. **3** the open end of a firearm. ● *v.tr.* **1** put a muzzle on (an animal etc.). **2** impose silence upon. **3** *Naut.* take in (a sail). □ **muzzle-loader** a gun that is loaded through the muzzle. **muzzle velocity** the velocity with which a projectile leaves the muzzle of a gun. □□ **muzzler** *n.* [ME f. OF *musel* ult. f. med.L *musum*: cf. MUSE[2]]
■ *n.* **1** snout, trunk, proboscis. ● *v.* **2** see SILENCE *v.*

muzzy /múzzi/ *adj.* (**muzzier, muzziest**) **1 a** mentally hazy; dull, spiritless. **b** stupid from drinking alcohol. **2** blurred, indistinct. □□ **muzzily** *adv.* **muzziness** *n.* [18th c.: orig. unkn.]
■ **1** see GROGGY. **2** see FAINT *adj.* 1.

MV *abbr.* **1** motor vessel. **2** muzzle velocity. **3** megavolt(s).

MVO *abbr.* (in the UK) Member of the Royal Victorian Order.

MW *abbr.* **1** megawatt(s). **2** medium wave.

mW *abbr.* milliwatt(s).

Mx. *abbr.* **1** maxwell(s). **2** Middlesex (a former county in England).

MY *abbr.* motor yacht.

my /mī/ *poss.pron.* (*attrib.*) **1** of or belonging to me or myself (*my house*; *my own business*). **2** as a form of address in affectionate, sympathetic, jocular, or patronizing contexts (*my dear boy*). **3** in various expressions of surprise (*my God!*; *oh my!*). **4** *Brit. colloq.* indicating the speaker's husband, wife, child, etc. (*my Johnny's ill again*). □ **my Lady** (or **Lord**) the form of address to certain titled persons. [ME *mī*, reduced f. *mīn* MINE[1]]

my- *comb. form* var. of MYO-.

myalgia /mīáljə/ *n.* a pain in a muscle or group of muscles. □□ **myalgic** *adj.* [mod.L f. Gk *mus* muscle]

myalism /mīəliz'm/ *n.* a kind of sorcery akin to obeah, practised esp. in the W. Indies. [*myal*, prob. of W.Afr. orig.]

myall /mīəl/ *n.* **1 a** any tree of the genus *Acacia*, esp. *A. pendula*, native to Australia. **b** the hard scented wood of this, used for fences and tobacco-pipes. **2** an Aboriginal living in a traditional way. [Aboriginal *maiāl*]

myasthenia /mīəss-theéniə/ *n.* a condition causing abnormal weakness of certain muscles . [mod.L f. Gk *mus* muscle: cf. ASTHENIA]

mycelium /mīseéliəm/ *n.* (*pl.* **mycelia** /-liə/) the vegetative part of a fungus, consisting of microscopic threadlike hyphae. □□ **mycelial** *adj.* [mod.L f. Gk *mukēs* mushroom, after EPITHELIUM]

Mycenaean /mīsineéən/ *adj.* & *n.* ● *adj. Archaeol.* of or relating to the late Bronze Age civilization in Greece (*c.*1580–1100 BC), depicted in the Homeric poems and represented by finds at Mycenae and elsewhere. ● *n.* an inhabitant of Mycenae or the Mycenaean world. [L *Mycenaeus*]

-mycin /mīsin/ *comb. form* used to form the names of antibiotic compounds derived from fungi. [Gk *mukēs* fungus + -IN]

mycology /mīkólləji/ *n.* **1** the study of fungi. **2** the fungi of a particular region. □□ **mycological** /-kəlójik'l/ *adj.* **mycologically** /-kəlójikəli/ *adv.* **mycologist** *n.* [Gk *mukēs* mushroom + -LOGY]

mycorrhiza /mīkərīzə/ *n.* (*pl.* **mycorrhizae** /-zee/) a symbiotic association of a fungus and the roots of a plant. □□ **mycorrhizal** *adj.* [mod.L f. Gk *mukēs* mushroom + *rhiza* root]

mycosis /mīkósiss/ *n.* any disease caused by a fungus, e.g. ringworm. □□ **mycotic** /-kóttik/ *adj.* [Gk *mukēs* mushroom + -OSIS]

mycotoxin /mīkətóksin/ *n.* any toxic substance produced by a fungus.

mycotrophy /mīkótrəfi/ *n.* the condition of a plant which has mycorrhizae and is perhaps helped to assimilate nutrients as a result. [G *Mykotrophie* f. Gk *mukēs* mushroom + *trophē* nourishment]

mydriasis /midrīəsiss/ *n.* excessive dilation of the pupil of the eye. [L f. Gk *mudriasis*]

myelin /mī-ilin/ *n.* a white substance which forms a sheath around certain nerve-fibres. □□ **myelination** /-náysh'n/ *n.* [Gk *muelos* marrow + -IN]

myelitis /mī-ilītiss/ *n.* inflammation of the spinal cord. [mod.L f. Gk *muelos* marrow]

myeloid /mī-iloyd/ *adj.* of or relating to bone marrow or the spinal cord. [Gk *muelos* marrow]

myeloma /mī́-ilṓmə/ *n.* (*pl.* **myelomas** or **myelomata** /-mətə/) a malignant tumour of the bone marrow. [mod.L, as MYELITIS + -OMA]

mylodon /mī́ləd'n/ *n.* an extinct gigantic ground sloth of the genus *Mylodon*, with cylindrical teeth and found in deposits formed during the ice age of the Pleistocene epoch in South America. [mod.L f. Gk *mulē* mill, molar + *odous odontos* tooth]

myna /mī́nə/ *n.* (also **mynah, mina**) any of various SE Asian starlings, esp. *Gracula religiosa* able to mimic the human voice. [Hindi *mainā*]

myo- /mī́ō/ *comb. form* (also **my-** before a vowel) muscle. [Gk *mus muos* muscle]

myocardium /mī́ōkaárdiəm/ *n.* (*pl.* **myocardia** /-diə/) the muscular tissue of the heart. ▫▫ **myocardiac** *adj.* **myocardial** *adj.* [MYO- + Gk *kardia* heart]

myofibril /mī́ōfībril/ *n.* any of the elongated contractile threads found in striated muscle cells.

myogenic /mī́əjénnik/ *adj.* originating in muscle tissue.

myoglobin /mī́ōglṓbin/ *n.* an oxygen-carrying protein containing iron and found in muscle cells.

myology /mīóllәji/ *n.* the study of the structure and function of muscles.

myope /mī́ōp/ *n.* a short-sighted person. [F f. LL *myops* f. Gk *muōps* f. *muō* shut + *ōps* eye]

myopia /mīṓpiə/ *n.* **1** short-sightedness. **2** lack of imagination or intellectual insight. ▫▫ **myopic** /mīóppik/ *adj.* **myopically** /mīóppikəli/ *adv.* [mod.L (as MYOPE)]

■ ▫▫ **myopic** see SHORT-SIGHTED 1, SMALL-MINDED.

myosis var. of MIOSIS.

myosotis /mī́əsṓtiss/ *n.* (also **myosote** /mī́əsōt/) any plant of the genus *Myosotis* with blue, pink, or white flowers, esp. a forget-me-not. [L f. Gk *muosōtis* f. *mus muos* mouse + *ous ōtos* ear]

myotonia /mī́ətṓniə/ *n.* the inability to relax voluntary muscle after vigorous effort. ▫▫ **myotonic** /-tónnik/ *adj.* [MYO- + Gk *tonos* tone]

myriad /mírriəd/ *n.* & *adj. literary* ● *n.* **1** an indefinitely great number. **2** ten thousand. ● *adj.* of an indefinitely great number. [LL *mirias miriad-* f. Gk *murias -ados* f. *murioi* 10,000]

■ *n.* **1** see LOT *n.* 1. ● *adj.* see UNLIMITED.

myriapod /mírriəpod/ *n.* & *adj.* ● *n.* any land-living arthropod of the group Myriapoda, with numerous leg-bearing segments, e.g. centipedes and millipedes. ● *adj.* of or relating to this group. [mod.L *Myriapoda* (as MYRIAD, Gk *pous podos* foot)]

myrmidon /múrmid'n/ *n.* **1** a hired ruffian. **2** a base servant. [L *Myrmidones* (pl.) f. Gk *Murmidones*, warlike Thessalian people who went with Achilles to Troy]

myrobalan /mīróbbələn/ *n.* **1** (in full **myrobalan plum**) = *cherry plum*. **2** (in full **myrobalan nut**) the fruit of an Asian tree, *Terminalia chebula*, used in medicines, for tanning leather, and to produce inks and dyes. [F *myrobolan* or L *myrobalanum* f. Gk *murobalanos* f. *muron* unguent + *balanos* acorn]

myrrh[1] /mur/ *n.* a gum resin from several trees of the genus *Commiphora* used, esp. in the Near East, in perfumery, medicine, incense, etc. ▫▫ **myrrhic** *adj.* **myrrhy** *adj.* [OE *myrra, myrre* f. L *myrr(h)a* f. Gk *murra*, of Semitic orig.]

myrrh[2] /mur/ *n.* = *sweet cicely*. [L *myrris* f. Gk *murris*]

myrtaceous /murtáyshəss/ *adj.* of or relating to the plant family Myrtaceae, including myrtles.

myrtle /múrt'l/ *n.* **1** an evergreen shrub of the genus *Myrtus* with aromatic foliage and white flowers, esp. *M. communis*, bearing purple-black ovoid berries. **2** *US* = PERIWINKLE[1]. [ME f. med.L *myrtilla, -us* dimin. of L *myrta, myrtus* f. Gk *murtos*]

myself /mīsélf/ *pron.* **1** *emphat. form* of I[2] or ME[1] (*I saw it myself; I like to do it myself*). **2** *refl. form* of ME[1] (*I was angry with myself; able to dress myself; as bad as myself*). **3** in my normal state of body and mind (*I'm not myself today*). **4** *poet.* = I[2]. ▫ **by myself** see *by oneself*. **I myself** I for my part (*I myself am doubtful*). [ME[1] + SELF: *my-* partly after *herself* with *her* regarded as poss. pron.]

mysterious /misteériəss/ *adj.* **1** full of or wrapped in mystery. **2** (of a person) delighting in mystery. ▫▫ **mysteriously** *adv.* **mysteriousness** *n.* [F *mystérieux* f. *mystère* f. OF (as MYSTERY[1])]

■ puzzling, enigmatic, baffling, insoluble, unsolvable, bewildering, confounding, confusing, perplexing, mystifying, weird, bizarre, strange, uncanny, curious; cryptic, arcane, secret, inscrutable, covert, hidden, furtive, unclear, dark, concealed, occult, inexplicable, incomprehensible, mystic(al), unknown, unfathomable, recondite, abstruse.

mystery[1] /místəri, -tri/ *n.* (*pl.* **-ies**) **1** a secret, hidden, or inexplicable matter (*the reason remains a mystery*). **2** secrecy or obscurity (*wrapped in mystery*). **3** (*attrib.*) secret, undisclosed (*mystery guest*). **4** the practice of making a secret of (esp. unimportant) things (*engaged in mystery and intrigue*). **5** (in full **mystery story**) a fictional work dealing with a puzzling event, esp. a crime (*a well-known mystery writer*). **6 a** a religious truth divinely revealed, esp. one beyond human reason. **b** *RC Ch.* a decade of the rosary. **7** (in *pl.*) **a** the secret religious rites of the ancient Greeks, Romans, etc. **b** *archaic* the Eucharist. ▫ **make a mystery of** treat as an impressive secret. **mystery play** a miracle play. **mystery tour** (or **trip**) a pleasure excursion to an unspecified destination. [ME f. OF *mistere* or L *mysterium* f. Gk *mustērion*, rel. to MYSTIC]

■ **1** puzzle, enigma, conundrum, riddle, question, secret. **2** obscurity, secrecy, indefiniteness, vagueness, nebulousness, ambiguity, ambiguousness, inscrutability, inscrutableness. **3** see SECRET *adj.* 1. **4** secrecy, intrigue, stealth, stealthiness, furtiveness, concealment, covertness, surreptitiousness, clandestinity. **5** detective story *or* novel, murder story *or* mystery, thriller, *colloq.* whodunit.

mystery[2] /místəri, -tri/ *n.* (*pl.* **-ies**) *archaic* a handicraft or trade, esp. as referred to in indentures etc. (*art and mystery*). [ME f. med.L *misterium* contr. of *ministerium* MINISTRY, assoc. with MYSTERY[1]]

mystic /místik/ *n.* & *adj.* ● *n.* a person who seeks by contemplation and self-surrender to obtain unity or identity with or absorption into the Deity or the ultimate reality, or who believes in the spiritual apprehension of truths that are beyond the understanding. ● *adj.* **1** mysterious and awe-inspiring. **2** spiritually allegorical or symbolic. **3** occult, esoteric. **4** of hidden meaning. ▫▫ **mysticism** /-tisiz'm/ *n.* [ME f. OF *mystique* or L *mysticus* f. Gk *mustikos* f. *mustēs* initiated person f. *muō* close the eyes or lips, initiate]

■ *adj.* **1, 3** see OCCULT *adj.* 1, 3. **4** see CRYPTIC 1c.

mystical /místik'l/ *adj.* of mystics or mysticism. ▫▫ **mystically** *adv.*

■ allegorical, symbolic(al), mystic, cabbalistic, arcane, unrevealed, secret, occult, supernatural, esoteric, other-worldly, preternatural, cryptic, concealed, hidden, clandestine, private, veiled, ineffable, mysterious.

mystify /místifī/ *v.tr.* (**-ies, -ied**) **1** bewilder, confuse. **2** hoax, take advantage of the credulity of. **3** wrap up in mystery. ▫▫ **mystification** /-fikáysh'n/ *n.* [F *mystifier* (irreg. formed as MYSTIC or MYSTERY[1])]

■ **1, 2** confuse, confound, mix up, bewilder, stump, puzzle, baffle, beat, *colloq.* flummox; fool, hoax, humbug, *colloq.* bamboozle.

mystique /misteék/ *n.* **1** an atmosphere of mystery and veneration attending some activity or person. **2** any skill or technique impressive or mystifying to the layman. [F f. OF (as MYSTIC)]

■ **1** mystery, magic, charisma, aura, inscrutability, charm, inscrutableness. **2** see MUMBO-JUMBO 2.

myth /mith/ *n.* **1** a traditional narrative usu. involving supernatural or imaginary persons and embodying popular ideas on natural or social phenomena etc. **2** such narratives collectively. **3** a widely held but false notion. **4** a fictitious person, thing, or idea. **5** an allegory (*the Platonic myth*). ▫▫

mythic *adj.* **mythical** *adj.* **mythically** *adv.* [mod.L *mythus* f. LL *mythos* f. Gk *muthos*]
■ **1, 2, 5** legend, fable, allegory, parable, (folk) tale, (folk) story, *literary* mythus. **3** see *misconception* (MISCONCEIVE). **4** fable, lie, (tall) tale, fiction, untruth, falsehood, fabrication, fairy story *or* tale, cock-and-bull story, *sl.* whopper. □□ **mythic, mythical** mythological, fabled, legendary, traditional, folkloric, romantic, fairy-tale, story-book, *literary* storied; allegorical, symbolic, parabolic(al); fanciful, imaginary, fictitious, make-believe, made-up, chimerical, untrue.

mythi *pl.* of MYTHUS.

mythicize /míthisīz/ *v.tr.* (also **-ise**) treat (a story etc.) as a myth; interpret mythically. □□ **mythicism** /-siz'm/ *n.* **mythicist** /-sist/ *n.*

mytho- /míthō/ *comb. form* myth.

mythogenesis /míthōjénnisiss/ *n.* the production of myths.

mythographer /mithógrəfər/ *n.* a compiler of myths.

mythography /mithógrəfi/ *n.* the representation of myths in plastic art.

mythology /mithólləji/ *n.* (*pl.* **-ies**) **1** a body of myths (*Greek mythology*). **2** the study of myths. □□ **mythologer** *n.* **mythologic** /-thəlójik/ *adj.* **mythological** /-thəlójik'l/ *adj.* **mythologically** /-thəlójikəli/ *adv.* **mythologist** *n.* **mythologize** *v.tr.* & *intr.* (also **-ise**). **mythologizer** *n.* [ME f. F *mythologie* or LL *mythologia* f. Gk *muthologia* (as MYTHO-, -LOGY)]
■ **1** myth(s), folklore, fable, legend, tradition, lore, stories.

mythomania /míthōmáyniə/ *n.* an abnormal tendency to exaggerate or tell lies. □□ **mythomaniac** /-niak/ *n.* & *adj.*

mythopoeia /míthōpéeə/ *n.* the making of myths. □□ **mythopoeic** *adj.* (also **mythopoetic** /-pō-éttik/).

mythus /míthəss/ *n.* (*pl.* **mythi** /-thī/) *literary* a myth. [mod.L: see MYTH]

myxo- /míksō/ *comb. form* (also **myx-** before a vowel) mucus. [Gk *muxa* mucus]

myxoedema /míksədéemə/ *n.* (*US* **myxedema**) a syndrome caused by hypothyroidism, resulting in thickening of the skin, weight gain, mental dullness, loss of energy, and sensitivity to cold.

myxoma /miksṓmə/ *n.* (*pl.* **myxomas** or **myxomata** /-mətə/) a benign tumour of mucous or gelatinous tissue. □□ **myxomatous** /-sómmətəss/ *adj.* [mod.L (as MYXO-, -OMA)]

myxomatosis /míksəmətṓsiss/ *n.* an infectious usu. fatal viral disease in rabbits, causing swelling of the mucous membranes.

myxomycete /miksōmīseet/ *n.* any of a group of small acellular organisms inhabiting damp areas.

myxovirus /miksōvīrəss/ *n.* any of a group of viruses including the influenza virus.

Nn

N[1] /en/ *n.* (also **n**) (*pl.* **Ns** or **N's**) **1** the fourteenth letter of the alphabet. **2** *Printing* en. **3** *Math.* an indefinite number. □ **to the nth** (or **nth degree**) **1** *Math.* to any required power. **2** to any extent; to the utmost.

N[2] *abbr.* (also **N.**) **1** North; Northern. **2** newton(s). **3** *Chess* knight. **4** New. **5** nuclear.

N[3] *symb. Chem.* the element nitrogen.

n *abbr.* (also **n.**) **1** name. **2** nano-. **3** neuter. **4** noon. **5** note. **6** noun.

'n *conj.* (also **'n'**) *colloq.* and. [abbr.]

-n[1] *suffix* see -EN[2].

-n[2] *suffix* see -EN[3].

Na *symb. Chem.* the element sodium.

na /nə/ *adv. Sc.* (in *comb.*; usu. with an auxiliary verb) = NOT (*I canna do it*; *they didna go*).

n/a *abbr.* **1** not applicable. **2** not available.

NAAFI /náffi/ *abbr. Brit.* **1** Navy, Army, and Air Force Institutes. **2** a canteen for servicemen run by the NAAFI.

nab /nab/ *v.tr.* (**nabbed, nabbing**) *sl.* **1** arrest; catch in wrongdoing. **2** seize, grab. [17th c., also *napp*, as in KIDNAP: orig. unkn.]

■ **1** catch, capture, arrest, put *or* place under arrest, seize, apprehend, pick up, bring in, take into custody, collar, nail, *colloq.* run in, *sl.* pinch, *Brit. sl.* nick.

nabob /náybob/ *n.* **1** *hist.* a Muslim official or governor under the Mughal empire. **2** (formerly) a conspicuously wealthy person, esp. one returned from India with a fortune. [Port. *nababo* or Sp. *nabab*, f. Urdu (as NAWAB)]

nacarat /nákkərat/ *n.* a bright orange-red colour. [F, perh. f. Sp. & Port. *nacardo* (*nacar* NACRE)]

nacelle /nəsél/ *n.* **1** the outer casing of the engine of an aircraft. **2** the car of an airship. [F, f. LL *navicella* dimin. of L *navis* ship]

nacho /náchō/ *n.* (*pl.* **-os**) (usu. in *pl.*) a tortilla chip, usu. topped with melted cheese and spices etc. [20th c.: orig. uncert.]

NACODS /náykodz/ *abbr.* (in the UK) National Association of Colliery Overmen, Deputies, and Shotfirers.

nacre /náykər/ *n.* mother-of-pearl from any shelled mollusc. □□ **nacred** *adj.* **nacreous** /náykriəss/ *adj.* **nacrous** /-krəss/ *adj.* [F]

nadir /náydeer, nád-/ *n.* **1** the part of the celestial sphere directly below an observer (opp. ZENITH). **2** the lowest point in one's fortunes; a time of deep despair. [ME f. OF f. Arab. *naẓīr* (*as-samt*) opposite (to the zenith)]

■ **2** abyss, down, low point, extreme; rock bottom; (*the nadir*) the depths (of despair), *sl.* the pits.

naevus /neévəss/ *n.* (*US* **nevus**) (*pl.* **naevi** /-vī/) **1** a birthmark in the form of a raised red patch on the skin. **2** = MOLE[2]. □□ **naevoid** *adj.* [L]

naff[1] /naf/ *v.intr. sl.* **1** (in *imper.*, foll. by *off*) go away. **2** (as **naffing** *adj.*) used as an intensive to express annoyance etc. [prob. euphem. for FUCK: cf. EFF]

naff[2] /naf/ *adj. sl.* **1** unfashionable; socially awkward. **2** worthless, rubbishy. [20th c.: orig. unkn.]

■ **1** see OBSOLETE, AWKWARD 2. **2** see WORTHLESS.

Naffy /náffi/ *n. sl.* = NAAFI. [phonet. sp.]

nag[1] /nag/ *v.* & *n.* ● *v.* (**nagged, nagging**) **1 a** *tr.* annoy or irritate (a person) with persistent fault-finding or continuous urging. **b** *intr.* (often foll. by *at*) find fault, complain, or urge, esp. persistently. **2** *intr.* (of a pain) ache dully but persistently. **3 a** *tr.* worry or preoccupy (a person, the mind, etc.) (*his mistake nagged him*). **b** *intr.* (often foll. by *at*) worry or gnaw. **c** (as **nagging** *adj.*) persistently worrying or painful. ● *n.* a persistently nagging person. □□ **nagger** *n.* **naggingly** *adv.* [of dial., perh. Scand. or LG, orig.: cf. Norw. & Sw. *nagga* gnaw, irritate, LG (*g*)*naggen* provoke]

■ *v.* **1, 3a, b** annoy, irritate, irk, pester, criticize, scold, carp at, upbraid, badger, harass, harry, vex, henpeck, torment, hector, pick at, goad, pick on, find fault with, berate, nettle, bully, provoke, worry, bother, chivvy, *US* ride, *colloq.* needle, plague, *Austral. colloq.* heavy. **3 c** (**nagging**) persistent, continuing, continual, unrelenting, relentless; worrying, distressing. ● *n.* pest, shrew, virago, termagant, harridan, *archaic* scold.

nag[2] /nag/ *n.* **1** *colloq.* a horse. **2** a small riding-horse or pony. [ME: orig. unkn.]

■ jade; horse, hack, pony, dobbin, bangtail, racehorse, thoroughbred, *Brit. colloq.* gee-gee.

Nah. *abbr.* Nahum (Old Testament).

Nahuatl /naáwaat'l/ *n.* & *adj.* ● *n.* **1** a member of a group of peoples native to S. Mexico and Central America, including the Aztecs. **2** the language of these people. ● *adj.* of or concerning the Nahuatl peoples or language. □□ **Nahuatlan** *adj.* [Sp. f. Nahuatl]

naiad /nīad/ *n.* (*pl.* **naiads** or **-des** /nīədeez/) **1** *Mythol.* a water-nymph. **2** the larva of a dragonfly etc. **3** any aquatic plant of the genus *Najas*, with narrow leaves and small flowers. [L *Naïas Naïad-* f. Gk *Naias -ados* f. *naō* flow]

nail /nayl/ *n.* & *v.* ● *n.* **1** a small usu. sharpened metal spike with a broadened flat head, driven in with a hammer to join things together or to serve as a peg, protection (cf. HOBNAIL), or decoration. **2 a** a horny covering on the upper surface of the tip of the human finger or toe. **b** a claw or talon. **c** a hard growth on the upper mandible of some soft-billed birds. **3** *hist.* a measure of cloth length (equal to $2\frac{1}{4}$ inches). ● *v.tr.* **1** fasten with a nail or nails (*nailed it to the beam*; *nailed the planks together*). **2** fix or keep (a person, attention, etc.) fixed. **3 a** secure, catch, or get hold of (a person or thing). **b** expose or discover (a lie or a liar). □ **hard as nails 1** callous; unfeeling. **2** in good physical condition. **nail-biting** causing severe anxiety or tension. **nail-brush** a small brush for cleaning the nails. **nail one's colours to the mast** persist; refuse to give in. **nail down 1** bind (a person) to a promise etc. **2** define precisely. **3** fasten (a thing) with nails. **nail enamel** *US* = *nail polish.* **nail-file** a roughened metal or emery strip used for smoothing the nails. **nail-head** *Archit.* an ornament like the head of a nail. **nail in a person's coffin** something thought to increase the risk of death. **nail polish** a varnish applied to the nails to colour them or make them shiny. **nail-punch** (or **-set**) a tool for sinking the head of a nail below a surface. **nail-scissors** small curved scissors for trimming the nails. **nail up 1** close (a door etc.) with nails. **2** fix (a thing) at a height with nails. **nail varnish** *Brit.* = *nail polish.* **on the nail** (esp. of payment) without delay (*cash on the nail*). □□ **nailed** *adj.* (also in *comb.*). **nailless** *adj.* [OE *nægel*, *næglan* f. Gmc]

■ *n.* **1** tack, clout, spike, (panel) pin; peg, fastener, fastening. **2** fingernail, toenail; claw, talon. ● *v.* **1** fasten, attach, secure, join, pin, tack, peg, clinch, clench, fix, rivet. **2** see HOLD[1] *v.* 7a. **3 a** see CATCH *v.* 1. **b** see EXPOSE 5. □ **hard as nails 1** cold, unsentimental, unsympathetic, unfeeling, callous. **2** see HARDY. **nail-biting** see *nerve-racking*. **nail down 1** see BIND *v.* 5. **2** see *pin down* 4. **3** see FASTEN 1. **on the nail** immediately, at once, straight *or* right away, promptly, without delay, on the spot.

nailer /náylər/ *n.* a nail-maker. □□ **nailery** *n.*

nainsook /náynsŏŏk/ *n.* a fine soft cotton fabric, orig. Indian. [Hindi *nainsukh* f. *nain* eye + *sukh* pleasure]

naira /nīrə/ *n.* the chief monetary unit of Nigeria. [contr. of *Nigeria*]

naïve /naa-éev, nī-éev/ *adj.* (also **naive**) **1** artless; innocent; unaffected. **2** foolishly credulous; simple. □□ **naïvely** *adv.* **naïveness** *n.* [F, fem. of *naïf* f. L *nativus* NATIVE]

■ innocent, unaffected, unsophisticated, artless, guileless, unpretentious, unpretending, candid, natural, ingenuous, childlike; unsuspecting, unsuspicious, trusting, trustful, credulous, gullible, green, inexperienced, unworldly, unenlightened, simple, simplistic, simple-minded.

naïvety /naa-éevti, nī-éev-/ *n.* (also **naivety**, ***naïveté*** /-éevtay, nī-éev-/) (*pl.* **-ies** or ***naïvetés***) **1** the state or quality of being naïve. **2** a naïve action. [F *naïveté* (as NAÏVE)]

■ **1** ingenuousness, innocence, credulity, credulousness, inexperience, trust, gullibility, artlessness, callowness, guilelessness, simplicity, unpretentiousness, candour, naturalness, frankness, openness, sincerity.

naked /náykid/ *adj.* **1** without clothes; nude. **2** plain; undisguised; exposed (*the naked truth*; *his naked soul*). **3** (of a light, flame, etc.) unprotected from the wind etc.; unshaded. **4** defenceless. **5** without addition, comment, support, evidence, etc. (*his naked word*; *naked assertion*). **6 a** (of landscape) barren; treeless. **b** (of rock) exposed; without soil etc. **7** (of a sword etc.) unsheathed. **8** (usu. foll. by *of*) devoid; without. **9** without leaves, hairs, scales, shell, etc. **10** (of a room, wall, etc.) without decoration, furnishings, etc.; empty, plain. □ **naked boys** (or **lady** or **ladies**) the meadow saffron, which flowers while leafless: also called *autumn crocus*. **the naked eye** unassisted vision, e.g. without a telescope, microscope, etc. □□ **nakedly** *adv.* **nakedness** *n.* [OE *nacod* f. Gmc]

■ **1** unclothed, undraped, bare, stripped, undressed, unclad, uncovered, bared, nude, in the nude, in the raw, in a state of nature, stark (naked), *colloq.* in the altogether, in the buff, *joc.* in one's birthday suit, *sl.* in the nuddy, *Austral. sl.* bollocky, *Brit. sl.* starkers. **2** plain, unadorned, unembellished, stark, overt, patent, obvious, conspicuous, manifest, sheer, exposed, undisguised, unvarnished, unmitigated, evident, palpable, unconcealed, in plain sight *or* view; blatant, barefaced, undeniable, glaring, flagrant; unmistakable, unalloyed, unmixed, blunt, unadulterated, pure. **3** see OPEN *adj.* 1–4, 13, 20. **5** unaided, unsupported, unassisted; see also BARE *adj.* 3. **7** unsheathed, drawn, bare.

naker /náykər/ *n. hist.* a kettledrum. [ME f. OF *nacre nacaire* f. Arab. *naḳḳāra* drum]

NALGO /nálgō/ *abbr.* (in the UK) National and Local Government Officers' Association.

namby-pamby /námbipámbi/ *adj.* & *n.* ● *adj.* **1** lacking vigour or drive; weak. **2** insipidly pretty or sentimental. ● *n.* (*pl.* **-ies**) **1** a namby-pamby person. **2** namby-pamby talk. [fanciful formulation on name of *Ambrose* Philips, Engl. pastoral writer d. 1749]

■ *adj.* **1** see WEAK *adj.* 3a. ● *n.* **1** see WEAKLING.

name /naym/ *n.* & *v.* ● *n.* **1 a** the word by which an individual person, animal, place, or thing is known, spoken of, etc. (*mentioned him by name*; *her name is Joanna*). **b** all who go under one name; a family, clan, or people in terms of its name (*the Scottish name*). **2 a** a usu. abusive term used of a person etc. (*called him names*). **b** a word denoting an object or esp. a class of objects, ideas, etc. (*what is the name of that kind of vase?*; *that sort of behaviour has no name*). **3** a famous person (*many great names were there*). **4** a reputation, esp. a good one (*has a name for honesty*; *their name is guarantee enough*). **5** something existing only nominally (opp. FACT, REALITY). **6** (*attrib.*) widely known (*a name brand of shampoo*). ● *v.tr.* **1** give a usu. specified name to (*named the dog Spot*). **2** call (a person or thing) by the right name (*named the man in the photograph*). **3** mention; specify; cite (*named his requirements*). **4** nominate, appoint, etc. (*was named the new chairman*). **5** specify as something desired (*named it as her dearest wish*). **6** *Brit. Parl.* (of the Speaker) mention (an MP) as disobedient to the chair. □ **by name** called (*Tom by name*). **have to one's name** possess. **in all but name** virtually. **in name** (or **name only**) as a mere formality; hardly at all (*is the leader in name only*). **in a person's name** = *in the name of*. **in the name of** calling to witness; invoking (*in the name of goodness*). **in one's own name** independently; without authority. **make a name for oneself** become famous. **name after** (*US* **for**) call (a person) by the name of (a specified person) (*named him after his uncle Roger*). **name-calling** abusive language. **name-child** (usu. foll. by *of*) one named after another person. **name-day 1** the feast-day of a saint after whom a person is named. **2** *Brit.* = *ticket-day*. **name the day** arrange a date (esp. of a woman fixing the date for her wedding). **name-drop** (**-dropped**, **-dropping**) indulge in name-dropping. **name-dropper** a person who name-drops. **name-dropping** the familiar mention of famous people as a form of boasting. **name names** mention specific names, esp. in accusation. **name of the game** *colloq.* the purpose or essence of an action etc. **name-part** the title role in a play etc. **name-plate** a plate or panel bearing the name of an occupant of a room etc. **name-tape** a tape fixed to a garment etc. and bearing the name of the owner. **of** (or **by**) **the name of** called. **put one's name down for 1** apply for. **2** promise to subscribe (a sum). **what's in a name?** names are arbitrary labels. **you name it** *colloq.* no matter what; whatever you like. □□ **nameable** *adj.* [OE *nama*, *noma*, *(ge)namian* f. Gmc, rel. to L *nomen*, Gk *onoma*]

■ *n.* **1, 2** designation, label, term, tag, style, *colloq.* handle, *formal* appellation, *sl.* moniker. **3** personage, somebody, celebrity, star, superstar, hero, VIP, dignitary, luminary, big name, *colloq.* big shot, bigwig, (big) cheese, big noise. **4** reputation; repute, honour, rank, standing, rating, pre-eminence, superiority, eminence, notability, prominence, prestige, distinction, renown, fame, popularity, celebrity. **6** (*attrib.*) see *well-known* (WELL[1]). ● *v.* **1** label, tag, style, call, dub, *archaic* entitle; christen, baptize. **3–5** choose, elect, select, delegate, nominate, designate, appoint; identify, denominate, pinpoint, specify; mention, cite. □ **by name** see CALL *v.* 7. **in all but name** see *virtually* (VIRTUAL). **name-calling** see ABUSE *n.* 2. **name of the game** see IDEA 3. **you name it** see *I'm easy* (EASY).

nameless /náymliss/ *adj.* **1** having no name or name-inscription. **2** inexpressible; indefinable (*a nameless sensation*). **3** unnamed; anonymous, esp. deliberately (*our informant, who shall be nameless*). **4** too loathsome or horrific to be named (*nameless vices*). **5** obscure; inglorious. **6** illegitimate. □□ **namelessly** *adv.* **namelessness** *n.*

■ **1, 3, 5** unnamed, innominate; unidentified, anonymous, incognito; unknown, unheard-of, unsung; obscure, inglorious. **2** inexpressible, indefinable, unidentifiable, unspecified, unspecifiable, ineffable. **4** ineffable, unutterable, unspeakable, unmentionable, abominable, horrible, indescribable, repulsive.

namely /náymli/ *adv.* that is to say; in other words.

■ specifically, that is (to say), i.e., in other words, videlicet, viz., scilicet, sc., to wit.

namesake /náymsayk/ *n.* a person or thing having the same name as another (*was her aunt's namesake*). [prob. f. phr. *for the name's sake*]

namma var. of GNAMMA.

nan /nan/ *n.* (also **nana**, **nanna** /nánnə/) *Brit. colloq.* grandmother. [childish pronunc.]

nana /naánə/ *n. sl.* a silly person; a fool. [perh. f. BANANA]

nancy /nánsi/ *n.* & *adj.* (also **nance** /nanss/) *sl.* ● *n.* (*pl.* **-ies**) (in full **nancy boy**) an effeminate man, esp. a homosexual. ● *adj.* effeminate. [pet-form of the name *Ann*]

nankeen /nangkeén/ *n.* **1** a yellowish cotton cloth. **2** a yellowish buff colour. **3** (in *pl.*) trousers of nankeen. [*Nankin(g)* in China, where orig. made]

nanna var. of NAN.

nanny /nánni/ *n.* & *v.* ● *n.* (*pl.* **-ies**) **1 a** a child's nurse. **b** an unduly protective person, institution, etc. (*the nanny State*). **2** = NAN. **3** (in full **nanny-goat**) a female goat. ● *v.tr.* (**-ies, -ied**) be unduly protective towards. [formed as NANCY]

■ *n.* **1 a** see MINDER 1.

nano- /nánnō, náynō/ *comb. form* denoting a factor of 10^{-9} (*nanosecond*). [L f. Gk *nanos* dwarf]

nanometre /nánnōmeetər/ *n.* one thousand-millionth of a metre. ¶ Abbr.: **nm**.

nanosecond /nánnōsekkənd/ *n.* one thousand-millionth of a second. ¶ Abbr.: **ns**.

naos /náyoss/ *n.* (*pl.* **naoi** /náyoy/) *Gk Hist.* the inner part of a temple. [Gk, = temple]

nap[1] /nap/ *v.* & *n.* ● *v.intr.* (**napped, napping**) sleep lightly or briefly. ● *n.* a short sleep or doze, esp. by day (*took a nap*). □ **catch a person napping 1** find a person asleep or off guard. **2** detect in negligence or error. [OE *hnappian*, rel. to OHG *(h)naffezan* to slumber]

■ *v.* sleep, doze, nod (off), catnap, *colloq.* catch *or* get forty winks, drop off, get some shut-eye, snooze, zizz, *Brit. sl.* kip, have a *or* some kip. ● *n.* sleep, doze, catnap, siesta, lie-down, *colloq.* forty winks, shut-eye, snooze, zizz, *Brit. sl.* kip. □ **catch a person napping 1** catch a person unawares *or* off guard *or* in an unguarded moment; see also SURPRISE *v.* 3, 4.

nap[2] /nap/ *n.* & *v.* ● *n.* **1** the raised pile on textiles, esp. velvet. **2** a soft downy surface. **3** *Austral. colloq.* blankets, bedding, swag. ● *v.tr.* (**napped, napping**) raise a nap on (cloth). □□ **napless** *adj.* [ME *noppe* f. MDu., MLG *noppe* nap, *noppen* trim nap from]

■ *n.* **1** pile, fibre, texture, weave, down, shag; see also TEXTURE *n.* 1, 2.

nap[3] /nap/ *n.* & *v.* ● *n.* **1 a** a form of whist in which players declare the number of tricks they expect to take, up to five. **b** a call of five in this game. **2 a** the betting of all one's money on one horse etc. **b** a tipster's choice for this. ● *v.tr.* (**napped, napping**) name (a horse etc.) as a probable winner. □ **go nap 1** attempt to take all five tricks in nap. **2** risk everything in one attempt. **3** win all the matches etc. in a series. **nap hand** a good winning position worth risking in a venture. **not go nap on** *Austral. colloq.* not be too keen on; not care much for. [abbr. of orig. name of game NAPOLEON]

napa var. of NAPPA.

napalm /náypaam/ *n.* & *v.* ● *n.* **1** a thickening agent produced from naphthenic acid, other fatty acids, and aluminium. **2** a jellied petrol made from this, used in incendiary bombs. ● *v.tr.* attack with napalm bombs. [NAPHTHENIC + *palmitic acid* in coconut oil]

nape /nayp/ *n.* the back of the neck. [ME: orig. unkn.]

napery /náypəri/ *n. Sc.* or *archaic* household linen, esp. table linen. [ME f. OF *naperie* f. *nape* (as NAPKIN)]

naphtha /náf-thə/ *n.* an inflammable oil obtained by the dry distillation of organic substances such as coal, shale, or petroleum. [L f. Gk, = inflammable volatile liquid issuing from the earth, of Oriental origin]

naphthalene /náf-thəleen/ *n.* a white crystalline aromatic substance produced by the distillation of coal tar and used in mothballs and the manufacture of dyes etc. □□ **naphthalic** /-thállik/ *adj.* [NAPHTHA + -ENE]

naphthene /náf-theen/ *n.* any of a group of cycloalkanes. [NAPHTHA + -ENE]

naphthenic /naf-theénik/ *adj.* of a naphthene or its radical. □ **naphthenic acid** any carboxylic acid resulting from the refining of petroleum.

Napierian logarithm /naypeérian/ *n.* see LOGARITHM. [J. *Napier*, Sc. mathematician d. 1617]

napkin /nápkin/ *n.* **1** (in full **table napkin**) a square piece of linen, paper, etc. used for wiping the lips, fingers, etc. at meals, or serving fish etc. on; a serviette. **2** *Brit.* a baby's nappy. **3** a small towel. □ **napkin-ring** a ring used to hold (and distinguish) a person's table napkin when not in use. [ME f. OF *nappe* f. L *mappa* (MAP)]

napoleon /nəpṓliən/ *n.* **1** *hist.* a gold twenty-franc piece minted in the reign of Napoleon I. **2** *hist.* a 19th-c. high boot. **3** = NAP[3]. **4** *US* = MILLEFEUILLE. □ **double napoleon** *hist.* a forty-franc piece. [F *napoléon* f. *Napoléon*, name of 19th-c. French emperors]

Napoleonic /nəpṓliónnik/ *adj.* of, relating to, or characteristic of Napoleon I or his time.

nappa /náppə/ *n.* (also **napa**) a soft leather made by a special process from the skin of sheep or goats. [*Napa* in California]

nappe /nap/ *n. Geol.* a sheet of rock that has moved sideways over neighbouring strata, usu. as a result of overthrust. [F *nappe* tablecloth]

napper /náppər/ *n. Brit. sl.* the head. [18th c.: orig. uncert.]

nappy /náppi/ *n.* (*pl.* **-ies**) *Brit.* a piece of towelling or other absorbent material wrapped round a baby to absorb or retain urine and faeces. □ **nappy rash** inflammation of a baby's skin, caused by prolonged contact with a damp nappy. [abbr. of NAPKIN]

■ *Brit.* napkin, *US* diaper.

narceine /naársi-een/ *n.* a narcotic alkaloid obtained from opium. [F *narcéine* f. Gk *narkē* numbness]

narcissism /naársisiz'm, naarsíss-/ *n. Psychol.* excessive or erotic interest in oneself, one's physical features, etc. □□ **narcissist** *n.* **narcissistic** /-sístik/ *adj.* **narcissistically** /-sístikəli/ *adv.* [*Narcissus* (Gk *Narkissos*), youth who fell in love with his reflection in water]

■ see VANITY 1. □□ **narcissistic** see VAIN 1.

narcissus /naarsíssəss/ *n.* (*pl.* **narcissi** /-sī/ or **narcissuses**) any bulbous plant of the genus *Narcissus*, esp. *N. poeticus* bearing a heavily scented single flower with an undivided corona edged with crimson and yellow. [L f. Gk *narkissos*, perh. f. *narkē* numbness, with ref. to its narcotic effects]

narcolepsy /naárkəlepsi/ *n. Med.* a disease with fits of sleepiness and drowsiness. □□ **narcoleptic** /-léptik/ *adj.* & *n.* [Gk *narkoō* make numb, after EPILEPSY]

narcosis /naarkṓsiss/ *n.* **1** *Med.* the working or effects of soporific narcotics. **2** a state of insensibility. [Gk *narkōsis* f. *narkoō* make numb]

narcoterrorism / naárkōtérrəriz'm/ *n.* violent crime associated with illicit drugs. □□ **narcoterrorist** *adj.* & *n.* [NARCOTIC + TERRORISM]

narcotic /naarkóttik/ *adj.* & *n.* ● *adj.* **1** (of a substance) inducing drowsiness, sleep, stupor, or insensibility. **2** (of a drug) affecting the mind. **3** of or involving narcosis. **4** soporific. ● *n.* a narcotic substance, drug, or influence. □□ **narcotically** *adv.* **narcotism** /naárkətiz'm/ *n.* **narcotize** /naárkətīz/ *v.tr.* (also **-ise**). **narcotization** /naárkətīzáysh'n/ *n.* [ME f. OF *narcotique* or med.L f. Gk *narkōtikos* (as NARCOSIS)]

■ *adj.* **1, 4** soporific, hypnotic, sedative, sleep-inducing, opiate, dulling, numbing, anaesthetic, stupefacient, stupefying, stupefactive, tranquillizing, Lethean. ● *n.* drug, soporific, hypnotic, sedative, opiate, anaesthetic, stupefacient, tranquillizer.

nard /naard/ *n.* **1** any of various plants yielding an aromatic balsam used by the ancients. **2** = SPIKENARD. [ME f. L *nardus* f. Gk *nardos* ult. f. Skr.]

nardoo /naardóó/ *n.* **1** a clover-like plant, *Marsilea drummondii*, native to Australia. **2** a food made from the spores of this plant. [Aboriginal]

nares /náireez/ *n.pl. Anat.* the nostrils. □□ **narial** *adj.* [pl. of L *naris*]

narghile /naárgili/ *n.* an oriental tobacco-pipe with the smoke drawn through water; a hookah. [Pers. *nārgīleh* (*nārgīl* coconut)]

nark /naark/ *n.* & *v. sl.* ● *n.* **1** *Brit.* a police informer or decoy. **2** *Austral.* an annoying person or thing. ● *v.tr.* (usu. in *passive*) *Brit.* annoy; infuriate (*was narked by their attitude*). □ **nark it!** stop that! [Romany *nāk* nose]
■ *n.* **1** see GRASS *n.* 6.

narky /naárki/ *adj.* (**narkier, narkiest**) *sl.* bad-tempered, irritable. [NARK]

narrate /nəráyt/ *v.tr.* (also *absol.*) **1** give a continuous story or account of. **2** provide a spoken commentary or accompaniment for (a film etc.). □□ **narratable** *adj.* **narration** /nəráysh'n/ *n.* [L *narrare narrat-*]
■ relate, tell, recount, report, give an account of, recite, rehearse, repeat, review, unfold, chronicle, describe, detail, reveal, retail; speak, read, *disp.* commentate. □□ **narration** telling; report, recital, recitation, rehearsal, relation, chronicle, description, portrayal, detailing, revelation, story, tale, narrative; reading, voice-over.

narrative /nárrətiv/ *n.* & *adj.* ● *n.* **1** a spoken or written account of connected events in order of happening. **2** the practice or art of narration. ● *adj.* in the form of, or concerned with, narration (*narrative verse*). □□ **narratively** *adv.* [F *narratif -ive* f. LL *narrativus* (as NARRATE)]
■ *n.* **1** story, tale, chronicle, description, revelation, portrayal, account, report, record, history, recital, statement. **2** storytelling.

narrator /nəráytər/ *n.* **1** an actor, announcer, etc. who delivers a commentary in a film, broadcast, etc. **2** a person who narrates. [L (as NARRATE)]
■ commentator, announcer, reader; reporter, storyteller, raconteur, taleteller, anecdotist, anecdotalist, relator, annalist, chronicler, describer, *Austral. sl.* magsman.

narrow /nárrō/ *adj.*, *n.*, & *v.* ● *adj.* (**narrower, narrowest**) **1 a** of small width in proportion to length; lacking breadth. **b** confined or confining; constricted (*within narrow bounds*). **2** of limited scope; restricted (*in the narrowest sense*). **3** with little margin (*a narrow escape*). **4** searching; precise; exact (*a narrow examination*). **5** = NARROW-MINDED. **6** (of a vowel) tense. **7** of small size. ● *n.* **1** (usu. in *pl.*) the narrow part of a strait, river, sound, etc. **2** a narrow pass or street. ● *v.* **1** *intr.* become narrow; diminish; contract; lessen. **2** *tr.* make narrow; constrict; restrict. □ **narrow boat** *Brit.* a canal boat, esp. one less than 7 ft. (2.1 metres) wide. **narrow circumstances** poverty. **narrow cloth** cloth less than 52 inches wide. **narrow gauge** a railway track that has a smaller gauge than the standard one. **narrow seas** the English Channel and the Irish Sea. **narrow squeak 1** a narrow escape. **2** a success barely attained. □□ **narrowish** *adj.* **narrowly** *adv.* **narrowness** *n.* [OE *nearu nearw-* f. Gmc]
■ *adj.* **1 a** slender, slim, thin, straitened, attenuated, narrowed; narrowing, tapering. **b** confined, confining, limited, cramped, close, meagre, pinched, tight, incommodious; constricted, restricted. **2** restricted, limited, circumscribed, prescribed, denotative; see also STRAIT *adj.* 1. **3** close, near, hairbreadth; lucky. **4** strict, careful, close, precise, exact, exacting, demanding, finicky, finical, fastidious, sharp, meticulous, scrupulous, fussy, rigid, stringent, rigorous, searching, critical. ● *n.* strait, channel, passage. ● *v.* **1** diminish, contract, lessen, decrease, reduce, get *or* become smaller *or* thinner *or* narrower. **2** constrict, limit, qualify, reduce, lessen, diminish, decrease, restrict, focus, confine, concentrate, narrow down. □□ **narrowly** barely, (only) just, scarcely, hardly, by a hair's breadth, by the skin of one's teeth, *colloq.* by a whisker; closely, carefully, meticulously, scrupulously, searchingly, critically.

narrow-minded /nárrōmīndid/ *adj.* rigid or restricted in one's views, intolerant, prejudiced, illiberal. □□ **narrow-mindedly** *adv.* **narrow-mindedness** *n.*
■ bigoted, prejudiced, illiberal, narrow, biased, opinionated, one-sided, intolerant, conservative, parochial, conventional, hidebound, petty, pettifogging, small-minded, puritanical, rigid, restricted, unprogressive, strait-laced, stuffy, close-minded, *sl.* square.

narthex /naártheks/ *n.* **1** a railed-off antechamber or porch etc. at the western entrance of some early Christian churches, used by catechumens, penitents, etc. **2** a similar antechamber in a modern church. [L f. Gk *narthēx* giant fennel, stick, casket, narthex]

narwhal /naárwəl/ *n.* an Arctic white whale, *Monodon monoceros*, the male of which has a long straight spirally fluted tusk developed from one of its teeth. Also called BELUGA. [Du. *narwal* f. Da. *narhval* f. *hval* whale: cf. ON *náhvalr* (perh. f. *nár* corpse, with ref. to its skin-colour)]

nary /náiri/ *adj. colloq.* or *dial.* not a; no (*nary a one*). [f. *ne'er a*]

NAS *abbr. Brit.* Noise Abatement Society.

NASA /nássə/ *abbr.* (in the US) National Aeronautics and Space Administration.

nasal /náyz'l/ *adj.* & *n.* ● *adj.* **1** of, for, or relating to the nose. **2** *Phonet.* (of a letter or a sound) pronounced with the breath passing through the nose, e.g. *m*, *n*, *ng*, or French *en*, *un*, etc. **3** (of the voice or speech) having an intonation caused by breathing through the nose. ● *n.* **1** *Phonet.* a nasal letter or sound. **2** *hist.* a nose-piece on a helmet. □□ **nasality** /-zálliti/ *n.* **nasalize** *v.intr.* & *tr.* (also **-ise**). **nasalization** /-záysh'n/ *n.* **nasally** *adv.* [F *nasal* or med.L *nasalis* f. L *nasus* nose]

nascent /náss'nt, náys-/ *adj.* **1** in the act of being born. **2** just beginning to be; not yet mature. **3** *Chem.* just being formed and therefore unusually reactive (*nascent hydrogen*). □□ **nascency** /nássənsi, náys-/ *n.* [L *nasci nascent-* be born]

naseberry /náyzbəri/ *n.* (*pl.* **-ies**) a sapodilla. [Sp. & Port. *néspera* medlar f. L (see MEDLAR): assim. to BERRY]

naso- /náyzō/ *comb. form* nose. [L *nasus* nose]

naso-frontal /náyzōfrúnt'l/ *adj.* of or relating to the nose and forehead.

nastic /nástik/ *adj. Bot.* (of the movement of plant parts) not determined by an external stimulus. [Gk *nastos* squeezed together f. *nassō* to press]

nasturtium /nəstúrshəm/ *n.* **1** (in general use) a trailing plant, *Tropaeolum majus*, with rounded edible leaves and bright orange, yellow, or red flowers. **2** any cruciferous plant of the genus *Nasturtium*, including watercress. [L]

nasty /naásti/ *adj.* & *n.* ● *adj.* (**nastier, nastiest**) **1 a** highly unpleasant (*a nasty experience*). **b** annoying; objectionable (*the car has a nasty habit of breaking down*). **2** difficult to negotiate; dangerous, serious (*a nasty fence*; *a nasty question*; *a nasty illness*). **3** (of a person or animal) ill-natured, ill-tempered, spiteful; violent, offensive (*nasty to his mother*; *turns nasty when he's drunk*). **4** (of the weather) foul, wet, stormy. **5 a** disgustingly dirty, filthy. **b** unpalatable; disagreeable (*nasty smell*). **c** (of a wound) septic. **6 a** obscene. **b** delighting in obscenity. ● *n.* (*pl.* **-ies**) *colloq.* a horror film, esp. one on video and depicting cruelty or killing. □ **a nasty bit** (or **piece**) **of work** *colloq.* an unpleasant or contemptible person. **a nasty one 1** a rebuff; a snub. **2** an awkward question. **3** a disabling blow etc. □□ **nastily** *adv.* **nastiness** *n.* [ME: orig. unkn.]
■ **1, 5a, b** disagreeable, unsavoury, painful, annoying, untoward, awkward, difficult, bad, serious; foul, filthy, dirty, unclean, offensive, disgusting, unpalatable, unpleasant, nauseating, revolting, horrible, loathsome, repugnant, repellent, vile, odious, obnoxious, objectionable, nauseous, sickening, fetid, mephitic, rank, stinking, malodorous, rancid, noxious, *literary* noisome. **2** bad, severe, acute, dangerous, critical, painful, serious; hard, tricky, problematical, difficult. **3** unpleasant, disagreeable, ugly, bad-tempered, vicious, violent, offensive, surly, abusive, spiteful, irascible, ill-natured, malicious, ill-tempered, cruel, mean, inconsiderate, rude, churlish, obnoxious, crotchety, curmudgeonly, cantankerous, crabbed, *esp. US* cranky. **4** see DIRTY *adj.* 6, FOUL *adj.* 7. **5c** septic. **6** obscene, dirty, filthy, pornographic, blue, smutty, lewd, vulgar, sordid, indecent, licentious, gross, coarse, crude, rude, ribald, bawdy, risqué, suggestive, *US* off colour, *colloq.* raunchy.

NAS/UWT *abbr.* (in the UK) National Association of Schoolmasters and Union of Women Teachers.

Nat. *abbr.* **1** National. **2** Nationalist. **3** Natural.

natal /náyt'l/ *adj.* of or from one's birth. [ME f. L *natalis* (as NATION)]
■ see INHERENT 1, INBORN.

natality /nətálliti/ *n.* (*pl.* **-ies**) birth rate. [F *natalité* (as NATAL)]

natation /nətáysh'n/ *n. formal* or *literary* the act or art of swimming. [L *natatio* f. *natare* swim]

natatorial /náytətóriəl, nát-/ *adj.* (also **natatory** /náytətəri, nətáytəri/) *formal* **1** swimming. **2** of or concerning swimming. [LL *natatorius* f. L *natator* swimmer (as NATATION)]

natatorium /náytətóriəm/ *n. US* a swimming-pool, esp. indoors. [LL neut. of *natatorius* (see NATATORIAL)]

natch /nach/ *adv. colloq.* = NATURALLY. [abbr.]

nates /náyteez/ *n.pl. Anat.* the buttocks. [L]

NATFHE *abbr.* (in the UK) National Association of Teachers in Further and Higher Education.

nathless /náythliss/ *adv.* (also **natheless**) *archaic* nevertheless. [ME f. OE *nā* not (f. *ne* not + *ā* ever) + THE + *lǣs* LESS]

nation /náysh'n/ *n.* **1** a community of people of mainly common descent, history, language, etc., forming a State or inhabiting a territory. **2** a tribe or confederation of tribes of N. American Indians. □ **law of nations** *Law* international law. □□ **nationhood** *n.* [ME f. OF f. L *natio -onis* f. *nasci nat-* be born]
■ **1** country, State, land, polity, domain, *formal esp. Law* realm.

national /náshən'l/ *adj.* & *n.* ● *adj.* **1** of or common to a nation or the nation. **2** peculiar to or characteristic of a particular nation. ● *n.* **1** a citizen of a specified country, usu. entitled to hold that country's passport (*French nationals*). **2** a fellow countryman. **3** (**the National**) = *Grand National.* □ **national anthem** a song adopted by a nation, expressive of its identity etc. and intended to inspire patriotism. **National Assembly 1** an elected house of legislature in various countries. **2** *hist.* the elected legislature in France 1789-91. **National Assistance** *hist.* **1** (in Britain) the former official name for supplementary benefits under National Insurance. **2** such benefits. **national bank** *US* a bank chartered under the federal government. **national convention** *US* a convention of a major political party, nominating candidates for the presidency etc. **national debt** the money owed by a State because of loans to it. **national football** *Austral.* Australian Rules football. **National Front** a UK political party with extreme reactionary views on immigration etc. **national grid** *Brit.* **1** the network of high-voltage electric power lines between major power stations. **2** the metric system of geographical coordinates used in maps of the British Isles. **National Guard** (in the US) the primary reserve force partly maintained by the States but available for federal use. **National Health** (or **Health Service**) (in the UK) a system of national medical care paid for mainly by taxation and started in 1948. **national income** the total money earned within a nation. **National Insurance** (in the UK) the system of compulsory payments by employed persons (supplemented by employers) to provide State assistance in sickness, unemployment, retirement, etc. **national park** an area of natural beauty protected by the State for the use of the general public. **national service** *Brit. hist.* service in the army etc. under conscription. **National Socialism** *hist.* the doctrines of nationalism, racial purity, etc., adopted by the Nazis. **National Socialist** *hist.* a member of the fascist party implementing National Socialism in Germany, 1933-45. **National Trust** (in the UK, Australia, etc.) an organization for maintaining and preserving historic buildings etc. □□ **nationally** *adv.* [F (as NATION)]
■ *adj.* nationwide, country-wide, State, governmental, civil, federal; public, popular. ● *n.* **1** citizen, subject, resident, native; voter. □ **national service** conscription, call-up, *US* draft, *US hist.* selective service.

nationalism /náshənəliz'm/ *n.* **1 a** patriotic feeling, principles, etc. **b** an extreme form of this; chauvinism. **2** a policy of national independence. □□ **nationalist** *n.* & *adj.* **nationalistic** /-lístik/ *adj.* **nationalistically** /-lístikəli/ *adv.*
■ **1 b** flag-waving, chauvinism; see also *jingoism* (JINGO). □□ **nationalist** (*n.*) see PATRIOT. **nationalistic** nationalist, patriotic, jingoistic, chauvinistic, xenophobic, isolationist.

nationality /náshənálliti/ *n.* (*pl.* **-ies**) **1 a** the status of belonging to a particular nation (*what is your nationality?*; *has British nationality*). **b** a nation (*people of all nationalities*). **2** the condition of being national; distinctive national qualities. **3** an ethnic group forming a part of one or more political nations. **4** existence as a nation; nationhood. **5** patriotic sentiment.
■ **1** citizenship. **3** race, nation, ethnic group, ethnic minority, clan, tribe; strain, stock, pedigree, heritage, extraction, bloodline, breed.

nationalize /náshənəlīz/ *v.tr.* (also **-ise**) **1** take over (railways, coal-mines, the steel industry, land, etc.) from private ownership on behalf of the State. **2 a** make national. **b** make into a nation. **3** naturalize (a foreigner). □□ **nationalization** /-záysh'n/ *n.* **nationalizer** *n.* [F *nationaliser* (as NATIONAL)]

nationwide /náysh'nwīd/ *adj.* extending over the whole nation.
■ see NATIONAL *adj.*

native /náytiv/ *n.* & *adj.* ● *n.* **1 a** (usu. foll. by *of*) a person born in a specified place, or whose parents are domiciled in that place at the time of the birth (*a native of Bristol*). **b** a local inhabitant. **2** often *offens.* **a** a member of a non-White indigenous people, as regarded by the colonial settlers. **b** *S.Afr.* a Black person. **3** (usu. foll. by *of*) an indigenous animal or plant. **4** an oyster reared in British waters, esp. in artificial beds (*a Whitstable native*). **5** *Austral.* a White person born in Australia. ● *adj.* **1** (usu. foll. by *to*) belonging to a person or thing by nature; inherent; innate (*spoke with the facility native to him*). **2** of one's birth or birthplace (*native dress*; *native country*). **3** belonging to one by right of birth. **4** (usu. foll. by *to*) belonging to a specified place (*the anteater is native to S. America*). **5 a** (esp. of a non-European) indigenous; born in a place. **b** of the natives of a place (*native customs*). **6** in a natural state; unadorned; simple. **7** *Geol.* (of metal etc.) found in a pure or uncombined state. **8** *Austral.* & *NZ* resembling an animal or plant familiar elsewhere (*native rabbit*). □ **go native** (of a settler) adopt the local way of life, esp. in a non-European country. **native bear** *Austral.* & *NZ* = KOALA. **native rock** rock in its original place. □□ **natively** *adv.* **nativeness** *n.* [ME (earlier as adj.) f. OF *natif -ive* or L *nativus* f. *nasci nat-* be born]
■ *n.* **1** aborigine, indigene, autochthon; national, citizen, resident, inhabitant; local. ● *adj.* **1** see INHERENT 1, INBORN. **2, 5** domestic, local, home, home-grown; indigenous, autochthonous, aboriginal; national, ethnic, clan, tribal; provincial, local. **3** inherited, hereditary; constitutional. **4** see INDIGENOUS. **6** unadorned, untouched, unaffected; simple, plain.

nativism /náytiviz'm/ *n. Philos.* the doctrine of innate ideas. □□ **nativist** *n.*

nativity /nətívviti/ *n.* (*pl.* **-ies**) **1** (esp. **the Nativity**) **a** the birth of Christ. **b** the festival of Christ's birth; Christmas. **2** a picture of the Nativity. **3** birth. **4** the horoscope at a person's birth. **5 a** the birth of the Virgin Mary or St John the Baptist. **b** the festival of the nativity of the Virgin (8 Sept.) or St John (24 June). □ **nativity play** a play usu. performed by children at Christmas dealing with the birth of Christ. [ME f. OF *nativité* f. LL *nativitas -tatis* f. L (as NATIVE)]
■ **3** see BIRTH *n.* 1

NATO /náytō/ *abbr.* (also **Nato**) North Atlantic Treaty Organization.

natron /náytrən/ *n.* a mineral form of hydrated sodium salts found in dried lake beds. [F f. Sp. *natrón* f. Arab. *naṭrūn* f. Gk *nitron* NITRE]

NATSOPA /natsṓpə/ *abbr.* (in the UK) National Society of Operative Printers, Graphical and Media Personnel (orig. Printers and Assistants).

natter /náttər/ *v.* & *n. colloq.* ● *v.intr.* **1** chatter idly. **2** grumble; talk fretfully. ● *n.* **1** aimless chatter. **2** grumbling talk. □□ **natterer** *n.* [orig. Sc., imit.]
■ *v.* **1** see CHATTER *v.* 1. ● *n.* **1** see CHAT[1] *n.* 2.

natterjack /náttərjak/ *n.* a toad, *Bufo calamita*, with a bright yellow stripe down its back, and moving by running not hopping. [perh. f. NATTER, from its loud croak, + JACK[1]]

nattier blue /náttiər/ *n.* a soft shade of blue. [much used by J. M. *Nattier*, Fr. painter d. 1766]

natty /nátti/ *adj.* (**nattier, nattiest**) *colloq.* **1 a** smartly or neatly dressed, dapper. **b** spruce; trim; smart (*a natty blouse*). **2** deft. □□ **nattily** *adv.* **nattiness** *n.* [orig. sl., perh. rel. to NEAT[1]]
■ **1** see SMART *adj.* 2.

natural /náchərəl/ *adj.* & *n.* ● *adj.* **1 a** existing in or caused by nature; not artificial (*natural landscape*). **b** uncultivated; wild (*existing in its natural state*). **2** in the course of nature; not exceptional or miraculous (*died of natural causes*; *a natural occurrence*). **3** (of human nature etc.) not surprising; to be expected (*natural for her to be upset*). **4 a** (of a person or a person's behaviour) unaffected, easy, spontaneous. **b** (foll. by *to*) spontaneous, easy (*friendliness is natural to him*). **5 a** (of qualities etc.) inherent; innate (*a natural talent for music*). **b** (of a person) having such qualities (*a natural linguist*). **6** not disguised or altered (as by make-up etc.). **7** lifelike; as if in nature (*the portrait looked very natural*). **8** likely by its or their nature to be such (*natural enemies*; *the natural antithesis*). **9** having a physical existence as opposed to what is spiritual, intellectual, etc. (*the natural world*). **10 a** related by nature, out of wedlock, esp. in a specified manner (*her natural son*). **b** illegitimate (*a natural child*). **11** based on the innate moral sense; instinctive (*natural justice*). **12** *Mus.* **a** (of a note) not sharpened or flattened (*B natural*). **b** (of a scale) not containing any sharps or flats. **13** not enlightened or communicated by revelation (*the natural man*). ● *n.* **1** *colloq.* (usu. foll. by *for*) a person or thing naturally suitable, adept, expert, etc. (*a natural for the championship*). **2** *archaic* a person mentally deficient from birth. **3** *Mus.* **a** a sign (♮) denoting a return to natural pitch after a sharp or a flat. **b** a natural note. **c** a white key on a piano. **4 a** *Cards* a hand making 21 in the first deal in pontoon. **b** a throw of 7 or 11 at craps. **5** a pale fawn colour. □ **natural-born** having a character or position by birth. **natural childbirth** *Med.* childbirth with minimal medical or technological intervention. **natural classification** a scientific classification according to natural features. **natural death** death by age or disease, not by accident, poison, violence, etc. **natural food** food without preservatives etc. **natural gas** an inflammable mainly methane gas found in the earth's crust, not manufactured. **natural historian** a writer or expert on natural history. **natural history 1** the study of animals or plants esp. as set forth for popular use. **2** an aggregate of the facts concerning the flora and fauna etc. of a particular place or class (*a natural history of the Isle of Wight*). **natural key** (or **scale**) *Mus.* a key or scale having no sharps or flats, i.e. C major and A minor. **natural language** a language that has developed naturally. **natural law 1** *Philos.* unchanging moral principles common to all people by virtue of their nature as human beings. **2** a correct statement of an invariable sequence between specified conditions and a specified phenomenon. **3** the laws of nature; regularity in nature (*where they saw chance, we see natural law*). **natural life** the duration of one's life on earth. **natural logarithm** see LOGARITHM. **natural magic** magic involving the supposed invocation of impersonal spirits. **natural note** *Mus.* a note that is neither sharp nor flat. **natural numbers** the integers 1, 2, 3, etc. **natural philosopher** *archaic* a physicist. **natural philosophy** *archaic* physics. **natural religion** a religion based on reason (opp. *revealed religion*); deism. **natural resources** materials or conditions occurring in nature and capable of economic exploitation. **natural science** the sciences used in the study of the physical world, e.g. physics, chemistry, geology, biology, botany. **natural selection** the Darwinian theory of the survival and propagation of organisms best adapted to their environment. **natural theology** the knowledge of God as gained by the light of natural reason. **natural uranium** unenriched uranium. **natural virtues** *Philos.* justice, prudence, temperance, fortitude. **natural year** the time taken by one revolution of the earth round the sun, 365 days 5 hours 48 minutes. □□ **naturalness** *n.* [ME f. OF *naturel* f. L *naturalis* (as NATURE)]
■ *adj.* **1a, 2, 3, 6** ordinary, common, commonplace, normal, standard, regular, usual, customary, unsurprising, unexceptional, routine, habitual, typical, everyday; reasonable, understandable, logical, sensible, accepted, obvious; expected; simple, basic, fundamental, real, genuine, unembellished, unadorned; true, actual, authentic, bona fide. **4** unstudied, unconstrained, candid, frank, spontaneous, unaffected, easy, honest, straight, straightforward, artless, guileless, impulsive, unpremeditated, ingenuous, unsophisticated. **5 a** see INHERENT 1, INBORN. **7** see LIFELIKE. **8** logical, reasonable, fitting, appropriate, expected, understandable, obvious. **10** see ILLEGITIMATE *adj.* 1. ● *n.* **2** see FOOL[1] *n.* 1. □ **natural history 1** ecology, biology, botany, zoology, geology.

naturalism /náchərəliz'm/ *n.* **1** the theory or practice in art and literature of representing nature, character, etc. realistically and in great detail. **2 a** *Philos.* a theory of the world that excludes the supernatural or spiritual. **b** any moral or religious system based on this theory. **3** action based on natural instincts. **4** indifference to conventions. [NATURAL, in Philos. after F *naturalisme*]

naturalist /náchərəlist/ *n.* & *adj.* ● *n.* **1** an expert in natural history. **2** a person who believes in or practises naturalism. ● *adj.* = NATURALISTIC.
■ *n.* **1** ecologist, biologist, botanist, zoologist, ornithologist, entomologist; natural historian, wildlife expert, bird-watcher, conservationist, environmentalist, ecologist, preservationist.

naturalistic /náchərəlístik/ *adj.* **1** imitating nature closely; lifelike. **2** of or according to naturalism. **3** of natural history. □□ **naturalistically** *adv.*
■ **1** see REALISTIC 1.

naturalize /náchərəlīz/ *v.* (also **-ise**) **1** *tr.* admit (a foreigner) to the citizenship of a country. **2** *tr.* introduce (an animal, plant, etc.) into another region so that it flourishes in the wild. **3** *tr.* adopt (a foreign word, custom, etc.). **4** *intr.* become naturalized. **5** *tr. Philos.* exclude from the miraculous; explain naturalistically. **6** *tr.* free from conventions; make natural. **7** *tr.* cause to appear natural. **8** *intr.* study natural history. □□ **naturalization** /-záysh'n/ *n.* [F *naturaliser* (as NATURAL)]

naturally /náchərəli/ *adv.* **1** in a natural manner. **2** as a natural result. **3** (qualifying a whole sentence) as might be expected; of course.
■ **1** normally, by nature, by character, genuinely; inherently, instinctively, innately, congenitally; unaffectedly, unpretentiously, easily, candidly, openly, simply, plainly, honestly, straightforwardly. **2, 3** (as a matter) of course, needless to say, to be sure, certainly, not unexpectedly, as expected, *disp.* as anticipated; obviously, clearly, logically.

nature /náychər/ *n.* **1** a thing's or person's innate or essential qualities or character (*not in their nature to be cruel*; *is the nature of iron to rust*). **2** (often **Nature**) **a** the physical power causing all the phenomena of the material world (*Nature is the best physician*). **b** these phenomena, including plants, animals, landscape, etc. (*nature gives him comfort*). **3** a kind, sort, or class (*things of this nature*). **4** = *human nature*. **5 a** a specified element of human character (*the rational nature*; *our animal nature*). **b** a person of a specified character (*even strong natures quail*). **6 a** an uncultivated or wild area, condition, community, etc. **b** the countryside, esp. when picturesque. **7** inherent impulses determining character or action. **8** heredity as an influence on or determinant of personality (opp. NURTURE). **9** a living thing's vital functions or needs (*such a diet will not support nature*). □ **against nature** unnatural; immoral. **against** (or **contrary to**) **nature** miraculous; miraculously. **back to nature** returning to a pre-civilized or natural state. **by nature** innately. **from nature** *Art* using natural objects as models. **human nature** general human characteristics, feelings, etc. **in nature 1** actually existing. **2** anywhere; at all. **in** (or **of**) **the nature of** characteristically resembling or belonging to the class of (*the answer was in the nature of an excuse*). **in a state of nature 1** in an uncivilized or uncultivated state. **2** totally naked. **3** in an unregenerate state. **law of nature** = *natural law* 2. **nature cure** = NATUROPATHY. **nature-printing** a method of producing a print of leaves etc. by pressing them on a prepared plate. **nature reserve** a tract of land managed so as to preserve its flora, fauna, physical features, etc. **nature study** the practical study of plant and animal life etc. as a school subject. **nature trail** a signposted path through the countryside designed to draw attention to natural phenomena. [ME f. OF f. L *natura* f. *nasci nat-* be born]

■ **1, 7** quality, properties, features, character, personality, make-up, essence, constitution, identity, reality, attributes, disposition, temperament, complexion. **2 a** Mother Nature. **b** wildlife, fauna and flora, environment, landscape, countryside. **3** kind, variety, description, sort, class, category, type, genre, species; stamp, cast, mould, kidney, colour, *US* stripe; character, constitution. **6** scenery, countryside, wilderness; wildness, primitiveness, simplicity. □ **by nature** see NATURALLY 1.

natured /náychərd/ *adj.* (in *comb.*) having a specified disposition (*good-natured*; *ill-natured*).

naturism /náychəriz'm/ *n.* **1** nudism. **2** naturalism in regard to religion. **3** the worship of natural objects. □□ **naturist** *n.*

naturopathy /náychəróppəthi/ *n.* **1** the treatment of disease etc. without drugs, usu. involving diet, exercise, massage, etc. **2** this regimen used preventively. □□ **naturopath** /náychərəpath/ *n.* **naturopathic** /náychərəpáthik/ *adj.*

naught /nawt/ *n.* & *adj.* ● *n.* **1** *archaic* or *literary* nothing, nought. **2** *US* = NOUGHT. ● *adj.* (usu. *predic.*) *archaic* or *literary* worthless; useless. □ **bring to naught** ruin; baffle. **come to naught** be ruined or baffled. **set at naught** disregard; despise. [OE *nāwiht*, *-wuht* f. *nā* (see NO[2]) + *wiht* WIGHT]

■ *n.* **1** nothing, nil, zero, *poet. or archaic* nought, *esp. US sl.* zilch.

naughty /náwti/ *adj.* (**naughtier**, **naughtiest**) **1** (esp. of children) disobedient; badly behaved. **2** *colloq. joc.* indecent. **3** *archaic* wicked. □□ **naughtily** *adv.* **naughtiness** *n.* [ME f. NAUGHT + -Y[1]]

■ **1** mischievous, impish, puckish, roguish, devilish, *colloq.* scampish; ill-behaved, disobedient, refractory, insubordinate, bad, perverse, wicked, fractious, unruly, wayward, wild, unmanageable, ungovernable, undisciplined, defiant, obstreperous. **2** improper, offensive, vulgar, rude, indecent, immoral, risqué, ribald, bawdy, blue, pornographic, smutty, lewd, obscene, dirty, *US* off colour, *colloq.* raunchy, near the knuckle.

nauplius /náwpliəss/ *n.* (*pl.* **nauplii** /-pli-ī/) the first larval stage of some crustaceans. [L, = a kind of shellfish, or f. Gk *Nauplios* son of Poseidon]

nausea /náwziə, -siə/ *n.* **1** a feeling of sickness with an inclination to vomit. **2** loathing; revulsion. [L f. Gk *nausia* f. *naus* ship]

■ **2** see DISGUST *n.* 1.

nauseate /náwziayt, -siayt/ *v.* **1** *tr.* affect with nausea (*was nauseated by the smell*); disgust. **2** *intr.* (usu. foll. by *at*) loathe food, an occupation, etc.; feel sick. □□ **nauseating** *adj.* **nauseatingly** *adv.* [L *nauseare* (as NAUSEA)]

■ **1** sicken, disgust, repel, revolt, offend. □□ **nauseating** see DISGUSTING.

nauseous /náwziəss, -siəss/ *adj.* **1** affected with nausea; sick. **2** causing nausea; offensive to the taste or smell. **3** disgusting; loathsome. □□ **nauseously** *adv.* **nauseousness** *n.* [L *nauseosus* (as NAUSEA)]

■ **2, 3** nauseating, loathsome, sickening, disgusting, repellent, offensive, revolting, repugnant, repulsive, abhorrent, nasty, foul, unpleasant, stomach-turning; emetic.

nautch /nawch/ *n.* a performance of professional Indian dancing-girls. □ **nautch-girl** a professional Indian dancing-girl. [Urdu (Hindi) *nāch* f. Prakrit *nachcha* f. Skr. *nṛitja* dancing]

nautical /náwtik'l/ *adj.* of or concerning sailors or navigation; naval; maritime. □ **nautical almanac** a yearbook containing astronomical and tidal information for navigators etc. **nautical mile** a unit of approx. 2,025 yards (1,852 metres): also called *sea mile*. □□ **nautically** *adv.* [F *nautique* or f. L *nauticus* f. Gk *nautikos* f. *nautēs* sailor f. *naus* ship]

■ maritime, marine, seafaring, seagoing; naval; boating, yachting, sailing; navigational.

nautilus /náwtiləss/ *n.* (*pl.* **nautiluses** or **nautili** /-lī/) **1** any cephalopod of the genus *Nautilus* with a light brittle spiral shell, esp. (**pearly nautilus**) one having a chambered shell with nacreous septa. **2** (in full **paper nautilus**) any small floating octopus of the genus *Argonauta*, of which the female has a very thin shell and webbed sail-like arms. [L f. Gk *nautilos*, lit. sailor (as NAUTICAL)]

Navajo /návvəhō/ *n.* (also **Navaho**) (*pl.* **-os**) **1** a member of an American Indian people native to New Mexico and Arizona. **2** the language of this people. [Sp., = pueblo]

naval /náyv'l/ *adj.* **1** of, in, for, etc. the navy or a navy. **2** of or concerning ships (*a naval battle*). □ **naval academy** a college for training naval officers. **naval architect** a designer of ships. **naval architecture** the designing of ships. **naval officer** an officer in a navy. **naval stores** all materials used in shipping. □□ **navally** *adv.* [L *navalis* f. *navis* ship]

■ see NAUTICAL.

navarin /návvəraN/ *n.* a casserole of mutton or lamb with vegetables. [F]

nave[1] /nayv/ *n.* the central part of a church, usu. from the west door to the chancel and excluding the side aisles. [med.L *navis* f. L *navis* ship]

nave[2] /nayv/ *n.* the hub of a wheel. [OE *nafu*, *nafa* f. Gmc, rel. to NAVEL]

navel /náyv'l/ *n.* **1** a depression in the centre of the belly caused by the detachment of the umbilical cord. **2** a central point. □ **navel orange** a large seedless orange with a navel-like formation at the top. [OE *nafela* f. Gmc, rel. to NAVE[2]]

■ **1** *Anat.* umbilicus, *colloq.* belly button. **2** centre, nub, *Gk Antiq.* omphalos; see also HUB.

navelwort /náyv'lwurt/ *n.* a pennywort.

navicular /navíkyoolər/ *adj.* & *n.* ● *adj.* boat-shaped. ● *n.* (in full **navicular bone**) a boat-shaped bone in the foot or hand. □ **navicular disease** an inflammatory disease of the navicular bone in horses, causing lameness. [F *naviculaire* or LL *navicularis* f. L *navicula* dimin. of *navis* ship]

navigable /návvigəb'l/ *adj.* **1** (of a river, the sea, etc.) affording a passage for ships. **2** (of a ship etc.) seaworthy (*in navigable condition*). **3** (of a balloon, airship, etc.) steerable. □□ **navigability** /-bílliti/ *n.* [F *navigable* or L *navigabilis* (as NAVIGATE)]

■ **1** passable, traversable, negotiable; unblocked, unobstructed, clear, open. **2, 3** seaworthy, sailable; manoeuvrable, controllable, steerable.

navigate /návvigayt/ *v.* **1** *tr.* manage or direct the course of (a ship, aircraft, etc.). **2** *tr.* **a** sail on (a sea, river, etc.). **b** travel or fly through (the air). **3** *intr.* (of a passenger in a vehicle) assist the driver by map-reading etc. **4** *intr.* sail a ship; sail in a ship. **5** *tr.* (often *refl.*) *colloq.* steer (oneself, a course, etc.) through a crowd etc. [L *navigare* f. *navis* ship + *agere* drive]

■ **1** manoeuvre, handle, sail, guide, pilot, steer, direct; skipper, captain, *Naut.* con. **2, 4** sail, voyage, cruise, journey; cross, traverse.

navigation /návvigáysh'n/ *n.* **1** the act or process of navigating. **2** any of several methods of determining or planning a ship's or aircraft's position and course by geometry, astronomy, radio signals, etc. **3** a voyage. □ **inland navigation** communication by canals and rivers. **navigation light** a light on a ship or aircraft at night, indicating its position and direction. □□ **navigational** *adj.* [F or f. L *navigatio* (as NAVIGATE)]

■ **1** pilotage, seamanship, steering, sailing.

navigator /návvigaytər/ *n.* **1** a person skilled or engaged in navigation. **2** an explorer by sea. [L (as NAVIGATE)]

■ **1** helmsman, seaman, steersman, skipper, *esp. US* wheelman, *archaic* pilot.

navvy /návvi/ *n.* & *v. Brit.* ● *n.* (*pl.* **-ies**) a labourer employed in building or excavating roads, canals, etc. ● *v.intr.* (**-ies, -ied**) work as a navvy. [abbr. of NAVIGATOR]

■ *n.* see LABOURER.

navy /náyvi/ *n.* (*pl.* **-ies**) **1** (often **the Navy**) **a** the whole body of a State's ships of war, including crews, maintenance systems, etc. **b** the officers and men of a navy. **2** (in full **navy blue**) a dark-blue colour as used in naval uniform. **3** *poet.* a fleet of ships. □ **Navy Department** *US* the government department in charge of the navy. **Navy List** *Brit.* an official list containing the names of all naval officers etc. **navy yard** *US* a government shipyard with civilian labour. [ME, = fleet f. OF *navie* ship, fleet f. Rmc & pop.L *navia* ship f. L *navis*]

■ **1a, 3** naval force(s); see also FLEET[1].

nawab /nəwaáb, -wawb/ *n.* **1** the title of a distinguished Muslim in Pakistan. **2** *hist.* the title of a governor or nobleman in India. [Urdu *nawwāb* pl. f. Arab. *nā'ib* deputy: cf. NABOB]

nay /nay/ *adv.* & *n.* ● *adv.* **1** or rather; and even; and more than that (*impressive, nay, magnificent*). **2** *archaic* = NO[2] *adv.* 1. ● *n.* **1** the word 'nay'. **2** a negative vote (*counted 16 nays*). [ME f. ON *nei* f. *ne* not + *ei* AYE[2]]

naysay /náysay/ *v.* (*3rd sing. present* **-says**; *past* and *past part.* **-said**) esp. *US* **1** *intr.* utter a denial or refusal. **2** *tr.* refuse or contradict. □□ **naysayer** *n.*

■ □□ **naysayer** denier, refuser, rejecter, dissenter, dissident, recusant.

Nazarene /názzəreén/ *n.* & *adj.* ● *n.* **1 a** (prec. by *the*) Christ. **b** (esp. in Jewish or Muslim use) a Christian. **2** a native or inhabitant of Nazareth. **3** a member of an early Jewish-Christian sect. ● *adj.* of or concerning Nazareth, the Nazarenes, etc. [ME f. LL *Nazarenus* f. Gk *Nazarēnos* f. *Nazaret* Nazareth]

Nazarite /názzərīt/ *n.* (also **Nazirite**) *hist.* a Hebrew who had taken certain vows of abstinence; an ascetic (Num. 6). [LL *Nazaraeus* f. Heb. *nāzīr* f. *nāzar* to separate or consecrate oneself]

Nazi /naátsi/ *n.* & *adj.* ● *n.* (*pl.* **Nazis**) **1** *hist.* a member of the German National Socialist party. **2** *derog.* a person holding extreme racist or authoritarian views or behaving brutally. **3** a person belonging to any organization similar to the Nazis. ● *adj.* of or concerning the Nazis, Nazism, etc. □□ **Nazidom** *n.* **Nazify** /-sifī/ *v.tr.* (**-ies, -ied**). **Naziism** /-si-iz'm/ *n.* **Nazism** /naátsiz'm/ *n.* [repr. pronunc. of *Nati-* in G *Nationalsozialist*]

■ *n.* **2** see SUPREMACIST. ● *adj.* see TOTALITARIAN *adj.*

Nazirite var. of NAZARITE.

NB *abbr.* **1** *US* Nebraska (in official postal use). **2** New Brunswick. **3** no ball. **4** Scotland (North Britain). **5** *nota bene.*

Nb *symb. Chem.* the element niobium.

NBC *abbr.* (in the US) National Broadcasting Company.

N. by E. *abbr.* North by East.

N. by W. *abbr.* North by West.

NC *abbr.* North Carolina (also in official postal use).

NCB *abbr. hist.* (in the UK) National Coal Board. ¶ Since 1987 officially called *British Coal.*

NCO *abbr.* non-commissioned officer.

NCU *abbr.* (in the UK) National Communications Union.

ND *abbr. US* North Dakota (in official postal use).

Nd *symb. Chem.* the element neodymium.

n.d. *abbr.* no date.

-nd[1] *suffix* forming nouns (*fiend*; *friend*). [OE *-ond*, orig. part. ending]

-nd[2] *suffix* see -AND, -END.

N.Dak. *abbr.* North Dakota.

NE *abbr.* **1** north-east. **2** north-eastern.

Ne *symb. Chem.* the element neon.

né /nay/ *adj.* born (indicating a man's previous name) (*Lord Beaconsfield, né Benjamin Disraeli*). [F, past part. of *naître* be born: cf. NÉE]

Neanderthal /niándərtaal/ *adj.* of or belonging to the type of human widely distributed in palaeolithic Europe, with a retreating forehead and massive brow-ridges. [*Neanderthal*, a region in Germany where remains were found]

neap /neep/ *n.* & *v.* ● *n.* (in full **neap tide**) a tide just after the first and third quarters of the moon when there is least difference between high and low water. ● *v.* **1** *intr.* (of a tide) tend towards or reach the highest point of a neap tide. **2** *tr.* (in *passive*) (of a ship) be kept aground, in harbour, etc., by a neap tide. [OE *nēpflōd* (cf. FLOOD), of unkn. orig.]

Neapolitan /neéəpóllit'n/ *n.* & *adj.* ● *n.* a native or citizen of Naples in Italy. ● *adj.* of or relating to Naples. □ **Neapolitan ice-cream** ice-cream made in layers of different colours. **Neapolitan violet** a sweet-scented double viola. [ME f. L *Neapolitanus* f. L *Neapolis* Naples f. Gk f. *neos* new + *polis* city]

near /neer/ *adv., prep., adj.,* & *v.* ● *adv.* **1** (often foll. by *to*) to or at a short distance in space or time; close by (*the time drew near; dropped near to them*). **2** closely (*as near as one can guess*). **3** *archaic* almost, nearly (*very near died*). **4** *archaic* parsimoniously; meanly (*lives very near*). ● *prep.* (compar. & superl. also used) **1** to or at a short distance (in space, time, condition, or resemblance) from (*stood near the back; occurs nearer the end; the sun is near setting*). **2** (in *comb.*) **a** that is almost (*near-hysterical; a near-Communist*). **b** intended as a substitute for; resembling (*near-beer*). ● *adj.* **1** (usu. *predic.*) close at hand; close to, in place or time (*the man nearest you; in the near future*). **2 a** closely related (*a near relation*). **b** intimate (*a near friend*). **3** (of a part of a vehicle, animal, or road) left (*the near fore leg; near side front wheel* (orig. of the side from which one mounted)) (opp. OFF). **4** close; narrow (*a near escape; a near guess*). **5** (of a road or way) direct. **6** niggardly, mean. ● *v.* **1** *tr.* approach; draw near to (*neared the harbour*). **2** *intr.* draw near (*could distinguish them as they neared*). □ **come** (or **go**) **near** (foll. by verbal noun, or *to* + verbal noun) be on the point of, almost succeed in (*came near to falling*). **go near** (foll. by *to* + infin.) narrowly fail. **near at hand 1** within easy reach. **2** in the immediate future. **the Near East** the region comprising the countries of the eastern Mediterranean. **Near Eastern** of the Near East. **near go** *colloq.* a narrow escape. **near the knuckle** *colloq.* verging on the indecent. **near miss 1** a bomb etc. which is close to the target. **2** a situation in which a collision is narrowly avoided. **3** an attempt which is almost but not quite successful. **near sight** esp. *US* = *short sight.* **near thing** a narrow escape. **near upon** *archaic* not far in time from. □□ **nearish** *adj.* **nearness** *n.* [ME f. ON *nær*, orig. compar. of *ná* = OE *nēah* NIGH]

■ *adv.* **1** close (by *or* at hand), not far (off *or* away), nearby, in the vicinity *or* neighbourhood, within reach, *archaic or dial.* nigh. **2** close, closely. **3** nearly, almost, just about, all but, virtually, practically, *archaic or rhet.* wellnigh; not quite. ● *prep.* **1** close to, in the vicinity *or* neighbourhood of, next to, adjacent to, within reach of, a stone's throw from, not far (away) from. ● *adj.* **1** close, imminent, immediate, impending, looming, coming, approaching, forthcoming, in the offing, at hand, *esp. US* upcoming; nearby, adjacent, next-door, adjoining, neighbouring, contiguous. **2 a** close, intimate, connected, related, attached. **b** see INTIMATE[1] *adj.* 1. **4** close, narrow, hairbreadth; lucky. **6** stingy, mean, niggardly, miserly, parsimonious, penurious, cheap, penny-pinching, cheese-paring, selfish, close, tight-fisted, close-fisted. ● *v.* approach, draw near, come close *or* closer to; verge on, approximate to, lean towards. □ **near at hand 1** see

NEARBY *adj.* **2** see SOON 1. **the Near East** the Levant. **near the knuckle** see RISQUÉ. **near miss 2** close *or* near thing, shave, narrow escape, narrow squeak, *colloq.* close shave. **near thing** see *near miss* above.

nearby *adj.* & *adv.* ● *adj.* /néerbī/ situated in a near position (*a nearby hotel*). ● *adv.* /neerbī/ close; not far away.
■ *adj.* close, within reach, handy, accessible, at *or* to hand, adjacent. ● *adv.* close by, close at hand, not far (off *or* away), in the vicinity *or* neighbourhood, within reach, about, around.

Nearctic /niáarktik/ *adj.* of or relating to the Arctic and the temperate parts of N. America as a zoogeographical region. [NEO- + ARCTIC]

nearly /néerli/ *adv.* **1** almost (*we are nearly there*). **2** closely (*they are nearly related*). □ **not nearly** nothing like; far from (*not nearly enough*).
■ **1** almost, not quite, about, approximately, around, approaching, nearing, close to, all but, just about, virtually, practically, as good as, more or less, next to, *archaic or rhet.* wellnigh, *colloq.* next; barely, hardly, scarcely.

nearside /néersīd/ *n.* (often *attrib.*) esp. *Brit.* the left side of a vehicle, animal, etc. (cf. OFFSIDE *n.*).

near-sighted /néersītid/ *adj.* esp. *US* = SHORT-SIGHTED. □□ **near-sightedly** *adv.* **near-sightedness** *n.*
■ short-sighted, myopic, dim-sighted.

neat[1] /neet/ *adj.* **1** tidy and methodical. **2** elegantly simple in form etc.; well-proportioned. **3** (of language, style, etc.) brief, clear, and pointed; epigrammatic. **4 a** cleverly executed (*a neat piece of work*). **b** deft; dexterous. **5** (of esp. alcoholic liquor) undiluted. **6** *US sl.* (as a general term of approval) good, pleasing, excellent. □□ **neatly** *adv.* **neatness** *n.* [F *net* f. L *nitidus* shining f. *nitēre* shine]
■ **1** tidy, orderly, clean, uncluttered, trim, spruce, fastidious, spick and span, shipshape, organized, well-organized, well-ordered, systematic, methodical, *archaic or dial.* trig, *colloq.* natty, *Brit. colloq.* dinky. **2** unembellished, unadorned, unornamented, simple, elegant, well-proportioned, graceful, smart, uncomplicated; regular, precise. **3** distinct, clear, witty, lucid, crisp, emphatic; see also *epigrammatic* (EPIGRAM). **4** deft, adroit, clever, efficient, ingenious, expert, practised, skilful, dexterous, *colloq.* nifty. **5** straight, unadulterated, unmixed, undiluted, unblended, pure, *US* uncut. **6** good, fine, wonderful, marvellous, splendid, excellent, exceptional, first-class, first-rate, *colloq.* far-out, capital, grand, great, smashing, keen, top-notch, A1, *Brit. colloq.* top-hole, *US colloq.* A-OK, swell, *sl.* crucial, def, ace, *esp. US sl.* cool, spiffy, *Brit. archaic sl.* spiffing, topping.

neat[2] /neet/ *n. archaic* **1** a bovine animal. **2** (as *pl.*) cattle. □ **neat's-foot oil** oil made from boiled cow-heel and used to dress leather. [OE *nēat* f. Gmc]

neaten /néet'n/ *v.tr.* make neat.
■ tidy (up), straighten (up *or* out), clean (up), spruce up, trim (up), (put in) order, smarten, *archaic or dial.* trig.

neath /neeth/ *prep. poet.* beneath. [BENEATH]

NEB *abbr.* **1** (in the UK) National Enterprise Board. **2** New English Bible.

Neb. *abbr.* Nebraska.

neb /neb/ *n. Sc.* & *N.Engl.* **1** a beak or bill. **2** a nose; a snout. **3** a tip, spout, or point. [OE *nebb* ult. f. Gmc: cf. NIB]

nebbish /nébbish/ *n.* & *adj. colloq.* ● *n.* a submissive or timid person. ● *adj.* submissive; timid. [Yiddish *nebach* poor thing!]

Nebr. *abbr.* Nebraska.

Nebuchadnezzar /nébyookədnézzər/ *n.* a wine bottle of about 20 times the standard size. [name of a king of Babylon (6th c. BC)]

nebula /nébyoolə/ *n.* (*pl.* **nebulae** /-lee/ or **nebulas**) **1** *Astron.* **a** a cloud of gas and dust, sometimes glowing and sometimes appearing as a dark silhouette against other glowing matter. **b** a bright area caused by a galaxy, or a large cloud of distant stars. **2** *Med.* a clouded spot on the cornea causing defective vision. [L, = mist]

nebular /nébyoolər/ *adj.* of or relating to a nebula or nebulae. □ **nebular theory** (or **hypothesis**) the theory that the solar and stellar systems were developed from a primeval nebula.

nebulous /nébyooləss/ *adj.* **1** cloudlike. **2 a** formless, clouded. **b** hazy, indistinct, vague (*put forward a few nebulous ideas*). **3** *Astron.* of or like a nebula or nebulae. □ **nebulous star** a small cluster of indistinct stars, or a star in a luminous haze. □□ **nebulosity** /-lóssiti/ *n.* **nebulously** *adv.* **nebulousness** *n.* [ME f. F *nébuleux* or L *nebulosus* (as NEBULA)]
■ **2** vague, hazy, clouded, unclear, obscure, indistinct, fuzzy, muddy, ill-defined, shapeless, amorphous, formless, blurred, indeterminate, murky, opaque, turbid, dim, foggy, faint, pale.

nebuly /nébyooli/ *adj. Heraldry* wavy in form; cloudlike. [F *nébulé* f. med.L *nebulatus* f. L NEBULA]

necessarian /néssisáiriən/ *n.* & *adj.* = NECESSITARIAN. □□ **necessarianism** *n.*

necessarily /néssəsərili, -sérrili/ *adv.* as a necessary result; inevitably.
■ inevitably, unavoidably, inescapably, incontrovertibly, automatically, naturally, (as a matter) of course, of necessity, as a result, by definition, axiomatically, certainly, surely, to be sure, willy-nilly, *archaic* perforce, *colloq.* like it or not, *literary nolens volens.*

necessary /néssəsəri/ *adj.* & *n.* ● *adj.* **1** requiring to be done, achieved, etc.; requisite, essential (*it is necessary to work*; *lacks the necessary documents*). **2** determined, existing, or happening by natural laws, predestination, etc., not by free will; inevitable (*a necessary evil*). **3** *Philos.* (of a concept or a mental process) inevitably resulting from or produced by the nature of things etc., so that the contrary is impossible. **4** *Philos.* (of an agent) having no independent volition. ● *n.* (*pl.* **-ies**) (usu. in *pl.*) any of the basic requirements of life, such as food, warmth, etc. □ **the necessary** *colloq.* **1** money. **2** an action, item, etc., needed for a purpose (*they will do the necessary*). [ME f. OF *necessaire* f. L *necessarius* f. *necesse* needful]
■ *adj.* **1** indispensable, essential, required, needed, compulsory, requisite, vital, demanded, imperative, obligatory, needful, of the essence. **2** sure, certain, predetermined, predestined, fated, inexorable; inevitable, unavoidable, inescapable, ineluctable. ● *n.* see NECESSITY 1a. □ **the necessary 1** see MONEY 3. **2** resources, means, material, essential(s), basics, requisite(s), tools, *colloq.* tne needful; (*have the necessary*) have potential, *colloq.* have what it takes.

necessitarian /niséssitáiriən/ *n.* & *adj. Philos.* ● *n.* a person who holds that all action is predetermined and free will is impossible. ● *adj.* of or concerning such a person or theory (opp. LIBERTARIAN). □□ **necessitarianism** *n.*

necessitate /niséssitayt/ *v.tr.* **1** make necessary (esp. as a result) (*will necessitate some sacrifice*). **2** *US* (usu. foll. by *to* + infin.) force or compel (a person) to do something. [med.L *necessitare* compel (as NECESSITY)]
■ **1** see ENTAIL *v.*

necessitous /niséssitəss/ *adj.* poor; needy. [F *nécessiteux* or f. NECESSITY + -OUS]
■ see POOR 1.

necessity /niséssiti/ *n.* (*pl.* **-ies**) **1 a** an indispensible thing; a necessary (*central heating is a necessity*). **b** (usu. foll. by *of*) indispensability (*the necessity of a warm overcoat*). **2** a state of things or circumstances enforcing a certain course (*there was a necessity to hurry*). **3** imperative need (*necessity is the mother of invention*). **4** want; poverty; hardship (*stole because of necessity*). **5** constraint or compulsion regarded as a natural law governing all human action. □ **of necessity** unavoidably. [ME f. OF *necessité* f. L *necessitas -tatis* f. *necesse* needful]
■ **1 a** requirement, essential, necessary, requisite, need, prerequisite, basic, fundamental, *sine qua non.* **b** indispensability, needfulness; unavoidability, inevitability, inexorability. **2, 3** urgency, need, emergency, crisis, misfortune, exigency. **4** poverty, want, indigence,

need, destitution, penury, straits, hardship, difficulty, difficulties, pauperism, neediness. □ **of necessity** see NECESSARILY.

neck /nek/ *n.* & *v.* ● *n.* **1 a** the part of the body connecting the head to the shoulders. **b** the part of a shirt, dress, etc. round or close to the neck. **2 a** something resembling a neck, such as the narrow part of a cavity or vessel, a passage, channel, pass, isthmus, etc. **b** the narrow part of a bottle near the mouth. **3** the part of a violin etc. bearing the finger-board. **4** the length of a horse's head and neck as a measure of its lead in a race. **5** the flesh of an animal's neck (*neck of lamb*). **6** *Geol.* solidified lava or igneous rock in an old volcano crater or pipe. **7** *Archit.* the lower part of a capital. **8** *sl.* impudence (*you've got a neck, asking that*). ● *v.* **1** *intr.* & *tr. colloq.* kiss and caress amorously. **2 a** *tr.* form a narrowed part in. **b** *intr.* form a narrowed part. □ **get it in the neck** *colloq.* **1** receive a severe reprimand or punishment. **2** suffer a fatal or severe blow. **neck and neck** running level in a race etc. **neck of the woods** *colloq.* a usu. remote locality. **neck or nothing** risking everything on success. **up to one's neck** (often foll. by *in*) *colloq.* very deeply involved; very busy. □□ **necked** *adj.* (also in *comb.*). **necker** *n.* (in sense 1 of *v.*). **neckless** *adj.* [OE *hnecca* ult. f. Gmc]
■ *n.* **2 a** see CAPE[2] *n.* ● *v.* **1** see KISS *v.* 1, 3. □ **neck and neck** see LEVEL *adj.* 5. **neck of the woods** see PART *n.* 11.

neckband /nékband/ *n.* a strip of material round the neck of a garment.

neckcloth /nék-kloth/ *n. hist.* a cravat.

neckerchief /nékkərchif/ *n.* a square of cloth worn round the neck.

necking /nékking/ *n. Archit.* = NECK *n.* 7.

necklace /nékləss/ *n.* & *v.* ● *n.* **1** a chain or string of beads, precious stones, links, etc., worn as an ornament round the neck. **2** *S.Afr.* a tyre soaked or filled with petrol, placed round a victim's neck, and set alight. ● *v.tr. S.Afr.* kill with a 'necklace'.
■ **1** beads, chain, choker, *hist.* torque.

necklet /néklit/ *n.* **1** = NECKLACE *n.* 1. **2** a strip of fur worn round the neck.

neckline /néklīn/ *n.* the edge or shape of the opening of a garment at the neck (*a square neckline*).

necktie /néktī/ *n.* esp. *US* = TIE *n.* 2. □ **necktie party** *sl.* a lynching or hanging.

neckwear /nékwair/ *n.* collars, ties, etc.

necro- /nékrō/ *comb. form* corpse. [from or after Gk *nekro-* f. *nekros* corpse]

necrobiosis /nékrōbīṓsiss/ *n.* decay in the tissues of the body, esp. swelling of the collagen bundles in the dermis. □□ **necrobiotic** /-bīóttik/ *adj.*

necrolatry /nekróllətri/ *n.* worship of, or excessive reverence towards, the dead.

necrology /nekrólləji/ *n.* (*pl.* **-ies**) **1** a list of recently dead people. **2** an obituary notice. □□ **necrological** /-rəlójik'l/ *adj.*

necromancy /nékrōmansi/ *n.* **1** the prediction of the future by the supposed communication with the dead. **2** witchcraft. □□ **necromancer** *n.* **necromantic** /-mántik/ *adj.* [ME f. OF *nigromancie* f. med.L *nigromantia* changed (by assoc. with L *niger nigri* black) f. LL *necromantia* f. Gk *nekromanteia* (as NECRO-, -MANCY)]
■ see MAGIC *n.* 1. □□ **necromancer** see MAGICIAN 1. **necromantic** see MAGIC *adj.* 1.

necrophilia /nékrəfilliə/ *n.* (also **necrophily** /nikróffili/) a morbid and esp. erotic attraction to corpses. □□ **necrophil** /nék-/ *n.* **necrophile** /nékrəfīl/ *n.* **necrophiliac** /-filliak/ *n.* **necrophilic** *adj.* **necrophilism** /-króffiliz'm/ *n.* **necrophilist** /-króffilist/ *n.* [NECRO- + Gk *-philia* loving]

necrophobia /nékrəfṓbiə/ *n.* an abnormal fear of death or dead bodies.

necropolis /nekróppəliss/ *n.* an ancient cemetery or burial place.
■ see GRAVEYARD.

necropsy /nékropsi/ *n.* (also **necroscopy** /-króskəpi/) (*pl.* **-ies**) = AUTOPSY 1. [NECRO- after AUTOPSY, or + -SCOPY]

necrosis /nekrṓsiss/ *n. Med.* & *Physiol.* the death of tissue caused by disease or injury, esp. as one of the symptoms of gangrene or pulmonary tuberculosis. □□ **necrose** /-krṓss/ *v.intr.* **necrotic** /-króttik/ *adj.* **necrotize** /nékrətīz/ *v.intr.* (also **-ise**). [mod.L f. Gk *nekrōsis* (as NECRO-, -OSIS)]

nectar /néktər/ *n.* **1** a sugary substance produced by plants and made into honey by bees. **2** (in Greek and Roman mythology) the drink of the gods. **3** a drink compared to this. □□ **nectarean** /-táiriən/ *adj.* **nectareous** /-táiriəss/ *adj.* **nectariferous** /-riffərəss/ *adj.* **nectarous** *adj.* [L f. Gk *nektar*]

nectarine /néktərin, -reen/ *n.* **1** a variety of peach with a thin brightly-coloured smooth skin and firm flesh. **2** the tree bearing this. [orig. as adj., = nectar-like, f. NECTAR + -INE[4]]

nectary /néktəri/ *n.* (*pl.* **-ies**) the nectar-secreting organ of a flower or plant. [mod.L *nectarium* (as NECTAR)]

NEDC *abbr.* (in the UK) National Economic Development Council.

neddy /néddi/ *n.* (*pl.* **-ies**) *colloq.* **1** a donkey. **2** (**Neddy**) = NEDC. [dimin. of *Ned*, pet-form of the name *Edward*]

Ned Kelly / ned kélli/ *n. Austral.* a person of reckless courage or unscrupulous business dealings. [the name of the most famous Australian bush-ranger (1857–80)]

née /nay/ *adj.* (*US* **nee**) (used in adding a married woman's maiden name after her surname) born (*Mrs Ann Smith, née Jones*). [F, fem. past part. of *naître* be born]

need /need/ *v.* & *n.* ● *v.* **1** *tr.* stand in want of; require (*needs a new coat*). **2** *tr.* (foll. by *to* + infin.; *3rd sing. present neg. or interrog.* **need** without *to*) be under the necessity or obligation (*it needs to be done carefully*; *he need not come*; *need you ask?*). **3** *intr. archaic* be necessary. ● *n.* **1 a** a want or requirement (*my needs are few*; *the need for greater freedom*). **b** a thing wanted (*my greatest need is a car*). **2** circumstances requiring some course of action; necessity (*there is no need to worry*; *if need arise*). **3** destitution; poverty. **4** a crisis; an emergency (*failed them in their need*). □ **at need** in time of need. **had need** *archaic* ought to (*had need remember*). **have need of** require; want. **have need to** require to (*has need to be warned*). **in need** requiring help. **in need of** requiring. **need not have** did not need to (but did). [OE *nēodian*, *nēd* f. Gmc]
■ *v.* **1** require, demand, want, be *or* stand in want of, be *or* stand in need of, call for, have need of, cry out for; lack, miss, have occasion for. **2** (*need to*) see GET *v.* 11b, *cannot choose but* (CHOOSE). ● *n.* **1, 2** necessity, requirement; call, demand, want; constraint; essential, necessary, requisite, prerequisite, basic(s), fundamental(s), *sine qua non*; lack, dearth, shortage, paucity, scarcity, insufficiency. **3, 4** distress, difficulty, trouble, (dire *or* desperate) straits, stress, crisis, emergency, exigency, extremity; neediness, needfulness; poverty, penury, impecuniousness, destitution, privation, deprivation, indigence, beggary. □ **have need of** see NEED *v.* 1 above. **in need** see *deprived* (DEPRIVE 2).

needful /néedfool/ *adj.* **1** requisite; necessary; indispensable. **2** (prec. by *the*) **a** what is necessary. **b** *colloq.* money or action needed for a purpose. □□ **needfully** *adv.* **needfulness** *n.*
■ **1** see NECESSARY *adj.* 1. **2 a** (*the needful*) see *the necessary* 2 (NECESSARY). **b** see MONEY 3. □□ **needfulness** see NECESSITY 1b.

needle /néed'l/ *n.* & *v.* ● *n.* **1 a** a very thin small piece of smooth steel etc. pointed at one end and with a slit (eye) for thread at the other, used in sewing. **b** a larger plastic, wooden, etc. slender stick without an eye, used in knitting. **c** a slender hooked stick used in crochet. **2** a pointer on a dial (see *magnetic needle*). **3** any of several small thin pointed instruments, esp.: **a** a surgical instrument for stitching. **b** the end of a hypodermic syringe. **c** = STYLUS. **d** an etching tool. **e** a steel pin exploding the cartridge of a breech-loading gun. **4 a** an obelisk (*Cleopatra's Needle*). **b** a pointed rock or peak. **5** the leaf of a fir or pine tree. **6** a beam used as a temporary support during underpinning. **7** *Brit. sl.* a fit of bad temper or nervousness (*got the needle while waiting*). ● *v.tr.* **1** *colloq.* incite or irritate; provoke (*the silence needled him*). **2** sew, pierce, or operate on with a needle. □ **needle game** (or **match** etc.) *Brit.* a contest that is very close or arouses personal grudges. **needle in a haystack** something almost impossible to find because it is concealed by so many other things etc. **needle-lace** lace made with needles not bobbins. **needle-point 1** a very sharp point. **2** = *needle-lace*. **3** = GROS or PETIT POINT. **needle's eye** (or **eye of a needle**) the least possible aperture, esp. with ref. to Matt. 19:24. **needle time** an agreed maximum allowance of time for broadcasting music from records. **needle valve** a valve closed by a thin tapering part. [OE *nǣdl* f. Gmc]

■ *n.* **2** see INDICATOR 1. **5** see SPINE 2. ● *v.* see IRRITATE 1.

needlecord /née'd'lkord/ *n.* a fine-ribbed corduroy fabric.

needlecraft /née'd'lkraaft/ *n.* skill in needlework.

needlefish /née'd'lfish/ *n.* a garfish.

needleful /née'd'lfool/ *n.* (*pl.* **-fuls**) the length of thread etc. put into a needle at one time.

needless /néedliss/ *adj.* **1** unnecessary. **2** uncalled-for; gratuitous. □ **needless to say** of course; it goes without saying. □□ **needlessly** *adv.* **needlessness** *n.*

■ unnecessary, non-essential, unessential, inessential, unneeded, unwanted, uncalled-for, gratuitous, superfluous, redundant, useless, excess, excessive, tautological, dispensable, expendable, supererogatory, *de trop*; pleonastic. □ **needless to say** (as a matter) of course, obviously, it goes without saying, manifestly, clearly; see also NATURALLY 2, 3. □□ **needlessly** see *unduly* (UNDUE).

needlewoman /née'd'lwoommən/ *n.* (*pl.* **-women**) **1** a seamstress. **2** a woman or girl with specified sewing skill (*a good needlewoman*).

needlework /née'd'lwurk/ *n.* sewing or embroidery.

needs /needz/ *adv. archaic* (usu. prec. or foll. by *must*) of necessity (*must needs decide*). [OE *nēdes* (as NEED, -s³)]

needy /néedi/ *adj.* (**needier, neediest**) **1** (of a person) poor; destitute. **2** (of circumstances) characterized by poverty. □□ **neediness** *n.*

■ **1** poor, indigent, poverty-stricken, destitute, impoverished, penniless, impecunious, necessitous, underprivileged, deprived, disadvantaged, in dire straits, in reduced circumstances, down-and-out, insolvent, hard up, pinched, on the breadline, *colloq.* on one's uppers, flat broke, strapped (for cash), up against it.

neep /neep/ *n. Sc.* & *N.Engl.* a turnip. [OE *nǣp* f. L *napus*]

ne'er /nair/ *adv. poet.* = NEVER. □ **ne'er-do-well** *n.* a good-for-nothing person. ● *adj.* good-for-nothing. [ME contr. of NEVER]

■ □ **ne'er-do-well** (*n.*) see *good-for-nothing n.* (*adj.*) see SHIFTLESS.

nefarious /nifáiriəss/ *adj.* wicked; iniquitous. □□ **nefariously** *adv.* **nefariousness** *n.* [L *nefarius* f. *nefas* wrong f. *ne-* not + *fas* divine law]

■ see EVIL *adj.* 1. □□ **nefariousness** see EVIL *n.* 2.

neg. *abbr.* negative.

negate /nigáyt/ *v.tr.* **1** nullify; invalidate. **2** imply, involve, or assert the non-existence of. **3** be the negation of. □□ **negator** *n.* [L *negare negat-* deny]

■ **1** see NEUTRALIZE.

negation /nigáysh'n/ *n.* **1** the absence or opposite of something actual or positive. **2 a** the act of denying. **b** an instance of this. **3** (usu. foll. by *of*) a refusal, contradiction, or denial. **4** a negative statement or doctrine. **5** a negative or unreal thing; a nonentity. **6** *Logic* the assertion that a certain proposition is false. □□ **negatory** /néggətəri/ *adj.* [F *negation* or L *negatio* (as NEGATE)]

■ **2** see DENIAL 1. **3** see DENIAL 3.

negative /néggətiv/ *adj.*, *n.* & *v.* ● *adj.* **1** expressing or implying denial, prohibition, or refusal (*a negative vote*; *a negative answer*). **2** (of a person or attitude): **a** lacking positive attributes; apathetic; pessimistic. **b** opposing or resisting; uncooperative. **3** marked by the absence of qualities (*a negative reaction*; *a negative result from the test*). **4** of the opposite nature to a thing regarded as positive (*debt is negative capital*). **5** *Algebra* (of a quantity) less than zero, to be subtracted from others or from zero (opp. POSITIVE). **6** *Electr.* **a** of the kind of charge carried by electrons (opp. POSITIVE). **b** containing or producing such a charge. ● *n.* **1** a negative statement, reply, or word (*hard to prove a negative*). **2** *Photog.* **a** an image with black and white reversed or colours replaced by complementary ones, from which positive pictures are obtained. **b** a developed film or plate bearing such an image. **3** a negative quality; an absence of something. **4** (prec. by *the*) a position opposing the affirmative. **5** *Logic* = NEGATION 6. ● *v.tr.* **1** refuse to accept or countenance; veto; reject. **2** disprove (an inference or hypothesis). **3** contradict (a statement). **4** neutralize (an effect). □ **in the negative** with negative effect; so as to reject a proposal etc.; no (*the answer was in the negative*). **negative evidence** (or **instance**) evidence of the non-occurrence of something. **negative feedback 1** the return of part of an output signal to the input, tending to decrease the amplification etc. **2** feedback that tends to diminish or counteract the process giving rise to it. **negative geotropism** see GEOTROPISM. **negative income tax** an amount credited as allowance to a taxed income, and paid as benefit when it exceeds debited tax. **negative pole** the south-seeking pole of a magnet. **negative proposition** *Logic* = NEGATION 6. **negative quantity** *joc.* nothing. **negative sign** a symbol (-) indicating subtraction or a value less than zero. **negative virtue** abstention from vice. □□ **negatively** *adv.* **negativeness** *n.* **negativity** /-tívviti/ *n.* [ME f. OF *negatif -ive* or LL *negativus* (as NEGATE)]

■ *adj.* **1** contradictory, anti, contrary, dissenting, opposing, denying. **2 a** apathetic, unenthusiastic, cool, cold, uninterested, unresponsive, *disp.* disinterested; pessimistic. **b** opposing, resisting, refusing, denying, gainsaying; uncooperative, disputatious, argumentative, adversarial, antagonistic, antipathetic, adverse. **3** see INERT 2. □ **in the negative** negatively; no.

negativism /néggətiviz'm/ *n.* **1** a negative position or attitude; extreme scepticism, criticism, etc. **2** denial of accepted beliefs. □□ **negativist** *n.* **negativistic** /-vístik/ *adj.*

neglect /niglékt/ *v.* & *n.* ● *v.tr.* **1** fail to care for or to do; be remiss about (*neglected their duty*; *neglected his children*). **2** (foll. by verbal noun, or *to* + infin.) fail; overlook or forget the need to (*neglected to inform them*; *neglected telling them*). **3** not pay attention to; disregard (*neglected the obvious warning*). ● *n.* **1** lack of caring; negligence (*the house suffered from neglect*). **2 a** the act of neglecting. **b** the state of being neglected (*the house fell into neglect*). **3** (usu. foll. by *of*) disregard. □□ **neglectful** *adj.* **neglectfully** *adv.* **neglectfulness** *n.* [L *neglegere neglect-* f. *neg-* not + *legere* choose, pick up]

■ *v.* **1, 2** disregard, let slide *or* pass, be remiss about, abandon, lose sight of, forget, shirk; fail to do, omit. **3** disregard, ignore, slight, pay no attention *or* heed to, be inattentive to, overlook; pass by, spurn, rebuff, scorn, disdain, cold-shoulder. ● *n.* **1** negligence, laxity, laxness, slackness, neglectfulness, lack of care, inactivity, inaction, dereliction, default, failure, failing, remissness. **3** disregard, disrespect, inattention, indifference, slighting, unconcern, oversight, heedlessness, neglectfulness, carelessness, inadvertence.

negligée /néglizhay/ *n.* (also **negligee, néglié**) **1** (usu. **negligee**) a woman's dressing-gown of thin fabric. **2** unceremonious or informal attire. [F, past part. of *négliger* NEGLECT]

■ **1** see WRAPPER 4.

negligence /néglijənss/ *n.* **1 a** a lack of proper care and attention; carelessness. **b** an act of carelessness. **2** *Law* = *contributory negligence*. **3** *Art* freedom from restraint or artificiality. □□ **negligent** *adj.* **negligently** *adv.* [ME f. OF *negligence* or L *negligentia* f. *negligere* = *neglegere*: see NEGLECT]

■ **1** inattention, inattentiveness, indifference, carelessness, unconcern, dereliction, failure, failing, heedlessness, laxity, laxness, disregard, oversight, omission, inadvertence, neglect, neglectfulness, remissness, forgetfulness, *formal* oscitation.

negligible /néglijib'l/ *adj.* not worth considering; insignificant. □ **negligible quantity** a person etc. that need not be considered. □□ **negligibility** /-bíliti/ *n.* **negligibly** *adv.* [obs. F f. *négliger* NEGLECT]
■ insignificant, minor, unimportant, trifling, trivial, inconsequential, inappreciable, small, slight, paltry, nugatory, worthless, petty, niggling, not worth mentioning *or* talking about, *colloq.* piddling, piffling.

negotiable /nigṓshəb'l, -siəb'l/ *adj.* **1** open to discussion or modification. **2** able to be negotiated. □□ **negotiability** /-bíliti/ *n.*
■ **2** see NAVIGABLE 1.

negotiate /nigṓshiayt, -siayt/ *v.* **1** *intr.* (usu. foll. by *with*) confer with others in order to reach a compromise or agreement. **2** *tr.* arrange (an affair) or bring about (a result) by negotiating (*negotiated a settlement*). **3** *tr.* find a way over, through, etc. (an obstacle, difficulty, fence, etc.). **4** *tr.* **a** transfer (a cheque etc.) to another for a consideration. **b** convert (a cheque etc.) into cash or notes. **c** get or give value for (a cheque etc.) in money. □□ **negotiant** /-shiənt, -siənt/ *n.* **negotiation** /-shiáysh'n, -siáysh'n/ *n.* **negotiator** *n.* [L *negotiari* f. *negotium* business f. *neg-* not + *otium* leisure]
■ **1** deal, bargain, haggle, chaffer, palter, *esp. US* dicker; discuss, debate, mediate, consult, parley, speak, talk, transact, come to terms. **2** arrange (for), organize, orchestrate, conduct, handle, manoeuvre, manage, engineer, work out, settle; get, obtain, bring off *or* about, accomplish, pull off, do, execute, effect, complete, conclude. **3** clear, manoeuvre one's way through *or* past *or* round *or* over, get through *or* past *or* round *or* over, pass, cross, *colloq.* make it through *or* past *or* round *or* over. □□ **negotiation** discussion, mediation, arbitration, bargaining, parley, talk; deal, bargain, transaction. **negotiator** arbitrator, arbiter, mediator, moderator, diplomat, ambassador, go-between, middleman, intercessor, interceder, intervener, agent, broker.

Negress /néegriss/ *n.* a female Negro (Black).

Negrillo /nigríllō/ *n.* (*pl.* **-os**) a member of a very small Negroid people native to Central and S. Africa. [Sp., dimin. of NEGRO]

Negrito /nigréetō/ *n.* (*pl.* **-os**) a member of a small Negroid people native to the Malayo-Polynesian region. [as NEGRILLO]

Negritude /néegrityōōd/ *n.* **1** the quality or state of being a Negro (Black). **2** the affirmation or consciousness of the value of Negro (Black) culture. [F *négritude* NIGRITUDE]

Negro /néegrō/ *n.* & *adj.* ● *n.* (*pl.* **-oes**) often *offens.* a member of a dark-skinned race orig. native to Africa. ● *adj.* **1** often *offens.* of or concerning Negroes. **2** (as **negro**) *Zool.* black or dark (*negro ant*). ¶ The term *Black* is usually preferred when referring to people. □ **Negro spiritual** a religious song derived from the musical traditions of Black people in the southern US. [Sp. & Port., f. L *niger nigri* black]
■ *adj.* **1** see BLACK *adj.* 3.

Negroid /néegroyd/ *adj.* & *n.* ● *adj.* **1** (of features etc.) characterizing a member of the Negro (Black) race, esp. in having dark skin, tightly curled hair, and a broad flattish nose. **2** of or concerning Negroes (Blacks). ● *n.* a Negro (Black). [NEGRO]
■ *adj.* see BLACK *adj.* 3.

Negus /néegəss/ *n. hist.* the title of the ruler of Ethiopia. [Amh. *n'gus* king]

negus /néegəss/ *n. hist.* a hot drink of port, sugar, lemon, and spice. [Col. F. *Negus* d. 1732, its inventor]

Neh. *abbr.* Nehemiah (Old Testament).

neigh /nay/ *n.* & *v.* ● *n.* **1** the high whinnying sound of a horse. **2** any similar sound, e.g. a laugh. ● *v.* **1** *intr.* make such a sound. **2** *tr.* say, cry, etc. with such a sound. [OE *hnægan*, of imit. orig.]

neighbour /náybər/ *n.* & *v.* (*US* **neighbor**) ● *n.* **1** a person living next door to or near or nearest another (*my next-door neighbour; his nearest neighbour is 12 miles away; they are neighbours*). **2 a** a person regarded as having the duties or claims of friendliness, consideration, etc., of a neighbour. **b** a fellow human being, esp. as having claims on friendship. **3** a person or thing near or next to another (*my neighbour at dinner*). **4** (*attrib.*) neighbouring. ● *v.* **1** *tr.* border on; adjoin. **2** *intr.* (often foll. by *on, upon*) border; adjoin. □□ **neighbouring** *adj.* **neighbourless** *adj.* **neighbourship** *n.* [OE *nēahgebūr* (as NIGH: *gebūr*, cf. BOOR)]
■ *v.* see BORDER *v.* 3a. □□ **neighbouring** nearby, adjacent, surrounding, adjoining, contiguous, bordering, next, nearest.

neighbourhood /náybərhōōd/ *n.* (*US* **neighborhood**) **1 a** district, esp. one forming a community within a town or city. **b** the people of a district; one's neighbours. **2** neighbourly feeling or conduct. □ **in the neighbourhood of** roughly; about (*paid in the neighbourhood of £100*). **neighbourhood watch** systematic local vigilance by householders to discourage crime, esp. against property.
■ **1** locality, community, area, region, vicinity, vicinage, environs, quarter, district, precinct(s), purlieus, locale; surroundings, confines. **2** neighbourliness. □ **in the neighbourhood of** approximately, about, around, nearly, practically, close to, almost, more or less, in the region of, as near as dammit to, not far off, *colloq.* getting on for, *US colloq.* in the ballpark of.

neighbourly /náybərli/ *adj.* (*US* **neighborly**) characteristic of a good neighbour; friendly; kind. □□ **neighbourliness** *n.*
■ friendly, cordial, warm, amiable, agreeable, affable, companionable, well-disposed, kindly, kind, sociable, social, harmonious, considerate, thoughtful, helpful, courteous, civil.

neither /nī́thər, néeth-/ *adj., pron., adv.,* & *conj.* ● *adj.* & *pron.* (foll. by sing. verb) **1** not the one nor the other (of two things); not either (*neither of the accusations is true; neither of them knows; neither wish was granted; neither went to the fair*). **2** *disp.* none of any number of specified things. ● *adv.* **1** not either; not on the one hand (foll. by *nor*; introducing the first of two or more things in the negative: *neither knowing nor caring; would neither come in nor go out; neither the teachers nor the parents nor the children*). **2** not either; also not (*if you do not, neither shall I*). **3** (with *neg.*) *disp.* either (*I don't know that neither*). ● *conj. archaic* nor yet; nor (*I know not, neither can I guess*). [ME *naither, neither* f. OE *nowther* contr. of *nōhwæther* (as NO², WHETHER): assim. to EITHER]

nek /nek/ *n. S.Afr.* = COL 1. [Du., = NECK]

nekton /néktən/ *n. Zool.* any aquatic animal able to swim and move independently. [G f. Gk *nēkton* neut. of *nēktos* swimming f. *nēkhō* swim]

nelly /nélli/ *n.* (*pl.* **-ies**) a silly or effeminate person. □ **not on your nelly** *Brit. sl.* certainly not. [perh. f. the name *Nelly*: idiom f. rhyming sl. *Nelly Duff* = puff = breath: cf. *not on your life*]

nelson /néls'n/ *n.* a wrestling-hold in which one arm is passed under the opponent's arm from behind and the hand is applied to the neck (**half nelson**), or both arms and hands are applied (**full nelson**). [app. f. the name *Nelson*]

nelumbo /nilúmbō/ *n.* (*pl.* **-os**) any water lily of the genus *Nelumbo*, native to India and China, bearing small pink flowers. Also called LOTUS. [mod.L f. Sinh. *nelum(bu)*]

nematocyst /nimáttəsist, némmə-/ *n.* a specialized cell in a jellyfish etc. containing a coiled thread that can be projected as a sting. [as NEMATODE + CYST]

nematode /némmətōd/ *n.* any parasitic or free-living worm of the phylum Nematoda, with a slender unsegmented cylindrical shape. Also called ROUNDWORM. [Gk *nēma -matos* thread + -ODE¹]

Nembutal /némbyootaal/ *n. propr.* a sodium salt of pentobarbitone, used as a sedative and anticonvulsant. [*Na* (= sodium) + 5-*e*thyl-5-(1-*m*ethyl*but*yl) barbiturate + -AL]

nem. con. *abbr.* with no one dissenting. [L *nemine contradicente*]

nemertean /nimértiən/ *n.* & *adj.* (also **nemertine** /-tīn/) ● *n.* any marine ribbon worm of the phylum Nemertea, often very long and brightly coloured, found in tangled knots in coastal waters of Europe and the Mediterranean. ● *adj.* of or relating to this class. [mod.L *Nemertes* f. Gk *Nēmertēs* name of a sea nymph]

nemesia /nimeézhə/ *n.* any S. African plant of the genus *Nemesia*, cultivated for its variously coloured and irregular flowers. [mod.L f. Gk *nemesion*, the name of a similar plant]

nemesis /némmisiss/ *n.* (*pl.* **nemeses** /-seez/) **1** retributive justice. **2 a** a downfall caused by this. **b** an agent of such a downfall. [Gk, = righteous indignation, personified as goddess of retribution f. *nemō* give what is due]

neo- /neé-ō/ *comb. form* **1** new, modern. **2** a new or revived form of. [Gk f. *neos* new]

neoclassical /neé-ōklássik'l/ *adj.* (also **neoclassic** /-sik/) of or relating to a revival of a classical style or treatment in art, literature, music, etc. □□ **neoclassicism** /-sisiz'm/ *n.* **neoclassicist** /-sisist/ *n.*

neocolonialism /neé-ōkəlóniəliz'm/ *n.* the use of economic, political, or other pressures to control or influence other countries, esp. former dependencies. □□ **neocolonialist** *n.* & *adj.*

neodymium /neéədímmiəm/ *n. Chem.* a silver-grey naturally-occurring metallic element of the lanthanide series used in colouring glass etc. ¶ Symb.: **Nd**. [NEO- + DIDYMIUM]

neolithic /neéəlíthik/ *adj.* of or relating to the later Stone Age, when ground or polished stone weapons and implements prevailed. [NEO- + Gk *lithos* stone]

neologism /nee-óllәjiz'm/ *n.* **1** a new word or expression. **2** the coining or use of new words. □□ **neologist** *n.* **neologize** /-jīz/ *v.intr.* (also **-ise**). [F *néologisme* (as NEO-, -LOGY, -ISM)]
■ coinage.

neomycin /neé-ōmísin/ *n.* an antibiotic related to streptomycin.

neon /neé-on/ *n. Chem.* an inert gaseous element occurring in traces in the atmosphere and giving an orange glow when electricity is passed through it in a sealed low-pressure tube, used in lights and illuminated advertisements (*neon light*; *neon sign*). ¶ Symb.: **Ne**. [Gk, neut. of *neos* new]

neonate /neéənayt/ *n.* a newborn child. □□ **neonatal** /-náyt'l/ *adj.* [mod.L *neonatus* (as NEO-, L *nasci nat-* be born)]

neophyte /neéəfīt/ *n.* **1** a new convert, esp. to a religious faith. **2** *RC Ch.* **a** a novice of a religious order. **b** a newly ordained priest. **3** a beginner; a novice. [eccl.L *neophytus* f. NT Gk *neophutos* newly planted (as NEO- *phuton* plant)]
■ **1** convert, proselyte. **2, 3** see NOVICE.

neoplasm /neé-ōplaz'm/ *n.* a new and abnormal growth of tissue in some part of the body, esp. a tumour. □□ **neoplastic** /-plástik/ *adj.* [NEO- + Gk *plasma* formation: see PLASMA]

Neoplatonism /neé-ōpláytəniz'm/ *n.* a philosophical and religious system developed by the followers of Plotinus in the third c., combining Platonic thought with oriental mysticism. □□ **Neoplatonic** /-plətónnik/ *adj.* **Neoplatonist** *n.*

neoprene /neé-ōpreen/ *n.* a synthetic rubber-like polymer. [NEO- + *chloroprene* etc. (perh. f. PROPYL + -ENE)]

neoteny /nióttini/ *n.* the retention of juvenile features in the adult form of some animals, e.g. an axolotl. □□ **neotenic** /neé-ōténnik/ *adj.* **neotenous** *adj.* [G *Neotenie* (as NEO- + Gk *teinō* extend)]

neoteric /neéətérrik/ *adj. literary* recent; newfangled; modern. [LL *neotericus* f. Gk *neōterikos* (*neōteros* compar. of *neos* new)]

neotropical /neé-ōtróppik'l/ *adj.* of or relating to tropical and S. America as a biogeographical region.

Nepalese /néppəleéz/ *adj.* & *n.* (*pl.* same) = NEPALI.

Nepali /nipáwli/ *n.* & *adj.* ● *n.* (*pl.* same or **Nepalis**) **1 a** a native or national of Nepal in Central Asia. **b** a person of Nepali descent. **2** the language of Nepal. ● *adj.* of or relating to Nepal or its language or people.

nepenthe /nipénthi/ *n.* = NEPENTHES 1. [var. of NEPENTHES, after It. *nepente*]

nepenthes /nipéntheez/ *n.* **1** *poet.* a drug causing forgetfulness of grief. **2** any pitcher-plant of the genus *Nepenthes*. [L f. Gk *nēpenthes* (*pharmakon* drug), neut. of *nēpenthēs* f. *nē-* not + *penthos* grief]

nephew /névyoo, néf-/ *n.* a son of one's brother or sister, or of one's brother-in-law or sister-in-law. [ME f. OF *neveu* f. L *nepos nepotis* grandson, nephew]

nephology /nifólləji/ *n.* the study of clouds. [Gk *nephos* cloud + -LOGY]

nephrite /néfrīt/ *n.* a green, yellow, or white calcium magnesium silicate form of jade. [G *Nephrit* f. Gk *nephros* kidney, with ref. to its supposed efficacy in treating kidney disease]

nephritic /nifríttik/ *adj.* **1** of or in the kidneys; renal. **2** of or relating to nephritis. [LL *nephriticus* f. Gk *nephritikos* (as NEPHRITIS)]

nephritis /nifrītiss/ *n.* inflammation of the kidneys. Also called *Bright's disease*. [LL f. Gk *nephros* kidney]

nephro- /néfrō/ *comb. form* (usu. **nephr-** before a vowel) kidney. [Gk f. *nephros* kidney]

ne plus ultra /náy plooss ooltraa/ *n.* **1** the furthest attainable point. **2** the culmination, acme, or perfection. [L, = not further beyond, the supposed inscription on the Pillars of Hercules (the Strait of Gibraltar) prohibiting passage by ships]

nepotism /néppətiz'm/ *n.* favouritism shown to relatives in conferring offices or privileges. □□ **nepotist** *n.* **nepotistic** /-tístik/ *adj.* [F *népotisme* f. It. *nepotismo* f. *nepote* NEPHEW: orig. with ref. to popes with illegitimate sons called nephews]
■ see FAVOURITISM.

Neptune /néptyoon/ *n.* a distant planet of the solar system, eighth from the sun, discovered in 1846 from mathematical computations. [ME f. F *Neptune* or L *Neptunus* god of the sea]

neptunium /neptyóoniəm/ *n. Chem.* a radioactive transuranic metallic element produced when uranium atoms absorb bombarding neutrons. ¶ Symb.: **Np**. [NEPTUNE, as the next planet beyond Uranus, + -IUM]

NERC *abbr.* (in the UK) Natural Environment Research Council.

nerd /nerd/ *n.* (also **nurd**) esp. *US sl.* a foolish, feeble, or uninteresting person. □□ **nerdy** *adj.* [20th c.: orig. uncert.]
■ see JERK[1] *n.* 4.

nereid /neéri-id/ *n. Mythol.* a sea-nymph. [L *Nereïs Nereïd-* f. Gk *Nērēis -idos* daughter of the sea-god Nereus]

nerine /nirīni/ *n.* any S. African plant of the genus *Nerine*, bearing flowers with usu. six narrow strap-shaped petals, often crimped and twisted. [mod.L f. the L name of a water-nymph]

neroli /neérəli/ *n.* (in full **neroli oil**) an essential oil from the flowers of the Seville orange, used in perfumery. [F *néroli* f. It. *neroli*, perh. f. the name of an Italian princess]

nervate /nérvayt/ *adj.* (of a leaf) having veins. □□ **nervation** /-váysh'n/ *n.* [NERVE + -ATE[2]]

nerve /nerv/ *n.* & *v.* ● *n.* **1 a** a fibre or bundle of fibres that transmits impulses of sensation or motion between the brain or spinal cord and other parts of the body. **b** the material constituting these. **2 a** coolness in danger; bravery; assurance. **b** *colloq.* impudence, audacity (*they've got a nerve*). **3** (in *pl.*) **a** the bodily state in regard to physical sensitiveness and the interaction between the brain and other parts. **b** a state of heightened nervousness or sensitivity; a condition of mental or physical stress (*need to calm my nerves*). **4** a rib of a leaf, esp. the midrib. **5** *poet. archaic* a sinew or tendon. ● *v.tr.* **1** (usu. *refl.*) brace (oneself) to face danger, suffering, etc. **2** give strength, vigour, or courage to. □ **get on a person's nerves** irritate or annoy a person. **have nerves of iron** (or **steel**) (of a person etc.) be not easily upset or frightened. **nerve-cell** an elongated branched cell transmitting impulses in nerve tissue. **nerve-centre 1** a group of closely connected nerve-cells associated in performing some function. **2** the centre of control of an organization etc. **nerve gas** a poisonous gas affecting the nervous system. **nerve-racking** stressful, frightening; straining the nerves. □□ **nerved** *adj.* (also in *comb.*). [ME, = sinew, f. L *nervus*, rel. to Gk *neuron*]
■ *n.* **1** (*attrib.*) nervo-, neuro-. **2 a** courage, coolness,

boldness, bravery, intrepidity, determination, valour, daring, fearlessness, nervelessness, dauntlessness, pluck, mettle, spirit, fortitude; assurance, will, tenacity, steadfastness, staunchness, firmness, resoluteness, *archaic or joc.* doughtiness, *colloq.* guts, grit, gumption, spunk, *US colloq.* sand, *Brit. sl.* bottle, *US sl.* moxie. **b** effrontery, brazenness, impertinence, impudence, insolence, audacity, brashness, presumption, presumptuousness, temerity, face, front, cheek, *colloq.* sauce, brass, *esp. Austral.* & *NZ colloq.* hide, *sl.* gall, chutzpah, crust. **3 b** (*nerves*) tension, nervousness, hysteria, anxiety, fretfulness, stress, worry, apprehension, fright, the shakes, *colloq.* the jitters, the willies, *sl.* the heebie-jeebies, jim-jams. □ **get on a person's nerves** annoy, irritate, upset; see also IRK. **nerve-racking** stressful, frightening, harrowing, worrying, nail-biting, agonizing, distressing, trying, vexing, vexatious, troublesome, worrisome, irksome, irritating.

nerveless /nérvliss/ *adj.* **1** inert, lacking vigour or spirit. **2** confident; not nervous. **3** (of style) diffuse. **4** *Bot.* & *Entomol.* without nervures. **5** *Anat.* & *Zool.* without nerves. □□ **nervelessly** *adv.* **nervelessness** *n.*

nervine /nérvīn/ *adj.* & *n.* ● *adj.* relieving nerve-disorders. ● *n.* a nervine drug. [F *nervin* (as NERVE)]

nervo- /nérvō/ *comb. form* (also **nerv-** before a vowel) a nerve or the nerves.

nervous /nérvəss/ *adj.* **1** having delicate or disordered nerves. **2** timid or anxious. **3 a** excitable; highly strung; easily agitated. **b** resulting from this temperament (*nervous tension*; *a nervous headache*). **4** affecting or acting on the nerves. **5** (foll. by *of* + verbal noun) reluctant, afraid (*am nervous of meeting them*). □ **nervous breakdown** a period of mental illness, usu. resulting from severe depression or anxiety. **nervous system** the body's network of specialized cells which transmit nerve impulses between parts of the body (cf. *central nervous system*, *peripheral nervous system*). **nervous wreck** *colloq.* a person suffering from mental stress, exhaustion, etc. □□ **nervously** *adv.* **nervousness** *n.* [ME f. L *nervosus* (as NERVE)]

■ **1–3, 5** highly-strung, excitable, sensitive, tense, agitated, overwrought, worked up, upset, flustered, ruffled, disturbed, perturbed, distressed, worried, anxious, troubled, concerned, disquieted, edgy, on edge, on tenterhooks, fidgety, fretful, uneasy, apprehensive, frightened, fearful, shaky, jumpy, nervy, scared, skittish, on pins and needles, *colloq.* jittery, windy, in a stew, all of a dither, in a sweat, in a tizzy, in a flap, uptight, *Austral. sl.* toey. **4** neurological.

nervure /nérvyoor/ *n.* **1** each of the hollow tubes that form the framework of an insect's wing; a venule. **2** the principal vein of a leaf. [F *nerf* nerve]

nervy /nérvi/ *adj.* (**nervier**, **nerviest**) **1** nervous; easily excited or disturbed. **2** *US* bold, impudent. **3** *archaic* sinewy, strong. □□ **nervily** *adv.* **nerviness** *n.*

■ **1** see NERVOUS 1–3, 5. **2** see IMPERTINENT 1.

nescient /néssiənt/ *adj. literary* (foll. by *of*) lacking knowledge; ignorant. □□ **nescience** *n.* [LL *nescientia* f. L *nescire* not know f. *ne-* not + *scire* know]

ness /ness/ *n.* a headland or promontory. [OE *næs*, rel. to OE *nasu* NOSE]

■ see CAPE².

-ness /niss/ *suffix* forming nouns from adjectives and occas. other words, expressing: **1** state or condition, or an instance of this (*bitterness*; *conceitedness*; *happiness*; *a kindness*). **2** something in a certain state (*wilderness*). [OE *-nes*, *-ness* f. Gmc]

nest /nest/ *n.* & *v.* ● *n.* **1** a structure or place where a bird lays eggs and shelters its young. **2** an animal's or insect's breeding-place or lair. **3** a snug or secluded retreat or shelter. **4** (often foll. by *of*) a place fostering something undesirable (*a nest of vice*). **5** a brood or swarm. **6** a group or set of similar objects, often of different sizes and fitting together for storage (*a nest of tables*). ● *v.* **1** *intr.* use or build a nest. **2** *intr.* take wild birds' nests or eggs. **3** *intr.* (of objects) fit together or one inside another. **4** *tr.* (usu. as **nested** *adj.*) establish in or as in a nest. □ **nest egg 1** a sum of money saved for the future. **2** a real or artificial egg left in a nest to induce hens to lay eggs there. □□ **nestful** *n.* (*pl.* **-fuls**). **nesting** *n.* (in sense 2 of *v.*). **nestlike** *adj.* [OE *nest*]

■ *n.* **1** roost, perch, eyrie. **2, 3** den, lair, nidus, snuggery, retreat, refuge, haunt, hideaway, nook, *colloq.* hide-out. **4** breeding-ground, den; cradle, nidus.

nestle /néss'l/ *v.* **1** *intr.* (often foll. by *down*, *in*, etc.) settle oneself comfortably. **2** *intr.* press oneself against another in affection etc. **3** *tr.* (foll. by *in*, *into*, etc.) push (a head or shoulder etc.) affectionately or snugly. **4** *intr.* lie half hidden or embedded. [OE *nestlian* (as NEST)]

■ **1, 2** cuddle, snuggle, huddle, curl up, nuzzle, settle down, snug down.

nestling /nésling, nést-/ *n.* a bird that is too young to leave its nest.

net¹ /net/ *n.* & *v.* ● *n.* **1** an open-meshed fabric of cord, rope, fibre, etc.; a structure resembling this. **2** a piece of net used esp. to restrain, contain, or delimit, or to catch fish or other animals. **3** a structure with net to enclose an area of ground, esp. in sport. **4 a** a structure with net used in various games, esp. forming the goal in football, netball, etc., and dividing the court in tennis etc. **b** (often in *pl.*) a practice-ground in cricket, surrounded by nets. **5** a system or procedure for catching or entrapping a person or persons. **6** = NETWORK. ● *v.* (**netted**, **netting**) **1** *tr.* **a** cover, confine, or catch with a net. **b** procure as with a net. **2** *tr.* hit (a ball) into the net, esp. of a goal. **3** *intr.* make netting. **4** *tr.* make (a purse, hammock, etc.) by knotting etc. threads together to form a net. **5** *tr.* fish with nets, or set nets, in (a river). **6** *tr.* (usu. as **netted** *adj.*) mark with a netlike pattern; reticulate. □□ **netful** *n.* (*pl.* **-fuls**). [OE *net*, *nett*]

■ *n.* **1** network, netting, mesh, mesh-work, web, webbing, openwork, lattice, lattice-work, trellis, trellis-work, lace-work, reticulum, reticle, plexus, grid, grid-work, grille, grate, grating, fretwork, *Anat.* rete. **2** trammel, trawl, trawl-net, fishing-net, cast-net, drag-net, drift-net, landing-net, butterfly net, mosquito-net. ● *v.* **1** catch, capture, trap, entrap, snare, ensnare, bag.

net² /net/ *adj.* & *v.* (also **nett**) ● *adj.* **1** (esp. of money) remaining after all necessary deductions, or free from deductions. **2** (of a price) to be paid in full; not reducible. **3** (of a weight) excluding that of the packaging or container etc. **4** (of an effect, result, etc.) ultimate, effective. ● *v.tr.* (**netted**, **netting**) gain or yield (a sum) as net profit. □ **net profit** the effective profit; the actual gain after working expenses have been paid. **net ton** see TON¹. [F *net* NEAT¹]

■ *adj.* **1** clear, after deductions, after taxes, take-home, final. **4** final, end, closing, concluding, conclusive, effective, ultimate. ● *v.* gain, yield, fetch; make, realize, clear, take home, bring in, earn, pocket, take in, get.

netball /nétbawl/ *n.* a team game in which goals are scored by throwing a ball through a high horizontal ring with a net suspended from it.

nether /nét͟hər/ *adj. archaic* = LOWER¹. □ **nether regions** (or **world**) hell; the underworld. □□ **nethermost** *adj.* [OE *nithera* etc. f. Gmc]

■ □ **nether regions** see HELL 1.

Netherlander /nét͟hərləndər/ *n.* **1** a native or national of the Netherlands. **2** a person of Dutch descent. □□ **Netherlandish** *adj.* [Du. *Nederlander*, *Nederlandsch*]

Netherlands /nét͟hərləndz/ *n.* **1** (usu. prec. by *the*) Holland. **2** *hist.* the Low Countries. [Du. *Nederland* (as NETHER, LAND)]

netsuke /nétsŏŏki/ *n.* (*pl.* same or **netsukes**) (in Japan) a carved button-like ornament, esp. of ivory or wood, formerly worn to suspend articles from a girdle. [Jap.]

nett var. of NET².

netting /nétting/ *n.* **1** netted fabric. **2** a piece of this.

■ see MESH *n.* 1–3a.

nettle /nétt'l/ *n.* & *v.* ● *n.* **1** any plant of the genus *Urtica*, esp. *U. dioica*, with jagged leaves covered with stinging hairs. **2** any of various plants resembling this. ● *v.tr.* **1** irritate, provoke, annoy. **2** sting with nettles. □ **nettle-rash** a skin eruption like nettle stings. [OE *netle*, *netele*]
■ *v.* **1** see IRRITATE 1.

nettlesome /nétt'lsəm/ *adj.* **1** awkward, difficult. **2** causing annoyance.
■ **1** see TROUBLESOME 1. **2** see TROUBLESOME 2.

network /nétwurk/ *n.* & *v.* ● *n.* **1** an arrangement of intersecting horizontal and vertical lines, like the structure of a net. **2** a complex system of railways, roads, canals, etc. **3** a group of people who exchange information, contacts, and experience for professional or social purposes. **4** a chain of interconnected computers, machines, or operations. **5** a system of connected electrical conductors. **6** a group of broadcasting stations connected for a simultaneous broadcast of a programme. ● *v.* **1** *tr.* broadcast on a network. **2** *intr.* establish a network. **3** *tr.* link (machines, esp. computers) to operate interactively. **4** *intr.* be a member of a network (see sense 3 of *n.*).
■ *n.* **1** see NET[1] *n.* 1. **2** system, arrangement, structure, organization, complex, grid, criss-cross, web, plexus; maze, labyrinth, jungle, tangle. **3** see UNION 2.

networker /nétwurkər/ *n.* **1** *Computing* a member of an organization or computer network who operates from home or from an external office. **2** a member of a professional or social network.

neume /nyoom/ *n.* (also **neum**) *Mus.* a sign in plainsong indicating a note or group of notes to be sung to a syllable. [ME f. OF *neume* f. med.L *neu(p)ma* f. Gk *pneuma* breath]

neural /nyoorəl/ *adj.* of or relating to a nerve or the central nervous system. □ **neural network** (or **neural net**) *Computing* a computer system modelled on the human brain and nervous system. □□ **neurally** *adv.* [Gk *neuron* nerve]

neuralgia /nyooráljə/ *n.* an intense intermittent pain along the course of a nerve, esp. in the head or face. □□ **neuralgic** *adj.* [as NEURAL + -ALGIA]

neurasthenia /nyoorəss-theéniə/ *n.* a general term for fatigue, anxiety, listlessness, etc. (not in medical use). □□ **neurasthenic** /-thénnik/ *adj.* & *n.* [Gk *neuron* nerve + ASTHENIA]

neuritis /nyoorītiss/ *n.* inflammation of a nerve or nerves. □□ **neuritic** /-ríttik/ *adj.* [formed as NEURO- + -ITIS]

neuro- /nyoorō/ *comb. form* a nerve or the nerves. [Gk *neuron* nerve]

neurogenesis /nyoorōjénnisiss/ *n.* the growth and development of nervous tissue.

neurogenic /nyoorōjénnik/ *adj.* caused by or arising in nervous tissue.

neuroglia /nyooróglia/ *n.* the connective tissue supporting the central nervous system. [NEURO- + Gk *glia* glue]

neurohormone /nyoorōhórmōn/ *n.* a hormone produced by nerve-cells and secreted into the circulation.

neurology /nyoorólləji/ *n.* the scientific study of nerve systems. □□ **neurological** /-rəlójik'l/ *adj.* **neurologically** /-rəlójikəli/ *adv.* **neurologist** *n.* [mod.L *neurologia* f. mod. Gk (as NEURO-, -LOGY)]

neuroma /nyoorṓmə/ *n.* (*pl.* **neuromas** or **neuromata** /-mətə/) a tumour on a nerve or in nerve-tissue. [Gk *neuron* nerve + -OMA]

neuromuscular /nyoorōmúskyoolər/ *adj.* of or relating to nerves and muscles.

neuron /nyooron/ *n.* (also **neurone** /-rōn/) a specialized cell transmitting nerve impulses; a nerve-cell. □□ **neuronal** /-rṓn'l/ *adj.* **neuronic** /-rónnik/ *adj.* [Gk *neuron* nerve]

neuropath /nyoorōpath/ *n.* a person affected by nervous disease, or with an abnormally sensitive nervous system. □□ **neuropathic** /-páthik/ *adj.* **neuropathy** /-róppəthi/ *n.*

neuropathology /nyoorōpəthólləji/ *n.* the pathology of the nervous system. □□ **neuropathologist** *n.*

neurophysiology /nyoorōfizziólləji/ *n.* the physiology of the nervous system. □□ **neurophysiological** /-ziəlójik'l/ *adj.* **neurophysiologist** *n.*

neuropteran /nyooróptərən/ *n.* any insect of the order Neuroptera, including lacewings, having four finely-veined membranous leaflike wings. □□ **neuropterous** *adj.* [NEURO- + Gk *pteron* wing]

neurosis /nyoorṓsiss/ *n.* (*pl.* **neuroses** /-seez/) a mental illness characterized by irrational or depressive thought or behaviour, caused by a disorder of the nervous system usu. without organic change. [mod.L (as NEURO-, -OSIS)]

neurosurgery /nyoorōsúrjəri/ *n.* surgery performed on the nervous system, esp. the brain and spinal cord. □□ **neurosurgeon** *n.* **neurosurgical** *adj.*

neurotic /nyooróttik/ *adj.* & *n.* ● *adj.* **1** caused by or relating to neurosis. **2** (of a person) suffering from neurosis. **3** *colloq.* abnormally sensitive or obsessive. ● *n.* a neurotic person. □□ **neurotically** *adv.* **neuroticism** /-tisiz'm/ *n.*
■ *adj.* **2, 3** psychoneurotic; unstable, disturbed, confused, irrational, disordered, maladjusted, distraught, oversensitive, overwrought, anxious, nervous, obsessive.

neurotomy /nyoorótt̄əmi/ *n.* (*pl.* **-ies**) the operation of cutting a nerve, esp. to produce sensory loss.

neurotransmitter /nyoorōtranzmíttər, -traanzmíttər/ *n.* *Biochem.* a chemical substance released from a nerve fibre that effects the transfer of an impulse to another nerve or muscle.

neuter /nyootər/ *adj.*, *n.*, & *v.* ● *adj.* **1** *Gram.* (of a noun etc.) neither masculine nor feminine. **2** (of a plant) having neither pistils nor stamen. **3** (of an insect, animal, etc.) sexually undeveloped; castrated or spayed. ● *n.* **1** *Gram.* a neuter word. **2 a** a non-fertile insect, esp. a worker bee or ant. **b** a castrated animal. ● *v.tr.* castrate or spay. [ME f. OF *neutre* or L *neuter* neither f. *ne-* not + *uter* either]
■ *adj.* **2** asexual, sexless. **3** asexual, sexless, neutral, androgyne, undeveloped, epicene; neutered, castrated, desexed, emasculated, gelded, caponized, spayed, *colloq.* doctored. ● *v.* desex, castrate, emasculate, cut, fix, geld, caponize, spay, *US* & *Austral.* alter, mark, *colloq.* doctor.

neutral /nyootrəl/ *adj.* & *n.* ● *adj.* **1** not helping or supporting either of two opposing sides, esp. States at war or in dispute; impartial. **2** belonging to a neutral party, State, etc. (*neutral ships*). **3** indistinct, vague, indeterminate. **4** (of a gear) in which the engine is disconnected from the driven parts. **5** (of colours) not strong or positive; grey or beige. **6** *Chem.* neither acid nor alkaline. **7** *Electr.* neither positive nor negative. **8** *Biol.* sexually undeveloped; asexual. ● *n.* **1 a** a neutral State or person. **b** a subject of a neutral State. **2** a neutral gear. □□ **neutrality** /-trálliti/ *n.* **neutrally** *adv.* [ME f. obs. F *neutral* or L *neutralis* of neuter gender (as NEUTER)]
■ *adj.* **1, 2** non-belligerent, non-combatant; unaligned, non-aligned, unaffiliated, uninvolved, unallied, non-allied, non-partisan, impartial, disinterested; indifferent, dispassionate, unbiased, uncommitted, noncommittal, aloof, withdrawn, detached, remote, removed. **3, 5** dull, drab, colourless, achromatic, toneless, washed out, pale, indefinite, indistinct, indistinguishable, indeterminate, vague; grey, beige, taupe, ecru.

neutralism /nyootrəliz'm/ *n.* a policy of political neutrality. □□ **neutralist** *n.*

neutralize /nyootrəlīz/ *v.tr.* (also **-ise**) **1** make neutral. **2** counterbalance; render ineffective by an opposite force or effect. **3** exempt or exclude (a place) from the sphere of hostilities. □□ **neutralization** /-záysh'n/ *n.* **neutralizer** *n.* [F *neutraliser* f. med.L *neutralizare* (as NEUTRAL)]
■ **2** void, annul, cancel (out), nullify, invalidate, negate, delete, undo, make *or* render ineffective, counterbalance, counteract, offset; equalize, even, square; compensate for, make up for.

neutrino /nyootreénō/ *n.* (*pl.* **-os**) any of a group of stable elementary particles with zero electric charge and probably zero mass, which travel at the speed of light. [It., dimin. of *neutro* neutral (as NEUTER)]

neutron /nyoōtron/ *n.* an elementary particle of about the same mass as a proton but without an electric charge, present in all atomic nuclei except those of ordinary hydrogen. □ **neutron bomb** a bomb producing neutrons and little blast, causing damage to life but little destruction to property. **neutron star** a very dense star composed mainly of neutrons. [NEUTRAL + -ON]

Nev. *abbr.* Nevada.

névé /névvay/ *n.* an expanse of granular snow not yet compressed into ice at the head of a glacier. [Swiss F, = glacier, ult. f. L *nix nivis* snow]

never /névvər/ *adv.* **1 a** at no time; on no occasion; not ever (*have never been to Paris*; *never saw them again*). **b** *colloq.* as an emphatic negative (*I never heard you come in*). **2** not at all (*never fear*). **3** *colloq.* (expressing surprise) surely not (*you never left the key in the lock!*). □ **never-ending** eternal, undying; immeasurable. **never-never** (often prec. by *the*) *Brit. colloq.* hire purchase. **never-never land** an imaginary utopian place. **never a one** none. **never say die** see DIE[1]. **well I never!** expressing great surprise. [OE *nǣfre* f. *ne* not + *ǣfre* EVER]

■ **1 a** at no time, not ever, not at any time, on no occasion, not at all. **1b, 2** by no means, on no account, by no chance, in no circumstances, under no circumstances *or* condition(s), *colloq.* no way, not in a million years; in no case, in no way, not in any way, not in the least, not in any degree, not under any condition(s), *US* nohow. □ **never-ending** see ENDLESS 1, 2; IMMEASURABLE. **well I never!** blow me down, good gracious, goodness me, you don't say, well I declare, *colloq.* well I'll be damned, *sl.* well I'll be blowed; see also BOY *int.*

nevermore /névvərmór/ *adv.* at no future time.

nevertheless /névvər<u>th</u>əléss/ *adv.* in spite of that; notwithstanding; all the same.

■ still, notwithstanding, yet, in spite of that, despite that, none the less, regardless, be that as it may, for all that, even so, but, however, just *or* all the same, anyway, in any case.

nevus *US* var. of NAEVUS.

new /nyoō/ *adj.* & *adv.* ● *adj.* **1 a** of recent origin or arrival. **b** made, invented, discovered, acquired, or experienced recently or now for the first time (*a new star*; *has many new ideas*). **2** in original condition; not worn or used. **3 a** renewed or reformed (*a new life*; *the new order*). **b** reinvigorated (*felt like a new person*). **4** different from a recent previous one (*has a new job*). **5** in addition to others already existing (*have you been to the new supermarket?*). **6** (often foll. by *to*) unfamiliar or strange (*a new sensation*; *the idea was new to me*). **7** (often foll. by *at*) (of a person) inexperienced, unaccustomed (to doing something) (*am new at this business*). **8** (usu. prec. by *the*) often *derog.* **a** later, modern. **b** newfangled. **c** given to new or modern ideas (*the new man*). **d** recently affected by social change (*the new rich*). **9** (often prec. by *the*) advanced in method or theory (*the new formula*). **10** (in place-names) discovered or founded later than and named after (*New York*; *New Zealand*). ● *adv.* (usu. in *comb.*) **1** newly, recently (*new-found*; *new-baked*). **2** anew, afresh. □ **New Age** a set of beliefs intended to replace traditional Western Culture, with alternative approaches to religion, medicine, the environment, music, etc. **new birth** *Theol.* spiritual regeneration. **new broom** see BROOM. **new deal** new arrangements or conditions, esp. when better than the earlier ones. **new-laid** (of an egg) freshly laid. **new look** a new or revised appearance or presentation, esp. of something familiar. **the new mathematics** (or **maths**) a system of teaching mathematics to children, with emphasis on investigation by them and on set theory. **new moon 1** the moon when first seen as a crescent after conjunction with the sun. **2** the time of its appearance. **a new one** (often foll. by *on*) *colloq.* an account or idea not previously encountered (by a person). **new potatoes** the earliest potatoes of a new crop. **new star** a nova. **new style** dating reckoned by the Gregorian Calendar. **New Testament** the part of the Bible concerned with the life and teachings of Christ and his earliest followers. **new town** *Brit.* a town established as a completely new settlement with government sponsorship. **new wave 1** = NOUVELLE VAGUE. **2** a style of rock music popular in the 1970s. **New World** North and South America regarded collectively in relation to Europe. **new year 1** the calendar year just begun or about to begin. **2** the first few days of a year. **New Year's Day** 1 January. **New Year's Eve** 31 December. □□ **newish** *adj.* **newness** *n.* [OE *nīwe* f. Gmc]

■ *adj.* **1 a** brand-new, recent, newly arrived. **b** novel, original, unique, different, fresh, innovative. **2** original, fresh, mint, unworn, unused. **3** revitalized, reinvigorated, reformed, reborn, renewed, rejuvenated, changed, altered, redone, restored, redesigned, remodelled. **4** different, fresh, (an)other. **5** further, additional, supplemental, supplementary. **6** unfamiliar, unknown, strange, different, unusual; unheard-of; uncharted, unexplored, untrodden; experimental. **7** inexperienced, green, fresh, callow, unfledged, untrained, unaccustomed; immature. **8, 9** latest, late, modern, avant-garde, innovative, contemporary, modish, stylish, fashionable, chic, *colloq.* mod, *colloq. often derog.* trendy, *formal* hodiernal, *sl.* hip; recent, advanced, up to date, brand-new; *derog.* newfangled.

newborn /nyoōbórn/ *adj.* **1** (of a child etc.) recently born. **2** spiritually reborn; regenerated.

newcomer /nyoōkummər/ *n.* **1** a person who has recently arrived. **2** a beginner in some activity.

■ **1** alien, immigrant, foreigner, outlander, stranger, settler, colonist, outsider. **2** beginner, amateur, novice, proselyte, neophyte, tiro, initiate, trainee, learner, fledgling, greenhorn, freshman, *Brit. colloq.* fresher.

newel /nyoōəl/ *n.* **1** the supporting central post of winding stairs. **2** the top or bottom supporting post of a stair-rail. [ME f. OF *noel*, *nouel*, knob f. med.L *nodellus* dimin. of L *nodus* knot]

newfangled /nyoōfángg'ld/ *adj. derog.* different from what one is used to; objectionably new. [ME *newfangle* (now dial.) liking what is new f. *newe* NEW *adv.* + *-fangel* f. OE *fangol* (unrecorded) inclined to take]

■ see MODERN *adj.*

Newfoundland /nyoofówndlənd/ *n.* (in full **Newfoundland dog**) **1** a dog of a very large breed with a thick coarse coat. **2** this breed. [the name of a Canadian province, an island at the mouth of the St Lawrence river]

newly /nyoōli/ *adv.* **1** recently (*a friend newly arrived*; *a newly-discovered country*). **2** afresh, anew (*newly painted*). **3** in a new or different manner (*newly arranged*). □ **newly-wed** a recently married person.

Newmarket /nyoōmaarkit/ *n.* a gambling card-game in which players seek to play cards that match those on the table. [*Newmarket* in S. England]

news /nyoōz/ *n.pl.* (usu. treated as *sing.*) **1** information about important or interesting recent events, esp. when published or broadcast. **2** (prec. by *the*) a broadcast report of news. **3** newly received or noteworthy information. **4** (foll. by *to*) *colloq.* information not previously known (to a person) (*that's news to me*). □ **news agency** an organization that collects and distributes news items. **news bulletin** a collection of items of news, esp. for broadcasting. **news conference** a press conference. **news-gatherer** *n.* a person who researches news items esp. for broadcast or publication. **news-gathering** this process. **news room** a room in a newspaper or broadcasting office where news is processed. **news-sheet** a simple form of newspaper; a newsletter. **news-stand** a stall for the sale of newspapers. **news-vendor** a newspaper-seller. □□ **newsless** *adj.* [ME, pl. of NEW after OF *noveles* or med.L *nova* neut. pl. of *novus* new]

■ **1, 3** word, information, advice, *archaic* intelligence, *colloq.* info, *literary* tidings; dispatch, report, account, story, communication, bulletin, flash, newsflash, communiqué, announcement, message, statement, (press) release, newsbrief; rumour, talk, gossip, hearsay, dirt, scandal, exposé, *colloq.* low-down, scuttlebutt, *sl.* dope; (good) copy, front-page news, (hot) item, scoop. **2** (*the news*) newscast, broadcast, telecast, news programme, newsreel; newsflash, newsbrief, (news) bulletin.

newsagent /nyóozayjənt/ *n. Brit.* a seller of or shop selling newspapers and usu. related items, e.g. stationery.

newsboy /nyóozboy/ *n.* a boy who sells or delivers newspapers.

newsbrief /nyóozbreef/ *n.* a short item of news, esp. on television; a newsflash.

newscast /nyóozkaast/ *n.* a radio or television broadcast of news reports.

newscaster /nyóozkaastər/ *n.* = NEWSREADER.
■ see ANNOUNCER.

newsdealer /nyóozdeelər/ *n. US* = NEWSAGENT.

newsflash /nyóozflash/ *n.* a single item of important news broadcast separately and often interrupting other programmes.
■ see BULLETIN 1.

newsgirl /nyóozgurl/ *n.* a girl who sells or delivers newspapers.

newsletter /nyóozlettər/ *n.* an informal printed report issued periodically to the members of a society, business, organization, etc.
■ see PUBLICATION 1b.

newsman /nyóozman/ *n.* (*pl.* **-men**) a newspaper reporter; a journalist.
■ see JOURNALIST.

newsmonger /nyóozmunggər/ *n.* a gossip.
■ see GOSSIP *n.* 3.

newspaper /nyóospaypər/ *n.* **1** a printed publication (usu. daily or weekly) containing news, advertisements, correspondence, etc. **2** the sheets of paper forming this (*wrapped in newspaper*).
■ **1** see PUBLICATION 1b.

newspaperman /nyóospaypərman/ *n.* (*pl.* **-men**) a journalist.
■ see JOURNALIST.

Newspeak /nyóospeek/ *n.* ambiguous euphemistic language used esp. in political propaganda. [an artificial official language in George Orwell's *Nineteen Eighty-Four* (1949)]

newsprint /nyóozprint/ *n.* a type of low-quality paper on which newspapers are printed.

newsreader /nyóozreedər/ *n.* a person who reads out broadcast news bulletins.
■ see ANNOUNCER.

newsreel /nyóozreel/ *n.* a short cinema film of recent events.

newsworthy /nyóozwurthi/ *adj.* topical; noteworthy as news. □□ **newsworthiness** *n.*

newsy /nyóozi/ *adj.* (**newsier**, **newsiest**) *colloq.* full of news.

newt /nyoot/ *n.* any of various small amphibians, esp. of the genus *Triturus*, having a well-developed tail. [ME f. *ewt*, with *n* from *an* (cf. NICKNAME): var. of *evet* EFT]

newton /nyóot'n/ *n. Physics* the SI unit of force that, acting on a mass of one kilogram, increases its velocity by one metre per second every second along the direction that it acts. ¶ Abbr.: **N.** [Sir Isaac *Newton*, Engl. scientist d. 1727]

Newtonian /nyootóniən/ *adj.* of or devised by Isaac Newton (see NEWTON). □ **Newtonian mechanics** the system of mechanics which relies on Newton's laws of motion concerning the relations between forces acting and motions occurring. **Newtonian telescope** a reflecting telescope with a small secondary mirror at 45° to the main beam of light to reflect it into a magnifying eyepiece.

New Zealander /zeéləndər/ *n.* **1** a native or national of New Zealand, an island group in the Pacific. **2** a person of New Zealand descent.

next /nekst/ *adj., adv., n.,* & *prep.* ● *adj.* **1** (often foll. by *to*) being or positioned or living nearest (*in the next house*; *the chair next to the fire*). **2** the nearest in order of time; the first or soonest encountered or considered (*next Friday*; *ask the next person you see*). ● *adv.* **1** (often foll. by *to*) in the nearest place or degree (*put it next to mine*; *came next to last*). **2** on the first or soonest occasion (*when we next meet*). ● *n.* the next person or thing. ● *prep. colloq.* next to. □ **next-best** the next in order of preference. **next door** see DOOR. **next of kin** the closest living relative or relatives. **next to** almost (*next to nothing left*). **the next world** see WORLD. [OE *nēhsta* superl. (as NIGH)]
■ *adj.* **1** see *adjoining* (ADJOIN). **2** see SUBSEQUENT. □ **next of kin** see FAMILY 1.

nexus /néksəss/ *n.* (*pl.* same) **1** a connected group or series. **2** a bond; a connection. [L f. *nectere nex-* bind]

NF *abbr.* (in the UK) National Front.

Nfld *abbr.* (also **NF**) Newfoundland.

NFU *abbr.* (in the UK) National Farmers' Union.

n.g. *abbr.* no good.

NGA *abbr.* (in the UK) National Graphical Association.

ngaio /nīō/ *n.* (*pl.* **-os**) a small New Zealand tree, *Myoporum laetum*, with edible fruit and light white timber. [Maori]

NGO *abbr.* non-governmental organization.

NH *abbr. US* New Hampshire (also in official postal use).

NHI *abbr.* (in the UK) National Health Insurance.

NHS *abbr.* (in the UK) National Health Service.

NI *abbr.* **1** (in the UK) National Insurance. **2** Northern Ireland.

Ni *symb. Chem.* the element nickel.

niacin /nīəsin/ *n.* = NICOTINIC ACID. [*nic*otinic *ac*id + -IN]

nib /nib/ *n.* & *v.* ● *n.* **1** the point of a pen, which touches the writing surface. **2** (in *pl.*) shelled and crushed coffee or cocoa beans. **3** the point of a tool etc. ● *v.* (**nibbed, nibbing**) **1** *tr.* provide with a nib. **2** *tr.* mend the nib of. **3** *tr.* & *intr.* nibble. [prob. f. MDu. *nib* or MLG *nibbe*, var. of *nebbe* NEB]
■ *n.* **1, 3** see TIP[1] *n.* 1.

nibble /níbb'l/ *v.* & *n.* ● *v.* **1** *tr.* & (foll. by *at*) *intr.* **a** take small bites at. **b** eat in small amounts. **c** bite at gently or cautiously or playfully. **2** *intr.* (foll. by *at*) show cautious interest in. ● *n.* **1** an instance of nibbling. **2** a very small amount of food. **3** *Computing* half a byte, i.e. 4 bits. □□ **nibbler** *n.* [prob. of LG or Du. orig.: cf. LG *nibbeln* gnaw]
■ *v.* **1** see *pick at* (PICK[1]). ● *n.* **2** see MORSEL.

niblick /níblik/ *n. Golf* an iron with a large round heavy head, used esp. for playing out of bunkers. [19th c.: orig. unkn.]

nibs /nibz/ *n.* □ **his nibs** *joc. colloq.* a mock title used with reference to an important or self-important person. [19th c.: orig. unkn. (cf. earlier *nabs*)]

nicad /nīcad/ *adj.* & *n.* ● *adj.* nickel and cadmium. ● *n.* a nickel and cadmium battery. [NICKEL + CADMIUM]

nice /nīss/ *adj.* **1** pleasant, agreeable, satisfactory. **2** (of a person) kind, good-natured. **3** *iron.* bad or awkward (*a nice mess you've made*). **4 a** fine or subtle (*a nice distinction*). **b** requiring careful thought or attention (*a nice problem*). **5** fastidious; delicately sensitive. **6** punctilious, scrupulous (*were not too nice about their methods*). **7** (foll. by an adj., often with *and*) satisfactory or adequate in terms of the quality described (*a nice long time*; *nice and warm*). □ **nice work** a task well done. □□ **nicely** *adv.* **niceness** *n.* **nicish** *adj.* (also **niceish**). [ME, = stupid, wanton f. OF, = silly, simple f. L *nescius* ignorant (as *nescience*: see NESCIENT)]
■ **1, 2** pleasant, agreeable, good, satisfactory, commendable, worthy, worthwhile; amiable, amicable, friendly, good-natured, cordial, warm, gracious, warm-hearted, kind, kindly, outgoing, charming, genial, delightful, courteous, polite, refined, gentlemanly, ladylike, winsome, likeable, attractive; trim, well turned out, tidy, neat, fine. **3** see AWFUL 1a, b. **4–6** fine, delicate, sensitive, exquisite, flawless, faultless, subtle; attentive, sharp, acute, keen, fastidious, hair-splitting, careful, strict, close, small, exact, minute, exacting, rigorous, precise, accurate, unerring, scrupulous, critical, meticulous, punctilious, discriminating, discriminative,

perceptive; complex, complicated, intricate. **7** pleasantly, delightfully, pleasingly, agreeably, enjoyably, gratifyingly, satisfyingly, comfortably, adequately, satisfactorily.

Nicene Creed /nī́seen/ *n.* a formal statement of Christian belief based on that adopted at the first Council of Nicaea in 325. [*Nicene* ME f. LL *Nicenus* of Nicaea in Asia Minor]

nicety /nī́siti/ *n.* (*pl.* **-ies**) **1** a subtle distinction or detail. **2** precision, accuracy. **3** intricate or subtle quality (*a point of great nicety*). **4** (in *pl.*) **a** minutiae; fine details. **b** refinements, trimmings. □ **to a nicety** with exactness. [ME f. OF *niceté* (as NICE)]

■ **2** see PRECISION 2. **3** see SUBTLETY 1.

niche /nich, neesh/ *n.* & *v.* ● *n.* **1** a shallow recess, esp. in a wall to contain a statue etc. **2** a comfortable or suitable position in life or employment. **3** an appropriate combination of conditions for a species to thrive. ● *v.tr.* (often as **niched** *adj.*) **1** place in a niche. **2** ensconce (esp. oneself) in a recess or corner. [F f. *nicher* make a nest, ult. f. L *nidus* nest]

■ *n.* **1** bay, slot, cell, hole, pigeon-hole, cubby-hole; see also NOOK. **2** pigeon-hole; see also PLACE *n.* 5.

Nichrome /nī́krōm/ *n. propr.* a group of nickel-chromium alloys used for making wire in heating elements etc. [NICKEL + CHROME]

Nick /nik/ *n.* □ **Old Nick** the Devil. [prob. f. a pet-form of the name *Nicholas*]

■ □ **Old Nick** see DEVIL *n.* 1, 2.

nick[1] /nik/ *n.* & *v.* ● *n.* **1** a small cut or notch. **2** *Brit. sl.* **a** a prison. **b** a police station. **3** (prec. by *in* with adj.) *Brit. colloq.* condition (*in reasonable nick*). **4** the junction between the floor and walls in a squash court. ● *v.tr.* **1** make a nick or nicks in. **2** *Brit. sl.* **a** steal. **b** arrest, catch. □ **in the nick of time** only just in time; just at the right moment. [ME: orig. uncert.]

■ *n.* **1** cut, notch, chip, gouge, gash, scratch, score; dent, indentation; flaw, mark, blemish, defect. **2 a** see PRISON *n.* 1. **b** police station, *US* station house, *sl.* cop-shop. **3** trim, (state of) health; see also CONDITION *n.* 2a. ● *v.* **1** cut, notch, chip, gouge, gash, scratch, dent, score. **2 a** steal, take, appropriate, make off with, *colloq.* lift, swipe, *formal or joc.* purloin, *sl.* pinch. **b** see ARREST *v.* 1a.

nick[2] /nik/ *v.intr. Austral. sl.* (foll. by *off, in,* etc.) move quickly or furtively. [19th c.: orig. uncert. (cf. NIP[1] 4)]

■ slip, hop, pop, *Brit. colloq.* nip; sneak, slink, steal, creep, edge; (*nick off*) depart, go *or* run off *or* away, take off, take to one's heels, beat a (hasty) retreat, *colloq.* skedaddle, show a clean pair of heels, make tracks, *sl.* beat it, split, *Brit. sl.* scarper.

nickel /níkk'l/ *n.* & *v.* ● *n.* **1** *Chem.* a malleable ductile silver-white metallic transition element, occurring naturally in various minerals and used in special steels, in magnetic alloys, and as a catalyst. ¶ Symb.: **Ni**. **2** *colloq.* a US five-cent coin. ● *v.tr.* (**nickelled, nickelling;** *US* **nickeled, nickeling**) coat with nickel. □ **nickel brass** an alloy of copper, zinc, and a small amount of nickel. **nickel-plated** coated with nickel by plating. **nickel silver** = *German silver*. **nickel steel** a type of stainless steel with chromium and nickel. □□ **nickelic** *adj.* **nickelous** *adj.* [abbr. of G *Kupfernickel* copper-coloured ore, from which nickel was first obtained, f. *Kupfer* copper + *Nickel* demon, with ref. to the ore's failure to yield copper]

nickelodeon /nikkəlṓdiən/ *n. US colloq.* a jukebox. [NICKEL + MELODEON]

nicker /níkkər/ *n.* (*pl.* same) *Brit. sl.* a pound (in money). [20th c.: orig. unkn.]

nick-nack var. of KNICK-KNACK.

nickname /níknaym/ *n.* & *v.* ● *n.* a familiar or humorous name given to a person or thing instead of or as well as the real name. ● *v.tr.* **1** give a nickname to. **2** call (a person or thing) by a nickname. [ME f. *eke-name*, with *n* from *an* (cf. NEWT): *eke* = addition, f. OE *ēaca* (as EKE)]

■ *n.* pet name, sobriquet, epithet, *colloq.* handle, tag, *formal* appellation, *sl.* moniker.

nicol /níkk'l/ *n.* (in full **nicol prism**) a device for producing plane-polarized light, consisting of two pieces of cut calcite cemented together with Canada balsam. [W. *Nicol*, Sc. physicist d. 1851, its inventor]

nicotine /níkkəteen/ *n.* a colourless poisonous alkaloid present in tobacco. □□ **nicotinism** *n.* **nicotinize** *v.tr.* (also **-ise**). [F f. mod.L *nicotiana* (*herba*) tobacco-plant, f. J. *Nicot*, Fr. diplomat & introducer of tobacco into France in the 16th c.]

nicotinic acid /níkkətínnik/ *n.* a vitamin of the B complex, found in milk, liver, and yeast, a deficiency of which causes pellagra. Also called NIACIN.

nictitate /níktitayt/ *v.intr.* close and open the eyes; blink or wink. □ **nictitating membrane** a clear membrane forming a third eyelid in amphibians, birds, and some other animals, that can be drawn across the eye to give protection without loss of vision. □□ **nictitation** /-táysh'n/ *n.* [med.L *nictitare* frequent. of L *nictare* blink]

nide /nīd/ *n.* (*Brit.* **nye** /nī/) a brood of pheasants. [F *nid* or L *nidus*: see NIDUS]

nidificate /níddifikayt/ *v.intr.* = NIDIFY.

nidify /níddifī/ *v.intr.* (**-ies, -ied**) (of a bird) build a nest. □□ **nidification** /-fikáysh'n/ *n.* [L *nidificare* f. NIDUS nest]

nidus /nī́dəss/ *n.* (*pl.* **nidi** /-dī/ or **niduses**) **1** a place in which an insect etc. deposits its eggs, or in which spores or seeds develop. **2** a place in which something is nurtured or developed. [L, rel. to NEST]

niece /neess/ *n.* a daughter of one's brother or sister, or of one's brother-in-law or sister-in-law. [ME f. OF ult. f. L *neptis* granddaughter]

niello /ni-éllō/ *n.* (*pl.* **nielli** /-lee/ or **-os**) **1** a black composition of sulphur with silver, lead, or copper, for filling engraved lines in silver or other metal. **2 a** such ornamental work. **b** an object decorated with this. □□ **nielloed** *adj.* [It. f. L *nigellus* dimin. of *niger* black]

niff /nif/ *n.* & *v. Brit. colloq.* ● *n.* a smell, esp. an unpleasant one. ● *v.intr.* smell, stink. □□ **niffy** *adj.* (**niffier, niffiest**). [orig. dial.]

nifty /nífti/ *adj.* (**niftier, niftiest**) *colloq.* **1** clever, adroit. **2** smart, stylish. □□ **niftily** *adv.* **niftiness** *n.* [19th c.: orig. uncert.]

■ **1** clever, adroit, skilful, neat; healthy, in good form, spry, energetic, agile, quick; apt, suitable; excellent, great, splendid, fine. **2** smart, stylish, modish, chic, spruce, elegant, well turned out, fashionable, snappy, *colloq.* swish; see also DAPPER 1.

niggard /níggərd/ *n.* & *adj.* ● *n.* a mean or stingy person. ● *adj. archaic* = NIGGARDLY. [ME, alt. f. earlier (obs.) *nigon*, prob. of Scand. orig.: cf. NIGGLE]

■ *n.* see MISER.

niggardly /níggərdli/ *adj.* & *adv.* ● *adj.* **1** stingy, parsimonious. **2** meagre, scanty. ● *adv.* in a stingy or meagre manner. □□ **niggardliness** *n.*

■ *adj.* **1** see MEAN[2] 1. **2** see MEAGRE 1. □□ **niggardliness** see THRIFT.

nigger /níggər/ *n. offens.* **1** a Black person. **2** a dark-skinned person. □ **a nigger in the woodpile** a hidden cause of trouble or inconvenience. [earlier *neger* f. F *nègre* f. Sp. *negro* NEGRO]

niggle /nígg'l/ *v.* & *n.* ● *v.* **1** *intr.* be over-attentive to details. **2** *intr.* find fault in a petty way. **3** *tr. colloq.* irritate; nag pettily. ● *n.* a trifling complaint or criticism; a worry or annoyance. [app. of Scand. orig.: cf. Norw. *nigla*]

■ *v.* **1, 2** find fault, moan, nag, carp, fuss, cavil, criticize; complain, *colloq.* grouse, bitch, *US sl.* kvetch.

niggling /nígling/ *adj.* **1** troublesome or irritating in a petty way. **2** trifling or petty. □□ **nigglingly** *adv.*

■ **1** irritating, worrying, worrisome, irksome, vexing, vexatious, annoying, troublesome, bothersome, *US colloq.* pesky. **2** petty, nugatory, trifling, trivial, insignificant, unimportant, inconsequential, frivolous, *US* picayune, *colloq.* piddling, piffling; nit-picking, fussy.

nigh /nī/ *adv., prep.,* & *adj. archaic* or *dial.* near. □ **nigh on** nearly, almost. [OE *nēh, nēah*]

night /nīt/ *n.* **1** the period of darkness between one day and the next; the time from sunset to sunrise. **2** nightfall (*shall not reach home before night*). **3** the darkness of night (*as black as night*). **4** a night or evening appointed for some activity, or spent or regarded in a certain way (*last night of the Proms; a great night out*). □ **night-blindness** = NYCTALOPIA. **night fighter** an aeroplane used for interception at night. **night-hawk 1** a nocturnal prowler, esp. a thief. **2** a nightjar. **night-life** entertainment available at night in a town. **night-light** a dim light kept on in a bedroom at night. **night-long** throughout the night. **night nurse** a nurse on duty during the night. **night-owl** *colloq.* a person active at night. **night safe** a safe with access from the outer wall of a bank for the deposit of money etc. when the bank is closed. **night school** an institution providing evening classes for those working by day. **night shift** a shift of workers employed during the night. **night-soil** the contents of cesspools etc. removed at night, esp. for use as manure. **night-time** the time of darkness. **night-watchman 1** a person whose job is to keep watch by night. **2** *Cricket* an inferior batsman sent in when a wicket falls near the close of a day's play. □□ **nightless** *adj.* [OE *neaht, niht* f. Gmc]

■ **1, 3** night-time, evening, dark; darkness, blackness, gloom. **2** nightfall, sunset, sundown, twilight, dusk, dark, evening, *archaic or poet.* eventide, *poet.* gloaming, vesper. □ **night-time** see NIGHT 1, 3 above.

nightbird /nītburd/ *n.* a person who habitually goes about at night.

nightcap /nītkap/ *n.* **1** *hist.* a cap worn in bed. **2** a hot or alcoholic drink taken at bedtime.

■ **2** see DRINK *n.* 2b.

nightclothes /nītklōthz/ *n.* clothes worn in bed.

nightclub /nītklub/ *n.* a club that is open at night and provides refreshment and entertainment.

■ see CABARET 2.

nightdress /nītdress/ *n.* a woman's or child's loose garment worn in bed.

nightfall /nītfawl/ *n.* the onset of night; the end of daylight.

■ see DUSK *n.* 1.

nightgown /nītgown/ *n.* **1** = NIGHTDRESS. **2** *hist.* a dressing-gown.

nightie /nīti/ *n. colloq.* a nightdress. [abbr.]

nightingale /nītinggayl/ *n.* any small reddish-brown bird of the genus *Luscinia*, esp. *L. megarhynchos*, of which the male sings melodiously, esp. at night. [OE *nihtegala* (whence obs. *nightgale*) f. Gmc: for *-n-* cf. FARTHINGALE]

nightjar /nītjaar/ *n.* any nocturnal bird of the family Caprimulgidae, having a characteristic harsh cry.

nightly /nītli/ *adj.* & *adv.* ● *adj.* **1** happening, done, or existing in the night. **2** recurring every night. ● *adv.* every night. [OE *nihtlic* (as NIGHT)]

■ *adj.* **1** night-time, nocturnal, bedtime. ● *adv.* every night, each (and every) night, night after night; after dark, after sunset; nocturnally.

nightmare /nītmair/ *n.* **1** a frightening or unpleasant dream. **2** *colloq.* a terrifying or very unpleasant experience or situation. **3** a haunting or obsessive fear. □□ **nightmarish** *adj.* **nightmarishly** *adv.* [an evil spirit (incubus) once thought to lie on and suffocate sleepers: OE *mære* incubus]

■ **2** see ORDEAL. **3** see FEAR *n.* 3. □□ **nightmarish** frightening, terrifying, alarming, horrific, horrible, dreadful, awful, ghastly, dismaying, agonizing, worrisome, exasperating, frustrating, Kafkaesque, *colloq.* creepy, scary.

nightshade /nītshayd/ *n.* any of various poisonous plants, esp. of the genus *Solanum*, including *S. nigrum* (**black nightshade**) with black berries, and *S. dulcamara* (**woody nightshade**) with red berries. □ **deadly nightshade** = BELLADONNA. [OE *nihtscada* app. formed as NIGHT + SHADE, prob. with ref. to its poisonous properties]

nightshirt /nītshurt/ *n.* a long shirt worn in bed.

nightspot /nītspot/ *n.* a nightclub.

■ see CABARET 2.

nightstick /nītstik/ *n. US* a policeman's truncheon.

nigrescent /nigréss'nt/ *adj.* blackish. □□ **nigrescence** *n.* [L *nigrescere* grow black f. *niger nigri* black]

nigritude /nígrityōōd/ *n.* blackness. [L *nigritudo* (as NIGRESCENT)]

nihilism /nī-iliz'm, nīhil-/ *n.* **1** the rejection of all religious and moral principles. **2** an extreme form of scepticism maintaining that nothing has a real existence. □□ **nihilist** *n.* **nihilistic** /-lístik/ *adj.* [L *nihil* nothing]

■ □□ **nihilist** sceptic, doubter, cynic.

nihility /nīhílliti/ *n.* (*pl.* **-ies**) **1** non-existence, nothingness. **2** a mere nothing; a trifle. [med.L *nihilitas* (as NIHILISM)]

■ **1** see OBLIVION.

nihil obstat /nīhil óbstat/ *n.* **1** *RC Ch.* a certificate that a book is not open to objection on doctrinal or moral grounds. **2** an authorization or official approval. [L, = nothing hinders]

-nik /nik/ *suffix* forming nouns denoting a person associated with a specified thing or quality (*beatnik; refusenik*). [Russ. (as SPUTNIK) and Yiddish]

nil /nil/ *n.* nothing; no number or amount (esp. as a score in games). [L, = *nihil* nothing]

■ nothing, zero, love, *Cricket* duck, *US* naught, goose-egg, *poet. or archaic* nought, *esp. US sl.* zilch.

Nile /nīl/ *n.* & *adj.* (in full **Nile-blue, Nile-green**) pale greenish blue or green. [the river *Nile* in NE Africa]

nilgai /neélgī/ *n.* a large short-horned Indian antelope, *Boselaphus tragocamelus*. [Hindi *nīlgāī* f. *nīl* blue + *gāī* cow]

Nilotic /nīlóttik/ *adj.* **1** of or relating to the Nile or the Nile region of Africa. **2** of or relating to a group of E. African Negroid peoples, or the languages spoken by them. [L *Niloticus* f. Gk *Neilōtikos* f. *Neilos* Nile]

nim /nim/ *n.* a game in which two players must alternately take one or more objects from one of several heaps and seek either to avoid taking or to take the last remaining object. [20th c.: perh. f. archaic *nim* take (as NIMBLE), or G *nimm* imper. of *nehmen* take]

nimble /nímb'l/ *adj.* (**nimbler, nimblest**) **1** quick and light in movement or action; agile. **2** (of the mind) quick to comprehend; clever, versatile. □□ **nimbleness** *n.* **nimbly** *adv.* [OE *næmel* quick to seize f. *niman* take f. Gmc, with *-b-* as in THIMBLE]

■ **1** agile, lively, active, light, lithe, limber, spry, sprightly, brisk, smart, energetic, rapid, quick, swift, adroit, deft, dexterous, *literary* volant. **2** agile, clever, versatile, alert, acute, quick-witted, quick, ready-witted, intelligent, keen, sharp, smart, brilliant.

nimbostratus /nímbōstráytəss, -straátəss/ *n.* (*pl.* **nimbostrati** /-tī/) *Meteorol.* a low dark-grey layer of cloud. [mod.L, f. NIMBUS + STRATUS]

nimbus /nímbəss/ *n.* (*pl.* **nimbi** /-bī/ or **nimbuses**) **1 a** a bright cloud or halo investing a deity or person or thing. **b** the halo of a saint etc. **2** *Meteorol.* a rain-cloud. □□ **nimbused** *adj.* [L, = cloud, aureole]

niminy-piminy /nímminipímmini/ *adj.* feeble, affected; lacking in vigour. [cf. MIMINY-PIMINY, NAMBY-PAMBY]

■ see AFFECTED 3, FEEBLE 2.

Nimrod /nímrod/ *n.* a great hunter or sportsman. [Heb. *Nimrōd* valiant: see Gen. 10:8-9]

nincompoop /níngkəmpōōp/ *n.* a simpleton; a fool. [17th c.: orig. unkn.]

■ see FOOL[1] *n.* 1.

nine /nīn/ *n.* & *adj.* ● *n.* **1** one more than eight, or one less than ten; the sum of five units and four units. **2** a symbol for this (9, ix, IX). **3** a size etc. denoted by nine. **4** a set or team of nine individuals. **5** the time of nine o'clock (*is it nine yet?*). **6** a card with nine pips. **7** (**the Nine**) the nine muses. ● *adj.* that amount to nine. □ **dressed up to the nines** dressed very elaborately. **nine days' wonder** a person or thing that is briefly famous. **nine times out of ten** nearly always. **nine to five** a designation of typical office hours. [OE *nigon* f. Gmc]

ninefold /nīnfōld/ *adj.* & *adv.* **1** nine times as much or as many. **2** consisting of nine parts.

ninepin /nīnpin/ *n.* **1** (in *pl.*; usu. treated as *sing.*) a game in which nine pins are set up at the end of an alley and bowled at in an attempt to knock them down. **2** a pin used in this game.

nineteen /nīnteen/ *n.* & *adj.* ● *n.* **1** one more than eighteen, nine more than ten. **2** the symbol for this (19, xix, XIX). **3** a size etc. denoted by nineteen. ● *adj.* that amount to nineteen. □ **talk nineteen to the dozen** see DOZEN. □□ **nineteenth** *adj.* & *n.* [OE *nigontȳne*]

ninety /nīnti/ *n.* & *adj.* ● *n.* (*pl.* **-ies**) **1** the product of nine and ten. **2** a symbol for this (90, xc, XC). **3** (in *pl.*) the numbers from 90 to 99, esp. the years of a century or of a person's life. ● *adj.* that amount to ninety. □ **ninety-first, -second**, etc. the ordinal numbers between ninetieth and hundredth. **ninety-one, -two**, etc. the cardinal numbers between ninety and a hundred. □□ **ninetieth** *adj.* & *n.* **ninetyfold** *adj.* & *adv.* [OE *nigontig*]

ninja /ninjə/ *n.* a person skilled in ninjutsu. [Jap.]

ninjutsu /ninjootsoo/ *n.* one of the Japanese martial arts, characterized by stealthy movement and camouflage. [Jap.]

ninny /ninni/ *n.* (*pl.* **-ies**) a foolish or simple-minded person. [perh. f. *innocent*]

■ see FOOL[1] *n.* 1.

ninon /neenon/ *n.* a lightweight silk dress fabric. [F]

ninth /nīnth/ *n.* & *adj.* ● *n.* **1** the position in a sequence corresponding to the number 9 in the sequence 1–9. **2** something occupying this position. **3** each of nine equal parts of a thing. **4** *Mus.* **a** an interval or chord spanning nine consecutive notes in the diatonic scale (e.g. C to D an octave higher). **b** a note separated from another by this interval. ● *adj.* that is the ninth. □□ **ninthly** *adv.*

niobium /nīōbiəm/ *n. Chem.* a rare grey-blue metallic transition element occurring naturally in several minerals and used in alloys for superconductors. ¶ Symb.: **Nb**. Also called COLUMBIUM. □□ **niobic** *adj.* **niobous** *adj.* [*Niobe* daughter of Tantalus: so called because first found in TANTALITE]

Nip /nip/ *n. sl. offens.* a Japanese person. [abbr. of NIPPONESE]

nip[1] /nip/ *v.* & *n.* ● *v.* (**nipped, nipping**) **1** *tr.* pinch, squeeze, or bite sharply. **2** *tr.* (often foll. by *off*) remove by pinching etc. **3** *tr.* (of the cold, frost, etc.) cause pain or harm to. **4** *intr.* (foll. by *in, out,* etc.) *Brit. colloq.* go nimbly or quickly. **5** *tr. US sl.* steal, snatch. ● *n.* **1 a** a pinch, a sharp squeeze. **b** a bite. **2 a** biting cold. **b** a check to vegetation caused by this. □ **nip and tuck** *US* neck and neck. **nip in the bud** suppress or destroy (esp. an idea) at an early stage. □□ **nipping** *adj.* [ME, prob. of LG or Du. orig.]

■ *v.* **1, 2** bite, nibble; pinch, snip, clip, cut, snap, tweak, twitch, trim, lop, crop, shear; grip, squeeze. **3** sting, bite, hurt, pain, pinch; grip. **4** dart, zip, dash, sprint, fly, shoot, speed, skip, hop, leap, flick, whisk, flash, hurry, pop, run, *Austral. sl.* nick. **5** see STEAL *v.* 1. ● *n.* **1** pinch, squeeze, tweak, snip; bite, nibble, morsel. **2a** chill, coldness, iciness, frost; sharpness, tang, bite. □ **nip and tuck** tied, equal, even, *Brit.* at level pegging, *colloq.* even Stephens; see also CLOSE[1] *adj.* 5. **nip in the bud** stop, arrest, check, thwart, obstruct, frustrate, stymie, forestall; quash, squash, crush, stamp on, squelch, suppress, extinguish, put down; scotch.

nip[2] /nip/ *n.* & *v.* ● *n.* a small quantity of spirits. ● *v.intr.* (**nipped, nipping**) drink spirits. [prob. abbr. of *nipperkin* small measure: cf. LG, Du. *nippen* to sip]

■ *n.* taste, drop, sip, soupçon, portion, swallow, gulp, mouthful, finger, tot, thimbleful, dram, draught, *Brit.* peg, *colloq.* snort, shot, *sl.* snifter.

nipa /neepə/ *n.* **1** an E. Indian palm-tree, *Nipa fruticans*, with a creeping trunk and large feathery leaves. **2** an alcoholic drink made from its sap. [Sp. & Port. f. Malay *nīpah*]

nipper /nippər/ *n.* **1** a person or thing that nips. **2** the claw of a crab, lobster, etc. **3** *Brit. colloq.* a young child. **4** (in *pl.*) any tool for gripping or cutting, e.g. forceps or pincers.

■ **3** see CHILD 1a. **4** (*nippers*) pincers, tweezers, pliers.

nipple /nipp'l/ *n.* **1** a small projection in which the mammary ducts of either sex of mammals terminate and from which in females milk is secreted for the young. **2** the teat of a feeding-bottle. **3** a device like a nipple in function, e.g. the tip of a grease-gun. **4** a nipple-like protuberance. **5** *US* a short section of pipe with a screw-thread at each end for coupling. [16th c., also *neble, nible*, perh. dimin. f. *neb*]

nipplewort /nipp'lwurt/ *n.* a yellow-flowered weed, *Lapsana communis*.

Nipponese /nippəneez/ *n.* & *adj.* ● *n.* (*pl.* same) a Japanese person. ● *adj.* Japanese. [Jap. *Nippon* Japan, lit. 'land of the rising sun']

nippy /nippi/ *adj.* (**nippier, nippiest**) *colloq.* **1** quick, nimble, active. **2** chilly, cold. □□ **nippily** *adv.* [NIP[1] + -Y[1]]

■ **2** see CHILLY 1.

NIREX /nīreks/ *abbr.* (in the UK) Nuclear Industry Radioactive Waste Executive.

nirvana /nurvaanə, neer-/ *n.* (in Buddhism) perfect bliss and release from karma, attained by the extinction of individuality. [Skr. *nirvāṇa* f. *nirvā* be extinguished f. *nis* out + *vā-* to blow]

■ see PARADISE 2.

nisei /neesay/ *n. US* an American whose parents were immigrants from Japan. [Jap., lit. 'second generation']

nisi /nīsī/ *adj. Law* that takes effect only on certain conditions (*decree nisi*). [L, = 'unless']

Nissen hut /niss'n/ *n.* a tunnel-shaped hut of corrugated iron with a cement floor. [P. N. *Nissen*, British engineer d. 1930, its inventor]

nit[1] /nit/ *n.* **1** the egg or young form of a louse or other parasitic insect esp. of human head-lice or body-lice. **2** *Brit. sl.* a stupid person. □ **nit-pick** *colloq.* indulge in nit-picking. **nit-picker** *colloq.* a person who nit-picks. **nit-picking** *n.* & *adj. colloq.* fault-finding in a petty manner. [OE *hnitu* f. WG]

■ **2** see FOOL[1] *n.* 1. □ **nit-pick** see QUIBBLE *v.* **nit-picking** (*adj.*) see OVERCRITICAL.

nit[2] /nit/ *int. Austral. sl.* used as a warning that someone is approaching. □ **keep nit** keep watch; act as guard. [19th c.: orig. unkn.: cf. NIX[3]]

niter *US* var. of NITRE.

nitinol /nittinol/ *n.* an alloy of nickel and titanium. [*Ni* + *Ti* + *N*aval *O*rdnance *L*aboratory, Maryland, US]

nitrate *n.* & *v.* ● *n.* /nītrayt/ **1** any salt or ester of nitric acid. **2** potassium or sodium nitrate when used as a fertilizer. ● *v.tr.* /nītráyt/ *Chem.* treat, combine, or impregnate with nitric acid. □□ **nitration** /-tráysh'n/ *n.* [F (as NITRE, -ATE[1])]

nitre /nītər/ *n.* (*US* **niter**) saltpetre, potassium nitrate. [ME f. OF f. L *nitrum* f. Gk *nitron*, of Semitic orig.]

nitric /nītrik/ *adj.* of or containing nitrogen, esp. in the quinquevalent state. □ **nitric acid** a colourless corrosive poisonous liquid. ¶ Chem. formula: HNO_3. **nitric oxide** a colourless gas. ¶ Chem. formula: NO. [F *nitrique* (as NITRE)]

nitride /nītrīd/ *n. Chem.* a binary compound of nitrogen with a more electropositive element. [NITRE + -IDE]

nitrify /nītrifī/ *v.tr.* (**-ies, -ied**) **1** impregnate with nitrogen. **2** convert (nitrogen, usu. in the form of ammonia) into nitrites or nitrates. □□ **nitrifiable** *adj.* **nitrification** /-fikáysh'n/ *n.* [F *nitrifier* (as NITRE)]

nitrile /nītrīl/ *n. Chem.* an organic compound consisting of an alkyl radical bound to a cyanide radical.

nitrite /nītrīt/ *n.* any salt or ester of nitrous acid.

nitro- /nītrō/ *comb. form* **1** of or containing nitric acid, nitre, or nitrogen. **2** made with or by use of any of these. **3** of or containing the monovalent $-NO_2$ group (*the nitro groups in TNT*). [Gk (as NITRE)]

nitrobenzene /nītrōbénzeen/ *n.* a yellow oily liquid made by the nitration of benzene and used to make aniline etc.

nitrocellulose /nītrōsélyoolōz, -lōss/ *n.* a highly flammable material made by treating cellulose with concentrated nitric acid, used in the manufacture of explosives and celluloid.

nitrogen /nītrəjən/ *n. Chem.* a colourless tasteless odourless gaseous element that forms four-fifths of the atmosphere and is an essential constituent of proteins and nucleic acids. ¶ Symb.: **N.** □ **nitrogen cycle** the interconversion of nitrogen and its compounds, usu. in the form of nitrates, in nature. **nitrogen fixation** a chemical process in which atmospheric nitrogen is assimilated into organic compounds in living organisms and hence into the nitrogen cycle. □□ **nitrogenous** /-trójinəss/ *adj.* [F *nitrogène* (as NITRO-, -GEN)]

nitroglycerine /nītrōglíssərin/ *n.* (also **nitroglycerin**) an explosive yellow liquid made by reacting glycerol with a mixture of concentrated sulphuric and nitric acids.

nitrous /nītrəss/ *adj.* of, like, or impregnated with nitrogen, esp. in the tervalent state. □ **nitrous acid** a weak acid existing only in solution and in the gas phase. ¶ Chem. formula: HNO_2. **nitrous oxide** a colourless gas used as an anaesthetic (= *laughing-gas*) and as an aerosol propellant. ¶ Chem. formula: N_2O. [L *nitrosus* (as NITRE), partly through F *nitreux*]

nitty-gritty /nittigritti/ *n. sl.* the realities or practical details of a matter. [20th c.: orig. uncert.]
■ see POINT *n.* 13a.

nitwit /nítwit/ *n. colloq.* a stupid person. □□ **nitwittery** /-witəri/ *n.* [perh. f. NIT[1] + WIT[1]]
■ see FOOL[1] *n.* 1.

nitwitted /nítwíttid/ *adj.* stupid. □□ **nitwittedness** /-wíttidniss/ *n.*

nix[1] /niks/ *n.* & *v. sl.* ● *n.* **1** nothing. **2** a denial or refusal. ● *v.tr.* **1** cancel. **2** reject. [G, colloq. var. of *nichts* nothing]
■ *n.* **1** see ZERO *n.* 1. ● *v.* **2** see VETO *v.*

nix[2] /niks/ *n.* (*fem.* **nixie** /níksi/) a water-elf. [G (fem. *Nixe*)]

nix[3] /niks/ *int. Brit. sl.* giving warning to confederates etc. that a person in authority is approaching. [19th c.: perh. = NIX[1]]

NJ *abbr. US* New Jersey (also in official postal use).

NM *abbr. US* New Mexico (in official postal use).

nm *abbr.* nanometre.

n.m. *abbr.* nautical mile.

N.Mex. *abbr.* New Mexico.

NMR *abbr.* (also **nmr**) nuclear magnetic resonance.

NNE *abbr.* north-north-east.

NNW *abbr.* north-north-west.

No[1] *symb. Chem.* the element nobelium.

No[2] var. of NOH.

No. *abbr.* **1** number. **2** *US* North. [sense 1 f. L *numero*, ablat. of *numerus* number]

no[1] /nō/ *adj.* **1** not any (*there is no excuse; no circumstances could justify it; no two of them are alike*). **2** not a, quite other than (*is no fool; is no part of my plan; caused no slight inconvenience*). **3** hardly any (*is no distance; did it in no time*). **4** used elliptically as a slogan, notice, etc., to forbid, reject, or deplore the thing specified (*no parking; no surrender*). □ **by no means** see MEANS. **no-account** unimportant, worthless. **no-ball** *Cricket n.* an unlawfully delivered ball (counting one to the batting side if not otherwise scored from). ● *v.tr.* pronounce (a bowler) to have bowled a no-ball. **no-claim** (or **-claims**) **bonus** a reduction of the insurance premium charged when the insured has not made a claim under the insurance during an agreed preceding period. **no date** (of a book etc.) not bearing a date of publication etc. **no dice** see DICE. **no doubt** see DOUBT. **no end** see END. **no entry** (of a notice) prohibiting vehicles or persons from entering a road or place. **no-fault** *US* (of insurance) valid regardless of the allocation of blame for an accident etc. **no fear** see FEAR. **no-frills** lacking ornament or embellishment. **no go** impossible, hopeless. **no-go area** an area forbidden to unauthorized people. **no good** see GOOD. **no-good** see GOOD. **no-hitter** *US Baseball* a game in which a team does not get a player to first base. **no-hoper** *sl.* a useless person. **no joke** see JOKE. **no joy** see JOY *n.* 3. **no little** see LITTLE. **no man** no person, nobody. **no man's land 1** *Mil.* the space between two opposing armies. **2** an area not assigned to any owner. **3** an area not clearly belonging to any one subject etc. **no-no** *colloq.* a thing not possible or acceptable. **no-nonsense** serious, without flippancy. **no place** *US* nowhere. **no-show** a person who has reserved a seat etc. but neither uses it nor cancels the reservation. **no side** *Rugby Football* **1** the end of a game. **2** the referee's announcement of this. **no small** see SMALL. **no sweat** *colloq.* no bother, no trouble. **no thoroughfare** an indication that passage along a street, path, etc., is blocked or prohibited. **no time** see TIME. **no trumps** (or **trump**) *Bridge* a declaration or bid involving playing without a trump suit. **no-trumper** *Bridge* a hand on which a no-trump bid can suitably be, or has been, made. **no way** *colloq.* **1** it is impossible. **2** I will not agree etc. **no whit** see WHIT. **no-win** of or designating a situation in which success is impossible. **no wonder** see WONDER. **... or no ...** regardless of the ... (*rain or no rain, I shall go out*). **there is no ...ing** it is impossible to ... (*there is no accounting for tastes; there was no mistaking what he meant*). [ME f. *nān, nōn* NONE[1], orig. only before consonants]
■ □ **no entry** no access, no right of way; no thoroughfare, no through road. **no-nonsense** serious, unfrivolous, businesslike, practical, down-to-earth.

no[2] /nō/ *adv.* & *n.* ● *adv.* **1** equivalent to a negative sentence: the answer to your question is negative, your request or command will not be complied with, the statement made or course of action intended or conclusion arrived at is not correct or satisfactory, the negative statement made is correct. **2** (foll. by *compar.*) by no amount; not at all (*no better than before*). **3** *Sc.* not (*will ye no come back again?*). ● *n.* (*pl.* **noes**) **1** an utterance of the word *no*. **2** a denial or refusal. **3** a negative vote. □ **is no more** has died or ceased to exist. **no better than she should be** morally suspect; sexually promiscuous. **no can do** *colloq.* I am unable to do it. **the noes have it** the negative voters are in the majority. **no less** (often foll. by *than*) **1** as much (*gave me £50, no less; gave me no less than £50; is no less than a scandal; a no less fatal victory*). **2** as important (*no less a person than the President*). **3** *disp.* no fewer (*no less than ten people have told me*). **no longer** not now or henceforth as formerly. **no more** *n.* nothing further (*have no more to say; want no more of it*). ● *adj.* not any more (*no more wine?*). ● *adv.* **1** no longer. **2** never again. **3** to no greater extent (*is no more a lord than I am; could no more do it than fly in the air*). **4** just as little, neither (*you did not come, and no more did he*). **no, no** an emphatic equivalent of a negative sentence (cf. sense 1 of *adv.*). **no-see-em** (or **-um**) *US* a small bloodsucking insect, esp. a midge of the family *Ceratopogonidae*. **no sooner ... than** see SOON. **not take no for an answer** persist in spite of refusals. **or no** or not (*pleasant or no, it is true*). **whether or no 1** in either case. **2** (as an indirect question) which of a case and its negative (*tell me whether or no*). [OE *nō, nā* f. *ne* not + *ō, ā* ever]

n.o. *abbr. Cricket* not out.

Noah's ark /nṓəz, nawz/ *n.* **1 a** the ship in which (according to the Bible) Noah, his family, and the animals were saved. **b** an imitation of this as a child's toy. **2** a large or cumbrous or old-fashioned trunk or vehicle. **3** a small bivalve mollusc, *Arca tetragona*, with a boat-shaped shell. [*Noah*, Hebrew patriarch in Gen. 6]

nob[1] /nob/ *n. Brit. sl.* a person of wealth or high social position. [orig. Sc. *knabb, nab*; 18th c., of unkn. orig.]
■ see SWELL *n.* 4.

nob[2] /nob/ *n. sl.* the head. □ **his nob** *Cribbage* a score of one point for holding the jack of the same suit as a card turned up by the dealer. [perh. var. of KNOB]

nobble /nóbb'l/ *v.tr. Brit. sl.* **1** tamper with (a racehorse) to prevent its winning. **2** get hold of (money etc.) dishonestly.

3 catch (a criminal). **4** secure the support of or weaken (a person) esp. by underhand means. **5** seize, grab. **6** try to influence (e.g. a judge) unfairly. [prob. = dial. *knobble*, *knubble* knock, beat, f. KNOB]

■ **2** see ROB 1.

nobbler /nóblər/ *n. Austral. sl.* a glass or drink of liquor. [19th c.: orig. unkn.]

Nobelist /nōbéllist/ *n. US* a winner of a Nobel prize.

nobelium /nōbeéliəm/ *n. Chem.* a radioactive transuranic metallic element. ¶ Symb.: **No**. [*Nobel* (see NOBEL PRIZE) + -IUM]

Nobel prize /nōbél/ *n.* any of six international prizes awarded annually for physics, chemistry, physiology or medicine, literature, economics, and the promotion of peace. [Alfred *Nobel* (d. 1896), Swedish chemist and engineer, who endowed them]

nobiliary /nəbílyəri/ *adj.* of the nobility. □ **nobiliary particle** a preposition forming part of a title of nobility (e.g. French *de*, German *von*). [F *nobiliaire* (as NOBLE)]

nobility /nōbílliti/ *n.* (*pl.* **-ies**) **1** nobleness of character, mind, birth, or rank. **2** (prec. by *a*, *the*) a class of nobles, an aristocracy. [ME f. OF *nobilité* or L *nobilitas* (as NOBLE)]

■ **1** nobleness, dignity, grandeur, illustriousness, greatness, glory, influence, authority, leadership, distinction; probity, integrity, excellence, goodness, character, rectitude, righteousness, ethics, honesty, honourableness, decency, justness, high-mindedness, magnanimity; prestige, loftiness, primacy, significance; rank, position, class, birth, blue blood. **2** (*the nobility*) the peerage, the élite, the aristocracy, the *noblesse*, the plutocracy, the ruling class(es), the Establishment, *US* four hundred, *colloq.* the upper crust.

noble /nṓb'l/ *adj.* & *n.* ● *adj.* (**nobler, noblest**) **1** belonging by rank, title, or birth to the aristocracy. **2** of excellent character; having lofty ideals; free from pettiness and meanness, magnanimous. **3** of imposing appearance, splendid, magnificent, stately. **4** excellent, admirable (*noble horse*; *noble cellar*). ● *n.* **1** a nobleman or noblewoman. **2** *hist.* a former English gold coin first issued in 1351. □ **noble gas** any gaseous element of a group that almost never combine with other elements. **noble metal** a metal (e.g. gold, silver, or platinum) that resists chemical action, does not corrode or tarnish in air or water, and is not easily attacked by acids. **noble savage** primitive man idealized as in Romantic literature. **the noble science** boxing. □□ **nobleness** *n.* **nobly** *adv.* [ME f. OF f. L *(g)nobilis*, rel. to KNOW]

■ *adj.* **1** high-born, high-class, upper-class, aristocratic, titled, high-ranking, lordly, patrician, blue-blood(ed). **2** upright, righteous, honourable, honest, virtuous, incorruptible, chivalrous, staunch, steadfast, true, loyal, faithful, trustworthy, true, principled, moral, good, decent, self-sacrificing, magnanimous, generous. **3, 4** splendid, magnificent, imposing, impressive, stately, fine, sublime, grand, striking, superb, excellent, admirable, elegant, rich, sumptuous, luxurious, *colloq.* stunning; dignified, eminent, distinguished, august, lofty, elevated, illustrious, prestigious, pre-eminent, noted, honoured, esteemed, celebrated, renowned, acclaimed, respected, venerated. ● *n.* **1** nobleman, noblewoman, aristocrat, patrician, lord, lady, peer, peeress.

nobleman /nṓb'lmən/ *n.* (*pl.* **-men**) a man of noble rank or birth, a peer.

■ see PEER² *n.* 1.

noblesse /nōbléss/ *n.* the class of nobles (esp. of a foreign country). □ ***noblesse oblige*** /obleézh/ privilege entails responsibility. [ME = nobility, f. OF (as NOBLE)]

noblewoman /nṓb'lwoomman/ *n.* (*pl.* **-women**) a woman of noble rank or birth, a peeress.

■ see PEER² *n.* 1.

nobody /nṓbədi/ *pron.* & *n.* ● *pron.* no person. ● *n.* (*pl.* **-ies**) a person of no importance, authority, or position. □ **like nobody's business** see BUSINESS. **nobody's fool** see FOOL. [ME f. NO¹ + BODY (= person)]

■ *pron.* no one, not anyone, no person. ● *n.* nonentity, unknown, zero, cipher, nothing; see also COG 2.

nock /nok/ *n.* & *v.* ● *n.* **1** a notch at either end of a bow for holding the string. **2 a** a notch at the butt-end of an arrow for receiving the bowstring. **b** a notched piece of horn serving this purpose. ● *v.tr.* set (an arrow) on the string. [ME, perh. = *nock* forward upper corner of some sails, f. MDu. *nocke*]

noctambulist /noktámbyoolist/ *n.* a sleepwalker. □□ **noctambulism** *n.* [L *nox noctis* night + *ambulare* walk]

noctule /nóktyool/ *n.* a large W. European bat, *Nyctalus noctula*. [F f. It. *nottola* bat]

nocturn /nókturn/ *n. RC Ch.* a part of matins orig. said at night. [ME f. OF *nocturne* or eccl.L *nocturnum* neut. of L *nocturnus*: see NOCTURNAL]

nocturnal /noktúrn'l/ *adj.* of or in the night; done or active by night. □ **nocturnal emission** involuntary emission of semen during sleep. □□ **nocturnally** *adv.* [LL *nocturnalis* f. L *nocturnus* of the night f. *nox noctis* night]

■ nightly, night-time, bedtime. □□ **nocturnally** see NIGHTLY *adv.*

nocturne /nókturn/ *n.* **1** *Mus.* a short composition of a romantic nature, usu. for piano. **2** a picture of a night scene. [F (as NOCTURN)]

nocuous /nókyooəss/ *adj. literary* noxious, harmful. [L *nocuus* f. *nocēre* hurt]

■ see *poisonous* (POISON).

nod /nod/ *v.* & *n.* ● *v.* (**nodded, nodding**) **1** *intr.* incline one's head slightly and briefly in greeting, assent, or command. **2** *intr.* let one's head fall forward in drowsiness; be drowsy. **3** *tr.* incline (one's head). **4** *tr.* signify (assent etc.) by a nod. **5** *intr.* (of flowers, plumes, etc.) bend downwards and sway, or move up and down. **6** *intr.* make a mistake due to a momentary lack of alertness or attention. **7** *intr.* (of a building etc.) incline from the perpendicular (*nodding to its fall*). ● *n.* a nodding of the head, esp. as a signal to proceed, etc. □ **get the nod** *US* be chosen or approved. **nodding acquaintance** (usu. foll. by *with*) a very slight acquaintance with a person or subject. **nod off** *colloq.* fall asleep. **nod through** *colloq.* **1** approve on the nod. **2** *Brit. Parl.* formally count (a Member of Parliament) as if having voted when unable to do so. **on the nod** *colloq.* **1** with merely formal assent and no discussion. **2** on credit. □□ **noddingly** *adv.* [ME *nodde*, of unkn. orig.]

■ *v.* **1, 4** say yes; consent, assent, agree, concur, acquiesce; (*nod at*) greet, acknowledge, recognize. **2** doze (off), nod off, nap, drowse, drop off, fall asleep. **3, 5, 7** see INCLINE *v.* 3, 4; SWAY *v.* 1. **6** slip (up), err, make a mistake, be mistaken *or* wrong; be careless *or* negligent *or* lax *or* inattentive. ● *n.* signal, sign, cue, indication, gesture; approval; consent, acquiescence, concurrence, assent, agreement, *colloq.* OK. □ **get the nod** see *make the grade* (GRADE). **nodding acquaintance** casual *or* slight *or* superficial *or* distant *or* passing acquaintance *or* knowledge *or* understanding; bowing acquaintance. **nod off** see NOD *v.* 2 above.

noddle¹ /nódd'l/ *n. colloq.* the head. [ME *nodle*, of unkn. orig.]

■ see HEAD *n.* 1.

noddle² /nódd'l/ *v.tr.* nod or wag (one's head). [NOD + -LE⁴]

noddy /nóddi/ *n.* (*pl.* **-ies**) **1** a simpleton. **2** any of various tropical sea birds of the genus *Anous*, resembling terns. [prob. f. obs. *noddy* foolish, which is perh. f. NOD]

■ **1** see SAP³.

node /nōd/ *n.* **1** *Bot.* **a** the part of a plant stem from which one or more leaves emerge. **b** a knob on a root or branch. **2** *Anat.* a natural swelling or bulge in an organ or part of the body. **3** *Astron.* either of two points at which a planet's orbit intersects the plane of the ecliptic or the celestial equator. **4** *Physics* a point of minimum disturbance in a standing wave system. **5** *Electr.* a point of zero current or voltage. **6** *Math.* **a** a point at which a curve intersects itself. **b** a vertex in a graph. **7** a component in a computer network. □□ **nodal** *adj.* **nodical** *adj.* (in sense 3). [L *nodus* knot]

■ **2** see SWELLING.

nodi *pl.* of NODUS.

nodose /nədṓss/ *adj.* knotty, knotted. ▫▫ **nodosity** /-dóssiti/ *n.* [L *nodosus* (as NODE)]

nodule /nódyo͞ol/ *n.* **1** a small rounded lump of anything, e.g. flint in chalk, carbon in cast iron, or a mineral on the seabed. **2** a small swelling or aggregation of cells, e.g. a small tumour, node, or ganglion, or a swelling on a root of a legume containing bacteria. ▫▫ **nodular** *adj.* **nodulated** *adj.* **nodulation** /-láysh'n/ *n.* **nodulose** *adj.* **nodulous** *adj.* [L *nodulus* dimin. of *nodus*: see NODUS]

■ **2** see SWELLING.

nodus /nṓdəss/ *n.* (*pl.* **nodi** /-dī/) a knotty point, a difficulty, a complication in the plot of a story etc. [L, = knot]

Noel /nō-él/ *n.* Christmas (esp. as a refrain in carols). [F f. L (as NATAL)]

noetic /nō-éttik, nō-éetik/ *adj.* & *n.* ● *adj.* **1** of the intellect. **2** purely intellectual or abstract. **3** given to intellectual speculation. ● *n.* (in *sing.* or *pl.*) the science of the intellect. [Gk *noētikos* f. *noētos* intellectual f. *noeō* apprehend]

nog[1] /nog/ *n.* & *v.* ● *n.* **1** a small block or peg of wood. **2** a snag or stump on a tree. **3** nogging. ● *v.tr.* (**nogged, nogging**) **1** secure with nogs. **2** build in the form of nogging. [17th c.: orig. unkn.]

nog[2] /nog/ *n.* **1** *Brit.* a strong beer brewed in East Anglia. **2** an egg-flip. [17th c.: orig. unkn.]

noggin /nóggin/ *n.* **1** a small mug. **2** a small measure, usu. ¼ pint, of spirits. **3** *sl.* the head. [17th c.: orig. unkn.]

■ **3** see HEAD *n.* 1.

nogging /nógging/ *n.* brickwork or timber braces in a timber frame. [NOG[1] + -ING[1]]

Noh /nō/ *n.* (also **No**) traditional Japanese drama with dance and song, evolved from Shinto rites. [Jap. *nō*]

nohow /nṓhow/ *adv.* **1** *US* in no way; by no means. **2** *dial.* out of order; out of sorts.

noil /noyl/ *n.* (in *sing.* or *pl.*) short wool-combings. [perh. f. OF *noel* f. med.L *nodellus* dimin. of L *nodus* knot]

noise /noyz/ *n.* & *v.* ● *n.* **1** a sound, esp. a loud or unpleasant or undesired one. **2** a series of loud sounds, esp. shouts; a confused sound of voices and movements. **3** irregular fluctuations accompanying a transmitted signal but not relevant to it. **4** (in *pl.*) conventional remarks, or speechlike sounds without actual words (*made sympathetic noises*). ● *v.* **1** *tr.* (usu. in *passive*) make public; spread abroad (a person's fame or a fact). **2** *intr. archaic* make much noise. ▫ **make a noise 1** (usu. foll. by *about*) talk or complain much. **2** be much talked of; attain notoriety. **noise-maker** a device for making a loud noise at a festivity etc. **noise pollution** harmful or annoying noise. **noises off** sounds made off stage to be heard by the audience of a play. [ME f. OF, = outcry, disturbance, f. L *nausea*: see NAUSEA]

■ *n.* **1, 2** sound, clamour, crash, clap, clash, clangour, din, thunder, thundering, rumble, rumbling, outcry, hubbub, uproar, hullabaloo, racket, charivari, rattle, caterwauling, blare, blast, blasting, bawling, babel, commotion, bedlam, fracas, tumult, pandemonium, turmoil; discordance, dissonance, cacophony, *esp. US* ruckus, shivaree, *colloq.* rumpus, ruction, ballyhoo, *joc.* alarums and excursions. ● *v.* **1** make public, make known, circulate, spread (abroad), rumour, bruit (abroad *or* about). ▫ **make a noise 1** see PROTEST *v.* 1. **2** see *make a splash* (SPLASH).

noiseless /nóyzliss/ *adj.* **1** silent. **2** making no avoidable noise. ▫▫ **noiselessly** *adv.* **noiselessness** *n.*

■ silent, mute, still, inaudible, soundless; muted, quiet, soft, hushed, muffled, deadened, dampened, damped.

noisette /nwaazét/ *n.* a small round piece of meat etc. [F, dimin. of *noix* nut]

noisome /nóysəm/ *adj. literary* **1** harmful, noxious. **2** evil-smelling. **3** objectionable, offensive. ▫▫ **noisomeness** *n.* [ME f. obs. *noy* f. ANNOY]

■ **1** see BAD *adj.* 3. **2** see SMELLY. **3** see OBNOXIOUS. ▫▫ **noisomeness** see STENCH.

noisy /nóyzi/ *adj.* (**noisier, noisiest**) **1** full of or attended with noise. **2** making or given to making much noise. **3** clamorous, turbulent. **4** (of a colour, garment, etc.) loud, conspicuous. ▫▫ **noisily** *adv.* **noisiness** *n.*

■ **1–3** loud, deafening, ear-splitting, jarring, grating, harsh, piercing, shrill, discordant, unmusical, dissonant, cacophonous, resounding, clarion, clamorous, clangorous, thunderous, uproarious, blaring, blasting, obstreperous, vociferous, boisterous, tumultuous, turbulent, riotous, *literary* clamant. **4** see LOUD *adj.* 2.

nolens volens /nṓlenz vṓlenz/ *adv. literary* willy-nilly, perforce. [L participles, = unwilling, willing]

nolle prosequi /nólli próssikwī/ *n. Law* **1** the relinquishment by a plaintiff or prosecutor of all or part of a suit. **2** the entry of this on record. [L, = refuse to pursue]

nom. *abbr.* nominal.

nomad /nṓmad/ *n.* & *adj.* ● *n.* **1** a member of a tribe roaming from place to place for pasture. **2** a wanderer. ● *adj.* **1** living as a nomad. **2** wandering. ▫▫ **nomadic** /-máddik/ *adj.* **nomadically** /-máddikəli/ *adv.* **nomadism** *n.* **nomadize** *v.intr.* (also **-ise**). [F *nomade* f. L *nomas nomad-* f. Gk *nomas -ados* f. *nemō* to pasture]

■ **2** see ROVER. ▫▫ **nomadic** see *travelling* (TRAVEL).

nombril /nómbril/ *n. Heraldry* the point halfway between fess point and the base of the shield. [F, = navel]

nom de guerre /nóm də gáir/ *n.* (*pl.* ***noms de guerre*** *pronunc.* same) an assumed name under which a person fights, plays, writes, etc. [F, = war-name]

■ see PSEUDONYM.

nom de plume /nóm də plo͞om/ *n.* (*pl.* ***noms de plume*** *pronunc.* same) an assumed name under which a person writes. [formed in E of F words, = pen-name, after NOM DE GUERRE]

■ see PSEUDONYM.

nomen /nṓmen/ *n.* an ancient Roman's second name, indicating the gens, as in Marcus *Tullius* Cicero. [L, = name]

nomenclature /nōménklachər, nṓmənklaychər/ *n.* **1** a person's or community's system of names for things. **2** the terminology of a science etc. **3** systematic naming. **4** a catalogue or register. ▫▫ **nomenclative** *adj.* **nomenclatural** /-kláchərəl/ *adj.* [F f. L *nomenclatura* f. *nomen* + *calare* call]

■ **2** see TERMINOLOGY.

nominal /nómmin'l/ *adj.* **1** existing in name only; not real or actual (*nominal and real prices; nominal ruler*). **2** (of a sum of money, rent, etc.) virtually nothing; much below the actual value of a thing. **3** of or in names (*nominal and essential distinctions*). **4** consisting of or giving the names (*nominal list of officers*). **5** of or as or like a noun. ▫ **nominal definition** a statement of all that is connoted in the name of a concept. **nominal value** the face value (of a coin, shares, etc.). ▫▫ **nominally** *adv.* [ME f. F *nominal* or L *nominalis* f. *nomen -inis* name]

■ **1** titular, in name only, formal, pretended, so-called, self-styled, *soi-disant*, professed, purported, supposed, would-be, representational, represented, supposititious; proposed, propositional; puppet, figurehead.
2 insignificant, trivial, trifling, minor, minuscule, tiny, small, insubstantial, minimal, inconsiderable, token; derisory.

nominalism /nómminəliz'm/ *n. Philos.* the doctrine that universals or general ideas are mere names (opp. REALISM). ▫▫ **nominalist** *n.* **nominalistic** /-lístik/ *adj.* [F *nominalisme* (as NOMINAL)]

nominalize /nómminəlīz/ *v.tr.* (also **-ise**) form a noun from (a verb, adjective, etc.), e.g. *output, truth,* from *put out, true.* ▫▫ **nominalization** /-záysh'n/ *n.*

nominate /nómminayt/ *v.tr.* **1** propose (a candidate) for election. **2** appoint to an office (*a board of six nominated and six elected members*). **3** name or appoint (a date or place). **4**

mention by name. **5** call by the name of, designate. □□ **nominator** *n.* [L *nominare nominat-* (as NOMINAL)]
■ **1–3** choose, select, name, appoint, designate, suggest, offer, submit, recommend, propose, present, put up *or* forward, forward, *formal* put forth.

nomination /nómmináysh'n/ *n.* **1** the act or an instance of nominating; the state of being nominated. **2** the right of nominating for an appointment (*have a nomination at your disposal*). [ME f. OF *nomination* or L *nominatio* (as NOMINATE)]
■ **1** see APPOINTMENT 2c.

nominative /nómminətiv/ *n.* & *adj.* ● *n. Gram.* **1** the case of nouns, pronouns, and adjectives, expressing the subject of a verb. **2** a word in this case. ● *adj.* **1** *Gram.* of or in this case. **2** /-naytiv/ of, or appointed by, nomination (as distinct from election). □□ **nominatival** /-tī́v'l/ *adj.* [ME f. OF *nominatif -ive* or L *nominativus* (as NOMINATE), transl. Gk *onomastikē* (*ptōsis* case)]
■ *n.* subjective (case).

nominee /nómminée/ *n.* **1** a person who is nominated for an office or as the recipient of a grant etc. **2** *Commerce* a person (not necessarily the owner) in whose name a stock etc. is registered. [NOMINATE]
■ **1** candidate, appointee; assignee.

nomogram /nómməgram, nṓm-/ *n.* (also **nomograph** /-graaf/) a graphical presentation of relations between quantities whereby the value of one may be found by simple geometrical construction (e.g. drawing a straight line) from those of others. □□ **nomographic** /-gráffik/ *adj.* **nomographically** /-gráffikəli/ *adv.* **nomography** /nəmógrəfi/ *n.* [Gk *nomo-* f. *nomos* law + -GRAM]

nomothetic /nómməthéttik, nṓm-/ *adj.* **1** stating (esp. scientific) laws. **2** legislative. [obs. *nomothete* legislator f. Gk *nomothetēs*]

-nomy /nəmi/ *comb. form* denoting an area of knowledge or the laws governing it (*aeronomy*; *economy*).

non- /non/ *prefix* giving the negative sense of words with which it is combined, esp.: **1** not doing or having or involved with (*non-attendance*; *non-payment*; *non-productive*). **2 a** not of the kind or class described (*non-alcoholic*; *non-member*; *non-event*). **b** forming terms used adjectivally (*non-union*; *non-party*). **3** a lack of (*non-access*). **4** (with adverbs) not in the way described (*non-aggressively*). **5** forming adjectives from verbs, meaning 'that does not' or 'that is not meant to (or to be)' (*non-skid*; *non-iron*). **6** used to form a neutral negative sense when a form in *in-* or *un-* has a special sense or (usu. unfavourable) connotation (*non-controversial*; *non-effective*; *non-human*). ¶ The number of words that can be formed with this prefix is unlimited; consequently only a selection, considered the most current or semantically noteworthy, can be given here. [from or after ME *no(u)n-* f. AF *noun-*, OF *non-*, *nom-* f. L *non* not]

nona- /nónnə/ *comb. form* nine. [L f. *nonus* ninth]

non-abstainer /nónnəbstáynər/ *n.* a person who does not abstain (esp. from alcohol).

non-acceptance /nónnəkséptənss/ *n.* a lack of acceptance.

non-access /nónnáksess/ *n.* a lack of access.

non-addictive /nónnədiktiv/ *adj.* (of a drug, habit, etc.) not causing addiction.

nonage /nṓnij, nón-/ *n.* **1** *hist.* the state of being under full legal age, minority. **2** a period of immaturity. [ME f. AF *nounage*, OF *nonage* (as NON-, AGE)]

nonagenarian /nṓnəjináiriən, nón-/ *n.* & *adj.* ● *n.* a person from 90 to 99 years old. ● *adj.* of this age. [L *nonagenarius* f. *nonageni* distributive of *nonaginta* ninety]

non-aggression /nónnəgrésh'n/ *n.* lack of or restraint from aggression (often *attrib.*: *non-aggression pact*).

nonagon /nónnəgən/ *n.* a plane figure with nine sides and angles. [L *nonus* ninth, after HEXAGON]

non-alcoholic /nónnalkəhóllik/ *adj.* (of a drink etc.) not containing alcohol.
■ see NON-INTOXICATING.

non-aligned /nónnəlī́nd/ *adj.* (of States etc.) not aligned with another (esp. major) power. □□ **non-alignment** *n.*
■ uncommitted, non-allied, non-affiliated, unaligned, unaffiliated, unallied; neutral, impartial.

non-allergic /nónnəlérjik/ *adj.* not causing allergy; not allergic.

non-ambiguous /nónnambígyooəss/ *adj.* not ambiguous. ¶ Neutral in sense: see NON- 6, UNAMBIGUOUS.

non-appearance /nónnəpéerənss/ *n.* failure to appear or be present.
■ see ABSENCE 1, 2.

non-art /nónnaárt/ *n.* something that avoids the normal forms of art.

nonary /nṓnəri/ *adj.* & *n.* ● *adj. Math.* (of a scale of notation) having nine as its base. ● *n.* (*pl.* **-ies**) a group of nine. [L *nonus* ninth]

non-Aryan /nón-áiriən/ *adj.* & *n.* ● *adj.* (of a person or language) not Aryan or of Aryan descent. ● *n.* a non-Aryan person.

non-attached /nónnətácht/ *adj.* that is not attached. ¶ Neutral in sense: see NON- 6, UNATTACHED.

non-attendance /nónnəténdənss/ *n.* failure to attend.
■ see ABSENCE 1, 2.

non-attributable /nónnətríbyootəb'l/ *adj.* that cannot or may not be attributed to a particular source etc. □□ **non-attributably** *adv.*

non-availability /nónnəváyləbílliti/ *n.* a state of not being available.

non-believer /nónbiléevər/ *n.* a person who does not believe or has no (esp. religious) faith.
■ unbeliever, disbeliever, cynic, doubting Thomas, doubter, sceptic, freethinker, agnostic, atheist, nullifidian; infidel, heathen, pagan.

non-belligerency /nónbəlíjərənsi/ *n.* a lack of belligerency.

non-belligerent /nónbəlíjərənt/ *adj.* & *n.* ● *adj.* not engaged in hostilities. ● *n.* a non-belligerent nation, State, etc.

non-biological /nónbī́əlójik'l/ *adj.* not concerned with biology or living organisms.

non-Black /nónblák/ *adj.* & *n.* ● *adj.* **1** (of a person) not Black. **2** of or relating to non-Black people. ● *n.* a non-Black person.

non-breakable /nónbráykəb'l/ *adj.* not breakable.
■ see INDESTRUCTIBLE.

non-capital /nónkáppit'l/ *adj.* (of an offence) not punishable by death.

non-Catholic /nónkáthəlik, -káthlik/ *adj.* & *n.* ● *adj.* not Roman Catholic. ● *n.* a non-Catholic person.

nonce /nonss/ *n.* □ **for the nonce** for the time being; for the present occasion. **nonce-word** a word coined for one occasion. [ME *for than anes* (unrecorded) = for the one, altered by wrong division (cf. NEWT)]
■ □ **for the nonce** see *for the time being* (TIME).

nonchalant /nónshələnt/ *adj.* calm and casual, unmoved, unexcited, indifferent. □□ **nonchalance** *n.* **nonchalantly** *adv.* [F, part. of *nonchaloir* f. *chaloir* be concerned]
■ cool, unexcited, unexcitable, unperturbed, imperturbable, undisturbed, untroubled, unruffled, dispassionate, unemotional, phlegmatic, detached, distant, unconcerned, indifferent, insouciant, uninterested, aloof, blasé, offhand, calm, collected, composed, serene, easygoing, free and easy, happy-go-lucky, casual, relaxed, at ease, *colloq.* unflappable, laid-back, together; unenthusiastic, apathetic.

non-Christian /nónkrístyən, -kriss-chən/ *adj.* & *n.* ● *adj.* not Christian. ● *n.* a non-Christian person.

non-citizen /nónsittiz'n/ *n.* a person who is not a citizen (of a particular State, town, etc.).

non-classified /nónklássifīd/ *adj.* (esp. of information) that is not classified. ¶ Neutral in sense: see NON- 6, UNCLASSIFIED.

non-clerical /nónklérrik'l/ *adj.* not doing or involving clerical work.

non-collegiate /nónkəleéjət/ *adj.* **1** not attached to a college. **2** not having colleges.

non-com /nónkom/ *n. colloq.* a non-commissioned officer. [abbr.]

non-combatant /nónkómbət'nt/ *n.* a person not fighting in a war, esp. a civilian, army chaplain, etc.

non-commissioned /nónkəmish'nd/ *adj. Mil.* (of an officer) not holding a commission.

noncommittal /nónkəmítt'l/ *adj.* avoiding commitment to a definite opinion or course of action. □□ **noncommittally** *adv.*

▪ wary, cautious, careful, gingerly, guarded, circumspect, watchful, prudent, canny, tentative, on guard, reserved, cool.

non-communicant /nónkəmyóonikənt/ *n.* a person who is not a communicant (esp. in the religious sense).

non-communicating /nónkəmyóonikayting/ *adj.* that does not communicate.

non-communist /nónkómyoonist/ *adj.* & *n.* (also **non-Communist** with ref. to a particular party) ● *adj.* not advocating or practising communism. ● *n.* a non-communist person.

non-compliance /nónkəmplíənss/ *n.* failure to comply; a lack of compliance.

▪ disobedience, nonconformity, non-observance, nonfeasance, disregard, non-cooperation, rejection, refusal, denial.

non compos mentis /nón komposs méntiss/ *adj.* (also ***non compos***) not in one's right mind. [L, = not having control of one's mind]

non-conductor /nónkəndúktər/ *n.* a substance that does not conduct heat or electricity. □□ **non-conducting** *adj.*

non-confidential /nónkonfidénsh'l/ *adj.* not confidential. □□ **non-confidentially** *adv.*

nonconformist /nónkənfórmist/ *n.* **1** a person who does not conform to the doctrine or discipline of an established Church, esp. (**Nonconformist**) a member of a (usu. Protestant) sect dissenting from the Anglican Church. **2** a person who does not conform to a prevailing principle. □□ **nonconformism** *n.* **Nonconformism** *n.*

▪ **2** renegade, maverick, rebel, radical, individualist, heretic, dissenter, dissident, iconoclast, loner, exception, anomaly; eccentric.

nonconformity /nónkənfórmiti/ *n.* **1 a** nonconformists as a body, esp. (**Nonconformity**) Protestants dissenting from the Anglican Church. **b** the principles or practice of nonconformists, esp. (**Nonconformity**) Protestant dissent. **2** (usu. foll. by *to*) failure to conform to a rule etc. **3** lack of correspondence between things.

▪ **2** see NON-COMPLIANCE. **3** see *disagreement* (DISAGREE).

non-contagious /nónkəntáyjəss/ *adj.* not contagious.

non-content /nónkəntent/ *n. Brit.* a negative voter in the House of Lords.

non-contentious /nónkənténshəss/ *adj.* not contentious.

non-contributory /nónkəntríbyootəri/ *adj.* not contributing or (esp. of a pension scheme) involving contributions.

non-controversial /nónkóntrəvérsh'l/ *adj.* not controversial. ¶ Neutral in sense: see NON- 6, UNCONTROVERSIAL.

non-cooperation /nónkō-ópperáysh'n/ *n.* failure to cooperate; a lack of cooperation.

▪ see NON-COMPLIANCE.

non-delivery /nóndilívvəri/ *n.* failure to deliver.

non-denominational /nóndinómminávshən'l/ *adj.* not restricted as regards religious denomination.

▪ ecumenical.

nondescript /nóndiskript/ *adj.* & *n.* ● *adj.* lacking distinctive characteristics, not easily classified, neither one thing nor another. ● *n.* a nondescript person or thing. □□ **nondescriptly** *adv.* **nondescriptness** *n.* [NON- + *descript* described f. L *descriptus* (as DESCRIBE)]

▪ *adj.* indescribable, unclassifiable, unclassified; ordinary, common, commonplace, unremarkable, colourless, drab, everyday, bland, uninteresting, insipid, characterless, undistinctive, unexceptional.

non-destructive /nóndistrúktiv/ *adj.* that does not involve destruction or damage.

non-drinker /nóndríngkər/ *n.* a person who does not drink alcoholic liquor.

▪ abstainer, teetotaller, *Austral. sl.* wowser.

non-driver /nóndrívər/ *n.* a person who does not drive a motor vehicle.

none[1] /nun/ *pron.*, *adj.*, & *adv.* ● *pron.* **1** (foll. by *of*) **a** not any of (*none of this concerns me*; *none of them have found it*; *none of your impudence!*). **b** not any one of (*none of them has come*). ¶ The verb following *none* in this sense can be singular or plural according to the sense. **2 a** no persons (*none but fools have ever believed it*). **b** no person (*none can tell*). ● *adj.* (usu. with a preceding noun implied) **1** no; not any (*you have money and I have none*; *would rather have a bad reputation than none at all*). **2** not to be counted in a specified class (*his understanding is none of the clearest*; *if a linguist is wanted, I am none*). ● *adv.* (foll. by *the* + compar., or *so*, *too*) by no amount; not at all (*am none the wiser*; *are none too fond of him*). □ **none the less** nevertheless. **none other** (usu. foll. by *than*) no other person. **none-so-pretty** London Pride. [OE *nān* f. *ne* not + *ān* ONE]

▪ *pron.* no one, not anyone, nobody, no person; not one; not any. □ **none the less** see NEVERTHELESS.

none[2] /nōn/ *n.* (also in *pl.*) **1** the office of the fifth of the canonical hours of prayer, orig. said at the ninth hour (3 p.m.). **2** this hour. [F f. L *nona* fem. sing. of *nonus* ninth: cf. NOON]

non-earning /nón-érning/ *adj.* not earning (esp. a regular wage or salary).

▪ unwaged.

non-effective /nónniféktiv/ *adj.* that does not have an effect. ¶ Neutral in sense: see NON- 6, INEFFECTIVE.

non-ego /nón-éegō/ *n. Philos.* all that is not the conscious self.

nonentity /nonéntiti/ *n.* (*pl.* **-ies**) **1** a person or thing of no importance. **2 a** non-existence. **b** a non-existent thing, a figment. [med.L *nonentitas* non-existence]

▪ **1** see NOBODY *n.*

nones /nōnz/ *n.pl.* in the ancient Roman calendar, the ninth day before the ides by inclusive reckoning, i.e. the 7th day of March, May, July, October, the 5th of other months. [OF *nones* f. L *nonae* fem. pl. of *nonus* ninth]

non-essential /nónnisénsh'l/ *adj.* not essential. ¶ Neutral in sense: see NON- 6, INESSENTIAL.

▪ unessential, inessential, non-requisite; dispensable, expendable; extra, optional; luxury.

nonesuch var. of NONSUCH.

nonet /nōnét/ *n.* **1** *Mus.* **a** a composition for nine voices or instruments. **b** the performers of such a piece. **2** a group of nine. [It. *nonetto* f. *nono* ninth f. L *nonus*]

nonetheless var. of *none the less*.

non-Euclidean /nónyooklíddiən/ *adj.* denying or going beyond Euclidean principles in geometry.

non-European /nónyoorəpéeən/ *adj.* & *n.* ● *adj.* not European. ● *n.* a non-European person.

non-event /nónnivént/ *n.* an unimportant or anticlimactic occurrence.

▪ anticlimax, damp squib, lead balloon, *colloq.* non-starter, *sl.* dud.

non-existent /nónnigzístənt/ *adj.* not existing. □□ **non-existence** *n.*

▪ unreal, imaginary, imagined, fictional, fictive, fanciful, fancied, mythical, fabulous, fabled, illusory, chimerical, delusive. □□ **non-existence** nonentity; see also NOTHING *n.* 4.

non-explosive /nónniksplósiv/ *adj.* (of a substance) that does not explode.

non-fattening /nónfátt'ning/ *adj.* (of food) that does not fatten.
■ low-calorie, low-fat, low-sugar; diet, light, healthy.
nonfeasance /nónféez'nss/ *n.* failure to perform an act required by law. [NON-: see MISFEASANCE]
non-ferrous /nónférrəss/ *adj.* (of a metal) other than iron or steel.
non-fiction /nónfiksh'n/ *n.* literary work other than fiction, including biography and reference books. ▫▫ **non-fictional** *adj.*
non-flam /nónflám/ *adj.* = NON-FLAMMABLE.
non-flammable /nónflámməb'l/ *adj.* not inflammable.
■ see INCOMBUSTIBLE.
non-fulfilment /nónfŏŏlfilmənt/ *n.* failure to fulfil (an obligation).
■ non-completion, breach; failure.
non-functional /nónfúngkshən'l/ *adj.* not having a function.
nong /nong/ *n. Austral. sl.* a foolish or stupid person. [20th c.: orig. unkn.]
■ see SILLY *n.*
non-governmental /nón-guvərnmént'l/ *adj.* not belonging to or associated with a government.
non-human /nónhyŏŏmən/ *adj.* & *n.* ● *adj.* (of a being) not human. ● *n.* a non-human being. ¶ Neutral in sense: see NON- 6, INHUMAN, UNHUMAN.
non-infectious /nónninfékshəss/ *adj.* (of a disease) not infectious.
non-inflected /nónninfléktid/ *adj.* (of a language) not having inflections.
non-interference /nónnintərféerənss/ *n.* a lack of interference.
■ see *laissez-faire.*
non-intervention /nónnintərvénsh'n/ *n.* the principle or practice of not becoming involved in others' affairs, esp. by one State in regard to another.
non-intoxicating /nónnintóksikayting/ *adj.* (of drink) not causing intoxication.
■ soft, non-alcoholic, dealcoholized; low-alcohol.
non-iron /nón-ī́rn/ *adj.* (of a fabric) that needs no ironing.
nonjoinder /nónjóyndər/ *n. Law* the failure of a partner etc. to become a party to a suit.
nonjuror /nónjŏŏrər/ *n.* a person who refuses to take an oath, esp. *hist.* a member of the clergy refusing to take the oath of allegiance to William and Mary in 1689. ▫▫ **nonjuring** *adj.*
non-jury /nónjŏŏri/ *adj.* (of a trial) without a jury.
non-linear /nónlinniər/ *adj.* not linear, esp. with regard to dimension.
non-literary /nónlíttərəri/ *adj.* (of writing, a text, etc.) not literary in character.
non-logical /nónlójik'l/ *adj.* not involving logic. ¶ Neutral in sense: see NON- 6, ILLOGICAL. ▫▫ **non-logically** *adv.*
non-magnetic /nónmagnéttik/ *adj.* (of a substance) not magnetic.
non-member /nónmémbər/ *n.* a person who is not a member (of a particular association, club, etc.). ▫▫ **non-membership** *n.*
■ see OUTSIDER 1, 2.
non-metal /nónmétt'l/ *adj.* not made of metal. ▫▫ **non-metallic** /-mitállik/ *adj.*
non-militant /nónmíllit'nt/ *adj.* not militant.
■ moderate, middle-of-the road; see also MEEK, MODERATE *adj.* 1.
non-military /nónmíllitəri, -tri/ *adj.* not military; not involving armed forces, civilian.
■ civil, civilian.
non-ministerial /nónministéeriəl/ *adj.* not ministerial (esp. in political senses).
non-moral /nónmórrəl/ *adj.* not concerned with morality. ¶ Neutral in sense: see NON- 6, AMORAL, IMMORAL. ▫▫ **non-morally** *adv.*
non-natural /nón-náchərəl/ *adj.* not involving natural means or processes. ¶ Neutral in sense: see NON- 6, UNNATURAL.
non-negotiable /nón-nigṓshəb'l, -siəb'l/ *adj.* that cannot be negotiated (esp. in financial senses).
■ see INALIENABLE.
non-net /nón-nét/ *adj.* (of a book) not subject to a minimum selling price.
non-nuclear /nón-nyŏŏkliər/ *adj.* **1** not involving nuclei or nuclear energy. **2** (of a State etc.) not having nuclear weapons.
non-observance /nónnəbzérv'nss/ *n.* failure to observe (esp. an agreement, requirement, etc.).
■ see NON-COMPLIANCE.
non-operational /nónnopəráyshən'l/ *adj.* **1** that does not operate. **2** out of order.
non-organic /nónnorgánnik/ *adj.* not organic. ¶ Neutral in sense: see NON- 6, INORGANIC.
nonpareil /nónpərəl, nónpəráyl/ *adj.* & *n.* ● *adj.* unrivalled or unique. ● *n.* such a person or thing. [F f. *pareil* equal f. pop.L *pariculus* dimin. of L *par*]
■ *n.* paragon, model, standard, *ne plus ultra*, exemplar, ideal, nonsuch, *colloq.* one-off, *Brit. sl.* oner.
non-participating /nónpaartíssipayting/ *adj.* not taking part.
non-partisan /nónpaartizán/ *adj.* not partisan.
■ non-aligned, unaligned, unaffiliated, independent, uncommitted, neutral, uninvolved, free, on the fence; impartial, even-handed, fair, just, objective, unbiased, unprejudiced, equitable, dispassionate, disinterested.
non-party /nónpaarti/ *adj.* independent of political parties.
non-payment /nónpáymənt/ *n.* failure to pay; a lack of payment.
■ see DEFAULT *n.* 1.
non-person /nónpers'n/ *n.* a person regarded as non-existent or insignificant (cf. UNPERSON).
non-personal /nónpérsən'l/ *adj.* not personal. ¶ Neutral in sense: see NON- 6, IMPERSONAL.
non-physical /nónfízzik'l/ *adj.* not physical. ▫▫ **non-physically** *adv.*
■ incorporeal, immaterial; mental, psychological; spiritual, ethereal; platonic.
non placet /non pláyset/ *n.* a negative vote in a Church or university assembly. [L, = it does not please]
non-playing /nónpláying/ *adj.* that does not play or take part (in a game etc.).
nonplus /nonplúss/ *v.* & *n.* ● *v.tr.* (**nonplussed, non-plussing**) completely perplex. ● *n.* a state of perplexity, a standstill (*at a nonplus; reduce to a nonplus*). [L *non plus* not more]
■ *v.* confound, perplex, puzzle, confuse, dismay, baffle, stop, check, stun, shock, dumbfound, take aback, astonish, astound, stump, *colloq.* faze, flummox.
non-poisonous /nónpóyzənəss/ *adj.* (of a substance) not poisonous.
■ see HARMLESS 1.
non-political /nónpəlíttik'l/ *adj.* not political; not involved in politics.
non-porous /nónpórəss/ *adj.* (of a substance) not porous.
non possumus /non póssyoomәss/ *n.* a statement of inability to act in a matter. [L, = we cannot]
non-productive /nónprədúktiv/ *adj.* not productive. ¶ Neutral in sense: see NON- 6, UNPRODUCTIVE. ▫▫ **non-productively** *adv.*
■ unproductive; non-operational.
non-professional /nónprəféshən'l/ *adj.* not professional (esp. in status). ¶ Neutral in sense: see NON- 6, UNPROFESSIONAL.
■ see AMATEUR *adj.*
non-profit /nónpróffit/ *adj.* not involving or making a profit.
■ see NON-PROFIT-MAKING.
non-profit-making /nónpróffitmayking/ *adj.* (of an enterprise) not conducted primarily to make a profit.

■ non-profit, self-financing, non-commercial, uncommercial, charitable.

non-proliferation /nónpralíffəráysh'n/ *n.* the prevention of an increase in something, esp. possession of nuclear weapons.

non-racial /nónráysh'l/ *adj.* not involving race or racial factors.

non-reader /nónreédər/ *n.* a person who cannot or does not read.

non-resident /nónrézzid'nt/ *adj.* & *n.* ● *adj.* **1** not residing in a particular place, esp. (of a member of the clergy) not residing where his or her duties require. **2** (of a post) not requiring the holder to reside at the place of work. ● *n.* a non-resident person, esp. a person using some of the facilities of a hotel. □□ **non-residence** *n.* **non-residential** /-dénsh'l/ *adj.*

non-resistance /nónrizístənss/ *n.* failure to resist; a lack of resistance.

non-returnable /nónritúrnəb'l/ *adj.* that may or need or will not be returned.

■ see DISPOSABLE *adj.* 1.

non-rigid /nónríjid/ *adj.* (esp. of materials) not rigid.

■ see FLEXIBLE.

non-scientific /nónsīəntíffik/ *adj.* not involving science or scientific methods. ¶ Neutral in sense: see NON- 6, UNSCIENTIFIC. □□ **non-scientist** /-sīəntist/ *n.*

non-sectarian /nónsektáiriən/ *adj.* not sectarian.

nonsense /nónsənss/ *n.* **1 a** (often as *int.*) absurd or meaningless words or ideas; foolish or extravagant conduct. **b** an instance of this. **2** a scheme, arrangement, etc., that one disapproves of. **3** (often *attrib.*) a form of literature meant to amuse by absurdity (*nonsense verse*). □□ **nonsensical** /-sénsik'l/ *adj.* **nonsensicality** /nónsensikálliti/ *n.* (*pl.* **-ies**). **nonsensically** /-sénsikəli/ *adv.*

■ **1** rubbish, drivel, gibberish, stuff and nonsense, garbage, twaddle, trash, babble, balderdash, moonshine, puffery, flummery, blather, cackle, bunkum, jargon, mumbo-jumbo, palaver, claptrap, jabberwocky, *colloq.* gobbledegook, piffle, hogwash, malarkey, tosh, gammon, tripe, *esp. Brit. colloq.* waffle, *Brit. colloq.* double Dutch, *sl.* poppycock, gas, bunk, rot, (Irish) bull, hooey, bosh, eyewash, bilge, boloney, hot air, *Brit sl.* (a load of (old)) cobblers; mischief, clowning, antics, capering, horseplay, pranks, tricks, jokes, silliness, foolishness, inanity, frivolity, tomfoolery, joking, jesting, waggishness, buffoonery, *colloq.* shenanigan(s), monkey business, monkey tricks, *US colloq.* monkeyshines. □□ **nonsensical** senseless, meaningless, absurd, ridiculous, ludicrous, laughable, preposterous, irrational, askew, mad, silly, foolish, hare-brained, asinine, idiotic, stupid, dumb, *colloq.* crazy, moronic, imbecilic, cock-eyed, *US colloq.* fool, *sl.* nutty, screwy, loony, *US sl.* screwball.

non sequitur /non sékwitər/ *n.* a conclusion that does not logically follow from the premisses. [L, = it does not follow]

non-sexual /nónséksyooəl, -sékshooəl/ *adj.* not based on or involving sex. □□ **non-sexually** *adv.*

■ see PLATONIC 2.

non-skid /nónskíd/ *adj.* **1** that does not skid. **2** that inhibits skidding.

non-slip /nónslíp/ *adj.* **1** that does not slip. **2** that inhibits slipping.

non-smoker /nónsmṓkər/ *n.* **1** a person who does not smoke. **2** a train compartment etc. in which smoking is forbidden. □□ **non-smoking** *adj.* & *n.*

non-soluble /nónsólyoob'l/ *adj.* (esp. of a substance) not soluble. ¶ Neutral in sense: see NON- 6, INSOLUBLE.

non-specialist /nónspéshəlist/ *n.* a person who is not a specialist (in a particular subject).

■ see AMATEUR *n.*

non-specific /nónspisíffik/ *adj.* that cannot be specified.

■ see VAGUE 1.

non-standard /nónstándərd/ *adj.* not standard.

non-starter /nónstaártər/ *n.* **1** a person or animal that does not start in a race. **2** *colloq.* a person or thing that is unlikely to succeed or be effective.

■ **2** see FAILURE *n.* 2.

non-stick /nónstík/ *adj.* **1** that does not stick. **2** that does not allow things to stick to it.

non-stop /nónstóp/ *adj.*, *adv.*, & *n.* ● *adj.* **1** (of a train etc.) not stopping at intermediate places. **2** (of a journey, performance, etc.) done without a stop or intermission. ● *adv.* without stopping or pausing. ● *n.* a non-stop train etc.

■ *adj.* uninterrupted, continuous, unbroken, direct; unending, endless, interminable, unceasing, ceaseless, continual, persistent, relentless, constant, unremitting, steady, round-the-clock, ongoing, continuing, unhesitating, unfaltering, tireless; regular, habitual. ● *adv.* unendingly, endlessly, interminably, unceasingly, ceaselessly, continually, continuously, uninterruptedly, persistently, relentlessly, constantly, unremittingly, steadily, round the clock, day in day out, tirelessly; regularly, habitually.

non-subscriber /nónsəbskrībər/ *n.* a person who is not a subscriber.

nonsuch /núnsuch/ *n.* (also **nonesuch**) **1** a person or thing that is unrivalled, a paragon. **2** a leguminous plant, *Medicago lupulina*, with black pods. [NONE[1] + SUCH, usu. now assim. to NON-]

nonsuit /nónsyo͞ot, -so͞ot/ *n.* & *v. Law* ● *n.* the stoppage of a suit by the judge when the plaintiff fails to make out a legal case or to bring sufficient evidence. ● *v.tr.* subject (a plaintiff) to a nonsuit. [ME f. AF *no(u)nsuit*]

non-swimmer /nónswímmər/ *n.* a person who cannot swim.

non-technical /nóntéknik'l/ *adj.* **1** not technical. **2** without technical knowledge.

■ **1** unspecialized, non-specialist, everyday, ordinary; understandable, accessible. **2** lay, amateur; uninitiated, untrained; unskilled.

non-toxic /nóntóksik/ *adj.* not toxic.

■ see HARMLESS 1.

non-transferable /nóntránsférəb'l, -traánsférəb'l/ *adj.* that may not be transferred.

non-U /nónyo͞o/ *adj. colloq.* not characteristic of the upper class. [NON- + U[2]]

non-uniform /nónyo͞oniform/ *adj.* not uniform.

non-union /nónyo͞oniən/ *adj.* **1** not belonging to a trade union. **2** not done or produced by members of a trade union.

non-usage /nónyo͞ozij, -yo͞ossij/ *n.* failure to use.

non-use /nónyo͞oss/ *n.* failure to use.

non-user /nónyo͞ozər/ *n. Law* the failure to use a right, by which it may be lost. [AF *nounuser* (unrecorded) (as NON-, USER)]

non-verbal /nónvérb'l/ *adj.* not involving words or speech. □□ **non-verbally** *adv.*

non-vintage /nónvíntij/ *adj.* (of wine etc.) not vintage.

non-violence /nónvīələnss/ *n.* the avoidance of violence, esp. as a principle. □□ **non-violent** *adj.*

■ non-resistance; ahimsa; pacifism; passive resistance, *Ind.* satyagraha. □□ **non-violent** see PEACEABLE 1.

non-volatile /nónvóllətīl/ *adj.* (esp. of a substance) not volatile.

non-voting /nónvṓting/ *adj.* not having or using a vote. □□ **non-voter** *n.*

non-White /nónwīt/ *adj.* & *n.* ● *adj.* **1** (of a person) not White. **2** of or relating to non-White people. ● *n.* a non-White person.

non-word /nónwurd/ *n.* an unrecorded or unused word.

noodle[1] /no͞od'l/ *n.* a strip or ring of pasta. [G *Nudel*]

noodle[2] /no͞od'l/ *n.* **1** a simpleton. **2** *sl.* the head. [18th c.: orig. unkn.]

■ **1** see SAP[3]. **2** see HEAD *n.* 1.

nook /no͝ok/ *n.* a corner or recess; a secluded place. □ **in every nook and cranny** everywhere. [ME *nok(e)* corner, of unkn. orig.]

■ cranny, recess, niche, alcove, corner, cavity, crevice,

crack, opening; retreat, bolt-hole, hideaway, nest, *colloq.* hide-out; inglenook.

nooky /nŏŏkki/ *n.* (also **nookie**) *sl.* sexual intercourse. [20th c.: perh. f. NOOK]

noon /nōōn/ *n.* **1** twelve o'clock in the day, midday. **2** the culminating point. [OE *nōn* f. L *nona (hora)* ninth hour: orig. = 3 p.m. (cf. NONE[2])]
▪ **1** twelve o'clock, midday, 1200 hours, twelve noon, noontide, noontime, noonday, high noon.

noonday /nŏŏnday/ *n.* midday.
▪ see NOON.

no one /nṓ wun/ *n.* no person; nobody.

noontide /nŏŏntīd/ *n.* (also **noontime** /-tīm/) midday.
▪ see NOON.

noose /nōōss/ *n.* & *v.* ● *n.* **1** a loop with a running knot, tightening as the rope or wire is pulled, esp. in a snare, lasso, or hangman's halter. **2** a snare or bond. **3** *joc.* the marriage tie. ● *v.tr.* **1** catch with or enclose in a noose, ensnare. **2 a** make a noose on (a cord). **b** (often foll. by *round*) arrange (a cord) in a noose. □ **put one's head in a noose** bring about one's own downfall. [ME *nose*, perh. f. OF *no(u)s* f. L *nodus* knot]
▪ *n.* **1** see LOOP *n.* **2** see SNARE *n.* 1.

nopal /nṓp'l/ *n.* any American cactus of the genus *Nopalea*, esp. *N. cochinellifera* grown in plantations for breeding cochineal. [F & Sp. f. Nahuatl *nopalli* cactus]

nope /nōp/ *adv. colloq.* = NO[2] *adv.* 1. [NO[2]]

nor /nor, nər/ *conj.* **1** and not; and not either (*neither one thing nor the other; not a man nor a child was to be seen; I said I had not seen it, nor had I; all that is true, nor must we forget ...; can neither read nor write*). **2** and no more; neither (*'I cannot go' – 'Nor can I'*). □ **nor ... nor ...** *poet.* or *archaic* neither ... nor ... [ME, contr. f. obs. *nother* f. OE *nawther*, *nāhwæther* (as NO[2], WHETHER)]

nor' /nor/ *n., adj.,* & *adv.* (esp. in compounds) = NORTH (*nor'ward; nor'wester*). [abbr.]

noradrenalin /nórədrénnəlin/ *n.* (also **noradrenaline**) a hormone released by the adrenal medulla and by sympathetic nerve endings as a neurotransmitter. [*nor*mal + ADRENALIN]

Nordic /nórdik/ *adj.* & *n.* ● *adj.* **1** of or relating to the tall blond dolichocephalic Germanic people found in N. Europe, esp. in Scandinavia. **2** of or relating to Scandinavia or Finland. **3** (of skiing) with cross-country work and jumping. ● *n.* a Nordic person, esp. a native of Scandinavia or Finland. [F *nordique* f. *nord* north]

Norfolk jacket /nórfək/ *n.* a man's loose belted jacket, with box pleats. [*Norfolk* in S. England]

nork /nork/ *n.* (usu. in *pl.*) *Austral. sl.* a woman's breast. [20th c.: orig. uncert.]
▪ (*norks*) see BREAST *n.* 1a.

norland /nórlənd/ *n. Brit.* a northern region. [contr. of NORTHLAND]

norm /norm/ *n.* **1** a standard or pattern or type. **2** a standard quantity to be produced or amount of work to be done. **3** customary behaviour etc. [L *norma* carpenter's square]
▪ model, standard, type, pattern, criterion, rule, measure, gauge, yardstick, benchmark; average, mean.

normal /nórm'l/ *adj.* & *n.* ● *adj.* **1** conforming to a standard; regular, usual, typical. **2** free from mental or emotional disorder. **3** *Geom.* (of a line) at right angles, perpendicular. **4** *Chem.* (of a solution) containing one gram-equivalent of solute per litre. ● *n.* **1 a** the normal value of a temperature etc., esp. blood-heat. **b** the usual state, level, etc. **2** *Geom.* a line at right angles. □ **normal distribution** *Statistics* a function that represents the distribution of many random variables as a symmetrical bell-shaped graph. **normal school** (in the US, France, etc.) a school or college for training teachers. □□ **normalcy** *n.* esp. *US.* **normality** /-málliti/ *n.* [F *normal* or L *normalis* (as NORM)]
▪ *adj.* **1** standard, regular, average, conventional, usual, run-of-the-mill, ordinary, routine, universal, general, common, customary, natural, typical, conformist, orthodox. **2** sane, stable, rational, reasonable, well-adjusted; healthy. □ **normal school** teacher training-college, *Brit.* college of education.

normalize /nórməlīz/ *v.* (also **-ise**) **1** *tr.* make normal. **2** *intr.* become normal. **3** *tr.* cause to conform. □□ **normalization** /-záysh'n/ *n.* **normalizer** *n.*
▪ regularize, standardize, regulate, control; conform.

normally /nórməli/ *adv.* **1** in a normal manner. **2** usually.
▪ **2** see *usually* (USUAL).

Norman /nórmən/ *n.* & *adj.* ● *n.* **1** a native or inhabitant of medieval Normandy. **2** a descendant of the people of mixed Scandinavian and Frankish origin established there in the 10th c., who conquered England in 1066. **3** Norman French. **4** *Archit.* the style of Romanesque architecture found in Britain under the Normans. **5** any of the English kings from William I to Stephen. ● *adj.* **1** of or relating to the Normans. **2** of or relating to the Norman style of architecture. □ **Norman Conquest** see CONQUEST. **Norman English** English as spoken or influenced by the Normans. **Norman French** French as spoken by the Normans or (after 1066) in English lawcourts. □□ **Normanesque** /-nésk/ *adj.* **Normanism** *n.* **Normanize** *v.tr.* & *intr.* (also **-ise**). [OF *Normans* pl. of *Normant* f. ON *Northmathr* (as NORTH, MAN)]

normative /nórmətiv/ *adj.* of or establishing a norm. □□ **normatively** *adv.* **normativeness** *n.* [F *normatif -ive* f. L *norma* (see NORM)]

Norn /norn/ *n.* any of three goddesses of destiny in Scandinavian mythology. [ON: orig. unkn.]

Norroy /nórroy/ *n.* (in full **Norroy and Ulster**) *Heraldry* (in the UK) the title given to the third King of Arms, with jurisdiction north of the Trent and (since 1943) in N. Ireland (cf. CLARENCEUX, *King of Arms*). [ME f. AF *norroi* (unrecorded) f. OF *nord* north, *roi* king]

Norse /norss/ *n.* & *adj.* ● *n.* **1 a** the Norwegian language. **b** the Scandinavian language-group. **2** (prec. by *the*; treated as *pl.*) **a** the Norwegians. **b** the Vikings. ● *adj.* of ancient Scandinavia, esp. Norway. □ **Old Norse 1** the Germanic language from which the Scandinavian languages are derived. **2** the language of Norway and its colonies until the 14th c. □□ **Norseman** *n.* (*pl.* **-men**). [Du. *noor(d)sch* f. *noord* north]

north /north/ *n., adj.,* & *adv.* ● *n.* **1 a** the point of the horizon 90° anticlockwise from east. **b** the compass point corresponding to this. **c** the direction in which this lies. **2** (usu. **the North**) **a** the part of the world or a country or a town lying to the north, esp. = *north country* or *Northern States*. **b** the Arctic. **c** the industrialized nations. **3** (**North**) *Bridge* a player occupying the position designated 'north'. ● *adj.* **1** towards, at, near, or facing north. **2** coming from the north (*north wind*). ● *adv.* **1** towards, at, or near the north. **2** (foll. by *of*) further north than. □ **North American** *adj.* of North America. ● *n.* a native or inhabitant of North America, esp. a citizen of the US or Canada. **north and south** lengthwise along a line from north to south. **north by east** (or **west**) between north and north-north-east (or north-north-west). **north country** the northern part of England (north of the Humber). **North-countryman** (*pl.* **-men**) a native of the north country. **north-east** *n.* **1** the point of the horizon midway between north and east. **2** the compass point corresponding to this. **3** the direction in which this lies. ● *adj.* of, towards, or coming from the north-east. ● *adv.* towards, at, or near the north-east. **North-East** the part of a country or town lying to the north-east. **north-easterly** *adj.* & *adv.* = *north-east.* **north-eastern** lying on the north-east side. **north-east passage** a passage for ships along the northern coast of Europe and Asia, formerly thought of as a possible route to the East. **north light** light from the north, esp. as desired by painters and in factory design. **north-north-east** the point or direction midway between north and north-east.

north-north-west the point or direction midway between north and north-west. **North Pole 1** the northernmost point of the earth's axis of rotation. **2** the northernmost point about which the stars appear to revolve. **North Sea** the sea between Britain, the Netherlands, Germany, and Scandinavia. **North Star** the pole star. **north-west** *n.* **1** the point of the horizon midway between north and west. **2** the compass point corresponding to this. **3** the direction in which this lies. ● *adj.* of, towards, or coming from the north-west. ● *adv.* towards, at, or near the north-west. **North-West** the part of a country or town lying to the north-west. **north-westerly** *adj.* & *adv.* = *north-west.* **north-western** lying on the north-west side. **north-west passage** a passage for ships along the northern coast of America, formerly thought of as a possible route from the Atlantic to the Pacific. **to the north** (often foll. by *of*) in a northerly direction. [OE f. Gmc]

Northants /nórthánts/ *abbr.* Northamptonshire.

northbound /nórthbownd/ *adj.* travelling or leading northwards.

northeaster /nórthe͞estər/ *n.* a north-east wind.

norther /nórthər/ *n. US* a strong cold north wind blowing in autumn and winter over Texas, Florida, and the Gulf of Mexico.

northerly /nórthərli/ *adj., adv.,* & *n.* ● *adj.* & *adv.* **1** in a northern position or direction. **2** (of wind) blowing from the north. ● *n.* (*pl.* **-ies**) (usu. in *pl.*) a wind blowing from the north.

■ *adj.* **1** north, northern, northward(s), northbound.

northern /nórthərn/ *adj.* **1** of or in the north; inhabiting the north. **2** lying or directed towards the north. □ **Northern hemisphere** the half of the earth north of the equator. **northern lights** the aurora borealis. **Northern States** the States in the north of the US. □□ **northernmost** *adj.* [OE *northerne* (as NORTH, -ERN)]

■ northerly, north; northward(s), northbound.

northerner /nórthərnər/ *n.* a native or inhabitant of the north.

northing /nórthing/ *n. Naut.* the distance travelled or measured northward.

Northland /nórthlənd/ *n. poet.* the northern lands; the northern part of a country. [OE (as NORTH, LAND)]

Northman /nórthmən/ *n.* (*pl.* **-men**) a native of Scandinavia, esp. of Norway. [OE]

Northumb. *abbr.* Northumberland.

Northumbrian /northúmbriən/ *adj.* & *n.* ● *adj.* of or relating to ancient Northumbria (England north of the Humber) or modern Northumberland. ● *n.* **1** a native of ancient Northumbria or modern Northumberland. **2** the dialect of ancient Northumbria or modern Northumberland. [obs. *Northumber*, persons living beyond the Humber, f. OE *Northhymbre*]

northward /nórthwərd/ *adj., adv.,* & *n.* ● *adj.* & *adv.* (also **northwards**) towards the north. ● *n.* a northward direction or region.

northwester /nórthwéstər/ *n.* a north-west wind.

Norway lobster /nórway/ *n.* a European lobster, *Nephrops norvegicus*, eaten as scampi. [*Norway* in N. Europe]

Norway rat /nórway/ *n.* the common brown rat, *Rattus norvegicus*.

Norwegian /norwe͞ejən/ *n.* & *adj.* ● *n.* **1 a** a native or national of Norway. **b** a person of Norwegian descent. **2** the language of Norway. ● *adj.* of or relating to Norway or its people or language. [med.L *Norvegia* f. ON *Norvegr* (as NORTH, WAY), assim. to *Norway*]

nor'-wester /nórwéstər/ *n.* **1** a northwester. **2** a glass of strong liquor. **3** an oilskin hat, a sou'wester. [contr.]

Nos. *abbr.* numbers. [cf. No.]

nose /nōz/ *n.* & *v.* ● *n.* **1** an organ above the mouth on the face or head of a human or animal, containing nostrils and used for smelling and breathing. **2 a** the sense of smell (*dogs have a good nose*). **b** the ability to detect a particular thing (*a nose for scandal*). **3** the odour or perfume of wine, tea, tobacco, hay, etc. **4** the open end or nozzle of a tube, pipe, pair of bellows, retort, etc. **5 a** the front end or projecting part of a thing, e.g. of a car or aircraft. **b** = NOSING. **6** *sl.* an informer of the police. ● *v.* **1** *tr.* (often foll. by *out*) **a** perceive the smell of, discover by smell. **b** detect. **2** *tr.* thrust or rub one's nose against or into, esp. in order to smell. **3** *intr.* (usu. foll. by *about*, *around*, etc.) pry or search. **4 a** *intr.* make one's way cautiously forward. **b** *tr.* make (one's or its way). □ **as plain as the nose on your face** easily seen. **by a nose** by a very narrow margin (*won the race by a nose*). **count noses** count those present, one's supporters, etc.; decide a question by mere numbers. **cut off one's nose to spite one's face** disadvantage oneself in the course of trying to disadvantage another. **get up a person's nose** *sl.* annoy a person. **keep one's nose clean** *sl.* stay out of trouble, behave properly. **keep one's nose to the grindstone** see GRINDSTONE. **nose-cone** the cone-shaped nose of a rocket etc. **nose-flute** a musical instrument blown with the nose in Fiji etc. **nose leaf** a fleshy part on the nostrils of some bats, used for echo location. **nose-monkey** the proboscis monkey. **nose-piece 1** = NOSEBAND. **2** the part of a helmet etc. protecting the nose. **3** the part of a microscope to which the object-glass is attached. **nose-rag** *sl.* a pocket handkerchief. **nose-to-tail** (of vehicles) moving or stationary one close behind another, esp. in heavy traffic. **nose-wheel** a landing-wheel under the nose of an aircraft. **on the nose 1** *US sl.* precisely. **2** *Austral. sl.* annoying. **3** *Austral. sl.* stinking. **put a person's nose out of joint** *colloq.* embarrass, disconcert, frustrate, or supplant a person. **rub a person's nose in it** see RUB. **see no further than one's nose** be short-sighted, esp. in foreseeing the consequences of one's actions etc. **speak through one's nose** pronounce words with a nasal twang. **turn up one's nose** (usu. foll. by *at*) *colloq.* show disdain. **under a person's nose** *colloq.* right before a person (esp. of defiant or unnoticed actions). **with one's nose in the air** haughtily. □□ **nosed** *adj.* (also in *comb.*). **noseless** *adj.* [OE *nosu*]

■ *n.* **3** see PERFUME *n.* 1. ● *v.* **3** see ROOT[2] *v.* 2a. □ **on the nose 1** see *spot on adv.* **put a person's nose out of joint** see OFFEND 1, 2; DISPOSSESS 1.

nosebag /nōzbag/ *n.* a bag containing fodder, hung on a horse's head.

noseband /nōzband/ *n.* the lower band of a bridle, passing over the horse's nose.

nosebleed /nōzbleed/ *n.* an instance of bleeding from the nose.

nosedive /nōzdīv/ *n.* & *v.* ● *n.* **1** a steep downward plunge by an aeroplane. **2** a sudden plunge or drop. ● *v.intr.* make a nosedive.

■ *n.* see PLUNGE *n.* ● *v.* see PLUNGE *v.* 1b.

nosegay /nōzgay/ *n.* a bunch of flowers, esp. a sweet-scented posy. [NOSE + GAY in obs. use = ornament]

■ see BOUQUET *n.* 1.

nosepipe /nōzpīp/ *n.* a piece of piping used as a nozzle.

nosering /nōzring/ *n.* a ring fixed in the nose of an animal (esp. a bull) for leading it, or of a person for ornament.

nosey var. of NOSY.

nosh /nosh/ *v.* & *n. sl.* ● *v.tr.* & *intr.* **1** eat or drink. **2** *US* eat between meals. ● *n.* **1** food or drink. **2** *US* a snack. □ **nosh-up** *Brit.* a large meal. [Yiddish]

■ *v.* **1** see EAT *v.* 1. **2** snack, nibble, pick. ● *n.* **1** see REFRESHMENT 2. **2** see SNACK *n.* 1, 2.

noshery /nóshəri/ *n.* (*pl.* **-ies**) *sl.* a restaurant or snack bar.

nosing /nōzing/ *n.* a rounded edge of a step, moulding, etc., or a metal shield for it.

nosography /nəsógrəfi/ *n.* the systematic description of diseases. [Gk *nosos* disease + -GRAPHY]

nosology /nəsólləji/ *n.* the branch of medical science dealing with the classification of diseases. □□ **nosological** /nóssəlójik'l/ *adj.* [Gk *nosos* disease + -LOGY]

nostalgia /nostáljiə, -jə/ *n.* **1** (often foll. by *for*) sentimental yearning for a period of the past. **2** regretful or wistful memory of an earlier time. **3** severe homesickness. □□ **nostalgic** *adj.* **nostalgically** *adv.* [mod.L f. Gk *nostos* return home]

■ **1, 2** see *sentimentality* (SENTIMENTAL), LONGING *n.* □□ **nostalgic** see HOMESICK, WISTFUL.

nostoc /nóstok/ *n.* any gelatinous blue-green unicellular alga of the genus *Nostoc*, that can fix nitrogen from the atmosphere. [name invented by Paracelsus]

Nostradamus /nóstrədaáməss/ *n.* a person who claims to foretell future events. [Latinized form of the name of M. de *Nostredame*, French astrologer and physician d. 1566]

nostril /nóstril/ *n.* either of two external openings of the nasal cavity in vertebrates that admit air to the lungs and smells to the olfactory nerves. □□ **nostrilled** *adj.* (also in *comb.*). [OE *nosthyrl*, *nosterl* f. *nosu* NOSE + *thȳr(e)l* hole: cf. THRILL]

nostrum /nóstrəm/ *n.* **1** a quack remedy, a patent medicine, esp. one prepared by the person recommending it. **2** a pet scheme, esp. for political or social reform. [L, neut. of *noster* our, used in sense 'of our own make']

■ **1** see MEDICINE 2, ELIXIR 1c.

nosy /nṓzi/ *adj.* & *n.* (also **nosey**) ● *adj.* (**nosier, nosiest**) **1** *colloq.* inquisitive, prying. **2** having a large nose. **3** having a distinctive (good or bad) smell. ● *n.* (*pl.* **-ies**) a person with a large nose. □ **Nosy Parker** esp. *Brit. colloq.* a busybody. □□ **nosily** *adv.* **nosiness** *n.*

■ *adj.* **1** curious, inquisitive, prying, meddlesome, spying, peeping, eavesdropping, *colloq.* snooping, snoopy. □ **Nosy Parker** see BUSYBODY 1.

not /not/ *adv.* expressing negation, esp.: **1** (also **n't** joined to a preceding verb) following an auxiliary verb or *be* or (in a question) the subject of such a verb (*I cannot say*; *she isn't there*; *didn't you tell me?*; *am I not right?*; *aren't we smart?*). ¶ Use with other verbs is now *archaic* (*I know not*; *fear not*), except with participles and infinitives (*not knowing, I cannot say*; *we asked them not to come*). **2** used elliptically for a negative sentence or verb or phrase (*Is she coming? — I hope not*; *Do you want it? — Certainly not!*). **3** used to express the negative of other words (*not a single one was left*; *Are they pleased? – Not they*; *he is not my cousin, but my nephew*). □ **not at all** (in polite reply to thanks) there is no need for thanks. **not but what** *archaic* **1** all the same; nevertheless (*I cannot do it; not but what a stronger man might*). **2** not such . . . or so . . . that . . . not (*not such a fool but what he can see it*). **not half** see HALF. **not least** with considerable importance, notably. **not much** see MUCH. **not quite 1** almost (*am not quite there*). **2** noticeably not (*not quite proper*). **not that** (foll. by clause) it is not to be inferred that (*if he said so - not that he ever did - he lied*). **not a thing** nothing at all. **not very** see VERY. [ME contr. of NOUGHT]

■ □ **not quite 1** see ALMOST. **2** see *a far cry* 2 (CRY).

nota bene /nṓtə bénnay/ *v.tr.* (as *imper.*) observe what follows, take notice (usu. drawing attention to a following qualification of what has preceded). [L, = note well]

notability /nṓtəbílliti/ *n.* (*pl.* **-ies**) **1** the state of being notable (*names of no historical notability*). **2** a prominent person. [ME f. OF *notabilité* or LL *notabilitas* (as NOTABLE)]

■ **1** see PROMINENCE 1.

notable /nṓtəb'l/ *adj.* & *n.* ● *adj.* worthy of note; striking, remarkable, eminent. ● *n.* an eminent person. □□ **notableness** *n.* **notably** *adv.* [ME f. OF f. L *notabilis* (as NOTE)]

■ *adj.* noteworthy, remarkable, different, distinctive, singular, unusual, uncommon, extraordinary, conspicuous, striking, pre-eminent, peerless, matchless, unmatched, unequalled, unparalleled, outstanding, memorable, unforgettable; noted, famous, famed, well-known, renowned, illustrious, important, prominent, eminent, great, distinguished, celebrated, acclaimed. ● *n.* dignitary, personage, notability, worthy, VIP; celebrity, luminary, (big) name, *colloq.* big shot, bigwig, big noise, *Brit. colloq.* brass hat, *sl.* big gun, (big) cheese, *Brit. sl.* nob, *US sl.* big wheel. □□ **notably** particularly, especially, markedly, noticeably, signally, distinctly, remarkably, unusually, uncommonly, outstandingly, conspicuously, clearly, obviously, evidently, manifestly, specifically, curiously, oddly, strangely, strikingly, shockingly, surprisingly, stunningly, *disp.* uniquely; meaningfully, significantly, importantly, prominently.

notarize /nṓtərīz/ *v.tr.* (also **-ise**) *US* certify (a document) as a notary.

■ see SANCTION *v.* 2.

notary /nṓtəri/ *n.* (*pl.* **-ies**) (in full **notary public**) a person authorized to perform certain legal formalities, esp. to draw up or certify contracts, deeds, etc. □□ **notarial** /nōtáiriəl/ *adj.* **notarially** /nōtáiriəli/ *adv.* [ME f. L *notarius* secretary (as NOTE)]

notate /nōtáyt/ *v.tr.* write in notation. [back-form. f. NOTATION]

notation /nōtáysh'n/ *n.* **1 a** the representation of numbers, quantities, pitch and duration etc. of musical notes, etc. by symbols. **b** any set of such symbols. **2** a set of symbols used to represent chess moves, dance steps, etc. **3** *US* **a** a note or annotation. **b** a record. **4** = *scale of notation* (see SCALE³). □□ **notational** *adj.* [F *notation* or L *notatio* (as NOTE)]

■ **1, 2** symbols, signs, code, characters; symbolism. **3** note, memorandum, jotting, record, reminder, minute(s), abstract, *colloq.* memo.

notch /noch/ *n.* & *v.* ● *n.* **1** a V-shaped indentation on an edge or surface. **2** a nick made on a stick etc. in order to keep count. **3** *colloq.* a step or degree (*move up a notch*). **4** *US* a deep gorge. ● *v.tr.* **1** make notches in. **2** (foll. by *up*) record or score with or as with notches. **3** secure or insert by notches. □□ **notched** *adj.* **notcher** *n.* **notchy** *adj.* (**notchier, notchiest**). [AF *noche* perh. f. a verbal form *nocher* (unrecorded), of uncert. orig.]

■ *n.* **1, 2** nick, cut, dent, indentation, groove, cleft, score, mark, gouge, gash. **3** step, grade, level, degree, stage, gradation, tier, echelon. ● *v.* **1** nick, cut, dent, indent, groove, score, mark, gash, gouge. **2** (*notch up*) score, gain, win, accomplish, achieve, register, mark (up), tally. □□ **notched** serrated, sawtooth(ed), crenellated, pinked, scalloped, zigzag, toothed, *Bot.* & *Zool.* crenate(d), dentate, *esp. Anat.*, *Biol.*, & *Zool.* serrate.

note /nōt/ *n.* & *v.* ● *n.* **1** a brief record of facts, topics, thoughts, etc., as an aid to memory, for use in writing, public speaking, etc. (often in *pl.*: *make notes*; *spoke without notes*). **2** an observation, usu. unwritten, of experiences etc. (*compare notes*). **3** a short or informal letter. **4** a formal diplomatic or parliamentary communication. **5** a short annotation or additional explanation in a book etc.; a footnote. **6 a** *Brit.* = BANKNOTE (*a five-pound note*). **b** a written promise or notice of payment of various kinds. **7 a** notice, attention (*worthy of note*). **b** distinction, eminence (*a person of note*). **8 a** a written sign representing the pitch and duration of a musical sound. **b** a single tone of definite pitch made by a musical instrument, the human voice, etc. **c** a key of a piano etc. **9 a** a bird's song or call. **b** a single tone in this. **10** a quality or tone of speaking, expressing mood or attitude etc.; a hint or suggestion (*sound a note of warning*; *ended on a note of optimism*). **11** a characteristic; a distinguishing feature. ● *v.tr.* **1** observe, notice; give or draw attention to. **2** (often foll. by *down*) record as a thing to be remembered or observed. **3** (in *passive*; often foll. by *for*) be famous or well known (for a quality, activity, etc.) (*were noted for their generosity*). □ **hit** (or **strike**) **the right note** speak or act in exactly the right manner. **of note** important, distinguished (*a person of note*). **take note** (often foll. by *of*) observe; pay attention (to). □□ **noted** *adj.* (in sense 3 of *v.*). **noteless** *adj.* [ME f. OF *note* (n.), *noter* (v.) f. L *nota* mark]

■ *n.* **1** memorandum, jotting, record, reminder, *aide-mémoire*, minute(s), abstract, *colloq.* memo. **2, 5** comment, remark, observation, explanation, annotation, footnote, end-note, side-note, gloss, critique, criticism, scholium, *Printing* shoulder-note; (*notes*) marginalia. **3** message, letter, communication, postcard,

card, word, line, memorandum, *colloq.* memo, *formal or joc.* epistle; fan letter, love-letter, bread-and-butter letter, thank-you note, *often joc.* billet-doux. **6 b** promissory note, letter of credit, (bank) draft, *Econ.* bill of exchange, *US* demand note. **7 a** heed, attention, notice, regard, respect, thought. **b** mark, consequence, substance, importance, moment, weight, distinction, merit, prestige, (high) rank *or* standing, eminence, prominence, repute, reputation, renown. **8** tone, sound; key. **10, 11** theme, characteristic, motif, element, quality, mood, tone, tenor; hint, suggestion, signal, cue, intimation, inkling, suspicion, clue, idea. ● *v.* **1** notice, observe, perceive, see, mark, think about, give thought to, consider, contemplate, study, pay attention to, attend to; call *or* draw attention to, remark on *or* about, mention, report, touch on, comment on *or* about. **2** record, register, write down, put *or* set down, put on record, jot down, put in writing, chronicle. □ **of note** see NOTABLE *adj.* **take note** take heed, attend, listen, pay attention, incline one's ear, beware; (*take note of*) see HEED *v.* □□ **noted** respected, eminent, distinguished, illustrious, esteemed, acclaimed; well-known, famous, famed, prominent, celebrated, notable, popular; notorious.

notebook /nṓtbŏŏk/ *n.* a small book for making or taking notes.
■ see TABLET 5.

notecase /nṓtkayss/ *n.* a wallet for holding banknotes.
■ see WALLET.

notelet /nṓtlit/ *n.* a small folded sheet of paper, usu. with a decorative design, for an informal letter.

notepaper /nṓtpaypər/ *n.* paper for writing letters.
■ writing-paper, letterhead, letter-paper, stationery, foolscap.

noteworthy /nṓtwurthi/ *adj.* worthy of attention; remarkable. □□ **noteworthiness** *n.*
■ notable, remarkable; exceptional, extraordinary, out of the ordinary, unusual, rare, uncommon, singular, different, *disp.* unique.

nothing /núthing/ *n.* & *adv.* ● *n.* **1** not anything (*nothing has been done*; *have nothing to do*). **2** no thing (often foll. by compl.: *I see nothing that I want*; *can find nothing useful*). **3 a** a person or thing of no importance or concern; a trivial event or remark (*was nothing to me*; *the little nothings of life*). **b** (*attrib.*) *colloq.* of no value; indeterminate (*a nothing sort of day*). **4** non-existence; what does not exist. **5** (in calculations) no amount; nought (*a third of nothing is nothing*). ● *adv.* **1** not at all, in no way (*helps us nothing*; *is nothing like enough*). **2** *US colloq.* not at all (*Is he ill? — Ill nothing, he's dead.*). □ **be nothing to 1** not concern. **2** not compare with. **be** (or **have**) **nothing to do with 1** have no connection with. **2** not be involved or associated with. **for nothing 1** at no cost; without payment. **2** to no purpose. **have nothing on 1** be naked. **2** have no engagements. **no nothing** *colloq.* (concluding a list of negatives) nothing at all. **nothing doing** *colloq.* **1 a** there is no prospect of success or agreement. **b** I refuse. **2** nothing is happening. **nothing** (or **nothing else**) **for it** (often foll. by *but to* + infin.) no alternative (*nothing for it but to pay up*). **nothing** (or **not much**) **in it** (or **to it**) **1** untrue or unimportant. **2** simple to do. **3** no (or little) advantage to be seen in one possibility over another. **nothing less than** at least (*nothing less than a disaster*). **think nothing of it** do not apologize or feel bound to show gratitude. [OE *nān thing* (as NO[1], THING)]
■ *n.* **1, 2** no thing, not anything, nil, *archaic or literary* naught, *poet. or archaic* nought, *sl.* nix, *Brit. sl.* (sweet) Fanny Adams *or* FA, *esp. US sl.* zilch. **3** cipher, zero, nobody, nonentity; trifle, bagatelle, *colloq.* peanuts. **4** non-existence, nothingness, nihility, nonentity, void, emptiness, vacuum. **5** see ZERO *n.* 1 □ **be** (or **have**) **nothing to do with 1** be remote from, be extrinsic to, be extraneous to, be unrelated to, be inapposite to, be irrelevant to, be unconnected with, be inappropriate to, be inapplicable to, be malapropos of. **2** have no truck with, be unknown to, be a stranger to, be unfamiliar with. **for nothing 2** to no avail; see also *in vain* (VAIN).

nothingness /núthingniss/ *n.* **1** non-existence; the non-existent. **2** worthlessness, triviality, insignificance.
■ **1** see OBLIVION.

notice /nṓtiss/ *n.* & *v.* ● *n.* **1** attention, observation (*it escaped my notice*). **2** a displayed sheet etc. bearing an announcement or other information. **3 a** an intimation or warning, esp. a formal one to allow preparations to be made (*give notice*; *at a moment's notice*). **b** (often foll. by *to* + infin.) a formal announcement or declaration of intention to end an agreement or leave employment at a specified time (*hand in one's notice*; *notice to quit*). **4** a short published review or comment about a new play, book, etc. ● *v.tr.* **1** (often foll. by *that*, *how*, etc. + clause) perceive, observe; take notice of. **2** remark upon; speak of. □ **at short** (or **a moment's**) **notice** with little warning. **notice-board** *Brit.* a board for displaying notices. **put a person on notice** *US* alert or warn a person. **take notice** (or **no notice**) show signs (or no signs) of interest. **take notice of 1** observe; pay attention to. **2** act upon. **under notice** served with a formal notice. [ME f. OF f. L *notitia* being known f. *notus* past part. of *noscere* know]
■ *n.* **1** attention, awareness, consciousness, perception, observation, cognizance; regard, consideration, respect, note, heed. **2** bill, handbill, broadsheet, *affiche*, leaflet, *US* flyer; see also SIGN *n.* 4. **3** notification, announcement; warning, intimation. **4** criticism, critique, *compte rendu*, review, comment, commentary, write-up. ● *v.* **1** note, take *or* make note of, take notice of, pay attention to, attend to, heed, take heed of, pay heed to, mark, remark, mind, observe, perceive, see, discern, detect, make out, identify, recognize, *colloq.* spot. □ **at short** (or **a moment's**) **notice** summarily, straight away, on the spur of the moment, on the spot, impromptu; see also PLUMP[2] *adv.* **notice-board** *US* bulletin-board. **put a person on notice** see WARN. **take notice of 1** see NOTICE *v.* above.

noticeable /nṓtisəb'l/ *adj.* **1** easily seen or noticed; perceptible. **2** noteworthy. □□ **noticeably** *adv.*
■ **1** discernible, perceivable, observable, perceptible, recognizable, distinguishable, visible, palpable, manifest, distinct, evident, clear, clear-cut, conspicuous, obvious; patent, unmistakable, undisguised, unconcealed. **2** noteworthy, notable, significant, signal, remarkable, important, singular, exceptional, pronounced, distinct, especial, considerable, major.

notifiable /nṓtifīəb'l/ *adj.* (of a disease) that must be notified to the health authorities.

notify /nṓtifī/ *v.tr.* (**-ies, -ied**) **1** (often foll. by *of*, or *that* + clause) inform or give notice to (a person). **2** make known; announce or report (a thing). □□ **notification** /-fikáysh'n/ *n.* [ME f. OF *notifier* f. L *notificare* f. *notus* known: see NOTICE]
■ **1** inform, tell, advise, alert, apprise, warn. **2** make known, announce, report, publish, declare, proclaim, give notice of. □□ **notification** word, intimation, warning, notice; see also ADVICE 2.

notion /nṓsh'n/ *n.* **1 a** a concept or idea; a conception (*it was an absurd notion*). **b** an opinion (*has the notion that people are honest*). **c** a vague view or understanding (*have no notion what you mean*). **2** an inclination, impulse, or intention (*has no notion of conforming*). **3** (in *pl.*) small, useful articles, esp. haberdashery. [L *notio* idea f. *notus* past part. of *noscere* know]
■ **1** idea, thought, concept, conception, image, impression, (mental) picture; view, understanding; opinion; inkling, clue. **2** fancy, whim, crotchet, whimsy, caprice, impulse, inclination, vagary, conceit; intention.

notional /nṓshən'l/ *adj.* **1 a** hypothetical, imaginary. **b** (of knowledge etc.) speculative; not based on experiment etc. **2** *Gram.* (of a verb) conveying its own meaning, not auxiliary.

□□ **notionally** *adv.* [obs. F *notional* or med.L *notionalis* (as NOTION)]

■ **1 a** see IMAGINARY.

notochord /nṓtəkord/ *n.* a cartilaginous skeletal rod supporting the body in all embryo and some adult chordate animals. [Gk *nōton* back + CHORD[2]]

notorious /nōtóriəss/ *adj.* well known, esp. unfavourably (*a notorious criminal; notorious for its climate*). □□ **notoriety** /-tərī́əti/ *n.* **notoriously** *adv.* [med.L *notorius* f. L *notus* (as NOTION)]

■ infamous, disreputable, dishonourable, disgraceful, shameful, shaming, embarrassing, discreditable, scandalous, flagrant, ignominious, opprobrious; celebrated, renowned, famous, well-known, fabled, legendary, memorable. □□ **notoriety** infamy, disrepute, dishonour, disgrace, shame, discredit, scandal, stain, blot, obloquy, ignominy, opprobrium; fame, renown.

notornis /nətórniss/ *n.* a rare flightless New Zealand bird, *Porphyrio mantelli*, with a large bill and brightly coloured plumage. Also called TAKAHE. [Gk *notos* south + *ornis* bird]

Notts. /nots/ *abbr.* Nottinghamshire.

notwithstanding /nótwithstánding, -with-/ *prep., adv., & conj.* ● *prep.* in spite of; without prevention by (*notwithstanding your objections; this fact notwithstanding*). ● *adv.* nevertheless; all the same. ● *conj.* (usu. foll. by *that* + clause) although. [ME, orig. absol. part. f. NOT + WITHSTAND + -ING[2]]

■ *prep.* despite, in spite of, regardless of, in the face of, against. ● *adv.* nevertheless, none the less, all the same, despite that, in spite of that, still, yet, anyway. ● *conj.* although, though, even though, despite the fact that.

nougat /nóogaa/ *n.* a sweet made from sugar or honey, nuts, and egg-white. [F f. Prov. *nogat* f. *noga* nut]

nought /nawt/ *n.* **1** the digit 0; a cipher. **2** *poet.* or *archaic* (in certain phrases) nothing (cf. NAUGHT). □ **noughts and crosses** a paper-and-pencil game with a square grid of nine squares, in which players seek to complete a row of three noughts or three crosses entered alternately. [OE *nōwiht* f. *ne* not + *ōwiht* var. of *āwiht* AUGHT[1]]

■ **1** see ZERO *n.* 1. **2** see NOTHING *n.* 1, 2. □ **noughts and crosses** *US* tic-tac-toe.

noun /nown/ *n. Gram.* a word (other than a pronoun) or group of words used to name or identify any of a class of persons, places, or things (**common noun**), or a particular one of these (**proper noun**). □□ **nounal** *adj.* [ME f. AF f. L *nomen* name]

nourish /núrrish/ *v.tr.* **1 a** sustain with food. **b** enrich; promote the development of (the soil etc.). **c** provide with intellectual or emotional sustenance or enrichment. **2** foster or cherish (a feeling etc.). □□ **nourisher** *n.* [ME f. OF *norir* f. L *nutrire*]

■ **1** feed, sustain, support, maintain, keep, provide for, care for, take care of, look after, nurture, nurse; strengthen, enrich, fortify, encourage, promote, stimulate, cultivate, help, advance, aid. **2** foster, cherish, nurse, maintain, harbour, keep, nurture, sustain.

nourishing /núrrishing/ *adj.* (esp. of food) containing much nourishment; sustaining. □□ **nourishingly** *adv.*

■ see WHOLESOME 1.

nourishment /núrrishmənt/ *n.* sustenance, food.

■ food, sustenance, nutriment, nutrition, victuals, *colloq.* grub.

nous /nowss/ *n.* **1** *colloq.* common sense; gumption. **2** *Philos.* the mind or intellect. [Gk]

■ **1** see GUMPTION 2. **2** see INTELLIGENCE 1b.

nouveau riche /nóovō reésh/ *n.* (*pl.* ***nouveaux riches*** *pronunc.* same) a person who has recently acquired (usu. ostentatious) wealth. [F, = new rich]

■ see PARVENU *n.*

nouvelle cuisine /nóovel kwizeén/ *n.* a modern style of cookery avoiding heaviness and emphasizing presentation. [F, = new cookery]

nouvelle vague /nóovel vaág/ *n.* a new trend, esp. in French film-making of the early 1960s. [F, fem. of *nouveau* new + *vague* wave]

Nov. *abbr.* November.

nova /nṓvə/ *n.* (*pl.* **novae** /-vee/ or **novas**) a star showing a sudden large increase of brightness which then subsides. [L, fem. of *novus* new, because orig. thought to be a new star]

■ see STAR *n.* 1.

novel[1] /nóvv'l/ *n.* **1** a fictitious prose story of book length. **2** (prec. by *the*) this type of literature. [It. *novella* (*storia* story) fem. of *novello* new f. L *novellus* f. *novus*]

■ story, tale, narrative, romance, fiction; novella, novelette, best-seller, *sl.* blockbuster.

novel[2] /nóvv'l/ *adj.* of a new kind or nature; strange; previously unknown. □□ **novelly** *adv.* [ME f. OF f. L *novellus* f. *novus* new]

■ new, unusual, unfamiliar, unconventional, fresh, different, original, creative; untested, untried, unknown, strange.

novelese /nóvvəleéz/ *n. derog.* a style characteristic of inferior novels.

novelette /nóvvəlét/ *n.* **1 a** a short novel. **b** *Brit. derog.* a light romantic novel. **2** *Mus.* a piano piece in free form with several themes.

novelettish /nóvvəléttish/ *adj. derog.* in the style of a light romantic novel; sentimental.

novelist /nóvvəlist/ *n.* a writer of novels. □□ **novelistic** /-lístik/ *adj.*

■ see WRITER 2.

novelize /nóvvəlīz/ *v.tr.* (also **-ise**) make into a novel. □□ **novelization** /-záysh'n/ *n.*

novella /nəvéllə/ *n.* (*pl.* **novellas**) a short novel or narrative story; a tale. [It.: see NOVEL[1]]

novelty /nóvvəlti/ *n.* & *adj.* ● *n.* (*pl.* **-ies**) **1 a** newness; new character. **b** originality. **2** a new or unusual thing or occurrence. **3** a small toy or decoration etc. of novel design. **4** (*attrib.*) having novelty (*novelty toys*). [ME f. OF *novelté* (as NOVEL[2])]

■ **1** originality, newness, uniqueness, freshness, innovativeness. **3** gimcrack, trifle, gewgaw, bauble, knick-knack, toy, trinket, ornament, plaything, kickshaw, *colloq.* gimmick. **4** (*attrib.*) see NEW *adj.* 1b.

November /nəvémbər/ *n.* the eleventh month of the year. [ME f. OF *novembre* f. L *November* f. *novem* nine (orig. the ninth month of the Roman year)]

novena /nəveénə/ *n. RC Ch.* a devotion consisting of special prayers or services on nine successive days. [med.L f. L *novem* nine]

novice /nóvviss/ *n.* **1 a** a probationary member of a religious order, before the taking of vows. **b** a new convert. **2** a beginner; an inexperienced person. **3** an animal that has not won a major prize in a competition. [ME f. OF f. L *novicius* f. *novus* new]

■ **1, 2** beginner, neophyte, newcomer, proselyte, tiro, noviciate, learner, amateur, initiate, apprentice, trainee, probationer, greenhorn, fledgling, freshman, *Brit. colloq.* fresher, *sl.* rookie.

noviciate /nəvíshiət/ *n.* (also **novitiate**) **1** the period of being a novice. **2** a religious novice. **3** novices' quarters. [F *noviciat* or med.L *noviciatus* (as NOVICE)]

Novocaine /nṓvəkayn/ *n.* (also **novocaine**) *propr.* a local anaesthetic derived from benzoic acid. [L *novus* new + COCAINE]

now /now/ *adv., conj.,* & *n.* ● *adv.* **1** at the present or mentioned time. **2** immediately (*I must go now*). **3** by this or that time (*it was now clear*). **4** under the present circumstances (*I cannot now agree*). **5** on this further occasion (*what do you want now?*). **6** in the immediate past (*just now*). **7** (esp. in a narrative or discourse) then, next (*the police now arrived; now to consider the next point*). **8** (without reference to time, giving various tones to a sentence) surely, I insist, I wonder, etc. (*now what do you mean by that?; oh come* *now!*). ● *conj.* (often foll. by *that* + clause) as a consequence of the fact (*now that I am older*; *now you mention it*). ● *n.* this time; the present (*should be there by now*; *has happened before now*). □ **as of now** from or at this time. **for now** until a later time (*goodbye for now*). **now and again** (or **then**) from time to time; intermittently. **now or never** an expression of urgency. [OE *nū*]

■ *adv.* **1, 4** at present, at the moment, just now, right now, as of now, at the present time *or* moment, at this (very) moment *or* minute *or* second *or* instant; these days, nowadays, today, in these times, in this day and age, under *or* in the present circumstances *or* conditions, in the present climate, things being what they are; contemporarily; any more, any longer. **2** at once, immediately, right away, straight away, without delay, instantly, promptly, *archaic* straightway, *archaic or joc.* instanter. **6** see JUST *adv.* 2. **7** then, next, at this *or* that point. ● *conj.* see FOR *conj.* ● *n.* the present, the time being, right now, this moment. □ **as of now** hence, henceforward, in (the) future, from now (on *or* onwards), hereafter. **for now** for the time being, for a little while, for the present. **now and again** occasionally, from time to time, at times, on occasion, sometimes, sporadically, once in a while, every now and then *or* again, randomly, intermittently; infrequently, seldom, rarely, once in a blue moon.

nowadays /nówədayz/ *adv.* & *n.* ● *adv.* at the present time or age; in these times. ● *n.* the present time.

■ *adv.* see NOW *adv.* 1, 4.

noway /nṓway/ *adv.* = NOWISE; (see *no way*).

Nowel (also **Nowell**) *archaic* var. of NOEL.

nowhere /nṓwair/ *adv.* & *pron.* ● *adv.* in or to no place. ● *pron.* no place. □ **be** (or **come in**) **nowhere** be unplaced in a race or competition. **come from nowhere** be suddenly evident or successful. **get nowhere** make or cause to make no progress. **in the middle of nowhere** *colloq.* remote from urban life. **nowhere near** not nearly. [OE *nāhwǣr* (as NO[1], WHERE)]

nowise /nṓwīz/ *adv.* in no manner; not at all.

■ see SCARCELY 2.

nowt /nowt/ *n. colloq.* or *dial.* nothing. [var. of NOUGHT]

noxious /nókshəss/ *adj.* harmful, unwholesome. □□ **noxiously** *adv.* **noxiousness** *n.* [f. L *noxius* f. *noxa* harm]

■ see HARMFUL. □□ **noxiousness** see *virulence* (VIRULENT).

noyau /nwáayō/ *n.* (*pl.* **noyaux** /-yōz/) a liqueur of brandy flavoured with fruit-kernels. [F, = kernel, ult. f. L *nux nucis* nut]

nozzle /nózz'l/ *n.* a spout on a hose etc. from which a jet issues. [NOSE + -LE[2]]

NP *abbr.* Notary Public.

Np *symb. Chem.* the element neptunium.

n.p. *abbr.* **1** new paragraph. **2** no place of publication.

NPA *abbr.* (in the UK) Newspaper Publishers' Association.

NPL *abbr.* (in the UK) National Physical Laboratory.

nr. *abbr.* near.

NS *abbr.* **1** new style. **2** new series. **3** Nova Scotia.

ns *abbr.* nanosecond.

NSB *abbr.* (in the UK) National Savings Bank.

NSC *abbr.* (in the US) National Security Council.

NSF *abbr.* (in the US) National Science Foundation.

NSPCC *abbr.* (in the UK) National Society for the Prevention of Cruelty to Children.

NSW *abbr.* New South Wales.

NT *abbr.* **1** New Testament. **2** Northern Territory (of Australia). **3** no trumps.

n't /ənt/ *adv.* (in *comb.*) = NOT (usu. with *is*, *are*, *have*, *must*, and the auxiliary verbs *can*, *do*, *should*, *would*: *isn't*; *mustn't*) (see also CAN'T, DON'T, WON'T). [contr.]

Nth. *abbr.* North.

nth see N[1].

NTP *abbr.* normal temperature and pressure.

nu /nyoo/ *n.* the thirteenth letter of the Greek alphabet (*N*, *ν*). [Gk]

nuance /nyoo-onss/ *n.* & *v.* ● *n.* a subtle difference in or shade of meaning, feeling, colour, etc. ● *v.tr.* give a nuance or nuances to. [F f. *nuer* to shade, ult. f. L *nubes* cloud]

■ *n.* see SHADE *n.* 11.

nub /nub/ *n.* **1** the point or gist (of a matter or story). **2** a small lump, esp. of coal. **3** a stub; a small residue. □□ **nubby** *adj.* [app. var. of *knub*, f. MLG *knubbe*, *knobbe* KNOB]

■ **1** essence, core, heart, nucleus, crux, point, gist, pith, kernel, nucleus, meat, (sum and) substance, main issue, gravamen. **2, 3** projection, protuberance, knob, boss, nubble, lump, bump, knop, protrusion, bulge, node, knot, stub; excrescence, swelling, tumescence.

nubble /núbb'l/ *n.* a small knob or lump. □□ **nubbly** *adj.* [dimin. of NUB]

nubile /nyoobīl/ *adj.* (of a woman) marriageable or sexually attractive. □□ **nubility** /-bílliti/ [L *nubilis* f. *nubere* become the wife of]

nuchal /nyook'l/ *adj.* of or relating to the nape of the neck. [*nucha* nape f. med.L *nucha* medulla oblongata f. Arab. *nukā'* spinal marrow]

nuci- /nyoossi/ *comb. form* nut. [L *nux nucis* nut]

nuciferous /nyoosíffərəss/ *adj. Bot.* bearing nuts.

nucivorous /nyoosívvərəss/ *adj.* nut-eating.

nuclear /nyookliər/ *adj.* **1** of, relating to, or constituting a nucleus. **2** using nuclear energy (*nuclear reactor*). **3** having nuclear weapons. □ **nuclear bomb** a bomb involving the release of energy by nuclear fission or fusion or both. **nuclear disarmament** the gradual or total reduction by a State of its nuclear weapons. **nuclear energy** energy obtained by nuclear fission or fusion. **nuclear family** a couple and their children, regarded as a basic social unit. **nuclear fission** a nuclear reaction in which a heavy nucleus splits spontaneously or on impact with another particle, with the release of energy. **nuclear force** a strong attractive force between nucleons in the atomic nucleus that holds the nucleus together. **nuclear-free** free from nuclear weapons, power, etc. **nuclear fuel** a substance that will sustain a fission chain reaction so that it can be used as a source of nuclear energy. **nuclear fusion** a nuclear reaction in which atomic nuclei of low atomic number fuse to form a heavier nucleus with the release of energy. **nuclear magnetic resonance** the absorption of electromagnetic radiation by a nucleus having a magnetic moment when in an external magnetic field, used mainly as an analytical technique and in body imaging for diagnosis. ¶ Abbr.: **NMR, nmr**. **nuclear physics** the physics of atomic nuclei and their interactions, esp. in the generation of nuclear energy. **nuclear power 1** electric or motive power generated by a nuclear reactor. **2** a country that has nuclear weapons. **nuclear reactor** a device in which a nuclear fission chain reaction is sustained and controlled in order to produce energy. **nuclear umbrella** supposed protection afforded by an alliance with a country possessing nuclear weapons. **nuclear warfare** warfare in which nuclear weapons are used. **nuclear waste** any radioactive waste material from the reprocessing of spent nuclear fuel. **nuclear winter** obstruction of sunlight as a potential result of nuclear warfare, causing extreme cold. [NUCLEUS + -AR[1]]

■ **2** atomic, fission, fusion; atom, hydrogen, neutron. □ **nuclear bomb** H-bomb, A-bomb, atom bomb, atomic bomb, hydrogen bomb, neutron bomb, the Bomb. **nuclear energy** nuclear power, atomic power, atomic energy.

nuclease /nyookliayz/ *n.* an enzyme that catalyses the breakdown of nucleic acids.

nucleate /nyookliayt/ *adj.* & *v.* ● *adj.* having a nucleus. ● *v.intr.* & *tr.* form or form into a nucleus. □□ **nucleation** /-áysh'n/ *n.* [LL *nucleare nucleat-* form a kernel (as NUCLEUS)]

nuclei *pl.* of NUCLEUS.

nucleic acid /nyookleé-ik, -kláyik/ *n.* either of two complex organic molecules (DNA and RNA), consisting of many nucleotides linked in a long chain, and present in all living cells.

nucleo- /nyŏŏkliō/ *comb. form* nucleus; nucleic acid (*nucleo-protein*).

nucleolus /nyookleéələss, -kliṓləss/ *n.* (*pl.* **nucleoli** /-lī/) a small dense spherical structure within a non-dividing nucleus. ▫▫ **nucleolar** *adj.* [LL, dimin. of L *nucleus*: see NUCLEUS]

nucleon /nyŏŏklion/ *n. Physics* a proton or neutron.

nucleonics /nyŏŏklióniks/ *n.pl.* (treated as *sing.*) the branch of science and technology concerned with atomic nuclei and nucleons, esp. the exploitation of nuclear power. ▫▫ **nucleonic** *adj.* [NUCLEAR, after *electronics*]

nucleoprotein /nyŏŏkliōprṓteen/ *n.* a complex of nucleic acid and protein.

nucleoside /nyŏŏkliəsīd/ *n. Biochem.* an organic compound consisting of a purine or pyrimidine base linked to a sugar, e.g. adenosine.

nucleotide /nyŏŏkliətīd/ *n. Biochem.* an organic compound consisting of a nucleoside linked to a phosphate group.

nucleus /nyŏŏkliəss/ *n.* (*pl.* **nuclei** /-li-ī/) **1 a** the central part or thing round which others are collected. **b** the kernel of an aggregate or mass. **2** an initial part meant to receive additions. **3** *Astron.* the solid part of a comet's head. **4** *Physics* the positively charged central core of an atom that contains most of its mass. **5** *Biol.* a large dense organelle of eukaryotic cells, containing the genetic material. **6** a discrete mass of grey matter in the central nervous system. [L, = kernel, inner part, dimin. of *nux nucis* nut]
▪ **1** core, heart, centre, kernel, pith, focus, nub.

nuclide /nyŏŏklīd/ *n. Physics* a certain type of atom characterized by the number of protons and neutrons in its nucleus. ▫▫ **nuclidic** /nyooklíddik/ *adj.* [NUCLEUS + Gk *eidos* form]

nuddy /núddi/ *n. sl.* nude (esp. *in the nuddy*). [prob. f. NUDE + -Y[2]]

nude /nyŏŏd/ *adj.* & *n.* ● *adj.* naked, bare, unclothed. ● *n.* **1** a painting, sculpture, photograph, etc. of a nude human figure; such a figure. **2** a nude person. **3** (prec. by *the*) **a** an unclothed state. **b** the representation of an undraped human figure as a genre in art. ▫ **nude contract** *Law* = *bare contract*. [L *nudus*]
▪ *adj.* unclothed, undressed, uncovered, bare, naked, in the nude, stark naked, undraped, without a stitch (on), *colloq.* in the buff, in the altogether, *joc.* in one's birthday suit, *sl.* in the nuddy, *Brit. sl.* starkers.

nudge /nuj/ *v.* & *n.* ● *v.tr.* **1** prod gently with the elbow to attract attention. **2** push gently or gradually. **3** give a gentle reminder or encouragement to (a person). ● *n.* the act or an instance of nudging; a gentle push. ▫▫ **nudger** *n.* [17th c.: orig. unkn.: cf. Norw. dial. *nugga*, *nyggja* to push, rub]
▪ *v.* jog, poke, elbow, jab, dig, bump, shove; prod, push, prompt, encourage; remind. ● *n.* jog, poke, elbow, jab, dig, bump, shove; prod, push, prompt, encouragement; reminder.

nudist /nyŏŏdist/ *n.* a person who advocates or practises going unclothed. ▫▫ **nudism** *n.*
▪ naturist.

nudity /nyŏŏditi/ *n.* the state of being nude; nakedness.

nugatory /nyŏŏgətəri/ *adj.* **1** futile, trifling, worthless. **2** inoperative; not valid. [L *nugatorius* f. *nugari* to trifle f. *nugae* jests]
▪ **1** see INSIGNIFICANT 1.

nugget /núggit/ *n.* **1 a** a lump of gold, platinum, etc., as found in the earth. **b** a lump of anything compared to this. **2** something valuable for its size (often abstract in sense: *a little nugget of information*). [app. f. dial. *nug* lump etc.]
▪ **1** see LUMP[1] *n.* 1, 2.

nuisance /nyŏŏss'nss/ *n.* **1** a person, thing, or circumstance causing trouble or annoyance. **2** anything harmful or offensive to the community or a member of it and for which a legal remedy exists. ▫ **nuisance value** an advantage resulting from the capacity to harass or frustrate. [ME f. OF, = hurt, f. *nuire nuis-* f. L *nocēre* to hurt]
▪ **1** annoyance, inconvenience, trial, ordeal, burden, irritation, irritant, thorn in one's flesh *or* side, difficulty, bother, *colloq.* pain (in the neck), headache, hassle, *Austral. sl.* nark, *esp. US sl.* pain in the butt; bore, pest, nag, tease, tormentor.

NUJ *abbr.* (in the UK) National Union of Journalists.

nuke /nyŏŏk/ *n.* & *v. colloq.* ● *n.* a nuclear weapon. ● *v.tr.* bomb or destroy with nuclear weapons. [abbr.]

null /nul/ *adj.* & *n.* ● *adj.* **1** (esp. **null and void**) invalid; not binding. **2** non-existent; amounting to nothing. **3** having or associated with the value zero. **4** *Computing* **a** empty; having no elements (*null list*). **b** all the elements of which are zeros (*null matrix*). **5** without character or expression. ● *n.* a dummy letter in a cipher. ▫ **null character** *Computing* a character denoting nothing, usu. represented by a zero. **null hypothesis** a hypothesis suggesting that the difference between statistical samples does not imply a difference between populations. **null instrument** an instrument used by adjustment to give a reading of zero. **null link** *Computing* a reference incorporated into the last item in a list to indicate there are no further items in the list. [F *nul nulle* or L *nullus* none f. *ne* not + *ullus* any]
▪ *adj.* **1** see INVALID[2].

nullah /núllə/ *n. Anglo-Ind.* a dry river-bed or ravine. [Hindi *nālā*]

nulla-nulla /núllənullə/ *n.* (also **nulla**) *Austral.* a hardwood club used by Aborigines. [Aboriginal]

nullifidian /núllifiddiən/ *n.* & *adj.* (a person) having no religious faith or belief. [med.L *nullifidius* f. L *nullus* none + *fides* faith]

nullify /núllifī/ *v.tr.* (**-ies**, **-ied**) make null; neutralize, invalidate, cancel. ▫▫ **nullification** /-fikáysh'n/ *n.* **nullifier** *n.*
▪ see NEUTRALIZE. ▫▫ **nullification** see CANCELLATION.

nullipara /nulíppərə/ *n.* a woman who has never borne a child. ▫▫ **nulliparous** *adj.* [mod.L f. L *nullus* none + *-para* fem. of *-parus* f. *parere* bear children]

nullipore /núllipor/ *n.* any of various seaweeds able to secrete lime. [L *nullus* none + PORE[1]]

nullity /núlliti/ *n.* (*pl.* **-ies**) **1** *Law* **a** being null; invalidity, esp. of marriage. **b** an act, document, etc., that is null. **2 a** nothingness. **b** a mere nothing; a nonentity. [F *nullité* or med.L *nullitas* f. L *nullus* none]

NUM *abbr.* (in the UK) National Union of Mineworkers.

Num. *abbr.* Numbers (Old Testament).

numb /num/ *adj.* & *v.* ● *adj.* (often foll. by *with*) deprived of feeling or the power of motion (*numb with cold*). ● *v.tr.* **1** make numb. **2** stupefy, paralyse. ▫ **numb-fish** = *electric ray*. ▫▫ **numbly** *adv.* **numbness** *n.* [ME *nome(n)* past part. of *nim* take: for *-b* cf. THUMB]
▪ *adj.* numbed, benumbed, insensible, insensate, dead, deadened, without feeling, senseless; asleep. ● *v.* benumb, anaesthetize, drug, deaden, dull, freeze, paralyse, immobilize, stun, stupefy. ▫▫ **numbness** anaesthesia, paralysis, torpidity; see also STUPOR.

numbat /númbat/ *n.* a small Australian marsupial, *Myrmecobius fasciatus*, with a bushy tail and black and white striped back. [Aboriginal]

number /númbər/ *n.* & *v.* ● *n.* **1 a** an arithmetical value representing a particular quantity and used in counting and making calculations. **b** a word, symbol, or figure representing this; a numeral. **c** an arithmetical value showing position in a series esp. for identification, reference, etc. (*registration number*). **2** (often foll. by *of*) the total count or aggregate (*the number of accidents has decreased*; *twenty in number*). **3 a** the study of the behaviour of numbers; numerical reckoning (*the laws of number*). **b** (in *pl.*) arithmetic (*not good at numbers*). **4 a** (in *sing.* or *pl.*) a quantity or amount; a total; a count (*a large number of people*; *only in small numbers*). **b** (in *pl.*) numerical preponderance (*force of*

numbers; there is safety in numbers). **5 a** a person or thing having a place in a series, esp. a single issue of a magazine, an item in a programme, etc. **b** a song, dance, musical item, etc. **6** company, collection, group (*among our number*). **7** *Gram.* **a** the classification of words by their singular or plural forms. **b** a particular such form. **8** *colloq.* a person or thing regarded familiarly or affectionately (usu. qualified in some way: *an attractive little number*). **9** (**Numbers**) the Old Testament book containing a census. ● *v.tr.* **1** include (*I number you among my friends*). **2** assign a number or numbers to. **3** have or amount to (a specified number). **4 a** count. **b** comprise (*numbering forty thousand men*). □ **by numbers** following simple instructions (as if) identified by numbers. **one's days are numbered** one does not have long to live. **have a person's number** *colloq.* understand a person's real motives, character, etc. **have a person's number on it** (of a bomb, bullet, etc.) be destined to hit a specified person. **number cruncher** *Computing* & *Math. sl.* a machine capable of complex calculations etc. **number crunching** the act or process of making these calculations. **one's number is up** *colloq.* one is finished or doomed to die. **a number of** some, several. ¶ Use with a plural verb is now standard: *a number of problems remain.* **number one** *n. colloq.* oneself (*always takes care of number one*). ● *adj.* most important (*the number one priority*). **number-plate** a plate on a vehicle displaying its registration number. **numbers game 1** usu. *derog.* action involving only arithmetical work. **2** *US* a lottery based on the occurrence of unpredictable numbers in the results of races etc. **Number Ten** 10 Downing Street, the official London home of the British Prime Minister. **number two** a second in command. **without number** innumerable. [ME f. OF *nombre* (n.), *nombrer* (v.) f. L *numerus, numerare*]
■ *n.* **1** numeral, integer, figure, digit. **2** see SUM *n.* 1, 2. **3 b** (*numbers*) see SUM *n.* 3b. **4** amount, quantity. **5 a** issue; edition, copy; item. **b** see ACT *n.* 3a. **6** see GROUP *n.* 1, COMPANY *n.* 1a. ● *v.* **1** see INCLUDE 3. **3** see AMOUNT *v.* 1. **4 a** see COUNT *v.* 1. **b** see INCLUDE 1. □ **a number of** see SEVERAL *adj.* **number-plate** *US* license-plate. **number two** deputy, second-in-command, lieutenant; see also AIDE. **without number** see NUMBERLESS.

numberless /númbərliss/ *adj.* innumerable.
■ uncountable, uncounted, countless, innumerable, incalculable, immeasurable, numerous, untold, without number, infinite, *literary* myriad.

numbles /númb'lz/ *n.pl. Brit. archaic* a deer's entrails. [ME f. OF *numbles, nombles* loin etc., f. L *lumbulus* dimin. of *lumbus* loin: cf. UMBLES]

numbskull var. of NUMSKULL.

numdah /númdaa/ *n.* an embroidered felt rug from India etc. [Urdu *namdā* f. Pers. *namad* carpet]

numen /nyo͞omen/ *n.* (*pl.* **numina** /-minə/) a presiding deity or spirit. [L *numen -minis*]

numerable /nyo͞omərəb'l/ *adj.* that can be counted. □□ **numerably** *adv.* [L *numerabilis* f. *numerare* NUMBER *v.*]

numeral /nyo͞omərəl/ *n.* & *adj.* ● *n.* a word, figure, or group of figures denoting a number. ● *adj.* of or denoting a number. [LL *numeralis* f. L (as NUMBER)]
■ *n.* see NUMBER *n.* 1.

numerate /nyo͞omərət/ *adj.* acquainted with the basic principles of mathematics. □□ **numeracy** *n.* [L *numerus* number + -ATE[2] after *literate*]

numeration /nyo͞oməráysh'n/ *n.* **1 a** a method or process of numbering or computing. **b** calculation. **2** the expression in words of a number written in figures. [ME f. L *numeratio* payment, in LL numbering (as NUMBER)]

numerator /nyo͞oməraytər/ *n.* **1** the number above the line in a vulgar fraction showing how many of the parts indicated by the denominator are taken (e.g. 2 in $^2/_3$). **2** a person or device that numbers. [F *numérateur* or LL *numerator* (as NUMBER)]

numerical /nyoomérrik'l/ *adj.* (also **numeric**) of or relating to a number or numbers (*numerical superiority*). □ **numerical analysis** the branch of mathematics that deals with the development and use of numerical methods for solving problems. □□ **numerically** *adv.* [med.L *numericus* (as NUMBER)]

numerology /nyo͞omərólləji/ *n.* (*pl.* **-ies**) the study of the supposed occult significance of numbers. □□ **numerological** /-rəlójik'l/ *adj.* **numerologist** *n.* [L *numerus* number + -LOGY]

numerous /nyo͞omərəss/ *adj.* **1** (with *pl.*) great in number (*received numerous gifts*). **2** consisting of many (*a numerous family*). □□ **numerously** *adv.* **numerousness** *n.* [L *numerosus* (as NUMBER)]
■ *adj.* **1** see MANY *adj.*

numina *pl.* of NUMEN.

numinous /nyo͞ominəss/ *adj.* **1** indicating the presence of a divinity. **2** spiritual. **3** awe-inspiring. [L *numen*: see NUMEN]

numismatic /nyo͞omizmáttik/ *adj.* of or relating to coins or medals. □□ **numismatically** *adv.* [F *numismatique* f. L *numisma* f. Gk *nomisma -atos* current coin f. *nomizō* use currently]

numismatics /nyo͞omizmáttiks/ *n.pl.* (usu. treated as *sing.*) the study of coins or medals. □□ **numismatist** /nyoomízmətist/ *n.*

numismatology /nyoomízmətólləji/ *n.* = NUMISMATICS.

nummulite /númyoolīt/ *n.* a disc-shaped fossil shell of a foraminiferous protozoan found in Tertiary strata. [L *nummulus* dimin. of *nummus* coin]

numnah /númnə/ *n.* a saddle-cloth or pad placed under a saddle. [Urdu *namdā*: see NUMDAH]

numskull /númskul/ *n.* (also **numbskull**) a stupid or foolish person. [NUMB + SKULL]
■ see FOOL[1] *n.* 1.

nun /nun/ *n.* a member of a community of women living apart under religious vows. □□ **nunhood** *n.* **nunlike** *adj.* **nunnish** *adj.* [ME f. OE *nunne* and OF *nonne* f. eccl.L *nonna* fem. of *nonnus* monk, orig. a title given to an elderly person]

nunatak /núnnətak/ *n.* an isolated peak of rock projecting above a surface of land ice or snow e.g. in Greenland. [Eskimo]

nun-buoy /núnboy/ *n.* a buoy circular in the middle and tapering to each end. [obs. *nun* child's top + BUOY]

nunc dimittis /núngk dimíttiss/ *n.* the Song of Simeon (Luke 2:29-32) used as a canticle. [f. the opening words *nunc dimittis* now let (your servant) depart]

nunciature /núnshətyoor/ *n. RC Ch.* the office or tenure of a nuncio. [It. *nunziatura* (as NUNCIO)]

nuncio /núnshiō, -siō/ *n.* (*pl.* **-os**) *RC Ch.* a papal ambassador. [It. f. L *nuntius* messenger]

nuncupate /núngkyoopayt/ *v.tr.* declare (a will or testament) orally, not in writing. □□ **nuncupation** /-páysh'n/ *n.* **nuncupative** /-pətiv/ *adj.* [L *nuncupare nuncupat-* name]

nunnery /núnnəri/ *n.* (*pl.* **-ies**) a religious house of nuns; a convent.

NUPE /nyo͞opi/ *abbr.* (in the UK) National Union of Public Employees.

nuptial /núpsh'l/ *adj.* & *n.* ● *adj.* of or relating to marriage or weddings. ● *n.* (usu. in *pl.*) a wedding. [F *nuptial* or L *nuptialis* f. *nuptiae* wedding f. *nubere nupt-* wed]
■ *adj.* bridal, matrimonial, wedding, wedded, marital, connubial, conjugal, *literary* hymeneal.

NUR *abbr.* (in the UK) National Union of Railwaymen. ¶ In 1990 merged with the NUS (sense 1) to form the RMT.

nurd var. of NERD.

nurse /nurss/ *n.* & *v.* ● *n.* **1** a person trained to care for the sick or infirm. **2** (formerly) a person employed or trained to take charge of young children. **3** *archaic* = *wet-nurse.* **4** *Forestry* a tree planted as a shelter to others. **5** *Zool.* a sexually imperfect bee, ant, etc., caring for a young brood; a worker. ● *v.* **1 a** *intr.* work as a nurse. **b** *tr.* attend to (a sick person). **c** *tr.* give medical attention to (an illness or injury). **2** *tr.* & *intr.* feed or be fed at the breast. **3** *tr.* (in *passive*; foll. by *in*) be brought up in (a specified condition) (*nursed in poverty*). **4** *tr.* hold or treat carefully or caressingly (*sat nursing my feet*). **5** *tr.* **a** foster; promote the development of (the arts, plants, etc.). **b** harbour or nurture (a grievance, hatred, etc.). **c** pay special attention to (*nursed the voters*). **6** *tr. Billiards* keep (the balls) together for a series of cannons. [reduced f. ME and OF *norice, nurice* f. LL *nutricia* fem. of L *nutricius* f. *nutrix -icis* f. *nutrire* NOURISH]

▪ *n.* **1** sister, matron, nursing officer, paramedic, health visitor, carer, attendant, ministering angel. ● *v.* **1 b** care for, look after, tend, attend, minister to, treat. **2** wet-nurse, suckle, breast-feed, nourish. **5** nurture, foster, cherish, preserve, keep alive, cultivate, develop; harbour; coddle, baby, pamper.

nurseling var. of NURSLING.

nursemaid /núrsmayd/ *n.* **1** a woman in charge of a child or children. **2** a person who watches over or guides another carefully.

▪ **1** child-minder, au pair, nursery nurse, nanny.

nursery /núrsəri/ *n.* (*pl.* **-ies**) **1 a** a room or place equipped for young children. **b** = *day nursery*. **2** a place where plants, trees, etc., are reared for sale or transplantation. **3** any sphere or place in or by which qualities or types of people are fostered or bred. **4** *Billiards* **a** grouped balls (see NURSE *v.* 6). **b** (in full **nursery cannon**) a cannon on three close balls. □ **nursery nurse** a person trained to take charge of babies and young children. **nursery rhyme** a simple traditional song or story in rhyme for children. **nursery school** a school for children between the ages of three and five. **nursery slopes** *Skiing* gentle slopes suitable for beginners. **nursery stakes** a race for two-year-old horses.

▪ □ **nursery school** kindergarten, playgroup.

nurseryman /núrsərimən/ *n.* (*pl.* **-men**) an owner of or worker in a plant nursery.

nursing /núrsing/ *n.* **1** the practice or profession of caring for the sick as a nurse. **2** (*attrib.*) concerned with or suitable for nursing the sick or elderly etc. (*nursing home; nursing sister*). □ **nursing officer** a senior nurse (see *senior nursing officer*).

nursling /núrsling/ *n.* (also **nurseling**) an infant that is being suckled.

nurture /núrchər/ *n.* & *v.* ● *n.* **1** the process of bringing up or training (esp. children); fostering care. **2** nourishment. **3** sociological factors as an influence on or determinant of personality (opp. NATURE). ● *v.tr.* **1** bring up; rear. **2** nourish. □□ **nurturer** *n.* [ME f. OF *nour(e)ture* (as NOURISH)]

▪ *n.* **1** see UPBRINGING. ● *v.* **1** see *bring up* 1. **2** see NOURISH. □□ **nurturer** see MOTHER *n.* 1.

NUS *abbr.* **1** (in the UK) National Union of Seamen. **2** (in the UK) National Union of Students.

NUT *abbr.* (in the UK) National Union of Teachers.

nut /nut/ *n.* & *v.* ● *n.* **1 a** a fruit consisting of a hard or tough shell around an edible kernel. **b** this kernel. **2** a pod containing hard seeds. **3** a small usu. square or hexagonal flat piece of metal or other material with a threaded hole through it for screwing on the end of a bolt to secure it. **4** *sl.* a person's head. **5** *sl.* **a** a crazy or eccentric person. **b** an obsessive enthusiast or devotee (*a health-food nut*). **6** a small lump of coal, butter, etc. **7 a** a device fitted to the bow of a violin for adjusting its tension. **b** the fixed ridge on the neck of a stringed instrument over which the strings pass. **8** (in *pl.*) *coarse sl.* the testicles. ● *v.intr.* (**nutted, nutting**) seek or gather nuts (*go nutting*). □ **do one's nut** *sl.* be extremely angry or agitated. **for nuts** *colloq.* even tolerably well (*cannot sing for nuts*). **nut cutlet** a cutlet-shaped portion of meat-substitute, made from nuts etc. **nut-house** *sl.* a mental home or hospital. **nut-oil** an oil obtained from hazelnuts and walnuts and used in paints and varnishes. **nuts and bolts** *colloq.* the practical details. **nut-tree** any tree bearing nuts, esp. a hazel. **off one's nut** *sl.* crazy. □□ **nutlike** *adj.* [OE *hnutu* f. Gmc]

▪ *n.* **1 b** see KERNEL 1, 2. **4** see HEAD *n.* 1. **5 a** see MADMAN. **b** see ENTHUSIAST.

nutant /nyóot'nt/ *adj. Bot.* nodding, drooping. [L *nutare* nod]

nutation /nyootáysh'n/ *n.* **1** the act or an instance of nodding. **2** *Astron.* a periodic oscillation of the earth's poles. **3** oscillation of a spinning top. **4** the spiral movement of a plant organ during growth. [L *nutatio* (as NUTANT)]

nutcase /nútkayss/ *n. sl.* a crazy or foolish person.

▪ see MADMAN.

nutcracker /nútkrakkər/ *n.* (usu. in *pl.*) a device for cracking nuts.

nutgall /nútgawl/ *n.* a gall found on dyer's oak, used as a dyestuff.

nuthatch /nút-hach/ *n.* any small bird of the family Sittidae, climbing up and down tree-trunks and feeding on nuts, insects, etc. [NUT + *hatch* rel. to HATCH[2]]

nutlet /nútlit/ *n.* a small nut or nutlike fruit.

nutmeg /nútmeg/ *n.* **1** an evergreen E. Indian tree, *Myristica fragrans*, yielding a hard aromatic spheroidal seed. **2** the seed of this used as a spice and in medicine. □ **nutmeg-apple** the fruit of this tree, yielding mace and nutmeg. [ME: partial transl. of OF *nois mug(u)ede* ult. f. L *nux* nut + LL *muscus* MUSK]

nutria /nyóotriə/ *n.* the skin or fur of a coypu. [Sp., = otter]

nutrient /nyóotriənt/ *n.* & *adj.* ● *n.* any substance that provides essential nourishment for the maintenance of life. ● *adj.* serving as or providing nourishment. [L *nutrire* nourish]

nutriment /nyóotrimənt/ *n.* **1** nourishing food. **2** an intellectual or artistic etc. nourishment or stimulus. □□ **nutrimental** /-mént'l/ *adj.* [L *nutrimentum* (as NUTRIENT)]

▪ **1** see NOURISHMENT. □□ **nutrimental** see NUTRITIOUS.

nutrition /nyootrísh'n/ *n.* **1 a** the process of providing or receiving nourishing substances. **b** food, nourishment. **2** the study of nutrients and nutrition. □□ **nutritional** *adj.* [F *nutrition* or LL *nutritio* (as NUTRIENT)]

▪ **1 b** see NOURISHMENT.

nutritionist /nyootríshənist/ *n.* a person who studies or is an expert on the processes of human nourishment.

nutritious /nyootríshəss/ *adj.* efficient as food; nourishing. □□ **nutritiously** *adv.* **nutritiousness** *n.* [L *nutritius* (as NURSE)]

▪ healthful, healthy, nutritive, nourishing, wholesome, life-giving, beneficial, salutary, alimentary, nutrimental.

nutritive /nyóotritiv/ *adj.* & *n.* ● *adj.* **1** of or concerned in nutrition. **2** serving as nutritious food. ● *n.* a nutritious article of food. [ME f. F *nutritif -ive* f. med.L *nutritivus* (as NUTRIENT)]

▪ *adj.* **2** see NUTRITIOUS.

nuts /nuts/ *adj.* & *int.* ● *adj. sl.* crazy, mad, eccentric. ● *int. sl.* an expression of contempt or derision (*nuts to you*). □ **be nuts about** (or **on**) *colloq.* be enthusiastic about or very fond of.

▪ *adj.* see CRAZY 1.

nutshell /nútshel/ *n.* the hard exterior covering of a nut. □ **in a nutshell** in a few words.

▪ □ **in a nutshell** see *in a word* (WORD).

nutter /núttər/ *n. Brit. sl.* a crazy or eccentric person.

▪ see MADMAN.

nutty /núttì/ *adj.* (**nuttier, nuttiest**) **1 a** full of nuts. **b** tasting like nuts. **2** *sl.* = NUTS *adj.* □□ **nuttiness** *n.*

▪ **2** see CRAZY 1. □□ **nuttiness** see FOLLY 1.

nux vomica /nuks vómmikə/ *n.* **1** an E. Indian tree, *Strychnos nux-vomica*, yielding a poisonous fruit. **2** the seeds of this tree, containing strychnine. [med.L f. L *nux* nut + *vomicus* f. *vomere* vomit]

nuzzle /núzz'l/ *v.* **1** *tr.* prod or rub gently with the nose. **2** *intr.* (foll. by *into, against, up to*) press the nose gently. **3** *tr.* (also *refl.*) nestle; lie snug. [ME f. NOSE + -LE[4]]

▪ **1, 2** see CARESS *v.* **3** see NESTLE.

NV *abbr. US* Nevada (in official postal use).

NW *abbr.* **1** north-west. **2** north-western.

NY *abbr. US* New York (also in official postal use).

nyala var. of INYALA.

NYC *abbr.* New York City.

nyctalopia /níktəlṓpiə/ *n.* the inability to see in dim light or at night. Also called *night-blindness.* [LL f. Gk *nuktalōps* f. *nux nuktos* night + *alaos* blind + *ōps* eye]

nyctitropic /níktitrṓpik/ *adj. Bot.* (of plant movements) occurring at night and caused by changes in light and temperature. [Gk *nukti-* comb. form of *nux nuktos* night + *tropos* turn]

nye var. of NIDE.

nylghau /nílgaw/ *n.* = NILGAI. [Hind. f. Pers. *nīlgāw* f. *nīl* blue + *gāw* cow]

nylon /nīlon/ *n.* **1** any of various synthetic polyamide fibres having a protein-like structure, with tough, lightweight, elastic properties, used in industry and for textiles etc. **2** a nylon fabric. **3** (in *pl.*) stockings made of nylon. [invented word, after *cotton, rayon*]

nymph /nimf/ *n.* **1** any of various mythological semi-divine spirits regarded as maidens and associated with aspects of nature, esp. rivers and woods. **2** *poet.* a beautiful young woman. **3 a** an immature form of some insects. **b** a young dragonfly or damselfly. □□ **nymphal** *adj.* **nymphean** /-féeən/ *adj.* **nymphlike** *adj.* [ME f. OF *nimphe* f. L *nympha* f. Gk *numphē*]
■ **2** see MISS^{2}, BEAUTY 3.

nymphae /nímfee/ *n.pl. Anat.* the labia minora. [L, pl. of *nympha*: see NYMPH]

nymphet /nímfét/ *n.* **1** a young nymph. **2** *colloq.* a sexually attractive young woman.
■ **2** see MISS^{2}.

nympho /nímfō/ *n.* (*pl.* **-os**) *colloq.* a nymphomaniac. [abbr.]

nympholepsy /nímfəlepsi/ *n.* ecstasy or frenzy caused by desire of the unattainable. [NYMPHOLEPT after *epilepsy*]

nympholept /nímfəlept/ *n.* a person inspired by violent enthusiasm esp. for an ideal. □□ **nympholeptic** /-léptik/ *adj.* [Gk *numpholēptos* caught by nymphs (as NYMPH, *lambanō* take)]

nymphomania /nímfəmáyniə/ *n.* excessive sexual desire in women. □□ **nymphomaniac** *n.* & *adj.* [mod.L (as NYMPH, -MANIA)]

nystagmus /nistágməss/ *n.* rapid involuntary movements of the eyes. □□ **nystagmic** *adj.* [Gk *nustagmos* nodding f. *nustazō* nod]

NZ *abbr.* New Zealand.

Oo

O[1] /ō/ *n.* (also **o**) (*pl.* **Os** or **O's**) **1** the fifteenth letter of the alphabet. **2** (**0**) nought, zero (in a sequence of numerals esp. when spoken). **3** a human blood type of the ABO system.

O[2] *abbr.* (also **O.**) Old.

O[3] *symb. Chem.* the element oxygen.

O[4] /ō/ *int.* **1** var. of OH[1]. **2** prefixed to a name in the vocative (*O God*). [ME, natural excl.]

O' /ō, ə/ *prefix* of Irish patronymic names (*O'Connor*). [Ir. *ó, ua*, descendant]

o' /ə/ *prep.* of, on (esp. in phrases: *o'clock*; *will-o'-the-wisp*). [abbr.]

-o /ō/ *suffix* forming usu. *sl.* or *colloq.* variants or derivatives (*beano*; *wino*). [perh. OH[1] as joc. suffix]

-o- /ō/ *suffix* the terminal vowel of combining forms (*spectro-*; *chemico-*; *Franco-*). ¶ Often elided before a vowel, as in *neuralgia*. [orig. Gk]

oaf /ōf/ *n.* (*pl.* **oafs**) **1** an awkward lout. **2** a stupid person. □□ **oafish** *adj.* **oafishly** *adv.* **oafishness** *n.* [orig. = elf's child, var. of obs. *auf* f. ON *álfr* elf]
■ **1** see HULK 3. **2** see FOOL[1] *n.* 1. □□ **oafish** see CLUMSY 1. **oafishness** see STUPIDITY.

oak /ōk/ *n.* **1** any tree or shrub of the genus *Quercus* usu. having lobed leaves and bearing acorns. **2** the durable wood of this tree, used esp. for furniture and in building. **3** (*attrib.*) made of oak (*oak table*). **4** a heavy outer door of a set of university college rooms. **5** (**the Oaks**) (treated as *sing.*) an annual race at Epsom for three-year-old fillies (from the name of a nearby estate). □ **oak-apple** (or **-gall**) an apple-like gall containing larvae of certain wasps, found on oak trees. □□ **oaken** *adj.* [OE *āc* f. Gmc]

oakum /ṓkəm/ *n.* a loose fibre obtained by picking old rope to pieces and used esp. in caulking. [OE *ǣcumbe, ācumbe*, lit. 'off-combings']

O. & M. *abbr.* organization and methods.

OAP *abbr. Brit.* old-age pensioner.
■ see PENSIONER.

oar /or/ *n.* **1** a pole with a blade used for rowing or steering a boat by leverage against the water. **2** a rower. □ **put** (or **stick**) **one's oar in** interfere, meddle. **rest** (*US* **lay**) **on one's oars** relax one's efforts. □□ **oared** *adj.* (also in *comb.*). **oarless** *adj.* [OE *ār* f. Gmc, perh. rel. to Gk *eretmos* oar]
■ **1** paddle, scull, sweep. **2** oarsman, oarswoman, sculler, rower, paddler. □ **put** (or **stick**) **one's oar in** see INTERFERE 2.

oarfish /órfish/ *n.* a ribbonfish, *Regalecus glesne*.

oarlock /órlok/ *n. US* a rowlock.

oarsman /órzmən/ *n.* (*pl.* **-men**; *fem.* **oarswoman**, *pl.* **-women**) a rower. □□ **oarsmanship** *n.*
■ see OAR 2.

oarweed /órweed/ *n.* (also **oreweed**) any large marine alga esp. of the genus *Laminaria*, often growing along shores.

OAS *abbr.* **1** Organization of American States. **2** on active service.

oasis /ō-áysiss/ *n.* (*pl.* **oases** /-seez/) **1** a fertile spot in a desert, where water is found. **2** an area or period of calm in the midst of turbulence. [LL f. Gk, app. of Egypt. orig.]
■ **1** watering-hole, water-hole, watering-place, *Austral.* gnamma, clay-pan. **2** haven, refuge, (safe) harbour, sanctuary, retreat, asylum, resort, *colloq.* sanctum.

oast /ōst/ *n.* a kiln for drying hops. □ **oast-house** a building containing this. [OE *āst* f. Gmc]

oat /ōt/ *n.* **1 a** a cereal plant, *Avena sativa*, cultivated in cool climates. **b** (in *pl.*) the grain yielded by this, used as food. **2** any other cereal of the genus *Avena*, esp. the wild oat, *A. fatua*. **3** *poet.* the oat-stem used as a musical pipe by shepherds etc., usu. in pastoral or bucolic poetry. **4** (in *pl.*) *sl.* sexual gratification. □ **feel one's oats** *colloq.* **1** be lively. **2** *US* feel self-important. **oat-grass** any of various grasses, esp. of the genus *Arrhenatherum*. **off one's oats** *colloq.* not hungry. **sow one's oats** (or **wild oats**) indulge in youthful excess or promiscuity. □□ **oaten** *adj.* [OE *āte*, pl. *ātan*, of unkn. orig.]

oatcake /ṓtkayk/ *n.* a thin unleavened biscuit-like food made of oatmeal, common in Scotland and N. England.

oath /ōth/ *n.* (*pl.* **oaths** /ō<u>th</u>z/) **1** a solemn declaration or undertaking (often naming God) as to the truth of something or as a commitment to future action. **2** a statement or promise contained in an oath (*oath of allegiance*). **3** a profane or blasphemous utterance; a curse. □ **on** (or **under**) **oath** having sworn a solemn oath. **take** (or **swear**) **an oath** make such a declaration or undertaking. [OE *āth* f. Gmc]
■ **1, 2** vow, avowal, pledge, promise, word (of honour), guarantee, guaranty, warranty, (sworn) statement, *archaic* plight, troth. **3** curse, profanity, blasphemy, imprecation, malediction, swear-word, expletive, four-letter word, obscenity, dirty word. □ **take** (or **swear**) **an oath** see SWEAR *v.* 1a, 2.

oatmeal /ṓtmeel/ *n.* **1** meal made from ground oats used esp. in porridge and oatcakes. **2** a greyish-fawn colour flecked with brown .

OAU *abbr.* Organization of African Unity.

OB *abbr. Brit.* outside broadcast.

ob. *abbr.* he or she died. [L *obiit*]

ob- /ob/ *prefix* (also **oc-** before *c*, **of-** before *f*, **op-** before *p*) occurring mainly in words of Latin origin, meaning: **1** exposure, openness (*object*; *obverse*). **2** meeting or facing (*occasion*; *obvious*). **3** direction (*oblong*; *offer*). **4** opposition, hostility, or resistance (*obstreperous*; *opponent*; *obstinate*). **5** hindrance, blocking, or concealment (*obese*; *obstacle*; *occult*). **6** finality or completeness (*obsolete*; *occupy*). **7** (in modern technical words) inversely; in a direction or manner contrary to the usual (*obconical*; *obovate*). [L f. *ob* towards, against, in the way of]

Obad. *abbr.* Obadiah (Old Testament).

obbligato /óbligaátō/ *n.* (*pl.* **-os**) *Mus.* an accompaniment, usu. special and unusual in effect, forming an integral part of a composition (*with violin obbligato*). [It., = obligatory, f. L *obligatus* past part. (as OBLIGE)]

obconical /obkónnik'l/ *adj.* (also **obconic**) in the form of an inverted cone.

obcordate /obkórdayt/ *adj. Biol.* in the shape of a heart and attached at the pointed end.

obdurate /óbdyoorət/ *adj.* **1** stubborn. **2** hardened against persuasion or influence. □□ **obduracy** *n.* **obdurately** *adv.*

obdurateness *n.* [ME f. L *obduratus* past part. of *obdurare* (as OB-, *durare* harden f. *durus* hard)]
■ **1** see OBSTINATE. **2** see DOGMATIC 1. □□ **obduracy** see *obstinacy* (OBSTINATE). **obdurateness** see *severity* (SEVERE).

OBE *abbr.* (in the UK) Officer of the Order of the British Empire.

obeah /ṓbiə/ *n.* (also **obi** /ṓbi/) a kind of sorcery practised esp. in the West Indies. [W. Afr.]

obeche /ōbéechi/ *n.* **1** a West African tree, *Triplochiton scleroxylon.* **2** the light-coloured timber from this. [Nigerian name]

obedience /ōbéediənss/ *n.* **1** obeying as an act or practice or quality. **2** submission to another's rule or authority. **3** compliance with a law or command. **4** *Eccl.* **a** compliance with a monastic rule. **b** a sphere of authority (*the Roman obedience*). □ **in obedience to** actuated by or in accordance with. [ME f. OF f. L *obedientia* (as OBEY)]
■ **1–3** compliance, dutifulness, observance, respect, respectfulness, tractability, conformity, conformance, yielding, conformability, adaptability, agreement, agreeableness, acquiescence, submissiveness, submission, subservience, docility, passiveness, passivity.

obedient /ōbéediənt/ *adj.* **1** obeying or ready to obey. **2** (often foll. by *to*) submissive to another's will; dutiful (*obedient to the law*). □□ **obediently** *adv.* [ME f. OF f. L *obediens -entis* (as OBEY)]
■ compliant, dutiful, observant, respectful, tractable, yielding, conformable, adaptable, agreeable, amenable, acquiescent, submissive, subservient, docile, passive, timid, biddable, pliant, *literary* duteous.

obeisance /ōbáys'nss/ *n.* **1** a bow, curtsy, or other respectful or submissive gesture (*make an obeisance*). **2** homage, submission, deference (*pay obeisance*). □□ **obeisant** *adj.* **obeisantly** *adv.* [ME f. OF *obeissance* (as OBEY)]
■ **1** see BOW[2] *n.* **2** deference, respect, respectfulness, homage, submission, reverence, honour.

obeli *pl.* of OBELUS.

obelisk /óbbəlisk/ *n.* **1 a** a tapering usu. four-sided stone pillar set up as a monument or landmark etc. **b** a mountain, tree, etc., of similar shape. **2** = OBELUS. [L *obeliscus* f. Gk *obeliskos* dimin. of *obelos* SPIT[2]]
■ pillar, needle.

obelize /óbbəlīz/ *v.tr.* (also **-ise**) mark with an obelus as spurious etc. [Gk *obelizō* f. *obelos*: see OBELISK]

obelus /óbbələss/ *n.* (*pl.* **obeli** /-lī/) **1** a dagger-shaped reference mark in printed matter. **2** a mark (— or ÷) used in ancient manuscripts to mark a word or passage, esp. as spurious. [L f. Gk *obelos* SPIT[2]]

obese /ōbéess/ *adj.* very fat; corpulent. □□ **obeseness** *n.* **obesity** *n.* [L *obesus* (as OB-, *edere* eat)]
■ fat, overweight, stout, fleshy, gross, corpulent, heavy, plump, portly, tubby, chubby, paunchy, rotund, abdominous, pot-bellied, podgy, *colloq.* pudgy, *Austral. colloq.* poddy. □□ **obesity** corpulence, plumpness, tubbiness, chubbiness, grossness, *embonpoint*, rotundity, portliness, paunchiness; size, bulk, weight, avoirdupois.

obey /ōbáy/ *v.* **1** *tr.* **a** carry out the command of (*you will obey me*). **b** carry out (a command) (*obey orders*). **2** *intr.* do what one is told to do. **3** *tr.* be actuated by (a force or impulse). □□ **obeyer** *n.* [ME f. OF *obeir* f. L *obedire* (as OB-, *audire* hear)]
■ comply (with), agree (to), consent (to), submit (to), abide by, observe, respect, adhere to, follow, conform (to *or* with), acquiesce (to *or* in), mind, accept, heed, defer (to), yield (to), knuckle down *or* under, give way (to), surrender (to), succumb (to), give in (to), truckle to, bow (to), bend (to), take *or* accept orders (from); discharge, execute, effect, carry out, fulfil, meet, satisfy, do, perform; serve, act.

obfuscate /óbfuskayt/ *v.tr.* **1** obscure or confuse (a mind, topic, etc.). **2** stupefy, bewilder. □□ **obfuscation** /-káysh'n/ *n.* **obfuscatory** *adj.* [LL *obfuscare* (as OB-, *fuscus* dark)]
■ **1** see OBSCURE *v.* 1, 2.

obi[1] var. of OBEAH.

obi[2] /ṓbi/ *n.* (*pl.* **obis**) a broad sash worn with a Japanese kimono. [Jap. *obi* belt]

obit /óbbit, ṓbit/ *n. colloq.* an obituary. [abbr.]

obiter dictum /óbbitər díktəm/ *n.* (*pl.* ***obiter dicta*** /-tə/) **1** a judge's expression of opinion uttered in court or giving judgement, but not essential to the decision and therefore without binding authority. **2** an incidental remark. [L f. *obiter* by the way + *dictum* a thing said]

obituary /əbítyoori/ *n.* (*pl.* **-ies**) **1** a notice of a death or deaths esp. in a newspaper. **2** an account of the life of a deceased person. **3** (*attrib.*) of or serving as an obituary. □□ **obituarial** /-tyoo-áiriəl/ *adj.* **obituarist** *n.* [med.L *obituarius* f. L *obitus* death f. *obire obit-* die (as OB-, *ire* go)]
■ necrology, death notice, *US* eulogy, *colloq.* obit.

object *n.* & *v.* ● *n.* /óbjikt/ **1** a material thing that can be seen or touched. **2** (foll. by *of*) a person or thing to which action or feeling is directed (*the object of attention*; *the object of our study*). **3** a thing sought or aimed at; a purpose. **4** *Gram.* a noun or its equivalent governed by an active transitive verb or by a preposition. **5** *Philos.* a thing external to the thinking mind or subject. **6** *derog.* a person or thing of esp. a pathetic or ridiculous appearance. **7** *Computing* a package of information and a description of its manipulation. ● *v.* /əbjékt/ **1** *intr.* (often foll. by *to, against*) express or feel opposition, disapproval, or reluctance; protest (*I object to being treated like this*; *objecting against government policies*). **2** *tr.* (foll. by *that* + clause) state as an objection (*objected that they were kept waiting*). **3** *tr.* (foll. by *to, against*, or *that* + clause) adduce (a quality or fact) as contrary or damaging (to a case). □ **no object** not forming an important or restricting factor (*money no object*). **object-ball** *Billiards* etc. that at which a player aims the cue-ball. **object-glass** the lens in a telescope etc. nearest to the object observed. **object language 1** a language described by means of another language (see METALANGUAGE). **2** *Computing* a language into which a program is translated by means of a compiler or assembler. **object-lesson** a striking practical example of some principle. **object of the exercise** the main point of an activity. □□ **objectless** /óbjiktliss/ *adj.* **objector** /əbjéktər/ *n.* [ME f. med.L *objectum* thing presented to the mind, past part. of L *objicere* (as OB-, *jacere ject-* throw)]
■ *n.* **1** thing, item; reality, entity. **2** focus, target, butt, aim, destination, quarry, goal. **3** purpose, end, intention, objective, reason, intent, idea, goal, plan, object of the exercise, *colloq.* name of the game. ● *v.* **1, 2** protest, raise objection(s), argue, take exception, disapprove, draw the line, complain, remonstrate, take a stand, refuse.

objectify /əbjéktifī/ *v.tr.* (**-ies, -ied**) **1** make objective; embody. **2** present as an object of perception. □□ **objectification** /-fikáysh'n/ *n.*

objection /əbjéksh'n/ *n.* **1** an expression or feeling of opposition or disapproval. **2** the act of objecting. **3** an adverse reason or statement. [ME f. OF *objection* or LL *objectio* (as OBJECT)]
■ protest, remonstration, remonstrance, demur, demurral, interference, opposition, disapproval, dislike, antipathy, exception, argument, challenge, complaint, question, doubt, stand, refusal, *Law* demurrer.

objectionable /əbjékshənəb'l/ *adj.* **1** open to objection. **2** unpleasant, offensive. □□ **objectionableness** *n.* **objectionably** /-bli/ *adv.*
■ **1** see EXCEPTIONABLE. **2** see OFFENSIVE *adj.* 1.

objective /əbjéktiv/ *adj.* & *n.* ● *adj.* **1** external to the mind; actually existing; real. **2** (of a person, writing, art, etc.) dealing with outward things or exhibiting facts uncoloured by feelings or opinions; not subjective. **3** *Gram.* (of a case or word) constructed as or appropriate to the object of a transitive verb or preposition (cf. ACCUSATIVE). **4** aimed at (*objective point*). **5** (of symptoms) observed by another and not only felt by the patient. ● *n.* **1** something sought or aimed at; an objective point. **2** *Gram.* the objective case. **3**

= *object-glass*. ▫▫ **objectival** /óbjektī́v'l/ *adj*. **objectively** *adv*. **objectiveness** *n*. **objectivity** /óbjektívviti/ *n*. **objectivize** /əbjéktivīz/ *v.tr.* (also **-ise**). **objectivization** /əbjéktivīzáysh'n/ *n*. [med.L *objectivus* (as OBJECT)]

▪ *adj*. **1** manifest, palpable, existing, real; see also FACTUAL, ACTUAL 1. **2** fair, impartial, just, judicious, equitable, neutral, disinterested, dispassionate, open-minded, detached, unbiased, unprejudiced, even-handed, uncoloured. ● *n*. **1** target, goal, object, aim, purpose, end, intent, intention, design, aspiration, ambition, hope. ▫▫ **objectivity, objectiveness** impartiality, fairness, fair-mindedness, equitableness, equitability, even-handedness, neutrality, disinterest, detachment, dispassion.

objectivism /əbjéktiviz'm/ *n*. **1** the tendency to lay stress on what is objective. **2** *Philos*. the belief that certain things (esp. moral truths) exist apart from human knowledge or perception of them. ▫▫ **objectivist** *n*. **objectivistic** /-vístik/ *adj*.

objet d'art /óbzhay daar/ *n*. (*pl*. ***objets d'art*** *pronunc*. same) a small decorative object. [F, lit. 'object of art']

objurgate /óbjərgayt/ *v.tr. literary* chide or scold. ▫▫ **objurgation** /-gáysh'n/ *n*. **objurgatory** /objúrgətəri/ *adj*. [L *objurgare objurgat-* (as OB-, *jurgare* quarrel f. *jurgium* strife)]

oblanceolate /oblaánsiələt/ *adj*. *Bot*. (esp. of leaves) lanceolate with the more pointed end at the base.

oblate[1] /óblayt/ *n*. a person dedicated to a monastic or religious life or work. [F f. med.L. *oblatus* f. *offerre oblat-* offer (as OB-, *ferre* bring)]

oblate[2] /óblayt/ *adj*. *Geom*. (of a spheroid) flattened at the poles (cf. PROLATE). [mod.L *oblatus* (as OBLATE[1])]

oblation /ōbláysh'n/ *n*. *Relig*. **1** a thing offered to a divine being. **2** the presentation of bread and wine to God in the Eucharist. ▫▫ **oblational** *adj*. **oblatory** /óblətəri/ *adj*. [ME f. OF *oblation* or LL *oblatio* (as OBLATE[1])]

▪ **1** see OFFERING.

obligate *v*. & *adj*. ● *v.tr.* /óbligayt/ **1** (usu. in *passive*; foll. by *to* + infin.) bind (a person) legally or morally. **2** *US* commit (assets) as security. ● *adj*. /óbligət/ *Biol*. that has to be as described (*obligate parasite*). ▫▫ **obligator** *n*. [L *obligare obligat-* (as OBLIGE)]

▪ *v*. **1** oblige, commit, bind; require, compel, constrain, force.

obligation /óbligáysh'n/ *n*. **1** the constraining power of a law, precept, duty, contract, etc. **2** a duty; a burdensome task. **3** a binding agreement, esp. one enforceable under legal penalty; a written contract or bond. **4 a** a service or benefit; a kindness done or received (*repay an obligation*). **b** indebtedness for this (*be under an obligation*). ▫ **day of obligation** *Eccl*. a day on which all are required to attend Mass or Communion. **of obligation** obligatory. ▫▫ **obligational** *adj*. [ME f. OF f. L *obligatio -onis* (as OBLIGE)]

▪ **1, 3** indebtedness, constraint, compulsion; requirement, demand; contract, promise, pledge, bond, agreement, covenant. **2** responsibility, duty, *archaic* devoir; charge, burden, onus; liability, trust. **4** debt, liability; see also KINDNESS 2.

obligatory /əblíggətəri, -tri/ *adj*. **1** legally or morally binding. **2** compulsory and not merely permissive. **3** constituting an obligation. ▫▫ **obligatorily** *adv*. [ME f. LL *obligatorius* (as OBLIGE)]

▪ required, demanded, necessary, requisite, compulsory, mandatory; incumbent; indispensable, essential.

oblige /əblī́j/ *v*. **1** *tr*. (foll. by *to* + infin.) constrain, compel. **2** *tr*. be binding on. **3** *tr*. **a** make indebted by conferring a favour. **b** (foll. by *with*, or *by* + verbal noun) gratify (*oblige me by leaving*). **c** perform a service for (often *absol*.: *will you oblige?*). **4** *tr*. (in *passive*; foll. by *to*) be indebted (*am obliged to you for your help*). **5** *intr*. *colloq*. (foll. by *with*) make a contribution of a specified kind (*Doris obliged with a song*). **6** *tr*. *archaic* or *Law* (foll. by *to*, or *to* + infin.) bind by oath, promise, contract, etc. ▫ **much obliged** an expression of thanks. ▫▫ **obliger** *n*. [ME f. OF *obliger* f. L *obligare* (as OB-, *ligare* bind)]

▪ **1, 2** make, require, demand, force, compel, constrain, coerce, bind, obligate. **3** accommodate, indulge, favour, serve, please, humour, gratify. **4** (*obliged*) thankful, grateful, appreciative, beholden, indebted, obligated. ▫ **much obliged** thank you, thanks, thanks a lot, thanks very much, *Brit. colloq*. thanks *or* ta (ever so *or joc*. muchly).

obligee /óblijeé/ *n*. *Law* a person to whom another is bound by contract or other legal procedure (cf. OBLIGOR).

obliging /əblī́jing/ *adj*. courteous, accommodating; ready to do a service or kindness. ▫▫ **obligingly** *adv*. **obligingness** *n*.

▪ accommodating, willing, indulgent, gracious, courteous, civil, considerate, polite, agreeable, amenable, kind, kindly, helpful, friendly, amiable, neighbourly, supportive.

obligor /óbligór/ *n*. *Law* a person who is bound to another by contract or other legal procedure (cf. OBLIGEE).

oblique /əbleék/ *adj*., *n*., & *v*. ● *adj*. **1 a** slanting; declining from the vertical or horizontal. **b** diverging from a straight line or course. **2** not going straight to the point; roundabout, indirect. **3** *Geom*. **a** (of a line, plane figure, or surface) inclined at other than a right angle. **b** (of an angle) acute or obtuse. **c** (of a cone, cylinder, etc.) with an axis not perpendicular to the plane of its base. **4** *Anat*. neither parallel nor perpendicular to the long axis of a body or limb. **5** *Bot*. (of a leaf) with unequal sides. **6** *Gram*. denoting any case other than the nominative or vocative. ● *n*. **1** an oblique stroke (/). **2** an oblique muscle. ● *v.intr.* (**obliques, obliqued, obliquing**) esp. *Mil*. advance obliquely. ▫ **oblique oration** (or **speech**) = *reported speech* (see REPORT). **oblique sphere** see SPHERE. ▫▫ **obliquely** *adv*. **obliqueness** *n*. **obliquity** /əblíkwiti/ *n*. [ME f. F f. L *obliquus*]

▪ *adj*. **1** slanting, slanted, sloping, aslant, slant, inclined, diagonal, inclining, angled, canted, banked, banking, cambered, crooked, askew, divergent, diverging, tilted, atilt, tilting. **2** roundabout, indirect, circuitous, circumlocutionary, evasive, sly, devious, sidelong, offhand, surreptitious, furtive, implied, clandestine, underhand(ed), deceitful, deceptive, false. ● *n*. **1** solidus, virgule, slash, stroke.

obliterate /əblíttərayt/ *v.tr.* **1 a** blot out; efface, erase, destroy. **b** leave no clear traces of. **2** deface (a postage stamp etc.) to prevent further use. ▫▫ **obliteration** /-ráysh'n/ *n*. **obliterative** /-rətiv/ *adj*. **obliterator** *n*. [L *obliterare* (as OB-, *litera* LETTER)]

▪ **1** erase, expunge, rub out, efface, eradicate, wipe *or* blot out, delete, strike off *or* out, block out, rule out, eliminate; annihilate, blot out, extirpate, destroy, kill, exterminate.

oblivion /əblívviən/ *n*. **1 a** the state of having or being forgotten. **b** disregard; an unregarded state. **2** an amnesty or pardon. ▫ **fall into oblivion** be forgotten or disused. [ME f. OF f. L *oblivio -onis* f. *oblivisci* forget]

▪ **1** blankness, blackness, darkness, obscurity, nothingness, nonentity, nihility, anonymity, extinction, non-existence, void, limbo; unawareness, obliviousness, forgetfulness, heedlessness, disregard, unconsciousness, insensibility.

oblivious /əblívviəss/ *adj*. **1** (often foll. by *of*) forgetful, unmindful. **2** (foll. by *to*, *of*) unaware or unconscious of. ▫▫ **obliviously** *adv*. **obliviousness** *n*. [ME f. L *obliviosus* (as OBLIVION)]

▪ absent-minded, forgetful, Lethean; unaware, unconscious, unmindful, disregardful, insensible, insensitive, distant, unconcerned, detached, removed, unfeeling, abstracted. ▫▫ **obliviousness** unawareness, heedlessness, disregard, unconsciousness, insensibility, oblivion; absent-mindedness, forgetfulness.

oblong /óblong/ *adj*. & *n*. ● *adj*. **1** deviating from a square form by having one long axis, esp. rectangular with adjacent sides unequal. **2** greater in breadth than in height. ● *n*. an oblong figure or object. [ME f. L *oblongus* longish (as OB-, *longus* long)]

obloquy /óbləkwi/ *n.* **1** the state of being generally ill spoken of. **2** abuse, detraction. [ME f. LL *obloquium* contradiction f. L *obloqui* deny (as OB-, *loqui* speak)]

■ **1** see *notoriety* (NOTORIOUS). **2** see ABUSE *n.* 2.

obnoxious /əbnókshəss/ *adj.* offensive, objectionable, disliked. □□ **obnoxiously** *adv.* **obnoxiousness** *n.* [orig. = vulnerable (to harm), f. L *obnoxiosus* or *obnoxius* (as OB-, *noxa* harm: assoc. with NOXIOUS)]

■ revolting, repulsive, repugnant, disgusting, offensive, objectionable, fulsome, vile, repellent, nauseous, nauseating, sickening, foul, noxious, mephitic, unsavoury, execrable, abominable, abhorrent, loathsome, detestable, hateful, odious, scurvy, base, obscene, despicable, awful, terrible, unpalatable, distasteful, unlikeable, disliked, unpleasant, nasty, *colloq.* beastly, *literary* noisome.

oboe /ṓbō/ *n.* **1 a** a woodwind double-reed instrument of treble pitch and plaintive incisive tone. **b** its player. **2** an organ stop with a quality resembling an oboe. □ **oboe d'amore** /damóray/ an oboe with a pear-shaped bell and mellow tone, pitched a minor third below a normal oboe, commonly used in baroque music. □□ **oboist** /ṓbō-ist/ *n.* [It. *oboe* or F *hautbois* f. *haut* high + *bois* wood: *d'amore* = of love]

obol /óbb'l/ *n.* an ancient Greek coin, equal to one-sixth of a drachma. [L *obolus* f. Gk *obolos*, var. of *obelos* OBELUS]

obovate /obṓvayt/ *adj. Biol.* (of a leaf) ovate with the narrower end at the base.

obscene /əbsẽen/ *adj.* **1** offensively or repulsively indecent, esp. by offending accepted sexual morality. **2** *colloq.* highly offensive or repugnant (*an obscene accumulation of wealth*). **3** *Brit. Law* (of a publication) tending to deprave or corrupt. □□ **obscenely** *adv.* **obsceneness** *n.* [F *obscène* or L *obsc(a)enus* ill-omened, abominable]

■ **1** improper, rude, shameless, shameful, indecent, immodest, indecorous, indelicate, risqué, vulgar, immoral, degenerate, amoral, dissolute, broad, suggestive, erotic, sensual, ribald, debauched, wanton, loose, libertine, bawdy, blue, X(-rated), scabrous, coarse, dirty, filthy, smutty, pornographic, hard-core, libidinous, lewd, licentious, lecherous, lustful, goatish, carnal, ruttish, lascivious, salacious, prurient, disgusting, offensive, repulsive, foul, abominable, vile, loathsome, gross, foul-mouthed, scurrilous, scatological, *US* off colour, *colloq.* near the knuckle, close to the wind; *euphem.* adult. **2** offensive, outrageous, repulsive, shocking, repellent, repugnant, obnoxious, off-putting, objectionable, intolerable, insufferable, unpalatable, distasteful, nauseous, nauseating, sickening, execrable, despicable, nasty, evil, wicked, heinous, atrocious, *colloq.* awful.

obscenity /əbsénniti/ *n.* (*pl.* **-ies**) **1** the state or quality of being obscene. **2** an obscene action, word, etc. [L *obscaenitas* (as OBSCENE)]

■ **1** see RIBALDRY. **2** see CURSE *n.* 3.

obscurantism /óbskyoorántiz'm/ *n.* opposition to knowledge and enlightenment. □□ **obscurant** /əbskyŏŏrənt/ *n.* **obscurantist** *n.* [*obscurant* f. G f. L *obscurans* f. *obscurare*: see OBSCURE]

obscure /əbskyŏŏr/ *adj.* & *v.* ● *adj.* **1** not clearly expressed or easily understood. **2** unexplained, doubtful. **3** dark, dim. **4** indistinct; not clear. **5** hidden; remote from observation. **6 a** unnoticed. **b** (of a person) undistinguished, hardly known. **7** (of a colour) dingy, dull, indefinite. ● *v.tr.* **1** make obscure, dark, indistinct, or unintelligible. **2** dim the glory of; outshine. **3** conceal from sight. □ **obscure vowel** = *indeterminate vowel.* □□ **obscuration** /-ráysh'n/ *n.* **obscurely** *adv.* [ME f. OF *obscur* f. L *obscurus* dark]

■ *adj.* **1, 2, 4** unclear, uncertain, ambiguous, vague, hazy, doubtful, dubious, equivocal, indefinite, indistinct, fuzzy, blurred, confused, confusing, Delphic, puzzling, enigmatic, perplexing, baffling, mystifying, mysterious, cryptic, unexplained, incomprehensible, unfamiliar, foreign, strange; abstruse, arcane, recondite, esoteric, intricate, complex, occult, out of the ordinary, unfamiliar, *sl.* far-out. **3** dark, unlit, gloomy, sombre, dismal, murky, dusky, black, dim, faint, blurred, veiled, shadowy, umbral, shady, hazy, foggy, befogged, clouded, nebulous, overcast, cloudy, *formal* subfusc, *literary* tenebrous. **5** secret, concealed, hidden, remote, out-of-the-way, inconspicuous, unnoticeable, secluded. **6** unknown, unheard-of, anonymous, unnamed, insignificant, unimportant, inconsequential, humble, lowly, mean, inglorious, inconspicuous, undistinguished, unnoticed, unsung, minor, little-known. **7** muddy, murky, dull, indefinite; see also SOBER *adj.* 5, DINGY. ● *v.* **1, 2** dim, cloud, becloud, dull, shroud, shade, darken, obfuscate, block, *poet.* bedim; eclipse, adumbrate, overshadow, outshine, put in the shade. **3** cover, conceal, hide, veil, shroud, cloak, mask, screen, disguise.

obscurity /əbskyŏŏriti/ *n.* (*pl.* **-ies**) **1** the state of being obscure. **2** an obscure person or thing. [F *obscurité* f. L *obscuritas* (as OBSCURE)]

■ **1** dimness, darkness, gloom, murk, murkiness, duskiness, dusk, blackness, faintness, blurriness, shade, shadow, haze, fog, cloudiness, nebulousness; abstruseness, ambiguousness, intricacy, complexity, unintelligibility; insignificance, unimportance, ingloriousness, inconspicuousness, anonymity, namelessness, limbo. **2** nobody, nonentity, nullity, nothing, zero, cipher, pawn, *colloq.* nebbish; mystery, arcanum, secret.

obsecration /óbsikráysh'n/ *n.* earnest entreaty. [ME f. L *obsecratio* f. *obsecrare* entreat (as OB-, *sacrare* f. *sacer sacri* sacred)]

obsequies /óbsikwiz/ *n.pl.* **1** funeral rites. **2** a funeral. □□ **obsequial** /əbsẽekwiəl/ *adj.* [ME, pl. of obs. *obsequy* f. AF *obsequie*, OF *obseque* f. med.L *obsequiae* f. L *exsequiae* funeral rites (see EXEQUIES): assoc. with *obsequium* (see OBSEQUIOUS)]

■ see FUNERAL *n.*

obsequious /əbsẽekwiəss/ *adj.* servilely obedient or attentive. □□ **obsequiously** *adv.* **obsequiousness** *n.* [ME f. L *obsequiosus* f. *obsequium* compliance (as OB-, *sequi* follow)]

■ low, cringing, toadying, toadyish, sycophantic, sycophantish, unctuous, truckling, grovelling, crawling, fawning, deferential, ingratiating, menial, flattering, servile, slavish, subservient, submissive, abject, mealy-mouthed, slimy, *colloq.* bootlicking, smarmy.

observance /əbzérv'nss/ *n.* **1** the act or process of keeping or performing a law, duty, custom, ritual, etc. **2** an act of a religious or ceremonial character; a customary rite. **3** the rule of a religious order. **4** *archaic* respect, deference. **5** *archaic* the act of observing or watching; observation. [ME f. OF f. L *observantia* (as OBSERVE)]

■ **1** observation, obedience, compliance, conformity, adherence, keeping, accordance, regard, recognition, respect, heed, attention. **2** ceremony, celebration, ceremonial, practice, rite, ritual, service, performance; form, custom, convention, tradition, formality, usage, habit, institution. **5** observation, examination, inspection, scrutiny, looking, watching.

observant /əbzérv'nt/ *adj.* & *n.* ● *adj.* **1 a** acute or diligent in taking notice. **b** (often foll. by *of*) carefully particular; heedful. **2** attentive in esp. religious observances (*an observant Jew*). ● *n.* (**Observant**) a member of the branch of the Franciscan order that observes the strict rule. □□ **observantly** *adv.* [F (as OBSERVE)]

■ **1 a** watchful, alert, attentive, vigilant, on the lookout, on the qui vive, on guard, regardful, mindful, aware, keen, keen-eyed, sharp-eyed, eagle-eyed, perceptive, sharp, shrewd, acute, diligent, *colloq.* wide awake. **b** heedful, attentive, particular. **2** obedient, compliant, respectful, conformist, adherent.

observation /óbzərváysh'n/ *n.* **1** the act or an instance of noticing; the condition of being noticed. **2** perception; the faculty of taking notice. **3** a remark or statement, esp. one that is of the nature of a comment. **4 a** the accurate watching and noting of phenomena as they occur in nature with regard to cause and effect or mutual relations. **b** the noting of the symptoms of a patient, the behaviour of a suspect, etc. **5** the taking of the sun's or another heavenly body's altitude to find a latitude or longitude. **6** *Mil.* the watching of a fortress or hostile position or movements. □ **observation car** esp. *US* a carriage in a train built so as to afford good views. **observation post** *Mil.* a post for watching the effect of artillery fire etc. **under observation** being watched. □□ **observational** *adj.* **observationally** *adv.* [ME f. L *observatio* (as OBSERVE)]

■ **1, 2, 4** watching, examination, scrutiny, inspection, viewing, survey, surveillance; notice, perception, discovery, attention, awareness. **3** comment, remark, note, reflection, opinion, sentiment, point of view, impression, feeling, commentary, criticism; utterance, word, announcement, pronouncement, proclamation, declaration.

observatory /əbzérvətəri, -tri/ *n.* (*pl.* **-ies**) a room or building equipped for the observation of natural, esp. astronomical or meteorological, phenomena. [mod.L *observatorium* f. L *observare* (as OBSERVE)]

observe /əbzérv/ *v.* **1** *tr.* (often foll. by *that, how* + clause) perceive, note; take notice of; become conscious of. **2** *tr.* watch carefully. **3** *tr.* **a** follow or adhere to (a law, command, method, principle, etc.). **b** keep or adhere to (an appointed time). **c** maintain (silence). **d** duly perform (a rite). **e** celebrate (an anniversary). **4** *tr.* examine and note (phenomena) without the aid of experiment. **5** *tr.* (often foll. by *that* + clause) say, esp. by way of comment. **6** *intr.* (foll. by *on*) make a remark or remarks about. □□ **observable** *adj.* **observably** *adv.* [ME f. OF *observer* f. L *observare* watch (as OB-, *servare* keep)]

■ **1** see NOTICE *v.* **2, 4** watch, look at, examine, monitor, scrutinize, study, regard, view, inspect, pore over, contemplate, consider, check (over), *US* check out, *sl.* case. **3 a, b** obey, abide by, comply with, be heedful of, attend to, conform to, regard, keep, follow, adhere to, respect, pay attention to. **c** see MAINTAIN 1, 2. **d, e** celebrate, keep, solemnize, mark, commemorate, memorialize, remember, recognize. **5** comment, remark, mention, say, note, make reference; state, declare. □□ **observable** perceptible, perceivable, noticeable, discernible, recognizable, detectable, visible, apparent, distinct, evident, manifest, plain, obvious, clear, explicit, transparent, patent, tangible, unmistakable.

observer /əbzérvər/ *n.* **1** a person who observes. **2** an interested spectator. **3** a person who attends a conference etc. to note the proceedings but does not participate. **4 a** a person trained to notice and identify aircraft. **b** a person carried in an aeroplane to note the enemy's position etc.

■ **1–3** witness, eyewitness, spectator, viewer, onlooker, beholder, watcher, looker-on; non-participant, bystander.

obsess /əbséss/ *v.tr.* (often in *passive*) preoccupy, haunt; fill the mind of (a person) continually. □□ **obsessive** *adj.* & *n.* **obsessively** *adv.* **obsessiveness** *n.* [L *obsidēre obsess-* (as OB-, *sedēre* sit)]

■ haunt, take control of, torment, take over, preoccupy, dominate, control, grip, possess, hold, *colloq.* plague. □□ **obsessive** (*adj.*) dominating, controlling, compulsive, addictive; haunting, harassing, tormenting.

obsession /əbsésh'n/ *n.* **1** the act of obsessing or the state of being obsessed. **2** a persistent idea or thought dominating a person's mind. **3** a condition in which such ideas are present. □□ **obsessional** *adj.* **obsessionalism** *n.* **obsessionally** *adv.* [L *obsessio* (as OBSESS)]

■ fixed idea, *idée fixe*, fixation, conviction, preoccupation, prepossession, passion, mania, phobia, *colloq.* thing, *sl.* hang-up.

obsidian /əbsíddiən/ *n.* a dark glassy volcanic rock formed from hardened lava. [L *obsidianus*, error for *obsianus* f. *Obsius*, the name (in Pliny) of the discoverer of a similar stone]

obsolescent /óbsəléss'nt/ *adj.* becoming obsolete; going out of use or date. □□ **obsolescence** *n.* [L *obsolescere obsolescent-* (as OB-, *solēre* be accustomed)]

■ fading, waning, on the wane, declining, dying, on the way out, on the decline; see also OBSOLETE.

obsolete /óbsəleet/ *adj.* **1** disused, discarded, antiquated. **2** *Biol.* less developed than formerly or than in a cognate species; rudimentary. □□ **obsoletely** *adv.* **obsoleteness** *n.* **obsoletism** *n.* [L *obsoletus* past part. (as OBSOLESCENT)]

■ **1** out of date, out of fashion, out-dated, *passé*, out, dead, outmoded, old, antiquated, ancient, superannuated, dated, archaic, old-fashioned, *démodé*, superseded, extinct, *colloq.* old hat, antediluvian; unused, disused, discarded.

obstacle /óbstək'l/ *n.* a person or thing that obstructs progress. □ **obstacle-race** a race in which various obstacles have to be negotiated. [ME f. OF f. L *obstaculum* f. *obstare* impede (as OB-, *stare* stand)]

■ impediment, hindrance, obstruction, hurdle, hitch, catch, snag, stumbling-block, barrier, bar, check.

obstetric /əbstétrik/ *adj.* (also **obstetrical**) of or relating to childbirth and associated processes. □□ **obstetrically** *adv.* **obstetrician** /-stətrísh'n/ *n.* [mod.L *obstetricus* for L *obstetricius* f. *obstetrix* midwife f. *obstare* be present (as OB-, *stare* stand)]

obstetrics /əbstétriks/ *n.pl.* (usu. treated as *sing.*) the branch of medicine and surgery concerned with childbirth and midwifery.

obstinate /óbstinət/ *adj.* **1** stubborn, intractable. **2** firmly adhering to one's chosen course of action or opinion despite dissuasion. **3** inflexible, self-willed. **4** unyielding; not readily responding to treatment etc. □□ **obstinacy** *n.* **obstinately** *adv.* [ME f. L *obstinatus* past part. of *obstinare* persist (as OB-, *stare* stand)]

■ stubborn, dogged, tenacious, persistent, mulish, perverse, headstrong, pigheaded, single-minded, wilful, strong-willed, self-willed, contrary, recalcitrant, uncooperative, rebellious, contumacious, refractory, intransigent, pertinacious, obdurate, fixed, inflexible, stony, adamant, set, unmoving, immovable, inexorable, intractable, unchangeable, resolute, steadfast, unyielding, persevering, stiff, rigid, hard, *archaic* froward, *colloq.* bloody-minded. □□ **obstinacy** stubbornness, doggedness, tenacity, persistence, persistency, mulishness, pigheadedness, wilfulness, contrariness, perverseness, perversity, recalcitrance, uncooperativeness, rebelliousness, contumacy, refractoriness, intractability, intransigence, pertinacity, pertinaciousness, obduracy, fixedness, stolidity, inflexibility, firmness, *archaic* frowardness, *colloq.* bloody-mindedness.

obstreperous /əbstréppərəss/ *adj.* **1** turbulent, unruly; noisily resisting control. **2** noisy, vociferous. □□ **obstreperously** *adv.* **obstreperousness** *n.* [L *obstreperus* f. *obstrepere* (as OB-, *strepere* make a noise)]

■ riotous, uproarious, tumultuous, boisterous, rowdy, tempestuous, unruly, disorderly, unmanageable, uncontrollable, uncontrolled, unrestrained, irrepressible, out of control, undisciplined, roisterous, wild, turbulent, *colloq.* rumbustious, *US colloq.* rambunctious; vociferous, clamorous, noisy, loud, raucous.

obstruct /əbstrúkt/ *v.tr.* **1** block up; make hard or impossible to pass. **2** prevent or retard the progress of; impede. □□ **obstructor** *n.* [L *obstruere obstruct-* (as OB-, *struere* build)]

■ **1** block (up), clog, stop (up), bar, blockade, barricade, shut off, get *or* stand in the way of. **2** baulk, block, check, hamper, slow, impede, retard, hinder, interrupt, delay, stay, stall, frustrate, inhibit, thwart, handicap, trammel, encumber.

obstruction /əbstrúksh'n/ *n.* **1** the act or an instance of blocking; the state of being blocked. **2** the act of making or the state of becoming more or less impassable. **3** an obstacle or blockage. **4** the retarding of progress by deliberate delays, esp. of Parliamentary business. **5** *Sport* the act of unlawfully obstructing another player. **6** *Med.* a blockage in a bodily passage, esp. in an intestine. □□ **obstructionism** *n.* (in sense 4). **obstructionist** *n.* (in sense 4). [L *obstructio* (as OBSTRUCT)]

■ **1, 2** blocking, barring, barricading; hindering, delaying, stalling; frustration. **3** obstacle, barrier, hurdle, bar, check, hindrance, impediment, constraint, restriction; blockage, bottleneck. **4** obstructiveness, delaying tactics.

obstructive /əbstrúktiv/ *adj.* & *n.* ● *adj.* causing or intended to cause an obstruction. ● *n.* an obstructive person or thing. □□ **obstructively** *adv.* **obstructiveness** *n.*

■ *adj.* see DIFFICULT 2.

obtain /əbtáyn/ *v.* **1** *tr.* acquire, secure; have granted to one. **2** *intr.* be prevalent or established or in vogue. □□ **obtainable** *adj.* **obtainability** /-táynəbílliti/ *n.* **obtainer** *n.* **obtainment** *n.* **obtention** /əbténsh'n/ *n.* [ME f. OF *obtenir* f. L *obtinēre obtent-* keep (as OB-, *tenēre* hold)]

■ **1** get, procure, acquire, come by, come into (the) possession of, secure, get hold of, lay *or* get one's hands on, grasp, capture, take possession of, seize; buy, purchase; earn, gain. **2** prevail, be in force, be in vogue, exist, have (a) place, be prevalent, be established, be customary, apply, be relevant.

obtrude /əbtróōd/ *v.* **1** *intr.* be or become obtrusive. **2** *tr.* (often foll. by *on*, *upon*) thrust forward (oneself, one's opinion, etc.) importunately. □□ **obtruder** *n.* **obtrusion** /-tróōzh'n/ *n.* [L *obtrudere obtrus-* (as OB-, *trudere* push)]

■ stick *or* stand out, impinge, trespass, push *or* shove *or* thrust forward *or* in, intrude, impose.

obtrusive /əbtróōssiv/ *adj.* **1** unpleasantly or unduly noticeable. **2** obtruding oneself. □□ **obtrusively** *adv.* **obtrusiveness** *n.* [as OBTRUDE]

■ **1** loud, showy, garish, *colloq.* flash; see also GLARING 1. **2** interfering, intrusive, meddling, officious, meddlesome, importunate, forward, presumptuous, forceful, *colloq.* pushy.

obtund /əbtúnd/ *v.tr.* blunt or deaden (a sense or faculty). [ME f. L *obtundere obtus-* (as OB-, *tundere* beat)]

obtuse /əbtyóōss/ *adj.* **1** dull-witted; slow to understand. **2** of blunt form; not sharp-pointed or sharp-edged. **3** (of an angle) more than 90° and less than 180°. **4** (of pain or the senses) dull; not acute. □□ **obtusely** *adv.* **obtuseness** *n.* **obtusity** *n.* [L *obtusus* past part. (as OBTUND)]

■ **1** dull, insensitive, unfeeling, imperceptive, thick-skinned, stolid, thick, dense, doltish, cloddish, thickheaded, dull-witted, dim-witted, slow-witted, boneheaded, lumpish, loutish, oafish, simple, simple-minded. **2** rounded; see also BLUNT *adj.* 1.

obverse /óbverss/ *n.* & *adj.* ● *n.* **1 a** the side of a coin or medal etc. bearing the head or principal design. **b** this design (cf. REVERSE). **2** the front or proper or top side of a thing. **3** the counterpart of a fact or truth. ● *adj.* **1** *Biol.* narrower at the base or point of attachment than at the apex or top (see OB- 7). **2** answering as the counterpart to something else. □□ **obversely** *adv.* [L *obversus* past part. (as OBVERT)]

■ *n.* **2** see FRONT *n.* 1.

obvert /əbvért/ *v.tr. Logic* alter (a proposition) so as to infer another proposition with a contradictory predicate, e.g. *no men are immortal* to *all men are mortal.* □□ **obversion** *n.* [L *obvertere obvers-* (as OB-, *vertere* turn)]

obviate /óbviayt/ *v.tr.* get round or do away with (a need, inconvenience, etc.). □□ **obviation** /-áysh'n/ *n.* [LL *obviare* oppose (as OB-, *via* way)]

■ see PRECLUDE 2. □□ **obviation** see *prevention* (PREVENT).

obvious /óbviəss/ *adj.* easily seen or recognized or understood; palpable, indubitable. □□ **obviously** *adv.* **obviousness** *n.* [L *obvius* f. *ob viam* in the way]

■ clear, plain, apparent, patent, perceptible, evident, self-evident, clear-cut, manifest, palpable, (much) in evidence, conspicuous, open, visible, overt, pronounced, prominent, glaring, undeniable, unconcealed, unhidden, unsubtle, distinct, simple, bald, bald-faced, straightforward, direct, self-explanatory, indisputable, indubitable, unmistakable; see also CERTAIN *adj.* 1b. □□ **obviously** clearly, plainly, apparently, patently, evidently, simply, certainly, of course, undeniably, unmistakably, indubitably, doubtless(ly).

OC *abbr.* Officer Commanding.

oc- /ok/ *prefix* assim. form of OB- before *c*.

ocarina /ókkəre͞enə/ *n.* a small egg-shaped ceramic (usu. terracotta) or metal wind instrument. [It. f. *oca* goose (from its shape)]

Occam's razor /ókkəmz/ *n.* the principle attributed to the English philosopher William of Occam (d. *c.*1350) that the fewest possible assumptions are to be made in explaining a thing.

occasion /əkáyzh'n/ *n.* & *v.* ● *n.* **1 a** a special or noteworthy event or happening (*dressed for the occasion*). **b** the time or occurrence of this (*on the occasion of their marriage*). **2** (often foll. by *for*, or *to* + infin.) a reason, ground, or justification (*there is no occasion to be angry*). **3** a juncture suitable for doing something; an opportunity. **4** an immediate but subordinate or incidental cause (*the assassination was the occasion of the war*). ● *v.tr.* **1** be the occasion or cause of; bring about esp. incidentally. **2** (foll. by *to* + infin.) cause (a person or thing to do something). □ **on occasion** now and then; when the need arises. **rise to the occasion** produce the necessary will, energy, ability, etc., in unusually demanding circumstances. **take occasion** (foll. by *to* + infin.) make use of the opportunity. [ME f. OF *occasion* or L *occasio* juncture, reason, f. *occidere occas-* go down (as OB-, *cadere* fall)]

■ *n.* **1 a** event, function, happening, occurrence, affair; observance, commemoration, ceremony, celebration. **2** reason, cause, call, justification, ground(s), warrant, provocation, stimulus, incitement, inducement. **3** time, moment, circumstance, opportunity, chance, opening, advantage. ● *v.* give rise to, bring about, cause, bring on, effect, prompt, provoke, evoke, call forth, elicit, call up, induce, impel, create, generate, engender, produce, make (for). □ **on occasion** see *occasionally* (OCCASIONAL).

occasional /əkáyzhən'l/ *adj.* **1** happening irregularly and infrequently. **2 a** made or meant for, or associated with, a special occasion. **b** (of furniture etc.) made or adapted for infrequent and varied use. **3** acting on a special occasion. □ **occasional cause** a secondary cause; an occasion (see OCCASION *n.* 4). **occasional table** a small table for infrequent and varied use. □□ **occasionality** /-nálliti/ *n.* **occasionally** *adv.*

■ **1** intermittent, irregular, periodic, random, sporadic, infrequent, casual, incidental. **2 a** special, particular, solemn, official; see also CEREMONIAL *adj.* 1. **b** additional, extra, spare, supplementary, incidental, auxiliary, accessory. □□ **occasionally** sometimes, on occasion, (every) now and then, from time to time, at times, (every) now and again, once in a while, every so often, periodically, intermittently, sporadically, irregularly, off and on.

Occident /óksid'nt/ *n. poet.* or *rhet.* **1** (prec. by *the*) the West. **2** western Europe. **3** Europe, America, or both, as distinct from the Orient. **4** European in contrast to Oriental civilization. [ME f. OF f. L *occidens -entis* setting, sunset, west (as OCCASION)]

occidental /óksidént'l/ *adj.* & *n.* ● *adj.* **1** of the Occident. **2** western. **3** of Western nations. ● *n.* (**Occidental**) a native of the Occident. □□ **occidentalism** *n.* **occidentalist** *n.* **occidentalize** *v.tr.* (also **-ise**). **occidentally** *adv.* [ME f. OF *occidental* or L *occidentalis* (as OCCIDENT)]

occipito- /oksíppitō/ *comb. form* the back of the head. [as OCCIPUT]

occiput /óksiput/ *n.* the back of the head. □□ **occipital** /-síppit'l/ *adj.* [ME f. L *occiput* (as OB-, *caput* head)]

Occitan /óksit'n/ *n.* (also *attrib.*) the Provençal language. □□ **Occitanian** /-táyniən/ *n.* & *adj.* [F: cf. LANGUE D'OC]

occlude /əklóōd/ *v.tr.* **1** stop up or close (pores or an orifice). **2** *Chem.* absorb and retain (gases or impurities). □ **occluded**

front *Meteorol.* a front resulting from occlusion. [L *occludere occlus-* (as OB-, *claudere* shut)]

occlusion /əklóozh'n/ *n.* **1** the act or process of occluding. **2** *Meteorol.* a phenomenon in which the cold front of a depression overtakes the warm front, causing upward displacement of warm air between them. **3** *Dentistry* the position of the teeth when the jaws are closed. **4** the blockage or closing of a hollow organ etc. (*coronary occlusion*). **5** *Phonet.* the momentary closure of the vocal passage. □□ **occlusive** *adj.*

occult *adj.* & *v.* ● *adj.* /okúlt, ókkult/ **1** involving the supernatural; mystical, magical. **2** kept secret; esoteric. **3** recondite, mysterious; beyond the range of ordinary knowledge. **4** *Med.* not obvious on inspection. ● *v.tr.* /okúlt/ *Astron.* (of a concealing body much greater in size than the concealed body) hide from view by passing in front; conceal by being in front. □ **the occult** occult phenomena generally. **occulting light** a lighthouse light that is cut off at regular intervals. □□ **occultation** /-táysh'n/ *n.* **occultism** *n.* **occultist** *n.* **occultly** *adv.* **occultness** *n.* [L *occulere occult-* (as OB-, *celare* hide)]

■ *adj.* **1, 3** magical, mystical, mystic, alchemic(al), unexplained, unexplainable, inexplicable, puzzling, baffling, perplexing, mystifying, mysterious, recondite, incomprehensible, inscrutable, indecipherable, impenetrable, unfathomable, transcendental, supernatural, preternatural. **2** secret, dark, concealed, private, hidden, obscure, veiled, obscured, shrouded, vague, abstruse, shadowy, mystical, mysterious, cabbalistic, esoteric, recondite, arcane, *archaic* privy. □ **the occult** the supernatural, the paranormal, the unknown, the black arts; arcana, cabbala; cabbalism, occultism, sorcery, witchcraft, (black) magic.

occupant /ókyoop'nt/ *n.* **1** a person who occupies, resides in, or is in a place etc. (*both occupants of the car were unhurt*). **2** a person holding property, esp. land, in actual possession. **3** a person who establishes a title by taking possession of something previously without an established owner. □□ **occupancy** *n.* (*pl.* **-ies**). [F *occupant* or L *occupans -antis* (as OCCUPY)]

■ **1, 2** resident, inhabitant, tenant, lessee, leaseholder, renter, owner, householder, owner-occupier, dweller, lodger, boarder, *Brit.* occupier, *US* roomer, *poet.* denizen; addressee; incumbent.

occupation /ókyoopáysh'n/ *n.* **1** what occupies one; a means of passing one's time. **2** a person's temporary or regular employment; a business, calling, or pursuit. **3** the act of occupying or state of being occupied. **4 a** the act of taking or holding possession of (a country, district, etc.) by military force. **b** the state or time of this. **5** tenure, occupancy. **6** (*attrib.*) for the sole use of the occupiers of the land concerned (*occupation road*). [ME f. AF *ocupaciou*n, OF *occupation* f. L *occupatio -onis* (as OCCUPY)]

■ **2** job, position, post, situation, appointment, employment, vocation, line (of work), career, field, calling, trade, pursuit, *métier*, craft, skill, profession, business, work. **3, 5** possession, tenure, occupancy; rule, control, suzerainty; subjugation, subjection, oppression, bondage. **4 a** conquest, seizure, appropriation, take-over.

occupational /ókyoopáyshən'l/ *adj.* **1** of or in the nature of an occupation or occupations. **2** (of a disease, hazard, etc.) rendered more likely by one's occupation. □ **occupational therapy** mental or physical activity designed to assist recovery from disease or injury.

■ **2** work-related.

occupier /ókyoopīər/ *n. Brit.* a person residing in a property as its owner or tenant.

■ see OCCUPANT.

occupy /ókyoopī/ *v.tr.* (**-ies, -ied**) **1** reside in; be the tenant of. **2** take up or fill (space or time or a place). **3** hold (a position or office). **4** take military possession of (a country, region, town, strategic position). **5** place oneself in (a building etc.) forcibly or without authority. **6** (usu. in *passive*; often foll. by *in*, *with*) keep busy or engaged. [ME f. OF *occuper* f. L *occupare* seize (as OB-, *capere* take)]

■ **1** live *or* reside in, tenant, be established *or* ensconced *or* situated in, establish *or* ensconce *or* situate oneself in, inhabit, be settled in *or* into, settle in *or* into, take up residence in, make one's home in, move in *or* into, *literary* dwell in; be located in. **2** take up, fill, cover, extend over, consume, use (up), eat up. **3** see HOLD[1] *v.* 3. **4** capture, seize, take possession of, conquer, invade, take over, overrun, garrison, dominate, hold. **6** engage, busy, absorb, monopolize, hold, take up *or* over, catch, grab, seize, grip; divert, amuse, entertain, distract, beguile, preoccupy, interest, engross, involve.

occur /əkúr/ *v.intr.* (**occurred, occurring**) **1** come into being as an event or process at or during some time; happen. **2** exist or be encountered in some place or conditions. **3** (foll. by *to*; usu. foll. by *that* + clause) come into the mind of, esp. as an unexpected or casual thought (*it occurred to me that you were right*). [L *occurrere* go to meet, present itself (as OB-, *currere* run)]

■ **1** happen, take place, arise, come about, come to pass, appear, surface, materialize, develop, become manifest, manifest itself, crop up, turn up, *colloq.* come off, *disp.* transpire, *poet.* befall. **3** (*occur to*) dawn on, strike, hit, come to, come to a person's mind, suggest itself to, cross a person's mind, enter a person's head.

occurrence /əkúrrənss/ *n.* **1** the act or an instance of occurring. **2** an incident or event. □ **of frequent occurrence** often occurring. [*occurrent* that occurs f. F f. L *occurrens -entis* (as OCCUR)]

■ **1** existence, instance, manifestation, materialization, appearance, development; frequency, incidence, rate, *Statistics* distribution. **2** happening, event, incident, phenomenon, affair, matter, experience.

ocean /ṓsh'n/ *n.* **1 a** a large expanse of sea, esp. each of the main areas called the Atlantic, Pacific, Indian, Arctic, and Antarctic Oceans. **b** these regarded cumulatively as the body of water surrounding the land of the globe. **2** (usu. prec. by *the*) the sea. **3** (often in *pl.*) a very large expanse or quantity of anything (*oceans of time*). □ **ocean-going** (of a ship) able to cross oceans. **ocean tramp** a merchant ship, esp. a steamer, running on no regular line or route. □□ **oceanward** *adv.* (also **-wards**). [ME f. OF *occean* f. L *oceanus* f. Gk *ōkeanos* stream encircling the earth's disc, Atlantic]

■ **1b, 2** (deep blue) sea, high sea(s), depths, *archaic or poet.* main, *colloq.* the drink, *poet.* the deep, *sl.* Davy Jones('s locker), *Brit. sl.* the briny. **3** (*oceans*) plenty, mass(es), an abundance, a multitude, a profusion, a flood, a plethora, *colloq.* loads, a lot, lots, tons, oodles, zillions, *US colloq.* scads.

oceanarium /ṓshənáiriəm/ *n.* (*pl.* **oceanariums** or **-ria** /-riə/) a large seawater aquarium for keeping sea animals. [OCEAN + -ARIUM, after *aquarium*]

Oceania /ṓsiáaniə/ *n.* the islands of the Pacific and adjacent seas. □□ **Oceanian** *adj.* & *n.* [mod.L f. F *Océanie* f. L (as OCEAN)]

oceanic /ṓshiánnik, ṓsi-/ *adj.* **1** of, like, or near the ocean. **2** (of a climate) governed by the ocean. **3** of the part of the ocean distant from the continents. **4** (**Oceanic**) of Oceania.

■ **1, 2** marine, pelagic, thalassic; salt-water, deep-water, aquatic, maritime, sea, ocean.

Oceanid /ōsééənid/ *n.* (*pl.* **Oceanids** or **-ides** /ṓsiánnideez/) (in Greek mythology) an ocean nymph. [Gk *ōkeanis -idos* daughter of Oceanus]

oceanography /ṓshənógrəfi/ *n.* the study of the oceans. □□ **oceanographer** *n.* **oceanographic** /-nəgráffik/ *adj.* **oceanographical** /-nəgráffik'l/ *adj.*

ocellus /osélləss/ *n.* (*pl.* **ocelli** /-lī/) **1** each of the simple, as opposed to compound, eyes of insects etc. **2** a spot of colour surrounded by a ring of a different colour on the wing of a butterfly etc. □□ **ocellar** *adj.* **ocellate** /óssilət/ *adj.* **ocellated** /óssilaytid/ *adj.* [L, dimin. of *oculus* eye]

ocelot /óssilot/ *n.* **1** a medium-sized feline, *Felis pardalis*, native to S. and Central America, having a deep yellow or orange coat with black striped and spotted markings. **2** its fur. [F f. Nahuatl *ocelotl* jaguar]

och /okh/ *int. Sc.* & *Ir.* expressing surprise or regret. [Gael. & Ir.]

oche /ókki/ *n.* (also **hockey** /ókki, hókki/) *Darts* the line behind which the players stand when throwing. [20th c.: orig. uncert. (perh. connected with OF *ocher* cut a deep notch in)]

ocher *US* var. of OCHRE.

ochlocracy /oklókrəsi/ *n.* (*pl.* **-ies**) mob rule. □□ **ochlocrat** /ókləkrat/ *n.* **ochlocratic** /ókləkráttik/ *adj.* [F *ochlocratie* f. Gk *okhlokratia* f. *okhlos* mob]

ochone /okhṓn/ *int.* (also **ohone**) *Sc.* & *Ir.* expressing regret or lament. [Gael. & Ir. *ochóin*]

ochre /ṓkər/ *n.* (*US* **ocher**) **1** a mineral of clay and ferric oxide, used as a pigment varying from light yellow to brown or red. **2** a pale brownish yellow. □□ **ochreish** *adj.* **ochreous** /ṓkriəss/ *adj.* **ochrous** /ṓkrəss/ *adj.* **ochry** /ṓkri/ *adj.* [ME f. OF *ocre* f. L *ochra* f. Gk *ōkhra* yellow ochre]

-ock /ək/ *suffix* forming nouns orig. with diminutive sense (*hillock*; *bullock*). [from or after OE *-uc*, *-oc*]

ocker /ókkər/ *n. Austral. sl.* a boorish or aggressive Australian (esp. as a stereotype). [20th c.: orig. uncert.]

o'clock /əklók/ *adv.* of the clock (used to specify the hour) (*6 o'clock*).

OCR *abbr.* optical character recognition.

Oct. *abbr.* October.

oct. *abbr.* octavo.

oct- /okt/ *comb. form* assim. form of OCTA-, OCTO- before a vowel.

octa- /óktə/ *comb. form* (also **oct-** before a vowel) eight. [Gk *okta-* f. *oktō* eight]

octad /óktad/ *n.* a group of eight. [LL *octas octad-* f. Gk *oktas -ados* f. *oktō* eight]

octagon /óktəgən/ *n.* **1** a plane figure with eight sides and angles. **2** an object or building with this cross-section. □□ **octagonal** /-tággən'l/ *adj.* **octagonally** /-tággənəli/ *adv.* [L *octagonos* f. Gk *octagōnos* (as OCTA-, -GON)]

octahedron /óktəhéedrən/ *n.* (*pl.* **octahedrons** or **octahedra** /-drə/) **1** a solid figure contained by eight (esp. triangular) plane faces. **2** a body, esp. a crystal, in the form of a regular octahedron. □ **regular octahedron** an octahedron contained by equal and equilateral triangles. □□ **octahedral** *adj.* [Gk *oktaedron* (as OCTA-, -HEDRON)]

octal /óktəl/ *adj.* reckoning or proceeding by eights (*octal scale*).

octamerous /oktámmərəss/ *adj.* **1** esp. *Bot.* having eight parts. **2** *Zool.* having organs arranged in eights.

octane /óktayn/ *n.* a colourless inflammable hydrocarbon of the alkane series. ¶ Chem. formula: C_8H_{18}. □ **high-octane** (of fuel used in internal-combustion engines) having good antiknock properties, not detonating readily during the power stroke. **octane number** (or **rating**) a figure indicating the antiknock properties of a fuel. [OCT- + -ANE[2]]

octant /óktənt/ *n.* **1** an arc of a circle equal to one eighth of the circumference. **2** such an arc with two radii, forming an area equal to one eighth of the circle. **3** each of eight parts into which three planes intersecting (esp. at right angles) at a point divide the space or the solid body round it. **4** *Astron.* a point in a body's apparent course 45° distant from a given point, esp. a point at which the moon is 45° from conjunction or opposition with the sun. **5** an instrument in the form of a graduated eighth of a circle, used in astronomy and navigation. [L *octans octant-* half-quadrant f. *octo* eight]

octaroon var. of OCTOROON.

octastyle /óktəstīl/ *adj.* & *n.* ● *adj.* having eight columns at the end or in front. ● *n.* an octastyle portico or building. [L *octastylus* f. Gk *oktastulos* (as OCTA- + *stulos* pillar)]

octavalent /óktəváylənt/ *adj. Chem.* having a valency of eight. [OCTA- + VALENCE[1]]

octave /óktiv/ *n.* **1** *Mus.* **a** a series of eight notes occupying the interval between (and including) two notes, one having twice or half the frequency of vibration of the other. **b** this interval. **c** each of the two notes at the extremes of this interval. **d** these two notes sounding together. **2** a group or stanza of eight lines; an octet. **3 a** the seventh day after a festival. **b** a period of eight days including a festival and its octave. **4** a group of eight. **5** the last of eight parrying positions in fencing. **6** *Brit.* a wine-cask holding an eighth of a pipe. [ME f. OF f. L *octava dies* eighth day (reckoned inclusively)]

octavo /oktáyvō, oktaávō/ *n.* (*pl.* **-os**) **1** a size of book or page given by folding a standard sheet three times to form a quire of eight leaves. **2** a book or sheet of this size. ¶ Abbr.: **8vo**. [L *in octavo* in an eighth f. *octavus* eighth]

octennial /okténniəl/ *adj.* **1** lasting eight years. **2** occurring every eight years. [LL *octennium* period of eight years (as OCT-, *annus* year)]

octet /oktét/ *n.* (also **octette**) **1** *Mus.* **a** a composition for eight voices or instruments. **b** the performers of such a piece. **2** a group of eight. **3** the first eight lines of a sonnet. **4** *Chem.* a stable group of eight electrons. [It. *ottetto* or G *Oktett*: assim. to OCT-, DUET, QUARTET]

octo- /óktō/ *comb. form* (also **oct-** before a vowel) eight. [L *octo* or Gk *oktō* eight]

October /oktṓbər/ *n.* the tenth month of the year. [OE f. L (as OCTO-): cf. DECEMBER, SEPTEMBER]

Octobrist /oktṓbrist/ *n. hist.* a member of the moderate party in the Russian Duma, supporting the Imperial Constitutional Manifesto of 30 Oct. 1905. [OCTOBER, after Russ. *oktyabrist*]

octocentenary /óktōsentéenəri/ *n.* & *adj.* ● *n.* (*pl.* **-ies**) **1** an eight-hundredth anniversary. **2** a celebration of this. ● *adj.* of or relating to an octocentenary.

octodecimo /óktōdéssimō/ *n.* (*pl.* **-os**) **1** a size of book or page given by folding a standard sheet into eighteen leaves. **2** a book or sheet of this size. [*in octodecimo* f. L *octodecimus* eighteenth]

octogenarian /óktōjináiriən/ *n.* & *adj.* ● *n.* a person from 80 to 89 years old. ● *adj.* of this age. [L *octogenarius* f. *octogeni* distributive of *octoginta* eighty]

octopod /óktəpod/ *n.* any cephalopod of the order Octopoda, with eight arms usu. having suckers, and a round saclike body, including octopuses. [Gk *oktōpous -podos* f. *oktō* eight + *pous* foot]

octopus /óktəpəss/ *n.* (*pl.* **octopuses**) **1** any cephalopod mollusc of the genus *Octopus* having eight suckered arms, a soft saclike body, and strong beaklike jaws. **2** an organized and usu. harmful ramified power or influence. [Gk *oktōpous*: see OCTOPOD]

octoroon /óktəroōn/ *n.* (also **octaroon**) the offspring of a quadroon and a White, a person of one-eighth Negro blood. [OCTO- after QUADROON]

octosyllabic /óktōsilábbik/ *adj.* & *n.* ● *adj.* having eight syllables. ● *n.* an octosyllabic verse. [LL *octosyllabus* (as OCTO-, SYLLABLE)]

octosyllable /óktəsílləb'l/ *n.* & *adj.* ● *n.* an octosyllabic verse or word. ● *adj.* = OCTOSYLLABIC.

octroi /óktrwaa/ *n.* **1** a duty levied in some European countries on goods entering a town. **2 a** the place where this is levied. **b** the officials by whom it is levied. [F f. *octroyer* grant, f. med.L *auctorizare*: see AUTHORIZE]

octuple /óktyoop'l/ *adj.*, *n.*, & *v.* ● *adj.* eightfold. ● *n.* an eightfold amount. ● *v.tr.* & *intr.* multiply by eight. [F *octuple* or L *octuplus* (adj.) f. *octo* eight: cf. DOUBLE]

ocular /ókyoolər/ *adj.* & *n.* ● *adj.* of or connected with the eyes or sight; visual. ● *n.* the eyepiece of an optical instrument. □ **ocular spectrum** see SPECTRUM. □□ **ocularly** *adv.* [F *oculaire* f. LL *ocularis* f. L *oculus* eye]

ocularist /ókyoolərist/ *n.* a maker of artificial eyes. [F *oculariste* (as OCULAR)]

oculate /ókyoolət/ *adj.* = OCELLATE (see OCELLUS). [L *oculatus* f. *oculus* eye]

oculist /ókyoolist/ *n.* a person who specializes in the medical treatment of eye disorders or defects. □□ **oculistic** /-lístik/ *adj.* [F *oculiste* f. L *oculus* eye]
■ eye-doctor, ophthalmologist.

oculo- /ókyoolō/ *comb. form* eye (*oculo-nasal*). [L *oculus* eye]

OD[1] *abbr.* ordnance datum.

OD[2] /ōdeé/ *n.* & *v.* esp. *US sl.* ● *n.* an overdose, esp. of a narcotic drug. ● *v.intr.* (**OD's, OD'd, OD'ing**) take an overdose. [abbr.]

od[1] /od/ *n.* a hypothetical power once thought to pervade nature and account for various scientific phenomena. [arbitrary term coined in G by Baron von Reichenbach, Ger. scientist d. 1869]

od[2] /od/ *n.* (as *int.* or in oaths) *archaic* = GOD. [corruption]

o.d. *abbr.* outer diameter.

odal var. of UDAL.

odalisque /ṓdəlisk/ *n. hist.* an Eastern female slave or concubine, esp. in the Turkish Sultan's seraglio. [F f. Turk. *odalik* f. *oda* chamber + *lik* function]

odd /od/ *adj.* & *n.* ● *adj.* **1** extraordinary, strange, queer, remarkable, eccentric. **2** casual, occasional, unconnected (*odd jobs; odd moments*). **3** not normally noticed or considered; unpredictable (*in some odd corner; picks up odd bargains*). **4** additional; beside the reckoning (*a few odd pence*). **5 a** (of numbers such as 3 and 5) not integrally divisible by two. **b** (of things or persons numbered consecutively) bearing such a number (*no parking on odd dates*). **6** left over when the rest have been distributed or divided into pairs (*have got an odd sock*). **7** detached from a set or series (*a few odd volumes*). **8** (appended to a number, sum, weight, etc.) somewhat more than (*forty odd; forty-odd people*). **9** by which a round number, given sum, etc., is exceeded (*we have 102 – what shall we do with the odd 2?*). ● *n. Golf* a handicap of one stroke at each hole. □ **odd job** a casual isolated piece of work. **odd job man** (or **odd jobber**) *Brit.* a person who does odd jobs. **odd man out 1** a person or thing differing from all the others in a group in some respect. **2** a method of selecting one of three or more persons e.g. by tossing a coin. □□ **oddish** *adj.* **oddly** *adv.* **oddness** *n.* [ME f. ON *odda-* in *odda-mathr* third man, odd man, f. *oddi* angle]
■ *adj.* **1** strange, peculiar, unusual, uncommon, different, unexpected, unfamiliar, extraordinary, remarkable, atypical, untypical, exotic, out of the ordinary, unparalleled, unconventional, exceptional, unique, singular, individual, anomalous, idiosyncratic, rare, deviant, outlandish, uncanny, queer, curious, bizarre, weird, eccentric, funny, quaint, fantastic, freak, abnormal, freakish, offbeat, kinky, freaky, *colloq.* oddball, *Brit. colloq.* rum, *sl.* screwy, bent, kooky. **2, 7** occasional, casual, part-time, irregular, random, sporadic, discontinuous, disconnected, unconnected, various, varied, miscellaneous, sundry, incidental. **4, 6, 9** leftover, surplus, remaining, unused, spare, superfluous, extra, additional; uneven, unmatched, unpaired.

oddball /ódbawl/ *n. colloq.* **1** an odd or eccentric person. **2** (*attrib.*) strange, bizarre.
■ **1** see ECCENTRIC *n.* 1. **2** (*attrib.*) see ODD *adj.* 1.

Oddfellow /ódfellō/ *n.* a member of a fraternity similar to the Freemasons.

oddity /ódditi/ *n.* (*pl.* **-ies**) **1** a strange person, thing, or occurrence. **2** a peculiar trait. **3** the state of being odd.
■ **1** peculiarity, curiosity, rarity, freak, original, phenomenon, character, eccentric, nonconformist, fish out of water, *rara avis*, misfit, round *or* square peg in a square *or* round hole, maverick, crank, *colloq.* card, weirdie, weirdo, oddball, odd fish, *Brit. sl.* oner, *US sl.* kook, screwball. **2** peculiarity, irregularity, anomaly, idiosyncrasy, eccentricity, deviation, quirk, mannerism, twist, kink. **3** peculiarity, strangeness, unnaturalness, curiousness, curiosity, incongruity, incongruousness, eccentricity, outlandishness, extraordinariness, unconventionality, bizarreness, weirdness, queerness, oddness, unusualness, individuality, singularity, distinctiveness, anomalousness, anomaly, *colloq.* kinkiness, *sl.* kookiness.

oddment /ódmənt/ *n.* **1** an odd article; something left over. **2** (in *pl.*) miscellaneous articles. **3** *Brit. Printing* matter other than the main text.
■ **2** (*oddments*) see *odds and ends*.

odds /odz/ *n.pl.* **1** the ratio between the amounts staked by the parties to a bet, based on the expected probability either way. **2** the chances or balance of probability in favour of or against some result (*the odds are against it; the odds are that it will rain*). **3** the balance of advantage (*the odds are in your favour; won against all the odds*). **4** an equalizing allowance to a weaker competitor. **5** a difference giving an advantage (*makes no odds*). □ **at odds** (often foll. by *with*) in conflict or at variance. **by all odds** certainly. **lay** (or **give**) **odds** offer a bet with odds favourable to the other better. **odds and ends** miscellaneous articles or remnants. **odds and sods** *colloq.* = *odds and ends*. **odds-on** a state when success is more likely than failure, esp. as indicated by the betting odds. **over the odds** above a generally agreed price etc. **take odds** offer a bet with odds unfavourable to the other better. **what's the odds?** *colloq.* what does it matter? [app. pl. of ODD *n.*: cf. NEWS]
■ **1, 2** chances, likelihood, probability. □ **at odds** at variance, at loggerheads, at daggers drawn, at sixes and sevens, at cross purposes, at each other's throats, in disagreement, in opposition, on bad terms; not in keeping, out of line, inharmonious, conflicting, clashing, disagreeing, differing. **odds and ends** oddments, fragments, leftovers, leavings, remnants, bits (and pieces *or* bobs), shreds, snippets, scraps, rummage, *Brit.* jumble, *colloq.* odds and sods.

ode /ōd/ *n.* **1** a lyric poem, usu. rhymed and in the form of an address, in varied or irregular metre. **2** *hist.* a poem meant to be sung. [F f. LL *oda* f. Gk *ōidē* Attic form of *aoidē* song f. *aeidō* sing]
■ see POEM.

-ode[1] /ōd/ *suffix* forming nouns meaning 'thing of the nature of' (*geode; trematode*). [Gk *-ōdēs* adj. ending]

-ode[2] /ōd/ *comb. form Electr.* forming names of electrodes, or devices having them (*cathode; diode*). [Gk *hodos* way]

odeum /ṓdiəm/ *n.* (*pl.* **odeums** or **odea** /-diə/) a building for musical performances, esp. among the ancient Greeks and Romans. [F *odéum* or L *odeum* f. Gk *ōideion* (as ODE)]

odious /ṓdiəss/ *adj.* hateful, repulsive. □□ **odiously** *adv.* **odiousness** *n.* [ME f. OF *odieus* f. L *odiosus* (as ODIUM)]
■ see REPULSIVE.

odium /ṓdiəm/ *n.* a general or widespread dislike or reprobation incurred by a person or associated with an action. [L, = hatred f. *odi* to hate]
■ see AVERSION 1.

odometer /ōdómmitər/ *n.* (also **hodometer** /hodóm-/) an instrument for measuring the distance travelled by a wheeled vehicle. □□ **odometry** *n.* [F *odomètre* f. Gk *hodos* way: see -METER]
■ milometer.

odonto- /ōdóntō/ *comb. form* tooth. [Gk *odous odont-* tooth]

odontoglossum /ōdóntəglóssəm/ *n.* any of various orchids bearing flowers with jagged edges like tooth-marks. [ODONTO- + Gk *glōssa* tongue]

odontoid /ōdóntoyd/ *adj.* toothlike. □ **odontoid process** a projection from the second cervical vertebra. [Gk *odontoeidēs* (as ODONTO- + Gk *eidos* form)]

odontology /ṓdontólləji/ *n.* the scientific study of the structure and diseases of teeth. □□ **odontological** /-təlójik'l/ *adj.* **odontologist** *n.*

odor *US* var. of ODOUR.

odoriferous /ṓdərífərəss/ *adj.* diffusing a scent, esp. an agreeable one; fragrant. □□ **odoriferously** *adv.* [ME f. L *odorifer* (as ODOUR)]

■ see FRAGRANT.

odorous /ṓdərəss/ *adj.* **1** having a scent. **2** = ODORIFEROUS. □□ **odorously** *adv.* [L *odorus* fragrant (as ODOUR)]
■ **1** redolent, aromatic.

odour /ṓdər/ *n.* (*US* **odor**) **1** the property of a substance that has an effect on the nasal sense of smell. **2** a lasting quality or trace attaching to something (*an odour of intolerance*). **3** regard, repute (*in bad odour*). □□ **odourless** *adj.* (in sense 1). [ME f. AF *odour*, OF *odor* f. L *odor -oris* smell, scent]
■ **1** smell, scent, aroma, bouquet, fragrance, perfume, redolence; stench, stink, fetor. **2** air, breath, hint, suggestion, whiff, atmosphere, spirit, quality, redolence, flavour, savour, aura, tone. **3** standing, esteem, repute, regard.

odyssey /óddisi/ *n.* (*pl.* **-eys**) a series of wanderings; a long adventurous journey. □□ **Odyssean** *adj.* [L *Odyssea* f. Gk *Odusseia*, title of an epic poem attributed to Homer describing the adventures of Odysseus (Ulysses) on his journey home from Troy]
■ see JOURNEY *n.*

OECD *abbr.* Organization for Economic Cooperation and Development.

OED *abbr.* Oxford English Dictionary.

oedema /ideémə/ *n.* (*US* **edema**) a condition characterized by an excess of watery fluid collecting in the cavities or tissues of the body. Also called DROPSY. □□ **oedematose** *adj.* **oedematous** *adj.* [LL f. Gk *oidēma -atos* f. *oideō* swell]

Oedipus complex /eédipəss/ *n. Psychol.* (according to Freud etc.) the complex of emotions aroused in a young (esp. male) child by a subconscious sexual desire for the parent of the opposite sex and wish to exclude the parent of the same sex. □□ **Oedipal** *adj.* [Gk *Oidipous*, legendary king of Thebes who unknowingly killed his father and married his mother]

oenology /eenólləji/ *n.* (*US* **enology**) the study of wines. □□ **oenological** /eénəlójik'l/ *adj.* **oenologist** *n.* [Gk *oinos* wine]

oenophile /eénəfīl/ *n.* a connoisseur of wines. □□ **oenophilist** /eenóffilist/ *n.* [as OENOLOGY]

o'er /ṓər/ *adv.* & *prep. poet.* = OVER. [contr.]

oersted /érsted/ *n.* a unit of magnetic field strength equivalent to 79.58 amperes per metre. [H. C. *Oersted*, Da. physicist d. 1851]

oesophagus /eesóffəgəss/ *n.* (*US* **esophagus**) (*pl.* **oesophagi** / -gī, -jī/ or **-guses**) the part of the alimentary canal from the mouth to the stomach; the gullet. □□ **oesophageal** /eesóffəjeéəl, eéssəfájiəl/ *adj.* [ME f. Gk *oisophagos*]

oestrogen /eéstrəjən/ *n.* (*US* **estrogen**) **1** any of various steroid hormones developing and maintaining female characteristics of the body. **2** this hormone produced artificially for use in oral contraceptives etc. □□ **oestrogenic** /-jénnik/ *adj.* **oestrogenically** /-jénnikəli/ *adv.* [OESTRUS + -GEN]

oestrus /eéstrəss/ *n.* (also **oestrum**, *US* **estrus, estrum**) a recurring period of sexual receptivity in many female mammals; heat. □□ **oestrous** *adj.* [Gk *oistros* gadfly, frenzy]

œuvre /ṓvrə/ *n.* the works of an author, painter, composer, etc., esp. regarded collectively. [F, = work, f. L *opera*]
■ see WORK *n.* 5.

of /ov, əv/ *prep.* connecting a noun (often a verbal noun) or pronoun with a preceding noun, adjective, adverb, or verb, expressing a wide range of relations broadly describable as follows: **1** origin, cause, or authorship (*paintings of Turner*; *people of Rome*; *died of malnutrition*). **2** the material or substance constituting or identifying a thing (*a house of cards*; *was built of bricks*). **3** belonging, connection, or possession (*a thing of the past*; *articles of clothing*; *the head of the business*; *the tip of the iceberg*). **4** identity or close relation (*the city of Rome*; *a pound of apples*; *a fool of a man*). **5** removal, separation, or privation (*north of the city*; *got rid of them*; *robbed us of £1000*). **6** reference, direction, or respect (*beware of the dog*; *suspected of lying*; *very good of you*; *short of money*; *the selling of goods*). **7** objective relation (*love of music*; *in search of peace*). **8** partition, classification, or inclusion (*no more of that*; *part of the story*; *a friend of mine*; *this sort of book*; *some of us will stay*). **9** description, quality, or condition (*the hour of prayer*; *a person of tact*; *a girl of ten*; *on the point of leaving*). **10** *US* time in relation to the following hour (*a quarter of three*). □ **be of** possess intrinsically; give rise to (*is of great interest*). **of all** designating the (nominally) least likely or expected example (*you of all people!*). **of all the nerve** (or **cheek** etc.) an exclamation of indignation at a person's impudence etc. **of an evening** (or **morning** etc.) *colloq.* **1** on most evenings (or mornings etc.). **2** at some time in the evenings (or mornings etc.). **of late** recently. **of old** formerly; long ago. [OE, unaccented form of *æf*, f. Gmc]

of- /of/ *prefix* assim. form of OB- before *f*.

ofay /ṓfay/ *n. US sl. offens.* a White person (esp. used by Blacks). [20th c.: prob. of Afr. orig.]

Off. *abbr.* **1** Office. **2** Officer.

off /of/ *adv.*, *prep.*, *adj.*, & *n.* ● *adv.* **1 a** away; at or to a distance (*drove off*; *is three miles off*). **b** distant or remote in fact, nature, likelihood, etc. **2** out of position; not on or touching or attached; loose, separate, gone (*has come off*; *take your coat off*). **3** so as to be rid of (*sleep it off*). **4** so as to break continuity or continuance; discontinued, stopped (*turn off the radio*; *take a day off*; *the game is off*). **5** not available as a choice, e.g. on a menu (*chips are off*). **6** to the end; entirely; so as to be clear (*clear off*; *finish off*; *pay off*). **7** situated as regards money, supplies, etc. (*is badly off*; *is not very well off*). **8** off-stage (*noises off*). **9 a** (of food etc.) beginning to decay. **b** in error; abnormal; odd. **10** (with preceding numeral) denoting a quantity produced or made at one time (esp. *one-off*). **11** away or free from a regular commitment (*How about tomorrow? I'm off then*). ● *prep.* **1 a** from; away or down or up from (*fell off the chair*; *took something off the price*; *jumped off the edge*). **b** not on (*was already off the pitch*). **2 a** (temporarily) relieved of or abstaining from (*off duty*; *am off my diet*). **b** not attracted by for the time being (*off their food*; *off smoking*). **c** not achieving or doing one's best in (*off form*; *off one's game*). **3** using as a source or means of support (*live off the land*). **4** leading from; not far from (*a street off the Strand*). **5** at a short distance to sea from (*sank off Cape Horn*). ● *adj.* **1** far, further (*the off side of the wall*). **2** (of a part of a vehicle, animal, or road) right (*the off front wheel*). **3** *Cricket* designating the half of the field (as divided lengthways through the pitch) to which the striker's feet are pointed. ● *n.* **1** *Cricket* the off side. **2** the start of a race. □ **a bit off** *Brit. colloq.* **1** rather annoying or unfair. **2** somewhat unwell (*am feeling a bit off*). **off and on** intermittently; now and then. **off-centre** not quite coinciding with a central position. **the off chance** see CHANCE. **off colour 1** not in good health. **2** *US* somewhat indecent. **off the cuff** see CUFF[1]. **off-day** a day when one is not at one's best. **off-drive** *Cricket* drive (the ball) to the off side. **off one's feet** see FOOT. **off form** see FORM. **off guard** see GUARD. **off one's hands** see HAND. **off one's head** see HEAD. **off-key 1** out of tune. **2** not quite suitable or fitting. **off-licence** *Brit.* **1** a shop selling alcoholic drink for consumption elsewhere. **2** a licence for this. **off limits** see LIMIT. **off-line** *Computing* (of a computer terminal or process) not directly controlled by or connected to a central processor. **off of** *sl. disp.* = OFF *prep.* (*picked it off of the floor*). **off-peak** used or for use at times other than those of greatest demand. **off the peg** see PEG. **off-piste** (of skiing) away from prepared ski runs. **off the point** *adj.* irrelevant. ● *adv.* irrelevantly. **off-putting** *Brit.* disconcerting; repellent. **off the record** see RECORD. **off-road** *attrib.adj.* **1** away from the road, on rough terrain. **2** (of a vehicle etc.) designed for rough terrain or for cross-country driving. **off-roading** driving on dirt tracks and other unmetalled surfaces as a sport or leisure activity. **off-season** a time when business etc. is slack. **off-stage** *adj.* & *adv.* not on the stage and so not visible or audible to the audience. **off-street** (esp. of parking vehicles) other than on a street. **off-time** a time when business etc. is

slack. **off the wall** see WALL. **off-white** white with a grey or yellowish tinge. [orig. var. of OF, to distinguish the sense]
▪ *adv.* **1 a** away, out, elsewhere; distant, afar, far-off. **2** away; loose, separate, removed, gone. **4** cancelled, postponed, discontinued, stopped. **6** up, entirely; see also THROUGH *adv.* **7** situated, fixed, supplied. **9 a** sour, mouldy, bad, rotten, rancid, turned, high. **b** incorrect, wrong, inaccurate, in error, mistaken, misguided, misled, off the mark; mad, insane, eccentric, *colloq.* dotty, dippy, crazy, nutty, potty; unlikely, odd, abnormal, *US sl.* off the wall. **11** off work, at leisure, idle, free; on holiday *or US* vacation. ● *prep.* **1** (away *or* down *or* up) from, out of. **2 c** not up to, not on. **3** on, by, from. **4, 5** near, adjoining, next to, connecting with, leading from, contiguous with, adjacent to, abutting, bordering. ● *adj.* **1** see FAR *adj.* □ **a bit off 1** not good enough, not up to scratch, unacceptable, unsatisfactory, below the belt, *sl.* out of order; see also UNWARRANTED 2. **off and on** on and off; see also *by fits and starts* (FIT[2]). **off colour 1** unwell, ill, off form, out of sorts, queasy, sick, run down, poorly, lousy, *colloq.* awful, under the weather, seedy, *sl.* rotten. **2** indelicate, risqué, ribald, bawdy, indecent, suggestive, broad, inelegant, improper, inappropriate, unseemly, blue, *colloq.* near the knuckle. **off-key 1** out of tune, tuneless, flat, unmelodic, unmusical; see also DISCORDANT 2. **2** see INCONGRUOUS. **off the point** see IRRELEVANT. **off-putting** see DISAGREEABLE 1.

offal /óff'l/ *n.* **1** the less valuable edible parts of a carcass, esp. the entrails and internal organs. **2** refuse or waste stuff. **3** carrion; putrid flesh. [ME f. MDu. *afval* f. *af* OFF + *vallen* FALL]
▪ **2** see RUBBISH 1.

offbeat *adj.* & *n.* ● *adj.* /ófbeét/ **1** not coinciding with the beat. **2** eccentric, unconventional. ● *n.* /ófbeet/ any of the unaccented beats in a bar.
▪ *adj.* **2** strange, eccentric, bizarre, weird, peculiar, odd, queer, unconventional, unorthodox, Bohemian, idiosyncratic, unusual, unexpected, *outré*, outlandish, deviant, novel, innovative, freaky, *colloq.* kinky, way-out, *sl.* off the wall, far out.

offcut /ófkut/ *n.* a remnant of timber, paper, etc., after cutting.

offence /əfénss/ *n.* (*US* **offense**) **1** an illegal act; a transgression or misdemeanour. **2** a wounding of the feelings; resentment or umbrage (*no offence was meant*). **3** the act of attacking or taking the offensive; aggressive action. □ **give offence** cause hurt feelings. **take offence** suffer hurt feelings. □□ **offenceless** *adj.* [orig. = stumbling, stumbling-block: ME & OF *offens* f. L *offensus* annoyance, and ME & F *offense* f. L *offensa* a striking against, hurt, displeasure, both f. *offendere* (as OB-, *fendere fens-* strike)]
▪ **1** violation, breach, crime, felony, misdemeanour, infraction, transgression, trespass, wrong, wrongdoing, sin, peccadillo, misdeed, fault, infringement, malefaction; dereliction, lapse, slip, error. **2** resentment, annoyance, umbrage. **3** see AGGRESSION 2. □ **give offence** injure, harm; see also OFFEND 1, 2. **take offence** take umbrage, feel displeased *or* annoyed *or* resentful *or or* indignant, be angered *or* enraged *or* hurt; see also *take exception* (EXCEPTION).

offend /əfénd/ *v.* **1** *tr.* cause offence to or resentment in; wound the feelings of. **2** *tr.* displease or anger. **3** *intr.* (often foll. by *against*) do wrong; transgress. □□ **offendedly** *adv.* **offender** *n.* **offending** *adj.* [ME f. OF *offendre* f. L (as OFFENCE)]
▪ **1, 2** hurt a person's feelings, affront, insult, slight, snub, give offence, hurt, pain, wound, displease, disgruntle, chagrin, humiliate, embarrass; pique, fret, gall, vex, annoy, irritate, nettle, needle, provoke, ruffle, outrage, anger, put out, get *or* put a person's back up, *colloq.* miff, rile, put a person's nose out of joint, tread on a person's toes, rattle; disgust, sicken, turn a person's stomach, nauseate, repel, repulse, revolt, *colloq.* turn off. **3** see TRANSGRESS. □□ **offender** criminal, malefactor, lawbreaker, outlaw, wrongdoer, culprit, miscreant, transgressor, sinner, evil-doer, *colloq.* crook.

offense *US* var. of OFFENCE.

offensive /əfénsiv/ *adj.* & *n.* ● *adj.* **1** giving or meant or likely to give offence; insulting (*offensive language*). **2** disgusting, foul-smelling, nauseous, repulsive. **3 a** aggressive, attacking. **b** (of a weapon) meant for use in attack. ● *n.* **1** an aggressive action or attitude (*take the offensive*). **2** an attack, an offensive campaign or stroke. **3** aggressive or forceful action in pursuit of a cause (*a peace offensive*). □□ **offensively** *adv.* **offensiveness** *n.* [F *offensif -ive* or med.L *offensivus* (as OFFENCE)]
▪ *adj.* **1** insulting, rude, disrespectful, uncivil, insolent, discourteous, impolite, unmannerly, impertinent, impudent, objectionable, displeasing. **2** disgusting, unsavoury, unpalatable, nauseating, nauseous, noxious, obnoxious, repugnant, repulsive, repellent, revolting, abominable, foul, loathsome, vile, sickening, fetid, rank, malodorous, mephitic, putrid, putrescent, putrefying, rancid, rotten, *literary* noisome. **3 a** antagonistic, hostile, contentious, quarrelsome, attacking, aggressive, threatening, provocative, combative, martial, belligerent, warlike, bellicose. ● *n.* **2, 3** attack, onslaught, drive, assault, offence, push.

offer /óffər/ *v.* & *n.* ● *v.* **1** *tr.* present for acceptance or refusal or consideration (*offered me a drink*; *was offered a lift*; *offer one's services*; *offer no apology*). **2** *intr.* (foll. by *to* + infin.) express readiness or show intention (*offered to take the children*). **3** *tr.* provide; give an opportunity for. **4** *tr.* make available for sale. **5** *tr.* (of a thing) present to one's attention or consideration (*each day offers new opportunities*). **6** *tr.* present (a sacrifice, prayer, etc.) to a deity. **7** *intr.* present itself; occur (*as opportunity offers*). **8** *tr.* give an opportunity for (battle) to an enemy. **9** *tr.* attempt, or try to show (violence, resistance, etc.). ● *n.* **1** an expression of readiness to do or give if desired, or to buy or sell (for a certain amount). **2** an amount offered. **3** a proposal (esp. of marriage). **4** a bid. □ **on offer** for sale at a certain (esp. reduced) price. □□ **offerer** *n.* **offeror** *n.* [OE *offrian* in religious sense, f. L *offerre* (as OB-, *ferre* bring)]
▪ *v.* **1** proffer, propose, tender; see also VENTURE *v.* 3. **2** volunteer, present oneself, step *or* come forward. **3, 5** proffer, provide, submit, put forward *or* forth, advance, present, tender, extend, make; suggest. **4** make available, present, put on the market, sell, put up for sale, put up, furnish. ● *n.* proposal, bid, tender, offering, presentation, proposition, *literary* proffer. □ **on offer** see *cut-price*.

offering /óffəring/ *n.* **1** a contribution, esp. of money, to a Church. **2** a thing offered as a religious sacrifice or token of devotion. **3** anything, esp. money, contributed or offered.
▪ contribution, donation, gift, present, sacrifice; *Relig.* oblation.

offertory /óffərtəri, -tri/ *n.* (*pl.* **-ies**) **1** *Eccl.* **a** the offering of the bread and wine at the Eucharist. **b** an anthem accompanying this. **2 a** the collection of money at a religious service. **b** the money collected. [ME f. eccl.L *offertorium* offering f. LL *offert-* for L *oblat-* past part. stem of *offerre* OFFER]

offhand *adj.* & *adv.* ● *adj.* /ófhánd/ curt or casual in manner. ● *adv.* /ofhánd/ **1** in an offhand manner. **2** without preparation or premeditation. □□ **offhanded** *adj.* **offhandedly** *adv.* **offhandedness** *n.*
▪ *adj.* curt, brusque, abrupt, perfunctory, ungracious, glib, smooth; casual, informal, nonchalant, cool, distant, aloof, easygoing, blasé, unceremonious, relaxed, easy, smooth, unconcerned, insouciant, light-hearted, uninterested, superficial, cursory, cavalier, careless; extempore, impromptu, unpremeditated, unstudied, extemporaneous, informal, off the cuff, ad lib. ● *adv.* **1** casually, informally, incidentally, by the way, offhandedly, by the by, parenthetically, in passing, *en*

passant, cursorily, superficially. **2** extempore, impromptu, extemporaneously, informally, off the cuff, ad lib, on the spur of the moment, at the drop of a hat.

office /óffiss/ *n.* **1** a room or building used as a place of business, esp. for clerical or administrative work. **2** a room or department or building for a particular kind of business (*ticket office*; *post office*). **3** the local centre of a large business (*our London office*). **4** *US* the consulting-room of a professional person. **5** a position with duties attached to it; a place of authority or trust or service, esp. of a public nature. **6** tenure of an official position, esp. that of a minister of State or of the party forming the Government (*hold office*; *out of office for 13 years*). **7** (**Office**) the quarters or staff or collective authority of a Government department etc. (*Foreign Office*). **8** a duty attaching to one's position; a task or function. **9** (usu. in *pl.*) a piece of kindness or attention; a service (esp. *through the good offices of*). **10** *Eccl.* **a** an authorized form of worship (*Office for the Dead*). **b** (in full **divine office**) the daily service of the Roman Catholic breviary (*say the office*). **11** a ceremonial duty. **12** (in *pl.*) *Brit.* the parts of a house devoted to household work, storage, etc. **13** *sl.* a hint or signal. □ **the last offices** rites due to the dead. **office-bearer** an official or officer. **office block** a large building designed to contain business offices. **office boy** (or **girl**) a young man (or woman) employed to do minor jobs in a business office. **office hours** the hours during which business is normally conducted. **office of arms** the College of Arms, or a similar body in another country. **office-worker** an employee in a business office. [ME f. OF f. L *officium* performance of a task (in med.L also office, divine service), f. *opus* work + *facere fic-* do]

▪ **1** workplace, workroom, studio, study; headquarters, station, base, centre. **2, 3, 7** commission, department, branch; section, division; business, organization, firm, house, establishment, company, corporation. **5, 6, 8** duty, obligation, responsibility, charge, commission, service, employment, occupation, position, post, appointment, assignment, chore, task, job, place, berth, work, role, function, purpose, part, bit. **9** (*offices*) intermediation, auspices, support, advocacy, aegis, help, aid, intercession, mediation, patronage, favour, backing, backup.

officer /óffisər/ *n.* & *v.* ● *n.* **1** a person holding a position of authority or trust, esp. one with a commission in the armed services, in the mercantile marine, or on a passenger ship. **2** a policeman or policewoman. **3** a holder of a post in a society (e.g. the president or secretary). **4** a holder of a public, civil, or ecclesiastical office; a sovereign's minister; an appointed or elected functionary (usu. with a qualifying word: *medical officer*; *probation officer*; *returning officer*). **5** a bailiff (*the sheriff's officer*). **6** a member of the grade below commander in the Order of the British Empire etc. ● *v.tr.* **1** provide with officers. **2** act as the commander of. □ **officer of arms** a herald or pursuivant. [ME f. AF *officer*, OF *officier* f. med.L *officiarius* f. L *officium*: see OFFICE]

▪ *n.* **1, 3, 4** (public) official, dignitary, office-holder, public servant, office-bearer, (political) appointee, (government) agent, bureaucrat, functionary, commissioner, administrator, manager, director, minister; *apparatchik.* **2** policeman, policewoman, police officer, officer of the law, constable, gendarme, *US* lawman, peace officer, *colloq.* tec, *US colloq.* G-man, *sl.* cop, dick, *Austral. sl.* demon, John Hop, *Brit. sl.* copper, fuzz.

official /əfish'l/ *adj.* & *n.* ● *adj.* **1** of or relating to an office (see OFFICE *n.* 5, 6) or its tenure or duties. **2** characteristic of officials and bureaucracy. **3** emanating from or attributable to a person in office; properly authorized. **4** holding office; employed in a public capacity. **5** *Med.* according to the pharmacopoeia, officinal. ● *n.* **1** a person holding office or engaged in official duties. **2** (in full **official principal**) the presiding officer or judge of an archbishop's, bishop's, or esp. archdeacon's court. □ **official birthday** *Brit.* a day in June chosen for the observance of the sovereign's birthday. **official secrets** confidential information involving national security. □□ **officialdom** *n.* **officialism** *n.* **officially** *adv.* [ME (as noun) f. OF f. L *officialis* (as OFFICE)]

▪ *adj.* **1, 2** ceremonial, formal, solemn, ritualistic, ceremonious, pompous, stiff, proper, seemly, decorous; bureaucratic. **3, 4** authorized, legitimate, lawful, legal, authentic, bona fide, proper, true, accredited, valid, documented, licensed, sanctioned, endorsed, certified, verified, recognized, accepted. ● *n.* **1** see OFFICER *n.* 1, 3, 4.

officialese /əfishəléez/ *n. derog.* the formal precise language characteristic of official documents.

officiant /əfish'nt/ *n.* a person who officiates at a religious ceremony.

officiate /əfishiayt/ *v.intr.* **1** act in an official capacity, esp. on a particular occasion. **2** perform a divine service or ceremony. □□ **officiation** *n.* **officiator** *n.* [med.L *officiare* perform a divine service (*officium*): see OFFICE]

▪ **1** umpire, referee, judge, adjudicate, moderate, mediate; (*officiate at*) preside (over), direct, manage, chair, conduct, oversee, head (up), run, lead, supervise, superintend.

officinal /óffiseén'l, əfissin'l/ *adj.* **1 a** (of a medicine) kept ready for immediate dispensing. **b** made from the pharmacopoeia recipe (cf. MAGISTRAL). **c** (of a name) adopted in the pharmacopoeia. **2** (of a herb or drug) used in medicine. □□ **officinally** *adv.* [med.L *officinalis* f. L *officina* workshop]

officious /əfishəss/ *adj.* **1** asserting one's authority aggressively; domineering. **2** intrusive or excessively enthusiastic in offering help etc.; meddlesome. **3** *Diplomacy* informal, unofficial. □□ **officiously** *adv.* **officiousness** *n.* [L *officiosus* obliging f. *officium*: see OFFICE]

▪ **1, 2** dictatorial, domineering, aggressive, insistent, persistent, demanding, importunate, intrusive, intruding, meddlesome, meddling, obtrusive, forward, bold, interfering.

offing /óffing/ *n.* the more distant part of the sea in view. □ **in the offing** not far away; likely to appear or happen soon. [perh. f. OFF + -ING[1]]

▪ □ **in the offing** see *impending* (IMPEND).

offish /óffish/ *adj. colloq.* inclined to be aloof. □□ **offishly** *adv.* **offishness** *n.* [OFF: cf. *uppish*]

offload /óflṓd/ *v.tr.* get rid of (esp. something unpleasant) by giving it to someone else.

off-price /ófprīss/ *adj. US* involving merchandise sold at a lower price than that recommended by the manufacturer.

offprint /ófprint/ *n.* a printed copy of an article etc. originally forming part of a larger publication.

offscreen *adj.* & *adv.* ● *adj.* /ófskreen/ not appearing on a cinema, television, or VDU screen. ● *adv.* /ofskreén/ **1** without use of a screen. **2** outside the view presented by a cinema-film scene.

offset *n.* & *v.* ● *n.* /ófset/ **1** a side-shoot from a plant serving for propagation. **2** an offshoot or scion. **3** a compensation; a consideration or amount diminishing or neutralizing the effect of a contrary one. **4** *Archit.* a sloping ledge in a wall etc. where the thickness of the part above is diminished. **5** a mountain-spur. **6** a bend in a pipe etc. to carry it past an obstacle. **7** (often *attrib.*) a method of printing in which ink is transferred from a plate or stone to a uniform rubber surface and from there to paper etc. (*offset litho*). **8** *Surveying* a short distance measured perpendicularly from the main line of measurement. ● *v.tr.* /ófsét/ (**-setting**; *past* and *past part.* **-set**) **1** counterbalance, compensate. **2** place out of line. **3** print by the offset process.

▪ *n.* **3** compensation, consideration, counterbalance, counteraction, check, equalizer, neutralizer. ● *v.* **1** compensate, counterbalance, countervail, counterpoise, counteract, balance (out), equalize, even (out *or* up), square, cancel (out), neutralize, nullify, make up (for), atone for, redress; repay, make amends *or* restitution for, make good, reimburse.

offshoot /ófshōōt/ *n.* **1 a** a side-shoot or branch. **b** a collateral branch or descendant of a family. **2** something derivative.
■ **1 a** branch, spur; shoot, limb, bough, twig, stem, appendage, sucker, sprout, sprig, tendril, scion, offset. **b** descendant, relation, relative, kin, kindred. **2** outgrowth, development, branch, spin-off, by-product, derivative.

offshore /ófshór/ *adj.* **1** situated at sea some distance from the shore. **2** (of the wind) blowing seawards. **3** (of goods, funds, etc.) made or registered abroad.

offside *adj.* & *n.* ● *adj.* /ófsīd/ *Sport* (of a player in a field game) in a position, usu. ahead of the ball, that is not allowed if it affects play. ● *n.* /ófsīd/ (often *attrib.*) esp. *Brit.* the right side of a vehicle, animal, etc. (cf. NEARSIDE).

offsider /ofsīdər/ *n. Austral. colloq.* a partner, assistant, or deputy.
■ see DEPUTY 1.

offspring /ófspring/ *n.* (*pl.* same) **1** a person's child or children or descendant(s). **2** an animal's young or descendant(s). **3** a result. [OE *ofspring* f. OF from + *springan* SPRING *v.*]
■ **1, 2** child(ren), progeny, youngster(s), brood, young, successor(s), heir(s), descendant(s), *Law* issue, *archaic* seed.

oft /oft/ *adv. archaic* or *literary* often (usu. in *comb.*: *oft-recurring*). □ **oft-times** often. [OE]

often /óff'n, óftən/ *adv.* (**oftener, oftenest**) **1 a** frequently; many times. **b** at short intervals. **2** in many instances. □ **as often as not** in roughly half the instances. [ME: extended f. OFT, prob. after *selden* = SELDOM]
■ frequently, regularly, much, many times, usually, habitually, commonly, ordinarily, again and again, over and over again, time after time, repeatedly, time and (time) again, in many cases *or* instances, on numerous occasions, day in (and) day out, continually, *archaic or literary* oft, *colloq.* a lot. □ **as often as not** many a time, every so often, frequently, many times, *archaic or literary* oft-times.

ogam var. of OGHAM.

ogdoad /ógdō-ad/ *n.* a group of eight. [LL *ogdoas ogdoad-* f. Gk *ogdoas -ados* f. *ogdoos* eighth f. *oktō* eight]

ogee /ṓjee, ōjée/ *adj.* & *n. Archit.* ● *adj.* showing in section a double continuous S-shaped curve. ● *n.* an S-shaped line or moulding. □ **ogee arch** an arch with two ogee curves meeting at the apex. □□ **ogee'd** *adj.* [app. f. OGIVE, as being the usu. moulding in groin-ribs]

ogham /óggəm/ *n.* (also **ogam**) **1** an ancient British and Irish alphabet of twenty characters formed by parallel strokes on either side of or across a continuous line. **2** an inscription in this alphabet. **3** each of its characters. [OIr. *ogam*, referred to *Ogma*, its supposed inventor]

ogive /ṓjīv, ōjīv/ *n.* **1** a pointed or Gothic arch. **2** one of the diagonal groins or ribs of a vault. **3** an S-shaped line. **4** *Statistics* a cumulative frequency graph. □□ **ogival** *adj.* [ME f. F, of unkn. orig.]

ogle /ṓg'l/ *v.* & *n.* ● *v.* **1** *tr.* eye amorously or lecherously. **2** *intr.* look amorously. ● *n.* an amorous or lecherous look. □□ **ogler** *n.* [prob. LG or Du.: cf. LG *oegeln*, frequent. of *oegen* look at]
■ *v.* **1** eye, make (sheep's) eyes at, leer at, *colloq.* give a person the glad eye, look a person over, eye a person up. **2** leer, gape, gaze, goggle, stare, *colloq.* gawk, *Brit. colloq.* gawp. ● *n.* leer, stare, gape, goggle, *colloq.* glad eye.

ogre /ṓgər/ *n.* (*fem.* **ogress** /ṓgriss/) **1** a man-eating giant in folklore etc. **2** a terrifying person. □□ **ogreish** *adj.* (also **ogrish**). [F, first used by Perrault in 1697, of unkn. orig.]
■ monster, giant, fiend, demon, troll, man-eater, bogey, bogeyman, spectre, gorgon, *archaic* bugbear; brute, sadist, villain, cad, scoundrel.

OH *abbr. US* Ohio (in official postal use).

oh[1] /ō/ *int.* (also **O**) expressing surprise, pain, entreaty, etc. (*oh, what a mess*; *oh for a holiday*). □ **oh boy** expressing surprise, excitement, etc. **oh well** expressing resignation. [var. of O[4]]

oh[2] /ō/ *n.* = O[1] 2.

o.h.c. *abbr.* overhead camshaft.

ohm /ōm/ *n. Electr.* the SI unit of resistance, transmitting a current of one ampere when subjected to a potential difference of one volt. ¶ Symb.: Ω. □□ **ohmage** *n.* [G. S. *Ohm*, Ger. physicist d. 1854]

ohmmeter /ṓm-meetər/ *n.* an instrument for measuring electrical resistance.

OHMS *abbr.* on Her (or His) Majesty's Service.

Ohm's law /ōmz/ *n. Electr.* a law stating that current is proportional to voltage and inversely proportional to resistance. [see OHM]

oho /ōhṓ/ *int.* expressing surprise or exultation. [ME f. O[4] + HO]

ohone var. of OCHONE.

OHP *abbr.* overhead projector.

o.h.p. *abbr.* overhead projector.

o.h.v. *abbr.* overhead valve.

oi /oy/ *int.* calling attention or expressing alarm etc. [var. of HOY[1]]

-oid /oyd/ *suffix* forming adjectives and nouns, denoting form or resemblance (*asteroid*; *rhomboid*; *thyroid*). □□ **-oidal** *suffix* forming adjectives. **-oidally** *suffix* forming adverbs. [mod.L *-oides* f. Gk *-oeidēs* f. *eidos* form]

oidium /ō-íddiəm/ *n.* (*pl.* **oidia** /-diə/) spores formed by the breaking up of fungal hyphae into cells. [mod.L f. Gk *ōion* egg + *-idion* dimin. suffix]

oil /oyl/ *n.* & *v.* ● *n.* **1** any of various thick, viscous, usu. inflammable liquids insoluble in water but soluble in organic solvents (see also *essential oil*, *fixed oil*, *mineral oil*, *volatile oil*). **2** *US* petroleum. **3** (in *comb.*) using oil as fuel (*oil-heater*). **4 a** (usu. in *pl.*) = *oil-paint*. **b** *colloq.* a picture painted in oil-paints. **5** (in *pl.*) = OILSKIN. ● *v.* **1** *tr.* apply oil to; lubricate. **2** *tr.* impregnate or treat with oil (*oiled silk*). **3** *tr.* & *intr.* supply with or take on oil as fuel. **4** *tr.* & *intr.* make (butter, grease, etc.) into or (of butter etc.) become an oily liquid. □ **oil-bird** a guacharo. **oil drum** a metal drum used for transporting oil. **oiled silk** silk made waterproof with oil. **oil engine** an engine driven by the explosion of vaporized oil mixed with air. **oil-fired** using oil as fuel. **oil a person's hand** (or **palm**) bribe a person. **oil-lamp** a lamp using oil as fuel. **oil-meal** ground oilcake. **oil of vitriol** see VITRIOL. **oil-paint** (or **-colour**) a mix of ground colour pigment and oil. **oil-painting 1** the art of painting in oil-paints. **2** a picture painted in oil-paints. **oil-palm** either of two trees, *Elaeis guineensis* of W. Africa, or *E. oleifera* of the US, from which palm oil is extracted. **oil-pan** an engine sump. **oil-paper** a paper made transparent or waterproof by soaking in oil. **oil-press** an apparatus for pressing oil from seeds etc. **oil rig** a structure with equipment for drilling an oil well. **oil-sand** a stratum of porous rock yielding petroleum. **oil-seed** any of various seeds from cultivated crops yielding oil, e.g. rape, peanut, or cotton. **oil-shale** a fine-grained rock from which oil can be extracted. **oil-slick** a smooth patch of oil, esp. one on the sea. **oil-tanker** a ship designed to carry oil in bulk. **oil one's tongue** say flattering or glib things. **oil well** a well from which mineral oil is drawn. **oil the wheels** help make things go smoothly. **well oiled** *colloq.* very drunk. □□ **oilless** *adj.* [ME *oli*, *oile* f. AF, ONF *olie* = OF *oile* etc. f. L *oleum* (olive) oil f. *olea* olive]
■ *n.* **1, 2** lubricant, grease, lubrication, unguent; fuel; petroleum. ● *v.* **1** lubricate, grease; see also SLICK *v.* □ **oil a person's hand** (or **palm**) see BRIBE *v.* **well oiled** see DRUNK *adj.* 1.

oilcake /óylkayk/ *n.* a mass of compressed linseed etc. left after oil has been extracted, used as fodder or manure.
■ linseed cake; cotton cake.

oilcan /óylkan/ *n.* a can containing oil, esp. one with a long nozzle for oiling machinery.

oilcloth /óylkloth/ *n.* **1** a fabric waterproofed with oil. **2** an oilskin. **3** a canvas coated with linseed or other oil and used to cover a table or floor.

oiler /óylər/ *n.* **1** an oilcan for oiling machinery. **2** an oil-tanker. **3** *US* **a** an oil well. **b** (in *pl.*) oilskin.

oilfield /óylfeeld/ *n.* an area yielding mineral oil.

oilman /óylmən/ *n.* (*pl.* **-men**) a person who deals in oil.

oilskin /óylskin/ *n.* **1** cloth waterproofed with oil. **2 a** a garment made of this. **b** (in *pl.*) a suit made of this.
■ **2 a** see SLICKER 2.

oilstone /óylstōn/ *n.* a fine-grained flat stone used with oil for sharpening flat tools, e.g. chisels, planes, etc. (cf. WHETSTONE).

oily /óyli/ *adj.* (**oilier**, **oiliest**) **1** of, like, or containing much oil. **2** covered or soaked with oil. **3** (of a manner etc.) fawning, insinuating, unctuous. ▫▫ **oilily** *adv.* **oiliness** *n.*
■ **1, 2** greasy, oleaginous, fat, fatty, adipose, sebaceous, soapy, buttery, *formal or joc.* pinguid; slippery, slimy, slithery, smooth, unctuous. **3** glib, smooth, unctuous, servile, fawning, obsequious, sycophantic, ingratiating, insinuating, flattering, hypocritical, *colloq.* smarmy, *joc.* saponaceous; suave, urbane, sophisticated.

oink /oyngk/ *v.intr.* (of a pig) make its characteristic grunt. [imit.]

ointment /óyntmənt/ *n.* a smooth greasy healing or cosmetic preparation for the skin. [ME *oignement*, *ointment*, f. OF *oignement* ult. f. L (as UNGUENT): *oint-* after obs. *oint* anoint f. OF, past part. of *oindre* ANOINT]
■ unguent, balm, salve, emollient, embrocation, demulcent, pomade, pomatum; *propr.* Vaseline; lotion, cream.

Oireachtas /érəkhthass/ *n.* the legislature of the Irish Republic: the President, Dáil, and Seanad. [Ir.]

OK[1] /ōkáy/ *adj.*, *adv.*, *n.*, & *v.* (also **okay**) *colloq.* ● *adj.* (often as *int.* expressing agreement or acquiescence) all right; satisfactory. ● *adv.* well, satisfactorily (*that worked out OK*). ● *n.* (*pl.* **OKs**) approval, sanction. ● *v.tr.* (**OK's, OK'd, OK'ing**) give an OK to; approve, sanction. [orig. US: prob. abbr. of *orl* (or *oll*) *korrect*, joc. form of 'all correct']
■ *adj.* satisfactory, acceptable, correct, suitable, all right, fine, good, in order, *Austral.* & *NZ sl.* jake; well, healthy, sound, in good condition, in fine fettle; adequate, mediocre, fair, middling, passable, tolerable, so so, pretty good, not bad. ● *adv.* all right, reasonably, passably, tolerably; see also WELL[1] *adv.* 1. ● *n.* approval, sanction, ratification, authorization, endorsement, agreement, support, permission, consent, go-ahead, thumbs up, *colloq.* green light. ● *v.* approve, sanction, ratify, authorize, endorse, support, allow, consent to, agree (to), rubber-stamp, give the go-ahead to, give the thumbs up to, *colloq.* give the green light to.

OK[2] *abbr. US* Oklahoma (in official postal use).

okapi /ōkaápi/ *n.* (*pl.* same or **okapis**) a ruminant mammal, *Okapia johnstoni*, native to N. and NE Zaïre, with a head resembling that of a giraffe and a body resembling that of a zebra, having a dark chestnut coat and transverse stripes on the hindquarters and upper legs only. [Mbuba]

okay var. of OK[1].

okey-dokey /ṓkidṓki/ *adj.* & *adv.* (also **okey-doke** /-dṓk/) *sl.* = OK[1]. [redupl.]

Okla. *abbr.* Oklahoma.

okra /ṓkrə, ókrə/ *n.* **1** a malvaceous African plant, *Abelmoschus esculentus*, yielding long ridged seed-pods. **2** the seed-pods eaten as a vegetable and used to thicken soups and stews. Also called GUMBO, *ladies' fingers*. [W.Afr. native name]

-ol[1] /ol/ *suffix Chem.* the termination of *alcohol*, used in names of alcohols or analogous compounds (*methanol*; *phenol*).

-ol[2] /ol/ *comb. form* = -OLE. [L *oleum* oil]

old /ōld/ *adj.* (**older**, **oldest**) (cf. ELDER, ELDEST). **1 a** advanced in age; far on in the natural period of existence. **b** not young or near its beginning. **2** made long ago. **3** long in use. **4** worn or dilapidated or shabby from the passage of time. **5** having the characteristics (experience, feebleness, etc.) of age (*the child has an old face*). **6** practised, inveterate (*an old offender*; *old in crime*). **7** belonging only or chiefly to the past; lingering on; former (*old times*; *haunted by old memories*). **8** dating from far back; long established or known; ancient, primeval (*old as the hills*; *old friends*; *an old family*). **9** (appended to a period of time) of age (*is four years old*; *a four-year-old boy*; *a four-year-old*). **10** (of language) as used in former or earliest times. **11** *colloq.* as a term of affection or casual reference (*good old Charlie*; *old shipmate*). **12** the former or first of two or more similar things (*our old house*; *wants his old job back*). ▫ **old age** the later part of normal life. **old-age pension** = *retirement pension*. **old-age pensioner** a person receiving this. **Old Bailey** the Central Criminal Court in London. **Old Bill** *Brit. sl.* the police. **old bird** a wary person. **old boy 1** a former male pupil of a school. **2** *colloq.* **a** an elderly man. **b** an affectionate form of address to a boy or man. **old boy network** *Brit. colloq.* preferment in employment of those from a similar social background, esp. fellow ex-pupils of public schools. **the old country** the native country of colonists etc. **Old English** the English language up to *c.*1150. **old-fashioned** in or according to a fashion or tastes no longer current; antiquated. **Old French** the French language of the period before *c.*1400. **old fustic** see FUSTIC. **old girl 1** a former female pupil of a school. **2** *colloq.* **a** an elderly woman. **b** an affectionate term of address to a girl or woman. **Old Glory** *US* the US national flag. **old gold** a dull brownish-gold colour. **old guard** the original or past or conservative members of a group. **old hand** a person with much experience. **old hat** *colloq. adj.* tediously familiar or out of date. ● *n.* something tediously familiar or out of date. **Old High German** High German (see GERMAN) up to *c.*1200. **old lady** *colloq.* one's mother or wife. **old lag** see LAG[3]. **old maid 1** *derog.* an elderly unmarried woman. **2** a prim and fussy person. **3** a card-game in which players try not to be left with an unpaired queen. **old-maidish** like an old maid. **old man** *colloq.* **1** one's husband or father. **2** one's employer or other person in authority over one. **3** an affectionate form of address to a boy or man. **old man's beard** a wild clematis, *Clematis vitalba*, with grey fluffy hairs round the seeds: also called *traveller's joy* (see TRAVELLER). **old master 1** a great artist of former times, esp. of the 13th–17th c. in Europe. **2** a painting by such a painter. **old moon** the moon in its last quarter, before the new moon. **Old Nick** *colloq.* the Devil. **Old Norse** see NORSE. **an old one** a familiar joke. **Old Pals Act** *Brit.* the principle that friends should always help one another. **Old Pretender** James Stuart (1688–1766), son of James II and claimant to the British throne. **old retainer** see RETAINER 3b. **old school 1** traditional attitudes. **2** people having such attitudes. **old school tie** *Brit.* **1** a necktie with a characteristic pattern worn by the pupils of a particular (usu. public) school. **2** the principle of excessive loyalty to traditional values. **old soldier** an experienced person, esp. in an arduous activity. **old stager** an experienced person, an old hand. **old style** of a date reckoned by the Julian calendar. **Old Testament** the part of the Christian Bible containing the scriptures of the Hebrews. **old-time** belonging to former times. **old-timer** *US* a person with long experience or standing. **old wives' tale** a foolish or unscientific tradition or belief. **old woman** *colloq.* **1** one's wife or mother. **2** a fussy or timid man. **old-womanish** fussy and timid. **Old World** Europe, Asia, and Africa. **old-world** belonging to or associated with old times. **old year** the year just ended or about to end. ▫▫ **oldish** *adj.* **oldness** *n.* [OE *ald* f. WG]
■ **1** elderly, ageing, aged, advanced in years *or* age, long-lived, past one's *or* its prime, grey, getting on (in years), hoary, superannuated, *archaic* full of years, *colloq.* over the hill, past it. **2, 3, 10** ancient, antiquated, old-fashioned, fossil, prehistoric, obsolete, antique, out-dated, out of date, old-time, dated, archaic, stale, out-moded, *passé*, *colloq.* antediluvian. **4** time-worn, decayed, dilapidated, ramshackle, disintegrated,

crumbling, shabby, worn out, dusty, broken-down, tumbledown; disused, unused, cast off, cast aside. **6** experienced, veteran, practised, (well-)versed, knowledgeable, proficient, accomplished, adept, skilled, expert, old-time; inveterate. **7, 12** previous, preceding, prior, former, quondam, erstwhile, one-time, sometime, ex-. **8** long-standing, well-established, enduring, lasting, age-old, time-honoured; former, bygone; early, ancient, primordial, primitive, *archaic* olden. □ **old age** see AGE *n.* 3. **old boy 2 b** friend, *colloq.* chum, pal, *Brit. sl.* old bean. **old-fashioned** old, antiquated, antique, *passé*, out-moded, out-dated, unfashionable, stale, dated, out of date, tired, old-time, obsolete, obsolescent, dead, superseded, replaced, disused, out, *colloq.* old hat. **old hand** past master; see also ADEPT *n.* **old hat** (*adj.*) see *old-fashioned* above.

olden /ṓldən/ *adj. archaic* of old; of a former age (esp. *in olden times*).

oldie /ṓldi/ *n. colloq.* an old person or thing.
■ old person, senior citizen, senior, geriatric; pensioner, OAP, old-age pensioner, *US* golden-ager, *colloq.* old-timer, old geezer, old fogey, *Austral. colloq.* geri, *sl. offens.* wrinkly.

oldster /ṓldstər/ *n.* an old person. [OLD + -STER, after *youngster*]

-ole /ōl/ *comb. form* forming names of esp. heterocyclic compounds (*indole*). [L *oleum* oil]

oleaceous /ṓliáyshəss/ *adj.* of the plant family Oleaceae, including olive and jasmine. [mod.L *Oleaceae* f. L *olea* olive-tree]

oleaginous /ṓliájinəss/ *adj.* **1** having the properties of or producing oil. **2** oily, greasy. **3** obsequious, ingratiating. [F *oléagineux* f. L *oleaginus* f. *oleum* oil]
■ **2** see OILY 1, 2.

oleander /ṓliándər/ *n.* an evergreen poisonous shrub, *Nerium oleander*, native to the Mediterranean and bearing clusters of white, pink, or red flowers. [med.L]

oleaster /ṓliástər/ *n.* any of various trees of the genus *Elaeagnus*, often thorny and with evergreen leathery foliage, esp. *E. angustifolia* bearing olive-shaped yellowish fruits. Also called *Russian olive*. [ME f. L f. *olea* olive-tree: see -ASTER]

olecranon /ōlékrənon, ṓlikráynən/ *n.* a bony prominence on the upper end of the ulna at the elbow. [Gk *ōle(no)kranon* f. *ōlenē* elbow + *kranion* head]

olefin /ṓlifin/ *n.* (also **olefine**) *Chem.* = ALKENE. [F *oléfiant* oil-forming (with ref. to oily ethylene dichloride)]

oleic acid /ōlée-ik/ *n.* an unsaturated fatty acid present in many fats and soaps. □□ **oleate** /ṓliət/ *n.* [L *oleum* oil]

oleiferous /ṓlee-íffərəss/ *adj.* yielding oil. [L *oleum* oil + -FEROUS]

oleo- /ólliō/ *comb. form* oil. [L *oleum* oil]

oleograph /ṓliəgraaf/ *n.* a print made to resemble an oil-painting.

oleomargarine /ṓliōmaárjəreen, -maargəreen/ *n.* **1** a fatty substance extracted from beef fat and often used in margarine. **2** *US* a margarine made from vegetable oils.

oleometer /ṓliómmitər/ *n.* an instrument for determining the density and purity of oils.

oleo-resin /ṓliō-rézzin/ *n.* a natural or artificial mixture of essential oils and a resin, e.g. balsam.

oleum /ṓliəm/ *n.* concentrated sulphuric acid containing excess sulphur trioxide in solution forming a dense corrosive liquid. [L, = oil]

O level /ō/ *n. Brit. hist.* = *ordinary level*. [abbr.]

olfaction /olfáksh'n/ *n.* the act or capacity of smelling; the sense of smell. □□ **olfactive** *adj.* [L *olfactus* a smell f. *olēre* to smell + *facere fact-* make]

olfactory /olfáktəri/ *adj.* of or relating to the sense of smell (*olfactory nerves*). [L *olfactare* frequent. of *olfacere* (as OLFACTION)]

olibanum /olíbbənəm/ *n.* an aromatic gum resin from any tree of the genus *Boswellia*, used as incense. [ME f. med.L f. LL *libanus* f. Gk *libanos* frankincense, of Semitic orig.]

oligarch /ólligaark/ *n.* a member of an oligarchy. [Gk *oligarkhēs* f. *oligoi* few + *arkhō* to rule]

oligarchy /ólligaarki/ *n.* (*pl.* **-ies**) **1** government by a small group of people. **2** a State governed in this way. **3** the members of such a government. □□ **oligarchic** /-gaárkik/ *adj.* **oligarchical** /-gaárkik'l/ *adj.* **oligarchically** /-gaárkikəli/ *adv.* [F *oligarchie* or med.L *oligarchia* f. Gk *oligarkhia* (as OLIGARCH)]

oligo- /ólligō/ *comb. form* few, slight. [Gk *oligos* small, *oligoi* few]

Oligocene /ólligəseen/ *adj.* & *n. Geol.* ● *adj.* of or relating to the third epoch of the Tertiary period, with evidence of the first primates. ¶ Cf. Appendix VII. ● *n.* this epoch or system. [as OLIGO- + Gk *kainos* new]

oligopoly /ólligóppəli/ *n.* (*pl.* **-ies**) a state of limited competition between a small number of producers or sellers. □□ **oligopolist** *n.* **oligopolistic** /-lístik/ *adj.* [OLIGO-, after MONOPOLY]

oligosaccharide /ólligōsákkərīd/ *n.* any carbohydrate whose molecules are composed of a relatively small number of monosaccharide units.

oligotrophic /ólligōtrṓfik/ *adj.* (of a lake etc.) relatively poor in plant nutrients. □□ **oligotrophy** /ólligótrəfi/ *n.*

olio /ṓliō/ *n.* (*pl.* **-os**) **1** a mixed dish; a stew of various meats and vegetables. **2** a hotchpotch or miscellany. [Sp. *olla* stew f. L *olla* cooking-pot]
■ **1** see STEW[1] *n.* 1. **2** see MISCELLANY.

olivaceous /ólliváyshəss/ *adj.* olive-green; of a dusky yellowish green.

olivary /ólliv*ə*ri/ *adj. Anat.* olive-shaped; oval. [L *olivarius* (as OLIVE)]

olive /ólliv/ *n.* & *adj.* ● *n.* **1** (in full **olive tree**) any evergreen tree of the genus *Olea*, having dark-green lance-shaped leathery leaves with silvery undersides, esp. *O. europaea* of the Mediterranean, and *O. africana* native to S. Africa. **2** the small oval fruit of this, having a hard stone and bitter flesh, green when unripe and bluish-black when ripe. **3** (in full **olive-green**) the greyish-green colour of an unripe olive. **4** the wood of the olive tree. **5** *Anat.* each of a pair of olive-shaped swellings in the medulla oblongata. **6 a** any olive-shaped gastropod of the genus *Oliva*. **b** the shell of this. **7** a slice of beef or veal made into a roll with stuffing inside and stewed. ● *adj.* **1** coloured like an unripe olive. **2** (of the complexion) yellowish-brown, sallow. □ **olive branch 1** the branch of an olive tree as a symbol of peace. **2** a gesture of reconciliation or friendship. **olive crown** a garland of olive leaves as a sign of victory. **olive drab** the dull olive colour of US army uniforms. **olive oil** an oil extracted from olives used esp. in cookery. [ME f. OF f. L *oliva* f. Gk *elaia* f. *elaion* oil]

olivine /ólliveen/ *n. Mineral.* a naturally occurring form of magnesium-iron silicate, usu. olive-green and found in igneous rocks.

olla podrida /óllə pədreedə/ *n.* = OLIO. [Sp., lit. 'rotten pot' (as OLIO + L *putridus*: cf. PUTRID]

olm /olm/ *n.* a blind cave-dwelling salamander, *Proteus anguinus*, native to SE Europe, usu. transparent but turning brown in light and having external gills. [G]

-ology /ólləji/ *comb. form* see -LOGY.

oloroso /ólləróssō/ *n.* (*pl.* **-os**) a heavy dark medium-sweet sherry. [Sp., lit. 'fragrant']

Olympiad /əlímpiad/ *n.* **1 a** a period of four years between Olympic games, used by the ancient Greeks in dating events. **b** a four-yearly celebration of the ancient Olympic Games. **2** a celebration of the modern Olympic Games. **3** a regular international contest in chess etc. [ME f. F *Olympiade* f. L *Olympias Olympiad-* f. Gk *Olumpias Olumpiad-* f. *Olumpios*: see OLYMPIAN, OLYMPIC]

Olympian /əlímpiən/ *adj.* & *n.* ● *adj.* **1 a** of or associated with Mount Olympus in NE Greece, traditionally the home of the Greek gods. **b** celestial, godlike. **2** (of manners etc.) magnificent, condescending, superior. **3 a** of or relating to ancient Olympia in S. Greece. **b** = OLYMPIC. ● *n.* **1** any of the pantheon of twelve gods regarded as living on Olympus. **2** a person of great attainments or of superhuman calm and detachment. [L *Olympus* or *Olympia*: see OLYMPIC]

■ *adj.* **2** see STANDOFFISH. ● *n.* **1** (*Olympians*) see IMMORTAL *n.* 1b.

Olympic /əlímpik/ *adj.* & *n.* ● *adj.* of ancient Olympia or the Olympic games. ● *n.pl.* (**the Olympics**) the Olympic games. □ **Olympic games 1** an ancient Greek festival held at Olympia every four years, with athletic, literary, and musical competitions. **2** a modern international revival of this as a sports festival held every four years since 1896 in different venues. [L *Olympicus* f. Gk *Olumpikos* of Olympus or Olympia (the latter being named from the games in honour of Zeus of *Olympus*)]

OM *abbr.* (in the UK) Order of Merit.

-oma /ṓmə/ *n.* forming nouns denoting tumours and other abnormal growths (*carcinoma*). [mod.L f. Gk *-ōma* suffix denoting the result of verbal action]

omasum /ōmáysəm/ *n.* (*pl.* **omasa** /-sə/) the third stomach of a ruminant. [L, = bullock's tripe]

ombre /ómbər/ *n.* a card-game for three, popular in Europe in the 17th–18th c. [Sp. *hombre* man, with ref. to one player seeking to win the pool]

ombré /ónbray/ *adj.* (of a fabric etc.) having gradual shading of colour from light to dark. [F, past part. of *ombrer* to shadow (as UMBER)]

ombro- /ómbrō/ *comb. form* rain. [Gk *ombros* rain-shower]

ombudsman /ómbŏŏdzmən/ *n.* (*pl.* **-men**) an official appointed by a government to investigate individuals' complaints against public authorities etc. [Sw., = legal representative]

-ome /ōm/ *suffix* forming nouns denoting objects or parts of a specified nature (*rhizome*; *trichome*). [var. of -OMA]

omega /ṓmigə/ *n.* **1** the last (24th) letter of the Greek alphabet (Ω, ω). **2** the last of a series; the final development. [Gk, *ō mega* = great O]

omelette /ómlit/ *n.* (also **omelet**) a dish of beaten eggs cooked in a frying-pan and served plain or with a savoury or sweet filling. [F *omelette*, obs. *amelette* by metathesis f. *alumette* var. of *alumelle* f. *lemele* knife-blade f. L *lamella*: see LAMELLA]

omen /ṓmən, ṓmen/ *n.* & *v.* ● *n.* **1** an occurrence or object regarded as portending good or evil. **2** prophetic significance (*of good omen*). ● *v.tr.* (usu. in *passive*) portend; foreshow. □□ **omened** *adj.* (also in *comb.*). [L *omen ominis*]

■ *n.* portent, augury, sign, token, foretoken, indication, harbinger, forewarning, premonition, foreshadowing, writing on the wall, prognostic, presage.

omentum /ōméntəm/ *n.* (*pl.* **omenta** /-tə/) a fold of peritoneum connecting the stomach with other abdominal organs. □□ **omental** *adj.* [L]

omertà /ōmairtaá/ *n.* a code of silence, esp. as practised by the Mafia. [It., = conspiracy of silence]

omicron /əmíkrən/ *n.* the fifteenth letter of the Greek alphabet (Ο, ο). [Gk, *o mikron* = small o]

ominous /ómminəss/ *adj.* **1** threatening; indicating disaster or difficulty. **2** of evil omen; inauspicious. **3** giving or being an omen. □□ **ominously** *adv.* **ominousness** *n.* [L *ominosus* (as OMEN)]

■ **1, 2** foreboding, threatening, fateful, dark, black, gloomy, lowering, menacing, sinister; unpropitious, unfavourable, ill-omened, ill-starred, unpromising, inauspicious, *archaic* star-crossed; minatory, warning, admonitory, cautionary. **3** portentous, prophetic, oracular, predictive, prognostic, augural, meaningful, premonitory, foreshadowing, foretelling, foretokening, indicative, *formal* vaticinal, mantic.

omission /əmísh'n/ *n.* **1** the act or an instance of omitting or being omitted. **2** something that has been omitted or overlooked. □□ **omissive** *adj.* [ME f. OF *omission* or LL *omissio* (as OMIT)]

■ **1, 2** non-inclusion, leaving out *or* off, dropping, skipping, exclusion, exception, deletion, elimination, excision; failure, default, neglect, dereliction, oversight, shortcoming, negligence.

omit /əmít/ *v.tr.* (**omitted, omitting**) **1** leave out; not insert or include. **2** leave undone. **3** (foll. by verbal noun or *to* + infin.) fail or neglect (*omitted saying anything*; *omitted to say*). □□ **omissible** *adj.* [ME f. L *omittere omiss-* (as OB-, *mittere* send)]

■ **1** leave out, exclude, skip, except, pass over. **2, 3** neglect, disregard, fail, forget, overlook, let slide, ignore.

ommatidium /ómmətíddiəm/ *n.* (*pl.* **ommatidia** /-diə/) a structural element in the compound eye of an insect. [mod.L f. Gk *ommatidion* dimin. of *omma ommat-* eye]

omni- /ómni/ *comb. form* **1** all; of all things. **2** in all ways or places. [L f. *omnis* all]

omnibus /ómnibəss/ *n.* & *adj.* ● *n.* **1** *formal* = BUS. **2** a volume containing several novels etc. previously published separately. ● *adj.* **1** serving several purposes at once. **2** comprising several items. [F f. L (dative pl. of *omnis*), = for all]

■ *n.* **1** see COACH *n.* 1.

omnicompetent /ómnikómpit'nt/ *adj.* **1** able to deal with all matters. **2** having jurisdiction in all cases. □□ **omnicompetence** *n.*

omnidirectional /ómnidirékshən'l/ *adj.* (of an aerial etc.) receiving or transmitting in all directions.

omnifarious /ómnifáiriəss/ *adj.* of all sorts or varieties. [LL *omnifarius* (as OMNI-): cf. MULTIFARIOUS]

omnipotent /omníppət'nt/ *adj.* **1** having great or absolute power. **2** having great influence. □□ **omnipotence** *n.* **omnipotently** *adv.* [ME f. OF f. L *omnipotens* (as OMNI-, POTENT[1])]

■ **1** see DICTATORIAL 1. □□ **omnipotence** see SUPREMACY 2.

omnipresent /ómniprézz'nt/ *adj.* **1** present everywhere at the same time. **2** widely or constantly encountered. □□ **omnipresence** *n.* [med.L *omnipraesens* (as OMNI-, PRESENT[1])]

■ **1** see UNIVERSAL *adj.* **2** see PREVALENT 1. □□ **omnipresence** see *prevalence* (PREVALENT).

omniscient /omníssiənt, -shiənt/ *adj.* knowing everything or much. □□ **omniscience** *n.* **omnisciently** *adv.* [med.L *omnisciens -entis* (as OMNI-, *scire* know)]

■ all-knowing.

omnium gatherum /ómniəm gáthərəm/ *n. colloq.* a miscellany or strange mixture. [mock L f. L *omnium* of all + GATHER]

omnivorous /omnívvərəss/ *adj.* **1** feeding on many kinds of food, esp. on both plants and flesh. **2** making use of everything available. □□ **omnivore** /ómnivor/ *n.* **omnivorously** *adv.* **omnivorousness** *n.* [L *omnivorus* (as OMNI-, -VOROUS)]

omphalo- /ómfəlō/ *comb. form* navel. [Gk (as OMPHALOS)]

omphalos /ómfəloss/ *n. Gk Antiq.* **1** a conical stone (esp. that at Delphi) representing the navel of the earth. **2** a boss on a shield. **3** a centre or hub. [Gk, = navel, boss, hub]

on /on/ *prep., adv., adj.,* & *n.* ● *prep.* **1** (so as to be) supported by or attached to or covering or enclosing (*sat on a chair*; *stuck on the wall*; *rings on her fingers*; *leaned on his elbow*). **2** carried with; about the person of (*have you a pen on you?*). **3** (of time) exactly at; during; contemporaneously with (*on 29 May*; *on the hour*; *on schedule*; *working on Tuesday*). **4** immediately after or before (*I saw them on my return*). **5** as a result of (*on further examination I found this*). **6** (so as to be) having membership etc. of or residence at or in (*she is on the board of directors*; *lives on the continent*). **7** supported financially by (*lives on £50 a week*; *lives on his wits*). **8** close to; just by (*a house on the sea*; *lives on the main road*). **9** in the direction of; against. **10** so as to threaten; touching or striking (*advanced on him*; *pulled a knife on me*; *a punch on the nose*). **11** having as an axis or pivot (*turned on his heels*). **12** having as a basis or motive (*works on a ratchet*; *arrested on suspicion*). **13** having as a standard, confirmation, or guarantee (*had it on good authority*; *did it on purpose*; *I promise on my word*). **14** concerning or about (*writes on frogs*). **15** using or engaged with (*is on the pill*; *here on business*). **16** so as to affect (*walked out on her*). **17** at the expense of (*the drinks are on me*; *the joke is on him*). **18** added to (*disaster on disaster*; *ten pence on a pint of beer*). **19** in a specified manner or style (often foll. by *the* + adj. or noun: *on the cheap*; *on the run*). ● *adv.* **1** (so as to be) covering or in contact with something, esp. of clothes (*put your boots on*). **2** in the appropriate direction; towards something (*look on*). **3** further forward; in an advanced position or state (*time is getting on*; *it happened later on*). **4** with continued movement or action (*went plodding on*; *keeps on complaining*). **5** in operation or activity (*the light is on*; *the chase was on*). **6** due to take place as planned (*is the party still on?*). **7** *colloq.* **a** (of a person) willing to participate or approve, or make a bet. **b** (of an idea, proposal, etc.) practicable or acceptable (*that's just not on*). **8** being shown or performed (*a good film on tonight*). **9** (of an actor) on stage. **10** (of an employee) on duty. **11** forward (*head on*). ● *adj. Cricket* designating the part of the field on the striker's side and in front of the wicket. ● *n. Cricket* the on side. □ **be on about** refer to or discuss esp. tediously or persistently (*what are they on about?*). **be on at** *colloq.* nag or grumble at. **be on to 1** realize the significance or intentions of. **2** get in touch with (esp. by telephone). **on and off** intermittently; now and then. **on and on** continually; at tedious length. **on-line** *Computing* (of equipment or a process) directly controlled by or connected to a central processor. **on-off 1** (of a switch) having two positions, 'on' and 'off'. **2** = *on and off*. **on-stage** *adj.* & *adv.* on the stage; visible to the audience. **on-street** (with ref. to parking vehicles) at the side of a street. **on time** punctual, punctually, on the dot, in good time. **on to** to a position or state on or in contact with (cf. ONTO). [OE *on*, *an* f. Gmc]

-on /on/ *suffix Physics*, *Biochem.*, & *Chem.* forming nouns denoting: **1** elementary particles (*meson*; *neutron*). **2** quanta (*photon*). **3** molecular units (*codon*). **4** substances (*interferon*; *parathion*). [ION, orig. in *electron*]

onager /ónnəgər/ *n.* **1** a wild ass, esp. *Equus hemionus* of Central Asia. **2** *hist.* an ancient military engine for throwing rocks. [ME f. L f. Gk *onagros* f. *onos* ass + *agrios* wild]

onanism /ṓnəniz'm/ *n.* **1** masturbation. **2** coitus interruptus. □□ **onanist** *n.* **onanistic** /-nístik/ *adj.* [F *onanisme* or mod.L *onanismus* f. *Onan* (Gen. 38:9)]

ONC *abbr.* (in the UK) Ordinary National Certificate.

once /wunss/ *adv.*, *conj.*, & *n.* ● *adv.* **1** on one occasion or for one time only (*did not once say please*; *have read it once*). **2** at some point or period in the past (*could once play chess*). **3** ever or at all (*if you once forget it*). **4** multiplied by one; by one degree. ● *conj.* as soon as (*once they have gone we can relax*). ● *n.* one time or occasion (*just the once*). □ **all at once 1** without warning; suddenly. **2** all together. **at once 1** immediately. **2** simultaneously. **for once** on this (or that) occasion, even if at no other. **once again** (or **more**) another time. **once and for all** (or **once for all**) (done) in a final or conclusive manner, esp. so as to end hesitation or uncertainty. **once** (or **every once**) **in a while** from time to time; occasionally. **once or twice** a few times. **once-over** *colloq.* **1** a rapid preliminary inspection or piece of work. **2** an appraising glance. **once upon a time** at some vague time in the past. [ME *ānes*, *ōnes*, genit. of ONE]

■ *adv.* **1** one time, on one occasion, a single time. **2** once upon a time, formerly, (at) one time, on a former occasion, previously, before, in days gone by, in the (good) old days, long ago, some time ago, years *or* ages ago, *archaic* in olden days, *literary* in days of yore. **3** see EVER 2. ● *conj.* as soon as, when, the minute *or* moment. □ **all at once** see *suddenly* (SUDDEN). **at once 1** immediately, straight away, right away, directly, without delay, promptly, instantly, post-haste; in a wink, in the twinkling of an eye, in a minute *or* moment *or* second *or* split second, in no time (at all), in a trice, in two shakes (of a lamb's tail), *colloq.* before you can say Jack Robinson, in a jiff *or* jiffy. **2** together, at the same time, simultaneously, at a stroke, in the same instant, in the same breath, *colloq.* at *or* in one go, at a go. **once again** (or **more**) again, one more time, another time, over (again), all over again. **once and for all** (or **once for all**) finally, positively, definitely, decidedly, conclusively, for good. **once** (or **every once**) **in a while** occasionally, (every) now and then, now and again, at times, sometimes, periodically, from time to time, at intervals, sporadically. **once-over** examination, assessment, check, inspection, survey, scrutiny, vetting, appraisal, evaluation; see also SCAN *n.* 1, LEER[1] *n.*

oncer /wúnsər/ *n.* **1** *Brit. hist. sl.* a one-pound note. **2** *colloq.* a thing that occurs only once. **3** *Austral. colloq.* an election of an MP likely to serve only one term.

onco- /óngkō/ *comb. form Med.* tumour. [Gk *ogkos* mass]

oncogene /óngkəjeen/ *n.* a gene which can transform a cell into a tumour cell. □□ **oncogenic** /-jénnik/ *adj.* **oncogenous** /-kójinəss/ *adj.*

oncology /ongkólləji/ *n. Med.* the study of tumours.

oncoming /ónkumming/ *adj.* & *n.* ● *adj.* approaching from the front. ● *n.* an approach or onset.

■ *adj.* advancing, arriving, coming, nearing, approaching, imminent. ● *n.* onset, beginning, nearing, arrival, advance, approach.

oncost /ónkost/ *n. Brit.* an overhead expense.

OND *abbr.* (in the UK) Ordinary National Diploma.

on dit /ON dée/ *n.* (*pl.* ***on dits*** *pronunc.* same) a piece of gossip or hearsay. [F, = they say]

one /wun/ *adj.*, *n.*, & *pron.* ● *adj.* **1** single and integral in number. **2** (with a noun implied) a single person or thing of the kind expressed or implied (*one of the best*; *a nasty one*). **3 a** particular but undefined, esp. as contrasted with another (*that is one view*; *one thing after another*). **b** *colloq.* (as an emphatic) a noteworthy example of (*that is one difficult question*). **4** only such (*the one man who can do it*). **5** forming a unity (*one and undivided*). **6** identical; the same (*of one opinion*). ● *n.* **1 a** the lowest cardinal number. **b** a thing numbered with it. **2** unity; a unit (*one is half of two*; *came in ones and twos*). **3** a single thing or person or example (often referring to a noun previously expressed or implied: *the big dog and the small one*). **4** *colloq.* an alcoholic drink (*have a quick one*; *have one on me*). **5** a story or joke (*the one about the frog*). ● *pron.* **1** a person of a specified kind (*loved ones*; *like one possessed*). **2** any person, as representing people in general (*one is bound to lose in the end*). **3** I, me (*one would like to help*). ¶ Often regarded as an affectation. □ **all one** (often foll. by *to*) a matter of indifference. **at one** in agreement. **for one** being one, even if the only one (*I for one do not believe it*). **for one thing** as a single consideration, ignoring others. **one and the same** the same; (the) identical. **one another** each the other or others (as a formula of reciprocity: *love one another*). **one-armed bandit** *colloq.* a fruit machine worked by a long handle at the side. **one by one** singly, successively. **one day 1** on an unspecified day. **2** at some unspecified future date. **one-horse 1** using a single horse. **2** *colloq.* small, poorly equipped. **one-liner** *colloq.* a single brief sentence, often witty or apposite. **one-man** involving, done, or operated by only one man. **one-night stand 1** a single performance of a play etc. in a place. **2** *colloq.* a sexual liaison lasting only one night. **one-off** *colloq.* *adj.* made or done as the only one; not repeated. ● *n.* the only example of a manufactured product; something not repeated. **one or two** see OR[1]. **one-piece** (of a bathing-suit etc.) made as a single garment. **one-sided 1** favouring one side in a dispute; unfair, partial. **2** having or occurring on one side only. **3** larger or more developed on one side. **one-sidedly** in a one-sided manner. **one-sidedness** the act or state of being one-sided. **one-time** former. **one-to-one** with one member of one group corresponding to one of another. **one-track mind** a mind preoccupied with one subject. **one-two** *colloq.* **1** *Boxing* the delivery of two punches in quick succession. **2** *Football* etc.

a series of reciprocal passes between two advancing players. **one-up** *colloq.* having a particular advantage. **one-upmanship** *colloq.* the art of maintaining a psychological advantage. **one-way** allowing movement or travel in one direction only. [OE *ān* f. Gmc]

■ *adj.* **4** single, lone, solitary, individual, sole, only. **3 a** a particular, a certain, a given, a specific. **b** *colloq.* some. **5** unified, united, inseparable, joined, undivided, one and the same, identical, equal, at one, harmonious, in unison, whole, entire, complete. ● *n.* **5** joke, story, anecdote, chestnut, one-liner, gag, *colloq.* funny. ● *pron.* **1, 2** a person, an individual, a man *or* a woman, everybody, everyone, anybody, anyone; people. □ **at one,** agreed, united, in accord *or* agreement, in harmony. **one by one** see *singly* (SINGLE). **one-off** *(adj.)* see UNIQUE *adj.* 1. *(n.)* rarity, special, exclusive, original. **one-sided 1** partial, biased, partisan, prejudiced, bigoted, unfair, unjust, inequitable, close-minded, narrow-minded, intolerant. **2** unilateral, independent; exclusionary, exclusive. **3** lopsided, unbalanced, unequal, unequalized, uneven, disproportionate; crooked, askew, *colloq.* cock-eyed. **one-time** see FORMER[1]. **one-up** ahead, in the lead, at an advantage, on top, one step ahead.

-one /ōn/ *suffix Chem.* forming nouns denoting various compounds, esp. ketones (*acetone*). [Gk *-ōnē* fem. patronymic]

onefold /wúnfōld/ *adj.* consisting of only one member or element; simple.

oneiric /ənīrik/ *adj.* of or relating to dreams or dreaming. [Gk *oneiros* dream]

oneiro- /ənīrō/ *comb. form* dream. [Gk *oneiros* dream]

oneiromancy /ənīrəmansi/ *n.* the interpretation of dreams.

oneness /wún-niss/ *n.* **1** the fact or state of being one; singleness. **2** uniqueness. **3** agreement; unity of opinion. **4** identity, sameness.

oner /wúnnər/ *n. Brit. sl.* **1** one pound (of money). **2** a remarkable person or thing.

onerous /ónnərəss, ṓn-/ *adj.* **1** burdensome; causing or requiring trouble. **2** *Law* involving heavy obligations. □□ **onerously** *adv.* **onerousness** *n.* [ME f. OF *onereus* f. L *onerosus* f. *onus oneris* burden]

■ **1** see *burdensome* (BURDEN). □□ **onerously** see *severely* (SEVERE). **onerousness** see *severity* (SEVERE).

oneself /wunsélf/ *pron.* the reflexive and (in apposition) emphatic form of *one* (*kill oneself*; *one has to do it oneself*).

onestep /wúnstep/ *n.* a vigorous kind of foxtrot in duple time.

onflow /ónflō/ *n.* an onward flow.

onglaze /ón-glayz/ *adj.* (of painting etc.) done on a glazed surface.

ongoing /ón-gṓing/ *adj.* **1** continuing to exist or be operative etc. **2** that is or are in progress (*ongoing discussions*). □□ **ongoingness** *n.*

■ developing, evolving, growing, successive, unfolding, progressing, progressive; continuing, continued, continuous, unbroken, uninterrupted, running.

onion /únyən/ *n.* **1** a liliaceous plant, *Allium cepa*, having a short stem and bearing greenish-white flowers. **2** the swollen bulb of this with many concentric skins used in cooking, pickling, etc. □ **know one's onions** be fully knowledgeable or experienced. **onion dome** a bulbous dome on a church, palace, etc. **onion-skin 1** the brown outermost skin or any outer skin of an onion. **2** thin smooth translucent paper. □□ **oniony** *adj.* [ME f. AF *union*, OF *oignon* ult. f. L *unio -onis*]

onkus /óngkəss/ *adj. Austral. colloq.* unpleasant; disorganized. [20th c.: orig. unkn.]

■ see HORRIBLE 2.

onlooker /ónlŏŏkkər/ *n.* a non-participating observer; a spectator. □□ **onlooking** *adj.*

■ spectator, observer, looker-on, eyewitness, witness, watcher, viewer; bystander, passer-by.

only /ṓnli/ *adv.*, *adj.*, & *conj.* ● *adv.* **1** solely, merely, exclusively; and no one or nothing more besides (*I only want to sit down*; *will only make matters worse*; *needed six only*; *is only a child*). **2** no longer ago than (*saw them only yesterday*). **3** not until (*arrives only on Tuesday*). **4** with no better result than (*hurried home only to find her gone*). ¶ In informal English *only* is usually placed between the subject and verb regardless of what it refers to (e.g. *I only want to talk to you*); in more formal English it is often placed more exactly, esp. to avoid ambiguity (e.g. *I want to talk only to you*). In speech, intonation usually serves to clarify the sense. ● *attrib.adj.* **1** existing alone of its or their kind (*their only son*). **2** best or alone worth knowing (*the only place to eat*). ● *conj. colloq.* **1** except that; but for the fact that (*I would go, only I feel ill*). **2** but then (as an extra consideration) (*he always makes promises, only he never keeps them*). □ **only-begotten** *literary* begotten as the only child. **only too** extremely (*is only too willing*). [OE *ānlic*, *ǣnlic*, ME *onliche* (as ONE, -LY[2])]

■ *adv.* **1** solely, just, exclusively, alone; merely, simply, barely, at best, at worst, at most, purely, not *or* no more than, not *or* no greater than. ● *attrib.adj.* sole, single, solitary, lone, one and only, exclusive, unique, nonpareil. ● *conj.* except (that), but, however, *archaic or poet.* save that. □ **only too** see *extremely* (EXTREME).

o.n.o. *abbr. Brit.* or near offer.

onomastic /ónnəmástik/ *adj.* relating to names or nomenclature. [Gk *onomastikos* f. *onoma* name]

onomastics /ónnəmástiks/ *n.pl.* (treated as *sing.*) the study of the origin and formation of (esp. personal) proper names.

onomatopoeia /ónnəmáttəpéeə/ *n.* **1** the formation of a word from a sound associated with what is named (e.g. *cuckoo*, *sizzle*). **2** the use of such words. □□ **onomatopoeic** *adj.* **onomatopoeically** *adv.* [LL f. Gk *onomatopoiia* word-making f. *onoma -matos* name + *poieō* make]

onrush /ónrush/ *n.* an onward rush.

■ see ONSET 1.

onscreen *adj.* & *adv.* ● *adj.* /ónskreen/ appearing on a cinema, television, or VDU screen. ● *adv.* /onskreen/ **1** on or by means of a screen. **2** within the view presented by a cinema-film scene.

onset /ónset/ *n.* **1** an attack. **2** a beginning, esp. an energetic or determined one.

■ **1** attack, assault, onrush, onslaught, charge, strike, hit, raid, storming, sally, sortie. **2** beginning, start, initiation, inauguration, launch, inception, dawn, origin, genesis, appearance, début, *formal* commencement, *rhet.* birth.

onshore /ónshór/ *adj.* **1** on the shore. **2** (of the wind) blowing from the sea towards the land.

onside /ónsīd/ *adj.* (of a player in a field game) in a lawful position; not offside.

onslaught /ónslawt/ *n.* a fierce attack. [earlier *anslaight* f. MDu. *aenslag* f. *aen* on + *slag* blow, with assim. to obs. *slaught* slaughter]

■ see ATTACK *n.* 1.

Ont. *abbr.* Ontario.

-ont /ont/ *comb. form Biol.* denoting an individual of a specified type (*symbiont*). [Gk *ōn ont-* being]

onto /óntoo/ *prep. disp.* to a position or state on or in contact with (cf. *on to*). ¶ The form *onto* is still not fully accepted in the way that *into* is, although it is in wide use. It is, however, useful in distinguishing sense as between *we drove on to the beach* (i.e. in that direction) and *we drove onto the beach* (i.e. in contact with it).

ontogenesis /óntəjénnisiss/ *n.* the origin and development of an individual (cf. PHYLOGENESIS). □□ **ontogenetic** /-jinéttik/ *adj.* **ontogenetically** /-jinéttikəli/ *adv.* [formed as ONTOGENY + Gk *genesis* birth]

ontogeny /ontójəni/ *n.* = ONTOGENESIS. □□ **ontogenic** /-təjénnik/ *adj.* **ontogenically** /-təjénnikəli/ *adv.* [Gk *ōn ont-* being, pres. part. of *eimi* be + -GENY]

ontology /ontólləji/ *n.* the branch of metaphysics dealing with the nature of being. □□ **ontological** /-təlójik'l/ *adj.* **ontologically** /-təlójikəli/ *adv.* **ontologist** *n.* [mod.L *ontologia* f. Gk *ōn ont-* being + -LOGY]

onus /ṓnəss/ *n.* (*pl.* **onuses**) a burden, duty, or responsibility. [L]
■ see BURDEN *n.* 1, 2.

onward /ónwərd/ *adv.* & *adj.* ● *adv.* (also **onwards**) **1** further on. **2** towards the front. **3** with advancing motion. ● *adj.* directed onwards.
■ *adv.* forward, ahead, in front, on, forth. ● *adj.* forward, advancing, progressive, progressing.

onyx /ónniks/ *n.* a semiprecious variety of agate with different colours in layers. □ **onyx marble** banded calcite etc. used as a decorative material. [ME f. OF *oniche, onix* f. L f. Gk *onux* fingernail, onyx]

oo- /ṓə/ *comb. form* (*US* **oö-**) *Biol.* egg, ovum. [Gk *ōion* egg]

oocyte /ṓəsīt/ *n.* an immature ovum in an ovary.

oodles /ṓṓd'lz/ *n.pl. colloq.* a very great amount. [19th-c. US: orig. unkn.]
■ see LOT *n.* 1.

oof /ōōf/ *n. sl.* money, cash. [Yiddish *ooftisch*, G *auf dem Tische* on the table (of money in gambling)]
■ see MONEY 1.

oofy /ṓṓfi/ *adj. sl.* rich, wealthy. □□ **oofiness** *n.*
■ see RICH 1.

oogamous /ō-óggəməss/ *adj.* reproducing by the union of mobile male and immobile female cells. □□ **oogamy** *n.*

oogenesis /ṓəjénnisiss/ *n.* the production or development of an ovum.

ooh /ōō/ *int.* expressing surprise, delight, pain, etc. [natural exclam.]

oolite /ṓəlīt/ *n.* **1** a sedimentary rock, usu. limestone, consisting of rounded grains made up of concentric layers. **2** = OOLITH. □□ **oolitic** /-líttik/ *adj.* [F *oölithe* (as OO-, -LITE)]

oolith /ṓəlith/ *n.* any of the rounded grains making up oolite.

oology /ō-ólləji/ *n.* the study or collecting of birds' eggs. □□ **oological** /ṓəlójik'l/ *adj.* **oologist** *n.*

oolong /ṓōlong/ *n.* a dark kind of cured China tea. [Chin. *wulong* black dragon]

oomiak var. of UMIAK.

oompah /ṓōmpaa/ *n. colloq.* the rhythmical sound of deep-toned brass instruments in a band. [imit.]

oomph /ṓōmf/ *n. sl.* **1** energy, enthusiasm. **2** attractiveness, esp. sexual appeal. [20th c.: orig. uncert.]
■ see VITALITY 1.

-oon /ōōn/ *suffix* forming nouns, orig. from French words in stressed *-on* (*balloon*; *buffoon*). ¶ Replaced by *-on* in recent borrowings and those with unstressed *-on* (*baron*). [L *-o -onis*, sometimes via It. *-one*]

oops /ōōps, ṓōps/ *int. colloq.* expressing surprise or apology, esp. on making an obvious mistake. [natural exclam.]

oosperm /ṓəsperm/ *n.* a fertilized ovum.

ooze[1] /ōōz/ *v.* & *n.* ● *v.* **1** *intr.* (of fluid) pass slowly through the pores of a body. **2** *intr.* trickle or leak slowly out. **3** *intr.* (of a substance) exude moisture. **4** *tr.* exude or exhibit (a feeling) liberally (*oozed sympathy*). ● *n.* **1** a sluggish flow or exudation. **2** an infusion of oak-bark or other vegetable matter, used in tanning. □□ **oozy** *adj.* **oozily** *adv.* **ooziness** *n.* [orig. as noun (sense 2), f. OE *wōs* juice, sap]
■ *v.* exude; weep, seep, secrete, bleed, leak, drain, trickle; discharge.

ooze[2] /ōōz/ *n.* **1** a deposit of wet mud or slime, esp. at the bottom of a river, lake, or estuary. **2** a bog or marsh; soft muddy ground. □□ **oozy** *adj.* [OE *wāse*]
■ **1** slime, muck, mud, mire, silt, sludge, sediment, slush, goo, *sl.* gunk, *US sl.* glop.

OP *abbr.* **1** *RC Ch.* Order of Preachers (Dominican). **2** observation post. **3** opposite prompt.

op /op/ *n. colloq.* operation (in surgical and military senses).

op. /op/ *abbr.* **1** *Mus.* opus. **2** operator.

o.p. *abbr.* **1** out of print. **2** overproof.

op- /op/ *prefix* assim. form of OB- before *p*.

opacify /ōpássifī/ *v.tr.* & *intr.* (**-ies, -ied**) make or become opaque. □□ **opacifier** *n.*

opacity /ōpássiti/ *n.* **1** the state of being opaque. **2** obscurity of meaning. **3** obtuseness of understanding. [F *opacité* f. L *opacitas -tatis* (as OPAQUE)]
■ **1** opaqueness, darkness, murkiness, dimness, obscurity, impermeability, impenetrability. **2** opaqueness, obscurity, density, impenetrability, unintelligibility, unintelligibleness, indefiniteness, vagueness, reconditeness, abstruseness, ambiguity, equivocation, mystification. **3** opaqueness, stupidity, dullness, denseness, obtuseness, *colloq.* thickness.

opah /ṓpə/ *n.* a large rare deep-sea fish, *Lampris guttatus*, usu. having a silver-blue back with white spots and crimson fins. Also called MOONFISH. [W. Afr. name]

opal /ṓp'l/ *n.* a quartzlike form of hydrated silica, usu. white or colourless and sometimes showing changing colours, often used as a gemstone. □ **opal glass** a semi-translucent white glass. [F *opale* or L *opalus* prob. ult. f. Skr. *upalas* precious stone]

opalescent /ṓpəléss'nt/ *adj.* showing changing colours like an opal. □□ **opalesce** *v.intr.* **opalescence** *n.*
■ opaline, iridescent, lustrous; nacreous, pearly.

opaline /ṓpəlīn/ *adj.* & *n.* ● *adj.* opal-like, opalescent, iridescent. ● *n.* opal glass.
■ *adj.* see OPALESCENT.

opaque /ōpáyk/ *adj.* & *n.* ● *adj.* (**opaquer, opaquest**) **1** not transmitting light. **2** impenetrable to sight. **3** obscure; not lucid. **4** obtuse, dull-witted. ● *n.* **1** an opaque thing or substance. **2** a substance for producing opaque areas on negatives. □□ **opaquely** *adv.* **opaqueness** *n.* [ME *opak* f. L *opacus*: spelling now assim. to F]
■ *adj.* **1, 2** dark, murky, dim, turbid, muddy, cloudy, obscure, obscured, obfuscated, black, impermeable, impenetrable, clouded, non-transparent, non-translucent, hazy, blurred, blurry, smoky. **3** unclear, vague, indefinite, obscure, unfathomable, unplumbable, baffling, mystifying, ambiguous, equivocal, impenetrable, cryptic, enigmatic, puzzling, perplexing, mysterious, elusive, abstruse, arcane, recondite. **4** unintelligent, dense, dull, obtuse, stupid, dull-witted, stolid, thickheaded, dunderheaded, slow, doltish, backward, cloddish, *colloq.* thick.

op art /op/ *n. colloq.* = *optical art*. [abbr.]

op. cit. *abbr.* in the work already quoted. [L *opere citato*]

OPEC /ṓpek/ *abbr.* Organization of Petroleum Exporting Countries.

open /ṓp'n/ *adj., v.,* & *n.* ● *adj.* **1** not closed or locked or blocked up; allowing entrance or passage or access. **2 a** (of a room, field, or other area) having its door or gate in a position allowing access, or part of its confining boundary removed. **b** (of a container) not fastened or sealed; in a position or with the lid etc. in a position allowing access to the inside part. **3** unenclosed, unconfined, unobstructed (*the open road*; *open views*). **4 a** uncovered, bare, exposed (*open drain*; *open wound*). **b** *Sport* (of a goal mouth or other object of attack) unprotected, vulnerable. **5** undisguised, public, manifest; not exclusive or limited (*open scandal*; *open hostilities*). **6** expanded, unfolded, or spread out (*had the map open on the table*). **7** (of a fabric) not close; with gaps or intervals. **8 a** (of a person) frank and communicative. **b** (of the mind) accessible to new ideas; unprejudiced or undecided. **c** generous. **9 a** (of an exhibition, shop, etc.) accessible to visitors or customers; ready for business. **b** (of a meeting) admitting all, not restricted to members etc. **10 a** (of a race, competition, scholarship, etc.) unrestricted as to who may compete. **b** (of a champion, scholar, etc.) having won such a contest. **11** (of government) conducted in an informative manner receptive to enquiry, criticism, etc., from the public. **12** (foll. by *to*) **a** willing to receive (*is open to offers*). **b** (of a choice, offer, or opportunity) still available (*there are three courses open to us*). **c** likely to suffer from or be affected by (*open to abuse*). **13 a** (of the mouth) with lips apart, esp. in surprise or incomprehension. **b** (of the ears or eyes) eagerly attentive. **14** *Mus.* **a** (of a string) allowed to vibrate along its whole length. **b** (of a pipe) unstopped at each end. **c** (of a note) sounded from an open string or pipe. **15** (of an electrical circuit) having a break in the conducting path. **16** (of the bowels) not constipated. **17** (of a return ticket) not restricted as to day of travel. **18** (of a cheque) not crossed. **19** (of a boat) without a deck. **20** (of a river or harbour) free of ice. **21** (of the weather or winter) free of frost. **22** *Phonet.* **a** (of a vowel) produced with a relatively wide opening of the mouth. **b** (of a syllable) ending in a vowel. **23** (of a town, city, etc.) not defended even if attacked. ● *v.* **1** *tr.* & *intr.* make or become open or more open. **2 a** *tr.* change from a closed or fastened position so as to allow access (*opened the door*; *opened the box*). **b** *intr.* (of a door, lid, etc.) have its position changed to allow access (*the door opened slowly*). **3** *tr.* remove the sealing or fastening element of (a container) to get access to the contents (*opened the envelope*). **4** *intr.* (foll. by *into*, *on to*, etc.) (of a door, room, etc.) afford access as specified (*opened on to a large garden*). **5 a** *tr.* start or establish or set going (a business, activity, etc.). **b** *intr.* be initiated; make a start (*the session opens tomorrow*; *the story opens with a murder*). **c** *tr.* (of a counsel in a lawcourt) make a preliminary statement in (a case) before calling witnesses. **6** *tr.* **a** spread out or unfold (a map, newspaper, etc.). **b** (often *absol.*) refer to the contents of (a book). **7** *intr.* (often foll. by *with*) (of a person) begin speaking, writing, etc. (*he opened with a warning*). **8** *intr.* (of a prospect) come into view; be revealed. **9** *tr.* **a** reveal or communicate (one's feelings, intentions, etc.). **b** make available, provide. **10** *tr.* make (one's mind, heart, etc.) more sympathetic or enlightened. **11** *tr.* ceremonially declare (a building etc.) to be completed and in use. **12** *tr.* break up (ground) with a plough etc. **13** *tr.* cause evacuation of (the bowels). **14** *Naut.* **a** *tr.* get a view of by change of position. **b** *intr.* come into full view. ● *n.* **1** (prec. by *the*) **a** open space or country or air. **b** public notice or view; general attention (esp. *into the open*). **2** an open championship, competition, or scholarship. □ **be open with** speak frankly to. **keep open house** see HOUSE. **open air** (usu. prec. by *the*) a free or unenclosed space outdoors. **open-air** (*attrib.*) out of doors. **open-and-shut** (of an argument, case, etc.) straightforward and conclusive. **open-armed** cordial; warmly receptive. **open book** a person who is easily understood. **Open College** a college offering training and vocational courses mainly by correspondence. **open day** a day when the public may visit a place normally closed to them. **open door** free admission of foreign trade and immigrants. **open-door** *adj.* open, accessible, public. **open the door to** see DOOR. **open-ended** having no pre-determined limit or boundary. **open a person's eyes** see EYE. **open-eyed 1** with the eyes open. **2** alert, watchful. **open-faced** having a frank or ingenuous expression. **open-handed** generous. **open-handedly** generously. **open-handedness** generosity. **open-hearted** frank and kindly. **open-heartedness** an open-hearted quality. **open-hearth process** a process of steel manufacture, using a shallow reverberatory furnace. **open-heart surgery** surgery with the heart exposed and the blood made to bypass it. **open house** welcome or hospitality for all visitors. **open ice** ice through which navigation is possible. **open letter** a letter, esp. of protest, addressed to an individual and published in a newspaper or journal. **open market** an unrestricted market with free competition of buyers and sellers. **open-minded** accessible to new ideas; unprejudiced. **open-mindedly** in an open-minded manner. **open-mindedness** the quality of being open-minded. **open-mouthed** with the mouth open, esp. in surprise. **open out 1** unfold; spread out. **2** develop, expand. **3** become communicative. **4** accelerate. **open-plan** (usu. *attrib.*) (of a house, office, etc.) having large undivided rooms. **open prison** a prison with the minimum of physical restraints on prisoners. **open question** a matter on which differences of opinion are legitimate. **open-reel** (of a tape recorder) having reels of tape requiring individual threading, as distinct from a cassette. **open sandwich** a sandwich without a top slice of bread. **open sea** an expanse of sea away from land. **open season** the season when restrictions on the killing of game etc. are lifted. **open secret** a supposed secret that is known to many people. **open sesame** see SESAME. **open shop 1** a business etc. where employees do not have to be members of a trade union (opp. *closed shop*). **2** this system. **open society** a society with wide dissemination of information and freedom of belief. **Open University** (in the UK) a university that teaches mainly by broadcasting and correspondence, and is open to those without formal academic qualifications. **open up 1** unlock (premises). **2** make accessible. **3** reveal; bring to notice. **4** accelerate esp. a motor vehicle. **5** begin shooting or sounding. **open verdict** a verdict affirming that a crime has been committed but not specifying the criminal or (in case of violent death) the cause. **with open arms** see ARM[1]. □□ **openable** *adj.* **openness** *n.* [OE *open*]

■ *adj.* **1–4, 13, 20** ajar, gaping, agape; unfastened, unlocked, unbarred, unbolted, unlatched, unclosed; yawning, uncovered, revealed, unsealed, exposed, bare, vulnerable; unprotected, unsheltered, undefended, unfortified; unwrapped, unsealed, unfastened; clear, unobstructed, wide open, uncluttered, roomy, spacious, extensive, expansive; treeless, uncrowded, unfenced; unenclosed, unconfined; ice-free, navigable, unblocked, passable; attentive. **5** exposed, public, well-known, widely known, unconcealed, undisguised; evident, obvious, conspicuous, manifest, clear, unconcealed, unequivocal, plain, palpable, apparent, patent, downright, out-and-out, blatant, flagrant, glaring, brazen. **6** unfolded, extended, spread (out), outstretched, outspread, expanded. **7** open-weave, loose, loosely woven, rough, coarse. **8 a** unreserved, candid, frank, outspoken, communicative, straightforward, forthright, direct, honest, sincere, guileless, artless, fair. **b** receptive, open-minded, flexible, amenable, persuasible, persuadable, pliant, willing, responsive. **c** generous, charitable, unreserved, open-handed, munificent, magnanimous, big-hearted, beneficent, unselfish, unstinting, humanitarian, altruistic, *poet.* bounteous. **9–11** free, accessible, public, available; obtainable; unrestricted, unobstructed, unencumbered, unimpeded, unhindered, unhampered, unregulated, unconditional, unqualified; unrestrained, unconstrained, uninhibited, unreserved; liberal. **12 b** available, accessible; unfilled, vacant; untaken. **c** liable, subject, susceptible, exposed, inclined, predisposed, disposed. **17** unscheduled, unbooked, unspoken for, unreserved, uncommitted, free, unpromised. ● *v.* **1–3** unlock, unbar, unlatch, unbolt, unfasten, open up; uncover; uncork, unseal; undo, untie, unwrap; pull out; unblock, clear, unobstruct, unclog, unstop. **4** (*open into* or *on to*) give access to, lead to, connect *or* communicate with. **5, 7** begin, start, get under way, *formal* commence; initiate, inaugurate, launch, put in *or* into operation, activate, get *or* set going, set in motion; establish, set up; *colloq.* get *or* start the ball rolling, get *or* put the show on the road, kick off. **6 a** expand, spread (out), stretch out, open out, unfurl, extend. **8** see APPEAR 1. **9 a** disclose, unveil, uncover, expose, display, show, exhibit, reveal, divulge, bring to light, communicate, bring out, explain, present, announce, release, publish, air, make known, advertise. **b** present, offer, furnish, provide, afford, yield, reveal, uncover, raise, contribute, introduce. □ **open-and-shut** see SIMPLE *adj.* 1. **open-armed** see CORDIAL *adj.* 2. **open-handed** philanthropic; see also BOUNTEOUS. **open-minded** catholic, unprejudiced, enlightened, undogmatic, *S.Afr.* verligte; see also LIBERAL *adj.* 3, 6. **open out 1** see OPEN *v.* 6a above. **open up 1** see OPEN *v.* 1–3 above. □□ **openness** see CANDOUR.

opencast /ōp'nkaast/ *adj. Brit.* (of a mine or mining) with removal of the surface layers and working from above, not from shafts.

opener /ṓp'nər/ *n.* **1** a device for opening tins, bottles, etc. **2** *colloq.* the first item on a programme etc. **3** *Cricket* an opening batsman. □ **for openers** *colloq.* to start with.

opening /ṓp'ning/ *n.* & *adj.* ● *n.* **1** an aperture or gap, esp. allowing access. **2** a favourable situation or opportunity. **3** a beginning; an initial part. **4** *Chess* a recognized sequence of moves at the beginning of a game. **5** a counsel's preliminary statement of a case in a lawcourt. ● *adj.* initial, first. □ **opening-time** *Brit.* the time at which public houses may legally open for custom.

■ *n.* **1** break, breach, rent, rift, cleft, crack, crevice, fissure, cranny, chink, pit, gap, split, slit, slot, aperture, hole, orifice, separation. **2** opportunity, chance, occasion, toe-hold, foothold, *colloq.* break; job, position, vacancy. **3** beginning, start, *formal* commencement; origin, outset, onset, inauguration, launch, send-off, initiation, presentation, début, *rhet.* birth; *US* start-off, start-up. ● *adj.* initiatory, first; see also INITIAL *adj.*

openly /ṓpənli/ *adv.* **1** frankly, honestly. **2** publicly; without concealment. [OE *openlīce* (as OPEN, -LY²)]

■ **1** frankly, honestly, unreservedly, plainly, forthrightly, candidly, directly, freely, outspokenly. **2** publicly, undisguisedly; brazenly, brashly, flagrantly, unabashedly, unashamedly, unreservedly, boldly, audaciously, flauntingly.

openwork /ṓp'nwurk/ *n.* a pattern with intervening spaces in metal, leather, lace, etc.

opera¹ /óppərə, óprə/ *n.* **1 a** a dramatic work in one or more acts, set to music for singers (usu. in costume) and instrumentalists. **b** this as a genre. **2** a building for the performance of opera. □ **opera-glasses** small binoculars for use at the opera or theatre. **opera-hat** a man's tall collapsible hat. **opera-house** a theatre for the performance of opera. [It. f. L, = labour, work]

■ □ **opera-glasses** see GLASS *n.* 3.

opera² *pl.* of OPUS.

operable /óppərəb'l/ *adj.* **1** that can be operated. **2** suitable for treatment by surgical operation. □□ **operability** /-bílliti/ *n.* [LL *operabilis* f. L (as OPERATE)]

■ **1** workable, practicable, serviceable, usable, functional, fit, operational, in working order *or* condition.

opera buffa /óppərə bóofə/ *n.* (esp. Italian) comic opera, esp. with characters drawn from everyday life. [It.]

opéra comique /ópperaá koméek/ *n.* (esp. French) opera on a light-hearted theme, with spoken dialogue. [F]

operand /óppərand/ *n. Math.* the quantity etc. on which an operation is to be done. [L *operandum* neut. gerundive of *operari*: see OPERATE]

opera seria /óppərə séeriə/ *n.* (esp. 18th-c. Italian) opera on a serious, usu. classical or mythological theme. [It.]

operate /óppərayt/ *v.* **1** *tr.* manage, work, control; put or keep in a functional state. **2** *intr.* be in action; function. **3** *intr.* produce an effect; exercise influence (*the tax operates to our disadvantage*). **4** *intr.* (often foll. by *on*) **a** perform a surgical operation. **b** conduct a military or naval action. **c** be active in business etc., esp. dealing in stocks and shares. **5** *intr.* (foll. by *on*) influence or affect (feelings etc.). **6** *tr.* bring about; accomplish. □ **operating system** the basic software that enables the running of a computer program. **operating theatre** (or **room**) a room for surgical operations. [L *operari* to work f. *opus operis* work]

■ **1** manage, run, direct, conduct, work, control, carry on, ply, manipulate, handle; drive. **2** go, run, perform; work, function, serve, act. **6** produce, accomplish, bring about, effect, effectuate.

operatic /óppəráttik/ *adj.* **1** of or relating to opera. **2** resembling or characteristic of opera. □□ **operatically** *adv.* [irreg. f. OPERA¹, after *dramatic*]

operatics /óppəráttiks/ *n.pl.* the production and performance of operas.

operation /óppəráysh'n/ *n.* **1 a** the action or process or method of working or operating. **b** the state of being active or functioning (*not yet in operation*). **c** the scope or range of effectiveness of a thing's activity. **2** an active process; a discharge of a function (*the operation of breathing*). **3** a piece of work, esp. one in a series (often in *pl.*: *begin operations*). **4** an act of surgery performed on a patient. **5 a** a strategic movement of troops, ships, etc. for military action. **b** preceding a code-name (*Operation Overlord*). **6** a financial transaction. **7** *Math.* the subjection of a number or quantity or function to a process affecting its value or form, e.g. multiplication, differentiation. □ **operations research** = *operational research.* [ME f. OF f. L *operatio -onis* (as OPERATE)]

■ **1, 2** function, functioning, working, running, performance, action, motion, movement; manipulation, handling, direction, running, control, management; manoeuvring. **3, 6** undertaking, enterprise, venture, project, affair, deal, job, task, procedure, proceeding, (day-to-day) business, transaction. **5 a** action, manoeuvre, mission, task, campaign, exercise.

operational /óppəráyshən'l/ *adj.* **1 a** of or used for operations. **b** engaged or involved in operations. **2** able or ready to function. □ **operational research** the application of scientific principles to business management, providing a quantitative basis for complex decisions. □□ **operationally** *adv.*

■ **2** see FUNCTIONAL 1.

operative /óppərətiv/ *adj.* & *n.* ● *adj.* **1** in operation; having effect. **2** having the principal relevance (*'may' is the operative word*). **3** of or by surgery. **4** *Law* expressing an intent to perform a transaction. ● *n.* **1** a worker, esp. a skilled one. **2** *US* an agent employed by a detective agency or secret service. □□ **operatively** *adv.* **operativeness** *n.* [LL *operativus* f. L (as OPERATE)]

■ *adj.* **1** functioning, working, in effect, in force, operating, operational, functional, effective. **2** significant, meaningful, important, telling, vital, critical, relevant; see also PERTINENT 1. ● *n.* **1** worker, hand, employee; craftsman, craftswoman, artisan, mechanic, machinist. **2** espionage *or* intelligence agent, counter-espionage *or* counter-intelligence agent, spy, counter-spy, undercover agent *or* man, (FBI *or* CIA) agent, *US colloq.* G-man; private detective, (private) investigator, *colloq.* private eye, eye, sleuth, sleuth-hound, snoop, snooper, *sl.* (private) dick, gumshoe, *US sl.* shamus, peeper.

operator /óppəraytər/ *n.* **1** a person operating a machine etc., esp. making connections of lines in a telephone exchange. **2** a person operating or engaging in business. **3** *colloq.* a person acting in a specified way (*a smooth operator*). **4** *Math.* a symbol or function denoting an operation (e.g. x, +). [LL f. L *operari* (as OPERATE)]

■ **1** driver; worker, operative, practitioner; switchboard. **2** businessman, businesswoman, business person, captain of industry, director, administrator, manager, supervisor, superintendent.

operculum /ōpérkyooləm/ *n.* (*pl.* **opercula** /-lə/) **1** *Zool.* **a** a flaplike structure covering the gills in a fish. **b** a platelike structure closing the aperture of a gastropod mollusc's shell when the organism is retracted. **c** any of various other parts covering or closing an aperture, such as a flap over the nostrils in some birds. **2** *Bot.* a lidlike structure of the spore-containing capsule of mosses. □□ **opercular** *adj.* **operculate** /-lət/ *adj.* **operculi-** *comb. form.* [L f. *operire* cover]

operetta /óppərέttə/ *n.* **1** a one-act or short opera. **2** a light opera. [It., dimin. of *opera*: see OPERA]

ophicleide /óffiklīd/ *n.* **1** an obsolete usu. bass brass wind instrument developed from the serpent. **2** a powerful organ reed-stop. [F *ophicléide* f. Gk *ophis* serpent + *kleis kleidos* key]

ophidian /ōfiddiən/ *n.* & *adj.* ● *n.* any reptile of the suborder Serpentes (formerly Ophidia), including snakes. ● *adj.* **1** of or relating to this group. **2** snakelike. [mod.L *Ophidia* f. Gk *ophis* snake]

ophio- /óffiō/ *comb. form* snake. [Gk *ophis* snake]

ophthalmia /of-thálmiə/ *n.* an inflammation of the eye, esp. conjunctivitis. [LL f. Gk f. *ophthalmos* eye]

ophthalmic /of-thálmik/ *adj.* of or relating to the eye and its diseases. □ **ophthalmic optician** an optician qualified

to prescribe as well as dispense spectacles and contact lenses. [L *ophthalmicus* f. Gk *ophthalmikos* (as OPHTHALMIA)]
ophthalmo- /of-thálmō/ *comb. form Optics* denoting the eye. [Gk *ophthalmos* eye]
ophthalmology /óf-thalmólləji/ *n.* the scientific study of the eye. □□ **ophthalmological** /-məlójik'l/ *adj.* **ophthalmologist** *n.*
■ □□ **ophthalmologist** eye-doctor, oculist.
ophthalmoscope /of-thálməskōp/ *n.* an instrument for inspecting the retina and other parts of the eye. □□ **ophthalmoscopic** /-skóppik/ *adj.*
-opia /ōpiə/ *comb. form* denoting a visual disorder (*myopia*). [Gk f. *ōps* eye]
opiate *adj.*, *n.*, & *v.* ● *adj.* /ṓpiət/ **1** containing opium. **2** narcotic, soporific. ● *n.* /ṓpiət/ **1** a drug containing opium, usu. to ease pain or induce sleep. **2** a thing which soothes or stupefies. ● *v.tr.* /ṓpiayt/ **1** mix with opium. **2** stupefy. [med.L *opiatus*, *-um*, *opiare* f. L *opium*: see OPIUM]
■ *adj.* **2** see NARCOTIC *adj.* 1, 4. ● *n.* **1** see NARCOTIC *n.* **2** see SEDATIVE *n.*
opine /ōpī́n/ *v.tr.* (often foll. by *that* + clause) hold or express as an opinion. [L *opinari* think, believe]
■ see COMMENT *v.* 1.
opinion /əpínyən/ *n.* **1** a belief or assessment based on grounds short of proof. **2** a view held as probable. **3** (often foll. by *on*) what one thinks about a particular topic or question (*my opinion on capital punishment*). **4 a** a formal statement of professional advice (*will get a second opinion*). **b** *Law* a formal statement of reasons for a judgement given. **5** an estimation (*had a low opinion of it*). □ **be of the opinion that** believe or maintain that. **in one's opinion** according to one's view or belief. **a matter of opinion** a disputable point. **opinion poll** = GALLUP POLL. **public opinion** views generally prevalent, esp. on moral questions. [ME f. OF f. L *opinio -onis* (as OPINE)]
■ **1, 3** belief, judgement, thought, sentiment, (point of) view, viewpoint, conviction, way of thinking, perception, idea, impression, notion, conception, theory, *idée reçue*. **5** evaluation, estimation, appraisal, impression.
opinionated /əpínyənaytid/ *adj.* conceitedly assertive or dogmatic in one's opinions. □□ **opinionatedly** *adv.* **opinionatedness** *n.* [obs. *opinionate* in the same sense f. OPINION]
■ stubborn, pigheaded, obstinate, doctrinaire, inflexible, dogmatic, cocksure, conceited, obdurate, dictatorial, dogged, mulish, bull-headed, overbearing; prejudiced, biased, bigoted, one-sided, jaundiced, coloured, partial, partisan.
opium /ṓpiəm/ *n.* **1** a reddish-brown heavy-scented addictive drug prepared from the juice of the opium poppy, used in medicine as an analgesic and narcotic. **2** anything regarded as soothing or stupefying. □ **opium den** a haunt of opium-smokers. **opium poppy** a poppy, *Papaver somniferum*, native to Europe and E. Asia, with white, red, pink, or purple flowers. [ME f. L f. Gk *opion* poppy-juice f. *opos* juice]
opopanax /ōpóppənaks/ *n.* **1 a** an umbelliferous plant, *Opopanax chironium*, with yellow flowers. **b** a resinous gum obtained from the roots of this plant and used in perfume. **2** = *sponge tree*. [ME f. L f. Gk f. *opos* juice + *panax* formed as PANACEA]
opossum /əpóssəm/ *n.* **1 a** any mainly tree-living marsupial of the family Didelphidae, native to America, having a prehensile tail and hind feet with an opposable thumb. **b** (in full **water opossum**) an opossum, *Chironectes minimus*, suited to an aquatic habitat and having webbed hind feet. Also called YAPOK. **2** *Austral.* & *NZ* = POSSUM 2. [Virginian Ind. *āpassūm*]
opp. *abbr.* opposite.
oppo /óppō/ *n.* (*pl.* **-os**) *Brit. colloq.* a colleague or friend. [*opposite number*]
opponent /əpṓnənt/ *n.* & *adj.* ● *n.* a person who opposes or belongs to an opposing side. ● *adj.* opposing, contrary, opposed. □ **opponent muscle** a muscle enabling the thumb to be placed front to front against a finger of the same hand. □□ **opponency** *n.* [L *opponere opponent-* (as OB-, *ponere* place)]
■ *n.* antagonist, adversary, disputant, contestant, competitor, contender, rival, enemy, *esp. poet. or formal* foe; (*opponents*) opposition, other side.
opportune /óppərtyōōn/ *adj.* **1** (of a time) well-chosen or especially favourable or appropriate (*an opportune moment*). **2** (of an action or event) well-timed; done or occurring at a favourable or useful time. □□ **opportunely** *adv.* **opportuneness** *n.* [ME f. OF *opportun -une* f. L *opportunus* (as OB-, *portus* harbour), orig. of the wind driving towards the harbour]
■ **1** favourable, advantageous, auspicious, good, appropriate, well-chosen, felicitous, happy, propitious, beneficial, helpful, fortunate, lucky, profitable. **2** timely, well-timed, seasonable, apt, appropriate, germane, pertinent, convenient, fitting, suitable.
opportunism /óppərtyṓōniz'm/ *n.* **1** the adaptation of policy or judgement to circumstances or opportunity, esp. regardless of principle. **2** the seizing of opportunities when they occur. □□ **opportunist** *n.* & *adj.* **opportunistic** /-nístik/ *adj.* **opportunistically** /-nístikəli/ *adv.* [OPPORTUNE after It. *opportunismo* and F *opportunisme* in political senses]
■ □□ **opportunistic** expedient, selfish, taking advantage, exploitive, exploitative, unprincipled, machiavellian, opportunist.
opportunity /óppərtyṓōniti/ *n.* (*pl.* **-ies**) **1** a good chance; a favourable occasion. **2** a chance or opening offered by circumstances. **3** good fortune. □ **opportunity knocks** an opportunity occurs. [ME f. OF *opportunité* f. L *opportunitas -tatis* (as OPPORTUNE)]
■ **1, 2** chance, occasion, opening, possibility, moment, time, *colloq.* break.
opposable /əpṓzəb'l/ *adj.* **1** able to be opposed. **2** *Zool.* (of the thumb in primates) capable of facing and touching the other digits on the same hand.
oppose /əpṓz/ *v.tr.* (often *absol.*) **1** set oneself against; resist, argue against. **2** be hostile to. **3** take part in a game, sport, etc., against (another competitor or team). **4** (foll. by *to*) place in opposition or contrast. □ **as opposed to** in contrast with. □□ **opposer** *n.* [ME f. OF *opposer* f. L *opponere*: see OPPONENT]
■ **1–2** resist, counter, object to, counteract, defy, take a stand against, withstand, combat, contest, attack, counter-attack, fight, grapple with, contend with; argue against, dispute, rebut, challenge. **3** meet, play; mark, pair with. **4** (*oppose to*) match *or* contrast with, offset *or* play off against. □ **as opposed to** as against, in contrast with; see also INSTEAD 1.
opposite /óppəzit/ *adj.*, *n.*, *adv.*, & *prep.* ● *adj.* **1** (often foll. by *to*) having a position on the other or further side, facing or back to back. **2** (often foll. by *to*, *from*) **a** of a contrary kind; diametrically different. **b** being the other of a contrasted pair. **3** (of angles) between opposite sides of the intersection of two lines. **4** *Bot.* (of leaves etc.) placed at the same height on the opposite sides of the stem, or placed straight in front of another organ. ● *n.* an opposite thing or person or term. ● *adv.* **1** in an opposite position (*the tree stands opposite*). **2** (of a leading theatrical etc. part) in a complementary role to (another performer). ● *prep.* in a position opposite to (*opposite the house is a tree*). □ **opposite number** a person holding an equivalent position in another group or organization. **opposite prompt** the side of a theatre stage usually to an actor's right. **the opposite sex** women in relation to men or vice versa. □□ **oppositely** *adv.* **oppositeness** *n.* [ME f. OF f. L *oppositus* past part. of *opponere*: see OPPONENT]
■ *adj.* **1** facing, *vis-à-vis*; back-to-back. **2 a** opposing, conflicting, contrary, contrasting, contradictory, antithetical, differing, different, divergent, diverse, antagonistic, inconsistent, irreconcilable. ● *n.* reverse,

converse, contrary, antithesis. ● *adv.* **1** *vis-à-vis*, in front. ● *prep.* facing, in front of, *vis-à-vis*. □ **opposite number** see LIKE[1] *n.* 1.

opposition /óppəzísh'n/ *n.* **1** resistance, antagonism. **2** the state of being hostile or in conflict or disagreement. **3** contrast or antithesis. **4 a** a group or party of opponents or competitors. **b** (**the Opposition**) *Brit.* the principal parliamentary party opposed to that in office. **5** the act of opposing or placing opposite. **6 a** diametrically opposite position. **b** *Astrol.* & *Astron.* the position of two heavenly bodies when their longitude differs by 180°, as seen from the earth. □□ **oppositional** *adj.* [ME f. OF f. L *oppositio* (as OB-, POSITION)]

■ **1–3** hostility, antagonism, unfriendliness, resistance, counteraction, conflict, defiance, contrast, antipathy, adversity; disapproval, objection, criticism, abuse, flak. **4 a** competition, opponents, adversaries, competitors, antagonists, enemy, enemies, rivals, other side, *esp. poet. or formal* foe(s).

oppress /əprés/ *v.tr.* **1** keep in subservience by coercion. **2** govern or treat harshly or with cruel injustice. **3** weigh down (with cares or unhappiness). □□ **oppressor** *n.* [ME f. OF *oppresser* f. med.L *oppressare* (as OB-, PRESS[1])]

■ **1, 2** crush, repress, put down, suppress, subjugate, tyrannize (over), subdue, overpower, enslave, persecute, maltreat, abuse, harry, harass, trample underfoot, ride roughshod over. **3** burden, afflict, trouble, weigh down, overload, encumber, wear (down), press, weary, overburden, overwhelm. □□ **oppressor** bully, tyrant, taskmaster, taskmistress, despot, autocrat, persecutor, slave-driver, dictator, overlord, iron hand, scourge, tormentor, torturer, intimidator.

oppression /əprésh'n/ *n.* **1** the act or an instance of oppressing; the state of being oppressed. **2** prolonged harsh or cruel treatment or control. **3** mental distress. [OF f. L *oppressio* (as OPPRESS)]

■ repression, suppression, subjugation, subjection, tyranny, despotism, enslavement; persecution, maltreatment, abuse, torment, torture, hardship, injury, pain, anguish; injustice.

oppressive /əpréssiv/ *adj.* **1** oppressing; harsh or cruel. **2** difficult to endure. **3** (of weather) close and sultry. □□ **oppressively** *adv.* **oppressiveness** *n.* [F *oppressif -ive* f. med.L *oppressivus* (as OPPRESS)]

■ **1, 2** oppressing, burdensome, overpowering, overwhelming, onerous, heavy, cumbersome, exhausting, racking, unbearable, intolerable, agonizing, unendurable, harsh, cruel, brutal, severe, tyrannical, repressive; dispiriting, depressing, disheartening, discouraging, grievous, distressing, miserable, harrowing, wretched, *literary or joc.* dolorous. **3** suffocating, stifling, stuffy, close, airless, unventilated, uncomfortable; sultry, muggy.

opprobrious /əprṓbriəss/ *adj.* (of language) severely scornful; abusive. □□ **opprobriously** *adv.* [ME f. LL *opprobriosus* (as OPPROBRIUM)]

■ see ABUSIVE 1, 2.

opprobrium /əprṓbriəm/ *n.* **1** disgrace or bad reputation attaching to some act or conduct. **2** a cause of this. [L f. *opprobrum* (as OB-, *probrum* disgraceful act)]

■ **1** see DISGRACE *n.*

oppugn /əpyóon/ *v.tr. literary* call into question; controvert. □□ **oppugner** *n.* [ME f. L *oppugnare* attack, besiege (as OB-, L *pugnare* fight)]

oppugnant /əpúgnənt/ *adj. formal* attacking; opposing. □□ **oppugnance** *n.* **oppugnancy** *n.* **oppugnation** /-náysh'n/ *n.*

opsimath /ópsimath/ *n. literary* a person who learns only late in life. □□ **opsimathy** /-símməthi/ *n.* [Gk *opsimathēs* f. *opse* late + *math-* learn]

opsonin /ópsənin/ *n.* an antibody which assists the action of phagocytes. □□ **opsonic** /opsónnik/ *adj.* [Gk *opsōnion* victuals + -IN]

opt /opt/ *v.intr.* (usu. foll. by *for*, *between*) exercise an option; make a choice. □ **opt out** (often foll. by *of*) choose not to participate (*opted out of the race*). [F *opter* f. L *optare* choose, wish]

■ see CHOOSE 3.

optant /óptənt/ *n.* **1** a person who may choose one of two nationalities. **2** a person who chooses or has chosen.

optative /optáytiv, óptətiv/ *adj.* & *n. Gram.* ● *adj.* expressing a wish. ● *n.* the optative mood. □ **optative mood** a set of verb-forms expressing a wish etc., distinct esp. in Sanskrit and Greek. □□ **optatively** *adv.* [F *optatif -ive* f. LL *optativus* (as OPT)]

optic /óptik/ *adj.* & *n.* ● *adj.* of or relating to the eye or vision (*optic nerve*). ● *n.* **1** a lens etc. in an optical instrument. **2** *archaic* or *joc.* the eye. **3** (**Optic**) *Brit. propr.* a device fastened to the neck of a bottle for measuring out spirits etc. □ **optic angle** the angle formed by notional lines from the extremities of an object to the eye, or by lines from the eyes to a given point. **optic axis 1** a line passing through the centre of curvature of a lens or spherical mirror and parallel to the axis of symmetry. **2** the direction in a doubly refracting crystal for which no double refraction occurs. **optic lobe** the dorsal lobe in the brain from which the optic nerve arises. [F *optique* or med.L *opticus* f. Gk *optikos* f. *optos* seen]

optical /óptik'l/ *adj.* **1** of sight; visual. **2 a** of or concerning sight or light in relation to each other. **b** belonging to optics. **3** (esp. of a lens) constructed to assist sight or on the principles of optics. □ **optical activity** *Chem.* the property of rotating the plane of polarization of plane-polarized light. **optical art** a style of painting that gives the illusion of movement by the precise use of pattern and colour. **optical brightener** any fluorescent substance used to produce a whitening effect on laundry. **optical character recognition** the identification of printed characters using photoelectric devices. **optical disc** see DISC. **optical fibre** thin glass fibre through which light can be transmitted. **optical glass** a very pure kind of glass used for lenses etc. **optical illusion 1** a thing having an appearance so resembling something else as to deceive the eye. **2** an instance of mental misapprehension caused by this. **optical microscope** a microscope using the direct perception of light (cf. *electron microscope*). □□ **optically** *adv.*

optician /optísh'n/ *n.* **1** a maker or seller of optical instruments, esp. spectacles and contact lenses. **2** a person trained in the detection and correction of poor eyesight (see OPTOMETRIST). [F *opticien* f. med.L *optica* (as OPTIC)]

optics /óptiks/ *n.pl.* (treated as *sing.*) the scientific study of sight and the behaviour of light, or of other radiation or particles (*electron optics*).

optima *pl.* of OPTIMUM.

optimal /óptim'l/ *adj.* best or most favourable, esp. under a particular set of circumstances. □□ **optimally** *adv.* [L *optimus* best]

■ see OPTIMUM *adj.*

optimism /óptimiz'm/ *n.* **1** an inclination to hopefulness and confidence (opp. PESSIMISM). **2** *Philos.* **a** the doctrine, esp. as set forth by Leibniz, that this world is the best of all possible worlds. **b** the theory that good must ultimately prevail over evil in the universe. □□ **optimist** *n.* **optimistic** /-místik/ *adj.* **optimistically** /-místikəli/ *adv.* [F *optimisme* f. L OPTIMUM]

■ **1** positivity, positiveness, hopefulness, confidence, sanguineness, cheerfulness. □□ **optimist** see *idealist* (IDEALISM). **optimistic** sanguine, positive, cheerful, buoyant, bright, hopeful, expectant, confident, bullish, idealistic, Pollyannaish.

optimize /óptimīz/ *v.* (also **-ise**) **1** *tr.* make the best or most effective use of (a situation, an opportunity, etc.). **2** *intr.* be an optimist. □□ **optimization** /-záysh'n/ *n.* [L *optimus* best]

optimum /óptiməm/ *n.* & *adj.* ● *n.* (*pl.* **optima** /-mə/ or **optimums**) **1 a** the most favourable conditions (for growth, reproduction, etc.). **b** the best or most favourable situation. **2**

the best possible compromise between opposing tendencies. ● *adj.* = OPTIMAL. [L, neut. (as n.) of *optimus* best]

■ *n.* **1** best, finest, most favourable; ideal, perfection, model, paragon, exemplar. **2** lesser evil. ● *adj.* best, finest, most favourable, ideal, perfect, choicest, optimal; first-rate, first-class, sterling, prime, capital, excellent, exceptional, superlative; extraordinary, unique, peerless, unequalled, unexcelled, unrivalled, unsurpassed.

option /ópsh'n/ *n.* **1 a** the act or an instance of choosing; a choice. **b** a thing that is or may be chosen (*those are the options*). **2** the liberty of choosing; freedom of choice. **3** *Stock Exch.* etc. the right, obtained by payment, to buy, sell, etc. specified stocks etc. at a specified price within a set time. □ **have no option but to** must. **keep** (or **leave**) **one's options open** not commit oneself. [F or f. L *optio*, stem of *optare* choose]

■ **1** choice, selection, alternative, recourse, opportunity, way out. **2** choice, privilege, election, opportunity, chance.

optional /ópshən'l/ *adj.* being an option only; not obligatory. □□ **optionality** /-nálliti/ *n.* **optionally** *adv.*

■ voluntary, discretionary, discretional, elective, free, spontaneous, unforced, non-compulsory, non-mandatory, unmandatory, non-requisite.

optometer /optómmitər/ *n.* an instrument for testing the refractive power and visual range of the eye. □□ **optometric** /óptəmétrik/ *adj.* **optometry** *n.* [Gk *optos* seen + -METER]

optometrist /optómmitrist/ *n.* esp. *US* **1** a person who practises optometry. **2** = *ophthalmic optician*.

optophone /óptəfōn/ *n.* an instrument converting light into sound, and so enabling the blind to read print etc. by ear. [Gk *optos* seen + -PHONE]

opulent /ópyoolənt/ *adj.* **1** ostentatiously rich; wealthy. **2** luxurious (*opulent surroundings*). **3** abundant; profuse. □□ **opulence** *n.* **opulently** *adv.* [L *opulens*, *opulent-* f. *opes* wealth]

■ **1** wealthy, affluent, rich, prosperous, well-to-do, well off, comfortable, in clover, on velvet, in velvet, *colloq.* flush, well-heeled, made of money, on Easy Street, *sl.* loaded, rolling in it, in the chips. **2** see PLUSH *adj.* **3** abundant, copious, bountiful, plentiful, prolific, profuse, *poet.* plenteous.

opuntia /ōpúnshiə/ *n.* any cactus of the genus *Opuntia*, with jointed cylindrical or elliptical stems and barbed bristles. Also called *prickly pear*. [L plant-name f. *Opus -untis* in Locris in ancient Greece]

opus /ṓpəss, óp-/ *n.* (*pl.* **opuses** or **opera** /óppərə/) **1** *Mus.* **a** a separate musical composition or set of compositions of any kind. **b** (also **op.**) used before a number given to a composer's work, usu. indicating the order of publication (*Beethoven, op. 15*). **2** any artistic work (cf. MAGNUM OPUS). □ **opus Dei** /dáyee/ *Eccl.* **1** liturgical worship regarded as man's primary duty to God. **2** (**Opus Dei**) a Roman Catholic organization of laymen and priests founded in Spain in 1928 with the aim of re-establishing Christian ideals in society. [L, = work]

■ work, composition, production, creation.

opuscule /əpúskyōōl/ *n.* (also **opusculum** /əpúskyooləm/) (*pl.* **opuscules** or **opuscula** /-lə/) a minor (esp. musical or literary) work. [F f. L *opusculum* dimin. of OPUS]

OR *abbr.* **1** operational research. **2** *US* Oregon (in official postal use). **3** other ranks.

or[1] /or, ər/ *conj.* **1 a** introducing the second of two alternatives (*white or black*). **b** introducing all but the first, or only the last, of any number of alternatives (*white or grey or black; white, grey, or black*). **2** (often prec. by *either*) introducing the only remaining possibility or choice given (*take it or leave it; either come in or go out*). **3** (prec. by *whether*) introducing the second part of an indirect question or conditional clause (*ask him whether he was there or not; must go whether I like or dislike it*). **4** introducing a synonym or explanation of a preceding word etc. (*suffered from vertigo or giddiness*). **5** introducing a significant afterthought (*he must know - or is he bluffing?*). **6** = *or else* (*run or you'll be late*). **7** *poet.* each of two; either (*or in the heart or in the head*). □ **not A or B** not A, and also not B. **one or two** (or **two or three** etc.) *colloq.* a few. **or else 1** otherwise (*do it now, or else you will have to do it tomorrow*). **2** *colloq.* expressing a warning or threat (*hand over the money or else*). **or rather** introducing a rephrasing or qualification of a preceding statement etc. (*he was there, or rather I heard that he was*). **or so** (after a quantity or a number) or thereabouts (*send me ten or so*). [reduced form of obs. *other* conj. (which superseded OE *oththe* or), of uncert. orig.]

or[2] /or/ *n.* & *adj.* *Heraldry* ● *n.* a gold or yellow colour. ● *adj.* (usu. following noun) gold or yellow (*a crescent or*). [F f. L *aurum* gold]

-or[1] /ər/ *suffix* forming nouns denoting a person or thing performing the action of a verb, or an agent more generally (*actor; escalator; tailor*) (see also -ATOR, -ITOR). [L *-or*, *-ator*, etc., sometimes via AF *-eour*, OF *-ëor*, *-ëur*]

-or[2] /ər/ *suffix* forming nouns denoting state or condition (*error; horror*). [L *-or -oris*, sometimes via (or after) OF *-or*, *-ur*]

-or[3] /ər/ *suffix* forming adjectives with comparative sense (*major; senior*). [AF *-our* f. L *-or*]

-or[4] /ər/ *suffix US* = -OUR[1].

orache /órrich/ *n.* (also **orach**) an edible plant, *Atriplex hortensis*, with red, yellow, or green leaves sometimes used as a substitute for spinach or sorrel. Also called SALTBUSH. [ME *arage* f. AF *arasche* f. L *atriplex* f. Gk *atraphaxus*]

oracle /órrək'l/ *n.* **1 a** a place at which advice or prophecy was sought from the gods in classical antiquity. **b** the usu. ambiguous or obscure response given at an oracle. **c** a prophet or prophetess at an oracle. **2 a** a person or thing regarded as an infallible guide to future action etc. **b** a saying etc. regarded as infallible guidance. **3** divine inspiration or revelation. **4** (**Oracle**) *Brit. propr. hist.* a teletext service provided by Independent Television. [ME f. OF f. L *oraculum* f. *orare* speak]

■ **1 b** prophecy, augury, prediction, divination, advice, prognostication, answer, message. **c** prophet, sibyl, seer, soothsayer, augur, fortune-teller, diviner, prognosticator, Cassandra, Nostradamus. **2 a** authority, guru, mastermind, mentor, wizard.

oracular /ərákyoolər/ *adj.* **1** of or concerning an oracle or oracles. **2** (esp. of advice etc.) mysterious or ambiguous. **3** prophetic. □□ **oracularity** /-lárriti/ *n.* **oracularly** *adv.* [L (as ORACLE)]

■ **2** see AMBIGUOUS. **3** see PROPHETIC.

oracy /órrəsi/ *n.* the ability to express oneself fluently in speech. [L *os oris* mouth, after *literacy*]

oral /órəl/ *adj.* & *n.* ● *adj.* **1** by word of mouth; spoken; not written (*the oral tradition*). **2** done or taken by the mouth (*oral contraceptive*). **3** of the mouth. **4** *Psychol.* of or concerning a supposed stage of infant emotional and sexual development, in which the mouth is of central interest. ● *n.* *colloq.* a spoken examination, test, etc. □ **oral sex** sexual activity in which the genitals of one partner are stimulated by the mouth of the other. **oral society** a society that has not reached the stage of literacy. □□ **orally** *adv.* [LL *oralis* f. L *os oris* mouth]

■ *adj.* **1** spoken, said, verbal, uttered, voiced, vocal, vocalized, enunciated, pronounced, articulated, word-of-mouth, viva voce. ● *n.* viva voce, *Brit. colloq.* viva.

Orange /órrinj/ *adj.* of or relating to Orangemen or their activities. □□ **Orangeism** *n.*

orange /órrinj/ *n.* & *adj.* ● *n.* **1 a** a large roundish juicy citrus fruit with a bright reddish-yellow tough rind. **b** any of various trees or shrubs of the genus *Citrus*, esp. *C. sinensis* or *C. aurantium*, bearing fragrant white flowers and yielding this fruit. **2** a fruit or plant resembling this. **3 a** the reddish-yellow colour of an orange. **b** orange pigment. ● *adj.* orange-coloured; reddish-yellow. □ **orange blossom** the flowers of the orange tree, traditionally worn by the bride at a wedding. **orange flower water** a solution of neroli in water. **orange peel 1** the skin of an orange. **2** a rough surface resembling this. **orange pekoe** tea made from very small leaves. **orange squash** *Brit.* a soft drink made from oranges and other ingredients, often sold in concentrated form. **orange-stick** a thin stick, pointed at one end and usu. of orange wood, for manicuring the fingernails. **orange-wood** the wood of the orange tree. [ME f. OF *orenge*, ult. f. Arab. *nāranj* f. Pers. *nārang*]

orangeade /órrinjáyd/ *n.* a usu. fizzy non-alcoholic drink flavoured with orange.

Orangeman /órrinjmən/ *n.* (*pl.* **-men**) a member of a political society formed in 1795 to support Protestantism in Ireland. [after William of *Orange* (William III)]

orangery /órrinjəri/ *n.* (*pl.* **-ies**) a place, esp. a special structure, where orange-trees are cultivated.

orang-utan /orángootán/ *n.* (also **orang-outang** /-táng/) a large red long-haired tree-living ape, *Pongo pygmaeus*, native to Borneo and Sumatra, with characteristic long arms and hooked hands and feet. [Malay *ōrang ūtan* wild man]

orate /oráyt/ *v.intr.* esp. *joc.* or *derog.* make a speech or speak, esp. pompously or at length. [back-form. f. ORATION]

oration /oráysh'n/ *n.* **1** a formal speech, discourse, etc., esp. when ceremonial. **2** *Gram.* a way of speaking; language. [ME f. L *oratio* discourse, prayer f. *orare* speak, pray]
■ **1** speech, declaration, address, lecture, recitation, monologue, declamation, *literary* discourse, *sl.* spiel; valedictory, eulogy, homily, panegyric.

orator /órrətər/ *n.* **1 a** a person making a speech. **b** an eloquent public speaker. **2** (in full **public orator**) an official speaking for a university on ceremonial occasions. ▫▫ **oratorial** /-tóriəl/ *adj.* [ME f. AF *oratour*, OF *orateur* f. L *orator -oris* speaker, pleader (as ORATION)]

oratorio /órrətóriō/ *n.* (*pl.* **-os**) a semi-dramatic work for orchestra and voices esp. on a sacred theme, performed without costume, scenery, or action. ▫▫ **oratorial** *adj.* [It. f. eccl.L *oratorium*, orig. of musical services at church of Oratory of St Philip Neri in Rome]

oratory /órrətəri, -tri/ *n.* (*pl.* **-ies**) **1** the art or practice of formal speaking, esp. in public. **2** exaggerated, eloquent, or highly coloured language. **3** a small chapel, esp. for private worship. **4** (**Oratory**) *RC Ch.* **a** a religious society of priests without vows founded in Rome in 1564 and providing plain preaching and popular services. **b** a branch of this in England etc. ▫▫ **oratorian** /-tóriən/ *adj.* & *n.* **oratorical** /-tórrik'l/ *adj.* [senses 1 and 2 f. L *ars oratoria* art of speaking; senses 3 and 4 ME f. AF *oratorie*, OF *oratoire* f. eccl.L *oratorium*: both f. L *oratorius* f. *orare* pray, speak]
■ **1, 2** public speaking, speech-making, eloquence, rhetoric, way with words, fluency, glibness, *colloq.* gift of the gab; grandiloquence, magniloquence, declamation.

orb /orb/ *n.* & *v.* ● *n.* **1** a globe surmounted by a cross esp. carried by a sovereign at a coronation. **2** a sphere; a globe. **3** *poet.* a heavenly body. **4** *poet.* an eyeball; an eye. ● *v.* **1** *tr.* enclose in (an orb); encircle. **2** *intr.* form or gather into an orb. [L *orbis* ring]
■ *n.* **2** sphere, ball, globe.

orbicular /orbíkyoolər/ *adj. formal* **1** circular and flat; disc-shaped; ring-shaped. **2** spherical; globular; rounded. **3** forming a complete whole. ▫▫ **orbicularity** /-lárriti/ *n.* **orbicularly** *adv.* [ME f. LL *orbicularis* f. L *orbiculus* dimin. of *orbis* ring]

orbiculate /orbíkyoolət/ *adj. Bot.* (of a leaf etc.) almost circular.

orbit /órbit/ *n.* & *v.* ● *n.* **1 a** the curved, usu. closed course of a planet, satellite, etc. **b** (prec. by *in*, *into*, *out of*, etc.) the state of motion in an orbit. **c** one complete passage around an orbited body. **2** the path of an electron round an atomic nucleus. **3** a range or sphere of action. **4 a** the eye socket. **b** the area around the eye of a bird or insect. ● *v.* (**orbited**, **orbiting**) **1** *intr.* **a** (of a satellite etc.) go round in orbit. **b** fly in a circle. **2** *tr.* move in orbit round. **3** *tr.* put into orbit. ▫▫ **orbiter** *n.* [L *orbita* course, track (in med.L eye-cavity): fem. of *orbitus* circular f. *orbis* ring]
■ *n.* **1 a, c** circuit, course, path, track, revolution, circle, round, cycle. ● *v.* **1, 2** revolve, turn; go round; circle, encircle.

orbital /órbit'l/ *adj.* & *n.* ● *adj.* **1** *Anat.*, *Astron.*, & *Physics* of an orbit or orbits. **2** (of a road) passing round the outside of a town. ● *n. Physics* a state or function representing the possible motion of an electron round an atomic nucleus. ▫ **orbital sander** a sander having a circular and not oscillating motion.

orca /órkə/ *n.* **1** any of various whales, esp. the killer whale. **2** any other large sea-animal or monster. [F *orque* or L *orca* a kind of whale]

Orcadian /orkáydiən/ *adj.* & *n.* ● *adj.* of or relating to the Orkney Islands off the N. coast of Scotland. ● *n.* a native of the Orkney Islands. [L *Orcades* Orkney Islands]

orch. *abbr.* **1** orchestrated by. **2** orchestra.

orchard /órchərd/ *n.* a piece of enclosed land with fruit-trees. ▫▫ **orchardist** *n.* [OE *ortgeard* f. L *hortus* garden + YARD²]

orcharding /órchərding/ *n.* the cultivation of fruit-trees.

orchardman /órchərdmən/ *n.* (*pl.* **-men**) a fruit-grower.

orchestra /órkistrə/ *n.* **1** a usu. large group of instrumentalists, esp. combining strings, woodwinds, brass, and percussion (*symphony orchestra*). **2 a** (in full **orchestra pit**) the part of a theatre, opera house, etc., where the orchestra plays, usu. in front of the stage and on a lower level. **b** *US* the stalls in a theatre. **3** the semicircular space in front of an ancient Greek theatre-stage where the chorus danced and sang. ▫ **orchestra stalls** the front of the stalls. ▫▫ **orchestral** /-késtrəl/ *adj.* **orchestrally** /-késtrəli/ *adv.* [L f. Gk *orkhēstra* f. *orkheomai* to dance (see sense 3)]

orchestrate /órkistrayt/ *v.tr.* **1** arrange, score, or compose for orchestral performance. **2** combine, arrange, or build up (elements of a situation etc.) for maximum effect. ▫▫ **orchestration** /-stráysh'n/ *n.* **orchestrator** *n.*
■ **1** see ARRANGE 6a. **2** see ARRANGE 1. ▫▫ **orchestration** see ARRANGEMENT 5, TACTICS 2a. **orchestrator** arranger; see also *tactician* (TACTICS).

orchid /órkid/ *n.* **1** any usu. epiphytic plant of the family Orchidaceae, bearing flowers in fantastic shapes and brilliant colours, usu. having one petal larger than the others and variously spurred, lobed, pouched, etc. **2** a flower of any of these plants. ▫▫ **orchidaceous** /-dáyshəss/ *adj.* **orchidist** *n.* **orchidology** /-dólləji/ *n.* [mod.L *Orchid(ac)eae* irreg. f. L *orchis*: see ORCHIS]

orchil /órchil/ *n.* (also **orchilla** /orchíllə/, **archil** /aárchil/) **1** a red or violet dye from lichen, esp. from *Roccella tinctoria*, often used in litmus. **2** the tropical lichen yielding this. [ME f. OF *orcheil* etc. perh. ult. f. L *herba urceolaris* a plant for polishing glass pitchers]

orchis /órkiss/ *n.* **1** any orchid of the genus *Orchis*, with a tuberous root and an erect fleshy stem having a spike of usu. purple or red flowers. **2** any of various wild orchids. [L f. Gk *orkhis*, orig. = testicle (with ref. to the shape of its tuber)]

orchitis /orkītiss/ *n.* inflammation of the testicles. [mod.L f. Gk *orkhis* testicle]

orcin /órsin/ *n.* (also **orcinol** /órsinol/) a crystalline substance, becoming red in air, extracted from any of several lichens and used to make dyes. [mod.L *orcina* f. It. *orcello* orchil]

ord. *abbr.* ordinary.

ordain /ordáyn/ *v.tr.* **1** confer holy orders on; appoint to the Christian ministry (*ordained him priest*; *was ordained in 1970*). **2 a** (often foll. by *that* + clause) decree (*ordained that he should go*). **b** (of God, fate, etc.) destine; appoint (*has ordained us to die*). ▫▫ **ordainer** *n.* **ordainment** *n.* [ME f. AF *ordeiner*, OF *ordein-* stressed stem of *ordener* f. L *ordinare* f. *ordo -inis* order]
■ **2 a** see DECREE *v.* **b** see DESTINE. ▫▫ **ordainment** see *inauguration* (INAUGURATE).

ordeal /ordeél/ *n.* **1** a painful or horrific experience; a severe trial. **2** *hist.* an ancient esp. Germanic test of guilt or innocence by subjection of the accused to severe pain or torture, survival of which was taken as divine proof of innocence. □ **ordeal tree** the tanghin. [OE *ordāl*, *ordēl* f. Gmc: cf. DEAL[1]]

■ **1** trial, test, tribulation, hardship, affliction, trouble, nightmare, misfortune, adversity, tragedy, disaster.

order /órdər/ *n.* & *v.* ● *n.* **1 a** the condition in which every part, unit, etc. is in its right place; tidiness (*restored some semblance of order*). **b** a usu. specified sequence, succession, etc. (*alphabetical order*; *the order of events*). **2** (in *sing.* or *pl.*) an authoritative command, direction, instruction, etc. (*only obeying orders*; *gave orders for it to be done*; *the judge made an order*). **3** a state of peaceful harmony under a constituted authority (*order was restored*; *law and order*). **4** (esp. in *pl.*) a social class, rank, etc., constituting a distinct group in society (*the lower orders*; *the order of baronets*). **5** a kind; a sort (*talents of a high order*). **6 a** a usu. written direction to a manufacturer, tradesman, waiter, etc. to supply something. **b** the quantity of goods etc. supplied. **7** the constitution or nature of the world, society, etc. (*the moral order*; *the order of things*). **8** *Biol.* a taxonomic rank below a class and above a family. **9** (esp. **Order**) a fraternity of monks and friars, or formerly of knights, bound by a common rule of life (*the Franciscan order*; *the order of Templars*). **10 a** any of the grades of the Christian ministry. **b** (in *pl.*) the status of a member of the clergy (*Anglican orders*). **11 a** any of the five classical styles of architecture (Doric, Ionic, Corinthian, Tuscan, and Composite) based on the proportions of columns, amount of decoration, etc. **b** any style or mode of architecture subject to uniform established proportions. **12** (esp. **Order**) **a** a company of distinguished people instituted esp. by a sovereign to which appointments are made as an honour or reward (*Order of the Garter*; *Order of Merit*). **b** the insignia worn by members of an order. **13** *Math.* **a** a degree of complexity of a differential equation (*equation of the first order*). **b** the order of the highest derivative in the equation. **14** *Math.* **a** the size of a matrix. **b** the number of elements of a finite group. **15** *Eccl.* the stated form of divine service (*the order of confirmation*). **16** the principles of procedure, decorum, etc., accepted by a meeting, legislative assembly, etc. or enforced by its president. **17** *Mil.* **a** a style of dress and equipment (*review order*). **b** (prec. by *the*) the position of a company etc. with arms ordered (see *order arms*). **18** a Masonic or similar fraternity. **19** any of the nine grades of angelic beings (seraphim, cherubim, thrones, dominations, principalities, powers, virtues, archangels, angels). **20** a pass admitting the bearer to a theatre, museum, private house, etc. free or cheap or as a privilege. ● *v.tr.* **1** (usu. foll. by *to* + infin., or *that* + clause) command; bid; prescribe (*ordered him to go*; *ordered that they should be sent*). **2** command or direct (a person) to a specified destination (*was ordered to Singapore*; *ordered them home*). **3** direct a manufacturer, waiter, tradesman, etc. to supply (*ordered a new suit*; *ordered dinner*). **4** put in order; regulate (*ordered her affairs*). **5** (of God, fate, etc.) ordain (*fate ordered it otherwise*). **6** *US* command (a thing) done or (a person) dealt with (*ordered it settled*; *ordered him expelled*). □ **by order** according to the proper authority. **holy orders** the status of a member of the clergy, esp. the grades of bishop, priest, and deacon. **in bad** (or **good** etc.) **order** not working (or working properly etc.). **in order 1** one after another according to some principle. **2** ready or fit for use. **3** according to the rules (of procedure at a meeting etc.). **in order that** with the intention; so that. **in order to** with the purpose of doing; with a view to. **keep order** enforce orderly behaviour. **made to order 1** made according to individual requirements, measurements, etc. (opp. *ready-made*). **2** exactly what is wanted. **minor orders** *RC Ch. hist.* the grades of members of the clergy below that of deacon. **not in order** not working properly. **of** (or **in** or **on**) **the order of 1** approximately. **2** having the order of magnitude specified by (*of the order of one in a million*). **on order** (of goods etc.) ordered but not yet received. **order about 1** dominate; command officiously. **2** send hither and thither. **order arms** *Mil.* hold a rifle with its butt on the ground close to one's right side. **order book 1** a book in which a tradesman enters orders. **2** the level of incoming orders. **order-form** a printed form in which details are entered by a customer. **Order in Council** *Brit.* a sovereign's order on an administrative matter given by the advice of the Privy Council. **Order of the Bath** (or **Garter** or **Merit**) each of several honours conferred by the sovereign for services etc. to the State. **order of the day 1** the prevailing state of things. **2** a principal topic of action or a procedure decided upon. **3** business set down for treatment; a programme. **order of magnitude** a class in a system of classification determined by size, usu. by powers of 10. **Order! Order!** *Parl.* a call for silence or calm, esp. by the Speaker of the House of Commons. **order-paper** esp. *Parl.* a written or printed order of the day; an agenda. **order to view** a house-agent's request for a client to be allowed to inspect premises. **out of order 1** not working properly. **2** not according to the rules (of a meeting, organization, etc.). **3** not in proper sequence. **take orders 1** accept commissions. **2** accept and carry out commands. **3** (also **take holy orders**) be ordained. □□ **orderer** *n.* [ME f. OF *ordre* f. L *ordo ordinis* row, array, degree, command, etc.]

■ *n.* **1** organization, uniformity, regularity, system, pattern, symmetry, harmony, tidiness, orderliness, neatness; shape, arrangement, grouping, disposition, form, structure, categorization, systematization, systemization, classification, codification, disposal, layout, array, sequence, set-up. **2** command, direction, directive, instruction, commandment, diktat, dictate, mandate, edict, request, demand, ukase, decree, fiat, proclamation, pronouncement; rule, regulation, law, ordinance, statute, requirement. **3** calm, peace, peacefulness, tranquillity, quiet, serenity, law and order, discipline. **4** category, class, caste, level, kind, sort, rank, group, scale, position, status, degree. **5** style, kind, genre; see also SORT *n.* 1. **6 a** purchase order, request, requisition, commission, instruction. **7** condition, state (of affairs), constitution, nature. **9, 18** brotherhood, fraternity, sisterhood, sorority, fellowship, sodality, association, organization, society, guild, sect, company, community, lodge, body. **16** procedure, proceeding(s), conduct, decorum; etiquette, protocol. ● *v.* **1, 2, 5, 6** direct, command, prescribe; instruct, charge, tell, require, enjoin, *archaic or literary* bid; demand, ordain; force, make. **3** requisition, ask for, send (away) for, call for, apply for, reserve, engage, commission, contract for. **4** put in order, regulate, organize, systematize, arrange, classify, categorize, codify, lay out, sort (out), straighten (out *or* up). □ **in order 1, 2** neat, clean, tidy, shipshape, orderly, (well-)organized, ready, prepared, arranged. **3** fitting, suitable, appropriate, correct, right, apt, called-for; required, demanded, needed. **in order that** so (that), with the aim *or* purpose *or* intention that, to the end that. **in order to** to, so as to, for the purpose of. **of** (or **in** or **on**) **the order of 1** roughly, somewhere near, something like, a matter of, say; see also NEARLY 1. **order about** see BOSS[1] *v.* 1. **out of order 1** out of commission, out of service, broken, in disrepair, non-functioning, non-functional, not working, broken-down, inoperative, out of kilter, down, *colloq.* haywire, bust(ed), shot, gone phut, *sl.* (gone) kaput, on the blink, *Brit. sl.* wonky, *US sl.* out of whack, on the fritz. **2** unseemly, out of place, improper, uncalled-for, unsuitable, indecorous, *Brit. colloq.* not cricket, *Austral.* & *NZ sl.* over the fence. **3** disordered, non-sequential, out of sequence, non-alphabetical, disorganized, unorganized, in disorder, chaotic.

orderly /órdərli/ *adj.* & *n.* ● *adj.* **1** methodically arranged; regular. **2** obedient to discipline; well-behaved; not unruly. **3** *Mil.* **a** of or concerned with orders. **b** charged with the conveyance or execution of orders. ● *n.* (*pl.* **-ies**) **1** an esp. male cleaner in a hospital. **2** a soldier who carries orders for

an officer etc. □ **orderly book** *Brit. Mil.* a regimental or company book for entering orders. **orderly officer** *Brit. Mil.* the officer of the day. **orderly room** *Brit. Mil.* a room in a barracks used for company business. □□ **orderliness** *n.*
■ *adj.* **1** in (good) order, (well-)organized, neat, shipshape, tidy, arranged, methodical, systematic, systematized, systemized, harmonious, symmetrical, regular, uniform. **2** well-behaved, disciplined, decorous, law-abiding, well-mannered, peaceable, tranquil, mannerly, polite, courteous, civil, civilized, non-violent. ● *n.* assistant, adjutant, attendant, messenger.

ordinal /órdin'l/ *n.* & *adj.* ● *n.* **1** (in full **ordinal number**) a number defining a thing's position in a series, e.g. 'first', 'second', 'third', etc. (cf. CARDINAL). **2** *Eccl.* a service-book, esp. one with the forms of service used at ordinations. ● *adj.* **1 a** of or relating to an ordinal number. **b** defining a thing's position in a series etc. **2** *Biol.* of or concerning an order (see ORDER *n.* 8). [ME f. LL *ordinalis* & med.L *ordinale* neut. f. L (as ORDER)]

ordinance /órdinənss/ *n.* **1** an authoritative order; a decree. **2** an enactment by a local authority. **3** a religious rite. **4** *archaic* = ORDONNANCE. [ME f. OF *ordenance* f. med.L *ordinantia* f. L *ordinare*: see ORDAIN]
■ **1** see DECREE *n.* 1. **2** see LAW 1a.

ordinand /órdinənd/ *n. Eccl.* a candidate for ordination. [L *ordinandus*, gerundive of *ordinare* ORDAIN]

ordinary /órdinəri, -dinri/ *adj.* & *n.* ● *adj.* **1 a** regular, normal, customary, usual (*in the ordinary course of events*). **b** boring; commonplace (*an ordinary little man*). **2** *Brit. Law* (esp. of a judge) having immediate or *ex officio* jurisdiction, not deputed. ● *n.* (*pl.* **-ies**) **1** *Brit. Law* a person, esp. a judge, having immediate or *ex officio* jurisdiction. **2** (**the Ordinary**) **a** an archbishop in a province. **b** a bishop in a diocese. **3** (usu. **Ordinary**) *RC Ch.* **a** those parts of a service, esp. the mass, which do not vary from day to day. **b** a rule or book laying down the order of divine service. **4** *Heraldry* a charge of the earliest, simplest, and commonest kind (esp. chief, pale, bend, fess, bar, chevron, cross, saltire). **5** (**Ordinary**) (also **Lord Ordinary**) any of the judges of the Court of Session in Scotland, constituting the Outer House. **6** esp. *US hist.* an early type of bicycle with one large and one very small wheel; a penny-farthing. **7** *Brit. hist.* **a** a public meal provided at a fixed time and price at an inn etc. **b** an establishment providing this. **8** *US* a tavern. **9** (prec. by *the*) *colloq.* the customary or usual condition, course, or degree. □ **in ordinary** *Brit.* by permanent appointment (esp. to the royal household) (*physician in ordinary*). **in the ordinary way** if the circumstances are or were not exceptional. **ordinary level** *Brit. hist.* the lowest of the three levels of the GCE examination. **ordinary scale** = *decimal scale.* **ordinary seaman** a sailor of the lowest rank, that below able-bodied seaman. **ordinary shares** *Brit.* shares entitling holders to a dividend from net profits (cf. *preference shares*). **out of the ordinary** unusual. □□ **ordinarily** *adv.* **ordinariness** *n.* [ME f. L *ordinarius* orderly (as ORDER)]
■ *adj.* **1** usual, normal, expected, common, general, customary, routine, typical, habitual, accustomed, traditional, regular, standard, average, everyday, familiar, set; humdrum, boring, commonplace, conventional, modest, plain, simple, prosaic, homespun, run-of-the-mill, everyday, unpretentious, workaday, mediocre, fair, passable, so so, undistinguished, unexceptional, unremarkable, uninspired, pedestrian, bourgeois, peasant, provincial, unrefined, *colloq.* common or garden. ● *n.* **9** standard, norm, average, status quo. □ **out of the ordinary** extraordinary, unusual, uncommon, strange, unfamiliar, different, unexpected, unconventional, curious, eccentric, peculiar, rare, exceptional, original, singular, unique, odd, bizarre, weird, offbeat, outlandish, striking, quaint, picturesque. □□ **ordinarily** usually, normally, as a rule, commonly, generally, in general, customarily, routinely, typically, habitually, by and large, for the most part.

ordinate /órdinit/ *n. Math.* a straight line from any point drawn parallel to one coordinate axis and meeting the other, usually a coordinate measured parallel to the vertical (cf. ABSCISSA). [L *linea ordinata applicata* line applied parallel f. *ordinare*: see ORDAIN]

ordination /órdináysh'n/ *n.* **1 a** the act of conferring holy orders esp. on a priest or deacon. **b** the admission of a priest etc. to church ministry. **2** the arrangement of things etc. in ranks; classification. **3** the act of decreeing or ordaining. [ME f. OF *ordination* or L *ordinatio* (as ORDAIN)]
■ **1** see INSTALLATION 1.

ordnance /órdnənss/ *n.* **1** mounted guns; cannon. **2** a branch of government service dealing esp. with military stores and materials. □ **ordnance datum** *Brit.* mean sea level as defined for Ordnance Survey. **Ordnance map** *Brit.* a map produced by Ordnance Survey. **Ordnance Survey** *Brit.* (in the UK) an official survey organization, orig. under the Master of the Ordnance, preparing large-scale detailed maps of the whole country. [ME var. of ORDINANCE]

ordonnance /órdənənss/ *n.* the systematic arrangement esp. of literary or architectural work. [F f. OF *ordenance*: see ORDINANCE]

Ordovician /órdəvíssiən, órdōvíshiən/ *adj.* & *n. Geol.* ● *adj.* of or relating to the second period of the Palaeozoic era, with evidence of the first vertebrates and an abundance of marine invertebrates. ¶ Cf. Appendix VII. ● *n.* this period or system. [L *Ordovices* ancient British tribe in N. Wales]

ordure /órdyoor/ *n.* **1** excrement; dung. **2** obscenity; filth; foul language. [ME f. OF f. *ord* foul f. L *horridus*: see HORRID]
■ **1** see MUCK *n.* 1, 2.

Ore. *abbr.* Oregon.

ore /or/ *n.* a naturally occurring solid material from which metal or other valuable minerals may be extracted. [OE *ōra* unwrought metal, *ār* bronze, rel. to L *aes* crude metal, bronze]

öre /ő̄rə/ *n.* (also **øre**) a Scandinavian monetary unit equal to one-hundredth of a krona or krone. [Swedish]

oread /óriad/ *n.* (in Greek and Roman mythology) a mountain nymph. [ME f. L *oreas -ados* f. Gk *oreias* f. *oros* mountain]

orectic /əréktik/ *adj. Philos.* & *Med.* of or concerning desire or appetite. [Gk *orektikos* f. *oregō* stretch out]

Oreg. *abbr.* Oregon.

oregano /órrigaánō/ *n.* the dried leaves of wild marjoram used as a culinary herb (cf. MARJORAM). [Sp., = ORIGANUM]

oreography var. of OROGRAPHY.

oreweed var. of OARWEED.

orfe /orf/ *n.* a golden-coloured ide. [G & F: cf. L *orphus* f. Gk *orphos* sea-perch]

organ /órgən/ *n.* **1 a** a usu. large musical instrument having pipes supplied with air from bellows, sounded by keys, and distributed into sets or stops which form partial organs, each with a separate keyboard (*choir organ*; *pedal organ*). **b** a smaller instrument without pipes, producing similar sounds electronically. **c** a smaller keyboard wind instrument with metal reeds; a harmonium. **d** = *barrel-organ.* **2 a** a usu. self-contained part of an organism having a special vital function (*vocal organs*; *digestive organs*). **b** esp. *joc.* the penis. **3** a medium of communication, esp. a newspaper, sectarian periodical, etc. **4** *archaic* a professionally trained singing voice. **5** *Phrenol. archaic* a region of the brain held to be the seat of a particular faculty. □ **organ-blower** a person or mechanism working the bellows of an organ. **organ-grinder** the player of a barrel-organ. **organ-loft** a gallery in a church or concert-room for an organ. **organ of Corti** see CORTI. **organ-pipe** any of the pipes on an organ. **organ-screen** an ornamental screen usu. between the choir and the nave of a church, cathedral, etc., on which the organ is placed. **organ-stop 1** a set of pipes of a similar tone in an organ. **2** the handle of the mechanism that brings it into action. [ME f. OE *organa* & OF *organe*, f. L *organum* f. Gk *organon* tool]

■ **2 a** device, instrument, implement, tool; member, part, element, unit, component, structure, process. **3** medium, vehicle, voice, mouthpiece, forum, publication; paper, magazine, newsletter, newspaper, annual, semi-annual, quarterly, monthly, fortnightly, weekly, daily, journal, periodical.

organdie /órgəndi, -gándi/ *n.* (*US* **organdy**) (*pl.* **-ies**) a fine translucent cotton muslin, usu. stiffened. [F *organdi*, of unkn. orig.]

organelle /órgənél/ *n. Biol.* any of various organized or specialized structures which form part of a cell. [mod.L *organella* dimin.; see ORGAN, -LE]

organic /orgánnik/ *adj.* **1 a** *Physiol.* of or relating to a bodily organ or organs. **b** *Med.* (of a disease) affecting the structure of an organ. **2** (of a plant or animal) having organs or an organized physical structure. **3** *Agriculture* produced or involving production without the use of chemical fertilizers, pesticides, etc. (*organic crop*; *organic farming*). **4** *Chem.* (of a compound etc.) containing carbon (opp. INORGANIC). **5 a** structural, inherent. **b** constitutional, fundamental. **6** organized, systematic, coordinated (*an organic whole*). □ **organic chemistry** the chemistry of carbon compounds. **organic law** a law stating the formal constitution of a country. □□ **organically** *adv.* [F *organique* f. L *organicus* f. Gk *organikos* (as ORGAN)]

■ **2** living, natural, biological, biotic, animate, breathing. **5** basic, elementary, essential, innate, inborn, natural, native, ingrained, primary, fundamental, visceral, constitutional, inherent, structural, integral. **6** organized, systematic, coherent, coordinated, integrated, structured, methodical, orderly, consistent.

organism /órgəniz'm/ *n.* **1** a living individual consisting of a single cell or of a group of interdependent parts sharing the life processes. **2 a** an individual live plant or animal. **b** the material structure of this. **3** a whole with interdependent parts compared to a living being. [F *organisme* (as ORGANIZE)]

■ living thing, structure, body, life-form; being, entity, creature.

organist /órgənist/ *n.* the player of an organ.

organization /órgənīzáysh'n/ *n.* (also **-isation**) **1** the act or an instance of organizing; the state of being organized. **2** an organized body, esp. a business, government department, charity, etc. **3** systematic arrangement; tidiness. □ **organization man** a man who subordinates his individuality and his personal life to the organization he serves. □□ **organizational** *adj.* **organizationally** *adv.*

■ **1** structuring, assembly, putting together, combination, coordination; systematization, classification, categorization, codification; structure, pattern, configuration, design, plan, scheme, order, system, organism, composition, arrangement, constitution, make-up, grouping, framework, format, form, shape. **2** body, institution, federation, confederacy, confederation, society, group, league, coalition, conglomerate, combine, consortium, syndicate, organism. **3** see ORDER *n.* 1.

organize /órgənīz/ *v.tr.* (also **-ise**) **1 a** give an orderly structure to, systematize. **b** bring the affairs of (another person or oneself) into order; make arrangements for (a person). **2 a** arrange for or initiate (a scheme etc.). **b** provide; take responsibility for (*organized some sandwiches*). **3** (often *absol.*) **a** enrol (new members) in a trade union, political party, etc. **b** form (a trade union or other political group). **4 a** form (different elements) into an organic whole. **b** form (an organic whole). **5** (esp. as **organized** *adj.*) make organic; make into a living being or tissue. □□ **organizable** *adj.* **organizer** *n.* [ME f. OF *organiser* f. med.L *organizare* f. L (as ORGAN)]

■ **1** structure, coordinate, systematize, systemize, order, arrange, sort (out), classify, categorize, codify, catalogue, group, tabulate, pigeon-hole, standardize. **2 a** form, found, set up, arrange for, establish, institute, start, begin, create, originate, initiate, put together, build, develop, pull together. **3b** see INSTITUTE *v.* 1, 2. **4** see STRUCTURE *v.*

organo- /órgənō/ *comb. form* **1** esp. *Biol.* organ. **2** *Chem.* organic. [Gk (as ORGAN)]

organoleptic /órgənōléptik/ *adj.* affecting the organs of sense. [ORGANO- + Gk *lēptikos* disposed to take f. *lambanō* take]

organometallic /orgánnōmitállik/ *adj.* (of a compound) organic and containing a metal.

organon /órgənon/ *n.* (also **organum** /órgənəm/) an instrument of thought, esp. a means of reasoning or a system of logic. [Gk *organon* & L *organum* (as ORGAN): *Organon* was the title of Aristotle's logical writings, and *Novum* (new) *Organum* that of Bacon's]

organotherapy /órgənōthérrəpi/ *n.* the treatment of disease with extracts of organs.

organza /orgánzə/ *n.* a thin stiff transparent silk or synthetic dress fabric. [prob. f. *Lorganza* (US trade name)]

organzine /órgənzeen, -gánzeen/ *n.* a silk thread in which the main twist is in a contrary direction to that of the strands. [F *organsin* f. It. *organzino*, of unkn. orig.]

orgasm /órgaz'm/ *n.* & *v.* ● *n.* **1 a** the climax of sexual excitement, esp. during sexual intercourse. **b** an instance of this. **2** violent excitement; rage. ● *v.intr.* experience a sexual orgasm. □□ **orgasmic** /-gázmik/ *adj.* **orgasmically** /-gázmikəli/ *adv.* **orgastic** /-gástik/ *adj.* **orgastically** /-gástikəli/ *adv.* [F *orgasme* or mod.L f. Gk *orgasmos* f. *orgaō* swell, be excited]

■ □□ **orgasmic** see ECSTATIC *adj.* 1, 2.

orgeat /órjiat, órzhaa/ *n.* a cooling drink made from barley or almonds and orange-flower water. [F f. Prov. *orjat* f. *ordi* barley f. L *hordeum*]

orgiastic /órjiástik/ *adj.* of or resembling an orgy. □□ **orgiastically** *adv.* [Gk *orgiastikos* f. *orgiastēs* agent-noun f. *orgiazō* hold an orgy]

■ see EPICUREAN *adj.* 2.

orgulous /órgyooləss/ *adj. archaic* haughty; splendid. [ME f. OF *orguillus* f. *orguill* pride f. Frank.]

orgy /órji/ *n.* (*pl.* **-ies**) **1** a wild drunken festivity, esp. one at which at which indiscriminate sexual activity takes place. **2** excessive indulgence in an activity. **3** (usu. in *pl.*) *Gk & Rom. Hist.* secret rites used in the worship of esp. Bacchus, celebrated with dancing, drunkenness, singing, etc. [orig. pl., f. F *orgies* f. L *orgia* f. Gk *orgia* secret rites]

■ **1** bacchanalia, bacchanal, saturnalia, debauch, carousal, carouse, revel, party, *archaic* wassail, *colloq.* spree, bust, *sl.* binge, booze-up, bender, jag, drunk. **2** overindulgence, fling, *colloq.* spree, splurge, *sl.* bender.

oribi /órribi/ *n.* (*pl.* same or **oribis**) a small S. African grazing antelope, *Ourebia ourebi*, having a reddish fawn back and white underparts. [prob. Khoisan]

oriel /óriəl/ *n.* **1** a large polygonal recess built out usu. from an upper storey and supported from the ground or on corbels. **2** (in full **oriel window**) **a** any of the windows in an oriel. **b** the projecting window of an upper storey. [ME f. OF *oriol* gallery, of unkn. orig.]

orient *n.*, *adj.*, & *v.* ● *n.* /óriənt/ **1** (**the Orient**) **a** *poet.* the east. **b** the countries E. of the Mediterranean, esp. E. Asia. **2** an orient pearl. ● *adj.* /óriənt/ **1** *poet.* oriental. **2** (of precious stones and esp. the finest pearls coming orig. from the East) lustrous; sparkling; precious. **3** *archaic* **a** radiant. **b** (of the sun, daylight, etc.) rising. ● *v.* /órient, órrient/ **1** *tr.* **a** place or exactly determine the position of with the aid of a compass; settle or find the bearings of. **b** (often foll. by *towards*) bring (oneself, different elements, etc.) into a clearly understood position or relationship; direct. **2** *tr.* **a** place or build (a church, building, etc.) facing towards the East. **b** bury (a person) with the feet towards the East. **3** *intr.* turn eastward or in a specified direction. □ **orient oneself** determine how one stands in relation to one's surroundings. [ME f. OF *orient*, *orienter* f. L *oriens -entis* rising, sunrise, east, f. *oriri* rise]

■ *n.* **1** east. ● *adj.* **1** oriental, eastern. ● *v.* **1** adjust, adapt, acclimatize, habituate, accommodate, condition, accustom, familiarize, assess, orientate, *US* acclimate. □ **orient oneself** feel one's way, get one's bearings, familiarize oneself, orientate oneself.

oriental /óriént'l, órri-/ *adj.* & *n.* ● *adj.* **1** (often **Oriental**) **a** of or characteristic of Eastern civilization etc. **b** of or concerning the East, esp. E. Asia. **2** (of a pearl etc.) orient. ● *n.* (esp. **Oriental**) a native of the Orient. □□ **orientalism** *n.* **orientalist** *n.* **orientalize** *v.intr.* & *tr.* (also **-ise**). **orientally** *adv.* [ME f. OF *oriental* or L *orientalis* (as ORIENT)]

orientate /órientayt, órri-/ *v.tr.* & *intr.* = ORIENT *v.* [prob. back-form. f. ORIENTATION]

orientation /órientáysh'n, órri-/ *n.* **1** the act or an instance of orienting; the state of being oriented. **2 a** a relative position. **b** a person's attitude or adjustment in relation to circumstances, esp. politically or psychologically. **3** an introduction to a subject or situation; a briefing. **4** the faculty by which birds etc. find their way home from a distance. □ **orientation course** esp. *US* a course giving information to newcomers to a university etc. □□ **orientational** *adj.* [app. f. ORIENT]

■ **1, 2** placement, bearings, attitude, alignment, adjustment, lie, placing, situation, layout, location, position, positioning, arrangement, set-up. **3** introduction, training, induction, initiation, briefing, familiarization, assimilation, acclimatization, preparation, instruction. □ **orientation course** induction course.

orienteering /órienteéring, órri-/ *n.* a competitive sport in which runners cross open country with a map, compass, etc. □□ **orienteer** *n.* & *v.intr.* [Sw. *orientering*]

orifice /órrifiss/ *n.* an opening, esp. the mouth of a cavity, a bodily aperture, etc. [F f. LL *orificium* f. *os oris* mouth + *facere* make]

■ see OPENING *n.* 1.

oriflamme /órriflam/ *n.* **1** *hist.* the sacred scarlet silk banner of St Denis given to early French kings by the abbot of St Denis on setting out for war. **2** a standard, a principle, or an ideal as a rallying-point in a struggle. **3** a bright conspicuous object, colour, etc. [ME f. OF f. L *aurum* gold + *flamma* flame]

origami /órrigaámi/ *n.* the Japanese art of folding paper into decorative shapes and figures. [Jap. f. *ori* fold + *kami* paper]

origan /órrigən/ *n.* (also **origanum** /ərig gənəm/) any plant of the genus *Origanum*, esp. wild marjoram (see MARJORAM). [(ME f. OF *origan*) f. L *origanum* f. Gk *origanon*]

origin /órrijin/ *n.* **1** a beginning or starting-point; a derivation; a source (*a word of Latin origin*). **2** (often in *pl.*) a person's ancestry (*what are his origins?*). **3** *Anat.* **a** a place at which a muscle is firmly attached. **b** a place where a nerve or blood vessel begins or branches from a main nerve or blood vessel. **4** *Math.* a fixed point from which coordinates are measured. [F *origine* or f. L *origo -ginis* f. *oriri* rise]

■ **1** source, derivation, rise, fountain-head, foundation, basis, base, well-spring, provenance, *US* provenience, *poet.* fount; creation, genesis, birth, birthplace, cradle, dawning, dawn, origination, start, beginning, outset, launch, launching, inception, inauguration, *formal* commencement. **2** (*origins*) parentage, ancestry, extraction, descent, lineage, pedigree, genealogy, stock, heritage.

original /ərijin'l/ *adj.* & *n.* ● *adj.* **1** existing from the beginning; innate. **2** novel; inventive; creative (*has an original mind*). **3** serving as a pattern; not derivative or imitative; firsthand (*in the original Greek*; *has an original Rembrandt*). ● *n.* **1** an original model, pattern, picture, etc. from which another is copied or translated (*kept the copy and destroyed the original*). **2** an eccentric or unusual person. **3 a** a garment specially designed for a fashion collection. **b** a copy of such a garment made to order. □ **original instrument** a musical instrument, or a copy of one, dating from the time the music played on it was composed. **original print** a print made directly from an artist's own woodcut, etching, etc., and printed under the artist's supervision. **original sin** the innate depravity of all mankind held to be a consequence of the Fall. □□ **originally** *adv.* [ME f. OF *original* or L *originalis* (as ORIGIN)]

■ *adj.* **1** initial, first, earliest, primary, beginning, starting, basic; native, innate, indigenous, autochthonous, aboriginal, primordial, primeval, primitive. **2** creative, novel, innovative, unique, imaginative, unusual, inventive, ingenious; fresh, underived, unprecedented, independent. **3** master, actual, primary, authentic, true, genuine, real, basic, firsthand; prototypic(al), archetypal, source. ● *n.* **1** prototype, archetype, source, model, pattern; master. **2** eccentric, nonconformist, individualist, *colloq.* case, card, character, one-off. □□ **originally** in *or* at *or* from the beginning, (at) first, from the first, initially, to begin with, at *or* from the outset, at *or* from the start, in the first place *or* instance, *colloq.* from the word go, from day one; creatively, unusually.

originality /ərijinálliti/ *n.* (*pl.* **-ies**) **1** the power of creating or thinking creatively. **2** newness or freshness (*this vase has originality*). **3** an original act, thing, trait, etc.

■ **1, 2** creativeness, creativity, inventiveness, ingenuity, innovativeness, innovation, novelty, newness, freshness, unorthodoxy, unconventionality, cleverness, daring, resourcefulness, independence, individuality, uniqueness, nonconformity. **3** innovation, novelty, invention.

originate /ərijinayt/ *v.* **1** *tr.* cause to begin; initiate. **2** *intr.* (usu. foll. by *from, in, with*) have as an origin; begin. □□ **origination** /-náysh'n/ *n.* **originative** /-nətiv/ *adj.* **originator** *n.* [med. L *originare* (as ORIGIN)]

■ **1** create, bring about, engender, give birth to, *literary* beget; conceive, initiate, inaugurate, start, begin, introduce, launch, found, set up, institute, establish, invent, coin, devise, pioneer, design, contrive, concoct, mastermind, compose, organize, formulate, form, generate, produce, develop, evolve. **2** arise, rise, begin, start, come, spring, stem, flow, issue, emerge, emanate, proceed, grow, develop, evolve, derive, result. □□ **origination** emergence, initiation; see also ORIGIN 1.

orinasal /órináyz'l/ *adj.* (esp. of French nasalized vowels) sounded with both the mouth and the nose. [L *os oris* mouth + NASAL]

o-ring /ṓ-ring/ *n.* a gasket in the form of a ring with a circular cross-section.

oriole /órióI/ *n.* **1** any Old World bird of the genus *Oriolus*, many of which have brightly coloured plumage (see *golden oriole*). **2** any New World bird of the genus *Icterus*, with similar coloration. [med.L *oriolus* f. OF *oriol* f. L *aureolus* dimin. of *aureus* golden f. *aurum* gold]

Orion /ərī́ən/ *n.* a brilliant constellation on the celestial equator visible from most parts of the earth. □ **Orion's belt** three bright stars in a short line across the middle of the constellation. **Orion's hound** Sirius. [ME f. L f. Gk *Ōriōn*, name of a legendary hunter]

orison /órriz'n/ *n.* (usu. in *pl.*) *archaic* a prayer. [ME f. AF *ureison*, OF *oreison* f. L (as ORATION)]

■ see PRAYER[1] 1a.

-orium /óriəm/ *suffix* forming nouns denoting a place for a particular function (*auditorium*; *crematorium*). [L, neut. of adjectives in *-orius*: see -ORY[1]]

Oriya /oreéə/ *n.* **1** a native of the State of Orissa in India. **2** the Indo-European language of this people. [Hindi]

orle /orl/ *n. Heraldry* a narrow band or border of charges near the edge of a shield. [F *o(u)rle* f. *ourler* to hem, ult. f. L *ora* edge]

Orlon /órlon/ *n. propr.* a man-made fibre and fabric for textiles and knitwear. [invented word, after NYLON]

orlop /órlop/ *n.* the lowest deck of a ship with three or more decks. [ME f. MDu. *overloop* covering f. *overloopen* run over (as OVER-, LEAP)]

ormer /órmər/ *n.* an edible univalve mollusc, *Haliotis tuberculata*, having a flattened shell with a series of holes of increasing size along the outer margin. Also called *sea-ear*. [Channel Islands F f. F *ormier* f. L *auris maris* ear of sea]

ormolu /órmələ͞o/ *n.* **1** (often *attrib.*) **a** a gilded bronze or gold-coloured alloy of copper, zinc, and tin used to decorate furniture, make ornaments, etc. **b** articles made of or decorated with these. **2** showy trash. [F *or moulu* powdered gold (for use in gilding)]

ornament *n.* & *v.* ● *n.* /órnəmənt/ **1 a** a thing used or serving to adorn, esp. a small trinket, vase, figure, etc. (*a mantelpiece crowded with ornaments*; *her only ornament was a brooch*). **b** a quality or person conferring adornment, grace, or honour (*an ornament to her profession*). **2** decoration added to embellish esp. a building (*a tower rich in ornament*). **3** (in *pl.*) *Mus.* embellishments and decorations made to a melody. **4** (usu. in *pl.*) the accessories of worship, e.g. the altar, chalice, sacred vessels, etc. ● *v.tr.* /órnəment/ adorn; beautify. ▫▫ **ornamentation** /-mentáysh'n/ *n.* [ME f. AF *urnement*, OF *o(u)rnement* f. L *ornamentum* equipment f. *ornare* adorn]

▪ *n.* **1, 2** enhancement, embellishment, adornment, decoration, ornamentation, gingerbread, trimming, garnish, garnishment, frill, embroidery, beautification, accessory; frippery; trinket, knick-knack, furbelow, bauble, gewgaw. **3** (*ornaments*) ornamentation, grace-notes. ● *v.* decorate, embellish, enhance, adorn, trim, garnish, embroider, elaborate, beautify, accessorize, deck (out), dress up.

ornamental /órnəmént'l/ *adj.* & *n.* ● *adj.* serving as an ornament; decorative. ● *n.* a thing considered to be ornamental, esp. a cultivated plant. ▫▫ **ornamentalism** *n.* **ornamentalist** *n.* **ornamentally** *adv.*

▪ *adj.* see FANCY *adj.* 1.

ornate /ornáyt/ *adj.* **1** elaborately adorned; highly decorated. **2** (of literary style) convoluted; flowery. ▫▫ **ornately** *adv.* **ornateness** *n.* [ME f. L *ornatus* past part. of *ornare* adorn]

▪ elaborate, florid, overdone, laboured, rococo, baroque, gingerbread, arabesque, fancy, lavish, rich, flowery, busy, convoluted, fussy, frilly, intricate; high-flown, euphuistic, bombastic, pompous, pretentious, affected, grandiose, fulsome, grandiloquent, flamboyant, *colloq.* highfalutin.

ornery /órnəri/ *adj.* *US colloq.* **1** cantankerous; unpleasant. **2** of poor quality. ▫▫ **orneriness** *n.* [var. of ORDINARY]

▪ **1** see TESTY.

ornithic /orníthik/ *adj.* of or relating to birds. [Gk *ornithikos* birdlike (as ORNITHO-)]

ornitho- /órnithō/ *comb. form* bird. [Gk f. *ornis ornithos* bird]

ornithology /órnithólləji/ *n.* the scientific study of birds. ▫▫ **ornithological** /-thəlójik'l/ *adj.* **ornithologically** /-thəlójikəli/ *adv.* **ornithologist** *n.* [mod.L *ornithologia* f. Gk *ornithologos* treating of birds (as ORNITHO-, -LOGY)]

ornithorhynchus /órnithō-ríngkəss/ *n.* = PLATYPUS. [ORNITHO- + Gk *rhugkhos* bill]

oro- /órō/ *comb. form* mountain. [Gk *oros* mountain]

orogeny /orójini/ *n.* (also **orogenesis** /órōjénnisiss/) the process of the formation of mountains. ▫▫ **orogenetic** /órōjinéttik/ *adj.* **orogenic** /órəjénnik/ *adj.*

orography /orógrəfi/ *n.* (also **oreography** /órriógrəfi/) the branch of physical geography dealing with mountains. ▫▫ **orographic** /órəgráffik/ *adj.* **orographical** /órəgráffik'l/ *adj.*

orotund /órrətund, órə-/ *adj.* **1** (of the voice or phrasing) full, round; imposing. **2** (of writing, style, expression, etc.) pompous; pretentious. [L *ore rotundo* with rounded mouth]

orphan /órf'n/ *n.* & *v.* ● *n.* (often *attrib.*) **1** a child bereaved of a parent or usu. both parents. **2** a person bereft of previous protection, advantages, etc. ● *v.tr.* bereave (a child) of its parents or a parent. ▫▫ **orphanhood** *n.* **orphanize** *v.tr.* (also **-ise**). [ME f. LL *orphanus* f. Gk *orphanos* bereaved]

orphanage /órfənij/ *n.* **1** a usu. residential institution for the care and education of orphans. **2** orphanhood.

Orphean /orfée̍ən/ *adj.* like the music of Orpheus, a legendary Greek poet and lyre-player; melodious; entrancing. [L *Orpheus* (adj.) f. Gk *Orpheios* f. *Orpheus*]

Orphic /órfik/ *adj.* **1** of or concerning Orpheus or the mysteries, doctrines, etc. associated with him; oracular; mysterious. **2** = ORPHEAN. ▫▫ **Orphism** *n.* [L *Orphicus* f. Gk *Orphikos* f. *Orpheus*]

orphrey /órfri/ *n.* (*pl.* **-eys**) an ornamental stripe or border or separate piece of ornamental needlework, esp. on ecclesiastical vestments. [ME *orfreis* (taken as pl.) (gold) embroidery f. OF f. med.L *aurifrisium* etc. f. L *aurum* gold + *Phrygius* Phrygian, also 'embroidered']

orpiment /órpimənt/ *n.* **1** a mineral form of arsenic trisulphide, formerly used as a dye and artist's pigment. Also called *yellow arsenic*. **2** (in full **red orpiment**) = REALGAR. [ME f. OF f. L *auripigmentum* f. *aurum* gold + *pigmentum* pigment]

orpine /órpin/ *n.* (also **orpin**) a succulent herbaceous purple-flowered plant, *Sedum telephium*. Also called LIVELONG[2]. [ME f. OF *orpine*, prob. alt. of ORPIMENT, orig. of a yellow-flowered species of the same genus]

orra /órrə/ *adj.* *Sc.* **1** not matched; odd. **2** occasional; extra. [18th c.: orig. unkn.]

orrery /órrəri/ *n.* (*pl.* **-ies**) a clockwork model of the solar system. [named after the fourth Earl of *Orrery*, for whom one was made]

orris /órriss/ *n.* **1** any plant of the genus *Iris*, esp. *I. florentina*. **2** = ORRISROOT. ▫ **orris-powder** powdered orrisroot. [16th c.: app. an unexpl. alt. of IRIS]

orrisroot /órrisrо͞ot/ *n.* the fragrant rootstock of the orris, used in perfumery and formerly in medicine.

ortanique /órtəne̍ek/ *n.* a citrus fruit produced by crossing an orange and a tangerine. [*or*ange + *tan*gerine + un*ique*]

ortho- /órthō/ *comb. form* **1 a** straight, rectangular, upright. **b** right, correct. **2** *Chem.* **a** relating to two adjacent carbon atoms in a benzene ring. **b** relating to acids and salts (e.g. *orthophosphates*) giving *meta-* compounds on removal of water. [Gk *orthos* straight]

orthocephalic /órthōsifállik/ *adj.* having a head with a medium ratio of breadth to height.

orthochromatic /órthōkrōmáttik/ *adj.* giving fairly correct relative intensity to colours in photography by being sensitive to all except red.

orthoclase /órthōklayss/ *n.* a common alkali feldspar usu. occurring as variously coloured crystals, used in ceramics and glass-making. [ORTHO- + Gk *klasis* breaking]

orthodontics /órthədóntiks/ *n.pl.* (treated as *sing.*) (also **orthodontia** /-dóntiə/) the treatment of irregularities in the teeth and jaws. ▫▫ **orthodontic** *adj.* **orthodontist** *n.* [ORTHO- + Gk *odous odont-* tooth]

orthodox /órthədoks/ *adj.* **1 a** holding correct or currently accepted opinions, esp. on religious doctrine, morals, etc. **b** not independent-minded; unoriginal; unheretical. **2** (of religious doctrine, standards of morality, etc.) generally accepted as right or true; authoritatively established; conventional. **3** (also **Orthodox**) (of Judaism) strictly keeping to traditional doctrine and ritual. ▫ **Orthodox Church** the Eastern Church, separated from the Western Church in the 11th c., having the Patriarch of Constantinople as its head, and including the national Churches of Russia, Romania, Greece, etc. ▫▫ **orthodoxly** *adv.* [eccl. L *orthodoxus* f. Gk *orthodoxos* f. *doxa* opinion]

▪ **1, 2** conformist, accepted, authoritative, authorized, recognized, received, official, standard, prevailing, prevalent, common, regular, popular, ordinary, doctrinal, unheretical, established, traditional, traditionalist, accustomed, conventional, customary, conservative, unoriginal.

orthodoxy /órthədoksi/ *n.* (*pl.* **-ies**) **1** the state of being orthodox. **2 a** the orthodox practice of Judaism. **b** the body of orthodox Jews. **3** esp. *Relig.* an authorized or generally accepted theory, doctrine, etc. [LL *orthodoxia* f. late Gk *orthodoxia* sound doctrine (as ORTHODOX)]

orthoepy /órthō-eepi, orthṓ-ipi/ *n.* the study of the (correct) pronunciation of words. ▫▫ **orthoepic** /-thō-éppik/ *adj.* **orthoepist** *n.* [Gk *orthoepeia* correct speech (as ORTHO-, *epos* word)]

orthogenesis /órthōjénnisiss/ *n.* a theory of evolution which proposes that variations follow a defined direction and are not merely sporadic and fortuitous. ▫▫ **orthogenetic** /-jinéttik/ *adj.* **orthogenetically** /-jinéttikəli/ *adv.*

orthognathous /orthógnəthəss/ *adj.* (of mammals, including man) having a jaw which does not project forwards and a facial angle approaching a right angle. [ORTHO- + Gk *gnathos* jaw]

orthogonal /orthóggən'l/ *adj.* of or involving right angles. [F f. *orthogone* (as ORTHO-, -GON)]

orthography /orthógrəfi/ *n.* (*pl.* **-ies**) **1 a** correct or conventional spelling. **b** spelling with reference to its correctness (*dreadful orthography*). **c** the study or science of spelling. **2 a** perspective projection used in maps and elevations in which the projection lines are parallel. **b** a map etc. so projected. ▫▫ **orthographer** *n.* **orthographic** /órthəgráffik/ *adj.* **orthographical** /órthəgráffik'l/ *adj.* **orthographically** /órthəgráffikəli/ *adv.* [ME f. OF *ortografie* f. L *orthographia* f. Gk *orthographia* (as ORTHO-, -GRAPHY)]

orthopaedics /órthəpeédiks/ *n.pl.* (treated as *sing.*) (*US* **-pedics**) the branch of medicine dealing with the correction of deformities of bones or muscles, orig. in children. ▫▫ **orthopaedic** *adj.* **orthopaedist** *n.* [F *orthopédie* (as ORTHO-, *pédie* f. Gk *paideia* rearing of children)]

orthopteran /orthóptərən/ *n.* any insect of the order Orthoptera, with straight narrow forewings, and hind legs modified for jumping etc., including grasshoppers and crickets. ▫▫ **orthopterous** *adj.* [ORTHO- + Gk *pteros* wing]

orthoptic /orthóptik/ *adj.* relating to the correct or normal use of the eyes. ▫▫ **orthoptist** *n.* [ORTHO- + Gk *optikos* of sight: see OPTIC]

orthoptics /orthóptiks/ *n. Med.* the study or treatment of irregularities of the eyes, esp. with reference to the eye-muscles.

orthorhombic /órthō-rómbik/ *adj. Crystallog.* (of a crystal) characterized by three mutually perpendicular axes which are unequal in length, as in topaz and talc.

orthotone /órthətōn/ *adj.* & *n.* • *adj.* (of a word) having an independent stress pattern, not enclitic nor proclitic. • *n.* a word of this kind.

ortolan /órtələn/ *n.* (in full **ortolan bunting**) *Zool.* a small European bird, *Emberiza hortulana*, eaten as a delicacy. [F f. Prov., lit. gardener, f. L *hortulanus* f. *hortulus* dimin. of *hortus* garden]

Orwellian /orwélliən/ *adj.* of or characteristic of the writings of George Orwell (E. A. Blair), English writer d. 1950, esp. with reference to the totalitarian development of the State as depicted in *1984* and *Animal Farm*.

-ory[1] /əri/ *suffix* forming nouns denoting a place for a particular function (*dormitory*; *refectory*). ▫▫ **-orial** /óriəl/ *suffix* forming adjectives. [L *-oria*, *-orium*, sometimes via ONF and AF *-orie*, OF *-oire*]

-ory[2] /əri/ *suffix* forming adjectives (and occasionally nouns) relating to or involving a verbal action (*accessory*; *compulsory*; *directory*). [L *-orius*, sometimes via AF *-ori(e)*, OF *-oir(e)*]

oryx /órriks/ *n.* any large straight-horned antelope of the genus *Oryx*, native to Africa and Arabia. [ME f. L f. Gk *orux* stonemason's pickaxe, f. its pointed horns]

OS *abbr.* **1** old style. **2** ordinary seaman. **3** (in the UK) Ordnance Survey. **4** outsize. **5** out of stock.

Os *symb. Chem.* the element osmium.

Osage orange /ősayj/ *n.* **1** a hardy thorny tree, *Maclura pomifera*, of the US, bearing inedible wrinkled orange-like fruit. **2** the durable orange-coloured timber from this. [name of a N. American Indian tribe]

Oscan /óskən/ *n.* & *adj.* • *n.* the ancient language of Campania in Italy, related to Latin and surviving only in inscriptions. • *adj.* relating to or written in Oscan. [L *Oscus*]

Oscar /óskər/ *n.* any of the statuettes awarded by the US Academy of Motion Picture Arts and Sciences for excellence in film acting, directing, etc. [the name *Oscar*]

oscillate /óssilayt/ *v.* **1** *intr.* & *tr.* **a** swing to and fro like a pendulum. **b** move to and fro between points. **2** *intr.* vacillate; vary between extremes of opinion, action, etc. **3** *intr. Physics* move with periodic regularity. **4** *intr. Electr.* (of a current) undergo high-frequency alternations as across a spark-gap or in a valve-transmitter circuit. **5** *intr.* (of a radio receiver) radiate electromagnetic waves owing to faulty operation. ▫▫ **oscillation** /-láysh'n/ *n.* **oscillator** *n.* **oscillatory** /osíllətəri, óssilaytəri/ *adj.* [L *oscillare oscillat-* swing]
■ **1, 2** fluctuate, vibrate, waver, see-saw, swing, sway; vacillate, equivocate, shilly-shally, hum and haw.

oscillo- /əsíllō/ *comb. form* oscillation, esp. of electric current.

oscillogram /əsílləgram/ *n.* a record obtained from an oscillograph.

oscillograph /əsílləgraaf/ *n.* a device for recording oscillations. ▫▫ **oscillographic** /-gráffik/ *adj.* **oscillography** /óssilógrəfi/ *n.*

oscilloscope /əsílləskōp/ *n.* a device for viewing oscillations by a display on the screen of a cathode-ray tube. ▫▫ **oscilloscopic** /-skóppik/ *adj.*

oscine /óssin/ *adj.* (also **oscinine** /óssineen/) of or relating to the suborder Oscines of passerine birds including many of the songbirds. [L *oscen -cinis* songbird (as OB-, *canere* sing)]

oscitation /óssitáysh'n/ *n. formal* **1** yawning; drowsiness. **2** inattention; negligence. [L *oscitatio* f. *oscitare* gape f. *os* mouth + *citare* move]

oscula *pl.* of OSCULUM.

oscular /óskyoolər/ *adj.* **1** of or relating to the mouth. **2** of or relating to kissing. [L *osculum* mouth, kiss, dimin. of *os* mouth]

osculate /óskyoolayt/ *v.* **1** *tr. Math.* (of a curve or surface) have contact of at least the second order with; have two branches with a common tangent, with each branch extending in both directions of the tangent. **2** *v.intr.* & *tr. joc.* kiss. **3** *intr. Biol.* (of a species etc.) be related through an intermediate species; have common characteristics with another or with each other. ▫▫ **osculant** *adj.* **osculation** /-láysh'n/ *n.* **osculatory** /óskyoolətəri/ *adj.* [L *osculari* kiss (as OSCULAR)]

osculum /óskyooləm/ *n.* (*pl.* **oscula** /-lə/) a mouthlike aperture, esp. of a sponge. [L: see OSCULAR]

-ose[1] /ōss/ *suffix* forming adjectives denoting possession of a quality (*grandiose*; *verbose*). ▫▫ **-osely** *suffix* forming adverbs. **-oseness** *suffix* forming nouns (cf. -OSITY). [from or after L *-osus*]

-ose[2] /ōss/ *suffix Chem.* forming names of carbohydrates (*cellulose*; *sucrose*). [after GLUCOSE]

osier /ṓziər/ *n.* **1** any of various willows, esp. *Salix viminalis*, with long flexible shoots used in basketwork. **2** a shoot of a willow. ▫ **osier-bed** a place where osiers are grown. [ME f. OF: cf. med.L *auseria* osier-bed]

-osis /ṓsiss/ *suffix* (*pl.* **-oses** /ṓseez/) denoting a process or condition (*apotheosis*; *metamorphosis*), esp. a pathological state (*acidosis*; *neurosis*; *thrombosis*). [L f. Gk *-ōsis* suffix of verbal nouns]

-osity /óssiti/ *suffix* forming nouns from adjectives in *-ose* (see -OSE[1]) and *-ous* (*verbosity*; *curiosity*). [F *-osité* or L *-ositas -ositatis*: cf. -ITY]

Osmanli /ozmánli, os-/ *adj.* & *n.* = OTTOMAN. [Turk. f. *Osman* f. Arab. *ʿuṯmān* (see OTTOMAN) + *-li* adj. suffix]

osmic /ózmik/ *adj.* of or relating to odours or the sense of smell. ▫▫ **osmically** *adv.* [Gk *osmē* smell, odour]

osmium /ózmiəm/ *n. Chem.* a hard bluish-white transition element, the heaviest known metal, occurring naturally in association with platinum and used in certain alloys. ¶ Symb.: **Os.** [Gk *osmē* smell (from the pungent smell of its tetroxide)]

osmosis /ozmṓsiss/ *n.* **1** *Biochem.* the passage of a solvent through a semi-permeable partition into a more concentrated solution. **2** any process by which something is acquired by absorption. ▫▫ **osmotic** /-móttik/ *adj.* **osmotically** /-móttikəli/ *adv.* [orig. *osmose*, after F f. Gk *ōsmos* push]

osmund /ózmənd/ *n.* (also **osmunda** /ozmúndə/) any fern of the genus *Osmunda*, esp. the royal fern, having large divided fronds. [ME f. AF, of uncert. orig.]

osprey /óspray, -pri/ *n.* (*pl.* **-eys**) **1** a large bird of prey, *Pandion haliaetus*, with a brown back and white markings, feeding on fish. Also called *fish-hawk*. **2** a plume on a woman's hat. [ME f. OF *ospres* app. ult. f. L *ossifraga* osprey f. *os* bone + *frangere* break]

ossein /óssi-in/ *n.* the collagen of bones. [L *osseus* (as OSSEOUS)]

osseous /óssiəss/ *adj.* **1** consisting of bone. **2** having a bony skeleton. **3** ossified. [L *osseus* f. *os ossis* bone]

ossicle /óssik'l/ *n.* **1** *Anat.* any small bone, esp. of the middle ear. **2** a small piece of bonelike substance. [L *ossiculum* dimin. (as OSSEOUS)]

Ossie var. of AUSSIE.

ossify /óssifī/ *v.tr.* & *intr.* (**-ies**, **-ied**) **1** turn into bone; harden. **2** make or become rigid, callous, or unprogressive. ▫▫ **ossific** /osíffik/ *adj.* **ossification** /-fikáysh'n/ *n.* [F *ossifier* f. L *os ossis* bone]

■ **1** see PETRIFY 2.

osso bucco /óssō bŏŏkkō/ *n.* shin of veal containing marrowbone stewed in wine with vegetables. [It., = marrowbone]

ossuary /óssyoori/ *n.* (*pl.* **-ies**) **1** a receptacle for the bones of the dead; a charnel-house; a bone-urn. **2** a cave in which ancient bones are found. [LL *ossuarium* irreg. f. *os ossis* bone]

osteitis /ósti-ī́tiss/ *n.* inflammation of the substance of a bone. [Gk *osteon* bone + -ITIS]

ostensible /osténsib'l/ *adj.* apparent but not necessarily real; professed (*his ostensible function was that of interpreter*). ▫▫ **ostensibly** *adv.* [F f. med.L *ostensibilis* f. L *ostendere ostens-* stretch out to view (as OB-, *tendere* stretch)]

■ see APPARENT 2, *alleged* (ALLEGE). ▫▫ **ostensibly** see *apparently* (APPARENT).

ostensive /osténsiv/ *adj.* **1** directly demonstrative. **2** (of a definition) indicating by direct demonstration that which is signified by a term. ▫▫ **ostensively** *adv.* **ostensiveness** *n.* [LL *ostensivus* (as OSTENSIBLE)]

■ **1** see TANGIBLE 2.

ostensory /osténsəri/ *n.* (*pl.* **-ies**) *RC Ch.* a receptacle for displaying the host to the congregation; a monstrance. [med.L *ostensorium* (as OSTENSIBLE)]

ostentation /óstentáysh'n/ *n.* **1** a pretentious and vulgar display esp. of wealth and luxury. **2** the attempt or intention to attract notice; showing off. ▫▫ **ostentatious** *adj.* **ostentatiously** *adv.* [ME f. OF f. L *ostentatio -onis* f. *ostentare* frequent. of *ostendere*: see OSTENSIBLE]

■ show, display, exhibition, exhibitionism, vanity, showing off, pretension, pretentiousness, flaunting, flashiness, flourish, flamboyance, parade, window-dressing. ▫▫ **ostentatious** showy, boastful, braggart, vain, flaunting, pretentious, flamboyant, theatrical, *colloq.* flash, *literary* vaunting, vainglorious.

osteo- /óstiō/ *comb. form* bone. [Gk *osteon*]

osteoarthritis /óstiō-aarthrī́tiss/ *n.* a degenerative disease of joint cartilage, esp. in the elderly. ▫▫ **osteoarthritic** /-thríttik/ *adj.*

osteogenesis /óstiōjénnisiss/ *n.* the formation of bone. ▫▫ **osteogenetic** /-jinéttik/ *adj.*

osteology /óstióllәji/ *n.* the study of the structure and function of the skeleton and bony structures. ▫▫ **osteological** /-tiəlójik'l/ *adj.* **osteologically** /-tiəlójikəli/ *adv.* **osteologist** *n.*

osteomalacia /óstiōməláyshə/ *n.* softening of the bones, often through a deficiency of vitamin D and calcium. ▫▫ **osteomalacic** /-lássik/ *adj.* [mod.L (as OSTEO-, Gk *malakos* soft)]

osteomyelitis /óstiōmī-ilī́tiss/ *n.* inflammation of the bone or of bone marrow, usu. due to infection.

osteopathy /óstióppəthi/ *n.* the treatment of disease through the manipulation of bones, esp. the spine, displacement of these being the supposed cause. ▫▫ **osteopath** /óstiəpath/ *n.* **osteopathic** /óstiəpáthik/ *adj.*

osteoporosis /óstiōpərṓsiss/ *n.* a condition of brittle and fragile bones caused by loss of bony tissue, esp. as a result of hormonal changes, or deficiency of calcium or vitamin D. [OSTEO- + Gk *poros* passage, pore]

ostinato /óstinaátō/ *n.* (*pl.* **-os**) (often *attrib.*) *Mus.* a persistent phrase or rhythm repeated through all or part of a piece. [It., = OBSTINATE]

ostler /óslər/ *n. Brit. hist.* a stableman at an inn. [f. earlier HOSTLER, *hosteler* f. AF *hostiler*, OF (*h*)*ostelier* (as HOSTEL)]

■ see GROOM *n.* 1.

Ostmark /óstmaark/ *n. hist.* the chief monetary unit of the Democratic Republic of Germany. [G, = east mark: see MARK²]

Ostpolitik /óstpoliteek/ *n. hist.* the foreign policy of many western European countries with reference to the former Communist bloc. [G f. *Ost* east + *Politik* politics]

ostracize /óstrəsīz/ *v.tr.* (also **-ise**) **1** exclude (a person) from a society, favour, common privileges, etc.; refuse to associate with. **2** (esp. in ancient Athens) banish (a powerful or unpopular citizen) for five or ten years by popular vote. ▫▫ **ostracism** /-siz'm/ *n.* [Gk *ostrakizō* f. *ostrakon* shell, potsherd (used to write a name on in voting)]

■ **1** blackball, blacklist, banish, exile, boycott, isolate, segregate, exclude, snub, shun, avoid, send to Coventry, cut, cold-shoulder, give a person the cold shoulder, *Eccl.* excommunicate. **2** banish, exile.

ostrich /óstrich/ *n.* **1** a large African swift-running flightless bird, *Struthio camelus*, with long legs and two toes on each foot. **2** a person who refuses to accept facts (from the belief that ostriches bury their heads in the sand when pursued). ▫ **ostrich-farm** a place that breeds ostriches for their feathers. **ostrich-plume** a feather or bunch of feathers of an ostrich. [ME f. OF *ostric(h)e* f. L *avis* bird + LL *struthio* f. Gk *strouthiōn* ostrich f. *strouthos* sparrow, ostrich]

Ostrogoth /óstrəgoth/ *n. hist.* a member of the Eastern branch of the Goths, who conquered Italy in the 5th–6th c. ▫▫ **Ostrogothic** /-góthik/ *adj.* [LL *Ostrogothi* (pl.) f. Gmc *austro-* (unrecorded) east + LL *Gothi* Goths: see GOTH]

OT *abbr.* Old Testament.

-ot¹ /ət/ *suffix* forming nouns, orig. diminutives (*ballot*; *chariot*; *parrot*). [F]

-ot² /ət/ *suffix* forming nouns denoting persons (*patriot*), e.g. natives of a place (*Cypriot*). [F *-ote*, L *-ota*, Gk *-ōtēs*]

OTC *abbr.* (in the UK) Officers' Training Corps.

other /úthər/ *adj.*, *n.* or *pron.*, & *adv.* ● *adj.* **1** not the same as one or some already mentioned or implied; separate in identity or distinct in kind (*other people*; *use other means*; *I assure you, my reason is quite other*). **2 a** further; additional (*a few other examples*). **b** alternative of two (*open your other eye*) (cf. *every other*). **3** (prec. by *the*) that remains after all except the one or ones in question have been considered, eliminated, etc. (*must be in the other pocket*; *where are the other two?*; *the other three men left*). **4** (foll. by *than*) apart from; excepting (*any person other than you*). ● *n.* or *pron.* (orig. an ellipt. use of the adj., now with pl. in *-s*) **1** an additional, different, or extra person, thing, example, etc. (*one or other of us will be there*; *some others have come*) (see also ANOTHER, *each other*). **2** (in *pl.*; prec. by *the*) the ones remaining (*where are the others?*). ● *adv.* (usu. foll. by *than*) *disp.* otherwise (*cannot react other than angrily*). ¶ In this sense *otherwise* is standard except in less formal use. ▫ **no**

other *archaic* nothing else (*I can do no other*). **of all others** out of the many possible or likely (*on this night of all others*). **on the other hand** see HAND. **the other day** (or **night** or **week** etc.) a few days etc. ago (*heard from him the other day*). **other-directed** governed by external circumstances and trends. **other half** *colloq.* one's wife or husband. **the other place** *Brit. joc.* Oxford University as regarded by Cambridge, and vice versa. **other ranks** soldiers other than commissioned officers. **the other thing** esp. *joc.* an unexpressed alternative (*if you don't like it, do the other thing*). **other things being equal** if conditions are or were alike in all but the point in question. **the other woman** a married man's mistress. **the other world** see WORLD. **someone** (or **something** or **somehow** etc.) **or other** some unspecified person, thing, manner, etc. [OE *ōther* f. Gmc]
■ *adj.* **2 a** see FURTHER *adj.* 2. **b** see ALTERNATIVE *adj.* 1. □ **on the other hand** see OTHERWISE *adv.* 1, 2.

otherness /úthərniss/ *n.* **1** the state of being different; diversity. **2** a thing or existence other than the thing mentioned and the thinking subject.

otherwhere /úthərwáir/ *adj. archaic* or *poet.* elsewhere.

otherwise /úthərwīz/ *adv.* & *adj.* ● *adv.* **1** else; or else; in the circumstances other than those considered etc. (*bring your umbrella, otherwise you will get wet*). **2** in other respects (*he is untidy, but otherwise very suitable*). **3** (often foll. by *than*) in a different way (*could not have acted otherwise; cannot react otherwise than angrily*). **4** as an alternative (*otherwise known as Jack*). ● *adj.* **1** (*predic.*) in a different state (*the matter is quite otherwise*). **2** *archaic* that would otherwise exist (*their otherwise dullness*). □ **and** (or **or**) **otherwise** the negation or opposite (of a specified thing) (*the merits or otherwise of the Bill; experiences pleasant and otherwise*). [OE *on ōthre wisan* (as OTHER, WISE²)]
■ *adv.* **1, 2** if not, (or) else; under *or* in other circumstances, in another situation, on the other hand; in other respects. **3** differently, in another manner *or* way, *disp.* other.

other-worldly /úthərwúrldli/ *adj.* **1** unworldly; impractical. **2** concerned with life after death etc. □□ **other-worldliness** *n.*

otic /ṓtik/ *adj.* of or relating to the ear. [Gk *ōtikos* f. *ous ōtos* ear]

-otic /óttik/ *suffix* forming adjectives and nouns corresponding to nouns in *-osis*, meaning 'affected with or producing or resembling a condition in *-osis*' or 'a person affected with this' (*narcotic; neurotic; osmotic*). □□ **-otically** *suffix* forming adverbs. [from or after F *-otique* f. L f. Gk *-ōtikos* adj. suffix]

otiose /ṓshiōss, ṓti-, -ōz/ *adj.* **1** serving no practical purpose; not required; functionless. **2** *archaic* indolent; futile. □□ **otiosely** *adv.* **otioseness** *n.* [L *otiosus* f. *otium* leisure]

otitis /ətītiss/ *n.* inflammation of the ear. [mod.L (as OTO-)]

oto- /ṓtō/ *comb. form* ear. [Gk *ōto-* f. *ous ōtos* ear]

otolaryngology /ṓtəlárringgólləji/ *n.* the study of diseases of the ear and throat. □□ **otolaryngological** /-gəlójik'l/ *adj.* **otolaryngologist** *n.*

otolith /ṓtəlith/ *n.* any of the small particles of calcium carbonate in the inner ear. □□ **otolithic** /-líthik/ *adj.*

otology /ōtólləji/ *n.* the study of the anatomy and diseases of the ear. □□ **otological** /ṓtəlójik'l/ *adj.* **otologist** *n.*

otorhinolaryngology /ṓtərīnōlárringgólləji/ *n.* the study of diseases of the ear, nose, and throat.

otoscope /ṓtəskōp/ *n.* an apparatus for examining the eardrum and the passage leading to it from the ear. □□ **otoscopic** /-skóppik/ *adj.*

OTT *abbr. colloq.* over-the-top.

ottava rima /otaávə reémə/ *n.* a stanza of eight lines of 10 or 11 syllables, rhyming *abababcc*. [It., lit. eighth rhyme]

otter /óttər/ *n.* **1 a** any of several aquatic fish-eating mammals of the family Mustelidae, esp. of the genus *Lutra*, having strong claws and webbed feet. **b** its fur or pelt. **2** = *sea otter*. **3** a piece of board used to carry fishing-bait in water. **4** a type of paravane, esp. as used on non-naval craft. □ **otter-board** a device for keeping the mouth of a trawl-net open. **otter-dog** (or **-hound**) a dog of a breed used in otter-hunting. [OE *otr, ot(t)or* f. Gmc]

otto var. of ATTAR.

Ottoman /óttəmən/ *adj.* & *n.* ● *adj. hist.* **1** of or concerning the dynasty of Osman or Othman I, the branch of the Turks to which he belonged, or the empire ruled by his descendants. **2** Turkish. ● *n.* (*pl.* **Ottomans**) an Ottoman person; a Turk. □ **the Ottoman Porte** see PORTE. [F f. Arab. *'uṯmānī* adj. of Othman (*'uṯmān*)]

ottoman /óttəmən/ *n.* (*pl.* **ottomans**) **1 a** an upholstered seat, usu. square and without a back or arms, sometimes a box with a padded top. **b** a footstool of similar design. **2** a heavy silken fabric with a mixture of cotton or wool. [F *ottomane* fem. (as OTTOMAN)]

OU *abbr. Brit.* **1** Open University. **2** Oxford University.

oubliette /ōōbli-ét/ *n.* a secret dungeon with access only through a trapdoor. [F f. *oublier* forget]

ouch /owch/ *int.* expressing pain or annoyance. [imit.: cf. G *autsch*]

ought[1] /awt/ *v.aux.* (usu. foll. by *to* + infin.; present and past indicated by the following infin.) **1** expressing duty or rightness (*we ought to love our neighbours*). **2** expressing shortcoming (*it ought to have been done long ago*). **3** expressing advisability or prudence (*you ought to go for your own good*). **4** expressing esp. strong probability (*he ought to be there by now*). □ **ought not** the negative form of *ought* (*he ought not to have stolen it*). [OE *āhte*, past of *āgan* OWE]
■ see MUST[1] *v.* 1, 3, 4.

ought[2] /awt/ *n.* (also **aught**) *colloq.* a figure denoting nothing; nought. [perh. f. *an ought* for a NOUGHT; cf. ADDER]

ought[3] var. of AUGHT[1].

oughtn't /áwt'nt/ *contr.* ought not.

Ouija /weéjə/ *n.* (in full **Ouija board**) *propr.* a board having letters or signs at its rim to which a planchette, movable pointer, or upturned glass points in answer to questions from attenders at a seance etc. [F *oui* yes + G *ja* yes]

ounce[1] /ownss/ *n.* **1 a** a unit of weight of one-sixteenth of a pound avoirdupois (approx. 28 grams). ¶ Abbr.: **oz. b** a unit of one-twelfth of a pound troy or apothecaries' measure, equal to 480 grains (approx. 31 grams). **2** a small quantity. □ **fluid ounce** *Brit.* **1** a unit of capacity equal to one-twentieth of a pint (approx. 0.028 litre). **2** *US* a unit of capacity equal to one-sixteenth of a pint (approx. 0.029 litre). [ME & OF *unce* f. L *uncia* twelfth part of pound or foot: cf. INCH[1]]

ounce[2] /ownss/ *n.* a large Asian feline, *Panthera uncia*, with leopard-like markings on a cream-coloured coat. Also called *mountain panther, snow leopard*. [ME f. OF *once* (earlier *lonce*) = It. *lonza* ult. f. L *lynx*: see LYNX]

OUP *abbr.* Oxford University Press.

our /owr/ *poss.pron.* (*attrib.*) **1** of or belonging to us or ourselves (*our house; our own business*). **2** of or belonging to all people (*our children's future*). **3** (esp. as **Our**) of Us the king or queen, emperor or empress, etc. (*given under Our seal*). **4** of us, the editorial staff of a newspaper etc. (*a foolish adventure in our view*). **5** *Brit. colloq.* indicating a relative, acquaintance, or colleague of the speaker (*our Barry works there*). □ **Our Father 1** the Lord's Prayer. **2** God. **Our Lady** the Virgin Mary. **Our Lord 1** Jesus Christ. **2** God. **Our Saviour** Jesus Christ. [OE *ūre* orig. genit. pl. of 1st pers. pron. = of us, later treated as possessive adj.]

-our[1] /ər/ *suffix* var. of -OR[2] surviving in some nouns (*ardour; colour; valour*).

-our[2] /ər/ *suffix* var. of -OR[1] (*saviour*).

ours /owrz/ *poss.pron.* the one or ones belonging to or associated with us (*it is ours; ours are over there*). □ **of ours** of or belonging to us (*a friend of ours*).

ourself /owrsélf/ *pron. archaic* a word formerly used instead of *myself* by a sovereign, newspaper editorial staff, etc. (cf. OUR 3, 4).

ourselves /owrsélvz/ *pron.* **1 a** *emphat. form* of WE or US (*we ourselves did it; made it ourselves; for our friends and* *ourselves*). **b** *refl. form* of US (*are pleased with ourselves*). **2** in our normal state of body or mind (*not quite ourselves today*). □ **be ourselves** act in our normal unconstrained manner. **by ourselves** see *by oneself*.

-ous /əss/ *suffix* **1** forming adjectives meaning 'abounding in, characterized by, of the nature of' (*envious*; *glorious*; *mountainous*; *poisonous*). **2** *Chem.* denoting a state of lower valence than the corresponding word in *-ic* (*ferrous*). □□ **-ously** *suffix* forming adverbs. **-ousness** *suffix* forming nouns. [from or after AF *-ous*, OF *-eus*, f. L *-osus*]

ousel var. of OUZEL.

oust /owst/ *v.tr.* **1** (usu. foll. by *from*) drive out or expel, esp. by forcing oneself into the place of. **2** (usu. foll. by *of*) *Law* put (a person) out of possession; deprive. [AF *ouster*, OF *oster* take away, f. L *obstare* oppose, hinder (as OB-, *stare* stand)]

■ **1** see EXPEL 1. **2** see DISPOSSESS 1.

ouster /ówstər/ *n.* **1** ejection as a result of physical action, judicial process, or political upheaval. **2** esp. *US* dismissal, expulsion.

out /owt/ *adv.*, *prep.*, *n.*, *adj.*, *int.*, & *v.* ● *adv.* **1** away from or not in or at a place etc. (*keep him out*; *get out of here*; *my son is out in Canada*). **2** (forming part of phrasal verbs) **a** indicating dispersal away from a centre etc. (*hire out*; *share out*; *board out*). **b** indicating coming or bringing into the open for public attention etc. (*call out*; *send out*; *shine out*; *stand out*). **c** indicating a need for attentiveness (*watch out*; *look out*; *listen out*). **3 a** not in one's house, office, etc. (*went out for a walk*). **b** no longer in prison. **4** to or at an end; completely (*tired out*; *die out*; *out of bananas*; *fight it out*; *typed it out*). **5** (of a fire, candle, etc.) not burning. **6** in error (*was 3% out in my calculations*). **7** *colloq.* unconscious (*she was out for five minutes*). **8 a** (of a tooth) extracted. **b** (of a joint, bone, etc.) dislocated (*put his shoulder out*). **9** (of a party, politician, etc.) not in office. **10** (of a jury) considering its verdict in secrecy. **11** (of workers) on strike. **12** (of a secret) revealed. **13** (of a flower) blooming, open. **14** (of a book) published. **15** (of a star) visible after dark. **16** unfashionable (*turn-ups are out*). **17** (of a batsman, batter, etc.) no longer taking part as such, having been caught, stumped, etc. **18 a** not worth considering; rejected (*that idea is out*). **b** not allowed. **19** *colloq.* (prec. by *superl.*) known to exist (*the best game out*). **20** (of a stain, mark, etc.) not visible, removed (*painted out the sign*). **21** (of time) not spent working (*took five minutes out*). **22** (of a rash, bruise, etc.) visible. **23** (of the tide) at the lowest point. **24** *Boxing* unable to rise from the floor (*out for the count*). **25** *archaic* (of a young upper-class woman) introduced into society. **26** (in a radio conversation etc.) transmission ends (*over and out*). ● *prep.* **1** out of (*looked out the window*). **2** *archaic* outside; beyond the limits of. ● *n.* **1** *colloq.* a way of escape; an excuse. **2** (**the outs**) the political party out of office. ● *adj.* **1** (of a match) played away. **2** (of an island) away from the mainland. ● *int.* a peremptory dismissal, reproach, etc. (*out, you scoundrel!*). ● *v.* **1** *tr.* **a** put out. **b** *colloq.* eject forcibly. **2** *intr.* come or go out; emerge (*murder will out*). **3** *tr. Boxing* knock out. **4** *tr. US colloq.* expose the homosexuality of (a prominent person). □ **at outs** at variance or enmity. **not out** *Cricket* (of a side or a batsman) not having been caught, bowled, etc. **out and about** (of a person, esp. after an illness) engaging in normal activity. **out and away** by far. **out and out 1** thorough; surpassing. **2** thoroughly; surpassingly. **out at elbows** see ELBOW. **out for** having one's interest or effort directed to; intent on. **out of 1** from within (*came out of the house*). **2** not within (*I was never out of England*). **3** from among (*nine people out of ten*; *must choose out of these*). **4** beyond the range of (*is out of reach*). **5** without or so as to be without (*was swindled out of his money*; *out of breath*; *out of sugar*). **6** from (*get money out of him*). **7** owing to; because of (*asked out of curiosity*). **8** by the use of (material) (*what did you make it out of?*). **9** at a specified distance from (a town, port, etc.) (*seven miles out of Liverpool*). **10** beyond (*something out of the ordinary*). **11** *Racing* (of an animal, esp. a horse) born of. **out of bounds** see BOUND[2]. **out of the closet** see CLOSET. **out of date** see DATE[1]. **out of doors** see DOOR. **out of drawing** see DRAWING. **out of hand** see HAND. **out of it 1** not included; forlorn. **2** *sl.* extremely drunk. **out of order** see ORDER. **out of pocket** see POCKET. **out of the question** see QUESTION. **out of sorts** see SORT. **out of temper** see TEMPER. **out of this world** see WORLD. **out of the way** see WAY. **out to** keenly striving to do. **out to lunch** *colloq.* crazy, mad. **out with** an exhortation to expel or dismiss (an unwanted person). **out with it** say what you are thinking. [OE *ūt*, OHG *ūz*, rel. to Skr. *ud-*]

■ *adv.* **1** away, abroad, elsewhere, not (at) home, absent. **2a, b, 3a, 12** outside, outdoors, in *or* into the open air; in *or* into the open, to *or* into public notice, for all to see, out of the closet; revealed, exposed, visible, discernible, manifest, in sight, in view. **3 b** free, at liberty, at large, loose, unconfined. **4** completely, thoroughly, effectively, entirely. **5** extinguished, unlit; off, doused; exhausted, gone, finished, ended; over, completed; inoperative, non-functioning. **6** inaccurate, incorrect, wrong, at fault, in error, faulty, off, wide of the mark; short, minus, missing, in default, out of pocket. **7, 24** *colloq.* (out) cold, out for the count; see also INSENSIBLE 1. **8a** pulled, removed, taken out, extracted, gone. **8b** out of place, out of joint, dislocated. **11** striking, on strike. **13** open, blooming, in flower *or* bloom *or* blossom. **14** in print, published, issued, produced. **16** dated, out-dated, out-moded, *passé*, old-fashioned, antiquated, old hat, *démodé*, obsolete, unfashionable. **18 a** see UNWELCOME. **b** unacceptable, forbidden, prohibited, not allowed, *colloq.* not on. ● *n.* **1** excuse, escape, loophole, evasion, alibi, *colloq.* get-out. ● *adj.* **2** outlying, distant, far-off; peripheral. □ **out and about** active, busy, back to normal, energetic, *colloq.* bustling. **out and out 1** complete, unmitigated, unalloyed, undiluted, pure, utter, perfect, consummate, surpassing, outright, total, downright, unqualified, thorough, thoroughgoing, dyed in the wool. **out for** interested in, intent *or* focused *or* bent on, aiming at *or* for, after, seeking, in search of, out to get. **out of it 1** left out, excluded, omitted; forlorn; see also ABANDONED 1a. **2** see DRUNK *adj.* 1. **out to** trying *or* aiming *or* keen *or* eager to. **out to lunch** see CRAZY 1.

out- /owt/ *prefix* added to verbs and nouns, meaning: **1** so as to surpass or exceed (*outdo*; *outnumber*). **2** external, separate (*outline*; *outhouse*; *outdoors*). **3** out of; away from; outward (*outspread*; *outgrowth*).

out-act /ówtákt/ *v.tr.* surpass in acting or performing.

outage /ówtij/ *n.* a period of time during which a power-supply etc. is not operating.

out-and-outer /ówtəndówtər/ *n. sl.* **1** a thorough or supreme person or thing. **2** an extremist.

outback /ówtbak/ *n.* esp. *Austral.* the remote and usu. uninhabited inland districts. □□ **outbacker** *n.*

■ see *back country*.

outbalance /ówtbállənss/ *v.tr.* **1** count as more important than. **2** outweigh.

outbid /ówtbíd/ *v.tr.* (**-bidding**; *past* and *past part.* **-bid**) **1** bid higher than (another person) at an auction. **2** surpass in exaggeration etc.

outblaze /ówtbláyz/ *v.* **1** *intr.* blaze out or outwards. **2** *tr.* blaze more brightly than.

outboard /ówtbord/ *adj.*, *adv.*, & *n.* ● *adj.* **1** (of a motor) portable and attachable to the outside of the stern of a boat. **2** (of a boat) having an outboard motor. ● *adj.* & *adv.* on, towards, or near the outside of esp. a ship, an aircraft, etc. ● *n.* **1** an outboard engine. **2** a boat with an outboard engine.

outbound /ówtbownd/ *adj.* outward bound.

outbrave /ówtbráyv/ *v.tr.* **1** outdo in bravery. **2** face defiantly.

outbreak /ówtbrayk/ *n.* **1** a usu. sudden eruption of war, disease, rebellion, etc. **2** an outcrop.

■ **1** see *eruption* (ERUPT).

outbreeding /ówtbreeding/ *n.* the theory or practice of breeding from animals not closely related. ▫▫ **outbreed** *v.intr.* & *tr.* (*past* and *past part.* **-bred**).

outbuilding /ówtbilding/ *n.* a detached shed, barn, garage, etc. within the grounds of a main building; an outhouse.

outburst /ówtburst/ *n.* **1** an explosion of anger etc., expressed in words. **2** an act or instance of bursting out. **3** an outcrop.
■ **1, 2** eruption, explosion, blow-up, flare-up, fulmination; upsurge, surge, outpouring, welling (forth), outflow(ing), rush, flood, effusion, effluence, efflux; fit, access, attack, spasm, paroxysm, seizure, tantrum.

outcast /ówtkaast/ *n.* & *adj.* ● *n.* **1** a person cast out from or rejected by his or her home, country, society, etc. **2** a tramp or vagabond. ● *adj.* rejected; homeless; friendless.
■ *n.* **1** pariah, exile, reject, *persona non grata*, leper, untouchable; expatriate, refugee, displaced person, DP, evacuee.

outcaste *n.* & *v.* ● *n.* /ówtkaast/ (also *attrib.*) **1** a person who has no caste, esp. in Hindu society. **2** a person who has lost his or her caste. ● *v.tr.* /ówtkaást/ cause (a person) to lose his or her caste.

outclass /ówtklaáss/ *v.tr.* **1** belong to a higher class than. **2** defeat easily.
■ **2** see SURPASS 1.

outcome /ówtkum/ *n.* a result; a visible effect.
■ result, consequence, end (result *or* product), after-effect, effect, upshot, sequel, development, outgrowth, aftermath, wake, follow-up, *Med.* sequela(e), *colloq.* bottom line, *sl.* pay-off.

outcrop /ówtkrop/ *n.* & *v.* ● *n.* **1 a** the emergence of a stratum, vein, or rock, at the surface. **b** a stratum etc. emerging. **2** a noticeable manifestation or occurrence. ● *v.intr.* (**-cropped**, **-cropping**) appear as an outcrop; crop out.
■ *n.* **1** see ROCK[1] 3a.

outcry /ówtkrī/ *n.* (*pl.* **-ies**) **1** the act or an instance of crying out. **2** an uproar. **3** a noisy or prolonged public protest.
■ protest, protestation, decrial, complaint, indignation, uproar, vociferation, clamour, clamouring, commotion, outburst, noise, hullabaloo, howl, hoot, boo, hiss.

outdance /ówtdaánss/ *v.tr.* surpass in dancing.

outdare /ówtdáir/ *v.tr.* **1** outdo in daring. **2** overcome by daring.

outdated /ówtdáytid/ *adj.* out of date; obsolete.

outdistance /ówtdístənss/ *v.tr.* leave (a competitor) behind completely.

outdo /ówtdóō/ *v.tr.* (*3rd sing. present* **-does**; *past* **-did**; *past part.* **-done**) exceed or excel in doing or performance; surpass.
■ exceed, surpass, excel, transcend, beat, outstrip, outshine, top, cap, trump, overcome, defeat, outweigh, overshadow, eclipse.

outdoor /ówtdor/ *adj.* done, existing, or used out of doors.
■ alfresco, open-air; see also OUTSIDE *adj.* 1.

outdoors /owtdórz/ *adv.* & *n.* ● *adv.* in or into the open air; out of doors. ● *n.* the world outside buildings; the open air.
■ *adv.* see OUTSIDE *adv.* 1–3.

outer /ówtər/ *adj.* & *n.* ● *adj.* **1** outside; external (*pierced the outer layer*). **2** farther from the centre or inside; relatively far out. **3** objective or physical, not subjective or psychical. ● *n.* **1 a** the division of a target furthest from the bull's-eye. **b** a shot that strikes this. **2** an outer garment or part of one. **3** *Austral. sl.* the part of a racecourse outside the enclosure. **4** an outer container for transport or display. ▫ **the outer bar** see BAR[1]. **outer garments** clothes worn over other clothes or outdoors. **Outer House** *Sc. Law* the hall where judges of the Court of Session sit singly. **outer man** (or **woman**) personal appearance; dress. **outer planet** a planet with an orbit outside the earth's. **outer space** the universe beyond the earth's atmosphere. **the outer world** people outside one's own circle. [ME f. OUT, replacing UTTER[1]]
■ *adj.* **1** see EXTERNAL *adj.* 1a, 3; 1b. **2** see OUTLYING.

outermost /ówtərmōst/ *adj.* furthest from the inside; the most far out.
■ see OUTLYING.

outerwear /ówtərwair/ *n.* = *outer garments*.

outface /ówtfáyss/ *v.tr.* disconcert or defeat by staring or by a display of confidence.

outfall /ówtfawl/ *n.* the mouth of a river, drain, etc., where it empties into the sea etc.
■ see MOUTH *n.* 3.

outfield /ówtfeeld/ *n.* **1** the outer part of a cricket or baseball field. **2** outlying land. ▫▫ **outfielder** *n.*

outfight /ówtfīt/ *v.tr.* fight better than; beat in a fight.

outfit /ówtfit/ *n.* & *v.* ● *n.* **1** a set of clothes worn or esp. designed to be worn together. **2** a complete set of equipment etc. for a specific purpose. **3** *colloq.* a group of people regarded as a unit, organization, etc.; a team. ● *v.tr.* (also *refl.*) (**-fitted**, **-fitting**) provide with an outfit, esp. of clothes.
■ *n.* **1** suit, costume, ensemble, *colloq.* get-up; garb, clothes, clothing, dress, *colloq.* togs, *formal* attire. **2** gear, rig, kit, equipment, equipage, apparatus, accoutrements, paraphernalia, trappings, tackle, tack, utensils. **3** firm, corporation, company, concern, business, organization, set-up, (military) unit, team; party, set, group. ● *v.* fit (out *or* up), equip, kit (out *or* up), provision, stock, accoutre, rig (out *or* up), supply, furnish; dress, clothe, *formal* attire.

outfitter /ówtfittər/ *n.* a supplier of equipment, esp. of men's clothing; a haberdasher.

outflank /ówtflángk/ *v.tr.* **1 a** extend one's flank beyond that of (an enemy). **b** outmanoeuvre (an enemy) in this way. **2** get the better of; confound (an opponent).

outflow /ówtflō/ *n.* **1** an outward flow. **2** the amount that flows out.
■ see OUTPOURING.

outfly /ówtflī/ *v.tr.* (**-flies**; *past* **-flew**; *past part.* **-flown**) **1** surpass in flying. **2** fly faster or farther than.

outfox /ówtfóks/ *v.tr. colloq.* outwit.

outgeneral /ówtjénnərəl/ *v.tr.* (**-generalled**, **-generalling**; *US* **-generaled**, **-generaling**) **1** outdo in generalship. **2** get the better of by superior strategy or tactics.

outgo *v.* & *n.* ● *v.tr.* /ówtgó/ (*3rd sing. present* **-goes**; *past* **-went**; *past part.* **-gone**) *archaic* go faster than; surpass. ● *n.* /ówtgō/ (*pl.* **-goes**) expenditure of money, effort, etc.

outgoing *adj.* & *n.* ● *adj.* /ówtgóing/ **1** friendly; sociable; extrovert. **2** retiring from office. **3** going out or away. ● *n.* /ówtgōing/ **1** (in *pl.*) expenditure. **2** the act or an instance of going out.
■ *adj.* **1** genial, friendly, amiable, cordial, warm, expansive, approachable, affable, accessible, amenable, easygoing, amicable, sociable, congenial, extrovert, familiar, informal, communicative. **2, 3** departing, retiring, ex-, former, past, emeritus; leaving, withdrawing.

outgrow /ówtgró/ *v.tr.* (*past* **-grew**; *past part.* **-grown**) **1** grow too big for (one's clothes). **2** leave behind (a childish habit, taste, ailment, etc.) as one matures. **3** grow faster or taller than (a person, plant, etc.). ▫ **outgrow one's strength** become lanky and weak through too rapid growth.

outgrowth /ówtgrōth/ *n.* **1** something that grows out. **2** an offshoot; a natural product. **3** the process of growing out.
■ **1** see PROMINENCE 2. **2** see OFFSHOOT 2.

outguess /ówtgéss/ *v.tr.* guess correctly what is intended by (another person).

outgun /ówtgún/ *v.tr.* (**-gunned**, **-gunning**) **1** surpass in military or other power or strength. **2** shoot better than.

outhouse /ówt-howss/ *n.* **1** a building, esp. a shed, lean-to, barn, etc. built next to or in the grounds of a house. **2** *US* an outdoor lavatory.

outing /ówting/ *n.* **1** a short holiday away from home, esp. of one day or part of a day; a pleasure-trip, an excursion. **2** any brief journey from home. **3** an appearance in an outdoor match, race, etc. **4** *US colloq.* the practice or policy of

exposing the homosexuality of a prominent person. [OUT *v.* = put out, go out + -ING[1]]
■ **1, 2** jaunt, junket, excursion, trip, expedition, tour, ride, drive, *colloq.* spin.

outjockey /ówtjókki/ *v.tr.* (**-eys, -eyed**) outwit by adroitness or trickery.

outjump /ówtjúmp/ *v.tr.* surpass in jumping.

outlander /ówtlandər/ *n.* a foreigner, alien, or stranger.
■ see STRANGER 1.

outlandish /owtlándish/ *adj.* **1** looking or sounding foreign. **2** bizarre, strange, unfamiliar. □□ **outlandishly** *adv.* **outlandishness** *n.* [OE *ūtlendisc* f. *ūtland* foreign country f. OUT + LAND]
■ unfamiliar, strange, odd, queer, offbeat, peculiar, curious, exotic, foreign, alien, unknown, unheard-of, different, exceptional, extraordinary, quaint, eccentric, bizarre, *outré*, weird, fantastic, unusual, singular, unique, freakish, grotesque, barbarous, far-out, kinky, *colloq.* camp(y).

outlast /ówtlaást/ *v.tr.* last longer than (a person, thing, or duration) (*outlasted its usefulness*).
■ survive, outlive; outwear; weather, endure; see also *sit out*.

outlaw /ówtlaw/ *n.* & *v.* ● *n.* **1** a fugitive from the law. **2** *hist.* a person deprived of the protection of the law. ● *v.tr.* **1** declare (a person) an outlaw. **2** make illegal; proscribe (a practice etc.). □ **outlaw strike** an unofficial strike. □□ **outlawry** *n.* [OE *ūtlaga, ūtlagian* f. ON *útlagi* f. *útlagr* outlawed, rel. to OUT, LAW]
■ *n.* **1** criminal, gangster, robber, desperado, bandit, highwayman, brigand, picaroon, pirate, fugitive, renegade, *hist.* footpad. ● *v.* **2** forbid, disallow, ban, interdict, bar, exclude, prohibit, proscribe.

outlay /ówtlay/ *n.* what is spent on something.
■ expense, cost, expenditure, spending, disbursement, payment.

outlet /ówtlet, -lit/ *n.* **1** a means of exit or escape. **2** (usu. foll. by *for*) a means of expression (of a talent, emotion, etc.) (*find an outlet for tension*). **3** an agency, distributor, or market for goods (*a new retail outlet in China*). **4** *US* a power point. [ME f. OUT- + LET[1]]
■ **1** way out, exit, egress, loophole, relief, escape, escape hatch, vent, opening, release, safety-valve, discharge. **3** retailer, boutique, booth, kiosk, stall, stand, booth, hypermarket, agency, distributor; see also MARKET *n.* 3, 4.

outlier /ówtlīər/ *n.* **1** (also *attrib.*) an outlying part or member. **2** *Geol.* a younger rock formation isolated in older rocks. **3** *Statistics* a result differing greatly from others in the same sample.

outline /ówtlīn/ *n.* & *v.* ● *n.* **1** a rough draft of a diagram, plan, proposal, etc. **2 a** a précis of a proposed novel, article, etc. **b** a verbal description of essential parts only; a summary. **3** a sketch containing only contour lines. **4** (in *sing.* or *pl.*) **a** lines enclosing or indicating an object (*the outline of a shape under the blankets*). **b** a contour. **c** an external boundary. **5** (in *pl.*) the main features or general principles (*the outlines of a plan*). **6** the representation of a word in shorthand. ● *v.tr.* **1** draw or describe in outline. **2** mark the outline of. □ **in outline** sketched or represented as an outline.
■ *n.* **1, 2** précis, synopsis, résumé, summary, digest, abstract, conspectus, survey, overview, recapitulation, review, (thumbnail) sketch, skeleton, (overall) plan, layout, framework, draft, scenario. **4** contour, periphery, boundary; footprint; profile, silhouette. ● *v.* trace, draft, sketch, rough out, profile, block (out), plan (out), lay out, define, delineate.

outlive /ówtlív/ *v.tr.* **1** live longer than (another person). **2** live beyond (a specified date or time). **3** live through (an experience).

outlook /ówtlŏŏk/ *n.* **1** the prospect for the future (*the outlook is bleak*). **2** one's mental attitude or point of view (*narrow in their outlook*). **3** what is seen on looking out.
■ **1** prospect, forecast, expectation(s), promise, hope, potentiality; see also FORECAST *n.* **2** view, position, point of view, viewpoint, prospect, perspective, slant, angle, standpoint, attitude, opinion, philosophy, *Weltanschauung*. **3** see VIEW *n.* 2a.

outlying /ówtlī-ing/ *adj.* situated far from a centre; remote.
■ distant, far-off, far-flung, outer, outermost, out-of-the-way, remote, far-away, peripheral; furthest, farthest.

outmanoeuvre /ówtmənōōvər/ *v.tr.* (*US* **-maneuver**) **1** use skill and cunning to secure an advantage over (a person). **2** outdo in manoeuvring.
■ **1** see OUTSMART.

outmatch /ówtmách/ *v.tr.* be more than a match for (an opponent etc.); surpass.

outmeasure /ówtmézhər/ *v.tr.* exceed in quantity or extent.

outmoded /ówtmōdid/ *adj.* **1** no longer in fashion. **2** obsolete. □□ **outmodedly** *adv.* **outmodedness** *n.*

outmost /ówtmōst/ *adj.* **1** outermost, furthest. **2** uttermost. [ME, var. of *utmest* UTMOST]

outnumber /ówtnúmbər/ *v.tr.* exceed in number.

outpace /ówtpáyss/ *v.tr.* **1** go faster than. **2** outdo in a contest.

out-patient /ówtpaysh'nt/ *n.* a hospital patient who is resident at home but attends regular appointments in hospital.

outperform /ówtpərfórm/ *v.tr.* **1** perform better than. **2** surpass in a specified field or activity. □□ **outperformance** *n.*
■ see SURPASS 1.

outplacement /ówtplaysmənt/ *n.* the act or process of finding new employment for esp. executive workers who have been dismissed or made redundant.

outplay /ówtpláy/ *v.tr.* surpass in playing; play better than.

outpoint /ówtpóynt/ *v.tr.* (in various sports, esp. boxing) score more points than.

outport /ówtport/ *n.* **1** a subsidiary port. **2** *Can.* a small remote fishing village.

outpost /ówtpōst/ *n.* **1** a detachment set at a distance from the main body of an army, esp. to prevent surprise. **2** a distant branch or settlement. **3** the furthest territory of an (esp. the British) empire.
■ **2** see SETTLEMENT 2.

outpouring /ówtporing/ *n.* **1** (usu. in *pl.*) a copious spoken or written expression of emotion. **2** what is poured out.
■ effusion, outflow, flow, outburst, flood, deluge, torrent, spate, emanation, spouting, spurt, gush, efflux, effluence, outrush, tide, cascade, cataract, debouchment.

output /ówtpŏŏt/ *n.* & *v.* ● *n.* **1** the product of a process, esp. of manufacture, or of mental or artistic work. **2** the quantity or amount of this. **3** the printout, results, etc. supplied by a computer. **4** the power etc. delivered by an apparatus. **5** a place where energy, information, etc. leaves a system. ● *v.tr.* (**-putting**; *past* and *past part.* **-put** or **-putted**) **1** put or send out. **2** (of a computer) supply (results etc.).
■ *n.* **1, 2** production, result, out-turn, turnout, yield, crop, harvest; achievement; see also WORK *n.* 3. **3** printout, results, dump. ● *v.* **1** put *or* send out, produce, generate, create, manufacture, yield, achieve, deliver; print out, transmit.

outrage /ówtrayj/ *n.* & *v.* ● *n.* **1** an extreme or shocking violation of others' rights, sentiments, etc. **2** a gross offence or indignity. **3** fierce anger or resentment (*a feeling of outrage*). ● *v.tr.* **1** subject to outrage. **2** injure, insult, etc. flagrantly. **3** shock and anger. [ME f. OF *outrage* f. *outrer* exceed f. *outre* f. L *ultra* beyond]
■ *n.* **1** violation, violence, atrocity, inhumanity, barbarism, enormity, evil, barbarity, savagery, brutality, malignity, malefaction, wrongdoing, evil-doing, maltreatment, abuse, cruelty, injury, harm, damage. **2** see INSULT *n.* **3** resentment, affront, bitterness, indignation, hurt, shock, anger, *literary* wrath, ire. ● *v.* **1** violate,

desecrate, defile, do violence to, injure, harm, abuse, damage; rape, violate, ravage, assault, ravish, attack. **2, 3** offend, insult, injure, affront, vex, displease, distress, nettle, chafe, infuriate, anger, enrage, madden, make a person's blood boil, make a person's hackles rise, *colloq.* rile; see also SHOCK[1] *v.* 1.

outrageous /owtráyjəss/ *adj.* **1** immoderate. **2** shocking. **3** grossly cruel. **4** immoral, offensive. □□ **outrageously** *adv.* **outrageousness** *n.* [ME f. OF *outrageus* (as OUTRAGE)]
■ **1, 2** excessive, extravagant, immoderate, fulsome, exorbitant, enormous, unreasonable, preposterous, shocking, *outré*, extreme, unwarranted, exaggerated, unconscionable, inordinate, intolerable, disgraceful, shameful, scandalous. **3** vicious, cruel, heinous, atrocious, barbaric, inhuman, abusive, beastly, horrible, horrid, horrendous, iniquitous, villainous, wicked, evil, egregious, flagrant, grievous, infamous, execrable, abominable, grisly, hideous, monstrous, vile, unthinkable, foul, unspeakable, appalling, *colloq.* awful. **4** indecent, offensive, immoral, rude, indelicate, obnoxious, profane, obscene, dirty, filthy, lewd, salacious, foul, smutty, scatological, pornographic, objectionable, repellent, repulsive, nauseating, nauseous, nasty, gross, revolting, shocking, repugnant, disgusting, perverted, depraved, dissolute, degenerate, dissipated, debauched, profligate; explicit, unrestrained; foul-mouthed, insulting; unseemly, inappropriate, indecorous, improper, appalling, embarrassing, *US* shy-making.

outran *past* of OUTRUN.

outrange /ówtráynj/ *v.tr.* (of a gun or its user) have a longer range than.

outrank /ówtrángk/ *v.tr.* **1** be superior in rank to. **2** take priority over.

outré /ōōtray/ *adj.* **1** outside the bounds of what is usual or proper. **2** eccentric or indecorous. [F, past part. of *outrer*: see OUTRAGE]
■ unconventional, unusual, extravagant, bizarre, weird, strange, odd, peculiar, grotesque, outlandish, freakish; outrageous; eccentric, indecorous.

outreach *v.* & *n.* ● *v.tr.* /ówtreéch/ **1** reach further than. **2** surpass. **3** *poet.* stretch out (one's arms etc.). ● *n.* /ówtreech/ **1 a** any organization's involvement with or influence in the community, esp. in the context of social welfare. **b** the extent of this. **2** the extent or length of reaching out (*an outreach of 38 metres*).

out-relief /ówtrileef/ *n. Brit. hist.* assistance given to very poor people not living in a workhouse etc.

outride /ówtríd/ *v.tr.* (*past* **-rode**; *past part.* **-ridden**) **1** ride better, faster, or further than. **2** (of a ship) come safely through (a storm etc.).

outrider /ówtrīdər/ *n.* **1** a mounted attendant riding ahead of, or with, a carriage etc. **2** a motor cyclist acting as a guard in a similar manner. **3** *US* a herdsman keeping cattle within bounds. □□ **outriding** *n.*

outrigged /ówtrigd/ *adj.* (of a boat etc.) having outriggers.

outrigger /ówtriggər/ *n.* **1** a beam, spar, or framework, rigged out and projecting from or over a ship's side for various purposes. **2** a similar projecting beam etc. in a building. **3** a log etc. fixed parallel to a canoe to stabilize it. **4 a** an extension of the splinter-bar of a carriage etc. to enable another horse to be harnessed outside the shafts. **b** a horse harnessed in this way. **5 a** an iron bracket bearing a rowlock attached horizontally to a boat's side to increase the leverage of the oar. **b** a boat fitted with these. [OUT- + RIG[1]: perh. partly after obs. (Naut.) *outligger*]

outright *adv.* & *adj.* ● *adv.* /owtrít/ **1** altogether, entirely (*proved outright*). **2** not gradually, nor by degrees, nor by instalments (*bought it outright*). **3** without reservation, openly (*denied the charge outright*). ● *adj.* /ówtrīt/ **1** downright, direct, complete (*their resentment turned to outright anger*). **2** undisputed, clear (*the outright winner*). □□ **outrightness** *n.*
■ *adv.* **1, 3** completely, altogether, entirely, thoroughly, quite, absolutely, totally, *in toto*, utterly; exactly, precisely, baldly, starkly, consummately, purely, directly, unhesitatingly, explicitly, categorically, straightforwardly, plainly, openly, forthrightly, unequivocally, unambiguously, candidly; unrestrictedly, unqualifiedly, unreservedly, unconditionally; peremptorily, out of hand. **2** directly, at once, immediately, instantaneously, instantly, then and there, there and then, straight *or* right away, right off, on the spot. ● *adj.* **1** undisguised, unmitigated, utter, consummate, pure, out-and-out, all-out, sheer, absolute, complete, stark, bald, thorough, arrant, thoroughgoing, downright, direct, definite, unmistakable. **2** unqualified, undisputed, total, unreserved, unrestricted, full, complete, unconditional, unequivocal, clear, direct, definite, unmistakable.

outrival /ówtrív'l/ *v.tr.* (**-rivalled, -rivalling**; *US* **-rivaled, -rivaling**) outdo as a rival.

outrode *past* of OUTRIDE.

outrun *v.* & *n.* ● *v.tr.* /ówtrún/ (**-running**; *past* **-ran**; *past part.* **-run**) **1 a** run faster or farther than. **b** escape from. **2** go beyond (a specified point or limit). ● *n.* /ówtrun/ *Austral.* a sheep-run distant from its homestead.

outrush /ówtrush/ *n.* **1** a rushing out. **2** a violent overflow.
■ see OUTPOURING.

outsail /ówtsáyl/ *v.tr.* sail better or faster than.

outsat *past* and *past part.* of OUTSIT.

outsell /ówtsél/ *v.tr.* (*past* and *past part.* **-sold**) **1** sell more than. **2** be sold in greater quantities than.

outset /ówtset/ *n.* the start, beginning. □ **at** (or **from**) **the outset** at or from the beginning.
■ beginning, start, inauguration, inception, *colloq.* kick-off, *formal* commencement. □ **at the outset** originally; see also *at first* (FIRST).

outshine /ówtshín/ *v.tr.* (*past* and *past part.* **-shone**) shine brighter than; surpass in ability, excellence, etc.

outshoot /ówtshōōt/ *v.tr.* (*past* and *past part.* **-shot**) **1** shoot better or further than (another person). **2** esp. *US* score more goals, points, etc. than (another player or team).

outside *n.*, *adj.*, *adv.*, & *prep.* ● *n.* /ówtsíd/ **1** the external side or surface; the outer parts (*painted blue on the outside*). **2** the external appearance; the outward aspect of a building etc. **3** (of a path) the side away from the wall or next to the road. **4** (also *attrib.*) all that is without; the world as distinct from the thinking subject (*learn about the outside world; viewed from the outside the problem is simple*). **5** a position on the outer side (*the gate opens from the outside*). **6** *colloq.* the highest computation (*it is a mile at the outside*). **7** an outside player in football etc. **8** (in *pl.*) the outer sheets of a ream of paper. ● *adj.* /ówtsīd/ **1** of or on or nearer the outside; outer. **2 a** not of or belonging to some circle or institution (*outside help; outside work*). **b** (of a broker) not a member of the Stock Exchange. **3** (of a chance etc.) remote; very unlikely. **4** (of an estimate etc.) the greatest or highest possible (*the outside price*). **5** (of a player in football etc.) positioned nearest to the edge of the field. ● *adv.* /owtsíd/ **1** on or to the outside. **2** in or to the open air. **3** not within or enclosed or included. **4** *sl.* not in prison. ● *prep.* /owtsíd/ (also *disp.* foll. by *of*) **1** not in; to or at the exterior of (*meet me outside the post office*). **2** external to, not included in, beyond the limits of (*outside the law*). **3** *colloq.* other than; apart from. □ **at the outside** (of an estimate etc.) at the most. **get outside of** *sl.* eat or drink. **outside and in** outside and inside. **outside broadcast** *Brit.* a broadcast made on location and not in a studio. **outside edge** (on an ice-skate) each of the edges facing outwards when both feet are together. **outside in** = *inside out*. **outside interest** a hobby; an interest not connected with one's work or normal way of life. **outside seat** a seat nearer the end of a row. **outside track** the outside lane of a sports track etc. which is longer because of the curve.

■ *n.* **1** exterior, face, facing, shell, skin, case, casing, surface, front; façade. **2** aspect, appearance, look, demeanour, face, front, façade, *literary* mien; mask, disguise, false front, pretence. **4** the outside *or* external *or* outer *or* manifest *or* physical world, the world at large; externals. **6** extreme, limit, most, maximum, utmost, best, worst, longest. ● *adj.* **1** exterior, external, outer; outdoor. **2 a** foreign, alien, outward; unconnected, excluded, uninvolved, separate, different; private, home, cottage, secondary, peripheral; independent, freelance. **3** faint; see also SLENDER 2. **4** maximum, maximal, highest, best, worst, greatest, most, largest, longest, furthest, farthest. ● *adv.* **1–3** on the outside, externally; out, outdoors, out of doors. □ **at the outside** at (the) maximum, at the most, at top, at the limit.

outsider /owtsī́dər/ *n.* **1 a** a non-member of some circle, party, profession, etc. **b** an uninitiated person, a layman. **2** a person without special knowledge, breeding, etc., or not fit to mix with good society. **3** a competitor, applicant, etc. thought to have little chance of success.
■ **1, 2** non-member, non-initiate, layman, laywoman, foreigner, alien, outlander, stranger; newcomer, guest, visitor, trespasser, interloper, intruder, squatter, invader, gatecrasher. **3** dark horse, *Austral. sl.* roughie.

outsit /ówtsít/ *v.tr.* (**-sitting**; *past* and *past part.* **-sat**) sit longer than (another person or thing).

outsize /ówtsīz/ *adj.* & *n.* ● *adj.* **1** unusually large. **2** (of garments etc.) of an exceptionally large size. ● *n.* an exceptionally large person or thing, esp. a garment. □□ **outsizeness** *n.*
■ *adj.* **1** see LARGE *adj.* 1, 2.

outskirts /ówtskurts/ *n.pl.* the outer border or fringe of a town, district, subject, etc.
■ periphery, edge, environs, vicinity, border(s), suburb(s), exurb(s), neighbourhood, purlieus, fringe(s), vicinage, *faubourg(s).*

outsmart /ówtsmaárt/ *v.tr. colloq.* outwit, be cleverer than.
■ outwit, out-think, outmanoeuvre, outmanipulate, outplay, steal a march on, get the better *or* best of, trick, dupe, hoodwink, fool, pull a fast one on, take in, deceive, hoax, gull, make a fool of, make a monkey (out) of, *colloq.* outfox; swindle, cheat, defraud, *colloq.* slip *or* put one over on, bamboozle, *literary* cozen, *sl.* con.

outsold *past* and *past part.* of OUTSELL.

outspan /ówtspan/ *v.* & *n. S.Afr.* ● *v.* (**-spanned, -spanning**) **1** *tr.* (also *absol.*) unharness (animals) from a cart, plough, etc. **2** *intr.* break a wagon journey. ● *n.* a place for grazing or encampment. [S.Afr. Du. *uit spannen* unyoke]

outspend /ówtspénd/ *v.tr.* (*past* and *past part.* **-spent**) spend more than (one's resources or another person).

outspoken /ówtspṓkən/ *adj.* given to or involving plain speaking; frank in stating one's opinions. □□ **outspokenly** *adv.* **outspokenness** *n.*
■ candid, frank, open, free, direct, unreserved, straightforward, forthright, explicit, specific, plain-spoken, plain-speaking, unequivocal, unceremonious, unambiguous, unsubtle, uninhibited, unshrinking, blunt, bold, brusque, brash, undiplomatic, tactless, crude.

outspread /ówtspréd/ *adj.* & *v.* ● *adj.*, spread out; fully extended or expanded. ● *v.tr.* & *intr.* (*past* and *past part.* **-spread**) spread out; expand.

outstanding /ówtstánding/ *adj.* **1 a** conspicuous, eminent, esp. because of excellence. **b** (usu. foll. by *at, in*) remarkable in (a specified field). **2** (esp. of a debt) not yet settled (*£200 still outstanding*). □□ **outstandingly** *adv.*
■ **1** prominent, eminent, renowned, famous, famed, unforgettable, memorable, celebrated, distinguished, special, choice, noteworthy, notable, noted, important, conspicuous, exceptional, excellent, superior, first-class, first-rate, superb, remarkable, extraordinary, marvellous, sensational, *colloq.* smashing, super. **2** unsettled, ongoing, unresolved, unpaid, due, owed, owing, receivable, payable; remaining, leftover.

outstare /ówtstáir/ *v.tr.* **1** outdo in staring. **2** abash by staring.

outstation /ówtstaysh'n/ *n.* **1** a branch of an organization, enterprise, or business in a remote area or at a considerable distance from headquarters. **2** esp. *Austral.* & *NZ* part of a farming estate separate from the main estate.

outstay /ówtstáy/ *v.tr.* **1** stay beyond the limit of (one's welcome, invitation, etc.). **2** stay or endure longer than (another person etc.).

outstep /ówtstép/ *v.tr.* (**-stepped, -stepping**) step outside or beyond.

outstretch /ówtstréch/ *v.tr.* **1** (usu. as **outstretched** *adj.*) reach out or stretch out (esp. one's hands or arms). **2** reach or stretch further than.

outstrip /ówtstríp/ *v.tr.* (**-stripped, -stripping**) **1** pass in running etc. **2** surpass in competition or relative progress or ability.
■ overcome, surpass, outdo, outperform, outshine, outclass, better, beat, transcend, best, worst, exceed, excel, outdistance, overtake, top, cap, put in the shade, eclipse, overshadow.

out-swinger /ówtswingər/ *n.* a ball that swings away from the batsman.

out-take /ówt-tayk/ *n.* a length of film or tape rejected in editing.

out-talk /ówt-táwk/ *v.tr.* outdo or overcome in talking.

out-think /ówt-thíngk/ *v.tr.* (*past* and *past part.* **-thought**) outwit; outdo in thinking.

out-thrust *adj., v.,* & *n.* ● *adj.* /ówt-thrúst/ extended; projected (*ran forward with out-thrust arms*). ● *v.tr.* /ówt-thrúst/ (*past* and *past part.* **-thrust**) thrust out. ● *n.* /ówt-thrust/ **1** the act or an instance of thrusting forcibly outward. **2** the act or an instance of becoming prominent or noticeable.

out-top /ówt-tóp/ *v.tr.* (**-topped, -topping**) surmount, surpass in height, extent, etc.

out-tray /ówt-tray/ *n.* a tray for outgoing documents, letters, etc.

out-turn /ówt-turn/ *n.* **1** the quantity produced. **2** the result of a process or sequence of events.

outvalue /ówtvályoo/ *v.tr.* (**-values, -valued, -valuing**) be of greater value than.

outvote /ówtvṓt/ *v.tr.* defeat by a majority of votes.

outwalk /ówtwáwk/ *v.tr.* **1** outdo in walking. **2** walk beyond.

outward /ówtwərd/ *adj., adv.,* & *n.* ● *adj.* **1** situated on or directed towards the outside. **2** going out (*on the outward voyage*). **3** bodily, external, apparent, superficial (*in all outward respects*). **4** *archaic* outer (*the outward man*). ● *adv.* (also **outwards**) in an outward direction; towards the outside. ● *n.* the outward appearance of something; the exterior. □ **outward bound 1** (of a ship, passenger, etc.) going away from home. **2** (**Outward Bound**) (in the UK) a movement to provide adventure training, naval training, and other outdoor activities for young people. **outward form** appearance. **outward things** the world around us. **to outward seeming** apparently. □□ **outwardly** *adv.* [OE *ūtweard* (as OUT, -WARD)]
■ *adj.* **1, 3** external, exterior, outer, outside, outlying, manifest, obvious, evident, apparent, visible, observable; superficial, surface, extrinsic, skin-deep, shallow, pretended, false, ostensible, formal, physical, bodily, fleshly, carnal, mundane, worldly, secular, temporal, terrestrial, material, non-spiritual. ● *adv.* outwards, outside, away, out, *archaic* without. □□ **outwardly** externally, apparently, visibly, superficially, ostensibly, evidently, seemingly, on the surface, to all appearances, to outward seeming.

outwardness /ówtwərdniss/ *n.* **1** external existence; objectivity. **2** an interest or belief in outward things, objective-mindedness.

outwards var. of OUTWARD *adv.*

outwash /ówtwosh/ *n.* the material carried from a glacier by melt water and deposited beyond the moraine.

outwatch /ówtwóch/ *v.tr.* **1** watch more than or longer than. **2** *archaic* keep awake beyond the end of (night etc.).

outwear *v.* & *n.* ● *v.tr.* /ówtwáir/ (*past* **-wore**; *past part.* **-worn**) **1** exhaust; wear out; wear away. **2** live or last beyond the duration of. **3** (as **outworn** *adj.*) out of date, obsolete. ● *n.* /ówtwair/ outer clothing.

▪ **3** (**outworn**) see *out of date* (DATE[1]).

outweigh /ówtwáy/ *v.tr.* exceed in weight, value, importance, or influence.

▪ overcome, outbalance, overbalance, tip the scales, preponderate over, surpass, prevail over, override, take precedence over, compensate for, (more than) make up for.

outwent *past* of OUTGO.

outwit /ówtwít/ *v.tr.* (**-witted**, **-witting**) be too clever or crafty for; deceive by greater ingenuity.

▪ see OUTSMART.

outwith /ówtwíth/ *prep. Sc.* outside, beyond.

outwore *past* of OUTWEAR.

outwork /ówtwurk/ *n.* **1** an advanced or detached part of a fortification. **2** work done outside the shop or factory which supplies it. ▫▫ **outworker** *n.* (in sense 2).

outworn *past part.* of OUTWEAR.

ouzel /ŏŏz'l/ *n.* (also **ousel**) **1** = *ring ouzel* (see RING[1]). **2** = *water ouzel.* **3** *archaic* a blackbird. [OE *ōsle* blackbird, of unkn. orig.]

ouzo /ŏŏzō/ *n.* (*pl.* **-os**) a Greek aniseed-flavoured spirit. [mod.Gk]

ova *pl.* of OVUM.

oval /ṓv'l/ *adj.* & *n.* ● *adj.* **1** egg-shaped, ellipsoidal. **2** having the outline of an egg, elliptical. ● *n.* **1** an egg-shaped or elliptical closed curve. **2** any object with an oval outline. **3** *Austral.* a ground for Australian Rules football. ▫ **Oval Office** the office of the US President in the White House. ▫▫ **ovality** /ōválliti/ *n.* **ovally** *adv.* **ovalness** *n.* [med.L *ovalis* (as OVUM)]

▪ *adj.* egg-shaped, ovoid, oviform, *Biol.* obovate, ovate; elliptical, ellipsoid(al), *Geom.* oblate.

ovary /ṓvəri/ *n.* (*pl.* **-ies**) **1** each of the female reproductive organs in which ova are produced. **2** the hollow base of the carpel of a flower, containing one or more ovules. ▫▫ **ovarian** /ōváiriən/ *adj.* **ovariectomy** /-ri-éktəmi/ *n.* (*pl.* **-ies**) (in sense 1). **ovariotomy** /-ri-óttəmi/ *n.* (*pl.* **-ies**) (in sense 1). **ovaritis** /-rī́tiss/ *n.* (in sense 1). [mod.L *ovarium* (as OVUM)]

ovate /ṓvayt/ *adj. Biol.* egg-shaped as a solid or in outline; oval. [L *ovatus* (as OVUM)]

ovation /ōváysh'n/ *n.* **1** an enthusiastic reception, esp. spontaneous and sustained applause. **2** *Rom. Antiq.* a lesser form of triumph. ▫ **standing ovation** prolonged applause during which the crowd or audience rise to their feet. ▫▫ **ovational** *adj.* [L *ovatio* f. *ovare* exult]

▪ **1** applause, acclamation, acclaim, plaudits, cheers, cheering, clapping, praise, *colloq.* (big) hand, *formal* laudation.

oven /úvv'n/ *n.* **1** an enclosed compartment of brick, stone, or metal for cooking food. **2** a chamber for heating or drying. **3** a small furnace or kiln used in chemistry, metallurgy, etc. ▫ **oven-ready** (of food) prepared before sale so as to be ready for immediate cooking in the oven. [OE *ofen* f. Gmc]

ovenbird /úvv'nburd/ *n.* any Central or S. American bird of the family Furnariidae, many of which make domed nests.

ovenproof /úvv'nprŏŏf/ *adj.* suitable for use in an oven; heat-resistant.

ovenware /úvv'nwair/ *n.* dishes that can be used for cooking food in the oven.

over /ṓvər/ *adv.*, *prep.*, *n.*, & *adj.* ● *adv.* expressing movement or position or state above or beyond something stated or implied: **1** outward and downward from a brink or from any erect position (*knocked the man over*). **2** so as to cover or touch a whole surface (*paint it over*). **3** so as to produce a fold, or reverse a position; with the effect of being upside down. **4 a** across a street or other space (*decided to cross over; came over from America*). **b** for a visit etc. (*invited them over last night*). **5** with transference or change from one hand or part to another (*went over to the enemy; swapped them over*). **6** with motion above something; so as to pass across something (*climb over; fly over; boil over*). **7 a** from beginning to end with repetition or detailed concentration (*think it over; did it six times over*). **b** esp. *US* again, once more. **8** in excess; more than is right or required (*left over*). **9** for or until a later time (*hold it over*). **10** at an end; settled (*the crisis is over; all is over between us*). **11** (in full **over to you**) (as *int.*) (in radio conversations etc.) said to indicate that it is the other person's turn to speak. **12** (as *int.*) *Cricket* an umpire's call to change ends. ● *prep.* **1** above, in, or to a position higher than; upon. **2** out and down from; down from the edge of (*fell over the cliff*). **3** so as to cover (*a hat over his eyes*). **4** above and across; so as to clear (*flew over the North Pole; a bridge over the Thames*). **5** concerning; engaged with; as a result of; while occupied with (*laughed over a good joke; fell asleep over the newspaper*). **6 a** in superiority of; superior to; in charge of (*a victory over the enemy; reign over three kingdoms*). **b** in preference to. **7** divided by. **8 a** throughout; covering the extent of (*travelled over most of Africa; a blush spread over his face*). **b** so as to deal with completely (*went over the plans*). **9 a** for the duration of (*stay over Saturday night*). **b** at any point during the course of (*I'll do it over the weekend*). **10** beyond; more than (*bids of over £50; are you over 18?*). **11** transmitted by (*heard it over the radio*). **12** in comparison with (*gained 20% last year*). **13** having recovered from (*am now over my cold; will get over it in time*). ● *n. Cricket* **1** a sequence of balls (now usu. six), bowled from one end of the pitch. **2** play resulting from this (*a maiden over*). ● *adj.* (see also OVER-). **1** upper, outer. **2** superior. **3** extra. ▫ **begin** (or **start** etc.) **over** *US* begin again. **get it over with** do or undergo something unpleasant etc. so as to be rid of it. **give over** (usu. as *int.*) *colloq.* stop talking. **not over** not very; not at all (*not over friendly*). **over again** once again, again from the beginning. **over against** in an opposite situation to; adjacent to, in contrast with. **over-age** over a certain age limit. **over all** taken as a whole. **over and above** in addition to; not to mention (*£100 over and above the asking price*). **over and over** so that the same thing or the same point comes up again and again (*said it over and over; rolled it over and over*). **over the fence** *Austral.* & *NZ sl.* unreasonable; unfair; indecent. **over one's head** see HEAD. **over the hill** see HILL. **over the moon** see MOON. **over-the-top** *colloq.* (esp. of behaviour, dress, etc.) outrageous, excessive. **over the way** (in a street etc.) facing or opposite. [OE *ofer* f. Gmc]

▪ *adv.* **1** down, to the ground *or* floor. **4** across. **7 a** see THROUGH *adv.* **b** (once) again, once more, one more time. **8** remaining, as a remainder, as surplus, outstanding. **10** over and done with, done (with), finished, terminated, concluded, ended, past, settled, closed, at an end, over with. ● *prep.* **1** above, on, upon, on top of, atop. **3, 4** across **5** see ABOUT *prep.* 1, *in the middle of* (MIDDLE). **8, 9** for, during, in *or* over *or* during the course of, throughout; (all) through, (all) about, all over. **10** more than, greater than, upwards of, in excess of, (over and) above, (over and) beyond; exceeding. ▫ **over and above** on top of, not to mention; see also BESIDES *prep.* **over and over** see *repeatedly* (REPEAT). **over the fence** see UNREASONABLE 1. **over-the-top** see UNREASONABLE 1, CAMP[2] *adj.* 3. **over the way** across the street, over the road, facing, opposite, on the other side.

over- /ṓvər/ *prefix* added to verbs, nouns, adjectives, and adverbs, meaning: **1** excessively; to an unwanted degree (*overheat; overdue*). **2** upper, outer, extra (*overcoat; overtime*). **3** 'over' in various senses (*overhang; overshadow*). **4** completely, utterly (*overawe; overjoyed*).

over-abundant /ṓvərəbúndənt/ *adj.* in excessive quantity. □□ **over-abound** /-əbównd/ *v.intr.* **over-abundance** *n.* **over-abundantly** *adv.*

overachieve /ṓvərəchéev/ *v.* **1** *intr.* do more than might be expected (esp. scholastically). **2** *tr.* achieve more than (an expected goal or objective etc.). □□ **overachievement** *n.* **overachiever** *n.*

overact /ṓvərákt/ *v.tr.* & *intr.* act in an exaggerated manner.
■ see OVERDO 1.

over-active /ṓvəráktiv/ *adj.* excessively active. □□ **over-activity** /-tívviti/ *n.*
■ see HECTIC *adj.* 1.

overage /ṓvərij/ *n.* a surplus or excess, esp. an amount greater than estimated.
■ see SURPLUS *n.*

overall *adj.*, *adv.*, & *n.* ● *adj.* /ṓvərawl/ **1** from end to end (*overall length*). **2** total, inclusive of all (*overall cost*). ● *adv.* /ṓvəráwl/ in all parts; taken as a whole (*overall, the performance was excellent*). ● *n.* /ṓvərawl/ **1** *Brit.* an outer garment worn to keep out dirt, wet, etc. **2** (in *pl.*) protective trousers, dungarees, or a combination suit, worn by workmen etc. **3** *Brit.* close-fitting trousers worn as part of army uniform. □□ **overalled** /ṓvərawld/ *adj.*
■ *adj.* **2** total, complete, comprehensive, all-inclusive, inclusive, whole, entire, all-embracing, blanket.

overambitious /ṓvərambíshəss/ *adj.* excessively ambitious. □□ **overambition** *n.* **overambitiously** *adv.*
■ see AMBITIOUS 1a.

over-anxious /ṓvərángkshəss/ *adj.* excessively anxious. □□ **over-anxiety** /-angzī́-iti/ *n.* **over-anxiously** *adv.*

overarch /ṓvəraárch/ *v.tr.* form an arch over. □□ **overarching** *adj.*

overarm /ṓvəraarm/ *adj.* & *adv.* **1** *Cricket* & *Tennis* etc. with the hand above the shoulder (*bowl it overarm; an overarm service*). **2** *Swimming* with one or both arms lifted out of the water during a stroke.

overate *past* of OVEREAT.

overawe /ṓvəráw/ *v.tr.* **1** restrain by awe. **2** keep in awe.
■ overwhelm, intimidate, cow, daunt, awe, bully, hector, browbeat, dominate, domineer, frighten, scare, terrify, disconcert, discomfit, abash.

overbalance /ṓvərbálləns/ *v.* & *n.* ● *v.* **1** *tr.* cause (a person or thing) to lose its balance and fall. **2** *intr.* fall over, capsize. **3** *tr.* outweigh. ● *n.* **1** an excess. **2** the amount of this.
■ *v.* **3** see OUTWEIGH.

overbear /ṓvərbáir/ *v.tr.* (*past* **-bore**; *past part.* **-borne**) **1** (as **overbearing** *adj.*) **a** domineering, masterful. **b** overpowering. **2** bear down; upset by weight, force, or emotional pressure. **3** put down or repress by power or authority. **4** surpass in importance etc., outweigh. □□ **overbearingly** *adv.* **overbearingness** *n.*
■ **1 a** (**overbearing**) repressive, domineering, masterful, bullying, imperious, officious, high and mighty, high-handed, overweening, magisterial, lordly, authoritarian, wilful, despotic, dogmatic, autocratic, tyrannical, dictatorial, peremptory, arbitrary, assertive, arrogant, cavalier, haughty, superior, supercilious, hoity-toity, *colloq.* bossy, pushy, highfalutin, snooty, snotty. □□ **overbearingly** see *imperatively* (IMPERATIVE).

overbid *v.* & *n.* ● *v.* /ṓvərbíd/ (**-bidding**; *past* and *past part.* **-bid**) **1** *tr.* make a higher bid than. **2** *tr.* (also *absol.*) *Bridge* **a** bid more on (one's hand) than warranted. **b** overcall. ● *n.* /ṓvərbid/ a bid that is higher than another, or higher than is justified. □□ **overbidder** *n.*

overblouse /ṓvərblowz/ *n.* a garment like a blouse, but worn without tucking it into a skirt or trousers.

overblown /ṓvərblṓn/ *adj.* **1** excessively inflated or pretentious. **2** (of a flower or a woman's beauty etc.) past its prime.
■ **1** see IMMODERATE.

overboard /ṓvərbórd/ *adv.* from on a ship into the water (*fall overboard*). □ **go overboard 1** be highly enthusiastic. **2** behave immoderately; go too far. **throw overboard** abandon, discard.

overbold /ṓvərbṓld/ *adj.* excessively bold.

overbook /ṓvərbŏ́ŏk/ *v.tr.* (also *absol.*) make too many bookings for (an aircraft, hotel, etc.).

overboot /ṓvərbōōt/ *n.* a boot worn over another boot or shoe.

overbore *past* of OVERBEAR.

overborne *past part.* of OVERBEAR.

overbought *past* and *past part.* of OVERBUY.

overbrim /ṓvərbrím/ *v.* (**-brimmed**, **-brimming**) **1** *tr.* flow over the brim of. **2** *intr.* (of a vessel or liquid) overflow at the brim.

overbuild /ṓvərbíld/ *v.tr.* (*past* and *past part.* **-built**) **1** build over or upon. **2** place too many buildings on (land etc.).

overburden /ṓvərbúrd'n/ *v.* & *n.* ● *v.tr.* burden (a person, thing, etc.) to excess. ● *n.* **1** rock etc. that must be removed prior to mining the mineral deposit beneath it. **2** an excessive burden. □□ **overburdensome** *adj.*
■ *v.* see OVERLOAD *v.* ● *n.* **2** see OVERLOAD *n.*

overbusy /ṓvərbízzi/ *adj.* excessively busy.

overbuy /ṓvərbī́/ *v.tr.* & *intr.* (*past* and *past part.* **-bought**) buy (a commodity etc.) in excess of immediate need.

overcall *v.* & *n.* ● *v.tr.* /ṓvərkáwl/ (also *absol.*) *Bridge* **1** make a higher bid than (a previous bid or opponent). **2** *Brit.* = OVERBID *v.* 2a. ● *n.* /ṓvərkawl/ an act or instance of overcalling.

overcame *past* of OVERCOME.

overcapacity /ṓvərkəpássiti/ *n.* a state of saturation or an excess of productive capacity.

overcapitalize /ṓvərkáppitəlīz/ *v.tr.* (also **-ise**) fix or estimate the capital of (a company etc.) too high.

overcareful /ṓvərkáirfŏŏl/ *adj.* excessively careful. □□ **overcarefully** *adv.*

overcast /ṓvərkaást/ *adj.*, *v.*, & *n.* ● *adj.* **1** (of the sky, weather, etc.) covered with cloud; dull and gloomy. **2** (in sewing) edged with stitching to prevent fraying. ● *v.tr.* (*past* and *past part.* **-cast**) **1** cover (the sky etc.) with clouds or darkness. **2** stitch over (a raw edge etc.) to prevent fraying. ● *n.* /ṓvərkaast/ a cloud covering part of the sky.
■ *adj.* **1** cloudy, clouded, sunless, moonless, starless, murky, grey, louring, dull, dark, darkened, dreary, sombre, gloomy, dismal, threatening, menacing.

overcautious /ṓvərkáwshəss/ *adj.* excessively cautious. □□ **overcaution** *n.* **overcautiously** *adv.* **overcautiousness** *n.*

overcharge /ṓvərchaárj/ *v.* & *n.* ● *v.tr.* **1 a** charge too high a price to (a person) or for (a thing). **b** charge (a specified sum) beyond the right price. **2** put too much charge into (a battery, gun, etc.). **3** put exaggerated or excessive detail into (a description, picture, etc.). ● *n.* an excessive charge (of explosive, money, etc.).
■ *v.* **1** see FLEECE *v.* 1.

overcheck /ṓvərchek/ *n.* **1** a combination of two different-sized check patterns. **2** a cloth with this pattern.

overcloud /ṓvərklówd/ *v.tr.* **1** cover with cloud. **2** mar, spoil, or dim, esp. as the result of anxiety etc. (*overclouded by uncertainties*). **3** make obscure.

overcoat /ṓvərkōt/ *n.* **1** a heavy coat, esp. one worn over indoor clothes for warmth outdoors in cold weather. **2** a protective coat of paint etc.
■ **1** see COAT *n.* 1.

overcome /ṓvərkúm/ *v.* (*past* **-came**; *past part.* **-come**) **1** *tr.* prevail over, master, conquer. **2** *tr.* (as **overcome** *adj.*) **a** exhausted, made helpless. **b** (usu. foll. by *with*, *by*) affected by (emotion etc.). **3** *intr.* be victorious. [OE *ofercuman* (as OVER-, COME)]
■ **1** beat, defeat, conquer, overpower, subdue, worst, triumph over, win over, prevail over, overthrow, overwhelm, get the better *or* best of, whip, drub, rout, break, subjugate, suppress, crush, master, *colloq.* lick, best, *literary* vanquish. **2** (**overcome**) beaten, defeated, exhausted, overwhelmed, subdued, worsted, bested;

affected, speechless, swept off one's feet, helpless, overpowered, moved, influenced, at a loss (for words), *colloq.* bowled over, flabbergasted, *sl.* gobsmacked.

overcompensate /ṓvərkómpensayt/ *v.* **1** *tr.* (usu. foll. by *for*) compensate excessively for (something). **2** *intr. Psychol.* strive for power etc. in an exaggerated way, esp. to make allowance or amends for a real or fancied grievance, defect, handicap, etc. ▫▫ **overcompensation** /-sáysh'n/ *n.* **overcompensatory** /-sáytəri/ *adj.*

overconfident /ṓvərkónfid'nt/ *adj.* excessively confident. ▫▫ **overconfidence** *n.* **overconfidently** *adv.*

■ brash, arrogant, cocksure, cocky, brazen, hubristic, swaggering, audacious, overbearing, *colloq.* pushy, *literary* vainglorious; heedless, foolhardy, thoughtless, short-sighted, hasty.

overcook /ṓvərkŏŏk/ *v.tr.* cook too much or for too long. ▫▫ **overcooked** *adj.*

■ see BURN[1] *v.* 5.

overcritical /ṓvərkríttik'l/ *adj.* excessively critical; quick to find fault.

■ supercritical, hypercritical, captious, carping, niggling, cavilling, querulous, fault-finding, finicky, fussy, hair-splitting, difficult, fastidious, harsh, severe, demanding, exacting, small, small-minded, *US* picayune, *colloq.* picky, nit-picking, pernickety.

overcrop /ṓvərkróp/ *v.tr.* (**-cropped, -cropping**) exhaust (the land) by the continuous growing of crops.

overcrowd /ṓvərkrówd/ *v.tr.* (often as **overcrowded** *adj.*) fill (a space, object, etc.) beyond what is usual or comfortable. ▫▫ **overcrowding** *n.*

■ see CRAM 1; (**overcrowded**) jammed, packed, crowded, congested.

over-curious /ṓvərkyŏŏriəss/ *adj.* excessively curious. ▫▫ **over-curiosity** /ṓvərkyooriόssiti/ *n.* **over-curiously** *adv.*

over-delicate /ṓvərdéllikət/ *adj.* excessively delicate. ▫▫ **over-delicacy** *n.*

overdevelop /ṓvərdivélləp/ *v.tr.* (**-developed, -developing**) **1** develop too much. **2** *Photog.* treat with developer for too long.

overdo /ṓvərdŏŏ/ *v.tr.* (*3rd sing. present* **-does**; *past* **-did**; *past part.* **-done**) **1** carry to excess, take too far, exaggerate (*I think you overdid the sarcasm*). **2** (esp. as **overdone** *adj.*) overcook. ▫ **overdo it** (or **things**) exhaust oneself. [OE *oferdōn* (as OVER-, DO[1])]

■ **1** take *or* carry to excess, take *or* carry to extremes, exaggerate, carry *or* take too far, not know when to stop, go overboard with, do to death; overindulge in. **2** see BURN[1] *v.* 5. ▫ **overdo it** (or **things**) overwork, do too much, overtax *or* overload *or* overburden oneself, exhaust oneself, bite off more than one can chew, burn the candle at both ends.

overdose /ṓvərdōss/ *n.* & *v.* ● *n.* an excessive dose (of a drug etc.). ● *v.tr.* give an excessive dose of (a drug etc.) or to (a person). ▫▫ **overdosage** /ṓvərdṓsij/ *n.*

overdraft /ṓvərdraaft/ *n.* **1** a deficit in a bank account caused by drawing more money than is credited to it. **2** the amount of this.

overdraw /ṓvərdráw/ *v.* (*past* **-drew**; *past part.* **-drawn**) **1** *tr.* **a** draw a sum of money in excess of the amount credited to (one's bank account). **b** (as **overdrawn** *adj.*) having overdrawn one's account. **2** *intr.* overdraw one's account. **3** *tr.* exaggerate in describing or depicting. ▫▫ **overdrawer** *n.* (in senses 1 & 2).

■ **3** see EXAGGERATE 1.

overdress *v.* & *n.* ● *v.* /ṓvərdréss/ **1** *tr.* dress with too much display or formality. **2** *intr.* overdress oneself. ● *n.* /ṓvərdress/ a dress worn over another dress or a blouse etc.

overdrink /ṓvərdríngk/ *v.intr.* & *refl.* (*past* **-drank**; *past part.* **-drunk**) drink too much.

overdrive /ṓvərdrīv/ *n.* **1 a** a mechanism in a motor vehicle providing a gear ratio higher than that of the usual gear. **b** an additional speed-increasing gear. **2** (usu. prec. by *in*, *into*) a state of high or excessive activity.

overdub *v.* & *n.* ● *v.tr.* /ṓvərdúb/ (**-dubbed, -dubbing**) (also *absol.*) impose (additional sounds) on an existing recording. ● *n.* /ṓvərdub/ the act or an instance of overdubbing.

overdue /ṓvərdyŏŏ/ *adj.* **1** past the time when due or ready. **2** not yet paid, arrived, born, etc., though after the expected time. **3** (of a library book etc.) retained longer than the period allowed.

■ late, tardy, behindhand, behind, unpunctual, belated, past due.

overeager /ṓvəreégər/ *adj.* excessively eager. ▫▫ **over-eagerly** *adv.* **overeagerness** *n.*

overeat /ṓvəreét/ *v.intr.* & *refl.* (*past* **-ate**; *past part.* **-eaten**) eat too much.

■ gorge, surfeit, gormandize, stuff oneself, overindulge, guzzle, feast, make a pig of oneself, *sl.* binge, *US sl.* pig out.

overelaborate /ṓvərilábbərət/ *adj.* excessively elaborate. ▫▫ **overelaborately** *adv.*

over-emotional /ṓvərimṓshən'l/ *adj.* excessively emotional. ▫▫ **over-emotionally** *adv.*

■ see SENTIMENTAL.

overemphasis /ṓvərémfəsiss/ *n.* excessive emphasis. ▫▫ **overemphasize** /-fəsīz/ *v.tr.* & *intr.* (also **-ise**).

■ see *exaggeration* (EXAGGERATE). ▫▫ **overemphasize** see EXAGGERATE 1.

overenthusiasm /ṓvərinthyŏŏziaz'm, -thŏŏziaz'm/ *n.* excessive enthusiasm. ▫▫ **overenthusiastic** /-ziástik/ *adj.* **overenthusiastically** /-ziástikəli/ *adv.*

overestimate /ṓvəréstimayt/ *v.* & *n.* ● *v.tr.* (also *absol.*) form too high an estimate of (a person, ability, cost, etc.). ● *n.* too high an estimate. ▫▫ **overestimation** /-máysh'n/ *n.*

■ *v.* see MISCALCULATE.

overexcite /ṓvəriksīt/ *v.tr.* excite excessively. ▫▫ **overexcitement** *n.*

over-exercise /ṓvəréksərsīz/ *v.* & *n.* ● *v.* **1** *tr.* use or exert (a part of the body, one's authority, etc.) too much. **2** *intr.* take too much exercise; overexert oneself. ● *n.* excessive exercise.

overexert /ṓvərigzért/ *v.tr.* & *refl.* exert too much. ▫▫ **overexertion** /-zérsh'n/ *n.*

overexpose /ṓvərikspṓz/ *v.tr.* (also *absol.*) **1** expose too much, esp. to the public eye. **2** *Photog.* expose (film) for too long a time. ▫▫ **overexposure** *n.*

overextend /ṓvərikstén d/ *v.tr.* **1** extend (a thing) too far. **2** (also *refl.*) take on (oneself) or impose on (another person) an excessive burden of work.

■ **1** see EXCEED 2. **2** see STRETCH *v.* 6.

overfall /ṓvərfawl/ *n.* **1** a turbulent stretch of sea etc. caused by a strong current or tide over a submarine ridge, or by a meeting of currents. **2** a place provided on a dam, weir, etc. for the overflow of surplus water.

overfamiliar /ṓvərfəmílliər/ *adj.* excessively familiar.

overfatigue /ṓvərfəteég/ *n.* excessive fatigue.

overfeed /ṓvərfeéd/ *v.tr.* (*past* and *past part.* **-fed**) feed excessively.

■ see STUFF *v.* 5a.

overfill /ṓvərfil/ *v.tr.* & *intr.* fill to excess or to overflowing.

■ see SATE 2.

overfine /ṓvərfīn/ *adj.* excessively fine; too precise.

overfish /ṓvərfish/ *v.tr.* deplete (a stream etc.) by too much fishing.

overflow *v.* & *n.* ● *v.* /ṓvərflṓ/ **1** *tr.* **a** flow over (the brim, limits, etc.). **b** flow over the brim or limits of. **2** *intr.* **a** (of a receptacle etc.) be so full that the contents overflow it (*until the cup was overflowing*). **b** (of contents) overflow a container. **3** *tr.* (of a crowd etc.) extend beyond the limits of (a room etc.). **4** *tr.* flood (a surface or area). **5** *intr.* (foll. by *with*) be full of. **6** *intr.* (of kindness, a harvest, etc.) be very abundant. ● *n.* /ṓvərflō/ (also *attrib.*) **1** what overflows or is superfluous (*mop up the overflow; put the overflow audience in another room*). **2** an instance of overflowing (*overflow occurs when* *both systems are run together*). **3** (esp. in a bath or sink) an outlet for excess water etc. **4** *Computing* the generation of a number having more digits than the assigned location. □ **overflow meeting** a meeting for those who cannot be accommodated at the main gathering. [OE *oferflōwan* (as OVER-, FLOW)]

■ *v.* **1** see *run over* 1. **2** see *brim over*. **3** see FILL *v.* 2. **4** see FLOOD *v.* 1. **5** (*overflow with*) see TEEM[1] *v.* 2. **6** (*overflow with*) see ABOUND 2. ● *n.* **1** see EXCESS *n.* 1. **2** see FLOOD *n.* 1.

overfly /ṓvərflī́/ *v.tr.* (**-flies**; *past* **-flew**; *past part.* **-flown**) fly over or beyond (a place or territory). □□ **overflight** /ṓvərflīt/ *n.*

overfold /ṓvərfōld/ *n.* a series of strata folded so that the middle part is upside down.

overfond /ṓvərfónd/ *adj.* (often foll. by *of*) having too great an affection or liking (for a person or thing) (*overfond of chocolate*; *an overfond parent*). □□ **overfondly** *adv.* **overfondness** *n.*

overfulfil /ṓvərfŏŏlfíl/ *v.tr.* (*US* **-fulfill**) (**-fulfilled, -fulfilling**) fulfil (a plan, quota, etc.) beyond expectation or before the appointed time. □□ **overfulfilment** *n.*

overfull /ṓvərfŏŏl/ *adj.* filled excessively or to overflowing.

overgeneralize /ṓvərjénnərəlīz/ *v.* (also **-ise**) **1** *intr.* draw general conclusions from inadequate data etc. **2** *intr.* argue more widely than is justified by the available evidence, by circumstances, etc. **3** *tr.* draw an over-general conclusion from (data, circumstances, etc.). □□ **overgeneralization** /-záysh'n/ *n.*

overgenerous /ṓvərjénnərəss/ *adj.* excessively generous. □□ **overgenerously** *adv.*

overglaze /ṓvərglayz/ *n.* & *adj.* ● *n.* **1** a second glaze applied to ceramic ware. **2** decoration on a glazed surface. ● *adj.* (of painting etc.) done on a glazed surface.

overground /ṓvərgrownd/ *adj.* **1** raised above the ground. **2** not underground.

overgrow /ṓvərgrṓ/ *v.tr.* (*past* **-grew**; *past part.* **-grown**) **1** (as **overgrown** *adj.* /ṓvərgrṓn/) **a** abnormally large (*a great overgrown child*). **b** wild; grown over with vegetation (*an overgrown pond*). **2** grow over, overspread, esp. so as to choke (*nettles have overgrown the pathway*). **3** grow too big for (one's strength etc.). □□ **overgrowth** *n.*

■ **1** (**overgrown**) **a** see ENORMOUS, TALL *adj.* 1. **b** covered, overrun, wild, overspread, luxuriant, weedy, abundant.

overhand /ṓvərhand/ *adj.* & *adv.* **1** (in cricket, tennis, baseball, etc.) thrown or played with the hand above the shoulder. **2** *Swimming* = OVERARM. **3 a** with the palm of the hand downward or inward. **b** with the hand above the object held. □ **overhand knot** a simple knot made by forming a loop and passing the free end through it.

overhang *v.* & *n.* ● *v.* /ṓvərháng/ (*past* and *past part.* **-hung**) **1** *tr.* & *intr.* project or hang over. **2** *tr.* menace, preoccupy, threaten. ● *n.* /ṓvərhang/ **1** the overhanging part of a structure or rock-formation. **2** the amount by which this projects.

■ *v.* **1** jut (out), beetle, bulge (out), project (out), protrude, stick out, loom (out), extend (out), impend, hang (out) over. **2** threaten, menace, imperil; preoccupy. ● *n.* ledge; projection, bulge, protrusion, extension.

overhaste /ṓvərháyst/ *n.* excessive haste. □□ **overhasty** *adj.* **overhastily** *adv.*

■ □□ **overhasty** see PREMATURE 1.

overhaul *v.* & *n.* ● *v.tr.* /ṓvərháwl/ **1 a** take to pieces in order to examine. **b** examine the condition of (and repair if necessary). **2** overtake. ● *n.* /ṓvərhawl/ a thorough examination, with repairs if necessary. [orig. Naut., = release (rope-tackle) by slackening]

■ *v.* **1** strip (down), take to pieces *or* bits, take apart; renovate, refurbish, recondition, rebuild, restore, repair, service, adjust, patch (up), mend, fix (up). **2** overtake, pass, gain on *or* upon, draw ahead of, catch up (with), get ahead of, outstrip, outdistance, leave behind, lap. ● *n.* reconditioning, overhauling, refurbishing, rebuilding, renovation, servicing, service, repair, adjustment, mending, fixing (up); see EXAMINATION 1, 2.

overhead *adv.*, *adj.*, & *n.* ● *adv.* /ṓvərhéd/ **1** above one's head. **2** in the sky or in the storey above. ● *adj.* /ṓvərhed/ **1** (of a driving mechanism etc.) above the object driven. **2** (of expenses) arising from general running costs, as distinct from particular business transactions. ● *n.* /ṓvərhed/ (in *pl.* or *US* in *sing.*) overhead expenses. □ **overhead projector** a device that projects an enlarged image of a transparency on to a surface above and behind the user.

■ *adv.* over *or* above one's head, (up) above, (up) in the air *or* sky, high up, on high, aloft, skyward(s). ● *adj.* **1** elevated, raised, upper. ● *n.* (basic *or* fixed *or* running) costs, operating cost(s), expense(s), outlay, disbursement(s), expenditure(s), maintenance.

overhear /ṓvərhéer/ *v.tr.* (*past* and *past part.* **-heard**) (also *absol.*) hear as an eavesdropper or as an unperceived or unintentional listener.

overheat /ṓvərhéet/ *v.* **1** *tr.* & *intr.* make or become too hot; heat to excess. **2** *tr.* (as **overheated** *adj.*) too passionate about a matter.

overindulge /ṓvərindúlj/ *v.tr.* & *intr.* indulge to excess. □□ **overindulgence** *n.* **overindulgent** *adj.*

■ see OVERDO 1. □□ **overindulgence** see EXCESS *n.* 4. **overindulgent** see DISSOLUTE.

overinsure /ṓvərinshóor/ *v.tr.* insure (property etc.) for more than its real value; insure excessively. □□ **overinsurance** *n.*

overissue *v.* & *n.* ● *v.tr.* /ṓvəríshōō/ (**-issues, -issued, -issuing**) issue (notes, shares, etc.) beyond the authorized amount, or the ability to pay. ● *n.* /ṓvərishōō, -issyōō/ the notes, shares, etc., or the amount so issued.

overjoyed /ṓvərjóyd/ *adj.* (often foll. by *at*, *to hear*, etc.) filled with great joy.

■ delighted, ecstatic, elated, happy, rapturous, euphoric, jubilant, thrilled, cock-a-hoop, transported, in seventh heaven, over the moon, *colloq.* tickled pink *or* to death, on cloud nine *or* seven.

overkill /ṓvərkil/ *n.* & *v.* ● *n.* **1** the amount by which destruction or the capacity for destruction exceeds what is necessary for victory or annihilation. **2** excess; excessive behaviour. ● *v.tr.* & *intr.* kill or destroy to a greater extent than necessary.

overladen /ṓvərláyd'n/ *adj.* bearing or carrying too large a load.

overlaid *past* and *past part.* of OVERLAY[1].

overlain *past part.* of OVERLIE.

overland /ṓvərland/ *adj.*, *adv.*, & *v.* ● *adj.* & *adv.* /also ṓvərlánd/ **1** by land. **2** not by sea. ● *v. Austral.* **1** *tr.* drive (livestock) overland. **2** *intr.* go a long distance overland.

overlander /ṓvərlandər/ *n. Austral.* & *NZ* **1** a person who drives livestock overland. **2** *sl.* a tramp, a sundowner.

■ see TRAMP *n.* 1.

overlap *v.* & *n.* ● *v.* /ṓvərláp/ (**-lapped, -lapping**) **1** *tr.* (of part of an object) partly cover (another object). **2** *tr.* cover and extend beyond. **3** *intr.* (of two things) partly coincide; not be completely separate (*where psychology and philosophy overlap*). ● *n.* /ṓvərlap/ **1** an instance of overlapping. **2** the amount of this.

■ *v.* **1, 2** lap (over), overlie, overlay, imbricate. **3** coincide, correspond, intersect; see also MEET[1] *v.* 3. ● *n.* lap, flap, overlay; imbrication.

over-large /ṓvərlaárj/ *adj.* too large.

overlay[1] *v.* & *n.* ● *v.tr.* /ṓvərláy/ (*past* and *past part.* **-laid**) **1** lay over. **2** (foll. by *with*) cover the surface of (a thing) with (a coating etc.). **3** overlie. ● *n.* /ṓvərlay/ **1** a thing laid over another. **2** (in printing, mapreading, etc.) a transparent sheet to be superimposed on another sheet. **3** *Computing* **a** the process of transferring a block of data etc. to replace what is already stored. **b** a section so transferred. **4** a coverlet, small tablecloth, etc.

■ *v.* **1, 3** see OVERLAP *v.* 1, 2. **2** see SPREAD *v.* 4a. ● *n.* **1** see SKIN *n.* 4, OVERLAP *n.*

overlay[2] *past* of OVERLIE.

overleaf /ṓvərleéf/ *adv.* on the other side of the leaf (of a book) (*see the diagram overleaf*).

overleap /ṓvərleép/ *v.tr.* (*past* and *past part.* **-leaped** or **-leapt**) **1** leap over, surmount. **2** omit, ignore. [OE *oferhlēapan* (as OVER, LEAP)]

overlie /ṓvərlī́/ *v.tr.* (**-lying**; *past* **-lay**; *past part.* **-lain**) **1** lie on top of. **2** smother (a child etc.) by lying on top.

■ **1** see OVERLAP *v.* 1, 2.

overload *v.* & *n.* ● *v.tr.* /ṓvərlṓd/ load excessively; force (a person, thing, etc.) beyond normal or reasonable capacity. ● *n.* /ṓvərlōd/ an excessive quantity; a demand etc. which surpasses capability or capacity.

■ *v.* weigh down, burden, overburden, load (up), overtax, saddle, tax, strain, impede, handicap, oppress, encumber, overcharge, *literary* cumber. ● *n.* surcharge, overcharge, overburden; dead weight, oppression, handicap, tax, load, encumbrance, impediment, hindrance.

over-long /ṓvərlóng/ *adj.* & *adv.* too or excessively long.

■ ● *adj.* see LENGTHY 2.

overlook *v.* & *n.* ● *v.tr.* /ṓvərlŏŏk/ **1** fail to notice; ignore, condone (an offence etc.). **2** have a view from above, be higher than. **3** supervise, oversee. **4** bewitch with the evil eye. ● *n.* /ṓvərlŏŏk/ *US* a commanding position or view. □□ **overlooker** /ṓvərlŏŏkkər/ *n.*

■ *v.* **1** miss, slip up on, omit, neglect, slight, disregard, fail to notice, ignore, pass over, leave out, forget, *colloq.* pass up; blink at, wink at, let go (by), let pass, let ride, turn a blind eye to, shut one's eyes to, pretend not to notice, take no notice of, disregard, forgive, pardon, excuse, permit, allow, forget about, write off, condone, make allowances for, gloss over. **2** command a view of, look over.

overlord /ṓvərlord/ *n.* a supreme lord. □□ **overlordship** *n.*

overly /ṓvərli/ *adv.* esp. *US* & *Sc.* excessively; too.

■ excessively, too, exceedingly, immoderately, disproportionately, unduly, inordinately, extraordinarily, very, *colloq.* damned.

overlying *pres. part.* of OVERLIE.

overman *v.* & *n.* ● *v.tr.* /ṓvərmán/ (**-manned, -manning**) provide with too large a crew, staff, etc. ● *n.* /ṓvərman/ (*pl.* **-men**) **1** an overseer in a colliery. **2** *Philos.* = SUPERMAN.

overmantel /ṓvərmant'l/ *n.* ornamental shelves etc. over a mantelpiece.

over-many /ṓvərménni/ *adj.* too many; an excessive number.

overmaster /ṓvərmaástər/ *v.tr.* master completely, conquer. □□ **overmastering** *adj.* **overmastery** *n.*

overmatch /ṓvərmách/ *v.tr.* be more than a match for; defeat by superior strength etc.

overmeasure /ṓvərmezhər/ *n.* an amount beyond what is proper or sufficient.

over-much /ṓvərmúch/ *adv.* & *adj.* ● *adv.* to too great an extent; excessively. ● *adj.* excessive; superabundant.

over-nice /ṓvərnī́ss/ *adj.* excessively fussy, punctilious, particular, etc. □□ **over-niceness** *n.* **over-nicety** *n.*

■ see FINICKY 1.

overnight *adv.* & *adj.* ● *adv.* /ṓvərnī́t/ **1** for the duration of a night (*stay overnight*). **2** during the course of a night. **3** suddenly, immediately (*the situation changed overnight*). ● *adj.* /ṓvərnīt/ **1** for use overnight (*an overnight bag*). **2** done etc. overnight (*an overnight stop*).

overnighter /ṓvərnī́tər/ *n.* **1** a person who stops at a place overnight. **2** an overnight bag.

overpaid *past* and *past part.* of OVERPAY.

overparted /ṓvərpaártid/ *adj. Theatr.* having too demanding a part to play; cast beyond one's ability.

over-particular /ṓvərpərtikyoolər/ *adj.* excessively particular or fussy.

■ see FINICKY 1.

overpass *n.* & *v.* ● *n.* /ṓvərpaass/ a road or railway line that passes over another by means of a bridge. ● *v.tr.* /ṓvərpaáss/ **1** pass over or across or beyond. **2** get to the end of; surmount. **3** (as **overpassed** or **overpast** *adj.*) that has gone by, past.

overpay /ṓvərpáy/ *v.tr.* (*past* and *past part.* **-paid**) recompense (a person, service, etc.) too highly. □□ **overpayment** *n.*

overpitch /ṓvərpích/ *v.tr.* **1** *Cricket* bowl (a ball) so that it pitches or would pitch too near the stumps. **2** exaggerate.

overplay /ṓvərpláy/ *v.tr.* play (a part) to excess; give undue importance to; overemphasize. □ **overplay one's hand** **1** be unduly optimistic about one's capabilities. **2** spoil a good case by exaggerating its value.

■ see EXAGGERATE 1.

overplus /ṓvərpluss/ *n.* a surplus, a superabundance. [ME, partial transl. of AF *surplus* or med.L *su(pe)rplus*]

overpopulated /ṓvərpópyoolaytid/ *adj.* having too large a population. □□ **overpopulation** /-láysh'n/ *n.*

■ see *overcrowded* (OVERCROWD).

overpower /ṓvərpówr/ *v.tr.* **1** reduce to submission, subdue. **2** make (a thing) ineffective or imperceptible by greater intensity. **3** (of heat, emotion, etc.) be too intense for, overwhelm. □□ **overpowering** *adj.* **overpoweringly** *adv.*

■ **1** overcome, overwhelm, beat, conquer, defeat, crush, put down, worst, prevail, master, quell, subdue, subjugate, *colloq.* best, *literary* vanquish. **3** overcome, overwhelm, dumbfound, daze, stagger, amaze, stun, stupefy, nonplus, strike, *colloq.* floor. □□ **overpowering** overwhelming, irresistible, powerful, telling, compelling, unendurable, unbearable, oppressive.

overprice /ṓvərprī́ss/ *v.tr.* price (a thing) too highly.

overprint *v.* & *n.* ● *v.tr.* /ṓvərprínt/ **1** print further matter on (a surface already printed, esp. a postage stamp). **2** print (further matter) in this way. **3** *Photog.* print (a positive) darker than was intended. **4** (also *absol.*) print too many copies of (a work). ● *n.* /ṓvərprint/ **1** the words etc. overprinted. **2** an overprinted postage stamp.

overproduce /ṓvərprədyŏŏss/ *v.tr.* (usu. *absol.*) **1** produce more of (a commodity) than is wanted. **2** produce to an excessive degree. □□ **overproduction** *n.*

overproof /ṓvərprŏŏf/ *adj.* containing more alcohol than proof spirit does.

overprotective /ṓvərprətéktiv/ *adj.* excessively protective, esp. of a person in one's charge.

overqualified /ṓvərkwóllifīd/ *adj.* too highly qualified (esp. for a particular job etc.).

overran *past* of OVERRUN.

overrate /ṓvəráyt/ *v.tr.* assess too highly.

■ overvalue, overestimate, make too much of, overprize.

overreach /ṓvəreéch/ *v.tr.* circumvent, outwit; get the better of by cunning or artifice. □ **overreach oneself** **1** strain oneself by reaching too far. **2** defeat one's object by going too far.

overreact /ṓvəriákt/ *v.intr.* respond more forcibly etc. than is justified. □□ **overreaction** *n.*

■ make too much of a thing, make a mountain out of a molehill, lose all *or* one's sense of proportion, go overboard, go too far.

overrefine /ṓvərifī́n/ *v.tr.* (also *absol.*) **1** refine too much. **2** make too subtle distinctions in (an argument etc.).

override *v.* & *n.* ● *v.tr.* /ṓvərī́d/ (*past* **-rode**; *past part.* **-ridden**) **1** (often as **overriding** *adj.*) have or claim precedence or superiority over (*an overriding consideration*). **2 a** intervene and make ineffective. **b** interrupt the action of (an automatic device) esp. to take manual control. **3 a** trample down or underfoot. **b** supersede arrogantly. **4** extend over, esp. (of a part of a fractured bone) overlap (another part). **5** ride over (enemy country). **6** exhaust (a horse etc.) by hard riding. ● *n.* /ṓvərīd/ **1** the action or process of suspending an automatic function. **2** a device for this.

■ *v.* **1** see OUTWEIGH; (**overriding**) dominant, dominating, predominant, prevailing, preponderant, primary, prime, overruling, principal, main, chief. **2 a** see REVERSE *v.* 2, 5.

overrider /ṓvərīdər/ *n. Brit.* each of a pair of projecting pieces on the bumper of a car.

overripe /ṓvərīp/ *adj.* (esp. of fruit etc.) past its best; excessively ripe; full-blown.

overrode *past* of OVERRIDE.

overruff *v.* & *n.* ● *v.tr.* /ṓvərúf/ (also *absol.*) overtrump. ● *n.* /ṓvəruf/ an instance of this.

overrule /ṓvəróol/ *v.tr.* **1** set aside (a decision, argument, proposal, etc.) by exercising a superior authority. **2** annul a decision by or reject a proposal of (a person) in this way.

overrun *v.* & *n.* ● *v.tr.* /ṓvərún/ (**-running**; *past* **-ran**; *past part.* **-run**) **1** (of vermin, weeds, etc.) swarm or spread over. **2** conquer or ravage (territory) by force. **3** (of time, expenditure, production, etc.) exceed (a fixed limit). **4** *Printing* carry over (a word etc.) to the next line or page. **5** *Mech.* rotate faster than. **6** flood (land). ● *n.* /ṓvərun/ **1** an instance of overrunning. **2** the amount of this. **3** the movement of a vehicle at a speed greater than is imparted by the engine. [OE *oferyrnan* (as OVER-, RUN)]
■ *v.* **1, 2** invade, defeat, attack, ravage, destroy, overwhelm, conquer, harry, vandalize, plunder, scourge, sack, strip, pillage, storm, *colloq.* blitz, *literary* despoil.

oversailing /ṓvərsáyling/ *adj.* (of a part of a building) projecting beyond what is below. [OVER + F *saillir* SALLY[1]]

oversaw *past* of OVERSEE.

overscrupulous /ṓvərskróopyooləss/ *adj.* excessively scrupulous or particular.
■ see *pedantic* (PEDANT).

overseas *adv.* & *adj.* ● *adv.* /ṓvərséez/ (also **oversea**) abroad (*was sent overseas for training*; *came back from overseas*). ● *adj.* /ṓvərseez/ (also **oversea**) **1** foreign; across or beyond the sea. **2** of or connected with movement or transport over the sea (*overseas postage rates*).
■ *adv.* see ABROAD 1. ● *adj.* **1** see EXTERNAL *adj.* 2.

oversee /ṓvərsée/ *v.tr.* (**-sees**; *past* **-saw**; *past part.* **-seen**) officially supervise (workers, work, etc.). [OE *oferséon* look at from above (as OVER-, SEE[1])]
■ direct, manage, watch (over), keep an eye on, administer, superintend, run, supervise; handle, control.

overseer /ṓvərseer/ *n.* a person who supervises others, esp. workers. □ **overseer of the poor** *Brit. hist.* a parish official who administered funds to the poor. [OVERSEE]
■ superintendent, supervisor, manager, foreman, forewoman, chief, superior, *US* straw boss, *colloq.* boss, super, *Brit. colloq.* gaffer, *US sl.* honcho.

oversell /ṓvərsél/ *v.tr.* (*past* and *past part.* **-sold**) (also *absol.*) **1** sell more of (a commodity etc.) than one can deliver. **2** exaggerate the merits of.
■ **2** see MAXIMIZE.

over-sensitive /ṓvərsénsitiv/ *adj.* excessively sensitive; easily hurt by, or too quick to react to, outside influences. □□ **over-sensitiveness** *n.* **over-sensitivity** /-tívviti/ *n.*
■ see TOUCHY 1. □□ **over-sensitivity** see SENSITIVITY.

overset /ṓvərsét/ *v.tr.* (**-setting**; *past* and *past part.* **-set**) **1** overturn, upset. **2** *Printing* set up (type) in excess of the available space.

oversew /ṓvərsṓ/ *v.tr.* (*past part.* **-sewn** or **-sewed**) **1** sew (two edges) with every stitch passing over the join. **2** join the sections of (a book) by a stitch of this type.

oversexed /ṓvərsékst/ *adj.* having unusually strong sexual desires.

overshadow /ṓvərsháddō/ *v.tr.* **1** appear much more prominent or important than. **2 a** cast into the shade; shelter from the sun. **b** cast gloom over; mar, spoil. [OE *ofersceadwian* (as OVER-, SHADOW)]
■ **1** dominate, outshine, eclipse, dwarf, diminish, minimize, put in *or* throw into *or* leave in the shade, steal the limelight from, tower over *or* above, excel. **2 b** spoil, blight, ruin, mar, take (all) the pleasure from *or* out of, put a damper on, take the edge off, impair, take the enjoyment out of.

overshoe /ṓvərshoo/ *n.* a shoe of rubber, felt, etc., worn over another as protection from wet, cold, etc.

overshoot *v.* & *n.* ● *v.tr.* /ṓvərshóot/ (*past* and *past part.* **-shot**) **1** pass or send beyond (a target or limit). **2** (of an aircraft) fly beyond or taxi too far along (the runway) when landing or taking off. ● *n.* /ṓvərshoot/ **1** the act of overshooting. **2** the amount of this. □ **overshoot the mark** go beyond what is intended or proper; go too far. **overshot wheel** a waterwheel operated by the weight of water falling into buckets attached to its periphery.
■ *v.* **1** see PASS[1] *v.* 4.

overside /ṓvərsīd/ *adv.* over the side of a ship (into a smaller boat, or into the sea).

oversight /ṓvərsīt/ *n.* **1** a failure to notice something. **2** an inadvertent mistake. **3** supervision.
■ **1** carelessness, heedlessness, inadvertence, neglect, laxity, laxness, failure, dereliction. **2** error, mistake, slip, fault, omission, blunder. **3** supervision, superintendence, surveillance, management, direction, guidance, administration; charge, care, custody, keeping, hands, protection, auspices.

oversimplify /ṓvərsímplifī/ *v.tr.* (**-ies**, **-ied**) (also *absol.*) distort (a problem etc.) by stating it in too simple terms. □□ **oversimplification** /-fikáysh'n/ *n.*

oversize /ṓvərsīz/ *adj.* (also **-sized** /-sīzd/) of more than the usual size.
■ see LARGE *adj.* 1, 2.

overskirt /ṓvərskurt/ *n.* an outer or second skirt.

overslaugh /ṓvərslaw/ *n.* & *v.* ● *n. Brit. Mil.* the passing over of one's turn of duty. ● *v.tr.* **1** *Brit. Mil.* pass over (one's duty) in consideration of another duty that takes precedence. **2** *US* pass over in favour of another. **3** *US* omit to consider. [Du. *overslag* (n.) f. *overslaan* omit (as OVER, *slaan* strike)]

oversleep /ṓvərsléep/ *v.intr.* & *refl.* (*past* and *past part.* **-slept**) **1** continue sleeping beyond the intended time of waking. **2** sleep too long.

oversleeve /ṓvərsleev/ *n.* a protective sleeve covering an ordinary sleeve.

oversold *past* and *past part.* of OVERSELL.

oversolicitous /ṓvərsəlíssitəss/ *adj.* excessively worried, anxious, eager, etc. □□ **oversolicitude** *n.*

oversoul /ṓvərsōl/ *n.* God as a spirit animating the universe and including all human souls.

overspecialize /ṓvərspéshəlīz/ *v.intr.* (also **-ise**) concentrate too much on one aspect or area. □□ **overspecialization** /-záysh'n/ *n.*

overspend /ṓvərspénd/ *v.* (*past* and *past part.* **-spent**) **1** *intr.* & *refl.* spend too much. **2** *tr.* spend more than (a specified amount).

overspill /ṓvərspil/ *n.* **1** what is spilt over or overflows. **2** the surplus population leaving a country or city to live elsewhere.

overspread /ṓvərspréd/ *v.tr.* (*past* and *past part.* **-spread**) **1** become spread or diffused over. **2** cover or occupy the surface of. **3** (as **overspread** *adj.*) (usu. foll. by *with*) covered (*high mountains overspread with trees*). [OE *ofersprǣdan* (as OVER-, SPREAD)]
■ **1** see SPREAD *v.* 4a. **2** see COVER *v.* 2.

overstaff /ṓvərstáaf/ *v.tr.* provide with too large a staff.

overstate /ṓvərstáyt/ *v.tr.* **1** state (esp. a case or argument) too strongly. **2** exaggerate. □□ **overstatement** *n.*
■ exaggerate, magnify, hyperbolize, embroider, overstress, colour, make (too) much of, overdraw, overemphasize, stretch, enlarge, inflate, blow up.

overstay /ṓvərstáy/ *v.tr.* stay longer than (one's welcome, a time limit, etc.).

oversteer /ṓvərstéer/ *v.* & *n.* ● *v.intr.* (of a motor vehicle) have a tendency to turn more sharply than was intended. ● *n.* this tendency.

overstep /ṓvərstép/ *v.tr.* (**-stepped, -stepping**) **1** pass beyond (a boundary or mark). **2** violate (certain standards of behaviour etc.).
■ **1** exceed, transcend, surpass, go beyond; see also PASS[1] *v.* 4.

overstock /ṓvərstók/ *v.tr.* stock excessively.
■ see GLUT *v.* 2, 3.

overstrain /ṓvərstráyn/ *v.tr.* strain too much.
■ see OVERWORK *v.* 2–4.

overstress /ṓvərstréss/ *v.* & *n.* ● *v.tr.* stress too much. ● *n.* an excessive degree of stress.
■ *v.* see EXAGGERATE 1.

overstretch /ṓvərstréch/ *v.tr.* **1** stretch too much. **2** (esp. as **overstretched** *adj.*) make excessive demands on (resources, a person, etc.).

overstrung *adj.* **1** /ṓvərstrúng/ (of a person, disposition, etc.) intensely strained, highly strung. **2** /ṓvərstrung/ (of a piano) with strings in sets crossing each other obliquely.

overstudy /ṓvərstúddi/ *v.tr.* (**-ies, -ied**) **1** study beyond what is necessary or desirable. **2** (as **overstudied** *adj.*) excessively deliberate; affected.
■ **2** (**overstudied**) see AFFECTED 2.

overstuff /ṓvərstúf/ *v.tr.* **1** stuff more than is necessary. **2** (as **overstuffed** *adj.*) (of furniture) made soft and comfortable by thick upholstery.
■ **1** see CRAM 1.

oversubscribe /ṓvərsəbskrī́b/ *v.tr.* (usu. as **oversubscribed** *adj.*) subscribe for more than the amount available of (a commodity offered for sale etc.) (*the offer was oversubscribed*).

oversubtle /ṓvərsútt'l/ *adj.* excessively subtle; not plain or clear.

oversupply /ṓvərsəplī́/ *v.* & *n.* ● *v.tr.* (**-ies, -ied**) supply with too much. ● *n.* an excessive supply.
■ *v.* see GLUT *v.* 2, 3. ● *n.* see SURPLUS *n.* 1.

oversusceptible /ṓvərsəséptib'l/ *adj.* too susceptible or vulnerable.

overt /ōvért, ṓvert/ *adj.* unconcealed; done openly. □□ **overtly** *adv.* **overtness** *n.* [ME f. OF past part. of *ovrir* open f. L *aperire*]
■ apparent, evident, plain, clear, obvious, manifest, clear-cut, unconcealed, patent, open, visible, observable, public. □□ **overtly** (out) in the open, for all to see, in plain *or* full view, straight (out); see also OPENLY 2.

overtake /ṓvərtáyk/ *v.tr.* (*past* **-took**; *past part.* **-taken**) **1** (also *absol.*) catch up with and pass in the same direction. **2** (of a storm, misfortune, etc.) come suddenly or unexpectedly upon. **3** become level with and exceed (a compared value etc.).
■ **1, 3** catch (up *or* up with *or esp. US* up to), reach, draw level *or* even with, overhaul, move by *or* past, pass, leave behind, outstrip, outdistance. **2** come upon, seize, catch (unprepared), strike, hit, *poet.* befall.

overtask /ṓvərtáask/ *v.tr.* **1** give too heavy a task to. **2** be too heavy a task for.

overtax /ṓvərtáks/ *v.tr.* **1** make excessive demands on (a person's strength etc.). **2** tax too heavily.
■ **1** see OVERLOAD *v.*

overthrow *v.* & *n.* ● *v.tr.* /ṓvərthrṓ/ (*past* **-threw**; *past part.* **-thrown**) **1** remove forcibly from power. **2** put an end to (an institution etc.). **3** conquer, overcome. **4** knock down, upset. ● *n.* /ṓvərthrō/ **1** a defeat or downfall. **2** *Cricket* **a** a fielder's return of the ball, not stopped near the wicket and so allowing further runs. **b** such a run. **3** *Archit.* a panel of decorated wrought-iron work in an arch or gateway.
■ *v.* **1–3** defeat, beat, rout, conquer, overcome, overpower, master, bring down, end, depose, oust, overwhelm, unseat, unhorse, topple, overturn, dethrone, thrash, worst, *colloq.* best. ● *n.* **1** defeat, rout, conquest, deposing, ousting, unseating, toppling, overturn, overturning, downfall, end, ruin, fall, collapse, destruction, suppression, quashing, crushing, subjugation, *US* ouster.

overthrust /ṓvərthrust/ *n. Geol.* the thrust of esp. lower strata on one side of a fault over those on the other side.

overtime /ṓvərtīm/ *n.* & *adv.* ● *n.* **1** the time during which a person works at a job in addition to the regular hours. **2** payment for this. **3** *US Sport* = *extra time.* ● *adv.* in addition to regular hours.

overtire /ṓvərtī́r/ *v.tr.* & *refl.* exhaust or wear out (esp. an invalid etc.).
■ see KILL[1] 3a.

overtone /ṓvərtōn/ *n.* **1** *Mus.* any of the tones above the lowest in a harmonic series. **2** a subtle or elusive quality or implication (*sinister overtones*). [OVER- + TONE, after G *Oberton*]
■ **2** undertone, connotation, hint, suggestion, innuendo, insinuation, intimation, indication, implication.

overtop /ṓvərtóp/ *v.tr.* (**-topped, -topping**) **1** be or become higher than. **2** surpass.

overtrain /ṓvərtráyn/ *v.tr.* & *intr.* subject to or undergo too much (esp. athletic) training with a consequent loss of proficiency.

overtrick /ṓvərtrik/ *n. Bridge* a trick taken in excess of one's contract.

overtrump /ṓvərtrúmp/ *v.tr.* (also *absol.*) play a higher trump than (another player).

overture /ṓvərtyoor/ *n.* **1** an orchestral piece opening an opera etc. **2** a one-movement composition in this style. **3** (usu. in *pl.*) **a** an opening of negotiations. **b** a formal proposal or offer (esp. *make overtures to*). **4** the beginning of a poem etc. [ME f. OF f. L *apertura* APERTURE]
■ **3** (*overtures*) approach, advance, offer, proposal, proposition, tender.

overturn *v.* & *n.* ● *v.* /ṓvərtúrn/ **1** *tr.* cause to fall down or over; upset. **2** *tr.* reverse; subvert; abolish; invalidate. **3** *intr.* fall down; fall over. ● *n.* /ṓvərturn/ a subversion, an act of upsetting.
■ *v.* **1, 3** turn over, tip over, capsize, up-end, upset, tumble, subvert, turn upside down, turn topsy-turvy, invert; knock down *or* over; turn turtle, fall down *or* over. **2** bring down, overthrow, throw over, upset, depose, unthrone, unseat, oust, eject; invalidate; see also ABOLISH. ● *n.* **3** subversion, overturning, overthrow, unseating, ousting, toppling, upsetting; fall, destruction, abolition, ruin, defeat, *US* ouster.

overuse *v.* & *n.* ● *v.tr.* /ṓvər-yṓoz/ use too much. ● *n.* /ṓvər-yṓoss/ excessive use.

overvalue /ṓvərvályoo/ *v.tr.* (**-values, -valued, -valuing**) value too highly; have too high an opinion of.

overview /ṓvərvyoo/ *n.* a general survey.

overweening /ṓvərwéening/ *adj.* arrogant, presumptuous, conceited, self-confident. □□ **overweeningly** *adv.* **overweeningness** *n.*
■ see ARROGANT. □□ **overweeningness** see PRIDE *n.* 2.

overweight *adj.*, *n.*, & *v.* ● *adj.* /ṓvərwáyt/ beyond an allowed or suitable weight. ● *n.* /ṓvərwayt/ excessive or extra weight; preponderance. ● *v.tr.* /ṓvərwáyt/ (usu. foll. by *with*) load unduly.
■ *adj.* see FAT *adj.* 1.

overwhelm /ṓvərwélm/ *v.tr.* **1** overpower with emotion. **2** (usu. foll. by *with*) overpower with an excess of business etc. **3** bring to sudden ruin or destruction; crush. **4** bury or drown beneath a huge mass, submerge utterly.
■ **1** overcome, overpower, stagger, astound, astonish, dumbfound, shock, stun, bewilder, confuse, confound, nonplus, surprise, take aback, *colloq.* bowl over, knock for six, knock off one's feet *or* pins, *US joc.* discombobulate, *sl.* blow a person's mind. **2, 4** overpower, inundate, overcome, engulf, submerge, drown, flood; deluge, swamp, bury, immerse. **3** overpower, overcome, overtax, devastate, stagger, crush, defeat, destroy, subdue, suppress, quash, quell,

conquer, beat, bring down, prostrate, weigh down, oppress.

overwhelming /ṓvərwélming/ *adj.* irresistible by force of numbers, influence, amount, etc. □□ **overwhelmingly** *adv.* **overwhelmingness** *n.*

■ overpowering, uncontrollable, irresistible, devastating, unendurable, unbearable, crushing, burdensome, formidable; awesome, awe-inspiring, stupefying, astounding, astonishing, staggering, bewildering, shattering, prodigious, *colloq.* mind-boggling, *sl.* mind-blowing.

overwind *v.* & *n.* ● *v.tr.* /ṓvərwī́nd/ (*past* and *past part.* **-wound**) wind (a mechanism, esp. a watch) beyond the proper stopping point. ● *n.* /ṓvərwīnd/ an instance of this.

overwinter /ṓvərwíntər/ *v.* **1** *intr.* (usu. foll. by *at*, *in*) spend the winter. **2** *intr.* (of insects, fungi, etc.) live through the winter. **3** *tr.* keep (animals, plants, etc.) alive through the winter.

overwork /ṓvərwúrk/ *v.* & *n.* ● *v.* **1** *intr.* work too hard. **2** *tr.* cause (another person) to work too hard. **3** *tr.* weary or exhaust with too much work. **4** *tr.* make excessive use of. ● *n.* excessive work.

■ *v.* **1** work too hard, do too much, overtax *or* overburden *or* overload oneself, exhaust oneself, overdo it, burn the candle at both ends, slave (away), burn the midnight oil. **2–4** overexert, overstrain, overburden, oppress, overtax, overload, overuse. ● *n.* overexertion, strain.

overwound *past* and *past part.* of OVERWIND.

overwrite /ṓvərī́t/ *v.* (*past* **-wrote**; *past part.* **-written**) **1** *tr.* write on top of (other writing). **2** *tr. Computing* destroy (data) in (a file etc.) by entering new data. **3** *intr.* (esp. as **overwritten** *adj.*) write too elaborately or too ornately. **4** *intr.* & *refl.* write too much; exhaust oneself by writing. **5** *tr.* write too much about. **6** *intr.* (esp. as **overwriting** *n.*) in shipping insurance, accept more risk than the premium income limits allow.

overwrought /ṓvəráwt/ *adj.* **1** overexcited, nervous, distraught. **2** overdone; too elaborate.

■ **1** tense, nervous, edgy, jumpy, fidgety, touchy, overexcited, on edge, over-stimulated, frantic, frenetic, distracted, distraught, strung up *or* out, *colloq.* jittery, all of a dither, in a tizzy, keyed up, worked up, wound up, uptight. **2** overdone, ornate, elaborate, baroque, rococo, florid, flowery, fussy, ostentatious, busy, gaudy, garish.

overzealous /ṓvərzélləss/ *adj.* too zealous in one's attitude, behaviour, etc.; excessively enthusiastic. □□ **overzeal** /-zéel/ *n.*

■ see AMBITIOUS *adj.* 1a.

ovi-[1] /ṓvi/ *comb. form* egg, ovum. [L *ovum* egg]

ovi-[2] /ṓvi/ *comb. form* sheep. [L *ovis* sheep]

ovibovine /ṓvibṓvīn/ *adj.* & *n. Zool.* ● *adj.* having characteristics intermediate between a sheep and an ox. ● *n.* such an animal, e.g. a musk-ox.

oviduct /ṓvidukt/ *n.* the tube through which an ovum passes from the ovary. □□ **oviducal** /-dyóok'l/ *adj.* **oviductal** /-dúktəl/ *adj.*

oviform /ṓviform/ *adj.* egg-shaped.

■ see OVAL *adj.*

ovine /ṓvīn/ *adj.* of or like sheep. [LL *ovinus* f. L *ovis* sheep]

oviparous /ōvíppərəss/ *adj. Zool.* producing young by means of eggs expelled from the body before they are hatched (cf. VIVIPAROUS). □□ **oviparity** /-párriti/ *n.* **oviparously** *adv.*

oviposit /ṓvipózzit/ *v.intr.* (**oviposited**, **ovipositing**) lay an egg or eggs, esp. with an ovipositor. □□ **oviposition** /-pəzísh'n/ *n.* [OVI-[1] + L *ponere posit-* to place]

ovipositor /ṓvipózzitər/ *n.* a pointed tubular organ with which a female insect deposits her eggs. [mod.L f. OVI-[1] + L *positor* f. *ponere posit-* to place]

ovoid /ṓvoyd/ *adj.* & *n.* ● *adj.* **1** (of a solid or of a surface) egg-shaped. **2** oval, with one end more pointed than the other. ● *n.* an ovoid body or surface. [F *ovoïde* f. mod.L *ovoides* (as OVUM)]

■ *adj.* see OVAL *adj.*

ovolo /ṓvəlō/ *n.* (*pl.* **ovoli**) /-lee/ *Archit.* a rounded convex moulding. [It. dimin. of *ovo* egg f. L OVUM]

ovotestis /ṓvətéstiss/ *n.* (*pl.* **-testes** /-teez/) *Zool.* an organ producing both ova and spermatozoa. [OVUM + TESTIS]

ovoviviparous /ṓvōvivíppərəss/ *adj. Zool.* producing young by means of eggs hatched within the body (cf. OVIPAROUS, VIVIPAROUS). □□ **ovoviviparity** /-párriti/ *n.* [OVUM + VIVIPAROUS]

ovulate /óvyoolayt/ *v.intr.* produce ova or ovules, or discharge them from the ovary. □□ **ovulation** /-láysh'n/ *n.* **ovulatory** *adj.* [mod.L *ovulum* (as OVULE)]

ovule /ṓvyool/ *n.* the part of the ovary of seed plants that contains the germ cell; an unfertilized seed. □□ **ovular** *adj.* [F f. med.L *ovulum*, dimin. of OVUM]

ovum /ṓvəm/ *n.* (*pl.* **ova** /ṓvə/) **1** a mature reproductive cell of female animals, produced by the ovary. **2** the egg cell of plants. [L, = egg]

■ **2** see SEED *n.* 1a.

ow /ow/ *int.* expressing sudden pain. [natural exclam.]

owe /ō/ *v.tr.* **1 a** be under obligation (to a person etc.) to pay or repay (money etc.) (*we owe you five pounds*; *owe more than I can pay*). **b** (*absol.*, usu. foll. by *for*) be in debt (*still owe for my car*). **2** (often foll. by *to*) be under obligation to render (gratitude etc., a person honour, gratitude, etc.) (*owe grateful thanks to*). **3** (usu. foll. by *to*) be indebted to a person or thing for (*we owe to Newton the principle of gravitation*). □ **owe a person a grudge** cherish resentment against a person. **owe it to oneself** (often foll. by *to* + infin.) need (to do) something to protect one's own interests. [OE *āgan* (see OUGHT[1]) f. Gmc]

■ be in debt to, be indebted to, be beholden to.

owing /ṓ-ing/ *predic.adj.* **1** owed; yet to be paid (*the balance owing*). **2** (foll. by *to*) **a** caused by; attributable to (*the cancellation was owing to ill health*). **b** (as *prep.*) because of (*trains are delayed owing to bad weather*).

■ **1** in arrears; see also OUTSTANDING 2. **2** (*owing to*) because of, on account of, thanks to; through, as a result of, caused by, attributable to.

owl /owl/ *n.* **1** any nocturnal bird of prey of the order Strigiformes, with large eyes and a hooked beak, including barn owls, tawny owls, etc. **2** *colloq.* a person compared to an owl, esp. in looking solemn or wise. □ **owl-light** dusk, twilight. **owl-monkey** (*pl.* **-eys**) a douroucouli. □□ **owlery** *n.* (*pl.* **-ies**). **owlish** *adj.* **owlishly** *adv.* **owlishness** *n.* (in sense 2). **owl-like** *adj.* [OE *ūle* f. Gmc]

owlet /ówlit/ *n.* a small or young owl.

own /ōn/ *adj.* & *v.* ● *adj.* (prec. by possessive) **1 a** belonging to oneself or itself; not another's (*saw it with my own eyes*). **b** individual, peculiar, particular (*a charm all of its own*). **2** used to emphasize identity rather than possession (*cooks his own meals*). **3** (*absol.*) **a** private property (*is it your own?*). **b** kindred (*among my own*). ● *v.* **1** *tr.* have as property; possess. **2 a** *tr.* confess; admit as valid, true, etc. (*own their faults*; *owns he did not know*). **b** *intr.* (foll. by *to*) confess to (*owned to a prejudice*). **3** *tr.* acknowledge paternity, authorship, or possession of. □ **come into one's own 1** receive one's due. **2** achieve recognition. **get one's own back** (often foll. by *on*) *colloq.* get revenge. **hold one's own** maintain one's position; not be defeated or lose strength. **of one's own** belonging to oneself alone. **on one's own 1** alone. **2** independently, without help. **own brand** (often *attrib.*) goods manufactured specially for a retailer and bearing the retailer's name. **own goal 1** a goal scored (usu. by mistake) against the scorer's own side. **2** an act or initiative that has the unintended effect of harming one's own interests. **own up** (often foll. by *to*) confess frankly. □□ **-owned** *adj.* (in *comb.*). [OE *āgen*, *āgnian*: see OWE]

■ *adj.* **1 b** see INDIVIDUAL *adj.* 2–4. **3 a** see PRIVATE *adj.* 1. ● *v.* **1** see POSSESS 1. **2** see CONFESS 1a. **3** see ACKNOWLEDGE 1.

owner /ṓnər/ *n.* **1** a person who owns something. **2** *sl.* the captain of a ship. □ **owner-occupier** a person who owns the house etc. he or she lives in. □□ **ownerless** *adj.* **ownership** *n.*

■ **1** possessor, holder; proprietor, proprietress; see also USER 1.

owt /owt/ *n. colloq.* or *dial.* anything. [var. of AUGHT[1]]

ox /oks/ *n.* (*pl.* **oxen** /óks'n/) **1** any bovine animal, esp. a large usu. horned domesticated ruminant used for draught, for supplying milk, and for eating as meat. **2** a castrated male of a domesticated species of cattle, *Bos taurus.* □ **ox-fence** a strong fence for keeping in cattle, consisting of railings, a hedge, and often a ditch. **ox-pecker** any African bird of the genus *Buphagus*, feeding on skin parasites living on animals. [OE *oxa* f. Gmc]

■ **1** (*oxen*) see CATTLE.

ox- var. of OXY-[2].

oxalic acid /oksállik/ *n. Chem.* a very poisonous and sour acid found in sorrel and rhubarb leaves. ¶ Chem. formula: $(COOH)_2$. □□ **oxalate** /óksəlayt/ *n.* [F *oxalique* f. L *oxalis* f. Gk *oxalis* wood sorrel]

oxalis /óksəliss, oksáa-/ *n.* any plant of the genus *Oxalis*, with trifoliate leaves and white or pink flowers. [L f. Gk f. *oxus* sour]

oxbow /óksbō/ *n.* **1** a U-shaped collar of an ox-yoke. **2 a** a loop formed by a horseshoe bend in a river. **b** a lake formed when the river cuts across the narrow end of the loop.

Oxbridge /óksbrij/ *n. Brit.* **1** (also *attrib.*) Oxford and Cambridge universities regarded together, esp. in contrast to newer institutions. **2** (often *attrib.*) the characteristics of these universities. [portmanteau word f. *Ox*(ford) + (Cam)*bridge*]

oxen *pl.* of OX.

oxer /óksər/ *n.* an ox-fence.

ox-eye /óksī/ *n.* a plant with a flower like the eye of an ox. □ **ox-eye daisy** *n.* a daisy, *Leucanthemum vulgare*, having flowers with white petals and a yellow centre: also called *white ox-eye*. □□ **ox-eyed** *adj.*

Oxf. *abbr.* Oxford.

Oxfam /óksfam/ *abbr.* Oxford Committee for Famine Relief.

Oxford bags /óksfərd/ *n.* wide baggy trousers. [*Oxford* in S. England]

Oxford blue /óksfərd/ *n.* & *adj.* ● *n.* a dark blue, sometimes with a purple tinge. ● *adj.* of this colour.

Oxford Group /óksfərd/ *n.* a religious movement founded at Oxford in 1921, with discussion of personal problems by groups.

Oxford Movement /óksfərd/ *n.* an Anglican High-Church movement started in Oxford in 1833, advocating traditional forms of worship.

oxherd /óks-herd/ *n.* a cowherd.

oxhide /óks-hīd/ *n.* **1** the hide of an ox. **2** leather made from this.

oxidant /óksid'nt/ *n.* an oxidizing agent. □□ **oxidation** /-dáysh'n/ *n.* **oxidational** /-dáyshən'l/ *adj.* **oxidative** /-daytiv/ *adj.* [F, part. of *oxider* (as OXIDE)]

oxide /óksīd/ *n.* a binary compound of oxygen. [F f. *oxygène* OXYGEN + *-ide* after *acide* ACID]

oxidize /óksidīz/ *v.* (also **-ise**) **1** *intr.* & *tr.* combine or cause to combine with oxygen. **2** *tr.* & *intr.* cover (metal) or (of metal) become covered with a coating of oxide; make or become rusty. **3** *intr.* & *tr.* undergo or cause to undergo a loss of electrons. □ **oxidized silver** the popular name for silver covered with a dark coat of silver sulphide. **oxidizing agent** *Chem.* a substance that brings about oxidation by being reduced and gaining electrons. □□ **oxidizable** *adj.* **oxidization** /-záysh'n/ *n.* **oxidizer** *n.*

oxlip /ókslip/ *n.* **1** a woodland primula, *Primula elatior*. **2** (in general use) a natural hybrid between a primrose and a cowslip.

Oxon. /óks'n/ *abbr.* **1** Oxfordshire. **2** of Oxford University or the diocese of Oxford. [abbr. of med.L *Oxoniensis* f. *Oxonia*: see OXONIAN]

Oxonian /oksṓniən/ *adj.* & *n.* ● *adj.* of or relating to Oxford or Oxford University. ● *n.* **1** a member of Oxford University. **2** a native or inhabitant of Oxford. [*Oxonia* Latinized name of *Ox(en)ford*]

oxtail /ókstayl/ *n.* the tail of an ox, often used in making soup.

oxter /ókstər/ *n. Sc.* & *N.Engl.* the armpit. [OE *ōhsta, ōxta*]

oxtongue /ókstung/ *n.* **1** the tongue of an ox, esp. cooked as food. **2** any composite plant of the genus *Picris*, with bright yellow flowers.

oxy-[1] /óksi/ *comb. form* denoting sharpness (*oxytone*). [Gk *oxu-* f. *oxus* sharp]

oxy-[2] /óksi/ *comb. form* (also **ox-** /oks/) *Chem.* oxygen (*oxyacetylene*). [abbr.]

oxyacetylene /óksiəséttileen/ *adj.* of or using a mixture of oxygen and acetylene, esp. in cutting or welding metals (*oxyacetylene burner*).

oxyacid /óksiássid/ *n. Chem.* an acid containing oxygen.

oxygen /óksijən/ *n. Chem.* a colourless tasteless odourless gaseous element, occurring naturally in air, water, and most minerals and organic substances, and essential to plant and animal life. ¶ Symb.: **O.** □ **oxygen mask** a mask placed over the nose and mouth to supply oxygen for breathing. **oxygen tent** a tentlike enclosure supplying a patient with air rich in oxygen. □□ **oxygenous** /oksíjinəss/ *adj.* [F *oxygène* acidifying principle (as OXY-[2]): it was at first held to be the essential principle in the formation of acids]

oxygenate /óksijənayt, oksíjə-/ *v.tr.* **1** supply, treat, or mix with oxygen; oxidize. **2** charge (blood) with oxygen by respiration. □□ **oxygenation** /-náysh'n/ *n.* [F *oxygéner* (as OXYGEN)]

oxygenator /óksijənaytər/ *n.* an apparatus for oxygenating the blood.

oxygenize /óksijənīz, oksíjə-/ (also **-ise**) *v.tr.* = OXYGENATE.

oxyhaemoglobin /óksiheéməglṓbin/ *n. Biochem.* a bright red complex formed when haemoglobin combines with oxygen.

oxymoron /óksimóron/ *n. rhet.* a figure of speech in which apparently contradictory terms appear in conjunction (e.g. *faith unfaithful kept him falsely true*). [Gk *oxumōron* neut. of *oxumōros* pointedly foolish f. *oxus* sharp + *mōros* foolish]

oxytocin /óksitṓsin/ *n.* **1** a hormone released by the pituitary gland that causes increased contraction of the womb during labour and stimulates the ejection of milk into the ducts of the breasts. **2** a synthetic form of this used to induce labour etc. [*oxytocic* accelerating parturition f. Gk *oxutokia* sudden delivery (as OXY-[1], *tokos* childbirth)]

oxytone /óksitōn/ *adj.* & *n.* ● *adj.* (esp. in ancient Greek) having an acute accent on the last syllable. ● *n.* a word of this kind. [Gk *oxutonos* (as OXY-[1], *tonos* tone)]

oyer and terminer /óyər ənd términər/ *n. hist.* a commission issued to judges on a circuit to hold courts. [ME f. AF *oyer et terminer* f. L *audire* hear + *et* and + *terminare* determine]

oyez /ō-yéss, ō-yéz/ *int.* (also **oyes**) uttered, usu. three times, by a public crier or a court officer to command silence and attention. [ME f. AF, OF *oiez, oyez*, imper. pl. of *oïr* hear f. L *audire*]

oyster /óystər/ *n.* **1** any of various bivalve molluscs of the family Ostreidae or Aviculidae, esp. an edible kind, *Ostrea edulus*, of European waters. **2** an oyster-shaped morsel of meat in a fowl's back. **3** something regarded as containing all that one desires (*the world is my oyster*). **4** (in full **oyster-white**) a white colour with a grey tinge. □ **oyster-bank** (or **-bed**) a part of the sea-bottom where oysters breed or are bred. **oyster-catcher** any usu. coastal wading bird of the genus *Haematopus*, with a strong orange-coloured bill, feeding on shellfish. **oyster-farm** an area of the seabed used for breeding oysters. **oyster-plant** **1** = SALSIFY. **2** a blue-flowered plant, *Mertensia maritima*, growing on beaches. [ME & OF *oistre* f. L *ostrea, ostreum* f. Gk *ostreon*]

Oz /oz/ *n. Austral. sl.* Australia. [abbr.]

oz. *abbr.* ounce(s). [It. f. *onza* ounce]

ozocerite /ōzṓkərīt/ *n.* (also **ozokerite**) a waxlike fossil paraffin used for candles, insulation, etc. [G *Ozokerit* f. Gk *ozō* smell + *kēros* wax]

ozone /ṓzōn/ *n.* **1** *Chem.* a colourless unstable gas with a pungent odour and powerful oxidizing properties, used for bleaching etc. ¶ Chem. formula: O_3. **2** *colloq.* **a** invigorating air at the seaside etc. **b** exhilarating influence. □ **ozone depletion** a reduction of ozone concentration in the stratosphere, caused by atmospheric pollution. **ozone-friendly** (of manufactured articles) containing chemicals that are not destructive to the ozone layer. **ozone hole** an area of the ozone layer in which depletion has occurred. **ozone layer** a layer of ozone in the stratosphere that absorbs most of the sun's ultraviolet radiation. □□ **ozonic** /ōzónnik/ *adj.* **ozonize** *v.tr.* (also **-ise**). **ozonization** /-nīzáysh'n/ *n.* **ozonizer** *n.* [G *Ozon* f. Gk, neut. pres. part. of *ozō* smell]

Ozzie var. of AUSSIE.

Pp

P[1] /pee/ *n.* (also **p**) (*pl.* **Ps** or **P's**) the sixteenth letter of the alphabet.

P[2] *abbr.* (also **P.**) **1** (on road signs) parking. **2** *Chess* pawn. **3** *Physics* poise (unit). **4** (also ®) proprietary.

P[3] *symb. Chem.* the element phosphorus.

p *abbr.* (also **p.**) **1** *Brit.* penny, pence. **2** page. **3** pico-. **4** piano (softly).

PA *abbr.* **1** personal assistant. **2** public address (esp. *PA system*). **3** Press Association. **4** *US* Pennsylvania (in official postal use).

Pa *symb. Chem.* the element protactinium.

pa /paa/ *n. colloq.* father. [abbr. of PAPA]

p.a. *abbr.* per annum.

pabulum /pábyooləm/ *n.* food, esp. for the mind (*mental pabulum*). [L f. *pascere* feed]

PABX *abbr. Brit.* private automatic branch exchange.

paca /pákkə/ *n.* any tailless rodent of the genus *Cuniculus*, esp. the spotted cavy of S. and Central America. [Sp. & Port., f. Tupi]

pace[1] /payss/ *n.* & *v.* ● *n.* **1 a** a single step in walking or running. **b** the distance covered in this (about 75 cm or 30 in.). **c** the distance between two successive stationary positions of the same foot in walking. **2** speed in walking or running. **3** *Theatr.* & *Mus.* speed or tempo in theatrical or musical performance (*played with great pace*). **4** a rate of progression. **5 a** a manner of walking or running; a gait. **b** any of various gaits, esp. of a trained horse etc. (*rode at an ambling pace*). ● *v.* **1** *intr.* **a** walk (esp. repeatedly or methodically) with a slow or regular pace (*pacing up and down*). **b** (of a horse) = AMBLE. **2** *tr.* traverse by pacing. **3** *tr.* set the pace for (a rider, runner, etc.). **4** *tr.* (often foll. by *out*) measure (a distance) by pacing. □ **keep pace** (often foll. by *with*) advance at an equal rate (as). **pace bowler** *Cricket* a bowler who delivers the ball at high speed without spin. **pace-setter 1** a leader. **2** = PACEMAKER 1. **put a person through his** (or **her**) **paces** test a person's qualities in action etc. **set the pace** determine the speed, esp. by leading. **stand** (or **stay**) **the pace** be able to keep up with others. □□ **-paced** *adj.* **pacer** *n.* [ME f. OF *pas* f. L *passus* f. *pandere pass-* stretch]

■ *n.* **1 a** footstep, step, stride, tread. **b** step, stride. **2** rate, tempo, speed, velocity, *colloq.* clip, *Austral.* & *NZ sl.* toe. ● *v.* **1** walk, stride, tread. **2** walk, stride, tread, traverse, perambulate. **4** measure, gauge, judge, rate, estimate, determine, reckon, figure, compute. □ **keep pace** keep up, keep in step *or* stride, stay level; compare, contend, compete, vie; (*keep pace with*) rival. **pace-setter 1** see PIONEER *n.* 1.

pace[2] /paáchay, páysi/ *prep.* (in stating a contrary opinion) with due deference to (the person named). [L, ablat. of *pax* peace]

pacemaker /páysmaykər/ *n.* **1** a competitor who sets the pace in a race. **2** a natural or artificial device for stimulating the heart muscle and determining the rate of its contractions.

pacha var. of PASHA.

pachinko /pəchíngkō/ *n.* a Japanese form of pinball. [Jap.]

pachisi /pəcheézi/ *n.* a four-handed Indian board-game with six cowries used like dice. [Hindi, = of 25 (the highest throw)]

pachyderm /pákkiderm/ *n.* any thick-skinned mammal, esp. an elephant or rhinoceros. □□ **pachydermatous** /-dérmətəss/ *adj.* [F *pachyderme* f. Gk *pakhudermos* f. *pakhus* thick + *derma -matos* skin]

pacific /pəsíffik/ *adj.* & *n.* ● *adj.* **1** characterized by or tending to peace; tranquil. **2** (**Pacific**) of or adjoining the Pacific. ● *n.* (**the Pacific**) the generally placid expanse of ocean between America to the east and Asia to the west. □ **Pacific Time** the standard time used in the Pacific region of Canada and the US. □□ **pacifically** *adv.* [F *pacifique* or L *pacificus* f. *pax pacis* peace]

pacification /pássifikáysh'n/ *n.* the act of pacifying or the process of being pacified. □□ **pacificatory** /pəsíffikətəri/ *adj.* [F f. L *pacificatio -onis* (as PACIFY)]

pacifier /pássifīər/ *n.* **1** a person or thing that pacifies. **2** *US* a baby's dummy.

pacifism /pássifiz'm/ *n.* the belief that war and violence are morally unjustified and that all disputes can be settled by peaceful means. □□ **pacifist** *n.* & *adj.* [F *pacifisme* f. *pacifier* PACIFY]

pacify /pássifī/ *v.tr.* (**-ies, -ied**) **1** appease (a person, anger, etc.). **2** bring (a country etc.) to a state of peace. [ME f. OF *pacifier* or L *pacificare* (as PACIFIC)]

pack[1] /pak/ *n.* & *v.* ● *n.* **1 a** a collection of things wrapped up or tied together for carrying. **b** = BACKPACK. **2** a set of items packaged for use or disposal together. **3** usu. *derog.* a lot or set (of similar things or persons) (*a pack of lies*; *a pack of thieves*). **4** *Brit.* a set of playing cards. **5 a** a group of hounds esp. for foxhunting. **b** a group of wild animals, esp. wolves, hunting together. **6** an organized group of Cub Scouts or Brownies. **7** *Rugby Football* a team's forwards. **8 a** a medicinal or cosmetic substance applied to the skin; = *face-pack*. **b** a hot or cold pad of absorbent material for treating a wound etc. **9** = *pack ice*. **10** a quantity of fish, fruit, etc., packed in a season etc. **11** *Med.* **a** the wrapping of a body or part of a body in a wet sheet etc. **b** a sheet etc. used for this. ● *v.* **1** *tr.* (often foll. by *up*) **a** fill (a suitcase, bag, etc.) with clothes and other items. **b** put (things) together in a bag or suitcase, esp. for travelling. **2** *intr.* & *tr.* come or put closely together; crowd or cram (*packed a lot into a few hours*; *passengers packed like sardines*). **3** *tr.* (in *passive*; often foll. by *with*) be filled (with); contain extensively (*the restaurant was packed*; *the book is packed with information*). **4** *tr.* fill (a hall, theatre, etc.) with an audience etc. **5** *tr.* cover (a thing) with something pressed tightly round. **6** *intr.* be suitable for packing. **7** *tr. colloq.* **a** carry (a gun etc.). **b** be capable of delivering (a punch) with skill or force. **8** *intr.* (of animals or Rugby forwards) form a pack. □ **pack-animal** an animal for carrying packs. **pack-drill** a military punishment of marching up and down carrying full equipment. **packed lunch** a lunch carried in a bag, box, etc., esp. to work, school, etc. **packed out** *colloq.* full, crowded. **pack ice** an area of large crowded pieces of floating ice in the sea. **pack it in** (or **up**) *colloq.* end or stop it. **pack off** send (a person) away, esp. abruptly or promptly. **pack-rat** *US* a large hoarding rodent. **pack-saddle** a saddle adapted for supporting packs. **pack up** *colloq.* **1** (esp. of a machine) stop functioning; break down. **2** retire from an activity, contest, etc. **send packing**

colloq. dismiss (a person) summarily. □□ **packable** *adj.* [ME f. MDu., MLG *pak, pakken*, of unkn. orig.]

▪ *n.* **1** parcel, package, packet, bundle, bale, load, backpack, knapsack, rucksack, haversack, kitbag, kit, duffle bag. **2** parcel, package, packet, bag, bale, load, lot, bunch. **3** group, collection, assembly, assemblage, congregation, gathering, crowd, number, throng, horde, mass, crew, gang, body, lot, load, band, company, party, set, flock, herd, drove, swarm, bevy, covey, circle, coterie, clique, *colloq.* mob. **4** deck, set, stack. **8** compress, poultice, compound; face-pack. ● *v.* **1 a** fill. **b** bundle, crowd, cram, jam, squeeze; stuff, ram, press. **2** bundle, crowd, cram, jam, squeeze, press, ram, stuff, wedge. **3, 4** crowd, cram, jam, squeeze, stuff. □ **packed out** filled, full, loaded, crowded, stuffed, jammed, crammed, brim-full, chock-a-block, chock-full, jam-packed, overloaded, overflowing, bursting, groaning, swollen, replete. **pack it in** (or **up**) stop (it), cease, end, finish, quit, give up, call it a day, *colloq.* chuck it (in), *sl.* cut it out. **pack off** dismiss, send off *or* away, bundle off *or* out, hustle off *or* out *or* away, get rid of, drive off *or* away, order off *or* away *or* out. **pack up** **1** stop, break down, fail, give out, stall, die, *archaic or colloq.* give up the ghost, *colloq.* conk (out), have had it. **2** see *pack it in* (*or up*) above.

pack[2] /pak/ *v.tr.* select (a jury etc.) or fill (a meeting) so as to secure a decision in one's favour. [prob. f. obs. verb *pact* f. PACT]

package /pákkij/ *n.* & *v.* ● *n.* **1 a** a bundle of things packed. **b** a parcel, box, etc., in which things are packed. **2** (in full **package deal**) a set of proposals or items offered or agreed to as a whole. **3** *Computing* a piece of software suitable for various applications rather than one which is custom-built. **4** *colloq.* = *package holiday.* ● *v.tr.* make up into or enclose in a package. □ **package holiday** (or **tour** etc.) a holiday or tour etc. with all arrangements made at an inclusive price. □□ **packager** *n.* [PACK[1] + -AGE]

▪ *n.* **1** packet, parcel, pack, box, container, case, carton, bundle. **2** combination, unit; proposals; deal, agreement, contract, arrangement, settlement, understanding, commitment, compact. ● *v.* wrap, pack, containerize, case, encase, enclose, include; combine, unite, couple, incorporate.

packaging /pákkijing/ *n.* **1** a wrapping or container for goods. **2** the process of packing goods.

packer /pákkər/ *n.* a person or thing that packs, esp. a dealer who prepares and packs food for transportation and sale.

packet /pákkit/ *n.* **1** a small package. **2** *colloq.* a large sum of money won, lost, or spent. **3** (in full **packet-boat**) *hist.* a mail-boat or passenger ship. [PACK[1] + -ET[1]]

▪ **1** package, pack, box, container, case, carton. **2** load(s), lot(s), great deal, (small) fortune, mint, king's ransom, *colloq.* pile(s), tidy sum, *iron.* pretty penny, *sl.* bundle, *Brit. sl.* bomb.

packhorse /pák-horss/ *n.* a horse for carrying loads.

packing /pákking/ *n.* **1** the act or process of packing. **2** material used as padding to pack esp. fragile articles. **3** material used to seal a join or assist in lubricating an axle. □ **packing-case** a case (usu. wooden) or framework for packing goods in.

packthread /pákthred/ *n.* stout thread for sewing or tying up packs.

pact /pakt/ *n.* an agreement or a treaty. [ME f. OF *pact(e)* f. L *pactum*, neut. past part. of *pacisci* agree]

▪ agreement, treaty, bargain, alliance, contract, compact, concord, covenant, concordat, entente, understanding, arrangement, deal.

pad[1] /pad/ *n.* & *v.* ● *n.* **1** a piece of soft material used to reduce friction or jarring, fill out hollows, hold or absorb liquid, etc. **2** a number of sheets of blank paper fastened together at one edge, for writing or drawing on. **3** = *ink-pad.* **4** the fleshy underpart of an animal's foot or of a human finger. **5** a guard for the leg and ankle in sports. **6** a flat surface for helicopter take-off or rocket-launching. **7** *colloq.* a lodging, esp. a bedsitter or flat. **8** the floating leaf of a water lily. ● *v.tr.* (**padded, padding**) **1** provide with a pad or padding; stuff. **2** (foll. by *out*) lengthen or fill out (a book etc.) with unnecessary material. □ **padded cell** a room with padded walls in a mental hospital. [prob. of LG or Du. orig.]

▪ *n.* **1** cushion, pillow, wad, wadding, stuffing, padding, filling, filler. **2** writing-pad, note-pad, drawing-pad, block (of paper), jotter. **7** flat, apartment, room(s), home, place, quarters, lodging(s), bedsitter, *Brit. colloq.* digs, diggings, *sl.* hang-out. ● *v.* **1** cushion, wad, stuff, fill; upholster. **2** (*pad out*) expand, inflate, stretch, dilate, lengthen, protract, extend, blow up, flesh out, puff up, augment, spin out, amplify.

pad[2] /pad/ *v.* & *n.* ● *v.* (**padded, padding**) **1** *intr.* walk with a soft dull steady step. **2 a** *tr.* tramp along (a road etc.) on foot. **b** *intr.* travel on foot. ● *n.* the sound of soft steady steps. [LG *padden* tread, *pad* PATH]

padding /pádding/ *n.* soft material used to pad or stuff with.

paddle[1] /pádd'l/ *n.* & *v.* ● *n.* **1** a short broad-bladed oar used without a rowlock. **2** a paddle-shaped instrument. **3** *Zool.* a fin or flipper. **4** each of the boards fitted round the circumference of a paddle-wheel or mill-wheel. **5** the action or a spell of paddling. ● *v.* **1** *intr.* & *tr.* move on water or propel a boat by means of paddles. **2** *intr.* & *tr.* row gently. **3** *tr.* esp. *US colloq.* spank. □ **paddle-boat** (or **-steamer** etc.) a boat, steamer, etc., propelled by a paddle-wheel. **paddle-wheel** a wheel for propelling a ship, with boards round the circumference so as to press backwards against the water. □□ **paddler** *n.* [15th c.: orig. unkn.]

▪ *n.* **1** oar, sweep, scull, blade. ● *v.* **1, 2** row, scull; propel, move. **3** spank, thrash, beat, whip, flog.

paddle[2] /pádd'l/ *v.* & *n.* ● *v.intr.* walk barefoot or dabble the feet or hands in shallow water. ● *n.* the action or a spell of paddling. □□ **paddler** *n.* [prob. of LG or Du. orig.: cf. LG *paddeln* tramp about]

▪ *v.* slosh, *colloq.* splosh; see also WADE *v.* 1.

paddock /páddək/ *n.* **1** a small field, esp. for keeping horses in. **2** a turf enclosure adjoining a racecourse where horses or cars are assembled before a race. **3** *Austral.* & *NZ* a field; a plot of land. [app. var. of (now dial.) *parrock* (OE *pearruc*): see PARK]

Paddy /páddi/ *n.* (*pl.* **-ies**) *colloq.* often *offens.* an Irishman. [pet-form of the Irish name *Padraig* (= Patrick)]

paddy[1] /páddi/ *n.* (*pl.* **-ies**) **1** (in full **paddy-field**) a field where rice is grown. **2** rice before threshing or in the husk. [Malay *pādī*]

paddy[2] /páddi/ *n.* (*pl.* **-ies**) *Brit. colloq.* a rage; a fit of temper. [PADDY]

▪ rage, (fit of) temper, fit, tantrum, *sl.* wax, *Brit. sl.* bate.

pademelon /páddimellən/ *n.* any small wallaby of the genus *Thylogale*, inhabiting the coastal scrub of Australia. [corrupt. of an Aboriginal name]

padlock /pádlok/ *n.* & *v.* ● *n.* a detachable lock hanging by a pivoted hook on the object fastened. ● *v.tr.* secure with a padlock. [ME f. LOCK[1]: first element unexpl.]

padouk /pədóok/ *n.* **1** any timber tree of the genus *Pterocarpus*, esp. *P. indicus.* **2** the wood of this tree, resembling rosewood. [Burmese]

padre /paadri, -dray/ *n.* a chaplain in any of the armed services. [It., Sp., & Port., = father, priest, f. L *pater patris* father]

padsaw /pádsaw/ *n.* a saw with a narrow blade, for cutting curves.

paean /peéən/ *n.* (*US* **pean**) a song of praise or triumph. [L f. Doric Gk *paian* hymn of thanksgiving to Apollo (under the name of *Paian*)]

paederast var. of PEDERAST.

paederasty var. of PEDERASTY.

paediatrics /peédiátriks/ *n.pl.* (treated as *sing.*) (*US* **pediatrics**) the branch of medicine dealing with children and their diseases. □□ **paediatric** *adj.* **paediatrician** /-diətrísh'n/ *n.* [PAEDO- + Gk *iatros* physician]

paedo- /péedō/ *comb. form* (*US* **pedo-**) child. [Gk *pais paid-* child]

paedophile /péedəfīl/ *n.* (*US* **pedophile**) a person who displays paedophilia.

paedophilia /péedəfílliə/ *n.* (*US* **pedophilia**) sexual desire directed towards children.

paella /pī-éllə/ *n.* a Spanish dish of rice, saffron, chicken, seafood, etc., cooked and served in a large shallow pan. [Catalan f. OF *paele* f. L *patella* pan]

paeon /péeən/ *n.* a metrical foot of one long syllable and three short syllables in any order. ▫▫ **paeonic** /pee-ónnik/ *adj.* [L f. Gk *paiōn*, the Attic form of *paian* PAEAN]

paeony var. of PEONY.

pagan /páygən/ *n.* & *adj.* ● *n.* a person not subscribing to any of the main religions of the world, esp. formerly regarded by Christians as unenlightened or heathen. ● *adj.* **1 a** of or relating to or associated with pagans. **b** irreligious. **2** identifying divinity or spirituality in nature; pantheistic. ▫▫ **paganish** *adj.* **paganism** *n.* **paganize** *v.tr.* & *intr.* (also **-ise**). [ME f. L *paganus* villager, rustic f. *pagus* country district: in Christian L = civilian, heathen]

▪ *n.* heathen, unbeliever, idolater, infidel. ● *adj.* **1** idolatrous, Gentile; see also HEATHEN *adj.*

page[1] /payj/ *n.* & *v.* ● *n.* **1 a** a leaf of a book, periodical, etc. **b** each side of this. **c** what is written or printed on this. **2 a** an episode that might fill a page in written history etc.; a record. **b** a memorable event. ● *v.tr.* paginate. [F f. L *pagina* f. *pangere* fasten]

▪ *n.* **1 a** leaf, sheet, folio. **b, c** side, verso, recto. **2** episode, phase, period, time, stage, point, era, epoch, age, record, event, chapter. ● *v.* paginate, number.

page[2] /payj/ *n.* & *v.* ● *n.* **1** a boy or man, usu. in livery, employed to run errands, attend to a door, etc. **2** a boy employed as a personal attendant of a person of rank, a bride, etc. **3** *hist.* a boy in training for knighthood and attached to a knight's service. ● *v.tr.* **1** (in hotels, airports, etc.) summon by making an announcement or by sending a messenger. **2** summon by means of a pager. ▫ **page-boy 1** = PAGE[2] *n.* 2. **2** a woman's hairstyle with the hair reaching to the shoulder and rolled under at the ends. [ME f. OF, perh. f. It. *paggio* f. Gk *paidion*, dimin. of *pais paidos* boy]

▪ *n.* **1, 2** attendant, page-boy, servant, errand-boy, messenger; *US* bellman, bellboy, *colloq.* buttons. ● *v.* summon (forth), send for *or* after, call, call for, call out, bleep.

pageant /pájənt/ *n.* **1 a** a brilliant spectacle, esp. an elaborate parade. **b** a spectacular procession, or play performed in the open, illustrating historical events. **c** a tableau etc. on a fixed stage or moving vehicle. **2** an empty or specious show. [ME *pagyn*, of unkn. orig.]

▪ **1** spectacle, display, tableau, show, parade, procession, ceremony, ritual, event, affair, extravaganza, presentation, gala.

pageantry /pájəntri/ *n.* (*pl.* **-ies**) **1** elaborate or sumptuous show or display. **2** an instance of this.

▪ **1** pomp, ceremony, display, magnificence, extravagance, showiness, show.

pager /páyjər/ *n.* a radio device with a bleeper, activated from a central point to alert the person wearing it.

paginal /pájin'l/ *adj.* **1** of pages (of books etc.). **2** corresponding page for page. ▫▫ **paginary** *adj.* [LL *paginalis* (as PAGE[1])]

paginate /pájinayt/ *v.tr.* assign numbers to the pages of a book etc. ▫▫ **pagination** /-náysh'n/ *n.* [F *paginer* f. L *pagina* PAGE[1]]

pagoda /pəgṓdə/ *n.* **1** a Hindu or Buddhist temple or sacred building, esp. a many-tiered tower, in India and the Far East. **2** an ornamental imitation of this. ▫ **pagoda-tree** any of various trees, esp. *Sophora japonica*, resembling a pagoda in shape. [Port. *pagode*, prob. ult. f. Pers. *butkada* idol temple]

pah /paa/ *int.* expressing disgust or contempt. [natural utterance]

Pahlavi /pa͞aləvi/ *n.* (also **Pehlevi** /páyləvi/) the writing system of Persia from the 2nd c. BC to the advent of Islam in the 7th c. AD. [Pers. *pahlawī* f. *pahlav* f. *parthava* Parthia]

paid *past* and *past part.* of PAY[1].

pail /payl/ *n.* **1** a bucket. **2** an amount contained in this. ▫▫ **pailful** *n.* (*pl.* **-fuls**). [OE *pægel* gill (cf. MDu. *pegel* gauge), assoc. with OF *paelle*: see PAELLA]

paillasse var. of PALLIASSE.

paillette /palyét, pīyét/ *n.* **1** a piece of bright metal used in enamel painting. **2** a spangle. [F, dimin. of *paille* f. L *palea* straw, chaff]

pain /payn/ *n.* & *v.* ● *n.* **1 a** the range of unpleasant bodily sensations produced by illness or by harmful physical contact etc. **b** a particular kind or instance of this (often in *pl.*: *suffering from stomach pains*). **2** mental suffering or distress. **3** (in *pl.*) careful effort; trouble taken (*take pains*; *got nothing for my pains*). **4** (also **pain in the neck** etc.) *colloq.* a troublesome person or thing; a nuisance. ● *v.tr.* **1** cause pain to. **2** (as **pained** *adj.*) expressing pain (*a pained expression*). ▫ **in pain** suffering pain. **on** (or **under**) **pain of** with (death etc.) as the penalty. [ME f. OF *peine* f. L *poena* penalty]

▪ *n.* **1** hurt, suffering, discomfort, distress, soreness, ache, aching, pang, spasm, smart, cramp. **2** anguish, agony, affliction, distress, grief, suffering, misery, wretchedness, despair, torment, tribulation, trial, torture, discomposure, ordeal, disquiet, *archaic or literary* woe, *literary* travail, dolour. **3** (*pains*) effort, trouble, exertion, toil, labour. **4** irritation, vexation, annoyance, bother, nuisance, pest, bore, *colloq.* headache, drag, *esp. US sl.* pain in the butt. ● *v.* **1** hurt, distress, grieve, wound, injure; trouble, depress, sadden, sorrow, cut (to the quick). **2** (**pained**) see HURT *adj.* ▫ **in pain** in agony *or* anguish *or* distress, agonized, hurt, wounded, tormented, sore, hurting, aching, suffering, racked (with pain), smarting, throbbing with pain, burning, stinging.

painful /páynfōōl/ *adj.* **1** causing bodily or mental pain or distress. **2** (esp. of part of the body) suffering pain. **3** causing trouble or difficulty; laborious (*a painful climb*). ▫▫ **painfully** *adv.* **painfulness** *n.*

▪ **1** hurting, grievous, hurtful, distressful, excruciating, torturous, agonizing, smarting, stinging, burning, piercing, stabbing, sharp; vexatious, annoying, harassing, irritating, irksome, galling, exasperating, unpleasant, afflictive, harrowing, worrisome, worrying, troubling, disquieting, disturbing, distressing, *disp.* aggravating. **2** hurting, grievous, hurtful, sore, excruciating, torturous, afflicted, agonizing, smarting, stinging, aching, achy, throbbing, burning, tender, sensitive, raw. **3** laborious, arduous, onerous, exacting, demanding, trying, troublesome. ▫▫ **painfully** agonizingly, distressingly, disagreeably, unpleasantly, unfortunately, sadly, woefully, lamentably, ruefully, unhappily; laboriously.

painkiller /páynkillər/ *n.* a medicine or drug for alleviating pain. ▫▫ **painkilling** *adj.*

▪ anodyne, analgesic, anaesthetic, sedative, palliative.

painless /páynliss/ *adj.* not causing or suffering pain. ▫▫ **painlessly** *adv.* **painlessness** *n.*

▪ trouble-free, easy, simple, comfortable, effortless, easy as pie, *colloq.* a piece of cake.

painstaking /páynztayking/ *adj.* careful, industrious, thorough. ▫▫ **painstakingly** *adv.* **painstakingness** *n.*

▪ see THOROUGH 2.

paint /paynt/ *n.* & *v.* ● *n.* **1 a** colouring matter, esp. in liquid form for imparting colour to a surface. **b** this as a dried film or coating (*the paint peeled off*). **2** *joc.* or *archaic* cosmetic make-up, esp. rouge or nail varnish. ● *v.tr.* **1 a** cover the surface of (a wall, object, etc.) with paint. **b** apply paint of a specified colour to (*paint the door green*). **2** depict (an object, scene, etc.) with paint; produce (a picture) by painting. **3** describe vividly as if by painting (*painted a gloomy picture of the future*). **4** *joc.* or *archaic* **a** apply liquid or cosmetic to (the face, skin, etc.). **b** apply (a liquid to the skin etc.). □ **painted lady** an orange-red butterfly, esp. *Cynthia cardui*, with black and white spots. **paint out** efface with paint. **paint shop** the part of a factory where goods are painted, esp. by spraying. **paint-stick** a stick of water-soluble paint used like a crayon. **paint the town red** *colloq.* enjoy oneself flamboyantly. □□ **paintable** *adj.* [ME f. *peint* past part. of OF *peindre* f. L *pingere pict-* paint]

■ *n.* **1** colour, tint, dye, colouring, pigment, stain; coating, coat, surface; enamel. **2** make-up, cosmetics, *maquillage*, greasepaint, *colloq.* warpaint. ● *v.* **1** coat, brush, cover, daub, colour, tint, dye, stain, decorate. **2** depict, portray, picture, show, represent, render, *archaic* limn. **3** depict, portray, picture, draw, characterize, describe. □ **paint the town red** make merry, carouse, revel, have a good time, go out on the town, step out, *colloq.* go on a spree, whoop it up, live it up, make whoopee.

paintbox /páyntboks/ *n.* a box holding dry paints for painting pictures.

paintbrush /páyntbrush/ *n.* a brush for applying paint.

painter[1] /páyntər/ *n.* a person who paints, esp. an artist or decorator. [ME f. OF *peintour* ult. f. L *pictor* (as PAINT)]

painter[2] /páyntər/ *n.* a rope attached to the bow of a boat for tying it to a quay etc. [ME, prob. f. OF *penteur* rope from a masthead: cf. G *Pentertakel* f. *pentern* fish the anchor]

painterly /páyntərli/ *adj.* **1 a** using paint well; artistic. **b** characteristic of a painter or paintings. **2** (of a painting) lacking clearly defined outlines.

painting /páynting/ *n.* **1** the process or art of using paint. **2** a painted picture.

paintwork /páyntwurk/ *n.* **1** a painted surface or area in a building etc. **2** the work of painting.

painty /páynti/ *adj.* (**paintier**, **paintiest**) **1** of or covered in paint. **2** (of a picture etc.) overcharged with paint.

pair /pair/ *n.* & *v.* ● *n.* **1** a set of two persons or things used together or regarded as a unit (*a pair of gloves*; *a pair of eyes*). **2** an article (e.g. scissors, trousers, or pyjamas) consisting of two joined or corresponding parts not used separately. **3 a** an engaged or married couple. **b** a mated couple of animals. **4** two horses harnessed side by side (*a coach and pair*). **5** the second member of a pair in relation to the first (*cannot find its pair*). **6** two playing cards of the same denomination. **7** either or both of two members of a legislative assembly on opposite sides absenting themselves from voting by mutual arrangement. ● *v.tr.* & *intr.* **1** (often foll. by *off*) arrange or be arranged in couples. **2 a** join or be joined in marriage. **b** (of animals) mate. **3** *Parl.* form a pair. □ **in pairs** in twos. **pair production** *Physics* the conversion of a radiation quantum into an electron and a positron. **pair royal** a set of three cards of the same denomination. [ME f. OF *paire* f. L *paria* neut. pl. of *par* equal]

■ *n.* **1** couple, twosome, two of a kind, set of two, duo, brace, tandem, twins, *Math.* dyad. **3** (courting *or* engaged *or* married) couple, twosome. **4** yoke, *US* span. **5** twin, double, doublet. ● *v.* **1** match (up), pair off *or* up, team (up), put together, partner, twin, double, join, unite, yoke. **2 a** marry, *formal or literary* wed; join *or* be joined in wedlock *or* (holy) matrimony. **b** mate.

paisa /pī́zə/ *n.* (*pl.* **paise** /-zay or -zə/) a coin and monetary unit of India, Pakistan, Nepal, and Bangladesh, equal to one-hundredth of a rupee or taka. [Hindi]

Paisley /páyzli/ *n.* (often *attrib.*) **1** a distinctive detailed pattern of curved feather-shaped figures. **2** a soft woollen garment having this pattern. [*Paisley* in Scotland]

pajamas *US* var. of PYJAMAS.

pakapoo / pákkəpōō, pakkəpōō/ *n.* (also **pakapu**) *Austral.* a Chinese form of lottery played with slips of paper marked with columns of characters. □ **pakapoo ticket** a piece of writing etc. that is illegible or difficult to decipher. [Chin. *bái gē piào* lit. 'white pigeon ticket', perh. referring to a Cantonese competition which involved releasing pigeons]

pakeha /pa̋akihaa/ *n.* *NZ* a White person as opposed to a Maori. [Maori]

Paki /pákki/ *n.* (*pl.* **Pakis**) *Brit. sl. offens.* a Pakistani, esp. an immigrant in Britain. [abbr.]

Pakistani /pa̋akista̋ani, pákki-/ *n.* & *adj.* ● *n.* **1** a native or national of Pakistan. **2** a person of Pakistani descent. ● *adj.* of or relating to Pakistan. [Hindu]

pakora /pəkórə/ *n.* a piece of cauliflower, carrot, or other vegetable, coated in seasoned batter and deep-fried. [Hind.]

pal /pal/ *n.* & *v.* ● *n.* *colloq.* a friend, mate, or comrade. ● *v.intr.* (**palled**, **palling**) (usu. foll. by *up*) associate; form a friendship. [Romany = brother, mate, ult. f. Skr. *bhrātr* BROTHER]

■ *n.* friend, comrade, *alter ego*, crony, mate, companion, playmate, classmate, *colloq.* chum, sidekick, *esp. US colloq. amigo*, buddy. ● *v.* associate, be *or* become friendly *or* friends, be *or* get *or* become on friendly *or* intimate terms, make friends, go (around *or* about), fraternize, consort, keep company, knock about *or* around, hang about *or* around, *sl.* hang out.

palace /pálliss/ *n.* **1** the official residence of a sovereign, president, archbishop, or bishop. **2** a splendid mansion; a spacious building. □ **palace revolution** (or **coup**) the (usu. non-violent) overthrow of a sovereign, government, etc. at the hands of senior officials. [ME f. OF *palais* f. L *Palatium* Palatine (hill) in Rome where the house of the emperor was situated]

■ **2** mansion, castle, stately home, manor (house), (country) estate, château, villa.

paladin /pálədin/ *n.* *hist.* **1** any of the twelve peers of Charlemagne's court, of whom the Count Palatine was the chief. **2** a knight errant; a champion. [F *paladin* f. It. *paladino* f. L *palatinus*: see PALATINE[1]]

Palaearctic /pálliaa̋rktik/ *adj.* *Zool.* of the Arctic and temperate parts of the old world. [PALAEO- + ARCTIC]

palaeo- /pálliō, páyliō/ *comb. form* (*US* **paleo-**) ancient, old; of ancient (esp. prehistoric) times. [Gk *palaios* ancient]

palaeobotany /pálliōbóttəni, páyliō-/ *n.* the study of fossil plants.

Palaeocene /pálliōseen, páyliō-/ *adj.* & *n.* (*US* **Paleocene**) *Geol.* ● *adj.* of or relating to the earliest epoch of the Tertiary period with evidence of the emergence and development of mammals. ● *n.* this epoch or system. ¶ Cf. Appendix VII. [PALAEO- + Gk *kainos* new]

palaeoclimatology /pálliōklī́mətólləji, páyliō-/ *n.* (*US* **paleoclimatology**) the study of the climate in geologically past times.

palaeogeography /pálliōjiógrəfi, páyliō-/ *n.* (*US* **paleogeography**) the study of the geographical features at periods in the geological past.

palaeography /pálliógrəfi, páyli-/ *n.* (*US* **paleography**) the study of writing and documents from the past. □□ **palaeographer** *n.* **palaeographic** /-liəgráffik/ *adj.* **palaeographical** /-liəgráffik'l/ *adj.* **palaeographically** /-liəgráffikəli/ *adv.* [F *paléographie* f. mod.L *palaeographia* (as PALAEO-, -GRAPHY)]

palaeolithic /pálliōlithik, páyliō-/ *adj.* (*US* **paleolithic**) *Archaeol.* of or relating to the early part of the Stone Age. [PALAEO- + Gk *lithos* stone]

palaeomagnetism /pálliōmágnitiz'm, páyliō-/ *n.* (*US* **paleomagnetism**) the study of the magnetism remaining in rocks.

palaeontology /pálliontólləji, páyli-/ *n.* (*US* **paleontology**) the study of life in the geological past. □□ **palaeontological** /-təlójikəl/ *adj.* **palaeontologist** *n.* [PALAEO- + Gk *onta* neut. pl. of *ōn* being, part. of *eimi* be + -LOGY]

Palaeozoic /pálliōzṓ-ik, páyliō-/ *adj.* & *n.* (also **Paleozoic**) *Geol.* ● *adj.* of or relating to an era of geological time marked by the appearance of marine and terrestrial plants and animals, esp. invertebrates. ¶ Cf. Appendix VII. ● *n.* this era (cf. CENOZOIC, MESOZOIC). [PALAEO- + Gk *zōē* life, *zōos* living]

palaestra /pəléestrə, -lī́strə/ *n.* (also **palestra** /-léstrə/) *Gk* & *Rom. Antiq.* a wrestling-school or gymnasium. [ME f. L *palaestra* f. Gk *palaistra* f. *palaiō* wrestle]

palais /pállay/ *n. colloq.* a public hall for dancing. [F *palais (de danse)* (dancing) hall]

palanquin /pállənkeén/ *n.* (also **palankeen**) (in India and the East) a covered litter for one passenger. [Port. *palanquim*: cf. Hindi *pālkī* f. Skr. *palyanka* bed, couch]

palatable /pállətəb'l/ *adj.* **1** pleasant to taste. **2** (of an idea, suggestion, etc.) acceptable, satisfactory. ▫▫ **palatability** /-bílliti/ *n.* **palatableness** *n.* **palatably** *adv.*

palatal /pállət'l/ *adj.* & *n.* ● *adj.* **1** of the palate. **2** (of a sound) made by placing the surface of the tongue against the hard palate (e.g. *y* in *yes*). ● *n.* a palatal sound. ▫▫ **palatalize** *v.tr.* (also **-ise**). **palatalization** /-līzáysh'n/ *n.* **palatally** *adv.* [F (as PALATE)]

palate /pállət/ *n.* **1** a structure closing the upper part of the mouth cavity in vertebrates. **2** the sense of taste. **3** a mental taste or inclination; liking. [ME f. L *palatum*]

palatial /pəláysh'l/ *adj.* (of a building) like a palace, esp. spacious and splendid. ▫▫ **palatially** *adv.* [L (as PALACE)]
■ luxurious, de luxe, magnificent, splendid, stately, sumptuous, opulent, majestic, grand, elegant, swanky, *colloq.* posh, ritzy, classy.

palatinate /pəláttinayt/ *n.* territory under the jurisdiction of a Count Palatine.

palatine[1] /pállətīn/ *adj.* (also **Palatine**) *hist.* **1** (of an official or feudal lord) having local authority that elsewhere belongs only to a sovereign (*Count Palatine*). **2** (of a territory) subject to this authority. [ME f. F *palatin -ine* f. L *palatinus* of the PALACE]

palatine[2] /pállətīn/ *adj.* & *n.* ● *adj.* of or connected with the palate. ● *n.* (in full **palatine bone**) each of two bones forming the hard palate. [F *palatin -ine* (as PALATE)]

palaver /pəlaávər/ *n.* & *v.* ● *n.* **1** fuss and bother, esp. prolonged. **2** profuse or idle talk. **3** cajolery. **4** *colloq.* a prolonged or tiresome business. **5** esp. *hist.* a parley between African or other natives and traders. ● *v.* **1** *intr.* talk profusely. **2** *tr.* flatter, wheedle. [Port. *palavra* word f. L (as PARABLE)]
■ *n.* **1** fuss, bother, trouble, red tape, commotion, bother, nonsense, *colloq.* song and dance, *Brit. sl.* carry-on, carrying-on. **2** chatter, babble, jabber, (empty *or* small) talk, blather, gossip, prating, prattle, *colloq.* natter, jaw, wittering, *Brit. colloq.* waffle, *sl.* hot air. **3** blarney, soft soap, weasel *or* honeyed words; see also *cajolery* (CAJOLE). **4** rigmarole, procedure, business, nuisance, to-do, *colloq.* performance. **5** parley, talk, conference, discussion, colloquy, conversation, confabulation, meeting, get-together, round table, powwow, *colloq.* confab, *sl.* chin-wag. ● *v.* **1** chatter, babble, jabber, blather, gossip, prattle, prate, gabble, witter, *colloq.* jaw, chit-chat, natter, *Brit. colloq.* waffle, *sl.* chin-wag, *sl. derog.* yack, yackety-yack. **2** see CAJOLE.

pale[1] /payl/ *adj.* & *v.* ● *adj.* **1** (of a person or complexion) of a whitish or ashen appearance. **2 a** (of a colour) faint; not dark or deep. **b** faintly coloured. **3** of faint lustre; dim. **4** lacking intensity, vigour, or strength (*pale imitation*). ● *v.* **1** *intr.* & *tr.* grow or make pale. **2** *intr.* (often foll. by *before*, *beside*) become feeble in comparison (with). ▫▫ **palely** *adv.* **paleness** *n.* **palish** *adj.* [ME f. OF *pale*, *palir* f. L *pallidus* f. *pallēre* be pale]
■ *adj.* **1** colourless, white, wan, sallow, waxen, livid, ashen, ashy, pallid, bloodless, whitish, pasty, whey-faced, washed out, anaemic, blanched, drained, ghostly, ghastly, peaky, peakish, cadaverous. **2** faint, light, dim, washed out, pastel. **3** see DIM *adj.* 1. **4** feeble, weak, flimsy, meagre, enfeebled, ineffective, ineffectual, puny, insignificant, paltry, lame, poor, inadequate, half-hearted, tame, spiritless, empty, sterile, lifeless, uninspired, anaemic, bloodless, *colloq.* half-baked. ● *v.* **1** blanch, dim, whiten. **2** diminish, lessen, fade (away), decrease, abate.

pale[2] /payl/ *n.* **1** a pointed piece of wood for fencing etc.; a stake. **2** a boundary or enclosed area. **3** *Heraldry* a vertical stripe in the middle of a shield. ▫ **beyond the pale** outside the bounds of acceptable behaviour. **in pale** *Heraldry* arranged vertically. [ME f. OF *pal* f. L *palus* stake]
■ **1** paling, palisade, picket, upright, post, stake. **2** boundary, limit(s), restriction, bounds, border(s), confines. ▫ **beyond the pale** improper, irregular, unseemly, unsuitable, indecent, unacceptable; inadmissible, forbidden, anathema, disallowed, prohibited, *verboten*, interdicted, taboo; unusual, bizarre, peculiar, *outré*, weird, abnormal, strange.

palea /páyliə/ *n.* (*pl.* **paleae** /-li-ee/) *Bot.* a chafflike bract, esp. in a flower of grasses. [L, = chaff]

paled /payld/ *adj.* having palings.

paleface /páylfayss/ *n.* a name supposedly used by the N. American Indians for the White man.

paleo- *comb. form US* var. of PALAEO-.

Paleocene *US* var. of PALAEOCENE.

Paleozoic *US* var. of PALAEOZOIC.

Palestinian /pállistínniən/ *adj.* & *n.* ● *adj.* of or relating to Palestine, a region (in ancient and modern times) and former mandated territory on the E. Mediterranean coast. ● *n.* **1** a native of Palestine in ancient or modern times. **2** an Arab, or a descendant of one, born or living in the area formerly called Palestine.

palestra var. of PALAESTRA.

palette /pállit/ *n.* **1** a thin board or slab or other surface, usu. with a hole for the thumb, on which an artist lays and mixes colours. **2** the range of colours used by an artist. ▫ **palette-knife 1** a thin steel blade with a handle for mixing colours or applying or removing paint. **2** a kitchen knife with a long blunt round-ended flexible blade. [F, dimin. of *pale* shovel f. L *pala* spade]

palfrey /páwlfri/ *n.* (*pl.* **-eys**) *archaic* a horse for ordinary riding, esp. for women. [ME f. OF *palefrei* f. med.L *palefredus*, LL *paraveredus* f. Gk *para* beside, extra, + L *veredus* light horse, of Gaulish orig.]

Pali /paáli/ *n.* an Indic language used in the canonical books of Buddhists. [Skr. *pāli-bhāsā* f. *pāli* canon + *bhāsā* language]

palimony /pállimәni/ *n.* esp. *US colloq.* an allowance made by one member of an unmarried couple to the other after separation. [PAL + ALIMONY]

palimpsest /pállimpsest/ *n.* **1** a piece of writing-material or manuscript on which the original writing has been effaced to make room for other writing. **2** a monumental brass turned and re-engraved on the reverse side. [L *palimpsestus* f. Gk *palimpsēstos* f. *palin* again + *psēstos* rubbed smooth]

palindrome /pállindrōm/ *n.* a word or phrase that reads the same backwards as forwards (e.g. *rotator*, *nurses run*). ▫▫ **palindromic** /-drómmik/ *adj.* **palindromist** *n.* [Gk *palindromos* running back again f. *palin* again + *drom-* run]

paling /páyling/ *n.* **1** a fence of pales. **2** a pale.

palingenesis /pállinjénnisiss/ *n. Biol.* the exact reproduction of ancestral characteristics in ontogenesis. ▫▫ **palingenetic** /-jənéttik/ *adj.* [Gk *palin* again + *genesis* birth, GENESIS]

palinode /pállinōd/ *n.* **1** a poem in which the writer retracts a view or sentiment expressed in a former poem. **2** a recantation. [F *palinode* or LL *palinodia* f. Gk *palinōidia* f. *palin* again + *ōidē* song]

palisade /pállisáyd/ *n.* & *v.* ● *n.* **1 a** a fence of pales or iron railings. **b** a strong pointed wooden stake used in a close row for defence. **2** *US* (in *pl.*) a line of high cliffs. ● *v.tr.* enclose or provide with a palisade. ▫ **palisade layer** *Bot.* a layer of elongated cells below the epidermis. [F *palissade* f. Prov. *palissada* f. *palissa* paling ult. f. L *palus* stake]

pall[1] /pawl/ *n.* **1** a cloth spread over a coffin, hearse, or tomb. **2** a shoulder-band with pendants, worn as an ecclesiastical vestment and sign of authority. **3** a dark covering (*a pall of darkness; a pall of smoke*). **4** *Heraldry* a Y-shaped bearing charged with crosses representing the front of an ecclesiastical pall. [OE *pæll*, f. L *pallium* cloak]
■ **3** see MANTLE *n.* 2.

pall[2] /pawl/ *v.* **1** *intr.* (often foll. by *on*) become uninteresting (to). **2** *tr.* satiate, cloy. [ME, f. APPAL]

■ **1** (*pall on*) bore, tire, weary, jade, irk, irritate, sicken. **2** see SATE 2.

palladia *pl.* of PALLADIUM[2].

Palladian /pəláydiən/ *adj. Archit.* in the neoclassical style of Palladio. □□ **Palladianism** *n.* [A. *Palladio*, It. architect d. 1580]

palladium[1] /pəláydiəm/ *n. Chem.* a white ductile metallic element occurring naturally in various ores and used in chemistry as a catalyst and for making jewellery. ¶ Symb.: **Pd**. [mod.L f. *Pallas*, an asteroid discovered (1803) just before the element, + -IUM; cf. CERIUM]

palladium[2] /pəláydiəm/ *n.* (*pl.* **palladia** /-diə/) a safeguard or source of protection. [ME f. L f. Gk *palladion* image of Pallas (Athene), a protecting deity]

pallbearer /páwlbairər/ *n.* a person helping to carry or officially escorting a coffin at a funeral.

pallet[1] /pállit/ *n.* **1** a straw mattress. **2** a mean or makeshift bed. [ME *pailet*, *paillet* f. AF *paillete* straw f. OF *paille* f. L *palea*]

pallet[2] /pállit/ *n.* **1** a flat wooden blade with a handle, used in ceramics to shape clay. **2** = PALETTE. **3** a portable platform for transporting and storing loads. **4** a projection transmitting motion from an escapement to a pendulum etc. **5** a projection on a machine-part, serving to change the mode of motion of a wheel. □□ **palletize** *v.tr.* (also **-ise**) (in sense 3). [F *palette*: see PALETTE]

pallia *pl.* of PALLIUM.

palliasse /pálliass/ *n.* (also **paillasse**) a straw mattress. [F *paillasse* f. It. *pagliaccio* ult. f. L *palea* straw]

palliate /pálliayt/ *v.tr.* **1** alleviate (disease) without curing it. **2** excuse, extenuate. □□ **palliation** /-áysh'n/ *n.* **palliator** *n.* [LL *palliare* to cloak f. *pallium* cloak]

palliative /pálliətiv/ *n.* & *adj.* ● *n.* anything used to alleviate pain, anxiety, etc. ● *adj.* serving to alleviate. □□ **palliatively** *adv.* [F *palliatif -ive* or med.L *palliativus* (as PALLIATE)]

pallid /pállid/ *adj.* pale, esp. from illness. □□ **pallidity** /-lídditi/ *n.* **pallidly** *adv.* **pallidness** *n.* [L *pallidus* PALE[1]]

pallium /pálliəm/ *n.* (*pl.* **palliums** or **pallia** /-liə/) **1** an ecclesiastical pall, esp. that sent by the Pope to an archbishop as a symbol of authority. **2** *hist.* a man's large rectangular cloak esp. as worn in antiquity. **3** *Zool.* the mantle of a mollusc or brachiopod . [L]

pall-mall /pálmál, pélmél/ *n. hist.* a game in which a ball was driven through an iron ring suspended in a long alley. [obs. F *pallemaille* f. It. *pallamaglio* f. *palla* ball + *maglio* mallet]

pallor /pállər/ *n.* pallidness, paleness. [L f. *pallēre* be pale]

pally /pálli/ *adj.* (**pallier, palliest**) *colloq.* like a pal; friendly.

palm[1] /paam/ *n.* **1** any usu. tropical tree of the family Palmae, with no branches and a mass of large pinnate or fan-shaped leaves at the top. **2** the leaf of this tree as a symbol of victory. **3 a** supreme excellence. **b** a prize for this. **4** a branch of various trees used instead of a palm in non-tropical countries, esp. in celebrating Palm Sunday. □ **palm oil** oil from the fruit of any of various palms. **Palm Sunday** the Sunday before Easter, celebrating Christ's entry into Jerusalem. **palm wine** an alcoholic drink made from fermented palm sap. □□ **palmaceous** /palmáyshəss/ *adj.* [OE *palm(a)* f. Gmc f. L *palma* PALM[2], its leaf being likened to a spread hand]

palm[2] /paam/ *n.* & *v.* ● *n.* **1** the inner surface of the hand between the wrist and fingers. **2** the part of a glove that covers this. **3** the palmate part of an antler. ● *v.tr.* conceal in the hand. □ **in the palm of one's hand** under one's control or influence. **palm off 1** (often foll. by *on*) **a** impose or thrust fraudulently (on a person). **b** cause a person to accept unwillingly or unknowingly (*palmed my old typewriter off on him*). **2** (often foll. by *with*) cause (a person) to accept unwillingly or unknowingly (*palmed him off with my old typewriter*). □□ **palmar** /pálmər/ *adj.* **palmed** *adj.* **palmful** *n.* (*pl.* **-fuls**). [ME *paume* f. OF *paume* f. L *palma*: later assim. to L]

palmate /pálmayt/ *adj.* **1** shaped like an open hand. **2** having lobes etc. like spread fingers. [L *palmatus* (as PALM[2])]

palmer /paámər/ *n.* **1** *hist.* **a** a pilgrim returning from the Holy Land with a palm branch or leaf. **b** an itinerant monk under a vow of poverty. **2** a hairy artificial fly used in angling. **3** (in full **palmer-worm**) a destructive hairy caterpillar of a European moth, *Euproctis chrysorrhoea*. [ME f. AF *palmer*, OF *palmier* f. med.L *palmarius* pilgrim]

palmette /palmét/ *n. Archaeol.* an ornament of radiating petals like a palm-leaf. [F, dimin. of *palme* PALM[1]]

palmetto /palméttō/ *n.* (*pl.* **-os**) a small palm tree, e.g. any of various fan palms of the genus *Sabal* or *Chamaerops*. [Sp. *palmito*, dimin. of *palma* PALM[1], assim. to It. words in *-etto*]

palmiped /pálmiped/ *adj.* & *n.* (also **palmipede** /-peed/) ● *adj.* web-footed. ● *n.* a web-footed bird. [L *palmipes -pedis* (as PALM[2], *pes pedis* foot)]

palmistry /paámistri/ *n.* supposed divination from lines and other features on the palm of the hand. □□ **palmist** *n.* [ME (orig. *palmestry*) f. PALM[2]: second element unexpl.]

palmy /paámi/ *adj.* (**palmier, palmiest**) **1** of or like or abounding in palms. **2** triumphant, flourishing (*palmy days*).

palmyra /palmírə/ *n.* an Asian palm, *Borassus flabellifer*, with fan-shaped leaves used for matting etc. [Port. *palmeira* palm-tree, assim. to *Palmyra* in Syria]

palomino /pálləmeénō/ *n.* (*pl.* **-os**) a golden or cream-coloured horse with a light-coloured mane and tail, orig. bred in the south-western US. [Amer. Sp. f. Sp. *palomino* young pigeon f. *paloma* dove f. L *palumba*]

paloverde /pállōvérdi/ *n.* any yellow-flowered thorny tree of the genus *Cercidium* in Arizona etc. [Amer. Sp., = green tree]

palp /palp/ *n.* (also **palpus** /pálpəss/) (*pl.* **palps** or **palpi** /-pī/) a segmented sense-organ at the mouth of an arthropod; a feeler. □□ **palpal** *adj.* [L *palpus* f. *palpare* feel]

palpable /pálpəb'l/ *adj.* **1** that can be touched or felt. **2** readily perceived by the senses or mind. □□ **palpability** /-bílliti/ *n.* **palpably** *adv.* [ME f. LL *palpabilis* (as PALPATE)]

palpate /palpáyt/ *v.tr.* examine (esp. medically) by touch. □□ **palpation** /-páysh'n/ *n.* [L *palpare palpat-* touch gently]

palpebral /pálpibrəl/ *adj.* of or relating to the eyelids. [LL *palpebralis* f. L *palpebra* eyelid]

palpitate /pálpitayt/ *v.intr.* **1** pulsate, throb. **2** tremble. □□ **palpitant** *adj.* [L *palpitare* frequent. of *palpare* touch gently]

palpitation /pálpitáysh'n/ *n.* **1** throbbing, trembling. **2** (often in *pl.*) increased activity of the heart due to exertion, agitation, or disease. [L *palpitatio* (as PALPITATE)]

palpus var. of PALP.

palsgrave /páwlzgrayv/ *n.* a Count Palatine. [Du. *paltsgrave* f. *palts* palatinate + *grave* count]

palstave /páwlstayv/ *n. Archaeol.* a type of chisel made of bronze etc. shaped to fit into a split handle. [Da. *paalstav* f. ON *pálstavr* f. *páll* hoe (cf. L *palus* stake) + *stafr* STAFF[1]]

palsy /páwlzi, pól-/ *n.* & *v.* ● *n.* (*pl.* **-ies**) **1** paralysis, esp. with involuntary tremors. **2 a** a condition of utter helplessness. **b** a cause of this. ● *v.tr.* (**-ies, -ied**) **1** affect with palsy. **2** render helpless. [ME *pa(r)lesi* f. OF *paralisie* ult. f. L *paralysis*: see PARALYSIS]

palter /páwltər, pól-/ *v.intr.* **1** haggle or equivocate. **2** trifle. □□ **palterer** *n.* [16th c.: orig. unkn.]

paltry /páwltri, pól-/ *adj.* (**paltrier, paltriest**) worthless, contemptible, trifling. □□ **paltriness** *n.* [16th c.: f. *paltry* trash app. f. *palt*, *pelt* rubbish + -RY (cf. *trumpery*): cf. LG *paltrig* ragged]

■ trifling, trivial, petty, small, insignificant, worthless, pitiful, pathetic, pitiable, puny, sorry, wretched, miserable, inconsequential, inconsiderable, unimportant, meagre, mean, beggarly, base, low, contemptible, *colloq.* piddling, piffling, *Brit. colloq.* twopenny, twopenny-halfpenny, mingy.

paludal /pəlyoód'l, pályoo-/ *adj.* **1** of a marsh. **2** malarial. □□ **paludism** *n.* (in sense 2). [L *palus -udis* marsh + -AL]

paly /páyli/ *adj. Heraldry* divided into equal vertical stripes. [OF *palé* f. *pal* PALE[2]]

palynology /pállinólləji/ *n.* the study of pollen, spores, etc., for rock-dating and the study of past environments. □□ **palynological** /-nəlójik'l/ *adj.* **palynologist** *n.* [Gk *palunō* sprinkle + -LOGY]

pampas /pámpəss/ *n.pl.* large treeless plains in S. America. □ **pampas-grass** a tall grass, *Cortaderia selloana*, from S. America, with silky flowering plumes. [Sp. f. Quechua *pampa* plain]

pamper /pámpər/ *v.tr.* **1** overindulge (a person, taste, etc.), cosset. **2** spoil (a person) with luxury. □□ **pamperer** *n.* [ME, prob. of LG or Du. orig.]

■ baby, coddle, cosset, (over)indulge, spoil, mollycoddle, pet.

pampero /pampáirō/ *n.* (*pl.* **-os**) a strong cold SW wind in S. America, blowing from the Andes to the Atlantic. [Sp. (as PAMPAS)]

pamphlet /pámflit/ *n.* & *v.* ● *n.* a small, usu. unbound booklet or leaflet containing information or a short treatise. ● *v.tr.* (**pamphleted, pamphleting**) distribute pamphlets to. [ME f. *Pamphilet*, the familiar name of the 12th-c. Latin love poem *Pamphilus seu de Amore*]

■ *n.* booklet, brochure, tract, leaflet, circular; handbill, bill, notice, bulletin, hand-out, *US* flyer.

pamphleteer /pámfliteér/ *n.* & *v.* ● *n.* a writer of (esp. political) pamphlets. ● *v.intr.* write pamphlets.

pan[1] /pan/ *n.* & *v.* ● *n.* **1 a** a vessel of metal, earthenware, or plastic, usu. broad and shallow, used for cooking and other domestic purposes. **b** the contents of this. **2** a panlike vessel in which substances are heated etc. **3** any similar shallow container such as the bowl of a pair of scales or that used for washing gravel etc. to separate gold. **4** *Brit.* the bowl of a lavatory. **5** part of the lock that held the priming in old guns. **6** a hollow in the ground (*salt-pan*). **7** a hard substratum of soil. **8** *US sl.* the face. ● *v.* (**panned, panning**) **1** *tr. colloq.* criticize severely. **2 a** *tr.* (often foll. by *off*, *out*) wash (gold-bearing gravel) in a pan. **b** *intr.* search for gold by panning gravel. **c** *intr.* (foll. by *out*) (of gravel) yield gold. □ **pan out** (of an action etc.) turn out well or in a specified way. □□ **panful** *n.* (*pl.* **-fuls**). **panlike** *adj.* [OE *panne*, perh. ult. f. L *patina* dish]

■ *n.* **1** saucepan, frying-pan, pot, casserole, *US* skillet. **4** bowl. **6** depression, indentation, concavity, cavity, hollow, pit, hole, crater. **8** face, façade, *literary* visage, mien, *sl.* kisser, mug. ● *v.* **1** criticize, censure, find fault with, put down, reject, flay, excoriate, roast, *colloq.* rubbish, *Brit. colloq.* slate, *US colloq.* trash, *sl.* knock. **2 a** wash, separate, sift. **b** see SEARCH *v.* 1, 3. □ **pan out** work out, turn out (well); result, come out, end (up), conclude, culminate, *formal* eventuate.

pan[2] /pan/ *v.* & *n.* ● *v.* (**panned, panning**) **1** *tr.* swing (a cine-camera) horizontally to give a panoramic effect or to follow a moving object. **2** *intr.* (of a cine-camera) be moved in this way. ● *n.* a panning movement. [abbr. of PANORAMA]

pan[3] /paan/ *n. Bot.* **1** a leaf of the betel. **2** this enclosing lime and areca-nut parings, chewed in India etc. [Hindi f. Skr. *parna* feather, leaf]

pan- /pan/ *comb. form* **1** all; the whole of. **2** relating to the whole or all the parts of a continent, racial group, religion, etc. (*pan-American*; *pan-African*; *pan-Hellenic*; *pan-Anglican*). [Gk f. *pan* neut. of *pas* all]

panacea /pánnəseéə/ *n.* a universal remedy. □□ **panacean** *adj.* [L f. Gk *panakeia* f. *panakēs* all-healing (as PAN-, *akos* remedy)]

panache /pənásh/ *n.* **1** assertiveness or flamboyant confidence of style or manner. **2** *hist.* a tuft or plume of feathers, esp. as a head-dress or on a helmet. [F f. It. *pennacchio* f. LL *pinnaculum* dimin. of *pinna* feather]

■ **1** flourish, dash, *élan*, éclat, chic, sophistication, *savoir faire*, *savoir vivre*, flamboyance, verve, style, vivacity, cultivation, flair, smartness, boldness, self-assurance, swagger, vigour, liveliness, spirit, brio, gusto, zest, animation, enthusiasm, energy.

panada /pənaádə/ *n.* **1** a thick paste of flour etc. **2** bread boiled to a pulp and flavoured. [Sp. ult. f. L *panis* bread]

panama /pánnəmaa/ *n.* a hat of strawlike material made from the leaves of a pine-tree. [*Panama* in Central America]

Panamanian /pánnəmáyniən/ *n.* & *adj.* ● *n.* **1** a native or national of the Republic of Panama in Central America. **2** a person of Panamanian descent. ● *adj.* of or relating to Panama.

panatella /pánnətéllə/ *n.* a long thin cigar. [Amer. Sp. *panatela*, = long thin biscuit f. It. *panatella* dimin. of *panata* (as PANADA)]

pancake /pánkayk/ *n.* & *v.* ● *n.* **1** a thin flat cake of batter usu. fried and turned in a pan and rolled up with a filling. **2** a flat cake of make-up etc. ● *v.* **1** *intr.* make a pancake landing. **2** *tr.* cause (an aircraft) to pancake. □ **flat as a pancake** completely flat. **Pancake Day** Shrove Tuesday (on which pancakes are traditionally eaten). **pancake landing** an emergency landing by an aircraft with its undercarriage still retracted, in which the pilot attempts to keep the aircraft in a horizontal position throughout. [ME f. PAN[1] + CAKE]

panchayat /punchī́ət/ *n.* a village council in India. [Hindi f. Skr. *pancha* five]

Panchen lama /pánchən laámə/ *n.* a Tibetan lama ranking next after the Dalai lama. [Tibetan *panchen* great learned one]

panchromatic /pánkrōmáttik/ *adj. Photog.* (of a film etc.) sensitive to all visible colours of the spectrum.

pancreas /pángkriəss/ *n.* a gland near the stomach supplying the duodenum with digestive fluid and secreting insulin into the blood. □□ **pancreatic** /-kriáttik/ *adj.* **pancreatitis** /-kriətī́tiss/ *n.* [mod.L f. Gk *pagkreas* (as PAN-, *kreas -atos* flesh)]

pancreatin /pángkriətin/ *n.* a digestive extract containing pancreatic enzymes, prepared from animal pancreases.

panda /pándə/ *n.* **1** (also **giant panda**) a large bearlike mammal, *Ailuropoda melanoleuca*, native to China and Tibet, having characteristic black and white markings. **2** (also **red panda**) a Himalayan racoon-like mammal, *Ailurus fulgens*, with reddish-brown fur and a long bushy tail. □ **panda car** *Brit.* a police patrol car (orig. white with black stripes on the doors). [Nepali name]

pandect /pándekt/ *n.* (usu. in *pl.*) **1** a complete body of laws. **2** *hist.* a compendium in 50 books of the Roman civil law made by order of Justinian in the 6th c. [F *pandecte* or L *pandecta pandectes* f. Gk *pandektēs* all-receiver (as PAN-, *dektēs* f. *dekhomai* receive)]

pandemic /pandémmik/ *adj.* & *n.* ● *adj.* (of a disease) prevalent over a whole country or the world. ● *n.* a pandemic disease. [Gk *pandēmos* (as PAN-, *dēmos* people)]

pandemonium /pándimṓniəm/ *n.* **1** uproar; utter confusion. **2** a scene of this. [mod.L (place of all demons in Milton's *Paradise Lost*) f. PAN- + Gk *daimōn* DEMON[1]]

■ bedlam, chaos, turmoil, disorder, tumult, frenzy, uproar, furore, confusion.

pander /pándər/ *v.* & *n.* ● *v.intr.* (foll. by *to*) gratify or indulge a person, a desire or weakness, etc. ● *n.* **1** a go-between in illicit love affairs; a procurer. **2** a person who encourages coarse desires. [*Pandare*, a character in Boccaccio and in Chaucer's *Troilus and Criseyde*, f. L *Pandarus* f. Gk *Pandaros*]

■ *v.* (*pander to*) satisfy, gratify, humour, indulge, fulfil, bow to, yield to, truckle to, cater to. ● *n.* **1** pimp, procurer, solicitor, *archaic* whoremonger, *Brit. sl.* ponce.

pandit var. of PUNDIT 1.

P. & O. *abbr.* Peninsular and Oriental Shipping Company (or Line).

Pandora's box /pandórəz/ *n.* a process that once activated will generate many unmanageable problems. [in Gk Mythol. the box from which the ills of mankind were released, Hope alone remaining: f. Gk *Pandōra* all-gifted (as PAN-, *dōron* gift)]

p. & p. *abbr. Brit.* postage and packing.

pane /payn/ *n.* **1** a single sheet of glass in a window or door. **2** a rectangular division of a chequered pattern etc. [ME f. OF *pan* f. L *pannus* piece of cloth]

■ **1** panel, sheet, glass, window-pane, light, bull's-eye.

panegyric /pánnijírrik/ *n.* a laudatory discourse; a eulogy. □□ **panegyrical** *adj.* [F *panégyrique* f. L *panegyricus* f. Gk *panēgurikos* of public assembly (as PAN-, *ēguris* = *agora* assembly)]

panegyrize /pánnijirīz/ *v.tr.* (also **-ise**) speak or write in praise of; eulogize. □□ **panegyrist** /-jírrist/ *n.* [Gk *panēgurizō* (as PANEGYRIC)]

■ □□ **panegyrist** eulogizer, eulogist, encomiast, *prôneur*; flatterer.

panel /pánn'l/ *n.* & *v.* ● *n.* **1 a** a distinct, usu. rectangular, section of a surface (e.g. of a wall, door, or vehicle). **b** a control panel (see CONTROL *n.* 5). **c** = *instrument panel.* **2** a strip of material as part of a garment. **3** a group of people forming a team in a broadcast game, discussion, etc. **4** *Brit. hist.* a list of medical practitioners registered in a district as accepting patients under the National Insurance Act. **5 a** a list of available jurors; a jury. **b** *Sc.* a person or persons accused of a crime. ● *v.tr.* (**panelled, panelling**; *US* **paneled, paneling**) **1** fit or provide with panels. **2** cover or decorate with panels. □ **panel-beater** one whose job is to beat out the metal panels of motor vehicles. **panel game** a broadcast quiz etc. played by a panel. **panel heating** the heating of rooms by panels in the wall etc. containing the sources of heat. **panel pin** a thin nail with a very small head. **panel saw** a saw with small teeth for cutting thin wood for panels. **panel truck** *US* a small enclosed delivery truck. [ME & OF, = piece of cloth, ult. f. L *pannus*: see PANE]

panelling /pánn'ling/ *n.* (*US* **paneling**) **1** panelled work. **2** wood for making panels.

panellist /pánn'list/ *n.* (*US* **panelist**) a member of a panel (esp. in broadcasting).

pang /pang/ *n.* (often in *pl.*) a sudden sharp pain or painful emotion. [16th c.: var. of earlier *prange* pinching f. Gmc]

■ pain, stab, ache, pinch, prick, twinge, stitch, spasm; qualm, hesitation, scruple, misgiving.

panga /pánggə/ *n.* a bladed African tool like a machete. [native name in E. Africa]

pangolin /panggṓlin/ *n.* any scaly anteater of the genus *Manis*, native to Asia and Africa, having a small head with elongated snout and tongue, and a tapering tail. [Malay *peng-gōling* roller (from its habit of rolling itself up)]

panhandle /pánhand'l/ *n.* & *v.* *US* ● *n.* a narrow strip of territory extending from one State into another. ● *v.tr.* & *intr. colloq.* beg for money in the street. □□ **panhandler** *n.*

panic[1] /pánnik/ *n.* & *v.* ● *n.* **1 a** sudden uncontrollable fear or alarm. **b** (*attrib.*) characterized or caused by panic (*panic buying*). **2** infectious apprehension or fright esp. in commercial dealings. ● *v.tr.* & *intr.* (**panicked, panicking**) (often foll. by *into*) affect or be affected with panic (*was panicked into buying*). □ **panic button** a button for summoning help in an emergency. **panic-monger** a person who fosters a panic. **panic stations** a state of emergency. **panic-stricken** (or **-struck**) affected with panic; very apprehensive. □□ **panicky** *adj.* [F *panique* f. mod.L *panicus* f. Gk *panikos* f. *Pan* a rural god causing terror]

■ *n.* terror, alarm, fear, fright, dread, horror, dismay, consternation, hysteria; anxiety, apprehension, apprehensiveness, nervousness. ● *v.* frighten, scare, alarm, terrify, unnerve; become terrified *or* alarmed *or* fearful *or* frightened, lose one's nerve, go to pieces, fall apart, *colloq.* chicken (out), *Brit. sl.* lose one's bottle. □ **panic-stricken** (or **-struck**) terrified, alarmed, horrified, aghast, terror-stricken *or* terror-struck, panicky, frenzied, in a frenzy, hysterical, beside oneself, fearful, afraid, scared (stiff), petrified, horror-struck *or* horror-stricken, frightened *or* scared out of one's wits, appalled, stunned, stupefied, perturbed, unnerved, nervous, distressed, upset, jumpy, worked up, in a cold sweat, *colloq.* in a flap *or* tizzy. □□ **panicky** see *panic-stricken* above.

panic[2] /pánnik/ *n.* any grass of the genus *Panicum*, including millet and other cereals. [OE f. L *panicum* f. *panus* thread on bobbin, millet-ear f. Gk *pēnos* web]

panicle /pánnik'l/ *n. Bot.* a loose branching cluster of flowers, as in oats. □□ **panicled** *adj.* [L *paniculum* dimin. of *panus* thread]

panjandrum /panjándrəm/ *n.* **1** a mock title for an important person. **2** a pompous or pretentious official etc. [app. invented in nonsense verse by S. Foote 1755]

panne /pan/ *n.* (in full **panne velvet**) a velvet-like fabric of silk or rayon with a flattened pile. [F]

pannier /pánniər/ *n.* **1** a basket, esp. one of a pair carried by a beast of burden. **2** each of a pair of bags or boxes on either side of the rear wheel of a bicycle or motor cycle. **3** *hist.* **a** part of a skirt looped up round the hips. **b** a frame supporting this. [ME f. OF *panier* f. L *panarium* bread-basket f. *panis* bread]

pannikin /pánnikin/ *n.* **1** *Brit.* a small metal drinking-cup. **2** *Brit.* the contents of this. **3** *Austral. sl.* the head (esp. *off one's pannikin*). □ **pannikin boss** *Austral. sl.* a minor overseer or foreman. [PAN[1] + -KIN, after *cannikin*]

■ **3** see HEAD *n.* 1; (*off one's pannikin*) see CRAZY 1.

panoply /pánnəpli/ *n.* (*pl.* **-ies**) **1** a complete or splendid array. **2** a complete suit of armour. □□ **panoplied** *adj.* [F *panoplie* or mod.L *panoplia* full armour f. Gk (as PAN-, *oplia* f. *hopla* arms)]

panoptic /panóptik/ *adj.* showing or seeing the whole at one view. [Gk *panoptos* seen by all, *panoptēs* all-seeing]

panorama /pánnəraámə/ *n.* **1** an unbroken view of a surrounding region. **2** a complete survey or presentation of a subject, sequence of events, etc. **3** a picture or photograph containing a wide view. **4** a continuous passing scene. □□ **panoramic** /-rámmik/ *adj.* **panoramically** /-rámmikəli/ *adv.* [PAN- + Gk *horama* view f. *horaō* see]

■ **1, 3** see VIEW *n.* 2. **2** see VIEW *n.* 3. □□ **panoramic** sweeping, commanding, extensive, comprehensive, wide, overall, scenic, far-reaching, all-embracing, far-ranging, all-encompassing, inclusive, bird's-eye, general.

pan-pipes /pánpīps/ *n.pl.* a musical instrument orig. associated with the Greek rural god Pan, made of a series of short pipes graduated in length and fixed together with the mouthpieces in line.

pansy /pánzi/ *n.* (*pl.* **-ies**) **1** any garden plant of the genus *Viola*, with flowers of various rich colours. **2** *colloq. derog.* **a** an effeminate man. **b** a male homosexual. [F *pensée* thought, pansy f. *penser* think f. L *pensare* frequent. of *pendere pens-* weigh]

pant /pant/ *v.* & *n.* ● *v.* **1** *intr.* breathe with short quick breaths. **2** *tr.* (often foll. by *out*) utter breathlessly. **3** *intr.* (often foll. by *for*) yearn or crave. **4** *intr.* (of the heart etc.) throb violently. ● *n.* **1** a panting breath. **2** a throb. □□ **pantingly** *adv.* [ME f. OF *pantaisier* ult. f. Gk *phantasioō* cause to imagine (as FANTASY)]

■ *v.* **1, 2** gasp, huff, puff, blow, heave, wheeze. **3** (*pant for*) crave, hanker after, hunger *or* thirst for *or* after, yearn for, ache for, want, desire, covet, wish for, long *or* pine *or* sigh for, have one's heart set on, die for, be dying for, *colloq.* have a yen for.

pantalets /pántəléts/ *n.pl.* (also **pantalettes**) *hist.* **1** long underpants worn by women and girls in the 19th c., with a frill at the bottom of each leg. **2** women's cycling trousers. [dimin. of PANTALOON]

pantaloon /pántəlṓōn/ *n.* **1** (in *pl.*) **a** *hist.* men's close-fitting breeches fastened below the calf or at the foot. **b** esp. *US* trousers. **2** (**Pantaloon**) a character in Italian comedy wearing pantaloons (in sense 1a). [F *pantalon* f. It. *pantalone*, a character in Italian comedy]

pantechnicon /panték-nikən/ *n. Brit.* a large van for transporting furniture. [PAN- + TECHNIC orig. as the name of a bazaar and then a furniture warehouse]

pantheism /pánthi-iz'm/ *n.* **1** the belief that God is identifiable with the forces of nature and with natural substances. **2** worship that admits or tolerates all gods. □□ **pantheist** *n.* **pantheistic** /-ístik/ *adj.* **pantheistical** /-ístik'l/ *adj.* **pantheistically** /-ístikəli/ *adv.* [PAN- + Gk *theos* god]

pantheon /pánthiən/ *n.* **1** a building in which illustrious dead are buried or have memorials. **2** the deities of a people collectively. **3** a temple dedicated to all the gods, esp. the circular one at Rome. [ME f. L f. Gk *pantheion* (as PAN-, *theion* holy f. *theos* god)]

panther /pánthər/ *n.* **1** a leopard, esp. with black fur. **2** *US* a puma. [ME f. OF *pantere* f. L *panthera* f. Gk *panthēr*]

pantie-girdle /pántigurd'l/ *n.* a woman's girdle with a crotch shaped like pants.

panties /pántiz/ *n.pl. colloq.* short-legged or legless underpants worn by women and girls. [dimin. of PANTS]

pantihose /pántihōz/ *n.* (*US* **panty hose**) (usu. treated as *pl.*) women's tights. [PANTIES + HOSE]

pantile /pántīl/ *n.* a roof-tile curved to form an S-shaped section, fitted to overlap. [PAN[1] + TILE]

panto /pántō/ *n.* (*pl.* **-os**) *Brit. colloq.* = PANTOMIME 1. [abbr.]

panto- /pántō/ *comb. form* all, universal. [Gk *pas pantos* all]

pantograph /pántəgraaf/ *n.* **1** *Art & Painting* an instrument for copying a plan or drawing etc. on a different scale by a system of jointed rods. **2** a jointed framework conveying a current to an electric vehicle from overhead wires. ▫▫ **pantographic** /-gráffik/ *adj.* [PANTO- + Gk *-graphos* writing]

pantomime /pántəmīm/ *n.* **1** *Brit.* a theatrical entertainment based on a fairy tale, with music, topical jokes, etc., usu. produced around Christmas. **2** the use of gestures and facial expression to convey meaning, esp. in drama and dance. **3** *colloq.* an absurd or outrageous piece of behaviour. ▫▫ **pantomimic** /-mímmik/ *adj.* [F *pantomime* or L *pantomimus* f. Gk *pantomimos* (as PANTO-, MIME)]

pantothenic acid /pántəthénnik/ *n.* a vitamin of the B complex, found in rice, bran, and many other foods, and essential for the oxidation of fats and carbohydrates. [Gk *pantothen* from every side]

pantry /pántri/ *n.* (*pl.* **-ies**) **1** a small room or cupboard in which crockery, cutlery, table linen, etc., are kept. **2** a larder. [ME f. AF *panetrie*, OF *paneterie* f. *panetier* baker ult. f. LL *panarius* bread-seller f. L *panis* bread]

pantryman /pántrimən/ *n.* (*pl.* **-men**) a butler or a butler's assistant.

pants /pants/ *n.pl.* **1** *Brit.* underpants or knickers. **2** *US* trousers or slacks. ▫ **bore** (or **scare** etc.) **the pants off** *colloq.* bore, scare, etc., to an intolerable degree. **pants** (or **pant**) **suit** esp. *US* a trouser suit. **with one's pants down** *colloq.* in an embarrassingly unprepared state. [abbr. of PANTALOONS]

■ **1** underpants, trunks, briefs, boxer shorts, *US* undershorts, *propr.* Y-fronts; knickers, drawers, *Brit.* camiknickers, *colloq.* panties, bloomers, *hist.* pantalets; underclothes, undergarments, lingerie, *colloq.* undies, underthings, *Brit. colloq.* smalls, *joc.* unmentionables. **2** see TROUSERS 1. ▫ **with one's pants down** see UNPREPARED.

panty hose *US* var. of PANTIHOSE.

panzer /pántsər, pánz-/ *n.* **1** (in *pl.*) armoured troops. **2** (*attrib.*) heavily armoured (*panzer division*). [G, = coat of mail]

pap[1] /pap/ *n.* **1 a** soft or semi-liquid food for infants or invalids. **b** a mash or pulp. **2** light or trivial reading matter; nonsense. ▫▫ **pappy** *adj.* [ME prob. f. MLG, MDu. *pappe*, prob. ult. f. L *pappare* eat]

pap[2] /pap/ *n. archaic* or *dial.* the nipple of a breast. [ME, of Scand. orig.: ult. imit. of sucking]

papa /pəpaá/ *n. archaic* father (esp. as a child's word). [F f. LL f. Gk *papas*]

papabile /pəpaábilay/ *adj.* suitable for high office. [It., = suitable to be pope, f. L *papa* pope]

papacy /páypəsi/ *n.* (*pl.* **-ies**) **1** a pope's office or tenure. **2** the papal system. [ME f. med.L *papatia* f. *papa* pope]

papain /pəpáyin/ *n.* an enzyme obtained from unripe pawpaws, used to tenderize meat and as a food supplement to aid digestion. [PAPAYA + -IN]

papal /páyp'l/ *adj.* of or relating to a pope or to the papacy. ▫ **Papal States** *hist.* the temporal dominions belonging to the Pope, esp. in central Italy. ▫▫ **papally** *adv.* [ME f. OF f. med.L *papalis* f. eccl.L *papa* POPE[1]]

paparazzo /páppəraátsō/ *n.* (*pl.* **paparazzi** /-si/) a freelance photographer who pursues celebrities to get photographs of them. [It.]

papaverous /pəpáyvərəss/ *adj.* like or related to the poppy. ▫▫ **papaveraceous** /-ráyshəss/ *adj.* [L *papaver* poppy]

papaw var. of PAWPAW.

papaya /pəpī́ə/ *n.* = PAWPAW 1. [earlier form of PAWPAW]

paper /páypər/ *n.* & *v.* ● *n.* **1** a material manufactured in thin sheets from the pulp of wood or other fibrous substances, used for writing or drawing or printing on, or as wrapping material etc. **2** (*attrib.*) **a** made of or using paper. **b** flimsy like paper. **3** = NEWSPAPER. **4 a** a document printed on paper. **b** (in *pl.*) documents attesting identity or credentials. **c** (in *pl.*) documents belonging to a person or relating to a matter. **5** *Commerce* **a** negotiable documents, e.g. bills of exchange. **b** (*attrib.*) recorded on paper though not existing (*paper profits*). **6 a** a set of questions to be answered at one session in an examination. **b** the written answers to these. **7** = WALLPAPER. **8** an essay or dissertation, esp. one read to a learned society or published in a learned journal. **9** a piece of paper, esp. as a wrapper etc. **10** *Theatr. sl.* free tickets or the people admitted by them (*the house is full of paper*). ● *v.tr.* **1** apply paper to, esp. decorate (a wall etc.) with wallpaper. **2** (foll. by *over*) **a** cover (a hole or blemish) with paper. **b** disguise or try to hide (a fault etc.). **3** *Theatr. sl.* fill (a theatre) by giving free passes. ▫ **on paper 1** in writing. **2** in theory; to judge from written or printed evidence. **paper-boy** (or **-girl**) a boy or girl who delivers or sells newspapers. **paper-chase** a cross-country run in which the runners follow a trail marked by torn-up paper. **paper-clip** a clip of bent wire or of plastic for holding several sheets of paper together. **paper-hanger** a person who decorates with wallpaper, esp. professionally. **paper-knife** a blunt knife for opening letters etc. **paper-mill** a mill in which paper is made. **paper money** money in the form of banknotes. **paper mulberry** a small Asiatic tree, *Broussonetia papyrifera*, of the mulberry family, whose bark is used for making paper and cloth. **paper nautilus** see NAUTILUS 2. **paper round 1** a job of regularly delivering newspapers. **2** a route taken doing this. **paper tape** *Computing* tape made of paper, esp. that on which data or instructions are represented by means of holes punched in it, for conveying to a processor etc. **paper tiger** an apparently threatening, but ineffectual, person or thing. ▫▫ **paperer** *n.* **paperless** *adj.* [ME f. AF *papir*, = OF *papier* f. L *papyrus*: see PAPYRUS]

■ *n.* **3** newspaper, tabloid, daily, weekly, journal, gazette, publication, periodical, newsletter, organ, *derog.* rag, sheet. **4** document(s), instrument, form, certificate, deed; credential(s), identification; docket, file, dossier, record, archive. **5 a** see NOTE *n.* 6b. **8** article, composition, essay, assignment, report, thesis, study, tract, analysis, critique, exegesis, treatise, monograph, dissertation, disquisition. ● *v.* **1** wallpaper, line; decorate. **2** (*paper over*) cover up; see also COVER *v.* 1. ▫ **on paper 1** in writing, on record, documented, in black and white. **2** see *ideally* (IDEAL).

paperback /páypərbak/ *adj.* & *n.* ● *adj.* (of a book) bound in stiff paper not boards. ● *n.* a paperback book.

paperweight /páypərwayt/ *n.* a small heavy object for keeping loose papers in place.

paperwork /páypərwurk/ *n.* **1** routine clerical or administrative work. **2** documents, esp. for a particular purpose.

papery /páypəri/ *adj.* like paper in thinness or texture.

papier mâché /pápyay máshay/ *n.* paper pulp used for moulding into boxes, trays, etc. [F, = chewed paper]

papilionaceous /pəpilyənáyshəss/ *adj.* (of a plant) with a corolla like a butterfly. [mod.L *papilionaceus* f. L *papilio -onis* butterfly]

papilla /pəpillə/ *n.* (*pl.* **papillae** /-lee/) **1** a small nipple-like protuberance in a part or organ of the body. **2** *Bot.* a small fleshy projection on a plant. ▫▫ **papillary** *adj.* **papillate** /páppilayt/ *adj.* **papillose** /páppilōss/ *adj.* [L, = nipple, dimin. of *papula*: see PAPULA]

papilloma /páppilṓmə/ *n.* (*pl.* **papillomas** or **papillomata** /-mətə/) a wartlike usu. benign tumour.

papillon /pəpilyən/ *n.* **1** a toy dog of a breed with ears suggesting the form of a butterfly. **2** this breed. [F, = butterfly, f. L *papilio -onis*]

papist /páypist/ *n.* & *adj.* often *derog.* ● *n.* **1** a Roman Catholic. **2** *hist.* an advocate of papal supremacy. ● *adj.* of or relating to Roman Catholics. ▫▫ **papistic** /pəpístik/ *adj.* **papistical** /pəpístik'l/ *adj.* **papistry** *n.* [F *papiste* or mod.L *papista* f. eccl.L *papa* POPE[1]]

papoose /pəpóoss/ *n.* a N. American Indian young child. [Algonquian]

pappus /páppəss/ *n.* (*pl.* **pappi** /-pī/) a group of hairs on the fruit of thistles, dandelions, etc. ▫▫ **pappose** *adj.* [L f. Gk *pappos*]

paprika /páprikə, pəpréekə/ *n.* **1** *Bot.* a red pepper. **2** a condiment made from it. [Magyar]

pap test /pap/ *n.* a test done by a cervical smear. [abbr. of G. N. *Papanicolaou*, US scientist d. 1962]

papula /pápyoolə/ *n.* (also **papule** /pápyool/) (*pl.* **papulae** /-lee/) **1** a pimple. **2** a small fleshy projection on a plant. ▫▫ **papular** *adj.* **papulose** *adj.* **papulous** *adj.* [L]

papyrology /páppiróllәji/ *n.* the study of ancient papyri. ▫▫ **papyrological** /-rəlójik'l/ *adj.* **papyrologist** *n.*

papyrus /pəpī́rəss/ *n.* (*pl.* **papyri** /-rī/) **1** an aquatic plant, *Cyperus papyrus*, with dark green stems topped with fluffy inflorescences. **2 a** a writing-material prepared in ancient Egypt from the pithy stem of this. **b** a document written on this. [ME f. L *papyrus* f. Gk *papuros*]

par[1] /paar/ *n.* **1** the average or normal amount, degree, condition, etc. (*be up to par*). **2** equality; an equal status or footing (*on a par with*). **3** *Golf* the number of strokes a first-class player should normally require for a hole or course. **4** *Stock Exch.* the face value of stocks and shares etc. (*at par*). **5** (in full **par of exchange**) the recognized value of one country's currency in terms of another's. ▫ **above par** *Stock Exch.* at a premium. **at par** *Stock Exch.* at face value. **below par 1** less good than usual in health or other quality. **2** *Stock Exch.* at a discount. **par for the course** *colloq.* what is normal or expected in any given circumstances. [L (adj. & n.) = equal, equality]

■ **1** standard, normal, average, norm, expectation. **2** level; see also PARITY[1] 1. ▫ **below par 1** below average, substandard, inferior, second-rate, mediocre, middling, poor, inadequate, unsatisfactory, wanting, bad, wretched, miserable, awful, terrible, not up to standard *or* scratch, *colloq.* lousy, not up to snuff; ill, sickly, poorly, unhealthy, unwell, not (very) well, not oneself, not in good *or* the best shape, in bad shape, off form, off colour, *colloq.* under the weather.

par[2] /paar/ *n. Brit.* esp. *Journalism colloq.* paragraph. [abbr.]

par. *abbr.* (also **para.**) paragraph.

par- /pər, par, paar/ *prefix* var. of PARA-[1] before a vowel or *h*; (*paraldehyde*; *parody*; *parhelion*).

para /párrə/ *n. colloq.* **1** a paratrooper. **2** a paragraph. [abbr.]

para-[1] /párrə/ *prefix* (also **par-**) **1** beside (*paramilitary*). **2** beyond (*paranormal*). **3** *Chem.* **a** modification of (*paraldehyde*). **b** relating to diametrically opposite carbon atoms in a benzene ring (*paradichlorobenzene*). [from or after Gk *para-* f. *para* beside, past, beyond]

para-[2] /párrə/ *comb. form* protect, ward off (*parachute*; *parasol*). [F f. It. f. L *parare* defend]

parabiosis /párrəbīṓsiss/ *n. Biol.* the natural or artificial joining of two individuals. ▫▫ **parabiotic** /-bīóttik/ *adj.* [mod.L, formed as PARA-[1] + Gk *biōsis* mode of life f. *bios* life]

parable /párrəb'l/ *n.* **1** a narrative of imagined events used to illustrate a moral or spiritual lesson. **2** an allegory. [ME f. OF *parabole* f. LL sense 'allegory, discourse' of L *parabola* comparison]

■ allegory, fable, lesson, morality tale.

parabola /pərábbələ/ *n.* an open plane curve formed by the intersection of a cone with a plane parallel to its side, resembling the path of a projectile under the action of gravity. [mod.L f. Gk *parabolē* placing side by side, comparison (as PARA-[1], *bolē* a throw f. *ballō*)]

parabolic /párrəbóllik/ *adj.* **1** of or expressed in a parable. **2** of or like a parabola. ▫▫ **parabolically** *adv.* [LL *parabolicus* f. Gk *parabolikos* (as PARABOLA)]

parabolical /párrəbóllik'l/ *adj.* = PARABOLIC 1.

paraboloid /pərábbəloyd/ *n.* **1** (in full **paraboloid of revolution**) a solid generated by the rotation of a parabola about its axis of symmetry. **2** a solid having two or more non-parallel parabolic cross-sections. ▫▫ **paraboloidal** *adj.*

paracetamol /párrəséttəmol, -séetəmol/ *n.* **1** a drug used to relieve pain and reduce fever. **2** a tablet of this. [*para-acetylaminophenol*]

parachronism /pərákrəniz'm/ *n.* an error in chronology, esp. by assigning too late a date. [PARA-[1] + Gk *khronos* time, perh. after *anachronism*]

parachute /párrəshoot/ *n.* & *v.* ● *n.* **1** a rectangular or umbrella-shaped apparatus allowing a person or heavy object attached to it to descend slowly from a height, esp. from an aircraft, or to retard motion in other ways. **2** (*attrib.*) dropped or to be dropped by parachute (*parachute troops*; *parachute flare*). ● *v.tr.* & *intr.* convey or descend by parachute. [F (as PARA-[2], CHUTE[1])]

parachutist /párrəshootist/ *n.* **1** a person who uses a parachute. **2** (in *pl.*) parachute troops.

Paraclete /párrəkleet/ *n.* the Holy Spirit as advocate or counsellor (John 14:16, 26, etc.). [ME f. OF *paraclet* f. LL *paracletus* f. Gk *paraklētos* called in aid (as PARA-[1], *klētos* f. *kaleō* call)]

parade /pəráyd/ *n.* & *v.* ● *n.* **1 a** a formal or ceremonial muster of troops for inspection. **b** = *parade-ground*. **2** a public procession. **3** ostentatious display (*made a parade of their wealth*). **4** a public square, promenade, or row of shops. ● *v.* **1** *intr.* assemble for parade. **2 a** *tr.* march through (streets etc.) in procession. **b** *intr.* march ceremonially. **3** *tr.* display ostentatiously. ▫ **on parade 1** taking part in a parade. **2** on display. **parade-ground** a place for the muster of troops. ▫▫ **parader** *n.* [F, = show, f. Sp. *parada* and It. *parata* ult. f. L *parare* prepare, furnish]

■ *n.* **2** procession, march, train, file, promenade, cortège; column. **3** exhibition, display, show, spectacle, array, splash. **4** promenade, walk, way, mall, esplanade, precinct; row. ● *v.* **2** march, pass in review, promenade, walk, file. **3** flaunt, show (off), brandish, wave, display, air, *literary* vaunt. ▫ **parade ground** parade, *Anglo-Ind. maidan*.

paradiddle /párrədidd'l/ *n.* a drum roll with alternate beating of sticks. [imit.]

paradigm /párrədīm/ *n.* an example or pattern, esp. a representative set of the inflections of a noun, verb, etc. ▫▫ **paradigmatic** /-digmáttik/ *adj.* **paradigmatically** /-digmáttikəli/ *adv.* [LL *paradigma* f. Gk *paradeigma* f. *paradeiknumi* show side by side (as PARA-[1], *deiknumi* show)]

paradise /párrədīss/ *n.* **1** (in some religions) heaven as the ultimate abode of the just. **2** a place or state of complete happiness. **3** (in full **earthly paradise**) the abode of Adam and Eve in the biblical account of the Creation; the garden of Eden. ▫▫ **paradisaical** /-disáyik'l/ *adj.* **paradisal** /párrədīs'l/ *adj.* **paradisiacal** /-disī́ək'l/ *adj.* **paradisical** /-díssik'l/ *adj.* [ME f. OF *paradis* f. LL *paradisus* f. Gk *paradeisos* f. Avestan *pairidaēza* park]

■ **1** heaven, Zion, Elysium, Elysian Fields, happy hunting-ground, the promised land, Valhalla. **2** heaven on earth, dreamland, seventh heaven, (Garden of) Eden, Utopia, Shangri-La; bliss, happiness, rapture, heaven, delight, blessedness, ecstasy, joy, nirvana.

parados /párrədoss, -dō/ *n.* an elevation of earth behind a fortified place as a protection against attack from the rear, esp. a mound along the back of a trench. [F (as PARA-[2], *dos* back f. L *dorsum*)]

paradox /párrədoks/ *n.* **1 a** a seemingly absurd or contradictory statement, even if actually well-founded. **b** a self-contradictory or essentially absurd statement. **2** a person or thing conflicting with a preconceived notion of what is reasonable or possible. **3** a paradoxical quality or character. [orig. = a statement contrary to accepted opinion, f. LL *paradoxum* f. Gk *paradoxon* neut. adj. (as PARA-[1], *doxa* opinion)]
▪ contradiction, self-contradiction, incongruity, inconsistency, absurdity, ambiguity, enigma, puzzle, mystery, quandary, problem, *disp.* dilemma; *rhet.* oxymoron.

paradoxical /párrədóksik'l/ *adj.* **1** of or like or involving paradox. **2** fond of paradox. ▫▫ **paradoxically** *adv.*
▪ **1** contradictory, self-contradictory, conflicting, impossible, improbable, incongruous, illogical, inconsistent, absurd, ambiguous, confusing, equivocal, enigmatic, puzzling, baffling, incomprehensible, bewildering, perplexing, mysterious, problematic.

paraffin /párrəfin/ *n.* **1** an inflammable waxy or oily substance obtained by distillation from petroleum or shale, used in liquid form (also **paraffin oil**) esp. as a fuel. **2** *Chem.* = ALKANE. ▫ **paraffin wax** paraffin in its solid form. [G (1830) f. L *parum* little + *affinis* related, from the small affinity it has for other substances]

paragoge /párrəgōji/ *n.* the addition of a letter or syllable to a word in some contexts or as a language develops (e.g. *t* in *peasant*). ▫▫ **paragogic** /-gójik/ *adj.* [LL f. Gk *paragōgē* derivation (as PARA-[1], *agōgē* f. *agō* lead)]

paragon /párrəgən/ *n.* **1 a** a model of excellence. **b** a supremely excellent person or thing. **2** (foll. by *of*) a model (of virtue etc.). **3** a perfect diamond of 100 carats or more. [obs. F f. It. *paragone* touchstone, f. med.Gk *parakonē* whetstone]
▪ **1, 2** epitome, archetype, model, prototype, quintessence, pattern, standard, exemplar, ideal, *beau idéal*, criterion.

paragraph /párrəgraaf/ *n.* & *v.* ● *n.* **1** a distinct section of a piece of writing, beginning on a new usu. indented line. **2** a symbol (usu. ¶) used to mark a new paragraph, and also as a reference mark. **3** a short item in a newspaper, usu. of only one paragraph. ● *v.tr.* arrange (a piece of writing) in paragraphs. ▫▫ **paragraphic** /-gráffik/ *adj.* [F *paragraphe* or med.L *paragraphus* f. Gk *paragraphos* short stroke marking a break in sense (as PARA-[1], *graphō* write)]

parakeet /párrəkeet/ *n.* (*US* also **parrakeet**) any of various small usu. long-tailed parrots. [OF *paroquet*, It. *parrocchetto*, Sp. *periquito*, perh. ult. f. dimin. of *Pierre* etc. Peter: cf. PARROT]

paralanguage /párrəlanggwij/ *n.* elements or factors in communication that are ancillary to language proper, e.g. intonation and gesture.

paraldehyde /pəráldihīd/ *n.* a cyclic polymer of acetaldehyde, used as a narcotic and sedative. [PARA-[1] + ALDEHYDE]

paralegal /párrəleeg'l/ *adj.* & *n.* esp. *US* ● *adj.* of or relating to auxiliary aspects of the law. ● *n.* a person trained in subsidiary legal matters. [PARA-[1] + LEGAL]

paralipomena /párrəlipómminə/ *n.pl.* (also **-leipomena** /párrəlī-/) **1** things omitted from a work and added as a supplement. **2** *Bibl.* the books of Chronicles in the Old Testament, containing particulars omitted from Kings. [ME f. eccl.L f. Gk *paraleipomena* f. *paraleipō* omit (as PARA-[1], *leipō* leave)]

paralipsis /párrəlípsiss/ *n.* (also **-leipsis** /-līpsiss/) (*pl.* **-ses** /-seez/) *Rhet.* **1** the device of giving emphasis by professing to say little or nothing of a subject, as in *not to mention their unpaid debts of several millions*. **2** an instance of this. [LL f. Gk *paraleipsis* passing over (as PARA-[1], *leipsis* f. *leipō* leave)]

parallax /párrəlaks/ *n.* **1** the apparent difference in the position or direction of an object caused when the observer's position is changed. **2** the angular amount of this. ▫▫ **parallactic** /-láktik/ *adj.* [F *parallaxe* f. mod.L *parallaxis* f. Gk *parallaxis* change f. *parallassō* to alternate (as PARA-[1], *allassō* exchange f. *allos* other)]

parallel /párrəlel/ *adj.*, *n.*, & *v.* ● *adj.* **1 a** (of lines or planes) side by side and having the same distance continuously between them. **b** (foll. by *to*, *with*) (of a line or plane) having this relation (to another). **2** (of circumstances etc.) precisely similar, analogous, or corresponding. **3 a** (of processes etc.) occurring or performed simultaneously. **b** *Computing* involving the simultaneous performance of operations. ● *n.* **1** a person or thing precisely analogous or equal to another. **2** a comparison (*drew a parallel between the two situations*). **3** (in full **parallel of latitude**) *Geog.* **a** each of the imaginary parallel circles of constant latitude on the earth's surface. **b** a corresponding line on a map (*the 49th parallel*). **4** *Printing* two parallel lines (‖) as a reference mark. ● *v.tr.* (**paralleled, paralleling**) **1** be parallel to; correspond to. **2** represent as similar; compare. **3** adduce as a parallel instance. ▫ **in parallel** (of electric circuits) arranged so as to join at common points at each end. **parallel bars** a pair of parallel rails on posts for gymnastics. ▫▫ **parallelism** *n.* [F *parallèle* f. L *parallelus* f. Gk *parallēlos* (as PARA-[1], *allēlos* one another)]
▪ *adj.* **2** similar, corresponding, congruent, analogous, analogical, correspondent, like, matching, homologous, coordinate, equivalent, proportional, proportionate, uniform, *archaic or literary* coequal. **3** contemporary, contemporaneous, simultaneous. ● *n.* **1** analogue, match, homologue, equivalent, counterpart, equal, *archaic or literary* coequal. **2** analogy, parallelism, equivalence, correspondence, symmetry, equality, parity, correlation, *archaic or literary* coequality; see also COMPARISON 3. ● *v.* **1** correspond to *or* with, match, equate to *or* with, be likened to, correlate to *or* with, compare with *or* to, imitate, repeat, echo, iterate, reiterate, duplicate, follow, agree with; keep pace with, conform to *or* with, balance, set off, offset, be accompanied by, coincide with, *US colloq.* jibe with. **2** match, equate, liken, compare, juxtapose, associate, correlate.

parallelepiped /párrəleléppiped, -ləpīpid/ *n. Geom.* a solid body of which each face is a parallelogram. [Gk *parallēlepipedon* (as PARALLEL, *epipedon* plane surface)]

parallelogram /párrəléllәgram/ *n. Geom.* a four-sided plane rectilinear figure with opposite sides parallel. ▫ **parallelogram of forces 1** a parallelogram illustrating the theorem that if two forces acting at a point are represented in magnitude and direction by two sides of a parallelogram meeting at that point, their resultant is represented by the diagonal drawn from that point. **2** this theorem. [F *parallélogramme* f. LL *parallelogrammum* f. Gk *parallēlogrammon* (as PARALLEL, *grammē* line)]

paralogism /pərállәjiz'm/ *n. Logic* **1** a fallacy. **2** illogical reasoning (esp. of which the reasoner is unconscious). ▫▫ **paralogist** *n.* **paralogize** *v.intr.* (also **-ise**). [F *paralogisme* f. LL *paralogismus* f. Gk *paralogismos* f. *paralogizomai* reason falsely f. *paralogos* contrary to reason (as PARA-[1], *logos* reason)]

paralyse /párrəlīz/ *v.tr.* (*US* **paralyze**) **1** affect with paralysis. **2** render powerless; cripple. ▫▫ **paralysation** /-záysh'n/ *n.* **paralysingly** *adv.* [F *paralyser* f. *paralysie*: cf. PALSY]
▪ **2** disable, cripple, incapacitate; immobilize, inactivate, deactivate, transfix; halt, stop.

paralysis /pərállisiss/ *n.* (*pl.* **paralyses** /-seez/) **1** a nervous condition with impairment or loss of esp. the motor function of the nerves. **2** a state of utter powerlessness. [L f. Gk *paralusis* f. *paraluō* disable (as PARA-[1], *luō* loosen)]

paralytic /párrəlíttik/ *adj.* & *n.* ● *adj.* **1** affected by paralysis. **2** *sl.* very drunk. ● *n.* a person affected by paralysis. ▫▫ **paralytically** *adv.* [ME f. OF *paralytique* f. L *paralyticus* f. Gk *paralutikos* (as PARALYSIS)]

paramagnetic /párrəmagnéttik/ *adj.* (of a body or substance) tending to become weakly magnetized so as to lie parallel to a magnetic field force. ▫▫ **paramagnetism** /-mágnitiz'm/ *n.*

paramatta var. of PARRAMATTA.

paramecium /párrəmeéssiəm/ *n.* (also **paramoecium**) any freshwater protozoan of the genus *Paramecium*, of a characteristic slipper-like shape covered with cilia. [mod.L f. Gk *paramēkēs* oval (as PARA-[1], *mēkos* length)]

paramedic /párrəméddik/ *n.* a paramedical worker.

paramedical /párrəméddik'l/ *adj.* (of services etc.) supplementing and supporting medical work.

parameter /pərámmitər/ *n.* **1** *Math.* a quantity constant in the case considered but varying in different cases. **2 a** an (esp. measurable or quantifiable) characteristic or feature. **b** (loosely) a constant element or factor, esp. serving as a limit or boundary. □□ **parametric** /párrəmétrik/ *adj.* **parametrize** *v.tr.* (also **-ise**). [mod.L f. Gk *para* beside + *metron* measure]

paramilitary /párrəmíllitəri, -tri/ *adj.* (of forces) ancillary to and similarly organized to military forces.

paramnesia /párrəmneéziə/ *n. Psychol.* = DÉJÀ VU. [PARA-[1] + AMNESIA]

paramo /párrəmō/ *n.* (*pl.* **-os**) a high treeless plateau in tropical S. America. [Sp. & Port. f. L *paramus*]

paramoecium var. of PARAMECIUM.

paramount /párrəmownt/ *adj.* **1** supreme; requiring first consideration; pre-eminent (*of paramount importance*). **2** in supreme authority. □□ **paramountcy** *n.* **paramountly** *adv.* [AF *paramont* f. OF *par* by + *amont* above: cf. AMOUNT]

▪ **1** pre-eminent, chief, supreme, dominant, main, predominant, cardinal, first, prime, primary, principal, essential, vital, requisite, basic. **2** see SUPREME *adj* 1.

paramour /párrəmoor/ *n. archaic* or *derog.* an illicit lover of a married person. [ME f. OF *par amour* by love]

▪ lover, love, inamorato, inamorata, mistress, gigolo, concubine, kept woman, (the) other woman, *sl.* sugar-daddy, *sl. derog.* fancy man *or* woman.

parang /párrang/ *n.* a large heavy Malayan knife used for clearing vegetation etc. [Malay]

paranoia /párrənóyə/ *n.* **1** a mental disorder esp. characterized by delusions of persecution and self-importance. **2** an abnormal tendency to suspect and mistrust others. □□ **paranoiac** *adj.* & *n.* **paranoiacally** *adv.* **paranoic** /-nṓ-ik, -nóyik/ *adj.* **paranoically** /-nṓ-ikəli, -nóyikəli/ *adv.* **paranoid** /párrənoyd/ *adj.* & *n.* [mod.L f. Gk f. *paranoos* distracted (as PARA-[1], *noos* mind)]

paranormal /párrənórm'l/ *adj.* beyond the scope of normal objective investigation or explanation. □□ **paranormally** *adv.*

parapet /párrəpit/ *n.* **1** a low wall at the edge of a roof, balcony, etc., or along the sides of a bridge. **2** a defence of earth or stone to conceal and protect troops. □□ **parapeted** *adj.* [F *parapet* or It. *parapetto* breast-high wall (as PARA-[2], *petto* breast f. L *pectus*)]

paraph /párrəf/ *n.* a flourish after a signature, orig. as a precaution against forgery. [ME f. F *paraphe* f. med.L *paraphus* for *paragraphus* PARAGRAPH]

paraphernalia /párrəfərnáyliə/ *n.pl.* (also treated as *sing.*) miscellaneous belongings, items of equipment, accessories, etc. [orig. = property owned by a married woman, f. med.L *paraphernalia* f. LL *parapherna* f. Gk *parapherna* property apart from a dowry (as PARA-[1], *pherna* f. *phernē* dower)]

▪ equipment, apparatus, accessories, outfit, kit, appliances, utensils, gear, rig, material(s), *matériel*, things, tackle, equipage, accoutrements, effects, chattels, possessions, belongings, appurtenances, trappings, property, baggage, impedimenta, supplies, stuff, junk, *esp. Brit.* rubbish, *Brit. sl.* clobber.

paraphrase /párrəfrayz/ *n.* & *v.* ● *n.* a free rendering or rewording of a passage. ● *v.tr.* express the meaning of (a passage) in other words. □□ **paraphrastic** /-frástik/ *adj.* [F *paraphrase* or L *paraphrasis* f. Gk *paraphrasis* f. *paraphrazō* (as PARA-[1] *phrazō* tell)]

▪ *n.* rephrasing, rewording, restatement, rewriting, rewrite, rehash, rendition, rendering, version. ● *v.* rephrase, metaphrase, reword, restate, rewrite, rehash.

paraplegia /párrəpleéjə/ *n.* paralysis of the legs and part or the whole of the trunk. □□ **paraplegic** *adj.* & *n.* [mod.L f. Gk *paraplēgia* f. *paraplēssō* (as PARA-[1], *plēssō* strike)]

parapsychology /párrəsīkólləji/ *n.* the study of mental phenomena outside the sphere of ordinary psychology (hypnosis, telepathy, etc.). □□ **parapsychological** /-sīkəlójik'l/ *adj.* **parapsychologist** *n.*

paraquat /párrəkwot/ *n.* a quick-acting herbicide, becoming inactive on contact with the soil. [PARA-[1] + QUATERNARY (from the position of the bond between the two parts of the molecule relative to quaternary nitrogen atom)]

parasailing / párrəsayling/ *n.* a sport in which participants wearing open parachutes are towed behind a motor boat. □□ **parasailer** *n.* **parasailor** *n.*

parascending /párrəsending/ *n.* a sport in which participants wearing open parachutes are towed behind a vehicle or motor boat to gain height before release for a conventional descent, usu. towards a predetermined target. □□ **parascender** *n.*

paraselene /párrəsileéni/ *n.* (*pl.* **paraselenae** /-nee/) a bright spot, esp. an image of the moon, on a lunar halo. Also called *mock moon*. [mod.L (as PARA-[1], Gk *selēnē* moon)]

parasite /párrəsīt/ *n.* **1** an organism living in or on another and benefiting at the expense of the other. **2** a person who lives off or exploits another or others. **3** *Philol.* an inorganic sound or letter developing from an adjacent one. □□ **parasitic** /-síttik/ *adj.* **parasitical** /-síttik'l/ *adj.* **parasitically** /-síttikəli/ *adv.* **parasiticide** /-síttisīd/ *n.* **parasitism** *n.* **parasitology** /-tólləji/ *n.* **parasitologist** /-tólləjist/ *n.* [L *parasitus* f. Gk *parasitos* one who eats at another's table (as PARA-[1], *sitos* food)]

▪ **2** leech, bloodsucker, hanger-on, sponger, sponge, cadger, scrounger, barnacle, *esp. US colloq.* moocher, *Austral.* & *NZ sl.* bludger, *US sl.* freeloader.

parasitize /párrəsitīz/ *v.tr.* (also **-ise**) infest as a parasite. □□ **parasitization** /-záysh'n/ *n.*

parasol /párrəsol/ *n.* a light umbrella used to give shade from the sun. [F f. It. *parasole* (as PARA-[2], *sole* sun f. L *sol*)]

parasympathetic /párrəsímpəthéttik/ *adj. Anat.* relating to the part of the nervous system that consists of nerves leaving the lower end of the spinal cord and connecting with those in or near the viscera (cf. SYMPATHETIC 9). [PARA-[1] + SYMPATHETIC, because some of these nerves run alongside sympathetic nerves]

parasynthesis /párrəsínthisiss/ *n. Philol.* a derivation from a compound, e.g. *black-eyed* from *black eye(s)* + *-ed*. □□ **parasynthetic** /-théttik/ *adj.* [Gk *parasunthesis* (as PARA-[1], SYNTHESIS)]

parataxis /párrətáksiss/ *n. Gram.* the placing of clauses etc. one after another, without words to indicate coordination or subordination, e.g. *Tell me, how are you?* □□ **paratactic** /-táktik/ *adj.* **paratactically** /-táktikəli/ *adv.* [Gk *parataxis* (as PARA-[1], *taxis* arrangement f. *tassō* arrange)]

parathion /párrəthīən/ *n.* a highly toxic agricultural insecticide. [PARA-[1] + THIO- + -ON]

parathyroid /párrəthīroyd/ *n.* & *adj. Anat.* ● *n.* a gland next to the thyroid, secreting a hormone that regulates calcium levels in the body. ● *adj.* of or associated with this gland.

paratroop /párrətrōōp/ *n.* (*attrib.*) of or consisting of paratroops (*paratroop regiment*).

paratrooper /párrətrōōpər/ *n.* a member of a body of paratroops.

paratroops /párrətrōōps/ *n.pl.* troops equipped to be dropped by parachute from aircraft. [contr. of PARACHUTE + TROOP]

paratyphoid /párrətīfoyd/ *n.* & *adj.* ● *n.* a fever resembling typhoid but caused by various different though related bacteria. ● *adj.* of, relating to, or caused by this fever.

paravane /párrəvayn/ *n.* a torpedo-shaped device towed at a depth regulated by its vanes or planes to cut the moorings of submerged mines.

par avion /paár avyóɴ/ *adv.* by airmail. [F, = by aeroplane]

parboil /pa͡arboyl/ *v.tr.* partly cook by boiling. [ME f. OF *parbo(u)illir* f. LL *perbullire* boil thoroughly (as PER-, *bullire* boil: confused with PART)]

parbuckle /pa͡arbukk'l/ *n.* & *v.* ● *n.* a rope arranged like a sling, for raising or lowering casks and cylindrical objects. ● *v.tr.* raise or lower with this. [earlier *parbunkle*, of unkn. orig.: assoc. with BUCKLE]

parcel /pa͡ars'l/ *n.* & *v.* ● *n.* **1 a** goods etc. wrapped up in a single package. **b** a bundle of things wrapped up, usu. in paper. **2** a piece of land, esp. as part of an estate. **3** a quantity dealt with in one commercial transaction. **4** *archaic* part. ● *v.tr.* (**parcelled, parcelling**; *US* **parceled, parceling**) **1** (foll. by *up*) wrap as a parcel. **2** (foll. by *out*) divide into portions. **3** cover (rope) with strips of canvas. □ **parcel post** the branch of the postal service dealing with parcels. [ME f. OF *parcelle* ult. f. L *particula* (as PART)]
■ *n.* **1** package, packet, carton, box, container, case; bundle, lot, group, batch, collection, pack, set. **2** portion, plot, piece, section, tract, *esp. US* lot, *US* plat. **3** set, group, number, quantity, assortment, lot, bunch, pack, bundle, collection, batch, assemblage. ● *v.* **1** (*parcel up*) see WRAP *v.* 1, BOX[1] *v.* 1. **2** (*parcel out*) apportion, allot, deal (out), dole (out), hand out, distribute, share (out), divide (out), *colloq.* divvy (up), *literary* mete (out).

parch /paarch/ *v.* **1** *tr.* & *intr.* make or become hot and dry. **2** *tr.* roast (peas, corn, etc.) slightly. [ME *perch*, *parche*, of unkn. orig.]
■ **1** dry (out *or* up), desiccate, dehydrate; scorch, sear, burn, bake, roast; shrivel (up), wither.

parched /paarcht/ *adj.* **1** hot and dry; dried out with heat. **2** *colloq.* thirsty.

parchment /pa͡archmənt/ *n.* **1 a** an animal skin, esp. that of a sheep or goat, prepared as a writing or painting surface. **b** a manuscript written on this. **2** (in full **vegetable parchment**) high-grade paper made to resemble parchment. [ME f. OF *parchemin*, ult. a blend of LL *pergamina* writing material from Pergamum (in Asia Minor) with *Parthica pellis* Parthian skin (leather)]

parclose /pa͡arklōz/ *n.* a screen or railing in a church, separating a side chapel. [ME f. OF *parclos* -*ose* past part. of *parclore* enclose]

pard /paard/ *n. archaic* or *poet.* a leopard. [ME f. OF f. L *pardus* f. Gk *pardos*]

pardalote /pa͡ardəlōt/ *n.* any small brightly-coloured Australian bird of the genus *Pardalotus*, with spotted plumage. Also called *diamond-bird*. [mod.L *Pardalotus* f. Gk *pardalōtos* spotted like a leopard (as PARD)]

pardner /pa͡ardnər/ *n. US colloq.* a partner or comrade. [corrupt.]

pardon /pa͡ard'n/ *n.*, *v.*, & *int.* ● *n.* **1** the act of excusing or forgiving an offence, error, etc. **2** (in full **free pardon**) a remission of the legal consequences of a crime or conviction. **3** *RC Ch.* an indulgence. ● *v.tr.* **1** release from the consequences of an offence, error, etc. **2** forgive or excuse a person for (an offence etc.). **3** make (esp. courteous) allowances for; excuse. ● *int.* (also **pardon me** or **I beg your pardon**) **1** a formula of apology or disagreement. **2** a request to repeat something said. □□ **pardonable** *adj.* **pardonably** *adv.* [ME f. OF *pardun*, *pardoner* f. med.L *perdonare* concede, remit (as PER-, *donare* give)]
■ *n.* **1** forgiveness, amnesty, remission, release, reprieve, absolution, excuse, excusal, allowance, overlooking, condonation, exoneration, *formal* exculpation. ● *v.* forgive, remit, release, reprieve, absolve, overlook, let off, excuse, condone, exonerate, *formal* exculpate. ● *int.* **1** excuse me, I'm sorry, I apologise, my apologies. **2** what (did you say)?, say (it) again, what (was that)?, eh? □□ **pardonable** see PERMISSIBLE.

pardoner /pa͡ard'nər/ *n. hist.* a person licensed to sell papal pardons or indulgences. [ME f. AF (as PARDON)]

pare /pair/ *v.tr.* **1 a** trim or shave (esp. fruit and vegetables) by cutting away the surface or edge. **b** (often foll. by *off*, *away*) cut off (the surface or edge). **2** (often foll. by *away*, *down*) diminish little by little. □□ **parer** *n.* [ME f. OF *parer* adorn, peel (fruit), f. L *parare* prepare]
■ **1 a** trim, peel, skin, shave; decorticate, excoriate. **b** trim *or* peel *or* shave off; excoriate. **2** reduce, diminish, decrease, cut (back *or* down), curtail, lower, lessen.

paregoric /párrigórrik/ *n.* (in full **paregoric elixir**) *hist.* a camphorated tincture of opium used to reduce pain. [LL *paregoricus* f. Gk *parēgorikos* soothing (as PARA-[1], -*agoros* speaking f. *agora* assembly)]

pareira /pəráirə/ *n.* a drug from the root of a Brazilian shrub, *Chondrodendron tomentosum*, used as a muscle relaxant in surgery etc. [Port. *parreira* vine trained against a wall]

parenchyma /pəréngkimə/ *n.* **1** *Anat.* the functional part of an organ as distinguished from the connective and supporting tissue. **2** *Bot.* the cellular material, usu. soft and succulent, found esp. in the softer parts of leaves, pulp of fruits, bark and pith of stems, etc. □□ **parenchymal** *adj.* **parenchymatous** /-kímmətəss/ *adj.* [Gk *paregkhuma* something poured in besides (as PARA-[1], *egkhuma* infusion f. *egkheō* pour in)]

parent /páirənt/ *n.* & *v.* ● *n.* **1** a person who has begotten or borne offspring; a father or mother. **2** a person who holds the position or exercises the functions of such a parent. **3** a forefather. **4** an animal or plant from which others are derived. **5** a source or origin. **6** an initiating organization or enterprise. ● *v.tr.* (also *absol.*) be a parent of. □ **parent company** a company of which other companies are subsidiaries. **parent–teacher association** a local organization of parents and teachers for promoting closer relations and improving educational facilities at a school. □□ **parental** /pərént'l/ *adj.* **parentally** /pəréntəli/ *adv.* **parenthood** *n.* [ME f. OF f. L *parens parentis* f. *parere* bring forth]
■ *n.* **1** father, mother, surrogate mother, progenitor, procreator, materfamilias, paterfamilias, *colloq.* old lady *or* woman, old man, *literary* begetter, *Brit. sl.* mater, pater. **2** adoptive parent *or* mother *or* father, foster-parent, foster-mother, foster-father, step-parent, stepmother, stepfather, guardian. **5** source, origin, originator, well-spring, fountain-head, root.

parentage /páirəntij/ *n.* lineage; descent from or through parents (*their parentage is unknown*). [ME f. OF (as PARENT)]
■ lineage, ancestry, line, family, extraction, descent, origin, pedigree, stock, birth, strain, bloodline, heritage, roots.

parenteral /pəréntərəl/ *adj. Med.* administered or occurring elsewhere than in the alimentary canal. □□ **parenterally** *adv.* [PARA-[1] + Gk *enteron* intestine]

parenthesis /pərénthəsiss/ *n.* (*pl.* **parentheses** /-seez/) **1 a** a word, clause, or sentence inserted as an explanation or afterthought into a passage which is grammatically complete without it, and usu. marked off by brackets or dashes or commas. **b** (in *pl.*) a pair of round brackets () used for this. **2** an interlude or interval. □ **in parenthesis** as a parenthesis or afterthought. [LL f. Gk *parenthesis* f. *parentithēmi* put in beside]

parenthesize /pərénthəsīz/ *v.tr.* (also **-ise**) **1** (also *absol.*) insert as a parenthesis. **2** put into brackets or similar punctuation.

parenthetic /párrənthéttik/ *adj.* **1** of or by way of a parenthesis. **2** interposed. □□ **parenthetical** *adj.* **parenthetically** *adv.* [PARENTHESIS after *synthesis*, *synthetic*, etc.]

parenting /páirənting/ *n.* the occupation or concerns of parents.
■ rearing, upbringing, raising, nurturing; parenthood.

parergon /pərérgən/ *n.* (*pl.* **parerga** /-gə/) **1** work subsidiary to one's main employment. **2** an ornamental accessory. [L f. Gk *parergon* (as PARA-[1], *ergon* work)]

paresis /pəréessis, párrisiss/ *n.* (*pl.* **pareses** /-seez/) *Med.* partial paralysis. □□ **paretic** /pərέttik/ *adj.* [mod.L f. Gk f. *pariēmi* let go (as PARA-[1], *hiēmi* let go)]

par excellence /pa͡ar eksəlónss/ *adv.* as having special excellence; being the supreme example of its kind (*the short story par excellence*). [F, = by excellence]

parfait /pa͞arfay/ *n.* **1** a rich iced pudding of whipped cream, eggs, etc. **2** layers of ice-cream, meringue, etc., served in a tall glass. [F *parfait* PERFECT *adj.*]

pargana /pərgúnnə/ *n.* (also **pergunnah, pergana**) (in India) a group of villages or a subdivision of a district. [Urdu *pargana* district]

parget /pa͞arjit/ *v.* & *n.* ● *v.tr.* (**pargeted, pargeting**) **1** plaster (a wall etc.) esp. with an ornamental pattern. **2** roughcast. ● *n.* **1** plaster applied in this way; ornamental plasterwork. **2** roughcast. [ME f. OF *pargeter, parjeter* f. *par* all over + *jeter* throw]

parhelion /paarhe͞eliən/ *n.* (*pl.* **parhelia** /-liə/) a bright spot on the solar halo. Also called *mock sun, sun-dog.* □□ **parheliacal** /-hilī́ək'l/ *adj.* **parhelic** *adj.* [L *parelion* f. Gk (as PARA-[1], *hēlios* sun)]

pariah /pərī́ə, párriə/ *n.* **1** a social outcast. **2** *hist.* a member of a low caste or of no caste in S. India. □ **pariah-dog** = PYE-DOG. [Tamil *paṛaiyar* pl. of *paṛaiyan* hereditary drummer f. *paṛai* drum]

parietal /pərī́ət'l/ *adj.* **1** *Anat.* of the wall of the body or any of its cavities. **2** *Bot.* of the wall of a hollow structure etc. **3** *US* relating to residence within a college. □ **parietal bone** either of a pair of bones forming the central part of the sides and top of the skull. [F *pariétal* or LL *parietalis* f. L *paries -etis* wall]

pari-mutuel /párrimyo͞otyooəl/ *n.* **1** a form of betting in which those backing the first three places divide the losers' stakes (less the operator's commission). **2** a totalizator. [F, = mutual stake]

paring /páiring/ *n.* a strip or piece cut off.

pari passu /pa͞ari pásso͞o, párri/ *adv.* **1** with equal speed. **2** simultaneously and equally. [L]

Paris commune see COMMUNE[1].

Paris green /párriss/ *n.* a poisonous chemical used as a pigment and insecticide. [*Paris* in France]

parish /párrish/ *n.* **1** an area having its own church and clergy. **2** (in full **civil parish**) a district constituted for purposes of local government. **3** the inhabitants of a parish. **4** *US* a county in Louisiana. □ **parish clerk** an official performing various duties concerned with the church. **parish council** *Brit.* the administrative body in a civil parish. **parish pump** (often *attrib.*) a symbol of a parochial or restricted outlook. **parish register** a book recording christenings, marriages, and burials, at a parish church. [ME *paroche, parosse* f. OF *paroche, paroisse* f. eccl.L *parochia, paroechia* f. Gk *paroikia* sojourning f. *paroikos* (as PARA-[1], *-oikos* -dwelling f. *oikeō* dwell)]

parishioner /pərishənər/ *n.* an inhabitant of a parish. [obs. *parishen* f. ME f. OF *parossien*, formed as PARISH]

Parisian /pərizziən/ *adj.* & *n.* ● *adj.* of or relating to Paris in France. ● *n.* **1** a native or inhabitant of Paris. **2** the kind of French spoken in Paris. [F *parisien*]

parison /párris'n/ *n.* a rounded mass of glass formed by rolling immediately after taking it from the furnace. [F *paraison* f. *parer* prepare f. L *parare*]

parity[1] /párriti/ *n.* **1** equality or equal status, esp. as regards status or pay. **2** parallelism or analogy (*parity of reasoning*). **3** equivalence of one currency with another; being at par. **4** (of a number) the fact of being even or odd. **5** *Physics* (of a quantity) the fact of changing its sign or remaining unaltered under a given transformation of coordinates etc. [F *parité* or LL *paritas* (as PAR[1])]

- **1** equality, equivalence, consistency, uniformity, congruity, similitude, conformity, congruence. **2** analogy, parallelism, likeness, similarity, proportion, balance, correspondence.

parity[2] /párriti/ *n. Med.* **1** the fact or condition of having borne children. **2** the number of children previously borne. [formed as -PAROUS + -ITY]

park /paark/ *n.* & *v.* ● *n.* **1** a large public garden in a town, for recreation. **2** a large enclosed piece of ground, usu. with woodland and pasture, attached to a country house etc. **3 a** a large area of land kept in its natural state for public recreational use. **b** a large enclosed area of land used to accommodate wild animals in captivity (*wildlife park*). **4** an area for motor vehicles etc. to be left in (*car park*). **5** the gear position or function in automatic transmission in which the gears are locked, preventing the vehicle's movement. **6** an area devoted to a specified purpose (*industrial park*). **7 a** *US* a sports ground. **b** (usu. prec. by *the*) a football pitch. ● *v.tr.* **1** (also *absol.*) leave (a vehicle) usu. temporarily, in a car park, by the side of the road, etc. **2** *colloq.* deposit and leave, usu. temporarily. □ **parking-light** a small light at the side of a vehicle, for use when the vehicle is parked at night. **parking-lot** *US* an outdoor area for parking vehicles. **parking-meter** a coin-operated meter which receives fees for vehicles parked in the street and indicates the time available. **parking-ticket** a notice, usu. attached to a vehicle, of a penalty imposed for parking illegally. **park oneself** *colloq.* sit down. [ME f. OF *parc* f. med.L *parricus* of Gmc orig., rel. to *pearruc*: see PADDOCK]

- *n.* **1–3** garden(s), green(s), common(s), preserve, reserve, parkland, woodland, estate, *Anglo-Ind. maidan, archaic or literary* greensward; playground. **4** car park, multi-storey car park, stand, rank, parking bay, *US* parking-lot. ● *v.* leave, store, *colloq.* stash, dump, *sl.* ditch; see also SET[1] *v.* 1, 3, 5.

parka /pa͞arkə/ *n.* **1** a skin jacket with hood, worn by Eskimos. **2** a similar windproof fabric garment worn by mountaineers etc. [Aleutian]

parkin /pa͞arkin/ *n. Brit.* a cake or biscuit made with oatmeal, ginger, and treacle or molasses. [perh. f. the name *Parkin*, dimin. of *Peter*]

Parkinsonism /pa͞arkinsəniz'm/ *n.* = PARKINSON'S DISEASE.

Parkinson's disease /pa͞arkins'nz/ *n.* a progressive disease of the nervous system with tremor, muscular rigidity, and emaciation. Also called PARKINSONISM. [J. *Parkinson*, Engl. surgeon d. 1824]

Parkinson's law /pa͞arkins'nz/ *n.* the notion that work expands so as to fill the time available for its completion. [C. N. *Parkinson*, Engl. writer b. 1909]

parkland /pa͞arkland/ *n.* open grassland with clumps of trees etc.

parkway /pa͞arkway/ *n.* **1** *US* an open landscaped highway. **2** *Brit.* a railway station with extensive parking facilities.

parky /pa͞arki/ *adj.* (**parkier, parkiest**) *Brit. colloq.* chilly. [19th c.: orig. unkn.]

Parl. *abbr. Brit.* **1** Parliament. **2** Parliamentary.

parlance /pa͞arlənss/ *n.* a particular way of speaking, esp. as regards choice of words, idiom, etc. [OF f. *parler* speak, ult. f. L *parabola* (see PARABLE): in LL = 'speech']

- way *or* manner of speaking, phrasing, phraseology, speech, wording, language, idiom, dialect, jargon, idiolect, *colloq.* lingo.

parlay /pa͞arlay/ *v.* & *n. US* ● *v.tr.* **1** use (money won on a bet) as a further stake. **2** increase in value by or as if by parlaying. ● *n.* **1** an act of parlaying. **2** a bet made by parlaying. [F *paroli* f. It. f. *paro* like f. L *par* equal]

parley /pa͞arli/ *n.* & *v.* ● *n.* (*pl.* **-eys**) a conference for debating points in a dispute, esp. a discussion of terms for an armistice etc. ● *v.intr.* (**-leys, -leyed**) (often foll. by *with*) hold a parley. [perh. f. OF *parlee*, fem. past part. of *parler* speak: see PARLANCE]

- *n.* conference, discussion, dialogue, negotiation, deliberation, meeting, colloquy, colloquium, confabulation, powwow, talk(s), *colloq.* huddle, confab, *esp. hist.* palaver. ● *v.* confer, discuss, deliberate, talk, negotiate, powwow.

parliament /pa͞arləmənt/ *n.* **1** (**Parliament**) **a** (in the UK) the highest legislature, consisting of the Sovereign, the House of Lords, and the House of Commons. **b** the members of this legislature for a particular period, esp. between one dissolution and the next. **2** a similar legislature in other nations and States. [ME f. OF *parlement* speaking (as PARLANCE)]

■ **1 a** (**Parliament**) Houses of Parliament, Westminster; House of Lords, House of Commons, the Commons, the Lords, the House, *Brit.* another place. **2** legislature, council, congress, diet, assembly, Upper *or* Lower House, upper *or* lower chamber.

parliamentarian /paárləmentáiriən/ *n.* & *adj.* ● *n.* **1** a member of a parliament, esp. one well-versed in its procedures. **2** *hist.* an adherent of Parliament in the English Civil War of the 17th c. ● *adj.* = PARLIAMENTARY.

parliamentary /paárləméntəri, -tri/ *adj.* **1** of or relating to a parliament. **2** enacted or established by a parliament. **3** (of language) admissible in a parliament; polite. □ **Parliamentary Commissioner for Administration** the official name of the ombudsman in the UK. **parliamentary private secretary** a member of parliament assisting a government minister.
■ **3** proper, polite, formal, ordered, orderly, acceptable.

parlour /paárlər/ *n.* (*US* **parlor**) **1** a sitting-room in a private house. **2** a room in a hotel, convent, etc., for the private use of residents. **3** esp. *US* a shop providing specified goods or services (*beauty parlour*; *ice-cream parlour*). **4** a room or building equipped for milking cows. **5** (*attrib.*) *derog.* denoting support for political views by those who do not try to practise them (*parlour socialist*). □ **parlour game** an indoor game, esp. a word game. **parlour-maid** *hist.* a maid who waits at table. [ME f. AF *parlur*, OF *parleor*, *parleur*: see PARLANCE]
■ **1, 2** living-room, drawing-room, sitting-room, morning-room, reception (room), lounge, *archaic* withdrawing-room.

parlous /paárləss/ *adj.* & *adv. archaic* or *joc.* ● *adj.* **1** dangerous or difficult. **2** hard to deal with. ● *adv.* extremely. □□ **parlously** *adv.* **parlousness** *n.* [ME, = PERILOUS]
■ *adj.* perilous, risky, precarious, uncertain, dangerous, hazardous, difficult, ticklish, awkward, chancy, *colloq.* iffy, *sl.* hairy.

Parma violet /paármə/ *n.* a variety of sweet violet with heavy scent and lavender-coloured flowers often crystallized for food decoration. [*Parma* in Italy]

Parmesan /paármizán/ *n.* a kind of hard dry cheese made orig. at Parma and used esp. in grated form. [F f. It. *parmegiano* of Parma in Italy]

Parnassian /paarnássiən/ *adj.* & *n.* ● *adj.* **1** of Parnassus, a mountain in central Greece, in antiquity sacred to the Muses. **2** poetic. **3** of or relating to a group of French poets in the late 19th c., emphasizing strictness of form, named from the anthology *Le Parnasse contemporain* (1866). ● *n.* a member of this group.

parochial /pərṓkiəl/ *adj.* **1** of or concerning a parish. **2** (of affairs, views, etc.) merely local, narrow or restricted in scope. □□ **parochialism** *n.* **parochiality** /-kiálliti/ *n.* **parochially** *adv.* [ME f. AF *parochiel*, OF *parochial* f. eccl.L *parochialis* (as PARISH)]
■ **1** regional, provincial, local. **2** narrow, insular, isolated, provincial, limited, restricted, narrow-minded, petty, short-sighted, hidebound, conservative, conventional, illiberal, bigoted, prejudiced, intolerant, one-sided, partial, biased, stubborn, opinionated, dogmatic, rigid, stiff, stiff-necked, immovable, intractable, unchangeable, unchanging, close-minded, unsophisticated, unworldly, uncultivated, uncultured.

parody /párrədi/ *n.* & *v.* ● *n.* (*pl.* **-ies**) **1** a humorous exaggerated imitation of an author, literary work, style, etc. **2** a feeble imitation; a travesty. ● *v.tr.* (**-ies, -ied**) **1** compose a parody of. **2** mimic humorously. □□ **parodic** /pəróddik/ *adj.* **parodist** *n.* [LL *parodia* or Gk *parōidia* burlesque poem (as PARA-[1], *ōidē* ode)]
■ *n.* **1** burlesque, lampoon, satire, caricature, mockery, *colloq.* take-off, spoof, *Brit. colloq.* send-up; mimicry. **2** travesty, mockery, feeble *or* poor imitation; distortion, perversion, corruption, debasement. ● *v.* burlesque, lampoon, satirize, caricature, mock, mimic, ape, ridicule, deride, laugh at, poke fun at, guy, scoff at, sneer at, rib, tease, twit, roast, pillory, make a laughing-stock (of), make sport of, make fun of, make a monkey (out) of, fleer, *colloq.* take off, spoof, *Brit. colloq.* send up, *sl.* take the mickey out of.

parol /pərṓl/ *adj.* & *n. Law* ● *adj.* **1** given orally. **2** (of a document) not given under seal. ● *n.* an oral declaration. [OF *parole* (as PAROLE)]

parole /pərṓl/ *n.* & *v.* ● *n.* **1 a** the release of a prisoner temporarily for a special purpose or completely before the expiry of a sentence, on the promise of good behaviour. **b** such a promise. **2** a word of honour. ● *v.tr.* put (a prisoner) on parole. □ **on parole** released on the terms of parole. □□ **parolee** /-lée/ *n.* [F, = word: see PARLANCE]

paronomasia /párrənəmáyziə/ *n.* a play on words; a pun. [L f. Gk *paronomasia* (as PARA-[1], *onomasia* naming f. *onomazō* to name f. *onoma* a name)]

paronym /párrənim/ *n.* **1** a word cognate with another. **2** a word formed from a foreign word. □□ **paronymous** /pərónniməss/ *adj.* [Gk *parōnumon*, neut. of *parōnumos* (as PARA-[1], *onuma* name)]

parotid /paróttid/ *adj.* & *n.* ● *adj.* situated near the ear. ● *n.* (in full **parotid gland**) a salivary gland in front of the ear. □ **parotid duct** a duct opening from the parotid gland into the mouth. [F *parotide* or L *parotis parotid-* f. Gk *parōtis -idos* (as PARA-[1], *ous ōtos* ear)]

parotitis /párrətī́tiss/ *n.* **1** inflammation of the parotid gland. **2** mumps. [PAROTID + -ITIS]

-parous /pərəss/ *comb. form* bearing offspring of a specified number or kind (*multiparous*; *viviparous*). [L *-parus* -bearing f. *parere* bring forth]

Parousia /pərṓōziə/ *n. Theol.* the supposed second coming of Christ. [Gk, = presence, coming]

paroxysm /párrəksiz'm/ *n.* **1** (often foll. by *of*) a sudden attack or outburst (of rage, laughter, etc.). **2** a fit of disease. □□ **paroxysmal** /-sízm'l/ *adj.* [F *paroxysme* f. med.L *paroxysmus* f. Gk *paroxusmos* f. *paroxunō* exasperate (as PARA-[1], *oxunō* sharpen f. *oxus* sharp)]
■ attack, fit, convulsion, spasm, throe, seizure, spell, outburst, eruption, explosion, flare-up.

paroxytone /pəróksitōn/ *adj.* & *n.* ● *adj.* (esp. in ancient Greek) having an acute accent on the last syllable but one. ● *n.* a word of this kind. [mod.L f. Gk *paroxutonos* (as PARA-[1], OXYTONE)]

parpen /paárp'n/ *n.* a stone passing through a wall from side to side, with two smooth vertical faces. [ME f. OF *parpain*, prob. ult. f. L *per* through + *pannus* piece of cloth, in Rmc 'piece of wall']

parquet /paárki, -kay/ *n.* & *v.* ● *n.* **1** a flooring of wooden blocks arranged in a pattern. **2** *US* the stalls of a theatre. ● *v.tr.* (**parqueted** /-kayd/; **parqueting** /-kaying/) furnish (a room) with a parquet floor. [F, = small compartment, floor, dimin. of *parc* PARK]

parquetry /paárkitri/ *n.* the use of wooden blocks to make floors or inlay for furniture.

parr /paar/ *n.* a young salmon with blue-grey finger-like markings on its sides, younger than a smolt. [18th c.: orig. unkn.]

parrakeet *US* var. of PARAKEET.

parramatta /párrəmáttə/ *n.* (also **paramatta**) a light dress fabric of wool and silk or cotton. [*Parramatta* in New South Wales, Australia]

parricide /párrisīd/ *n.* **1** the killing of a near relative, esp. of a parent. **2** an act of parricide. **3** a person who commits parricide. □□ **parricidal** /-sī́d'l/ *adj.* [F *parricide* or L *parricida* (= sense 3), *parricidium* (= sense 1), of uncert. orig., assoc. in L with *pater* father and *parens* parent]

parrot /párrət/ *n.* & *v.* ● *n.* **1** any of various mainly tropical birds of the order Psittaciformes, with a short hooked bill, often having vivid plumage and able to mimic the human voice. **2** a person who mechanically repeats the words or actions of another. ● *v.tr.* (**parroted, parroting**) repeat mechanically. □ **parrot-fashion** (learning or repeating) mechanically without understanding. **parrot-fish** any fish of the genus *Scarus*, with a mouth like a parrot's bill and forming a protective mucous cocoon against predators. [prob. f. obs. or dial. F *perrot* parrot, dimin. of *Pierre* Peter: cf. PARAKEET]

■ *n.* **2** imitator, mimic, *colloq.* copycat. ● *v.* imitate, mimic, ape; echo, repeat, reiterate.

parry /párri/ *v.* & *n.* ● *v.tr.* (**-ies, -ied**) **1** avert or ward off (a weapon or attack), esp. with a countermove. **2** deal skilfully with (an awkward question etc.). ● *n.* (*pl.* **-ies**) an act of parrying. [prob. repr. F *parez* imper. of *parer* f. It. *parare* ward off]

parse /paarz/ *v.tr.* **1** describe (a word in context) grammatically, stating its inflection, relation to the sentence, etc. **2** resolve (a sentence) into its component parts and describe them grammatically. □□ **parser** *n.* esp. *Computing*. [perh. f. ME *pars* parts of speech f. OF *pars*, pl. of *part* PART, infl. by L *pars* part]

parsec /paarsek/ *n.* a unit of stellar distance, equal to about 3.25 light years (3.08 x 10^{16} metres), the distance at which the mean radius of the earth's orbit subtends an angle of one second of arc. [PARALLAX + SECOND²]

Parsee /paarseé/ *n.* **1** an adherent of Zoroastrianism. **2** a descendant of the Persians who fled to India from Muslim persecution in the 7th–8th c. **3** = PAHLAVI. □□ **Parseeism** *n.* [Pers. *pārsī* Persian f. *pārs* Persia]

parsimony /paarsiməni/ *n.* **1** carefulness in the use of money or other resources. **2** meanness, stinginess. □ **law of parsimony** the assertion that no more causes or forces should be assumed than are necessary to account for the facts. □□ **parsimonious** /-mṓniəss/ *adj.* **parsimoniously** /-mṓniəsli/ *adv.* **parsimoniousness** /-mṓniəsniss/ *n.* [ME f. L *parsimonia, parcimonia* f. *parcere pars-* spare]

parsley /paarsli/ *n.* a biennial herb, *Petroselinum crispum*, with white flowers and crinkly aromatic leaves, used for seasoning and garnishing food. □ **parsley fern** a fern, *Cryptogramma crispa*, with leaves like parsley. **parsley-piert** a dwarf annual herb, *Aphanes arvensis*. [ME *percil, per(e)sil* f. OF *peresil*, and OE *petersilie* ult. f. L *petroselinum* f. Gk *petroselinon*; *parsley-piert* prob. corrupt. of F *perce-pierre* pierce stone]

parsnip /paarsnip/ *n.* **1** a biennial umbelliferous plant, *Pastinaca sativa*, with yellow flowers and a large pale-yellow tapering root. **2** this root eaten as a vegetable. [ME *pas(se)nep* (with assim. to *nep* turnip) f. OF *pasnaie* f. L *pastinaca*]

parson /paars'n/ *n.* **1** a rector. **2** a vicar or any beneficed member of the clergy. **3** *colloq.* any (esp. Protestant) member of the clergy. □ **parson's nose** the piece of fatty flesh at the rump of a fowl. □□ **parsonical** /-sónnik'l/ *adj.* [ME *person(e), parson* f. OF *persone* f. L *persona* PERSON (in med.L rector)]

parsonage /paarsənij/ *n.* a church house provided for a parson.

part /paart/ *n., v.,* & *adv.* ● *n.* **1** some but not all of a thing or number of things. **2** an essential member or constituent of anything (*part of the family; a large part of the job*). **3** a component of a machine etc. (*spare parts; needs a new part*). **4 a** a portion of a human or animal body. **b** (in *pl.*) *colloq.* = *private parts*. **5** a division of a book, broadcast serial, etc., esp. as much as is issued or broadcast at one time. **6** each of several equal portions of a whole (*the recipe has 3 parts sugar to 2 parts flour*). **7 a** a portion allotted; a share. **b** a person's share in an action or enterprise (*will have no part in it*). **c** one's duty (*was not my part to interfere*). **8 a** a character assigned to an actor on stage. **b** the words spoken by an actor on stage. **c** a copy of these. **9** *Mus.* a melody or other constituent of harmony assigned to a particular voice or instrument. **10** each of the sides in an agreement or dispute. **11** (in *pl.*) a region or district (*am not from these parts*). **12** (in *pl.*) abilities (*a man of many parts*). **13** *US* = PARTING 2. ● *v.* **1** *tr.* & *intr.* divide or separate into parts (*the crowd parted to let them through*). **2** *intr.* **a** leave one another's company (*they parted the best of friends*). **b** (foll. by *from*) say goodbye to. **3** *tr.* cause to separate (*they fought hard and had to be parted*). **4** *intr.* (foll. by *with*) give up possession of; hand over. **5** *tr.* separate (the hair of the head on either side of the parting) with a comb. ● *adv.* to some extent; partly (*is part iron and part wood; a lie that is part truth*). □ **for the most part** see MOST. **for one's part** as far as one is concerned. **in part** (or **parts**) to some extent; partly. **look the part** appear suitable for a role. **on the part of** on the behalf or initiative of (*no objection on my part*). **part and parcel** (usu. foll. by *of*) an essential part. **part company** see COMPANY. **part-exchange** *n.* a transaction in which goods are given as part of the payment for other goods, with the balance in money. ● *v.tr.* give (goods) in such a transaction. **part of speech** *n.* each of the categories to which words are assigned in accordance with their grammatical and semantic functions (in English esp. noun, pronoun, adjective, adverb, verb, preposition, conjunction, and interjection). **part-song** a song with three or more voice-parts, often without accompaniment, and harmonic rather than contrapuntal in character. **part time** less than the full time required by an activity. **part-time** *adj.* occupying or using only part of one's working time. **part-timer** a person employed in part-time work. **part-work** *Brit.* a publication appearing in several parts over a period of time. **play a part 1** be significant or contributory. **2** act deceitfully. **3** perform a theatrical role. **take in good part** see GOOD. **take part** (often foll. by *in*) assist or have a share (in). **take the part of 1** support; back up. **2** perform the role of. **three parts** three quarters. [ME f. OF f. L *pars partis* (n.), *partire, partiri* (v.)]

■ *n.* **1** some, a few, not all. **2** piece, portion, division, segment, section. **3** component, constituent, element, ingredient, unit. **4 a** member, organ, limb. **5** episode, instalment, chapter. **6** portion, measure, unit, share. **7 a** allotment, share, percentage, participation, interest, parcel. **b** share, interest, participation, say, voice, influence. **c** role, function, duty, responsibility, share, business. **8 a** role, character. **b, c** lines, script, words. **10** side, interest, cause, faction, party. **11** (*parts*) neighbourhood, quarter, section, district, region, area, corner, vicinity, vicinage, *colloq.* neck of the woods. **12** (*parts*) accomplishment(s), capability; see also TALENT 1. ● *v.* **1, 3** separate, divide, split (up); put *or* pull apart, *literary* put asunder. **2** separate, part company, split (up), go one's way, break up, say goodbye, *archaic or literary* bid goodbye *or* farewell; leave, depart, go (away *or* off). **4** (*part with*) give up, yield, relinquish, release, sacrifice, forgo, go without, renounce, forsake, let go, surrender. ● *adv.* see *in part* (PART) below. □ **in part** partly, partially, part, to some extent *or* degree, in some measure; relatively, comparatively, somewhat. **on the part of** on the behalf of; by; as regards, with regard to. **take part** participate, join in, be (a) party, play a part *or* role, be involved *or* associated, have *or* take a hand, have *or* take a share, partake, contribute, assist. **take the part of 1** stand *or* stick up for, take the side of; see also SUPPORT *v.* 4, 6, 7.

partake /paartáyk/ *v.intr.* (*past* **partook** /-to͝ok/; *past part.* **partaken** /-táykən/) **1** (foll. by *of, in*) take a share or part. **2** (foll. by *of*) eat or drink some or *colloq.* all (of a thing). **3** (foll. by *of*) have some (of a quality etc.) (*their manner partook of insolence*). □□ **partakable** *adj.* **partaker** *n.* [16th c.: back-form. f. *partaker, partaking* = part-taker etc.]

■ **1** share, participate, take (a) part, enter. **2** (*partake of*) receive, get, have (a share *or* portion *or* part *or* bit of); see also EAT 1a, DRINK *v.* 1. **3** (*partake of*) evoke, suggest, hint at, intimate, imply; have the *or* a quality of.

parterre /paartáir/ *n.* **1** a level space in a garden occupied by flower-beds arranged formally. **2** *US* the ground floor of a theatre auditorium, esp. the pit overhung by balconies. [F, = *par terre* on the ground]

parthenogenesis /paarthinōjénnisiss/ *n. Biol.* reproduction from an ovum without fertilization, esp. as a normal process in invertebrates and lower plants. □□ **parthenogenetic** /-jinéttik/ *adj.* **parthenogenetically**

/-jinéttikəli/ *adv.* [mod.L f. Gk *parthenos* virgin + *genesis* as GENESIS]

Parthian shot /paárthiən/ *n.* a remark or glance etc. reserved for the moment of departure. [*Parthia*, an ancient kingdom in W. Asia: from the custom of a retreating Parthian horseman firing a shot at the enemy]

partial /paársh'l/ *adj.* & *n.* ● *adj.* **1** not complete; forming only part (*a partial success*). **2** biased, unfair. **3** (foll. by *to*) having a liking for. ● *n. Mus.* any of the constituents of a musical sound. □ **partial eclipse** an eclipse in which only part of the luminary is covered or darkened. **partial verdict** a verdict finding a person guilty of part of a charge. □□ **partially** *adv.* **partialness** *n.* [ME f. OF *parcial* f. LL *partialis* (as PART)]

■ *adj.* **1** incomplete, fragmentary, imperfect; see also INCOMPLETE. **2** prejudiced, biased, partisan, inclined, influenced, one-sided, jaundiced, unfair, discriminatory. **3** (*partial to*) in favour of, predisposed to *or* towards, fond of, with a liking *or* taste *or* predilection *or* fondness *or* weakness *or* soft spot for. □□ **partially** partly, in part, to some extent *or* degree, to a limited extent *or* degree, to a certain extent *or* degree, not totally *or* wholly *or* entirely, restrictedly, incompletely, in some measure, relatively, comparatively, moderately, (up) to a point, somewhat.

partiality /paárshiálliti/ *n.* **1** bias, favouritism. **2** (foll. by *for*) fondness. [ME f. OF *parcialité* f. med.L *partialitas* (as PARTIAL)]

■ **1** prejudice, bias, inclination, favouritism, predilection, predisposition, leaning, preference. **2** preference, taste, relish, liking, fondness, appreciation, fancy, love, eye, weakness, soft spot, penchant; fetish.

participant /paartíssip'nt/ *n.* a participator.

■ participator, partaker, sharer, party, contributor.

participate /paartíssipayt/ *v.intr.* **1** (often foll. by *in*) take a part or share (in). **2** *literary* or *formal* (foll. by *of*) have a certain quality (*the speech participated of wit*). □□ **participation** /-páysh'n/ *n.* **participator** *n.* **participatory** *adj.* [L *participare* f. *particeps -cipis* taking part, formed as PART + *-cip-* = *cap-* stem of *capere* take]

■ **1** take part, partake, have *or* take a hand, get *or* become involved; (*participate in*) engage in, share in, join in, enter into, be *or* become associated with, contribute to. □□ **participation** see VOICE *n.* 2c.

participle /paártisip'l, paartíssip'l/ *n. Gram.* a word formed from a verb (e.g. *going, gone, being, been*) and used in compound verb-forms (e.g. *is going, has been*) or as an adjective (e.g. *working woman, burnt toast*). □□ **participial** /-síppiəl/ *adj.* **participially** /-síppiəli/ *adv.* [ME f. OF, by-form of *participe* f. L *participium* (as PARTICIPATE)]

particle /paártik'l/ *n.* **1** a minute portion of matter. **2** the least possible amount (*not a particle of sense*). **3** *Gram.* **a** a minor part of speech, esp. a short indeclinable one. **b** a common prefix or suffix such as *in-, -ness*. [ME f. L *particula* (as PART)]

■ **1** atom, molecule. **2** atom, molecule, scintilla, spark, mote, suggestion, hint, suspicion, gleam, bit, crumb, jot, tittle, whit, mite, speck, dot, spot, iota, grain, morsel, shred, sliver, scrap, *colloq.* smidgen.

particoloured /paártikúllərd/ *adj.* partly of one colour, partly of another or others. [PARTY[2] + COLOURED]

■ motley, variegated, pied, mottled.

particular /pərtíkyoolər/ *adj.* & *n.* ● *adj.* **1** relating to or considered as one thing or person as distinct from others; individual (*in this particular instance*). **2** more than is usual; special, noteworthy (*took particular trouble*). **3** scrupulously exact; fastidious. **4** detailed (*a full and particular account*). **5** *Logic* (of a proposition) in which something is asserted of some but not all of a class (opp. UNIVERSAL). ● *n.* **1** a detail; an item. **2** (in *pl.*) points of information; a detailed account. □ **in particular** especially, specifically. [ME f. OF *particuler* f. L *particularis* (as PARTICLE)]

■ *adj.* **1** certain, specific, special, peculiar, singular, single, isolated, individual, distinct, discrete, separate, definite, precise, express. **2** marked, special, especial, exceptional, remarkable, noteworthy, notable, outstanding, unusual. **3** fussy, meticulous, finicky, finical, fastidious, discriminating, selective, demanding, hypercritical, critical, *colloq.* pernickety, choosy, picky. **4** detailed, itemized, item-by-item, thorough, minute, precise, exact, exacting, painstaking, nice, rigorous, close, blow-by-blow. ● *n.* **1** detail, fine point, item, specific, element, fact, circumstance. **2** (*particulars*) information, minutiae, details, facts, circumstances, account. □ **in particular** particularly, specifically, precisely, exactly, especially, specially.

particularism /pərtíkyooləriz'm/ *n.* **1** exclusive devotion to one party, sect, etc. **2** the principle of leaving political independence to each State in an empire or federation. **3** the theological doctrine of individual election or redemption. □□ **particularist** *n.* [F *particularisme*, mod.L *particularismus*, and G *Partikularismus* (as PARTICULAR)]

particularity /pərtíkyoolárriti/ *n.* **1** the quality of being individual or particular. **2** fullness or minuteness of detail in a description.

particularize /pərtíkyoolərīz/ *v.tr.* (also **-ise**) *tr.* (also *absol.*) **1** name specially or one by one. **2** specify (items). □□ **particularization** /-záysh'n/ *n.* [F *particulariser* (as PARTICULAR)]

particularly /pərtíkyoolərli/ *adv.* **1** especially, very. **2** specifically (*they particularly asked for you*). **3** in a particular or fastidious manner.

■ **1** especially, specially, exceptionally, peculiarly, singularly, distinctively, uniquely, unusually, uncommonly, notably, outstandingly, markedly, extraordinarily, very, extremely, strikingly, surprisingly, amazingly. **2** in particular, specifically, especially, principally, mainly, exceptionally, expressly, explicitly, notably, markedly; only, solely. **3** just so, neatly, tidily, systematically, perfectly, accurately; see also PRECISELY 1.

particulate /pərtíkyoolayt, -lət/ *adj.* & *n.* ● *adj.* in the form of separate particles. ● *n.* matter in this form. [L *particula* PARTICLE]

parting /paárting/ *n.* **1** a leave-taking or departure (often *attrib.*: *parting words*). **2** *Brit.* the dividing line of combed hair. **3** a division; an act of separating. □ **parting shot** = PARTHIAN SHOT.

■ **1** leave-taking, farewell, saying goodbye, departure, leaving, going (away), making one's adieus *or* adieux; valediction; (*attrib.*) closing, final, concluding, last, departing, farewell, valedictory; deathbed, dying. **2** *US* part. **3** splitting, dividing, breaking (up *or* apart); separation, split, division, break-up, rift, rupture, partition.

parti pris /paárti prée/ *n.* & *adj.* ● *n.* a preconceived view; a bias. ● *adj.* prejudiced, biased. [F, = side taken]

partisan /paártizán/ *n.* & *adj.* (also **partizan**) ● *n.* **1** a strong, esp. unreasoning, supporter of a party, cause, etc. **2** *Mil.* a guerrilla in wartime. ● *adj.* **1** of or characteristic of partisans. **2** loyal to a particular cause; biased. □□ **partisanship** *n.* [F f. It. dial. *partigiano* etc. f. *parte* PART]

■ *n.* **1** devotee, follower, supporter, adherent, backer, champion, enthusiast, fan, zealot, fanatic, *US sl.* rooter. **2** guerrilla, freedom fighter, underground *or* resistance fighter, irregular. ● *adj.* **1** guerrilla, freedom, underground, resistance, irregular. **2** one-sided, factional, biased, sectarian, opinionated, partial, bigoted, prejudiced, parochial, myopic, short-sighted, narrow, narrow-minded, limited, *esp. US* near-sighted, *derog.* tendentious; see also LOYAL.

partita /paartéetə/ *n.* (*pl.* **partite** /-tay/) *Mus.* **1** a suite. **2** an air with variations. [It., fem. past part. of *partire* divide, formed as PART]

partite /paártīt/ *adj.* **1** divided (esp. in *comb.*: *tripartite*). **2** *Bot.* & *Zool.* divided to or nearly to the base. [L *partitus* past part. of *partiri* PART *v.*]

partition /paartísh'n/ *n.* & *v.* ● *n.* **1** division into parts, esp. *Polit.* of a country with separate areas of government. **2** a structure dividing a space into two parts, esp. a light interior wall. ● *v.tr.* **1** divide into parts. **2** (foll. by *off*) separate (part of a room etc.) with a partition. □□ **partitioned** *adj.* **partitioner** *n.* **partitionist** *n.* [ME f. OF f. L *partitio -onis* (as PARTITE)]
■ *n.* **1** separation, division, splitting (up), split-up, break-up, segmentation. **2** (room) divider, (dividing) wall, barrier, screen, separator. ● *v.* **1** divide (up), separate, cut up, subdivide, split (up). **2** (*partition off*) divide (off), separate (off), wall off, screen (off), fence off.

partitive /paártitiv/ *adj.* & *n. Gram.* ● *adj.* (of a word, form, etc.) denoting part of a collective group or quantity. ● *n.* a partitive word (e.g. *some, any*) or form. □ **partitive genitive** a genitive used to indicate a whole divided into or regarded in parts, expressed in English by *of* as in *most of us.* □□ **partitively** *adv.* [F *partitif -ive* or med.L *partitivus* (as PARTITE)]

partizan var. of PARTISAN.

partly /paártli/ *adv.* **1** with respect to a part or parts. **2** to some extent.
■ **2** see *partially* (PARTIAL).

partner /paártnər/ *n.* & *v.* ● *n.* **1** a person who shares or takes part with another or others, esp. in a business firm with shared risks and profits. **2** a companion in dancing. **3** a player (esp. one of two) on the same side in a game. **4** either member of a married couple, or of an unmarried couple living together. ● *v.tr.* **1** be the partner of. **2** associate as partners. □□ **partnerless** *adj.* [ME, alt. of *parcener* joint heir, after PART]
■ *n.* **1** sharer, partaker, associate, colleague, participant, accomplice, accessory, confederate, comrade, ally, collaborator, companion, mate, helpmate, fellow, *alter ego*, friend, *US* cohort, *colloq.* pal, sidekick, *Austral. colloq.* offsider, *esp. US colloq.* buddy. **3** team-mate. **4** wife, husband, spouse, helpmate, consort, *colloq.* mate, other *or* better half, *sl.* Dutch; lover, live-in lover *or* partner, cohabitant, cohabitee, cohabitor; common-law husband *or* wife.

partnership /paártnərship/ *n.* **1** the state of being a partner or partners. **2** a joint business. **3** a pair or group of partners.

partook *past* of PARTAKE.

partridge /paártrij/ *n.* (*pl.* same or **partridges**) **1** any game-bird of the genus *Perdix*, esp. *P. perdix* of Europe and Asia. **2** any other of various similar birds of the family Phasianidae, including the snow partridge. [ME *partrich* etc. f. OF *perdriz* etc. f. L *perdix -dicis*: for *-dge* cf. CABBAGE]

parturient /paartyóoriənt/ *adj.* about to give birth. [L *parturire* be in labour, incept. f. *parere part-* bring forth]

parturition /paártyoorísh'n/ *n. Med.* the act of bringing forth young; childbirth. [LL *parturitio* (as PARTURIENT)]

party[1] /paárti/ *n.* & *v.* ● *n.* (*pl.* **-ies**) **1** a social gathering, usu. of invited guests. **2** a body of persons engaged in an activity or travelling together (*fishing party; search party*). **3** a group of people united in a cause, opinion, etc., esp. a political group organized on a national basis. **4** a person or persons forming one side in an agreement or dispute. **5** (foll. by *to*) *Law* an accessory (to an action). **6** *colloq.* a person. ● *v.tr.* & *intr.* (**-ies, -ied**) entertain at or attend a party. □ **party line 1** the policy adopted by a political party. **2** a telephone line shared by two or more subscribers. **party pooper** esp. *US sl.* a person whose manner or behaviour inhibits other people's enjoyment; a killjoy. **party-wall** a wall common to two adjoining buildings or rooms. [ME f. OF *partie* ult. f. L *partire*: see PART]
■ *n.* **1** (social) gathering, celebration, fête, function, reception, soirée, festivity, festival, frolic, romp, carousal, carouse, saturnalia, bacchanalia, debauch, orgy, ball, dance, at-home, *archaic or US* levee, *colloq.* get-together, shindig, shindy, do, rave(-up), spree, bust, hop, bop, *Austral. colloq.* shivoo, *Brit. colloq.* beanfeast, knees-up, *sl.* bash, blast, *Austral. sl.* ding, *Brit. sl.* beano, *esp. US sl.* wingding. **2** group, company, band, body, corps, gang, crew, commando, team, squad, troop, platoon, detachment, detail, cadre, unit, *colloq.* bunch, outfit. **3** side, interest, faction, league, club, coalition, bloc, division, sect, denomination, clique, coterie, set, cabal, junta, adherents, confederacy, confederation, federation, conference, congress, lobby, *US* caucus. **4** individual, person, litigant, plaintiff, defendant, side, part, interest, signer, signatory, co-signatory, participant; interested party. **5** participant, participator, confederate, associate, ally, accomplice, accessory, abetter, supporter, backer, aid, helper, seconder.

party[2] /paárti/ *adj. Heraldry* divided into parts of different colours. [ME f. OF *parti* f. L (as PARTY[1])]

parvenu /paárvənoo/ *n.* & *adj.* ● *n.* (*fem.* **parvenue**) **1** a person of obscure origin who has gained wealth or position. **2** an upstart. ● *adj.* **1** associated with or characteristic of such a person. **2** upstart. [F, past part. of *parvenir* arrive f. L *pervenire* (as PER-, *venire* come)]
■ *n.* upstart, *arriviste, nouveau riche*, adventurer, social climber; intruder. ● *adj. nouveau riche*, upstart, social-climbing, status-seeking.

parvis /paárviss/ *n.* (also **parvise**) **1** an enclosed area in front of a cathedral, church, etc. **2** a room over a church porch. [ME f. OF *parvis* ult. f. LL *paradisus* PARADISE, a court in front of St Peter's, Rome]

pas /paa/ *n.* (*pl.* same) a step in dancing, esp. in classical ballet. □ ***pas de chat*** /də shaá/ a leap in which each foot in turn is raised to the opposite knee. ***pas de deux*** /də dő/ a dance for two persons. ***pas glissé*** see GLISSÉ. ***pas seul*** /sől/ a solo dance. [F, = step]

pascal *n.* **1** /pásk'l/ the SI unit of pressure, equal to one newton per square metre. **2** (**Pascal**) /paskaál/ *Computing* a programming language esp. used in education. [B. *Pascal*, Fr. scientist d. 1662: sense 2 so named because he built a calculating machine]

paschal /pásk'l/ *adj.* **1** of or relating to the Jewish Passover. **2** of or relating to Easter. □ **paschal lamb 1** a lamb sacrificed at Passover. **2** Christ. [ME f. OF *pascal* f. eccl.L *paschalis* f. *pascha* f. Gk *paskha* f. Aram. *pasḥa*, rel. to Heb. *pesaḥ* PASSOVER]

pash /pash/ *n. sl.* a brief infatuation. [abbr. of PASSION]

pasha /paáshə/ *n.* (also **pacha**) *hist.* the title (placed after the name) of a Turkish officer of high rank, e.g. a military commander, the governor of a province, etc. [Turk. *paşa*, prob. = *başa* f. *baş* head, chief]

pashm /páshəm/ *n.* the under-fur of some Tibetan animals, esp. that of goats as used for Cashmere shawls.

Pashto /púshtō/ *n.* & *adj.* ● *n.* the official language of Afghanistan, also spoken in areas of Pakistan. ● *adj.* of or in this language. [Pashto]

paso doble /pássō dőblay/ *n.* **1** a ballroom dance based on a Latin American style of marching. **2** this style of marching. [Sp., = double step]

pasque-flower /páskflowr/ *n.* a ranunculaceous plant, *Pulsatilla vulgaris*, with bell-shaped purple flowers and fernlike foliage. Also called ANEMONE. [earlier *passe-flower* f. F *passe-fleur*: assim. to *pasque* = obs. *pasch* (as PASCHAL), Easter]

pasquinade /páskwináyd/ *n.* a lampoon or satire, orig. one displayed in a public place. [It. *pasquinata* f. *Pasquino*, a statue in Rome on which abusive Latin verses were annually posted]

pass[1] /paass/ *v.* & *n.* ● *v.* (*past part.* **passed**) (see also PAST). **1** *intr.* (often foll. by *along, by, down, on*, etc.) move onward; proceed, esp. past some point of reference (*saw the procession passing*). **2** *tr.* **a** go past; leave (a thing etc.) on one side or behind in proceeding. **b** overtake, esp. in a vehicle. **c** go across (a frontier, mountain range, etc.). **3** *intr.* & *tr.* be transferred or cause to be transferred from one person or place to another (*pass the butter; the title passes to his son*). **4** *tr.* surpass; be too great for (*it passes my comprehension*). **5** *intr.* get through; effect a passage. **6** *intr.* **a** be accepted as adequate; go uncensured (*let the matter pass*). **b** (foll. by *as*, *for*) be accepted or currently known as. **c** *US* (of a person with some Black ancestry) be accepted as White. **7** *tr.* move; cause to go (*passed her hand over her face; passed a rope round it*). **8 a** *intr.* (of a candidate in an examination) be successful. **b** *tr.* be successful in (an examination). **c** *tr.* (of an examiner) judge the performance of (a candidate) to be satisfactory. **9 a** *tr.* (of a bill) be examined and approved by (a parliamentary body or process). **b** *tr.* cause or allow (a bill) to proceed to further legislative processes. **c** *intr.* (of a bill or proposal) be approved. **10** *intr.* **a** occur, elapse (*the remark passed unnoticed; time passes slowly*). **b** happen; be done or said (*heard what passed between them*). **11 a** *intr.* circulate; be current. **b** *tr.* put into circulation (*was passing forged cheques*). **12** *tr.* spend or use up (a certain time or period) (*passed the afternoon reading*). **13** *tr.* (also *absol.*) (in field games) send (the ball) to another player of one's own side. **14** *intr.* forgo one's turn or chance in a game etc. **15** *intr.* (foll. by *to, into*) change from one form (to another). **16** *intr.* come to an end. **17** *tr.* discharge from the body as or with excreta. **18** *tr.* (foll. by *on, upon*) **a** utter (criticism) about. **b** pronounce (a judicial sentence) on. **19** *intr.* (often foll. by *on, upon*) adjudicate. **20** *tr.* not declare or pay (a dividend). **21** *tr.* cause (troops etc.) to go by esp. ceremonially. ● *n.* **1** an act or instance of passing. **2 a** success in an examination. **b** *Brit.* the status of a university degree without honours. **3** written permission to pass into or out of a place, or to be absent from quarters. **4 a** a ticket or permit giving free entry or access etc. **b** = *free pass*. **5** (in field games) a transference of the ball to another player on the same side. **6** a thrust in fencing. **7** a juggling trick. **8** an act of passing the hands over anything, as in conjuring or hypnotism. **9** a critical position (*has come to a fine pass*). □ **in passing 1** by the way. **2** in the course of speech, conversation, etc. **make a pass at** *colloq.* make amorous or sexual advances to. **pass away 1** *euphem.* die. **2** cease to exist; come to an end. **pass by 1** go past. **2** disregard, omit. **passed pawn** *Chess* a pawn that has advanced beyond the pawns on the other side. **pass** (or **run**) **one's eye over** see EYE. **pass muster** see MUSTER. **pass off 1** (of feelings etc.) disappear gradually. **2** (of proceedings) be carried through (in a specified way). **3** (foll. by *as*) misrepresent (a person or thing) as something else. **4** evade or lightly dismiss (an awkward remark etc.). **pass on 1** proceed on one's way. **2** *euphem.* die. **3** transmit to the next person in a series. **pass out 1** become unconscious. **2** *Brit. Mil.* complete one's training as a cadet. **3** distribute. **pass over 1** omit, ignore, or disregard. **2** ignore the claims of (a person) to promotion or advancement. **3** *euphem.* die. **pass round 1** distribute. **2** send or give to each of a number in turn. **pass through** experience. **pass the time of day** see TIME. **pass up** *colloq.* refuse or neglect (an opportunity etc.). **pass water** urinate. □□ **passer** *n.* [ME f. OF *passer* ult. f. L *passus* PACE[1]]

■ *v.* **1** proceed, move (onwards), go (ahead), progress, extend, lie; run, flow, fly, roll, course, stream, drift, sweep. **2** proceed *or* move past, go by *or* past; overtake; cross, go across, traverse. **3, 11, 13** give, hand round *or* along *or* over, transfer, circulate, pass on *or* over, deliver, convey, toss, throw, release. **4** surpass, exceed, outdo, transcend, go beyond, overshoot, outstrip, outrun, surmount, outdistance. **5** go *or* travel *or* voyage *or* make one's way past *or* through *or* by, progress, make headway, advance. **6 a** see STAND *v.* 9. **b** (*pass for* or *as*) be taken for, be mistaken for, be regarded as, be accepted as. **7** see PUT[1] *v.* 1. **8 a** qualify, pass muster, get *or* come through, succeed. **9 b** allow, permit, approve, sanction, accept, authorize, endorse, carry, agree to, confirm. **10 a** go (by), expire, elapse; slip by *or* away, fly; crawl, creep, drag. **b** *formal* eventuate; see also OCCUR 1. **12** spend, devote, use (up), expend, employ, occupy, fill, while away; dissipate, waste, fritter away, kill. **14** decline, abstain, go *or* do without. **15** see RESOLVE *v.* 4, 6. **16** go away, disappear, vanish, evaporate, fade away, melt away, blow over, evanesce, cease (to exist), (come to an) end, die out, go by the board, terminate. **17** evacuate, void, eliminate, excrete. **18** utter, express, issue, declare, pronounce, deliver, set forth, offer. ● *n.* **1** manoeuvre, approach; passage, flight, fly-by, transit. **2 a** see SUCCESS 1. **3** authorization, permit, licence, approval, safe conduct, protection; permission, freedom, liberty, authority, sanction, clearance, go-ahead, *colloq.* green light, OK. **4 a** permit, ticket. **5** transfer, toss, throw, ball. **9** state (of affairs), condition, situation, stage, juncture, status, crux; predicament, crisis. □ **in passing** by the way, incidentally, by the by, parenthetically, *en passant*. **make a pass at** court, pay court to, make advances to, *archaic* make love to. **pass away 1** die, expire, perish, succumb, breathe one's last, *archaic or colloq.* give up the ghost, *colloq.* turn up one's toes, *euphem.* pass on *or* over, *sl.* go west, croak, kick the bucket, bite the dust. **2** vanish, disappear, go away, stop, cease, end. **pass off 1** evaporate, disappear, evanesce. **2** come about, shape up, come to pass, be accomplished; see also *pan out*. **3** camouflage, misrepresent, disguise, dress up, disimulate. **4** see DISMISS 4. **pass on 1** see PROCEED 1. **2** see *pass away* 1 above. **3** see PASS[1] *v.* 3, 11, 13 above. **pass out 1** faint, collapse, black out, drop, keel over, *colloq.* conk (out), *literary* swoon. **3** see DISTRIBUTE 1. **pass over 1** let pass, let go (by), overlook, disregard, ignore, pay no heed to, omit, skip. **3** see *pass away* 1 above. **pass round 1** see DISTRIBUTE 1. **2** see CIRCULATE 2a, b. **pass through** see UNDERGO. **pass up** reject, decline, refuse, waive, turn down, dismiss, spurn, renounce; deny (oneself), skip, give up, forgo, let go (by), abandon, forswear, forsake, let pass, ignore, pay no heed, disregard, omit, neglect. **pass water** see URINATE.

pass[2] /paass/ *n.* **1** a narrow passage through mountains. **2** a navigable channel, esp. at the mouth of a river. □ **sell the pass** betray a cause. [ME, var. of PACE[1], infl. by F *pas* and by PASS[1]]

■ **1** defile, gorge, col, cut, canyon, notch, gap, gully, couloir; passage, opening, way, route, road.

passable /paássəb'l/ *adj.* **1** barely satisfactory; just adequate. **2** (of a road, pass, etc.) that can be passed. □□ **passableness** *n.* **passably** *adv.* [ME f. OF (as PASS[1])]

■ **1** satisfactory, acceptable, tolerable, all right, adequate, admissible, allowable, presentable, average, fair (enough), (fair to) middling, fairly good, not bad, unexceptional, sufficient, indifferent, so so, *colloq.* OK. **2** traversable, navigable, negotiable, open, unobstructed, unblocked. □□ **passably** see FAIRLY 2, PRETTY *adv.*

passacaglia /pássəkaáliə/ *n. Mus.* an instrumental piece usu. with a ground bass. [It. f. Sp. *pasacalle* f. *pasar* pass + *calle* street: orig. often played in the streets]

passage[1] /pássij/ *n.* **1** the process or means of passing; transit. **2** = PASSAGEWAY. **3** the liberty or right to pass through. **4 a** the right of conveyance as a passenger by sea or air. **b** a journey by sea or air. **5** a transition from one state to another. **6 a** a short extract from a book etc. **b** a section of a piece of music. **7** the passing of a bill etc. into law. **8** (in *pl.*) an interchange of words etc. **9** *Anat.* a duct etc. in the body. □ **passage of** (or **at**) **arms** a fight or dispute. **work one's passage** earn a right (orig. of passage) by working for it. [ME f. OF (as PASS[1])]

■ **1** movement, moving, going, transition, transit, traversal, traverse, progress, crossing, passing. **3** safe conduct, protection, permission, right of way, privilege, liberty, freedom, visa, authorization, allowance. **4** voyage, trip, journey, cruise, crossing, sail, run, travel, travelling. **5** transition, change, mutation, shift, conversion, progression, passing; progress, flow, march, advance. **6** extract, excerpt, selection, section, part, snippet, portion, text, paragraph, canto, stanza, verse, line, sentence, phrase; citation, quotation. **7** enactment, ratification, sanction, approval, acceptance, passing, adoption, endorsement, legitimatization, legitimization, legalization, legislation. **9** duct; aperture, hole, orifice, opening; entry, access, inlet; exit, outlet.

passage[2] /pássij/ *v.* **1** *intr.* (of a horse or rider) move sideways, by the pressure of the rein on the horse's neck and of the rider's leg on the opposite side. **2** *tr.* make (a horse) do this. [F *passager*, earlier *passéger* f. It. *passeggiare* to walk, pace f. *passeggio* walk f. L *passus* PACE[1]]

passageway /pássijway/ *n.* a narrow way for passing along, esp. with walls on either side; a corridor.
■ corridor, hall, passage, hallway, lobby; way, route, avenue, course, channel; road, thoroughfare.

passant /páss'nt/ *adj. Heraldry* (of an animal) walking and looking to the dexter side, with three paws on the ground and the right forepaw raised. [ME f. OF, part. of *passer* PASS[1]]

passband /paásband/ *n.* a frequency band within which signals are transmitted by a filter without attenuation.

passbook /paásbo͝ok/ *n.* a book issued by a bank or building society etc. to an account-holder recording sums deposited and withdrawn.

passé /pássay/ *adj.* (*fem.* ***passée***) **1** behind the times; out of date. **2** past its prime. [F, past part. of *passer* PASS[1]]
■ **1** old-fashioned, unfashionable, dated, out of date, behind the times, outmoded, obsolete, obsolescent, antiquated, archaic, *démodé*, quaint, antique, superseded, *colloq.* out, old hat.

passementerie /pásməntri/ *n.* a trimming of gold or silver lace, braid, beads, etc. [F f. *passement* gold lace etc. f. *passer* PASS[1]]

passenger /pássinjər/ *n.* **1** a traveller in or on a public or private conveyance (other than the driver, pilot, crew, etc.). **2** *colloq.* a member of a team, crew, etc., who does no effective work. **3** (*attrib.*) for the use of passengers (*passenger seat*). □ **passenger-mile** one mile travelled by one passenger, as a unit of traffic. **passenger-pigeon** an extinct wild pigeon of N. America, capable of long flight. [ME f. OF *passager* f. OF *passager* (adj.) passing (as PASSAGE[1]): *-n-* as in *messenger* etc.]
■ **1** rider, fare, traveller, voyager, commuter.

passe-partout /páspaarto͞o, paás-/ *n.* **1** a master-key. **2** a picture-frame (esp. for mounted photographs) consisting of two pieces of glass stuck together at the edges with adhesive tape. **3** adhesive tape or paper used for this. [F, = passes everywhere]
■ **1** skeleton key, passkey.

passer-by /paássərbī́/ *n.* (*pl.* **passers-by**) a person who goes past, esp. by chance.

passerine /pássəreen/ *n.* & *adj.* ● *n.* any perching bird of the order Passeriformes, having feet with three toes pointing forward and one pointing backwards, including sparrows and most land birds. ● *adj.* **1** of or relating to this order. **2** of the size of a sparrow. [L *passer* sparrow]

passible /pássib'l/ *adj. Theol.* capable of feeling or suffering. □□ **passibility** /-bílliti/ *n.* [ME f. OF *passible* or LL *passibilis* f. L *pati pass-* suffer]

passim /pássim/ *adv.* (of allusions or references in a published work) to be found at various places throughout the text. [L f. *passus* scattered f. *pandere* spread]

passing /paássing/ *adj.* & *n.* ● *adj.* **1** in senses of PASS *v.* **2** transient, fleeting (*a passing glance*). **3** cursory, incidental (*a passing reference*). ● *n.* **1** in senses of PASS *v.* **2** *euphem.* the death of a person (*mourned his passing*). □ **passing note** *Mus.* a note not belonging to the harmony but interposed to secure a smooth transition. **passing shot** *Tennis* a shot aiming the ball beyond and out of reach of the other player. □□ **passingly** *adv.*
■ *adj.* **2** disappearing, vanishing, ephemeral, brief, going, fading (away), slipping away, short-lived, expiring, transient, transitory, temporary, momentary, fleeting, transitional, impermanent. **3** hasty, superficial, cursory, incidental, casual, quick, fleeting, brief, summary, abrupt, dismissive; glancing. ● *n.* **2** death, dying, demise, end, loss, expiry, expiration.

passion /pásh'n/ *n.* **1** strong barely controllable emotion. **2** an outburst of anger (*flew into a passion*). **3 a** intense sexual love. **b** a person arousing this. **4 a** strong enthusiasm (*has a passion for football*). **b** an object arousing this. **5** (**the Passion**) **a** *Relig.* the suffering of Christ during his last days. **b** a narrative of this from the Gospels. **c** a musical setting of any of these narratives. □ **passion-flower** any climbing plant of the genus *Passiflora*, with a flower that was supposed to suggest the instruments of the Crucifixion. **passion-fruit** the edible fruit of some species of passion-flower, esp. *Passiflora edulis*: also called GRANADILLA. **passion-play** a miracle play representing Christ's Passion. **Passion Sunday** the fifth Sunday in Lent. **Passion Week 1** the week between Passion Sunday and Palm Sunday. **2** = *Holy Week*. □□ **passionless** *adj.* [ME f. OF f. LL *passio -onis* f. L *pati pass-* suffer]
■ **1, 3a, 4a** ardour, ardency, eagerness, intensity, fervour, fervency, fervidness, zeal, zealousness, avidity, avidness, zest, zestfulness, vivacity, vivaciousness, gusto, verve, emotion, feeling, animation, spirit, spiritedness, vigour, enthusiasm, zealotry, fanaticism, feverishness; infatuation, mania, obsession, craze, craving, lust, thirst, hunger, itch, yearning, longing, desire, love, affection, compulsion, fondness, predilection, keenness, fancy, fascination, partiality, liking, interest, weakness, *colloq.* pash, yen, crush, *formal* concupiscence. **2** fit, outburst, frenzy, paroxysm, fury, furore. **3 b** love, heart's desire, beloved, idol, hero, heroine, obsession, infatuation, *colloq.* crush, heartthrob. **4 b** see ENTHUSIASM 2. **5 a** (**Passion**) pain, suffering, agony, martyrdom.

passional /páshən'l/ *adj.* & *n.* ● *adj. literary* of or marked by passion. ● *n.* a book of the sufferings of saints and martyrs.

passionate /páshənət/ *adj.* **1** dominated by or easily moved to strong feeling, esp. love or anger. **2** showing or caused by passion. □□ **passionately** *adv.* **passionateness** *n.* [ME f. med.L *passionatus* (as PASSION)]
■ ardent, eager, intense, fervid, zealous, avid, earnest, zestful, feverish, fanatic(al), vehement, impassioned, emotional, animated, spirited, enthusiastic, vigorous, invigorated, energetic, *literary* passional; quick-tempered, irascible, hotheaded, fiery, testy, huffy, huffish, peevish, peppery, choleric, touchy, bilious, snappish, volatile, cross, temperamental, irritable, quarrelsome, pugnacious, argumentative, contentious, belligerent, *esp. US* cranky, *literary* atrabilious; aroused, lustful, lecherous, erotic, sexual, amorous, sensual, hot, randy, sexy.

Passiontide /pásh'ntīd/ *n.* the last two weeks of Lent.

passivate /pássivayt/ *v.tr.* make (esp. metal) passive (see PASSIVE). □□ **passivation** /-váysh'n/ *n.*

passive /pássiv/ *adj.* **1** suffering action; acted upon. **2** offering no opposition; submissive. **3 a** not active; inert. **b** (of a metal) abnormally unreactive. **4** *Gram.* designating the voice in which the subject undergoes the action of the verb (e.g. in *they were killed*). **5** (of a debt) incurring no interest payment. □ **passive obedience 1** surrender to another's will without cooperation. **2** compliance with commands irrespective of their nature. **passive resistance** a non-violent refusal to cooperate. **passive smoking** the involuntary inhaling, esp. by a non-smoker, of smoke from others' cigarettes etc. □□ **passively** *adv.* **passiveness** *n.* **passivity** /-sívviti/ *n.* [ME f. OF *passif -ive* or L *passivus* (as PASSION)]
■ **2** submissive, repressed, deferential, yielding, compliant, complaisant, receptive, flexible, malleable, pliable, tractable, docile, subdued, lamblike, tame, gentle, meek, patient, unresisting, unassertive, forbearing, tolerant, resigned, long-suffering. **3 a** inactive, non-aggressive, inert, motionless, unresponsive, quiet, calm, tranquil, serene, placid, still, idle, unmoving, unmoved, impassive, untouched, cool, indifferent, phlegmatic, uninterested, uninvolved, dispassionate, apathetic, lifeless, listless, quiescent, unperturbed, unaffected, imperturbable, unshaken, *colloq.* laid-back.

passkey /paáskee/ *n.* **1** a private key to a gate etc. for special purposes. **2** a master-key.

passmark /paásmaark/ *n.* the minimum mark needed to pass an examination.

Passover /pàassōvər/ *n.* **1** the Jewish spring festival commemorating the liberation of the Israelites from Egyptian bondage, held from the 14th to the 21st day of the seventh month of the Jewish year. **2** = *paschal lamb.* [*pass over* = pass without touching, with ref. to the exemption of the Israelites from the death of the first-born (Exod. 12)]

passport /pàasport/ *n.* **1** an official document issued by a government certifying the holder's identity and citizenship, and entitling the holder to travel under its protection to and from foreign countries. **2** (foll. by *to*) a thing that ensures admission or attainment (*a passport to success*). [F *passeport* (as PASS[1], PORT[1])]

password /pàaswurd/ *n.* a selected word or phrase securing recognition, admission, etc., when used by those to whom it is disclosed.
■ watchword, open sesame, sign, countersign.

past /paast/ *adj., n., prep.,* & *adv.* ● *adj.* **1** gone by in time and no longer existing (*in past years; the time is past*). **2** recently completed or gone by (*the past month; for some time past*). **3** relating to a former time (*past president*). **4** *Gram.* expressing a past action or state. ● *n.* **1** (prec. by *the*) **a** past time. **b** what has happened in past time (*cannot undo the past*). **2** a person's past life or career, esp. if discreditable (*a man with a past*). **3** a past tense or form. ● *prep.* **1** beyond in time or place (*is past two o'clock; ran past the house*). **2** beyond the range, duration, or compass of (*past belief; past endurance*). ● *adv.* so as to pass by (*hurried past*). □ **not put it past a person** believe it possible of a person. **past it** *colloq.* incompetent or unusable through age. **past master 1** a person who is especially adept or expert in an activity, subject, etc. **2** a person who has been a master in a guild, Freemason's lodge, etc. **past perfect** = PLUPERFECT. [past part. of PASS[1] *v.*]
■ *adj.* **1** over, done, finished, (over and) done with, gone (and forgotten), dead (and buried *or* gone), defunct. **2** last, recent. **3** late, former, one-time, sometime, previous, prior, erstwhile, quondam, ex-, *archaic* whilom. ● *n.* **1** (*the past*) days *or* years *or* times gone by, old times, former times, the (good) old days, days of old, yesterday, yesteryear, *Sc.* (auld) lang syne, *archaic* olden times *or* days. **2** history, background, life, career, biography. ● *prep.* **1** beyond, across, over; after. **2** beyond, surpassing, exceeding. ● *adv.* on, by, along, away. □ **past it** see OLD 1, 4, STALE *adj.* 1.

pasta /pástə/ *n.* **1** a dried flour paste used in various shapes in cooking (e.g. lasagne, spaghetti). **2** a cooked dish made from this. [It., = PASTE]

paste /payst/ *n.* & *v.* ● *n.* **1** any moist fairly stiff mixture, esp. of powder and liquid. **2** a dough of flour with fat, water, etc., used in baking. **3** an adhesive of flour, water, etc., esp. for sticking paper and other light materials. **4** an easily spread preparation of ground meat, fish, etc. (*anchovy paste*). **5** a hard vitreous composition used in making imitation gems. **6** a mixture of clay, water, etc., used in making ceramic ware, esp. a mixture of low plasticity used in making porcelain. ● *v.tr.* **1** fasten or coat with paste. **2** *sl.* **a** beat or thrash. **b** bomb or bombard heavily. □ **paste-up** a document prepared for copying etc. by combining and pasting various sections on a backing. □□ **pasting** *n.* (esp. in sense 2 of *v.*). [ME f. OF f. LL *pasta* small square medicinal lozenge f. Gk *pastē* f. *pastos* sprinkled]

pasteboard /páystbord/ *n.* **1** a sheet of stiff material made by pasting together sheets of paper. **2** (*attrib.*) **a** flimsy, unsubstantial. **b** fake.

pastel /pást'l/ *n.* **1** a crayon consisting of powdered pigments bound with a gum solution. **2** a work of art in pastel. **3** a light and subdued shade of a colour. □□ **pastelist** *n.* **pastellist** *n.* [F *pastel* or It. *pastello*, dimin. of *pasta* PASTE]

pastern /pástərn/ *n.* **1** the part of a horse's foot between the fetlock and the hoof. **2** a corresponding part in other animals. [ME *pastron* f. OF *pasturon* f. *pasture* hobble ult. f. L *pastorius* of a shepherd: see PASTOR]

pasteurize /pàastyərīz, -chərīz, páss-/ *v.tr.* (also **-ise**) subject (milk etc.) to the process of partial sterilization by heating. □□ **pasteurization** /-záysh'n/ *n.* **pasteurizer** *n.* [L. *Pasteur*, Fr. chemist d. 1895]

pasticcio /pastíchō/ *n.* (*pl.* **-os**) = PASTICHE. [It.: see PASTICHE]

pastiche /pasteésh/ *n.* **1** a medley, esp. a picture or a musical composition, made up from or imitating various sources. **2** a literary or other work of art composed in the style of a well-known author. [F f. It. *pasticcio* ult. f. LL *pasta* PASTE]
■ **1** mixture, medley, blend, compound, composite, patchwork, olio, olla podrida, pot-pourri, motley, miscellany, *mélange*, *pasticcio*, gallimaufry, farrago, mishmash, hotchpotch, tangle, *colloq.* omnium gatherum, *derog.* mess. **2** parody, *pasticcio*, take-off.

pastille /pástil/ *n.* **1** a small sweet or lozenge. **2** a small roll of aromatic paste burnt as a fumigator etc. □ **pastille-burner** an ornamental ceramic container in which an aromatic pastille may be burnt. [F f. L *pastillus* little loaf, lozenge f. *panis* loaf]

pastime /pàastīm/ *n.* **1** a pleasant recreation or hobby. **2** a sport or game. [PASS[1] + TIME]
■ **1** hobby, avocation, recreation, diversion, distraction, amusement, entertainment, fun, play, relaxation, leisure, divertissement. **2** game, sport.

pastis /pástiss/ *n.* an aniseed-flavoured aperitif. [F]

pastor /pàastər/ *n.* **1** a minister in charge of a church or a congregation. **2** a person exercising spiritual guidance. **3** a pink starling, *Sturnus roseus.* □□ **pastorship** *n.* [ME f. AF & OF *pastour* f. L *pastor -oris* shepherd f. *pascere past-* feed, graze]
■ **1** vicar, clergyman, clergywoman, parson, minister, churchman, churchwoman, rector, canon, reverend, father, divine, ecclesiastic, priest, bishop.

pastoral /pàastərəl/ *adj.* & *n.* ● *adj.* **1** of, relating to, or associated with shepherds or flocks and herds. **2** (of land) used for pasture. **3** (of a poem, picture, etc.) portraying country life, usu. in a romantic or idealized form. **4** of or appropriate to a pastor. ● *n.* **1** a pastoral poem, play, picture, etc. **2** a letter from a pastor (esp. a bishop) to the clergy or people. □ **pastoral staff** a bishop's crosier. **pastoral theology** that considering religious truth in relation to spiritual needs. □□ **pastoralism** *n.* **pastorality** /-rálliti/ *n.* **pastorally** *adv.* [ME f. L *pastoralis* (as PASTOR)]
■ *adj.* **1** country, rural, rustic, provincial, farming, agricultural, agrarian; humble. **3** bucolic, idyllic, innocent, simple, tranquil, serene, quiet, restful, peaceful, peaceable, placid, pacific, harmonious, uncomplicated, Arcadian. **4** clerical, ministerial, ecclesiastic(al), church(ly). ● *n.* **1** idyll, eclogue, pastorale.

pastorale /pástəraál, -li/ *n.* (*pl.* **pastorales** or **pastorali** /-li/) **1** a slow instrumental composition in compound time, usu. with drone notes in the bass. **2** a simple musical play with a rural subject. [It. (as PASTORAL)]

pastoralist /pàastərəlist/ *n. Austral.* a farmer of sheep or cattle.

pastorate /pàastərət/ *n.* **1** the office or tenure of a pastor. **2** a body of pastors.

pastrami /pastraámi/ *n.* seasoned smoked beef. [Yiddish]

pastry /páystri/ *n.* (*pl.* **-ies**) **1** a dough of flour, fat, and water baked and used as a base and covering for pies etc. **2 a** food, esp. cake, made wholly or partly of this. **b** a piece or item of this food. □ **pastry-cook** a cook who specializes in pastry, esp. for public sale. [PASTE after OF *pastaierie*]

pasturage /pàass-chərij/ *n.* **1** land for pasture. **2** the process of pasturing cattle etc. [OF (as PASTURE)]

pasture /pàass-chər/ *n.* & *v.* ● *n.* **1** land covered with grass etc. suitable for grazing animals, esp. cattle or sheep. **2** herbage for animals. ● *v.* **1** *tr.* put (animals) to graze in a pasture. **2** *intr.* & *tr.* (of animals) graze. [ME f. OF f. LL *pastura* (as PASTOR)]
■ *n.* **1** meadow, meadow-land, pasture land, pasturage, grassland, grass, range, *poet.* lea.

pasty[1] /pásti/ *n.* (*pl.* **-ies**) a pastry case with a sweet or savoury filling, baked without a dish to shape it. [ME f. OF *pasté* ult. f. LL *pasta* PASTE]

pasty[2] /páysti/ *adj.* (**pastier, pastiest**) **1** of or like or covered with paste. **2** unhealthily pale (esp. in complexion) (*pasty-faced*). □□ **pastily** *adv.* **pastiness** *n.*
■ **1** moist, damp, sticky, gummy, clammy, viscous, slimy. **2** wan, pallid, pasty-faced, sallow, pale, pale-faced, whey-faced, sickly, anaemic.

Pat /pat/ *n.* a nickname for an Irishman. [abbr. of the name *Patrick*]

Pat. *abbr.* Patent.

pat[1] /pat/ *v.* & *n.* ● *v.* (**patted, patting**) **1** *tr.* strike gently with the hand or a flat surface. **2** *tr.* flatten or mould by patting. **3** *tr.* strike gently with the inner surface of the hand, esp. as a sign of affection, sympathy, or congratulation. **4** *intr.* (foll. by *on, upon*) beat lightly. ● *n.* **1** a light stroke or tap, esp. with the hand in affection etc. **2** the sound made by this. **3** a small mass (esp. of butter) formed by patting. □ **pat-a-cake** a child's game with the patting of hands (the first words of a nursery rhyme). **pat on the back** a gesture of approval or congratulation. **pat a person on the back** congratulate a person. [ME, prob. imit.]
■ *v.* **1** strike, tap, touch, dab. **3** pet, stroke, caress. ● *n.* **1, 2** tap, touch, dab; stroke, caress. **3** piece, patty, lump, cake, portion. □ **pat on the back** commendation, praise, compliment, flattery, encouragement, credit, reassurance, approval, endorsement, recognition. **pat a person on the back** congratulate, commend, praise, compliment, encourage, reassure.

pat[2] /pat/ *adj.* & *adv.* ● *adj.* **1** known thoroughly and ready for any occasion. **2** apposite or opportune, esp. unconvincingly so (*gave a pat answer*). ● *adv.* **1** in a pat manner. **2** appositely, opportunely. □ **have off pat** know or have memorized perfectly. **stand pat** esp. *US* **1** stick stubbornly to one's opinion or decision. **2** *Poker* retain one's hand as dealt; not draw other cards. □□ **patly** *adv.* **patness** *n.* [16th c.: rel. to PAT[1]]
■ *adj.* **1** see READY *adj.* 1, 2. **2** apt, suitable, apposite, ready, appropriate, fitting, relevant; well-rehearsed; glib, slick. ● *adv.* **1** thoroughly, perfectly, exactly, precisely, faultlessly, flawlessly, just so *or* right, readily; off pat; slickly, glibly. **2** aptly, suitably, appositely, opportunely, appropriately, fittingly, relevantly. □ **have off pat** see KNOW 1a.

pat[3] /pat/ *n.* □ **on one's pat** *Austral. sl.* on one's own. [*Pat Malone*, rhyming slang for *own*]
■ □ **on one's pat** see ALONE 1.

patagium /páttəjī́əm/ *n.* (*pl.* **patagia** /-jī́ə/) *Zool.* **1** the wing-membrane of a bat or similar animal. **2** a scale covering the wing-joint in moths and butterflies. [med.L use of L *patagium* f. Gk *patageion* gold edging]

patball /pátbawl/ *n.* **1** a simple game of ball played between two players. **2** *derog.* lawn tennis.

patch /pach/ *n.* & *v.* ● *n.* **1** a piece of material or metal etc. used to mend a hole or as reinforcement. **2** a pad worn to protect an injured eye. **3** a dressing etc. put over a wound. **4** a large or irregular distinguishable area on a surface. **5** *colloq.* a period of time in terms of its characteristic quality (*went through a bad patch*). **6** a piece of ground. **7** *colloq.* an area assigned to or patrolled by an authorized person, esp. a police officer. **8** a number of plants growing in one place (*brier patch*). **9** a scrap or remnant. **10** a temporary electrical connection. **11** *hist.* a small disc etc. of black silk attached to the face, worn esp. by women in the 17th–18th c. for adornment. **12** *Mil.* a piece of cloth on a uniform as the badge of a unit. ● *v.tr.* **1** (often foll. by *up*) repair with a patch or patches; put a patch or patches on. **2** (of material) serve as a patch to. **3** (often foll. by *up*) put together, esp. hastily or in a makeshift way. **4** (foll. by *up*) settle (a quarrel etc.) esp. hastily or temporarily. □ **not a patch on** *colloq.* greatly inferior to. **patch cord** an insulated lead with a plug at each end, for use with a patchboard. **patch panel** = PATCHBOARD. **patch pocket** one made of a piece of cloth sewn on a garment. **patch test** a test for allergy by applying to the skin patches containing allergenic substances. □□ **patcher** *n.* [ME *pacche, patche*, perh. var. of *peche* f. OF *pieche* dial. var. of *piece* PIECE]
■ *n.* **1** piece, scrap, reinforcement. **2** eye-patch. **3** pad, bandage, dressing, plaster. **4** area, region, zone, stretch, section, segment. **5** period, time, interval, spell, bit, stage, episode; experience. **6** plot, tract, ground, parcel, field, *US* plat, lot. **7** responsibility, area, territory, round, beat, *US* precinct, *Law or joc.* bailiwick, *Brit. colloq.* manor. **8** border, bed, garden. **9** piece, scrap, shred, snip, snippet, tatter. ● *v.* **1, 2** patch up *or* over, mend, repair, vamp, revamp, darn, sew (up), reinforce, cover. **3** patch up, fix (up), improvise, knock together *or* up, *Naut.* jury-rig, *colloq.* doctor. **4** (*patch up*) settle, set right *or* straight, straighten out, reconcile, resolve, heal.

patchboard /páchbord/ *n.* a board with electrical sockets linked to enable changeable permutations of connection.

patchouli /pəchōōli, páchōōli/ *n.* **1** a strongly scented E. Indian plant, *Pogostemon cablin.* **2** the perfume obtained from this. [a native name in Madras]

patchwork /páchwurk/ *n.* **1** needlework using small pieces of cloth with different designs, forming a pattern. **2** a thing composed of various small pieces or fragments.
■ **2** pastiche, pasticcio, mixture, confusion, hotchpotch, gallimaufry, olio, olla podrida, mishmash, jumble, mosaic, *mélange*, medley, hash, mixed bag *or* bunch, pot-pourri.

patchy /páchi/ *adj.* (**patchier, patchiest**) **1** uneven in quality. **2** having or existing in patches. □□ **patchily** *adv.* **patchiness** *n.*

pate /payt/ *n. archaic* or *colloq.* the head, esp. representing the seat of intellect. [ME: orig. unkn.]

pâté /páttay/ *n.* a rich paste or spread of mashed and spiced meat or fish etc. □ ***pâté de foie gras*** /də fwaa gráa/ a paste of fatted goose liver. [F f. OF *pasté* (as PASTY[1])]

pâte /paat/ *n.* the paste of which porcelain is made. [F, = PASTE]

patella /pətéllə/ *n.* (*pl.* **patellae** /-lee/) the kneecap. □□ **patellar** *adj.* **patellate** /-lət/ *adj.* [L, dimin. of *patina*: see PATEN]

paten /pátt'n/ *n.* **1** a shallow dish used for the bread at the Eucharist. **2** a thin circular plate of metal. [ME ult. f. OF *patene* or L *patena, patina* shallow dish f. Gk *patanē* a plate]

patent /páyt'nt, pát-/ *n., adj.,* & *v.* ● *n.* **1** a government authority to an individual or organization conferring a right or title, esp. the sole right to make or use or sell some invention. **2** a document granting this authority. **3** an invention or process protected by it. ● *adj.* **1** /páyt'nt/ obvious, plain. **2** conferred or protected by patent. **3 a** made and marketed under a patent; proprietary. **b** to which one has a proprietary claim. **4** such as might be patented; ingenious, well-contrived. **5** (of an opening etc.) allowing free passage. ● *v.tr.* obtain a patent for (an invention). □ **letters patent** an open document from a sovereign or government conferring a patent or other right. **patent leather** leather with a glossy varnished surface. **patent medicine** medicine made and marketed under a patent and available without prescription. **patent office** an office from which patents are issued. **Patent Roll** (in the UK) a list of patents issued in a year. □□ **patency** *n.* **patentable** *adj.* **patently** /páytəntli/ *adv.* (in sense 1 of *adj.*). [ME f. OF *patent* and L *patēre* lie open]
■ *n.* **1, 2** letters patent, trade name, (registered) trade mark, copyright, licence, permit, charter, franchise, grant. **3** see INVENTION 2. ● *adj.* **1** obvious, clear, transparent, manifest, apparent, plain, evident, self-evident, unmistakable, unequivocal, explicit, palpable, tangible, physical, conspicuous, flagrant, blatant, prominent. **2, 3** protected, proprietary. **4** see INGENIOUS. □ **letters patent** see PATENT *n.* 1, 2 above. □□ **patently** see *manifestly* (MANIFEST[1]).

patentee /páytəntée/ *n.* **1** a person who takes out or holds a patent. **2** a person for the time being entitled to the benefit of a patent.

patentor /páytəntər/ *n.* a person or body that grants a patent.

pater /páytər/ *n. Brit. sl.* father. ¶ Now only in jocular or affected use. [L]

paterfamilias /páytərfəmílliass/ *n.* the male head of a family or household. [L, = father of the family]

paternal /pətérn'l/ *adj.* **1** of or like or appropriate to a father. **2** fatherly. **3** related through the father. **4** (of a government etc.) limiting freedom and responsibility by well-meant regulations. □□ **paternally** *adv.* [LL *paternalis* f. L *paternus* f. *pater* father]

■ **1, 2** fatherly, kindly, indulgent, solicitous, fond, concerned, devoted, loving; patriarchal. **3** patrilineal, patrimonial. **4** paternalistic.

paternalism /pətérnəliz'm/ *n.* the policy of governing in a paternal way, or behaving paternally to one's associates or subordinates. □□ **paternalist** *n.* **paternalistic** /-lístik/ *adj.* **paternalistically** /-lístikəli/ *adv.*

paternity /pətérniti/ *n.* **1** fatherhood. **2** one's paternal origin. **3** the source or authorship of a thing. □ **paternity suit** a lawsuit held to determine whether a certain man is the father of a certain child. **paternity test** a blood test to determine whether a man may be or cannot be the father of a particular child. [ME f. OF *paternité* or LL *paternitas*]

■ **1** fatherhood, fathership. **2** parentage, descent, heritage, line, lineage, extraction, family, stock, strain, blood.

paternoster /páttərnóstər/ *n.* **1 a** the Lord's Prayer, esp. in Latin. **b** a rosary bead indicating that this is to be said. **2** a lift consisting of a series of linked doorless compartments moving continuously on a circular belt. [OE f. L *pater noster* our father]

path /paath/ *n.* (*pl.* **paths** /paathz/) **1** a way or track laid down for walking or made by continual treading. **2** the line along which a person or thing moves (*flight path*). **3** a course of action or conduct. **4** a sequence of movements or operations taken by a system. □□ **pathless** *adj.* [OE *pæth* f. WG]

■ **1** footpath, pathway, track, trail, walk, walkway, footway, pavement, *US* sidewalk. **2** way, course, track, route, road, orbit, trajectory, circuit, *Math.* locus. **3** course, approach, channel, direction, procedure, process, way, avenue, means, method, technique, strategy, scheme, plan, scenario, *esp. US* game plan.

-path /path/ *comb. form* forming nouns denoting: **1** a practitioner of curative treatment (*homoeopath*; *osteopath*). **2** a person who suffers from a disease (*psychopath*). [back-form. f. -PATHY, or f. Gk *-pathēs* -sufferer (as PATHOS)]

Pathan /pətaán/ *n.* a member of a Pashto-speaking people inhabiting NW Pakistan and SE Afghanistan. [Hindi]

pathetic /pəthéttik/ *adj.* **1** arousing pity or sadness or contempt. **2** *Brit. colloq.* miserably inadequate. **3** *archaic* of the emotions. □ **pathetic fallacy** the attribution of human feelings and responses to inanimate things, esp. in art and literature. □□ **pathetically** *adv.* [F *pathétique* f. LL *patheticus* f. Gk *pathētikos* (as PATHOS)]

■ **1** moving, stirring, affecting, affective, touching, emotional, emotive, poignant, tragic, heart-rending, heartbreaking, pitiful, pitiable, piteous, plaintive, wretched, miserable, sorrowful, grievous, sad, doleful, mournful, woeful, *literary* lamentable, *literary or joc.* dolorous. **2** meagre, paltry, feeble, inadequate, poor, petty, puny, sorry, *colloq.* piddling, measly, crummy. □ **pathetic fallacy** anthropomorphism.

pathfinder /paáthfīndər/ *n.* **1** a person who explores new territory, investigates a new subject, etc. **2** an aircraft or its pilot sent ahead to locate and mark the target area for bombing.

■ **1** pioneer, trail-blazer.

patho- /páthō/ *comb. form* disease. [Gk *pathos* suffering: see PATHOS]

pathogen /páthəjən/ *n.* an agent causing disease. □□ **pathogenic** /-jénnik/ *adj.* **pathogenous** /-thójənəss/ *adj.* [PATHO- + -GEN]

pathogenesis /páthəjénnisiss/ *n.* (also **pathogeny** /pəthójəni/) the manner of development of a disease. □□ **pathogenetic** /-jinéttik/ *adj.*

pathological /páthəlójik'l/ *adj.* **1** of pathology. **2** of or caused by a physical or mental disorder (*a pathological fear of spiders*). □□ **pathologically** *adv.*

pathology /pəthólləji/ *n.* **1** the science of bodily diseases. **2** the symptoms of a disease. □□ **pathologist** *n.* [F *pathologie* or mod.L *pathologia* (as PATHO-, -LOGY)]

pathos /páythoss/ *n.* a quality in speech, writing, events, etc., that excites pity or sadness. [Gk *pathos* suffering, rel. to *paskhō* suffer, *penthos* grief]

pathway /paáthway/ *n.* **1** a path or its course. **2** *Biochem.* etc. a sequence of reactions undergone in a living organism.

-pathy /pəthi/ *comb. form* forming nouns denoting: **1** curative treatment (*allopathy*; *homoeopathy*). **2** feeling (*telepathy*). [Gk *patheia* suffering]

patience /páysh'nss/ *n.* **1** calm endurance of hardship, provocation, pain, delay, etc. **2** tolerant perseverance or forbearance. **3** the capacity for calm self-possessed waiting. **4** esp. *Brit.* a game for one player in which cards taken in random order have to be arranged in certain groups or sequences. □ **have no patience with 1** be unable to tolerate. **2** be irritated by. [ME f. OF f. L *patientia* (as PATIENT)]

■ **1, 3** tolerance, forbearance, restraint, toleration, stoicism, fortitude, endurance, sufferance, submission, resignation, self-control, imperturbability, even temper, unflappability, composure, calmness, serenity, equanimity. **2** diligence, tenacity, doggedness, indefatigability, endurance, assiduity, perseverance, constancy, persistence, steadfastness, pertinacity, determination, resolve, resolution, firmness; forbearance. **4** *US* solitaire.

patient /páysh'nt/ *adj.* & *n.* ● *adj.* having or showing patience. ● *n.* a person receiving or registered to receive medical treatment. □□ **patiently** *adv.* [ME f. OF f. L *patiens -entis* pres. part. of *pati* suffer]

■ *adj.* resigned, submissive, stoical, long-suffering, compliant, acquiescent, passive, self-possessed, philosophical, serene; forbearing, tolerant, forgiving, accommodating; diligent, dogged, tenacious, persistent, assiduous, sedulous, steadfast, staunch, perseverant, unwavering, unswerving, constant, unfaltering, unfailing, untiring, tireless, indefatigable, pertinacious, determined, resolved, resolute, firm, unyielding. ● *n.* invalid, sufferer, case, client.

patina /páttinə/ *n.* (*pl.* **patinas**) **1** a film, usu. green, formed on the surface of old bronze. **2** a similar film on other surfaces. **3** a gloss produced by age on woodwork. □□ **patinated** /-naytid/ *adj.* **patination** /-náysh'n/ *n.* [It. f. L *patina* dish]

patio /páttiō/ *n.* (*pl.* **-os**) **1** a paved usu. roofless area adjoining and belonging to a house. **2** an inner court open to the sky in a Spanish or Spanish-American house. [Sp.]

patisserie /pəteéssəri/ *n.* **1** a shop where pastries are made and sold. **2** pastries collectively. [F *pâtisserie* f. med.L *pasticium* pastry f. *pasta* PASTE]

Patna rice /pátnə/ *n.* a variety of rice with long firm grains. [*Patna* in India, where it was orig. grown]

patois /pátwaa/ *n.* (*pl.* same /-waaz/) the dialect of the common people in a region, differing fundamentally from the literary language. [F, = rough speech, perh. f. OF *patoier* treat roughly f. *patte* paw]

■ dialect, vernacular.

patrial /páytriəl/ *adj.* & *n. Brit. hist.* ● *adj.* having the right to live in the UK through the British birth of a parent or a grandparent. ● *n.* a person with this right. □□ **patriality** /-riálliti/ *n.* [obs. F *patrial* or med.L *patrialis* f. L *patria* fatherland f. *pater* father]

patriarch /páytriaark/ *n.* **1** the male head of a family or tribe. **2** (often in *pl.*) *Bibl.* any of those regarded as fathers of the human race, esp. the sons of Jacob, or Abraham,

Isaac, and Jacob, and their forefathers. **3** *Eccl.* **a** the title of a chief bishop, esp. those presiding over the Churches of Antioch, Alexandria, Constantinople, and (formerly) Rome; now also the title of the heads of certain autocephalous Orthodox Churches. **b** (in the Roman Catholic Church) a bishop ranking next above primates and metropolitans, and immediately below the pope. **c** the head of a Uniate community. **4 a** the founder of an order, science, etc. **b** a venerable old man. **c** the oldest member of a group. ▫▫ **patriarchal** /-áark'l/ *adj.* **patriarchally** /-áarkəli/ *adv.* [ME f. OF *patriarche* f. eccl.L *patriarcha* f. Gk *patriarkhēs* f. *patria* family f. *patēr* father + *-arkhēs* -ruler]
▪ **4 a** (founding) father. **b** *archaic* greybeard.

patriarchate /páytriaarkət/ *n.* **1** the office, see, or residence of an ecclesiastical patriarch. **2** the rank of a tribal patriarch. [med.L *patriarchatus* (as PATRIARCH)]

patriarchy /páytriaarki/ *n.* (*pl.* **-ies**) a system of society, government, etc., ruled by a man or men and with descent through the male line. ▫▫ **patriarchism** *n.* [med.L *patriarchia* f. Gk *patriarkhia* (as PATRIARCH)]

patrician /pətrísh'n/ *n.* & *adj.* ● *n.* **1** *hist.* a member of the ancient Roman nobility (cf. PLEBEIAN). **2** *hist.* a nobleman in some Italian republics. **3** an aristocrat. ● *adj.* **1** noble, aristocratic. **2** *hist.* of the ancient Roman nobility. [ME f. OF *patricien* f. L *patricius* having a noble father f. *pater patris* father]

patriciate /pətríshət/ *n.* **1** a patrician order; an aristocracy. **2** the rank of patrician. [L *patriciatus* (as PATRICIAN)]

patricide /pátrisīd/ *n.* = PARRICIDE (esp. with reference to the killing of one's father). ▫▫ **patricidal** /-sīd'l/ *adj.* [LL *patricida, patricidium,* alt. of L *parricida, parricidium* (see PARRICIDE) after *pater* father]

patrilineal /pátrilínniəl/ *adj.* of or relating to, or based on kinship with, the father or descent through the male line. [L *pater patris* father + LINEAL]

patrimony /pátriməni/ *n.* (*pl.* **-ies**) **1** property inherited from one's father or ancestor. **2** a heritage. **3** the endowment of a church etc. ▫▫ **patrimonial** /-mṓniəl/ *adj.* [ME *patrimoigne* f. OF *patrimoine* f. L *patrimonium* f. *pater patris* father]

patriot /páytriət, pát-/ *n.* a person who is devoted to and ready to support or defend his or her country. ▫▫ **patriotic** /-trióttik/ *adj.* **patriotically** /-trióttikəli/ *adv.* **patriotism** *n.* [F *patriote* f. LL *patriota* f. Gk *patriōtēs* f. *patrios* of one's fathers f. *patēr patros* father]
▪ nationalist, loyalist; flag-waver, jingo, jingoist, chauvinist.

patristic /pətrístik/ *adj.* of the early Christian writers or their work. ▫▫ **patristics** *n.pl.* (usu. treated as *sing.*). [G *patristisch* f. L *pater patris* father]

patrol /pətrṓl/ *n.* & *v.* ● *n.* **1** the act of walking or travelling around an area, esp. at regular intervals, in order to protect or supervise it. **2** one or more persons or vehicles assigned or sent out on patrol, esp. a detachment of guards, police, etc. **3 a** a detachment of troops sent out to reconnoitre. **b** such reconnaissance. **4** a routine operational voyage of a ship or aircraft. **5** a routine monitoring of astronomical or other phenomena. **6** *Brit.* an official controlling traffic where children cross the road. **7** a unit of six to eight Scouts or Guides. ● *v.* (**patrolled, patrolling**) **1** *tr.* carry out a patrol of. **2** *intr.* act as a patrol. ▫ **patrol car** a police car used in patrolling roads and streets. **patrol wagon** esp. *US* a police van for transporting prisoners. ▫▫ **patroller** *n.* [F *patrouiller* paddle in mud f. *patte* paw: (n.) f. G *Patrolle* f. F *patrouille*]
▪ *n.* **1** rounds, policing, patrolling, beat; protection, (safe)guarding, defence, watchfulness, vigilance, watch. **2** guard, sentry, sentinel, patrolman, *archaic or hist.* watchman, *hist.* watch; see also SQUAD. **6** *Brit. colloq.* lollipop man *or* lady *or* woman. ● *v.* **1** police, guard, protect, defend, watch over, stand *or* keep guard over, stand *or* keep watch over. **2** walk a beat, make *or* do the rounds, be on *or* stand *or* keep guard, be on *or* stand *or* keep watch, keep vigil. ▫ **patrol car** police car, squad car, *Brit.* panda car, *US* prowl car. **patrol wagon** *sl.* Black Maria.

patrolman /pətrṓlmən/ *n.* (*pl.* **-men**) *US* a policeman of the lowest rank.
▪ *Brit.* (police) constable, PC.

patrology /pətróllәji/ *n.* (*pl.* **-ies**) **1** the study of the writings of the Fathers of the Church. **2** a collection of such writings. ▫▫ **patrological** /pátrəlójik'l/ *adj.* **patrologist** *n.* [Gk *patēr patros* father]

patron /páytrən/ *n.* (*fem.* **patroness**) **1** a person who gives financial or other support to a person, cause, work of art, etc., esp. one who buys works of art. **2** a usu. regular customer of a shop etc. **3** *Rom. Antiq.* **a** the former owner of a freed slave. **b** the protector of a client. **4** *Brit.* a person who has the right of presenting a member of the clergy to a benefice. ▫ **patron saint** the protecting or guiding saint of a person, place, etc. [ME f. OF f. L *patronus* protector of clients, defender f. *pater patris* father]
▪ **1** benefactor, philanthropist, Maecenas, protector, supporter, defender, advocate, champion, guardian (angel), sponsor, backer, promoter, sympathizer, friend (at court), *colloq.* booster, *sl.* angel. **2** customer, client, purchaser, buyer, patronizer, *habitué*, regular, frequenter.

patronage /pátrənij/ *n.* **1** the support, promotion, or encouragement given by a patron. **2** a patronizing or condescending manner. **3** *Rom. Antiq.* the rights and duties or position of a patron. **4** *Brit.* the right of presenting a member of the clergy to a benefice etc. **5** a customer's support for a shop etc. [ME f. OF (as PATRON)]
▪ **1** sponsorship, support, backing, promotion, encouragement, boosting, aid, help, sympathy, financing, auspices, protection, guardianship, aegis. **2** condescension, disdain, scorn, patronizing, stooping, deigning, superiority, superciliousness, snobbishness. **5** trade, business, custom; trading, traffic.

patronal /pátrən'l, páy-, pətrṓn'l/ *adj.* of or relating to a patron saint (*the patronal festival*). [F *patronal* or LL *patronalis* (as PATRON)]

patronize /pátrənīz/ *v.tr.* (also **-ise**) **1** treat condescendingly. **2** act as a patron towards (a person, cause, artist, etc.); support; encourage. **3** frequent (a shop etc.) as a customer. ▫▫ **patronization** /-záysh'n/ *n.* **patronizer** *n.* **patronizing** *adj.* **patronizingly** *adv.* [obs. F *patroniser* or med.L *patronizare* (as PATRON)]
▪ **1** look down on *or* upon, scorn, look down one's nose at, talk down to; disdain, demean, put down, humiliate, treat *de haut en bas*. **2** sponsor, support, back, promote, encourage, aid, assist, help, fund, contribute *or* subscribe to, underwrite, foster, *colloq.* boost. **3** deal *or* trade with, do *or* transact business with, buy *or* purchase from, frequent, shop at, be a customer *or* client of, go to *or* attend regularly.

patronymic /pátrənímmik/ *n.* & *adj.* ● *n.* a name derived from the name of a father or ancestor, e.g. *Johnson, O'Brien, Ivanovich.* ● *adj.* (of a name) so derived. [LL *patronymicus* f. Gk *patrōnumikos* f. *patrōnumos* f. *patēr patros* father + *onuma, onoma* name]

patroon /pətrṓōn/ *n.* *US hist.* a landowner with manorial privileges under the Dutch governments of New York and New Jersey. [Du., = PATRON]

patsy /pátsi/ *n.* (*pl.* **-ies**) esp. *US sl.* a person who is deceived, ridiculed, tricked, etc. [20th c.: orig. unkn.]

pattée /páttay, -ti/ *adj.* (of a cross) having almost triangular arms becoming very broad at the ends so as to form a square. [F f. *patte* paw]

patten /pátt'n/ *n.* *hist.* a shoe or clog with a raised sole or set on an iron ring, for walking in mud etc. [ME f. OF *patin* f. *patte* paw]

patter¹ /páttər/ *v.* & *n.* ● *v.* **1** *intr.* make a rapid succession of taps, as of rain on a window-pane. **2** *intr.* run with quick short steps. **3** *tr.* cause (water etc.) to patter. ● *n.* a rapid succession of taps, short light steps, etc. [PAT¹]

■ *v.* **1** spatter, tap; beat, pelt. **2** tiptoe, scurry, scuttle, skip, trip, scamper. **3** spatter. ● *n.* spatter, pit-a-pat, pitter-patter, tapping, tattoo, drum, thrum, beat, beating, tap, rat-tat, ratatat.

patter[2] /páttər/ *n.* & *v.* ● *n.* **1 a** the rapid speech used by a comedian or introduced into a song. **b** the words of a comic song. **2** the words used by a person selling or promoting a product; a sales pitch. **3** the special language or jargon of a profession, class, etc. **4** *colloq.* mere talk; chatter. ● *v.* **1** *tr.* repeat (prayers etc.) in a rapid mechanical way. **2** *intr.* talk glibly or mechanically. [ME f. *pater* = PATERNOSTER]
■ *n.* **2** pitch, sales talk, *colloq.* line, *sl.* spiel. **3** see JARGON[1] 1, 2. **4** chatter, prattle, prate, babble, gabble, cackle, palaver, jabber, jabbering, small talk, gossip, blather, blether, gibberish, gibber, *colloq.* gab, natter, chit-chat, *sl.* gas, hot air, *sl. derog.* (yackety-)yack. ● *v.* **1** jabber, gabble, babble. **2** chatter, prattle, prate, babble, gabble, cackle, palaver, jabber, rattle (on), blather, gibber, *colloq.* chit-chat, natter (on), witter (on), gas, *sl. derog.* (yackety-)yack.

pattern /páttərn/ *n.* & *v.* ● *n.* **1** a repeated decorative design on wallpaper, cloth, a carpet, etc. **2** a regular or logical form, order, or arrangement of parts (*behaviour pattern*; *the pattern of one's daily life*). **3** a model or design, e.g. of a garment, from which copies can be made. **4** an example of excellence; an ideal; a model (*a pattern of elegance*). **5** a wooden or metal figure from which a mould is made for a casting. **6** a sample (of cloth, wallpaper, etc.). **7** the marks made by shots, bombs, etc. on a target or target area. **8** a random combination of shapes or colours. ● *v.tr.* **1** (usu. foll. by *after*, *on*) model (a thing) on a design etc. **2** decorate with a pattern. □ **pattern bombing** bombing over a large area, not on a single target. [ME *patron* (see PATRON): differentiated in sense and spelling since the 16th–17th c.]
■ *n.* **1** figure, motif, design, device; decoration, ornament. **2** system, order, arrangement, plan, theme; repetition, consistency, orderliness, regularity, sequence, cycle, habit. **3** model, original, blueprint, diagram, plan, layout, design, draft, guide, template, stencil, mould, matrix. **4** model, archetype, prototype, exemplar, paragon, ideal, standard, yardstick, criterion, gauge, measure. **6** sample, example, instance, specimen. **8** layout, configuration, formation, composition. ● *v.* **1** (*pattern after* or *on*) model on; see also IMITATE 1, 2. **2** decorate, figure, ornament; see also EMBELLISH 1.

patty /pátti/ *n.* (*pl.* **-ies**) **1** a little pie or pastry. **2** *US* a small flat cake of minced meat etc. [F *pâté* PASTY[1]]

pattypan /páttipan/ *n.* a pan for baking a patty.

patulous /pátyooləss/ *adj.* **1** (of branches etc.) spreading. **2** *formal* open; expanded. □□ **patulously** *adj.* **patulousness** *n.* [L *patulus* f. *patēre* be open]

paua /pówə/ *n.* **1** a large edible New Zealand shellfish of the genus *Haliotis*. **2** its ornamental shell. **3** a fish-hook made from this. [Maori]

paucity /páwsiti/ *n.* smallness of number or quantity. [ME f. OF *paucité* or f. L *paucitas* f. *paucus* few]

Pauli exclusion principle /pówli/ *n. Physics* the assertion that no two fermions can have the same quantum number. [W. *Pauli*, Austrian physicist d. 1958]

Pauline /páwlīn/ *adj.* of or relating to St Paul (*the Pauline epistles*). [ME f. med.L *Paulinus* f. L *Paulus* Paul]

Paul Jones /pawl jōnz/ *n.* a ballroom dance in which partners are exchanged according to a pattern. [the name of an Amer. naval officer d. 1792]

paulownia /pawlṓniə/ *n.* any Chinese tree of the genus *Paulownia*, with fragrant purple flowers. [Anna *Paulovna*, Russian princess d. 1865]

paunch /pawnch/ *n.* & *v.* ● *n.* **1** the belly or stomach, esp. when protruding. **2** a ruminant's first stomach; the rumen. **3** *Naut.* a thick strong mat. ● *v.tr.* disembowel (an animal). □□ **paunchy** *adj.* (**paunchier, paunchiest**). **paunchiness** *n.* [ME f. AF *pa(u)nche*, ONF *panche* ult. f. L *pantex panticis* bowels]
■ *n.* **1** belly, pot-belly, stomach, *colloq.* tummy, gut, *joc.* corporation, *sl.* beer-belly.

pauper /páwpər/ *n.* **1** a person without means; a beggar. **2** *hist.* a recipient of poor-law relief. **3** *Law* a person who may sue *in forma pauperis*. □□ **pauperdom** /-pərdəm/ *n.* **pauperism** /-riz'm/ *n.* **pauperize** *v.tr.* (also **-ise**). **pauperization** /-rīzáysh'n/ *n.* [L, = poor]
■ **1** indigent, down-and-out, bankrupt, insolvent, *colloq.* have-not; beggar, mendicant.

pause /pawz/ *n.* & *v.* ● *n.* **1** an interval of inaction, esp. when due to hesitation; a temporary stop. **2** a break in speaking or reading; a silence. **3** *Mus.* a mark (⌒) over a note or rest that is to be lengthened by an unspecified amount. ● *v.* **1** *intr.* make a pause; wait. **2** *intr.* (usu. foll. by *upon*) linger over (a word etc.). **3** *tr.* cause to hesitate or pause. □ **give pause to** cause (a person) to hesitate. [ME f. OF *pause* or L *pausa* f. Gk *pausis* f. *pauō* stop]
■ *n.* hesitation, interruption, delay, lull, lapse, moratorium, hold-up, wait, break, rest, breathing-space, interval, stop, discontinuity, lacuna, gap, hiatus, abeyance, discontinuation, discontinuance, *Mus.* fermata, *Prosody* caesura, *colloq.* let-up, breather. ● *v.* **1, 3** delay, break, hesitate, wait, mark time, falter, rest, *colloq.* take a breather; interrupt, hold up, suspend, discontinue, intermit.

pavage /páyvij/ *n.* **1** paving. **2** a tax or toll towards the paving of streets. [ME f. OF f. *paver* PAVE]

pavane /pəvaán/ *n.* (also **pavan** /pávv'n/) *hist.* **1** a stately dance in elaborate clothing. **2** the music for this. [F *pavane* f. Sp. *pavana*, perh. f. *pavon* peacock]

pave /payv/ *v.tr.* **1** cover (a street, floor, etc.) with paving etc. **2** cover or strew (a floor etc.) with anything (*paved with flowers*). □ **pave the way for** prepare for; facilitate. **paving-stone** a large flat usu. rectangular piece of stone etc. for paving. □□ **paver** *n.* **paving** *n.* **pavior** /páyvyər/ *n.* (also **paviour**). [ME f. OF *paver*, back-form. (as PAVEMENT)]
■ **1** cover, surface, floor; tile, flag, concrete; macadamize, tarmac, asphalt. **2** cover, strew, bestrew, scatter, litter. □ **pave the way for** facilitate, ease; see also PREPARE 1.

pavé /pávvay/ *n.* **1** a paved street, road, or path. **2** a setting of jewels placed closely together. [F, past part. of *paver*: see PAVE]

pavement /páyvmənt/ *n.* **1** *Brit.* a paved path for pedestrians at the side of and a little higher than a road. **2** the covering of a street, floor, etc., made of tiles, wooden blocks, asphalt, and esp. of rectangular stones. **3** *US* a roadway. **4** *Zool.* a pavement-like formation of close-set teeth, scales, etc. □ **pavement artist 1** *Brit.* an artist who draws on paving-stones with coloured chalks, hoping to be given money by passers-by. **2** *US* an artist who displays paintings for sale on a pavement. [ME f. OF f. L *pavimentum* f. *pavire* beat, ram]
■ **1** walk, footpath, footway, *US* sidewalk. **3** road, roadway.

pavilion /pəvílyən/ *n.* & *v.* ● *n.* **1** *Brit.* a building at a cricket or other sports ground used for changing, refreshments, etc. **2** a summerhouse or other decorative building in a garden. **3** a tent, esp. a large one with crenellated decorations at a show, fair, etc. **4** a building used for entertainments. **5** a temporary stand at an exhibition. **6** a detached building at a hospital. **7** a usu. highly decorated subdivision of a building. **8** the part of a cut gemstone below the girdle. ● *v.tr.* enclose in or provide with a pavilion. [ME f. OF *pavillon* f. L *papilio -onis* butterfly, tent]

pavior, paviour see PAVE.

pavlova /pavlṓvə/ *n.* a meringue cake with cream and fruit. [A. *Pavlova*, Russ. ballerina d. 1931]

Pavlovian /pavlṓviən/ *adj.* of or relating to I. P. Pavlov, Russian physiologist d. 1936, or his work, esp. on conditioned reflexes.

pavonine /pávvənīn/ *adj.* of or like a peacock. [L *pavoninus* f. *pavo -onis* peacock]

paw /paw/ *n.* & *v.* ● *n.* **1** a foot of an animal having claws or nails. **2** *colloq.* a person's hand. ● *v.* **1** *tr.* strike or scrape with a paw or foot. **2** *intr.* scrape the ground with a paw or hoof. **3** *tr. colloq.* fondle awkwardly or indecently. [ME *pawe*, *powe* f. OF *poue* etc. ult. f. Frank.]

pawky /páwki/ *adj.* (**pawkier, pawkiest**) *Sc.* & *dial.* **1** drily humorous. **2** shrewd. □□ **pawkily** *adv.* **pawkiness** *n.* [Sc. & N.Engl. dial. *pawk* trick, of unkn. orig.]

pawl /pawl/ *n.* & *v.* ● *n.* **1** a lever with a catch for the teeth of a wheel or bar. **2** *Naut.* a short bar used to lock a capstan, windlass, etc., to prevent it from recoiling. ● *v.tr.* secure (a capstan etc.) with a pawl. [perh. f. LG & Du. *pal*, rel. to *pal* fixed]

pawn[1] /pawn/ *n.* **1** *Chess* a piece of the smallest size and value. **2** a person used by others for their own purposes. [ME f. AF *poun*, OF *peon* f. med.L *pedo -onis* foot-soldier f. L *pes pedis* foot: cf. PEON]

■ **2** tool, cat's-paw, puppet, instrument, dupe, *colloq.* dummy, stooge.

pawn[2] /pawn/ *v.* & *n.* ● *v.tr.* **1** deposit an object, esp. with a pawnbroker, as security for money lent. **2** pledge or wager (one's life, honour, word, etc.). ● *n.* **1** an object left as security for money etc. lent. **2** anything or any person left with another as security etc. □ **in** (or **at**) **pawn** (of an object etc.) held as security. [ME f. OF *pan*, *pand*, *pant*, pledge, security f. WG]

■ *v.* pledge, mortgage, hypothecate, deposit, *archaic* plight, gage, *esp. US colloq.* hock, *sl.* pop. ● *n.* collateral, guaranty, guarantee, pledge, surety, security, assurance, deposit; bond, bail. □ **in** (or **at**) **pawn** *esp. US colloq.* in hock.

pawnbroker /páwnbrōkər/ *n.* a person who lends money at interest on the security of personal property pawned. □□ **pawnbroking** *n.*

pawnshop /páwnshop/ *n.* a shop where pawnbroking is conducted.

pawpaw /páwpaw/ *n.* (also **papaw** /pəpáw/, **papaya** /pəpī́ə/) **1 a** an elongated melon-shaped fruit with edible orange flesh and small black seeds. **b** a tropical tree, *Carica papaya*, bearing this and producing a milky sap from which papain is obtained. **2** *US* a N. American tree, *Asimina triloba*, with purple flowers and edible fruit. [earlier *papay(a)* f. Sp. & Port. *papaya*, of Carib orig.]

PAX *abbr.* private automatic (telephone) exchange.

pax /paks/ *n.* **1** the kiss of peace. **2** (as *int.*) *Brit. sl.* a call for a truce (used esp. by schoolchildren). [ME f. L, = peace]

pay[1] /pay/ *v.* & *n.* ● *v.tr.* (*past* and *past part.* **paid** /payd/) **1** (also *absol.*) give (a person etc.) what is due for services done, goods received, debts incurred, etc. (*paid him in full*; *I assure you I have paid*). **2 a** give (a usu. specified amount) for work done, a debt, a ransom, etc. (*they pay £6 an hour*). **b** (foll. by *to*) hand over the amount of (a debt, wages, recompense, etc.) to (*paid the money to the assistant*). **3 a** give, bestow, or express (attention, respect, a compliment, etc.) (*paid them no heed*). **b** make (a visit, a call, etc.) (*paid a visit to their uncle*). **4** (also *absol.*) (of a business, undertaking, attitude, etc.) be profitable or advantageous to (a person etc.). **5** reward or punish (*can never pay you for what you have done for us*; *I shall pay you for that*). **6** (usu. as **paid** *adj.*) recompense (work, time, etc.) (*paid holiday*). **7** (usu. foll. by *out*, *away*) let out (a rope) by slackening it. ● *n.* wages; payment. □ **in the pay of** employed by. **paid holidays** an agreed holiday period for which wages are paid as normal. **paid-up member** (esp. of a trade-union member) a person who has paid the subscriptions in full. **pay-as-you-earn** *Brit.* the deduction of income tax from wages at source. **pay-bed** a hospital bed for private patients. **pay-claim** a demand for an increase in pay, esp. by a trade union. **pay-day** a day on which payment, esp. of wages, is made or expected to be made. **pay dearly** (usu. foll. by *for*) **1** obtain at a high cost, great effort, etc. **2** suffer for a wrongdoing etc. **pay dirt** (or **gravel**) *US* **1** *Mineral.* ground worth working for ore. **2** a financially promising situation. **pay envelope** *US* = *pay-packet*. **pay for 1** hand over the price of. **2** bear the cost of. **3** suffer or be punished for (a fault etc.). **pay in** pay (money) into a bank account. **paying guest** a boarder. **pay its** (or **one's**) **way** cover costs; not be indebted. **pay one's last respects** show respect towards a dead person by attending the funeral. **pay off 1** dismiss (workers) with a final payment. **2** *colloq.* yield good results; succeed. **3** pay (a debt) in full. **4** (of a ship) turn to leeward through the movement of the helm. **pay-off** *n. sl.* **1** an act of payment. **2** a climax. **3** a final reckoning. **4** *colloq.* a bribe; bribery. **pay out** (or **back**) punish or be revenged on. **pay-packet** *Brit.* a packet or envelope containing an employee's wages. **pay phone** a coin-box telephone. **pay the piper and call the tune** pay for, and therefore have control over, a proceeding. **pay one's respects** make a polite visit. **pay station** *US* = *pay phone*. **pay through the nose** *colloq.* pay much more than a fair price. **pay up** pay the full amount, or the full amount of. **put paid to** *colloq.* **1** deal effectively with (a person). **2** terminate (hopes etc.). □□ **payee** /payée/ *n.* **payer** *n.* [ME f. OF *paie*, *payer* f. L *pacare* appease f. *pax pacis* peace]

■ *v.* **1** recompense, compensate, remunerate, reward, indemnify, repay, reimburse. **2** repay, refund, reimburse, pay off, pay out, pay up, satisfy, clear, remit, discharge, liquidate, settle, honour, meet; disburse, expend, spend, contribute, lay out, *colloq.* shell out, *sl.* fork out *or* up, cough up. **3** extend, bestow, transmit, pass on, give, deliver; make, do; express. **4** benefit, profit, avail, help, advantage; (*absol.*) be *or* prove profitable, be *or* prove worthwhile, yield a return, be advantageous, produce results, show a profit, pay off; see also SUCCEED 1b. **5** pay back *or* out, repay, settle (accounts) with, requite; take *or* get revenge on, avenge oneself on, hit *or* strike *or* get back at, even the score with, make a person pay for, punish, chastise, castigate, get even with. **7** (*pay out*) release, loosen, let out, slack *or* slacken off (on). ● *n.* remuneration, consideration, reward, money, wage(s), salary, fee, honorarium, remittance, allowance, stipend, income, take-home pay, *Brit. sl.* screw; payment, compensation, recompense, defrayment, settlement, pay-off, return; gain, profit; takings, *esp. US* take. □ **pay for 3** suffer for, answer for, make amends for, atone for, get one's (just) deserts for, be punished for. **pay in** see DEPOSIT *v.* 2. **pay off 1** see DISMISS 2. **2** see PAY[1] *v.* 4 above. **3** see PAY[1] *v.* 2 above. **pay-off 1** see PAY[1] *n.* above. **2, 3** result, outcome, upshot, conclusion, wind-up, settlement, (final) reckoning, climax, (grand) finale, punch-line, *colloq.* crunch. **4** bribe, rebate, *colloq.* graft; ransom, blood-money, *esp. US* payola, *colloq.* kickback, hush money, *esp. US colloq.* plugola. **pay out** (or **back**) see PAY[1] *v.* 5 above. **pay up** see PAY[1] *v.* 2 above. **put paid to 1** see *dispose of* 1a, c. **2** see END *v.* 1.

pay[2] /pay/ *v.tr.* (*past* and *past part.* **payed**) *Naut.* smear (a ship) with pitch, tar, etc. as a defence against wet. [OF *peier* f. L *picare* f. *pix picis* PITCH[2]]

payable /páyəb'l/ *adj.* **1** that must be paid; due (*payable in April*). **2** that may be paid. **3** (of a mine etc.) profitable.

■ **1** due, owed, owing, outstanding, unpaid, receivable, mature.

payback /páybak/ *n.* **1** a financial return; a reward. **2** the profit from an investment etc., esp. one equal to the initial outlay. □ **payback period** the length of time required for an investment to pay for itself in terms of profits or savings.

PAYE *abbr. Brit.* pay-as-you-earn.

payload /páylōd/ *n.* **1** the part of an aircraft's load from which revenue is derived. **2 a** the explosive warhead carried by an aircraft or rocket. **b** the instruments etc. carried by a spaceship.

paymaster /páymaastər/ *n.* **1** an official who pays troops, workmen, etc. **2** a person, organization, etc., to whom another owes duty or loyalty because of payment given. **3** (in full **Paymaster General**) *Brit.* the minister at the head of the Treasury department responsible for payments.

payment /páymənt/ *n.* **1** the act or an instance of paying. **2** an amount paid. **3** reward, recompense. [ME f. OF *paiement* (as PAY[1])]
■ **1** remuneration, compensation, settlement. **2** expenditure, disbursement, distribution, outlay, fee, contribution, charge, expense. **3** see PAY[1] *n.*

paynim /páynim/ *n. archaic* **1** a pagan. **2** a non-Christian, esp. a Muslim. [ME f. OF *pai(e)nime* f. eccl.L *paganismus* heathenism (as PAGAN)]

payola /payṓlə/ *n.* esp. *US* **1** a bribe offered in return for unofficial promotion of a product etc. in the media. **2** the practice of such bribery. [PAY[1] + *-ola* as in *Victrola*, make of gramophone]

payroll /páyrōl/ *n.* a list of employees receiving regular pay.

paysage /payzaázh/ *n.* **1** a rural scene; a landscape. **2** landscape painting. □□ ***paysagist*** /páyzaajist/ *n.* [F f. *pays* country: see PEASANT]

Pb *symb. Chem.* the element lead. [L *plumbum*]

PBX *abbr.* private branch exchange (private telephone switchboard).

PC *abbr.* **1** (in the UK) police constable. **2** (in the UK) Privy Counsellor. **3** personal computer. **4** political correctness, politically correct.
■ **1** see *police officer*. **3** (personal) computer, micro, microcomputer, work station.

p.c. *abbr.* **1** per cent. **2** postcard.

PCB *abbr.* **1** *Computing* printed circuit board. **2** *Chem.* polychlorinated biphenyl, any of several toxic aromatic compounds containing two benzene molecules in which hydrogens have been replaced by chlorine atoms, formed as waste in industrial processes.

PCM *abbr.* pulse code modulation.

pct. *abbr. US* per cent.

PD *abbr. US* Police Department.

Pd *symb. Chem.* the element palladium.

pd. *abbr.* paid.

p.d.q. *abbr. colloq.* pretty damn quick.
■ see FAST[1] *adv.* 1.

PDT *abbr. US* Pacific Daylight Time.

PE *abbr.* physical education.

p/e *abbr.* price/earnings (ratio).

pea /pee/ *n.* **1 a** a hardy climbing plant, *Pisum sativum*, with seeds growing in pods and used for food. **b** its seed. **2** any of several similar plants (*sweet pea*; *chick-pea*). □ **pea-brain** *colloq.* a stupid or dim-witted person. **pea-green** bright green. **pea-souper** *Brit. colloq.* a thick yellowish fog. [back-form. f. PEASE (taken as pl.: cf. CHERRY)]
■ □ **pea-souper** see FOG[1] *n.* 1.

peace /peess/ *n.* **1 a** quiet; tranquillity (*needs peace to work well*). **b** mental calm; serenity (*peace of mind*). **2 a** (often *attrib.*) freedom from or the cessation of war (*peace talks*). **b** (esp. **Peace**) a treaty of peace between two States etc. at war. **3** freedom from civil disorder. **4** *Eccl.* a ritual liturgical greeting. □ **at peace 1** in a state of friendliness. **2** serene. **3** *euphem.* dead. **hold one's peace** keep silence. **keep the peace** prevent, or refrain from, strife. **make one's peace** (often foll. by *with*) re-establish friendly relations. **make peace** bring about peace; reconcile. **the peace** (or **the queen's peace**) peace existing within a realm; civil order. **Peace Corps** *US* an organization sending young people to work as volunteers in developing countries. **peace dividend** public money which becomes available when defence spending is reduced. **peace-offering 1** a propitiatory or conciliatory gift. **2** *Bibl.* an offering presented as a thanksgiving to God. **peace-pipe** a tobacco-pipe as a token of peace among US Indians. [ME f. AF *pes*, OF *pais* f. L *pax pacis*]
■ **1** serenity, tranquillity, calm, calmness, placidity, placidness, peace of mind, quiet, peacefulness, peaceableness, stillness. **2** harmony, accord, harmoniousness, concord, amity, peacefulness, peacetime; cease-fire, armistice, truce. □ **at peace 1** see FRIENDLY *adj.* 2. **2** see SERENE. **3** see DEAD 1.

peaceable /péessəb'l/ *adj.* **1** disposed to peace; unwarlike. **2** free from disturbance; peaceful. □□ **peaceableness** *n.* **peaceably** *adv.* [ME f. OF *peisible*, *plaisible* f. LL *placibilis* pleasing f. L *placēre* please]
■ **1** pacific, inoffensive, dovish, peace-loving, mild, non-violent, peaceful, non-belligerent, unwarlike, non-warring, non-combative, temperate, agreeable, compatible, congenial, genial, friendly, amiable, amicable, cordial, civil. **2** see PEACEFUL 1.

peaceful /péesfŏŏl/ *adj.* **1** characterized by peace; tranquil. **2** not violating or infringing peace (*peaceful coexistence*). **3** belonging to a state of peace. □□ **peacefully** *adv.* **peacefulness** *n.*
■ **1** peaceable, serene, placid, calm, quiet, quiescent, gentle, restful, tranquil, untroubled, undisturbed, unruffled. **2** see PEACEABLE 1.

peacemaker /péesmaykər/ *n.* a person who brings about peace. □□ **peacemaking** *n.* & *adj.*
■ conciliator, pacifier, reconciler, propitiator, placater, pacificator, mediator, arbitrator, intermediator, intermediary, diplomat, appeaser, interceder, intercessor, go-between; referee, umpire, adjudicator; peacemonger.

peacetime /péestīm/ *n.* a period when a country is not at war.
■ see PEACE 2.

peach[1] /peech/ *n.* **1 a** a round juicy stone-fruit with downy cream or yellow skin flushed with red. **b** the tree, *Prunus persica*, bearing it. **2** the yellowish-pink colour of a peach. **3** *colloq.* **a** a person or thing of superlative quality. **b** often *offens.* an attractive young woman. □ **peach-bloom** an oriental porcelain-glaze of reddish pink, usu. with green markings. **peach-blow 1** a delicate purplish-pink colour. **2** = *peach-bloom*. **peaches and cream** (of a complexion) creamy skin with downy pink cheeks. **peach Melba** see MELBA. □□ **peachy** *adj.* (**peachier**, **peachiest**). **peachiness** *n.* [ME f. OF *peche*, *pesche*, f. med.L *persica* f. L *persicum (malum)*, lit. Persian apple]
■ **3 a** see BEAUTY 2a. **b** see BEAUTY 3. □ **peaches and cream** see FAIR[1] *adj.* 2. □□ **peachy** see FINE[1] *adj.* 2b.

peach[2] /peech/ *v.* **1** *intr.* (usu. foll. by *against*, *on*) *colloq.* turn informer; inform. **2** *tr. archaic* inform against. [ME f. *appeach* f. AF *enpecher*, OF *empechier* IMPEACH]
■ see INFORM 2.

pea-chick /péechik/ *n.* a young peafowl. [formed as PEACOCK + CHICK[1]]

peacock /péekok/ *n.* **1** a male peafowl, having brilliant plumage and a tail (with eyelike markings) that can be expanded erect in display like a fan. **2** an ostentatious strutting person. □ **peacock blue** the lustrous greenish-blue of a peacock's neck. **peacock butterfly** a butterfly, *Inachis io*, with eyelike markings on its wings. [ME *pecock* f. OE *pēa* f. L *pavo* + COCK[1]]
■ **2** see BRAGGART *n.*

peafowl /péefowl/ *n.* **1** a peacock or peahen. **2** a pheasant of the genus *Pavo*.

peahen /péehen/ *n.* a female peafowl.

pea-jacket /péejakkit/ *n.* a sailor's short double-breasted overcoat of coarse woollen cloth. [prob. f. Du. *pijjakker* f. *pij* coat of coarse cloth + *jekker* jacket: assim. to JACKET]

peak[1] /peek/ *n.* & *v.* ● *n.* **1** a projecting usu. pointed part, esp.: **a** the pointed top of a mountain. **b** a mountain with a peak. **c** a stiff brim at the front of a cap. **d** a pointed beard. **e** the narrow part of a ship's hold at the bow or stern (*forepeak*; *after-peak*). **f** *Naut.* the upper outer corner of a sail extended by a gaff. **2 a** the highest point in a curve (*on the peak of the wave*). **b** the time of greatest success (in a career etc.). **c** the highest point on a graph etc. ● *v.intr.* reach the highest value, quality, etc. (*output peaked in September*). □ **peak hour** the time of the most intense traffic etc. **peak-load** the maximum of electric power demand etc. □□ **peaked** *adj.* **peaky** *adj.* **peakiness** *n.* [prob. back-form. f. *peaked* var. of dial. *picked* pointed (PICK[2])]

■ *n.* **1 a, b** top, pinnacle, crest, ridge, tor, mountain top, summit; mountain, eminence, elevation, hill. **c** visor, brim. **d** goatee. **2** top, tip, apex, acme, culmination, pinnacle, apogee, zenith, high point, crown, *colloq.* tiptop; extreme, utmost, uttermost, perfection, *ne plus ultra*, consummation, climax. ● *v.* crest, culminate, (reach a) climax, reach a peak, top (out); come to a head. □ **peak hour** rush hour; prime time.

peak[2] /peek/ *v.intr.* **1** waste away. **2** (as **peaked** *adj.*) esp. *US* sharp-featured; pinched, sickly-looking. [16th c.: orig. unkn.]

■ **2** (**peaked**) see PEAKY.

peaky /péeki/ *adj.* (**peakier**, **peakiest**) **1** sickly; puny. **2** white-faced. □ **peakish** *adj.*

■ peakish, pinched, unhealthy, sickly, ailing, ill, unwell, infirm, unwholesome, pale, pallid, wan, waxen, anaemic, pasty, sallow, whey-faced, ashen, washed out, drained, emaciated, wasted, gaunt, hollow-eyed, haggard, drawn, weak, feeble, *esp. US* peaked.

peal[1] /peel/ *n.* & *v.* ● *n.* **1 a** the loud ringing of a bell or bells, esp. a series of changes. **b** a set of bells. **2** a loud repeated sound, esp. of thunder, laughter, etc. ● *v.* **1** *intr.* sound forth in a peal. **2** *tr.* utter sonorously. **3** *tr.* ring (bells) in peals. [ME *pele* f. *apele* APPEAL]

■ *n.* ringing, ring, carillon, chime, toll, tolling, tinkle, tinkling, tintinnabulation; changes; clang, clangour, clamour, reverberation; knell; clap, crash, roar, rumble, thunder. ● *v.* ring, toll, chime, clang, reverberate, resonate, resound; knell; boom, crash, roar, roll, rumble, thunder.

peal[2] /peel/ *n.* a salmon grilse. [16th c.: orig. unkn.]

pean[1] /peen/ *n. Heraldry* fur represented as sable spotted with or. [16th c.: orig. unkn.]

pean[2] *US* var. of PAEAN.

peanut /péenut/ *n.* **1** a leguminous plant, *Arachis hypogaea*, bearing pods that ripen underground and contain seeds used as food and yielding oil. **2** the seed of this plant. **3** (in *pl.*) *colloq.* a paltry or trivial thing or amount, esp. of money. □ **peanut butter** a paste of ground roasted peanuts.

■ **1** pignut, earth-nut, monkey nut, *Brit.* groundnut. **3** (*peanuts*) see PITTANCE.

pear /pair/ *n.* **1** a yellowish or brownish-green fleshy fruit, tapering towards the stalk. **2** any of various trees of the genus *Pyrus* bearing it, esp. *P. communis*. □ **pear-drop** a small sweet with the shape of a pear. [OE *pere*, *peru* ult. f. L *pirum*]

pearl[1] /perl/ *n.* & *v.* ● *n.* **1 a** (often *attrib.*) a usu. white or bluish-grey hard mass formed within the shell of a pearl-oyster or other bivalve mollusc, highly prized as a gem for its lustre (*pearl necklace*). **b** an imitation of this. **c** (in *pl.*) a necklace of pearls. **d** = *mother-of-pearl* (cf. *seed-pearl*). **2** a precious thing; the finest example. **3** anything resembling a pearl, e.g. a dewdrop, tear, etc. ● *v.* **1** *tr. poet.* **a** sprinkle with pearly drops. **b** make pearly in colour etc. **2** *tr.* reduce (barley etc.) to small rounded grains. **3** *intr.* fish for pearl-oysters. **4** *intr. poet.* form pearl-like drops. □ **cast pearls before swine** offer a treasure to a person unable to appreciate it. **pearl ash** commercial potassium carbonate. **pearl barley** barley reduced to small round grains by grinding. **pearl bulb** a translucent electric light bulb. **pearl button** a button made of mother-of-pearl or an imitation of it. **pearl-diver** a person who dives for pearl-oysters. **pearl millet** a tall cereal, *Pennisetum typhoides*. **pearl onion** a very small onion used in pickles. **pearl-oyster** any of various marine bivalve molluscs of the genus *Pinctada*, bearing pearls. □□ **pearler** *n.* [ME f. OF *perle* prob. f. L *perna* leg (applied to leg-of-mutton-shaped bivalve)]

■ *n.* **2** gem, treasure, prize, flower, wonder, nonpareil.

pearl[2] /perl/ *n. Brit.* = PICOT. [var. of PURL[1]]

pearled /perld/ *adj.* **1** adorned with pearls. **2** formed into pearl-like drops or grains. **3** pearl-coloured.

pearlescent /perléss'nt/ *adj.* having or producing the appearance of mother-of-pearl.

pearlite var. of PERLITE.

pearlized /pérlīzd/ *adj.* treated so as to resemble mother-of-pearl.

pearlware /pérlwair/ *n.* a fine white glazed earthenware.

pearlwort /pérlwurt/ *n. Bot.* any small herbaceous plant of the genus *Sagina*, inhabiting rocky and sandy areas.

pearly /pérli/ *adj.* & *n.* ● *adj.* (**pearlier**, **pearliest**) **1** resembling a pearl; lustrous. **2** containing pearls or mother-of-pearl. **3** adorned with pearls. ● *n.* (*pl.* **-ies**) (in *pl.*) *Brit.* **1** pearly kings and queens. **2** a pearly king's or queen's clothes or pearl buttons. □ **Pearly Gates** *colloq.* the gates of Heaven. **pearly king** (or **queen**) *Brit.* a London costermonger (or his wife) wearing clothes covered with pearl buttons. **pearly nautilus** see NAUTILUS. □□ **pearliness** *n.*

■ *adj.* **1, 2** nacreous, pearl-like, lustrous; mother-of-pearl.

pearmain /páirmayn, pér-/ *n.* a variety of apple with firm white flesh. [ME, = warden pear, f. OF *parmain*, *permain*, prob. ult. f. L *parmensis* of *Parma* in Italy]

peart /pert/ *adj. US* lively; cheerful. [var. of PERT]

peasant /pézz'nt/ *n.* **1** esp. *colloq.* a countryman or countrywoman; a rustic. **2 a** a worker on the land, esp. a labourer or smallholder. **b** *hist.* a member of an agricultural class dependent on subsistence farming. **3** *derog.* a lout; a boorish person. □□ **peasantry** *n.* (*pl.* **-ies**). **peasanty** *adj.* [ME f. AF *paisant*, OF *païsent*, earlier *païsence* f. *païs* country ult. f. L *pagus* canton]

■ rustic, countryman, countrywoman, farmer, provincial, (farm) worker, (country) bumpkin, bucolic, yokel, boor, peon, fellah, oaf, lout, *archaic* swain, churl, clown, *esp. US colloq.* hick, *US colloq.* hayseed, rube, *US colloq. often derog.* hill-billy, *hist.* muzhik, serf, hind, *offens.* mean white, poor white (trash), *US offens.* cracker.

pease /peez/ *n.pl. archaic* peas. □ **pease-pudding** boiled split peas (served esp. with boiled ham). [OE *pise* pea, pl. *pisan*, f. LL *pisa* f. L *pisum* f. Gk *pison*: cf. PEA]

peashooter /péeshōōtər/ *n.* a small tube for blowing dried peas through as a toy.

peat /peet/ *n.* **1** vegetable matter decomposed in water and partly carbonized, used for fuel, in horticulture, etc. **2** a cut piece of this. □□ **peaty** *adj.* [ME f. AL *peta*, perh. f. Celt.: cf. PIECE]

peatbog /péetbog/ *n.* a bog composed of peat.

peatmoss /péetmoss/ *n.* **1** a peatbog. **2** any of various mosses of the genus *Sphagnum*, which grow in damp conditions and form peat as they decay.

peau-de-soie /pṓdəswaá/ *n.* a smooth finely-ribbed satiny fabric of silk or rayon. [F, = skin of silk]

pebble /pébb'l/ *n.* **1** a small smooth stone worn by the action of water. **2 a** a type of colourless transparent rock-crystal used for spectacles. **b** a lens of this. **c** (*attrib.*) *colloq.* (of a spectacle-lens) very thick and convex. **3** an agate or other gem, esp. when found as a pebble in a stream etc. **4** esp. *Austral. sl.* a high-spirited person or animal, esp. one hard to control. □ **not the only pebble on the beach** (esp. of a person) easily replaced. **pebble-dash** mortar with pebbles in it used as a coating for external walls. □□ **pebbly** *adj.* [OE *papel-stān* pebble-stone, *pyppelrīpig* pebble-stream, of unkn. orig.]

■ □□ **pebbly** see STONY 1.

p.e.c. *abbr.* photoelectric cell.

pecan /péekən/ *n.* **1** a pinkish-brown smooth nut with an edible kernel. **2** a hickory, *Carya illinoensis*, of the southern US, producing this. [earlier *paccan*, of Algonquian orig.]

peccable /pékkəb'l/ *adj. formal* liable to sin. □□ **peccability** /-bílliti/ *n.* [F, f. med.L *peccabilis* f. *peccare* sin]

peccadillo /pékkədíllō/ *n.* (*pl.* **-oes** or **-os**) a trifling offence; a venial sin. [Sp. *pecadillo*, dimin. of *pecado* sin f. L (as PECCANT)]

■ slip, error, lapse, mistake, infraction, violation, misdeed, shortcoming, misstep, blunder, *faux pas*, indiscretion, gaffe, botch, stumble, fault, petty sin, transgression, trespass, *colloq.* slip-up, *sl.* goof.

peccant /pékkənt/ *adj. formal* **1** sinning. **2** inducing disease; morbid. □□ **peccancy** *n.* [F *peccant* or L *peccare* sin]

peccary /pékkəri/ *n.* (*pl.* **-ies**) any American wild pig of the family Tayassuidae, esp. *Tayassu tajacu* and *T. pecari.* [Carib *pakira*]

peccavi /pekaávi/ *int.* & *n.* ● *int.* expressing guilt. ● *n.* (*pl.* **peccavis**) a confession of guilt. [L, = I have sinned]

pêche Melba /pesh mélbə/ *n.* = *peach Melba* (see MELBA). [F]

peck[1] /pek/ *v.* & *n.* ● *v.tr.* **1** strike or bite (something) with a beak. **2** kiss (esp. a person's cheek) hastily or perfunctorily. **3 a** make (a hole) by pecking. **b** (foll. by *out*, *off*) remove or pluck out by pecking. **4** *colloq.* (also *absol.*) eat (food) listlessly; nibble at. **5** mark with short strokes. **6** (usu. foll. by *up*, *down*) break with a pick etc. ● *n.* **1 a** a stroke or bite with a beak. **b** a mark made by this. **2** a hasty or perfunctory kiss. **3** *sl.* food. □ **peck at 1** eat (food) listlessly; nibble. **2** carp at; nag. **3** strike (a thing) repeatedly with a beak. **pecking** (or **peck**) **order** a social hierarchy, orig. as observed among hens. [ME prob. f. MLG *pekken*, of unkn. orig.]

■ *v.* **1** see TAP[2] *v.* 1, 2. **2** see KISS *v.* 1. **4** see *pick at* 1 (PICK[1]). ● *n.* **1 a** see TAP[2] *n.* **2** see KISS *n.* 1. □ **peck at 1** see *pick at* 1 (PICK[1]). **2** see *pick on* 1 (PICK[1]).

peck[2] /pek/ *n.* **1** a measure of capacity for dry goods, equal to 2 gallons or 8 quarts. **2** a vessel used to contain this amount. □ **a peck of** a large number or amount of (troubles, dirt, etc.). [ME f. AF *pek*, of unkn. orig.]

pecker /pékkər/ *n.* **1** a bird that pecks (*woodpecker*). **2** *US coarse sl.* the penis. □ **keep your pecker up** *Brit. colloq.* remain cheerful.

peckish /pékkish/ *adj. colloq.* **1** hungry. **2** *US* irritable.

■ **1** see HUNGRY 1.

pecorino /pékkəréenō/ *n.* (*pl.* **-os**) an Italian cheese made from ewes' milk. [It. f. *pecorino* (adj.) of ewes f. *pecora* sheep]

pecten /péktin/ *n.* (*pl.* **pectens** or **pectines** /-tineez/) *Zool.* **1** a comblike structure of various kinds in animal bodies. **2** any bivalve mollusc of the genus *Pecten.* Also called SCALLOP. □□ **pectinate** /-nət/ *adj.* **pectinated** /-naytid/ *adj.* **pectination** /-náysh'n/ *n.* (all in sense 1). [L *pecten pectinis* comb]

pectin /péktin/ *n. Biochem.* any of various soluble gelatinous polysaccharides found in ripe fruits etc. and used as a setting agent in jams and jellies. □□ **pectic** *adj.* [Gk *pēktos* congealed f. *pēgnumi* make solid]

pectoral /péktərəl/ *adj.* & *n.* ● *adj.* **1** of or relating to the breast or chest; thoracic (*pectoral fin*; *pectoral muscle*). **2** worn on the chest (*pectoral cross*). ● *n.* **1** (esp. in *pl.*) a pectoral muscle. **2** a pectoral fin. **3** an ornamental breastplate esp. of a Jewish high priest. [ME f. OF f. L *pectorale* (n.), *pectoralis* (adj.) f. *pectus pectoris* breast, chest]

pectose /péktōss/ *n. Biochem.* an insoluble polysaccharide derivative found in unripe fruits and converted into pectin by ripening, heating, etc. [*pectic* (see PECTIN) + -OSE[2]]

peculate /pékyoolayt/ *v.tr.* & *intr.* embezzle (money). □□ **peculation** /-láysh'n/ *n.* **peculator** *n.* [L *peculari* rel. to *peculium*: see PECULIAR]

■ see EMBEZZLE. □□ **peculator** see THIEF.

peculiar /pikyōōliər/ *adj.* & *n.* ● *adj.* **1** strange; odd; unusual (*a peculiar flavour*; *is a little peculiar*). **2 a** (usu. foll. by *to*) belonging exclusively (*a fashion peculiar to the time*). **b** belonging to the individual (*in their own peculiar way*). **3** particular; special (*a point of peculiar interest*). ● *n.* **1** a peculiar property, privilege, etc. **2** a parish or church exempt from the jurisdiction of the diocese in which it lies. [ME f. L *peculiaris* of private property f. *peculium* f. *pecu* cattle]

■ *adj.* **1** odd, curious, strange, queer, bizarre, weird, unusual, abnormal, anomalous, aberrant, deviant, eccentric, uncommon, outlandish, exceptional, extraordinary, out of the ordinary, offbeat, unorthodox, atypical, idiosyncratic, unconventional, out of the way, quaint, unique, singular, *sui generis*, distinct, special, particular, quirky, funny, freakish, freaky, far-out, *colloq.* way-out, *Brit. colloq.* rum. **2 a** (*peculiar to*) typical of, characteristic of, characterized by, natural to, symptomatic of, appropriate to *or* for, distinctive of, restricted to, specific to, indicative of, denotative of, limited to, individual to, personal to, special to, unique to; local to, native to, indigenous to. **3** see PARTICULAR *adj.* 1.

peculiarity /pikyōōliárriti/ *n.* (*pl.* **-ies**) **1 a** idiosyncrasy; unusualness; oddity. **b** an instance of this. **2** a characteristic or habit (*meanness is his peculiarity*). **3** the state of being peculiar.

■ **1** idiosyncrasy, oddity, unusualness, eccentricity, abnormality, irregularity, quirk, kink. **2** feature, characteristic, habit, property, quality, trait, attribute, earmark, hallmark, mark, particularity, singularity, speciality, *esp. US* specialty.

peculiarly /pikyōōliərli/ *adv.* **1** more than usually; especially (*peculiarly annoying*). **2** oddly. **3** as regards oneself alone; individually (*does not affect him peculiarly*).

■ **1** see ESPECIALLY.

pecuniary /pikyōōniəri/ *adj.* **1** of, concerning, or consisting of, money (*pecuniary aid*; *pecuniary considerations*). **2** (of an offence) entailing a money penalty or fine. □□ **pecuniarily** *adv.* [L *pecuniarius* f. *pecunia* money f. *pecu* cattle]

■ **1** see FINANCIAL 1.

pedagogue /péddəgog/ *n. archaic* or *derog.* a schoolmaster; a teacher. □□ **pedagogic** /-góggik, -gójik/ *adj.* **pedagogical** /-góggik'l, -gójik'l/ *adj.* **pedagogically** /-góggikəli, -gójikəli/ *adv.* **pedagogism** *n.* (also **pedagoguism**). [ME f. L *paedagogus* f. Gk *paidagōgos* f. *pais paidos* boy + *agōgos* guide]

■ see TEACHER. □□ **pedagogic** see *pedantic* (PEDANT). **pedagogical** see *educational* (EDUCATION).

pedagogy /péddəgoji, -gogi/ *n.* the science of teaching. □□ **pedagogics** /-gójiks, -gōjiks/ *n.* [F *pédagogie* f. Gk *paidagōgia* (as PEDAGOGUE)]

pedal[1] /pédd'l/ *n.* & *v.* ● *n.* **1** any of several types of foot-operated levers or controls for mechanisms, esp.: **a** either of a pair of levers for transmitting power to a bicycle or tricycle wheel etc. **b** any of the foot-operated controls in a motor vehicle. **c** any of the foot-operated keys of an organ used for playing notes, or for drawing out several stops at once etc. **d** each of the foot-levers on a piano etc. for making the tone fuller or softer. **e** each of the foot-levers on a harp for altering the pitch of the strings. **2** a note sustained in one part, usu. the bass, through successive harmonies, some of which are independent of it. ● *v.* (**pedalled, pedalling**; *US* **pedaled, pedaling**) **1** *intr.* operate a cycle, organ, etc. by using the pedals. **2** *tr.* work (a bicycle etc.) with the pedals. □ **pedal cycle** a bicycle. [F *pédale* f. It. *pedale* f. L (as PEDAL[2])]

pedal[2] /pédd'l, peéd'l/ *adj. Zool.* of the foot or feet (esp. of a mollusc). [L *pedalis* f. *pes pedis* foot]

pedalo /péddəlō/ *n.* (*pl.* **-os**) a pedal-operated pleasure-boat.

pedant /pédd'nt/ *n.* **1** a person who insists on strict adherence to formal rules or literal meaning at the expense of a wider view. **2** a person who rates academic learning or technical knowledge above everything. **3** a person who is obsessed by a theory; a doctrinaire. □□ **pedantic** /pidántik/ *adj.* **pedantically** /pidántikəli/ *adv.* **pedantize** *v.intr.* & *tr.* (also **-ise**). **pedantry** *n.* (*pl.* **-ies**). [F *pédant* f. It. *pedante*: app. formed as PEDAGOGUE]

■ **1** see PURIST. □□ **pedantic** didactic, doctrinaire, donnish, pedantical, professorial, bookish, sententious, pompous, stuffy, stilted, stiff, dry, *archaic or derog.* pedagogic, *colloq.* preachy; perfectionist, scrupulous, overscrupulous, finicky, finicking, finical, fussy, punctilious, fastidious, meticulous, exact, hair-splitting, quibbling, *colloq.* nit-picking. **pedantry** see LEGALISM.

pedate /péddayt/ *adj.* **1** *Zool.* having feet. **2** *Bot.* (of a leaf) having divisions like toes or a bird's claws. [L *pedatus* f. *pes pedis* foot]

peddle /pédd'l/ *v.* **1** *tr.* **a** sell (goods), esp. in small quantities, as a pedlar. **b** advocate or promote (ideas, a philosophy, a way of life, etc.). **2** *tr.* sell (drugs) illegally. **3** *intr.* engage in selling, esp. as a pedlar. [back-form. f. PEDLAR]

■ sell, hawk, market, vend, huckster, *colloq.* push, *Brit. sl.* flog.

peddler /pédlər/ *n.* **1** a person who sells drugs illegally. **2** *US* var. of PEDLAR.

■ **1** dealer, pusher.

pederast /péddərast/ *n.* (also **paederast**) a man who performs pederasty.

pederasty /péddərasti/ *n.* (also **paederasty**) anal intercourse between a man and a boy. [mod.L *paederastia* f. Gk *paiderastia* f. *pais paidos* boy + *erastēs* lover]

pedestal /péddist'l/ *n.* & *v.* ● *n.* **1** a base supporting a column or pillar. **2** the stone etc. base of a statue etc. **3** either of the two supports of a knee-hole desk or table, usu. containing drawers. ● *v.tr.* (**pedestalled, pedestalling**; *US* **pedestaled, pedestaling**) set or support on a pedestal. □ **pedestal table** a table with a single central support. **put** (or **set**) **on a pedestal** regard as highly admirable, important, etc.; venerate. [F *piédestal* f. It. *piedestallo* f. *piè* foot f. L *pes pedis* + *di* of + *stallo* STALL[1]]

■ *n.* **1, 2** foundation, base, platform, stand, substructure, mounting, pier, foot, leg, support, plinth, dado, *Archit.* socle. □ **put on a pedestal** glorify, exalt, worship, deify, revere, idolize, dignify, venerate, apotheosize, ennoble, elevate, raise.

pedestrian /pidéstriən/ *n.* & *adj.* ● *n.* **1** (often *attrib.*) a person who is walking, esp. in a town (*pedestrian crossing*). **2** a person who walks competitively. ● *adj.* prosaic; dull; uninspired. □ **pedestrian crossing** *Brit.* a specified part of a road where pedestrians have right of way to cross. **pedestrian precinct** an area of a town restricted to pedestrians. □□ **pedestrianism** *n.* **pedestrianize** *v.tr.* & *intr.* (also **-ise**). **pedestrianization** /-nīzáysh'n/ *n.* [F *pédestre* or L *pedester -tris*]

■ *n.* **1** walker, stroller, rambler, footslogger. ● *adj.* boring, dull, banal, tiresome, commonplace, mundane, tedious, unimaginative, uninteresting, monotonous, run-of-the-mill, humdrum, stock, prosaic, insipid, dry, flat, jejune, colourless, dreary, pale, ordinary, hackneyed, trite, vapid, stale, uninspired, uninspiring, spiritless, lifeless, dead.

pediatrics *US* var. of PAEDIATRICS.

pedicab /péddikab/ *n.* a pedal-operated rickshaw.

pedicel /péddis'l/ *n.* (also **pedicle** /péddik'l/) **1** a small (esp. subordinate) stalklike structure in a plant or animal (cf. PEDUNCLE). **2** *Surgery* part of a graft left temporarily attached to its original site. □□ **pedicellate** /-səlayt/ *adj.* **pediculate** /pidíkyoolət/ *adj.* [mod.L *pedicellus* & L *pediculus* dimin. of *pes pedis* foot]

■ **1** see STEM[1] *n.* 2.

pedicular /pidíkyoolər/ *adj.* (also **pediculous** /-ləss/) infested with lice. □□ **pediculosis** /-lṓsiss/ *n.* [L *pedicularis*, *-losus* f. *pediculus* louse]

■ see LOUSY 1.

pedicure /péddikyoor/ *n.* & *v.* ● *n.* **1** the care or treatment of the feet, esp. of the toenails. **2** a person practising this, esp. professionally. ● *v.tr.* treat (the feet) by removing corns etc. [F *pédicure* f. L *pes pedis* foot + *curare*: see CURE]

pedigree /péddigree/ *n.* **1** (often *attrib.*) a recorded line of descent of a person or esp. a pure-bred domestic or pet animal. **2** the derivation of a word. **3** a genealogical table. **4** *colloq.* the 'life history' of a person, thing, idea, etc. □□ **pedigreed** *adj.* [ME *pedegru* etc. f. AF f. OF *pie de grue* (unrecorded) crane's foot, a mark denoting succession in pedigrees]

■ **1** (line of) descent, ancestry, genealogy, blood, bloodline, line, extraction, lineage, stock, heritage, family, derivation, birth, parentage, strain, roots. **2** etymology. **3** family tree.

pediment /péddimənt/ *n.* **1 a** the triangular front part of a building in Grecian style, surmounting esp. a portico of columns. **b** a similar part of a building in Roman or Renaissance style. **2** *Geol.* a broad flattish rock surface at the foot of a mountain slope. □□ **pedimental** /-mént'l/ *adj.* **pedimented** *adj.* [earlier *pedament*, *periment*, perh. corrupt. of PYRAMID]

pedlar /pédlər/ *n.* (*US* **peddler**) **1** a travelling seller of small items esp. carried in a pack etc. **2** (usu. foll. by *of*) a retailer of gossip etc. □□ **pedlary** *n.* [ME *pedlere* alt. of *pedder* f. *ped* pannier, of unkn. orig.]

■ **1** hawker, (door-to-door) salesman, cheapjack, vendor, huckster, seller, *US* peddler, *esp. US colloq.* drummer, *hist.* chapman.

pedo- *comb. form US* var. of PAEDO-.

pedology /pidólləji/ *n.* the scientific study of soil, esp. its formation, nature, and classification. □□ **pedological** /péddəlójik'l/ *adj.* **pedologist** *n.* [Russ. *pedologiya* f. Gk *pedon* ground]

pedometer /pidómmitər/ *n.* an instrument for estimating the distance travelled on foot by recording the number of steps taken. [F *pédomètre* f. L *pes pedis* foot]

peduncle /pidúngk'l/ *n.* **1** *Bot.* the stalk of a flower, fruit, or cluster, esp. a main stalk bearing a solitary flower or subordinate stalks (cf. PEDICEL). **2** *Zool.* a stalklike projection in an animal body. □□ **peduncular** /-kyoolər/ *adj.* **pedunculate** /-kyoolət/ *adj.* [mod.L *pedunculus* f. L *pes pedis* foot: see -UNCLE]

■ **1** see STEM[1] *n.* 2.

pee /pee/ *v.* & *n. colloq.* ● *v.* (**pees, peed**) **1** *intr.* urinate. **2** *tr.* pass (urine, blood, etc.) from the bladder. ● *n.* **1** urination. **2** urine. [initial letter of PISS]

■ *v.* **1** see URINATE. ● *n.* **2** see PIDDLE *n.*

peek /peek/ *v.* & *n.* ● *v.intr.* (usu. foll. by *in*, *out*, *at*) look quickly or slyly; peep. ● *n.* a quick or sly look. [ME *pike*, *pyke*, of unkn. orig.]

■ *v.* see PEEP[1] *v.* ● *n.* see PEEP[1] *n.*

peekaboo /peékəbōō/ *adj.* & *n.* ● *adj.* **1** (of a garment etc.) transparent or having a pattern of small holes. **2** (of a hairstyle) concealing one eye with a fringe or wave. ● *n.* *US* = BO-PEEP. [PEEK + BOO]

■ *adj.* **1** see *see-through*.

peel[1] /peel/ *v.* & *n.* ● *v.* **1** *tr.* **a** strip the skin, rind, bark, wrapping, etc. from (a fruit, vegetable, tree, etc.). **b** (usu. foll. by *off*) strip (skin, peel, wrapping, etc.) from a fruit etc. **2** *intr.* **a** (of a tree, an animal's or person's body, a painted surface, etc.) become bare of bark, skin, paint, etc. **b** (often foll. by *off*) (of bark, a person's skin, paint, etc.) flake off. **3** *intr.* (often foll. by *off*) *colloq.* (of a person) strip for exercise etc. **4** *tr.* *Croquet* send (another player's ball) through the hoops. ● *n.* the outer covering of a fruit, vegetable, prawn, etc.; rind. □ **peel off 1** veer away and detach oneself from a group of marchers, a formation of aircraft, etc. **2** *colloq.* strip off one's clothes. □□ **peeler** *n.* (in sense 1 of *v.*). [earlier *pill*, *pele* (orig. = plunder) f. ME *pilien* etc. f. OE *pilian* (unrecorded) f. L *pilare* f. *pilus* hair]

■ *v.* **1, 2** skin, strip (off), pare, flay, flake (off), descale, decorticate, excoriate; hull, bark, scale, *US* shuck; *Med.* desquamate. **3** undress, disrobe, *colloq.* peel off; see also STRIP[1] *v.* 2. ● *n.* skin, rind, coating, peeling. □ **peel off 1** part (company), separate, veer *or* go away, split (up), deviate. **2** see STRIP[1] *v.* 2.

peel[2] /peel/ *n.* a shovel, esp. a baker's shovel for bringing loaves etc. into or out of an oven. [ME & OF *pele* f. L *pala*, rel. to *pangere* fix]

peel[3] /peel/ *n.* (also **pele**) *hist.* a small square tower built in the 16th c. in the border counties of England and Scotland for defence against raids. [ME *pel* stake, palisade, f. AF & OF *pel* f. L *palus* stake: cf. PALE[2]]

peeler /peélər/ *n. Brit. archaic sl.* or *dial.* a policeman. [Sir Robert *Peel*, Engl. statesman d. 1850]

■ see *police officer*.

peeling /peéling/ *n.* a strip of the outer skin of a vegetable, fruit, etc. (*potato peelings*).

■ peel, skin, rind.

peen /peen/ *n.* & *v.* ● *n.* the wedge-shaped or thin or curved end of a hammer-head (opp. FACE *n.* 5a). ● *v.tr.* **1** hammer with a peen. **2** treat (sheet metal) with a stream of metal shot in order to shape it. [17th c.: also *pane*, app. f. F *panne* f. Du. *pen* f. L *pinna* point]

peep[1] /peep/ *v.* & *n.* ● *v.intr.* **1** (usu. foll. by *at, in, out, into*) look through a narrow opening; look furtively. **2** (usu. foll. by *out*) **a** (of daylight, a flower beginning to bloom, etc.) come slowly into view; emerge. **b** (of a quality etc.) show itself unconsciously. ● *n.* **1** a furtive or peering glance. **2** the first appearance (*at peep of day*). □ **peep-bo** = BO-PEEP. **peep-hole** a small hole that may be looked through. **peeping Tom** a furtive voyeur. **peep-show** a small exhibition of pictures etc. viewed through a lens or hole set into a box etc. **peep-sight** the aperture backsight of some rifles. **peep-toe** (or **-toed**) (of a shoe) leaving the toes partly bare. [ME: cf. PEEK, PEER[1]]

■ *v.* **1** peer, peek, glimpse. look, squint, *Sc.* keek, *Brit. colloq.* have *or* take a shufti, *sl.* take *or* have a gander, *Brit. sl.* take *or* have a dekko, *rhyming sl.* take *or* have a butcher's. ● *n.* **1** look, glimpse, peek, glance, squint, *Sc.* keek, *colloq.* look-see, *Brit. colloq.* shufti, *sl.* gander, *Brit. sl.* dekko, *rhyming sl.* butcher's.

peep[2] /peep/ *v.* & *n.* ● *v.intr.* make a shrill feeble sound as of young birds, mice, etc.; squeak; chirp. ● *n.* **1** such a sound, a cheep, **2** the slightest sound or utterance, esp. of protest etc. [imit.: cf. CHEEP]

■ *v.* **1** chirp, tweet, cheep, squeak, twitter, pipe, chirrup, chirr. ● *n.* **1** chirp, tweet, cheep, squeak, twitter, pipe, chirrup, chirr. **2** sound, complaint, outcry, protest, protestation, grumble, murmur.

peeper /péepər/ *n.* **1** a person who peeps. **2** *colloq.* an eye. **3** *US sl.* a private detective.

■ **1** peeping Tom, voyeur; see also BUSYBODY 1. **3** see DETECTIVE *n.*

peepul /peép'l/ *n.* (also **pipal**) = BO-TREE. [Hindi *pīpal* f. Skr. *pippala*]

peer[1] /peer/ *v.intr.* **1** (usu. foll. by *into, at,* etc.) look keenly or with difficulty (*peered into the fog*). **2** appear; peep out. **3** *archaic* come into view. [var. of *pire*, LG *pīren*; perh. partly f. APPEAR]

■ **1** peep, peek, squint, look; see also EYE *v.* **2** peep through *or* out, break through, show, emerge; see also APPEAR 1, 2.

peer[2] /peer/ *n.* & *v.* ● *n.* **1 a** (*fem.* **peeress**) a member of one of the degrees of the nobility in Britain, i.e. a duke, marquis, earl, viscount, or baron. **b** a noble of any country. **2** a person who is equal in ability, standing, rank, or value; a contemporary (*tried by a jury of his peers*). ● *v.intr.* & *tr.* (usu. foll. by *with*) rank or cause to rank equally. □ **peer group** a group of people of the same age, status, interests, etc. **peer of the realm** (or **the United Kingdom**) any of the class of peers whose adult members may all sit in the House of Lords. □□ **peerless** *adj.* [ME f. AF & OF *pe(e)r*, *perer* f. LL *pariare* f. L *par* equal]

■ *n.* **1** noble, nobleman, noblewoman, lord, lady, aristocrat; duke, duchess, marquess, marquis, marchioness, earl, countess, viscount, viscountess, baron, baroness; count; life peer. **2** equal, compeer, *archaic or literary* coequal; like, match; confrère, associate, colleague. □□ **peerless** without equal, unequalled, matchless, unmatched, unrivalled, unique, incomparable, beyond compare, unparalleled, nonpareil, inimitable, unsurpassed, superior, superb, excellent, supreme, superlative, finest, best, sovereign, consummate, pre-eminent, paramount.

peerage /peérij/ *n.* **1** peers as a class; the nobility. **2** the rank of peer or peeress (*was given a life peerage*). **3** a book containing a list of peers with their genealogy etc.

■ **1** nobility, aristocracy.

peeve /peev/ *v.* & *n. colloq.* ● *v.tr.* (usu. as **peeved** *adj.*) annoy; vex; irritate. ● *n.* **1** a cause of annoyance. **2** vexation. [back-form. f. PEEVISH]

■ *v.* see IRRITATE 1; (**peeved**) see DISGRUNTLED.

peevish /péevish/ *adj.* querulous; irritable. □□ **peevishly** *adv.* **peevishness** *n.* [ME, = foolish, mad, spiteful, etc., of unkn. orig.]

■ irritable, testy, touchy, fretful, ill-humoured, waspish, petulant, crabbed, churlish, querulous, short-tempered, ill-natured, tetchy, cross, bad-tempered, ill-tempered, fault-finding, captious, carping, cavilling, crusty, curmudgeonly, crotchety, cantankerous, grumpy, pettish, acrimonious, splenetic, bilious, *esp. US* cranky, *colloq.* grumpish.

peewit /péewit/ *n.* (also **pewit**) **1** a lapwing. **2** its cry. [imit.]

peg /peg/ *n.* & *v.* ● *n.* **1 a** a usu. cylindrical pin or bolt of wood or metal, often tapered at one end, and used for holding esp. two things together. **b** such a peg attached to a wall etc. and used for hanging garments etc. on. **c** a peg driven into the ground and attached to a rope for holding up a tent. **d** a bung for stoppering a cask etc. **e** each of several pegs used to tighten or loosen the strings of a violin etc. **f** a small peg, matchstick, etc. stuck into holes in a board for calculating the scores at cribbage. **2** *Brit.* = *clothes-peg*. **3** *Brit.* a measure of spirits or wine. ● *v.tr.* (**pegged, pegging**) **1** (usu. foll. by *down, in, out,* etc.) fix (a thing) with a peg. **2** *Econ.* **a** stabilize (prices, wages, exchange rates, etc.). **b** prevent the price of (stock etc.) from falling or rising by freely buying or selling at a given price. **3** mark (the score) with pegs on a cribbage-board. **4** (usu. foll. by *at*) throw (a missile etc.). □ **off the peg** (of clothes) ready-made. **peg away** (often foll. by *at*) work consistently and esp. for a long period. **peg down** restrict (a person etc.) to rules, a commitment, etc. **peg-leg 1** an artificial leg. **2** a person with an artificial leg. **peg on** = *peg away*. **peg out 1** *sl.* die. **2** score the winning point at cribbage. **3** *Croquet* hit the peg with the ball as the final stroke in a game. **4** mark the boundaries of (land etc.). **a peg to hang an idea** etc. **on** a suitable occasion or pretext etc. for it. **a round** (or **square**) **peg in a square** (or **round**) **hole** a misfit. **take a person down a peg or two** humble a person. [ME, prob. of LG or Du. orig.: cf. MDu. *pegge*, Du. dial. *peg*, LG *pigge*]

■ *n.* **1, 2** pin, dowel, rod, stick, bolt; thole(-pin); clothes-peg, hook. ● *v.* **1** fasten, secure, make fast, fix, attach, pin. **2** stabilize, fix, attach, pin, set (by), control by, limit by, restrict, confine, freeze, bind, regulate, govern. **4** toss, throw, shy, flip, sling, cast. □ **off the peg** ready-made, ready-to-wear, stock. **peg away, peg on** (*peg away* or *on at*) work (away) at, persevere at *or* with, apply oneself to, persist at *or* with, keep at, stick to *or* with *or* at, stay with *or* at, carry on with *or* at, hammer (away) at, *colloq.* plug (away) at, beaver (away) at. **peg down** see TIE *v.* 3. **peg out 1** see DIE[1] 1. **a round** (or **square**) **peg in a square** (or **round**) **hole** see MISFIT. **take a person down a peg or two** humble, diminish, lower, subdue, downgrade, mortify, humiliate, put down, abase, debase, devalue.

pegboard /pégbord/ *n.* a board having a regular pattern of small holes for pegs, used for commercial displays, games, etc.

pegmatite /pégmətīt/ *n.* a coarsely crystalline type of granite. [Gk *pēgma -atos* thing joined together f. *pēgnumi* fasten]

pegtop /pégtop/ *n.* a pear-shaped spinning-top with a metal pin or peg forming the point, spun by the rapid uncoiling of a string wound round it.

Pehlevi var. of PAHLAVI.

PEI *abbr.* Prince Edward Island.

peignoir /páynwaar/ *n.* a woman's loose dressing-gown. [F f. *peigner* to comb]

■ see WRAPPER 4.

pejorative /pijórrətiv, peéjərə-/ *adj.* & *n.* ● *adj.* (of a word, an expression, etc.) depreciatory. ● *n.* a depreciatory word. □□ **pejoratively** *adv.* [F *péjoratif -ive* f. LL *pejorare* make worse (*pejor*)]

pekan /pékkən/ *n.* a N. American flesh-eating mammal, *Martes pennanti*, valued for its fur. [Can.F f. Abnaki *pékané*]

peke /peek/ *n. colloq.* a Pekingese dog. [abbr.]

Pekingese /peékineéz/ *n.* & *adj.* (also **Pekinese**) ● *n.* (*pl.* same) **1 a** a lap-dog of a short-legged breed with long hair and a snub nose. **b** this breed. **2** a citizen of Peking (Beijing) in China. **3** the form of the Chinese language used in Beijing. ● *adj.* of or concerning Beijing or its language or citizens.

pekoe /peékō/ *n.* a superior kind of black tea. [Chin. dial. *pek-ho* f. *pek* white + *ho* down, leaves being picked young with down on them]

pelage /péllij/ *n.* the fur, hair, wool, etc. of a mammal. [F f. *poil* hair]

Pelagian /piláyjiən/ *adj.* & *n.* ● *adj.* of or concerning the monk Pelagius (4th–5th c.) or his theory denying the doctrine of original sin. ● *n.* a follower of Pelagius. ▫▫ **Pelagianism** *n.* [eccl.L *Pelagianus* f. *Pelagius*]

pelagian /piláyjiən/ *adj.* & *n.* ● *adj.* inhabiting the open sea. ● *n.* an inhabitant of the open sea. [L *pelagius* f. Gk *pelagios* of the sea (*pelagos*)]

pelagic /pilájik/ *adj.* **1** of or performed on the open sea (*pelagic whaling*). **2** (of marine life) belonging to the upper layers of the open sea. [L *pelagicus* f. Gk *pelagikos* (as PELAGIAN)]

■ **1** see MARINE *adj.* 1.

pelargonium /péllərgṓniəm/ *n.* any plant of the genus *Pelargonium*, with red, pink, or white flowers and fragrant leaves. Also called GERANIUM. [mod.L f. Gk *pelargos* stork: cf. GERANIUM]

pele var. of PEEL[3].

pelf /pelf/ *n. derog.* or *joc.* money; wealth. [ME f. ONF f. OF *pelfre*, *peufre* spoils, of unkn. orig.: cf. PILFER]

■ see MONEY 1.

pelham /pélləm/ *n.* a horse's bit combining a curb and a snaffle. [the surname *Pelham*]

pelican /péllikən/ *n.* any large gregarious waterfowl of the family Pelecanidae with a large bill and a pouch in the throat for storing fish. ▫ **pelican crossing** (in the UK) a pedestrian crossing with traffic lights operated by pedestrians. [OE *pellican* & OF *pelican* f. LL *pelicanus* f. Gk *pelekan* prob. f. *pelekus* axe, with ref. to its bill]

pelisse /pileéss/ *n. hist.* **1** a woman's cloak with armholes or sleeves, reaching to the ankles. **2** a fur-lined cloak, esp. as part of a hussar's uniform. [F f. med.L *pellicia* (*vestis*) (garment) of fur f. *pellis* skin]

■ see MANTLE *n.* 1.

pelite /peélīt/ *n.* a rock composed of claylike sediment. [Gk *pēlos* clay, mud]

pellagra /pilágrə, -láygrə/ *n.* a disease caused by deficiency of nicotinic acid, characterized by cracking of the skin and often resulting in insanity. ▫▫ **pellagrous** *adj.* [It. f. *pelle* skin, after PODAGRA]

pellet /péllit/ *n.* & *v.* ● *n.* **1** a small compressed ball of paper, bread, etc. **2** a pill. **3 a** a small mass of bones, feathers, etc. regurgitated by a bird of prey. **b** a small hard piece of animal, usu. rodent, excreta. **4 a** a piece of small shot. **b** an imitation bullet for a toy gun. ● *v.tr.* (**pelleted, pelleting**) **1** make into a pellet or pellets. **2** hit with (esp. paper) pellets. ▫▫ **pelletize** *v.tr.* (also **-ise**). [ME f. OF *pelote* f. L *pila* ball]

■ *n.* **2** see PILL 1a. **4** see SHOT[1] 3.

pellicle /péllik'l/ *n.* a thin skin, membrane, or film. ▫▫ **pellicular** /-líkyoolər/ *adj.* [F *pellicule* f. L *pellicula*, dimin. of *pellis* skin]

■ see SKIN *n.* 4.

pellitory /péllitəri/ *n.* any of several wild plants, esp.: **1** (in full **pellitory of Spain**) a composite plant, *Anacyclus pyrethrum*, with a pungent-flavoured root, used as a local irritant etc. **2** (in full **pellitory of the wall**) a low bushy plant, *Parietaria judaica*, with greenish flowers growing on or at the foot of walls. [(sense 1) alt. f. ME f. OF *peletre*, *peretre* f. L *pyrethrum* f. Gk *purethron* feverfew: (sense 2) ult. f. OF *paritaire* f. LL *parietaria* f. L *paries -etis* wall]

pell-mell /pélmél/ *adv.*, *adj.*, & *n.* ● *adv.* **1** headlong, recklessly (*rushed pell-mell out of the room*). **2** in disorder or confusion (*stuffed the papers together pell-mell*). ● *adj.* confused, tumultous. ● *n.* confusion; a mixture. [F *pêle-mêle*, OF *pesle mesle*, *mesle pesle*, etc., redupl. of *mesle* f. *mesler* mix]

■ *adv.* **1** headlong, helter-skelter, recklessly, heedlessly, slapdash, slap-bang, feverishly, incautiously, wildly, impulsively, impetuously, hastily, hurriedly, hell for leather, precipitately. **2** confusedly, chaotically, in disorder; see also HELTER-SKELTER *adv.* ● *adj.* helter-skelter, feverish, confused, disordered, disorderly, disorganized, slapdash, wild, mad, chaotic, tumultuous, panicky, impulsive, reckless, precipitate, impetuous, hasty, hurried; see also TOPSY-TURVY *adj.* 2. ● *n.* confusion, disorder, chaos, tumult, pandemonium, turmoil, mêlée, uproar, furore, commotion, bedlam, brouhaha, hubbub, excitement; see also MIXTURE 2.

pellucid /piloͦossid, -lyoͦossid/ *adj.* **1** (of water, light, etc.) transparent, clear. **2** (of style, speech, etc.) not confused; clear. **3** mentally clear. ▫▫ **pellucidity** /-sídditi/ *n.* **pellucidly** *adv.* [L *pellucidus* f. *perlucēre* (as PER-, *lucēre* shine)]

■ **1** see TRANSPARENT 1. **2, 3** see CLEAR *adj.* 6.

▫▫ **pellucidity** see CLARITY.

Pelmanism /pélməniz'm/ *n.* **1** a system of memory-training orig. devised by the Pelman Institute for the Scientific Development of Mind, Memory and Personality in London. **2** a card-game based on this. ▫▫ **Pelmanize** *v.tr.* (also **-ise**).

pelmet /pélmit/ *n.* a narrow border of cloth, wood, etc. above esp. a window, concealing the curtain rail. [prob. f. F PALMETTE]

■ valance, swag, *US* lambrequin.

pelorus /pilórəss/ *n.* a sighting device like a ship's compass for taking bearings. [perh. f. *Pelorus*, reputed name of Hannibal's pilot]

pelota /pilóttə, pilṓtə/ *n.* a Basque or Spanish game played in a walled court with a ball and basket-like rackets attached to the hand. [Sp., = ball, augment. of *pella* f. L *pila*]

pelt[1] /pelt/ *v.* & *n.* ● *v.* **1** *tr.* (usu. foll. by *with*) **a** hurl many small missiles at. **b** strike repeatedly with missiles. **c** assail (a person etc.) with insults, abuse, etc. **2** *intr.* (usu. foll. by *down*) (of rain etc.) fall quickly and torrentially. **3** *intr.* run fast. **4** *intr.* (often foll. by *at*) fire repeatedly. ● *n.* the act or an instance of pelting. ▫ **at full pelt** as fast as possible. [16th c.: orig. unkn.]

■ *v.* **1** bombard, shower, bomb, pepper, strafe, batter, shell, assail, assault, attack, pummel, pommel, belabour, pound. **2** (*pelt down*) come down in sheets *or* buckets, sheet down, pour (down), rain cats and dogs, bucket down. **3** hurry, rush, run, shoot, scurry, *colloq.* scoot; see also DASH *v.* 1. ● *n.* stroke, blow, hit, smack, slap, bang, thump, *colloq.* whack, thwack, *sl.* wallop, belt, whop; see also DASH *n.* 1. ▫ **at full pelt** see BREAKNECK.

pelt[2] /pelt/ *n.* **1** the undressed skin of a fur-bearing mammal. **2** the skin of a sheep, goat, etc. with short wool, or stripped ready for tanning. **3** *joc.* the human skin. ▫▫ **peltry** *n.* [ME f. obs. *pellet* skin, dimin. of *pel* f. AF *pell*, OF *pel*, or back-form. f. *peltry*, AF *pelterie*, OF *peleterie* f. *peletier* furrier, ult. f. L *pellis* skin]

■ **1, 2** skin, hide, coat, fur, fleece.

pelta /péltə/ *n.* (*pl.* **peltae** /-tee/) **1** a small light shield used by the ancient Greeks, Romans, etc. **2** *Bot.* a shieldlike structure. ▫▫ **peltate** *adj.* [L f. Gk *peltē*]

pelvic /pélvik/ *adj.* of or relating to the pelvis. ▫ **pelvic girdle** the bony or cartilaginous structure in vertebrates to which the posterior limbs are attached.

pelvis /pélviss/ *n.* (*pl.* **pelvises** or **pelves** /-veez/) **1** a basin-shaped cavity at the lower end of the torso of most vertebrates, formed from the innominate bone with the sacrum and other vertebrae. **2** the basin-like cavity of the kidney. [L, = basin]

Pembs. *abbr.* Pembrokeshire (a former county in Wales).

pemmican /pémmikən/ *n.* **1** a cake of dried pounded meat mixed with melted fat, orig. made by N. American Indians. **2** beef so treated and flavoured with currants etc. for use by Arctic travellers etc. [Cree *pimecan* f. *pime* fat]

pemphigus /pémfigəss/ *n. Med.* the formation of watery blisters or eruptions on the skin. ▫▫ **pemphigoid** *adj.* **pemphigous** *adj.* [mod.L f. Gk *pemphix -igos* bubble]

PEN *abbr.* International Association of Poets, Playwrights, Editors, Essayists, and Novelists.

Pen. *abbr.* Peninsula.

pen[1] /pen/ *n.* & *v.* ● *n.* **1** an instrument for writing or drawing with ink, orig. consisting of a shaft with a sharpened quill or metal nib, now more widely applied. **2 a** (usu. prec. by *the*) the occupation of writing. **b** a style of writing. **3** *Zool.* the internal feather-shaped cartilaginous shell of certain cuttlefish, esp. squid. ● *v.tr.* (**penned**, **penning**) **1** write. **2** compose and write. ▫ **pen and ink** *n.* **1** the instruments of writing. **2** writing. **pen-and-ink** *adj.* drawn or written with ink. **pen-feather** a quill-feather of a bird's wing. **pen-friend** a friend communicated with by letter only. **pen-light** a small electric torch shaped like a fountain-pen. **pen-name** a literary pseudonym. **pen-pal** *colloq.* = *pen-friend.* **pen-pusher** *colloq. derog.* a clerical worker. **pen-pushing** *colloq. derog.* clerical work. **put pen to paper** begin writing. [ME f. OF *penne* f. L *penna* feather]

■ *n.* **1** fountain-pen, ball-point (pen), rollerball, *Brit propr.* Biro; quill. ● *v.* **1** write (down *or* out), jot down, make a note of, note, put on paper, commit to paper, commit to writing, put in writing, scribble, scrawl, scratch, *formal or joc.* indite. **2** draft, compose; see *draw up* 1. ▫ **pen and ink** (*n.*) **2** see WRITING 2. **pen-pusher** see WRITER 1, 3, 4.

pen[2] /pen/ *n.* & *v.* ● *n.* **1** a small enclosure for cows, sheep, poultry, etc. **2** a place of confinement. **3** an enclosure for sheltering submarines. **4** a Jamaican farm or plantation. ● *v.tr.* (**penned**, **penning**) (often foll. by *in*, *up*) enclose or shut in a pen. [OE *penn*, of unkn. orig.]

■ *n.* **1** coop, enclosure, hutch, sty, pound, fold, stall, confine, *US* corral. ● *v.* **2** enclose, confine, coop up, shut up *or* in, impound, corral.

pen[3] /pen/ *n.* a female swan. [16th c.: orig. unkn.]

pen[4] /pen/ *n. US sl.* = PENITENTIARY *n.* 1. [abbr.]

penal /peén'l/ *adj.* **1 a** of or concerning punishment or its infliction (*penal laws*; *a penal sentence*; *a penal colony*). **b** (of an offence) punishable, esp. by law. **2** extremely severe (*penal taxation*). ▫ **penal servitude** *hist.* imprisonment with compulsory labour. ▫▫ **penally** *adv.* [ME f. OF *penal* or L *poenalis* f. *poena* PAIN]

■ **1 a** correctional, punitive, disciplinary. **2** see HARSH 2.

penalize /peénəlīz/ *v.tr.* (also **-ise**) **1** subject (a person) to a penalty or comparative disadvantage. **2** make or declare (an action) penal. ▫▫ **penalization** /-záysh'n/ *n.*

■ **1** discipline, mulct, fine, impose a penalty on, *Law* amerce; see also PUNISH 1.

penalty /pénnəlti/ *n.* (*pl.* **-ies**) **1 a** a punishment, esp. a fine, for a breach of law, contract, etc. **b** a fine paid. **2** a disadvantage, loss, etc., esp. as a result of one's own actions (*paid the penalty for his carelessness*). **3 a** a disadvantage imposed on a competitor or side in a game etc. for a breach of the rules etc. **b** (*attrib.*) awarded against a side incurring a penalty (*penalty kick*; *penalty goal*). **4** *Bridge* etc. points gained by opponents when a contract is not fulfilled. ▫ **penalty area** *Football* the ground in front of the goal in which a foul by defenders involves the award of a penalty kick. **penalty box** *Ice Hockey* an area reserved for penalized players and some officials. **the penalty of** a disadvantage resulting from (a quality etc.). **penalty rate** *Austral.* an increased rate of pay for overtime. **under** (or **on**) **penalty of** under the threat of (dismissal etc.). [AF *penalte* (unrecorded), F *pénalité* f. med.L *penalitas* (as PENAL)]

■ **1** punishment, discipline, penance, sentence; forfeit, toll, exaction, fine, mulct, *Law* amercement. **2** price; loss, disadvantage, handicap; sacrifice. ▫ **under penalty of** on *or* under pain of, under threat of.

penance /pénnənss/ *n.* & *v.* ● *n.* **1** an act of self-punishment as reparation for guilt. **2 a** (in the RC and Orthodox Church) a sacrament including confession of and absolution for a sin. **b** a penalty imposed esp. by a priest, or undertaken voluntarily, for a sin. ● *v.tr.* impose a penance on. ▫ **do penance** perform a penance. [ME f. OF f. L *paenitentia* (as PENITENT)]

■ *n.* **1** (self-)punishment, penalty, repentance, penitence; reparation, atonement, regret, contrition. ▫ **do penance** pay, suffer; make amends *or* reparation(s), atone, wear sackcloth and ashes *or* a hair shirt.

penannular /penányoolər/ *adj.* almost ringlike. [L *paene* almost + ANNULAR]

penates /pinaáteez, -tayz/ *n.pl.* (in Roman mythology) the household gods, esp. of the storeroom (see LARES). [L f. *penus* provision of food]

pence *pl.* of PENNY.

penchant /pónshon/ *n.* an inclination or liking (*has a penchant for old films*). [F, pres. part. of *pencher* incline]

■ inclination, bent, proclivity, leaning, bias, predisposition, predilection, partiality, proneness, propensity, tendency, affinity, liking, preference, fondness, taste.

pencil /pénsil/ *n.* & *v.* ● *n.* **1** (often *attrib.*) **a** an instrument for writing or drawing, usu. consisting of a thin rod of graphite etc. enclosed in a wooden cylinder (*a pencil sketch*). **b** a similar instrument with a metal or plastic cover and retractable lead. **c** a cosmetic in pencil form. **2** (*attrib.*) resembling a pencil in shape (*pencil skirt*). **3** *Optics* a set of rays meeting at a point. **4** *Geom.* a figure formed by a set of straight lines meeting at a point. **5** a draughtsman's art or style. ● *v.tr.* (**pencilled**, **pencilling**; *US* **penciled**, **penciling**) **1** tint or mark with or as if with a pencil. **2** (usu. foll. by *in*) **a** write, esp. tentatively or provisionally (*have pencilled in the 29th for our meeting*). **b** (esp. as **pencilled** *adj.*) fill (an area) with soft pencil strokes (*pencilled in her eyebrows*). ▫ **pencil-case** a container for pencils etc. **pencil-pusher** *colloq. derog.* a clerical worker. **pencil-pushing** *colloq. derog.* clerical work. **pencil-sharpener** a device for sharpening a pencil by rotating it against a cutting edge. ▫▫ **penciller** *n.* [ME f. OF *pincel* ult. f. L *penicillum* paintbrush, dimin. of *peniculus* brush, dimin. of *penis* tail]

pendant /péndənt/ *n.* (also **pendent**) **1** a hanging jewel etc., esp. one attached to a necklace, bracelet, etc. **2** a light fitting, ornament, etc., hanging from a ceiling. **3** *Naut.* **a** a short rope hanging from the head of a mast etc., used for attaching tackles. **b** = PENNANT 1. **4** the shank and ring of a pocket-watch by which it is suspended. **5** /péndənt, póndon/ (usu. foll. by *to*) a match, companion, parallel, complement, etc. [ME f. OF f. *pendre* hang f. L *pendere*]

■ **1** ornament, lustre, medallion, locket, ear-drop, tear-drop, drop. **5** see PARALLEL *n.* 1.

pendent /péndənt/ *adj.* (also **pendant**) **1 a** hanging. **b** overhanging. **2** undecided; pending. **3** *Gram.* (esp. of a sentence) incomplete; not having a finite verb (*pendent nominative*). ▫▫ **pendency** *n.* [ME (as PENDANT)]

■ **1** see PENDULOUS 1.

pendente lite /pendénti līti/ *adv. Law* during the progress of a suit. [L]

pendentive /pendéntiv/ *n. Archit.* a curved triangle of vaulting formed by the intersection of a dome with its supporting arches. [F *pendentif -ive* (adj.) (as PENDANT)]

pending /pénding/ *adj.* & *prep.* ● *predic.adj.* **1** awaiting decision or settlement, undecided (*a settlement was pending*). **2** about to come into existence (*patent pending*). ● *prep.* **1** during (*pending these negotiations*). **2** until (*pending his return*). ▫ **pending-tray** a tray for documents, letters, etc., awaiting attention. [after F *pendant* (see PENDENT)]

■ *predic.adj.* **1** unsettled, undetermined, undecided, unconfirmed, unfinished, inconclusive, (up) in the air, in the balance, abeyant, on hold, deferred, *colloq.* on ice; see also ABEYANCE. **2** forthcoming, impending, in the offing, *archaic or dial.* nigh; see also IMMINENT. ● *prep.* **1** see THROUGHOUT *prep.* **2** awaiting, waiting (for), till, until.

pendragon /pendrággən/ *n. hist.* an ancient British or Welsh prince (often as a title). [Welsh, = chief war-leader, f. *pen* head + *dragon* standard]

penduline /péndyoolīn/ *adj.* **1** (of a nest) suspended. **2** (of a bird) of a kind that builds such a nest. [F (as PENDULOUS)]

pendulous /péndyooləss/ *adj.* **1** (of ears, breasts, flowers, bird's nests, etc.) hanging down; drooping and esp. swinging. **2** oscillating. □□ **pendulously** *adv.* [L *pendulus* f. *pendēre* hang]

■ **1** pendent, hanging, drooping, sagging, dangling, suspended, pensile. **2** swinging, swaying, oscillating, oscillatory.

pendulum /péndyooləm/ *n.* a weight suspended so as to swing freely, esp. a rod with a weighted end regulating the movement of a clock's works. □ **swing of the pendulum** the tendency of public opinion to oscillate between extremes, esp. between political parties. [L neut. adj. (as PENDULOUS)]

peneplain /péeniplayn/ *n. Geol.* a fairly flat area of land produced by erosion. [L *paene* almost + PLAIN[1]]

penetralia /pénnitráyliə/ *n.pl.* **1** innermost shrines or recesses. **2** secret or hidden parts; mysteries. [L, neut. pl. of *penetralis* interior (as PENETRATE)]

■ **1** see RECESS *n.* 2.

penetrate /pénnitrayt/ *v.* **1** *tr.* **a** find access into or through, esp. forcibly. **b** (usu. foll. by *with*) imbue (a person or thing) with; permeate. **2** *tr.* see into, find out, or discern (a person's mind, the truth, a meaning, etc.). **3** *tr.* see through (darkness, fog, etc.) (*could not penetrate the gloom*). **4** *intr.* be absorbed by the mind (*my hint did not penetrate*). **5** *tr.* (as **penetrating** *adj.*) **a** having or suggesting sensitivity or insight (*a penetrating remark*). **b** (of a voice etc.) easily heard through or above other sounds; piercing. **c** (of a smell) sharp, pungent. **6** *tr.* (of a man) put the penis into the vagina of (a woman). **7** *intr.* (usu. foll. by *into, through, to*) make a way. □□ **penetrable** /-trəb'l/ *adj.* **penetrability** /-trəbílliti/ *n.* **penetrant** *adj.* & *n.* **penetratingly** *adv.* **penetration** /-tráysh'n/ *n.* **penetrative** /-trətiv/ *adj.* **penetrator** *n.* [L *penetrare* place or enter within f. *penitus* interior]

■ **1 a** enter, go through *or* into, pass through *or* into, pierce, bore (into), lance, spear, probe, perforate; reach, get to, get at, touch, affect. **b** permeate, suffuse, pervade, filter through *or* into, seep through *or* into, percolate through, spread throughout, soak into, be absorbed by; see also CHARGE *v.* 9. **2** see into, understand, sense, become aware *or* conscious of, see (through), gain insight into, discern, uncover, discover, find (out), comprehend, grasp, work out, unravel, fathom, perceive, figure out, *esp. US* figure, *sl.* dig, *Brit. sl.* suss out. **4** sink in, be absorbed, be understood, register, get through, become clear, come across, be realized, *colloq.* soak in. **5** (**penetrating**) **a** incisive, trenchant, keen, searching, deep, acute, sharp, perceptive, perspicuous, percipient, quick, discriminating, intelligent, sensitive, clever, smart, discerning. **b** audible; piercing, shrill, strident, ear-splitting, ear-shattering, pervasive. **c** pungent, harsh, sharp, biting, mordant, strong, stinging. □□ **penetration** perforation, incision; insight, keenness, perception, percipience, intelligence, perspicacity, perspicuity, perspicaciousness, perceptiveness, incisiveness, sensitivity, sentience, understanding, acuteness, discernment, discrimination, cleverness, shrewdness, wit, quick-wittedness; pungency; shrillness.

penguin /pénggwin/ *n.* any flightless sea bird of the family Spheniscidae of the southern hemisphere, with black upper-parts and white under-parts, and wings developed into scaly flippers for swimming underwater. [16th c., orig. = great auk: orig. unkn.]

penholder /pénhōldər/ *n.* the esp. wooden shaft of a pen with a metal nib.

penicillate /pénnisilət, -síllit/ *adj. Biol.* **1** having or forming a small tuft or tufts. **2** marked with streaks as of a pencil or brush. [L *penicillum*: see PENCIL]

penicillin /pénnisíllin/ *n.* any of various antibiotics produced naturally by moulds of the genus *Penicillium*, or synthetically, and able to prevent the growth of certain disease-causing bacteria. [mod.L *Penicillium* genus name f. L *penicillum*: see PENCIL]

penile /péenīl/ *adj.* of or concerning the penis. [mod.L *penilis*]

penillion *pl.* of PENNILL.

peninsula /pinínsyoolə/ *n.* a piece of land almost surrounded by water or projecting far into a sea or lake etc. □□ **peninsular** *adj.* [L *paeninsula* f. *paene* almost + *insula* island]

■ see POINT *n.* 22.

penis /péeniss/ *n.* (*pl.* **penises** or **penes** /-neez/) **1** the male organ of copulation and (in mammals) urination. **2** the male copulatory organ in lower vertebrates. [L, = tail, penis]

■ **1** phallus, *archaic* membrum virile, *esp. joc.* organ, *Brit. sl.* willy.

penitent /pénnit'nt/ *adj.* & *n.* ● *adj.* regretting and wishing to atone for sins etc.; repentant. ● *n.* **1** a repentant sinner. **2** a person doing penance under the direction of a confessor. **3** (in *pl.*) various RC orders associated for mutual discipline etc. □□ **penitence** *n.* **penitently** *adv.* [ME f. OF f. L *paenitens* f. *paenitēre* repent]

■ *adj.* regretful, repentant, remorseful, sorrowful, sorry, rueful, contrite, apologetic, shamefaced, self-reproachful, conscience-stricken. □□ **penitence** contrition, regret, repentance, regretfulness, compunction, remorse, shame, ruefulness, shamefacedness, self-reproach.

penitential /pénniténsh'l/ *adj.* of or concerning penitence or penance. □ **penitential psalms** seven psalms (6, 32, 38, 51, 102, 130, 143) expressing penitence. □□ **penitentially** *adv.* [OF *penitencial* f. LL *paenitentialis* f. *paenitentia* penitence (as PENITENT)]

■ see SORRY 1, *compensatory* (COMPENSATE).

penitentiary /pénniténshəri/ *n.* & *adj.* ● *n.* (*pl.* **-ies**) **1** *US* a reformatory prison. **2** an office in the papal court deciding questions of penance, dispensations, etc. ● *adj.* **1** of or concerning penance. **2** of or concerning reformatory treatment. **3** *US* (of an offence) making a culprit liable to a prison sentence. □ **Grand Penitentiary** a cardinal presiding over the penitentiary. [ME f. med.L *paenitentiarius* (adj. & n.) (as PENITENT)]

■ *n.* **1** see PRISON *n.* 1.

penknife /pén-nīf/ *n.* a small folding knife, esp. for carrying in a pocket.

■ knife, pocket knife; clasp-knife.

penman /pénmən/ *n.* (*pl.* **-men**) **1** a person who writes by hand with a specified skill (*a good penman*). **2** an author. □□ **penmanship** *n.*

■ **2** see AUTHOR *n.* 1, SCRIBE *n.* 4. □□ **penmanship** calligraphy, handwriting, script, writing, chirography.

Penn. *abbr.* (also **Penna.**) Pennsylvania.

pennant /pénnənt/ *n.* **1** *Naut.* a tapering flag, esp. that flown at the masthead of a vessel in commission. **2** = PENDANT 3a. **3** = PENNON. **4** *US* a flag denoting a sports championship etc. [blend of PENDANT and PENNON]

■ **1, 3** flag, banner, pennon, streamer, banderole, gonfalon, ensign, colours, standard, labarum, jack, burgee, *Rom.Antiq.* vexillum.

penniless /pénniliss/ *adj.* having no money; destitute. □□ **pennilessly** *adv.* **pennilessness** *n.*

■ see DESTITUTE 1.

pennill /pénnil/ *n.* (*pl.* **penillion** /penílyən/) (usu. in *pl.*) an improvised stanza sung to a harp accompaniment at an eisteddfod etc. [Welsh f. *penn* head]

pennon /pénnən/ *n.* **1** a long narrow flag, triangular or swallow-tailed, esp. as the military ensign of lancer regiments. **2** *Naut.* a long pointed streamer on a ship. **3** a flag. □□ **pennoned** *adj.* [ME f. OF f. L *penna* feather]

■ see FLAG[1] *n.*

penn'orth var. of PENNYWORTH.

Pennsylvania Dutch /pénsilváyniə/ *n.* **1** a dialect of High German spoken by descendants of 17th–18th-c. German and Swiss immigrants to Pennsylvania etc. **2** (as *pl.*) these settlers or their descendants.

Pennsylvanian /pénsilváyniən/ *n.* & *adj.* ● *n.* **1** a native or inhabitant of Pennsylvania, a State of the US. **2** (prec. by *the*) esp. *US Geol.* the upper Carboniferous period or system. ● *adj.* **1** of or relating to Pennsylvania. **2** esp. *US Geol.* of or relating to the upper Carboniferous period or system..

penny /pénni/ *n.* (*pl.* for separate coins **-ies,** for a sum of money **pence** /penss/) **1** a British coin and monetary unit equal to one-hundredth of a pound. ¶ Abbr.: **p. 2** *hist.* a former British bronze coin and monetary unit equal to one-two-hundred-and-fortieth of a pound. ¶ Abbr.: **d. 3** *US colloq.* a one-cent coin. **4** *Bibl.* a denarius. □ **in for a penny, in for a pound** an exhortation to total commitment to an undertaking. **like a bad penny** continually returning when unwanted. **pennies from heaven** unexpected benefits. **penny-a-liner** a hack writer. **penny black** the first adhesive postage stamp (1840, value one penny). **penny cress** *Bot.* a plant, *Thlaspi arvense*, with flat round pods. **penny dreadful** *Brit.* a cheap sensational comic or storybook. **the penny drops** *colloq.* one begins to understand at last. **penny farthing** *Brit.* an early type of bicycle with one large and one small wheel. **a penny for your thoughts** a request to a thoughtful person to confide in the speaker. **penny-in-the-slot** (of a machine) activated by a coin pushed into a slot. **penny-pincher** a niggardly person. **penny-pinching** *n.* meanness. ● *adj.* mean. **penny post** *Brit. hist.* the system of carrying letters etc. at a standard charge of 1d. regardless of distance. **penny whistle** a tin pipe with six holes giving different notes. **penny wise** too careful in saving small amounts. **penny wise and pound foolish** mean in small expenditures but wasteful of large amounts. **a pretty penny** a large sum of money. **two a penny** almost worthless though easily obtained. [OE *penig*, *penning* f. Gmc, perh. rel. to PAWN[2]]

■ □ **penny-pinching** (*n.*) meanness, miserliness, stinginess. (*adj.*) see MEAN[2] 1. **penny wise and pound foolish** see WASTEFUL. **two a penny** see COMMON *adj.* 1.

-penny /pəni/ *comb. form Brit.* forming attributive adjectives meaning 'costing . . . pence' (esp. in pre-decimal currency) (*fivepenny*).

pennyroyal /pénniróyəl/ *n.* **1** a creeping mint, *Mentha pulegium*, cultivated for its supposed medicinal properties. **2** *US* an aromatic plant, *Hedeoma pulegioides*. [app. f. earlier *puliol(e) ryall* f. AF *puliol*, OF *pouliol* ult. f. L *pulegium* + real ROYAL]

pennyweight /pénniwayt/ *n.* a unit of weight, 24 grains or one-twentieth of an ounce troy.

pennywort /pénniwurt/ *n.* any of several wild plants with rounded leaves, esp.: **1** (**wall pennywort**) *Umbilicus rupestris*, growing in crevices. **2** (**marsh** or **water pennywort**) *Hydrocotyle vulgaris*, growing in marshy places. [ME, f. PENNY + WORT]

pennyworth /pénniwurth/ *n.* (also **penn'orth** /pénnərth/) **1** as much as can be bought for a penny. **2** a bargain of a specified kind (*a bad pennyworth*). □ **not a pennyworth** not the least bit.

penology /peenólləji/ *n.* the study of the punishment of crime and of prison management. □□ **penological** /-nəlójik'l/ *adj.* **penologist** *n.* [L *poena* penalty + -LOGY]

pensée /ponsáy/ *n.* a thought or reflection put into literary form; an aphorism. [F]

pensile /pénsīl/ *adj.* **1** hanging down; pendulous. **2** (of a bird etc.) building a pensile nest. [L *pensilis* f. *pendēre pens-* hang]

■ **1** see PENDULOUS 1.

pension[1] /pénsh'n/ *n.* & *v.* ● *n.* **1 a** a regular payment made by a government to people above a specified age, to widows, or to the disabled. **b** similar payments made by an employer etc. on the retirement of an employee. **2 a** a pension paid to a scientist, artist, etc. for services to the state, or to fund work. **b** any pension paid esp. by a government on charitable grounds. ● *v.tr.* **1** grant a pension to. **2** bribe with a pension. □ **pension off 1** dismiss with a pension. **2** cease to employ or use. □□ **pensionless** *adj.* [ME f. OF f. L *pensio -onis* payment f. *pendere pens-* pay]

■ *n.* **1** superannuation, social security, *colloq.* golden handshake. **2** benefit, allowance, annuity, subsistence, allotment. □ **pension off 1** (cause to) retire, superannuate, shelve, put on the shelf; see also DISMISS 2.

pension[2] /ponsyón/ *n.* a European, esp. French, boarding-house providing full or half board at a fixed rate. □ ***en pension*** /on/ as a boarder. [F: see PENSION[1]]

pensionable /pénshənəb'l/ *adj.* **1** entitled to a pension. **2** (of a service, job, etc.) entitling an employee to a pension. □□ **pensionability** /-bílliti/ *n.*

pensionary /pénshənəri/ *adj.* & *n.* ● *adj.* of or concerning a pension. ● *n.* (*pl.* **-ies**) **1** a pensioner. **2** a creature; a hireling. □ **Grand Pensionary** *hist.* the first minister of Holland and Zealand (1619-1794). [med.L *pensionarius* (as PENSION[1])]

pensioner /pénshənər/ *n.* a recipient of a pension, esp. the retirement pension. [ME f. AF *pensionner*, OF *pensionnier* (as PENSION[1])]

■ old-age pensioner, retirer, veteran, senior citizen, oldster, *Brit.* OAP, *esp. US* retiree, *US* golden-ager, *colloq.* oldie.

pensive /pénsiv/ *adj.* **1** deep in thought. **2** sorrowfully thoughtful. □□ **pensively** *adv.* **pensiveness** *n.* [ME f. OF *pensif, -ive* f. *penser* think f. L *pensare* frequent. of *pendere pens-* weigh]

■ **1** thoughtful, meditative, musing, cogitative, absorbed, contemplative, reflective, preoccupied, ruminative, day-dreaming; in a trance, in a reverie, in a brown study. **2** brooding, sober, serious, grave; wistful.

penstemon var. of PENTSTEMON.

penstock /pénstok/ *n.* **1** a sluice; a floodgate. **2** *US* a channel for conveying water to a water-wheel. [PEN[2] in sense 'mill-dam' + STOCK]

pent /pent/ *adj.* (often foll. by *in, up*) closely confined; shut in (*pent-up feelings*). [past part. of *pend* var. of PEN[2] *v.*]

■ (*pent-up*) restrained, constrained, repressed, stifled, bottled-up, held in, checked, held back, shut in, curbed, inhibited, restricted.

penta- /péntə/ *comb. form* **1** five. **2** *Chem.* (forming the names of compounds) containing five atoms or groups of a specified kind (*pentachloride*; *pentoxide*). [Gk f. *pente* five]

pentachord /péntəkord/ *n.* **1** a musical instrument with five strings. **2** a series of five musical notes.

pentacle /péntək'l/ *n.* a figure used as a symbol, esp. in magic, e.g. a pentagram. [med.L *pentaculum* (as PENTA-)]

pentad /péntad/ *n.* **1** the number five. **2** a group of five. [Gk *pentas -ados* f. *pente* five]

pentadactyl /péntədáktil/ *adj. Zool.* having five toes or fingers.

pentagon /péntəgən/ *n.* **1** a plane figure with five sides and angles. **2** (**the Pentagon**) **a** the pentagonal Washington headquarters of the US defence forces. **b** the leaders of the US defence forces. □□ **pentagonal** /-tággən'l/ *adj.* [F *pentagone* or f. LL *pentagonus* f. Gk *pentagōnon* (as PENTA-, -GON)]

pentagram /péntəgram/ *n.* a five-pointed star formed by extending the sides of a pentagon both ways until they intersect, formerly used as a mystic symbol. [Gk *pentagrammon* (as PENTA-, -GRAM)]

pentagynous /pentájinəss/ *adj. Bot.* having five pistils.

pentahedron /péntəhe͞edrən/ *n.* a solid figure with five faces. □□ **pentahedral** *adj.*

pentamerous /pentámmərəss/ *adj.* **1** *Bot.* having five parts in a flower-whorl. **2** *Zool.* having five joints or parts.

pentameter /pentámmitər/ *n.* **1** a verse of five feet, e.g. English iambic verse of ten syllables. **2** a form of Gk or Latin dactylic verse composed of two halves each of two feet and a long syllable, used in elegiac verse. [L f. Gk *pentametros* (as PENTA-, -METER)]

pentandrous /pentándrəss/ *adj. Bot.* having five stamens.

pentane /péntayn/ *n. Chem.* a hydrocarbon of the alkane series. ¶ Chem. formula: C_5H_{12}. [Gk *pente* five + ALKANE]

pentangle /péntangg'l/ *n.* = PENTAGRAM. [ME perh. f. med.L *pentaculum* PENTACLE, assim. to L *angulus* ANGLE[1]]

pentanoic acid /péntənṓ-ik/ *n. Chem.* a colourless liquid carboxylic acid used in making perfumes. [PENTANE]

pentaprism /péntəpriz'm/ *n.* a five-sided prism with two silvered surfaces used in a viewfinder to obtain a constant deviation of all rays of light through 90°.

Pentateuch /péntətyōōk/ *n.* the first five books of the Old Testament, traditionally ascribed to Moses. ▫▫ **pentateuchal** /-tyṓōk'l/ *adj.* [eccl.L *pentateuchus* f. eccl.Gk *pentateukhos* (as PENTA-, *teukhos* implement, book)]

pentathlon /pentáthlən/ *n.* an athletic event comprising five different events for each competitor. ▫▫ **pentathlete** /-táthleet/ *n.* [Gk f. *pente* five + *athlon* contest]

pentatonic /péntətónnik/ *adj. Mus.* **1** consisting of five notes. **2** relating to such a scale.

pentavalent /péntəváylənt/ *adj. Chem.* having a valency of five; quinquevalent.

Pentecost /péntikost/ *n.* **1 a** Whit Sunday. **b** a festival celebrating the descent of the Holy Spirit on Whit Sunday. **2 a** the Jewish harvest festival, on the fiftieth day after the second day of Passover (Lev. 23:15–16). **b** a synagogue ceremony on the anniversary of the giving of the Law on Mount Sinai. [OE *pentecosten* & OF *pentecoste*, f. eccl.L *pentecoste* f. Gk *pentēkostē* (*hēmera*) fiftieth (day)]

Pentecostal /péntikóst'l/ *adj.* & *n.* • *adj.* (also **pentecostal**) **1** of or relating to Pentecost. **2** of or designating Christian sects and individuals who emphasize the gifts of the Holy Spirit, are often fundamentalist in outlook, and express religious feelings by clapping, shouting, dancing, etc. • *n.* a Pentecostalist. ▫▫ **Pentecostalism** *n.* **Pentecostalist** *adj.* & *n.*

penthouse /pént-howss/ *n.* **1** a house or flat on the roof or the top floor of a tall building. **2** a sloping roof, esp. of an outhouse built on to another building. **3** an awning, a canopy. [ME *pentis* f. OF *apentis*, *-dis*, f. med.L *appendicium*, in LL = appendage, f. L (as APPEND): infl. by HOUSE]

pentimento /péntiméntō/ *n.* (*pl.* **pentimenti** /-ti/) the phenomenon of earlier painting showing through a layer or layers of paint on a canvas. [It., = repentance]

pentobarbitone /péntəbaárbitōn/ *n.* (*US* **pentobarbital** /-tal/) a narcotic and sedative barbiturate drug formerly used to relieve insomnia. [PENTA-, BARBITONE, BARBITAL]

pentode /péntōd/ *n.* a thermionic valve having five electrodes. [Gk *pente* five + *hodos* way]

pentose /péntōz/ *n. Biochem.* any monosaccharide containing five carbon atoms, including ribose. [PENTA- + -OSE[2]]

pent-roof /péntrōōf/ *n.* a roof sloping in one direction only. [PENTHOUSE + ROOF]

pentstemon /pentstéemən, péntstəmən/ *n.* (also **penstemon** /penstéemən/) any American herbaceous plant of the genus *Penstemon*, with showy flowers and five stamens, one of which is sterile. [mod.L, irreg. f. PENTA- + Gk *stēmōn* warp, used for 'stamen']

pentyl /péntil/ *n.* = AMYL. [PENTANE + -YL]

penult /pinúlt, péenult/ *n.* & *adj.* • *n.* the last but one (esp. syllable). • *adj.* last but one. [abbr. of L *paenultimus* (see PENULTIMATE) or of PENULTIMATE]

penultimate /pinúltimət/ *adj.* & *n.* • *adj.* last but one. • *n.* **1** the last but one. **2** the last syllable but one. [L *paenultimus* f. *paene* almost + *ultimus* last, after *ultimate*]

penumbra /pinúmbrə/ *n.* (*pl.* **penumbrae** /-bree/ or **penumbras**) **1 a** the partly shaded region around the shadow of an opaque body, esp. that around the total shadow of the moon or earth in an eclipse. **b** the less dark outer part of a sunspot. **2** a partial shadow. ▫▫ **penumbral** *adj.* [mod.L f. L *paene* almost + UMBRA shadow]

penurious /pinyóoriəss/ *adj.* **1** poor; destitute. **2** stingy; grudging. **3** scanty. ▫▫ **penuriously** *adv.* **penuriousness** *n.* [med.L *penuriosus* (as PENURY)]

▪ **1** poor, poverty-stricken, destitute, impoverished, penniless, indigent, needy, impecunious, necessitous, beggarly, bankrupt, hard up, *Brit. sl.* stony-broke; see also BROKE. **2** stingy, mean, penny-pinching, miserly, tight, tight-fisted, close-fisted, cheese-paring, niggardly, ungenerous, parsimonious, skinflinty, begrudging, grudging, Scrooge-like, near, close, costive, sordid, *Brit. colloq.* mingy.

penury /pényoori/ *n.* (*pl.* **-ies**) **1** destitution; poverty. **2** a lack; scarcity. [ME f. L *penuria*, perh. rel. to *paene* almost]

▪ **1** see POVERTY 1.

peon /péeən/ *n.* **1 a** a Spanish American day labourer or farm-worker. **b** a poor or destitute South American. **2** /also pyōōn/ an Indian office messenger, attendant, or orderly. **3** a bullfighter's assistant. **4** *hist.* a worker held in servitude in the southern US. ▫▫ **peonage** *n.* [Port. *peão* & Sp. *peon* f. med.L *pedo -onis* walker f. L *pes pedis* foot: cf. PAWN[1]]

▪ **1, 4** see PEASANT.

peony /péeəni/ *n.* (also **paeony**) (*pl.* **-ies**) any herbaceous plant of the genus *Paeonia*, with large globular red, pink, or white flowers, often double in cultivated varieties. [OE *peonie* f. L *peonia* f. Gk *paiōnia* f. *Paiōn*, physician of the gods]

people /péep'l/ *n.* & *v.* • *n.* **1** (usu. as *pl.*) **a** persons composing a community, tribe, race, nation, etc. (*the English people*; *a warlike people*; *the peoples of the Commonwealth*). **b** a group of persons of a usu. specified kind (*the chosen people*; *these people here*; *right-thinking people*). **2** (prec. by *the*; treated as *pl.*) **a** the mass of people in a country etc. not having special rank or position. **b** these considered as an electorate (*the people will reject it*). **3** parents or other relatives (*my people are French*). **4 a** subjects, armed followers, a retinue, etc. **b** a congregation of a parish priest etc. **5** persons in general (*people do not like rudeness*). • *v.tr.* (usu. foll. by *with*) **1** fill with people, animals, etc.; populate. **2** (esp. as **peopled** *adj.*) inhabit; occupy; fill (*thickly peopled*). ▫ **people's democracy** a political system, esp. in E. Europe, with power regarded as invested in the people. [ME f. AF *poeple*, *people*, OF *pople*, *peuple*, f. L *populus*]

▪ *n.* **1 a** race, community, clan, tribe, folk, nation, population, society. **2** masses, (general) public, *hoi polloi*, multitude, populace, common people, common man *or* woman, commoners, subjects, citizenry, plebeians, proletariat, rank and file, the crowd, commonalty, commonage, the rabble, silent majority, *colloq. derog.* proles, *colloq. usu. derog.* plebs, *derog.* ragtag and bobtail, common herd; electorate, voters, voting public, grass roots; man in the street, Everyman, Mr *or* Mrs Average, *Brit. colloq.* Joe Bloggs. **3** parents, relations, relatives, kin, kinsmen, kinsfolk, family, kith and kin; ancestors, forebears. **4 b** flock, congregation. **5** persons, individuals, human beings; living souls, mortals, bodies. • *v.* **1, 2** populate, colonize, settle, occupy, inhabit; fill.

PEP *abbr. Brit.* **1** Political and Economic Planning. **2** Personal Equity Plan.

pep /pep/ *n.* & *v. colloq.* • *n.* vigour; go; spirit. • *v.tr.* (**pepped**, **pepping**) (usu. foll. by *up*) fill with vigour. ▫ **pep pill** a pill containing a stimulant drug. **pep talk** a usu. short talk intended to enthuse, encourage, etc. [abbr. of PEPPER]

▪ *n.* vigour, vim (and vigour), spirit, animation, go, vivacity, energy, verve, zest, fire, sprightliness, life, effervescence, sparkle, ebullience, dash, enthusiasm, brio, *élan*, zip, *colloq.* zing, get-up-and-go. • *v.* (*pep up*) stimulate, invigorate, animate, enliven, vitalize, vivify, energize, exhilarate, quicken, arouse, breathe (some) life into, inspire, activate, fire, cheer up, spark, fire up, *colloq.* buck up. ▫ **pep pill** *sl.* upper.

peperino /péppəréénō/ *n.* a light porous (esp. brown) volcanic rock formed of small grains of sand, cinders, etc. [It. f. *pepere* pepper]

peperoni var. of PEPPERONI.

peplum /pépləm/ *n.* **1** a short flounce etc. at waist level, esp. of a blouse or jacket over a skirt. **2** *Gk Antiq.* a woman's outer garment. [L f. Gk *peplos*]

▪ **1** see FLOUNCE[2] *n.*

pepo /péépō/ *n.* (*pl.* **-os**) any fleshy fruit of the melon or cucumber type, with numerous seeds and surrounded by a hard skin. [L, = pumpkin, f. Gk *pepōn* abbr. of *pepōn sikuos* ripe gourd]

pepper /péppər/ *n.* & *v.* ● *n.* **1 a** a hot aromatic condiment from the dried berries of certain plants used whole or ground. **b** any climbing vine of the genus *Piper*, esp. *P. nigrum*, yielding these berries. **2** anything hot or pungent. **3 a** any plant of the genus *Capsicum*, esp. *C. annuum*. **b** the fruit of this used esp. as a vegetable or salad ingredient. **4** = CAYENNE. ● *v.tr.* **1** sprinkle or treat with or as if with pepper. **2 a** pelt with missiles. **b** hurl abuse etc. at. **3** punish severely. □ **black pepper** the unripe ground or whole berries of *Piper nigrum* as a condiment. **green pepper** the unripe fruit of *Capsicum annuum*. **pepper-mill** a device for grinding pepper by hand. **pepper-pot 1** a small container with a perforated lid for sprinkling pepper. **2** a W. Indian dish of meat etc. stewed with cayenne pepper. **3** *colloq.* a Jamaican. **red** (or **yellow**) **pepper** the ripe fruit of *Capsicum annuum*. **sweet pepper** a pepper with a relatively mild taste. **white pepper** the ripe or husked ground or whole berries of *Piper nigrum* as a condiment. [OE *piper*, *pipor* f. L *piper* f. Gk *peperi* f. Skr. *pippalī-* berry, peppercorn]

▪ *v.* **1** sprinkle, scatter, dot, speckle, fleck, spot, spray, spatter, stipple, mottle. **2 a** see PELT[1] *v.* 1. **b** see ABUSE *v.* 2. **3** see PUNISH 1.

pepperbox /péppərboks/ *n.* = *pepper-pot* 1.

peppercorn /péppərkorn/ *n.* **1** the dried berry of *Piper nigrum* as a condiment. **2** (in full **peppercorn rent**) a nominal rent.

peppermint /péppərmint/ *n.* **1 a** a mint plant, *Mentha piperita*, grown for the strong-flavoured oil obtained from its leaves. **b** the oil from this. **2** a sweet flavoured with peppermint. **3** *Austral.* any of various eucalyptuses yielding oil with a similar flavour. □□ **pepperminty** *adj.*

pepperoni /péppərṓni/ *n.* (also **peperoni**) beef and pork sausage seasoned with pepper. [It. *peperone* chilli]

pepperwort /péppərwurt/ *n.* any cruciferous plant of the genus *Lepidium*, esp. garden cress.

peppery /péppəri/ *adj.* **1** of, like, or containing much, pepper. **2** hot-tempered. **3** pungent; stinging. □□ **pepperiness** *n.*

▪ **1** see SPICY 1. **2** see PASSIONATE. **3** see PUNGENT 1.

peppy /péppi/ *adj.* (**peppier**, **peppiest**) *colloq.* vigorous, energetic, bouncy. □□ **peppily** *adv.* **peppiness** *n.*

▪ see ENERGETIC 1, 2.

pepsin /pépsin/ *n.* an enzyme contained in the gastric juice, which hydrolyses proteins. [G f. Gk *pepsis* digestion]

peptic /péptik/ *adj.* concerning or promoting digestion. □ **peptic glands** glands secreting gastric juice. **peptic ulcer** an ulcer in the stomach or duodenum. [Gk *peptikos* able to digest (as PEPTONE)]

peptide /péptīd/ *n. Biochem.* any of a group of organic compounds consisting of two or more amino acids bonded in sequence. [G *Peptid*, back-form. (as POLYPEPTIDE)]

peptone /péptōn/ *n.* a protein fragment formed by hydrolysis in the process of digestion. □□ **peptonize** /-tənīz/ *v.tr.* (also **-ise**). [G *Pepton* f. Gk *peptos*, neut. *pepton* cooked]

per /per/ *prep.* **1** for each; for every (*two sweets per child*; *five miles per hour*). **2** by means of; by; through (*per post*; *per rail*). **3** (in full **as per**) in accordance with (*as per instructions*). **4** *Heraldry* in the direction of. □ **as per usual** *colloq.* as usual. [L]

per- /per, pər/ *prefix* **1** forming verbs, nouns, and adjectives meaning: **a** through; all over (*perforate*; *perforation*; *pervade*). **b** completely; very (*perfervid*; *perturb*). **c** to destruction; to the bad (*pervert*; *perdition*). **2** *Chem.* having the maximum of some element in combination, esp.: **a** in the names of binary compounds in *-ide* (*peroxide*). **b** in the names of oxides, acids, etc. in *-ic* (*perchloric*; *permanganic*). **c** in the names of salts of these acids (*perchlorate*; *permanganate*). [L *per-* (as PER)]

peradventure /pərədvénchər, pér-/ *adv.* & *n. archaic* or *joc.* ● *adv.* perhaps. ● *n.* uncertainty; chance; conjecture; doubt (esp. *beyond* or *without peradventure*). [ME f. OF *per* or *par auenture* by chance (as PER, ADVENTURE)]

▪ *adv.* see PERHAPS.

perambulate /pərámbyoolayt/ *v.* **1** *tr.* walk through, over, or about (streets, the country, etc.). **2** *intr.* walk from place to place. **3** *tr.* **a** travel through and inspect (territory). **b** formally establish the boundaries of (a parish etc.) by walking round them. □□ **perambulation** /-láysh'n/ *n.* **perambulatory** *adj.* [L *perambulare perambulat-* (as PER-, *ambulare* walk)]

▪ **1, 2** see WALK *v.* 1, 2. □□ **perambulation** see TOUR *n.* 1b.

perambulator /pərámbyoolaytər/ *n. Brit. formal* = PRAM[1]. [PERAMBULATE]

per annum /pər ánnəm/ *adv.* for each year. [L]

▪ see YEARLY *adv.*

percale /pərkáyl/ *n.* a closely woven cotton fabric like calico. [F, of uncert. orig.]

per capita /pər káppitə/ *adv.* & *adj.* (also **per caput** /káppŏŏt/) for each person. [L, = by heads]

perceive /pərséév/ *v.tr.* **1** apprehend, esp. through the sight; observe. **2** (usu. foll. by *that*, *how*, etc. + clause) apprehend with the mind; understand. **3** regard mentally in a specified manner (*perceives the universe as infinite*). □□ **perceivable** *adj.* **perceiver** *n.* [ME f. OF *perçoivre*, f. L *percipere* (as PER-, *capere* take)]

▪ **1** see, make out, discern, catch sight of, glimpse, spot, apprehend, take in, notice, note, discover, observe, mark, identify, distinguish, detect, *literary* espy, descry. **2** apprehend, understand, gather, comprehend, appreciate, grasp, feel, sense, deduce, infer, figure out, ascertain, determine, conclude, decipher, *colloq.* catch on, *sl.* dig. **3** regard, view, look on, consider, judge, believe, think, *formal* deem.

per cent /pər sént/ *adv.* & *n.* (*US* **percent**) ● *adv.* in every hundred. ● *n.* **1** percentage. **2** one part in every hundred (*half a per cent*). **3** (in *pl.*) *Brit.* public securities yielding interest of so much per cent (*three per cents*).

percentage /pərséntij/ *n.* **1** a rate or proportion per cent. **2** a proportion. **3** *colloq.* personal benefit or advantage.

▪ **2** share, part, portion, proportion, interest, piece, commission, *colloq.* cut.

percentile /pərséntīl/ *n. Statistics* one of 99 values of a variable dividing a population into 100 equal groups as regards the value of that variable.

percept /pérsept/ *n. Philos.* **1** an object of perception. **2** a mental concept resulting from perceiving, esp. by sight. [L *perceptum* perceived (thing), neut. past part. of *percipere* PERCEIVE, after *concept*]

perceptible /pərséptib'l/ *adj.* capable of being perceived by the senses or intellect. □□ **perceptibility** /-bílliti/ *n.* **perceptibly** *adv.* [OF *perceptible* or LL *perceptibilis* f. L (as PERCEIVE)]

▪ discernible, detectable, observable, perceivable, noticeable, distinguishable, recognizable, apparent, evident, notable, obvious, patent, manifest, palpable, plain, clear, prominent, unmistakable.

perception /pərsépsh'n/ *n.* **1 a** the faculty of perceiving. **b** an instance of this. **2** (often foll. by *of*) **a** the intuitive recognition of a truth, aesthetic quality, etc. **b** an instance of this (*a sudden perception of the true position*). **3** *Philos.* the ability of the mind to refer sensory information to an external object as its cause. □□ **perceptional** *adj.* **perceptual** /pərséptyooəl/ *adj.* **perceptually** /pərséptyooəli/ *adv.* [ME f. L *perceptio* (as PERCEIVE)]

■ **2** appreciation, recognition, grasp, awareness, consciousness, realization, apprehension, understanding, comprehension, knowledge; intuition, insight, feeling, sense, impression, idea, notion.

perceptive /pərséptiv/ *adj.* **1** capable of perceiving. **2** sensitive; discerning; observant (*a perceptive remark*). ▫▫ **perceptively** *adv.* **perceptiveness** *n.* **perceptivity** /-tívviti/ *n.* [med.L *perceptivus* (as PERCEIVE)]
■ **2** astute, alert, attentive, quick, alive, quick-witted, intelligent, acute, sharp, sensitive, sensible, percipient, discerning, perspicacious, incisive, *colloq.* on the ball; see also OBSERVANT 1a.

perch[1] /perch/ *n.* & *v.* ● *n.* **1** a usu. horizontal bar, branch, etc. used by a bird to rest on. **2** a usu. high or precarious place for a person or thing to rest on. **3** a measure of length, esp. for land, of 5½ yards (see also ROD, POLE). ● *v.intr.* & *tr.* (usu. foll. by *on*) settle or rest, or cause to settle or rest on or as if on a perch etc. (*the bird perched on a branch*; *a town perched on a hill*). ▫ **knock a person off his or her perch 1** vanquish, destroy. **2** make less confident or secure. **square perch** 30¼ sq. yards. [ME f. OF *perche*, *percher* f. L *pertica* pole]
■ *n.* **2** spot, location, position, place, site, vantage point, perspective. ● *v.* roost, rest, sit, nest; place, put, set, situate, locate, position, site. ▫ **knock a person off his or her perch 1** destroy, defeat, disgrace; see also RUIN *v.* 1a. **2** see DEMORALIZE 1.

perch[2] /perch/ *n.* (*pl.* same or **perches**) any spiny-finned freshwater edible fish of the genus *Perca*, esp. *P. fluviatilis* of Europe. [ME f. OF *perche* f. L *perca* f. Gk *perkē*]

perchance /pərchaánss/ *adv. archaic* or *poet.* **1** by chance. **2** possibly; maybe. [ME f. AF *par chance* f. *par* by, CHANCE]
■ **2** see MAYBE.

percher /pérchər/ *n.* any bird with feet adapted for perching; a passerine.

percheron /páirshəron/ *n.* a powerful breed of cart-horse. [F, orig. bred in le *Perche*, a district of N. France]

perchlorate /pərklórayt/ *n. Chem.* a salt or ester of perchloric acid.

perchloric acid /pərklórik/ *n. Chem.* a strong liquid acid containing heptavalent chlorine. [PER- + CHLORINE]

percipient /pərsíppiənt/ *adj.* & *n.* ● *adj.* **1** able to perceive; conscious. **2** discerning; observant. ● *n.* a person who perceives, esp. something outside the range of the senses. ▫▫ **percipience** *n.* **percipiently** *adv.* [L (as PERCEIVE)]
■ *adj.* **2** see PERCEPTIVE. ▫▫ **percipience** see INSIGHT.

percolate /pérkəlayt/ *v.* **1** *intr.* (often foll. by *through*) **a** (of liquid etc.) filter or ooze gradually (esp. through a porous surface). **b** (of an idea etc.) permeate gradually. **2** *tr.* prepare (coffee) by repeatedly passing boiling water through ground beans. **3** *tr.* ooze through; permeate. **4** *tr.* strain (a liquid, powder, etc.) through a fine mesh etc. ▫▫ **percolation** /-láysh'n/ *n.* [L *percolare* (as PER-, *colare* strain f. *colum* strainer)]
■ **1** seep, transfuse, leach, drip, drain, strain, filter, infuse, ooze, transude, filtrate, trickle, sink in. **3** suffuse, penetrate; see also PERMEATE.

percolator /pérkəlaytər/ *n.* a machine for making coffee by circulating boiling water through ground beans.

per contra /per kóntrə/ *adv.* on the opposite side (of an account, assessment, etc.); on the contrary. [It.]

percuss /pərkúss/ *v.tr. Med.* tap (a part of the body) gently with a finger or an instrument as part of a diagnosis. [L *percutere percuss-* strike (as PER-, *cutere* = *quatere* shake)]

percussion /pərkúsh'n/ *n.* **1** *Mus.* **a** (often *attrib.*) the playing of music by striking instruments with sticks etc. (*a percussion band*). **b** the section of such instruments in an orchestra (*asked the percussion to stay behind*). **2** *Med.* the act or an instance of percussing. **3** the forcible striking of one esp. solid body against another. ▫ **percussion cap** a small amount of explosive powder contained in metal or paper and exploded by striking, used esp. in toy guns and formerly in some firearms. ▫▫ **percussionist** *n.* **percussive** *adj.* **percussively** *adv.* **percussiveness** *n.* [F *percussion* or L *percussio* (as PERCUSS)]

percutaneous /pérkyootáyniəss/ *adj.* esp. *Med.* made or done through the skin. [L *per cutem* through the skin]

per diem /pər dée-em, dī́em/ *adv.*, *adj.*, & *n.* ● *adv.* & *adj.* for each day. ● *n.* an allowance or payment for each day. [L]

perdition /pərdísh'n/ *n.* eternal death; damnation. [ME f. OF *perdiciun* or eccl.L *perditio* f. L *perdere* destroy (as PER-, *dere dit-* = *dare* give)]
■ damnation, hell, hell-fire, doom, ruin, condemnation, destruction, ruination, downfall.

perdurable /pərdyoórəb'l/ *adj. formal* permanent; eternal; durable. ▫▫ **perdurability** /-bílliti/ *n.* **perdurably** *adv.* [ME f. OF f. LL *perdurabilis* (as PER-, DURABLE)]

père /pair/ *n.* (added to a surname to distinguish a father from a son) the father, senior (cf. FILS). [F, = father]

Père David's deer /páir dáyvidz/ *n.* a large slender-antlered deer, *Elaphurus davidianus*. [after Father A. *David*, Fr. missionary d. 1900]

peregrinate /pérrigrinayt/ *v.intr. archaic* or *joc.* travel; journey, esp. extensively or at leisure. ▫▫ **peregrination** /-náysh'n/ *n.* **peregrinator** *n.* [L *peregrinari* (as PEREGRINE)]
■ see JOURNEY *v.* ▫▫ **peregrination** see JOURNEY *n.* **peregrinator** see MIGRANT *n.*

peregrine /pérrigrin/ *n.* & *adj.* ● *n.* (in full **peregrine falcon**) a kind of falcon much used for hawking. ● *adj. archaic* imported from abroad; foreign; outlandish. [L *peregrinus* f. *peregre* abroad f. *per* through + *ager* field]

peremptory /pərémptəri, pérrimp-, -tri/ *adj.* **1** (of a statement or command) admitting no denial or refusal. **2** (of a person, a person's manner, etc.) dogmatic; imperious; dictatorial. **3** *Law* not open to appeal or challenge; final. **4** absolutely fixed; essential. ▫ **peremptory challenge** *Law* a defendant's objection to a proposed juror, made without needing to give a reason. ▫▫ **peremptorily** *adv.* **peremptoriness** *n.* [AF *peremptorie*, OF *peremptoire* f. L *peremptorius* deadly, decisive, f. *perimere perempt-* destroy, cut off (as PER-, *emere* take, buy)]
■ **1** commanding, imperative, emphatic, positive, firm, insistent, compelling. **2** imperious, dogmatic, authoritative, tyrannical, despotic, dictatorial, autocratic, domineering, *colloq.* bossy. **3** decisive, final, preclusive, incontrovertible, irrefutable, categorical, unequivocal, unconditional, unreserved, flat, out and out, outright, unqualified, unmitigated, unchallengeable, *esp. Law* unappealable. **4** see IMPERATIVE 2.

perennial /pərénniəl/ *adj.* & *n.* ● *adj.* **1** lasting through a year or several years. **2** (of a plant) lasting several years (cf. ANNUAL). **3** lasting a long time or for ever. **4** (of a stream) flowing through all seasons of the year. ● *n.* a perennial plant (*a herbaceous perennial*). ▫▫ **perenniality** /-niálliti/ *n.* **perennially** *adv.* [L *perennis* (as PER-, *annus* year)]
■ *adj.* **3** lasting, continuing, enduring, lifelong, persistent; endless, unending, ceaseless, unceasing, imperishable, undying, constant, perpetual, continual, everlasting, timeless, eternal, immortal, permanent, unfailing, never-failing, *rhet.* sempiternal.

perestroika /pérrestróykə/ *n. hist.* (in the Soviet Union) the policy or practice of restructuring or reforming the economic and political system. [Russ. *perestroĭka* = restructuring]
■ see REFORM *n.*

perfect *adj.*, *v.*, & *n.* ● *adj.* /pérfikt/ **1** complete; not deficient. **2 a** faultless (*a perfect diamond*). **b** blameless in morals or behaviour. **3 a** very satisfactory (*a perfect evening*). **b** (often foll. by *for*) most appropriate, suitable. **4** exact; precise (*a perfect circle*). **5** entire; unqualified (*a perfect stranger*). **6** *Math.* (of a number) equal to the sum of its divisors. **7** *Gram.* (of a tense) denoting a completed action or event in the past, formed in English with *have* or *has* and the past participle, as in *they have eaten*. **8** *Mus.* (of pitch) absolute. **9** *Bot.* **a** (of a flower) having all four types of whorl. **b** (of a fungus) in the stage where the sexual spores are formed. **10** (often foll. by *in*) thoroughly trained or skilled (*is perfect in geometry*). ● *v.tr.* /pərfékt/ **1** make perfect; improve. **2** carry through; complete. **3** complete (a sheet) by printing the other side. ● *n.* /pérfikt/ *Gram.* the perfect tense. □ **perfect binding** a form of bookbinding in which the leaves are attached to the spine by gluing rather than sewing. **perfect interval** *Mus.* a fourth or fifth as it would occur in a major or minor scale starting on the lower note of the interval, or octave. **perfect pitch** = *absolute pitch* 1. □□ **perfecter** *n.* **perfectible** /pərféktib'l/ *adj.* **perfectibility** /pərféktibílliti/ *n.* **perfectness** *n.* [ME and OF *parfit*, *perfet* f. L *perfectus* past part. of *perficere* complete (as PER-, *facere* do)]

■ *adj.* **1** complete, absolute, finished, (fully) realized, fulfilled, consummate, pure, entire, whole, perfected, best, ideal. **2 a** flawless, faultless, sublime, ideal, superb, supreme, superlative, pre-eminent, excellent, exquisite, unexcelled, unrivalled, unequalled, unmatched, matchless, incomparable, nonpareil, peerless, inimitable. **b** blameless, righteous, holy, faultless, flawless, spotless, pure, immaculate. **3 a** see DELIGHTFUL. **b** fitting, appropriate, (just) right, apt, suitable, correct, proper, made to order, *Brit. colloq.* spot on. **4** precise, exact, accurate, correct, unerring, true, *Brit. colloq.* spot on. **5** utter, entire, complete, thorough, out and out, unqualified, unalloyed, unmitigated, 24-carat; see also ABSOLUTE *adj.* 1. **10** expert, proficient, accomplished, experienced, practised, skilful, skilled, gifted, talented, adept, deft, adroit, polished, professional, masterly, masterful. ● *v.* **1** refine, polish, cultivate, better, bring to perfection, *formal* ameliorate; see also IMPROVE 1a. **2** complete, finish, realize, fulfil, consummate, accomplish, achieve, effect, execute, carry out *or* through, bring to completion.

perfecta /pərféktə/ *n. US* a form of betting in which the first two places in a race must be predicted in the correct order . [Amer. Sp. *quiniela perfecta* perfect quinella]

perfection /pərféksh'n/ *n.* **1** the act or process of making perfect. **2** the state of being perfect; faultlessness, excellence. **3** a perfect person, thing, or example. **4** an accomplishment. **5** full development; completion. □ **to perfection** exactly; completely. [ME f. OF f. L *perfectio -onis* (as PERFECT)]

■ **1** refinement, enhancement; improvement, *formal* amelioration. **2** purity, flawlessness, faultlessness, sublimity, superiority, pre-eminence, transcendence; see also EXCELLENCE 1. **3** ideal, paragon, model, archetype, pattern, mould, standard, idealization, essence, quintessence, acme, pinnacle, summit. **4** accomplishment, attainment, achievement; endowment, talent, ability, aptitude, gift, skill, faculty, flair. **5** completion, completeness, fulfilment, realization, consummation; maturity, ripeness, fullness, readiness, mellowness. □ **to perfection** see *completely* (COMPLETE).

perfectionism /pərfékshəniz'm/ *n.* **1** the uncompromising pursuit of excellence. **2** *Philos.* the belief that religious or moral perfection is attainable. □□ **perfectionist** *n.* & *adj.* [PERFECT]

■ **1** strictness, fastidiousness, rigourousness, stringency. □□ **perfectionist** (*n.*) purist, pedant, precisian, precisionist, stickler, *colloq.* fusspot, nit-picker. (*adj.*) meticulous, precise, punctilious, scrupulous, exacting, particular, demanding, fastidious, obsessive, *colloq.* picky, nit-picking; see also FUSSY 3.

perfective /pərféktiv/ *adj.* & *n. Gram.* ● *adj.* (of an aspect of a verb etc.) expressing the completion of an action (opp. IMPERFECTIVE). ● *n.* the perfective aspect or form of a verb. [med.L *perfectivus* (as PERFECT)]

perfectly /pérfiktli/ *adv.* **1** completely; absolutely (*I understand you perfectly*). **2** quite, completely (*is perfectly capable of doing it*). **3** in a perfect way. **4** very (*you know perfectly well*).

■ **1, 2** completely, entirely, absolutely, utterly, totally, wholly, consummately, thoroughly, quite, definitely, positively, unambiguously, unequivocally, unmistakably, explicitly, extremely, extraordinarily, remarkably; exactly, precisely, accurately. **3** superbly, superlatively, flawlessly, faultlessly, impeccably, inimitably, incomparably, sublimely, exquisitely, marvellously, admirably, wonderfully. **4** very, full, quite, *archaic* right, *colloq.* jolly, damned.

perfecto /pərféktō/ *n.* (*pl.* **-os**) orig. *US* a large thick cigar pointed at each end. [Sp., = perfect]

perfervid /pərférvid/ *adj. literary* very fervid. □□ **perfervidly** *adv.* **perfervidness** *n.* [mod.L *perfervidus* (as PER-, FERVID)]

■ see *fanatical* (FANATIC).

perfidy /pérfidi/ *n.* breach of faith; treachery. □□ **perfidious** /-fíddiəss/ *adj.* **perfidiously** /-fíddiəsli/ *adv.* [L *perfidia* f. *perfidus* treacherous (as PER-, *fidus* f. *fides* faith)]

■ perfidiousness, treachery, deceit, traitorousness, treason, disloyalty, faithlessness, falseness, falsity, unfaithfulness, infidelity, hypocrisy, betrayal. □□ **perfidious** treacherous, deceitful, traitorous, treasonous, treasonable, disloyal, faithless, false, unfaithful, untrue, insidious, hypocritical, corrupt, dishonest.

perfoliate /pərfṓliət/ *adj.* (of a plant) having the stalk apparently passing through the leaf. [mod.L *perfoliatus* (as PER-, FOLIATE)]

perforate *v.* & *adj.* ● *v.* /pérfərayt/ **1** *tr.* make a hole or holes through; pierce. **2** *tr.* make a row of small holes in (paper etc.) so that a part may be torn off easily. **3** *tr.* make an opening into; pass into or extend through. **4** *intr.* (usu. foll. by *into*, *through*, etc.) penetrate. ● *adj.* /pérfərət/ perforated. □□ **perforation** /-ráysh'n/ *n.* **perforative** /pérfərətiv/ *adj.* **perforator** /pérfəraytər/ *n.* [L *perforare* (as PER-, *forare* pierce)]

■ *v.* **1** puncture, drill, bore; see also PIERCE 1a, b. **3, 4** enter, penetrate, pass into *or* through, go into; see also PENETRATE 1a.

perforce /pərfórss/ *adv. archaic* unavoidably; necessarily. [ME f. OF *par force* by FORCE[1]]

■ see NECESSARILY.

perform /pərfórm/ *v.* **1** *tr.* (also *absol.*) carry into effect; be the agent of; do (a command, promise, task, etc.). **2** *tr.* (also *absol.*) go through, execute (a public function, play, piece of music, etc.). **3** *intr.* act in a play; play music, sing, etc. (*likes performing*). **4** *intr.* (of a trained animal) execute tricks etc. at a public show. **5** *intr.* operate, function. □□ **performable** *adj.* **performability** /-fórməbílliti/ *n.* **performatory** *adj.* & *n.* (*pl.* **-ies**). **performer** *n.* **performing** *adj.* [ME f. AF *parfourmer* f. OF *parfournir* (assim. to *forme* FORM) f. *par* PER- + *fournir* FURNISH]

■ **1** carry out, complete, bring off *or* about, accomplish, do, fulfil; see also EFFECT *v.* 1, 2. **2** execute, discharge, dispatch, conduct, carry on, go through, do; present, stage, produce, put on, mount. **5** do, act, behave, operate, function, run, work, go, respond. □□ **performer** actor, actress, artiste, Thespian, trouper, player, entertainer, *formal* executant.

performance /pərfórmənss/ *n.* **1** (usu. foll. by *of*) **a** the act or process of performing or carrying out. **b** the execution or fulfilment (of a duty etc.). **2** a staging or production (of a drama, piece of music, etc.) (*the afternoon performance*). **3** a person's achievement under test conditions etc. (*put up a good performance*). **4** *colloq.* a fuss; a scene; a public exhibition (*made such a performance about leaving*). **5 a** the capabilities of a machine, esp. a car or aircraft. **b** (*attrib.*) of high capability (*a performance car*).

■ **1** execution, accomplishment, effectuation, discharge, dispatch, conduct, fulfilment, completion. **2** show, showing, play, production, staging, act; concert, *colloq.* gig. **4** scene, show, exhibition, display, act; see also FUSS *n.* 1, 2a. **5 a** capability, capabilities, power, capacity, potential.

performative /pərfórmətiv/ *adj.* & *n.* ● *adj.* **1** of or relating to performance. **2** denoting an utterance that effects an action by being spoken or written (e.g. *I bet*, *I apologize*). ● *n.* a performative utterance.

performing arts /pərfórming/ *n.pl.* the arts, such as drama, music, and dance, that require performance for their realization.

perfume /pérfyōōm/ *n.* & *v.* ● *n.* **1** a sweet smell. **2** fluid containing the essence of flowers etc.; scent. ● *v.tr.* /also pərfyōōm/ (usu. as **perfumed** *adj.*) impart a sweet scent to; impregnate with a sweet smell. ▫▫ **perfumy** *adj.* [F *parfum, parfumer* f. obs. It. *parfumare, perfumare* (as PER-, *fumare* smoke, FUME): orig. of smoke from a burning substance]
■ *n.* **1** fragrance, aroma, odour, smell, bouquet, nose, redolence, balm. **2** eau-de-Cologne, toilet water, fragrance, scent, balm, essence. ● *v.* scent; (**perfumed**) see FRAGRANT.

perfumer /pərfyōōmər/ *n.* a maker or seller of perfumes. ▫▫ **perfumery** *n.* (*pl.* **-ies**).

perfunctory /pərfúngktəri, -tri/ *adj.* **1 a** done merely for the sake of getting through a duty. **b** done in a cursory or careless manner. **2** superficial; mechanical. ▫▫ **perfunctorily** *adv.* **perfunctoriness** *n.* [LL *perfunctorius* careless f. L *perfungi perfunct-* (as PER-, *fungi* perform)]
■ routine, mechanical, automatic, robot-like, unthinking, superficial, dismissive, inattentive, uninvolved, apathetic, indifferent, unconcerned, removed, distant, *dégagé*, offhand, heedless, uninterested; hasty, hurried, fleeting, rushed, cursory; careless, slipshod, slovenly, negligent, sketchy.

perfuse /pərfyōōz/ *v.tr.* **1** (often foll. by *with*) **a** besprinkle (with water etc.). **b** cover or suffuse (with radiance etc.). **2** pour or diffuse (water etc.) through or over. **3** *Med.* cause a fluid to pass through (an organ etc.). ▫▫ **perfusion** /-fyōōzh'n/ *n.* **perfusive** /-fyōōssiv/ *adj.* [L *perfundere perfus-* (as PER-, *fundere* pour)]

pergana var. of PARGANA.

pergola /pérgələ/ *n.* an arbour or covered walk, formed of growing plants trained over trellis-work. [It. f. L *pergula* projecting roof f. *pergere* proceed]

pergunnah var. of PARGANA.

perhaps /pərháps/ *adv.* **1** it may be; possibly (*perhaps it is lost*). **2** introducing a polite request (*perhaps you would open the window?*). [PER + HAP]
■ **1** maybe, possibly, it is possible (that), conceivably, it may be, *archaic* mayhap, *archaic or joc.* peradventure, *archaic or poet.* perchance, *N.Engl. dial.* happen.

peri /péeri/ *n.* (*pl.* **peris**) **1** (in Persian mythology) a fairy; a good (orig. evil) genius. **2** a beautiful or graceful being. [Pers. *pārī*]

peri- /pérri/ *prefix* **1** round, about. **2** *Astron.* the point nearest to (*perigee; perihelion*). [Gk *peri* around, about]

perianth /pérrianth/ *n.* the outer part of a flower. [F *périanthe* f. mod.L *perianthium* (as PERI- + Gk *anthos* flower)]

periapt /pérriapt/ *n.* a thing worn as a charm; an amulet. [F *périapte* f. Gk *periapton* f. *haptō* fasten]
■ see TALISMAN.

pericardium /pérrikaárdiəm/ *n.* (*pl.* **pericardia** /-diə/) the membranous sac enclosing the heart. ▫▫ **pericardiac** /-diak/ *adj.* **pericardial** *adj.* **pericarditis** /-dítiss/ *n.* [mod.L f. Gk *perikardion* (as PERI- + *kardia* heart)]

pericarp /pérrikaarp/ *n.* the part of a fruit formed from the wall of the ripened ovary. [F *péricarpe* f. Gk *perikarpion* pod, shell (as PERI-, *karpos* fruit)]

perichondrium /pérrikóndriəm/ *n.* the membrane enveloping cartilage tissue (except at the joints). [PERI- + Gk *khondros* cartilage]

periclase /pérriklayss/ *n.* a pale mineral consisting of magnesia. [mod.L *periclasia*, erron. f. Gk *peri* exceedingly + *klasis* breaking, from its perfect cleavage]

periclinal /pérriklín'l/ *adj.* *Geol.* (of a mound etc.) sloping down in all directions from a central point. [Gk *periklinēs* sloping on all sides (as PERI-, CLINE)]

pericope /pəríkkəpi/ *n.* a short passage or paragraph, esp. a portion of Scripture read in public worship. [LL f. Gk *perikopē* (as PERI-, *kopē* cutting f. *koptō* cut)]
■ see EXCERPT *n.*

pericranium /pérrikráyniəm/ *n.* the membrane enveloping the skull. [mod.L f. Gk (as PERI-, *kranion* skull)]

peridot /pérridot/ *n.* a green variety of olivine, used esp. as a semiprecious stone. [ME f. OF *peritot*, of unkn. orig.]

perigee /pérrijee/ *n.* the point in a celestial body's orbit where it is nearest the earth (opp. APOGEE). ▫▫ **perigean** /pérrijéeən/ *adj.* [F *périgée* f. mod.L f. Gk *perigeion* round the earth (as PERI-, *gē* earth)]

periglacial /pérrigláysh'l, -gláysiəl/ *adj.* of or relating to a region adjoining a glacier.

perigynous /pəríjinəss/ *adj.* (of stamens) situated around the pistil or ovary. [mod.L *perigynus* (as PERI-, -GYNOUS)]

perihelion /pérrihéeliən/ *n.* (*pl.* **perihelia** /-liə/) the point of a planet's or comet's orbit nearest to the sun's centre. [Graecized f. mod.L *perihelium* (as PERI-, Gk *hēlios* sun)]

peril /pérril/ *n.* & *v.* ● *n.* serious and immediate danger. ● *v.tr.* (**perilled, perilling**; *US* **periled, periling**) threaten; endanger. ▫ **at one's peril** at one's own risk. **in peril of** with great risk to (*in peril of your life*). **peril point** *US Econ.* a critical threshold or limit. [ME f. OF f. L *peric(u)lum*]
■ *n.* danger, threat, risk, jeopardy, exposure, vulnerability, susceptibility, insecurity. ● *v.* see ENDANGER.

perilous /pérriləss/ *adj.* **1** full of risk; dangerous; hazardous. **2** exposed to imminent risk of destruction etc. ▫▫ **perilously** *adv.* **perilousness** *n.* [ME f. OF *perillous* f. L *periculosus* f. *periculum*: see PERIL]
■ **1** risky, hazardous, unsafe; see also DANGEROUS.
2 vulnerable, susceptible, exposed, at risk, in danger, in jeopardy.

perilune /pérrilōōn, -lyōōn/ *n.* the point in a body's lunar orbit where it is closest to the moon's centre (opp. APOLUNE). [PERI- + L *luna* moon, after *perigee*]

perilymph /pérrilimf/ *n.* the fluid in the labyrinth of the ear.

perimeter /pərímmitər/ *n.* **1 a** the circumference or outline of a closed figure. **b** the length of this. **2 a** the outer boundary of an enclosed area. **b** a defended boundary. **3** an instrument for measuring a field of vision. ▫▫ **perimetric** /pérrimétrik/ *adj.* [F *périmètre* or f. L *perimetrus* f. Gk *perimetros* (as PERI-, *metros* f. *metron* measure)]
■ **2** boundary, border, borderline, margin, periphery, limit(s), bounds, ambit, circumference, edge, verge, fringe(s), *archaic* bourn.

perinatal /pérrináyt'l/ *adj.* of or relating to the time immediately before and after birth.

perineum /pérrinéeəm/ *n.* the region of the body between the anus and the scrotum or vulva. ▫▫ **perineal** *adj.* [LL f. Gk *perinaion*]

period /péeriəd/ *n.* & *adj.* ● *n.* **1** a length or portion of time (*showers and bright periods*). **2** a distinct portion of history, a person's life, etc. (*the Georgian period; Picasso's Blue Period*). **3** *Geol.* a time forming part of a geological era (*the Quaternary period*). **4 a** an interval between recurrences of an astronomical or other phenomenon. **b** the time taken by a planet to rotate about its axis. **5** the time allowed for a lesson in school. **6** an occurrence of menstruation. **7 a** a complete sentence, esp. one consisting of several clauses. **b** (in *pl.*) rhetorical language. **8** esp. *US* **a** = *full stop* (see FULL[1]). **b** used at the end of a sentence etc. to indicate finality, absoluteness, etc. (*we want the best, period*). **9 a** a set of figures marked off in a large number to assist in reading. **b** a set of figures repeated in a recurring decimal. **c** the smallest interval over which a function takes the same value. **10** *Chem.* a sequence of elements between two noble gases forming a row in the periodic table. ● *adj.* belonging to or characteristic of some past period (*period furniture*). ▫ **of the period** of the era under discussion (*the custom of the period*). **period piece** an object or work whose main interest

lies in its historical etc. associations. [ME f. OF *periode* f. L *periodus* f. Gk *periodos* (as PERI-, *odos* = *hodos* way)]
■ *n.* **1** interval, time, term, span, duration, spell, space, stretch, *colloq.* patch; while. **2** time, era, days, epoch, aeon, age, years. **5** lesson, class, session.

periodate /pərīədayt/ *n. Chem.* a salt or ester of periodic acid.

periodic /peerióddik/ *adj.* **1** appearing or occurring at regular intervals. **2** of or concerning the period of a celestial body (*periodic motion*). **3** (of diction etc.) expressed in periods (see PERIOD *n.* 7a). □ **periodic decimal** *Math.* a set of figures repeated in a recurring decimal. **periodic function** *Math.* a function returning to the same value at regular intervals. **periodic table** an arrangement of elements in order of increasing atomic number and in which elements of similar chemical properties appear at regular intervals. □□ **periodicity** /-riədíssiti/ *n.* [F *périodique* or L *periodicus* f. Gk *periodikos* (as PERIOD)]
■ **1** periodical, regular, recurrent, cyclical, cyclic, repeated.

periodic acid /pérīóddik/ *n. Chem.* a hygroscopic solid acid containing heptavalent iodine. [PER- + IODINE]

periodical /peerióddik'l/ *n.* & *adj.* ● *n.* a newspaper, magazine, etc. issued at regular intervals, usu. monthly or weekly. ● *adj.* **1** published at regular intervals. **2** periodic, occasional. □□ **periodically** *adv.*
■ *n.* magazine, journal, newspaper, paper, publication, newsletter, organ, serial, weekly, monthly, quarterly, yearbook, almanac. ● *adj.* **2** see PERIODIC.

periodization /peeriədīzáysh'n/ *n.* the division of history into periods.

periodontics /pérriədóntiks/ *n.pl.* (treated as *sing.*) the branch of dentistry concerned with the structures surrounding and supporting the teeth. □□ **periodontal** *adj.* **periodontist** *n.* [PERI- + Gk *odous odont-* tooth]

periodontology /pérriədontólləji/ *n.* = PERIODONTICS.

periosteum /pérriósti əm/ *n.* (*pl.* **periostea** /-tiə/) a membrane enveloping the bones where no cartilage is present. □□ **periosteal** *adj.* **periostitis** /-stītiss/ *n.* [mod.L f. Gk *periosteon* (as PERI-, *osteon* bone)]

peripatetic /pérripətéttik/ *adj.* & *n.* ● *adj.* **1** (of a teacher) working in more than one school or college etc. **2** going from place to place; itinerant. **3** (**Peripatetic**) Aristotelian (from Aristotle's habit of walking in the Lyceum whilst teaching). ● *n.* a peripatetic person, esp. a teacher. □□ **peripatetically** *adv.* **peripateticism** /-tisiz'm/ *n.* [ME f. OF *peripatetique* or L *peripateticus* f. Gk *peripatētikos* f. *peripateō* (as PERI-, *pateō* walk)]
■ *adj.* **1, 2** see *travelling* (TRAVEL).

peripeteia /pérripitīə, -teeə/ *n.* a sudden change of fortune in a drama or in life. [Gk (as PERI-, *pet-* f. *piptō* fall)]

peripheral /pəríffərəl/ *adj.* & *n.* ● *adj.* **1** of minor importance; marginal. **2** of the periphery; on the fringe. **3** *Anat.* near the surface of the body, with special reference to the circulation and nervous system. **4** (of equipment) used with a computer etc. but not an integral part of it. ● *n.* a peripheral device or piece of equipment. □ **peripheral nervous system** *Anat.* the nervous system outside the brain and spinal cord. □□ **peripherally** *adv.*
■ *adj.* **1** incidental, unimportant, marginal, minor, secondary, inessential, unessential, non-essential, unnecessary, superficial, tangential, irrelevant, beside the point; see also IMMATERIAL 1. **2** circumferential, external, perimetric, outside, outer, border.

periphery /pəríffəri/ *n.* (*pl.* **-ies**) **1** the boundary of an area or surface. **2** an outer or surrounding region (*built on the periphery of the old town*). [LL *peripheria* f. Gk *periphereia* circumference (as PERI-, *phereia* f. *phero* bear)]
■ **1** perimeter, circumference, border, edge, rim, brim, boundary, margin. **2** see OUTSKIRTS.

periphrasis /pərífrəsiss/ *n.* (*pl.* **periphrases** /-seez/) **1** a roundabout way of speaking; circumlocution. **2** a roundabout phrase. [L f. Gk f. *periphrazō* (as PERI-, *phrazō* declare)]

periphrastic /pérrifrástik/ *adj.* **1** of or involving periphrasis. **2** *Gram.* (of a case, tense, etc.) formed by combination of words rather than by inflection (e.g. *did go*, *of the people* rather than *went*, *the people's*). □□ **periphrastically** *adv.* [Gk *periphrastikos* (as PERIPHRASIS)]
■ **1** see RAMBLING 2.

peripteral /pəríptərəl/ *adj.* (of a temple) surrounded by a single row of columns. [Gk *peripteron* (as PERI-, Gk *pteron* wing)]

periscope /pérriskōp/ *n.* an apparatus with a tube and mirrors or prisms, by which an observer in a trench, submerged submarine, or at the rear of a crowd etc., can see things otherwise out of sight.

periscopic /pérriskóppik/ *adj.* of a periscope. □ **periscopic lens** a lens allowing distinct vision over a wide angle. □□ **periscopically** *adv.*

perish /pérrish/ *v.* **1** *intr.* be destroyed; suffer death or ruin. **2 a** *intr.* (esp. of rubber, a rubber object, etc.) lose its normal qualities; deteriorate, rot. **b** *tr.* cause to rot or deteriorate. **3** *tr.* (in *passive*) suffer from cold or exposure (*we were perished standing outside*). □ **perish the thought** an exclamation of horror against an unwelcome idea. □□ **perishless** *adj.* [ME f. OF *perir* f. L *perire* pass away (as PER-, *ire* go)]
■ **1** expire, lose one's life, be killed, be lost, meet one's death, be destroyed; see also DIE[1] 1. **2** deteriorate, rot, decay, disintegrate, weaken, fall apart, crumble, corrode. □ **perish the thought** God forbid.

perishable /pérrishəb'l/ *adj.* & *n.* ● *adj.* liable to perish; subject to decay. ● *n.* a thing, esp. a foodstuff, subject to speedy decay. □□ **perishability** /-bílliti/ *n.* **perishableness** *n.*

perisher /pérrishər/ *n. Brit. sl.* an annoying person.

perishing /pérrishing/ *adj.* & *adv. colloq.* ● *adj.* **1** confounded. **2** freezing cold, extremely chilly. ● *adv.* confoundedly. □□ **perishingly** *adv.*
■ *adj.* **1** infernal, confounded; see also FLAMING 3b, TIRESOME 2. **2** see *freezing* (FREEZE).

perisperm /pérrisperm/ *n.* a mass of nutritive material outside the embryo-sac in some seeds. [PERI- + Gk *sperma* seed]

peristalsis /pérristálsiss/ *n.* an involuntary muscular wave-like movement by which the contents of the alimentary canal etc. are propelled along. □□ **peristaltic** *adj.* **peristaltically** *adv.* [mod.L f. Gk *peristellō* wrap around (as PERI-, *stellō* place)]

peristome /pérristōm/ *n.* **1** *Bot.* a fringe of small teeth around the mouth of a capsule in mosses and certain fungi. **2** *Zool.* the parts surrounding the mouth of various invertebrates. [mod.L *peristoma* f. PERI- + Gk *stoma* mouth]

peristyle /pérristīl/ *n.* a row of columns surrounding a temple, court, cloister, etc.; a space surrounded by columns. [F *péristyle* f. L *peristylum* f. Gk *peristulon* (as PERI-, *stulos* pillar)]

peritoneum /pérritəneeəm/ *n.* (*pl.* **peritoneums** or **peritonea** /-neeə/) the serous membrane lining the cavity of the abdomen. □□ **peritoneal** *adj.* [LL f. Gk *peritonaion* (as PERI-, *tonaion* f. *-tonos* stretched)]

peritonitis /pérritənītiss/ *n.* an inflammatory disease of the peritoneum.

periwig /pérriwig/ *n.* esp. *hist.* a wig. □□ **periwigged** *adj.* [alt. of PERUKE, with *-wi-* for F *-u-* sound]

periwinkle[1] /pérriwingk'l/ *n.* **1** any plant of the genus *Vinca*, esp. an evergreen trailing plant with blue or white flowers. **2** a tropical shrub, *Catharanthus roseus*, native to Madagascar. [ME f. AF *pervenke*, OF *pervenche* f. LL *pervinca*, assim. to PERIWINKLE[2]]

periwinkle[2] /pérriwingk'l/ *n.* = WINKLE. [16th c.: orig. unkn.]

perjure /pérjər/ *v.refl. Law* **1** wilfully tell an untruth when on oath. **2** (as **perjured** *adj.*) guilty of or involving perjury. □□ **perjurer** *n.* [ME f. OF *parjurer* f. L *perjurare* (as PER-, *jurare* swear)]

■ **1** see LIE² *v.* □□ **perjurer** see LIAR.

perjury /pérjəri/ *n.* (*pl.* **-ies**) *Law* **1** a breach of an oath, esp. the act of wilfully telling an untruth when on oath. **2** the practice of this. □□ **perjurious** /-jóoriəss/ *adj.* [ME f. AF *perjurie* f. OF *parjurie* f. L *perjurium* (as PERJURE)]
■ **2** lying, mendacity, mendaciousness, falsification, deception, untruthfulness, dishonesty, duplicity.

perk¹ /perk/ *v.* & *adj.* ● *v.tr.* raise (one's head etc.) briskly. ● *adj.* perky; pert. □ **perk up 1** recover confidence, courage, life, or zest. **2** restore confidence or courage or liveliness in (esp. another person). **3** smarten up. [ME, perh. f. var. of PERCH¹]
■ *adj.* see PERKY 2, JAUNTY. □ **perk up 1** cheer up, become jaunty, brighten, liven up, quicken, revive, *colloq.* buck up. **2** invigorate, revitalize, vitalize, revive, inspirit, *colloq.* pep up, buck up. **3** see SPRUCE¹ *v.*

perk² /perk/ *n. Brit. colloq.* a perquisite. [abbr.]
■ see PERQUISITE.

perk³ /perk/ *v. colloq.* **1** *intr.* (of coffee) percolate, make a bubbling sound in the percolator. **2** *tr.* percolate (coffee). [abbr. of PERCOLATE]

perky /pérki/ *adj.* (**perkier**, **perkiest**) **1** self-assertive; saucy; pert. **2** lively; cheerful. □□ **perkily** *adv.* **perkiness** *n.*
■ **1** see PERT 1. **2** lively, cheery, cheerful, jaunty, bouncy, bright, perk, vigorous, vitalized, spirited, energetic, zestful, sprightly, frisky, animated, vivacious, effervescent, bubbly, buoyant, gay, *colloq.* full of pep, peppy.

perlite /pérlīt/ *n.* (also **pearlite**) a glassy type of vermiculite, expandable to a solid form by heating, used for insulation etc. [F f. *perle* pearl]

perm¹ /perm/ *n.* & *v.* ● *n.* a permanent wave. ● *v.tr.* give a permanent wave to (a person or a person's hair). [abbr.]

perm² /perm/ *n.* & *v. colloq.* ● *n.* a permutation. ● *v.tr.* make a permutation of. [abbr.]

permafrost /pérməfrost/ *n.* subsoil which remains below freezing-point throughout the year, as in polar regions. [PERMANENT + FROST]

permalloy /pérməloy/ *n.* an alloy of nickel and iron that is easily magnetized and demagnetized. [PERMEABLE + ALLOY]

permanent /pérmənənt/ *adj.* lasting, or intended to last or function, indefinitely (opp. TEMPORARY). □ **permanent magnet** a magnet retaining its magnetic properties without continued excitation. **Permanent Secretary** (or **Under-secretary** etc.) *Brit.* a senior grade in the Civil Service, often a permanent adviser to a minister. **permanent set 1** the irreversible deformation of a substance after being subjected to stress. **2** the amount of this. **permanent tooth** a tooth succeeding a milk tooth in a mammal, and lasting most of the mammal's life. **permanent wave** an artificial wave in the hair, intended to last for some time. **permanent way** *Brit.* the finished roadbed of a railway. □□ **permanence** *n.* **permanency** *n.* **permanentize** *v.tr.* (also **-ise**). **permanently** *adv.* [ME f. OF *permanent* or L *permanēre* (as PER-, *manēre* remain)]
■ unchanging, invariable, changeless, fixed, unchangeable, immutable, unalterable, inalterable, stable, persistent, lasting, long-lasting, enduring, indefinite, perennial; everlasting, eternal, unending, endless, perpetual, undying, imperishable, indestructible. □□ **permanence, permanency** fixedness, changelessness, unalterableness, immutability, unchangeableness, longevity, endurance, perenniality, persistence, dependability, reliability, stability, durability. **permanently** for ever, for good, once and for all, always, eternally, everlastingly, *esp. US* forevermore.

permanganate /permánggənayt, -nət/ *n. Chem.* any salt of permanganic acid, esp. potassium permanganate.

permanganic acid /pérmanggánnik/ *n. Chem.* an acid containing heptavalent manganese. [PER- + MANGANIC: see MANGANESE]

permeability /pérmiəbílliti/ *n.* **1** the state or quality of being permeable. **2** a quantity measuring the influence of a substance on the magnetic flux in the region it occupies.

permeable /pérmiəb'l/ *adj.* capable of being permeated. [L *permeabilis* (as PERMEATE)]
■ see POROUS 1, 2.

permeate /pérmiayt/ *v.* **1** *tr.* penetrate throughout; pervade; saturate. **2** *intr.* (usu. foll. by *through*, *among*, etc.) diffuse itself. □□ **permeance** *n.* **permeant** *adj.* **permeation** /-áysh'n/ *n.* **permeator** *n.* [L *permeare permeat-* (as PER-, *meare* pass, go)]
■ **1** imbue, penetrate, pervade, infiltrate, enter, spread through(out), saturate, seep through(out), percolate (through), soak through.

Permian /pérmiən/ *adj.* & *n. Geol.* ● *adj.* of or relating to the last period of the Palaeozoic era with evidence of the development of reptiles and amphibians, and deposits of sandstone. ¶ Cf. Appendix VII. ● *n.* this period or system. [*Perm* in Russia]

per mille /per mílli/ *adv.* (also **per mil** /mil/) in every thousand. [L]

permissible /pərmíssib'l/ *adj.* allowable. □□ **permissibility** /-bílliti/ *n.* **permissibly** *adv.* [ME f. F or f. med.L *permissibilis* (as PERMIT)]
■ allowable, admissible, acceptable, allowed, permitted, tolerable, legal, licit, lawful, legitimate, authorized, proper, (all) right, *colloq.* OK, kosher, legit; pardonable, excusable, venial.

permission /pərmísh'n/ *n.* (often foll. by *to* + infin.) consent; authorization. [ME f. OF or f. L *permissio* (as PERMIT)]
■ consent, assent, leave, licence, sanction, acceptance, authorization, approval, approbation, countenance, allowance, indulgence, *formal* permit.

permissive /pərmíssiv/ *adj.* **1** tolerant; liberal, esp. in sexual matters (*the permissive society*). **2** giving permission. □ **permissive legislation** legislation giving powers but not enjoining their use. □□ **permissively** *adv.* **permissiveness** *n.* [ME f. OF (*-if -ive*) or med.L *permissivus* (as PERMIT)]
■ **1** indulgent, lenient, latitudinarian, lax, easygoing, liberal, tolerant, non-restrictive, libertarian. **2** assenting, consenting, acquiescent; see also AGREEABLE 2.

permit *v.* & *n.* ● *v.* /pərmít/ (**permitted**, **permitting**) **1** *tr.* give permission or consent to; authorize (*permit me to say*). **2 a** *tr.* allow as possible; give an opportunity to (*permit the traffic to flow again*). **b** *intr.* give an opportunity (*circumstances permitting*). **3** *intr.* (foll. by *of*) admit; allow for. ● *n.* /pérmit/ **1 a** a document giving permission to act in a specified way (*was granted a work permit*). **b** a document etc. which allows entry into a specified zone. **2** *formal* permission. □□ **permittee** /pérmitée/ *n.* **permitter** *n.* [L *permittere* (as PER-, *mittere miss-* let go)]
■ *v.* **1** see AUTHORIZE 1, 2a. **2 a** enable, allow, entitle. ● *n.* **1** licence, authorization, warrant; pass, passport, visa. **2** see PERMISSION.

permittivity /pérmitívviti/ *n. Electr.* a quantity measuring the ability of a substance to store electrical energy in an electric field.

permutate /pérmyootayt/ *v.tr.* change the order or arrangement of. [as PERMUTE, or back-form. f. PERMUTATION]

permutation /pérmyootáysh'n/ *n.* **1 a** an ordered arrangement or grouping of a set of numbers, items, etc. **b** any one of the range of possible groupings. **2** any combination or selection of a specified number of things from a larger group, esp. *Brit.* matches in a football pool. □□ **permutational** *adj.* [ME f. OF or f. L *permutatio* (as PERMUTE)]
■ **1** see VARIATION 1.

permute /pərmyoot/ *v.tr.* alter the sequence or arrangement of. [ME f. L *permutare* (as PER-, *mutare* change)]
■ see TRANSFORM *v.*

Permutit /pérmyootit/ *n. propr.* an artificial zeolite used as an ion exchanger esp. for the softening of water. [G f. L *permutare* to exchange]

pernicious /pərníshəss/ *adj.* destructive; ruinous; fatal. □ **pernicious anaemia** see ANAEMIA. □□ **perniciously** *adv.* **perniciousness** *n.* [L *perniciosus* f. *pernicies* ruin f. *nex necis* death]
■ see DESTRUCTIVE 1. □□ **perniciousness** see *virulence* (VIRULENT).

pernickety /pərníkkiti/ *adj. colloq.* **1** fastidious. **2** precise or over-precise. **3** ticklish, requiring tact or careful handling. [19th-c. Sc.: orig. unkn.]
■ **1** see FASTIDIOUS 1.

pernoctate /pərnóktayt/ *v.intr. formal* pass or spend the night. □□ **pernoctation** /-táysh'n/ *n.* [LL *pernoctatio* f. L *pernoctare pernoctat-* (as PER-, *noctare* f. *nox noctis* night)]

peroneal /pérrənéeəl/ *adj. Anat.* relating to or near the fibula. [mod.L *peronaeus* peroneal muscle f. *perone* fibula f. Gk *peronē* pin, fibula]

perorate /pérrərayt/ *v.intr.* **1** sum up and conclude a speech. **2** speak at length. [L *perorare perorat-* (as PER-, *orare* speak)]
■ **2** see RANT *v.* 2, 3.

peroration /pérrəráysh'n/ *n.* the concluding part of a speech, forcefully summing up what has been said.

peroxidase /pəróksidayz, -dayss/ *n. Biochem.* any of a class of enzymes found esp. in plants, which catalyze the oxidation of a substrate by hydrogen peroxide.

peroxide /pəróksīd/ *n.* & *v.* ● *n. Chem.* **1 a** = *hydrogen peroxide.* **b** (often *attrib.*) a solution of hydrogen peroxide used to bleach the hair or as an antiseptic. **2** a compound of oxygen with another element containing the greatest possible proportion of oxygen. **3** any salt or ester of hydrogen peroxide. ● *v.tr.* bleach (the hair) with peroxide. [PER- + OXIDE]

perpendicular /pérpəndíkyoolər/ *adj.* & *n.* ● *adj.* **1 a** at right angles to the plane of the horizon. **b** (usu. foll. by *to*) *Geom.* at right angles (to a given line, plane, or surface). **2** upright, vertical. **3** (of a slope etc.) very steep. **4** (**Perpendicular**) *Archit.* of the third stage of English Gothic (15th–16th c.) with vertical tracery in large windows. **5** *joc.* in a standing position. ● *n.* **1** a perpendicular line. **2** a plumb-rule or a similar instrument. **3** (prec. by *the*) a perpendicular line or direction (*is out of the perpendicular*). □□ **perpendicularity** /-lárriti/ *n.* **perpendicularly** *adv.* [ME f. L *perpendicularis* f. *perpendiculum* plumb-line f. PER- + *pendēre* hang]
■ *adj.* **1** (*perpendicular to*) at right angles to, at 90 degrees to. **2** erect, upright, vertical, plumb, straight (up and down). **3** precipitous, sheer; see also STEEP[1] *adj.* 1.

perpetrate /pérpitrayt/ *v.tr.* commit or perform (a crime, blunder, or anything outrageous). □□ **perpetration** /-tráysh'n/ *n.* **perpetrator** *n.* [L *perpetrare perpetrat-* (as PER-, *patrare* effect)]
■ commit, execute, perform, carry out *or* through, effect, effectuate, accomplish, do; practise.

perpetual /pərpétyooəl/ *adj.* **1** eternal; lasting for ever or indefinitely. **2** continuous, uninterrupted. **3** *colloq.* frequent, much repeated (*perpetual interruptions*). **4** permanent during life (*perpetual secretary*). □ **perpetual calendar** a calendar which can be adjusted to show any combination of day, month, and year. **perpetual check** *Chess* the position of play when a draw is obtained by repeated checking of the king. **perpetual motion** the motion of a hypothetical machine which once set in motion would run for ever unless subject to an external force or to wear. □□ **perpetualism** *n.* **perpetually** *adv.* [ME f. OF *perpetuel* f. L *perpetualis* f. *perpetuus* f. *perpes -etis* continuous]
■ **1** eternal, everlasting, never-ending, unending, perennial, ageless, timeless, long-lived, permanent, indefinite, unceasing, lasting, enduring; unvarying, unchanging, immutable, invariable, undeviating, *rhet.* sempiternal. **2** constant, uninterrupted, continuous, incessant, persistent, unremitting, unending, non-stop, endless, recurrent. **3** frequent, constant, numerous, many, countless, innumerable, *sl.* umpteen; repeated, continual.

perpetuate /pərpétyoo-ayt/ *v.tr.* **1** make perpetual. **2** preserve from oblivion. □□ **perpetuance** *n.* **perpetuation** /-áysh'n/ *n.* **perpetuator** *n.* [L *perpetuare* (as PERPETUAL)]
■ **2** continue, maintain, extend, keep (on *or* up), keep going, preserve, memorialize, immortalize, eternalize.

perpetuity /pérpityóo-iti/ *n.* (*pl.* **-ies**) **1** the state or quality of being perpetual. **2** a perpetual annuity. **3** a perpetual possession or position. □ **in** (or **to** or **for**) **perpetuity** for ever. [ME f. OF *perpetuité* f. L *perpetuitas -tatis* (as PERPETUAL)]
■ **1** permanence, constancy, timelessness, everlastingness, unendingness; eternity, infinity. □ **in** (or **to** or **for**) **perpetuity** for ever, for all time, till the end of time, till doomsday, *esp. US* forevermore, *colloq.* till the cows come home, till kingdom come.

perpetuum mobile /perpétyooəm mṓbili/ *n.* **1** = *perpetual motion.* **2** *Mus.* = MOTO PERPETUO. [L *perpetuus* continuous + *mobilis* movable, after PRIMUM MOBILE]

perplex /pərpléks/ *v.tr.* **1** puzzle, bewilder, or disconcert (a person, a person's mind, etc.). **2** complicate or confuse (a matter). **3** (as **perplexed** *adj.*) *archaic* entangled, intertwined. □□ **perplexedly** /-pléksidli/ *adv.* **perplexing** *adj.* **perplexingly** *adv.* [back-form. f. *perplexed* f. obs. *perplex* (adj.) f. OF *perplexe* or L *perplexus* (as PER-, *plexus* past part. of *plectere* plait)]
■ **1** confuse, bewilder, puzzle, mystify, distract, baffle, befuddle, confound, muddle, disconcert, stump, nonplus, stymie, stupefy, stun, daze, dumbfound, *archaic* wilder, *colloq.* throw, bamboozle, flabbergast, *US joc.* discombobulate. **2** see COMPLICATE 1. **3** (**perplexed**) entangled, intertwined, intertwisted, interwoven, ensnarled, knotty, tangled, twisted, entwined. □□ **perplexing** confusing, bewildering, puzzling, mystifying, baffling, disconcerting, enigmatic, paradoxical, incomprehensible, unfathomable, impenetrable, recondite, arcane; labyrinthine, complex, complicated, Byzantine, intricate, involved, convoluted, twisted, knotty, Gordian.

perplexity /pərpléksiti/ *n.* (*pl.* **-ies**) **1** bewilderment; the state of being perplexed. **2** a thing which perplexes. **3** the state of being complicated. **4** *archaic* an entangled state. [ME f. OF *perplexité* or LL *perplexitas* (as PERPLEX)]
■ **1** confusion, bewilderment, bafflement, befuddlement, puzzlement, bemusement, doubt, difficulty. **2** puzzle, enigma, mystery, problem, paradox, quandary, predicament, *esp. US* bind, *colloq.* catch-22, *disp.* dilemma. **3** intricacy, complexity, complicatedness, arcaneness, reconditeness, impenetrability, impenetrableness, involvement, unfathomability, obscurity, difficulty.

per pro. /per prṓ/ *abbr.* through the agency of (used in signatures). ¶ The correct sequence is A *per pro.* B, where B is signing on behalf of A. [L *per procurationem*]

perquisite /pérkwizit/ *n.* **1** an extra profit or allowance additional to a main income etc. **2** a customary extra right or privilege. **3** an incidental benefit attached to employment etc. **4** a thing which has served its primary use and to which a subordinate or servant has a customary right. [ME f. med.L *perquisitum* f. L *perquirere* search diligently for (as PER-, *quaerere* seek)]
■ **1–3** consideration, emolument, bonus, added attraction *or* extra, reward, (fringe) benefit, extra, dividend, appanage, token (of appreciation), *colloq.* perk; right, privilege.

Perrier /pérriay/ *n. propr.* an effervescent natural mineral water. [the name of a spring at Vergèze, France, its source]

perron /pérrən/ *n.* an exterior staircase leading up to a main entrance to a church or other (usu. large) building. [ME f. OF ult. f. L *petra* stone]

perry /pérri/ *n.* (*pl.* **-ies**) *Brit.* a drink like cider, made from the fermented juice of pears. [ME *pereye* etc. f. OF *peré*, ult. f. L *pirum* pear]

per se /per sáy/ *adv.* by or in itself; intrinsically. [L]

persecute /pérsikyoot/ *v.tr.* **1** subject (a person etc.) to hostility or ill-treatment, esp. on the grounds of political or religious belief. **2** harass; worry. **3** (often foll. by *with*) bombard (a person) with questions etc. □□ **persecutor** *n.* **persecutory** *adj.* [ME f. OF *persecuter* back-form. f. *persecuteur* persecutor f. LL *persecutor* f. L *persequi* (as PER-, *sequi secut-* follow, pursue)]
■ **1** oppress, maltreat, ill-treat, abuse, molest, victimize, tyrannize, afflict, punish, martyr, torment, torture. **2** bother, annoy, pester, plague, hector, bully, badger, harry, harass, irritate, worry, vex, trouble, importune, hound, *Austral. colloq.* heavy.

persecution /pérsikyóosh'n/ *n.* the act or an instance of persecuting; the state of being persecuted. □ **persecution complex** (or **mania**) an irrational obsessive fear that others are scheming against one.
■ oppression, maltreatment, ill-treatment, abuse, molestation, victimization, tyrannization, punishment, torment, torture; hectoring, bullying, badgering, harassment.

perseverance /pérsivéeranss/ *n.* **1** the steadfast pursuit of an objective. **2** (often foll. by *in*) constant persistence (in a belief etc.). [ME f. OF f. L *perseverantia* (as PERSEVERE)]
■ **1** persistence, steadfastness, determination, resolution, resolve, decision, firmness, purposefulness, pertinacity, staying power, stamina, sedulousness, assiduity, tirelessness, indefatigability, endurance, diligence, devotion, tenacity, doggedness.

perseverate /pərsévvərayt/ *v.intr.* **1** continue action etc. for an unusually or excessively long time. **2** *Psychol.* tend to prolong or repeat a response after the original stimulus has ceased. □□ **perseveration** /-ráysh'n/ *n.* [L *perseverare* (as PERSEVERE)]
■ **1** see PERSIST 1.

persevere /pérsivéer/ *v.intr.* (often foll. by *in*, *at*, *with*) continue steadfastly or determinedly; persist. [ME f. OF *perseverer* f. L *perseverare* persist f. *perseverus* very strict (as PER-, *severus* severe)]
■ persist, continue, be steadfast *or* staunch *or* constant, keep going, stand fast *or* firm, show determination, stop at nothing, go the distance, keep at it, stick to (it), *colloq.* stick at it, stick it out, hang on, soldier on, *US colloq.* hang in (there); (*persevere in* or *with* or *at*) endure, carry on *or* through, keep at *or* on *or* up, see through, cling to, stick to, go on with, *colloq.* stick with *or* at.

Persian /pérsh'n, -zh'n/ *n.* & *adj.* ● *n.* **1 a** a native or inhabitant of ancient or modern Persia (now Iran). **b** a person of Persian descent. **2** the language of ancient Persia or modern Iran. ¶ With modern reference the preferred terms are *Iranian* and *Farsi*. **3** (in full **Persian cat**) **a** a cat of a breed with long silky hair and a thick tail. **b** this breed. ● *adj.* of or relating to Persia or its people or language. □ **Persian carpet** (or **rug**) a carpet or rug of a traditional pattern made in Persia. **Persian lamb** the silky tightly curled fur of a young karakul, used in clothing. [ME f. OF *persien* f. med.L]

persiennes /pérsi-énz/ *n.pl.* window shutters, or outside blinds, with louvres. [F, fem. pl. of obs. *persien* Persian]

persiflage /pérsiflaazh/ *n.* light raillery, banter. [F *persifler* banter, formed as PER- + *siffler* whistle]
■ see RAILLERY.

persimmon /persímmən/ *n.* **1** any usu. tropical evergreen tree of the genus *Diospyros* bearing edible tomato-like fruits. **2** the fruit of this. [corrupt. of an Algonquian word]

persist /pərsíst/ *v.intr.* **1** (often foll. by *in*) continue firmly or obstinately (in an opinion or a course of action) esp. despite obstacles, remonstrance, etc. **2** (of an institution, custom, phenomenon, etc.) continue in existence; survive. [L *persistere* (as PER-, *sistere* stand)]
■ **1** be persistent, insist, stand firm *or* fast, be steadfast *or* staunch; perseverate; see also PERSEVERE. **2** remain, continue, endure, carry on, keep up *or* on, last, linger, stay; see also SURVIVE 1.

persistent /pərsístənt/ *adj.* **1** continuing obstinately; persisting. **2** enduring. **3** constantly repeated (*persistent nagging*). **4** *Biol.* (of horns, leaves, etc.) remaining instead of falling off in the normal manner. □□ **persistence** *n.* **persistency** *n.* **persistently** *adv.*
■ **1** persisting, persevering, tenacious, steadfast, firm, fast, fixed, staunch, resolute, resolved, determined, unfaltering, unswerving, undeviating, unflagging, tireless, untiring, indefatigable, dogged, unwavering, stubborn, obstinate, obdurate, inflexible, rigid. **2, 3** continuing, enduring, lasting, persisting; constant, continuous, continual, unending, interminable, unremitting, unrelenting, perpetual, incessant, unceasing, non-stop. □□ **persistence** perseverance, resolve, determination, resolution, steadfastness, tenacity, constancy, assiduity, stamina, tirelessness, indefatigability, patience, diligence, pertinacity, doggedness, stubbornness, obstinacy, obduracy; perseveration.

person /pérs'n/ *n.* **1** an individual human being (*a cheerful and forthright person*). **2** the living body of a human being (*hidden about your person*). **3** *Gram.* any of three classes of personal pronouns, verb-forms, etc.: the person speaking (**first person**); the person spoken to (**second person**); the person spoken of (**third person**). **4** (in *comb.*) used to replace *-man* in offices open to either sex (*salesperson*). **5** (in Christianity) God as Father, Son, or Holy Ghost (*three persons in one God*). **6** *euphem.* the genitals (*expose one's person*). **7** a character in a play or story. □ **in one's own person** oneself; as oneself. **in person** physically present. **person-to-person 1** between individuals. **2** (of a phone call) booked through the operator to a specified person. [ME f. OF *persone* f. L *persona* actor's mask, character in a play, human being]
■ **1** individual, human (being), being, (living) soul; *Brit. colloq.* bod; mortal, *archaic* wight; (*persons*) people. □ **in person** physically, personally, bodily, actually, in the flesh, *in propria persona*, *colloq.* large as life; oneself.

persona /persónə/ *n.* (*pl.* **personae** /-nee/) **1** an aspect of the personality as shown to or perceived by others (opp. ANIMA). **2** *Literary criticism* an author's assumed character in his or her writing. □ ***persona grata*** /graátə/ a person, esp. a diplomat, acceptable to certain others. ***persona non grata*** /non, nōn graátə/ a person not acceptable. [L (as PERSON)]
■ **1** face, front, façade, mask, guise, exterior, role, part, character, identity; self.

personable /pérsənəb'l/ *adj.* pleasing in appearance and behaviour. □□ **personableness** *n.* **personably** *adv.*

personage /pérsənij/ *n.* **1** a person, esp. of rank or importance. **2** a character in a play etc. [ME f. PERSON + -AGE, infl. by med.L *personagium* effigy & F *personnage*]
■ **1** celebrity, luminary, VIP, name, notable, somebody, personality, star, magnate, mogul, big noise, *colloq.* big shot, hot stuff, *esp. US colloq.* hotshot, *US sl.* big wheel; see also BIGWIG.

personal /pérsən'l/ *adj.* **1** one's own; individual; private. **2** done or made in person (*made a personal appearance*; *my personal attention*). **3** directed to or concerning an individual (*a personal letter*). **4 a** referring (esp. in a hostile way) to an individual's private life or concerns (*making personal remarks*; *no need to be personal*). **b** close, intimate (*a personal friend*). **5** of the body and clothing (*personal hygiene*; *personal appearance*). **6** existing as a person, not as an abstraction or thing (*a personal God*). **7** *Gram.* of or denoting one of the three persons (*personal pronoun*). □ **personal column** the part of a newspaper devoted to private advertisements or messages. **personal computer** a computer designed for use by a single individual, esp. in an office or business environment. **personal equation 1** the allowance for an individual person's time of reaction in making observations, esp. in astronomy. **2** a bias or prejudice. **personal equity plan** a scheme for limited personal investment in shares, unit trusts, etc. **personal identification number** a number allocated to an individual, serving as a password esp. for a cash dispenser, computer, etc. **personal organizer 1** a loose-leaf notebook with sections for various kinds of information, including a diary etc. **2** a hand-held microcomputer serving the same purpose. **personal pronoun** a pronoun replacing the subject, object, etc., of a clause etc., e.g. *I*, *we*, *you*, *them*, *us*. **personal property** (or **estate**) *Law* all one's property except land and those interests in land that pass to one's heirs (cf. REAL[1] *adj.* 3). **personal service** individual service given to a customer. **personal stereo** a small portable audio cassette player, often with radio, or compact disc player, used with lightweight headphones. **personal touch** a way of treating a matter characteristic of or designed for an individual. [ME f. OF f. L *personalis* (as PERSON)]

■ **1** private, particular; see also INDIVIDUAL *adj.* 2–4. **2** physical, bodily, actual, live. **3** private, confidential, intimate; unofficial. **4 a** see FAMILIAR *adj.* 4. **b** see INTIMATE[1] *adj.* 1. □ **personal property** (or **estate**) *Law* personalty.

personality /pérsənálliti/ *n.* (*pl.* **-ies**) **1** the distinctive character or qualities of a person, often as distinct from others (*an attractive personality*). **2** a famous person; a celebrity (*a TV personality*). **3** a person who stands out from others by virtue of his or her character (*is a real personality*). **4** personal existence or identity; the condition of being a person. **5** (usu. in *pl.*) personal remarks. □ **have personality** have a lively character or noteworthy qualities. **personality cult** the extreme adulation of an individual. [ME f. OF *personalité* f. LL *personalitas -tatis* (as PERSONAL)]

■ **1** character, nature, temperament, disposition, make-up, persona; identity. **2** celebrity, luminary, star, superstar, name, somebody, *US* headliner. **3** see CHARACTER *n.* 4.

personalize /pérsənəlīz/ *v.tr.* (also **-ise**) **1** make personal, esp. by marking with one's name etc. **2** personify. □□ **personalization** /-záysh'n/ *n.*

■ **1** monogram, initial, individualize; sign, autograph. **2** humanize, personify, anthropomorphize.

personally /pérsənəli/ *adv.* **1** in person (*see to it personally*). **2** for one's own part (*speaking personally*). **3** in the form of a person (*a God existing personally*). **4** in a personal manner (*took the criticism personally*). **5** as a person; on a personal level.

■ **1** in person, oneself. **2** in one's (own) view *or* opinion, for one's part, for oneself, as far as one is concerned, from one's own viewpoint, from where one stands, as one sees it, as for oneself. **3** in the flesh, bodily, physically; actually. **5** as an individual, as a person.

personalty /pérsənəlti/ *n.* (*pl.* **-ies**) *Law* one's personal property or estate (opp. REALTY). [AF *personalté* (as PERSONAL)]

personate /pérsənayt/ *v.tr.* **1** play the part of (a character in a drama etc.; another type of person). **2** pretend to be (another person), esp. for fraudulent purposes; impersonate. □□ **personation** /-náysh'n/ *n.* **personator** *n.* [LL *personare personat-* (as PERSON)]

■ see ACT *v.* 5a.

personhood /pérsənhood/ *n.* the quality or condition of being an individual person.

personification /pərsónnifikáysh'n/ *n.* **1** the act of personifying. **2** (foll. by *of*) a person or thing viewed as a striking example of (a quality etc.) (*the personification of ugliness*).

■ **2** see *embodiment* (EMBODY).

personify /pərsónnifī/ *v.tr.* (**-ies, -ied**) **1** attribute a personal nature to (an abstraction or thing). **2** symbolize (a quality etc.) by a figure in human form. **3** (usu. as **personified** *adj.*) embody (a quality) in one's own person; exemplify typically (*has always been kindness personified*). □□ **personifier** *n.* [F *personnifier* (as PERSON)]

■ **1** humanize, personalize, anthropomorphize. **3** embody, typify, exemplify, epitomize, be the embodiment of, manifest, represent, stand for, symbolize, incarnate.

personnel /pérsənél/ *n.* a body of employees, persons involved in a public undertaking, armed forces, etc. □ **personnel carrier** an armoured vehicle for transporting troops etc. **personnel department** etc. the part of an organization concerned with the appointment, training, and welfare of employees. [F, orig. adj. = personal]

■ see STAFF[1] *n.* 2.

perspective /pərspéktiv/ *n.* & *adj.* ● *n.* **1 a** the art of drawing solid objects on a two-dimensional surface so as to give the right impression of relative positions, size, etc. **b** a picture drawn in this way. **2** the apparent relation between visible objects as to position, distance, etc. **3** a mental view of the relative importance of things (*keep the right perspective*). **4** a geographical or imaginary prospect. ● *adj.* of or in perspective. □ **in perspective 1** drawn or viewed according to the rules of perspective. **2** correctly regarded in terms of relative importance. □□ **perspectival** /-tīv'l/ *adj.* **perspectively** *adv.* [ME f. med.L *perspectiva* (*ars* art) f. *perspicere perspect-* (as PER-, *specere spect-* look)]

■ *n.* **3** attitude, position, angle, approach, sentiment, outlook, lookout. **4** (point of) view, viewpoint, standpoint, prospect, vantage point, position, angle.

Perspex /pérspeks/ *n. propr.* a tough light transparent acrylic thermoplastic used instead of glass. [L *perspicere* look through (as PER-, *specere* look)]

perspicacious /pérspikáyshəss/ *adj.* having mental penetration or discernment. □□ **perspicaciously** *adv.* **perspicaciousness** *n.* **perspicacity** /-kássiti/ *n.* [L *perspicax -acis* (as PERSPEX)]

■ see SHREWD. □□ **perspicaciousness, perspicacity** see INSIGHT.

perspicuous /pərspíkyooəss/ *adj.* **1** easily understood; clearly expressed. **2** (of a person) expressing things clearly. □□ **perspicuity** /pérspikyoo-iti/ *n.* **perspicuously** *adv.* **perspicuousness** *n.* [ME, = transparent f. L *perspicuus* (as PERSPECTIVE)]

■ see CLEAR *adj.* 6b. □□ **perspicuity, perspicuousness** see WISDOM 2, 3.

perspiration /pérspiráysh'n/ *n.* **1** = SWEAT. **2** sweating. □□ **perspiratory** /-spírrətəri, -tri/ *adj.* [F (as PERSPIRE)]

■ **1** sweat, dampness, wetness. **2** sweating, *Med.* diaphoresis.

perspire /pərspír/ *v.* **1** *intr.* sweat or exude perspiration, esp. as the result of heat, exercise, anxiety, etc. **2** *tr.* sweat or exude (fluid etc.). [F *perspirer* f. L *perspirare* (as PER-, *spirare* breathe)]

■ sweat, glow.

persuade /pərswáyd/ *v.tr.* & *refl.* **1** (often foll. by *of*, or *that* + clause) cause (another person or oneself) to believe; convince (*persuaded them that it would be helpful*; *tried to persuade me of its value*). **2 a** (often foll. by *to* + infin.) induce (another person or oneself) (*persuaded us to join them*; *managed to persuade them at last*). **b** (foll. by *away from*, *down to*, etc.) lure, attract, entice, etc. (*persuaded them away from the pub*). □□ **persuadable** *adj.* **persuadability** /-swáydəbílliti/ *n.* **persuasible** *adj.* [L *persuadēre* (as PER-, *suadēre suas-* advise)]

■ **1** convince; bring round, win over, convert; assure. **2 a** induce, prevail (up)on, exhort, importune, prompt, sway. **b** see LURE[1] *v.*

persuader /pərswáydər/ *n.* **1** a person who persuades. **2** *sl.* a gun or other weapon.

persuasion /pərswáyzh'n/ *n.* **1** persuading (*yielded to persuasion*). **2** persuasiveness (*use all your persuasion*). **3** a belief or conviction (*my private persuasion*). **4** a religious belief, or the group or sect holding it (*of a different persuasion*). **5** *colloq.* any group or party (*the male persuasion*). [ME f. L *persuasio* (as PERSUADE)]

■ **1** inducement, influence, exhortation; see also *encouragement* (ENCOURAGE). **3** opinion, creed, faith, conviction, set of beliefs; see also BELIEF 1. **4** religion, (religious) conviction; sect, denomination, faction, school (of thought), affiliation, group. **5** see SET[2] 3.

persuasive /pərswáysiv/ *adj.* able to persuade. ▫▫ **persuasively** *adv.* **persuasiveness** *n.* [F *persuasif -ive* or med.L *persuasivus*, (as PERSUADE)]
■ convincing, influential, effective, productive, impressive, efficacious, cogent, weighty, compelling, forceful, valid, winning, authoritative.

PERT *abbr.* programme evaluation and review technique.

pert /pert/ *adj.* **1** saucy or impudent, esp. in speech or conduct. **2** (of clothes etc.) neat and suggestive of jauntiness. **3** = PEART. ▫▫ **pertly** *adv.* **pertness** *n.* [ME f. OF *apert* f. L *apertus* past part. of *aperire* open & f. OF *aspert* f. L *expertus* EXPERT]
■ **1** forward, brash, brazen, cheeky, insolent, impertinent, flippant, saucy, bold, presumptuous, impudent, disrespectful, out of line, audacious, rude, impolite, uncivil, ill-mannered, unmannerly, brassy, *archaic* malapert, *colloq.* fresh, flip, wise-guy, *sl.* smart-arsed. **2** lively, neat, dapper, sprightly, brisk, cheerful, bright, perky; see also JAUNTY.

pertain /pərtáyn/ *v.intr.* **1** (foll. by *to*) **a** relate or have reference to. **b** belong to as a part or appendage or accessory. **2** (usu. foll. by *to*) be appropriate to. [ME f. OF *partenir* f. L *pertinēre* (as PER-, *tenēre* hold)]
■ **1 a** (*pertain to*) concern, refer to, have reference *or* relation to, apply to, relate to, include, cover, affect, appertain to, bear on, have bearing on. **2** be appropriate to, be fitting for, befit, suit.

pertinacious /pértináyshəss/ *adj.* stubborn; persistent; obstinate (in a course of action etc.). ▫▫ **pertinaciously** *adv.* **pertinaciousness** *n.* **pertinacity** /-nássiti/ *n.* [L *pertinax* (as PER-, *tenax* tenacious)]
■ see STUBBORN. ▫▫ **pertinaciousness, pertinacity** see *obstinacy* (OBSTINATE).

pertinent /pértinənt/ *adj.* **1** (often foll. by *to*) relevant to the matter in hand; apposite. **2** to the point. ▫▫ **pertinence** *n.* **pertinency** *n.* **pertinently** *adv.* [ME f. OF *pertinent* or L *pertinēre* (as PERTAIN)]
■ **1** fitting, suitable, apt, relevant, germane, apropos, apposite; see APPROPRIATE *adj.* **2** see INCISIVE 2.

perturb /pərtúrb/ *v.tr.* **1** throw into confusion or disorder. **2** disturb mentally; agitate. **3** *Physics* & *Math.* subject (a physical system, or a set of equations, or its solution) to a perturbation. ▫▫ **perturbable** *adj.* **perturbative** /pərtúrbətiv, pértərbaytiv/ *adj.* **perturbingly** *adv.* [ME f. OF *pertourber* f. L (as PER-, *turbare* disturb)]
■ **1** see DISORDER *v.* **2** upset, disturb, fluster, ruffle, unsettle, disconcert, make uneasy, discomfit, vex, worry, agitate, shake up, alarm, disquiet, confuse, discompose, unnerve.

perturbation /pértərbáysh'n/ *n.* **1** the act or an instance of perturbing; the state of being perturbed. **2** a cause of disturbance or agitation. **3** *Physics* a slight alteration of a physical system, e.g. of the electrons in an atom, caused by a secondary influence. **4** *Astron.* a minor deviation in the course of a celestial body, caused by the attraction of a neighbouring body.
■ **1** see FLUSTER *n.*

pertussis /pərtússiss/ *n.* whooping cough. [mod.L f. PER- + L *tussis* cough]

peruke /pəro͞ok/ *n. hist.* a wig. [F *perruque* f. It. *perrucca parrucca*, of unkn. orig.]

peruse /pəro͞oz/ *v.tr.* **1** (also *absol.*) read or study, esp. thoroughly or carefully. **2** examine (a person's face etc.) carefully. ▫▫ **perusal** *n.* **peruser** *n.* [ME, orig. = use up, prob. f. AL f. Rmc (as PER-, USE)]
■ read, study, scrutinize, examine, inspect, review, look over *or* through, go over *or* through; scan, run one's eye over; search, explore, survey, appraise. ▫▫ **perusal** reading, scrutiny, check, examination, study, inspection, scanning, review.

Peruvian /pəro͞oviən/ *n.* & *adj.* ● *n.* **1** a native or national of Peru. **2** a person of Peruvian descent. ● *adj.* of or relating to Peru. ▫ **Peruvian bark** the bark of the cinchona tree. [mod.L *Peruvia* Peru]

perv /perv/ *n.* & *v.* (also **perve**) *sl.* ● *n.* **1** a sexual pervert. **2** *Austral.* an erotic gaze. ● *v.intr.* **1** act like a sexual pervert. **2** (foll. by *at, on*) *Austral.* gaze with erotic interest. [abbr.]

pervade /pərváyd/ *v.tr.* **1** spread throughout, permeate. **2** (of influences etc.) become widespread among or in. **3** be rife among or through. ▫▫ **pervasion** /-váyzh'n/ *n.* [L *pervadere* (as PER-, *vadere vas-* go)]
■ **1, 2** see PERMEATE. **3** see INFEST.

pervasive /pərváysiv/ *adj.* **1** pervading. **2** able to pervade. ▫▫ **pervasively** *adv.* **pervasiveness** *n.*
■ **1** penetrating, pervading, permeating, omnipresent, general, inescapable, prevalent, universal, widespread, ubiquitous.

perve var. of PERV.

perverse /pərvérss/ *adj.* **1** (of a person or action) deliberately or stubbornly departing from what is reasonable or required. **2** persistent in error. **3** wayward; intractable; peevish. **4** perverted; wicked. **5** (of a verdict etc.) against the weight of evidence or the judge's direction. ▫▫ **perversely** *adv.* **perverseness** *n.* **perversity** *n.* (*pl.* **-ies**). [ME f. OF *pervers perverse* f. L *perversus* (as PERVERT)]
■ **2** wrong, wrong-headed, awry, contrary, wayward, incorrect, irregular, improper, contradictory. **3** stubborn, self-willed, wayward, wrong-headed, intractable, wilful, obdurate, obstinate, pigheaded, adamant, inflexible, unbending, refractory, unyielding; cantankerous, testy, curmudgeonly, churlish, crusty, crotchety, bad-tempered, awkward, petulant, captious, cross, cross-grained, peevish, waspish, snappish, bilious, splenetic, fractious, ill-tempered, quarrelsome, irascible, sullen, contentious, touchy, obstreperous, crabby, crabbed, irritable, surly, *esp. US* cranky, *colloq.* grouchy, *Brit. colloq.* stroppy. **4** see ROTTEN 2a.

perversion /pərvérsh'n/ *n.* **1** an act of perverting; the state of being perverted. **2** a perverted form of an act or thing. **3 a** preference for an abnormal form of sexual activity. **b** such an activity. [ME f. L *perversio* (as PERVERT)]
■ **1** deviation, diversion, misdirection, corruption, subversion, distortion, twisting, falsification, misrepresentation. **3 b** deviation, deviance, deviancy, abnormality, depravity, debauchery, *colloq.* kinkiness; unnatural act, vice, aberration.

pervert *v.* & *n.* ● *v.tr.* /pərvért/ **1** turn (a person or thing) aside from its proper use or nature. **2** misapply or misconstrue (words etc.). **3** lead astray (a person, a person's mind, etc.) from right opinion or conduct, or esp. religious belief. **4** (as **perverted** *adj.*) showing perversion. ● *n.* /pérvert/ **1** a perverted person. **2** a person showing sexual perversion. ▫▫ **perversive** /pərvérsiv/ *adj.* **pervertedly** /pərvértidli/ *adv.* **perverter** /-vértər/ *n.* [ME f. OF *pervertir* or f. L *pervertere* (as PER-, *vertere vers-* turn): cf. CONVERT]
■ *v.* **1, 2** deflect, divert, sidetrack, turn aside *or* away, subvert, misdirect, distort, twist, abuse, falsify, misapply, misconstrue, misrepresent, corrupt. **3** lead astray, degrade, corrupt, *archaic* demoralize. **4** (**perverted**) deviant, deviate, abnormal, amoral, unmoral, immoral, bad, depraved, unnatural, warped, twisted, profligate, dissolute, delinquent, degenerate, evil, wicked, malign, malicious, malevolent, evil-minded, sinful, iniquitous, base, foul, corrupt, unprincipled, *literary* malefic. ● *n.* **1** see WEIRDO. **2** deviant, degenerate, debauchee, deviate.

pervious /pérviəss/ *adj.* **1** permeable. **2** (usu. foll. by *to*) **a** affording passage. **b** accessible (to reason etc.). ▫▫ **perviousness** *n.* [L *pervius* (as PER-, *vius* f. *via* way)]
■ **1** see POROUS 1, 2. **2 b** see RECEPTIVE.

Pesach /páysaakh/ *n.* the Passover festival. [Heb. *Pesaḥ*]

peseta /pəsáytə/ *n.* the chief monetary unit of Spain, orig. a silver coin. [Sp., dimin. of *pesa* weight f. L *pensa* pl. of *pensum*: see POISE[1]]

pesky /péski/ *adj.* (**peskier**, **peskiest**) esp. *US colloq.* troublesome; confounded; annoying. ▫▫ **peskily** *adv.* **peskiness** *n.* [18th c.: perh. f. PEST]

■ see TROUBLESOME 2.

peso /páysō/ *n.* (*pl.* **-os**) **1** the chief monetary unit of several Latin American countries and of the Philippines. **2** a note or coin worth one peso. [Sp., = weight, f. L *pensum*: see POISE[1]]

pessary /péssəri/ *n.* (*pl.* **-ies**) *Med.* **1** a device worn in the vagina to support the uterus or as a contraceptive. **2** a vaginal suppository. [ME f. LL *pessarium*, *pessulum* f. *pessum*, *pessus* f. Gk *pessos* oval stone]

pessimism /péssimiz'm/ *n.* **1** a tendency to take the worst view or expect the worst outcome. **2** *Philos.* a belief that this world is as bad as it could be or that all things tend to evil (opp. OPTIMISM). □□ **pessimist** *n.* **pessimistic** /-místik/ *adj.* **pessimistically** /-místikəli/ *adv.* [L *pessimus* worst, after OPTIMISM]
■ **1** defeatism, negativity, cynicism; discouragement, gloom, melancholy, despondency, hopelessness, despair. □□ **pessimist** see MISERY 3. **pessimistic** gloomy, negative, despairing, depressed, despondent, dejected, downhearted, heavy-hearted, defeatist, glum, unhappy, cheerless, joyless, cynical, bleak, hopeless, forlorn.

pest /pest/ *n.* **1** a troublesome or annoying person or thing; a nuisance. **2** a destructive animal, esp. an insect which attacks crops, livestock, etc. **3** *archaic* a pestilence; a plague. □ **pest-house** *hist.* a hospital for sufferers from the plague etc. [F *peste* or L *pestis* plague]
■ **1** nuisance, annoyance, nag, irritant, bother, gadfly, bane, trial, vexation, curse, thorn in one's flesh *or* side, *colloq.* pain (in the neck), *esp. US sl.* pain in the butt. **3** see PLAGUE *n.* 1.

pester /péstər/ *v.tr.* trouble or annoy, esp. with frequent or persistent requests. □□ **pesterer** *n.* [prob. f. *impester* f. F *empestrer* encumber: infl. by PEST]
■ annoy, nag, irritate, irk, bother, get at *or* to, badger, plague, vex, fret, hector, harass, harry, heckle, nettle, chafe, pique, provoke, exasperate, bedevil, get *or* grate on a person's nerves, torment, persecute, chivvy, *colloq.* drive a person up the wall, get under a person's skin, get in a person's hair, hassle, needle, give a person the needle, peeve, *sl.* bug; trouble, importune.

pesticide /péstisīd/ *n.* a substance used for destroying insects or other organisms harmful to cultivated plants or to animals. □□ **pesticidal** /-sīd'l/ *adj.*

pestiferous /pestíffərəss/ *adj.* **1** noxious; pestilent. **2** harmful; pernicious; bearing moral contagion. [L *pestifer*, *-ferus* (as PEST)]
■ pestilential; see also HARMFUL.

pestilence /péstilənss/ *n.* **1** a fatal epidemic disease, esp. bubonic plague. **2** something evil or destructive. [ME f. OF f. L *pestilentia* (as PESTILENT)]
■ **1** plague, epidemic, pandemic, Black Death, *archaic* pest. **2** scourge, blight, curse, cancer, canker, bane, affliction.

pestilent /péstilənt/ *adj.* **1** destructive to life, deadly. **2** harmful or morally destructive. **3** *colloq.* troublesome; annoying. □□ **pestilently** *adv.* [L *pestilens*, *pestilentus* f. *pestis* plague]

pestilential /péstilénsh'l/ *adj.* **1** of or relating to pestilence. **2** dangerous; troublesome; pestilent. □□ **pestilentially** *adv.* [ME f. med.L *pestilentialis* f. L *pestilentia* (as PESTILENT)]
■ **2** see HARMFUL, TROUBLESOME 2.

pestle /péss'l/ *n.* & *v.* ● *n.* **1** a club-shaped instrument for pounding substances in a mortar. **2** an appliance for pounding etc. ● *v.* **1** *tr.* pound with a pestle or in a similar manner. **2** *intr.* use a pestle. [ME f. OF *pestel* f. L *pistillum* f. *pinsare pist-* to pound]

pestology /pestólləji/ *n.* the scientific study of pests (esp. harmful insects) and of methods of dealing with them. □□ **pestological** /-stəlójik'l/ *adj.* **pestologist** *n.*

Pet. *abbr.* Peter (New Testament).

pet[1] /pet/ *n.*, *adj.*, & *v.* ● *n.* **1** a domestic or tamed animal kept for pleasure or companionship. **2** a darling, a favourite (often as a term of endearment). ● *attrib.adj.* **1** kept as a pet (*pet lamb*). **2** of or for pet animals (*pet food*). **3** often *joc.* favourite or particular (*pet aversion*). **4** expressing fondness or familiarity (*pet name*). ● *v.tr.* (**petted, petting**) **1** treat as a pet. **2** (also *absol.*) fondle, esp. erotically. □□ **petter** *n.* [16th-c. Sc. & N.Engl. dial.: orig. unkn.]
■ *n.* **2** darling, favourite, idol, apple of one's eye, *Brit. colloq. usu. derog.* blue-eyed boy, *derog.* minion. ● *attrib.adj.* **1** tame, trained, domesticated; broken, house-broken, house-trained. **3** favourite, favoured, preferred, cherished, special, particular; prized, treasured, precious, dearest, adored, darling. ● *v.* **1** pamper, favour, baby, coddle, cosset, mollycoddle, spoil, indulge, dote on. **2** caress, fondle, stroke, pat; cuddle, snuggle, *colloq.* neck, smooch, canoodle, *Austral.* & *NZ* smoodge.

pet[2] /pet/ *n.* a feeling of petty resentment or ill-humour (esp. *be in a pet*). [16th c.: orig. unkn.]
■ (bad *or* ill) temper, fit of pique, sulk, (bad) mood, fume, *Brit. colloq.* paddy, *sl.* wax.

peta- /péttə/ *comb. form* denoting a factor of 10^{15}. [perh. f. PENTA-]

petal /pétt'l/ *n.* each of the parts of the corolla of a flower. □□ **petaline** /-līn, -lin/ *adj.* **petalled** *adj.* (also in *comb.*). **petal-like** *adj.* **petaloid** *adj.* [mod.L *petalum*, in LL metal plate f. Gk *petalon* leaf f. *petalos* outspread]

petard /pitaárd/ *n. hist.* **1** a small bomb used to blast down a door etc. **2** a kind of firework or cracker. □ **hoist with one's own petard** affected oneself by one's schemes against others. [F *pétard* f. *péter* break wind]

petasus /péttəsəss/ *n.* an ancient Greek hat with a low crown and broad brim, esp. (in Greek mythology) as worn by Hermes. [L f. Gk *petasos*]

petaurist /pətáwrist/ *n.* any flying squirrel of the genus *Petaurista*, native to E. Asia. [Gk *petauristēs* performer on a springboard (*petauron*)]

Pete /peet/ *n.* □ **for Pete's sake** see SAKE[1]. [abbr. of the name *Peter*]

petechia /piteékiə/ *n.* (*pl.* **petechiae** /-ki-ee/) *Med.* a small red or purple spot as a result of bleeding into the skin. □□ **petechial** *adj.* [mod.L f. It. *petecchia* a freckle or spot on one's face]

peter[1] /peétər/ *v.* & *n.* ● *v.intr.* **1** (foll. by *out*) (orig. of a vein of ore etc.) diminish, come to an end. **2** *Bridge* play an echo. ● *n. Bridge* an echo. [19th c.: orig. unkn.]
■ *v.* **1** (*peter out*) diminish, evaporate, wane, come to nothing, die out, disappear, fail, fade (out *or* away), dwindle, run out, give out, flag, melt away.

peter[2] /peétər/ *n. sl.* **1** a prison cell. **2** a safe. [perh. f. the name *Peter*]

peterman /peétərmən/ *n.* (*pl.* **-men**) *sl.* a safe-breaker.

Peter Pan /peétər pán/ *n.* a person who retains youthful features, or who is immature. [hero of J. M. Barrie's play of the same name (1904)]

Peter Principle /peétər/ *n. joc.* the principle that members of a hierarchy are promoted until they reach the level at which they are no longer competent. [L. J. *Peter*, its propounder, b. 1919]

petersham /peétərshəm/ *n.* thick corded silk ribbon used for stiffening in dressmaking etc. [Lord *Petersham*, Engl. army officer d. 1851]

Peter's pence /peétərz/ *n.pl. RC Ch.* **1** *hist.* an annual tax of one penny, formerly paid to the papal see. **2** (since 1860) a voluntary payment to the papal treasury. [St *Peter*, as first pope]

pethidine /péthideen/ *n.* a synthetic soluble analgesic used esp. in childbirth. [perh. f. PIPERIDINE (from which the drug is derived) + ETHYL]

petiole /péttiōl/ *n.* the slender stalk joining a leaf to a stem. □□ **petiolar** *adj.* **petiolate** /péttiəlayt/ *adj.* [F *pétiole* f. L *petiolus* little foot, stalk]

petit /pétti/ *adj.* esp. *Law* petty; small; of lesser importance. □ **petit jury** = *petty jury*. [ME f. OF, = small, f. Rmc, perh. imit. of child's speech]

petit bourgeois /pétti bóorzhwaa/ *n.* (*pl.* **petits bourgeois** *pronunc.* same) a member of the lower middle classes. [F]

petite /pәtéet/ *adj.* (of a woman) of small and dainty build. □ **petite bourgeoisie** the lower middle classes. [F, fem. of PETIT]
■ delicate, dainty, diminutive, small, little, slight, tiny, small-boned, *Brit. colloq.* dinky.

petit four /pétti fór/ *n.* (*pl.* **petits fours** /fórz/) a very small fancy cake, biscuit, or sweet. [F, = little oven]

petition /pitísh'n/ *n.* & *v.* ● *n.* **1** a supplication or request. **2** a formal written request, esp. one signed by many people, appealing to authority in some cause. **3** *Law* an application to a court for a writ etc. ● *v.* **1** *tr.* make or address a petition to (*petition your MP*). **2** *intr.* (often foll. by *for*, *to*) appeal earnestly or humbly. □ **Petition of Right 1** *hist.* a parliamentary declaration of rights and liberties of the people assented to by Charles I in 1628. **2** *Law* a common-law remedy against the crown for the recovery of property. □□ **petitionable** *adj.* **petitionary** *adj.* **petitioner** *n.* [ME f. OF f. L *petitio -onis*]
■ *n.* **1** request, application, solicitation, suit, entreaty, supplication, plea, appeal. ● *v.* **1** request, ask, apply to, solicit, call upon. **2** supplicate, plead; (*petition for* or *to*) entreat, beseech, implore, importune, pray; see also APPEAL *v.* 1.

petitio principii /pitíshiō prinkíppi-ī/ *n.* a logical fallacy in which a conclusion is taken for granted in the premiss; begging the question. [L, = assuming a principle: see PETITION]

petit-maître /pәtimáytrә/ *n.* a dandy or coxcomb. [F, = little master]

petit mal /pétti mál/ *n.* a mild form of epilepsy with only momentary loss of consciousness (cf. GRAND MAL). [F, = little sickness]

petit point /pәti pwáɴ, pétti póynt/ *n.* **1** embroidery on canvas using small stitches. **2** tent-stitch. [F, = little point]

petits pois /pétti pwaá/ *n.pl.* small green peas. [F]

Petrarchan /pitraárkәn/ *adj.* denoting a sonnet of the kind used by the Italian poet Petrarch (d. 1374), with an octave rhyming abbaabba, and a sestet usu. rhyming cdcdcd or cdecde.

petrel /pétrәl/ *n.* any of various sea birds of the family Procellariidae or Hydrobatidae, usu. flying far from land. [17th c. (also *pitteral*), of uncert. orig.: later assoc. with St Peter (Matt. 14:30)]

Petri dish /pétri, péet-/ *n.* a shallow covered dish used for the culture of bacteria etc. [J. R. *Petri*, Ger. bacteriologist d. 1921]

petrifaction /pétrifáksh'n/ *n.* **1** the process of fossilization whereby organic matter is turned into a stony substance. **2** a petrified substance or mass. **3** a state of extreme fear or terror. [PETRIFY after *stupefaction*]

petrify /pétrifī/ *v.* (**-ies, -ied**) **1** *tr.* (also as **petrified** *adj.*) paralyse with fear, astonishment, etc. **2** *tr.* change (organic matter) into a stony substance. **3** *intr.* become like stone. **4** *tr.* deprive (the mind, a doctrine, etc.) of vitality; deaden. [F *pétrifier* f. med.L *petrificare* f. L *petra* rock f. Gk]
■ **1** frighten, scare, horrify, terrify, paralyse, numb, benumb; shock, dumbfound, strike dumb, stun, astonish, astound, amaze, confound, disconcert, stupefy, appal, *colloq.* flabbergast; (**petrified**) horrified, horror-struck, terrified, terror-stricken, panic-stricken, frightened, afraid, scared, paralysed, numbed, benumbed, frozen; shocked, speechless, dumbfounded, dumbstruck, stunned, thunderstruck, astonished, astounded, stupefied, appalled, aghast, *colloq.* flabbergasted. **2** ossify, fossilize, turn to stone. **4** see DEADEN.

petro- /pétrō/ *comb. form* **1** rock. **2** petroleum (*petrochemistry*). [Gk *petros* stone or *petra* rock]

petrochemical /pétrōkémmik'l/ *n.* & *adj.* ● *n.* a substance industrially obtained from petroleum or natural gas. ● *adj.* of or relating to petrochemistry or petrochemicals.

petrochemistry /pétrōkémmistri/ *n.* **1** the chemistry of rocks. **2** the chemistry of petroleum.

petrodollar /pétrōdollәr/ *n.* a notional unit of currency earned by a petroleum-exporting country.

petroglyph /pétrōglif/ *n.* a rock-carving, esp. a prehistoric one. [PETRO- + Gk *glyphē* carving]

petrography /petrógrәfi/ *n.* the scientific description of the composition and formation of rocks. □□ **petrographer** *n.* **petrographic** /-rәgráffik/ *adj.* **petrographical** /-rәgráffik'l/ *adj.*

petrol /pétrәl/ *n. Brit.* **1** refined petroleum used as a fuel in motor vehicles, aircraft, etc. **2** (*attrib.*) concerned with the supply of petrol (*petrol pump*; *petrol station*). □ **petrol bomb** a simple bomb made of a petrol-filled bottle and a wick. [F *pétrole* f. med.L *petroleum*: see PETROLEUM]

petrolatum /pétrәláytәm/ *n. US* petroleum jelly. [mod.L f. PETROL + *-atum*]

petroleum /pitrṓliәm/ *n.* a hydrocarbon oil found in the upper strata of the earth, refined for use as a fuel for heating and in internal-combustion engines, for lighting, dry-cleaning, etc. □ **petroleum ether** a volatile liquid distilled from petroleum, consisting of a mixture of hydrocarbons. **petroleum jelly** a translucent solid mixture of hydrocarbons used as a lubricant, ointment, etc. [med.L f. L *petra* rock f. Gk + L *oleum* oil]

petrolic /pitróllik/ *adj.* of or relating to petrol or petroleum.

petrology /pitróllәji/ *n.* the study of the origin, structure, composition, etc., of rocks. □□ **petrologic** /pétrәlójik/ *adj.* **petrological** /pétrәlójik'l/ *adj.* **petrologist** *n.*

petrous /pétrәss/ *adj.* **1** *Anat.* denoting the hard part of the temporal bone protecting the inner ear. **2** *Geol.* of, like, or relating to rock. [L *petrosus* f. L *petra* rock f. Gk]

petticoat /péttikōt/ *n.* **1** a woman's or girl's skirted undergarment hanging from the waist or shoulders. **2** *sl.* **a** a woman or girl. **b** (in *pl.*) the female sex. **3** (*attrib.*) often *derog.* feminine; associated with women (*petticoat pedantry*). □□ **petticoated** *adj.* **petticoatless** *adj.* [ME f. *petty coat*]

pettifog /péttifog/ *v.intr.* (**pettifogged, pettifogging**) **1** practise legal deception or trickery. **2** quibble or wrangle about petty points. [back-form. f. PETTIFOGGER]
■ **2** see QUIBBLE *v.*

pettifogger /péttifoggәr/ *n.* **1** a rascally lawyer; an inferior legal practitioner. **2** a petty practitioner in any activity. □□ **pettifoggery** *n.* **pettifogging** *adj.* [PETTY + *fogger* underhand dealer, prob. f. *Fugger* family of merchants in Augsburg in the 15th–16th c.]
■ □□ **pettifogging** see *legalistic* (LEGALISM).

pettish /péttish/ *adj.* peevish, petulant; easily put out. □□ **pettishly** *adv.* **pettishness** *n.* [PET[2] + -ISH[1]]
■ see PETULANT.

petty /pétti/ *adj.* (**pettier, pettiest**) **1** unimportant; trivial. **2** mean, small-minded; contemptible. **3** minor; inferior; on a small scale (*petty princes*). **4** *Law* (of a crime) of lesser importance (*petty sessions*) (cf. COMMON, GRAND). □ **petty bourgeois** = PETIT BOURGEOIS. **petty bourgeoisie** = *petite bourgeoisie*. **petty cash** money from or for small items of receipt or expenditure. **petty jury** a jury of 12 persons who try the final issue of fact in civil or criminal cases and pronounce a verdict. **petty officer** a naval NCO. **petty treason** see TREASON. □□ **pettily** *adv.* **pettiness** *n.* [ME *pety*, var. of PETIT]
■ **1** insignificant, unimportant, trivial, paltry, niggling, trifling, negligible, puny, inessential, non-essential, inconsequential, slight, nugatory, *Brit.* twopenny-halfpenny, *US* picayune, dinky, *colloq.* piddling. **2** miserly, mean, stingy, cheese-paring, grudging, small-minded, cheap, niggardly, parsimonious, ungenerous, tight, tight-fisted, close, close-fisted, *US* picayune, *Brit. colloq.* mingy. **3** inferior, *colloq.* measly, small-time; see also MINOR *adj.*

petulant /pétyoolәnt/ *adj.* peevishly impatient or irritable. □□ **petulance** *n.* **petulantly** *adv.* [F *pétulant* f. L *petulans -antis* f. *petere* seek]

■ peevish, pettish, impatient, ill-humoured, testy, waspish, irascible, choleric, cross, captious, ill-tempered, bad-tempered, splenetic, moody, sour, bilious, crabby, crabbed, irritable, huffish, huffy, perverse, snappish, crotchety, cantankerous, curmudgeonly, grumpy, *colloq.* grouchy.

petunia /pityōōniə/ *n.* **1** any plant of the genus *Petunia* with white, purple, red, etc., funnel-shaped flowers. **2** a dark violet or purple colour. [mod.L f. F *petun* f. Guarani *petȳ* tobacco]

petuntse /pitōōntsi, -túntsi/ *n.* a white variable feldspathic mineral used for making porcelain. [Chin. *baidunzi* f. *bai* white + *dun* stone + suffix *-zi*]

pew /pyōō/ *n.* & *v.* ● *n.* **1** (in a church) a long bench with a back; an enclosed compartment. **2** *Brit. colloq.* a seat (esp. *take a pew*). ● *v.tr.* furnish with pews. ▫▫ **pewage** *n.* **pewless** *adj.* [ME *pywe*, *puwe* f. OF *puye* balcony f. L *podia* pl. of PODIUM]

pewit var. of PEEWIT.

pewter /pyōōtər/ *n.* **1** a grey alloy of tin with copper and antimony (formerly tin and lead). **2** utensils made of this. **3** *sl.* a tankard etc. as a prize. ▫▫ **pewterer** *n.* [ME f. OF *peutre*, *peualtre* f. Rmc, of unkn. orig.]

peyote /payṓti/ *n.* **1** any Mexican cactus of the genus *Lophophora*, esp. *L. williamsii* having no spines and button-like tops when dried. **2** a hallucinogenic drug containing mescaline prepared from this. [Amer. Sp. f. Nahuatl *peyotl*]

Pf. *abbr.* pfennig.

Pfc. *abbr. US* Private First Class.

pfennig /pfénnig, fénnig/ *n.* a small German coin, worth one-hundredth of a mark. [G, rel. to PENNY]

PG *abbr.* **1** (of films) classified as suitable for children subject to parental guidance. **2** paying guest.

pH /peé-áych/ *n. Chem.* a logarithm of the reciprocal of the hydrogen-ion concentration in moles per litre of a solution, giving a measure of its acidity or alkalinity. [G, f. *Potenz* power + *H* (symbol for hydrogen)]

phaeton /fáyt'n/ *n.* **1** a light open four-wheeled carriage, usu. drawn by a pair of horses. **2** *US* a touring-car. [F *phaéton* f. L *Phaethon* f. Gk *Phaethōn*, son of Helios the sun god who was allowed to drive the sun-chariot for a day, with disastrous results]

phage /fayj, faazh/ *n.* = BACTERIOPHAGE. [abbr.]

phagocyte /fággəsīt/ *n.* a type of cell capable of engulfing and absorbing foreign matter, esp. a leucocyte ingesting bacteria in the body. ▫▫ **phagocytic** /-síttik/ *adj.* [Gk *phag-* eat + -CYTE]

phagocytosis /fággəsītṓsiss/ *n.* the ingestion of bacteria etc. by phagocytes. ▫▫ **phagocytize** *v.tr.* (also **-ise**). **phagocytose** *v.tr.*

-phagous /fəgəss/ *comb. form* that eats (as specified) (*ichthyophagous*). [L *-phagus* f. Gk *-phagos* f. *phagein* eat]

-phagy /fəji/ *comb. form* the eating of (specified food) (*ichthyophagy*). [Gk *-phagia* (as -PHAGOUS)]

phalange /fállanj/ *n.* **1** *Anat.* = PHALANX 4. **2** (**Phalange**) a right-wing activist Maronite party in Lebanon (cf. FALANGE). [F f. L *phalanx*: see PHALANX]

phalangeal /fəlánjiəl/ *adj. Anat.* of or relating to a phalanx.

phalanger /fəlánjər/ *n.* any of various marsupials of the family Phalangeridae, including cuscuses and possums. [F f. Gk *phalaggion* spider's web, f. the webbed toes of its hind feet]

phalanx /fállangks/ *n.* (*pl.* **phalanxes** or **phalanges** /fəllánjeez/) **1** *Gk Antiq.* a line of battle, esp. a body of Macedonian infantry drawn up in close order. **2** a set of people etc. forming a compact mass, or banded for a common purpose. **3** a bone of the finger or toe. **4** *Bot.* a bundle of stamens united by filaments. [L f. Gk *phalagx -ggos*]

phalarope /fállərōp/ *n.* any small wading or swimming bird of the subfamily Phalaropodidae, with a straight bill and lobed feet. [F f. mod.L *Phalaropus*, irreg. f. Gk *phalaris* coot + *pous podos* foot]

phalli *pl.* of PHALLUS.

phallic /fállik/ *adj.* **1** of, relating to, or resembling a phallus. **2** *Psychol.* denoting the stage of male sexual development characterized by preoccupation with the genitals. ▫▫ **phallically** *adv.* [F *phallique* & Gk *phallikos* (as PHALLUS)]

phallocentric /fállōséntrik/ *adj.* centred on the phallus or on male attitudes. ▫▫ **phallocentricity** /-trísiti/ *n.* **phallocentrism** /-triz'm/ *n.*

phallus /fálləss/ *n.* (*pl.* **phalli** /-lī/ or **phalluses**) **1** the (esp. erect) penis. **2** an image of this as a symbol of generative power in nature. ▫▫ **phallicism** /-lisiz'm/ *n.* **phallism** *n.* [LL f. Gk *phallos*]

phanariot /fənárriət/ *n. hist.* a member of a class of Greek officials in Constantinople under the Ottoman Empire. [mod.Gk *phanariōtēs* f. *Phanar* the part of the city where they lived f. Gk *phanarion* lighthouse (on the Golden Horn)]

phanerogam /fánnərəgam/ *n. Bot.* a plant that has stamens and pistils, a flowering plant (cf. CRYPTOGAM). ▫▫ **phanerogamic** /-gámmik/ *adj.* **phanerogamous** /-róggəməss/ *adj.* [F *phanérogame* f. Gk *phaneros* visible + *gamos* marriage]

phantasize var. of FANTASIZE.

phantasm /fántaz'm/ *n.* **1** an illusion, a phantom. **2** (usu. foll. by *of*) an illusory likeness. **3** a supposed vision of an absent (living or dead) person. ▫▫ **phantasmal** /-tázm'l/ *adj.* **phantasmic** /-tázmik/ *adj.* [ME f. OF *fantasme* f. L f. Gk *phantasma* f. *phantazō* make visible f. *phainō* show]

■ **1** see ILLUSION 4. **3** see VISION *n.* 2. ▫▫ **phantasmal** see INSUBSTANTIAL 2.

phantasmagoria /fántazməgóriə/ *n.* **1** a shifting series of real or imaginary figures as seen in a dream. **2** an optical device for rapidly varying the size of images on a screen. ▫▫ **phantasmagoric** /-górrik/ *adj.* **phantasmagorical** /-górrik'l/ *adj.* [prob. f. F *fantasmagorie* (as PHANTASM + fanciful ending)]

■ **1** see ILLUSION 4. ▫▫ **phantasmagorical** see INSUBSTANTIAL 2.

phantast var. of FANTAST.

phantasy var. of FANTASY.

phantom /fántəm/ *n.* & *adj.* ● *n.* **1** a ghost; an apparition; a spectre. **2** a form without substance or reality; a mental illusion. **3** *Med.* a model of the whole or part of the body used to practise or demonstrate operative or therapeutic methods. ● *adj.* merely apparent; illusory. ▫ **phantom circuit** an arrangement of telegraph or other electrical wires equivalent to an extra circuit. **phantom limb** a continuing sensation of the presence of a limb which has been amputated. **phantom pregnancy** *Med.* the symptoms of pregnancy in a person not actually pregnant. [ME f. OF *fantosme* ult. f. Gk *phantasma* (as PHANTASM)]

■ *n.* **1** apparition, spectre, ghost, spirit, phantasm, wraith, revenant, vision, eidolon, *colloq.* spook, *literary* shade. **2** figment (of the imagination), delusion, phantasm, chimera, hallucination, fancy, mirage; see also ILLUSION 3, 4. ● *adj.* see ILLUSORY.

Pharaoh /fáirō/ *n.* **1** the ruler of ancient Egypt. **2** the title of this ruler. ▫ **Pharaoh's serpent** an indoor firework burning and uncoiling in serpentine form. ▫▫ **Pharaonic** /fáirayónnik/ *adj.* [OE f. eccl.L *Pharao* f. Gk *Pharaō* f. Heb. *par'ōh* f. Egypt. *pr-'o* great house]

Pharisee /fárrisee/ *n.* **1** a member of an ancient Jewish sect, distinguished by strict observance of the traditional and written law. **2** a person of the spirit or disposition attributed to the Pharisees in the New Testament; a self-righteous person; a hypocrite. ▫▫ **Pharisaic** /fárrisáyik/ *adj.* **Pharisaical** /fárrisáyik'l/ *adj.* **Pharisaism** /fárrisayiz'm/ *n.* [OE *fariseus* & OF *pharise* f. eccl.L *pharisaeus* f. Gk *Pharisaios* f. Aram. *p'rīšayyâ* pl. f. Heb. *pārûš* separated]

■ **2** hypocrite, pretender, dissembler, humbug, fraud, whited sepulchre, pietist, charlatan, prig, *colloq.* goody, goody-goody. ▫▫ **Pharisaic, Pharisaical** hypocritical, insincere, self-righteous, pretentious, sanctimonious, pietistical, priggish, pietistic, *colloq.* goody-goody, holier-than-thou, smarmy.

pharmaceutical /fáarməsyóotik'l/ *adj.* & *n.* ● *adj.* **1** of or engaged in pharmacy. **2** of the use or sale of medicinal drugs. ● *n.* a medicinal drug. □□ **pharmaceutically** *adv.* **pharmaceutics** *n.* [LL *pharmaceuticus* f. Gk *pharmakeutikos* f. *pharmakeutēs* druggist f. *pharmakon* drug]
■ *n.* see MEDICINE. □□ **pharmaceutics** pharmacy.

pharmacist /fáarməsist/ *n.* a person qualified to prepare and dispense drugs.
■ pharmacologist, *Brit.* chemist, *esp. US* druggist, *archaic* apothecary.

pharmacognosy /fáarməkógnəsi/ *n.* the science of drugs, esp. relating to medicinal products in their natural or unprepared state. [Gk *pharmakon* drug + *gnōsis* knowledge]

pharmacology /fáarməkólləji/ *n.* the science of the action of drugs on the body. □□ **pharmacological** /-kəlójik'l/ *adj.* **pharmacologically** /-kəlójikəli/ *adv.* **pharmacologist** *n.* [mod.L *pharmacologia* f. Gk *pharmakon* drug]

pharmacopoeia /fáarməkəpéeə/ *n.* **1** a book, esp. one officially published, containing a list of drugs with directions for use. **2** a stock of drugs. □□ **pharmacopoeial** *adj.* [mod.L f. Gk *pharmakopoiia* f. *pharmakopoios* drug-maker (as PHARMACOLOGY + *-poios* making)]

pharmacy /fáarməsi/ *n.* (*pl.* **-ies**) **1** the preparation and the (esp. medicinal) dispensing of drugs. **2** a pharmacist's shop, a dispensary. [ME f. OF *farmacie* f. med.L *pharmacia* f. Gk *pharmakeia* practice of the druggist f. *pharmakeus* f. *pharmakon* drug]
■ **1** pharmaceutics. **2** dispensary, *Brit.* chemist, dispensing chemist, chemist's (shop), *esp. US* druggist, *US* drugstore, *archaic* apothecary.

pharos /fáiross/ *n.* a lighthouse or a beacon to guide sailors. [L f. Gk *Pharos* island off Alexandria where a famous lighthouse stood]

pharyngo- /fəringgō/ *comb. form* denoting the pharynx.

pharyngotomy /fárringgóttəmi/ *n.* (*pl.* **-ies**) an incision into the pharynx.

pharynx /fárringks/ *n.* (*pl.* **pharynges** /-rinjeez/) a cavity, with enclosing muscles and mucous membrane, behind the nose and mouth, and connecting them to the oesophagus. □□ **pharyngal** /-ringg'l/ *adj.* **pharyngeal** /-rinjéeəl/ *adj.* **pharyngitis** /-rinjītiss/ *n.* [mod.L f. Gk *pharugx -ggos*]

phase /fayz/ *n.* & *v.* ● *n.* **1** a distinct period or stage in a process of change or development. **2** each of the aspects of the moon or a planet, according to the amount of its illumination, esp. the new moon, the first quarter, the last quarter, and the full moon. **3** *Physics* a stage in a periodically recurring sequence, esp. of alternating electric currents or light vibrations. **4** a difficult or unhappy period, esp. in adolescence. **5** a genetic or seasonal variety of an animal's coloration etc. **6** *Chem.* a distinct and homogeneous form of matter separated by its surface from other forms. ● *v.tr.* carry out (a programme etc.) in phases or stages. □ **in phase** having the same phase at the same time. **out of phase** not in phase. **phase in** (or **out**) bring gradually into (or out of) use. **phase rule** *Chem.* a rule relating numbers of phases, constituents, and degrees of freedom. **three-phase** (of an electric generator, motor, etc.) designed to supply or use simultaneously three separate alternating currents of the same voltage, but with phases differing by a third of a period. □□ **phasic** *adj.* [F *phase* & f. earlier *phasis* f. Gk *phasis* appearance f. *phainō phan-* show]
■ *n.* **1** see STAGE *n.* 1. **2** stage, state, form, shape, aspect, appearance, look. **4** stage, step, spell, period. **5** variety, race, form; coat, plumage. □ **phase in** (gradually) introduce, usher in, work in, inject, insert, insinuate, include, incorporate. **phase out** ease off, wind up, put a stop to, (gradually) eliminate, remove, withdraw, discontinue, end.

phatic /fáttik/ *adj.* (of speech etc.) used to convey general sociability rather than to communicate a specific meaning, e.g. 'nice morning, isn't it?' [Gk *phatos* spoken f. *phēmi phan-* speak]

Ph.D. *abbr.* Doctor of Philosophy. [L *philosophiae doctor*]

pheasant /fézz'nt/ *n.* any of several long-tailed game-birds of the family Phasianidae, orig. from Asia. □□ **pheasantry** *n.* (*pl.* **-ies**). [ME f. AF *fesaunt* f. OF *faisan* f. L *phasianus* f. Gk *phasianos* (bird) of the river *Phasis* in Asia Minor]

phenacetin /finássitin/ *n.* an acetyl derivative of phenol used to treat fever etc. [PHENO- + ACETYL + -IN]

pheno- /féenō/ *comb. form* **1** *Chem.* derived from benzene (*phenol*; *phenyl*). **2** showing (*phenocryst*). [Gk *phainō* shine (with ref. to substances used for illumination), show]

phenobarbitone /féenōbaárbitōn/ *n.* (*US* **phenobarbital** /-bit'l/) a narcotic and sedative barbiturate drug used esp. to treat epilepsy.

phenocryst /féenəkrist/ *n.* a large or conspicuous crystal in porphyritic rock. [F *phénocryste* (as PHENO-, CRYSTAL)]

phenol /féenol/ *n.* *Chem.* **1** the monohydroxyl derivative of benzene used in dilute form as an antiseptic and disinfectant. Also called CARBOLIC. ¶ Chem. formula: C_6H_5OH. **2** any hydroxyl derivative of an aromatic hydrocarbon. □□ **phenolic** /finóllik/ *adj.* [F *phénole* f. *phène* benzene (formed as PHENO-)]

phenolphthalein /féenolthávleen/ *n.* *Chem.* a white crystalline solid used in solution as an acid-base indicator and medicinally as a laxative. [PHENOL + *phthal* f. NAPHTHALENE + -IN]

phenomena *pl.* of PHENOMENON.

phenomenal /finómmin'l/ *adj.* **1** of the nature of a phenomenon. **2** extraordinary, remarkable, prodigious. **3** perceptible by, or perceptible only to, the senses. □□ **phenomenalize** *v.tr.* (also **-ise**). **phenomenally** *adv.*
■ **2** outstanding, remarkable, exceptional, extraordinary, unusual, freakish, rare, uncommon, singular, unorthodox, unprecedented, unheard-of, unparalleled, unbelievable, marvellous, wonderful, amazing, astonishing, astounding, staggering, prodigious, miraculous, fantastic, surprising, *colloq.* stunning, mind-boggling, incredible.

phenomenalism /finómminəliz'm/ *n.* *Philos.* **1** the doctrine that human knowledge is confined to the appearances presented to the senses. **2** the doctrine that appearances are the foundation of all our knowledge. □□ **phenomenalist** *n.* **phenomenalistic** /-lístik/ *adj.*

phenomenology /finómminólləji/ *n.* *Philos.* **1** the science of phenomena. **2** the description and classification of phenomena. □□ **phenomenological** /-nəlójik'l/ *adj.* **phenomenologically** /-nəlójikəli/ *adv.*

phenomenon /finómminən/ *n.* (*pl.* **phenomena** /-nə/) **1** a fact or occurrence that appears or is perceived, esp. one of which the cause is in question. **2** a remarkable person or thing. **3** *Philos.* the object of a person's perception; what the senses or the mind notice. [LL f. Gk *phainomenon* neut. pres. part. of *phainomai* appear f. *phainō* show]
■ **1** event, happening, occurrence, incident, occasion, experience, fact. **2** wonder, curiosity, spectacle, sight, sensation, marvel, rarity, exception, miracle, *US* standout, *colloq.* one-off, *Brit. sl.* oner. **3** *Philos.* percept.

phenotype /féenōtīp/ *n.* *Biol.* a set of observable characteristics of an individual or group as determined by its genotype and environment. □□ **phenotypic** /-típpik/ *adj.* **phenotypical** /-típpik'l/ *adj.* **phenotypically** /-típpikəli/ *adv.* [G *Phaenotypus* (as PHENO-, TYPE)]

phenyl /féenīl, -nil/ *n.* *Chem.* the univalent radical formed from benzene by the removal of a hydrogen atom. [PHENO- + -YL]

phenylalanine /féenīlálləneen/ *n.* *Biochem.* an amino acid widely distributed in plant proteins and essential in the human diet. [PHENYL + ALANINE]

phenylketonuria /féenīlkéetənyoóriə/ *n.* an inherited inability to metabolize phenylalanine, ultimately leading to mental deficiency if untreated. [PHENYL + KETONE + -URIA]

pheromone /férrəmōn/ *n.* a chemical substance secreted and released by an animal for detection and response by another usu. of the same species. ▫▫ **pheromonal** /-mṓn'l/ *adj.* [Gk *pherō* convey + HORMONE]

phew /fyōō/ *int.* an expression of impatience, discomfort, relief, astonishment, or disgust. [imit. of puffing]

phi /fī/ *n.* the twenty-first letter of the Greek alphabet (Φ, φ). ▫ **Phi Beta Kappa 1** (in the US) an intercollegiate honorary society to which distinguished scholars may be elected (from the initial letters of a Greek motto, = philosophy is the guide to life). **2** a member of this society. [Gk]

phial /fīəl/ *n.* a small glass bottle, esp. for liquid medicine. [ME f. OF *fiole* f. L *phiola phiala* f. Gk *phialē*, a broad flat vessel: cf. VIAL]

Phil. *abbr.* **1** Philadelphia. **2** Philharmonic. **3** Philippians (New Testament). **4** Philosophy.

phil- *comb. form* var. of PHILO-.

-phil *comb. form* var. of -PHILE.

philabeg var. of FILIBEG.

philadelphus /filədélfəss/ *n.* any highly-scented deciduous flowering shrub of the genus *Philadelphus*, esp. the mock orange. [mod.L f. Gk *philadelphon*]

philander /filándər/ *v.intr.* (often foll. by *with*) flirt or have casual affairs with women; womanize. ▫▫ **philanderer** *n.* [*philander* (n.) used in Gk literature as the proper name of a lover, f. Gk *philandros* fond of men f. *anēr* male person: see PHIL-]

▪ play about *or* around, flirt, womanize, carry on, dally, tease, toy, *colloq.* play the field, gallivant. ▫▫ **philanderer** gallant, roué, rake, debauchee, Casanova, Lothario, libertine, seducer, Don Juan, Romeo, womanizer, *US* sport, *colloq.* stud; see also FLIRT *n.*

philanthrope /filənthrōp/ *n.* = PHILANTHROPIST (see PHILANTHROPY). [Gk *philanthrōpos* (as PHIL-, *anthrōpos* human being)]

philanthropic /filənthróppik/ *adj.* loving one's fellow men; benevolent. ▫▫ **philanthropically** *adv.* [F *philanthropique* (as PHILANTHROPE)]

▪ charitable, eleemosynary, generous, magnanimous, munificent, benevolent, open-handed, ungrudging, unstinting, beneficent, humanitarian, altruistic, humane.

philanthropy /filánthrəpi/ *n.* **1** a love of mankind. **2** practical benevolence, esp. charity on a large scale. ▫▫ **philanthropism** *n.* **philanthropist** *n.* **philanthropize** *v.tr.* & *intr.* (also **-ise**). [LL *philanthropia* f. Gk *philanthrōpia* (as PHILANTHROPE)]

▪ **1** see ALTRUISM. **2** generosity, benevolence, magnanimity, charitableness, public-spiritedness, big-heartedness, largesse, thoughtfulness, kind-heartedness, beneficence, benignity, liberality, open-handedness; charity, patronage, *hist.* alms-giving. ▫▫ **philanthropist** philanthrope, contributor, donor, benefactor, benefactress, patron, patroness, sponsor, Maecenas, Good Samaritan, humanitarian, altruist; Lady Bountiful.

philately /filáttəli/ *n.* the collection and study of postage stamps. ▫▫ **philatelic** /filətéllik/ *adj.* **philatelically** /filətéllikəli/ *adv.* **philatelist** *n.* [F *philatélie* f. Gk *ateleia* exemption from payment f. *a-* not + *telos* toll, tax]

-phile /fīl/ *comb. form* (also **-phil** /fil/) forming nouns and adjectives denoting fondness for what is specified (*bibliophile*; *Francophile*). [Gk *philos* dear, loving]

Philem. *abbr.* Philemon (New Testament).

philharmonic /filhaarmónnik/ *adj.* **1** fond of music. **2** used characteristically in the names of orchestras, choirs, etc. (*Royal Philharmonic Orchestra*). [F *philharmonique* f. It. *filarmonico* (as PHIL-, HARMONIC)]

philhellene /filheleen, -hélleen/ *n.* (often *attrib.*) **1** a lover of Greece and Greek culture. **2** *hist.* a supporter of the cause of Greek independence. ▫▫ **philhellenic** /-leénik/ *adj.* **philhellenism** /-hélliniz'm/ *n.* **philhellenist** /-héllinist/ *n.* [Gk *philellēn* (as PHIL-, HELLENE)]

-philia /filliə/ *comb. form* **1** denoting (esp. abnormal) fondness or love for what is specified (*necrophilia*). **2** denoting undue inclination (*haemophilia*). ▫▫ **-philiac** /-liak/ *comb. form* forming nouns and adjectives. **-philic** *comb. form* forming adjectives. **-philous** *comb. form* forming adjectives. [Gk f. *philos* loving]

philippic /filíppik/ *n.* a bitter verbal attack or denunciation. [L *philippicus* f. Gk *philippikos* the name of Demosthenes' speeches against Philip II of Macedon and Cicero's against Mark Antony]

▪ see TIRADE.

Philippine /fillipeen/ *adj.* of or relating to the Philippine Islands or their people; Filipino. [*Philip* II of Spain]

Philistine /fillistīn/ *n.* & *adj.* ● *n.* **1** a member of a people opposing the Israelites in ancient Palestine. **2** (usu. **philistine**) a person who is hostile or indifferent to culture, or one whose interests or tastes are commonplace or material. ● *adj.* hostile or indifferent to culture, commonplace, prosaic. ▫▫ **philistinism** /-stiniz'm/ *n.* [ME f. F *Philistin* or LL *Philistinus* f. Gk *Philistinos* = *Palaistinos* f. Heb. *pᵉlištî*]

▪ *n.* **2** vulgarian, ignoramus, Babbitt, materialist, barbarian, boor, yahoo, lowbrow, lout, oaf, clod, lubber, churl. ● *adj.* uncultured, uncultivated, unenlightened, unrefined, unread, unlettered, untaught, uneducated, untutored, unlearned, narrow-minded, anti-intellectual, boorish, lowbrow, prosaic, commonplace, bourgeois, commercial, materialistic.

Phillips /fillips/ *n.* (usu. *attrib.*) *propr.* denoting a screw with a cross-shaped slot for turning, or a corresponding screwdriver. [name of the original US manufacturer]

phillumenist /filyóōmənist, filóō-/ *n.* a collector of matchbox labels. ▫▫ **phillumeny** *n.* [PHIL- + L *lumen* light]

Philly /filli/ *n. US sl.* Philadelphia. [abbr.]

philo- /fillō/ *comb. form* (also **phil-** before a vowel or *h*) denoting a liking for what is specified.

philodendron /fillōdéndrən/ *n.* (*pl.* **philodendrons** or **philodendra** /-drə/) any tropical American climbing plant of the genus *Philodendron*, with bright foliage. [PHILO- + Gk *dendron* tree]

philogynist /filójənist/ *n.* a person who likes or admires women. [PHILO- + Gk *gunē* woman]

philology /filólləji/ *n.* **1** the science of language, esp. in its historical and comparative aspects. **2** the love of learning and literature. ▫▫ **philologian** /-ləlṓjən/ *n.* **philologist** *n.* **philological** /-ləlójik'l/ *adj.* **philologically** /-ləlójikəli/ *adv.* **philologize** *v.intr.* (also **-ise**). [F *philologie* f. L *philologia* love of learning f. Gk (as PHILO-, -LOGY)]

Philomel /filləmel/ *n.* (also **Philomela** /filləmeélə/) *poet.* the nightingale. [earlier *philomene* f. med.L *philomena* f. L *philomela* nightingale f. Gk *philomēla*: cap. with ref. to the myth of *Philomela*]

philoprogenitive /fillōprōjénnitiv/ *adj.* **1** prolific. **2** loving one's offspring.

philosopher /filóssəfər/ *n.* **1** a person engaged or learned in philosophy or a branch of it. **2** a person who lives by philosophy. **3** a person who shows philosophic calmness in trying circumstances. ▫ **philosophers'** (or **philosopher's**) **stone** the supreme object of alchemy, a substance supposed to change other metals into gold or silver. [ME f. AF *philosofre* var. of OF, *philosophe* f. L *philosophus* f. Gk *philosophos* (as PHILO-, *sophos* wise)]

philosophical /filləsóffik'l/ *adj.* (also **philosophic**) **1** of or according to philosophy. **2** skilled in or devoted to philosophy or learning; learned (*philosophical society*). **3** wise; serene; temperate. **4** calm in adverse circumstances. ▫▫ **philosophically** *adv.* [LL *philosophicus* f. L *philosophia* (as PHILOSOPHY)]

▪ **1, 2** rational, logical, reasoned, argued; see also LEARNED 2–4. **3, 4** detached, unconcerned, unemotional, unimpassioned, composed, thoughtful, reflective, meditative, cogitative, contemplative, judicious, sober, level-headed, realistic, practical, pragmatical, pragmatic, down-to-earth, cool, calm, serene, placid, stoical, patient, unruffled, cool-headed, tranquil, unperturbed, even-tempered, temperate, moderate, equable, equanimous, imperturbable; see also WISE *adj*. 1.

philosophize /filóssəfīz/ *v*. (also **-ise**) **1** *intr*. reason like a philosopher. **2** *intr*. moralize. **3** *intr*. speculate; theorize. **4** *tr*. render philosophic. ▫▫ **philosophizer** *n*. [app. f. F *philosopher*]

philosophy /filóssəfi/ *n*. (*pl*. **-ies**) **1** the use of reason and argument in seeking truth and knowledge of reality, esp. of the causes and nature of things and of the principles governing existence, the material universe, perception of physical phenomena, and human behaviour. **2 a** a particular system or set of beliefs reached by this. **b** a personal rule of life. **3** advanced learning in general (*doctor of philosophy*). **4** serenity; calmness; conduct governed by a particular philosophy. [ME f. OF *filosofie* f. L *philosophia* wisdom f. Gk (as PHILO-, *sophos* wise)]

▪ **1** metaphysics, epistemology, logic, rationalism, reason, thinking; argument. **2** viewpoint, (point of) view, outlook, opinion, attitude, feeling, sentiment, idea, notion, ideology, (set of) beliefs *or* values, tenets, credo, *Weltanschauung*, world-view. **4** composure, calmness, serenity, sang-froid, control, self-control, restraint, coolness, placidity, cool-headedness, equanimity, thoughtfulness, imperturbability, self-possession, aplomb, dispassion, patience, stoicism, resignation.

philtre /filtər/ *n*. (*US* **philter**) a drink supposed to excite sexual love in the drinker. [F *philtre* f. L *philtrum* f. Gk *philtron* f. *phileō* to love]

-phily /filli/ *comb. form* = -PHILIA.

phimosis /fīmṓsiss/ *n*. a constriction of the foreskin, making it difficult to retract. ▫▫ **phimotic** /-móttik/ *adj*. [mod.L f. Gk, = muzzling]

phiz /fiz/ *n*. (also **phizog** /fizzog/) *Brit. colloq*. **1** the face. **2** the expression on a face. [abbr. of *phiznomy* = PHYSIOGNOMY]

▪ **1** see FACE *n*. 1. **2** see FACE *n*. 2a.

phlebitis /flibī́tiss/ *n*. inflammation of the walls of a vein. ▫▫ **phlebitic** /-bíttik/ *adj*. [mod.L f. Gk f. *phleps phlebos* vein]

phlebotomy /flibóttəmi/ *n*. **1** the surgical opening or puncture of a vein. **2** esp. *hist*. blood-letting as a medical treatment. ▫▫ **phlebotomist** *n*. **phlebotomize** *v.tr*. (also **-ise**). [ME f. OF *flebothomie* f. LL *phlebotomia* f. Gk f. *phleps phlebos* vein + -TOMY]

phlegm /flem/ *n*. **1** the thick viscous substance secreted by the mucous membranes of the respiratory passages, discharged by coughing. **2 a** coolness and calmness of disposition. **b** sluggishness or apathy (supposed to result from too much phlegm in the constitution). **3** *archaic* phlegm regarded as one of the four bodily humours. ▫▫ **phlegmy** *adj*. [ME & OF *fleume* f. LL *phlegma* f. Gk *phlegma -atos* inflammation f. *phlegō* burn]

▪ **2 a** see SANG-FROID. **b** see *sluggishness* (SLUGGISH).

phlegmatic /flegmáttik/ *adj*. stolidly calm; unexcitable, unemotional. ▫▫ **phlegmatically** *adv*.

▪ stoical, stoic, unemotional, unexcitable, apathetic, uninvolved, unfeeling, uncaring, unresponsive, stolid, unmoved, insensitive, unaffected, insensible, indifferent, unconcerned, uninterested; self-possessed, self-controlled, controlled, restrained, composed, calm, tranquil, placid, cool-headed, equable, equanimous, cool, undisturbed, unperturbed, unruffled, imperturbable, even-tempered, philosophical; listless, indolent, inactive, passive.

phloem /flṓ-em/ *n*. *Bot*. the tissue conducting food material in plants (cf. XYLEM). [Gk *phloos* bark]

phlogiston /fləjístən, -gístən/ *n*. a substance formerly supposed to exist in all combustible bodies, and to be released in combustion. [mod.L f. Gk *phlogizō* set on fire f. *phlox phlogos* flame]

phlox /floks/ *n*. any cultivated plant of the genus *Phlox*, with scented clusters of esp. white, blue, and red flowers. [L f. Gk *phlox*, the name of a plant (lit. flame)]

-phobe /fōb/ *comb. form* forming nouns and adjectives denoting a person having a fear or dislike of what is specified (*xenophobe*). [F f. L *-phobus* f. Gk *-phobos* f. *phobos* fear]

phobia /fṓbiə/ *n*. an abnormal or morbid fear or aversion. ▫▫ **phobic** *adj*. & *n*. [-PHOBIA used as a separate word]

▪ fear, horror, terror, dread, hatred, detestation, abhorrence, loathing, execration, aversion, revulsion, repugnance, dislike, distaste, antipathy; nervousness, distrust, suspicion.

-phobia /fṓbiə/ *comb. form* forming abstract nouns denoting a fear or dislike of what is specified (*agoraphobia*; *xenophobia*). ▫▫ **-phobic** *comb. form* forming adjectives. [L f. Gk]

phoebe /féebi/ *n*. any American flycatcher of the genus *Sayornis*. [imit.: infl. by the name]

Phoenician /fənísh'n, fənée-/ *n*. & *adj*. ● *n*. a member of a Semitic people of ancient Phoenicia in S. Syria or of its colonies. ● *adj*. of or relating to Phoenicia. [ME f. OF *phenicien* f. L *Phoenicia* f. L *Phoenice* f. Gk *Phoinikē* Phoenicia]

phoenix /féeniks/ *n*. **1** a mythical bird, the only one of its kind, that after living for five or six centuries in the Arabian desert, burnt itself on a funeral pyre and rose from the ashes with renewed youth to live through another cycle. **2** a unique person or thing. [OE & OF *fenix* f. L *phoenix* f. Gk *phoinix* Phoenician, purple, phoenix]

pholas /fṓləss/ *n*. a piddock, esp. of the genus *Pholas*. [mod.L f. Gk *phōlas* that lurks in a hole (*phōleos*)]

phon /fon/ *n*. a unit of the perceived loudness of sounds. [Gk *phōnē* sound]

phonate /fṓnayt/ *v.intr*. utter a vocal sound. ▫▫ **phonation** /-náysh'n/ *n*. **phonatory** /fṓnətəri/ *adj*. [Gk *phōnē* voice]

phone[1] /fōn/ *n*. & *v.tr*. & *intr*. *colloq*. = TELEPHONE. ▫ **phone book** = *telephone directory*. **phone-in** *n*. a broadcast programme during which the listeners or viewers telephone the studio etc. and participate. [abbr.]

phone[2] /fōn/ *n*. a simple vowel or consonant sound. [formed as PHONEME]

-phone /fōn/ *comb. form* forming nouns and adjectives meaning: **1** an instrument using or connected with sound (*telephone*; *xylophone*). **2** a person who uses a specified language (*anglophone*). [Gk *phōnē* voice, sound]

phonecard /fṓnkaard/ *n*. a card containing prepaid units for use with a Cardphone.

phoneme /fṓneem/ *n*. any of the units of sound in a specified language that distinguish one word from another (e.g. *p*, *b*, *d*, *t* as in pad, pat, bad, bat, in English). ▫▫ **phonemic** /-néemik/ *adj*. **phonemics** /-néemiks/ *n*. [F *phonème* f. Gk *phōnēma* sound, speech f. *phōneō* speak]

phonetic /fənéttik/ *adj*. **1** representing vocal sounds. **2** (of a system of spelling etc.) having a direct correspondence between symbols and sounds. **3** of or relating to phonetics. ▫▫ **phonetically** *adv*. **phoneticism** /-tisiz'm/ *n*. **phoneticist** /-tisist/ *n*. **phoneticize** /-tisīz/ *v.tr*. (also **-ise**). [mod.L *phoneticus* f. Gk *phōnētikos* f. *phōneō* speak]

phonetics /fənéttiks/ *n.pl*. (usu. treated as *sing*.) **1** vocal sounds and their classification. **2** the study of these. ▫▫ **phonetician** /fṓnitísh'n/ *n*.

phonetist /fṓnitist/ *n*. **1** a person skilled in phonetics. **2** an advocate of phonetic spelling.

phoney /fṓni/ *adj*. & *n*. (also **phony**) *colloq*. ● *adj*. (**phonier**, **phoniest**) **1** sham; counterfeit. **2** fictitious; fraudulent. ● *n*. (*pl*. **-eys** or **-ies**) a phoney person or thing. ▫▫ **phonily** *adv*. **phoniness** *n*. [20th c.: orig. unkn.]

▪ *adj*. unreal, fake, pretend, synthetic, artificial, factitious, false, fictitious, fraudulent, imitation, bogus, spurious, counterfeit, mock, ersatz, pseudo, sham; pretended, insincere, hypocritical, dissimulating, deceitful, dishonest, *colloq*. pseud. ● *n*. fake, fraud, imitation, counterfeit, forgery, hoax, sham; trickster, faker, humbug, impostor, pretender, charlatan, mountebank, double-dealer, counterfeiter, quack, deceiver, *colloq*. pseud, con man.

phonic /fónnik, fṓ-/ *adj*. & *n*. ● *adj*. of sound; acoustic; of vocal sounds. ● *n*. (in *pl*.) a method of teaching reading based on sounds. ▫▫ **phonically** *adv*. [Gk *phōnē* voice]

phono- /fṓnō/ *comb. form* denoting sound. [Gk *phōnē* voice, sound]

phonogram /fṓnəgram/ *n.* a symbol representing a spoken sound.

phonograph /fṓnəgraaf/ *n.* **1** *Brit.* an early form of gramophone using cylinders and able to record as well as reproduce sound. **2** *US* a gramophone.

phonography /fənógrəfi/ *n.* **1** writing in esp. shorthand symbols, corresponding to the sounds of speech. **2** the recording of sounds by phonograph. □□ **phonographic** /fṓnəgráffik/ *adj.*

phonology /fənólləji/ *n.* the study of sounds in a language. □□ **phonological** /fṓnəlójik'l, fón-/ *adj.* **phonologically** /fṓnəlójikəli, fón-/ *adv.* **phonologist** *n.*
■ phonemics; phonetics.

phonon /fṓnon/ *n. Physics* a quantum of sound or elastic vibrations. [Gk *phōnē* sound, after PHOTON]

phony var. of PHONEY.

phooey /fóo-i/ *int.* an expression of disgust or disbelief. [imit.]

-phore /for/ *comb. form* forming nouns meaning 'bearer' (*ctenophore*; *semaphore*). □□ **-phorous** /fərəss/ *comb. form* forming adjectives. [mod.L f. Gk *-phoros -phoron* bearing, bearer f. *pherō* bear]

phoresy /foreéssi, fórrəsi/ *n. Biol.* an association in which one organism is carried by another, without being a parasite. □□ **phoretic** /foréttik/ *adj.* [F *phorésie* f. Gk *phorēsis* being carried]

phormium /fórmiəm/ *n.* **1** a liliaceous plant, *Phormium tenax*, yielding a leaf-fibre that is used commercially. **2** New Zealand flax. [mod.L f. Gk *phormion* a species of plant]

phosgene /fózjeen/ *n.* a colourless poisonous gas (carbonyl chloride), formerly used in warfare. ¶ Chem. formula: $COCl_2$. [Gk *phōs* light + -GEN, with ref. to its orig. production by the action of sunlight on chlorine and carbon monoxide]

phosphatase /fósfətayz, -tayss/ *n. Biochem.* any enzyme that catalyses the synthesis or hydrolysis of an organic phosphate.

phosphate /fósfayt/ *n.* **1** any salt or ester of phosphoric acid, esp. used as a fertilizer. **2** an effervescent drink containing a small amount of phosphate. □□ **phosphatic** /-fáttik/ *adj.* [F f. *phosphore* PHOSPHORUS]

phosphene /fósfeen/ *n.* the sensation of rings of light produced by pressure on the eyeball due to irritation of the retina. [irreg. f. Gk *phōs* light + *phainō* show]

phosphide /fósfīd/ *n. Chem.* a binary compound of phosphorus with another element or group.

phosphine /fósfeen/ *n. Chem.* a colourless ill-smelling gas, phosphorus trihydride. ¶ Chem. formula: PH_3. □□ **phosphinic** /-fínnik/ *adj.* [PHOSPHO- + -INE[4], after *amine*]

phosphite /fósfīt/ *n. Chem.* any salt or ester of phosphorous acid. [F (as PHOSPHO-)]

phospho- /fósfō/ *comb. form* denoting phosphorus. [abbr.]

phospholipid /fósfəlíppid/ *n. Biochem.* any lipid consisting of a phosphate group and one or more fatty acids.

phosphor /fósfər/ *n.* **1** = PHOSPHORUS. **2** a synthetic fluorescent or phosphorescent substance esp. used in cathode-ray tubes. □ **phosphor bronze** a tough hard bronze alloy containing a small amount of phosphorus, used esp. for bearings. [G f. L *phosphorus* PHOSPHORUS]

phosphorate /fósfərayt/ *v.tr.* combine or impregnate with phosphorus.

phosphorescence /fósfəréss'nss/ *n.* **1** radiation similar to fluorescence but detectable after excitation ceases. **2** the emission of light without combustion or perceptible heat. □□ **phosphoresce** *v.intr.* **phosphorescent** *adj.*
■ **2** see GLOW *n.* 1. □□ **phosphoresce** see GLOW *v.* 1.

phosphorite /fósfərīt/ *n.* a non-crystalline form of apatite.

phosphorus /fósfərəss/ *n. Chem.* a non-metallic element occurring naturally in various phosphate rocks and existing in allotropic forms, esp. as a poisonous whitish waxy substance burning slowly at ordinary temperatures and so appearing luminous in the dark, and a reddish form used in matches, fertilizers, etc. ¶ Symb.: **P.** □□ **phosphoric** /-fórrik/ *adj.* **phosphorous** *adj.* [L, = morning star, f. Gk *phōsphoros* f. *phōs* light + *-phoros* -bringing]

phosphorylate /fosfórrilayt/ *v.tr. Chem.* introduce a phosphate group into (an organic molecule etc.). □□ **phosphorylation** /-láysh'n/ *n.*

phossy jaw /fóssi/ *n. colloq. hist.* gangrene of the jawbone caused by phosphorus poisoning. [abbr.]

phot /fot, fōt/ *n.* a unit of illumination equal to one lumen per square centimetre. [Gk *phōs phōtos* light]

photic /fṓtik/ *adj.* **1** of or relating to light. **2** (of ocean layers) reached by sunlight.

photism /fṓtiz'm/ *n.* a hallucinatory sensation or vision of light. [Gk *phōtismos* f. *phōtizō* shine f. *phōs phōtos* light]

photo /fṓtō/ *n.* & *v.* ● *n.* (*pl.* **-os**) = PHOTOGRAPH *n.* ● *v.tr.* (**-oes, -oed**) = PHOTOGRAPH *v.* □ **photo-call** an occasion on which theatrical performers, famous personalities, etc., pose for photographers by arrangement. **photo finish** a close finish of a race or contest, esp. one where the winner is only distinguishable on a photograph. **photo opportunity** = *photo-call*. [abbr.]

photo- /fṓtō/ *comb. form* denoting: **1** light (*photosensitive*). **2** photography (*photocomposition*). [Gk *phōs phōtos* light, or as abbr. of PHOTOGRAPH]

photobiology /fṓtōbīólləji/ *n.* the study of the effects of light on living organisms.

photocell /fṓtōsel/ *n.* = *photoelectric cell*.

photochemistry /fṓtōkémmistri/ *n.* the study of the chemical effects of light. □□ **photochemical** *adj.*

photocomposition /fṓtōkómpəzísh'n/ *n.* = FILMSETTING.

photoconductivity /fṓtōkónduktívviti/ *n.* conductivity due to the action of light. □□ **photoconductive** /-kəndúktiv/ *adj.* **photoconductor** /-kəndúktər/ *n.*

photocopier /fṓtōkoppiər/ *n.* a machine for producing photocopies.

photocopy /fṓtōkoppi/ *n.* & *v.* ● *n.* (*pl.* **-ies**) a photographic copy of printed or written material produced by a process involving the action of light on a specially prepared surface. ● *v.tr.* (**-ies, -ied**) make a photocopy of. □□ **photocopiable** *adj.*
■ copy, *propr.* Xerox, Photostat.

photodiode /fṓtōdīōd/ *n.* a semiconductor diode responding electrically to illumination.

photoelectric /fṓtō-iléktrik/ *adj.* marked by or using emissions of electrons from substances exposed to light. □ **photoelectric cell** a device using this effect to generate current. □□ **photoelectricity** /-tríssiti/ *n.*

photoelectron /fṓtō-iléktron/ *n.* an electron emitted from an atom by interaction with a photon, esp. one emitted from a solid surface by the action of light.

photoemission /fṓtō-imísh'n/ *n.* the emission of electrons from a surface by the action of light incident on it. □□ **photoemitter** *n.*

photofit /fṓtōfit/ *n.* a reconstructed picture of a person (esp. one sought by the police) made from composite photographs of facial features (cf. IDENTIKIT).

photogenic /fṓtōjénnik, -jeénik/ *adj.* **1** (esp. of a person) having an appearance that looks pleasing in photographs. **2** *Biol.* producing or emitting light. □□ **photogenically** *adv.*

photogram /fṓtōgram/ *n.* **1** a picture produced with photographic materials but without a camera. **2** *archaic* a photograph.

photogrammetry /fṓtōgrámmitri/ *n.* the use of photography for surveying. □□ **photogrammetrist** *n.*

photograph /fṓtəgraaf/ *n.* & *v.* ● *n.* a picture taken by means of the chemical action of light or other radiation on sensitive film. ● *v.tr.* (also *absol.*) take a photograph of (a person etc.). □□ **photographable** *adj.* **photographer** /fətógrəfər/ *n.* **photographically** /-gráffikəli/ *adv.*

■ *n.* snapshot, print, picture, snap, photo, shot, *archaic* photogram, *colloq.* pic. ● *v.* take a picture of, shoot, film, take, snap; take a person's picture. □□ **photographer** cameraman, cinematographer, *paparazzo*.

photographic /fōtəgráffik/ *adj.* **1** of, used in, or produced by photography. **2** having the accuracy of a photograph (*photographic likeness*).
■ **1** cinematic, filmic; pictorial. **2** vivid, natural, realistic, graphic, accurate, exact, precise, faithful, detailed, lifelike, true to life.

photography /fətógrəfi/ *n.* the taking and processing of photographs.

photogravure /fṓtōgrəvyoor/ *n.* **1** an image produced from a photographic negative transferred to a metal plate and etched in. **2** this process . [F (as PHOTO-, *gravure* engraving)]

photojournalism /fṓtōjúrnəliz'm/ *n.* the art or practice of relating news by photographs, with or without an accompanying text, esp. in magazines etc. □□ **photojournalist** *n.*

photolithography /fṓtōlithógrəfi/ *n.* (also **photolitho** /-lī́thō/) lithography using plates made photographically. □□ **photolithographer** *n.* **photolithographic** /-thəgráffik/ *adj.* **photolithographically** /-thəgráffikəli/ *adv.*

photolysis /fōtóllisiss/ *n.* decomposition or dissociation of molecules by the action of light. □□ **photolyse** /fṓtəlīz/ *v.tr.* & *intr.* **photolytic** /-təlíttik/ *adj.*

photometer /fōtómmitər/ *n.* an instrument for measuring light. □□ **photometric** /fṓtōmétrik/ *adj.* **photometry** /-tómmitri/ *n.*

photomicrograph /fṓtōmī́krəgraaf/ *n.* a photograph of an image produced by a microscope. □□ **photomicrography** /-krógrəfi/ *n.*

photon /fṓton/ *n.* a quantum of electromagnetic radiation energy, proportional to the frequency of radiation. [Gk *phōs phōtos* light, after *electron*]

photonovel /fṓtōnovv'l/ *n.* a novel told in a series of photographs with superimposed speech bubbles.

photo-offset /fṓtō-ófset/ *n.* offset printing with plates made photographically.

photoperiod /fṓtōpeeriəd/ *n.* the period of daily illumination which an organism receives. □□ **photoperiodic** /-ióddik/ *adj.*

photoperiodism /fṓtōpeeriədiz'm/ *n.* the response of an organism to changes in the lengths of the daily periods of light.

photophobia /fṓtōfṓbiə/ *n.* an abnormal fear of or aversion to light. □□ **photophobic** *adj.*

photoreceptor /fṓtō-riséptər/ *n.* any living structure that responds to incident light.

photosensitive /fṓtōsénsitiv/ *adj.* reacting chemically, electrically, etc., to light. □□ **photosensitivity** /-tívviti/ *n.*

photosetting /fṓtōsetting/ *n.* = FILMSETTING. □□ **photoset** *v.tr.* (*past* and *past part.* **-set**). **photosetter** *n.*

photosphere /fṓtōsfeer/ *n.* the luminous envelope of a star from which its light and heat radiate. □□ **photospheric** /-sférrik/ *adj.*

Photostat /fṓtōstat/ *n.* & *v.* ● *n. propr.* **1** a type of machine for making photocopies. **2** a copy made by this means. ● *v.tr.* (**photostat**) (**-statted, -statting**) make a Photostat of. □□ **photostatic** /-státtik/ *adj.*
■ *n.* **1** photocopier. **2** photocopy, copy, *propr.* Xerox. ● *v.* photocopy, copy, *propr.* Xerox.

photosynthesis /fṓtōsínthisiss/ *n.* the process in which the energy of sunlight is used by organisms, esp. green plants, to synthesize carbohydrates from carbon dioxide and water. □□ **photosynthesize** *v.tr.* & *intr.* (also **-ise**). **photosynthetic** /-théttik/ *adj.* **photosynthetically** /-thét tikəli/ *adv.*

phototransistor /fṓtōtranzístər, -traanzístər/ *n.* a transistor that responds to incident light by generating and amplifying an electric current.

phototropism /fṓtōtrṓpiz'm, fətótrəpiz'm/ *n.* the tendency of a plant etc. to bend or turn towards or away from a source of light. □□ **phototropic** /-tróppik/ *adj.*

photovoltaic /fṓtōvoltáyik/ *adj.* relating to the production of electric current at the junction of two substances exposed to light.

phrasal /fráyz'l/ *adj. Gram.* consisting of a phrase. □ **phrasal verb** an idiomatic phrase consisting of a verb and an adverb (e.g. *break down*), a verb and a preposition (e.g. *see to*), or a combination of both (e.g. *look down on*).

phrase /frayz/ *n.* & *v.* ● *n.* **1** a group of words forming a conceptual unit, but not a sentence. **2** an idiomatic or short pithy expression. **3** a manner or mode of expression (*a nice turn of phrase*). **4** *Mus.* a group of notes forming a distinct unit within a larger piece. ● *v.tr.* **1** express in words (*phrased the reply badly*). **2** (esp. when reading aloud or speaking) divide (sentences etc.) into units so as to convey the meaning of the whole. **3** *Mus.* divide (music) into phrases etc. in performance. □ **phrase book** a book for tourists etc. listing useful expressions with their equivalent in a foreign language. □□ **phrasing** *n.* [earlier *phrasis* f. L f. Gk f. *phrazō* declare, tell]
■ *n.* **1** clause, word-group, collocation, locution. **2** expression, idiom, idiomatic expression, proverb, motto, slogan, saying, catch-phrase, adage, maxim, axiom, saw, colloquialism, cliché. **3** phraseology, wording, language, way *or* manner of speaking, style, choice of words, vocabulary. ● *v.* **1** express, word, put into words, put, frame, formulate, couch, put *or* set forth, verbalize, articulate, voice, utter, say, write.

phraseogram /fráyziəgram/ *n.* a written symbol representing a phrase, esp. in shorthand.

phraseology /fráyziólləji/ *n.* (*pl.* **-ies**) **1** a choice or arrangement of words. **2** a mode of expression. □□ **phraseological** /-ziəlójik'l/ *adj.* [mod.L *phraseologia* f. Gk *phraseōn* genit. pl. of *phrasis* PHRASE]
■ wording, phrasing, expression, language, style, diction, usage, speech, delivery.

phreatic /friáttik/ *adj. Geol.* **1** (of water) situated underground in the zone of saturation; ground water. **2** (of a volcanic eruption or explosion) caused by the heating and expansion of underground water. [Gk *phrear phreatos* well]

phrenetic /frinéttik/ *adj.* **1** frantic. **2** fanatic. □□ **phrenetically** *adv.* [ME, var. of FRENETIC]

phrenic /frénnik/ *adj. Anat.* of or relating to the diaphragm. [F *phrénique* f. Gk *phrēn phrenos* diaphragm, mind]

phrenology /frinólləji/ *n. hist.* the study of the shape and size of the cranium as a supposed indication of character and mental faculties. □□ **phrenological** /-nəlójik'l/ *adj.* **phrenologist** *n.*

Phrygian /fríjiən/ *n.* & *adj.* ● *n.* **1** a native or inhabitant of ancient Phrygia in central Asia Minor. **2** the language of this people. ● *adj.* of or relating to Phrygia or its people or language. □ **Phrygian bonnet** (or **cap**) an ancient conical cap with the top bent forwards, now identified with the cap of liberty. **Phrygian mode** *Mus.* the mode represented by the natural diatonic scale E–E.

phthalic acid /fthállik/ *n. Chem.* one of three isomeric dicarboxylic acids derived from benzene. □□ **phthalate** /-layt/ *n.* [abbr. of NAPHTHALIC: see NAPHTHALENE]

phthisis /fthī́siss, thī́-/ *n.* any progressive wasting disease, esp. pulmonary tuberculosis. □□ **phthisic** *adj.* **phthisical** *adj.* [L f. Gk f. *phthinō* to decay]

phut /fut/ *n.* a dull abrupt sound as of an impact or explosion. □ **go phut** *colloq.* (esp. of a scheme or plan) collapse, break down. [perh. f. Hindi *phaṭnā* to burst]

phycology /fīkólləji/ *n.* the study of algae. □□ **phycological** /-kəlójik'l/ *adj.* **phycologist** *n.* [Gk *phukos* seaweed + -LOGY]

phycomycete /fī́kōmī́seet/ *n.* any of various fungi which typically form non-septate mycelium. [Gk *phukos* seaweed + pl. of Gk *mukēs* mushroom]

phyla *pl.* of PHYLUM.

phylactery /filáktəri/ *n.* (*pl.* **-ies**) **1** a small leather box containing Hebrew texts on vellum, worn by Jewish men at morning prayer as a reminder to keep the law. **2** an amulet; a charm. **3** a usu. ostentatious religious observance. **4** a fringe; a border. [ME f. OF f. LL *phylacterium* f. Gk *phulaktērion* amulet f. *phulassō* guard]

phyletic /filéttik/ *adj. Biol.* of or relating to the development of a species or other group. [Gk *phuletikos* f. *phuletēs* tribesman f. *phulē* tribe]

phyllo- /fillō/ *comb. form* leaf. [Gk *phullo-* f. *phullon* leaf]

phyllode /fillōd/ *n.* a flattened leaf-stalk resembling a leaf. [mod.L *phyllodium* f. Gk *phullōdēs* leaflike (as PHYLLO-)]

phyllophagous /filóffəgəss/ *adj.* feeding on leaves.

phylloquinone /fílōkwinnōn/ *n.* one of the K vitamins, found in cabbage, spinach, and other leafy green vegetables, and essential for the blood clotting process. Also called *vitamin* K_1.

phyllostome /fillōstōm/ *n.* any bat of the family Phyllostomatidae having a nose leaf. [PHYLLO- + Gk *stoma* mouth]

phyllotaxis /fillōtáksiss/ *n.* (also **phyllotaxy** /-táksi/) the arrangement of leaves on an axis or stem. ▫▫ **phyllotactic** *adj.*

phylloxera /fillokseérə, filóksərə/ *n.* any plant-louse of the genus *Phylloxera*, esp. of a species attacking vines. [mod.L f. Gk *phullon* leaf + *xēros* dry]

phylo- /fílō/ *comb. form Biol.* denoting a race or tribe. [Gk *phulon*, *phulē*]

phylogenesis /fīlōjénnisiss/ *n.* (also **phylogeny** /fīlójəni/) **1** the evolutionary development of an organism or groups of organisms. **2** a history of this. ▫▫ **phylogenetic** /-jinéttik/ *adj.* **phylogenic** /-jénnik/ *adj.*

▪ see EVOLUTION.

phylum /fíləm/ *n.* (*pl.* **phyla** /-lə/) *Biol.* a taxonomic rank below kingdom comprising a class or classes and subordinate taxa. [mod.L f. Gk *phulon* race]

physalis /físálliss/ *n.* any plant of the genus *Physalis*, bearing fruit surrounded by lantern-like calyxes (see *Chinese lantern* 2). [Gk *phusallis* bladder, with ref. to the inflated calyx]

physic /fizzik/ *n.* & *v.* esp. *archaic.* ● *n.* **1** a medicine (*a dose of physic*). **2** the art of healing. **3** the medical profession. ● *v.tr.* (**physicked, physicking**) dose with physic. ▫ **physic garden** a garden for cultivating medicinal herbs etc. [ME f. OF *fisique* medicine f. L *physica* f. Gk *phusikē* (*epistēmē*) (knowledge) of nature]

▪ *n.* **1** see MEDICINE 2.

physical /fizzik'l/ *adj.* & *n.* ● *adj.* **1** of or concerning the body (*physical exercise*; *physical education*). **2** of matter; material (*both mental and physical force*). **3 a** of, or according to, the laws of nature (*a physical impossibility*). **b** belonging to physics (*physical science*). ● *n.* (in full **physical examination**) a medical examination to determine physical fitness. ▫ **physical chemistry** the application of physics to the study of chemical behaviour. **physical geography** geography dealing with natural features. **physical jerks** *colloq.* physical exercises. **physical science** the sciences used in the study of inanimate natural objects, e.g. physics, chemistry, astronomy, etc. **physical training** exercises promoting bodily fitness and strength. ▫▫ **physicality** /-kálliti/ *n.* **physically** *adv.* **physicalness** *n.* [ME f. med.L *physicalis* f. L *physica* (as PHYSIC)]

▪ *adj.* **1** bodily, corporal. **2** material, corporeal, tangible, palpable, real, actual, true, concrete, manifest, solid; fleshly, incarnate, carnal, animal, mortal, earthly, natural, somatic, worldly; non-spiritual.

physician /fizísh'n/ *n.* **1 a** a person legally qualified to practise medicine and surgery. **b** a specialist in medical diagnosis and treatment. **c** any medical practitioner. **2** a healer (*work is the best physician*). [ME f. OF *fisicien* (as PHYSIC)]

▪ **1** doctor, medical practitioner, general practitioner, GP, *Mil.* surgeon, *colloq.* doc, medico, medic, *sl.* quack, sawbones; specialist, *esp. US* diplomate, *US* internist.

physicist /fizzisist/ *n.* a person skilled or qualified in physics.

physico- /fizzikō/ *comb. form* **1** physical (and). **2** of physics (and). [Gk *phusikos* (as PHYSIC)]

physico-chemical /fizzikōkémmik'l/ *adj.* relating to physics and chemistry or to physical chemistry.

physics /fizziks/ *n.* the science dealing with the properties and interactions of matter and energy. [pl. of *physic* physical (thing), after L *physica*, Gk *phusika* natural things f. *phusis* nature]

physio /fizziō/ *n.* (*pl.* **-os**) *colloq.* a physiotherapist. [abbr.]

physio- /fizziō/ *comb. form* nature; what is natural. [Gk *phusis* nature]

physiocracy /fizziókrəsi/ *n.* (*pl.* **-ies**) *hist.* **1** government according to the natural order, esp. as advocated by some 18th-c. economists. **2** a society based on this. ▫▫ **physiocrat** /-ziəkrat/ *n.* **physiocratic** /-ziəkráttik/ *adj.* [F *physiocratie* (as PHYSIO-, -CRACY)]

physiognomy /fizziónnəmi/ *n.* (*pl.* **-ies**) **1 a** the cast or form of a person's features, expression, body, etc. **b** the art of supposedly judging character from facial characteristics etc. **2** the external features of a landscape etc. **3** a characteristic, esp. moral, aspect. ▫▫ **physiognomic** /-ziənómmik/ *adj.* **physiognomical** /-ziənómmik'l/ *adj.* **physiognomically** /-ziənómmikəli/ *adv.* **physiognomist** *n.* [ME *fisnomie* etc. f. OF *phisonomie* f. med.L *phisonomia* f. Gk *phusiognōmonia* judging of a man's nature (by his features) (as PHYSIO-, *gnōmōn* judge)]

▪ **1 a** see FEATURE *n.* 2.

physiography /fizziógrəfi/ *n.* the description of nature, of natural phenomena, or of a class of objects; physical geography. ▫▫ **physiographer** *n.* **physiographic** /-ziəgráffik/ *adj.* **physiographical** /-ziəgráffik'l/ *adj.* **physiographically** /-ziəgráffikəli/ *adv.* [F *physiographie* (as PHYSIO-, -GRAPHY)]

physiological /fizziəlójik'l/ *adj.* (also **physiologic**) of or concerning physiology. ▫ **physiological salt solution** a saline solution having a concentration about equal to that of body fluids. ▫▫ **physiologically** *adv.*

physiology /fizzióllәji/ *n.* **1** the science of the functions of living organisms and their parts. **2** these functions. ▫▫ **physiologist** *n.* [F *physiologie* or L *physiologia* f. Gk *phusiologia* (as PHYSIO-, -LOGY)]

physiotherapy /fizziōthérrəpi/ *n.* the treatment of disease, injury, deformity, etc., by physical methods including manipulation, massage, infrared heat treatment, remedial exercise, etc., not by drugs. ▫▫ **physiotherapist** *n.*

physique /fizeék/ *n.* the bodily structure, development, and organization of an individual (*an undernourished physique*). [F, orig. adj. (as PHYSIC)]

▪ build, figure, body, frame, shape, form.

-phyte /fīt/ *comb. form* forming nouns denoting a vegetable or plantlike organism (*saprophyte*; *zoophyte*). ▫▫ **-phytic** /fittik/ *comb. form* forming adjectives. [Gk *phuton* plant f. *phuō* come into being]

phyto- /fītō/ *comb. form* denoting a plant.

phytochemistry /fītōkémmistri/ *n.* the chemistry of plant products. ▫▫ **phytochemical** *adj.* **phytochemist** *n.*

phytochrome /fītōkrōm/ *n. Biochem.* a blue-green pigment found in many plants, and regulating various developmental processes according to the nature and timing of the light it absorbs. [PHYTO- + Gk *khrōma* colour]

phytogenesis /fītōjénnisiss/ *n.* (also **phytogeny** /-tójini/) the science of the origin or evolution of plants.

phytogeography /fītōjiógrəfi/ *n.* the geographical distribution of plants.

phytopathology /fītōpəthólləji/ *n.* the study of plant diseases.

phytophagous /fītóffəgəss/ *adj.* feeding on plants.

phytoplankton /fītōplángktən/ *n.* plankton consisting of plants.

phytotomy /fītóttəmi/ *n.* the dissection of plants.

phytotoxic /fītōtóksik/ *adj.* poisonous to plants.

phytotoxin /fītōtóksin/ *n.* **1** any toxin derived from a plant. **2** a substance poisonous or injurious to plants, esp. one produced by a parasite.

pi[1] /pī/ *n.* **1** the sixteenth letter of the Greek alphabet (Π, π). **2** (as π) the symbol of the ratio of the circumference of a circle to its diameter (approx. 3.14159). □ **pi-meson** = PION. [Gk: sense 2 f. Gk *periphereia* circumference]

pi[2] /pī/ *adj. Brit. sl.* pious. □ **pi jaw** a long moralizing lecture or reprimand. [abbr.]
■ see SANCTIMONIOUS.

pi[3] *US* var. of PIE[3].

piacular /pīákyoolər/ *adj. formal* **1** expiatory. **2** needing expiation. [L *piacularis* f. *piaculum* expiation f. *piare* appease]
■ **1** see *compensatory* (COMPENSATE).

piaffe /piáf/ *v.intr.* (of a horse etc.) move as in a trot, but slower. [F *piaffer* to strut]

piaffer /piáffər/ *n.* the action of piaffing.

pia mater /pīə máytər/ *n. Anat.* the delicate innermost membrane enveloping the brain and spinal cord (see MENINX). [med.L, = tender mother, transl. of Arab. *al-'umm al-raḳīḳa*: cf. DURA MATER]

piani *pl.* of PIANO[2].

pianism /péeəniz'm/ *n.* **1** the art or technique of piano-playing. **2** the skill or style of a composer of piano music. □□ **pianistic** /-nístik/ *adj.* **pianistically** /-nístikəli/ *adv.*

pianissimo /péeənissimō/ *adj., adv.,* & *n. Mus.* ● *adj.* performed very softly. ● *adv.* very softly. ● *n.* (*pl.* **-os** or **pianissimi** /-mi/) a passage to be performed very softly. [It., superl. of PIANO[2]]

pianist /péeənist/ *n.* the player of a piano. [F *pianiste* (as PIANO[1])]

piano[1] /piánnō/ *n.* (*pl.* **-os**) a large musical instrument played by pressing down keys on a keyboard and causing hammers to strike metal strings, the vibration from which is stopped by dampers when the keys are released. □ **piano-accordion** an accordion with the melody played on a small vertical keyboard like that of a piano. **piano organ** a mechanical piano constructed like a barrel-organ. **piano-player** **1** a pianist. **2** a contrivance for playing a piano automatically. [It., abbr. of PIANOFORTE]

piano[2] /pyáanō/ *adj., adv.,* & *n.* ● *adj.* **1** *Mus.* performed softly. **2** subdued. ● *adv.* **1** *Mus.* softly. **2** in a subdued manner. ● *n.* (*pl.* **-os** or **piani** /-ni/) *Mus.* a piano passage. [It. f. L *planus* flat, (of sound) soft]

pianoforte /piánnōfórti/ *n. Mus. formal* or *archaic* a piano. [It., earlier *piano e forte* soft and loud, expressing its gradation of tone]

Pianola /péeənólə/ *n.* **1** *propr.* a kind of automatic piano; a player-piano. **2** (**pianola**) *Bridge* an easy hand needing no skill. **3** (**pianola**) an easy task. [app. dimin. of PIANO[1]]

piano nobile /pyáanō nóbilay/ *n. Archit.* the main storey of a large house. [It., = noble floor]

piassava /péeəsaávə/ *n.* **1** a stout fibre obtained from the leaf-stalks of various American and African palm-trees. **2** any of these trees. [Port. f. Tupi *piaçába*]

piastre /piástər/ *n.* (*US* **piaster**) a small coin and monetary unit of several Middle Eastern countries. [F *piastre* f. It. *piastra* (*d'argento*) plate (of silver), formed as PLASTER]

piazza /piátsə/ *n.* **1** a public square or market-place esp. in an Italian town. **2** *US* the veranda of a house. [It., formed as PLACE]
■ **1** see SQUARE *n.* 3a.

pibroch /péebrokh, -brok/ *n.* a series of esp. martial or funerary variations on a theme for the bagpipes. [Gael. *piobaireachd* art of piping f. *piobair* piper f. *piob* f. E PIPE]

pic /pik/ *n. colloq.* a picture, esp. a cinema film. [abbr.]
■ see FILM *n.* 3a, b, PICTURE *n.* 1a.

pica[1] /pīkə/ *n. Printing* **1** a unit of type-size (1/6 inch). **2** a size of letters in typewriting (10 per inch). [AL *pica* 15th-c. book of rules about church feasts, perh. formed as PIE[2]]

pica[2] /pīkə/ *n. Med.* the eating of substances other than normal food. [mod.L or med.L, = magpie]

picador /píkkədor/ *n.* a mounted man with a lance who goads the bull in a bullfight. [Sp. f. *picar* prick]

picaresque /píkkərésk/ *adj.* (of a style of fiction) dealing with the episodic adventures of rogues etc. [F f. Sp. *picaresco* f. *pícaro* rogue]

picaroon /píkkəroōn/ *n.* **1 a** a rogue. **b** a thief. **2 a** a pirate. **b** a pirate ship. [Sp. *picarón* (as PICARESQUE)]
■ **1 a** see ROGUE *n.* 1. **b** see THIEF. **2 a** see PIRATE *n.* 1a.

picayune /píkkəyoōn/ *n.* & *adj. US* ● *n.* **1** *colloq.* a small coin of little value, esp. a 5-cent piece. **2** an insignificant person or thing. ● *adj.* mean; contemptible; petty. [F *picaillon* Piedmontese coin, cash, f. Prov. *picaioun*, of unkn. orig.]
■ *adj.* see PETTY 1, 2.

piccalilli /píkkəlílli/ *n.* (*pl.* **piccalillis**) a pickle of chopped vegetables, mustard, and hot spices. [18th c.: perh. f. PICKLE + CHILLI]

piccaninny /píkkənínni/ *n.* & *adj.* (*US* **pickaninny**) ● *n.* (*pl.* **-ies**) often *offens.* a small Black or Australian Aboriginal child. ● *adj. archaic* very small. [W.Ind. Negro f. Sp. *pequeño* or Port. *pequeno* little]

piccolo /píkkəlō/ *n.* (*pl.* **-os**) **1** a small flute sounding an octave higher than the ordinary one. **2** its player. [It., = small (flute)]

pichiciago /píchisiáygō/ *n.* (*pl.* **-os**) a small S. American armadillo, *Chlamyphorus truncatus*. [Sp. *pichiciego* perh. f. Guarani *pichey* armadillo + Sp. *ciego* blind f. L *caecus*]

pick[1] /pik/ *v.* & *n.* ● *v.tr.* **1** (also *absol.*) choose carefully from a number of alternatives (*picked the pink one*; *picked a team*; *picked the right moment to intervene*). **2** detach or pluck (a flower, fruit, etc.) from a stem, tree, etc. **3 a** probe (the teeth, nose, ears, a pimple, etc.) with the finger, an instrument, etc. to remove unwanted matter. **b** clear (a bone, carcass, etc.) of scraps of meat etc. **4** (also *absol.*) (of a person) eat (food, a meal, etc.) in small bits; nibble without appetite. **5** (also *absol.*) esp. *US* pluck the strings of (a banjo etc.). **6** remove stalks etc. from (esp. soft fruit) before cooking. **7 a** select (a route or path) carefully over difficult terrain by foot. **b** place (one's steps etc.) carefully. **8** pull apart (*pick oakum*). **9** (of a bird) take up (grains etc.) in the beak. ● *n.* **1** the act or an instance of picking. **2 a** a selection or choice. **b** the right to select (*had first pick of the prizes*). **3** (usu. foll. by *of*) the best (*the pick of the bunch*). □ **pick and choose** select carefully or fastidiously. **pick at 1** eat (food) without interest; nibble. **2** = *pick on* 1 (PICK[1]). **pick a person's brains** extract ideas, information, etc., from a person for one's own use. **pick holes** (or **a hole**) **in 1** make holes in (material etc.) by plucking, poking, etc. **2** find fault with (an idea etc.). **pick a lock** open a lock with an instrument other than the proper key, esp. with intent to steal. **pick-me-up 1** a tonic for the nerves etc. **2** a good experience, good news, etc. that cheers. **pick off 1** pluck (leaves etc.) off. **2** shoot (people etc.) one by one without haste. **3** eliminate (opposition etc.) singly. **pick on 1** find fault with; nag at. **2** select. **pick out 1** take from a larger number (*picked him out from the others*). **2** distinguish from surrounding objects or at a distance (*can just pick out the church spire*). **3** play (a tune) by ear on the piano etc. **4** (often foll. by *in*, *with*) **a** highlight (a painting etc.) with touches of another colour. **b** accentuate (decoration, a painting, etc.) with a contrasting colour (*picked out the handles in red*). **5** make out (the meaning of a passage etc.). **pick over** select the best from. **pick a person's pockets** steal the contents of a person's pockets. **pick a quarrel** start an argument or a fight deliberately. **pick to pieces** = *take to pieces* (see PIECE). **pick up 1** grasp and raise (from the ground etc.) (*picked up his hat*). **2** gain or acquire by chance or without effort (*picked up a cold*). **3 a** fetch (a person, animal, or thing) left in another person's charge. **b** stop for and take along with one, esp. in a vehicle (*pick me up on the corner*). **4** make the acquaintance of (a person) casually, esp. as a sexual overture. **5** (of one's health, the weather, share prices, etc.) recover, prosper, improve. **6** (of a motor engine etc.) recover speed; accelerate. **7** (of the police etc.) take into charge; arrest. **8** detect by scrutiny or with a telescope, searchlight, radio, etc. (*picked up most of the mistakes*; *picked up a distress signal*). **9** (often foll. by *with*) form or renew a friendship. **10** accept the responsibility of paying (a bill etc.). **11** (*refl.*) raise (oneself etc.) after a fall etc. **12** raise (the feet etc.) clear of the ground. **13** *Golf* pick up one's ball, esp. when conceding a hole. **pick-up 1** *sl.* a person met casually, esp. for sexual purposes. **2** a small open motor truck. **3 a** the part of a record-player carrying the stylus. **b** a detector of vibrations etc. **4 a** the act of picking up. **b** something picked up. **5** *colloq.* = *pick-me-up* 1 above. **pick-your-own** (usu. *attrib.*) (of commercially grown fruit and vegetables) dug or picked by the customer at the place of production. **take one's pick** make a choice. ▫▫ **pickable** *adj.* [ME, earlier *pike*, of unkn. orig.]

▪ *v.* **1** select, choose, pick out, pick on, cull, sort out, single out, opt for, fix *or* decide upon, go for, elect, settle upon *or* on, screen out, sift out. **2** pluck, gather, collect, harvest, bring *or* take in, garner. **4** pick at, nibble, peck; snack. ● *n.* **2 a** selection, choice, option, preference. **3** choicest, best, *crème de la crème*, cream, finest, first. ▫ **pick at 1** nibble (at), peck at; play *or* toy *or* mess *or* fiddle with. **pick holes** (or **a hole**) **in 2** see CRITICIZE 1. **pick off 2, 3** shoot (down), kill; see also ELIMINATE 1. **pick on 1** bully, intimidate, abuse, browbeat, badger, harry, hector, tease, taunt, needle, torment, *US* ride; criticize, carp at, find fault with, cavil at, quibble at, pick at, nag (at), niggle (at), harass, pester, annoy, irritate, bother. **2** see PICK *v.* 1 above. **pick out 1** see PICK *v.* 1 above. **2** discern, distinguish, make out, recognize, discriminate. **pick a quarrel** start a quarrel, pick *or* start a fight. **pick up 1** raise (up), lift (up), take up. **2** acquire, learn, become acquainted with, *colloq.* get the hang of; find, come by, get hold of, obtain; catch, come down with, contract, get, develop, fall ill with, *Brit.* go down with. **3** fetch; call for, give a lift *or* ride to, collect, come *or* go for. **4** meet, introduce oneself to, strike up an acquaintance with; make advances to; see also APPROACH *v.* 3. **5** improve, get better, make headway, recover, perk up, rally, (make) progress, move ahead, increase, prosper, make a comeback. **6** recover, revive, accelerate, speed up. **7** arrest, apprehend, detain, take into custody *or* charge, collar, *colloq.* run in, pull in, *esp. US colloq.* bust, *sl.* pinch, nab, *Brit. sl.* nick.

pick[2] /pik/ *n.* & *v.* ● *n.* **1** a long-handled tool having a usu. curved iron bar pointed at one or both ends, used for breaking up hard ground, masonry, etc. **2** *colloq.* a plectrum. **3** any instrument for picking, such as a toothpick. ● *v.tr.* **1** break the surface of (the ground etc.) with or as if with a pick. **2** make (holes etc.) in this way. [ME, app. var. of PIKE[2]]

pickaback var. of PIGGYBACK.

pickaninny *US* var. of PICCANINNY.

pickaxe /píkkaks/ *n.* & *v.* (*US* **pickax**) ● *n.* = PICK[2] *n.* 1. ● *v.* **1** *tr.* break (the ground etc.) with a pickaxe. **2** *intr.* work with a pickaxe. [ME *pikois* f. OF *picois*, rel. to PIKE[2]: assim. to AXE]

pickelhaube /píkk'lhowbə/ *n. hist.* a German soldier's spiked helmet. [G]

picker /píkkər/ *n.* **1** a person or thing that picks. **2** (often in *comb.*) a person who gathers or collects (*hop-picker*; *rag-picker*).

pickerel /píkkərəl/ *n.* (*pl.* same or **pickerels**) a young pike. [ME, dimin. of PIKE[1]]

picket /píkkit/ *n.* & *v.* ● *n.* **1** a person or group of people outside a place of work, intending to persuade esp. workers not to enter during a strike etc. **2** a pointed stake or peg driven into the ground to form a fence or palisade, to tether a horse, etc. **3** (also **picquet**, **piquet**) *Mil.* **a** a small body of troops or a single soldier sent out to watch for the enemy, held in readiness, etc. **b** a party of sentries. **c** an outpost. **d** a camp-guard on police duty in a garrison town etc. ● *v.* (**picketed**, **picketing**) **1 a** *tr.* & *intr.* station or act as a picket. **b** *tr.* beset or guard (a factory, workers, etc.) with a picket or pickets. **2** *tr.* secure with stakes. **3** *tr.* tether (an animal). ▫ **picket line** a boundary established by workers on strike, esp. at the entrance to the place of work, which others are asked not to cross. ▫▫ **picketer** *n.* [F *piquet* pointed stake f. *piquer* prick, f. *pic* PICK[2]]

▪ *n.* **1** picketer, demonstrator, protester, striker. **2** stake, pale, post, peg, stanchion, upright, rod, palisade, paling. **3 a, b** guard, patrol, watch; sentry, sentinel, scout, observer, vedette, *archaic or hist.* watchman. ● *v.* **1** protest, demonstrate; blockade; see also STRIKE *v.* 17a. **2** enclose, shut in, wall in, fence (in), hem in, box in. **3** see TETHER *v.*

pickings /píkkingz/ *n.pl.* **1** perquisites; pilferings (*rich pickings*). **2** remaining scraps; gleanings.

▪ **1** see SPOIL *n.* 1. **2** see SCRAP *n.* 6a.

pickle /píkk'l/ *n.* & *v.* ● *n.* **1 a** (often in *pl.*) food, esp. vegetables, preserved in brine, vinegar, mustard, etc. and used as a relish. **b** the brine, vinegar, etc. in which food is preserved. **2** *colloq.* a plight (*a fine pickle we are in!*). **3** *Brit. colloq.* a mischievous child. **4** an acid solution for cleaning metal etc. ● *v.tr.* **1** preserve in pickle. **2** treat with pickle. **3** (as **pickled** *adj.*) *sl.* drunk. [ME *pekille*, *pykyl*, f. MDu., MLG *pekel*, of unkn. orig.]

▪ *n.* **2** see PLIGHT[1]. ● *v.* **3** (**pickled**) see DRUNK *adj.* 1.

pickler /píklər/ *n.* **1** a person who pickles vegetables etc. **2** a vegetable suitable for pickling.

picklock /píklok/ *n.* **1** a person who picks locks. **2** an instrument for this.

▪ **1** see THIEF.

pickpocket /píkpokkit/ *n.* a person who steals from the pockets of others.

▪ **1** see THIEF.

Pickwickian /pikwíkkiən/ *adj.* **1** of or like Mr Pickwick in Dickens's *Pickwick Papers*, esp. in being jovial, plump, etc. **2** (of words or their sense) misunderstood or misused, esp. to avoid offence.

picky /píkki/ *adj.* (**pickier**, **pickiest**) *colloq.* excessively fastidious; choosy. ▫▫ **pickiness** *n.*

▪ see FASTIDIOUS 1.

picnic /píknik/ *n.* & *v.* ● *n.* **1** an outing or excursion including a packed meal eaten out of doors. **2** any meal eaten out of doors or without preparation, tables, chairs, etc. **3** (usu. with *neg.*) *colloq.* something agreeable or easily accomplished etc. (*it was no picnic organizing the meeting*). ● *v.intr.* (**picnicked**, **picnicking**) take part in a picnic. ▫▫ **picnicker** *n.* **picnicky** *adj. colloq.* [F *pique-nique*, of unkn. orig.]

▪ *n.* **2** garden party, barbecue, *US* cookout. **3** child's play, *colloq.* pushover, cinch, piece of cake, *esp. US colloq.* breeze; see also BREEZE[1] *n.* 5; (*no picnic*) torture, agony, *colloq.* a pain in the neck, *esp. US sl.* pain in the butt; difficult, arduous, torturous, agonizing, painful, disagreeable, tough, hard, rough, unpleasant.

pico- /píkō, péekō/ *comb. form* denoting a factor of 10^{-12} (*picometre*). [Sp. *pico* beak, peak, little bit]

picot /péekō/ *n.* a small loop of twisted thread in a lace edging etc. [F, dimin. of *pic* peak, point]

picotee /píkkətée/ *n.* a type of carnation of which the flowers have a light ground and dark-edged petals. [F *picoté -ée* past part. of *picoter* prick (as PICOT)]

picquet var. of PICKET 3.

picric acid /píkrik/ *n.* a very bitter yellow compound used in dyeing and surgery and in explosives. ▫▫ **picrate** /-rayt/ *n.* [Gk *pikros* bitter]

Pict /pikt/ *n.* a member of an ancient people of N. Britain. ▫▫ **Pictish** *adj.* [ME f. LL *Picti* perh. f. *pingere pict-* paint, tattoo]

pictograph /píktəgraaf/ *n.* (also **pictogram** /píktəgram/) **1 a** a pictorial symbol for a word or phrase. **b** an ancient record consisting of these. **2** a pictorial representation of statistics etc. on a chart, graph, etc. ▫▫ **pictographic** /-gráffik/ *adj.* **pictography** /-tógrəfi/ *n.* [L *pingere pict-* paint]

pictorial /piktóriəl/ *adj.* & *n.* ● *adj.* **1** of or expressed in a picture or pictures. **2** illustrated. **3** picturesque. ● *n.* a journal, postage stamp, etc., with a picture or pictures as the main feature. ▫▫ **pictorially** *adv.* [LL *pictorius* f. L *pictor* painter (as PICTURE)]

■ *adj.* **3** see PICTURESQUE 1.

picture /píkchər/ *n.* & *v.* ● *n.* **1 a** (often *attrib.*) a painting, drawing, photograph, etc., esp. as a work of art (*picture frame*). **b** a portrait, esp. a photograph, of a person (*does not like to have her picture taken*). **c** a beautiful object (*her hat is a picture*). **2 a** a total visual or mental impression produced; a scene (*the picture looks bleak*). **b** a written or spoken description (*drew a vivid picture of moral decay*). **3 a** a film. **b** (in *pl.*) *Brit.* a showing of films at a cinema (*went to the pictures*). **c** (in *pl.*) films in general. **4** an image on a television screen. **5** *colloq.* **a** esp. *iron.* a person or thing exemplifying something (*he was the picture of innocence*). **b** a person or thing resembling another closely (*the picture of her aunt*). ● *v.tr.* **1** represent in a picture. **2** (also *refl.*; often foll. by *to*) imagine, esp. visually or vividly (*pictured it to herself*). **3** describe graphically. ▫ **get the picture** *colloq.* grasp the tendency or drift of circumstances, information, etc. **in the picture** fully informed or noticed. **out of the picture** uninvolved, inactive; irrelevant. **picture-book** a book containing many illustrations. **picture-card** a court-card. **picture-gallery** a place containing an exhibition or collection of pictures. **picture-goer** a person who frequents the cinema. **picture hat** a woman's wide-brimmed highly decorated hat as in pictures by Reynolds and Gainsborough. **picture-moulding 1** woodwork etc. used for framing pictures. **2** a rail on a wall used for hanging pictures from. **picture-palace** (or **-theatre**) *Brit. archaic* a cinema. **picture postcard** a postcard with a picture on one side. **picture window** a very large window consisting of one pane of glass. **picture-writing** a mode of recording events etc. by pictorial symbols as in early hieroglyphics etc. [ME f. L *pictura* f. *pingere pict-* paint]

■ *n.* **1 a** drawing, painting, portrait, depiction, representation, illustration, sketch, photograph, photo. **2** impression, idea, notion, understanding, image; see also SCENE 6. **3** film, *Brit. colloq.* flick, *esp. US colloq.* movie; cinema, *Brit. colloq.* flicks, *esp. US colloq.* movies. **5 a** model, prototype, epitome, essence, embodiment, incarnation, personification, perfect example. **b** image, (perfect *or* exact) likeness, double, duplicate, twin, (exact) replica, facsimile, dead ringer, *colloq.* spitting image. ● *v.* **1** depict, draw, portray, paint, represent, show, illustrate. **2** envision, envisage, visualize, imagine, fancy, conceive (of), see in the mind's eye, contemplate. ▫ **get the picture** get the gist *or* drift; see also UNDERSTAND 7. **in the picture** see INFORMED 1; (*put in the picture*) inform *or* advise fully, *colloq.* fill in. **out of the picture** see IRRELEVANT. **picture-palace** (or **-theatre**) cinema, theatre, *esp. US colloq.* movie-house, *S.Afr. sl.* bioscope; flea-pit.

picturesque /píkchərésk/ *adj.* **1** (of landscape etc.) beautiful or striking, as in a picture. **2** (of language etc.) strikingly graphic; vivid. ▫▫ **picturesquely** *adv.* **picturesqueness** *n.* [F *pittoresque* f. It. *pittoresco* f. *pittore* painter f. L (as PICTORIAL): assim. to PICTURE]

■ **1** beautiful, charming, idyllic, fetching, attractive, pretty, lovely, quaint, delightful, pleasing, scenic, interesting, striking. **2** colourful, graphic, realistic, vivid, striking.

piddle /pídd'l/ *v.* & *n.* ● *v.intr.* **1** *colloq.* urinate (used esp. to or by children). **2** work or act in a trifling way. **3** (as **piddling** *adj.*) *colloq.* trivial; trifling. ● *n. colloq.* **1** urination. **2** urine (used esp. to or by children). ▫▫ **piddler** *n.* [sense 1 prob. f. PISS + PUDDLE: sense 2 perh. f. PEDDLE]

■ *v.* **1** see URINATE. **3** (**piddling**) see TRIFLING. ● *n.* **2** urine, *colloq.* pee, widdle, *esp. Brit. sl.* wee.

piddock /píddək/ *n.* any rock-boring bivalve mollusc of the family Pholadidae, used for bait. [18th c.: orig. unkn.]

pidgin /píjin/ *n.* a simplified language containing vocabulary from two or more languages, used for communication between people not having a common language. ▫ **pidgin English** a pidgin in which the chief language is English, used orig. between Chinese and Europeans. [corrupt. of *business*]

pi-dog var. of PYE-DOG.

pie[1] /pī/ *n.* **1** a baked dish of meat, fish, fruit, etc., usu. with a top and base of pastry. **2** anything resembling a pie in form (*a mud pie*). ▫ **easy as pie** very easy. **pie chart** a circle divided into sectors to represent relative quantities. **pie-eater** *Austral. sl.* a person of little account. **pie-eyed** *sl.* drunk. **pie in the sky** an unrealistic prospect of future happiness after present suffering; a misleading promise. [ME, perh. = PIE[2] f. miscellaneous contents compared to objects collected by a magpie]

■ **1** see TART[1] 2. ▫ **pie-eyed** see DRUNK *adj.* 1.

pie[2] /pī/ *n. archaic* **1** a magpie. **2** a pied animal. [ME f. OF f. L *pica*]

pie[3] /pī/ *n.* & *v.* (*US* **pi**) ● *n.* **1** a confused mass of printers' type. **2** chaos. ● *v.tr.* (**pieing**) muddle up (type). [perh. transl. F PÂTÉ = PIE[1]]

pie[4] /pī/ *n. hist.* a former monetary unit of India equal to one-twelfth of an anna. [Hind. etc. *pā'ī* f. Skr. *pad, padī* quarter]

piebald /píbawld/ *adj.* & *n.* ● *adj.* **1** (usu. of an animal, esp. a horse) having irregular patches of two colours, esp. black and white. **2** motley; mongrel. ● *n.* a piebald animal, esp. a horse.

■ *adj.* **1** see *dapple grey* 1. ● *n.* see DAPPLE *n.* 2.

piece /peess/ *n.* & *v.* ● *n.* **1 a** (often foll. by *of*) one of the distinct portions forming part of or broken off from a larger object; a bit; a part (*a piece of string*). **b** each of the parts of which a set or category is composed (*a five-piece band; a piece of furniture*). **2** a coin of specified value (*50p piece*). **3 a** a usu. short literary or musical composition or a picture. **b** a theatrical play. **4** an item, instance, or example (*a piece of impudence; a piece of news*). **5 a** any of the objects used to make moves in board-games. **b** a chessman (strictly, other than a pawn). **6** a definite quantity in which a thing is sold. **7** (often foll. by *of*) an enclosed portion (of land etc.). **8** *sl. derog.* a woman. **9** *US* (foll. by *of*) *sl.* a financial share or investment in (*has a piece of the new production*). ● *v.tr.* **1** (usu. foll. by *together*) form into a whole; put together; join (*finally pieced his story together*). **2** (usu. foll. by *out*) **a** eke out. **b** form (a theory etc.) by combining parts etc. **3** (usu. foll. by *up*) patch. **4** join (threads) in spinning. ▫ **break to pieces** break into fragments. **by the piece** (paid) according to the quantity of work done. **go to pieces** collapse emotionally; suffer a breakdown. **in one piece 1** unbroken. **2** unharmed. **in pieces** broken. **of a piece** (often foll. by *with*) uniform, consistent, in keeping. **piece-goods** fabrics, esp. Lancashire cottons, woven in standard lengths. **a piece of the action** *sl.* a share of the profits; a share in the excitement. **a piece of cake** see CAKE. **piece of eight** *hist.* a Spanish dollar, equivalent to 8 reals. **piece of goods** *sl. derog.* a woman. **a piece of one's mind** a sharp rebuke or lecture. **piece of water** a small lake etc. **piece of work** a thing made by working (cf. *nasty piece of work*). **piece-rates** a rate paid according to the amount produced. **piece-work** work paid for by the amount produced. **say one's piece** give one's opinion or make a prepared statement. **take to pieces 1** break up or dismantle. **2** criticize harshly. ▫▫ **piecer** *n.* (in sense 4 of *v.*). [ME f. AF *pece*, OF *piece* f. Rmc, prob. of Gaulish orig.: cf. PEAT]

■ *n.* **1 a** bit, morsel, scrap, chunk, hunk, sliver, lump, particle, fragment, shred, shard, wedge, slice; share, portion, part, segment, section, percentage, proportion; serving, helping. **3** work, composition; (short) story, article, essay, poem; piece of music, opus, (musical) number, arrangement, tune, melody, song, air, jingle, ditty; production, play, drama, sketch, show. **4** item, instance; see also EXAMPLE *n.* 1. **5** man, token; chessman, draughtsman, checkerman, *US* checker. **8** see *bit of fluff* (FLUFF). **9** share, investment, interest, holding, percentage, stake, quota, portion. ● *v.* **1** (*piece together*) assemble, put together; join, fix, unite, mend; make sense of. **2** (*piece out*) **a** see SHARE[1] *v.* 1, 2, 5. ▫ **break to pieces** fall apart, disintegrate, crumble, shatter; see also BREAK[1] *v.* 1a. **go to pieces** collapse, be shattered, have a nervous breakdown, disintegrate, go out of *or* lose control, break down, *colloq.* crack up. **in one piece 2** see UNSCATHED. **in pieces** smashed, destroyed, ruined, shattered, broken. **of a piece** similar, alike, of the same sort *or* kind *or* type; uniform, consistent; in harmony, in agreement, harmonious, in keeping. **piece of goods** see *bit of fluff* (FLUFF). **a piece of one's mind** scolding, rebuke, lecture, reprimand, tongue-lashing, ticking-off, telling-off, chiding, rap over *or* on the knuckles, *colloq.* what for, dressing-down. **say one's piece** have one's say, give one's opinion, say what is on one's mind; vent one's spleen, *colloq.* get a load *or* thing off one's chest. **take to pieces 1** strip (down), dismantle, take apart. **2** see ATTACK *v.* 3.

pièce de résistance /pyéss də rayzeéstonss/ *n.* (*pl.* ***pièces de résistance*** *pronunc.* same) **1** the most important or remarkable item. **2** the most substantial dish at a meal. [F]

■ **1** highlight, (special *or* main) feature, (special *or* main) attraction, speciality, *esp. US* specialty; masterpiece, *chef-d'œuvre*.

piecemeal /peésmeel/ *adv.* & *adj.* ● *adv.* piece by piece; gradually. ● *adj.* partial; gradual; unsystematic. [ME f. PIECE + *-meal* f. OE *mǣlum* (instr. dative pl. of *mǣl* MEAL[1])]

■ *adv.* piece by piece, little by little, inch by inch, bit by bit, inchmeal, gradually, by degrees, slowly; by fits and starts, fitfully, intermittently, sporadically, disjointedly. ● *adj.* partial, inchmeal, gradual; disjointed, fragmentary, sporadic, unsystematic.

piecrust /pīkrust/ *n.* the baked pastry crust of a pie. □ **piecrust table** a table with an indented edge like a piecrust.

pied /pīd/ *adj.* particoloured. □ **Pied Piper** a person enticing followers esp. to their doom. [ME f. PIE[2], orig. of friars]

■ see *mottled* (MOTTLE).

pied-à-terre /pyáydaatáir/ *n.* (*pl.* ***pieds-à-terre*** *pronunc.* same) a usu. small flat, house, etc. kept for occasional use. [F, lit. 'foot to earth']

piedmont /peédmont/ *n.* a gentle slope leading from the foot of mountains to a region of flat land. [It. *piemonte* mountain foot, name of a region at the foot of the Alps]

pie-dog var. of PYE-DOG.

pieman /pīmən/ *n.* (*pl.* **-men**) a pie seller.

pier /peer/ *n.* **1 a** a structure of iron or wood raised on piles and leading out to sea, a lake, etc., used as a promenade and landing-stage, and often with entertainment arcades etc. **b** a breakwater; a mole. **2 a** a support of an arch or of the span of a bridge; a pillar. **b** solid masonry between windows etc. □ **pier-glass** a large mirror, used orig. to fill wall-space between windows. [ME *per* f. AL *pera*, of unkn. orig.]

■ **1 a** landing-stage, jetty, quay, *US* levee; wharf. **2 a** pillar, column, support, pile, piling, post, upright; see also BUTTRESS *n.*

pierce /peerss/ *v.* **1** *tr.* **a** (of a sharp instrument etc.) penetrate the surface of. **b** (often foll. by *with*) prick with a sharp instrument, esp. to make a hole in. **c** make (a hole etc.) (*pierced a hole in the belt*). **d** (of cold, grief, etc.) affect keenly or sharply. **e** (of a light, glance, sound, etc.) penetrate keenly or sharply. **2** (as **piercing** *adj.*) (of a glance, intuition, high noise, bright light, etc.) keen, sharp, or unpleasantly penetrating. **3** *tr.* force (a way etc.) through or into (something) (*pierced their way through the jungle*). **4** *intr.* (usu. foll. by *through, into*) penetrate. □□ **piercer** *n.* **piercingly** *adv.* [ME f. OF *percer* f. L *pertundere* bore through (as PER-, *tundere tus-* thrust)]

■ **1 a, b** puncture, penetrate, thrust *or* poke into, lance, spear, spit, run through *or* into, skewer, impale, fix, transfix; bore into *or* through, drill into *or* through, perforate, hole. **c** see PUNCH[1] *v.* 3. **d** touch, move, melt, stir, rouse, strike; pain, cut to the quick, wound. **2** (**piercing**) strident, shrill, harsh, ear-splitting, high-pitched, loud, blaring; probing, searching, penetrating, sharp, keen; icy, frosty, frigid, chilling, freezing, cold, numbing, wintry, raw, bitter, fierce, biting, nipping, *colloq.* arctic, nippy; stabbing, shooting, excruciating, acute, sharp, severe, agonizing, fierce, intense, painful, racking. **4** (*pierce through* or *into*) see PENETRATE 1a.

pierrot /peérō/ *n.* (*fem.* **pierrette** /peerét/) *Theatr.* **1** a white-faced entertainer in pier shows etc. with a loose white clown's costume. **2** a French pantomime character so dressed. [F, dimin. of *Pierre* Peter]

■ see FOOL[1] *n.* 2.

pietà /pi-etaá/ *n.* a picture or sculpture of the Virgin Mary holding the dead body of Christ on her lap or in her arms. [It. f. L (as PIETY)]

pietas /pīətaass/ *n.* respect due to an ancestor, a forerunner, etc. [L: see PIETY]

pietism /pīətiz'm/ *n.* **1 a** pious sentiment. **b** an exaggerated or affected piety. **2** (esp. as **Pietism**) *hist.* a movement for the revival of piety in the Lutheran Church in the 17th c. □□ **pietist** *n.* **pietistic** /-tístik/ *adj.* **pietistical** /-tístik'l/ *adj.* [G *Pietismus* (as PIETY)]

■ **1** see PIETY. □□ **pietistic, pietistical** see PIOUS 2.

piety /pī-iti/ *n.* (*pl.* **-ies**) **1** the quality of being pious. **2** a pious act. [ME f. OF *pieté* f. L *pietas -tatis* dutifulness (as PIOUS)]

■ **1** devotion, devotedness, respect, deference, dedication, dutifulness, loyalty, affection; piousness, reverence, veneration, devoutness, holiness, godliness, pietism, observance, religiousness, sanctity; sanctimoniousness, sanctimony.

piezoelectricity /pī-eézō-íllektríssiti/ *n.* electric polarization in a substance resulting from the application of mechanical stress, esp. in certain crystals. □□ **piezoelectric** /-iléktrik/ *adj.* **piezoelectrically** /-iléktrikəli/ *adv.* [Gk *piezō* press + ELECTRIC]

piezometer /pī-izómmitər/ *n.* an instrument for measuring the magnitude or direction of pressure.

piffle /píff'l/ *n.* & *v. colloq.* ● *n.* nonsense; empty speech. ● *v.intr.* talk or act feebly; trifle. □□ **piffler** *n.* [imit.]

■ see RUBBISH *n.* 3.

piffling /pifling/ *adj. colloq.* trivial; worthless.

pig /pig/ *n.* & *v.* ● *n.* **1 a** any omnivorous hoofed bristly mammal of the family Suidae, esp. a domesticated kind, *Sus scrofa*. **b** *US* a young pig; a piglet. **c** (often in *comb.*) any similar animal (*guinea-pig*). **2** the flesh of esp. a young or sucking pig as food (*roast pig*). **3** *colloq.* **a** a greedy, dirty, obstinate, sulky, or annoying person. **b** an unpleasant, awkward, or difficult thing, task, etc. **4** an oblong mass of metal (esp. iron or lead) from a smelting-furnace. **5** *sl. derog.* a policeman. ● *v.* (**pigged, pigging**) **1** *tr.* (also *absol.*) (of a sow) bring forth (piglets). **2** *tr. colloq.* eat (food) greedily. **3** *intr.* herd together or behave like pigs. □ **bleed like a pig** (or **stuck pig**) bleed copiously. **buy a pig in a poke** buy, accept, etc. something without knowing its value or esp. seeing it. **in pig** (of a sow) pregnant. **in a pig's eye** *colloq.* certainly not. **make a pig of oneself** overeat. **make a pig's ear of** *colloq.* make a mess of; bungle. **pig in the middle** a person who is placed in an awkward situation between two others (after a ball game for three with one in the middle). **pig-iron** crude iron from a smelting-furnace. **Pig Island** *Austral.* & *NZ sl.* New Zealand. **pig it** live in a disorderly, untidy, or filthy fashion. **pig-jump** *Austral. sl.* *n.* a jump made by a horse from all four legs. ● *v.intr.* (of a horse) jump in this manner. **pig Latin** a made-up jargon. **pig-meat** *Brit.* pork, ham, or bacon. **pig out** (often foll. by *on*) esp. *US sl.* eat gluttonously. **pigs might fly** *iron.* an expression of disbelief. **pig-sticker** a long sharp knife. **pig's wash** = PIGSWILL. □□ **piggish** *adj.* **piggishly** *adv.* **piggishness** *n.* **piglet** *n.* **piglike** *adj.* **pigling** *n.* [ME *pigge* f. OE *pigga* (unrecorded)]

■ *n.* **3 a** see GLUTTON 1, SLOB, STINKER. **5** see *police officer*. ● *v.* **2** see OVEREAT. □ **pig out** see OVEREAT. □□ **piggish** see GREEDY 1. **piggishness** see GREED.

pigeon[1] /píjin/ *n.* **1** any of several large usu. grey and white birds of the family Columbidae, esp. *Columba livia*, often domesticated and bred and trained to carry messages etc.; a dove (cf. *rock-pigeon*). **2** a person easily swindled; a simpleton. □ **pigeon-breast** (or **-chest**) a deformed human chest with a projecting breastbone. **pigeon-breasted** (or **-chested**) having a pigeon-breast. **pigeon-fancier** a person who keeps and breeds fancy pigeons. **pigeon-fancying** this pursuit. **pigeon-hawk** = MERLIN. **pigeon-hearted** cowardly. **pigeon-hole** *n.* **1** each of a set of compartments in a cabinet or on a wall for papers, letters, etc. **2** a small recess for a pigeon to nest in. ● *v.tr.* **1** deposit (a document) in a pigeon-hole. **2** put (a matter) aside for future consideration or to forget it. **3** assign (a person or thing) to a preconceived category. **pigeon pair** *Brit.* **1** boy and girl twins. **2** a boy and girl as sole children. **pigeon's milk 1** a secretion from the oesophagus with which pigeons feed their young. **2** an imaginary article for which children are sent on a fool's errand. **pigeon-toed** (of a person) having the toes turned inwards. □□ **pigeonry** *n.* (*pl.* **-ies**). [ME f. OF *pijon* f. LL *pipio -onis* (imit.)]

■ **2** see DUPE *n.* □□ **pigeon-hole** (*v.*) **2** see DELAY *v.* 1. **3** see LABEL *v.* 2.

pigeon[2] /píjin/ *n.* **1** = PIDGIN. **2** *colloq.* a particular concern, job, or business (*that's not my pigeon*).

piggery /píggəri/ *n.* (*pl.* **-ies**) **1** a pig-breeding farm etc. **2** = PIGSTY. **3** piggishness.

piggy /píggi/ *n.* & *adj.* ● *n.* (also **piggie**) *colloq.* **1** a little pig. **2 a** a child's word for a pig. **b** a child's word for a toe. **3** *Brit.* the game of tipcat. ● *adj.* (**piggier, piggiest**) **1** like a pig. **2** (of features etc.) like those of a pig (*little piggy eyes*). □ **piggy bank** a pig-shaped money box. **piggy in the middle** = *pig in the middle*.

piggyback /píggibak/ *n.* & *adv.* (also **pickaback** /píkkəbak/) ● *n.* a ride on the back and shoulders of another person. ● *adv.* **1** on the back and shoulders of another person. **2** on the back or top of a larger object. [16th c.: orig. unkn.]

pigheaded /píg-héddid/ *adj.* obstinate. □□ **pigheadedly** *adv.* **pigheadedness** *n.*

■ see OBSTINATE. □□ **pigheadedness** see *obstinacy* (OBSTINATE).

pigment /pígmənt/ *n.* & *v.* ● *n.* **1** colouring-matter used as paint or dye, usu. as an insoluble suspension. **2** the natural colouring-matter of animal or plant tissue, e.g. chlorophyll, haemoglobin. ● *v.tr.* colour with or as if with pigment. □□ **pigmental** /-mént'l/ *adj.* **pigmentary** *adj.* [ME f. L *pigmentum* f. *pingere* paint]

■ *n.* see COLOUR *n.* 3. ● *v.* see COLOUR *v.* 1.

pigmentation /pigmәntáysh'n/ *n.* **1** the natural colouring of plants, animals, etc. **2** the excessive colouring of tissue by the deposition of pigment.

■ **1** see COLOUR *n.* 3, 5a.

pigmy var. of PYGMY.

pignut /pígnut/ *n.* = *earth-nut*.

pigpen /pígpen/ *n. US* = PIGSTY.

pigskin /pígskin/ *n.* **1** the hide of a pig. **2** leather made from this. **3** *US* a football.

pigsticking /pígstikking/ *n.* **1** the hunting of wild boar with a spear on horseback. **2** the butchering of pigs.

pigsty /pígstī/ *n.* (*pl.* **-ies**) **1** a pen or enclosure for a pig or pigs. **2** a filthy house, room, etc.

■ **2** see SHAMBLES 1.

pigswill /pígswil/ *n.* kitchen refuse and scraps fed to pigs.

■ see SWILL *n.* 2, 4.

pigtail /pígtayl/ *n.* **1** a plait of hair hanging from the back of the head, or either of a pair at the sides. **2** a thin twist of tobacco. □□ **pigtailed** *adj.*

■ **1** braid, plait. **2** chew, plug, twist, quid.

pigwash /pígwosh/ *n.* = PIGSWILL.

pigweed /pígweed/ *n.* any herb of the genus *Amaranthus*, grown for grain or fodder.

pika /pīkə/ *n.* any small rabbit-like mammal of the genus *Ochotona*, with small ears and no tail. [Tungus *piika*]

pike[1] /pīk/ *n.* (*pl.* same) **1** a large voracious freshwater fish, *Esox lucius*, with a long narrow snout and sharp teeth. **2** any other fish of the family Esocidae. □ **pike-perch** any of various pikelike perches of the genus *Lucioperca* or *Stizostedion*. [ME, = PIKE[2] (because of its pointed jaw)]

pike[2] /pīk/ *n.* & *v.* ● *n.* **1** *hist.* an infantry weapon with a pointed steel or iron head on a long wooden shaft. **2** *N.Engl.* the peaked top of a hill, esp. in names of hills in the Lake District. ● *v.tr.* thrust through or kill with a pike. □ **pike on** *colloq.* withdraw timidly from. [OE *pīc* point, prick: sense 2 perh. f. ON]

■ *n.* **1** see LANCE *n.* 1.

pike[3] /pīk/ *n.* **1** a toll-gate; a toll. **2** a turnpike road. [abbr. of TURNPIKE]

■ **2** see ROAD[1] 1.

pike[4] /pīk/ *n.* a jackknife position in diving or gymnastics. [20th c.: orig. unkn.]

pikelet /pīklit/ *n. N.Engl.* a thin kind of crumpet. [Welsh (*bara*) *pyglyd* pitchy (bread)]

pikeman /pīkmən/ *n.* (*pl.* **-men**) the keeper of a turnpike.

piker /pīkər/ *n.* a cautious, timid, or mean person.

pikestaff /pīkstaaf/ *n.* **1** the wooden shaft of a pike. **2** a walking-stick with a metal point. □ **plain as a pikestaff** quite plain or obvious (orig. *packstaff*, a smooth staff used by a pedlar).

pilaster /pilástər/ *n.* a rectangular column, esp. one projecting from a wall. □□ **pilastered** *adj.* [F *pilastre* f. It. *pilastro* f. med.L *pilastrum* f. L *pila* pillar]

■ see PILLAR 1.

pilau /pilów/ *n.* (also **pilaff** /piláf/, **pilaw** /piláw/) a Middle Eastern or Indian dish of spiced rice or wheat with meat, fish, vegetables, etc. [Turk. *pilâv*]

pilch /pilch/ *n. archaic* a baby's usu. waterproof garment worn over a nappy. [OE *pyl(e)ce* f. LL *pellicia*: see PELISSE]

pilchard /pílchərd/ *n.* a small marine fish, *Sardinia pilchardus* of the herring family (see SARDINE). [16th-c. *pilcher* etc.: orig. unkn.]

pile[1] /pīl/ *n.* & *v.* ● *n.* **1** a heap of things laid or gathered upon one another (*a pile of leaves*). **2 a** a large imposing building (*a stately pile*). **b** a large group of tall buildings. **3** *colloq.* **a** a large quantity. **b** a large amount of money; a fortune (*made his pile*). **4 a** a series of plates of dissimilar metals laid one on another alternately to produce an electric current. **b** = *atomic pile*. **5** a funeral pyre. ● *v.* **1** *tr.* **a** (often foll. by *up, on*) heap up (*piled the plates on the table*). **b** (foll. by *with*) load (*piled the bed with coats*). **2** *intr.* (usu. foll. by *in, into, on, out of*, etc.) crowd hurriedly or tightly (*all piled into the car; piled out of the restaurant*). □ **pile arms** *hist.* place (usu. four) rifles with their butts on the ground and the muzzles together. **pile it on** *colloq.* exaggerate. **pile on the agony** *colloq.* exaggerate for effect or to gain sympathy etc. **pile up 1** accumulate; heap up. **2** *colloq.* run (a ship) aground or cause (a vehicle etc.) to crash. **pile-up** *n. colloq.* a multiple crash of road vehicles. [ME f. OF f. L *pila* pillar, pier, mole]

■ *n.* **1** heap, mound, stack, accumulation, stockpile, mass, mountain, collection, assemblage, batch, hoard, aggregation, congeries, agglomeration, amassment. **3 a** large *or* great amount, a lot, *colloq.* great *or* good deal, *Austral. colloq.* big bickies; (*piles*) ocean(s), lots, masses, stack(s), *colloq.* oodles, tons, bags, heaps, loads. **b** money, fortune, wealth, wad, *sl.* bundle, loot; *colloq.* packet, tidy sum; see also MINT[2] *n.* 2. ● *v.* **1** stack (up), heap (up), mound; accumulate, pile up *or* with, stockpile, amass, collect, assemble, hoard, aggregate, cumulate; load (up). **2** (*pile in* or *into*) crowd in, pack in, jam in, crush in, cram into, jump in. □ **pile it on** see EXAGGERATE 1. **pile up 1** see PILE *v.* 1 above. **2** see CRASH[1] *v.* 3a. **pile-up** (road) accident, crash, (multiple) collision, *colloq.* smash-up.

pile[2] /pīl/ *n.* & *v.* ● *n.* **1** a heavy beam driven vertically into the bed of a river, soft ground, etc., to support the foundations of a superstructure. **2** a pointed stake or post. **3** *Heraldry* a wedge-shaped device. ● *v.tr.* **1** provide with piles. **2** drive (piles) into the ground etc. □ **pile-driver** a machine for driving piles into the ground. **pile-dwelling** a dwelling built on piles, esp. in a lake. [OE *pīl* f. L *pilum* javelin]

pile[3] /pīl/ *n.* **1** the soft projecting surface on velvet, plush, etc., or esp. on a carpet; nap. **2** soft hair or down, or the wool of a sheep. [ME prob. f. AF *pyle, peile,* OF *poil* f. L *pilus* hair]
■ nap, shag, plush; fuzz, down, fleece.

piles /pīlz/ *n.pl. colloq.* haemorrhoids. [ME prob. f. L *pila* ball, f. the globular form of external piles]

pileus /pīliəss/ *n.* (*pl.* **pilei** /-li-ī/) the caplike part of a mushroom or other fungus. ▫▫ **pileate** /-liət/ *adj.* **pileated** /-liaytid/ *adj.* [L, = felt cap]

pilewort /pīlwurt/ *n.* the lesser celandine. [PILES, f. its reputed efficacy against piles]

pilfer /pilfər/ *v.tr.* (also *absol.*) steal (objects) esp. in small quantities. ▫▫ **pilferage** /-rij/ *n.* **pilferer** *n.* [ME f. AF & OF *pelfrer* pillage, of unkn. orig.: assoc. with archaic *pill* plunder: PELF]
■ steal, rob, plunder, thieve, filch, take, snatch, grab, *colloq.* walk off with, lift, snaffle, swipe, rip off, *formal or joc.* purloin, *sl.* hook, snitch, pinch, *Brit. sl.* nick; see also APPROPRIATE *v.* 1.

pilgrim /pilgrim/ *n.* & *v.* ● *n.* **1** a person who journeys to a sacred place for religious reasons. **2** a person regarded as journeying through life etc. **3** a traveller. ● *v.intr.* (**pilgrimed, pilgriming**) wander like a pilgrim. ▫ **Pilgrim Fathers** English Puritans who founded the colony of Plymouth, Massachusetts, in 1620. ▫▫ **pilgrimize** *v.intr.* (also **-ise**). [ME *pilegrim* f. Prov. *pelegrin* f. L *peregrinus* stranger: see PEREGRINE]
■ *n.* **1** hajji, *hist.* palmer.

pilgrimage /pilgrimij/ *n.* & *v.* ● *n.* **1** a pilgrim's journey (*go on a pilgrimage*). **2** life viewed as a journey. **3** any journey taken for nostalgic or sentimental reasons. ● *v.intr.* go on a pilgrimage. [ME f. Prov. *pilgrinatge* (as PILGRIM)]
■ *n.* **1** hajj, holy expedition. **3** expedition, journey, trek, voyage, tour, trip, excursion.

Pilipino /pillipeénō/ *n.* the national language of the Philippines. [Tagalog f. Sp. *Filipino*]

pill /pil/ *n.* **1 a** a solid medicine formed into a ball or a flat disc for swallowing whole. **b** (usu. prec. by *the*) *colloq.* a contraceptive pill. **2** an unpleasant or painful necessity; a humiliation (*a bitter pill; must swallow the pill*). **3** *colloq.* or *joc.* a ball, e.g. a football, a cannon-ball. **4** *sl.* a bore. ▫ **pill-popper** *colloq.* a person who takes pills freely; a drug addict. **pill-pusher** *colloq.* a drug pusher. **sugar** (or **sweeten**) **the pill** make an unpleasant necessity acceptable. [MDu., MLG *pille* prob. f. L *pilula* dimin. of *pila* ball]
■ **1 a** tablet, capsule, bolus, pellet, pilule; pastille, lozenge, troche. **2** see DISCOMFORT *n.* 1a, BURDEN *n.* 1, 2. **4** nuisance, bore, pest, *colloq.* pain (in the neck), crank, drag. ▫ **pill-popper** see ADDICT *n.* 1. **sugar the pill** ease the pain, lighten the load.

pillage /pillij/ *v.* & *n.* ● *v.tr.* (also *absol.*) plunder; sack (a place or a person). ● *n.* **1** the act or an instance of pillaging, esp. in war. **2** *hist.* goods plundered. ▫▫ **pillager** *n.* [ME f. OF f. *piller* plunder]
■ *v.* plunder, raid, ravage, sack, rob, loot, ransack, rifle, maraud, vandalize, *literary* despoil. ● *n.* **1** plunder, despoliation, looting, robbery, sack, ransacking, brigandage, piracy, banditry, depredation, vandalization, destruction, *literary* despoiling, *rhet.* rapine. **2** plunder, loot, booty, spoils.

pillar /pillər/ *n.* **1 a** a usu. slender vertical structure of wood, metal, or esp. stone used as a support for a roof etc. **b** a similar structure used for ornament. **c** a post supporting a structure. **2** a person regarded as a mainstay or support (*a pillar of the faith; a pillar of strength*). **3** an upright mass of air, water, rock, etc. (*pillar of salt*). **4** a solid mass of coal etc. left to support the roof of a mine. ▫ **from pillar to post** (driven etc.) from one place to another; to and fro. **pillar-box** *Brit.* a public postbox shaped like a pillar. **pillar-box red** a bright red colour, as of pillar-boxes. **Pillars of Hercules 1** two rocks on either side of the Strait of Gibraltar. **2** the ultimate limit. ▫▫ **pillared** *adj.* **pillaret** *n.* [ME & AF *piler,* OF *pilier* ult. f. L *pila* pillar]
■ **1** column, pilaster, pile, piling, pier, upright, post, shaft, prop. **2** mainstay, support(er), upholder, backbone, lynchpin; leader. ▫ **from pillar to post** to and fro, up and down, back and forth, *literary or dial.* hither and yon; all over (the place).

pillbox /pilboks/ *n.* **1** a small shallow cylindrical box for holding pills. **2** a hat of a similar shape. **3** *Mil.* a small partly underground enclosed concrete fort used as an outpost.

pillion /pilyən/ *n.* **1** seating for a passenger behind a motor cyclist. **2** *hist.* **a** a woman's light saddle. **b** a cushion attached to the back of a saddle for a usu. female passenger. ▫ **ride pillion** travel seated behind a motor cyclist etc. [Gael. *pillean, pillin* dimin. of *pell* cushion f. L *pellis* skin]

pilliwinks /pilliwingks/ *n. hist.* an instrument of torture used for squeezing the fingers. [ME *pyrwykes, pyrewinkes,* of unkn. orig.]

pillock /pillək/ *n. Brit. sl.* a stupid person; a fool. [16th c., = penis (var. of *pillicock*): 20th c. in sense defined]
■ see FOOL[1] *n.* 1.

pillory /pilləri/ *n.* & *v.* ● *n.* (*pl.* **-ies**) *hist.* a wooden framework with holes for the head and hands, enabling the public to assault or ridicule a person so imprisoned. ● *v.tr.* (**-ies, -ied**) **1** expose (a person) to ridicule or public contempt. **2** *hist.* put in the pillory. [ME f. AL *pillorium* f. OF *pilori* etc.: prob. f. Prov. *espilori* of uncert. orig.]
■ *v.* **1** see DENOUNCE 1, RIDICULE *v.*

pillow /pillō/ *n.* & *v.* ● *n.* **1 a** a usu. oblong support for the head, esp. in bed, with a cloth cover stuffed with feathers, flock, foam rubber, etc. **b** any pillow-shaped block or support. **2** = *lace-pillow.* ● *v.tr.* **1** rest (the head etc.) on or as if on a pillow (*pillowed his head on his arms*). **2** serve as a pillow for (*moss pillowed her head*). ▫ **pillow-fight** a mock fight with pillows, esp. by children. **pillow-lace** lace made on a lace-pillow. **pillow lava** lava forming rounded masses. **pillow talk** romantic or intimate conversation in bed. ▫▫ **pillowy** *adj.* [OE *pyle, pylu,* ult. f. L *pulvinus* cushion]
■ *n.* **1** bolster, pad, cushion.

pillowcase /pillōkayss/ *n.* a washable cotton etc. cover for a pillow.

pillowslip /pillōslip/ *n.* = PILLOWCASE.

pillule var. of PILULE.

pillwort /pilwurt/ *n.* an aquatic fern, *Pilularia globulifera,* with small globular spore-producing bracts.

pilose /pīlōz/ *adj.* (also **pilous** /pīləss/) covered with hair. ▫▫ **pilosity** /pīlóssiti/ *n.* [L *pilosus* f. *pilus* hair]

pilot /pīlət/ *n.* & *v.* ● *n.* **1** a person who operates the flying controls of an aircraft. **2** a person qualified to take charge of a ship entering or leaving harbour. **3** (usu. *attrib.*) an experimental undertaking or test, esp. in advance of a larger one (*a pilot project*). **4** a guide; a leader. **5** *archaic* a steersman. ● *v.tr.* (**piloted, piloting**) **1** act as a pilot on (a ship) or of (an aircraft). **2** conduct, lead, or initiate as a pilot (*piloted the new scheme*). ▫ **pilot balloon** a small balloon used to track air currents etc. **pilot-bird** a rare dark-brown Australian babbler, *Pycnoptilus floccosus,* with a distinctive loud cry. **pilot chute** a small parachute used to bring the main one into operation. **pilot-cloth** thick blue woollen cloth for seamen's coats etc. **pilot-fish** a small fish, *Naucrates ductor,* said to act as a pilot leading a shark to food. **pilot-house** = *wheel-house.* **pilot-jacket** = PEA-JACKET. **pilot-light 1** a small gas burner kept alight to light another. **2** an electric indicator light or control light. **pilot officer** *Brit.* the lowest commissioned rank in the RAF. ▫▫ **pilotage** *n.* **pilotless** *adj.* [F *pilote* f. med.L *pilotus, pedot(t)a* f. Gk *pēdon* oar]
■ *n.* **1** captain, aviator, aviatrix, airman, airwoman, *colloq.* flyer. **2, 5** steersman, helmsman, navigator, *US* wheelsman. **3** see TRIAL 2a–c. **4** leader, cicerone, conductor; see also GUIDE *n.* 1–4. ● *v.* steer, navigate, drive; fly; conduct, guide, run, control, lead; initiate; see also DIRECT *v.* 1.

Pilsner /pílznər, píls-/ *n.* (also **Pilsener**) a lager beer brewed or like that brewed at *Pilsen* (Plzeň) in the Czech Republic.

pilule /pílyōōl/ *n.* (also **pillule**) a small pill. □□ **pilular** *adj.* **pilulous** *adj.* [F f. L *pilula*: see PILL]
■ see PILL 1a.

pimento /piméntō/ *n.* (*pl.* **-os**) **1** a small tropical tree, *Pimenta dioica*, native to Jamaica. **2** the unripe dried berries of this, usu. crushed for culinary use. Also called ALLSPICE. **3** = PIMIENTO. [Sp. *pimiento* (as PIMIENTO)]

pimiento /pímmi-éntō/ *n.* (*pl.* **-os**) = *sweet pepper* (see PEPPER). [Sp. f. L *pigmentum* PIGMENT, in med.L = spice]

pimp /pimp/ *n.* & *v.* ● *n.* a man who lives off the earnings of a prostitute or a brothel; a pander; a ponce. ● *v.intr.* act as a pimp. [17th c.: orig. unkn.]
■ *n.* procurer, pander, souteneur, *archaic* whoremonger, whoremaster, *Brit. sl.* ponce, *sl. derog.* fancy man. ● *v.* procure.

pimpernel /pímpərnel/ *n.* any plant of the genus *Anagallis*, esp. = *scarlet pimpernel*. [ME f. OF *pimpernelle*, *piprenelle* ult. f. L *piper* PEPPER]

pimping /pímping/ *adj.* **1** small or mean. **2** sickly. [17th c.: orig. unkn.]

pimple /pímp'l/ *n.* **1** a small hard inflamed spot on the skin. **2** anything resembling a pimple, esp. in relative size. □□ **pimpled** *adj.* **pimply** *adj.* [ME nasalized f. OE *piplian* break out in pustules]
■ **1** spot, pustule, papula, blackhead, pock, *Med.* comedo, *colloq.* whitehead,, *esp. US sl.* zit; boil, swelling, eruption, carbuncle, excrescence.

PIN /pin/ *n.* personal identification number (as issued by a bank etc. to validate electronic transactions). [abbr.]

pin /pin/ *n.* & *v.* ● *n.* **1 a** a small thin pointed piece of esp. steel wire with a round or flattened head used (esp. in sewing) for holding things in place, attaching one thing to another, etc. **b** any of several types of pin (*drawing-pin*; *safety pin*; *hairpin*). **c** a small brooch (*diamond pin*). **d** a badge fastened with a pin. **2** a peg of wood or metal for various purposes, e.g. a wooden skittle in bowling. **3** something of small value (*don't care a pin*; *for two pins I'd resign*). **4** (in *pl.*) *colloq.* legs (*quick on his pins*). **5** *Med.* a steel rod used to join the ends of fractured bones while they heal. **6** *Chess* a position in which a piece is pinned to another. **7** *Golf* a stick with a flag placed in a hole to mark its position. **8** *Mus.* a peg round which one string of a musical instrument is fastened. **9** a half-firkin cask for beer. ● *v.tr.* (**pinned, pinning**) **1 a** (often foll. by *to*, *up*, *together*) fasten with a pin or pins (*pinned up the hem*; *pinned the papers together*). **b** transfix with a pin, lance, etc. **2** (usu. foll. by *on*) fix (blame, responsibility, etc.) on a person etc. (*pinned the blame on his friend*). **3** (often foll. by *against*, *on*, etc.) seize and hold fast. **4** *Chess* prevent (an opposing piece) from moving except by exposing a more valuable piece to capture. □ **on pins and needles** in an agitated state of suspense. **pin down 1** (often foll. by *to*) bind (a person etc.) to a promise, arrangement, etc. **2** force (a person) to declare his or her intentions. **3** restrict the actions or movement of (an enemy etc.). **4** specify (a thing) precisely (*could not pin down his unease to a particular cause*). **5** hold (a person etc.) down by force. **pin one's faith** (or **hopes** etc.) **on** rely implicitly on. **pin-feather** *Zool.* an ungrown feather. **pin-high** *Golf* (of a ball) at the same distance ahead as the pin. **pin-money 1** *hist.* an allowance to a woman for dress etc. from her husband. **2** a very small sum of money, esp. for spending on inessentials (*only works for pin-money*). **pins and needles** a tingling sensation in a limb recovering from numbness. **pin-table** a table used in playing pinball. **pin-tuck** a very narrow ornamental tuck. **pin-up 1** a photograph of a popular or sexually attractive person, designed to be hung on the wall. **2** a person shown in such a photograph. **pin-wheel** a small Catherine wheel. **split pin** a metal cotter pin passed through a hole and held in place by its gaping split end. [OE *pinn* f. L *pinna* point etc., assoc. with *penna* PEN[1]]
■ *n.* **1a, b, 2** tack, nail, peg, dowel, bolt, thole, spike, rivet, stud; tin-tack, *Brit.* drawing-pin, *esp. US* thumbtack. **1 c, d** brooch, clip, badge; tie-pin, *US* stickpin. **3** two figs, a fig, a rap, a stiver, *archaic* a groat, *sl.* a hoot, two hoots. ● *v.* **1** fasten, secure, tack, hold, staple, clip; attach, fix, affix, stick; see also TRANSFIX 1. **2** (*pin the blame on*) blame, hold responsible *or* accountable, point the finger at, accuse, lay at the door of. □ **on pins and needles** see TENSE[1] *adj.* 1. **pin down 1** keep, bind, hold, commit, oblige. **3** confine, hold (down), immobilize, tie down, constrain, restrict. **4** specify, pinpoint, name, identify, determine, put *or* lay one's finger on, home *or* zero in on. **pin one's faith on** see RELY. **pin-money 2** pocket money, spending money; *colloq.* peanuts. **pin-up 2** see STAR *n.* 8a.

pina colada /péenə kəlaádə/ *n.* a drink made from pineapple juice, rum, and coconut. [Sp., lit. 'strained pineapple']

pinafore /pínnəfor/ *n.* esp. *Brit.* **1 a** an apron, esp. with a bib. **b** a woman's sleeveless wraparound washable covering for the clothes, tied at the back. **2** (in full **pinafore dress**) a collarless sleeveless dress worn over a blouse or jumper. [PIN + AFORE (because orig. pinned on the front of a dress)]

pinaster /pīnástər/ *n.* = *cluster pine*. [L, = wild pine f. *pinus* pine + -ASTER]

pinball /pínbawl/ *n.* a game in which small metal balls are shot across a board and score points by striking pins with lights etc.

pince-nez /pánsnay, PANsnáy/ *n.* (*pl.* same) a pair of eyeglasses with a nose-clip instead of earpieces. [F, lit. = pinch-nose]

pincers /pínsərz/ *n.pl.* **1** (also **pair of pincers**) a gripping-tool resembling scissors but with blunt usu. concave jaws to hold a nail etc. for extraction. **2** the front claws of lobsters and some other crustaceans. □ **pincer movement** *Mil.* a movement by two wings of an army converging on the enemy. [ME *pinsers*, *pinsours* f. AF f. OF *pincier* PINCH]
■ **1** pliers, nippers, tweezers.

pincette /PANsét/ *n.* small pincers; tweezers. [F]

pinch /pinch/ *v.* & *n.* ● *v.* **1** *tr.* **a** grip (esp. the skin of part of the body or of another person) tightly, esp. between finger and thumb (*pinched my finger in the door*; *stop pinching me*). **b** (often *absol.*) (of a shoe, garment, etc.) constrict (the flesh) painfully. **2** *tr.* (of cold, hunger, etc.) grip (a person) painfully (*she was pinched with cold*). **3** *tr. sl.* **a** steal; take without permission. **b** arrest (a person) (*pinched him for loitering*). **4** (as **pinched** *adj.*) (of the features) drawn, as with cold, hunger, worry, etc. **5 a** *tr.* (usu. foll. by *in*, *of*, *for*, etc.) stint (a person). **b** *intr.* be niggardly with money, food, etc. **6** *tr.* (usu. foll. by *out*, *back*, *down*) *Hort.* remove (leaves, buds, etc.) to encourage bushy growth. **7** *intr.* sail very close to the wind. ● *n.* **1** the act or an instance of pinching etc. the flesh. **2** an amount that can be taken up with fingers and thumb (*a pinch of snuff*). **3** the stress or pain caused by poverty, cold, hunger, etc. **4** *sl.* **a** an arrest. **b** a theft. □ **at** (or **in**) **a pinch** in an emergency; if necessary. **feel the pinch** experience the effects of poverty. **pinch-hitter** *US* **1** a baseball player who bats instead of another in an emergency. **2** a person acting as a substitute. [ME f. AF & ONF *pinchier* (unrecorded), OF *pincier*, ult. f. L *pungere punct-* prick]
■ *v.* **1** squeeze, nip, tweak, compress, constrict, grip, crush. **3 a** steal, thieve, rob, take, shoplift, filch, pilfer, snatch, grab, *colloq.* lift, swipe, *formal or joc.* purloin, *sl.* knock off, *Brit. sl.* nick; see also APPROPRIATE *v.* 1. **b** arrest, apprehend, take into custody, collar, *colloq.* run in, *esp. US colloq.* bust, *sl.* nab, *Brit. sl.* nick. **4** (**pinched**) see DRAWN. **5 b** see STINT *v.* 1. ● *n.* **1** squeeze, nip, tweak, twinge. **2** see BIT[1] 1, DASH *n.* 7. **4 a** see ARREST *n.* 1. **b** see THEFT. □ **at** (or **in**) **a pinch** in a predicament *or* emergency *or* crisis *or* difficulty, in a ticklish *or* delicate situation, *colloq.* in a pickle *or* jam *or* scrape, in a crunch; if necessary *or* required *or* needed, if the worst comes to the worst, if all else fails, *faute de mieux*. **pinch-hitter 2** see SUBSTITUTE *n.* 1a.

pinchbeck /pinchbek/ *n.* & *adj.* ● *n.* an alloy of copper and zinc resembling gold and used in cheap jewellery etc. ● *adj.* **1** counterfeit; sham. **2** cheap; tawdry. [C. *Pinchbeck*, Engl. watchmaker d. 1732]
■ *adj.* **1** see FAKE[1] *adj.* **2** see SHODDY *adj.* 1.

pinchpenny /pinchpenni/ *n.* (*pl.* **-ies**) (also *attrib.*) a miserly person.
■ see MISER.

pincushion /pinkŏŏsh'n/ *n.* a small cushion for holding pins.

pine[1] /pīn/ *n.* **1** any evergreen tree of the genus *Pinus* native to northern temperate regions, with needle-shaped leaves growing in clusters. **2** the soft timber of this, often used to make furniture. Also called DEAL[2]. **3** (*attrib.*) made of pine. **4** = PINEAPPLE. □ **pine cone** the cone-shaped fruit of the pine tree. **pine marten** a weasel-like mammal, *Martes martes*, native to Europe and America, with a dark brown coat and white throat and stomach. **pine nut** the edible seed of various pine trees. □□ **pinery** *n.* (*pl.* **-ies**). [ME f. OE *pīn* & OF *pin* f. L *pinus*]

pine[2] /pīn/ *v.intr.* **1** (often foll. by *away*) decline or waste away, esp. from grief, disease, etc. **2** (usu. foll. by *for*, *after*, or *to* + infin.) long eagerly; yearn. [OE *pīnian*, rel. to obs. E *pine* punishment, f. Gmc f. med.L *pena*, L *poena*]
■ **2** see YEARN.

pineal /pinniəl, pī-/ *adj.* shaped like a pine cone. □ **pineal body** (or **gland**) a pea-sized conical mass of tissue behind the third ventricle of the brain, secreting a hormone-like substance in some mammals. [F *pinéal* f. L *pinea* pine cone: see PINE[1]]

pineapple /pīnapp'l/ *n.* **1** a tropical plant, *Ananas comosus*, with a spiral of sword-shaped leaves and a thick stem bearing a large fruit developed from many flowers. **2** the fruit of this, consisting of yellow flesh surrounded by a tough segmented skin and topped with a tuft of stiff leaves. □ **the rough end of the pineapple** *Austral. colloq.* a raw deal. [PINE[1], from the fruit's resemblance to a pine cone]

pinetum /pīneetəm/ *n.* (*pl.* **pineta** /-tə/) a plantation of pine-trees or other conifers for scientific or ornamental purposes. [L f. *pinus* pine]

pinfold /pinfōld/ *n.* & *v.* ● *n.* a pound for stray cattle etc. ● *v.tr.* confine (cattle) in a pinfold. [OE *pundfald* (as POUND[3], FOLD[2])]

ping /ping/ *n.* & *v.* ● *n.* a single short high ringing sound. ● *v.intr.* make a ping. [imit.]

pinger /pingər/ *n.* **1** a device that transmits pings at short intervals for purposes of detection or measurement etc. **2** a device to ring a bell.

pingo /pinggō/ *n.* (*pl.* **-os**) *Geol.* a dome-shaped mound found in permafrost areas. [Eskimo]

ping-pong /pingpong/ *n.* = *table tennis*. [imit. f. the sound of a bat striking a ball]

pinguid /pinggwid/ *adj. formal* or *joc.* fat, oily, or greasy. [L *pinguis* fat]
■ see OILY 1, 2.

pinhead /pinhed/ *n.* **1** the flattened head of a pin. **2** a very small thing. **3** *colloq.* a stupid or foolish person.
■ **3** see FOOL[1] *n.* 1.

pinheaded /pinhéddid/ *adj. colloq.* stupid, foolish. □□ **pinheadedness** *n.*
■ see STUPID *adj.* 1, 5.

pinhole /pinhōl/ *n.* **1** a hole made by a pin. **2** a hole into which a peg fits. □ **pinhole camera** a camera with a pinhole aperture and no lens.
■ **1** see PRICK *n.* 2.

pinion[1] /pinyən/ *n.* & *v.* ● *n.* **1** the outer part of a bird's wing, usu. including the flight feathers. **2** *poet.* a wing; a flight-feather. ● *v.tr.* **1** cut off the pinion of (a wing or bird) to prevent flight. **2 a** bind the arms of (a person). **b** (often foll. by *to*) bind (the arms, a person, etc.) esp. to a thing. [ME f. OF *pignon* ult. f. L *pinna*: see PIN]
■ *v.* **2** see TIE *v.* 1a.

pinion[2] /pinyən/ *n.* **1** a small cog-wheel engaging with a larger one. **2** a cogged spindle engaging with a wheel. [F *pignon* alt. f. obs. *pignol* f. L *pinea* pine-cone (as PINE[1])]

pink[1] /pingk/ *n.* & *adj.* ● *n.* **1** a pale red colour (*decorated in pink*). **2 a** any cultivated plant of the genus *Dianthus*, with sweet-smelling white, pink, crimson, etc. flowers. **b** the flower of this plant. **3** (prec. by *the*) the most perfect condition etc. (*the pink of elegance*). **4** (also **hunting pink**) **a** a fox-hunter's red coat. **b** the cloth for this. **c** a fox-hunter. ● *adj.* **1** (often in *comb.*) of a pale red colour of any of various shades (*rose-pink*; *salmon-pink*). **2** esp. *derog.* tending to socialism. □ **in the pink** *colloq.* in very good health. **pink-collar** (usu. *attrib.*) (of a profession etc.) traditionally associated with women (cf. *white-collar*, *blue-collar* (see BLUE[1])). **pink disease** a disease of young children with pink discoloration of the extremities. **pink elephants** *colloq.* hallucinations caused by alcoholism. **pink-eye 1** a contagious fever in horses. **2** contagious ophthalmia in humans and some livestock. **pink gin** gin flavoured with angostura bitters. □□ **pinkish** *adj.* **pinkly** *adv.* **pinkness** *n.* **pinky** *adj.* [perh. f. dial. *pink-eyed* having small eyes]
■ *adj.* **1** rosy, rose, rose-coloured, pinkish, flesh-coloured, flesh, salmon, carnation, magnolia, *poet.* incarnadine. **2** socialist, left, left-wing, bolshie, *colloq.* red. □ **in the pink** at one's best, healthy, (hale and) hearty, in the best of health, in top form, in good shape, *colloq.* in tiptop condition, *US colloq.* in great shape.

pink[2] /pingk/ *v.tr.* **1** pierce slightly with a sword etc. **2** cut a scalloped or zigzag edge on. **3** (often foll. by *out*) ornament (leather etc.) with perforations. **4** adorn; deck. □ **pinking shears** (or **scissors**) a dressmaker's serrated shears for cutting a zigzag edge. [ME, perh. f. LG or Du.: cf. LG *pinken* strike, peck]
■ **1** perforate, puncture, prick, pierce. **2** serrate, notch, scallop.

pink[3] /pingk/ *v.intr.* (of a vehicle engine) emit a series of high-pitched explosive sounds caused by faulty combustion. [imit.]

pink[4] /pingk/ *n. hist.* a sailing-ship, esp. with a narrow stern, orig. small and flat-bottomed. [ME f. MDu. *pin(c)ke*, of unkn. orig.]

pink[5] /pingk/ *n.* a yellowish lake pigment made by combining vegetable colouring matter with a white base (*brown pink*; *French pink*). [17th c.: orig. unkn.]

pink[6] /pingk/ *n. Brit.* **1** a young salmon. **2** *dial.* a minnow. [15th c. *penk*, of unkn. orig.]

pinkie[1] /pingki/ *n.* esp. *US* & *Sc.* the little finger. [cf. dial. *pink* small, half-shut (eye)]

pinkie[2] / pingki/ *n.* **1** esp. *Austral. sl.* cheap red wine. **2** *Black sl.* a White person.

Pinkster /pingkstər/ *n. US* Whitsuntide. □ **pinkster flower** the pink azalea, *Rhododendron nudiflorum*. [Du., = Pentecost]

pinna /pinnə/ *n.* (*pl.* **pinnae** /-nee/ or **pinnas**) **1** the auricle; the external part of the ear. **2** a primary division of a pinnate leaf. **3** a fin or finlike structure, feather, wing, etc. [L, = *penna* feather, wing, fin]

pinnace /pinniss/ *n. Naut.* a warship's or other ship's small boat, usu. motor-driven, orig. schooner-rigged or eight-oared. [F *pinnace*, *pinasse* ult. f. L *pinus* PINE[1]]

pinnacle /pinnək'l/ *n.* & *v.* ● *n.* **1** the culmination or climax (of endeavour, success, etc.). **2** a natural peak. **3** a small ornamental turret usu. ending in a pyramid or cone, crowning a buttress, roof, etc. ● *v.tr.* **1** set on or as if on a pinnacle. **2** form the pinnacle of. **3** provide with pinnacles. [ME *pinacle* f. OF *pin(n)acle* f. LL *pinnaculum* f. *pinna* wing, point (as PIN, -CULE)]
■ *n.* **1** culmination, peak, apex, acme, summit, zenith, climax, crowning point, consummation, utmost, extreme. **2** peak, top, summit, tip, cap, crest, crown.
● *v.* **2** see TOP[1] *v.* 1.

pinnae *pl.* of PINNA.

pinnate /pínnayt/ *adj.* **1** (of a compound leaf) having leaflets arranged on either side of the stem, usu. in pairs opposite each other. **2** having branches, tentacles, etc., on each side of an axis. □□ **pinnated** *adj.* **pinnately** *adv.* **pinnation** /-náysh'n/ *n.* [L *pinnatus* feathered (as PINNA)]

pinni- /pínni/ *comb. form* wing, fin. [L *pinna*]

pinniped /pínniped/ *adj.* & *n.* ● *adj.* denoting any aquatic mammal with limbs ending in fins. ● *n.* a pinniped mammal. [L *pinna* fin + *pes ped-* foot]

pinnule /pínyōōl/ *n.* **1** the secondary division of a pinnate leaf. **2** a part or organ like a small wing or fin. □□ **pinnular** *adj.* [L *pinnula* dimin. of *pinna* fin, wing]

pinny /pínni/ *n.* (*pl.* **-ies**) *colloq.* a pinafore. [abbr.]

pinochle /péenok'l/ *n.* *US* **1** a card-game with a double pack of 48 cards (nine to ace only). **2** the combination of queen of spades and jack of diamonds in this game. [19th c.: orig. unkn.]

pinole /pinṓli/ *n.* *US* flour made from parched cornflour, esp. mixed with sweet flour made of mesquite beans, sugar, etc. [Amer. Sp. f. Aztec *pinolli*]

piñon /peenyṓn/ *n.* **1** a pine, *Pinus cembra*, bearing edible seeds. **2** the seed of this, a type of pine nut. [Sp. f. L *pinea* pine cone]

pinpoint /pínpoynt/ *n.* & *v.* ● *n.* **1** the point of a pin. **2** something very small or sharp. **3** (*attrib.*) **a** very small. **b** precise, accurate. ● *v.tr.* locate with precision (*pinpointed the target*).

■ *v.* see LOCATE 1, 3.

pinprick /pínprik/ *n.* **1** a prick caused by a pin. **2** a trifling irritation.

■ **1** see PRICK *n.* 2.

pinstripe /pínstrīp/ *n.* **1** a very narrow stripe in (esp. worsted or serge) cloth. **2** a fabric or garment with this.

pint /pīnt/ *n.* **1** a measure of capacity for liquids etc., one-eighth of a gallon or 20 fluid oz. (0.568 litre). **2** *Brit.* **a** *colloq.* a pint of beer. **b** a pint of a liquid, esp. milk. **3** *Brit.* a measure of shellfish, being the amount containable in a pint mug (*bought a pint of whelks*). □ **pint-pot** a pot, esp. of pewter, holding one pint, esp. of beer. **pint-sized** *colloq.* very small, esp. of a person. [ME f. OF *pinte*, of unkn. orig.]

■ **2 a** see DRINK *n.* 2b. □ **pint-sized** see SMALL *adj.* 1.

pinta /pī́ntə/ *n.* *Brit. colloq.* a pint of milk. [corrupt. of *pint of*]

pintail /píntayl/ *n.* a duck, esp. *Anas acuta*, or grouse with a pointed tail.

pintle /pínt'l/ *n.* a pin or bolt, esp. one on which some other part turns. [OE *pintel* penis, of unkn. orig.: cf. OFris. etc. *pint*]

■ see PIVOT *n.* 1.

pinto /píntō, péen-/ *adj.* & *n.* *US* ● *adj.* piebald. ● *n.* (*pl.* **-os**) a piebald horse. [Sp., = mottled, ult. f. L *pictus* past part. of *pingere* paint]

■ *adj.* see *dapple grey*. ● *n.* see DAPPLE *n.* 2.

pinworm /pínwurm/ *n.* a small parasitic nematode worm, *Enterobius vermicularis*, of which the female has a pointed tail.

piny /pīni/ *adj.* of, like, or full of pines.

Pinyin /pinyín/ *n.* a system of romanized spelling for transliterating Chinese. [Chin. *pīn-yīn*, lit. 'spell sound']

piolet /pyōláy/ *n.* a two-headed ice-axe for mountaineering. [F]

pion /pī́on/ *n.* *Physics* a meson having a mass approximately 270 times that of an electron. Also called *pi-meson* (see PI[1]). □□ **pionic** /pīónnik/ *adj.* [PI[1] (the letter used as a symbol for the particle) + -ON]

pioneer /pī́əneer/ *n.* & *v.* ● *n.* **1** an initiator of a new enterprise, an inventor, etc. **2** an explorer or settler; a colonist. **3** *Mil.* a member of an infantry group preparing roads, terrain, etc. for the main body of troops. ● *v.* **1 a** *tr.* initiate or originate (an enterprise etc.). **b** *intr.* act or prepare the way as a pioneer. **2** *tr. Mil.* open up (a road etc.) as a pioneer. **3** *tr.* go before, lead, or conduct (another person or persons). [F *pionnier* foot-soldier, pioneer, OF *paonier*, *peon(n)ier* (as PEON)]

■ *n.* **1** initiator, ground-breaker, innovator, inventor, leader, trend-setter, pacemaker, pace-setter, trail-blazer. **2** explorer, pathfinder, frontiersman, trail-blazer, colonist, (early) settler; navigator, conquistador, conqueror. ● *v.* **1** create, originate, invent, initiate, take the first step in, introduce, institute, inaugurate, launch, establish, found, set up, develop, set *or* put in motion, open up; lay the groundwork *or* foundation, take the lead, lead *or* show the way, blaze the trail, be a prime mover. **3** see LEAD[1] *v.* 1.

pious /pī́əss/ *adj.* **1** devout; religious. **2** hypocritically virtuous; sanctimonious. **3** dutiful. □ **pious fraud** a deception intended to benefit those deceived, esp. religiously. □□ **piously** *adv.* **piousness** *n.* [L *pius* dutiful, pious]

■ **1** devout, religious, reverent, reverential, God-fearing, godly, faithful, holy, dedicated, devoted, spiritual, moral, good, virtuous, saintly, angelic, seraphic, Christ-like, godlike, *archaic* worshipful. **2** hypocritical, sanctimonious, pietistic, pietistical, self-righteous, Pharisaic, *colloq.* goody-goody. **3** see DUTIFUL.

pip[1] /pip/ *n.* & *v.* ● *n.* the seed of an apple, pear, orange, grape, etc. ● *v.tr.* (**pipped, pipping**) remove the pips from (fruit etc.). □□ **pipless** *adj.* [abbr. of PIPPIN]

pip[2] /pip/ *n.* *Brit.* a short high-pitched sound, usu. mechanically produced, esp. as a radio time signal. [imit.]

pip[3] /pip/ *n.* **1** any of the spots on a playing-card, dice, or domino. **2** *Brit.* a star (1–3 according to rank) on the shoulder of an army officer's uniform. **3** a single blossom of a clustered head of flowers. **4** a diamond-shaped segment of the surface of a pineapple. **5** an image of an object on a radar screen. [16th c. *peep*, of unkn. orig.]

pip[4] /pip/ *n.* **1** a disease of poultry etc. causing thick mucus in the throat and white scale on the tongue. **2** *colloq.* a fit of disgust or bad temper (esp. *give one the pip*). [ME f. MDu. *pippe*, MLG *pip* prob. ult. f. corrupt. of L *pituita* slime]

pip[5] /pip/ *v.tr.* (**pipped, pipping**) *Brit. colloq.* **1** hit with a shot. **2** defeat. **3** blackball. □ **pip at the post** defeat at the last moment. **pip out** die. [PIP[2] or PIP[1]]

pipa /píppə/ *n.* an aquatic toad, *Pipa pipa*, having a flat body with long webbed feet, the female of which carries her eggs and tadpoles in pockets on her back. Also called SURINAM TOAD. [Surinam Negro *pipál* (masc.), *pipá* (fem.)]

pipal var. of PEEPUL.

pipe /pīp/ *n.* & *v.* ● *n.* **1** a tube of metal, plastic, wood, etc. used to convey water, gas, etc. **2** (also **tobacco-pipe**) **a** a narrow wooden or clay etc. tube with a bowl at one end containing burning tobacco, the smoke from which is drawn into the mouth. **b** the quantity of tobacco held by this (*smoked a pipe*). **3** *Mus.* **a** a wind instrument consisting of a single tube. **b** any of the tubes by which sound is produced in an organ. **c** (in *pl.*) = BAGPIPES. **d** (in *pl.*) a set of pipes joined together, e.g. pan-pipes. **4** a tubal organ, vessel, etc. in an animal's body. **5** a high note or song, esp. of a bird. **6** a cylindrical vein of ore. **7** a cavity in cast metal. **8 a** a boatswain's whistle. **b** the sounding of this. **9** a cask for wine, esp. as a measure of two hogsheads, usu. equivalent to 105 gallons (about 477 litres). **10** *archaic* the voice, esp. in singing. ● *v.tr.* **1** (also *absol.*) play (a tune etc.) on a pipe or pipes. **2 a** convey (oil, water, gas, etc.) by pipes. **b** provide with pipes. **3** transmit (music, a radio programme, etc.) by wire or cable. **4** (usu. foll. by *up*, *on*, *to*, etc.) *Naut.* **a** summon (a crew) to a meal, work, etc. **b** signal the arrival of (an officer etc.) on board. **5** utter in a shrill voice; whistle. **6 a** arrange (icing, cream, etc.) in decorative lines or twists on a cake etc. **b** ornament (a cake etc.) with piping. **7** trim (a dress etc.) with piping. **8** lead or bring (a person etc.) by the sound of a pipe. **9** propagate (pinks etc.) by taking cuttings at the joint of a stem. □ **pipe away** give a signal for (a boat) to start. **pipe-cleaner** a piece of flexible covered wire for cleaning a tobacco-pipe. **pipe down 1** *colloq.* be quiet or less insistent. **2** *Naut.* dismiss from duty. **pipe-fish** any of various long slender fish of the family Syngnathidae, with an elongated snout. **pipe-light** a spill for lighting a pipe. **pipe major** an NCO commanding regimental pipers. **pipe-organ** *Mus.* an organ using pipes instead of or as well as reeds. **pipe-rack** a rack for holding tobacco-pipes. **pipe-rolls** *hist.* the annual records of the British Exchequer from the 12th–19th c. (prob. because subsidiary documents were rolled in pipe form). **pipe-stem** the shaft of a tobacco-pipe. **pipe-stone** a hard red clay used by US Indians for tobacco-pipes. **pipe up** begin to play, sing, speak, etc. **put that in your pipe and smoke it** *colloq.* a challenge to another to accept something frank or unwelcome. □□ **pipeful** *n.* (*pl.* **-fuls**). **pipeless** *adj.* **pipy** *adj.* [OE *pīpe*, *pīpian* & OF *piper* f. Gmc ult. f. L *pipare* peep, chirp]

■ *n.* **1** pipeline, tube, duct, hose, line, main, conduit, channel. **2 a** brier, meerschaum, chibouk; hookah, narghile, calumet, hubble-bubble. ● *v.* **1** tootle, skirl, whistle. **2 a** transmit, deliver, channel, conduct, convey. **3** see BROADCAST *v.* 1a. □ **pipe down 1** be quiet, quiet down, make less noise, tone (it) down, hush (up), shush, *Brit.* quieten down, *colloq.* shut up, *sl.* shut your face *or* head *or* mouth *or* trap, *Brit. sl.* put a sock in it, belt up. **pipe up** speak (up), raise one's voice, make oneself heard.

pipeclay /pī́pklay/ *n.* & *v.* ● *n.* a fine white clay used for tobacco-pipes, whitening leather, etc. ● *v.tr.* **1** whiten (leather etc.) with this. **2** put in order.

pipedream /pī́pdreem/ *n.* an unattainable or fanciful hope or scheme. [orig. as experienced when smoking an opium pipe]

■ see FANTASY *n.* 2.

pipeline /pī́plīn/ *n.* **1** a long, usu. underground, pipe for conveying esp. oil. **2** a channel supplying goods, information, etc. □ **in the pipeline** awaiting completion or processing.

■ **1** pipe, tube, duct, hose, line, main, conduit, passage, channel. □ **in the pipeline** on the way, under way, in preparation, in the offing, ready, imminent, coming, *colloq.* in the works, cooking, *US* in work.

pip emma /pip émmə/ *adv.* & *n. Brit. colloq.* = P.M. [formerly signallers' names for letters PM]

piper /pī́pər/ *n.* **1** a bagpipe-player. **2** a person who plays a pipe, esp. an itinerant musician. [OE *pīpere* (as PIPE)]

piperidine /pipérrideen/ *n. Chem.* a peppery-smelling liquid formed by the reduction of pyridine. [L *piper* pepper + -IDE + -INE[4]]

pipette /pipét/ *n.* & *v.* ● *n.* a slender tube for transferring or measuring small quantities of liquids esp. in chemistry. ● *v.tr.* transfer or measure (a liquid) using a pipette. [F, dimin. of *pipe* PIPE]

piping /pī́ping/ *n.* & *adj.* ● *n.* **1** the act or an instance of piping, esp. whistling or singing. **2** a thin pipelike fold used to edge hems or frills on clothing, seams on upholstery, etc. **3** ornamental lines of icing, cream, potato, etc. on a cake or other dish. **4** lengths of pipe, or a system of pipes, esp. in domestic use. ● *adj.* (of a noise) high; whistling. □ **piping hot** very or suitably hot (esp. as required of food, water, etc.).

■ *adj.* see SHRILL *adj.* □ **piping hot** see HOT *adj.* 1.

pipistrelle /píppistrél/ *n.* any bat of the genus *Pipistrellus*, native to temperate regions and feeding on insects . [F f. It. *pipistrello*, *vip-*, f. L *vespertilio* bat f. *vesper* evening]

pipit /píppit/ *n.* **1** any of various birds of the family Motacillidae, esp. of the genus *Anthus*, found worldwide and having brown plumage often heavily streaked with a lighter colour. **2** = *meadow pipit*. [prob. imit.]

pipkin /pípkin/ *n.* a small earthenware pot or pan. [16th c.: orig. unkn.]

pippin /píppin/ *n.* **1 a** an apple grown from seed. **b** a red and yellow dessert apple. **2** *colloq.* an excellent person or thing; a beauty. [ME f. OF *pepin*, of unkn. orig.]

pipsqueak /pípskweek/ *n. colloq.* an insignificant or contemptible person or thing. [imit.]

piquant /peékənt, -kaant/ *adj.* **1** agreeably pungent, sharp, or appetizing. **2** pleasantly stimulating, or disquieting, to the mind. □□ **piquancy** *n.* **piquantly** *adv.* [F, pres. part. of *piquer* (as PIQUE[1])]

■ **1** see PUNGENT 1. **2** keen, acute, intense, incisive, sharp, stinging, pointed, piercing, penetrating, barbed, cutting, caustic, acid, acerbic, bitter, biting; see also *stimulating* (STIMULATE), WITTY. □□ **piquancy** see SPICE *n.* 3a.

pique[1] /peek/ *v.* & *n.* ● *v.tr.* (**piques, piqued, piquing**) **1** wound the pride of, irritate. **2** arouse (curiosity, interest, etc.). **3** (*refl.*; usu. foll. by *on*) pride or congratulate oneself. ● *n.* ill-feeling; enmity; resentment (*in a fit of pique*). [F *piquer* prick, irritate, f. Rmc]

■ *v.* **1** see IRRITATE 1. **2** see EXCITE 1a, b. ● *n.* see RESENTMENT.

pique[2] /peek/ *n.* & *v.* ● *n.* the winning of 30 points on cards and play in piquet before one's opponent scores anything. ● *v.* (**piques, piqued, piquing**) **1** *tr.* score a pique against. **2** *intr.* score a pique. [F *pic*, of unkn. orig.]

piqué /peékay/ *n.* a stiff ribbed cotton or other fabric. [F, past part. of *piquer*: see PIQUE[1]]

piquet[1] /pikét/ *n.* a game for two players with a pack of 32 cards (seven to ace only). [F, of unkn. orig.]

piquet[2] var. of PICKET 3.

piracy /pī́rəsi/ *n.* (*pl.* **-ies**) **1** the practice or an act of robbery of ships at sea. **2** a similar practice or act in other forms, esp. hijacking. **3** the infringement of copyright. [med.L *piratia* f. Gk *pirateia* (as PIRATE)]

■ **3** see PLAGIARISM 1.

piragua /pirágwə/ *n.* **1** a long narrow canoe made from a single tree-trunk. **2** a two-masted sailing barge. [Sp. f. Carib, = dug-out]

piranha /piraánə, -raányə/ *n.* (also **piraya** /-raáyə/) any of various freshwater predatory fish of the genera *Pygocentrus*, *Rooseveltiella*, or *Serrasalmus*, native to S. America and having sharp cutting teeth. [Port. f. Tupi, var. of *piraya* scissors]

pirate /pī́rət/ *n.* & *v.* ● *n.* **1 a** a person who commits piracy. **b** a ship used by pirates. **2** a person who infringes another's copyright or other business rights; a plagiarist. **3** (often *attrib.*) a person, organization, etc., that broadcasts without official authorization (*pirate radio station*). ● *v.tr.* **1** appropriate or reproduce (the work or ideas etc. of another) without permission, for one's own benefit. **2** plunder. □□ **piratic** /-ráttik/ *adj.* **piratical** /-ráttik'l/ *adj.* **piratically** /-ráttikəli/ *adv.* [ME f. L *pirata* f. Gk *peiratēs* f. *peiraō* attempt, assault]

■ *n.* **1 a** buccaneer, rover, corsair, freebooter, sea robber, *esp. US* filibuster, picaroon, *hist.* rapparee. **2** plagiarist, plagiarizer, infringer. ● *v.* **1** plagiarize, copy, reproduce, steal, appropriate, poach, *colloq.* lift, crib, *sl.* pinch. **2** see PLUNDER *v.* 2.

piraya var. of PIRANHA.

piripiri /pírripirri/ *n.* (*pl.* **piripiris**) *NZ* a rosaceous plant, *Acaena anserinifolia*, native to New Zealand and having prickly burs. [Maori]

pirogue /pirṓg/ *n.* = PIRAGUA. [F, prob. f. Galibi]

pirouette /pírroo-ét/ *n.* & *v.* ● *n.* a dancer's spin on one foot or the point of the toe. ● *v.intr.* perform a pirouette. [F, = spinning-top]

■ *n.* spin, whirl, twirl, turn, revolution. ● *v.* spin, whirl, twirl, turn (round), revolve, pivot.

pis aller /peez aláy/ *n.* a course of action followed as a last resort. [F f. *pis* worse + *aller* go]

piscary /pískəri/ *n.* □ **common of piscary** the right of fishing in another's water in common with the owner and others. [ME f. med.L *piscaria* neut. pl. of L *piscarius* f. *piscis* fish]

piscatorial /pískətóriəl/ *adj.* = PISCATORY 1. □□ **piscatorially** *adv.*

piscatory /pískətəri, -tri/ *adj.* **1** of or concerning fishermen or fishing. **2** addicted to fishing. [L *piscatorius* f. *piscator* fisherman f. *piscis* fish]

■ **1** piscatorial, fishy, piscine, fishlike.

Pisces /pī́seez, pískeez/ *n.* (*pl.* same) **1** a constellation, traditionally regarded as contained in the figure of fishes . **2 a** the twelfth sign of the zodiac (the Fishes). **b** a person born when the sun is in this sign. □□ **Piscean** /pī́siən/ *n.* & *adj.* [ME f. L, pl. of *piscis* fish]

pisciculture /píssikulchər/ *n.* the artificial rearing of fish. □□ **piscicultural** /-kúlchərəl/ *adj.* **pisciculturist** /-kúlchərist/ *n.* [L *piscis* fish, after *agriculture* etc.]

piscina /pisee̋nə, -sī́nə/ *n.* (*pl.* **piscinae** /-nee/ or **piscinas**) **1** a stone basin near the altar in RC and pre-Reformation churches for draining water used in the Mass. **2** a fish-pond. **3** *hist.* a Roman bathing-pond. [L f. *piscis* fish]

piscine[1] /píssīn/ *adj.* of or concerning fish. [L *piscis* fish]
■ piscatory, piscatorial, *joc. or poet.* fishy.

piscine[2] /piséen/ *n.* a bathing-pool. [F (as PISCINA)]

piscivorous /pisívvərəss/ *adj.* fish-eating. [L *piscis* fish + -VOROUS]

pish /pish/ *int.* & *n.* ● *int.* an expression of contempt, impatience, or disgust. ● *n.* nonsense, rubbish. [imit.]

pisiform /píssiform/ *adj.* pea-shaped. □ **pisiform bone** a small bone in the wrist in the upper row of the carpus. [mod.L *pisiformis* f. *pisum* pea]

pismire /písmīr/ *n. dial.* an ant. [ME f. PISS (from smell of anthill) + obs. *mire* ant]

piss /piss/ *v.* & *n. coarse sl.* ¶ Usually considered a taboo word. ● *v.* **1** *intr.* urinate. **2** *tr.* **a** discharge (blood etc.) when urinating. **b** wet with urine. **3** *tr.* (as **pissed** *adj.*) *Brit.* drunk. ● *n.* **1** urine. **2** an act of urinating. □ **piss about** fool or mess about. **piss artist 1** a drunkard. **2** a person who fools about. **3** a glib person. **piss down** rain heavily. **piss off** *Brit.* **1** go away. **2** (often as **pissed off** *adj.*) annoy; depress. **piss-pot** a chamber-pot. **piss-taker** a person who mocks. **piss-taking** mockery. **piss-up** a drinking spree. **take the piss** (often foll. by *out of*) mock; deride. [ME f. OF *pisser* (imit.)]

pissoir /peeswaár/ *n.* a public urinal. [F]
■ see TOILET 1.

pistachio /pistaáshiō/ *n.* (*pl.* **-os**) **1** an evergreen tree, *Pistacia vera*, bearing small brownish-green flowers and ovoid reddish fruit. **2** (in full **pistachio nut**) the edible pale-green seed of this. **3** a pale green colour. [It. *pistaccio* and Sp. *pistacho* f. L *pistacium* f. Gk *pistakion* f. Pers. *pistah*]

piste /peest/ *n.* a ski-run of compacted snow. [F, = racetrack]

pistil /pístil/ *n.* the female organs of a flower, comprising the stigma, style, and ovary. □□ **pistillary** *adj.* **pistilliferous** /-líffərəss/ *adj.* **pistilline** /-līn/ *adj.* [F *pistile* or L *pistillum* PESTLE]

pistillate /pístilət/ *adj.* **1** having pistils. **2** having pistils but no stamens.

pistol /píst'l/ *n.* & *v.* ● *n.* **1** a small hand-held firearm. **2** anything of a similar shape. ● *v.tr.* (**pistolled, pistolling**; *US* **pistoled, pistoling**) shoot with a pistol. □ **hold a pistol to a person's head** coerce a person by threats. **pistol-grip** a handle shaped like a pistol-butt. **pistol-shot 1** the range of a pistol. **2** a shot fired from a pistol. **pistol-whip** (**-whipped, -whipping**) beat with a pistol. [obs. F f. G *Pistole* f. Czech *pišťal*]
■ *n.* **1** gun, handgun, revolver, six-shooter, *esp. US colloq.* shooting-iron, *sl.* gat, heater, shooter, *US sl.* rod, roscoe. □ **hold a pistol to a person's head** see BLACKMAIL *v.*

pistole /pistṓl/ *n. hist.* a foreign (esp. Spanish) gold coin. [F *pistole* abbr. of *pistolet*, of uncert. orig.]

pistoleer /pistəléer/ *n.* a soldier armed with a pistol.

piston /pístən/ *n.* **1** a disc or short cylinder fitting closely within a tube in which it moves up and down against a liquid or gas, used in an internal-combustion engine to impart motion, or in a pump to receive motion. **2** a sliding valve in a trumpet etc. □ **piston-ring** a ring on a piston sealing the gap between the piston and the cylinder wall. **piston-rod** a rod or crankshaft attached to a piston to drive a wheel or to impart motion. [F f. It. *pistone* var. of *pestone* augment. of *pestello* PESTLE]

pit[1] /pit/ *n.* & *v.* ● *n.* **1 a** a usu. large deep hole in the ground. **b** a hole made in digging for industrial purposes, esp. for coal (*chalk pit*; *gravel pit*). **c** a covered hole as a trap for esp. wild animals. **2 a** an indentation left after smallpox, acne, etc. **b** a hollow in a plant or animal body or on any surface. **3** *Brit. Theatr.* **a** = *orchestra pit*. **b** usu. *hist.* seating at the back of the stalls. **c** the people in the pit. **4 a** (**the pit** or **bottomless pit**) hell. **b** (**the pits**) *sl.* a wretched or the worst imaginable place, situation, person, etc. **5 a** an area at the side of a track where racing cars are serviced and refuelled. **b** a sunken area in a workshop floor for access to a car's underside. **6** *US* the part of the floor of an exchange allotted to special trading (*wheat-pit*). **7** = COCKPIT. **8** *Brit. sl.* a bed. ● *v.* (**pitted, pitting**) **1** *tr.* (usu. foll. by *against*) **a** set (one's wits, strength, etc.) in opposition or rivalry. **b** set (a cock, dog, etc.) to fight, orig. in a pit, against another. **2** *tr.* (usu. as **pitted** *adj.*) make pits, esp. scars, in. **3** *intr.* (of the flesh etc.) retain the impression of a finger etc. when touched. **4** *tr. Hort.* put (esp. vegetables etc. for storage) into a pit. □ **dig a pit for** try to ensnare. **pit bull terrier** a small American dog noted for its ferocity. **pit-head 1** the top of a mineshaft. **2** the area surrounding this. **pit of the stomach 1** the floor of the stomach. **2** the depression below the bottom of the breastbone. **pit pony** *hist.* a pony kept underground for haulage in coal-mines. **pit-prop** a balk of wood used to support the roof of a coal mine. **pit-saw** a large saw for use in a saw-pit. **pit viper** any US snake of the family Crotalidae with a pit between the eye and the nostril. [OE *pytt* ult. f. L *puteus* well]
■ *n.* **1** hole, shaft, cavity, mine, well, mine-shaft, quarry, working, ditch, trench, trough; abyss, chasm, crater. **2** hollow, depression, dent, indentation, dimple, pock-mark, pock. **4 a** (**the pit** or **bottomless pit**) see HELL 1. **b** (**the pits**) lowest of the low, rock bottom; the worst, awful, terrible, *sl.* lousy. **8** bed, *sl. esp. US* flop, *Brit. sl.* doss, kip. ● *v.* **1** (*pit against*) match, set against; see also OPPOSE 1–3. **2** dent, pock-mark, scar; (**pitted**) pock-marked, defaced, marred, marked. □ **dig a pit for** set a trap for; see also AMBUSH *v.*

pit[2] /pit/ *n.* & *v. US* ● *n.* the stone of a fruit. ● *v.tr.* (**pitted, pitting**) remove pits from (fruit). [perh. Du., rel. to PITH]
■ *n.* see STONE *n.* 6a.

pita var. of PITTA.

pit-a-pat /píttəpát/ *adv.* & *n.* (also **pitter-patter** /píttərpáttər/) ● *adv.* **1** with a sound like quick light steps. **2** with a faltering sound (*heart went pit-a-pat*). ● *n.* such a sound. [imit.]
■ *n.* see PATTER[1] *n.*

pitch[1] /pich/ *v.* & *n.* ● *v.* **1** *tr.* (also *absol.*) erect and fix (a tent, camp, etc.). **2** *tr.* **a** throw; fling. **b** (in games) throw (a flat object) towards a mark. **3** *tr.* fix or plant (a thing) in a definite position. **4** *tr.* express in a particular style or at a particular level (*pitched his argument at the most basic level*). **5** *intr.* (often foll. by *against*, *into*, etc.) fall heavily, esp. headlong. **6** *intr.* (of a ship etc.) plunge in a longitudinal direction (cf. ROLL *v.* 8a). **7** *tr. Mus.* set at a particular pitch. **8** *intr.* (of a roof etc.) slope downwards. **9** *intr.* (often foll. by *about*) move with a vigorous jogging motion, as in a train, carriage, etc. **10** *Cricket* **a** *tr.* cause (a bowled ball) to strike the ground at a specified point etc. **b** *intr.* (of a bowled ball) strike the ground. **11** *tr. colloq.* tell (a yarn or a tale). **12** *tr. Golf* play (a ball) with a pitch shot. **13** *tr.* pave (a road) with stones. ● *n.* **1 a** the area of play in a field-game. **b** *Cricket* the area between the creases. **2** height, degree, intensity, etc. (*the pitch of despair*; *nerves were strung to a pitch*). **3 a** the steepness of a slope, esp. of a roof, stratum, etc. **b** the degree of such a pitch. **4** *Mus.* **a** that quality of a sound which is governed by the rate of vibrations producing it; the degree of highness or lowness of a tone. **b** = *concert pitch*. **5** the pitching motion of a ship etc. **6** *Cricket* the act or mode of delivery in bowling, or the spot where the ball bounces. **7** *colloq.* a salesman's advertising or selling approach. **8** *Brit.* a place where a street vendor sells wares, has a stall, etc. **9** (also **pitch shot**) *Golf* a high approach shot with a short run. **10** *Mech.* the distance between successive corresponding points or lines, e.g. between the teeth of a cog-wheel etc. **11** the height to which a falcon etc. soars before swooping on its prey. **12** the delivery of a baseball by a pitcher. □ **pitch-and-toss** a gambling game in which coins are pitched at a mark and then tossed. **pitched battle 1** a vigorous argument etc. **2** *Mil.* a battle planned beforehand and fought on chosen ground. **pitched roof** a sloping roof. **pitch in** *colloq.* **1** set to work vigorously. **2** assist, cooperate. **pitch into** *colloq.* **1** attack forcibly with blows, words, etc. **2** assail (food, work, etc.) vigorously. **pitch on** (or **upon**) happen to select. **pitch-pipe** *Mus.* a small pipe blown to set the pitch for singing or tuning. **pitch up** *Cricket* bowl (a ball) to bounce near the batsman. **pitch wickets** *Cricket* fix the stumps in the ground and place the bails. [ME *pic(c)he*, perh. f. OE *picc(e)an* (unrecorded: cf. *picung* stigmata)]

■ *v.* **1** erect, raise, set *or* put up, position, fix, place. **2 a** toss, throw, cast, fling, hurl, sling, fire, launch, shoot, send, let fly, lob, *colloq.* chuck. **4** see DIRECT *v.* 4. **5** plunge, fall (headlong), dive, drop, plummet, (take a) nosedive. **6** toss about, lurch, plunge, go head over heels. **9** see LURCH[1] *v.* ● *n.* **1** playing-field, field, ground; court. **2** see HEIGHT 7. **3** see SLANT *n.* 1. **8** see PATCH *n.* 6, 7. □ **pitched battle 1** see ARGUMENT 1. **pitch in 1** see *put one's shoulder to the wheel* (SHOULDER). **2** contribute, cooperate, help, assist, *colloq.* chip in. **pitch into 1** attack, lay into, assail, lash out at, abuse, rail against, tear into, *colloq.* jump down a person's throat, jump on; assault, set upon, belabour, *colloq.* light into, sail into, tear into. **pitch on** or **upon** decide on, select, pick, choose, opt for, elect for, name; *colloq.* light on; see also *hit on*.

pitch[2] /pich/ *n.* & *v.* ● *n.* **1** a sticky resinous black or dark-brown substance obtained by distilling tar or turpentine, semi-liquid when hot, hard when cold, and used for caulking the seams of ships etc. **2** any of various bituminous substances including asphalt. ● *v.tr.* cover, coat, or smear with pitch. □ **pitch-black** (or **-dark**) very or completely dark. **pitch-pine** any of various pine-trees, esp. *Pinus rigida* or *P. palustris*, yielding much resin. [OE *pic* f. Gmc f. L *pix picis*]

■ *n.* tar, bitumen, asphalt. □ **pitch-black** (or **-dark**) black, dark, ebony, inky, coal-black, sooty, jet-black, raven, *esp. poet.* sable; unlit, unlighted, moonless, starless, *literary* Stygian.

pitchblende /píchblend/ *n.* a mineral form of uranium oxide occurring in pitchlike masses and yielding radium. [G *Pechblende* (as PITCH[2], BLENDE)]

pitcher[1] /píchər/ *n.* **1** a large usu. earthenware jug with a lip and a handle, for holding liquids. **2** a modified leaf in pitcher form. **3** (in *pl.*) broken pottery crushed and reused. □ **pitcher-plant** any of various plants, esp. of the family Nepenthaceae or Sarraceniaceae, with pitcher leaves that can hold liquids, trap insects, etc. □□ **pitcherful** *n.* (*pl.* **-fuls**). [ME f. OF *pichier*, *pechier*, f. Frank.]

■ **1** see JUG *n.* 1, 2.

pitcher[2] /píchər/ *n.* **1** a person or thing that pitches. **2** *Baseball* a player who delivers the ball to the batter. **3** a stone used for paving.

pitchfork /píchfork/ *n.* & *v.* ● *n.* a long-handled two-pronged fork for pitching hay etc. ● *v.tr.* **1** throw with or as if with a pitchfork. **2** (usu. foll. by *into*) thrust (a person) forcibly into a position, office, etc. [in ME *pickfork*, prob. f. PICK[1] + FORK, assoc. with PITCH[1]]

pitchstone /píchstōn/ *n.* obsidian etc. resembling pitch.

pitchy /píchi/ *adj.* (**pitchier**, **pitchiest**) of, like, or dark as pitch.

piteous /píttiəss/ *adj.* deserving or causing pity; wretched. □□ **piteously** *adv.* **piteousness** *n.* [ME *pito(u)s* etc. f. AF *pitous*, OF *pitos* f. Rmc (as PIETY)]

■ pitiable, pathetic, pitiful, plaintive, miserable, heart-rending, poignant, distressing, grievous, heartbreaking, moving, painful, lamentable, deplorable, regrettable; wretched, mournful, sad, doleful, tearful, rueful, woeful, *literary or joc.* dolorous.

pitfall /pítfawl/ *n.* **1** an unsuspected snare, danger, or drawback. **2** a covered pit for trapping animals etc.

■ **1** danger, peril, hazard, catch, difficulty, snag; snare, trap. **2** trap, pit.

pith /pith/ *n.* & *v.* ● *n.* **1** spongy white tissue lining the rind of an orange, lemon, etc. **2** the essential part; the quintessence (*came to the pith of his argument*). **3** *Bot.* the spongy cellular tissue in the stems and branches of dicotyledonous plants. **4 a** physical strength; vigour. **b** force; energy. **5** importance, weight. **6** *archaic* spinal cord. ● *v.tr.* **1** remove the pith or marrow from. **2** slaughter or immobilize (an animal) by severing the spinal cord. □ **pith helmet** a lightweight sun-helmet made from the dried pith of the sola etc. □□ **pithless** *adj.* [OE *pitha* f. WG]

■ *n.* **2** core, heart, kernel, nucleus, crux, focus, focal point, essence, meat, marrow, nub, point, spirit, substance, quintessence. **4** see VIGOUR 1. **5** weight, burden, gravamen, gravity, force, moment, import, importance, significance, substance, depth, matter.

pithecanthrope /píthikánthrōp/ *n.* any prehistoric apelike human of the extinct genus *Pithecanthropus*, now considered to be part of the genus *Homo* (see also JAVA MAN). [Gk *pithēkos* ape + *anthrōpos* man]

pithos /píthoss/ *n.* (*pl.* **pithoi** /-thoy/) *Archaeol.* a large storage jar. [Gk]

pithy /píthi/ *adj.* (**pithier**, **pithiest**) **1** (of style, speech, etc.) condensed, terse, and forcible. **2** of, like, or containing much pith. □□ **pithily** *adv.* **pithiness** *n.*

■ **1** see TERSE 1. □□ **pithiness** see BREVITY.

pitiable /píttiəb'l/ *adj.* **1** deserving or causing pity. **2** contemptible. □□ **pitiableness** *n.* **pitiably** *adv.* [ME f. OF *piteable*, *pitoiable* (as PITY)]

■ **1** see PITEOUS. **2** see CONTEMPTIBLE.

pitiful /píttifōōl/ *adj.* **1** causing pity. **2** contemptible. **3** *archaic* compassionate. □□ **pitifully** *adv.* **pitifulness** *n.*

■ **1** see PITEOUS. **2** beggarly, sorry, mean, contemptible; small, little, insignificant, trifling, pathetic.

pitiless /píttiliss/ *adj.* showing no pity (*the pitiless heat of the desert*). □□ **pitilessly** *adv.* **pitilessness** *n.*

■ see MERCILESS. □□ **pitilessly** see ROUGHLY 1. **pitilessness** see *severity* (SEVERE).

pitman /pítmən/ *n.* **1** (*pl.* **-men**) a collier. **2** *US* (*pl.* **-mans**) a connecting rod in machinery.

piton /peéton/ *n.* a peg or spike driven into a rock or crack to support a climber or a rope. [F, = eye-bolt]

Pitot tube /peétō/ *n.* a device consisting of an open-ended right-angled tube used to measure the speed or flow of a fluid. [H. *Pitot*, Fr. physicist d. 1771]

pitpan /pítpan/ *n.* a Central American boat made from a tree-trunk. [Miskito]

pitta /píttə/ *n.* (also **pita**) a flat hollow unleavened bread which can be split and filled with salad etc. [mod.Gk, = a cake]

pittance /pítt'nss/ *n.* **1** a scanty or meagre allowance, remuneration, etc. (*paid him a mere pittance*). **2** a small number or amount. **3** *hist.* a pious bequest to a religious house for extra food etc. [ME f. OF *pitance* f. med.L *pi(e)tantia* f. L *pietas* PITY]

■ **2** *colloq.* peanuts, chicken-feed, small potatoes.

pitter-patter var. of PIT-A-PAT.

pittosporum /píttōspórəm/ *n.* any evergreen shrub of the family Pittosporaceae, chiefly native to Australasia with many species having fragrant foliage. [Gk *pitta* PITCH[2] + *sporos* seed]

pituitary /pityōō-itəri, -tri/ *n.* & *adj.* ● *n.* (*pl.* **-ies**) (also **pituitary gland** or **body**) a small ductless gland at the base of the brain secreting various hormones essential for growth and other bodily functions. ● *adj.* of or relating to this gland. [L *pituitarius* secreting phlegm f. *pituita* phlegm]

pity /pítti/ *n.* & *v.* ● *n.* (*pl.* **-ies**) **1** sorrow and compassion aroused by another's condition (*felt pity for the child*). **2** something to be regretted; grounds for regret (*what a pity!*; *the pity of it is that he didn't mean it*). ● *v.tr.* (**-ies, -ied**) feel (often contemptuous) pity for (*they are to be pitied*; *I pity you if you think that*). □ **for pity's sake** an exclamation of urgent supplication, anger, etc. **more's the pity** so much the worse. **take pity on** feel or act compassionately towards. □□ **pitying** *adj.* **pityingly** *adv.* [ME f. OF *pité* f. L *pietas* (as PIETY)]

▪ *n.* **1** sympathy, sorrow, compassion; commiseration, condolence. **2** (crying) shame; disgrace, sin, sacrilege, *colloq.* crime. ● *v.* sympathize with, feel for, commiserate with, feel sorry for, bleed for, weep for, be moved by, take pity on; have one's heart go out to. □ **for pity's sake** for Christ's *or* God's *or* goodness' *or* Heaven's sake.

pityriasis /píttirī́əsiss/ *n.* any of a group of skin diseases characterized by the shedding of branlike scales. [mod.L f. Gk *pituriasis* f. *pituron* bran]

più /pyōō/ *adv. Mus.* more (*più piano*). [It.]

pivot /pívvət/ *n.* & *v.* ● *n.* **1** a short shaft or pin on which something turns or oscillates. **2** a crucial or essential person, point, etc., in a scheme or enterprise. **3** *Mil.* the man or men about whom a body of troops wheels. ● *v.* (**pivoted, pivoting**) **1** *intr.* turn on or as if on a pivot. **2** *intr.* (foll. by *on*, *upon*) hinge on; depend on. **3** *tr.* provide with or attach by a pivot. □□ **pivotable** *adj.* **pivotability** /-təbílliti/ *n.* **pivotal** *adj.* [F, of uncert. orig.]

▪ *n.* **1** fulcrum, pintle, gudgeon, hinge, swivel, kingpin, spindle. **2** centre, heart, focal point, hub, crux; see also KEYSTONE. ● *v.* **1** rotate, revolve, turn, spin, twirl, whirl, swivel. **2** hinge, depend, hang, be contingent, rely; (*pivot on*) revolve around; see also TURN *v.* 17. □□ **pivotal** critical, central, focal, crucial, significant, important, essential, vital.

pix[1] /piks/ *n.pl. colloq.* pictures, esp. photographs. [abbr.: cf. PIC]

pix[2] var. of PYX.

pixel /píks'l/ *n. Electronics* any of the minute areas of uniform illumination of which an image on a display screen is composed. [abbr. of *picture element*: cf. PIX[1]]

pixie /píksi/ *n.* (also **pixy**) (*pl.* **-ies**) a being like a fairy; an elf. □ **pixie hat** (or **hood**) a child's hat with a pointed crown. [17th c.: orig. unkn.]

▪ see IMP *n.* 2.

pixilated /píksilaytid/ *adj.* (also **pixillated**) **1** bewildered; crazy. **2** drunk. [var. of *pixie-led* (as PIXIE, LED)]

▪ **1** see *in a daze* (DAZE). **2** see DRUNK *adj.* 1.

pizazz /pizáz/ *n.* (also **pizzazz, pzazz** etc.) *sl.* verve, energy, liveliness, sparkle.

▪ see VERVE.

pizza /péetsə/ *n.* a flat round base of dough with a topping of tomatoes, cheese, onions, etc. [It., = pie]

pizzeria /péetsəréeə/ *n.* a place where pizzas are made or sold. [It. (as PIZZA)]

pizzicato /pítsikaátō/ *adv.*, *adj.*, & *n. Mus.* ● *adv.* plucking the strings of a violin etc. with the finger. ● *adj.* (of a note, passage, etc.) performed pizzicato. ● *n.* (*pl.* **pizzicatos** or **pizzicati** /-ti/) a note, passage, etc. played pizzicato. [It., past part. of *pizzicare* twitch f. *pizzare* f. *pizza* edge]

pizzle /pízz'l/ *n.* esp. *Austral.* the penis of an animal, esp. a bull, formerly used as a whip. [LG *pesel*, dimin. of MLG *pēse*, MDu. *pēze*]

pk. *abbr.* **1** park. **2** peak. **3** peck(s).

pl. *abbr.* **1** plural. **2** place. **3** plate. **4** esp. *Mil.* platoon.

PLA *abbr.* (in the UK) Port of London Authority.

placable /plákkəb'l/ *adj.* easily placated; mild; forgiving. □□ **placability** /-bílliti/ *n.* **placably** *adv.* [ME f. OF *placable* or L *placabilis* f. *placare* appease]

placard /plákkaard/ *n.* & *v.* ● *n.* a printed or handwritten poster esp. for advertising. ● *v.tr.* **1** set up placards on (a wall etc.). **2** advertise by placards. **3** display (a poster etc.) as a placard. [ME f. OF *placquart* f. *plaquier* to plaster f. MDu. *placken*]

▪ *n.* see POSTER.

placate /pləkáyt/ *v.tr.* pacify; conciliate. □□ **placatingly** *adv.* **placation** /pləkáysh'n/ *n.* **placatory** /pləkáytəri/ *adj.* [L *placare placat-*]

▪ see CALM *v.* □□ **placation** conciliation, appeasement, propitiation, pacification. **placatory** see PROPITIATORY.

place /playss/ *n.* & *v.* ● *n.* **1 a** a particular portion of space. **b** a portion of space occupied by a person or thing (*it has changed its place*). **c** a proper or natural position (*he is out of his place*; *take your places*). **d** situation, circumstances (*put yourself in my place*). **2** a city, town, village, etc. (*was born in this place*). **3** a residence; a dwelling (*has a place in the country*; *come round to my place*). **4 a** a group of houses in a town etc., esp. a square. **b** a country house with its surroundings. **5** a person's rank or status (*know their place*; *a place in history*). **6** a space, esp. a seat, for a person (*two places in the coach*). **7** a building or area for a specific purpose (*place of worship*; *bathing-place*). **8 a** a point reached in a book etc. (*lost my place*). **b** a passage in a book. **9** a particular spot on a surface, esp. of the skin (*a sore place on his wrist*). **10 a** employment or office, esp. government employment (*lost his place at the Ministry*). **b** the duties or entitlements of office etc. (*is his place to hire staff*). **11** a position as a member of a team, a student in a college, etc. **12** *Brit.* any of the first three or sometimes four positions in a race, esp. other than the winner (*backed it for a place*). **13** the position of a figure in a series indicated in decimal or similar notation (*calculated to 50 decimal places*). ● *v.tr.* **1** put (a thing etc.) in a particular place or state; arrange. **2** identify, classify, or remember correctly (*cannot place him*). **3** assign to a particular place; locate. **4 a** appoint (a person, esp. a member of the clergy) to a post. **b** find a situation, living, etc. for. **c** (usu. foll. by *with*) consign to a person's care etc. (*placed her with her aunt*). **5** assign rank, importance, or worth to (*place him among the best teachers*). **6 a** dispose of (goods) to a customer. **b** make (an order for goods etc.). **7** (often foll. by *in*, *on*, etc.) have (confidence etc.). **8** invest (money). **9** *Brit.* state the position of (any of the first three or sometimes four runners) in a race. **10** *tr.* (as **placed** *adj.*) **a** *Brit.* among the first three or sometimes four in a race. **b** *US* second in a race. **11** *Football* get (a goal) by a place-kick. □ **all over the place** in disorder; chaotic. **give place to 1** make room for. **2** yield precedence to. **3** be succeeded by. **go places** *colloq.* be successful. **in place** in the right position; suitable. **in place of** in exchange for; instead of. **in places** at some places or in some parts, but not others. **keep a person in his** or **her place** suppress a person's pretensions. **out of place 1** in the wrong position. **2** unsuitable. **place-bet 1** *Brit.* a bet on a horse to come first, second, third, or sometimes fourth in a race. **2** *US* a bet on a horse to come second. **place-brick** an imperfectly burnt brick from the windward side of the kiln. **place card** a card marking a person's place at a table etc. **place in the sun** a favourable situation, position, etc. **place-kick** *Football* a kick made when the ball is previously placed on the ground. **place-mat** a small mat on a table underneath a person's plate. **place-name** the name of a town, village, hill, field, lake, etc. **place-setting** a set of plates, cutlery, etc. for one person at a meal. **put oneself in another's place** imagine oneself in another's position. **put a person in his** or **her place** deflate or humiliate a person. **take place** occur. **take one's place** go to one's correct position, be seated, etc. **take the place of** be substituted for; replace. □□ **placeless** *adj.* **placement** *n.* [ME f. OF f. L *platea* f. Gk *plateia* (*hodos*) broad (way)]

▪ *n.* **1 a, b** location, site, position, point, spot, locus, area, locale, scene, setting. **d** position, situation, circumstances, condition. **2** locale, area, neighbourhood, vicinity, district, section, quarter, region; city, town, village, hamlet. **3** home, house, flat, apartment, room(s), quarters, lodgings, residence, domicile, abode, *colloq.* pad, *Brit. colloq.* digs, diggings, *formal* dwelling(-place).

5 status, station, standing, grade, rank, position, niche, slot, situation, state, *archaic or literary* estate. **6** seat, chair, position, spot. **10 a** position, job, post, appointment, situation, *colloq.* billet, berth; employment, occupation. **b** function, role, part, purpose, duty, obligation, task, responsibility, charge, burden, concern, mission. ● *v.* **1** put (out), position, dispose, arrange, order, set (out), lay, lodge, deposit, *colloq.* stick. **2** put one's finger on; recall, remember, recognize; see IDENTIFY 1, 2. **3** locate, station, post; see also SITUATE *v.* **4** see APPOINT 1. **5** class, classify, rank, group, categorize, bracket, grade; regard, view, see, consider; put, set, assign. □ **all over the place** see *chaotic* (CHAOS). **go places** succeed, become successful, get ahead, advance, prosper, thrive, flourish, go up in the world, make good, *colloq.* strike it rich. **in place** *in situ*, in position, ready, in order, *colloq.* all set; fitting, suitable, appropriate, right, proper, correct. **in place of** instead of, in lieu of, in exchange for. **out of place 2** unsuitable, inappropriate, wrong, improper, misplaced. **put a person in his** or **her place** deflate, humiliate, humble, mortify, bring down, squelch, take a person down a peg (or two), *colloq.* cut a person down to size. **take place** happen, go on, come about; arise, *disp.* transpire; see also OCCUR 1. **take the place of** see REPLACE 2. □□ **placement** arrangement, placing, position, distribution, array, disposition, deployment, positioning, stationing, organization, order, ordering, location, emplacement; employment, appointment, engagement.

placebo /pləseébō/ *n.* (*pl.* **-os**) **1 a** a pill, medicine, etc. prescribed more for psychological than for any physiological effect. **b** a placebo used as a control in testing new drugs etc. **c** a blank sample in a test. **2** *RC Ch.* the opening antiphon of the vespers for the dead. [L, = I shall be acceptable or pleasing f. *placēre* please, first word of Ps. 114:9]

placenta /pləséntə/ *n.* (*pl.* **placentae** /-tee/ or **placentas**) **1** a flattened circular organ in the uterus of pregnant mammals nourishing and maintaining the foetus through the umbilical cord and expelled after birth. **2** (in flowers) part of the ovary wall carrying the ovules. □□ **placental** *adj.* [L f. Gk *plakous -ountos* flat cake f. the root of *plax plakos* flat plate]

placer /pláysər, plássər/ *n.* a deposit of sand, gravel, etc., in the bed of a stream etc., containing valuable minerals in particles. [Amer. Sp., rel. to *placel* sandbank f. *plaza* PLACE]

placet /pláyset/ *n.* an affirmative vote in a church or university assembly. [L, = it pleases]

placid /plássid/ *adj.* **1** (of a person) not easily aroused or disturbed; peaceful. **2** mild; calm; serene. □□ **placidity** /pləsídditi/ *n.* **placidly** *adv.* **placidness** *n.* [F *placide* or L *placidus* f. *placēre* please]

■ see SERENE. □□ **placidity, placidness** see CALM *n.* 1.

placket /plákkit/ *n.* **1** an opening or slit in a garment, for fastenings or access to a pocket. **2** the flap of fabric under this. [var. of PLACARD]

placoid /plákkoyd/ *adj.* & *n.* ● *adj.* **1** (of a fish-scale) consisting of a hard base embedded in the skin and a spiny backward projection (cf. CTENOID). **2** (of a fish) covered with these scales. ● *n.* a placoid fish, e.g. a shark. [Gk *plax plakos* flat plate]

plafond /plafóN/ *n.* **1 a** an ornately decorated ceiling. **b** such decoration. **2** an early form of contract bridge. [F f. *plat* flat + *fond* bottom]

plagal /pláyg'l/ *adj. Mus.* (of a church mode) having sounds between the dominant and its octave (cf. AUTHENTIC). □ **plagal cadence** (or **close**) a cadence in which the chord of the subdominant immediately precedes that of the tonic. [med.L *plagalis* f. *plaga* plagal mode f. L *plagius* f. med. Gk *plagios* (in anc. Gk = oblique) f. Gk *plagos* side]

plage /plaazh/ *n.* **1** *Astron.* an unusually bright region on the sun. **2** a sea beach, esp. at a fashionable resort. [F, = beach]

plagiarism /pláyjəriz'm/ *n.* **1** the act or an instance of plagiarizing. **2** something plagiarized. □□ **plagiarist** *n.* **plagiaristic** /-rístik/ *adj.*

■ **1** plagiary, piracy, theft, stealing, appropriation, thievery, usurpation, infringement, borrowing. **2** borrowing, *colloq.* crib.

plagiarize /pláyjərīz/ *v.tr.* (also **-ise**) (also *absol.*) **1** take and use (the thoughts, writings, inventions, etc. of another person) as one's own. **2** pass off the thoughts etc. of (another person) as one's own. □□ **plagiarizer** *n.* [L *plagiarius* kidnapper f. *plagium* a kidnapping f. Gk *plagion*]

■ see PIRATE *v.* 1. □□ **plagiarizer** see PIRATE *n.* 2.

plagio- /pláyjiō/ *comb. form* oblique. [Gk *plagios* oblique f. *plagos* side]

plagioclase /pláyjiōklayz/ *n.* a series of feldspar minerals forming glassy crystals. [PLAGIO- + Gk *klasis* cleavage]

plague /playg/ *n.*, *v.*, & *int.* ● *n.* **1** a deadly contagious disease spreading rapidly over a wide area. **2** (foll. by *of*) an unusual infestation of a pest etc. (*a plague of frogs*). **3 a** great trouble. **b** an affliction, esp. as regarded as divine punishment. **4** *colloq.* a nuisance. ● *v.tr.* (**plagues, plagued, plaguing**) **1** affect with plague. **2** *colloq.* pester or harass continually. ● *int. joc.* or *archaic* a curse etc. (*a plague on it!*). □□ **plaguesome** *adj.* [ME f. L *plaga* stroke, wound prob. f. Gk *plaga, plēgē*]

■ *n.* **1** epidemic, pestilence, pandemic, *archaic* pest. **3** scourge, affliction, misfortune, curse, bane, calamity, evil, blight, adversity. **4** irritation, annoyance, nuisance, pest, vexation, bother, thorn in one's side *or* flesh, torment, *colloq.* pain (in the neck), headache, hassle, drag, *disp.* aggravation, *sl.* bitch, *esp. US sl.* pain in the butt. ● *v.* **2** badger, harry, hound, pester, bother, harass, nag, torment, torture, anguish, distress, chivvy, pursue. ● *int.* curse; see also BOTHER *int.*

plaice /playss/ *n.* (*pl.* same) **1** a European flatfish, *Pleuronectes platessa*, having a brown back with orange spots and a white underside, much used for food. **2** (in full **American plaice**) a N. Atlantic fish, *Hippoglossoides platessoides*. [ME f. OF *plaïz* f. LL *platessa* app. f. Gk *platus* broad]

plaid /plad/ *n.* **1** (often *attrib.*) chequered or tartan, esp. woollen, twilled cloth (*a plaid skirt*). **2** a long piece of plaid worn over the shoulder as part of Highland Scottish costume. □□ **plaided** *adj.* [Gael. *plaide*, of unkn. orig.]

■ **1** tartan, chequered, checked.

plain[1] /playn/ *adj.*, *adv.*, & *n.* ● *adj.* **1** clear; evident (*is plain to see*). **2** readily understood; simple (*in plain words*). **3 a** (of food, sewing, decoration, etc.) uncomplicated; not elaborate; unembellished; simple. **b** without a decorative pattern. **4** (esp. of a woman or girl) ugly. **5** outspoken; straightforward. **6** (of manners, dress, etc.) unsophisticated; homely (*a plain man*). **7** (of drawings etc.) not coloured (*penny plain, twopence coloured*). **8** not in code. ● *adv.* **1** clearly; unequivocally (*to speak plain, I don't approve*). **2** simply (*that is plain stupid*). ● *n.* **1** a level tract of esp. treeless country. **2** a basic knitting stitch made by putting the needle through the back of the stitch and passing the wool round the front of the needle (opp. PURL[1]). □ **as plain as day** obvious. **be plain with** speak bluntly to. **plain card** neither a trump nor a court-card. **plain chocolate** dark chocolate without added milk. **plain clothes** ordinary clothes worn esp. as a disguise by policemen etc. **plain-clothes** (*attrib.*) wearing plain clothes. **plain cook** a person competent in plain English cooking. **plain dealing** candour; straightforwardness. **plain sailing 1** sailing a straightforward course. **2** an uncomplicated situation or course of action. **plain service** *Eccl.* a church service without music. **plain-spoken** outspoken; blunt. **plain suit** a suit that is not trumps. **plain text** a text not in cipher or code. **plain time** time not paid for at overtime rates. **plain weaving** weaving with the weft alternately over and under the warp. □□ **plainly** *adv.* **plainness** /pláyn-niss/ *n.* [ME f. OF *plain* (adj. & n.) f. L *planus* (adj.), *planum* (n.)]

■ *adj.* **1, 2** clear, evident, simple, distinct, crystal clear, lucid, vivid, transparent, apparent, obvious, patent, self-evident, manifest, unmistakable, unequivocal, unambiguous, understandable, intelligible, direct. **3** unadorned, undecorated, unembellished, unostentatious, unpretentious, uncomplicated, homely, basic, austere, stark, bare, unvarnished, featureless, Spartan; see also SIMPLE *adj.* 2. **4** unattractive, ordinary-looking, unlovely, ugly, *US* homely. **5** open, honest, straightforward, forthright, plain-spoken, direct, frank, candid, blunt, outspoken, unreserved, sincere, guileless, artless. ● *adv.* **1** see *clearly* (CLEAR). **2** see SIMPLY 2. ● *n.* **1** prairie, grassland, pasture, meadow-land, pampas, llano, savannah, steppe, tundra, *S.Afr.* veld, *literary* champaign, *poet. or archaic* mead; heath, wold, moor, moorland; plateau. □ **plain dealing** see CANDOUR. **plain-spoken** see BLUNT *adj.* 2.

plain^2 /playn/ *v.intr. archaic* or *poet.* **1** mourn. **2** complain. **3** make a plaintive sound. [ME f. OF *plaindre* (stem *plaign-*) f. L *plangere planct-* lament]

plainchant /pláynchaant/ *n.* = PLAINSONG.

plainsman /pláynzmən/ *n.* (*pl.* **-men**) a person who lives on a plain, esp. in N. America.

plainsong /pláynsong/ *n.* unaccompanied church music sung in unison in medieval modes and in free rhythm corresponding to the accentuation of the words (cf. GREGORIAN CHANT).

plaint /playnt/ *n.* **1** *Brit. Law* an accusation; a charge. **2** *literary* or *archaic* a complaint; a lamentation. [ME f. OF *plainte* fem. past part. of *plaindre*, and OF *plaint* f. L *planctus* (as PLAIN^2)]

■ see GRIEVANCE.

plaintiff /pláyntif/ *n. Law* a person who brings a case against another into court (opp. DEFENDANT). [ME f. OF *plaintif* (adj.) (as PLAINTIVE)]

■ see LITIGANT *n.*

plaintive /pláyntiv/ *adj.* **1** expressing sorrow; mournful. **2** mournful-sounding. □□ **plaintively** *adv.* **plaintiveness** *n.* [ME f. OF (*-if, -ive*) f. *plainte* (as PLAINT)]

■ see PITEOUS.

plait /plat/ *n.* & *v.* ● *n.* **1** a length of hair, straw, etc., in three or more interlaced strands. **2** = PLEAT. ● *v.tr.* form (hair etc.) into a plait. [ME f. OF *pleit* fold ult. f. L *plicare* fold]

■ *n.* **1** braid, pigtail, *esp. Brit.* queue. ● *v.* see BRAID *v.* 1.

plan /plan/ *n.* & *v.* ● *n.* **1 a** a formulated and esp. detailed method by which a thing is to be done; a design or scheme. **b** an intention or proposed proceeding (*my plan was to distract them; plan of campaign*). **2** a drawing or diagram made by projection on a horizontal plane, esp. showing a building or one floor of a building (cf. ELEVATION). **3** a large-scale detailed map of a town or district. **4 a** a table etc. indicating times, places, etc. of intended proceedings. **b** a scheme or arrangement (*prepared the seating plan*). **5** an imaginary plane perpendicular to the line of vision and containing the objects shown in a picture. ● *v.* (**planned, planning**) **1** *tr.* (often foll. by *that* + clause or *to* + infin.) arrange (a procedure etc.) beforehand; form a plan (*planned to catch the evening ferry*). **2** *tr.* **a** design (a building, new town, etc.). **b** make a plan of (an existing building, an area, etc.). **3** *tr.* (as **planned** *adj.*) in accordance with a plan (*his planned arrival; planned parenthood*). **4** *intr.* make plans. □ **planning permission** *Brit.* formal permission for building development etc., esp. from a local authority. **plan on** *colloq.* aim at doing; intend. □□ **planning** *n.* [F f. earlier *plant*, f. It. *pianta* plan of building: cf. PLANT]

■ *n.* **1 a** scheme, method, procedure, system, arrangement, programme, project, formula, pattern; see also DESIGN *n.* 1a. **b** see INTENTION 1. **2** drawing, sketch, design, layout, blueprint, chart, map, diagram, arrangement, scheme. ● *v.* **1** intend, expect, aim, contrive, devise; envisage, envision, foresee, contemplate, propose; see also ARRANGE 2, 3. **2** see DESIGN *v.* 1. □ **plan on** see INTEND 1, 2.

planar /pláynər/ *adj. Math.* of, relating to, or in the form of a plane.

planarian /plənáiriən/ *n.* any flatworm of the class Turbellaria, usu. living in fresh water. [mod.L *Planaria* the genus-name, fem. of L *planarius* lying flat]

planchet /plánshit/ *n.* a plain metal disc from which a coin is made. [dimin. of *planch* slab of metal f. OF *planche*: see PLANK]

planchette /plaanshét/ *n.* a small usu. heart-shaped board on castors with a pencil that is supposedly caused to write spirit messages when a person's fingers rest lightly on it. [F, dimin. of *planche* PLANK]

Planck's constant /plangks/ *n.* (also **Planck constant**) a fundamental constant, equal to the energy of quanta of electromagnetic radiation divided by its frequency, with a value of 6.626×10^{-34} joules. [M. *Planck*, Ger. physicist d. 1947]

plane^1 /playn/ *n., adj.,* & *v.* ● *n.* **1 a** a flat surface on which a straight line joining any two points on it would wholly lie. **b** an imaginary flat surface through or joining etc. material objects. **2** a level surface. **3** *colloq.* = AEROPLANE. **4** a flat surface producing lift by the action of air or water over and under it (usu. in *comb.*: *hydroplane*). **5** (often foll. by *of*) a level of attainment, thought, knowledge, etc. **6** a flat thin object such as a tabletop. ● *adj.* **1** (of a surface etc.) perfectly level. **2** (of an angle, figure, etc.) lying in a plane. ● *v.intr.* **1** (often foll. by *down*) travel or glide in an aeroplane. **2** (of a speedboat etc.) skim over water. **3** soar. □ **plane chart** a chart on which meridians and parallels of latitude are represented by equidistant straight lines, used in plane sailing. **plane polarization** a process restricting the vibrations of electromagnetic radiation, esp. light, to one direction. **plane sailing 1** the practice of determining a ship's position on the theory that she is moving on a plane. **2** = *plain sailing* (see PLAIN^1). **plane-table** a surveying instrument used for direct plotting in the field, with a circular drawing-board and pivoted alidade. [L *planum* flat surface, neut. of *planus* PLAIN^1 (different. f. PLAIN^1 in 17th c.): adj. after F *plan, plane*]

■ *n.* **2** flat, level. **3** aircraft, airliner, jet (plane), *esp. Brit.* aeroplane, *US* airplane. **5** see DEGREE 10. ● *adj.* **1** flat, even, level, horizontal; smooth. ● *v.* **2** glide, skim, skate, slip, slide.

plane^2 /playn/ *n.* & *v.* ● *n.* **1** a tool consisting of a wooden or metal block with a projecting steel blade, used to smooth a wooden surface by paring shavings from it. **2** a similar tool for smoothing metal. ● *v.tr.* **1** smooth (wood, metal, etc.) with a plane. **2** (often foll. by *away, down*) pare (irregularities) with a plane. **3** *archaic* level (*plane the way*). [ME f. OF var. of *plaine* f. LL *plana* f. L *planus* PLAIN^1]

plane^3 /playn/ *n.* (in full **plane-tree**) any tree of the genus *Platanus* often growing to great heights, with maple-like leaves and bark which peels in uneven patches. [ME f. OF f. L *platanus* f. Gk *platanos* f. *platus* broad]

planet /plánnit/ *n.* **1** a celestial body moving in an elliptical orbit round a star; the earth. **2** esp. *Astrol. hist.* a celestial body distinguished from the fixed stars by having an apparent motion of its own (including the moon and sun), esp. with reference to its supposed influence on people and events. □□ **planetology** /-tólləji/ *n.* [ME f. OF *planete* f. LL *planeta, planetes* f. Gk *planētēs* wanderer, planet f. *planaomai* wander]

planetarium /plánnitáiriəm/ *n.* (*pl.* **planetariums** or **planetaria** /-riə/) **1** a domed building in which images of stars, planets, constellations, etc. are projected for public entertainment or education. **2** the device used for such projection. **3** = ORRERY. [mod.L (as PLANET)]

planetary /plánnitəri, -tri/ *adj.* **1** of or like planets (*planetary influence*). **2** terrestrial; mundane. **3** wandering; erratic. □ **planetary nebula** a ring-shaped nebula formed by an expanding shell of gas round a star. [LL *planetarius* (as PLANET)]

■ **3** see ERRATIC 2.

planetesimal /plánnitéssim'l/ *n.* any of a vast number of minute planets or planetary bodies. □ **planetesimal hypothesis** the theory that planets were formed by the accretion of planetesimals in a cold state. [PLANET, after *infinitesimal*]

planetoid /plánnitoyd/ *n.* = ASTEROID.

plangent /plánjənt/ *adj.* **1** (of a sound) loud and reverberating. **2** (of a sound) plaintive; sad. □□ **plangency** *n.* [L *plangere plangent-* lament]

planimeter /plənímmitər/ *n.* an instrument for mechanically measuring the area of a plane figure. □□ **planimetric** /plánnimétrik/ *adj.* **planimetrical** /plánnimétrik'l/ *adj.* **planimetry** *n.* [F *planimètre* f. L *planus* level]

planish /plánnish/ *v.tr.* flatten (sheet metal, coining-metal, etc.) with a smooth-faced hammer or between rollers. □□ **planisher** *n.* [ME f. OF *planir* smooth f. *plain* PLANE[1] *adj.*]

planisphere /plánnisfeer/ *n.* a map formed by the projection of a sphere or part of a sphere on a plane, esp. to show the appearance of the heavens at a specific time or place. □□ **planispheric** /-sférrik/ *adj.* [ME f. med.L *planisphaerium* (as PLANE[1], SPHERE): infl. by F *planisphère*]

plank /plangk/ *n.* & *v.* ● *n.* **1** a long flat piece of timber used esp. in building, flooring, etc. **2** an item of a political or other programme (cf. PLATFORM). ● *v.tr.* **1** provide, cover, or floor, with planks. **2** (usu. foll. by *down*; also *absol.*) esp. *US colloq.* **a** put (a thing, person, etc.) down roughly or violently. **b** pay (money) on the spot or abruptly (*planked down £5*). □ **plank bed** a bed of boards without a mattress, esp. in prison. **walk the plank** *hist.* (of a pirate's captive etc.) be made to walk blindfold along a plank over the side of a ship to one's death in the sea. [ME f. ONF *planke*, OF *planche* f. LL *planca* board f. *plancus* flat-footed]

■ *n.* **1** board, timber, slab. ● *v.* **2 a** slap, slam, dump, fling, toss, throw, sling.

planking /plángking/ *n.* planks as flooring etc.

■ flooring, boarding.

plankton /plángktən/ *n.* the chiefly microscopic organisms drifting or floating in the sea or fresh water (see BENTHOS, NEKTON). □□ **planktonic** /-tónnik/ *adj.* [G f. Gk *plagktos* wandering f. *plazomai* wander]

planner /plánnər/ *n.* **1** a person who controls or plans the development of new towns, designs buildings, etc. **2** a person who makes plans. **3** a list, table, etc., with information helpful in planning.

■ **2** see MASTERMIND *n.*

plano- /pláynō/ *comb. form* level, flat. [L *planus* flat]

planoconcave /pláynōkónkayv/ *adj.* (of a lens etc.) with one surface plane and the other concave.

planoconvex /pláynōkónveks/ *adj.* (of a lens etc.) with one surface plane and the other convex.

planographic /pláynəgráffik/ *adj.* relating to or produced by a process in which printing is done from a plane surface. □□ **planography** /plənógrəfi/ *n.*

planometer /plənómmitər/ *n.* a flat plate used as a gauge for plane surfaces in metalwork.

plant /plaant/ *n.* & *v.* ● *n.* **1 a** any living organism of the kingdom Plantae, usu. containing chlorophyll enabling it to live wholly on inorganic substances and lacking specialized sense organs and the power of voluntary movement. **b** a small organism of this kind, as distinguished from a shrub or tree. **2 a** machinery, fixtures, etc., used in industrial processes. **b** a factory. **3 a** *colloq.* something, esp. incriminating or compromising, positioned or concealed so as to be discovered later. **b** *sl.* a spy or detective; hidden police officers. ● *v.tr.* **1** place (a seed, bulb, or growing thing) in the ground so that it may take root and flourish. **2** (often foll. by *in*, *on*, etc.) put or fix in position. **3** deposit (young fish, spawn, oysters, etc.) in a river or lake. **4** station (a person etc.), esp. as a spy or source of information. **5** *refl.* take up a position (*planted myself by the door*). **6** cause (an idea etc.) to be established esp. in another person's mind. **7** deliver (a blow, kiss, etc.) with a deliberate aim. **8 a** *colloq.* position or conceal (something incriminating or compromising) for later discovery. **b** *sl.* post or infiltrate (a person) as a spy. **9 a** settle or people (a colony etc.). **b** found or establish (a city, community, etc.). **10** bury. □ **plant-louse** a small insect that infests plants, esp. an aphis. **plant out** transfer (a plant) from a pot or frame to the open ground; set out (seedlings) at intervals. □□ **plantable** *adj.* **plantlet** *n.* **plantlike** *adj.* [OE *plante* & F *plante* f. L *planta* sprout, slip, cutting]

■ *n.* **2 a** machinery, apparatus; gear, fixtures; see also EQUIPMENT. **b** factory, mill, works, workshop. **3 b** spy, (undercover *or* secret) agent, informer, informant. ● *v.* **1** bed (out), sow, seed, set (out). **2** place, put, position, station, situate, set (out), *colloq.* stick. **6** implant, establish, root, fix, ingrain, lodge, sow, instil, insinuate, introduce, impress, imprint. **8 a** hide, conceal; see also SECRETE[2].

Plantagenet /plantájinit/ *adj.* & *n.* ● *adj.* of or relating to the kings of England from Henry II to Richard II. ● *n.* any of these kings. [= sprig of broom (L *planta genista*) worn as a distinctive mark, the origin of their surname]

plantain[1] /plántin/ *n.* any shrub of the genus *Plantago*, with broad flat leaves spread out close to the ground and seeds used as food for birds and as a mild laxative. □ **plantain lily** = HOSTA. [ME f. OF f. L *plantago -ginis* f. *planta* sole of the foot (from its broad prostrate leaves)]

plantain[2] /plántin/ *n.* **1** a banana plant, *Musa paradisiaca*, widely grown for its fruit. **2** the starchy fruit of this containing less sugar than a dessert banana and chiefly used in cooking. [earlier *platan* f. Sp. *plá(n)tano* plane-tree, prob. assim. f. Galibi *palatana* etc.]

plantar /plántər/ *adj.* of or relating to the sole of the foot. [L *plantaris* f. *planta* sole]

plantation /plantáysh'n, plaan-/ *n.* **1** an estate on which cotton, tobacco, etc. is cultivated, esp. in former colonies, formerly by slave labour. **2** an area planted with trees etc. **3** *hist.* a colony; colonization. □ **plantation song** a song of the kind formerly sung by Blacks on American plantations. [ME f. OF *plantation* or L *plantatio* (as PLANT)]

planter /plaántər/ *n.* **1** a person who cultivates the soil. **2** the manager or occupier of a coffee, cotton, tobacco, etc. plantation. **3** a large container for decorative plants. **4** a machine for planting seeds etc. (*potato-planter*).

■ **3** flowerpot, plant-pot.

plantigrade /plántigrayd/ *adj.* & *n.* ● *adj.* (of an animal) walking on the soles of its feet. ● *n.* a plantigrade animal, e.g. humans or bears (cf. DIGITIGRADE). [F f. mod.L *plantigradus* f. L *planta* sole + *-gradus* -walking]

plaque /plak, plaak/ *n.* **1** an ornamental tablet of metal, porcelain, etc., esp. affixed to a building in commemoration. **2** a deposit on teeth where bacteria proliferate. **3** *Med.* **a** a patch or eruption of skin etc. as a result of damage. **b** a fibrous lesion in atherosclerosis. **4** a small badge of rank in an honorary order. □□ **plaquette** /plakét/ *n.* [F f. Du. *plak* tablet f. *plakken* stick]

■ **1** tablet, medallion, plate, panel, marker, slab, plaquette. **4** badge, pin, patch, medallion, medal, insignia.

plash[1] /plash/ *n.* & *v.* ● *n.* **1** a splash; a plunge. **2 a** a marshy pool. **b** a puddle. ● *v.* **1** *tr.* & *intr.* splash. **2** *tr.* strike the surface of (water). □□ **plashy** *adj.* [OE *plæsc*, prob. imit.]

■ *v.* **1** see GURGLE *v.*, SPLASH *v.* 3.

plash[2] /plash/ *v.tr.* **1** bend down and interweave (branches, twigs, etc.) to form a hedge. **2** make or renew (a hedge) in this way. [ME f. OF *pla(i)ssier* ult. f. L *plectere* plait: cf. PLEACH]

plasma /plázmə/ *n.* (also **plasm** /plázz'm/) **1** the colourless fluid part of blood, lymph, or milk, in which corpuscles or fat-globules are suspended. **2** = PROTOPLASM. **3** a gas of positive ions and free electrons with an approximately equal positive and negative charge. **4** a green variety of quartz used in mosaic and for other decorative purposes. □□ **plasmatic** /-máttik/ *adj.* **plasmic** *adj.* [LL, = mould f. Gk *plasma -atos* f. *plassō* to shape]

plasmodesma /plázmədézmə/ *n.* (*pl.* **plasmodesmata** /-mətə/) a narrow thread of cytoplasm that passes through cell walls and affords communication between plant cells. [PLASMA + Gk *desma* bond, fetter]

plasmodium /plazmṓdiəm/ *n.* (*pl.* **plasmodia** /-diə/) **1** any parasitic protozoan of the genus *Plasmodium*, including those causing malaria in man. **2** a form within the life cycle of various micro-organisms including slime moulds, usu. consisting of a mass of naked protoplasm containing many nuclei. ▫▫ **plasmodial** *adj.* [mod.L f. PLASMA[1] + *-odium*: see -ODE[1]]

plasmolyse /plázməlīz/ *v.intr.* & *tr.* (*US* **plasmolyze**) undergo or subject to plasmolysis.

plasmolysis /plazmóllisiss/ *n.* contraction of the protoplast of a plant cell as a result of loss of water from the cell. [mod.L (as PLASMA, -LYSIS)]

plaster /plaástər/ *n.* & *v.* ● *n.* **1** a soft pliable mixture esp. of lime putty with sand or Portland cement etc. for spreading on walls, ceilings, etc., to form a smooth hard surface when dried. **2** *Brit.* = *sticking-plaster* (see STICK[2]). **3** *hist.* a curative or protective substance spread on a bandage etc. and applied to the body (*mustard plaster*). ● *v.tr.* **1** cover (a wall etc.) with plaster or a similar substance. **2** (often foll. by *with*) coat thickly or to excess; bedaub (*plastered the bread with jam*; *the wall was plastered with slogans*). **3** stick or apply (a thing) thickly like plaster (*plastered glue all over it*). **4** (often foll. by *down*) make (esp. hair) smooth with water, cream, etc.; fix flat. **5** (as **plastered** *adj.*) *sl.* drunk. **6** apply a medical plaster or plaster cast to. **7** *sl.* bomb or shell heavily. ▫ **plaster cast 1** a bandage stiffened with plaster of Paris and applied to a broken limb etc. **2** a statue or mould made of plaster. **plaster of Paris** fine white plaster made of gypsum and used for making plaster casts etc. **plaster saint** *iron.* a person regarded as being without moral faults or human frailty. ▫▫ **plasterer** *n.* **plastery** *adj.* [ME f. OE & OF *plastre* or F *plastrer* f. med.L *plastrum* f. L *emplastrum* f. Gk *emplastron*]

■ *v.* **2** smear, daub, bedaub, spread, coat, cover, overlay, smother. **3** smear, stick, daub, spread. **5** (**plastered**) see DRUNK *adj.* 1 **7** see SHELL *v.* 2.

plasterboard /plaástərbord/ *n.* two boards with a filling of plaster used to form or line the inner walls of houses etc.

plastic /plástik/ *n.* & *adj.* ● *n.* **1** any of a number of synthetic polymeric substances that can be given any required shape. **2** (*attrib.*) made of plastic (*plastic bag*); made of cheap materials. **3** = *plastic money*. ● *adj.* **1 a** capable of being moulded; pliant; supple. **b** susceptible, impressionable. **2** moulding or giving form to clay, wax, etc. **3** *Biol.* exhibiting an adaptability to environmental changes. **4** (esp. in philosophy) formative, creative. ▫ **plastic arts** art forms involving modelling or moulding, e.g. sculpture and ceramics, or art involving the representation of solid objects with three-dimensional effects. **plastic bomb** a bomb containing plastic explosive. **plastic explosive** a putty-like explosive capable of being moulded by hand. **plastic money** *colloq.* a credit card, charge card, or other plastic card that can be used in place of money. **plastic surgeon** a qualified practitioner of plastic surgery. **plastic surgery** the process of reconstructing or repairing parts of the body by the transfer of tissue, either in the treatment of injury or for cosmetic reasons. ▫▫ **plastically** *adv.* **plasticity** /-tíssiti/ *n.* **plasticize** /-tisīz/ *v.tr.* (also **-ise**). **plasticization** /-tisīzáysh'n/ *n.* **plasticizer** /-tisīzər/ *n.* **plasticky** *adj.* [F *plastique* or L *plasticus* f. Gk *plastikos* f. *plassō* mould]

■ *n.* **2** (*attrib.*) cheap, inferior, worthless, pinchbeck, shoddy, chintzy, gaudy, *colloq.* crummy. ● *adj.* **1 a** mouldable, pliable, shapable, soft, waxy, malleable, workable, ductile, flexible, pliant, supple. **b** impressionable, receptive, open, persuadable *or* persuasible, susceptible, tractable, compliant, responsive, manageable; unformed, inexperienced. **4** see SEMINAL 4.

Plasticine /plástiseen/ *n. propr.* a soft plastic material used, esp. by children, for modelling. [PLASTIC + -INE[4]]

plastid /plástid/ *n.* any small organelle in the cytoplasm of a plant cell, containing pigment or food. [G f. Gk *plastos* shaped]

plastron /plástrən/ *n.* **1 a** a fencer's leather-covered breastplate. **b** a lancer's breast-covering of facings-cloth. **2 a** an ornamental front on a woman's bodice. **b** a man's starched shirt-front. **3 a** the ventral part of the shell of a tortoise or turtle. **b** the corresponding part in other animals. **4** *hist.* a steel breastplate. ▫▫ **plastral** *adj.* [F f. It. *piastrone* augment. of *piastra* breastplate, f. L *emplastrum* PLASTER]

plat[1] /plat/ *n. US* **1** a plot of land. **2** a plan of an area of land. [16th c.: collateral form of PLOT]

■ **1** see PLOT *n.* 1.

plat[2] /plat/ *n.* & *v.* ● *n.* = PLAIT *n.* 1. ● *v.tr.* (**platted**, **platting**) = PLAIT *v.*

platan /plátt'n/ *n.* = PLANE[3]. [ME f. L *platanus*: see PLANE[3]]

plat du jour /plaá dōō zhóor/ *n.* a dish specially featured on a day's menu. [F, = dish of the day]

plate /playt/ *n.* & *v.* ● *n.* **1 a** a shallow vessel, usu. circular and of earthenware or china, from which food is eaten or served. **b** the contents of this (*ate a plate of sandwiches*). **2** a similar vessel usu. of metal or wood, used esp. for making a collection in a church etc. **3** *US* a main course of a meal, served on one plate. **4** *Austral.* & *NZ* a contribution of cakes, sandwiches, etc., to a social gathering. **5 a** (*collect.*) utensils of silver, gold, or other metal. **b** (*collect.*) objects of plated metal. **c** = PLATING. **6** a piece of metal with a name or inscription for affixing to a door, container, etc. **7** an illustration on special paper in a book. **8** a thin sheet of metal, glass, etc., coated with a sensitive film for photography. **9** a flat thin usu. rigid sheet of metal etc. with an even surface and uniform thickness, often as part of a mechanism. **10 a** a smooth piece of metal etc. for engraving. **b** an impression made from this. **11 a** a silver or gold cup as a prize for a horse-race etc. **b** a race with this as a prize. **12 a** a thin piece of plastic material, moulded to the shape of the mouth and gums, to which artificial teeth or another orthodontic appliance are attached. **b** *colloq.* a complete denture or orthodontic appliance. **13** *Geol.* each of several rigid sheets of rock thought to form the earth's outer crust. **14** *Biol.* a thin flat organic structure or formation. **15** a light shoe for a racehorse. **16** a stereotype, electrotype, or plastic cast of a page of composed movable types, or a metal or plastic copy of filmset matter, from which sheets are printed. **17** *US Baseball* a flat piece of whitened rubber marking the station of a batter or pitcher. **18** *US* the anode of a thermionic valve. **19** a horizontal timber laid along the top of a wall to support the ends of joists or rafters (*window-plate*). ● *v.tr.* **1** apply a thin coat esp. of silver, gold, or tin to (another metal). **2** cover (esp. a ship) with plates of metal, esp. for protection. **3** make a plate of (type etc.) for printing. ▫ **on a plate** *colloq.* available with little trouble to the recipient. **on one's plate** for one to deal with or consider. **plate armour** armour of metal plates, for a man, ship, etc. **plate glass** thick fine-quality glass for shop windows etc., orig. cast in plates. **plate-mark** a hallmark. **plate-rack** *Brit.* a rack in which plates are placed to drain. **plate tectonics** *Geol.* the study of the earth's surface based on the concept of moving 'plates' (see sense 13 of *n.*) forming its structure. **plate tracery** *Archit.* tracery with perforations in otherwise continuous stone. ▫▫ **plateful** *n.* (*pl.* **-fuls**). **plateless** *adj.* **plater** *n.* [ME f. OF f. med.L *plata* plate armour f. *platus* (adj.) ult. f. Gk *platus* flat]

■ *n.* **1 a** platter, dish, bowl, *archaic* charger, *hist.* trencher. **b** plateful, serving, portion, dish, platter. **6** see PLAQUE 1. **7** illustration, picture, print, vignette. **9** layer, leaf, sheet, pane, panel, lamina, slab. ● *v.* **1** cover, coat, overlay, face, laminate.

plateau /pláttō/ *n.* & *v.* ● *n.* (*pl.* **plateaux** /-tōz/ or **plateaus**) **1** an area of fairly level high ground. **2** a state of little variation after an increase. ● *v.intr.* (**plateaus**, **plateaued**) (often foll. by *out*) reach a level or stable state after an increase. [F f. OF *platel* dimin. of *plat* flat surface]

■ *n.* **1** tableland, table, upland, plain. ● *v.* see LEVEL *v.* 1.

platelayer /pláytlayər/ *n. Brit.* a person employed in fixing and repairing railway rails.

platelet /pláytlit/ *n.* a small colourless disc of protoplasm found in blood and involved in clotting.

platen /plátt'n/ *n.* **1** a plate in a printing-press which presses the paper against the type. **2** a cylindrical roller in a typewriter against which the paper is held. [OF *platine* a flat piece f. *plat* flat]

plateresque /pláttərésk/ *adj.* richly ornamented in a style suggesting silverware. [Sp. *plateresco* f. *platero* silversmith f. *plata* silver]

platform /plátform/ *n.* **1** a raised level surface; a natural or artificial terrace. **2** a raised surface from which a speaker addresses an audience. **3** *Brit.* a raised elongated structure along the side of a track in a railway station. **4** the floor area at the entrance to a bus. **5** a thick sole of a shoe. **6** the declared policy of a political party. □ **platform ticket** a ticket allowing a non-traveller access to a station platform. [F *plateforme* ground-plan f. *plate* flat + *forme* FORM]

■ **2** stand, dais, stage, podium, rostrum. **6** policy, party line, principle(s), tenet(s), programme, manifesto.

plating /pláyting/ *n.* **1** a coating of gold, silver, etc. **2** racing for plates.

■ **1** plate, coat, coating, layer, lamination.

platinic /plətínnik/ *adj.* of or containing (esp. tetravalent) platinum.

platinize /pláttinīz/ *v.tr.* (also **-ise**) coat with platinum. □□ **platinization** /-záysh'n/ *n.*

platinoid /pláttinoyd/ *n.* an alloy of copper, zinc, nickel, and tungsten.

platinum /pláttinəm/ *n. Chem.* a ductile malleable silvery-white metallic element occurring naturally in nickel and copper ores, unaffected by simple acids and fusible only at a very high temperature, used in making jewellery and laboratory apparatus. ¶ Symb.: **Pt.** □ **platinum black** platinum in powder form like lampblack. **platinum blonde** (or **blond**) *adj.* silvery-blond. ● *n.* a person with silvery-blond hair. **platinum metal** any metallic element found with and resembling platinum e.g. osmium, iridium, and palladium. [mod.L f. earlier *platina* f. Sp., dimin. of *plata* silver]

platitude /pláttityōōd/ *n.* **1** a trite or commonplace remark, esp. one solemnly delivered. **2** the use of platitudes; dullness, insipidity. □□ **platitudinize** /-tyōōdinīz/ *v.intr.* (also **-ise**). **platitudinous** /-tyōōdinəss/ *adj.* [F f. *plat* flat, after *certitude*, *multitudinous*, etc.]

■ **1** see CLICHÉ. □□ **platitudinous** see BANAL.

Platonic /plətónnik/ *adj.* **1** of or associated with the Greek philosopher Plato (d. 347 BC) or his ideas. **2** (**platonic**) (of love or friendship) purely spiritual, not sexual. **3** (**platonic**) confined to words or theory; not leading to action; harmless. □ **Platonic solid** (or **body**) any of the five regular solids (tetrahedron, cube, octahedron, dodecahedron, icosahedron). □□ **Platonically** *adv.* [L *Platonicus* f. Gk *Platōnikos* f. *Platōn* Plato]

■ **2** (**platonic**) non-physical, asexual, non-sexual, chaste, dispassionate, detached, spiritual, friendly. **3** (**platonic**) see ABSTRACT *adj.* 1a.

Platonism /pláytəniz'm/ *n.* the philosophy of Plato or his followers. □□ **Platonist** *n.*

platoon /plətōōn/ *n.* **1** *Mil.* a subdivision of a company, a tactical unit commanded by a lieutenant and usu. divided into three sections. **2** a group of persons acting together. [F *peloton* small ball, dimin. of *pelote*: see PELLET, -OON]

■ company, squad, squadron, group, patrol, team, cadre, body, formation, unit, *colloq.* outfit.

platteland /plaátəlaant/ *n. S.Afr.* remote country districts. □□ **plattelander** *n.* [Afrik., = flat land]

platter /pláttər/ *n.* **1** a large flat dish or plate, esp. for food. **2** *colloq.* a gramophone record. □ **on a platter** = *on a plate* (see PLATE). [ME & AF *plater* f. AF *plat* PLATE]

■ **1** serving dish, server, plate, dish, salver, tray.

platy- /plátti/ *comb. form* broad, flat. [Gk *platu-* f. *platus* broad, flat]

platyhelminth /pláttihélminth/ *n.* any invertebrate of the phylum Platyhelminthes, including flatworms, flukes, and tapeworms.

platypus /pláttipəss/ *n.* an Australian aquatic egg-laying mammal, *Ornithorhynchus anatinus*, having a pliable duck-like bill, webbed feet, and sleek grey fur. Also called DUCKBILL.

platyrrhine /pláttirīn/ *adj.* & *n.* ● *adj.* (of primates) having nostrils far apart and directed forwards or sideways (cf. CATARRHINE). ● *n.* such an animal. [PLATY- + Gk *rhis rhin-* nose]

plaudit /pláwdit/ *n.* (usu. in *pl.*) **1** a round of applause. **2** an emphatic expression of approval. [shortened f. L *plaudite* applaud, imper. pl. of *plaudere plaus-* applaud, said by Roman actors at the end of a play]

■ **1** see APPLAUSE 1. **2** see APPLAUSE 2.

plausible /pláwzib'l/ *adj.* **1** (of an argument, statement, etc.) seeming reasonable or probable. **2** (of a person) persuasive but deceptive. □□ **plausibility** /-bílliti/ *n.* **plausibly** *adv.* [L *plausibilis* (as PLAUDIT)]

■ **1** likely, believable, cogent, convincing, reasonable, feasible, credible, creditable, tenable, conceivable, thinkable, probable, imaginable, possible, admissible, compelling, sound, rational, logical, acceptable. **2** specious, meretricious, misleading, deceitful, casuistic, sophistical, smooth; see also DECEPTIVE.

play /play/ *v.* & *n.* ● *v.* **1** *intr.* (often foll. by *with*) occupy or amuse oneself pleasantly with some recreation, game, exercise, etc. **2** *intr.* (foll. by *with*) act light-heartedly or flippantly (with feelings etc.). **3** *tr.* **a** perform on or be able to perform on (a musical instrument). **b** perform (a piece of music etc.). **c** cause (a record, record-player, etc.) to produce sounds. **4 a** *intr.* (foll. by *in*) perform a role in (a drama etc.). **b** *tr.* perform (a drama or role) on stage, or in a film or broadcast. **c** *tr.* give a dramatic performance at (a particular theatre or place). **5** *tr.* act in real life the part of (*play truant*; *play the fool*). **6** *tr.* (foll. by *on*) perform (a trick or joke etc.) on (a person). **7** *tr.* (foll. by *for*) regard (a person) as (something specified) (*played me for a fool*). **8** *intr. colloq.* participate, cooperate; do what is wanted (*they won't play*). **9** *intr.* gamble. **10** *tr.* gamble on. **11** *tr.* **a** take part in (a game or recreation). **b** compete with (another player or team) in a game. **c** occupy (a specified position) in a team for a game. **d** (foll. by *in*, *on*, *at*, etc.) assign (a player) to a position. **12** *tr.* move (a piece) or display (a playing-card) in one's turn in a game. **13** *tr.* (also *absol.*) strike (a ball etc.) or execute (a stroke) in a game. **14** *intr.* move about in a lively or unrestrained manner. **15** *intr.* (often foll. by *on*) **a** touch gently. **b** emit light, water, etc. (*fountains gently playing*). **16** *tr.* allow (a fish) to exhaust itself pulling against a line. **17** *intr.* (often foll. by *at*) **a** engage in a half-hearted way (in an activity). **b** pretend to be. **18** *intr.* (of a cricket ground etc.) be conducive to play as specified (*the pitch is playing fast*). **19** *intr. colloq.* act or behave (as specified) (*play fair*). **20** *tr.* (foll. by *in*, *out*, etc.) accompany (a person) with music (*were played out with bagpipes*). ● *n.* **1** recreation, amusement, esp. as the spontaneous activity of children and young animals. **2 a** the playing of a game. **b** the action or manner of this. **c** the status of the ball etc. in a game as being available to be played according to the rules (*in play*; *out of play*). **3** a dramatic piece for the stage etc. **4** activity or operation (*are in full play*; *brought into play*). **5 a** freedom of movement. **b** space or scope for this. **6** brisk, light, or fitful movement. **7** gambling. **8** an action or manoeuvre, esp. in or as in a game. □ **at play** engaged in recreation. **in play** for amusement; not seriously. **make play** act effectively. **make a play for** *colloq.* make a conspicuous attempt to acquire. **make play with** use ostentatiously. **play about** (or **around**) **1** behave irresponsibly. **2** philander. **play along** pretend to cooperate. **play back** play (sounds recently recorded), esp. to monitor recording quality etc.

play-back *n.* a playing back of a sound or sounds. **play ball** see BALL[1]. **play by ear 1** perform (music) without the aid of a score. **2** (also **play it by ear**) proceed instinctively or step by step according to results and circumstances. **play one's cards right** (or **well**) make good use of opportunities; act shrewdly. **play down** minimize the importance of. **play ducks and drakes with** see DUCK[1]. **played out** exhausted of energy or usefulness. **play false** act, or treat a (person), deceitfully or treacherously. **play fast and loose** act unreliably; ignore one's obligations. **play the field** see FIELD. **play for time** seek to gain time by delaying. **play the game** see GAME[1]. **play God** see GOD. **play havoc with** see HAVOC. **play hell with** see HELL. **play hookey** see HOOKEY. **play into a person's hands** act so as unwittingly to give a person an advantage. **play it cool** *colloq.* **1** affect indifference. **2** be relaxed or unemotional. **play the man** = *be a man* (see MAN). **play the market** speculate in stocks etc. **play off** (usu. foll. by *against*) **1** oppose (one person against another), esp. for one's own advantage. **2** play an extra match to decide a draw or tie. **play-off** *n.* a match played to decide a draw or tie. **play on 1** continue to play. **2** take advantage of (a person's feelings etc.). **play oneself in** become accustomed to the prevailing conditions in a game etc. **play on words** a pun. **play-pen** a portable enclosure for young children to play in. **play possum** see POSSUM. **play safe** (or **for safety**) avoid risks. **play-suit** a garment for a young child. **play to the gallery** see GALLERY. **play up 1** behave mischievously. **2** cause trouble; be irritating (*my rheumatism is playing up again*). **3** obstruct or annoy in this way (*played the teacher up*). **4** put all one's energy into a game. **5** make the most of; emphasize. **play up to** flatter, esp. to win favour. **play with fire** take foolish risks. □□ **playable** *adj.* **playability** /pláyabilliti/ *n.* [OE *plega* (n.), *pleg(i)an* (v.), orig. = (to) exercise]

■ *v.* **1** amuse oneself, frolic, caper, sport, have fun, have a good time, enjoy oneself, disport (oneself). **2** see TOY *v.* 1. **3 a** perform upon *or* on. **c** operate; put *or* turn on. **4 a** perform, act; appear. **b** put on, perform; act, take the role *or* part of, appear as. **7** see TAKE *v.* 20. **8** participate, take part, join in, cooperate, play the game, play ball, play along. **9, 10** gamble, bet; see also SPECULATE 3. **11 a** take part in, join in, participate in, be occupied in *or* with, occupy oneself in *or* with, engage in; take up. **b** engage (with), contend with, compete with *or* against, challenge, vie with, pit oneself against, take on. **17 b** sham, feign, pretend, fake, dissemble; (*play at*) fake, feign, simulate, affect. **19** see BEHAVE 1a. ● *n.* **1** amusement, frivolity, entertainment, recreation, fun, pleasure, sport, merrymaking, revelry; tomfoolery, horseplay, skylarking. **3** drama, stage play, show, piece, production, entertainment. **4** see OPERATION 1, 2. **5** flexibility, looseness, freedom, leeway, margin, room, space, movement, motion, give. **8** move, action; see also MANOEUVRE *n.* 1, 3. □ **in play** in jest, in fun, jokingly, teasingly, playfully, tongue in cheek, for a laugh. **make a play for** see *go for* 4. **play about** or **around 1** fool around *or* about, monkey about, horse about, act up, mess about, misbehave, cause trouble; tease. **2** dally, flirt, be unfaithful; philander, womanize; *colloq.* fool around, run around, sleep around, play the field. **play along** (*play along with*) cooperate with, go along with; see also OBLIGE 3. **play by ear 2** improvise, ad lib; take it as it comes. **play down** belittle, minimize, diminish, make light of, de-emphasize, brush off, shrug off, laugh off, pooh-pooh. **played out** see *exhausted* (EXHAUST *v.* 2). **play for time** delay, procrastinate, stall, temporize, hesitate, drag one's feet *or* heels, hold back. **play on 2** trade on, exploit, take advantage of, use, make use of, misuse, abuse. **play up 1** see MISBEHAVE. **2** give *or* cause trouble, malfunction, *sl.* go on the blink. **5** stress, emphasize, underscore, underline, accentuate, call attention to, highlight, spotlight, dramatize, build up. **play up to** curry favour with, toady to, ingratiate oneself with, truckle to, court, fawn on, *colloq.* soft-soap, butter up, suck up to, bootlick; see also FLATTER 1. **play with fire** undertake a risk *or* hazard *or* peril, run a risk, risk a thing *or* everything, imperil *or* endanger a thing, tempt fate, live dangerously, sail close to the wind.

playa /plaáyə/ *n.* a flat dried-up area, esp. a desert basin from which water evaporates quickly. [Sp., = beach, f. LL *plagia*]

play-act /pláyakt/ *v.* **1** *intr.* act in a play. **2** *intr.* behave affectedly or insincerely. **3** *tr.* act (a scene, part, etc.). □□ **play-acting** *n.* **play-actor** *n.*

■ **2** act, put on an act; see also SHAM *v.* 1. □□ **play-acting** see MASQUERADE *n.* 1.

playbill /pláybil/ *n.* **1** a poster announcing a theatrical performance. **2** *US* a theatre programme.

playboy /pláyboy/ *n.* an irresponsible pleasure-seeking man, esp. a wealthy one.

■ man about town, roué, rake, debauchee, womanizer, Don Juan, Casanova, Lothario, lady-killer.

player /pláyər/ *n.* **1 a** a person taking part in a sport or game. **b** a gambler. **2** a person playing a musical instrument. **3** a person who plays a part on the stage; an actor. **4** = *record-player.* □ **player-piano** a piano fitted with an apparatus enabling it to be played automatically. [OE *plegere* (as PLAY)]

■ **1 a** contestant, participant, competitor, contender; athlete, sportswoman, sportsman. **b** gambler, better, gamester, speculator, *Brit.* punter. **2** musician, instrumentalist, performer. **3** actor, actress, performer, entertainer, trouper, Thespian.

playfellow /pláyfellō/ *n.* a playmate.

■ see PLAYMATE.

playful /pláyfo͝ol/ *adj.* **1** fond of or inclined to play. **2** done in fun; humorous, jocular. □□ **playfully** *adv.* **playfulness** *n.*

■ **1** fun-loving, sportive, gamesome, frolicsome, puppyish, kittenish, *archaic* frolic, wanton. **2** humorous, jocular, jocose, teasing, humorous, tongue-in-cheek.

playgoer /pláygōər/ *n.* a person who goes often to the theatre.

playground /pláygrownd/ *n.* an outdoor area for children to play on.

playgroup /pláygro͞op/ *n.* a group of preschool children who play regularly together at a particular place under supervision.

playhouse /pláyhowss/ *n.* **1** a theatre. **2** a toy house for children to play in.

■ **1** see THEATRE 1a.

playing-card /pláyingkaard/ *n.* each of a set of usu. 52 oblong pieces of card or other material with an identical pattern on one side and different values represented by numbers and symbols on the other, used to play various games.

playing-field /pláyingfeeld/ *n.* a field used for outdoor team games.

■ field, pitch, ground.

playlet /pláylit/ *n.* a short play or dramatic piece.

playmate /pláymayt/ *n.* a child's companion in play.

■ playfellow, friend, *colloq.* pal, *esp. US colloq.* buddy; see also CHUM[1].

plaything /pláything/ *n.* **1** a toy or other thing to play with. **2** a person treated as a toy.

■ **1** toy, game, gewgaw, *archaic* whim-wham. **2** pawn, puppet, toy, tool, cat's-paw, sport.

playtime /pláytīm/ *n.* time for play or recreation.

■ break, rest period.

playwright /pláyrīt/ *n.* a person who writes plays.

■ dramatist, dramaturge, scriptwriter, screenwriter, scenarist.

plaza /plaázə/ *n.* a market-place or open square (esp. in a Spanish town). [Sp., = place]

■ see SQUARE *n.* 3a.

plc *abbr.* (also **PLC**) Public Limited Company.

plea /plee/ *n.* **1** an earnest appeal or entreaty. **2** *Law* a formal statement by or on behalf of a defendant. **3** an argument or excuse. □ **plea bargaining** *US* an arrangement between prosecutor and defendant whereby the defendant pleads guilty to a lesser charge in the expectation of leniency. [ME & AF *ple, plai*, OF *plait, plaid* agreement, discussion f. L *placitum* a decree, neut. past part. of *placēre* to please]

■ **1** entreaty, appeal, petition, request, supplication, suit, cry, solicitation. **2** answer, defence, argument; case. **3** argument, explanation, justification; pretext; see also EXCUSE *n.* 1, 2.

pleach /pleech/ *v.tr.* entwine or interlace (esp. branches to form a hedge). [ME *pleche* f. OF (as PLASH[2])]
■ see TWIST *v.* 2.

plead /pleed/ *v.* (*past* and *past part.* **pleaded** or esp. *US, Sc., & dial.* **pled** /pled/) **1** *intr.* (foll. by *with*) make an earnest appeal to. **2** *intr. Law* address a lawcourt as an advocate on behalf of a party. **3** *tr.* maintain (a cause) esp. in a lawcourt. **4** *tr. Law* declare to be one's state as regards guilt in or responsibility for a crime (*plead guilty; plead insanity*). **5** *tr.* offer or allege as an excuse (*pleaded forgetfulness*). **6** *intr.* make an appeal or entreaty. □□ **pleadable** *adj.* **pleader** *n.* **pleadingly** *adv.* [ME f. AF *pleder*, OF *plaidier* (as PLEA)]
■ **1** (*plead with*) request, entreat, appeal to, petition, apply to, implore, beseech, beg, importune, solicit, supplicate (to). **3** argue, maintain, put forward. **6** (*plead for*) appeal for, cry for, ask (for), seek, beg (for), pray for, request, supplicate for.

pleading /pléeding/ *n.* (usu. in *pl.*) a formal statement of the cause of an action or defence.
■ see *supplication* (SUPPLICATE).

pleasance /plézz'nss/ *n.* a secluded enclosure or part of a garden, esp. one attached to a large house. [ME f. OF *plaisance* (as PLEASANT)]

pleasant /plézz'nt/ *adj.* (**pleasanter**, **pleasantest**) pleasing to the mind, feelings, or senses. □□ **pleasantly** *adv.* **pleasantness** *n.* [ME f. OF *plaisant* (as PLEASE)]
■ pleasing, pleasurable, nice, enjoyable, satisfying, good, lovely, attractive, gratifying, delightful, charming, agreeable, acceptable, enjoyable, salubrious, savoury, beautiful, *esp. literary* delectable; friendly, affable, amiable, amicable, sweet, companionable, engaging, winning, congenial, genial, likeable, cordial, *Sc. & N.Engl.* canny.

pleasantry /plézzəntri/ *n.* (*pl.* **-ies**) **1** a pleasant or amusing remark, esp. made in casual conversation. **2** a humorous manner of speech. **3** jocularity. [F *plaisanterie* (as PLEASANT)]
■ **2, 3** see BANTER *n.*

please /pleez/ *v.* **1** *tr.* (also *absol.*) be agreeable to; make glad; give pleasure to (*the gift will please them; anxious to please*). **2** *tr.* (in *passive*) **a** (foll. by *to* + infin.) be glad or willing to (*am pleased to help*). **b** (often foll. by *about, at, with*) derive pleasure or satisfaction (from). **3** *tr.* (with *it* as subject; usu. foll. by *to* + infin.) be the inclination or wish of (*it did not please them to attend*). **4** *intr.* think fit; have the will or desire (*take as many as you please*). **5** *tr.* (short for **may it please you**) used in polite requests (*come in, please*). □ **if you please** if you are willing, esp. *iron.* to indicate unreasonableness (*then, if you please, we had to pay*). **pleased as Punch** see PUNCH[4]. **please oneself** do as one likes. □□ **pleased** *adj.* **pleasing** *adj.* **pleasingly** *adv.* [ME *plaise* f. OF *plaisir* f. L *placēre*]
■ **1** delight, gratify, humour, content, cheer, gladden, amuse, divert, interest, entertain. **2 a** (*be pleased*) be content, be glad, be willing, be happy, be delighted. **4** like, prefer, choose, desire, want, see fit, wish, will. □□ **pleased** happy, delighted, glad, gratified, satisfied, contented, thrilled.

pleasurable /plézhərəb'l/ *adj.* causing pleasure; agreeable. □□ **pleasurableness** *n.* **pleasurably** *adv.* [PLEASURE + -ABLE, after *comfortable*]
■ see PLEASANT.

pleasure /plézhər/ *n.* & *v.* ● *n.* **1** a feeling of satisfaction or joy. **2** enjoyment. **3** a source of pleasure or gratification (*painting was my chief pleasure; it is a pleasure to talk to them*). **4** *formal* a person's will or desire (*what is your pleasure?*). **5** sensual gratification or enjoyment (*a life of pleasure*). **6** (*attrib.*) done or used for pleasure (*pleasure-ground*). ● *v.* **1** *tr.* give (esp. sexual) pleasure to. **2** *intr.* (often foll. by *in*) take pleasure. □ **take pleasure in** like doing. **with pleasure** gladly. [ME & OF *plesir, plaisir* PLEASE, used as a noun]
■ *n.* **1, 2** happiness, delight, joy; satisfaction, fulfilment, contentment, enjoyment, gratification. **3** comfort, solace; recreation, amusement, entertainment, diversion. **4** desire, wish, will, preference, inclination; discretion. **5** hedonism, debauchery, libertinism, indulgence, self-indulgence, self-gratification, profligacy, dissipation. ● *v.* **2** see REJOICE 1–3; (*pleasure in*) ENJOY 1. □ **take pleasure in** see ENJOY 1. **with pleasure** gladly, willingly, happily, readily.

pleat /pleet/ *n.* & *v.* ● *n.* a fold or crease, esp. a flattened fold in cloth doubled upon itself. ● *v.tr.* make a pleat or pleats in. [ME, var. of PLAIT]

pleb /pleb/ *n. colloq.* usu. *derog.* an ordinary insignificant person. □□ **plebby** *adj.* [abbr. of PLEBEIAN]
■ see PLEBEIAN *n.*

plebeian /plibéeən/ *n.* & *adj.* ● *n.* a commoner, esp. in ancient Rome. ● *adj.* **1** of low birth; of the common people. **2** uncultured. **3** coarse, ignoble. □□ **plebeianism** *n.* [L *plebeius* f. *plebs plebis* the common people]
■ *n.* **3** proletarian, common man *or* woman, commoner, *colloq. usu. derog.* pleb, prole. ● *adj.* **1** proletarian, working-class, blue-collar, low-class, lower-class, lowly, low-born, mean, humble, *derog.* common. **2** unrefined, uncultured, uncultivated, lowbrow, unpolished, provincial, rustic, popular, commonplace, undistinguished. **3** uncouth, crass, coarse, vulgar, ignoble, brutish, barbaric, philistine.

plebiscite /plébbisit, -sīt/ *n.* **1** the direct vote of all the electors of a State etc. on an important public question, e.g. a change in the constitution. **2** the public expression of a community's opinion, with or without binding force. **3** *Rom.Hist.* a law enacted by the plebeians' assembly. □□ **plebiscitary** /-bissitəri/ *adj.* [F *plébiscite* f. L *plebiscitum* f. *plebs plebis* the common people + *scitum* decree f. *sciscere* vote for]
■ **2** popular vote *or* ballot, referendum, poll.

plectrum /pléktrəm/ *n.* (*pl.* **plectrums** or **plectra** /-trə/) **1** a thin flat piece of plastic or horn etc. held in the hand and used to pluck a string, esp. of a guitar. **2** the corresponding mechanical part of a harpsichord etc. [L f. Gk *plēktron* f. *plēssō* strike]

pled see PLEAD.

pledge /plej/ *n.* & *v.* ● *n.* **1** a solemn promise or undertaking. **2** a thing given as security for the fulfilment of a contract, the payment of a debt, etc., and liable to forfeiture in the event of failure. **3** a thing put in pawn. **4** a thing given as a token of love, favour, or something to come. **5** the drinking of a person's health; a toast. **6** a solemn undertaking to abstain from alcohol (*sign the pledge*). **7** the state of being pledged (*goods lying in pledge*). ● *v.tr.* **1 a** deposit as security. **b** pawn. **2** promise solemnly by the pledge of (one's honour, word, etc.). **3** (often *refl.*) bind by a solemn promise. **4** drink to the health of. □ **pledge one's troth** see TROTH. □□ **pledgeable** *adj.* **pledger** *n.* **pledgor** *n.* [ME *plege* f. OF *plege* f. LL *plebium* f. *plebire* assure]
■ *n.* **1** promise, oath, vow, word (of honour), covenant, bond, agreement, assurance, guaranty, guarantee. **2** gage, bond, guaranty, guarantee; collateral, security, earnest, surety. **5** salutation, toast, tribute, health. ● *v.* **1** deposit, pawn, *archaic* gage, *esp. US colloq.* hock. **2** swear, vow, promise, undertake, *archaic* plight, vouch. **3** see BIND *v.* 5. **4** salute, toast, drink to; drink a person's health.

pledgee /plejée/ *n.* a person to whom a pledge is given.

pledget /pléjit/ *n.* a small wad of lint etc. [16th c.: orig. unkn.]

pleiad /plīəd/ *n.* a brilliant group of (usu. seven) persons or things. [named after PLEIADES]

Pleiades /plīədeez/ *n.pl.* a cluster of stars in the constellation Taurus, usu. known as 'the Seven Sisters'. [ME f. L *Pleïas* f. Gk *Plēias -ados*]

Pleistocene /plīstəseen/ *adj.* & *n. Geol.* ● *adj.* of or relating to the first epoch of the Quaternary period marked by great fluctuations in temperature with glacial periods followed by interglacial periods. ● *n.* this epoch or system. Also called

Ice age. ¶ Cf. Appendix VII. [Gk *pleistos* most + *kainos* new]

plenary /pleénəri/ *adj.* **1** entire, unqualified, absolute (*plenary indulgence*). **2** (of an assembly) to be attended by all members. [LL *plenarius* f. *plenus* full]
■ **1** see FULL[1] *adj.* 3, 6.

plenipotentiary /plénnipəténshəri/ *n.* & *adj.* ● *n.* (*pl.* **-ies**) a person (esp. a diplomat) invested with the full power of independent action. ● *adj.* **1** having this power. **2** (of power) absolute. [med.L *plenipotentiarius* f. *plenus* full + *potentia* power]
■ *n.* see AMBASSADOR.

plenitude /plénnityood/ *n. literary* **1** fullness, completeness. **2** abundance. [ME f. OF f. LL *plenitudo* f. *plenus* full]
■ **2** see ABUNDANCE 1.

plenteous /pléntiəss/ *adj. poet.* plentiful. □□ **plenteously** *adv.* **plenteousness** *n.* [ME f. OF *plentivous* f. *plentif -ive* f. *plenté* PLENTY: cf. *bounteous*]
■ see PLENTIFUL. □□ **plenteousness** see PLENTY *n.* 2.

plentiful /pléntifool/ *adj.* abundant, copious. □□ **plentifully** *adv.* **plentifulness** *n.*
■ ample, abundant, profuse, copious, lavish, bountiful, generous, fruitful, productive, bumper, luxuriant, thriving, prolific, *poet.* bounteous, plenteous.

plenty /plénti/ *n.*, *adj.*, & *adv.* ● *n.* **1** (often foll. by *of*) a great or sufficient quantity or number (*we have plenty*; *plenty of time*). **2** abundance (*in great plenty*). ● *adj. colloq.* existing in an ample quantity. ● *adv. colloq.* fully, entirely (*it is plenty large enough*). [ME *plenteth*, *plente* f. OF *plentet* f. L *plenitas -tatis* f. *plenus* full]
■ *n.* **1** see LOT *n.* 1. **2** plentifulness, copiousness, abundance, wealth, profusion, lavishness, prodigality, bountifulness, *literary* plenitude, *poet.* plenteousness.

plenum /pleénəm/ *n.* **1** a full assembly of people or a committee etc. **2** *Physics* space filled with matter. [L, neut. of *plenus* full]

pleochroic /pleéəkrṓ-ik/ *adj.* showing different colours when viewed in different directions. □□ **pleochroism** *n.* [Gk *pleiōn* more + *-khroos* f. *khrōs* colour]

pleomorphism /pleéəmórfiz'm/ *n. Biol.*, *Chem.*, & *Mineral.* the occurrence of more than one distinct form. □□ **pleomorphic** *adj.* [Gk *pleiōn* more + *morphē* form]

pleonasm /pleéənaz'm/ *n.* the use of more words than are needed to give the sense (e.g. *see with one's eyes*). □□ **pleonastic** /-nástik/ *adj.* **pleonastically** /-nástikəli/ *adv.* [LL *pleonasmus* f. Gk *pleonasmos* f. *pleonazō* be superfluous]
■ see TAUTOLOGY. □□ **pleonastic** see REPETITIOUS.

plesiosaurus /pleéssiəsáwrəss/ *n.* (also **plesiosaur** /pleéssiəsawr/) any of a group of extinct marine reptiles with a broad flat body, short tail, long flexible neck, and large paddle-like limbs. [mod.L f. Gk *plēsios* near + *sauros* lizard]

plessor var. of PLEXOR.

plethora /pléthərə/ *n.* **1** an oversupply, glut, or excess. **2** *Med.* **a** an abnormal excess of red corpuscles in the blood. **b** an excess of any body fluid. □□ **plethoric** /also plithórrik/ *adj.* **plethorically** /plithórrikəli/ *adv.* [LL f. Gk *plēthōrē* f. *plēthō* be full]
■ **1** see EXCESS *n.* 1.

pleura[1] /plóorə/ *n.* (*pl.* **pleurae** /-ree/) **1** each of a pair of serous membranes lining the thorax and enveloping the lungs in mammals. **2** lateral extensions of the body-wall in arthropods. □□ **pleural** *adj.* [med.L f. Gk, = side of the body, rib]

pleura[2] *pl.* of PLEURON.

pleurisy /plóorisi/ *n.* inflammation of the pleura, marked by pain in the chest or side, fever, etc. □□ **pleuritic** /-ríttik/ *adj.* [ME f. OF *pleurisie* f. LL *pleurisis* alt. f. L *pleuritis* f. Gk (as PLEURA[1])]

pleuro- /plóorō/ *comb. form* **1** denoting the pleura. **2** denoting the side.

pleuron /plóoron/ *n.* (*pl.* **pleura** /-rə/) = PLEURA[1] 2. [Gk, = side of the body, rib]

pleuropneumonia /plóorōnyoomṓniə/ *n.* pneumonia complicated with pleurisy.

Plexiglas /pléksiglaass/ *n. propr.* = PERSPEX. [formed as PLEXOR + GLASS]

plexor /pléksər/ *n.* (also **plessor** /pléssər/) *Med.* a small hammer used to test reflexes and in percussing. [irreg. f. Gk *plēxis* percussion + -OR[1]]

plexus /pléksəss/ *n.* (*pl.* same or **plexuses**) **1** *Anat.* a network of nerves or vessels in an animal body (*gastric plexus*). **2** any network or weblike formation. □□ **plexiform** *adj.* [L f. *plectere plex-* plait]
■ **2** see NETWORK *n.* 2.

pliable /plī́əb'l/ *adj.* **1** bending easily; supple. **2** yielding, compliant. □□ **pliability** /-bílliti/ *n.* **pliableness** *n.* **pliably** *adv.* [F f. *plier* bend: see PLY[1]]
■ **1** flexible, pliant, elastic, plastic, malleable, willowy, bendable, ductile, *colloq.* bendy; supple, lithe, limber. **2** tractable, adaptable, flexible, pliant, yielding, compliant, persuadable, persuasible, impressionable, susceptible, responsive, receptive, manageable.

pliant /plī́ənt/ *adj.* = PLIABLE 1. □□ **pliancy** *n.* **pliantly** *adv.* [ME f. OF (as PLIABLE)]

plicate /plī́kayt/ *adj. Biol.* & *Geol.* folded, crumpled, corrugated. □□ **plicated** /plikáytid/ *adj.* [L *plicatus* past part. of *plicare* fold]

plication /plikáysh'n/ *n.* **1** the act of folding. **2** a fold; a folded condition. [ME f. med.L *plicatio* or L *plicare* fold, after *complication*]

plié /pleé-ay/ *n. Ballet* a bending of the knees with the feet on the ground. [F, past part. of *plier* bend: see PLY[1]]

pliers /plī́ərz/ *n.pl.* pincers with parallel flat usu. serrated surfaces for holding small objects, bending wire, etc. [(dial.) *ply* bend (as PLIABLE)]

plight[1] /plīt/ *n.* a condition or state, esp. an unfortunate one. [ME & AF *plit* = OF *pleit* fold: see PLAIT: *-gh-* by confusion with PLIGHT[2]]
■ condition, state, circumstances, situation, case; difficulty, predicament, quandary, trouble, extremity; mess, *esp. US* bind, *colloq.* hole, jam, pickle, spot, scrape, fix, *disp.* dilemma.

plight[2] /plīt/ *v.* & *n. archaic* ● *v.tr.* **1** pledge or promise solemnly (one's faith, loyalty, etc.). **2** (foll. by *to*) engage, esp. in marriage. ● *n.* an engagement or act of pledging. □ **plight one's troth** see TROTH. [orig. as noun, f. OE *pliht* danger f. Gmc]

plimsoll /plíms'l/ *n.* (also **plimsole**) *Brit.* a rubber-soled canvas sports shoe. [prob. from the resemblance of the side of the sole to a PLIMSOLL LINE]
■ pump, sports shoe, *Brit.* trainer, *sl.* sneaker.

Plimsoll line /plíms'l/ *n.* (also **Plimsoll mark**) a marking on a ship's side showing the limit of legal submersion under various conditions. [S. *Plimsoll*, Engl. politician d. 1898, promoter of the Merchant Shipping Act of 1876]

plinth /plinth/ *n.* **1** the lower square slab at the base of a column. **2** a base supporting a vase or statue etc. [F *plinthe* or L *plinthus* f. Gk *plinthos* tile, brick, squared stone]
■ see PEDESTAL *n.*

Pliocene /plī́əseen/ *adj.* & *n. Geol.* ● *adj.* of or relating to the last epoch of the Tertiary period with evidence of the extinction of many mammals, and the development of hominids. ● *n.* this epoch or system. ¶ Cf. Appendix VII. [Gk *pleiōn* more + *kainos* new]

plissé /pleéssay/ *adj.* & *n.* ● *adj.* (of cloth etc.) treated so as to cause permanent puckering. ● *n.* material treated in this way. [F, past part. of *plisser* pleat]

PLO *abbr.* Palestine Liberation Organization.

plod /plod/ *v.* & *n.* ● *v.* (**plodded**, **plodding**) **1** *intr.* (often foll. by *along*, *on*, etc.) walk doggedly or laboriously; trudge. **2** *intr.* (often foll. by *at*) work slowly and steadily. **3** *tr.* tread or make (one's way) laboriously. ● *n.* the act or a spell of plodding. □□ **plodder** *n.* **ploddingly** *adv.* [16th c.: prob. imit.]

■ *v.* **1** trudge, tramp, lumber, labour, *colloq.* galumph. **2** labour, work, drudge, toil, slave (away), grind (away), grub (on *or* along), peg away (at), *colloq.* plug (along *or* away), *archaic* moil.

-ploid /ployd/ *comb. form Biol.* forming adjectives denoting the number of sets of chromosomes in a cell (*diploid*; *polyploid*). [after HAPLOID]

ploidy /plóydi/ *n.* the number of sets of chromosomes in a cell. [after DIPLOIDY, POLYPLOIDY, etc.]

plonk[1] /plongk/ *v.* & *n.* ● *v.tr.* **1** set down hurriedly or clumsily. **2** (usu. foll. by *down*) set down firmly. ● *n.* **1** an act of plonking. **2** a heavy thud. [imit.]
■ *v.* see SET[1] 1, 3, 5.

plonk[2] /plongk/ *n. colloq.* cheap or inferior wine. [orig. Austral.: prob. corrupt. of *blanc* in F *vin blanc* white wine]

plonker /plóngkər/ *n. coarse sl.* a stupid person.

plonko / plóngkō/ *n.* (*pl.* **-os**) *Austral. sl.* an excessive drinker of cheap wine; an alcoholic.

plop /plop/ *n.*, *v.*, & *adv.* ● *n.* **1** a sound as of a smooth object dropping into water without a splash. **2** an act of falling with this sound. ● *v.* (**plopped**, **plopping**) *intr.* & *tr.* fall or drop with a plop. ● *adv.* with a plop. [19th c.: imit.]
■ *v.* see PLUMP[2] *v.* 1.

plosion /plṓzh'n/ *n. Phonet.* the sudden release of breath in the pronunciation of a stop consonant. [EXPLOSION]

plosive /plṓsiv/ *adj.* & *n. Phonet.* ● *adj.* pronounced with a sudden release of breath. ● *n.* a plosive sound. [EXPLOSIVE]

plot /plot/ *n.* & *v.* ● *n.* **1** a defined and usu. small piece of ground. **2** the interrelationship of the main events in a play, novel, film, etc. **3** a conspiracy or secret plan, esp. to achieve an unlawful end. **4** esp. *US* a graph or diagram. **5** a graph showing the relation between two variables. ● *v.* (**plotted**, **plotting**) *tr.* **1** make a plan or map of (an existing object, a place or thing to be laid out, constructed, etc.). **2** (also *absol.*) plan or contrive secretly (a crime, conspiracy, etc.). **3** mark (a point or course etc.) on a chart or diagram. **4 a** mark out or allocate (points) on a graph. **b** make (a curve etc.) by marking out a number of points. □□ **plotless** *adj.* **plotlessness** *n.* **plotter** *n.* [OE and f. OF *complot* secret plan: both of unkn. orig.]
■ *n.* **1** patch, tract, acreage, area, allotment, *esp. US* lot, *US* plat. **2** story, story-line, scenario. **3** scheme, plan, intrigue, machination, cabal, conspiracy, stratagem. **4** chart, diagram, graph; table, tabulation. ● *v.* **1, 3** draw, plan, map (out); diagram, lay down, outline, represent, figure, chart; mark, indicate, designate, label. **2** scheme, plan, intrigue, machinate, cabal, collude, conspire, hatch, devise, design, arrange, organize, concoct, dream up, conceive, *colloq.* cook up.

plough /plow/ *n.* & *v.* (esp. *US* **plow**) ● *n.* **1** an implement with a cutting blade fixed in a frame drawn by a tractor or by horses, for cutting furrows in the soil and turning it up. **2** an implement resembling this and having a comparable function (*snowplough*). **3** ploughed land. **4** (**the Plough**) the constellation Ursa Major or its seven bright stars. ● *v.* **1** *tr.* (also *absol.*) turn up (the earth) with a plough, esp. before sowing. **2** *tr.* (foll. by *out*, *up*, *down*, etc.) turn or extract (roots, weeds, etc.) with a plough. **3** *tr.* furrow or scratch (a surface) as if with a plough. **4** *tr.* produce (a furrow or line) in this way. **5** *intr.* (foll. by *through*) advance laboriously, esp. through work, a book, etc. **6** *intr.* (foll. by *through*, *into*) move like a plough violently. **7** *intr.* & *tr. Brit. colloq.* fail in an examination. □ **plough back 1** plough (grass etc.) into the soil to enrich it. **2** reinvest (profits) in the business producing them. **Plough Monday** the first Monday after the Epiphany. **put one's hand to the plough** undertake a task (Luke 9:62). □□ **ploughable** *adj.* **plougher** *n.* [OE *plōh* f. ON *plógr* f. Gmc]
■ *v.* **1** till, cultivate, furrow, harrow, rib. **5** see PROCEED 1. **6** drive, plunge, push, career, bulldoze, lunge, dive, lurch, hurtle, crash. **7** see FAIL *v.* 1, 2a.

ploughman /plówmən/ *n.* (*pl.* **-men**) a person who uses a plough. □ **ploughman's lunch** a meal of bread and cheese with pickle or salad. **ploughman's spikenard** a composite fragrant plant, *Inula conyzae*, with purplish-yellow flowerheads.

ploughshare /plówshair/ *n.* the cutting blade of a plough.

plover /plúvvər/ *n.* any plump-breasted wading bird of the family Charadriidae, including the lapwing, usu. having a pigeon-like bill. [ME & AF f. OF *plo(u)vier* ult. f. L *pluvia* rain]

plow *US* var. of PLOUGH.

ploy /ploy/ *n. colloq.* a stratagem; a cunning manoeuvre to gain an advantage. [orig. Sc., 18th c.: orig. unkn.]
■ see STRATAGEM 1.

PLP *abbr.* (in the UK) Parliamentary Labour Party.

PLR *abbr.* (in the UK) Public Lending Right.

pluck /pluk/ *v.* & *n.* ● *v.* **1** *tr.* (often foll. by *out*, *off*, etc.) remove by picking or pulling out or away. **2** *tr.* strip (a bird) of feathers. **3** *tr.* pull at, twitch. **4** *intr.* (foll. by *at*) tug or snatch at. **5** *tr.* sound (the string of a musical instrument) with the finger or plectrum etc. **6** *tr.* plunder. **7** *tr.* swindle. ● *n.* **1** courage, spirit. **2** an act of plucking; a twitch. **3** the heart, liver, and lungs of an animal as food. □ **pluck up** summon up (one's courage, spirits, etc.). □□ **plucker** *n.* **pluckless** *adj.* [OE *ploccian*, *pluccian*, f. Gmc]
■ *v.* **1** pick; snatch, grab, yank off, tear (off *or* away); (*pluck out*) remove, withdraw, draw out, extract, pull *or* take out. **3, 4** tug (at), pull (at), catch (at), clutch (at), jerk, twitch, snatch, *colloq.* yank. **6** see PLUNDER *v.* 2. **7** see SWINDLE *v.* ● *n.* **1** courage, spirit, bravery, boldness, intrepidity, backbone, mettle, determination, gameness, resolve, resolution, steadfastness, hardiness, sturdiness, stout-heartedness, stoutness, fortitude, manfulness, nerve, *colloq.* gumption, guts, spunk, grit, *US colloq.* sand, *Brit. sl.* bottle, *US sl.* moxie. □ **pluck up** see *summon up*.

plucky /plúkki/ *adj.* (**pluckier**, **pluckiest**) brave, spirited. □□ **pluckily** *adv.* **pluckiness** *n.*
■ see BRAVE *adj.* 1.

plug /plug/ *n.* & *v.* ● *n.* **1** a piece of solid material fitting tightly into a hole, used to fill a gap or cavity or act as a wedge or stopper. **2 a** a device of metal pins in an insulated casing fitting into holes in a socket for making an electrical connection, esp. between an appliance and the mains. **b** *colloq.* an electric socket. **3** = *sparking-plug* (see SPARK[1]). **4** *colloq.* a piece of (often free) publicity for an idea, product, etc. **5** a mass of solidified lava filling the neck of a volcano. **6** a cake or stick of tobacco; a piece of this for chewing. **7** = *fire-plug*. ● *v.* (**plugged**, **plugging**) **1** *tr.* (often foll. by *up*) stop (a hole etc.) with a plug. **2** *tr. sl.* shoot or hit (a person etc.). **3** *tr. colloq.* seek to popularize (an idea, product, etc.) by constant recommendation. **4** *intr. colloq.* (often foll. by *at*) work steadily away (at). □ **plug in** connect electrically by inserting a plug in a socket. **plug-in** *adj.* able to be connected by means of a plug. **plug-ugly** *US sl.* *n.* (*pl.* **-ies**) a thug or ruffian. ● *adj.* villainous-looking. □□ **plugger** *n.* [MDu. & MLG *plugge*, of unkn. orig.]
■ *n.* **1** stopper, stopple, bung, cork. **4** mention, promotion, recommendation, puff; advertisement, *colloq.* promo, *Brit. colloq.* advert; (*plugs*) publicity, *sl.* hype. **6** chew, twist, quid, pigtail. ● *v.* **1** stop (up), close (up *or* off), seal (off *or* up), cork, stopper, stopple, bung, block (up *or* off), dam (up). **2** see SHOOT *v.* 1c. **3** publicize, mention, promote, beat the drum for, push, advertise, puff, commend, *colloq.* boost. **4** see PLOD *v.* 2. □ **plug-ugly** (*n.*) see THUG.

plugola / plugṓlə/ *n.* esp. *US colloq.* **1** a bribe offered in return for incidental or surreptitious promotion of a person or product, esp. on radio or television. **2** the practice of such bribery. [PLUG + *-ola*, prob. after PAYOLA]

plum /plum/ *n.* **1 a** an oval fleshy fruit, usu. purple or yellow when ripe, with sweet pulp and a flattish pointed stone. **b** any deciduous tree of the genus *Prunus* bearing this. **2** a reddish-purple colour. **3** a dried grape or raisin used in cooking. **4** *colloq.* the best of a collection; something especially prized (often *attrib.*: *a plum job*). □ **plum cake** a cake containing raisins, currants, etc. **plum duff** a plain flour pudding with raisins or currants. **plum pudding** a rich

boiled suet pudding with raisins, currants, spices, etc. [OE *plūme* f. med.L *pruna* f. L *prunum*]
■ **4** find, catch, coup, prize, treasure; (*attrib.*) prized, esteemed, favoured, *often joc.* pet.

plumage /plŏŏmij/ *n.* a bird's feathers. □□ **plumaged** *adj.* (usu. in *comb.*). [ME f. OF (as PLUME)]

plumassier /plŏŏmaseer/ *n.* a person who trades or works in ornamental feathers. [F f. *plumasse* augment. of *plume* PLUME]

plumb[1] /plum/ *n.*, *adv.*, *adj.*, & *v.* ● *n.* a ball of lead or other heavy material, esp. one attached to the end of a line for finding the depth of water or determining the vertical on an upright surface. ● *adv.* **1** exactly (*plumb in the centre*). **2** vertically. **3** *US sl.* quite, utterly (*plumb crazy*). ● *adj.* **1** vertical. **2** downright, sheer (*plumb nonsense*). **3** *Cricket* (of the wicket) level, true. ● *v.tr.* **1 a** measure the depth of (water) with a plumb. **b** determine (a depth). **2** test (an upright surface) to determine the vertical. **3** reach or experience in extremes (*plumb the depths of fear*). **4** learn in detail the facts about (a matter). □ **out of plumb** not vertical. **plumb-line** a line with a plumb attached. **plumb-rule** a mason's plumb-line attached to a board. [ME, prob. ult. f. L *plumbum* lead, assim. to OF *plomb* lead]
■ *n.* weight, bob, plummet, sinker. ● *adv.* **1** exactly, precisely, dead, right, directly, slap, *colloq.* (slap) bang. **2** vertically, perpendicularly, straight up and down. **3** see DOWNRIGHT *adv.* ● *adj.* **1** see PERPENDICULAR 2. **2** see ABSOLUTE *adj.* 1. ● *v.* **1** sound, fathom, probe; measure, gauge, test; determine. **3** reach, experience, go through, go into, explore, probe, delve into, penetrate; see also TASTE *v.* 4.

plumb[2] /plum/ *v.* **1** *tr.* provide (a building or room etc.) with plumbing. **2** *tr.* (often foll. by *in*) fit as part of a plumbing system. **3** *intr.* work as a plumber. [back-form. f. PLUMBER]

plumbago /plumbáygō/ *n.* (*pl.* **-os**) **1** = GRAPHITE. **2** any plant of the genus *Plumbago*, with grey or blue flowers. Also called LEADWORT. [L f. *plumbum* LEAD[2]]

plumbeous /plúmbiəss/ *adj.* **1** of or like lead. **2** lead-glazed. [L *plumbeus* f. *plumbum* LEAD[2]]

plumber /plúmmər/ *n.* a person who fits and repairs the apparatus of a water-supply, heating, etc. [ME *plummer* etc. f. OF *plommier* f. L *plumbarius* f. *plumbum* LEAD[2]]

plumbic /plúmbik/ *adj.* **1** *Chem.* containing lead esp. in its tetravalent form. **2** *Med.* due to the presence of lead. □□ **plumbism** *n.* (in sense 2). [L *plumbum* lead]

plumbing /plúmming/ *n.* **1** the system or apparatus of water-supply, heating, etc., in a building. **2** the work of a plumber. **3** *colloq.* lavatory installations.

plumbless /plúmliss/ *adj.* (of a depth of water etc.) that cannot be plumbed.

plumbous /plúmbəss/ *n. Chem.* containing lead in its divalent form.

plume /plŏŏm/ *n.* & *v.* ● *n.* **1** a feather, esp. a large one used for ornament. **2** an ornament of feathers etc. attached to a helmet or hat or worn in the hair. **3** something resembling this (*a plume of smoke*). **4** *Zool.* a feather-like part or formation. ● *v.* **1** *tr.* decorate or provide with a plume or plumes. **2** *refl.* (foll. by *on*, *upon*) pride (oneself on esp. something trivial). **3** *tr.* (of a bird) preen (itself or its feathers). □□ **plumeless** *adj.* **plumelike** *adj.* **plumery** *n.* [ME f. OF f. L *pluma* down]
■ *v.* **3** see PREEN 1.

plummet /plúmmit/ *n.* & *v.* ● *n.* **1** a plumb or plumb-line. **2** a sounding-line. **3** a weight attached to a fishing-line to keep the float upright. ● *v.intr.* (**plummeted**, **plummeting**) fall or plunge rapidly. [ME f. OF *plommet* dimin. (as PLUMB[1])]
■ *v.* see PLUNGE *v.* 1b.

plummy /plúmmi/ *adj.* (**plummier**, **plummiest**) **1** abounding or rich in plums. **2** *colloq.* **a** (of a voice) sounding affectedly rich or deep in tone. **b** snobbish. **3** *colloq.* good, desirable.
■ **3** see DESIRABLE 1.

plumose /plŏŏmōss/ *adj.* **1** feathered. **2** feather-like. [L *plumosus* (as PLUME)]

plump[1] /plump/ *adj.* & *v.* ● *adj.* (esp. of a person or animal or part of the body) having a full rounded shape; fleshy; filled out. ● *v.tr.* & *intr.* (often foll. by *up*, *out*) make or become plump; fatten. □□ **plumpish** *adj.* **plumply** *adv.* **plumpness** *n.* **plumpy** *adj.* [ME *plompe* f. MDu. *plomp* blunt, MLG *plump*, *plomp* shapeless etc.]
■ *adj.* plump, chubby, stout, fleshy, full-bodied, portly, tubby, rotund, round, squat, chunky, buxom, corpulent, roly-poly, hippy, beefy, fat, overweight, podgy, *colloq.* pudgy, well-covered, porky, *Austral. colloq.* poddy, *joc.* well-upholstered. ● *v.* puff up *or* out; fatten, fill out; see also PAD[1] *v.* 2.

plump[2] /plump/ *v.*, *n.*, *adv.*, & *adj.* ● *v.* **1** *intr.* & *tr.* (often foll. by *down*) drop or fall abruptly (*plumped down on the chair*; *plumped it on the floor*). **2** *intr.* (foll. by *for*) decide definitely in favour of (one of two or more possibilities). **3** *tr.* (often foll. by *out*) utter abruptly; blurt out. ● *n.* an abrupt plunge; a heavy fall. ● *adv. colloq.* **1** with a sudden or heavy fall. **2** directly, bluntly (*I told him plump*). ● *adj. colloq.* direct, unqualified (*answered with a plump 'no'*). [ME f. MLG *plumpen*, MDu. *plompen*: orig. imit.]
■ *v.* **1** drop, plummet, fall, plunge, dive, sink, collapse, flop (down); deposit, set *or* put (down), plonk, plop, dump. **2** (*plump for*) go for, opt for, choose, select, pick (out), settle on, pitch on; back, favour, side with, campaign for. **3** see BLURT. ● *n.* plunge, fall, drop, plonk, flop, thump, clunk, clump, thud, bump, clonk. ● *adv.* **2** abruptly, suddenly, directly, at once, unexpectedly, without warning, bang; see also STRAIGHT *adv.* 1. ● *adj.* direct, unequivocal, unqualified, unmistakable, unambiguous, definite, definitive, blunt, simple, plain, forthright, downright, straight.

plumule /plŏŏmyōōl/ *n.* **1** the rudimentary shoot or stem of an embryo plant. **2** a down feather on a young bird. □□ **plumulaceous** /plŏŏmyooláyshəss/ *adj.* (in sense 2). **plumular** /plŏŏmyoolər/ *adj.* (in sense 1). [F *plumule* or L *plumula*, dimin. (as PLUME)]

plumy /plŏŏmi/ *adj.* (**plumier**, **plumiest**) **1** plumelike, feathery. **2** adorned with plumes.

plunder /plúndər/ *v.* & *n.* ● *v.tr.* **1** rob (a place or person) forcibly of goods, e.g. as in war. **2** rob systematically. **3** (also *absol.*) steal or embezzle (goods). ● *n.* **1** the violent or dishonest acquisition of property. **2** property acquired by plundering. **3** *colloq.* profit, gain. □□ **plunderer** *n.* [LG *plündern* lit. 'rob of household goods' f. MHG *plunder* clothing etc.]
■ *v.* **2** pillage, loot, rob, ravage, ransack, rifle (through), pirate, sack, strip, pluck, maraud, lay waste, *archaic or literary* spoil, *literary* despoil. **3** see STEAL *v.* 1. ● *n.* **1** pillage, looting, robbery, depredation, spoliation, ransacking, brigandage, piracy, banditry, *literary* despoliation, *rhet.* rapine. **2** booty, loot, spoils, takings, *Bibl. or archaic* prey, *hist.* pillage, *sl.* boodle, swag. **3** see PROFIT *n.* 2.

plunge /plunj/ *v.* & *n.* ● *v.* **1** (usu. foll. by *in*, *into*) **a** *tr.* thrust forcefully or abruptly. **b** *intr.* dive; propel oneself forcibly. **c** *intr.* & *tr.* enter or cause to enter a certain condition or embark on a certain course abruptly or impetuously (*they plunged into a lively discussion*; *the room was plunged into darkness*). **2** *tr.* immerse completely. **3** *intr.* **a** move suddenly and dramatically downward. **b** (foll. by *down*, *into*, etc.) move with a rush (*plunged down the stairs*). **c** diminish rapidly (*share prices have plunged*). **4** *intr.* (of a horse) start violently forward. **5** *intr.* (of a ship) pitch. **6** *intr. colloq.* gamble heavily; run into debt. ● *n.* a plunging action or movement; a dive. □ **plunging** (or **plunge**) **neckline** a low-cut neckline. **take the plunge** *colloq.* commit oneself to a (usu. risky) course of action. [ME f. OF *plungier* ult. f. L *plumbum* plummet]
■ *v.* **1 a** see THRUST *v.* 1. **b** descend, drop, plummet, fall (headlong); dive, pitch, nosedive, catapult *or* hurl oneself. **c** see LAUNCH[1] *v.* 1, 3, 4; 5. **2** submerge, sink; see also IMMERSE 1. **3 c** see DROP *v.* 8a. **5** see PITCH[1] *v.* 6. ● *n.* dive, nosedive, fall, pitch, drop, descent; submersion,

immersion. □ **plunging** (or **plunge**) **neckline** *décolletage, décolleté*. **take the plunge** gamble, wager, bet, risk; jump in at the deep end, give it one's all, give it all one has, *colloq.* go for it, go all out, *sl.* go for broke.

plunger /plúnjər/ *n.* **1** a part of a mechanism that works with a plunging or thrusting movement. **2** a rubber cup on a handle for clearing blocked pipes by a plunging and sucking action. **3** *colloq.* a reckless gamble.

plunk /plungk/ *n.* & *v.* ● *n.* **1** the sound made by the sharply plucked string of a stringed instrument. **2** *US* a heavy blow. **3** *US* = PLONK[1] *n.* ● *v.* **1** *intr.* & *tr.* sound or cause to sound with a plunk. **2** *tr.* *US* hit abruptly. **3** *tr.* *US* = PLONK[1] *v.* [imit.]

pluperfect /plo͞opérfikt/ *adj.* & *n.* *Gram.* ● *adj.* (of a tense) denoting an action completed prior to some past point of time specified or implied, formed in English by *had* and the past participle, as: *he had gone by then.* ● *n.* the pluperfect tense. [mod.L *plusperfectum* f. L *plus quam perfectum* more than perfect]

plural /plóorəl/ *adj.* & *n.* ● *adj.* **1** more than one in number. **2** *Gram.* (of a word or form) denoting more than one, or (in languages with dual number) more than two. ● *n.* *Gram.* **1** a plural word or form. **2** the plural number. □□ **plurally** *adv.* [ME f. OF *plurel* f. L *pluralis* f. *plus pluris* more]

pluralism /plóorəliz'm/ *n.* **1** holding more than one office, esp. an ecclesiastical office or benefice, at a time. **2** a form of society in which the members of minority groups maintain their independent cultural traditions. **3** *Philos.* a system that recognizes more than one ultimate principle (cf. MONISM 2). □□ **pluralist** *n.* **pluralistic** /-lístik/ *adj.* **pluralistically** /-lístikəli/ *adv.*

plurality /ploorálliti/ *n.* (*pl.* **-ies**) **1** the state of being plural. **2** = PLURALISM 1. **3** a large or the greater number. **4** *US* a majority that is not absolute. [ME f. OF *pluralité* f. LL *pluralitas* (as PLURAL)]

pluralize /plóorəlīz/ *v.* (also **-ise**) **1** *tr.* & *intr.* make or become plural. **2** *tr.* express in the plural. **3** *intr.* hold more than one ecclesiastical office or benefice.

pluri- /plóori/ *comb. form* several. [L *plus pluris* more, *plures* several]

plurry / plúrri/ *adj.* & *adv.* *Austral.* & *NZ sl.* bloody, damn. [alt. of BLOODY]

plus /pluss/ *prep.*, *adj.*, *n.*, & *conj.* ● *prep.* **1** *Math.* with the addition of (*3 plus 4 equals 7*). ¶ Symbol: +. **2** (of temperature) above zero (*plus 2° C*). **3** *colloq.* with; having gained; newly possessing (*returned plus a new car*). ● *adj.* **1** (after a number) at least (*fifteen plus*). **2** (after a grade etc.) rather better than (*beta plus*). **3** *Math.* positive. **4** having a positive electrical charge. **5** (*attrib.*) additional, extra (*plus business*). ● *n.* **1** = *plus sign.* **2** *Math.* an additional or positive quantity. **3** an advantage (*experience is a definite plus*). ● *conj.* *colloq. disp.* also; and furthermore (*they arrived late, plus they were hungry*). □ **plus sign** the symbol +, indicating addition or a positive value. [L, = more]
■ *prep.* **1** and, added to, increased by, with the addition of, with an increment of, (coupled) with, together with. ● *adj.* **5** added, additional, supplementary, extra. ● *n.* **3** benefit, asset, advantage, addition, bonus, extra.

plus-fours /plúsfórz/ *n.* long wide men's knickerbockers usu. worn for golf etc. [20th c.: so named because the overhang at the knee requires an extra four inches]

plush /plush/ *n.* & *adj.* ● *n.* cloth of silk or cotton etc., with a long soft nap. ● *adj.* **1** made of plush. **2** plushy. □□ **plushly** *adv.* **plushness** *n.* [obs. F *pluche* contr. f. *peluche* f. OF *peluchier* f. It. *peluzzo* dimin. of *pelo* f. L *pilus* hair]
■ *adj.* **2** luxurious, costly, de luxe, palatial, lavish, rich, opulent, sumptuous, regal, elegant, swanky, *colloq.* ritzy, classy, posh, plushy, *esp. US colloq.* swank.

plushy /plúshi/ *adj.* (**plushier**, **plushiest**) *colloq.* stylish, luxurious. □□ **plushiness** *n.*
■ see STYLISH 1, LUXURIOUS 1.

plutarchy /plo͞otaarki/ *n.* (*pl.* **-ies**) plutocracy. [Gk *ploutos* wealth + *-arkhia* -rule]

Pluto /plo͞otō/ *n.* the outermost known planet of the solar system. [L f. Gk *Ploutōn* god of the underworld]

plutocracy /plo͞otókrəsi/ *n.* (*pl.* **-ies**) **1 a** government by the wealthy. **b** a State governed in this way. **2** a wealthy élite or ruling class. □□ **plutocratic** /plo͞otəkráttik/ *adj.* **plutocratically** /plo͞otəkráttikəli/ *adv.* [Gk *ploutokratia* f. *ploutos* wealth + -CRACY]

plutocrat /plo͞otəkrat/ *n.* *derog.* or *joc.* **1** a member of a plutocracy or wealthy élite. **2** a wealthy and influential person.

pluton /plo͞ot'n/ *n.* *Geol.* a body of plutonic rock. [back-form. f. PLUTONIC]

Plutonian /plo͞otṓniən/ *adj.* **1** infernal. **2** of the infernal regions. [L *Plutonius* f. Gk *Ploutōnios* (as PLUTO)]

plutonic /plo͞otónnik/ *adj.* **1** *Geol.* (of rock) formed as igneous rock by solidification below the surface of the earth. **2** (**Plutonic**) = PLUTONIAN. [formed as PLUTONIAN]

plutonium /plo͞otṓniəm/ *n.* *Chem.* a dense silvery radioactive metallic transuranic element of the actinide series, used in some nuclear reactors and weapons. ¶ Symb.: **Pu**. [PLUTO (as the next planet beyond Neptune) + -IUM]

pluvial /plo͞oviəl/ *adj.* & *n.* ● *adj.* **1** of rain; rainy. **2** *Geol.* caused by rain. ● *n.* a period of prolonged rainfall. □□ **pluvious** *adj.* (in sense 1). [L *pluvialis* f. *pluvia* rain]

pluviometer /plo͞oviómmitər/ *n.* a rain-gauge. □□ **pluviometric** /-viəmétrik/ *adj.* **pluviometrical** /-viəmétrik'l/ *adj.* **pluviometrically** /-viəmétrikəli/ *adv.* [L *pluvia* rain + -METER]

ply[1] /plī/ *n.* (*pl.* **-ies**) **1** a thickness or layer of certain materials, esp. wood or cloth (*three-ply*). **2** a strand of yarn or rope etc. [ME f. F *pli* f. *plier*, *pleier* f. L *plicare* fold]
■ **1** layer, leaf, thickness, fold.

ply[2] /plī/ *v.* (**-ies**, **-ied**) **1** *tr.* use or wield vigorously (a tool, weapon, etc.). **2** *tr.* work steadily at (one's business or trade). **3** *tr.* (foll. by *with*) **a** supply (a person) continuously (with food, drink, etc.). **b** approach repeatedly (with questions, demands, etc.). **4 a** *intr.* (often foll. by *between*) (of a vehicle etc.) travel regularly (to and fro between two points). **b** *tr.* work (a route) in this way. **5** *intr.* (of a taxi-driver, boatman, etc.) attend regularly for custom (*ply for trade*). **6** *intr.* sail to windward. [ME *plye*, f. APPLY]

Plymouth Brethren /plímməth/ *n.pl.* a strict Calvinistic religious body formed at Plymouth in Devon *c.*1830, having no formal creed and no official order of ministers.

plywood /plī́wo͝od/ *n.* a strong thin board consisting of two or more layers glued and pressed together with the direction of the grain alternating.

PM *abbr.* **1** Prime Minister. **2** post-mortem. **3** Provost Marshal.
■ **1** see PREMIER *n.*

Pm *symb.* *Chem.* the element promethium.

p.m. *abbr.* after noon. [L *post meridiem*]

PMG *abbr.* **1** Paymaster General. **2** Postmaster General.

PMS *abbr.* premenstrual syndrome.

PMT *abbr.* premenstrual tension.

PNdB *abbr.* perceived noise decibel(s).

pneumatic /nyoomáttik/ *adj.* & *n.* ● *adj.* **1** of or relating to air or wind. **2** containing or operated by compressed air. **3** connected with or containing air cavities esp. in the bones of birds or in fish. □ **pneumatic drill** a drill driven by compressed air, for breaking up a hard surface. **pneumatic trough** a shallow container used in laboratories to collect gases in jars over the surface of water or mercury. □□ **pneumatically** *adv.* **pneumaticity** /nyo͞omətíssiti/ *n.* [F *pneumatique* or L *pneumaticus* f. Gk *pneumatikos* f. *pneuma* wind f. *pneō* breathe]

pneumatics /nyoomáttiks/ *n.pl.* (treated as *sing.*) the science of the mechanical properties of gases.

pneumato- /nyo͞omətō/ *comb. form* denoting: **1** air. **2** breath. **3** spirit. [Gk f. *pneuma* (as PNEUMATIC)]

pneumatology /nyo͞omətólləji/ *n.* **1** the branch of theology concerned with the Holy Ghost and other spiritual concepts. **2** *archaic* psychology. □□ **pneumatological** /-təlójik'l/ *adj.*

pneumatophore /nyo͞omətəfor/ *n.* **1** the gaseous cavity of various hydrozoa, such as the Portuguese man-of-war. **2** an aerial root specialized for gaseous exchange found in various plants growing in swampy areas.

pneumo- /nyo͝omō/ *comb. form* denoting the lungs. [abbr. of *pneumono-* f. Gk *pneumōn* lung]

pneumoconiosis /nyo͞omōkónniṓsiss/ *n.* a lung disease caused by inhalation of dust or small particles. [PNEUMO- + Gk *konis* dust]

pneumogastric /nyo͞omōgástrik/ *adj.* of or relating to the lungs and stomach.

pneumonectomy /nyo͞omənéktəmi/ *n.* (*pl.* **-ies**) *Surgery* the surgical removal of a lung or part of a lung.

pneumonia /nyoomṓniə/ *n.* a bacterial inflammation of one lung (**single pneumonia**) or both lungs (**double pneumonia**) causing the air sacs to fill with pus and become solid. ▫▫ **pneumonic** /nyoomónnik/ *adj.* [L f. Gk f. *pneumōn* lung]

pneumonitis /nyo͞omənī́tiss/ *n.* inflammation of the lungs usu. caused by a virus.

pneumothorax /nyo͞omōthóraks/ *n.* the presence of air or gas in the cavity between the lungs and the chest wall.

PNG *abbr.* Papua New Guinea.

PO *abbr.* **1** Post Office. **2** postal order. **3** Petty Officer. **4** Pilot Officer.

Po *symb. Chem.* the element polonium.

po /pō/ *n.* (*pl.* **pos**) *Brit. colloq.* a chamber-pot.

POA *abbr.* (in the UK) Prison Officers' Association.

poach[1] /pōch/ *v.tr.* **1** cook (an egg) without its shell in or over boiling water. **2** cook (fish etc.) by simmering in a small amount of liquid. ▫▫ **poacher** *n.* [ME f. OF *pochier* f. *poche* POKE[2]]

poach[2] /pōch/ *v.* **1** *tr.* (also *absol.*) catch (game or fish) illegally. **2** *intr.* (often foll. by *on*) trespass or encroach (on another's property, ideas, etc.). **3** *tr.* appropriate illicitly or unfairly (a person, thing, idea, etc.). **4** *tr. Tennis* etc. take (a shot) in one's partner's portion of the court. **5 a** *tr.* trample or cut up (turf) with hoofs. **b** *intr.* (of land) become sodden by being trampled. ▫▫ **poacher** *n.* [earlier *poche*, perh. f. F *pocher* put in a pocket (as POACH[1])]

▪ **3** see PIRATE *v.* 1.

pochard /pṓchərd/ *n.* any duck of the genus *Aythya*, esp. *A. ferina*, the male of which has a bright reddish-brown head and neck and a grey breast. [16th c.: orig. unkn.]

pochette /poshét/ *n.* a woman's envelope-shaped handbag. [F, dimin. of *poche* pocket: see POKE[2]]

pock /pok/ *n.* (also **pock-mark**) **1** a small pus-filled spot on the skin, esp. caused by chickenpox or smallpox. **2** a mark resembling this. ▫ **pock-marked** bearing marks resembling or left by such spots. ▫▫ **pocky** *adj.* [OE *poc* f. Gmc]

pocket /pókkit/ *n.* & *v.* ● *n.* **1** a small bag sewn into or on clothing, for carrying small articles. **2** a pouchlike compartment in a suitcase, car door, etc. **3** one's financial resources (*it is beyond my pocket*). **4** an isolated group or area (*a few pockets of resistance remain*). **5 a** a cavity in the earth containing ore, esp. gold. **b** a cavity in rock, esp. filled with foreign matter. **6** a pouch at the corner or on the side of a billiard- or snooker-table into which balls are driven. **7** = *air pocket*. **8** (*attrib.*) **a** of a suitable size and shape for carrying in a pocket. **b** smaller than the usual size. ● *v.tr.* (**pocketed, pocketing**) **1** put into one's pocket. **2** appropriate, esp. dishonestly. **3** confine as in a pocket. **4** submit to (an injury or affront). **5** conceal or suppress (one's feelings). **6** *Billiards* etc. drive (a ball) into a pocket. ▫ **in pocket 1** having gained in a transaction. **2** (of money) available. **in a person's pocket 1** under a person's control. **2** close to or intimate with a person. **out of pocket** having lost in a transaction. **out-of-pocket expenses** the actual outlay of cash incurred. **pocket battleship** *hist.* a warship armoured and equipped like, but smaller than, a battleship. **pocket borough** *Brit. hist.* a borough in which the election of political representatives was controlled by one person or family. **pocket gopher** = GOPHER[1] 1. **pocket knife** a knife with a folding blade or blades, for carrying in the pocket. **pocket money 1** money for minor expenses. **2** *Brit.* an allowance of money made to a child. **put one's hand in one's pocket** spend or provide money. ▫▫ **pocketable** *adj.* **pocketless** *adj.* **pockety** *adj.* (in sense 5 of *n.*). [ME f. AF *poket(e)* dimin. of *poke* POKE[2]]

▪ *n.* **1** pouch, sack, bag. **3** see MEANS 2. **4** area, island, centre, cluster, concentration, group. **5 b** pit, hollow, crater; see also CAVITY. **8 b** see SMALL *adj.* 1. ● *v.* **2** take, appropriate, keep; filch, embezzle, steal, thieve, pilfer, help oneself to, *colloq.* swipe, walk off *or* away with, rip off, lift, snaffle, *formal or joc.* purloin, *sl.* pinch, hook, snitch, *Brit. sl.* nick. **5** see SUPPRESS 2. ▫ **put one's hand in one's pocket** see PRESENT[2] *v.* 2.

pocketbook /pókkitbo͝ok/ *n.* **1** a notebook. **2** a booklike case for papers or money carried in a pocket. **3** *US* a purse or handbag. **4** *US* a paperback or other small book.

▪ **2** see WALLET. **3** see PURSE *n.* 1, 2.

pocketful /pókkitfo͝ol/ *n.* (*pl.* **-fuls**) as much as a pocket will hold.

▪ see WAD *n.* 3.

poco /pṓkō/ *adv. Mus.* a little; rather (*poco adagio*). [It.]

pod /pod/ *n.* & *v.* ● *n.* **1** a long seed-vessel esp. of a leguminous plant, e.g. a pea. **2** the cocoon of a silkworm. **3** the case surrounding locust eggs. **4** a narrow-necked eel-net. **5** a compartment suspended under an aircraft for equipment etc. ● *v.* (**podded, podding**) **1** *intr.* bear or form pods. **2** *tr.* remove (peas etc.) from pods. ▫ **in pod** *colloq.* pregnant. [back-form. f. dial. *podware*, *podder* field crops, of unkn. orig.]

▪ *n.* **1** shell, hull, case, husk, skin, *US* shuck.

podagra /pədágrə, póddəgrə/ *n. Med.* gout of the foot, esp. the big toe. ▫▫ **podagral** *adj.* **podagric** *adj.* **podagrous** *adj.* [L f. Gk *pous podos* foot + *agra* seizure]

poddy / póddi/ *adj.*, *n.*, & *v. colloq.* ● *adj.* **1** corpulent, obese. **2** *Austral.* (of a calf, lamb, etc.) fed by hand. ● *n.* (*pl.* **-ies**) *Austral.* **1** an unbranded calf. **2** a calf fed by hand. ● *v.tr. Austral.* feed (a young animal) by hand. [E dial. word: f. POD + -Y[1]]

podgy /póji/ *adj.* (**podgier, podgiest**) **1** (of a person) short and fat. **2** (of a face etc.) plump, fleshy. ▫▫ **podginess** *n.* [19th c.: f. *podge* a short fat person]

▪ see PLUMP[1] *adj.* ▫▫ **podginess** see FAT *n.*

podiatry /pədī́ətri/ *n. US* = CHIROPODY. ▫▫ **podiatrist** *n.* [Gk *pous podos* foot + *iatros* physician]

podium /pṓdiəm/ *n.* (*pl.* **podiums** or **podia** /-diə/) **1** a continuous projecting base or pedestal round a room or house etc. **2** a raised platform round the arena of an amphitheatre. **3** a platform or rostrum. [L f. Gk *podion* dimin. of *pous pod-* foot]

▪ **2, 3** see PLATFORM 2.

podzol /pódzol/ *n.* (also **podsol** /-sol/) a soil with minerals leached from its surface layers into a lower stratum. ▫▫ **podzolize** *v.tr.* & *intr.* (also **-ise**). [Russ. f. *pod* under, *zola* ashes]

poem /pṓ-im/ *n.* **1** a metrical composition, usu. concerned with feeling or imaginative description. **2** an elevated composition in verse or prose. **3** something with poetic qualities (*a poem in stone*). [F *poème* or L *poema* f. Gk *poēma* = *poiēma* f. *poieō* make]

▪ **1** verse, lyric, rhyme, song, ode, ballad, sonnet, *Gk. Antiq.* rhapsody, *archaic* poesy.

poesy /pṓ-izi, -si/ *n. archaic* **1** poetry. **2** the art or composition of poetry. [ME f. OF *poesie* ult. f. L *poesis* f. Gk *poēsis* = *poiēsis* making, poetry (as POEM)]

▪ **1** poetry, verse, versification. **2** poetics.

poet /pṓ-it/ *n.* (*fem.* **poetess** /pṓ-itiss/) **1** a writer of poems. **2** a person possessing high powers of imagination or expression etc. ▫ **Poet Laureate** a poet appointed to write poems for State occasions. **Poets' Corner** part of Westminster Abbey where several poets are buried or commemorated. [ME f. OF *poete* f. L *poeta* f. Gk *poētēs* = *poiētēs* maker, poet (as POEM)]

▪ versifier, rhymester, lyricist, lyrist, rhymer, minstrel, poetaster, *usu. derog.* sonneteer, *poet.* bard.

poetaster /pṓ-itástər/ *n.* a paltry or inferior poet. [mod.L (as POET): see -ASTER]

▪ see POET.

poetic /pō-éttik/ *adj.* (also **poetical** /-tik'l/) **1 a** of or like poetry or poets. **b** written in verse. **2** elevated or sublime in expression. ▫ **poetic justice** well-deserved unforeseen retribution or reward. **poetic licence** a writer's or artist's transgression of established rules for effect. ▫▫ **poetically** *adv.* [F *poétique* f. L *poeticus* f. Gk *poētikos* (as POET)]

▪ **1 b** lyrical, lyric, metrical, rhapsodic. **2** elevated, artistic, fine, aesthetic, Parnassian; see SUBLIME *adj.* 1.

poeticize /pō-éttisīz/ *v.tr.* (also **-ise**) make (a theme) poetic.

poetics /pō-éttiks/ *n.* **1** the art of writing poetry. **2** the study of poetry and its techniques.

poetize /pṓ-itīz/ *v.* (also **-ise**) **1** *intr.* play the poet. **2** *intr.* compose poetry. **3** *tr.* treat poetically. **4** *tr.* celebrate in poetry. [F *poétiser* (as POET)]

poetry /pṓ-itri/ *n.* **1** the art or work of a poet. **2** poems collectively. **3** a poetic or tenderly pleasing quality. **4** anything compared to poetry. [ME f. med.L *poetria* f. L *poeta* POET, prob. after *geometry*]

▪ **1, 2** verse, versification, *archaic* poesy.

po-faced /pṓfáyst/ *adj.* **1** solemn-faced, humourless. **2** smug. [20th c.: perh. f. PO, infl. by *poker-faced*]

▪ **1** austere, dour, disapproving, severe, stern, grave, solemn, sombre, humourless, grim, forbidding; expressionless, impassive, poker-faced. **2** see SMUG.

pogo /pṓgō/ *n.* (*pl.* **-os**) (also **pogo stick**) a toy consisting of a spring-loaded stick with rests for the feet, for springing about on. [20th c.: orig. uncert.]

pogrom /pógrəm, -rom/ *n.* an organized massacre (orig. of Jews in Russia). [Russ., = devastation f. *gromit'* destroy]

▪ see MASSACRE *n.* 1.

poignant /póynyənt/ *adj.* **1** painfully sharp to the emotions or senses; deeply moving. **2** arousing sympathy. **3** sharp or pungent in taste or smell. **4** pleasantly piquant. **5** *archaic* (of words etc.) sharp, severe. ▫▫ **poignance** *n.* **poignancy** *n.* **poignantly** *adv.* [ME f. OF, pres. part. of *poindre* prick f. L *pungere*]

▪ **1, 2** distressing, upsetting, agonizing, grievous, painful, woeful, sad, sorrowful, heart-rending, heart-breaking, excruciating, pathetic, pitiable, piteous, pitiful, moving, touching, stirring, emotional. **3** see PUNGENT 1. **5** keen, acute, intense, incisive, sharp, stinging, pointed, piercing, penetrating, barbed, cutting, caustic, acid, acerbic, bitter, biting, hurtful, mordant, sarcastic, sardonic, severe.

poikilotherm /póykilləthərm/ *n.* an organism that regulates its body temperature by behavioural means, such as basking or burrowing; a cold-blooded organism (cf. HOMOEOTHERM). ▫▫ **poikilothermal** /-thérm'l/ *adj.* **poikilothermia** /-thérmiə/ *n.* **poikilothermic** /-thérmik/ *adj.* **poikilothermy** *n.* [Gk *poikilos* multicoloured, changeable + *thermē* heat]

poilu /pwaalṓō/ *n. hist.* a French private soldier, esp. as a nickname. [F, lit. hairy f. *poil* hair]

poinciana /póynsiáanə/ *n.* any tropical tree of the genus *Poinciana*, with bright showy red flowers. [mod.L f. M. de *Poinci*, 17th-c. governor in the West Indies + *-ana* fem. suffix]

poind /poynd/ *v.* & *n. Sc.* ● *v.tr.* distrain upon; impound. ● *n.* **1** an act of poinding. **2** an animal or chattel poinded. [ME f. OE *pyndan* impound]

poinsettia /poynséttiə/ *n.* a shrub, *Euphorbia pulcherrima*, with large showy scarlet or pink bracts surrounding small yellow flowers. [mod.L f. J. R. *Poinsett*, Amer. diplomat d. 1851]

point /poynt/ *n.* & *v.* ● *n.* **1** the sharp or tapered end of a tool, weapon, pencil, etc. **2** a tip or extreme end. **3** that which in geometry has position but not magnitude, e.g. the intersection of two lines. **4** a particular place or position (*Bombay and points east*; *point of contact*). **5 a** a precise or particular moment (*at the point of death*). **b** the critical or decisive moment (*when it came to the point, he refused*). **6** a very small mark on a surface. **7 a** a dot or other punctuation mark, esp. = *full point* (see FULL[1]). **b** a dot or small stroke used in Semitic languages to indicate vowels or distinguish consonants. **8** = *decimal point*. **9** a stage or degree in progress or increase (*abrupt to the point of rudeness*; *at that point we gave up*). **10** a level of temperature at which a change of state occurs (*freezing-point*). **11** a single item; a detail or particular (*we differ on these points*; *it is a point of principle*). **12 a** a unit of scoring in games or of measuring value etc. **b** an advantage or success in less quantifiable contexts such as an argument or discussion. **c** a unit of weight (2 mg) for diamonds. **d** a unit (of varying value) in quoting the price of stocks etc. **13 a** (usu. prec. by *the*) the significant or essential thing; what is actually intended or under discussion (*that was the point of the question*). **b** (usu. with *neg.* or *interrog.*; often foll. by *in*) sense or purpose; advantage or value (*saw no point in staying*). **c** (usu. prec. by *the*) a salient feature of a story, joke, remark, etc. (*don't see the point*). **14** a distinctive feature or characteristic (*it has its points*; *tact is not his good point*). **15** pungency, effectiveness (*their comments lacked point*). **16 a** each of 32 directions marked at equal distances round a compass. **b** the corresponding direction towards the horizon. **17** (usu. in *pl.*) *Brit.* a junction of two railway lines, with a pair of linked tapering rails that can be moved laterally to allow a train to pass from one line to the other. **18** *Brit.* = *power point*. **19** (usu. in *pl.*) each of a set of electrical contacts in the distributor of a motor vehicle. **20** *Cricket* **a** a fielder on the off side near the batsman. **b** this position. **21** the tip of the toe in ballet. **22** a promontory. **23** the prong of a deer's antler. **24** the extremities of a dog, horse, etc. **25** *Printing* a unit of measurement for type bodies (in the UK and US 0.351 mm, in Europe 0.376 mm). **26** *Hunting* **a** a spot to which a straight run is made. **b** such a run. **27** *Heraldry* any of nine particular positions on a shield used for specifying the position of charges etc. **28** *Boxing* the tip of the chin as a spot for a knockout blow. **29** *Mil.* a small leading party of an advanced guard. **30** *hist.* a tagged lace for lacing a bodice, attaching a hose to a doublet, etc. **31** *Naut.* a short piece of cord at the lower edge of a sail for tying up a reef. **32** the act or position of a dog in pointing. ● *v.* **1** (usu. foll. by *to*, *at*) **a** *tr.* direct or aim (a finger, weapon, etc.). **b** *intr.* direct attention in a certain direction (*pointed to the house across the road*). **2** *intr.* (foll. by *at*, *towards*) **a** aim or be directed to. **b** tend towards. **3** *intr.* (foll. by *to*) indicate; be evidence of (*it all points to murder*). **4** *tr.* give point or force to (words or actions). **5** *tr.* fill in or repair the joints of (brickwork) with smoothly finished mortar or cement. **6** *tr.* **a** punctuate. **b** insert points in (written Hebrew etc.). **c** mark (Psalms etc.) with signs for chanting. **7** *tr.* sharpen (a pencil, tool, etc.). **8** *tr.* (also *absol.*) (of a dog) indicate the presence of (game) by acting as pointer. ▫ **at all points** in every part or respect. **at the point of** (often foll. by verbal noun) on the verge of; about to do (the action specified). **beside the point** irrelevant or irrelevantly. **case in point** an instance that is relevant or (prec. by *the*) under consideration. **have a point** be correct or effective in one's contention. **in point** apposite, relevant. **in point of fact** see FACT. **make** (or **prove**) **a** (or **one's**) **point** establish a proposition; prove one's contention. **make a point of** (often foll. by verbal noun) insist on; treat or regard as essential. **nine points** nine tenths, i.e. nearly the whole (esp. *possession is nine points of the law*). **on** (or **upon**) **the point of** (foll. by verbal noun) about to do (the action specified). **point-duty** the positioning of a police officer or traffic warden at a crossroad or other point to control traffic. **point lace** thread lace made wholly with a needle. **point of honour** an action or circumstance that affects one's reputation. **point of no return** a point in a journey or enterprise at which it becomes essential or more practical to continue to the end. **point of order** a query in a debate etc. as to whether correct procedure is being followed. **point-of-sale** (usu. *attrib.*) denoting publicity etc. associated with the place at which goods are retailed. **point of view 1** a position from which a thing is viewed. **2** a particular way of considering a matter. **point out** (often foll. by *that* + clause) indicate, show; draw attention to. **point-to-point** a steeplechase over a marked course for horses used regularly in hunting. **point up** emphasize; show as important. **score points off** get the better of in an argument etc. **take a person's point** concede that a person has made a valid contention. **to the point** relevant or relevantly. **up to a point** to some extent but not completely. **win on points** *Boxing* win by scoring more points, not by a knockout. [ME f. OF *point, pointer* f. L *punctum* f. *pungere punct-* prick]

■ *n.* **1** spike, spur, prong, sharp end. **2** tip, peak, apex, end. **4** place, site, position; location, locale, spot. **5 a** time, moment, instant, juncture. **6** dot, mark, speck, spot, fleck. **7, 8** dot, (full) stop, full point, decimal point, *esp. US* period. **9** see STAGE *n.* 1. **11** detail, particular, item, element, aspect, facet, matter, issue, subject, question. **13 a** focus, essence, meat, pith, substance, heart, nucleus, crux, nub, core, bottom, details, *sl.* brass tacks, nitty-gritty. **b, c** purpose, intent, intention, aim, goal, object, objective, sense, thrust, drift, theme, import, implication, significance, meaning; application, applicability, relevancy, relevance, appropriateness; advantage, value. **14** attribute, characteristic, feature, aspect, trait, quality, property. **15** pungency, acuteness, sharpness, keenness; effectiveness. **22** promontory, projection, headland, cape, peninsula, bluff, ness. ● *v.* **1 a** direct, level, aim, train. **b** (*point to*) see INDICATE,1, 4. **3** (*point to*) see SUGGEST 2. □ **at the point of** on the point of, on the verge *or* brink of, just about to. **beside the point** irrelevant, incidental, immaterial, unimportant, inconsequential. **have a point** have something. **make a point of** make an effort to, put *or* place emphasis on, go out of one's way to; emphasize, single out, stress, highlight; see also *insist on*. **point of view 1** viewpoint, perspective, approach, position, angle, slant, orientation, outlook, stance, standpoint, vantage point. **2** opinion, view, belief, (way of) thinking, principle, doctrine, tenet. **point out** designate, call *or* direct *or* draw attention to, show, indicate, identify; bring up, mention, emphasize, stress, point up, single out. **point up** emphasize, stress, accentuate, underline, underscore, accent, spotlight. **to the point** relevant, pertinent, appropriate, fitting, apropos, germane, apt, applicable, apposite.

point-blank /póyntblángk/ *adj.* & *adv.* ● *adj.* **1 a** (of a shot) aimed or fired horizontally at a range very close to the target. **b** (of a distance or range) very close. **2** (of a remark, question, etc.) blunt, direct. ● *adv.* **1** at very close range. **2** directly, bluntly. [prob. f. POINT + BLANK = white spot in the centre of a target]

■ *adj.* **1 b** close, short, near. **2** direct, straight, blunt, flat, straightforward, abrupt, categorical, explicit, uncompromising, unmitigated, unalloyed, downright, outright, absolute, unreserved. ● *adv.* **2** directly, straight away, right away, bluntly, flatly, abruptly, categorically, unqualifiedly, explicitly, uncompromisingly, unmitigatedly, outright, unreservedly, plainly, frankly, openly, candidly, straight, *colloq.* flat.

pointed /póyntid/ *adj.* **1** sharpened or tapering to a point. **2** (of a remark etc.) having point; penetrating, cutting. **3** emphasized; made evident. □□ **pointedly** *adv.* **pointedness** *n.*

■ **1** sharp, barbed, spined, pointy, *Biol.* acuminate, *Bot.* & *Zool.* spiculate, mucronate. **2** piercing, cutting, sharp, pungent, keen, penetrating, trenchant, biting, barbed; see also INCISIVE 3. **3** see EXPLICIT 1.

pointer /póyntər/ *n.* **1** a thing that points, e.g. the index hand of a gauge etc. **2** a rod for pointing to features on a map, chart, etc. **3** *colloq.* a hint, clue, or indication. **4 a** a dog of a breed that on scenting game stands rigid looking towards it. **b** this breed. **5** (in *pl.*) two stars in the Great Bear in line with the pole star.

■ **1** indicator, arrow, hand; cursor. **3** tip, hint, clue, suggestion, recommendation, piece of advice.

pointillism /pwántiliz'm, póyn-/ *n. Art* a technique of impressionist painting using tiny dots of various pure colours, which become blended in the viewer's eye. □□ **pointillist** *n.* & *adj.* **pointillistic** /-lístik/ *adj.* [F *pointillisme* f. *pointiller* mark with dots]

pointing /póynting/ *n.* **1** cement or mortar filling the joints of brickwork. **2** facing produced by this. **3** the process of producing this.

pointless /póyntliss/ *adj.* **1** without a point. **2** lacking force, purpose, or meaning. **3** (in games) without a point scored. □□ **pointlessly** *adv.* **pointlessness** *n.*

■ **2** purposeless, aimless, worthless, meaningless, futile, ineffectual, ineffective, unproductive, fruitless, useless, vain, senseless, absurd, silly, empty, hollow, *archaic* bootless.

pointsman /póyntsmən/ *n.* (*pl.* **-men**) *Brit.* **1** a person in charge of railway points. **2** a policeman or traffic warden on point-duty.

pointy /póynti/ *adj.* (**pointier, pointiest**) having a noticeably sharp end; pointed.

poise[1] /poyz/ *n.* & *v.* ● *n.* **1** composure or self-possession of manner. **2** equilibrium; a stable state. **3** carriage (of the head etc.). ● *v.* **1** *tr.* balance; hold suspended or supported. **2** *tr.* carry (one's head etc. in a specified way). **3** *intr.* be balanced; hover in the air etc. [ME f. OF *pois, peis, peser* ult. f. L *pensum* weight f. *pendere pens-* weigh]

■ *n.* **1** composure, control, self-possession, aplomb, assurance, dignity, equanimity, sang-froid, cool-headedness, imperturbability, presence of mind, coolness, calmness, serenity, *sl.* cool. **2** balance, equilibrium, equipoise, counterpoise. ● *v.* **1** balance, hold, steady, suspend; equilibrate. **3** balance, hover, hang, float.

poise[2] /poyz/ *n. Physics* a unit of dynamic viscosity, such that a tangential force of one dyne per square centimetre causes a velocity change one centimetre per second between two parallel planes in a liquid separated by one centimetre. [J. L. M. *Poiseuille*, Fr. physician d. 1869]

poised /poyzd/ *adj.* **1** composed, self-assured. **2** (often foll. by *for*, or *to* + infin.) ready for action.

■ **1** composed, controlled, self-assured, self-possessed, self-confident, assured, dignified, cool-headed, imperturbable, unruffled, cool, reserved, calm, serene, *colloq.* unflappable, together. **2** ready, standing by, waiting, prepared, *colloq.* all set.

poison /póyz'n/ *n.* & *v.* ● *n.* **1** a substance that when introduced into or absorbed by a living organism causes death or injury, esp. one that kills by rapid action even in a small quantity. **2** *colloq.* a harmful influence or principle etc. **3** *Physics* & *Chem.* a substance that interferes with the normal progress of a nuclear reaction, chain reaction, catalytic reaction, etc. ● *v.tr.* **1** administer poison to (a person or animal). **2** kill or injure or infect with poison. **3** infect (air, water, etc.) with poison. **4** (esp. as **poisoned** *adj.*) treat (a weapon) with poison. **5** corrupt or pervert (a person or mind). **6** spoil or destroy (a person's pleasure etc.). **7** render (land etc.) foul and unfit for its purpose by a noxious application etc. □ **poison gas** = GAS *n.* 4. **poison ivy** a N. American climbing plant, *Rhus toxicodendron*, secreting an irritant oil from its leaves. **poison-pen letter** an anonymous libellous or abusive letter. □□ **poisoner** *n.* **poisonous** *adj.* **poisonously** *adv.* [ME f. OF *poison, poisonner* (as POTION)]

■ *n.* **1** toxin, venom, *archaic* virus, bane; mephitis, *archaic* miasma. **2** cancer, canker, virus, bad influence, blight, contagion. ● *v.* **3** defile, adulterate, envenom, infect, taint, pollute, contaminate, debase. **5** pervert, corrupt, vitiate, subvert, warp, degrade, deprave. **6** taint, destroy; see also SPOIL *v.* 1. □□ **poisonous** toxic, virulent, venomous, noxious, mephitic, pernicious, deleterious, lethal, deadly, fatal, mortal, *archaic* miasmic, *literary* nocuous; malicious, malevolent, malignant, corruptive, vicious, ugly, baleful, evil, foul.

Poisson distribution /pwússon/ *n. Statistics* a discrete frequency distribution which gives the probability of events occurring in a fixed time. [S. D. *Poisson*, French mathematician d. 1840]

poke[1] /pōk/ *v.* & *n.* ● *v.* **1** (foll. by *in*, *up*, *down*, etc.) **a** *tr.* thrust or push with the hand, point of a stick, etc. **b** *intr.* be thrust forward. **2** *intr.* (foll. by *at* etc.) make thrusts with a stick etc. **3** *tr.* thrust the end of a finger etc. against. **4** *tr.* (foll. by *in*) produce (a hole etc. in a thing) by poking. **5** *tr.* thrust forward, esp. obtrusively. **6** *tr.* stir (a fire) with a poker. **7** *intr.* **a** (often foll. by *about*, *around*) move or act desultorily; potter. **b** (foll. by *about*, *into*) pry; search casually. **8** *tr. coarse sl.* have sexual intercourse with. **9** *tr.* (foll. by *up*) *colloq.* confine (esp. oneself) in a poky place. ● *n.* **1** the act or an instance of poking. **2** a thrust or nudge. **3** a device fastened on cattle etc. to prevent them breaking through fences. **4 a** a projecting brim or front of a woman's bonnet or hat. **b** (in full **poke-bonnet**) a bonnet having this. □ **poke fun at** ridicule, tease. **poke** (or **stick**) **one's nose into** *colloq.* pry or intrude into (esp. a person's affairs). [ME f. MDu. and MLG *poken*, of unkn. orig.]

■ *v.* **1 a** jab, prod, dig (into), stab, push, elbow, butt, shove, stick; see also PUNCH *v.* 1. **7 a** see *mess about*. **b** (*poke about*) pry, nose (about *or* around), intrude; meddle, interfere; *colloq.* snoop (about); (*poke into*) dig into, tamper with, probe into, *colloq.* poke *or* stick one's nose into. **9** (*poke oneself up*) see HIDE[1] *v.* 2. ● *n.* **2** jab, prod, dig, stab, thrust, push, nudge, jog, shove; see also PUNCH *n.* 1. □ **poke fun at** tease, ridicule, mock, make fun of, jeer at, chaff at, taunt, guy, gibe at, twit, make sport of, laugh at, *colloq.* rib, *Brit. colloq.* send up, *sl.* take the mickey out of. **poke** (or **stick**) **one's nose into** pry *or* dig *or* probe into, meddle *or* interfere in, nose around, intrude on.

poke[2] /pōk/ *n. dial.* a bag or sack. □ **buy a pig in a poke** see PIG. [ME f. ONF *poke*, *poque* = OF *poche*: cf. POUCH]

poker[1] /pṓkər/ *n.* a stiff metal rod with a handle for stirring an open fire. □ **poker-work 1** the technique of burning designs on white wood etc. with a heated metal rod. **2** a design made in this way.

poker[2] /pṓkər/ *n.* a card-game in which bluff is used as players bet on the value of their hands. □ **poker-dice** dice with card designs from ace to nine instead of spots. **poker-face 1** the impassive countenance appropriate to a poker-player. **2** a person with this. **poker-faced** having a poker-face. [19th c.: orig. unkn.: cf. G *pochen* to brag, *Pochspiel* bragging game]

■ □ **poker-faced** serious; see also WOODEN 3b, IMPASSIVE 1b.

pokeweed /pṓkweed/ *n.* a tall hardy American plant, *Phytolacca americana*, with spikes of cream flowers and purple berries that yield emetics and purgatives. [*poke*, Amer. Ind. word + WEED]

pokey /pṓki/ *n. US sl.* prison. [perh. f. POKY]

■ see PRISON *n.* 1.

poky /pṓki/ *adj.* (**pokier**, **pokiest**) (of a room etc.) small and cramped. □□ **pokily** *adv.* **pokiness** *n.* [POKE[1] (in colloq. sense 'confine') + -Y[1]]

polack /pṓlak/ *n. US sl. offens.* a person of Polish origin. [F *Polaque* and G *Polack* f. Pol. *Polak*]

polar /pṓlər/ *adj.* **1 a** of or near a pole of the earth or a celestial body, or of the celestial sphere. **b** (of a species or variety) living in the north polar region. **2** having magnetic polarity. **3 a** (of a molecule) having a positive charge at one end and a negative charge at the other. **b** (of a compound) having electric charges. **4** *Geom.* of or relating to a pole. **5** directly opposite in character or tendency. **6** *colloq.* (esp. of weather) very cold. □ **polar bear** a white bear, *Ursus maritimus*, of the Arctic regions. **polar body** a small cell produced from an oocyte during the formation of an ovum, which does not develop further. **polar circle** each of the circles parallel to the equator at a distance of 23° 27′ from either pole. **polar coordinates** a system by which a point can be located with reference to two angles. **polar curve** a curve related in a particular way to a given curve and to a fixed point called a *pole*. **polar distance** the angular distance of a point on a sphere from the nearest pole. **polar star** = POLE STAR. □□ **polarly** *adv.* [F *polaire* or mod.L *polaris* (as POLE[2])]

■ **5** opposite, opposed, antithetical, contrary, contradictory, antipodal. **6** frigid, glacial, freezing, frozen, numbing, wintry, chilling, chilly, *colloq.* Siberian, arctic, nippy, perishing; see also ICY 1.

polari- /pṓləri/ *comb. form* polar. [mod.L *polaris* (as POLAR)]

polarimeter /pṓlərímmitər/ *n.* an instrument used to measure the polarization of light or the effect of a substance on the rotation of the plane of polarized light. □□ **polarimetric** /-métrik/ *adj.* **polarimetry** *n.*

polariscope /pōlárriskōp/ *n.* = POLARIMETER. □□ **polariscopic** /-skóppik/ *adj.*

polarity /pəlárriti/ *n.* (*pl.* **-ies**) **1** the tendency of a lodestone, magnetized bar, etc., to point with its extremities to the magnetic poles of the earth. **2** the condition of having two poles with contrary qualities. **3** the state of having two opposite tendencies, opinions, etc. **4** the electrical condition of a body (positive or negative). **5** a magnetic attraction towards an object or person.

polarize /pṓləriz/ *v.* (also **-ise**) **1** *tr.* restrict the vibrations of (a transverse wave, esp. light) to one direction. **2** *tr.* give magnetic or electric polarity to (a substance or body). **3** *tr.* reduce the voltage of (an electric cell) by the action of electrolysis products. **4** *tr.* & *intr.* divide into two groups of opposing opinion etc. □□ **polarizable** *adj.* **polarization** /-záysh'n/ *n.* **polarizer** *n.*

polarography /pṓlərógrəfi/ *n. Chem.* the analysis by measurement of current-voltage relationships in electrolysis between mercury electrodes. □□ **polarographic** /-ərəgráffik/ *adj.*

Polaroid /pṓləroyd/ *n. propr.* **1** material in thin plastic sheets that produces a high degree of plane polarization in light passing through it. **2** a type of camera with internal processing that produces a finished print rapidly after each exposure. **3** (in *pl.*) sunglasses with lenses made from Polaroid. [POLARI- + -OID]

polder /pṓldər/ *n.* a piece of low-lying land reclaimed from the sea or a river, esp. in the Netherlands. [MDu. *polre*, Du. *polder*]

Pole /pōl/ *n.* **1** a native or national of Poland. **2** a person of Polish descent. [G f. Pol. *Polanie*, lit. field-dwellers f. *pole* field]

pole[1] /pōl/ *n.* & *v.* ● *n.* **1** a long slender rounded piece of wood or metal, esp. with the end placed in the ground as a support etc. **2** a wooden shaft fitted to the front of a vehicle and attached to the yokes or collars of the draught animals. **3** = PERCH[3]. ● *v.tr.* **1** provide with poles. **2** (usu. foll. by *off*) push off (a punt etc.) with a pole. □ **pole position** the most favourable position at the start of a motor race (orig. next to the inside boundary-fence). **pole-vault** (or **-jump**) *n.* the athletic sport of vaulting over a high bar with the aid of a long flexible pole held in the hands and giving extra spring. ● *v.intr.* take part in this sport. **pole-vaulter** a person who pole-vaults. **under bare poles** *Naut.* with no sail set. **up the pole** *sl.* **1** crazy, eccentric. **2** in difficulty. [OE *pāl* ult. f. L *palus* stake]

■ **1** rod, stick, staff, spar, shaft, mast, upright. □ **up the pole 1** see CRAZY 1. **2** see *in trouble* 1 (TROUBLE).

pole[2] /pōl/ *n.* **1** (in full **north pole, south pole**) **a** each of the two points in the celestial sphere about which the stars appear to revolve. **b** each of the extremities of the axis of rotation of the earth or another body. **c** see *magnetic pole*. ¶ The spelling is *North Pole* and *South Pole* when used as geographical designations. **2** each of the two opposite points on the surface of a magnet at which magnetic forces are strongest. **3** each of two terminals (positive and negative) of an electric cell or battery etc. **4** each of two opposed principles or ideas. **5** *Geom.* each of two points in which the axis of a circle cuts the surface of a sphere. **6** a fixed point to which others are referred. **7** *Biol.* an extremity of the main axis of any spherical or oval organ. □ **be poles apart** differ greatly, esp. in nature or opinion. □□ **poleward** *adj.* **polewards** *adj.* & *adv.* [ME f. L *polus* f. Gk *polos* pivot, axis, sky]

■ **4** extremity, end, limit, extreme. □ **poles apart** (very *or* completely) different, as different as chalk and cheese, worlds apart, at opposite extremes, at opposite ends of the earth; irreconcilable.

poleaxe /pṓlaks/ *n.* & *v.* ● *n.* **1** a battleaxe. **2** a butcher's axe. ● *v.tr.* hit or kill with or as if with a poleaxe . [ME *pol(l)ax, -ex* f. MDu. *pol(l)aex*, MLG *pol(l)exe* (as POLL[1], AXE)]

polecat /pṓlkat/ *n.* **1** *Brit.* a small European brownish-black fetid flesh-eating mammal, *Mustela putorius*, of the weasel family. **2** *US* a skunk. [*pole* (unexplained) + CAT]

polemic /pəlémmik/ *n.* & *adj.* ● *n.* **1** a controversial discussion. **2** *Polit.* a verbal or written attack, esp. on a political opponent. ● *adj.* (also **polemical**) involving dispute; controversial. □□ **polemically** *adv.* **polemicist** /-misist/ *n.* **polemicize** *v.tr.* (also **-ise**). **polemize** /póllimīz/ *v.tr.* (also **-ise**). [med.L *polemicus* f. Gk *polemikos* f. *polemos* war]

■ *n.* **1** see DEBATE *n.* 1. ● *adj.* see DEBATABLE.

polemics /pəlémmiks/ *n.pl.* the art or practice of controversial discussion.

polenta /pəléntə/ *n.* porridge made of maize meal etc. [It. f. L, = pearl barley]

pole star *n.* **1** *Astron.* a star in Ursa Minor now about 1° distant from the celestial north pole. **2 a** a thing or principle serving as a guide. **b** a centre of attraction.

■ **1** North star, lodestar. **2** see GUIDE *n.* 5.

police /pəléess/ *n.* & *v.* ● *n.* **1** (usu. prec. by *the*) the civil force of a State, responsible for maintaining public order. **2** (as *pl.*) the members of a police force (*several hundred police*). **3** a force with similar functions of enforcing regulations (*military police; railway police*). ● *v.tr.* **1** control (a country or area) by means of police. **2** provide with police. **3** keep order in; control; monitor. □ **police constable** see CONSTABLE. **police dog** a dog, esp. an Alsatian, used in police work. **police officer** a policeman or policewoman. **police State** a totalitarian State controlled by political police supervising the citizens' activities. **police station** the office of a local police force. [F f. med.L *politia* POLICY[1]]

■ *n.* **1, 2** constabulary, the (long arm of the) law, *Brit.* boys in blue, *colloq.* law, *hist.* Bow Street runner, *sl.* fuzz, *Brit. sl.* the (Old) Bill, *derog. sl.* filth, *US sl.* the Man; policemen, policewomen, police officers. ● *v.* **1** patrol, guard, watch, protect; see also CONTROL *v.* 1, 2. **3** enforce, regulate, administer, oversee, control, observe, supervise, monitor. □ **police officer** officer (of the law), policeman, policewoman, gendarme, *Brit.* (police) constable, PC, WPC, *US* lawman, patrolman, patrolwoman, *colloq.* flattie, *Brit. colloq.* bobby, *sl.* cop, fuzz, flatfoot, busy, finger, jack, *Austral. sl.* demon, John Hop, walloper, *Brit. sl.* copper, rozzer, *Brit. archaic sl. or dial* peeler, *sl. derog.* pig.

policeman /pəléesmən/ *n.* (*pl.* **-men**; *fem.* **policewoman**, *pl.* **-women**) a member of a police force.

■ see *police officer*.

policy[1] /póllisi/ *n.* (*pl.* **-ies**) **1** a course or principle of action adopted or proposed by a government, party, business, or individual etc. **2** prudent conduct; sagacity. [ME f. OF *policie* f. L *politia* f. Gk *politeia* citizenship f. *politēs* citizen f. *polis* city]

■ **1** course, approach, procedure, plan, design, scheme, action, strategy, tactic(s), principle(s), programme, method, system, practice, *esp. US* game plan. **2** see *prudence* (PRUDENT).

policy[2] /póllisi/ *n.* (*pl.* **-ies**) **1** a contract of insurance. **2** a document containing this. [F *police* bill of lading, contract of insurance, f. Prov. *poliss(i)a* prob. f. med.L *apodissa, apodixa*, f. L *apodixis* f. Gk *apodeixis* evidence, proof (as APO-, *deiknumi* show)]

policyholder /póllisihōldər/ *n.* a person or body holding an insurance policy.

polio /pṓliō/ *n.* = POLIOMYELITIS. [abbr.]

poliomyelitis /pṓliōmī-ilītiss/ *n. Med.* an infectious viral disease that affects the central nervous system and which can cause temporary or permanent paralysis. [mod.L f. Gk *polios* grey + *muelos* marrow]

Polish /pṓlish/ *adj.* & *n.* ● *adj.* **1** of or relating to Poland. **2** of the Poles or their language. ● *n.* the language of Poland. □ **Polish notation** *Math.* a system of formula notation without brackets and punctuation. [POLE + -ISH[1]]

polish /póllish/ *v.* & *n.* ● *v.* **1** *tr.* & *intr.* make or become smooth or glossy by rubbing. **2** (esp. as **polished** *adj.*) refine or improve; add finishing touches to. ● *n.* **1** a substance used for polishing. **2** smoothness or glossiness produced by friction. **3** the act or an instance of polishing. **4** refinement or elegance of manner, conduct, etc. □ **polish off 1** finish (esp. food) quickly. **2** *colloq.* kill, murder. **polish up** revise or improve (a skill etc.). □□ **polishable** *adj.* **polisher** *n.* [ME f. OF *polir* f. L *polire polit-*]

■ *v.* **1** shine, brighten, burnish, buff, furbish, wax, clean, gloss. **2** (**polished**) accomplished, finished, masterful, masterly, virtuoso, outstanding; flawless, faultless, perfect, impeccable; refined, elegant, cultivated, graceful, debonair, sophisticated, urbane, *soigné*, courtly, genteel, cultured, civilized, well-bred, well-mannered, polite. ● *n.* **1** wax, beeswax, oil. **2** gloss, shine, lustre, sheen, glossiness, smoothness, glaze, brilliance, sparkle, gleam. **4** see REFINEMENT 3. □ **polish off 1** dispose of, put away, eat up, gobble (up), consume, wolf (down), *joc.* demolish. **2** see MURDER *v.* 1. **polish up** refine, improve, perfect, cultivate, enhance, *formal* ameliorate; study, review, revise, *archaic* con, *colloq.* bone up (on), *Brit. colloq.* swot up (on).

politburo /póllitbyoorō/ *n.* (*pl.* **-os**) the principal policy-making committee of a Communist party, esp. in the former USSR. [Rus. *politbyuro* f. *politícheskoe byuró* political bureau]

polite /pəlī́t/ *adj.* (**politer, politest**) **1** having good manners; courteous. **2** cultivated, cultured. **3** refined, elegant (*polite letters*). □□ **politely** *adv.* **politeness** *n.* [L *politus* (as POLISH)]

■ **1** civil, respectful, well-mannered, mannerly, courteous, diplomatic, considerate, tactful, formal, proper, cordial. **2** see *polished* (POLISH).

politesse /póllitéss/ *n.* formal politeness. [F f. It. *politezza, pulitezza* f. *pulito* polite]

■ see ETIQUETTE 1.

politic /póllitik/ *adj.* & *v.* ● *adj.* **1** (of an action) judicious, expedient. **2** (of a person:) **a** prudent, sagacious. **b** scheming, sly. **3** political (now only in *body politic*). ● *v.intr.* (**politicked, politicking**) engage in politics. □□ **politicly** *adv.* [ME f. OF *politique* f. L *politicus* f. Gk *politikos* f. *politēs* citizen f. *polis* city]

■ *adj.* **1** see JUDICIOUS. **2 a** prudent, tactful, diplomatic, discreet, judicious, wise, sage, sagacious, sensible, percipient, discriminating, far-sighted, perceptive. **b** ingenious, shrewd, crafty, canny, cunning, designing, scheming, clever, sly, wily, foxy, tricky, artful, machiavellian, evasive, *colloq.* shifty, cagey.

political /pəlíttik'l/ *adj.* **1 a** of or concerning the State or its government, or public affairs generally. **b** of, relating to, or engaged in politics. **c** belonging to or forming part of a civil administration. **2** having an organized form of society or government. **3** taking or belonging to a side in politics or in controversial matters. **4** relating to or affecting interests of status or authority in an organization rather than matters of principle (*a political decision*). □ **political asylum** see ASYLUM. **political correctness** (esp. in the US) avoidance of forms of expression and action that exclude or marginalize racial and cultural minorities; advocacy of this. **political economist** a student of or expert in political economy. **political economy** the study of the economic aspects of government. **political geography** that dealing with boundaries and the possessions of States. **political prisoner** a person imprisoned for political beliefs or actions. **political science** the study of the State and systems of

government. **political scientist** a specialist in political science. ▫▫ **politically** *adv.* [L *politicus* (as POLITIC)]
■ **1** governmental, State, public, national; civic, civil; administrative, bureaucratic. **3** partisan, factional, factious; active, involved, committed, militant.

politician /póllitísh'n/ *n.* **1** a person engaged in or concerned with politics, esp. as a practitioner. **2** a person skilled in politics. **3** *US derog.* a person with self-interested political concerns.
■ **1** legislator, lawmaker, statesman, stateswoman; minister, Member of Parliament, MP, senator, congressman, congresswoman, representative, *Austral.* & *US* polly; public servant, administrator, official, bureaucrat, office-bearer *or* -holder; *colloq.* politico.

politicize /pəlíttisīz/ *v.* (also **-ise**) **1** *tr.* **a** give a political character to. **b** make politically aware. **2** *intr.* engage in or talk politics. ▫▫ **politicization** /-záysh'n/ *n.*

politico /pəlíttikō/ *n.* (*pl.* **-os**) *colloq.* a politician or political enthusiast. [Sp. or It. (as POLITIC)]
■ see POLITICIAN.

politico- /pəlíttikō/ *comb. form* **1** politically. **2** political and (*politico-social*). [Gk *politikos*: see POLITIC]

politics /póllitiks/ *n.pl.* **1** (treated as *sing.* or *pl.*) **a** the art and science of government. **b** public life and affairs as involving authority and government. **2** (usu. treated as *pl.*) **a** a particular set of ideas, principles, or commitments in politics (*what are their politics?*). **b** activities concerned with the acquisition or exercise of authority or government. **c** an organizational process or principle affecting authority, status, etc. (*the politics of the decision*).
■ **1** political science, government, statecraft, diplomacy, statesmanship; public affairs *or* life, civil affairs. **2 a** belief, conviction, persuasion; see also LEANING. **b** manipulation, machination, manoeuvring, *esp. US* wirepulling; see also GOVERNMENT 1.

polity /pólliti/ *n.* (*pl.* **-ies**) **1** a form or process of civil government or constitution. **2** an organized society; a State as a political entity. [L *politia* f. Gk *politeia* f. *politēs* citizen f. *polis* city]
■ **2** see NATION.

polka /pólkə, pṓlkə/ *n.* & *v.* ● *n.* **1** a lively dance of Bohemian origin in duple time. **2** the music for this. ● *v.intr.* (**polkas, polkaed** /-kəd/ or **polka'd, polkaing** /-kəing/) dance the polka. ▫ **polka dot** a round dot as one of many forming a regular pattern on a textile fabric etc. [F and G f. Czech *půlka* half-step f. *půl* half]

poll[1] /pōl/ *n.* & *v.* ● *n.* **1 a** the process of voting at an election. **b** the counting of votes at an election. **c** the result of voting. **d** the number of votes recorded (*a heavy poll*). **2** = GALLUP POLL, *opinion poll.* **3 a** a human head. **b** the part of this on which hair grows (*flaxen poll*). **4** a hornless animal, esp. one of a breed of hornless cattle. ● *v.* **1** *tr.* **a** take the vote or votes of. **b** (in *passive*) have one's vote taken. **c** (of a candidate) receive (so many votes). **d** give (a vote). **2** *tr.* record the opinion of (a person or group) in an opinion poll. **3** *intr.* give one's vote. **4** *tr.* cut off the top of (a tree or plant), esp. make a pollard of. **5** *tr.* (esp. as **polled** *adj.*) cut the horns off (cattle). **6** *tr. Computing* check the status of (a computer system) at intervals. ▫ **poll tax 1** *hist.* a tax levied on every adult. **2** = *community charge.* ▫▫ **pollee** /pōlée/ *n.* (in sense 2 of *n.*). **pollster** *n.* [ME, perh. f. LG or Du.]
■ *n.* **1 c** voting, vote, return, tally, figures, ballot, count. **2** opinion poll, survey, canvass, census. **4** pollard. ● *v.* **1 a** ballot. **c** receive, get, win, register, tally. **2** canvass, ballot, sample, survey.

poll[2] /pol/ *n.* a tame parrot (*Pretty poll!*). ▫ **poll parrot** a user of conventional or clichéd phrases and arguments. [*Poll*, a conventional name for a parrot, alt. f. *Moll*, a familiar form of *Mary*]

pollack /póllək/ *n.* (also **pollock**) a European marine fish, *Pollachius pollachius*, with a characteristic protruding lower jaw, used for food. [earlier (Sc.) *podlock*: orig. unkn.]

pollan /póllən/ *n.* a freshwater fish, *Coregonus pollan*, found in Irish lakes. [perh. f. Ir. *poll* deep water]

pollard /póllərd/ *n.* & *v.* ● *n.* **1** an animal that has lost or cast its horns; an ox, sheep, or goat of a hornless breed. **2** a tree whose branches have been cut off to encourage the growth of new young branches, esp. a riverside willow. **3 a** the bran sifted from flour. **b** a fine bran containing some flour. ● *v.tr.* make (a tree) a pollard. [POLL[1] + -ARD]

pollen /póllən/ *n.* the fine dustlike grains discharged from the male part of a flower containing the gamete that fertilizes the female ovule. ▫ **pollen analysis** = PALYNOLOGY. **pollen count** an index of the amount of pollen in the air, published esp. for the benefit of those allergic to it. ▫▫ **pollenless** *adj.* **pollinic** /pəlínnik/ *adj.* [L *pollen pollinis* fine flour, dust]

pollex /pólleks/ *n.* (*pl.* **pollices** /-liseez/) the innermost digit of a forelimb, usu. the thumb in primates. [L, = thumb or big toe]

pollie var. of POLLY[2].

pollinate /póllinayt/ *v.tr.* (also *absol.*) sprinkle (a stigma) with pollen. ▫▫ **pollination** /-náysh'n/ *n.* **pollinator** *n.*
■ see FERTILIZE 2.

polling /pṓling/ *n.* the registering or casting of votes. ▫ **polling-booth** a compartment in which a voter stands to mark the ballot-paper. **polling-day** the day of a local or general election. **polling-station** a building, often a school, where voting takes place during an election.

pollinic see POLLEN.

polliniferous /póllinífərəss/ *adj.* bearing or producing pollen.

polliwog /pólliwog/ *n.* (also **pollywog**) *US dial.* a tadpole. [earlier *polwigge*, *polwygle* f. POLL[1] + WIGGLE]

pollock var. of POLLACK.

pollute /pəlóót/ *v.tr.* **1** contaminate or defile (the environment). **2** make foul or filthy. **3** destroy the purity or sanctity of. ▫▫ **pollutant** *adj.* & *n.* **polluter** *n.* **pollution** *n.* [ME f. L *polluere pollut-*]
■ **1** defile, poison; see also CONTAMINATE 1. **2** foul, soil, taint, stain, dirty, grime, *poet.* befoul, sully; see also DIRTY *v.* **3** corrupt, desecrate, profane, defile, violate. ▫▫ **pollution** contamination, adulteration, dirtying; vitiation, corruption, debasement; see also SACRILEGE.

polly[1] /pólli/ *n.* (*pl.* **-ies**) *colloq.* a bottle or glass of Apollinaris water. [abbr.]

polly[2] /pólli/ *n.* (also **pollie**) (*pl.* **-ies**) *Austral.* & *US* a politician. [abbr.]

Pollyanna /pólliánnə/ *n.* a cheerful optimist; an excessively cheerful person. ▫▫ **Pollyannaish** *adj.* **Pollyannaism** *n.* [character in a novel (1913) by E. Porter]

pollywog var. of POLLIWOG.

polo /pṓlō/ *n.* a game of Eastern origin like hockey played on horseback with a long-handled mallet. ▫ **polo-neck** a high round turned-over collar. **polo-stick** a mallet for playing polo. [Balti, = ball]

polonaise /póllənáyz/ *n.* & *adj.* ● *n.* **1** a dance of Polish origin in triple time. **2** the music for this. **3** *hist.* a woman's dress consisting of a bodice and a skirt open from the waist downwards to show an underskirt. ● *adj.* cooked in a Polish style. [F, fem. of *polonais* Polish f. med.L *Polonia* Poland]

polonium /pəlṓniəm/ *n. Chem.* a rare radioactive metallic element, occurring naturally in uranium ores. ¶ Symb.: **Po**. [F & mod.L f. med.L *Polonia* Poland (the discoverer's native country) + -IUM]

polony /pəlṓni/ *n.* (*pl.* **-ies**) *Brit.* = BOLOGNA SAUSAGE. [app. corrupt.]

poltergeist /póltərgīst/ *n.* a noisy mischievous ghost, esp. one manifesting itself by physical damage. [G f. *poltern* create a disturbance + *Geist* GHOST]
■ see GHOST *n.* 1.

poltroon /poltróon/ *n.* a spiritless coward. ▫▫ **poltroonery** *n.* [F *poltron* f. It. *poltrone* perh. f. *poltro* sluggard]
■ see COWARD *n.*

poly /pólli/ *n.* (*pl.* **polys**) *colloq.* polytechnic. [abbr.]

poly-[1] /pólli/ *comb. form* denoting many or much. [Gk *polu-* f. *polus* much, *polloi* many]

poly-[2] /pólli/ *comb. form Chem.* polymerized (*polyunsaturated*). [POLYMER]

polyadelphous /pólliədélfəss/ *adj. Bot.* having numerous stamens grouped into three or more bundles.

polyamide /pólliámmīd/ *n. Chem.* any of a class of condensation polymers produced from the interaction of an amino group of one molecule and a carboxylic acid group of another, and which includes many synthetic fibres such as nylon.

polyandry /pólliandri/ *n.* **1** polygamy in which a woman has more than one husband. **2** *Bot.* the state of having numerous stamens. □□ **polyandrous** /-ándrəss/ *adj.* [POLY-[1] + *andry* f. Gk *anēr andros* male]

polyanthus /pólliánthəss/ *n.* (*pl.* **polyanthuses**) a flower cultivated from hybridized primulas. [mod.L, formed as POLY-[1] + Gk *anthos* flower]

polycarbonate /póllikaárbənayt/ *n.* any of a class of polymers in which the units are linked through a carbonate group, mainly used as moulding materials.

polychaete /póllikeet/ *n.* any aquatic annelid worm of the class Polychaeta, including lugworms and ragworms, having numerous bristles on the fleshy lobes of each body segment. □□ **polychaetan** /-keét'n/ *adj.* **polychaetous** /-keétəss/ *adj.*

polychromatic /póllikrōmáttik/ *adj.* **1** many-coloured. **2** (of radiation) containing more than one wavelength. □□ **polychromatism** /-krṓmətiz'm/ *n.*
■ **1** see *variegated* (VARIEGATE).

polychrome /póllikrōm/ *adj.* & *n.* ● *adj.* painted, printed, or decorated in many colours. ● *n.* **1** a work of art in several colours, esp. a coloured statue. **2** varied colouring. □□ **polychromic** /-krṓmik/ *adj.* **polychromous** /-krṓməss/ *adj.* [F f. Gk *polukhrōmos* as POLY-[1], *khrōma* colour]
■ *adj.* see *variegated* (VARIEGATE).

polychromy /póllikrōmi/ *n.* the art of painting in several colours, esp. as applied to ancient pottery, architecture, etc. [F *polychromie* (as POLYCHROME)]

polyclinic /pólliklinik/ *n.* a clinic devoted to various diseases; a general hospital.

polycrystalline /póllikrístəlīn/ *adj.* (of a solid substance) consisting of many crystalline parts at various orientations, e.g. a metal casting.

polycyclic /póllisīklik/ *adj. Chem.* having more than one ring of atoms in the molecule.

polydactyl /póllidáktil/ *adj.* & *n.* ● *adj.* (of an animal) having more than five fingers or toes. ● *n.* a polydactyl animal.

polyester /pólli-éstər/ *n.* any of a group of condensation polymers used to form synthetic fibres such as Terylene or to make resins.

polyethene /pólli-étheen/ *n. Chem.* = POLYTHENE.

polyethylene /pólli-éthileen/ *n.* = POLYTHENE.

polygamous /pəlíggəməss/ *adj.* **1** having more than one wife or husband at the same time. **2** having more than one mate. **3** bearing some flowers with stamens only, some with pistils only, some with both, on the same or different plants. □□ **polygamic** /pólligámmik/ *adj.* **polygamist** *n.* **polygamously** *adv.* **polygamy** *n.* [Gk *polugamos* (as POLY-[1], *-gamos* marrying)]

polygene /póllijeen/ *n. Biol.* each of a group of independent genes that collectively affect a characteristic.

polygenesis /póllijénnisiss/ *n.* the (usu. postulated) origination of a race or species from several independent stocks. □□ **polygenetic** /-jinéttik/ *adj.*

polygeny /pəlíggəni/ *n.* the theory that mankind originated from several independent pairs of ancestors. □□ **polygenism** *n.* **polygenist** *n.*

polyglot /pólliglot/ *adj.* & *n.* ● *adj.* **1** of many languages. **2** (of a person) speaking or writing several languages. **3** (of a book, esp. the Bible) with the text translated into several languages. ● *n.* **1** a polyglot person. **2** a polyglot book, esp. a Bible. □□ **polyglottal** /-glótt'l/ *adj.* **polyglottic** /-glóttik/ *adj.* **polyglottism** *n.* [F *polyglotte* f. Gk *poluglōttos* (as POLY-[1], *glōtta* tongue)]

polygon /pólligən/ *n.* a plane figure with many (usu. a minimum of three) sides and angles. □ **polygon of forces** a polygon that represents by the length and direction of its sides all the forces acting on a body or point. □□ **polygonal** /pəlíggən'l/ *adj.* [LL *polygonum* f. Gk *polugōnon* (neut. adj.) (as POLY-[1] + *-gōnos* angled)]

polygonum /pəlíggənəm/ *n.* any plant of the genus *Polygonum*, with small bell-shaped flowers. Also called KNOTGRASS, KNOTWEED. [mod.L f. Gk *polugonon*]

polygraph /pólligraaf/ *n.* a machine designed to detect and record changes in physiological characteristics (e.g. rates of pulse and breathing), used esp. as a lie-detector.

polygyny /pəlíjini/ *n.* polygamy in which a man has more than one wife. □□ **polygynous** /pəlíjinəss/ *adj.* [POLY-[1] + *gyny* f. Gk *gunē* woman]

polyhedron /pólliheédrən/ *n.* (*pl.* **polyhedra** /-drə/) a solid figure with many (usu. more than six) faces. □□ **polyhedral** *adj.* **polyhedric** *adj.* [Gk *poluedron* neut. of *poluedros* (as POLY-[1], *hedra* base)]

polyhistor /póllihístər/ *n.* = POLYMATH.

polymath /póllimath/ *n.* **1** a person of much or varied learning. **2** a great scholar. □□ **polymathic** /póllimáthik/ *adj.* **polymathy** /pəlímməthi/ *n.* [Gk *polumathēs* (as POLY-[1], *math-* stem *manthanō* learn)]
■ see INTELLECTUAL *n.*

polymer /póllimər/ *n.* a compound composed of one or more large molecules that are formed from repeated units of smaller molecules. □□ **polymeric** /-mérrik/ *adj.* **polymerism** *n.* **polymerize** *v.intr.* & *tr.* (also **-ise**). **polymerization** /-rīzáysh'n/ *n.* [G f. Gk *polumeros* having many parts (as POLY-[1], *meros* share)]

polymerous /pəlímmərəss/ *adj. Biol.* having many parts.

polymorphism /póllimórfiz'm/ *n.* **1 a** *Biol.* the existence of various different forms in the successive stages of the development of an organism. **b** = PLEOMORPHISM. **2** *Chem.* = ALLOTROPY. □□ **polymorphic** *adj.* **polymorphous** *adj.*
■ □□ **polymorphic, polymorphous** see PROTEAN 1.

Polynesian /póllineézh'n/ *adj.* & *n.* ● *adj.* of or relating to Polynesia, a group of Pacific islands including New Zealand, Hawaii, Samoa, etc. ● *n.* **1 a** a native of Polynesia. **b** a person of Polynesian descent. **2** the family of languages including Maori, Hawaiian, and Samoan. [as POLY-[1] + Gk *nēsos* island]

polyneuritis /póllinyoorítiss/ *n.* any disorder that affects many of the peripheral nerves. □□ **polyneuritic** /-ríttik/ *adj.*

polynomial /póllinṓmiəl/ *n.* & *adj. Math.* ● *n.* an expression of more than two algebraic terms, esp. the sum of several terms that contain different powers of the same variable(s). ● *adj.* of or being a polynomial. [POLY-[1] after *multinomial*]

polynya /pəlínyə/ *n.* a stretch of open water surrounded by ice, esp. in the Arctic seas. [Russ. f. *pole* field]

polyp /póllip/ *n.* **1** *Zool.* an individual coelenterate. **2** *Med.* a small usu. benign growth protruding from a mucous membrane. [F *polype* (as POLYPUS)]

polypary /pólliрəri/ *n.* (*pl.* **-ies**) the common stem or support of a colony of polyps. [mod.L *polyparium* (as POLYPUS)]

polypeptide /póllipéptīd/ *n. Biochem.* a peptide formed by the combination of about ten or more amino acids. [G *Polypeptid* (as POLY-[2], PEPTONE)]

polyphagous /pəlíffəgəss/ *adj. Zool.* able to feed on various kinds of food.

polyphase /póllifayz/ *adj. Electr.* (of a device or circuit) designed to supply or use simultaneously several alternating currents of the same voltage but with different phases.

polyphone /póllifōn/ *n. Phonet.* a symbol or letter that represents several different sounds.

polyphonic /póllifónnik/ *adj.* **1** *Mus.* (of vocal music etc.) in two or more relatively independent parts; contrapuntal. **2** *Phonet.* (of a letter etc.) representing more than one sound. □□ **polyphonically** *adv.* [Gk *poluphōnos* (as POLY-[1], *phōnē* voice, sound)]

polyphony /pəlíffəni/ *n.* (*pl.* **-ies**) **1** *Mus.* **a** a polyphonic style in musical composition; counterpoint. **b** a composition written in this style. **2** *Philol.* the symbolization of different vocal sounds by the same letter or character. ▫▫ **polyphonous** *adj.*

polypi *pl.* of POLYPUS.

polyploid /pólliployd/ *n.* & *adj.* *Biol.* ● *n.* a nucleus or organism that contains more than two sets of chromosomes. ● *adj.* of or being a polyploid. ▫▫ **polyploidy** *n.* [G (as POLY-[1], -PLOID)]

polypod /póllipod/ *adj.* & *n.* *Zool.* ● *adj.* having many feet. ● *n.* a polypod animal. [F *polypode* (adj.) f. Gk (as POLYPUS)]

polypody /póllipōdi/ *n.* (*pl.* **-ies**) any fern of the genus *Polypodium*, usu. found in woods growing on trees, walls, and stones. [ME f. L *polypodium* f. Gk *polupodion* (as POLYPUS)]

polypoid /póllipoyd/ *adj.* of or like a polyp. ▫▫ **polypous** /-pəss/ *adj.*

polypropene /pólliprṓpeen/ *n.* = POLYPROPYLENE.

polypropylene /pólliprṓpileen/ *n.* *Chem.* any of various polymers of propylene including thermoplastic materials used for films, fibres, or moulding materials. Also called POLYPROPENE.

polypus /póllipəss/ *n.* (*pl.* **polypi** /-pī/ or **polypuses**) *Med.* = POLYP 2. [ME f. L *polypus* f. Gk *pōlupos*, *polupous* cuttlefish, polyp (as POLY-[1], *pous podos* foot)]

polysaccharide /póllisákkərid/ *n.* any of a group of carbohydrates whose molecules consist of long chains of monosaccharides.

polysemy /pólliseémi/ *n.* *Philol.* the existence of many meanings (of a word etc.). ▫▫ **polysemic** /-seémik/ *adj.* **polysemous** /-seéməss/ *adj.* [POLY-[1] + Gk *sēma* sign]

polystyrene /póllistī́reen/ *n.* a thermoplastic polymer of styrene, usu. hard and colourless or expanded with a gas to produce a lightweight rigid white substance, used for insulation and in packaging.

polysyllabic /póllisilábbik/ *adj.* **1** (of a word) having many syllables. **2** characterized by the use of words of many syllables. ▫▫ **polysyllabically** *adv.*

polysyllable /póllisilləb'l/ *n.* a polysyllabic word.

polytechnic /pólliteknik/ *n.* & *adj.* ● *n.* an institution of higher education offering courses in many (esp. vocational) subjects at degree level or below. ● *adj.* dealing with or devoted to various vocational or technical subjects. [F *polytechnique* f. Gk *polutekhnos* (as POLY-[1] *tekhnē* art)]
■ *adj.* see TECHNICAL 1.

polytetrafluoroethylene /póllitétrəflóorō-éthileen/ *n.* *Chem.* a tough translucent polymer resistant to chemicals and used to coat cooking utensils etc. ¶ Abbr.: **PTFE**. [POLY-[2] + TETRA- + FLUORO- + ETHYLENE]

polytheism /póllitheé-iz'm/ *n.* the belief in or worship of more than one god. ▫▫ **polytheist** *n.* **polytheistic** /-ístik/ *adj.* [F *polythéisme* f. Gk *polutheos* of many gods (as POLY-[1], *theos* god)]

polythene /póllitheen/ *n.* *Chem.* a tough light thermoplastic polymer of ethylene, usu. translucent and flexible or opaque and rigid, used for packaging and insulating materials. Also called POLYETHYLENE, POLYETHENE.

polytonality /póllitōnálliti/ *n.* *Mus.* the simultaneous use of two or more keys in a composition. ▫▫ **polytonal** /-tṓn'l/ *adj.*

polyunsaturated /pólliunsáchəraytid, -sátyooraytid/ *adj.* *Chem.* (of a compound, esp. a fat or oil molecule) containing several double or triple bonds and therefore capable of further reaction.

polyurethane /pólliyóorəthayn/ *n.* any polymer containing the urethane group, used in adhesives, paints, plastics, rubbers, foams, etc.

polyvalent /pólliváylənt/ *adj.* *Chem.* having a valency of more than two, or several valencies. ▫▫ **polyvalence** *n.*

polyvinyl acetate /póllivī́nil/ *n.* *Chem.* a soft plastic polymer used in paints and adhesives. ¶ Abbr.: **PVA**.

polyvinyl chloride /póllivī́nil/ *n.* a tough transparent solid polymer of vinyl chloride, easily coloured and used for a wide variety of products including pipes, flooring, etc. ¶ Abbr.: **PVC**.

polyzoan /póllizṓən/ *n.* = BRYOZOAN.

pom /pom/ *n.* **1** a Pomeranian dog. **2** *Austral.* & *NZ sl. offens.* = POMMY. [abbr.]

pomace /púmmiss/ *n.* **1** the mass of crushed apples in cider-making before or after the juice is pressed out. **2** the refuse of fish etc. after the oil has been extracted, generally used as a fertilizer. [ME f. med.L *pomacium* cider f. L *pomum* apple]

pomade /pəmaád/ *n.* & *v.* ● *n.* scented dressing for the hair and the skin of the head. ● *v.tr.* anoint with pomade. [F *pommade* f. It. *pomata* f. med.L f. L *pomum* apple (from which it was orig. made)]

pomander /pəmándər/ *n.* **1** a ball of mixed aromatic substances placed in a cupboard etc. or *hist.* carried in a box, bag, etc. as a protection against infection. **2** a (usu. spherical) container for this. **3** a spiced orange etc. similarly used. [earlier *pom(e)amber* f. AF f. OF *pome d'embre* f. med.L *pomum de ambra* apple of ambergris]

pomatum /pəmaátəm/ *n.* & *v.tr.* = POMADE. [mod.L f. L *pomum* apple]

pome /pōm/ *n.* a firm-fleshed fruit in which the carpels from the central core enclose the seeds, e.g. the apple, pear, and quince. ▫▫ **pomiferous** /pəmíffərəss/ *adj.* [ME f. OF ult. f. *poma* pl. of L *pomum* fruit, apple]

pomegranate /pómmigrannit, pómgrannit/ *n.* **1** **a** an orange-sized fruit with a tough golden-orange outer skin containing many seeds in a red pulp. **b** the tree bearing this fruit, *Punica granatum*, native to N. Africa and W. Asia. **2** an ornamental representation of a pomegranate. [ME f. OF *pome grenate* (as POME, L *granatum* having many seeds f. *granum* seed)]

pomelo /púmməlō/ *n.* (*pl.* **-os**) **1** = SHADDOCK. **2** *US* = GRAPEFRUIT. [19th c.: orig. unkn.]

Pomeranian /pómməráyniən/ *n.* **1** a small dog with long silky hair, a pointed muzzle, and pricked ears. **2** this breed. [*Pomerania* in Germany and Poland]

pomfret /pómfrit/ *n.* **1** any of various fish of the family Stromateidae of the Indian and Pacific Oceans. **2** a dark-coloured deep-bodied marine fish, *Brama brama*, used as food. [app. f. Port. *pampo*]

pomfret-cake /púmfrit, póm-/ *n.* (also **Pontefract-cake** /póntifrakt/) *Brit.* a small round flat liquorice sweetmeat orig. made at Pontefract (earlier *Pomfret*) in Yorkshire.

pomiculture /pómmikulchər/ *n.* fruit-growing. [L *pomum* fruit + CULTURE]

pommel /púmm'l/ *n.* & *v.* ● *n.* **1** a knob, esp. at the end of a sword-hilt. **2** the upward projecting front part of a saddle. ● *v.tr.* (**pommelled, pommelling**; *US* **pommeled, pommeling**) = PUMMEL. ▫ **pommel horse** a vaulting horse fitted with a pair of curved handgrips . [ME f. OF *pomel* f. Rmc *pomellum* (unrecorded), dimin. of L *pomum* fruit, apple]

pommy /pómmi/ *n.* (also **pommie**) (*pl.* **-ies**) *Austral.* & *NZ sl. offens.* a British person, esp. a recent immigrant. [20th c.: orig. uncert.]

pomology /pəmólləji/ *n.* the science of fruit-growing. ▫▫ **pomological** /pómməlójik'l/ *adj.* **pomologist** *n.* [L *pomum* fruit + -LOGY]

pomp /pomp/ *n.* **1** a splendid display; splendour. **2** (often in *pl.*) vainglory (*the pomps and vanities of this wicked world*). [ME f. OF *pompe* f. L *pompa* f. Gk *pompē* procession, pomp f. *pempō* send]
■ **1** glory, grandeur, magnificence, splendour, show, pageantry, ceremony, spectacle, brilliance, ceremoniousness. **2** see VANITY 1, OSTENTATION.

pompadour /pómpədoor/ *n.* a woman's hairstyle with the hair in a high turned-back roll round the face. [f. Marquise de *Pompadour*, the mistress of Louis XV of France d. 1764]

pompano /pompaánō/ *n.* (*pl.* **-os**) any of various fish of the family Carangidae or Stromateidae of the Atlantic and Pacific Oceans, used as food. [Sp. *pámpano*]

pom-pom /pómpom/ *n.* an automatic quick-firing gun esp. on a ship. [imit.]

pompon /pómpon/ *n.* (also **pompom**) **1** an ornamental ball or bobble made of wool, silk, or ribbons, usu. worn on women's or children's hats or clothing. **2** the round tuft on a soldier's cap, the front of a shako, etc. **3** (often *attrib.*) a dahlia or chrysanthemum with small tightly-clustered petals. [F, of unkn. orig.]

pompous /pómpəss/ *adj.* **1** self-important, affectedly grand or solemn. **2** (of language) pretentious; unduly grand in style. **3** *archaic* magnificent; splendid. □□ **pomposity** /pompóssiti/ *n.* (*pl.* **-ies**). **pompously** *adv.* **pompousness** *n.* [ME f. OF *pompeux* f. LL *pomposus* (as POMP)]
■ **1** self-important, vain, proud, arrogant, haughty, overbearing, conceited, egotistical, boastful, braggart, snobbish, magisterial, imperious, pontifical, stuffy, affected, high-hat, *colloq.* uppity, highfalutin, stuck-up, hoity-toity, la-di-da, *literary* vainglorious, *Brit. sl.* toffee-nosed. **2** bombastic, pretentious, ostentatious, showy, grandiose, flowery, inflated, grandiloquent, pedantic, fustian, orotund, ornate, embroidered, flatulent, turgid, high-flown, euphuistic, *colloq.* windy.

'pon /pon/ *prep. archaic* = UPON. [abbr.]

ponce /ponss/ *n.* & *v. Brit. sl.* ● *n.* **1** a man who lives off a prostitute's earnings; a pimp. **2** *offens.* a homosexual; an effeminate man. ● *v.intr.* act as a ponce. □ **ponce about** move about effeminately or ineffectually. □□ **poncey** *adj.* (also **poncy**) (in sense 2 of *n.*). [perh. f. POUNCE[1]]
■ *n.* **1** see PIMP *n.* □□ **poncey** see EFFEMINATE.

poncho /pónchō/ *n.* (*pl.* **-os**) **1** a S. American cloak made of a blanket-like piece of cloth with a slit in the middle for the head. **2** a garment in this style. [S.Amer. Sp., f. Araucan]
■ see CLOAK *n.* 1.

pond /pond/ *n.* & *v.* ● *n.* **1** a fairly small body of still water formed naturally or by hollowing or embanking. **2** *joc.* the sea. ● *v.* **1** *tr.* hold back, dam up (a stream etc.). **2** *intr.* form a pond. □ **pond-life** animals (esp. invertebrates) that live in ponds. [ME var. of POUND[3]]
■ *n.* **1** pool, tarn, lake, *archaic or poet.* mere. **2** see SEA 1.

ponder /póndər/ *v.* **1** *tr.* weigh mentally; think over; consider. **2** *intr.* (usu. foll. by *on*, *over*) think; muse. [ME f. OF *ponderer* f. L *ponderare* f. *pondus -eris* weight]
■ brood over *or* upon, mull over, deliberate over, meditate upon *or* on, think over *or* on *or* about, ruminate over, chew over, reflect on *or* over, *literary* muse over *or* on; contemplate, consider, cogitate.

ponderable /póndərəb'l/ *adj. literary* having appreciable weight or significance. □□ **ponderability** /-bílliti/ *n.* [LL *ponderabilis* (as PONDER)]
■ see TANGIBLE 2.

ponderation /póndəráysh'n/ *n. literary* the act or an instance of weighing, balancing, or considering. [L *ponderatio* (as PONDER)]

ponderosa /póndərṓsə/ *n. US* **1** a N. American pine-tree, *Pinus ponderosa*. **2** the red timber of this tree. [mod.L, fem. of L *ponderosus*: see PONDEROUS]

ponderous /póndərəss/ *adj.* **1** heavy; unwieldy. **2** laborious. **3** (of style etc.) dull; tedious. □□ **ponderosity** /-róssiti/ *n.* **ponderously** *adv.* **ponderousness** *n.* [ME f. L *ponderosus* f. *pondus -eris* weight]
■ **1** weighty, unwieldy, heavy, cumbersome, cumbrous, elephantine. **2** tiresome, difficult; see also LABORIOUS 1. **3** laboured, turgid, dull, pedestrian, stilted, inflated, wordy, verbose, prolix, pompous, grandiloquent, overdone, *colloq.* windy; see also TEDIOUS.

pondweed /póndweed/ *n.* any of various aquatic plants, esp. of the genus *Potamogeton*, growing in still or running water.

pone[1] /pōn/ *n. US* **1** unleavened maize bread, esp. as made by N. American Indians. **2** a fine light bread made with milk, eggs, etc. **3** a cake or loaf of this. [Algonquian, = bread]

pone[2] /pṓni/ *n.* the dealer's opponent in two-handed card games. [L, 2nd sing. imper. of *ponere* place]

pong /pong/ *n.* & *v. Brit. colloq.* ● *n.* an unpleasant smell. ● *v.intr.* stink. □□ **pongy** /póngi/ *adj.* (**pongier, pongiest**). [20th c.: orig. unkn.]
■ *n.* see SMELL *n.* 3. ● *v.* see SMELL *v.* 5. □□ **pongy** see STINKING *adj.* 1.

pongal /póngg'l/ *n.* **1** the Tamil New Year festival at which new rice is cooked. **2** a dish of cooked rice. [Tamil *poṅkal* boiling]

pongee /ponjeé, pun-/ *n.* **1** a soft usu. unbleached type of Chinese silk fabric. **2** an imitation of this in cotton etc. [perh. f. Chin. dial. *pun-chī* own loom, i.e. home-made]

pongid /pónjid/ *n.* & *adj.* ● *n.* any ape of the family Pongidae, including gorillas, chimpanzees, and orang-utans. ● *adj.* of or relating to this family. [mod.L *Pongidae* f. *Pongo* the genus-name: see PONGO[1]]

pongo[1] /pónggō/ *n.* (*pl.* **-os**) **1** an orang-utan. **2** *Naut. sl.* a soldier. [Congolese *mpongo*, orig. of African apes]

pongo[2] /pónggō/ *n.* (*pl.* **-os**) *Austral.* & *NZ sl. offens.* an Englishman. [20th c.: orig. unkn.]

poniard /pónyərd/ *n. literary* a small slim dagger. [F *poignard* f. OF *poignal* f. med.L *pugnale* f. L *pugnus* fist]
■ see DAGGER 1.

pons /ponz/ *n.* (*pl.* **pontes** /pónteez/) *Anat.* (in full **pons Varolii**) /vərṓli-ī/ the part of the brain stem that links the medulla oblongata and the thalamus. □ **pons asinorum** /ássinórəm/ any difficult proposition, orig. a rule of geometry from Euclid ('bridge of asses'). [L, = bridge: *Varolii* f. C. *Varoli*, It. anatomist d. 1575]

pont /pont/ *n. S.Afr.* a flat-bottomed ferry-boat. [Du.]

Pontefract-cake var. of POMFRET-CAKE.

pontes *pl.* of PONS.

pontifex /póntifeks/ *n.* (*pl.* **pontifices** /pontíffiseez/) **1** = PONTIFF. **2** *Rom. Antiq.* a member of the principal college of priests in Rome. □ **Pontifex Maximus** the head of this. [L *pontifex -ficis* f. *pons pontis* bridge + *-fex* f. *facere* make]

pontiff /póntif/ *n. RC Ch.* (in full **sovereign** or **supreme pontiff**) the Pope. [F *pontife* (as PONTIFEX)]

pontifical /pontíffik'l/ *adj.* & *n.* ● *adj.* **1** *RC Ch.* of or befitting a pontiff; papal. **2** pompously dogmatic; with an attitude of infallibility. ● *n.* **1** an office-book of the Western Church containing rites to be performed by the Pope or bishops. **2** (in *pl.*) the vestments and insignia of a bishop, cardinal, or abbot. □ **pontifical mass** a high mass, usu. celebrated by a cardinal, bishop, etc. □□ **pontifically** *adv.* [ME f. F *pontifical* or L *pontificalis* (as PONTIFEX)]
■ *adj.* **2** see DOGMATIC.

pontificate *v.* & *n.* ● *v.intr.* /pontíffikayt/ **1 a** play the pontiff; pretend to be infallible. **b** be pompously dogmatic. **2** *RC Ch.* officiate as bishop, esp. at mass. ● *n.* /pontíffikət/ **1** the office of pontifex, bishop, or pope. **2** the period of this. [L *pontificatus* (as PONTIFEX)]
■ *v.* **1** see PREACH 2, RANT *v.* 2, 3.

pontifices *pl.* of PONTIFEX.

pontoon[1] /pontóon/ *n. Brit.* **1** a card-game in which players try to acquire cards with a face value totalling 21 and no more. **2** = NATURAL *n.* 4a. [prob. corrupt.]

pontoon[2] /pontóon/ *n.* & *v.* ● *n.* **1** a flat-bottomed boat. **2 a** each of several boats, hollow metal cylinders, etc., used to support a temporary bridge. **b** a bridge so formed; a floating platform. **3** = CAISSON 1,2. ● *v.tr.* cross (a river) by means of pontoons. [F *ponton* f. L *ponto -onis* f. *pons pontis* bridge]
■ *n.* **1** punt. **2 a** float.

pony /pṓni/ *n.* (*pl.* **-ies**) **1** a horse of any small breed. **2** a small drinking-glass. **3** (in *pl.*) *sl.* racehorses. **4** *Brit. sl.* £25. □ **pony-tail** a person's hair drawn back, tied, and hanging down like a pony's tail. **pony-trekker** a person who travels across country on a pony for pleasure. **pony-trekking** this as a hobby or activity. [perh. f. *poulney* (unrecorded) f. F *poulenet* dimin. of *poulain* foal]

pooch /po͞och/ *n.* esp. *US sl.* a dog. [20th c.: orig. unkn.]

poodle /po͞od'l/ *n.* **1 a** a dog of a breed with a curly coat that is usually clipped. **b** this breed. **2** a lackey or servile follower. [G *Pudel(hund)* f. LG *pud(d)eln* splash in water: cf. PUDDLE]

poof /po͝of, po͞of/ *n.* (also **pouf, poove** /po͞ov/) *Brit. sl. derog.* **1** an effeminate man. **2** a male homosexual. □□ **poofy** /po͝offi/ *adj.* [19th c.: cf. PUFF in sense 'braggart']

poofter /po͝oftər, po͞of-/ *n. sl. derog.* = POOF.

pooh /po͞o/ *int.* & *n.* (**poo**) ● *int.* expressing impatience or contempt. ● *n. sl.* **1** excrement. **2** an act of defecation. [imit.]

Pooh-Bah /po͞obaa/ *n.* (also **pooh-bah**) a holder of many offices at once. [a character in W. S. Gilbert's *The Mikado* (1885)]

pooh-pooh /po͞opo͞o/ *v.tr.* express contempt for; ridicule; dismiss (an idea etc.) scornfully. [redupl. of POOH]
■ see BELITTLE, DISMISS 4.

pooja var. of PUJA.

pooka /po͞okə/ *n. Ir.* a hobgoblin. [Ir. *púca*]

pool[1] /po͞ol/ *n.* & *v.* ● *n.* **1** a small body of still water, usu. of natural formation. **2** a small shallow body of any liquid. **3** = *swimming-pool* (see SWIM). **4** a deep place in a river. ● *v.* **1** *tr.* form into a pool. **2** *intr.* (of blood) become static. [OE *pōl*, MLG, MDu. *pōl*, OHG *pfuol* f. WG]
■ *n.* **1** pond, lake, tarn, *archaic or poet.* mere.

pool[2] /po͞ol/ *n.* & *v.* ● *n.* **1 a** (often *attrib.*) a common supply of persons, vehicles, commodities, etc. for sharing by a group of people (*a typing pool*; *a pool car*). **b** a group of persons sharing duties etc. **2 a** the collective amount of players' stakes in gambling etc. **b** a receptacle for this. **3 a** a joint commercial venture, esp. an arrangement between competing parties to fix prices and share business to eliminate competition. **b** the common funding for this. **4 a** *US* a game on a billiard-table with usu. 16 balls. **b** *Brit.* a game on a billiard-table in which each player has a ball of a different colour with which he tries to pocket the others in fixed order, the winner taking all of the stakes. **5** a group of contestants who compete against each other in a tournament for the right to advance to the next round. ● *v.tr.* **1** put (resources etc.) into a common fund. **2** share (things) in common. **3** (of transport or organizations etc.) share (traffic, receipts). **4** *Austral. sl.* **a** involve (a person) in a scheme etc., often by deception. **b** implicate, inform on. □ **the pools** *Brit.* = *football pool.* [F *poule* (= hen) in same sense: assoc. with POOL[1]]
■ *n.* **2 a** pot, jackpot, kitty, stakes, bank, purse. **3 a** syndicate, combine, cartel, trust, group, consortium. ● *v.* **1** combine, merge, consolidate, amalgamate. **4 b** see INFORM 2.

poolroom /po͞olro͞om, -ro͝om/ *n. US* **1** a betting shop. **2** a place for playing pool.

poon[1] /po͞on/ *n.* any E. Indian tree of the genus *Calophyllum.* □ **poon oil** an oil from the seeds of this tree, used in medicine and for lamps. [Sinh. *pūna*]

poon[2] / po͞on/ *n.* esp. *Austral. sl.* a simple or foolish person. [orig. unkn.]

poop[1] /po͞op/ *n.* & *v.* ● *n.* the stern of a ship; the aftermost and highest deck. ● *v.tr.* **1** (of a wave) break over the stern of (a ship). **2** (of a ship) receive (a wave) over the stern. [ME f. OF *pupe, pope* ult. f. L *puppis*]

poop[2] /po͞op/ *v.tr.* (esp. as **pooped** *adj.*) *US colloq.* exhaust; tire out. [20th c.: orig. unkn.]
■ (**pooped**) see *exhausted* (EXHAUST).

poop[3] /po͞op/ *n. US sl.* up to date or inside information; the low-down, the gen. [20th c.: orig. unkn.]

poor /poor/ *adj.* **1** lacking adequate money or means to live comfortably. **2 a** (foll. by *in*) deficient in (a possession or quality) (*the poor in spirit*). **b** (of soil, ore, etc.) unproductive. **3 a** scanty, inadequate (*a poor crop*). **b** less good than is usual or expected (*poor visibility*; *is a poor driver*; *in poor health*). **c** paltry; inferior (*poor condition*; *came a poor third*). **4 a** deserving pity or sympathy; unfortunate (*you poor thing*). **b** with reference to a dead person (*as my poor father used to say*). **5** spiritless; despicable (*is a poor creature*). **6** often *iron.* or *joc.* humble; insignificant (*in my poor opinion*). □ **poor-box** a collection-box, esp. in church, for the relief of the poor. **poor law** *hist.* a law relating to the support of paupers. **poor man's** an inferior or cheaper substitute for. **poor man's weather-glass** the pimpernel. **poor-rate** *hist.* a rate or assessment for relief or support of the poor. **poor relation** an inferior or subordinate member of a family or any other group. **poor-spirited** timid; cowardly. **poor White** *offens.* a member of a socially inferior group of White people. **take a poor view of** regard with disfavour or pessimism. [ME & OF *pov(e)re, poure* f. L *pauper*]
■ **1** needy, destitute, indigent, penniless, poverty-stricken, impoverished, badly off, necessitous, impecunious, financially embarrassed, down and out, hard up, *colloq.* on one's uppers, *Brit. sl.* skint; see also BROKE. **2 a** (*poor in*) deficient *or* low in; lacking (in), wanting. **b** barren, unproductive, unfruitful, infertile, sterile; depleted, exhausted, impoverished, low-yielding. **3 a** low, skimpy, meagre, scant, scanty, inadequate, insufficient, sparse. **b, c** bad, awful, inadequate, unsatisfactory, unacceptable, inefficient, amateurish, unprofessional, inferior, paltry, inconsequential, second-rate, third-rate, low-grade, shoddy, mediocre, defective, faulty, flawed, substandard, sorry, slipshod, below *or* under par, *colloq.* lousy. **4 a** unfortunate, unlucky, pathetic, luckless, pitiful, pitiable, ill-fated, miserable, wretched, hapless. **6** see INFERIOR *adj.* 1, 2. □ **poor-spirited** see COWARDLY *adj.* **take a poor view of** see DISAPPROVE.

poorhouse /poorhowss/ *n. hist.* = WORKHOUSE 1.

poorly /poorli/ *adv.* & *adj.* ● *adv.* **1** scantily; defectively. **2** with no great success. **3** meanly; contemptibly. ● *predic.adj.* unwell.
■ *adv.* **1** defectively, scantily, skimpily, badly, inadequately, unsatisfactorily, incompetently, inexpertly, improperly, crudely, shoddily, unprofessionally, amateurishly, inefficiently. ● *predic.adj.* unwell, indisposed, ailing, sick, off-colour, indisposed, *colloq.* under the weather; see also ILL *adj.*

poorness /poorniss/ *n.* **1** defectiveness. **2** the lack of some good quality or constituent.

poove var. of POOF.

POP *abbr.* Post Office Preferred (size of envelopes etc.).

pop[1] /pop/ *n.*, *v.*, & *adv.* ● *n.* **1** a sudden sharp explosive sound as of a cork when drawn. **2** *colloq.* an effervescent sweet drink. ● *v.* (**popped, popping**) **1** *intr.* & *tr.* make or cause to make a pop. **2** *intr.* & *tr.* (foll. by *in, out, up, down,* etc.) go, move, come, or put unexpectedly or in a quick or hasty manner (*pop out to the shops*; *pop in for a visit*; *pop it on your head*). **3 a** *intr.* & *tr.* burst, making a popping sound. **b** *tr.* heat (popcorn etc.) until it pops. **4** *intr.* (often foll. by *at*) *colloq.* fire a gun (at birds etc.). **5** *tr. sl.* pawn. **6** *tr. sl.* take or inject (a drug etc.). **7** *intr.* (often foll. by *up*) (of a cricket-ball) rise sharply off the pitch. ● *adv.* with the sound of a pop (*heard it go pop*). □ **in pop** *Brit. sl.* in pawn. **pop off** *colloq.* **1** die. **2** quietly slip away (cf. sense 2 of *v.*). **pop one's clogs** *sl.* die. **pop the question** *colloq.* propose marriage. **pop-shop** *Brit. sl.* a pawnbroker's shop. **pop-up 1** (of a toaster etc.) operating so as to move the object (toast when ready etc.) quickly upwards. **2** (of a book, greetings card, etc.) containing three-dimensional figures, illustrations, etc., that rise up when the page is turned. **3** *Computing* (of a menu) able to be superimposed on the screen being worked on and suppressed rapidly. [ME: imit.]
■ *n.* **1** explosion, bang, report, crack, snap. **2** fizzy *or* carbonated drink, *Brit.* mineral(s), *esp. US* soda. ● *v.* **1, 3** burst; explode, bang, go off. **2** nip, run; (*pop in* or *by*) visit, pay a visit, stop (by), call, come by, *colloq.* drop in *or* by. **4** open fire, shoot, *colloq.* blast. **5** pledge, *esp. US colloq.* hock; see also PAWN[2] *v.* □ **pop off 1** see DIE 1. **pop one's clogs** see DIE 1. **pop the question** propose, ask for a person's hand (in marriage).

pop[2] /pop/ *adj.* & *n. colloq.* ● *adj.* **1** in a popular or modern style. **2** performing popular music etc. (*pop group*; *pop star*). ● *n.* **1** pop music. **2** a pop record or song (*top of the pops*). □ **pop art** art based on modern popular culture and the mass media, esp. as a critical comment on traditional fine art values. **pop culture** commercial culture based on popular taste. **pop festival** a festival at which popular music etc. is performed. [abbr.]

pop[3] /pop/ *n.* esp. *US colloq.* father. [abbr. of POPPA]

pop. *abbr.* population.

popadam var. of POPPADAM.

popcorn /pópkorn/ *n.* **1** Indian corn which bursts open when heated. **2** these kernels when popped.

pope[1] /pōp/ *n.* **1** (as title usu. **Pope**) the head of the Roman Catholic Church (also called the Bishop of Rome). **2** the head of the Coptic Church. **3** = RUFF[2]. □ **pope's eye 1** a lymphatic gland surrounded with fat in the middle of a sheep's leg. **2** *Sc.* a cut of steak. □□ **popedom** *n.* **popeless** *adj.* [OE f. eccl.L *pāpa* bishop, pope f. eccl.Gk *papas* = Gk *pappas* father: cf. PAPA]

pope[2] /pōp/ *n.* a parish priest of the Orthodox Church in Russia etc. [Russ. *pop* f. OSlav. *popŭ* f. WG f. eccl.Gk (as POPE[1])]

popery /pṓpəri/ *n. derog.* the papal system; the Roman Catholic Church.

pop-eyed /póppīd/ *adj. colloq.* **1** having bulging eyes. **2** wide-eyed (with surprise etc.).

popgun /pópgun/ *n.* **1** a child's toy gun which shoots a pellet etc. by the compression of air with a piston. **2** *derog.* an inefficient firearm.

popinjay /póppinjay/ *n.* **1** a fop, a conceited person, a coxcomb. **2 a** *archaic* a parrot. **b** *hist.* a figure of a parrot on a pole as a mark to shoot at. [ME f. AF *papeiaye*, OF *papingay* etc. f. Sp. *papagayo* f. Arab. *babaġā*: assim. to JAY]
■ **1** see DUDE 1.

popish /pṓpish/ *adj. derog.* Roman Catholic. □□ **popishly** *adv.*

poplar /póplər/ *n.* **1** any tree of the genus *Populus*, with a usu. rapidly growing trunk and tremulous leaves. **2** *US* = *tulip-tree*. [ME f. AF *popler*, OF *poplier* f. *pople* f. L *populus*]

poplin /póplin/ *n.* a plain-woven fabric usu. of cotton, with a corded surface. [obs. F *papeline* perh. f. It. *papalina* (fem.) PAPAL, f. the papal town Avignon where it was made]

popliteal /poplíttiəl/ *adj.* of the hollow at the back of the knee. [mod.L *popliteus* f. L *poples -itis* this hollow]

poppa /póppə/ *n. US colloq.* father (esp. as a child's word). [var. of PAPA]

poppadam /póppədəm/ *n.* (also **poppadom, popadam**) *Ind.* a thin, crisp, spiced bread eaten with curry etc. [Tamil *pappaḍam*]

popper /póppər/ *n.* **1** *Brit. colloq.* a press-stud. **2** a person or thing that pops. **3** *colloq.* a small vial of amyl nitrite used for inhalation.

poppet /póppit/ *n.* **1** *Brit. colloq.* (esp. as a term of endearment) a small or dainty person. **2** (in full **poppet-head**) the head of a lathe. **3** a small square piece of wood fitted inside the gunwale or washstrake of a boat. □ **poppet-head** *Brit.* the frame at the top of a mine-shaft supporting pulleys for the ropes used in hoisting. **poppet-valve** *Engin.* a mushroom-shaped valve, lifted bodily from its seat rather than hinged. [ME *popet(te)*, ult. f. L *pup(p)a*: cf. PUPPET]
■ **1** see DEAR *n.*

popping-crease /póppingkreess/ *n. Cricket* a line four feet in front of and parallel to the wicket, within which the batsman must keep the bat or one foot grounded to avoid the risk of being stumped. [POP[1], perh. in obs. sense 'strike']

popple /pópp'l/ *v.* & *n.* ● *v.intr.* (of water) tumble about, toss to and fro. ● *n.* the act or an instance of rolling, tossing, or rippling of water. □□ **popply** *adj.* [ME prob. f. MDu. *popelen* murmur, quiver, of imit. orig.]

poppy /póppi/ *n.* (*pl.* **-ies**) any plant of the genus *Papaver*, with showy often red flowers and a milky sap with narcotic properties. □ **Poppy Day** = *Remembrance Sunday*. **poppy-head 1** the seed capsule of the poppy. **2** an ornamental top on the end of a church pew. □□ **poppied** *adj.* [OE *popig*, *papæg*, etc. f. med.L *papauum* f. L *papaver*]

poppycock /póppikok/ *n. sl.* nonsense. [Du. dial. *pappekak*]
■ see RUBBISH *n.* 3.

popsy /pópsi/ *n.* (also **popsie**) (*pl.* **-ies**) *colloq.* (usu. as a term of endearment) a young woman. [shortening of POPPET]
■ see WOMAN 1, DEAR *n.*

populace /pópyooləss/ *n.* **1** the common people. **2** *derog.* the rabble. [F f. It. *popolaccio* f. *popolo* people + *-accio* pejorative suffix]
■ **1** (common *or* ordinary) people, masses, commonalty, commonality, (general) public, commoners, multitude, *hoi polloi*, peasantry, proletariat, common folk, working class, rank and file. **2** rabble, riff-raff, *canaille*, *colloq.* the great unwashed, *colloq. usu. derog.* the plebs, *usu. derog.* mob, *derog.* ragtag and bobtail.

popular /pópyoolər/ *adj.* **1** liked or admired by many people or by a specified group (*popular teachers*; *a popular hero*). **2 a** of or carried on by the general public (*popular meetings*). **b** prevalent among the general public (*popular discontent*). **3** adapted to the understanding, taste, or means of the people (*popular science*; *popular medicine*). □ **popular front** a party or coalition representing left-wing elements. **popular music** songs, folk tunes, etc., appealing to popular tastes. □□ **popularism** *n.* **popularity** /-lárriti/ *n.* **popularly** *adv.* [ME f. AF *populer*, OF *populeir* or L *popularis* f. *populus* people]
■ **1** favourite, favoured, well-received, well-liked; see also FASHIONABLE. **3** lay, non-professional; public, general, universal, average, everyday, ordinary, common. □□ **popularity** acceptance, reputation; vogue, trend, stylishness, *colloq. often derog.* trendiness. **popularly** commonly, generally, ordinarily, usually, universally, widely, regularly, customarily, habitually.

popularize /pópyooləriz/ *v.tr.* (also **-ise**) **1** make popular. **2** cause (a person, principle, etc.) to be generally known or liked. **3** present (a technical subject, specialized vocabulary, etc.) in a popular or readily understandable form. □□ **popularization** /-záysh'n/ *n.* **popularizer** *n.*

populate /pópyoolayt/ *v.tr.* **1** inhabit; form the population of (a town, country, etc.). **2** supply with inhabitants; people (*a densely populated district*). [med.L *populare populat-* (as PEOPLE)]
■ **1** inhabit, reside in, live in, occupy, *literary* dwell in. **2** colonize, settle, people.

population /pópyooláysh'n/ *n.* **1 a** the inhabitants of a place, country, etc. referred to collectively. **b** any specified group within this (*the Irish population of Liverpool*). **2** the total number of any of these (*a population of eight million*; *the seal population*). **3** the act or process of supplying with inhabitants (*the population of forest areas*). **4** *Statistics* any finite or infinite collection of items under consideration. □ **population explosion** a sudden large increase of population. [LL *populatio* (as PEOPLE)]
■ **1 a** people, populace, inhabitants, residents, natives, citizenry, citizens, folk, *poet.* denizens. **3** colonization, settlement, settling, populating.

populist /pópyoolist/ *n.* & *adj.* ● *n.* a member or adherent of a political party seeking support mainly from the ordinary people. ● *adj.* of or relating to such a political party. □□ **populism** *n.* **populistic** /-lístik/ *adj.* [L *populus* people]

populous /pópyooləss/ *adj.* thickly inhabited. □□ **populously** *adv.* **populousness** *n.* [ME f. LL *populosus* (as PEOPLE)]
■ crowded, heavily populated, teeming, thronged, jam-packed, packed.

porbeagle /pórbeeg'l/ *n.* a large shark, *Lamna nasus*, having a pointed snout. [18th-c. Corn. dial., of unkn. orig.]

porcelain /pórsəlin/ *n.* **1** a hard vitrified translucent ceramic. **2** objects made of this. □ **porcelain clay** kaolin. **porcelain-shell** cowrie. □□ **porcellaneous** /pórsəláyniəss/

adj. **porcellanous** /porsélənəss/ *adj.* [F *porcelaine* cowrie, porcelain f. It. *porcellana* f. *porcella* dimin. of *porca* sow (a cowrie being perh. likened to a sow's vulva) f. L *porca* fem. of *porcus* pig]

■ **2** see POTTERY 1.

porch /porch/ *n.* **1** a covered shelter for the entrance of a building. **2** *US* a veranda. **3** (**the Porch**) = *the Stoa* (see STOA 2). □□ **porched** *adj.* **porchless** *adj.* [ME f. OF *porche* f. L *porticus* (transl. Gk *stoa*) f. *porta* passage]

porcine /pórsīn/ *adj.* of or like pigs. [F *porcin* or f. L *porcinus* f. *porcus* pig]

porcupine /pórkyoopīn/ *n.* **1** any rodent of the family Hystricidae native to Africa, Asia, and SE Europe, or the family Erethizontidae native to America, having defensive spines or quills. **2** (*attrib.*) denoting any of various animals or other organisms with spines. □ **porcupine fish** a marine fish, *Diodon hystrix*, covered with sharp spines and often distending itself into a spherical shape. □□ **porcupinish** *adj.* **porcupiny** *adj.* [ME f. OF *porc espin* f. Prov. *porc espi(n)* ult. f. L *porcus* pig + *spina* thorn]

pore[1] /por/ *n.* esp. *Biol.* a minute opening in a surface through which gases, liquids, or fine solids may pass. [ME f. OF f. L *porus* f. Gk *poros* passage, pore]

■ opening, orifice, hole, aperture, vent, perforation, *Biol.* spiracle, *Bot.* stoma.

pore[2] /por/ *v.intr.* (foll. by *over*) **1** be absorbed in studying (a book etc.). **2** meditate on, think intently about (a subject). [ME *pure* etc. perh. f. OE *puriān* (unrecorded): cf. PEER[1]]

■ (*pore over*) study, examine, scrutinize, peruse, read, go over; see also MEDITATE 2.

porgy /pórgi/ *n.* (*pl.* **-ies**) *US* any usu. marine fish of the family Sparidae, used as food. Also called *sea bream.* [18th c.: orig. uncert.: cf. Sp. & Port. *pargo*]

porifer /pórifər/ *n.* any aquatic invertebrate of the phylum Porifera, including sponges. [mod.L *Porifera* f. L *porus* PORE[1] + *-fer* bearing]

pork /pork/ *n.* the (esp. unsalted) flesh of a pig, used as food. □ **pork-barrel** *US colloq.* government funds as a source of political benefit. **pork-butcher** a person who slaughters pigs for sale, or who sells pork rather than other meats. **pork pie** a pie of minced pork etc. eaten cold. **pork pie hat** a hat with a flat crown and a brim turned up all round. [ME *porc* f. OF *porc* f. L *porcus* pig]

porker /pórkər/ *n.* **1** a pig raised for food. **2** a young fattened pig.

porkling /pórkling/ *n.* a young or small pig.

porky[1] /pórki/ *adj.* & *n.* ● *adj.* (**porkier, porkiest**) **1** *colloq.* fleshy, fat. **2** of or like pork. ● *n. rhyming sl.* a lie (short for *porky pie*).

■ *adj.* see PLUMP[1] *adj.*

porky[2] /pórki/ *n.* (*pl.* **-ies**) *US colloq.* a porcupine. [abbr.]

porn /porn/ *n. colloq.* pornography. [abbr.]

porno /pórnō/ *n.* & *adj. colloq.* ● *n.* pornography. ● *adj.* pornographic. [abbr.]

pornography /pornógrəfi/ *n.* **1** the explicit description or exhibition of sexual activity in literature, films, etc., intended to stimulate erotic rather than aesthetic or emotional feelings. **2** literature etc. characterized by this. □□ **pornographer** *n.* **pornographic** /-nəgráffik/ *adj.* **pornographically** /-nəgráffikəli/ *adv.* [Gk *pornographos* writing of harlots f. *pornē* prostitute + *graphō* write]

■ **2** erotica, curiosa, *colloq.* porn, porno; smut, filth, dirt. □□ **pornographic** obscene, lewd, offensive, indecent, prurient, smutty, blue, dirty, salacious, licentious, nasty, *colloq.* porno, *euphem.* curious, adult.

porous /pórəss/ *adj.* **1** full of pores. **2** letting through air, water, etc. **3** (of an argument, security system, etc.) leaky, admitting infiltration. □□ **porosity** /poróssiti/ *n.* **porously** *adv.* **porousness** *n.* [ME f. OF *poreux* f. med.L *porosus* f. L *porus* PORE[1]]

■ **1, 2** spongy, spongelike; permeable, pervious, penetrable. **3** see DEFICIENT 2.

porphyria /porfírriə/ *n.* any of a group of genetic disorders associated with abnormal metabolism of various pigments. [mod.L f. *porphyrin* purple substance excreted by porphyria patients f. Gk *porphura* purple]

porphyry /pórfiri/ *n.* (*pl.* **-ies**) **1** a hard rock quarried in ancient Egypt, composed of crystals of white or red feldspar in a red matrix. **2** *Geol.* an igneous rock with large crystals scattered in a matrix of much smaller crystals. □□ **porphyritic** /-ríttik/ *adj.* [ME ult. f. med.L *porphyreum* f. Gk *porphuritēs* f. *porphura* purple]

porpoise /pórpəss/ *n.* any of various small toothed whales of the family Phocaenidae, esp. of the genus *Phocaena*, with a low triangular dorsal fin and a blunt rounded snout. [ME *porpays* etc. f. OF *po(u)rpois* etc. ult. f. L *porcus* pig + *piscis* fish]

porridge /pórrij/ *n.* **1** a dish consisting of oatmeal or another meal or cereal boiled in water or milk. **2** *Brit. sl.* imprisonment. □□ **porridgy** *adj.* [16th c.: alt. of POTTAGE]

porringer /pórrinjər/ *n.* a small bowl, often with a handle, for soup, stew, etc. [earlier *pottinger* f. OF *potager* f. *potage* (see POTTAGE): -n- as in *messenger* etc.]

port[1] /port/ *n.* **1** a harbour. **2** a place of refuge. **3** a town or place possessing a harbour, esp. one where customs officers are stationed. □ **port of call** a place where a ship or a person stops on a journey. **Port of London Authority** the corporate body controlling the London harbour and docks. [OE f. L *portus* & ME prob. f. OF f. L *portus*]

■ harbour, haven; seaport.

port[2] /port/ *n.* (in full **port wine**) a strong, sweet, dark-red (occas. brown or white) fortified wine of Portugal. [shortened form of *Oporto*, city in Portugal from which port is shipped]

port[3] /port/ *n.* & *v.* ● *n.* the left-hand side (looking forward) of a ship, boat, or aircraft (cf. STARBOARD). ● *v.tr.* (also *absol.*) turn (the helm) to port. □ **port tack** see TACK[1] 4. **port watch** see WATCH *n.* 3b. [prob. orig. the side turned towards PORT[1]]

port[4] /port/ *n.* **1 a** an opening in the side of a ship for entrance, loading, etc. **b** a porthole. **2** an aperture for the passage of steam, water, etc. **3** *Electr.* a socket or aperture in an electronic circuit, esp. in a computer network, where connections can be made with peripheral equipment. **4** an aperture in a wall etc. for a gun to be fired through. **5** esp. *Sc.* a gate or gateway, esp. of a walled town. [ME & OF *porte* f. L *porta*]

port[5] /port/ *v.* & *n.* ● *v.tr. Mil.* carry (a rifle, or other weapon) diagonally across and close to the body with the barrel etc. near the left shoulder (esp. *port arms!*). ● *n.* **1** *Mil.* this position. **2** external deportment; carriage; bearing. [ME f. OF *port* ult. f. L *portare* carry]

port[6] /port/ *n. Austral.* **1** a suitcase or travelling bag. **2** a shopping bag, sugar bag, etc. [abbr. of PORTMANTEAU]

portable /pórtəb'l/ *adj.* & *n.* ● *adj.* **1** easily movable, convenient for carrying (*portable TV*; *portable computer*). **2** (of a right, privilege, etc.) capable of being transferred or adapted in altered circumstances (*portable pension*). ● *n.* a portable object, e.g. a radio, typewriter, etc. (*decided to buy a portable*). □□ **portability** /-bílliti/ *n.* **portableness** *n.* **portably** *adv.* [ME f. OF *portable* or LL *portabilis* f. L *portare* carry]

■ *adj.* **1** transportable, manageable, handy, light, lightweight, compact.

portage /pórtij/ *n.* & *v.* ● *n.* **1** the carrying of boats or goods between two navigable waters. **2** a place at which this is necessary. **3 a** the act or an instance of carrying or transporting. **b** the cost of this. ● *v.tr.* convey (a boat or goods) between navigable waters. [ME f. OF f. *porter*: see PORT[5]]

Portakabin /pórtəkabbin/ *n. propr.* a portable room or building designed for quick assembly. [PORTABLE + CABIN]

portal[1] /pórt'l/ *n.* a doorway or gate etc., esp. a large and elaborate one. [ME f. OF f. med.L *portale* (neut. adj.): see PORTAL[2]]

portal[2] /pórt'l/ *adj.* **1** of or relating to an aperture in an organ through which its associated vessels pass. **2** of or relating to the portal vein. □ **portal vein** a vein conveying blood to the liver from the spleen, stomach, pancreas, and intestines. [mod.L *portalis* f. L *porta* gate]

portamento /pórtəméntō/ *n.* (*pl.* **portamenti** /-ti/) *Mus.* **1** the act or an instance of gliding from one note to another in singing, playing the violin, etc. **2** piano-playing in a manner intermediate between legato and staccato. [It., = carrying]

portative /pórtətiv/ *adj.* **1** serving to carry or support. **2** *Mus. hist.* (esp. of a small pipe-organ) portable. [ME f. OF *portatif*, app. alt. of *portatil* f. med.L *portatilis* f. L *portare* carry]

portcullis /portkúlliss/ *n.* **1** a strong heavy grating sliding up and down in vertical grooves, lowered to block a gateway in a fortress etc. **2** (**Portcullis**) *Heraldry* one of the four pursuivants of the English College of Arms, with this as a badge. □□ **portcullised** *adj.* [ME f. OF *porte coleïce* sliding door f. *porte* door f. L *porta* + *col(e)ïce* fem. of *couleïs* sliding ult. f. L *colare* filter]

Porte /port/ *n.* (in full **the Sublime** or **Ottoman Porte**) *hist.* the Ottoman court at Constantinople. [F (*la Sublime Porte* = the exalted gate), transl. of Turk. title of the central office of the Ottoman government]

porte-cochère /pórtkosháir/ *n.* **1** a porch large enough for vehicles to pass through, usu. into a courtyard. **2** *US* a roofed structure extending from the entrance of a building over a place where vehicles stop to discharge passengers. [F f. *porte* PORT[4] + *cochère* (fem. adj.) f. *coche* COACH]

portend /porténd/ *v.tr.* **1** foreshadow as an omen. **2** give warning of. [ME f. L *portendere portent-* f. *por-* PRO-[1] + *tendere* stretch]

■ see FORESHADOW, SPELL[1] 2b.

portent /pórtent, -t'nt/ *n.* **1** an omen, a sign of something to come, esp. something of a momentous or calamitous nature. **2** a prodigy; a marvellous thing. [L *portentum* (as PORTEND)]

■ see OMEN *n.*

portentous /porténtəss/ *adj.* **1** like or serving as a portent. **2** pompously solemn. □□ **portentously** *adv.*

■ **1** ominous, threatening, fateful, menacing, foreboding, louring, unpromising, unpropitious, ill-omened, inauspicious, ill-starred, ill-fated, *archaic* star-crossed. **2** solemn, dignified, stately, courtly, majestic, august, imperial.

porter[1] /pórtər/ *n.* **1 a** a person employed to carry luggage etc., esp. a railway, airport, or hotel employee. **b** a hospital employee who moves equipment, trolleys, etc. **2** a dark-brown bitter beer brewed from charred or browned malt (app. orig. made esp. for porters). **3** *US* a sleeping-car attendant. □□ **porterage** *n.* [ME f. OF *port(e)our* f. med.L *portator -oris* f. *portare* carry]

■ **1 a** bearer, (baggage) carrier *or* attendant, *US* redcap.

porter[2] /pórtər/ *n. Brit.* a gatekeeper or doorkeeper, esp. of a large building. [ME & AF, OF *portier* f. LL *portarius* f. *porta* door]

■ doorkeeper, watchman, doorman, gatekeeper, concierge; caretaker, janitor.

porterhouse /pórtərhowss/ *n.* esp. *US* **1** *hist.* a house at which porter and other drinks were retailed. **2** a house where steaks, chops, etc. were served. □ **porterhouse steak** a thick steak cut from the thick end of a sirloin.

portfire /pórtfīr/ *n.* a device for firing rockets, igniting explosives in mining, etc. [after F *porte-feu* f. *porter* carry + *feu* fire]

portfolio /portfṓliō/ *n.* (*pl.* **-os**) **1** a case for keeping loose sheets of paper, drawings, etc. **2** a range of investments held by a person, a company, etc. **3** the office of a minister of State (cf. *Minister without Portfolio*). **4** samples of an artist's work. [It. *portafogli* f. *portare* carry + *foglio* leaf f. L *folium*]

porthole /pórt-hōl/ *n.* **1** an (esp. glazed) aperture in a ship's or aircraft's side for the admission of light. **2** *hist.* an aperture for pointing a cannon through.

portico /pórtikō/ *n.* (*pl.* **-oes** or **-os**) a colonnade; a roof supported by columns at regular intervals usu. attached as a porch to a building. [It. f. L *porticus* PORCH]

■ porch, veranda, gallery, colonnade, stoa.

portière /pórtiáir/ *n.* a curtain hung over a door or doorway. [F f. *porte* door f. L *porta*]

■ see DRAPERY.

portion /pórsh'n/ *n.* & *v.* ● *n.* **1** a part or share. **2** the amount of food allotted to one person. **3** a specified or limited quantity. **4** one's destiny or lot. **5** a dowry. ● *v.tr.* **1** divide (a thing) into portions. **2** (foll. by *out*) distribute. **3** give a dowry to. **4** (foll. by *to*) assign (a thing) to (a person). □□ **portionless** *adj.* (in sense 5 of *n.*). [ME f. OF *porcion portion* f. L *portio -onis*]

■ *n.* **1** share, allotment, quota, ration, apportionment, allowance, allocation, percentage, measure; segment, part, section, division, subdivision, parcel. **2** helping, serving; ration, share; piece. **4** see DESTINY 2. ● *v.* **1** partition, divide, split up, carve up, cut up, break up, section, *colloq.* divvy up. **2** (*portion out*) share out, allocate, ration, allot, dole out, deal (out), parcel out, distribute, administer, dispense, disperse. **4** see ASSIGN 1a.

Portland cement /pórtlənd/ *n.* a cement manufactured from chalk and clay which when hard resembles Portland stone in colour.

Portland stone /pórtlənd/ *n.* a limestone from the Isle of Portland in Dorset, used in building.

portly /pórtli/ *adj.* (**portlier**, **portliest**) **1** corpulent; stout. **2** *archaic* of a stately appearance. □□ **portliness** *n.* [PORT[5] (in the sense 'bearing') + -LY[1]]

■ **1** see STOUT *adj.* 1. □□ **portliness** see FAT *n.* 3.

portmanteau /portmántō/ *n.* (*pl.* **portmanteaus** /-tōz/ or **portmanteaux**) a leather trunk for clothes etc., opening into two equal parts. □ **portmanteau word** a word blending the sounds and combining the meanings of two others, e.g. *motel*, *Oxbridge*. [F *portmanteau* f. *porter* carry f. L *portare* + *manteau* MANTLE]

portolan /pórtəlan/ *n.* (also **portolano** /pórtəlaánō/) (*pl.* **portolans** or **portolanos**) *hist.* a book of sailing directions with charts, descriptions of harbours, etc. [It. *portolano* f. *porto* PORT[1]]

portrait /pórtrit/ *n.* **1** a representation of a person or animal, esp. of the face, made by drawing, painting, photography, etc. **2** a verbal picture; a graphic description. **3** a person etc. resembling or typifying another (*is the portrait of his father*). **4** (in graphic design etc.) a format in which the height of an illustration etc. is greater than the width (cf. LANDSCAPE). [F, past part. of OF *portraire* PORTRAY]

■ **1** picture, likeness, vignette, image, representation, rendition, portrayal; sketch, drawing, painting. **2** description, profile, portrayal; account, characterization. **3** picture, spitting image; see also IMAGE *n.* 5.

portraitist /pórtritist/ *n.* a person who takes or paints portraits.

portraiture /pórtrichər/ *n.* **1** the art of painting or taking portraits. **2** graphic description. **3** a portrait. [ME f. OF (as PORTRAIT)]

portray /portráy/ *v.tr.* **1** represent (an object) by a painting, carving, etc; make a likeness of. **2** describe graphically. **3** represent dramatically. □□ **portrayable** *adj.* **portrayal** *n.* **portrayer** *n.* [ME f. OF *portraire* f. *por-* = PRO-[1] + *traire* draw f. L *trahere*]

■ **1, 2** represent, picture, show, depict, render, characterize, describe, delineate. **3** act *or* play (the part of), take the part *or* role of, represent. □□ **portrayal** see PORTRAIT 1, 2, RENDERING 1a.

Port Salut /pór səlōō/ *n.* a pale mild type of cheese. [after the Trappist monastery in France where it was first produced]

Portuguese /pórtyoogeéz, pórchoo-/ *n.* & *adj.* ● *n.* (*pl.* same) **1 a** a native or national of Portugal. **b** a person of Portuguese descent. **2** the language of Portugal. ● *adj.* of or relating to Portugal or its people or language. □ **Portuguese man-of-war** a dangerous tropical or sub-tropical marine hydrozoan of the genus *Physalia* with a large crest and a poisonous sting. [Port. *portuguez* f. med.L *portugalensis*]

POS *abbr.* point-of-sale.

pose[1] /pōz/ *v.* & *n.* ● *v.* **1** *intr.* assume a certain attitude of body, esp. when being photographed or being painted for a portrait. **2** *intr.* (foll. by *as*) set oneself up as or pretend to be (another person etc.) (*posing as a celebrity*). **3** *intr.* behave affectedly in order to impress others. **4** *tr.* put forward or present (a question etc.). **5** *tr.* place (an artist's model etc.) in a certain attitude or position. ● *n.* **1** an attitude of body or mind. **2** an attitude or pretence, esp. one assumed for effect (*his generosity is a mere pose*). [F *poser* (v.), *pose* (n.) f. LL *pausare* PAUSE: some senses by confusion with L *ponere* place (cf. COMPOSE)]

■ *v.* **1** sit, model. **2** (*pose as*) impersonate, be disguised as, masquerade as, pretend *or* profess to be, pass for, imitate, mimic. **3** attitudinize, posture, put on airs; see also *show off*. **4** set, put (forward), ask, submit, broach, advance, present, raise. **5** see POSITION *v.* ● *n.* **1** position, posture, stance; see also ATTITUDE. **2** affectation, act, pretence, affectedness, display, façade, show; attitude.

pose[2] /pōz/ *v.tr.* puzzle (a person) with a question or problem. [obs. *appose* f. OF *aposer* var. of *oposer* OPPOSE]

poser /pṓzər/ *n.* **1** a person who poses (see POSE[1] *v.* 3). **2** a puzzling question or problem.

■ **2** see PUZZLE *n.*

poseur /pōzṓr/ *n.* (*fem.* **poseuse** /pōzṓz/) a person who poses for effect or behaves affectedly. [F f. *poser* POSE[1]]

■ posturer, exhibitionist, pseudo, *colloq.* show-off, pseud.

posh /posh/ *adj.* & *adv. colloq.* ● *adj.* **1** smart; stylish. **2** of or associated with the upper classes (*spoke with a posh accent*). ● *adv.* in a stylish or upper-class way (*talk posh; act posh*). □ **posh up** smarten up. □□ **poshly** *adv.* **poshness** *n.* [20th c.: perh. f. sl. *posh* a dandy: *port out starboard home* (referring to the more comfortable accommodation on ships to and from the East) is a later association and not the true origin]

■ *adj.* **1** smart, stylish, up-market, high-class, de luxe, plush, luxurious, elegant, grand, swanky, *colloq.* classy, ritzy, top drawer, plushy, *esp. US colloq.* swank, *US colloq.* tony, *sl.* snazzy. **2** upper-class, snobby, snobbish, *colloq.* upper-crust, plummy, *esp. Brit. colloq.* U, *Brit. sl.* Sloaney. □ **posh up** see PRIMP 2.

posit /pózzit/ *v.* & *n.* ● *v.tr.* (**posited, positing**) **1** assume as a fact, postulate. **2** put in place or position. ● *n. Philos.* a statement which is made on the assumption that it will prove valid. [L *ponere posit-* place]

■ *v.* **1** postulate, hypothesize, propound, put *or* set forth, put forward, advance, pose, predicate. **2** see POSITION *v.*

position /pəzísh'n/ *n.* & *v.* ● *n.* **1** a place occupied by a person or thing. **2** the way in which a thing or its parts are placed or arranged (*sitting in an uncomfortable position*). **3** the proper place (*in position*). **4** the state of being advantageously placed (*jockeying for position*). **5** a person's mental attitude; a way of looking at a question (*changed their position on nuclear disarmament*). **6** a person's situation in relation to others (*puts one in an awkward position*). **7** rank or status; high social standing. **8** paid employment. **9** a place where troops etc. are posted for strategical purposes (*the position was stormed*). **10** the configuration of chessmen etc. during a game. **11** a specific pose in ballet etc. (*hold first position*). **12** *Logic* **a** a proposition. **b** a statement of a proposition. ● *v.tr.* place in position. □ **in a position to** enabled by circumstances, resources, information, etc. to (do, state, etc.). **position paper** orig. *US* (in business etc.) a written report of attitude or intentions. **position vector** *Math.* a vector which determines the position of a point. □□ **positional** *adj.* **positionally** *adv.* **positioner** *n.* [ME f. OF *position* or L *positio -onis* (as POSIT)]

■ *n.* **1** spot, location, site, situation; whereabouts. **2** posture, attitude, stance, pose; disposition, arrangement, configuration. **3** see PLACE *n.* 1a, b. **5** viewpoint, point of view, outlook, attitude, stance, stand, standpoint, opinion, way of thinking, angle, slant, inclination, leaning, bent, sentiment, feeling. **6** condition, state, situation; circumstances. **7** class, place, rank, standing, station, status. **8** job, occupation, situation, post, office, place, appointment, *colloq.* billet, berth. **12** hypothesis, thesis, tenet, principle, contention, assertion, predication, belief, proposition, postulate. ● *v.* put, place, lay, lie, situate, site, locate, establish, set, fix, settle, pose, posit, dispose, arrange.

positive /pózzitiv/ *adj.* & *n.* ● *adj.* **1** formally or explicitly stated; definite, unquestionable (*positive proof*). **2** (of a person) convinced, confident, or overconfident in his or her opinion (*positive that I was not there*). **3 a** absolute; not relative. **b** *Gram.* (of an adjective or adverb) expressing a simple quality without comparison (cf. COMPARATIVE, SUPERLATIVE). **4** *colloq.* downright; complete (*it would be a positive miracle*). **5 a** constructive; directional (*positive criticism; positive thinking*). **b** favourable; optimistic (*positive reaction; positive outlook*). **6** marked by the presence rather than absence of qualities or *Med.* symptoms (*the test was positive*). **7** esp. *Philos.* dealing only with matters of fact; practical (cf. POSITIVISM 1). **8** tending in a direction naturally or arbitrarily taken as that of increase or progress (*clockwise rotation is positive*). **9** greater than zero (*positive and negative integers*) (opp. NEGATIVE). **10** *Electr.* of, containing, or producing the kind of electrical charge produced by rubbing glass with silk; an absence of electrons. **11** (of a photographic image) showing lights and shades or colours true to the original (opp. NEGATIVE). ● *n.* a positive adjective, photograph, quantity, etc. □ **positive discrimination** the practice of making distinctions in favour of groups considered to be underprivileged. **positive feedback 1** a constructive response to an experiment, questionnaire, etc. **2** *Electronics* the return of part of an output signal to the input, tending to increase the amplification etc. **positive geotropism** see GEOTROPISM. **positive pole** the north-seeking pole. **positive ray** *Physics* a canal ray. **positive sign** = *plus sign.* **positive vetting** *Brit.* an exhaustive inquiry into the background and character of a candidate for a post in the Civil Service that involves access to secret material. □□ **positively** *adv.* **positiveness** *n.* **positivity** /pózzitívviti/ *n.* [ME f. OF *positif -ive* or L *positivus* (as POSIT)]

■ *adj.* **1** sure, certain, definite, unequivocal, categorical, absolute, unqualified, unambiguous, unmistakable, clear-cut, clear, firm, explicit, express, decisive, indisputable, indubitable, unquestionable, incontestable, undeniable, reliable, persuasive, convincing, irrefutable. **2** sure, certain, confident, convinced, satisfied, decided; overconfident, dogmatic, pontifical, opinionated, pigheaded, stubborn, obstinate, obdurate, arbitrary, overwheening, arrogant, assertive. **4** complete, utter, downright, total, perfect, out and out, consummate, unmitigated, thorough, thoroughgoing, outright; see also ABSOLUTE *adj.* 1. **5 a** constructive, productive, useful, practical, functional, pragmatic; directional. **b** beneficial, favourable, complimentary, productive, encouraging, supportive, constructive, reassuring, enthusiastic, affirmative; promising, encouraging, optimistic, cheerful, confident, *colloq.* bullish, upbeat. **6** affirmative, confirming. □□ **positively** definitely, absolutely, unquestionably, certainly, assuredly, undeniably, undoubtedly, surely, emphatically, unmistakably, categorically, indisputably, beyond *or* without a doubt, indubitably, beyond question; constructively; see also *utterly* (UTTER).

positivism /pózzitiviz'm/ *n.* **1** *Philos.* the philosophical system of Auguste Comte, recognizing only non-metaphysical facts and observable phenomena, and rejecting metaphysics and theism. **2** a religious system founded on this. **3** = *logical positivism.* □□ **positivist** *n.* **positivistic** /-vístik/ *adj.* **positivistically** /-vístikəli/ *adv.* [F *positivisme* (as POSITIVE)]

positron /pózzitron/ *n. Physics* an elementary particle with a positive charge equal to the negative charge of an electron and having the same mass as an electron. [POSITIVE + -TRON]

posology /pəsólləji/ *n.* the study of the dosage of medicines. □□ **posological** /póssəlójik'l/ *adj.* [F *posologie* f. Gk *posos* how much]

posse /póssi/ *n.* **1** a strong force or company or assemblage. **2** (in full **posse comitatus** /kómmitáytəss/) **a** a body of constables, law-enforcers, etc. **b** esp. *US* a body of men summoned by a sheriff etc. to enforce the law. [med.L, = power f. L *posse* be able: *comitatus* = of the county]

possess /pəzéss/ *v.tr.* **1** hold as property; own. **2** have a faculty, quality, etc. (*they possess a special value for us*). **3** (also *refl.*; foll. by *in*) maintain (oneself, one's soul, etc.) in a specified state (*possess oneself in patience*). **4 a** (of a demon etc.) occupy; have power over (a person etc.) (*possessed by the devil*). **b** (of an emotion, infatuation, etc.) dominate, be an obsession of (*possessed by fear*). **5** have sexual intercourse with (esp. a woman). □ **be possessed of** own, have. **possess oneself of** take or get for one's own. **what possessed you?** an expression of incredulity. □□ **possessor** *n.* **possessory** *adj.* [OF *possesser* f. L *possidēre possess-* f. *potis* able + *sedēre* sit]

■ **1** be in possession of, be possessed of, have, own, enjoy, be blessed *or* endowed with. **2** have, hold, contain, embody, embrace, include. **3** see MAINTAIN 1, 2. **4 a** occupy, take over, take control of, have power over, bedevil, captivate, enchant, cast a spell on *or* over, enthral; see also BEWITCH 2. **b** dominate, control, govern, influence, hold, consume, take control of, preoccupy, obsess, haunt, eat up. **5** see LAY[1] *v.* 16. □ **possess oneself of** acquire, achieve, get, win, obtain, procure, secure, take, seize, take *or* gain possession of.

possession /pəzésh'n/ *n.* **1** the act or state of possessing or being possessed. **2 a** the thing possessed. **b** a foreign territory subject to a state or ruler. **3** the act or state of actual holding or occupancy. **4** *Law* power or control similar to lawful ownership but which may exist separately from it (*prosecuted for possession of narcotic drugs*). **5** (in *pl.*) property, wealth, subject territory, etc. **6** *Football* etc. temporary control of the ball by a particular player. □ **in possession 1** (of a person) possessing. **2** (of a thing) possessed. **in possession of 1** having in one's possession. **2** maintaining control over (*in possession of one's wits*). **in the possession of** held or owned by. **possession order** an order made by a court directing that possession of a property be given to the owner. **take possession** (often foll. by *of*) become the owner or possessor (of a thing). □□ **possessionless** *adj.* [ME f. OF *possession* or L *possessio -onis* (as POSSESS)]

■ **1, 3** ownership, proprietorship; control, hold, tenure, keeping, care, custody, guardianship, protection; occupancy. **2 b** holding, territory, province, dominion, colony, protectorate. **5** (*possessions*) belongings, property, effects, chattels, assets, worldly goods, things. □ **take possession** (*take possession of*) seize, capture, take, get, conquer, occupy, acquire, win, possess oneself of, secure, obtain.

possessive /pəzéssiv/ *adj.* & *n.* ● *adj.* **1** showing a desire to possess or retain what one already owns. **2** showing jealous and domineering tendencies towards another person. **3** *Gram.* indicating possession. ● *n.* (in full **possessive case**) *Gram.* the case of nouns and pronouns expressing possession. □ **possessive pronoun** each of the pronouns indicating possession (*my*, *your*, *his*, *their*, etc.) or the corresponding absolute forms (*mine*, *yours*, *his*, *theirs*, etc.). □□ **possessively** *adv.* **possessiveness** *n.* [L *possessivus* (as POSSESS), transl. Gk *ktētikē* (*ptōsis* case)]

■ *adj.* **1** greedy, selfish, ungenerous, stingy, niggardly, materialistic, covetous, acquisitive. **2** overprotective, controlling, domineering, overbearing; jealous.

posset /póssit/ *n. hist.* a drink made of hot milk curdled with ale, wine, etc., often flavoured with spices, formerly much used as a remedy for colds etc. [ME *poshote*: orig. unkn.]

possibility /póssibílliti/ *n.* (*pl.* **-ies**) **1** the state or fact of being possible, or an occurrence of this (*outside the range of possibility*; *saw no possibility of going away*). **2** a thing that may exist or happen (*there are three possibilities*). **3** (usu. in *pl.*) the capability of being used, improved, etc.; the potential of an object or situation (esp. *have possibilities*). [ME f. OF *possibilité* or LL *possibilitas -tatis* (as POSSIBLE)]

■ **1** conceivability, feasibility, plausibility, admissibility; likelihood, chance, prospect. **3** (*possibilities*) potentiality, potential, promise; capability, capacity.

possible /póssib'l/ *adj.* & *n.* ● *adj.* **1** capable of existing or happening; that may be managed, achieved, etc. (*came as early as possible*; *did as much as possible*). **2** that is likely to happen etc. (*few thought their victory possible*). **3** acceptable; potential (*a possible way of doing it*). ● *n.* **1** a possible candidate, member of a team, etc. **2** (prec. by *the*) whatever is likely, manageable, etc. **3** the highest possible score, esp. in shooting etc. [ME f. OF *possible* or L *possibilis* f. *posse* be able]

■ *adj.* **1** feasible, plausible, imaginable, conceivable, thinkable, credible, believable, tenable, admissible. **2** realizable, achievable, attainable, reachable, accomplishable; likely, probable.

possibly /póssibli/ *adv.* **1** perhaps. **2** in accordance with possibility (*cannot possibly refuse*).

■ **1** maybe, perhaps, if possible, *archaic* mayhap, *archaic or joc.* peradventure, *archaic or poet.* perchance. **2** in any way, under any circumstances, at all, by any chance, ever.

possum /póssəm/ *n.* **1** *colloq.* = OPOSSUM 1. **2** *Austral.* & *NZ colloq.* a phalanger resembling an American opossum. □ **play possum 1** pretend to be asleep or unconscious when threatened. **2** feign ignorance. [abbr.]

post[1] /pōst/ *n.* & *v.* ● *n.* **1** a long stout piece of timber or metal set upright in the ground etc.: **a** to support something, esp. in building. **b** to mark a position, boundary, etc. **c** to carry notices. **2** a pole etc. marking the start or finish of a race. ● *v.tr.* **1** (often foll. by *up*) **a** attach (a paper etc.) in a prominent place; stick up (*post no bills*). **b** announce or advertise by placard or in a published text. **2** publish the name of (a ship etc.) as overdue or missing. **3** placard (a wall etc.) with bills etc. **4** *US* achieve (a score in a game etc.). □ **post-mill** a windmill pivoted on a post and turning to catch the wind. [OE f. L *postis*: in ME also f. OF etc.]

■ *n.* **1** pole, stake, upright, column, pillar, pale, picket, shaft, pier, pylon, pile, piling, strut, shore, stanchion. ● *v.* **1 a** put *or* pin *or* tack *or* stick *or* hang up, affix. **b** advertise, announce, proclaim, publish, propagate, promulgate.

post[2] /pōst/ *n.*, *v.*, & *adv.* ● *n.* **1** *Brit.* the official conveyance of parcels, letters, etc. (*send it by post*). **2** *Brit.* a single collection, dispatch, or delivery of these; the letters etc. dispatched (*has the post arrived yet?*). **3** *Brit.* a place where letters etc. are dealt with; a post office or postbox (*take it to the post*). **4** *hist.* **a** one of a series of couriers who carried mail on horseback between fixed stages. **b** a letter-carrier; a mail cart. ● *v.* **1** *tr.* put (a letter etc.) in the post. **2** *tr.* (esp. as **posted** *adj.*) (often foll. by *up*) supply a person with information (*keep me posted*). **3** *tr.* **a** enter (an item) in a ledger. **b** (often foll. by *up*) complete (a ledger) in this way. **c** carry (an entry) from an auxiliary book to a more formal one, or from one account to another. **4** *intr.* **a** travel with haste, hurry. **b** *hist.* travel with relays of horses. ● *adv.* express; with haste. □ **post-chaise** *hist.* a travelling carriage hired from stage to stage or drawn by horses hired in this manner. **post exchange** *US Mil.* a shop at a military camp etc. **post-free** *Brit.* carried by post free of charge or with the postage prepaid. **post-haste** with great speed. **post-horn** a valveless horn formerly used to announce the arrival of the post. **Post Office 1** the public department or corporation responsible for postal services and (in some countries) telecommunication. **2** (**post office**) **a** a room or building where postal business is carried on. **b** *US* = *postman's knock*. **post-office box** a numbered place in a post office where letters are kept until called for. **post-paid** on which postage has been paid. **post room** the department of a company that deals with incoming and outgoing mail. **post-town** a town with a post office, esp. one that is not a sub-office of another. [F *poste* (fem.) f. It. *posta* ult. f. L *ponere posit-* place]

■ *n.* **1** postal service, mail. **2** collection, dispatch, delivery; letters, mail, correspondence. ● *v.* **1** send (off), dispatch, *esp. US* mail. **2** (*keep a person posted*) advise, brief, notify, *colloq.* fill in; see also INFORM 1. **3 a** record, enter, register, list. ● *adv.* see FAST[1] *adv.* 1. □ **post-haste** post, quickly, at once, without delay, immediately, directly, straight away, right away, promptly, speedily, swiftly, instantly, rapidly, in a wink, in a trice, in the twinkling of an eye, chop-chop, *colloq.* pronto, before you can say knife *or* Jack Robinson, p.d.q., like greased lightning; see also FAST[1] *adv.* 1.

post[3] /pōst/ *n.* & *v.* ● *n.* **1** a place where a soldier is stationed or which he patrols. **2** a place of duty. **3 a** a position taken up by a body of soldiers. **b** a force occupying this. **c** a fort. **4** a situation, paid employment. **5** = *trading post*. **6** *Naut. hist.* a commission as an officer in command of a vessel of 20 guns or more. ● *v.tr.* **1** place or station (soldiers, an employee, etc.). **2** appoint to a post or command. □ **first post** *Brit.* the earliest of several bugle-calls giving notice of the hour of retiring at night. **last post** *Brit.* the final such bugle-call, also blown at military funerals etc. [F *poste* (masc.) f. It. *posto* f. Rmc *postum* (unrecorded) f. L *ponere posit-* place]

■ *n.* **4** assignment, appointment, position, situation, job, place; employment, work. ● *v.* **1** place, put, station, position, situate, set, locate. **2** see APPOINT 1.

post- /pōst/ *prefix* after in time or order. [from or after L *post* (adv. & prep.)]

postage /pṓstij/ *n.* the amount charged for sending a letter etc. by post, usu. prepaid in the form of a stamp (*£25 including postage & packing*). □ **postage meter** *US* a franking-machine. **postage stamp** an official stamp affixed to or imprinted on a letter etc. indicating the amount of postage paid.

■ see CARRIAGE 3b.

postal /pṓst'l/ *adj.* & *n.* ● *adj.* **1** of the post. **2** by post (*postal vote*). ● *n.* *US* a postcard. □ **postal card** *US* = POSTCARD. **postal code** = POSTCODE. **postal meter** a franking-machine. **postal note** *Austral.* & *NZ* = *postal order*. **postal order** a money order issued by the Post Office, payable to a specified person. **Postal Union** a union of the governments of various countries for the regulation of international postage. □□ **postally** *adv.* [F (*poste* POST[2])]

postbag /pṓstbag/ *n. Brit.* = MAILBAG.

postbox /pṓstboks/ *n. Brit.* a letter-box.

postcard /pṓstkaard/ *n.* a card, often with a photograph on one side, for sending a short message by post without an envelope.

post-classical /pōstklássik'l/ *adj.* (esp. of Greek and Roman literature) later than the classical period.

postcode /pṓstkōd/ *n.* a group of letters or letters and figures which are added to a postal address to assist sorting.

post-coital /pōstkṓ-it'l/ *adj.* occurring or existing after sexual intercourse. □□ **post-coitally** *adv.*

postdate *v.* & *n.* ● *v.tr.* /pōstdáyt/ affix or assign a date later than the actual one to (a document, event, etc.). ● *n.* /pṓstdayt/ such a date.

post-doctoral /pōstdóktərəl/ *adj.* of or relating to research undertaken after the completion of doctoral research.

post-entry /pōsténtri/ *n.* (*pl.* **-ies**) a late or subsequent entry, esp. in a race or in bookkeeping.

poster /pṓstər/ *n.* **1** a placard in a public place. **2** a large printed picture. **3** a billposter. □ **poster paint** a gummy opaque paint.

■ **1** placard, notice, bill; see also SIGN *n.* 4. **2** print, picture, reproduction.

poste restante /pōst restónt/ *n.* **1** a direction on a letter to indicate that it should be kept at a specified post office until collected by the addressee. **2** the department in a post office where such letters are kept. [F, = letter(s) remaining]

posterior /postéeriər/ *adj.* & *n.* ● *adj.* **1** later; coming after in series, order, or time. **2** situated at the back. ● *n.* (in *sing.* or *pl.*) the buttocks. □□ **posteriority** /postéeriórriti/ *n.* **posteriorly** *adv.* [L, compar. of *posterus* following f. *post* after]

■ *adj.* **1** later, ensuing, following, succeeding; see also SUBSEQUENT. **2** hind, rear, back, hinder, rearward. ● *n.* rump, seat, *colloq.* bottom, *colloq. euphem. derrière*, *Brit. sl.* bum, *esp. US sl.* tush; see also BUTTOCK.

posterity /postérriti/ *n.* **1** all succeeding generations. **2** the descendants of a person. [ME f. OF *posterité* f. L *posteritas -tatis* f. *posterus*: see POSTERIOR]

■ **2** descendants, successors, heirs, children, offspring, issue, progeny.

postern /póstərn, pṓ-/ *n.* **1** a back door. **2** a side way or entrance. [ME f. OF *posterne*, *posterle*, f. LL *posterula* dimin. of *posterus*: see POSTERIOR]

postfix *n.* & *v.* ● *n.* /pṓstfiks/ a suffix. ● *v.tr.* /pōstfíks/ append (letters) at the end of a word.

postglacial /pōstgláysh'l, -gláysiəl/ *adj.* & *n.* ● *adj.* formed or occurring after a glacial period. ● *n.* a postglacial period or deposit.

postgraduate *adj.* & *n.* ● *adj.* /pōstgrádyooət/ **1** (of a course of study) carried on after taking a first degree. **2** of or relating to students following this course of study (*postgraduate accommodation*). ● *n.* /pōstgrádyooət/ a postgraduate student.

posthumous /póstyooməss/ *adj.* **1** occurring after death. **2** (of a child) born after the death of its father. **3** (of a book etc.) published after the author's death. □□ **posthumously** *adv.* [L *postumus* last (superl. f. *post* after): in LL *posth-* by assoc. with *humus* ground]

postiche /postéesh/ *n.* a coil of false hair, worn as an adornment. [F, = false, f. It. *posticcio*]

postie /pṓsti/ *n. colloq.* a postman or postwoman. [abbr.]

postil /póstil/ *n. hist.* **1** a marginal note or comment, esp. on a text of Scripture. **2** a commentary. [ME f. OF *postille* f. med.L *postilla*, of uncert. orig.]

postilion /postílyən/ *n.* (also **postillion**) the rider on the near (left-hand side) horse drawing a coach etc. when there is no coachman. [F *postillon* f. It. *postiglione* post-boy f. *posta* POST[2]]

post-impressionism /pōstimpréshəniz'm/ *n.* artistic aims and methods developed as a reaction against impressionism and intending to express the individual artist's conception of the objects represented rather than the ordinary observer's view. □□ **post-impressionist** *n.* & *adj.* **post-impressionistic** /-nístik/ *adj.*

postindustrial /pōstindústriəl/ *adj.* relating to or characteristic of a society or economy which no longer relies on heavy industry.

postliminy /pōstlímmini/ *n.* **1** (in international law) the restoration to their former status of persons and things taken in war. **2** (in Roman law) the right of a banished person or captive to resume civic privileges on return from exile. [L *postliminium* (as POST-, *limen liminis* threshold)]

postlude /pṓstlood/ *n. Mus.* a concluding voluntary. [POST-, after PRELUDE]

postman /pṓstmən/ *n.* (*pl.* **-men**; *fem.* **postwoman**, *pl.* **-women**) a person who is employed to deliver and collect letters etc. □ **postman's knock** *Brit.* a parlour game in which imaginary letters are delivered in exchange for kisses.

postmark /pṓstmaark/ *n.* & *v.* ● *n.* an official mark stamped on a letter, esp. one giving the place, date, etc. of dispatch or arrival, and serving to cancel the stamp. ● *v.tr.* mark (an envelope etc.) with this.

postmaster /pṓstmaastər/ *n.* a man in charge of a post office. □ **postmaster general** the head of a country's postal service. ¶ The office was abolished in the UK in 1969.

post-millennial /pōstmilénniəl/ *adj.* following the millennium.

post-millennialism /pṓstmilénniəliz'm/ *n.* the doctrine that a second Advent will follow the millennium. ▫▫ **post-millennialist** *n.*

postmistress /pṓstmistriss/ *n.* a woman in charge of a post office.

post-modern /pṓstmóddərn/ *adj.* (in literature, architecture, the arts, etc.) denoting a movement reacting against modern tendencies, esp. by drawing attention to former conventions. ▫▫ **post-modernism** *n.* **post-modernist** *n.* & *adj.*

post-mortem *n.*, *adv.*, & *adj.* ● *n.* /pōstmórtəm/ **1** (in full **post-mortem examination**) an examination made after death, esp. to determine its cause. **2** *colloq.* a discussion analysing the course and result of a game, election, etc. ● *adv.* /pōstmórtəm/ *adj.* /pṓstmórtəm/ after death. [L]
■ *n.* **1** autopsy, necropsy. **2** see ANALYSIS 1.

postnatal /pṓstnáyt'l/ *adj.* characteristic of or relating to the period after childbirth.

post-nuptial /pṓstnúpsh'l/ *adj.* after marriage.

post-obit *n.* & *adj.* ● *n.* /pōstṓbit/ a bond given to a lender by a borrower securing a sum for payment on the death of another person from whom the borrower expects to inherit. ● *adj.* /pṓstṓbit/ taking effect after death. [L *post obitum* f. *post* after + *obitus* decease f. *obire* die]

post-partum /pṓstpaártəm/ *adj.* following parturition.

postpone /pōstpṓn, pəspṓn/ *v.tr.* cause or arrange (an event etc.) to take place at a later time. ▫▫ **postponable** *adj.* **postponement** *n.* **postponer** *n.* [L *postponere* (as POST-, *ponere posit-* place)]
■ delay, adjourn, defer, keep in abeyance, put off *or* aside *or* back, lay aside, suspend, shelve, table, *colloq.* put on the back burner, put *or* keep on ice. ▫▫ **postponement** delay, adjournment, suspension, deferment, deferral; stay; moratorium.

postposition /pṓstpəzísh'n/ *n.* **1** a word or particle, esp. an enclitic, placed after the word it modifies, e.g. *-ward* in *homeward* and *at* in *the books we looked at*. **2** the use of a postposition. ▫▫ **postpositional** *adj.* & *n.* **postpositive** /pṓstpózzitiv/*adj.* /pōstpózzitiv/ *n.* **postpositively** /-pózzitivli/ *adv.* [LL *postpositio* (as POSTPONE)]

postprandial /pṓstprándiəl/ *adj. formal* or *joc.* after dinner or lunch. [POST- + L *prandium* a meal]

postscript /pṓstskript, pṓskript/ *n.* **1** an additional paragraph or remark, usu. at the end of a letter after the signature and introduced by 'PS'. **2** any additional information, action, etc. [L *postscriptum* neut. past part. of *postscribere* (as POST-, *scribere* write)]
■ **2** see SUPPLEMENT *n.* 1, 2.

post-tax /pṓst-táks/ *adj.* (of income) after the deduction of taxes.

postulant /póstyoolənt/ *n.* a candidate, esp. for admission into a religious order. [F *postulant* or L *postulans -antis* (as POSTULATE)]

postulate *v.* & *n.* ● *v.tr.* /póstyoolayt/ **1** (often foll. by *that* + clause) assume as a necessary condition, esp. as a basis for reasoning; take for granted. **2** claim. **3** (in ecclesiastical law) nominate or elect to a higher rank. ● *n.* /póstyoolət/ **1** a thing postulated. **2** a fundamental prerequisite or condition. **3** *Math.* an assumption used as a basis for mathematical reasoning. ▫▫ **postulation** /póstyooláysh'n/ *n.* [L *postulare postulat-* demand]
■ *v.* **1** see PRESUME 1. **2** see PROPOUND. ● *n.* **1, 2** see PREMISS. ▫▫ **postulation** see PRESUMPTION 2.

postulator /póstyoolaytər/ *n.* **1** a person who postulates. **2** *RC Ch.* a person who presents a case for canonization or beatification.

posture /póss-chər/ *n.* & *v.* ● *n.* **1** the relative position of parts, esp. of the body (*in a reclining posture*). **2** carriage or bearing (*improved by good posture and balance*). **3** a mental or spiritual attitude or condition. **4** the condition or state (of affairs etc.) (*in more diplomatic postures*). ● *v.* **1** *intr.* assume a mental or physical attitude, esp. for effect (*inclined to strut and posture*). **2** *tr.* pose (a person). ▫▫ **postural** *adj.* **posturer** *n.* [F f. It. *postura* f. L *positura* f. *ponere posit-* place]
■ *n.* **1** pose, position, attitude, stance. **2** see CARRIAGE 6. **3** attitude, stance, position, feeling, sentiment, outlook, (point of) view, viewpoint, orientation, disposition, frame of mind, mood. **4** position, condition, situation, state, disposition, circumstance, status. ● *v.* **1** pose, attitudinize, put on airs, put on a show, do for effect, *colloq.* show off.

postwar /pṓstwáwr/ *adj.* occurring or existing after a war (esp. the most recent major war).

posy /pṓzi/ *n.* (*pl.* **-ies**) **1** a small bunch of flowers. **2** *archaic* a short motto, line of verse, etc., inscribed within a ring. ▫ **posy-ring** a ring with this inscription. [alt. f. POESY]
■ **1** bouquet, nosegay, spray.

pot[1] /pot/ *n.* & *v.* ● *n.* **1** a vessel, usu. rounded, of ceramic ware or metal or glass for holding liquids or solids or for cooking in. **2 a** a coffee-pot, flowerpot, glue-pot, jam-pot, teapot, etc. **b** = *chimney-pot*. **c** = *lobster-pot*. **3** a drinking vessel of pewter etc. **4** the contents of a pot (*ate a whole pot of jam*). **5** the total amount of the bet in a game etc. **6** *colloq.* a large sum (*pots of money*). **7** *sl.* a vessel given as a prize in an athletic contest, esp. a silver cup. **8** = *pot-belly*. ● *v.tr.* (**potted, potting**) **1** place in a pot. **2** (usu. as **potted** *adj.*) preserve in a sealed pot (*potted shrimps*). **3** sit (a young child) on a chamber pot. **4** pocket (a ball) in billiards etc. **5** shoot at, hit, or kill (an animal) with a pot-shot. **6** seize or secure. **7** abridge or epitomize (*in a potted version*; *potted wisdom*). ▫ **go to pot** *colloq.* deteriorate; be ruined. **pot-bellied** having a pot-belly. **pot-belly** (*pl.* **-ies**) **1** a protruding stomach. **2** a person with this. **3** a small bulbous stove. **pot-boiler 1** a work of literature or art done merely to make the writer or artist a living. **2** a writer or artist who does this. **pot-bound** (of a plant) having roots which fill the flowerpot, leaving no room to expand. **pot cheese** *US* cottage cheese. **pot-herb** any herb grown in a kitchen garden. **pot-hook 1** a hook over a hearth for hanging a pot etc. on, or for lifting a hot pot. **2** a curved stroke in handwriting, esp. as made in learning to write. **pot-hunter 1** a person who hunts for game at random. **2** a person who takes part in a contest merely for the sake of the prize. **pot luck** whatever (hospitality etc.) is available. **pot of gold** an imaginary reward; an ideal; a jackpot. **pot pie** a pie of meat etc. or fruit with a crust baked in a pot. **pot plant** a plant grown in a flowerpot. **pot roast** a piece of meat cooked slowly in a covered dish. **pot-roast** *v.tr.* cook (a piece of meat) in this way. **pot-shot 1** a random shot. **2** a shot aimed at an animal etc. within easy reach. **3** a shot at a game-bird etc. merely to provide a meal. **pot-valiant** courageous because of drunkenness. **pot-valour** this type of courage. **put a person's pot on** *Austral.* & *NZ sl.* inform on a person. ▫▫ **potful** *n.* (*pl.* **-fuls**). [OE *pott*, corresp. to OFris., MDu., MLG *pot*, f. pop.L]
■ *n.* **1** pan, saucepan, cauldron, casserole, cook-pot, stewpot. **5** jackpot, bank, kitty, stakes, pool. **6** see LOT *n.* 1. ● *v.* **5** see SHOOT *v.* 1c. **6** see SECURE *v.* 3. **7** see ABRIDGE 1. ▫ **go to pot** see DETERIORATE. **pot-bellied** rotund, tubby, portly, paunchy; see also FAT *adj.* 1. **pot-belly 1** pot, paunch, gut, *Brit. colloq.* spare tyre, *joc.* corporation, *sl.* beer-belly. **pot-valour** Dutch courage.

pot[2] /pot/ *n. sl.* marijuana. ▫ **pot-head** one who smokes this. [prob. f. Mex. Sp. *potiguaya*]

pot[3] /pot/ *n.* & *v. Austral.* & *NZ* ● *n.* a dropped goal in rugby football. ● *v.tr.* (**potted, potting**) score (a dropped goal). [perh. f. pot-shot]

potable /pṓtəb'l/ *adj.* drinkable. ▫▫ **potability** /-bílliti/ *n.* [F *potable* or LL *potabilis* f. L *potare* drink]

potage /potaázh/ *n.* thick soup. [F (as POTTAGE)]

potamic /pətámmik/ *adj.* of rivers. ▫▫ **potamology** /póttəmólliji/ *n.* [Gk *potamos* river]

potash /póttash/ *n.* an alkaline potassium compound, usu. potassium carbonate or hydroxide. [17th-c. *pot-ashes* f. Du.

pot-asschen (as POT[1], ASH[1]): orig. obtained by leaching vegetable ashes and evaporating the solution in iron pots]

potassium /pətássiəm/ *n. Chem.* a soft silver-white metallic element occurring naturally in seawater and various minerals, an essential element for living organisms, and forming many useful compounds used industrially. ¶ Symb.: **K.** □ **potassium chloride** a white crystalline solid used as a fertilizer and in photographic processing. **potassium cyanide** a highly toxic solid that can be hydrolysed to give poisonous hydrogen cyanide gas: also called CYANIDE. **potassium iodide** a white crystalline solid used as an additive to table salt to prevent iodine deficiency. **potassium permanganate** a purple crystalline solid that is used in solution as an oxidizing agent and disinfectant. □□ **potassic** *adj.* [POTASH + -IUM]

potation /pōtáysh'n/ *n.* **1** a drink. **2** the act or an instance of drinking. **3** (usu. in *pl.*) the act or an instance of tippling. □□ **potatory** /-táytəri/ *adj.* [ME f. OF *potation* or L *potatio* f. *potare* drink]
■ **1** see DRINK *n.* 1a.

potato /pətáytō/ *n.* (*pl.* **-oes**) **1** a starchy plant tuber that is cooked and used for food. **2** the plant, *Solanum tuberosum*, bearing this. **3** *colloq.* a hole in (esp. the heel of) a sock or stocking. □ **potato chip** = CHIP *n.* 3. **potato crisp** *Brit.* = CRISP *n.* 1. [Sp. *patata* var. of Taino *batata*]

pot-au-feu /póttōfố/ *n.* **1** a large cooking pot of the kind common in France. **2** the soup or broth cooked in it. **3** the traditional French recipe associated with this. [F, = pot on the fire]

potch /poch/ *n.* an opal of inferior quality. [19th c.: orig. unkn.]

poteen /potéen/ *n.* (also **potheen** /-chéen/) *Ir.* alcohol made illicitly, usu. from potatoes. [Ir. *poitín* dimin. of *pota* POT[1]]
■ moonshine, home-brew, *US colloq.* hooch.

potent[1] /pṓt'nt/ *adj.* **1** powerful; strong. **2** (of a reason) cogent; forceful. **3** (of a male) capable of sexual erection or orgasm. **4** *literary* mighty. □□ **potence** *n.* **potency** *n.* **potently** *adv.* [L *potens -entis* pres. part. of *posse* be able]
■ **1** powerful, strong, mighty, vigorous, forceful, formidable, influential, *literary or archaic* puissant. **2** forceful, effective, convincing, cogent, persuasive, compelling, efficacious, sound, valid, impressive, weighty, authoritative, influential. **3** virile, masculine, manly.

potent[2] /pṓt'nt/ *adj.* & *n. Heraldry* ● *adj.* **1** with a crutch-head shape. **2** (of a fur) formed by a series of such shapes. ● *n.* this fur. [ME f. OF *potence* crutch f. L *potentia* power (as POTENT[1])]

potentate /pṓt'ntayt/ *n.* a monarch or ruler. [ME f. OF *potentat* or L *potentatus* dominion (as POTENT[2])]
■ see MONARCH 1, 2.

potential /pəténsh'l/ *adj.* & *n.* ● *adj.* capable of coming into being or action; latent. ● *n.* **1** the capacity for use or development; possibility (*achieved its highest potential*). **2** usable resources. **3** *Physics* the quantity determining the energy of mass in a gravitational field or of charge in an electric field. □ **potential barrier** a region of high potential impeding the movement of particles etc. **potential difference** the difference of electric potential between two points. **potential energy** a body's ability to do work by virtue of its position relative to others, stresses within itself, electric charge, etc. □□ **potentiality** /-shiálliti/ *n.* **potentialize** *v.tr.* (also **-ise**). **potentially** *adv.* [ME f. OF *potencial* or LL *potentialis* f. *potentia* (as POTENT[1])]
■ *adj.* possible, likely, latent, implicit, implied, imminent, developing, budding, embryonic, dormant, quiescent, future, unrealized. ● *n.* **1** capacity, capability, possibility, aptitude, potency; (*have potential*) *colloq.* have what it takes, have the necessary. **2** see *the necessary* 2 (NECESSARY).

potentiate /pəténshiayt/ *v.tr.* **1** make more powerful, esp. increase the effectiveness of (a drug). **2** make possible. [as POTENT[1] after SUBSTANTIATE]

potentilla /pōtəntíllə/ *n.* any plant or shrub of the genus *Potentilla*; a cinquefoil. [med.L, dimin. of L *potens* POTENT[1]]

potentiometer /pəténshiómmitər/ *n.* an instrument for measuring or adjusting small electrical potentials. □□ **potentiometric** /-shiəmétrik/ *adj.* **potentiometry** /-shiómmitri/ *n.*

potheen var. of POTEEN.

pother /pó*th*ər/ *n.* & *v. literary* ● *n.* a noise; commotion; fuss. ● *v.* **1** *tr.* fluster, worry. **2** *intr.* make a fuss. [16th c.: orig. unkn.]
■ *n.* see FUSS *n.* 1, 2a.

pothole /pót-hōl/ *n.* & *v.* ● *n.* **1** *Geol.* a deep hole or system of caves and underground river-beds formed by the erosion of rock esp. by the action of water. **2** a deep hole in the ground or a river-bed. **3** a hole in a road surface caused by wear or subsidence. ● *v.intr. Brit.* explore potholes. □□ **potholed** *adj.* **potholer** *n.* **potholing** *n.*
■ *n.* **2, 3** see HOLE *n.* 1.

potion /pṓsh'n/ *n.* a liquid medicine, drug, poison, etc. [ME f. OF f. L *potio -onis* f. *potus* having drunk]
■ draught, brew, potation, *formal* beverage, *joc.* libation; philtre, elixir, tonic, concoction; dose.

potlatch /pótlach/ *n.* (among N. American Indians) a ceremonial giving away or destruction of property to enhance status. [Chinook f. Nootka *patlatsh* gift]

potoroo /póttəroo͞/ *n. Austral.* any small marsupial of the genus *Potorus*, native to Australia and Tasmania; a rat kangaroo. [Aboriginal]

pot-pourri /pōpoóri, -rée/ *n.* **1** a mixture of dried petals and spices used to perfume a room etc. **2** a musical or literary medley. [F, = rotten pot]
■ **2** mixture, medley, miscellany, assortment, olla podrida, gallimaufry, salmagundi, patchwork, collection, hotchpotch, *mélange*, pastiche, pasticcio.

potrero /potráirō/ *n.* (*pl.* **-os**) **1** (in the SW US and S. America) a paddock or pasture for horses or cattle. **2** (in the SW US) a narrow steep-sided plateau. [Sp. f. *potro* colt, pony]

potsherd /pótsherd/ *n.* a broken piece of ceramic material, esp. one found on an archaeological site.
■ shard, sherd.

pottage /póttij/ *n. archaic* soup, stew. [ME f. OF *potage* (as POT[1])]

potter[1] /póttər/ *v.* (*US* **putter** /púttər/) **1** *intr.* **a** (often foll. by *about*, *around*) work or occupy oneself in a desultory but pleasant manner (*likes pottering about in the garden*). **b** (often foll. by *at*, *in*) dabble in a subject or occupation. **2** *intr.* go slowly, dawdle, loiter (*pottered up to the pub*). **3** *tr.* (foll. by *away*) fritter away (one's time etc.). □□ **potterer** *n.* [frequent. of dial. *pote* push f. OE *potian*]
■ **1 a** see *mess about*. **b** dabble, tinker, experiment, *US* putter. **2** amble, saunter, stroll, dawdle, wander, loiter, *sl.* mosey. **3** (*potter away*) fritter (away), squander; see also WASTE *v.* 1.

potter[2] /póttər/ *n.* a maker of ceramic vessels. □ **potter's field** a burial place for paupers, strangers, etc. (after Matt. 27:7). **potter's wheel** a horizontal revolving disc to carry clay for making pots. [OE *pottere* (as POT[1])]

pottery /póttəri/ *n.* (*pl.* **-ies**) **1** vessels etc. made of fired clay. **2** a potter's work. **3** a potter's workshop. □ **the Potteries** a district in N. Staffordshire, where the English pottery industry is centred. [ME f. OF *poterie* f. *potier* POTTER[2]]
■ **1** earthenware, ceramics, terracotta, crockery, stoneware, porcelain, china.

potting shed /pótting/ *n.* a building in which plants are potted and tools etc. are stored.

pottle /pótt'l/ *n.* **1** a small punnet or carton for strawberries etc. **2** *archaic* **a** a measure for liquids; a half gallon. **b** a pot etc. containing this. [ME f. OF *potel* (as POT[1])]

potto /póttō/ *n.* (*pl.* **-os**) **1** a W. African lemur-like mammal, *Perodicticus potto*. **2** a kinkajou. [perh. f. Guinea dial.]

Pott's fracture /pots/ *n.* a fracture of the lower end of the fibula, usu. with dislocation of the ankle. [P. *Pott*, Engl. surgeon d. 1788]

potty[1] /pótti/ *adj.* (**pottier, pottiest**) *Brit. sl.* **1** foolish or crazy. **2** insignificant, trivial (esp. *potty little*). □□ **pottiness** *n.* [19th c.: orig. unkn.]

■ **1** see FOOLISH.

potty[2] /pótti/ *n.* (*pl.* **-ies**) *colloq.* a chamber-pot, esp. for a child.

pouch /powch/ *n.* & *v.* ● *n.* **1** a small bag or detachable outside pocket. **2** a baggy area of skin underneath the eyes etc. **3 a** a pocket-like receptacle in which marsupials carry their young during lactation. **b** any of several similar structures in various animals, e.g. in the cheeks of rodents. **4** a soldier's leather ammunition bag. **5** a lockable bag for mail or dispatches. **6** *Bot.* a baglike cavity, esp. the seed-vessel, in a plant. ● *v.tr.* **1** put or make into a pouch. **2** take possession of; pocket. **3** make (part of a dress etc.) hang like a pouch. □□ **pouched** *adj.* **pouchy** *adj.* [ME f. ONF *pouche*: cf. POKE[2]]

■ *n.* **1** pocket, sack, bag, purse, *dial.* poke, *usu. hist.* reticule. ● *v.* **2** see POCKET *v.* 2.

pouf var. of POOF.

pouffe /pōōf/ *n.* (also **pouf**) a large firm cushion used as a low seat or footstool. [F *pouf*; ult. imit.]

poulard /pōōlaard/ *n.* a domestic hen that has been spayed and fattened for eating. [F *poularde* f. *poule* hen]

poult[1] /pōlt/ *n.* a young domestic fowl, turkey, pheasant, etc. [ME, contr. f. PULLET]

poult[2] /pōōlt/ *n.* (in full **poult-de-soie** /pōōdəswaa/) a fine corded silk or taffeta, usu. coloured. [F, of unkn. orig.]

poulterer /pṓltərər/ *n.* a dealer in poultry and usu. game. [ME *poulter* f. OF *pouletier* (as PULLET)]

poultice /pṓltiss/ *n.* & *v.* ● *n.* a soft medicated and usu. heated mass applied to the body and kept in place with muslin etc., for relieving soreness and inflammation. ● *v.tr.* apply a poultice to. [orig. *pultes* (pl.) f. L *puls pultis* pottage, pap, etc.]

poultry /pṓltri/ *n.* domestic fowls (ducks, geese, turkeys, chickens, etc.), esp. as a source of food. [ME f. OF *pouletrie* (as POULTERER)]

pounce[1] /pownss/ *v.* & *n.* ● *v.intr.* **1** spring or swoop, esp. as in capturing prey. **2** (often foll. by *on, upon*) **a** make a sudden attack. **b** seize eagerly upon an object, remark, etc. (*pounced on what we said*). ● *n.* **1** the act or an instance of pouncing. **2** the claw or talon of a bird of prey. □□ **pouncer** *n.* [perh. f. PUNCHEON[1]]

■ *v.* **1, 2a** spring, leap, swoop down (on *or* upon), jump; (*pounce on*) fall upon, take by surprise *or* unawares, attack, ambush, mug. **2 b** seize, leap, fasten, dive, sweep down. ● *n.* **1** spring, swoop, dive, sweep, leap, jump.

pounce[2] /pownss/ *n.* & *v.* ● *n.* **1** a fine powder formerly used to prevent ink from spreading on unglazed paper. **2** powdered charcoal etc. dusted over a perforated pattern to transfer the design to the object beneath. ● *v.tr.* **1** dust with pounce. **2** transfer (a design etc.) by use of pounce. **3** smooth (paper etc.) with pounce or pumice. □□ **pouncer** *n.* [F *ponce, poncer* f. L *pumex* PUMICE]

pouncet-box /pównsitboks/ *n.* *archaic* a small box with a perforated lid for perfumes etc. [16th c.: perh. orig. erron. f. *pounced* (= perforated) *box*]

pound[1] /pownd/ *n.* **1** a unit of weight equal to 16 oz. avoirdupois (0.4536 kg), or 12 oz. troy (0.3732 kg). **2** (in full **pound sterling**) (*pl.* same or **pounds**) the chief monetary unit of the UK and several other countries. □ **pound cake** a rich cake containing a pound (or equal weights) of each chief ingredient. **pound coin** (or **note**) a coin or note worth one pound sterling. **pound of flesh** any legitimate but crippling demand. **pound Scots** *hist.* 1s. 8d. **pound sign** the sign £, representing a pound. [OE *pund* ult. f. L *pondo* Roman pound weight of 12 ounces]

■ **2** sovereign, *Brit. sl.* nicker, oner, quid.

pound[2] /pownd/ *v.* & *n.* ● *v.* **1** *tr.* **a** crush or beat with repeated heavy blows. **b** thump or pummel, esp. with the fists. **c** grind to a powder or pulp. **2** *intr.* (foll. by *at, on*) deliver heavy blows or gunfire. **3** *intr.* (foll. by *along* etc.) make one's way heavily or clumsily. **4** *intr.* (of the heart) beat heavily. ● *n.* a heavy blow or thump; the sound of this. □ **pound into** instil (an attitude, behaviour, etc.) forcefully (*pounded into me*). **pound out 1** produce with or as if with heavy blows. **2** remove (an attitude, behaviour, etc.) forcefully (*pounded out of him*). □□ **pounder** *n.* [OE *pūnian*, rel. to Du. *puin*, LG *pün* rubbish]

■ *v.* **1 a, b** batter, pelt, hammer, pummel; thump, belabour, thrash, bludgeon, cudgel, strike, *colloq.* lambaste, give a person the works, work over, *sl.* paste, clobber, give a person a pasting; see also BEAT *v.* 1. **c** crush, grind, powder, pulverize, triturate, mash, pulp, *archaic* bray. **3** see TRAMP *v.* 1a. **4** beat, throb, hammer, thump, pulse, pulsate, palpitate. ● *n.* pounding, beat, beating, thump, thumping. □ **pound into** instil, din *or* drill *or* drub *or* hammer *or* beat into. **pound out 1** beat out, hammer out, produce. **2** remove, rid, expel, clear, empty, purge, beat out, hammer out, *usu. formal* cleanse.

pound[3] /pownd/ *n.* & *v.* ● *n.* **1** an enclosure where stray animals or officially removed vehicles are kept until redeemed. **2** a place of confinement. ● *v.tr.* enclose (cattle etc.) in a pound. □ **pound lock** a lock with two gates to confine water and often a side reservoir to maintain the water level. [ME f. OE *pund-* in *pundfald*: see PINFOLD]

■ **1** pen, compound, confine, yard; see also ENCLOSURE 2.

poundage /pówndij/ *n.* **1** a commission or fee of so much per pound sterling or weight. **2** a percentage of the total earnings of a business, paid as wages. **3** a person's weight, esp. that which is regarded as excess.

poundal /pównd'l/ *n.* *Physics* a unit of force equal to the force required to give a mass of one pound an acceleration of one foot per second per second. [POUND[1] + *-al* perh. after *quintal*]

pounder /pówndər/ *n.* (usu. in *comb.*) **1** a thing or person weighing a specified number of pounds (*a five-pounder*). **2** a gun carrying a shell of a specified number of pounds. **3** a thing worth, or a person possessing, so many pounds sterling.

pour /por/ *v.* **1** *intr.* & *tr.* (usu. foll. by *down, out, over*, etc.) flow or cause to flow esp. downwards in a stream or shower. **2** *tr.* dispense (a drink, e.g. tea) by pouring. **3** *intr.* (of rain, or with *it* as subject) fall heavily. **4** *intr.* (usu. foll. by *in, out*, etc.) come or go in profusion or rapid succession (*the crowd poured out; letters poured in; poems poured from her fertile mind*). **5** *tr.* discharge or send freely (*poured forth arrows*). **6** *tr.* (often foll. by *out*) utter at length or in a rush (*poured out their story; poured scorn on my attempts*). □ **it never rains but it pours** misfortunes rarely come singly. **pour cold water on** see COLD. **pour oil on the waters** (or **on troubled waters**) calm a disagreement or disturbance, esp. with conciliatory words. □□ **pourable** *adj.* **pourer** *n.* [ME: orig. unkn.]

■ **1** flow, run, gush, rush, flood, stream, course, spout, spurt, spew out *or* forth, cascade; discharge, let out, let flow. **3** rain, teem down, fall, come down in buckets *or* by the bucketful *or* in sheets, sheet down, bucket down, rain cats and dogs, pelt down. **4** stream, swarm, crowd, throng, gush, teem, issue (forth), go (forth), *archaic* sally forth.

pourboire /poorbwaar/ *n.* a gratuity or tip. [F, = *pour boire* (money) for drinking]

■ see TIP[3] *n.* 1.

poussin /pōōssaN/ *n.* a young chicken bred for eating. [F]

pout[1] /powt/ *v.* & *n.* ● *v.* **1** *intr.* **a** push the lips forward as an expression of displeasure or sulking. **b** (of the lips) be pushed forward. **2** *tr.* push (the lips) forward in pouting. ● *n.* **1** such an action or expression. **2** (**the pouts**) a fit of sulking. □□ **pouter** *n.* **poutingly** *adv.* **pouty** *adj.* [ME, perh. f. OE *putian* (unrecorded) be inflated: cf. POUT[2]]

■ *v.* **1 a** make a moue, pull a long face, frown, lour, knit one's brows; mope, brood, sulk. ● *n.* **1** moue, (long) face, grimace, mouth, scowl, frown. **2** (**the pouts**) sulk, huff, mood; the sulks.

pout[2] /powt/ *n.* **1** = BIB[1] 3. **2** = EELPOUT. [OE *-puta* in *æ lepūta* eelpout, f. WG]

pouter /pówtər/ *n.* **1** a person who pouts. **2** a kind of pigeon able to inflate its crop considerably.

poverty /póvvərti/ *n.* **1** the state of being poor; want of the necessities of life. **2** (often foll. by *of, in*) scarcity or lack. **3** inferiority, poorness, meanness. **4** *Eccl.* renunciation of the right to individual ownership of property. □ **poverty line** the minimum income level needed to secure the necessities of life. **poverty-stricken** extremely poor. **poverty trap** a situation in which an increase of income incurs a loss of State benefits, making real improvement impossible. [ME f. OF *poverte, poverté* f. L *paupertas -tatis* f. *pauper* poor]
■ **1** want, penury, indigence, destitution, pauperism, impecuniousness, neediness, beggary, narrow *or* reduced circumstances, necessity, need. **2** scarcity, scarceness, want, need, lack, insufficiency, shortage, dearth, paucity, inadequacy. **3** see INFERIORITY. □ **poverty-stricken** see POOR 1.

POW *abbr.* prisoner of war.

pow /pow/ *int.* expressing the sound of a blow or explosion. [imit.]

powder /pówdər/ *n.* & *v.* ● *n.* **1** a substance in the form of fine dry particles. **2** a medicine or cosmetic in this form. **3** = GUNPOWDER. ● *v.tr.* **1 a** apply powder to. **b** sprinkle or decorate with or as with powder. **2** (esp. as **powdered** *adj.*) reduce to a fine powder (*powdered milk*). □ **keep one's powder dry** be cautious and alert. **powder blue** pale blue. **powder-flask** *hist.* a small case for carrying gunpowder. **powder-keg 1** a barrel of gunpowder. **2** a dangerous or volatile situation. **powder metallurgy** the production of metal as fine powders to make objects. **powder-monkey** *hist.* a boy employed on board ship to carry powder to the guns. **powder-puff** a soft pad for applying powder to the skin, esp. the face. **powder-room** a women's cloakroom or lavatory in a public building. **powder snow** loose dry snow on a ski-run etc. **take a powder** *sl.* depart quickly. □□ **powdery** *adj.* [ME f. OF *poudre* f. L *pulvis pulveris* dust]
■ *n.* **1** dust; talc. ● *v.* **1** dust; dredge, flour. **2** pulverize, grind, crush, pound, granulate, levigate, triturate, *archaic* bray. □ **keep one's powder dry** see *watch out.* **powder-keg 2** time-bomb, precipice; dynamite. **powder-room** toilets, lavatory, ladies' room, *Brit.* Ladies, (public) conveniences, *esp. US* rest room, bathroom, *US* washroom, *Brit. colloq.* loo, *Brit. euphem.* cloakroom, *US euphem.* comfort station. **take a powder** abscond, escape, vanish, disappear, do a moonlight flit, *sl.* do a runner, *Brit. sl.* scarper, *US sl.* take it on the lam; see also RUN *v.* 2.

power /powr/ *n.* & *v.* ● *n.* **1** the ability to do or act (*will do all in my power; has the power to change colour*). **2** a particular faculty of body or mind (*lost the power of speech; powers of persuasion*). **3 a** government, influence, or authority. **b** political or social ascendancy or control (*the party in power; Black Power*). **4** authorization; delegated authority (*power of attorney; police powers*). **5** (often foll. by *over*) personal ascendancy. **6** an influential person, group, or organization (*the press is a power in the land*). **7 a** military strength. **b** a State having international influence, esp. based on military strength (*the leading powers*). **8** vigour, energy. **9** an active property or function (*has a high heating power*). **10** *colloq.* a large number or amount (*has done me a power of good*). **11** the capacity for exerting mechanical force or doing work (*horsepower*). **12** mechanical or electrical energy as distinct from hand-labour (often *attrib.*: *power tools; power steering*). **13 a** a public supply of (esp. electrical) energy. **b** a particular source or form of energy (*hydroelectric power*). **14** a mechanical force applied e.g. by means of a lever. **15** *Physics* the rate of energy output. **16** the product obtained when a number is multiplied by itself a certain number of times (*2 to the power of 3 = 8*). **17** the magnifying capacity of a lens. **18 a** a deity. **b** (in *pl.*) the sixth order of the ninefold celestial hierarchy. ● *v.tr.* **1** supply with mechanical or electrical energy. **2** (foll. by *up, down*) increase or decrease the power supplied to (a device); switch on or off. □ **in the power of** under the control of. **more power to your elbow!** an expression of encouragement or approval. **power behind the throne** a person who asserts authority or influence without having formal status. **power block** a group of nations constituting an international political force. **power cut** a temporary withdrawal or failure of an electric power supply. **power-dive** *n.* a steep dive of an aircraft with the engines providing thrust. ● *v.intr.* perform a power-dive. **power line** a conductor supplying electrical power, esp. one supported by pylons or poles. **power of attorney** see ATTORNEY. **power pack 1** a unit for supplying power. **2** the equipment for converting an alternating current (from the mains) to a direct current at a different (usu. lower) voltage. **power play 1** tactics involving the concentration of players at a particular point. **2** similar tactics in business, politics, etc., involving a concentration of resources, effort, etc. **power point** *Brit.* a socket in a wall etc. for connecting an electrical device to the mains. **power politics** political action based on power or influence. **power-sharing** a policy agreed between parties or within a coalition to share responsibility for decision-making and political action. **power station** a building where electrical power is generated for distribution. **the powers that be** those in authority (Rom. 13:1). **power stroke** the stroke of an internal-combustion engine, in which the piston is moved downward by the expansion of gases. □□ **powered** *adj.* (also in *comb.*). [ME & AF *poer* etc., OF *poeir* ult. f. L *posse* be able]
■ *n.* **2** capacity, capability, ability, potential, faculty, competence, potentiality, energies; talent, skill, ability, gift, aptitude, genius, knack. **3a, 5** control, dominance, authority, mastery, rule, influence, government, command, ascendancy, sovereignty, dominion, *archaic* puissance; weight, sway, pull, *colloq.* clout, *US sl.* drag. **4** authority, right, authorization, warrant; see also LICENCE 2, PERMISSION. **8** strength, might, vigour, energy, force, mightiness, potency, forcefulness, brawn, muscle, *archaic* puissance. **10** see LOT *n.* 1. **13** energy; electricity. **14** energy, momentum, impetus, drive, force. **18 a** see GOD 1a. ● *v.* **2** see *turn on* 1, *turn off* 1. □ **in the power of** under a person's thumb, at the mercy of. **power behind the throne** kingmaker, *éminence grise*, grey eminence. **power cut** power failure, blackout; outage. **power point** socket, *Brit.* point(s), *US* outlet. **the powers that be** Establishment, government, administration, authorities.

powerboat /pówrbōt/ *n.* a powerful motor boat.

powerful /pówrfŏŏl/ *adj.* **1** having much power or strength. **2** politically or socially influential. □□ **powerfully** *adv.* **powerfulness** *n.*
■ **1** potent, strong, mighty, vigorous, robust, energetic, sturdy, stalwart, tough, resilient, dynamic; intense, substantial, great, high. **2** influential, strong, compelling, forceful, potent, substantial, weighty, authoritative, effective, persuasive; important, impressive, effectual, formidable.

powerhouse /pówrhowss/ *n.* **1** = *power station.* **2** a person or thing of great energy.

powerless /pówrliss/ *adj.* **1** without power or strength. **2** (often foll. by *to* + infin.) wholly unable (*powerless to help*). □□ **powerlessly** *adv.* **powerlessness** *n.*
■ **1** helpless, ineffectual, ineffective, incapacitated, weak, feeble, debilitated. **2** (*powerless to*) unable *or* not able to, unfit *or* incompetent *or* unqualified to, incapable of.

powerplant /pówrplaant/ *n.* an apparatus or an installation which provides power for industry, a machine, etc.

powwow /pów-wow/ *n.* & *v.* ● *n.* a conference or meeting for discussion (orig. among N. American Indians). ● *v.tr.*

hold a powwow. [Algonquian *powah*, *powwaw* magician (lit. 'he dreams')]

■ *n.* see DISCUSSION 1, PALAVER *n.* 5. ● *v.* see CONFER 2.

pox /poks/ *n.* **1** any virus disease producing a rash of pimples that become pus-filled and leave pock-marks on healing. **2** *colloq.* = SYPHILIS. **3** a plant disease that causes pocklike spots. □ **a pox on** *archaic* an exclamation of anger or impatience with (a person). [alt. spelling of *pocks* pl. of POCK]

poxy /póksi/ *adj.* (**poxier**, **poxiest**) **1** infected by pox. **2** *sl.* of poor quality; worthless.

pozzolana /pótsəlaánə/ *n.* (also **puzzolana**) a volcanic ash used for mortar or hydraulic cement. [It., f. *pozz(u)olano* (adj.) of *Pozzuoli* near Naples]

pp *abbr.* pianissimo.

pp. *abbr.* pages.

p.p. *abbr.* (also **pp**) *per pro.*

PPE *abbr. Brit.* philosophy, politics, and economics (as a degree course at Oxford University).

p.p.m. *abbr.* parts per million.

PPS *abbr. Brit.* **1** Parliamentary Private Secretary. **2** additional postscript.

PR *abbr.* **1** public relations. **2** proportional representation. **3** *US* Puerto Rico.

Pr *symb. Chem.* the element praseodymium.

pr. *abbr.* pair.

PRA *abbr.* (in the UK) President of the Royal Academy.

praam var. of PRAM².

practicable /práktikəb'l/ *adj.* **1** that can be done or used. **2** possible in practice. □□ **practicability** /-bílliti/ *n.* **practicableness** *n.* **practicably** *adv.* [F *praticable* f. *pratiquer* put into practice (as PRACTICAL)]

■ possible, feasible, workable, performable, doable, achievable, attainable, accomplishable, viable.

practical /práktik'l/ *adj.* & *n.* ● *adj.* **1** of or concerned with practice or use rather than theory. **2** suited to use or action; designed mainly to fulfil a function (*practical shoes*). **3** (of a person) inclined to action rather than speculation; able to make things function well. **4 a** that is such in effect though not nominally (*for all practical purposes*). **b** virtual (*in practical control*). **5** feasible; concerned with what is actually possible (*practical politics*). ● *n.* a practical examination or lesson. □ **practical joke** a humorous trick played on a person. **practical joker** a person who plays practical jokes. □□ **practicality** /-kálliti/ *n.* (*pl.* **-ies**). **practicalness** *n.* [earlier *practic* f. obs. F *practique* or LL *practicus* f. Gk *praktikos* f. *prassō* do, act]

■ *adj.* **1** empirical, pragmatic, empiric, experimental, applied, field, hands on. **2** pragmatic, functional, useful, usable, utilitarian, serviceable; appropriate, suitable, expedient; everyday, ordinary. **3** down-to-earth, pragmatic, hard-headed, realistic, businesslike, commonsensical, sensible, efficient, matter-of-fact, no-nonsense, *colloq.* hard-nosed. **4 b** virtual, effective, essential. □ **practical joke** see PRANK.

practically /práktikəli/ *adv.* **1** virtually, almost (*practically nothing*). **2** in a practical way.

■ **1** almost, (very) nearly, virtually, just about, more or less, *archaic or rhet.* wellnigh. **2** realistically, in fact, in reality; empirically, experimentally; sensibly, efficiently, matter-of-factly.

practice /práktiss/ *n.* & *v.* ● *n.* **1** habitual action or performance (*the practice of teaching*; *makes a practice of saving*). **2** a habit or custom (*has been my regular practice*). **3 a** repeated exercise in an activity requiring the development of skill (*to sing well needs much practice*). **b** a session of this (*time for target practice*). **4** action or execution as opposed to theory. **5** the professional work or business of a doctor, lawyer, etc. (*has a practice in town*). **6** an established method of legal procedure. **7** procedure generally, esp. of a specified kind (*bad practice*). ● *v.tr.* & *intr. US* var. of PRACTISE. □ **in practice 1** when actually applied; in reality. **2** skilful because of recent exercise in a particular pursuit. **out of practice** lacking a former skill from lack of recent practice. **put into practice** actually apply (an idea, method, etc.). [ME f. PRACTISE, after *advice*, *device*]

■ *n.* **2, 7** custom, habit, praxis, *formal or joc.* wont; routine, convention, tradition, rule, procedure, mode, style, way, *modus operandi*, m.o., technique. **3** exercise, discipline, drill, repetition, rehearsal, training, preparation; workout. **4** action, execution, operation, enactment, reality, actuality, fact, truth. □ **in practice 1** practically, actually, in reality, realistically, in real life. **out of practice** unpractised, unaccustomed, rusty; out of touch. **put into practice** see APPLY 3a.

practician /praktísh'n/ *n.* a worker; a practitioner. [obs. F *practicien* f. *practique* f. med.L *practica* f. Gk *praktikē* fem. of *praktikos*: see PRACTICAL]

practise /práktiss/ *v.* (*US* **practice**) **1** *tr.* perform habitually; carry out in action (*practise the same method*; *practise what you preach*). **2** *tr.* & (foll. by *in*, *on*) *intr.* do repeatedly as an exercise to improve a skill; exercise oneself in or on (an activity requiring skill) (*had to practise in the art of speaking*; *practise your reading*). **3** *tr.* (as **practised** *adj.*) experienced, expert (*a practised liar*; *with a practised hand*). **4** *tr.* **a** pursue or be engaged in (a profession, religion, etc.). **b** (as **practising** *adj.*) currently active or engaged in (a profession or activity) (*a practising Christian*; *a practising lawyer*). **5** *intr.* (foll. by *on*, *upon*) take advantage of; impose upon. **6** *intr. archaic* scheme, contrive (*when first we practise to deceive*). □□ **practiser** *n.* [ME f. OF *pra(c)tiser* or med.L *practizare* alt. f. *practicare* (as PRACTICAL)]

■ **1** carry out, make a practice of, perform, do, act, put into practice. **2** exercise, work out, train, prepare, rehearse, study; run through, go through. **3** (**practised**) accomplished, proficient, expert, skilled, experienced, capable, adept, seasoned, able, qualified, gifted, talented, skilful, masterful, consummate, well-trained, well-versed. **5** (*practise on* or *upon*) see IMPOSE 3.

practitioner /praktíshənər/ *n.* a person practising a profession, esp. medicine (*general practitioner*). [obs. *practitian* = PRACTICIAN]

prad / prad/ *n.* esp. *Austral. sl.* a horse. [by metathesis f. Du. *paard* f. LL *paraveredus*; see PALFREY]

prae- /pree/ *prefix* = PRE- (esp. in words regarded as Latin or relating to Roman antiquity). [L: see PRE-]

praecipe /préessipi/ *n.* **1** a writ demanding action or an explanation of non-action. **2** an order requesting a writ. [L (the first word of the writ), imper. of *praecipere* enjoin: see PRECEPT]

praecocial /prikṓsh'l/ *adj.* & *n.* (*US* **precocial**) ● *adj.* (of a bird) having young that can feed themselves as soon as they are hatched. ● *n.* a praecocial bird (cf. ALTRICIAL). [L *praecox -cocis* (as PRECOCIOUS)]

praemunire /préemoonéeri/ *n. hist.* a writ charging a sheriff to summon a person accused of asserting or maintaining papal jurisdiction in England. [med.L, = forewarn, for L *praemonēre* (as PRAE-, *monēre* warn): the words *praemunire facias* that you warn (a person to appear) occur in the writ]

praenomen /preenṓmen/ *n.* an ancient Roman's first or personal name (e.g. *Marcus* Tullius Cicero). [L f. *prae* before + *nomen* name]

praepostor /pripóstər/ *n.* (also **prepostor**) *Brit.* (at some public schools) a prefect or monitor. [*praepositor* alt. f. L *praepositus* past part. of *praeponere* set over (as PRAE-, *ponere posit-* place)]

praesidium var. of PRESIDIUM.

praetor /préetər, -tor/ *n.* (*US* **pretor**) *Rom.Hist.* each of two ancient Roman magistrates ranking below consul. □□ **praetorial** /-tóriəl/ *adj.* **praetorship** *n.* [ME f. F *préteur* or L *praetor* (perh. as PRAE-, *ire it-* go)]

praetorian /preetóriən/ *adj.* & *n.* (*US* **pretorian**) *Rom.Hist.* ● *adj.* of or having the powers of a praetor. ● *n.* a man of praetorian rank. □ **praetorian guard** the bodyguard of the Roman emperor. [ME f. L *praetorianus* (as PRAETOR)]

pragmatic /pragmáttik/ *adj.* **1** dealing with matters with regard to their practical requirements or consequences. **2** treating the facts of history with reference to their practical lessons. **3** *hist.* of or relating to the affairs of a State. **4** (also **pragmatical**) **a** concerning pragmatism. **b** meddlesome. **c** dogmatic. □ **pragmatic sanction** *hist.* an imperial or royal ordinance issued as a fundamental law, esp. regarding a question of royal succession. □□ **pragmaticality** /-kálliti/ *n.* **pragmatically** *adv.* [LL *pragmaticus* f. Gk *pragmatikos* f. *pragma -matos* deed]
■ **1** see PRACTICAL 1–3.

pragmatics /pragmáttiks/ *n.pl.* (usu. treated as *sing.*) the branch of linguistics dealing with language in use.

pragmatism /prágmətiz'm/ *n.* **1** a pragmatic attitude or procedure. **2** a philosophy that evaluates assertions solely by their practical consequences and bearing on human interests. □□ **pragmatist** *n.* **pragmatistic** /-tístik/ *adj.* [Gk *pragma*: see PRAGMATIC]

pragmatize /prágmətīz/ *v.tr.* (also **-ise**) **1** represent as real. **2** rationalize (a myth).

prahu var. of PROA.

prairie /práiri/ *n.* a large area of usu. treeless grassland esp. in N. America. □ **prairie chicken** (or **hen**) a N. American grouse, *Tympanuchus cupido.* **prairie dog** any N. American rodent of the genus *Cynomys*, living in burrows and making a barking sound. **prairie oyster** a seasoned raw egg, often served in spirits and swallowed in one as a cure for a hangover. **prairie schooner** *US* a covered wagon used by the 19th-c. pioneers in crossing the N. American prairies. **prairie wolf** = COYOTE. [F f. OF *praerie* ult. f. L *pratum* meadow]
■ see PLAIN[1] *n.* 1.

praise /prayz/ *v.* & *n.* ● *v.tr.* **1** express warm approval or admiration of. **2** glorify (God) in words. ● *n.* the act or an instance of praising; commendation (*won high praise; were loud in their praises*). □ **praise be!** an exclamation of pious gratitude. **sing the praises of** commend (a person) highly. □□ **praiseful** *adj.* **praiser** *n.* [ME f. OF *preisier* price, prize, praise, f. LL *pretiare* f. L *pretium* price: cf. PRIZE[1]]
■ *v.* **1** acclaim, laud, applaud, pay tribute to, compliment, commend, eulogize, extol, honour, sing the praises of, pay homage to, endorse. **2** worship, revere, reverence, exalt, glorify, venerate, hallow. ● *n.* acclaim, approval, approbation, applause, plaudits, acclamation, tribute, compliments, commendation, glory, *colloq.* kudos; honour, glorification, adoration, exaltation, worship, veneration, adulation, reverence. □ **sing the praises of** see PRAISE *v.* 1 above.

praiseworthy /práyzwurthi/ *adj.* worthy of praise; commendable. □□ **praiseworthily** *adv.* **praiseworthiness** *n.*
■ commendable, laudable, admirable, creditable, worthy, meritorious, deserving, exemplary.

Prakrit /praákrit/ *n.* any of the (esp. ancient or medieval) vernacular dialects of North and Central India existing alongside or derived from Sanskrit. [Skr. *prākṛta* unrefined: cf. SANSKRIT]

praline /praáleen/ *n.* a sweet made by browning nuts in boiling sugar. [F f. Marshal de Plessis-*Praslin*, Fr. soldier d. 1675, whose cook invented it]

pralltriller /praáltrillər/ *n.* a musical ornament consisting of one rapid alternation of the written note with the note immediately above it. [G f. *prallen* rebound + *Triller* TRILL]

pram[1] /pram/ *n. Brit.* a four-wheeled carriage for a baby, pushed by a person on foot. [abbr. of PERAMBULATOR]
■ *Brit. formal* perambulator, *US* baby carriage.

pram[2] /praam/ *n.* (also **praam**) **1** a flat-bottomed gunboat or Baltic cargo-boat. **2** a Scandinavian ship's dinghy. [MDu. *prame, praem*, MLG *prām(e)*, f. OSlav. *pramŭ*]

prana /praánə/ *n.* **1** (in Hinduism) breath as a life-giving force. **2** the breath; breathing. [Skr.]

prance /praanss/ *v.* & *n.* ● *v.intr.* **1** (of a horse) raise the forelegs and spring from the hind legs. **2** (often foll. by *about*) walk or behave in an elated or arrogant manner. ● *n.* **1** the act of prancing. **2** a prancing movement. □□ **prancer** *n.* [ME: orig. unkn.]
■ *v.* **1** curvet, capriole, caper, skip, frisk, jump, spring, bound. ● *n.* **2** see CAPER[1] *n.* 1.

prandial /prándiəl/ *adj. formal* or *joc.* of dinner or lunch. [L *prandium* meal]

prang /prang/ *v.* & *n. Brit. sl.* ● *v.tr.* **1** crash or damage (an aircraft or vehicle). **2** bomb (a target) successfully. ● *n.* the act or an instance of pranging. [imit.]
■ *v.* **1** crash, smash, bump, dent, damage. **2** see BOMB *v.* 1. ● *n.* see COLLISION 1.

prank /prangk/ *n.* a practical joke; a piece of mischief. □□ **prankful** *adj.* **prankish** *adj.* **pranksome** *adj.* [16th c.: orig. unkn.]
■ trick, practical joke, frolic, escapade, antic, caper, stunt, jape, *Austral.* goak; (*pranks*) mischief, *colloq.* lark, monkey business *or* tricks, shenanigans, *US colloq.* monkeyshines.

prankster /prángkstər/ *n.* a person fond of playing pranks.
■ see JOKER 1.

prase /prayz/ *n.* a translucent leek-green type of quartz. [F f. L *prasius* f. Gk *prasios* (adj.) leek-green f. *prason* leek]

praseodymium /práyziədímmiəm/ *n. Chem.* a soft silvery metallic element of the lanthanide series, occurring naturally in various minerals and used in catalyst mixtures. ¶ Symb.: **Pr**. [G *Praseodym* f. Gk *prasios* (see PRASE) from its green salts, + G *Didym* DIDYMIUM]

prat /prat/ *n. sl.* **1** *Brit.* a silly or foolish person. **2** the buttocks. [16th-c. cant (in sense 2): orig. unkn.]
■ **1** see FOOL[1] *n.* 1. **2** see BUTTOCKS.

prate /prayt/ *v.* & *n.* ● *v.* **1** *intr.* chatter; talk too much. **2** *intr.* talk foolishly or irrelevantly. **3** *tr.* tell or say in a prating manner. ● *n.* prating; idle talk. □□ **prater** *n.* **prating** *adj.* [ME f. MDu., MLG *praten*, prob. imit.]
■ *v.* see CHATTER *v.* 1. ● *n.* see CHATTER *n.* 1.

pratfall /prátfawl/ *n. US sl.* **1** a fall on the buttocks. **2** a humiliating failure.

pratie /práyti/ *n.* esp. *Ir.* a potato. [corrupt.]

pratincole /práttingkōl/ *n.* any of various birds of the subfamily Glareolinae, inhabiting sandy and stony areas and feeding on insects. [mod.L *pratincola* f. L *pratum* meadow + *incola* inhabitant]

pratique /prateek/ *n.* a licence to have dealings with a port, granted to a ship after quarantine or on showing a clean bill of health. [F, = practice, intercourse, f. It. *pratica* f. med.L *practica*: see PRACTICIAN]

prattle /prátt'l/ *v.* & *n.* ● *v.intr.* & *tr.* chatter or say in a childish or inconsequential way. ● *n.* **1** childish chatter. **2** inconsequential talk. □□ **prattler** *n.* **prattling** *adj.* [MLG *pratelen* (as PRATE)]
■ *v.* prate, babble, blather, gibber, jabber, palaver, tattle, twaddle, gabble, chatter, patter, drivel on, twitter, rattle on, go on (and on), run (on), *colloq.* natter, witter (on), gas, gab, jaw, *Brit. colloq.* rabbit (on), *sl.* shoot one's mouth off, *sl. derog.* yack, yackety-yack. ● *n.* prate, prating, talk, babble, blather, gibber, jabber, palaver, tattle, twaddle, chatter, gabble, patter, drivel, cackle, clack, *colloq.* gab, *sl. derog.* yackety-yack.

prau var. of PROA.

prawn /prawn/ *n.* & *v.* ● *n.* any of various marine crustaceans, resembling a shrimp but usu. larger. ● *v.intr.* fish for prawns. □ **come the raw prawn** see RAW. [ME *pra(y)ne*, of unkn. orig.]

praxis /práksiss/ *n.* **1** accepted practice or custom. **2** the practising of an art or skill. [med.L f. Gk, = doing, f. *prassō* do]
■ **1** see PRACTICE *n.* 2, 7.

pray /pray/ *v.* (often foll. by *for* or *to* + infin. or *that* + clause) **1** *intr.* (often foll. by *to*) say prayers (to God etc.); make devout supplication. **2 a** *tr.* entreat, beseech. **b** *tr.* & *intr.* ask earnestly (*prayed to be released*). **3** *tr.* (as *imper.*) *archaic* & *formal* please (*pray tell me*). □ **praying mantis**

see MANTIS. [ME f. OF *preier* f. LL *precare* f. L *precari* entreat]

■ **1** say one's prayers, offer a prayer. **2 a** beseech, ask, call upon *or* on, entreat, implore, appeal to, plead (with), beg, importune, solicit, petition, supplicate. **b** see ASK 2, BEG 2.

prayer[1] /prair/ *n.* **1 a** a solemn request or thanksgiving to God or an object of worship (*say a prayer*). **b** a formula or form of words used in praying (*the Lord's prayer*). **c** the act of praying (*be at prayer*). **d** a religious service consisting largely of prayers (*morning prayers*). **2 a** an entreaty to a person. **b** a thing entreated or prayed for. □ **not have a prayer** *US colloq.* have no chance (of success etc.). **prayer-book** a book containing the forms of prayer in regular use, esp. the Book of Common Prayer. **prayer-mat** a small carpet used by Muslims when praying. **prayer-wheel** a revolving cylindrical box inscribed with or containing prayers, used esp. by Tibetan Buddhists. □□ **prayerless** *adj.* [ME f. OF *preiere* ult. f. L *precarius* obtained by entreaty f. *prex precis* prayer]

■ **1 a** invocation, intercession, *archaic* orison; puja; see also LITANY 1. **c, d** devotion, praying, intercession, worship; (divine) service. **2 a** petition, supplication, request, entreaty, plea, suit, appeal, obsecration. □ **not have a prayer** have *or* stand no chance, not have *or* stand a chance, *colloq.* not have a hope (in hell), *Austral.* & *NZ colloq.* not have a Buckley's.

prayer[2] /práyər/ *n.* a person who prays.

prayerful /práirfŏŏl/ *adj.* **1** (of a person) given to praying; devout. **2** (of speech, actions, etc.) characterized by or expressive of prayer. □□ **prayerfully** *adv.* **prayerfulness** *n.*

pre- /pree/ *prefix* before (in time, place, order, degree, or importance). [from or after L *prae-* f. *prae* (adv. & prep.)]

preach /preech/ *v.* **1 a** *intr.* deliver a sermon or religious address. **b** *tr.* deliver (a sermon); proclaim or expound (the Gospel etc.). **2** *intr.* give moral advice in an obtrusive way. **3** *tr.* advocate or inculcate (a quality or practice etc.). □□ **preachable** *adj.* [ME f. OF *prechier* f. L *praedicare* proclaim, in eccl.L preach (as PRAE-, *dicare* declare)]

■ **1 a** deliver a sermon, sermonize, *colloq.* preachify. **b** teach, proclaim, evangelize, expound, propagate, explain; see also INTERPRET 1, 2. **2** moralize, sermonize, lecture, pontificate, *colloq.* preachify; see also RANT *v.* 2, 3. **3** urge, inculcate, advocate, instil, teach; see also CHAMPION *v.*

preacher /préechər/ *n.* a person who preaches, esp. a minister of religion. [ME f. AF *prech(o)ur*, OF *prech(e)or* f. eccl.L *praedicator* (as PREACH)]

■ orator, rhetorician, speech-maker, *usu. derog.* rhetor; minister, clergyman, clergywoman, cleric, ecclesiastic, reverend, divine, *colloq.* tub-thumper.

preachify /préechifī/ *v.intr.* (**-ies**, **-ied**) *colloq.* preach or moralize tediously.

preachment /préechmənt/ *n.* usu. *derog.* preaching, sermonizing.

preachy /préechi/ *adj.* (**preachier**, **preachiest**) *colloq.* inclined to preach or moralize. □□ **preachiness** *n.*

■ priggish, prescriptive; see also *pedantic* (PEDANT), PURITAN *adj.* 2.

preadolescent /prée-adəléss'nt/ *adj.* & *n.* ● *adj.* **1** (of a child) having nearly reached adolescence. **2** of or relating to the two or three years preceding adolescence. ● *n.* a preadolescent child. □□ **preadolescence** *n.*

preamble /prée-ámb'l/ *n.* **1** a preliminary statement or introduction. **2** the introductory part of a statute or deed etc. □□ **preambular** /-ámbyoolər/ *adj.* [ME f. OF *preambule* f. med.L *praeambulum* f. LL *praeambulus* (adj.) going before (as PRE-, AMBLE)]

■ **1** introduction, foreword, prologue, preface; proem, prolegomenon, exordium.

pre-amp /prée-ámp/ *n.* = PREAMPLIFIER. [abbr.]

preamplifier /prée-ámplifīər/ *n.* an electronic device that amplifies a very weak signal (e.g. from a microphone or pickup) and transmits it to a main amplifier. □□ **preamplified** *adj.*

prearrange /préeəráynj/ *v.tr.* arrange beforehand. □□ **prearrangement** *n.*

■ see ARRANGE 2, 3. □□ **prearrangement** see PROVISION *n.* 1a.

preatomic /préeətómmik/ *adj.* existing or occurring before the use of atomic energy.

Preb. *abbr.* Prebendary.

prebend /prébb'nd/ *n.* **1** the stipend of a canon or member of chapter. **2** a portion of land or tithe from which this is drawn. □□ **prebendal** *adj.* [ME f. OF *prebende* f. LL *praebenda* pension, neut.pl. gerundive of L *praebēre* grant f. *prae* forth + *habēre* hold]

prebendary /prébbəndəri/ *n.* (*pl.* **-ies**) **1** the holder of a prebend. **2** an honorary canon. □□ **prebendaryship** *n.* [ME f. med.L *praebendarius* (as PREBEND)]

Precambrian /préekámbriən/ *adj.* & *n. Geol.* ● *adj.* of or relating to the earliest era of geological time from the formation of the earth to the first forms of life. ¶ Cf. Appendix VII. ● *n.* this era.

precarious /prikáiriəss/ *adj.* **1** uncertain; dependent on chance (*makes a precarious living*). **2** insecure, perilous (*precarious health*). □□ **precariously** *adv.* **precariousness** *n.* [L *precarius*: see PRAYER[1]]

■ uncertain, unreliable, unsure, unpredictable, insecure, unstable, unsteady, unsettled, shaky, doubtful, dubious, questionable, delicate, (hanging) in the balance, hanging by a thread; perilous, risky, hazardous, treacherous, dangerous, difficult, problematic, chancy, *colloq.* dodgy, *sl.* dicey, hairy.

precast /préekaást/ *adj.* (of concrete) cast in its final shape before positioning.

precative /prékkətiv/ *adj.* (of a word or form) expressing a wish or request. [LL *precativus* f. *precari* pray]

precaution /prikáwsh'n/ *n.* **1** an action taken beforehand to avoid risk or ensure a good result. **2** (in *pl.*) *colloq.* the use of contraceptives. **3** caution exercised beforehand; prudent foresight. □□ **precautionary** *adj.* [F *précaution* f. LL *praecautio -onis* f. L *praecavēre* (as PRAE-, *cavēre caut-* beware of)]

■ **1** preventive measure, safety measure, safeguard. **3** foresight, prudence, providence, forethought, caution, cautiousness, circumspection, care, attention, watchfulness, vigilance, alertness, wariness, chariness, apprehension, far-sightedness, anticipation.

precede /priséed/ *v.tr.* **1 a** (often as **preceding** *adj.*) come or go before in time, order, importance, etc. (*preceding generations*; *the preceding paragraph*; *sons of barons precede baronets*). **b** walk etc. in front of (*preceded by our guide*). **2** (foll. by *by*) cause to be preceded (*must precede this measure by milder ones*). [OF *preceder* f. L *praecedere* (as PRAE-, *cedere cess-* go)]

■ **1** come *or* go before, go ahead *or* in advance of, lead, pave the way for, herald, usher in, introduce; foreshadow, antedate, predate; (**preceding**) foregoing, former, previous, prior, earlier, above-mentioned, aforementioned, above, above-stated, above-named; *formal* prevenient.

precedence /préssid'nss/ *n.* (also **precedency**) **1** priority in time, order, or importance, etc. **2** the right of preceding others on formal occasions. □ **take precedence** (often foll. by *over*, *of*) have priority (over).

■ **1** pre-eminence, preference, privilege, primacy; see also PRIORITY.

precedent *n.* & *adj.* ● *n.* /préssid'nt/ a previous case or legal decision etc. taken as a guide for subsequent cases or as a justification. ● *adj.* /priséed'nt, préssi-/ preceding in time, order, importance, etc. □□ **precedently** /préessidəntli, préssi-/ *adv.* [ME f. OF (n. & adj.) (as PRECEDE)]

■ *n.* yardstick, criterion, standard, prototype, model, example, exemplar, pattern, paradigm, lead, guide.

precedented /préssidentid/ *adj.* having or supported by a precedent.

precent /prisént/ *v.* **1** *intr.* act as a precentor. **2** *tr.* lead the singing of (a psalm etc.). [back-form. f. PRECENTOR]

precentor /priséntər/ *n.* **1** a person who leads the singing or (in a synagogue) the prayers of a congregation. **2** a minor canon who administers the musical life of a cathedral. □□ **precentorship** *n.* [F *précenteur* or L *praecentor* f. *praecinere* (as PRAE-, *canere* sing)]

precept /préessept/ *n.* **1** a command; a rule of conduct. **2 a** moral instruction (*example is better than precept*). **b** a general or proverbial rule; a maxim. **3 a** a writ or warrant. **b** *Brit.* an order for collection or payment of money under a local rate. □□ **preceptive** /priséptiv/ *adj.* [ME f. L *praeceptum* neut. past part. of *praecipere praecept-* warn, instruct (as PRAE-, *capere* take)]

■ **1** rule, guide, principle, law, unwritten law, canon, guideline, dictate, code, injunction, commandment, instruction, directive, prescription, mandate, charge. **2 b** maxim, proverb, axiom, motto, slogan, saying, byword, aphorism, apophthegm.

preceptor /priséptər/ *n.* a teacher or instructor. □□ **preceptorial** /préesseptóriəl/ *adj.* **preceptorship** *n.* **preceptress** /-triss/ *n.* [L *praeceptor* (as PRECEPT)]

■ see INSTRUCTOR.

precession /prisésh'n/ *n.* the slow movement of the axis of a spinning body around another axis. □ **precession of the equinoxes 1** the slow retrograde motion of equinoctial points along the ecliptic. **2** the resulting earlier occurrence of equinoxes in each successive sidereal year. □□ **precessional** *adj.* [LL *praecessio* (as PRECEDE)]

pre-Christian /preékristiən, -kríss-chən/ *adj.* before Christ or the advent of Christianity.

precinct /préessingkt/ *n.* **1** an enclosed or clearly defined area, e.g. around a cathedral, college, etc. **2** a specially designated area in a town, esp. with the exclusion of traffic (*shopping precinct*). **3** (in *pl.*) **a** the surrounding area or environs. **b** the boundaries. **4** *US* **a** a subdivision of a county, city, etc., for police or electoral purposes. **b** (in *pl.*) a neighbourhood. [ME f. med.L *praecinctum* neut. past part. of *praecingere* encircle (as PRAE-, *cingere* gird)]

■ **3** (*precincts*) environs, suburbs; purlieus, outskirts; boundaries, borders, bounds, confines. **4 b** (*precincts*) area, territory, region, province, sphere, neighbourhood, zone, sector, section, quarter, district, locale.

preciosity /préshióssiti/ *n.* overrefinement in art or language, esp. in the choice of words. [OF *préciosité* f. L *pretiositas* f. *pretiosus* (as PRECIOUS)]

precious /préshəss/ *adj.* & *adv.* ● *adj.* **1** of great value or worth. **2** beloved; much prized (*precious memories*). **3** affectedly refined, esp. in language or manner. **4** *colloq.* often *iron.* **a** considerable (*a precious lot you know about it*). **b** expressing contempt or disdain (*you can keep your precious flowers*). ● *adv. colloq.* extremely, very (*tried precious hard; had precious little left*). □ **precious metals** gold, silver, and platinum. **precious stone** a piece of mineral having great value esp. as used in jewellery. □□ **preciously** *adv.* **preciousness** *n.* [ME f. OF *precios* f. L *pretiosus* f. *pretium* price]

■ *adj.* **1** valuable, invaluable, costly, expensive, high-priced, priceless. **2** cherished, beloved, esteemed, valued, prized, choice, dear, dearest, adored, loved, revered, venerated, hallowed. **3** precise, overrefined, chichi, over-nice, studied, artificial, affected, overdone, pretentious, euphuistic, *Brit. usu. derog.* twee. **4 a** *colloq. iron.* fat. ● *adv.* see VERY *adv.*

precipice /préssipiss/ *n.* **1** a vertical or steep face of a rock, cliff, mountain, etc. **2** a dangerous situation. [F *précipice* or L *praecipitium* falling headlong, precipice (as PRECIPITOUS)]

■ **1** escarpment, bluff, *Brit.* crag; see also CLIFF. **2** powder-keg, time-bomb; dynamite.

precipitant /prisíppit'nt/ *adj.* & *n.* ● *adj.* = PRECIPITATE *adj.* ● *n. Chem.* a substance that causes another substance to precipitate. □□ **precipitance** *n.* **precipitancy** *n.* [obs. F *précipitant* pres. part. of *précipiter* (as PRECIPITATE)]

precipitate *v.*, *adj.*, & *n.* ● *v.tr.* /prisíppitayt/ **1** hasten the occurrence of; cause to occur prematurely. **2** (foll. by *into*) send rapidly into a certain state or condition (*were precipitated into war*). **3** throw down headlong. **4** *Chem.* cause (a substance) to be deposited in solid form from a solution. **5** *Physics* **a** cause (dust etc.) to be deposited from the air on a surface. **b** condense (vapour) into drops and so deposit it. ● *adj.* /prisíppitət/ **1** headlong; violently hurried (*precipitate departure*). **2** (of a person or act) hasty, rash, inconsiderate. ● *n.* /prisíppitət/ **1** *Chem.* a substance precipitated from a solution. **2** *Physics* moisture condensed from vapour by cooling and depositing, e.g. rain or dew. □□ **precipitable** /prisíppitəb'l/ *adj.* **precipitability** /prisíppitəbílliti/ *n.* **precipitately** /prisíppitətli/ *adv.* **precipitateness** /prisíppitətniss/ *n.* **precipitator** /prisíppitaytər/ *n.* [L *praecipitare praecipitat-* f. *praeceps praecipitis* headlong (as PRAE-, *caput* head)]

■ *v.* **1** accelerate, hasten, speed (up), advance, hurry, quicken, expedite, bring on *or* about, trigger, provoke, instigate, incite, facilitate, further, push forward. **2, 3** throw, catapult, hurl, fling, cast, launch, project. ● *adj.* **1** headlong, violent, hurried, rapid, swift, quick, speedy, meteoric, fast; sudden, abrupt, unannounced, unexpected, unanticipated. **2** rash, impetuous, hasty, careless, reckless, incautious, inconsiderate, injudicious, harum-scarum, foolhardy, impulsive, unrestrained; volatile, hotheaded.

precipitation /prisíppitáysh'n/ *n.* **1** the act of precipitating or the process of being precipitated. **2** rash haste. **3 a** rain or snow etc. falling to the ground. **b** a quantity of this. [F *précipitation* or L *praecipitatio* (as PRECIPITATE)]

■ **2** see HASTE *n.* 2. **3 a** showers, drizzle, rain, rainfall; snow, snowfall, hail, sleet.

precipitous /prisíppitəss/ *adj.* **1 a** of or like a precipice. **b** dangerously steep. **2** = PRECIPITATE *adj.* □□ **precipitously** *adv.* **precipitousness** *n.* [obs. F *précipiteux* f. L *praeceps* (as PRECIPITATE)]

■ **1** perpendicular, abrupt, steep, sheer, bluff, vertical.

précis /práysee/ *n.* & *v.* ● *n.* (*pl.* same /-seez/) a summary or abstract, esp. of a text or speech. ● *v.tr.* (**précises** /-seez/; **précised** /-seed/; **précising** /-seeing/) make a précis of. [F, = PRECISE (as n.)]

■ *n.* outline, summary, synopsis, *aperçu*, résumé, conspectus, survey, overview, abstract, abridgement, digest, compendium. ● *v.* see ABBREVIATE.

precise /prisīss/ *adj.* **1 a** accurately expressed. **b** definite, exact. **2 a** punctilious; scrupulous in being exact, observing rules, etc. **b** often *derog.* rigid; fastidious. **3** identical, exact (*at that precise moment*). □□ **preciseness** *n.* [F *précis -ise* f. L *praecidere praecis-* cut short (as PRAE-, *caedere* cut)]

■ **1** correct, exact, definite, accurate, unerring, strict, meticulous, faithful, perfect, true, absolute, truthful, error-free. **2 a** punctilious, strict, meticulous, scrupulous, careful, conscientious, exact, particular, nice, exacting, critical, demanding. **b** fastidious; rigorous, rigid, puritanical, unbending, inflexible, unyielding, demanding, severe, finicky, finical, fussy, prim. **3** identical, very same; see also VERY *adj.* 1a.

precisely /prisīsli/ *adv.* **1** in a precise manner; exactly. **2** (as a reply) quite so; as you say.

■ **1** exactly, correctly, absolutely, punctiliously, minutely, carefully, meticulously, scrupulously, conscientiously, strictly; in all respects, in every way. **2** see ABSOLUTELY 6.

precisian /prisízh'n/ *n.* a person who is rigidly precise or punctilious, esp. in religious observance. □□ **precisianism** *n.*

■ see PURIST. □□ **precisianism** see LEGALISM.

precision /prisízh'n/ *n.* **1** the condition of being precise; accuracy. **2** the degree of refinement in measurement etc. **3** (*attrib.*) marked by or adapted for precision (*precision instruments; precision timing*). □□ **precisionism** *n.* **precisionist** *n.* [F *précision* or L *praecisio* (as PRECISE)]

■ **1** correctness, accuracy, exactness, exactitude, fidelity, faithfulness, preciseness, perfection, flawlessness, faultlessness, unerringness. **2** nicety, rigour, rigorousness, strictness, meticulousness, punctiliousness, scrupulousness; see also CARE *n.* 3.

preclassical /preéklássik'l/ *adj.* before a period regarded as classical, esp. in music and literature.

preclinical /preéklínnik'l/ *adj.* **1** of or relating to the first, chiefly theoretical, stage of a medical education. **2** (of a stage in a disease) before symptoms can be identified.

preclude /priklóod/ *v.tr.* **1** (foll. by *from*) prevent, exclude (*precluded from taking part*). **2** make impossible; remove (*so as to preclude all doubt*). ▫▫ **preclusion** /-kloózh'n/ *n.* **preclusive** /-kloóssiv/ *adj.* [L *praecludere praeclus-* (as PRAE-, *claudere* shut)]

■ **1** bar, prevent, stop, exclude, prohibit, debar, obstruct, impede, inhibit. **2** remove, forestall, rule out, obviate, avoid, get rid of.

precocial *US* var. of PRAECOCIAL.

precocious /prikṓshəss/ *adj.* **1** often *derog.* (of a person, esp. a child) prematurely developed in some faculty or characteristic. **2** (of an action etc.) indicating such development. **3** (of a plant) flowering or fruiting early. ▫▫ **precociously** *adv.* **precociousness** *n.* **precocity** /-kóssiti/ *n.* [L *praecox -cocis* f. *praecoquere* ripen fully (as PRAE-, *coquere* cook)]

■ **1** advanced, forward, bright, gifted, intelligent, smart, quick.

precognition /preékognísh'n/ *n.* **1** (supposed) foreknowledge, esp. of a supernatural kind. **2** *Sc.* the preliminary examination of witnesses etc., esp. to decide whether there is ground for a trial. ▫▫ **precognitive** /-kógnitiv/ *adj.* [LL *praecognitio* (as PRE-, COGNITION)]

■ **1** see ANTICIPATION 1.

precoital /preékṓ-it'l/ *adj.* preceding sexual intercourse. ▫▫ **precoitally** *adv.*

pre-Columbian /preékəlúmbiən/ *adj.* before the discovery of America by Columbus.

preconceive /preékənseév/ *v.tr.* (esp. as **preconceived** *adj.*) form (an idea or opinion etc.) beforehand; anticipate in thought.

■ (**preconceived**) prejudged, predetermined, prejudiced, biased, anticipatory.

preconception /preékənsépsh'n/ *n.* **1** a preconceived idea. **2** a prejudice.

■ prejudgement, presupposition, assumption, presumption, *idée fixe*, preconceived notion *or* idea; prejudice, bias.

preconcert /preékənsért/ *v.tr.* arrange or organize beforehand.

precondition /preékəndísh'n/ *n.* & *v.* ● *n.* a prior condition, that must be fulfilled before other things can be done. ● *v.tr.* bring into a required condition beforehand.

■ *n.* prerequisite, stipulation, condition, essential, must, *sine qua non*, imperative, requirement, proviso, qualification.

preconize /preékənīz/ *v.tr.* (also **-ise**) **1** proclaim or commend publicly. **2** summon by name. **3** *RC Ch.* (of the Pope) approve publicly the appointment of (a bishop). ▫▫ **preconization** /-záysh'n/ *n.* [ME f. med.L *praeconizare* f. L *praeco -onis* herald]

preconscious *adj.* & *n. Psychol.* ● *adj.* /preékónshəss/ **1** preceding consciousness. **2** of or associated with a part of the mind below the level of immediate conscious awareness, from which memories and emotions can be recalled. ● *n.* /preekónshəss/ this part of the mind. ▫▫ **preconsciousness** *n.*

precook /preékóok/ *v.tr.* cook in advance.

precool /preékóol/ *v.tr.* cool in advance.

precordial /preékórdiəl/ *adj.* in front of or about the heart.

precostal /preékóst'l/ *adj.* in front of the ribs.

precursor /prikúrsər/ *n.* **1 a** a forerunner. **b** a person who precedes in office etc. **2** a harbinger. **3** a substance from which another is formed by decay or chemical reaction etc. [L *praecursor* f. *praecurrere praecurs-* (as PRAE-, *currere* run)]

■ **1** forerunner, predecessor, antecedent; progenitor, foregoer. **2** harbinger, herald, forerunner, envoy, messenger.

precursory /prikúrsəri/ *adj.* (also **precursive** /-siv/) **1** preliminary, introductory. **2** (foll. by *of*) serving as a harbinger of. [L *praecursorius* (as PRECURSOR)]

precut /preékút/ *v.tr.* (*past* and *past part.* **-cut**) cut in advance.

predacious /pridáyshəss/ *adj.* (also **predaceous**) **1** (of an animal) predatory. **2** relating to such animals (*predacious instincts*). ▫▫ **predaciousness** *n.* **predacity** /-dássiti/ *n.* [L *praeda* booty: cf. *audacious*]

■ see PREDATORY 1, RAPACIOUS. ▫▫ **predaciousness** see *rapacity* (RAPACIOUS).

predate /preédáyt/ *v.tr.* exist or occur at a date earlier than.

■ see PRECEDE.

predation /pridáysh'n/ *n.* **1** (usu. in *pl.*) = DEPREDATION. **2** *Zool.* the natural preying of one animal on others. [L *praedatio -onis* taking of booty f. L *praeda* booty]

predator /préddətər/ *n.* **1** an animal naturally preying on others. **2** a person, State, etc., compared to this. [L *praedator* plunderer f. *praedari* seize as plunder f. *praeda* booty (as PREDACIOUS)]

predatory /préddətəri, -tri/ *adj.* **1** (of an animal) preying naturally upon others. **2** (of a nation, State, or individual) plundering or exploiting others. ▫▫ **predatorily** *adv.* **predatoriness** *n.* [L *praedatorius* (as PREDATOR)]

■ **1** predacious, carnivorous, preying, raptorial. **2** ravenous, piratical, vulturine, exploitative, parasitic, parasitical; see also RAPACIOUS.

predecease /preédiseéss/ *v.* & *n.* ● *v.tr.* die earlier than (another person). ● *n.* a death preceding that of another.

predecessor /preédisessər/ *n.* **1** a former holder of an office or position with respect to a later holder (*my immediate predecessor*). **2** an ancestor. **3** a thing to which another has succeeded (*the new plan will share the fate of its predecessor*). [ME f. OF *predecesseur* f. LL *praedecessor* (as PRAE-, *decessor* retiring officer, as DECEASE)]

■ **1, 3** forerunner, antecedent, precursor. **2** forebear, forefather, ancestor, antecedent.

pre-decimal /preédéssim'l/ *adj.* of or relating to a time before the introduction of a decimal system, esp. of coinage.

predella /pridéllə/ *n.* **1** an altar-step, or raised shelf at the back of an altar. **2** a painting or sculpture on this, or any picture forming an appendage to a larger one esp. beneath an altarpiece. [It., = stool]

predestinarian /pridéstináiriən/ *n.* & *adj.* ● *n.* a person who believes in predestination. ● *adj.* of or relating to predestination.

predestinate *v.* & *adj.* ● *v.tr.* /pridéstinayt/ = PREDESTINE. ● *adj.* /pridéstinət/ predestined. [ME f. eccl.L *praedestinare praedestinat-* (as PRAE-, *destinare* establish)]

predestination /preédestináysh'n/ *n. Theol.* (as a belief or doctrine) the divine foreordaining of all that will happen, esp. with regard to the salvation of some and not others. [ME f. eccl.L *praedestinatio* (as PREDESTINATE)]

■ destiny; doom, fate, lot, kismet, karma; foreordination; predetermination.

predestine /preédéstin/ *v.tr.* **1** determine beforehand. **2** ordain in advance by divine will or as if by fate. [ME f. OF *predestiner* or eccl.L *praedestinare* PREDESTINATE *v.*]

■ see DESTINE.

predetermine /preéditérmin/ *v.tr.* **1** determine or decree beforehand. **2** predestine. ▫▫ **predeterminable** *adj.* **predeterminate** /-nət/ *adj.* **predetermination** /-náysh'n/ *n.* [LL *praedeterminare* (as PRAE-, DETERMINE)]

■ **1** fix, prearrange, pre-establish, preplan, pre-set, set up; see also ARRANGE 2, 3. **2** fate, doom, destine, predestine, predestinate, predoom, ordain, foreordain, preordain; see also DESTINE. ▫▫ **predetermination** see PREDESTINATION.

predial /préediəl/ *adj.* & *n. hist.* ● *adj.* **1 a** of land or farms. **b** rural, agrarian. **c** (of a slave, tenant, etc.) attached to farms or the land. **2** (of a tithe) consisting of agricultural produce. ● *n.* a predial slave. [med.L *praedialis* f. L *praedium* farm]

predicable /préddikəb'l/ *adj.* & *n.* ● *adj.* that may be predicated or affirmed. ● *n.* **1** a predicable thing. **2** (in *pl.*) *Logic* the five classes to which predicates belong: genus, species, difference, property, and accident. ▫▫ **predicability** /-bílliti/ *n.* [med.L *praedicabilis* that may be affirmed (as PREDICATE)]

predicament /pridíkkəmənt/ *n.* **1** a difficult, unpleasant, or embarrassing situation. **2** *Philos.* a category in (esp. Aristotelian) logic. [ME (in sense 2) f. LL *praedicamentum* thing predicated: see PREDICATE]
■ **1** quandary, difficulty, trial, imbroglio, emergency, crisis, impasse, *esp. US* bind, *US* box, *colloq.* pickle, state, jam, fix, scrape, mess, spot, corner, hole, *disp.* dilemma.

predicant /préddikənt/ *adj.* & *n.* ● *adj. hist.* (of a religious order, esp. the Dominicans) engaged in preaching. ● *n.* **1** *hist.* a predicant person, esp. a Dominican friar. **2** *S.Afr.* = PREDIKANT. [L *praedicans* part. of *praedicare* (as PREDICATE)]

predicate *v.* & *n.* ● *v.tr.* /préddikayt/ **1** assert or affirm as true or existent. **2** (foll. by *on*) found or base (a statement etc.) on. ● *n.* /préddikət/ **1** *Gram.* what is said about the subject of a sentence etc. (e.g. *went home* in *John went home*). **2** *Logic* **a** what is predicated. **b** what is affirmed or denied of the subject by means of the copula (e.g. *mortal* in *all men are mortal*). ▫▫ **predication** /-káysh'n/ *n.* [L *praedicare praedicat-* proclaim (as PRAE-, *dicare* declare)]
■ *v.* **1** assume, propose, postulate, posit, assert, affirm, suppose, presuppose, surmise. **2** see BASE[1] *v.* 1. ▫▫ **predication** hypothesis, thesis, principle, contention, assertion, belief, proposition, postulate.

predicative /pridíkkətiv/ *adj.* **1** *Gram.* (of an adjective or noun) forming or contained in the predicate, as *old* in *the dog is old* (but not in *the old dog*) and *house* in *there is a large house* (opp. ATTRIBUTIVE). **2** that predicates. ▫▫ **predicatively** *adv.* [L *praedicativus* (as PREDICATE)]

predict /pridíkt/ *v.tr.* (often foll. by *that* + clause) make a statement about the future; foretell, prophesy. ▫▫ **predictive** *adj.* **predictively** *adv.* **predictor** *n.* [L *praedicere praedict-* (as PRAE-, *dicere* say)]
■ foretell, prophesy, forecast, foresee, augur, prognosticate, presage, *formal* vaticinate, *literary* previse; intimate, hint, suggest.

predictable /pridíktəb'l/ *adj.* that can be predicted or is to be expected. ▫▫ **predictability** /-bílliti/ *n.* **predictably** *adv.*
■ foreseeable, expected, anticipated, imaginable.

prediction /pridíksh'n/ *n.* **1** the art of predicting or the process of being predicted. **2** a thing predicted; a forecast. [L *praedictio -onis* (as PREDICT)]
■ **2** see FORECAST *n.*

predigest /préedījést/ *v.tr.* **1** render (food) easily digestible before being eaten. **2** make (reading matter) easier to read or understand. ▫▫ **predigestion** /-jéss-chən/ *n.*

predikant /práydeekaánt/ *n. S.Afr.* a minister of the Dutch Reformed Church. [Du. (as PREDICANT)]

predilection /préedilékshʼn/ *n.* (often foll. by *for*) a preference or special liking. [F *prédilection* ult. f. L *praediligere praedilect-* prefer (as PRAE-, *diligere* select): see DILIGENT]
■ see LIKING 2.

predispose /préedispṓz/ *v.tr.* **1** influence favourably in advance. **2** (foll. by *to*, or *to* + infin.) render liable or inclined beforehand. ▫▫ **predisposition** /-pəzísh'n/ *n.*
■ **1** see INCLINE *v.* 1. **2** see INCLINE *v.* 2. ▫▫ **predisposition** see INCLINATION 1.

prednisone /prédnizōn/ *n.* a synthetic drug similar to cortisone, used to relieve rheumatic and allergic conditions and to treat leukaemia. [perh. f. *pregnant* + *diene* + cort*isone*]

predominant /pridómminənt/ *adj.* **1** predominating. **2** being the strongest or main element. ▫▫ **predominance** *n.* **predominantly** *adv.*
■ **1** dominant, predominating, controlling, sovereign, ruling, pre-eminent, preponderant, preponderating, ascendant, superior, supreme, transcendent. **2** main, primary, leading, chief, prevailing, prevalent; see also CHIEF *adj.* 2. ▫▫ **predominance** superiority, influence, dominance, pre-eminence, preponderance, transcendence, transcendency, ascendancy, supremacy, power, hold, hegemony, mastery, control, dominion, sovereignty, authority.

predominate /pridómminayt/ *v.intr.* **1** (foll. by *over*) have or exert control. **2** be superior. **3** be the strongest or main element; preponderate (*a garden in which dahlias predominate*). [med.L *praedominari* (as PRAE-, DOMINATE)]
■ **1** control, rule, reign, get *or* have the upper hand, be in charge, hold sway; see also DOMINATE 1. **3** preponderate, dominate, obtain, prevail, be in the majority, stick out, stand out; be prevalent *or* widespread *or* current, be the order of the day.

predominately /pridómminətli/ *adv.* = PREDOMINANTLY (see PREDOMINANT). [rare *predominate* (adj.) = PREDOMINANT]

predoom /préedóóm/ *v.tr.* doom beforehand.

predorsal /préedórs'l/ *adj.* in front of the dorsal region.

predynastic /préedinástik/ *adj.* of or relating to a period before the normally recognized dynasties (esp. of ancient Egypt).

pre-echo /prée-ékkō/ *n.* (*pl.* **-oes**) **1** a faint copy heard just before an actual sound in a recording, caused by the accidental transfer of signals. **2** a foreshadowing.

pre-eclampsia /prée-iklámpsiə/ *n.* a condition of pregnancy characterized by high blood pressure and other symptoms associated with eclampsia. ▫▫ **pre-eclamptic** *adj.* & *n.*

pre-elect /prée-ilékt/ *v.tr.* elect beforehand.

pre-election /prée-iléksh'n/ *n.* **1** an election held beforehand. **2** (*attrib.*) (esp. of an act or undertaking) done or given before an election.

pre-embryo /pree-émbriō/ *n. Med.* a human embryo in the first fourteen days after fertilization. ▫▫ **pre-embryonic** /-briónnik/ *adj.*

pre-eminent /prée-émminənt/ *adj.* **1** excelling others. **2** outstanding; distinguished in some quality. **3** principal, leading; predominant. ▫▫ **pre-eminence** *n.* **pre-eminently** *adv.* [ME f. L *praeeminens* (as PRAE-, EMINENT)]
■ **2** peerless, excellent, distinguished, eminent, inimitable, superb, unequalled, matchless, incomparable, outstanding, unique, unrivalled, unsurpassed, supreme, superior. **3** see CHIEF *adj.* 2. ▫▫ **pre-eminence** peerlessness, magnificence, excellence, distinction, eminence, inimitability, superiority, greatness. **pre-eminently** manifestly, eminently, notably, conspicuously, prominently, signally, uniquely, matchlessly, incomparably, outstandingly; primarily, principally, chiefly, mainly, mostly.

pre-empt /prée-émpt/ *v.* **1** *tr.* **a** forestall. **b** acquire or appropriate in advance. **2** *tr.* prevent (an attack) by disabling the enemy. **3** *tr.* obtain by pre-emption. **4** *tr. US* take for oneself (esp. public land) so as to have the right of pre-emption. **5** *intr. Bridge* make a pre-emptive bid. ▫▫ **preemptor** *n.* **preemptory** *adj.* [back-form. f. PRE-EMPTION]
■ **1 a** see ANTICIPATE 3. **b** appropriate, usurp, arrogate, take over, assume, take possession of, seize, acquire, take, possess, expropriate.

pre-emption /prée-émpsh'n/ *n.* **1 a** the purchase or appropriation by one person or party before the opportunity is offered to others. **b** the right to purchase (esp. public land) in this way. **2** prior appropriation or acquisition. [med.L *praeemptio* (as PRAE-, *emere empt-* buy)]

pre-emptive /prée-émptiv/ *adj.* **1** pre-empting; serving to pre-empt. **2** (of military action) intended to prevent attack by disabling the enemy (*a pre-emptive strike*). **3** *Bridge* (of a bid) intended to be high enough to discourage further bidding.

preen /preen/ *v.tr.* & *refl.* **1** (of a bird) tidy (the feathers or itself) with its beak. **2** (of a person) smarten or admire (oneself, one's hair, clothes, etc.). **3** (often foll. by *on*) congratulate or pride (oneself). □ **preen gland** a gland situated at the base of a bird's tail and producing oil used in preening. □□ **preener** *n.* [ME, app. var. of earlier *prune* (perh. rel. to PRUNE[2]): assoc. with Sc. & dial. *preen* pierce, pin]

■ **1** plume, groom, prink, trim, clean. **2** primp, smarten, dress up, prettify, beautify, prink, spruce up, doll up, *colloq.* titivate, *Brit. colloq.* tart up. **3** (*preen oneself on*) see PRIDE *v.*

pre-engage /pree-in-gáyj/ *v.tr.* engage beforehand. □□ **pre-engagement** *n.*

pre-establish /pree-istáblish/ *v.tr.* establish beforehand.

pre-exist /pree-igzíst/ *v.intr.* exist at an earlier time. □□ **pre-existence** *n.* **pre-existent** *adj.*

pref. *abbr.* **1** prefix. **2** preface. **3 a** preference. **b** preferred.

prefab /preefab/ *n. Brit. colloq.* a prefabricated building, esp. a small house. [abbr.]

prefabricate /preefábrikayt/ *v.tr.* **1** manufacture sections of (a building etc.) prior to their assembly on a site. **2** produce in an artificially standardized way. □□ **prefabrication** /-káysh'n/ *n.*

preface /préffəss/ *n.* & *v.* ● *n.* **1** an introduction to a book stating its subject, scope, etc. **2** the preliminary part of a speech. **3** *Eccl.* the introduction to the central part of the Eucharistic service. ● *v.tr.* **1** (foll. by *with*) introduce or begin (a speech or event) (*prefaced my remarks with a warning*). **2** provide (a book etc.) with a preface. **3** (of an event etc.) lead up to (another). □□ **prefatorial** /-fətóriəl/ *adj.* **prefatory** /-fətəri/ *adj.* [ME f. OF f. med.L *praefatia* for L *praefatio* f. *praefari* (as PRAE-, *fari* speak)]

■ *n.* **1, 2** introduction, foreword, prologue, preamble, proem, prolegomenon, exordium. ● *v.* **1** prefix, prologue, begin, open, start off; see also INTRODUCE 8. **3** see *lead up to* 1. □□ **prefatory** see INTRODUCTORY.

prefect /preefekt/ *n.* **1** the chief administrative officer of certain departments, esp. in France. **2** esp. *Brit.* a senior pupil in a school etc. authorized to enforce discipline. **3** *Rom. Antiq.* a senior magistrate or military commander. □□ **prefectoral** /-féktərəl/ *adj.* **prefectorial** /-tóriəl/ *adj.* [ME f. OF f. L *praefectus* past part. of *praeficere* set in authority over (as PRAE-, *facere* make)]

prefecture /preefektyoor/ *n.* **1** a district under the government of a prefect. **2 a** a prefect's office or tenure. **b** his official residence. □□ **prefectural** /priféktyoorəl/ *adj.* [F *préfecture* or L *praefectura* (as PREFECT)]

prefer /prifér/ *v.tr.* (**preferred, preferring**) **1** (often foll. by *to*, or *to* + infin.) choose rather; like better (*would prefer to stay*; *prefers coffee to tea*). **2** submit (information, an accusation, etc.) for consideration. **3** promote or advance (a person). □ **preferred shares** (or **stock**) = *preference shares* or *stock*. [ME f. OF *preferer* f. L *praeferre* (as PRAE-, *ferre lat-* bear)]

■ **1** favour, like better, lean *or* incline towards, be inclined towards, be partial to. **2** present, offer, propose, proffer, advance, submit, tender, put forward, file, lodge, enter. **3** see PROMOTE 1.

preferable /préffərəb'l, *disp.* prifér-/ *adj.* **1** to be preferred. **2** more desirable. □□ **preferably** *adv.*

■ preferred, better, best, advantageous, beneficial, desirable, convenient, favourable, promising, propitious. □□ **preferably** see RATHER 1.

preference /préffərənss/ *n.* **1** the act or an instance of preferring or being preferred. **2** a thing preferred. **3 a** the favouring of one person etc. before others. **b** *Commerce* the favouring of one country by admitting its products at a lower import duty. **4** *Law* a prior right, esp. to the payment of debts. □ **in preference to** as a thing preferred over (another). **preference shares** (or **stock**) *Brit.* shares or stock whose entitlement to dividend takes priority over that of ordinary shares. [F *préférence* f. med.L *praeferentia* (as PREFER)]

■ **1** partiality, proclivity, predilection, liking; predisposition, bent, inclination, leaning. **2** favourite, choice, selection, pick, desire, option. **3 a** see FAVOURITISM.

preferential /préffərénsh'l/ *adj.* **1** of or involving preference (*preferential treatment*). **2** giving or receiving a favour. **3** *Commerce* (of a tariff etc.) favouring particular countries. **4** (of voting) in which the voter puts candidates in order of preference. □□ **preferentially** *adv.* [as PREFERENCE, after *differential*]

■ **1** privileged, better, favoured, superior, advantageous, favourable; biased, prejudiced, partial.

preferment /prifέrmənt/ *n.* promotion to office.

■ promotion, advance, rise, elevation.

prefigure /preefiggər/ *v.tr.* **1** represent beforehand by a figure or type. **2** imagine beforehand. □□ **prefiguration** /-ráysh'n/ *n.* **prefigurative** /-rətiv/ *adj.* **prefigurement** *n.* [ME f. eccl.L *praefigurare* (as PRAE-, FIGURE)]

prefix /preefiks/ *n.* & *v.* ● *n.* **1** a verbal element placed at the beginning of a word to adjust or qualify its meaning (e.g. *ex-*, *non-*, *re-*) or (in some languages) as an inflectional formative. **2** a title placed before a name (e.g. *Mr*). ● *v.tr.* (often foll. by *to*) **1** add as an introduction. **2** join (a word or element) as a prefix. □□ **prefixation** /-fiksáysh'n/ *n.* **prefixion** /-fiksh'n/ *n.* [earlier as verb: ME f. OF *prefixer* (as PRE-, FIX): (n.) f. L *praefixum*]

■ *v.* **1** see PREFACE *v.* 1.

preflight /preeflīt/ *attrib.adj.* occurring or provided before an aircraft flight.

preform /preefórm/ *v.tr.* form beforehand. □□ **preformation** /-máysh'n/ *n.*

preformative /preefórmətiv/ *adj.* & *n.* ● *adj.* **1** forming beforehand. **2** prefixed as the formative element of a word. ● *n.* a preformative syllable or letter.

prefrontal /preefrúnt'l/ *adj.* **1** in front of the frontal bone of the skull. **2** in the forepart of the frontal lobe of the brain.

preglacial /preegláysh'l, -gláysiəl/ *adj.* before a glacial period.

pregnable /prégnəb'l/ *adj.* able to be captured etc.; not impregnable. [ME f. OF *prenable* takable: see IMPREGNABLE[1]]

pregnancy /prégnənsi/ *n.* (*pl.* **-ies**) the condition or an instance of being pregnant.

pregnant /prégnənt/ *adj.* **1** (of a woman or female animal) having a child or young developing in the uterus. **2** full of meaning; significant or suggestive (*a pregnant pause*). **3** (esp. of a person's mind) imaginative, inventive. **4** (foll. by *with*) plentifully provided (*pregnant with danger*). □ **pregnant construction** *Gram.* one in which more is implied than the words express (e.g. *not have a chance* implying *of success* etc.). □□ **pregnantly** *adv.* (in sense 2). [ME f. F *prégnant* or L *praegnans -antis*, earlier *praegnas* (prob. as PRAE-, (*g*)*nasci* be born)]

■ **1** expectant, impregnate, *archaic* in a delicate *or* interesting condition, *enceinte*, *literary* with child, *literary or Zool.* gravid, *colloq.* in the family way, in pod, *sl.* up the spout, *Brit. sl.* in the (pudding) club; (*be pregnant*) *colloq.* be expecting, *sl.* have a bun in the oven. **2** charged, fraught, loaded, weighty, significant, meaningful, suggestive, expressive, pointed. **3** fertile, fecund, fruitful, productive; see also IMAGINATIVE 1. **4** (*pregnant with*) see ABUNDANT 2.

preheat /preeheet/ *v.tr.* heat beforehand.

prehensile /preehénsīl/ *adj. Zool.* (of a tail or limb) capable of grasping. □□ **prehensility** /-sílliti/ *n.* [F *préhensile* f. L *prehendere prehens-* (as PRE-, *hendere* grasp)]

prehension /prihénsh'n/ *n.* **1** grasping, seizing. **2** mental apprehension. [L *prehensio* (as PREHENSILE)]

prehistoric /preehistórrik/ *adj.* **1** of or relating to the period before written records. **2** *colloq.* utterly out of date. □□

prehistorian /-stórian/ *n.* **prehistorically** *adv.* **prehistory** /-hístari/ *n.* [F *préhistorique* (as PRE-, HISTORIC)]
■ **1** primordial, primal, primeval, primitive, earliest, early, antediluvian, ancient. **2** out of date, out-dated, old-fashioned, *passé*; see also ANTIQUATED.

prehuman /preéhyoóman/ *adj.* existing before the time of man.

pre-ignition /preé-ignish'n/ *n.* the premature firing of the explosive mixture in an internal-combustion engine.

prejudge /preéjúj/ *v.tr.* **1** form a premature judgement on (a person, issue, etc.). **2** pass judgement on (a person) before a trial or proper enquiry. □□ **prejudgement** *n.* **prejudication** /-joodikáysh'n/ *n.*
■ □□ **prejudgement** see PRECONCEPTION.

prejudice /préjoodiss/ *n.* & *v.* ● *n.* **1 a** a preconceived opinion. **b** (usu. foll. by *against, in favour of*) bias or partiality. **c** intolerance of or discrimination against a person or group, esp. on account of race, religion, or gender; bigotry (*racial prejudice*). **2** harm or injury that results or may result from some action or judgement (*to the prejudice of*). ● *v.tr.* **1** impair the validity or force of (a right, claim, statement, etc.). **2** (esp. as **prejudiced** *adj.*) cause (a person) to have a prejudice. □ **without prejudice** (often foll. by *to*) without detriment (to any existing right or claim). [ME f. OF *prejudice* f. L *praejudicium* (as PRAE-, *judicium* judgement)]
■ *n.* **1 a, b** preconception, prejudgement, preconceived notion; partiality, bias, leaning, warp, twist, predisposition, predilection; favouritism, partisanship, prepossession. **c** bigotry, bias, partisanship, discrimination, intolerance, inequality; racism, racialism, apartheid, sexism, (male) chauvinism, *US* Jim Crowism. **2** see DETRIMENT. ● *v.* **1** bias, influence, warp, twist, distort, slant; colour, jaundice, poison. **2** (**prejudiced**) predisposed, partial, prepossessed; unfair, one-sided, biased, jaundiced, opinionated, partisan, non-objective, unobjective, bigoted, intolerant, narrow-minded, parochial, chauvinistic.

prejudicial /préjoodísh'l/ *adj.* causing prejudice; detrimental. □□ **prejudicially** *adv.* [ME f. OF *prejudiciel* (as PREJUDICE)]
■ injurious, damaging, detrimental, harmful, unfavourable, inimical, deleterious, disadvantageous, counter-productive, pernicious.

prelacy /préllasi/ *n.* (*pl.* **-ies**) **1** church government by prelates. **2** (prec. by *the*) prelates collectively. **3** the office or rank of prelate. [ME f. AF *prelacie* f. med.L *prelatia* (as PRELATE)]

prelapsarian /preélapsáirian/ *adj.* before the Fall of man.

prelate /préllat/ *n.* **1** a high ecclesiastical dignitary, e.g. a bishop. **2** *hist.* an abbot or prior. □□ **prelatic** /prilátik/ *adj.* **prelatical** /prilátik'l/ *adj.* [ME f. OF *prelat* f. med.L *praelatus* past part.: see PREFER]

prelature /préllatyoor/ *n.* **1** the office of prelate. **2** (prec. by *the*) prelates collectively. [F *prélature* f. med.L *praelatura* (as PRELATE)]

prelim /preélim, prilím/ *n. colloq.* **1** a preliminary examination, esp. at a university. **2** (in *pl.*) the pages preceding the text of a book. [abbr.]
■ **2** (*prelims*) introduction, preface, foreword, preamble, prologue, front matter, proem, exordium, prolegomenon.

preliminary /prilímminari/ *adj.*, *n.*, & *adv.* ● *adj.* introductory, preparatory. ● *n.* (*pl.* **-ies**) (usu. in *pl.*) **1** a preliminary action or arrangement (*dispense with the preliminaries*). **2** a preliminary trial or contest. ● *adv.* (foll. by *to*) preparatory to; in advance of (*was completed preliminary to the main event*). □□ **preliminarily** *adv.* [mod.L *praeliminaris* or F *préliminaire* (as PRE-, L *limen liminis* threshold)]
■ *adj.* introductory, initial, opening, preparatory, prefatory, preceding, precursory, antecedent, initiatory, preambular, preludial; exploratory, premonitory; *Med.* prodromal, prodromic. ● *n.* **1** introduction, beginning, opening, preparation, prelude, overture, prologue. **2** trial, round; see also HEAT *n.* 6. ● *adv.* (*preliminary to*) in advance of, preparatory to, prior to, ahead of; see also BEFORE *prep.* 2.

preliterate /preélittarat/ *adj.* of or relating to a society or culture that has not developed the use of writing.

prelude /prélyood/ *n.* & *v.* ● *n.* (often foll. by *to*) **1** an action, event, or situation serving as an introduction. **2** the introductory part of a poem etc. **3 a** an introductory piece of music, often preceding a fugue or forming the first piece of a suite or beginning an act of an opera. **b** a short piece of music of a similar type, esp. for the piano. ● *v.tr.* **1** serve as a prelude to. **2** introduce with a prelude. □□ **preludial** /prilyoódial/ *adj.* [F *prélude* or med.L *praeludium* f. L *praeludere praelus-* (as PRAE-, *ludere* play)]
■ *n.* **1** see PRELIMINARY *n.* 1. **2** see FOREWORD.

premarital /preémárrit'l/ *adj.* existing or (esp. of sexual relations) occurring before marriage. □□ **premaritally** *adv.*

premature /prémmatyoór/ *adj.* **1 a** occurring or done before the usual or proper time; too early (*a premature decision*). **b** too hasty (*must not be premature*). **2** (of a baby, esp. a viable one) born (esp. three or more weeks) before the end of the full term of gestation. □□ **prematurely** *adv.* **prematureness** *n.* **prematurity** /-tyoóriti/ *n.* [L *praematurus* very early (as PRAE-, MATURE)]
■ **1** untimely, unready, early, unseasonable, too soon, hasty, ill-timed, overhasty, impulsive. **2** preterm. □□ **prematurely** preterm, before one's *or* its time, ahead of time, too soon, too early, hastily, overhastily, at half cock, *archaic* untimely.

premaxillary /preémaksíllari/ *adj.* in front of the upper jaw.

premed /preeméd/ *n. colloq.* **1** = PREMEDICATION. **2** a premedical course or student. [abbr.]

premedical /preeméddik'l/ *adj.* of or relating to study in preparation for a course in medicine.

premedication /preémedikáysh'n/ *n.* medication to prepare for an operation or other treatment.

premeditate /preeméddittayt/ *v.tr.* (often as **premeditated** *adj.*) think out or plan (an action) beforehand (*premeditated murder*). □□ **premeditation** /-táysh'n/ *n.* [L *praemeditari* (as PRAE-, MEDITATE)]
■ (**premeditated**) planned, conscious, intentional, intended, wilful, deliberate, studied, purposive, aforethought, *esp. Law* prepense; contrived, preplanned, calculated, preconceived. □□ **premeditation** planning, pre-planning, forethought, intent; criminal intent, *mens rea*.

premenstrual /preeménstrooal/ *adj.* of, occurring, or experienced before menstruation (*premenstrual tension*). □ **premenstrual syndrome** any of a complex of symptoms (including tension, fluid retention, etc.) experienced by some women in the days immediately preceding menstruation. □□ **premenstrually** *adv.*

premier /prémmiar/ *n.* & *adj.* ● *n.* a prime minister or other head of government. ● *adj.* **1** first in importance, order, or time. **2** of earliest creation (*premier earl*). □□ **premiership** *n.* [ME f. OF = first, f. L (as PRIMARY)]
■ *n.* prime minister, PM, head of government, chief executive, president, chancellor. ● *adj.* **1** première, first, prime, primary, chief, principal, head, main, foremost, top-ranking, high-ranking, senior, leading, top, pre-eminent, *US* ranking.

première /prémmiair/ *n.*, *adj.*, & *v.* ● *n.* the first performance or showing of a play or film. ● *adj.* = PREMIER *adj.* 1 ● *v.tr.* give a première of. [F, fem. of *premier* (adj.) (as PREMIER)]
■ *n.* first night, opening (night). ● *v.* open, launch.

premillennial /preémiléniial/ *adj.* existing or occurring before the millennium, esp. with reference to the supposed second coming of Christ. □□ **premillennialism** *n.* **premillennialist** *n.*

premise *n.* & *v.* ● *n.* /prémmiss/ **1** *Logic* = PREMISS. **2** (in *pl.*) **a** a house or building with its grounds and appurtenances. **b** *Law* houses, lands, or tenements previously specified in a document etc. ● *v.* /primíz/ **1** *tr.* say or write by way of

introduction. **2** *tr.* & *intr.* assert or assume as a premise. □ **on the premises** in the building etc. concerned. [ME f. OF *premisse* f. med.L *praemissa (propositio)* (proposition) set in front f. L *praemittere praemiss-* (as PRAE-, *mittere* send)]
▪ *v.* **2** assume, propose, postulate, hypothesize, hypothecate, conjecture, posit, assert, suppose, presuppose, theorize, surmise, put *or* set forth, predicate, argue.

premiss /prémmiss/ *n. Logic* a previous statement from which another is inferred. [var. of PREMISE]
▪ assumption, proposition, postulate, hypothesis, conjecture, assertion, supposition, thesis, presupposition, proposal, surmise, basis, ground(s); see also PRESUMPTION 2.

premium /préemiəm/ *n.* **1** an amount to be paid for a contract of insurance. **2 a** a sum added to interest, wages, etc.; a bonus. **b** a sum added to ordinary charges. **3** a reward or prize. **4** (*attrib.*) (of a commodity) of best quality and therefore more expensive. **5** an item offered free or cheaply as an incentive to buy, sample, or subscribe to something. □ **at a premium 1** highly valued; above the usual or nominal price. **2** scarce and in demand. **Premium Bond** (or **Savings Bond**) *Brit.* a government security without interest but with a draw for cash prizes. **put a premium on 1** provide or act as an incentive to. **2** attach special value to. [L *praemium* booty, reward (as PRAE-, *emere* buy, take)]
▪ **2** extra, dividend, perquisite; see also BONUS 2. **3** see REWARD *n.* 1a. **4** see CHOICE *adj.* **5** incentive, inducement, stimulus, incitement, lure, bait, spur, goad, reward, *esp. US colloq.* freebie, *colloq.* come-on. □ **at a premium 1** costly, expensive, dear, high-priced, up-market; valuable, precious, priceless; *Stock Exchange* above par. **2** scarce, rare, hard to come by, in short supply, thin on the ground.

premolar *adj.* & *n.* ● *adj.* /préemṓlər/ in front of a molar tooth. ● *n.* /preemṓlər/ (in an adult human) each of eight teeth situated in pairs between each of the four canine teeth and each first molar.

premonition /prémmənísh'n, prée-/ *n.* a forewarning; a presentiment. □□ **premonitor** /primónnitər/ *n.* **premonitory** /primónnitəri, -tri/ *adj.* [F *prémonition* or LL *praemonitio* f. L *praemonēre praemonit-* (as PRAE-, *monēre* warn)]
▪ foreboding, presentiment, forewarning, suspicion, feeling, hunch, sneaking suspicion, *colloq.* funny feeling.

Premonstratensian /primónstrəténsiən/ *adj.* & *n. hist.* ● *adj.* of or relating to an order of regular canons founded at Prémontré in France in 1120, or of the corresponding order of nuns. ● *n.* a member of either of these orders. [med.L *Praemonstratensis* f. *Praemonstratus* the abbey of Prémontré (lit. = foreshown)]

premorse /préemórss/ *adj. Bot.* & *Zool.* with the end abruptly terminated. [L *praemordēre praemors-* bite off (as PRAE-, *mordēre* bite)]

prenatal /préenáyt'l/ *adj.* of or concerning the period before birth. □□ **prenatally** *adv.*

prentice /préntiss/ *n.* & *v. archaic* ● *n.* = APPRENTICE. ● *v.tr.* (as **prenticed** *adj.*) apprenticed. □ **prentice hand** an inexperienced hand. □□ **prenticeship** *n.* [ME f. APPRENTICE]

preoccupation /prée-ókyoopáysh'n/ *n.* **1** the state of being preoccupied. **2** a thing that engrosses the mind. [F *préoccupation* or L *praeoccupatio* (as PREOCCUPY)]
▪ **2** see OBSESSION.

preoccupy /prée-ókyoopī/ *v.tr.* (**-ies, -ied**) **1** (of a thought etc.) dominate or engross the mind of (a person) to the exclusion of other thoughts. **2** (as **preoccupied** *adj.*) otherwise engrossed; mentally distracted. **3** occupy beforehand. [PRE- + OCCUPY, after L *praeoccupare* seize beforehand]
▪ **1** see OCCUPY 6. **2** (**preoccupied**) engrossed, rapt, thoughtful, pensive, absorbed, meditative, cogitative; distracted, abstracted, oblivious, unaware, wrapped up, immersed, *distrait*.

preocular /prée-ókyoolər/ *adj.* in front of the eye.

preordain /prée-ordáyn/ *v.tr.* ordain or determine beforehand.
▪ see DESTINE.

prep /prep/ *n. colloq.* **1** *Brit.* **a** the preparation of school work by a pupil. **b** the period when this is done. **2** *US* a student in a preparatory school. [abbr. of PREPARATION]
▪ **1 a** homework.

prep. *abbr.* preposition.

prepack /préepák/ *v.tr.* (also **pre-package** /-pákkij/) pack (goods) on the site of production or before retail.

prepaid *past* and *past part.* of PREPAY.

preparation /préppəráysh'n/ *n.* **1** the act or an instance of preparing; the process of being prepared. **2** (often in *pl.*) something done to make ready. **3** a specially prepared substance, esp. a food or medicine. **4** work done by school pupils to prepare for a lesson. **5** *Mus.* the sounding of the discordant note in a chord in the preceding chord where it is not discordant, lessening the effect of the discord. [ME f. OF f. L *praeparatio -onis* (as PREPARE)]
▪ **1** organization, planning; groundwork, spadework; training, education, teaching, instruction, tuition, briefing. **2** (*preparations*) plans, arrangements, provision(s), measures, programme, schedule, itinerary. **3** substance, compound, concoction, mixture, product, material, composition.

preparative /pripárrətiv/ *adj.* & *n.* ● *adj.* preparatory. ● *n.* **1** *Mil.* & *Naut.* a signal on a drum, bugle, etc., as an order to make ready. **2** a preparatory act. □□ **preparatively** *adv.* [ME f. OF *preparatif -ive* f. med.L *praeparativus* (as PREPARE)]
▪ *adj.* see INTRODUCTORY.

preparatory /pripárrətəri, -tri/ *adj.* & *adv.* ● *adj.* (often foll. by *to*) serving to prepare; introductory. ● *adv.* (often foll. by *to*) in a preparatory manner (*was packing preparatory to departure*). □ **preparatory school** a usu. private school preparing pupils for a higher school or *US* for college or university. □□ **preparatorily** *adv.* [ME f. LL *praeparatorius* (as PREPARE)]
▪ *adj.* preparative, preliminary, prefatory, initial; see also INTRODUCTORY. ● *adv.* (*preparatory to*) in preparation for, preceding; see also BEFORE *prep.* 1a, b, 2.

prepare /pripáir/ *v.* **1** *tr.* make or get ready for use, consideration, etc. **2** *tr.* make ready or assemble (food, a meal, etc.) for eating. **3 a** *tr.* make (a person or oneself) ready or disposed in some way (*prepares students for university*; *prepared them for a shock*). **b** *intr.* put oneself or things in readiness, get ready (*prepare to jump*). **4** *tr.* make (a chemical product etc.) by a regular process; manufacture. **5** *tr. Mus.* lead up to (a discord). □ **be prepared** (often foll. by *for*, or *to* + infin.) be disposed or willing to. □□ **preparer** *n.* [ME f. F *préparer* or L *praeparare* (as PRAE-, *parare* make ready)]
▪ **1** (get *or* make) ready, arrange, lay, set, (put in) order, organize, provide for, make provision(s) for, lay the groundwork for. **2** cook (up), make, do, whip up, *US colloq.* fix. **3 a** (get *or* make) ready, prime, make fit, fit (out), equip, outfit, adapt; brace, steel; train, groom, brief. **4** process, produce, make, treat; manufacture, fabricate, put out, build, construct, assemble, put together, turn out, fashion, forge, mould. □ **be prepared** be willing *or* disposed *or* predisposed *or* inclined *or* of a mind.

preparedness /pripáiridniss/ *n.* a state of readiness, esp. for war.
▪ vigilance, alertness, readiness, fitness.

prepay /préepáy/ *v.tr.* (*past* and *past part.* **prepaid**) **1** pay (a charge) in advance. **2** pay postage on (a letter or parcel etc.) before posting. □□ **prepayable** *adj.* **prepayment** *n.*
▪ □□ **prepayment** advance.

prepense /pripénss/ *adj.* (usu. placed after noun) esp. *Law* deliberate, intentional (*malice prepense*). □□ **prepensely** *adv.* [earlier *prepensed* past part. of obs. *prepense* (v.) alt. f. earlier *purpense* f. AF & OF *purpenser* (as PUR-, *penser*): see PENSIVE]

preplan /preéplán/ *v.tr.* (**preplanned, preplanning**) plan in advance.

preponderant /pripóndərənt/ *adj.* surpassing in influence, power, number, or importance; predominant, preponderating. □□ **preponderance** *n.* **preponderantly** *adv.*
■ see PREDOMINANT 1. □□ **preponderance** dominance, predominance, primacy, ascendancy, superiority, supremacy; majority, bulk, mass.

preponderate /pripóndərayt/ *v.intr.* (often foll. by *over*) **1 a** be greater in influence, quantity, or number. **b** predominate. **2 a** be of greater importance. **b** weigh more. [L *praeponderare* (as PRAE-, PONDER)]
■ **1** see PREDOMINATE 3. **2 a** (*preponderate over*) see OUTWEIGH.

preposition /préppəzísh'n/ *n. Gram.* a word governing (and usu. preceding) a noun or pronoun and expressing a relation to another word or element, as in: 'the man *on* the platform', 'came *after* dinner', 'what did you do it *for*?'. □□ **prepositional** *adj.* **prepositionally** *adv.* [ME f. L *praepositio* f. *praeponere praeposit-* (as PRAE-, *ponere* place)]

prepositive /preépózzitiv/ *adj. Gram.* (of a word, particle, etc.) that should be placed before or prefixed. [LL *praepositivus* (as PREPOSITION)]

prepossess /preépəzéss/ *v.tr.* **1** (usu. in *passive*) (of an idea, feeling, etc.) take possession of (a person); imbue. **2 a** prejudice (usu. favourably and spontaneously). **b** (as **prepossessing** *adj.*) attractive, appealing. □□ **prepossession** /-zésh'n/ *n.*
■ **2 a** see BIAS *v.* **b** (**prepossessing**) attractive, appealing, pleasing, engaging, charming, captivating, fascinating, winsome, winning, magnetic, alluring, bewitching, fetching, inviting, good-looking, handsome, lovely, beautiful. □□ **prepossession** see OBSESSION, PRECONCEPTION.

preposterous /pripóstərəss/ *adj.* **1** utterly absurd; outrageous. **2** contrary to nature, reason, or common sense. □□ **preposterously** *adv.* **preposterousness** *n.* [L *praeposterus* reversed, absurd (as PRAE-, *posterus* coming after)]
■ absurd, ridiculous, ludicrous, laughable, risible, senseless, mad, irrational, incredible, unbelievable, outrageous, extreme, outlandish, nonsensical, fatuous, mindless, *colloq.* moronic, insane, crazy, idiotic, imbecilic; weird, bizarre.

prepostor var. of PRAEPOSTOR.

prepotent /pripṓt'nt/ *adj.* **1** greater than others in power, influence, etc. **2 a** having a stronger fertilizing influence. **b** dominant in transmitting hereditary qualities. □□ **prepotence** *n.* **prepotency** *n.* [ME f. L *praepotens -entis*, part. of *praeposse* (as PRAE-, *posse* be able)]

preppy /préppi/ *n.* & *adj. US colloq.* ● *n.* (*pl.* **-ies**) a person attending an expensive private school or who looks like such a person (with short hair, blazer, etc.). ● *adj.* (**preppier, preppiest**) **1** like a preppy. **2** neat and fashionable. [PREP (SCHOOL) + -Y²]

preprandial /preéprándiəl/ *adj. formal* or *joc.* before dinner or lunch. [PRE- + L *prandium* a meal]

pre-preference /preépréffərənss/ *adj. Brit.* (of shares, claims, etc.) ranking before preference shares etc.

preprint /preéprint/ *n.* a printed document issued in advance of general publication.

preprocessor /preeprṓsessər/ *n.* a computer program that modifies data to conform with the input requirements of another program.

prep school /prep/ *n.* = PREPARATORY SCHOOL. [abbr. of PREPARATORY]

prepubescence / preépyoobéss'nss/ *n.* the time, esp. the last two or three years, before puberty. □□ **prepubescent** *adj.*
■ see CHILDHOOD.

prepublication /preépublikáysh'n/ *adj.* & *n.* ● *attrib.adj.* produced or occurring before publication. ● *n.* publication in advance or beforehand.

prepuce /preépyōōss/ *n.* **1** = FORESKIN. **2** the fold of skin surrounding the clitoris. □□ **preputial** /preépyōōsh'l/ *adj.* [ME f. L *praeputium*]

prequel /preékwəl/ *n.* a story, film, etc., whose events or concerns precede those of an existing work. [PRE- + SEQUEL]

Pre-Raphaelite /preé-ráffəlīt/ *n.* & *adj.* ● *n.* a member of a group of English 19th-c. artists, including Holman Hunt, Millais, and D. G. Rossetti, emulating the work of Italian artists before the time of Raphael. ● *adj.* **1** of or relating to the Pre-Raphaelites. **2** (**pre-Raphaelite**) (esp. of a woman) like a type painted by a Pre-Raphaelite (e.g. with long thick curly auburn hair). □ **Pre-Raphaelite Brotherhood** the chosen name of the Pre-Raphaelites. □□ **pre-Raphaelitism** *n.*

pre-record /preé-rikórd/ *v.tr.* record (esp. material for broadcasting) in advance.

prerequisite /preé-rékwizit/ *adj.* & *n.* ● *adj.* required as a precondition. ● *n.* a prerequisite thing.
■ *adj.* essential, necessary, requisite, imperative, indispensable, obligatory, required. ● *n.* precondition, requirement, requisite, condition, stipulation, *sine qua non*, proviso, necessity.

prerogative /priróggətiv/ *n.* **1** a right or privilege exclusive to an individual or class. **2** (in full **royal prerogative**) *Brit.* the right of the sovereign, theoretically subject to no restriction. [ME f. OF *prerogative* or L *praerogativa* privilege (orig. to vote first) f. *praerogativus* asked first (as PRAE-, *rogare* ask)]
■ **1** privilege, right, liberty, power, due, advantage, licence, authority.

Pres. *abbr.* President.

presage /préssij/ *n.* & *v.* ● *n.* **1** an omen or portent. **2** a presentiment or foreboding. ● *v.tr.* /also prisáyj/ **1** portend, foreshadow. **2** give warning of (an event etc.) by natural means. **3** (of a person) predict or have a presentiment of. □□ **presageful** /prisáyjfōōl/ *adj.* **presager** *n.* [ME f. F *présage*, *présager* f. L *praesagium* f. *praesagire* forebode (as PRAE-, *sagire* perceive keenly)]
■ *n.* **1** see OMEN *n.* **2** see FOREBODING. ● *v.* **1** see FORESHADOW. **2** see SPELL¹. **3** see PREDICT.

presbyopia /prézbiṓpiə/ *n.* long-sightedness caused by loss of elasticity of the eye lens, occurring esp. in middle and old age. □□ **presbyopic** /-bióppik/ *adj.* [mod.L f. Gk *presbus* old man + *ōps ōpos* eye]
■ □□ **presbyopic** see FAR-SIGHTED 2.

presbyter /prézbitər/ *n.* **1** an elder in the early Christian Church. **2** (in the Episcopal Church) a minister of the second order; a priest. **3** (in the Presbyterian Church) an elder. □□ **presbyteral** /-bíttərəl/ *adj.* **presbyterate** /-bíttərət/ *n.* **presbyterial** /-teériəl/ *adj.* **presbytership** *n.* [eccl.L f. Gk *presbuteros* elder, compar. of *presbus* old]

Presbyterian /prézbiteériən/ *adj.* & *n.* ● *adj.* (of a church) governed by elders all of equal rank, esp. with reference to the national Church of Scotland. ● *n.* **1** a member of a Presbyterian Church. **2** an adherent of the Presbyterian system. □□ **Presbyterianism** *n.* [eccl.L *presbyterium* (as PRESBYTERY)]

presbytery /prézbitəri, -tri/ *n.* (*pl.* **-ies**) **1** the eastern part of a chancel beyond the choir; the sanctuary. **2 a** a body of presbyters, esp. a court next above a Kirk-session. **b** a district represented by this. **3** the house of a Roman Catholic priest. [ME f. OF *presbiterie* f. eccl.L f. Gk *presbuterion* (as PRESBYTER)]

preschool /preéskōōl/ *adj.* of or relating to the time before a child is old enough to go to school. □□ **preschooler** /-skōōlər/ *n.*

prescient /préssiənt/ *adj.* having foreknowledge or foresight. □□ **prescience** *n.* **presciently** *adv.* [L *praescire praescient-* know beforehand (as PRAE-, *scire* know)]
■ clairvoyant; see also FAR-SIGHTED 1. □□ **prescience** clairvoyance, prevision, vision, foresight, foreknowledge.

prescind /prisínd/ *v.* **1** *tr.* (foll. by *from*) cut off (a part from a whole), esp. prematurely or abruptly. **2** *intr.* (foll. by *from*) leave out of consideration. [L *praescindere* (as PRAE-, *scindere* cut)]

prescribe /priskrī́b/ *v.* **1** *tr.* **a** advise the use of (a medicine etc.), esp. by an authorized prescription. **b** recommend, esp. as a benefit (*prescribed a change of scenery*). **2** *tr.* lay down or impose authoritatively. **3** *intr.* (foll. by *to*, *for*) assert a prescriptive right or claim. □□ **prescriber** *n.* [L *praescribere praescript-* direct in writing (as PRAE-, *scribere* write)]

■ **1 b** see ADVISE 1, 2. **2** ordain, order, dictate, decree, enjoin, rule, set down, stipulate, specify, impose, lay down.

prescript /preéskript/ *n.* an ordinance, law, or command. [L *praescriptum* neut. past part.: see PRESCRIBE]

prescription /priskrípsh'n/ *n.* **1** the act or an instance of prescribing. **2 a** a doctor's (usu. written) instruction for the composition and use of a medicine. **b** a medicine prescribed. **3** (in full **positive prescription**) uninterrupted use or possession from time immemorial or for the period fixed by law as giving a title or right. **4 a** an ancient custom viewed as authoritative. **b** a claim founded on long use. □ **negative prescription** the time limit within which an action or claim can be raised. [ME f. OF f. L *praescriptio -onis* (as PRESCRIBE)]

■ **1** see INSTRUCTION 1. **2 a** formula, recipe. **b** remedy, medication, medicine, drug, preparation, medicament.

prescriptive /priskríptiv/ *adj.* **1** prescribing. **2** *Linguistics* concerned with or laying down rules of usage. **3** based on prescription (*prescriptive right*). **4** prescribed by custom. □□ **prescriptively** *adv.* **prescriptiveness** *n.* **prescriptivism** *n.* **prescriptivist** *n.* & *adj.* [LL *praescriptivus* (as PRESCRIBE)]

■ **1** dictatorial, constrictive, didactic, restrictive, dogmatic, authoritarian, overbearing, autocratic, imperious.

preselect /preéssilékt/ *v.tr.* select in advance. □□ **preselection** *n.*

preselective /preéssiléktiv/ *adj.* that can be selected or set in advance.

preselector /preéssiléktər/ *n.* any of various devices for selecting a mechanical or electrical operation in advance of its execution, e.g. of a gear-change in a motor vehicle.

presence /prézz'nss/ *n.* **1 a** the state or condition of being present (*your presence is requested*). **b** existence; location (*the presence of a hospital nearby*). **2** a place where a person is (*was admitted to their presence*). **3 a** a person's appearance or bearing, esp. when imposing (*an august presence*). **b** a person's force of personality (esp. *have presence*). **4** a person or thing that is present (*the royal presence*; *there was a presence in the room*). **5** representation for reasons of political influence (*maintained a presence*). □ **in the presence of** in front of; observed by. **presence chamber** a room in which a monarch or other distinguished person receives visitors. **presence of mind** calmness and self-command in sudden difficulty etc. [ME f. OF f. L *praesentia* (as PRESENT[1])]

■ **1 a** attendance, company, companionship, society, fellowship, coming. **b** existence; location, situation. **3** bearing, carriage, deportment, air, aspect, aura, appearance, *literary* comportment; personality. **4** being, manifestation; spirit, wraith, spectre. □ **presence of mind** self-possession, self-control, self-assurance, coolness, cool-headedness, composure, imperturbability, sang-froid, calm, equanimity, level-headedness.

present[1] /prézz'nt/ *adj.* & *n.* ● *adj.* **1** (usu. *predic.*) being in the place in question (*was present at the trial*). **2 a** now existing, occurring, or being such (*the present Duke*; *during the present season*). **b** now being considered or discussed etc. (*in the present case*). **3** *Gram.* expressing an action etc. now going on or habitually performed (*present participle*; *present tense*). ● *n.* (prec. by *the*) **1** the time now passing (*no time like the present*). **2** *Gram.* the present tense. □ **at present** now. **by these presents** *Law* by this document (*know all men by these presents*). **for the present 1** just now. **2** as far as the present is concerned. **present company excepted** excluding those who are here now. **present-day** *adj.* of this time; modern. [ME f. OF f. L *praesens -entis* part. of *praeesse* be at hand (as PRAE-, *esse* be)]

■ *adj.* **2 a** current, contemporary, present-day, existing, existent. ● *n.* **1** (*the present*) the time being, right now, this moment; see also NOW *adv.* 1, 4. □ **at present** right *or* just now, currently, at this point, at this *or* the moment, *esp. US* & *Sc.* presently, *colloq.* at this point *or* moment in time; see also NOW *adv.* 1, 4. **for the present 2** for the time being, for the nonce, for now, for a little while, for the moment; see also *temporarily* (TEMPORARY). **present-day** see MODERN *adj.*

present[2] /prizént/ *v.* & *n.* ● *v.tr.* **1** introduce, offer, or exhibit, esp. for public attention or consideration. **2 a** (with a thing as object, usu. foll. by *to*) offer, give, or award as a gift (to a person), esp. formally or ceremonially. **b** (with a person as object, foll. by *with*) make available to; cause to have (*presented them with a new car*; *that presents us with a problem*). **3 a** (of a company, producer, etc.) put (a form of entertainment) before the public. **b** (of a performer, compère, etc.) introduce or put before an audience . **4** introduce (a person) formally (*may I present my fiancé?*; *was presented at court*). **5** offer, give (compliments etc.) (*may I present my card*; *present my regards to your family*). **6 a** (of a circumstance) reveal (some quality etc.) (*this presents some difficulty*). **b** exhibit (an appearance etc.) (*presented a rough exterior*). **7** (of an idea etc.) offer or suggest itself. **8** deliver (a cheque, bill, etc.) for acceptance or payment. **9 a** (usu. foll. by *at*) aim (a weapon). **b** hold out (a weapon) in a position for aiming. **10** (*refl.* or *absol.*) *Med.* (of a patient or illness etc.) come forward for or undergo initial medical examination. **11** (*absol.*) *Med.* (of a part of a foetus) be directed toward the cervix at the time of delivery. **12** (foll. by *to*) *Law* bring formally under notice, submit (an offence, complaint, etc.). **13** (foll. by *to*) *Eccl.* recommend (a clergyman) to a bishop for institution to a benefice. ● *n.* the position of presenting arms in salute. □ **present arms** hold a rifle etc. vertically in front of the body as a salute. **present oneself 1** appear. **2** come forward for examination etc. □□ **presenter** *n.* (in sense 3 of *v.*). [ME f. OF *presenter* f. L *praesentare* (as PRESENT[1])]

■ *v.* **1** introduce, bring in *or* up, proffer, tender, produce, submit, set forth, put forward *or* up, offer, *formal* put forth; exhibit, display. **2** offer, give (out), award, bestow, grant, confer, turn *or* hand over; provide, furnish, supply; dispense, distribute, dole out, pass out, deal out, mete out. **3 a** give, stage, show, exhibit, put on, mount, produce. **b** introduce, host, give, offer, *Brit.* compère, *colloq.* emcee; announce. **4** introduce, make known, acquaint. **5** see VENTURE *v.* 3. **6 b** see EXHIBIT *v.* 1, 2a. □ **present oneself 1** see ARRIVE 1, APPEAR 2. **2** come *or* step forward, volunteer, offer oneself, put oneself forward.

present[3] /prézz'nt/ *n.* a gift; a thing given or presented. □ **make a present of** give as a gift. [ME f. OF (as PRESENT[1]), orig. in phr. *mettre une chose en present à quelqu'un* put a thing into the presence of a person]

■ gift, donation, offering, bounty, donative, *archaic* boon, propitiation, *colloq.* pressie.

presentable /prizéntəb'l/ *adj.* **1** of good appearance; fit to be presented to other people. **2** fit for presentation. □□ **presentability** /-bílliti/ *n.* **presentableness** *n.* **presentably** *adv.*

■ **1** decent, respectable; see also SMART *adj.* 2. **2** fit, fitting, suitable, acceptable, satisfactory, adequate, passable, tolerable, admissible, all right, allowable, up to par *or* standard, up to scratch, *colloq.* OK, up to snuff.

presentation /prézzəntáysh'n/ *n.* **1 a** the act or an instance of presenting; the process of being presented. **b** a thing presented. **2** the manner or quality of presenting. **3** a demonstration or display of materials, information, etc.; a lecture. **4** an exhibition or theatrical performance. **5** a formal introduction. **6** the position of the foetus in relation to the cervix at the time of delivery. □□ **presentational** *adj.* **presentationally** *adv.* [ME f. OF f. LL *praesentatio -onis* (as PRESENT[2])]

■ **1** bestowal, donation, *esp. US* conferral, *US* conferment; hand-over, transfer, giving; see also ENDOWMENT 1. **2** delivery, *archaic* address; appearance; production. **3** see DEMONSTRATION 3, LECTURE *n.* 1. **4** performance, show, showing, play, production, staging.

presentationism /prézzəntáyshəniz'm/ *n. Philos.* the doctrine that in perception the mind has immediate cognition of the object. ▫▫ **presentationist** *n.*

presentative /prizéntətiv/ *adj.* **1** *Philos.* subject to direct cognition. **2** *hist.* (of a benefice) to which a patron has the right of presentation. [prob. f. med.L (as PRESENTATION)]

presentee /prézzəntée/ *n.* **1** the recipient of a present. **2** a person presented. [ME f. AF (as PRESENT[2])]

presentient /prisénsh'nt, -zénsh'nt/ *adj.* (often foll. by *of*) having a presentiment. [L *praesentiens* (as PRAE-, SENTIENT)]

presentiment /prizéntimənt, -séntimənt/ *n.* a vague expectation; a foreboding (esp. of misfortune). [obs. F *pressentiment* (as PRE-, SENTIMENT)]

■ see FOREBODING.

presently /prézzəntli/ *adv.* **1** soon; after a short time. **2** esp. *US* & *Sc.* at the present time; now.

■ **1** soon, by and by, in a little while, shortly, after a short time, in due course, after a while *or* time, before long, in a moment *or* minute *or* while, in two shakes (of a lamb's tail), (at) any moment, (at) any moment now, *US* momentarily, *archaic or literary* anon, *colloq.* in a jiffy. **2** see NOW *n.* 1, 4.

presentment /prizéntmənt/ *n.* the act of presenting information, esp. a statement on oath by a jury of a fact known to them. [ME f. OF *presentement* (as PRESENT[2])]

preservation /prézzərváysh'n/ *n.* **1** the act of preserving or process of being preserved. **2** a state of being well or badly preserved (*in an excellent state of preservation*). [ME f. OF f. med.L *praeservatio -onis* (as PRESERVE)]

■ **1** upkeep, maintenance, care, conservation; retention, perpetuation, continuation, safe keeping, safeguarding, protection.

preservationist /prézzərváyshənist/ *n.* a supporter or advocate of preservation, esp. of antiquities and historic buildings.

■ conservationist, protectionist.

preservative /prizérvətiv/ *n.* & *adj.* ● *n.* a substance for preserving perishable foodstuffs, wood, etc. ● *adj.* tending to preserve. [ME f. OF *preservatif -ive* f. med.L *praeservativus -um* (as PRESERVE)]

preserve /prizérv/ *v.* & *n.* ● *v.tr.* **1 a** keep safe or free from harm, decay, etc. **b** keep alive (a name, memory, etc.). **2** maintain (a thing) in its existing state. **3** retain (a quality or condition). **4 a** treat or refrigerate (food) to prevent decomposition or fermentation. **b** prepare (fruit) by boiling it with sugar, for long-term storage. **5** keep (game, a river, etc.) undisturbed for private use. ● *n.* (in *sing.* or *pl.*) **1** preserved fruit; jam. **2** a place where game or fish etc. are preserved. **3** a sphere or area of activity regarded as a person's own. ▫ **well-preserved** (of an elderly person) showing little sign of ageing. ▫▫ **preservable** *adj.* **preserver** *n.* [ME f. OF *preserver* f. LL *praeservare* (as PRAE-, *servare* keep)]

■ *v.* **1 a** keep safe, protect, guard, safeguard, shield, shelter, defend, spare. **2** keep (up), conserve; see also MAINTAIN 4. **3** retain, keep, sustain, hold; see MAINTAIN 1, 2. **4 a** conserve, pickle, cure, smoke, kipper, salt, corn, marinate, can, freeze, freeze-dry, refrigerate, dry, irradiate. ● *n.* **1** conserve, jam, jelly, marmalade. **2** (game) reserve, sanctuary, park. **3** see SPHERE *n.* 4a.

pre-set /préesét/ *v.tr.* (**-setting**; *past* and *past part.* **-set**) **1** set or fix (a device) in advance of its operation. **2** settle or decide beforehand.

preshrunk /préeshrúngk/ *adj.* (of a fabric or garment) treated so that it shrinks during manufacture and not in use.

preside /prizíd/ *v.intr.* **1** (often foll. by *at, over*) be in a position of authority, esp. as the chairperson or president of a meeting. **2 a** exercise control or authority. **b** (foll. by *at*) *colloq.* play an instrument in company (*presided at the piano*). [F *présider* f. L *praesidēre* (as PRAE-, *sedēre* sit)]

■ **1** (*preside over* or *at*) chair, administer, officiate at; manage, handle, supervise, run, oversee, head (up), control, direct, administrate, regulate. **2 a** see CHAIR *v.*

presidency /prézzidənsi/ *n.* (*pl.* **-ies**) **1** the office of president. **2** the period of this. [Sp. & Port. *presidencia*, It. *presidenza* f. med.L *praesidentia* (as PRESIDE)]

■ premiership, leadership, rule, command; *colloq.* driver's seat, saddle; administration.

president /prézzid'nt/ *n.* **1** the elected head of a republican State. **2** the head of a society or council etc. **3** the head of certain colleges. **4** *US* **a** the head of a university. **b** the head of a company, etc. **5** a person in charge of a meeting, council, etc. ▫▫ **presidential** /-dénsh'l/ *adj.* **presidentially** /-dénshəli/ *adv.* **presidentship** *n.* [ME f. OF f. L (as PRESIDE)]

■ **1–3** chief, leader, principal, *colloq.* boss, *sl.* (big) cheese, *Brit. sl.* guv'nor, guv, *US sl.* (chief) honcho, Mr Big. **4 a** *US sl.* prex, prexy; see also PRINCIPAL *n.* 2. **b** director, managing director, MD. **5** chair, chairman, chairwoman, chairperson.

presidium /prisíddiəm, -zíddiəm/ *n.* (also **praesidium**) a standing executive committee in a Communist country, esp. *hist.* in the former USSR. [Russ. *prezidium* f. L *praesidium* protection etc. (as PRESIDE)]

presocratic /préessəkráttik/ *adj.* (of philosophy) of the time before Socrates.

press[1] /press/ *v.* & *n.* ● *v.* **1** *tr.* apply steady force to (a thing in contact) (*press a switch; pressed the two surfaces together*). **2** *tr.* **a** compress or apply pressure to a thing to flatten, shape, or smooth it, as by ironing (*got the curtains pressed*). **b** squeeze (a fruit etc.) to extract its juice. **c** manufacture (a gramophone record etc.) by moulding under pressure. **3** *tr.* (foll. by *out of, from*, etc.) squeeze (juice etc.). **4** *tr.* embrace or caress by squeezing (*pressed my hand*). **5** *intr.* (foll. by *on, against*, etc.) exert pressure. **6** *intr.* be urgent; demand immediate action (*time was pressing*). **7** *intr.* (foll. by *for*) make an insistent demand. **8** *intr.* (foll. by *up, round*, etc.) form a crowd. **9** *intr.* (foll. by *on, forward*, etc.) hasten insistently. **10** *tr.* (often in *passive*) (of an enemy etc.) bear heavily on. **11** *tr.* (often foll. by *for*, or *to* + infin.) urge or entreat (*pressed me to stay; pressed me for an answer*). **12** *tr.* (foll. by *on, upon*) **a** put forward or urge (an opinion, claim, or course of action). **b** insist on the acceptance of (an offer, a gift, etc.). **13** *tr.* insist on (*did not press the point*). **14** *intr.* (foll. by *on*) produce a strong mental or moral impression; oppress; weigh heavily. **15** *intr. Golf* try too hard for a long shot etc. and so strike the ball imperfectly. ● *n.* **1** the act or an instance of pressing (*give it a slight press*). **2 a** a device for compressing, flattening, shaping, extracting juice, etc. (*trouser press; flower press; wine press*). **b** a machine that applies pressure to a workpiece by means of a tool, in order to punch shapes, bend it, etc. **3** = *printing-press*. **4** (prec. by *the*) **a** the art or practice of printing. **b** newspapers, journalists, etc., generally or collectively (*read it in the press; pursued by the press*). **5** a notice or piece of publicity in newspapers etc. (*got a good press*). **6** (**Press**) **a** a printing house or establishment. **b** a publishing company (*Athlone Press*). **7 a** crowding. **b** a crowd (of people etc.). **8** the pressure of affairs. **9** esp. *Ir.* & *Sc.* a large usu. shelved cupboard for clothes, books, etc., esp. in a recess. ▫ **at** (or **in**) **press** (or **the press**) being printed. **be pressed for** have barely enough (time etc.). **go** (or **send**) **to press** go or send to be printed. **press agent** a person employed to attend to advertising and press publicity. **press-box** a reporters' enclosure esp. at a sports event. **press the button** **1** set machinery in motion. **2** *colloq.* take a decisive initial step. **press-button** *adj.* = *push-button*. **press conference** an interview given to journalists to make an announcement or answer questions. **press gallery** a gallery for reporters esp. in a legislative assembly. **press-on** (of a material) that can be pressed or ironed on. **press release**

an official statement issued to newspapers for information. **press-stud** a small fastening device engaged by pressing its two halves together. **press-up** an exercise in which the prone downward-facing body is raised from the legs or trunk upwards by pressing down on the hands to straighten the arms. [ME f. OF *presser*, *presse* f. L *pressare* frequent. of *premere press-*]

■ *v.* **1** squeeze, compress, push; depress, press *or* push down. **2 a** iron, smooth, flatten, *esp. Brit hist.* put through a mangle. **b** squeeze, crush, compress, mash; cream, purée. **3** see EXPRESS[1] 4. **4** clasp, embrace, hug, hold (close *or* tight), take in one's arms, throw one's arms about *or* around, grip, clip. **5** exert pressure *or* force, jab, prod, dig, poke, nudge, depress. **7** (*press for*) cry out for, call for, insist on; see ASK 4a. **8** crowd, flock, gather, mill, swarm, throng, seethe, cluster, congregate, converge, huddle. **9** (*press on* or *forward*) see HURRY *v.* 1. **11** urge, pressure, pressurize, importune, beseech, ask, request, beg, entreat. **12 b** push, force; see also THRUST *v.* 2. **13** pursue; see also LABOUR *v.* 3a. **14** (*press on*) see OPPRESS 3. ● *n.* **1** push, squeeze, nudge, shove, thrust. **4 b** (*the press*) the newspapers, the papers, Fleet Street, *joc.* the fourth estate; newspapermen, newsmen, reporters, ladies *or* gentlemen of the press, journalists, paparazzi, news-hounds, *Austral. colloq.* journos. **5** review(s); see also NOTICE *n.* 4. **7 b** crowd, throng, swarm, cluster, huddle, pack, herd, host, mob, crush, *usu. derog.* horde. **8** pressure, stress; urgency, haste, hurry, (hustle and) bustle, hurly-burly. □ **be pressed for** (*be pressed for time*) be busy, be run *or* rushed off one's feet, *colloq.* be pushed (for time), be up to one's neck.

press[2] /press/ *v.* & *n.* ● *v.tr.* **1** *hist.* force to serve in the army or navy. **2** bring into use as a makeshift (*was pressed into service*). ● *n. hist.* compulsory enlistment esp. in the navy. [alt. f. obs. *prest* (v. & n.) f. OF *prest* loan, advance pay f. *prester* f. L *praestare* furnish (as PRAE-, *stare* stand)]

press-gang /présgang/ *n.* & *v.* ● *n.* **1** *hist.* a body of men employed to press men into service in the army or navy. **2** any group using similar coercive methods. ● *v.tr.* force into service.

pressie /prézzi/ *n.* (also **prezzie**) *colloq.* a present or gift. [abbr.]

pressing /préssing/ *adj.* & *n.* ● *adj.* **1** urgent (*pressing business*). **2 a** urging strongly (*a pressing invitation*). **b** persistent, importunate (*since you are so pressing*). ● *n.* **1** a thing made by pressing, esp. a gramophone record. **2** a series of these made at one time. **3** the act or an instance of pressing a thing, esp. a gramophone record or grapes etc. (*all at one pressing*). □□ **pressingly** *adv.*

■ *adj.* **1** urgent, compelling, pivotal, major, important, vital, high-priority, critical, portentous, momentous, significant, *colloq. disp.* crucial. **2 b** see INSISTENT 1.

pressman /présmən/ *n.* (*pl.* **-men**) **1** a journalist. **2** an operator of a printing-press.

■ **1** see JOURNALIST.

pressmark /présmaark/ *n.* a library shelf-mark showing the location of a book etc.

pressure /préshər/ *n.* & *v.* ● *n.* **1 a** the exertion of continuous force on or against a body by another in contact with it. **b** the force exerted. **c** the amount of this (expressed by the force on a unit area) (*atmospheric pressure*). **2** urgency; the need to meet a deadline etc. (*work under pressure*). **3** affliction or difficulty (*under financial pressure*). **4** constraining influence (*if pressure is brought to bear*). ● *v.tr.* **1** apply (esp. moral) pressure to. **2 a** coerce. **b** (often foll. by *into*) persuade (*was pressured into attending*). □ **pressure-cook** cook in a pressure-cooker. **pressure-cooker** an airtight pan for cooking quickly under steam pressure. **pressure gauge** a gauge showing the pressure of steam etc. **pressure group** a group or association formed to promote a particular interest or cause by influencing public policy. **pressure point 1** a point where an artery can be pressed against a bone to inhibit bleeding. **2** a point on the skin sensitive to pressure. **3** a target for political pressure or influence. **pressure suit** an inflatable suit for flying at a high altitude. [ME f. L *pressura* (as PRESS[1])]

■ *n.* **1 a, b** force, compression, tension; weight, power, strength. **2, 3** stress, strain, constraint; urgency, demand(s); affliction, oppression, press, weight, burden, load; difficulty. **4** influence, power, sway; insistence, coercion, inducement, persuasion, *colloq.* arm-twisting. ● *v.* **1** bring pressure to bear on, apply pressure on *or* to, pressurize, *colloq.* lean on, twist a person's arm, turn the heat on, put the screws on; intimidate, constrain. **2 a** see FORCE[1] *v.* 1. **b** persuade, prevail upon *or* on, induce, get.

pressurize /préshərīz/ *v.tr.* (also **-ise**) **1** (esp. as **pressurized** *adj.*) maintain normal atmospheric pressure in (an aircraft cabin etc.) at a high altitude. **2** raise to a high pressure. **3** pressure (a person). □ **pressurized-water reactor** a nuclear reactor in which the coolant is water at high pressure. □□ **pressurization** /-záysh'n/ *n.*

■ **3** see PRESSURE *v.*

Prestel /préstel/ *n. propr.* (in the UK) the computerized visual information system operated by British Telecom. [PRESS[1] + TELECOMMUNICATION]

prestidigitator /préstidíjitaytər/ *n. formal* a conjuror. □□ **prestidigitation** /-táysh'n/ *n.* [F *prestidigitateur* f. *preste* nimble (as PRESTO) + L *digitus* finger]

■ conjuror, illusionist. □□ **prestidigitation** see MAGIC *n.* 2.

prestige /presteézh/ *n.* **1** respect, reputation, or influence derived from achievements, power, associations, etc. **2** (*attrib.*) having or conferring prestige. □□ **prestigeful** *adj.* [F, = illusion, glamour, f. LL *praestigium* (as PRESTIGIOUS)]

■ **1** status, respect, reputation, standing, rank, stature, influence, eminence, esteem, pre-eminence, distinction, renown, regard, fame, cachet, repute, glamour.

prestigious /prestíjəss/ *adj.* having or showing prestige. □□ **prestigiously** *adv.* **prestigiousness** *n.* [orig. = deceptive, f. L *praestigiosus* f. *praestigiae* juggler's tricks]

■ prestigeful, distinguished, august, dignified, illustrious, acclaimed, respected, celebrated, renowned, eminent, estimable, influential, impressive, pre-eminent, famous, famed, well-known, noted, notable, noteworthy, outstanding; (*attrib.*) prestige.

prestissimo /prestíssimō/ *adv.* & *n. Mus.* ● *adv.* in a very quick tempo. ● *n.* (*pl.* **-os**) a movement or passage played in this way. [It., superl. (as PRESTO 1)]

presto /préstō/ *adv.* & *n.* ● *adv.* **1** *Mus.* in quick tempo. **2** (in a conjuror's formula in performing a trick) quickly (*hey presto!*). ● *n.* (*pl.* **-os**) *Mus.* a movement to be played in a quick tempo. [It. f. LL *praestus* f. L *praesto* ready]

■ *adv.* **1** see FAST[1] *adv.* 1.

prestressed /preéstrést/ *adj.* strengthened by stressing in advance, esp. of concrete by means of stretched rods or wires put in during manufacture.

presumably /prizyóóməbli/ *adv.* as may reasonably be presumed.

■ probably, in all likelihood, (very *or* most) likely, in all probability, as likely as not.

presume /prizyóóm/ *v.* **1** *tr.* (often foll. by *that* + clause) suppose to be true; take for granted. **2** *tr.* (often foll. by *to* + infin.) **a** take the liberty; be impudent enough (*presumed to question their authority*). **b** dare, venture (*may I presume to ask?*). **3** *intr.* be presumptuous; take liberties. **4** *intr.* (foll. by *on*, *upon*) take advantage of or make unscrupulous use of (a person's good nature etc.). □□ **presumable** *adj.* **presumedly** *adv.* [ME f. OF *presumer* f. L *praesumere praesumpt-* anticipate, venture (as PRAE-, *sumere* take)]

■ **1** assume, take for granted, suppose, surmise, infer, presuppose, take it; postulate, posit. **2** take the liberty, be so presumptuous as, make so bold as, have the audacity *or* effrontery, go so far as; dare, venture. **4** (*presume on* or *upon*) take advantage of, abuse, misemploy, misuse, impose on *or* upon, take liberties with, *colloq.* put upon, *usu. derog.* exploit.

presuming /prizyóóming/ *adj.* presumptuous. □□ **presumingly** *adv.* **presumingness** *n.*

■ see PRESUMPTUOUS.

presumption /prizúmpsh'n/ *n.* **1** arrogance; presumptuous behaviour. **2 a** the act of presuming a thing to be true. **b** a thing that is or may be presumed to be true; a belief based on reasonable evidence. **3** a ground for presuming (*a strong presumption against their being guilty*). **4** *Law* an inference from known facts. [ME f. OF *presumpcion* f. L *praesumptio -onis* (as PRESUME)]

■ **1** arrogance, effrontery, hubris, audacity, boldness, brazenness, impudence, impertinence, insolence, temerity, overconfidence, presumptuousness, forwardness, immodesty, cheek, cheekiness, *colloq.* nerve, *sl.* gall, chutzpah, brass, brass neck. **2** assumption, supposition, presupposition, preconception, surmise, proposition, postulation; premise; belief, thought, feeling, conviction, inference, deduction, guess, theory, hypothesis, conjecture. **3** see ARGUMENT 2.

presumptive /prizúmptiv/ *adj.* **1** based on presumption or inference. **2** giving reasonable grounds for presumption (*presumptive evidence*). ▫▫ **presumptively** *adv.* [F *présomptif -ive* f. LL *praesumptivus* (as PRESUME)]

■ **1** inferred, presumed, assumed, supposed, understood, predicted, predicated. **2** likely, reasonable, plausible, tenable, believable, credible, conceivable, acceptable, justifiable, sensible, rational, sound.

presumptuous /prizúmptyooəss/ *adj.* unduly or overbearingly confident and presuming. ▫▫ **presumptuously** *adv.* **presumptuousness** *n.* [ME f. OF *presumptueux* f. LL *praesumptuosus, -tiosus* (as PRESUME)]

■ arrogant, proud, prideful, overconfident, overweening, forward, egotistical, presuming, audacious, bold, brazen, impertinent, insolent, cheeky, *esp. Brit. colloq.* uppish.

presuppose /préessəpṓz/ *v.tr.* (often foll. by *that* + clause) **1** assume beforehand. **2** require as a precondition; imply. [ME f. OF *presupposer*, after med.L *praesupponere* (as PRE-, SUPPOSE)]

■ **1** see PRESUME 1. **2** see IMPLY 3, REQUIRE 1.

presupposition /préessúppəzísh'n/ *n.* **1** the act or an instance of presupposing. **2** a thing assumed beforehand as the basis of argument etc. [med.L *praesuppositio* (as PRAE-, *supponere* as SUPPOSE)]

■ **1** see PRESUMPTION 2. **2** see PREMISE *n.*

pre-tax /préetáks/ *adj.* (of income or profits) before the deduction of taxes.

■ gross.

pre-teen /préeteén/ *adj.* of or relating to a child just under the age of thirteen.

pretence /priténss/ *n.* (*US* **pretense**) **1** pretending, make-believe. **2 a** a pretext or excuse (*on the slightest pretence*). **b** a false show of intentions or motives (*under the pretence of friendship*; *under false pretences*). **3** (foll. by *to*) a claim, esp. a false or ambitious one (*has no pretence to any great talent*). **4 a** affectation, display. **b** pretentiousness, ostentation (*stripped of all pretence*). [ME f. AF *pretense* ult. f. med.L *pretensus* pretended (as PRETEND)]

■ **1** make-believe, fiction, pretending, fabrication, invention. **2 a** pretext, pretension, blind; see also EXCUSE *n.* 1, 2. **b** front, façade, appearance, show, cover, cloak, veil, mask; hoax, artifice, sham, pose, cover-up, masquerade, guise, ruse, dodge, blind. **3** claim; right, title. **4** affectation, display, ostentation, show, airs, pretentiousness, pretension, posturing; hypocrisy, fakery, humbuggery, humbug, deception, artifice, falseness.

pretend /priténd/ *v.* & *adj.* ● *v.* **1** *tr.* claim or assert falsely so as to deceive (*pretend knowledge*; *pretended that they were foreigners*). **2 a** *tr.* imagine to oneself in play (*pretended to be monsters*; *pretended it was night*). **b** *absol.* make pretence, esp. in imagination or play; make believe (*they're just pretending*). **3** *tr.* **a** profess, esp. falsely or extravagantly (*does not pretend to be a scholar*). **b** (as **pretended** *adj.*) falsely claim to be such (*a pretended friend*). **4** *intr.* (foll. by *to*) **a** lay claim to (a right or title etc.). **b** profess to have (a quality etc.). **5** *tr.* (foll. by *to*) aspire or presume; venture (*I cannot pretend to guess*). ● *adj. colloq.* pretended; in pretence (*pretend money*). [ME f. F *prétendre* or f. L (as PRAE-, *tendere tent-*, later *tens-* stretch)]

■ *v.* **1** see COUNTERFEIT *v.* 2, *make believe* (BELIEVE). **2 b** make believe, act, play, play-act, put on an act; dissemble, sham. **3 a** profess, (lay) claim, make a pretence, purport; maintain, declare. **b** (**pretended**) self-styled, so-called, alleged, professed, ostensible, purported, sham, false, fake, feigned, bogus, counterfeit, spurious, pseudo, *colloq.* phoney, pretend. **5** try, attempt, endeavour, venture, presume, aspire, undertake. ● *adj.* see PRETEND *v.* 3b above.

pretender /priténdər/ *n.* **1** a person who claims a throne or title etc. **2** a person who pretends.

■ **1** claimant, aspirant, candidate, suitor, seeker.

pretense *US* var. of PRETENCE.

pretension /priténsh'n/ *n.* **1** (often foll. by *to*) **a** an assertion of a claim. **b** a justifiable claim (*has no pretensions to the name*; *has some pretensions to be included*). **2** pretentiousness. [med.L *praetensio, -tio* (as PRETEND)]

■ **1 a** claim; aspiration(s), ambitiousness; see also AMBITION 2. **b** claim, right, title. **2** pretence, pretentiousness, ostentation, affectation, hypocrisy, show, artifice, falseness, fakery, *Austral.* & *NZ sl.* guiver.

pretentious /priténshəss/ *adj.* **1** making an excessive claim to great merit or importance. **2** ostentatious. ▫▫ **pretentiously** *adv.* **pretentiousness** *n.* [F *prétentieux* (as PRETENSION)]

■ **1** pompous, self-aggrandizing, self-important, affected, *colloq.* highfalutin; snobbish, lofty, haughty, hoity-toity, *colloq.* high-hat, snotty, *Brit. sl.* toffee-nosed. **2** ostentatious, showy, superficial, grandiose, grandiloquent, extravagant, magniloquent; bombastic, inflated, high-flown, exaggerated, flowery, fustian, orotund, ornate, flatulent, turgid, euphuistic, *colloq.* windy.

preter- /préetər/ *comb. form* more than. [L *praeter* (adv. & prep.), = past, beyond]

preterite /préttərit/ *adj.* & *n.* (*US* **preterit**) *Gram.* ● *adj.* expressing a past action or state. ● *n.* a preterite tense or form. [ME f. OF *preterite* or L *praeteritus* past part. of *praeterire* pass (as PRETER-, *ire it-* go)]

preterm *adj.* /préetérm/ *adv.* /preetérm/ born or occurring prematurely.

pretermit /préetərmit/ *v.tr.* (**pretermitted, pretermitting**) *formal* **1** omit to mention (a fact etc.). **2** omit to do or perform; neglect. **3** leave off (a custom or continuous action) for a time. ▫▫ **pretermission** /-mísh'n/ *n.* [L *praetermittere* (as PRETER-, *mittere miss-* let go)]

■ **1, 2** see DISREGARD *v.* 1, NEGLECT *v.* 1, 2. ▫▫ **pretermission** see DISREGARD *n.*, NEGLECT *n.*

preternatural /préetərnáchərəl/ *adj.* outside the ordinary course of nature; supernatural. ▫▫ **preternaturalism** *n.* **preternaturally** *adv.*

■ see SUPERNATURAL *adj.* ▫▫ **preternaturalism** see MYSTIQUE 1.

pretext /préetekst/ *n.* **1** an ostensible or alleged reason or intention. **2** an excuse offered. ▫ **on** (or **under**) **the pretext** (foll. by *of*, or *that* + clause) professing as one's object or intention. [L *praetextus* outward display f. *praetexere praetext-* (as PRAE-, *texere* weave)]

■ pretence, guise; rationalization, explanation; see also EXCUSE *n.* 1, 2.

pretor *US* var. of PRAETOR.

pretorian *US* var. of PRAETORIAN.

prettify /príttifī/ *v.tr.* (**-ies, -ied**) make (a thing or person) pretty esp. in an affected way. ▫▫ **prettification** /-fikáysh'n/ *n.* **prettifier** *n.*

■ see PREEN 2.

pretty /prítti/ *adj.*, *n.*, *v.*, & *adv.* ● *adj.* (**prettier, prettiest**) **1** attractive in a delicate way without being truly beautiful or handsome (*a pretty child*; *a pretty dress*; *a pretty tune*). **2** fine or good of its kind (*a pretty wit*). **3** *iron.* considerable, fine (*a pretty penny*; *a pretty mess you have made*). ● *adv.*

colloq. fairly, moderately; considerably (*am pretty well*; *find it pretty difficult*). ● *n.* (*pl.* **-ies**) a pretty person (esp. as a form of address to a child). ● *v.tr.* (**-ies, -ied**) (often foll. by *up*) make pretty or attractive. □ **pretty much** (or **nearly** or **well**) *colloq.* almost; very nearly. **pretty-pretty** too pretty. **sitting pretty** *colloq.* in a favourable or advantageous position. □□ **prettily** *adv.* **prettiness** *n.* **prettyish** *adj.* **prettyism** *n.* [OE *prættig* f. WG]

■ *adj.* **1** comely, attractive, good-looking, nice-looking, appealing, lovely, fair, fetching, charming, winsome, *esp. US* & *N.Engl.* bonny, *esp. US colloq.* cute; sweet, melodic, melodious, dulcet, musical, harmonious, mellifluous, euphonious, *colloq.* easy on the eye(s) *or* ear(s). **2** see FINE[1] *adj.* 2. ● *adv.* rather, quite, fairly, moderately, reasonably, tolerably, somewhat; considerably, very, extremely, unbelievably, incredibly. □ **pretty much** (or **nearly** or **well**) see ALMOST.

pretzel /préts'l/ *n.* (also **bretzel** /brét-/) a crisp knot-shaped or stick-shaped salted biscuit. [G]

prevail /priváyl/ *v.intr.* **1** (often foll. by *against, over*) be victorious or gain mastery. **2** be the more usual or predominant. **3** exist or occur in general use or experience; be current. **4** (foll. by *on, upon*) persuade. **5** (as **prevailing** *adj.*) predominant; generally current or accepted (*prevailing opinion*). □ **prevailing wind** the wind that most frequently occurs at a place. □□ **prevailingly** *adv.* [ME f. L *praevalēre* (as PRAE-, *valēre* have power), infl. by AVAIL]

■ **1** win (out), succeed, triumph, gain *or* achieve victory, prove superior, gain mastery *or* control. **2, 3** predominate, preponderate, dominate; be prevalent *or* widespread *or* current, be the order of the day, hold sway. **4** (*prevail on* or *upon*) persuade, induce, sway, convince, prompt. **5** (**prevailing**) dominant, predominant, prevalent, common(est), usual, customary, universal, general, accepted, popular, shared.

prevalent /prévvələnt/ *adj.* **1** generally existing or occurring. **2** predominant. □□ **prevalence** *n.* **prevalently** *adv.* [as PREVAIL]

■ **1** current, general, universal, catholic, common, frequent, ubiquitous, pervasive, omnipresent, extensive, widespread, established. **2** prevailing, dominant, governing, ruling; see also PREDOMINANT 1. □□ **prevalence** frequency, commonness, currency, universality, ubiquitousness, ubiquity, pervasiveness, omnipresence, extensiveness, popularity; predominance; primacy.

prevaricate /privárrikayt/ *v.intr.* **1** speak or act evasively or misleadingly. **2** quibble, equivocate. ¶ Often confused with *procrastinate*. □□ **prevarication** /-káysh'n/ *n.* **prevaricator** *n.* [L *praevaricari* walk crookedly, practise collusion, in eccl.L transgress (as PRAE-, *varicari* straddle f. *varus* bent, knock-kneed)]

■ see EQUIVOCATE. □□ **prevarication** see EVASION 2, FLANNEL *n.* 3.

prevenient /priveéniənt/ *adj. formal* preceding something else. [L *praeveniens* pres. part of *praevenire* (as PREVENT)]

prevent /privént/ *v.tr.* **1** (often foll. by *from* + verbal noun) stop from happening or doing something; hinder; make impossible (*the weather prevented me from going*). **2** *archaic* go or arrive before, precede. □□ **preventable** *adj.* (also **preventible**). **preventability** /-véntəbílliti/ *n.* (also **preventibility**). **preventer** *n.* **prevention** *n.* [ME = anticipate, f. L *praevenire praevent-* come before, hinder (as PRAE-, *venire* come)]

■ **1** stop, put a stop to, arrest, (bring to a) halt; hinder, impede, curb, restrain, hamper, obstruct, inhibit, delay, retard, slow, thwart, foil, frustrate, check, block, baulk, control; preclude, forestall, avert, avoid, ward *or* fend *or* stave off; prohibit, ban, bar, forbid, interdict, taboo, debar. **2** see PRECEDE. □□ **prevention** preclusion, avoidance; prohibition, forbiddance, interdiction; obstruction, hindrance; stopping, arrest, halt; restraint, retardation, control.

preventative /privéntətiv/ *adj.* & *n.* = PREVENTIVE. □□ **preventatively** *adv.*

preventive /privéntiv/ *adj.* & *n.* ● *adj.* serving to prevent, esp. preventing disease, breakdown, etc. (*preventive medicine*; *preventive maintenance*). ● *n.* a preventive agent, measure, drug, etc. □ **preventive detention** the imprisonment of a criminal for corrective training etc. □□ **preventively** *adv.*

■ *adj.* preventative, inhibitive, inhibitory, restrictive, preclusive, interdictory; prophylactic, precautionary; protective; counteractive. ● *n.* preventative, inhibitor, hindrance, curb, block, barrier, obstacle; prophylactic, protection, shield, safeguard, prevention, countermeasure.

preview /preévyoo/ *n.* & *v.* ● *n.* **1** the act of seeing in advance. **2 a** the showing of a film, play, exhibition, etc., before it is seen by the general public. **b** (*US* **prevue**) a film trailer. ● *v.tr.* see or show in advance.

■ *n.* **2 a** advance showing, private viewing.

previous /preéviəss/ *adj.* & *adv.* ● *adj.* **1** (often foll. by *to*) coming before in time or order. **2** done or acting hastily. ● *adv.* (foll. by *to*) before (*had called previous to writing*). □ **previous question** *Parl.* a motion concerning the vote on a main question. □□ **previously** *adv.* **previousness** *n.* [L *praevius* (as PRAE-, *via* way)]

■ *adj.* **1** former, prior, past, earlier, sometime, erstwhile, *archaic* whilom; above, preceding, antecedent, anterior, aforementioned, aforesaid, above-mentioned, above-named, aforestated, *formal* prevenient. **2** see PREMATURE 1. ● *adv.* (*previous to*) previously to, prior to, in advance of; see also BEFORE *prep.* 1a, b, 2. □□ **previously** before, once, formerly, earlier, at one time, then, beforehand, hitherto, thitherto, *formal* heretofore, theretofore; in the past, in days gone by, in days of old, in days *or* times past, in the old days, some time ago, a while ago, once upon a time, *archaic* in olden days *or* times, *literary* in days of yore.

previse /privíz/ *v.tr. literary* foresee or forecast (an event etc.). □□ **prevision** /-vízh'n/ *n.* **previsional** /-vízhən'l/ *adj.* [L *praevidēre praevis-* (as PRAE-, *vidēre* see)]

■ □□ **prevision** clairvoyance, foresight, vision, foreknowledge, prescience.

prevue *US* var. of PREVIEW *n.* 2b.

pre-war /preéwáwr/ *adj.* existing or occurring before a war (esp. the most recent major war).

prex /preks/ *n.* (also **prexy**) *US sl.* a president (esp. of a college). [abbr.]

prey /pray/ *n.* & *v.* ● *n.* **1** an animal that is hunted or killed by another for food. **2** (often foll. by *to*) a person or thing that is influenced by or vulnerable to (something undesirable) (*became a prey to morbid fears*). **3** *Bibl.* or *archaic* plunder, booty, etc. ● *v.intr.* (foll. by *on, upon*) **1** seek or take as prey. **2** make a victim of. **3** (of a disease, emotion, etc.) exert a harmful influence (*fear preyed on his mind*). □ **beast** (or **bird**) **of prey** an animal (or bird) which hunts animals for food. □□ **preyer** *n.* [ME f. OF *preie* f. L *praeda* booty]

■ *n.* **1** quarry, kill; victim; game. **2** victim, target, objective; dupe, *Brit.* mug, *colloq.* mark, *sl.* fall guy, pushover. ● *v.* (*prey on* or *upon*) **1** live off, feed on *or* upon, eat, consume, devour; stalk, pursue, hunt. **2** victimize, go after, exploit, use, take advantage of, intimidate, bully. **3** oppress, weigh on *or* upon, burden, depress, strain, vex, worry, gnaw (at), plague, trouble, torment.

prezzie var. of PRESSIE.

priapic /prīáppik/ *adj.* phallic. [*Priapos* (as PRIAPISM) + -IC]

priapism /príəpiz'm/ *n.* **1** lewdness, licentiousness. **2** *Med.* persistent erection of the penis. [F *priapisme* f. LL *priapismus* f. Gk *priapismos* f. *priapizō* be lewd f. *Priapos* god of procreation]

price /prīss/ *n.* & *v.* ● *n.* **1 a** the amount of money or goods for which a thing is bought or sold. **b** value or worth (*a pearl of great price*; *beyond price*). **2** what is or must be given, done, sacrificed, etc., to obtain or achieve something. **3** the odds in betting (*starting price*). **4** a sum of money offered or given as a reward, esp. for the capture or killing of a person. ● *v.tr.* **1** fix or find the price of (a thing for sale). **2** estimate the value of. □ **above** (or **beyond** or **without**) **price** so valuable that no price can be stated. **at any price** no matter what the cost, sacrifice, etc. (*peace at any price*). **at a price** at a high cost. **price-fixing** the maintaining of prices at a certain level by agreement between competing sellers. **price-list** a list of current prices of items on sale. **price on a person's head** a reward for a person's capture or death. **price oneself out of the market** lose to one's competitors by charging more than customers are willing to pay. **price-ring** a group of traders acting illegally to control certain prices. **price tag 1** the label on an item showing its price. **2** the cost of an enterprise or undertaking. **price war** fierce competition among traders cutting prices. **set a price on** declare the price of. **what price . . .?** (often foll. by verbal noun) *colloq.* **1** what is the chance of . . .? (*what price your finishing the course?*). **2** *iron.* the expected or much boasted . . . proves disappointing (*what price your friendship now?*). □□ **priced** *adj.* (also in *comb.*). **pricer** *n.* [(n.) ME f. OF *pris* f. L *pretium*: (v.) var. of *prise* = PRIZE[1]]

■ *n.* **1 a** charge, cost, expense, expenditure, outlay, payment, amount, figure, fee, *sl.* damage. **b** value, worth; appraisal, valuation, evaluation. **2** sacrifice, toll, penalty, cost; see also LOSS 2, 3. **4** reward, bounty, premium, prize, payment, bonus, *poet.* guerdon. ● *v.* **2** value, evaluate, rate, cost. □ **above price** see PRICELESS 1.

priceless /príssliss/ *adj.* **1** invaluable; beyond price. **2** *colloq.* very amusing or absurd. □□ **pricelessly** *adv.* **pricelessness** *n.*

■ **1** costly, dear, expensive, high-priced, valuable, invaluable, precious, above *or* beyond *or* without price. **2** hilarious, (screamingly) funny, side-splitting, *colloq.* hysterical; absurd, ridiculous, droll, comical.

pricey /prísi/ *adj.* (also **pricy**) (**pricier**, **priciest**) *colloq.* expensive. □□ **priciness** *n.*

■ costly, dear, expensive; overpriced, exorbitant, outrageous, excessive.

prick /prik/ *v.* & *n.* ● *v.* **1** *tr.* pierce slightly; make a small hole in. **2** *tr.* (foll. by *off*, *out*) mark (esp. a pattern) with small holes or dots. **3** *tr.* trouble mentally (*my conscience is pricking me*). **4** *intr.* feel a pricking sensation. **5** *intr.* (foll. by *at*, *into*, etc.) make a thrust as if to prick. **6** *tr.* (foll. by *in*, *off*, *out*) plant (seedlings etc.) in small holes pricked in the earth. **7** *tr. Brit. archaic* mark off (a name in a list, esp. to select a sheriff) by pricking. **8** *tr. archaic* spur or urge on (a horse etc.). ● *n.* **1** the act or an instance of pricking. **2** a small hole or mark made by pricking. **3** a pain caused as by pricking. **4** a mental pain (*felt the pricks of conscience*). **5** *coarse sl.* **a** the penis. **b** *derog.* (as a term of contempt) a person. ¶ Usually considered a taboo use. **6** *archaic* a goad for oxen. □ **kick against the pricks** persist in futile resistance. **prick up one's ears 1** (of a dog etc.) make the ears erect when on the alert. **2** (of a person) become suddenly attentive. □□ **pricker** *n.* [OE *prician* (v.), *pricca* (n.)]

■ *v.* **1, 2** puncture, pierce, punch, perforate, penetrate. **3** see TROUBLE *v.* 1, 3. **4** smart, sting, stab, tingle, tickle, prickle, pinch, hurt. ● *n.* **2** pinhole, pinprick; hole, perforation, mark; see also LEAK *n.* 1a. **3** sting, pinch, twinge, prickle, tingle, smart. **4** see PANG.

pricket /príkkit/ *n.* **1** *Brit.* a male fallow deer in its second year, having straight unbranched horns. **2** a spike for holding a candle. [ME f. AL *prikettus* -*um*, dimin. of PRICK]

prickle /príkk'l/ *n.* & *v.* ● *n.* **1 a** a small thorn. **b** *Bot.* a thornlike process developed from the epidermis of a plant. **2** a hard-pointed spine of a hedgehog etc. **3** a prickling sensation. ● *v.tr.* & *intr.* affect or be affected with a sensation as of pricking. [OE *pricel* PRICK: (v.) also dimin. of PRICK]

■ *n.* **1, 2** spine, bristle, barb, thorn, needle, spike. **3** prickliness, itch, itchiness, sting, tingling, prick, tingle. ● *v.* tingle, sting, itch, smart; jab, prick.

prickly /príkli/ *adj.* (**pricklier**, **prickliest**) **1** (esp. in the names of plants and animals) having prickles. **2 a** (of a person) ready to take offence. **b** (of a topic, argument, etc.) full of contentious or complicated points; thorny. **3** tingling. □ **prickly heat** an itchy inflammation of the skin, causing a tingling sensation and common in hot countries. **prickly pear 1** any cactus of the genus *Opuntia*, native to arid regions of America, bearing barbed bristles and large pear-shaped prickly fruits. **2** its fruit. **prickly poppy** a tropical poppy-like plant, *Argemone mexicana*, with prickly leaves and yellow flowers. □□ **prickliness** *n.*

■ **1** bristly, thorny, brambly, spiny, barbed, briery, spiky, *Biol.* setose, *Bot.* spinous, spinose, aculeate, spiculate, *Bot.* & *Zool.* setaceous. **2 a** touchy, irritable, petulant, cantankerous, testy, peevish, fractious, spiky, short-tempered, quick-tempered, inflammable, *esp. US* cranky. **b** nettlesome, thorny, ticklish, touchy, troublesome, intricate, complicated, complex, knotty, hard, difficult, contentious. **3** tingling, tingly, stinging, pricking, prickling, itchy, scratchy.

pricy var. of PRICEY.

pride /prīd/ *n.* & *v.* ● *n.* **1 a** a feeling of elation or satisfaction at achievements or qualities or possessions etc. that do one credit. **b** an object of this feeling. **2** a high or overbearing opinion of one's worth or importance. **3** (in full **proper pride**) a proper sense of what befits one's position; self-respect. **4** a group or company (of animals, esp. lions). **5** the best condition; the prime. ● *v.refl.* (foll. by *on*, *upon*) be proud of. □ **my, his,** etc. **pride and joy** a thing of which one is very proud. **pride of the morning** a mist or shower at sunrise, supposedly indicating a fine day to come. **pride of place** the most important or prominent position. **take pride** (or **a pride**) **in 1** be proud of. **2** maintain in good condition or appearance. □□ **prideful** *adj.* **pridefully** *adv.* **prideless** *adj.* [OE *prȳtu*, *prȳte*, *prȳde* f. *prūd* PROUD]

■ *n.* **1 b** boast, prize, pride and joy, treasure, jewel, gem, delight, joy, darling, ideal. **2** self-satisfaction, conceit, proudness, egotism, egocentricity, self-importance, haughtiness, hauteur, vanity, hubris, arrogance, overconfidence, overweeningness, self-admiration, self-love, smugness. **3** honour, self-esteem, self-respect, *amour propre*, dignity; credit. **5** see PRIME[1] *n.* 1. ● *v.* (*pride oneself on*) be proud of, take pride in, plume oneself on, preen oneself on, delight in, revel in, celebrate, glory in. □ **my, his,** etc. **pride and joy** see PRIDE *n.* 1b above. **take (a) pride in 1** see PRIZE[1] *v.* **2** see CHERISH 1.

prie-dieu /preedyő/ *n.* (*pl.* **prie-dieux** *pronunc.* same) a kneeling-desk for prayer. [F, = pray God]

priest /preest/ *n.* **1** an ordained minister of the Roman Catholic or Orthodox Church, or of the Anglican Church (above a deacon and below a bishop), authorized to perform certain rites and administer certain sacraments. **2** an official minister of a non-Christian religion. □ **priest's hole** *hist.* a hiding-place for a Roman Catholic priest during times of religious persecution. □□ **priestless** *adj.* **priestlike** *adj.* **priestling** *n.* [OE *prēost*, ult. f. eccl.L *presbyter*: see PRESBYTER]

■ **1** clergyman, clergywoman, ecclesiastic, cleric, churchman, reverend, vicar, divine, man of the cloth, man of God, confessor, minister, servant of God, Father, holy man, padre.

priestcraft /préestkraaft/ *n.* usu. *derog.* the work and influence of priests.

priestess /préestiss/ *n.* a female priest of a non-Christian religion.

priesthood /préest-hŏŏd/ *n.* (usu. prec. by *the*) **1** the office or position of priest. **2** priests in general.

■ see MINISTRY 2, 3.

priestly /préestli/ *adj.* of or associated with priests. □□ **priestliness** *n.* [OE *prēostlic* (as PRIEST)]

■ clerical, ecclesiastical, pastoral, hieratic, sacerdotal, ministerial.

prig /prig/ *n.* a self-righteously correct or moralistic person. □□ **priggery** *n.* **priggish** *adj.* **priggishly** *adv.* **priggishness** *n.* [16th-c. cant, = tinker: orig. unkn.]

■ prude, purist, pedant, puritan, moralist, (Mrs) Grundy, precisionist, precisian, conformist, *colloq.* stuffed shirt, goody-goody. ▫▫ **priggish** prim, demure, prudish, prissy, puristic, moralistic, pedantic, strait-laced, stiff-necked, puritanical, old-maidish, (Mrs) Grundyish, punctilious, formal, strict, over-nice, *colloq.* goody-goody, school-marmish, stuffy, *US colloq.* uptight.

prim /prim/ *adj.* & *v.* ● *adj.* (**primmer, primmest**) **1** (of a person or manner) stiffly formal and precise. **2** (of a woman or girl) demure. **3** prudish. ● *v.tr.* (**primmed, primming**) **1** form (the face, lips, etc.) into a prim expression. **2** make prim. ▫▫ **primly** *adv.* **primness** *n.* [17th c.: prob. orig. cant f. OF *prin prime* excellent f. L *primus* first]

■ *adj.* **1** see FORMAL *adj.* 4. **2** see RESERVED. **3** see *prudish* (PRUDE). ▫▫ **primness** see *prudery* (PRUDE).

prima ballerina /préemə bálləréenə/ *n.* the chief female dancer in a ballet or ballet company. [It.]

■ see LEAD[1] *n.* 6.

primacy /prīməsi/ *n.* (*pl.* **-ies**) **1** pre-eminence. **2** the office of a primate. [ME f. OF *primatie* or med.L *primatia* (as PRIMATE)]

■ **1** see SUPERIORITY.

prima donna /préemə dónnə/ *n.* (*pl.* **prima donnas**) **1** the chief female singer in an opera or opera company. **2** a temperamentally self-important person. ▫▫ **prima donna-ish** *adj.* [It.]

■ diva, leading lady; see also LEAD[1] *n.* 6.

primaeval var. of PRIMEVAL.

prima facie /prīmə fáyshee/ *adv.* & *adj.* ● *adv.* at first sight; from a first impression (*seems prima facie to be guilty*). ● *adj.* (of evidence) based on the first impression (*can see a prima facie reason for it*). [ME f. L, fem. ablat. of *primus* first, *facies* FACE]

primal /prīm'l/ *adj.* **1** primitive, primeval. **2** chief, fundamental. ▫▫ **primally** *adv.* [med.L *primalis* f. L *primus* first]

■ **1** see PRIMITIVE *adj.* 1. **2** see FUNDAMENTAL *adj.*

primary /prīməri/ *adj.* & *n.* ● *adj.* **1 a** of the first importance; chief (*that is our primary concern*). **b** fundamental, basic. **2** earliest, original; first in a series. **3** of the first rank in a series; not derived (*the primary meaning of a word*). **4** designating any of the colours red, green, and blue, or for pigments red, blue, and yellow, from which all other colours can be obtained by mixing. **5** (of a battery or cell) generating electricity by irreversible chemical reaction. **6** (of education) for young children, esp. below the age of 11. **7** (**Primary**) *Geol.* of the lowest series of strata. **8** *Biol.* belonging to the first stage of development. **9** (of an industry or source of production) concerned with obtaining or using raw materials. **10** *Gram.* (of a tense in Latin and Greek) present, future, perfect, or future perfect (cf. HISTORIC). ● *n.* (*pl.* **-ies**) **1** a thing that is primary. **2** (in full **primary election**) (in the US) a preliminary election to appoint delegates to a party conference or to select the candidates for a principal (esp. presidential) election. **3** = *primary planet*. **4** (**Primary**) *Geol.* the Primary period. **5** = *primary feather*. **6** = *primary coil*. ▫ **primary coil** a coil to which current is supplied in a transformer. **primary feather** a large flight-feather of a bird's wing. **primary industry** industry (such as mining, forestry, agriculture, etc.) that provides raw materials for conversion into commodities and products for the consumer. **primary planet** a planet that directly orbits the sun (cf. *secondary planet*). **primary school** a school where young children are taught, esp. below the age of 11. ▫▫ **primarily** /prīmərili, *disp.* prīmáirili/ [ME f. L *primarius* f. *primus* first]

■ *adj.* **1 a** first, prime, principal, chief, main, leading, pre-eminent, predominant; cardinal. **b** fundamental, basic, essential, rudimentary, elemental, first, primitive. **2** earliest, first, original, initial, primitive, primeval, germinal, beginning. ▫ **primary school** see *elementary school*. ▫▫ **primarily** principally, mainly, chiefly, at bottom, first of all, pre-eminently, basically, essentially, fundamentally, mostly, predominantly, generally.

primate /prīmayt/ *n.* **1** any animal of the order Primates, the highest order of mammals, including tarsiers, lemurs, apes, monkeys, and man. **2** an archbishop. ▫ **Primate of All England** the Archbishop of Canterbury. **Primate of England** the Archbishop of York. ▫▫ **primatial** /-máysh'l/ *adj.* **primatology** /-mətólləji/ *n.* (in sense 1). [ME f. OF *primat* f. L *primas -atis* (adj.) of the first rank f. *primus* first, in med.L = primate]

primavera /préeməvérrə/ *n.* **1** a Central American tree, *Cybistax donnellsmithii*, bearing yellow blooms. **2** the hard light-coloured timber from this. [Sp., = spring (the season) f. L *primus* first + *ver* SPRING]

prime[1] /prīm/ *adj.* & *n.* ● *adj.* **1** chief, most important (*the prime agent*; *the prime motive*). **2** (esp. of cattle and provisions) first-rate, excellent. **3** primary, fundamental. **4** *Math.* **a** (of a number) divisible only by itself and unity (e.g. 2, 3, 5, 7, 11). **b** (of numbers) having no common factor but unity. ● *n.* **1** the state of the highest perfection of something (*in the prime of life*). **2** (prec. by *the*; foll. by *of*) the best part. **3** the beginning or first age of anything. **4** *Eccl.* **a** the second canonical hour of prayer, appointed for the first hour of the day (i.e. 6 a.m.). **b** the office of this. **c** *archaic* this time. **5** a prime number. **6** *Printing* a symbol (′) added to a letter etc. as a distinguishing mark, or to a figure as a symbol for minutes or feet. **7** the first of eight parrying positions in fencing. ▫ **prime cost** the direct cost of a commodity in terms of materials, labour, etc. **prime meridian 1** the meridian from which longitude is reckoned, esp. that passing through Greenwich. **2** the corresponding line on a map. **prime minister** the head of an elected government; the principal minister of a sovereign or State. **prime mover 1** an initial natural or mechanical source of motive power. **2** the author of a fruitful idea. **prime rate** the lowest rate at which money can be borrowed commercially. **prime time** the time at which a radio or television audience is expected to be at its highest. **prime vertical** the great circle of the heavens passing through the zenith and the E. and W. points of the horizon. ▫▫ **primeness** *n.* [(n.) OE *prīm* f. L *prima* (*hora*) first (hour), & MF f. OF *prime*: (adj.) ME f. OF f. L *primus* first]

■ *adj.* **1** see MAIN[1] *adj.* 1. **2** first-rate, first-class, excellent, choice, select, superior, pre-eminent, leading, unparalleled, matchless, peerless, noteworthy, outstanding, admirable, worthy, exceptional. **3** primary, original, fundamental, basic, elemental, elementary, primitive. ● *n.* **1** best years, heyday; springtime, *poet.* springtide; pinnacle, acme, peak, zenith. **3** see BEGINNING. ▫ **prime minister** see PREMIER *n.* **prime mover 2** see AUTHOR *n.* 2.

prime[2] /prīm/ *v.tr.* **1** prepare (a thing) for use or action. **2** prepare (a gun) for firing or (an explosive) for detonation. **3 a** pour (a liquid) into a pump to prepare it for working. **b** inject petrol into (the cylinder or carburettor of an internal-combustion engine). **4** prepare (wood etc.) for painting by applying a substance that prevents paint from being absorbed. **5** equip (a person) with information etc. **6** ply (a person) with food or drink in preparation for something. [16th c.: orig. unkn.]

■ **1** see PREPARE 1, 3a. **5** educate, teach, instruct, coach, train, tutor, drill; inform, brief, apprise.

primer[1] /prīmər/ *n.* **1** a substance used to prime wood etc. **2** a cap, cylinder, etc., used to ignite the powder of a cartridge etc.

primer[2] /prīmər/ *n.* **1** an elementary textbook for teaching children to read. **2** an introductory book. [ME f. AF f. med.L *primarius -arium* f. L *primus* first]

■ see TEXT 6.

primeval /prīméev'l/ *adj.* (also **primaeval**) **1** of or relating to the first age of the world. **2** ancient, primitive. ▫▫ **primevally** *adv.* [L *primaevus* f. *primus* first + *aevum* age]

▪ **1** see PREHISTORIC 1. **2** see ANCIENT[1] *adj.*

primigravida /preémigrávvidə, prími-/ *n.* (*pl.* **primigravidae** /-dee/) a woman who is pregnant for the first time. [mod.L fem. f. L *primus* first + *gravidus* pregnant: see GRAVID]

priming[1] /príming/ *n.* **1** a mixture used by painters for a preparatory coat. **2** a preparation of sugar added to beer. **3 a** gunpowder placed in the pan of a firearm. **b** a train of powder connecting the fuse with the charge in blasting etc.

priming[2] /príming/ *n.* an acceleration of the tides taking place from the neap to the spring tides. [*prime* (v.) f. PRIME[1] + -ING[1]]

primipara /prīmíppərə/ *n.* (*pl.* **primiparae** /-ree/) a woman who is bearing a child for the first time. ▫▫ **primiparous** *adj.* [mod.L fem. f. *primus* first + *-parus* f. *parere* bring forth]

primitive /prímmitiv/ *adj.* & *n.* ● *adj.* **1** early, ancient; at an early stage of civilization (*primitive man*). **2** undeveloped, crude, simple (*primitive methods*). **3** original, primary. **4** *Gram.* & *Philol.* (of words or language) radical; not derivative. **5** *Math.* (of a line, figure, etc.) from which another is derived, from which some construction begins, etc. **6** (of a colour) primary. **7** *Geol.* of the earliest period. **8** *Biol.* appearing in the earliest or a very early stage of growth or evolution. ● *n.* **1 a** a painter of the period before the Renaissance. **b** a modern imitator of such. **c** an untutored painter with a direct naïve style. **d** a picture by such a painter. **2** a primitive word, line, etc. ▫ **the Primitive Church** the Christian Church in its earliest times. ▫▫ **primitively** *adv.* **primitiveness** *n.* [ME f. OF *primitif -ive* or L *primitivus* first of its kind f. *primitus* in the first place f. *primus* first]

▪ *adj.* **1** antediluvian, ancient, aboriginal, early, primordial, primal, primeval, pristine, prehistoric, *archaic* olden. **2** crude, rude, raw, barbaric, uncultured, barbarian, coarse, rough, uncivilized, savage, uncultivated, unsophisticated, uncouth; simple, basic, naïve, undeveloped, unrefined, unpolished, untutored, untaught, untrained, unschooled, childlike. **3** germinal, first; see also ORIGINAL *adj.* 1. **7, 8** lower, early; primordial, ancestral, unspecialized, undeveloped.

primitivism /prímmitiviz'm/ *n.* **1** primitive behaviour. **2** belief in the superiority of what is primitive. **3** the practice of primitive art. ▫▫ **primitivist** *n.* & *adj.*

primo /preémō/ *n.* (*pl.* **-os**) *Mus.* the leading or upper part in a duet etc.

primogenitor /prīmōjénnitər/ *n.* **1** the earliest ancestor of a people etc. **2** an ancestor. [var. of *progenitor*, after PRIMOGENITURE]

▪ see ANCESTOR 1.

primogeniture /prīmōjénnichər/ *n.* **1** the fact or condition of being the first-born child. **2** (in full **right of primogeniture**) the right of succession belonging to the first-born, esp. the feudal rule by which the whole real estate of an intestate passes to the eldest son. ▫▫ **primogenital** *adj.* **primogenitary** *adj.* [med.L *primogenitura* f. L *primo* first + *genitura* f. *gignere genit-* beget]

primordial /prīmórdiəl/ *adj.* **1** existing at or from the beginning, primeval. **2** original, fundamental. ▫▫ **primordiality** /-diálliti/ *n.* **primordially** *adv.* [ME f. LL *primordialis* (as PRIMORDIUM)]

▪ **1** see PREHISTORIC 1. **2** see ORIGINAL *adj.* 1.

primordium /prīmórdiəm/ *n.* (*pl.* **primordia** /-diə/) *Biol.* an organ or tissue in the early stages of development. [L, neut. of *primordius* original f. *primus* first + *ordiri* begin]

primp /primp/ *v.tr.* **1** make (the hair, one's clothes, etc.) tidy. **2** *refl.* make (oneself) smart. [dial. var. of PRIM]

▪ **1** groom, tidy, preen, prink. **2** (*primp oneself*) preen *or* prink *or* prettify *or* plume oneself, spruce oneself (up), deck *or* fig oneself out, trick oneself out *or* up, smarten oneself (up), smarten up, doll (oneself) up, get (oneself) dolled up, dress (oneself) up, put on one's best bib and tucker, *colloq.* titivate oneself, *esp. Brit. colloq.* tart oneself up.

primrose /prímrōz/ *n.* **1 a** any plant of the genus *Primula*, esp. *P. vulgaris*, bearing pale yellow flowers. **b** the flower of this. **2** a pale yellow colour. ▫ **primrose path** the pursuit of pleasure, esp. with disastrous consequences (with ref. to Shakesp. *Hamlet* I. iii. 50). [ME *primerose*, corresp. to OF *primerose* and med.L *prima rosa*, lit. first rose: reason for the name unkn.]

primula /prímyoolə/ *n.* any plant of the genus *Primula*, bearing primrose-like flowers in a wide variety of colours during the spring, including primroses, cowslips, and polyanthuses. [med.L, fem. of *primulus* dimin. of *primus* first]

primum mobile /prīmōōm mōbili/ *n.* **1** the central or most important source of motion or action. **2** *Astron.* in the medieval version of the Ptolemaic system, an outer sphere supposed to move round the earth in 24 hours carrying the inner spheres with it. [med.L, = first moving thing]

Primus /prīməss/ *n. propr.* a brand of portable stove burning vaporized oil for cooking etc. [L (as PRIMUS)]

primus /prīməss/ *n.* the presiding bishop of the Scottish Episcopal Church. [L, = first]

primus inter pares /preéməss íntər paáreez/ *n.* a first among equals; the senior or representative member of a group. [L]

prince /prinss/ *n.* (as a title usu. **Prince**) **1** a male member of a royal family other than a reigning king. **2** (in full **prince of the blood**) a son or grandson of a British monarch. **3** a ruler of a small State, actually or nominally subject to a king or emperor. **4** (as an English rendering of foreign titles) a noble usu. ranking next below a duke. **5** (as a courtesy title in some connections) a duke, marquess, earl. **6** (often foll. by *of*) the chief or greatest (*the prince of novelists*). ▫ **Prince Charming** an idealized young hero or lover. **prince consort 1** the husband of a reigning female sovereign who is himself a prince. **2** the title conferred on him. **Prince of Darkness** Satan. **Prince of Peace** Christ. **Prince of Wales** the heir apparent to the British throne, as a title conferred by the monarch. **Prince Regent** a prince who acts as regent, esp. George (afterwards IV) as regent 1811–20. **prince royal** the eldest son of the reigning monarch. **prince's feather** a tall plant, *Amaranthus hypochondriacus*, with feathery spikes of small red flowers. **prince's metal** a brasslike alloy of copper and zinc. ▫▫ **princedom** *n.* **princelet** *n.* **princelike** *adj.* **princeship** *n.* [ME f. OF f. L *princeps principis* first, chief, sovereign f. *primus* first + *capere* take]

▪ ▫ **Prince of Darkness** see DEVIL *n.* 1, 2. **Prince of Peace** see SAVIOUR 2. ▫▫ **princelike** see PRINCELY 1a.

princeling /prínsling/ *n.* a young or petty prince.

princely /prínsli/ *adj.* (**princelier, princeliest**) **1 a** of or worthy of a prince. **b** held by a prince. **2 a** sumptuous, generous, splendid. **b** (of a sum of money) substantial. ▫▫ **princeliness** *n.*

▪ **1 a** royal, noble, regal, sovereign, majestic, imperial. **2** lavish, bountiful, generous, liberal, ample; magnificent, splendid, luxurious, majestic, sumptuous, swanky, plush, *colloq.* ritzy, plushy, *esp. US colloq.* swank; substantial, considerable, huge, enormous, large.

princess /prinséss/ *n.* (as a title usu. **Princess** /prínsess/) **1** the wife of a prince. **2** a female member of a royal family other than a reigning queen. **3** (in full **princess of the blood**) a daughter or granddaughter of a British monarch. **4** a pre-eminent woman or thing personified as a woman. ▫ **Princess Regent 1** a princess who acts as regent. **2** the wife of a Prince Regent. **Princess Royal** a monarch's eldest daughter, as a title conferred by the monarch. [ME f. OF *princesse* (as PRINCE)]

principal /prínsip'l/ *adj.* & *n.* ● *adj.* **1** (usu. *attrib.*) first in rank or importance; chief (*the principal town of the district*). **2** main, leading (*a principal cause of my success*). **3** (of money) constituting the original sum invested or lent. ● *n.* **1** a head, ruler, or superior. **2** the head of some schools, colleges, and universities. **3** the leading performer in a concert, play, etc. **4** a capital sum as distinguished from interest or income. **5** a person for whom another acts as agent etc. **6** (in the UK) a civil servant of the grade below Secretary. **7** the person actually responsible for a crime. **8** a person for whom another is surety. **9** each of the combatants in a duel. **10 a** a main rafter supporting purlins. **b** a main girder. **11** an organ stop sounding an octave above the diapason. **12** *Mus.* the leading player in each section of an orchestra. □ **principal boy** (or **girl**) an actress who takes the leading male (or female) part in a pantomime. **principal clause** *Gram.* a clause to which another clause is subordinate. **principal in the first degree** a person directly responsible for a crime as its actual perpetrator. **principal in the second degree** a person directly responsible for a crime as aiding in its perpetration. **principal parts** *Gram.* the parts of a verb from which all other parts can be deduced. □□ **principalship** *n.* [ME f. OF f. L *principalis* first, original (as PRINCE)]

■ *adj.* **1, 2** chief, primary, prime, paramount, main, first, foremost, prominent, leading, key, pre-eminent, predominant, dominant, prevailing; leading, starring, important. **3** capital, original, basic, initial. ● *n.* **1** director, head, president, chief, employer, chief executive, ruler, superior, manager, manageress, superintendent, overseer, supervisor, *colloq.* boss. **2** dean, director, headmaster, headmistress, master, mistress, provost, rector, chancellor, vice-chancellor, *US* president, *US sl.* prex(y). **3** star, lead, leading lady *or* man, leading role, main part. **4** capital, capital funds, resources, investment, reserves, assets.

principality /prínsipálliti/ *n.* (*pl.* **-ies**) **1** a State ruled by a prince. **2** the government of a prince. **3** (in *pl.*) the fifth order of the ninefold celestial hierarchy. **4** (**the Principality**) *Brit.* Wales. [ME f. OF *principalité* f. LL *principalitas -tatis* (as PRINCIPAL)]

principally /prínsipəli/ *adv.* for the most part; chiefly.

■ chiefly, mainly, first (and foremost), primarily, above all, in the main, mostly, for the most part, largely, predominantly, on the whole, at bottom, in essence, essentially, basically, fundamentally; especially, particularly.

principate /prínsipət/ *n.* **1** a State ruled by a prince. **2** *Rom.Hist.* the rule of the early emperors during which some republican forms were retained. [ME f. OF *principat* or L *principatus* first place]

principle /prínsip'l/ *n.* **1** a fundamental truth or law as the basis of reasoning or action (*arguing from first principles; moral principles*). **2 a** a personal code of conduct (*a person of high principle*). **b** (in *pl.*) such rules of conduct (*has no principles*). **3** a general law in physics etc. (*the uncertainty principle*). **4** a law of nature forming the basis for the construction or working of a machine etc. **5** a fundamental source; a primary element (*held water to be the first principle of all things*). **6** *Chem.* a constituent of a substance, esp. one giving rise to some quality, etc. □ **in principle** as regards fundamentals but not necessarily in detail. **on principle** on the basis of a moral attitude (*I refuse on principle*). [ME f. OF *principe* f. L *principium* source, (in pl.) foundations (as PRINCE)]

■ **1** truth, given, precept, tenet, fundamental, law, rule, dictum, canon, doctrine, teaching, dogma, proposition, (basic) assumption, postulate, axiom, maxim, standard, criterion, model. **2** honour, uprightness, honesty, morality, morals, probity, integrity, conscience; (*principles*) philosophy, attitude, (point of) view, viewpoint, sentiment, belief, credo, creed, notion, ethics; sense of right and wrong. **5** see ORIGIN 1. □ **in principle** in theory, theoretically, ideally; fundamentally, at bottom, in essence, essentially.

principled /prínsip'ld/ *adj.* based on or having (esp. praiseworthy) principles of behaviour.

■ moral, righteous, right-minded, virtuous, noble, high-minded, ethical, honourable, proper, correct, right, just, upright, honest, scrupulous.

prink /pringk/ *v.* **1** *tr.* (usu. *refl.*) **a** make (oneself etc.) smart. **b** (foll. by *up*) smarten (oneself) up. **c** (of a bird) preen. **2** *intr.* dress oneself up. [16th c.: prob. f. *prank* dress, adorn, rel. to MLG *prank* pomp, Du. *pronk* finery]

■ **1a, b, 2** see PREEN 2. **1 c** see PREEN 1.

print /print/ *n.* & *v.* ● *n.* **1** an indentation or mark on a surface left by the pressure of a thing in contact with it (*fingerprint; footprint*). **2 a** printed lettering or writing (*large print*). **b** words in printed form. **c** a printed publication, esp. a newspaper. **d** the quantity of a book etc. printed at one time. **e** the state of being printed. **3** a picture or design printed from a block or plate. **4** *Photog.* a picture produced on paper from a negative. **5** a printed cotton fabric. ● *v.tr.* **1 a** produce or reproduce (a book, picture, etc.) by applying inked types, blocks, or plates, to paper, vellum, etc. **b** (of an author, publisher, or editor) cause (a book or manuscript etc.) to be produced or reproduced in this way. **2** express or publish in print. **3 a** (often foll. by *on, in*) impress or stamp (a mark or figure on a surface). **b** (often foll. by *with*) impress or stamp (a soft surface, e.g. of butter or wax, with a seal, die, etc.). **4** (often *absol.*) write (words or letters) without joining, in imitation of typography. **5** (often foll. by *off, out*) *Photog.* produce (a picture) by the transmission of light through a negative. **6** (usu. foll. by *out*) (of a computer etc.) produce output in printed form. **7** mark (a textile fabric) with a decorative design in colours. **8** (foll. by *on*) impress (an idea, scene, etc. on the mind or memory). **9** transfer (a coloured or plain design) from paper etc. to the unglazed or glazed surface of ceramic ware. □ **appear in print** have one's work published. **in print 1** (of a book etc.) available from the publisher. **2** in printed form. **out of print** no longer available from the publisher. **printed circuit** an electric circuit with thin strips of conductor on a flat insulating sheet, usu. made by a process like printing. □□ **printable** *adj.* **printability** /printəbílliti/ *n.* **printless** *adj.* (in sense 1 of *n.*). [ME f. OF *priente, preinte*, fem. past part. of *preindre* press f. L *premere*]

■ *n.* **1** indentation, impression; see also MARK[1] *n.* 1. **2 a, b** text, printed matter; see also TYPE *n.* 6. **3** reproduction, copy, replica, facsimile; picture, illustration; design, pattern, motif. **4** see PHOTOGRAPH *n.* ● *v.* **1, 2** publish, issue, run off, put out. **3** see STAMP *v.* 2.

printer /príntər/ *n.* **1** a person who prints books, magazines, advertising matter, etc. **2** the owner of a printing business. **3** a device that prints, esp. as part of a computer system. □ **printer's devil** an errand-boy in a printer's office. **printer's mark** a device used as a printer's trade mark. **printer's pie** = PIE[3] *n.*

printery /príntəri/ *n.* (*pl.* **-ies**) *US* a printer's office or works.

printhead /print-hed/ *n.* the component in a printer (see PRINTER 3) that assembles and prints the characters on the paper.

printing /prínting/ *n.* **1** the production of printed books etc. **2** a single impression of a book. **3** printed letters or writing imitating them. □ **printing-press** a machine for printing from types or plates etc.

■ **2** see IMPRESSION 5.

printmaker /príntmaykər/ *n.* a person who makes a print. □□ **printmaking** *n.*

printout /príntowt/ *n.* computer output in printed form.

printworks /príntwurks/ *n.* a factory where fabrics are printed.

prior /prī́ər/ *adj., adv.,* & *n.* ● *adj.* **1** earlier. **2** (often foll. by *to*) coming before in time, order, or importance. ● *adv.* (foll. by *to*) before (*decided prior to their arrival*). ● *n.* **1** the superior officer of a religious house or order. **2** (in an abbey) the officer next under the abbot. □□ **priorate** /-rət/ *n.* **prioress** *n.* **priorship** *n.* [L, = former, elder, compar. of OL *pri* = L *prae* before]

■ *adj.* **1** former, previous, earlier; see also FOREGOING. ● *adv.* (*prior to*) previous to, previously to; see also BEFORE *prep.* 2.

priority /prīórriti/ *n.* (*pl.* **-ies**) **1** the fact or condition of being earlier or antecedent. **2** precedence in rank etc. **3** an interest having prior claim to consideration. □□ **prioritize**

v.tr. (also **-ise**). **prioritization** /-tīzáysh'n/ *n.* [ME f. OF *priorité* f. med.L *prioritas -tatis* f. L *prior* (as PRIOR)]
■ **2** precedence, precedency, preference; primacy, urgency, predominance, pre-eminence, rank, superiority, prerogative, right, seniority, importance, weight.

priory /prīəri/ *n.* (*pl.* **-ies**) a monastery governed by a prior or a nunnery governed by a prioress. [ME f. AF *priorie*, med.L *prioria* (as PRIOR)]

prise /prīz/ *v.* & *n.* (also **prize**) ● *v.tr.* force open or out by leverage (*prised up the lid; prised the box open*). ● *n.* leverage, purchase. [ME & OF *prise* levering instrument (as PRIZE[1])]
■ *v.* see FORCE[1] *v.* 2.

prism /prízz'm/ *n.* **1** a solid geometric figure whose two ends are similar, equal, and parallel rectilinear figures, and whose sides are parallelograms. **2** a transparent body in this form, usu. triangular with refracting surfaces at an acute angle with each other, which separates white light into a spectrum of colours. □□ **prismal** /prízm'l/ *adj.* [LL *prisma* f. Gk *prisma prismatos* thing sawn f. *prizō* to saw]

prismatic /prizmáttik/ *adj.* **1** of, like, or using a prism. **2 a** (of colours) distributed by or as if by a transparent prism. **b** (of light) displayed in the form of a spectrum. □□ **prismatically** *adv.* [F *prismatique* f. Gk *prisma* (as PRISM)]

prismoid /prízmoyd/ *n.* a body like a prism, with similar but unequal parallel polygonal ends. □□ **prismoidal** /-móyd'l/ *adj.*

prison /prízz'n/ *n.* & *v.* ● *n.* **1** a place in which a person is kept in captivity, esp. a building to which persons are legally committed while awaiting trial or for punishment; a jail. **2** custody, confinement (*in prison*). ● *v.tr. poet.* (**prisoned, prisoning**) put in prison. □ **prison-breaking** escape from prison. **prison camp** a camp for prisoners of war or of State. [ME f. OF *prisun, -on* f. L *prensio -onis* f. *prehensio* f. *prehendere prehens-* lay hold of]
■ *n.* **1** jail, lock-up, penal institution, guardhouse, bagnio, *US* penitentiary, brig, calaboose, correctional facility, *archaic* bridewell, house of correction, *hist.* bastille, roundhouse, *sl.* clink, can, cooler, jug, stir, slammer, big house, *Brit. sl.* glasshouse, nick, quod, choky, *US sl.* pokey, pen, hoosegow, slam. **2** confinement, detention, custody; (*in prison*) see *behind bars* (BAR[1]). ● *v.* see IMPRISON 1.

prisoner /príznər/ *n.* **1** a person kept in prison. **2** (in full **prisoner at the bar**) a person in custody on a criminal charge and on trial. **3** a person or thing confined by illness, another's grasp, etc. **4** (in full **prisoner of war**) a person who has been captured in war. □ **prisoner of conscience** see CONSCIENCE. **prisoner of State** (or **State prisoner**) a person confined for political reasons. **prisoner's base** a game played by two parties of boys etc., each occupying a distinct base or home. **take prisoner** seize and hold as a prisoner. [ME f. AF *prisoner*, OF *prisonier* (as PRISON)]
■ **1** convict, inmate, internee, detainee, jailbird, *sl.* con, (old) lag, *US sl.* yardbird.

prissy /príssi/ *adj.* (**prissier, prissiest**) prim, prudish. □□ **prissily** *adv.* **prissiness** *n.* [perh. f. PRIM + SISSY]
■ precious, over-nice, strait-laced, old-maidish, prim (and proper), prudish, *colloq.* school-marmish.

pristine /prísteen, prístīn/ *adj.* **1** in its original condition; unspoilt. **2** *disp.* spotless; fresh as if new. **3** ancient, primitive. [L *pristinus* former]
■ **1** uncorrupted, pure, unsullied, undefiled, virginal, virgin, chaste, untouched, unspoiled, unpolluted, untarnished, immaculate, natural. **2** spotless, clean, gleaming, shiny, polished, unspotted, spick and span; immaculate, fresh, as new; mint. **3** ancient, original, primal, basic, primeval, primitive, primordial, earliest, first, initial.

prithee /príthee/ *int. archaic* pray, please. [= *I pray thee*]

privacy /prívvəsi, prī-/ *n.* **1 a** the state of being private and undisturbed. **b** a person's right to this. **2** freedom from intrusion or public attention. **3** avoidance of publicity.
■ **1** seclusion, retirement, solitude, isolation, reclusion, solitariness, reclusiveness, separation; monasticism. **3** secretiveness, confidentiality; see also SECRECY.

private /prīvət/ *adj.* & *n.* ● *adj.* **1** belonging to an individual; one's own; personal (*private property*). **2** confidential; not to be disclosed to others (*private talks*). **3** kept or removed from public knowledge or observation. **4 a** not open to the public. **b** for an individual's exclusive use (*private room*). **5** (of a place) secluded; affording privacy. **6** (of a person) not holding public office or an official position. **7** (of education or medical treatment) conducted outside the State system, at the individual's expense. **8** (of a person) retiring; reserved; unsociable. ● *n.* **1** a private soldier. **2** (in *pl.*) *colloq.* the genitals. □ **in private** privately; in private company or life. **private bill** a parliamentary bill affecting an individual or corporation only. **private company** *Brit.* a company with restricted membership and no issue of shares. **private detective** a detective engaged privately, outside an official police force. **private enterprise 1** a business or businesses not under State control. **2** individual initiative. **private eye** *colloq.* a private detective. **private first class** *US* a soldier ranking above an ordinary private but below officers. **private hotel** a hotel not obliged to take all comers. **private house** the dwelling-house of a private person, as distinct from a shop, office, or public building. **private law** a law relating to individual persons and private property. **private life** life as a private person, not as an official, public performer, etc. **private means** income from investments etc., apart from earned income. **private member** a member of a legislative body not holding a government office. **private member's bill** a bill introduced by a private member, not part of government legislation. **private parts** the genitals. **private patient** *Brit.* a patient treated by a doctor other than under the National Health Service. **private practice** *Brit.* medical practice that is not part of the National Health Service. **private press** a printing establishment operated by a private person or group not primarily for profit and usu. on a small scale. **private school 1** *Brit.* a school supported wholly by the payment of fees. **2** *US* a school not supported mainly by the State. **private secretary** a secretary dealing with the personal and confidential concerns of a businessman or businesswoman. **private sector** the part of the economy free of direct State control. **private soldier** an ordinary soldier other than the officers (and *US* other than recruits). **private view** the viewing of an exhibition (esp. of paintings) before it is open to the public. **private war 1** a feud between persons or families disregarding the law of murder etc. **2** hostilities against members of another State without the sanction of one's own government. **private wrong** an offence against an individual but not against society as a whole. □□ **privately** *adv.* [ME f. L *privatus*, orig. past part. of *privare* deprive]
■ *adj.* **1** personal, individual, one's own, *archaic* proper. **2** (top) secret, confidential, clandestine, hidden, concealed, covert, surreptitious, *colloq.* hush-hush; unofficial. **3, 5** hidden, secluded, concealed, secret; undisclosed, sneaking, undeclared, unspoken. **4** restrictive, restricted, exclusive, special, reserved. **8** solitary, seclusive, reclusive, withdrawn, retiring, reticent, ungregarious, non-gregarious, unsocial, unsociable, antisocial, reserved, uncommunicative, hermitic(al), hermit-like, eremitic(al); sequestered, secluded, retired. ● *n.* **1** private soldier, infantryman, foot-soldier, *poilu*, *US* enlisted man, *Brit. colloq.* Tommy, *Brit. Mil. sl.* squaddie, *US* GI. **2** (*privates*) genitals, private parts, sexual *or* sex organs, genitalia, pudenda, *euphem.* one's person. □ **in private** in secret, secretly, privately, *sub rosa*, personally, in confidence, confidentially, behind closed doors, in camera, off the record; clandestinely, secretively, sneakily, sneakingly, surreptitiously, furtively, covertly, on the sly, on the quiet, *colloq.* on the q.t. **private detective** see DETECTIVE *n.* **private eye** see DETECTIVE *n.* **private parts** see

PRIVATE *n.* 2 above. **private soldier** see PRIVATE *n.* 1 above.

privateer /prīvəteér/ *n.* **1** an armed vessel owned and officered by private individuals holding a government commission and authorized for war service. **2 a** a commander of such a vessel. **b** (in *pl.*) its crew. □□ **privateering** *n.* [PRIVATE, after *volunteer*]

privateersman /prīvəteérzmən/ *n.* (*pl.* **-men**) = PRIVATEER 2.

privation /prīváysh'n/ *n.* **1** lack of the comforts or necessities of life (*suffered many privations*). **2** (often foll. by *of*) loss or absence (of a quality). [ME f. L *privatio* (as PRIVATE)]

■ **1** deprivation, hardship, indigence, poverty, penury, destitution, pauperism, beggary, neediness, necessity, need, want; distress, misery. **2** see LACK *n.*, LOSS 1.

privative /prívvətiv/ *adj.* **1** consisting in or marked by the loss or removal or absence of some quality or attribute. **2** (of a term) denoting the privation or absence of a quality etc. **3** *Gram.* (of a particle etc.) expressing privation, as Gk *a-* = 'not'. □□ **privatively** *adv.* [F *privatif -ive* or L *privativus* (as PRIVATION)]

privatize /prīvətīz/ *v.tr.* (also **-ise**) make private, esp. assign (a business etc.) to private as distinct from State control or ownership; denationalize. □□ **privatization** /-záysh'n/ *n.*

privet /prívvit/ *n.* any evergreen shrub of the genus *Ligustrum*, esp. *L. vulgare* bearing small white flowers and black berries, and much used for hedges. [16th c.: orig. unkn.]

privilege /prívvilij/ *n.* & *v.* ● *n.* **1 a** a right, advantage, or immunity, belonging to a person, class, or office. **b** the freedom of members of a legislative assembly when speaking at its meetings. **2** a special benefit or honour (*it is a privilege to meet you*). **3** a monopoly or patent granted to an individual, corporation, etc. **4** *US Stock Exch.* an option. ● *v.tr.* **1** invest with a privilege. **2** (foll. by *to* + infin.) allow (a person) as a privilege (to do something). **3** (often foll. by *from*) exempt (a person from a liability etc.). [ME f. OF *privilege* f. L *privilegium* bill or law affecting an individual, f. *privus* private + *lex legis* law]

■ *n.* **1 a** benefit, advantage, right, prerogative, concession, freedom, liberty, franchise; permission, consent, leave, authorization, sanction, authority, licence, allowance, indulgence; immunity, exemption, dispensation. **2** honour, pleasure; see also HONOUR *n.* 5. ● *v.* **3** see EXEMPT *v.*

privileged /prívvilijd/ *adj.* **1 a** invested with or enjoying a certain privilege or privileges; honoured, favoured. **b** exempt from standard regulations or procedures. **c** powerful, affluent. **2** (of information, etc.) confidential, restricted.

■ **1 a** favoured, élite, special, honoured, advantaged. **b** protected, immune; licensed, authorized, chartered. **c** wealthy, rich, affluent, advantaged, well off, *colloq.* comfortable, well-heeled; powerful, empowered, well-connected. **2** confidential, secret, private, restricted, off the record, *archaic* privy, *colloq.* hush-hush.

privity /prívviti/ *n.* (*pl.* **-ies**) **1** *Law* a relation between two parties that is recognized by law, e.g. that of blood, lease, or service. **2** (often foll. by *to*) the state of being privy (to plans etc.). [ME f. OF *priveté* f. med.L *privitas -tatis* f. L *privus* private]

privy /prívvi/ *adj.* & *n.* ● *adj.* **1** (foll. by *to*) sharing in the secret of (a person's plans etc.). **2** *archaic* hidden, secret. ● *n.* (*pl.* **-ies**) **1** *US* or *archaic* a lavatory. **2** *Law* a person having a part or interest in any action, matter, or thing. □ **Privy Council 1** (in the UK) a body of advisers appointed by the sovereign (now chiefly on an honorary basis and including present and former government ministers etc.). **2** usu. *hist.* a sovereign's or governor-general's private counsellors. **privy counsellor** (or **councillor**) a private adviser, esp. a member of a Privy Council. **privy purse** *Brit.* **1** an allowance from the public revenue for the monarch's private expenses. **2** the keeper of this. **privy seal** (in the UK) a seal formerly affixed to documents that are afterwards to pass the Great Seal or that do not require it. □□ **privily** *adv.* [ME f. OF *privé* f. L *privatus* PRIVATE]

■ *adj.* **1** (*privy to*) aware of, in on, sharing (in), cognizant of, apprised of, informed *or* advised about *or* of, *colloq.* wise to, *sl.* hip to. **2** see SECRET *adj.* 1. ● *n.* **1** lavatory, toilet, latrine, water-closet, WC, *Brit.* convenience, *esp. US* bathroom, *US* outhouse, can, *Brit. colloq.* loo, lav, *Brit. euphem.* cloakroom, *US euphem.* comfort station, *Brit. sl.* bog, *US sl.* john, *esp. Austral. sl.* dyke, *Austral. & NZ sl.* dunny.

prize[1] /prīz/ *n.* & *v.* ● *n.* **1** something that can be won in a competition or lottery etc. **2** a reward given as a symbol of victory or superiority. **3** something striven for or worth striving for (*missed all the great prizes of life*). **4** (*attrib.*) **a** to which a prize is awarded (*a prize bull; a prize poem*). **b** supremely excellent or outstanding of its kind. ● *v.tr.* value highly (*a much prized possession*). □ **prize-giving** an award of prizes, esp. formally at a school etc. **prize-money** money offered as a prize. **prize-ring 1** an enclosed area (now usu. a square) for prizefighting. **2** the practice of prizefighting. [(n.) ME, var. of PRICE: (v.) ME f. OF *pris-* stem of *preisier* PRAISE]

■ *n.* **2** reward, award, trophy, premium; honour, accolade, *poet.* guerdon; winnings, jackpot. **4 b** (*attrib.*) choice, excellent, winning, champion, outstanding, select, superior, superlative, first-rate, first-class. ● *v.* value, treasure, esteem, cherish, appreciate, rate highly, hold dear.

prize[2] /prīz/ *n.* & *v.* ● *n.* **1** a ship or property captured in naval warfare. **2** a find or windfall. ● *v.tr.* make a prize of. □ **prize-court** a department of an admiralty court concerned with prizes. [ME f. OF *prise* taking, booty, fem. past part. of *prendre* f. L *prehendere prehens-* seize: later identified with PRIZE[1]]

■ *n.* **1** loot, booty, spoil(s), trophy, plunder, pickings. **2** find, gain, haul, *esp. US* take; see also WINDFALL.

prize[3] var. of PRISE.

prizefight /prīzfīt/ *n.* a boxing-match fought for prize-money. □□ **prizefighter** *n.*

■ see BOUT 2a. □□ **prizefighter** see PUGILIST.

prizeman /prīzmən/ *n.* (*pl.* **-men**) a winner of a prize, esp. a specified academic one.

prizewinner /prīzwinnər/ *n.* a winner of a prize. □□ **prizewinning** *adj.*

■ see WINNER 1.

PRO *abbr.* **1** Public Record Office. **2** public relations officer.

pro[1] /prō/ *n.* & *adj. colloq.* ● *n.* (*pl.* **-os**) a professional. ● *adj.* professional. □ **pro-am** involving professionals and amateurs. [abbr.]

■ *n.* see PROFESSIONAL *n.* ● *adj.* see PROFESSIONAL *adj.*

pro[2] /prō/ *adj.*, *n.*, & *prep.* ● *adj.* (of an argument or reason) for; in favour. ● *n.* (*pl.* **-os**) a reason or argument for or in favour. ● *prep.* in favour of. □ **pros and cons** reasons or considerations for and against a proposition etc. [L, = for, on behalf of]

■ *adj.* & *prep.* see *in favour* (FAVOUR), FOR *prep.* 2. ● *n.* see ADVANTAGE *n.* 1, 3.

pro-[1] /prō/ *prefix* **1** favouring or supporting (*pro-government*). **2** acting as a substitute or deputy for (*proconsul*). **3** forwards (*produce*). **4** forwards and downwards (*prostrate*). **5** onwards (*proceed; progress*). **6** in front of (*protect*). [L *pro* in front (of), for, on behalf of, instead of, on account of]

pro-[2] /prō/ *prefix* before in time, place, order, etc. (*problem; proboscis; prophet*). [Gk *pro* before]

proa /prṓə/ *n.* (also **prau**, **prahu** /praá-ōō/) a Malay boat, esp. with a large triangular sail and a canoe-like outrigger. [Malay *prāū, prāhū*]

proactive /prō-áktiv/ *adj.* **1** (of a person, policy, etc.) creating or controlling a situation by taking the initiative. **2** of or relating to mental conditioning or a habit etc. which has been learned. □□ **proaction** /-áksh'n/ *n.* **proactively** *adv.* **proactivity** /-tívviti/ *n.* [PRO-[2], after REACTIVE]

probability /próbbəbílliti/ *n.* (*pl.* **-ies**) **1** the state or condition of being probable. **2** the likelihood of something happening. **3** a probable or most probable event (*the*

probability is that they will come). **4** *Math.* the extent to which an event is likely to occur, measured by the ratio of the favourable cases to the whole number of cases possible. □ **in all probability** most probably. [F *probabilité* or L *probabilitas* (as PROBABLE)]
■ **2, 3** likelihood, likeliness, odds, (good) chance, (strong *or* distinct) possibility, good prospect. □ **in all probability** (most *or* very) probably, almost certainly, (most *or* very) likely, in all likelihood, as likely as not, presumably.

probable /próbbəb'l/ *adj.* & *n.* ● *adj.* (often foll. by *that* + clause) that may be expected to happen or prove true; likely (*the probable explanation*; *it is probable that they forgot*). ● *n.* a probable candidate, member of a team, etc. □□ **probably** *adv.* [ME f. OF f. L *probabilis* f. *probare* prove]
■ *adj.* (most) likely, possible, plausible, feasible, believable, credible, conceivable, tenable, expected, *disp.* anticipated. □□ **probably** (very) likely, in all likelihood, in all probability; presumably, as likely as not.

proband /prṓband/ *n.* a person forming the starting-point for the genetic study of a family etc. [L *probandus*, gerundive of *probare* test]

probang /prṓbang/ *n. Surgery* a strip of flexible material with a sponge or button etc. at the end for introducing into the throat. [17th c. (named *provang* by its inventor): orig. unkn., perh. alt. after *probe*]

probate /prṓbayt, -bət/ *n.* & *v.* ● *n.* **1** the official proving of a will. **2** a verified copy of a will with a certificate as handed to the executors. ● *v.tr. US* establish the validity of (a will). [ME f. L *probatum* neut. past part. of *probare* PROVE]

probation /prəbáysh'n/ *n.* **1** *Law* a system of suspending the sentence on an offender subject to a period of good behaviour under supervision. **2** a process or period of testing the character or abilities of a person in a certain role, esp. of a new employee. **3** a moral trial or discipline. □ **on probation** undergoing probation, esp. legal supervision. **probation officer** an official supervising offenders on probation. □□ **probational** *adj.* **probationary** *adj.* [ME f. OF *probation* or L *probatio* (as PROVE)]

probationer /prəbáyshənər/ *n.* **1** a person on probation, e.g. a newly appointed nurse, teacher, etc. **2** an offender on probation. □□ **probationership** *n.*

probative /prṓbətiv/ *adj.* affording proof; evidential. [L *probativus* (as PROVE)]
■ see DEMONSTRATIVE *adj.* 2.

probe /prōb/ *n.* & *v.* ● *n.* **1** a penetrating investigation. **2** any small device, esp. an electrode, for measuring, testing, etc. **3** a blunt-ended surgical instrument usu. of metal for exploring a wound etc. **4** (in full **space probe**) an unmanned exploratory spacecraft transmitting information about its environment. ● *v.* **1** *tr.* examine or enquire into closely. **2** *tr.* explore (a wound or part of the body) with a probe. **3** *tr.* penetrate with or as with a sharp instrument, esp. in order to explore. **4** *intr.* make an investigation with or as with a probe (*the detective probed into her past life*). □□ **probeable** *adj.* **prober** *n.* **probingly** *adv.* [LL *proba* proof, in med.L = examination, f. L *probare* test]
■ *n.* **1** investigation, examination, exploration, scrutiny, search, study, inquiry, enquiry. ● *v.* **1** explore, examine, scrutinize, investigate, search (into), look into, go into, study; dig into, delve into, poke into. **3** explore, examine; plumb, poke, prod, dig.

probit /próbbit/ *n. Statistics* a unit of probability based on deviation from the mean of a standard distribution. [*probability unit*]

probity /prṓbiti, prób-/ *n.* uprightness, honesty. [F *probité* or L *probitas* f. *probus* good]
■ integrity, uprightness, honesty, morality, rectitude, virtue, goodness, decency, righteousness, right-mindedness, sincerity, trustworthiness, honour, equity, justness, justice, fairness.

problem /próbləm/ *n.* **1** a doubtful or difficult matter requiring a solution (*how to prevent it is a problem*; *the problem of ventilation*). **2** something hard to understand or accomplish or deal with. **3** (*attrib.*) **a** causing problems; difficult to deal with (*problem child*). **b** (of a play, novel, etc.) in which a social or other problem is treated. **4 a** *Physics* & *Math.* an inquiry starting from given conditions to investigate or demonstrate a fact, result, or law. **b** *Geom.* a proposition in which something has to be constructed (cf. THEOREM). **5 a** (in various games, esp. chess) an arrangement of men, cards, etc., in which the solver has to achieve a specified result. **b** a puzzle or question for solution. [ME f. OF *probleme* or L *problema* f. Gk *problēma -matos* f. *proballō* (as PRO-[2], *ballō* throw)]
■ **1, 2** difficulty, trouble, complication, knot, question, Gordian knot, hornet's nest, *colloq.* can of worms, facer, proposition, hard *or* tough nut to crack, *disp.* dilemma. **3 a** (*attrib.*) unruly, unmanageable, intractable, uncontrollable, difficult, ungovernable, refractory, incorrigible, obstreperous, delinquent, maladjusted, disturbed. **5 b** puzzle, conundrum, poser, riddle, question, enigma, puzzler.

problematic /próbləmáttik/ *adj.* (also **problematical**) **1** attended by difficulty. **2** doubtful or questionable. **3** *Logic* enunciating or supporting what is possible but not necessarily true. □□ **problematically** *adv.* [F *problématique* or LL *problematicus* f. Gk *problēmatikos* (as PROBLEM)]
■ **1** see DIFFICULT 1. **2** uncertain, questionable, doubtful, debatable, disputable, moot, controversial, tricky, touchy, sensitive, delicate.

proboscidean /próbbəsíddiən/ *adj.* & *n.* (also **proboscidian**) ● *adj.* **1** having a proboscis. **2** of or like a proboscis. **3** of the mammalian order Proboscidea, including elephants and their extinct allies. ● *n.* a mammal of this order. [mod.L *Proboscidea* (as PROBOSCIS)]

proboscis /prōbóssiss/ *n.* **1** the long flexible trunk or snout of some mammals, e.g. an elephant or tapir. **2** the elongated mouth parts of some insects. **3** the sucking organ in some worms. **4** *joc.* the human nose. □ **proboscis monkey** a monkey, *Nasalis larvatus*, native to Borneo, the male of which has a large pendulous nose. □□ **proboscidiferous** /-sidíffərəss/ *adj.* **proboscidiform** /-síddiform/ *adj.* [L *proboscis -cidis* f. Gk *proboskis* f. *proboskō* (as PRO-[2], *boskō* feed)]

procaine /prṓkayn/ *n.* (also **procain**) a synthetic compound used as a local anaesthetic. [PRO-[1] + COCAINE]

procaryote var. of PROKARYOTE.

procedure /prəséedyər, -séejər/ *n.* **1** a way of proceeding, esp. a mode of conducting business or a legal action. **2** a mode of performing a task. **3** a series of actions conducted in a certain order or manner. **4** a proceeding. **5** *Computing* = SUBROUTINE. □□ **procedural** *adj.* **procedurally** *adv.* [F *procédure* (as PROCEED)]
■ **1–3** conduct, course, action, course of action, process, methodology, form, system, approach, strategy, plan (of action), scheme, *modus operandi*; routine, drill, practice, method, *colloq.* MO (= 'modus operandi'), SOP (= 'standard operating procedure'). **4** see PROCEEDING 1.

proceed /prəséed/ *v.intr.* **1** (often foll. by *to*) go forward or on further; make one's way. **2** (often foll. by *with*, or *to* + infin.) continue; go on with an activity (*proceeded with their work*; *proceeded to tell the whole story*). **3** (of an action) be carried on or continued (*the case will now proceed*). **4** adopt a course of action (*how shall we proceed?*). **5** go on to say. **6** (foll. by *against*) start a lawsuit (against a person). **7** (often foll. by *from*) come forth or originate (*shouts proceeded from the bedroom*). **8** (foll. by *to*) *Brit.* take the degree of (MA etc.). [ME f. OF *proceder* f. L *procedere process-* (as PRO-[1], *cedere* go)]
■ **1** go *or* move on *or* ahead *or* forward, advance, progress, move along, push *or* press on *or* onward(s), forge ahead, make one's way. **2** continue; pass on, go on; see also *carry on* 1. **4** go on, continue; see also START *v.* 1, 2. **7** result, arise, come (forth), stem, spring, develop, issue, derive, descend, emerge, grow, originate, begin, start.

proceeding /prəséeding/ *n.* **1** an action or piece of conduct (*a high-handed proceeding*). **2** (in *pl.*) (in full **legal proceedings**) an action at law; a lawsuit. **3** (in *pl.*) a published

report of discussions or a conference. **4** (in *pl.*) business, actions, or events in progress (*the proceedings were enlivened by a dog running on to the pitch*).
■ **1** measure, act, (course of) action, move, step, undertaking, deed, procedure, process, operation, transaction, manoeuvre, feat, accomplishment. **2 legal proceedings** suit, lawsuit, action, case, process, cause, trial; litigation. **3** (*proceedings*) transactions, procès-verbal, report(s), minutes, record(s), annals, account(s), archives. **4** (*proceedings*) affairs, dealings, business; events, goings-on, doings; celebration(s); performance(s).

proceeds /prṓseedz/ *n.pl.* money produced by a transaction or other undertaking. [pl. of obs. *proceed* (n.) f. PROCEED]
■ profit(s), gain, yield; income, takings, receipts, return(s), gate, gate-money, *esp. US* take.

process[1] /prṓsess/ *n.* & *v.* ● *n.* **1** a course of action or proceeding, esp. a series of stages in manufacture or some other operation. **2** the progress or course of something (*in process of construction*). **3** a natural or involuntary operation or series of changes (*the process of growing old*). **4** an action at law; a summons or writ. **5** *Anat.*, *Zool.*, & *Bot.* a natural appendage or outgrowth on an organism. ● *v.tr.* **1** handle or deal with by a particular process. **2** treat (food, esp. to prevent decay) (*processed cheese*). **3** *Computing* operate on (data) by means of a program. □ **in process of time** as time goes on. **process server** a sheriff's officer who serves writs. □□ **processable** *adj.* [ME f. OF *proces* f. L *processus* (as PROCEED)]
■ *n.* **1** proceeding, operation, system, method, approach, technique; course of action; see also PROCEDURE 1–3. **2** course, progress; midst, middle. **3** see OPERATION 1, 2. **4** see ACTION *n.* 8, WARRANT *n.* 2. ● *v.* **1** handle, take care of, deal with, manage, look after; prepare, make or get ready; answer. **2** treat, prepare.

process[2] /prōséss/ *v.intr.* walk in procession. [back-form. f. PROCESSION]

procession /prəsésh'n/ *n.* **1** a number of people or vehicles etc. moving forward in orderly succession, esp. at a ceremony, demonstration, or festivity. **2** the movement of such a group (*go in procession*). **3** a regular succession of things; a sequence. **4** a race in which no competitor is able to overtake another. **5** *Theol.* the emanation of the Holy Spirit. □□ **processionist** *n.* [ME f. OF f. L *processio -onis* (as PROCEED)]
■ **1** parade, march, cortège, column, line, file, train, cavalcade, motorcade. **3** succession, cycle, sequence, string, train, chain, series, course, run, progression.

processional /prəséshən'l/ *adj.* & *n.* ● *adj.* **1** of processions. **2** used, carried, or sung in processions. ● *n. Eccl.* an office-book of processional hymns etc. [med.L *processionalis* (adj.), *-ale* (n.) (as PROCESSION)]

processor /prṓsessər/ *n.* a machine that processes things, esp.: **1** = *central processor*. **2** = *food processor*.

procès-verbal /próssayverbaál/ *n.* (*pl.* **procès-verbaux** /-bṓ/) a written report of proceedings; minutes. [F]

prochronism /prṓkrəniz'm/ *n.* the action of referring an event etc. to an earlier date than the true one. [PRO-[2] + Gk *khronos* time]
■ see ANACHRONISM 1.

proclaim /prəkláym/ *v.tr.* **1** (often foll. by *that* + clause) announce or declare publicly or officially. **2** declare (a person) to be (a king, traitor, etc.). **3** reveal as being (*an accent that proclaims you a Scot*). □□ **proclaimer** *n.* **proclamation** /prókləmáysh'n/ *n.* **proclamatory** /-klámmətəri, -tri/ *adj.* [ME *proclame* f. L *proclamare* cry out (as PRO-[1], CLAIM)]
■ **1** announce, declare, pronounce, make known, bruit (about), trumpet, publish, advertise, broadcast, promulgate, herald; profess, assert. **2** brand, accuse of being, stigmatize as, pronounce, characterize as, declare, announce, decree. □□ **proclamation** announcement, declaration, publication, promulgation, statement, advertisement, manifesto, notification.

proclitic /prəklíttik/ *adj.* & *n. Gram.* ● *adj.* (of a monosyllable) closely attached in pronunciation to a following word and having itself no accent. ● *n.* such a word, e.g. *at* in *at home*. □□ **proclitically** *adv.* [mod.L *procliticus* f. Gk *proklinō* lean forward, after LL *encliticus*: see ENCLITIC]

proclivity /prəklívviti/ *n.* (*pl.* **-ies**) a tendency or inclination. [L *proclivitas* f. *proclivis* inclined (as PRO-[1], *clivus* slope)]
■ see TENDENCY.

proconsul /prōkóns'l/ *n.* **1** *Rom.Hist.* a governor of a province, in the later republic usu. an ex-consul. **2** a governor of a modern colony etc. **3** a deputy consul. □□ **proconsular** /-kónsyoolər/ *adj.* **proconsulate** /-kónsyoolət/ *n.* **proconsulship** *n.* [ME f. L, earlier *pro consule* (one acting) for the consul]

procrastinate /prōkrástinayt/ *v.intr.* defer action; be dilatory. ¶ Often confused with *prevaricate*. □□ **procrastination** /-náysh'n/ *n.* **procrastinative** /-nətiv/ *adj.* **procrastinator** *n.* **procrastinatory** *adj.* [L *procrastinare procrastinat-* (as PRO-[1], *crastinus* of tomorrow f. *cras* tomorrow)]
■ temporize, play for time, dally, delay, stall, take one's time, dilly-dally; hesitate, pause, waver, vacillate, shilly-shally, dither, be undecided.

procreate /prṓkriayt/ *v.tr.* (often *absol.*) bring (offspring) into existence by the natural process of reproduction. □□ **procreant** /prṓkriənt/ *adj.* **procreative** *adj.* **procreation** /-kriáysh'n/ *n.* **procreator** *n.* [L *procreare procreat-* (as PRO-[1], *creare* create)]
■ see REPRODUCE 3. □□ **procreant, procreative** reproductive, sexual, progenitive, propagative. **procreation** see GENERATION 6. **procreator** see PARENT *n.* 1, 5.

Procrustean /prōkrústiən/ *adj.* seeking to enforce uniformity by forceful or ruthless methods. [Gk *Prokroustēs*, lit. stretcher, f. *prokrouō* beat out: the name of a legendary robber who fitted victims to a bed by stretching them or cutting off parts of them]

proctology /proktólləji/ *n.* the branch of medicine concerned with the anus and rectum. □□ **proctological** /-təlójik'l/ *adj.* **proctologist** *n.* [Gk *prōktos* anus + -LOGY]

proctor /próktər/ *n.* **1** *Brit.* an officer (usu. one of two) at certain universities, appointed annually and having mainly disciplinary functions. **2** *US* a supervisor of students in an examination etc. **3** *Law* a person managing causes in a court (now chiefly ecclesiastical) that administers civil or canon law. **4** a representative of the clergy in the Church of England convocation. □ **Queen's** (or **King's**) **Proctor** (in the UK) an official who has the right to intervene in probate, divorce, and nullity cases when collusion or the suppression of facts is alleged. □□ **proctorial** /-tóriəl/ *adj.* **proctorship** *n.* [ME, syncopation of PROCURATOR]

proctoscope /próktəskōp/ *n.* a medical instrument for inspecting the rectum. [Gk *prōktos* anus + -SCOPE]

procumbent /prəkúmb'nt/ *adj.* **1** lying on the face; prostrate. **2** *Bot.* growing along the ground. [L *procumbere* fall forwards (as PRO-[1], *cumbere* lay oneself)]
■ **1** see PROSTRATE *adj.* 1. **2** creeping, low-growing, prostrate, *Bot.* repent, *Bot.* & *Zool.* decumbent.

procuration /prókyooráysh'n/ *n.* **1** *formal* the action of procuring, obtaining, or bringing about. **2** the function or an authorized action of an attorney. [ME f. OF *procuration* or L *procuratio* (as PROCURE)]

procurator /prókyooraytər/ *n.* **1** an agent or proxy, esp. one who has power of attorney. **2** *Rom.Hist.* a treasury officer in an imperial province. □ **procurator fiscal** (in Scotland) a local coroner and public prosecutor. □□ **procuratorial** /-rətóriəl/ *adj.* **procuratorship** *n.* [ME f. OF *procurateur* or L *procurator* administrator, finance-agent (as PROCURE)]

procure /prəkyŏŏr/ *v.tr.* **1** obtain, esp. by care or effort; acquire (*managed to procure a copy*). **2** bring about (*procured their dismissal*). **3** (also *absol.*) obtain (women) for prostitution. □□ **procurable** *adj.* **procural** *n.* **procurement** *n.* [ME f. OF *procurer* f. L *procurare* take care of, manage (as PRO-[1], *curare* see to)]

■ **1** obtain, acquire, get, come by, secure, get *or* lay one's hands on, get (a) hold of, pick up, appropriate, requisition; buy, purchase. **2** accomplish, effect, cause, produce; see also *bring about*.

procurer /prəkyŏŏrər/ *n.* (*fem.* **procuress** /-kyŏŏriss/) a person who obtains women for prostitution. [ME f. AF *procurour*, OF *procureur* f. L *procurator*: see PROCURATOR]

■ pander, *archaic* whoremaster, whoremonger; madam, procuress, bawd, brothel-keeper; see also PIMP *n.*

prod /prod/ *v.* & *n.* ● *v.* (**prodded, prodding**) **1** *tr.* poke with the finger or a pointed object. **2** *tr.* stimulate or goad to action. **3** *intr.* (foll. by *at*) make a prodding motion. ● *n.* **1** a poke or thrust. **2** a stimulus to action. **3** a pointed instrument. ▫▫ **prodder** *n.* [16th c.: perh. imit.]

■ *v.* **1** jab, dig, poke, nudge, thrust, job, elbow. **2** spur, urge, impel, push, prompt, rouse, stir, incite, move, motivate, provoke, encourage, stimulate; incite, goad, pester, harass, hector, badger, plague, nag. ● *n.* **1** jab, dig, poke, nudge, thrust, job, push. **2** stimulus, push, shove, prompt; see also SPUR *n.* 2.

prodigal /próddig'l/ *adj.* & *n.* ● *adj.* **1** recklessly wasteful. **2** (foll. by *of*) lavish. ● *n.* **1** a prodigal person. **2** (in full **prodigal son**) a repentant wastrel, returned wanderer, etc. (Luke 15:11–32). ▫▫ **prodigality** /-gálliti/ *n.* **prodigally** *adv.* [med.L *prodigalis* f. L *prodigus* lavish]

■ *adj.* **1** wasteful, extravagant, spendthrift, profligate, immoderate, intemperate, wanton, improvident, reckless. **2** generous, bountiful, copious, profuse, excessive, lavish, liberal, luxuriant, abundant, abounding, rich, plentiful, *poet.* bounteous, plenteous. ● *n.* **1** wastrel, spendthrift, squanderer, waster, big spender; see also PROFLIGATE *n.* ▫▫ **prodigality** wastefulness, extravagance, excessiveness, immoderation, intemperateness, wantonness, recklessness, profligacy, improvidence, dissipation, squandering; lavishness, luxuriousness, luxuriance, abundance, bounty, bountifulness, copiousness, profusion, profuseness, sumptuousness, richness, plentifulness, *poet.* bounteousness, plenteousness.

prodigious /prədíjəss/ *adj.* **1** marvellous or amazing. **2** enormous. **3** abnormal. ▫▫ **prodigiously** *adv.* **prodigiousness** *n.* [L *prodigiosus* (as PRODIGY)]

■ **1** amazing, astonishing, astounding, startling, extraordinary, exceptional, marvellous, wonderful, incredible, phenomenal, spectacular, sensational, unusual, staggering, remarkable, noteworthy, notable, *colloq.* fabulous, fantastic, mind-boggling, *poet.* wondrous. **2** vast, immeasurable, colossal, enormous, tremendous, huge, massive, immense; giant, gigantic, mammoth, monumental, stupendous, titanic, gargantuan, leviathan, monstrous, *sl.* humongous, *Brit. sl.* ginormous. **3** see ABNORMAL.

prodigy /próddiji/ *n.* (*pl.* **-ies**) **1** a person endowed with exceptional qualities or abilities, esp. a precocious child. **2** a marvellous thing, esp. one out of the ordinary course of nature. **3** (foll. by *of*) a wonderful example (of a quality). [L *prodigium* portent]

■ **1** genius, mastermind, mental giant, wizard, virtuoso, *colloq.* brain, wunderkind, Einstein, whiz-kid, whiz, walking dictionary *or* encyclopedia. **2** marvel, phenomenon, sensation, miracle; see also WONDER *n.* 2.

prodrome /prṓdrōm/ *n.* **1** a preliminary book or treatise. **2** *Med.* a premonitory symptom. ▫▫ **prodromal** /prōdrṓm'l/ *adj.* **prodromic** /prōdrómmik/ *adj.* [F f. mod.L f. Gk *prodromos* precursor (as PRO-[2], *dromos* running)]

■ ▫▫ **prodromal, prodromic** see PRELIMINARY *adj.*

produce *v.* & *n.* ● *v.tr.* /prədyŏŏss/ **1** bring forward for consideration, inspection, or use (*will produce evidence*). **2** manufacture (goods) from raw materials etc. **3** bear or yield (offspring, fruit, a harvest, etc.). **4** bring into existence. **5** cause or bring about (a reaction, sensation, etc.). **6** *Geom.* extend or continue (a line). **7 a** bring (a play, performer, book, etc.) before the public. **b** supervise the production of (a film, broadcast, etc.). ● *n.* /pródyooss/ **1 a** what is produced, esp. agricultural and natural products collectively (*dairy produce*). **b** an amount of this. **2** (often foll. by *of*) a result (of labour, efforts, etc.). **3** a yield, esp. in the assay of ore. ▫▫ **producible** /prədyŏŏssib'l/ *adj.* **producibility** /prədyŏŏssibílliti/ *n.* [ME f. L *producere* (as PRO-[1], *ducere duct-* lead)]

■ *v.* **1** bring forward *or* out, introduce, present, offer, show, exhibit, display; disclose, reveal, bring to light. **2** make, manufacture, fabricate, turn out, put *or* bring out; construct, assemble, put together, compose. **3** put out *or* forth, generate; see also BEAR[1] 3. **4, 5** give rise to, cause, bring forth, spark off, initiate, occasion, bring about, prompt, evoke, *literary* beget; create, generate, give birth to. ● *n.* **1** goods, merchandise, products, commodities, stock, staples, wares. **2** see RESULT *n.*

producer /prədyŏŏssər/ *n.* **1 a** *Econ.* a person who produces goods or commodities. **b** a person who or thing which produces something or someone. **2 a** a person generally responsible for the production of a film or play (apart from the direction of the acting). **b** *Brit.* the director of a play or broadcast programme. ▫ **producer gas** a combustible gas formed by passing air, or air and steam, through red-hot carbon.

■ **1** maker, manufacturer, fabricator, processor; creator, grower. **2 a** promoter, impresario, administrator, manager, stage-manager, showman. **b** director, regisseur.

product /próddukt/ *n.* **1** a thing or substance produced by natural process or manufacture. **2** a result (*the product of their labours*). **3** *Math.* a quantity obtained by multiplying quantities together. [ME f. L *productum*, neut. past part. of *producere* PRODUCE]

■ **1** artefact, commodity; (*products*) see PRODUCE *n.* 1. **2** result, consequence, outcome, issue, effect, yield, upshot.

production /prədúksh'n/ *n.* **1** the act or an instance of producing; the process of being produced. **2** the process of being manufactured, esp. in large quantities (*go into production*). **3** a total yield. **4** a thing produced, esp. a literary or artistic work, a film, play, etc. ▫ **production line** a systematized sequence of mechanical or manual operations involved in producing a commodity. ▫▫ **productional** *n.* [ME f. OF f. L *productio -onis* (as PRODUCT)]

■ **1** manufacture, manufacturing, making, fabrication, preparation, creation, development; formation, assembly, building, construction; artistry, direction, staging; presentation. **4** product; show, performance; work, opus; play, film.

productive /prədúktiv/ *adj.* **1** of or engaged in the production of goods. **2 a** producing much (*productive soil*; *a productive writer*). **b** (of the mind) inventive, creative. **3** *Econ.* producing commodities of exchangeable value (*productive labour*). **4** (foll. by *of*) producing or giving rise to (*productive of great annoyance*). ▫▫ **productively** *adv.* **productiveness** *n.* [F *productif -ive* or LL *productivus* (as PRODUCT)]

■ **2 a** fruitful, fertile, rich, fecund, plentiful, abundant, bountiful, prolific, dynamic, *poet.* bounteous, plenteous. **b** imaginative, creative, inventive, resourceful, generative, ingenious, fertile, vigorous.

productivity /pródduktívviti/ *n.* **1** the capacity to produce. **2** the quality or state of being productive. **3** the effectiveness of productive effort, esp. in industry. **4** production per unit of effort.

■ **3** efficiency, productiveness.

proem /prṓ-im/ *n.* **1** a preface or preamble to a book or speech. **2** a beginning or prelude. ▫▫ **proemial** /prō-éemiəl/ *adj.* [ME f. OF *proeme* or L *prooemium* f. Gk *prooimion* prelude (as PRO-[2], *oimē* song)]

■ **1** see PREAMBLE. **2** see PRELIMINARY *n.* 1.

Prof. *abbr.* Professor.

prof /prof/ *n. colloq.* a professor. [abbr.]

profane /prəfáyn/ *adj.* & *v.* ● *adj.* **1** not belonging to what is sacred or biblical; secular. **2 a** irreverent, blasphemous. **b** vulgar, obscene. **3** (of a rite etc.) heathen. **4** not initiated into religious rites or any esoteric knowledge. ● *v.tr.* **1** treat (a sacred thing) with irreverence or disregard. **2** violate or pollute (what is entitled to respect). □□ **profanation** /próffənáysh'n/ *n.* **profanely** *adv.* **profaneness** *n.* **profaner** *n.* [ME *prophane* f. OF *prophane* or med.L *prophanus* f. L *profanus* before (i.e. outside) the temple, not sacred (as PRO-[1], *fanum* temple)]

■ *adj.* **1** non-religious, laic, lay, non-clerical, secular, temporal; unsanctified, unconsecrated, unhallowed. **2 a** irreverent, sacrilegious, blasphemous, idolatrous, irreligious, unbelieving, disbelieving, impious, godless, ungodly, unholy, disrespectful; bad, taboo; non-halal, *Judaism* trefa, not kosher. **b** impure, unclean, dirty, filthy, smutty, foul, foul-mouthed, obscene, vulgar, coarse, uncouth, rude, low, bawdy, ribald, scurrilous, immodest, improper, indecent, unmentionable, indecorous, indelicate, common, *US* off colour, *colloq. joc.* naughty. **3** see HEATHEN *adj.* ● *v.* **2** debase, contaminate, pollute, taint, vitiate, degrade, defile, desecrate, violate, pervert, corrupt, prostitute.

profanity /prəfánniti/ *n.* (*pl.* **-ies**) **1** a profane act. **2** profane language; blasphemy. [LL *profanitas* (as PROFANE)]

■ **1** see SACRILEGE. **2** blasphemy, obscenity, cursing, swearing, foul *or* bad language.

profess /prəféss/ *v.* **1** *tr.* claim openly to have (a quality or feeling). **2** *tr.* (foll. by *to* + infin.) pretend. **3** *tr.* (often foll. by *that* + clause; also *refl.*) declare (*profess ignorance; professed herself satisfied*). **4** *tr.* affirm one's faith in or allegiance to. **5** *tr.* receive into a religious order under vows. **6** *tr.* have as one's profession or business. **7 a** *tr.* teach (a subject) as a professor. **b** *intr.* perform the duties of a professor. [ME f. L *profitēri profess-* declare publicly (as PRO-[1], *fatēri* confess)]

■ **2** (*profess to*) pretend to, lay claim to, purport to, claim to, make a pretence of. **3** assert, claim, asseverate, state, affirm, confirm, confess, declare, maintain, set forth, put forward, pronounce, announce, *archaic* vow, *formal* aver.

professed /prəfést/ *adj.* **1** self-acknowledged (*a professed Christian*). **2** alleged, ostensible. **3** claiming to be duly qualified. **4** (of a monk or nun) having taken the vows of a religious order. □□ **professedly** /-féssidli/ *adv.* (in senses 1, 2).

■ **1** sworn, acknowledged, confirmed, self-acknowledged, certified, declared. **2** supposed, ostensible, apparent, alleged, purported, so-called. **3** see SELF-STYLED.

profession /prəfésh'n/ *n.* **1** a vocation or calling, esp. one that involves some branch of advanced learning or science (*the medical profession*). **2** a body of people engaged in a profession. **3** a declaration or avowal. **4** a declaration of belief in a religion. **5 a** the declaration or vows made on entering a religious order. **b** the ceremony or fact of being professed in a religious order. □ **the oldest profession** *colloq.* or *joc.* prostitution. □□ **professionless** *adj.* [ME f. OF f. L *professio -onis* (as PROFESS)]

■ **1** occupation, calling, work, field, vocation, employment, *métier*, trade, business, craft, line, sphere, speciality, job, position. **3** confession, affirmation, statement, assertion, asseveration, declaration, testimony, averment, announcement; admission, avowal.

professional /prəféshən'l/ *adj.* & *n.* ● *adj.* **1** of or belonging to or connected with a profession. **2 a** having or showing the skill of a professional, competent. **b** worthy of a professional (*professional conduct*). **3** engaged in a specified activity as one's main paid occupation (cf. AMATEUR) (*a professional boxer*). **4** *derog.* engaged in a specified activity regarded with disfavour (*a professional agitator*). ● *n.* a professional person. □ **professional foul** a deliberate foul in football etc., esp. to prevent an opponent from scoring. □□ **professionally** *adv.*

■ *adj.* **2** trained, practised, veteran, experienced, qualified, licensed, official, seasoned; competent, able, skilled, skilful, expert, masterful, masterly, efficient, adept, proficient, polished, finished, thorough, authoritative, businesslike. ● *n.* master, expert, specialist, authority, proficient, adept, *esp. Brit. colloq.* dab hand, *US colloq.* maven.

professionalism /prəféshənəliz'm/ *n.* the qualities or typical features of a profession or of professionals, esp. competence, skill, etc. □□ **professionalize** *v.tr.* (also **-ise**).

professor /prəféssər/ *n.* **1 a** (often as a title) a university academic of the highest rank; the holder of a university chair. **b** *US* a university teacher. **2** a person who professes a religion. □□ **professorate** *n.* **professorial** /próffisóriəl/ *adj.* **professorially** /próffisóriəli/ *adv.* **professoriate** /próffisóriət/ *n.* **professorship** *n.* [ME f. OF *professeur* or L *professor* (as PROFESS)]

■ **1** see TEACHER. □□ **professorship** see CHAIR *n* 2a, b.

proffer /próffər/ *v.* & *n.* ● *v.tr.* (esp. as **proffered** *adj.*) offer (a gift, services, a hand, etc.). ● *n. literary* an offer or proposal. [ME f. AF & OF *proffrir* (as PRO-[1], *offrir* OFFER)]

■ *v.* see OFFER *v.* 1, 3, 5. ● *n.* see OFFER *n.*

proficient /prəfish'nt/ *adj.* & *n.* ● *adj.* (often foll. by *in*, *at*) adept, expert. ● *n.* a person who is proficient. □□ **proficiency** /-shənsi/ *n.* **proficiently** *adv.* [L *proficiens proficient-* (as PROFIT)]

■ *adj.* skilful, skilled, adept, expert, experienced, practised, well-versed, trained, professional, qualified, capable, able, accomplished, dexterous, competent, knowledgeable. □□ **proficiency** skill, adeptness, expertise, expertness, know-how, skilfulness, aptitude, capability, ability, competence, competency.

profile /prṓfīl/ *n.* & *v.* ● *n.* **1 a** an outline (esp. of a human face) as seen from one side. **b** a representation of this. **2 a** a short biographical or character sketch. **b** a report, esp. one written by a teacher on a pupil's academic and social progress. **3** *Statistics* a representation by a graph or chart of information (esp. on certain characteristics) recorded in a quantified form. **4** a characteristic personal manner or attitude. **5** a vertical cross-section of a structure. **6** a flat outline piece of scenery on stage. ● *v.tr.* **1** represent in profile. **2** give a profile to. **3** write a profile on. □ **in profile** as seen from one side. **keep a low profile** remain inconspicuous. □□ **profiler** *n.* **profilist** *n.* [obs. It. *profilo*, *profilare* (as PRO-[1], *filare* spin f. L *filare* f. *filum* thread)]

■ *n.* **1** outline, contour, silhouette, side-view. **2 a** biography, (biographical *or* thumbnail *or* character) sketch, portrait, vignette. **3** picture, idea, impression, notion, understanding; see also CHART *n.* 2. **4** see CHARACTERISTIC *n.* ● *v.* **1** describe, draw, sketch, characterize, portray, paint, depict, style. **3** describe, detail, give an account of; outline, sketch. □ **keep a low profile** keep low *or* down, adopt a softly softly approach, soft-pedal; see also *dummy up*.

profit /próffit/ *n.* & *v.* ● *n.* **1** an advantage or benefit. **2** financial gain; excess of returns over outlay. ● *v.* (**profited, profiting**) **1** *tr.* (also *absol.*) be beneficial to. **2** *intr.* obtain an advantage or benefit (*profited by the experience*). **3** *intr.* make a profit. □ **at a profit** with financial gain. **profit and loss account** an account in which gains are credited and losses debited so as to show the net profit or loss at any time. **profit margin** the profit remaining in a business after costs have been deducted. **profit-sharing** the sharing of profits esp. between employer and employees. **profit-taking** the sale of shares etc. at a time when profit will accrue. □□ **profitless** *adj.* [ME f. OF f. L *profectus* progress, profit f. *proficere profect-* advance (as PRO-[1], *facere* do)]

■ *n.* **1** advantage, avail, good, benefit, gain, value, interest, use, usefulness, *archaic* behoof. **2** net profit, net, return(s), gain, yield, payback, revenue, proceeds, surplus, *esp. US* take, *sl.* clean-up. ● *v.* **1** advance, further, be of profit *or* advantage to, benefit, promote, aid, help, be advantageous *or* beneficial to, serve, avail. **2** (*profit from* or *by*) take advantage of, turn to advantage *or* account, exploit, utilize, make (good) use of, make capital (out) of, capitalize on, maximize, make the most of, *colloq.* cash in on. **3** profiteer, make a killing, *colloq.* make a packet, rake it in, *sl.* clean up, make a bundle.

profitable /próffitəb'l/ *adj.* **1** yielding profit; lucrative. **2** beneficial; useful. ▫▫ **profitability** /-bílliti/ *n.* **profitableness** *n.* **profitably** *adv.* [ME f. OF (as PROFIT)]
■ **1** productive, lucrative, fruitful, well-paid, cost-effective, gainful, remunerative, money-making, rewarding, payable, rentable, *colloq.* juicy, *Brit. colloq.* jammy. **2** beneficial, helpful, useful, utilitarian, valuable, worthwhile, advantageous, productive, rewarding, serviceable.

profiteer /próffiteér/ *v.* & *n.* ● *v.intr.* make or seek to make excessive profits, esp. illegally or in black market conditions. ● *n.* a person who profiteers.
■ *v.* see PROFIT *v.* 3. ● *n.* racketeer, exploiter, extortionist, extortioner, blackmarketeer, bloodsucker.

profiterole /prəfíttərōl/ *n.* a small hollow case of choux pastry usu. filled with cream and covered with chocolate sauce. [F, dimin. of *profit* PROFIT]

profligate /prófligət/ *adj.* & *n.* ● *adj.* **1** licentious; dissolute. **2** recklessly extravagant. ● *n.* a profligate person. ▫▫ **profligacy** /-gəsi/ *n.* **profligately** *adv.* [L *profligatus* dissolute, past part. of *profligare* overthrow, ruin (as PRO-[1], *fligere* strike down)]
■ *adj.* **1** dissolute, degenerate, loose, licentious, depraved, debauched, immoral, unprincipled, shameless, dissipative, corrupt, promiscuous, lascivious, libertine, wanton, unrestrained, sybaritic. **2** extravagant, prodigal, wasteful, reckless, improvident, spendthrift, immoderate, excessive. ● *n.* debauchee, degenerate, reprobate, libertine, wanton, sybarite, voluptuary, sensualist; prodigal, spendthrift, wastrel, waster, squanderer. ▫▫ **profligacy** debauchery, immorality, dissipation, dissoluteness, degeneracy, licentiousness, depravity, corruption, promiscuity, lasciviousness, lewdness, libertinism, wantonness, unrestraint, sybaritism, voluptuousness; prodigality, extravagance, wastefulness, recklessness, lavishness, improvidence.

pro forma /prō fórmə/ *adv.*, *adj.*, & *n.* ● *adv.* & *adj.* as or being a matter of form. ● *n.* (in full **pro-forma invoice**) an invoice sent in advance of goods supplied. [L]
■ *adj.* see FORMAL *adj.* 1, 2, 7.

profound /prəfównd/ *adj.* & *n.* ● *adj.* (**profounder**, **profoundest**) **1 a** having or showing great knowledge or insight (*a profound treatise*). **b** demanding deep study or thought (*profound doctrines*). **2** (of a state or quality) deep, intense, unqualified (*a profound sleep*; *profound indifference*). **3** at or extending to a great depth (*profound crevasses*). **4** (of a sigh) deep-drawn. **5** (of a disease) deep-seated. ● *n.* (prec. by *the*) *poet.* the vast depth (of the ocean, soul, etc.). ▫▫ **profoundly** *adv.* **profoundness** *n.* **profundity** /prəfúnditi/ *n.* (*pl.* **-ies**). [ME f. AF & OF *profund*, *profond* f. L *profundus* deep (as PRO-[1], *fundus* bottom)]
■ *adj.* **1 a** learned, scholarly, intellectual, erudite, discerning, astute, sagacious, sage, wise, penetrating, insightful, analytical, knowledgeable, informed, well-informed, well-read. **b** deep, unfathomable, abstruse, recondite, arcane, esoteric, intricate, knotty, involved, tricky, inscrutable, obscure, subtle. **2** deep, great, intense; keen, acute, extreme, overpowering, overwhelming; utter, complete, unqualified, total, perfect, absolute, thorough, thoroughgoing, out-and-out, downright, consummate. **3** see DEEP *adj.* 1. ● *n.* (*the profound*) see DEEP *n.* 1, *depths* (DEPTH 5). ▫▫ **profoundly** deeply, greatly, very, extremely, keenly, acutely, intensely, *colloq.* terribly, awfully. **profoundness**, **profundity** depth, intensity, abstruseness, reconditeness, arcaneness, intricacy, subtlety, complexity, complicatedness, difficulty, inscrutability, involvement, involvedness; erudition, discernment, scholarship, scholarliness, sagacity, wisdom, astuteness, insightfulness, knowledgeableness, knowledgeability.

profuse /prəfyo͞oss/ *adj.* **1** (often foll. by *in*, *of*) lavish; extravagant (*was profuse in her generosity*). **2** (of a thing) exuberantly plentiful; abundant (*profuse bleeding*; *a profuse variety*). ▫▫ **profusely** *adv.* **profuseness** *n.* **profusion** /prəfyo͞ozh'n/ *n.* [ME f. L *profusus* past part. of *profundere profus-* (as PRO-[1], *fundere fus-* pour)]
■ **1** generous, lavish, extravagant, unsparing, unselfish, unstinting, exuberant, magnanimous, ungrudging, liberal, bountiful, *poet.* bounteous. **2** abundant, ample, plentiful, copious, prolific, superabundant, lush, overflowing, productive, fruitful, rich; excessive, considerable. ▫▫ **profuseness**, **profusion** abundance, bounty, plenty, plentifulness, copiousness, superabundance, wealth, plethora; superfluity, glut, surplus, oversupply, surfeit, *poet.* plenteousness.

progenitive /prōjénnitiv/ *adj.* capable of or connected with the production of offspring.
■ reproductive, procreative, procreant, propagative; sexual.

progenitor /prōjénnitər/ *n.* **1** the ancestor of a person, animal, or plant. **2** a political or intellectual predecessor. **3** the origin of a copy. ▫▫ **progenitorial** /-tóriəl/ *adj.* **progenitorship** *n.* [ME f. OF *progeniteur* f. L *progenitor -oris* f. *progignere progenit-* (as PRO-[1], *gignere* beget)]
■ **1** see ANCESTOR 1. **2** predecessor, forerunner, precursor, antecedent, foregoer. **3** origin, original, prototype, archetype, source, originator, pattern.

progeniture /prōjénnityoor/ *n.* **1** the act or an instance of procreation. **2** young, offspring.

progeny /prójini/ *n.* **1** the offspring of a person or other organism. **2** a descendant or descendants. **3** an outcome or issue. [ME f. OF *progenie* f. L *progenies* f. *progignere* (as PROGENITOR)]
■ **1** progeniture, offspring, children, young, sons and daughters, *derog.* spawn; see also ISSUE *n.* 5. **2** descendants, posterity, heirs, scions, successors; see also SUCCESSION 2c. **3** see OUTCOME.

progesterone /prōjéstərōn/ *n.* a steroid hormone released by the corpus luteum which stimulates the preparation of the uterus for pregnancy (see also PROGESTOGEN). [*progestin* (as PRO-[2], GESTATION) + luteo*sterone* f. CORPUS LUTEUM + STEROL]

progestogen /prōjéstəjin/ *n.* **1** any of a group of steroid hormones (including progesterone) that maintain pregnancy and prevent further ovulation during it. **2** a similar hormone produced synthetically.

proglottis /prōglóttiss/ *n.* (*pl.* **proglottides** /-glóttideez/) each segment in the strobile of a tapeworm that contains a complete reproductive system. [mod.L f. Gk *proglōssis* (as PRO-[2], *glōssis* f. *glōssa*, *glōtta* tongue), from its shape]

prognathous /prognáythəss, prógnəthəss/ *adj.* **1** having a projecting jaw. **2** (of a jaw) projecting. ▫▫ **prognathic** /prognáthik/ *adj.* **prognathism** *n.* [PRO-[2] + Gk *gnathos* jaw]

prognosis /prognṓsiss/ *n.* (*pl.* **prognoses** /-seez/) **1** a forecast; a prognostication. **2** a forecast of the course of a disease. [LL f. Gk *prognōsis* (as PRO-[2], *gignōskō* know)]
■ **1** forecast, prognostication, prediction, prophecy, projection.

prognostic /prognóstik/ *n.* & *adj.* ● *n.* **1** (often foll. by *of*) an advance indication or omen, esp. of the course of a disease etc. **2** a prediction; a forecast. ● *adj.* foretelling; predictive (*prognostic of a good result*). ▫▫ **prognostically** *adv.* [ME f. OF *pronostique* f. L *prognosticum* f. Gk *prognōstikon* neut. of *prognōstikos* (as PROGNOSIS)]
■ *n.* **1** see INDICATION 1b, OMEN *n.* **2** see FORECAST *n.* ● *adj.* see PROPHETIC.

prognosticate /prognóstikayt/ *v.tr.* **1** (often foll. by *that* + clause) foretell; foresee; prophesy. **2** (of a thing) betoken; indicate (future events etc.). ▫▫ **prognosticable** /-kəb'l/ *adj.* **prognostication** /-káysh'n/ *n.* **prognosticative** /-kətiv/ *adj.* **prognosticator** *n.* **prognosticatory** *adj.* [med.L *prognosticare* (as PROGNOSTIC)]
■ **1** predict, foretell, prophesy, forecast, foresee, presage, divine. **2** betoken, augur, herald, forebode, foreshadow, foretoken, portend, harbinger, signal, indicate.

programme /prṓgram/ *n.* & *v.* (*US* **program**) ● *n.* **1** a usu. printed list of a series of events, performers, etc. at a public function etc. **2** a radio or television broadcast. **3** a plan of future events (*the programme is dinner and an early night*). **4** a course or series of studies, lectures, etc.; a syllabus. **5** (usu. **program**) a series of coded instructions to control the operation of a computer or other machine. ● *v.tr.* (**programmed, programming**; *US* **programed, programing**) **1** make a programme or definite plan of. **2** (usu. **program**) express (a problem) or instruct (a computer) by means of a program. □ **programme music** a piece of music intended to tell a story, evoke images, etc. □□ **programmable** *adj.* **programmability** /-gramәbílliti/ *n.* **programmatic** /-grәmáttik/ *adj.* **programmatically** /-grәmáttikәli/ *adv.* **programmer** *n.* [LL *programma* f. Gk *programma -atos* f. *prographō* write publicly (as PRO-², *graphō* write): spelling after F *programme*]

■ *n.* **1, 3** schedule, agenda, list, outline, calendar; plan, order of the day. **2** broadcast, production, show, presentation, telecast. **4** course, curriculum, syllabus; timetable, schedule. ● *v.* **1** prearrange, plan, lay out, map (out), set up, schedule, *US* slate.

progress *n.* & *v.* ● *n.* /prṓgress/ **1** forward or onward movement towards a destination. **2** advance or development towards completion, betterment, etc.; improvement (*has made little progress this term*; *the progress of civilization*). **3** *Brit. archaic* a State journey or official tour, esp. by royalty. ● *v.* /prәgréss/ **1** *intr.* move or be moved forward or onward; continue (*the argument is progressing*). **2** *intr.* /prәgréss/ advance or develop towards completion, improvement, etc. (*science progresses*). **3** *tr.* cause (work etc.) to make regular progress. □ **in progress** in the course of developing; going on. **progress-chaser** a person employed to check the regular progress of manufacturing work. **progress report** an account of progress made. [ME f. L *progressus* f. *progredi* (as PRO-¹, *gradi* walk: (v.) readopted f. US after becoming obs. in Brit. use in the 17th c.]

■ *n.* **1** forward *or* onward movement *or* motion, progression, advancement; headway, moving. **2** advancement, advance, promotion, development, spread, furtherance, improvement, betterment, evolution, maturation; elevation, rise; growth, expansion, extension. ● *v.* **1** advance, move *or* go (forward(s) *or* onward(s) *or* on), proceed, continue, go *or* forge ahead, go *or* move along, make one's *or* its way, make headway. **2** advance, improve, get better, develop, grow, expand, increase, evolve, mature, spread; rise, move up. □ **in progress** under way, ongoing, going on, taking place, at work, in operation, in the pipeline, awaiting completion, *colloq.* in the works.

progression /prәgrésh'n/ *n.* **1** the act or an instance of progressing (*a mode of progression*). **2** a succession; a series. **3** *Math.* **a** = *arithmetic progression*. **b** = *geometric progression*. **c** = *harmonic progression*. **4** *Mus.* passing from one note or chord to another. □□ **progressional** *adj.* [ME f. OF *progression* or L *progressio* (as PROGRESS)]

■ **1** forward movement, advance, advancement, progress, development; ascension, rise, elevation. **2** order, sequence, succession, train, chain, concatenation, course, flow; series, set.

progressionist /prәgréshәnist/ *n.* **1** an advocate of or believer in esp. political or social progress. **2** a person who believes in the theory of gradual progression to higher forms of life.

progressive /prәgréssiv/ *adj.* & *n.* ● *adj.* **1** moving forward (*progressive motion*). **2** proceeding step by step; cumulative (*progressive drug use*). **3 a** (of a political party, government, etc.) favouring or implementing rapid progress or social reform. **b** modern; efficient (*this is a progressive company*). **4** (of disease, violence, etc.) increasing in severity or extent. **5** (of taxation) at rates increasing with the sum taxed. **6** (of a card-game, dance, etc.) with periodic changes of partners. **7** *Gram.* (of an aspect) expressing an action in progress, e.g. *am writing*, *was writing*. **8** (of education) informal and without strict discipline, stressing individual needs. ● *n.* (also **Progressive**) an advocate of progressive political policies. □□ **progressively** *adv.* **progressiveness** *n.* **progressivism** *n.* **progressivist** *n.* & *adj.* [F *progressif -ive* or med.L *progressivus* (as PROGRESS)]

■ *adj.* **2, 4** continuing, developing, increasing, growing, ongoing; cumulative, step by step, gradual. **3 a** forward-looking, advanced, reformist, progressivist, left-wing, radical, liberal, avant-garde, dynamic, *S.Afr. verligte*. **b** forward-looking, advanced, modern, new, go-ahead, enterprising, *colloq.* go; see also CAPABLE 1. **8** child-centred, liberal, individualistic; open, informal. ● *n.* reformist, reformer; regressionist; leftist, left-winger; see also LIBERAL *n.*

pro hac vice /prṓ haak vī́si/ *adv.* for this occasion (only). [L]

prohibit /prәhíbbit/ *v.tr.* (**prohibited, prohibiting**) (often foll. by *from* + verbal noun) **1** formally forbid, esp. by authority. **2** prevent; make impossible (*his accident prohibits him from playing football*). □ **prohibited degrees** degrees of blood relationship within which marriage is forbidden. □□ **prohibiter** *n.* **prohibitor** *n.* [ME f. L *prohibēre* (as PRO-¹, *habēre* hold)]

■ **1** forbid, bar, ban, disallow, interdict, outlaw, taboo, debar. **2** prevent, stop, obstruct, block, impede, hinder, hamper, inhibit, restrain; preclude, rule out.

prohibition /prṓhibísh'n, prṓ-ibísh'n/ *n.* **1** the act or an instance of forbidding; a state of being forbidden. **2** *Law* **a** an edict or order that forbids. **b** a writ from a superior court forbidding an inferior court from proceeding in a suit deemed to be beyond its cognizance. **3** (usu. **Prohibition**) the prevention by law of the manufacture and sale of alcohol, esp. in the US (1920–33). □□ **prohibitionary** *adj.* **prohibitionist** *n.* [ME f. OF *prohibition* or L *prohibitio* (as PROHIBIT)]

■ **1** forbiddance, banning, disallowance, interdiction, outlawry, debarment, proscription; bar, interdict, injunction, embargo, ban.

prohibitive /prōhíbbitiv/ *adj.* **1** prohibiting. **2** (of prices, taxes, etc.) so high as to prevent purchase, use, abuse, etc. (*published at a prohibitive price*). □□ **prohibitively** *adv.* **prohibitiveness** *n.* **prohibitory** *adj.* [F *prohibitif -ive* or L *prohibitivus* (as PROHIBIT)]

■ **1** suppressive, repressive, restrictive, prohibitory; inhibitory, restraining, obstructive. **2** excessive, high, extortionate, exorbitant, outrageous, outlandish, insupportable, scandalous, *colloq.* criminal.

project *n.* & *v.* ● *n.* /prójekt/ **1** a plan; a scheme. **2** a planned undertaking. **3** a usu. long-term task undertaken by a student to be submitted for assessment. ● *v.* /prәjékt/ **1** *tr.* plan or contrive (a course of action, scheme, etc.). **2** *intr.* protrude; jut out. **3** *tr.* throw; cast; impel (*projected the stone into the water*). **4** *tr.* extrapolate (results etc.) to a future time; forecast (*I project that we shall produce two million next year*). **5** *tr.* cause (light, shadow, images, etc.) to fall on a surface, screen, etc. **6** *tr.* cause (a sound, esp. the voice) to be heard at a distance. **7** *tr.* (often *refl.* or *absol.*) express or promote (oneself or a positive image) forcefully or effectively. **8** *tr. Geom.* **a** draw straight lines from a centre or parallel lines through every point of (a given figure) to produce a corresponding figure on a surface or a line by intersecting it. **b** draw (such lines). **c** produce (such a corresponding figure). **9** *tr.* make a projection of (the earth, sky, etc.). **10** *tr. Psychol.* **a** (also *absol.*) attribute (an emotion etc.) to an external object or person, esp. unconsciously. **b** (*refl.*) project (oneself) into another's feelings, the future, etc. [ME f. L *projectum* neut. past part. of *projicere* (as PRO-¹, *jacĕre* throw)]

■ *n.* **1** proposal, idea, plan, scheme, programme, design. **2** activity, enterprise, programme, undertaking, venture, assignment; contract, engagement. ● *v.* **1** plan, scheme, propose, present, outline, devise, think up, contemplate, contrive, invent, work up *or* out, design, draft, draw up, delineate, describe, put forward, *formal* put forth. **2** jut out, stick out, protrude, overhang, stand out, bulge (out), extend (out), poke out, beetle (out). **3** cast, hurl, fling, toss, launch, propel, impel, lob, discharge, *colloq.* chuck; see also THROW *v.* 1, 2. **4** extrapolate; estimate, reckon, calculate, predict; see also FORECAST *v.* **5** reflect, transmit, cast, throw, shed, let fall, scatter, spread. **7** see COMMUNICATE 1a; (*project oneself*) carry on, conduct oneself, present oneself, express oneself, put oneself across; see also BEHAVE 1a. **10 a** see ATTRIBUTE *v.*

projectile /prəjéktīl/ *n.* & *adj.* ● *n.* **1** a missile, esp. fired by a rocket. **2** a bullet, shell, etc. fired from a gun. **3** any object thrown as a weapon. ● *adj.* **1** capable of being projected by force, esp. from a gun. **2** projecting or impelling. [mod.L *projectilis* (adj.), *-ile* (n.) (as PROJECT)]

■ *n.* **1, 2** missile, brickbat; shell, bullet, cartridge, shot, rocket.

projection /prəjéksh'n/ *n.* **1** the act or an instance of projecting; the process of being projected. **2** a thing that projects or obtrudes. **3** the presentation of an image etc. on a surface or screen. **4 a** a forecast or estimate based on present trends (*a projection of next year's profits*). **b** this process. **5 a** a mental image or preoccupation viewed as an objective reality. **b** the unconscious transfer of one's own impressions or feelings to external objects or persons. **6** *Geom.* the act or an instance of projecting a figure. **7** the representation on a plane surface of any part of the surface of the earth or a celestial sphere (*Mercator projection*). □□ **projectionist** *n.* (in sense 3). [L *projectio* (as PROJECT)]

■ **2** protrusion, protuberance, bulge, extension, overhang, ledge, *Engin.* flange; prominence, spur, outcrop, *Brit.* crag. **4** estimate, forecast, prediction, prognostication, calculation, reckoning; forecasting, planning, estimation; extrapolation. **5 b** transference, ascription; see also *attribution* (ATTRIBUTE).

projective /prəjéktiv/ *adj.* **1** *Geom.* **a** relating to or derived by projection. **b** (of a property of a figure) unchanged by projection. **2** *Psychol.* mentally projecting or projected (*a projective imagination*). □ **projective geometry** the study of the projective properties of geometric figures. □□ **projectively** *adv.*

projector /prəjéktər/ *n.* **1 a** an apparatus containing a source of light and a system of lenses for projecting slides or film on to a screen. **b** an apparatus for projecting rays of light. **2** a person who forms or promotes a project. **3** *archaic* a promoter of speculative companies.

prokaryote /prōkárriət/ *n.* (also **procaryote**) an organism in which the chromosomes are not separated from the cytoplasm by a membrane; a bacterium (cf. EUKARYOTE). □□ **prokaryotic** /-rióttik/ *adj.* [PRO-² + KARYO- + *-ote* as in ZYGOTE]

prolactin /prōláktin/ *n.* a hormone released from the anterior pituitary gland that stimulates milk production after childbirth. [PRO-¹ + LACTATION]

prolapse /prṓlaps/ *n.* & *v.* ● *n.* (also **prolapsus** /-lápsəss/) **1** the forward or downward displacement of a part or organ. **2** the prolapsed part or organ, esp. the womb or rectum. ● *v.intr.* undergo prolapse. [L *prolabi prolaps-* (as PRO-¹, *labi* slip)]

prolate /prṓlayt/ *adj.* **1** *Geom.* (of a spheroid) lengthened in the direction of a polar diameter (cf. OBLATE²). **2** growing or extending in width. **3** widely spread. **4** *Gram.* = PROLATIVE. □□ **prolately** *adv.* [L *prolatus* past part. of *proferre* prolong (as PRO-¹, *ferre* carry)]

prolative /prəláytiv/ *adj. Gram.* serving to continue or complete a predication, e.g. *go* (prolative infinitive) in *you may go.*

prole /prōl/ *adj.* & *n. derog. colloq.* ● *adj.* proletarian. ● *n.* a proletarian. [abbr.]

■ *adj.* see PLEBEIAN *adj.* 1. ● *n.* see PLEBEIAN *n.*

proleg /prṓleg/ *n.* a fleshy abdominal limb of a caterpillar or other larva. [PRO-¹ + LEG]

prolegomenon /prṓligómminən/ *n.* (*pl.* **prolegomena**) (usu. in *pl.*) an introduction or preface to a book etc., esp. when critical or discursive. □□ **prolegomenary** *adj.* **prolegomenous** *adj.* [L f. Gk, neut. passive pres. part. of *prolegō* (as PRO-², *legō* say)]

■ see PREFACE *n.* 1, 2.

prolepsis /prōlépsiss, -leépsiss/ *n.* (*pl.* **prolepses** /-seez/) **1** the anticipation and answering of possible objections in rhetorical speech. **2** anticipation. **3** the representation of a thing as existing before it actually does or did so, as in *he was a dead man when he entered.* **4** *Gram.* the anticipatory use of adjectives, as in *paint the town red.* □□ **proleptic** *adj.* [LL f. Gk *prolēpsis* f. *prolambanō* anticipate (as PRO-², *lambanō* take)]

proletarian /prṓlitáiriən/ *adj.* & *n.* ● *adj.* of or concerning the proletariat. ● *n.* a member of the proletariat. □□ **proletarianism** *n.* **proletarianize** *v.tr.* (also **-ise**). [L *proletarius* one who served the State not with property but with offspring (*proles*)]

■ *adj.* see PLEBEIAN *adj.* 1. ● *n.* see PLEBEIAN *n.* 3.

proletariat /prṓlitáiriət/ *n.* (also **proletariate**) **1 a** *Econ.* wage-earners collectively, esp. those without capital and dependent on selling their labour. **b** esp. *derog.* the lowest class of the community, esp. when considered as uncultured. **2** *Rom.Hist.* the lowest class of citizens. [F *prolétariat* (as PROLETARIAN)]

■ **1 b** see PEOPLE *n.* 2.

pro-life /prṓlíf/ *adj.* in favour of preserving life, esp. in opposing abortion.

proliferate /prəlíffərayt/ *v.* **1** *intr.* reproduce; increase rapidly in numbers; grow by multiplication. **2** *tr.* produce (cells etc.) rapidly. □□ **proliferation** /-ráysh'n/ *n.* **proliferative** /-rətiv/ *adj.* [back-form. f. *proliferation* f. F *prolifération* f. *prolifère* (as PROLIFEROUS)]

■ **1** grow, increase, multiply, mushroom, snowball, flourish, *literary* burgeon; breed, reproduce. □□ **proliferation** growth, increase, escalation, multiplication, expansion, spread, build-up, rise.

proliferous /prəlíffərəss/ *adj.* **1** (of a plant) producing many leaf or flower buds; growing luxuriantly. **2** growing or multiplying by budding. **3** spreading by proliferation. [L *proles* offspring + -FEROUS]

prolific /prəlíffik/ *adj.* **1** producing many offspring or much output. **2** (often foll. by *of*) abundantly productive. **3** (often foll. by *in*) abounding, copious. □□ **prolificacy** *n.* **prolifically** *adv.* **prolificness** *n.* [med.L *prolificus* (as PROLIFEROUS)]

■ **1** productive, creative, fertile, fecund, fruitful, proliferative, proliferous. **3** abundant, copious, profuse, plentiful, bountiful, *poet.* bounteous, plenteous; lush, rich; rife.

prolix /prṓliks, prəlíks/ *adj.* (of speech, writing, etc.) lengthy; tedious. □□ **prolixity** /-líksiti/ *n.* **prolixly** *adv.* [ME f. OF *prolixe* or L *prolixus* poured forth, extended (as PRO-¹, *liquēre* be liquid)]

■ see LENGTHY 2. □□ **prolixity** see RHETORIC 2.

prolocutor /prōlókyootər/ *n.* **1** *Eccl.* the chairperson esp. of the lower house of convocation of either province of the Church of England. **2** a spokesman. □□ **prolocutorship** *n.* [ME f. L f. *proloqui prolocut-* (as PRO-¹, *loqui* speak)]

prologize /prṓlogīz/ *v.intr.* (also **prologuize, -ise**) write or speak a prologue. [med.L *prologizare* f. Gk *prologizō* speak prologue (as PROLOGUE)]

prologue /prṓlog/ *n.* & *v.* ● *n.* **1 a** a preliminary speech, poem, etc., esp. introducing a play (cf. EPILOGUE). **b** the actor speaking the prologue. **2** (usu. foll. by *to*) any act or event serving as an introduction. ● *v.tr.* (**prologues, prologued, prologuing**) introduce with or provide with a prologue. [ME *prolog* f. OF *prologue* f. L *prologus* f. Gk *prologos* (as PRO-², *logos* speech)]

■ *n.* **1 a** see FOREWORD. **2** see PRELIMINARY *n.* 1.

prolong /prəlóng/ *v.tr.* **1** extend (an action, condition, etc.) in time or space. **2** lengthen the pronunciation of (a syllable etc.). **3** (as **prolonged** *adj.*) lengthy, esp. tediously so. □□ **prolongation** /prṓlonggáysh'n/ *n.* **prolongedly** /-lóngidli/ *adv.* **prolonger** *n.* [ME f. OF *prolonger* & f. LL *prolongare* (as PRO-¹, *longus* long)]

■ **1** extend, lengthen, elongate, stretch (out), draw *or* drag out, drag (on), keep up, string out, protract, continue. **3** (**prolonged**) see LENGTHY 2.

prolusion /prəlyo͞ozh'n, -lo͞ozh'n/ *n. formal* **1** a preliminary essay or article. **2** a first attempt. □□ **prolusory** /-lyo͞ossəri, -lo͞ossəri/ *adj.* [L *prolusio* f. *proludere prolus-* practise beforehand (as PRO-[1], *ludere lus-* play)]

prom /prom/ *n. colloq.* **1** *Brit.* = PROMENADE *n.* 1a. **2** *Brit.* = *promenade concert*. **3** *US* = PROMENADE *n.* 3. [abbr.]

promenade /prómmənaád/ *n.* & *v.* ● *n.* **1 a** *Brit.* a paved public walk along the sea front at a resort. **b** any paved public walk. **2** a walk, or sometimes a ride or drive, taken esp. for display, social intercourse, etc. **3** *US* a school or university ball or dance. **4** a march of dancers in country dancing etc. ● *v.* **1** *intr.* make a promenade. **2** *tr.* lead (a person etc.) about a place esp. for display. **3** *tr.* make a promenade through (a place). □ **promenade concert** a concert at which the audience, or part of it, can stand, sit on the floor, or move about. **promenade deck** an upper deck on a passenger ship where passengers may promenade. [F f. *se promener* walk, refl. of *promener* take for a walk]

■ *n.* **1** walk, parade, esplanade. **2** walk, stroll, saunter, ramble, turn, constitutional, airing; ride, drive. ● *v.* **1** walk, stroll, saunter, amble, ramble, perambulate, take a walk *or* stroll. **2** parade, display, flaunt, show (off), make an exhibit *or* a spectacle of, advertise.

promenader /prómmənaádər/ *n.* **1** a person who promenades. **2** *Brit.* a person who attends a promenade concert, esp. regularly.

promethazine /prōméthəzeen/ *n.* an antihistamine drug used to treat allergies, motion sickness, etc. [PROPYL + di*methy*lamine + phenothi*azine*]

Promethean /prəmeéthiən/ *adj.* daring or inventive like Prometheus, who in Greek myth was punished for stealing fire from the gods and giving it to the human race along with other skills.

promethium /prəmeéthiəm/ *n. Chem.* a radioactive metallic element of the lanthanide series occurring in nuclear-waste material. ¶ Symb.: **Pm**. [*Prometheus*: see PROMETHEAN]

prominence /prómminənss/ *n.* **1** the state of being prominent. **2** a prominent thing, esp. a jutting outcrop, mountain, etc. **3** *Astron.* a stream of incandescent gas projecting above the sun's chromosphere. [obs.F f. L *prominentia* jutting out (as PROMINENT)]

■ **1** celebrity, eminence, fame, distinction, notability, reputation, pre-eminence, standing, position, rank, prestige, renown, repute, importance, weight, influence, account, name, consequence. **2** hill, hillock, rise, hummock, outcrop, spur, tor, peak, arête, spine, ridge, pinnacle, *Brit.* crag; headland, point, promontory; protuberance, projection, protrusion, extrusion, outshoot, outgrowth, bulge.

prominent /prómminənt/ *adj.* **1** jutting out; projecting. **2** conspicuous. **3** distinguished; important. □□ **prominency** *n.* **prominently** *adv.* [L *prominēre* jut out: cf. EMINENT]

■ **1** protuberant, protruding, protrusive, projecting, jutting; bulging, raised, elevated. **2** conspicuous, noticeable, pronounced, obvious, evident, recognizable, discernible, distinguishable, identifiable, eye-catching, striking, outstanding. **3** eminent, pre-eminent, distinguished, notable, noteworthy, noted, well-known, famed, illustrious, famous, celebrated, renowned, acclaimed, honoured, esteemed, honourable, respected, well-thought-of, prestigious, reputable, creditable; significant, important.

promiscuous /prəmískyooəss/ *adj.* **1 a** (of a person) having frequent and diverse sexual relationships, esp. transient ones. **b** (of sexual relationships) of this kind. **2** of mixed and indiscriminate composition or kinds; indiscriminate (*promiscuous hospitality*). **3** *colloq.* carelessly irregular; casual. □□ **promiscuity** /prómmiskyo͞o-iti/ *n.* **promiscuously** *adv.* **promiscuousness** *n.* [L *promiscuus* (as PRO-[1], *miscēre* mix)]

■ **1 a** lax, loose, wanton, wild, uninhibited, unrestrained, uncontrolled, unbridled, uncurbed, immoderate, abandoned, libertine, licentious, dissipated, dissolute, depraved, profligate, debauched, fast, sluttish, *colloq.* tarty. **2, 3** indiscriminate, undiscriminating; mixed, miscellaneous, heterogeneous, random; careless, cursory, haphazard, unsystematic, indifferent, disregardful, slipshod, slovenly, sloppy, irresponsible, unthinking, thoughtless, unconsidered.

promise /prómmiss/ *n.* & *v.* ● *n.* **1** an assurance that one will or will not undertake a certain action, behaviour, etc. (*a promise of help; gave a promise to be generous*). **2** a sign or signs of future achievements, good results, etc. (*a writer of great promise*). ● *v.tr.* **1** (usu. foll. by *to* + infin., or *that* + clause; also *absol.*) make (a person) a promise, esp. to do, give, or procure (a thing) (*I promise you a fair hearing; they promise not to be late; promised that he would be there; cannot positively promise*). **2 a** afford expectations of (*the discussions promise future problems; promises to be a good cook*). **b** (foll. by *to* + infin.) seem likely to (*is promising to rain*). **3** *colloq.* assure, confirm (*I promise you, it will not be easy*). **4** (usu. in *passive*) *archaic* betroth (*she is promised to another*). □ **the promised land 1** *Bibl.* Canaan (Gen. 12:7 etc.). **2** any desired place, esp. heaven. **promise oneself** look forward to (a pleasant time etc.). **promise well** (or **ill** etc.) hold out good (or bad etc.) prospects. □□ **promisee** /-seé/ *n.* esp. *Law.* **promiser** *n.* **promisor** *n.* esp. *Law.* [ME f. L *promissum* neut. past part. of *promittere* put forth, promise (as PRO-[1], *mittere* send)]

■ *n.* **1** assurance, word (of honour), pledge, vow, oath, bond, guarantee; undertaking, engagement, commitment; agreement, contract, covenant, compact. **2** potential, capability, capacity, aptitude; expectation, likelihood, probability; see also ABILITY. ● *v.* **1** give one's word (of honour), pledge, swear, vow, take an oath, undertake, commit oneself, guarantee, cross one's heart (and hope to die). **2 a** give (an *or* every) indication of, hint at, suggest, foretell, augur, indicate, betoken, bespeak, be evidence of. **b** (*promise to*) show signs of, look like, seem *or* appear likely to, bid fair to. **3** assure, swear, confirm. **4** engage, betroth, *literary* affiance. □ **the promised land 2** see HEAVEN 2. **promise well** bode well, augur well, prospect well, have good prospects, look good *or* rosy.

promising /prómmising/ *adj.* likely to turn out well; hopeful; full of promise (*a promising start*). □□ **promisingly** *adv.*

■ hopeful, encouraging, favourable, auspicious, positive, rosy, optimistic, propitious, cheering, reassuring, heartening.

promissory /prómmisəri/ *adj.* **1** conveying or implying a promise. **2** (often foll. by *of*) full of promise. □ **promissory note** a signed document containing a written promise to pay a stated sum to a specified person or the bearer at a specified date or on demand. [med.L *promissorius* f. L *promissor* (as PROMISE)]

■ □ **promissory note** letter of credit, (bank) draft, *Econ.* bill of exchange, *US* demand note.

promo /prṓmō/ *n.* & *adj. colloq.* ● *n.* (*pl.* **-os**) **1** publicity, advertising. **2** a trailer for a television programme. ● *adj.* promotional. [abbr.]

promontory /prómməntəri, -tri/ *n.* (*pl.* **-ies**) **1** a point of high land jutting out into the sea etc.; a headland. **2** *Anat.* a prominence or protuberance in the body. [med.L *promontorium* alt. (after *mons montis* mountain) f. L *promunturium* (perh. f. PRO-[1], *mons*)]

■ **1** see POINT *n.* 22.

promote /prəmṓt/ *v.tr.* **1** (often foll. by *to*) advance or raise (a person) to a higher office, rank, etc. (*was promoted to captain*). **2** help forward; encourage; support actively (a cause, process, desired result, etc.) (*promoted women's suffrage*). **3** publicize and sell (a product). **4** attempt to ensure the passing of (a private act of parliament). **5** *Chess* raise (a pawn) to the rank of queen etc. when it reaches the opponent's end of the board. □□ **promotable** *adj.* **promotability** /-mṓtəbílliti/ *n.* **promotion** /-mṓsh'n/ *n.* **promotional** /-mṓshən'l/ *adj.* **promotive** *adj.* [ME f. L *promovēre promot-* (as PRO-[1], *movēre* move)]

■ **1** advance, move up, prefer, raise, upgrade, elevate; create. **2** help, further, encourage, assist, advance, support, forward, advantage, abet, aid, foster, nurture, develop, inspirit, strengthen, stimulate, inspire, *colloq.* boost; endorse, sponsor, espouse, commend, advocate, champion, speak for, side with, call attention to. **3** advertise, publicize, push, market, beat the drum for, *chiefly US* ballyhoo, *colloq.* plug, *sl.* hype. □□ **promotion** furtherance, advancement, encouragement, support, development, improvement, stimulation; advance, rise, preferment, elevation; espousal, commendation, advocacy, championship; advertising, marketing, publicity, advertisement, public relations, propaganda, puffery, *sl.* (media) hype.

promoter /prəmṓtər/ *n.* **1** a person who promotes. **2** a person who finances, organizes, etc. a sporting event, theatrical production, etc. **3** (in full **company promoter**) a person who promotes the formation of a joint-stock company. **4** *Chem.* an additive that increases the activity of a catalyst. [earlier *promotour* f. AF f. med.L *promotor* (as PROMOTE)]
■ **2** see *backer* (BACK).

prompt /prompt/ *adj.*, *adv.*, *v.*, & *n.* ● *adj.* **1 a** acting with alacrity; ready. **b** made, done, etc. readily or at once (*a prompt reply*). **2 a** (of a payment) made forthwith. **b** (of goods) for immediate delivery and payment. ● *adv.* punctually (*at six o'clock prompt*). ● *v.tr.* **1** (usu. foll. by *to*, or *to* + infin.) incite; urge (*prompted them to action*). **2 a** (also *absol.*) supply a forgotten word, sentence, etc., to (an actor, reciter, etc.). **b** assist (a hesitating speaker) with a suggestion. **3** give rise to; inspire (a feeling, thought, action, etc.). ● *n.* **1 a** an act of prompting. **b** a thing said to help the memory of an actor etc. **c** = PROMPTER 2. **d** *Computing* an indication or sign on a VDU screen to show that the system is waiting for input. **2** the time limit for the payment of an account, stated on a prompt note. □ **prompt-book** a copy of a play for a prompter's use. **prompt-box** a box in front of the footlights beneath the stage where the prompter sits. **prompt-note** a note sent to a customer as a reminder of payment due. **prompt side** the side of the stage where the prompter sits, usu. to the actor's left. □□ **prompting** *n.* **promptitude** *n.* **promptly** *adv.* **promptness** *n.* [ME f. OF *prompt* or L *promptus* past part. of *promere prompt-* produce (as PRO-[1], *emere* take)]
■ *adj.* **1 a** alert, eager, ready, quick, expeditious, ready and willing, disposed, predisposed, unhesitating, keen, avid. **b** quick, ready, immediate, instantaneous, unhesitating, rapid, fast, swift, speedy, punctual, timely, instant, summary, brisk. ● *adv.* on the dot, *Austral.* & *NZ colloq.* on the knocker, see also SHARP *adv.* 1. ● *v.* **1** urge, egg (on), prod, nudge, spur, incite, induce, impel, provoke, rouse, arouse, encourage, work *or* stir *or* fire up, move, motivate. **2** cue, remind, feed lines to. **3** bring about, inspire, occasion, give rise to, elicit, evoke, provoke, call forth, stimulate, awaken. ● *n.* **1 a** reminder, cue, hint, stimulus, refresher, suggestion. □□ **promptly** quickly, at once, straight away, directly, right away, immediately, without delay *or* hesitation, unhesitatingly, swiftly, speedily, readily, instantly, instantaneously, punctually, expeditiously, *US* momentarily; by return (of post).

prompter /prómptər/ *n.* **1** a person who prompts. **2** *Theatr.* a person seated out of sight of the audience who prompts the actors.

promulgate /prómməlgayt/ *v.tr.* **1** make known to the public; disseminate; promote (a cause etc.). **2** proclaim (a decree, news, etc.). □□ **promulgation** /-gáysh'n/ *n.* **promulgator** *n.* [L *promulgare* (as PRO-[1], *mulgēre* milk, cause to come forth)]
■ see PROMOTE 3, PROCLAIM 1. □□ **promulgation** see *proclamation* (PROCLAIM).

promulge /prōmúlj/ *v.tr. archaic* = PROMULGATE. [PROMULGATE]

pronaos /prōnáyoss/ *n.* (*pl.* **pronaoi** /-náyoy/) *Gk Antiq.* the space in front of the body of a temple, enclosed by a portico and projecting side walls. [L f. Gk *pronaos* hall of a temple (as PRO-[2], NAOS)]

pronate /prṓnayt/ *v.tr.* put (the hand, forearm, etc.) into a prone position (with the palm etc. downwards) (cf. SUPINATE). □□ **pronation** /-náysh'n/ *n.* [back-form. f. *pronation* (as PRONE)]

pronator /prōnáytər/ *n. Anat.* any muscle producing or assisting in pronation.

prone /prōn/ *adj.* **1 a** lying face downwards (cf. SUPINE). **b** lying flat; prostrate. **c** having the front part downwards, esp. the palm of the hand. **2** (usu. foll. by *to*, or *to* + infin.) disposed or liable, esp. to a bad action, condition, etc. (*is prone to bite his nails*). **3** (usu. in *comb.*) more than usually likely to suffer (*accident-prone*). **4** *archaic* with a downward slope or direction. □□ **pronely** *adv.* **proneness** /prṓn-niss/ *n.* [ME f. L *pronus* f. *pro* forwards]
■ **1 a, b** face down *or* downwards; prostrate, reclining, recumbent, horizontal, procumbent, *Bot.* & *Zool.* decumbent. **2** inclined, apt, disposed, predisposed, of a mind, subject, given, tending, leaning, *disp.* liable.

proneur /prōnṓr/ *n.* a person who extols; a flatterer. [F *prôneur* f. *prôner* eulogize f. *prône* place in church where addresses were delivered]

prong /prong/ *n.* & *v.* ● *n.* each of two or more projecting pointed parts at the end of a fork etc. ● *v.tr.* **1** pierce or stab with a fork. **2** turn up (soil) with a fork. □ **prong-buck** (or **-horn** or **-horned antelope**) a N. American deerlike ruminant, *Antilocapra americana*, the male of which has horns with forward-pointing prongs. **three-pronged attack** an attack on three separate points at once. □□ **pronged** *adj.* (also in *comb.*). [ME (also *prang*), perh. rel. to MLG *prange* pinching instrument]
■ *n.* tine.

pronominal /prōnómmin'l/ *adj.* of, concerning, or being, a pronoun. □□ **pronominalize** *v.tr.* (also **-ise**). **pronominally** *adv.* [LL *pronominalis* f. L *pronomen* (as PRO-[1], *nomen*, *nominis* noun)]

pronoun /prṓnown/ *n.* a word used instead of and to indicate a noun already mentioned or known, esp. to avoid repetition (e.g. *we*, *their*, *this*, *ourselves*). [PRO-[1], + NOUN, after F *pronom*, L *pronomen* (as PRO-[1], *nomen* name)]

pronounce /prənównss/ *v.* **1** *tr.* (also *absol.*) utter or speak (words, sounds, etc.) in a certain way. **2** *tr.* **a** utter or deliver (a judgement, sentence, curse, etc.) formally or solemnly. **b** proclaim or announce officially (*I pronounce you man and wife*). **3** *tr.* state or declare, as being one's opinion (*the apples were pronounced excellent*). **4** *intr.* (usu. foll. by *on*, *for*, *against*, *in favour of*) pass judgement; give one's opinion (*pronounced for the defendant*). □□ **pronounceable** /-nównsəb'l/ *adj.* **pronouncement** *n.* **pronouncer** *n.* [ME f. OF *pronuncier* f. L *pronuntiare* (as PRO-[1], *nuntiare* announce f. *nuntius* messenger)]
■ **1** utter, say, voice, express, articulate, enunciate, vocalize; put into words. **2 a** see PASS[1] *v.* 18. **b** declare, proclaim, announce, assert, say to be, decree. **3** declare, judge, adjudge, proclaim; accuse of being, stigmatize as, characterize as. □□ **pronouncement** statement, assertion, announcement, proclamation, declaration, avowal, affirmation, asseveration, averment, promulgation; opinion, judgement; decree, edict, dictum, order, ordinance.

pronounced /prənównst/ *adj.* **1** (of a word, sound, etc.) uttered. **2** strongly marked; decided (*a pronounced flavour*; *a pronounced limp*). □□ **pronouncedly** /-nównsidli/ *adv.*
■ **2** definite, distinct, unmistakable, marked, strong, clear, plain, well-defined, decided, conspicuous, noticeable, recognizable, identifiable, obvious, striking, prominent, notable.

pronto /próntō/ *adv. colloq.* promptly, quickly. [Sp. f. L (as PROMPT)]
■ see *quickly* (QUICK).

pronunciation /prənúnsiáysh'n/ *n.* **1** the way in which a word is pronounced, esp. with reference to a standard. **2** the act or an instance of pronouncing. **3** a person's way of

pronouncing words etc. [ME f. OF *prononciation* or L *pronuntiatio* (as PRONOUNCE)]
■ **1, 3** enunciation, articulation, elocution, diction, speech, speech pattern, manner of speaking, delivery, accent.

proof /pro͞of/ *n.*, *adj.*, & *v.* ● *n.* **1** facts, evidence, argument, etc. establishing or helping to establish a fact (*proof of their honesty*; *no proof that he was there*). **2** *Law* the spoken or written evidence in a trial. **3** a demonstration or act of proving (*not capable of proof*; *in proof of my assertion*). **4** a test or trial (*put them to the proof*; *the proof of the pudding is in the eating*). **5** the standard of strength of distilled alcoholic liquors. **6** *Printing* a trial impression taken from type or film, used for making corrections before final printing. **7** the stages in the resolution of a mathematical or philosophical problem. **8** each of a limited number of impressions from an engraved plate before the ordinary issue is printed and usu. (in full **proof before letters**) before an inscription or signature is added. **9** a photographic print made for selection etc. **10** *Sc. Law* a trial before a judge instead of by a jury. ● *adj.* **1** impervious to penetration, ill effects, etc. (*proof against the severest weather*; *his soul is proof against corruption*). **2** (*in comb.*) able to withstand damage or destruction by a specified agent (*soundproof*; *childproof*). **3** being of proof alcoholic strength. **4** (of armour) of tried strength. ● *v.tr.* **1** make (something) proof, esp. make (fabric) waterproof. **2** make a proof of (a printed work, engraving, etc.). □ **above proof** (of alcohol) having a stronger than standard strength. **proof-plane** a small flat conductor on an insulating handle for measuring the electrification of a body. **proof positive** absolutely certain proof. **proof-sheet** a sheet of printer's proof. **proof spirit** a mixture of alcohol and water having proof strength. □□ **proofless** *adj.* [ME *prōf prōve*, earlier *prēf* etc. f. OF *proeve*, *prueve* f. LL *proba* f. L *probare* (see PROVE; adj. and sometimes v. formed app. by ellipsis f. phr. *of proof* = proved to be impenetrable]
■ *n.* **1** evidence, documentation, facts, data, certification, testimony, ammunition. **3** verification, corroboration, confirmation, validation, authentication, ratification, substantiation. **4** test, trial; measure; standard, touchstone, criterion. ● *adj.* **1** protected, resistant; impervious, impenetrable, impregnable.

proofread /pro͞ofreed/ *v.tr.* (*past* and *past part.* **-read** /-red/) read (printer's proofs) and mark any errors. □□ **proofreader** *n.* **proofreading** *n.*

prop[1] /prop/ *n.* & *v.* ● *n.* **1** a rigid support, esp. one not an integral part of the thing supported. **2** a person who supplies support, assistance, comfort, etc. **3** *Rugby Football* a forward at either end of the front row of a scrum. **4** esp. *Austral.* a horse's action of propping. ● *v.* (**propped**, **propping**) **1** *tr.* (often foll. by *against*, *up*, etc.) support with or as if with a prop (*propped him against the wall*; *propped it up with a brick*). **2** *intr.* esp. *Austral.* (of a horse etc.) come to a dead stop with the forelegs rigid. [ME prob. f. MDu. *proppe*: cf. MLG, MDu. *proppen* (v.)]
■ *n.* **1** support, brace, stay, buttress, mainstay, upright, vertical, shore, post, pier. **2** see SUPPORT *n.* 2. ● *v.* **1** (*prop up*) support, brace, hold (up), buttress, stay, bolster, uphold, sustain, shore up; lean, stand, rest.

prop[2] /prop/ *n. Theatr. colloq.* **1** = PROPERTY 3. **2** (in *pl.*) a property man or mistress. [abbr.]

prop[3] /prop/ *n. colloq.* an aircraft propeller. □ **prop-jet** a turboprop. [abbr.]

prop. *abbr.* **1** proprietor. **2** proposition.

propaedeutic /prṓpidyo͞otik/ *adj.* & *n.* ● *adj.* serving as an introduction to higher study; introductory. ● *n.* (esp. in *pl.*) preliminary learning; a propaedeutic subject, study, etc. □□ **propaedeutical** *adj.* [PRO-[2] + Gk *paideutikos* of teaching, after Gk *propaideuō* teach beforehand]

propaganda /próppəgándə/ *n.* **1 a** an organized programme of publicity, selected information, etc., used to propagate a doctrine, practice, etc. **b** usu. *derog.* the information, doctrines, etc., propagated in this way. **2** (**Propaganda**) *RC Ch.* a committee of cardinals responsible for foreign missions. [It. f. mod.L *congregatio de propaganda fide* congregation for propagation of the faith]
■ **1 b** advertising, promotion, publicity; ballyhoo, puffery, *sl.* hype; agitprop, disinformation, Newspeak, rumours, lies.

propagandist /próppəgándist/ *n.* a member or agent of a propaganda organization; a person who spreads propaganda. □□ **propagandism** *n.* **propagandistic** /-dístik/ *adj.* **propagandistically** /-dístikəli/ *adv.* **propagandize** *v.intr.* & *tr.* (also **-ise**).

propagate /próppəgayt/ **1** *tr.* **a** breed specimens of (a plant, animal, etc.) by natural processes from the parent stock. **b** (*refl.* or *absol.*) (of a plant, animal, etc.) reproduce itself. **2 a** *tr.* disseminate; spread (a statement, belief, theory, etc.). **b** *intr.* grow more widespread or numerous; spread. **3** *tr.* hand down (a quality etc.) from one generation to another. **4** *tr.* extend the operation of; transmit (a vibration, earthquake, etc.). □□ **propagation** /-gáysh'n/ *n.* **propagative** *adj.* [L *propagare propagat-* multiply plants from layers, f. *propago* (as PRO-[1], *pangere* fix, layer)]
■ **1 b** breed, generate, reproduce, multiply, proliferate, procreate. **2 a** publicize, disseminate, dispense, distribute, spread, publish, broadcast, circulate, promulgate, transmit, disperse, propagandize; proclaim, make known, bruit about, noise abroad. **b** multiply, increase, spread, grow, develop.

propagator /próppəgaytər/ *n.* **1** a person or thing that propagates. **2** a small box that can be heated, used for germinating seeds or raising seedlings.

propane /prṓpayn/ *n.* a gaseous hydrocarbon of the alkane series used as bottled fuel. ¶ Chem. formula: C_3H_8. [PROPIONIC (ACID) + -ANE[1]]

propanoic acid /prṓpənṓ-ik/ *n. Chem.* = PROPIONIC ACID. [PROPANE + -IC]

propanone /prṓpənōn/ *n. Chem.* = ACETONE. [PROPANE + -ONE]

propel /prəpél/ *v.tr.* (**propelled**, **propelling**) **1** drive or push forward. **2** urge on; encourage. □ **propelling pencil** a pencil with a replaceable lead moved upward by twisting the outer case. [ME, = expel, f. L *propellere* (as PRO-[1], *pellere puls-* drive)]
■ **1** drive, impel, move, actuate, set in motion, get moving, push *or* thrust forward, launch. **2** see SPUR *v.*

propellant /prəpéllənt/ *n.* **1** a thing that propels. **2** an explosive that fires bullets etc. from a firearm. **3** a substance used as a reagent in a rocket engine etc. to provide thrust.

propellent /prəpéllənt/ *adj.* propelling; capable of driving or pushing forward.

propeller /prəpéllər/ *n.* **1** a person or thing that propels. **2** a revolving shaft with blades, esp. for propelling a ship or aircraft (cf. *screw-propeller*). □ **propeller shaft** a shaft transmitting power from an engine to a propeller or to the driven wheels of a motor vehicle. **propeller turbine** a turbo-propeller.

propene /prṓpeen/ *n. Chem.* = PROPYLENE. [PROPANE + ALKENE]

propensity /prəpénsiti/ *n.* (*pl.* **-ies**) an inclination or tendency (*has a propensity for wandering*). [*propense* f. L *propensus* inclined, past part. of *propendēre* (as PRO-[1], *pendēre* hang)]
■ see TENDENCY.

proper /próppər/ *adj.*, *adv.*, & *n.* ● *adj.* **1 a** accurate, correct (*in the proper sense of the word*; *gave him the proper amount*). **b** fit, suitable, right (*at the proper time*; *do it the proper way*). **2** decent; respectable, esp. excessively so (*not quite proper*). **3** (usu. foll. by *to*) belonging or relating exclusively or distinctively; particular, special (*with the respect proper to them*). **4** (usu. placed after noun) strictly so called; real; genuine (*this is the crypt, not the cathedral proper*). **5** *colloq.* thorough; complete (*had a proper row about it*). **6** (usu. placed after noun) *Heraldry* in the natural, not conventional, colours (*a peacock proper*). **7** *archaic* (of a person) handsome; comely. **8** (usu. with possessive pronoun) *archaic* own (*with my proper eyes*). ● *adv. Brit. dial.* or *colloq.* **1** completely;

very (*felt proper daft*). **2** (with reference to speech) in a genteel manner (*learn to talk proper*). ● *n. Eccl.* the part of a service that varies with the season or feast. □ **proper fraction** a fraction that is less than unity, with the numerator less than the denominator. **proper motion** *Astron.* the part of the apparent motion of a fixed star etc. that is due to its actual movement in space relative to the sun. **proper noun** (or **name**) *Gram.* a name used for an individual person, place, animal, country, title, etc., and spelt with a capital letter, e.g. Jane, London, Everest. **proper psalms** (or **lessons** etc.) psalms or lessons etc. appointed for a particular day. □□ **properness** *n.* [ME f. OF *propre* f. L *proprius* one's own, special]

■ *adj.* **1 a** correct, accurate, exact, right, precise, orthodox, formal, accepted, established. **b** fitting, suitable, correct, right, appropriate, apt, fit, apposite, *archaic* meet. **2** decorous, dignified, genteel, decent, seemly, correct, *comme il faut*; gentlemanly, ladylike, polite, refined, punctilious, respectable, formal. **3** belonging, relating, own, individual, separate, distinct, correct, specific, special, particular, respective; characteristic, distinctive, peculiar, singular, unique; see also DUE *adj.* 2, 3. **4** see REAL[1] *adj.* 2. **5** complete, perfect, utter, thorough, thoroughgoing, out-and-out, unmitigated, absolute. **7** see BEAUTIFUL 1. **8** (very) own, personal, individual; private. ● *adv.* **1** see VERY *adv.* **2** genteelly, nicely, well, politely, respectably, correctly, fittingly.

properly /próppərli/ *adv.* **1** fittingly; suitably (*do it properly*). **2** accurately; correctly (*properly speaking*). **3** rightly (*he very properly refused*). **4** with decency; respectably (*behave properly*). **5** *colloq.* thoroughly (*they were properly ashamed*).

■ **1** fittingly, duly, appropriately, well, suitably, rightly, correctly, aptly. **2** correctly, accurately, precisely, exactly, strictly, technically. **4** politely, decently, decorously, nicely, respectably, courteously, with decorum, genteelly, fittingly, correctly, well, becomingly. **5** see *thoroughly* (THOROUGH).

propertied /própportid/ *adj.* having property, esp. land.

property /própporti/ *n.* (*pl.* **-ies**) **1 a** something owned; a possession, esp. a house, land, etc. **b** *Law* the right to possession, use, etc. **c** possessions collectively, esp. real estate (*has money in property*). **2** an attribute, quality, or characteristic (*has the property of dissolving grease*). **3** a moveable object used on a theatre stage, in a film, etc. **4** *Logic* a quality common to a whole class but not necessary to distinguish it from others. □ **common property** a thing known by most people. **property man** (or **mistress**) a man (or woman) in charge of theatrical properties. **property qualification** a qualification for office, or for the exercise of a right, based on the possession of property. **property tax** a tax levied directly on property. [ME through AF f. OF *propriété* f. L *proprietas -tatis* (as PROPER)]

■ **1 c** land, acreage, ground(s), *Law* real estate, realty; see also ESTATE 3. **2** characteristic, attribute, quality, feature, trait, mark, hallmark.

prophase /prṓfayz/ *n. Biol.* the phase in cell division in which chromosomes contract and each becomes visible as two chromatids. [PRO-[2] + PHASE]

prophecy /próffisi/ *n.* (*pl.* **-ies**) **1 a** a prophetic utterance, esp. Biblical. **b** a prediction of future events (*a prophecy of massive inflation*). **2** the faculty, function, or practice of prophesying (*the gift of prophecy*). [ME f. OF *profecie* f. LL *prophetia* f. Gk *prophēteia* (as PROPHET)]

■ **1 b** see FORECAST *n.* **2** prediction, fortune-telling, divination, soothsaying, augury, prognostication, crystal-gazing, *formal* vaticination.

prophesy /próffisī/ *v.* (**-ies, -ied**) **1** *tr.* (usu. foll. by *that, who*, etc.) foretell (an event etc.). **2** *intr.* speak as a prophet; foretell future events. **3** *intr. archaic* expound the Scriptures. □□ **prophesier** /-sīər/ *n.* [ME f. OF *profecier* (as PROPHECY)]

■ **1** predict, foretell, forecast, forewarn, prognosticate, *formal* vaticinate; augur, presage, foreshadow, portend, bode, harbinger, herald, promise.

prophet /próffit/ *n.* (*fem.* **prophetess** /-tiss/) **1** a teacher or interpreter of the supposed will of God, esp. any of the Old Testament or Hebrew prophets. **2 a** a person who foretells events. **b** a person who advocates and speaks innovatively for a cause (*a prophet of the new order*). **3** (**the Prophet**) **a** Muhammad. **b** Joseph Smith, founder of the Mormons, or one of his successors. **c** (in *pl.*) the prophetic writings of the Old Testament. **4** *colloq.* a tipster. □□ **prophethood** *n.* **prophetism** *n.* **prophetship** *n.* [ME f. OF *prophete* f. L *propheta, prophetes* f. Gk *prophētēs* spokesman (as PRO-[2], *phētēs* speaker f. *phēmi* speak)]

■ **2 a** prophesier, oracle, forecaster, seer, soothsayer, clairvoyant, prognosticator, fortune-teller, augur, diviner, haruspex; sibyl, *formal* vaticinator; (*prophet of doom*) Cassandra, Calamity Jane. **b** see ADVOCATE *n.* 1. **4** tipster, *US* tout, touter.

prophetic /prəféttik/ *adj.* **1** (often foll. by *of*) containing a prediction; predicting. **2** of or concerning a prophet. □□ **prophetical** *adj.* **prophetically** *adv.* **propheticism** /-tisiz'm/ *n.* [F *prophétique* or LL *propheticus* f. Gk *prophētikos* (as PROPHET)]

■ **1** prophetical, predictive, prognostic, divinatory, oracular, inspired, prescient, sibylline, apocalyptic, revelatory, fateful, *formal* vatic.

prophylactic /próffiláktik/ *adj.* & *n.* ● *adj.* tending to prevent disease. ● *n.* **1** a preventive medicine or course of action. **2** esp. *US* a condom. [F *prophylactique* f. Gk *prophulaktikos* f. *prophulassō* (as PRO-[2], *phulassō* guard)]

■ *adj.* see PREVENTIVE *adj.* ● *n.* **1** see PREVENTIVE *n.* **2** condom, sheath, *propr.* Durex, *colloq.* rubber, *Brit. colloq.* French letter.

prophylaxis /próffiláksiss/ *n.* (*pl.* **prophylaxes** /-seez/) preventive treatment against disease. [mod.L f. PRO-[2] + Gk *phulaxis* act of guarding]

propinquity /prəpíngkwiti/ *n.* **1** nearness in space; proximity. **2** close kinship. **3** similarity. [ME f. OF *propinquité* or L *propinquitas* f. *propinquus* near f. *prope* near to]

■ **1** see PROXIMITY. **3** see LIKENESS 1.

propionic acid /prṓpiónnik/ *n.* a colourless sharp-smelling liquid carboxylic acid used for inhibiting the growth of mould in bread. ¶ Chem. formula: C_2H_5COOH. Also called PROPANOIC ACID. □□ **propionate** /prṓpiənayt/ *n.* [F *propionique*, formed as PRO-[2] + Gk *piōn* fat, as being the first in the series of 'true' fatty acids]

propitiate /prəpíshiayt/ *v.tr.* appease (an offended person etc.). □□ **propitiator** *n.* [L *propitiare* (as PROPITIOUS)]

■ make amends to, placate, answer, compensate; see also HUMOUR *v.* □□ **propitiator** see PEACEMAKER.

propitiation /prəpíshiáysh'n/ *n.* **1** appeasement. **2** *Bibl.* atonement, esp. Christ's. **3** *archaic* a gift etc. meant to propitiate. [ME f. LL *propitiatio* (as PROPITIATE)]

■ **1, 2** see ATONEMENT.

propitiatory /prəpíshiətəri, -tri/ *adj.* serving or intended to propitiate (*a propitiatory smile*). □□ **propitiatorily** *adv.* [ME f. LL *propitiatorius* (as PROPITIATE)]

■ conciliatory, pacifying, appeasing, expiatory, placative, pacificatory, placatory, propitiative.

propitious /prəpíshəss/ *adj.* **1** (of an omen etc.) favourable. **2** (often foll. by *for, to*) (of the weather, an occasion, etc.) suitable. **3** well-disposed (*the fates were propitious*). □□ **propitiously** *adv.* **propitiousness** *n.* [ME f. OF *propicieus* or L *propitius*]

■ **1** favourable, auspicious, promising, advantageous, lucky, fortunate, happy, providential, bright, encouraging, rosy. **2** suitable, apt, fitting, timely, well-timed; fair, favourable, auspicious, benign; see also OPPORTUNE 2. **3** see FAVOURABLE 1a, 3.

propolis /próppəliss/ *n.* a red or brown resinous substance collected by bees from buds for use in constructing hives. [L f. Gk *propolis* suburb, bee-glue, f. PRO-[2] + *polis* city]

proponent /prəpṓnənt/ *n.* & *adj.* ● *n.* a person advocating a motion, theory, or proposal. ● *adj.* proposing or advocating a theory etc. [L *proponere* (as PROPOUND)]

■ *n.* proposer, promoter, supporter, upholder, backer, subscriber, patron, espouser, adherent, enthusiast, champion, friend, partisan, defender, advocate, exponent, pleader, apologist, spokesman, spokeswoman, spokesperson.

proportion /prəpórsh'n/ *n.* & *v.* ● *n.* **1 a** a comparative part or share (*a large proportion of the profits*). **b** a comparative ratio (*the proportion of births to deaths*). **2** the correct or pleasing relation of things or parts of a thing (*the house has fine proportions; exaggerated out of all proportion*). **3** (in *pl.*) dimensions; size (*large proportions*). **4** *Math.* **a** an equality of ratios between two pairs of quantities, e.g. 3:5 and 9:15. **b** a set of such quantities. **c** *Math.* = *rule of three*; see also *direct proportion, inverse proportion.* ● *v.tr.* (usu. foll. by *to*) make (a thing etc.) proportionate (*must proportion the punishment to the crime*). □ **in proportion 1** by the same factor. **2** without exaggerating (importance etc.) (*must get the facts in proportion*). □□ **proportioned** *adj.* (also in *comb.*). **proportionless** *adj.* **proportionment** *n.* [ME f. OF *proportion* or L *proportio* (as PRO-[1], PORTION)]

■ *n.* **1 a** portion, division, share, part, percentage, quota, ration, *colloq.* cut. **b** ratio, relation, relationship, comparison, correlation. **2** balance, agreement, concord, harmony, symmetry, congruity, correspondence, correlation, arrangement. **3** (*proportions*) size, magnitude, dimensions, measurements, extent; volume, capacity, mass, bulk, expanse, scope, range. ● *v.* adjust, modify, change, modulate, poise, balance, shape, fit, match, conform.

proportionable /prəpórshənəb'l/ *adj.* = PROPORTIONAL. □□ **proportionably** *adv.*

proportional /prəpórshən'l/ *adj.* & *n.* ● *adj.* in due proportion; comparable (*a proportional increase in the expense; resentment proportional to his injuries*). ● *n. Math.* each of the terms of a proportion. □ **proportional representation** an electoral system in which all parties gain seats in proportion to the number of votes cast for them. □□ **proportionality** /-nálliti/ *n.* **proportionally** *adv.*

■ *adj.* proportionate, proportioned, comparable, analogous, analogical, relative, related, correlated, corresponding, compatible, harmonious, consistent, commensurate, in accordance with; balanced, symmetrical.

proportionalist /prəpórshənəlist/ *n.* an advocate of proportional representation.

proportionate /prəpórshənət/ *adj.* = PROPORTIONAL. □□ **proportionately** *adv.*

proposal /prəpṓz'l/ *n.* **1 a** the act or an instance of proposing something. **b** a course of action etc. so proposed (*the proposal was never carried out*). **2** an offer of marriage.

■ **1** offer, presentation, bid, tender, motion, overture, proposition, programme, project, suggestion, recommendation, *literary* proffer; plan, scheme, draft, layout.

propose /prəpṓz/ *v.* **1** *tr.* (also *absol.*) put forward for consideration or as a plan. **2** *tr.* (usu. foll. by *to* + infin., or verbal noun) intend; purpose (*propose to open a restaurant*). **3** *intr.* (usu. foll. by *to*) offer oneself in marriage. **4** *tr.* nominate (a person) as a member of a society, for an office, etc. **5** *tr.* offer (a person's health, a person, etc.) as a subject for a toast. □□ **proposer** *n.* [ME f. OF *proposer* f. L *proponere* (as PROPOUND)]

■ **1** offer, tender, proffer; submit, advance, set forth, put forward, propound, recommend, suggest, come up with; table. **2** mean, intend, plan, resolve, have a mind, expect, aim; purpose. **3** ask for a person's hand (in marriage), *colloq.* pop the question. **4** see NOMINATE.

proposition /próppəzísh'n/ *n.* & *v.* ● *n.* **1** a statement or assertion. **2** a scheme proposed; a proposal. **3** *Logic* a statement consisting of subject and predicate that is subject to proof or disproof. **4** *colloq.* a problem, opponent, prospect, etc. that is to be dealt with (*a difficult proposition*). **5** *Math.* a formal statement of a theorem or problem, often including the demonstration. **6 a** an enterprise etc. with regard to its likelihood of commercial etc. success. **b** a person regarded similarly. **7** *colloq.* a sexual proposal. ● *v.tr. colloq.* make a proposal (esp. of sexual intercourse) to (*he propositioned her*). □ **not a proposition** unlikely to succeed. □□ **propositional** *adj.* [ME f. OF *proposition* or L *propositio* (as PROPOUND)]

■ *n.* **1** see STATEMENT 1–3. **2** see SCHEME *n.* 1a. **4** see PROBLEM 1, 2. ● *v.* accost, solicit, make advances *or* overtures to, make a proposition to, *colloq.* make a pass at.

propound /prəpównd/ *v.tr.* **1** offer for consideration; propose. **2** *Law* produce (a will etc.) before the proper authority so as to establish its legality. □□ **propounder** *n.* [earlier *propoune, propone* f. L *proponere* (as PRO-[1], *ponere posit-* place): cf. *compound, expound*]

■ **1** put forward, set forth, propose, offer, proffer, suggest, submit, table.

proprietary /prəprī́ətəri, -tri/ *adj.* **1 a** of, holding, or concerning property (*the proprietary classes*). **b** of or relating to a proprietor (*proprietary rights*). **2** held in private ownership. □ **proprietary medicine** any of several drugs, medicines, etc. produced by private companies under brand names. **proprietary name** (or **term**) a name of a product etc. registered by its owner as a trade mark and not usable by another without permission. [LL *proprietarius* (as PROPERTY)]

proprietor /prəprī́ətər/ *n.* (*fem.* **proprietress**) **1** a holder of property. **2** the owner of a business etc., esp. of a hotel. □□ **proprietorial** /-tóriəl/ *adj.* **proprietorially** /-tóriəli/ *adv.* **proprietorship** *n.*

■ **1** owner, landowner, landlady, landlord, landholder, property owner. **2** owner, landlord, landlady, innkeeper, hotel-keeper, hotelier, manager.

propriety /prəprī́-iti/ *n.* (*pl.* **-ies**) **1** fitness; rightness (*doubt the propriety of refusing him*). **2** correctness of behaviour or morals (*highest standards of propriety*). **3** (in *pl.*) the details or rules of correct conduct (*must observe the proprieties*). [ME, = ownership, peculiarity f. OF *propriété* PROPERTY]

■ **1** correctness, properness, rightness, appropriateness, fitness, seemliness, decorum; advisability, wisdom. **2** decorum, politeness, courtesy, *politesse*, refinement, sedateness, dignity, decency, breeding, respectability, gentility, grace, mannerliness. **3** (*proprieties*) protocol, good *or* proper form, punctilio, etiquette, social graces, civilities, formality *or* formalities, social convention(s) *or* niceties, *convenances*, tradition.

proprioceptive /prṓpriəséptiv/ *adj.* relating to stimuli produced and perceived within an organism, esp. relating to the position and movement of the body. [L *proprius* own + RECEPTIVE]

proptosis /proptṓsiss/ *n. Med.* protrusion or displacement, esp. of an eye. [LL f. Gk *proptōsis* (as PRO-[2], *piptō* fall)]

propulsion /prəpúlsh'n/ *n.* **1** the act or an instance of driving or pushing forward. **2** an impelling influence. □□ **propulsive** /-púlsiv/ *adj.* [med.L *propulsio* f. L *propellere* (as PROPEL)]

■ **2** drive, impulse, impetus, thrust, power, driving force, momentum, push.

propyl /prṓpil/ *n. Chem.* the univalent radical of propane. ¶ Chem. formula: C_3H_7-. [PROPIONIC (ACID) + -YL]

propyla *pl.* of PROPYLON.

propylaeum /próppilééəm/ *n.* (*pl.* **propylaea** /-lééə/) **1** the entrance to a temple. **2** (**the Propylaeum**) the entrance to the Acropolis at Athens. [L f. Gk *propulaion* (as PRO-[2], *pulē* gate)]

propylene /prṓpileen/ *n. Chem.* a gaseous hydrocarbon of the alkene series used in the manufacture of chemicals. ¶ Chem. formula: C_3H_6.

propylon /próppilon/ *n.* (*pl.* **propylons** or **propyla** /-lə/) = PROPYLAEUM. [L f. Gk *propulon* (as PRO-[2], *pulē* gate)]

pro rata /prō raátə, ráytə/ *adj.* & *adv.* ● *adj.* proportional. ● *adv.* proportionally. [L, = according to the rate]

prorate /pró-ráyt/ *v.tr.* allocate or distribute *pro rata.* □□ **proration** *n.*

prorogue /prərṓg/ *v.* (**prorogues, prorogued, proroguing**) **1** *tr.* discontinue the meetings of (a parliament

etc.) without dissolving it. **2** *intr.* (of a parliament etc.) be prorogued. □□ **prorogation** /prṓrəgáysh'n/ *n.* [ME *proroge* f. OF *proroger, -guer* f. L *prorogare* prolong (as PRO-[1], *rogare* ask)]
■ **1** see SUSPEND 2.

pros- /pross/ *prefix* **1** to, towards. **2** in addition. [Gk f. *pros* (prep.)]

prosaic /prəzáyik/ *adj.* **1** like prose, lacking poetic beauty. **2** unromantic; dull; commonplace (*took a prosaic view of life*). □□ **prosaically** *adv.* **prosaicness** *n.* [F *prosaïque* or LL *prosaicus* (as PROSE)]
■ **2** dull, banal, tedious, prosy, commonplace, pedestrian, flat, routine, everyday, ordinary, common, workaday, mediocre, undistinguished, bland, characterless, plain, trite, tired, lifeless, dead, dry, jejune, boring, tiresome, unimaginative, unpoetic, unromantic, uninspiring, uninspired, insipid, uninteresting, humdrum, monotonous, run-of-the-mill, *colloq.* ho-hum, mouldy.

prosaist /prṓzayist/ *n.* **1** a prose-writer. **2** a prosaic person. □□ **prosaism** *n.* [F *prosaïste* f. L *prosa* PROSE]

proscenium /prəséeniəm/ *n.* (*pl.* **prosceniums** or **proscenia** /-niə/) **1** the part of the stage in front of the drop or curtain, usu. with the enclosing arch. **2** the stage of an ancient theatre. [L f. Gk *proskēnion* (as PRO-[2], *skēnē* stage)]

prosciutto /prōshóotō/ *n.* (*pl.* **-os**) Italian ham, esp. cured and eaten as an hors-d'œuvre. [It.]

proscribe /prəskrī́b/ *v.tr.* **1** banish, exile (*proscribed from the club*). **2** put (a person) outside the protection of the law. **3** reject or denounce (a practice etc.) as dangerous etc. □□ **proscription** /-skrípsh'n/ *n.* **proscriptive** /-skríptiv/ *adj.* [L *proscribere* (as PRO-[1], *scribere script-* write)]
■ **1** see EXPEL 1–3. **3** see FORBID 2. □□ **proscription** see PROHIBITION.

prose /prōz/ *n.* & *v.* ● *n.* **1** the ordinary form of the written or spoken language (opp. POETRY, VERSE) (*Milton's prose works*). **2** a passage of prose, esp. for translation into a foreign language. **3** a tedious speech or conversation. **4** a plain matter-of-fact quality (*the prose of existence*). **5** *Eccl.* = SEQUENCE 8. ● *v.* **1** *intr.* (usu. foll. by *about, away*, etc.) talk tediously (*was prosing away about his dog*). **2** *tr.* turn (a poem etc.) into prose. □ **prose idyll** a short description in prose of a picturesque, esp. rustic, incident, character, etc. **prose poem** (or **poetry**) a piece of imaginative poetic writing in prose. □□ **proser** *n.* [ME f. OF f. L *prosa* (*oratio*) straightforward (discourse), fem. of *prosus*, earlier *prorsus* direct]
■ *v.* **1** see SPOUT *v.* 2. **2** prosify.

prosector /prəséktər/ *n.* a person who dissects dead bodies in preparation for an anatomical lecture etc. [LL = anatomist, f. *prosecare prosect-* (as PRO-[1], *secare* cut), perh. after F *prosecteur*]

prosecute /próssikyoot/ *v.tr.* **1** (also *absol.*) **a** institute legal proceedings against (a person). **b** institute a prosecution with reference to (a claim, crime, etc.) (*decided not to prosecute*). **2** follow up, pursue (an inquiry, studies, etc.). **3** carry on (a trade, pursuit, etc.). □□ **prosecutable** *adj.* [ME f. L *prosequi prosecut-* (as PRO-[1], *sequi* follow)]
■ **1 a** arraign, indict, charge, put on trial, bring to trial, try, take to court, sue, bring suit *or* action against, put in the dock. **2** pursue, follow up *or* through, see *or* carry through, persist with, go on with. **3** carry on *or* out, perform, do, conduct, follow, engage in, practise, continue.

prosecution /próssikyóosh'n/ *n.* **1 a** the institution and carrying on of a criminal charge in a court. **b** the carrying on of legal proceedings against a person. **c** the prosecuting party in a court case (*the prosecution denied this*). **2** the act or an instance of prosecuting (*met her in the prosecution of his hobby*). [OF *prosecution* or LL *prosecutio* (as PROSECUTE)]
■ **2** see EXECUTION 2.

prosecutor /próssikyootər/ *n.* (*fem.* **prosecutrix** /-triks/) a person who prosecutes, esp. in a criminal court. □□ **prosecutorial** /-tóriəl/ *adj.*

proselyte /próssilīt/ *n.* & *v.* ● *n.* **1** a person converted, esp. recently, from one opinion, creed, party, etc., to another. **2** a Gentile convert to Judaism. ● *v.tr.* *US* = PROSELYTIZE. □□ **proselytism** /-litiz'm/ *n.* [ME f. LL *proselytus* f. Gk *prosēluthos* stranger, convert (as PROS-, stem *ēluth-* of *erkhomai* come)]
■ *n.* convert, neophyte.

proselytize /próssilitīz/ *v.tr.* (also **-ise**) (also *absol.*) convert (a person or people) from one belief etc. to another, esp. habitually. □□ **proselytizer** *n.*
■ □□ **proselytizer** see MISSIONARY *n.*

prosenchyma /proséngkimə/ *n.* a plant tissue of elongated cells with interpenetrating tapering ends, occurring esp. in vascular tissue. □□ **prosenchymal** *adj.* **prosenchymatous** /-kímmətəss/ *adj.* [Gk *pros* toward + *egkhuma* infusion, after *parenchyma*]

prosify /prṓzifī/ *v.* (**-ies, -ied**) **1** *tr.* turn into prose. **2** *tr.* make prosaic. **3** *intr.* write prose.

prosit /prṓzit/ *int.* an expression used in drinking a person's health etc. [G f. L, = may it benefit]

prosody /próssədi/ *n.* **1** the theory and practice of versification; the laws of metre. **2** the study of speech-rhythms. □□ **prosodic** /prəsóddik/ *adj.* **prosodist** *n.* [ME f. L *prosodia* accent f. Gk *prosōidia* (as PROS-, ODE)]

prosopography /próssəpógrəfi/ *n.* (*pl.* **-ies**) **1** a description of a person's appearance, personality, social and family connections, career, etc. **2** the study of such descriptions, esp. in Roman history. □□ **prosopographer** *n.* **prosopographic** /-pəgráffik/ *adj.* **prosopographical** /-pəgráffik'l/ *adj.* [mod.L *prosopographia* f. Gk *prosōpon* face, person]
■ **1** see RÉSUMÉ 2, PROFILE *n.* 2a.

prosopopoeia /próssəpəpéeə/ *n.* the rhetorical introduction of a pretended speaker or the personification of an abstract thing. [L f. Gk *prosōpopoiia* f. *prosōpon* person + *poieō* make]

prospect *n.* & *v.* ● *n.* /próspekt/ **1 a** (often in *pl.*) an expectation, esp. of success in a career etc. (*his prospects were brilliant; offers a gloomy prospect; no prospect of success*). **b** something one has to look forward to (*don't relish the prospect of meeting him*). **2** an extensive view of landscape etc. (*a striking prospect*). **3** a mental picture (*a new prospect in his mind*). **4 a** a place likely to yield mineral deposits. **b** a sample of ore for testing. **c** the resulting yield. **5** a possible or probable customer, subscriber, etc. ● *v.* /prəspékt/ **1** *intr.* (usu. foll. by *for*) **a** explore a region for gold etc. **b** look out for or search for something. **2** *tr.* **a** explore (a region) for gold etc. **b** work (a mine) experimentally. **c** (of a mine) promise (a specified yield). □ **in prospect 1** in sight, within view. **2** within the range of expectation, likely. **prospect well** (or **ill** etc.) (of a mine) promise well (or ill etc.). □□ **prospectless** *adj.* **prospector** /prəspéktər/ *n.* [ME f. L *prospectus*: see PROSPECTUS]
■ *n.* **1 a** (*prospects*) expectation(s); future, outlook, chances, hopes, possibilities, opportunities. **2** view, scene, panorama, landscape, vista, sight, spectacle. ● *v.* **1** (*prospect for*) search for, look for, seek, quest after *or* for, pursue, hunt (for), try to find, be after. □ **in prospect** in *or* within sight *or* view, in the offing, on the horizon, in store, in the wind, projected, likely, probable, possible, *Brit.* on the cards, on the table, *US* in the cards.

prospective /prəspéktiv/ *adj.* **1** concerned with or applying to the future (*implies a prospective obligation*) (cf. RETROSPECTIVE). **2** some day to be; expected; future (*prospective bridegroom*). □□ **prospectively** *adv.* **prospectiveness** *n.* [obs. F *prospectif -ive* or LL *prospectivus* (as PROSPECTUS)]
■ **2** expected, future, forthcoming, coming, approaching, imminent, nearing, pending, impending, destined, incipient, -to-be, *disp.* anticipated.

prospectus /prəspéktəss/ *n.* a printed document advertising or describing a school, commercial enterprise, forthcoming book, etc. [L, = prospect f. *prospicere* (as PRO-[1], *specere* look)]

▪ brochure, pamphlet, booklet, leaflet; *US* catalog.

prosper /próspər/ *v.* **1** *intr.* succeed; thrive (*nothing he touches prospers*). **2** *tr.* make successful (*Heaven prosper him*). [ME f. OF *prosperer* or L *prosperare* (as PROSPEROUS)]

▪ **1** flourish, thrive, succeed, progress, get ahead, grow, develop, *literary* fare well; profit, gain, become wealthy, grow rich, make one's fortune, make good, *colloq.* make it, make one's pile.

prosperity /prospérriti/ *n.* a state of being prosperous; wealth or success.

▪ success, (good) fortune, wealth, riches, affluence, money, plenty, prosperousness, opulence, bounty, *literary* weal.

prosperous /próspərəss/ *adj.* **1** successful; rich (*a prosperous merchant*). **2** flourishing; thriving (*a prosperous enterprise*). **3** auspicious (*a prosperous wind*). ▫▫ **prosperously** *adv.* **prosperousness** *n.* [ME f. obs. F *prospereus* f. L *prosper(us)*]

▪ **1** rich, wealthy, moneyed, affluent, well-to-do, well off, *colloq.* well-heeled, flush, *sl.* loaded; successful, fortunate, halcyon; (*be prosperous*) be in clover, be on velvet, *colloq.* be rolling (in it *or* money), be in the money, be on Easy Street. **2** thriving, flourishing, booming, prospering, thrifty; see also SUCCESSFUL. **3** see BENIGN 2, 3.

prostaglandin /próstəglándin/ *n.* any of a group of hormone-like substances causing contraction of the muscles in mammalian (esp. uterine) tissues etc. [G f. PROSTATE + GLAND[1] + -IN]

prostate /próstayt/ *n.* (in full **prostate gland**) a gland surrounding the neck of the bladder in male mammals and releasing a fluid forming part of the semen. ▫▫ **prostatic** /-státtik/ *adj.* [F f. mod.L *prostata* f. Gk *prostatēs* one that stands before (as PRO-[2], *statos* standing)]

prosthesis /próss-thisiss, -theéssiss/ *n.* (*pl.* **prostheses** /-seez/) **1 a** an artificial part supplied to remedy a deficiency, e.g. a false breast, leg, tooth, etc. **b** the branch of surgery supplying and fitting prostheses. **2** *Gram.* the addition of a letter or syllable at the beginning of a word, e.g. *be-* in *beloved*. ▫▫ **prosthetic** /-théttik/ *adj.* **prosthetically** /-théttikəli/ *adv.* [LL f. Gk *prosthesis* f. *prostithēmi* (as PROS-, *tithēmi* place)]

prosthetics /pross-théttiks/ *n.pl.* (usu. treated as *sing.*) = PROSTHESIS 1b.

prostitute /próstityoot/ *n.* & *v.* • *n.* **1 a** a woman who engages in sexual activity for payment. **b** (usu. **male prostitute**) a man or boy who engages in sexual activity, esp. with homosexual men, for payment. **2** a person who debases himself or herself for personal gain. • *v.tr.* **1** (esp. *refl.*) make a prostitute of (esp. oneself). **2 a** misuse (one's talents, skills, etc.) for money. **b** offer (oneself, one's honour, etc.) for unworthy ends, esp. for money. ▫▫ **prostitution** /-tyóosh'n/ *n.* **prostitutor** *n.* [L *prostituere prostitut-* offer for sale (as PRO-[1], *statuere* set up, place)]

▪ *n.* **1 a** whore, call-girl, streetwalker, trollop, drab, *fille de joie*, lady of the night, lady of easy virtue, fallen *or* loose woman, *archaic* cocotte, wench, trull, woman of the streets, harlot, *archaic or rhet.* strumpet, *derog.* scarlet woman, *literary* hetaera, courtesan, doxy, *sl.* tart, hustler, pro, moll, hooker, *Austral. sl.* chromo, *US sl.* working girl, *sl.derog.* slag. **b** catamite, rent-boy; gigolo. • *v.* **2 a** misuse, devalue, abuse, corrupt, misemploy, misapply, pervert. **b** degrade, demean, lower, cheapen, debase, defile, discredit, shame, disgrace; see also PROFANE *v.* ▫▫ **prostitution** whoredom, *archaic* harlotry, *colloq. or joc.* the oldest profession; degradation, debasement, profanation, defilement, desecration, misuse, abuse, devaluation, lowering, corruption.

prostrate *adj.* & *v.* • *adj.* /próstrayt/ **1 a** lying face downwards, esp. in submission. **b** lying horizontally. **2** overcome, esp. by grief, exhaustion, etc. (*prostrate with self-pity*). **3** *Bot.* growing along the ground. • *v.tr.* /prostráyt/ **1** lay (a person etc.) flat on the ground. **2** (*refl.*) throw (oneself) down in submission etc. **3** (of fatigue, illness, etc.) overcome; reduce to extreme physical weakness. ▫▫ **prostration** /prostráysh'n/ *n.* [ME f. L *prostratus* past part. of *prosternere* (as PRO-[1], *sternere strat-* lay flat)]

▪ *adj.* **1** prone, horizontal, stretched out, procumbent, recumbent. **2** overwhelmed, overcome, overpowered, crushed, brought *or* laid low, paralysed, brought down, humbled, helpless, powerless, impotent, defenceless, disarmed; exhausted, drained, fatigued, spent, worn out, wearied, weary, tired (out). **3** *Bot.* procumbent, repent, *Bot.* & *Zool.* decumbent. • *v.* **1** see LAY[1] *v.* 1. **2** (*prostrate oneself*) throw oneself down, lie down, kowtow, bow (down), bow and scrape, grovel, kneel, fall to *or* on one's knees, submit. **3** overwhelm, overcome, overpower, crush, lay *or* bring low, paralyse, bring down, make helpless, *colloq.* floor; exhaust, fatigue, weary, wear down *or* out, tire (out). ▫▫ **prostration** submission, servility; weariness, exhaustion, tiredness, weakness, debility, feebleness, enervation, lassitude, paralysis; despair, misery, desolation, desperation, dejection, depression, despondency, wretchedness, unhappiness, grief, woefulness, *archaic or literary* woe.

prostyle /prṓstīl/ *n.* & *adj.* • *n.* a portico with not more than four columns. • *adj.* (of a building) having such a portico. [L *prostylos* having pillars in front (as PRO-[2], STYLE)]

prosy /prṓzi/ *adj.* (**prosier**, **prosiest**) tedious; commonplace; dull (*prosy talk*). ▫▫ **prosily** *adv.* **prosiness** *n.*

▪ see TEDIOUS.

Prot. *abbr.* **1** Protectorate. **2** Protestant.

protactinium /prṓtaktínniəm/ *n. Chem.* a radioactive metallic element whose chief isotope yields actinium by decay. ¶ Symb.: **Pa**. [G (as PROTO-, ACTINIUM)]

protagonist /prōtággənist/ *n.* **1** the chief person in a drama, story, etc. **2** the leading person in a contest etc.; a principal performer. **3** (usu. foll. by *of*, *for*) *disp.* an advocate or champion of a cause, course of action, etc. (*a protagonist of women's rights*). [Gk *prōtagōnistēs* (as PROTO-, *agōnistēs* actor)]

▪ **1, 2** hero, heroine; principal, lead, leading role, title role; (*be the protagonist*) play first fiddle, take the lead. **3** leader, supporter, advocate, prime mover, moving spirit, champion, standard-bearer, exponent.

protamine /prṓtəmeen/ *n.* any of a group of proteins found in association with chromosomal DNA in the sperm of birds and fish. [PROTO- + AMINE]

protasis /próttəsiss/ *n.* (*pl.* **protases** /-seez/) the clause expressing the condition in a conditional sentence. ▫▫ **protatic** /prōtáttik/ *adj.* [L, f. Gk *protasis* proposition (as PRO-[2], *teinō* stretch)]

protea /prṓtiə/ *n.* any shrub of the genus *Protea* native to S. Africa, with conelike flower-heads. [mod.L f. PROTEUS, with ref. to the many species]

protean /prṓtiən, -teéən/ *adj.* **1** variable, taking many forms. **2** (of an artist, writer, etc.) versatile. [after *Proteus*: see PROTEUS]

▪ **1** variable, ever-changing, multiform, changeable, polymorphous, polymorphic, *literary* mutable. **2** see VERSATILE 1.

protease /prṓtiayss/ *n.* any enzyme able to hydrolyse proteins and peptides by proteolysis. [PROTEIN + -ASE]

protect /prətékt/ *v.tr.* **1** (often foll. by *from*, *against*) keep (a person, thing, etc.) safe; defend; guard (*goggles protected her eyes from dust*; *guards protected the queen*). **2** *Econ.* shield (home industry) from competition by imposing import duties on foreign goods. **3** *Brit.* provide funds to meet (a bill, draft, etc.). **4** provide (machinery etc.) with appliances to prevent injury from it. [L *protegere protect-* (as PRO-[1], *tegere* cover)]

▪ **1** defend, guard, safeguard, keep safe, shield, cover, screen; care for, preserve, keep, shelter, watch over, take care of, conserve.

protection /prətéksh'n/ *n.* **1 a** the act or an instance of protecting. **b** the state of being protected; defence (*affords protection against the weather*). **c** a thing, person, or animal that provides protection (*bought a dog as protection*). **2** (also

protectionism /-niz'm/) *Econ.* the theory or practice of protecting home industries. **3** *colloq.* **a** immunity from molestation obtained by payment to gangsters etc. under threat of violence. **b** (in full **protection money**) the money so paid, esp. on a regular basis. **4** = *safe conduct.* **5** *archaic* the keeping of a woman as a mistress. ▫▫ **protectionist** *n.* [ME f. OF *protection* or LL *protectio* (as PROTECT)]
■ **1 a** care, guardianship, custody, charge, safe keeping. **b, c** defence, screen, shield, barrier, aegis, guard, bulwark, buffer, shelter, refuge, haven, sanctuary, tower; security, safety, immunity, preservation. **3 b** see BLACKMAIL *n.* 1.

protective /prətéktiv/ *adj.* & *n.* ● *adj.* **1 a** protecting; intended or intending to protect. **b** (of a person) tending to protect in a possessive way. **2** (of food) protecting against deficiency diseases. ● *n.* something that protects, esp. a condom. ▫ **protective clothing** clothing worn to shield the body from dangerous substances or a hostile environment. **protective colouring** colouring disguising or camouflaging a plant or animal. **protective custody** the detention of a person for his or her own protection. ▫▫ **protectively** *adv.* **protectiveness** *n.*
■ *adj.* **1 a** protecting, preservative, defensive. **b** overprotective, possessive; jealous.

protector /prətéktər/ *n.* (*fem.* **protectress** /-triss/) **1 a** a person who protects. **b** a guardian or patron. **2** *hist.* a regent in charge of a kingdom during the minority, absence, etc. of the sovereign. **3** (often in *comb.*) a thing or device that protects (*chest-protector*). **4** (**Protector**) (in full **Lord Protector of the Commonwealth**) *hist.* the title of Oliver Cromwell 1653–58 and his son Richard Cromwell 1658–59. ▫▫ **protectoral** *adj.* **protectorship** *n.* [ME f. OF *protecteur* f. LL *protector* (as PROTECT)]
■ **1** defender, guardian (angel), champion, knight in shining armour, bodyguard, *sl.* minder; patron.

protectorate /prətéktərət/ *n.* **1 a** a State that is controlled and protected by another. **b** such a relation of one State to another. **2** *hist.* **a** the office of the protector of a kingdom or State. **b** the period of this, esp. in England under the Cromwells 1653–59.

protégé /próttizhay, prṓ-/ *n.* (*fem.* **protégée** *pronunc.* same) a person under the protection, patronage, tutelage, etc. of another. [F, past part. of *protéger* f. L *protegere* PROTECT]
■ ward, charge, dependant, fosterling; student, pupil.

protein /prṓteen/ *n.* any of a group of organic compounds composed of one or more chains of amino acids and forming an essential part of all living organisms. ▫▫ **proteinaceous** /-teenáyshəss/ *adj.* **proteinic** /-téenik/ *adj.* **proteinous** /-téenəss, -tée-inəss/ *adj.* [F *protéine*, G *Protein* f. Gk *prōteios* primary]

pro tem /prō tém/ *adj.* & *adv. colloq.* = PRO TEMPORE. [abbr.]

pro tempore /prō témpəri/ *adj.* & *adv.* for the time being. [L]
■ *adj.* see TEMPORARY *adj.* ● *adv.* see *temporarily* (TEMPORARY).

proteolysis /prōtióllisiss/ *n.* the splitting of proteins or peptides by the action of enzymes esp. during the process of digestion. ▫▫ **proteolytic** /-tiəlíttik/ *adj.* [mod.L f. PROTEIN + -LYSIS]

Proterozoic /prṓtərōzṓ-ik/ *adj.* & *n. Geol.* ● *adj.* of or relating to the later part of the Precambrian era, characterized by the oldest forms of life. ● *n.* this time. [Gk *proteros* former + *zōē* life, *zōos* living]

protest *n.* & *v.* ● *n.* /prṓtest/ **1** a statement of dissent or disapproval; a remonstrance (*made a protest*). **2** (often *attrib.*) a usu. public demonstration of objection to government etc. policy (*marched in protest; protest demonstration*). **3** a solemn declaration. **4** *Law* a written declaration, usu. by a notary public, that a bill has been presented and payment or acceptance refused. ● *v.* /prətést/ **1** *intr.* (usu. foll. by *against, at, about,* etc.) make a protest against an action, proposal, etc. **2** *tr.* (often foll. by *that* + clause; also *absol.*) affirm (one's innocence etc.) solemnly, esp. in reply to an accusation etc. **3** *tr. Law* write or obtain a protest in regard to (a bill). **4** *tr. US* object to (a decision etc.). ▫ **under protest** unwillingly. ▫▫ **protester** *n.* **protestingly** *adv.* **protestor** *n.* [ME f. OF *protest* (n.), *protester* (v.), f. L *protestari* (as PRO-[1], *testari* assert f. *testis* witness)]
■ *n.* **1** remonstrance, objection, complaint, outcry, clamour, grumble, squawk, fuss, grievance, protestation, demur, demurral, expostulation, *Law* demurrer, *colloq.* gripe, grouse, *sl.* beef. **3** see ASSERTION 1, 2. ● *v.* **1** object, complain, grumble, dissent, demur, demonstrate, expostulate, remonstrate, declaim, rebel, make a fuss, make *or* kick up a row, *colloq.* gripe, grouse, *sl.* beef, squeal; (*protest at* or *against* or *about*) kick against, take issue with. **2** assert, declare, asseverate, affirm, announce, profess, insist on, *archaic or rhet.* avouch, *formal* aver. ▫ **under protest** unwillingly, reluctantly, involuntarily, begrudgingly, grudgingly, without good grace, against one's better judgement; under duress.

Protestant /próttistənt/ *n.* & *adj.* ● *n.* **1** a member or follower of any of the western Christian Churches that are separate from the Roman Catholic Church in accordance with the principles of the Reformation. **2** (**protestant**) /also prətéstənt/ a protesting person. ● *adj.* **1** of or relating to any of the Protestant Churches or their members etc. **2** (**protestant**) /also prətéstənt/ protesting. ▫▫ **Protestantism** *n.* **Protestantize** *v.tr.* & *intr.* (also **-ise**). [mod.L *protestans*, part. of L *protestari* (see PROTEST)]

protestation /próttistáysh'n/ *n.* **1** a strong affirmation. **2** a protest. [ME f. OF *protestation* or LL *protestatio* (as PROTESTANT)]
■ **1** see ASSERTION 1, 2. **2** see PROTEST *n.* 1.

Proteus /prṓtiəss, -tyōōss/ *n.* **1** a changing or inconstant person or thing. **2** (**proteus**) **a** any bacterium of the genus *Proteus*, usu. found in the intestines and faeces of animals. **b** = OLM. [L f. Gk *Prōteus* a sea-god able to take various forms at will]

prothalamium /prṓthəláymiəm/ *n.* (also **prothalamion** /-miən/) (*pl.* **prothalamia** /-miə/) a song or poem to celebrate a forthcoming wedding. [title of a poem by Spenser, after *epithalamium*]

prothallium /prōthálliəm/ *n.* (*pl.* **prothallia** /-liə/) = PROTHALLUS. [mod.L f. PRO-[2] + Gk *thallion* dimin. of *thallos*: see PROTHALLUS]

prothallus /prōthálləss/ *n.* (*pl.* **prothalli** /-lī/) *Bot.* the gametophyte of certain plants, esp. a fern. [mod.L f. PRO-[2] + Gk *thallos* green shoot]

prothesis /próthisiss/ *n.* (*pl.* **protheses** /-seez/) **1** *Eccl.* **a** the placing of the Eucharistic elements on the credence table. **b** a credence table. **c** the part of a church where this stands. **2** *Gram.* = PROSTHESIS 2. ▫▫ **prothetic** /prəthéttik/ *adj.* [Gk f. *protithēmi* (as PRO-[2], *tithēmi* place)]

prothonotary var. of PROTONOTARY.

protist /prṓtist/ *n.* any usu. unicellular organism of the kingdom Protista, with both plant and animal characteristics, including bacteria, algae, and protozoa. ▫▫ **protistology** /-tistólləji/ *n.* [mod.L *Protista* f. Gk *prōtista* neut. pl. superl. f. *prōtos* first]

protium /prṓtiəm/ *n.* the ordinary isotope of hydrogen as distinct from heavy hydrogen (cf. DEUTERIUM, TRITIUM). [mod.L f. PROTO- + -IUM]

proto- /prṓtō/ *comb. form* **1** original, primitive (*proto-Germanic; proto-Slavic*). **2** first, original (*protomartyr; protophyte*). [Gk *prōto-* f. *prōtos* first]

protocol /prṓtəkol/ *n.* & *v.* ● *n.* **1 a** official, esp. diplomatic, formality and etiquette observed on State occasions etc. **b** the rules, formalities, etc. of any procedure, group, etc. **2** the original draft of a diplomatic document, esp. of the terms of a treaty agreed to in conference and signed by the parties. **3** a formal statement of a transaction. **4** the official formulae at the beginning and end of a charter, papal bull, etc. **5** *US* a record of experimental observations etc. ● *v.* (**protocolled, protocolling**) **1** *intr.* draw up a protocol or protocols. **2** *tr.* record in a protocol. [orig. Sc. *prothocoll* f. OF *prothocole* f. med.L *protocollum* f. Gk *protokollon* flyleaf (as PROTO-, *kolla* glue)]

■ *n.* **1** rule(s) *or* code(s) *or* standard(s) of behaviour, conventions, customs, formality, form, etiquette, *politesse*, manners, practice, usage. **2** draft, outline.

protomartyr /prṓtōmaártər/ *n.* the first martyr in any cause, esp. the first Christian martyr St Stephen.

proton /prṓton/ *n. Physics* a stable elementary particle with a positive electric charge, equal in magnitude to that of an electron, and occurring in all atomic nuclei. □□ **protonic** /prətónnik/ *adj.* [Gk, neut. of *prōtos* first]

protonotary /prṓtənṓtəri, prətónnə-/ *n.* (*pl.* **-ies**) (also **prothonotary** /prṓthō-, prəthónnə-/) a chief clerk in some law courts, orig. in the Byzantine court. □ **Protonotary Apostolic** (or **Apostolical**) a member of the college of prelates who register papal acts, direct the canonization of saints, etc. [med.L *protonotarius* f. late Gk *protonotarios* (as PROTO-, NOTARY)]

protopectin /prṓtəpéktin/ *n.* = PECTOSE.

protophyte /prṓtəfīt/ *n.* a unicellular plant bearing gametes.

protoplasm /prṓtəplaz'm/ *n.* the material comprising the living part of a cell, consisting of a nucleus embedded in membrane-enclosed cytoplasm. □□ **protoplasmal** /-plázm'l/ *adj.* **protoplasmatic** /-máttik/ *adj.* **protoplasmic** /-plázmik/ *adj.* [Gk *protoplasma* (as PROTO-, PLASMA)]

protoplast /prṓtəplast/ *n.* the protoplasm of one cell. □□ **protoplastic** /-plástik/ *adj.* [F *protoplaste* or LL *protoplastus* f. Gk *protoplastos* (as PROTO-, *plassō* mould)]

prototherian /prṓtōthéeriən/ *n.* & *adj.* ● *n.* any mammal of the subclass Prototheria, including monotremes. ● *adj.* of or relating to this subclass. [PROTO- + Gk *thēr* wild beast]

prototype /prṓtətīp/ *n.* **1** an original thing or person of which or whom copies, imitations, improved forms, representations, etc. are made. **2** a trial model or preliminary version of a vehicle, machine, etc. **3** a thing or person representative of a type; an exemplar. □□ **prototypal** *adj.* **prototypic** /-típpik/ *adj.* **prototypical** /-típpik'l/ *adj.* **prototypically** /-tippikəli/ *adv.* [F *prototype* or LL *prototypus* f. Gk *prototupos* (as PROTO-, TYPE)]

■ **1** model, archetype, pattern, exemplar, first, original, source; master. **3** example, instance, illustration, sample, norm, paragon, epitome, exemplar, model, standard.

protozoan /prṓtəzṓən/ *n.* & *adj.* ● *n.* (also **protozoon** /-zṓ-on/) (*pl.* **protozoa** /-zṓə/ or **protozoans**) any usu. unicellular and microscopic organism of the subkingdom Protozoa, including amoebae and ciliates. ● *adj.* (also **protozoic** /-zṓ-ik/) of or relating to this phylum. □□ **protozoal** *adj.* [mod.L (as PROTO-, Gk *zōion* animal)]

protract /prətrákt/ *v.tr.* **1 a** prolong or lengthen in space or esp. time (*protracted their stay for some weeks*). **b** (as **protracted** *adj.*) of excessive length or duration (*a protracted illness*). **2** draw (a plan of ground etc.) to scale. □□ **protractedly** *adv.* **protractedness** *n.* [L *protrahere protract-* (as PRO-[1], *trahere* draw)]

■ **1 a** see LENGTHEN 1. **b** (**protracted**) long, long-drawn-out, interminable, prolonged, over-long, never-ending, extended, stretched out, marathon, endless, everlasting, long-winded.

protractile /prətráktīl/ *adj.* (of a part of the body etc.) capable of being protruded or extended.

protraction /prətráksh'n/ *n.* **1** the act or an instance of protracting; the state of being protracted. **2** a drawing to scale. **3** the action of a protractor muscle. [F *protraction* or LL *protractio* (as PROTRACT)]

protractor /prətráktər/ *n.* **1** an instrument for measuring angles, usu. in the form of a graduated semicircle. **2** a muscle serving to extend a limb etc.

protrude /prətrṓōd/ *v.* **1** *intr.* extend beyond or above a surface; project. **2** *tr.* thrust or cause to thrust forth. □□ **protrudent** *adj.* **protrusible** *adj.* **protrusion** /-trṓōzh'n/ *n.* **protrusive** *adj.* [L *protrudere* (as PRO-[1], *trudere trus-* thrust)]

■ **1** stick out, jut (out), project, extend, poke out, stand out, thrust out *or* forward; bulge, balloon, bag (out), belly (out); pop, goggle. □□ **protrusion** projection, protuberance, prominence, swelling, excrescence, outgrowth, tumescence, bump, lump, knob, bulge.

protrusile /prətrṓōssīl/ *adj.* (of a limb etc.) capable of being thrust forward. [PRO-[1] + EXTRUSILE: see EXTRUDE]

protuberant /prətyṓōbərənt/ *adj.* bulging out; prominent (*protuberant eyes*; *a protuberant fact*). □□ **protuberance** *n.* [LL *protuberare* (as PRO-[1], *tuber* bump)]

■ protrusive, protruding, bulging, gibbous, bulbous; extrusive, excrescent, extruding, projecting, overhanging; prominent; undeniable.

proud /prowd/ *adj.* **1** feeling greatly honoured or pleased (*am proud to know him*; *proud of his friendship*). **2 a** (often foll. by *of*) valuing oneself, one's possessions, etc. highly, or esp. too highly; haughty; arrogant (*proud of his ancient name*). **b** (often in *comb.*) having a proper pride; satisfied (*house-proud*; *proud of a job well done*). **3 a** (of an occasion etc.) justly arousing pride (*a proud day for us*; *a proud sight*). **b** (of an action etc.) showing pride (*a proud wave of the hand*). **4** (of a thing) imposing; splendid. **5** slightly projecting from a surface etc. (*the nail stood proud of the plank*). **6** (of flesh) overgrown round a healing wound. **7** (of water) swollen in flood. □ **do proud** *colloq.* **1** treat (a person) with lavish generosity or honour (*they did us proud on our anniversary*). **2** (*refl.*) act honourably or worthily. **proud-hearted** haughty; arrogant. □□ **proudly** *adv.* **proudness** *n.* [OE *prūt*, *prūd* f. OF *prud*, *prod* oblique case of *pruz* etc. valiant, ult. f. LL *prode* f. L *prodesse* be of value (as PRO-[1], *esse* be)]

■ **1** pleased, well-pleased, satisfied, contented, glad, happy, delighted, elated; honoured, gratified. **2 a** conceited, self-satisfied, self-important, vain, prideful, self-centred, complacent, haughty, smug, arrogant, boastful, braggart, *literary* vainglorious. **3** lofty, dignified, lordly, noble, great, respected, honoured, honourable, glorious, august, illustrious, estimable, creditable, distinguished, noteworthy. **4** stately, majestic, magnificent, splendid, grand, impressive, imposing, great. □ **proud-hearted** see ARROGANT.

Prov. *abbr.* **1** Proverbs (Old Testament). **2** Province. **3** Provençal.

prove /prōōv/ *v.* (*past part.* **proved** or **proven** /prṓōv'n, prṓ-/) **1** *tr.* (often foll. by *that* + clause) demonstrate the truth of by evidence or argument. **2** *intr.* **a** (usu. foll. by *to* + infin.) be found (*it proved to be untrue*). **b** emerge incontrovertibly as (*will prove the winner*). **3** *tr. Math.* test the accuracy of (a calculation). **4** *tr.* establish the genuineness and validity of (a will). **5** *intr.* (of dough) rise in bread-making. **6** *tr.* = PROOF 6. **7** *tr.* subject (a gun etc.) to a testing process. **8** *tr. archaic* test the qualities of; try. □ **not proven** (in Scottish Law) a verdict that there is insufficient evidence to establish guilt or innocence. **prove oneself** show one's abilities, courage, etc. □□ **provable** *adj.* **provability** /prṓōvəbílliti/ *n.* **provably** *adv.* [ME f. OF *prover* f. L *probare* test, approve, demonstrate f. *probus* good]

■ **1** verify, authenticate, confirm, make good, corroborate, demonstrate, show, validate, establish, substantiate, certify; support, sustain, back (up), uphold. **2** turn out, be found, be shown, be established; end up, emerge (as), result. **8** examine, check, analyse; try; see also TEST[1] *v.* 1.

provenance /próvvinənss/ *n.* **1** the place of origin or history, esp. of a work of art etc. **2** origin. [F f. *provenir* f. L *provenire* (as PRO-[1], *venire* come)]

■ see ORIGIN 1.

Provençal /próvvonsaál, próvvonsál/ *adj.* & *n.* ● *adj.* of or concerning the language, inhabitants, landscape, etc. of Provence, a former province of SE France. ● *n.* **1** a native of Provence. **2** the language of Provence. [F (as PROVINCIAL f. *provincia* as L colloq. name for southern Gaul under Roman rule)]

provender /próvvindər/ *n.* **1** animal fodder. **2** *joc.* food for human beings. [ME f. OF *provendre, provende* ult. f. L *praebenda* (see PREBEND)]
■ **1** fodder, forage, feed. **2** provisions, food, supplies, victuals, foodstuffs, nourishment, sustenance, groceries, edibles, *colloq.* grub, eats, *formal* aliment, *formal or joc.* comestibles, *sl.* nosh.

provenience /prəvéeniənss/ *n. US* = PROVENANCE. [L *provenire* f. *venire* come]

proverb /próvverb/ *n.* **1** a short pithy saying in general use, held to embody a general truth. **2** a person or thing that is notorious (*he is a proverb for inaccuracy*). **3** (**Proverbs** or **Book of Proverbs**) a didactic poetic Old Testament book of maxims attributed to Solomon and others. [ME f. OF *proverbe* or L *proverbium* (as PRO-[1], *verbum* word)]
■ **1** saying, maxim, aphorism, saw, adage, apophthegm, axiom, dictum, gnome.

proverbial /prəvérbiəl/ *adj.* **1** (esp. of a specific characteristic etc.) as well-known as a proverb; notorious (*his proverbial honesty*). **2** of or referred to in a proverb (*the proverbial ill wind*). □□ **proverbiality** /-biálliti/ *n.* **proverbially** *adv.* [ME f. L *proverbialis* (as PROVERB)]
■ **1** acknowledged, axiomatic, time-honoured, notorious; see also *well-known* 1. **2** axiomatic, aphoristic, epigrammatic, apophthegmatic, gnomic; well-known, celebrated, notorious.

provide /prəvíd/ *v.* **1** *tr.* supply; furnish (*provided them with food; provided food for them; provided a chance for escape*). **2** *intr.* **a** (usu. foll. by *for, against*) make due preparation (*provided for any eventuality; provided against invasion*). **b** (usu. foll. by *for*) prepare for the maintenance of a person etc. **3** *tr.* (also *refl.*) equip with necessities (*they had to provide themselves*). **4** *tr.* (usu. foll. by *that*) stipulate in a will, statute, etc. **5** *tr.* (usu. foll. by *to*) *Eccl. hist.* **a** appoint (an incumbent) to a benefice. **b** (of the Pope) appoint (a successor) to a benefice not yet vacant. [ME f. L *providēre* (as PRO-[1], *vidēre vis-* see)]
■ **1** supply, furnish, equip, outfit, fix up with, provision; produce, yield, afford, lend, give, present, offer, accord. **2 a** make provision(s), arrange, cater, prepare, make *or* get ready, plan, take precautions, take measures; (*provide for*) anticipate. **b** (*provide for*) look after, care for, support, take care of, take under one's wing, minister to, attend (to). **4** stipulate, lay down, require, demand, specify, state.

provided /prəvídid/ *adj.* & *conj.* ● *adj.* supplied, furnished. ● *conj.* (often foll. by *that*) on the condition or understanding (that).
■ *conj.* providing (that), on (the) condition (that), if (only), only if, as long as, with the proviso that, with *or* on the understanding (that).

providence /próvvid'nss/ *n.* **1** the protective care of God or nature. **2** (**Providence**) God in this aspect. **3** timely care or preparation; foresight; thrift. □ **special providence** a particular instance of God's providence. [ME f. OF *providence* or L *providentia* (as PROVIDE)]
■ **1** protection, care, concern, beneficence, direction, control, divine intervention, guidance. **3** foresight, forethought, preparation, anticipation, far-sightedness, discretion, prudence, care; thrift, frugality, husbandry, thriftiness, conservation, economy.

provident /próvvid'nt/ *adj.* having or showing foresight; thrifty. □ **Provident Society** *Brit.* = *Friendly Society*. □□ **providently** *adv.* [ME f. L (as PROVIDE)]
■ far-sighted, long-headed, far-seeing, thoughtful, anticipatory, wise, shrewd, sagacious, sage, judicious; frugal, economical, thrifty; canny, prudent.

providential /próvvidénsh'l/ *adj.* **1** of or by divine foresight or interposition. **2** opportune, lucky. □□ **providentially** *adv.* [PROVIDENCE + -IAL, after *evidential* etc.]
■ **2** fortunate, lucky, blessed, felicitous, happy, opportune, timely.

provider /prəvídər/ *n.* **1** a person or thing that provides. **2** the breadwinner of a family etc.
■ **1** see DONOR.

providing /prəvíding/ *conj.* = PROVIDED *conj.*

province /próvvinss/ *n.* **1** a principal administrative division of a country etc. **2** (**the provinces**) the whole of a country outside the capital, esp. regarded as uncultured, unsophisticated, etc. **3** a sphere of action; business (*outside my province as a teacher*). **4** a branch of learning etc. (*in the province of aesthetics*). **5** *Eccl.* a district under an archbishop or a metropolitan. **6** *Rom.Hist.* a territory outside Italy under a Roman governor. [ME f. OF f. L *provincia* charge, province]
■ **1** territory, state, zone, region, area, district, domain, county. **2** (**the provinces**) (the) outlying districts, the countryside, the hinterland, the backwoods, *colloq.* the sticks, *US sl.* the boonies, the boondocks; see also *back country*. **3** sphere *or* area (of responsibility), responsibility, concern, function, charge, business, field, *joc.* bailiwick. **4** see BRANCH *n.* 2, 3, FIELD *n.* 8.

provincial /prəvínsh'l/ *adj.* & *n.* ● *adj.* **1 a** of or concerning a province. **b** of or concerning the provinces. **2** unsophisticated or uncultured in manner, speech, opinion, etc. ● *n.* **1** an inhabitant of a province or the provinces. **2** an unsophisticated or uncultured person. **3** *Eccl.* the head or chief of a province or of a religious order in a province. □□ **provinciality** /-shiálliti/ *n.* **provincialize** *v.tr.* (also **-ise**). **provincially** *adv.* [ME f. OF f. L *provincialis* (as PROVINCE)]
■ *adj.* **1** see LOCAL *adj.* 1–3. **2** uncultured, uncultivated, unsophisticated, limited, uninformed, naive, innocent, ingenuous, unpolished, unrefined, homespun, rustic, rude, country, parochial, insular, narrow-minded, parish pump, small-town, *colloq.* hick. ● *n.* **2** rustic, (country) bumpkin, yokel, out-of-towner, *esp. US colloq.* hick, *US colloq.* hayseed, *often derog.* country cousin.

provincialism /prəvínshəliz'm/ *n.* **1** provincial manners, fashion, mode of thought, etc., esp. regarded as restricting or narrow. **2** a word or phrase peculiar to a provincial region. **3** concern for one's local area rather than one's country. □□ **provincialist** *n.*
■ **1** narrow-mindedness, insularity, parochialism, narrowness, benightedness; unsophisticatedness, simplicity, naïvety, ingenuousness, innocence, inexperience. **2** localism, regionalism.

provision /prəvízh'n/ *n.* & *v.* ● *n.* **1 a** the act or an instance of providing (*made no provision for his future*). **b** something provided (*a provision of bread*). **2** (in *pl.*) food, drink, etc., esp. for an expedition. **3 a** a legal or formal statement providing for something. **b** a clause of this. **4** *Eccl. hist.* an appointment to a benefice not yet vacant (cf. PROVIDE 5). ● *v.tr.* supply (an expedition etc.) with provisions. □□ **provisioner** *n.* **provisionless** *adj.* **provisionment** *n.* [ME f. OF f. L *provisio -onis* (as PROVIDE)]
■ *n.* **1 a** preparation(s), prearrangement, arrangement(s), plan(s); equipment; see also STEP *n.* 3. **2** (*provisions*) supplies, stores, stock(s); food, foodstuffs, eatables, edibles, victuals, rations, groceries, staples, *formal* viands, *formal or joc.* comestibles, *joc.* provender, *Austral. colloq.* tucker. **3 b** clause, term, stipulation, proviso, condition, restriction, qualification, demand, requirement. ● *v.* stock, victual; see also EQUIP.

provisional /prəvízhən'l/ *adj.* & *n.* ● *adj.* **1** providing for immediate needs only; temporary. **2** (**Provisional**) designating the unofficial wing of the IRA established in 1970, advocating terrorism. ● *n.* (**Provisional**) a member of the Provisional wing of the IRA. □□ **provisionality** /-nálliti/ *n.* **provisionally** *adv.* **provisionalness** *n.*
■ *adj.* **1** temporary, interim, transitional, stopgap, *pro tempore*, *colloq.* pro tem; conditional, contingent.

proviso /prəvízō/ *n.* (*pl.* **-os**) **1** a stipulation. **2** a clause of stipulation or limitation in a document. [L, neut. ablat. past part. of *providēre* PROVIDE, in med.L phr. *proviso quod* it being provided that]
■ see CONDITION *n.* 1.

provisor /prəvízər/ *n. Eccl.* **1** a deputy of a bishop or archbishop. **2** *hist.* the holder of a provision (see PROVISION *n.* 4). [ME f. AF *provisour* f. L *provisor -oris* (as PROVIDE)]

provisory /prəvízəri/ *adj.* **1** conditional; having a proviso. **2** making provision (*provisory care*). ▫▫ **provisorily** *adv.* [F *provisoire* or med.L *provisorius* (as PROVISOR)]
■ **1** conditional, contingent.

Provo /próvō/ *n.* (*pl.* **-os**) *colloq.* a member of the Provisional IRA. [abbr.]

provocation /próvvəkáysh'n/ *n.* **1** the act or an instance of provoking; a state of being provoked (*did it under severe provocation*). **2** a cause of annoyance. **3** *Law* an action, insult, etc. held to be likely to provoke physical retaliation. [ME f. OF *provocation* or L *provocatio* (as PROVOKE)]
■ **1** incitement, instigation. **2** insult, offence, taunt, irritation; ground(s), reason, cause, justification, stimulus, incentive, motivation, motive, inducement.

provocative /prəvókkətiv/ *adj.* & *n.* ● *adj.* **1** (usu. foll. by *of*) tending to provoke, esp. anger or sexual desire. **2** intentionally annoying. ● *n.* a provocative thing. ▫▫ **provocatively** *adv.* **provocativeness** *n.* [ME f. obs. F *provocatif -ive* f. LL *provocativus* (as PROVOKE)]
■ *adj.* **1** alluring, seductive, stimulating, suggestive, erotic, arousing, exciting, outrageous, sexy. **2** irritating, annoying, galling, irksome, nettlesome, exasperating, infuriating, maddening.

provoke /prəvṓk/ *v.tr.* **1 a** (often foll. by *to*, or *to* + infin.) rouse or incite (*provoked him to fury*). **b** (often as **provoking** *adj.*) annoy, irritate; exasperate. **2** call forth; instigate (indignation, an inquiry, a storm, etc.). **3** (usu. foll. by *into* + verbal noun) irritate or stimulate (a person) (*the itch provoked him into scratching*). **4** tempt; allure. **5** cause, give rise to (*will provoke fermentation*). ▫▫ **provokable** *adj.* **provokingly** *adv.* [ME f. OF *provoquer* f. L *provocare* (as PRO-[1], *vocare* call)]
■ **1 a** rouse, stir, stimulate, incite, move, motivate, prompt, induce, encourage, push, impel, drive, spur (on), goad, force, compel. **b** irritate, annoy, irk, pester, vex, pique, anger, enrage, madden, incense, infuriate, gall, rile, nettle, harass, hector, plague, badger, exasperate, get on one's nerves, try one's patience, frustrate, upset, disturb, perturb, distress, outrage, offend, insult, affront; (**provoking**) see TRYING. **2** start, incite, instigate, produce, foment, kindle, work up, call forth. **4** see TEMPT 2. **5** see CAUSE *v.* 1.

provost /próvvəst/ *n.* **1** *Brit.* the head of some colleges esp. at Oxford or Cambridge. **2** *Eccl.* **a** the head of a chapter in a cathedral. **b** *hist.* the head of a religious community. **3** *Sc.* the head of a municipal corporation or burgh. **4** the Protestant minister of the principal church of a town etc. in Germany etc. **5** *US* a high administrative officer in a university. **6** = *provost marshal.* ▫ **provost guard** *US* a body of soldiers under a provost marshal. **provost marshal 1** the head of military police in camp or on active service. **2** the master-at-arms of a ship in which a court-martial is to be held. ▫▫ **provostship** *n.* [ME f. OE *profost* & AF *provost*, *prevost* f. med.L *propositus* for *praepositus*: see PRAEPOSTOR]

prow /prow/ *n.* **1** the fore-part or bow of a ship adjoining the stem. **2** a pointed or projecting front part. [F *proue* f. Prov. *proa* or It. dial. *prua* f. L *prora* f. Gk *prōira*]
■ **1** bow(s).

prowess /prówiss/ *n.* **1** skill; expertise. **2** valour; gallantry. [ME f. OF *proesce* f. *prou* valiant]
■ **1** expertise, ability, skill, skilfulness, aptitude, adroitness, dexterity, dexterousness, adeptness, facility, mastery, know-how, capability, proficiency, competence. **2** bravery, valour, courage, boldness, daring, intrepidity, dauntlessness, mettle, stout-heartedness, lion-heartedness, fearlessness, gallantry, fortitude, *archaic or joc.* doughtiness.

prowl /prowl/ *v.* & *n.* ● *v.* **1** *tr.* roam (a place) in search or as if in search of prey, plunder, etc. **2** *intr.* (often foll. by *about*, *around*) move about like a hunter. ● *n.* the act or an instance of prowling. ▫ **on the prowl** moving about secretively or rapaciously, esp. in search of sexual contact etc. **prowl car** *US* a police squad car. ▫▫ **prowler** *n.* [ME *prolle*, of unkn. orig.]
■ *v.* **1** scour, scavenge, range over, rove, roam, patrol, cruise. **2** lurk, sneak, skulk, steal, slink, creep; lie in wait. ▫ **on the prowl** searching, hunting, tracking, stalking, cruising. **prowl car** patrol car, squad car, *Brit.* panda car.

prox. *abbr.* proximo.

prox. acc. *abbr. proxime accessit.*

proxemics /proksé́emiks/ *n. Sociol.* the study of socially conditioned spatial factors in ordinary human relations. [PROXIMITY + *-emics*: cf. *phonemics*]

proximal /próksim'l/ *adj.* situated towards the centre of the body or point of attachment. ▫▫ **proximally** *adv.* [L *proximus* nearest]

proximate /próksimət/ *adj.* **1** nearest or next before or after (in place, order, time, causation, thought process, etc.). **2** approximate. ▫▫ **proximately** *adv.* [L *proximatus* past part. of *proximare* draw near (as PROXIMAL)]
■ **1** see IMMEDIATE 2. **2** see APPROXIMATE *adj.* 1.

proxime accessit /próksimi əkséessit/ *n.* **1** second place in an examination etc. **2** a person gaining this. [L, = came very near]

proximity /proksímmiti/ *n.* nearness in space, time, etc. (*sat in close proximity to them*). ▫ **proximity fuse** an electronic device causing a projectile to explode when near its target. **proximity of blood** kinship. [ME f. F *proximité* or L *proximitas* (as PROXIMAL)]
■ nearness, closeness, adjacency, contiguity, contiguousness, propinquity.

proximo /próksimō/ *adj. Commerce* of next month (*the third proximo*). [L *proximo mense* in the next month]

proxy /próksi/ *n.* (*pl.* **-ies**) (also *attrib.*) **1** the authorization given to a substitute or deputy (*a proxy vote*; *was married by proxy*). **2** a person authorized to act as a substitute etc. **3 a** a document giving the power to act as a proxy, esp. in voting. **b** a vote given by this. [ME f. obs. *procuracy* f. med.L *procuratia* (as PROCURATION)]
■ **2** substitute, agent, delegate, surrogate, representative, factor.

PRS *abbr.* **1** (in the UK) President of the Royal Society. **2** Performing Rights Society.

prude /prōōd/ *n.* a person having or affecting an attitude of extreme propriety or modesty esp. in sexual matters. ▫▫ **prudery** *n.* (*pl.* **-ies**). **prudish** *adj.* **prudishly** *adv.* **prudishness** *n.* [F, back form. f. *prudefemme* fem. of *prud'homme* good man and true f. *prou* worthy]
■ prig, puritan, (Mrs) Grundy, *colloq.* goody-goody. ▫▫ **prudery, prudishness** priggishness, puritanicalness, puritanism, Grundyism, primness, stuffiness, old-maidishness. **prudish** priggish, puritanical, old-maidish, prissy, prim, strait-laced, stiff, over-nice, proper, demure, formal, moralistic, stiff-necked, *colloq.* goody-goody, school-marmish, *US colloq.* uptight.

prudent /prōōd'nt/ *adj.* **1** (of a person or conduct) careful to avoid undesired consequences; circumspect. **2** discreet. ▫▫ **prudence** *n.* **prudently** *adv.* [ME f. OF *prudent* or L *prudens* = *providens* PROVIDENT]
■ **1** careful, cautious, circumspect, watchful, wise, sage, sagacious, sensible, reasonable, canny, shrewd. **2** discreet, politic, judicious, discriminating; see also TACTFUL. ▫▫ **prudence** discretion, wisdom, sagacity, discrimination, common sense, providence, canniness, presence of mind, awareness, care, tact, carefulness, caution, cautiousness, circumspection; foresightedness, forethought, foresight, far-sightedness.

prudential /proodénsh'l/ *adj.* & *n.* ● *adj.* of, involving, or marked by prudence (*prudential motives*). ● *n.* (in *pl.*) **1** prudential considerations or matters. **2** *US* minor administrative or financial matters. ▫▫ **prudentialism** *n.* **prudentialist** *n.* **prudentially** *adv.* [PRUDENT + -IAL, after *evidential* etc.]
■ *adj.* see PRUDENT.

pruinose /prōō-inōss/ *adj.* esp. *Bot.* covered with white powdery granules; frosted in appearance. [L *pruinosus* f. *pruina* hoar-frost]

prune[1] /proōn/ *n.* **1** a dried plum. **2** *colloq.* a silly or disliked person. [ME f. OF ult. f. L *prunum* f. Gk *prou(m)non* plum]

prune[2] /proōn/ *v.tr.* **1 a** (often foll. by *down*) trim (a tree etc.) by cutting away dead or overgrown branches etc. **b** (usu. foll. by *off*, *away*) lop (branches etc.) from a tree. **2** reduce (costs etc.) (*must try to prune expenses*). **3 a** (often foll. by *of*) clear (a book etc.) of superfluities. **b** remove (superfluities). □ **pruning-hook** a long-handled hooked cutting tool used for pruning. □□ **pruner** *n.* [ME *prouyne* f. OF *pro(o)ignier* ult. f. L *rotundus* ROUND]
■ **1 a** trim (down), clip, cut back, pare (down). **b** lop (off), dock, chop (off), cut (off), clip, shear, snip (off). **2** see CUT *v.* 6.

prunella[1] /proōnéllə/ *n.* any plant of the genus *Prunella*, esp. *P. vulgaris*, bearing pink, purple, or white flower spikes, and formerly thought to cure quinsy. Also called SELF HEAL. [mod.L, = quinsy: earlier *brunella* dimin. of med.L *brunus* brown]

prunella[2] /proōnéllə/ *n.* a strong silk or worsted fabric used formerly for barristers' gowns, the uppers of women's shoes, etc. [perh. f. F *prunelle*, of uncert. orig.]

prurient /proóriənt/ *adj.* **1** having an unhealthy obsession with sexual matters. **2** encouraging such an obsession. □□ **prurience** *n.* **pruriency** *n.* **pruriently** *adv.* [L *prurire* itch, be wanton]
■ **1** voyeuristic, lubricious, salacious. **2** dirty, lewd, filthy, pornographic, smutty, obscene, foul, scurrilous, vile, gross, lurid, blue, bawdy, ribald, titillating, suggestive, coarse, vulgar, rude, low, crude.

prurigo /proorígō/ *n.* a skin disease marked by severe itching. □□ **pruriginous** /prooríjinəss/ *adj.* [L *prurigo -ginis* f. *prurire* to itch]

pruritus /prooritəss/ *n.* severe itching of the skin. □□ **pruritic** /-ríttik/ *adj.* [L, = itching (as PRURIGO)]

Prussian /prúsh'n/ *adj.* & *n.* ● *adj.* of or relating to Prussia, a former German State, or relating to its rigidly militaristic tradition. ● *n.* a native of Prussia. □ **Old Prussian** the language spoken in Prussia until the 17th c. **Prussian blue** a deep blue pigment, ferric ferrocyanide, used in painting and dyeing.

prussic /prússik/ *adj.* of or obtained from Prussian blue. □ **prussic acid** hydrocyanic acid. [F *prussique* f. *Prusse* Prussia]

pry[1] /prī/ *v.intr.* (**pries, pried**) **1** (usu. foll. by *into*) inquire impertinently (into a person's private affairs etc.). **2** (usu. foll. by *into*, *about*, etc.) look or peer inquisitively. □□ **prying** *adj.* **pryingly** *adv.* [ME *prie*, of unkn. orig.]
■ intrude, meddle, interfere, be nosy, nose about *or* around, poke about *or* around, ferret about, peer, peek, *colloq.* snoop; (*pry into*) *colloq.* poke *or* stick one's nose in *or* into, *Austral.* & *NZ sl.* stickybeak.

pry[2] /prī/ *v.tr.* (**pries, pried**) *US* (often foll. by *out of*, *open*, etc.) = PRISE. [PRISE taken as *pries* 3rd sing. pres.]

PS *abbr.* **1** Police Sergeant. **2** postscript. **3** private secretary. **4** prompt side.

Ps. *abbr.* (*pl.* **Pss.**) Psalm, Psalms (Old Testament).

psalm /saam/ *n.* **1 a** (also **Psalm**) any of the sacred songs contained in the Book of Psalms, esp. when set for metrical chanting in a service. **b** (**the Psalms** or **the Book of Psalms**) the book of the Old Testament containing the Psalms. **2** a sacred song or hymn. □ **psalm-book** a book containing the Psalms, esp. with metrical settings for worship. □□ **psalmic** *adj.* [OE *(p)sealm* f. LL *psalmus* f. Gk *psalmos* song sung to a harp f. *psallō* pluck]

psalmist /saámist/ *n.* **1** the author or composer of a psalm. **2** (**the Psalmist**) David or the author of any of the Psalms. [LL *psalmista* (as PSALM)]

psalmody /saámədi, sál-/ *n.* **1** the practice or art of singing psalms, hymns, etc., esp. in public worship. **2 a** the arrangement of psalms for singing. **b** the psalms so arranged. □□ **psalmodic** /salmóddik/ *adj.* **psalmodist** *n.* **psalmodize** *v.intr.* (also **-ise**). [ME f. LL *psalmodia* f. Gk *psalmōidia* singing to a harp (as PSALM, *ōidē* song)]

psalter /sáwltər, sól-/ *n.* **1 a** the Book of Psalms. **b** a version of this (*the English Psalter*; *Prayer-Book Psalter*). **2** a copy of the Psalms, esp. for liturgical use. [ME f. AF *sauter*, OF *sautier*, & OE *(p)saltere* f. LL *psalterium* f. Gk *psaltērion* stringed instrument (*psallō* pluck), in eccl.L Book of Psalms]

psalterium /sawltéeriəm, sol-/ *n.* the third stomach of a ruminant, the omasum. [L (see PSALTER): named from its booklike form]

psaltery /sáwltəri, sól-/ *n.* (*pl.* **-ies**) an ancient and medieval instrument like a dulcimer but played by plucking the strings with the fingers or a plectrum. [ME f. OF *sauterie* etc. f. L (as PSALTER)]

PSBR *abbr. Brit.* public sector borrowing requirement.

psephology /sefólləji, psef-/ *n.* the statistical study of elections, voting, etc. □□ **psephological** /-fəlójik'l/ *adj.* **psephologically** /-fəlójikəli/ *adv.* **psephologist** *n.* [Gk *psēphos* pebble, vote + -LOGY]

pseud /syoōd/ *adj.* & *n. colloq.* ● *adj.* intellectually or socially pretentious; not genuine. ● *n.* such a person; a poseur. [abbr. of PSEUDO]
■ *adj.* see PHONEY *adj.* ● *n.* see PHONEY *n.*

pseud- var. of PSEUDO-.

pseudepigrapha /syoōdipígrəfə/ *n.pl.* **1** Jewish writings ascribed to various Old Testament prophets etc. but written during or just before the early Christian period. **2** spurious writings. □□ **pseudepigraphal** *adj.* **pseudepigraphic** /-gráffik/ *adj.* **pseudepigraphical** /-gráffik'l/ *adj.* [neut. pl. of Gk *pseudepigraphos* with false title (as PSEUDO-, EPIGRAPH)]

pseudo /syoōdō/ *adj.* & *n.* ● *adj.* **1** sham; spurious. **2** insincere. ● *n.* (*pl.* **-os**) a pretentious or insincere person. [see PSEUDO-]
■ *adj.* **1** see SPURIOUS. **2** see INSINCERE.

pseudo- /syoōdō/ *comb. form* (also **pseud-** before a vowel) **1** supposed or purporting to be but not really so; false; not genuine (*pseudo-intellectual*; *pseudepigrapha*). **2** resembling or imitating (often in technical applications) (*pseudo-language*; *pseudo-acid*). [Gk f. *pseudēs* false, *pseudos* falsehood]

pseudocarp /syoōdōkaarp/ *n.* a fruit formed from parts other than the ovary, e.g. the strawberry or fig. [PSEUDO- + Gk *karpos* fruit]

pseudomorph /syoōdəmorf/ *n.* **1** a crystal etc. consisting of one mineral with the form proper to another. **2** a false form. □□ **pseudomorphic** /-mórfik/ *adj.* **pseudomorphism** /-mórfiz'm/ *n.* **pseudomorphous** /-mórfəss/ *adj.* [PSEUDO- + Gk *morphē* form]

pseudonym /syoōdənim/ *n.* a fictitious name, esp. one assumed by an author. [F *pseudonyme* f. Gk *pseudōnymos* (as PSEUDO-, *-ōnumos* f. *onoma* name)]
■ *nom de plume*, *nom de guerre*, alias, pen-name, stage name, incognito.

pseudonymous /syoodónniməss/ *adj.* writing or written under a false name. □□ **pseudonymity** /syoōdənímmiti/ *n.* **pseudonymously** *adv.*

pseudopod /syoōdōpod/ *n.* = PSEUDOPODIUM. [mod.L (as PSEUDOPODIUM)]

pseudopodium /syoōdōpōdiəm/ *n.* (*pl.* **pseudopodia** /-diə/) (in amoeboid cells) a temporary protrusion of protoplasm for movement, feeding, etc. [mod.L (as PSEUDO-, PODIUM)]

pseudo-science /syoōdōsīənss/ *n.* a pretended or spurious science. □□ **pseudo-scientific** /-sīəntíffik/ *adj.*

pshaw /pshaw, shaw/ *int. archaic* an expression of contempt or impatience. [imit.]

psi /psī/ *n.* **1** the twenty-third letter of the Greek alphabet (Ψ, ψ). **2** supposed parapsychological faculties, phenomena, etc. regarded collectively. [Gk]

p.s.i. *abbr.* pounds per square inch.

psilocybin /síllәsībin/ *n.* a hallucinogenic alkaloid found in Mexican mushrooms of the genus *Psilocybe*. [*Psilocybe* f. Gk *psilos* bald + *kubē* head]

psilosis /sīlṓsiss/ *n.* = SPRUE[2]. [Gk *psilōsis* f. *psilos* bare]

psittacine /síttəsīn/ *adj.* of or relating to parrots; parrot-like. [L *psittacinus* f. *psittacus* f. Gk *psittakos* parrot]

psittacosis /síttəkṓsiss/ *n.* a contagious viral disease of birds transmissible (esp. from parrots) to human beings as a form of pneumonia. [mod.L f. L *psittacus* (as PSITTACINE) + -OSIS]

psoas /sṓəss/ *n.* either of two muscles used in flexing the hip joint. [Gk, accus. pl. of *psoa*, taken as sing.]

psoriasis /sərī́əsiss/ *n.* a skin disease marked by red scaly patches. ▫▫ **psoriatic** /sóriáttik/ *adj.* [mod.L f. Gk *psōriasis* f. *psōriaō* have an itch f. *psōra* itch]

psst /pst/ *int.* (also **pst**) a whispered exclamation seeking to attract a person's attention surreptitiously. [imit.]

PST *abbr. US* Pacific Standard Time.

PSV *abbr. Brit.* public service vehicle.

psych /sīk/ *v.tr. colloq.* **1** (usu. foll. by *up*; often *refl.*) prepare (oneself or another person) mentally for an ordeal etc. **2 a** (usu. foll. by *out*) analyse (a person's motivation etc.) for one's own advantage (*can't psych him out*). **b** subject to psychoanalysis. **3** (often foll. by *out*) influence a person psychologically, esp. negatively; intimidate, frighten. ▫ **psych out** break down mentally; become confused or deranged. [abbr.]
■ **1** set; see also PREPARE 1, 3a. **3** see DISTURB 2.

psyche /sīki/ *n.* **1** the soul; the spirit. **2** the mind. [L f. Gk *psukhē* breath, life, soul]
■ **1** soul, spirit, life-force, anima, (inner) self, subconscious, unconscious, inner man *or* woman. **2** mind, intellect.

psychedelia /sīkidéeliə/ *n.pl.* **1** psychedelic articles, esp. posters, paintings, etc. **2** psychedelic drugs.

psychedelic /sīkidéllik/ *adj.* & *n.* ● *adj.* **1 a** expanding the mind's awareness etc., esp. through the use of hallucinogenic drugs. **b** (of an experience) hallucinatory; bizarre. **c** (of a drug) producing hallucinations. **2** *colloq.* **a** producing an effect resembling that of a psychedelic drug; having vivid colours or designs etc. **b** (of colours, patterns, etc.) bright, bold and often abstract. ● *n.* a hallucinogenic drug. ▫▫ **psychedelically** *adv.* [irreg. f. Gk (as PSYCHE, *dēlos* clear, manifest)]

psychiatry /sīkī́ətri/ *n.* the study and treatment of mental disease. ▫▫ **psychiatric** /-kiátrik/ *adj.* **psychiatrical** /-kiátrik'l/ *adj.* **psychiatrically** /-kiátrikəli/ *adv.* **psychiatrist** *n.* [as PSYCHE + *iatreia* healing f. *iatros* healer]
■ ▫▫ **psychiatrist** see *therapist* (THERAPY).

psychic /sīkik/ *adj.* & *n.* ● *adj.* **1 a** (of a person) considered to have occult powers, such as telepathy, clairvoyance, etc. **b** (of a faculty, phenomenon, etc.) inexplicable by natural laws. **2** of the soul or mind. **3** *Bridge* (of a bid) made on the basis of a hand not usually considered strong enough to support it. ● *n.* **1** a person considered to have psychic powers; a medium. **2** *Bridge* a psychic bid. **3** (in *pl.*) the study of psychic phenomena. [Gk *psukhikos* (as PSYCHE)]
■ *adj.* **1 a** telepathic, clairvoyant; see also PROPHETIC. **b** psychical, extrasensory, supernatural, occult, magical, telepathic, telekinetic, preternatural, spiritualistic, unearthly, extramundane, supermundane, metaphysical. **2** psychical, mental, spiritual, psychological, intellectual. ● *n.* **1** medium, spiritualist, clairvoyant, mind-reader, telepathist; seer, seeress, crystal-gazer, soothsayer, fortune-teller, prophet, prophetess, sibyl.

psychical /sīkik'l/ *adj.* **1** concerning psychic phenomena or faculties (*psychical research*). **2** of the soul or mind. ▫▫ **psychically** *adv.* **psychicism** /-kisiz'm/ *n.* **psychicist** /-kisist/ *n.*
■ **1** see PSYCHIC *adj.* 1b. **2** see SPIRITUAL *adj.* 1, 4.

psycho /sīkō/ *n.* & *adj. colloq.* ● *n.* (*pl.* **-os**) a psychopath. ● *adj.* psychopathic. [abbr.]
■ *n.* see PSYCHOTIC *n.*

psycho- /sīkō/ *comb. form* relating to the mind or psychology. [Gk *psukho-* (as PSYCHE)]

psychoactive /sīkō-áktiv/ *adj.* affecting the mind.

psychoanalysis /sīkōənállisiss/ *n.* a therapeutic method of treating mental disorders by investigating the interaction of conscious and unconscious elements in the mind and bringing repressed fears and conflicts into the conscious mind. ▫▫ **psychoanalyse** /-ánnəlīz/ *v.tr.* **psychoanalyst** /-ánnəlist/ *n.* **psychoanalytic** /-ənəlíttik/ *adj.* **psychoanalytical** /-ənəlíttik'l/ *adj.* **psychoanalytically** /-ənəlíttikəli/ *adv.*
■ see THERAPY 2b. ▫▫ **psychoanalyst** see *therapist* (THERAPY).

psychobabble /sīkōbabb'l/ *n. US colloq. derog.* jargon used in popular psychology.

psychodrama /sīkōdraamə/ *n.* **1** a form of psychotherapy in which patients act out events from their past. **2** a play or film etc. in which psychological elements are the main interest.

psychodynamics /sīkōdīnámmiks/ *n.pl.* (treated as *sing.*) the study of the activity of and the interrelation between the various parts of an individual's personality or psyche. ▫▫ **psychodynamic** *adj.* **psychodynamically** *adv.*

psychogenesis /sīkōjénnisiss/ *n.* the study of the origin of the mind's development.

psychokinesis /sīkōkinéessiss/ *n.* the movement of objects supposedly by mental effort without the action of natural forces.

psycholinguistics /sīkōlinggwistiks/ *n.pl.* (treated as *sing.*) the study of the psychological aspects of language and language-learning. ▫▫ **psycholinguist** /-línggwist/ *n.* **psycholinguistic** *adj.*

psychological /sīkəlójik'l/ *adj.* **1** of, relating to, or arising in the mind. **2** of or relating to psychology. **3** *colloq.* (of an ailment etc.) having a basis in the mind; imaginary (*her cold is psychological*). ▫ **psychological block** a mental inability or inhibition caused by emotional factors. **psychological moment** the most appropriate time for achieving a particular effect or purpose. **psychological warfare** a campaign directed at reducing an opponent's morale. ▫▫ **psychologically** *adv.*
■ **1** mental, non-physical, psychosomatic, intellectual, psychical, psychic, subconscious, unconscious, subliminal. **3** see IMAGINARY.

psychology /sīkólləji/ *n.* (*pl.* **-ies**) **1** the scientific study of the human mind and its functions, esp. those affecting behaviour in a given context. **2** a treatise on or theory of this. **3 a** the mental characteristics or attitude of a person or group. **b** the mental factors governing a situation or activity (*the psychology of crime*). ▫▫ **psychologist** *n.* **psychologize** *v.tr.* & *intr.* (also **-ise**). [mod.L *psychologia* (as PSYCHO-, -LOGY)]
■ **3 a** (mental) make-up, constitution, attitude, behaviour, thought processes, thinking, psyche, nature, feeling(s), emotion(s), rationale, reasoning.

psychometrics /sīkōmétriks/ *n.pl.* (treated as *sing.*) the science of measuring mental capacities and processes.

psychometry /sīkómmitri/ *n.* **1** the supposed divination of facts about events, people, etc., from inanimate objects associated with them. **2** the measurement of mental abilities. ▫▫ **psychometric** /-kəmétrik/ *adj.* **psychometrically** /-kəmétrikəli/ *adv.* **psychometrist** *n.*

psychomotor /sīkōmōtər/ *adj.* concerning the study of movement resulting from mental activity.

psychoneurosis /sīkōnyoorṓsiss/ *n.* neurosis, esp. with the indirect expression of emotions. ▫▫ **psychoneurotic** *adj.*

psychopath /sīkəpath/ *n.* **1** a person suffering from chronic mental disorder esp. with abnormal or violent social behaviour. **2** a mentally or emotionally unstable person. ▫▫ **psychopathic** /-páthik/ *adj.* **psychopathically** /-páthikəli/ *adv.*
■ see PSYCHOTIC *n.* ▫▫ **psychopathic** see PSYCHOTIC *adj.*

psychopathology /sīkōpəthólləji/ *n.* **1** the scientific study of mental disorders. **2** a mentally or behaviourally disordered state. ▫▫ **psychopathological** /-pathəlójik'l/ *adj.*

psychopathy /sīkóppəthi/ *n.* psychopathic or psychologically abnormal behaviour.

psychophysics /sīkōfízziks/ *n.* the science of the relation between the mind and the body. ▫▫ **psychophysical** *adj.*

psychophysiology /sīkōfizziólləji/ *n.* the branch of physiology dealing with mental phenomena. ◻◻ **psychophysiological** /-ziəlójik'l/ *adj.*

psychosexual /sīkōséksyooəl, -sékshooəl/ *adj.* of or involving the psychological aspects of the sexual impulse. ◻◻ **psychosexually** *adv.*

psychosis /sīkōsiss/ *n.* (*pl.* **psychoses** /-seez/) a severe mental derangement, esp. when resulting in delusions and loss of contact with external reality. [Gk *psukhōsis* f. *psukhoō* give life to (as PSYCHE)]
■ see *insanity* (INSANE).

psychosocial /sīkōsōsh'l/ *adj.* of or involving the influence of social factors or human interactive behaviour. ◻◻ **psychosocially** *adv.*

psychosomatic /sīkōsəmáttik/ *adj.* **1** (of an illness etc.) caused or aggravated by mental conflict, stress, etc. **2** of the mind and body together. ◻◻ **psychosomatically** *adv.*

psychosurgery /sīkōsúrjəri/ *n.* brain surgery as a means of treating mental disorder. ◻◻ **psychosurgical** *adj.*

psychotherapy /sīkōthérrəpi/ *n.* the treatment of mental disorder by psychological means. ◻◻ **psychotherapeutic** /-pyōōtik/ *adj.* **psychotherapist** *n.*
■ see THERAPY 2b. ◻◻ **psychotherapist** see *therapist* (THERAPY).

psychotic /sīkóttik/ *adj.* & *n.* ● *adj.* of or characterized by a psychosis. ● *n.* a person suffering from a psychosis. ◻◻ **psychotically** *adv.*
■ *adj.* mad, insane, psychopathic, deranged, demented, lunatic, unbalanced, (mentally) ill *or* sick, disturbed, of unsound mind, certifiable, unhinged, *colloq.* mental. ● *n.* mental patient, madman, madwoman, maniac, lunatic, psychopath, *colloq.* mental.

psychotropic /sīkōtróppik/ *n.* (of a drug) acting on the mind. [PSYCHO- + Gk *tropē* turning: see TROPIC]

psychrometer /sīkrómmitər/ *n.* a thermometer consisting of a dry bulb and a wet bulb for measuring atmospheric humidity. [Gk *psukhros* cold + -METER]

PT *abbr.* physical training.

Pt *symb. Chem.* the element platinum.

pt. *abbr.* **1** part. **2** pint. **3** point. **4** port.

PTA *abbr.* **1** parent-teacher association. **2** Passenger Transport Authority.

ptarmigan /taármigən/ *n.* any of various game-birds of the genus *Lagopus*, esp. *L. mutus*, with grouselike appearance and black or grey plumage in the summer and white in the winter. [Gael. *tàrmachan*: *p-* after Gk words in *pt-*]

PT boat *n. US* a motor torpedo-boat. [*P*atrol *T*orpedo]

Pte. *abbr.* Private (soldier).

pteridology /térridólləji/ *n.* the study of ferns. ◻◻ **pteridological** /-dəlójik'l/ *adj.* **pteridologist** *n.* [Gk *pteris -idos* fern + -LOGY]

pteridophyte /térridəfīt/ *n.* any flowerless plant of the division Pteridophyta, including ferns, club-mosses, and horsetails. [Gk *pteris -idos* fern + *phuton* plant]

ptero- /térrō/ *comb. form* wing. [Gk *pteron* wing]

pterodactyl /térrədáktil/ *n.* a large extinct flying birdlike reptile with a long slender head and neck.

pteropod /térrəpod/ *n.* a marine gastropod with the middle part of its foot expanded into a pair of winglike lobes. [PTERO- + Gk *pous podos* foot]

pterosaur /térrəsawr/ *n.* any of a group of extinct flying reptiles with large bat-like wings, including pterodactyls. [PTERO- + Gk *saura* lizard]

pteroylglutamic acid /térrō-īlglōōtámmik/ *n.* = FOLIC ACID. [*ptero*ic acid + -YL + GLUTAMIC (ACID)]

pterygoid process /térrigoyd/ *adj.* each of a pair of processes from the sphenoid bone in the skull. [Gk *pterux -ugos* wing]

PTFE *abbr.* polytetrafluoroethylene.

ptisan /tízz'n, tizán/ *n.* a nourishing drink, esp. barley water. [ME & OF *tizanne* etc. f. L *ptisana* f. Gk *ptisanē* peeled barley]

PTO *abbr.* please turn over.

Ptolemaic /tóllimáyik/ *adj. hist.* **1** of or relating to Ptolemy, a 2nd-c. Alexandrian astronomer, or his theories. **2** of or relating to the Ptolemies, Macedonian rulers of Egypt from the death of Alexander the Great (323 BC) to the death of Cleopatra (30 BC). ◻ **Ptolemaic system** the theory that the earth is the stationary centre of the Universe (cf. COPERNICAN SYSTEM). [L *Ptolemaeus* f. Gk *Ptolemaios*]

ptomaine /tōmayn/ *n.* any of various amine compounds, some toxic, in putrefying animal and vegetable matter. ◻ **ptomaine poisoning** *archaic* food poisoning. [F *ptomaïne* f. It. *ptomaina* irreg. f. Gk *ptōma* corpse]

ptosis /tōsiss/ *n.* a drooping of the upper eyelid due to paralysis etc. ◻◻ **ptotic** /tōtik/ *adj.* [Gk *ptōsis* f. *piptō* fall]

Pty. *abbr. Austral.*, *NZ*, & *S.Afr.* proprietary.

ptyalin /tīəlin/ *n.* an enzyme which hydrolyses certain carbohydrates and is found in the saliva of humans and some other animals. [Gk *ptualon* spittle]

Pu *symb. Chem.* the element plutonium.

pub /pub/ *n. colloq.* **1** *Brit.* a public house. **2** *Austral.* a hotel. ◻ **pub-crawl** *Brit. colloq.* a drinking tour of several pubs. [abbr.]
■ **1** public house, inn, taproom, *Austral.* & *NZ* hotel, *Brit.* beerhouse, *US* bar-room, bar, saloon, *archaic or literary* hostelry, *Brit. colloq.* local, boozer, public, *hist.* alehouse, *literary* tavern, *sl.* watering-hole, joint, *Austral. sl.* rub-a-dub(-dub), rubbity(-dub). **2** see HOTEL 1. ◻ **pub-crawl** see JAG[2] 1.

puberty /pyōōbərti/ *n.* the period during which adolescents reach sexual maturity and become capable of reproduction. ◻ **age of puberty** the age at which puberty begins, in law usu. 14 in boys and 12 in girls. ◻◻ **pubertal** *adj.* [ME f. F *puberté* or L *pubertas* f. *puber* adult]
■ pubescence, sexual maturity, adolescence, teens, young manhood, young womanhood, the awkward age.

pubes[1] /pyōōbeez/ *n.* (*pl.* same) the lower part of the abdomen at the front of the pelvis, covered with hair from puberty. [L]

pubes[2] *pl.* of PUBIS.

pubescence /pyoobéss'nss/ *n.* **1** the time when puberty begins. **2** *Bot.* soft down on the leaves and stems of plants. **3** *Zool.* soft down on various parts of animals, esp. insects. ◻◻ **pubescent** *adj.* [F *pubescence* or med.L *pubescentia* f. L *pubescere* reach puberty]
■ **1** see PUBERTY. ◻◻ **pubescent** see ADOLESCENT *adj.*

pubic /pyōōbik/ *adj.* of or relating to the pubes or pubis.

pubis /pyōōbiss/ *n.* (*pl.* **pubes** /-beez/) either of a pair of bones forming the two sides of the pelvis. [L *os pubis* bone of the PUBES]

public /públik/ *adj.* & *n.* ● *adj.* **1** of or concerning the people as a whole (*a public holiday; the public interest*). **2** open to or shared by all the people (*public baths; public library; public meeting*). **3** done or existing openly (*made his views public; a public protest*). **4 a** (of a service, funds, etc.) provided by or concerning local or central government (*public money; public records; public expenditure*). **b** (of a person) in government (*had a distinguished public career*). **5** well-known; famous (*a public institution*). **6** *Brit.* of, for, or acting for, a university (*public examination*). ● *n.* **1** (as *sing.* or *pl.*) the community in general, or members of the community. **2** a section of the community having a particular interest or in some special connection (*the reading public; my public demands my loyalty*). **3** *Brit. colloq.* **a** = *public bar.* **b** = *public house.* ◻ **go public** become a public company. **in public** openly, publicly. **in the public domain** belonging to the public as a whole, esp. not subject to copyright. **in the public eye** famous or notorious. **make public** publicize, make known; publish. **public act** an act of legislation affecting the public as a whole. **public-address system** loudspeakers, microphones, amplifiers, etc., used in addressing large audiences. **public bar** *Brit.* the least expensive bar in a public house. **public bill** a bill of legislation affecting the public as a whole. **public company** *Brit.* a company that sells shares to all buyers on the open market. **public enemy** a notorious wanted criminal. **public figure** a famous person. **public health** the provision of adequate sanitation, drainage, etc. by government. **public house 1** *Brit.* an inn providing alcoholic drinks for consumption on the premises. **2** an inn. **public law 1** the law of relations between individuals and the State. **2** = *public act*. **public lending right** the right of authors to payment when their books etc. are lent by public libraries. **public libel** a published libel. **public nuisance 1** an illegal act against the public generally. **2** *colloq.* an obnoxious person. **public opinion** views, esp. moral, prevalent among the general public. **public ownership** the State ownership of the means of production, distribution, and exchange. **public prosecutor** a law officer conducting criminal proceedings on behalf of the State or in the public interest. **Public Record Office** an institution keeping official archives, esp. birth, marriage, and death certificates, for public inspection. **public relations** the professional maintenance of a favourable public image, esp. by a company, famous person, etc. **public relations officer** a person employed by a company etc. to promote a favourable public image. **public school 1** *Brit.* a private fee-paying secondary school, esp. for boarders. **2** *US*, *Austral.*, & *Sc.* etc. any non-fee-paying school. **public sector** that part of an economy, industry, etc., that is controlled by the State. **public servant** a State official. **public spirit** a willingness to engage in community action. **public-spirited** having a public spirit. **public-spiritedly** in a public-spirited manner. **public-spiritedness** the quality of being public-spirited. **public transport** buses, trains, etc., charging set fares and running on fixed routes, esp. when State-owned. **public utility** an organization supplying water, gas, etc. to the community. **public works** building operations etc. done by or for the State on behalf of the community. **public wrong** an offence against society as a whole. ▫▫ **publicly** *adv.* [ME f. OF *public* or L *publicus* f. *pubes* adult]

■ *adj.* **1** communal, community, common, general, collective, universal, popular, national, civil, civic, societal. **2** accessible, open, free, unrestricted, non-exclusive, communal. **3** open, known, manifest, visible, viewable, conspicuous, exposed, overt; projected, acknowledged, admitted. **4 a** government, local-authority, state, national, federal, civic, civil. **5** well-known, prominent, eminent, celebrated, famous, renowned, notable; influential, illustrious. ● *n.* **1** community, people (at large *or* in general), citizenry, citizens, nation, populace, population, society, voters; plebeians, proletariat, rank and file, commonalty, masses, multitude, *hoi polloi*, man *or* woman in the street, Mr *or* Mrs Average. **2** sector, segment, group, crowd; see also WORLD 7. ▫ **in public** publicly, openly, in the open, *coram populo*; see also *on the level* (LEVEL), *above-board*. **in the public eye** see *well-known* 1, NOTORIOUS. **make public** see PUBLISH. **public figure** see CELEBRITY 1. **public house 1** see PUB 1. **public nuisance 2** see PEST 1. **public servant** see OFFICER *n.* 1, 3, 4. **public-spirited** see CHARITABLE 1. **public-spiritedness** see ALTRUISM.

publican /públikən/ *n.* **1 a** *Brit.* the keeper of a public house. **b** *Austral.* the keeper of a hotel. **2** *Rom.Hist.* & *Bibl.* a tax-collector or tax-farmer. [ME f. OF *publicain* f. L *publicanus* f. *publicum* public revenue (as PUBLIC)]

■ **1 a** see LANDLORD 2.

publication /públikáysh'n/ *n.* **1 a** the preparation and issuing of a book, newspaper, engraving, music, etc. to the public. **b** a book etc. so issued. **2** the act or an instance of making something publicly known. [ME f. OF f. L *publicatio* -*onis* (as PUBLISH)]

■ **1 b** book, booklet, pamphlet, brochure, leaflet, periodical, magazine, journal, newsletter, newspaper, paper. **2** dissemination, promulgation, publicizing, publishing, proclamation, reporting, announcement, advertisement, pronouncement, revelation, declaration, appearance.

publicist /públisist/ *n.* **1** a publicity agent or public relations officer. **2** a journalist, esp. concerned with current affairs. **3** *archaic* a writer or other person skilled in international law. ▫▫ **publicism** *n.* **publicistic** /-sístik/ *adj.* [F *publiciste* f. L (*jus*) *publicum* public law]

publicity /publíssiti/ *n.* **1 a** the professional exploitation of a product, company, person, etc., by advertising or popularizing. **b** material or information used for this. **2** public exposure; notoriety. ▫ **publicity agent** a person employed to produce or heighten public exposure. [F *publicité* (as PUBLIC)]

■ **1 a** advertising, public relations, marketing, promotion; see also ADVERTISEMENT 2. **b** see ADVERTISEMENT 1. **2** see ATTENTION *n.* 1c.

publicize /públisīz/ *v.tr.* (also **-ise**) advertise; make publicly known.

■ promote, advertise, push, give publicity to, *colloq.* beat the drum for, plug, *sl.* hype; make public *or* known, air, broadcast, circulate, announce, put out, release; disclose, reveal, expose.

publish /públish/ *v.tr.* **1** (also *absol.*) (of an author, publisher, etc.) prepare and issue (a book, newspaper, engraving, etc.) for public sale. **2** make generally known. **3** announce (an edict etc.) formally; read (marriage banns). **4** *Law* communicate (a libel etc.) to a third party. ▫▫ **publishable** *adj.* [ME *puplise* etc. f. OF *puplier*, *publier* f. L *publicare* (as PUBLIC)]

■ **2** make public, put out, broadcast, circulate, release, spread (about *or* around), advertise, make known, let a thing be known, tell, announce, publicize, report, proclaim, promulgate, bruit about, noise about; reveal, divulge, disclose.

publisher /públishər/ *n.* **1** a person or esp. a company that produces and distributes copies of a book, newspaper, etc. for sale. **2** *US* a newspaper proprietor. **3** a person or thing that publishes.

puce /pyo͞oss/ *adj.* & *n.* dark red or purple-brown. [F, = flea(-colour) f. L *pulex -icis*]

puck[1] /puk/ *n.* a rubber disc used as a ball in ice hockey. [19th c.: orig. unkn.]

puck[2] /puk/ *n.* **1** a mischievous or evil sprite. **2** a mischievous child. ▫▫ **puckish** *adj.* **puckishly** *adv.* **puckishness** *n.* **pucklike** *adj.* [OE *pūca*: cf. Welsh *pwca*, Ir. *púca*]

■ **1** see IMP *n.* 2. **2** see IMP *n.* 1. ▫▫ **puckish** see MISCHIEVOUS 1, 2.

pucka var. of PUKKA.

pucker /púkkər/ *v.* & *n.* ● *v.tr.* & *intr.* (often foll. by *up*) gather or cause to gather into wrinkles, folds, or bulges (*puckered her eyebrows*; *this seam is puckered up*). ● *n.* such a wrinkle, bulge, fold, etc. ▫▫ **puckery** *adj.* [prob. frequent., formed as POKE[2], POCKET (cf. PURSE)]

■ *v.* gather, draw together, compress, purse, crinkle, ruck, ruffle, furrow, wrinkle, crease, screw up, tighten, contract, squeeze. ● *n.* gather, tuck, pleat, ruffle, ruck, wrinkle, fold, crinkle, *Brit.* ruckle.

pud /po͝od/ *n. colloq.* = PUDDING. [abbr.]

pudding /po͝odding/ *n.* **1 a** any of various sweet cooked dishes (*plum pudding*; *rice pudding*). **b** a savoury dish containing flour, suet, etc. (*Yorkshire pudding*; *steak and kidney pudding*). **c** *Brit.* the sweet course of a meal. **d** the intestines of a pig etc. stuffed with oatmeal, spices, blood, etc. (*black pudding*). **2** *colloq.* a person or thing resembling a pudding. **3** (*Naut.* **puddening** /po͝odd'ning/) a pad or tow binding to prevent chafing etc. ▫ **in the pudding club** *sl.* pregnant. **pudding-cloth** a cloth used for tying up some puddings for boiling. **pudding face** *colloq.* a large fat face. **pudding-head** *colloq.* a stupid person. **pudding-stone** a conglomerate rock consisting of rounded pebbles in a siliceous matrix. ▫▫ **puddingy** *adj.* [ME *poding* f. OF *boudin* black pudding ult. f. L *botellus* sausage: see BOWEL]

■ **1 a, c** see SWEET *n.* 2.

puddle /púdd'l/ *n.* & *v.* ● *n.* **1** a small pool, esp. of rainwater on a road etc. **2** clay and sand mixed with water and used as a watertight covering for embankments etc. **3** a circular patch of disturbed water made by the blade of an oar at each stroke. ● *v.* **1** *tr.* **a** knead (clay and sand) into puddle. **b** line (a canal etc.) with puddle. **2** *intr.* make puddle from clay etc. **3** *tr.* stir (molten iron) to produce wrought iron by expelling carbon. **4** *intr.* **a** dabble or wallow in mud or shallow water. **b** busy oneself in an untidy way. **5** *tr.* make (water etc.) muddy. **6** *tr.* work (mixed water and clay) to separate gold or opal. □□ **puddler** *n.* **puddly** *adj.* [ME *podel*, *puddel*, dimin. of OE *pudd* ditch]

pudency /pyoódənsi/ *n. literary* modesty; shame. [LL *pudentia* (as PUDENDUM)]

pudendum /pyoodéndəm/ *n.* (*pl.* **pudenda** /-də/) (usu. in *pl.*) the genitals, esp. of a woman. □□ **pudendal** *adj.* **pudic** /pyoódik/ *adj.* [L *pudenda* (*membra* parts), neut. pl. of gerundive of *pudēre* be ashamed]

pudgy /púji/ *adj.* (**pudgier**, **pudgiest**) *colloq.* (esp. of a person) plump, thickset. □□ **pudge** *n.* **pudgily** *adv.* **pudginess** *n.* [cf. PODGY]

■ see PLUMP[1] *adj.*

pueblo /pwéblō/ *n.* (*pl.* **-os**) a town or village in Latin America, esp. an Indian settlement. [Sp., = people, f. L *populus*]

puerile /pyoóril/ *adj.* **1** trivial, childish, immature. **2** of or like a child. □ **puerile breathing** breathing characterized by a loud pulmonary murmur as in children, a sign of disease in an adult. □□ **puerilely** *adv.* **puerility** /-rílliti/ *n.* (*pl.* **-ies**). [F *puéril* or L *puerilis* f. *puer* boy]

■ **1** childish, immature, babyish, infantile, juvenile, adolescent, *US* sophomoric; trivial, ridiculous, shallow, inconsequential, insignificant. **2** childish, childlike, boyish, girlish, youthful, infantile, babyish, *US* sophomoric.

puerperal /pyoo-érpərəl/ *adj.* of or caused by childbirth. □ **puerperal fever** fever following childbirth and caused by uterine infection. [L *puerperus* f. *puer* child + *-parus* bearing]

Puerto Rican /pwértō reékən/ *n.* & *adj.* ● *n.* **1** a native of Puerto Rico, an island of the Greater Antilles. **2** a person of Puerto Rican descent. ● *adj.* of or relating to Puerto Rico or its inhabitants.

puff /puf/ *n.* & *v.* ● *n.* **1 a** a short quick blast of breath or wind. **b** the sound of this; a similar sound. **c** a small quantity of vapour, smoke, etc., emitted in one blast; an inhalation or exhalation from a cigarette, pipe, etc. (*went up in a puff of smoke*; *took a puff from his cigarette*). **2** a cake etc. containing jam, cream, etc., and made of light esp. puff pastry. **3** a gathered mass of material in a dress etc. (*puff sleeve*). **4** a rolled protuberant mass of hair. **5 a** an extravagantly enthusiastic review of a book etc., esp. in a newspaper. **b** an advertisement for goods etc., esp. in a newspaper. **6** = *powder-puff*. **7** *US* an eiderdown. **8** *colloq.* one's life (*in all my puff*). ● *v.* **1** *intr.* emit a puff of air or breath; blow with short blasts. **2** *intr.* (usu. foll. by *away*, *out*, etc.) (of a person smoking, a steam engine, etc.) emit or move with puffs (*puffing away at his cigar*; *a train puffed out of the station*). **3** *tr.* (usu. in *passive*; often foll. by *out*) put out of breath (*arrived somewhat puffed*; *completely puffed him out*). **4** *intr.* breathe hard; pant. **5** *tr.* utter pantingly (*'No more,' he puffed*). **6** *intr.* & *tr.* (usu. foll. by *up*, *out*) become or cause to become inflated; swell (*his eye was inflamed and puffed up*; *puffed up the balloon*). **7** *tr.* (usu. foll. by *out*, *up*, *away*) blow or emit (dust, smoke, a light object, etc.) with a puff. **8** *tr.* smoke (a pipe etc.) in puffs. **9** *tr.* (usu. as **puffed up** *adj.*) elate; make proud or boastful. **10** *tr.* advertise or promote (goods, a book, etc.) with exaggerated or false praise. □ **puff-adder** a large venomous African viper, *Bitis arietans*, which inflates the upper part of its body and hisses when excited. **puff and blow** = sense 4 of *v.* **puff-ball** any of various fungi having a ball-shaped spore case. **puff pastry** light flaky pastry. **puff-puff** *Brit.* a childish word for a steam-engine or train. **puff up** = sense 9 of *v.* [ME *puf*, *puffe*, perh. f. OE, imit. of the sound of breath]

■ *n.* **1** blow, breath, wind, whiff, gust, blast; draw, pull, *sl.* drag. **5 b** advertisement, notice, *colloq.* plug, *Brit. colloq.* advert. **7** eiderdown, duvet, coverlet, bedspread, quilt, *US* comforter. **8** life, existence, lifetime, lifespan, time, duration, days. ● *v.* **1** blow (out), exhale, breathe (out). **2** (*puff at* or *on*) draw on, pull at *or* on, smoke, drag on. **3** (*puffed out*) see *exhausted* (EXHAUST *v.* 2). **4** huff, pant, gasp, wheeze, blow, breathe. **6** inflate, distend, bloat, swell (up *or* out), stretch, balloon, expand, pump up. **7** see EXHALE 1. **9** (**puffed up**) see PROUD 2a. **10** publicize, advertise, promote, push, trumpet, blow up, ballyhoo, extol, commend, praise, *colloq.* plug, beat the drum for.

puffer /púffər/ *n.* **1** a person or thing that puffs. **2** = *puff-puff*. □ **puffer-fish** = *globe-fish*. □□ **puffery** *n.*

puffin /púffin/ *n.* any of various sea birds of the family Alcidae native to the N. Atlantic and N. Pacific, esp. *Fratercula arctica*, having a large head with a brightly coloured triangular bill, and black and white plumage. [ME *poffin*, *pophyn*, of unkn. orig.]

puffy /púffi/ *adj.* (**puffier**, **puffiest**) **1** swollen, esp. of the face etc. **2** fat. **3** gusty. **4** short-winded; puffed out. □□ **puffily** *adv.* **puffiness** *n.*

■ **1** see SWELL *v.* 6.

pug[1] /pug/ *n.* **1** (in full **pug-dog**) **a** a dwarf breed of dog like a bulldog with a broad flat nose and deeply wrinkled face. **b** a dog of this breed. **2** a fox. **3** *Brit.* a small locomotive for shunting etc. □ **pug-nose** a short squat or snub nose. **pug-nosed** having such a nose. □□ **puggish** *adj.* **puggy** *adj.* [16th c.: perh. f. LG or Du.]

pug[2] /pug/ *n.* & *v.* ● *n.* loam or clay mixed and prepared for making bricks, pottery, etc. ● *v.tr.* (**pugged**, **pugging**) **1** prepare (clay) thus. **2** pack (esp. the space under the floor to deaden sound) with pug, sawdust, etc. □ **pug-mill** a mill for preparing pug. □□ **pugging** *n.* [19th c.: orig. unkn.]

pug[3] /pug/ *n. sl.* a boxer. [abbr. of PUGILIST]

■ see PUGILIST.

pug[4] /pug/ *n.* & *v.* ● *n.* the footprint of an animal. ● *v.tr.* (**pugged**, **pugging**) track by pugs . [Hindi *pag* footprint]

puggaree /púggəri/ *n.* **1** an Indian turban. **2** a thin muslin scarf tied round a sun-helmet etc. and shielding the neck. [Hindi *pagṛī* turban]

pugilist /pyoójilist/ *n.* a boxer, esp. a professional. □□ **pugilism** *n.* **pugilistic** /-lístik/ *adj.* [L *pugil* boxer]

■ boxer, prizefighter, fighter, battler, combatant, *colloq.* bruiser, *US* slugger, *sl.* pug. □□ **pugilism** boxing, prizefighting, fisticuffs.

pugnacious /pugnáyshəss/ *adj.* quarrelsome; disposed to fight. □□ **pugnaciously** *adv.* **pugnaciousness** *n.* **pugnacity** /-nássiti/ *n.* [L *pugnax -acis* f. *pugnare* fight f. *pugnus* fist]

■ aggressive, belligerent, combative, quarrelsome, bellicose, antagonistic, argumentative, hostile, litigious, contentious, disputatious, disagreeable, hot-tempered, unfriendly, curmudgeonly, short-tempered.

puisne /pyoóni/ *adj. Law* denoting a judge of a superior court inferior in rank to chief justices. [OF f. *puis* f. L *postea* afterwards + *né* born f. L *natus*: cf. PUNY]

puissance /pyoó-is'nss, pwís-/ *n.* **1** /also pweesónss/ a test of a horse's ability to jump large obstacles in showjumping. **2** *archaic* great power, might, or influence. [ME (in sense 2) f. OF (as PUISSANT)]

■ **2** see POWER *n.* 3a, 5, 8.

puissant /pyoó-is'nt, pweés-, pwís-/ *adj. literary* or *archaic* having great power or influence; mighty. □□ **puissantly** *adv.* [ME f. OF f. L *posse* be able: cf. POTENT[1]]

■ see POWERFUL.

puja /poójə/ *n.* (also **pooja**) a Hindu rite of worship; a prayer. [Skr.]

puke /pyoōk/ *v.* & *n. sl.* ● *v.tr.* & *intr.* vomit. ● *n.* vomit. □□ **pukey** *adj.* [16th c.: prob. imit.]

■ *v.* see VOMIT *v.* 1. ● *n.* vomit, *Brit. colloq.* sick, *Austral. sl.* chunder.

pukeko /pŏŏkekō/ *n.* (*pl.* **-os**) *Austral.* & *NZ* a rail, *Porphyrio porphyrio*, with blue, black, and white plumage. [Maori]

pukka /púkkə/ *adj.* (also **pukkah, pucka**) *Anglo-Ind.* **1** genuine. **2** of good quality; reliable (*did a pukka job*). **3** of full weight. [Hindi *pakkā* cooked, ripe, substantial]

■ **1** see GENUINE. **2** good-quality, well-made; see also RELIABLE.

pulchritude /púlkrityōōd/ *n. literary* beauty. □□ **pulchritudinous** /-tyōōdinəss/ *adj.* [ME f. L *pulchritudo -dinis* f. *pulcher -chri* beautiful]

■ see BEAUTY 1.

pule /pyōōl/ *v.intr. literary* cry querulously or weakly; whine, whimper. [16th c.: prob. imit.: cf. F *piauler*]

■ see CRY *v.* 2a.

Pulitzer prize /pŏŏlitsər, pyōō-/ *n.* each of 13 annual awards for achievements in American journalism, literature, and music. [J. *Pulitzer*, Amer. newspaper-publisher d. 1911]

pull /pŏŏl/ *v.* & *n.* ● *v.* **1** *tr.* exert force upon (a thing) tending to move it to oneself or the origin of the force (*stop pulling my hair*). **2** *tr.* cause to move in this way (*pulled it nearer*; *pulled me into the room*). **3** *intr.* exert a pulling force (*the horse pulls well*; *the engine will not pull*). **4** *tr.* extract (a cork or tooth) by pulling. **5** *tr.* damage (a muscle etc.) by abnormal strain. **6 a** *tr.* move (a boat) by pulling on the oars. **b** *intr.* (of a boat etc.) be caused to move, esp. in a specified direction. **7** *intr.* (often foll. by *up*) proceed with effort (up a hill etc.). **8** *tr.* (foll. by *on*) bring out (a weapon) for use against (a person). **9 a** *tr.* check the speed of (a horse), esp. so as to make it lose the race. **b** *intr.* (of a horse) strain against the bit. **10** *tr.* attract or secure (custom or support). **11** *tr.* draw (liquor) from a barrel etc. **12** *intr.* (foll. by *at*) tear or pluck at. **13** *intr.* (often foll. by *on, at*) inhale deeply; draw or suck (on a pipe etc.). **14** *tr.* (often foll. by *up*) remove (a plant) by the root. **15** *tr.* **a** *Cricket* strike (the ball) to the leg side. **b** *Golf* strike (the ball) widely to the left. **16** *tr.* print (a proof etc.). **17** *tr. colloq.* achieve or accomplish (esp. something illicit). **18** *tr. sl.* pick up or attract (a person) for sexual purposes. ● *n.* **1** the act of pulling. **2** the force exerted by this. **3** a means of exerting influence; an advantage. **4** something that attracts or draws attention. **5** a deep draught of liquor. **6** a prolonged effort, e.g. in going up a hill. **7** a handle etc. for applying a pull. **8** a spell of rowing. **9** a printer's rough proof. **10** *Cricket* & *Golf* a pulling stroke. **11** a suck at a cigarette. □ **pull about 1** treat roughly. **2** pull from side to side. **pull apart** (or **to pieces**) = *take to pieces* (see PIECE). **pull away** withdraw, move away. **pull back** retreat or cause to retreat. **pull-back** *n.* **1** a retarding influence. **2** a withdrawal of troops. **pull down 1** demolish (esp. a building). **2** humiliate. **3** *colloq.* earn (a sum of money) as wages etc. **pull a face** assume a distinctive or specified (e.g. sad or angry) expression. **pull a fast one** see FAST[1]. **pull in 1** (of a bus, train, etc.) arrive to take passengers. **2** (of a vehicle) move to the side of or off the road. **3** earn or acquire. **4** *colloq.* arrest. **pull-in** *n. Brit.* a roadside café or other stopping-place. **pull a person's leg** deceive a person playfully. **pull off 1** remove by pulling. **2** succeed in achieving or winning. **pull oneself together** recover control of oneself. **pull the other one** *colloq.* expressing disbelief (with ref. to *pull a person's leg*). **pull out 1** take out by pulling. **2** depart. **3** withdraw from an undertaking. **4** (of a bus, train, etc.) leave with its passengers. **5** (of a vehicle) move out from the side of the road, or from its normal position to overtake. **pull-out** *n.* something that can be pulled out, esp. a section of a magazine. **pull over** (of a vehicle) pull in. **pull the plug on** *colloq.* defeat, discomfit. **pull one's punches** avoid using one's full force. **pull rank** take unfair advantage of one's seniority. **pull round** (or **through**) recover or cause to recover from an illness. **pull strings** exert (esp. clandestine) influence. **pull the strings** be the real actuator of what another does. **pull together** work in harmony. **pull up 1** stop or cause to stop moving. **2** pull out of the ground. **3** reprimand. **4** check oneself. **pull one's weight** do one's fair share of work. **pull wires** esp. *US* = *pull strings*. □□ **puller** *n.* [OE (*ā*)*pullian*, perh. rel. to LG *pūlen*, MDu. *polen* to shell]

■ *v.* **1** jerk, pull at, pluck, tug, *colloq.* yank; wrench. **2** draw, haul, drag, lug, tow, trail; see also TUG *v.* 1. **4** see EXTRACT *v.* 1. **5** tear, stretch, strain, rip, wrench, sprain, *archaic or rhet.* rend. **10, 18** attract, draw, pull in; secure, get, obtain; lure, entice, allure, seduce. **12** see PLUCK *v.* 3, 4. **13** draw, drag, puff, suck; see also INHALE. **14** pull out, pluck (out), extract, uproot, pick (up *or* out), withdraw, tear *or* rip out *or* up, take out, remove, dig up *or* out, *literary* deracinate. **17** see *pull off* 2 below. ● *n.* **1** see TUG *n.* 1. **2, 4** magnetism, appeal, pulling power, seductiveness, seduction; attraction, draw, lure. **3** influence, authority, weight, leverage, *colloq.* clout. **5** see DRAUGHT *n.* 5. **7** lever, grip; see also HANDLE *n.* 1. **11** puff, draw, inhalation, *sl.* drag. □ **pull away** withdraw, draw *or* drive *or* go *or* move away. **pull back** withdraw, draw back, back off *or* away, recoil, shrink (away *or* back), shy away, flinch, jump back, start, (beat a) retreat, take flight, flee, turn tail. **pull-back 1** see IMPEDIMENT. **2** see RETREAT *n.* 1a. **pull down 1** raze, level, destroy, wreck; see also DEMOLISH 1a. **2** lower, humiliate, debase, reduce, degrade, dishonour, disgrace, discredit. **3** earn, draw, receive, get, be paid, take home, clear, pocket, net, bring in, pull in. **pull in 1, 2** draw up *or* in *or* over; see also ARRIVE 1. **3** see EARN 1, ACQUIRE 1. **4** arrest, apprehend, take into custody, collar, *esp. US colloq.* bust, *sl.* pinch, nab, lag, *Brit. sl.* nick. **pull a person's leg** tease, chaff, rib, twit, make fun of, *colloq.* have on, rag; see also *poke fun at* (POKE[1]). **pull off 1** detach, rip *or* tear off, wrench off *or* away; see also SEPARATE *v.* 1. **2** bring off, accomplish, do, complete, succeed in, carry out, manage, perform. **pull oneself together** get a grip (on oneself), *colloq.* buck up, *sl.* snap out of it; recover, get over it, recuperate. **pull the other one** see *go on!* (GO[1]). **pull out 1** uproot, extract, withdraw, pull; pull up, take out; see also PULL *v.* 14 above. **2, 4** see LEAVE[1] *v.* 1b, 3, 4. **3** withdraw, give up; retreat, beat a retreat, draw back, run away *or* off, *colloq.* cry off, *sl.* beat it, *Brit. sl.* do a bunk. **pull the plug on** see BEAT *v.* 3a. **pull rank** pull strings, *esp. US* pull wires, *colloq.* throw one's weight around. **pull round** recover, improve, get better, get over it; live, survive. **pull strings** use *or* exert influence, use connections, *esp. US* pull wires. **pull the strings** be in control *or* command, be behind it all, be in the driving seat, hold the reins; see also DOMINATE. **pull through** see *pull round* above. **pull together** cooperate, agree, *colloq.* jell; see also *get along* 1. **pull up 1** see STOP *v.* 3. **2** see PULL *v.* 14 above. **3** see REPRIMAND *v.* **4** stop, control oneself, check oneself, get a grip on *or* of oneself, get (a) hold on *or* of oneself, pull oneself together, (re)gain control of oneself, snap out of it. **pull one's weight** do one's fair share, perform, *colloq.* do one's bit, deliver the goods.

pullet /pŏŏlit/ *n.* a young hen, esp. one less than one year old. [ME f. OF *poulet* dimin. of *poule* ult. fem. of L *pullus* chicken]

pulley /pŏŏli/ *n.* & *v.* ● *n.* (*pl.* **-eys**) **1** a grooved wheel or set of wheels for a cord etc. to pass over, set in a block and used for changing the direction of a force. **2** a wheel or drum fixed on a shaft and turned by a belt, used esp. to increase speed or power. ● *v.tr.* (**-eys, -eyed**) **1** hoist or work with a pulley. **2** provide with a pulley. [ME f. OF *polie* prob. ult. f. med. Gk *polidion* (unrecorded) pivot, dimin. of *polos* POLE[2]]

■ *v.* **1** hoist, pull *or* lift up, haul up, elevate, raise, heave up, uplift, winch.

Pullman /pŏŏlmən/ *n.* **1** a railway carriage or motor coach affording special comfort. **2** a sleeping-car. [G. M. *Pullman*, Amer. designer d. 1897]

pullover /pŏŏllōvər/ *n.* a knitted garment put on over the head and covering the top half of the body.

pullulate /púlyoolayt/ *v.intr.* **1** (of a seed, shoot, etc.) bud, sprout, germinate. **2** (esp. of an animal) swarm, throng; breed prolifically. **3** develop; spring up; come to life. **4** (foll.

by *with*) abound. ▫▫ **pullulant** *adj.* **pullulation** /-láysh'n/ *n.* [L *pullulare* sprout f. *pullulus* dimin. of *pullus* young of an animal]

pulmonary /púlmənəri, -mənri/ *adj.* **1** of or relating to the lungs. **2** having lungs or lunglike organs. **3** affected with or susceptible to lung disease. ▫ **pulmonary artery** the artery conveying blood from the heart to the lungs. **pulmonary tuberculosis** a form of tuberculosis caused by inhaling the tubercle bacillus into the lungs. **pulmonary vein** the vein carrying oxygenated blood from the lungs to the heart. ▫▫ **pulmonate** /-nət/ *adj.* [L *pulmonarius* f. *pulmo -onis* lung]

pulmonic /pulmónnik/ *adj.* = PULMONARY 1. [F *pulmonique* or f. mod.L *pulmonicus* f. L *pulmo* (as PULMONARY)]

pulp /pulp/ *n.* & *v.* ● *n.* **1** the soft fleshy part of fruit etc. **2** any soft thick wet mass. **3** a soft shapeless mass derived from rags, wood, etc., used in paper-making. **4** (often *attrib.*) poor quality (often sensational) writing orig. printed on rough paper (*pulp fiction*). **5** vascular tissue filling the interior cavity and root canals of a tooth. **6** *Mining* pulverized ore mixed with water. ● *v.* **1** *tr.* reduce to pulp. **2** *tr.* withdraw (a publication) from the market, usu. recycling the paper. **3** *tr.* remove pulp from. **4** *intr.* become pulp. ▫▫ **pulper** *n.* **pulpless** *adj.* **pulpy** *adj.* **pulpiness** *n.* [L *pulpa*]

▪ *n.* **1** marrow, flesh, soft part. **2** mush, paste, mash, pap, pomace, mass. **4** (*attrib.*) bad, poor quality, shoddy, rubbishy, cheap; sensational, lurid. ● *v.* **1** mash, squash, pulverize, triturate, grind down, levigate.

pulpit /pŏŏlpit/ *n.* **1** a raised enclosed platform in a church etc. from which the preacher delivers a sermon. **2** (prec. by *the*) preachers or preaching collectively. [ME f. L *pulpitum* scaffold, platform]

▪ **2** see MINISTRY 2, 3.

pulpwood /púlpwŏŏd/ *n.* timber suitable for making pulp.

pulque /pŏŏlkay, pŏŏlki/ *n.* a Mexican fermented drink made from the sap of the maguey. ▫ **pulque brandy** a strong intoxicant made from pulque. [17th c.: Amer. Sp., of unkn. orig.]

pulsar /púlsaar/ *n.* *Astron.* a cosmic source of regular and rapid pulses of radiation usu. at radio frequencies, e.g. a rotating neutron star. [*puls*ating star, after *quasar*]

pulsate /pulsáyt, púl-/ *v.intr.* **1** expand and contract rhythmically; throb. **2** vibrate, quiver, thrill. ▫▫ **pulsation** /-sáysh'n/ *n.* **pulsator** /-sáytər/ *n.* **pulsatory** /púlsətəri/ *adj.* [L *pulsare* frequent. of *pellere puls-* drive, beat]

▪ beat, pulse, throb, pound, thrum, drum, thump, thud, reverberate, hammer, palpitate, vibrate, oscillate, quiver, thrill.

pulsatile /púlsətīl/ *adj.* **1** of or having the property of pulsation. **2** (of a musical instrument) played by percussion. [med.L *pulsatilis* (as PULSATE)]

pulsatilla /púlsətíllə/ *n.* any plant of the genus *Pulsatilla*, esp. the pasque-flower. [mod.L dimin. of *pulsata* fem. past part. (as PULSATE), because it quivers in the wind]

pulse[1] /pulss/ *n.* & *v.* ● *n.* **1 a** a rhythmical throbbing of the arteries as blood is propelled through them, esp. as felt in the wrists, temples, etc. **b** each successive beat of the arteries or heart. **2** a throb or thrill of life or emotion. **3** a latent feeling. **4** a single vibration of sound, electric current, light, etc., esp. as a signal. **5** a musical beat. **6** any regular or recurrent rhythm, e.g. of the stroke of oars. ● *v.intr.* **1** pulsate. **2** (foll. by *out*, *in*, etc.) transmit etc. by rhythmical beats. ▫ **pulse code** coding information in pulses. **pulse code modulation** a pulse modulation technique of representing a signal by a sequence of binary codes. **pulse modulation** a type of modulation in which pulses are varied to represent a signal. ▫▫ **pulseless** *adj.* [ME f. OF *pous* f. L *pulsus* f. *pellere puls-* drive, beat]

▪ *n.* **2** see THRILL *n.* 2. **5, 6** beat, beating, throb, throbbing, pulsation, pounding, drumming, reverberation, hammering, palpitation, vibration; rhythm. ● *v.* **1** see PULSATE.

pulse[2] /pulss/ *n.* (as *sing.* or *pl.*) **1** the edible seeds of various leguminous plants, e.g. chick-peas, lentils, beans, etc. **2** the plant or plants producing this. [ME f. OF *pols* f. L *puls pultis* porridge of meal etc.]

pulsimeter /pulsímmitər/ *n.* an instrument for measuring the rate or force of a pulse.

pulverize /púlvərīz/ *v.* (also **-ise**) **1** *tr.* reduce to fine particles. **2** *tr.* & *intr.* crumble to dust. **3** *colloq.* *tr.* **a** demolish. **b** defeat utterly. ▫▫ **pulverizable** *adj.* **pulverization** /-záysh'n/ *n.* **pulverizator** *n.* **pulverizer** *n.* [ME f. LL *pulverizare* f. *pulvis pulveris* dust]

▪ **1, 2** powder, comminute, grind, crush, mill, granulate, crumble, break up, pound, triturate, levigate, *archaic* bray. **3** devastate, destroy, demolish, crush, smash, shatter, ruin, wreck, annihilate; see also BEAT *v.* 3a.

pulverulent /pulvérroolənt/ *adj.* **1** consisting of fine particles; powdery. **2** likely to crumble. [L *pulverulentus* (as PULVERIZE)]

puma /pyŏŏmə/ *n.* a large American feline, *Felis concolor*, usu. with a plain greyish-brown coat. Also called COUGAR, PANTHER, *mountain lion*. [Sp. f. Quechua]

pumice /púmmiss/ *n.* & *v.* ● *n.* (in full **pumice-stone**) **1** a light porous volcanic rock often used as an abrasive in cleaning or polishing substances. **2** a piece of this used for removing hard skin etc. ● *v.tr.* rub or clean with a pumice. ▫▫ **pumiceous** /pyoomíshəss/ *adj.* [ME f. OF *pomis* f. L *pumex pumicis* (dial. *pom-*): cf. POUNCE[2]]

pummel /púmm'l/ *v.tr.* (**pummelled, pummelling**; *US* **pummeled, pummeling**) strike repeatedly esp. with the fist. [alt. f. POMMEL]

▪ see BEAT *v.* 1, 2a.

pump[1] /pump/ *n.* & *v.* ● *n.* **1** a machine, usu. with rotary action or the reciprocal action of a piston, for raising or moving liquids, compressing gases, inflating tyres, etc. **2** an instance of pumping; a stroke of a pump. ● *v.* **1** *tr.* (often foll. by *in*, *out*, *into*, *up*, etc.) raise or remove (liquid, gas, etc.) with a pump. **2** *tr.* (often foll. by *up*) fill (a tyre etc.) with air. **3** *tr.* **a** remove (water etc.) with a pump. **b** (foll. by *out*) remove liquid from (a place, well, etc.) with a pump. **4** *intr.* work a pump. **5** *tr.* (often foll. by *out*) cause to move, pour forth, etc., as if by pumping. **6** *tr.* question (a person) persistently to obtain information. **7** *tr.* **a** move vigorously up and down. **b** shake (a person's hand) effusively. **8** *tr.* (usu. foll. by *up*) arouse, excite. ▫ **pump-brake** a handle of a pump, esp. with a transverse bar for several people to work at. **pump-handle** *colloq.* shake (a person's hand) effusively. **pump iron** *colloq.* exercise with weights. **pump-priming 1** introduce fluid etc. into a pump to prepare it for working. **2** esp. *US* the stimulation of commerce etc. by investment. **pump room 1** a room where fuel pumps etc. are stored or controlled. **2** a room at a spa etc. where medicinal water is dispensed. [ME *pumpe*, *pompe* (orig. Naut.): prob. imit.]

▪ *v.* **1, 3a, 5** send, deliver, push; (*pump out*) drive *or* force out, draw off *or* out, siphon (out *or* off), drain, tap, extract, withdraw. **2** (*pump up*) see INFLATE 1. **3 b** (*pump out*) pump dry *or* empty, empty, drain, bail out. **6** interrogate, question, examine, cross-examine, quiz, probe, grill, give a person the third degree. **8** (*pump up*) arouse, excite, inspire, stimulate, animate, inspirit, electrify, galvanize, energize, motivate, *colloq.* enthuse.

pump[2] /pump/ *n.* **1** a plimsoll. **2** a light shoe for dancing etc. **3** *US* a court shoe. [16th c.: orig. unkn.]

pumpernickel /púmpərnikk'l, pŏŏmp-/ *n.* German wholemeal rye bread. [G, earlier = lout, bumpkin, of uncert. orig.]

pumpkin /púmpkin/ *n.* **1** any of various plants of the genus *Cucurbita*, esp. *C. maxima*, with large lobed leaves and tendrils. **2** the large rounded yellow fruit of this with a thick rind and edible flesh. [alt. f. earlier *pompon*, *pumpion* f. obs. F *po(m)pon* f. L *pepo -onis* f. Gk *pepōn* large melon: see PEPO]

pun[1] /pun/ *n.* & *v.* ● *n.* the humorous use of a word to suggest different meanings, or of words of the same sound and different meanings. ● *v.intr.* (**punned, punning**) (foll. by *on*) make a pun or puns with (words). ▫▫ **punningly** *adv.* [17th c.: perh. f. obs. *pundigrion*, a fanciful formation]

■ *n.* play on words, quibble, *double entendre*, innuendo, equivoque, paronomasia; wordplay; quip, witticism, *bon mot*.

pun[2] /pun/ *v.tr.* (**punned, punning**) *Brit.* consolidate (earth or rubble) by pounding or ramming. ▫▫ **punner** *n.* [dial. var. of POUND[2]]

puna /po͞onə/ *n.* **1** a high plateau in the Peruvian Andes. **2** = *mountain sickness*. [Quechua, in sense 1]

punch[1] /punch/ *v.* & *n.* ● *v.tr.* **1** strike bluntly, esp. with a closed fist. **2** prod or poke with a blunt object. **3 a** pierce a hole in (metal, paper, a ticket, etc.) as or with a punch. **b** pierce (a hole) by punching. **4** *US* drive (cattle) by prodding with a stick etc. ● *n.* **1** a blow with a fist. **2** the ability to deliver this. **3** *colloq.* vigour, momentum; effective force. ▫ **punch** (or **punched**) **card** (or **tape**) a card or paper tape perforated according to a code, for conveying instructions or data to a data processor etc. **punch-drunk** stupefied from or as though from a series of heavy blows. **punching-bag** *US* a suspended stuffed bag used as a punchball. **punch-line** words giving the point of a joke or story. **punch-up** *Brit. colloq.* a fist-fight; a brawl. ▫▫ **puncher** *n.* [ME, var. of POUNCE[1]]

■ *v.* **1** hit, clip, jab, smack, box, strike, clout, thump, cuff, poke, *US* slug, *archaic or literary* smite, *colloq.* whack, sock, thwack, bop, *Austral.* & *NZ colloq.* dong, *sl.* wallop, biff, belt. **2** see POKE[1] *v.* 1a. **3 a** puncture, perforate, penetrate, go through, rupture. **b** pierce, prick. ● *n.* **1** clip, jab, smack, blow, box, cuff, thump, upper-cut, clout, hit, poke, *US* slug, *colloq.* sock, whack, thwack, bop, *sl.* wallop, belt, biff, haymaker. **3** effect, impact, effectiveness, force, momentum, impetus, forcefulness, power, vitality, gusto, vigour, life, vim, zest, zip, *colloq.* zing, *sl.* oomph. ▫ **punch-up** see FIGHT *n.* 1a.

punch[2] /punch/ *n.* **1** any of various devices or machines for punching holes in materials (e.g. paper, leather, metal, plaster). **2** a tool or machine for impressing a design or stamping a die on a material. [perh. an abbr. of PUNCHEON[1], or f. PUNCH[1]]

■ **1** awl, auger, bodkin, perforator.

punch[3] /punch/ *n.* a drink of wine or spirits mixed with water, fruit juices, spices, etc., and usu. served hot. ▫ **punch-bowl 1** a bowl in which punch is mixed. **2** a deep round hollow in a hill. [17th c.: orig. unkn.]

punch[4] /punch/ *n.* **1** (**Punch**) a grotesque humpbacked figure in a puppet-show called *Punch and Judy*. **2** (in full **Suffolk punch**) a short-legged thickset draught horse. ▫ **as pleased as Punch** showing great pleasure. [abbr. of PUNCHINELLO]

punchball /púnchbawl/ *n.* **1** a stuffed or inflated ball suspended or mounted on a stand, for punching as a form of exercise. **2** *US* a ball game in which a rubber ball is punched with the fist or head.

puncheon[1] /púnchən/ *n.* **1** a short post, esp. one supporting a roof in a coal-mine. **2** = PUNCH[2]. [ME f. OF *poinson*, *po(i)nchon*, ult. f. L *pungere punct-* prick]

puncheon[2] /púnchən/ *n. hist.* a large cask for liquids etc. holding from 72 to 120 gallons. [ME f. OF *poinson*, *po(i)nchon*, of unkn. orig. (prob. not the same as in PUNCHEON[1])]

Punchinello /púnchinéllō/ *n.* (*pl.* **-os**) **1** the chief character in a traditional Italian puppet show. **2** a short stout person of comical appearance. [Neapolitan dial. *Polecenella*, It. *Pulcinella*, perh. dimin. of *pollecena*, young turkey-cock with a hooked beak f. *pulcino* chicken ult. f. L *pullus*]

punchy /púnchi/ *adj.* (**punchier, punchiest**) having punch or vigour; forceful. ▫▫ **punchily** *adv.* **punchiness** *n.*

■ see FORCEFUL.

puncta *pl.* of PUNCTUM.

punctate /púngktayt/ *adj. Biol.* marked or studded with points, dots, spots, etc. ▫▫ **punctation** /-táysh'n/ *n.* [L *punctum* (as POINT)]

punctilio /pungktílliō/ *n.* (*pl.* **-os**) **1** a delicate point of ceremony or honour. **2** the etiquette of such points. **3** petty formality. [It. *puntiglio* & Sp. *puntillo* dimin. of *punto* POINT]

■ **2** see ETIQUETTE 1, see FORMALITY 2, 4.

punctilious /pungktílliəss/ *adj.* **1** attentive to formality or etiquette. **2** precise in behaviour. ▫▫ **punctiliously** *adv.* **punctiliousness** *n.* [F *pointilleux* f. *pointille* f. It. (as PUNCTILIO)]

■ **1** see FORMAL *adj.* 4. **2** see PRECISE 2. ▫▫ **punctiliously** see PRECISELY 1. **punctiliousness** see PRECISION 2.

punctual /púngktyooəl/ *adj.* **1** observant of the appointed time. **2** neither early nor late. **3** *Geom.* of a point. ▫▫ **punctuality** /-tyoo-álliti/ *n.* **punctually** *adv.* [ME f. med.L *punctualis* f. L *punctum* POINT]

■ **1, 2** on time, timely, prompt; on target.

punctuate /púngktyoo-ayt/ *v.tr.* **1** insert punctuation marks in. **2** interrupt at intervals (*punctuated his tale with heavy sighs*). [med.L *punctuare punctuat-* (as PUNCTUAL)]

■ **2** interrupt, break; intersperse, interlard, pepper, sprinkle, besprinkle, dot.

punctuation /púngktyoo-áysh'n/ *n.* **1** the system or arrangement of marks used to punctuate a written passage. **2** the practice or skill of punctuating. ▫ **punctuation mark** any of the marks (e.g. full stop and comma) used in writing to separate sentences and phrases etc. and to clarify meaning. [med.L *punctuatio* (as PUNCTUATE)]

punctum /púngktəm/ *n.* (*pl.* **puncta** /-tə/) *Biol.* a speck, dot, spot of colour, etc., or an elevation or depression on a surface. [L, = POINT]

puncture /púngkchər/ *n.* & *v.* ● *n.* **1** a prick or pricking, esp. the accidental piercing of a pneumatic tyre. **2** a hole made in this way. ● *v.* **1** *tr.* make a puncture in. **2** *intr.* undergo puncture. **3** *tr.* prick or pierce. **4** *tr.* cause (hopes, confidence, etc.) to collapse; dash, deflate. [ME f. L *punctura* f. *pungere punct-* prick]

■ *n.* **1** perforation, holing, piercing; prick. **2** see LEAK *n.* 1a. ● *v.* **1, 3** hole, pierce, penetrate, go through, prick, nick. **4** deflate, disillusion, discourage, dash, destroy, ruin.

pundit /púndit/ *n.* **1** (also **pandit**) a Hindu learned in Sanskrit and in the philosophy, religion, and jurisprudence of India. **2** often *iron.* a learned expert or teacher. ▫▫ **punditry** *n.* [Hind. *paṇḍit* f. Skr. *paṇḍita* learned]

■ **2** see EXPERT *n.*

pungent /púnjənt/ *adj.* **1** having a sharp or strong taste or smell, esp. so as to produce a pricking sensation. **2** (of remarks) penetrating, biting, caustic. **3** mentally stimulating. **4** *Biol.* having a sharp point. ▫▫ **pungency** *n.* **pungently** *adv.* [L *pungent-* pres. part. of *pungere* prick]

■ **1** spicy, hot, sharp, strong, penetrating, aromatic, seasoned, peppery, piquant, tangy, flavourful, tasty, *literary* sapid. **2** sharp, biting, penetrating, stinging, caustic, severe, astringent, stern, acrid, harsh, acid, acrimonious, bitter, cutting, keen, barbed, trenchant, scathing, incisive, mordant, sarcastic. **3** see *stimulating* (STIMULATE).

Punic /pyo͞onik/ *adj.* & *n.* ● *adj.* of or relating to ancient Carthage in N. Africa. ● *n.* the language of Carthage, related to Phoenician. ▫ **Punic faith** treachery. [L *Punicus*, *Poenicus* f. *Poenus* f. Gk *Phoinix* Phoenician]

punish /púnnish/ *v.tr.* **1** cause (an offender) to suffer for an offence. **2** inflict a penalty for (an offence). **3** *colloq.* inflict severe blows on (an opponent). **4 a** tax severely; subject to severe treatment. **b** abuse or treat improperly. ▫▫ **punishable** *adj.* **punisher** *n.* **punishing** *adj.* (in sense 4a). **punishingly** *adv.* [ME f. OF *punir* f. L *punire* = *poenire* f. *poena* penalty]

■ **1** penalize, chastise, castigate, discipline, chasten, amerce, scold, rebuke, take to task, reprove, drop on, admonish, correct, pepper, trounce, teach a person a lesson, rap on the knuckles, give a person a slap on the wrist, have on the carpet, make a person pay for, *Bibl.* visit, *colloq.* throw the book at, dress down, give it to a person, give a person hell, lay into; tar and feather; flog, beat, scourge, spank, whip, cane, birch, bastinado. **3** rough up, knock about *or* around, thrash, trounce, batter, beat up; see also BEAT *v.* 1. **4** abuse,

maltreat, mistreat, hurt, harm, injure, damage.
□□ **punishing** gruelling, hard, arduous, strenuous, exhausting, tiring, taxing, demanding, burdensome, back-breaking, torturous.

punishment /púnnishmənt/ *n.* **1** the act or an instance of punishing; the condition of being punished. **2** the loss or suffering inflicted in this. **3** *colloq.* severe treatment or suffering. [ME f. AF & OF *punissement* f. *punir*]
■ **1, 2** chastisement, castigation, discipline, scolding, rebuke, reproof, admonishment, admonition, correction, sentencing, punitive measures; penance, penalty, sentence; (just) deserts, *colloq.* comeuppance; stick; flogging, beating, whipping, scourging, spanking, caning, birching. **3** injury, harm, damage, abuse, maltreatment, suffering, torture; beating, thrashing, battering; pounding; *colloq.* stick.

punitive /pyóonitiv/ *adj.* (also **punitory** /-təri/) **1** inflicting or intended to inflict punishment. **2** (of taxation etc.) extremely severe. **3** *Law* (of damages etc.) = VINDICTIVE. □□ **punitively** *adv.* [F *punitif -ive* or med.L *punitivus* (as PUNISHMENT)]
■ **1** chastening, castigatory, disciplinary, retributive, correctional. **2** see HARSH 2.

Punjabi /poonjaábi/ *n.* & *adj.* ● *n.* (*pl.* **Punjabis**) **1** a native of the Punjab in India. **2** the language of this people. ● *adj.* of or relating to the Punjab. [Hindi *pañjābī*]

punk /pungk/ *n.* & *adj.* ● *n.* **1 a** a worthless person or thing (often as a general term of abuse). **b** nonsense. **2 a** (in full **punk rock**) a loud fast-moving form of rock music with crude and aggressive effects. **b** (in full **punk rocker**) a devotee of this. **3** *US* a hoodlum or ruffian. **4** *US* a passive male homosexual. **5** *US* an inexperienced person; a novice. **6** soft crumbly wood that has been attacked by fungus, used as tinder. ● *adj.* **1** worthless, poor in quality. **2** denoting punk rock and its associations. **3** *US* (of wood) rotten, decayed. □□ **punky** *adj.* [18th c.: orig. unkn.: cf. SPUNK]
■ *n.* **1 a** see WRETCH 2. **b** see NONSENSE. **3** ruffian, hooligan, delinquent, tough, thug, vandal, yahoo, barbarian, *US sl.* mug; see also HOODLUM. **5** see NOVICE. ● *adj.* **1** inferior, unimportant, bad, poor, *colloq.* lousy, awful, *sl.* rotten; see also WORTHLESS.

punkah /púngkə/ *n.* **1** (in India) a fan usu. made from the leaf of the palmyra. **2** a large swinging cloth fan on a frame worked by a cord or electrically. □ **punkah-wallah** a person who works a punkah. [Hindi *pankhā* fan f. Skr. *pakṣaka* f. *pakṣa* wing]

punnet /púnnit/ *n. Brit.* a small light basket or container for fruit or vegetables. [19th c.: perh. dimin. of dial. *pun* POUND[1]]

punster /púnstər/ *n.* a person who makes puns, esp. habitually.

punt[1] /punt/ *n.* & *v.* ● *n.* a long narrow flat-bottomed boat, square at both ends, used mainly for pleasure on rivers and propelled by a long pole. ● *v.* **1** *tr.* propel (a punt) with a pole. **2** *intr.* & *tr.* travel or convey in a punt. □□ **punter** *n.* [ME f. MLG *punte*, *punto* & MDu. *ponte* ferry-boat f. L *ponto* Gaulish transport vessel]

punt[2] /punt/ *v.* & *n.* ● *v.tr.* kick (a ball, esp. in rugby) after it has dropped from the hands and before it reaches the ground. ● *n.* such a kick. □□ **punter** *n.* [prob. f. dial. *punt* push forcibly: cf. BUNT[3]]

punt[3] /punt/ *v.* & *n.* ● *v.intr.* **1** (in some card-games) lay a stake against the bank. **2** *Brit. colloq.* **a** bet on a horse etc. **b** speculate in shares etc. ● *n.* **1** a bet. **2** a point in faro. **3** a person who plays against the bank in faro. [F *ponter* f. *ponte* player against the bank f. Sp. *punto* POINT]
■ *v.* **2 a** bet, wager, gamble, speculate, lay a bet *or* wager. ● *n.* **1** wager, stake; see also BET *n.* 1, 2.

punt[4] /poont/ *n.* the chief monetary unit of the Republic of Ireland. [Ir., = pound]

punter /púntər/ *n.* **1** a person who gambles or lays a bet. **2 a** *colloq.* a customer or client; a member of an audience. **b** *colloq.* a participant in any activity; a person. **c** *sl.* a prostitute's client. **3** a point in faro.
■ **1** better, gambler, gamester, player, speculator, punt. **2 a** customer, buyer, shopper, client; patron. **b** fellow, chap, person, individual, man in the street, woman in the street; *colloq.* guy, *sl.* geezer, *Brit. sl.* bloke.

puny /pyóoni/ *adj.* (**punier, puniest**) **1** undersized. **2** weak, feeble. **3** petty. □□ **punily** *adv.* **puniness** *n.* [phonetic spelling of PUISNE]
■ **1, 2** small, little, diminutive, tiny, minute, undersized, stunted, dwarf, midget, pygmy; weak, feeble, frail, sickly, weakly, underfed, undernourished. **3** insignificant, petty, unimportant, inconsequential, paltry, trivial, trifling, minor, negligible, nugatory, small, little, worthless, useless, *colloq.* piddling.

pup /pup/ *n.* & *v.* ● *n.* **1** a young dog. **2** a young wolf, rat, seal, etc. **3** *Brit.* an unpleasant or arrogant young man. ● *v.tr.* (**pupped, pupping**) (also *absol.*) (of a bitch etc.) bring forth (young). □ **in pup** (of a bitch) pregnant. **sell a person a pup** swindle a person, esp. by selling something worthless. [back-form. f. PUPPY as if a dimin. in -Y[2]]
■ *n.* **1** puppy, whelp. **3** puppy, whelp, upstart, whippersnapper, cub, *archaic* jackanapes. □ **sell a person a pup** see SWINDLE *v.*

pupa /pyóopə/ *n.* (*pl.* **pupae** /-pee/) an insect in the stage of development between larva and imago. □□ **pupal** *adj.* [mod.L f. L *pupa* girl, doll]

pupate /pyoopáyt/ *v.intr.* become a pupa. □□ **pupation** *n.*

pupil[1] /pyóopil, -p'l/ *n.* **1** a person who is taught by another, esp. a schoolchild or student in relation to a teacher. **2** *Sc. Law* a boy less than 14 or a girl less than 12 years in age. □□ **pupillage** *n.* (also **pupilage**). **pupillary** *adj.* (also **pupilary**). [ME, orig. = orphan, ward f. OF *pupille* or L *pupillus, -illa*, dimin. of *pupus* boy, *pupa* girl]
■ **1** student, learner, schoolchild, schoolgirl, schoolboy; disciple, apprentice; chela.

pupil[2] /pyóopil, -p'l/ *n.* the dark circular opening in the centre of the iris of the eye, varying in size to regulate the passage of light to the retina. □□ **pupillar** *adj.* (also **pupilar**). **pupillary** *adj.* (also **pupilary**). [OF *pupille* or L *pupilla*, dimin. of *pūpa* doll (as PUPIL[1]): so called from the tiny images visible in the eye]

pupiparous /pyoopíppərəss/ *adj. Entomol.* bringing forth young which are already in a pupal state. [mod.L *pupipara* neut. pl. of *pupiparus* (as PUPA, *parere* bring forth)]

puppet /púppit/ *n.* **1** a small figure representing a human being or animal and moved by various means as entertainment. **2** a person whose actions are controlled by another. □ **puppet State** a country that is nominally independent but actually under the control of another power. □□ **puppetry** *n.* [later form of POPPET]
■ **2** figurehead, cat's-paw, pawn, dupe, tool, instrument, *colloq.* yes-man, stooge.

puppeteer /púppitéer/ *n.* a person who works puppets.

puppy /púppi/ *n.* (*pl.* **-ies**) **1** a young dog. **2** a conceited or arrogant young man. □ **puppy-fat** temporary fatness of a child or adolescent. **puppy love** = *calf-love* (see CALF[1]). □□ **puppyhood** *n.* **puppyish** *adj.* [ME perh. f. OF *po(u)pee* doll, plaything, toy f. Rmc (as POPPET)]
■ **2** see PUP *n.* 3.

pur- /pur/ *prefix* = PRO-[1] (*purchase*; *pursue*). [AF f. OF *por-*, *pur-*, *pour-* f. L *por-*, *pro-*]

Purana /pooraánə/ *n.* any of a class of Sanskrit sacred writings on Hindu mythology, folklore, etc. □□ **Puranic** *adj.* [Skr. *purāṇa* ancient legend, ancient, f. *purā* formerly]

Purbeck marble /púrbek/ *n.* (also **Purbeck stone**) *Archit.* a hard usu. polished limestone from Purbeck in Dorset, used in pillars, effigies, etc.

purblind /púrblīnd/ *adj.* **1** partly blind; dim-sighted. **2** obtuse, dim-witted. □□ **purblindness** *n.* [ME *pur(e) blind* f. PURE orig. in sense 'utterly', with assim. to PUR-]

■ **1** partially sighted, visually handicapped. **2** see DIM *adj.* 3.

purchase /púrchiss/ *v.* & *n.* ● *v.tr.* **1** acquire by payment; buy. **2** obtain or achieve at some cost. **3** *Naut.* haul up (an anchor etc.) by means of a pulley, lever, etc. ● *n.* **1** the act or an instance of buying. **2** something bought. **3** *Law* the acquisition of property by one's personal action and not by inheritance. **4 a** a firm hold on a thing to move it or to prevent it from slipping; leverage. **b** a device or tackle for moving heavy objects. **5** the annual rent or return from land. □ **purchase tax** *Brit. hist.* a tax on goods bought, levied at higher rates for non-essential or luxury goods. □□ **purchasable** *adj.* **purchaser** *n.* [ME f. AF *purchacer*, OF *pourchacier* seek to obtain (as PUR-, CHASE[1])]

■ *v.* **1** buy, acquire, procure, obtain, get, secure, pay for. **2** win, gain, achieve, realize, attain, obtain. ● *n.* **1** acquisition, buying, purchasing, procurement. **2** acquisition, *colloq.* buy. **4 a** grip, hold, support, toe-hold, foothold, grasp, footing; leverage; position, advantage, edge.

purdah /púrdə/ *n. Ind.* **1** a system in certain Muslim and Hindu societies of screening women from strangers by means of a veil or curtain. **2** a curtain in a house, used for this purpose. [Urdu & Pers. *pardah* veil, curtain]

pure /pyoor/ *adj.* **1** unmixed, unadulterated (*pure white*; *pure alcohol*). **2** of unmixed origin or descent (*pure-blooded*). **3** chaste. **4** morally or sexually undefiled; not corrupt. **5** conforming absolutely to a standard of quality; faultless. **6** guiltless. **7** sincere. **8** mere, simple, nothing but, sheer (*it was pure malice*). **9** (of a sound) not discordant, perfectly in tune. **10** (of a subject of study) dealing with abstract concepts and not practical application. **11 a** (of a vowel) not joined with another in a diphthong. **b** (of a consonant) not accompanied by another. □ **pure science** a science depending on deductions from demonstrated truths (e.g. mathematics or logic), or one studied without practical applications. □□ **pureness** *n.* [ME f. OF *pur* pure f. L *purus*]

■ **1, 2** unmixed, unadulterated, uncontaminated, clear, unalloyed, entire, true, perfect; 24-carat, sterling, solid. **3, 4** chaste, virginal, virgin, intact, maidenly, vestal, immaculate, undefiled, uncorrupted, wholesome, unpolluted, spotless, unblemished, untainted, unsullied; virtuous, good, modest, moral, correct, proper, sinless, impeccable, honourable, (highly) principled, righteous, upright, honest, high-minded, pious, worthy, ethical. **5** faultless, flawless, correct, errorless, perfect. **6** guiltless, innocent, above suspicion, above reproach, blameless. **7** see SINCERE. **8** sheer, utter, absolute, unqualified, complete, total, perfect, thorough, outright, downright, out-and-out, mere, unalloyed, simple, unmitigated, nothing but. **10** abstract, conceptual, theoretical, hypothetical, conjectural, speculative, notional, philosophical, academic.

purée /pyóoray/ *n.* & *v.* ● *n.* a pulp of vegetables or fruit etc. reduced to a smooth cream. ● *v.tr.* (**purées, puréed**) make a purée of. [F]

purely /pyóorli/ *adv.* **1** in a pure manner. **2** merely, solely, exclusively.

■ **2** see *merely* (MERE[1]).

purfle /púrf'l/ *n.* & *v.* ● *n.* **1** an ornamental border, esp. on a violin etc. **2** *archaic* the ornamental or embroidered edge of a garment. ● *v.tr.* **1** decorate with a purfle. **2** (often foll. by *with*) ornament (the edge of a building). **3** beautify. □□ **purfling** *n.* [ME f. OF *porfil*, *porfiler* ult. f. L *filum* thread]

purgation /purgáysh'n/ *n.* **1** purification. **2** purging of the bowels. **3** spiritual cleansing, esp. (*RC Ch.*) of a soul in purgatory. **4** *hist.* the cleansing of oneself from accusation or suspicion by an oath or ordeal. [ME f. OF *purgation* or L *purgatio* (as PURGE)]

purgative /púrgətiv/ *adj.* & *n.* ● *adj.* **1** serving to purify. **2** strongly laxative. ● *n.* **1** a purgative thing. **2** a laxative. [ME f. OF *purgatif -ive* or LL *purgativus* (as PURGE)]

■ *adj.* **1** cathartic, depurative, purifying. **2** laxative, cathartic, aperient, evacuant. ● *n.* **1** purifier, depurative, purge. **2** laxative, cathartic, aperient, purge, depurative.

purgatory /púrgətəri, -tri/ *n.* & *adj.* ● *n.* (*pl.* **-ies**) **1** the condition or supposed place of spiritual cleansing, esp. (*RC Ch.*) of those dying in the grace of God but having to expiate venial sins etc. **2** a place or state of temporary suffering or expiation. ● *adj.* purifying. □□ **purgatorial** /-tóriəl/ *adj.* [ME f. AF *purgatorie*, OF *-oire* f. med.L *purgatorium*, neut. of LL *purgatorius* (as PURGE)]

purge /purj/ *v.* & *n.* ● *v.tr.* **1** (often foll. by *of*, *from*) make physically or spiritually clean. **2** remove by a cleansing process. **3 a** rid (an organization, party, etc.) of persons regarded as undesirable. **b** remove (a person regarded as undesirable) from an organization, party, etc., often violently or by force. **4 a** empty (the bowels). **b** empty the bowels of. **5** *Law* atone for or wipe out (an offence, esp. contempt of court). ● *n.* **1 a** the act or an instance of purging. **b** the removal, often in a forcible or violent manner, of people regarded as undesirable from an organization, party, etc. **2** a purgative. □□ **purger** *n.* [ME f. OF *purg(i)er* f. L *purgare* purify f. *purus* pure]

■ *v.* **1** purify, clean (out), make clean, scour (out), depurate, wash (out), *usu. formal* cleanse; clear, exonerate, absolve, *formal* exculpate. **3 a** rid, free from, clear. **b** eject, expel, eliminate, get rid of, dismiss, clear out *or* away, sweep away *or* out, oust, remove, rout out, weed out, root out. **4 a** see EMPTY *v.* 1. **5** see ATONE. ● *n.* **1** cleansing, purification; ousting, ouster, removal, ejection, expulsion, elimination. **2** see PURGATIVE *n.* 2.

purify /pyóorifī/ *v.tr.* (**-ies, -ied**) **1** (often foll. by *of*, *from*) cleanse or make pure. **2** make ceremonially clean. **3** clear of extraneous elements. □□ **purification** /-fikáysh'n/ *n.* **purificatory** /-fikáytəri/ *adj.* **purifier** *n.* [ME f. OF *purifier* f. L *purificare* (as PURE)]

■ **1** clean, clarify, refine, wash, sanitize, depurate, decontaminate, freshen, disinfect, *usu. formal* cleanse.

Purim /pyóorim, pyooréem/ *n.* a Jewish spring festival commemorating the defeat of Haman's plot to massacre the Jews (Esth. 9). [Heb., pl. of *pūr*, perh. = LOT *n.* 2]

purine /póoreen/ *n.* **1** *Chem.* an organic nitrogenous base forming uric acid on oxidation. **2** any of a group of derivatives with purine-like structure, including the nucleotide constituents adenine and guanine. [G *Purin* L *purus* pure + *uricum* uric acid + *-in* -INE[4]]

purist /pyóorist/ *n.* a stickler for or advocate of scrupulous purity, esp. in language or art. □□ **purism** *n.* **puristic** /-ristik/ *adj.* [F *puriste* f. *pur* PURE]

■ pedant, precisionist, formalist, stickler, prescriptivist, *colloq.* die-hard.

puritan /pyóorit'n/ *n.* & *adj.* ● *n.* **1** (**Puritan**) *hist.* a member of a group of English Protestants who regarded the Reformation of the Church under Elizabeth as incomplete and sought to simplify and regulate forms of worship. **2** a purist member of any party. **3** a person practising or affecting extreme strictness in religion or morals. ● *adj.* **1** *hist.* of or relating to the Puritans. **2** scrupulous and austere in religion or morals. □□ **puritanism** *n.* [LL *puritas* (as PURITY) after earlier *Catharan* (as CATHAR)]

■ *n.* **3** moralist, pietist, purist, precisian; religionist, fanatic, zealot, *Austral. sl.* wowser; see also PRIG. ● *adj.* **2** prudish, puritanical, prim, proper, strait-laced, ascetic, austere, moralistic, pietistic, intolerant, disapproving, bigoted, narrow-minded, stuffy, stiff-necked, rigid, uncompromising, hard-line, stern, severe, strict, *US colloq.* uptight.

puritanical /pyóoritánnik'l/ *adj.* often *derog.* practising or affecting strict religious or moral behaviour. □□ **puritanically** *adv.*

■ see PURITAN *adj.*

purity /pyóoriti/ *n.* **1** pureness, cleanness. **2** freedom from physical or moral pollution. [ME f. OF *pureté*, with assim. to LL *puritas -tatis* f. L *purus* pure]

■ **1** pureness, cleanness, cleanliness, clarity; healthfulness, wholesomeness, salubrity. **2** pureness, faultlessness, correctness, flawlessness, perfection, spotlessness; chastity, chasteness, virginity, virtuousness, virtue, modesty, morality, propriety, honesty, integrity, rectitude, properness, innocence, guilelessness, blamelessness, sinlessness.

purl[1] /purl/ *n.* & *v.* ● *n.* **1** a knitting stitch made by putting the needle through the front of the previous stitch and passing the yarn round the back of the needle. **2** a cord of twisted gold or silver wire for bordering. **3** a chain of minute loops; a picot. **4** the ornamental edges of lace, ribbon, etc. ● *v.tr.* (also *absol.*) knit with a purl stitch. [orig. *pyrle, pirle* f. Sc. *pirl* twist: the knitting sense may be f. a different word]

purl[2] /purl/ *v.* & *n.* ● *v.intr.* (of a brook etc.) flow with a swirling motion and babbling sound. ● *n.* this motion or sound. [16th c.: prob. imit.: cf. Norw. *purla* bubble up]
■ *v.* see GURGLE *v.* ● *n.* see GURGLE *n.*

purler /púrlər/ *n. Brit. colloq.* a headlong fall. [*purl* upset, rel. to PURL[1]]

purlieu /púrlyōō/ *n.* (*pl.* **purlieus**) **1** a person's bounds or limits. **2** a person's usual haunts. **3** *Brit. hist.* a tract on the border of a forest, esp. one earlier included in it and still partly subject to forest laws. **4** (in *pl.*) the outskirts; an outlying region. [ME *purlew*, prob. alt. after F *lieu* place f. AF *purale(e)*, OF *pourallee* a going round to settle the boundaries f. *po(u)raler* traverse]
■ **2** see TERRITORY 3. **4** (*purlieus*) see OUTSKIRTS.

purlin /púrlin/ *n.* a horizontal beam along the length of a roof, resting on principals and supporting the common rafters or boards. [ME: orig. uncert.]

purloin /pərlóyn/ *v.tr. formal* or *joc.* steal, pilfer. □□ **purloiner** *n.* [ME f. AF *purloigner* put away, do away with (as PUR-, *loign* far f. L *longe*)]
■ see PILFER. □□ **purloiner** see THIEF.

purple /púrp'l/ *n.*, *adj.*, & *v.* ● *n.* **1** a colour intermediate between red and blue. **2** (in full **Tyrian purple**) a crimson dye obtained from some molluscs. **3** a purple robe, esp. as the dress of an emperor or senior magistrate. **4** the scarlet official dress of a cardinal. **5** (prec. by *the*) a position of rank, authority, or privilege. ● *adj.* of a purple colour. ● *v.tr.* & *intr.* make or become purple. □ **born in the purple 1** born into a reigning family. **2** belonging to the most privileged class. **purple emperor** a large butterfly, *Apatura iris*, with purple wings. **purple heart** *Brit. colloq.* a heart-shaped stimulant tablet, esp. of amphetamine. **Purple Heart** (in the US) a decoration for those wounded in action. **purple passage** (or **patch**) **1** an ornate or elaborate passage in a literary composition. **2** *Austral. colloq.* a piece of luck or success. □□ **purpleness** *n.* **purplish** *adj.* **purply** *adj.* [OE alt. f. *purpure purpuran* f. L *purpura* (as PURPURA)]

purport *v.* & *n.* ● *v.tr.* /pərpórt/ **1** profess; be intended to seem (*purports to be the royal seal*). **2** (often foll. by *that* + clause) (of a document or speech) have as its meaning; state. ● *n.* /púrport/ **1** the ostensible meaning of something. **2** the sense or tenor (of a document or statement). □□ **purportedly** /pərpórtidli/ *adv.* [ME f. AF & OF *purport, porport* f. *purporter* f. med.L *proportare* (as PRO-[1], *portare* carry)]
■ *v.* **1** profess, pretend, (lay) claim, make a pretence. ● *n.* see MEANING *n.* 1, 2. □□ **purportedly** see *seemingly* (SEEMING[1]).

purpose /púrpəss/ *n.* & *v.* ● *n.* **1** an object to be attained; a thing intended. **2** the intention to act. **3** resolution, determination. **4** the reason for which something is done or made. ● *v.tr.* have as one's purpose; design, intend. □ **on purpose** intentionally. **purpose-built** (or **-made**) built or made for a specific purpose. **to no purpose** with no result or effect. **to the purpose 1** relevant. **2** useful. [ME f. OF *porpos, purpos* f. L *proponere* (as PROPOUND)]
■ *n.* **1** object, intention, intent, end, goal, ambition, objective, target, aim; rationale, reason, motive, motivation. **2** intent, intention, scheme, plan, design. **3** resolution, firmness, determination, persistence, drive, single-mindedness, deliberation, deliberateness, purposefulness, steadfastness, tenacity, doggedness, will, resolve, resoluteness, perseverance. **4** use, practicality, avail, effect, utility, usefulness; advantage, profit, gain, good, benefit; *raison d'être*. ● *v.* plan, intend, design, resolve, mean, aim, have in mind *or* view, have a mind, propose. □ **on purpose** purposely, intentionally, deliberately, wilfully, by design, consciously, knowingly, designedly, wittingly. **to the purpose 1** see RELEVANT. **2** see USEFUL.

purposeful /púrpəsfōōl/ *adj.* **1** having or indicating purpose. **2** intentional. **3** resolute. □□ **purposefully** *adv.* **purposefulness** *n.*
■ **2** intentional, intended, planned, deliberate, wilful, intended. **3** resolved, settled, determined, resolute, decided, sure, certain, positive, definite, staunch, steadfast, persistent, strong-willed, dogged, tenacious, pertinacious, purposive, unfailing, unfaltering, firm, fixed.

purposeless /púrpəsliss/ *adj.* having no aim or plan. □□ **purposelessly** *adv.* **purposelessness** *n.*
■ aimless, undirected, directionless; erratic, haphazard; pointless, meaningless, senseless.

purposely /púrpəsli/ *adv.* on purpose; intentionally.
■ see *on purpose* (PURPOSE).

purposive /púrpəsiv/ *adj.* **1** having or serving a purpose. **2** done with a purpose. **3** (of a person or conduct) having purpose or resolution; purposeful. □□ **purposively** *adv.* **purposiveness** *n.*
■ **3** see RESOLUTE.

purpura /púrpyoorə/ *n.* **1** a disease characterized by purple or livid spots on the skin, due to internal bleeding from small blood vessels. **2** any mollusc of the genus *Purpura*, some of which yield a purple dye. □□ **purpuric** /-pyóorik/ *adj.* [L f. Gk *porphura* purple]

purpure /púrpyoor/ *n.* & *adj. Heraldry* purple. [OE *purpure* & OF *purpre* f. L *purpura* (as PURPURA)]

purpurin /púrpyoorin/ *n.* a red colouring-matter occurring naturally in madder roots, or manufactured synthetically.

purr /pur/ *v.* & *n.* ● *v.* **1** *intr.* (of a cat) make a low vibratory sound expressing contentment. **2** *intr.* (of machinery etc.) make a similar sound. **3** *intr.* (of a person) express pleasure. **4** *tr.* utter or express (words or contentment) in this way. ● *n.* a purring sound. [imit.]
■ *v.* **2** see HUM[1] *v.* 1. ● *n.* see HUM[1] *n.*

purse /purss/ *n.* & *v.* ● *n.* **1** a small pouch of leather etc. for carrying money on the person. **2** *US* a handbag. **3** a receptacle resembling a purse in form or purpose. **4** money, funds. **5** a sum collected as a present or given as a prize in a contest. ● *v.* **1** *tr.* (often foll. by *up*) pucker or contract (the lips). **2** *intr.* become contracted and wrinkled. □ **hold the purse-strings** have control of expenditure. **the public purse** the national treasury. [OE *purs* f. med.L *bursa, byrsa* purse f. Gk *bursa* hide, leather]
■ *n.* **1** pouch, bag, money-bag, wallet, *US* pocketbook, *dial.* poke. **2** bag, handbag, *US* pocketbook. **4** money, wealth, resources, funds, finances, capital, revenue, income, means, cash, riches, pocket. **5** prize, reward, award, present, gift. ● *v.* **1** pucker (up), contract, wrinkle, compress, press together.

purser /púrsər/ *n.* an officer on a ship who keeps the accounts, esp. the head steward in a passenger vessel. □□ **pursership** *n.*

purslane /púrslin/ *n.* any of various plants of the genus *Portulaca*, esp. *P. oleracea*, with green or golden leaves, used as a herb and salad vegetable. [ME f. OF *porcelaine* (cf. PORCELAIN) alt. f. L *porcil(l)aca, portulaca*]

pursuance /pərsyóōənss/ *n.* (foll. by *of*) the carrying out or observance (of a plan, idea, etc.).

■ see EXECUTION 2.

pursuant /pərsyóōənt/ *adj.* & *adv.* ● *adj.* pursuing. ● *adv.* (foll. by *to*) conforming to or in accordance with. □□ **pursuantly** *adv.* [ME, = prosecuting, f. OF *po(u)rsuiant* part. of *po(u)rsu(iv)ir* (as PURSUE): assim. to AF *pursuer* and PURSUE]

pursue /pərsyóō/ *v.* (**pursues, pursued, pursuing**) **1** *tr.* follow with intent to overtake or capture or do harm to. **2** *tr.* continue or proceed along (a route or course of action). **3** *tr.* follow or engage in (study or other activity). **4** *tr.* proceed in compliance with (a plan etc.). **5** *tr.* seek after, aim at. **6** *tr.* continue to investigate or discuss (a topic). **7** *tr.* seek the attention or acquaintance of (a person) persistently. **8** *tr.* (of misfortune etc.) persistently assail. **9** *tr.* persistently attend, stick to. **10** *intr.* go in pursuit. □□ **pursuable** *adj.* **pursuer** *n.* [ME f. AF *pursiwer*, *-suer* = OF *porsivre* etc. ult. f. L *prosequi* follow after]

■ **1** follow, chase, go *or* run after, hunt (after *or* for), trail, track, run down, dog, stalk, shadow, chivvy, *colloq.* tail. **2, 9** follow (on with), keep to; carry on with, continue, push, devote *or* dedicate oneself to, undertake, practise, persist *or* persevere in, maintain, proceed with, adhere to, stay with, apply oneself to, *colloq.* stick with, plug at. **3** follow, take; see also ENGAGE 8. **5** aspire to, aim at *or* for, work for *or* toward(s), try *or* strive for, seek, search for, go in search of, quest after *or* for, be intent on, be bent upon *or* on. **7** go after, woo, pay court to, court, pay suit *or* court to, set one's cap at; follow, hound; see also CHASE[1] *v.* 1, 4.

pursuit /pərsyóōt/ *n.* **1** the act or an instance of pursuing. **2** an occupation or activity pursued. □ **in pursuit of** pursuing. [ME f. OF *poursuite* (as PUR-, SUIT)]

■ **1** hunt, tracking, stalking, chase; pursuance. **2** work, line (of work), activity, field, area, business, profession, trade, vocation, calling, career, life's-work, *colloq.* avocation; hobby, pastime, interest.

pursuivant /púrsiv'nt/ *n.* **1** *Brit.* an officer of the College of Arms ranking below a herald. **2** *archaic* a follower or attendant. [ME f. OF *pursivant* pres. part. of *pursivre* (as PURSUE)]

pursy /púrsi/ *adj.* **1** short-winded; puffy. **2** corpulent. □□ **pursiness** *n.* [ME, earlier *pursive* f. AF *porsif* f. OF *polsif* f. *polser* breathe with difficulty f. L *pulsare* (as PULSATE)]

purulent /pyóōroolənt/ *adj.* **1** consisting of or containing pus. **2** discharging pus. □□ **purulence** *n.* **purulency** *n.* **purulently** *adv.* [F *purulent* or L *purulentus* (as PUS)]

purvey /pərváy/ *v.* **1** *tr.* provide or supply (articles of food) as one's business. **2** *intr.* (often foll. by *for*) **a** make provision. **b** act as supplier. □□ **purveyor** *n.* [ME f. AF *purveier*, OF *porveiir* f. L *providēre* PROVIDE]

■ see SUPPLY[1] *v.* 1, 2.

purveyance /pərváyənss/ *n.* **1** the act of purveying. **2** *Brit. hist.* the right of the sovereign to provisions etc. at a fixed price. [ME f. OF *porveance* f. L *providentia* PROVIDENCE]

■ **1** see SUPPLY[1] *n.* 1.

purview /púrvyōō/ *n.* **1** the scope or range of a document, scheme, etc. **2** the range of physical or mental vision. [ME f. AF *purveü*, OF *porveü* past part. of *porveiir* (as PURVEY)]

■ **2** see HORIZON.

pus /puss/ *n.* a thick yellowish or greenish liquid produced from infected tissue. [L *pus puris*]

■ see DISCHARGE *n.* 5.

push /pōōsh/ *v.* & *n.* ● *v.* **1** *tr.* exert a force on (a thing) to move it away from oneself or from the origin of the force. **2** *tr.* cause to move in this direction. **3** *intr.* exert such a force (*do not push against the door*). **4** *tr.* press, depress (*push the button for service*). **5** *intr.* & *tr.* **a** thrust forward or upward. **b** project or cause to project (*pushes out new roots*; *the cape pushes out into the sea*). **6** *intr.* move forward by force or persistence. **7** *tr.* make (one's way) by pushing. **8** *intr.* exert oneself, esp. to surpass others. **9** *tr.* (often foll. by *to*, *into*, or *to* + infin.) urge or impel. **10** *tr.* tax the abilities or tolerance of; press (a person) hard. **11** *tr.* pursue (a claim etc.). **12** *tr.* promote the use or sale or adoption of, e.g. by advertising. **13** *intr.* (foll. by *for*) demand persistently (*pushed hard for reform*). **14** *tr. colloq.* sell (a drug) illegally. ● *n.* **1** the act or an instance of pushing; a shove or thrust. **2** the force exerted in this. **3** a vigorous effort. **4** a military attack in force. **5** enterprise, determination to succeed. **6** the use of influence to advance a person. **7** the pressure of affairs. **8** a crisis. **9** (prec. by *the*) *colloq.* dismissal, esp. from employment. **10** *Austral. sl.* a group of people with a common interest; a clique. □ **be pushed for** *colloq.* have very little of (esp. time). **get the push** *colloq.* be dismissed or sent away. **give a person the push** *colloq.* dismiss or send away a person. **push along** (often in *imper.*) *colloq.* depart, leave. **push around** *colloq.* bully. **push-bike** *Brit. colloq.* a bicycle worked by pedals. **push-button 1** a button to be pushed esp. to operate an electrical device. **2** (*attrib.*) operated in this way. **push one's luck 1** take undue risks. **2** act presumptuously. **push off 1** push with an oar etc. to get a boat out into a river etc. **2** (often in *imper.*) *colloq.* go away. **push-pull 1** operated by pushing and pulling. **2** *Electr.* consisting of two valves etc. operated alternately. **push-start** *n.* the starting of a motor vehicle by pushing it to turn the engine. ● *v.tr.* start (a vehicle) in this way. **push through** get (a scheme, proposal, etc.) completed or accepted quickly. **push-up** = *press-up*. [ME f. OF *pousser*, *pou(l)ser* f. L *pulsare* (as PULSATE)]

■ *v.* **1** thrust, shove, drive, move, get moving, propel; press. **4** press, depress. **5 b** see PROJECT *v.* 2. **6** (*push on* or *forward*) move onward *or* ahead *or* forward, continue, proceed, advance, press on *or* onward. **7** shove, thrust, elbow, shoulder, force, jostle. **9** urge, encourage, press, induce, persuade, prod, spur, goad, rouse, prompt, incite, move, motivate, stimulate; impel, compel, force, dragoon, coerce, constrain; badger, hound, pester, plague, nag. **10** see TAX *v.* 3. **11** see PURSUE 2, 9. **12** promote, publicize, advertise, propagandize, puff, *colloq.* boost, plug, *sl.* ballyhoo, hype. **13** (*push for*) see *insist on*. **14** see PEDDLE. ● *n.* **1** shove, thrust, nudge; press. **2** drive, thrust; see also FORCE[1] *n.* 1. **3** see ATTEMPT *n.* **4** campaign, attack, assault, advance, offensive, charge, onslaught, foray, sortie, invasion, incursion, raid, sally, blitzkrieg, strike, *colloq.* blitz. **5** enterprise, ambition, initiative, resourcefulness, determination, energy, dynamism, drive, vigour, spirit, zip, zeal, verve, *colloq.* get-up-and-go, zing, gumption, go. **6** see PULL *n.* 3. **8** crisis, turning-point, critical time *or* moment. **9** (*the push*) see *dismissal* (DISMISS). □ **give a person the push** see DISMISS 1, 2. **push along** see *beat it*. **push around** intimidate, bully, domineer, tyrannize, torment. **push off 2** leave, go away, take off, *colloq.* light out, push along, skedaddle, scram, make oneself scarce, *sl.* hit the road; see also *beat it*. **push through** force through, press through, *esp. US* railroad through; see also EXPEDITE 1.

pushcart /pōōshkaart/ *n.* a handcart or barrow.

pushchair /pōōshchair/ *n. Brit.* a folding chair on wheels, for pushing a child in.

pusher /pōōshər/ *n.* **1** *colloq.* an illegal seller of drugs. **2** *colloq.* a pushing or pushy person. **3** a child's utensil for pushing food on to a spoon etc.

pushful /pōōshfōōl/ *adj.* pushy; arrogantly self-assertive. □□ **pushfully** *adv.*

pushing /pōōshing/ *adj.* **1** pushy; aggressively ambitious. **2** *colloq.* having nearly reached (a specified age). □□ **pushingly** *adv.*

■ **1** see PUSHY. **2** see ALMOST.

pushover /pōōshōvər/ *n. colloq.* **1** something that is easily done. **2** a person who can easily be overcome, persuaded, etc.

■ **1** walk-over, child's play, *colloq.* piece of cake, picnic, cinch, *Brit. colloq.* doddle, *Austral. sl.* snack, *US sl.* snap, duck soup; see also BREEZE[1] *n.* 5. **2** putty in a person's hands, *colloq.* soft touch, *sl.* (easy) mark, sucker, sap, *Brit. sl.* mug, *esp. US sl.* patsy.

pushrod /pōōshrod/ *n.* a rod operated by cams, that opens and closes the valves in an internal-combustion engine.

Pushtu /púshtōō/ *n.* & *adj.* = PASHTO. [Pers. *puštū*]

pushy /pōōshi/ *adj.* (**pushier**, **pushiest**) *colloq.* **1** excessively or unpleasantly self-assertive. **2** selfishly determined to succeed. ▫▫ **pushily** *adv.* **pushiness** *n.*

▪ forward, self-assertive, assertive, self-seeking, forceful, aggressive, domineering, overbearing, ambitious, bumptious, brassy, brazen, impertinent, insolent, pushing, pushful, presumptuous, officious, loud, cocky, brash, bold, *colloq.* bossy, go-getting.

pusillanimous /pyōōssilánnimǝss/ *adj.* lacking courage; timid. ▫▫ **pusillanimity** /-lǝnímmiti/ *n.* **pusillanimously** *adv.* [eccl.L *pusillanimis* f. *pusillus* very small + *animus* mind]

▪ see TIMID. ▫▫ **pusillanimity** see COWARDICE.

puss /pōōss/ *n. colloq.* **1** a cat (esp. as a form of address). **2** a playful or coquettish girl. **3** a hare. ▫ **puss moth** a large European moth, *Cerura vinula*. [prob. f. MLG *pūs*, Du. *poes*, of unkn. orig.]

pussy /pōōssi/ *n.* (*pl.* **-ies**) **1** (also **pussy-cat**) *colloq.* a cat. **2** *coarse sl.* the vulva. ¶ Usually considered a taboo use. ▫ **pussy willow** any of various willows, esp. *Salix discolor*, with furry catkins.

pussyfoot /pōōssifōōt/ *v.intr.* **1** move stealthily or warily. **2** act cautiously or noncommittally. ▫▫ **pussyfooter** *n.*

▪ **1** sneak, creep, slink, prowl, steal, tiptoe. **2** beat about the bush, hem *or* hum and haw, equivocate, be evasive, tergiversate, evade the issue, prevaricate, shilly-shally, dither, hesitate; sit on the fence.

pustulate *v.* & *adj.* ● *v.tr.* & *intr.* /pústyoolayt/ form into pustules. ● *adj.* /pústyoolǝt/ of or relating to a pustule or pustules. ▫▫ **pustulation** /-láysh'n/ *n.* [LL *pustulare* f. *pustula*: see PUSTULE]

pustule /pústyōōl/ *n.* a pimple containing pus. ▫▫ **pustular** *adj.* **pustulous** *adj.* [ME f. OF *pustule* or L *pustula*]

▪ see PIMPLE.

put[1] /pōōt/ *v.* & *n.* ● *v.* (**putting**; *past* and *past part.* **put**) **1** *tr.* move to or cause to be in a specified place or position (*put it in your pocket*; *put the children to bed*; *put your signature here*). **2** *tr.* bring into a specified condition, relation, or state (*puts me in great difficulty*; *an accident put the car out of action*). **3** *tr.* **a** (often foll. by *on*) impose or assign (*put a tax on beer*; *where do you put the blame?*). **b** (foll. by *on, to*) impose or enforce the existence of (*put a veto on it*; *put a stop to it*). **4** *tr.* **a** cause (a person) to go or be, habitually or temporarily (*put them at their ease*; *put them on the right track*). **b** *refl.* imagine (oneself) in a specified situation (*put yourself in my shoes*). **5** *tr.* (foll. by *for*) substitute (one thing for another). **6** *tr.* express (a thought or idea) in a specified way (*to put it mildly*). **7** *tr.* (foll. by *at*) estimate (an amount etc. at a specified amount) (*put the cost at £50*). **8** *tr.* (foll. by *into*) express or translate in (words, or another language). **9** *tr.* (foll. by *into*) invest (money in an asset, e.g. land). **10** *tr.* (foll. by *on*) stake (money) on (a horse etc.). **11** *tr.* (foll. by *to*) apply or devote to a use or purpose (*put it to good use*). **12** *tr.* (foll. by *to*) submit for consideration or attention (*let me put it to you another way*; *shall now put it to a vote*). **13** *tr.* (foll. by *to*) subject (a person) to (death, suffering, etc.). **14** *tr.* throw (esp. a shot or weight) as an athletic sport or exercise. **15** *tr.* (foll. by *to*) couple (an animal) with (another of the opposite sex) for breeding. **16** *intr.* (foll. by *back, off, out*, etc.) (of a ship etc.) proceed or follow a course in a specified direction. **17** *intr. US* (foll. by *in, out of*) (of a river) flow in a specified direction. ● *n.* **1** a throw of the shot or weight. **2** *Stock Exch.* the option of selling stock at a fixed price at a given date. ▫ **not know where to put oneself** feel deeply embarrassed. **put about 1** spread (information, rumour, etc.). **2** *Naut.* turn round; put (a ship) on the opposite tack. **3** trouble, distress. **put across 1** make acceptable or effective. **2** express in an understandable way. **3** (often in **put it** (or **one**) **across**) achieve by deceit. **put aside 1** = *put by*. **2** set aside, ignore. **put away 1** put (a thing) back in the place where it is normally kept. **2** lay (money etc.) aside for future use. **3 a** confine or imprison. **b** commit to a home or mental institution. **4** consume (food and drink), esp. in large quantities. **5** put (an old or sick animal) to death. **put back 1** restore to its proper or former place. **2** change (a planned event) to a later date or time. **3** move back the hands of (a clock or watch). **4** check the advance of. **put a bold** etc. **face on it** see FACE. **put the boot in** see BOOT[1]. **put by** lay (money etc.) aside for future use. **put down 1** suppress by force or authority. **2** *colloq.* snub or humiliate. **3** record or enter in writing. **4** enter the name of (a person) on a list, esp. as a member or subscriber. **5** (foll. by *as, for*) account or reckon. **6** (foll. by *to*) attribute (*put it down to bad planning*). **7** put (an old or sick animal) to death. **8** preserve or store (eggs etc.) for future use. **9** pay (a specified sum) as a deposit. **10** put (a baby) to bed. **11** land (an aircraft). **12** stop to let (passengers) get off. **put-down** *n. colloq.* a snub or humiliating criticism. **put an end to** see END. **put one's foot down** see FOOT. **put one's foot in it** see FOOT. **put forth 1** (of a plant) send out (buds or leaves). **2** *formal* submit or put into circulation. **put forward 1** suggest or propose. **2** advance the hands of (a clock or watch). **3** (often *refl.*) put into a prominent position; draw attention to. **put in 1 a** enter or submit (a claim etc.). **b** (foll. by *for*) submit a claim for (a specified thing). **2** (foll. by *for*) be a candidate for (an appointment, election, etc.). **3** spend (time). **4** perform (a spell of work) as part of a whole. **5** interpose (a remark, blow, etc.). **6** insert as an addition. **put in an appearance** see APPEARANCE. **put a person in mind of** see MIND. **put it to a person** (often foll. by *that* + clause) challenge a person to deny. **put one's mind to** see MIND. **put off 1 a** postpone. **b** postpone an engagement with (a person). **2** (often foll. by *with*) evade (a person) with an excuse etc. **3** hinder or dissuade. **4** offend, disconcert; cause (a person) to lose interest in something. **put on 1** clothe oneself with. **2** cause (an electrical device, light, etc.) to function. **3** cause (esp. transport) to be available; provide. **4** stage (a play, show, etc.). **5** advance the hands of (a clock or watch). **6 a** pretend to be affected by (an emotion). **b** assume, take on (a character or appearance). **c** (**put it on**) exaggerate one's feelings etc. **7** increase one's weight by (a specified amount). **8** send (a cricketer) on to bowl. **9** (foll. by *to*) make aware of or put in touch with (*put us on to their new accountant*). **10** *colloq.* tease, play a trick on. **put-on** *n. colloq.* a deception or hoax. **put out 1 a** (often as **put out** *adj.*) disconcert or annoy. **b** (often *refl.*) inconvenience (*don't put yourself out*). **2** extinguish (a fire or light). **3** cause (a batsman or side) to be out. **4** dislocate (a joint). **5** exert (strength etc.). **6** lend (money) at interest. **7** allocate (work) to be done off the premises. **8** blind (a person's eyes). **9** issue, publish. **put out of its** etc. **misery** see MISERY. **put over 1** make acceptable or effective. **2** express in an understandable way. **3** *US* postpone. **4** *US* achieve by deceit. **put one over** (usu. foll. by *on*) get the better of, outsmart, trick. **put a sock in it** see SOCK[1]. **put store by** see STORE. **put through 1** carry out or complete (a task or transaction). **2** (often foll. by *to*) connect (a person) by telephone to another subscriber. **put to flight** see FLIGHT[2]. **put together 1** assemble (a whole) from parts. **2** combine (parts) to form a whole. **put under** render unconscious by anaesthetic etc. **put up 1** build or erect. **2** raise (a price etc.). **3** take or provide accommodation for (*friends put me up for the night*). **4** engage in (a fight, struggle, etc.) as a form of resistance. **5** present (a proposal). **6 a** present oneself for election. **b** propose for election. **7** provide (money) as a backer in an enterprise. **8** display (a notice). **9** publish (banns). **10** offer for sale or competition. **11** cause (game) to rise from cover. **12** put (a sword) back in its sheath. **put-up** *adj.* fraudulently presented or devised. **put upon** *colloq.* make unfair or excessive demands on; take advantage of (a person). **put a person up to 1** inform or instruct a person about. **2** (usu. foll. by verbal noun) instigate a person in (*put them up to stealing the money*). **put up with** endure, tolerate; submit to. **put the wind up** see WIND[1]. **put a person wise** see WISE. **put words into a person's mouth** see MOUTH. ▫▫ **putter** *n.* [ME f. an unrecorded OE form *putian*, of unkn. orig.]

■ *v.* **1** place, position, situate, set, lay, station, stand, deposit, rest, settle. **3 a** place, assign, attribute, lay, pin, attach, fix; impose, raise, levy, exact. **4 b** imagine, consider, regard, picture, envisage. **5** exchange, substitute, change, swap, switch. **6, 8** express, word, phrase; say, utter; translate. **7** see GAUGE *v.* 3. **10** bet, gamble, wager, stake, chance, risk, hazard. **12** (*put to*) present to, set before; refer to; see also SUBMIT 2. **13** (*put to*) subject to, cause to undergo *or* suffer, consign to, send to. **14** throw, heave, toss, fling, cast, pitch, bowl, lob, shy, shoot, catapult. ● *n.* **1** see THROW *n.* 1. □ **put about 1** broadcast, publish, make known, publicize, announce, spread about *or* around. **2** turn, turn round, turn about. **3** see DISTRESS *v.* **put across 2** make clear, get across, make understood, explain, spell out, convey, communicate. **put aside 1** see *put by* below. **2** set aside, disregard, ignore, pay no heed to, push aside, shrug off. **put away 1** return, replace, put back; store. **2** see *put by* below. **3 a** jail, incarcerate, *Brit.* send down, *US* send up, *sl.* jug; confine; see also IMPRISON 1. **b** commit, institutionalize. **4** consume, devour, gorge, gormandize, polish off, dispose of, eat up, wolf (down), *joc.* demolish. **5** see *put down* 7 below. **put back 1** return, replace, restore, put away. **2** see POSTPONE. **put by** lay aside *or* by, set aside; put away *or* aside; save, store, hoard, stow *or* squirrel away, cache, bank, *sl.* salt away. **put down 1** suppress, quash, quell, put an end to, topple, crush, overthrow, subdue, check. **2** abash, humiliate, crush, silence, mortify, lower, take a person down a peg or two, shame; snub, deflate, slight, reject, dismiss, ignore; belittle, diminish, disparage, deprecate, depreciate, criticize. **3, 4** record, register, write down, set down, enter, list; log, note (down), jot down, make a note *or* notation of; enrol. **5** take, reckon, account, count, categorize, regard, assess. **6** ascribe, assign, attribute, impute. **7** destroy, put to death, put to sleep, put out of its misery, put away *or* down, do away with. **12** let off, drop off. **put-down** snub, disparaging remark, slight, insult, criticism, *colloq.* dig. **put forth 1** grow, produce, send out *or* forth. **2** propose, offer, set forth, advance, suggest, put forward; promulgate, issue, publish, make known, make public, send out, put into circulation, air, announce. **put forward 1** propose, present, tender, recommend, suggest, offer, set forth, submit, proffer, propound, *formal* put forth. **put in 1 a** see SUBMIT 2. **b** (*put in for*) seek, apply for, pursue, file for, request, ask for, petition for. **3** devote, pass; see also SPEND 2a. **4** do, perform, effect, carry out. **5, 6** see INSERT *v.* **put off 1 a** postpone, delay, defer, put back, stay, hold off, shelve, put *or* set aside, table, *US* put over. **3** see DETER. **4** disconcert, upset, offend, disturb, perturb, *colloq.* throw, rattle, knock back; discourage, give (someone) the brush-off. **put on 1** don, get dressed in, change *or* slip into. **2** turn on, switch on. **3** see PROVIDE 1. **4** stage, mount, produce, present; perform. **6 a** assume, take on, pretend, affect, feign, make a show of. **c** (**put it on**) see EXAGGERATE 1. **7** gain. **10** tease, mock, *colloq.* kid, pull (a person's) leg, rib, rag, *Brit* have on. **put-on** deception, hoax, trick, jest, (practical) joke, prank, pretence, *colloq.* spoof, leg-pull. **put out 1 a** annoy, vex, irritate, exasperate, irk, perturb, disconcert, offend. **b** inconvenience, discommode, disturb, trouble, bother; impose upon *or* on, give trouble, create difficulties for, *colloq.* put on the spot. **2** turn off; snuff out, extinguish, blow out, douse, quench, smother. **5** exert, expend, use. **9** publish, issue, broadcast, make public, circulate, spread, make known, release. **put over 2** put *or* get across, convey, communicate, make clear, set forth, relate. **3** see *put off* 1 above. **put one over** (*put one over on*) fool, mislead, pull a person's leg, pull the wool over a person's eyes, trick, hoodwink; see also DECEIVE 1. **put through 1** carry out *or* through, execute, (put into) effect, bring off, accomplish, complete, finish, conclude, pull off. **2** connect, hook up. **put together** see ASSEMBLE 3. **put up 1** erect, build, construct, raise, set up, put together, fabricate. **2** increase, raise, elevate, *colloq.* boost. **3** accommodate, lodge, board, house, take in, quarter, *Mil.* billet. **5** see PRESENT[2] *v.* 1. **7** contribute, pledge, give, supply, donate, advance, pay, offer. **8** see DISPLAY *v.* 1. **10** see OFFER 4. **put-up** (*put-up job*) see DECEIT 2. **put upon** see IMPOSE 3, TROUBLE 1, 3. **put a person up to 2** incite to, urge to, spur to, encourage to, prompt to, instigate in. **put up with** tolerate, take, stand (for), stomach, accept, bear, endure, swallow, submit to, *colloq.* stick, *literary* brook.

put[2] var. of PUTT.

putative /pyo͞otətiv/ *adj.* reputed, supposed (*his putative father*). □□ **putatively** *adv.* [ME f. OF *putatif -ive* or LL *putativus* f. L *putare* think]
■ see *supposed* (SUPPOSE 6).

putlog /pútlog/ *n.* (also **putlock** /-lok/) a short horizontal timber projecting from a wall, on which scaffold floorboards rest. [17th c.: orig. uncert.]

put-put /pútpút/ *n.* & *v.* ● *n.* the rapid intermittent sound of a small petrol engine. ● *v.intr.* (**put-putted, put-putting**) make this sound. [imit.]

putrefy /pyo͞otrifī/ *v.* (**-ies, -ied**) **1** *intr.* & *tr.* become or make putrid; go bad. **2** *intr.* fester, suppurate. **3** *intr.* become morally corrupt. □□ **putrefacient** /-fáysh'nt/ *adj.* **putrefaction** /-fáksh'n/ *n.* **putrefactive** /-fáktiv/ *adj.* [ME f. L *putrefacere* f. *puter putris* rotten]
■ **1** rot, decompose, decay, moulder, go bad, deteriorate, go off. **2** suppurate, fester, decompose; see also ROT *v.* 1a.

putrescent /pyootréss'nt/ *adj.* **1** in the process of rotting. **2** of or accompanying this process. □□ **putrescence** *n.* [L *putrescere* incept. of *putrēre* (as PUTRID)]
■ see ROTTEN 1. □□ **putrescence** see ROT *n.* 1.

putrid /pyo͞otrid/ *adj.* **1** decomposed, rotten. **2** foul, noxious. **3** corrupt. **4** *sl.* of poor quality; contemptible; very unpleasant. □□ **putridity** /-ríddititi/ *n.* **putridly** *adv.* **putridness** *n.* [L *putridus* f. *putrēre* to rot f. *puter putris* rotten]
■ **1** rotten, rotting, decomposed, decomposing, decayed, decaying, mouldy, putrefacient, putrescent. **2** fetid, rank, noxious; see also FOUL *adj.* 1, 4a. **3** tainted, corrupt; see also DEGENERATE *adj.* **4** see AWFUL 1a, b.

putsch /po͞och/ *n.* an attempt at political revolution; a violent uprising. [Swiss G, = thrust, blow]
■ see UPRISING.

putt /put/ *v.* & *n.* (also **put**) ● *v.tr.* (**putted, putting**) strike (a golf ball) gently to get it into or nearer to a hole on a putting-green. ● *n.* a putting stroke. □ **putting-green** (in golf) the smooth area of grass round a hole. [differentiated f. PUT[1]]

puttee /pútti/ *n.* **1** a long strip of cloth wound spirally round the leg from ankle to knee for protection and support. **2** *US* a leather legging. [Hindi *paṭṭī* band, bandage]

putter[1] /púttər/ *n.* **1** a golf club used in putting. **2** a golfer who putts.

putter[2] /púttər/ *n.* & *v.* = PUT-PUT. [imit.]

putter[3] *US* var. of POTTER[1].

putto /po͞ottō/ *n.* (*pl.* **putti** /-ti/) a representation of a naked child (esp. a cherub or a cupid) in (esp. Renaissance) art. [It., = boy, f. L *putus*]

putty /pútti/ *n.* & *v.* ● *n.* (*pl.* **-ies**) **1** a cement made from whiting and raw linseed oil, used for fixing panes of glass, filling holes in woodwork, etc. **2** a fine white mortar of lime and water, used in pointing brickwork, etc. **3** a polishing powder usu. made from tin oxide, used in jewellery work. ● *v.tr.* (**-ies, -ied**) cover, fix, join, or fill up with putty. □ **putty in a person's hands** someone who is overcompliant, or easily influenced. [F *potée*, lit. potful]

puy /pwee/ *n.* a small extinct volcanic cone, esp. in the Auvergne, France. [F, = hill, f. L *podium*: see PODIUM]

puzzle /púzz'l/ *n.* & *v.* ● *n.* **1** a difficult or confusing problem; an enigma. **2** a problem or toy designed to test knowledge or ingenuity. ● *v.* **1** *tr.* confound or disconcert mentally. **2** *intr.* (usu. foll. by *over* etc.) be perplexed (about). **3** *tr.* (usu. as **puzzling** *adj.*) require much thought to comprehend (*a puzzling situation*). **4** *tr.* (foll. by *out*) solve or understand by hard thought. □□ **puzzlement** *n.* **puzzlingly** *adv.* [16th c.: orig. unkn.]

■ *n.* **1** enigma, problem, question, paradox, poser, mystery. **2** poser, riddle, conundrum, *colloq.* brain-teaser, brain-twister. ● *v.* **1** baffle, bewilder, confuse, confound, mystify, perplex, nonplus, stump, *archaic* wilder, *colloq.* flummox. **2** be confused *or* baffled *or* bewildered *or* perplexed; (*puzzle over*) study, ponder (over), mull over, contemplate, meditate on *or* upon *or* over, consider, reflect on *or* over, think about *or* over, *literary* muse over *or* on. **3** (**puzzling**) mystifying, enigmatic, bewildering, baffling, perplexing, confusing, ambiguous, contradictory; abstruse, obscure. **4** (*puzzle out*) solve, decipher, crack, unravel, work out, figure out, think through, sort out.

puzzler /púzlər/ *n.* a difficult question or problem.

■ see PROBLEM 1, 2, 5b.

puzzolana var. of POZZOLANA.

PVA *abbr.* polyvinyl acetate.

PVC *abbr.* polyvinyl chloride.

Pvt. *abbr.* **1** private. **2** *US* private soldier.

PW *abbr.* policewoman.

p.w. *abbr.* per week.

PWA *abbr.* person with Aids.

PWR *abbr.* pressurized-water reactor.

PX *abbr. US* post exchange.

pyaemia /pī-éemiə/ *n.* (*US* **pyemia**) blood-poisoning caused by the spread of pus-forming bacteria in the bloodstream from a source of infection. □□ **pyaemic** *adj.* [mod.L f. Gk *puon* pus + *haima* blood]

pycnic var. of PYKNIC.

pye-dog /pídog/ *n.* (also **pie-dog, pi-dog**) a vagrant mongrel, esp. in Asia. [Anglo-Ind. *pye, paë*, Hindi *pāhī* outsider + DOG]

pyelitis /pīəlītiss/ *n.* inflammation of the renal pelvis. [Gk *puelos* trough, basin + -ITIS]

pyemia *US* var. of PYAEMIA.

pygmy /pígmi/ *n.* (also **pigmy**) (*pl.* **-ies**) **1** a member of a dwarf people of equatorial Africa and parts of SE Asia. **2** a very small person, animal, or thing. **3** an insignificant person. **4** (*attrib.*) **a** of or relating to pygmies. **b** (of a person, animal, etc.) dwarf. □□ **pygmaean** /-meéən/ *adj.* **pygmean** /-meéən/ *adj.* [ME f. L *pygmaeus* f. Gk *pugmaios* dwarf f. *pugmē* the length from elbow to knuckles, fist]

■ **2** dwarf, midget, runt. **4 b** see UNDERSIZED.

pyjamas /pijaáməz/ *n.pl.* (*US* **pajamas**) **1** a suit of loose trousers and jacket for sleeping in. **2** loose trousers tied round the waist, worn by both sexes in some Asian countries. **3** (**pyjama**) (*attrib.*) designating parts of a suit of pyjamas (*pyjama jacket; pyjama trousers*). [Urdu *pā(ē)jāma* f. Pers. *pae, pay* leg + Hindi *jāma* clothing]

pyknic /píknik/ *adj.* & *n.* (also **pycnic**) *Anthropol.* ● *adj.* characterized by a thick neck, large abdomen, and relatively short limbs. ● *n.* a person of this bodily type. [Gk *puknos* thick]

■ *adj.* see STOCKY.

pylon /pīlən/ *n.* **1** a tall structure erected as a support (esp. for electric-power cables) or boundary or decoration. **2** a gateway, esp. of an ancient Egyptian temple. **3** a structure marking a path for aircraft. **4** a structure supporting an aircraft engine. [Gk *pulōn* f. *pulē* gate]

pylorus /pīlórəss/ *n.* (*pl.* **pylori** /-rī/) *Anat.* the opening from the stomach into the duodenum. □□ **pyloric** /-lórrik/ *adj.* [LL f. Gk *pulōros, pulouros* gatekeeper f. *pulē* gate + *ouros* warder]

pyorrhoea /pīreéə/ *n.* (*US* **pyorrhea**) **1** a disease of periodontal tissue causing shrinkage of the gums and loosening of the teeth. **2** any discharge of pus. [Gk *puo-* f. *puon* pus + *rhoia* flux f. *rheō* flow]

pyracantha /pīrəkánthə/ *n.* any evergreen thorny shrub of the genus *Pyracantha*, having white flowers and bright red or yellow berries. [L f. Gk *purakantha*]

pyramid /pírrəmid/ *n.* **1** a monumental structure, usu. of stone, with a square base and sloping sides meeting centrally at an apex, esp. an ancient Egyptian royal tomb. **2** a solid of this type with a base of three or more sides. **3** a pyramid-shaped thing or pile of things. **4** (in *pl.*) a game played on a billiard-table with (usu. 15) coloured balls and a cue-ball. □ **pyramid selling** a system of selling goods in which agency rights are sold to an increasing number of distributors at successively lower levels. □□ **pyramidal** /-rámmid'l/ *adj.* **pyramidally** /-rámmidəli/ *adv.* **pyramidic** /-míddik/ *adj.* (also **pyramidical** /-míddik'l/). **pyramidically** /-míddikəli/ *adv.* **pyramidwise** *adj.* [ME f. L *pyramis* f. Gk *puramis -idos*]

pyre /pīr/ *n.* a heap of combustible material esp. a funeral pile for burning a corpse. [L *pyra* f. Gk *pura* f. *pur* fire]

pyrethrin /pīreéthrin/ *n.* any of several active constituents of pyrethrum flowers used in the manufacture of insecticides.

pyrethrum /pīreéthrəm/ *n.* **1** any of several aromatic chrysanthemums of the genus *Tanacetum*, esp. *T. coccineum*. **2** an insecticide made from the dried flowers of these plants, esp. *Tanacetum cinerariifolium*. [L f. Gk *purethron* feverfew]

pyretic /pīréttik, pi-/ *adj.* of, for, or producing fever. [mod.L *pyreticus* f. Gk *puretos* fever]

■ pyrogenic; see also FEVERISH 1.

Pyrex /pīreks/ *n. propr.* a hard heat-resistant type of glass, often used for cookware. [invented word]

pyrexia /pīréksiə, pi-/ *n. Med.* = FEVER. □□ **pyrexial** *adj.* **pyrexic** *adj.* **pyrexical** *adj.* [mod.L f. Gk *purexis* f. *puressō* be feverish f. *pur* fire]

pyridine /pírrədeen/ *n. Chem.* a colourless volatile odorous liquid, formerly obtained from coal tar, used as a solvent and in chemical manufacture. ¶ Chem. formula: C_5H_5N. [Gk *pur* fire + -ID[4] + -INE[4]]

pyridoxine /pirridóksin/ *n.* a vitamin of the B complex found in yeast, and important in the body's use of unsaturated fatty acids. Also called *vitamin* B_6. [PYRIDINE + OX- + -INE[4]]

pyrimidine /pirímmideen/ *n.* **1** *Chem.* an organic nitrogenous base. **2** any of a group of derivatives with similar structure, including the nucleotide constituents uracil, thymine, and cytosine. [G *Pyrimidin* f. *Pyridin* (as PYRIDINE, IMIDE)]

pyrite /pīrīt/ *n.* = PYRITES. [F *pyrite* or L (as PYRITES)]

pyrites /pīrīteez/ *n.* (in full **iron pyrites**) a yellow lustrous form of iron disulphide. □□ **pyritic** /-ríttik/ *adj.* **pyritiferous** /-ritíffərəss/ *adj.* **pyritize** /pīritīz/ *v.tr.* (also **-ise**). **pyritous** /pīritəss/ *adj.* [L f. Gk *puritēs* of fire (*pur*)]

pyro /pīrō/ *n. colloq.* = PYROGALLIC ACID.

pyro- /pīrō/ *comb. form* **1** denoting fire. **2** *Chem.* denoting a new substance formed from another by elimination of water (*pyrophosphate*). **3** *Mineral.* denoting a mineral etc. showing some property or change under the action of heat, or having a fiery red or yellow colour. [Gk *puro-* f. *pur* fire]

pyroclastic /pīrōklástik/ *adj.* (of rocks etc.) formed as the result of a volcanic eruption. □□ **pyroclast** *n.*

pyroelectric /pīrō-iléktrik/ *adj.* having the property of becoming electrically charged when heated. □□ **pyroelectricity** /-trίssiti/ *n.*

pyrogallic acid /pīrōgállik/ *n.* a weak acid used as a developer in photography, etc.

pyrogallol /pīrōgállol/ *n.* = PYROGALLIC ACID.

pyrogenic /pīrōjénnik/ *adj.* (also **pyrogenous** /pīrójinəss/) **1 a** producing heat, esp. in the body. **b** producing fever. **2** produced by combustion or volcanic processes.

pyrography /pīrógrəfi/ *n.* = *poker-work* (see POKER[1]).

pyroligneous /pīrōlígniəss/ *adj.* produced by the action of fire or heat on wood.

pyrolyse /pīrəlīz/ *v.tr.* (*US* **pyrolyze**) decompose by pyrolysis. [PYROLYSIS after *analyse*]

pyrolysis /pīróllisiss/ *n.* chemical decomposition brought about by heat. □□ **pyrolytic** /pīrəlíttik/ *adj.*

pyromania /pīrōmáyniə/ *n.* an obsessive desire to set fire to things. □□ **pyromaniac** *n.*

■ □□ **pyromaniac** arsonist, *Brit.* fire-raiser.

pyrometer /pīrómmitər/ *n.* an instrument for measuring high temperatures, esp. in furnaces and kilns. □□ **pyrometric** /-rəmétrik/ *adj.* **pyrometrically** /-rəmétrikəli/ *adv.* **pyrometry** /-rómmitri/ *n.*

pyrope /pīrōp/ *n.* a deep red variety of garnet. [ME f. OF *pirope* f. L *pyropus* f. Gk *purōpos* gold-bronze, lit. fiery-eyed, f. *pur* fire + *ōps* eye]

pyrophoric /pīrōfórrik/ *adj.* (of a substance) liable to ignite spontaneously on exposure to air. [mod.L *pyrophorus* f. Gk *purophoros* fire-bearing f. *pur* fire + *pherō* bear]

pyrosis /pīrōsiss/ *n. Med.* a burning sensation in the lower part of the chest, combined with the return of gastric acid to the mouth. [mod.L f. Gk *purōsis* f. *puroō* set on fire f. *pur* fire]

pyrotechnic /pīrōtéknik/ *adj.* **1** of or relating to fireworks. **2** (of wit etc.) brilliant or sensational. □□ **pyrotechnical** *adj.* **pyrotechnist** *n.* **pyrotechny** *n.* [PYRO- + Gk *tekhnē* art]

pyrotechnics /pīrōtékniks/ *n.pl.* **1** the art of making fireworks. **2** a display of fireworks. **3** any brilliant display.
■ **3** see *virtuosity* (VIRTUOSO).

pyroxene /pīrókseen/ *n.* any of a group of minerals commonly found as components of igneous rocks, composed of silicates of calcium, magnesium, and iron. [PYRO- + Gk *xenos* stranger (because supposed to be alien to igneous rocks)]

pyroxylin /pīróksilin/ *n.* a form of nitrocellulose, soluble in ether and alcohol, used as a basis for lacquers, artificial leather, etc. [F *pyroxyline* (as PYRO-, Gk *xulon* wood)]

pyrrhic[1] /pírrik/ *adj.* (of a victory) won at too great a cost to be of use to the victor. [*Pyrrhus* of Epirus, who defeated the Romans at Asculum in 279 BC, but sustained heavy losses]
■ see HOLLOW *adj.* 4.

pyrrhic[2] /pírrik/ *n.* & *adj.* ● *n.* a metrical foot of two short or unaccented syllables. ● *adj.* written in or based on pyrrhics. [L *pyrrhichius* f. Gk *purrhikhios* (*pous*) pyrrhic (foot)]

Pyrrhonism /pírrəniz'm/ *n.* **1** the philosophy of Pyrrho of Elis (*c.*300 BC), maintaining that certainty of knowledge is unattainable. **2** scepticism; philosophic doubt. □□ **Pyrrhonist** *n.* [Gk *Purrhōn* Pyrrho]
■ **2** see *scepticism* (SCEPTIC). □□ **Pyrrhonist** see SCEPTIC 1.

pyruvate /pīrōōvayt/ *n. Biochem.* any salt or ester of pyruvic acid.

pyruvic acid /pīrōōvik/ *n.* an organic acid occurring as an intermediate in many stages of metabolism. [as PYRO- + L *uva* grape]

Pythagoras' theorem /pīthággərəss/ *n.* the theorem attributed to Pythagoras (see PYTHAGOREAN) that the square on the hypotenuse of a right-angled triangle is equal to the sum of the squares on the other two sides.

Pythagorean /pīthággəreéən/ *adj.* & *n.* ● *adj.* of or relating to the Greek philosopher Pythagoras (6th c. BC) or his philosophy, esp. regarding the transmigration of souls. ● *n.* a follower of Pythagoras.

Pythian /píthiən/ *adj.* of or relating to Delphi (in central Greece) or its ancient oracle of Apollo. [L *Pythius* f. Gk *Puthios* f. *Puthō*, an older name of Delphi]

python /pīthən/ *n.* any constricting snake of the family Pythonidae, esp. of the genus *Python*, found throughout the tropics in the Old World. □□ **pythonic** /-thónnik/ *adj.* [L f. Gk *Puthōn* a huge serpent or monster killed by Apollo]

pythoness /pīthəniss/ *n.* **1** the Pythian priestess. **2** a witch. [ME f. OF *phitonise* f. med.L *phitonissa* f. LL *pythonissa* fem. of *pytho* f. Gk *puthōn* soothsaying demon: cf. PYTHON]

pyuria /pīyóoriə/ *n. Med.* the presence of pus in urine. [Gk *puon* pus + -URIA]

pyx /piks/ *n.* (also **pix**) **1** *Eccl.* the vessel in which the consecrated bread of the Eucharist is kept. **2** (in the UK) a box at the Royal Mint in which specimen gold and silver coins are deposited to be tested annually. [ME f. L (as PYXIS)]

pyxidium /piksíddiəm/ *n.* (*pl.* **pyxidia** /-diə/) *Bot.* a seed-capsule with a top that comes off like the lid of a box. [mod.L f. Gk *puxidion*, dimin. of *puxis*: see PYXIS]

pyxis /píksiss/ *n.* (*pl.* **pyxides** /-sideez/) **1** a small box or casket. **2** = PYXIDIUM. [ME f. L f. Gk *puxis* f. *puxos* BOX[3]]

pzazz var. of PIZAZZ.

Qq

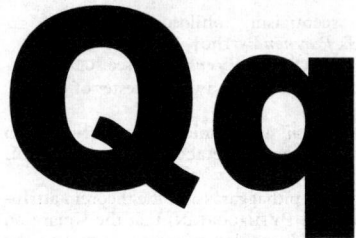

Q[1] /kyōō/ *n.* (also **q**) (*pl.* **Qs** or **Q's**) the seventeenth letter of the alphabet.

Q[2] *abbr.* (also **Q.**) **1** Queen, Queen's. **2** question.

Qantas /kwóntəss/ *n.* the international airline of Australia. [abbr. of *Q*ueensland *a*nd *N*orthern *T*erritory *A*erial *S*ervices]

QARANC *abbr.* Queen Alexandra's Royal Army Nursing Corps.

QB *abbr.* Queen's Bench.

QC *abbr. Law* Queen's Counsel.

QED *abbr. quod erat demonstrandum.*

Q fever /kyōō/ *n.* a mild febrile disease caused by rickettsiae. [*Q* = query]

qibla var. of KIBLAH.

Qld. *abbr.* Queensland.

QM *abbr.* quartermaster.

QMG *abbr.* Quartermaster General.

QMS *abbr.* Quartermaster Sergeant.

QPM *abbr.* (in the UK) Queen's Police Medal.

qr. *abbr.* quarter(s).

Q-ship /kyōōship/ *n.* an armed and disguised merchant ship used as a decoy or to destroy submarines. [*Q* = query]

QSO *abbr.* quasi-stellar object, quasar.

qt. *abbr.* quart(s).

q.t. *n. colloq.* quiet (esp. *on the q.t.*). [abbr.]
■ (*on the q.t.*) see *secretly* (SECRET).

qu. *abbr.* **1** query. **2** question.

qua /kwaa/ *conj.* in the capacity of; as being (*Napoleon qua general*). [L, ablat. fem. sing. of *qui* who (rel. pron.)]

quack[1] /kwak/ *v.* & *n.* ● *n.* the harsh sound made by ducks. ● *v.intr.* **1** utter this sound. **2** *colloq.* talk loudly and foolishly. [imit.: cf. Du. *kwakken*, G *quacken* croak, quack]

quack[2] /kwak/ *n.* **1 a** an unqualified practiser of medicine. **b** (*attrib.*) of or characteristic of unskilled medical practice (*quack cure*). **2 a** a charlatan. **b** (*attrib.*) of or characteristic of a charlatan; fraudulent, sham. **3** *sl.* any doctor or medical officer. □□ **quackery** *n.* **quackish** *adj.* [abbr. of *quacksalver* f. Du. (prob. f. obs. *quacken* prattle + *salf* SALVE[1])]
■ **2 a** charlatan, impostor, pretender, faker, fraud, *colloq.* phoney. **b** (*attrib.*) fake, fraudulent, sham, counterfeit, *colloq.* phoney. **3** see DOCTOR *n.* 1a.

quad[1] /kwod/ *n. colloq.* a quadrangle. [abbr.]

quad[2] /kwod/ *n. colloq.* = QUADRUPLET 1. [abbr.]

quad[3] /kwod/ *n. Printing* a piece of blank metal type used in spacing. [abbr. of earlier QUADRAT]

quad[4] /kwod/ *n.* & *adj.* ● *n.* quadraphony. ● *adj.* quadraphonic. [abbr.]

quadragenarian /kwódrəjináiriən/ *n.* & *adj.* ● *n.* a person from 40 to 49 years old. ● *adj.* of this age. [LL *quadragenarius* f. *quadrageni* distrib. of *quadraginta* forty]

Quadragesima /kwódrəjéssimə/ *n.* the first Sunday in Lent. [LL, fem. of L *quadragesimus* fortieth f. *quadraginta* forty, Lent having 40 days]

quadragesimal /kwódrəjéssim'l/ *adj.* **1** (of a fast, esp. in Lent) lasting forty days. **2** Lenten.

quadrangle /kwódrangg'l/ *n.* **1** a four-sided plane figure, esp. a square or rectangle. **2 a** a four-sided court, esp. enclosed by buildings, as in some colleges. **b** such a court with the buildings round it. □□ **quadrangular** /-ránggyoolər/ *adj.* [ME f. OF f. LL *quadrangulum* square, neut. of *quadrangulus* (as QUADRI-, ANGLE[1])]
■ **2** *colloq.* quad; see also AREA 5, SQUARE *n.* 3a.

quadrant /kwódrənt/ *n.* **1** a quarter of a circle's circumference. **2** a plane figure enclosed by two radii of a circle at right angles and the arc cut off by them. **3** a quarter of a sphere etc. **4 a** a thing, esp. a graduated strip of metal, shaped like a quarter-circle. **b** an instrument graduated (esp. through an arc of 90°) for taking angular measurements. □□ **quadrantal** /-dránt'l/ *adj.* [ME f. L *quadrans -antis* quarter f. *quattuor* four]

quadraphonic /kwódrəfónnik/ *adj.* (also **quadrophonic**) (of sound reproduction) using four transmission channels. □□ **quadraphonically** *adv.* **quadraphonics** *n.pl.* **quadraphony** /-róffəni/ *n.* [QUADRI- + STEREOPHONIC]

quadrat /kwódrət/ *n. Ecol.* a small area marked out for study. [var. of QUADRATE]

quadrate *adj.*, *n.*, & *v.* ● *adj.* /kwódrət/ esp. *Anat.* & *Zool.* square or rectangular (*quadrate bone*; *quadrate muscle*). ● *n.* /kwódrət/ **1** a quadrate bone or muscle. **2** a rectangular object. ● *v.* /kwodráyt/ **1** *tr.* make square. **2** *intr.* & *tr.* (often foll. by *with*) conform or make conform. [ME f. L *quadrare quadrat-* make square f. *quattuor* four]

quadratic /kwodráttik/ *adj.* & *n. Math.* ● *adj.* **1** involving the second and no higher power of an unknown quantity or variable (*quadratic equation*). **2** square. ● *n.* **1** a quadratic equation. **2** (in *pl.*) the branch of algebra dealing with these. [F *quadratique* or mod.L *quadraticus* (as QUADRATE)]

quadrature /kwódrəchər/ *n.* **1** *Math.* the process of constructing a square with an area equal to that of a figure bounded by a curve, e.g. a circle. **2** *Astron.* **a** each of two points at which the moon is 90° from the sun as viewed from earth. **b** the position of a heavenly body in relation to another 90° away. [F *quadrature* or L *quadratura* (as QUADRATE)]

quadrennial /kwodrénniəl/ *adj.* **1** lasting four years. **2** recurring every four years. □□ **quadrennially** *adv.* [as QUADRENNIUM]

quadrennium /kwodrénniəm/ *n.* (*pl.* **quadrenniums** or **quadrennia** /-niə/) a period of four years. [L *quadriennium* (as QUADRI-, *annus* year)]

quadri- /kwódri/ *comb. form* denoting four. [L f. *quattuor* four]

quadric /kwódrik/ *adj.* & *n. Geom.* ● *adj.* (of a surface) described by an equation of the second degree. ● *n.* a quadric surface. [L *quadra* square]

quadriceps /kwódriseps/ *n. Anat.* a four-headed muscle at the front of the thigh. [mod.L (as QUADRI-, BICEPS)]

quadrifid /kwódrifid/ *adj. Bot.* having four divisions or lobes. [L *quadrifidus* (as QUADRI-, *findere fid-* cleave)]

quadrilateral /kwódriláttərəl/ *adj.* & *n.* ● *adj.* having four sides. ● *n.* a four-sided figure. [LL *quadrilaterus* (as QUADRI-, *latus lateris* side)]

quadrille[1] /kwodríl/ *n.* **1** a square dance containing usu. five figures. **2** the music for this. [F f. Sp. *cuadrilla* troop, company f. *cuadra* square or It. *quadriglia* f. *quadra* square]

quadrille[2] /kwodríl/ *n.* a card game for four players with forty cards, fashionable in the 18th c. [F, perh. f. Sp. *cuartillo* f. *cuarto* fourth, assim. to QUADRILLE[1]]

quadrillion /kwodrílyən/ *n.* (*pl.* same or **quadrillions**) a thousand raised to the fifth (or formerly, esp. *Brit.*, the eighth) power (10^{15} and 10^{24} respectively). [F (as QUADRI-, MILLION)]

quadrinomial /kwódrinṓmiəl/ *n.* & *adj. Math.* ● *n.* an expression of four algebraic terms. ● *adj.* of or being a quadrinomial. [QUADRI- + Gk *nomos* part, portion]

quadripartite /kwódripaártīt/ *adj.* **1** consisting of four parts. **2** shared by or involving four parties.

quadriplegia /kwódripleéjiə, -jə/ *n. Med.* paralysis of all four limbs. ▫▫ **quadriplegic** *adj.* & *n.* [mod.L (as QUADRI-, Gk *plēgē* blow, strike)]

quadrivalent /kwódriváylənt/ *adj. Chem.* having a valency of four.

quadrivium /kwodrívviəm/ *n. hist.* a medieval university course of arithmetic, geometry, astronomy, and music. [L, = the place where four roads meet (as QUADRI-, *via* road)]

quadroon /kwodrṓōn/ *n.* the offspring of a White person and a mulatto; a person of one quarter Negro blood. [Sp. *cuarterón* f. *cuarto* fourth, assim. to QUADRI-]

quadrophonic var. of QUADRAPHONIC.

quadrumanous /kwodrṓōmənəss/ *adj.* (of primates other than humans) four-handed, i.e. with opposable digits on all four limbs. [mod.L *quadrumana* neut. pl. of *quadrumanus* (as QUADRI-, L *manus* hand)]

quadruped /kwódrooped/ *n.* & *adj.* ● *n.* a four-footed animal, esp. a four-footed mammal. ● *adj.* four-footed. ▫▫ **quadrupedal** /-rṓōpid'l/ *adj.* [F *quadrupède* or L *quadrupes -pedis* f. *quadru-* var. of QUADRI- + L *pes ped-* foot]

quadruple /kwódroop'l/ *adj.*, *n.*, & *v.* ● *adj.* **1** fourfold. **2 a** having four parts. **b** involving four participants (*quadruple alliance*). **3** being four times as many or as much. **4** (of time in music) having four beats in a bar. ● *n.* a fourfold number or amount. ● *v.tr.* & *intr.* multiply by four; increase fourfold. ▫▫ **quadruply** *adv.* [F f. L *quadruplus* (as QUADRI-, *-plus* as in *duplus* DUPLE)]

quadruplet /kwódrooplit, -drṓōplit/ *n.* **1** each of four children born at one birth. **2** a set of four things working together. **3** *Mus.* a group of four notes to be performed in the time of three. [QUADRUPLE, after *triplet*]

quadruplicate *adj.* & *v.* ● *adj.* /kwodrṓōplikət/ **1** fourfold. **2** of which four copies are made. ● *v.tr.* /kwodrṓōplikayt/ **1** multiply by four. **2** make four identical copies of. ▫ **in quadruplicate** in four identical copies. ▫▫ **quadruplication** /-káysh'n/ *n.* [L *quadruplicare* f. *quadruplex -plicis* fourfold: cf. QUADRUPED, DUPLEX]

quadruplicity /kwódrooplíssiti/ *n.* the state of being fourfold. [L *quadruplex -plicis* (see QUADRUPLICATE), after *duplicity*]

quaestor /kweéstər/ *n.* either of two ancient Roman magistrates with mainly financial responsibilities. ▫▫ **quaestorial** /-stóriəl/ *adj.* **quaestorship** *n.* [ME f. L f. *quaerere quaesit-* seek]

quaff /kwof, kwaaf/ *v. literary* **1** *tr.* & *intr.* drink deeply. **2** *tr.* drain (a cup etc.) in long draughts. ▫▫ **quaffable** *adj.* **quaffer** *n.* [16th c.: perh. imit.]

■ **1** see DRINK *v.* 1. **2** drink up *or* down, drain, swallow, finish.

quag /kwag, kwog/ *n.* a marshy or boggy place. ▫▫ **quaggy** *adj.* [rel. to dial. *quag* (v.) = shake: prob. imit.]

quagga /kwággə/ *n.* an extinct zebra-like mammal, *Equus quagga*, formerly native to S. Africa, with yellowish-brown stripes on the head, neck, and forebody. [Xhosa-Kaffir *iqwara*]

quagmire /kwógmīr, kwág-/ *n.* **1** a soft boggy or marshy area that gives way underfoot. **2** a hazardous or awkward situation. [QUAG + MIRE]

■ **1** see MARSH. **2** see MORASS 1.

quahog /kwáwhog/ *n.* (*US* **quahaug** /-hawg/) any of various edible clams of the Atlantic coast of N. America. [Narragansett Indian]

quaich /kwaykh/ *n.* (also **quaigh**) *Sc.* a kind of drinking-cup, usu. of wood and with two handles. [Gael. *cuach* cup, prob. f. L *caucus*]

quail[1] /kwayl/ *n.* (*pl.* same or **quails**) any small migratory bird of the genus *Coturnix*, with a short tail and allied to the partridge. [ME f. OF *quaille* f. med.L *coacula* (prob. imit.)]

quail[2] /kwayl/ *v.intr.* flinch; be apprehensive with fear. [ME, of unkn. orig.]

■ see FLINCH[1] *v.*

quaint /kwaynt/ *adj.* **1** piquantly or attractively unfamiliar or old-fashioned. **2** daintily odd. ▫▫ **quaintly** *adv.* **quaintness** *n.* [earlier senses 'wise, cunning': ME f. OF *cointe* f. L *cognitus* past part. of *cognoscere* ascertain]

■ **1** old-fashioned, outmoded, antiquated, out-dated, antique; picturesque, sweet, bijou, twee, *esp. US colloq.* cute. **2** curious, odd, strange, bizarre, peculiar, unusual, queer, uncommon, singular, eccentric, whimsical, offbeat, fanciful, outlandish, unconventional, fantastic.

quake /kwayk/ *v.* & *n.* ● *v.intr.* **1** shake, tremble. **2** rock to and fro. **3** (of a person) shake or shudder (*was quaking with fear*). ● *n.* **1** *colloq.* an earthquake. **2** an act of quaking. ▫ **quaking-grass** any grass of the genus *Briza*, having slender stalks and trembling in the wind: also called *dodder-grass*. ▫▫ **quaky** *adj.* (**quakier**, **quakiest**). [OE *cwacian*]

■ *v.* **1, 3** tremble, shake, quiver, shudder; vibrate. ● *n.* **1** earthquake, tremor. **2** shiver, tremble, shudder; see also SHAKE *n.* 1, 2.

Quaker /kwáykər/ *n.* a member of the Society of Friends, a Christian movement devoted to peaceful principles and eschewing formal doctrine, sacraments, and ordained ministers. ▫▫ **Quakerish** *adj.* **Quakerism** *n.* [QUAKE + -ER[1]]

■ Friend.

qualification /kwóllifikáysh'n/ *n.* **1** the act or an instance of qualifying. **2** (often in *pl.*) **a** a quality, skill, or accomplishment fitting a person for a position or purpose. **b** an award gained on successful completion of a course of education or training (*left school without any qualifications*). **3 a** a circumstance, condition, etc., that modifies or limits (*the statement had many qualifications*). **b** a thing that detracts from completeness or absoluteness (*their relief had one qualification*). **4** a condition that must be fulfilled before a right can be acquired etc. **5** an attribution of a quality (*the qualification of our policy as opportunist is unfair*). ▫▫ **qualificatory** /kwóllifikaytəri/ *adj.* [F *qualification* or med.L *qualificatio* (as QUALIFY)]

■ **2 a** (*qualifications*) ability, aptitude, competence, capacity, proficiency, skill(s), knowledge, *colloq.* know-how. **3 a** limitation, restriction, modification, reservation, caveat, condition, stipulation, proviso; prerequisite, requirement. **b** see DRAWBACK.

qualify /kwóllifī/ *v.* (**-ies**, **-ied**) **1** *tr.* make competent or fit for a position or purpose. **2** *tr.* make legally entitled. **3** *intr.* (foll. by *for* or *as*) (of a person) satisfy the conditions or requirements for (a position, award, competition, etc.). **4** *tr.* add reservations to; modify or make less absolute (a statement or assertion). **5** *tr. Gram.* (of a word, esp. an adjective) attribute a quality to another word, esp. a noun. **6** *tr.* moderate, mitigate; make less severe or extreme. **7** *tr.* alter the strength or flavour of. **8** *tr.* (foll. by *as*) attribute a specified quality to, describe as (*the idea was qualified as absurd*). **9** *tr.* (as **qualifying** *adj.*) serving to determine those that qualify (*qualifying examination*). **10** (as **qualified** *adj.*) **a** having the qualifications necessary for a particular office or function. **b** dependent on other factors; not definite (*a qualified 'yes'*). ▫▫ **qualifiable** *adj.* **qualifier** *n.* [F *qualifier* f. med.L *qualificare* f. L *qualis* such as]

■ **1** equip, fit, ready, prepare, condition, make eligible. **2** certify. **3** be eligible, meet the requirements, have the qualifications, be fit *or* equipped *or* ready *or* prepared, *colloq.* make the grade. **4** modulate; restrict, limit; see also MODIFY 1. **6** temper, moderate; see also MITIGATE. **8** see DESCRIBE 1b. **10** (**qualified**) **a** experienced, practised, knowledgeable, competent, able, suitable, capable, fit, fitted, trained, proficient, accomplished, expert, talented, adept, skilful, skilled, well-informed. **b** contingent, conditional, restricted, modified, limited, provisional. □□ **qualifier** see HEAT *n.* 6.

qualitative /kwóllitətiv, -taytiv/ *adj.* concerned with or depending on quality (*led to a qualitative change in society*). □ **qualitative analysis** *Chem.* detection of the constituents, as elements, functional groups, etc., present in a substance (opp. *quantitative analysis*). □□ **qualitatively** *adv.* [LL *qualitativus* (as QUALITY)]

quality /kwólliti/ *n.* (*pl.* **-ies**) **1** the degree of excellence of a thing (*of good quality; poor in quality*). **2 a** general excellence (*their work has quality*). **b** (*attrib.*) of high quality (*a quality product*). **3** a distinctive attribute or faculty; a characteristic trait. **4** the relative nature or kind or character of a thing (*is made in three qualities*). **5** the distinctive timbre of a voice or sound. **6** *archaic* high social standing (*people of quality*). **7** *Logic* the property of a proposition's being affirmative or negative. □ **quality control** a system of maintaining standards in manufactured products by testing a sample of the output against the specification. [ME f. OF *qualité* f. L *qualitas -tatis* f. *qualis* of what kind]

■ **1** grade, calibre, rank, value, worth. **2 a** see EXCELLENCE 1. **b** see *first-rate adj.* **3** property, attribute, characteristic, mark, faculty, distinction, trait. **6** eminence, prominence, importance, superiority, distinction, standing, dignity, nobility.

qualm /kwaam, kwawm/ *n.* **1** a misgiving; an uneasy doubt esp. about one's own conduct. **2** a scruple of conscience. **3** a momentary faint or sick feeling. □□ **qualmish** *adj.* [16th c.: orig. uncert.]

■ **1** second thought(s), doubt, uncertainty, misgiving, hesitation, uneasiness, reluctance, disinclination, queasiness, sinking feeling, apprehension, apprehensiveness, worry, concern, *colloq.* funny feeling. **2** scruple, compunction, twinge, pang.

quandary /kwóndəri, -dri/ *n.* (*pl.* **-ies**) **1** a state of perplexity. **2** a difficult situation; a practical dilemma. [16th c.: orig. uncert.]

■ confusion; predicament, difficulty, plight; see also DILEMMA.

quango /kwánggō/ *n.* (*pl.* **-os**) a semi-public body with financial support from and senior appointments made by the government. [abbr. of *qua*si (or *qua*si-*a*utonomous) *n*on-*g*overnment(al) *o*rganization]

quant /kwont/ *n.* & *v.* ● *n. Brit.* a punting-pole with a prong at the bottom to prevent it sinking into the mud, as used by Norfolk bargemen etc. ● *v.tr.* (also *absol.*) propel (a boat) with a quant. [15th c.: perh. f. L *contus* f. Gk *kontos* boat-pole]

quanta *pl.* of QUANTUM.

quantal /kwónt'l/ *adj.* **1** composed of discrete units; varying in steps, not continuously. **2** of or relating to a quantum or quantum theory. □□ **quantally** *adv.* [L *quantus* how much]

quantic /kwóntik/ *n. Math.* a rational integral homogeneous function of two or more variables.

quantify /kwóntifī/ *v.tr.* (**-ies, -ied**) **1** determine the quantity of. **2** measure or express as a quantity. **3** *Logic* define the application of (a term or proposition) by the use of *all*, *some*, etc., e.g. 'for all *x* if *x* is A then *x* is B'. □□ **quantifiable** *adj.* **quantifiability** /-fīəbílliti/ *n.* **quantification** /kwóntifikáysh'n/ *n.* **quantifier** *n.* [med.L *quantificare* (as QUANTAL)]

■ **1** see COUNT[1] *v.* 1, CALCULATE 1.

quantitative /kwóntitətiv, -taytiv/ *adj.* **1 a** concerned with quantity. **b** measured or measurable by quantity. **2** of or based on the quantity of syllables. □ **quantitative analysis** *Chem.* measurement of the amounts of the constituents of a substance (opp. QUALITATIVE ANALYSIS). □□ **quantitatively** *adv.* [med.L *quantitativus* (as QUANTITY)]

quantitive /kwóntitiv/ *adj.* = QUANTITATIVE. □□ **quantitively** *adv.*

quantity /kwóntiti/ *n.* (*pl.* **-ies**) **1** the property of things that is measurable. **2** the size or extent or weight or amount or number. **3** a specified or considerable portion or number or amount (*buys in quantity; the quantity of heat in a body*). **4** (in *pl.*) large amounts or numbers; an abundance (*quantities of food; is found in quantities on the shore*). **5** the length or shortness of vowel sounds or syllables. **6** *Math.* **a** a value, component, etc. that may be expressed in numbers. **b** the figure or symbol representing this. □ **quantity mark** a mark put over a vowel etc. to indicate its length. **quantity surveyor** a person who measures and prices building work. **quantity theory** the hypothesis that prices correspond to changes in the monetary supply. [ME f. OF *quantité* f. L *quantitas -tatis* f. *quantus* how much]

■ **2** amount, extent, volume; sum, number, total; weight, measure. **3** see BULK *n.* 1a, AMOUNT *n.* 1. **4** see LOT *n.* 1.

quantize /kwóntīz/ *v.tr.* (also **-ise**) **1** form into quanta. **2** apply quantum mechanics to. □□ **quantization** /-záysh'n/ *n.*

quantum /kwóntəm/ *n.* (*pl.* **quanta** /-tə/) **1** *Physics* **a** a discrete quantity of energy proportional in magnitude to the frequency of radiation it represents. **b** an analogous discrete amount of any other physical quantity. **2 a** a required or allowed amount. **b** a share or portion. □ **quantum jump** (or **leap**) **1** a sudden large increase or advance. **2** *Physics* an abrupt transition in an atom or molecule from one quantum state to another. **quantum mechanics** (or **theory**) *Physics* a system or theory using the assumption that energy exists in discrete units. [L, neut. of *quantus* how much]

quaquaversal /kwáykwəvérs'l/ *adj. Geol.* pointing in every direction. [LL *quaquaversus* f. *quaqua* wheresoever + *versus* towards]

quarantine /kwórrənteen/ *n.* & *v.* ● *n.* **1** isolation imposed on persons or animals that have arrived from elsewhere or been exposed to, and might spread, infectious or contagious disease. **2** the period of this isolation. ● *v.tr.* impose such isolation on, put in quarantine. [It. *quarantina* forty days f. *quaranta* forty]

quark[1] /kwaark/ *n. Physics* any of several postulated components of elementary particles. [invented word, assoc. with 'Three quarks for Muster Mark' in Joyce's *Finnegans Wake* (1939)]

quark[2] /kwaark/ *n.* a type of low-fat curd cheese. [G]

quarrel[1] /kwórrəl/ *n.* & *v.* ● *n.* **1** a violent contention or altercation between individuals or with others. **2** a rupture of friendly relations. **3** an occasion of complaint against a person, a person's actions, etc. ● *v.intr.* (**quarrelled, quarrelling**; *US* **quarreled, quarreling**) **1** (often foll. by *with*) take exception; find fault. **2** fall out; have a dispute; break off friendly relations. □□ **quarreller** *n.* [ME f. OF *querele* f. L *querel(l)a* complaint f. *queri* complain]

■ *n.* **1** dispute, argument, disagreement, debate, controversy, difference (of opinion), contention, wrangle, tiff, squabble, altercation, fight, falling out, *colloq.* set-to, row, scrap, *Brit. colloq.* barney, *US colloq.* spat. **2** see RIFT *n.* 3. **3** complaint, objection, grudge, *colloq.* gripe, *sl.* beef. ● *v.* **1** see OBJECT *v.*, OPPOSE 1–3. **2** argue, disagree, dispute, altercate, have an altercation, differ, wrangle, be at odds *or* loggerheads, clash, squabble, feud, fight, fall out, *colloq.* scrap.

quarrel[2] /kwórrəl/ *n. hist.* a short heavy square-headed arrow or bolt used in a crossbow or arbalest. [ME f. OF *quar(r)el* ult. f. LL *quadrus* square]

quarrelsome /kwórrəlsəm/ *adj.* given to or characterized by quarrelling. □□ **quarrelsomely** *adv.* **quarrelsomeness** *n.*

■ argumentative, querulous, contrary, combative, antagonistic, pugnacious, bellicose, belligerent, contentious, disputatious, irascible, cross, choleric, curmudgeonly, irritable, disagreeable, peevish, *esp. US* cranky, *colloq.* grouchy.

quarrian /kwórriən/ *n.* (also **quarrion**) a cockatiel. [prob. Aboriginal]

quarry[1] /kwórri/ *n.* & *v.* ● *n.* (*pl.* **-ies**) **1** an excavation made by taking stone etc. for building etc. from its bed. **2** a place from which stone etc. may be extracted. **3** a source of information, knowledge, etc. ● *v.* (**-ies, -ied**) **1** *tr.* extract (stone) from a quarry. **2** *tr.* extract (facts etc.) laboriously from books etc. **3** *intr.* laboriously search documents etc. [ME f. med.L *quare(r)ia* f. OF *quarriere* f. L *quadrum* square]

■ *n.* **2** working. **3** see MINE[2] *n.* 2. ● *v.* **2** mine, extract, obtain, get, cull. **3** see SCRUTINIZE.

quarry[2] /kwórri/ *n.* (*pl.* **-ies**) **1** the object of pursuit by a bird of prey, hounds, hunters, etc. **2** an intended victim or prey. [ME f. AF f. OF *cuiree, couree* (assim. to *cuir* leather and *curer* disembowel) ult. f. L *cor* heart: orig. = parts of deer placed on hide and given to hounds]

■ prey, game, victim; prize, object, target.

quarry[3] /kwórri/ *n.* (*pl.* **-ies**) **1** a diamond-shaped pane of glass as used in lattice windows. **2** (in full **quarry tile**) an unglazed floor-tile. [a later form of QUARREL[2] in the same sense]

quarryman /kwórrimən/ *n.* (*pl.* **-men**) a worker in a quarry.

quart /kwawrt/ *n.* **1** a liquid measure equal to a quarter of a gallon; two pints. **2** a vessel containing this amount. **3** *US* a unit of dry measure, equivalent to one-thirty-second of a bushel (1.1 litre). **4** /kaart/ (also **quarte**) the fourth of eight parrying positions in fencing. □ **a quart into a pint pot 1** a large amount etc. fitted into a small space. **2** something difficult or impossible to achieve. [ME f. OF *quarte* f. L *quarta* fem. of *quartus* fourth f. *quattuor* four]

quartan /kwáwrt'n/ *adj.* (of a fever etc.) recurring every fourth day. [ME f. OF *quartaine* f. L (*febris* fever) *quartana* f. *quartus* fourth]

quarte var. of QUART 4.

quarter /kwáwrtər/ *n.* & *v.* ● *n.* **1** each of four equal parts into which a thing is or might be divided. **2** a period of three months, usu. for which payments become due on the quarter day. **3** a point of time 15 minutes before or after any hour. **4** a school or *US* university term. **5 a** 25 US or Canadian cents. **b** a coin of this denomination. **6** a part of a town, esp. as occupied by a particular class or group (*residential quarter*). **7 a** a point of the compass. **b** a region at such a point. **8** the direction, district, or source of supply etc. (*help from any quarter*; *came from all quarters*). **9** (in *pl.*) **a** lodgings; an abode. **b** *Mil.* the living accommodation of troops etc. **10 a** one fourth of a lunar month. **b** the moon's position between the first and second (**first quarter**) or third and fourth (**last quarter**) of these. **11 a** each of the four parts into which an animal's or bird's carcass is divided, each including a leg or wing. **b** (in *pl.*) *hist.* the four parts into which a traitor etc. was cut after execution. **c** (in *pl.*) = HINDQUARTERS. **12** mercy offered or granted to an enemy in battle etc. on condition of surrender. **13 a** *Brit.* a grain measure equivalent to 8 bushels. **b** one-fourth of a hundredweight (28 lb. or *US* 25 lb.). **14 a** each of four divisions on a shield. **b** a charge occupying this, placed in chief. **15** either side of a ship abaft the beam. **16** (in American and Australian football) each of four equal periods into which a match is divided. ● *v.tr.* **1** divide into quarters. **2** *hist.* divide (the body of an executed person) in this way. **3 a** put (troops etc.) into quarters. **b** station or lodge in a specified place. **4** (foll. by *on*) impose (a person) on another as a lodger. **5** cut (a log) into quarters, and these into planks so as to show the grain well. **6** (esp. of a dog) range or traverse (the ground) in every direction. **7** *Heraldry* **a** place or bear (charges or coats of arms) on the four quarters of a shield's surface. **b** add (another's coat) to one's hereditary arms. **c** (foll. by *with*) place in alternate quarters with. **d** divide (a shield) into four or more parts by vertical and horizontal lines. □ **quarter-binding** the type of bookbinding in which the spine is bound in one material (usu. leather) and the sides in another. **quarter day** one of four days on which quarterly payments are due, tenancies begin and end, etc. **quarter-final** a match or round preceding the semifinal. **quarter-hour 1** a period of 15 minutes. **2** = sense 3 of *n.* **quarter-light** *Brit.* a window in the side of a motor vehicle, closed carriage, etc. other than the main door-window. **quarter-line** *Rugby Football* a space enclosed by a line across the ground 22 metres from the goal-line. **quarter note** esp. *US Mus.* a crotchet. **quarter-plate 1** a photographic plate or film 8.3 x 10.8 cm. **2** a photograph reproduced from it. **quarter sessions** *hist.* (in the UK) a court of limited criminal and civil jurisdiction and of appeal, usu. held quarterly. **quarter-tone** *Mus.* half a semitone. [ME f. AF *quarter*, OF *quartier* f. L *quartarius* fourth part (of a measure) f. *quartus* fourth]

■ *n.* **6** area, region, district, zone, section, division, territory, neighbourhood, locality, locale. **8** source, place, location, point, spot, area; direction. **9** (*quarters*) **a** living quarters, lodging(s), accommodation(s), rooms, residence, habitation, domicile, home, house, abode, *Brit. colloq.* digs, diggings, *formal* dwelling(-place). **b** billet, barracks, cantonment. **12** mercy, compassion, mercifulness, clemency, leniency, forgiveness, favour, humanity, pity. ● *v.* **3** billet, lodge, accommodate, house, board, shelter, put up; post, station.

quarterage /kwáwrtərij/ *n.* **1** a quarterly payment. **2** a quarter's wages, allowance, pension, etc.

quarterback /kwáwrtərbak/ *n.* a player in American football who directs attacking play.

quarterdeck /kwáwrtərdek/ *n.* **1** part of a ship's upper deck near the stern, usu. reserved for officers. **2** the officers of a ship or the navy.

quartering /kwáwrtəring/ *n.* **1** (in *pl.*) the coats of arms marshalled on a shield to denote the alliances of a family with the heiresses of others. **2** the provision of quarters for soldiers. **3** the act or an instance of dividing, esp. into four equal parts. **4** timber sawn into lengths, used for high-quality floor-boards etc.

quarterly /kwáwrtərli/ *adj.*, *adv.*, & *n.* ● *adj.* **1** produced or occurring once every quarter of a year. **2** (of a shield) quartered. ● *adv.* **1** once every quarter of a year. **2** in the four, or in two diagonally opposite, quarters of a shield. ● *n.* (*pl.* **-ies**) a quarterly review or magazine.

■ *adj.* **1** tri-monthly, three-monthly, trimestral, trimestrial. ● *adv.* **1** every three months, four times a year.

quartermaster /kwáwrtərmaastər/ *n.* **1** a regimental officer in charge of quartering, rations, etc. **2** a naval petty officer in charge of steering, signals, etc. □ **Quartermaster General** the head of the army department in charge of quartering etc. **quartermaster sergeant** a sergeant assisting an army quartermaster.

quartern /kwáwrtərn/ *n. Brit. archaic* a quarter of a pint. □ **quartern loaf** a four-pound loaf. [ME, = quarter f. AF *quartrun*, OF *quart(e)ron* f. QUART fourth or *quartier* QUARTER]

quarterstaff /kwáwrtərstaaf/ *n. hist.* a stout pole 6–8 feet long, formerly used as a weapon.

quartet /kwawrtét/ *n.* (also **quartette**) **1** *Mus.* **a** a composition for four voices or instruments. **b** the performers of such a piece. **2** any group of four. [F *quartette* f. It. *quartetto* f. *quarto* fourth f. L *quartus*]

quartic /kwaártik/ *adj.* & *n. Math.* ● *adj.* involving the fourth and no higher power of an unknown quantity or variable. ● *n.* a quartic equation. [L *quartus* fourth]

quartile /kwáwrtīl/ *adj.* & *n.* ● *adj. Astrol.* relating to the aspect of two celestial bodies 90° apart. ● *n.* **1** a quartile aspect. **2** *Statistics* one of three values of a variable dividing a population into four equal groups as regards the value of that variable. [med.L *quartilis* f. L *quartus* fourth]

quarto /kwáwrtō/ *n.* (*pl.* **-os**) *Printing* **1** the size given by folding a (usu. specified) sheet of paper twice. **2** a book consisting of sheets folded in this way. ¶ Abbr.: **4to.** □ **quarto paper** paper folded in this way and cut into sheets. [L (*in*) *quarto* (in) the fourth (of a sheet), ablat. of *quartus* fourth]

quartz /kwawrts/ *n.* a mineral form of silica that crystallizes as hexagonal prisms. □ **quartz clock** a clock operated by vibrations of an electrically driven quartz crystal. **quartz lamp** a quartz tube containing mercury vapour and used as a light source. [G *Quarz* f. WSlav. *kwardy*]

quartzite /kwáwrtsīt/ *n.* a metamorphic rock consisting mainly of quartz.

quasar /kwáyzaar, -saar/ *n. Astron.* any of a class of starlike celestial objects having a spectrum with a large red-shift. [*quasi*-stellar]

quash /kwosh/ *v.tr.* **1** annul; reject as not valid, esp. by a legal procedure. **2** suppress; crush (a rebellion etc.). [ME f. OF *quasser*, *casser* annul f. LL *cassare* f. *cassus* null, void or f. L *cassare* frequent. of *quatere* shake]

▪ **1** annul, nullify, void, declare *or* render null and void, invalidate, revoke, set aside, rescind, cancel, reject, throw out, reverse, overthrow, discharge, overrule, overturn, *Law* vacate. **2** suppress, subdue, quell, put down, squelch, stamp on, repress, overthrow, crush, overwhelm, put an end to.

quasi /kwáyzī, kwaázi/ *adv.* (introducing an exclamation) that is to say; as it were. [L, = as if, almost]

quasi- /kwáyzī, kwaázi/ *comb. form* **1** seemingly; apparently but not really (*quasi-scientific*). **2** being partly or almost (*quasi-independent*). [L *quasi* as if, almost]

▪ **1** pseudo-; seemingly; see also *apparently* (APPARENT). **2** partly, to some extent; virtually; see also ALMOST.

quassia /kwóshə/ *n.* **1** an evergreen tree, *Quassia amara*, native to S. America. **2** the wood, bark, or root of this tree, yielding a bitter medicinal tonic and insecticide. [G. *Quassi*, 18th-c. Surinam slave, who discovered its medicinal properties]

quatercentenary /kwáttərsenteéenəri/ *n.* & *adj.* ● *n.* (*pl.* **-ies**) **1** a four-hundredth anniversary. **2** a festival marking this. ● *adj.* of this anniversary. [L *quater* four times + CENTENARY]

quaternary /kwətérnəri/ *adj.* & *n.* ● *adj.* **1** having four parts. **2** (**Quaternary**) *Geol.* of or relating to the most recent period in the Cenozoic era with evidence of many species of present-day plants and animals (cf. PLEISTOCENE, HOLOCENE). ¶ Cf. Appendix VII. ● *n.* (*pl.* **-ies**) **1** a set of four things. **2** (**Quaternary**) *Geol.* the Quaternary period or system. [ME f. L *quaternarius* f. *quaterni* distrib. of *quattuor* four]

quaternion /kwətérniən/ *n.* **1** a set of four. **2** *Math.* a complex number of the form $w + xi + yj + zk$, where w, x, y, z are real numbers and i, j, k are imaginary units that satisfy certain conditions. [ME f. LL *quaternio -onis* (as QUATERNARY)]

quatorzain /káttərzayn/ *n.* any fourteen-line poem; an irregular sonnet. [F *quatorzaine* f. *quatorze* fourteen f. L *quattuordecim*]

quatorze /kətórz/ *n.* a set of four aces, kings, queens, or jacks, in one hand at piquet, scoring fourteen. [F: see QUATORZAIN]

quatrain /kwótrayn/ *n.* a stanza of four lines, usu. with alternate rhymes. [F f. *quatre* four f. L *quattuor*]

quatrefoil /kátrəfoyl/ *n.* a four-pointed or four-leafed figure, esp. as an ornament in architectural tracery, resembling a flower or clover leaf. [ME f. AF f. *quatre* four: see FOIL[2]]

quattrocento /kwátrōchéntō/ *n.* the style of Italian art of the 15th c. ▫▫ **quattrocentist** *n.* [It., = 400 used with reference to the years 1400–99]

quaver /kwáyvər/ *v.* & *n.* ● *v.* **1** *intr.* **a** (esp. of a voice or musical sound) vibrate, shake, tremble. **b** use trills or shakes in singing. **2** *tr.* **a** sing (a note or song) with quavering. **b** (often foll. by *out*) say in a trembling voice. ● *n.* **1** *Mus.* a note having the time value of an eighth of a semibreve or half a crotchet and represented by a large dot with a hooked stem. Also called *eighth note*. **2** a trill in singing. **3** a tremble in speech. ▫▫ **quaveringly** *adv.* [ME f. *quave*, perh. f. OE *cwafian* (unrecorded: cf. *cwacian* QUAKE)]

▪ *v.* **1 a** tremble, quiver, shake, shiver, vibrate, waver, shudder, oscillate, flutter. ● *n.* **3** trembling, tremble, quiver, tremor, shaking, vibration, wavering, fluctuation, oscillation.

quavery /kwáyvəri/ *adj.* (of a voice etc.) tremulous. ▫▫ **quaveriness** *n.*

quay /kee/ *n.* a solid stationary artificial landing-place lying alongside or projecting into water for loading and unloading ships. ▫▫ **quayage** *n.* [ME *key(e)*, *kay* f. OF *kay* f. Gaulish *caio* f. OCelt.]

▪ see LANDING 1c.

quayside /keéssīd/ *n.* the land forming or near a quay.

Que. *abbr.* Quebec.

quean /kween/ *n. archaic* an impudent or ill-behaved girl or woman. [OE *cwene* woman: cf. QUEEN]

▪ hussy, minx, vixen.

queasy /kweézi/ *adj.* (**-ier, -iest**) **1 a** (of a person) feeling nausea. **b** (of a person's stomach) easily upset, weak of digestion. **2** (of the conscience etc.) overscrupulous, tender. **3** (of a feeling, thought, etc.) uncomfortable, uneasy. ▫▫ **queasily** *adv.* **queasiness** *n.* [ME *queysy*, *coisy* perh. f. AF & OF, rel. to OF *coisir* hurt]

▪ **1 a** sick, nauseous, nauseated, ill, bilious, queer, groggy. **3** uncomfortable, uneasy, nervous, apprehensive.

Quechua /kéchwə/ *n.* (also **Quichua** /kích-/) a S. American Indian language widely spoken in Peru and neighbouring countries. ▫▫ **Quechuan** *adj.* [Sp. f. Quechua]

queen /kween/ *n.* & *v.* ● *n.* **1** (as a title usu. **Queen**) a female sovereign etc., esp. the hereditary ruler of an independent State. **2** (in full **queen consort**) a king's wife. **3** a woman, country, or thing pre-eminent or supreme in a specified area or of its kind (*tennis queen*; *the queen of roses*). **4** the fertile female among ants, bees, etc. **5** the most powerful piece in chess. **6** a court card with a picture of a queen. **7** *sl.* a male homosexual, esp. an effeminate one. **8 a** an honoured female, e.g. the Virgin Mary (*Queen of Heaven*). **b** an ancient goddess (*Venus, Queen of love*). **9** a belle or mock sovereign on some occasion (*beauty queen*; *queen of the May*). **10** a person's sweetheart, wife, or mistress. **11** (**the Queen**) (in the UK) the national anthem when there is a female sovereign. ● *v.tr.* **1** make (a woman) queen. **2** *Chess* convert (a pawn) into a queen when it reaches the opponent's side of the board. ▫ **Queen-Anne** in the style of English architecture, furniture, etc., in or about Queen Anne's time, the early 18th c. **Queen Anne's lace** cow-parsley. **queen bee 1** the fertile female in a hive. **2** the chief or controlling woman in an organization or social group. **queen-cake** a small soft cake often with raisins etc. **queen dowager** the widow of a king. **queen it** play the queen. **queen mother** the dowager who is mother of the sovereign. **queen of the meadows** meadowsweet. **queen of puddings** a pudding made with bread, jam, and meringue. **queen-post** one of two upright timbers between the tie-beam and principal rafters of a roof-truss. **Queen's bench** see BENCH. **queen's bishop, knight**, etc. *Chess* (of pieces which exist in pairs) the piece starting on the queen's side of the board. **Queen's bounty** see BOUNTY. **Queen's colour** see COLOUR. **Queen's Counsel** see COUNSEL. **the Queen's English** see ENGLISH. **Queen's evidence** see EVIDENCE. **Queen's Guide** see GUIDE. **Queen's highway** see HIGHWAY. **queen-size** (or **-sized**) of an extra-large size, usu. smaller than king-size. **Queen's Messenger** see MESSENGER. **queen's pawn** *Chess* the pawn in front of the queen at the beginning of a game. **Queen's Proctor** see PROCTOR. **Queen's Scout** see SCOUT[1]. **Queen's speech** see SPEECH. **queen's-ware** cream-coloured Wedgwood. ▫▫ **queendom** *n.* **queenhood** *n.* **queenless** *adj.* **queen-like** *adj.* **queenship** *n.* [OE *cwēn* f. Gmc; cf. QUEAN]

▪ *n.* **1** sovereign, monarch, ruler; empress. **2** queen consort. **3** star; ideal, epitome, paragon, nonpareil. **10** see SWEETHEART 1.

queenie /kweéni/ *n. sl.* = QUEEN *n.* 7.

queenly /kweénli/ *adj.* (**queenlier, queenliest**) **1** fit for or appropriate to a queen. **2** majestic; queenlike. ▫▫ **queenliness** *n.*

▪ see ROYAL *adj.* 5.

Queensberry Rules /kweénzbəri/ *n.pl.* the standard rules, esp. of boxing. [the 8th Marquis of *Queensberry*, Engl.

nobleman d. 1900, who supervised the preparation of boxing laws in 1867]

queer /kweer/ *adj.*, *n.*, & *v.* ● *adj.* **1** strange; odd; eccentric. **2** shady; suspect; of questionable character. **3 a** slightly ill; giddy; faint. **b** *Brit. sl.* drunk. **4** *derog. sl.* (esp. of a man) homosexual. **5** *colloq.* (of a person or behaviour) crazy; unbalanced; slightly mad. ● *n. derog. sl.* a homosexual. ● *v.tr. sl.* spoil; put out of order. □ **in Queer Street** *sl.* in a difficulty, in debt or trouble or disrepute. **queer a person's pitch** spoil a person's chances, esp. secretly or maliciously. □□ **queerish** *adj.* **queerly** *adv.* **queerness** *n.* [perh. f. G *quer* oblique (as THWART)]

■ *adj.* **1** odd, strange, peculiar, eccentric, funny, curious, uncommon, unconventional, unorthodox, atypical, singular, exceptional, anomalous, extraordinary, unusual, bizarre, uncanny, unnatural, freakish, remarkable, offbeat, irregular, unparalleled, incongruous, outlandish, *outré*, fey, quaint, absurd, *colloq.* weird. **2** questionable, dubious, shady, suspect, doubtful, puzzling, mysterious, *sl.* fishy. **3 a** (slightly) ill, queasy, sick, unwell, off colour, out of sorts, poorly, faint, dizzy, giddy, light-headed, *colloq.* under the weather. **b** see DRUNK *adj.* 1. **5** mad, unbalanced, unhinged, demented, deranged, insane, touched, *colloq.* crazy, dotty, potty, nutty, nuts, batty, cracked, *esp. Brit. colloq.* daft, *sl.* loony. ● *v.* ruin, spoil, bungle, mess up, botch, muff, wreck, make a mess of, *colloq.* make a hash of, make a pig's ear of, *Brit. colloq.* muck up, fluff, *sl.* blow, screw up, louse up, goof up, *Brit. sl.* cock up. □ **in Queer Street** see *in trouble* 1 (TROUBLE).

quell /kwel/ *v.tr.* **1 a** crush or put down (a rebellion etc.). **b** reduce (rebels etc.) to submission. **2** suppress or alleviate (fear, anger, etc.). □□ **queller** *n.* (also in *comb.*). [OE *cwellan* kill f. Gmc]

■ **1** suppress, put down, repress, subdue, quash, overcome, crush, squelch, overwhelm, defeat. **2** restrain, control, hold in check, hold back; moderate, mollify, soothe, assuage, alleviate, mitigate, allay, quiet, calm, *Brit.* quieten; pacify, tranquillize, compose; see also SUPPRESS 2.

quench /kwench/ *v.tr.* **1** satisfy (thirst) by drinking. **2** extinguish (a fire or light etc.). **3** cool, esp. with water (heat, a heated thing). **4** esp. *Metallurgy* cool (a hot substance) in cold water, air, oil, etc. **5 a** stifle or suppress (desire etc.). **b** *Physics* & *Electronics* inhibit or prevent (oscillation, luminescence, etc.) by counteractive means. **6** *sl.* reduce (an opponent) to silence. □□ **quenchable** *adj.* **quencher** *n.* **quenchless** *adj.* [ME f. OE *-cwencan* causative f. *-cwincan* be extinguished]

■ **1** satisfy, slake, sate, satiate, allay, appease, assuage, gratify. **2** put out, extinguish, douse, smother, snuff out. **5 a** stifle, suppress, squelch, quell, repress, overcome, subdue; kill, destroy, get rid of.

quenelle /kənél/ *n.* a seasoned ball or roll of pounded fish or meat. [F, of unkn. orig.]

querist /kwéerist/ *n. literary* a person who asks questions; a questioner. [L *quaerere* ask]

quern /kwern/ *n.* **1** a hand-mill for grinding corn. **2** a small hand-mill for pepper etc. □ **quern-stone** a millstone. [OE *cweorn(e)* f. Gmc]

■ mill, grinder, crusher, roller.

querulous /kwérrooləss/ *adj.* complaining, peevish. □□ **querulously** *adj.* **querulousness** *n.* [LL *querulosus* or L *querulus* f. *queri* complain]

■ complaining, critical, hypercritical, finicky, finical, fussy, over-particular, censorious, *colloq.* pernickety; petulant, peevish, testy, touchy, irritable, irascible, fractious, perverse, quarrelsome, ill-natured, ill-humoured, cantankerous, curmudgeonly, crusty, crotchety, fretful, bad-tempered, ill-tempered, waspish, crabby, cross, splenetic, choleric, grumpy.

query /kwéeri/ *n.* & *v.* ● *n.* (*pl.* **-ies**) **1** a question, esp. expressing doubt or objection. **2** a question mark, or the word *query* spoken or written to question accuracy or as a mark of interrogation. ● *v.* (**-ies, -ied**) **1** *tr.* (often foll. by *whether*, *if*, etc. + clause) ask or inquire. **2** *tr.* call (a thing) in question in speech or writing. **3** *tr.* dispute the accuracy of. **4** *intr.* put a question. [Anglicized form of *quaere* f. L *quaerere* ask, after INQUIRY]

■ *n.* **1** question, inquiry, enquiry; doubt, uncertainty, reservation, problem. ● *v.* **1** ask (about), enquire *or* inquire (about). **3** challenge, doubt, dispute, take issue with, question, contest.

quest /kwest/ *n.* & *v.* ● *n.* **1** a search or the act of seeking. **2** the thing sought, esp. the object of a medieval knight's pursuit. ● *v.* **1** *intr.* (often foll. by *about*) **a** (often foll. by *after*, *for*) go about in search of something. **b** (of a dog etc.) search about for game. **2** *tr. poet.* search for, seek out. □ **in quest of** seeking. □□ **quester** *n.* **questingly** *adv.* [ME f. OF *queste*, *quester* ult. f. L *quaerere quaest-* seek]

■ *n.* **1** search, pursuit, exploration, expedition, voyage (of discovery); chase, hunt. ● *v.* **1 a** (*quest* (*about*) *after* or *for*) seek (after *or* for), search after *or* for, seek out, hunt (for), pursue, look for.

question /kwéss-chən/ *n.* & *v.* ● *n.* **1** a sentence worded or expressed so as to seek information. **2 a** doubt about or objection to a thing's truth, credibility, advisability, etc. (*allowed it without question*). **b** the raising of such doubt etc. **3** a matter to be discussed or decided or voted on. **4** a problem requiring an answer or solution. **5** (foll. by *of*) a matter or concern depending on conditions (*it's a question of money*). ● *v.tr.* **1** ask questions of; interrogate. **2** subject (a person) to examination. **3** throw doubt upon; raise objections to. **4** seek information from the study of (phenomena, facts). □ **be a question of time** be certain to happen sooner or later. **beyond all question** undoubtedly. **call in** (or **into**) **question** make a matter of dispute; query. **come into question** be discussed; become of practical importance. **in question 1** that is being discussed or referred to (*the person in question*). **2** in dispute (*that was never in question*). **is not the question** is irrelevant. **out of the question** too impracticable etc. to be worth discussing; impossible. **put the question** require supporters and opponents of a proposal to record their votes, divide a meeting. **question mark** a punctuation mark (?) indicating a question. **question-master** *Brit.* a person who presides over a quiz game etc. **question time** *Parl.* a period during parliamentary proceedings when MPs may question ministers. **without question** see *beyond all question* above. □□ **questioner** *n.* **questioningly** *adv.* **questionless** *adj.* [ME f. AF *questiun*, OF *question*, *questionner* f. L *quaestio -onis* f. *quaerere quaest-* seek]

■ *n.* **2** query, demur, objection; see also DOUBT *n.* 1. **3, 5** issue, point, concern; see also MATTER *n.* 7. **4** problem, difficulty, doubt, uncertainty, query. ● *v.* **1** ask, interrogate, query, interview, sound out, quiz, pump, grill, give a person the third degree. **3** call in *or* into question, doubt, query, mistrust, distrust, cast doubt upon, dispute, suspect, have one's doubts about. □ **beyond all question** beyond (the shadow of) a doubt, without question, without a doubt, indubitably, undoubtedly, definitely, certainly, assuredly. **call in** *or* **into question** question, doubt, query, challenge, dispute, harbour *or* entertain *or* have doubts *or* suspicions about, suspect, cast doubt *or* suspicion on. **in question 1** under discussion *or* consideration, at issue. **2** questionable, debatable, in dispute, disputable, at issue, in doubt, doubtful, open to debate. **out of the question** unthinkable, impossible, absurd, ridiculous, preposterous, inconceivable, beyond consideration.

questionable /kwéss-chənəb'l/ *adj.* **1** doubtful as regards truth or quality. **2** not clearly in accordance with honesty, honour, wisdom, etc. □□ **questionability** /kwéss-chənəbílliti/ *n.* **questionableness** *n.* **questionably** *adv.*

■ **1** doubtful, dubious, debatable, moot, disputable, borderline, ambiguous, open to question, in dispute, problematic(al), uncertain, arguable, unsure. **2** suspect, shady; see also QUEER *adj.* 2.

questionary /kwéss-chənəri/ *n.* (*pl.* **-ies**) = QUESTIONNAIRE. [med.L *quaestionarium* or F (as QUESTIONNAIRE)]

questionnaire /kwéss-chənáir, késtyə-/ *n.* **1** a formulated series of questions, esp. for statistical study. **2** a document containing these. [F f. *questionner* QUESTION + *-aire* -ARY[1]]

quetzal /kwéts'l/ *n.* **1** any of various brilliantly coloured birds of the family Trogonidae, esp. the Central and S. American *Pharomachrus mocinno*, the male of which has long green tail coverts. **2** the chief monetary unit of Guatemala. [Sp. f. Aztec f. *quetzalli* the bird's tail-feather]

queue /kyōō/ *n.* & *v.* esp. *Brit.* ● *n.* **1** a line or sequence of persons, vehicles, etc., awaiting their turn to be attended to or to proceed. **2** a pigtail or plait of hair. ● *v.intr.* (**queues, queued, queuing** or **queueing**) (often foll. by *up*) (of persons etc.) form a queue; take one's place in a queue. □ **queue-jump** *Brit.* push forward out of turn in a queue. [F f. L *cauda* tail]

■ *n.* **1** line, row, file, column, string, *Brit. colloq.* crocodile; train, cortège, procession, succession, chain; tail, *Brit.* tailback. **2** pigtail, pony-tail, horsetail; braid, plait. ● *v.* line up, get in *or* into line, form a line *or* queue.

quibble /kwíbb'l/ *n.* & *v.* ● *n.* **1** a petty objection; a trivial point of criticism. **2** a play on words; a pun. **3** an evasion; an insubstantial argument which relies on an ambiguity etc. ● *v.intr.* use quibbles. □□ **quibbler** *n.* **quibbling** *adj.* **quibblingly** *adv.* [dimin. of obs. *quib* prob. f. L *quibus* dative & ablat. pl. of *qui* who (familiar from use in legal documents)]

■ *n.* **1** cavil, nicety, quiddity; trifle. **2** see PUN[1] *n.* **3** evasion, sophism, quip, equivocation. ● *v.* **1** equivocate, split hairs, evade the issue, be evasive, palter, chop logic, cavil, pettifog, find fault, *colloq.* nit-pick.

quiche /keesh/ *n.* an open flan or tart with a savoury filling. [F]

Quichua var. of QUECHUA.

quick /kwik/ *adj.*, *adv.*, & *n.* ● *adj.* **1** taking only a short time (*a quick worker*; *a quick visit*). **2 a** arriving after a short time, prompt (*quick action*; *quick results*). **b** (of an action, occurrence, etc.) sudden; hasty; abrupt. **3** with only a short interval (*in quick succession*). **4** lively, intelligent. **5 a** acute, alert (*has a quick ear*). **b** agile, nimble; energetic. **6** (of a temper) easily roused. **7** *archaic* living, alive (*the quick and the dead*). ● *adv.* **1** quickly, at a rapid rate. **2** (as *int.*) come, go, etc., quickly. ● *n.* **1** the soft flesh below the nails, or the skin, or a sore. **2** the seat of feeling or emotion (*cut to the quick*). □ **be quick** act quickly. **quick-fire 1** (of repartee etc.) rapid. **2** firing shots in quick succession. **quick-freeze 1** freeze (food) rapidly so as to preserve its natural qualities. **2** this process. **quick march** *Mil.* **1** a march in quick time. **2** the command to begin this. **quick one** *colloq.* a drink taken quickly. **quick-tempered** quick to lose one's temper; irascible. **quick step** *Mil.* a step used in quick time (cf. QUICKSTEP). **quick time** *Mil.* marching at about 120 paces per minute. **quick trick** *Bridge* **1** a trick in the first two rounds of a suit. **2** the card that should win this. **quick with child** *archaic* at a stage of pregnancy when movements of the foetus have been felt. □□ **quickly** *adv.* **quickness** *n.* [OE *cwic(u)* alive f. Gmc]

■ *adj.* **1** rapid, fast, speedy, swift, *poet. or literary* fleet; expeditious, express, high-speed. **2 a** immediate, timely, instantaneous; see also PROMPT *adj.* 1b. **b** sudden, precipitate, hasty, brisk, short, abrupt, hurried, perfunctory, summary, brief. **4** lively, vivacious, animated; intelligent, bright, adept, adroit, dexterous, apt, able, astute, clever, shrewd, smart, ingenious, perceptive, perspicacious, discerning, far-sighted, responsive, nimble-witted, quick-witted. **5** alert, keen, sharp, acute; agile, nimble, energetic, spry, light. **6** short, excitable, touchy, testy, impatient. **7** see ALIVE 1. ● *adv.* **1** see *quickly* below. ● *n.* **2** see CORE *n.* 2a.
□ **quick-tempered** excitable, impulsive, temperamental, hot-tempered, waspish, choleric, splenetic, impatient, short-tempered, touchy, irascible, irritable, snappish, abrupt, short, quarrelsome, testy, volatile, hot-blooded, bad-tempered, ill-tempered, churlish, highly-strung, high strung. □□ **quickly** quick, rapidly, swiftly, speedily, fast, in a trice *or* wink *or* twinkle, in the twinkling of an eye, in a flash, in two shakes (of a lamb's *or* dog's tail); post-haste, *tout de suite*, at *or* on the double, with all speed, quick, *archaic or joc.* instanter, *colloq.* lickety-split, p.d.q., like a shot, *literary* apace; instantly, promptly, hastily, at once, instantaneously, unhesitatingly, spontaneously, immediately, straight away, right away, (right) now, here and now, then and there, there and then, on the spot, this (very) minute *or* second *or* instant, directly, forthwith, shortly, without delay *or* hesitation, without more ado, (very) soon, hurriedly, *US* momentarily, *colloq.* pronto, in a jiffy.

quicken /kwíkkən/ *v.* **1** *tr.* & *intr.* make or become quicker; accelerate. **2** *tr.* give life or vigour to; rouse; animate; stimulate. **3** *intr.* **a** (of a woman) reach a stage in pregnancy when movements of the foetus can be felt. **b** (of a foetus) begin to show signs of life. **4** *tr. archaic* kindle; make (a fire) burn brighter. **5** *intr.* come to life.

■ **1** accelerate, hasten, speed up, expedite, hurry, rush. **2** stimulate, arouse, kindle, spark, invigorate, excite, animate, vitalize, vivify, galvanize, enliven, awaken, energize, rouse. **4** see KINDLE 1.

quickie /kwíkki/ *n. colloq.* **1** a thing done or made quickly or hastily. **2** a drink taken quickly.

quicklime /kwíklīm/ *n.* = LIME[1] *n.* 1.

quicksand /kwíksand/ *n.* **1** loose wet sand that sucks in anything placed or falling into it. **2** a bed of this.

quickset /kwíkset/ *adj.* & *n.* ● *adj.* (of a hedge) formed of slips of plants, esp. hawthorn set in the ground to grow. ● *n.* **1** such slips. **2** a hedge formed in this way.

quicksilver /kwíksilvər/ *n.* & *v.* ● *n.* **1** mercury. **2** mobility of temperament or mood. ● *v.tr.* coat (a mirror-glass) with an amalgam of tin.

quickstep /kwíkstep/ *n.* & *v.* ● *n.* a fast foxtrot (cf. *quick step*). ● *v.intr.* (**-stepped, -stepping**) dance the quickstep.

quickthorn /kwíkthorn/ *n.* a common hawthorn, *Crataegus monogyna*.

quick-witted /kwíkwíttid/ *adj.* quick to grasp a situation, make repartee, etc. □□ **quick-wittedness** *n.*

■ quick, acute, sharp, clever, smart, nimble-witted, alert, keen, astute, perceptive, perspicacious, bright, intelligent.

quid[1] /kwid/ *n.* (*pl.* same) *Brit. sl.* one pound sterling. □ **not the full quid** *Austral. sl.* mentally deficient. **quids in** *sl.* in a position of profit. [prob. f. *quid* the nature of a thing f. L *quid* what, something]

quid[2] /kwid/ *n.* a lump of tobacco for chewing. [dial. var. of CUD]

■ plug, chew, twist, pigtail.

quiddity /kwídditi/ *n.* (*pl.* **-ies**) **1** *Philos.* the essence of a person or thing; what makes a thing what it is. **2** a quibble; a trivial objection. [med.L *quidditas* f. L *quid* what]

quidnunc /kwídnungk/ *n. archaic* a newsmonger, a person given to gossip. [L *quid* what + *nunc* now]

■ see GOSSIP *n.* 3.

quid pro quo /kwíd prō kwṓ/ *n.* **1** a thing given as compensation. **2** return made (for a gift, favour, etc.). [L, = something for something]

■ return, recompense, compensation, payment, requital, (just) deserts, *poet.* guerdon.

quiescent /kwi-éss'nt/ *adj.* **1** motionless, inert. **2** silent, dormant. □□ **quiescence** *n.* **quiescency** *n.* **quiescently** *adv.* [L *quiescere* f. *quies* QUIET]

■ **1** see INERT 1. **2** see QUIET *adj.* 1.

quiet /kwī́ət/ *adj.*, *n.*, & *v.* ● *adj.* (**quieter, quietest**) **1** with little or no sound or motion. **2 a** of gentle or peaceful disposition. **b** shy; reticent; reserved. **3** (of a colour, piece of clothing, etc.) unobtrusive; not showy. **4** not overt; private; disguised (*quiet resentment*). **5** undisturbed; uninterrupted; free or far from vigorous action (*a quiet time for* *prayer*). **6** informal; simple (*just a quiet wedding*). **7** enjoyed in quiet (*a quiet smoke*). **8** tranquil; not anxious or remorseful. ● *n.* **1** silence; stillness. **2** an undisturbed state; tranquillity. **3** a state of being free from urgent tasks or agitation (*a period of quiet*). **4** a peaceful state of affairs (*could do with some quiet*). ● *v.* **1** *tr.* soothe, make quiet. **2** *intr.* (often foll. by *down*) become quiet or calm. □ **be quiet** (esp. in *imper.*) cease talking etc. **keep quiet 1** refrain from making a noise. **2** (often foll. by *about*) suppress or refrain from disclosing information etc. **on the quiet** unobtrusively; secretly. □□ **quietly** *adv.* **quietness** *n.* [ME f. AF *quiete* f. OF *quiet(e)*, *quieté* f. L *quietus* past part. of *quiescere*: see QUIESCENT]

■ *adj.* **1** silent, soundless, noiseless, hushed, quiescent; still, smooth, motionless, unmoving, at rest; inactive. **2 a** see GENTLE *adj.* 1. **b** see SHY[1] *adj.* 1. **3** see UNOBTRUSIVE. **4** see PRIVATE *adj.* 2. **5** see PEACEFUL 1. **6** see MODEST 5. **8** serene, peaceful, unperturbed, calm, tranquil, placid, pacific, restful, unagitated, temperate, unexcited. ● *n.* **1** silence, stillness, still, soundlessness, noiselessness, hush, quietness, quietude. **2** calmness, serenity, tranquillity, peace; see also CALM *n.* 1. **3, 4** ease, rest, repose; see also PEACE 1. ● *v.* see CALM *v.* □ **be quiet** see HUSH *int.*, *wrap up* 3. **keep quiet 2** see HIDE[1] *v.* 3. **on the quiet** see *secretly* (SECRET). □□ **quietly** silently, soundlessly, noiselessly, inaudibly, softly, in hushed tones, in whispers; peacefully, calmly, serenely, peaceably, meekly, mildly; unobtrusively; privately, secretly, in private.

quieten /kwī́ət'n/ *v.tr.* & *intr. Brit.* (often foll. by *down*) make or become quiet.

■ (*quieten down*) quiet (down), hush, calm (down), lull, soothe, still, silence.

quietism /kwī́ətiz'm/ *n.* **1** a passive attitude towards life, with devotional contemplation and abandonment of the will, as a form of religious mysticism. **2** the principle of non-resistance. □□ **quietist** *n.* & *adj.* **quietistic** /-tístik/ *adj.* [It. *quietismo* (as QUIET)]

quietude /kwī́-ityood/ *n.* a state of quiet.

■ see QUIET *n.* 1.

quietus /kwī-éetəss/ *n.* **1** something which quiets or represses. **2** discharge or release from life; death, final riddance. [med.L *quietus est* he is quit (QUIET) used as a form of receipt]

quiff /kwif/ *n. Brit.* **1** a man's tuft of hair, brushed upward over the forehead. **2** a curl plastered down on the forehead. [20th c.: orig. unkn.]

quill /kwil/ *n.* & *v.* ● *n.* **1** (in full **quill-feather**) a large feather in a wing or tail. **2** the hollow stem of this. **3** (in full **quill pen**) a pen made of a quill. **4** (usu. in *pl.*) the spines of a porcupine. **5** a musical pipe made of a hollow stem. ● *v.tr.* form into cylindrical quill-like folds; goffer. □ **quill-coverts** the feathers covering the base of quill-feathers. [ME prob. f. (M)LG *quiele*]

quilling / kwílling/ *n.* the art or craft of paper filigree. [QUILL]

quilt[1] /kwilt/ *n.* & *v.* ● *n.* **1** a bed-covering made of padding enclosed between layers of cloth etc. and kept in place by cross lines of stitching. **2** a bedspread of similar design (*patchwork quilt*). ● *v.tr.* **1** cover or line with padded material. **2** make or join together (pieces of cloth with padding between) after the manner of a quilt. **3** sew up (a coin, letter, etc.) between two layers of a garment etc. **4** compile (a literary work) out of extracts or borrowed ideas. □□ **quilter** *n.* **quilting** *n.* [ME f. OF *coilte*, *cuilte* f. L *culcita* mattress, cushion]

■ *n.* **1** duvet, *Brit.* continental quilt. **2** bedspread, eiderdown, counterpane, coverlet, bed-cover, cover, *US* comforter, throw.

quilt[2] /kwilt/ *v.tr. Austral. sl.* thrash; clout. [perh. f. QUILT[1]]

■ see BEAT *v.* 1.

quim /kwim/ *n. coarse sl.* the female genitals. [18th c.: orig. unkn.]

quin /kwin/ *n.* esp. *Brit. colloq.* a quintuplet. [abbr.]

quinacrine /kwínnəkreen, -krin/ *n.* an anti-malarial drug derived from acridine. [*quin*ine + *acridine*]

quinary /kwī́nəri/ *adj.* **1** of the number five. **2** having five parts. [L *quinarius* f. *quini* distrib. of *quinque* five]

quinate /kwī́nayt/ *adj. Bot.* (of a leaf) having five leaflets. [L *quini* (as QUINARY)]

quince /kwinss/ *n.* **1** a hard acid pear-shaped fruit used as a preserve or flavouring. **2** any shrub or small tree of the genus *Cydonia*, esp. *C. oblonga*, bearing this fruit. [ME, orig. collect. pl. of obs. *quoyn*, *coyn*, f. OF *cooin* f. L *cotoneum* var. of *cydoneum* (apple) of *Cydonia* in Crete]

quincentenary /kwínsentéenəri/ *n.* & *adj.* ● *n.* (*pl.* **-ies**) **1** a five-hundredth anniversary. **2** a festival marking this. ● *adj.* of this anniversary. □□ **quincentennial** /-ténniəl/ *adj.* & *n.* [irreg. f. L *quinque* five + CENTENARY]

quincunx /kwínkungks/ *n.* **1** five objects set so that four are at the corners of a square or rectangle and the fifth is at its centre, e.g. the five on dice or cards. **2** this arrangement, esp. in planting trees. □□ **quincuncial** /kwinkúnsh'l/ *adj.* **quincuncially** /-kúnshəli/ *adv.* [L, = five-twelfths f. *quinque* five, *uncia* twelfth]

quinella /kwinéllə/ *n.* a form of betting in which the better must select the first two place-winners in a race, not necessarily in the correct order. [Amer. Sp. *quiniela*]

quinine /kwínneen, kwinéen/ *n.* **1** an alkaloid found esp. in cinchona bark. **2** a bitter drug containing this, used as a tonic and to reduce fever. [*quina* cinchona bark f. Sp. *quina* f. Quechua *kina* bark]

quinol /kwínnol/ *n.* = HYDROQUINONE.

quinoline /kwínnəleen/ *n. Chem.* an oily amine obtained from the distillation of coal tar or by synthesis and used in the preparation of drugs etc.

quinone /kwínnōn, kwinṓn/ *n. Chem.* **1** a yellow crystalline derivative of benzene with the hydrogen atoms on opposite carbon atoms replaced by two of oxygen. **2** any in a class of similar compounds.

quinquagenarian /kwíngkwəjináiriən/ *n.* & *adj.* ● *n.* a person from 50 to 59 years old. ● *adj.* of or relating to this age. [L *quinquagenarius* f. *quinquageni* distrib. of *quinquaginta* fifty]

Quinquagesima /kwíngkwəjéssimə/ *n.* (in full **Quinquagesima Sunday**) the Sunday before the beginning of Lent. [med.L, fem. of L *quinquagesimus* fiftieth f. *quinquaginta* fifty, after QUADRAGESIMA]

quinque- /kwíngkwi/ *comb. form* five. [L f. *quinque* five]

quinquennial /kwinkwénniəl/ *adj.* **1** lasting five years. **2** recurring every five years. □□ **quinquennially** *adv.* [L *quinquennis* (as QUINQUENNIUM)]

quinquennium /kwinkwénniəm/ *n.* (*pl.* **quinquenniums** or **quinquennia** /-niə/) a period of five years. [L f. *quinque* five + *annus* year]

quinquereme /kwíngkwireem/ *n.* an ancient Roman galley with five files of oarsmen on each side. [L *quinqueremis* (as QUINQUE-, *remus* oar)]

quinquevalent /kwíngkwəváylənt/ *adj.* having a valency of five.

quinsy /kwínzi/ *n.* an inflammation of the throat, esp. an abscess in the region around the tonsils. □□ **quinsied** *adj.* [ME f. OF *quinencie* f. med.L *quinancia* f. Gk *kunagkhē* f. *kun-* dog + *agkhō* throttle]

quint /kwint/ *n.* **1** a sequence of five cards in the same suit in piquet etc. **2** *US* a quintuplet. □ **quint major** a quint headed by an ace. [F *quinte* f. L *quinta* fem. of *quintus* fifth f. *quinque* five]

quintain /kwíntin/ *n. hist.* **1** a post set up as a mark in tilting, and often provided with a sandbag to swing round and strike an unsuccessful tilter. **2** the medieval military exercise of tilting at such a mark. [ME f. OF *quintaine* perh. ult. f. L *quintana* camp market f. *quintus* (*manipulus*) fifth (maniple)]

quintal /kwínt'l/ *n.* **1** a weight of about 100 lb. **2** a hundredweight (112 lb.). **3** a weight of 100 kg. [ME f. OF *quintal*, med.L *quintale* f. Arab. *ḳinṭār*]

quintan /kwíntən/ *adj.* (of a fever etc.) recurring every fifth day. [L *quintana* f. *quintus* fifth]

quinte /kaNt/ *n.* the fifth of eight parrying positions in fencing. [F: see QUINT]

quintessence /kwintéss'nss/ *n.* **1** the most essential part of any substance; a refined extract. **2** (usu. foll. by *of*) the purest and most perfect, or most typical, form, manifestation, or embodiment of some quality or class. **3** (in Ancient Philosophy) a fifth substance (beside the four elements) forming heavenly bodies and pervading all things. □□ **quintessential** /kwíntisénsh'l/ *adj.* **quintessentially** /kwíntisénshəli/ *adv.* [ME (in sense 3) f. F f. med.L *quinta essentia* fifth ESSENCE]

■ **1** essence, heart, core, quiddity, pith, marrow, nub, *Philos.* haecceity. **2** epitome, embodiment, incarnation, personification, model, prototype, exemplar, ideal, *beau idéal*, paragon, pinnacle.

quintet /kwintét/ *n.* (also **quintette**) **1** *Mus.* **a** a composition for five voices or instruments. **b** the performers of such a piece. **2** any group of five. [F *quintette* f. It. *quintetto* f. *quinto* fifth f. L *quintus*]

quintillion /kwintílyən/ *n.* (*pl.* same or **quintillions**) a thousand raised to the sixth (or formerly, esp. *Brit.*, the tenth) power (10^{18} and 10^{30} respectively). □□ **quintillionth** *adj.* & *n.* [L *quintus* fifth + MILLION]

quintuple /kwíntyoop'l/ *adj.*, *n.*, & *v.* ● *adj.* **1** fivefold; consisting of five parts. **2** involving five parties. **3** (of time in music) having five beats in a bar. ● *n.* a fivefold number or amount. ● *v.tr.* & *intr.* multiply by five; increase fivefold. □□ **quintuply** *adv.* [F *quintuple* f. L *quintus* fifth, after QUADRUPLE]

quintuplet /kwíntyooplit, -tyoo͝plit/ *n.* **1** each of five children born at one birth. **2** a set of five things working together. **3** *Mus.* a group of five notes to be performed in the time of three or four. [QUINTUPLE, after QUADRUPLET, TRIPLET]

quintuplicate *adj.* & *v.* ● *adj.* /kwintyoo͝plikət/ **1** fivefold. **2** of which five copies are made. ● *v.tr.* & *intr.* /kwintyoo͝plikayt/ multiply by five. □ **in quintuplicate 1** in five identical copies. **2** in groups of five. [F *quintuple* f. L *quintus* fifth, after QUADRUPLICATE]

quip /kwip/ *n.* & *v.* ● *n.* **1** a clever saying; an epigram; a sarcastic remark etc. **2** a quibble; an equivocation. ● *v.intr.* (**quipped**, **quipping**) make quips. □□ **quipster** *n.* [abbr. of obs. *quippy* perh. f. L *quippe* forsooth]

■ *n.* **1** *bon mot*, witticism, sally, aphorism, epigram, apophthegm; jest, joke, gag, *colloq.* one-liner, crack, wisecrack, wheeze, chestnut. **2** quibble, equivocation, evasion, sophism. ● *v.* see JOKE *v.* 1.

quipu /kéepoo͞, kwée-/ *n.* the ancient Peruvians' substitute for writing by variously knotting threads of various colours. [Quechua, = knot]

quire /kwīr/ *n.* **1** four sheets of paper etc. folded to form eight leaves, as often in medieval manuscripts. **2** any collection of leaves one within another in a manuscript or book. **3** 25 (also 24) sheets of paper. □ **in quires** unbound; in sheets. [ME f. OF *qua(i)er* ult. f. L *quaterni* set of four (as QUATERNARY)]

quirk /kwurk/ *n.* **1** a peculiarity of behaviour. **2** a trick of fate; a freak. **3** a flourish in writing. **4** (often *attrib.*) *Archit.* a hollow in a moulding. □□ **quirkish** *adj.* **quirky** *adj.* (**quirkier**, **quirkiest**). **quirkily** *adv.* **quirkiness** *n.* [16th c.: orig. unkn.]

■ **1** peculiarity, caprice, vagary, whim, idiosyncrasy, oddity, eccentricity, fancy, aberration, kink, characteristic. **2** trick, twist; oddity, kink, aberration; fluke, accident.

quirt /kwurt/ *n.* & *v.* ● *n.* a short-handled riding-whip with a braided leather lash. ● *v.tr.* strike with this. [Sp. *cuerda* CORD]

quisling /kwízling/ *n.* **1** a person cooperating with an occupying enemy; a collaborator or fifth-columnist. **2** a traitor. □□ **quislingite** *adj.* & *n.* [V. *Quisling*, renegade Norwegian Army officer d. 1945]

■ see TRAITOR.

quit /kwit/ *v.* & *adj.* ● *v.tr.* (**quitting**; *past* and *past part.* **quitted** or **quit**) **1** (also *absol.*) give up; let go; abandon (a task etc.). **2** *US* cease; stop (*quit grumbling*). **3 a** leave or depart from (a place, person, etc.). **b** (*absol.*) (of a tenant) leave occupied premises (esp. *notice to quit*). **4** (*refl.*) acquit; behave (*quit oneself well*). ● *predic.adj.* (foll. by *of*) rid (*glad to be quit of the problem*). □ **quit hold of** loose. [ME f. OF *quitte, quitter* f. med.L *quittus* f. L *quietus* QUIET]

■ *v.* **1** let go, resign, give up, relinquish, leave, renounce, retire from, withdraw from, abandon, forsake. **2** cease, stop, discontinue, leave off, *literary* desist from. **3 a** depart from, go (away) from, get away from, flee; see also LEAVE[1] *v.* 1b, 3, 4. **b** leave, move, move out, *colloq.* up sticks. **4** see BEHAVE 1a. ● *predic.adj.* free, clear, discharged, rid, released, exempt; (*be* or *get quit of*) wash one's hands of, get rid of, be done with, get a thing off one's hands, *sl.* be *or* get shot of. □ **quit hold of** see LOOSE *v.* 1.

quitch /kwich/ *n.* (in full **quitch-grass**) = COUCH[2]. [OE *cwice*, perh. rel. to QUICK]

quite /kwīt/ *adv.* **1** completely; entirely; wholly; to the utmost extent; in the fullest sense. **2** somewhat; rather; to some extent. **3** (often foll. by *so*) said to indicate agreement. **4** absolutely; definitely; very much. □ **quite another** (or **other**) very different (*that's quite another matter*). **quite a few** *colloq.* a fairly large number of. **quite something** a remarkable thing. [ME f. obs. *quite* (adj.) = QUIT]

■ **1** completely, very, totally, utterly, entirely, fully, wholly, absolutely, perfectly, altogether, thoroughly. **2** rather, fairly, moderately, somewhat, relatively, to some *or* a certain extent, to some *or* a certain degree. **3** (*quite so*) see ABSOLUTELY 6. **4** very much, totally, entirely, wholly, altogether; really, actually, truly, definitely, positively, undoubtedly, indubitably, absolutely, unequivocally, certainly, unreservedly, honestly. □ **quite another** (*quite another matter*) a (completely) different kettle of fish, something else (altogether), *esp. US colloq.* a whole new ball game. **quite a few** quite a lot, a fair number *or* few, a good number *or* few.

quits /kwits/ *predic.adj.* on even terms by retaliation or repayment (*then we'll be quits*). □ **call it** (or **cry**) **quits** acknowledge that things are now even; agree not to proceed further in a quarrel etc. [perh. colloq. abbr. of med.L *quittus*: see QUIT]

■ (*be quits*) be even *or* square *or* equal with.

quittance /kwítt'nss/ *n.* *archaic* or *poet.* **1** (foll. by *from*) a release. **2** an acknowledgement of payment; a receipt. [ME f. OF *quitance* f. *quiter* QUIT]

quitter /kwíttər/ *n.* **1** a person who gives up easily. **2** a shirker.

quiver[1] /kwívvər/ *v.* & *n.* ● *v.* **1** *intr.* tremble or vibrate with a slight rapid motion, esp.: **a** (usu. foll. by *with*) as the result of emotion (*quiver with anger*). **b** (usu. foll. by *in*) as the result of air currents etc. (*quiver in the breeze*). **2** *tr.* (of a bird, esp. a skylark) make (its wings) quiver. ● *n.* a quivering motion or sound. □□ **quiveringly** *adv.* **quivery** *adj.* [ME f. obs. *quiver* nimble: cf. QUAVER]

■ *v.* **1** shake, tremble, vibrate, shiver, quaver; shudder, tremor, oscillate. ● *n.* tremble, quaver, shudder, spasm, shake, tremor, shiver.

quiver[2] /kwívvər/ *n.* a case for holding arrows. □ **have an arrow** (or **shaft**) **left in one's quiver** not be resourceless. [ME f. OF *quivre* f. WG (cf. OE *cocor*)]

quiverful /kwívvərfoo͝l/ *n.* (*pl.* **-fuls**) **1** as much as a quiver can hold. **2** many children of one parent (Ps. 127:5). [QUIVER[2]]

qui vive /kee véev/ *n.* □ **on the qui vive** on the alert; watching for something to happen. [F, = lit. '(long) live who?', i.e. on whose side are you?, as a sentry's challenge]

■ □ **on the qui vive** see *on the alert* (ALERT).

quixotic /kwiksóttik/ *adj.* **1** extravagantly and romantically chivalrous; regardless of material interests in comparison with honour or devotion. **2** visionary; pursuing lofty but unattainable ideals. **3** *derog.* ridiculously impractical; preposterous; foolhardy. □□ **quixotically** *adv.* **quixotism** /kwíksətiz'm/ *n.* **quixotry** /kwíksətri/ *n.* [Don *Quixote*, hero of Cervantes' romance f. Sp. *quixote* thigh armour]

■ **1** romantic, chivalrous, gallant; sentimental. **2** idealistic, visionary, utopian, impractical, unpractical, unrealistic, romantic, heady, fantastic(al), starry-eyed. **3** absurd, mad, foolhardy, reckless, wild, preposterous, ridiculous; impracticable, unrealizable, impractical; chimerical, fanciful, dreamlike.

quiz[1] /kwiz/ *n.* & *v.* ● *n.* (*pl.* **quizzes**) **1** a test of knowledge, esp. between individuals or teams as a form of entertainment. **2** an interrogation, examination, or questionnaire. ● *v.tr.* (**quizzed**, **quizzing**) examine by questioning. □ **quiz-master** a person who presides over a quiz. [19th-c. dial.: orig. unkn.]

■ *n.* **2** examination, test, exam; interrogation, questioning; questionnaire, questionary. ● *v.* question, interrogate, ask, examine, interview, ask the opinion of, grill, pump.

quiz[2] /kwiz/ *v.* & *n.* *archaic* ● *v.tr.* (**quizzed**, **quizzing**) **1** look curiously at; observe the ways or oddities of; survey through an eyeglass. **2** make sport of; regard with a mocking air. ● *n.* (*pl.* **quizzes**) **1** a hoax, a thing done to burlesque or expose another's oddities. **2 a** an odd or eccentric person; a person of ridiculous appearance. **b** a person given to quizzing. □□ **quizzer** *n.* [18th c.: orig. unkn.]

quizzical /kwízzik'l/ *adj.* **1** expressing or done with mild or amused perplexity. **2** strange; comical. □□ **quizzicality** /-kálliti/ *n.* **quizzically** *adv.* **quizzicalness** *n.*

■ **1** perplexed, bemused, puzzled, enquiring, questioning. **2** curious, queer, comical, strange; see ODD *adj.* 1.

quod /kwod/ *n.* *Brit. sl.* prison. [17th c.: orig. unkn.]

■ see PRISON *n.* 1.

quod erat demonstrandum /kwod érrat démmənstrándōōm/ (esp. at the conclusion of a proof etc.) which was the thing to be proved. ¶ Abbr.: **QED**. [L]

quodlibet /kwódlibet/ *n.* **1** *hist.* **a** a topic for philosophical or theological discussion. **b** an exercise on this. **2** a light-hearted medley of well-known tunes. □□ **quodlibetarian** /-bitáiriən/ *n.* **quodlibetical** /-béttik'l/ *adj.* **quodlibetically** /-béttikəli/ *adv.* [ME f. L f. *quod* what + *libet* it pleases one]

quod vide /kwod veéday/ which see (in cross-references etc.). ¶ Abbr.: **q.v.** [L]

quoin /koyn/ *n.* & *v.* ● *n.* **1** an external angle of a building. **2** a stone or brick forming an angle; a cornerstone. **3** a wedge used for locking type in a forme. **4** a wedge for raising the level of a gun, keeping the barrel from rolling, etc. ● *v.tr.* secure or raise with quoins. □□ **quoining** *n.* [var. of COIN]

quoit /koyt/ *n.* & *v.* ● *n.* **1** a heavy flattish sharp-edged iron ring thrown to encircle an iron peg or to land as near as possible to the peg. **2** (in *pl.*) a game consisting of aiming and throwing these. **3** a ring of rope, rubber, etc. for use in a similar game. **4 a** the flat stone of a dolmen. **b** the dolmen itself. ● *v.tr.* fling like a quoit. [ME: orig. unkn.]

■ *n.* **1, 3** ring, hoop.

quokka /kwókkə/ *n.* a small Australian short-tailed wallaby, *Setonix brachyurus*. [Aboriginal name]

quondam /kwóndam/ *predic.adj.* that once was; sometime; former. [L (adv.), = formerly]

■ see FORMER[1] 1.

Quonset /kwónsit/ *n.* *US propr.* a prefabricated metal building with a semicylindrical corrugated roof. [*Quonset* Point, Rhode Island, where it was first made]

quorate /kwórət, -rayt/ *adj.* *Brit.* (of a meeting) attended by a quorum. [QUORUM]

quorum /kwórəm/ *n.* the fixed minimum number of members that must be present to make the proceedings of an assembly or society valid. [L, = of whom (we wish that you be two, three, etc.), in the wording of commissions]

quota /kwṓtə/ *n.* **1** the share that an individual person or company is bound to contribute to or entitled to receive from a total. **2** a quantity of goods etc. which under official controls must be manufactured, exported, imported, etc. **3** the number of yearly immigrants allowed to enter a country, students allowed to enrol for a course, etc. [med.L *quota* (*pars*) how great (a part), fem. of *quotus* f. *quot* how many]

■ **1** apportionment, portion, allotment, allocation, allowance, ration, share, part, proportion, percentage, *colloq.* cut.

quotable /kwṓtəb'l/ *adj.* worth, or suitable for, quoting. □□ **quotability** /-bílliti/ *n.*

quotation /kwōtáysh'n/ *n.* **1** the act or an instance of quoting or being quoted. **2** a passage or remark quoted. **3** *Mus.* a short passage or tune taken from one piece of music to another. **4** *Stock Exch.* an amount stated as the current price of stocks or commodities. **5** a contractor's estimate. □ **quotation mark** each of a set of punctuation marks, single (' ') or double (" "), used to mark the beginning and end of a quoted passage, a book title, etc., or words regarded as slang or jargon. [med.L *quotatio* (as QUOTE)]

■ **2** passage, citation, reference, extract, excerpt, sound bite, *colloq.* quote. **4** (market) price, charge, rate, cost, *colloq.* quote; value. □ **quotation mark** inverted comma; (*quotation marks*) *colloq.* quotes.

quote /kwōt/ *v.* & *n.* ● *v.tr.* **1** cite or appeal to (an author, book, etc.) in confirmation of some view. **2** repeat a statement by (another person) or copy out a passage from (*don't quote me*). **3** (often *absol.*) **a** repeat or copy out (a passage) usu. with an indication that it is borrowed. **b** (foll. by *from*) cite (an author, book, etc.). **4** (foll. by *as*) cite (an author etc.) as proof, evidence, etc. **5 a** enclose (words) in quotation marks. **b** (as *int.*) (in dictation, reading aloud, etc.) indicate the presence of opening quotation marks (*he said, quote, 'I shall stay'*). **6** (often foll. by *at*) state the price of (a commodity, bet, etc.) (*quoted at 200 to 1*). **7** *Stock Exch.* regularly list the price of. ● *n.* *colloq.* **1** a passage quoted. **2** a price quoted. **3** (usu. in *pl.*) quotation marks. [ME, earlier 'mark with numbers', f. med.L *quotare* f. *quot* how many, or as QUOTA]

■ *v.* **1** cite; appeal to, refer to. **3** cite, recite, repeat; extract, excerpt. **4** instance, name, identify, denominate, pinpoint. ● *n.* **1** see QUOTATION *n.* 2. **2** see QUOTATION *n.* 4. **3** (*quotes*) see *quotation mark*.

quoth /kwōth/ *v.tr.* (only in 1st and 3rd person) *archaic* said. [OE *cwæth* past of *cwethan* say f. Gmc]

quotidian /kwotíddiən/ *adj.* & *n.* ● *adj.* **1** daily, of every day. **2** commonplace, trivial. ● *n.* (in full **quotidian fever**) a fever recurring every day. [ME f. OF *cotidien* & L *cotidianus* f. *cotidie* daily]

■ *adj.* **1** diurnal, daily, everyday, *Physiol.* circadian.

quotient /kwṓsh'nt/ *n.* a result obtained by dividing one quantity by another. [ME f. L *quotiens* how many times f. *quot* how many, by confusion with -ENT]

Qur'an var. of KORAN.

q.v. *abbr.* *quod vide*.

qwerty /kwérti/ *attrib.adj.* denoting the standard keyboard on English-language typewriters, word processors, etc., with *q*, *w*, *e*, *r*, *t*, and *y* as the first keys on the top row of letters.

qy. *abbr.* query.

Rr

R[1] /aar/ *n.* (also **r**) (*pl.* **Rs** or **R's**) the eighteenth letter of the alphabet. □ **the r months** the months with r in their names (September to April) as the season for oysters.

R[2] *abbr.* (also **R.**) **1** *Regina* (*Elizabeth R*). **2** *Rex*. **3** River. **4** (also ®) registered as a trademark. **5** (in names of societies etc.) Royal. **6** *Chess* rook. **7** Railway. **8** rand. **9** Regiment. **10** Réaumur. **11** radius. **12** roentgen.

r. *abbr.* (also **r**) **1** right. **2** recto. **3** run(s). **4** radius.

RA *abbr.* **1 a** (in the UK) Royal Academy. **b** (in the UK) Royal Academician. **2** (in the UK) Royal Artillery. **3** right ascension.

Ra *symb. Chem.* the element radium.

RAAF *abbr.* Royal Australian Air Force.

rabbet /rábbit/ *n.* & *v.* ● *n.* a step-shaped channel etc. cut along the edge or face or projecting angle of a length of wood etc., usu. to receive the edge or tongue of another piece. ● *v.tr.* (**rabbeted, rabbeting**) **1** join or fix with a rabbet. **2** make a rabbet in. □ **rabbet plane** a plane for cutting a groove along an edge. [ME f. OF *rab(b)at* abatement, recess f. *rabattre* REBATE]

rabbi /rábbī/ *n.* (*pl.* **rabbis**) **1** a Jewish scholar or teacher, esp. of the law. **2** a person appointed as a Jewish religious leader. □ **Chief Rabbi** the religious head of the Jewish communities in Britain. □□ **rabbinate** /rábbinət/ *n.* [ME & OE f. eccl.L f. Gk *rhabbi* f. Heb. *rabbî* my master f. *rab̲* master + pronominal suffix]

rabbinical /rəbínnik'l/ *adj.* of or relating to rabbis, or to Jewish law or teaching. □□ **rabbinically** *adv.*

rabbit /rábbit/ *n.* & *v.* ● *n.* **1 a** any of various burrowing gregarious plant-eating mammals of the hare family, esp. *Oryctolagus cuniculus*, with long ears and a short tail, varying in colour from brown in the wild to black and white, and kept as a pet or for meat. **b** *US* a hare. **c** the fur of the rabbit. **2** *Brit. colloq.* a poor performer in any sport or game. ● *v.intr.* (**rabbited, rabbiting**) **1** hunt rabbits. **2** (often foll. by *on, away*) *Brit. colloq.* talk excessively or pointlessly; chatter (*rabbiting on about his holiday*). □ **rabbit punch** a short chop with the edge of the hand to the nape of the neck. **rabbit's foot** the foot of a rabbit, carried to bring luck. **rabbit warren** an area in which rabbits have their burrows, or are kept for meat etc. □□ **rabbity** *adj.* [ME perh. f. OF: cf. F dial. *rabotte*, Walloon *robète*, Flem. *robbe*]
■ *v.* **2** see CHATTER *v.* 1.

rabble[1] /rább'l/ *n.* **1** a disorderly crowd; a mob. **2** a contemptible or inferior set of people. **3** (prec. by *the*) the lower or disorderly classes of the populace. □ **rabble-rouser** a person who stirs up the rabble or a crowd of people in agitation for social or political change. **rabble-rousing** *adj.* tending to arouse the emotions of a crowd. ● *n.* the act or process of doing this. [ME: orig. uncert.]
■ **1** mob, crowd, horde, throng, swarm, gang. **2** vermin, trash, dregs (of society), *colloq.* scum. **3** (*the rabble*) populace, people (at large), masses, proletariat, *hoi polloi*, commoners, peasantry, commonalty, rank and file, lower classes, working class, *colloq.* great unwashed, *colloq. derog.* proles, *usu. derog.* ragtag and bobtail, riff-raff, *canaille*, plebs, mob. □ **rabble-rouser** agitator, demagogue, inciter, firebrand, incendiary, troublemaker, *agent provocateur*, revolutionary, insurrectionist, hell-raiser.

rabble[2] /rább'l/ *n.* an iron bar with a bent end for stirring molten metal etc. [F *râble* f. med.L *rotabulum*, L *rutabulum* fire-shovel f. *ruere rut-* rake up]

Rabelaisian /rábbəláyziən/ *adj.* & *n.* ● *adj.* **1** of or like Rabelais or his writings. **2** marked by exuberant imagination and language, coarse humour, and satire. ● *n.* an admirer or student of Rabelais. [F. *Rabelais*, Fr. satirist d. 1553]
■ *adj.* **2** see BAWDY *adj.*, SATIRICAL.

rabid /rábbid, ráy-/ *adj.* **1** furious, violent (*rabid hate*). **2** unreasoning; headstrong; fanatical (*a rabid anarchist*). **3** (esp. of a dog) affected with rabies; mad. **4** of or connected with rabies. □□ **rabidity** /rəbídditi/ *n.* **rabidly** *adv.* **rabidness** *n.* [L *rabidus* f. *rabere* rave]
■ **1** raging, furious; see also VIOLENT 2a. **2** unreasonable, unreasoning, extreme, fanatical, headstrong. **3** crazed, frenzied, maniacal, wild, mad, raving, berserk.

rabies /ráybeez/ *n.* a contagious and fatal viral disease esp. of dogs, transmissible through the saliva to humans etc. and causing madness and convulsions; hydrophobia. [L f. *rabere* rave]

RAC *abbr.* **1** (in the UK) Royal Automobile Club. **2** (in the UK) Royal Armoured Corps.

raccoon var. of RACOON.

race[1] /rayss/ *n.* & *v.* ● *n.* **1** a contest of speed between runners, horses, vehicles, ships, etc. **2** (in *pl.*) a series of these for horses, dogs, etc. at a fixed time on a regular course. **3** a contest between persons to be first to achieve something. **4 a** a strong or rapid current flowing through a narrow channel in the sea or a river (*a tide race*). **b** the channel of a stream etc. (*a mill-race*). **5** each of two grooved rings in a ball-bearing or roller bearing. **6** *Austral.* a fenced passageway for drafting sheep etc. **7** a passageway along which football players etc. run to enter the field. **8** (in weaving) the channel along which the shuttle moves. **9** *archaic* **a** the course of the sun or moon. **b** the course of life (*has run his race*). ● *v.* **1** *intr.* take part in a race. **2** *tr.* have a race with. **3** *tr.* try to surpass in speed. **4** *intr.* (foll. by *with*) compete in speed with. **5** *tr.* cause (a horse, car, etc.) to race. **6 a** *intr.* move swiftly; go at full or (of an engine, propeller, the pulse, etc.) excessive speed. **b** *tr.* cause (a person or thing) to do this (*raced the bill through the House*). **7** *intr.* (usu. as **racing** *adj.*) follow or take part in horse-racing (*a racing man*). □ **not in the race** *Austral. sl.* having no chance. **race meeting** a sequence of horse-races at one place. **racing car** a motor car built for racing on a prepared track. [ME, = running, f. ON *rás*]
■ *n.* **1** competition, contest. **2** (*races*) race meeting, meeting, meet; *Brit. colloq.* the dogs. **4 b** sluice, flume, chute, watercourse, course, channel, bed, raceway. ● *v.* **6 a** speed, hurry, hasten, dash, sprint, fly, rush, scramble, step lively, *colloq.* tear, rip, zip, step on the gas, step on it, hop to it, get a move on, *Brit* hare, *esp. US sl.* get a wiggle on. **b** rush, push, press, drive; urge, egg.

race[2] /rayss/ *n.* **1** each of the major divisions of humankind, having distinct physical characteristics. **2** a tribe, nation, etc., regarded as of a distinct ethnic stock. **3** the fact or concept of division into races (*discrimination based on race*). **4** a genus, species, breed, or variety of animals, plants, or micro-organisms. **5** a group of persons, animals, or plants connected by common descent. **6** any great division of living creatures (*the feathered race*; *the four-footed race*). **7** descent; kindred (*of noble race*; *separate in language and race*). **8** a class of persons etc. with some common feature (*the race of poets*). □ **race relations** relations between members of different races usu. in the same country. **race riot** an outbreak of violence due to racial antagonism. [F f. It. *razza*, of unkn. orig.]

■ **1, 2** stock, tribe, nation, people, folk, clan, family. **7** blood, descent, breed, kin, kindred, family, stock, line, lineage. **8** see CLASS *n.* 1.

race[3] /rayss/ *n.* a ginger root. [OF *rais*, *raiz* f. L *radix radicis* root]

racecard /ráyskaard/ *n.* a programme of races.

racecourse /ráyskorss/ *n.* a ground or track for horse-racing.

■ racetrack, *esp. US* raceway.

racegoer /ráysgōər/ *n.* a person who frequents horse-races.

racehorse /ráyss-horss/ *n.* a horse bred or kept for racing.

racemate /rássimayt/ *n. Chem.* a racemic mixture.

raceme /rəseém/ *n. Bot.* a flower cluster with the separate flowers attached by short equal stalks at equal distances along a central stem (cf. CYME). [L *racemus* grape-bunch]

racemic /rəseémik, -sémmik/ *adj. Chem.* composed of equal numbers of dextrorotatory and laevorotatory molecules of a compound. □□ **racemize** /rássimīz/ *v.tr.* & *intr.* (also **-ise**). [RACEME + -IC, orig. of tartaric acid in grape-juice]

racemose /rássimōss/ *adj.* **1** *Bot.* in the form of a raceme. **2** *Anat.* (of a gland etc.) clustered. [L *racemosus* (as RACEME)]

racer /ráysər/ *n.* **1** a horse, yacht, bicycle, etc., of a kind used for racing. **2** a circular horizontal rail along which the traversing-platform of a heavy gun moves. **3** a person or thing that races.

racetrack /ráystrak/ *n.* **1** = RACECOURSE. **2** a track for motor-racing.

raceway /ráysway/ *n.* **1** a track or channel along which something runs, esp.: **a** a channel for water. **b** a groove in which ball-bearings run. **c** a pipe or tubing enclosing electrical wires. **2** esp. *US* **a** a track for trotting, pacing, or harness racing. **b** a racecourse.

■ **1 a** see RACE[1] *n.* 4b.

rachis /ráykiss/ *n.* (*pl.* **rachides** /-kideez/) **1** *Bot.* **a** a stem of grass etc. bearing flower-stalks at short intervals. **b** the axis of a compound leaf or frond. **2** *Anat.* the vertebral column or the cord from which it develops. **3** *Zool.* a feather-shaft, esp. the part bearing the barbs. □□ **rachidial** /rəkíddiəl/ *adj.* [mod.L f. Gk *rhakhis* spine: the E pl. *-ides* is erron.]

rachitis /rəkītiss/ *n.* rickets. □□ **rachitic** /-kíttik/ *adj.* [mod.L f. Gk *rhakhitis* (as RACHIS)]

Rachmanism /rákmәniz'm/ *n. Brit.* the exploitation and intimidation of slum tenants by unscrupulous landlords. [P. *Rachman*, London landlord of the early 1960s]

racial /ráysh'l/ *adj.* **1** of or concerning race (*racial diversities*; *racial minority*). **2** on the grounds of or connected with difference in race (*racial discrimination*; *racial tension*). □□ **racially** *adv.*

■ **1** ethnic, genetic, ethnological, tribal; national.

racialism /ráyshəliz'm/ *n.* = RACISM 1. □□ **racialist** *n.* & *adj.*

racism /ráysiz'm/ *n.* **1 a** a belief in the superiority of a particular race; prejudice based on this. **b** antagonism towards other races, esp. as a result of this. **2** the theory that human abilities etc. are determined by race. □□ **racist** *n.* & *adj.*

■ **1** racialism, apartheid, Jim Crowism, chauvinism, bigotry. □□ **racist** (*n.*) see SUPREMACIST *n.* (*adj.*) racialist, prejudiced, chauvinistic, bigoted.

rack[1] /rak/ *n.* & *v.* ● *n.* **1 a** a framework usu. with rails, bars, hooks, etc., for holding or storing things. **b** a frame for holding animal fodder. **2** a cogged or toothed bar or rail engaging with a wheel or pinion etc., or using pegs to adjust the position of something. **3 a** *hist.* an instrument of torture stretching the victim's joints by the turning of rollers to which the wrists and ankles were tied. **b** a cause of suffering or anguish. ● *v.tr.* **1** (of disease or pain) inflict suffering on. **2** *hist.* torture (a person) on the rack. **3** place in or on a rack. **4** shake violently. **5** injure by straining. **6** oppress (tenants) by exacting excessive rent. **7** exhaust (the land) by excessive use. □ **on the rack** in distress or under strain. **rack one's brains** make a great mental effort (*racked my brains for something to say*). **rack-railway** a railway with a cogged rail between the bearing rails. **rack-rent** *n.* **1** a high rent, annually equalling the full value of the property to which it relates. **2** an extortionate rent. ● *v.tr.* exact this from (a tenant) or for (land). **rack-renter** a tenant paying or a landlord exacting an extortionate rent. **rack-up** *US* accumulate or achieve (a score etc.). **rack-wheel** a cog-wheel. [ME *rakke* f. MDu., MLG *rak*, *rek*, prob. f. *recken* stretch]

■ *n.* **1** framework, frame, trestle, holder, support; stand, scaffold. **3 b** torment, torture, agony, anguish, pain, misery, distress, affliction, scourge. ● *v.* **1** distress, torment, torture, agonize, oppress, pain, persecute, anguish, beleaguer, plague, gnaw at, harrow. **4** see SHAKE *v.* 1, 2, 5. **5** strain, wrench, tear, pull, rick, sprain. □ **on the rack** in distress, under stress *or* pressure *or* strain, *esp. US colloq.* stressed out; see also *worried* (WORRY *v.* 4).

rack[2] /rak/ *n.* destruction (esp. *rack and ruin*). [var. of WRACK, WRECK]

■ see DESTRUCTION 1.

rack[3] /rak/ *n.* a joint of lamb etc. including the front ribs. [perh. f. RACK[1]]

rack[4] /rak/ *v.tr.* (often foll. by *off*) draw off (wine, beer, etc.) from the lees. [ME f. Prov. *arracar* f. *raca* stems and husks of grapes, dregs]

rack[5] /rak/ *n.* & *v.* ● *n.* driving clouds. ● *v.intr.* (of clouds) be driven before the wind. [ME, prob. of Scand. orig.: cf. Norw. and Sw. dial. *rak* wreckage etc. f. *reka* drive]

rack[6] /rak/ *n.* & *v.* ● *n.* a horse's gait between a trot and a canter. ● *v.intr.* progress in this way.

racket[1] /rákkit/ *n.* (also **racquet**) **1** a bat with a round or oval frame strung with catgut, nylon, etc., used in tennis, squash, etc. **2** (in *pl.*) a ball game for two or four persons played with rackets in a plain four-walled court. **3** a snow shoe resembling a racket. □ **racket-ball** a small hard orig. kid-covered ball of cork and string. **racket-press** a press for keeping rackets taut and in shape. **racket-tail** a S. American humming-bird, *Loddigesia mirabilis*, with a racket-shaped tail. [F *racquette* f. It. *racchetta* f. Arab. *rāḥa* palm of the hand]

racket[2] /rákkit/ *n.* **1 a** a disturbance; an uproar; a din. **b** social excitement; gaiety. **2** *sl.* **a** a scheme for obtaining money or attaining other ends by fraudulent and often violent means. **b** a dodge; a sly game. **3** *colloq.* an activity; a way of life; a line of business (*starting up a new racket*). □□ **rackety** *adj.* [16th c.: perh. imit.]

■ **1 a** noise, din, uproar, disturbance, clamour, hubbub, hullabaloo, ballyhoo, fuss, ado, commotion, to-do, hue and cry, outcry, brouhaha, tumult, babel, *colloq.* row, rumpus, *joc.* alarums and excursions. **b** see GAIETY 2. **2** trick, dodge, scheme, swindle, stratagem, artifice, game, ruse, fraud, *Austral. colloq.* lurk, *sl.* gyp, con, *Brit. sl.* ramp, *US sl.* scam. **3** business, line (of business), profession, occupation, trade, vocation, calling, job, employment.

racketeer /rákkiteér/ *n.* a person who operates a dishonest business. □□ **racketeering** *n.*

■ gangster, *sl.* mobster; see also *swindler* (SWINDLE).

racon /ráykon/ *n.* esp. *US* a radar beacon that can be identified and located by its response to a radar signal from a ship etc. [*radar* + *beacon*]

raconteur /rákkontőr/ *n.* (*fem.* **raconteuse** /-tőz/) a teller of anecdotes. [F f. *raconter* relate, RECOUNT]

■ storyteller, anecdotalist, anecdotist, taleteller; chronicler, narrator, *Austral. sl.* magsman.

racoon /rəkóon/ *n.* (also **raccoon**) **1** any greyish-brown furry N. American nocturnal flesh-eating mammal of the genus *Procyon*, with a bushy tail and sharp snout. **2** the fur of the racoon. [Algonquian dial.]

racquet var. of RACKET[1].

racy /ráysi/ *adj.* (**racier, raciest**) **1** lively and vigorous in style. **2** risqué, suggestive. **3** having characteristic qualities in a high degree (*a racy flavour*). □□ **racily** *adv.* **raciness** *n.* [RACE[2] + -Y[1]]

■ **1** fresh, lively, vigorous, bouncy, animated, spirited, sprightly, vivacious, energetic, dynamic, zestful, stimulating, *colloq.* peppy. **2** risqué, suggestive, ribald, bawdy, naughty, lusty, earthy, gross, salty, immodest, indelicate, improper, indecent, blue, smutty, lewd, salacious, vulgar, dirty, filthy, pornographic, obscene, rude, crude, coarse, spicy, *US* off colour, *colloq.* raunchy. **3** strong, sharp, spicy, piquant, tasty, flavourful, pungent, savoury, zesty, tangy.

rad[1] /rad/ *n.* (*pl.* same) radian. [abbr.]

rad[2] /rad/ *n. sl.* a political radical. [abbr.]

rad[3] /rad/ *n. Physics* a unit of absorbed dose of ionizing radiation, corresponding to the absorption of 0.01 joule per kilogram of absorbing material. [*r*adiation *a*bsorbed *d*ose]

RADA /raádə/ *abbr.* (in the UK) Royal Academy of Dramatic Art.

radar /ráydaar/ *n.* **1** a system for detecting the direction, range, or presence of aircraft, ships, and other (usu. moving) objects, by sending out pulses of high frequency electromagnetic waves. **2** the apparatus used for this. □ **radar trap** the use of radar to detect vehicles exceeding a speed limit. [*ra*dio *d*etection *a*nd *r*anging]

RADC *abbr.* (in the UK) Royal Army Dental Corps.

raddle /rádd'l/ *n.* & *v.* ● *n.* red ochre (often used to mark sheep). ● *v.tr.* **1** colour with raddle or too much rouge. **2** (as **raddled** *adj.*) worn out; untidy, unkempt. [var. of RUDDLE]

■ *v.* **2** (**raddled**) see DILAPIDATED, UNTIDY.

radial /ráydiəl/ *adj.* & *n.* ● *adj.* **1** of, concerning, or in rays. **2 a** arranged like rays or radii; having the position or direction of a radius. **b** having spokes or radiating lines. **c** acting or moving along lines diverging from a centre. **3** *Anat.* relating to the radius (*radial artery*). **4** (in full **radial-ply**) (of a vehicle tyre) having the core fabric layers arranged radially at right angles to the circumference and the tread strengthened. ● *n.* **1** *Anat.* the radial nerve or artery. **2** a radial-ply tyre. □ **radial engine** an engine having cylinders arranged along radii. **radial symmetry** symmetry occurring about any number of lines or planes passing through the centre of an organism etc. **radial velocity** esp. *Astron.* the speed of motion along a radial line, esp. between a star etc. and an observer. □□ **radially** *adv.* [med.L *radialis* (as RADIUS)]

radian /ráydiən/ *n. Geom.* a unit of angle, equal to an angle at the centre of a circle the arc of which is equal in length to the radius. [RADIUS + -AN]

radiant /ráydiənt/ *adj.* & *n.* ● *adj.* **1** emitting rays of light. **2** (of eyes or looks) beaming with joy or hope or love. **3** (of beauty) splendid or dazzling. **4** (of light) issuing in rays. **5** operating radially. **6** extending radially; radiating. ● *n.* **1** the point or object from which light or heat radiates, esp. in an electric or gas heater. **2** *Astron.* a radiant point. □ **radiant heat** heat transmitted by radiation, not by conduction or convection. **radiant heater** a heater that works by this method. **radiant point 1** a point from which rays or radii proceed. **2** *Astron.* the apparent focal point of a meteor shower. □□ **radiance** *n.* **radiancy** *n.* **radiantly** *adv.* [ME f. L *radiare* (as RADIUS)]

■ *adj.* **1** shining, bright, beaming, burning, blazing, brilliant, luminous, resplendent, splendid, lustrous, gleaming, glowing, shimmering, incandescent, sparkling, dazzling, glittering, scintillating, twinkling, *literary* effulgent, refulgent. **2** happy, overjoyed, ecstatic, rapturous, delighted, joyful, blissful, glad, joyous, gay, jubilant, elated, rhapsodic, exultant, exhilarated, *colloq.* beatific, *poet.* blithe, blithesome; warm, lovely. **3** see *dazzling* (DAZZLE). □□ **radiance, radiancy** splendour, brightness, brilliance, resplendence, luminosity, luminousness, dazzle, sparkle, coruscation, scintillation, twinkle, incandescence, glow, lustre, shimmer, *literary* effulgence, refulgence; warmth, gladness, joy, pleasure, happiness, cheerfulness, delight.

radiate *v.* & *adj.* ● *v.* /ráydiayt/ **1** *intr.* **a** emit rays of light, heat, or other electromagnetic waves. **b** (of light or heat) be emitted in rays. **2** *tr.* emit (light, heat, or sound) from a centre. **3** *tr.* transmit or demonstrate (life, love, joy, etc.) (*radiates happiness*). **4** *intr.* & *tr.* diverge or cause to diverge or spread from a centre. **5** *tr.* (as **radiated** *adj.*) with parts arranged in rays. ● *adj.* /ráydiət/ having divergent rays or parts radially arranged. □□ **radiately** /-diətli/ *adv.* **radiative** /-diətiv/ *adj.* [L *radiare radiat-* (as RADIUS)]

■ *v.* **1 a** shine, burn, blaze, gleam, glow, shimmer, glisten, sparkle, glitter, coruscate, scintillate, twinkle. **2** emanate, shed, send out, emit, give off *or* out. **3** transmit, give out, disseminate, disperse, spread, diffuse. **4** diverge, fan out, spread out, extend, unfurl.

radiation /ráydiáysh'n/ *n.* **1** the act or an instance of radiating; the process of being radiated. **2** *Physics* **a** the emission of energy as electromagnetic waves or as moving particles. **b** the energy transmitted in this way, esp. invisibly. **3** (in full **radiation therapy**) treatment of cancer and other diseases using radiation, such as X-rays or ultraviolet light. □ **radiation chemistry** the study of the chemical effects of radiation on matter. **radiation sickness** sickness caused by exposure to radiation, such as X-rays or gamma rays. □□ **radiational** *adj.* **radiationally** *adv.* [L *radiatio* (as RADIATE)]

■ **1** emission, emanation, diffusion, dispersal.

radiator /ráydiaytər/ *n.* **1** a person or thing that radiates. **2 a** a device for heating a room etc., consisting of a metal case through which hot water or steam circulates. **b** a usu. portable oil or electric heater resembling this. **3** an engine-cooling device in a motor vehicle or aircraft with a large surface for cooling circulating water. □ **radiator grille** a grille at the front of a motor vehicle allowing air to circulate to the radiator.

radical /ráddik'l/ *adj.* & *n.* ● *adj.* **1** of the root or roots; fundamental (*a radical error*). **2** far-reaching; thorough; going to the root (*radical change*). **3 a** advocating thorough reform; holding extreme political views; leftwing, revolutionary. **b** (of a measure etc.) advanced by or according to principles of this kind. **4** forming the basis; primary (*the radical idea*). **5** *Math.* of the root of a number or quantity. **6** (of surgery etc.) seeking to ensure the removal of all diseased tissue. **7** of the roots of words. **8** *Mus.* belonging to the root of a chord. **9** *Bot.* of, or springing direct from, the root. **10** *hist.* belonging to an extreme section of the Liberal party. **11** *US hist.* seeking extreme anti-South action at the time of the Civil War. ● *n.* **1** a person holding radical views or belonging to a radical party. **2** *Chem.* **a** a free radical. **b** an element or atom or a group of these normally forming part of a compound and remaining unaltered during the compound's ordinary chemical changes. **3** the root of a word. **4** a fundamental principle; a basis. **5** *Math.* **a** a quantity forming or expressed as the root of another. **b** a radical sign. □ **radical sign** $\sqrt{}$, $\sqrt[3]{}$, etc., indicating the square, cube, etc., root of the number following. □□ **radicalism** *n.* **radicalize** *v.tr.* & *intr.* (also **-ise**). **radicalization** /-līzáysh'n/ *n.* **radically** *adv.* **radicalness** *n.* [ME f. LL *radicalis* f. L *radix radicis* root]

■ *adj.* **1** basic, fundamental, elementary, inherent, constitutional, elemental, essential, cardinal, deep, deep-seated, deep-rooted, structural, profound, underlying, organic, natural. **2** far-reaching, thorough, thoroughgoing, complete, entire, total, exhaustive, sweeping, all-inclusive, comprehensive, all-embracing, out-and-out, drastic. **3** extremist, revolutionary, fanatical, militant, extreme; left-wing, leftist, socialist, communist, Bolshevik, *colloq.* red, *esp. derog.* pink, *sl.* Bolshie. **4** see PRIMARY *adj.* 1b. ● *n.* **1** extremist, revolutionary, fanatic, zealot, militant; leftist, left-winger, communist, red, Bolshevik, Bolshevist, *colloq.* red, *sl.* Bolshy. **4** see BASIS 1, 2.

radicchio /rədéekiō/ *n.* (*pl.* **-os**) a variety of chicory with dark red-coloured leaves. [It., = chicory]

radices *pl.* of RADIX.

radicle /ráddik'l/ *n.* **1** the part of a plant embryo that develops into the primary root; a rootlet. **2** a rootlike subdivision of a nerve or vein. □□ **radicular** /rədíkyoolər/ *adj.* [L *radicula* (as RADIX)]
■ **1** see ROOT[1] *n.* 1a.

radii *pl.* of RADIUS.

radio /ráydiō/ *n.* & *v.* ● *n.* (*pl.* **-os**) **1** (often *attrib.*) **a** the transmission and reception of sound messages etc. by electromagnetic waves of radio-frequency (cf. WIRELESS). **b** an apparatus for receiving, broadcasting, or transmitting radio signals. **c** a message sent or received by radio. **2 a** sound broadcasting in general (*prefers the radio*). **b** a broadcasting station or channel (*Radio One*). ● *v.* (**-oes, -oed**) **1** *tr.* **a** send (a message) by radio. **b** send a message to (a person) by radio. **2** *intr.* communicate or broadcast by radio. □ **radio astronomy** the branch of astronomy concerned with the radio-frequency range of the electromagnetic spectrum. **radio cab** (or **car**) a cab or car equipped with a two-way radio. **radio fix** the position of an aircraft, ship, etc., found by radio. **radio galaxy** a galaxy emitting radiation in the radio-frequency range of the electromagnetic spectrum. **radio ham** see HAM. **radio star** a small star etc. emitting strong radio waves. **radio telescope** a directional aerial system for collecting and analysing radiation in the radio-frequency range from stars etc. [short for *radio-telegraphy* etc.]
■ *n.* **1 b** receiver, *esp. Brit.* wireless (set), transistor (radio), *esp. Brit. colloq.* tranny, *sl.* ghetto-blaster. ● *v.* **1 a** send, transmit, broadcast, air; announce, present. **b** contact, get through to, communicate with.

radio- /ráydiō/ *comb. form* **1** denoting radio or broadcasting. **2 a** connected with radioactivity. **b** denoting artificially prepared radioisotopes of elements (*radio-caesium*). **3** connected with rays or radiation. **4** *Anat.* belonging to the radius in conjunction with some other part (*radio-carpal*). [RADIUS + -O- or f. RADIO]

radioactive /ráydiō-áktiv/ *adj.* of or exhibiting radioactivity. □□ **radioactively** *adv.*

radioactivity /ráydiō-aktívviti/ *n.* the spontaneous disintegration of atomic nucleii, with the emission of usu. penetrating radiation or particles.

radio-assay /ráydiōəsáy/ *n.* an analysis of a substance based on radiation from a sample.

radiobiology /ráydiōbīólləji/ *n.* the biology concerned with the effects of radiation on organisms and the application in biology of radiological techniques. □□ **radiobiological** /-bīəlójik'l/ *adj.* **radiobiologically** /-bīəlójikəli/ *adv.* **radiobiologist** *n.*

radiocarbon /ráydiōkaárb'n/ *n.* a radioactive isotope of carbon. □ **radiocarbon dating** = *carbon dating.*

radiochemistry /ráydiōkémmistri/ *n.* the chemistry of radioactive materials. □□ **radiochemical** *adj.* **radiochemist** *n.*

radio-controlled /ráydiōkəntrṓld/ *adj.* (of a model aircraft etc.) controlled from a distance by radio.

radio-element /ráydiō-éllimənt/ *n.* a natural or artificial radioactive element or isotope.

radio-frequency /ráydiōfreékwənsi/ *n.* (*pl.* **-ies**) the frequency band of telecommunication, ranging from 10^4-10^{11} or 10^{12} Hz.

radiogenic /ráydiōjénnik/ *adj.* **1** produced by radioactivity. **2** suitable for broadcasting by radio. □□ **radiogenically** *adv.*

radio-goniometer /ráydiōgṓniómmitər/ *n.* an instrument for finding direction using radio waves.

radiogram /ráydiōgram/ *n.* **1** *Brit.* a combined radio and record-player. **2** a picture obtained by X-rays, gamma rays, etc. **3** a radio-telegram. [RADIO- + -GRAM, GRAMOPHONE]
■ **3** see TELEGRAM.

radiograph /ráydiōgraaf/ *n.* & *v.* ● *n.* **1** an instrument recording the intensity of radiation. **2** = RADIOGRAM 2. ● *v.tr.* obtain a picture of by X-ray, gamma ray, etc. □□ **radiographer** /-diógrəfər/ *n.* **radiographic** /-diəgráffik/ *adj.* **radiographically** /-diəgráffikəli/ *adv.* **radiography** /-diógrəfi/ *n.*

radioimmunology /ráydiō-ímyoonólləji/ *n.* the application of radiological techniques in immunology.

radioisotope /ráydiō-ī́sətōp/ *n.* a radioactive isotope. □□ **radioisotopic** /-tóppik/ *adj.* **radioisotopically** /-tóppikəli/ *adv.*

radiolarian /ráydiōláiriən/ *n.* any marine protozoan of the order Radiolaria, having a siliceous skeleton and radiating pseudopodia. [mod.L *radiolaria* f. L *radiolus* dimin. of RADIUS]

radiology /ráydiólləji/ *n.* the scientific study of X-rays and other high-energy radiation, esp. as used in medicine. □□ **radiologic** /-diəlójik/ *adj.* **radiological** /-diəlójik'l/ *adj.* **radiologist** *n.*

radiometer /ráydiómmitər/ *n.* an instrument for measuring the intensity or force of radiation. □□ **radiometry** *n.*

radiometric /ráydiōmétrik/ *adj.* of or relating to the measurement of radioactivity. □ **radiometric dating** a method of dating geological specimens by determining the relative proportions of the isotopes of a radioactive element present in a sample.

radionics /ráydiónniks/ *n.pl.* (usu. treated as *sing.*) the study and interpretation of radiation believed to be emitted from substances, esp. as a form of diagnosis. [RADIO- + *-onics*, after ELECTRONICS]

radionuclide /ráydiōnyṓōklīd/ *n.* a radioactive nuclide.

radiopaque /ráydiōpáyk/ *adj.* (also **radio-opaque**) opaque to X-rays or similar radiation. □□ **radiopacity** /-pássiti/ *n.* [RADIO- + OPAQUE]

radiophonic /ráydiōfónnik/ *adj.* of or relating to synthetic sound, esp. music, produced electronically.

radioscopy /ráydiósk əpi/ *n.* the examination by X-rays etc. of objects opaque to light. □□ **radioscopic** /-diəskóppik/ *adj.*

radiosonde /ráydiōsond/ *n.* a miniature radio transmitter broadcasting information about pressure, temperature, etc., from various levels of the atmosphere, carried esp. by balloon. [RADIO- + G *Sonde* probe]

radio-telegram /ráydiōtélligram/ *n.* a telegram sent by radio, usu. from a ship to land.

radio-telegraphy /ráydiōtilégrəfi/ *n.* telegraphy using radio transmission. □□ **radio-telegraph** /-télligraaf/ *n.*

radio-telephony /ráydiōtiléffəni/ *n.* telephony using radio transmission. □□ **radio-telephone** /-téllifōn/ *n.* **radio-telephonic** /-telifónnik/ *adj.*

radiotelex /ráydiōtélleks/ *n.* a telex sent usu. from a ship to land.

radiotherapy /ráydiōthérrəpi/ *n.* the treatment of disease by X-rays or other forms of radiation. □□ **radiotherapeutic** /-pyṓōtik/ *adj.* **radiotherapist** *n.*

radish /ráddish/ *n.* **1** a cruciferous plant, *Raphanus sativus*, with a fleshy pungent root. **2** this root, eaten esp. raw in salads etc. [OE *rædic* f. L *radix radicis* root]

radium /ráydiəm/ *n. Chem.* a radioactive metallic element orig. obtained from pitchblende etc., used esp. in luminous materials and in radiotherapy. ¶ Symb.: **Ra.** □ **radium bomb** a container holding a large quantity of radium and used in radiotherapy as a source of gamma rays. **radium emanation** = RADON. **radium therapy** the treatment of disease by the use of radium. [L *radius* ray]

radius /ráydiəss/ *n.* & *v.* ● *n.* (*pl.* **radii** /-di-ī/ or **radiuses**) **1** *Math.* **a** a straight line from the centre to the circumference of a circle or sphere. **b** a radial line from the focus to any point of a curve. **c** the length of the radius of a circle etc. **2** a usu. specified distance from a centre in all directions (*within a radius of 20 miles*; *has a large radius of action*). **3 a** the thicker and shorter of the two bones in the human forearm (cf. ULNA). **b** the corresponding bone in a vertebrate's foreleg or a bird's wing. **4** any of the five arm-like structures of a starfish. **5 a** any of a set of lines diverging from a point like the radii of a circle. **b** an object of this kind, e.g. a spoke. **6 a** the outer rim of a composite flower-head, e.g. a daisy. **b** a radiating branch of an umbel. ● *v.tr.* give a rounded form to (an edge etc.). □ **radius vector** *Math.* a variable line drawn from a fixed point to an orbit or other curve, or to any point as an indication of the latter's position. [L, = staff, spoke, ray]

■ *n.* **2** see RANGE *n.* 1a–c.

radix /ráydiks/ *n.* (*pl.* **radices** /-diseez/) **1** *Math.* a number or symbol used as the basis of a numeration scale (e.g. ten in the decimal system). **2** (usu. foll. by *of*) a source or origin. [L, = root]

radome /ráydōm/ *n.* a dome or other structure, transparent to radio waves, protecting radar equipment, esp. on the outer surface of an aircraft. [*radar* + *dome*]

radon /ráydon/ *n. Chem.* a gaseous radioactive inert element arising from the disintegration of radium, and used in radiotherapy. ¶ Symb.: **Rn**. [RADIUM after *argon* etc.]

radula /rádyoolə/ *n.* (*pl.* **radulae** /-lee/) a filelike structure in molluscs for scraping off food particles and drawing them into the mouth. □□ **radular** *adj.* [L, = scraper f. *radere* scrape]

RAF *abbr.* /*colloq.* raf/ (in the UK) Royal Air Force.

Rafferty's rules /ráffərtiz/ *n. Austral.* & *NZ colloq.* no rules at all, esp. in boxing. [E dial. corrupt. of *refractory*]

raffia /ráffiə/ *n.* (also **raphia**) **1** a palm-tree, *Raphia ruffia*, native to Madagascar, having very long leaves. **2** the fibre from its leaves used for making hats, baskets, etc., and for tying plants etc. [Malagasy]

raffinate /ráffinayt/ *n. Chem.* a refined liquid oil produced by solvent extraction of impurities. [F *raffiner* + -ATE[1]]

raffish /ráffish/ *adj.* **1** disreputable; rakish. **2** tawdry. □□ **raffishly** *adv.* **raffishness** *n.* [as RAFT[2] + -ISH[1]]

■ **1** see RAKISH[1]. **2** see GAUDY[1].

raffle[1] /ráff'l/ *n.* & *v.* ● *n.* a fund-raising lottery with goods as prizes. ● *v.tr.* (often foll. by *off*) dispose of by means of a raffle. [ME, a kind of dice-game, f. OF *raf(f)le*, of unkn. orig.]

■ *n.* lottery, draw.

raffle[2] /ráff'l/ *n.* **1** rubbish; refuse. **2** lumber; debris. [ME, perh. f. OF *ne rifle, ne rafle* nothing at all]

raft[1] /raaft/ *n.* & *v.* ● *n.* **1** a flat floating structure of timber or other materials for conveying persons or things. **2** a lifeboat or small (often inflatable) boat, esp. for use in emergencies. **3** a floating accumulation of trees, ice, etc. ● *v.* **1** *tr.* transport as or on a raft. **2** *tr.* cross (water) on a raft. **3** *tr.* form into a raft. **4** *intr.* (often foll. by *across*) work a raft (across water etc.). [ME f. ON *raptr* RAFTER]

raft[2] /raaft/ *n. colloq.* **1** a large collection. **2** (foll. by *of*) a crowd. [*raff* rubbish, perh. of Scand. orig.]

■ see HEAP *n.* 1, 2.

rafter[1] /ráaftər/ *n.* each of the sloping beams forming the framework of a roof. □□ **raftered** *adj.* [OE *ræfter*, rel. to RAFT[1]]

■ see BEAM *n.* 1.

rafter[2] /ráaftər/ *n.* **1** a person who rafts timber. **2** a person who travels by raft.

raftsman /ráaftsmən/ *n.* (*pl.* **-men**) a worker on a raft.

rag[1] /rag/ *n.* **1 a** a torn, frayed, or worn piece of woven material. **b** one of the irregular scraps to which cloth etc. is reduced by wear and tear. **2 a** (in *pl.*) old or worn clothes. **b** (usu. in *pl.*) *colloq.* a garment of any kind. **3** (*collect.*) scraps of cloth used as material for paper, stuffing, etc. **4** *derog.* **a** a newspaper. **b** a flag, handkerchief, curtain, etc. **5** (usu. with *neg.*) the smallest scrap of cloth etc. (*not a rag to cover him*). **6** an odd scrap; an irregular piece. **7** a jagged projection, esp. on metal. □ **in rags 1** much torn. **2** in old torn clothes. **rag-and-bone man** *Brit.* an itinerant dealer in old clothes, furniture, etc. **rag-bag 1** a bag in which scraps of fabric etc. are kept for use. **2** a miscellaneous collection. **3** *sl.* a sloppily-dressed woman. **rag bolt** a bolt with barbs to keep it tight when it has been driven in. **rag book** a children's book made of untearable cloth. **rag doll** a stuffed doll made of cloth. **rag paper** paper made from rags. **rag-picker** a collector and seller of rags. **rags to riches** poverty to affluence. **rag trade** *colloq.* the business of designing, making, and selling women's clothes. [ME, prob. back-form. f. RAGGED]

■ **2 b** (*rags*) clothes, clothing, dress, garments, *formal* attire, *sl.* duds. **4 a** paper, newspaper, periodical, magazine, publication, journal, daily. **6** shred, scrap, fragment, bit, piece, *dial.* clout. □ **in rags 1** in tatters, torn; see also TATTERED. **rag-bag 2** see HOTCHPOTCH 1. **3** slattern, slut, sloven. **rag trade** garment-industry, clothing business, fashion industry.

rag[2] /rag/ *n.* & *v.* ● *n. Brit.* **1** a fund-raising programme of stunts, parades, and entertainment organized by students. **2** *colloq.* a prank. **3 a** a rowdy celebration. **b** a noisy disorderly scene. ● *v.* (**ragged**, **ragging**) **1** *tr.* tease; torment; play rough jokes on. **2** *tr.* scold; reprove severely. **3** *intr. Brit.* engage in rough play; be noisy and riotous. [18th c.: orig. unkn.: cf. BALLYRAG]

■ *n.* **2** see PRANK. **3 b** see TUMULT 1, 2. ● *v.* **1** tease, taunt, twit, ridicule, mock, make fun of, joke, poke fun at, pull a person's leg, rally, *colloq.* kid; see also TORMENT *v.* 2. **2** see SCOLD *v.* 1.

rag[3] /rag/ *n.* **1** a large coarse roofing-slate. **2** any of various kinds of hard coarse sedimentary stone that break into thick slabs. [ME: orig. unkn., but assoc. with RAG[1]]

rag[4] /rag/ *n. Mus.* a ragtime composition or tune. [perh. f. RAGGED: see RAGTIME]

raga /ráagə/ *n.* (also **rag** /raag/) *Ind. Mus.* **1** a pattern of notes used as a basis for improvisation. **2** a piece using a particular raga. [Skr., = colour, musical tone]

ragamuffin /rággəmuffin/ *n.* a person in ragged dirty clothes, esp. a child. [prob. based on RAG[1]: cf. 14th-c. *ragamoffyn* the name of a demon]

■ (street) urchin, waif, gamin, stray, guttersnipe, *hist.* mudlark.

rage /rayj/ *n.* & *v.* ● *n.* **1** fierce or violent anger. **2** a fit of this (*flew into a rage*). **3** the violent action of a natural force (*the rage of the storm*). **4** (foll. by *for*) **a** a vehement desire or passion. **b** a widespread temporary enthusiasm or fashion. **5** *poet.* poetic, prophetic, or martial enthusiasm or ardour. **6** *sl.* a lively frolic. ● *v.intr.* **1** be full of anger. **2** (often foll. by *at*, *against*) speak furiously or madly; rave. **3** (of wind, battle, fever, etc.) be violent; be at its height; continue unchecked. **4** *Austral. sl.* seek enjoyment; go on a spree. □ **all the rage** popular, fashionable. [ME f. OF *rager* ult. f. L RABIES]

■ *n.* **1** fury, *literary* wrath, ire; see also ANGER *n.* **2** fury, frenzy, hysterics, tantrum, fit, temper, *Brit. colloq.* paddy, wobbly. **3** violence, fury, strength; see also FORCE[1] *n.* 1. **4 a** see THIRST *n.* 2. **b** fashion, craze, vogue, mode, fad, trend. ● *v.* **1, 2** rant, rave, rant and rave, rail; storm, be beside oneself (with anger *or* fury), fulminate, fume, foam at the mouth, stew, smoulder, seethe, simmer. □ **all the rage** popular; the last word, the *dernier cri*; see also FASHIONABLE.

ragee /ráagee/ *n.* (also **raggee**) a coarse cereal, *Eleusine coracana*, forming a staple food in parts of India etc. [Hindi *rāgī*]

ragged /rággid/ *adj.* **1 a** (of clothes etc.) torn; frayed. **b** (of a place) dilapidated. **2** rough; shaggy; hanging in tufts. **3** (of a person) in ragged clothes. **4** with a broken or jagged outline or surface. **5** faulty; imperfect. **6 a** lacking finish, smoothness, or uniformity (*ragged rhymes*). **b** (of a sound) harsh, discordant. **7** exhausted (esp. *be run ragged*). □ **ragged robin** a pink-flowered campion, *Lychnis flos-cuculi*,

with tattered petals. □□ **raggedly** *adv.* **raggedness** *n.* **raggedy** *adj.* [ME f. ON *roggvathr* tufted]
■ **1a, 3** rough, shaggy, tattered, scraggy, torn, rent, ripped, frayed, worn (out), threadbare, patched, *colloq.* tatty; unkempt, shabby, seedy, down at heel. **1 b** run-down, battered, broken-down, neglected, deteriorated, dilapidated, *colloq.* beat-up. **4** rough, uneven, irregular, jagged; serrated, zigzag, notched, ridged. **5** faulty, imperfect, uneven, bad, poor, shabby, patchy, shoddy. **6 a** see ROUGH *adj.* 10. **b** rough, harsh, discordant, grating, rasping, hoarse, scratchy, croaking. **7** (*run ragged*) wear out, exhaust, weary; see also TIRE[1] 1.

raggee var. of RAGEE.

raggle-taggle /rágg'ltagg'l/ *adj.* (also **wraggle-taggle**) ragged; rambling, straggling. [app. fanciful var. of RAGTAG]

raglan /ráglən/ *n.* (often *attrib.*) an overcoat without shoulder seams, the sleeves running up to the neck. □ **raglan sleeve** a sleeve of this kind. [Lord *Raglan*, Brit. commander d. 1855]

ragman /rágmən/ *n.* a person who collects or deals in rags, old clothes, etc.
■ rag-dealer, rag-picker, scrap dealer, *Brit.* rag-and-bone man, knacker, *US* junk dealer, junkman.

ragout /ragóō/ *n.* & *v.* ● *n.* meat in small pieces stewed with vegetables and highly seasoned. ● *v.tr.* cook (food) in this way . [F *ragoût* f. *ragoûter* revive the taste of]
■ *n.* see STEW[1] *n.* 1. ● *v.* see STEW[1] *v.* 1.

ragstone /rágstōn/ *n.* = RAG[3] 2.

ragtag /rágtag/ *n.* (in full **ragtag and bobtail**) *derog.* the rabble or common people. [earlier *tag-rag*, *tag and rag*, f. RAG[1] + TAG[1]]
■ (**ragtag and bobtail**) see RABBLE[1] 3.

ragtime /rágtīm/ *n.* & *adj.* ● *n.* music characterized by a syncopated melodic line and regularly-accented accompaniment, evolved by American Black musicians in the 1890s and played esp. on the piano. ● *adj. sl.* disorderly, disreputable, inferior (*a ragtime army*). [prob. f. RAG[4]]

raguly /rágyooli/ *adj. Heraldry* like a row of sawn-off branches. [perh. f. RAGGED after *nebuly*]

ragweed /rágweed/ *n.* **1** = RAGWORT. **2** *US* any plant of the genus *Ambrosia*, with allergenic pollen.

ragwort /rágwurt/ *n.* any yellow-flowered ragged-leaved plant of the genus *Senecio*.

rah /raa/ *int.* esp. *US colloq.* an expression of encouragement, approval, etc. [shortening of HURRAH]

rai /rī/ *n* a style of rock music which fuses Arabic and Algerian folk elements with Western rock styles. [Algerian or Moroccan Arab.]

raid /rayd/ *n.* & *v.* ● *n.* **1** a rapid surprise attack, esp.: **a** by troops, aircraft, etc. in warfare. **b** to commit a crime or do harm. **2** a surprise attack by police etc. to arrest suspected persons or seize illicit goods. **3** *Stock Exch.* an attempt to lower prices by the concerted selling of shares. **4** (foll. by *on*, *upon*) a forceful or insistent attempt to make a person or thing provide something. ● *v.tr.* **1** make a raid on (a person, place, or thing). **2** plunder, deplete. □□ **raider** *n.* [ME, Sc. form of OE *rād* ROAD[1]]
■ *n.* **1** (surprise) attack, incursion, invasion, onset, onslaught, sortie, sally, *colloq.* blitz. **2** *esp. US colloq.* bust. ● *v.* **1** attack, invade, assault, storm, set upon, descend upon, swoop down on *or* upon, pounce upon. **2** sack, plunder, pillage, forage, loot, ransack, rifle, maraud, *esp. US colloq.* bust; deplete, strip.

rail[1] /rayl/ *n.* & *v.* ● *n.* **1** a level or sloping bar or series of bars: **a** used to hang things on. **b** running along the top of a set of banisters. **c** forming part of a fence or barrier as protection against contact, falling over, etc. **2** a steel bar or continuous line of bars laid on the ground, usu. as one of a pair forming a railway track. **3** (often *attrib.*) a railway (*send it by rail*; *rail fares*). **4** (in *pl.*) the inside boundary fence of a racecourse. **5** a horizontal piece in the frame of a panelled door etc. (cf. STILE[2]). ● *v.tr.* **1** furnish with a rail or rails. **2** (usu. foll. by *in*, *off*) enclose with rails (*a small space was railed off*). **3** convey (goods) by rail. □ **off the rails** disorganized; out of order; deranged. **over the rails** over the side of a ship. **rail fence** esp. *US* a fence made of posts and rails. **rail gun** an electromagnetic projectile launcher used esp. as an anti-missile weapon. □□ **railage** *n.* **railless** *adj.* [ME f. OF *reille* iron rod f. L *regula* RULE]
■ *n.* **1** bar, rod; railing, banisters, balustrade; fence, barrier. **3** (*by rail*) by train, by railway, *esp. US* by railroad. □ **off the rails** see *chaotic* (CHAOS), MAD *adj.* 1.

rail[2] /rayl/ *v.intr.* (often foll. by *at*, *against*) complain using abusive language; rant. □□ **railer** *n.* **railing** *n.* & *adj.* [ME f. F *railler* f. Prov. *ralhar* jest, ult. f. L *rugire* bellow]
■ (*rail at* or *against*) rant at, fulminate against, rage at, rant and rave at; revile, attack, berate, scold, upbraid, criticize, have a go at, censure, decry, condemn, denounce, *colloq.* go on at.

rail[3] /rayl/ *n.* any bird of the family Rallidae, often inhabiting marshes, esp. the corncrake and water rail. [ME f. ONF *raille* f. Rmc, perh. imit.]

railcar /ráylkaar/ *n.* a railway vehicle consisting of a single powered coach.

railcard /ráylkaard/ *n. Brit.* a pass entitling the holder to reduced rail fares.

railhead /ráylhed/ *n.* **1** the furthest point reached by a railway under construction. **2** the point on a railway at which road transport of goods begins.

railing /ráyling/ *n.* **1** (usu. in *pl.*) a fence or barrier made of rails. **2** the material for these.
■ **1** see FENCE *n.* 1.

raillery /ráyləri/ *n.* (*pl.* **-ies**) **1** good-humoured ridicule; rallying. **2** an instance of this. [F *raillerie* (as RAIL[2])]
■ **1** banter, *badinage*, persiflage, repartee, frivolity, joking, jesting, chaffing, teasing, ridicule, *colloq.* kidding.

railman /ráylmən/ *n.* (*pl.* **-men**) = RAILWAYMAN.

railroad /ráylrōd/ *n.* & *v.* ● *n.* esp. *US* = RAILWAY. ● *v.tr.* **1** (often foll. by *to*, *into*, *through*, etc.) rush or coerce (a person or thing) (*railroaded me into going too*). **2** send (a person) to prison by means of false evidence.
■ *v.* **1** force, urge, compel, coerce, intimidate, push, press, pressurize, pressure, drive, stampede, bully, hector, tyrannize, dragoon, browbeat, *colloq.* bulldoze.

railway /ráylway/ *n.* **1** a track or set of tracks made of steel rails upon which goods trucks and passenger trains run. **2** such a system worked by a single company (*Great Western Railway*). **3** the organization and personnel required for its working. **4** a similar set of tracks for other vehicles etc. □ **railway-yard** the area where rolling-stock is kept and made up into trains.
■ **1–3** rail, *esp. US* railroad.

railwayman /ráylwaymən/ *n.* (*pl.* **-men**) a railway employee.

raiment /ráymənt/ *n. archaic* clothing. [ME f. obs. *arrayment* (as ARRAY)]
■ see CLOTHES.

rain /rayn/ *n.* & *v.* ● *n.* **1 a** the condensed moisture of the atmosphere falling visibly in separate drops. **b** the fall of such drops. **2** (in *pl.*) **a** rainfalls. **b** (prec. by *the*) the rainy season in tropical countries. **3 a** falling liquid or solid particles or objects. **b** the rainlike descent of these. **c** a large or overwhelming quantity (*a rain of congratulations*). ● *v.* **1** *intr.* (prec. by *it* as subject) rain falls (*it is raining*; *if it rains*). **2 a** *intr.* fall in showers or like rain (*tears rained down their cheeks*; *blows rain upon him*). **b** *tr.* (prec. by *it* as subject) send in large quantities (*it rained blood*; *it is raining invitations*). **3** *tr.* send down like rain; lavishly bestow (*rained benefits on us*; *rained blows upon him*). **4** *intr.* (of the sky, the clouds, etc.) send down rain. □ **rain cats and dogs** see CAT. **rain check** *US* **1** a ticket given for later use when a sporting fixture or other outdoor event is interrupted or postponed by rain. **2** a promise that an offer will be maintained though deferred. **rain-cloud** a cloud bringing rain. **rain forest** luxuriant tropical forest with heavy rainfall. **rain-gauge** an instrument measuring rainfall. **rain-making** the action of attempting to increase rainfall by artificial means. **rain off** (or *US* **out**) (esp. in *passive*) cause (an event etc.) to be terminated or cancelled because of rain. **rain or shine** whether it rains or not. **rain-shadow** a region shielded from rain by mountains etc. **rain-wash 1** loose material carried away by rain. **2** the movement of this. **rain-worm** the common earthworm. □□ **rainless** *adj.* **raintight** *adj.* [OE *regn, rēn, regnian* f. Gmc]

■ *n.* **1** precipitation, drizzle, mizzle. **3 c** flood, torrent, shower, volley, stream, outpouring, deluge. ● *v.* **1** pour (down), drizzle, spit, mizzle. **2 a** trickle, shower, pour, run, fall, spatter, splash, sprinkle; come down, descend. **3** bestow, lavish; pour down, hail.

rainbird /ráynburd/ *n.* a bird said to foretell rain by its cry, esp. the green woodpecker.

rainbow /ráynbō/ *n.* & *adj.* ● *n.* **1** an arch of colours (conventionally red, orange, yellow, green, blue, indigo, violet) formed in the sky (or across a cataract etc.) opposite the sun by reflection, twofold refraction, and dispersion of the sun's rays in falling rain or in spray or mist. **2** a similar effect formed by the moon's rays. ● *adj.* many-coloured. □ **rainbow lorikeet** a small brightly coloured Polynesian parrot, *Trichoglossus haematodus.* **rainbow trout** a large trout, *Salmo gairdneri*, orig. of the Pacific coast of N. America. **secondary rainbow** an additional arch with the colours in reverse order formed inside or outside a rainbow by twofold reflection and twofold refraction. [OE *regnboga* (as RAIN, BOW[1])]

raincoat /ráynkōt/ *n.* a waterproof or water-resistant coat.

■ anorak, cagoule, *Brit.* mackintosh, *Brit. colloq.* mac.

raindrop /ráyndrop/ *n.* a single drop of rain. [OE *regndropa*]

rainfall /ráynfawl/ *n.* **1** a fall of rain. **2** the quantity of rain falling within a given area in a given time.

■ **1** shower, cloudburst, downpour, rainstorm, deluge, monsoon; see also PRECIPITATION 3a. **2** precipitation.

rainproof /ráynproof/ *adj.* (esp. of a building, garment, etc.) resistant to rainwater.

rainstorm /ráynstorm/ *n.* a storm with heavy rain.

■ shower, cloudburst, downpour, deluge, monsoon, thunder-shower, thunderstorm.

rainwater /ráynwawtər/ *n.* water obtained from collected rain, as distinct from a well etc.

rainy /ráyni/ *adj.* (**rainier, rainiest**) **1** (of weather, a climate, day, region, etc.) in or on which rain is falling or much rain usually falls. **2** (of cloud, wind, etc.) laden with or bringing rain. □ **rainy day** a time of special need in the future. □□ **rainily** *adv.* **raininess** *n.* [OE *rēnig* (as RAIN)]

■ **1** see WET *adj.* 2.

raise /rayz/ *v.* & *n.* ● *v.tr.* **1** put or take into a higher position. **2** (often foll. by *up*) cause to rise or stand up or be vertical; set upright. **3** increase the amount or value or strength of (*raised their prices*). **4** (often foll. by *up*) construct or build up. **5** levy or collect or bring together (*raise money*; *raise an army*). **6** cause to be heard or considered (*raise a shout*; *raise an objection*). **7** set going or bring into being; arouse (*raise a protest*; *raise hopes*). **8** bring up; educate. **9** breed or grow (*raise one's own vegetables*). **10** promote to a higher rank. **11** (foll. by *to*) *Math.* multiply a quantity to a specified power. **12** cause (bread) to rise with yeast. **13** *Cards* **a** bet more than (another player). **b** increase (a stake). **c** *Bridge* make a bid contracting for more tricks in the same suit as (one's partner); increase (a bid) in this way. **14** abandon or force an enemy to abandon (a siege or blockade). **15** remove (a barrier or embargo). **16** cause (a ghost etc.) to appear (opp. LAY[1] 6b). **17** *colloq.* find (a person etc. wanted). **18** establish contact with (a person etc.) by radio or telephone. **19** (usu. as **raised** *adj.*) cause (pastry etc.) to stand without support (*a raised pie*). **20** *Naut.* come in sight of (land, a ship, etc.). **21** make a nap on (cloth). **22** extract from the earth. ● *n.* **1** *Cards* an increase in a stake or bid (cf. sense 13 of *v.*). **2** esp. *US* an increase in salary. □ **raise Cain** see CAIN. **raised beach** *Geol.* a beach lying above water level owing to changes since its formation. **raise the devil** *colloq.* make a disturbance. **raise a dust 1** cause turmoil. **2** obscure the truth. **raise one's eyebrows** see EYEBROW. **raise one's eyes** see EYE. **raise from the dead** restore to life. **raise one's glass to** drink the health of. **raise one's hand to** make as if to strike (a person). **raise one's hat** (often foll. by *to*) remove it momentarily as a gesture of courtesy or respect. **raise hell** *colloq.* make a disturbance. **raise a laugh** cause others to laugh. **raise a person's spirits** give him or her new courage or cheerfulness. **raise one's voice** speak, esp. louder. **raise the wind** *Brit.* procure money for a purpose. □□ **raisable** *adj.* [ME f. ON *reisa*, rel. to REAR[2]]

■ *v.* **1** lift (up), elevate, upraise, take up; hoist, pull up, haul up. **3** increase, advance, put up, run up, *colloq.* jack (up). **4** erect, put up, construct, build, put together, assemble, frame, run up, produce, create. **5** assemble, gather, bring *or* gather together, muster, amass, mobilize, round up, rally, collect, convene, recruit, put together, *colloq.* pull together; levy. **6** introduce, broach, bring up, bring *or* put forward, present, suggest, mention, moot, set forth; utter, express, let out. **7** occasion, put *or* set in motion, institute, prompt, initiate, engender, stir up, instigate, inspire, give rise to, bring about, arouse, originate; rouse, buoy, lift, uplift, cheer, invigorate, stimulate, animate, vivify, *colloq.* boost; foster, nurture, heighten, quicken, encourage, develop. **8** bring up, nurture, rear; parent; see also EDUCATE 1, 2. **9** farm, grow, cultivate, plant, nurture, harvest, propagate; breed. **10** see PROMOTE 1. **15** remove, lift, abandon, discontinue, (bring to an) end, terminate. ● *n.* **2** see INCREASE *n.* 3. □ **raise from the dead** revive, resurrect, resuscitate; reanimate, recall. **raise one's glass to** see TOAST *v.* 4. **raise hell** raise a dust, make a disturbance, raise Cain, *colloq.* raise the devil; see also STORM *v.* 1.

raisin /ráyz'n/ *n.* a partially dried grape. □□ **raisiny** *adj.* [ME f. OF ult. f. L *racemus* grape-bunch]

raison d'être /ráyzon détrə/ *n.* (*pl.* ***raisons d'être*** *pronunc.* same) a purpose or reason that accounts for or justifies or originally caused a thing's existence. [F, = reason for being]

■ purpose, reason, function, role.

raj /raaj/ *n.* (prec. by *the*) *hist.* British sovereignty in India. [Hindi *rāj* reign]

raja /raajə/ *n.* (also **rajah**) *hist.* **1** an Indian king or prince. **2** a petty dignitary or noble in India. **3** a Malay or Javanese chief. □□ **rajaship** *n.* [Hindi *rājā* f. Skr. *rājan* king]

raja yoga /raajə/ *n.* a form of yoga intended to achieve control over the mind and emotions. [Skr. f. *rājan* king + YOGA]

Rajput /raajpoot/ *n.* (also **Rajpoot**) a member of a Hindu soldier caste claiming Kshatriya descent. [Hindi *rājpūt* f. Skr. *rājan* king + *putrá* son]

rake[1] /rayk/ *n.* & *v.* ● *n.* **1 a** an implement consisting of a pole with a crossbar toothed like a comb at the end, or with several tines held together by a crosspiece, for drawing together hay etc. or smoothing loose soil or gravel. **b** a wheeled implement for the same purpose. **2** a similar implement used for other purposes, e.g. by a croupier drawing in money at a gaming-table. ● *v.* **1** *tr.* (usu. foll. by *out, together, up*, etc.) collect or gather or remove with or as with a rake. **2** *tr.* make tidy or smooth with a rake (*raked it level*). **3** *intr.* use a rake. **4** *tr.* & *intr.* search with or as with a rake, search thoroughly, ransack. **5** *tr.* **a** direct gunfire along (a line) from end to end. **b** sweep with the eyes. **c** (of a window etc.) have a commanding view of. **6** *tr.* scratch or scrape. □ **rake in** *colloq.* amass (profits etc.). **rake it in** *colloq.* make much money. **rake-off** *colloq.* a commission or share, esp. in a disreputable deal. **rake up** (or **over**) revive the memory of (past quarrels, grievances, etc.). □□ **raker** *n.* [OE *raca, racu* f. Gmc, partly f. ON *raka* scrape, rake]

■ *v.* **1** (*rake together*) gather, collect, draw *or* drag together; (*rake out*) sift (out), remove, take out, clear (out), clean; (*rake up*) scrape up, pick up, dig up, dredge up, find, unearth. **2** see SMOOTH *v.* 1. **4** (*rake through*) search, probe, ransack, scour, comb, rummage through, pick through *or* over, go through, rifle (through). **6** scrape, scratch, grate, graze, rasp. □ **rake in** amass, collect, gather (up *or* in), pull in, accumulate. **rake it in** coin money, make money (hand-over-fist), become wealthy. **rake-off** commission, share, *colloq.* cut, kickback, *US sl.* piece. **rake up** revive, resuscitate, resurrect, raise, bring up, recall, go over; dredge up, unearth, dig up.

rake[2] /rayk/ *n.* a dissolute man of fashion. □ **rake's progress** a progressive deterioration, esp. through self-indulgence (the title of a series of engravings by Hogarth 1735). [short for archaic *rakehell* in the same sense]
▪ debauchee, voluptuary, roué, libertine, profligate, prodigal, Lothario, womanizer, lecher, playboy, ladies' man, lady-killer, Don Juan, Casanova, *sl.* wolf; young blood, fop, man about town; see also DANDY *n.*

rake[3] /rayk/ *v.* & *n.* ● *v.* **1** *tr.* & *intr.* set or be set at a sloping angle. **2** *intr.* **a** (of a mast or funnel) incline from the perpendicular towards the stern. **b** (of a ship or its bow or stern) project at the upper part of the bow or stern beyond the keel. ● *n.* **1** a raking position or build. **2** the amount by which a thing rakes. **3** the slope of the stage or the auditorium in a theatre. **4** the slope of a seat-back etc. **5** the angle of the edge or face of a cutting tool. [17th c.: prob. rel. to G *ragen* project, of unkn. orig.]

raki /rəkeé, rákki/ *n.* (*pl.* **rakis**) any of various spirits made in E. Europe and the Middle East. [Turk. *raqi*]

rakish[1] /ráykish/ *adj.* of or like a rake (see RAKE[2]); dashing; jaunty. □□ **rakishly** *adv.* **rakishness** *n.*
▪ dashing, jaunty, dapper, spruce, debonair, raffish, smart, flashy, chic, fashionable, elegant, dandyish, foppish, *colloq.* sharp.

rakish[2] /ráykish/ *adj.* (of a ship) smart and fast-looking, seemingly built for speed and therefore open to suspicion of piracy. [RAKE[3], assoc. with RAKE[2]]

raku /raákoo/ *n.* a kind of Japanese earthenware, usu. lead-glazed. [Jap., lit. enjoyment]

rale /raal/ *n.* an abnormal rattling sound heard in the auscultation of unhealthy lungs. [F f. *râler* to rattle]

rall. /ral/ *adv.* & *adj.* & *n.* = RALLENTANDO. [abbr.]

rallentando /rállәntándō/ *adv.*, *adj.*, & *n.* *Mus.* ● *adv.* & *adj.* with a gradual decrease of speed. ● *n.* (*pl.* **-os** or **rallentandi** /-di/) a passage to be performed in this way. [It.]

ralli car /rálli/ *n.* (also **ralli cart**) *hist.* a light two-wheeled horse-drawn vehicle for four persons. [*Ralli*, name of the first purchaser 1885]

ralline /rállīn/ *adj.* of the bird-family Rallidae (see RAIL[3]). [mod.L *rallus* RAIL[3]]

rally[1] /rálli/ *v.* & *n.* ● *v.* (**-ies, -ied**) **1** *tr.* & *intr.* (often foll. by *round, behind, to*) bring or come together as support or for concentrated action. **2** *tr.* & *intr.* bring or come together again after a rout or dispersion. **3 a** *intr.* renew a conflict. **b** *tr.* cause to do this. **4 a** *tr.* revive (courage etc.) by an effort of will. **b** *tr.* rouse (a person or animal) to fresh energy. **c** *intr.* pull oneself together. **5** *intr.* recover after illness or prostration or fear, regain health or consciousness, revive. **6** *intr.* (of share-prices etc.) increase after a fall. ● *n.* (*pl.* **-ies**) **1** an act of reassembling forces or renewing conflict; a reunion for fresh effort. **2** a recovery of energy after or in the middle of exhaustion or illness. **3** a mass meeting of supporters or persons having a common interest. **4** a competition for motor vehicles, usu. over public roads. **5** (in lawn tennis etc.) an extended exchange of strokes between players. □ **rally-cross** motor racing over roads and cross-country. □□ **rallier** *n.* [F *rallier* (as RE-, ALLY[1])]
▪ *v.* **1, 2** (*rally round*) bring *or* call together, round up, marshal, mobilize, summon, gather, muster; get together, assemble, convene, group, congregate, come together; regroup, reform. **4 a** mobilize, summon, muster, marshal; revive. **b** see ROUSE 2a. **5** revive, recover, improve, get better, take a turn for the better, recuperate, perk up, pick up, make a comeback, come to. ● *n.* **1** see GATHERING. **2** recovery, improvement, revival, turn for the better, recuperation. **3** gathering, (mass) meeting, convocation, convention, assemblage, assembly.

rally[2] /rálli/ *v.tr.* (**-ies, -ied**) subject to good-humoured ridicule. [F *railler*: see RAIL[2]]

RAM *abbr.* **1** (in the UK) Royal Academy of Music. **2** *Computing* random-access memory.

ram /ram/ *n.* & *v.* ● *n.* **1** an uncastrated male sheep, a tup. **2** (**the Ram**) the zodiacal sign or constellation Aries. **3** *hist.* **a** = *battering ram* (see BATTER[1]). **b** a beak projecting from the bow of a battleship, for piercing the sides of other ships. **c** a battleship with such a beak. **4** the falling weight of a pile-driving machine. **5 a** a hydraulic water-raising or lifting machine. **b** the piston of a hydrostatic press. **c** the plunger of a force-pump. **6** *Austral. sl.* an accomplice in petty crime. ● *v.tr.* (**rammed, ramming**) **1** force or squeeze into place by pressure. **2** (usu. foll. by *down, in, into*) beat down or drive in by heavy blows. **3** (of a ship, vehicle, etc.) strike violently, crash against. **4** (foll. by *against, at, on, into*) dash or violently impel. □ **ram home** stress forcefully (an argument, lesson, etc.). **ram-raid** a form of robbery in which the front of a shop is rammed using a large vehicle, and the occupants of the vehicle then loot the shop and escape in the vehicle. □□ **rammer** *n.* [OE *ram(m)*, perh. rel. to ON *rammr* strong]
▪ *n.* **6** see ACCOMPLICE. ● *v.* **1** jam, force, drive, cram, crowd, pack, compress, stuff, squeeze, thrust. **2** pound, hammer, beat, tamp, bash, bang. **3** butt, bump, strike, hit, collide with, dash against, crash into, slam into.
□ **ram home** see STRESS *v.* 1.

Ramadan /rámmədan/ *n.* (also **Ramadhan**) the ninth month of the Muslim year, during which strict fasting is observed from sunrise to sunset. [Arab. *ramaḍān* f. *ramaḍa* be hot; reason for name uncert.]

ramal /ráym'l/ *adj.* *Bot.* of or proceeding from a branch. [L *ramus* branch]

Raman effect /raámən/ *n.* the change of frequency in the scattering of radiation in a medium, used in spectroscopic analysis. [Sir C. V. *Raman*, Ind. physicist d. 1970]

ramble /rámb'l/ *v.* & *n.* ● *v.intr.* **1** walk for pleasure, with or without a definite route. **2** wander in discourse, talk or write disconnectedly. ● *n.* a walk taken for pleasure. [prob. f. MDu. *rammelen* (of an animal) wander about in sexual excitement, frequent. of *rammen* copulate with, rel. to RAM]
▪ *v.* **1** amble, meander, wander, stroll, saunter, walk, perambulate, range, rove, hike, trek, *sl.* mosey. **2** wander, digress, maunder, get off the point, lose the thread; (*ramble on*) babble, chatter, gibber, rattle on, *colloq.* go on (and on), witter on. ● *n.* stroll, amble, saunter, walk, promenade, constitutional, turn, tour, hike, trek.

rambler /rámblər/ *n.* **1** a person who rambles. **2** a straggling or climbing rose (*crimson rambler*).
▪ **1** walker, hiker, backpacker.

rambling /rámbling/ *adj.* **1** peripatetic, wandering. **2** disconnected, desultory, incoherent. **3** (of a house, street, etc.) irregularly arranged. **4** (of a plant) straggling, climbing. □□ **ramblingly** *adv.*
▪ **1** roving, wandering, travelling, peripatetic, itinerant, wayfaring, migratory, nomadic. **2** discursive, roundabout, circuitous, tortuous, incoherent, diffuse, disconnected, disjointed, disorganized, unorganized, desultory, illogical, maundering, aimless, confused, muddled, jumbled, unintelligible, inarticulate, periphrastic, circumlocutory, circumlocutional, circumlocutionary, wordy, verbose, prolix. **3** straggling, irregular, sprawling, spread out, straggly.

rambunctious /rambúngkshəs/ *adj.* *US colloq.* **1** uncontrollably exuberant. **2** unruly. □□ **rambunctiously** *adv.* **rambunctiousness** *n.* [19th c.: orig. unkn.]
▪ see BOISTEROUS 1.

rambutan /rambóot'n/ *n.* **1** a red plum-sized prickly fruit. **2** an East Indian tree, *Nephelium lappaceum*, that bears this. [Malay *rambūtan* f. *rambut* hair, in allusion to its spines]

RAMC *abbr.* (in the UK) Royal Army Medical Corps.

ramekin /rámmikin/ *n.* **1** (in full **ramekin case** or **dish**) a small dish for baking and serving an individual portion of food. **2** food served in such a dish, esp. a small quantity of cheese baked with breadcrumbs, eggs, etc. [F *ramequin*, of LG or Du. orig.]

ramie /rámmi/ *n.* **1** any of various tall East Asian plants of the genus *Boehmeria*, esp. *B. nivea*. **2** a strong fibre obtained from this, woven into cloth. [Malay *rāmī*]

ramification /rámmifikáysh'n/ *n.* **1** the act or an instance of ramifying; the state of being ramified. **2** a subdivision of a complex structure or process comparable to a tree's branches. **3** a consequence, esp. when complex or unwelcome. [F f. *ramifier*: see RAMIFY]

■ **2** branch, extension, outgrowth, subdivision, offshoot. **3** consequence, result, effect, upshot, implication.

ramify /rámmifī/ *v.* (**-ies, -ied**) **1** *intr.* form branches or subdivisions or offshoots, branch out. **2** *tr.* (usu. in *passive*) cause to branch out; arrange in a branching manner. [F *ramifier* f. med.L *ramificare* f. L *ramus* branch]

■ **1** see BRANCH *v.* 2.

ramin /raméen/ *n.* **1** any Malaysian tree of the genus *Gonystylus*, esp. *G. bancanus*. **2** the light-coloured hardwood obtained from this tree. [Malay]

ramjet /rámjet/ *n.* a type of jet engine in which air is drawn in and compressed by the forward motion of the engine.

rammer see RAM.

rammies /rámmiz/ *n.pl. Austral.* & *S.Afr. sl.* trousers. [orig. uncert.]

rammy /rámmi/ *n.* (*pl.* **-ies**) *Sc. sl.* a brawl, a fight (esp. between gangs); a quarrel. [perh. f. Sc. *rammle* row, uproar, var. of RAMBLE]

ramose /rámmōss, ráy-/ *adj.* branched; branching. [L *ramosus* f. *ramus* branch]

ramp[1] /ramp/ *n.* & *v.* ● *n.* **1** a slope or inclined plane, esp. for joining two levels of ground, floor, etc. **2** movable stairs for entering or leaving an aircraft. **3** an upward bend in a stair-rail. **4** *Brit.* a transverse ridge in a road to control the speed of vehicles. ● *v.* **1** *tr.* furnish or build with a ramp. **2** *intr.* **a** assume or be in a threatening posture. **b** (often foll. by *about*) storm, rage, rush. **c** *Heraldry* be rampant. **3** *intr. Archit.* (of a wall) ascend or descend to a different level. [ME (as verb in heraldic sense) f. F *rampe* f. OF *ramper* creep, crawl]

■ *n.* **1** slope, grade, gradient, incline; rise, acclivity; dip, declivity. ● *v.* **2 b** see STORM *v.* 2.

ramp[2] /ramp/ *n.* & *v. Brit. sl.* ● *n.* a swindle or racket, esp. one conducted by the levying of exorbitant prices. ● *v.* **1** *intr.* engage in a ramp. **2** *tr.* subject (a person etc.) to a ramp. [16th c.: orig. unkn.]

rampage /rampáyj/ *v.* & *n.* ● *v.intr.* **1** (often foll. by *about*) rush wildly or violently about. **2** rage, storm. ● *n.* /often rámpayj/ wild or violent behaviour. □ **on the rampage** rampaging. □□ **rampageous** *adj.* **rampager** *n.* [18th c., perh. f. RAMP[1]]

■ *v.* **1** career, charge, storm, ramp (about); see also TEAR[1] *v.* 5. **2** storm, rant, rave, run amok, ramp (about); see also RAGE *v.* ● *n.* recklessness, riotness, frenzy, fury, rage, furore, outburst. □ **on the rampage** (*go on the rampage*) go berserk, run amok, run wild, go out of control, *sl.* flip one's lid.

rampant /rámp'nt/ *adj.* **1** (placed after noun) *Heraldry* (of an animal) standing on its left hind foot with its forepaws in the air (*lion rampant*). **2** unchecked, flourishing excessively (*rampant violence*). **3** violent or extravagant in action or opinion (*rampant theorists*). **4** rank, luxuriant. □□ **rampancy** *n.* **rampantly** *adv.* [ME f. OF, part. of *ramper*: see RAMP[1]]

■ **2** unchecked, unrestrained, uncontrolled, unbridled, uncontrollable, unbounded, abounding, flourishing, rife, widespread, pandemic, prevalent; indiscriminate. **3** violent, wild, frenzied; see also FURIOUS 3. **4** rank, luxuriant; see also PROFUSE 2.

rampart /rámpaart/ *n.* & *v.* ● *n.* **1 a** a defensive wall with a broad top and usu. a stone parapet. **b** a walkway on top of such a wall. **2** a defence or protection. ● *v.tr.* fortify or protect with or as with a rampart. [F *rempart*, *rempar* f. *remparer* fortify f. *emparer* take possession of, ult. f. L *ante* before + *parare* prepare]

■ *n.* **1 a** defence, fortification, bulwark, barricade, wall; earthwork, parados. **2** defence, protection, shelter, cover, guard, shield, barrier, buffer.

rampion /rámpiən/ *n.* **1** a bellflower, *Campanula rapunculus*, with white tuberous roots used as a salad. **2** any of various plants of the genus *Phyteuma*, with clusters of hornlike buds and flowers. [ult. f. med.L *rapuncium*, *rapontium*, prob. f. L *rapum* RAPE[2]]

ramrod /rámrod/ *n.* **1** a rod for ramming down the charge of a muzzle-loading firearm. **2** a thing that is very straight or rigid.

ramshackle /rámshakk'l/ *adj.* (usu. of a house or vehicle) tumbledown, rickety. [earlier *ramshackled* past part. of obs. *ransackle* RANSACK]

■ dilapidated, tumbledown, crumbling, broken-down, rickety, jerry-built, decrepit, flimsy, shaky, unstable, tottering, insubstantial, ruined, run-down, neglected, derelict.

ramsons /rámz'nz/ *n.* (usu. treated as *sing.*) **1** a broad-leaved garlic, *Allium ursinum*, with elongate pungent-smelling bulbous roots. **2** the root of this, eaten as a relish. [OE *hramsan* pl. of *hramsa* wild garlic, later taken as sing.]

RAN *abbr.* Royal Australian Navy.

ran *past* of RUN.

ranch /raanch/ *n.* & *v.* ● *n.* **1 a** a cattle-breeding establishment esp. in the US and Canada. **b** a farm where other animals are bred (*mink ranch*). **2** *US* a single-storey or split-level house. ● *v.intr.* farm on a ranch. [Sp. *rancho* group of persons eating together]

■ **1** see SPREAD *n.* 12.

rancher /raánchər/ *n.* **1** a person who farms on a ranch. **2** *US* a modern single-storey house.

ranchero /raancháirō/ *n.* (*pl.* **-os**) a person who farms or works on a ranch, esp. in Mexico. [Sp. (as RANCH)]

rancid /ránsid/ *adj.* smelling or tasting like rank stale fat. □□ **rancidity** /-sídditi/ *n.* **rancidness** *n.* [L *rancidus* stinking]

■ stinking, foul-smelling, fetid, ill-smelling, evil-smelling, mephitic, smelly, rank, malodorous, fusty, *archaic* miasmal, miasmatic, miasmic, *literary* noisome; rotten, decayed, bad, high, gamy, putrid, off, stale.

rancour /rángkər/ *n.* (*US* **rancor**) inveterate bitterness, malignant hate, spitefulness. □□ **rancorous** *adj.* **rancorously** *adv.* [ME f. OF f. LL *rancor -oris* (as RANCID)]

■ hatred, antipathy, spitefulness, resentment, resentfulness, antagonism, hostility, malignity, bitterness, malevolence, venomousness, vindictiveness, vengefulness, acrimony, animus, ill feeling, animosity, enmity, bad feeling, hate, spite, malice, venom, spleen. □□ **rancorous** hateful, spiteful, resentful, hostile, bitter, malevolent, malicious, venomous, vindictive, vengeful, splenetic, acrimonious.

rand[1] /rand, raant/ *n.* **1** the chief monetary unit of South Africa and some neighbouring countries. **2** *S.Afr.* a ridge of high ground on either side of a river. [Afrik., = edge, rel. to RAND[2]: sense 1 f. *the Rand*, gold-field district near Johannesburg]

rand[2] /rand/ *n.* a levelling-strip of leather between the heel and sides of a shoe or boot. [OE f. Gmc]

R & B *abbr.* (also **R. & B.**) rhythm and blues.

R & D *abbr.* (also **R. & D.**) research and development.

random /rándəm/ *adj.* **1** made, done, etc., without method or conscious choice (*random selection*). **2** *Statistics* **a** with equal chances for each item. **b** given by a random process. **3** (of masonry) with stones of irregular size and shape. □ **at random** without aim or purpose or principle. **random-access** *Computing* (of a memory or file) having all parts directly accessible, so that it need not be read sequentially. **random error** *Statistics* an error in measurement caused by factors which vary from one measurement to another.

□□ **randomize** *v.tr.* (also **-ise**). **randomization** /-mīzáysh'n/ *n.* **randomly** *adv.* **randomness** *n.* [ME f. OF *randon* great speed f. *randir* gallop]

■ **1** haphazard, chance, fortuitous, aleatory, aleatoric, arbitrary, casual, indiscriminate, non-specific, unspecific, unspecified, unordered, unorganized, undirected, unpremeditated, unplanned, accidental, uncalculated, unsystematic, adventitious, incidental, hit-or-miss. □ **at random** randomly, haphazardly, by chance, arbitrarily, casually, erratically, indiscriminately, unsystematically, adventitiously, unpremeditatedly.

R and R *abbr.* (also **R. and R.**) **1** rescue and resuscitation. **2** rest and recreation. **3** rock and roll.

■ **2** see LEISURE 2.

randy /rándi/ *adj.* (**randier**, **randiest**) **1** lustful; eager for sexual gratification. **2** *Sc.* loud-tongued, boisterous, lusty. □□ **randily** *adv.* **randiness** *n.* [perh. f. obs. *rand* f. obs. Du. *randen*, *ranten* RANT]

■ **1** aroused, lustful, lecherous, sexy, libidinous, hot, *formal* concupiscent, *sl.* horny. **2** see BOISTEROUS 1.

ranee /raáni/ *n.* (also **rani**) *hist.* a raja's wife or widow; a Hindu queen. [Hindi *rānī* = Skr. *rājnī* fem. of *rājan* king]

rang *past* of RING².

rangatira /ránggətéérə/ *n.* *NZ* a Maori chief or noble. [Maori]

range /raynj/ *n.* & *v.* ● *n.* **1 a** the region between limits of variation, esp. as representing a scope of effective operation (*a voice of astonishing range*; *the whole range of politics*). **b** such limits. **c** a limited scale or series (*the range of the thermometer readings is about 10 degrees*). **d** a series representing variety or choice; a selection. **2** the area included in or concerned with something. **3 a** the distance attainable by a gun or projectile (*the enemy are out of range*). **b** the distance between a gun or projectile and its objective. **4** a row, series, line, or tier, esp. of mountains or buildings. **5 a** an open or enclosed area with targets for shooting. **b** a testing-ground for military equipment. **6 a** a fireplace with ovens and hotplates for cooking. **b** *US* an electric or gas cooker. **7** the area over which a thing, esp. a plant or animal, is distributed (*gives the ranges of all species*). **8** the distance that can be covered by a vehicle or aircraft without refuelling. **9** the distance between a camera and the subject to be photographed. **10** the extent of time covered by a forecast etc. **11 a** a large area of open land for grazing or hunting. **b** a tract over which one wanders. **12** lie, direction (*the range of the strata is east and west*). ● *v.* **1** *intr.* **a** reach; lie spread out; extend; be found or occur over a specified district; vary between limits (*ages ranging from twenty to sixty*). **b** run in a line (*ranges north and south*). **2** *tr.* (usu. in *passive* or *refl.*) place or arrange in a row or ranks or in a specified situation or order or company (*ranged their troops*; *ranged themselves with the majority party*; *trees ranged in ascending order of height*). **3** *intr.* rove, wander (*ranged through the woods*; *his thoughts range over past, present, and future*). **4** *tr.* traverse in all directions (*ranging the woods*). **5** *Printing* **a** *tr. Brit.* make (type) lie flush at the ends of successive lines. **b** *intr.* (of type) lie flush. **6** *intr.* **a** (often foll. by *with*) be level. **b** (foll. by *with*, *among*) rank; find one's right place (*ranges with the great writers*). **7** *intr.* **a** (of a gun) send a projectile over a specified distance (*ranges over a mile*). **b** (of a projectile) cover a specified distance. **c** obtain the range of a target by adjustment after firing past it or short of it. □ **ranging-pole** (or **-rod**) *Surveying* a pole or rod for setting a straight line. [ME f. OF *range* row, rank f. *ranger* f. *rang* RANK¹]

■ *n.* **1 a–c** scope, sweep, reach, limit, round, extent, span, area, radius, distance, compass, latitude, stretch, sphere, orbit. **d** assortment, series, collection, lot, spread, selection, choice, number, variety, kind, sort, scale, gamut, register. **2** see AREA 4. **4** row, tier, rank, line, file, series, string, chain. **6 b** stove, cooking-stove, *Brit.* cooker, *propr.* Aga. **7** distribution, dispersal, spread. ● *v.* **1 a** vary, fluctuate; run the gamut, extend, reach, stretch, run, go. **2** line up, rank, order, align, array, arrange; organize, categorize, catalogue, classify, sort, class, group, bracket, file, index, grade. **3** roam, rove; see also WANDER *v.* 1. **4** cover, traverse, travel over *or* across, go *or* pass over; extend over. **6 b** see RANK¹ *v.* 1.

rangé /rONzháy/ *adj.* (*fem.* **rangée**) domesticated, orderly, settled. [F]

rangefinder /ráynjfīndər/ *n.* an instrument for estimating the distance of an object, esp. one to be shot at or photographed.

ranger /ráynjər/ *n.* **1** a keeper of a royal or national park, or of a forest. **2** a member of a body of armed men, esp.: **a** a mounted soldier. **b** *US* a commando. **3** (**Ranger**) *Brit.* a senior Guide. **4** a wanderer. □□ **rangership** *n.*

rangy /ráynji/ *adj.* (**rangier**, **rangiest**) **1** (of a person) tall and slim. **2** *Austral.* hilly, mountainous.

■ **1** see LANKY.

rani var. of RANEE.

rank¹ /rangk/ *n.* & *v.* ● *n.* **1 a** a position in a hierarchy, a grade of advancement. **b** a distinct social class, a grade of dignity or achievement (*people of all ranks*; *in the top rank of performers*). **c** high social position (*persons of rank*). **d** a place in a scale. **2** a row or line. **3** a single line of soldiers drawn up abreast. **4** *Brit.* a place where taxis stand to await customers. **5** order, array. **6** *Chess* a row of squares across the board (cf. FILE²). ● *v.* **1** *intr.* have rank or place (*ranks next to the king*). **2** *tr.* classify, give a certain grade to. **3** *tr.* arrange (esp. soldiers) in a rank or ranks. **4** *US* **a** *tr.* take precedence of (a person) in respect to rank. **b** *intr.* have the senior position among the members of a hierarchy etc. □ **break rank** fail to remain in line. **close ranks** maintain solidarity. **keep rank** remain in line. **other ranks** soldiers other than commissioned officers. **rank and fashion** high society. **rank and file** ordinary undistinguished people (orig. = *the ranks*). **the ranks** the common soldiers, i.e. privates and corporals. **rise from the ranks 1** (of a private or a non-commissioned officer) receive a commission. **2** (of a self-made man or woman) advance by one's own exertions. [OF *ranc*, *renc*, f. Gmc, rel. to RING¹]

■ *n.* **1 a** position, place, level, echelon, grade. **b** class, social class, caste; status, standing; situation, circumstances, position, grade, level. **c** nobility, title, high birth, aristocracy, dignity, prestige, prominence, (blue) blood; weight, authority, power, superiority, seniority, influence, eminence. **2** line, row, string, file, column, tier. ● *v.* **1** have (one's) place, rate, count, stand, have standing *or* value. **2** grade, rate, classify, class, categorize. **3** arrange, array, align, range, organize, order, dispose, sort. □ **rank and fashion** see SOCIETY 5a. **rank and file** see PEOPLE *n.* 2. **rise from the ranks** pull oneself up by one's bootstraps.

rank² /rangk/ *adj.* **1** too luxuriant; choked with or apt to produce weeds or excessive foliage. **2 a** foul-smelling, offensive. **b** loathsome, indecent, corrupt. **3** flagrant, virulent, gross, complete, unmistakable, strongly marked (*rank outsider*). □□ **rankly** *adv.* **rankness** *n.* [OE *ranc* f. Gmc]

■ **1** lush, luxuriant, abundant, flourishing, profuse, prolific, dense, superabundant, exuberant, fertile. **2 a** offensive, loathsome, disgusting, vile, horrible, gross, foul, foul-smelling, smelly, rancid, stinking, reeky, reeking, mephitic, fetid, noxious, rotten, putrid, musty, stale, *archaic* miasmic, miasmal, miasmatic, *literary* noisome. **b** corrupt, foul, low, base, gross; offensive, loathsome, disgusting, indecent, shocking, lurid, outrageous. **3** gross, downright, utter, complete, sheer, absolute, out-and-out, blatant, flagrant, virulent; unmistakable.

ranker /rángkər/ *n.* **1** a soldier in the ranks. **2** a commissioned officer who has been in the ranks.

ranking /rángking/ *n.* & *adj.* ● *n.* ordering by rank; classification. ● *adj.* *US* having a high rank or position.

■ *n.* rating; see also SCALE³ *n.* 1. ● *adj.* see CHIEF *adj.* 1.

rankle /rángk'l/ *v.intr.* **1** (of envy, disappointment, etc., or their cause) cause persistent annoyance or resentment. **2** *archaic* (of a wound, sore, etc.) fester, continue to be painful.

[ME (in sense 2) f. OF *rancler* f. *rancle*, *draoncle* festering sore f. med.L *dranculus*, *dracunculus* dimin. of *draco* serpent]
■ **1** grate, hurt, chafe, smoulder, fester; (*rankle with*) irk, vex, plague, nettle, torment, pain, anger, exasperate, get (to), upset. **2** fester, suppurate; see also SMART *v.*

ransack /ránsak/ *v.tr.* **1** pillage or plunder (a house, country, etc.). **2** thoroughly search (a place, a receptacle, a person's pockets, one's conscience, etc.). □□ **ransacker** *n.* [ME f. ON *rannsaka* f. *rann* house + *-saka* f. *sœkja* seek]
■ **1** rob, plunder, pillage, sack, loot, strip, ravage, maraud, lay waste, *archaic or literary* spoil, *literary* despoil. **2** search, examine, go through *or* over, comb, rake *or* rummage *or* rifle through, scour, scrutinize, turn inside out.

ransom /ránsəm/ *n.* & *v.* ● *n.* **1** a sum of money or other payment demanded or paid for the release of a prisoner. **2** the liberation of a prisoner in return for this. ● *v.tr.* **1** buy the freedom or restoration of; redeem. **2** hold to ransom. **3** release for a ransom. □□ **ransomer** *n.* (in sense 1 of *v.*). [ME f. OF *ransoun(er)* f. L *redemptio -onis* REDEMPTION]
■ *n.* **1** payment, payout, *sl.* pay-off. **2** release, liberation, freedom; rescue, deliverance. ● *v.* **1, 3** redeem, rescue, release, deliver, free, liberate. **2** hold hostage; see also KIDNAP.

rant /rant/ *v.* & *n.* ● *v.* **1** *intr.* use bombastic language. **2** *tr.* & *intr.* declaim, recite theatrically. **3** *tr.* & *intr.* preach noisily. **4** *intr.* (often foll. by *about*, *on*) speak vehemently or intemperately. ● *n.* **1** a piece of ranting, a tirade. **2** empty turgid talk. □□ **ranter** *n.* **rantingly** *adv.* [Du. *ranten* rave]
■ *v.* **2, 3** declaim, hold forth, expound, expatiate, perorate, pontificate, trumpet, preach, lecture, deliver a tirade *or* diatribe. **4** vociferate, bluster, rave, rant and rave, bellow, rage. ● *n.* **1** tirade, philippic, verbal attack, diatribe, harangue, declamation, onslaught, screed, stream of abuse. **2** bluster, flatulence, rhetoric, bombast, pomposity, turgidity, theatrics.

ranunculaceous /rənúngkyooláyshəss/ *adj.* of or relating to the family Ranunculaceae of flowering plants, including clematis and delphiniums.

ranunculus /rənúngkyooləss/ *n.* (*pl.* **ranunculuses** or **ranunculi** /-lī/) any plant of the genus *Ranunculus*, usu. having bowl-shaped flowers with many stamens and carpels, including buttercups and crowfoots. [L, orig. dimin. of *rana* frog]

RAOC *abbr.* (in the UK) Royal Army Ordnance Corps.

rap[1] /rap/ *n.* & *v.* ● *n.* **1** a smart slight blow. **2** a knock, a sharp tapping sound. **3** *sl.* blame, censure, or punishment. **4** *sl.* a conversation. **5 a** a rhyming monologue recited rhythmically to prerecorded music. **b** (in full **rap music**) a style of pop music with a pronounced beat and words recited rather than sung. ● *v.* (**rapped**, **rapping**) **1** *tr.* strike smartly. **2** *intr.* knock; make a sharp tapping sound (*rapped on the table*). **3** *tr.* criticize adversely. **4** *intr. sl.* talk. □ **beat the rap** *US* escape punishment. **rap on** (or **over**) **the knuckles** ● *n.* a reprimand or reproof. ● *v.* reprimand, reprove. **rap out 1** utter (an oath, order, pun, etc.) abruptly or on the spur of the moment. **2** *Spiritualism* express (a message or word) by raps. **take the rap** suffer the consequences. □□ **rapper** *n.* [ME, prob. imit.]
■ *n.* **1** hit, blow, crack, stroke, cuff, punch, thump, clout, *US* slug, *colloq.* whack, thwack, sock, *sl.* belt, biff. **2** see TAP[2] *n.* **3** censure; responsibility; punishment, sentence; see also BLAME *n.* 2. **4** conversation, discussion, chat, confabulation, talk, dialogue, colloquy, *US* bull session, *colloq.* confab, *literary* discourse, *sl.* chin-wag. ● *v.* **1** see STRIKE *v.* 1. **2** knock, tap, hammer. **3** criticize, scold, reprimand, rap over the knuckles, *colloq.* tick off, *Brit. colloq.* slate, *sl.* knock; see also REBUKE *v.* **4** converse, talk, chat, gossip, *colloq.* gab, *sl.* chew the fat *or* rag. □ **beat the rap** get off, *US sl.* walk. **rap on** (or **over**) **the knuckles** (*n.*) see REPRIMAND *n.* (*v.*) see RAP[1] *v.* 3 above. **take the rap** suffer the consequences, accept responsibility, take what is coming to one.

rap[2] /rap/ *n.* a small amount, the least bit (*don't care a rap*). [Ir. *ropaire* Irish counterfeit coin]

rapacious /rəpáyshəss/ *adj.* grasping, extortionate, predatory. □□ **rapaciously** *adv.* **rapaciousness** *n.* **rapacity** /rəpássiti/ *n.* [L *rapax -acis* f. *rapere* snatch]
■ greedy, covetous, grasping, avaricious, acquisitive, predatory, predacious, ravenous, wolfish, wolflike, lupine, vulturine, extortionate. □□ **rapacity** predaciousness, rapaciousness; greed, greediness, cupidity, avarice, covetousness, acquisitiveness.

RAPC *abbr.* (in the UK) Royal Army Pay Corps.

rape[1] /rayp/ *n.* & *v.* ● *n.* **1 a** the act of forcing a woman to have sexual intercourse against her will. **b** forcible sodomy. **2** (often foll. by *of*) violent assault, forcible interference, violation. **3** *poet.* carrying off (esp. of a woman) by force. **4** an instance of rape. ● *v.tr.* **1** commit rape on (a person, usu. a woman). **2** violate, assault, pillage. **3** *poet.* take by force. [ME f. AF *rap(er)* f. L *rapere* seize]
■ *n.* **1** ravishment, violation, sexual assault. **2** violation, pillage, depredation, ravagement, ravaging, plundering, sack, sacking, looting, ransacking, defloration, deflowering, defilement, *literary* despoliation, despoilment. **3** abduction, kidnapping, seizure, capture. ● *v.* **1** violate, ravish, sexually assault. **2** violate, assault, pillage, deflower, defile, ravage, plunder, sack, loot, *literary* despoil. **3** see ABDUCT.

rape[2] /rayp/ *n.* a plant, *Brassica napus*, grown as food for livestock and for its seed, from which oil is made. Also called COLZA, COLE. □ **rape-cake** rape-seed pressed into a flat shape after the extraction of oil and used as manure or food for livestock. **rape-oil** an oil made from rape-seed and used as a lubricant and in foodstuffs. [ME f. L *rapum*, *rapa* turnip]

rape[3] /rayp/ *n. hist.* (in the UK) any of the six ancient divisions of Sussex. [OE, var. of *rāp* ROPE, with ref. to the fencing-off of land]

rape[4] /rayp/ *n.* **1** the refuse of grapes after wine-making, used in making vinegar. **2** a vessel used in vinegar-making. [F *râpe*, med.L *raspa*]

raphia var. of RAFFIA.

raphide /ráyfīd/ *n.* a needle-shaped crystal of an irritant substance such as oxalic acid formed in a plant. [back-form. f. *raphides* pl. of *raphis* f. Gk *rhaphis -idos* needle]

rapid /ráppid/ *adj.* & *n.* ● *adj.* (**rapider**, **rapidest**) **1** quick, swift. **2** acting or completed in a short time. **3** (of a slope) descending steeply. **4** *Photog.* fast. ● *n.* (usu. in *pl.*) a steep descent in a river-bed, with a swift current. □ **rapid eye-movement** a type of jerky movement of the eyes during periods of dreaming. **rapid-fire** (*attrib.*) fired, asked, etc., in quick succession. **rapid transit** (*attrib.*) denoting high-speed urban transport of passengers. □□ **rapidity** /rəpídditi/ *n.* **rapidly** *adv.* **rapidness** *n.* [L *rapidus* f. *rapere* seize]
■ *adj.* **1, 2** quick, fast, swift, speedy, high-speed, brisk, expeditious, prompt, express, lightning, *literary* volant, *poet. or literary* fleet; hurried, hasty, precipitate, instantaneous, instant, sudden. □□ **rapidity** quickness, swiftness, speed, speediness, briskness, expeditiousness, promptness, promptitude, alacrity, dispatch; suddeness, hastiness, *archaic or literary* celerity. **rapidly** quickly, quick, fast, swiftly, speedily, briskly, expeditiously, like a shot, at the speed of light, at full speed, in a flash *or* twinkle, double-quick, like a bat out of hell, at a gallop, *colloq.* like (greased) lightning, like mad *or* crazy, lickety-split, before you can say Jack Robinson, in two shakes of a lamb's tail, *joc.* in (less than) no time, *sl.* like blazes; promptly, without delay, at once, straight away, right away, *archaic or joc.* instanter.

rapier /ráypiər/ *n.* a light slender sword used for thrusting. [prob. f. Du. *rapier* or LG *rappir*, f. F *rapière*, of unkn. orig.]

rapine /ráppīn, -pin/ *n. rhet.* plundering, robbery. [ME f. OF or f. L *rapina* f. *rapere* seize]

■ see PILLAGE *n.*1.

rapist /ráypist/ *n.* a person who commits rape.

rapparee /ráppəreé/ *n. hist.* a 17th-c. Irish irregular soldier or freebooter. [Ir. *rapaire* short pike]

rappee /rapeé/ *n.* a coarse kind of snuff. [F (*tabac*) *râpé* rasped (tobacco)]

rappel /rapél/ *n.* & *v.intr.* (**rappelled, rappelling;** *US* **rappeled, rappeling**) = ABSEIL. [F, = recall, f. *rappeler* (as RE-, APPEAL)]

rapport /rapór/ *n.* **1** relationship or communication, esp. when useful and harmonious (*in rapport with; establish a rapport*). **2** *Spiritualism* communication through a medium. [F f. *rapporter* (as RE-, AP-, *porter* f. L *portare* carry)]

■ **1** empathy, relationship, affinity, accord, bond, (mutual) understanding.

rapporteur /rápportőr/ *n.* a person who prepares an account of the proceedings of a committee etc. for a higher body. [F (as RAPPORT)]

rapprochement /rapróshmon/ *n.* the resumption of harmonious relations, esp. between States. [F f. *rapprocher* (as RE-, APPROACH)]

■ understanding, settlement; *détente*; see also *reconciliation* (RECONCILE).

rapscallion /rapskályən/ *n. archaic* or *joc.* a rascal, scamp, or rogue. [earlier *rascallion*, perh. f. RASCAL]

■ see RASCAL.

rapt /rapt/ *adj.* **1** fully absorbed or intent, enraptured (*listen with rapt attention*). **2** carried away with joyous feeling or lofty thought. **3** carried away bodily. □□ **raptly** *adv.* **raptness** *n.* [ME f. L *raptus* past part. of *rapere* seize]

■ **1** enraptured, entranced, fascinated, spellbound, engrossed, enthralled, bewitched, absorbed, transported, captivated. **2** elated, happy, blissful, overjoyed, rapturous, joyous, joyful, beatific, ecstatic; uplifted, elevated.

raptor /ráptər/ *n.* any bird of prey, e.g. an owl, falcon, etc. [L, = ravisher, plunderer f. *rapere rapt-* seize]

raptorial /raptóriəl/ *adj.* & *n.* ● *adj.* (of a bird or animal) adapted for seizing prey; predatory. ● *n.* **1** = RAPTOR. **2** a predatory animal. [L *raptor*: see RAPTOR]

■ *adj.* see PREDATORY 1.

rapture /rápchər/ *n.* **1 a** ecstatic delight, mental transport. **b** (in *pl.*) great pleasure or enthusiasm or the expression of it. **2** *archaic* the act of transporting a person from one place to another. □ **go into** (or **be in**) **raptures** be enthusiastic; talk enthusiastically. □□ **rapturous** *adj.* **rapturously** *adv.* **rapturousness** *n.* [obs. F *rapture* or med.L *raptura* (as RAPT)]

■ **1 a** ecstasy, delight, joy, joyfulness, joyousness, pleasure, exaltation, elation, thrill, enchantment, euphoria, ecstasy. □ **go into raptures** wax lyrical; see also GUSH *v.* 2. □□ **rapturous** ecstatic, delighted, joyful, joyous, elated, thrilled, euphoric, overjoyed, rhapsodic.

rara avis /ráirə áyviss, ra͡arə ávviss/ *n.* (*pl.* ***rarae aves*** /-ri -veez/) a rarity; a kind of person or thing rarely encountered. [L, = rare bird]

■ see RARITY 2.

rare[1] /rair/ *adj.* (**rarer, rarest**) **1** seldom done or found or occurring, uncommon, unusual, few and far between. **2** exceptionally good (*had a rare time*). **3** of less than the usual density, with only loosely packed substance (*the rare atmosphere of the mountain tops*). □ **rare bird** = RARA AVIS. **rare earth 1** a lanthanide element. **2** an oxide of such an element. **rare gas** = *noble gas.* □□ **rareness** *n.* [ME f. L *rarus*]

■ **1** uncommon, unfamiliar, unusual, exceptional, out of the ordinary, extraordinary, atypical; scarce, infrequent, few and far between, sparse, scanty, limited, thin on the ground; unparalleled, choice, recherché, unique, singular. **2** fine, good, admirable, excellent, first-rate, first-class, exquisite, superior, superlative, peerless, unequalled, matchless, incomparable, outstanding.

rare[2] /rair/ *adj.* (**rarer, rarest**) (of meat) underdone. [var. of obs. *rear* half-cooked (of eggs), f. OE *hrēr*]

■ underdone, undercooked.

rarebit /ráirbit/ *n.* = *Welsh rabbit.* [RARE[1] + BIT[1]]

raree-show /ráireeshō/ *n.* **1** a show or spectacle. **2** a show carried about in a box; a peep-show. [app. = *rare show* as pronounced by Savoyard showmen]

rarefy /ráirifī/ *v.* (**-ies, -ied**) (esp. as **rarefied** *adj.*) **1** *tr.* & *intr.* make or become less dense or solid (*rarefied air*). **2** *tr.* purify or refine (a person's nature etc.). **3** *tr.* **a** make (an idea etc.) subtle. **b** (as **rarefied** *adj.*) refined, subtle; elevated, exalted; select. □□ **rarefaction** /-fáksh'n/ *n.* **rarefactive** /-fáktiv/ *adj.* **rarefication** /-fikáysh'n/ *n.* [ME f. OF *rarefier* or med.L *rarificare* f. L *rarefacere* f. *rarus* rare + *facere* make]

■ **1** (**rarefied**) thin, diluted, insubstantial, sparse, tenuous, scant, scanty. **3 b** (**rarefied**) cliquish, exclusive, private, select; esoteric.

rarely /ráirli/ *adv.* **1** seldom; not often. **2** in an unusual degree; exceptionally. **3** exceptionally well.

■ **1** seldom, infrequently, on rare occasions, hardly (ever), scarcely (ever), almost never, once in a blue moon. **3** see *admirably* (ADMIRABLE).

raring /ráiring/ *adj.* (foll. by *to* + infin.) *colloq.* enthusiastic, eager (*raring to go*). [part. of *rare*, dial. var. of ROAR or REAR[2]]

rarity /ráiriti/ *n.* (*pl.* **-ies**) **1** rareness. **2** an uncommon thing, esp. one valued for being rare. [F *rareté* or L *raritas* (as RARE[1])]

■ **1** unusualness, uncommonness, rareness, uniqueness, scarcity, sparseness, scantiness, infrequency. **2** curiosity, oddity, curio, collector's item, find, treasure, conversation piece; rare bird, *rara avis*, *colloq.* one-off, *Brit. sl.* oner.

rascal /ra͡ask'l/ *n.* often *joc.* a dishonest or mischievous person, esp. a child. □□ **rascaldom** *n.* **rascalism** *n.* **rascality** /-skálliti/ *n.* (*pl.* **-ies**). **rascally** *adj.* [ME f. OF *rascaille* rabble, prob. ult. f. L *radere ras-* scrape]

■ imp, devil, mischief-maker, scallywag, rogue, knave, good-for-nothing, ne'er-do-well, wastrel, scapegrace, *archaic or joc.* rapscallion, *colloq.* vagabond, scamp.

rase var. of RAZE.

rash[1] /rash/ *adj.* reckless, impetuous, hasty; acting or done without due consideration. □□ **rashly** *adv.* **rashness** *n.* [ME, prob. f. OE *ræsc* (unrecorded) f. Gmc]

■ reckless, impetuous, impulsive, unthinking, thoughtless, foolhardy, unconsidered, ill-considered, ill-advised, injudicious, imprudent, indiscreet, precipitate, hasty, careless, heedless, wild, madcap, hare-brained, hotheaded.

rash[2] /rash/ *n.* **1** an eruption of the skin in spots or patches. **2** (usu. foll. by *of*) a sudden widespread phenomenon, esp. of something unwelcome (*a rash of strikes*). [18th c.: prob. rel. to OF *ra(s)che* eruptive sores, = It. *raschia* itch]

■ **1** eruption, redness, efflorescence; see also INFLAMMATION 2. **2** profusion, outbreak, series, succession, spate, wave, flood, deluge, plague, epidemic.

rasher /ráshər/ *n.* a thin slice of bacon or ham. [16th c.: orig. unkn.]

rasp /raasp/ *n.* & *v.* ● *n.* **1** a coarse kind of file having separate teeth. **2** a rough grating sound. ● *v.* **1** *tr.* **a** scrape with a rasp. **b** scrape roughly. **c** (foll. by *off, away*) remove by scraping. **2 a** *intr.* make a grating sound. **b** *tr.* say gratingly or hoarsely. **3** *tr.* grate upon (a person or a person's feelings), irritate. □□ **raspingly** *adv.* **raspy** *adj.* [ME f. OF *raspe(r)* ult. f. WG]

■ *n.* **1** file, grater, rasper. **2** grating, scrape, scraping, scratch, scratching, grinding, stridulation. ● *v.* **1** scrape, abrade, grate, file. **2** croak, grate; see also JAR[2] *v.* 1, 2. **3** jar (upon), grate upon *or* against, wear on; get on a person's nerves, nettle, irk, annoy, vex; see also IRRITATE 1.

raspberry /raázbəri/ *n.* (*pl.* **-ies**) **1 a** a bramble, *Rubus idaeus*, having usu. red berries consisting of numerous drupels on a conical receptacle. **b** this berry. **2** any of various red colours. **3** *colloq.* **a** a sound made with the lips expressing dislike, derision, or disapproval (orig. *raspberry tart*, rhyming sl. = *fart*). **b** a show of strong disapproval (*got a raspberry from the audience*). □ **raspberry-cane** a raspberry plant. **raspberry vinegar** a kind of syrup made from raspberries. [16th-c. *rasp* (now dial.) f. obs. *raspis*, of unkn. orig., + BERRY]

rasper /raáspər/ *n.* **1** a person or thing that rasps. **2** *Hunting* a high difficult fence.

Rasta /rástə/ *n.* & *adj.* = RASTAFARIAN. [abbr.]

Rastafarian /rástəfáiriən/ *n.* & *adj.* ● *n.* a member of a sect of Jamaican origin regarding Blacks as a chosen people and the former Emperor Haile Selassie of Ethiopia (d. 1975, entitled *Ras Tafari*) as God. ● *adj.* of or relating to this sect. □□ **Rastafarianism** *n.*

raster /rástər/ *n.* a pattern of scanning lines for a cathode-ray tube picture. [G, = screen, f. L *rastrum* rake f. *radere ras-* scrape]

rat /rat/ *n.* & *v.* ● *n.* **1 a** any of several rodents of the genus *Rattus* (*brown rat*). **b** any similar rodent (*muskrat*; *water-rat*). **2** a deserter from a party, cause, difficult situation, etc.; a turncoat (from the superstition that rats desert a sinking ship). **3** *colloq.* an unpleasant person. **4** a worker who refuses to join a strike, or who blacklegs. **5** (in *pl.*) *sl.* an exclamation of contempt, annoyance, etc. ● *v.intr.* (**ratted, ratting**) **1** (of a person or dog) hunt or kill rats. **2** *colloq.* desert a cause, party, etc. **3** *colloq.* (foll. by *on*) **a** betray; let down. **b** inform on. □ **rat-catcher** a person who rids buildings of rats etc. **rat kangaroo** *Austral.* any of various small ratlike marsupials of the family Potoroidae, having kangaroo-like hind limbs for jumping. **rat race** a fiercely competitive struggle for position, power, etc. **rat's tail** a thing shaped like a rat's tail, e.g. a tapering cylindrical file. **rat-tail 1** the grenadier fish. **2** a horse with a hairless tail. **3** such a tail. **rat-tail** (or **-tailed**) **spoon** a spoon with a tail-like moulding from the handle to the back of the bowl. [OE *ræt* & OF *rat*]

■ *n.* **2** see *deserter* (DESERT[1]). **3** see WRETCH 2. **5** (*rats*) damn, blast, *esp. Brit.* bother, *colloq.* hell, drat, shoot, *esp. Brit. colloq.* botheration, *euphem.* sugar, *esp. US sl.* tarnation. ● *v.* **2** see DESERT[1] *v.* 2, 4. **3 a** see BETRAY 2. **b** see INFORM 2.

rata /raátə/ *n.* any large tree of the genus *Metrosideros*, esp. *M. robusta* of New Zealand, with crimson flowers and hard red wood. [Maori]

ratable var. of RATEABLE.

ratafia /ráttəféeə/ *n.* **1** a liqueur flavoured with almonds or kernels of peach, apricot, or cherry. **2** a kind of biscuit similarly flavoured. [F, perh. rel. to TAFIA]

ratan var. of RATTAN.

rataplan /ráttəplán/ *n.* & *v.* ● *n.* a drumming sound. ● *v.* (**rataplanned, rataplanning**) **1** *tr.* play (a tune) on or as on a drum. **2** *intr.* make a rataplan. [F: imit.]

ratatat (also **rat-a-tat**) var. of RAT-TAT.

ratatouille /ráttətóo-i, -twée/ *n.* a vegetable dish made of stewed onions, courgettes, tomatoes, aubergines, and peppers. [F dial.]

ratbag /rátbag/ *n. sl.* an unpleasant or disgusting person.

ratch /rach/ *n.* **1** a ratchet. **2** a ratchet-wheel. [perh. f. G *Ratsche*: cf. RATCHET]

ratchet /ráchit/ *n.* & *v.* ● *n.* **1** a set of teeth on the edge of a bar or wheel in which a device engages to ensure motion in one direction only. **2** (in full **ratchet-wheel**) a wheel with a rim so toothed. ● *v.* (**ratcheted, ratcheting**) **1** *tr.* **a** provide with a ratchet. **b** make into a ratchet. **2** *tr.* & *intr.* move as under the control of a ratchet. [F *rochet* blunt lance-head, bobbin, ratchet, etc., prob. ult. f. Gmc]

rate[1] /rayt/ *n.* & *v.* ● *n.* **1** a stated numerical proportion between two sets of things (the second usu. expressed as unity), esp. as a measure of amount or degree (*moving at a rate of 50 miles per hour*) or as the basis of calculating an amount or value (*rate of taxation*). **2** a fixed or appropriate charge or cost or value; a measure of this (*postal rates*; *the rate for the job*). **3** rapidity of movement or change (*travelling at a great rate*; *prices increasing at a dreadful rate*). **4** class or rank (*first-rate*). **5** *Brit.* **a** an assessment levied by local authorities at so much per pound of the assessed value of buildings and land owned or leased. **b** (in *pl.*) the amount payable by this. ● *v.* **1** *tr.* **a** estimate the worth or value of (*I do not rate him very highly*; *how do you rate your chances of winning the race?*). **b** assign a fixed value to (a coin or metal) in relation to a monetary standard. **c** assign a value to (work, the power of a machine, etc.). **2** *tr.* consider; regard as (*I rate them among my benefactors*). **3** *intr.* (foll. by *as*) rank or be rated. **4** *tr. Brit.* **a** subject to the payment of a local rate. **b** value for the purpose of assessing rates. **5** *tr.* be worthy of, deserve. **6** *tr. Naut.* place in a specified class (cf. RATING[1]). □ **at any rate** in any case, whatever happens. **at this** (or **that**) **rate** if this example is typical or this assumption is true. **rate-capping** *Brit.* the imposition of an upper limit on the rate leviable by a local authority. [ME f. OF f. med.L *rata* f. L *pro rata parte* or *portione* according to the proportional share f. *ratus* past part. of *rēri* reckon]

■ *n.* **1** scale, proportion; measure, level. **2** charge, price, fee, tariff, figure, amount; toll. **3** pace, gait, speed, velocity, *colloq.* clip. **4** rank, grade, place, position, class, rating, worth, value. ● *v.* **1 a** rank, grade, class, position, place; evaluate, estimate, calculate, compute, count, reckon, judge, gauge, assess, appraise, measure. **2** see CONSIDER 6. **3** count, be placed; see also RANK[1] *v.* 1. **5** merit, be entitled to, deserve, be worthy of, have a claim to. □ **at any rate** in any case, in any event, anyway, at all events, anyhow, under *or* in any circumstances, regardless, notwithstanding, whatever (else) happens.

rate[2] /rayt/ *v.tr.* scold angrily. [ME: orig. unkn.]

■ berate, reprimand, rebuke, reproach, reprove, take to task, upbraid, censure, *colloq.* bawl out, dress down, *US colloq.* chew out; see also SCOLD *v.* 1.

rate[3] var. of RET.

rateable /ráytəb'l/ *adj.* (also **ratable**) **1** *Brit.* liable to payment of rates. **2** able to be rated or estimated. □ **rateable value** the value formerly ascribed to a building for the assessment of local rates. □□ **rateability** /-bíliti/ *n.* **rateably** *adv.*

ratel /ráyt'l, raá-/ *n.* an African and Indian nocturnal flesh-eating burrowing mammal, *Mellivora capensis*. Also called *honey-badger*. [Afrik., of unkn. orig.]

ratepayer /ráytpayər/ *n. Brit.* a person liable to pay rates.

ratfink /rátfingk/ *n.* esp. *US sl.* = FINK.

rathe /rayth/ *adj. poet.* coming, blooming, etc., early in the year or day. □ **rathe-ripe 1** ripening early. **2** precocious. [OE *hræth*, *hræd* f. Gmc]

rather /raáthər/ *adv.* **1** (often foll. by *than*) by preference; for choice (*would rather not go*; *would rather stay than go*). **2** (usu. foll. by *than*) more truly; as a more likely alternative (*is stupid rather than honest*). **3** more precisely (*a book, or rather, a pamphlet*). **4** slightly; to some extent; somewhat (*became rather drunk*; *I rather think you know him*). **5** /raathér/ *Brit.* (as an emphatic response) indeed, assuredly (*Did you like it? – Rather!*). □ **had rather** would rather. [ME f. OE *hrathor*, compar. of *hræthe* (adv.) f. *hræth* (adj.): see RATHE]

■ **1** preferably, sooner, more readily *or* willingly, by choice. **4** quite, somewhat, fairly, moderately, to a certain extent *or* degree, to some extent, slightly, *colloq.* sort of, kind of, pretty. **5** see ABSOLUTELY 6. □ **had rather** had sooner, would rather *or* sooner, prefer *or* choose to.

rathskeller /raátskellər/ *n. US* a beer-hall or restaurant in a basement. [G, = (restaurant in) town-hall cellar]

■ beer-cellar, beer hall; brasserie.

ratify /ráttifī/ *v.tr.* (**-ies, -ied**) confirm or accept (an agreement made in one's name) by formal consent, signature, etc. □□ **ratifiable** *adj.* **ratification** /-fikáysh'n/ *n.*

ratifier *n.* [ME f. OF *ratifier* f. med.L *ratificare* (as RATE[1])]
▪ confirm, approve, sanction, endorse, support, corroborate, uphold, back (up), certify, affirm; sign.

rating[1] /ráyting/ *n.* **1** the act or an instance of placing in a rank or class or assigning a value to. **2** the estimated standing of a person as regards credit etc. **3** *Naut.* **a** *Brit.* a non-commissioned sailor. **b** a person's position or class on a ship's books. **4** *Brit.* an amount fixed as a local rate. **5** the relative popularity of a broadcast programme as determined by the estimated size of the audience. **6** *Naut.* any of the classes into which racing yachts are distributed by tonnage.
▪ **1** see SCALE[3] *n.* 1.

rating[2] /ráyting/ *n.* an angry reprimand.

ratio /ráyshiō/ *n.* (*pl.* **-os**) the quantitative relation between two similar magnitudes determined by the number of times one contains the other integrally or fractionally (*in the ratio of three to two*; *the ratios 1:5 and 20:100 are the same*). [L (as RATE[1])]
▪ proportion, correlation, relation.

ratiocinate /ráttióssinayt, ráshi-/ *v.intr. literary* go through logical processes, reason, esp. using syllogisms. ▫▫ **ratiocination** /-náysh'n/ *n.* **ratiocinative** /-nətiv/ *adj.* **ratiocinator** *n.* [L *ratiocinari* (as RATIO)]
▪ see REASON *v.* 1. ▫▫ **ratiocination** see *reasoning* (REASON). **ratiocinative** see RATIONAL 1.

ration /rásh'n/ *n.* & *v.* ● *n.* **1** a fixed official allowance of food, clothing, etc., in a time of shortage. **2** (foll. by *of*) a single portion of provisions, fuel, clothing, etc. **3** (usu. in *pl.*) a fixed daily allowance of food, esp. in the armed forces (and formerly of forage for animals). **4** (in *pl.*) provisions. ● *v.tr.* **1** limit (persons or provisions) to a fixed ration. **2** (usu. foll. by *out*) share out (food etc.) in fixed quantities. ▫ **given out with the rations** *Mil. sl.* awarded without regard to merit. **ration book** (or **card**) a document entitling the holder to a ration. [F f. It. *razione* or Sp. *ración* f. L *ratio -onis* reckoning, RATIO]
▪ *n.* **1** allowance, share, quota, allotment, allocation, portion, helping, percentage, measure, apportionment. **4** (*rations*) supplies, provisions, food, victuals, edibles, commons, *formal* viands, *formal or joc.* comestibles, *joc.* provender. ● *v.* **1** budget, restrict, confine, control, limit. **2** (*ration out*) allot, apportion, dole (out), give out, distribute, deal out, parcel out, measure out, admeasure, hand out, distribute, share out, dispense, *literary* mete out.

rational /ráshən'l/ *adj.* **1** of or based on reasoning or reason. **2** sensible, sane, moderate; not foolish or absurd or extreme. **3** endowed with reason, reasoning. **4** rejecting what is unreasonable or cannot be tested by reason in religion or custom. **5** *Math.* (of a quantity or ratio) expressible as a ratio of whole numbers. ▫ **rational dress** *hist.* a style of dress adopted by some women in the late nineteenth century, including bloomers or knickerbockers. **rational horizon** see HORIZON 1c. ▫▫ **rationality** /-nálliti/ *n.* **rationally** *adv.* [ME f. L *rationalis* (as RATION)]
▪ **1** reasoned, logical, practical, pragmatic, *literary* ratiocinative. **2** sensible, common-sense, commonsensical, practical, pragmatic, down-to-earth, reasonable, well-balanced, sane, sound, normal, clear-headed, clear-eyed, sober, moderate, measured. **3** discriminating, intelligent, thinking, enlightened, prudent, wise, knowledgeable, informed.

rationale /ráshənaàl/ *n.* **1** (often foll. by *for*) the fundamental reason or logical basis of anything. **2** a reasoned exposition; a statement of reasons. [mod.L, neut. of L *rationalis*: see RATIONAL]
▪ reason, basis, ground(s), reasoning, philosophy, principle, theory, thinking, *raison d'être*; explanation, exposition.

rationalism /ráshənəliz'm/ *n.* **1** *Philos.* the theory that reason is the foundation of certainty in knowledge (opp. EMPIRICISM (see EMPIRIC), SENSATIONALISM). **2** *Theol.* the practice of treating reason as the ultimate authority in religion. **3** a belief in reason rather than religion as a guiding principle in life. ▫▫ **rationalist** *n.* **rationalistic** /-lístik/ *adj.* **rationalistically** /-lístikəli/ *adv.*

rationalize /ráshənəlīz/ *v.* (also **-ise**) **1 a** *tr.* offer or subconsciously adopt a rational but specious explanation of (one's behaviour or attitude). **b** *intr.* explain one's behaviour or attitude in this way. **2** *tr.* make logical and consistent. **3** *tr.* make (a business etc.) more efficient by reorganizing it to reduce or eliminate waste of labour, time, or materials. **4** *tr.* (often foll. by *away*) explain or explain away rationally. **5** *tr. Math.* clear of surds. **6** *intr.* be or act as a rationalist. ▫▫ **rationalization** /-záysh'n/ *n.* **rationalizer** *n.*
▪ **1a, 4** make acceptable *or* reasonable, make excuses for, account for, justify, excuse, reason away, explain (away). **2** think through, reason out; apply logic to, *literary* ratiocinate. **3** reorganize, realign, remodel, streamline, make efficient, simplify.

ratite /ráttīt/ *adj.* & *n.* ● *adj.* (of a bird) having a keelless breastbone, and unable to fly (opp. CARINATE). ● *n.* a flightless bird, e.g. an ostrich, emu, cassowary, etc. [L *ratis* raft]

ratline /rátlin/ *n.* (also **ratlin**) (usu. in *pl.*) any of the small lines fastened across a sailing-ship's shrouds like ladder-rungs. [ME: orig. unkn.]

ratoon /rətōōn/ *n.* & *v.* ● *n.* a new shoot springing from a root of sugar cane etc. after cropping. ● *v.intr.* send up ratoons. [Sp. *retoño* sprout]

ratsbane /rátsbayn/ *n.* anything poisonous to rats, esp. a plant.

rattan /rətán/ *n.* (also **ratan**) **1** any East Indian climbing palm of the genus *Calamus* etc. with long thin jointed pliable stems. **2** a piece of rattan stem used as a walking-stick etc. [earlier *rot(t)ang* f. Malay *rōtan* prob. f. *raut* pare]

rat-tat /rat-tát/ *n.* (also **rat-tat-tat** /ráttat-tát/, **ratatat**, **rat-a-tat** /ráttətát/) a rapping sound, esp. of a knocker. [imit.]

ratter /ráttər/ *n.* **1** a dog or other animal that hunts rats. **2** *sl.* a person who betrays a cause, party, friend, etc.

rattle /rátt'l/ *v.* & *n.* ● *v.* **1 a** *intr.* give out a rapid succession of short sharp hard sounds. **b** *tr.* make (a chair, window, crockery, etc.) do this. **c** *intr.* cause such sounds by shaking something (*rattled at the door*). **2 a** *intr.* move with a rattling noise. **b** *intr.* drive a vehicle or ride or run briskly. **c** *tr.* cause to move quickly (*the bill was rattled through Parliament*). **3 a** *tr.* (usu. foll. by *off*) say or recite rapidly. **b** *intr.* (usu. foll. by *on*) talk in a lively thoughtless way. **4** *tr. colloq.* disconcert, alarm, fluster, make nervous, frighten. ● *n.* **1** a rattling sound. **2** an instrument or plaything made to rattle esp. in order to amuse babies or to give an alarm. **3** the set of horny rings in a rattlesnake's tail. **4** a plant with seeds that rattle in their cases when ripe (*red rattle*; *yellow rattle*). **5** uproar, bustle, noisy gaiety, racket. **6 a** a noisy flow of words. **b** empty chatter, trivial talk. **7** *archaic* a lively or thoughtless incessant talker. ▫ **rattle the sabre** threaten war. ▫▫ **rattly** *adj.* [ME, prob. f. MDu. & LG *ratelen* (imit.)]
▪ *v.* **1 a** clatter, jangle. **1b, 2a** shake, vibrate, joggle, jiggle; jounce, bounce, bump, jolt; clank. **2 b** speed, hurtle, race, rush. **c** race, rush, speed, expedite, push, press, drive. **3 a** (*rattle off*) recite, list, utter, reel off, run through, enumerate, call off. **b** chatter, babble, jabber, gibber, prate, prattle, blabber, blather, ramble, maunder, *colloq.* witter, rabbit, natter. **4** unnerve, disconcert, discomfit, disturb, perturb, shake, discountenance, upset, agitate, alarm, fluster, put off, *colloq.* faze, throw. ● *n.* **1** clatter, crackle, crackling; rale. **2** sistrum, noise-maker. **5** see RACKET[2] 1a. **6** see BABBLE *n.* 1. **7** see BLABBER *n.*

rattlebox /rátt'lboks/ *n.* **1** a rattle consisting of a box with objects inside. **2** a rickety old vehicle etc.

rattler /rátlər/ *n.* **1** a thing that rattles, esp. an old or rickety vehicle. **2** *colloq.* a rattlesnake. **3** *sl.* a remarkably good specimen of anything.
▪ **1** see RATTLETRAP *n.*

rattlesnake /rátt'lsnayk/ *n.* any of various poisonous American snakes of the family Viperidae, esp. of the genus

Crotalus or *Sistrurus*, with a rattling structure of horny rings in its tail.

rattletrap /ráttʹltrap/ *n.* & *adj. colloq.* ● *n.* a rickety old vehicle etc. ● *adj.* rickety.
■ *n.* rattler, boneshaker, wreck, *colloq.* jalopy, (old) crock, tin Lizzie, *Brit. sl.* (old) banger, *US sl.* flivver.

rattling /rátling/ *adj.* & *adv.* ● *adj.* **1** that rattles. **2** brisk, vigorous (*a rattling pace*). ● *adv.* remarkably (*a rattling good story*).
■ *adj.* **2** see BRISK *adj.* 1. ● *adv.* see EXCEEDINGLY 1.

ratty /rátti/ *adj.* (**rattier, rattiest**) **1** relating to or infested with rats. **2** *colloq.* irritable or angry. **3** *colloq.* **a** wretched, nasty. **b** unkempt; seedy, dirty. □□ **rattily** *adv.* **rattiness** *n.*
■ **2** irritable, cross, testy, touchy, crabby, crabbed, angry, short-tempered, impatient, disagreeable. **3 a** see NASTY 1, 5a, b. **b** dirty, greasy, straggly, unkempt, matted; see also SEEDY 3.

raucous /ráwkəss/ *adj.* harsh-sounding, loud and hoarse. □□ **raucously** *adv.* **raucousness** *n.* [L *raucus*]
■ harsh, rasping, rough, husky, hoarse, grating, scratchy, discordant, dissonant, jarring, strident, shrill, noisy, loud, ear-splitting, piercing, penetrating.

raunchy /ráwnchi/ *adj.* (**raunchier, raunchiest**) *colloq.* **1** coarse, earthy, boisterous; sexually provocative. **2** esp. *US* slovenly, grubby. □□ **raunchily** *adv.* **raunchiness** *n.* [20th c.: orig. unkn.]
■ **1** see BAWDY *adj.*

ravage /rávvij/ *v.* & *n.* ● *v.tr.* & *intr.* devastate, plunder. ● *n.* **1** the act or an instance of ravaging; devastation, damage. **2** (usu. in *pl.*; foll. by *of*) destructive effect (*survived the ravages of winter*). □□ **ravager** *n.* [F *ravage(r)* alt. f. *ravine* rush of water]
■ *v.* lay waste, devastate, ruin, destroy, demolish, raze, wreck, wreak havoc on; pillage, plunder, ransack, sack, loot, rape, maraud, *literary* despoil. ● *n.* **1** destruction, damage, depredation(s), ruin, devastation. **2** (*ravages*) ill effects, scars; see also DEPREDATION.

rave[1] /rayv/ *v.* & *n.* ● *v.* **1** *intr.* talk wildly or furiously in or as in delirium. **2** *intr.* (usu. foll. by *about, of, over*) speak with rapturous admiration; go into raptures. **3** *tr.* bring into a specified state by raving (*raved himself hoarse*). **4** *tr.* utter with ravings (*raved their grief*). **5** *intr.* (of the sea, wind, etc.) howl, roar. **6** *tr.* & *intr. colloq.* enjoy oneself freely (esp. *rave it up*). ● *n.* **1** (usu. *attrib.*) *colloq.* a highly enthusiastic review of a film, play, etc. (*a rave review*). **2** *sl.* **a** an infatuation. **b** a temporary fashion or craze. **3** (also **rave-up**) *colloq.* a lively party. **4** the sound of the wind etc. raving. [ME, prob. f. ONF *raver*, rel. to (M)LG *reven* be senseless, rave]
■ *v.* **1** rant, rant and rave, rage, storm, fulminate, roar, thunder, bellow, shout; fume, seethe. **2** (*rave about*) praise, sing the praises of, rhapsodize over *or* about, applaud, gush over, go into raptures about, be thrilled about, eulogize, extol, laud, *colloq.* go on about. **5** howl, rage, roar. **6** see *enjoy oneself*. ● *n.* **1** enthusiastic reception, tribute, testimonial, encomium, bouquet, plaudit, accolade. **2 a** crush, infatuation, obsession; passion, *colloq.* pash. **b** rage, fashion, vogue, trend, thing, last word, *dernier cri*, craze, mania, *colloq.* fad. **3** party, fête, *colloq.* do, shindig, *Brit. colloq.* knees-up, *sl.* bash, blast, *Austral. sl.* ding, *esp. US sl.* wingding; see also JAMBOREE.

rave[2] /rayv/ *n.* **1** a rail of a cart. **2** (in *pl.*) a permanent or removable framework added to the sides of a cart to increase its capacity. [var. of dial. *rathe* (15th c., of unkn. orig.)]

ravel /rávvʹl/ *v.* & *n.* ● *v.* (**ravelled, ravelling**; *US* **raveled, raveling**) **1** *tr.* & *intr.* entangle or become entangled or knotted. **2** *tr.* confuse or complicate (a question or problem). **3** *intr.* fray out. **4** *tr.* (often foll. by *out*) disentangle, unravel, distinguish the separate threads or subdivisions of. ● *n.* **1** a tangle or knot. **2** a complication. **3** a frayed or loose end. [prob. f. Du. *ravelen* tangle, fray out, unweave]
■ *v.* **1** see TANGLE[1] *v.* 1. **2** see COMPLICATE 1. **3** see FRAY[1]. **4** see FREE *v.* 3, SEPARATE *v.* 6a. ● *n.* **1** see TANGLE[1] *n.* 1. **2** see TANGLE[1] *n.* 2.

ravelin /rávlin/ *n. hist.* an outwork of fortifications, with two faces forming a salient angle. [F f. obs. It. *ravellino*, of unkn. orig.]

ravelling /rávvʹling/ *n.* a thread from fabric which is frayed or unravelled.

raven[1] /ráyvʹn/ *n.* & *adj.* ● *n.* a large glossy blue-black crow, *Corvus corax*, feeding chiefly on carrion etc., having a hoarse cry. ● *adj.* glossy black (*raven tresses*). [OE *hræfn* f. Gmc]
■ *adj.* see BLACK *adj.* 1.

raven[2] /rávvʹn/ *v.* **1** *intr.* **a** plunder. **b** (foll. by *after*) seek prey or booty. **c** (foll. by *about*) go plundering. **d** prowl for prey (*ravening beast*). **2 a** *tr.* devour voraciously. **b** *intr.* (usu. foll. by *for*) have a ravenous appetite. **c** *intr.* (often foll. by *on*) feed voraciously. [OF *raviner* ravage ult. f. L *rapina* RAPINE]

ravenous /rávvənəss/ *adj.* **1** very hungry, famished. **2** (of hunger, eagerness, etc., or of an animal) voracious. **3** rapacious. □□ **ravenously** *adv.* **ravenousness** *n.* [ME f. OF *ravineus* (as RAVEN[2])]
■ **1** hungry, famished, starving, starved. **2** insatiable, eager; see also VORACIOUS. **3** see RAPACIOUS.

raver /ráyvər/ *n.* **1** *colloq.* an uninhibited pleasure-loving person. **2** a person who raves; a madman or madwoman.

ravin /rávvin/ *n. poet.* or *rhet.* **1** robbery, plundering. **2** the seizing and devouring of prey. **3** prey. □ **beast of ravin** a beast of prey. [ME f. OF *ravine* f. L *rapina* RAPINE]

ravine /rəveén/ *n.* a deep narrow gorge or cleft. □□ **ravined** *adj.* [F (as RAVIN)]
■ gorge, canyon, pass, cleft, defile, chine, gully, valley, flume, couloir, *dial.* clough, *Anglo-Ind.* nullah, *Brit.* gill, *S.Afr.* sloot, kloof, donga, *Sc.* linn, *US* coulée, gap, gulch, arroyo.

raving /ráyving/ *n.*, *adj.*, & *adv.* ● *n.* (usu. in *pl.*) wild or delirious talk. ● *adj.* delirious, frenzied. ● *adj.* & *adv. colloq.* as an intensive (*a raving beauty*; *raving mad*). □□ **ravingly** *adv.*
■ *n.* (*ravings*) ranting, bombast, grandiloquence, magniloquence, rhetoric, bluster, blustering, babbling, hyperbole, fustian; delirium. ● *adj.* mad, insane, raging, crazed, irrational, manic, maniacal, frantic, frenzied, delirious, hysterical, *colloq.* crazy. ● *adj.* & *adv.* real, outstanding, rare, phenomenal, great, extraordinary, remarkable, *colloq.* stunning; completely, totally, absolutely.

ravioli /ràvviṓli/ *n.* small pasta envelopes containing minced meat etc. [It.]

ravish /rávvish/ *v.tr.* **1** commit rape on (a woman). **2** enrapture; fill with delight. **3** *archaic* **a** carry off (a person or thing) by force. **b** (of death, circumstances, etc.) take from life or from sight. □□ **ravisher** *n.* **ravishment** *n.* [ME f. OF *ravir* ult. f. L *rapere* seize]
■ **1** rape; see also VIOLATE 4. **2** enrapture, delight, captivate, enthral, fascinate, charm, entrance, spellbind, bewitch, transport. **3 a** carry off, seize, *poet.* rape; see also ABDUCT.

ravishing /rávvishing/ *adj.* entrancing, delightful; very beautiful. □□ **ravishingly** *adv.*
■ dazzling, beautiful, gorgeous, striking, radiant, charming, alluring, attractive, entrancing, delightful, captivating, enthralling, bewitching, *colloq.* stunning.

raw /raw/ *adj.* & *n.* ● *adj.* **1** (of food) uncooked. **2** in the natural state; not processed or manufactured (*raw sewage*). **3** (of alcoholic spirit) undiluted. **4** (of statistics etc.) not analysed or processed. **5** (of a person) inexperienced, untrained; new to an activity (*raw recruits*). **6 a** stripped of skin; having the flesh exposed. **b** sensitive to the touch from having the flesh exposed. **c** sensitive to emotional pain etc. **7** (of the atmosphere, day, etc.) chilly and damp. **8 a** crude in artistic quality; lacking finish. **b** unmitigated; brutal. **9** (of the edge of cloth) without hem or selvage. **10** (of silk) as reeled from cocoons. **11** (of grain) unmalted. ● *n.* a raw place on a person's or horse's body. □ **come the raw prawn** *Austral. sl.* attempt to deceive. **in the raw 1** in its natural state without mitigation (*life in the raw*). **2** naked. **raw-boned** gaunt and bony. **raw deal** harsh or unfair treatment. **raw material** that from which the process of manufacture makes products. **raw sienna** a brownish-yellow ferruginous earth used as a pigment. **raw umber** umber in its natural state, dark yellow in colour. **touch on the raw** upset (a person) on a sensitive matter. □□ **rawish** *adj.* **rawly** *adv.* **rawness** *n.* [OE *hrēaw* f. Gmc]

■ *adj.* **1** uncooked, fresh. **2** unprocessed, untreated, unrefined, unfinished, natural, crude. **5** new, inexperienced, unseasoned, immature, green, untried, fresh, untrained, unskilled, untested. **6a, b** exposed, unprotected, uncovered, open; sore, tender, inflamed, painful, sensitive. **6 c** sensitive, tender, susceptible. **7** chilly, chilling, cold, damp, freezing, biting, stinging, sharp, keen, piercing, penetrating, icy, bitter, *colloq.* nippy, *literary* chill. **8 a** see CRUDE *adj.* 1b. **b** brutal, frank, candid, blunt, direct, unvarnished, unmollified, unmitigated, unembellished, realistic, honest, plain, unreserved, unrestrained, uninhibited, straightforward. □ **come the raw prawn** see DECEIVE 1. **in the raw 2** naked, stark naked, undressed, unclothed, nude, in the nude, *colloq.* in the buff, in the altogether, *joc.* in one's birthday suit, *Brit. sl.* starkers. **raw-boned** gaunt, lean, gangling, thin, skinny, spare, meagre, scrawny, underfed, bony, emaciated, half-starved, hollow-cheeked. **touch on the raw** see DISCOMFIT 1a.

rawhide /ráwhīd/ *n.* **1** untanned hide. **2** a rope or whip of this.

■ **2** see WHIP *n.*

Rawlplug /ráwlplug/ *n. propr.* a thin cylindrical plug for holding a screw or nail in masonry. [*Rawl*ings, name of the engineers who introduced it]

ray[1] /ray/ *n.* & *v.* ● *n.* **1** a single line or narrow beam of light from a small or distant source. **2** a straight line in which radiation travels to a given point. **3** (in *pl.*) radiation of a specified type (*gamma rays*; *X-rays*). **4** a trace or beginning of an enlightening or cheering influence (*a ray of hope*). **5 a** any of a set of radiating lines or parts or things. **b** any of a set of straight lines passing through one point. **6** the marginal portion of a composite flower, e.g. a daisy. **7 a** a radial division of a starfish. **b** each of a set of bones etc. supporting a fish's fin. ● *v.* **1** *intr.* (foll. by *forth, out*) (of light, thought, emotion, etc.) issue in or as if in rays. **2** *intr.* & *tr.* radiate. □ **ray gun** (esp. in science fiction) a gun causing injury or damage by the emission of rays. □□ **rayed** *adj.* **rayless** *adj.* **raylet** *n.* [ME f. OF *rai* f. L *radius*: see RADIUS]

■ *n.* **1** beam, shaft, streak, gleam, flash. **4** glimmer, trace, spark, scintilla, flicker. ● *v.* **1** see BEAM *v.* 2a. **2** see RADIATE *v.*

ray[2] /ray/ *n.* a large cartilaginous fish of the order Batoidea, with a broad flat body, winglike pectoral fins and a long slender tail, used as food. [ME f. OF *raie* f. L *raia*]

ray[3] /ray/ *n.* (also **re**) *Mus.* **1** (in tonic sol-fa) the second note of a major scale. **2** the note D in the fixed-doh system. [ME *re* f. L *resonare*: see GAMUT]

rayon /ráyon/ *n.* any of various textile fibres or fabrics made from cellulose. [arbitrary f. RAY[1]]

raze /rayz/ *v.tr.* (also **rase**) **1** completely destroy; tear down (esp. *raze to the ground*). **2** erase; scratch out (esp. in abstract senses). [ME *rase* = wound slightly f. OF *raser* shave close ult. f. L *radere ras-* scrape]

■ **1** tear *or* pull *or* bring *or* knock *or* throw down, demolish, destroy, level, flatten, bulldoze.

razoo / raazóó/ *n.* (also **brass razoo**) *Austral.* & *NZ sl.* an imaginary coin of trivial value; a very small sum of money (*I hadn't a brass razoo*). [20th c.: orig. unkn.]

razor /ráyzər/ *n.* & *v.* ● *n.* an instrument with a sharp blade used in cutting hair esp. from the skin. ● *v.tr.* **1** use a razor on. **2** shave; cut down close. □ **razor-back** an animal with a sharp ridged back, esp. a rorqual. **razor-bill** an auk, *Alca torda*, with a sharp-edged bill. **razor-blade** a blade used in a razor, esp. a flat piece of metal with a sharp edge or edges used in a safety razor. **razor-cut** a haircut made with a razor. **razor-** (or **razor's**) **edge 1** a keen edge. **2** a sharp mountain-ridge. **3** a critical situation (*found themselves on a razor-edge*). **4** a sharp line of division. **razor-fish** (or **-shell**) any of various bivalve molluscs of the family Solenidae, with a shell like the handle of a cutthroat razor. [ME f. OF *rasor* (as RAZE)]

razz /raz/ *n.* & *v.* *US sl.* ● *n.* = RASPBERRY 3. ● *v.tr.* tease, ridicule. [*razzberry*, corrupt. of RASPBERRY]

■ *v.* see RIDICULE *v.*

razzle-dazzle /rázz'ldázz'l/ *n.* (also **razzle**) *sl.* **1 a** glamorous excitement; bustle. **b** a spree. **2** extravagant publicity. [redupl. of DAZZLE]

■ **1 a** see GLITTER *n.* 2, FLURRY *n.* 3. **2** *sl.* (media) hype.

razzmatazz /rázmətáz/ *n.* (also **razzamatazz** /rázzəmə-/) *colloq.* **1** = RAZZLE-DAZZLE. **2** insincere actions; humbug. [prob. alt. f. RAZZLE-DAZZLE]

■ **2** see MOONSHINE 1.

Rb *symb. Chem.* the element rubidium.

RC *abbr.* **1** Roman Catholic. **2** Red Cross. **3** reinforced concrete.

RCA *abbr.* **1** (in the UK) Royal College of Art. **2** (in the US) Radio Corporation of America.

RCAF *abbr.* Royal Canadian Air Force.

RCM *abbr.* (in the UK) Royal College of Music.

RCMP *abbr.* Royal Canadian Mounted Police.

RCN *abbr.* **1** (in the UK) Royal College of Nursing. **2** Royal Canadian Navy.

RCP *abbr.* (in the UK) Royal College of Physicians.

RCS *abbr.* (in the UK): **1** Royal College of Scientists. **2** Royal College of Surgeons. **3** Royal Corps of Signals.

RCVS *abbr.* (in the UK) Royal College of Veterinary Surgeons.

RD *abbr.* **1** refer to drawer. **2** (in the UK) Royal Naval Reserve Decoration.

Rd. *abbr.* Road (in names).

RDC *abbr. Brit. hist.* Rural District Council.

RDF *abbr.* radio direction-finder.

RE *abbr.* **1** (in the UK) Royal Engineers. **2** religious education.

Re *symb. Chem.* the element rhenium.

re[1] /ray, ree/ *prep.* **1** in the matter of (as the first word in a heading, esp. of a legal document). **2** *colloq.* about, concerning. [L, ablat. of *res* thing]

■ see CONCERNING.

re[2] var. of RAY[3].

re- /ree, ri, re/ *prefix* **1** attachable to almost any verb or its derivative, meaning: **a** once more; afresh, anew (*readjust*; *renumber*). **b** back; with return to a previous state (*reassemble*; *reverse*). ¶ A hyphen is normally used when the word begins with *e* (*re-enact*), or to distinguish the compound from a more familiar one-word form (*re-form* = form again). **2** (also **red-** before a vowel, as in *redolent*) in verbs and verbal derivatives denoting: **a** in return; mutually (*react*; *resemble*). **b** opposition (*repel*; *resist*). **c** behind or after (*relic*; *remain*). **d** retirement or secrecy (*recluse*; *reticence*). **e** off, away, down (*recede*; *relegate*; *repress*). **f** frequentative or intensive force (*redouble*; *refine*; *resplendent*). **g** negative force (*recant*; *reveal*). [L *re-*, *red-*, again, back, etc.]

reabsorb /reéəbsórb, -zórb/ *v.tr.* absorb again. □□ **reabsorption** *n.*

reaccept /reéəksépt/ *v.tr.* accept again. □□ **reacceptance** *n.*

reaccustom /reéəkústəm/ *v.tr.* accustom again.

reach /reech/ *v.* & *n.* ● *v.* **1** *intr.* & *tr.* (often foll. by *out*) stretch out; extend. **2** *intr.* stretch out a limb, the hand, etc.; make a reaching motion or effort. **3** *intr.* (often foll. by *for*) make a motion or effort to touch or get hold of, or to attain (*reached for his pipe*). **4** *tr.* get as far as; arrive at (*reached Lincoln at lunch-time*; *your letter reached me today*). **5** *tr.* get to or attain (a specified point) on a scale (*the temperature reached 90°; the number of applications reached 100*). **6** *intr.* (foll. by *to*) attain to; be adequate for (*my income will not reach to it*). **7** *tr.* succeed in achieving; attain (*have reached agreement*). **8** *tr.* make contact with the hand etc., or by telephone etc. (*was out all day and could not be reached*). **9** *tr.* succeed in influencing or having the required effect on (*could not manage to reach their audience*). **10** *tr.* hand, pass (*reach me that book*). **11** *tr.* take with an outstretched hand. **12** *intr. Naut.* sail with the wind abeam or abaft the beam. ● *n.* **1** the extent to which a hand etc. can be reached out, influence exerted, motion carried out, or mental powers used. **2** an act of reaching out. **3** a continuous extent, esp. a stretch of river between two bends, or the part of a canal between locks. **4** *Naut.* a distance traversed in reaching. □ **out of reach** not able to be reached or attained. **reach-me-down** ready-made; second-hand; inferior. □□ **reachable** *adj.* **reacher** *n.* [OE *rǣcan* f. WG]

■ *v.* **1, 2** (*reach out*) hold out, extend, stretch (out), stick out, thrust out, outstretch, *poet.* outreach. **4** arrive at, get to, come to, get as far as, end up at *or* in, land at *or* in, *colloq.* make it to, make. **5** come *or* go *or* get up to, amount to, attain, climb to, rise to, run to; live to. **7** attain, achieve, accomplish, get *or* come to, get *or* come as far as. **8** contact, get, get in touch with, communicate with, establish *or* make contact with, get through to, get (a) hold of. **9** get through *or* across to, register with, communicate with, influence, sway, move, stir, carry weight with. **10** convey, hand (over), pass (over). ● *n.* **1** range, extent, ambit, scope, orbit, compass; control, influence; capability, capacity. □ **reach-me-down** ready-made, off the peg, ready-to-wear; derivative, inferior; see also STALE[1] *adj.* 2, *used* (USE 5).

reacquaint /réeəkwáynt/ *v.tr.* & *refl.* (usu. foll. by *with*) make (a person or oneself) acquainted again. □□ **reacquaintance** *n.*

reacquire /réeəkwír/ *v.tr.* acquire anew. □□ **reacquisition** /rée-akwizísh'n/ *n.*

react /riákt/ *v.* **1** *intr.* (foll. by *to*) respond to a stimulus; undergo a change or show behaviour due to some influence (*how did they react to the news?*). **2** *intr.* (often foll. by *against*) be actuated by repulsion to; tend in a reverse or contrary direction. **3** *intr.* (often foll. by *upon*) produce a reciprocal or responsive effect; act upon the agent (*they react upon each other*). **4** *intr.* (foll. by *with*) *Chem.* & *Physics* (of a substance or particle) be the cause of activity or interaction with another (*nitrous oxide reacts with the metal*). **5** *tr.* (foll. by *with*) *Chem.* cause (a substance) to react with another. **6** *intr. Mil.* make a counter-attack. **7** *intr. Stock Exch.* (of shares) fall after rising. [RE- + ACT or med.L *reagere react-* (as RE-, L *agere* do, act)]

■ **1** respond; act, behave, conduct oneself; retaliate, reciprocate.

re-act /rée-ákt/ *v.tr.* act (a part) again.

reactance /riáktənss/ *n. Electr.* a component of impedance in an AC circuit, due to capacitance or inductance or both.

reactant /riáktənt/ *n. Chem.* a substance that takes part in, and undergoes change during a reaction.

reaction /riáksh'n/ *n.* **1** the act or an instance of reacting; a responsive or reciprocal action. **2 a** a responsive feeling (*what was your reaction to the news?*). **b** an immediate or first impression. **3** the occurrence of a (physical or emotional) condition after a period of its opposite. **4** a bodily response to an external stimulus, e.g. a drug. **5** a tendency to oppose change or to advocate return to a former system, esp. in politics. **6** the interaction of substances undergoing chemical change. **7** propulsion by emitting a jet of particles etc. in the direction opposite to that of the intended motion. □□ **reactionist** *n.* & *adj.* [REACT + -ION or med.L *reactio* (as RE-, ACTION)]

■ **1** reply, answer; reciprocation; see also RESPONSE 1. **2** see RESPONSE 2. **3** counteraction, counterbalance, compensation.

reactionary /riákshənəri, -shənri/ *adj.* & *n.* ● *adj.* tending to oppose (esp. political) change and advocate return to a former system. ● *n.* (*pl.* **-ies**) a reactionary person.

■ *adj.* ultra-conservative, conservative, rightist, right-wing, blimpish, traditionalist, traditional, conventional, old-fashioned, *S.Afr. verkrampte.* ● *n.* ultra-conservative, conservative, rightist, Tory, right-winger, (Colonel) Blimp, traditionalist, *S.Afr. verkrampte.*

reactivate /riáktivayt/ *v.tr.* restore to a state of activity; bring into action again. □□ **reactivation** /-váysh'n/ *n.*

■ see REVIVE 2.

reactive /riáktiv/ *adj.* **1** showing reaction. **2** of or relating to reactance. □□ **reactivity** /-tívviti/ *n.*

■ **1** see RESPONSIVE.

reactor /riáktər/ *n.* **1** a person or thing that reacts. **2** (in full **nuclear reactor**) an apparatus or structure in which a controlled nuclear chain reaction releases energy. **3** *Electr.* a component used to provide reactance, esp. an inductor. **4** an apparatus for the chemical reaction of substances. **5** *Med.* a person who has a reaction to a drug etc.

read /reed/ *v.* & *n.* ● *v.* (*past* and *past part.* **read** /red/) **1** *tr.* (also *absol.*) reproduce mentally or (often foll. by *aloud, out, off,* etc.) vocally the written or printed words of (a book, author, etc.) by following the symbols with the eyes or fingers. **2** *tr.* convert or be able to convert into the intended words or meaning (written or other symbols or the things expressed in this way). **3** *tr.* interpret mentally. **4** *tr.* deduce or declare an (esp. accurate) interpretation of (*read the expression on my face*). **5** *tr.* (often foll. by *that* + clause) find (a thing) recorded or stated in print etc. (*I read somewhere that you are leaving*). **6** *tr.* interpret (a statement or action) in a certain sense (*my silence is not to be read as consent*). **7** *tr.* (often foll. by *into*) assume as intended or deducible from a writer's words; find (implications) (*you read too much into my letter*). **8** *tr.* bring into a specified state by reading (*read myself to sleep*). **9** *tr.* (of a meter or other recording instrument) show (a specified figure etc.) (*the thermometer reads 20°*). **10** *intr.* convey meaning in a specified manner when read (*it reads persuasively*). **11** *intr.* sound or affect a hearer or reader as specified when read (*the book reads like a parody*). **12 a** *tr.* study by reading (esp. a subject at university). **b** *intr.* carry out a course of study by reading (*is reading for the Bar*). **13** *tr.* (as **read** /red/ *adj.*) versed in a subject (esp. literature) by reading (*a well-read person; was widely read in law*). **14** *tr.* **a** (of a computer) copy or transfer (data). **b** (foll. by *in, out*) enter or extract (data) in an electronic storage device. **15** *tr.* **a** understand or interpret (a person) by hearing words or seeing signs, gestures, etc. **b** interpret (cards, a person's hand, etc.) as a fortune-teller. **c** interpret (the sky) as an astrologer or meteorologist. **16** *tr. Printing* check the correctness of and emend (a proof). **17** *tr.* (of an editor or text) give as the word or words probably used or intended by an author. ● *n.* **1** a spell of reading. **2** *colloq.* a book etc. as regards its readability (*is a really good read*). □ **read between the lines** look for or find hidden meaning (in a document etc.). **read-in** the entry of data in an electronic storage device. **read a person like a book** understand a person's motives etc. **read-only memory** *Computing* a memory read at high speed but not capable of being changed by program instructions. **read out 1** read aloud. **2** *US* expel from a political party etc. **read-out** information retrieved from a computer. **read up** make a special study of (a subject). **read-write** *Computing* capable of reading existing data and accepting alterations or further input (cf. *read-only memory*). [OE *rǣdan* advise, consider, discern f. Gmc]

■ *v.* **1** peruse, study, look over, pore over; (*read out* or *aloud*) see *read out* 1 below. **2** understand, know, be familiar with, comprehend; translate, decode. **3, 6** see INTERPRET 1, 2; 4. **7** assign, impute, infer, assume, presume, conclude, find. **11** come over *or* across, appear; see also SOUND[1] *v.* 3. **12 a** study, take, *US* major in.

13 (*adj.*) see KNOWLEDGEABLE. □ **read out 1** recite, read *or* say aloud, quote, read. **2** see EXPEL 2, 3. **read up** see STUDY *v.* 1, 3.

readable /réedəb'l/ *adj.* **1** able to be read; legible. **2** interesting or pleasant to read. □□ **readability** /-bílliti/ *n.* **readableness** *n.* **readably** *adv.*
■ **1** legible, decipherable, distinct; intelligible, comprehensible, understandable, easy to understand, easily understood, plain. **2** entertaining, easy to read, enjoyable, pleasurable, absorbing, interesting, engaging, stimulating.

readapt /réeədápt/ *v.intr.* & *tr.* become or cause to become adapted anew. □□ **readaptation** /rée-adaptáysh'n/ *n.*

readdress /réeədréss/ *v.tr.* **1** change the address of (a letter or parcel). **2** address (a problem etc.) anew. **3** speak or write to anew.

reader /réedər/ *n.* **1** a person who reads or is reading. **2** a book of extracts for learning, esp. a language. **3** a device for producing an image that can be read from microfilm etc. **4** *Brit.* a university lecturer of the highest grade below professor. **5** a publisher's employee who reports on submitted manuscripts. **6** a printer's proof-corrector. **7** a person appointed to read aloud, esp. parts of a service in a church. **8** a person entitled to use a particular library. [OE (as READ)]

readership /réedərship/ *n.* **1** the readers of a newspaper etc. **2** the number or extent of these.

readily /réddili/ *adv.* **1** without showing reluctance; willingly. **2 a** without difficulty. **b** without delay.
■ **1** willingly, eagerly, ungrudgingly, unhesitatingly, freely, gladly, happily, cheerfully. **2 a** effortlessly, smoothly, without difficulty; see also EASILY 1. **b** promptly, quickly, speedily, swiftly, at once, without delay, in no time, immediately, instantly, instantaneously, straight away, right away, at *or* on short notice, *archaic or joc.* instanter, *colloq* pronto, *literary* apace.

reading /réeding/ *n.* **1 a** the act or an instance of reading or perusing (*the reading of the will*). **b** matter to be read (*have plenty of reading with me*). **c** the specified quality of this (*it made exciting reading*). **2** (in *comb.*) used for reading (*reading-lamp*; *reading-room*). **3** literary knowledge (*a person of wide reading*). **4** an entertainment at which a play, poems, etc., are read (*poetry reading*). **5** a figure etc. shown by a meter or other recording instrument. **6** an interpretation or view taken (*what is your reading of the facts?*). **7** an interpretation made (of drama, music, etc.). **8** each of the successive occasions on which a bill must be presented to a legislature for acceptance (see also *first reading*, *second reading*, *third reading*). **9** the version of a text, or the particular wording, conjectured or given by an editor etc. □ **reading age** reading ability expressed as the age for which the same ability is calculated as average (*has a reading age of eight*). [OE (as READ)]
■ **1 a** see *perusal* (PERUSE), RECITAL 1, 3. **6, 7** see *interpretation* (INTERPRET).

readjust /réeəjúst/ *v.tr.* adjust again or to a former state. □□ **readjustment** *n.*

readmit /réeədmít/ *v.tr.* (**readmitted**, **readmitting**) admit again. □□ **readmission** *n.*

readopt /réeədópt/ *v.tr.* adopt again. □□ **readoption** *n.*

ready /réddi/ *adj.*, *adv.*, *n.*, & *v.* ● *adj.* (**readier**, **readiest**) (usu. *predic.*) **1** with preparations complete (*dinner is ready*). **2** in a fit state (*are you ready to go?*). **3** willing, inclined, or resolved (*he is always ready to complain*; *I am ready for anything*; *a ready accomplice*). **4** within reach; easily secured (*a ready source of income*). **5** fit for immediate use (*was ready to hand*). **6** immediate, unqualified (*found ready acceptance*). **7** prompt, quick, facile (*is always ready with excuses*; *has a ready wit*). **8** (foll. by *to* + infin.) about to do something (*a bud just ready to burst*). **9** provided beforehand. ● *adv.* **1** beforehand. **2** so as not to require doing when the time comes for use (*the cases are ready packed*). ● *n.* (*pl.* **-ies**) *sl.* **1** (prec. by *the*) = *ready money*. **2** (in *pl.*) bank notes. ● *v.tr.* (**-ies**, **-ied**) make ready; prepare. □ **at the ready** ready for action. **make ready** prepare. **ready-made** (or **-to-wear**) **1** (esp. of clothes) made in a standard size, not to measure. **2** already available; convenient (*a ready-made excuse*). **ready-mix** (or **-mixed**) (of concrete, paint, food, etc.) having some or all of the constituents already mixed together. **ready money 1** actual coin or notes. **2** payment on the spot. **ready reckoner** a book or table listing standard numerical calculations as used esp. in commerce. **ready, steady** (or **get set**), **go** the usual formula for starting a race. □□ **readiness** *n.* [ME *rædi(g)*, *re(a)di*, f. OE *rǣde* f. Gmc]
■ *adj.* **1, 2** prepared, (all) set, in readiness, primed, ripe, fit; *colloq.* psyched (up). **3** apt, likely, inclined, disposed, given, prone; willing, pleased, content; prepared, resolved; consenting, agreeable, acquiescent, eager, keen, *colloq.* game. **4** on *or* at *or* to hand, handy, available, accessible, at one's fingertips, at the ready, close at hand, convenient, within reach. **6** see IMMEDIATE 1. **7** prompt, rapid, quick, speedy, swift; (*of the mind*) clever, keen, sharp, agile, bright, intelligent, perceptive; (*of wit*) facile, fluent, glib. **8** about, likely, apt, *disp.* liable; (*ready to*) on the verge of, subject to, in danger of, on the brink of, on the point of, close to. ● *n.* **2** see BILL[1] *n.* 5. ● *v.* make *or* get ready, set, equip, *colloq.* psych up; see also PREPARE 1, 3a. □ **at the ready** in position, poised, *esp. US* on deck, *colloq.* on tap; see also READY *adj.* 4 above. **make ready** see PREPARE 1, 3a. **ready-made 1** finished, off the peg, reach-me-down, stock. **2** convenient, serviceable, usable, handy, useful, suitable, adaptable; see also STALE[1] *adj.* 2. **ready money 1** see CASH[1] *n.* 1. □□ **readiness** willingness, eagerness, enthusiasm, keenness; promptness, quickness, speediness; facility, ease, skill, proficiency.

reaffirm /réeəfúrm/ *v.tr.* affirm again. □□ **reaffirmation** /-afərmáysh'n/ *n.*
■ see RENEW 4.

reafforest /réeəfórrist/ *v.tr.* replant (former forest land) with trees. □□ **reafforestation** /-stáysh'n/ *n.*

reagency /ree-áyjənsi/ *n.* reactive power or operation.

reagent /ree-áyjənt/ *n. Chem.* **1** a substance used to cause a reaction, esp. to detect another substance. **2** a reactive substance or force. [RE- + AGENT: cf. REACT]

real[1] /reel/ *adj.* & *adv.* ● *adj.* **1** actually existing as a thing or occurring in fact. **2** genuine; rightly so called; not artificial or merely apparent. **3** *Law* consisting of or relating to immovable property such as land or houses (*real estate*) (cf. *personal property*). **4** appraised by purchasing power; adjusted for changes in the value of money (*real value*; *income in real terms*). **5** *Philos.* having an absolute and necessary and not merely contingent existence. **6** *Math.* (of a quantity) having no imaginary part (see IMAGINARY 2). **7** *Optics* (of an image etc.) such that light actually passes through it. ● *adv. Sc.* & *US colloq.* really, very. □ **for real** *colloq.* as a serious or actual concern; in earnest. **real ale** beer regarded as brewed in a traditional way, with secondary fermentation in the cask. **real life** that lived by actual people, as distinct from fiction, drama, etc. **real live** (*attrib.*) often *joc.* actual; not pretended or simulated (*a real live burglar*). **the real McCoy** see McCOY. **real money** current coin or notes; cash. **real tennis** the original form of tennis played on an indoor court. **the real thing** (of an object or emotion) genuine, not inferior. **real time** the actual time during which a process or event occurs. **real-time** (*attrib.*) *Computing* (of a system) in which the response time is of the order of milliseconds, e.g. in an airline booking system. □□ **realness** *n.* [AF = OF *reel*, LL *realis* f. L *res* thing]
■ *adj.* **1** genuine, actual, true, existent, authentic, natural; material, physical, tangible, palpable, corporeal. **2** genuine, true, actual, proper, authentic, verified, verifiable, legitimate, bona fide, official; sincere, heartfelt, unfeigned, unaffected, earnest, honest, truthful; intrinsic. ● *adv.* see REALLY 2. □ **for real** see *in earnest* (EARNEST[1]). **real money** see CASH[1] *n.* 1.

real[2] /rayaál/ *n. hist.* a former coin and monetary unit of various Spanish-speaking countries. [Sp., noun use of *real* (adj.) (as ROYAL)]

realgar /riálgər/ *n.* a mineral of arsenic sulphide used as a pigment and in fireworks. [ME f. med.L f. Arab. *rahj al-ġār* dust of the cave]

realign /reéəlín/ *v.tr.* **1** align again. **2** regroup in politics etc. ▫▫ **realignment** *n.*

■ ▫▫ **realignment** see *shake-up.*

realism /reéəliz'm/ *n.* **1** the practice of regarding things in their true nature and dealing with them as they are. **2** fidelity to nature in representation; the showing of life etc. as it is in fact. **3** *Philos.* **a** the doctrine that universals or abstract concepts have an objective existence (opp. NOMINALISM). **b** the belief that matter as an object of perception has real existence. ▫▫ **realist** *n.*

realistic /reéəlístik/ *adj.* **1** regarding things as they are; following a policy of realism. **2** based on facts rather than ideals. ▫▫ **realistically** *adv.*

■ **1** natural, lifelike, true to life, naturalistic, vivid, graphic; factual. **2** practical, matter-of-fact, down-to-earth, pragmatic, sensible, reasonable, level-headed, rational, sane, hard-headed, businesslike, no-nonsense, unromantic, unsentimental, tough, tough-minded, hard-boiled, *colloq.* hard-nosed.

reality /riálliti/ *n.* (*pl.* **-ies**) **1** what is real or existent or underlies appearances. **2** (foll. by *of*) the real nature of (a thing). **3** real existence; the state of being real. **4** resemblance to an original (*the model was impressive in its reality*). ▫ **in reality** in fact. [med.L *realitas* or F *réalité* (as REAL[1])]

■ **1** actuality, fact, truth, genuineness, authenticity. **2** see NATURE 1, 7. ▫ **in reality** see *in fact* 1 (FACT).

realize /reéəlīz/ *v.tr.* (also **-ise**) **1** (often foll. by *that* + clause) (also *absol.*) be fully aware of; conceive as real. **2** (also *absol.*) understand clearly. **3** present as real; make realistic; give apparent reality to (*the story was powerfully realized on stage*). **4** convert into actuality; achieve (*realized a childhood dream*). **5 a** convert into money. **b** acquire (profit). **c** be sold for (a specified price). **6** *Mus.* reconstruct (a part) in full from a figured bass. ▫▫ **realizable** *adj.* **realizability** /-līzəbílliti/ *n.* **realization** /-záysh'n/ *n.* **realizer** *n.*

■ **1** be *or* become aware (of), appreciate, be conscious *or* appreciative (of); see also KNOW *v.* 1b. **2** understand, comprehend, grasp, perceive, discern, recognize, see, *colloq.* catch on to, cotton on to, *Brit* twig. **4** make real, effect, bring about, make happen, make a reality, produce, actualize, accomplish, achieve, fulfil, materialize, effectuate. **5 b** acquire, return, gain, clear, make, earn, bring *or* take in, net, produce, get. ▫▫ **realization 1** conception, understanding, comprehension, apprehension, awareness, appreciation, perception, recognition, cognizance; actualization, consummation, accomplishment, achievement, establishment, fulfilment, materialization, effectuation.

reallocate /reé-álləkayt/ *v.tr.* allocate again or differently. ▫▫ **reallocation** /-káysh'n/ *n.*

reallot /reéəlót/ *v.tr.* (**reallotted, reallotting**) allot again or differently. ▫▫ **reallotment** *n.*

really /reéəli/ *adv.* **1** in reality; in fact. **2** positively, assuredly (*really useful*). **3** (as a strong affirmative) indeed, I assure you. **4** an expression of mild protest or surprise. **5** (in *interrog.*) (expressing disbelief) is that so? (*They're musicians. — Really?*).

■ **1** in reality, in actuality, in (point of) fact, genuinely, actually, truly, honestly, as a matter of fact, indeed, definitely; in effect. **2** positively, assuredly, unqualifiedly, categorically, unquestionably, undeniably; very, extremely, exceptionally, remarkably, unusually, uncommonly, extraordinarily, exceedingly, *Sc.* & *US* real. **3** indeed, absolutely; see also DEFINITELY *adv.* 2. **5** well, I declare; well blow *or* knock me down with a feather, well I never, you don't say so, is that so, go on, *archaic* go to, *colloq.* well I'm damned, *sl.* I'll be blowed.

realm /relm/ *n.* **1** *formal* esp. *Law* a kingdom. **2** a sphere or domain (*the realm of imagination*). [ME f. OF *realme, reaume*, f. L *regimen -minis* (see REGIMEN): infl. by OF *reiel* ROYAL]

■ **1** domain, kingdom, empire, principality, palatinate, duchy. **2** sphere, limits, domain, confines, bounds; territory, area.

realpolitik /rayaálpoliteék/ *n.* politics based on realities and material needs, rather than on morals or ideals. [G]

realtor /reéəltər/ *n. US* a real-estate agent, esp. (**Realtor**) a member of the National Association of Realtors.

realty /reéəlti/ *n. Law* real estate (opp. PERSONALTY).

■ see PROPERTY 1c.

ream[1] /reem/ *n.* **1** twenty quires or 500 (formerly 480) sheets of paper (or a larger number, to allow for waste). **2** (in *pl.*) a large quantity of paper or writing (*wrote reams about it*). [ME *rēm, rīm* f. OF *raime* etc., ult. f. Arab. *rizma* bundle]

ream[2] /reem/ *v.tr.* **1** widen (a hole in metal etc.) with a borer. **2** turn over the edge of (a cartridge-case etc.). **3** *Naut.* open (a seam) for caulking. **4** *US* squeeze the juice from (fruit). ▫▫ **reamer** *n.* [19th c.: orig. uncert.]

■ **1** widen, broaden, extend, drill out, bore out, open up.

reanimate /reé-ánnimayt/ *v.tr.* **1** restore to life. **2** restore to activity or liveliness. ▫▫ **reanimation** /-máysh'n/ *n.*

■ **1** see RESURRECT 4. **2** see REJUVENATE. ▫▫ **reanimation** see REVIVAL 1, 3; 4a.

reap /reep/ *v.tr.* **1** cut or gather (a crop, esp. grain) as a harvest. **2** harvest the crop of (a field etc.). **3** receive as the consequence of one's own or others' actions. [OE *ripan, reopan*, of unkn. orig.]

■ **1** harvest, garner, glean, gather (in), take in. **3** receive, bring in, gain, procure, acquire, get, obtain, take in.

reaper /reépər/ *n.* **1** a person who reaps. **2** a machine for reaping. ▫ **the Reaper** (or **grim Reaper**) death personified.

reappear /reéəpeér/ *v.intr.* appear again or as previously. ▫▫ **reappearance** *n.*

■ see RETURN *v.* 1. ▫▫ **reappearance** see RETURN *n.* 1.

reapply /reéəplī́/ *v.tr.* & *intr.* (**-ies, -ied**) apply again, esp. submit a further application (for a position etc.). ▫▫ **reapplication** /reé-aplikáysh'n/ *n.*

reappoint /reéəpóynt/ *v.tr.* appoint again to a position previously held. ▫▫ **reappointment** *n.*

reapportion /reéəpórsh'n/ *v.tr.* apportion again or differently. ▫▫ **reapportionment** *n.*

reappraise /reéəpráyz/ *v.tr.* appraise or assess again. ▫▫ **reappraisal** *n.*

rear[1] /reer/ *n.* & *adj.* ● *n.* **1** the back part of anything. **2** the space behind, or position at the back of, anything (*a large house with a terrace at the rear*). **3** the hindmost part of an army or fleet. **4** *colloq.* the buttocks. ● *adj.* at the back. ▫ **bring up the rear** come last. **in the rear** behind; at the back. **rear admiral** a naval officer ranking below vice admiral. **rear commodore** a yacht-club officer below vice commodore. **rear-lamp** (or **-light**) a usu. red light at the rear of a vehicle. **rear sight** the sight nearest to the stock on a firearm. **rear-view mirror** a mirror fixed inside the windscreen of a motor vehicle enabling the driver to see traffic etc. behind. **take in the rear** *Mil.* attack from behind. [prob. f. (*in the*) REARWARD OR REARGUARD]

■ *n.* **1** back, back end, end, hind part, tail(-end), *Naut.* stern. **2** (*at* or *in the rear*) see BEHIND *prep.* 1a, b. **4** seat, hindquarters, posterior, rump, buttocks, rear end, *colloq.* bottom, behind, backside, *Brit. sl.* bum, *esp. US sl.* tush. ● *adj.* back, end, rearmost. ▫ **in the rear** see BEHIND *prep.* 1a, b.

rear[2] /reer/ *v.* **1** *tr.* **a** bring up and educate (children). **b** breed and care for (animals). **c** cultivate (crops). **2** *intr.* (of a horse etc.) raise itself on its hind legs. **3** *tr.* **a** set upright. **b** build. **c** hold upwards (*rear one's head*). **4** *intr.* extend to a great height. ▫▫ **rearer** *n.* [OE *rǣran* f. Gmc]

■ **1 a** raise, bring up, nurture; cultivate, educate, train. **b** breed, raise; care for, look after, tend. **c** see CULTIVATE 2a. **3 b** erect, raise, build, put up, construct, fabricate. **c** raise, lift, put up, upraise, uplift, hold up.

rearguard /reérgaard/ *n.* **1** a body of troops detached to protect the rear, esp. in retreats. **2** a defensive or conservative element in an organization etc. □ **rearguard action 1** *Mil.* an engagement undertaken by a rearguard. **2** a defensive stand in argument etc., esp. when losing. [OF *rereguarde* (as RETRO-, GUARD)]

rearm /reé-aárm/ *v.tr.* (also *absol.*) arm again, esp. with improved weapons. □□ **rearmament** *n.*

rearmost /reérmōst/ *adj.* furthest back.
■ see LAST[1] *adj.* 1, 5.

rearrange /reéəráynj/ *v.tr.* arrange again in a different way. □□ **rearrangement** *n.*
■ arrange, adjust, alter, reposition, shuffle, reshuffle, rejig, scramble, change, sort out; see also TIDY *v.*

rearrest /reéərést/ *v.* & *n.* ● *v.tr.* arrest again. ● *n.* an instance of rearresting or being rearrested.

rearward /reérwərd/ *n.*, *adj.*, & *adv.* ● *n.* rear, esp. in prepositional phrases (*to the rearward of*; *in the rearward*). ● *adj.* to the rear. ● *adv.* (also **rearwards**) towards the rear. [AF *rerewarde* = REARGUARD]
■ *adj.* see BACKWARD *adj.* 1. ● *adv.* see BACKWARDS 2.

reascend /reéəsénd/ *v.tr.* & *intr.* ascend again or to a former position. □□ **reascension** *n.*

reason /reéz'n/ *n.* & *v.* ● *n.* **1** a motive, cause, or justification (*has good reasons for doing this*; *there is no reason to be angry*). **2** a fact adduced or serving as this (*I can give you my reasons*). **3** the intellectual faculty by which conclusions are drawn from premisses. **4** sanity (*has lost his reason*). **5** *Logic* a premiss of a syllogism, esp. a minor premiss when given after the conclusion. **6** a faculty transcending the understanding and providing a priori principles; intuition. **7** sense; sensible conduct; what is right or practical or practicable; moderation. ● *v.* **1** *intr.* form or try to reach conclusions by connected thought. **2** *intr.* (foll. by *with*) use an argument (with a person) by way of persuasion. **3** *tr.* (foll. by *that* + clause) conclude or assert in argument. **4** *tr.* (foll. by *why*, *whether*, *what* + clause) discuss; ask oneself. **5** *tr.* (foll. by *into*, *out of*) persuade or move by argument (*I reasoned them out of their fears*). **6** *tr.* (foll. by *out*) think or work out (consequences etc.). **7** *tr.* (often as **reasoned** *adj.*) express in logical or argumentative form. **8** *tr.* embody reason in (an amendment etc.). □ **by reason of** owing to. **in** (or **within**) **reason** within the bounds of sense or moderation. **it stands to reason** (often foll. by *that* + clause) it is evident or logical. **listen to reason** be persuaded to act sensibly. **see reason** acknowledge the force of an argument. **with reason** justifiably. □□ **reasoner** *n.* **reasoning** *n.* **reasonless** *adj.* [ME f. OF *reisun*, *res(o)un*, *raisoner*, ult. f. L *ratio -onis* f. *rēri rat-* consider]
■ *n.* **1, 2** cause, motive, purpose, aim, intention, objective, goal; justification, argument, case, explanation, rationale, ground(s), pretext, basis, defence; excuse, rationalization. **3** reasoning, logic, rationality, thought; mind, intellect, intelligence. **4** see SANITY 1. **6** judgement, insight, perspicacity, percipience, understanding; see also INTUITION. **7** common sense; moderation; see also SENSE *n.* 4, 5. ● *v.* **1** think rationally *or* logically, use (one's) judgement *or* common sense, think it through, use one's head, put two and two together, *literary* ratiocinate. **2** (*reason with*) argue with, remonstrate with, debate with, discuss with, talk with, plead with, prevail (up)on. **3, 6** argue, assert; conclude, calculate, reckon, estimate, figure (out), work out, deduce, think out *or* through. **7** (**reasoned**) see LOGICAL 2, 3. □ **by reason of** because of, on account of, owing to, by virtue of, as a result of, *disp.* due to. **in** (or **within**) **reason** reasonable, sensible, justifiable, rational, fitting, proper, acceptable. **with reason** see WELL[1] *adv.* 7. □□ **reasoning** thinking, logic, rationality, thought, analysis, rationalization; reasons, arguments, rationale, explanation, explication, *Logic* premises, premisses, *literary* ratiocination.

reasonable /reézənəb'l/ *adj.* **1** having sound judgement; moderate; ready to listen to reason. **2** in accordance with reason; not absurd. **3 a** within the limits of reason; not greatly less or more than might be expected. **b** inexpensive; not extortionate. **c** tolerable, fair. **4** *archaic* endowed with the faculty of reason. □□ **reasonableness** *n.* **reasonably** *adv.* [ME f. OF *raisonable* (as REASON) after L *rationabilis*]
■ **1** sensible, rational, sane, logical, sober, moderate, sound, judicious, wise, intelligent. **2** tenable, reasoned, well-thought-out, logical, well-grounded, justifiable, justified, valid, sensible. **3 a, c** appropriate, suitable, moderate, tolerable, acceptable, within reason, average, normal; equitable, fair. **b** see INEXPENSIVE.

reassemble /reéəsémb'l/ *v.intr.* & *tr.* assemble again or into a former state. □□ **reassembly** *n.*

reassert /reéəsért/ *v.tr.* assert again. □□ **reassertion** *n.*
■ see RENEW 4.

reassess /reéəséss/ *v.tr.* assess again, esp. differently. □□ **reassessment** *n.*
■ see REVIEW *v.* 2, 5. □□ **reassessment** see REVIEW *n.* 3.

reassign /reéəsín/ *v.tr.* assign again or differently. □□ **reassignment** *n.*

reassume /reéəsyóōm/ *v.tr.* take on oneself or undertake again. □□ **reassumption** /-súmpsh'n/ *n.*

reassure /reéəshóor/ *v.tr.* **1** restore confidence to; dispel the apprehensions of. **2** confirm in an opinion or impression. □□ **reassurance** *n.* **reassurer** *n.* **reassuring** *adj.* **reassuringly** *adv.*
■ **1** comfort, encourage, hearten, buoy (up), bolster, cheer, uplift, inspirit, support, restore confidence to, set *or* put a person's mind at rest, set *or* put at ease.

reattach /reéətách/ *v.tr.* attach again or in a former position. □□ **reattachment** *n.*

reattain /reéətáyn/ *v.tr.* attain again. □□ **reattainment** *n.*

reattempt /reéətémpt/ *v.tr.* attempt again, esp. after failure.

Réaumur /ráyōmyoor/ *adj.* expressed in or related to the scale of temperature at which water freezes at 0° and boils at 80° under standard conditions. □ **Réaumur scale** this scale. [R. de *Réaumur*, Fr. physicist d. 1757]

reave /reev/ *v.* (*past* and *past part.* **reft** /reft/) *archaic* **1** *tr.* **a** (foll. by *of*) forcibly deprive of. **b** (foll. by *away*, *from*) take by force or carry off. **2** *intr.* make raids; plunder; = REIVE. [OE *rēafian* f. Gmc: cf. ROB]

reawaken /reéəwáykən/ *v.tr.* & *intr.* awaken again.
■ see REVIVE.

rebarbative /ribaárbətiv/ *adj. literary* repellent, unattractive. [F *rébarbatif -ive* f. *barbe* beard]

rebate[1] /reébayt/ *n.* & *v.* ● *n.* **1** a partial refund of money paid. **2** a deduction from a sum to be paid; a discount. ● *v.tr.* pay back as a rebate. □□ **rebatable** *adj.* **rebater** *n.* [earlier = diminish: ME f. OF *rabattre* (as RE-, ABATE)]
■ *n.* discount, reduction, deduction, allowance, mark-down, refund, repayment. ● *v.* refund, give back, pay back; see also REPAY 1, 3.

rebate[2] /reébayt/ *n.* & *v.tr.* = RABBET. [respelling of RABBET, after REBATE[1]]

rebec /reébek/ *n.* (also **rebeck**) *Mus.* a medieval usu. three-stringed instrument played with a bow. [F *rebec* var. of OF *rebebe rubebe* f. Arab. *rabāb*]

rebel *n.*, *adj.*, & *v.* ● *n.* /rébb'l/ **1** a person who fights against, resists, or refuses allegiance to, the established government. **2** a person or thing that resists authority or control. ● *adj.* /rébb'l/ (*attrib.*) **1** rebellious. **2** of or concerning rebels. **3** in rebellion. ● *v.intr.* /ribél/ (**rebelled**, **rebelling**; *US* **rebeled**, **rebeling**) (usu. foll. by *against*) **1** act as a rebel; revolt. **2** feel or display repugnance. [ME f. OF *rebelle*, *rebeller* f. L *rebellis* (as RE-, *bellum* war)]
■ *n.* revolutionary, revolutionist, insurgent, insurrectionist, mutineer, resister, resistance fighter, freedom fighter, guerrilla; heretic, nonconformist, dissenter, recusant. ● *adj.* **1** see REBELLIOUS 1. ● *v.* **1** revolt, mutiny, rise up, dissent; (*rebel against*) defy, flout, challenge, disobey.

rebellion /ribélyən/ *n.* open resistance to authority, esp. (an) organized armed resistance to an established government. [ME f. OF f. L *rebellio -onis* (as REBEL)]

■ uprising, revolution, mutiny, insurrection, revolt, insurgence, insurgency; insubordination, disobedience, defiance, resistance, rebelliousness, contumacy.

rebellious /ribélyəss/ *adj.* **1** tending to rebel, insubordinate. **2** in rebellion. **3** defying lawful authority. **4** (of a thing) unmanageable, refractory. □□ **rebelliously** *adv.* **rebelliousness** *n.* [ME f. REBELLION + -OUS or f. earlier *rebellous* + -IOUS]

■ **1** rebel, insubordinate, defiant, mutinous, revolutionary, contumacious, insurgent, insurrectionary, seditious; unmanageable, disobedient, difficult, refractory, incorrigible, ungovernable, unruly, stubborn, obstinate, recalcitrant. **4** unmanageable, difficult, refractory.

rebid /reébid/ *v.* & *n.* ● *v.* (**rebidding**; *past* and *past part.* **rebid**) *Cards* **1** *intr.* bid again. **2** *tr.* bid (a suit) again at a higher level. ● *n.* **1** the act of rebidding. **2** a bid made in this way.

rebind /reébīnd/ *v.tr.* (*past* and *past part.* **rebound**) bind (esp. a book) again or differently.

rebirth /reébúrth/ *n.* **1** a new incarnation. **2** spiritual enlightenment. **3** a revival (*the rebirth of learning*). □□ **reborn** /reébórn/ *adj.*

■ **1** see REINCARNATION. **2** see *illumination* (ILLUMINATE). **3** renaissance, renascence, revival, renewal, reawakening, resurgence, resurrection, regeneration, rejuvenation, restoration.

reboot /reébo͞ot/ *v.tr.* (often *absol.*) *Computing* boot up (a system) again.

rebore *v.* & *n.* ● *v.tr.* /reébór/ make a new boring in, esp. widen the bore of (the cylinder in an internal-combustion engine). ● *n.* /reébor/ **1** the process of doing this. **2** a rebored engine.

rebound[1] *v.* & *n.* ● *v.intr.* /ribównd/ **1** spring back after action or impact. **2** (foll. by *upon*) (of an action) have an adverse effect upon (the doer). ● *n.* /reébownd/ **1** the act or an instance of rebounding; recoil. **2** a reaction after a strong emotion. □ **on the rebound** while still recovering from an emotional shock, esp. rejection by a lover. □□ **rebounder** *n.* [ME f. OF *rebonder*, *rebondir* (as RE-, BOUND[1])]

■ *v.* **1** spring back, bounce, recoil, ricochet, resile. ● *n.* **1** bounce, recoil, ricochet, return, comeback. **2** see BACKLASH 1.

rebound[2] /reébównd/ *past* and *past part.* of REBIND.

rebroadcast /reébráwdkaast/ *v.* & *n.* ● *v.tr.* (*past* **rebroadcast** or **rebroadcasted**; *past part.* **rebroadcast**) broadcast again. ● *n.* a repeat broadcast.

■ repeat, rerun.

rebuff /ribúf/ *n.* & *v.* ● *n.* **1** a rejection of one who makes advances, proffers help or sympathy, shows interest or curiosity, makes a request, etc. **2** a repulse; a snub. ● *v.tr.* give a rebuff to. [obs. F *rebuffe(r)* f. It. *ribuffo*, *ribuffare*, *rabbuffo*, *rabbuffare* (as RE-, *buffo* puff)]

■ *n.* rejection, discouragement, snub, repulse, refusal, dismissal, brush-off, repudiation, slight, cut, *colloq.* put-down, knock-back. ● *v.* reject, snub, repel, drive away, spurn, repulse, refuse, dismiss, repudiate, slight, ignore, give a person the cold shoulder, cut (dead), brush off, give a person the brush-off, *colloq.* put down, knock back, *US colloq.* freeze out.

rebuild /reébíld/ *v.tr.* (*past* and *past part.* **rebuilt**) build again or differently.

■ see RESTORE 1.

rebuke /ribyo͞ok/ *v.* & *n.* ● *v.tr.* reprove sharply; subject to protest or censure. ● *n.* **1** the act of rebuking. **2** the process of being rebuked. **3** a reproof. □□ **rebuker** *n.* **rebukingly** *adv.* [ME f. AF & ONF *rebuker* (as RE-, OF *buchier* beat, orig. cut down wood f. *busche* log)]

■ *v.* scold, reproach, admonish, reprove, reprimand, lecture, censure, reprehend, berate, castigate, criticize, take to task, upbraid, have a go at, revile, give a piece of one's mind, haul *or* rake over the coals, *archaic or literary* chide, *colloq.* dress down, bawl out, give a person hell *or* what for, tell off, carpet, tear a person off a strip, tick off, wig, give a person a wigging, *US colloq.* chew out; see also CASTIGATE. ● *n.* censure, reprehension, castigation, criticism, upbraiding, revilement; scolding, reproach, admonition, reproof, lecture, tongue-lashing, *colloq.* dressing-down, wigging; see also REPRIMAND *n.*

rebury /reébérri/ *v.tr.* (**-ies, -ied**) bury again. □□ **reburial** *n.*

rebus /reébəss/ *n.* **1** an enigmatic representation of a word (esp. a name), by pictures etc. suggesting its parts. **2** *Heraldry* a device suggesting the name of its bearer. [F *rébus* f. L *rebus*, ablat. pl. of *res* thing]

rebut /ribút/ *v.tr.* (**rebutted**, **rebutting**) **1** refute or disprove (evidence or a charge). **2** force or turn back; check. □□ **rebutment** *n.* **rebuttable** *adj.* **rebuttal** *n.* [ME f. AF *rebuter*, OF *rebo(u)ter* (as RE-, BUTT[1])]

■ **1** refute, deny, disprove, confute, invalidate, negate, discredit, belie, contradict, controvert, puncture, expose, destroy, shoot down, knock the bottom out of. **2** force back, turn back; see also CHECK[1] *v.* 2a. □□ **rebuttal** counter-argument, riposte, retaliation, denial, refutation, contradiction, confutation, negation, rejection; retort, response, rejoinder.

rebutter /ribúttər/ *n.* **1** a refutation. **2** *Law* a defendant's reply to the plaintiff's surrejoinder. [AF *rebuter* (as REBUT)]

■ see ANSWER *n.* 1.

recalcitrant /rikálsitrənt/ *adj.* & *n.* ● *adj.* **1** obstinately disobedient. **2** objecting to restraint. ● *n.* a recalcitrant person. □□ **recalcitrance** *n.* **recalcitrantly** *adv.* [L *recalcitrare* (as RE-, *calcitrare* kick out with the heels f. *calx calcis* heel)]

■ *adj.* **1** stubborn, disobedient, obstinate, wilful, defiant, refractory, headstrong, perverse, contrary, contumacious, mutinous, rebellious, fractious, unruly, unmanageable, ungovernable, uncontrollable, wayward, insubordinate. **2** intractable, unsubmissive, unyielding, unbending, immovable, inflexible, firm.

recalculate /reékálkyoolayt/ *v.tr.* calculate again. □□ **recalculation** /-láysh'n/ *n.*

recalesce /reékəléss/ *v.intr.* grow hot again (esp. of iron allowed to cool from white heat, whose temperature rises at a certain point for a short time). □□ **recalescence** *n.* [L *recalescere* (as RE-, *calescere* grow hot)]

recall /rikáwl/ *v.* & *n.* ● *v.tr.* **1** summon to return from a place or from a different occupation, inattention, a digression, etc. **2** recollect, remember. **3** bring back to memory; serve as a reminder of. **4** revoke or annul (an action or decision). **5** cancel or suspend the appointment of (an official sent overseas etc.). **6** revive, resuscitate. **7** take back (a gift). ● *n.* /also reékawl/ **1** the act or an instance of recalling, esp. a summons to come back. **2** the act of remembering. **3** the ability to remember. **4** the possibility of recalling, esp. in the sense of revoking (*beyond recall*). **5** *US* removal of an elected official from office. □□ **recallable** *adj.*

■ *v.* **1** call back, summon (back); rally, rouse. **2** remember, recollect, call to mind; think back to, reminisce over *or* about. **4** rescind, suspend, annul, nullify, retract, withdraw, revoke, recant, take back; see also CANCEL *v.* 1a, 4. **6** see REVIVE 2. ● *n.* **1** withdrawal, retraction, return; summons. **2, 3** memory, recollection; remembrance, reminiscence. **4** withdrawal, recantation, cancellation, revocation, annulment, nullification, rescission, retraction, repeal. **5** see *dismissal* (DISMISS).

recant /rikánt/ *v.* **1** *tr.* withdraw and renounce (a former belief or statement) as erroneous or heretical. **2** *intr.* disavow a former opinion, esp. with a public confession of error. □□ **recantation** /reékantáysh'n/ *n.* **recanter** *n.* [L *recantare* revoke (as RE-, *cantare* sing, chant)]

■ **1** recall, forswear, deny, rescind, repudiate, disavow, disclaim, withdraw, revoke, retract, forsake, abandon, renounce, abjure, take back, reverse, renege. **2** apostatize; see also RENEGE 1a.

recap /reékap/ *v.* & *n.* *colloq.* ● *v.tr.* & *intr.* (**recapped**, **recapping**) recapitulate. ● *n.* recapitulation. [abbr.]

■ *v.* see RECAPITULATE. ● *n.* see RÉSUMÉ 1.

recapitalize /reekáppitəlīz/ *v.tr.* (also **-ise**) capitalize (shares etc.) again. ▫▫ **recapitalization** /-záysh'n/ *n.*

recapitulate /reekəpítyoolayt/ *v.tr.* **1** go briefly through again; summarize. **2** go over the main points or headings of. ▫▫ **recapitulative** /-lətiv/ *adj.* **recapitulatory** /-lətəri/ *adj.* [L *recapitulare* (as RE-, *capitulum* CHAPTER)]
■ summarize, sum up; repeat, go over (again), reiterate, restate, review, *colloq.* recap; recount, enumerate, recite, relate, list.

recapitulation /reekəpítyooláysh'n/ *n.* **1** the act or an instance of recapitulating. **2** *Biol.* the reappearance in embryos of successive type-forms in the evolutionary line of development. **3** *Mus.* part of a movement, esp. in sonata form, in which themes from the exposition are restated. [ME f. OF *recapitulation* or LL *recapitulatio* (as RECAPITULATE)]
■ **1** see RÉSUMÉ 1.

recapture /reekápchər/ *v.* & *n.* ● *v.tr.* **1** capture again; recover by capture. **2** re-experience (a past emotion etc.). ● *n.* the act or an instance of recapturing.
■ *v.* **1** see RECOVER *v.* 1. **2** relive, re-experience, retrieve, recall.

recast /reekaast/ *v.* & *n.* ● *v.tr.* (*past* and *past part.* **recast**) **1** put into a new form. **2** improve the arrangement of. **3** change the cast of (a play etc.). ● *n.* **1** the act or an instance of recasting. **2** a recast form.
■ *v.* **1, 2** see MODIFY 2.

recce /rékki/ *n.* & *v. colloq.* ● *n.* a reconnaissance. ● *v.tr.* & *intr.* (**recced, recceing**) reconnoitre. [abbr.]
■ *n.* see RECONNAISSANCE. ● *v.* see RECONNOITRE *v.*

recd. *abbr.* received.

recede /riséed/ *v.intr.* **1** go or shrink back or further off. **2** be left at an increasing distance by an observer's motion. **3** slope backwards (*a receding chin*). **4** decline in force or value. **5** (foll. by *from*) withdraw from (an engagement, opinion, etc.). **6** (of a man's hair) cease to grow at the front, sides, etc. [ME f. L *recedere* (as RE-, *cedere cess-* go)]
■ **1** ebb, subside, fall *or* go *or* move back, shrink back, abate, withdraw, retreat. **4** diminish, lessen, dwindle, shrink, wane, fade, become less likely; see also DECLINE *v.* 1, 7. **5** see WITHDRAW 5.

re-cede /reesséed/ *v.tr.* cede back to a former owner.

receipt /riséet/ *n.* & *v.* ● *n.* **1** the act or an instance of receiving or being received into one's possession (*will pay on receipt of the goods*). **2** a written acknowledgement of this, esp. of the payment of money. **3** (usu. in *pl.*) an amount of money etc. received. **4** *archaic* a recipe. ● *v.tr.* place a written or printed receipt on (a bill). [ME *receit(e)* f. AF & ONF *receite*, OF *reçoite*, *recete* f. med.L *recepta* fem. past part. of L *recipere* RECEIVE: *-p-* inserted after L]
■ *n.* **1** delivery, acceptance; arrival, appearance. **2** sales slip, ticket, stub, counterfoil, proof of purchase, voucher. **3** (*receipts*) income, proceeds, gate, takings, return, *esp. US* take.

receive /riséev/ *v.tr.* **1** take or accept (something offered or given) into one's hands or possession. **2** acquire; be provided with or given (*have received no news; will receive a small fee*). **3** accept delivery of (something sent). **4** have conferred or inflicted on one (*received many honours; received a heavy blow on the head*). **5 a** stand the force or weight of. **b** bear up against; encounter with opposition. **6** consent to hear (a confession or oath) or consider (a petition). **7** (also *absol.*) accept or have dealings with (stolen property knowing of the theft). **8** admit; consent or prove able to hold; provide accommodation for (*received many visitors*). **9** (of a receptacle) be able to hold (a specified amount or contents). **10** greet or welcome, esp. in a specified manner (*how did they receive your offer?*). **11** entertain as a guest etc. **12** admit to membership of a society, organization, etc. **13** be marked more or less permanently with (an impression etc.). **14** convert (broadcast signals) into sound or pictures. **15** *Tennis* be the player to whom the server serves (the ball). **16** (often as **received** *adj.*) give credit to; accept as authoritative or true (*received opinion*). **17** eat or drink (the Eucharistic bread and wine). ▫ **be at** (or **on**) **the receiving end** *colloq.* bear the brunt of something unpleasant. **received pronunciation** (or **Received Standard**) the form of spoken English based on educated speech in southern England. **receiving-order** *Brit.* an order of a court authorizing a receiver (see RECEIVER 3) to act. ▫▫ **receivable** *adj.* [ME f. OF *receivre*, *reçoivre* f. L *recipere recept-* (as RE-, *capere* take)]
■ **1, 2** get, obtain, come by, be provided with, collect, take (into one's possession), accept, be given, acquire, come into, inherit, gain; hear, learn, ascertain, be told, be informed *or* notified of, find out, pick up; see also EARN 1. **4** (*of honours*) accept, collect, earn, gain, win; (*of a blow*) experience, undergo, endure, suffer, bear, sustain, be subjected to, meet with. **8, 12** show in, let in; see also ADMIT 3, ACCOMMODATE 1. **9** see HOLD[1] *v.* 2. **10** greet, meet, welcome; respond to, react to. **11** see ENTERTAIN 2a. **16** (**received**) see ORTHODOX.

receiver /riséevər/ *n.* **1** a person or thing that receives. **2** the part of a machine or instrument that receives sound, signals, etc. (esp. the part of a telephone that contains the earpiece). **3** (in full **official receiver**) a person appointed by a court to administer the property of a bankrupt or insane person, or property under litigation. **4** a radio or television receiving apparatus. **5** a person who receives stolen goods. **6** *Chem.* a vessel for collecting the products of distillation, chromatography, etc.
■ **1** see RECIPIENT *n.* **4** see RADIO *n.*, TELEVISION 2.

receivership /riséevərship/ *n.* **1** the office of official receiver. **2** the state of being dealt with by a receiver (esp. *in receivership*).

recension /risénsh'n/ *n.* **1** the revision of a text. **2** a particular form or version of a text resulting from such revision. [L *recensio* f. *recensēre* revise (as RE-, *censēre* review)]

recent /reess'nt/ *adj.* & *n.* ● *adj.* **1** not long past; that happened, appeared, began to exist, or existed lately. **2** not long established; lately begun; modern. **3** (**Recent**) *Geol.* = HOLOCENE. ● *n. Geol.* = HOLOCENE. ▫▫ **recency** *n.* **recently** *adv.* **recentness** *n.* [L *recens recentis* or F *récent*]
■ *adj.* **2** new, current, modern, up to date.

receptacle /riséptək'l/ *n.* **1** a containing vessel, place, or space. **2** *Bot.* **a** the common base of floral organs. **b** the part of a leaf or thallus in some algae where the reproductive organs are situated. [ME f. OF *receptacle* or L *receptaculum* (as RECEPTION)]
■ **1** container, holder, repository; box, tin, can, case, casket, chest, vessel, bag, basket.

reception /risépsh'n/ *n.* **1** the act or an instance of receiving or the process of being received, esp. of a person into a place or group. **2** the manner in which a person or thing is received (*got a cool reception*). **3** a social occasion for receiving guests, esp. after a wedding. **4** a formal or ceremonious welcome. **5** a place where guests or clients etc. report on arrival at a hotel, office, etc. **6 a** the receiving of broadcast signals. **b** the quality of this (*we have excellent reception*). ▫ **reception order** an order authorizing the entry of a patient into a mental hospital. **reception room** a room available or suitable for receiving company or visitors. [ME f. OF *reception* or L *receptio* (as RECEIVE)]
■ **2** welcome, greeting, treatment; reaction, response. **3** party, social (event), function,, *archaic or US* levee, *colloq.* do. ▫ **reception room** see PARLOUR.

receptionist /risépshənist/ *n.* a person employed in a hotel, office, etc., to receive guests, clients, etc.

receptive /riséptiv/ *adj.* **1** able or quick to receive impressions or ideas. **2** concerned with receiving stimuli etc. ▫▫ **receptively** *adv.* **receptiveness** *n.* **receptivity** /reesseptívviti/ *n.* [F *réceptif -ive* or med.L *receptivus* (as RECEPTION)]
■ **1** open, responsive, impressionable, susceptive, amenable, recipient, sensitive, willing, tractable, flexible, pliant; quick, sharp, alert, perceptive, astute, bright.

receptor /riséptər/ *n.* (often *attrib.*) *Biol.* **1** an organ able to respond to an external stimulus such as light, heat, or a drug, and transmit a signal to a sensory nerve. **2** a region of a cell, tissue, etc., that responds to a molecule or other substance. [OF *receptour* or L *receptor* (as RECEPTIVE)]

■ **recess** /risés, réesess/ *n.* & *v.* ● *n.* **1** a space set back in a wall; a niche. **2** (often in *pl.*) a remote or secret place (*the innermost recesses*). **3** a temporary cessation from work, esp. of Parliament, or *US* of a lawcourt or during a school day. **4** *Anat.* a fold or indentation in an organ. **5** *Geog.* a receding part of a mountain chain etc. ● *v.* **1** *tr.* make a recess in. **2** *tr.* place in a recess; set back. **3** *US* & *Austral.* **a** *intr.* take a recess; adjourn. **b** *tr.* order a temporary cessation from the work of (a court etc.). [L *recessus* (as RECEDE)]

■ *n.* **1** alcove, niche, nook, cranny, bay, hollow. **2** (*recesses*) innermost reaches, corners, secret places, depths, penetralia. **3** respite, rest, interlude, break, intermission, breathing-space, pause, cessation, *colloq.* breather; holiday, vacation. ● *v.* **3 a** take a break, break, stop, rest, pause, adjourn, *colloq.* take a breather.

recession /riséshʼn/ *n.* **1** a temporary decline in economic activity or prosperity. **2** a receding or withdrawal from a place or point. **3** a receding part of an object; a recess. □□ **recessionary** *adj.* [L *recessio* (as RECESS)]

■ **1** (economic) downturn, slump, decline, dip, depression, set-back.

recessional /riséshənʼl/ *adj.* & *n.* ● *adj.* sung while the clergy and choir withdraw after a service. ● *n.* a recessional hymn.

recessive /risésiv/ *adj.* **1** tending to recede. **2** *Phonet.* (of an accent) falling near the beginning of a word. **3** *Genetics* (of an inherited characteristic) appearing in offspring only when not masked by a dominant characteristic inherited from one parent. □□ **recessively** *adv.* **recessiveness** *n.* [RECESS after *excessive*]

recharge *v.* & *n.* ● *v.tr.* /reécha̋arj/ **1** charge again. **2** reload. ● *n.* /réechaarj/ **1** a renewed charge. **2** material etc. used for this. □□ **rechargeable** /reécha̋arjəbʼl/ *adj.*

réchauffé /rishṓfay/ *n.* **1** a warmed-up dish. **2** a rehash. [F past part. of *réchauffer* (as RE-, CHAFE)]

recheck *v.* & *n.* ● *v.tr.* & *intr.* /reechék/ check again. ● *n.* /réechek/ a second or further check or inspection.

recherché /rəsháirshay/ *adj.* **1** carefully sought out; rare or exotic. **2** far-fetched, obscure. [F, past part. of *rechercher* (as RE-, *chercher* seek)]

■ **1** see RARE[1] 1. **2** see *far-fetched*.

rechristen /reekríssʼn/ *v.tr.* **1** christen again. **2** give a new name to.

recidivist /risíddivist/ *n.* a person who relapses into crime. □□ **recidivism** *n.* **recidivistic** /-vístik/ *adj.* [F *récidiviste* f. *récidiver* f. med.L *recidivare* f. L *recidivus* f. *recidere* (as RE-, *cadere* fall)]

recipe /réssipi/ *n.* **1** a statement of the ingredients and procedure required for preparing cooked food. **2** an expedient; a device for achieving something. **3** a medical prescription. [2nd sing. imper. (as used in prescriptions) of L *recipere* take, RECEIVE]

■ **1** formula, *archaic* receipt. **2** expedient; plan, procedure, method, approach, technique, way, means, system, programme, *modus operandi*.

recipient /risíppiənt/ *n.* & *adj.* ● *n.* a person who receives something. ● *adj.* **1** receiving. **2** receptive. □□ **recipiency** *n.* [F *récipient* f. It. *recipiente* or L *recipiens* f. *recipere* RECEIVE]

■ *n.* receiver, beneficiary, heir, heiress, legatee. ● *adj.* **2** see RECEPTIVE.

reciprocal /risíprəkʼl/ *adj.* & *n.* ● *adj.* **1** in return (*offered a reciprocal greeting*). **2** mutual (*their feelings are reciprocal*). **3** *Gram.* (of a pronoun) expressing mutual action or relation (as in *each other*). **4** inversely correspondent; complementary (*natural kindness matched by a reciprocal severity*). ● *n.* *Math.* an expression or function so related to another that their product is unity ($^1/_2$ is the reciprocal of 2). □□ **reciprocality** /-kálliti/ *n.* **reciprocally** *adv.* [L *reciprocus* ult. f. *re-* back + *pro* forward]

■ *adj.* **2** mutual; common, shared, joint. **4** complementary, correlative, matching, corresponding, correspondent.

reciprocate /risíprəkayt/ *v.* **1** *tr.* return or requite (affection etc.). **2** *intr.* (foll. by *with*) offer or give something in return (*reciprocated with an invitation to lunch*). **3** *tr.* give and receive mutually; interchange. **4 a** *intr.* (of a part of a machine) move backwards and forwards. **b** *tr.* cause to do this. □ **reciprocating engine** an engine using a piston or pistons moving up and down in cylinders. □□ **reciprocation** /-káyshʼn/ *n.* **reciprocator** *n.* [L *reciprocare reciprocat-* (as RECIPROCAL)]

■ **1** repay, requite, return, match, equal. **2** see RESPOND *v.* 2. **3** exchange, interchange; swap, trade.

reciprocity /réssiprόssiti/ *n.* **1** the condition of being reciprocal. **2** mutual action. **3** give and take, esp. the interchange of privileges between countries and organizations. [F *réciprocité* f. *réciproque* f. L *reciprocus* (as RECIPROCATE)]

■ **3** see *give and take*.

recirculate /reessúrkyoolayt/ *v.tr.* & *intr.* circulate again, esp. make available for reuse. □□ **recirculation** /-láyshʼn/ *n.*

recital /rísītʼl/ *n.* **1** the act or an instance of reciting or being recited. **2** the performance of a programme of music by a solo instrumentalist or singer or by a small group. **3** (foll. by *of*) a detailed account of (connected things or facts); a narrative. **4** *Law* the part of a legal document that states the facts. □□ **recitalist** *n.*

■ **1, 3** narration, recitation, description, relation, reading, telling, recounting; report, account, narrative, version, recapitulation, *colloq.* recap. **2** concert, performance; *colloq.* gig.

recitation /réssitáyshʼn/ *n.* **1** the act or an instance of reciting. **2** a thing recited. [OF *recitation* or L *recitatio* (as RECITE)]

■ see RECITAL 1, 3.

recitative /réssitəteév/ *n.* **1** musical declamation of the kind usual in the narrative and dialogue parts of opera and oratorio. **2** the words or part given in this form. [It. *recitativo* (as RECITE)]

recite /risī́t/ *v.* **1** *tr.* repeat aloud or declaim (a poem or passage) from memory, esp. before an audience. **2** *intr.* give a recitation. **3** *tr.* mention in order; enumerate. □□ **reciter** *n.* [ME f. OF *reciter* or L *recitare* (as RE-, CITE)]

■ **1** repeat, quote, say aloud, read out *or* aloud, declaim. **2** declaim, hold forth, speak, *esp. joc. or derog.* orate. **3** enumerate, spell out, detail, chronicle, list, recount, relate, report, repeat.

reck /rek/ *v. archaic* or *poet.* (only in *neg.* or *interrog.*) **1** *tr.* (foll. by *of*) pay heed to; take account of; care about. **2** *tr.* pay heed to. **3** *intr.* (usu. with *it* as subject) be of importance (*it recks little*). [OE *reccan*, rel. to OHG *ruohhen*]

reckless /rékliss/ *adj.* disregarding the consequences or danger etc.; lacking caution; rash. □□ **recklessly** *adv.* **recklessness** *n.* [OE *recceléas* (as RECK)]

■ careless, rash, thoughtless, incautious, heedless, foolhardy, imprudent, unwise, injudicious, impulsive, irresponsible, negligent, unmindful, foolish, devil-may-care, wild, madcap, mad, hare-brained, *esp. US* wildcat.

reckon /rékkən/ *v.* **1** *tr.* count or compute by calculation. **2** *tr.* (foll. by *in*) count in or include in computation. **3** *tr.* (often foll. by *as* or *to be*) consider or regard (*reckon him wise*; *reckon them to be beyond hope*). **4** *tr.* **a** (foll. by *that* + clause) conclude after calculation; be of the considered opinion. **b** *colloq.* (foll. by *to* + infin.) expect (*reckons to finish by Friday*). **5** *intr.* make calculations; add up an account or sum. **6** *intr.* (foll. by *on*, *upon*) rely on, count on, or base plans on. **7** *intr.* (foll. by *with*) **a** take into account. **b** settle accounts with. □ **reckon up 1** count up; find the total of. **2** settle accounts. **to be reckoned with** of considerable importance; not to be ignored. [OE (*ge*)*recenian* f. WG]

■ **1** calculate, compute; add (up), figure (up), tally (up), sum up, total (up), work out *or* up, reckon up. **2** include, count, number, enumerate, list, name, enter. **3** consider, account, judge, look upon, regard, view, think of, hold, gauge, estimate, appraise, *formal* deem. **4 a** suppose, think, assume, presume, guess, imagine, consider, conclude, be of the opinion. **b** see EXPECT 1a, 2. **6** (*reckon on*) count on, rely on, depend on, trust in, take for granted, bank on, take as read. **7** (*reckon with*) **a** take into account *or* consideration, consider, account for, remember, bear in mind, allow for. **b** reckon up with, settle (accounts) with, sort it out with; see also *attend to* (ATTEND 4). □ **reckon up 1** see RECKON 1 above. **2** see RECKON 7b above. **to be reckoned with** see IMPORTANT 1.

reckoner /rékkənər/ *n.* = *ready reckoner.*

reckoning /rékkəning/ *n.* **1** the act or an instance of counting or calculating. **2** a consideration or opinion. **3 a** the settlement of an account. **b** an account. □ **day of reckoning** the time when something must be atoned for or avenged.

■ **1** counting, calculating, calculation, computation, enumeration. **2** see OPINION 1, 3. **3 a** payment, settlement, return, *sl.* pay-off. **b** bill, account, invoice, *US colloq.* tab. □ **day of reckoning** judgement day, day of atonement, day of judgement; retribution, final account(ing) *or* settlement, doom.

reclaim /rikláym/ *v.* & *n.* ● *v.tr.* **1** seek the return of (one's property). **2** claim in return or as a rebate etc. **3** bring under cultivation, esp. from a state of being under water. **4 a** win back or away from vice or error or a waste condition; reform. **b** tame, civilize. ● *n.* the act or an instance of reclaiming; the process of being reclaimed. □□ **reclaimable** *adj.* **reclaimer** *n.* **reclamation** /rékləmáysh'n/ *n.* [ME f. OF *reclamer reclaim-* f. L *reclamare* cry out against (as RE-, *clamare* shout)]

■ *v.* **1, 3** take back, recover, redeem, salvage, save, regain, retrieve; regenerate, rejuvenate, restore. **4 a** reform; win back, rescue; see also SAVE[1] *v.* 1. **b** tame, civilize, enlighten, refine, improve.

reclassify /reéklássifī/ *v.tr.* (**-ies, -ied**) classify again or differently. □□ **reclassification** /-fikáysh'n/ *n.*

reclinate /réklinayt/ *adj. Bot.* bending downwards. [L *reclinatus*, past part. of *reclinare* (as RECLINE)]

recline /riklīn/ *v.* **1** *intr.* assume or be in a horizontal or leaning position, esp. in resting. **2** *tr.* cause to recline or move from the vertical. □□ **reclinable** *adj.* [ME f. OE *recliner* or L *reclinare* bend back, recline (as RE-, *clinare* bend)]

■ **1** lie down, lie back, lean back, stretch out, rest, repose, lounge.

recliner /riklīnər/ *n.* **1** a comfortable chair for reclining in. **2** a person who reclines.

reclothe /reéklōth/ *v.tr.* clothe again or differently.

recluse /riklōōss/ *n.* & *adj.* ● *n.* a person given to or living in seclusion or isolation, esp. as a religious discipline; a hermit. ● *adj.* favouring seclusion; solitary. □□ **reclusion** /riklōōzh'n/ *n.* **reclusive** *adj.* [ME f. OF *reclus recluse* past part. of *reclure* f. L *recludere reclus-* (as RE-, *claudere* shut)]

■ *n.* hermit, anchorite, anchoress, eremite; loner, lone wolf. ● *adj.* see *reclusive* below. □□ **reclusive** recluse, seclusive, solitary, lone, secluded, isolated, eremitic(al), hermitic, anchoritic, monastic, cloistered, sequestered, retiring.

recognition /rékkəgnísh'n/ *n.* the act or an instance of recognizing or being recognized. □□ **recognitory** /rikógnitəri, -tri/ *adj.* [L *recognitio* (as RECOGNIZE)]

■ identification, detection; acknowledgement, acceptance, awareness, perception, admission; honour.

recognizance /rikógniz'nss/ *n.* **1** a bond by which a person undertakes before a court or magistrate to observe some condition, e.g. to appear when summoned. **2** a sum pledged as surety for this. [ME f. OF *recon(n)issance* (as RE-, COGNIZANCE)]

recognizant /rikógniz'nt/ *adj.* (usu. foll. by *of*) **1** showing recognition (of a favour etc.). **2** conscious or showing consciousness (of something).

recognize /rékkəgnīz/ *v.tr.* (also **-ise**) **1** identify (a person or thing) as already known; know again. **2** realize or discover the nature of. **3** (foll. by *that*) realize or admit. **4** acknowledge the existence, validity, character, or claims of. **5** show appreciation of; reward. **6** (foll. by *as*, *for*) treat or acknowledge. **7** (of a chairperson etc.) allow (a person) to speak in a debate etc. □□ **recognizable** *adj.* **recognizability** /-nīzəbílliti/ *n.* **recognizably** *adv.* **recognizer** *n.* [OF *recon(n)iss-* stem of *reconnaistre* f. L *recognoscere recognit-* (as RE-, *cognoscere* learn)]

■ **1** identify, detect, place, recall, remember, recollect, know (again). **2** realize, perceive, understand, be *or* become aware of, discover, know, appreciate, be conscious *or* appreciative (of). **3** acknowledge, realize, see, admit, accept, own, concede, allow, grant, appreciate. **4** acknowledge, approve, sanction, validate, ratify, endorse; see also SUPPORT *v.* 5. **5** honour, give recognition to, salute, show gratitude *or* appreciation of, reward, distinguish, pay respect to, pay homage to. **6** acknowledge, treat, accept.

recoil /rikóyl/ *v.* & *n.* ● *v.intr.* **1** suddenly move or spring back in fear, horror, or disgust. **2** shrink mentally in this way. **3** rebound after an impact. **4** (foll. by *on*, *upon*) have an adverse reactive effect on (the originator). **5** (of a gun) be driven backwards by its discharge. **6** retreat under an enemy's attack. **7** *Physics* (of an atom etc.) move backwards by the conservation of momentum on emission of a particle. ● *n.* /also reékoyl/ **1** the act or an instance of recoiling. **2** the sensation of recoiling. [ME f. OF *reculer* (as RE-, L *culus* buttocks)]

■ *v.* **1, 2** jerk *or* jump *or* spring back, start, flinch, wince, shrink, blench, balk, shy away; (*recoil from*) see AVOID. **3** rebound, bounce *or* spring back, resile, kick back, ricochet. **6** see RETREAT *v.* 1a. ● *n.* **1** flinch, wince, shrinking, start; kick, rebound, comeback, return; backlash.

recollect /rékkəlékt/ *v.tr.* **1** remember. **2** succeed in remembering; call to mind. [L *recolligere recollect-* (as RE-, COLLECT[1])]

■ **1** recall, remember, retain; call to mind. **2** see REMEMBER 2a.

re-collect /reékəlékt/ *v.tr.* **1** collect again. **2** (*refl.*) recover control of (oneself).

recollection /rékkəléksh'n/ *n.* **1** the act or power of recollecting. **2** a thing recollected. **3 a** a person's memory (*to the best of my recollection*). **b** the time over which memory extends (*happened within my recollection*). □□ **recollective** *adj.* [F *recollection* or med.L *recollectio* (as RECOLLECT)]

■ **2** memory, remembrance; reminiscence.

recolonize /reékóllənīz/ *v.tr.* (also **-ise**) colonize again. □□ **recolonization** /-záysh'n/ *n.*

recolour /reékúllər/ *v.tr.* colour again or differently.

recombinant /reekómbinənt/ *adj.* & *n. Biol.* ● *adj.* (of a gene etc.) formed by recombination. ● *n.* a recombinant organism or cell. □ **recombinant DNA** DNA that has been recombined using constituents from different sources.

recombination /reékombináysh'n/ *n. Biol.* the rearrangement, esp. by crossing over in chromosomes, of nucleic acid molecules forming a new sequence of the constituent nucleotides.

recombine /reékəmbīn/ *v.tr.* & *intr.* combine again or differently.

recommence /reékəménss/ *v.tr.* & *intr.* begin again. □□ **recommencement** *n.*

■ see RENEW 3.

recommend /rékkəménd/ *v.tr.* **1 a** suggest as fit for some purpose or use. **b** suggest (a person) as suitable for a particular position. **2** (often foll. by *that* + clause or *to* + infin.) advise as a course of action etc. (*I recommend that you stay where you are*). **3** (of qualities, conduct, etc.) make acceptable or desirable. **4** (foll. by *to*) commend or entrust (to a person or a person's care). □□ **recommendable** *adj.* **recommendation** /-dáysh'n/ *n.* **recommendatory** /-dətəri/ *adj.* **recommender** *n.* [ME (in sense 4) f. med.L *recommendare* (as RE-, COMMEND)]

■ **1 a** see SUGGEST 1. **b** endorse, propose, commend, support, promote, vouch for, second, back, push, favour, approve, stand up for. **2** counsel, advise, urge, exhort; suggest, advocate. **3** favour, make attractive *or* interesting *or* acceptable, back, support; see also ADVOCATE *v.* **4** see ENTRUST 1. □□ **recommendation** counsel, advice, exhortation, direction, encouragement, suggestion, advocacy, proposal; endorsement, commendation, blessing, approval, approbation, support, good word.

recommit /réekəmít/ *v.tr.* (**recommitted, recommitting**) **1** commit again. **2** return (a bill etc.) to a committee for further consideration. □□ **recommitment** *n.* **recommittal** *n.*

recompense /rékkəmpenss/ *v.* & *n.* ● *v.tr.* **1** make amends to (a person) or for (a loss etc.). **2** requite; reward or punish (a person or action). ● *n.* **1** a reward; requital. **2** retribution; satisfaction given for an injury. [ME f. OF *recompense*(*r*) f. LL *recompensare* (as RE-, COMPENSATE)]

■ *v.* **1** see COMPENSATE 1, 2. **2** see REQUITE. ● *n.* **1** see *requital* (REQUITE). **2** see RETRIBUTION.

recompose /réekəmpṓz/ *v.tr.* compose again or differently.

reconcile /rékkənsīl/ *v.tr.* **1** make friendly again after an estrangement. **2** (usu. in *refl.* or *passive*; foll. by *to*) make acquiescent or contentedly submissive to (something disagreeable or unwelcome) (*was reconciled to failure*). **3** settle (a quarrel etc.). **4 a** harmonize; make compatible. **b** show the compatibility of by argument or in practice (*cannot reconcile your views with the facts*). □□ **reconcilable** *adj.* **reconcilability** /-sīləbílliti/ *n.* **reconcilement** *n.* **reconciler** *n.* **reconciliation** /-siliáysh'n/ *n.* **reconciliatory** /-sílliətəri, -tri/ *adj.* [ME f. OF *reconcilier* or L *reconciliare* (as RE-, *conciliare* CONCILIATE)]

■ **1** get *or* bring (back) together, unite, reunite, settle *or* resolve differences between, restore harmony between, make peace between, placate. **2** (*be reconciled*) see RESIGN 4a. **3** sort out, smooth over; see also SETTLE[1] 5–7, 8b. □□ **reconciliation** conciliation, appeasement, propitiation, pacification, placation, *rapprochement*, reconcilement, understanding, *détente*, reunion; compromise, settlement, agreement.

recondite /rékkəndīt, rikón-/ *adj.* **1** (of a subject or knowledge) abstruse; out of the way; little known. **2** (of an author or style) dealing in abstruse knowledge or allusions; obscure. □□ **reconditely** *adv.* **reconditeness** *n.* [L *reconditus* (as RE-, *conditus* past part. of *condere* hide)]

■ **1** abstruse, arcane, obscure, little known, esoteric, deep, profound, incomprehensible, unfathomable, impenetrable, undecipherable, opaque, dark, inexplicable, enigmatic.

recondition /réekəndísh'n/ *v.tr.* **1** overhaul, refit, renovate. **2** make usable again. □□ **reconditioner** *n.*

■ see OVERHAUL *v.* 1.

reconfigure /réekənfiggər/ *v.tr.* configure again or differently. □□ **reconfiguration** /-ráysh'n/ *n.*

reconfirm /réekənfúrm/ *v.tr.* confirm, establish, or ratify anew. □□ **reconfirmation** /-konfərmáysh'n/ *n.*

■ see RENEW 4.

reconnaissance /rikónnis'nss/ *n.* **1** a survey of a region, esp. a military examination to locate an enemy or ascertain strategic features. **2** a preliminary survey or inspection. [F (earlier *-oissance*) f. stem of *reconnaître* (as RECONNOITRE)]

■ reconnoitre, survey, examination, patrol, exploration, investigation, inspection, scrutiny, *colloq.* recce.

reconnect /réekənékt/ *v.tr.* connect again. □□ **reconnection** *n.*

reconnoitre /rékkənóytər/ *v.* & *n.* (*US* **reconnoiter**) ● *v.* **1** *tr.* make a reconnaissance of (an area, enemy position, etc.). **2** *intr.* make a reconnaissance. ● *n.* a reconnaissance. [obs. F *reconnoître* f. L *recognoscere* RECOGNIZE]

■ *v.* **1** survey, examine, scout (out), scan, explore, investigate, inspect, scrutinize, check out, check up (on), *colloq.* recce. ● *n.* see RECONNAISSANCE.

reconquer /réekóngkər/ *v.tr.* conquer again. □□ **reconquest** *n.*

reconsider /réekənsíddər/ *v.tr.* & *intr.* consider again, esp. for a possible change of decision. □□ **reconsideration** /-ráysh'n/ *n.*

■ see REVIEW *v.* 2, 5. □□ **reconsideration** see REVIEW *n.* 3.

reconsign /réekənsín/ *v.tr.* consign again or differently. □□ **reconsignment** *n.*

reconsolidate /réekənsóllidayt/ *v.tr.* & *intr.* consolidate again. □□ **reconsolidation** /-dáysh'n/ *n.*

reconstitute /réekónstityoot/ *v.tr.* **1** build up again from parts; reconstruct. **2** reorganize. **3** restore the previous constitution of (dried food etc.) by adding water. □□ **reconstitution** /-tyoosh'n/ *n.*

reconstruct /réekənstrúkt/ *v.tr.* **1** build or form again. **2 a** form a mental or visual impression of (past events) by assembling the evidence for them. **b** re-enact (a crime). **3** reorganize. □□ **reconstructable** *adj.* (also **reconstructible**). **reconstruction** *n.* **reconstructive** *adj.* **reconstructor** *n.*

■ **1** see RESTORE 1. **3** see MODIFY 2. □□ **reconstruction** see RESTORATION 1a.

reconvene /réekənvéen/ *v.tr.* & *intr.* convene again, esp. (of a meeting etc.) after a pause in proceedings.

reconvert /réekənvért/ *v.tr.* convert back to a former state. □□ **reconversion** *n.*

■ □□ **reconversion** see RESTORATION 1a.

record *n.* & *v.* ● *n.* /rékkord/ **1 a** a piece of evidence or information constituting an (esp. official) account of something that has occurred, been said, etc. **b** a document preserving this. **2** the state of being set down or preserved in writing or some other permanent form (*is a matter of record*). **3 a** (in full **gramophone record**) a thin plastic disc carrying recorded sound in grooves on each surface, for reproduction by a record-player. **b** a trace made on this or some other medium, e.g. magnetic tape. **4 a** an official report of the proceedings and judgement in a court of justice. **b** a copy of the pleadings etc. constituting a case to be decided by a court (see also *court of record*). **5 a** the facts known about a person's past (*has an honourable record of service*). **b** a list of a person's previous criminal convictions. **6** the best performance (esp. in sport) or most remarkable event of its kind on record (often *attrib.*: *a record attempt*). **7** an object serving as a memorial of a person or thing; a portrait. **8** *Computing* a number of related items of information which are handled as a unit. ● *v.tr.* /rikórd/ **1** set down in writing or some other permanent form for later reference, esp. as an official record. **2** convert (sound, a broadcast, etc.) into permanent form for later reproduction. **3** establish or constitute a historical or other record of. □ **break** (or **beat**) **the record** outdo all previous performances etc. **for the record** as an official statement etc. **go on record** state one's opinion or judgement openly or officially, so that it is recorded. **have a record** be known as a criminal. **a matter of record** a thing established as a fact by being recorded. **off the record** as an unofficial or confidential statement etc. **on record** officially recorded; publicly known. **put** (or **get** or **set** etc.) **the record straight** correct a misapprehension. **recorded delivery** a Post Office service in which the dispatch and receipt of a letter or parcel are recorded. **recording angel** an angel that supposedly registers each person's good and bad actions. **record-player** an apparatus for reproducing sound from gramophone records. □□ **recordable** *adj.* [ME f. OF *record* remembrance, *recorder* record, f. L *recordari* remember (as RE-, *cor cordis* heart)]

■ *n.* **1** (*record* or *records*) documentation, data, information, evidence; report, document, archive(s), log, journal, memorandum, note, minute(s), annals, chronicle, diary, register, list, catalogue. **3 a** disc, album, release, LP, forty-five, single, *colloq.* platter. **5** history, reputation, track record, past, background, life; accomplishment(s), deed(s); *sl.* form. **6** (best) performance; (*attrib.*) record-breaking. **7** see MEMENTO, PORTRAIT 1. ● *v.* **1** write (down), transcribe, document, register, note, make a note of, take down, put *or* set down, log, chronicle, report, itemize, list, enumerate, catalogue. □ **off the record** confidential, unofficial, secret, private, between you and me; unofficially, privately, confidentially, not for publication, in (strict) confidence, *sub rosa.* **on record** see *well-known* 2 (WELL[1]). **record-player** gramophone, *US* phonograph.

recorder /rikórdər/ *n.* **1** an apparatus for recording, esp. a tape recorder. **2 a** a keeper of records. **b** a person who makes an official record. **3** *Brit.* **a** a barrister or solicitor of at least ten years' standing, appointed to serve as a part-time judge. **b** *hist.* a judge in certain courts. **4** *Mus.* a woodwind instrument like a flute but blown through the end and having a more hollow tone. □□ **recordership** *n.* (in sense 3). [ME f. AF *recordour*, OF *recordeur* & f. RECORD (in obs. sense 'practise a tune')]

recording /rikórding/ *n.* **1** the process by which audio or video signals are recorded for later reproduction. **2** material or a programme recorded.
■ **2** CD, compact disc; see also RECORD *n.* 3a, TAPE *n.* 4.

recordist /rikórdist/ *n.* a person who records sound.

recount /rikównt/ *v.tr.* **1** narrate. **2** tell in detail. [ONF & AF *reconter* (as RE-, COUNT[1])]
■ **1** relate, narrate, tell, recite, communicate, impart, unfold. **2** particularize, review, detail, describe, enumerate, specify, itemize, go over.

re-count *v.* & *n.* ● *v.* /re͞ekównt/ *tr.* count again. ● *n.* /re͞ekownt/ a re-counting, esp. of votes in an election.

recoup /riko͞op/ *v.tr.* **1** recover or regain (a loss). **2** compensate or reimburse for a loss. **3** *Law* deduct or keep back (part of a sum due). □ **recoup oneself** recover a loss. □□ **recoupable** *adj.* **recoupment** *n.* [F *recouper* (as RE-, *couper* cut)]
■ **1** regain, make good, make up (for), repay, recover, redeem. **2** recompense, reimburse, compensate, repay, refund, pay back, remunerate.

recourse /rikórss/ *n.* **1** resorting to a possible source of help. **2** a person or thing resorted to. □ **have recourse to** turn to (a person or thing) for help. **without recourse** a formula used by the endorser of a bill etc. to disclaim responsibility for payment. [ME f. OF *recours* f. L *recursus* (as RE-, COURSE)]
■ resort, access; backup, reserve, refuge, alternative, remedy.

recover /rikúvvər/ *v.* & *n.* ● *v.* **1** *tr.* regain possession or use or control of, reclaim. **2** *intr.* return to health or consciousness or to a normal state or position (*have recovered from my illness; the country never recovered from the war*). **3** *tr.* obtain or secure (compensation etc.) by legal process. **4** *tr.* retrieve or make up for (a loss, set-back, etc.). **5** *refl.* regain composure or consciousness or control of one's limbs. **6** *tr.* retrieve (reusable substances) from industrial waste. ● *n.* the recovery of a normal position in fencing etc. □□ **recoverable** *adj.* **recoverability** /-vərəbílliti/ *n.* **recoverer** *n.* [ME f. AF *recoverer*, OF *recovrer* f. L *recuperare* RECUPERATE]
■ *v.* **1** reclaim, retrieve, regain, get *or* take *or* win back (again), repossess, retake, recapture, bring back; save, salvage, rescue, restore. **2** get well *or* better, recuperate, convalesce, return to health, regain one's strength *or* health, be on the mend, improve, revive, rally, take a turn for the better, pull through, get over it; survive, live. **4** retrieve, make up (for), recoup, redeem, make good. **5** (*recover oneself*) see *pull oneself together*.

re-cover /re͞ekúvvər/ *v.tr.* **1** cover again. **2** provide (a chair etc.) with a new cover.

recovery /rikúvvəri/ *n.* (*pl.* **-ies**) **1** the act or an instance of recovering; the process of being recovered. **2** *Golf* a stroke bringing the ball out of a bunker etc. [ME f. AF *recoverie*, OF *reco(u)vree* (as RECOVER)]
■ **1** recuperation, convalescence, improvement, rally, turn for the better, comeback; revival, advance, gain, advancement, *formal* amelioration; retrieval, repossession, retaking, reclamation, recapture, redemption, salvage, delivery, deliverance, rescue, return.

recreant /rékriənt/ *adj.* & *n. literary* ● *adj.* **1** craven, cowardly. **2** apostate. ● *n.* **1** a coward. **2** an apostate. □□ **recreancy** *n.* **recreantly** *adv.* [ME f. OF, part. of *recroire* f. med.L (*se*) *recredere* yield in trial by combat (as RE-, *credere* entrust)]
■ *adj.* **1** see COWARDLY *adj.* **2** see DISLOYAL.

re-create /re͞ekriáyt/ *v.tr.* create over again. □□ **re-creation** *n.*
■ see REPRODUCE 1, 2.

recreation /rékriáysh'n/ *n.* **1** the process or means of refreshing or entertaining oneself. **2** a pleasurable activity. □ **recreation-ground** public land for games etc. □□ **recreational** *adj.* **recreationally** *adv.* **recreative** /rékriaytiv/ *adj.* [ME f. OF f. L *recreatio -onis* f. *recreare* create again, renew]
■ entertainment, amusement, enjoyment, diversion, distraction, fun and games, leisure, relaxation, sport, play, R and R; leisure activity, pastime, hobby.

recriminate /rikrímminayt/ *v.intr.* make mutual or counter accusations. □□ **recrimination** /-náysh'n/ *n.* **recriminative** /-nətiv/ *adj.* **recriminatory** /-nətəri/ *adj.* [med.L *recriminare* (as RE-, *criminare* accuse f. *crimen* CRIME)]
■ □□ **recrimination** counter-accusation, countercharge, retaliation, counter-attack, reprisal.

recross /re͞ekróss/ *v.tr.* & *intr.* cross or pass over again.

recrudesce /re͞ekro͞odéss, rék-/ *v.intr.* (of a disease or difficulty etc.) break out again, esp. after a dormant period. □□ **recrudescence** *n.* **recrudescent** *adj.* [back-form. f. *recrudescent*, *-ence* f. L *recrudescere* (as RE-, *crudus* raw)]

recruit /rikro͞ot/ *n.* & *v.* ● *n.* **1** a serviceman or servicewoman newly enlisted and not yet fully trained. **2** a new member of a society or organization. **3** a beginner. ● *v.* **1** *tr.* enlist (a person) as a recruit. **2** *tr.* form (an army etc.) by enlisting recruits. **3** *intr.* get or seek recruits. **4** *tr.* replenish or reinvigorate (numbers, strength, etc.). □□ **recruitable** *adj.* **recruiter** *n.* **recruitment** *n.* [earlier = reinforcement, f. obs. F dial. *recrute* ult. f. F *recroître* increase again f. L *recrescere*]
■ *n.* **1, 2** conscript, trainee, apprentice, *US* draftee, *sl.* rookie; initiate, new boy, newcomer, freshman, *Brit. colloq.* fresher. **3** beginner, novice, neophyte, greenhorn, tiro, tenderfoot, fledgling, learner. ● *v.* **1** induct, enlist, enrol. **2** muster, raise, form; see also MOBILIZE. **4** replenish, restock, refill, fill *or* top up, reinvigorate.

recrystallize /re͞ekrístəlīz/ *v.tr.* & *intr.* (also **-ise**) crystallize again. □□ **recrystallization** /-záysh'n/ *n.*

recta *pl.* of RECTUM.

rectal /réktəl/ *adj.* of or by means of the rectum. □□ **rectally** *adv.*

rectangle /réktangg'l/ *n.* a plane figure with four straight sides and four right angles, esp. one with the adjacent sides unequal. [F *rectangle* or med.L *rectangulum* f. LL *rectiangulum* f. L *rectus* straight + *angulus* ANGLE[1]]

rectangular /rektánggyoolər/ *adj.* **1 a** shaped like a rectangle. **b** having the base or sides or section shaped like a rectangle. **2 a** placed at right angles. **b** having parts or lines placed at right angles. □ **rectangular coordinates** coordinates measured along axes at right angles. **rectangular hyperbola** a hyperbola with rectangular asymptotes. □□ **rectangularity** /-lárriti/ *n.* **rectangularly** *adv.*

recti *pl.* of RECTUS.

rectifier /réktifīər/ *n.* **1** a person or thing that rectifies. **2** *Electr.* an electrical device that allows a current to flow preferentially in one direction by converting an alternating current into a direct one.

rectify /réktifī/ *v.tr.* (**-ies, -ied**) **1** adjust or make right; correct, amend. **2** purify or refine, esp. by repeated

distillation. **3** find a straight line equal in length to (a curve). **4** convert (alternating current) to direct current. □□ **rectifiable** *adj.* **rectification** /-fikáysh'n/ *n.* [ME f. OF *rectifier* f. med.L *rectificare* f. L *rectus* right]
■ **1** correct, redress, amend, put *or* set right, cure, repair, remedy, improve, emend, square, reconcile, adjust, *formal* ameliorate. **2** see REFINE 1.

rectilinear /réktilínniər/ *adj.* (also **rectilineal** /-niəl/) **1** bounded or characterized by straight lines. **2** in or forming a straight line. □□ **rectilinearity** /-niárriti/ *n.* **rectilinearly** *adv.* [LL *rectilineus* f. L *rectus* straight + *linea* LINE[1]]

rectitude /réktityood/ *n.* **1** moral uprightness. **2** righteousness. **3** correctness. [ME f. OF *rectitude* or LL *rectitudo* f. L *rectus* right]
■ propriety, correctness, morality, uprightness, probity, virtue, decency, goodness, honesty, integrity, incorruptibility, righteousness, principle, good character, respectability.

recto /réktō/ *n.* (*pl.* **-os**) **1** the right-hand page of an open book. **2** the front of a printed leaf of paper or manuscript (opp. VERSO). [L *recto* (*folio*) on the right (leaf)]

rector /réktər/ *n.* **1** (in the Church of England) the incumbent of a parish where all tithes formerly passed to the incumbent (cf. VICAR). **2** *RC Ch.* a priest in charge of a church or religious institution. **3 a** the head of some schools, universities, and colleges. **b** (in Scotland) an elected representative of students on a university's governing body. □□ **rectorate** /-rət/ *n.* **rectorial** /-tóriəl/ *adj.* **rectorship** *n.* [ME f. OF *rectour* or L *rector* ruler f. *regere rect-* rule]
■ **1, 2** see CLERGYMAN. **3 a** see PRINCIPAL *n.* 2.

rectory /réktəri, -tri/ *n.* (*pl.* **-ies**) **1** a rector's house. **2** (in the Church of England) a rector's benefice. [AF & OF *rectorie* or med.L *rectoria* (as RECTOR)]

rectrix /réktriks/ *n.* (*pl.* **rectrices** /-triseez/) a bird's strong tail-feather directing flight. [L, fem. of *rector* ruler: see RECTOR]

rectum /réktəm/ *n.* (*pl.* **rectums** or **recta** /-tə/) the final section of the large intestine, terminating at the anus. [L *rectum* (*intestinum*) straight (intestine)]

rectus /réktəss/ *n.* (*pl.* **recti** /-tī/) *Anat.* a straight muscle. [L, = straight]

recumbent /rikúmb'nt/ *adj.* lying down; reclining. □□ **recumbency** *n.* **recumbently** *adv.* [L *recumbere* recline (as RE-, *cumbere* lie)]
■ reclining, horizontal, reposing, supine, prone, prostrate, procumbent.

recuperate /rikóopərayt/ *v.* **1** *intr.* recover from illness, exhaustion, loss, etc. **2** *tr.* regain (health, something lost, etc.). □□ **recuperable** *adj.* **recuperation** /-ráysh'n/ *n.* **recuperative** /-rətiv/ *adj.* **recuperator** *n.* [L *recuperare recuperat-* recover]
■ **1** improve, recover, convalesce, get better, rally, revive, regain one's health *or* strength. **2** see RECOVER *v.* 1.

recur /rikúr/ *v.intr.* (**recurred, recurring**) **1** occur again; be repeated. **2** (of a thought, idea, etc.) come back to one's mind. **3** (foll. by *to*) go back in thought or speech. □ **recurring decimal** a decimal fraction in which the same figures are repeated indefinitely. [L *recurrere recurs-* (as RE-, *currere* run)]
■ **1** return, happen *or* occur again, reoccur, be repeated, repeat itself, come (back) again, reappear.

recurrent /rikúrrənt/ *adj.* **1** recurring; happening repeatedly. **2** (of a nerve, vein, branch, etc.) turning back so as to reverse direction. □□ **recurrence** *n.* **recurrently** *adv.*
■ **1** repeated, recurring, frequent, periodic, regular, repetitive, repetitious, persistent.

recursion /rikúrsh'n/ *n.* **1** the act or an instance of returning. **2** *Math.* the repeated application of a procedure or definition to a previous result to obtain a series of values. □ **recursion formula** *Math.* an expression giving successive terms of a series etc. □□ **recursive** *adj.* [LL *recursio* (as RECUR)]

recurve /rikúrv/ *v.tr.* & *intr.* bend backwards. □□ **recurvate** /-vət/ *adj.* **recurvature** *n.* [L *recurvare recurvat-* (as RE-, *curvare* bend)]

recusant /rékyooz'nt/ *n.* & *adj.* ● *n.* a person who refuses submission to an authority or compliance with a regulation, esp. *hist.* one who refused to attend services of the Church of England. ● *adj.* of or being a recusant. □□ **recusance** *n.* **recusancy** *n.* [L *recusare* refuse]
■ *n.* see REBEL *n.*

recycle /reessík'l/ *v.tr.* return (material) to a previous stage of a cyclic process, esp. convert (waste) to reusable material. □□ **recyclable** *adj.*
■ reuse, reclaim.

red /red/ *adj.* & *n.* ● *adj.* **1** of or near the colour seen at the least-refracted end of the visible spectrum, of shades ranging from that of blood to pink or deep orange. **2** flushed in the face with shame, anger, etc. **3** (of the eyes) bloodshot or red-rimmed with weeping. **4** (of the hair) reddish-brown, orange, tawny. **5** involving or having to do with bloodshed, burning, violence, or revolution. **6** *colloq.* communist or socialist. **7** (**Red**) Soviet or (formerly) Russian (*the Red Army*). **8** (of wine) made from dark grapes and coloured by their skins. ● *n.* **1** a red colour or pigment. **2** red clothes or material (*dressed in red*). **3** *colloq.* a communist or socialist. **4 a** a red ball, piece, etc., in a game or sport. **b** the player using such pieces. **5** the debit side of an account (*in the red*). **6** a red light. □ **red admiral** a butterfly, *Vanessa atalanta*, with red bands on each pair of wings. **red bark** a red kind of cinchona. **red biddy** *colloq.* a mixture of cheap wine and methylated spirits. **red-blooded** virile, vigorous. **red-bloodedness** vigour, spirit. **red card** *Football* a card shown by the referee to a player being sent off the field. **red carpet** privileged treatment of an eminent visitor. **red cedar** an American juniper, *Juniperus virginiana*. **red cell** (or **corpuscle**) an erythrocyte. **red cent** *US* the smallest (orig. copper) coin; a trivial sum. **Red Crescent** an organization like the Red Cross in Muslim countries. **red cross 1** St George's cross, the national emblem of England. **2** the Christian side in the crusades. **Red Cross 1** an international organization (originally medical) bringing relief to victims of war or natural disaster. **2** the emblem of this organization. **red deer** a deer, *Cervus elaphus*, with a rich red-brown summer coat turning dull-brown in winter. **red duster** *Brit. colloq.* = *red ensign*. **red dwarf** an old relatively cool star. **red ensign** see ENSIGN. **red-eye 1** = RUDD. **2** *US sl.* cheap whisky. **red-faced** embarrassed, ashamed. **red flag 1** the symbol of socialist revolution. **2** a warning of danger. **red fox** a native British fox, *Vulpes vulpes*, having a characteristic deep red or fawn coat. **red giant** a relatively cool giant star. **red grouse** a subspecies of the willow grouse, native to Britain and familiar as a game-bird. **Red Guard** *hist.* a member of a militant youth movement in China (1966-76). **red gum 1** a teething-rash in children. **2 a** a reddish resin. **b** any of various kinds of eucalyptus yielding this. **red-handed** in or just after the act of committing a crime, doing wrong, etc. **red hat 1** a cardinal's hat. **2** the symbol of a cardinal's office. **red-headed 1** (of a person) having red hair. **2** (of birds etc.) having a red head. **red heat 1** the temperature or state of something so hot as to emit red light. **2** great excitement. **red herring 1** dried smoked herring. **2** a misleading clue or distraction (so called from the practice of using the scent of red herring in training hounds). **red-hot 1** heated until red. **2** highly exciting. **3** (of news) fresh; completely new. **4** intensely excited. **5** enraged. **red-hot poker** any plant of the genus *Kniphofia*, with spikes of usually red or yellow flowers. **Red Indian** *offens.* an American Indian. **red lead** a red form of lead oxide used as a pigment. **red-letter day** a day that is pleasantly noteworthy or memorable (orig. a festival marked in red on the calendar). **red light 1** a signal to stop on a road, railway, etc. **2** a warning or refusal. **red-light district** a district containing many brothels. **red man** = *Red Indian*. **red meat** meat that is red when raw (e.g. beef or lamb). **red mullet** a marine fish, *Mullus surmuletus*, valued as food. **red pepper 1** cayenne pepper. **2** the ripe fruit of the capsicum plant, *Capsicum annuum*. **red rag** something that excites a person's rage (so called because red is supposed to provoke bulls). **red rattle** a pink-flowered marsh plant, *Pedicularis palustris*. **red roan** see ROAN[1]. **red rose** the emblem of Lancashire or the Lancastrians. **red shift** the displacement of the spectrum to longer wavelengths in the light coming from distant galaxies etc. in recession. **red spider** any of various mites of the family Tetranychidae infesting hothouse plants esp. vines. **red squirrel** the common Eurasian squirrel, *Sciurus vulgaris*, with reddish fur. **Red Star** the emblem of some Communist countries. **red tape** excessive bureaucracy or adherence to formalities esp. in public business. **red-water** **1** a bacterial disease of calves, a symptom of which is the passing of reddish urine. **2** a mass of water made red by pigmented plankton, esp. *Gonyanlax tamarensis*. □□ **reddish** *adj.* **reddy** *adj.* **redly** *adv.* **redness** *n.* [OE *rēad* f. Gmc]

■ *adj.* **1** crimson, scarlet, vermilion, burgundy, cherry, wine, nacarat, ruby; *Bot. & Zool.* testaceous, *Heraldry* gules, *Heraldry or literary* sanguine; see also ROSY 1. **2** blushing, red-faced, red in the face, shamefaced, discountenanced, embarrassed, abashed. **4** orange, ginger, sandy, strawberry blonde, tawny, chestnut, copper, auburn, foxy, reddish-brown. **6** see LEFT[1] *adj.* 3. ● *n.* **1** see RED *adj.* 1 above. **3** see *left-winger* (LEFT[1]). **5** (*in the red*) see DEBT. □ **red-blooded** see TOUGH *adj.* 2. **red-bloodedness** see VIGOUR 1. **red-eye 2** see LIQUOR *n.* 1. **red-faced** see ASHAMED 1. **red-handed** in the (very) act, *in flagrante (delicto)*, *colloq.* with one's hand in the till. **red herring 2** see *misinformation* (MISINFORM). **red-hot 1** see HOT *adj.* 1. **2** see EXCITING. **3** see *brand-new*. **4** see HOT *adj.* 5a. **5** see FURIOUS 1, 2. **red light 2** see WARNING 1, REFUSAL 1. **red rag** see PROVOCATION 1. **red tape** see BUREAUCRACY. □□ **reddish** see ROSY 1. **redness** see FLUSH[1] *n.* 1.

redact /ridákt/ *v.tr.* put into literary form; edit for publication. □□ **redactor** *n.* [L *redigere redact-* (as RE-, *agere* bring)]

■ see EDIT *v.* 1. □□ **redactor** see EDITOR 1.

redaction /ridáksh'n/ *n.* **1** preparation for publication. **2** revision, editing, rearrangement. **3** a new edition. □□ **redactional** *adj.* [F *rédaction* f. LL *redactio* (as REDACT)]

■ **2** see REVISION 1.

redan /ridán/ *n.* a fieldwork with two faces forming a salient angle. [F f. *redent* notching (as RE-, *dent* tooth)]

redbreast /rédbrest/ *n. colloq.* a robin.

redbrick /rédbrik/ *adj.* esp. *Brit.* (of a university) founded relatively recently.

redbud /rédbud/ *n.* any American tree of the genus *Cercis*, with pale pink flowers.

redcap /rédkap/ *n.* **1** *Brit.* a member of the military police. **2** *US* a railway porter.

redcoat /rédkōt/ *n. hist.* a British soldier (so called from the scarlet uniform of most regiments).

redcurrant /rédkúrrənt/ *n.* **1** a widely cultivated shrub, *Ribes rubrum*. **2** a small red edible berry of this plant.

redd /red/ *v.tr.* (*past* and *past part.* **redd**) *dial.* **1** clear up. **2** arrange, tidy, compose, settle. [ME: cf. MLG, MDu. *redden*]

redden /rédd'n/ *v.tr.* & *intr.* make or become red.

■ go red; see also FLUSH[1] *v.* 1a.

reddle /rédd'l/ *n.* red ochre; ruddle. [var. of RUDDLE]

rede /reed/ *n.* & *v. archaic* ● *n.* advice, counsel. ● *v.tr.* **1** advise. **2** read (a riddle or dream). [OE *rǣd* f. Gmc, rel. to READ (of which the verb is a ME var. retained for archaic senses)]

redecorate /reédékkərayt/ *v.tr.* decorate again or differently. □□ **redecoration** /-ráysh'n/ *n.*

■ see DECORATE 2.

redeem /rideém/ *v.tr.* **1** buy back; recover by expenditure of effort or by a stipulated payment. **2** make a single payment to discharge (a regular charge or obligation). **3** convert (tokens or bonds etc.) into goods or cash. **4** (of God or Christ) deliver from sin and damnation. **5** make up for; be a compensating factor in (*has one redeeming feature*). **6** (foll. by *from*) save from (a defect). **7** *refl.* save (oneself) from blame. **8** purchase the freedom of (a person). **9** save (a person's life) by ransom. **10** save or rescue or reclaim. **11** fulfil (a promise). □□ **redeemable** *adj.* [ME f. OF *redimer* or L *redimere redempt-* (as RE-, *emere* buy)]

■ **1** reclaim, recover, regain, repossess, retrieve, get back, buy back, repurchase. **2** see PAY[1] *v.* 2. **3** exchange, convert, cash (in), collect on, trade in. **4** save, rescue, absolve, deliver (from evil). **5** reinstate, restore to favour, rehabilitate, make amends for; make up for, atone for, redress, compensate for, offset, make restitution for. **8** ransom, reclaim, deliver, free, liberate, set free, emancipate, release. **9, 10** see RECLAIM *v.* 1, 3. **11** perform, fulfil, keep, make good, discharge, satisfy, abide by, keep faith with, be faithful to, hold to, carry out, see through.

redeemer /rideémər/ *n.* a person who redeems. □ **the Redeemer** Christ.

■ see SAVIOUR 1.

redefine /reédifín/ *v.tr.* define again or differently. □□ **redefinition** /-definísh'n/ *n.*

redemption /ridémpsh'n/ *n.* **1** the act or an instance of redeeming; the process of being redeemed. **2** man's deliverance from sin and damnation. **3** a thing that redeems. □□ **redemptive** *adj.* [ME f. OF f. L *redemptio* (as REDEEM)]

■ **1** see RECOVERY. □□ **redemptive** redeeming, compensating, compensatory, qualifying, extenuating, extenuatory.

redeploy /reédiplóy/ *v.tr.* send (troops, workers, etc.) to a new place or task. □□ **redeployment** *n.*

redesign /reédizín/ *v.tr.* design again or differently.

■ see MODIFY 2.

redetermine /reéditérmin/ *v.tr.* determine again or differently. □□ **redetermination** /-náysh'n/ *n.*

redevelop /reédivélləp/ *v.tr.* develop anew (esp. an urban area, with new buildings). □□ **redeveloper** *n.* **redevelopment** *n.*

redfish /rédfish/ *n.* **1** a male salmon in the spawning season. **2** a rose-fish.

redhead /rédhed/ *n.* a person with red hair.

redial /reédíəl/ *v.tr.* & *intr.* (**redialled**, **redialling**; *US* **redialed**, **redialing**) dial again.

redid *past* of REDO.

rediffusion /reédifyóozh'n/ *n.* the relaying of broadcast programmes esp. by cable from a central receiver.

redingote /réddinggōt/ *n.* a woman's long coat with a cutaway front or a contrasting piece on the front. [F f. E *riding-coat*]

redintegrate /ridíntigrayt/ *v.tr.* **1** restore to wholeness or unity. **2** renew or re-establish in a united or perfect state. □□ **redintegration** /-gráysh'n/ *n.* **redintegrative** *adj.* [ME f. L *redintegrare* (as RE-, INTEGRATE)]

redirect /reédīrékt, -dirékt/ *v.tr.* direct again, esp. change the address of (a letter). □□ **redirection** *n.*

■ see DIVERT 1a.

rediscover /reédiskúvvər/ *v.tr.* discover again. □□ **rediscovery** *n.* (*pl.* **-ies**).

redissolve /reédizólv/ *v.tr.* & *intr.* dissolve again. □□ **redissolution** /-disəlóosh'n/ *n.*

redistribute /reédistríbyoot, *disp.* reédís-/ *v.tr.* distribute again or differently. □□ **redistribution** /-byóosh'n/ *n.* **redistributive** /-tríbyootiv/ *adj.*

redivide /reédivíd/ *v.tr.* divide again or differently. □□ **redivision** /-vízh'n/ *n.*

redivivus /rédditiveévəss/ *adj.* (placed after noun) come back to life. [L (as RE-, *vivus* living)]

redneck /rédnek/ *n. US* often *derog.* a working-class White in the southern US, esp. a politically conservative one.

redo /reédóo/ *v.tr.* (*3rd sing. present* **redoes**; *past* **redid**; *past part.* **redone**) **1** do again or differently. **2** redecorate.

redolent /réddələnt/ *adj.* **1** (foll. by *of*, *with*) strongly reminiscent or suggestive or mentally associated. **2** fragrant.

3 having a strong smell; odorous. □□ **redolence** *n.* **redolently** *adv.* [ME f. OF *redolent* or L *redolēre* (as RE-, *olēre* smell)]

■ **1** (*redolent with* or *of*) reminiscent of, suggestive of, evocative of, remindful of, similar to, comparable with *or* to. **2** fragrant, sweet-smelling, aromatic, perfumed, scented, odoriferous, ambrosial, sweet-scented. **3** odorous, aromatic, smelly.

redouble /reédúbb'l/ *v.* & *n.* ● *v.* **1** *tr.* & *intr.* make or grow greater or more intense or numerous; intensify, increase. **2** *intr. Bridge* double again a bid already doubled by an opponent. ● *n. Bridge* the redoubling of a bid. [F *redoubler* (as RE-, DOUBLE)]

redoubt /ridówt/ *n. Mil.* an outwork or fieldwork usu. square or polygonal and without flanking defences. [F *redoute* f. obs. It. *ridotta* f. med.L *reductus* refuge f. past part. of L *reducere* withdraw (see REDUCE): *-b-* after DOUBT (cf. REDOUBTABLE)]

redoubtable /ridówtəb'l/ *adj.* formidable, esp. as an opponent. □□ **redoubtably** *adv.* [ME f. OF *redoutable* f. *redouter* fear (as RE-, DOUBT)]

redound /ridównd/ *v.intr.* **1** (foll. by *to*) (of an action etc.) make a great contribution to (one's credit or advantage etc.). **2** (foll. by *upon, on*) come as the final result to; come back or recoil upon. [ME, orig. = overflow, f. OF *redonder* f. L *redundare* surge (as RE-, *unda* wave)]

redox /réddoks, reé-/ *n. Chem.* (often *attrib.*) oxidation and reduction. [*red*uction + *ox*idation]

redpoll /rédpōl/ *n.* a finch, *Acanthis flammea*, with a red forehead, similar to a linnet.

redraft /reédraáft/ *v.tr.* draft (a writing or document) again.

redraw /reédráw/ *v.tr.* (*past* **redrew**; *past part.* **redrawn**) draw again or differently.

redress /ridréss/ *v.* & *n.* ● *v.tr.* **1** remedy or rectify (a wrong or grievance etc.). **2** readjust; set straight again. ● *n.* **1** reparation for a wrong. **2** (foll. by *of*) the act or process of redressing (a grievance etc.). □ **redress the balance** restore equality. □□ **redressable** *adj.* **redressal** *n.* **redresser** *n.* (also **redressor**). [ME f. OF *redresse(r)*, *redrecier* (as RE-, DRESS)]

re-dress /reédréss/ *v.tr.* & *intr.* dress again or differently.

redshank /rédshangk/ *n.* either of two sandpipers, *Tringa totanus* and *T. erythropus*, with bright-red legs.

redskin /rédskin/ *n. colloq. offens.* an American Indian.

redstart /rédstaart/ *n.* **1** any European red-tailed songbird of the genus *Phoenicurus*. **2** any of various similar American warblers of the family Parulidae. [RED + OE *steort* tail]

reduce /ridyoóss/ *v.* **1** *tr.* & *intr.* make or become smaller or less. **2** *tr.* (foll. by *to*) bring by force or necessity (to some undesirable state or action) (*reduced them to tears; were reduced to begging*). **3** *tr.* convert to another (esp. simpler) form (*reduced it to a powder*). **4** *tr.* convert (a fraction) to the form with the lowest terms. **5** *tr.* (foll. by *to*) bring or simplify or adapt by classification or analysis (*the dispute may be reduced to three issues*). **6** *tr.* make lower in status or rank. **7** *tr.* lower the price of. **8** *intr.* lessen one's weight or size. **9** *tr.* weaken (*is in a very reduced state*). **10** *tr.* impoverish. **11** *tr.* subdue; bring back to obedience. **12** *Chem. intr.* & *tr.* **a** combine or cause to combine with hydrogen. **b** undergo or cause to undergo addition of electrons. **13** *tr. Chem.* convert (oxide etc.) to metal. **14** *tr.* **a** (in surgery) restore (a dislocated etc. part) to its proper position. **b** remedy (a dislocation etc.) in this way. **15** *tr. Photog.* make (a negative or print) less dense. **16** *tr. Cookery* boil off excess liquid from. □ **reduced circumstances** poverty after relative prosperity. **reduce to the ranks** demote (an NCO) to the rank of private. **reducing agent** *Chem.* a substance that brings about reduction by oxidation and losing electrons. □□ **reducer** *n.* **reducible** *adj.* **reducibility** /-səbílliti/ *n.* [ME in sense 'restore to original or proper position', f. L *reducere reduct-* (as RE-, *ducere* bring)]

■ **1** decrease, diminish, abate, lessen; ease (up on), let up (on), moderate, tone down, slacken up (on); cut (back), cut down, shorten, crop, trim, compress. **2** (*reduce to*) bring to, force to, push *or* drive to. **3** turn, convert; break down *or* up; see also CHANGE *v.* 1. **6** demote, degrade, lower, downgrade, reduce to the ranks, relegate, *Mil.* break, *Naut.* disrate, *esp. US colloq.* bust. **7** cut, decrease, bring down, lower, drop, mark down, slash, *colloq.* knock down. **8** lose *or* shed weight, slim (down), diet, trim down, slenderize. **9** see WEAKEN 1. **10** see RUIN *v.* 1a. **11** see SUBDUE 1. **14 a** set, adjust, reset. **16** boil down, distil; see also CONCENTRATE *v.* 3. □ **reduced circumstances** see POVERTY 1. **reduce to the ranks** see REDUCE 6 above.

reductio ad absurdum /ridúktiō ad absúrdəm/ *n.* a method of proving the falsity of a premiss by showing that the logical consequence is absurd; an instance of this. [L, = reduction to the absurd]

reduction /ridúksh'n/ *n.* **1** the act or an instance of reducing; the process of being reduced. **2** an amount by which prices etc. are reduced. **3** a reduced copy of a picture etc. **4** an arrangement of an orchestral score for piano etc. □□ **reductive** *adj.* [ME f. OF *reduction* or L *reductio* (as REDUCE)]

reductionism /ridúkshəniz'm/ *n.* **1** the tendency to or principle of analysing complex things into simple constituents. **2** often *derog.* the doctrine that a system can be fully understood in terms of its isolated parts, or an idea in terms of simple concepts. □□ **reductionist** *n.* **reductionistic** /-nístik/ *adj.*

redundant /ridúndənt/ *adj.* **1** superfluous; not needed. **2** that can be omitted without any loss of significance. **3** (of a person) no longer needed at work and therefore unemployed. **4** *Engin.* & *Computing* (of a component) not needed but included in case of failure in another component. □□ **redundancy** *n.* (*pl.* **-ies**). **redundantly** *adv.* [L *redundare redundant-* (as REDOUND)]

■ **1** superfluous, unnecessary, surplus, inessential, unessential, non-essential, unneeded, unwanted, *de trop*. **3** see UNEMPLOYED 1.

reduplicate /ridyoóplikayt/ *v.tr.* **1** make double. **2** repeat. **3** repeat (a letter or syllable or word) exactly or with a slight change (e.g. hurly-burly, see-saw). □□ **reduplication** /-káysh'n/ *n.* **reduplicative** /-kətiv/ *adj.* [LL *reduplicare* (as RE-, DUPLICATE)]

redwing /rédwing/ *n.* a thrush, *Turdus iliacus*, with red underwings showing in flight.

redwood /rédwŏŏd/ *n.* **1** an exceptionally large Californian conifer, *Sequoia sempervirens*, yielding red wood. **2** any tree yielding red wood.

reebok /reébok/ *n.* (also **rhebok**) a small S. African antelope, *Pelea capreolus*, with sharp horns. [Du., = roebuck]

re-echo /reé-ékkō/ *v.intr.* & *tr.* (**-oes, -oed**) **1** echo. **2** echo repeatedly; resound.

reed[1] /reed/ *n.* & *v.* ● *n.* **1 a** any of various water or marsh plants with a firm stem, esp. of the genus *Phragmites*. **b** a tall straight stalk of this. **2** (*collect.*) reeds growing in a mass or used as material esp. for thatching. **3** *Brit.* wheat-straw prepared for thatching. **4** a pipe of reed or straw. **5 a** the vibrating part of the mouthpiece of some wind instruments, e.g. the oboe and clarinet, made of reed or other material and producing the sound. **b** (esp. in *pl.*) a reed instrument. **6** a weaver's comblike implement for separating the threads of the warp and correctly positioning the weft. **7** (in *pl.*) a set of semicylindrical adjacent mouldings like reeds laid together. ● *v.tr.* **1** thatch with reed. **2** make (straw) into reed. **3** fit (a musical instrument) with a reed. **4** decorate with a moulding of reeds. □ **reed bunting** a small brown bird, *Emberiza schoeniclus*, frequenting reed-beds. **reed-mace** a tall reedlike water-plant, *Typha latifolia*, with straplike leaves and a head of numerous tiny red-brown flowers. **reed-organ** a harmonium etc. with the sound produced by metal reeds. **reed-pipe 1** a wind instrument with sound produced by a reed. **2** an organ-pipe with a reed. **reed-stop** a reeded organ-stop. **reed-warbler** any bird of the genus *Acrocephalus*, esp. *A. scirpaceus*, frequenting reed-beds. [OE *hrēod* f. WG]

reed[2] /reed/ *n.* the fourth stomach of a ruminant; the abomasum. [OE *rēada*]

reedbuck /réedbuk/ *n.* an antelope, *Redunca redunca*, native to W. Africa.

reeded /réedid/ *adj. Mus.* (of an instrument) having a vibrating reed.

reeding /réeding/ *n. Archit.* a small semicylindrical moulding or ornamentation (cf. REED[1] *n.* 7).

re-edit /rée-éddit/ *v.tr.* (**-edited, -editing**) edit again or differently. □□ **re-edition** /rée-idísh'n/ *n.*

reedling /réedling/ *n.* a bearded tit. [REED[1]]

re-educate /rée-édyookayt/ *v.tr.* educate again, esp. to change a person's views or beliefs. □□ **re-education** /-káysh'n/ *n.*

reedy /réedi/ *adj.* (**reedier, reediest**) **1** full of reeds. **2** like a reed, esp. in weakness or slenderness. **3** (of a voice) like a reed instrument in tone; not full. □□ **reediness** *n.*

reef[1] /reef/ *n.* **1** a ridge of rock or coral etc. at or near the surface of the sea. **2 a** a lode of ore. **b** the bedrock surrounding this. [earlier *riff(e)* f. MDu., MLG *rif*, *ref*, f. ON *rif* RIB]

reef[2] /reef/ *n.* & *v. Naut.* ● *n.* each of several strips across a sail, for taking it in or rolling it up to reduce the surface area in a high wind. ● *v.tr.* **1** take in a reef or reefs of (a sail). **2** shorten (a topmast or a bowsprit). □ **reefing-jacket** a thick close-fitting double-breasted jacket. **reef-knot** a double knot made symmetrically to hold securely and cast off easily. **reef-point** each of several short pieces of rope attached to a sail to secure it when reefed. [ME *riff*, *refe* f. Du. *reef*, *rif* f. ON *rif* RIB, in the same sense: cf. REEF[1]]

reefer /réefər/ *n.* **1** *sl.* a marijuana cigarette. **2** = *reefing-jacket* (see REEF[2]). **3 a** a person who reefs. **b** *colloq.* a midshipman. [REEF[2] (in sense 1, = a thing rolled) + -ER[1]]

reek /reek/ *v.* & *n.* ● *v.intr.* (often foll. by *of*) **1** smell strongly and unpleasantly. **2** have unpleasant or suspicious associations (*this reeks of corruption*). **3** give off smoke or fumes. ● *n.* **1** a foul or stale smell. **2** esp. *Sc.* smoke. **3** vapour; a visible exhalation (esp. from a chimney). □□ **reeky** *adj.* [OE *rēocan* (v.), *rēc* (n.), f. Gmc]

■ *v.* **1** stink, smell, *Brit. colloq.* pong, hum. **2** (*reek of*) be redolent of, suggest, smell of, smack of, savour of, imply. **3** smoke, steam, give off smoke, fume. ● *n.* **1** stink, stench, fetor, mephitis, odour, smell, *archaic* miasma, *Brit. colloq.* hum, pong. **2, 3** fumes, smoke, steam, vapour, cloud, mist, exhalation.

reel /reel/ *n.* & *v.* ● *n.* **1** a cylindrical device on which thread, silk, yarn, paper, film, wire, etc., are wound. **2** a quantity of thread etc. wound on a reel. **3** a device for winding and unwinding a line as required, esp. in fishing. **4** a revolving part in various machines. **5 a** a lively folk or Scottish dance, of two or more couples facing each other. **b** a piece of music for this. ● *v.* **1** *tr.* wind (thread, a fishing-line, etc.) on a reel. **2** *tr.* (foll. by *in*, *up*) draw (fish etc.) in or up by the use of a reel. **3** *intr.* stand or walk or run unsteadily. **4** *intr.* be shaken mentally or physically. **5** *intr.* rock from side to side, or swing violently. **6** *intr.* dance a reel. □ **reel off** say or recite very rapidly and without apparent effort. □□ **reeler** *n.* [OE *hrēol*, of unkn. orig.]

■ *v.* **3** stagger, totter, waver, stumble, lurch, falter, flounder. **5** roll, rock, sway, pitch, swing, lurch. □ **reel off** list, recite, rattle off, enumerate, review, itemize, read off, call off, run through, run over.

re-elect /rée-ilékt/ *v.tr.* elect again, esp. to a further term of office. □□ **re-election** /-iléksh'n/ *n.* **re-eligible** /-éllijib'l/ *adj.*

re-embark /rée-imbaárk/ *v.intr.* & *tr.* go or put on board ship again. □□ **re-embarkation** /-káysh'n/ *n.*

re-emerge /rée-imérj/ *v.intr.* emerge again; come back out. □□ **re-emergence** *n.* **re-emergent** *adj.*

re-emphasize /rée-émfəsīz/ *v.tr.* place renewed emphasis on. □□ **re-emphasis** /-émfəsiss/ *n.*

re-employ /rée-implóy/ *v.tr.* employ again. □□ **re-employment** *n.*

re-enact /rée-inákt/ *v.tr.* act out (a past event). □□ **re-enactment** *n.*

re-enlist /rée-inlíst/ *v.intr.* enlist again, esp. in the armed services. □□ **re-enlister** *n.*

re-enter /rée-éntər/ *v.tr.* & *intr.* enter again; go back in. □□ **re-entrance** /-éntrənss/ *n.*

re-entrant /rée-éntrənt/ *adj.* & *n.* ● *adj.* **1** esp. *Fortification* (of an angle) pointing inwards (opp. SALIENT). **2** *Geom.* reflex. ● *n.* a re-entrant angle.

re-entry /rée-éntri/ *n.* (*pl.* **-ies**) **1** the act of entering again, esp. (of a spacecraft, missile, etc.) re-entering the earth's atmosphere. **2** *Law* an act of retaking or repossession.

re-equip /rée-ikwíp/ *v.tr.* & *intr.* (**-equipped, -equipping**) provide or be provided with new equipment.

re-erect /rée-irékt/ *v.tr.* erect again.

re-establish /rée-istáblish/ *v.tr.* establish again or anew. □□ **re-establishment** *n.*

re-evaluate /rée-iválуoo-ayt/ *v.tr.* evaluate again or differently. □□ **re-evaluation** /-áysh'n/ *n.*

reeve[1] /reev/ *n.* **1** *hist.* **a** the chief magistrate of a town or district. **b** an official supervising a landowner's estate. **c** any of various minor local officials. **2** *Can.* the president of a village or town council. [OE *(ge)rēfa*, *girǣfa*]

reeve[2] /reev/ *v.tr.* (*past* **rove** /rōv/ or **reeved**) *Naut.* **1** (usu. foll. by *through*) thread (a rope or rod etc.) through a ring or other aperture. **2** pass a rope through (a block etc.). **3** fasten (a rope or block) in this way. [prob. f. Du. *rēven* REEF[2]]

reeve[3] /reev/ *n.* a female ruff (see RUFF[1]). [17th c.: orig. unkn.]

re-examine /rée-igzámmin/ *v.tr.* examine again or further (esp. a witness after cross-examination). □□ **re-examination** /-náysh'n/ *n.*

re-export *v.* & *n.* ● *v.tr.* /rée-iksport/ export again (esp. imported goods after further processing or manufacture). ● *n.* /rée-éksport/ **1** the process of re-exporting. **2** something re-exported. □□ **re-exportation** /-táysh'n/ *n.* **re-exporter** /rée-ikspórtər/ *n.*

ref /ref/ *n. colloq.* a referee in sports. [abbr.]

ref. *abbr.* **1** reference. **2** refer to.

reface /réefáyss/ *v.tr.* put a new facing on (a building).

refashion /réefásh'n/ *v.tr.* fashion again or differently.

refection /rifékshʼn/ *n. literary* **1** refreshment by food or drink (*we took refection*). **2** a light meal. [ME f. OF f. L *refectio -onis* f. *reficere* (as REFECTORY)]

refectory /riféktəri, réffiktəri, -tri/ *n.* (*pl.* **-ies**) a room used for communal meals, esp. in a monastery or college. □ **refectory table** a long narrow table. [LL *refectorium* f. L *reficere* refresh (as RE-, *facere* make)]

refer /rifér/ *v.* (**referred, referring**) (usu. foll. by *to*) **1** *tr.* trace or ascribe (to a person or thing as a cause or source) (*referred their success to their popularity*). **2** *tr.* consider as belonging (to a certain date or place or class). **3** *tr.* send on or direct (a person, or a question for decision) (*the matter was referred to arbitration*; *referred him to her previous answer*). **4** *intr.* make an appeal or have recourse to (some authority or source of information) (*referred to his notes*). **5** *tr.* send (a person) to a medical specialist etc. **6** *tr.* (foll. by *back to*) send (a proposal etc.) back to (a lower body, court, etc.). **7** *intr.* (foll. by *to*) (of a person speaking) make an allusion or direct the hearer's attention (*decided not to refer to our other problems*). **8** *intr.* (foll. by *to*) (of a statement etc.) have a particular relation; be directed (*this paragraph refers to the events of last year*). **9** *tr.* (foll. by *to*) interpret (a statement) as being directed to (a particular context etc.). **10** *tr.* fail (a candidate in an examination). □ **referred pain** pain felt in a part of the body other than its actual source. **refer to drawer** a banker's note suspending payment of a cheque. □□ **referable** /riférəb'l, réffər-/ *adj.* **referrer** *n.* [ME f. OF *referer* f. L *referre* carry back (as RE-, *ferre* bring)]

■ **1** see ATTRIBUTE *v.* **3** hand over, pass on *or* over, send on, assign, commit; direct, point. **4** (*refer to*) look at, study, check, consult, resort to, have recourse to, turn to, appeal to, confer with; talk to, ask, inquire *or* enquire of, apply to. **7, 8** (*refer to*) allude to, make reference to, mention, make mention of, touch on, bring up, speak of, talk *or* write about, turn *or* call *or* direct attention to, indicate, point to, specify, pick out, single out, quote, cite, *literary* advert to.

referee /réffərée/ *n.* & *v.* ● *n.* **1** an umpire esp. in football or boxing. **2** a person whose opinion or judgement is sought in some connection, or who is referred to for a decision in a dispute etc. **3** a person willing to testify to the character of an applicant for employment etc. ● *v.* (**referees, refereed**) **1** *intr.* act as referee. **2** *tr.* be the referee of (a game etc.).

reference /réffərənss, réfrənss/ *n.* & *v.* ● *n.* **1** the referring of a matter for decision or settlement or consideration to some authority. **2** the scope given to this authority. **3** (foll. by *to*) **a** a relation or respect or correspondence (*success seems to have little reference to merit*). **b** an allusion (*made no reference to our problems*). **c** a direction to a book etc. (or a passage in it) where information may be found. **d** a book or passage so cited. **4 a** the act of looking up a passage etc. or looking in a book for information. **b** the act of referring to a person etc. for information. **5 a** a written testimonial supporting an applicant for employment etc. **b** a person giving this. ● *v.tr.* provide (a book etc.) with references to authorities. □ **reference book** a book intended to be consulted for information on individual matters rather than read continuously. **reference library** a library in which the books are for consultation not loan. **with** (or **in**) **reference to** regarding; as regards; about. **without reference to** not taking account of. □□ **referential** /réffərénsh'l/ *adj.*

■ *n.* **1** referral, *Law* appeal. **3 a** regard, concern, connection, respect, relation, correspondence, relevance, pertinence. **b** allusion, mention, remark; hint, intimation, innuendo, insinuation. **c** direction, indication, specification, quotation, citation, note, notation. **5 a** endorsement, recommendation, testimonial. **b** referee.

referendum /réffəréndəm/ *n.* (*pl.* **referendums** or **referenda** /-də/) **1** the process of referring a political question to the electorate for a direct decision by general vote. **2** a vote taken by referendum. [L, gerund or neut. gerundive of *referre*: see REFER]

referent /réffərənt/ *n.* the idea or thing that a word etc. symbolizes. [L *referens* (as REFERENDUM)]

referral /rifërəl/ *n.* the referring of an individual to an expert or specialist for advice, esp. the directing of a patient by a GP to a medical specialist.

refill *v.* & *n.* ● *v.tr.* /reéfil/ **1** fill again. **2** provide a new filling for. ● *n.* /reéfil/ **1** a new filling. **2** the material for this. □□ **refillable** /-filləb'l/ *adj.*

refine /rifín/ *v.* **1** *tr.* free from impurities or defects; purify, clarify. **2** *tr.* & *intr.* make or become more polished or elegant or cultured. **3** *tr.* & *intr.* make or become more subtle or delicate in thought, feelings, etc. □□ **refinable** *adj.* [RE- + FINE[1] *v.*]

■ **1** clear, clarify, decontaminate, *usu. formal* cleanse; see also PURIFY. **2** cultivate, civilize, polish, improve, elevate, perfect. **3** hone, sharpen, concentrate, focus, subtilize; see also ENHANCE.

refined /rifínd/ *adj.* **1** characterized by polish or elegance or subtlety. **2** purified; clarified.

■ **1** cultivated, cultured, civilized, polished, sophisticated, urbane, elegant, well-bred, genteel, courtly, ladylike, gentlemanly, polite, courteous, mannerly, well-mannered, gracious, dignified, elevated, *colloq.* posh; subtle, discriminating, discerning, sensitive, fastidious, nice, precise, exacting, educated, advanced. **2** purified, clarified, pure, clean, *usu. formal* cleansed; filtered, distilled.

refinement /rifínmənt/ *n.* **1** the act of refining or the process of being refined. **2** fineness of feeling or taste. **3** polish or elegance in behaviour or manner. **4** an added development or improvement (*a car with several refinements*). **5** a piece of subtle reasoning. **6** a fine distinction. **7** a subtle or ingenious example or display (*all the refinements of reasoning*). [REFINE + -MENT, after F *raffinement*]

■ **1** improvement, betterment, enhancement, development, perfection; purification, clarification, cleaning, filtration, distillation, *usu. formal* cleansing. **2** fineness, delicacy, discrimination, discernment, sensitivity, finesse. **3** culture, polish, elegance, sophistication, urbanity, urbaneness, breeding, cultivation, gentility, propriety, courtliness, civility, politeness, tact, diplomacy, finesse, suavity, suaveness, good taste. **4** see IMPROVEMENT 1, 2. **6** subtlety, nicety, nuance, distinction, detail, fine point, minutia.

refiner /rifínər/ *n.* a person or firm whose business is to refine crude oil, metal, sugar, etc.

refinery /rifínəri/ *n.* (*pl.* **-ies**) a place where oil etc. is refined.

refit *v.* & *n.* ● *v.tr.* & *intr.* /reéfit/ (**refitted, refitting**) make or become fit or serviceable again (esp. of a ship undergoing renewal and repairs). ● *n.* /reéfit/ the act or an instance of refitting; the process of being refitted. □□ **refitment** *n.*

reflag /reéflág/ *v.tr.* (**reflagged, reflagging**) change the national registration of (a ship).

reflate /reéfláyt/ *v.tr.* cause reflation of (a currency or economy etc.). [RE- after *inflate, deflate*]

reflation /reéfláysh'n/ *n.* the inflation of a financial system to restore its previous condition after deflation. □□ **reflationary** *adj.* [RE- after *inflation, deflation*]

reflect /riflékt/ *v.* **1** *tr.* **a** (of a surface or body) throw back (heat, light, sound, etc.). **b** cause to rebound (*reflected light*). **2** *tr.* (of a mirror) show an image of; reproduce to the eye or mind. **3** *tr.* correspond in appearance or effect to; have as a cause or source (*their behaviour reflects a wish to succeed*). **4** *tr.* **a** (of an action, result, etc.) show or bring (credit, discredit, etc.). **b** (*absol.*; usu. foll. by *on, upon*) bring discredit on. **5 a** *intr.* (often foll. by *on, upon*) meditate on; think about. **b** *tr.* (foll. by *that, how*, etc. + clause) consider; remind oneself. **6** *intr.* (usu. foll. by *upon, on*) make disparaging remarks. □ **reflecting telescope** = REFLECTOR. [ME f. OF *reflecter* or L *reflectere* (as RE-, *flectere flex-* bend)]

■ **1 a** mirror, send *or* throw back, return; echo. **3** show, demonstrate, exhibit, illustrate, exemplify, reveal, lay bare, expose, display, disclose, bring to light, uncover, point to, indicate, suggest, evidence. **4 a** bring, attract, cast, throw. **5 a** (*reflect on* or *upon*) think about *or* over *or* on, contemplate, consider, ponder about *or* over *or* on, deliberate on *or* over, ruminate *or* meditate about *or* on *or* over, cogitate about *or* on *or* over, mull over, *literary* muse about *or* on. **b** remind oneself, remember; see also CONSIDER 1.

reflection /rifléksh'n/ *n.* (also **reflexion**) **1** the act or an instance of reflecting; the process of being reflected. **2 a** reflected light, heat, or colour. **b** a reflected image. **3** meditation; reconsideration (*on reflection*). **4** (often foll. by *on*) discredit or a thing bringing discredit. **5** (often foll. by *on, upon*) an idea arising in the mind; a comment or apophthegm. **6** (usu. foll. by *of*) a consequence; evidence (*a reflection of how she feels*). □ **angle of reflection** *Physics* the angle made by a reflected ray with a perpendicular to the reflecting surface. □□ **reflectional** *adj.* [ME f. OF *reflexion* or LL *reflexio* (as REFLECT), with assim. to *reflect*]

■ **1** image, echo. **3** thought, thinking, meditation, consideration, cogitation, rumination, deliberation, pondering, cerebration; reconsideration, second thoughts. **4** see DISCREDIT *n.* 1. **5** see THOUGHT[1] 4, COMMENT *n.* 1. **6** result, consequence; sign, token, symbol, mark; evidence, testimony, testament, proof, substantiation, corroboration.

reflective /rifléktiv/ *adj.* **1** (of a surface etc.) giving a reflection or image. **2** (of mental faculties) concerned in

reflection or thought. **3** (of a person or mood etc.) thoughtful; given to meditation. □□ **reflectively** *adv.* **reflectiveness** *n.*
■ **3** thoughtful, pensive, contemplative, meditative, cogitative, ruminative, deliberative.

reflector /rifléktər/ *n.* **1** a piece of glass or metal etc. for reflecting light in a required direction, e.g. a red one on the back of a motor vehicle or bicycle. **2 a** a telescope etc. using a mirror to produce images. **b** the mirror itself.

reflet /rəfláy/ *n.* lustre or iridescence, esp. on pottery. [F f. It. *riflesso* reflection, REFLEX]

reflex /réefleks/ *adj.* & *n.* ● *adj.* **1** (of an action) independent of the will, as an automatic response to the stimulation of a nerve (e.g. a sneeze). **2** (of an angle) exceeding 180°. **3** bent backwards. **4** (of light) reflected. **5** (of a thought etc.) introspective; directed back upon itself or its own operations. **6** (of an effect or influence) reactive; coming back upon its author or source. ● *n.* **1** a reflex action. **2** a sign or secondary manifestation (*law is a reflex of public opinion*). **3** reflected light or a reflected image. **4** a word formed by development from an earlier stage of a language. □ **reflex arc** *Anat.* the sequence of nerves involved in a reflex action. **reflex camera** a camera with a ground-glass focusing screen on which the image is formed by a combination of lens and mirror, enabling the scene to be correctly composed and focused. □□ **reflexly** *adv.* [L *reflexus* (as REFLECT)]

reflexible /rifléksib'l/ *adj.* capable of being reflected. □□ **reflexibility** /-bílliti/ *n.*

reflexion var. of REFLECTION.

reflexive /rifléksiv/ *adj.* & *n. Gram.* ● *adj.* **1** (of a word or form) referring back to the subject of a sentence (esp. of a pronoun, e.g. *myself*). **2** (of a verb) having a reflexive pronoun as its object (as in *to wash oneself*). ● *n.* a reflexive word or form, esp. a pronoun. □□ **reflexively** *adv.* **reflexiveness** *n.* **reflexivity** /-sívviti/ *n.*

reflexology /réefleksólləji/ *n.* **1** a system of massage through reflex points on the feet, hands, and head, used to relieve tension and treat illness. **2** *Psychol.* the scientific study of reflexes. □□ **reflexologist** *n.*

refloat /reeflốt/ *v.tr.* set (a stranded ship) afloat again.

refluent /réflooənt/ *adj.* flowing back (*refluent tide*). □□ **refluence** *n.* [ME f. L *refluere* (as RE-, *fluere* flow)]

reflux /réefluks/ *n.* & *v.* ● *n.* **1** a backward flow. **2** *Chem.* a method of boiling a liquid so that any vapour is liquefied and returned to the boiler. ● *v.tr.* & *intr. Chem.* boil or be boiled under reflux.

refocus /reefṓkəss/ *v.tr.* (**refocused, refocusing** or **refocussed, refocussing**) adjust the focus of (esp. a lens).

reforest /reefórrist/ *v.tr.* = REAFFOREST. □□ **reforestation** /-stáysh'n/ *n.*

reforge /reefórj/ *v.tr.* forge again or differently.

reform /rifórm/ *v.* & *n.* ● *v.* **1** *tr.* & *intr.* make or become better by the removal of faults and errors. **2** *tr.* abolish or cure (an abuse or malpractice). **3** *tr. US* correct (a legal document). **4** *tr. Chem.* convert (a straight-chain hydrocarbon) by catalytic reaction to a branched-chain form for use as petrol. ● *n.* **1** the removal of faults or abuses, esp. of a moral or political or social kind. **2** an improvement made or suggested. □ **Reformed Church** a Church that has accepted the principles of the Reformation, esp. a Calvinist Church (as distinct from Lutheran). **Reform Judaism** a simplified and rationalized form of Judaism. **reform school** an institution to which young offenders are sent to be reformed. □□ **reformable** *adj.* [ME f. OF *reformer* or L *reformare* (as RE-, FORM)]
■ *v.* **1** improve, better, emend, rectify, correct, mend, repair, fix, remedy, revise, revolutionize, rehabilitate, remodel, refashion, renovate, reorganize, rebuild, *formal* ameliorate, *literary* meliorate; mend one's ways, turn over a new leaf, go straight. **2** see ABOLISH. ● *n.* **1** improvement, betterment, emendation, rectification, correction, rehabilitation, modification, reorganization, renovation, *formal* amelioration, *literary* melioration; change. □ **reform school** *Brit.* youth custody centre, community home, *hist.* approved school, *Brit. hist.* Borstal, *US* & *hist.* reformatory.

re-form /reefórm/ *v.tr.* & *intr.* form again.

reformat /reefórmat/ *v.tr.* (**reformatted, reformatting**) format anew.

reformation /réffərmáysh'n/ *n.* the act of reforming or process of being reformed, esp. a radical change for the better in political or religious or social affairs. □ **the Reformation** *hist.* a 16th-c. movement for the reform of abuses in the Roman Church ending in the establishment of the Reformed and Protestant Churches. □□ **Reformational** *adj.* [ME f. OF *reformation* or L *reformatio* (as REFORM)]

re-formation /reeformáysh'n/ *n.* the process or an instance of forming or being formed again.

reformative /rifórmətiv/ *adj.* tending or intended to produce reform. [OF *reformatif -ive* or med.L *reformativus* (as REFORM)]

reformatory /rifórmətəri, -tri/ *n.* & *adj.* ● *n.* (*pl.* **-ies**) *US* & *hist.* = *reform school.* ● *adj.* reformative.

reformer /rifórmər/ *n.* a person who advocates or brings about (esp. political or social) reform.

reformism /rifórmiz'm/ *n.* a policy of reform rather than abolition or revolution. □□ **reformist** *n.*
■ gradualism, Fabianism, *often derog.* revisionism.

reformulate /reefórmyoolayt/ *v.tr.* formulate again or differently. □□ **reformulation** /-láysh'n/ *n.*

refract /rifrákt/ *v.tr.* **1** (of water, air, glass, etc.) deflect (a ray of light etc.) at a certain angle when it enters obliquely from another medium. **2** determine the refractive condition of (the eye). [L *refringere refract-* (as RE-, *frangere* break)]

refraction /rifráksh'n/ *n.* the process by which or the extent to which light is refracted. □ **angle of refraction** the angle made by a refracted ray with the perpendicular to the refracting surface. [F *réfraction* or LL *refractio* (as REFRACT)]

refractive /rifráktiv/ *adj.* of or involving refraction. □ **refractive index** the ratio of the velocity of light in a vacuum to its velocity in a specified medium.

refractometer /rífraktómmitər/ *n.* an instrument for measuring a refractive index. □□ **refractometric** /-təmétrik/ *adj.* **refractometry** *n.*

refractor /rifráktər/ *n.* **1** a refracting medium or lens. **2** a telescope using a lens to produce an image.

refractory /rifráktəri/ *adj.* & *n.* ● *adj.* **1** stubborn, unmanageable, rebellious. **2 a** (of a wound, disease, etc.) not yielding to treatment. **b** (of a person etc.) resistant to infection. **3** (of a substance) hard to fuse or work. ● *n.* (*pl.* **-ies**) a substance especially resistant to heat, corrosion, etc. □□ **refractorily** *adv.* **refractoriness** *n.* [alt. of obs. *refractary* f. L *refractarius* (as REFRACT)]

refrain[1] /rifráyn/ *v.intr.* (foll. by *from*) avoid doing (an action); forbear, desist (*refrain from smoking*). □□ **refrainment** *n.* [ME f. OF *refrener* f. L *refrenare* (as RE-, *frenum* bridle)]
■ (*refrain from*) keep from, abstain from, avoid, *literary* forbear from, eschew; stop, cease, give up, discontinue, leave off, renounce, *US* quit, *literary* desist from, *sl.* stow.

refrain[2] /rifráyn/ *n.* **1** a recurring phrase or number of lines, esp. at the ends of stanzas. **2** the music accompanying this. [ME f. OF *refrain* (earlier *refrait*) ult. f. L *refringere* (as RE-, *frangere* break), because the refrain 'broke' the sequence]
■ **1** chorus, burden, reprise, tag.

refrangible /rifránjib'l/ *adj.* that can be refracted. □□ **refrangibility** /-bílliti/ *n.* [mod.L *refrangibilis* f. *refrangere* = L *refringere*: see REFRACT]

refreeze /reefréez/ *v.tr.* & *intr.* (*past* **refroze**; *past part.* **refrozen**) freeze again.

refresh /rifrésh/ *v.tr.* **1 a** (of food, rest, amusement, etc.) give fresh spirit or vigour to. **b** (esp. *refl.*) revive with food, rest, etc. (*refreshed myself with a short sleep*). **2** revive or stimulate (the memory), esp. by consulting the source of one's information. **3** make cool. **4** restore to a certain

condition, esp. by provision of fresh supplies, equipment, etc.; replenish. [ME f. OF *refreschi(e)r* f. *fres fresche* FRESH]
■ **1** enliven, renew, revive, freshen (up), resuscitate, bring back to life, breathe new life into, invigorate, vitalize, energize, brace, fortify, exhilarate, revitalize, reinvigorate, reanimate. **2** revive, renew, stimulate, jog, activate, prod. **4** renew, restock, restore, replenish; fix up, repair, redo, revamp, overhaul, spruce up, recondition, renovate, refurbish, refurnish.

refresher /rifréshər/ *n.* **1** something that refreshes, esp. a drink. **2** *Law* an extra fee payable to counsel in a prolonged case. □ **refresher course** a course reviewing or updating previous studies.

refreshing /rifréshing/ *adj.* **1** serving to refresh. **2** welcome or stimulating because sincere or untypical (*refreshing innocence*). □□ **refreshingly** *adv.*
■ **1** invigorating, stimulating, bracing, exhilarating, tonic, rejuvenating, enlivening, revitalizing, restorative; cool, thirst-quenching.

refreshment /rifréshmənt/ *n.* **1** the act of refreshing or the process of being refreshed in mind or body. **2** (usu. in *pl.*) food or drink that refreshes. **3** something that refreshes or stimulates the mind. [ME f. OF *refreschement* (as REFRESH)]
■ **1** stimulation, invigoration, exhilaration, rejuvenation, enlivenment, restoration, renewal, resuscitation. **2** (*refreshments*) food, drink(s), edibles, eatables, snack(s), titbit(s), *colloq.* grub, eats, *sl.* chow, nosh. **3** stimulation, restorative; see also TONIC *n.*

refrigerant /rifríjərənt/ *n.* & *adj.* ● *n.* **1** a substance used for refrigeration. **2** *Med.* a substance that cools or allays fever. ● *adj.* cooling. [F *réfrigérant* or L *refrigerant-* (as REFRIGERATE)]

refrigerate /rifríjərayt/ *v.* **1** *tr.* & *intr.* make or become cool or cold. **2** *tr.* subject (food etc.) to cold in order to freeze or preserve it. □□ **refrigeration** /-ráysh'n/ *n.* **refrigerative** /-rətiv/ *adj.* [L *refrigerare* (as RE-, *frigus frigoris* cold)]
■ cool, chill, keep cool *or* cold *or* chilled, ice, freeze.

refrigerator /rifríjəraytər/ *n.* a cabinet or room in which food etc. is kept cold.

refrigeratory /rifríjərətəri/ *adj.* & *n.* ● *adj.* serving to cool. ● *n.* (*pl.* **-ies**) *hist.* a cold-water vessel attached to a still for condensing vapour. [mod.L *refrigeratorium* (n.), L *refrigeratorius* (adj.) (as REFRIGERATE)]

refringent /rifrínjənt/ *adj.* *Physics* refracting. □□ **refringence** *n.* **refringency** *n.* [L *refringere*: see REFRACT]

refroze *past* of REFREEZE.

refrozen *past part.* of REFREEZE.

reft *past part.* of REAVE.

refuel /reéfyōōəl/ *v.* (**refuelled, refuelling**; *US* **refueled, refueling**) **1** *intr.* replenish a fuel supply. **2** *tr.* supply with more fuel.

refuge /réfyōōj/ *n.* **1** a shelter from pursuit or danger or trouble. **2** a person or place etc. offering this. **3 a** a person, thing, or course resorted to in difficulties. **b** a pretext, an excuse. **4** a traffic island. [ME f. OF f. L *refugium* (as RE-, *fugere* flee)]
■ **1, 2** sanctuary, shelter, haven, asylum, protection, cover, retreat, harbour, security; safe house, stronghold, citadel, bolt-hole, hideaway, *colloq.* hidey-hole, hide-out. **3 a** resort, recourse. **b** excuse, pretext, ruse, trick, stratagem, subterfuge, dodge, evasion, expedient.

refugee /réfyoojeé/ *n.* a person taking refuge, esp. in a foreign country from war or persecution or natural disaster. [F *réfugié* past part. of *(se) réfugier* (as REFUGE)]
■ fugitive, runaway, escapee, displaced person, DP, exile, émigré.

refulgent /rifúljənt/ *adj. literary* shining; gloriously bright. □□ **refulgence** *n.* **refulgently** *adv.* [L *refulgēre* (as RE-, *fulgēre* shine)]

refund *v.* & *n.* ● *v.* /rifúnd/ *tr.* (also *absol.*) **1** pay back (money or expenses). **2** reimburse (a person). ● *n.* /reéfund/ **1** an act of refunding. **2** a sum refunded; a repayment. □□ **refundable** /rifúndəb'l/ *adj.* **refunder** /rifúndər/ *n.* [ME in sense 'pour back', f. OF *refonder* or L *refundere* (as RE-, *fundere* pour), later assoc. with FUND]

re-fund /reéfúnd/ *v.tr.* fund (a debt etc.) again.

refurbish /rifúrbish/ *v.tr.* **1** brighten up. **2** restore and redecorate. □□ **refurbishment** *n.*
■ **2** restore, refurnish, redecorate, clean (up), polish, renew, renovate, spruce up, remodel, refit, overhaul, repair, recondition, revamp, rebuild, *colloq.* do up.

refurnish /reéfúrnish/ *v.tr.* furnish again or differently.

refusal /rifyōōz'l/ *n.* **1** the act or an instance of refusing; the state of being refused. **2** (in full **first refusal**) the right or privilege of deciding to take or leave a thing before it is offered to others.
■ **1** denial, rejection, rebuff, *colloq.* knock-back. **2** option, choice, pick, selection, preference.

refuse[1] /rifyōōz/ *v.* **1** *tr.* withhold acceptance of or consent to (*refuse an offer*; *refuse orders*). **2** *tr.* (often foll. by *to* + infin.) indicate unwillingness (*I refuse to go*; *the car refuses to start*; *I refuse!*). **3** *tr.* (often with double object) not grant (a request) made by (a person) (*refused me a day off*; *I could not refuse them*). **4** *tr.* (also *absol.*) (of a horse) be unwilling to jump (a fence etc.). □□ **refusable** *adj.* **refuser** *n.* [ME f. OF *refuser* prob. ult. f. L *recusare* (see RECUSANT) after *refutare* REFUTE]
■ **1** decline, reject, spurn, repudiate, turn down, rebuff, give the thumbs down, *colloq.* pass by *or* up, knock back. **3** deny, deprive (of); reject, turn down, decline.

refuse[2] /réfyōōss/ *n.* items rejected as worthless; waste. [ME, perh. f. OF *refusé* past part. (as REFUSE)]
■ rubbish, sweepings, waste, litter, dirt, dross, garbage, debris, junk, *Austral. or dial.* mullock, *esp. US* trash.

re-fuse /reéfyōōz/ *v.tr.* fuse again; provide with a new fuse.

refusenik /rifyōōznik/ *n. hist.* a Jew refused permission to emigrate to Israel from the former Soviet Union. [REFUSE[1] + -NIK]

refute /rifyōōt/ *v.tr.* **1** prove the falsity or error of (a statement etc. or the person advancing it). **2** rebut or repel by argument. **3** *disp.* deny or contradict (without argument). ¶ Often confused in this sense with *repudiate*. □□ **refutable** *adj.* **refutal** *n.* **refutation** /réfyootáysh'n/ *n.* **refuter** *n.* [L *refutare* (as RE-: cf. CONFUTE)]
■ **1, 2** rebut, confute. **3** deny, contradict, reject, repudiate.

reg /rej/ *n. colloq.* = *registration mark*. [abbr.]

regain /rigáyn/ *v.tr.* obtain possession or use of after loss (*regain consciousness*). [F *regagner* (as RE-, GAIN)]

regal /reég'l/ *adj.* **1** royal; of or by a monarch or monarchs. **2** fit for a monarch; magnificent. □□ **regally** *adv.* [ME f. OF *regal* or L *regalis* f. *rex regis* king]
■ **1** royal, kingly, queenly, princely, sovereign, imperial, stately. **2** majestic, splendid, magnificent, grand, resplendent, palatial, exalted; see also ROYAL *adj.* 6.

regale /rigáyl/ *v.tr.* **1** entertain lavishly with feasting. **2** (foll. by *with*) entertain or divert with (talk etc.). **3** (of beauty, flowers, etc.) give delight to. □□ **regalement** *n.* [F *régaler* f. OF *gale* pleasure]
■ **1** entertain, feast, wine and dine, indulge, feed, treat, banquet. **2** entertain, amuse, delight, divert, indulge, please, gratify, captivate, fascinate, entrance, enchant, spellbind, bewitch, charm, enrapture.

regalia /rigáyliə/ *n.pl.* **1** the insignia of royalty used at coronations. **2** the insignia of an order or of civic dignity. **3** any distinctive or elaborate clothes, accoutrements, etc.; trappings, finery. [med.L, = royal privileges, f. L neut. pl. of *regalis* REGAL]
■ **1, 2** decorations, insignia, emblems, badges; see also SYMBOL *n.* **3** accoutrements, apparatus, gear, paraphernalia, trappings, tackle, appurtenances, equipment, equipage; finery.

regalism /reégəliz'm/ *n.* the doctrine of a sovereign's ecclesiastical supremacy.

regality /rigálliti/ *n.* (*pl.* **-ies**) **1** the state of being a king or queen. **2** an attribute of sovereign power. **3** a royal privilege. [ME f. OF *regalité* or med.L *regalitas* (as REGAL)]

regard /rigaárd/ *v.* & *n.* ● *v.tr.* **1** gaze on steadily (usu. in a specified way) (*regarded them suspiciously*). **2** give heed to; take into account; let one's course be affected by. **3** look upon or contemplate mentally in a specified way (*I regard them kindly*; *I regard it as an insult*). **4** (of a thing) have relation to; have some connection with. ● *n.* **1** a gaze; a steady or significant look. **2** (foll. by *to*, *for*) attention or care. **3** (foll. by *for*) esteem; kindly feeling; respectful opinion. **4 a** a respect; a point attended to (*in this regard*). **b** (usu. foll. by *to*) reference; connection, relevance. **5** (in *pl.*) an expression of friendliness in a letter etc.; compliments (*sent my best regards*). □ **as regards** about, concerning; in respect of. **in** (or **with**) **regard to** as concerns; in respect of. [ME f. OF *regard* f. *regarder* (as RE-, *garder* GUARD)]
■ *v.* **1** view, look at *or* upon *or* on, observe, watch, eye, gaze at *or* upon, contemplate, stare at. **2** pay heed *or* attention to, esteem, account, take into account, allow for, take into consideration, consider, take note of, notice, have regard for *or* to. **3** consider, perceive, view, look upon *or* on, see, treat, think of, judge, rate, *formal* deem; (*regard highly*) respect, esteem, value, admire. **4** concern, relate to, be relevant to, pertain to, refer to, affect, have (a) bearing on, bear on *or* upon, involve, have *or* be to do with. ● *n.* **1** see GAZE *n.* **2** care, concern, heed, attention, thought, notice. **3** respect, consideration, concern, thought, sympathy, feeling, reverence, veneration, deference, honour, esteem, high opinion, approval, approbation, appreciation, admiration, affection, fondness. **4 a** point, particular, respect, aspect, detail, matter. **b** reference, relevance, relevancy, association, pertinence, application, bearing, connection, link, tie-in. **5** (*regards*) best wishes, good wishes, compliments, greetings, respects, salutations, attentions, remembrances, *archaic* devoirs. □ **as regards** see CONCERNING. **in** (or **with**) **regard to** with reference to, in relation to, as concerns, in respect of; see also CONCERNING.

regardant /rigaárd'nt/ *adj. Heraldry* looking backwards. [AF & OF (as REGARD)]

regardful /rigaárdfōōl/ *adj.* (foll. by *of*) mindful of; paying attention to.

regarding /rigaárding/ *prep.* about, concerning; in respect of.
■ concerning, about, respecting, with regard to, with respect to, in respect of, with reference to, in *or* on the matter of, pertaining to, on the subject of, apropos, *archaic or Sc. or US* anent, *colloq.* re.

regardless /rigaárdliss/ *adj.* & *adv.* ● *adj.* (foll. by *of*) without regard or consideration for (*regardless of the expense*). ● *adv.* without paying attention (*carried on regardless*). □□ **regardlessly** *adv.* **regardlessness** *n.*
■ *adj.* (*regardless of*) despite, notwithstanding, in spite of, heedless of, irrespective of, *US dial. or joc.* irregardless of. ● *adv.* nevertheless, no matter what, in any event, in any case, anyway, anyhow, irrespectively, *US dial. or joc.* irregardless.

regather /reégáthər/ *v.tr.* & *intr.* **1** gather or collect again. **2** meet again.

regatta /rigáttə/ *n.* a sporting event consisting of a series of boat or yacht races. [It. (Venetian)]

regd. *abbr.* registered.

regelate /reéjiláyt, réj-/ *v.intr.* freeze again (esp. of pieces of ice etc. frozen together after temporary thawing of the surfaces). □□ **regelation** /-láysh'n/ *n.* [RE- + L *gelare* freeze]

regency /reéjənsi/ *n.* (*pl.* **-ies**) **1** the office of regent. **2** a commission acting as regent. **3 a** the period of office of a regent or regency commission. **b** (**Regency**) a particular period of a regency, esp. (in Britain) from 1811 to 1820, and (in France) from 1715 to 1723 (often *attrib.*: *Regency costume*). [ME f. med.L *regentia* (as REGENT)]

regenerate *v.* & *adj.* ● *v.* /rijénnərayt/ **1** *tr.* & *intr.* bring or come into renewed existence; generate again. **2** *tr.* improve the moral condition of. **3** *tr.* impart new, more vigorous, and spiritually greater life to (a person or institution etc.). **4** *intr.* reform oneself. **5** *tr.* invest with a new and higher spiritual nature. **6** *intr.* & *tr. Biol.* regrow or cause (new tissue) to regrow to replace lost or injured tissue. **7** *tr.* & *intr. Chem.* restore or be restored to an initial state of reaction or process. ● *adj.* /rijénnərət/ **1** spiritually born again. **2** reformed. □□ **regeneration** /-ráysh'n/ *n.* **regenerative** /-rətiv/ *adj.* **regeneratively** /-rətivli/ *adv.* **regenerator** *n.* [L *regenerare* (as RE-, GENERATE)]

regent /reéjənt/ *n.* & *adj.* ● *n.* **1** a person appointed to administer a State because the monarch is a minor or is absent or incapacitated. **2** *US* a member of the governing body of a State university. ● *adj.* (placed after noun) acting as regent (*Prince Regent*). □ **regent-bird** an Australian bower bird, *Sericulus chrysocephalus*. [ME f. OF *regent* or L *regere* rule]

regerminate /reéjérminayt/ *v.tr.* & *intr.* germinate again. □□ **regermination** /-náysh'n/ *n.*

reggae /réggay/ *n.* a W. Indian style of music with a strongly accented subsidiary beat. [W.Ind.]

regicide /réjisīd/ *n.* **1** a person who kills or takes part in killing a king. **2** the act of killing a king. □□ **regicidal** /-sīd'l/ *adj.* [L *rex regis* king + -CIDE]

regild /reégild/ *v.tr.* gild again, esp. to renew faded or worn gilding.

regime /rayzhéem/ *n.* (also **régime**) **1 a** a method or system of government. **b** *derog.* a particular government. **2** a prevailing order or system of things. **3** the conditions under which a scientific or industrial process occurs. **4** = REGIMEN 1. [F *régime* (as REGIMEN)]
■ **1** government, rule, administration, leadership, system, *archaic* regimen, regiment. **2** see ORDER *n.* 1.

regimen /réjimen/ *n.* **1** esp. *Med.* a prescribed course of exercise, way of life, and diet. **2** *archaic* a system of government. [L f. *regere* rule]
■ **1** see DIET[1] *n.* 2. **2** see REGIME 1.

regiment *n.* & *v.* ● *n.* /réjimənt/ **1 a** a permanent unit of an army usu. commanded by a colonel and divided into several companies or troops or batteries and often into two battalions. **b** an operational unit of artillery etc. **2** (usu. foll. by *of*) a large array or number. **3** *archaic* rule, government. ● *v.tr.* /réjiment/ **1** organize (esp. oppressively) in groups or according to a system. **2** form into a regiment or regiments. □□ **regimented** *adj.* **regimentation** /-táysh'n/ *n.* [ME (in sense 3) f. OF f. LL *regimentum* (as REGIMEN)]
■ *n.* **2** see LOT *n.* 1. ● *v.* **1** discipline, order, organize, systematize, lick *or* knock *or* whip into shape, regulate, control. □□ **regimented** see UNIFORM *adj.* 1, 2.

regimental /réjimént'l/ *adj.* & *n.* ● *adj.* of or relating to a regiment. ● *n.* (in *pl.*) military uniform, esp. of a particular regiment. □□ **regimentally** *adv.*

Regina /rijīnə/ *n.* the reigning queen (following a name or in the titles of lawsuits, e.g. *Regina v. Jones* the Crown versus Jones). [L, = queen f. *rex regis* king]

region /reéjən/ *n.* **1** an area of land, or division of the earth's surface, having definable boundaries or characteristics (*a mountainous region*; *the region between London and the coast*). **2** an administrative district esp. in Scotland. **3** a part of the body round or near some organ etc. (*the lumbar region*). **4** a sphere or realm (*the region of metaphysics*). **5 a** a separate part of the world or universe. **b** a layer of the atmosphere or the sea according to its height or depth. □ **in the region of** approximately. □□ **regional** *adj.* **regionalism** *n.* **regionalist** *n.* & *adj.* **regionalize** *v.tr.* (also **-ise**). **regionally** *adv.* [ME f. OF f. L *regio -onis* direction, district f. *regere* direct]
■ **1** see AREA 2. **2** district, zone, division, locality, sector, precinct, province, quarter, department. **4** sphere, domain, realm, province, field, ambit, jurisdiction. □ **in the region of** see *approximately* (APPROXIMATE). □□ **regional** see LOCAL *adj.* 1–3. **regionalism** localism, provincialism, parochialism; insularity, narrowness, narrow-mindedness.

regisseur /ráyzhisőr/ *n.* the director of a theatrical production, esp. a ballet. [F *régisseur* stage-manager]

register /réjistər/ *n.* & *v.* ● *n.* **1** an official list e.g. of births, marriages, and deaths, of shipping, of professionally qualified persons, or of qualified voters in a constituency. **2** a book in which items are recorded for reference. **3** a device recording speed, force, etc. **4** (in electronic devices) a location in a store of data, used for a specific purpose and with quick access time. **5 a** the compass of a voice or instrument. **b** a part of this compass (*lower register*). **6** an adjustable plate for widening or narrowing an opening and regulating a draught, esp. in a fire-grate. **7 a** a set of organ pipes. **b** a sliding device controlling this. **8** = *cash register* (see CASH[1]). **9** *Linguistics* each of several forms of a language (colloquial, formal, literary, etc.) usually used in particular circumstances. **10** *Printing* the exact correspondence of the position of printed matter on the two sides of a leaf. **11** *Printing* & *Photog.* the correspondence of the position of colour-components in a printed positive. ● *v.* **1** *tr.* set down (a name, fact, etc.) formally; record in writing. **2** *tr.* make a mental note of; notice. **3** *tr.* enter or cause to be entered in a particular register. **4** *tr.* entrust (a letter etc.) to a post office for transmission by registered post. **5** *intr.* & *refl.* put one's name on a register, esp. as an eligible voter or as a guest in a register kept by a hotel etc. **6** *tr.* (of an instrument) record automatically; indicate. **7 a** *tr.* express (an emotion) facially or by gesture (*registered surprise*). **b** *intr.* (of an emotion) show in a person's face or gestures. **8** *intr.* make an impression on a person's mind (*did not register at all*). **9** *intr.* & *tr.* *Printing* correspond or cause to correspond exactly in position. **10** *tr.* make known formally or publicly; cause (an opinion, grievance, etc.) to be recorded or noted (*I wish to register my disapproval*). □ **registered nurse** a nurse with a State certificate of competence. **registered post** a postal procedure with special precautions for safety and for compensation in case of loss. **register office** *Brit.* a State office where civil marriages are conducted and births, marriages, and deaths are recorded with the issue of certificates. ¶ The name in official use, and generally preferred to *registry office*. □□ **registrable** *adj.* [ME & OF *regestre*, *registre* or med.L *regestrum*, *registrum*, alt. of *regestum* f. LL *regesta* things recorded (as RE-, L *gerere gest-* carry)]

■ *n.* **1** record, roll, catalogue, annal(s), archive, calendar, chronicle, schedule, programme, directory, file, index, inventory, list, listing. ● *v.* **1** record, write *or* take *or* put *or* set down, list, enter, catalogue, log, index, chronicle, note, make *or* take note of. **2** see NOTICE *v.* **5** check in, sign in, log in; sign on *or* up, enrol. **6** record, indicate, mark, measure, point to, exhibit, show. **7 a** show, display, express, indicate, manifest, reveal, betray, reflect. **8** sink in, make an impression, penetrate; (*register with*) dawn on, occur to. **10** make known, transmit, communicate, record.

registrar /réjistraár/ *n.* **1** an official responsible for keeping a register or official records. **2** the chief administrative officer in a university. **3** a middle-ranking hospital doctor undergoing training as a specialist. **4** (in the UK) the judicial and administrative officer of the High Court etc. □ **Registrar General** a government official responsible for holding a population census. □□ **registrarship** *n.* [med.L *registrarius* f. *registrum* REGISTER]

registrary /réjistrəri/ *n.* (*pl.* **-ies**) the registrar of Cambridge University.

registration /réjistráysh'n/ *n.* the act or an instance of registering; the process of being registered. □ **registration mark** (or **number**) a combination of letters and figures identifying a motor vehicle etc. [obs. F *régistration* or med.L *registratio* (as REGISTRAR)]

registry /réjistri/ *n.* (*pl.* **-ies**) **1** a place or office where registers or records are kept. **2** registration. □ **registry office** = *register office*. [obs. *registery* f. med.L *registerium* (as REGISTER)]

Regius professor /réejiəss/ *n. Brit.* the holder of a chair founded by a sovereign (esp. one at Oxford or Cambridge instituted by Henry VIII) or filled by Crown appointment. [L, = royal, f. *rex regis* king]

reglaze /réegláyz/ *v.tr.* glaze (a window etc.) again.

reglet /réglit/ *n.* **1** *Archit.* a narrow strip separating mouldings. **2** *Printing* a thin strip of wood or metal separating type. [F *réglet* dimin. of *règle* (as RULE)]

regnal /régn'l/ *adj.* of a reign. □ **regnal year** a year reckoned from the date or anniversary of a sovereign's accession. [AL *regnalis* (as REIGN)]

regnant /régnənt/ *adj.* **1** reigning (*Queen regnant*). **2** (of things, qualities, etc.) predominant, prevalent. [L *regnare* REIGN]

regolith /réggəlith/ *n. Geol.* unconsolidated solid material covering the bedrock of a planet. [erron. f. Gk *rhēgos* rug, blanket + -LITH]

regorge /rigórj/ *v.* **1** *tr.* bring up or expel again after swallowing. **2** *intr.* gush or flow back from a pit, channel, etc. [F *regorger* or RE- + GORGE]

regrade /reegráyd/ *v.tr.* grade again or differently.

regress *v.* & *n.* ● *v.* /rigréss/ **1** *intr.* move backwards, esp. (in abstract senses) return to a former state. **2** *intr.* & *tr.* *Psychol.* return or cause to return mentally to a former stage of life, esp. through hypnosis or mental illness. ● *n.* /réegress/ **1** the act or an instance of going back. **2** reasoning from effect to cause. [ME (as n.) f. L *regressus* f. *regredi regress-* (as RE-, *gradi* step)]

regression /rigrésh'n/ *n.* **1** a backward movement, esp. a return to a former state. **2** a relapse or reversion. **3** *Psychol.* a return to an earlier stage of development, esp. through hypnosis or mental illness. **4** *Statistics* a measure of the relation between the mean value of one variable (e.g. output) and corresponding values of other variables (e.g. time and cost). [L *regressio* (as REGRESS)]

regressive /rigréssiv/ *adj.* **1** regressing; characterized by regression. **2** (of a tax) proportionally greater on lower incomes. □□ **regressively** *adv.* **regressiveness** *n.*

regret /rigrét/ *v.* & *n.* ● *v.tr.* (**regretted, regretting**) **1** (often foll. by *that* + clause) feel or express sorrow or repentance or distress over (an action or loss etc.) (*I regret that I forgot*; *regretted your absence*). **2** (often foll. by *to* + infin. or *that* + clause) acknowledge with sorrow or remorse (*I regret to say that you are wrong*; *regretted he would not be attending*). ● *n.* **1** a feeling of sorrow, repentance, disappointment, etc., over an action or loss etc. **2** (often in *pl.*) an (esp. polite or formal) expression of disappointment or sorrow at an occurrence, inability to comply, etc. (*refused with many regrets*; *heard with regret of her death*). □ **give** (or **send**) **one's regrets** formally decline an invitation. [ME f. OF *regreter* bewail]

■ *v.* rue, mourn, lament, bemoan, bewail; be *or* feel sorry for, repent, feel remorse for, be *or* feel upset about. ● *n.* **1** repentance, guilt, sorrow, disappointment, contrition, remorse, regretfulness, ruefulness, grief, sadness, mournfulness, *archaic* rue, *archaic or literary* woe, *literary* dolour; (*regrets*) qualms, second thoughts. □ **give** (or **send**) **one's regrets** refuse, decline, say no, give the thumbs down.

regretful /rigrétfo͝ol/ *adj.* feeling or showing regret. □□ **regretfully** *adv.* **regretfulness** *n.*

■ sorry, sorrowful, rueful, mournful, sad, repentant, guilty, disappointed, contrite, remorseful, penitent. □□ **regretfully** see *sadly* (SAD).

regrettable /rigréttəb'l/ *adj.* (of events or conduct) undesirable, unwelcome; deserving censure. □□ **regrettably** *adv.*

■ undesirable, unwelcome, lamentable, woeful, sad, distressing, upsetting, unhappy, unfortunate, unlucky; deplorable, reprehensible, wrong, shameful, *colloq.* terrible, awful.

regroup /reegro͞op/ *v.tr.* & *intr.* group or arrange again or differently. □□ **regroupment** *n.*

regrow /reegró/ *v.intr.* & *tr.* grow again, esp. after an interval. □□ **regrowth** *n.*

Regt. *abbr.* Regiment.

regulable /régyooləb'l/ *adj.* able to be regulated.

regular /régyoolər/ *adj.* & *n.* ● *adj.* **1** conforming to a rule or principle; systematic. **2 a** (of a structure or arrangement) harmonious, symmetrical (*regular features*). **b** (of a surface, line, etc.) smooth, level, uniform. **3** acting or done or recurring uniformly or calculably in time or manner; habitual, constant, orderly. **4** conforming to a standard of etiquette or procedure; correct; according to convention. **5** properly constituted or qualified; not defective or amateur; pursuing an occupation as one's main pursuit (*cooks as well as a regular cook*; *has no regular profession*). **6** *Gram.* (of a noun, verb, etc.) following the normal type of inflection. **7** *colloq.* complete, thorough, absolute (*a regular hero*). **8** *Geom.* **a** (of a figure) having all sides and all angles equal. **b** (of a solid) bounded by a number of equal figures. **9** *Eccl.* (placed before or after noun) **a** bound by religious rule. **b** belonging to a religious or monastic order (*canon regular*). **10** (of forces or troops etc.) relating to or constituting a permanent professional body (*regular soldiers*; *regular police force*). **11** (of a person) defecating or menstruating at predictable times. **12** *Bot.* (of a flower) having radial symmetry. **13** *US colloq.* likeable; normal; reliable (esp. as *regular guy*). ● *n.* **1** a regular soldier. **2** *colloq.* a regular customer, visitor, etc. **3** *Eccl.* one of the regular clergy. **4** *colloq.* a person permanently employed. □ **keep regular hours** do the same thing, esp. going to bed and getting up, at the same time each day. □□ **regularity** /-lárriti/ *n.* **regularize** *v.tr.* (also **-ise**). **regularization** /-rīzáysh'n/ *n.* **regularly** *adv.* [ME *reguler*, *regular* f. OF *reguler* f. L *regularis* f. *regula* RULE]

■ *adj.* **1** scheduled, systematic, ordered, steady, consistent, uniform, logical. **2 a** symmetrical, uniform, even, harmonious, well-proportioned, classic. **b** even, smooth, level, straight, uniform, uninterrupted, unvarying, continuous, flat, plane, plumb. **3** routine, customary, accustomed, wonted, normal, usual, time-honoured, habitual, constant, expected, familiar, standard, predictable; periodic, rhythmic(al), cyclic(al); dependable, methodical, well-regulated, well-ordered, orderly. **4** proper, correct, legal, official, bona fide, legitimate, established, recognized, orthodox, approved, *colloq.* kosher. **5** permanent, career; see also PROFESSIONAL *adj.* **7** complete, utter, out and out, thoroughgoing, unmitigated, unalloyed, unqualified, consummate, perfect, thorough, absolute; acknowledged, real, genuine. **8 a** even-sided, equal-sided, equilateral, equal-angled, equiangular. **13** estimable, fine, good, likeable, aimiable, easy-going, nice, popular, pleasant, acceptable, accepted; reliable, dependable; normal. ● *n.* **2** fixture, *habitué*, (steady) customer, patron, client, frequenter. □□ **regularity** consistency, constancy, uniformity, evenness, sameness, symmetry, balance, harmony, harmoniousness, orderliness, order, stability, predictability, routine, reliability, dependability, steadiness, invariability.

regulate /régyoolayt/ *v.tr.* **1** control by rule. **2** subject to restrictions. **3** adapt to requirements. **4** alter the speed of (a machine or clock) so that it may work accurately. □□ **regulative** /-lətiv/ *adj.* **regulator** *n.* **regulatory** /-lətəri/ *adj.* [LL *regulare regulat-* f. L *regula* RULE]

■ **1** control, monitor; govern, run, operate, administer, handle, guide, steer, conduct, direct, oversee, manage. **2** see RESTRICT. **4** adjust, modify, modulate, control, balance, set, fix.

regulation /régyooláysh'n/ *n.* **1** the act or an instance of regulating; the process of being regulated. **2** a prescribed rule; an authoritative direction. **3** (*attrib.*) **a** in accordance with regulations; of the correct type etc. (*the regulation speed*; *a regulation tie*). **b** *colloq.* usual (*the regulation soup*).

■ **1** adjustment, modification, modulation, control; see also DISCIPLINE *n.* 1a. **2** rule, ruling, law, edict, order, ordinance, statute, decree, directive, dictate, pronouncement, fiat. **3** (*attrib.*) **a** standard, accepted, official, required, prescribed, proper, correct, right. **b** see USUAL.

regulo /régyoolō/ *n.* (usu. foll. by a numeral) each of the numbers of a scale denoting temperature in a gas oven (*cook at regulo 6*). [*Regulo*, propr. term for a thermostatic gas oven control]

regulus /régyooləss/ *n.* (*pl.* **reguluses** or **reguli** /-lī/) *Chem.* **1** the purer or metallic part of a mineral that separates by sinking on reduction. **2** an impure metallic product formed during the smelting of various ores. □□ **reguline** /-līn/ *adj.* [L, dimin. of *rex regis* king: orig. of a metallic form of antimony, so called because of its readiness to combine with gold]

regurgitate /rigúrjitayt/ *v.* **1** *tr.* bring (swallowed food) up again to the mouth. **2** *tr.* cast or pour out again (*required by the exam to regurgitate facts*). **3** *intr.* be brought up again; gush back. □□ **regurgitation** /-táysh'n/ *n.* [med.L *regurgitare* (as RE-, L *gurges gurgitis* whirlpool)]

■ **1** vomit, disgorge, spew up, *colloq.* throw up, *sl.* puke, *US sl.* upchuck. **2** reiterate, repeat, restate.

rehab /reéhab/ *n. colloq.* rehabilitation. [abbr.]

rehabilitate /reéhəbíllitayt/ *v.tr.* **1** restore to effectiveness or normal life by training etc., esp. after imprisonment or illness. **2** restore to former privileges or reputation or a proper condition. □□ **rehabilitation** /-táysh'n/ *n.* **rehabilitative** /-tətiv/ *adj.* [med.L *rehabilitare* (as RE-, HABILITATE)]

■ **1** restore, re-establish, re-educate, reintegrate, reorient, reform, straighten out. **2** reinstate; renew, renovate, refurbish, restore, fix (up), repair, reconstruct, rebuild; change, transform.

rehandle /reéhánd'l/ *v.tr.* **1** handle again. **2** give a new form or arrangement to.

rehang /reéháng/ *v.tr.* (*past* and *past part.* **rehung**) hang (esp. a picture or a curtain) again or differently.

rehash *v.* & *n.* ● *v.tr.* /reéhásh/ put (old material) into a new form without significant change or improvement. ● *n.* /reéhash/ **1** material rehashed. **2** the act or an instance of rehashing.

■ *v.* rework, go over again, restate, redo, rearrange, reshuffle, reuse. ● *n.* **2** reworking, restatement, rearrangement, reshuffle, reuse, rewording.

rehear /reéheér/ *v.tr.* (*past* and *past part.* **reheard** /reéhérd/) hear again.

rehearsal /rihérs'l/ *n.* **1** the act or an instance of rehearsing. **2** a trial performance or practice of a play, recital, etc.

■ **1** relation, recital, telling, description, enumeration, listing, account, narration, repetition, repeat. **2** practice, run-through, dummy run, read-through, *colloq.* dry run.

rehearse /rihérss/ *v.* **1** *tr.* practise (a play, recital, etc.) for later public performance. **2** *intr.* hold a rehearsal. **3** *tr.* train (a person) by rehearsal. **4** *tr.* recite or say over. **5** *tr.* give a list of; enumerate. □□ **rehearser** *n.* [ME f. AF *rehearser*, OF *reherc(i)er*, perh. formed as RE- + *hercer* to harrow f. *herse* harrow: see HEARSE]

■ **1** practise, run through *or* over, go through *or* over. **3** see TRAIN *v.* 1a. **4** repeat, relate, recite, tell, describe, recount, review, go through *or* over, say over, recapitulate, *colloq.* recap. **5** see LIST[1] *v.* 1, ENUMERATE 1.

reheat *v.* & *n.* ● *v.tr.* /reéheét/ heat again. ● *n.* /reéheet/ the process of using the hot exhaust to burn extra fuel in a jet engine and produce extra power. □□ **reheater** /-heétər/ *n.*

reheel /reéheél/ *v.tr.* fit (a shoe etc.) with a new heel.

rehoboam /reéhəbŏŏəm/ *n.* a wine bottle of about six times the standard size. [*Rehoboam* King of Israel (1 Kings 11–14)]

rehouse /reéhówz/ *v.tr.* provide with new housing.

rehung *past* and *past part.* of REHANG.

rehydrate /reéhīdráyt/ *v.* **1** *intr.* absorb water again after dehydration. **2** *tr.* add water to (esp. food) again to restore to a palatable state. □□ **rehydratable** *adj.* **rehydration** /-dráysh'n/ *n.*

Reich /rīkh/ *n.* the former German State, esp. the Third Reich. □ **First Reich** the Holy Roman Empire, 962–1806. **Second Reich** the German Empire 1871–1918. **Third**

Reich the Nazi regime, 1933–45. ¶ Only *Third Reich* is normal historical terminology. [G, = empire]

Reichstag /ríkhstaag/ *n. hist.* **1** the main legislature of the German State under the Second and Third Reichs. **2** the building in which this met. [G]

reify /reé-ifī/ *v.tr.* (**-ies, -ied**) convert (a person, abstraction, etc.) into a thing; materialize. ▫▫ **reification** /-fikáysh'n/ *n.* **reificatory** /-fikáytəri/ *adj.* [L *res* thing + -FY]

reign /rayn/ *v.* & *n.* ● *v.intr.* **1** hold royal office; be king or queen. **2** have power or predominance; prevail; hold sway (*confusion reigns*). **3** (as **reigning** *adj.*) (of a winner, champion, etc.) currently holding the title etc. ● *n.* **1** sovereignty, rule. **2** the period during which a sovereign rules. [ME f. OF *reigne* kingdom f. L *regnare* f. *rex regis* king]

■ *v.* **1** rule, command, govern, wear the crown, wield the sceptre, occupy the throne, be king *or* queen. **2** prevail, be prevalent, predominate, hold sway, obtain, be rampant; win (out), prove superior, gain mastery *or* control, triumph, succeed; *colloq.* run the show, rule the roost, *sl.* call the shots. ● *n.* **1** rule, sovereignty, ascendancy, power, hegemony, command, jurisdiction, leadership, government, direction, control, domination, mastery.

reignite /reé-ignīt/ *v.tr.* & *intr.* ignite again.

Reilly var. of RILEY.

reimburse /reé-imbúrss/ *v.tr.* **1** repay (a person who has expended money). **2** repay (a person's expenses). ▫▫ **reimbursable** *adj.* **reimbursement** *n.* **reimburser** *n.* [RE- + obs. *imburse* put in a purse f. med.L *imbursare* (as IM-, PURSE)]

■ **1** repay, recompense, pay back, compensate, remunerate, indemnify.

reimport *v.* & *n.* ● *v.tr.* /reé-impórt/ import (goods processed from exported materials). ● *n.* /reé-import/ **1** the act or an instance of reimporting. **2** a reimported item. ▫▫ **reimportation** /-táysh'n/ *n.*

reimpose /reé-impṓz/ *v.tr.* impose again, esp. after a lapse. ▫▫ **reimposition** /-pəzish'n/ *n.*

rein /rayn/ *n.* & *v.* ● *n.* (in *sing.* or *pl.*) **1** a long narrow strap with each end attached to the bit, used to guide or check a horse etc. in riding or driving. **2** a similar device used to restrain a young child. **3** (a means of) control or guidance; a curb, a restraint. ● *v.tr.* **1** check or manage with reins. **2** (foll. by *up*, *back*) pull up or back with reins. **3** (foll. by *in*) hold in as with reins; restrain. **4** govern, restrain, control. ▫ **draw rein 1** stop one's horse. **2** pull up. **3** abandon an effort. **give free rein to** remove constraints from; allow full scope to. **keep a tight rein on** allow little freedom to. ▫▫ **reinless** *adj.* [ME f. OF *rene*, *reigne*, earlier *resne*, ult. f. L *retinēre* RETAIN]

■ *n.* **3** check, curb, control, restraint, constraint, limitation, harness, bridle, brake; (*hold the reins*) be in control *or* command; be at the tiller *or* helm; see also DOMINATE 1. ● *v.* **3, 4** (*rein in*) (keep under *or* in) check, curb, (keep *or* hold in) control, restrain, govern, limit, harness, bridle, restrict, hold in *or* back. ▫ **draw rein 3** see *give up* 1. **give free rein to** see INDULGE. **keep a tight rein on** see RESTRAIN 1.

reincarnation /reé-inkaarnáysh'n/ *n.* (in some beliefs) the rebirth of a soul in a new body. ▫▫ **reincarnate** /-kaárnayt/ *v.tr.* **reincarnate** /-kaárnət/ *adj.*

■ rebirth, transmigration, metempsychosis. ▫▫ **reincarnate** (*adj.*) reincarnated, reborn, redivivus.

reincorporate /reé-inkórpərayt/ *v.tr.* incorporate afresh. ▫▫ **reincorporation** /-ráysh'n/ *n.*

reindeer /ráyndeer/ *n.* (*pl.* same or **reindeers**) a subarctic deer, *Rangifer tarandus*, of which both sexes have large antlers, used domestically for drawing sledges and as a source of milk, flesh, and hide. ▫ **reindeer moss** an arctic lichen, *Cladonia rangiferina*, with short branched stems growing in clumps. [ME f. ON *hreindýri* f. *hreinn* reindeer + *dýr* DEER]

reinfect /reé-infékt/ *v.tr.* infect again. ▫▫ **reinfection** /reé-infékshʼn/ *n.*

reinforce /reé-infórss/ *v.tr.* strengthen or support, esp. with additional personnel or material or by an increase of numbers or quantity or size etc. ▫ **reinforced concrete** concrete with metal bars or wire etc. embedded to increase its tensile strength. ▫▫ **reinforcer** *n.* [earlier *renforce* f. F *renforcer*]

■ strengthen, buttress, bolster, support, fortify, prop (up), shore up, brace, hold up, *archaic* stay.

reinforcement /reé-infórsmənt/ *n.* **1** the act or an instance of reinforcing; the process of being reinforced. **2** a thing that reinforces. **3** (in *pl.*) reinforcing personnel or equipment etc.

■ **2** buttress, support, prop, brace, stay, bolster, reinforcer, strengthener. **3** (*reinforcements*) reserves, auxiliaries; help, aid, backup, support.

reinsert /reé-insért/ *v.tr.* insert again. ▫▫ **reinsertion** /-sérsh'n/ *n.*

reinstate /reé-instáyt/ *v.tr.* **1** replace in a former position. **2** restore (a person etc.) to former privileges. ▫▫ **reinstatement** *n.*

reinsure /reé-inshoór/ *v.tr.* & *intr.* insure again (esp. of an insurer securing the risk by transferring some or all of it to another insurer). ▫▫ **reinsurance** *n.* **reinsurer** *n.*

reintegrate /reé-intigrayt/ *v.tr.* **1** = REDINTEGRATE. **2** integrate back into society. ▫▫ **reintegration** /-gráysh'n/ *n.*

reinter /reé-intér/ *v.tr.* inter (a corpse) again. ▫▫ **reinterment** *n.*

reinterpret /reé-intérprit/ *v.tr.* (**reinterpreted, reinterpreting**) interpret again or differently. ▫▫ **reinterpretation** /-táysh'n/ *n.*

reintroduce /reé-intrədyoóss/ *v.tr.* introduce again. ▫▫ **reintroduction** /-dúksh'n/ *n.*

reinvest /reé-invést/ *v.tr.* invest again (esp. money in other property etc.). ▫▫ **reinvestment** *n.*

reinvigorate /reé-invíggərayt/ *v.tr.* impart fresh vigour to. ▫▫ **reinvigoration** /-ráysh'n/ *n.*

reissue *v.* & *n.* ● *v.tr.* /reé-ishōō, -issyōō/ (**reissues, reissued, reissuing**) issue again or in a different form. ● *n.* /ree-íshōō, -syōō/ a new issue, esp. of a previously published book.

reiterate /ree-íttərayt/ *v.tr.* say or do again or repeatedly. ▫▫ **reiteration** /-ráysh'n/ *n.* **reiterative** /-rətiv/ *adj.* [L *reiterare* (as RE-, ITERATE)]

■ repeat, restate, iterate; labour, belabour, harp on about, dwell on.

reive /reev/ *v.intr.* esp. *Sc.* make raids; plunder. ▫▫ **reiver** *n.* [var. of REAVE]

reject *v.* & *n.* ● *v.tr.* /rijékt/ **1** put aside or send back as not to be used or done or complied with etc. **2** refuse to accept or believe in. **3** rebuff or snub (a person). **4** (of a body or digestive system) cast up again; vomit, evacuate. **5** *Med.* show an immune response to (a transplanted organ or tissue) so that it fails to survive. ● *n.* /reéjekt/ a thing or person rejected as unfit or below standard. ▫▫ **rejectable** /rijéktəb'l/ *adj.* **rejecter** /rijéktər/ *n.* (also **rejector**). **rejection** /rijéksh'n/ *n.* **rejective** *adj.* [ME f. L *rejicere reject-* (as RE-, *jacere* throw)]

■ *v.* **1** decline, refuse, disallow, spurn, veto, turn down, say no to, give the thumbs down, set *or* put aside, sweep aside, *Austral.* & *NZ sl.* wipe; throw away *or* out, discard, disown, jettison, eliminate, scrap, junk, scratch. **2** see DISMISS 4, RENOUNCE 1. **3** rebuff, shun, brush aside, snub, refuse, repel, repulse, spurn, turn down, give a person the cold shoulder, turn one's back on, ignore, give a person the brush-off, *Austral.* & *NZ sl.* wipe; jilt, throw over, *colloq.* drop, chuck. ● *n.* second, irregular, discard, cast-off; (*rejects*) defective *or* imperfect merchandise *or* goods. ▫▫ **rejection** refusal, denial, repudiation, renunciation, rebuff, turn-down.

rejig /reejíg/ *v.tr.* (**rejigged, rejigging**) **1** re-equip (a factory etc.) for a new kind of work. **2** rearrange.

rejoice /rijóyss/ *v.* **1** *intr.* feel great joy. **2** *intr.* (foll. by *that* + clause or *to* + infin.) be glad. **3** *intr.* (foll. by *in, at*) take delight. **4** *intr.* celebrate some event. **5** *tr.* cause joy to. □□ **rejoicer** *n.* **rejoicingly** *adv.* [ME f. OF *rejoir rejoiss-* (as RE-, JOY)]
■ **1–3** delight, exult, glory, revel, be happy *or* delighted *or* overjoyed, be tickled. **4** exult; jump for joy, celebrate, revel, glory, delight.

rejoin[1] /reéjóyn/ *v.* **1** *tr.* & *intr.* join together again; reunite. **2** *tr.* join (a companion etc.) again.

rejoin[2] /rijóyn/ *v.* **1** *tr.* say in answer, retort. **2** *intr.* *Law* reply to a charge or pleading in a lawsuit. [ME f. OF *rejoindre rejoign-* (as RE-, JOIN)]

rejoinder /rijóyndər/ *n.* **1** what is said in reply. **2** a retort. **3** *Law* a reply by rejoining. [AF *rejoinder* (unrecorded: as REJOIN[2])]

rejuvenate /rijóóvinayt/ *v.tr.* make young or as if young again. □□ **rejuvenation** /-náysh'n/ *n.* **rejuvenator** *n.* [RE- + L *juvenis* young]
■ restore, refresh, reinvigorate, revitalize, revivify, renew, reanimate, regenerate, recharge, breathe new life into.

rejuvenesce /rijóóvinéss/ *v.* **1** *intr.* become young again. **2** *Biol.* **a** *intr.* (of cells) gain fresh vitality. **b** *tr.* impart fresh vitality to (cells). □□ **rejuvenescent** *adj.* **rejuvenescence** *n.* [LL *rejuvenescere* (as RE-, L *juvenis* young)]

rekindle /reékínd'l/ *v.tr.* & *intr.* kindle again.

-rel /rəl/ *suffix* with diminutive or derogatory force (*cockerel*; *scoundrel*). [from or after OF *-erel(le)*]

relabel /reéláyb'l/ *v.tr.* (**relabelled, relabelling**; *US* **relabeled, relabeling**) label (esp. a commodity) again or differently.

relapse /riláps/ *v.* & *n.* • *v.intr.* (usu. foll. by *into*) fall back or sink again (into a worse state after an improvement). • *n.* /also reélaps/ the act or an instance of relapsing, esp. a deterioration in a patient's condition after a partial recovery. □ **relapsing fever** a bacterial infectious disease with recurrent periods of fever. □□ **relapser** *n.* [L *relabi relaps-* (as RE-, *labi* slip)]
■ *v.* fall back, decline, deteriorate, weaken, degenerate, fail, fade, sink again *or* back (down), sicken, worsen, get *or* become worse, slip back, regress; backslide, lapse, retrogress; (*relapse into*) get back into, go back *or* return *or* revert to. • *n.* decline, deterioration, weakening, degeneration, fading, sinking, worsening; backsliding, falling *or* going back, lapse, return, reversion, regression, retrogression.

relate /riláyt/ *v.* **1** *tr.* narrate or recount (incidents, a story, etc.). **2** *tr.* (in *passive*; often foll. by *to*) be connected by blood or marriage. **3** *tr.* (usu. foll. by *to, with*) bring into relation (with one another); establish a connection between (*cannot relate your opinion to my own experience, a related problem*). **4** *intr.* (foll. by *to*) have reference to; concern (*see only what relates to themselves*). **5** *intr.* (foll. by *to*) **a** bring oneself into relation to; associate with. **b** feel emotionally or sympathetically involved or connected; respond (*they relate well to one another*). □□ **relatable** *adj.* [L *referre relat-* bring back: see REFER]
■ **1** narrate, recount, tell, report, describe, recite, detail, set forth, communicate, impart, delineate, give an account of. **3** associate, connect, link, tie, correlate, coordinate. **4** (*relate to*) apply to, concern, coordinate with, respect, regard, have a bearing on, have reference to, have to do *or* be with, pertain to, refer to, appertain to, belong with *or* to. **5 b** (*relate to*) understand, empathize *or* sympathize with, comprehend, identify with, be in rapport *or en rapport* with, be tuned in to.

related /riláytid/ *adj.* **1** connected by blood or marriage. **2** having (mutual) relation; associated, connected. □□ **relatedness** *n.*
■ **1** kin, akin; kindred, consanguineous, cognate, agnate. **2** associated, affiliated, connected, linked, coupled, affiliate; allied, correlated, coordinated, interconnected, interrelated, interdependent.

relater /riláytər/ *n.* (also **relator**) a person who relates something, esp. a story; a narrator.

relation /riláysh'n/ *n.* **1 a** what one person or thing has to do with another. **b** the way in which one person stands or is related to another. **c** the existence or effect of a connection, correspondence, contrast, or feeling prevailing between persons or things, esp. when qualified in some way (*bears no relation to the facts; enjoyed good relations for many years*). **2** a relative; a kinsman or kinswoman. **3** (in *pl.*) **a** (foll. by *with*) dealings (with others). **b** sexual intercourse. **4** = RELATIONSHIP. **5 a** narration (*his relation of the events*). **b** a narrative. **6** *Law* the laying of information. □ **in relation to** as regards. [ME f. OF *relation* or L *relatio* (as RELATE)]
■ **1 a, c** relationship, connection, interrelation, interrelationship, association, link, tie, tie-in, interconnection, interdependence, correspondence, kinship; pertinence. **b** see LINK[1] *n.* 2b. **2** relative, kinsman, kinswoman, blood relative, in-law, member of the family. **3** (*relations*) **a** dealings, intercourse, link(s), association(s), liaison, relationship, truck, doings. **b** sexual intercourse, coitus, sex; *Law* carnal knowledge, knowledge. **5 a** narration, telling, recounting, description, reporting, recital, recitation, delineation, portrayal, recapitulation. **b** narrative, description, recital, delineation, portrayal, story, report. □ **in relation to** as regards, concerning, about, regarding, respecting, pertaining to, with regard to, with respect to, referring to, in *or* with reference to, in the matter of, on the subject of, *vis-à-vis*, apropos, *archaic or Sc. or US* anent, *colloq.* re.

relational /riláyshən'l/ *adj.* **1** of, belonging to, or characterized by relation. **2** having relation. □ **relational database** *Computing* a database structured to recognize the relation of stored items of information.

relationship /riláyshənship/ *n.* **1** the fact or state of being related. **2** *colloq.* **a** a connection or association (*enjoyed a good working relationship*). **b** an emotional (esp. sexual) association between two people. **3** a condition or character due to being related. **4** kinship.
■ **1, 2a** see ASSOCIATION 4. **2b** see *love affair*. **3** see AFFINITY 2–4.

relative /réllətiv/ *adj.* & *n.* • *adj.* **1** considered or having significance in relation to something else (*relative velocity*). **2** (also foll. by *to*) existing or quantifiable only in terms of individual perception or consideration; not absolute or independent (*truth is relative to your perspective; it's all relative, though, isn't it?*). **3** (foll. by *to*) proportioned to (something else) (*growth is relative to input*). **4** implying comparison or contextual relation (*'heat' is a relative word*). **5** comparative; compared one with another (*their relative advantages*). **6** having mutual relations; corresponding in some way; related to each other. **7** (foll. by *to*) having reference or relating (*the facts relative to the issue*). **8** involving a different but corresponding idea (*the concepts of husband and wife are relative to each other*). **9** *Gram.* **a** (of a word, esp. a pronoun) referring to an expressed or implied antecedent and attaching a subordinate clause to it, e.g. *which, who*. **b** (of a clause) attached to an antecedent by a relative word. **10** *Mus.* (of major and minor keys) having the same key signature. **11** (of a service rank) corresponding in grade to another in a different service. **12** pertinent, relevant; related to the subject (*need more relative proof*). • *n.* **1** a person connected by blood or marriage. **2** a species related to another by common origin (*the apes, man's closest relatives*). **3** *Gram.* a relative word, esp. a pronoun. **4** *Philos.* a relative thing or term. □ **relative atomic mass** the ratio of the average mass of one atom of an element to one twelfth of the mass of an atom of carbon-12: also called *atomic weight*. **relative density** *Chem.* the ratio of the density of a substance to the density of a standard, usu. water for a liquid or solid, and air for a gas. **relative molecular mass** the ratio of the average mass of one molecule of an element or compound to one twelfth of the mass of an atom of carbon-12: also called *molecular weight*. □□ **relatival** /-tīv'l/

adj. (in sense 3 of *n.*). **relatively** *adv.* **relativeness** *n.* [ME f. OF *relatif -ive* or LL *relativus* having reference or relation (as RELATE)]

■ *adj.* **2** (*relative to*) dependent on, contingent on, reliant on, subject to, conditioned by, subordinate to, provisional on. **3** proportionate, proportional; (*relative to*) commensurate to *or* with. **4** comparative, contextual. **5** comparative, related; see also PROPORTIONAL *adj.* **6** related, allied, affiliated, associated, correlated, corresponding. **7** (*relative to*) related *or* connected to, connected with, associated with, allied *or* affiliated to, interconnected with, interrelated to, pertinent *or* relevant *or* germane *or* applicable *or* appurtenant to. **8** see LIKE[1] *adj.* 1a. **12** pertinent, relevant, germane, related, appurtenant; see also APPLICABLE. ● *n.* **1** see RELATION 2. □□ **relatively** more or less, somewhat, comparatively, rather, to some degree, to some extent.

relativism /rélləṭiviz'm/ *n.* the doctrine that knowledge is relative, not absolute. □□ **relativist** *n.*

relativistic /rélləṭivístik/ *adj. Physics* (of phenomena etc.) accurately described only by the theory of relativity. □□ **relativistically** *adv.*

relativity /rélləṭívviti/ *n.* **1** the fact or state of being relative. **2** *Physics* **a** (**special theory of relativity**) a theory based on the principle that all motion is relative and that light has constant velocity, regarding space-time as a four-dimensional continuum, and modifying previous conceptions of geometry. **b** (**general theory of relativity**) a theory extending this to gravitation and accelerated motion.

relator /riláytər/ *n.* **1** var. of RELATER. **2** *Law* a person who makes a relation (see RELATION 6). [L (as RELATE)]

relax /riláks/ *v.* **1 a** *tr.* & *intr.* (of the body, a muscle, etc.) make or become less stiff or rigid (*his frown relaxed into a smile*). **b** *tr.* & *intr.* make or become loose or slack; diminish in force or tension (*relaxed my grip*). **c** *tr.* & *intr.* (also as *int.*) make or become less tense or anxious. **2** *tr.* & *intr.* make or become less formal or strict (*rules were relaxed*). **3** *tr.* reduce or abate (one's attention, efforts, etc.). **4** *intr.* cease work or effort. **5** *tr.* (as **relaxed** *adj.*) at ease; unperturbed. □□ **relaxedly** *adv.* **relaxedness** *n.* **relaxer** *n.* [ME f. L *relaxare* (as RE-, LAX)]

■ **1 a, b** loosen, ease, slacken, release; let go. **c** calm *or* quiet *or* cool down, stay calm *or* cool, ease off *or* up, take it easy, unwind, *sl.* cool it. **2** modify, tone down, moderate, modulate, lighten, check, temper, curb; lighten up (on). **3** reduce, diminish, decrease, lessen, weaken, ease, moderate, ease up on, slacken; abate, remit. **4** ease up, slow down, let up, rest, take it easy, unwind, *colloq.* put one's feet up, *sl.* cool it. **5** (**relaxed**) easygoing, nonchalant, calm, peaceful, tranquil, serene, mellow, at ease, composed, cool, collected, pacific, carefree, insouciant, unperturbed, free and easy, happy-go-lucky.

relaxant /riláks'nt/ *n.* & *adj.* ● *n.* a drug etc. that relaxes and reduces tension. ● *adj.* causing relaxation.

relaxation /reélaksáysh'n/ *n.* **1** the act of relaxing or state of being relaxed. **2** recreation or rest, esp. after a period of work. **3** a partial remission or relaxing of a penalty, duty, etc. **4** a lessening of severity, precision, etc. **5** *Physics* the restoration of equilibrium following disturbance. [L *relaxatio* (as RELAX)]

■ **2** recreation, rest, repose, leisure, amusement, entertainment, fun, pleasure, diversion, R and R. **3, 4** mitigation, moderation, slackening, weakening, easing (up *or* off), alleviation, letting up, diminution, lessening, abatement, remission, *colloq.* let-up.

relay /reélay/ *n.* & *v.* ● *n.* **1** a fresh set of people or horses substituted for tired ones. **2** a gang of workers, supply of material, etc., deployed on the same basis (*operated in relays*). **3** = *relay race.* **4** a device activating changes in an electric circuit etc. in response to other changes affecting itself. **5 a** a device to receive, reinforce, and transmit a telegraph message, broadcast programme, etc. **b** a relayed message or transmission. ● *v.tr.* /also riláy/ **1** receive (a message, broadcast, etc.) and transmit it to others. **2 a** arrange in relays. **b** provide with or replace by relays. □ **relay race** a race between teams of which each member in turn covers part of the distance. [ME f. OF *relai* (n.), *relayer* (v.) (as RE-, *laier* ult. f. L *laxare*): cf. RELAX]

re-lay /reéláy/ *v.tr.* (*past* and *past part.* **re-laid**) lay again or differently.

relearn /reélérn/ *v.tr.* learn again.

release /riléess/ *v.* & *n.* ● *v.tr.* **1** (often foll. by *from*) set free; liberate, unfasten. **2** allow to move from a fixed position. **3 a** make (information, a recording, etc.) publicly or generally available. **b** issue (a film etc.) for general exhibition. **4** *Law* **a** remit (a debt). **b** surrender (a right). **c** make over (property or money) to another. ● *n.* **1** deliverance or liberation from a restriction, duty, or difficulty. **2** a handle or catch that releases part of a mechanism. **3** a document or item of information made available for publication (*press release*). **4 a** a film or record etc. that is released. **b** the act or an instance of releasing or the process of being released in this way. **5** *Law* **a** the act of releasing (property, money, or a right) to another. **b** a document effecting this. □□ **releasable** *adj.* **releasee** /-seé/ *n.* (in sense 4 of *v.*). **releaser** *n.* **releasor** *n.* (in sense 4 of *v.*). [ME f. OF *reles* (n.), *relesser* (v.), *relaiss(i)er* f. L *relaxare*: see RELAX]

■ *v.* **1** let go, (set) free, liberate, (let) loose, set *or* turn loose, unloose, untie, unfasten, unchain, unfetter, unshackle, deliver, let out, discharge, emancipate, *hist.* manumit, *literary* disenthral. **3** issue, publish, make available, put out, pass out, hand out, come out with, circulate, distribute, disseminate; launch. ● *n.* **1** freeing, releasing, liberating, loosing, unloosing, delivering, emancipating, freedom, liberation, deliverance, discharge, emancipation, *hist.* manumission, manumitting. **3** press release, announcement, notice, story, report.

relegate /rélligayt/ *v.tr.* **1** consign or dismiss to an inferior or less important position; demote. **2** transfer (a sports team) to a lower division of a league etc. **3** banish or send into exile. **4** (foll. by *to*) **a** transfer (a matter) for decision or implementation. **b** refer (a person) for information. □□ **relegable** *adj.* **relegation** /-gáysh'n/ *n.* [L *relegare relegat-* (as RE-, *legare* send)]

■ **1** demote; see also DOWNGRADE *v.* 1. **3** see BANISH 1. **4 a** assign, commit, hand over, transfer, pass on, send on. **b** refer, pass on, hand over, send on, direct, point.

relent /rilént/ *v.intr.* **1** abandon a harsh intention. **2** yield to compassion. **3** relax one's severity; become less stern. [ME f. med.L *relentare* (unrecorded), formed as RE- + L *lentāre* bend f. *lentus* flexible]

■ relax, soften, yield, give way, give ground, compromise, capitulate, be merciful, show pity *or* compassion *or* mercy, melt, succumb, come round.

relentless /riléntliss/ *adj.* **1** unrelenting; insistent and uncompromising. **2** continuous; oppressively constant (*the pressure was relentless*). □□ **relentlessly** *adv.* **relentlessness** *n.*

■ **1** unyielding, inexorable, unstoppable, unrelenting, dogged, implacable, inflexible, unbending, unrelieved, stiff-necked, rigid, obstinate, adamant, obdurate, intransigent, determined, unswerving, undeviating, intractable, persevering, steely, tough, unsparing, uncompromising, pitiless, unforgiving, ruthless, merciless, cruel, unmerciful, remorseless; unmoved. **2** non-stop, persistent, incessant, unrelenting, unremitting, unstoppable, perpetual, unflagging, unrelieved, unabated, unbroken, continual, continuous, ceaseless, constant, unceasing, steady.

re-let /reélét/ *v.tr.* (**-letting**; *past* and *past part.* **-let**) let (a property) for a further period or to a new tenant.

relevant /rélliv'nt/ *adj.* (often foll. by *to*) bearing on or having reference to the matter in hand. □□ **relevance** *n.* **relevancy** *n.* **relevantly** *adv.* [med.L *relevans*, part. of L *relevare* RELIEVE]

■ pertinent, appropriate, apt, related, relative, significant, applicable, germane, apposite; to the point.
□□ **relevance, relevancy** appropriateness, aptness, pertinence, connection, tie-in, relation, significance, applicability, application.

reliable /rilī́əb'l/ *adj.* **1** that may be relied on. **2** of sound and consistent character or quality. □□ **reliability** /-bílliti/ *n.* **reliableness** *n.* **reliably** *adv.*
■ dependable, trustworthy, trusted, sound, safe, infallible, *archaic or joc.* trusty; honest, responsible, principled, conscientious, honourable, unfailing, reputable; credible, believable.

reliance /rilī́ənss/ *n.* **1** (foll. by *in, on*) trust, confidence (*put full reliance in you*). **2** a thing relied upon. □□ **reliant** *adj.*
■ **1** (*reliance in* or *on*) confidence in, trust in, faith in, belief in, dependence on.

relic /réllik/ *n.* **1** an object interesting because of its age or association. **2** a part of a deceased holy person's body or belongings kept as an object of reverence. **3** a surviving custom or belief etc. from a past age. **4** a memento or souvenir. **5** (in *pl.*) what has survived destruction or wasting or use. **6** (in *pl.*) the dead body or remains of a person. [ME *relike, relique*, etc. f. OF *relique* f. L *reliquiae*: see RELIQUIAE]
■ **4** memento, souvenir, keepsake, remembrance, token, reminder, trophy. **5** (*relics*) remains, traces, remnants, fragments, pieces; embers, wreckage, rubble, debris, ruins. **6** see CORPSE.

relict /réllikt/ *n.* **1 a** a geological or other object surviving in its primitive form. **b** an animal or plant known to have existed in the same form in previous geological ages. **2** (foll. by *of*) *archaic* a widow. [L *relinquere relict-* leave behind (as RE-, *linquere* leave): sense 2 f. OF *relicte* f. L *relicta*]

relief /rile͞ef/ *n.* **1 a** the alleviation of or deliverance from pain, distress, anxiety, etc. **b** the feeling accompanying such deliverance. **2** a feature etc. that diversifies monotony or relaxes tension. **3** assistance (esp. financial) given to those in special need or difficulty (*rent relief*). **4 a** the replacing of a person or persons on duty by another or others. **b** a person or persons replacing others in this way. **5** (usu. *attrib.*) a thing supplementing another in some service, esp. an extra vehicle providing public transport at peak times. **6 a** a method of moulding or carving or stamping in which the design stands out from the surface, with projections proportioned and more (**high relief**) or less (**low relief**) closely approximating to those of the objects depicted (cf. ROUND *n.* 9). **b** a piece of sculpture etc. in relief. **c** a representation of relief given by an arrangement of line or colour or shading. **7** vividness, distinctness (*brings the facts out in sharp relief*). **8** (foll. by *of*) the reinforcement (esp. the raising of a siege) of a place. **9** esp. *Law* the redress of a hardship or grievance. □ **relief map 1** a map indicating hills and valleys by shading etc. rather than by contour lines alone. **2** a map-model showing elevations and depressions, usu. on an exaggerated relative scale. **relief printing** = LETTERPRESS 2. **relief road** a road taking traffic around a congested (esp. urban) area. [ME f AF *relef*, OF *relief* (in sense 6 F *relief* f. It. *rilievo*) f. *relever*: see RELIEVE]
■ **1 a** easing, abatement, deliverance, alleviation, release, remission, assuagement, liberation, freedom. **b** see EASE *n.* 2a. **3** aid, help, support, assistance, succour, benefit, reinforcement, backing; subsidy. **4 a** see SUBSTITUTE *n.* 1a, CHANGE *n.* 4. **b** substitute, surrogate, replacement, stand-in, double, *esp. US* alternate, *colloq.* locum, *esp. Theatr.* understudy. **7** vividness, distinctness, sharpness, focus, precision, clarity. **9** redress, reparation, (legal) remedy, litigation.

relieve /rile͞ev/ *v.tr.* **1** bring or provide aid or assistance to. **2** alleviate or reduce (pain, suffering, etc.). **3** mitigate the tedium or monotony of. **4** bring military support for (a besieged place). **5** release (a person) from a duty by acting as or providing a substitute. **6** (foll. by *of*) take (a burden or responsibility) away from (a person). **7** bring into relief; cause to appear solid or detached. □ **relieve one's feelings** use strong language or vigorous behaviour when annoyed. **relieve oneself** urinate or defecate. □□ **relievable** *adj.* **reliever** *n.* [ME f. OF *relever* f. L *relevare* (as RE-, *levis* light)]
■ **1** see ASSIST *v.* 1. **2** alleviate, ease, reduce, lessen, diminish, mitigate, palliate, soften, soothe. **3** see MITIGATE. **4** help, aid, assist, support, succour, rescue, save. **5** stand in for, replace, substitute for, take over for *or* from, spell, *colloq.* sub for. **6** (*relieve of*) disburden of, free of, rid of, liberate of, disencumber of, unburden of, rescue from, save from, release from. □ **relieve oneself** see URINATE.

relieved /rile͞evd/ *predic.adj.* freed from anxiety or distress (*am very relieved to hear it*). □□ **relievedly** *adv.*

relievo /rile͞evō/ *n.* (also **rilievo** /reelyáyvō/) (*pl.* **-os**) = RELIEF 6. [It. *rilievo* RELIEF 6]

relight /re͞elī́t/ *v.tr.* light (a fire etc.) again.

religio- /rilíggiō, rilíjiō/ *comb. form* **1** religion. **2** religious.

religion /rilíjən/ *n.* **1** the belief in a superhuman controlling power, esp. in a personal God or gods entitled to obedience and worship. **2** the expression of this in worship. **3** a particular system of faith and worship. **4** life under monastic vows (*the way of religion*). **5** a thing that one is devoted to (*football is their religion*). □ **freedom of religion** the right to follow whatever religion one chooses. □□ **religionless** *adj.* [ME f. AF *religiun*, OF *religion* f. L *religio -onis* obligation, bond, reverence]
■ **1, 3, 5** creed, belief, faith.

religionism /rilíjəniz'm/ *n.* excessive religious zeal. □□ **religionist** *n.*

religiose /rilíjiōss/ *adj.* excessively religious. [L *religiosus* (as RELIGIOUS)]

religiosity /rilíjiόssiti/ *n.* the condition of being religious or religiose. [ME f. L *religiositas* (as RELIGIOUS)]

religious /rilíjəss/ *adj.* & *n.* ● *adj.* **1** devoted to religion; pious, devout. **2** of or concerned with religion. **3** of or belonging to a monastic order. **4** scrupulous, conscientious (*a religious attention to detail*). ● *n.* (*pl.* same) a person bound by monastic vows. □□ **religiously** *adv.* **religiousness** *n.* [ME f. AF *religius*, OF *religious* f. L *religiosus* (as RELIGION)]
■ *adj.* **1** devout, churchgoing, pious, God-fearing, holy, spiritual. **2** see SPIRITUAL *adj.* 2. **4** scrupulous, exact, precise, conscientious, rigorous, strict, fastidious, meticulous, faithful, punctilious.

reline /re͞elī́n/ *v.tr.* renew the lining of (a garment etc.).

relinquish /rilíngkwish/ *v.tr.* **1** surrender or resign (a right or possession). **2** give up or cease from (a habit, plan, belief, etc.). **3** relax hold of (an object held). □□ **relinquishment** *n.* [ME f. OF *relinquir* f. L *relinquere* (as RE-, *linquere* leave)]
■ **1, 2** yield, cede, waive; give up, abandon, drop, forsake, forswear, desert, abdicate, resign, renounce, let go of, surrender; cease from. **3** release, free; see also *let go* 2 (LET[1]).

reliquary /réllikwəri/ *n.* (*pl.* **-ies**) esp. *Relig.* a receptacle for relics. [F *reliquaire* (as RELIC)]

reliquiae /rilíkwi-ee/ *n.pl.* **1** remains. **2** *Geol.* fossil remains of animals or plants. [L f. *reliquus* remaining, formed as RE- + *linquere liq-* leave]

relish /réllish/ *n.* & *v.* ● *n.* **1** (often foll. by *for*) **a** a great liking or enjoyment. **b** keen or pleasurable longing (*had no relish for travelling*). **2 a** an appetizing flavour. **b** an attractive quality (*fishing loses its relish in winter*). **3** a condiment eaten with plainer food to add flavour, esp. a piquant sauce, pickle, etc. **4** (foll. by *of*) a distinctive taste or tinge. ● *v.tr.* **1 a** get pleasure out of; enjoy greatly. **b** look forward to, anticipate with pleasure (*did not relish what lay before her*). **2** add relish to. □□ **relishable** *adj.* [alt. (with assim. to -ISH[2]) of obs. *reles* f. OF *reles, relais* remainder f. *relaisser*: see RELEASE]
■ *n.* **1 a** enjoyment, pleasure, delight, liking, appreciation, fondness, eagerness, avidity, partiality, preference, *archaic* gusto. **b** taste, zest, fancy; see also APPETITE 2. **2 a** see TANG[1] 1. **b** see APPEAL *n.* 4. **3** sauce, condiment, dressing, seasoning, flavouring. ● *v.* **1 a** enjoy, delight in, take

pleasure in, fancy, be partial to, appreciate, savour. **b** look forward to, eagerly await. **2** season, garnish.

relive /reéliv/ *v.tr.* live (an experience etc.) over again, esp. in the imagination.

reload /reélṓd/ *v.tr.* (also *absol.*) load (esp. a gun) again.

relocate /reélōkáyt/ *v.* **1** *tr.* locate in a new place. **2** *tr.* & *intr.* move to a new place (esp. to live or work). □□ **relocation** /-káysh'n/ *n.*

reluctant /rilúktənt/ *adj.* (often foll. by *to* + infin.) unwilling or disinclined (*most reluctant to agree*). □□ **reluctance** *n.* **reluctantly** *adv.* [L *reluctari* (as RE-, *luctari* struggle)]

▪ unwilling, disinclined, unenthusiastic, hesitant; indisposed, loath; averse, opposed. □□ **reluctance** unwillingness, disinclination, aversion, dislike, disrelish, distaste, hesitancy.

rely /rilī́/ *v.intr.* (**-ies, -ied**) (foll. by *on, upon*) **1** depend on with confidence or assurance (*am relying on your judgement*). **2** be dependent on (*relies on her for everything*). [ME (earlier senses 'rally, be a vassal of') f. OF *relier* bind together f. L *religare* (as RE-, *ligare* bind)]

▪ (*rely on* or *upon*) depend on *or* upon, count on *or* upon, trust in, swear by, bank on *or* upon, bet on, have confidence in, be sure *or* certain of; lean on *or* upon.

REM *abbr.* rapid eye-movement.

rem /rem/ *n.* (*pl.* same) a unit of effective absorbed dose of ionizing radiation in human tissue, equivalent to one roentgen of X-rays. [*r*oentgen *e*quivalent *m*an]

remade *past* and *past part.* of REMAKE.

remain /rimáyn/ *v.intr.* **1 a** be left over after others or other parts have been removed or used or dealt with. **b** (of a period of time) be still to elapse. **2** be in the same place or condition during further time; continue to exist or stay; be left behind (*remained at home; it will remain cold*). **3** (foll. by compl.) continue to be (*remained calm; remains President*). **4** (as **remaining** *adj.*) left behind; not having been used or dealt with. [ME f. OF *remain-* stressed stem of *remanoir* or f. OF *remaindre* ult. f. L *remanēre* (as RE-, *manēre* stay)]

▪ **1** stay behind; be left (behind *or* over). **2** linger, wait, *archaic or literary* tarry, *colloq.* stay put; see also STAY[1] *v.* 1. **3** stay, continue to be *or* as, carry on as, persist as. **4** (**remaining**) left (over), extant, outstanding, leftover, surviving, residual, remanent; unused, uneaten, unconsumed.

remainder /rimáyndər/ *n.* & *v.* ● *n.* **1** a part remaining or left over. **2** remaining persons or things. **3** a number left after division or subtraction. **4** the copies of a book left unsold when demand has fallen. **5** *Law* an interest in an estate that becomes effective in possession only when a prior interest (devised at the same time) ends. ● *v.tr.* dispose of (a remainder of books) at a reduced price. [ME (in sense 5) f. AF, = OF *remaindre*: see REMAIN]

▪ *n.* **1, 2** rest, balance, residue, residuum; remains, leftovers, remnants; excess, overage, surplus.

remains /rimáynz/ *n.pl.* **1** what remains after other parts have been removed or used etc. **2** relics of antiquity, esp. of buildings (*Roman remains*). **3** a person's body after death. **4** an author's (esp. unpublished) works left after death.

▪ **1** vestiges, relics, remnants, leavings, crumbs, leftovers, scraps, *reliquiae*; odds and ends. **2** see RELIC 5. **3** body, corpse, carcass, *esp. Med.* cadaver, *archaic* corse, *sl.* stiff.

remake *v.* & *n.* ● *v.tr.* /reémáyk/ (*past* and *past part.* **remade**) make again or differently. ● *n.* /reémayk/ a thing that has been remade, esp. a cinema film.

reman /reémán/ *v.tr.* (**remanned, remanning**) **1** equip (a fleet etc.) with new personnel. **2** make courageous again.

remand /rimaánd/ *v.* & *n.* ● *v.tr.* return (a prisoner) to custody, esp. to allow further inquiries to be made. ● *n.* a recommittal to custody. □ **on remand** in custody pending trial. **remand centre** (in the UK) an institution to which accused persons are remanded pending trial. [ME f. LL *remandare* (as RE-, *mandare* commit)]

remanent /rémmənənt/ *adj.* **1** remaining, residual. **2** (of magnetism) remaining after the magnetizing field has been removed. □□ **remanence** *n.* [ME f. L *remanēre* REMAIN]

remark /rimaárk/ *v.* & *n.* ● *v.* **1** *tr.* (often foll. by *that* + clause) **a** say by way of comment. **b** take notice of; regard with attention. **2** *intr.* (usu. foll. by *on, upon*) make a comment. ● *n.* **1** a written or spoken comment; anything said. **2 a** the act of noticing or observing (*worthy of remark*). **b** the act of commenting (*let it pass without remark*). [F *remarque, remarquer* (as RE-, MARK[1])]

▪ *v.* **1 a** comment, say, observe, reflect, mention, declare, state, assert. **b** note, notice, observe, perceive, regard, look at, take notice *or* note of. **2** comment (on *or* upon), reflect (on *or* upon), deliberate (over); (*remark on* or *upon*) discuss, talk about *or* over, chat about, review, examine. ● *n.* **1** see COMMENT *n.* 1. **2 a** see COMMENT *n.* 2a.

remarkable /rimaárkəb'l/ *adj.* **1** worth notice; exceptional, extraordinary. **2** striking, conspicuous. □□ **remarkableness** *n.* **remarkably** *adv.* [F *remarquable* (as REMARK)]

▪ **1** extraordinary, unusual, singular, exceptional, outstanding, noteworthy, signal, notable, distinguished, uncommon, incredible, unbelievable, impressive, phenomenal, astonishing, astounding; strange, different, odd, peculiar. **2** striking, conspicuous, distinctive, curious, special, wonderful, marvellous, out of the ordinary, unique, significant, outstanding, rare, memorable, unforgettable, never-to-be-forgotten.

remarry /reémárri/ *v.intr.* & *tr.* (**-ies, -ied**) marry again. □□ **remarriage** *n.*

remaster /reémaástər/ *v.tr.* make a new master of (a recording), esp. to improve the sound quality.

rematch /reémach/ *n.* a return match or game.

REME /reémee/ *abbr.* (in the UK) Royal Electrical and Mechanical Engineers.

remeasure /reémézhər/ *v.tr.* measure again. □□ **remeasurement** *n.*

remedial /rimeédiəl/ *adj.* **1** affording or intended as a remedy (*remedial therapy*). **2** (of teaching) for slow or backward children. □□ **remedially** *adv.* [LL *remedialis* f. L *remedium* (as REMEDY)]

remedy /rémmidi/ *n.* & *v.* ● *n.* (*pl.* **-ies**) (often foll. by *for, against*) **1** a medicine or treatment (for a disease etc.). **2** a means of counteracting or removing anything undesirable. **3** redress; legal or other reparation. **4** the margin within which coins as minted may differ from the standard fineness and weight. ● *v.tr.* (**-ies, -ied**) **1** rectify; make good. **2** heal, cure (a person, diseased part, etc.) □□ **remediable** /rimeédiəb'l/ *adj.* [ME f. AF *remedie*, OF *remede* or L *remedium* (as RE-, *medēri* heal)]

▪ *n.* **1** cure, treatment, therapy, antidote, medicament, medicine, prescription, drug, pharmaceutical, cure-all, panacea, nostrum, restorative, *archaic* specific. **2** cure, antidote, cure-all, panacea, nostrum, countermeasure, answer, solution. **3** redress, legal remedy, reparation. ● *v.* **1** correct, rectify, reform, improve, redress, repair, make good, put *or* set right, straighten out, *formal* ameliorate. **2** cure, treat, heal, mend, restore, relieve, soothe, control, ease.

remember /rimémbər/ *v.tr.* **1** keep in the memory; not forget. **2 a** (also *absol.*) bring back into one's thoughts, call to mind (knowledge or experience etc.). **b** (often foll. by *to* + infin. or *that* + clause) have in mind (a duty, commitment, etc.) (*will you remember to lock the door?*). **3** think of or acknowledge (a person) in some connection, esp. in making a gift etc. **4** (foll. by *to*) convey greetings from (one person) to (another) (*remember me to your mother*). **5** mention (in prayer). □ **remember oneself** recover one's manners or intentions after a lapse. □□ **rememberer** *n.* [ME f. OF *remembrer* f. LL *rememorari* (as RE-, L *memor* mindful)]

▪ **1** retain, keep *or* bear in mind, recall, call to mind; think back to. **2 a** call to mind; recall, recollect, reminisce over *or* about, think back on *or* to, *literary* muse on *or* about. **b** mind; not forget. **3** think of, acknowledge, tip, reward, remunerate, recompense, requite.

remembrance /rimémbrənss/ *n.* **1** the act of remembering or process of being remembered. **2** a memory or recollection. **3** a keepsake or souvenir. **4** (in *pl.*) greetings conveyed through a third person. □ **Remembrance Day 1** = *Remembrance Sunday*. **2** *hist.* Armistice Day. **Remembrance Sunday** (in the UK) the Sunday nearest 11 Nov., when those who were killed in the wars of 1914–18 and 1939–45 are commemorated. [ME f. OF (as REMEMBER)]
■ **1** memory, recollection, retention; reminiscing. **2** memory, recollection, reminiscence, thought. **3** memento, reminder, souvenir, keepsake, token, relic, trophy. **4** (*remembrances*) greetings, regards, best wishes.

remex /reéemeks/ *n.* (*pl.* **remiges** /rémmijeez/) a primary or secondary feather in a bird's wing. [L, = rower, f. *remus* oar]

remind /rimínd/ *v.tr.* **1** (foll. by *of*) cause (a person) to remember or think of. **2** (foll. by *to* + infin. or *that* + clause) cause (a person) to remember (a commitment etc.) (*remind them to pay their subscriptions*).
■ **1** (*remind of*) cause to remember, put in mind of, make a person think of, take *or* carry back to. **2** prompt, encourage, urge; jog a person's memory.

reminder /rimíndər/ *n.* **1 a** a thing that reminds, esp. a letter or bill. **b** a means of reminding; an *aide-mémoire*. **2** (often foll. by *of*) a memento or souvenir.
■ **1 b** mnemonic, *aide-mémoire*; cue, prompt. **2** memento, souvenir, keepsake, remembrance, relic, trophy, token.

remindful /rimíndfōōl/ *adj.* (often foll. by *of*) acting as a reminder; reviving the memory.

reminisce /rémminíss/ *v.intr.* (often foll. by *about*) indulge in reminiscence. □□ **reminiscer** *n.* [back-form. f. REMINISCENCE]
■ remember, recollect, think back, look back, turn *or* cast one's mind *or* thoughts back, hark back, take a trip down memory lane.

reminiscence /rémminíss'nss/ *n.* **1** the act of remembering things past; the recovery of knowledge by mental effort. **2 a** a past fact or experience that is remembered. **b** the process of narrating this. **3** (in *pl.*) a collection in literary form of incidents and experiences that a person remembers. **4** *Philos.* (esp. in Platonism) the theory of the recovery of things known to the soul in previous existences. **5** a characteristic of one thing reminding or suggestive of another. □□ **reminiscential** /-nisénsh'l/ *adj.* [LL *reminiscentia* f. L *reminisci* remember]
■ **1, 2** recollection, memory, remembrance; thought. **3** (*reminiscences*) memories, reflections, memoirs.

reminiscent /rémminíss'nt/ *adj.* **1** (foll. by *of*) tending to remind one of or suggest. **2** concerned with reminiscence. **3** (of a person) given to reminiscing. □□ **reminiscently** *adv.*
■ **1** (*reminiscent of*) redolent of, evocative of, suggestive of, similar to, comparable with *or* to.

remise /rimeéz/ *v.* & *n.* ● *v.intr.* **1** *Law* surrender or make over (a right or property). **2** *Fencing* make a remise. ● *n.* *Fencing* a second thrust made after the first has failed. [F f. *remis, remise* past part. of *remettre* put back: cf. REMIT]

remiss /rimíss/ *adj.* careless of duty; lax, negligent. □□ **remissly** *adv.* **remissness** *n.* [ME f. L *remissus* past part. of *remittere* slacken: see REMIT]
■ slack, careless, negligent, neglectful, heedless, unheeding, inattentive, unmindful, thoughtless, forgetful, unthinking, lax, indolent, lazy, dilatory.

remissible /rimíssib'l/ *adj.* that may be remitted. [F *rémissible* or LL *remissibilis* (as REMIT)]

remission /rimísh'n/ *n.* **1** the reduction of a prison sentence on account of good behaviour. **2** the remitting of a debt or penalty etc. **3** a diminution of force, effect, or degree (esp. of disease or pain). **4** (often foll. by *of*) forgiveness (of sins etc.). □□ **remissive** *adj.* [ME f. OF *remission* or L *remissio* (as REMIT)]
■ **3** diminution, abatement, decrease, lessening, subsidence, alleviation, mitigation, assuagement, ebbing, easing. **4** forgiveness, deliverance, absolution; exoneration, *formal* exculpation.

remit *v.* & *n.* ● *v.* /rimít/ (**remitted, remitting**) **1** *tr.* cancel or refrain from exacting or inflicting (a debt or punishment etc.). **2** *intr.* & *tr.* abate or slacken; cease or cease from partly or entirely. **3** *tr.* send (money etc.) in payment. **4** *tr.* cause to be conveyed by post. **5** *tr.* **a** (foll. by *to*) refer (a matter for decision etc.) to some authority. **b** *Law* send back (a case) to a lower court. **6** *tr.* **a** (often foll. by *to*) postpone or defer. **b** (foll. by *in, into*) send or put back into a previous state. **7** *tr.* *Theol.* (usu. of God) pardon (sins etc.). ● *n.* /reémit, rimít/ **1** the terms of reference of a committee etc. **2** an item remitted for consideration. □□ **remittable** /rimíttəb'l/ *adj.* **remittal** /rimítt'l/ *n.* **remittee** /rímmiteé/ *n.* **remitter** /rimíttər/ *n.* [ME f. L *remittere remiss-* (as RE-, *mittere* send)]
■ *v.* **2** subside, ebb, dwindle, ease up *or* off, fall off; assuage; abate, diminish, slacken, decrease, reduce, lessen, alleviate, ease, mitigate. **3** see PAY[1] *v.* 2. **5 a** see REFER 3. **6 a** see POSTPONE.

remittance /rimítt'nss/ *n.* **1** money sent, esp. by post, for goods or services or as an allowance. **2** the act of sending money. □ **remittance man** *hist.* an emigrant subsisting on remittances from home.
■ **1** see PAY[1] *n.*

remittent /rimítt'nt/ *adj.* (of a fever) that abates at intervals. [L *remittere* (as REMIT)]

remix *v.* & *n.* ● *v.tr.* /reémíks/ mix again. ● *n.* /reémiks/ a sound recording that has been remixed.

remnant /rémnənt/ *n.* **1** a small remaining quantity. **2** a piece of cloth etc. left when the greater part has been used or sold. **3** (foll. by *of*) a surviving trace (*a remnant of empire*). [ME (earlier *remenant*) f. OF *remenant* f. *remenoir* REMAIN]
■ **1** leftover, vestige, trace, scrap, fragment, relic, remains. **2** scrap, shred, fragment, end, bit, piece. **3** trace, relic, vestige; see also MEMENTO.

remodel /reémódd'l/ *v.tr.* (**remodelled, remodelling**; *US* **remodeled, remodeling**) **1** model again or differently. **2** reconstruct.

remodify /reémóddifī/ *v.tr.* (**-ies, -ied**) modify again. □□ **remodification** /-fikáysh'n/ *n.*

remold *US* var. of REMOULD.

remonetize /reémúnnitīz/ *v.tr.* (also **-ise**) restore (a metal etc.) to its former position as legal tender. □□ **remonetization** /-záysh'n/ *n.*

remonstrance /rimónstrənss/ *n.* **1** the act or an instance of remonstrating. **2** an expostulation or protest. [ME f. obs. F *remonstrance* or med.L *remonstrantia* (as REMONSTRATE)]

remonstrate /rémmənstrayt/ *v.* **1** *intr.* (foll. by *with*) make a protest; argue forcibly (*remonstrated with them over the delays*). **2** *tr.* (often foll. by *that* + clause) urge protestingly. □□ **remonstrant** /rimónstrənt/ *adj.* **remonstration** /-stráysh'n/ *n.* **remonstrative** /rimónstrətiv/ *adj.* **remonstrator** *n.* [med.L *remonstrare* (as RE-, *monstrare* show)]

remontant /rimóntənt/ *adj.* & *n.* ● *adj.* blooming more than once a year. ● *n.* a remontant rose. [F f. *remonter* REMOUNT]

remora /rémmərə/ *n.* *Zool.* any of various marine fish of the family Echeneidae, which attach themselves by modified sucker-like fins to other fish and to ships. [L, = hindrance (as RE-, *mora* delay, from the former belief that the fish slowed ships down)]

remorse /rimórss/ *n.* **1** deep regret for a wrong committed. **2** compunction; a compassionate reluctance to inflict pain (esp. in *without remorse*). [ME f. OF *remors* f. med.L *remorsus* f. L *remordēre remors-* vex (as RE-, *mordēre* bite)]
■ regret, repentance, ruefulness, pangs *or* prickings of conscience, contrition, contriteness, penitence, compunction, guilt, self-reproach, shame, uneasiness of mind.

remorseful /rimórsfōōl/ *adj.* filled with repentance. □□ **remorsefully** *adv.*
■ regretful, repentant, rueful, sorry, apologetic, guilty, conscience-stricken, contrite, penitent, guilt-ridden, shamefaced, shameful, ashamed, *colloq.* bad.

remorseless /rimórsliss/ *adj.* **1** without compassion or compunction. **2** relentless; unabating. □□ **remorselessly** *adv.* **remorselessness** *n.*
■ **1** cruel, heartless, callous, harsh, hard-hearted, stony-hearted, merciless, unmerciful, pitiless, ruthless. **2** relentless, unrelenting, unremitting, unabating, unstoppable, inexorable, implacable.

remortgage /reémórgij/ *v.* & *n.* ● *v.tr.* (also *absol.*) mortgage again; revise the terms of an existing mortgage on (a property). ● *n.* a different or altered mortgage.

remote /rimṓt/ *adj.* (**remoter, remotest**) **1** far away in place or time. **2** out of the way; situated away from the main centres of population, society, etc. **3** distantly related (*a remote ancestor*). **4** slight, faint (esp. in *not the remotest chance, idea*, etc.). **5** (of a person) aloof; not friendly. **6** (foll. by *from*) widely different; separate by nature (*ideas remote from the subject*). □ **remote control** control of a machine or apparatus from a distance by means of signals transmitted from a radio or electronic device. **remote-controlled** (of a machine etc.) controlled at a distance. □□ **remotely** *adv.* **remoteness** *n.* [ME f. L *remotus* (as REMOVE)]
■ **1** distant, far-away, far-off, removed, outlying, inaccessible. **2** lonely, isolated, secluded, out of the way, sequestered, God-forsaken. **3** far-removed, distant; early, ancient. **4** slight, faint, foggy; small, meagre, slim, slender, poor, inconsiderable, negligible, improbable, unlikely, implausible. **5** aloof, detached, withdrawn, standoffish, reserved, preoccupied, abstracted, indifferent. **6** (*remote from*) unrelated to, irrelevant to, unconnected to, outside, *Sc.* outwith.

remould *v.* & *n.* (*US* **remold**) ● *v.tr.* /reémṓld/ **1** mould again; refashion. **2** re-form the tread of (a tyre). ● *n.* /reémōld/ a remoulded tyre.

remount *v.* & *n.* ● *v.* /reémównt/ **1 a** *tr.* mount (a horse etc.) again. **b** *intr.* get on horseback again. **2** *tr.* get on to or ascend (a ladder, hill, etc.) again. **3** *tr.* provide (a person) with a fresh horse etc. **4** *tr.* put (a picture) on a fresh mount. ● *n.* /reémownt/ **1** a fresh horse for a rider. **2** a supply of fresh horses for a regiment.

removal /rimoóv'l/ *n.* **1** the act or an instance of removing; the process of being removed. **2** the transfer of furniture and other contents on moving house. **3 a** dismissal from an office or post; deposition. **b** (an act of) murder.
■ **1** removing, taking away, elimination, eradication. **2** move, moving (house). **3 a** dismissal, transfer, transferral, discharge, throwing out, deposition, unseating, dethroning, dethronement, displacement, expulsion, ousting, riddance, purge, departure, move, *esp. US* ouster, *colloq.* sacking, *sl.* firing. **b** extermination, murder, elimination, killing, assassination, execution, liquidation, eradication, *colloq.* doing away with, *sl.* bumping off, *esp. US sl.* rubbing out, wasting.

remove /rimoóv/ *v.* & *n.* ● *v.* **1** *tr.* take off or away from the place or position occupied; detach (*remove the top carefully*). **2** *tr.* **a** move or take to another place; change the situation of (*will you remove the tea things?*). **b** get rid of; eliminate (*will remove all doubts*). **3** *tr.* cause to be no longer present or available; take away (*all privileges were removed*). **4** *tr.* (often foll. by *from*) dismiss (from office). **5** *tr. colloq.* kill, assassinate. **6** *tr.* (in *passive*; foll. by *from*) distant or remote in condition (*the country is not far removed from anarchy*). **7** *tr.* (as **removed** *adj.*) (esp. of cousins) separated by a specified number of steps of descent (*a first cousin twice removed* = a grandchild of a first cousin). **8** *formal* **a** *intr.* (usu. foll. by *from, to*) change one's home or place of residence. **b** *tr.* conduct the removal of. ● *n.* **1** a degree of remoteness; a distance. **2** a stage in a gradation; a degree (*is several removes from what I expected*). **3** *Brit.* a form or division in some schools. □□ **removable** *adj.* **removability** /-moóvəbílliti/ *n.* **remover** *n.* (esp. in sense 8b of *v.*). [ME f. OF *removeir* f. L *removēre remot-* (as RE-, *movēre* move)]
■ *v.* **1** take off, shed, strip *or* peel off, discard, *literary* doff; take out, unfasten, detach, disconnect, separate, undo. **2 a** take away, get rid of, carry away *or* off, shift; see also CONFISCATE. **b** obliterate, eradicate, eliminate, get rid of; wipe *or* rub out, erase, efface; wipe *or* rub off, take off, delete, expunge. **4** discharge, dismiss, displace, expel, oust, turn out, get rid of, purge, depose, unseat, kick out, *colloq.* sack, *sl.* fire. **5** murder, assassinate, kill, execute, eliminate, liquidate, dispose of, get rid of, *colloq.* do away with, *sl.* wipe out, do in, bump off, *esp. US sl.* rub out, *US sl.* waste. **8 a** see MOVE *v.* 7. **b** relocate, move, transfer, shift. ● *n.* **1** see DISTANCE *n.* 2. **2** degree, level; see also STAGE *n.* 1.

remunerate /rimyoónərayt/ *v.tr.* **1** reward; pay for services rendered. **2** serve as or provide recompense for (toil etc.) or to (a person). □□ **remuneration** /-ráysh'n/ *n.* **remunerative** /-rətiv/ *adj.* **remuneratory** /-rətəri/ *adj.* [L *remunerari* (as RE-, *munus muneris* gift)]
■ □□ **remuneration** payment, compensation, salary, wages, earnings, emolument, income, pay, stipend, consideration, reward; recompense, repayment, reimbursement, restitution, reparation, damages, indemnity, indemnification; redress.

Renaissance /rináys'nss, -SONSS/ *n.* **1** the revival of art and literature under the influence of classical models in the 14th–16th c. **2** the period of this. **3** the culture and style of art, architecture, etc. developed during this era. **4** (**renaissance**) any similar revival. [F *renaissance* (as RE-, F *naissance* birth f. L *nascentia* or F *naître naiss-* be born f. Rmc: cf. NASCENT)]
■ **4** (**renaissance**) renascence, rebirth, revival, reawakening, renewal, resurgence, regeneration, rejuvenation, new dawn, new birth.

renal /reén'l/ *adj.* of or concerning the kidneys. [F *rénal* f. LL *renalis* f. L *renes* kidneys]

rename /reénáym/ *v.tr.* name again; give a new name to.

renascence /rináss'nss/ *n.* **1** rebirth; renewal. **2** = RENAISSANCE. [RENASCENT]

renascent /rináss'nt/ *adj.* springing up anew; being reborn. [L *renasci* (as RE-, *nasci* be born)]

rencontre /renkóntər/ *n. archaic* = RENCOUNTER. [F (as RENCOUNTER)]

rencounter /renkówntər/ *n.* & *v.* ● *n.* **1** an encounter; a chance meeting. **2** a battle, skirmish, or duel. ● *v.tr.* encounter; meet by chance. [F *rencontre(r)* (as RE-, ENCOUNTER)]

rend /rend/ *v.* (*past* and *past part.* **rent** /rent/) *archaic* or *rhet.* **1** *tr.* (foll. by *off, from, away*, etc.; also *absol.*) tear or wrench forcibly. **2** *tr.* & *intr.* split or divide in pieces or into factions (*a country rent by civil war*). **3** *tr.* cause emotional pain to (the heart etc.). □ **rend the air** sound piercingly. **rend one's garments** (or **hair**) display extreme grief or rage. [OE *rendan*, rel. to MLG *rende*]
■ **1** see WRENCH *v.* 1a. **2** split, tear *or* rip (to pieces *or* apart), divide, separate, shred, slice, *archaic or poet.* rive, *literary* cleave, tear *or* rip asunder; lacerate. **3** pain, distress, pierce, stab, wound, lacerate, afflict, torment, wring, hurt, *archaic or literary* smite. □ **rend one's garments** (or **hair**) tear one's hair out; see also FRET[1] *v.* 1a.

render /réndər/ *v.tr.* **1** cause to be or become; make (*rendered us helpless*). **2** give or pay (money, service, etc.), esp. in return or as a thing due (*render thanks*; *rendered good for evil*). **3** (often foll. by *to*) **a** give (assistance) (*rendered aid to the injured man*). **b** show (obedience etc.). **c** do (a service etc.). **4 a** submit; send in; present (an account, reason, etc.). **b** *Law* (of a judge or jury) deliver formally (a judgement or verdict). **5 a** represent or portray artistically, musically, etc. **b** act (a role); represent (a character, idea, etc.) (*the dramatist's conception was well rendered*). **c** *Mus.* perform; execute. **6** translate (*rendered the poem into French*). **7** (often foll. by *down*) melt down (fat etc.) esp. to clarify; extract by melting. **8** cover (stone or brick) with a coat of plaster. **9** *archaic* **a** give back; hand over; deliver, give up, surrender (*render unto Caesar the things that are Caesar's*). **b** show (obedience). □ **render-set** *v.tr.* (**-setting**; *past* and *past part.* **-set**) plaster (a wall etc.) with two coats. ● *n.* a plastering of two coats. ● *adj.* of two coats. ▫▫ **renderer** *n.* [ME f. OF *rendre* ult. f. L *reddere reddit-* (as RE-, *dare* give)]

■ **1** make, cause to be *or* become. **2** give (back), pay (back), reciprocate, return, repay; see also OFFER *v.* 3, 5. **3 a** give, offer, extend, proffer; see also PROVIDE 1. **c** do, perform, provide, offer, carry out, fulfil. **4 a** submit, deliver, hand in, present, offer, proffer, furnish, provide, tender. **b** deliver, return, *US* hand down. **5 a** depict, represent, reproduce, portray, create, produce, do, execute, make. **b** see ACT *v.* 5a. **c** see PERFORM 2. **6** translate, put, interpret; transcribe, convert; restate, reword, rephrase. **7** melt (down); clarify, purify, clean; extract. **9 a** give up *or* back, yield (up), surrender, relinquish, cede, deliver, hand over, tender, offer, proffer, present, furnish, provide.

rendering /réndəring/ *n.* **1 a** the act or an instance of performing music, drama, etc.; an interpretation or performance (*an excellent rendering of the part*). **b** a translation. **2 a** the act or an instance of plastering stone, brick, etc. **b** this coating. **3** the act or an instance of giving, yielding, or surrendering.

■ **1 a** interpretation, conception, construction, understanding, concept, reading, performance, depiction, delineation, portrayal, rendition, representation, version, reading. **b** translation, interpretation.

rendezvous /róndivōō, -dayvōō/ *n.* & *v.* ● *n.* (*pl.* same /-vōōz/) **1** an agreed or regular meeting-place. **2** a meeting by arrangement. **3** a place appointed for assembling troops, ships, etc. ● *v.intr.* (**rendezvouses** /-vōōz/; **rendezvoused** /-vōōd/; **rendezvousing** /-vōōing/) meet at a rendezvous. [F *rendez-vous* present yourselves f. *rendre*: see RENDER]

rendition /rendísh'n/ *n.* (often foll. by *of*) **1** an interpretation or rendering of a dramatic role, piece of music, etc. **2** a visual representation. [obs. F f. *rendre* RENDER]

■ **1** performance, interpretation, conception, concept, understanding, construction, reading, rendering, depiction, portrayal, delineation, representation, version. **2** representation, picture, version, execution, depiction, portrayal, delineation.

renegade /rénnigayd/ *n.*, *adj.*, & *v.* ● *n.* **1** a person who deserts a party or principles. **2** an apostate; a person who abandons one religion for another. ● *adj.* traitorous, heretical. ● *v.intr.* be a renegade. [Sp. *renegado* f. med.L *renegatus* (as RE-, L *negare* deny)]

■ *n.* **1** deserter, turncoat, heretic, defector, traitor, apostate, *archaic* renegado. **2** see DISSIDENT *n.* ● *adj.* traitorous, treacherous, perfidious, treasonous, apostate, heretical, disloyal.

renegado /rénnigáydō/ *n.* (*pl.* **-oes**) *archaic* = RENEGADE. [Sp. (as RENEGADE)]

renege /rinéeg, -nég, -náyg/ *v.* (also **renegue**) **1** *intr.* **a** go back on one's word; change one's mind; recant. **b** (foll. by *on*) go back on (a promise or undertaking or contract). **2** *tr.* deny, renounce, abandon (a person, faith, etc.). **3** *intr.* *Cards* revoke. ▫▫ **reneger** *n.* **reneguer** *n.* [med.L *renegare* (as RE-, L *negare* deny)]

■ **1 a** back out, default, go back on one's word, change one's mind, break one's word, break one's promise, recant. **b** (*renege on*) back out of, default on, welsh on; see also *go back on* (BACK). **2** deny, recant, renounce, abjure; see also ABANDON *v.* 2a.

renegotiate /réenigṓshiayt/ *v.tr.* (also *absol.*) negotiate again or on different terms. ▫▫ **renegotiable** *adj.* **renegotiation** /-áysh'n/ *n.*

renew /rinyṓō/ *v.tr.* **1** revive; regenerate; make new again; restore to the original state. **2** reinforce; resupply; replace. **3** repeat or re-establish, resume after an interruption (*renewed our acquaintance*; *a renewed attack*). **4** get, begin, make, say, give, etc., anew. **5** (also *absol.*) grant or be granted a continuation of or continued validity of (a licence, subscription, lease, etc.). **6** recover (one's youth, strength, etc.). ▫▫ **renewable** *adj.* **renewability** /-nyṓōəbílliti/ *n.* **renewal** *n.* **renewer** *n.*

■ **1** revive, regenerate, refresh, rejuvenate, revitalize, reinvigorate, resuscitate; restore, revamp, redo, refurbish, refurnish, renovate, refit, overhaul, recondition, modernize, redecorate, *colloq.* do over. **2** reinforce, resupply, restock, replenish, fill *or* top up, refill; replace. **3** resume, resurrect, pick *or* take up (again), recommence, restart, return to, reopen, re-establish. **4** repeat, reiterate, reaffirm, confirm, reconfirm, restate, reassert.

reniform /réeniform/ *adj.* esp. *Med.* kidney-shaped. [L *ren* kidney + -FORM]

rennet /rénnit/ *n.* **1** curdled milk found in the stomach of an unweaned calf, used in curdling milk for cheese, junket, etc. **2** a preparation made from the stomach-membrane of a calf or from certain fungi, used for the same purpose. [ME, prob. f. an OE form *rynet* (unrecorded), rel. to RUN]

rennin /rénnin/ *n.* *Biochem.* an enzyme secreted into the stomach of unweaned mammals causing the clotting of milk. [RENNET + -IN]

renominate /reenómminayt/ *v.tr.* nominate for a further term of office. ▫▫ **renomination** /-náysh'n/ *n.*

renounce /rinównss/ *v.* **1** *tr.* consent formally to abandon; surrender; give up (a claim, right, possession, etc.). **2** *tr.* repudiate; refuse to recognize any longer (*renouncing their father's authority*). **3** *tr.* **a** decline further association or disclaim relationship with (*renounced my former friends*). **b** withdraw from; discontinue; forsake. **4** *intr.* *Law* refuse or resign a right or position esp. as an heir or trustee. **5** *intr.* *Cards* follow with a card of another suit when having no card of the suit led (cf. REVOKE). ▫ **renounce the world** abandon society or material affairs. ▫▫ **renounceable** *adj.* **renouncement** *n.* **renouncer** *n.* [ME f. OF *renoncer* f. L *renuntiare* (as RE-, *nuntiare* announce)]

■ **1** give up, forswear, surrender, abjure, abandon, desert, deny, forgo, abstain from, forsake, reject, repudiate, spurn, throw off *or* out, *colloq.* swear off, *literary* eschew. **2, 3a** repudiate, reject, spurn, disown, scorn, abandon, discard, turn one's back on; see also SPURN *v.* ▫ **renounce the world** retreat, withdraw, turn one's back on the world, become a hermit, cloister or seclude *or* sequester oneself, hide away *or* out, shut *or* cut oneself off.

renovate /rénnəvayt/ *v.tr.* **1** restore to good condition; repair. **2** make new again. ▫▫ **renovation** /-váysh'n/ *n.* **renovative** *adj.* **renovator** *n.* [L *renovare* (as RE-, *novus* new)]

■ **1** redecorate, modernize, refurbish, refurnish, refit, recondition, restore, repair, revamp, overhaul, *US* remodel, *colloq.* do over, do up. **2** see RENEW 1.

renown /rinówn/ *n.* fame; high distinction; celebrity (*a city of great renown*). [ME f. AF *ren(o)un*, OF *renon*, *renom* f. *renomer* make famous (as RE-, L *nominare* NOMINATE)]

■ fame, celebrity, prestige, repute, glory, distinction, acclaim, prominence, eminence, note; éclat, lustre, illustriousness; stardom.

renowned /rinównd/ *adj.* famous; celebrated.

■ famous, famed, celebrated, distinguished, acclaimed, prominent, eminent, well-known, noted, notable, illustrious.

rent[1] /rent/ *n.* & *v.* ● *n.* **1** a tenant's periodical payment to an owner or landlord for the use of land or premises. **2** payment for the use of a service, equipment, etc. ● *v.* **1** *tr.* (often foll. by *from*) take, occupy, or use at a rent (*rented a cottage from the local farmer*). **2** *tr.* (often foll. by *out*) let or hire (a thing) for rent. **3** *intr.* (foll. by *at*) be let or hired out at a specified rate (*the land rents at £100 per month*). ▫ **for rent** *US* available to be rented. **rent-a-** (in *comb.*) often *joc.* denoting availability for hire (*rent-a-van*; *rent-a-crowd*). **rent-boy** a young male prostitute. **rent-free** with exemption from rent. **rent-roll** the register of a landlord's lands etc. with the rents due from them; the sum of one's income from rent. [ME f. OF *rente* f. Rmc (as RENDER)]

■ *n.* **2** rental, hire, (hire) charge, lease; fee, cost, price, rate. ● *v.* **2, 3** let (out), lease, hire (out), charter.

rent[2] /rent/ *n.* **1** a large tear in a garment etc. **2** an opening in clouds etc. **3** a cleft, fissure, or gorge. [obs. *rent* var. of REND]

■ **1** tear, rip, split, gash, slash, hole, slit. **3** cleft, fissure; see also GORGE *n.* 1.

rent[3] *past* and *past part.* of REND.

rentable /réntəb'l/ *adj.* **1** available or suitable for renting. **2** giving an adequate ratio of profit to capital. □□ **rentability** /-bílliti/ *n.*

rental /rént'l/ *n.* **1** the amount paid or received as rent. **2** the act of renting. **3** an income from rents. **4** *US* a rented house etc. □ **rental library** *US* a library which rents books for a fee. [ME f. AF *rental* or AL *rentale* (as RENT[1])]

renter /réntər/ *n.* **1** a person who rents. **2** *Cinematog.* (in the UK) a person who distributes cinema films. **3** *sl.* a male prostitute.

■ **3** rent-boy.

rentier /róntiay/ *n.* a person living on dividends from property, investments, etc. [F f. *rente* dividend]

renumber /reenúmbər/ *v.tr.* change the number or numbers given or allocated to.

renunciation /rinúnsiáysh'n/ *n.* **1** the act or an instance of renouncing or giving up. **2** self-denial. **3** a document expressing renunciation. □□ **renunciant** /rinúnsiənt/ *n.* & *adj.* **renunciative** /rinúnsiətiv/ *adj.* **renunciatory** /rinúnshətəri/ *adj.* [ME f. OF *renonciation* or LL *renuntiatio* (as RENOUNCE)]

renvoi /RONVWÚ/ *n. Law* the act or an instance of referring a case, dispute, etc. to a different jurisdiction. [F f. *renvoyer* send back]

reoccupy /reé-ókyoopī/ *v.tr.* (**-ies, -ied**) occupy again. □□ **reoccupation** /-páysh'n/ *n.*

reoccur /reéəkúr/ *v.intr.* (**reoccurred, reoccurring**) occur again or habitually. □□ **reoccurrence** /-kúrrənss/ *n.*

reopen /reé-ṓp'n/ *v.tr.* & *intr.* open again.

reorder /reé-órdər/ *v.* & *n.* ● *v.tr.* order again. ● *n.* a renewed or repeated order for goods.

reorganize /reé-órgənīz/ *v.tr.* (also **-ise**) organize differently. □□ **reorganization** /-záysh'n/ *n.* **reorganizer** *n.*

reorient /reé-órient, -órrient/ *v.tr.* **1** give a new direction to (ideas etc.); redirect (a thing). **2** help (a person) find his or her bearings again. **3** change the outlook of (a person). **4** (refl., often foll. by *to*) adjust oneself to or come to terms with something.

reorientate /reé-óriəntayt, -órriəntayt/ *v.tr.* = REORIENT. □□ **reorientation** /-táysh'n/ *n.*

Rep. *abbr. US* **1** a Representative in Congress. **2** a Republican.

rep[1] /rep/ *n. colloq.* a representative, esp. a commercial traveller. [abbr.]

rep[2] /rep/ *n. colloq.* **1** repertory. **2** a repertory theatre or company. [abbr.]

rep[3] /rep/ *n.* (also **repp**) a textile fabric with a corded surface, used in curtains and upholstery. [F *reps*, of unkn. orig.]

rep[4] /rep/ *n. US sl.* reputation. [abbr.]

repack /reepák/ *v.tr.* pack again.

repackage /reepákkij/ *v.tr.* **1** package again or differently. **2** present in a new form. □□ **repackaging** *n.*

repaginate /reepájinayt/ *v.tr.* paginate again; renumber the pages of. □□ **repagination** /-náysh'n/ *n.*

repaid *past* and *past part.* of REPAY.

repaint *v.* & *n.* ● *v.tr.* /reepáynt/ **1** paint again or differently. **2** restore the paint or colouring of. ● *n.* /reepaynt/ **1** the act of repainting. **2** a repainted thing, esp. a golf ball.

repair[1] /ripáir/ *v.* & *n.* ● *v.tr.* **1** restore to good condition after damage or wear. **2** renovate or mend by replacing or fixing parts or by compensating for loss or exhaustion. **3** set right or make amends for (loss, wrong, error, etc.). ● *n.* **1** the act or an instance of restoring to sound condition (*in need of repair*; *closed during repair*). **2** the result of this (*the repair is hardly visible*). **3** good or relative condition for working or using (*must be kept in repair*; *in good repair*). □□ **repairable** *adj.* **repairer** *n.* [ME f. OF *reparer* f. L *reparare* (as RE-, *parare* make ready)]

■ *v.* **1, 2** put *or* set right, restore, fix (up), service, put (back) in *or* into working order, renovate, mend, patch (up), vamp, revamp, adjust. ● *n.* **1** restoration, fixing (up), servicing, adjustment, renovation, revamping. **2** mend; patch, darn. **3** form, condition, fettle, working order, shape, *Brit. colloq.* nick.

repair[2] /ripáir/ *v.* & *n.* ● *v.intr.* (foll. by *to*) resort; have recourse; go often or in great numbers or for a specific purpose (*repaired to Spain*). ● *n. archaic* **1** resort (*have repair to*). **2** a place of frequent resort. **3** popularity (*a place of great repair*). [ME f. OF *repaire(r)* f. LL *repatriare* REPATRIATE]

repairman /ripáirmən/ *n.* (*pl.* **-men**) a man who repairs machinery etc.

repand /ripánd/ *adj. Bot.* with an undulating margin; wavy. [L *repandus* (as RE-, *pandus* bent)]

repaper /reepáypər/ *v.tr.* paper (a wall etc.) again.

reparable /réppərəb'l/ *adj.* (of a loss etc.) that can be made good. □□ **reparability** /-bílliti/ *n.* **reparably** *adv.* [F f. L *reparabilis* (as REPAIR[1])]

reparation /réppəráysh'n/ *n.* **1** the act or an instance of making amends. **2 a** compensation. **b** (esp. in *pl.*) compensation for war damage paid by the defeated State. **3** the act or an instance of repairing or being repaired. □□ **reparative** /réppərətiv, ripárrətiv/ *adj.* [ME f. OF f. LL *reparatio -onis* (as REPAIR)]

repartee /réppaarteé/ *n.* **1** the practice or faculty of making witty retorts; sharpness or wit in quick reply. **2 a** a witty retort. **b** witty retorts collectively. [F *repartie* fem. past part. of *repartir* start again, reply promptly (as RE-, *partir* PART)]

■ **2b** banter, *badinage*, patter, raillery, persiflage, word-play.

repartition /reepaartísh'n/ *v.tr.* partition again.

repass /reepaáss/ *v.tr.* & *intr.* pass again, esp. on the way back. [ME f. OF *repasser*]

repast /ripaást/ *n. formal* **1** a meal, esp. of a specified kind (*a light repast*). **2** food and drink supplied for or eaten at a meal. [ME f. OF *repaistre* f. LL *repascere repast-* feed]

repat /reepát/ *n. colloq.* **1** a repatriate. **2** repatriation. [abbr.]

repatriate /reepátriayt/ *v.* & *n.* ● *v.* **1** *tr.* restore (a person) to his or her native land. **2** *intr.* return to one's own native land. ● *n.* a person who has been repatriated. □□ **repatriation** /-áysh'n/ *n.* [LL *repatriare* (as RE-, L *patria* native land)]

repay /reepáy/ *v.* (*past* and *past part.* **repaid**) **1** *tr.* pay back (money). **2** *tr.* return (a blow, visit, etc.). **3** *tr.* make repayment to (a person). **4** *tr.* make return for; requite (a service, action, etc.) (*must repay their kindness*; *the book repays close study*). **5** *tr.* (often foll. by *for*) give in recompense. **6** *intr.* make repayment. □□ **repayable** *adj.* **repayment** *n.* [OF *repaier* (as RE-, PAY[1])]

■ **1** pay back, refund, square, give back, return. **2** return, pay back, reciprocate. **3** pay back, refund, recompense, compensate, reward, reimburse, settle up with, indemnify. **4** requite, reciprocate; return the compliment to, return the favour to. **5** pay back, recompense; see also PAY[1] *v.* 5.

repeal /ripeél/ *v.* & *n.* ● *v.tr.* revoke, rescind, or annul (a law, act of parliament, etc.). ● *n.* the act or an instance of repealing. □□ **repealable** *adj.* [ME f. AF *repeler*, OF *rapeler* (as RE-, APPEAL)]

■ *v.* revoke, recall, rescind, reverse, cancel, annul, nullify, invalidate, void, set aside, abolish, abrogate, *Law* vacate. ● *n.* revocation, recall, rescission, rescindment, reversal, cancellation, annulment, nullification, invalidation, voiding, abolition, abrogation.

repeat /ripeét/ *v.* & *n.* ● *v.* **1** *tr.* say or do over again. **2** *tr.* recite, rehearse, report, or reproduce (something from memory) (*repeated a poem*). **3** *tr.* imitate (an action etc.). **4 a** *intr.* recur; appear again, perhaps several times (*a repeating pattern*). **b** *refl.* recur in the same or a similar form (*history repeats itself*). **5** *tr.* used for emphasis (*am not, repeat not, going*). **6** *intr.* (of food) be tasted intermittently for some time after being swallowed as a result of belching or indigestion. **7** *intr.* (of a watch etc.) strike the last quarter etc. over again when required. **8** *intr.* (of a firearm) fire several shots without reloading. **9** *intr. US* illegally vote more than once in an election. ● *n.* **1 a** the act or an instance of repeating. **b** a thing repeated (often *attrib.*: *repeat prescription*). **2** a repeated broadcast. **3** *Mus.* **a** a passage intended to be repeated. **b** a mark indicating this. **4** a pattern repeated in wallpaper etc. **5** *Commerce* **a** a consignment similar to a previous one. **b** an order given for this; a reorder. □ **repeating decimal** a recurring decimal. **repeat oneself** say or do the same thing over again. □□ **repeatable** *adj.* **repeatability** /-peétəbílliti/ *n.* **repeatedly** *adv.* [ME f. OF *repeter* f. L *repetere* (as RE-, *petere* seek)]

■ *v.* **1** say again, reiterate, restate, retell, recapitulate, *colloq.* recap; echo; do again. **2** recite, quote, rehearse, report, reproduce, replicate, duplicate. **3** imitate, copy, duplicate, replicate, ape, mimic, parrot, monkey, emulate, simulate, impersonate, do an impression of. **4 a** see RECUR. **b** reproduce, replicate, duplicate. ● *n.* **1 a** repetition; duplication, replication, reproduction; duplicate, copy, replica. **2** rerun, rebroadcast. □□ **repeatedly** again and again, over again, over and again, over and over, frequently, often, time and (time) again, time after time, recurrently, repetitively, repetitiously.

repeater /ripeétər/ *n.* **1** a person or thing that repeats. **2** a firearm which fires several shots without reloading. **3** a watch or clock which repeats its last strike when required. **4** a device for the automatic re-transmission or amplification of an electrically transmitted message. **5** a signal lamp indicating the state of another that is invisible.

repêchage /réppishaázh/ *n.* (in rowing etc.) an extra contest in which the runners-up in the eliminating heats compete for a place in the final. [F *repêcher* fish out, rescue]

repel /ripél/ *v.tr.* (**repelled, repelling**) **1** drive back; ward off; repulse. **2** refuse admission or approach or acceptance to (*repel an assailant*). **3** be repulsive or distasteful to. □□ **repeller** *n.* [ME f. L *repellere* (as RE-, *pellere puls-* drive)]

■ **1** repulse, reject, fend off, ward off, hold off, rebuff, resist, withstand, drive back *or* away *or* off; hold *or* keep at bay, keep at arm's length. **3** revolt, repulse, offend, disgust, sicken, nauseate, turn a person's stomach, make a person's skin crawl, *colloq.* give a person the creeps, turn off.

repellent /ripéllənt/ *adj.* & *n.* ● *adj.* **1** that repels. **2** disgusting, repulsive. ● *n.* a substance that repels esp. insects etc. □□ **repellence** *n.* **repellency** *n.* **repellently** *adv.* [L *repellere* (as REPEL)]

■ *adj.* repulsive, repelling, revolting, disgusting, nauseating, nauseous, stomach-turning, sickening, offensive, loathsome, repugnant, distasteful, disagreeable, obnoxious, off-putting, *colloq.* sick-making.

repent[1] /ripént/ *v.* **1** *intr.* (often foll. by *of*) feel deep sorrow about one's actions etc. **2** *tr.* (also *absol.*) wish one had not done, regret (one's wrong, omission, etc.); resolve not to continue (a wrongdoing etc.). **3** *refl.* (often foll. by *of*) *archaic* feel regret or penitence about (*now I repent me*). □□ **repentance** *n.* **repentant** *adj.* **repenter** *n.* [ME f. OF *repentir* (as RE-, *pentir* ult. f. L *paenitēre*)]

■ regret, feel contrition, lament, bemoan, bewail, be sorry, rue, feel remorse, feel remorseful *or* penitent, show penitence. □□ **repentant** regretful, contrite, rueful, remorseful, apologetic, sorry, ashamed, penitent.

repent[2] /reép'nt/ *adj. Bot.* creeping, esp. growing along the ground or just under the surface. [L *repere* creep]

repeople /reépeép'l/ *v.tr.* people again; increase the population of.

repercussion /reépərkúsh'n/ *n.* **1** (often foll. by *of*) an indirect effect or reaction following an event or action (*consider the repercussions of moving*). **2** the recoil after impact. **3** an echo or reverberation. □□ **repercussive** /-kússiv/ *adj.* [ME f. OF *repercussion* or L *repercussio* (as RE-, PERCUSSION)]

■ **1** effect, consequence, after-effect, result; outcome, conclusion, upshot. **3** reverberation, echo, echoing, reverberating, re-echo, re-echoing, resonating, ring; roll, boom, peal.

repertoire /réppərtwaar/ *n.* **1** a stock of pieces etc. that a company or a performer knows or is prepared to give. **2** a stock of regularly performed pieces, regularly used techniques, etc. (*went through his repertoire of excuses*). [F *répertoire* f. LL (as REPERTORY)]

■ **1** repertory, *US* stock.

repertory /réppərtəri, -tri/ *n.* (*pl.* **-ies**) **1** = REPERTOIRE. **2** the theatrical performance of various plays for short periods by one company. **3 a** a repertory company. **b** repertory theatres regarded collectively. **4** a store or collection, esp. of information, instances, etc. □ **repertory company** a theatrical company that performs plays from a repertoire. [LL *repertorium* f. L *reperire repert-* find]

■ **4** repertoire, store, reservoir, collection, hoard, stock, supply, stockpile.

repetend /réppitend/ *n.* **1** the recurring figures of a decimal. **2** the recurring word or phrase; a refrain. [L *repetendum* (as REPEAT)]

répétiteur /repéttitőr/ *n.* **1** a tutor or coach of musicians, esp. opera singers. **2** a person who supervises ballet rehearsals etc. [F]

repetition /réppitish'n/ *n.* **1 a** the act or an instance of repeating or being repeated. **b** the thing repeated. **2** a copy or replica. **3** a piece to be learned by heart. **4** the ability of a musical instrument to repeat a note quickly. □□ **repetitional** *adj.* **repetitionary** *adj.* [F *répétition* or L *repetitio* (as REPEAT)]

■ **1** reiteration, duplication, tautology, repeating, duplicating, recapitulation, replication, rereading, retelling, recital, rerunning, echoing; repeat, rehearsal, restatement, rerun, echo. **2** see COPY *n.* 1.

repetitious /réppitíshəss/ *adj.* characterized by repetition, esp. when unnecessary or tiresome. □□ **repetitiously** *adv.* **repetitiousness** *n.*

■ tiresome, tedious, boring, redundant, prolix, long-winded, wordy, tautological, pleonastic, *colloq.* windy.

repetitive /ripéttitiv/ *adj.* characterized by, or consisting of, repetition; monotonous. □ **repetitive strain injury** injury arising from the continued repeated use of particular muscles, esp. during keyboarding, etc. □□ **repetitively** *adv.* **repetitiveness** *n.*

■ repetitious, prolix, long-winded, wordy, tautological, pleonastic, *colloq.* windy; repeated, redundant; monotonous, humdrum, boring, tiresome, tedious.

rephrase /reéfráyz/ *v.tr.* express in an alternative way.

■ reword, reformulate.

repine /ripín/ *v.intr.* (often foll. by *at, against*) fret; be discontented. [RE- + PINE[2], after *repent*]

repique /ripeék/ *n.* & *v.* ● *n.* (in piquet) the winning of 30 points on cards alone before beginning to play. ● *v.* (**repiques, repiqued, repiquing**) **1** *intr.* score repique. **2** *tr.* score repique against (another person). [F *repic* (as RE-, PIQUE[2])]

replace /ripláyss/ *v.tr.* **1** put back in place. **2** take the place of; succeed; be substituted for. **3** find or provide a substitute for; renew. **4** (often foll. by *with, by*) fill up the place of. **5** (in *passive*, often foll. by *by*) be succeeded or have one's place filled by another; be superseded. □□ **replaceable** *adj.* **replacer** *n.*

■ **1** restore, return, put back. **2** take the place of, supplant, succeed, supersede, take over from, substitute for; be substituted for, be put in place of. **3** change, renew. **4** see SUBSTITUTE *v.* **5** (*be replaced by*) be succeeded *or* superseded *or* supplanted *or* followed by.

replacement /ripláysmənt/ *n.* **1** the act or an instance of replacing or being replaced. **2** a person or thing that takes the place of another.
■ see SUBSTITUTE *n.* 1a.

replan /reeplán/ *v.tr.* (**replanned, replanning**) plan again or differently.

replant /reeplaant/ *v.tr.* **1** transfer (a plant etc.) to a larger pot, a new site, etc. **2** plant (ground) again; provide with new plants.

replay *v.* & *n.* ● *v.tr.* /reepláy/ play (a match, recording, etc.) again. ● *n.* /reeplay/ the act or an instance of replaying a match, a recording, or a recorded incident in a game etc.

replenish /riplénnish/ *v.tr.* **1** (often foll. by *with*) fill up again. **2** renew (a supply etc.). **3** (as **replenished** *adj.*) filled; fully stored or stocked; full. ▫▫ **replenisher** *n.* **replenishment** *n.* [ME f. OF *replenir* (as RE-, *plenir* f. *plein* full f. L *plenus*)]
■ **1, 2** restock, refill, replace, fill *or* top up, reinforce; renew.

replete /ripleet/ *adj.* (often foll. by *with*) **1** filled or well-supplied with. **2** stuffed; gorged; sated. ▫▫ **repleteness** *n.* **repletion** *n.* [ME f. OF *replet replete* or L *repletus* past part. of *replēre* (as RE-, *plēre plet-* fill)]
■ **1** well supplied *or* provided *or* stocked, chock-full, crammed *or* jammed, brim-full, chock-a-block, overflowing, brimming, bursting, teeming, loaded, overloaded, full, stuffed, *colloq.* jam-packed, gorged, lousy; filled up. **2** stuffed, gorged, sated, satisfied, full, *archaic* satiated; filled up.

replevin /riplévvin/ *n. Law* **1** the provisional restoration or recovery of distrained goods pending the outcome of trial and judgement. **2** a writ granting this. **3** the action arising from this process. [ME f. AF f. OF *replevir* (as REPLEVY)]

replevy /riplévvi/ *v.tr.* (**-ies, -ied**) *Law* recover by replevin. [OF *replevir* recover f. Gmc]

replica /répliкə/ *n.* **1** a duplicate of a work made by the original artist. **2 a** a facsimile, an exact copy. **b** (of a person) an exact likeness, a double. **3** a copy or model, esp. on a smaller scale. [It. f. *replicare* REPLY]
■ **2 a** copy, duplicate, facsimile, reproduction, replication; carbon copy, photocopy, duplication. **b** twin, clone, (dead) ringer, double, *doppelgänger*, exact *or* perfect likeness, *colloq.* picture, spitting image. **3** see MODEL *n.* 1, 3.

replicate *v.*, *adj.*, & *n.* ● *v.tr.* /réplikayt/ **1** repeat (an experiment etc.). **2** make a replica of. **3** fold back. ● *adj.* /réplikət/ *Bot.* folded back on itself. ● *n.* /réplikət/ *Mus.* a tone one or more octaves above or below the given tone. ▫▫ **replicable** /-kəb'l/ *adj.* (in sense 1 of *v.*). **replicability** /-kəbílliti/ *n.* (in sense 1 of *v.*). **replicative** /-kətiv/ *adj.* [L *replicare* (as RE-, *plicare* fold)]

replication /réplikáysh'n/ *n.* **1** a reply or response, esp. a reply to an answer. **2** *Law* the plaintiff's reply to the defendant's plea. **3 a** the act or an instance of copying. **b** a copy. **c** the process by which genetic material or a living organism gives rise to a copy of itself. [ME f. OF *replicacion* f. L *replicatio -onis* (as REPLICATE)]

reply /riplī́/ *v.* & *n.* ● *v.* (**-ies, -ied**) **1** *intr.* (often foll. by *to*) make an answer, respond in word or action. **2** *tr.* say in answer (*he replied, 'Please yourself'*). ● *n.* (*pl.* **-ies**) **1** the act of replying (*what did they say in reply?*). **2** what is replied; a response. **3** *Law* = REPLICATION. ▫ **reply coupon** a coupon exchangeable for stamps in any country for prepaying the reply to a letter. **reply paid 1** *hist.* (of a telegram) with the cost of a reply prepaid by the sender. **2** (of an envelope etc.) for which the addressee undertakes to pay postage. ▫▫ **replier** *n.* [ME f. OF *replier* f. L (as REPLICATE)]
■ *v.* **1** answer, respond; counter, answer back, riposte, *US* come back. **2** answer, respond, retort, rejoin, return, fling *or* hurl (back), *US* come back. ● *n.* **1** response, reaction, answer, explanation, explication. **2** answer, response, rejoinder, retort, riposte, reaction, *sl.* comeback.

repoint /reepóynt/ *v.tr.* point (esp. brickwork) again.

repolish /reepóllish/ *v.tr.* polish again.

repopulate /reepópyoolayt/ *v.tr.* populate again or increase the population of. ▫▫ **repopulation** /-láysh'n/ *n.*

report /ripórt/ *v.* & *n.* ● *v.* **1** *tr.* **a** bring back or give an account of. **b** state as fact or news, narrate or describe or repeat, esp. as an eyewitness or hearer etc. **c** relate as spoken by another. **2** *tr.* make an official or formal statement about. **3** *tr.* (often foll. by *to*) name or specify (an offender or offence) (*shall report you for insubordination*; *reported them to the police*). **4** *intr.* (often foll. by *to*) present oneself as having returned or arrived (*report to the manager on arrival*). **5** *tr.* (also *absol.*) take down word for word or summarize or write a description of for publication. **6** *intr.* make or draw up or send in a report. **7** *intr.* (often foll. by *to*) be responsible (to a superior, supervisor, etc.) (*reports directly to the managing director*). **8** *tr. Parl.* (of a committee chairman) announce that the committee has dealt with (a bill). **9** *intr.* (often foll. by *of*) give a report to convey that one is well, badly, etc. impressed (*reports well of the prospects*). **10** *intr.* (usu. foll. by *on*) investigate or scrutinize for a journalistic report; act as a reporter. ● *n.* **1** an account given or opinion formally expressed after investigation or consideration. **2** a description, summary, or reproduction of an event or speech or law case, esp. for newspaper publication or broadcast. **3** common talk; rumour. **4** the way a person or thing is spoken of (*I hear a good report of you*). **5** a periodical statement on (esp. a school pupil's) work, conduct, etc. **6** the sound of an explosion. ▫ **report back** deliver a report to the person, organization, etc. for whom one acts etc. **reported speech** the speaker's words with the changes of person, tense, etc. usual in reports, e.g. *he said that he would go* (opp. *direct speech*). **report progress** state what has been done so far. **report stage** (in the UK) the debate on a bill in the House of Commons or House of Lords after it is reported. ▫▫ **reportable** *adj.* **reportedly** *adv.* [ME f. OF *reporter* f. L *reportare* (as RE-, *portare* bring)]
■ *v.* **1 a, b** relate, recount, describe, narrate, tell of, detail, give an account of, communicate, set forth; document. **c** relate, recount, recite, communicate, give an account of. **2** publish, promulgate, publicize, put out, announce, set forth, reveal, disclose, divulge, circulate, make public, broadcast. **4** present *or* announce oneself, make oneself known. **10** (*report on*) investigate, cover, examine, explore, look into, inquire into, check into *or* on, check up on, research, study, probe, scrutinize, *US* check out, *Brit. sl.* suss out. ● *n.* **1** see ACCOUNT *n.* 1. **2** description, story, article, piece, statement, dispatch, communication, communiqué, announcement, narrative, record, *colloq.* write-up. **3** piece of gossip *or* hearsay, *on dit*; see also RUMOUR *n.* 1. **5** assessment, evaluation, appraisal, record (of achievement). **6** explosion, bang, boom, shot, gunshot, crack, blast, detonation.

reportage /répportaazh/ *n.* **1** the describing of events, esp. the reporting of news etc. for the press and for broadcasting. **2** the typical style of this. **3** factual presentation in a book etc. [REPORT, after F]

reporter /ripórtər/ *n.* **1** a person employed to report news etc. for newspapers or broadcasts. **2** a person who reports.
■ **1** journalist, newspaperman, newsman, correspondent, columnist, newswriter, gentleman *or* lady of the press, pressman, news-hound, news-hawk, *colloq.* stringer, *Austral. colloq.* journo, *joc.* gentleman *or* lady of the fourth estate.

reportorial /rípportóriəl/ *adj. US* of newspaper reporters. ▫▫ **reportorially** *adv.* [REPORTER, after *editorial*]

repose[1] /ripṓz/ *n.* & *v.* ● *n.* **1** the cessation of activity or excitement or toil. **2** sleep. **3** a peaceful or quiescent state; stillness; tranquillity. **4** *Art* a restful effect; harmonious combination. **5** composure or ease of manner. ● *v.* **1** *intr.* & *refl.* lie down in rest (*reposed on a sofa*). **2** *tr.* (often foll. by *on*) lay (one's head etc.) to rest (on a pillow etc.). **3** *intr.* (often foll. by *in*, *on*) lie, be lying or laid, esp. in sleep or death. **4** *tr.* give rest to; refresh with rest. **5** *intr.* (foll. by

on, upon) be supported or based on. **6** *intr.* (foll. by *on*) (of memory etc.) dwell on. ▫▫ **reposal** *n.* **reposeful** *adj.* **reposefully** *adv.* **reposefulness** *n.* [ME f. OF *repos(er)* f. LL *repausare* (as RE-, *pausare* PAUSE)]
■ *n.* **1** inactivity, quiet, peace (and quiet); breathing-space, break, breather, interval, intermission. **2** see SLEEP *n.* 2. **3** calm, tranquillity, quiet, stillness, still, restfulness, peace, relaxation. **5** composure, calmness, calm, serenity, equanimity, poise, self-possession. ● *v.* **1, 2** see LIE[1] *v.* 1, REST[1] *v.* 1, 2. **3** see REST[1] *v.* 2. **5** rest, be supported *or* based.

repose[2] /ripṓz/ *v.tr.* (foll. by *in*) place (trust etc.) in. ▫▫ **reposal** *n.* [RE- + POSE[1] after L *reponere reposit-*]

reposition /reépəzísh'n/ *v.* **1** *tr.* move or place in a different position. **2** *intr.* adjust or alter one's position.

repository /ripózzitəri, -tri/ *n.* (*pl.* **-ies**) **1** a place where things are stored or may be found, esp. a warehouse or museum. **2** a receptacle. **3** (often foll. by *of*) **a** a book, person, etc. regarded as a store of information etc. **b** the recipient of confidences or secrets. [obs. F *repositoire* or L *repositorium* (as REPOSE[2])]
■ **3a** mine, storehouse, treasure trove.

repossess /reépəzéss/ *v.tr.* regain possession of (esp. property or goods on which repayment of a debt is in arrears). ▫▫ **repossession** *n.* **repossessor** *n.*

repot /reépót/ *v.tr.* (**repotted, repotting**) put (a plant) in another, esp. larger, pot.

repoussé /rəpṓossay/ *adj.* & *n.* ● *adj.* hammered into relief from the reverse side. ● *n.* ornamental metalwork fashioned in this way. [F, past part. of *repousser* (as RE-, *pousser* PUSH)]

repp var. of REP[3].

repped /rept/ *adj.* having a surface like rep.

repr. *abbr.* **1** represent, represented, etc. **2** reprint, reprinted.

reprehend /réprihénd/ *v.tr.* rebuke; blame; find fault with. ▫▫ **reprehension** *n.* [ME f. L *reprehendere* (as RE-, *prehendere* seize)]

reprehensible /réprihénsib'l/ *adj.* deserving censure or rebuke; blameworthy. ▫▫ **reprehensibility** /-bílliti/ *n.* **reprehensibly** *adv.* [LL *reprehensibilis* (as REPREHEND)]

represent /réprizént/ *v.tr.* **1** stand for or correspond to (*the comment does not represent all our views*). **2** (often in *passive*) be a specimen or example of; exemplify (*all types of people were represented in the audience*). **3** act as an embodiment of; symbolize (*the sovereign represents the majesty of the State; numbers are represented by letters*). **4** call up in the mind by description or portrayal or imagination; place a likeness of before the mind or senses. **5** serve or be meant as a likeness of. **6 a** state by way of expostulation or persuasion (*represented the rashness of it*). **b** (foll. by *to*) try to bring (the facts influencing conduct) home to (*represented the risks to his client*). **7 a** (often foll. by *as, to be*) describe or depict as; declare or make out (*represented them as martyrs; not what you represent it to be*). **b** (often *refl.*; usu. foll by *as*) portray; assume the guise of, pose as (*represents himself as an honest broker*). **8** (foll. by *that* + clause) allege. **9** show, or play the part of, on stage. **10** fill the place of; be a substitute or deputy for; be entitled to act or speak for (*the Queen was represented by the Princess of Wales*). **11** be elected as a member of Parliament, a legislature, etc. by (*represents a rural constituency*). ▫▫ **representable** *adj.* **representability** /-zéntəbílliti/ *n.* [ME f. OF *representer* or f. L *repraesentare* (as RE-, PRESENT[2])]
■ **1** stand for, typify, exemplify, embody, illustrate, epitomize; correspond to, fit, match. **2** see EXEMPLIFY. **3** see SYMBOLIZE. **4** evoke, capture; see also CHARACTERIZE 1, 2. **5** show, present, display, exhibit; see also SYMBOLIZE. **6 a** argue, urge, plead, affirm, set forth. **7 a** present, depict, describe, delineate, show, characterize, define, sketch, note, picture, portray, draw, paint, report; declare, make out, pretend, assert, state, allege. **b** (*represent oneself as*) present oneself as, depict oneself as, put *or* set oneself forth as, masquerade as, take (on) *or* assume the guise of, take (on) the role *or* part of as, impersonate, pretend to be, pose as. **8** see ALLEGE. **9** present, show, stage, produce, put on, mount, do, play, perform; see also ACT *v.* 5a. **10** substitute for, stand (in) for, deputize for, replace, act for *or* on behalf of, take the place of, be substituted for, be put in place of.

representation /réprizentáysh'n/ *n.* **1** the act or an instance of representing or being represented. **2** a thing (esp. a painting etc.) that represents another. **3** (esp. in *pl.*) a statement made by way of allegation or to convey opinion. [ME f. OF *representation* or L *repraesentatio* (as REPRESENT)]
■ **2** reproduction, replica; image, portrait, likeness, picture, model, figure, figurine, statue, statuette, bust, head, effigy; depiction, portrayal, manifestation. **3** allegation, deposition, statement; declaration, account, exposition, assertion.

representational /réprizentáyshən'l/ *adj.* of representation. ▫ **representational art** art seeking to portray the physical appearance of a subject. ▫▫ **representationalism** *n.* **representationalist** *adj.* & *n.*

representationism /réprizentáyshəniz'm/ *n.* the doctrine that perceived objects are only a representation of real external objects. ▫▫ **representationist** *n.*

representative /réprizéntətiv/ *adj.* & *n.* ● *adj.* **1** typical of a class or category. **2** containing typical specimens of all or many classes (*a representative sample*). **3 a** consisting of elected deputies etc. **b** based on the representation of a nation etc. by such deputies (*representative government*). **4** (foll. by *of*) serving as a portrayal or symbol of (*representative of their attitude to work*). **5** that presents or can present ideas to the mind (*imagination is a representative faculty*). **6** (of art) representational. ● *n.* **1** (foll. by *of*) a sample, specimen, or typical embodiment or analogue of. **2 a** the agent of a person or society. **b** a commercial traveller. **3** a delegate; a substitute. **4** a deputy in a representative assembly. ▫▫ **representatively** *adv.* **representativeness** *n.* [ME f. OF *representatif -ive* or med.L *repraesentativus* (as REPRESENT)]
■ *adj.* **1, 2** typical, characteristic, illustrative, exemplary; archetypal, paradigmatic. **3 b** elected, chosen, democratic, popular. **4** (*representative of*) typical of, characteristic of, illustrative of, symbolic of, emblematic of, in character with *or* of, like, indicative of; symptomatic of. ● *n.* **1** see SPECIMEN, *embodiment* (EMBODY). **2 a** see AGENT 1a. **b** commercial traveller, salesman *or* saleswoman, travelling salesman, *colloq.* rep. **3** delegate, substitute, deputy, ambassador, spokesman, spokeswoman, proxy, envoy, emissary; missionary, *RC Ch.* (papal) nuncio, *archaic* legate. **4** Member of Parliament, MP, Member of Congress, congressman, congresswoman; councillor.

repress /ripréss/ *v.tr.* **1 a** check; restrain; keep under; quell. **b** suppress; prevent from sounding, rioting, or bursting out. **2** *Psychol.* actively exclude (an unwelcome thought) from conscious awareness. **3** (usu. as **repressed** *adj.*) subject (a person) to the suppression of his or her thoughts or impulses. ▫▫ **represser** *n.* **repressible** *adj.* **repression** /-présh'n/ *n.* **repressive** *adj.* **repressively** *adv.* **repressiveness** *n.* **repressor** *n.* [ME f. L *reprimere* (as RE-, *premere* PRESS[1])]
■ **1** suppress, put down, (keep in) check, curb, quash, stifle, squelch, (keep under) control, contain, restrain, constrain, limit, keep back *or* in, quell, hold back *or* in, subdue, inhibit; deter, frustrate, discourage, disallow. **2** inhibit, suppress, stifle, control, keep under control, restrain, keep back *or* in, hold back *or* in; discourage, disallow. **3** (**repressed**) see PENT. ▫▫ **repression** restraint, suppression, subjugation, checking, squelching, control, inhibition, stifling; frustration, frustrating, deterrence, deterring. **repressive** tyrannical, oppressive, dictatorial, despotic, brutal, suppressive, authoritarian, totalitarian.

reprice /reéprī́ss/ *v.tr.* price again or differently.

reprieve /ripreév/ *v.* & *n.* ● *v.tr.* **1** remit, commute, or postpone the execution of (a condemned person). **2** give respite to. ● *n.* **1 a** the act or an instance of reprieving or being reprieved. **b** a warrant for this. **2** respite; a respite or temporary escape. [ME as past part. *repryed* f. AF & OF *repris* past part. of *reprendre* (as RE-, *prendre* f. L *prehendere* take): 16th-c. *-v-* unexpl.]

■ *v.* remit, let off, spare, pardon; *Law* commute; respite, postpone. ● *n.* **1a, 2** remission; respite, stay (of execution), postponement, delay, suspension, extension; amnesty, pardon.

reprimand /réprimaand/ *n.* & *v.* ● *n.* (often foll. by *for*) an official or sharp rebuke (for a fault etc.). ● *v.tr.* administer this to. [F *réprimande(r)* f. Sp. *reprimenda* f. L *reprimenda* neut. pl. gerundive of *reprimere* REPRESS]

■ *n.* scolding, reproof, rebuke, admonition, upbraiding, castigation, reproach, lecture, tongue-lashing, rap on *or* over the knuckles, *colloq.* dressing-down, talking-to, telling-off, ticking-off, slap on the wrist, wigging, *Brit. colloq.* slating, *Austral. sl.* serve. ● *v.* scold, reprove, rebuke, admonish, upbraid, castigate, reproach, berate, lecture, censure, criticize, find fault with, attack, flay, flay alive, reprehend, read a person the Riot Act, give a person a rap on *or* over the knuckles, take to task, haul over the coals, give a person a piece of one's mind, *archaic or literary* chide, *colloq.* bawl out, dress down, give a person a dressing-down, give a person a slap on the wrist, tell off, tick off, carpet, wig, give a person a row, *Brit. colloq.* slate, send a person away *or* off with a flea in his *or* her ear, tell a person a thing or two, *US colloq.* chew out.

reprint *v.* & *n.* ● *v.tr.* /reéprint/ print again. ● *n.* /reéprint/ **1** the act or an instance of reprinting a book etc. **2** the book etc. reprinted. **3** the quantity reprinted. □□ **reprinter** *n.*

reprisal /riprī́z'l/ *n.* **1** (an act of) retaliation. **2** *hist.* the forcible seizure of a foreign subject or his or her goods as an act of retaliation. [ME (in sense 2) f. AF *reprisaille* f. med.L *reprisalia* f. *repraehensalia* (as REPREHEND)]

■ **1** retaliation, requital; revenge, retribution, vengeance, repayment, getting even.

reprise /ripreéz/ *n.* **1** a repeated passage in music. **2** a repeated item in a musical programme. [F, fem. past part. of *reprendre* (see REPRIEVE)]

repro /reéprō/ *n.* (*pl.* **-os**) (often *attrib.*) a reproduction or copy. [abbr.]

reproach /riprṓch/ *v.* & *n.* ● *v.tr.* **1** express disapproval to (a person) for a fault etc. **2** scold; rebuke; censure. **3** *archaic* rebuke (an offence). ● *n.* **1** a rebuke or censure (*heaped reproaches on them*). **2** (often foll. by *to*) a thing that brings disgrace or discredit (*their behaviour is a reproach to us all*). **3** a disgraced or discredited state (*live in reproach and ignominy*). **4** (in *pl.*) *RC Ch.* a set of antiphons and responses for Good Friday representing the reproaches of Christ to his people. □ **above** (or **beyond**) **reproach** perfect. □□ **reproachable** *adj.* **reproacher** *n.* **reproachingly** *adv.* [ME f. OF *reproche(r)* f. Rmc (as RE-, L *prope* near)]

reproachful /riprṓchfŏŏl/ *adj.* full of or expressing reproach. □□ **reproachfully** *adv.* **reproachfulness** *n.*

■ fault-finding, critical, censorious, disapproving, disparaging, upbraiding, reproving, scolding, admonitory, condemnatory, hypercritical.

reprobate /réprəbayt/ *n.*, *adj.*, & *v.* ● *n.* **1** an unprincipled person; a person of highly immoral character. **2** a person who is condemned by God. ● *adj.* **1** immoral. **2** hardened in sin. ● *v.tr.* **1** express or feel disapproval of; censure. **2** (of God) condemn; exclude from salvation. □□ **reprobation** /-báysh'n/ *n.* [ME f. L *reprobare reprobat-* disapprove (as RE-, *probare* approve)]

■ *n.* **1** scoundrel, blackguard, miscreant, rake, profligate, roué, wastrel, degenerate, unprincipled person, evil-doer, debauchee, libertine, good-for-nothing, ne'er-do-well, cur, knave, scallywag, *archaic or joc.* rapscallion, *colloq.* scamp, *often joc.* rascal. ● *adj.* **1, 2** unprincipled, immoral, amoral, abandoned, depraved, despicable, dissolute, low, base, mean, debased, cursed, degenerate, profligate, shameful, shameless, vile, evil, wicked, villainous, sinful, irredeemable, iniquitous, reprehensible, *colloq.* accursed, damned.

reprocess /reéprṓsess/ *v.tr.* process again or differently.

reproduce /reéprədyŏŏss/ *v.* **1** *tr.* produce a copy or representation of. **2** *tr.* cause to be seen or heard etc. again (*tried to reproduce the sound exactly*). **3** *intr.* produce further members of the same species by natural means. **4** *refl.* produce offspring (*reproduced itself several times*). **5** *intr.* give a specified quality or result when copied (*reproduces badly in black and white*). **6** *tr. Biol.* form afresh (a lost part etc. of the body). □□ **reproducer** *n.* **reproducible** *adj.* **reproducibility** /-dyŏŏssəbílliti/ *n.* **reproducibly** *adv.*

■ **1, 2** duplicate, copy, replicate, recreate, repeat, simulate; imitate. **3** breed, multiply, propagate, procreate, spawn, proliferate. **5** duplicate, copy, photocopy, *propr.* xerox.

reproduction /reéprədúksh'n/ *n.* **1** the act or an instance of reproducing. **2** a copy of a work of art, esp. a print or photograph of a painting. **3** (*attrib.*) (of furniture etc.) made in imitation of a certain style or of an earlier period. □□ **reproductive** *adj.* **reproductively** *adv.* **reproductiveness** *n.*

■ **1** duplication, copying, printing; propagation, breeding, spawning, proliferation, production. **2** print, imitation, copy, facsimile, replica; photograph. **3** see IMITATION *adj.*

reprogram /reéprṓgram/ *v.tr.* (also **reprogramme**) (**reprogrammed, reprogramming**; *US* **reprogramed, reprograming**) program (esp. a computer) again or differently. □□ **reprogramable** *adj.* (also **reprogrammable**).

reprography /riprógrəfi/ *n.* the science and practice of copying documents by photography, xerography, etc. □□ **reprographer** *n.* **reprographic** /reéprəgráffik/ *adj.* **reprographically** /reéprəgráffikəli/ *adv.* [REPRODUCE + -GRAPHY]

reproof[1] /riprŏŏf/ *n.* **1** blame (*a glance of reproof*). **2** a rebuke; words expressing blame. [ME f. OF *reprove* f. *reprover* REPROVE]

■ **1** see BLAME *n.* 1. **2** see REBUKE *n.*

reproof[2] /reéprŏŏf/ *v.tr.* **1** render (a coat etc.) waterproof again. **2** make a fresh proof of (printed matter etc.).

reprove /riprŏŏv/ *v.tr.* rebuke (a person, a person's conduct, etc.). □□ **reprovable** *adj.* **reprover** *n.* **reprovingly** *adv.* [ME f. OF *reprover* f. LL *reprobare* disapprove: see REPROBATE]

■ see REPRIMAND *v.*

reptant /réptənt/ *adj.* (of a plant or animal) creeping. [L *reptare reptant-* frequent. of *repere* crawl]

reptile /réptīl/ *n.* & *adj.* ● *n.* **1** any cold-blooded scaly animal of the class Reptilia, including snakes, lizards, crocodiles, turtles, tortoises, etc. **2** a mean, grovelling, or repulsive person. ● *adj.* **1** (of an animal) creeping. **2** mean, grovelling. □□ **reptilian** /-tílliən/ *adj.* & *n.* [ME f. LL *reptilis* f. L *repere rept-* crawl]

republic /ripúblik/ *n.* **1** a State in which supreme power is held by the people or their elected representatives or by an elected or nominated president, not by a monarch etc. **2** a society with equality between its members (*the literary republic*). □ **Republic Day** the day on which the foundation of a republic is commemorated; in India 26 January. [F *république* f. L *respublica* f. *res* concern + *publicus* PUBLIC]

republican /ripúblikən/ *adj.* & *n.* ● *adj.* **1** of or constituted as a republic. **2** characteristic of a republic. **3** advocating or supporting republican government. ● *n.* **1** a person advocating or supporting republican government. **2** (**Republican**) (in the US) a member or supporter of the Republican Party. **3** an advocate of a united Ireland. □ **Republican Party** one of the two main US political parties, favouring only a moderate degree of central power (cf. *Democratic Party*). □□ **republicanism** *n.*

republish /reépúblish/ *v.tr.* (also *absol.*) publish again or in a new edition etc. □□ **republication** /-likáysh'n/ *n.*

repudiate /ripyŏŏdiayt/ *v.tr.* **1 a** disown; disavow; reject. **b** refuse dealings with. **c** deny. **2** refuse to recognize or obey (authority or a treaty). **3** refuse to discharge (an obligation or debt). **4** (esp. of the ancients or non-Christians) divorce (one's wife). □□ **repudiable** *adj.* **repudiation** /-áysh'n/ *n.* **repudiator** *n.* [L *repudiare* f. *repudium* divorce]

■ **1 a** disown, disavow, reject, scorn, renounce, retract, rescind, reverse, abandon, abrogate, forswear, forgo, deny, discard. **2** see DISOBEY.

repugnance /ripúgnənss/ *n.* (also **repugnancy**) **1** (usu. foll. by *to*, *against*) antipathy; aversion. **2** (usu. foll. by *of*, *between*, *to*, *with*) inconsistency or incompatibility of ideas, statements, etc. [ME (in sense 2) f. F *répugnance* or L *repugnantia* f. *repugnare* oppose (as RE-, *pugnare* fight)]

repugnant /ripúgnənt/ *adj.* **1** (often foll. by *to*) extremely distasteful. **2** (often foll. by *to*) contradictory. **3** (often foll. by *with*) incompatible. **4** *poet.* refractory; resisting. □□ **repugnantly** *adv.* [ME f. F *répugnant* or L (as REPUGNANCE)]

■ **1** repulsive, abhorrent, disgusting, off-putting, offensive, repellent, revolting, vile, abominable, loathsome, foul, distasteful, unpalatable, unsavoury, execrable, intolerable, obnoxious, nauseating, nauseous, sickening, unpleasant, objectionable, *literary* noisome. **2** see CONTRADICTORY. **3** see INCOMPATIBLE 1, 3.

repulse /ripúlss/ *v.* & *n.* ● *v.tr.* **1** drive back (an attack or attacking enemy) by force of arms. **2 a** rebuff (friendly advances or their maker). **b** refuse (a request or offer or its maker). **3** be repulsive to, repel. **4** foil in controversy. ● *n.* **1** the act or an instance of repulsing or being repulsed. **2** a rebuff. [L *repellere repuls-* drive back (as REPEL)]

■ *v.* **1** repel, drive back, ward off, fight *or* beat off, check. **2 a** see REBUFF *v.* **b** see REFUSE[1] 1. **3** see REPEL 3. ● *n.* rejection, rebuff, refusal, denial, snub, cold shoulder, spurning.

repulsion /ripúlsh'n/ *n.* **1** aversion; disgust. **2** esp. *Physics* the force by which bodies tend to repel each other or increase their mutual distance (opp. ATTRACTION). [LL *repulsio* (as REPEL)]

repulsive /ripúlsiv/ *adj.* **1** causing aversion or loathing; loathsome, disgusting. **2** *Physics* exerting repulsion. **3** *archaic* (of behaviour etc.) cold, unsympathetic. □□ **repulsively** *adv.* **repulsiveness** *n.* [F *répulsif -ive* or f. REPULSE]

■ **1** disgusting, revolting, abhorrent, loathsome, repugnant, repellent, offensive, obnoxious, objectionable, unsavoury, distasteful, nasty, unpleasant, displeasing, disagreeable, ugly, off-putting, sickening, nauseating, nauseous, vile, foul, odious, hideous, horrible, horrid, abominable, execrable, *sl.* gross.

repurchase /reépúrchiss/ *v.* & *n.* ● *v.tr.* purchase again. ● *n.* the act or an instance of purchasing again.

repurify /reépyoórifī/ *v.tr.* (**-ies**, **-ied**) purify again. □□ **repurification** /-fikáysh'n/ *n.*

reputable /répyootəb'l, *disp.* ripyoōt-/ *adj.* of good repute; respectable. □□ **reputably** *adv.* [obs. F or f. med.L *reputabilis* (as REPUTE)]

■ respectable, honourable, well-thought-of, estimable, esteemed, respected, trustworthy, trusted, honest, reliable, dependable, principled, virtuous, good, worthy.

reputation /répyootáysh'n/ *n.* **1** what is generally said or believed about a person's or thing's character or standing (*has a reputation for dishonesty*). **2** the state of being well thought of; distinction; respectability (*have my reputation to think of*). **3** (foll. by *of*, *for* + verbal noun) credit or discredit (*has the reputation of driving hard bargains*). [ME f. L *reputatio* (as REPUTE)]

■ **1** name. **2** repute, name, standing, stature, position, status. **3** see HONOUR *v.* 1, DISCREDIT *v.* 1.

repute /ripyoōt/ *n.* & *v.* ● *n.* reputation (*known by repute*). ● *v.tr.* **1** (as **reputed** *adj.*) (often foll. by *to* + infin.) be generally considered or reckoned (*is reputed to be the best*). **2** (as **reputed** *adj.*) passing as being, but probably not being (*his reputed father*). □□ **reputedly** *adv.* [ME f. OF *reputer* or L *reputare* (as RE-, *putare* think)]

■ *v.* **1** (**reputed**) rumoured, said, held, regarded, viewed, looked on *or* upon, judged, considered, thought, believed, *formal* deemed; alleged, purported. **2** (**reputed**) see *supposed* (SUPPOSE 6).

request /rikwést/ *n.* & *v.* ● *n.* **1** the act or an instance of asking for something; a petition (*came at his request*). **2** a thing asked for. **3** the state of being sought after; demand (*in great request*). **4** a letter etc. asking for a particular record etc. to be played on a radio programme, often with a personal message. ● *v.tr.* **1** ask to be given or allowed or favoured with (*request a hearing*; *requests your presence*). **2** (foll. by *to* + infin.) ask a person to do something (*requested her to answer*). **3** (foll. by *that* + clause) ask that. □ **by** (or **on**) **request** in response to an expressed wish. **request programme** a programme composed of items requested by the audience. **request stop** a bus-stop at which a bus stops only on a person's request. □□ **requester** *n.* [ME f. OF *requeste(r)* ult. f. L *requaerere* (as REQUIRE)]

■ *n.* **1, 2** solicitation, entreaty, plea, petition, application, requisition, call, demand. **3** (*in request*) see *in demand* (DEMAND). ● *v.* **1** ask for, seek, plead for, apply for, put in for, requisition, call for, demand, insist on, solicit, beg, entreat, beseech. **2** ask, call on, require, appeal to, beg, entreat, beseech, importune.

requiem /rékwi-em/ *n.* **1** (**Requiem**) (also *attrib.*) *chiefly RC Ch.* a mass for the repose of the souls of the dead. **2** *Mus.* the musical setting for this. [ME f. accus. of L *requies* rest, the initial word of the mass]

requiescat /rékwi-éskat/ *n.* a wish or prayer for the repose of a dead person. [L, = may he or she rest (in peace)]

require /rikwī́r/ *v.tr.* **1** need; depend on for success or fulfilment (*the work requires much patience*). **2** lay down as an imperative (*did all that was required by law*). **3** command; instruct (a person etc.). **4** order; insist on (an action or measure). **5** (often foll. by *of*, *from*, or *that* + clause) demand (of or from a person) as a right. **6** wish to have (*is there anything else you require?*). □□ **requirer** *n.* **requirement** *n.* [ME f. OF *requere* ult. f. L *requirere* (as RE-, *quaerere* seek)]

■ **1** need, necessitate, demand, ask *or* call for, cry out for; rely *or* depend on. **2** see DECREE *v.* **3** order, command, ask (for), call (for), instruct, coerce, force, compel, make; insist, demand. **6** need, want, desire, lack, be lacking, be missing, be short of. □□ **requirement** requisite, prerequisite, demand, precondition, condition, qualification, stipulation, *sine qua non*, provision, proviso, necessity, essential, desideratum, must; need, want, demand, wish.

requisite /rékwizit/ *adj.* & *n.* ● *adj.* required by circumstances; necessary to success etc. ● *n.* (often foll. by *for*) a thing needed (for some purpose). □□ **requisitely** *adv.* [ME f. L *requisitus* past part. (as REQUIRE)]

requisition /rékwizísh'n/ *n.* & *v.* ● *n.* **1** an official order laying claim to the use of property or materials. **2** a formal written demand that some duty should be performed. **3** being called or put into service. ● *v.tr.* demand the use or supply of, esp. by requisition order. □ **under** (or **in**) **requisition** being used or applied. □□ **requisitioner** *n.* **requisitionist** *n.* [F *réquisition* or L *requisitio* (as REQUIRE)]

■ *n.* **2** see ORDER *n.* 2. ● *v.* request, order, demand, call for, mandate; seize, appropriate, confiscate, take possession of, take (over), occupy; expropriate.

requite /rikwī́t/ *v.tr.* **1** make return for (a service). **2** (often foll. by *with*) reward or avenge (a favour or injury). **3** (often foll. by *for*) make return to (a person). **4** (often foll. by *for*, *with*) repay with good or evil (*requite like for like*; *requite hate with love*). □□ **requital** *n.* [RE- + *quite* var. of QUIT]

■ **1** reciprocate, return, match, equal, complement. **2** reward, repay, reciprocate, recompense; avenge, revenge, pay back for, give tit for tat for. **3** repay, reward, recompense, pay back, compensate. □□ **requital** repayment, return, payment, quid pro quo, a Roland for an Oliver; recompense, remuneration; revenge, retribution, vengeance; retaliation.

reran *past* of RERUN.

reread /reé-reéd/ *v.* & *n.* ● *v.tr.* (*past* and *past part.* **reread** /-réd/) read again. ● *n.* an instance of reading again. ▫▫ **re-readable** *adj.*

reredos /reérdoss/ *n. Eccl.* an ornamental screen covering the wall at the back of an altar. [ME f. AF f. OF *areredos* f. *arere* behind + *dos* back: cf. ARREARS]

re-release /reé-rileéss/ *v.* & *n.* ● *v.tr.* release (a record, film, etc.) again. ● *n.* a re-released record, film, etc.

re-route /reé-ro͞ot/ *v.tr.* (**-routeing**) send or carry by a different route.

rerun *v.* & *n.* ● *v.tr.* /reé-rún/(**rerunning**; *past* **reran**; *past part.* **rerun**) run (a race, film, etc.) again. ● *n.* /reé-run/ **1** the act or an instance of rerunning. **2** a film etc. shown again.

resale /reéssáyl/ *n.* the sale of a thing previously bought. ▫ **resale price maintenance** a manufacturer's practice of setting a minimum resale price for goods. ▫▫ **resalable** *adj.*

resat *past* and *past part.* of RESIT.

reschedule /reéshédyool, -skédyool/ *v.tr.* alter the schedule of; replan.

rescind /risínd/ *v.tr.* abrogate, revoke, cancel. ▫▫ **rescindable** *adj.* **rescindment** *n.* **rescission** /-sízh'n/ *n.* [L *rescindere resciss-* (as RE-, *scindere* cut)]

rescript /reéskrípt/ *n.* **1** a Roman emperor's written reply to an appeal for guidance, esp. on a legal point. **2** *RC Ch.* the Pope's decision on a question of doctrine or papal law. **3** an official edict or announcement. **4 a** the act or an instance of rewriting. **b** the thing rewritten. [L *rescriptum*, neut. past part. of *rescribere rescript-* (as RE-, *scribere* write)]

rescue /réskyo͞o/ *v.* & *n.* ● *v.tr.* (**rescues, rescued, rescuing**) **1** (often foll. by *from*) save or set free or bring away from attack, custody, danger, or harm. **2** *Law* **a** unlawfully liberate (a person). **b** forcibly recover (property). ● *n.* the act or an instance of rescuing or being rescued; deliverance. ▫ **rescue bid** *Bridge* a bid made to get one's partner out of a difficult situation. ▫▫ **rescuable** *adj.* **rescuer** *n.* [ME *rescowe* f. OF *rescoure* f. Rmc, formed as RE- + L *excutere* (as EX-[1], *quatere* shake)]

■ *v.* **1** save, deliver, (set) free, liberate, let go, release, (let) loose. ● *n.* freeing, liberation, release, liberating; deliverance, saving.

reseal /reésseél/ *v.tr.* seal again. ▫▫ **resealable** *adj.*

research /risérch, *disp.* reésserch/ *n.* & *v.* ● *n.* **1 a** the systematic investigation into and study of materials, sources, etc., in order to establish facts and reach new conclusions. **b** (usu. in *pl.*) an endeavour to discover new or collate old facts etc. by the scientific study of a subject or by a course of critical investigation. **2** (*attrib.*) engaged in or intended for research (*research assistant*). ● *v.* **1** *tr.* do research into or for. **2** *intr.* make researches. ▫ **research and development** (in industry etc.) work directed towards the innovation, introduction, and improvement of products and processes. ▫▫ **researchable** *adj.* **researcher** *n.* [obs. F *recerche* (as RE-, SEARCH)]

■ *n.* **1** investigation(s), investigating(s), exploration(s), delving(s), digging(s), examination(s), inspection(s), probing(s), experimentation(s); analysis, analyses, inquiry, enquiries; fact-finding, scrutiny. ● *v.* investigate, explore, delve (into), dig (into), enquire *or* inquire (into), study, analyse, inspect, check (into), check up (on), probe, experiment (with); scrutinize, examine, *US* check out.

reseat /reésseét/ *v.tr.* **1** (also *refl.*) seat (oneself, a person, etc.) again. **2** provide with a fresh seat or seats.

resect /risékt/ *v.tr. Surgery* **1** cut out part of (a lung etc.). **2** pare down (bone, cartilage, etc.). ▫▫ **resection** *n.* **resectional** *adj.* **resectionist** *n.* [L *resecare resect-* (as RE-, *secare* cut)]

reseda /réssidə/ *n.* **1** any plant of the genus *Reseda*, with sweet-scented flowers, e.g. a mignonette. **2** /also réz-/ the pale green colour of mignonette flowers. [L, perh. f. imper. of *resedare* assuage, with ref. to its supposed curative powers]

reselect /reéssilékt/ *v.tr.* select again or differently. ▫▫ **reselection** *n.*

resell /reéssél/ *v.tr.* (*past* and *past part.* **resold**) sell (an object etc.) after buying it.

resemblance /rizémblənss/ *n.* (often foll. by *to*, *between*, *of*) a likeness or similarity. ▫▫ **resemblant** *adj.* [ME f. AF (as RESEMBLE)]

■ likeness, similarity; correspondence, congruity, coincidence, conformity, accord, agreement, equivalence, analogy, comparableness, comparability, comparison.

resemble /rizémb'l/ *v.tr.* be like; have a similarity to, or features in common with, or the same appearance as. ▫▫ **resembler** *n.* [ME f. OF *resembler* (as RE-, *sembler* f. L *similare* f. *similis* like)]

■ be *or* seem *or* look *or* sound *or* taste like, be similar to, bear (a) resemblance to, approximate (to), smack of, correspond to, have (all) the hallmarks *or* earmarks of, take after, *colloq.* favour.

resent /rizént/ *v.tr.* show or feel indignation at; be aggrieved by (a circumstance, action, or person) (*we resent being patronized*). [obs. F *resentir* (as RE-, L *sentire* feel)]

■ feel embittered *or* bitter about, feel envious *or* jealous of, begrudge, have hard feelings about, be displeased *or* disgruntled at, be angry about.

resentful /rizéntfo͝ol/ *adj.* feeling resentment. ▫▫ **resentfully** *adv.* **resentfulness** *n.*

■ embittered, bitter, acrimonious, envious, jealous, begrudging, indignant, displeased, disgruntled, dissatisfied, unsatisfied, unhappy, peeved, irritated, irked, annoyed, provoked, riled, angry, piqued, irate, furious, incensed, upset, worked up, agitated, antagonistic, hostile.

resentment /rizéntmənt/ *n.* (often foll. by *at*, *of*) indignant or bitter feelings; anger. [It. *risentimento* or F *ressentiment* (as RESENT)]

■ bitterness, acrimony, rancour, envy, jealousy, indignation, displeasure, dissatisfaction, unhappiness, irritation, annoyance, pique, anger, fury, ill will, malice, antagonism, hostility, animosity, enmity, antipathy, hate, *literary* ire.

reserpine /risérpeen/ *n.* an alkaloid obtained from plants of the genus *Rauwolfia*, used as a tranquillizer and in the treatment of hypertension. [G *Reserpin* f. mod.L *Rauwolfia* (f. L. *Rauwolf*, Ger. botanist d. 1596) *serpentina*]

reservation /rézzərváysh'n/ *n.* **1** the act or an instance of reserving or being reserved. **2** a booking (of a room, berth, seat, etc.). **3** the thing booked, e.g. a room in a hotel. **4** an express or tacit limitation or exception to an agreement etc. (*had reservations about the plan*). **5** *Brit.* a strip of land between the carriageways of a road. **6** an area of land reserved for occupation by American Indians, South African Blacks, or Australian Aboriginals, etc. **7 a** a right or interest retained in an estate being conveyed. **b** the clause reserving this. **8** *Eccl.* **a** the practice of retaining for some purpose a portion of the Eucharistic elements (esp. the bread) after celebration. **b** *RC Ch.* the power of absolution reserved to a superior. **c** *RC Ch.* the right reserved to the Pope of nomination to a vacant benefice. [ME f. OF *reservation* or LL *reservatio* (as RESERVE)]

■ *n.* **1, 2** booking, order, arrangement. **4** qualm, scruple; objection, *Law* demurrer; condition, proviso, provision; hesitancy, reticence, reluctance, hesitation; (*without reservation*) without reserve *or* demur *or* exception *or* limitation *or* qualification *or* restraint. **6** sanctuary, reserve.

reserve /rizérv/ *v.* & *n.* ● *v.tr.* **1** postpone, put aside, keep back for a later occasion or special use. **2** order to be specially retained or allocated for a particular person or at a particular time. **3** retain or secure, esp. by formal or legal stipulation (*reserve the right to*). **4** postpone delivery of (judgement etc.) (*reserved my comments until the end*). ● *n.* **1** a thing reserved for future use; an extra stock or amount (*a great reserve of strength*; *huge energy reserves*). **2** a limitation, qualification, or exception attached to something (*accept your offer without reserve*). **3 a** self-restraint; reticence; lack of cordiality (*difficult to overcome his reserve*). **b** (in artistic or literary expression) absence from exaggeration or ill-proportioned effects. **4** a company's profit added to capital. **5** (in *sing.* or *pl.*) assets kept readily available as cash or at a central bank, or as gold or foreign exchange (*reserve currency*). **6** (in *sing.* or *pl.*) **a** troops withheld from action to reinforce or protect others. **b** forces in addition to the regular army, navy, airforce, etc., but available in an emergency. **7** a member of the military reserve. **8** an extra player chosen to be a possible substitute in a team. **9** a place reserved for special use, esp. as a habitat for a native tribe or for wildlife (*game reserve*; *nature reserve*). **10** the intentional suppression of the truth (*exercised a certain amount of reserve*). **11** (in the decoration of ceramics or textiles) an area which still has the original colour of the material or the colour of the background. □ **in reserve** unused and available if required. **reserve grade** *Austral.* a second-grade team. **reserve price** the lowest acceptable price stipulated for an item sold at an auction. **with all** (or **all proper**) **reserve** without endorsing. □□ **reservable** *adj.* **reserver** *n.* [ME f. OF *reserver* f. L *reservare* (as RE-, *servare* keep)]

■ *v.* **1, 4** keep *or* hold back, withhold, save, set *or* put aside, keep to *or* for oneself, hold over, postpone, delay, put off, defer; retain, conserve, preserve. **2** order, hold, keep, book, save, put *or* set aside, secure. **3** see RETAIN 1. ● *n.* **1** store, stock, stockpile, supply, reservoir, fund; hoard, cache. **2** see RESERVATION 4. **3** reticence, (self-)restraint, (self-)control, taciturnity, formality, coolness, aloofness, guardedness, standoffishness, remoteness, detachment. **6** backup; (*reserves*) auxiliaries, reinforcements. **9** reservation, sanctuary, conservation area, national park; preserve. □ **in reserve** ready, on hand, available, on call, accessible, in readiness, in store, *colloq.* on tap.

re-serve /réessérv/ *v.tr.* & *intr.* serve again.

reserved /rizérvd/ *adj.* **1** reticent; slow to reveal emotion or opinions; uncommunicative. **2 a** set apart, destined for some use or fate. **b** (often foll. by *for*, *to*) left by fate for; falling first or only to. □ **reserved occupation** an occupation from which a person will not be taken for military service. □□ **reservedly** /-vidli/ *adv.* **reservedness** *n.*

■ **1** reticent, restrained, silent, taciturn, uncommunicative, unforthcoming, close-mouthed, unresponsive, undemonstrative, unemotional, cool, formal, aloof, guarded, standoffish, unsocial, antisocial, distant, remote, detached, retiring, withdrawn, demure, rigid, icy, frigid, ice-cold.

reservist /rizérvist/ *n.* a member of the reserve forces.

reservoir /rézzərvwaar/ *n.* **1** a large natural or artificial lake used as a source of water supply. **2 a** any natural or artificial receptacle esp. for or of fluid. **b** a place where fluid etc. collects. **3** a part of a machine etc. holding fluid. **4** (usu. foll. by *of*) a reserve or supply esp. of information. [F *réservoir* f. *réserver* RESERVE]

reset /réessét/ *v.tr.* (**resetting**; *past* and *past part.* **reset**) set (a broken bone, gems, a mechanical device, etc.) again or differently. □□ **resettable** *adj.* **resettability** /-séttəbílliti/ *n.*

resettle /réessétt'l/ *v.tr.* & *intr.* settle again. □□ **resettlement** *n.*

reshape /réesháyp/ *v.tr.* shape or form again or differently.

reshuffle /réeshúff'l/ *v.* & *n.* ● *v.tr.* **1** shuffle (cards) again. **2** interchange the posts of (government ministers etc.). ● *n.* the act or an instance of reshuffling.

reside /rizíd/ *v.intr.* **1** (often foll. by *at*, *in*, *abroad*, etc.) (of a person) have one's home, dwell permanently. **2** (of power, a right, etc.) rest or be vested in. **3** (of an incumbent official) be in residence. **4** (foll. by *in*) (of a quality) be present or inherent in. [ME, prob. back-form. f. RESIDENT infl. by F *résider* or L *residēre* (as RE-, *sedēre* sit)]

residence /rézzid'nss/ *n.* **1** the act or an instance of residing. **2 a** the place where a person resides; an abode. **b** a mansion; the official house of a government minister etc. **c** a house, esp. one of considerable pretension (*returned to their London residence*). □ **in residence** dwelling at a specified place, esp. for the performance of duties or work. [ME f. OF *residence* or med.L *residentia* f. L *residēre*: see RESIDE]

■ **1** residency, stay, sojourn, visit, stop, stopoff, layover, stopover; tenancy, occupancy. **2 a** abode, home, domicile, residency, place, house, habitation, *formal* dwelling(-place). **b** see SEAT *n.* 10. **c** villa, manor (house), stately home, estate, château, hall. □ **in residence** see RESIDENT *adj.* 1.

residency /rézzidənsi/ *n.* (*pl.* **-ies**) **1** = RESIDENCE 1, 2a. **2** *US* a period of specialized medical training; the position of a resident. **3** *hist.* the official residence of the Governor-General's representative or other government agent at an Indian native court; the territory supervised by this official. **4** a musician's regular engagement at a club etc. **5** a group or organization of intelligence agents in a foreign country.

resident /rézzid'nt/ *n.* & *adj.* ● *n.* **1** (often foll. by *of*) **a** a permanent inhabitant (of a town or neighbourhood). **b** a bird belonging to a species that does not migrate. **2** a guest in a hotel etc. staying overnight. **3** *hist.* a British government agent in any semi-independent State, esp. the Governor-General's agent at an Indian native court. **4** *US* a medical graduate engaged in specialized practice under supervision in a hospital. **5** an intelligence agent in a foreign country. ● *adj.* **1** residing; in residence. **2 a** having quarters on the premises of one's work etc. (*resident housekeeper*; *resident doctor*). **b** working regularly in a particular place. **3** located in; inherent (*powers of feeling are resident in the nerves*). **4** (of birds etc.) non-migratory. □□ **residentship** *n.* (in sense 3 of *n.*). [ME f. OF *resident* or L: see RESIDE]

■ *n.* **1 a** dweller, inhabitant, citizen, local, *poet.* denizen; householder, home-owner; tenant, occupant. ● *adj.* **1** in residence, residing, living, staying, dwelling, *archaic* abiding. **3** situated *or* located *or* positioned, lodged *or* placed, found; see also INHERENT 1.

residential /rézzidénsh'l/ *adj.* **1** suitable for or occupied by private houses (*residential area*). **2** used as a residence (*residential hotel*). **3** based on or connected with residence (*the residential qualification for voters*; *a residential course of study*). □□ **residentially** *adv.*

residentiary /rèzzidénshəri/ *adj.* & *n.* ● *adj.* of, subject to, or requiring, official residence. ● *n.* (*pl.* **-ies**) an ecclesiastic who must officially reside in a place. [med.L *residentiarius* (as RESIDENCE)]

residua *pl.* of RESIDUUM.

residual /rizídyooəl/ *adj.* & *n.* ● *adj.* **1** remaining; left as a residue or residuum. **2** *Math.* resulting from subtraction. **3** (in calculation) still unaccounted for or not eliminated. ● *n.* **1** a quantity left over or *Math.* resulting from subtraction. **2** an error in calculation not accounted for or eliminated. □□ **residually** *adv.*

■ *adj.* **1** remaining, leftover, surplus, spare, extra, residuary. ● *n.* **1** see DIFFERENCE *n.* 4b.

residuary /rizídyoori/ *adj.* **1** of the residue of an estate (*residuary bequest*). **2** of or being a residuum; residual; still remaining.

residue /rézzidyoo/ *n.* **1** what is left over or remains; a remainder; the rest. **2** *Law* what remains of an estate after the payment of charges, debts, and bequests. **3** esp. *Chem.* a residuum. [ME f. OF *residu* f. L *residuum*: see RESIDUUM]

■ **1** remainder, leftovers, remains, rest, surplus, excess, dregs, residuum.

residuum /rizídyooəm/ *n.* (*pl.* **residua** /-dyooə/) **1** *Chem.* a substance left after combustion or evaporation. **2** a remainder or residue. [L, neut. of *residuus* remaining f. *residēre*: see RESIDE]

resign /rizín/ *v.* **1** *intr.* **a** (often foll. by *from*) give up office, one's employment, etc. (*resigned from the Home Office*). **b** (often foll. by *as*) retire (*resigned as chief executive*). **2** *tr.* (often foll. by *to*, *into*) give up (office, one's employment, etc.); surrender; hand over (a right, charge, task, etc.). **3** *tr.* give up (hope etc.). **4** *refl.* (usu. foll. by *to*) **a** reconcile (oneself, one's mind, etc.) to the inevitable (*have resigned myself to the idea*). **b** surrender (oneself to another's guidance). **5** *intr. Chess* etc. discontinue play and admit defeat. □□ **resigner** *n.* [ME f. OF *resigner* f. L *resignare* unseal, cancel (as RE-, *signare* sign, seal)]

■ **1 a** leave, go, give notice, demit. **b** retire, stop *or* give up work(ing), quit, give up, stop. **2** surrender, hand over, yield up, abdicate, let go (of), release, deliver up, turn over; see also QUIT *v.* 1. **3** see RELINQUISH 1, 2. **4 a** (*resign oneself*) reconcile oneself *or* one's mind, be *or* become resigned *or* reconciled, accommodate oneself, adjust (oneself), adapt (oneself), acclimatize (oneself), *US* acclimate (oneself), submit (oneself). **b** surrender, abandon, give up, hand over, yield up, deliver up, turn over.

re-sign /reéssín/ *v.tr.* & *intr.* sign again.

resignation /rézzignáysh'n/ *n.* **1** the act or an instance of resigning, esp. from one's job or office. **2** the document etc. conveying this intention. **3** the state of being resigned; the uncomplaining endurance of a sorrow or difficulty. [ME f. OF f. med.L *resignatio* (as RESIGN)]

■ **1** notice; abdication, abandonment, resigning, demission, renunciation, forgoing, relinquishment, surrender, yielding up. **3** reconciliation, reconcilement, adjustment, adaptation, acclimatization, submission, acceptance, compliance, abandonment, acquiescence; endurance, tolerance.

resigned /rizínd/ *adj.* (often foll. by *to*) having resigned oneself; submissive, acquiescent. □□ **resignedly** /-zínidli/ *adv.* **resignedness** *n.*

resile /rizíl/ *v.intr.* **1** (of something stretched or compressed) recoil to resume a former size and shape; spring back. **2** have or show resilience or recuperative power. **3** (usu. foll. by *from*) withdraw from a course of action. [obs. F *resilir* or L *resilire* (as RE-, *salire* jump)]

resilient /rizílliənt/ *adj.* **1** (of a substance etc.) recoiling; springing back; resuming its original shape after bending, stretching, compression, etc. **2** (of a person) readily recovering from shock, depression, etc.; buoyant. □□ **resilience** *n.* **resiliency** *n.* **resiliently** *adv.* [L *resiliens resilient-* (as RESILE)]

■ **1** see ELASTIC *adj.* 1, 2. **2** see BUOYANT 2. □□ **resilience** bounce, elasticity, springiness, spring, flexibility, suppleness; buoyancy.

resin /rézzin/ *n.* & *v.* ● *n.* **1** an adhesive inflammable substance insoluble in water, secreted by some plants, and often extracted by incision, esp. from fir and pine (cf. GUM[1]). **2** (in full **synthetic resin**) a solid or liquid organic compound made by polymerization etc. and used in plastics etc. ● *v.tr.* (**resined, resining**) rub or treat with resin. □□ **resinate** /-nət/ *n.* **resinate** /-nayt/ *v.tr.* **resinoid** *adj.* & *n.* **resinous** *adj.* [ME *resyn, rosyn* f. L *resina* & med.L *rosina, rosinum*]

resist /rizíst/ *v.* & *n.* ● *v.* **1** *tr.* withstand the action or effect of; repel. **2** *tr.* stop the course or progress of; prevent from reaching, penetrating, etc. **3** *tr.* abstain from (pleasure, temptation, etc.). **4** *tr.* strive against; try to impede; refuse to comply with (*resist arrest*). **5** *intr.* offer opposition; refuse to comply. ● *n.* a protective coating of a resistant substance, applied esp. to parts of calico that are not to take dye or to parts of pottery that are not to take glaze or lustre. □ **cannot** (or **could not** etc.) **resist 1** (foll. by verbal noun) feel obliged or strongly inclined to (*cannot resist teasing me about it*). **2** is certain to be amused, attracted, etc., by (*can't resist children's clothes*). □□ **resistant** *adj.* **resister** *n.* **resistible** *adj.* **resistibility** /-zístəbílliti/ *n.* [ME f. OF *resister* or L *resistere* (as RE-, *sistere* stop, redupl. of *stare* stand)]

■ *v.* **1, 2** withstand, hold out against, be proof against, keep *or* hold at bay, hold the line against, countervail against, counteract, stand up to *or* against; weather, endure, outlast; stop, hinder, repel, thwart, impede, block, obstruct, restrain, check, control, curb. **3** refuse, turn down, decline, forgo, abstain from, reject, dismiss; see also AVOID 1. **4** strive *or* struggle against, combat, fight (against), battle against, oppose, defy, counteract, countervail against. **5** see BATTLE *v.* 1, PROTEST *v.* 1. □ **cannot** (or **could not** etc.) **resist** see LOVE *v.* 2–4. □□ **resistant** recalcitrant, defiant, stubborn, obstinate, intransigent, rebellious, immovable, intractable, refractory, wilful, ungovernable, unmanageable, unruly, uncooperative; impenetrable; (*resistant to*) impervious to, proof against, unaffected by; opposed to, averse to, defiant of.

resistance /rizístənss/ *n.* **1** the act or an instance of resisting; refusal to comply. **2** the power of resisting (*showed resistance to wear and tear*). **3** *Biol.* the ability to withstand adverse conditions. **4** the impeding, slowing, or stopping effect exerted by one material thing on another. **5** *Physics* **a** the property of hindering the conduction of electricity, heat, etc. **b** the measure of this in a body. ¶ Symb.: **R. 6** a resistor. **7** (in full **resistance movement**) a secret organization resisting authority, esp. in an occupied country. [ME f. F *résistance, résistence* f. LL *resistentia* (as RESIST)]

■ **1** opposition, defiance, obstruction, intransigence, rebelliousness, recalcitrance, stubbornness; refusal. **3** resilience, hardiness, endurance; immunity, insusceptibility, unsusceptibility; (*resistance to*) defences against. **4** see OBSTRUCTION 3. **7** see UNDERGROUND *n.* 2.

resistive /rizístiv/ *adj.* **1** able to resist. **2** *Electr.* of or concerning resistance.

resistivity /rízzistívviti/ *n. Electr.* a measure of the resisting power of a specified material to the flow of an electric current.

resistless /rizístliss/ *adj. archaic poet.* **1** irresistible; relentless. **2** unresisting. □□ **resistlessly** *adv.*

resistor /rizístər/ *n. Electr.* a device having resistance to the passage of an electrical current.

resit *v.* & *n.* ● *v.tr.* /reéssit/ (**resitting**; *past* and *past part.* **resat**) sit (an examination) again after failing. ● *n.* /reéssit/ **1** the act or an instance of resitting an examination. **2** an examination held specifically to enable candidates to resit.

re-site /reesít/ *v.tr.* place on another site; relocate.

resold *past* and *past part.* of RESELL.

resoluble /rizólyoob'l/ *adj.* **1** that can be resolved. **2** (foll. by *into*) analysable. [F *résoluble* or L *resolubilis* (as RESOLVE, after *soluble*)]

re-soluble /reéssólyoob'l/ *adj.* that can be dissolved again.

resolute /rézzəlo͞ot, -lyo͞ot/ *adj.* (of a person or a person's mind or action) determined; decided; firm of purpose; not vacillating. □□ **resolutely** *adv.* **resoluteness** *n.* [L *resolutus* past part. of *resolvere* (see RESOLVE)]

■ resolved, determined, purposeful, stubborn, adamant, set, decided, dogged, persevering, persistent, pertinacious, tenacious, single-minded, dedicated, devoted, bold, purposive, deliberate, inflexible; steadfast, firm, unwavering, unshakeable, unshaken, unfaltering, unhesitating, unswerving, undeviating, unchanging, changeless, unchangeable, immutable, unalterable.

resolution /rézzəlo͞osh'n, -lyo͞osh'n/ *n.* **1** a resolute temper or character; boldness and firmness of purpose. **2** a thing resolved on; an intention (*New Year's resolutions*). **3 a** a formal expression of opinion or intention by a legislative body or public meeting. **b** the formulation of this (*passed a resolution*). **4** (usu. foll. by *of*) the act or an instance of solving doubt or a problem or question (*towards a resolution of the difficulty*). **5 a** separation into components; decomposition. **b** the replacing of a single force etc. by two or more jointly equivalent to it. **6** (foll. by *into*) analysis; conversion into another form. **7** *Mus.* the act or an instance of causing discord to pass into concord. **8** *Physics* etc. the smallest interval measurable by a scientific instrument; the resolving power. **9** *Med.* the disappearance of inflammation etc. without suppuration. **10** *Prosody* the substitution of two short syllables for one long. [ME f. L *resolutio* (as RESOLVE)]

■ **1** resolve, resoluteness, determination, purpose, purposefulness, steadfastness, firmness, decidedness, decision, staunchness, doggedness, stubbornness, obstinacy, perseverance, persistence, pertinacity, boldness, tenacity, single-mindedness, dedication, devotion, constancy, devotedness, deliberation, deliberateness, inflexibility, unshakeability, fixedness, changelessness, unchangeability, immutability, unalterability. **2** commitment, pledge, promise, word of honour, oath, vow, undertaking, obligation; intention. **3** proposal, proposition, plan; motion, *US* resolve; verdict, judgement, decision, ruling, decree, settlement, conclusion, *Law* determination. **4** answer, answering, solution, solving, unravelling, disentanglement, sorting out. **6** analysis, assay, breakdown, division. **8** acutance, sharpness, precision, accuracy, exactness, exactitude, fineness, discrimination, detailing, distinguishability, resolving power.

resolutive /rézzəlōōtiv, -lyōōtiv/ *adj. Med.* having the power or ability to dissolve. □ **resolutive condition** *Law* a condition whose fulfilment terminates a contract etc. [med.L *resolutivus* (as RESOLVE)]

resolve /rizólv/ *v.* & *n.* ● *v.* **1** *intr.* make up one's mind; decide firmly (*resolve to do better*). **2** *tr.* (of circumstances etc.) cause (a person) to do this (*events resolved him to leave*). **3** *tr.* (foll. by *that* + clause) (of an assembly or meeting) pass a resolution by vote (*the committee resolved that immediate action should be taken*). **4** *intr.* & *tr.* (often foll. by *into*) separate or cause to separate into constituent parts; disintegrate; analyse; dissolve. **5** *tr.* (of optical or photographic equipment) separate or distinguish between closely adjacent objects. **6** *tr.* & *intr.* (foll. by *into*) convert or be converted. **7** *tr.* & *intr.* (foll. by *into*) reduce by mental analysis into. **8** *tr.* solve; explain; clear up; settle (doubt, argument, etc.). **9** *tr.* & *intr. Mus.* convert or be converted into concord. **10** *tr. Med.* remove (inflammation etc.) without suppuration. **11** *tr. Prosody* replace (a long syllable) by two short syllables. **12** *tr. Mech.* replace (a force etc.) by two or more jointly equivalent to it. ● *n.* **1 a** a firm mental decision or intention; a resolution (*made a resolve not to go*). **b** *US* a formal resolution by a legislative body or public meeting. **2** resoluteness; steadfastness. □ **resolving power** an instrument's ability to distinguish very small or very close objects. □□ **resolvable** *adj.* **resolvability** /-zólvəbílliti/ *n.* **resolver** *n.* [ME f. L *resolvere resolut-* (as RE-, SOLVE)]

■ *v.* **1** determine, decide, make up one's mind, agree, undertake, conclude. **2** see CAUSE *v.* 2. **3** decide, vote, move; see also RULE *v.* 3. **4, 6** (*resolve into*) change into, convert into, alter into, transform into, transmute into, metamorphose into, dissolve (into), break down (into), liquefy (into), disintegrate (into), reduce to *or* into; become, be converted into; analyse into. **7** see ANALYSE 2b. **8** explain, work out, figure out, solve, settle, clear up, answer. ● *n.* **1 a** see RESOLUTION 2. **b** see RESOLUTION 3. **2** see RESOLUTION 1. □ **resolving power** see RESOLUTION 8.

resolved /rizólvd/ *adj.* resolute, determined. □□ **resolvedly** /-zólvidli/ *adv.* **resolvedness** *n.*

resolvent /rizólv'nt/ *adj.* & *n.* esp. *Med.* ● *adj.* (of a drug, application, substance, etc.) effecting the resolution of a tumour etc. ● *n.* such a drug etc.

resonance /rézzənənss/ *n.* **1** the reinforcement or prolongation of sound by reflection or synchronous vibration. **2** *Mech.* a condition in which an object or system is subjected to an oscillating force having a frequency close to its own natural frequency. **3** *Chem.* the property of a molecule having a structure best represented by two or more forms rather than a single structural formula. **4** *Physics* a short-lived elementary particle that is an excited state of a more stable particle. [OF f. L *resonantia* echo (as RESONANT)]

resonant /rézzənənt/ *adj.* **1** (of sound) echoing, resounding; continuing to sound; reinforced or prolonged by reflection or synchronous vibration. **2** (of a body, room, etc.) tending to reinforce or prolong sounds esp. by synchronous vibration. **3** (often foll. by *with*) (of a place) resounding. **4** of or relating to resonance. □□ **resonantly** *adv.* [F *résonnant* or L *resonare resonant-* (as RE-, *sonare* sound)]

■ **1** vibrating, vibrant, (re-)echoing, reverberating, reverberant, ringing, resounding; booming, thundering, thunderous, loud.

resonate /rézzənayt/ *v.intr.* produce or show resonance; resound. [L *resonare resonat-* (as RESONANT)]

resonator /rézzənaytər/ *n. Mus.* **1** an instrument responding to a single note and used for detecting it in combinations. **2** an appliance for giving resonance to sound or other vibrations.

resorb /risórb/ *v.tr.* absorb again. □□ **resorbence** *n.* **resorbent** *adj.* [L *resorbēre resorpt-* (as RE-, *sorbēre* absorb)]

■ reabsorb. □□ **resorbence** reabsorption, resorption. **resorbent** resorptive.

resorcin /rizórsin/ *n.* = RESORCINOL. [RESIN + ORCIN]

resorcinol /rizórsinol/ *n. Chem.* a crystalline organic compound usu. made by synthesis and used in the production of dyes, drugs, resins, etc.

resorption /rizórpsh'n/ *n.* **1** the act or an instance of resorbing; the state of being resorbed. **2** the absorption of tissue within the body. □□ **resorptive** /-zórptiv/ *adj.* [RESORB after *absorption*]

resort /rizórt/ *n.* & *v.* ● *n.* **1** a place frequented esp. for holidays or for a specified purpose or quality (*seaside resort; health resort*). **2 a** a thing to which one has recourse; an expedient or measure (*a taxi was our best resort*). **b** (foll. by *to*) recourse to; use of (*without resort to violence*). **3** a tendency to frequent or be frequented (*places of great resort*). ● *v.intr.* **1** (foll. by *to*) turn to as an expedient (*resorted to threats*). **2** (foll. by *to*) go often or in large numbers to. □ **in the** (or **as a**) **last resort** when all else has failed. □□ **resorter** *n.* [ME f. OF *resortir* (as RE-, *sortir* come or go out)]

■ *n.* **2 a** alternative, remedy, resource, recourse, backup, reserve, refuge. ● *v.* (*resort to*) **1** have recourse to, turn to, look to, fall back on, repair to, take to. **2** frequent, patronize, visit, go to, haunt, *sl.* hang out in.

re-sort /reé-sórt/ *v.tr.* sort again or differently.

resound /rizównd/ *v.* **1** *intr.* (often foll. by *with*) (of a place) ring or echo (*the hall resounded with laughter*). **2** *intr.* (of a voice, instrument, sound, etc.) produce echoes; go on sounding; fill the place with sound. **3** *intr.* **a** (of fame, a reputation, etc.) be much talked of. **b** (foll. by *through*) produce a sensation (*the call resounded through Europe*). **4** *tr.* (often foll. by *of*) proclaim or repeat loudly (the praises) of a person or thing (*resounded the praises of Greece*). **5** *tr.* (of a place) re-echo (a sound). [ME f. RE- + SOUND[1] *v.*, after OF *resoner* or L *resonare*: see RESONANT]

■ **1, 2** resonate, (re-)echo, reverberate, ring, boom, pulsate; ring out, boom out, thunder (out).

resounding /rizównding/ *adj.* **1** in senses of RESOUND. **2** unmistakable; emphatic (*was a resounding success*). □□ **resoundingly** *adv.*

resource /risórss, -zórss/ *n.* **1** an expedient or device (*escape was their only resource*). **2** (usu. in *pl.*) **a** the means available to achieve an end, fulfil a function, etc. **b** a stock or supply that can be drawn on. **c** *US* available assets. **3** (in *pl.*) a country's collective wealth or means of defence. **4** a leisure occupation (*reading is a great resource*). **5 a** (often in *pl.*) skill in devising expedients (*a person of great resource*). **b** practical ingenuity; quick wit (*full of resource*). **6** *archaic* the possibility of aid (*lost without resource*). □ **one's own resources** one's own abilities, ingenuity, etc. □□ **resourceful** *adj.* **resourcefully** *adv.* **resourcefulness** *n.* **resourceless** *adj.* **resourcelessness** *n.* [F *ressource*, *ressourse*, fem. past part. of OF dial. *resourdre* (as RE-, L *surgere* rise)]

■ **1** expedient, device, means, measure, contrivance; see also RESORT *n.* **2 a, c** (*resources*) see ASSET 2a, MEANS 2. **b** (*resources*) see STOCK *n.* 1, 2. **3** (*resources*) prosperity, wealth, riches; stockpile, stocks, reserves. **5 a** initiative, ingenuity, talent, inventiveness, originality, imagination, imaginativeness, cleverness, capability, resourcefulness, aptitude, flair, strength, quality, *colloq.* gumption, guts. □□ **resourceful** ingenious, inventive, imaginative, clever, enterprising, creative, skilful, smart, slick.

respect /rispékt/ *n.* & *v.* ● *n.* **1** deferential esteem felt or shown towards a person or quality. **2 a** (foll. by *of*, *for*) heed or regard. **b** (foll. by *to*) attention to or consideration of (*without respect to the results*). **3** an aspect, detail, particular, etc. (*correct except in this one respect*). **4** reference, relation (*a morality that has no respect to religion*). **5** (in *pl.*) a person's polite messages or attentions (*give my respects to your mother*). ● *v.tr.* **1** regard with deference, esteem, or honour. **2 a** avoid interfering with, harming, degrading, insulting, injuring, or interrupting. **b** treat with consideration. **c** refrain from offending, corrupting, or tempting (a person, a person's feelings, etc.). □ **in respect of** as concerns; with reference to. **in respect that** because. **with** (or **with all due**) **respect** a mollifying formula preceding an expression of one's disagreement with another's views. □□ **respecter** *n.* [ME f. OF *respect* or L *respectus* f. *respicere* (as RE-, *specere* look at) or f. *respectare* frequent. of *respicere*]

■ *n.* **1** admiration, esteem, regard; consideration, appreciation, deference, reverence, veneration, courtesy, politeness, civility, attentiveness. **2** see REGARD *n.* 2. **3** detail, point, aspect, particular, characteristic, feature, quality, trait, matter, attribute, property, element. **4** reference, regard, relation, connection, comparison, bearing. **5** (*respects*) regards, good *or* best wishes, greetings, compliments, salutations, *archaic* devoirs. ● *v.* **1** admire, esteem, honour, appreciate, value, defer to, pay homage to, think highly *or* well *or* much of, look up to, revere, reverence, venerate. **2 b, c** heed, obey, be considerate *or* polite *or* courteous to; show consideration *or* regard for, pay attention to, attend to, defer to. □ **in respect of** see CONCERNING.

respectability /rispéktəbílliti/ *n.* **1** the state of being respectable. **2** those who are respectable.

respectable /rispéktəb'l/ *adj.* **1** deserving or enjoying respect (*an intellectually respectable hypothesis*, *a respectable elder statesman*). **2 a** (of people) of good social standing or reputation (*comes from a respectable middle-class family*). **b** characteristic of or associated with people of such status or character (*a respectable neighbourhood*; *a respectable profession*). **3 a** honest and decent in character or conduct. **b** characterized by (a sense of) convention or propriety; socially acceptable (*respectable behaviour*; *a respectable publication*). **c** *derog.* highly conventional; prim. **4 a** commendable, meritorious (*an entirely respectable ambition*). **b** comparatively good or competent; passable, tolerable (*a respectable effort*; *speaks respectable French*). **5** reasonably good in condition or appearance; presentable. **6** appreciable in number, size, amount, etc. (*earns a very respectable salary*). **7** accepted or tolerated on account of prevalence (*materialism has become respectable again*). □□ **respectably** *adv.*

■ **1** estimable, worthy, respected, creditable; good, great, eminent; tenable, solid, sound, credible. **2** genteel, good, proper; dignified, worthy, estimable. **3 a, b** dignified, moral, decent, upright, straight, honest; seemly, proper, genteel, demure, refined; reputable, unimpeachable, law-abiding, above-board. **c** see SQUARE *adj.* 12. **4 a** laudable, commendable, creditable, meritorious, exemplary, worthy, praiseworthy, good, estimable, admirable. **b** decent, tolerable, passable, competent, fair, fairly good, not bad. **5** see SMART *adj.* 2. **6** moderate, appreciable, goodly, reasonable, fair, not inconsiderable, considerable, tolerable, satisfactory, sizeable, good-sized, substantial, not insignificant, significant, *colloq.* tidy.

respectful /rispéktfŏŏl/ *adj.* showing deference (*stood at a respectful distance*). □□ **respectfully** *adv.* **respectfulness** *n.*

■ courteous, polite, well-mannered, well-behaved, mannerly, civil, cordial, gentlemanly, ladylike, gracious, obliging, accommodating, considerate, thoughtful.

respecting /rispékting/ *prep.* with reference or regard to; concerning.

respective /rispéktiv/ *adj.* concerning or appropriate to each of several individually; proper to each (*go to your respective places*). [F *respectif -ive* f. med.L *respectivus* (as RESPECT)]

■ separate, individual, personal, own, particular, several, pertinent, specific, special, relevant, corresponding.

respectively /rispéktivli/ *adv.* for each separately or in turn, and in the order mentioned (*she and I gave £10 and £1 respectively*).

■ separately, individually, singly, severally.

respell /reéspél/ *v.tr.* (*past* and *past part.* **respelt** or **respelled**) spell again or differently, esp. phonetically.

respirable /réspərəb'l, rispírəb'l/ *adj.* (of air, gas, etc.) able or fit to be breathed. [F *respirable* or LL *respirabilis* (as RESPIRE)]

respirate /réspirayt/ *v.tr.* subject to artificial respiration. [back-form. f. RESPIRATION]

respiration /réspiráysh'n/ *n.* **1 a** the act or an instance of breathing. **b** a single inspiration or expiration; a breath. **2** *Biol.* in living organisms, the process involving the release of energy and carbon dioxide from the oxidation of complex organic substances. [ME f. F *respiration* or L *respiratio* (as RESPIRE)]

respirator /réspiraytər/ *n.* **1** an apparatus worn over the face to prevent poison gas, cold air, dust particles, etc., from being inhaled. **2** *Med.* an apparatus for maintaining artificial respiration.

respire /rispír/ *v.* **1** *intr.* breathe air. **2** *intr.* inhale and exhale air. **3** *intr.* (of a plant) carry out respiration. **4** *tr.* breathe (air etc.). **5** *intr.* breathe again; take a breath. **6** *intr.* get rest or respite; recover hope or spirit. □□ **respiratory** /rispírrətəri, -tri, réspəraytəri/ *adj.* [ME f. OF *respirer* or f. L *respirare* (as RE-, *spirare* breathe)]

respite /réspīt, -pit/ *n.* & *v.* ● *n.* **1** an interval of rest or relief. **2** a delay permitted before the discharge of an obligation or the suffering of a penalty. ● *v.tr.* **1** grant respite to; reprieve (a condemned person). **2** postpone the execution or exaction of (a sentence, obligation, etc.). **3** give temporary relief from (pain or care) or to (a sufferer). [ME f. OF *respit* f. L *respectus* RESPECT]

■ *n.* **1** rest; interval, intermission, break, breather, interruption. **2** reprieve, stay, postponement, extension; pause, delay, hiatus. ● *v.* **1** reprieve, let off; see also SPARE *v.* 2. **2** see POSTPONE.

resplendent /rispléndənt/ *adj.* brilliant, dazzlingly or gloriously bright. □□ **resplendence** *n.* **resplendency** *n.* **resplendently** *adv.* [ME f. L *resplendēre* (as RE-, *splendēre* glitter)]

respond /rispónd/ *v.* & *n.* ● *v.* **1** *intr.* answer, give a reply. **2** *intr.* act or behave in an answering or corresponding manner. **3** *intr.* (usu. foll. by *to*) show sensitiveness to by behaviour or change (*does not respond to kindness*). **4** *intr.* (of a congregation) make answers to a priest etc. **5** *intr.* *Bridge* make a bid on the basis of a partner's preceding bid. **6** *tr.* say (something) in answer. ● *n.* **1** *Archit.* a half-pillar or half-pier attached to a wall to support an arch, esp. at the end of an arcade. **2** *Eccl.* a responsory; a response to a versicle. □□ **respondence** *n.* **respondency** *n.* **responder** *n.* [ME f. OF *respondre* answer ult. f. L *respondēre respons-* answer (as RE-, *spondēre* pledge)]

■ *v.* **1** answer (back), reply, (make a) retort, riposte, *US* come back; counter. **2** react, reciprocate; behave, conduct oneself, act; retaliate. **3** be responsive, react, be affected *or* moved *or* touched. **6** answer, reply, return, rejoin, retort, fling *or* hurl (back), *US* come back.

respondent /rispóndənt/ *n.* & *adj.* ● *n.* **1** a defendant, esp. in an appeal or divorce case. **2** a person who makes an answer or defends an argument etc. ● *adj.* **1** making answer. **2** (foll. by *to*) responsive. **3** in the position of defendant.

response /rispóns/ *n.* **1** an answer given in word or act; a reply. **2** a feeling, movement, change, etc., caused by a

stimulus or influence. **3** (often in *pl.*) *Eccl.* any part of the liturgy said or sung in answer to the priest; a responsory. **4** *Bridge* a bid made in responding. [ME f. OF *respons(e)* or L *responsum* neut. past part. of *respondēre* RESPOND]
■ **1** answer, reply, retort, rejoinder, reaction, *sl.* comeback; reaction, feedback. **2** reaction, effect; result, consequence, outcome, upshot.

responsibility /rispónsibílliti/ *n.* (*pl.* **-ies**) **1 a** (often foll. by *for, of*) the state or fact of being responsible (*refuses all responsibility for it; will take the responsibility of doing it*). **b** authority; the ability to act independently and make decisions (*a job with more responsibility*). **2** the person or thing for which one is responsible (*the food is my responsibility*). □ **on one's own responsibility** without authorization.
■ **1 a** accountability, liability, chargeability, answerability, obligation; blame, guilt, culpability; see also *responsibleness* (RESPONSIBLE). **b** see POWER *n.* 3a, 5, INDEPENDENCE. **2** charge, duty, onus, burden, job, task, trust.

responsible /rispónsib'l/ *adj.* **1** (often foll. by *to, for*) liable to be called to account (to a person or for a thing). **2** morally accountable for one's actions; capable of rational conduct. **3** of good credit, position, or repute; respectable; evidently trustworthy. **4** (often foll. by *for*) being the primary cause (*a short circuit was responsible for the power failure*). **5** (of a ruler or government) not autocratic. **6** involving responsibility (*a responsible job*). □□ **responsibleness** *n.* **responsibly** *adv.* [obs. F f. L *respondēre*: see RESPOND]
■ **1, 2** accountable, answerable, liable, chargeable, (legally *or* statutorily) bound. **3** reliable, respectable, reputable, trustworthy, dependable, stable, creditable, accountable, ethical, honest. **4** guilty, to blame, at fault, culpable. **5** democratic, representative, popular; elected, chosen. **6** authoritative, important, top, leading, decision-making. □□ **responsibleness** responsibility; dependability, respectability, reputability, reliability, trustworthiness, stability, creditability; accountability.

responsive /rispónsiv/ *adj.* **1** (often foll. by *to*) responding readily (to some influence). **2** sympathetic; impressionable. **3 a** answering. **b** by way of answer. **4** (of a liturgy etc.) using responses. □□ **responsively** *adv.* **responsiveness** *n.* [F *responsif -ive* or LL *responsivus* (as RESPOND)]
■ **1, 2** alert, alive, (wide-awake), reactive, communicative, sharp, keen, receptive, sensitive, open, sympathetic, impressionable.

responsory /rispónsəri/ *n.* (*pl.* **-ies**) an anthem said or sung by a soloist and choir after a lesson. [ME f. LL *responsorium* (as RESPOND)]

respray *v.* & *n.* ● *v.tr.* /reésprάy/ spray again (esp. to change the colour of the paint on a vehicle). ● *n.* /reéspray/ the act or an instance of respraying.

rest[1] /rest/ *v.* & *n.* ● *v.* **1** *intr.* cease, abstain, or be relieved from exertion, action, movement, or employment; be tranquil. **2** *intr.* be still or asleep, esp. to refresh oneself or recover strength. **3** *tr.* give relief or repose to; allow to rest (*a chair to rest my legs*). **4** *intr.* (foll. by *on, upon, against*) lie on; be supported by; be spread out on; be propped against. **5** *intr.* (foll. by *on, upon*) depend, be based, or rely on. **6** *intr.* (foll. by *on, upon*) (of a look) alight or be steadily directed on. **7** *tr.* (foll. by *on, upon*) place for support or foundation. **8** *intr.* (of a problem or subject) be left without further investigation or discussion (*let the matter rest*). **9** *intr.* **a** lie in death. **b** (foll. by *in*) lie buried in (a churchyard etc.). **10** *tr.* (as **rested** *adj.*) refreshed or reinvigorated by resting. **11** *intr. US* conclude the calling of witnesses in a law case (*the prosecution rests*). **12** *intr.* (of land) lie fallow. **13** *intr.* (foll. by *in*) repose trust in (*am content to rest in God*). ● *n.* **1** repose or sleep, esp. in bed at night (*get a good night's rest*). **2** freedom from or the cessation of exertion, worry, activity, etc. (*give the subject a rest*). **3** a period of resting (*take a 15-minute rest*). **4** a support or prop for holding or steadying something. **5** *Mus.* **a** an interval of silence of a specified duration. **b** the sign denoting this. **6** a place of resting or abiding, esp. a lodging place or shelter provided for sailors, cabmen, etc. **7** a pause in elocution. **8** a caesura in verse. □ **at rest** not moving; not agitated or troubled; dead. **be resting** *Brit. euphem.* (of an actor) be out of work. **rest-baulk** a ridge left unploughed between furrows. **rest one's case** conclude one's argument etc. **rest-cure** a rest usu. of some weeks as a medical treatment. **rest-day 1** a day spent in rest. **2** = *day of rest*. **rest** (or **God rest**) **his** (or **her**) **soul** may God grant his (or her) soul repose. **rest-home** a place where old or frail people can be cared for. **rest-house** *Ind.* a house for travellers to rest in. **resting-place** a place provided or used for resting. **rest mass** *Physics* the mass of a body when at rest. **rest on one's laurels** see LAUREL. **rest on one's oars** see OAR. **rest room** esp. *US* a public lavatory in a factory, shop, etc. **rest up** *US* rest oneself thoroughly. **set at rest** settle or relieve (a question, a person's mind, etc.). □□ **rester** *n.* [OE *ræst, rest* (n.), *ræstan, restan* (v.)]
■ *v.* **1** relax, repose, take a rest, take one's ease, unwind, take it easy, *Austral.* spell, *colloq.* put one's feet up; loll, languish, laze about, be idle, idle about, lounge (about). **2** (go to) sleep, doze, take a rest, (take one's) repose, lie down, go *or* take to one's bed, (take a) nap, *colloq.* snooze, (take *or* have a) zizz, catch *or* grab some shut-eye, hit the sack *or* hay, get *or* take forty winks, *Brit. sl.* kip, doss down. **4** see LIE *v.* 1; (*resting on* or *upon* or *against*) supported by, spread out on, spread *or* extended over, propped (up) against, overlying. **5** (*rest on* or *upon*) see DEPEND 1. **8** drop, cease, end, stop, lie. **10** (**rested**) see REFRESH 1. ● *n.* **1** repose, sleep, nap, doze, siesta, lie-down, *colloq.* zizz, snooze, *poet. rhet.* slumber; shut-eye. **2** relaxation, ease, breathing-space, respite, time off *or* out, leisure; see also BREAK[1] *n.* 2. **3** intermission, interval, interlude, entr'acte, rest period, cessation, break, recess, *colloq.* breather, *Austral.* & *NZ colloq.* smoko; holiday, *US* vacation. **4** prop, holder, trestle; see also SUPPORT *n.* 2. **6** see SHELTER *n.* 2a. □ **at rest** see CALM *adj.* 1, DEAD *adj.* 1. **be resting** see UNEMPLOYED 1. **rest room** see LAVATORY. **set at rest** see SETTLE[1] 5–7, 8b.

rest[2] /rest/ *n.* & *v.* ● *n.* (prec. by *the*) **1** the remaining part or parts; the others; the remainder of some quantity or number (*finish what you can and leave the rest*). **2** *Brit. Econ.* the reserve fund, esp. of the Bank of England. **3** *hist.* a rally in tennis. ● *v.intr.* **1** remain in a specified state (*rest assured*). **2** (foll. by *with*) be left in the hands or charge of (*the final arrangements rest with you*). □ **and all the rest** (or **the rest of it**) and all else that might be mentioned; et cetera. **for the rest** as regards anything else. [ME f. OF *reste rester* f. L *restare* (as RE-, *stare* stand)]
■ *n.* **1** remainder, balance; remains, remnants, leftovers, residue, residuum, excess, surplus, overage. ● *v.* **1** (continue to) be, remain, keep on being. **2** reside, be situated, be lodged, lie, be placed, be found, remain. □ **and all the rest** (or **the rest of it**) et cetera, and so on (and so forth), and so forth, and the like.

restart *v.* & *n.* ● *v.tr.* & *intr.* /reéstaárt/ begin again. ● *n.* /reéstaart/ a new beginning.

restate /reéstáyt/ *v.tr.* express again or differently, esp. more clearly or convincingly. □□ **restatement** *n.*

restaurant /réstəront, -RON/ *n.* public premises where meals or refreshments may be had. □ **restaurant car** *Brit.* a dining-car on a train. [F f. *restaurer* RESTORE]

restaurateur /réstərətőr/ *n.* a restaurant-keeper. [F (as RESTAURANT)]

restful /réstfōōl/ *adj.* **1** favourable to quiet or repose. **2** free from disturbing influences. **3** soothing. □□ **restfully** *adv.* **restfulness** *n.*
■ **1** tranquil, calm, peaceful, quiet, still, serene, pacific; relaxed, reposeful. **3** relaxing, soothing, comforting, tranquillizing, sedative, calming, sleep-inducing, hypnotic, soporific, somnolent.

rest-harrow /rést-harrō/ *n.* any tough-rooted plant of the genus *Ononis*, native to Europe and the Mediterranean. [obs. *rest* (v.) = ARREST (in sense 'stop') + HARROW]

restitution /réstityóosh'n/ *n.* **1** (often foll. by *of*) the act or an instance of restoring a thing to its proper owner. **2** reparation for an injury (esp. *make restitution*). **3** esp. *Theol.* the restoration of a thing to its original state. **4** the resumption of an original shape or position because of elasticity. □□ **restitutive** /réstityootiv/ *adj.* [ME f. OF *restitution* or L *restitutio* f. *restituere restitut-* restore (as RE-, *statuere* establish)]

■ **1** restoration, return, recovery, replacement, replacing, restoring; reinstatement, re-establishment. **2** amends, compensation, redress, remuneration, reparation, requital, indemnification, indemnity.

restive /réstiv/ *adj.* **1** fidgety; restless. **2** (of a horse) refusing to advance, stubbornly standing still or moving backwards or sideways; jibbing; refractory. **3** (of a person) unmanageable; rejecting control. □□ **restively** *adv.* **restiveness** *n.* [ME f. OF *restif -ive* f. Rmc (as REST²)]

■ **1** see RESTLESS 2, 3. **2** see DISOBEDIENT. **3** see UNGOVERNABLE.

restless /réstliss/ *adj.* **1** finding or affording no rest. **2** uneasy; agitated. **3** constantly in motion, fidgeting, etc. □□ **restlessly** *adv.* **restlessness** *n.* [OE *restlēas* (as REST, -LESS)]

■ **1** sleepless, wakeful; see also UNSETTLED 1. **2** restive, uneasy, edgy, on edge, on tenterhooks, nervous, excitable, highly-strung, high-strung, worked up, agitated, jumpy, skittish, fretful, apprehensive, jittery, uptight, *US colloq.* antsy, *Austral. sl.* toey; (*be restless*) champ at the bit, *colloq.* have itchy feet, have ants in one's pants. **3** fidgety, jumpy, restive, skittish, *US colloq.* antsy; (*be restless*) *colloq.* have ants in one's pants, have itchy feet.

restock /reéstók/ *v.tr.* (also *absol.*) stock again or differently.

restoration /réstəráysh'n/ *n.* **1 a** the act or an instance of restoring (a building etc.) or of being restored. **b** = RESTITUTION 1. **2** a model or drawing representing the supposed original form of an extinct animal, ruined building, etc. **3 a** the re-establishment of a monarch etc. **b** the period of this. **4** (**Restoration**) *hist.* **a** (prec. by *the*) the re-establishment of Charles II as king of England in 1660. **b** (often *attrib.*) the literary period following this (*Restoration comedy*). [17th-c. alt. (after RESTORE) of *restauration*, ME f. OF *restauration* or LL *restauratio* (as RESTORE)]

■ **1 a** renovation, refurbishment, repair, reconstruction, reconversion; resurrection. **3 a** re-establishment, rehabilitation, reinstatement.

restorative /ristórrətiv/ *adj.* & *n.* ● *adj.* tending to restore health or strength. ● *n.* a restorative medicine, food, etc. (*needs a restorative*). □□ **restoratively** *adv.* [ME var. of obs. *restaurative* f. OF *restauratif -ive* (as RESTORE)]

■ analeptic, tonic.

restore /ristór/ *v.tr.* **1** bring back or attempt to bring back to the original state by rebuilding, repairing, repainting, emending, etc. **2** bring back to health etc.; cure. **3** give back to the original owner etc.; make restitution of. **4** reinstate; bring back to dignity or right. **5** replace; put back; bring back to a former condition. **6** make a representation of the supposed original state of (a ruin, extinct animal, etc.). **7** reinstate by conjecture (missing words in a text, missing pieces, etc.). □□ **restorable** *adj.* **restorer** *n.* [ME f. OF *restorer* f. L *restaurare*]

■ **1** renovate, refurbish, make good, repair, reconstruct, rebuild; resurrect; mend, fix, touch (up). **2** make better, cure; see also HEAL 2. **3** give *or* hand *or* put *or* bring *or* pay back, return, replace, make good, make restitution of; repay. **4** reinstate, rehabilitate, re-establish, bring back. **5** replace, put back, re-establish, bring back.

restrain /ristráyn/ *v.tr.* **1** (often *refl.*, usu. foll. by *from*) check or hold in; keep in check or under control or within bounds. **2** repress; keep down. **3** confine; imprison. □□ **restrainable** *adj.* **restrainer** *n.* [ME f. OF *restrei(g)n-* stem of *restreindre* f. L *restringere restrict-* (as RE-, *stringere* tie)]

■ **1** (keep under *or* in) control, (keep *or* hold in) check, hold (back *or* in), curb, govern; limit, restrict, inhibit, regulate, curtail, hinder, interfere with, hamper, handicap. **2** keep down, stifle; see also REPRESS 2. **3** (place under) arrest, confine, imprison, incarcerate, detain, lock up, jail, shut up.

re-strain /reéstráyn/ *v.tr.* strain again.

restrainedly /ristráynidli/ *adv.* with self-restraint.

restraint /ristráynt/ *n.* **1** the act or an instance of restraining or being restrained. **2** a stoppage; a check; a controlling agency or influence. **3 a** self-control; avoidance of excess or exaggeration. **b** austerity of literary expression. **4** reserve of manner. **5** confinement, esp. because of insanity. **6** something which restrains or holds in check; bondage, shackles. □ **in restraint of** in order to restrain. **restraint of trade** action seeking to interfere with free-market conditions. [ME f. OF *restreinte* fem. past part. of *restreindre*: see RESTRAIN]

■ **2** control, check, curb, rein, bridle, restriction, constraint, limit, limitation, stoppage, curtailment, delimitation, bound. **3a, 4** control, reserve, self-control, self-possession, poise, equanimity, self-discipline, self-restraint. **5** duress, captivity, *archaic* durance; see also *imprisonment* (IMPRISON). **6** bondage, bonds, fetters, shackles, handcuffs, bilboes, pinions, manacles, strait-jacket, *colloq.* cuffs, *sl.* bracelets.

restrict /ristríkt/ *v.tr.* (often foll. by *to*, *within*) **1** confine, bound, limit (*restricted parking*; *restricted them to five days a week*). **2** subject to limitation. **3** withhold from general circulation or disclosure. □ **restricted area 1** *Brit.* an area in which there is a special speed limit for vehicles. **2** *US* an area which military personnel are not allowed to enter. □□ **restrictedly** *adv.* **restrictedness** *n.* [L *restringere*: see RESTRAIN]

■ **1, 2** limit, confine, bound, circumscribe, delimit, mark off, demarcate, regulate, restrain, crib, impede.

restriction /ristríksh'n/ *n.* **1** the act or an instance of restricting; the state of being restricted. **2** a thing that restricts. **3** a limitation placed on action. □□ **restrictionist** *adj.* & *n.* [ME f. OF *restriction* or L *restrictio* (as RESTRICT)]

■ **2** see RESTRAINT 2. **3** condition, provision, proviso, qualification; see also *stipulation* (STIPULATE¹).

restrictive /ristríktiv/ *adj.* imposing restrictions. □ **restrictive clause** *Gram.* a relative clause, usu. without surrounding commas. **restrictive practice** *Brit.* an agreement to limit competition or output in industry. □□ **restrictively** *adv.* **restrictiveness** *n.* [ME f. OF *restrictif -ive* or med.L *restrictivus* (as RESTRICT)]

restring /reéstríng/ *v.tr.* (*past* and *past part.* **restrung**) **1** fit (a musical instrument) with new strings. **2** thread (beads etc.) on a new string.

restructure /reéstrúkchər/ *v.tr.* give a new structure to; rebuild; rearrange.

restudy /reéstúddi/ *v.tr.* (**-ies**, **-ied**) study again.

restyle /reéstíl/ *v.tr.* **1** reshape; remake in a new style. **2** give a new designation to (a person or thing).

result /rizúlt/ *n.* & *v.* ● *n.* **1** a consequence, issue, or outcome of something. **2** a satisfactory outcome; a favourable result (*gets results*). **3** a quantity, formula, etc., obtained by calculation. **4** (in *pl.*) a list of scores or winners etc. in an examination or sporting event. ● *v.intr.* **1** (often foll. by *from*) arise as the actual consequence or follow as a logical consequence (from conditions, causes, etc.). **2** (often foll. by *in*) have a specified end or outcome (*resulted in a large profit*). □ **without result** in vain; fruitless. □□ **resultful** *adj.* **resultless** *adj.* [ME f. med.L *resultare* f. L (as RE-, *saltare* frequent. of *salire* jump)]

■ *n.* **1** consequence, effect, development; issue, fruit, conclusion, upshot, end (result), denouement. ● *v.* **1** develop, emerge, follow, happen, occur, come (about), come to pass, arise, evolve, be produced. **2** end, conclude, culminate, terminate, finish up. □ **without result** see *in vain* (VAIN), FRUITLESS 2.

resultant /rizúlt'nt/ *adj.* & *n.* ● *adj.* resulting, esp. as the total outcome of more or less opposed forces. ● *n. Math.* a force etc. equivalent to two or more acting in different directions at the same point.

resume /rizyóóm/ *v.* & *n.* ● *v.* **1** *tr.* & *intr.* begin again or continue after an interruption. **2** *tr.* & *intr.* begin to speak, work, or use again; recommence. **3** *tr.* get back; take back; recover; reoccupy (*resume one's seat*). ● *n.* = RÉSUMÉ. □□ **resumable** *adj.* [ME f. OF *resumer* or L *resumere resumpt-* (as RE-, *sumere* take)]
■ *v.* **1** see CONTINUE 2, *carry on* 1. **2** recommence, restart, pick *or* take up (again), reopen, resurrect. **3** take back, reoccupy; see also RECOVER *v.* 1.

résumé /rézyoomay/ *n.* **1** a summary. **2** *US* a curriculum vitae. [F past part. of *résumer* (as RESUME)]
■ **1** summary, digest, abstract, synopsis, précis, outline, recapitulation, epitome, recap. **2** curriculum vitae, work *or* job history, biography, career description, prosopography.

resumption /rizúmpsh'n/ *n.* the act or an instance of resuming (*ready for the resumption of negotiations*). □□ **resumptive** *adj.* [ME f. OF *resumption* or LL *resumptio* (as RESUME)]

resupinate /risyóópinət/ *adj.* (of a leaf etc.) upside down. [L *resupinatus* past part. of *resupinare* bend back: see SUPINE]

resurface /reéssúrfiss/ *v.* **1** *tr.* lay a new surface on (a road etc.). **2** *intr.* rise or arise again; turn up again.

resurgent /risúrjənt/ *adj.* **1** rising or arising again. **2** tending to rise again. □□ **resurgence** *n.* [L *resurgere resurrect-* (as RE-, *surgere* rise)]
■ renascent, on the rise; see also *on the increase* (INCREASE). □□ **resurgence** renaissance, renascence, rebirth, revival, reawakening, renewal, return, resurrection, regeneration, rejuvenation.

resurrect /rézzərékt/ *v.* **1** *tr. colloq.* revive the practice, use, or memory of. **2** *tr.* take from the grave; exhume. **3** *tr.* dig up. **4** *tr.* & *intr.* raise or rise from the dead. [back-form. f. RESURRECTION]
■ **1** revive, bring back, reintroduce, restore, renew, resuscitate. **2, 3** see DIG *v.* 4. **4** restore to life, raise (from the dead), resuscitate, breathe new life into, reanimate, reincarnate, regenerate; reawaken, rise.

resurrection /rézzəréksh'n/ *n.* **1** the act or an instance of rising from the dead. **2** (**Resurrection**) **a** Christ's rising from the dead. **b** the rising of the dead at the Last Judgement. **3** a revival after disuse, inactivity, or decay. **4** exhumation. **5** the unearthing of a lost or forgotten thing; restoration to vogue or memory. □ **resurrection plant** any of various plants, including clubmosses of the genus *Selaginella* and the Rose of Jericho, unfolding when moistened after being dried. □□ **resurrectional** *adj.* [ME f. OF f. LL *resurrectio -onis* (as RESURGENT)]

resurvey *v.* & *n.* ● *v.tr.* /reéssurváy/ survey again; reconsider. ● *n.* /reesúrvay/ the act or an instance of resurveying.

resuscitate /risússitayt/ *v.tr.* & *intr.* **1** revive from unconsciousness or apparent death. **2** return or restore to vogue, vigour, or vividness. □□ **resuscitation** /-táysh'n/ *n.* **resuscitative** *adj.* **resuscitator** *n.* [L *resuscitare* (as RE-, *suscitare* raise)]

ret /ret/ *v.* (also **rate** /rayt/) (**retted, retting**) **1** *tr.* soften (flax, hemp, etc.) by soaking or by exposure to moisture. **2** *intr.* (often as **retted** *adj.*) (of hay etc.) be spoilt by wet or rot. [ME, rel. to ROT]

ret. *abbr.* retired; returned.

retable /ritáyb'l/ *n.* **1** a frame enclosing decorated panels above the back of an altar. **2** a shelf. [F *rétable, retable* f. Sp. *retablo* f. med.L *retrotabulum* rear table (as RETRO-, TABLE)]

retail /reétayl/ *n.*, *adj.*, *adv.*, & *v.* ● *n.* the sale of goods in relatively small quantities to the public, and usu. not for resale (cf. WHOLESALE). ● *adj.* & *adv.* by retail; at a retail price (*do you buy wholesale or retail?*). ● *v.* /also ritáyl/ **1** *tr.* sell (goods) in retail trade. **2** *intr.* (often foll. by *at*, *of*) (of goods) be sold in this way (esp. for a specified price) (*retails at £4.95*). **3** *tr.* recount; relate details of. □ **retail price index** an index of the variation in the prices of retail goods. □□ **retailer** *n.* [ME f. OF *retaille* a piece cut off f. *retaillier* (as RE-, TAIL[2])]

retain /ritáyn/ *v.tr.* **1 a** keep possession of; not lose; continue to have, practise, or recognize. **b** not abolish, discard, or alter. **2** keep in one's memory. **3 a** keep in place; hold fixed. **b** hold (water etc.). **4** secure the services of (a person, esp. a barrister) with a preliminary payment. □ **retaining fee** a fee paid to secure a person, service, etc. **retaining wall** a wall supporting and confining a mass of earth or water. □□ **retainable** *adj.* **retainability** /-táynəbílliti/ *n.* **retainment** *n.* [ME f. AF *retei(g)n-* f. stem of OF *retenir* ult. f. L *retinēre retent-* (as RE-, *tenēre* hold)]
■ **1** keep (possession of), hold on to, save, reserve, preserve, *colloq.* hang on to. **2** remember, keep in mind, memorize, impress on the memory. **3 a** see FIX *v.* 1. **b** hold (back), contain, absorb, soak up. **4** secure, engage, hire, employ, commission, take on. □ **retaining fee** *Law* retainer.

retainer /ritáynər/ *n.* **1** a person or thing that retains. **2** *Law* a fee for retaining a barrister etc. **3 a** *hist.* a dependant or follower of a person of rank. **b** *joc.* an old and faithful friend or servant (esp. *old retainer*). **4** *Brit.* a reduced rent paid to retain accommodation during a period of non-occupancy.

retake *v.* & *n.* ● *v.tr.* /reétáyk/ (*past* **retook**; *past part.* **retaken**) **1** take again. **2** recapture. ● *n.* /reétayk/ **1 a** the act or an instance of retaking. **b** a thing retaken, e.g. an examination. **2 a** the act or an instance of filming a scene or recording music etc. again. **b** the scene or recording obtained in this way.

retaliate /ritálliayt/ *v.* **1** *intr.* repay an injury, insult, etc., in kind; attack in return; make reprisals. **2** *tr.* **a** (usu. foll. by *upon*) cast (an accusation) back upon a person. **b** repay (an injury or insult) in kind. □□ **retaliation** /-áysh'n/ *n.* **retaliative** /-tályətiv/ *adj.* **retaliator** *n.* **retaliatory** /-tályətəri, -tri/ *adj.* [L *retaliare* (as RE-, *talis* such)]
■ **1** counter, strike back, take revenge, wreak vengeance, revenge oneself, reciprocate, settle a score, give a Roland for an Oliver, give tit for tat, take an eye for an eye (and a tooth for a tooth), give as good as one gets, *colloq.* get one's own back. **2 b** avenge, revenge, repay, requite, pay back (in kind); (*retaliate against*) give a person a taste of his *or* her own medicine, get even with, strike back at, take revenge on, wreak revenge on, settle a score with, get back at.

retard /ritaárd/ *v.* & *n.* ● *v.tr.* **1** make slow or late. **2** delay the progress, development, arrival, or accomplishment of. ● *n.* **1** retardation. **2** /reétard/ *US sl.* usu. *derog.* a person with a mental handicap. □ **in retard** delayed, in the rear. □□ **retardant** *adj.* & *n.* **retardation** /reétaardáysh'n/ *n.* **retardative** *adj.* **retardatory** *adj.* **retarder** *n.* **retardment** *n.* [F *retarder* f. L *retardare* (as RE-, *tardus* slow)]
■ *v.* slow (down *or* up), hold up *or* back, delay; set back, hinder, impede, keep back, thwart, baulk, block, restrict, hold in check, frustrate, interfere with. ● *n.* **1** see DELAY *n.* 1, 2.

retardate /ritaárdayt/ *adj.* & *n. US* ● *adj.* mentally retarded. ● *n.* a mentally retarded person. [L *retardare*: see RETARD]

retarded /ritaárdid/ *adj.* backward in mental or physical development.

retch /rech, reech/ *v.* & *n.* ● *v.intr.* make a motion of vomiting esp. involuntarily and without effect. ● *n.* such a motion or the sound of it. [var. of (now dial.) *reach* f. OE *hræcan* spit, ON *hrækja* f. Gmc, of imit. orig.]

retd. *abbr.* **1** retired. **2** returned.

rete /reéti/ *n.* (*pl.* **retia** /-tiə, -shiə/) *Anat.* an elaborate network or plexus of blood vessels and nerve cells. [L *rete* net]

reteach /reéteéch/ *v.tr.* (*past* and *past part.* **retaught**) teach again or differently.

retell /reétél/ *v.tr.* (*past* and *past part.* **retold**) tell again or in a different version.

retention /riténsh'n/ *n.* **1 a** the act or an instance of retaining; the state of being retained. **b** the ability to retain things experienced or learned; memory. **2** *Med.* the failure to evacuate urine or another secretion. [ME f. OF *retention* or L *retentio* (as RETAIN)]

retentive /riténtiv/ *adj.* **1** (often foll. by *of*) tending to retain (moisture etc.). **2** (of memory or a person) not forgetful. **3** *Surgery* (of a ligature etc.) serving to keep something in place. □□ **retentively** *adv.* **retentiveness** *n.* [ME f. OF *retentif -ive* or med.L *retentivus* (as RETAIN)]

retexture /reétéks-chər/ *v.tr.* treat (material, a garment, etc.) so as to restore its original texture.

rethink *v.* & *n.* ● *v.tr.* /reéthíngk/ (*past* and *past part.* **rethought**) think about (something) again, esp. with a view to making changes. ● *n.* /reéthingk/ a reassessment; a period of rethinking.

retia *pl.* of RETE.

retiarius /réttiaáriəss/ *n.* (*pl.* **retiarii** /-ri-ī/) a Roman gladiator using a net to trap his opponent. [L f. *rete* net]

reticence /réttis'nss/ *n.* **1** the avoidance of saying all one knows or feels, or of saying more than is necessary; reserve in speech. **2** a disposition to silence; taciturnity. **3** the act or an instance of holding back some fact. **4** abstinence from overemphasis in art. □□ **reticent** *adj.* **reticently** *adv.* [L *reticentia* f. *reticēre* (as RE-, *tacēre* be silent)]

■ **1, 2** see RESERVE *n.* 3. □□ **reticent** quiet, shy, timid, retiring, reserved; taciturn, silent, unresponsive, tight-lipped, unforthcoming.

reticle /réttik'l/ *n.* a network of fine threads or lines in the focal plane of an optical instrument to help accurate observation. [L *reticulum*: see RETICULUM]

reticula *pl.* of RETICULUM.

reticulate *v.* & *adj.* ● *v.tr.* & *intr.* /ritíkyoolayt/ **1** divide or be divided in fact or appearance into a network. **2** arrange or be arranged in small squares or with intersecting lines. ● *adj.* /ritíkyoolət/ reticulated. □□ **reticulately** /ritíkyoolətli/ *adv.* **reticulation** /-láysh'n/ *n.* [L *reticulatus* reticulated (as RETICULUM)]

reticule /réttikyōōl/ *n.* **1** = RETICLE. **2** usu. *hist.* a woman's netted or other bag, esp. with a drawstring, carried or worn to serve the purpose of a pocket. [F *réticule* f. L (as RETICULUM)]

reticulum /ritíkyooləm/ *n.* (*pl.* **reticula** /-lə/) **1** a netlike structure; a fine network, esp. of membranes etc. in living organisms. **2** a ruminant's second stomach. □□ **reticular** *adj.* **reticulose** *adj.* [L, dimin. of *rete* net]

retie /reétī/ *v.tr.* (**retying**) tie again.

retiform /reétiform/ *adj.* netlike, reticulated. [L *rete* net + -FORM]

retina /réttinə/ *n.* (*pl.* **retinas, retinae** /-nee/) a layer at the back of the eyeball sensitive to light, and triggering nerve impulses via the optic nerve to the brain where the visual image is formed. □□ **retinal** *adj.* [ME f. med.L f. L *rete* net]

retinitis /réttinītiss/ *n.* inflammation of the retina.

retinol /réttinol/ *n.* a vitamin found in green and yellow vegetables, egg-yolk, and fish-liver oil, essential for growth and vision in dim light. Also called *vitamin A.* [RETINA + -OL[1]]

retinue /réttinyōō/ *n.* a body of attendants accompanying an important person. [ME f. OF *retenue* fem. past part. of *retenir* RETAIN]

■ entourage, escort, convoy, cortège, company, train, suite.

retiral /ritīrəl/ *n.* esp. *Sc.* retirement from office etc.

retire /ritīr/ *v.* **1 a** *intr.* leave office or employment, esp. because of age (*retire from the army*; *retire on a pension*). **b** *tr.* cause (a person) to retire from work. **2** *intr.* withdraw; go away; retreat. **3** *intr.* seek seclusion or shelter. **4** *intr.* go to bed. **5** *tr.* withdraw (troops). **6** *intr.* & *tr.* *Cricket* (of a batsman) voluntarily end or be compelled to suspend one's innings (*retired hurt*). **7** *tr.* *Econ.* withdraw (a bill or note) from circulation or currency. □ **retire from the world** become a recluse. **retire into oneself** become uncommunicative or unsociable. **retiring age** the age at which most people normally retire from work. □□ **retiree** *n.* esp. *US.* **retirer** *n.* [F *retirer* (as RE-, *tirer* draw)]

■ **1 a** stop *or* give up work(ing), leave one's employment, go on a pension, *colloq.* take a golden handshake. **b** pension off, superannuate, put out to grass *or* pasture, *colloq.* give a person a golden handshake. **2, 3** withdraw, retreat, hibernate, seclude *or* sequester *or* cloister oneself; go off *or* away, take off; rusticate. **4** go to bed *or* sleep, go *or* take to one's bed, withdraw, call it a day, lie down, *colloq.* hit the hay *or* sack, turn in, *Brit. sl.* kip (down). **5** retreat, remove; see also WITHDRAW 3. □ **retire from the world** see *renounce the world*. **retire into oneself** see WITHDRAW 5. □□ **retiree, retirer** see PENSIONER.

retired /ritīrd/ *adj.* **1 a** having retired from employment (*a retired teacher*). **b** relating to a retired person (*received retired pay*). **2** withdrawn from society or observation; secluded (*lives a retired life*). □□ **retiredness** *n.*

retirement /ritīrmənt/ *n.* **1 a** the act or an instance of retiring. **b** the condition of having retired. **2 a** seclusion or privacy. **b** a secluded place. □ **retirement pension** *Brit.* a pension paid by the State to retired people above a certain age.

retiring /ritīring/ *adj.* shy; fond of seclusion. □□ **retiringly** *adv.*

■ shy, bashful, coy, demure, modest, diffident, timid, unassuming, humble, self-effacing, timorous, meek, reticent, reserved, unsocial, unsociable, aloof, removed, standoffish, distant, reclusive, eremitic(al).

retold *past* and *past part.* of RETELL.

retook *past* of RETAKE.

retool /reétōōl/ *v.tr.* equip (a factory etc.) with new tools.

retort[1] /ritórt/ *n.* & *v.* ● *n.* **1** an incisive or witty or angry reply. **2** the turning of a charge or argument against its originator. **3** a retaliation. ● *v.* **1 a** *tr.* say by way of a retort. **b** *intr.* make a retort. **2** *tr.* repay (an insult or attack) in kind. **3** *tr.* (often foll. by *on*, *upon*) return (mischief, a charge, sarcasm, etc.) to its originator. **4** *tr.* (often foll. by *against*) make (an argument) tell against its user. **5** *tr.* (as **retorted** *adj.*) recurved; twisted or bent backwards. [L *retorquēre retort-* (as RE-, *torquēre* twist)]

■ *n.* **1, 3** response, reply, rejoinder, answer; retaliation, a Roland for an Oliver, riposte, quip, sally, gibe, barb, *colloq.* wisecrack, put-down, *sl.* comeback. ● *v.* **1** fling *or* hurl (back), rejoin, return; answer back, counter, respond, answer, reply, *US* come back (with); riposte. **2** avenge, revenge, requite, repay, pay back, retaliate.

retort[2] /ritórt/ *n.* & *v.* ● *n.* **1** a vessel usu. of glass with a long recurved neck used in distilling liquids. **2** a vessel for heating mercury for purification, coal to generate gas, or iron and carbon to make steel. ● *v.tr.* purify (mercury) by heating in a retort. [F *retorte* f. med.L *retorta* fem. past part. of *retorquēre*: see RETORT[1]]

retortion /ritórsh'n/ *n.* **1** the act or an instance of bending back; the condition of being bent back. **2** retaliation by a State on the subjects of another. [RETORT[1], perh. after *contortion*]

retouch /reétúch/ *v.* & *n.* ● *v.tr.* improve or repair (a composition, picture, photographic negative or print, etc.) by fresh touches or alterations. ● *n.* the act or an instance of retouching. □□ **retoucher** *n.* [prob. f. F *retoucher* (as RE-, TOUCH)]

■ *v.* touch up, correct; restore, repair, recondition, refresh, adjust, improve, finish, titivate, put the finishing touches to, add *or* give (the) finishing touches to.

retrace /ritráyss/ *v.tr.* **1** go back over (one's steps etc.). **2** trace back to a source or beginning. **3** recall the course of in one's memory. [F *retracer* (as RE-, TRACE[1])]

retract /ritrákt/ *v.* **1** *tr.* (also *absol.*) withdraw or revoke (a statement or undertaking). **2 a** *tr.* & *intr.* (esp. with ref. to part of the body) draw or be drawn back or in. **b** *tr.* draw (an undercarriage etc.) into the body of an aircraft. □□

retractable *adj.* **retraction** *n.* **retractive** *adj.* [L *retrahere* or (in sense 1) *retractare* (as RE-, *trahere tract-* draw)]
■ **1** take back, withdraw, rescind, revoke, repeal, deny, disavow, recant, renounce, abjure, cancel, forswear, repudiate, disclaim, disown, reverse. **2 a** withdraw, pull *or* draw *or* take back.

retractile /ritráktīl/ *adj.* capable of being retracted. □□ **retractility** /-tílliti/ *n.* [RETRACT, after *contractile*]

retractor /ritráktər/ *n.* **1** a muscle used for retracting. **2** a device for retracting.

retrain /reetráyn/ *v.tr.* & *intr.* train again or further, esp. for new work.

retral /reetrəl/ *adj. Biol.* hinder, posterior; at the back. [RETRO- + -AL]

retranslate /reetranzláyt, reetraanz-/ *v.tr.* translate again, esp. back into the original language. □□ **retranslation** *n.*

retransmit /reetranzmít, reetraanz-/ *v.tr.* (**retransmitted, retransmitting**) transmit (esp. radio signals or broadcast programmes) back again or to a further distance. □□ **retransmission** /-mísh'n/ *n.*

retread *v.* & *n.* ● *v.tr.* /reetréd/ (*past* **retrod**; *past part.* **retrodden**) **1** tread (a path etc.) again. **2** put a fresh tread on (a tyre). ● *n.* /reetred/ a retreaded tyre.

retreat /ritreet/ *v.* & *n.* ● *v.* **1 a** *intr.* (esp. of military forces) go back, retire; relinquish a position. **b** *tr.* cause to retreat; move back. **2** *intr.* (esp. of features) recede; slope back. ● *n.* **1 a** the act or an instance of retreating. **b** *Mil.* a signal for this. **2** withdrawal into privacy or security. **3** a place of shelter or seclusion. **4** a period of seclusion for prayer and meditation. **5** *Mil.* a bugle-call at sunset. **6** a place for the reception of the elderly or others in need of care. [ME f. OF *retret* (n.), *retraiter* (v.) f. L *retrahere*: see RETRACT]
■ *v.* **1 a** decamp, fall *or* go back, give *or* lose ground, flee, take flight, run (away), turn tail, depart, retire, move back, recoil. **b** withdraw, pull *or* draw *or* move back, pull out, retire, evacuate. **2** see RECEDE 1. ● *n.* **1 a** decampment, retirement, withdrawal, falling back, evacuation, rout, flight. **2** retirement, seclusion, withdrawal, rustication, separation, escape, departure. **3** sanctuary, refuge, shelter, den, haven, asylum, hideaway, hiding place, *colloq.* sanctum, hide-out. **6** old people's home, nursing home, home, rest-home.

retrench /ritrénch/ *v.* **1 a** *tr.* reduce the amount of (costs). **b** *intr.* cut down expenses; introduce economies. **2** *tr.* shorten or abridge. □□ **retrenchment** *n.* [obs. F *retrencher* (as RE-, TRENCH)]

retrial /reetrīəl/ *n.* a second or further (judicial) trial.

retribution /rétribyoosh'n/ *n.* requital usu. for evil done; vengeance. □□ **retributive** /ritríbyootiv/ *adj.* **retributory** /ritríbyootəri/ *adj.* [ME f. LL *retributio* (as RE-, *tribuere tribut-* assign)]
■ vengeance, revenge, reprisal, retaliation, requital, recompense, redress, punishment; justice.

retrieve /ritreev/ *v.* & *n.* ● *v.tr.* **1 a** regain possession of. **b** recover by investigation or effort of memory. **2 a** restore to knowledge or recall to mind. **b** obtain (information stored in a computer etc.). **3** (of a dog) find and bring in (killed or wounded game etc.). **4** (foll. by *from*) recover or rescue (esp. from a bad state). **5** restore to a flourishing state; revive. **6** repair or set right (a loss or error etc.) (*managed to retrieve the situation*). ● *n.* the possibility of recovery (*beyond retrieve*). □□ **retrievable** *adj.* **retrieval** *n.* [ME f. OF *retroeve-* stressed stem of *retrover* (as RE-, *trover* find)]
■ *v.* **1 a** reclaim, regain; see also RECOVER *v.* 1. **2 a** recall, remember, call to mind, summon back, recollect. **3** bring *or* get (back *or* in), fetch, come back with. **4** see DELIVER 2. **5** see REVIVE 2. **6** recoup, make up, recover, cover, redeem, get back, regain, be repaid *or* reimbursed for; repair, set right.

retriever /ritreevər/ *n.* **1 a** a dog of a breed used for retrieving game. **b** this breed. **2** a person who retrieves something.

retro /rétrō/ *adj.* & *n. sl.* ● *adj.* reviving or harking back to the past. ● *n.* a retro fashion or style.

retro- /rétrō/ *comb. form* **1** denoting action back or in return (*retroact*; *retroflex*). **2** *Anat.* & *Med.* denoting location behind. [L *retro* backwards]

retroact /rétrō-ákt/ *v.intr.* **1** operate in a backward direction. **2** have a retrospective effect. **3** react. □□ **retroaction** *n.*

retroactive /rétrō-áktiv/ *adj.* (esp. of legislation) having retrospective effect. □□ **retroactively** *adv.* **retroactivity** /-tívviti/ *n.*

retrocede /rétrōseed/ *v.* **1** *intr.* move back; recede. **2** *tr.* cede back again. □□ **retrocedence** *n.* **retrocedent** *adj.* **retrocession** /-sésh'n/ *n.* **retrocessive** /-séssiv/ *adj.* [L *retrocedere* (as RETRO-, *cedere cess-* go)]

retrochoir /rétrōkwīr/ *n.* the part of a cathedral or large church behind the high altar. [med.L *retrochorus* (as RETRO-, CHOIR)]

retrod *past* of RETREAD.

retrodden *past part.* of RETREAD.

retrofit /rétrōfit/ *v.tr.* (**-fitted, -fitting**) modify (machinery, vehicles, etc.) to incorporate changes and developments introduced after manufacture. [RETROACTIVE + REFIT]

retroflex /rétrəfleks/ *adj.* (also **retroflexed**) **1** *Anat.*, *Med.*, & *Bot.* turned backwards. **2** *Phonet.* = CACUMINAL. □□ **retroflexion** /-fléksh'n/ *n.* [L *retroflectere retroflex-* (as RETRO-, *flectere* bend)]

retrogradation /rétrōgrədáysh'n/ *n. Astron.* **1** the apparent backward motion of a planet in the zodiac. **2** the apparent motion of a celestial body from east to west. **3** backward movement of the lunar nodes on the ecliptic. [LL *retrogradatio* (as RETRO-, GRADATION)]

retrograde /rétrəgrayd/ *adj.*, *n.*, & *v.* ● *adj.* **1** directed backwards; retreating. **2** reverting esp. to an inferior state; declining. **3** inverse, reversed (*in retrograde order*). **4** *Astron.* in or showing retrogradation. ● *n.* a degenerate person. ● *v.intr.* **1** move backwards; recede, retire. **2** decline, revert. **3** *Astron.* show retrogradation. □□ **retrogradely** *adv.* [ME f. L *retrogradus* (as RETRO-, *gradus* step, *gradi* walk)]

retrogress /rétrəgréss/ *v.intr.* **1** go back; move backwards. **2** deteriorate. □□ **retrogressive** *adj.* [RETRO-, after PROGRESS *v.*]

retrogression /rétrəgrésh'n/ *n.* **1** backward or reversed movement. **2** a return to a less advanced state; a reversal of development; a decline or deterioration. **3** *Astron.* = RETROGRADATION. □□ **retrogressive** /-gréssiv/ *adj.* **retrogressively** *adv.* [RETRO-, after *progression*]

retroject /rétrōjekt/ *v.tr.* throw back (usu. opp. PROJECT). [RETRO-, after PROJECT *v.*]

retro-rocket /rétrō-rokkit/ *n.* an auxiliary rocket for slowing down a spacecraft etc., e.g. when re-entering the earth's atmosphere.

retrorse /ritrórss/ *adj. Biol.* turned back or down. □□ **retrorsely** *adv.* [L *retrorsus* = *retroversus* (as RETRO-, *versus* past part. of *vertere* turn)]

retrospect /rétrəspekt/ *n.* **1** (foll. by *to*) regard or reference to precedent or authority, or to previous conditions. **2** a survey of past time or events. □ **in retrospect** when looked back on. [RETRO-, after PROSPECT *n.*]
■ **2** review, survey, re-examination, reconsideration, reassessment. □ **in retrospect** with hindsight, on reconsideration.

retrospection /rétrəspéksh'n/ *n.* **1** the action of looking back esp. into the past. **2** an indulgence or engagement in retrospect. [prob. f. *retrospect* (v.) (as RETROSPECT)]

retrospective /rétrəspéktiv/ *adj.* & *n.* ● *adj.* **1** looking back on or dealing with the past. **2** (of an exhibition, recital, etc.) showing an artist's development over his or her lifetime. **3** (of a statute etc.) applying to the past as well as the future; retroactive. **4** (of a view) lying to the rear. ● *n.* a retrospective exhibition, recital, etc. □□ **retrospectively** *adv.*

retrosternal /rétrōstérn'l/ *adj. Anat.* & *Med.* behind the breastbone.

retroussé /rətroōssay/ *adj.* (of the nose) turned up at the tip. [F, past part. of *retrousser* tuck up (as RE-, TRUSS)]

retrovert /rétrōvert/ *v.tr.* **1** turn backwards. **2** *Med.* (as **retroverted** *adj.*) (of the womb) having a backward inclination. ▫▫ **retroversion** /-vérsh'n/ *n.* [LL *retrovertere* (as RETRO-, *vertere vers-* turn)]

retrovirus /rétrōvīrəss/ *n. Biol.* any of a group of RNA viruses which form DNA during the replication of their RNA. [mod.L f. initial letters of *reverse transcriptase* + VIRUS]

retry /réetrī/ *v.tr.* (**-ies, -ied**) try (a defendant or lawsuit) a second or further time. ▫▫ **retrial** *n.*

retsina /retséenə/ *n.* a Greek white wine flavoured with resin. [mod. Gk]

retune /réetyoōn/ *v.tr.* **1** tune (a musical instrument) again or differently. **2** tune (a radio etc.) to a different frequency.

returf /réetúrf/ *v.tr.* provide with new turf.

return /ritúrn/ *v.* & *n.* ● *v.* **1** *intr.* come or go back. **2** *tr.* bring or put or send back to the person or place etc. where originally belonging or obtained (*returned the fish to the river; have you returned my scissors?*). **3** *tr.* pay back or reciprocate; give in response (*decided not to return the compliment*). **4** *tr.* yield (a profit). **5** *tr.* say in reply; retort. **6** *tr.* (in cricket or tennis etc.) hit or send (the ball) back after receiving it. **7** *tr.* state or mention or describe officially, esp. in answer to a writ or formal demand. **8** *tr.* (of an electorate) elect as an MP, government, etc. **9** *tr. Cards* **a** lead (a suit) previously led or bid by a partner. **b** lead (a suit or card) after taking a trick. **10** *tr. Archit.* continue (a wall etc.) in a changed direction, esp. at right angles. ● *n.* **1** the act or an instance of coming or going back. **2 a** the act or an instance of giving or sending or putting or paying back. **b** a thing given or sent back. **3** (in full **return ticket**) esp. *Brit.* a ticket for a journey to a place and back to the starting-point. **4** (in *sing.* or *pl.*) **a** the proceeds or profit of an undertaking. **b** the acquisition of these. **5** a formal report or statement compiled or submitted by order (*an income-tax return*). **6** (in full **return match** or **game**) a second match etc. between the same opponents. **7** *Electr.* a conductor bringing a current back to its source. **8** *Brit.* a sheriff's report on a writ. **9** esp. *Brit.* **a** a person's election as an MP etc. **b** a returning officer's announcement of this. **10** *Archit.* a part receding from the line of the front, e.g. the side of a house or of a window-opening. ▫ **by return** (**of post**) by the next available post in the return direction. **in return** as an exchange or reciprocal action. **many happy returns** (**of the day**) a greeting on a birthday. **return crease** *Cricket* each of two lines joining the popping-crease and bowling-crease at right angles to the bowling-crease and extending beyond it. **returning officer** *Brit.* an official conducting an election in a constituency and announcing the results. **return thanks** express thanks esp. in a grace at meals or in response to a toast or condolence. ▫▫ **returnable** *adj.* **returner** *n.* **returnless** *adj.* [ME f. OF *returner* (as RE-, TURN)]

■ *v.* **1** come back, reappear, resurface, turn up again, make *or* put in an appearance again, *colloq.* show up again; recur, reoccur, crop up again, pop up again; go back, revert, turn back. **2** replace, restore, put *or* give *or* bring *or* carry *or* take back. **3** pay back, reciprocate, requite, repay. **4** earn, gain; see also YIELD *v.* 1. **5** see REPLY *v.* 2. **7** deliver, give, turn in, state, offer, proffer, report. **8** see VOTE *v.* 1. ● *n.* **1** home-coming; recurrence, reappearance, repetition, renewal, recrudescence, resurfacing, re-emergence; comeback. **2 a** replacement, replacing, restoration, restoring, restitution, reciprocation, repayment, recompense, reimbursement, compensation, payment, reparation, indemnity, indemnification, consideration, amends, redress, requital. **4 a** yield, earnings, profit, gain, income, revenue, proceeds, takings. **5** report, statement, record. **9** see ELECTION 1. ▫ **in return** in exchange, again; see also BACK *adv.* 2b.

returnee /ritturnée/ *n.* a person who returns home from abroad, esp. after war service.

retuse /rityoōss/ *adj.* esp. *Bot.* having a broad end with a central depression. [L *retundere retus-* (as RE-, *tundere* beat)]

retying *pres. part.* of RETIE.

retype /réetīp/ *v.tr.* type again, esp. to correct errors.

reunify /rée-yoōnifī/ *v.tr.* (**-ies, -ied**) restore (esp. separated territories) to a political unity. ▫▫ **reunification** /-fikáysh'n/ *n.*

reunion /ree-yoōnyən/ *n.* **1 a** the act or an instance of reuniting. **b** the condition of being reunited. **2** a social gathering esp. of people formerly associated. [F *réunion* or AL *reunio* f. L *reunire* unite (as RE-, UNION)]

reunite /rée-yoonīt/ *v.tr.* & *intr.* bring or come back together.

reupholster /rée-uphṓlstər/ *v.tr.* upholster anew. ▫▫ **reupholstery** *n.*

reuse *v.* & *n.* ● *v.tr.* /rée-yoōz/ use again or more than once. ● *n.* /rée-yoōss/ a second or further use. ▫▫ **reusable** /-yoōzəb'l/ *adj.*

reutilize /rée-yoōtilīz/ *v.tr.* (also **-ise**) utilize again or for a different purpose. ▫▫ **reutilization** /-záysh'n/ *n.*

Rev. *abbr.* **1** Reverend. **2** Revelation (New Testament).

rev /rev/ *n.* & *v. colloq.* ● *n.* (in *pl.*) the number of revolutions of an engine per minute (*running at 3,000 revs*). ● *v.* (**revved, revving**) **1** *intr.* (of an engine) revolve; turn over. **2** *tr.* (also *absol.*; often foll. by *up*) cause (an engine) to run quickly. ▫ **rev counter** = *revolution counter*. [abbr.]

revaccinate /réeváksinayt/ *v.tr.* vaccinate again. ▫▫ **revaccination** /-náysh'n/ *n.*

revalue /réeválуoō/ *v.tr.* (**revalues, revalued, revaluing**) *Econ.* give a different value to, esp. give a higher value to, (a currency) in relation to other currencies or gold (opp. DEVALUE). ▫▫ **revaluation** /-vályoo-áysh'n/ *n.*

revamp /réevámp/ *v.tr.* **1** renovate, revise, improve. **2** patch up. [RE- + VAMP[1]]

■ overhaul, redo, recondition, renovate, repair, fix, refit, refurbish, restore, *colloq.* do up; revise, improve; see also REPAIR[1] *v.*

revanchism /ribánchiz'm/ *n. Polit.* a policy of seeking to retaliate, esp. to recover lost territory. ▫▫ **revanchist** *n.* & *adj.* [F *revanche* (as REVENGE)]

revarnish /réevaárnish/ *v.tr.* varnish again.

Revd *abbr.* Reverend.

reveal[1] /rivéel/ *v.tr.* **1** display or show; allow to appear. **2** (often as **revealing** *adj.*) disclose, divulge, betray (*revealed his plans; a revealing remark*). **3** *tr.* (in *refl.* or *passive*) come to sight or knowledge. **4** *Relig.* (esp. of God) make known by inspiration or supernatural means. ▫ **revealed religion** a religion based on revelation (opp. *natural religion*). ▫▫ **revealable** *adj.* **revealer** *n.* **revealingly** *adv.* [ME f. OF *reveler* or L *revelare* (as RE-, *velum* veil)]

■ **1** expose, display, show, present, exhibit, unveil, uncover, lay bare. **2** divulge, disclose, make known, communicate, give vent to, air, ventilate, let out, give away, let slip, betray, leak, *colloq.* let on.

reveal[2] /rivéel/ *n.* an internal side surface of an opening or recess, esp. of a doorway or window-aperture. [obs. *revale* (v.) lower f. OF *revaler* f. *avaler* (as RE-, VAIL)]

reveille /riválli, -vélli/ *n.* a military waking-signal sounded in the morning on a bugle or drums etc. [F *réveillez* imper. pl. of *réveiller* awaken (as RE-, *veiller* f. L *vigilare* keep watch)]

revel /révv'l/ *v.* & *n.* ● *v.* (**revelled, revelling;** *US* **reveled, reveling**) **1** *intr.* have a good time; be extravagantly festive. **2** *intr.* (foll. by *in*) take keen delight in. **3** *tr.* (foll. by *away*) throw away (money or time) in revelry. ● *n.* (in *sing.* or *pl.*) the act or an instance of revelling. ▫▫ **reveller** *n.* **revelry** *n.* (*pl.* **-ies**). [ME f. OF *reveler* riot f. L *rebellare* REBEL *v.*]

■ *v.* **1** make merry, celebrate, rollick, roister, roit, cut loose, (go on a) spree, *colloq.* live it up, whoop it up, make whoopee, paint the town red, party, push the boat out, have a rave *or* rave-up. **2** (*revel in*) (take) delight in, take pleasure in, rejoice in, luxuriate in, bask in, wallow in, lap up, glory in, savour, relish. ● *n.* party, celebration, debauch, romp, fling, carnival, jamboree, bacchanal, saturnalia, *colloq.* spree, *sl.* ball; festival, fête, gala. □□ **revelry** merrymaking, fun, revelling, gaiety, festivity, jollity, mirth, celebrations, high jinks, *colloq.* spree, rave, rave-up, *sl.* ball.

revelation /révvəláysh'n/ *n.* **1 a** the act or an instance of revealing, esp. the supposed disclosure of knowledge to humankind by a divine or supernatural agency. **b** knowledge disclosed in this way. **2** a striking disclosure (*it was a revelation to me*). **3** (**Revelation** or *colloq.* **Revelations**) (in full **the Revelation of St John the Divine**) the last book of the New Testament, describing visions of heaven. □□ **revelational** *adj.* [ME f. OF *revelation* or LL *revelatio* (as REVEAL[1])]

■ **2** admission, confession; declaration, announcement, pronouncement, proclamation, statement; leak, discovery, unveiling, disclosure, exposé.

revelationist /révvəláyshənist/ *n.* a believer in divine revelation.

revelatory /révvəláytəri/ *adj.* serving to reveal, esp. something significant. [L *revelare*: see REVEAL[1]]

revenant /révvənənt/ *n.* a person who has returned, esp. supposedly from the dead. [F, pres. part. of *revenir*: see REVENUE]

revenge /rivénj/ *n.* & *v.* ● *n.* **1** retaliation for an offence or injury. **2** an act of retaliation. **3** the desire for this; a vindictive feeling. **4** (in games) a chance to win after an earlier defeat. ● *v.* **1** *tr.* (in *refl.* or *passive*; often foll. by *on*, *upon*) inflict retaliation for an offence. **2** *tr.* take revenge for (an offence). **3** *tr.* avenge (a person). **4** *intr.* take vengeance. □□ **revenger** *n.* [ME f. OF *revenger*, *revencher* f. LL *revindicare* (as RE-, *vindicare* lay claim to)]

■ *n.* **1** vengeance, retaliation, reprisal, retribution, repayment, satisfaction. **2** see BACKLASH 1. **3** vengeance, spitefulness, vindictiveness; see also RANCOUR. ● *v.* **1** settle a score *or* an old score with, get even with, punish, *colloq.* get. **2** avenge, get even for, take revenge for, make reprisal for, right, exact retribution *or* payment *or* repayment for. **4** settle a score *or* an old score, get even, give a Roland for an Oliver, give tit for tat, take an eye for an eye (and a tooth for a tooth), give a person a taste of his *or* her own medicine, *colloq.* get one's own back, give a person his *or* her comeuppance.

revengeful /rivénjfōōl/ *adj.* eager for revenge. □□ **revengefully** *adv.* **revengefulness** *n.*

revenue /révvənyōō/ *n.* **1 a** income, esp. of a large amount, from any source. **b** (in *pl.*) items constituting this. **2** a State's annual income from which public expenses are met. **3** the department of the civil service collecting this. □ **revenue tax** a tax imposed to raise revenue, rather than to affect trade. [ME f. OF *revenu(e)* past part. of *revenir* f. L *revenire* return (as RE-, *venire* come)]

■ **1** income, proceeds, receipts, return(s), yield, profit(s), gain, gate, gate-money, *esp. US* take.

reverb /rivérb, réeverb/ *n. Mus. colloq.* **1** reverberation. **2** a device to produce this. [abbr.]

reverberate /rivérbərayt/ *v.* **1 a** *intr.* (of sound, light, or heat) be returned or echoed or reflected repeatedly. **b** *tr.* return (a sound etc.) in this way. **2** *intr.* (of a story, rumour, etc.) be heard much or repeatedly. □ **reverberating furnace** a furnace constructed to throw heat back on to the substance exposed to it. □□ **reverberant** *adj.* **reverberantly** *adv.* **reverberation** /-ráysh'n/ *n.* **reverberative** /-rətiv/ *adj.* **reverberator** *n.* **reverberatory** /-rətəri/ *adj.* [L *reverberare* (as RE-, *verberare* lash f. *verbera* (pl.) scourge)]

revere /riveér/ *v.tr.* hold in deep and usu. affectionate or religious respect; venerate. [F *révérer* or L *reverēri* (as RE-, *verēri* fear)]

■ adore, reverence, venerate, glorify, esteem, admire, respect, honour, worship, idolize, enshrine, sanctify.

reverence /révvərənss/ *n.* & *v.* ● *n.* **1 a** the act of revering or the state of being revered (*hold in reverence*; *feel reverence for*). **b** the capacity for revering (*lacks reverence*). **2** *archaic* a gesture showing that one reveres; a bow or curtsy. **3** (**Reverence**) a title used of or to some members of the clergy. ● *v.tr.* regard or treat with reverence. [ME f. OF f. L *reverentia* (as REVERE)]

■ *n.* **1 a** honour, respect, esteem, admiration, veneration, idolization, awe; glorification, beatification, sanctification, worship, adoration, homage, obeisance, deference. ● *v.* see REVERE.

reverend /révvərənd/ *adj.* & *n.* ● *adj.* (esp. as the title of a clergyman) deserving reverence. ● *n. colloq.* a clergyman. □ **Most Reverend** the title of an archbishop or an Irish Roman Catholic bishop. **Reverend Mother** the title of the Mother Superior of a convent. **Right Reverend** the title of a bishop. **Very Reverend** the title of a dean etc. [ME f. OF *reverend* or L *reverendus* gerundive of *reverēri*: see REVERE]

reverent /révvərənt/ *adj.* feeling or showing reverence. □□ **reverently** *adv.* [ME f. L *reverens* (as REVERE)]

reverential /révvərénsh'l/ *n.* of the nature of, due to, or characterized by reverence. □□ **reverentially** *adv.* [med.L *reverentialis* (as REVERE)]

reverie /révvəri/ *n.* **1** a fit of abstracted musing (*was lost in a reverie*). **2** *archaic* a fantastic notion or theory; a delusion. **3** *Mus.* an instrumental piece suggesting a dreamy or musing state. [obs. F *resverie* f. OF *reverie* rejoicing, revelry f. *rever* be delirious, of unkn. orig.]

■ **1** day-dream, brown study; see also FANTASY *n.* 2.

revers /riveér/ *n.* (*pl.* same /-veérz/) **1** the turned-back edge of a garment revealing the under-surface. **2** the material on this surface. [F, = REVERSE]

reverse /rivérss/ *v.*, *adj.*, & *n.* ● *v.* **1** *tr.* turn the other way round or up or inside out. **2** *tr.* change to the opposite character or effect (*reversed the decision*). **3** *intr.* & *tr.* travel or cause to travel backwards. **4** *tr.* make (an engine etc.) work in a contrary direction. **5** *tr.* revoke or annul (a decree, act, etc.). **6** *intr.* (of a dancer, esp. in a waltz) revolve in the opposite direction. ● *adj.* **1** placed or turned in an opposite direction or position. **2** opposite or contrary in character or order; inverted. ● *n.* **1** the opposite or contrary (*the reverse is the case*; *is the reverse of the truth*). **2** the contrary of the usual manner. **3** an occurrence of misfortune; a disaster, esp. a defeat in battle (*suffered a reverse*). **4** reverse gear or motion. **5** the reverse side of something. **6 a** the side of a coin or medal etc. bearing the secondary design. **b** this design (cf. OBVERSE). **7** the verso of a leaf. □ **reverse arms** hold a rifle with the butt upwards. **reverse the charges** *Brit.* make the recipient of a telephone call responsible for payment. **reverse gear** a gear used to make a vehicle etc. travel backwards. **reversing light** a white light at the rear of a vehicle operated when the vehicle is in reverse gear. **reverse Polish notation** see *Polish notation*. **reverse strata** *Geol.* a fault in which the overlying side of a mass of rock is displaced upward in relation to the underlying side. □□ **reversal** *n.* **reversely** *adv.* **reverser** *n.* **reversible** *adj.* **reversibility** /-vérsəbílliti/ *n.* **reversibly** *adv.* [ME f. OF *revers* (n.), *reverser* (v.), f. L *revertere revers-* (as RE-, *vertere* turn)]

■ *v.* **1** invert, overturn, turn upside down, turn over, up-end; transpose, switch. **2, 5** overturn, overthrow, quash, override, annul, nullify, revoke, annul, negate, declare null and void, disaffirm, invalidate, cancel, repeal, rescind, overrule, countermand, undo, *Law* vacate; renounce, recant, take back. **3** back up, go backwards *or* backward, backtrack, *Naut.* make sternway; move backwards *or* backward. ● *adj.* **1** opposite, contrary, inverse, converse; inverted, upside down, mirror, reversed, backward. ● *n.* **1** opposite, contrary, converse, antithesis. **3** misfortune, reversal, vicissitude, set-back, disappointment, mishap, misadventure, disaster, catastrophe, débâcle, rout, defeat, *colloq.* wash-out. **5** back, rear, wrong side, verso, underside, underneath; B-side, *colloq.* flip side. □□ **reversal** turn-about, turn-round, U-turn, change, volte-face, switch, about-turn, about-face; annulment, nullification, cancellation, revocation, repeal, rescission; see also REVERSE *n.* 3 above.

reversion /rivérsh'n/ *n.* **1 a** the legal right (esp. of the original owner, or his or her heirs) to possess or succeed to property on the death of the present possessor. **b** property to which a person has such a right. **2** *Biol.* a return to ancestral type. **3** a return to a previous state, habit, etc. **4** a sum payable on a person's death, esp. by way of life insurance. ▫▫ **reversional** *adj.* **reversionary** *adj.* [ME f. OF *reversion* or L *reversio* (as REVERSE)]

revert /rivért/ *v.* **1** *intr.* (foll. by *to*) return to a former state, practice, opinion, etc. **2** *intr.* (of property, an office, etc.) return by reversion. **3** *intr.* fall back into a wild state. **4** *tr.* turn (one's eyes or steps) back. ▫▫ **reverter** *n.* (in sense 2). [ME f. OF *revertir* or L *revertere* (as REVERSE)]

■ **1** (*revert to*) return to, come *or* go back to, take *or* pick up again, lapse (back) into, backslide into, relapse into.

revertible /rivértib'l/ *adj.* (of property) subject to reversion.

revet /rivét/ *v.tr.* (**revetted**, **revetting**) face (a rampart, wall, etc.) with masonry, esp. in fortification. [F *revêtir* f. OF *revestir* f. LL *revestire* (as RE-, *vestire* clothe f. *vestis*)]

revetment /rivétmənt/ *n.* a retaining wall or facing. [F *revêtement* (as REVET)]

review /rivyóo/ *n.* & *v.* ● *n.* **1** a general survey or assessment of a subject or thing. **2** a retrospect or survey of the past. **3** revision or reconsideration (*is under review*). **4** a display and formal inspection of troops etc. **5** a published account or criticism of a book, play, etc. **6** a periodical publication with critical articles on current events, the arts, etc. **7** a second view. ● *v.tr.* **1** survey or look back on. **2** reconsider or revise. **3** hold a review of (troops etc.). **4** write a review of (a book, play, etc.). **5** view again. ▫ **court of review** a court before which sentences etc. come for revision. ▫▫ **reviewable** *adj.* **reviewal** *n.* **reviewer** *n.* [obs. F *reveue* f. *revoir* (as RE-, *voir* see)]

■ *n.* **1** survey, assessment, examination, study, inspection, analysis, consideration, scrutiny. **3** re-examination, reconsideration, reassessment, revaluation, revision, reappraisal. **4** inspection, parade, procession, array, march past; fly-past, *US* flyover. **5** criticism, critique, review article, *compte rendu*, assessment, judgement, evaluation, commentary, study, comment, notice. **6** see PERIODICAL *n.* ● *v.* **1** survey, examine, regard, look at *or* over, study, look back on, consider, weigh, inspect, scrutinize. **2, 5** re-examine, revise, go over again, look at *or* over again; reassess, reconsider. **4** criticize, critique, give one's opinion of, comment on *or* upon, discuss, judge.

revile /rivīl/ *v.* **1** *tr.* abuse; criticize abusively. **2** *intr.* talk abusively; rail. ▫▫ **revilement** *n.* **reviler** *n.* **reviling** *n.* [ME f. OF *reviler* (as RE-, VILE)]

revise /rivīz/ *v.* & *n.* ● *v.tr.* **1** examine or re-examine and improve or amend (esp. written or printed matter). **2** consider and alter (an opinion etc.). **3** (also *absol.*) *Brit.* read again (work learnt or done) to improve one's knowledge, esp. for an examination. ● *n. Printing* a proof-sheet including corrections made in an earlier proof. ▫ **Revised Standard Version** a revision in 1946–52 of the Authorized Version of the Bible. **Revised Version** a revision in 1881–5 of the Authorized Version of the Bible. ▫▫ **revisable** *adj.* **revisal** *n.* **reviser** *n.* **revisory** *adj.* [F *réviser* look at, or L *revisere* (as RE-, *visere* intensive of *vidēre vis-* see)]

■ *v.* **1** edit, emend, improve, correct; revamp, rework, re-examine, overhaul, update; rewrite, reinterpret. **2** alter, change, amend, modify, adjust; see also *think better of*. **3** go over again; reread, practise, *archaic* con, *Brit. colloq.* swot up on, *Brit. sl.* mug up on; see also STUDY *v.* 2, 4.

revision /rivízh'n/ *n.* **1** the act or an instance of revising; the process of being revised. **2** a revised edition or form. ▫▫ **revisionary** *adj.* [OF *revision* or LL *revisio* (as REVISE)]

■ **1** editing, revising, redaction, emendation, improvement, correction, modification, revamping, reworking, overhaul, overhauling, updating, update; rewriting, reinterpretation. **2** rewrite, revised *or* new edition, revised *or* new version.

revisionism /rivízhəniz'm/ *n.* often *derog.* a policy of revision or modification, esp. of Marxism on evolutionary socialist (rather than revolutionary) or pluralist principles. ▫▫ **revisionist** *n.* & *adj.*

revisit /reevízzit/ *v.tr.* (**revisited**, **revisiting**) visit again.

revitalize /reevītəlīz/ *v.tr.* (also **-ise**) imbue with new life and vitality. ▫▫ **revitalization** /-záysh'n/ *n.*

revival /rivīv'l/ *n.* **1** the act or an instance of reviving; the process of being revived. **2** a new production of an old play etc. **3** a revived use of an old practice, custom, etc. **4 a** a reawakening of religious fervour. **b** a series of evangelistic meetings to promote this. **5** restoration to bodily or mental vigour or to life or consciousness.

■ **1, 3** resurrection, resuscitation, renewal, restoration, return, reanimation, revitalization, resurfacing; comeback. **4 a** rebirth, renascence, reanimation, resurgence, awakening, reawakening. **5** recovery, improvement, advance; increase, upsurge, upturn, upswing, rise, escalation, *colloq.* boost.

revivalism /rivīvəliz'm/ *n.* belief in or the promotion of a revival, esp. of religious fervour. ▫▫ **revivalist** *n.* **revivalistic** /-lístik/ *adj.*

revive /rivīv/ *v.intr.* & *tr.* **1** come or bring back to consciousness or life or strength. **2** come or bring back to existence, use, notice, etc. ▫▫ **revivable** *adj.* [ME f. OF *revivre* or LL *revivere* (as RE-, L *vivere* live)]

■ **1** (re)awaken, wake (up), waken; come (a)round, recover, gain consciousness; bring (a)round, resuscitate; revivify, revitalize. **2** reawaken, resume, reopen; stir up again, renew, bring back, reactivate, resurrect, recall, re-establish, revitalize, breathe new life into, reinvigorate.

reviver /rivīvər/ *n.* **1** a person or thing that revives. **2** *colloq.* a stimulating drink. **3** a preparation used for restoring faded colours etc.

revivify /rivívvifī/ *v.tr.* (**-ies**, **-ied**) restore to animation, activity, vigour, or life. ▫▫ **revivification** /-fikáysh'n/ *n.* [F *revivifier* or LL *revivificare* (as RE-, VIVIFY)]

revoke /rivṓk/ *v.* & *n.* ● *v.* **1** *tr.* rescind, withdraw, or cancel (a decree or promise etc.). **2** *intr. Cards* fail to follow suit when able to do so. ● *n. Cards* the act of revoking. ▫▫ **revocable** /révvəkəb'l/ *adj.* **revocability** /révvəkəbílliti/ *n.* **revocation** /révvəkáysh'n/ *n.* **revocatory** /révvəkətəri/ *adj.* **revoker** *n.* [ME f. OF *revoquer* or L *revocare* (as RE-, *vocare* call)]

■ *v.* **1** cancel, invalidate, annul, declare null and void, void, nullify, negate, rescind, repeal, recall, quash, veto, abrogate, abolish; withdraw, take back, retract.

revolt /rivṓlt/ *v.* & *n.* ● *v.* **1** *intr.* **a** rise in rebellion against authority. **b** (as **revolted** *adj.*) having revolted. **2 a** *tr.* (often in *passive*) affect with strong disgust; nauseate (*was revolted by the thought of it*). **b** *intr.* (often foll. by *at*, *against*) feel strong disgust. ● *n.* **1** an act of rebelling. **2** a state of insurrection (*in revolt*). **3** a sense of loathing. **4** a mood of protest or defiance. [F *révolter* f. It. *rivoltare* ult. f. L *revolvere* (as REVOLVE)]

■ *v.* **1 a** rebel, rise (up), mutiny, take up arms, kick over the traces; protest. **2 a** repel, offend, disgust, repulse, nauseate, sicken, shock, horrify. ● *n.* **1** rebellion, revolution, uprising, mutiny, insurrection, *coup d'état*, putsch, take-over.

revolting /rivṓlting/ *adj.* disgusting, horrible. ▫▫ **revoltingly** *adv.*

■ sickening, nauseating, nauseous, loathsome, abhorrent, nasty, obnoxious, repulsive, offensive, objectionable, disagreeable, unpleasant, repellent, disgusting, foul, horrid, horrible, vile, abominable, appalling, *Brit.* off-putting; stomach-turning, vomit-provoking, *colloq.* sick-making, beastly, icky, *sl.* gross, rotten, yucky.

revolute /révvəloot/ *adj. Bot.* etc. having a rolled-back edge. [L *revolutus* past part. of *revolvere*: see REVOLVE]

revolution /révvəlo͞osh'n/ *n.* **1 a** the forcible overthrow of a government or social order, in favour of a new system. **b** (in Marxism) the replacement of one ruling class by another; the class struggle which is expected to lead to political change and the triumph of communism. **2** any fundamental change or reversal of conditions. **3** the act or an instance of revolving. **4 a** motion in orbit or a circular course or round an axis or centre; rotation. **b** the single completion of an orbit or rotation. **c** the time taken for this. **5** a cyclic recurrence. □ **revolution counter** a device for indicating the number or rate of revolutions of an engine etc. □□ **revolutionism** *n.* **revolutionist** *n.* [ME f. OF *revolution* or LL *revolutio* (as REVOLVE)]
- **1 a** revolt, rebellion, coup, mutiny, *coup d'état*, uprising, insurgency, insurrection, putsch, take-over, overthrow; counter-revolution. **2** upheaval, cataclysm, transformation, (radical *or* major) change, sea change, reversal, metamorphosis. **3, 4** rotation, turn, gyration; wheel, whirl, pirouette, spin; orbit, circle, circuit, lap, round. **5** cycle, phase, period; see also TURN *n.* 1.

revolutionary /révvəlo͞oshənəri, -shənri/ *adj.* & *n.* ● *adj.* **1** involving great and often violent change or innovation. **2** of or causing political revolution. **3** (**Revolutionary**) of or relating to a particular revolution, esp. the War of American Independence. ● *n.* (*pl.* **-ies**) an instigator or supporter of political revolution.
- *adj.* **1** novel, innovative, creative, new, different, original, avant-garde. **2** mutinous, rebellious, insurgent, insurrectionist, insurrectionary, radical, seditious, subversive; rebel. ● *n.* rebel, mutineer, insurgent, insurrectionist, insurrectionary, revolutionist, sansculotte, radical, anarchist, extremist, Jacobin.

revolutionize /révvəlo͞oshənīz/ *v.tr.* (also **-ise**) introduce fundamental change to.

revolve /rivólv/ *v.* **1** *intr.* & *tr.* turn or cause to turn round, esp. on an axis; rotate. **2** *intr.* move in a circular orbit. **3** *tr.* ponder (a problem etc.) in the mind. □ **revolve on** depend on. **revolving credit** credit that is automatically renewed as debts are paid off. **revolving door** a door with usu. four partitions turning round a central axis. □□ **revolvable** *adj.* [ME f. L *revolvere* (as RE-, *volvere* roll)]
- **1, 2** spin (round), turn (round), whirl (round), twirl (round), swivel (round); pivot, rotate, gyrate, reel, wheel, go (a)round, circle, orbit, cycle. **3** turn over (in one's mind), ponder, weigh, consider, meditate upon *or* on, think about, reflect upon *or* on, ruminate over *or* on, chew over, contemplate. □ **revolve on** turn *or* depend *or* pivot *or* rely on.

revolver /rivólvər/ *n.* a pistol with revolving chambers enabling several shots to be fired without reloading.
- pistol, gun, firearm, handgun, *esp. US colloq.* shooting-iron, *sl.* gat, *US sl.* rod, roscoe; (*revolvers*) side-arms.

revue /rivyo͞o/ *n.* a theatrical entertainment of a series of short usu. satirical sketches and songs. [F, = REVIEW *n.*]

revulsion /rivúlsh'n/ *n.* **1** abhorrence; a sense of loathing. **2** a sudden violent change of feeling. **3** a sudden reaction in taste, fortune, trade, etc. **4** *Med.* counterirritation; the treatment of one disordered organ etc. by acting upon another. [F *revulsion* or L *revulsio* (as RE-, *vellere vuls-* pull)]
- **1** loathing, detestation, disgust, repugnance, abomination, abhorrence, aversion, hatred, antipathy, odium.

revulsive /rivúlsiv/ *adj.* & *n. Med.* ● *adj.* producing revulsion. ● *n.* a revulsive substance.

reward /riwáwrd/ *n.* & *v.* ● *n.* **1 a** a return or recompense for service or merit. **b** requital for good or evil; retribution. **2** a sum offered for the detection of a criminal, the restoration of lost property, etc. ● *v.tr.* give a reward to (a person) or for (a service etc.). □□ **rewardless** *adj.* [ME f. AF, ONF *reward* = OF *reguard* REGARD]
- *n.* **1 a** prize, award, tribute, honour, award, return, recompense, compensation, payment, pay, requital, *poet.* guerdon. **b** requital, retribution; (just) deserts. **2** see BOUNTY 2. ● *v.* recompense, compensate, pay, repay, remunerate, requite.

rewarding /riwáwrding/ *adj.* (of an activity etc.) well worth doing; providing satisfaction. □□ **rewardingly** *adv.*
- satisfying, gratifying, worthwhile, enriching, fruitful, profitable, advantageous, productive, gainful.

rewarewa /ráywəráywə/ *n.* a tall red-flowered tree, *Knightia excelsa*, of New Zealand. [Maori]

rewash /reéwósh/ *v.tr.* wash again.

reweigh /reéwáy/ *v.tr.* weigh again.

rewind /reéwīnd/ *v.tr.* (*past* and *past part.* **rewound**) wind (a film or tape etc.) back to the beginning. □□ **rewinder** *n.*

rewire /reéwīr/ *v.tr.* provide (a building etc.) with new wiring. □□ **rewirable** *adj.*

reword /reéwúrd/ *v.tr.* change the wording of.
- paraphrase, rephrase, put into different words *or* terms, put another way, express differently, rewrite, reformulate.

rework /reéwúrk/ *v.tr.* revise; refashion, remake.

rewound *past* and *past part.* of REWIND.

rewrap /reé-ráp/ *v.tr.* (**rewrapped**, **rewrapping**) wrap again or differently.

rewrite *v.* & *n.* ● *v.tr.* /reé-rīt/ (*past* **rewrote**; *past part.* **rewritten**) write again or differently. ● *n.* /reé-rīt/ **1** the act or an instance of rewriting. **2** a thing rewritten.

Rex /reks/ *n.* the reigning king (following a name or in the titles of lawsuits, e.g. *Rex v. Jones* the Crown versus Jones). [L]

Rexine /rékseen/ *n. propr.* an artificial leather used in upholstery, bookbinding, etc. [20th c.: orig. unkn.]

Reynard /rénnaard, ráy-/ *n.* a fox (esp. as a proper name in stories). [ME f. OF *Renart* name of a fox in the *Roman de Renart*]

Reynolds number /rénn'ldz/ *n. Physics* a quantity indicating the degree of turbulence of flow past an obstacle etc. [O. *Reynolds*, Engl. physicist d. 1912]

Rf *symb. Chem.* the element rutherfordium.

r.f. *abbr.* radio frequency.

RFA *abbr.* (in the UK) Royal Fleet Auxiliary.

RFC *abbr.* **1** Rugby Football Club. **2** *hist.* Royal Flying Corps.

RGS *abbr.* Royal Geographical Society.

Rh[1] *symb. Chem.* the element rhodium.

Rh[2] *abbr.* **1** Rhesus. **2** Rhesus factor.

r.h. *abbr.* right hand.

RHA *abbr.* (in the UK) Royal Horse Artillery.

rhabdomancy /rábdəmansi/ *n.* the use of a divining-rod, esp. for discovering subterranean water or mineral ore. [Gk *rhabdomanteia* f. *rhabdos* rod: see -MANCY]

Rhadamanthine /ráddəmánthīn/ *adj.* stern and incorruptible in judgement. [*Rhadamanthus* f. L f. Gk *Rhadamanthos*, name of a judge in the underworld]

Rhaeto-Romance /reétō-rōmánss/ *adj.* & *n.* (also **Rhaeto-Romanic** /-mánnik/) ● *adj.* of or in any of the Romance dialects of SE Switzerland and Tyrol, esp. Romansh and Ladin. ● *n.* any of these dialects. [L *Rhaetus* of Rhaetia in the Alps + ROMANIC]

rhapsode /rápsōd/ *n.* a reciter of epic poems, esp. of Homer in ancient Greece. [Gk *rhapsōidos* f. *rhaptō* stitch + *ōidē* song, ODE]

rhapsodist /rápsədist/ *n.* **1** a person who rhapsodizes. **2** = RHAPSODE.

rhapsodize /rápsədīz/ *v.intr.* (also **-ise**) talk or write rhapsodies.

rhapsody /rápsədi/ *n.* (*pl.* **-ies**) **1** an enthusiastic, ecstatic, or extravagant utterance or composition. **2** *Mus.* a piece of music in one extended movement, usu. emotional in character. **3** *Gk Antiq.* an epic poem, or part of it, of a length for one recitation. □□ **rhapsodic** /rapsóddik/ *adj.*

rhapsodical /rapsóddik'l/ *adj.* (in senses 1, 2). [L *rhapsodia* f. Gk *rhapsōidia* (as RHAPSODE)]
■ □□ **rhapsodic, rhapsodical** ecstatic, enthusiastic, elated, overjoyed, effusive, rapturous, thrilled, blissful, transported, orgasmic, intoxicated, euphoric, delighted; walking on air, happy as a sandboy, in seventh heaven, *colloq.* on top of the world.

rhatany /ráttəni/ *n.* (*pl.* **-ies**) **1** either of two American shrubs, *Krameria trianda* and *K. argentea*, having an astringent root when dried. **2** the root of either of these. [mod.L *rhatania* f. Port. *ratanha*, Sp. *ratania*, f. Quechua *rataña*]

rhea /réeə/ *n.* any of several S. American flightless birds of the family Rheidae, like but smaller than an ostrich. [mod.L genus name f. L f. Gk *Rhea* mother of Zeus]

rhebok var. of REEBOK.

Rhenish /réenish, rén-/ *adj.* & *n.* ● *adj.* of the Rhine and the regions adjoining it. ● *n.* wine from this area. [ME *rynis, rynisch* etc., f. AF *reneis*, OF *r(a)inois* f. L *Rhenanus* f. *Rhenus* Rhine]

rhenium /réeniəm/ *n. Chem.* a rare metallic element of the manganese group, occurring naturally in molybdenum ores and used in the manufacture of superconducting alloys. ¶ Symb.: **Re**. [mod.L f. L *Rhenus* Rhine]

rheology /ree-ólləji/ *n.* the science dealing with the flow and deformation of matter. □□ **rheological** /réeəlójik'l/ *adj.* **rheologist** *n.* [Gk *rheos* stream + -LOGY]

rheostat /réeəstat/ *n. Electr.* an instrument used to control a current by varying the resistance. □□ **rheostatic** /-státtik/ *adj.* [Gk *rheos* stream + -STAT]

rhesus /réessəss/ *n.* (in full **rhesus monkey**) a small catarrhine monkey, *Macaca mulatta*, common in N. India. □ **rhesus baby** an infant with a haemolytic disorder caused by the incompatibility of its own rhesus-positive blood with its mother's rhesus-negative blood. **rhesus factor** an antigen occurring on the red blood cells of most humans and some other primates (as in the rhesus monkey, in which it was first observed). **rhesus negative** lacking the rhesus factor. **rhesus positive** having the rhesus factor. [mod.L, arbitrary use of L *Rhesus* f. Gk *Rhēsos*, mythical King of Thrace]

rhetor /réetər/ *n.* **1** an ancient Greek or Roman teacher or professor of rhetoric. **2** usu. *derog.* an orator. [ME f. LL *rethor* f. L *rhetor* f. Gk *rhētōr*]

rhetoric /réttərik/ *n.* **1** the art of effective or persuasive speaking or writing. **2** language designed to persuade or impress (often with an implication of insincerity or exaggeration etc.). [ME f. OF *rethorique* f. L *rhetorica, -ice* f. Gk *rhētorikē (tekhnē)* (art) of rhetoric (as RHETOR)]
■ **1** eloquence, expressiveness, elocution, way with words, *colloq.* gift of the gab. **2** bombast, bluster, fustian, rodomontade, grandiloquence, magniloquence, oratory, wordiness, verbosity, prolixity, long-windedness, turgidity, flatulence, puffery, *colloq.* windiness, *sl.* hot air.

rhetorical /ritórrik'l/ *adj.* **1 a** expressed with a view to persuasive or impressive effect; artificial or extravagant in language. **b** (of a question) assuming a preferred answer. **2** of the nature of rhetoric. **3 a** of or relating to the art of rhetoric. **b** given to rhetoric; oratorical. □ **rhetorical question** a question asked not for information but to produce an effect, e.g. *who cares?* for *nobody cares.* □□ **rhetorically** *adv.* [ME f. L *rhetoricus* f. Gk *rhētorikos* (as RHETOR)]
■ **1 a** pretentious, bombastic, flamboyant, extravagant, florid, fustian, high-flown, inflated, grandiose, euphuistic, turgid, grandiloquent, magniloquent, long-winded, orotund, wordy, prolix, *colloq.* windy, highfalutin. **b** artificial, contrived, for effect, unanswerable, not literal. **2, 3** oratorical, stylistic, linguistic, poetic, expressive.

rhetorician /réttərísh'n/ *n.* **1** an orator. **2** a teacher of rhetoric. **3** a rhetorical speaker or writer. [ME f. OF *rethoricien* (as RHETORICAL)]

rheum /rōōm/ *n.* a watery discharge from a mucous membrane, esp. of the eyes or nose. □□ **rheumy** *adj.* [ME f. OF *reume* ult. f. Gk *rheuma -atos* stream f. *rheō* flow]

rheumatic /roomáttik/ *adj.* & *n.* ● *adj.* **1** of, relating to, or suffering from rheumatism. **2** producing or produced by rheumatism. ● *n.* a person suffering from rheumatism. □ **rheumatic fever** a non-infectious fever with inflammation and pain in the joints. □□ **rheumatically** *adv.* **rheumaticky** *adj. colloq.* [ME f. OF *reumatique* or L *rheumaticus* f. Gk *rheumatikos* (as RHEUM)]

rheumatics /roomáttiks/ *n.pl.* (treated as *sing.*; often prec. by *the*) *colloq.* rheumatism.

rheumatism /rōōmətiz'm/ *n.* any disease marked by inflammation and pain in the joints, muscles, or fibrous tissue, esp. rheumatoid arthritis. [F *rhumatisme* or L *rheumatismus* f. Gk *rheumatismos* f. *rheumatizō* f. *rheuma* stream]

rheumatoid /rōōmətoyd/ *adj.* having the character of rheumatism. □ **rheumatoid arthritis** a chronic progressive disease causing inflammation and stiffening of the joints.

rheumatology /rōōmətólləji/ *n.* the study of rheumatic diseases. □□ **rheumatological** /-təlójik'l/ *adj.* **rheumatologist** *n.*

RHG *abbr.* (in the UK) Royal Horse Guards.

rhinal /rín'l/ *adj. Anat.* of a nostril or the nose. [Gk *rhis rhin-*: see RHINO-]

rhinestone /rínstōn/ *n.* an imitation diamond. [*Rhine*, river and region in Germany + STONE]

rhinitis /rinítiss/ *n.* inflammation of the mucous membrane of the nose. [Gk *rhis rhinos* nose]

rhino[1] /rínō/ *n.* (*pl.* same or **-os**) *colloq.* a rhinoceros. [abbr.]

rhino[2] /rínō/ *n. Brit. sl.* money. [17th c.: orig. unkn.]

rhino- /rínō/ *comb. form Anat.* the nose. [Gk *rhis rhinos* nostril, nose]

rhinoceros /rīnóssərəss/ *n.* (*pl.* same or **rhinoceroses**) any of various large thick-skinned plant-eating ungulates of the family Rhinocerotidae of Africa and S. Asia, with one horn or in some cases two horns on the nose and plated or folded skin. □ **rhinoceros bird** = *ox-pecker*. **rhinoceros horn** a mass of keratinized fibres, reputed to have medicinal or aphrodisiac powers. □□ **rhinocerotic** /rīnóssəróttik/ *adj.* [ME f. L f. Gk *rhinokerōs* (as RHINO-, *keras* horn)]

rhinopharyngeal /rínōfərínjiəl/ *adj.* of or relating to the nose and pharynx.

rhinoplasty /rínōplasti/ *n.* plastic surgery of the nose. □□ **rhinoplastic** *adj.*

rhizo- /rízō/ *comb. form Bot.* a root. [Gk *rhiza* root]

rhizocarp /rízōkaarp/ *n.* a plant with a perennial root but stems that wither. [RHIZO- + Gk *karpos* fruit]

rhizoid /rízoyd/ *adj.* & *n. Bot.* ● *adj.* rootlike. ● *n.* a root-hair or filament in mosses, ferns, etc.

rhizome /rízōm/ *n.* an underground rootlike stem bearing both roots and shoots. [Gk *rhizōma* f. *rhizoō* take root (as RHIZO-)]

rhizopod /rízōpod/ *n.* any protozoa of the class Rhizopodea, forming rootlike pseudopodia.

rho /rō/ *n.* the seventeenth letter of the Greek alphabet (P, ρ). [Gk]

rhodamine /rōdəmin/ *n. Chem.* any of various red synthetic dyes used to colour textiles. [RHODO- + AMINE]

Rhode Island Red /rōd/ *n.* an orig. American breed of reddish-black domestic fowl.

Rhodes Scholarship /rōdz/ *n.* any of several scholarships awarded annually and tenable at Oxford University by students from certain Commonwealth countries, South Africa, the United States, and Germany. □□ **Rhodes Scholar** *n.* [Cecil *Rhodes*, Brit. statesman d. 1902, who founded them]

rhodium /rōdiəm/ *n. Chem.* a hard white metallic element of the platinum group, occurring naturally in platinum ores and used in making alloys and plating jewellery. ¶ Symb.:

Rh. [Gk *rhodon* rose (from the colour of the solution of its salts)]

rhodo- /rṓdō/ *comb. form* esp. *Mineral.* & *Chem.* rose-coloured. [Gk *rhodon* rose]

rhodochrosite /rṓdōkrṓsīt/ *n.* a mineral form of manganese carbonate occurring in rose-red crystals. [Gk *rhodokhrous* rose-coloured]

rhododendron /rṓdədéndrən/ *n.* any evergreen shrub of the genus *Rhododendron*, with large clusters of trumpet-shaped flowers. [L, = oleander, f. Gk (as RHODO-, *dendron* tree)]

rhodopsin /rōdópsin/ *n.* = *visual purple*. [Gk *rhodon* rose + *opsis* sight]

rhodora /rədórə/ *n.* a N. American pink-flowered shrub, *Rhodora canadense*. [mod.L f. L plant-name f. Gk *rhodon* rose]

rhomb /rom/ *n.* = RHOMBUS. □□ **rhombic** *adj.* [F *rhombe* or L *rhombus*]

rhombi *pl.* of RHOMBUS.

rhombohedron /rómbəhe͞edrən/ *n.* (*pl.* **-hedrons** or **-hedra** /-drə/) **1** a solid bounded by six equal rhombuses. **2** a crystal in this form. □□ **rhombohedral** *adj.* [RHOMBUS, after *polyhedron* etc.]

rhomboid /rómboyd/ *adj.* & *n.* ● *adj.* (also **rhomboidal** /-bóyd'l/) having or nearly having the shape of a rhombus. ● *n.* a quadrilateral of which only the opposite sides and angles are equal. [F *rhomboïde* or LL *rhomboides* f. Gk *rhomboeidēs* (as RHOMB)]

rhomboideus /rombóydiəss/ *n.* (*pl.* **rhomboidei** /-di-ī/) *Anat.* a muscle connecting the shoulder-blade to the vertebrae. [mod.L *rhomboideus* RHOMBOID]

rhombus /rómbəss/ *n.* (*pl.* **rhombuses** or **rhombi** /-bī/) *Geom.* a parallelogram with oblique angles and equal sides. [L f. Gk *rhombos*]

RHS *abbr.* **1** Royal Historical Society. **2** Royal Horticultural Society. **3** Royal Humane Society.

rhubarb /ro͞obaarb/ *n.* **1 a** any of various plants of the genus *Rheum*, esp. *R. rhaponticum*, producing long fleshy dark-red leaf-stalks used cooked as food. **b** the leaf-stalks of this. **2 a** a root of a Chinese and Tibetan plant of the genus *Rheum*. **b** a purgative made from this. **3 a** *colloq.* a murmurous conversation or noise, esp. the repetition of the word 'rhubarb' by crowd actors. **b** *sl.* nonsense; worthless stuff. **4** *US sl.* a heated dispute. [ME f. OF *r(e)ubarbe*, shortening of med.L *r(h)eubarbarum*, alt. (by assoc. with Gk *rhēon* rhubarb) of *rhabarbarum* foreign 'rha', ult. f. Gk *rha* + *barbaros* foreign]

rhumb /rum/ *n. Naut.* **1** any of the 32 points of the compass. **2** the angle between two successive compass-points. **3** (in full **rhumb-line**) **a** a line cutting all meridians at the same angle. **b** the line followed by a ship sailing in a fixed direction. [F *rumb* prob. f. Du. *ruim* room, assoc. with L *rhombus*: see RHOMBUS]

rhumba var. of RUMBA.

rhyme /rīm/ *n.* & *v.* ● *n.* **1** identity of sound between words or the endings of words, esp. in verse. **2** (in *sing.* or *pl.*) verse having rhymes. **3 a** the use of rhyme. **b** a poem having rhymes. **4** a word providing a rhyme. ● *v.* **1** *intr.* **a** (of words or lines) produce a rhyme. **b** (foll. by *with*) act as a rhyme (with another). **2** *intr.* make or write rhymes; versify. **3** *tr.* put or make (a story etc.) into rhyme. **4** *tr.* (foll. by *with*) treat (a word) as rhyming with another. □ **rhyming slang** slang that replaces words by rhyming words or phrases, e.g. *stairs* by *apples and pears*, often with the rhyming element omitted (as in TITFER). **without rhyme or reason** lacking discernible sense or logic. □□ **rhymeless** *adj.* **rhymer** *n.* **rhymist** *n.* [ME *rime* f. OF *rime* f. med.L *rithmus*, *rythmus* f. L f. Gk *rhuthmos* RHYTHM]

■ □ **rhyme or reason** (common) sense, logic, meaning, wisdom, rationality, rationale.

rhymester /rīmstər/ *n.* a writer of (esp. simple) rhymes.

rhyolite /rīəlīt/ *n.* a fine-grained volcanic rock of granitic composition. [G *Rhyolit* f. Gk *rhuax* lava-stream + *lithos* stone]

rhythm /ríthəm/ *n.* **1** a measured flow of words and phrases in verse or prose determined by various relations of long and short or accented and unaccented syllables. **2** the aspect of musical composition concerned with periodical accent and the duration of notes. **3** *Physiol.* movement with a regular succession of strong and weak elements. **4** a regularly recurring sequence of events. **5** *Art* a harmonious correlation of parts. □ **rhythm and blues** popular music with a blues theme and a strong rhythm. **rhythm method** birth control by avoiding sexual intercourse when ovulation is likely to occur. **rhythm section** the part of a dance band or jazz band mainly supplying rhythm, usu. consisting of piano, bass, and drums. □□ **rhythmless** *adj.* [F *rhythme* or L *rhythmus* f. Gk *rhuthmos*, rel. to *rhēo* flow]

■ **1, 2** accent, measure, metre, stress, stress pattern, arsis; rhythmic pattern, tempo, beat, lilt; pulse, time, *Mus.* downbeat. **4** see CYCLE *n.* 1a.

rhythmic /ríthmik/ *adj.* (also **rhythmical**) **1** relating to or characterized by rhythm. **2** regularly occurring. □□ **rhythmically** *adv.* [F *rhythmique* or L *rhythmicus* (as RHYTHM)]

■ measured, cadenced, regular, steady, paced, even.

rhythmicity /rithmíssiti/ *n.* **1** rhythmical quality or character. **2** the capacity for maintaining a rhythm.

RI *abbr.* **1** King and Emperor. **2** Queen and Empress. **3** *US* Rhode Island (also in official postal use). **4** Royal Institute or Institution. [sense 1 f. L *rex et imperator*: sense 2 f. L *regina et imperatrix*]

ria /re͞eə/ *n. Geog.* a long narrow inlet formed by the partial submergence of a river valley. [Sp. *ría* estuary]

rial /re͞e-aal/ *n.* (also **riyal**) the monetary unit of Iran, equal to 100 dinars. [Pers. f. Arab. *riyal* f. Sp. *real* ROYAL]

rib /rib/ *n.* & *v.* ● *n.* **1** each of the curved bones articulated in pairs to the spine and protecting the thoracic cavity and its organs. **2** a joint of meat from this part of an animal. **3** a ridge or long raised piece often of stronger or thicker material across a surface or through a structure serving to support or strengthen it. **4** any of a ship's transverse curved timbers forming the framework of the hull. **5** *Knitting* a combination of plain and purl stitches producing a ribbed somewhat elastic fabric. **6** each of the hinged rods supporting the fabric of an umbrella. **7** a vein of a leaf or an insect's wing. **8** *Aeron.* a structural member in an aerofoil. ● *v.tr.* (**ribbed**, **ribbing**) **1** provide with ribs; act as the ribs of. **2** *colloq.* make fun of; tease. **3** mark with ridges. **4** plough with spaces between the furrows. □□ **ribless** *adj.* [OE *rib*, *ribb* f. Gmc]

RIBA *abbr.* Royal Institute of British Architects.

ribald /ríbb'ld/ *adj.* & *n.* ● *adj.* (of language or its user) coarsely or disrespectfully humorous; scurrilous. ● *n.* a user of ribald language. [ME (earlier sense 'low-born retainer') f. OF *ribau(l)d* f. *riber* pursue licentious pleasures f. Gmc]

ribaldry /ríbbəldri/ *n.* ribald talk or behaviour.

■ vulgarity, immodesty, impudicity, indelicacy, indecency, coarseness, bawdiness, wantonness, raciness, shamelessness, rakishness, dissoluteness, lubricity, lasciviousness, looseness, scurrilousness, lewdness, salaciousness, licentiousness, grossness, offensiveness, rankness, rudeness, smuttiness, smut, dirt, filth, foulness, obscenity, *colloq. joc.* naughtiness.

riband /ríbb'nd/ *n.* a ribbon. [ME f. OF *riban*, prob. f. a Gmc compound of BAND[1]]

ribbed /ribd/ *adj.* having ribs or riblike markings.

ribbing /ríbbing/ *n.* **1** ribs or a riblike structure. **2** *colloq.* the act or an instance of teasing.

ribbon /ríbb'n/ *n.* **1 a** a narrow strip or band of fabric, used esp. for trimming or decoration. **b** material in this form. **2** a ribbon of a special colour etc. worn to indicate some honour or membership of a sports team etc. **3** a long narrow strip of anything, e.g. impregnated material forming the inking agent in a typewriter. **4** (in *pl.*) ragged strips (*torn to ribbons*). □ **ribbon development** the building of houses along a main road, usu. one leading out of a town or village. **ribbon worm** a nemertean. □□ **ribboned** *adj.* [var. of RIBAND]

ribbonfish /ríbb'nfish/ *n.* any of various long slender flat fishes of the family Trachypteridae.

ribcage /ríbkayj/ *n.* the wall of bones formed by the ribs round the chest.

riboflavin /rībōfláyvin/ *n.* (also **riboflavine** /-veen/) a vitamin of the B complex, found in liver, milk, and eggs, essential for energy production. Also called *vitamin* B_2. [RIBOSE + L *flavus* yellow]

ribonucleic acid /rībənyooklée-ik/ *n.* a nucleic acid yielding ribose on hydrolysis, present in living cells, esp. in ribosomes where it is involved in protein synthesis. ¶ Abbr.: **RNA**. [RIBOSE + NUCLEIC ACID]

ribose /rībōss/ *n.* a sugar found in many nucleosides and in several vitamins and enzymes. [G, alt. f. *Arabinose* a related sugar]

ribosome /rībəsōm/ *n. Biochem.* each of the minute particles consisting of RNA and associated proteins found in the cytoplasm of living cells, concerned with the synthesis of proteins. □□ **ribosomal** *adj.* [RIBONUCLEIC (ACID) + -SOME[3]]

ribwort /ríbwurt/ *n.* a kind of plantain (see PLANTAIN[1]) with long narrow ribbed leaves.

rice /rīss/ *n.* & *v.* *n.* **1** a swamp grass, *Oryza sativa*, cultivated in marshes, esp. in Asia. **2** the grains of this, used as cereal food. ● *v.tr. US* sieve (cooked potatoes etc.) into thin strings. □ **rice-bowl** an area producing much rice. **rice-paper** edible paper made from the pith of an oriental tree and used for painting and in cookery. □□ **ricer** *n.* [ME *rys* f. OF *ris* f. It. *riso*, ult. f. Gk *oruza*, of oriental orig.]

ricercar /réeshairkaar/ *n.* (also **ricercare** /-kaare/) an elaborate contrapuntal instrumental composition in fugal or canonic style, esp. of the 16th–18th c. [It., = seek out]

rich /rich/ *adj.* **1** having much wealth. **2** (often foll. by *in*, *with*) splendid, costly, elaborate (*rich tapestries*; *rich with lace*). **3** valuable (*rich offerings*). **4** copious, abundant, ample (*a rich harvest*; *a rich supply of ideas*). **5** (often foll. by *in*, *with*) (of soil or a region etc.) abounding in natural resources or means of production; fertile (*rich in nutrients*; *rich with vines*). **6** (of food or diet) containing much fat or spice etc. **7** (of the mixture in an internal-combustion engine) containing a high proportion of fuel. **8** (of colour or sound or smell) mellow and deep, strong and full. **9 a** (of an incident or assertion etc.) highly amusing or ludicrous; outrageous. **b** (of humour) earthy. □□ **richen** *v.intr.* & *tr.* **richness** *n.* [OE *rīce* f. Gmc f. Celt., rel. to L *rex* king: reinforced in ME f. OF *riche* rich, powerful, of Gmc orig.]

■ **1** wealthy, affluent, prosperous, well-to-do, well off, well provided for, opulent, moneyed, in clover, on velvet, *colloq.* flush, on Easy Street, rolling in it *or* money *or* wealth, in the money, well-heeled, *sl.* in the chips, loaded, oofy, *Austral.* & *NZ sl.* financial. **2** costly, expensive, dear, valuable, invaluable, precious, priceless; lavish, sumptuous, lush, luxurious, palatial, elaborate, splendid, exquisite, superb, elegant. **3** valuable, precious, invaluable, priceless, costly, high-priced, beyond *or* without price. **4** productive, plentiful, abundant, ample, bountiful, fruitful, fertile, fecund, copious, prolific, profitable, potent. **5** abundant, overflowing, fertile, fecund, productive, copious, abounding, well supplied, well stocked, rife, replete, profuse. **6** fatty, fat, fattening, heavy, creamy; spicy. **8** intense, dark, deep, warm, vibrant, strong; mellow, mellifluous, resonant, sonorous, full; aromatic, savoury, fragrant, redolent, pungent, strong; ambrosial. **9 a** hilarious, comic(al), side-splitting; ridiculous, preposterous, ludicrous, laughable, funny, absurd, nonsensical; outrageous, outlandish. **b** earthy; see also COARSE 2.

riches /ríchiz/ *n.pl.* abundant means; valuable possessions. [ME *richesse* f. OF *richeise* f. *riche* RICH, taken as pl.]

■ wealth, affluence, opulence, plenty, prosperity, abundance, fortune, means, resources, *derog.* or *joc.* pelf.

richly /ríchli/ *adv.* **1** in a rich way. **2** fully, thoroughly (*richly deserves success*).

■ **1** sumptuously, lavishly, luxuriously, splendidly, elaborately, exquisitely, elegantly, superbly. **2** well, thoroughly, amply, fully; condignly; see also WHOLLY 1.

Richter scale /ríktər/ *n.* a scale of 0 to 10 for representing the strength of an earthquake. [C. F. *Richter*, Amer. seismologist d. 1985]

ricin /ríssin/ *n.* a toxic substance obtained from castor oil beans and causing gastroenteritis, jaundice, and heart failure. [mod.L *ricinus communis* castor oil]

rick[1] /rik/ *n.* & *v.* ● *n.* a stack of hay, corn, etc., built into a regular shape and usu. thatched. ● *v.tr.* form into a rick or ricks. [OE *hrēac*, of unkn. orig.]

rick[2] /rik/ *n.* & *v.* (also **wrick**) ● *n.* a slight sprain or strain. ● *v.tr.* sprain or strain slightly. [ME *wricke* f. MLG *wricken* move about, sprain]

rickets /ríkkits/ *n.* (treated as *sing.* or *pl.*) a disease of children with softening of the bones (esp. the spine) and bow-legs, caused by a deficiency of vitamin D. [17th c.: orig. uncert., but assoc. by medical writers with Gk *rhakhitis* RACHITIS]

rickettsia /rikétsiə/ *n.* a parasitic micro-organism of the genus *Rickettsia* causing typhus and other febrile diseases. □□ **rickettsial** *adj.* [mod.L f. H. T. *Ricketts*, Amer. pathologist d. 1910]

rickety /ríkkiti/ *adj.* **1 a** insecure or shaky in construction; likely to collapse. **b** feeble. **2 a** suffering from rickets. **b** resembling or of the nature of rickets. □□ **ricketiness** *n.* [RICKETS + -Y[1]]

■ **1 a** wobbly, unsteady, shaky, tottering, teetering, precarious, insecure. **b** broken-down, decrepit, ramshackle, flimsy, frail, dilapidated, in (a state of) disrepair; feeble.

rickey /ríkki/ *n.* (*pl.* **-eys**) a drink of spirit (esp. gin), lime-juice, etc. [20th c.: prob. f. the surname *Rickey*]

rickrack var. of RICRAC.

rickshaw /ríkshaw/ *n.* (also **ricksha** /-shə/) a light two-wheeled hooded vehicle drawn by one or more persons. [abbr. of *jinricksha*, *jinrikshaw* f. Jap. *jinrikisha* f. *jin* person + *riki* power + *sha* vehicle]

ricochet /ríkkəshay, -shet/ *n.* & *v.* ● *n.* **1** the action of a projectile, esp. a shell or bullet, in rebounding off a surface. **2** a hit made after this. ● *v.intr.* (**ricocheted** /-shayd/; **ricocheting** /-shaying/ or **ricochetted** /-shetid/; **ricochetting** /-sheting/) (of a projectile) rebound one or more times from a surface. [F, of unkn. orig.]

ricotta /rikóttə/ *n.* a soft Italian cheese. [It., = recooked, f. L *recoquere* (as RE-, *coquere* cook)]

ricrac /ríkrak/ *n.* (also **rickrack**) a zigzag braided trimming for garments. [redupl. of RACK[1]]

RICS *abbr.* Royal Institution of Chartered Surveyors.

rictus /ríktəss/ *n. Anat.* & *Zool.* the expanse or gape of a mouth or beak. □□ **rictal** *adj.* [L, = open mouth f. *ringi rict-* to gape]

rid /rid/ *v.tr.* (**ridding**; *past* and *past part.* **rid** or *archaic* **ridded**) (foll. by *of*) make (a person or place) free of something unwanted. □ **be** (or **get**) **rid of** be freed or relieved of (something unwanted); dispose of. [ME, earlier = 'clear (land etc.)' f. ON *rythja*]

■ (*rid of*) deliver from, relieve of, free from *or* of, rescue from, save from. □ **be** (*or* **get**) **rid of** be freed or relieved of, send away, banish, exile, expel, eject, eliminate, reject, dismiss, shake off, *colloq.* unload; dispose of, throw out, discard, junk, dispense with; throw away.

riddance /rídd'nss/ *n.* the act of getting rid of something. □ **good riddance** welcome relief from an unwanted person or thing.

ridden *past part.* of RIDE.

riddle[1] /rídd'l/ *n.* & *v.* ● *n.* **1** a question or statement testing ingenuity in divining its answer or meaning. **2** a puzzling fact or thing or person. ● *v.* **1** *intr.* speak in or propound riddles. **2** *tr.* solve or explain (a riddle). □□ **riddler** *n.* [OE *rǣdels*, *rǣdelse* opinion, riddle, rel. to READ]

■ *n.* conundrum, puzzle, poser, problem, brain-teaser, *colloq.* brain-twister; koan; enigma, mystery. ● *v.* **2** see DECIPHER 2.

riddle[2] /ridd'l/ *v.* & *n.* ● *v.tr.* (usu. foll. by *with*) **1** make many holes in, esp. with gunshot. **2** (in *passive*) fill; spread through; permeate (*was riddled with errors*). **3** pass through a riddle. ● *n.* a coarse sieve. [OE *hriddel*, earlier *hrīder*: cf. *hrīdrian* sift]

■ *v.* **1** perforate, pepper, puncture, pierce, honeycomb. **2** fill, infest, pervade, permeate, spread through, infect. ● *n.* sieve, colander, sifter.

riddling /ridling/ *adj.* expressed in riddles; puzzling. ▫▫ **riddlingly** *adv.*

ride /rīd/ *v.* & *n.* ● *v.* (*past* **rode** /rōd/; *past part.* **ridden** /ridd'n/) **1** *tr.* travel or be carried on (a bicycle etc.) or esp. *US* in (a vehicle). **2** *intr.* (often foll. by *on, in*) travel or be conveyed (on a bicycle or in a vehicle). **3** *tr.* sit on and control or be carried by (a horse etc.). **4** *intr.* (often foll. by *on*) be carried (on a horse etc.). **5** *tr.* be carried or supported by (*the ship rides the waves*). **6** *tr.* **a** traverse on horseback etc., ride over or through (*ride 50 miles; rode the prairie*). **b** compete or take part in on horseback etc. (*rode a good race*). **7** *intr.* **a** lie at anchor; float buoyantly. **b** (of the moon) seem to float. **8** *intr.* (foll. by *in, on*) rest in or on while moving. **9** *tr.* yield to (a blow) so as to reduce its impact. **10** *tr.* give a ride to; cause to ride (*rode the child on his back*). **11** *tr.* (of a rider) cause (a horse etc.) to move forward (*rode their horses at the fence*). **12** *tr.* **a** (in *passive*; foll. by *by, with*) be oppressed or dominated by; be infested with (*was ridden with guilt*). **b** (as **ridden** *adj.*) infested or afflicted (usu. in *comb.*: *a rat-ridden cellar*). **13** *intr.* (of a thing normally level or even) project or overlap. **14** *tr.* mount (a female) in copulation. **15** *tr. US* annoy or seek to annoy. ● *n.* **1** an act or period of travel in a vehicle. **2** a spell of riding on a horse, bicycle, person's back, etc. **3** a path (esp. through woods) for riding on. **4** the quality of sensations when riding (*gives a bumpy ride*). ▫ **let a thing ride** leave it alone; let it take its natural course. **ride again** reappear, esp. unexpectedly and reinvigorated. **ride down** overtake or trample on horseback. **ride for a fall** act recklessly risking defeat or failure. **ride herd on** see HERD. **ride high** be elated or successful. **ride out** come safely through (a storm etc., or a danger or difficulty). **ride roughshod over** see ROUGHSHOD. **ride to hounds** see HOUND. **ride up** (of a garment, carpet, etc.) work or move out of its proper position. **take for a ride 1** *colloq.* hoax or deceive. **2** *sl.* abduct in order to murder. ▫▫ **ridable** *adj.* [OE *rīdan*]

■ *v.* **1** see DRIVE *v.* 3a, b. **2, 8** sit, travel, journey, go, proceed; be borne *or* carried *or* conveyed. **7** float, lie, rest, sit. **9** yield to, take, go *or* roll *or* stay with. **12 a** (*be ridden by* or *with*) be oppressed *or* plagued by *or* with, be dominated *or* tyrannized *or* terrorized by, be tormented *or* nagged *or* pestered by *or* with. **b** (**ridden**) afflicted, infested, infected. **14** mount, cover, mate *or* couple *or* copulate with. ● *n.* **1** drive, journey, trip, excursion, tour, jaunt, outing, expedition, *colloq.* spin. ▫ **let a thing ride** leave it, leave it alone, let it be. **ride high** fly (high); see also ACHIEVE 3, BOOM[2] *v.* **ride out** see through, spend, pass; see also ENDURE 1. **take for a ride 1** hoax, delude, swindle, trick, deceive, defraud, humbug, gull, take in, cheat, *colloq.* bamboozle. **2** (kidnap and) murder *or* kill *or* execute, *sl.* do in, bump off, *esp. US sl.* (snatch and) rub out, *US sl.* waste.

rider /rīdər/ *n.* **1** a person who rides (esp. a horse). **2 a** an additional clause amending or supplementing a document. **b** *Brit. Parl.* an addition or amendment to a bill at its third reading. **c** a corollary. **d** *Brit.* a recommendation etc. added to a judicial verdict. **3** *Math.* a problem arising as a corollary of a theorem etc. **4** a piece in a machine etc. that surmounts or bridges or works on or over others. **5** (in *pl.*) an additional set of timbers or iron plates strengthening a ship's frame. ▫▫ **riderless** *adj.* [OE *rīdere* (as RIDE)]

ridge /rij/ *n.* & *v.* ● *n.* **1** the line of the junction of two surfaces sloping upwards towards each other (*the ridge of a roof*). **2** a long narrow hilltop, mountain range, or watershed. **3** any narrow elevation across a surface. **4** *Meteorol.* an elongated region of high barometric pressure. **5** *Agriculture* a raised strip of arable land, usu. one of a set separated by furrows. **6** *Hort.* a raised hotbed for melons etc. ● *v.* **1** *tr.* mark with ridges. **2** *tr. Agriculture* break up (land) into ridges. **3** *tr. Hort.* plant (cucumbers etc.) in ridges. **4** *tr.* & *intr.* gather into ridges. ▫ **ridge-piece** (or **-tree**) a beam along the ridge of a roof. **ridge-pole 1** the horizontal pole of a long tent. **2** = *ridge-piece*. **ridge-tile** a tile used in making a roof-ridge. ▫▫ **ridgy** *adj.* [OE *hrycg* f. Gmc]

■ *n.* **1** line, strip, top edge, angle; crest, peak. **2** mountain range, arête; watershed; see also PROMINENCE 2.

ridgeway /rijway/ *n.* a road or track along a ridge.

ridicule /riddikyōōl/ *n.* & *v.* ● *n.* subjection to derision or mockery. ● *v.tr.* make fun of; subject to ridicule; laugh at. [F or f. L *ridiculum* neut. of *ridiculus* laughable f. *ridēre* laugh]

■ *n.* derision, deriding, jeering, taunting, mockery, mocking, gibing, raillery, *Austral.* mullock, *colloq.* ribbing, *sl.* joshing, *US sl.* razzing. ● *v.* deride, jeer at, taunt, tease, mock, gibe at, guy, chaff, laugh at, caricature, poke fun at, make fun *or* sport of, lampoon, burlesque, travesty, parody, make a laughing-stock of, *colloq.* rib, *Brit. colloq.* send up, *sl.* take the mickey out of, josh, *US sl.* razz.

ridiculous /ridíkyooləss/ *adj.* **1** deserving or inviting ridicule. **2** unreasonable, absurd. ▫▫ **ridiculously** *adv.* **ridiculousness** *n.* [L *ridiculosus* (as RIDICULE)]

■ absurd, laughable, comical, funny, humorous, ludicrous, farcical, droll, amusing, hilarious, side-splitting, risible; unreasonable, ludicrous, preposterous, silly, nonsensical, foolish, stupid, outlandish, bizarre, grotesque, queer, zany, wild, far-out, *colloq.* crazy, insane.

riding[1] /rīding/ *n.* **1** in senses of RIDE *v.* **2** the practice or skill of riders of horses. **3** = RIDE *n.* 3. ▫ **riding-light** (or **-lamp**) a light shown by a ship at anchor. **riding-school** an establishment teaching skills in horsemanship.

riding[2] /rīding/ *n.* **1** each of three former administrative divisions (**East Riding, North Riding, West Riding**) of Yorkshire. **2** an electoral division of Canada. [OE *thriding* (unrecorded) f. ON *thrithjungr* third part f. *thrithi* THIRD: *th-* was lost owing to the preceding *-t* or *-th* of *east* etc.]

Riesling /reézling, reés-/ *n.* **1** a kind of dry white wine produced in Germany, Austria, and elsewhere. **2** the variety of grape from which this is produced. [G]

rife /rīf/ *predic.adj.* **1** of common occurrence; widespread. **2** (foll. by *with*) abounding in; teeming with. ▫▫ **rifeness** *n.* [OE *rȳfe* prob. f. ON *rífr* acceptable f. *reifa* enrich, *reifr* cheerful]

riff /rif/ *n.* & *v.* ● *n.* a short repeated phrase in jazz etc. ● *v.intr.* play riffs. [20th c.: abbr. of RIFFLE *n.*]

riffle /riff'l/ *v.* & *n.* ● *v.* **1** *tr.* **a** turn (pages) in quick succession. **b** shuffle (playing-cards) esp. by flexing and combining the two halves of a pack. **2** *intr.* (often foll. by *through*) leaf quickly (through pages). ● *n.* **1** the act or an instance of riffling. **2** (in gold-washing) a groove or slat set in a trough or sluice to catch gold particles. **3** *US* **a** a shallow part of a stream where the water flows brokenly. **b** a patch of waves or ripples on water. [perh. var. of RUFFLE]

riff-raff /rifraf/ *n.* (often prec. by *the*) rabble; disreputable or undesirable persons. [ME *riff and raff* f. OF *rif et raf*]

■ rabble, *hoi polloi, canaille*; *colloq.* scum, *derog.* ragtag and bobtail; (*the riff-raff*) the dregs (of society *or* humanity), *colloq.* the great unwashed.

rifle[1] /rīf'l/ *n.* & *v.* ● *n.* **1** a gun with a long rifled barrel, esp. one fired from shoulder-level. **2** (in *pl.*) riflemen. ● *v.tr.* make spiral grooves in (a gun or its barrel or bore) to make a bullet spin. ▫ **rifle bird** any dark green Australian bird of paradise of the genus *Ptiloris*. **rifle-range** a place for rifle-practice. **rifle-shot 1** the distance coverable by a shot from a rifle. **2** a shot fired with a rifle. [OF *rifler* graze, scratch f. Gmc]

rifle[2] /rīf'l/ *v.tr.* & (foll. by *through*) *intr.* **1** search and rob, esp. of all that can be found. **2** carry off as booty. [ME f. OF *rifler* graze, scratch, plunder f. ODu. *riffelen*]
■ **1** rob, ransack, plunder, pillage, loot, *literary* despoil; (*rifle through*) see RANSACK 2.

rifleman /rīf'lmən/ *n.* (*pl.* **-men**) **1** a soldier armed with a rifle. **2** a small yellow and green New Zealand bird, *Acanthisitta chloris*.

rifling /rīfling/ *n.* the arrangement of grooves on the inside of a gun's barrel.

rift /rift/ *n.* & *v.* ● *n.* **1 a** a crack or split in an object. **b** an opening in a cloud etc. **2** a cleft or fissure in earth or rock. **3** a disagreement; a breach in friendly relations. ● *v.tr.* tear or burst apart. □ **rift-valley** a steep-sided valley formed by subsidence of the earth's crust between nearly parallel faults. □□ **riftless** *adj.* **rifty** *adj.* [ME, of Scand. orig.]
■ *n.* **1** split, tear, rent, opening, hole, crack, chink, cleavage. **2** fissure, crevice, cleft, gulf, gap; see also CRACK *n.* 3, CREVASSE. **3** disagreement, schism, conflict, difference; breach, separation, break, split, disruption, break-up, division, alienation; gulf, gap, distance.

rig[1] /rig/ *v.* & *n.* ● *v.tr.* (**rigged, rigging**) **1 a** provide (a sailing ship) with sails, rigging, etc. **b** prepare ready for sailing. **2** (often foll. by *out*, *up*) fit with clothes or other equipment. **3** (foll. by *up*) set up hastily or as a makeshift. **4** assemble and adjust the parts of (an aircraft). ● *n.* **1** the arrangement of masts, sails, rigging, etc., of a sailing ship. **2** equipment for a special purpose, e.g. a radio transmitter. **3** = *oil rig*. **4** a person's or thing's look as determined by clothing, equipment, etc., esp. uniform. □ **in full rig** *colloq.* smartly or ceremonially dressed. **rig-out** *Brit. colloq.* an outfit of clothes. □□ **rigged** *adj.* (also in *comb.*). [ME, perh. of Scand. orig.: cf. Norw. *rigga* bind or wrap up]
■ *v.* **2** equip, set up, outfit, supply, provision, accoutre, caparison, kit out; (*rig out* or *up*) fit out *or* up. ● *n.* **2** equipment, equipage, gear, tackle, apparatus, outfit, kit, accoutrements, paraphernalia, *colloq.* things, stuff. □ **in full rig** (*be in full rig*) be in full fig, *colloq.* be (all) togged up, *joc.* wear *or* be in one's Sunday best, be dressed up to the nines, be dressed to kill, be (all) kitted out. **rig-out** outfit, *colloq.* get-up, togs, costume; see also ENSEMBLE 2, DRESS *n.* 2.

rig[2] /rig/ *v.* & *n.* ● *v.tr.* (**rigged, rigging**) manage or conduct fraudulently (*they rigged the election*). ● *n.* **1** a trick or dodge. **2** a way of swindling. □ **rig the market** cause an artificial rise or fall in prices. □□ **rigger** *n.* [19th c.: orig. unkn.]
■ *v.* falsify, manipulate, juggle with, tamper with, fake, *colloq.* doctor, fix, cook, *sl.* fiddle (with).

rigadoon /rìggədōōn/ *n.* **1** a lively dance in duple or quadruple time for two persons. **2** the music for this. [F *rigodon, rigaudon*, perh. f. its inventor *Rigaud*]

rigger /ríggər/ *n.* **1** a person who rigs or who arranges rigging. **2** (of a rowing-boat) = OUTRIGGER 5a. **3** a ship rigged in a specified way. **4** a worker on an oil rig.

rigging /rígging/ *n.* **1** a ship's spars, ropes, etc., supporting and controlling the sails. **2** the ropes and wires supporting the structure of an airship or biplane.

right /rīt/ *adj.*, *n.*, *v.*, *adv.*, & *int.* ● *adj.* **1** (of conduct etc.) just, morally or socially correct (*it is only right to tell you*; *I want to do the right thing*). **2** true, correct; not mistaken (*the right time*; *you were right about the weather*). **3** less wrong or not wrong (*which is the right way to town?*). **4** more or most suitable or preferable (*the right person for the job*; *along the right lines*). **5** in a sound or normal condition; physically or mentally healthy; satisfactory (*the engine doesn't sound right*). **6 a** on or towards the side of the human body which corresponds to the position of east if one regards oneself as facing north. **b** on or towards that part of an object which is analogous to a person's right side or (with opposite sense) which is nearer to a spectator's right hand. **7** (of a side of fabric etc.) meant for display or use (*turn it right side up*). **8** *colloq.* or *archaic* real; properly so called (*made a right mess of it*; *a right royal welcome*). ● *n.* **1** that which is morally or socially correct or just; fair treatment (often in *pl.*: *the rights and wrongs of the case*). **2** (often foll. by *to*, or *to* + infin.) a justification or fair claim (*has no right to speak like that*). **3** a thing one may legally or morally claim; the state of being entitled to a privilege or immunity or authority to act (*a right of reply*; *human rights*). **4** the right-hand part or region or direction. **5** *Boxing* **a** the right hand. **b** a blow with this. **6** (often **Right**) *Polit.* **a** a group or section favouring conservatism (orig. the more conservative section of a continental legislature, seated on the president's right). **b** such conservatives collectively. **7** the side of a stage which is to the right of a person facing the audience. **8** (esp. in marching) the right foot. **9** the right wing of an army. ● *v.tr.* **1** (often *refl.*) restore to a proper or straight or vertical position. **2 a** correct (mistakes etc.); set in order. **b** avenge (a wrong or a wronged person); make reparation for or to. **c** vindicate, justify, rehabilitate. ● *adv.* **1** straight (*go right on*). **2** *colloq.* immediately; without delay (*I'll be right back*; *do it right now*). **3 a** (foll. by *to*, *round*, *through*, etc.) all the way (*sank right to the bottom*; *ran right round the block*). **b** (foll. by *off*, *out*, etc.) completely (*came right off its hinges*; *am right out of butter*). **4** exactly, quite (*right in the middle*). **5** justly, properly, correctly, truly, satisfactorily (*did not act right*; *not holding it right*; *if I remember right*). **6** on or to the right side. **7** *archaic* very; to the full (*am right glad to hear it*; *dined right royally*). ● *int. colloq.* expressing agreement or assent. □ **as right as rain** perfectly sound and healthy. **at right angles** placed to form a right angle. **by right** (or **rights**) if right were done. **do right by** act dutifully towards (a person). **in one's own right** through one's own position or effort etc. **in the right** having justice or truth on one's side. **in one's right mind** sane; competent to think and act. **of** (or **as of**) **right** having legal or moral etc. entitlement. **on the right side of 1** in the favour of (a person etc.). **2** somewhat less than (a specified age). **put** (or **set**) **right 1** restore to order, health, etc. **2** correct the mistaken impression etc. of (a person). **put** (or **set**) **to rights** make correct or well ordered. **right about** (or **about-turn** or **about-face**) **1** a right turn continued to face the rear. **2** a reversal of policy. **3** a hasty retreat. **right and left** (or **right, left, and centre**) on all sides. **right angle** an angle of 90°, made by lines meeting with equal angles on either side. **right-angled 1** containing or making a right angle. **2** involving right angles, not oblique. **right arm** one's most reliable helper. **right ascension** see ASCENSION. **right away** (or **off**) immediately. **right bank** the bank of a river on the right facing downstream. **right bower** see BOWER[3]. **right field** *Baseball* the part of the outfield to the right of the batter as he faces the pitcher. **right hand 1** = *right-hand man*. **2** the most important position next to a person (*stand at God's right hand*). **right-hand** *adj.* **1** on or towards the right side of a person or thing (*right-hand drive*). **2** done with the right hand (*right-hand blow*). **3** (of a screw) = RIGHT-HANDED 4b. **right-hand man** an indispensable or chief assistant. **Right Honourable** *Brit.* a title given to certain high officials, e.g. Privy Counsellors. **right-minded** (or **-thinking**) having sound views and principles. **right of search** *Naut.* see SEARCH. **right of way 1** a right established by usage to pass over another's ground. **2** a path subject to such a right. **3** the right of one vehicle to proceed before another. **right oh!** (or **ho!**) = RIGHTO. **right on!** *colloq.* an expression of strong approval or encouragement. **a right one** *Brit. colloq.* a silly or foolish person. **Right Reverend** see REVEREND. **right sphere** *Astron.* see SPHERE. **right turn** a turn that brings one's front to face as one's right side did before. **right whale** any large-headed whale of the family Balaenidae, rich in whalebone and easily captured. **right wing 1** the right side of a football etc. team on the field. **2** the conservative section of a political party or system. **right-wing** *adj.* conservative or reactionary. **right-winger** a person on the right wing. **right you are!** *colloq.* an exclamation of assent. **she's** (or **she'll be**) **right** *Austral. colloq.* that will be all right. **too right** *sl.* an expression of agreement. **within one's rights** not exceeding one's authority or entitlement. □□ **rightable**

adj. **righter** *n.* **rightish** *adj.* **rightless** *adj.* **rightlessness** *n.* **rightness** *n.* [OE *riht* (adj.), *rihtan* (v.), *rihte* (adv.)]

■ *adj.* **1** just, moral, good, proper, sound, correct, legal, lawful, licit, honest, upright, righteous, virtuous, ethical, fair, true, honourable, right-minded, principled, open, above-board. **2** true, correct, not mistaken, accurate, exact, precise, perfect, valid, *Brit. colloq.* bang on, spot on. **4** fitting, suitable, proper, perfect, preferred, preferable, promising, advantageous, beneficial; (of time) favourable, propitious, convenient, auspicious, strategic. **5** sound, sane, normal, rational, lucid, healthy; satisfactory, *colloq.* OK. **6 b** right-hand, dextral, *esp. Heraldry* dexter. **7** upper, front; (*right side*) face, surface, top, outside. **8** utter, complete, perfect, unmitigated, out and out, thorough, thoroughgoing, pure, absolute, real, *colloq.* proper. ● *n.* **1** justice, reason, truth, fairness, equity, good, goodness, integrity, virtue, virtuousness, honesty, honourableness, morality, propriety, rectitude, right-mindedness, nobility, uprightness. **2** see CAUSE *n.* 1c. **3** privilege, prerogative, licence, power, claim, freedom, liberty; (*right to*) title to. **6** right wing, conservatives; Conservatives, Tories. ● *v.* **1** straighten (out), straighten up, set upright. **2 a** righten, put *or* set right, make right, put *or* set to rights, correct, straighten out, sort out, repair, fix; redress, amend, rectify. **b** avenge, get even for, requite, make up for; see also REVENGE *v.* 2. **c** vindicate, rehabilitate; see also JUSTIFY 1, 2, 4. ● *adv.* **2** directly, straightaway, right away *or* off, forthwith, unhesitatingly, immediately, promptly, at once, instantly, without hesitation, without delay, quickly, swiftly, speedily, *archaic* straight, *colloq.* pronto, straight off; just. **4** exactly, quite, precisely, just; see also SLAP *adv.* **5** correctly, accurately, justly, truly, properly, precisely, well, sensibly, fittingly, suitably, aptly, satisfactorily, advantageously, profitably, favourably, opportunely. ● *int.* certainly, definitely, absolutely, *colloq.* OK, sure, *esp. US colloq.* sure thing, *US sl.* you got it. □ **as right as rain** fine; see also OK[1] *adj.* **by right(s)** to be just *or* fair, in fairness. **in the right** right, just, justified; see also RIGHTEOUS. **in one's right mind** see SANE 1. **put** (*or* **set**) **right** straighten out; see also STRAIGHTEN. **put** (*or* **set**) **to rights** straighten out; see also STRAIGHTEN. **right away** (*or* **off**) immediately, forthwith; see also *at once* 1 (ONCE). **right-minded** (*or* **-thinking**) politically correct; see also CONSCIENTIOUS. **right on!** excellent, *sl.* ace, first-rate; see also DIVINE *adj.* 2b, FABULOUS 2. **a right one** see DOLT. **right wing** right, conservatives, Conservatives, Tories. **right-wing** rightist, right-wing, conservative, Conservative, reactionary, Tory. **right-winger** rightist, conservative, Conservative, Tory; see also REACTIONARY *n.* **right you are!** see ABSOLUTELY 6.

righten /rī́t'n/ *v.tr.* make right or correct.

■ see RIGHT *v.* 2a.

righteous /rī́chəss/ *adj.* (of a person or conduct) morally right; virtuous, law-abiding. □□ **righteously** *adv.* **righteousness** *n.* [OE *rihtwīs* (as RIGHT *n.* + -WISE or RIGHT *adj.* + WISE[2]), assim. to *bounteous* etc.]

■ moral, just, virtuous, upstanding, upright, good, honest, ethical, honourable, fair, reputable, trustworthy; right, correct, justifiable, justified, appropriate, condign, fitting, apt.

rightful /rī́tfōōl/ *adj.* **1 a** (of a person) legitimately entitled to (a position etc.) (*the rightful heir*). **b** (of status or property etc.) that one is entitled to. **2** (of an action etc.) equitable, fair. □□ **rightfully** *adv.* **rightfulness** *n.* [OE *rihtful* (as RIGHT *n.*)]

■ **1** legal, lawful, legitimate, licit, correct, proper, true, right; *de jure*; bona fide, valid, authorized. **2** see EQUITABLE.

right-handed /rī́t-hándid/ *adj.* **1** using the right hand by preference as more serviceable than the left. **2** (of a tool etc.) made to be used with the right hand. **3** (of a blow) struck with the right hand. **4 a** turning to the right; towards the right. **b** (of a screw) advanced by turning to the right (clockwise). □□ **right-handedly** *adv.* **right-handedness** *n.*

right-hander /rī́t-hándər/ *n.* **1** a right-handed person. **2** a right-handed blow.

rightism /rī́tiz'm/ *n. Polit.* the principles or policy of the right. □□ **rightist** *n.* & *adj.*

rightly /rī́tli/ *adv.* justly, properly, correctly, justifiably.

rightmost /rī́tmōst/ *adj.* furthest to the right.

righto /rī́tṓ/ *int. Brit. colloq.* expressing agreement or assent.

rightward /rī́twərd/ *adv.* & *adj.* ● *adv.* (also **rightwards** /-wərdz/) towards the right. ● *adj.* going towards or facing the right.

rigid /ríjid/ *adj.* **1** not flexible; that cannot be bent (*a rigid frame*). **2** (of a person, conduct, etc.) **a** inflexible, unbending, harsh (*a rigid disciplinarian; rigid economy*). **b** strict, precise, punctilious. □□ **rigidity** /-jídditi/ *n.* **rigidly** *adv.* **rigidness** *n.* [F *rigide* or L *rigidus* f. *rigēre* be stiff]

■ **1** stiff, inflexible, unbending, inelastic, unbendable, firm, hard, strong. **2 a** inflexible, unyielding, undeviating, unbending, firm, unwavering, unswerving, strong, uncompromising, iron, unrelenting, intransigent, stringent, severe, strict, rigorous, stern, harsh, austere, hard; obstinate, stubborn, pigheaded, immovable, adamant, adamantine, fixed, obdurate, wilful, headstrong, dogged, persevering, determined, resolute, steadfast, resolved, tenacious, relentless, unrelenting, uncompromising, unadaptable, mulish. **b** exact, precise, demanding, strict, hard and fast, literal, nice, close, thorough, scrupulous, careful, conscientious, painstaking, meticulous, punctilious, exacting, strait-laced.

rigidify /rijíddifī/ *v.tr.* & *intr.* (**-ies**, **-ied**) make or become rigid.

rigmarole /rígmərōl/ *n.* **1** a lengthy and complicated procedure. **2 a** a rambling or meaningless account or tale. **b** such talk. [orig. *ragman roll* = a catalogue, of unkn. orig.]

■ **1** ceremony, ritual, procedure; bother, *colloq.* hassle. **2b** mumbo-jumbo, gobbledegook, waffle, balderdash, rubbish, nonsense, bunkum, *sl.* bunk.

rigor[1] /ríggər, rī́gor/ *n. Med.* **1** a sudden feeling of cold with shivering accompanied by a rise in temperature, preceding a fever etc. **2** rigidity of the body caused by shock or poisoning etc. [ME f. L f. *rigēre* be stiff]

rigor[2] *US* var. of RIGOUR.

rigor mortis /ríggər mórtiss/ *n.* stiffening of the body after death. [L, = stiffness of death]

rigorous /ríggərəss/ *adj.* **1** characterized by or showing rigour; strict, severe. **2** strictly exact or accurate. **3** (of the weather) cold, severe. □□ **rigorously** *adv.* **rigorousness** *n.* [OF *rigorous* or LL *rigorosus* (as RIGOR[1])]

rigour /ríggər/ *n.* (*US* **rigor**) **1 a** severity, strictness, harshness. **b** (often in *pl.*) severity of weather or climate; extremity of cold. **c** (in *pl.*) harsh measures or conditions. **2** logical exactitude. **3** strict enforcement of rules etc. (*the utmost rigour of the law*). **4** austerity of life; puritanical discipline. [ME f. OF *rigour* f. L *rigor* (as RIGOR[1])]

■ **1 a** strictness, harshness; see also *severity* (SEVERE). **b** inclemency, inhospitableness; bitterness, cold. **c** (*rigours*) austerities, asceticism; see also HARDSHIP. **3** strictness, rigidity, precision, preciseness, literalness, exactness, meticulousness, stringency, inflexibility. **4** harshness, severity, hardship, austerity, sternness, strictness, asceticism, discipline, rigidity, stringency.

Rig-Veda /rigváydə, -veédə/ *n.* the oldest and principal of the Hindu Vedas (see VEDA). [Skr. *ṛigvēda* f. *ṛic* praise + *vēda* VEDA]

rile /rīl/ *v.tr.* **1** *colloq.* anger, irritate. **2** *US* make (water) turbulent or muddy. [var. of ROIL]

Riley /rī́li/ *n.* (also **Reilly**) □ **the life of Riley** *colloq.* a carefree existence. [20th c.: orig. unkn.]

rilievo var. of RELIEVO.

rill /ril/ *n.* **1** a small stream. **2** a shallow channel cut in the surface of soil or rocks by running water. **3** var. of RILLE. [LG *ril*, *rille*]

rille /ril/ *n.* (also **rill**) *Astron.* a cleft or narrow valley on the moon's surface. [G (as RILL)]

rim /rim/ *n.* & *v.* ● *n.* **1 a** a raised edge or border. **b** a margin or verge, esp. of something circular. **2** the part of a pair of spectacles surrounding the lenses. **3** the outer edge of a wheel, on which the tyre is fitted. **4** a boundary line (*the rim of the horizon*). ● *v.tr.* (**rimmed, rimming**) **1 a** provide with a rim. **b** be a rim for or to. **2** edge, border. □ **rim-brake** a brake acting on the rim of a wheel. □□ **rimless** *adj.* **rimmed** *adj.* (also in *comb.*). [OE *rima* edge: cf. ON *rimi* ridge (the only known cognate)]
■ *n.* **1 a** edge, brim, lip, border, perimeter. **b** margin, verge; see also EDGE *n.* 1.

rime[1] /rīm/ *n.* & *v.* ● *n.* **1** frost, esp. formed from cloud or fog. **2** *poet.* hoar-frost. ● *v.tr.* cover with rime. [OE *hrīm*]

rime[2] *archaic* var. of RHYME.

rimose /rī́mōz/ *adj.* (also **rimous** /-məss/) esp. *Bot.* full of chinks or fissures. [L *rimosus* f. *rima* chink]

rimu /reémoo/ *n.* *NZ* a softwood tree, *Dacrydium cupressinum*, native to New Zealand. [Maori]

rimy /rī́mi/ *adj.* (**rimier, rimiest**) frosty; covered with frost.

rind /rīnd/ *n.* & *v.* ● *n.* **1** the tough outer layer or covering of fruit and vegetables, cheese, bacon, etc. **2** the bark of a tree or plant. ● *v.tr.* strip the bark from. □□ **rinded** *adj.* (also in *comb.*). **rindless** *adj.* [OE *rind(e)*]
■ *n.* **1** peel, skin, husk, pod, hull, shell; see also CASE[2] *n.* 1, 3.

rinderpest /rindərpest/ *n.* a virulent infectious disease of ruminants (esp. cattle). [G f. *Rinder* cattle + *Pest* PEST]

ring[1] /ring/ *n.* & *v.* ● *n.* **1** a circular band, usu. of precious metal, worn on a finger as an ornament or a token of marriage or betrothal. **2** a circular band of any material. **3** the rim of a cylindrical or circular object, or a line or band round it. **4** a mark or part having the form of a circular band (*had rings round his eyes*; *smoke rings*). **5** = *annual ring*. **6 a** an enclosure for a circus performance, betting at races, the showing of cattle, etc. **b** (prec. by *the*) bookmakers collectively. **c** a roped enclosure for boxing or wrestling. **7 a** a group of people or things arranged in a circle. **b** such an arrangement. **8** a combination of traders, bookmakers, spies, politicians, etc. acting together usu. illicitly for the control of operations or profit. **9** a circular or spiral course. **10** = *gas ring*. **11** *Astron.* **a** a thin band or disc of particles etc. round a planet. **b** a halo round the moon. **12** *Archaeol.* a circular prehistoric earthwork usu. of a bank and ditch. **13** *Chem.* a group of atoms each bonded to two others in a closed sequence. **14** *Math.* a set of elements with two binary operations, addition and multiplication, the second being distributive over the first and associative. ● *v.tr.* **1** make or draw a circle round. **2** (often foll. by *round*, *about*, *in*) encircle or hem in (game or cattle). **3** put a ring on (a bird etc.) or through the nose of (a pig, bull, etc.). **4** cut (fruit, vegetables, etc.) into rings. □ **ring-binder** a loose-leaf binder with ring-shaped clasps that can be opened to pass through holes in the paper. **ring circuit** an electrical circuit serving a number of power points with one fuse in the supply to the circuit. **ring-dove 1** the woodpigeon. **2** the collared dove. **ringed plover** either of two small plovers, *Charadrius hiaticula* and *C. dubius*. **ring finger** the finger next to the little finger, esp. of the left hand, on which the wedding ring is usu. worn. **ring main 1** an electrical supply serving a series of consumers and returning to the original source, so that each consumer has an alternative path in the event of a failure. **2** = *ring circuit*. **ring-neck** any of various ring-necked birds esp. a type of pheasant, *Phasianus colchicus*, with a white neck-ring. **ring-necked** *Zool.* having a band or bands of colour round the neck. **ring ouzel** a thrush, *Turdus torquatus*, with a white crescent across its breast. **ring-pull** (of a tin) having a ring for pulling to break its seal. **ring road** a bypass encircling a town. **ring-tailed 1** (of monkeys, lemurs, racoons, etc.) having a tail ringed in alternate colours. **2** with the tail curled at the end. **run** (or **make**) **rings round** *colloq.* outclass or outwit (another person). □□ **ringed** *adj.* (also in *comb.*). **ringless** *adj.* [OE *hring* f. Gmc]
■ *n.* **2** circle, necklace, bracelet, armlet, crown, coronet, tiara, diadem, *hist.* torque; bandeau, fillet, loop, band, circlet, belt, girdle, *literary* cincture; hoop, quoit; halo, aureole, nimbus; wreath, garland; *Anat.* cingulum. **6 a** enclosure, rink, arena, bullring, *Rom. Antiq.* circus. **8** organization, group, circle, team, crew; cartel, bloc, gang, band, pack, cell, coterie, set, clan, clique, junta, camarilla, cabal, faction, *colloq.* mob; fraternity, brotherhood, sisterhood, guild, (secret) society, league, alliance, federation, confederacy, confederation, combination, coalition, union. **9** see COIL[1] *n.*, SPIRAL *n.* ● *v.* **1** encircle, circle, loop, circumscribe, *literary* gird. **2** encircle, surround, hem in, *literary* compass. □ **run** (or **make**) **rings round** outclass, outwit, baffle, nonplus; see also MYSTIFY.

ring[2] /ring/ *v.* & *n.* ● *v.* (*past* **rang** /rang/; *past part.* **rung** /rung/) **1** *intr.* (often foll. by *out* etc.) give a clear resonant or vibrating sound of or as of a bell (*a shot rang out*; *a ringing laugh*; *the telephone rang*). **2** *tr.* **a** make (esp. a bell) ring. **b** (*absol.*) call for service or attention by ringing a bell (*you rang, madam?*). **3** *tr.* (also *absol.*; often foll. by *up*) *Brit.* call by telephone (*will ring you on Monday*; *did you ring?*). **4** *intr.* (usu. foll. by *with*, *to*) (of a place) resound or be permeated with a sound, or an attribute, e.g. fame (*the theatre rang with applause*). **5** *intr.* (of the ears) be filled with a sensation of ringing. **6** *tr.* **a** sound (a peal etc.) on bells. **b** (of a bell) sound (the hour etc.). **7** *tr.* (foll. by *in*, *out*) usher in or out with bell-ringing (*ring in the May*; *rang out the Old Year*). **8** *intr.* (of sentiments etc.) convey a specified impression (*words rang hollow*). ● *n.* **1** a ringing sound or tone. **2 a** the act of ringing a bell. **b** the sound caused by this. **3** *colloq.* a telephone call (*give me a ring*). **4** a specified feeling conveyed by an utterance (*had a melancholy ring*). **5** a set of esp. church bells. □ **ring back** make a return telephone call to (a person who has telephoned earlier). **ring a bell** see BELL[1]. **ring the changes** (**on**) see CHANGE. **ring down** (or **up**) **the curtain 1** cause the curtain to be lowered or raised. **2** (foll. by *on*) mark the end or the beginning of (an enterprise etc.). **ring in 1** report or make contact by telephone. **2** *Austral.* & *NZ sl.* substitute fraudulently. **ring in one's ears** (or **heart** etc.) linger in the memory. **ringing tone** a sound heard by a telephone caller when the number dialled is being rung. **ring off** *Brit.* end a telephone call by replacing the receiver. **ring true** (or **false**) convey an impression of truth or falsehood. **ring up 1** *Brit.* call by telephone. **2** record (an amount etc.) on a cash register. □□ **ringed** *adj.* (also in *comb.*). **ringer** *n.* **ringing** *adj.* **ringingly** *adv.* [OE *hringan*]
■ *v.* **1** peal, chime (out), toll, knell, dong, *archaic* knoll; sound, resound, echo, re-echo, reverberate, resonate; clang, jangle; tinkle, jingle. **3** telephone, ring up, call; *colloq.* phone, give a person a ring, get a person on the blower, *Brit. colloq.* give a person a tinkle, *sl.* buzz, give a person a buzz. **4** resound, echo, re-echo; see also ROLL *v.* 11. **6 b** toll, sound; see also CHIME[1] *v.* 1. ● *n.* **1** ringing, clang, clanging, jangle, jangling, tinkle, tinkling, jingle, jingling. **2 b** ringing, peal, pealing, chime, chiming, toll, tolling, knell, sounding, *archaic* knoll. **3** (telephone *or* phone) call, *Brit. colloq.* tinkle *sl.* buzz. **4** see UNDERCURRENT 2. □ **ring up the curtain 2** see LAUNCH[1] *v.* 1, 3, 4. **ring in 1** report, make contact, get in touch, call in. **ring off** hang up. **ring up 1** call, telephone, *colloq.* phone; see also BUZZ *v.* 2b.

ringbark /ríngbaark/ *v.tr.* cut a ring in the bark of (a tree) to kill it or retard its growth and thereby improve fruit production.

ringbolt /ríngbōlt/ *n.* a bolt with a ring attached for fitting a rope to etc.

ringer /ríngər/ *n. sl.* **1 a** esp. *US* an athlete or horse entered in a competition by fraudulent means, esp. as a substitute.

b a person's double, esp. an impostor. **2** *Austral.* **a** the fastest shearer in a shed. **b** a stockman or station hand. **3** a person who rings, esp. a bell-ringer. □ **be a ringer** (or **dead ringer**) **for** resemble (a person) exactly. [RING[2] + -ER[1]]

ringhals /ring-halss/ *n.* a large venomous snake, *Hemachatus hemachatus*, of Southern Africa, with a white ring or two across the neck. [Afrik. *rinkhals* f. *ring* RING[1] + *hals* neck]

ringleader /ríngleedər/ *n.* a leading instigator in an illicit or illegal activity.

ringlet /rínglit/ *n.* **1** a curly lock of hair, esp. a long one. **2** a butterfly, *Aphantopus hyperantus*, with spots on its wings. □□ **ringleted** *adj.* **ringlety** *adj.*

ringmaster /ríngmaastər/ *n.* the person directing a circus performance.

ringside /ríngsīd/ *n.* (often *attrib.*) **1** the area immediately beside a boxing ring or circus ring etc. **2** an advantageous position from which to observe or monitor something. □□ **ringsider** *n.*

ringster /ríngstər/ *n.* a person who participates in a political or commercial ring (see RING[1] *n.* 8).

ringtail /ríngtayl/ *n.* **1** a ring-tailed opossum, lemur, or phalanger. **2** a golden eagle up to its third year. **3** a female hen-harrier.

ringworm /ríngwurm/ *n.* any of various fungous infections of the skin causing circular inflamed patches, esp. on a child's scalp.

rink /ringk/ *n.* **1** an area of natural or artificial ice for skating or the game of curling etc. **2** an enclosed area for roller-skating. **3** a building containing either of these. **4** *Bowls* a strip of the green used for playing a match. **5** a team in bowls or curling. [ME (orig. Sc.), = jousting-ground: perh. orig. f. OF *renc* RANK[1]]

rinse /rinss/ *v.* & *n.* ● *v.tr.* (often foll. by *through*, *out*) **1** wash with clean water. **2** apply liquid to. **3** wash lightly. **4** put (clothes etc.) through clean water to remove soap or detergent. **5** (foll. by *out*, *away*) clear (impurities) by rinsing. **6** treat (hair) with a rinse. ● *n.* **1** the act or an instance of rinsing (*give it a rinse*). **2** a solution for cleansing the mouth. **3** a dye for the temporary tinting of hair (*a blue rinse*). □□ **rinser** *n.* [ME f. OF *rincer*, *raincier*, of unkn. orig.]

■ *v.* **1** wash, clean, *usu. formal* cleanse; see also FLUSH[1] *v.* 3a. **5** (*rinse out* or *away*) wash out *or* away *or* off, clear (out), clean out, swill out *or* away, flush out. **6** highlight; see also TINT *v.* ● *n.* **1** rinsing, wash, washing, cleaning, ablution, flushing, *usu. formal* cleansing. **3** tint, dye.

riot /rī́ət/ *n.* & *v.* ● *n.* **1 a** a disturbance of the peace by a crowd; an occurrence of public disorder. **b** (*attrib.*) involved in suppressing riots (*riot police*; *riot shield*). **2** uncontrolled revelry; noisy behaviour. **3** (foll. by *of*) a lavish display or enjoyment (*a riot of emotion*; *a riot of colour and sound*). **4** *colloq.* a very amusing thing or person. ● *v.intr.* **1** make or engage in a riot. **2** live wantonly; revel. □ **read the Riot Act** put a firm stop to insubordination etc.; give a severe warning (from the name of a former act partly read out to disperse rioters). **run riot 1** throw off all restraint. **2** (of plants) grow or spread uncontrolled. □□ **rioter** *n.* **riotless** *adj.* [ME f. OF *riote*, *rioter*, *rihoter*, of unkn. orig.]

■ *n.* **1 a** disturbance, uproar, tumult, fracas, fray, affray, mêlée, Donnybrook, brawl, commotion, to-do, *colloq.* row, ruction, rumpus, imbroglio, *Brit. colloq.* punch-up, *esp. US* ruckus. **4** funny man *or* woman, comedian, comedienne; *sl.* gas; see also LAUGH *n.* 2. ● *v.* **1** rebel, revolt, create *or* cause a disturbance, brawl, fight, rampage, go on the rampage, run riot, storm, *US* go on a rampage. **2** see REVEL *v.* 1.

riotous /rī́ətəss/ *adj.* **1** marked by or involving rioting. **2** characterized by wanton conduct. **3** wildly profuse. □□ **riotously** *adv.* **riotousness** *n.* [ME f. OF (as RIOT)]

■ **1** tumultuous, wild, noisy, uncontrollable, unmanageable, chaotic, disorderly, lawless, turbulent, violent, brawling, obstreperous, uncontrolled. **2** rowdy, boisterous, unruly, uproarious, rollicking, roisterous, wild, unrestrained, uninhibited, *colloq.* rumbustious, no-holds-barred, *US colloq.* rambunctious. **3** extravagant, wild; see also PROFUSE 2.

RIP *abbr.* may he or she or they rest in peace. [L *requiescat* (pl. *requiescant*) *in pace*]

rip[1] /rip/ *v.* & *n.* ● *v.tr.* & *intr.* (**ripped**, **ripping**) **1** *tr.* tear or cut (a thing) quickly or forcibly away or apart (*ripped out the lining*; *ripped the book up*). **2** *tr.* **a** make (a hole etc.) by ripping. **b** make a long tear or cut in. **3** *intr.* come violently apart; split. **4** *intr.* rush along. ● *n.* **1** a long tear or cut. **2** an act of ripping. □ **let rip** *colloq.* **1** act or proceed without restraint. **2** speak violently. **3** not check the speed of or interfere with (a person or thing). **rip-cord** a cord for releasing a parachute from its pack. **rip into** attack (a person) verbally. **rip off** *colloq.* defraud, steal. **rip-off** *n. colloq.* **1** a fraud or swindle. **2** financial exploitation. [ME: orig. unkn.]

■ *v.* **1** tear, cut, *archaic or rhet.* rend; see also SLIT *v.* **2** tear, slash, slit, cut open, gash. **3** see SPLIT *v.* 1a. ● *n.* **1** tear, rent, split, slash, gash, cut. □ **rip into** see ATTACK *v.* 3. **rip off** defraud, rob, cheat, swindle, trick, fleece, dupe, deceive, rook, *colloq.* bamboozle, *sl.* con, bilk, skin, gyp; steal, snatch, pilfer, filch, take, *colloq.* lift, swipe, *formal or joc.* purloin, *sl.* pinch, *Brit. sl.* nick. **rip-off 1** swindle, confidence trick, cheat, fraud, deception; embezzlement, *Law* defalcation, *sl.* con, con job *or* trick. **2** overcharging, exploitation, *colloq.* daylight robbery.

rip[2] /rip/ *n.* a stretch of rough water in the sea or in a river, caused by the meeting of currents. □ **rip current** (or **tide**) **1** a strong surface current from the shore. **2** a state of conflicting psychological forces. [18th c.: perh. rel. to RIP[1]]

rip[3] /rip/ *n.* **1** a dissolute person. **2** a rascal. **3** a worthless horse. [perh. f. *rep*, abbr. of REPROBATE]

riparian /rīpáiriən/ *adj.* & *n.* esp. *Law* ● *adj.* of or on a river-bank (*riparian rights*). ● *n.* an owner of property on a river-bank. [L *riparius* f. *ripa* bank]

ripe /rīp/ *adj.* **1** (of grain, fruit, cheese, etc.) ready to be reaped or picked or eaten. **2** mature; fully developed (*ripe in judgement*; *a ripe beauty*). **3** (of a person's age) advanced. **4** (often foll. by *for*) fit or ready (*when the time is ripe*; *land ripe for development*). **5** (of the complexion etc.) red and full like ripe fruit. □□ **ripely** *adv.* **ripeness** *n.* [OE *rīpe* f. WG]

■ **1** mature, matured, seasoned, fully grown, (well-)ripened, mellow, ready, *US* (fully) aged. **2** mature, seasoned, sage, wise, sophisticated, informed, qualified, ready, experienced, prepared, veteran; fully grown; ripened, matured, mellow, seasoned, aged. **3** advanced, mature, adult. **4** right, ideal, apt, proper, suitable, suitably advanced, ready, prepared, fit.

ripen /rī́p'n/ *v.tr.* & *intr.* make or become ripe.

■ mature, develop; age, season, come to maturity; bring to maturity.

ripieno /ripyáynō/ *n.* (*pl.* **-os** or **ripieni** /-ni/) *Mus.* a body of accompanying instruments in baroque concerto music. [It. (as RE-, *pieno* full)]

riposte /ripóst/ *n.* & *v.* ● *n.* **1** a quick sharp reply or retort. **2** a quick return thrust in fencing. ● *v.intr.* deliver a riposte. [F *ri(s)poste*, *ri(s)poster* f. It. *risposta* RESPONSE]

ripper /ríppər/ *n.* **1** a person or thing that rips. **2** a murderer who rips the victims' bodies.

ripping /rípping/ *adj. Brit. archaic sl.* very enjoyable (*a ripping good yarn*). □□ **rippingly** *adv.*

■ fine, splendid, marvellous, excellent, exciting, thrilling, stirring.

ripple[1] /ripp'l/ *n.* & *v.* ● *n.* **1** a ruffling of the water's surface, a small wave or series of waves. **2 a** a gentle lively sound that rises and falls, e.g. of laughter or applause. **b** a brief wave of emotion, excitement, etc. (*the new recruit caused a ripple of interest in the company*). **3** a wavy appearance in hair, material, etc. **4** *Electr.* a slight variation in the strength of a current etc. **5** ice-cream with added syrup giving a coloured ripple effect (*raspberry ripple*). **6** *US* a riffle in a stream. ● *v.* **1 a** *intr.* form ripples; flow in ripples. **b** *tr.*

cause to do this. **2** *intr.* show or sound like ripples. □ **ripple mark** a ridge or ridged surface left on sand, mud, or rock by the action of water or wind. □□ **ripplet** *n.* **ripply** *adj.* [17th c.: orig. unkn.]

■ *n.* **1** wavelet, wave, ruffle, ruffling, undulation, purling, *US* riffle. **2 b** flurry, flutter, wave, disturbance, stir. ● *v.* **1** ruffle, undulate, purl. **2** see GURGLE *v.*

ripple[2] /rípp'l/ *n.* & *v.* ● *n.* a toothed implement used to remove seeds from flax. ● *v.tr.* treat with a ripple. [corresp. to MDu. & MLG *repel(en)*, OHG *riffila, rifilōn*]

riprap /ríprap/ *n. US* a collection of loose stone as a foundation for a structure. [redupl. of RAP[1]]

rip-roaring /ríproring/ *adj.* **1** wildly noisy or boisterous. **2** excellent, first-rate. □□ **rip-roaringly** *adv.*

ripsaw /rípsaw/ *n.* a coarse saw for sawing wood along the grain.

ripsnorter /rípsnortər/ *n. colloq.* an energetic, remarkable, or excellent person or thing. □□ **ripsnorting** *adj.* **ripsnortingly** *adv.*

rise /rīz/ *v.* & *n.* ● *v.intr.* (*past* **rose** /rōz/; *past part.* **risen** /rízz'n/) **1** move from a lower position to a higher one; come or go up. **2** grow, project, expand, or incline upwards; become higher. **3** (of the sun, moon, or stars) appear above the horizon. **4 a** get up from lying or sitting or kneeling (*rose to their feet; rose from the table*). **b** get out of bed, esp. in the morning (*do you rise early?*). **5** recover a standing or vertical position; become erect (*rose to my full height*). **6** (of a meeting etc.) cease to sit for business; adjourn (*Parliament rises next week; the court will rise*). **7** reach a higher position or level or amount (*the flood has risen; prices are rising*). **8** develop greater intensity, strength, volume, or pitch (*the colour rose in her cheeks; the wind is rising; their voices rose with excitement*). **9** make progress; reach a higher social position (*rose from the ranks*). **10 a** come to the surface of liquid (*bubbles rose from the bottom; waited for the fish to rise*). **b** (of a person) react to provocation (*rise to the bait*). **11** become or be visible above the surroundings etc., stand prominently (*mountains rose to our right*). **12 a** (of buildings etc.) undergo construction from the foundations (*office blocks were rising all around*). **b** (of a tree etc.) grow to a (usu. specified) height. **13** come to life again (*rise from the ashes; risen from the dead*). **14** (of dough) swell by the action of yeast etc. **15** (often foll. by *up*) cease to be quiet or submissive; rebel (*rise in arms*). **16** originate; have as its source (*the river rises in the mountains*). **17** (of wind) start to blow. **18** (of a person's spirits) become cheerful. **19** (of a barometer) show a higher atmospheric pressure. **20** (of a horse) rear (*rose on its hind legs*). **21** (of a bump, blister, etc.) form. **22** (of the stomach) show nausea. ● *n.* **1** an act or manner or amount of rising. **2** an upward slope or hill or movement (*a rise in the road; the house stood on a rise; the rise and fall of the waves*). **3** an increase in sound or pitch. **4 a** an increase in amount, extent, etc. (*a rise in unemployment*). **b** *Brit.* an increase in salary, wages, etc. **5** an increase in status or power. **6** social, commercial, or political advancement; upward progress. **7** the movement of fish to the surface. **8** origin. **9 a** the vertical height of a step, arch, incline, etc. **b** = RISER 2. □ **get** (or **take**) **a rise out of** *colloq.* provoke an emotional reaction from (a person), esp. by teasing. **on the rise** on the increase. **rise above 1** be superior to (petty feelings etc.). **2** show dignity or strength in the face of (difficulty, poor conditions, etc.). **rise and shine** (usu. as *imper.*) *colloq.* get out of bed smartly; wake up. **rise in the world** attain a higher social position. **rise to** develop powers equal to (an occasion). **rise with the sun** (or **lark**) get up early in the morning. [OE *rīsan* f. Gmc]

■ *v.* **1** lift, climb, soar, mount, *esp. archaic* & *poet.* arise; fly, take flight, take wing, take to the air, take off. **2** slant *or* incline *or* slope (upwards), ascend, climb, go uphill, *colloq.* surface. **3** ascend, come up, appear, come out. **4a, 5, 20** get up, stand (up), *esp. archaic* & *poet.* arise; get to one's feet; rear (up). **4 b** get up, awaken, waken, wake up, start *or* begin the day, *colloq.* turn out, *esp. archaic* & *poet.* arise. **6** see DISSOLVE *v.* 3b. **7** swell, flood, increase, grow, wax; increase, grow, go up, climb, escalate, ascend, snowball; see also *go up* (GO[1]). **8** see DEEPEN. **9** advance, improve a person's lot *or* position, progress, get ahead, go somewhere, succeed, make something of oneself, be promoted, prosper, thrive, make good, *colloq.* get somewhere, make it, make the grade, go places. **10 a** ascend, climb, come *or* go *or* move up, mount, lift, surface. **b** (*rise to*) react to, respond to, succumb to, be tempted by. **11** see *stand out*. **12 a** ascend, be elevated, climb, lift, go up, mount, *esp. archaic* & *poet.* arise. **13** come back, return, resurface, arise, turn up again, reappear, be resurrected; see also RESURRECT 4. **15** rebel, revolt, mutiny, kick over the traces, take up arms. **16** start, begin, originate, arise, be produced, be generated, be created, spring up, be engendered; grow, occur, happen, take place. **18** lift, improve, get better. ● *n.* **1** ascent, ascension, elevation, flight, climb, take-off. **2** ascent, hill, hillock, knoll, eminence, prominence, elevation, upland, highland, (upward)slope *or* incline, acclivity, *US* upgrade. **3** increase, intensification, amplification, build-up, strengthening, raising, heightening. **4 a** see INCREASE *n.* 1, 2. **b** increase, increment, gain, addition, *esp. US* raise. **5, 6** see PROGRESS *n.* 2. **8** see ORIGIN 1. □ **get** (or **take**) **a rise out of** provoke, stimulate, incite, instigate, foment, goad, encourage, press, push, shake up, waken, awaken, move, motivate, activate, agitate, stir (up), inflame, impassion. **on the rise** see *on the increase* (INCREASE). **rise above** see TRANSCEND 2. **rise in the world** see PROGRESS *v.* **rise to** come *or* measure up to, meet, be equal to, prove adequate to.

riser /rīzər/ *n.* **1** a person who rises esp. from bed (*an early riser*). **2** a vertical section between the treads of a staircase. **3** a vertical pipe for the flow of liquid or gas.

rishi /ríshi/ *n.* (*pl.* **rishis**) a Hindu sage or saint. [Skr. *ṛṣi*]

risible /rízzib'l/ *adj.* **1** laughable, ludicrous. **2** inclined to laugh. **3** *Anat.* relating to laughter (*risible nerves*). □□ **risibility** /-bílliti/ *n.* **risibly** *adv.* [LL *risibilis* f. L *ridēre ris-* laugh]

rising /rīzing/ *adj.* & *n.* ● *adj.* **1** going up; getting higher. **2** increasing (*rising costs*). **3** advancing to maturity or high standing (*the rising generation; a rising young lawyer*). **4** approaching a specified age (*the rising fives*). **5** (of ground) sloping upwards. ● *n.* a revolt or insurrection. □ **rising damp** moisture absorbed from the ground into a wall.

risk /risk/ *n.* & *v.* ● *n.* **1** a chance or possibility of danger, loss, injury, or other adverse consequences (*a health risk; a risk of fire*). **2** a person or thing causing a risk or regarded in relation to risk (*is a poor risk*). ● *v.tr.* **1** expose to risk. **2** accept the chance of (*could not risk getting wet*). **3** venture on. □ **at risk** exposed to danger. **at one's** (**own**) **risk** accepting responsibility, agreeing to make no claims. **at the risk of** with the possibility of (an adverse consequence). **put at risk** expose to danger. **risk capital** money put up for speculative business investment. **risk one's neck** put one's own life in danger. **run a** (or **the**) **risk** (often foll. by *of*) expose oneself to danger or loss etc. **take** (or **run**) **a risk** chance the possibility of danger etc. [F *risque, risquer* f. It. *risco* danger, *riscare* run into danger]

■ *n.* **1** danger, peril; hazard, chance. **2** danger, gamble, hazard, liability; threat, menace. ● *v.* **1** endanger, imperil, hazard, jeopardize. **2** chance. □ **at risk** in danger, in jeopardy; in peril. **put at risk** see ENDANGER.

risky /ríski/ *adj.* (**riskier, riskiest**) **1** involving risk. **2** = RISQUÉ. □□ **riskily** *adv.* **riskiness** *n.*

■ **1** dangerous, perilous, hazardous, chancy, touch-and-go, precarious, *colloq.* iffy, dodgy, *sl.* dicey.

Risorgimento /risórjiméntō/ *n. hist.* a movement for the unification and independence of Italy (achieved in 1870). [It., = resurrection]

risotto /rizóttō/ *n.* (*pl.* **-os**) an Italian dish of rice cooked in stock with meat, onions, etc. [It.]

risqué /rískay, riskáy/ *adj.* (of a story etc.) slightly indecent or liable to shock. [F, past part. of *risquer* RISK]
■ risky, indelicate, unrefined, indecorous, indecent, improper, broad, naughty, spicy, salty, racy, bawdy, suggestive, blue, ribald, daring, *US* off colour, *colloq.* near the knuckle.

rissole /ríssōl/ *n.* a compressed mixture of meat and spices, coated in breadcrumbs and fried. [F f. OF *ruissole, roussole* ult. f. LL *russeolus* reddish f. L *russus* red]

rit. /rit/ *abbr. Mus.* ritardando.

ritardando /ríttaardándō/ *adv.* & *n. Mus.* (*pl.* **-os** or **ritardandi** /-di/) = RALLENTANDO. [It.]

rite /rīt/ *n.* **1** a religious or solemn observance or act (*burial rites*). **2** an action or procedure required or usual in this. **3** a body of customary observances characteristic of a Church or a part of it (*the Latin rite*). □ **rite of passage** (often in *pl.*) a ritual or event marking a stage of a person's advance through life, e.g. marriage. □□ **riteless** *adj.* [ME f. OF *rit, rite* or L *ritus* (esp. religious) usage]
■ **1** observance, solemnity. **2** ceremony, ritual, ceremonial, observance, formality, custom, convention, practice, routine, procedure, solemnity.

ritenuto /ríttənóotō/ *adv.* & *n. Mus.* ● *adv.* with immediate reduction of speed. ● *n.* (*pl.* **-os** or **ritenuti** /-ti/) a passage played in this way. [It.]

ritornello /ríttornéllō/ *n. Mus.* (*pl.* **-os** or **ritornelli** /-li/) a short instrumental refrain, interlude, etc., in a vocal work. [It., dimin. of *ritorno* RETURN]

ritual /rítyooəl/ *n.* & *adj.* ● *n.* **1** a prescribed order of performing rites. **2** a procedure regularly followed. ● *adj.* of or done as a ritual or rites (*ritual murder*). □□ **ritualize** *v.tr.* & *intr.* (also **-ise**). **ritualization** /-līzáysh'n/ *n.* (also **-isation**). **ritually** *adv.* [L *ritualis* (as RITE)]
■ *n.* **1** routine, practice, procedure, protocol. **2** see RITE 2. ● *adj.* ceremonial, ceremonious, sacramental; procedural, formal, conventional, customary, habitual, routine, prescribed, usual, automatic.

ritualism /rítyooəliz'm/ *n.* the regular or excessive practice of ritual. □□ **ritualist** *n.* **ritualistic** /-lístik/ *adj.* **ritualistically** /-lístikəli/ *adv.*

ritzy /rítsi/ *adj.* (**ritzier**, **ritziest**) *colloq.* **1** high-class, luxurious. **2** ostentatiously smart. □□ **ritzily** *adv.* **ritziness** *n.* [*Ritz*, the name of luxury hotels f. C. *Ritz*, Swiss hotel-owner d. 1918]

rival /rī́v'l/ *n.* & *v.* ● *n.* **1** a person competing with another for the same objective. **2** a person or thing that equals another in quality. **3** (*attrib.*) being a rival or rivals (*a rival firm*). ● *v.tr.* (**rivalled**, **rivalling**; *US* **rivaled**, **rivaling**) **1** be the rival of or comparable to. **2** seem or claim to be as good as. [L *rivalis*, orig. = using the same stream, f. *rivus* stream]
■ *n.* **1** competitor, opponent, contender, challenger, antagonist, adversary; opposition. **2** match, equal; see also EQUIVALENT *n.* 1. ● *v.* **1, 2** compete with, contend with, challenge, compare with, equal, measure up to, match, be a match for, vie with, oppose.

rivalry /rī́vəlri/ *n.* (*pl.* **-ies**) the state or an instance of being rivals; competition.
■ competition, conflict, struggle, controversy; competitiveness, contention, vying, feuding, strife, dissension, discord.

rive /rīv/ *v.* (*past* **rived**; *past part.* **riven** /rívv'n/) *archaic* or *poet.* **1** *tr.* split or tear apart violently. **2 a** *tr.* split (wood or stone). **b** *intr.* be split. [ME f. ON *rífa*]

river /rívvər/ *n.* **1** a copious natural stream of water flowing in a channel to the sea or a lake etc. **2** a copious flow (*a river of lava; rivers of blood*). **3** (*attrib.*) (in the names of animals, plants, etc.) living in or associated with the river. □ **river blindness** a tropical disease of the skin caused by a parasitic worm, the larvae of which can migrate into the eye and cause blindness. **river capture** the diversion of the upper headwaters of a mountain stream into a more powerful one. **sell down the river** *colloq.* betray or let down. □□ **rivered** *adj.* (also in *comb.*). **riverless** *adj.* [ME f. AF *river, rivere*, OF *riviere* river or river-bank ult. f. L *riparius* f. *ripa* bank]
■ **1** watercourse, tributary, stream, waterway, *esp. US* creek, *US dial.* kill. **2** stream, flood, torrent, quantity, cataract, cascade. □ **sell down the river** see BETRAY 2.

riverine /rívvərīn/ *adj.* of or on a river or river-bank; riparian.

riverside /rívvərsīd/ *n.* the ground along a river-bank.

rivet /rívvit/ *n.* & *v.* ● *n.* a nail or bolt for holding together metal plates etc., its headless end being beaten out or pressed down when in place. ● *v.tr.* (**riveted**, **riveting**) **1 a** join or fasten with rivets. **b** beat out or press down the end of (a nail or bolt). **c** fix; make immovable. **2 a** (foll. by *on, upon*) direct intently (one's eyes or attention etc.). **b** (esp. as **riveting** *adj.*) engross (a person or the attention). □□ **riveter** *n.* [ME f. OF f. *river* clench, of unkn. orig.]
■ *v.* **1 c** fix, make secure; see also ANCHOR *v.* 1, 2. **2 a** see FIX *v.* 5a, b. **b** (**riveting**) spellbinding, engrossing, hypnotic, hypnotizing, transfixing, fascinating, enthralling, gripping, captivating, absorbing.

riviera /rívviáirə/ *n.* a coastal region with a subtropical climate, vegetation, etc., esp. that of SE France and NW Italy. [It., = sea-shore]

rivière /reevyáir, rívviair/ *n.* a gem necklace, esp. of more than one string. [F, = RIVER]

rivulet /rívyoolit/ *n.* a small stream. [obs. *riveret* f. F, dimin. of *rivière* RIVER, perh. after It. *rivoletto* dimin. of *rivolo* dimin. of *rivo* f. L *rivus* stream]
■ see STREAM *n.* 1.

riyal var. of RIAL.

RL *abbr.* Rugby League.

rly. *abbr.* railway.

RM *abbr.* **1** (in the UK) Royal Marines. **2** Resident Magistrate. **3** (in the UK) Royal Mail.

rm. *abbr.* room.

RMA *abbr.* Royal Military Academy.

r.m.s. *abbr. Math.* root-mean-square.

RMT *abbr.* National Union of Rail, Maritime, and Transport Workers.

RN *abbr.* **1** (in the UK) Royal Navy. **2** (in the UK) Registered Nurse.

Rn *symb. Chem.* the element radon.

RNA *abbr.* ribonucleic acid.

RNAS *abbr.* (in the UK) Royal Naval Air Service (or Station).

RNLI *abbr.* (in the UK) Royal National Lifeboat Institution.

RNZAF *abbr.* Royal New Zealand Air Force.

RNZN *abbr.* Royal New Zealand Navy.

roach[1] /rōch/ *n.* (*pl.* same) a small freshwater fish, esp. *Rutilus rutilus*, allied to the carp. [ME f. OF *roc(h)e*, of unkn. orig.]

roach[2] /rōch/ *n.* **1** *US colloq.* a cockroach. **2** *sl.* the butt of a marijuana cigarette. [abbr.]

roach[3] /rōch/ *n. Naut.* an upward curve in the foot of a square sail. [18th c.: orig. unkn.]

road[1] /rōd/ *n.* **1 a** a path or way with a specially prepared surface, used by vehicles, pedestrians, etc. **b** the part of this used by vehicles (*don't step in the road*). **2 a** one's way or route (*our road took us through unexplored territory*). **b** a method or means of accomplishing something. **3** an underground passage in a mine. **4** *US* a railway. **5** (usu. in *pl.*) a partly sheltered piece of water near the shore in which ships can ride at anchor. □ **by road** using transport along roads. **get out of the** (or **my** etc.) **road** *colloq.* cease to obstruct a person. **in the** (or **my** etc.) **road** *colloq.* obstructing a person or thing. **one for the road** *colloq.* a final (esp. alcoholic) drink before departure. **on the road** travelling, esp. as a firm's representative, itinerant performer, or vagrant. **road fund** *Brit. hist.* a fund for the construction and maintenance of roads and bridges. **road fund licence** *Brit.* a disc displayed on a vehicle certifying payment of road tax. **road-hog** *colloq.* a reckless or inconsiderate road-user, esp. a motorist. **road-holding** the capacity of a moving vehicle to remain stable when cornering at high speeds etc. **road-house** an inn or club on a major road. **road hump** = *sleeping policeman* (see SLEEP). **road-manager** the organizer and supervisor of a musicians' tour. **road-map** a map showing the roads of a country or area. **road-metal** broken stone used in road-making or for railway ballast. **road sense** a person's capacity for safe behaviour on the road, esp. in traffic. **road show 1 a** a performance given by a touring company, esp. a group of pop musicians. **b** a company giving such performances. **2** a radio or television programme done on location. **road sign** a sign giving information or instructions to road users. **road tax** a periodic tax payable on road vehicles. **road test** a test of the performance of a vehicle on the road. **road-test** *v.tr.* test (a vehicle) on the road. **the road to** the way of getting to or achieving (*the road to London*; *the road to ruin*). **road train** a large lorry pulling one or more trailers. **rule of the road** the custom or law regulating which side of the road is to be taken by vehicles (also riders or ships) meeting or passing each other. **take the road** set out. □□ **roadless** *adj.* [OE *rād* f. *rīdan* RIDE]

■ **1** thoroughfare, way, byway, roadway, low road, avenue, boulevard, street, lane, alley, alley-way; highway, high road, pike, parkway, *Autobahn*, *autostrada*, *autoroute*, *Brit.* motorway, carriageway, *US* superhighway, turnpike, expressway, freeway, throughway. **2 a** way, route; see also PATH 2. **b** way, means, approach, route, procedure, technique, method, course. **4** railway, *esp. US* railroad . □ **take the road** see *set forth* 1 (SET[1]).

road[2] /rōd/ *v.tr.* (also *absol.*) (of a dog) follow up (a game-bird) by the scent of its trail. [19th c.: orig. unkn.]

roadbed /rṓdbed/ *n.* **1** the foundation structure of a railway. **2** the material laid down to form a road. **3** *US* the part of a road on which vehicles travel.

roadblock /rṓdblok/ *n.* a barrier or barricade on a road, esp. one set up by the authorities to stop and examine traffic.

roadie /rṓdi/ *n. colloq.* an assistant employed by a touring band of musicians to erect and maintain equipment.

roadman /rṓdmən/ *n.* (*pl.* **-men**) a man employed to repair or maintain roads.

roadroller /rṓdrōlər/ *n.* a motor vehicle with a heavy roller, used in road-making.

roadrunner /rṓdrunnər/ *n.* a bird of Mexican and US deserts, *Geococcyx californianus*, related to the cuckoo, and a poor flier but fast runner.

roadside /rṓdsīd/ *n.* the strip of land beside a road.

roadstead /rṓdsted/ *n.* = ROAD[1] 5. [ROAD[1] + *stead* in obs. sense 'place']

roadster /rṓdstər/ *n.* **1** an open car without rear seats. **2** a horse or bicycle for use on the road.

roadway /rṓdway/ *n.* **1** a road. **2** = ROAD[1] 1b. **3** the part of a bridge or railway used for traffic.

■ **1** see ROAD[1] 1.

roadwork /rṓdwurk/ *n.* **1** (in *pl.*) the construction or repair of roads, or other work involving digging up a road surface. **2** athletic exercise or training involving running on roads.

roadworthy /rṓdwurthi/ *adj.* **1** fit to be used on the road. **2** (of a person) fit to travel. □□ **roadworthiness** *n.*

roam /rōm/ *v.* & *n.* ● *v.* **1** *intr.* ramble, wander. **2** *tr.* travel unsystematically over, through, or about. ● *n.* an act of roaming; a ramble. □□ **roamer** *n.* [ME: orig. unkn.]

■ *v.* wander, rove (around), range, drift, meander, ramble; walk *or* stroll *or* amble *or* saunter *or* perambulate (around *or* about), travel *or* voyage (around *or* about), *archaic or joc.* peregrinate, *formal* circumambulate, *sl.* mosey (around *or* about).

roan[1] /rōn/ *adj.* & *n.* ● *adj.* (of an animal, esp. a horse or cow) having a coat of which the prevailing colour is thickly interspersed with hairs of another colour, esp. bay or sorrel or chestnut mixed with white or grey. ● *n.* a roan animal. □ **blue roan** *adj.* black mixed with white. ● *n.* a blue roan animal. **red roan** *adj.* bay mixed with white or grey. ● *n.* a red roan animal. **strawberry roan** *adj.* chestnut mixed with white or grey. ● *n.* a strawberry roan animal. [OF, of unkn. orig.]

roan[2] /rōn/ *n.* soft sheepskin leather used in bookbinding as a substitute for morocco. [ME, perh. f. *Roan*, old name of *Rouen* in N. France]

roar /ror/ *n.* & *v.* ● *n.* **1** a loud deep hoarse sound, as made by a lion, a person in pain or rage or excitement, thunder, a loud engine, etc. **2** a loud laugh. ● *v.* **1** *intr.* **a** utter or make a roar. **b** utter loud laughter. **c** (of a horse) make a loud noise in breathing as a symptom of disease. **2** *intr.* travel in a vehicle at high speed, esp. with the engine roaring. **3** *tr.* (often foll. by *out*) say, sing, or utter (words, an oath, etc.) in a loud tone. □□ **roarer** *n.* [OE *rārian*, of imit. orig.]

■ *n.* **1** roaring, bellow, thunder, rumble, boom; howl, squall, cry, yell, yowl, clamour, outcry. **2** guffaw, howl, hoot. ● *v.* **1 b** laugh, guffaw, howl, howl with laughter, hoot. **3** bellow, thunder, bawl (out), cry (out), yell, bark, bay, snarl, growl.

roaring /róring/ *adj.* in senses of ROAR *v.* □ **roaring drunk** very drunk and noisy. **roaring forties** stormy ocean tracts between lat. 40° and 50° S. **roaring trade** (or **business**) very brisk trade or business. **roaring twenties** the decade of the 1920s (with ref. to its postwar buoyancy). □□ **roaringly** *adv.*

■ see THUNDEROUS.

roast /rōst/ *v.*, *adj.*, & *n.* ● *v.* **1** *tr.* **a** cook (food, esp. meat) in an oven or by exposure to open heat. **b** heat (coffee beans) before grinding. **2** *tr.* heat (the ore of metal) in a furnace. **3** *tr.* **a** expose (a torture victim) to fire or great heat. **b** *tr.* & *refl.* expose (oneself or part of oneself) to warmth. **4** *tr.* criticize severely, denounce. **5** *intr.* undergo roasting. ● *attrib.adj.* (of meat or a potato, chestnut, etc.) roasted. ● *n.* **1 a** roast meat. **b** a dish of this. **c** a piece of meat for roasting. **2** the process of roasting. **3** *US* a party where roasted food is eaten. [ME f. OF *rost*, *rostir*, f. Gmc]

■ *v.* **3 b** warm, toast, cook. **4** see CRITICIZE 1, TAUNT *v.*

roaster /rṓstər/ *n.* **1** a person or thing that roasts. **2 a** an oven or dish for roasting food in. **b** an ore-roasting furnace. **c** a coffee-roasting apparatus. **3** something fit for roasting, e.g. a fowl, a potato, etc.

roasting /rṓsting/ *adj.* & *n.* ● *adj.* very hot. ● *n.* **1** in senses of ROAST *v.* **2** a severe criticism or denunciation.

■ *adj.* see HOT *adj.* 1. ● *n.* **2** see REPRIMAND *n.*

rob /rob/ *v.tr.* (**robbed**, **robbing**) (often foll. by *of*) **1** take unlawfully from, esp. by force or threat of force (*robbed the safe*; *robbed her of her jewels*). **2** deprive of what is due or normal (*was robbed of my sleep*). **3** (*absol.*) commit robbery. **4** *colloq.* cheat, swindle. □ **rob Peter to pay Paul** take away from one to give to another, discharge one debt by incurring another. [ME f. OF *rob(b)er* f. Gmc: cf. REAVE]

■ **1** loot, rifle, ransack, plunder, raid, pillage, sack; burgle, *US* burglarize; hold up, mug, *colloq.* stick up, *sl.* roll; (*rob of*) strip of, *colloq.* do out of. **2** deny, refuse; (*rob of*) deprive of, strip of. **4** cheat, swindle, defraud, fleece, mulct, rook, *colloq.* rip off, diddle, *sl.* bilk, gyp.

robber /róbbər/ *n.* a person who commits robbery. □ **robber baron 1** a plundering feudal lord. **2** an unscrupulous plutocrat. [ME f. AF & OF (as ROB)]

■ thief, pickpocket, sneak-thief, shoplifter; housebreaker, burglar, cat burglar; bandit, brigand, highwayman; pirate, freebooter, buccaneer, corsair; mugger, hold-up man, *esp. US sl.* stick-up man; safe-breaker, safe-cracker, *sl.* cracksman.

robbery /róbbəri/ *n.* (*pl.* **-ies**) **1 a** the act or process of robbing, esp. with force or threat of force. **b** an instance of this. **2** excessive financial demand or cost (*set us back £20 - it was sheer robbery*). [ME f. OF *roberie* (as ROB)]

■ **1 a** robbing, thieving, theft, stealing, thievery, pilfering, *sl.* pinching, *Brit. sl.* nicking; plunder, sack, looting, plundering, sacking, ransacking, depredation, pillage, pillaging; breaking and entering; burglary, larceny; mugging; *colloq.* ripping-off. **b** theft, burglary, looting, sacking, ransacking, depredation; *US sl.* heist; hold-up, mugging, *colloq.* stick-up. **2** overcharging, exploitation, *colloq.* rip-off.

robe /rōb/ *n.* & *v.* ● *n.* **1** a long loose outer garment. **2** esp. *US* a dressing-gown. **3** a baby's outer garment esp. at a christening. **4** (often in *pl.*) a long outer garment worn as an indication of the wearer's rank, office, profession, etc.; a gown or vestment. **5** *US* a blanket or wrap of fur. ● *v.* **1** *tr.* clothe (a person) in a robe; dress. **2** *intr.* put on one's robes or vestments. [ME f. OF f. Gmc (as ROB, orig. sense 'booty')]

■ *n.* **1** cloak, wrapper, mantle, cape, wrap, poncho. **2** dressing-gown, lounging robe, housecoat, kimono, peignoir, *US* bathrobe. **4** (*robes*) costume, uniform, garb, vestments, livery, garments, accoutrements, regalia, finery, trappings, equipage, *archaic* habit, raiment, *colloq.* gear, *formal* attire, apparel, *poet.* vesture. ● *v.* **1** see DRESS *v.* 1a. **2** enrobe, dress, get dressed up, dress oneself up; dress up.

robin /róbbin/ *n.* **1** (also **robin redbreast**) a small brown European bird, *Erithacus rubecula*, the adult of which has a red throat and breast. **2** *US* a red-breasted thrush, *Turdus migratorius.* **3** a bird similar in appearance etc. to either of these. □ **Robin Hood** (with ref. to the legend of the medieval forest outlaw) a person who acts illegally or unfavourably towards the rich for the benefit of the poor. [ME f. OF, familiar var. of the name *Robert*]

robinia /rəbínniə/ *n.* any N. American tree or shrub of the genus *Robinia*, e.g. a locust tree or false acacia. [mod.L, f. J. *Robin*, 17th-c. French gardener]

roborant /rṓbərənt, rób-/ *adj.* & *n. Med.* ● *adj.* strengthening. ● *n.* a strengthening drug. [L *roborare* f. *robur -oris* strength]

■ *adj.* see TONIC *adj.* ● *n.* see TONIC *n.*

robot /rṓbot/ *n.* **1** a machine with a human appearance or functioning like a human. **2** a machine capable of carrying out a complex series of actions automatically. **3** a person who works mechanically and efficiently but insensitively. **4** *S.Afr.* an automatic traffic-signal. □□ **robotic** /-bóttik/ *adj.* **robotize** *v.tr.* (also **-ise**). [Czech (in K. Čapek's play *R.U.R.* (*Rossum's Universal Robots*) 1920), f. *robota* forced labour]

■ **1, 2** mechanical man *or* monster, android, automaton. **3** automaton; drudge.

robotics /rōbóttiks/ *n.pl.* the study of robots; the art or science of their design and operation.

robust /rōbúst/ *adj.* (**robuster, robustest**) **1** (of a person, animal, or thing) strong and sturdy, esp. in physique or construction. **2** (of exercise, discipline, etc.) vigorous, requiring strength. **3** (of intellect or mental attitude) straightforward, not given to nor confused by subtleties. **4** (of a statement, reply, etc.) bold, firm, unyielding. **5** (of wine etc.) full-bodied. □□ **robustly** *adv.* **robustness** *n.* [F *robuste* or L *robustus* firm and hard f. *robus*, *robur* oak, strength]

■ **1** sound, sturdy, strong; healthy, fit, hale (and hearty), hardy, hearty, stout, tough, strapping, brawny, sinewy, muscular, powerful, athletic, vigorous; in fine fettle, husky. **2** see SEVERE 1, 5. **3** see SOLID *adj.* 6a, SIMPLE *adj.* 6. **4** see FIRM[1] *adj.* 2a, b **5** strong, flavourful, full-bodied, *literary* sapid.

ROC *abbr.* (in the UK) Royal Observer Corps.

roc /rok/ *n.* a gigantic bird of Eastern legend. [Sp. *rocho* ult. f. Arab *ruḵ*]

rocaille /rōkī́/ *n.* **1** an 18th-c. style of ornamentation based on rock and shell motifs. **2** a rococo style. [F f. *roc* (as ROCK[1])]

rocambole /rókkəmbōl/ *n.* an alliaceous plant, *Allium scorodoprasum*, with a garlic-like bulb used for seasoning. [F f. G *Rockenbolle*]

roche moutonnée /rósh mōōtónnay/ *n. Geol.* a small bare outcrop of rock shaped by glacial erosion. [F, = fleecy rock]

rochet /róchit/ *n.* a vestment resembling a surplice, used chiefly by bishops and abbots. [ME f. OF, dimin. f. Gmc]

rock[1] /rok/ *n.* **1 a** the hard material of the earth's crust, exposed on the surface or underlying the soil. **b** a similar material on other planets. **2** *Geol.* any natural material, hard or soft (e.g. clay), consisting of one or more minerals. **3 a** a mass of rock projecting and forming a hill, cliff, reef, etc. **b** (**the Rock**) Gibraltar. **4** a large detached stone. **5** *US* a stone of any size. **6** a firm and dependable support or protection. **7** a source of danger or destruction. **8** *Brit.* a hard usu. cylindrical stick of confectionery made from sugar with flavouring esp. of peppermint. **9** (in *pl.*) *US sl.* money. **10** *sl.* a precious stone, esp. a diamond. **11** *sl.* a solid form of cocaine. **12** (in *pl.*) *coarse sl.* the testicles. □ **get one's rocks off** *coarse sl.* **1** achieve sexual satisfaction. **2** obtain enjoyment. **on the rocks** *colloq.* **1** short of money. **2** broken down. **3** (of a drink) served undiluted with ice-cubes. **rock-bed** a base of rock or a rocky bottom. **rock-bottom** *adj.* (of prices etc.) the very lowest. ● *n.* the very lowest level. **rock-bound** (of a coast) rocky and inaccessible. **rock-cake** a small currant cake with a hard rough surface. **rock-candy** *US* = sense 8 of *n.* **rock cress** = ARABIS. **rock-crystal** transparent colourless quartz usu. in hexagonal prisms. **rock-dove** a wild dove, *Columba livia*, frequenting rocks, supposed ancestor of the domestic pigeon. **rock-face** a vertical surface of natural rock. **rock-fish** a rock-frequenting goby, bass, wrasse, catfish, etc. **rock-garden** an artifical mound or bank of earth and stones planted with rock-plants etc.; a garden in which rockeries are the chief feature. **rock-pigeon** = *rock-dove.* **rock-pipit** a species of pipit, *Anthus spinoletta*, frequenting rocky shores. **rock-plant** any plant growing on or among rocks. **rock python** any large snake of the family Boidae, esp. the African python *Python sebae.* **rock-rabbit** any of several species of hyrax. **rock rose** any plant of the genus *Cistus*, *Helianthemum*, etc., with rose-like flowers. **rock-salmon 1** any of several fishes, esp. *Brit.* (as a commercial name) the catfish and dogfish. **2** *US* an amberjack. **rock-salt** common salt as a solid mineral. **rock-wool** inorganic material made into matted fibre esp. for insulation or soundproofing. □□ **rockless** *adj.* **rocklet** *n.* **rocklike** *adj.* [ME f. OF *ro(c)que*, *roche*, med.L *rocca*, of unkn. orig.]

■ **3 a** tor, *Brit.* crag, outcrop, *US* outcropping; see also CLIFF. **4** stone, pebble, *Austral. sl.* goolie; boulder. **6** pillar *or* tower of strength, mainstay, backbone, *sl.* brick. □ **on the rocks 1** see DESTITUTE 1. **2** in ruins, ruined, broken-down, beyond repair, in tatters *or* shreds, in pieces, *colloq.* in (a) shambles; destroyed, shattered, in disarray. **3** with ice, on ice.

rock[2] /rok/ *v.* & *n.* ● *v.* **1** *tr.* move gently to and fro in or as if in a cradle; set or maintain such motion (*rock him to sleep*; *the ship was rocked by the waves*). **2** *intr.* be or continue in such motion (*sat rocking in his chair*; *the ship was rocking on the waves*). **3 a** *intr.* sway from side to side; shake, oscillate, reel (*the house rocks*). **b** *tr.* cause to do this (*an earthquake rocked the house*). **4** *tr.* distress, perturb. **5** *intr.* dance to or play rock music. ● *n.* **1** a rocking movement (*gave the chair a rock*). **2** a spell of rocking (*had a rock in his chair*). **3 a** = *rock and roll.* **b** any of a variety of types of modern popular music with a rocking or swinging beat, derived from rock and roll. □ **rock and** (or **rock 'n'**) **roll** a type of popular dance-music originating in the 1950s, characterized by a heavy beat and simple melodies, often with a blues element. **rock and** (or **rock 'n'**) **roller** a devotee of rock and roll. **rock the boat** *colloq.* disturb the equilibrium of a situation. **rocking-chair** a chair mounted on rockers or springs for gently rocking in. **rocking-horse** a model of a horse on rockers or springs for a child to rock on. **rocking-stone** a poised boulder easily rocked. **rock-shaft** a shaft that oscillates about an axis without making complete revolutions. [OE *roccian*, prob. f. Gmc]

■ *v.* **1** sway, swing, move to and fro, move back and forth, move backwards and forwards; lull. **2, 3a** toss; roll, reel, lurch, swing, sway, shake, oscillate; wobble. **3 b** sway, roll, swing, move, shake, shudder, rattle. **4** astound, astonish, shock, distress, surprise, jar, stagger, amaze, stun, dumbfound, daze, stupefy, overwhelm, disconcert, unnerve, disturb, perturb, *colloq.* throw, rattle, shake, shake up.

rockabilly /rókkəbilli/ *n.* a type of popular music combining elements of rock and roll and hill-billy music. [blend of *rock and roll* and *hill-billy*]

rockburst /rókburst/ *n.* a sudden rupture or collapse of highly stressed rock in a mine.

rocker /rókkər/ *n.* **1** a person or thing that rocks. **2** a curved bar or similar support, on which something can rock. **3** a rocking-chair. **4** *Brit.* a young devotee of rock music, characteristically associated with leather clothing and motor cycles. **5** a skate with a highly curved blade. **6** a switch constructed on a pivot mechanism operating between the 'on' and 'off' positions. **7** any rocking device forming part of a mechanism. □ **off one's rocker** *sl.* crazy.
■ □ **off one's rocker** see CRAZY 1.

rockery /rókkəri/ *n.* (*pl.* **-ies**) a heaped arrangement of rough stones with soil between them for growing rock-plants on.

rocket[1] /rókkit/ *n.* & *v.* ● *n.* **1** a cylindrical projectile that can be propelled to a great height or distance by combustion of its contents, used esp. as a firework or signal. **2** an engine using a similar principle but not dependent on air intake for its operation. **3** a rocket-propelled missile, spacecraft, etc. **4** *Brit. sl.* a severe reprimand. ● *v.* (**rocketed, rocketing**) **1** *tr.* bombard with rockets. **2** *intr.* **a** move rapidly upwards or away. **b** increase rapidly (*prices rocketed*). [F *roquette* f. It. *rochetto* dimin. of *rocca* ROCK[2], with ref. to its cylindrical shape]
■ *n.* **4** see *tongue-lashing*. ● *v.* **2 a** see SPEED *v.* **b** sky-rocket, shoot up, climb, soar, spiral (upwards), *colloq.* go through the roof.

rocket[2] /rókkit/ *n.* **1** (also **sweet rocket**) any of various fast-growing plants, esp. of the genus *Hesperis* or *Sisymbrium.* **2** a cruciferous annual plant, *Eruca sativa*, grown for salad. □ **wall-rocket** a yellow-flowered weed, *Diplotaxis muralis*, emitting a foul smell when crushed. **yellow rocket** winter cress. [F *roquette* f. It. *rochetta*, *ruchetta* dimin. of *ruca* f. L *eruca* downy-stemmed plant]

rocketeer /rókkiteér/ *n.* **1** a discharger of rockets. **2** a rocket expert or enthusiast.

rocketry /rókkitri/ *n.* the science or practice of rocket propulsion.

rockfall /rókfawl/ *n.* **1** a descent of loose rocks. **2** a mass of fallen rock.

rockhopper /rók-hoppər/ *n.* a small penguin, *Eudyptes crestatus*, of the Antarctic and New Zealand, with a crest of feathers on the forehead.

rockling /rókling/ *n.* any of various small marine fish of the cod family, esp. of the genus *Ciliata* and *Rhinomenus*, found in pools among rocks.

rocky[1] /rókki/ *adj.* & *n.* ● *adj.* (**rockier, rockiest**) **1** of or like rock. **2** full of or abounding in rock or rocks (*a rocky shore*). **3 a** firm as a rock; determined, steadfast. **b** unfeeling, cold, hard. ● *n.* (**the Rockies**) the Rocky Mountains in western N. America. □□ **rockiness** *n.*
■ *adj.* **1, 2** stony, pebbly, shingly, shingled; boulder-strewn, craggy; hard, bumpy, uncomfortable. **3 a** stony, adamant, adamantine, firm, unyielding, rocklike, tough, unbending, flinty, firm, solid, steadfast, steady, unfaltering, staunch, unflinching, determined, resolute, unwavering, unchanging, unvarying, reliable, dependable, sure, certain. **b** stony, flinty, unfeeling, unsympathetic, unemotional, emotionless, impassive, cold, cool, apathetic, indifferent, uncaring, detached, callous, thick-skinned, tough, hard.

rocky[2] /rókki/ *adj.* (**rockier, rockiest**) *colloq.* unsteady, tottering. □□ **rockily** *adv.* **rockiness** *n.* [ROCK[2]]
■ unstable, unsteady, tottering, teetering, shaky, rickety, unsure, uncertain, weak, flimsy, wobbly, vacillating, dubious, doubtful, questionable, *colloq.* iffy.

rococo /rəkṓkō/ *adj.* & *n.* ● *adj.* **1** of a late baroque style of decoration prevalent in 18th-c. continental Europe, with asymmetrical patterns involving scroll-work, shell motifs, etc. **2** (of literature, music, architecture, and the decorative arts) highly ornamented, florid. ● *n.* the rococo style. [F, joc. alt. f. ROCAILLE]
■ *adj.* **2** see ORNATE.

rod /rod/ *n.* **1** a slender straight bar esp. of wood or metal. **2** this as a symbol of office. **3 a** a stick or bundle of twigs used in caning or flogging. **b** (prec. by *the*) the use of this; punishment, chastisement. **4 a** = *fishing-rod.* **b** an angler using a rod. **5 a** a slender straight round stick growing as a shoot on a tree. **b** this when cut. **6** (as a measure) a perch or square perch (see PERCH[1]). **7** *US sl.* = *hot rod.* **8** *US sl.* a pistol or revolver. **9** *Anat.* any of numerous rod-shaped structures in the eye, detecting dim light. □ **make a rod for one's own back** act in a way that will bring one trouble later. □□ **rodless** *adj.* **rodlet** *n.* **rodlike** *adj.* [OE *rodd*, prob. rel. to ON *rudda* club]
■ **1** bar, pole, baton, wand, staff, stick. **2** see STAFF[1] *n.* 1a, b. **3 a** cane, birch, birch-rod, switch. **b** (*the rod*) (corporal) punishment, chastisement, castigation, discipline, chastening, correction; birching, caning.

rode[1] *past* of RIDE.

rode[2] /rōd/ *v.intr.* **1** (of wildfowl) fly landwards in the evening. **2** (of woodcock) fly in the evening during the breeding season. [18th c.: orig. unkn.]

rodent /rṓd'nt/ *n.* & *adj.* ● *n.* any mammal of the order Rodentia with strong incisors and no canine teeth, e.g. rat, mouse, squirrel, beaver, porcupine. ● *adj.* **1** of the order Rodentia. **2** gnawing (esp. *Med.* of slow-growing ulcers). □ **rodent officer** *Brit.* an official dealing with rodent pests. □□ **rodential** /-dénsh'l/ *adj.* [L *rodere ros-* gnaw]

rodenticide /rədéntisīd/ *n.* a poison used to kill rodents.

rodeo /rṓdiō, rədáyō/ *n.* (*pl.* **-os**) **1** an exhibition or entertainment involving cowboys' skills in handling animals. **2** an exhibition of other skills, e.g. in motor cycling. **3 a** a round-up of cattle on a ranch for branding etc. **b** an enclosure for this. [Sp. f. *rodear* go round ult. f. L *rotare* ROTATE[1]]

rodham /róddəm/ *n.* a raised bank in the Fen district of E. Anglia, formed on the bed of a dry river-course. [20th c.: orig. uncert.]

rodomontade /róddəmontáyd/ *n.*, *adj.*, & *v.* ● *n.* **1** boastful or bragging talk or behaviour. **2** an instance of this. ● *adj.* boastful or bragging. ● *v.intr.* brag, talk boastfully. [F f. obs. It. *rodomontada* f. F *rodomont* & It. *rodomonte* f. the name of a boastful character in the *Orlando* epics]
■ *n.* **1** see BRAVADO. **2** see BOAST *n.* 1.

roe[1] /rō/ *n.* **1** (also **hard roe**) the mass of eggs in a female fish's ovary. **2** (also **soft roe**) the milt of a male fish. □ **roe-stone** oolite. □□ **roed** *adj.* (also in *comb.*). [ME *row(e)*, *rough*, f. MLG, MDu. *roge(n)*, OHG *rogo*, *rogan*, ON *hrogn*]

roe[2] /rō/ *n.* (*pl.* same or **roes**) (also **roe-deer**) a small European and Asian deer, *Capreolus capreolus.* [OE *rā(ha)*]

roebuck /rṓbuk/ *n.* a male roe.

roentgen /rúntgən/ *n.* a unit of ionizing radiation, the amount producing one electrostatic unit of positive or negative ionic charge in one cubic centimetre of air under standard conditions. □ **roentgen rays** X-rays. [W. C. *Röntgen*, Ger. physicist d. 1923, discoverer of X-rays]

roentgenography /rúntgənógrəfi/ *n.* photography using X-rays.

roentgenology /rúntgənólləji/ *n.* = RADIOLOGY.

rogation /rōgáysh'n/ *n.* (usu. in *pl.*) *Eccl.* a solemn supplication consisting of the litany of the saints chanted on the three days before Ascension day. □ **Rogation Days** the three days before Ascension Day. **Rogation Sunday** the Sunday preceding these. □□ **rogational** *adj.* [ME f. L *rogatio* f. *rogare* ask]

roger /rójər/ *int.* & *v.* ● *int.* **1** your message has been received and understood (used in radio communication etc.). **2** *sl.* I agree. ● *v. coarse sl.* **1** *intr.* have sexual intercourse. **2** *tr.* have sexual intercourse with (a woman). [the name *Roger*, code for *R*]

rogue /rōg/ *n.* & *v.* ● *n.* **1** a dishonest or unprincipled person. **2** *joc.* a mischievous person, esp. a child. **3** (usu. *attrib.*) **a** a wild animal driven away or living apart from the herd and of fierce temper (*rogue elephant*). **b** a stray, irresponsible, or undisciplined person or thing (*rogue trader*). **4** an inferior or defective specimen among many acceptable ones. ● *v.tr.* remove rogues (sense 4 of *n.*) from. □ **rogues' gallery** a collection of photographs of known criminals etc., used for identification of suspects. [16th-c. cant word: orig. unkn.]

■ *n.* **1** trickster, swindler, cheat, cad, ne'er-do-well, wastrel, good-for-nothing, miscreant, scoundrel, blackguard, knave, scapegrace, cur, villain, wretch, charlatan, mountebank, rip, *archaic or joc.* rapscallion, *colloq.* scamp, rat, *colloq. or joc.* bounder, *Brit. colloq.* blighter, *esp. US colloq.* son of a gun, *often joc.* rascal, *sl.* louse, stinker, bastard, son of a bitch, *Austral. sl.* illywhacker, *esp. Brit. sl.* rotter, *esp. US sl.* SOB *or* s.o.b., *US sl.* bum. **2** see RASCAL. **3** (*attrib.*) **a** undisciplined, uncontrollable, ungovernable, unmanageable, disobedient, fractious, self-willed, unruly, intractable, unrestrained, wild, lawless, strong-willed, headstrong, refractory, contumacious, recalcitrant, cross-grained, rampageous. **b** *colloq.* cowboys.

roguery /rṓgəri/ *n.* (*pl.* **-ies**) conduct or an action characteristic of rogues.

■ see DEVILRY.

roguish /rṓgish/ *adj.* **1** playfully mischievous. **2** characteristic of rogues. □□ **roguishly** *adv.* **roguishness** *n.*

■ **1** see MISCHIEVOUS 1, 2. **2** see WICKED 1.

roil /royl/ *v.tr.* **1** make (a liquid) turbid by agitating it. **2** *US* = RILE 1. [perh. f. OF *ruiler* mix mortar f. LL *regulare* regulate]

■ **1** see AGITATE 3.

roister /róystər/ *v.intr.* (esp. as **roistering** *adj.*) revel noisily; be uproarious. □□ **roisterer** *n.* **roistering** *n.* **roisterous** *adj.* [obs. *roister* roisterer f. F *rustre* ruffian var. of *ruste* f. L *rusticus* RUSTIC]

■ see REVEL *v.* 1.

Roland /rṓlənd/ *n.* □ **a Roland for an Oliver 1** an effective retort. **2** a well-balanced combat or exchange. [name of the legendary nephew of Charlemagne celebrated with his comrade Oliver in the *Chanson de Roland*]

■ □ **a Roland for an Oliver 1** see RETORT[1] *n.* 1, 3. **2** see *requital* (REQUITE).

role /rōl/ *n.* (also **rôle**) **1** an actor's part in a play, film, etc. **2** a person's or thing's characteristic or expected function (*the role of the tape recorder in language-learning*). □ **role model** a person looked to by others as an example in a particular role. **role-playing** an exercise in which participants act the part of another character, used in psychotherapy, language-teaching, etc. [F *rôle* and obs. F *roule, rolle,* = ROLL *n.*]

■ **1** part, character. **2** function, place, part, job; duty, task, responsibility.

roll /rōl/ *v.* & *n.* ● *v.* **1 a** *intr.* move or go in some direction by turning over and over on an axis or by a rotary movement (*the ball rolled under the table*; *a barrel started rolling*). **b** *tr.* cause to do this (*rolled the barrel into the cellar*). **2** *tr.* make revolve between two surfaces (*rolled the clay between his palms*). **3 a** *intr.* (foll. by *along, by,* etc.) move or advance on or (of time etc.) as if on wheels etc. (*the bus rolled past*; *the pram rolled off the pavement*; *the years rolled by*). **b** *tr.* cause to do this (*rolled the tea trolley into the kitchen*). **c** *intr.* (of a person) be conveyed in a vehicle (*the farmer rolled by on his tractor*). **4 a** *tr.* turn over and over on itself to form a more or less cylindrical or spherical shape (*rolled a newspaper*). **b** *tr.* make by forming material into a cylinder or ball (*rolled a cigarette*; *rolled a huge snowball*). **c** *tr.* accumulate into a mass (*rolled the dough into a ball*). **d** *intr.* (foll. by *into*) make a specified shape of itself (*the hedgehog rolled into a ball*). **5** *tr.* flatten or form by passing a roller etc. over or by passing between rollers (*roll the lawn*; *roll pastry*; *roll thin foil*). **6** *intr.* & *tr.* change or cause to change direction by rotatory movement (*his eyes rolled*; *he rolled his eyes*). **7** *intr.* **a** wallow, turn about in a fluid or a loose medium (*the dog rolled in the dust*). **b** (of a horse etc.) lie on its back and kick about, esp. in an attempt to dislodge its rider. **8** *intr.* **a** (of a moving ship, aircraft, or vehicle) sway to and fro on an axis parallel to the direction of motion. **b** walk with an unsteady swaying gait (*they rolled out of the pub*). **9 a** *intr.* undulate, show or go with an undulating surface or motion (*rolling hills*; *rolling mist*; *the waves roll in*). **b** *tr.* carry or propel with such motion (*the river rolls its waters to the sea*). **10 a** *intr.* (of machinery) start functioning or moving (*the cameras rolled*; *the train began to roll*). **b** *tr.* cause (machinery) to do this. **11** *intr.* & *tr.* sound or utter with a vibratory or trilling effect (*words rolled off his tongue*; *thunder rolled in the distance*; *he rolls his rs*). **12** *US sl.* **a** *tr.* overturn (a car etc.). **b** *intr.* (of a car etc.) overturn. **13** *tr.* *US* throw (dice). **14** *tr. sl.* rob (esp. a helpless victim). ● *n.* **1** a rolling motion or gait; rotation, spin; undulation (*the roll of the hills*). **2 a** a spell of rolling (*a roll in the mud*). **b** a gymnastic exercise in which the body is rolled into a tucked position and turned in a forward or backward circle. **c** (esp. **a roll in the hay**) *colloq.* an act of sexual intercourse or erotic fondling. **3** the continuous rhythmic sound of thunder or a drum. **4** *Aeron.* a complete revolution of an aircraft about its longitudinal axis. **5 a** a cylinder formed by turning flexible material over and over on itself without folding (*a roll of carpet*; *a roll of wallpaper*). **b** a filled cake or pastry of similar form (*fig roll*; *sausage roll*). **6 a** a small portion of bread individually baked. **b** this with a specified filling (*ham roll*). **7** a more or less cylindrical or semicylindrical straight or curved mass of something (*rolls of fat*; *a roll of hair*). **8 a** an official list or register (*the electoral roll*). **b** the total numbers on this (*the schools' rolls have fallen*). **c** a document, esp. an official record, in scroll form. **9** a cylinder or roller, esp. to shape metal in a rolling-mill. **10** *Archit.* **a** a moulding of convex section. **b** a spiral scroll of an Ionic capital. **11** *US* & *Austral.* money, esp. as banknotes rolled together. □ **be rolling** *colloq.* be very rich. **be rolling in** *colloq.* have plenty of (esp. money). **on a roll** *US sl.* experiencing a bout of success or progress; engaged in a period of intense activity. **roll back** *US* cause (esp. prices) to decrease. **roll-back** *n.* a reduction (esp. in price). **roll bar** an overhead metal bar strengthening the frame of a vehicle (esp. in racing) and protecting the occupants if the vehicle overturns. **roll-call** a process of calling out a list of names to establish who is present. **rolled gold** gold in the form of a thin coating applied to a baser metal by rolling. **rolled into one** combined in one person or thing. **rolled oats** oats that have been husked and crushed. **roll in 1** arrive in great numbers or quantity. **2** wallow, luxuriate in. **rolling barrage** = *creeping barrage*. **rolling drunk** swaying or staggering from drunkenness. **rolling-mill** a machine or factory for rolling metal into shape. **rolling-pin** a cylinder for rolling out pastry, dough, etc. **rolling-stock 1** the locomotives, carriages, or other vehicles, used on a railway. **2** *US* the road vehicles of a company. **rolling stone** a person who is unwilling to settle for long in one place. **rolling strike** industrial action through a series of limited strikes by consecutive groups. **roll-neck** (of a garment) having a high loosely turned-over neck. **roll of honour** a list of those honoured, esp. the dead in war. **roll on** *v.tr.* **1** put on or apply by rolling. **2** (in *imper.*) *colloq.* (of a time, in eager expectation) come quickly (*roll on Friday!*). **roll-on** (*attrib.*) (of deodorant etc.) applied by means of a rotating ball in the neck of the container. ● *n.* a light elastic corset. **roll-on roll-off** (of a ship, a method of transport, etc.) in which vehicles are driven directly on at the start of the voyage and off at the end of it. **roll out** unroll, spread out. **roll over 1** send (a person) sprawling or rolling. **2** *Econ.* finance the repayment of (maturing stock etc.) by an issue of new stock. **roll-over** *n.* **1** *Econ.* the extension or transfer of a debt or other financial relationship. **2** *colloq.* the overturning of a vehicle etc. **roll-top desk** a desk with a flexible cover sliding in curved grooves. **roll up 1** *colloq.* arrive in a vehicle; appear on the scene. **2** make into or form a roll. **3** *Mil.* drive the flank of (an enemy line) back and round so that the line is shortened or surrounded. **roll-up** (or **roll-your-own**) *n.* a hand-rolled cigarette. **roll up one's sleeves** see SLEEVE. **strike off the rolls** debar (esp. a solicitor) from practising after dishonesty etc. □□ **rollable** *adj.* [ME f. OF *rol(l)er, rouler, ro(u)lle* f. L *rotulus* dimin. of *rota* wheel]

■ *v.* **1** wheel *or* trundle along, spin along; rotate, cycle, turn, turn over (and over), turn round (and round); go (a)round, orbit, tumble, somersault, roll over; see also SPIN *v.* 1. **3 a** bowl, be carried *or* conveyed, cruise, coast; float (by *or* past), sail (by *or* past), fly (by *or* past), flit *or* glide *or* slide by *or* past; pass, go, flow, slip by *or* past, move on; expire, elapse, disappear, vanish, evaporate. **b** wheel, trundle. **5** roll out, flatten, level (off *or* out), smooth (out), even (out). **7 a** see WALLOW *v.* 1. **8b** see STAGGER *v.* 1a. **9 a** undulate, billow, rise and fall; see also WAVE *v.* 2. **11** rumble, reverberate, resound, echo, re-echo, boom, peal, resonate. **12** see OVERTURN *v.* 1, 3. **14** see ROB 1. ● *n.* **1** rolling, billowing, wave, billow, undulation, pitching, rocking, tossing; rotation, spin, toss, whirl, twirl. **3** rumble, reverberation, boom, echo, clap, crash, roar; tattoo, rataplan, rub-a-dub. **5 a** reel, spool, cylinder, scroll. **6 a** bun, *Brit.* bread-roll, bap, bagel, *Brit. sl.* wad. **8 a** list, register, record, directory, listing, catalogue. **11** wad, *US* bankroll, *sl.* bundle. □ **roll-back** reduction, decrease, fall, drop, mark-down, cut. **roll in 1** arrive, come in, pour in, flow in, turn up, *colloq.* show up. **2** luxuriate in, revel in, wallow in, savour, bask in, delight in, take pleasure in, indulge in, rejoice in, relish. **roll out** unroll, unfurl, spread (out), unfold, uncoil, uncurl, unwind, open (out). **roll up 1** see ARRIVE 1. **2** furl, coil, curl, wind up; see also WIND[2] *v.* 4.

rollaway /rṓləway/ *adj. US* (of a bed etc.) that can be removed on wheels or castors.

roller /rṓlər/ *n.* **1 a** a hard revolving cylinder for smoothing the ground, spreading ink or paint, crushing or stamping, rolling up cloth on, hanging a towel on, etc., used alone or as a rotating part of a machine. **b** a cylinder for diminishing friction when moving a heavy object. **2** a small cylinder on which hair is rolled for setting. **3** a long swelling wave. **4** (also **roller bandage**) a long surgical bandage rolled up for convenient application. **5** a kind of tumbler-pigeon. **6 a** any brilliantly plumaged bird of the family Coraciidae, with characteristic tumbling display-flight. **b** a breed of canary with a trilling song. □ **roller bearing** a bearing like a ball-bearing but with small cylinders instead of balls. **roller-coaster** *n.* a switchback at a fair etc. ● *adj.* that goes up and down, or changes, suddenly and repeatedly. ● *v.intr.* (or **roller-coast**) go up and down or change in this way. **roller-skate** see SKATE[1]. **roller-skater** a person who roller-skates. **roller towel** a towel with the ends joined, hung on a roller.

■ **1 a** drum, cylinder; calender; wringer, *esp. Brit. hist.* mangle; windlass. **3** see WAVE *n.* 1, 2.

rollerball /rṓlərbawl/ *n.* a ball-point pen using thinner ink than other ball-points.

rollick /róllik/ *v.* & *n.* ● *v.intr.* (esp. as **rollicking** *adj.*) be jovial or exuberant, indulge in high spirits, revel. ● *n.* **1** exuberant gaiety. **2** a spree or escapade. [19th-c., prob. dial.: perh. f. ROMP + FROLIC]

■ *v.* see REVEL *v.* 1.

rollmop /rṓlmop/ *n.* a rolled uncooked pickled herring fillet. [G *Rollmops*]

roly-poly /rṓlipṓli/ *n.* & *adj.* ● *n.* (*pl.* **-ies**) **1** (also **roly-poly pudding**) a pudding made of a strip of suet pastry covered with jam etc., formed into a roll, and boiled or baked. **2** *US* a tumbler toy. **3** *Austral.* a bushy plant, esp. *Salsola kali*, that breaks off and is rolled by the wind. ● *adj.* (usu. of a child) podgy, plump. [prob. formed on ROLL]

■ *adj.* see PLUMP[1] *adj.*

ROM /rom/ *n. Computing* read-only memory. [abbr.]

Rom /rom/ *n.* (*pl.* **Roma** /rómmə/) a male gypsy. [Romany, = man, husband]

Rom. *abbr.* Romans (New Testament).

rom. *abbr.* roman (type).

Romaic /rōmáyik/ *n.* & *adj.* ● *n.* the vernacular language of modern Greece. ● *adj.* of or relating to this language. [Gk *Rhōmaikos* Roman (used esp. of the Eastern Empire)]

romaine /rəmáyn/ *n. US* a cos lettuce. [F, fem. of *romain* (as ROMAN)]

romaji /rṓməji/ *n.* a system of Romanized spelling used to transliterate Japanese. [Jap.]

Roman /rṓmən/ *adj.* & *n.* ● *adj.* **1 a** of ancient Rome or its territory or people. **b** *archaic* of its language. **2** of medieval or modern Rome. **3** of papal Rome, esp. = ROMAN CATHOLIC. **4** of a kind ascribed to the early Romans (*Roman honesty; Roman virtue*). **5** surviving from a period of Roman rule (*Roman road*). **6** (**roman**) (of type) of a plain upright kind used in ordinary print. **7** (of the alphabet etc.) based on the ancient Roman system with letters A–Z. ● *n.* **1 a** a citizen of the ancient Roman Republic or Empire. **b** a soldier of the Roman Empire. **2** a citizen of modern Rome. **3** = ROMAN CATHOLIC. **4** (**roman**) roman type. **5** (in *pl.*) the Christians of ancient Rome. □ **Holy Roman Empire** the Western part of the Roman Empire as revived by Charlemagne in 800. **Roman candle** a firework discharging a series of flaming coloured balls and sparks. **Roman Empire** *hist.* that established by Augustus in 27 BC and divided by Theodosius in AD 395 into the Western or Latin and Eastern or Greek Empire. **Roman holiday** enjoyment derived from others' discomfiture. **Roman law** the law-code developed by the ancient Romans and forming the basis of many modern codes. **Roman nose** one with a high bridge; an aquiline nose. **roman numeral** any of the Roman letters representing numbers: I = 1, V = 5, X = 10, L = 50, C = 100, D = 500, M = 1000. [ME f. OF *Romain* (n. & adj.) f. L *Romanus* f. *Roma* Rome]

roman-à-clef /rōmaánaakláy/ *n.* (*pl.* ***romans-à-clef*** *pronunc.* same) a novel in which real persons or events appear with invented names. [F, = novel with a key]

Roman Catholic *adj.* & *n.* ● *adj.* of the part of the Christian Church acknowledging the Pope as its head. ● *n.* a member of this Church. □□ **Roman Catholicism** *n.* [17th-c. transl. L (*Ecclesia*) *Romana Catholica* (*et Apostolica*), app. orig. as a conciliatory term: see ROMAN, CATHOLIC]

■ *n.* Catholic, Romanist.

romance /rōmánss/ *n., adj.,* & *v.* ● *n.* /also *disp.* rṓmanss/ **1** an atmosphere or tendency characterized by a sense of remoteness from or idealization of everyday life. **2 a** a prevailing sense of wonder or mystery surrounding the mutual attraction in a love affair. **b** sentimental or idealized love. **c** a love affair. **3 a** a literary genre with romantic love or highly imaginative unrealistic episodes forming the central theme. **b** a work of this genre. **4** a medieval tale, usu. in verse, of some hero of chivalry, of the kind common in the Romance languages. **5 a** exaggeration or picturesque falsehood. **b** an instance of this. **6** (**Romance**) the languages descended from Latin regarded collectively. **7** *Mus.* a short informal piece. ● *adj.* (**Romance**) of any of the languages descended from Latin (French, Italian, Spanish, etc.). ● *v.* **1** *intr.* exaggerate or distort the truth, esp. fantastically. **2** *tr.* court, woo; court the favour of, esp. by flattery. [ME f. OF *romanz, -ans, -ance*, ult. f. L *Romanicus* ROMANIC]

■ *n.* **1** fantasy, mystery, nostalgia; glamour, colour, colourfulness, exoticism. **2 a** mystery, intrigue, excitement, fascination, wonder, sentiment. **c** (love) affair, amour, *affaire*, liaison, relationship, dalliance, *archaic* intrigue. **3 a** fantasy, melodrama, Gothic, Gothic horror. **b** love story, idyll; mystery (story), thriller, horror story, ghost story, fantasy, melodrama, Gothic novel *or* tale, fairy story *or* tale, epic, legend. **5 a** fantasy, fiction, imagination; see also *exaggeration* (EXAGGERATE). **b** tall story, tall tale, fantasy, fabrication, fairy story *or* tale; exaggeration, concoction, flight of fancy, fiction. **6** Romanic. ● *v.* **1** exaggerate, *colloq.* lay it on thick, lay it on with a trowel, pile it on. **2** court, woo, chase, pursue, *archaic* make love to; pander to, flatter, curry favour with, toady (up) to, *colloq.* butter up, soft-soap.

romancer /rōmánsər/ *n.* **1** a writer of romances, esp. in the medieval period. **2** a liar who resorts to fantasy.

Romanesque /rṓmənésk/ *n.* & *adj.* ● *n.* a style of architecture prevalent in Europe *c.* 900–1200, with massive vaulting and round arches (cf. NORMAN). ● *adj.* of the Romanesque style of architecture. [F f. *roman* ROMANCE]

roman-fleuve /rṓmonflṓv/ *n.* (*pl.* ***romans-fleuves*** *pronunc.* same) **1** a novel featuring the leisurely description of the lives of members of a family etc. **2** a sequence of self-contained novels. [F, = river novel]

Romanian /rōmáyniən/ *n.* & *adj.* (also **Rumanian** /roo-/) ● *n.* **1 a** a native or national of Romania in E. Europe. **b** a person of Romanian descent. **2** the language of Romania. ● *adj.* of or relating to Romania or its people or language.

Romanic /rōmánnik/ *n.* & *adj.* ● *n.* = ROMANCE *n.* 6. ● *adj.* **1 a** of or relating to Romance. **b** Romance-speaking. **2** descended from the ancient Romans or inheriting aspects of their social or political life. [L *Romanicus* (as ROMAN)]

Romanism /rṓmənizʼm/ *n.* Roman Catholicism.

Romanist /rṓmənist/ *n.* **1** a student of Roman history or law or of the Romance languages. **2 a** a supporter of Roman Catholicism. **b** a Roman Catholic. [mod.L *Romanista* (as ROMAN)]

romanize /rṓmənīz/ *v.tr.* (also **-ise**) **1** make Roman or Roman Catholic in character. **2** put into the Roman alphabet or into roman type. ▫▫ **romanization** /-záyshʼn/ *n.*

Romano /rōmaánō/ *n.* a strong-tasting hard cheese, orig. made in Italy . [It., = ROMAN]

Romano- /rōmaánō/ *comb. form* Roman; Roman and (*Romano-British*).

Romansh /rōmánsh, -maánsh/ *n.* & *adj.* (also **Rumansh** /roo-/) ● *n.* the Rhaeto-Romanic dialects, esp. as spoken in the Swiss canton of Grisons. ● *adj.* of these dialects. [Romansh *Ruman(t)sch*, *Roman(t)sch* f. med.L *romanice* (adv.) (as ROMANCE)]

romantic /rōmántik/ *adj.* & *n.* ● *adj.* **1** of, characterized by, or suggestive of an idealized, sentimental, or fantastic view of reality; remote from experience (*a romantic picture*; *a romantic setting*). **2** inclined towards or suggestive of romance in love (*a romantic woman*; *a romantic evening*; *romantic words*). **3** (of a person) imaginative, visionary, idealistic. **4 a** (of style in art, music, etc.) concerned more with feeling and emotion than with form and aesthetic qualities; preferring grandeur or picturesqueness to finish and proportion. **b** (also **Romantic**) of or relating to the 18th–19th-c. romantic movement or style in the European arts. **5** (of a project etc.) unpractical, fantastic. ● *n.* **1** a romantic person. **2** a romanticist. ▫▫ **romantically** *adv.* [*romant* tale of chivalry etc. f. OF f. *romanz* ROMANCE]

■ *adj.* **1** imaginary, imagined, fictitious, fictional, ideal, idealized, fancied, fabulous, made-up, dreamed-up, dreamt-up, fantasized, fanciful, fairy-tale, mythical, idyllic, Utopian, illusory; picturesque, exotic, glamorous; sentimental, mawkish, maudlin, saccharine, mushy, sloppy, *Brit. colloq.* soppy, sugary. **2** sentimental, emotional; see also TENDER[1] 5. **3** see IMAGINATIVE 2, *idealistic* (IDEALISM). **5** impractical, visionary, unpractical, unrealistic, ideal, abstract, quixotic, chimerical, absurd, extravagant, wild, mad, *sl.* crackpot. ● *n.* **1** Don Quixote, visionary, idealist; sentimentalist; see also DREAMER.

romanticism /rōmántisizʼm/ *n.* (also **Romanticism**) adherence to a romantic style in art, music, etc.

romanticist /rōmántisist/ *n.* (also **Romanticist**) a writer or artist of the romantic school.

romanticize /rōmántisīz/ *v.* (also **-ise**) **1** *tr.* **a** make or render romantic or unreal (*a romanticized account of war*). **b** describe or portray in a romantic fashion. **2** *intr.* indulge in romantic thoughts or actions. ▫▫ **romanticization** /-záyshʼn/ *n.*

■ **1** see IDEALIZE. **2** see FANTASIZE 1.

Romany /rómməni, rṓ-/ *n.* & *adj.* ● *n.* (*pl.* **-ies**) **1** a Gypsy. **2** the Indo-European language of the Gypsies. ● *adj.* **1** of or concerning Gypsies. **2** of the Romany language. [Romany *Romani* fem. and pl. of *Romano* (adj.) (ROM)]

Romeo /rṓmiō/ *n.* (*pl.* **-os**) a passionate male lover or seducer. [the hero of Shakesp. *Romeo and Juliet*]

■ see GALLANT *n.* 1.

Romish /rṓmish/ *adj.* usu. *derog.* Roman Catholic.

romneya /rómniə/ *n.* any shrub of the genus *Romneya*, bearing poppy-like flowers. [T. *Romney* Robinson, Brit. astronomer d. 1882]

romp /romp/ *v.* & *n.* ● *v.intr.* **1** play about roughly and energetically. **2** (foll. by *along*, *past*, etc.) *colloq.* proceed without effort. ● *n.* a spell of romping or boisterous play. ▫ **romp in** (or **home**) *colloq.* finish as the easy winner. ▫▫ **rompingly** *adv.* **rompy** *adj.* (**rompier**, **rompiest**). [perh. var. of RAMP[1]]

■ *v.* **1** see FROLIC *v.* **2** sail, skip, coast, sweep. ● *n.* see FROLIC *n.* 1, 3, 5.

romper /rómpər/ *n.* (usu. in *pl.*) (also **romper suit**) a young child's one-piece garment covering legs and trunk.

rondavel /rondaável/ *n. S.Afr.* **1** a round tribal hut usu. with a thatched conical roof. **2** a similar building, esp. as a holiday cottage, or as an outbuilding on a farm etc. [Afrik. *rondawel*]

ronde /rond/ *n.* **1** a dance in which the dancers move in a circle. **2** a course of talk, activity, etc. [F, fem. of *rond* ROUND *adj.*]

rondeau /róndō/ *n.* (*pl.* **rondeaux** *pronunc.* same or /-dōz/) a poem of ten or thirteen lines with only two rhymes throughout and with the opening words used twice as a refrain. [F, earlier *rondel*: see RONDEL]

rondel /róndʼl/ *n.* a rondeau, esp. one of special form. [ME f. OF f. *rond* ROUND: cf. ROUNDEL]

rondo /róndō/ *n.* (*pl.* **-os**) *Mus.* a form with a recurring leading theme, often found in the final movement of a sonata or concerto etc. [It. f. F *rondeau*: see RONDEAU]

rone /rōn/ *n. Sc.* a gutter for carrying off rain from a roof.

ronin /rṓnin/ *n. hist.* (in feudal Japan) a lordless wandering samurai; an outlaw. [Jap.]

röntgen etc. var. of ROENTGEN etc.

roo /ro͞o/ *n.* (also **'roo**) *Austral. colloq.* a kangaroo. [abbr.]

rood /ro͞od/ *n.* **1** a crucifix, esp. one raised on a screen or beam at the entrance to the chancel. **2** a quarter of an acre. ▫ **rood-loft** a gallery on top of a rood-screen. **rood-screen** a wooden or stone carved screen separating nave and chancel. [OE *rōd*]

■ **1** crucifix, cross.

roof /ro͞of/ *n.* & *v.* ● *n.* (*pl.* **roofs** or *disp.* **rooves** /ro͞ovz/) **1 a** the upper covering of a building, usu. supported by its walls. **b** the top of a covered vehicle. **c** the top inner surface of an oven, refrigerator, etc. **2** the overhead rock in a cave or mine etc. **3** the branches or the sky etc. overhead. **4** (of prices etc.) the upper limit or ceiling. ● *v.tr.* **1** (often foll. by *in*, *over*) cover with or as with a roof. **2** be the roof of. ▫ **go through the roof** *colloq.* (of prices etc.) reach extreme or unexpected heights. **hit** (or **go through** or **raise**) **the roof** *colloq.* become very angry. **roof-garden** a garden on the flat roof of a building. **roof of the mouth** the palate. **a roof over one's head** somewhere to live. **roof-rack** a framework for carrying luggage etc. on the roof of a vehicle. **roof-tree** the ridge-piece of a roof. **under one roof** in the same building. **under a person's roof** in a person's house (esp. with ref. to hospitality). ▫▫ **roofed** *adj.* (also in *comb.*). **roofless** *adj.* [OE *hrōf*]

roofage /ro͞ofij/ *n.* the expanse of a roof or roofs.

roofer /ro͞ofər/ *n.* a person who constructs or repairs roofs.

roofing /ro͞ofing/ *n.* **1** material for constructing a roof. **2** the process of constructing a roof or roofs.

roofscape /ro͞ofskayp/ *n.* a scene or view of roofs.

rooftop /rōōftop/ *n.* **1** the outer surface of a roof. **2** (esp. in *pl.*) the level of a roof.

rooibos /róyboss/ *n. S.Afr.* **1** an evergreen shrub of the genus *Aspalathus*, with leaves used to make tea. **2** a shrub or small tree, *Combretum apiculatum*, with spikes of scented yellow flowers. [Afrik., = red bush]

rooinek /róynek, rṓ-/ *n. S.Afr. sl. offens.* a British or English-speaking South African. [Afrik., = red-neck]

rook[1] /rōōk/ *n.* & *v.* ● *n.* **1** a black European and Asiatic bird, *Corvus frugilegus*, of the crow family, nesting in colonies in tree-tops. **2** a sharper, esp. at dice or cards; a person who lives off inexperienced gamblers etc. ● *v.tr.* **1** charge (a customer) extortionately. **2** win money from (a person) at cards etc. esp. by swindling. [OE *hrōc*]
▪ *v.* **1** see FLEECE *v.* 1. **2** see SWINDLE *v.* 1.

rook[2] /rōōk/ *n.* a chess piece with its top in the shape of a battlement. [ME f. OF *roc(k)* ult. f. Arab. *rukk*, orig. sense uncert.]

rookery /rōōkkəri/ *n.* (*pl.* **-ies**) **1 a** a colony of rooks. **b** a clump of trees having rooks' nests. **2** a colony of sea birds (esp. penguins) or seals.

rookie /rōōkki/ *n. sl.* **1** a new recruit, esp. in the army or police. **2** *US* a new member of a sports team. [corrupt. of *recruit*, after ROOK[1]]
▪ **1** see RECRUIT *n.* 1, 2.

room /rōōm, rōōm/ *n.* & *v.* ● *n.* **1 a** space that is or might be occupied by something; capaciousness or ability to accommodate contents (*it takes up too much room; there is plenty of room; we have no room here for idlers*). **b** space in or on (*houseroom; shelf-room*). **2 a** a part of a building enclosed by walls or partitions, floor and ceiling. **b** (in *pl.*) a set of these occupied by a person or family; apartments or lodgings. **c** persons present in a room (*the room fell silent*). **3** (in *comb.*) a room or area for a specified purpose (*auction-room*). **4** (foll. by *for*, or *to* + infin.) opportunity or scope (*room to improve things; no room for dispute*). ● *v.intr. US* have a room or rooms; lodge, board. □ **make room** (often foll. by *for*) clear a space (for a person or thing) by removal of others; make way, yield place. **not** (or **no**) **room to swing a cat** a very confined space. **rooming-house** a lodging house. **room-mate** a person occupying the same room as another. **room service** (in a hotel etc.) service of food or drink taken to a guest's room. □□ **-roomed** *adj.* (in *comb.*). **roomful** *n.* (*pl.* **-fuls**). [OE *rūm* f. Gmc]
▪ *n.* **1 a, b** see SPACE *n.* 1c. **2 a** see CELL 1. **b** (*rooms*) quarters, lodgings, apartments; see also PLACE *n.* 3. **4** allowance, latitude, leeway, margin; see also OCCASION *n.* 3, SCOPE[1]. ● *v.* lodge, board; live, reside, stay, *archaic* abide, *literary* dwell. □ **rooming-house** lodging-house, boarding house; see also HOTEL 1.

roomer /rōōmər, rōōmmər/ *n. US* a lodger occupying a room or rooms without board.
▪ see GUEST *n.* 2.

roomette /roomét/ *n. US* **1** a private single compartment in a sleeping-car. **2** a small bedroom for letting.

roomie /rōōmi/ *n. US colloq.* a room-mate.

roomy /rōōmi/ *adj.* (**roomier, roomiest**) having much room, spacious. □□ **roomily** *adv.* **roominess** *n.*
▪ spacious, capacious, commodious, large, sizeable, big, ample.

roost[1] /rōōst/ *n.* & *v.* ● *n.* **1** a branch or other support on which a bird perches, esp. a place where birds regularly settle to sleep. **2** a place offering temporary sleeping-accommodation. ● *v.* **1** *intr.* **a** (of a bird) settle for rest or sleep. **b** (of a person) stay for the night. **2** *tr.* provide with a sleeping-place. □ **come home to roost** (of a scheme etc.) recoil unfavourably upon the originator. [OE *hrōst*]
▪ *n.* **1** perch. ● *v.* **1** perch, sit, rest, sleep; *sl.* crash (out); nest.

roost[2] /rōōst/ *n.* a tidal race in the Orkneys and Shetlands. [ON *röst*]

rooster /rōōstər/ *n.* esp. *US* a domestic cock.

root[1] /rōōt/ *n.* & *v.* ● *n.* **1 a** the part of a plant normally below the ground, attaching it to the earth and conveying nourishment to it from the soil. **b** (in *pl.*) such a part divided into branches or fibres. **c** the corresponding organ of an epiphyte; the part attaching ivy to its support. **d** the permanent underground stock of a plant. **e** any small plant with a root for transplanting. **2 a** any plant, e.g. a turnip or carrot, with an edible root. **b** such a root. **3** (in *pl.*) the sources of or reasons for one's long-standing emotional attachment to a place, community, etc. **4 a** the embedded part of a bodily organ or structure, e.g. hair, tooth, nail, etc. **b** the part of a thing attaching it to a greater or more fundamental whole. **c** (in *pl.*) the base of a mountain etc. **5 a** the basic cause, source, or origin (*love of money is the root of all evil; has its roots in the distant past*). **b** (*attrib.*) (of an idea etc.) from which the rest originated. **6** the basis of something, its means of continuance or growth (*has its root(s) in selfishness; has no root in the nature of things*). **7** the essential substance or nature of something (*get to the root of things*). **8** *Math.* **a** a number or quantity that when multiplied by itself a usu. specified number of times gives a specified number or quantity (*the cube root of eight is two*). **b** a square root. **c** a value of an unknown quantity satisfying a given equation. **9** *Philol.* any ultimate unanalysable element of language; a basis, not necessarily surviving as a word in itself, on which words are made by the addition of prefixes or suffixes or by other modification. **10** *Mus.* the fundamental note of a chord. **11** *Bibl.* a scion, an offshoot (*there shall be a root of Jesse*). **12** *Austral.* & *NZ coarse sl.* **a** an act of sexual intercourse. **b** a (female) sexual partner. ● *v.* **1 a** *intr.* take root or grow roots. **b** *tr.* cause to do this (*take care to root them firmly*). **2** *tr.* **a** fix firmly; establish (*fear rooted him to the spot*). **b** (as **rooted** *adj.*) firmly established (*her affection was deeply rooted; rooted objection to*). **3** *tr.* (usu. foll. by *out, up*) drag or dig up by the roots. **4** *tr. Austral. coarse sl.* **a** have sexual intercourse with (a woman). **b** exhaust, frustrate. □ **pull up by the roots 1** uproot. **2** eradicate, destroy. **put down roots 1** begin to draw nourishment from the soil. **2** become settled or established. **root and branch** thorough(ly), radical(ly). **root beer** *US* an effervescent drink made from an extract of roots. **root-mean-square** *Math.* the square root of the arithmetic mean of the squares of a set of values. **root out** find and get rid of. **root sign** *Math.* = *radical sign*. **strike at the root** (or **roots**) **of** set about destroying. **strike** (or **take**) **root 1** begin to grow and draw nourishment from the soil. **2** become fixed or established. □□ **rootage** *n.* **rootedness** *n.* **rootless** *adj.* **rootlet** *n.* **rootlike** *adj.* **rooty** *adj.* [OE *rōt* f. ON *rót*, rel. to WORT & L *radix*: see RADIX]
▪ *n.* **1 a** rootstock, tap root, rootlet, tuber, radicle, rhizome, rhizomorph. **b** (*roots*) rootstock, rhizome. **3** (*roots*) origins; heritage; family; antecedents, ancestors, predecessors; birthplace, native land *or* country, native soil. **5a, 6** base, basis, foundation, source, seat, cause, fountain-head, origin, well-spring, *poet.* fount. **7** see ESSENCE 1. ● *v.* **1 b** plant, embed, bed (out), set (out), sow, fix. **2 b** (**rooted**) established, set, fixed, fast, firm, deep-rooted, deep-seated, entrenched, ingrained, engrained, (firmly) embedded, implanted, instilled; inbred, inherent, intrinsic, fundamental, basic, *colloq. disp.* chronic. **4 a** see HAVE *v.* 14. **b** see TIRE[1] 1, ANNOY 1. □ **pull up by the roots 1** see UPROOT 1. **2** see UPROOT 3. **put down roots 2** see SETTLE[1] 1, 2a, b. **root and branch** thorough(ly), radical(ly), complete(ly), utter(ly), entire(ly), total(ly). **root out** find, uncover, discover, dig up *or* out, unearth, turn up, bring to light; eradicate, eliminate, destroy, extirpate, exterminate. **strike** (*or* **take**) **root 1** germinate, sprout, strike, grow, develop, thrive, flourish, *literary* burgeon. **2** become set *or* established *or* settled, catch on, take hold.

root[2] /rōōt/ *v.* **1 a** *intr.* (of an animal, esp. a pig) turn up the ground with the snout, beak, etc., in search of food. **b** *tr.* (foll. by *up*) turn up (the ground) by rooting. **2 a** *intr.* (foll. by *around, in*, etc.) rummage. **b** *tr.* (foll. by *out* or *up*) find or extract by rummaging. **3** *intr.* (foll. by *for*) *US sl.* encourage by applause or support. ▫▫ **rooter** *n.* (in sense 3). [earlier *wroot* f. OE *wrōtan* & ON *róta*: rel. to OE *wrōt* snout]

■ **2 a** forage, dig, nose, poke, ferret, burrow, rummage, delve, search, *Brit.* rootle; (*root about, in, etc.*) ransack. **3** (*root for*) cheer (for), applaud (for); support, encourage, urge on, *colloq.* boost.

rootle /rōōt'l/ *v.intr.* & *tr. Brit.* = ROOT[2] 1, 2. [ROOT[2]]

rootstock /rōōtstok/ *n.* **1** a rhizome. **2** a plant into which a graft is inserted. **3** a primary form from which offshoots have arisen.

rooves see ROOF.

rope /rōp/ *n.* & *v.* ● *n.* **1 a** stout cord made by twisting together strands of hemp, sisal, flax, cotton, nylon, wire, or similar material. **b** a piece of this. **c** *US* a lasso. **2** (foll. by *of*) a quantity of onions, ova, or pearls strung together. **3** (in *pl.*, prec. by *the*) **a** the conditions in some sphere of action (*know the ropes*; *show a person the ropes*). **b** the ropes enclosing a boxing- or wrestling-ring or cricket ground. **4** (prec. by *the*) **a** a halter for hanging a person. **b** execution by hanging. ● *v.* **1** *tr.* fasten, secure, or catch with rope. **2** *tr.* (usu. foll. by *off*, *in*) enclose (a space) with rope. **3** *Mountaineering* **a** *tr.* connect (a party) with a rope; attach (a person) to a rope. **b** (*absol.*) put on a rope. **c** *intr.* (foll. by *down*, *up*) climb down or up using a rope. ▫ **give a person plenty of rope** (or **enough rope to hang himself** or **herself**) give a person enough freedom of action to bring about his or her own downfall. **on the rope** *Mountaineering* roped together. **on the ropes 1** *Boxing* forced against the ropes by the opponent's attack. **2** near defeat. **rope in** persuade to take part. **rope into** persuade to take part in (*was roped into doing the washing-up*). **rope-ladder** two long ropes connected by short crosspieces, used as a ladder. **rope-moulding** a moulding cut spirally in imitation of rope-strands. **rope of sand** delusive security. **rope's end** *hist.* a short piece of rope used to flog (formerly, esp. a sailor) with. **rope-walk** a long piece of ground where ropes are made. **rope-walker** a performer on a tightrope. **rope-walking** the action of performing on a tightrope. **rope-yard** a rope-making establishment. **rope-yarn 1** material obtained by unpicking rope-strands, or used for making them. **2** a piece of this. **3** a mere trifle. [OE *rāp* f. Gmc]

■ *n.* **1 a** see CABLE *n.* 1. **2** see STRING *n.* 6. **3 a** (*the ropes*) the routine, the procedure, *colloq.* the score. ● *v.* **1** tie, bind, lash, hitch, fasten, secure, tether. ▫ **rope in** attract, draw (in), tempt, entice, lure, persuade.

ropeable /rṓpəb'l/ *adj.* (also **ropable**) **1** capable of being roped. **2** *Austral.* & *NZ sl.* angry.

■ **2** see ANGRY 1.

ropemanship /rṓpmənship/ *n.* skill in rope-walking or climbing with ropes.

ropeway /rṓpway/ *n.* a cable railway.

roping /rṓping/ *n.* a set or arrangement of ropes.

ropy /rṓpi/ *adj.* (also **ropey**) (**ropier**, **ropiest**) **1** *Brit. colloq.* **a** poor in quality. **b** unwell. **2** (of wine, bread, etc.) forming viscous or gelatinous threads. **3** like a rope. ▫▫ **ropily** *adv.* **ropiness** *n.*

■ **1 a** inadequate, inferior, deficient, indifferent, mediocre, substandard, unsatisfactory, poor. **b** see ILL *adj.* 1. **2** viscous, viscid, glutinous, mucilaginous, gluey, gummy; stringy, thready, fibrous, filamentous.

roque /rōk/ *n. US* croquet played on a hard court surrounded by a bank. [alt. form of ROQUET]

Roquefort /rókfor/ *n. propr.* **1** a soft blue cheese made from ewes' milk. **2** a salad-dressing made of this. [*Roquefort* in S. France]

roquet /rṓkay, -ki/ *v.* & *n. Croquet* ● *v.* (**roqueted**, **roqueting**) **1** *tr.* **a** cause one's ball to strike (another ball). **b** (of a ball) strike (another). **2** *intr.* strike another ball thus. ● *n.* an instance of roqueting. [app. arbitr. f. CROQUET *v.*, orig. used in the same sense]

ro-ro /rṓ-rō/ *adj.* roll-on roll-off. [abbr.]

rorqual /rórkwəl/ *n.* any of various whales of the family Balaenopteridae esp. *Balaenoptera musculus*, having a dorsal fin. Also called *fin-back*, *fin whale*. [F f. Norw. *røyrkval* f. OIcel. *reythr* the specific name + *hvalr* WHALE[1]]

Rorschach test /rórshaak/ *n. Psychol.* a type of personality test in which a standard set of ink-blots is presented one by one to the subject, who is asked to describe what they suggest or resemble. [H. *Rorschach*, Swiss psychiatrist d. 1922]

rort /rort/ *n. Austral. sl.* **1** a trick, a fraud; a dishonest practice. **2** a wild party. [back-form. f. RORTY]

■ **1** see FRAUD 2. **2** see JAMBOREE.

rorty /rórti/ *adj.* (**rortier**, **rortiest**) *Brit. sl.* **1** splendid; boisterous, rowdy (*had a rorty time*). **2** coarse, earthy. [19th c.: orig. unkn.]

rosace /rṓzayss/ *n.* **1** a rose-window. **2** a rose-shaped ornament or design. [F f. L *rosaceus*: see ROSACEOUS]

rosaceous /rōzáyshəss/ *adj. Bot.* of the large plant family Rosaceae, which includes the rose. [L *rosaceus* f. *rosa* rose]

rosaline /rṓzəleen/ *n.* a variety of fine needlepoint or pillow lace. [prob. F]

rosaniline /rōzánnileen, -lin, -līn/ *n.* **1 a** an organic base derived from aniline. **b** a red dye obtained from this. **2** fuchsine. [ROSE[1] + ANILINE]

rosarian /rəzáiriən/ *n.* a person who cultivates roses, esp. professionally. [L *rosarium* ROSARY]

rosarium /rəzáiriəm/ *n.* a rose-garden. [L (as ROSARY)]

rosary /rṓzəri/ *n.* (*pl.* **-ies**) **1** *RC Ch.* **a** a form of devotion in which five (or fifteen) decades of Hail Marys are repeated, each decade preceded by an Our Father and followed by a Glory Be. **b** a string of 55 (or 165) beads for keeping count in this. **c** a book containing this devotion. **2** a similar form of bead-string used in other religions. **3** a rose-garden or rose-bed. [ME f. L *rosarium* rose-garden, neut. of *rosarius* (as ROSE[1])]

roscoe /róskō/ *n. US sl.* a gun, esp. a pistol or revolver. [the name *Roscoe*]

■ see PISTOL *n.*

rose[1] /rōz/ *n.*, *adj.*, & *v.* ● *n.* **1** any prickly bush or shrub of the genus *Rosa*, bearing usu. fragrant flowers generally of a red, pink, yellow, or white colour. **2** this flower. **3** any flowering plant resembling this (*Christmas rose*; *rock rose*). **4 a** a light crimson colour, pink. **b** (usu. in *pl.*) a rosy complexion (*roses in her cheeks*). **5 a** a representation of the flower in heraldry or decoration (esp. as the national emblem of England). **b** a rose-shaped design, e.g. on a compass card or on the sound-hole of a lute etc. **6** the sprinkling-nozzle of a watering-can or hose. **7** a circular mounting on a ceiling through which the wiring of an electric light passes. **8 a** a rose diamond. **b** a rose-window. **9** (in *pl.*) used in various phrases to express favourable circumstances, ease, success, etc. (*roses all the way*; *everything's roses*). **10** an excellent person or thing, esp. a beautiful woman (*English rose*; *rose between two thorns*; *not the rose but near it*). ● *adj.* = *rose-coloured* 1. ● *v.tr.* (esp. as **rosed** *adj.*) make (one's face, a snow-slope, etc.) rosy. ▫ **rose-apple 1** a tropical tree of the genus *Eugenia*, cultivated for its foliage and fragrant fruit. **2** this fruit. **rose-bush** a rose plant. **rose-chafer** a green or copper-coloured beetle, *Cetonia aurata*, frequenting roses. **rose-colour** the colour of a pale red rose, warm pink. **rose-coloured 1** of rose-colour. **2** optimistic, sanguine, cheerful (*takes rose-coloured views*). **rose comb** a flat fleshy comb of a fowl. **rose-cut** cut as a rose diamond. **rose diamond** a hemispherical diamond with the curved part cut in triangular facets. **rose-engine** an appendage to a lathe for engraving curved patterns. **rose-fish** a bright red food fish, *Sebastes marinus*, of the N. Atlantic. **rose geranium** a pink-flowered sweet-scented pelargonium, *Pelargonium graveolus*. **rose-hip** = HIP[2]. **rose-leaf** (*pl.* **-leaves**) **1** a petal of a rose. **2** a leaf of a rose. **rose madder** a pale pink pigment. **rose-mallow** = HIBISCUS. **rose nail** a nail with a head shaped like a rose diamond. **rose of Jericho** a resurrection plant, *Anastatica hierochuntica*. **rose**

of Sharon 1 a species of hypericum, *Hypericum calycinum*, with dense foliage and golden-yellow flowers: also called AARON'S BEARD. **2** *Bibl.* a flowering plant of unknown identity. **rose-pink** = *rose-colour, rose-coloured*. **rose-point** a point lace with a design of roses. **rose-red** *adj.* red like a rose, rose-coloured. ● *n.* this colour. **rose-root** a yellow-flowered plant, *Rhodiola rosea*, with roots smelling like a rose when dried or bruised. **rose-tinted** = *rose-coloured*. **rose-tree** a rose plant, esp. a standard rose. **rose-water** perfume made from roses. **rose-window** a circular window, usu. with roselike or spokelike tracery. **see through rose-coloured** (or **-tinted**) **spectacles** regard (circumstances etc.) with unfounded favour or optimism. **under the rose** in confidence; under pledge of secrecy. **Wars of the Roses** *hist.* the 15th-c. civil wars between Yorkists with a white rose as an emblem and Lancastrians with a red rose. □□ **roseless** *adj.* **roselike** *adj.* [ME f. OE *rōse* f. L *rosa*]

rose[2] *past* of RISE.

rosé /rṓzay/ *n.* any light pink wine, coloured by only brief contact with red grape-skins. [F, = pink]

roseate /rṓziət/ *adj.* **1** = *rose-coloured* (see ROSE[1]). **2** having a partly pink plumage (*roseate spoonbill*; *roseate tern*). [L *roseus* rosy (as ROSE[1])]

rosebay /rṓzbay/ *n.* an oleander, rhododendron, or willow-herb.

rosebowl /rṓzbōl/ *n.* a bowl for displaying cut roses.

rosebud /rṓzbud/ *n.* **1** a bud of a rose. **2** a pretty young woman.

rosella /rəzéllə/ *n.* **1** any brightly coloured Australian parakeet of the genus *Platycercus*. **2** *Austral.* an easily-shorn sheep. [corrupt. of *Rosehill*, NSW, where the bird was first found]

rosemaling /rṓzəmaaling, -mawling/ *n.* the art of painting wooden furniture etc. with flower motifs. [Norw., = rose painting]

rosemary /rṓzməri/ *n.* an evergreen fragrant shrub, *Rosmarinus officinalis*, with leaves used as a culinary herb, in perfumery, etc., and taken as an emblem of remembrance. [ME, earlier *rosmarine* ult. f. L *ros marinus* f. *ros* dew + *marinus* MARINE, with assim. to ROSE[1] and *Mary* name of the Virgin]

roseola /rōzéeələ/ *n.* **1** a rosy rash in measles and similar diseases. **2** a mild febrile disease of infants. □□ **roseolar** *adj.* **roseolous** *adj.* [mod. var. of RUBEOLA f. L *roseus* rose-coloured]

rosery /rṓzəri/ *n.* (*pl.* **-ies**) a rose-garden.

Rosetta stone /rōzéttə/ *n.* a key to previously unattainable understanding. [a stone found near *Rosetta* in Egypt, with a trilingual inscription of the 2nd c. BC in Egyptian hieroglyphs, demotic, and Greek, important in the decipherment of hieroglyphs]

rosette /rōzét/ *n.* **1** a rose-shaped ornament made usu. of ribbon and worn esp. as a supporter's badge, or as an award or the symbol of an award in a competition, esp. by a prizewinning animal. **2** *Archit.* **a** a carved or moulded ornament resembling or representing a rose. **b** a rose-window. **3** an object or symbol or arrangement of parts resembling a rose. **4** *Biol.* **a** a roselike cluster of parts. **b** markings resembling a rose. **5** a rose diamond. □□ **rosetted** *adj.* [F dimin. of *rose* ROSE[1]]

rosewood /rṓzwŏŏd/ *n.* any of several fragrant close-grained woods used in making furniture.

Rosh Hashana /rosh haáshaanaá, rōsh həshṓnō/ *n.* (also **Rosh Hashanah**) the Jewish New Year. [Heb., = beginning (lit. 'head') of the year]

Roshi /rṓshi/ *n.* (*pl.* **Roshis**) the spiritual leader of a community of Zen Buddhist monks. [Jap.]

Rosicrucian /rṓzikrṓōsh'n/ *n.* & *adj.* ● *n.* **1** *hist.* a member of a 17th–18th-c. society devoted to the study of metaphysical and mystical lore (said to have been founded in 1484 by Christian Rosenkreuz). **2** a member of any of several later organizations deriving from this. ● *adj.* of or relating to the Rosicrucians. □□ **Rosicrucianism** *n.* [mod.L *rosa crucis* (or *crux*), as Latinization of G *Rosenkreuz*]

rosin /rózzin/ *n.* & *v.* ● *n.* resin, esp. the solid residue after distillation of oil of turpentine from crude turpentine. ● *v.tr.* (**rosined, rosining**) **1** rub (esp. the bow of a violin etc.) with rosin. **2** smear or seal up with rosin. □□ **rosiny** *adj.* [ME, alt. f. RESIN]

rosolio /rəzṓliō/ *n.* (also **rosoglio**) (*pl.* **-os**) a sweet cordial of spirits, sugar, and flavouring. [It., f. mod.L *ros solis* dew of the sun]

RoSPA /róspə/ *abbr.* (in the UK) Royal Society for the Prevention of Accidents.

roster /róstər, rṓstər/ *n.* & *v.* ● *n.* a list or plan showing turns of duty or leave for individuals or groups esp. of a military force. ● *v.tr.* place on a roster. [Du. *rooster* list, orig. gridiron f. *roosten* ROAST, with ref. to its parallel lines]

■ *n. esp. Brit.* rota.

rostra *pl.* of ROSTRUM.

rostral /róstrəl/ *adj.* **1** *Zool.* & *Bot.* of or on the rostrum. **2** *Anat.* **a** nearer the hypophysial area in the early embryo. **b** nearer the region of the nose and mouth in post-embryonic life. **3** (of a column etc.) adorned with the beaks of ancient war-galleys or with representations of these. □□ **rostrally** *adv.*

rostrated /rostráytid/ *adj.* **1** *Zool.* & *Bot.* having or ending in a rostrum. **2** = ROSTRAL 3. [L *rostratus* (as ROSTRUM)]

rostrum /róstrəm/ *n.* (*pl.* **rostra** /-strə/ or **rostrums**) **1 a** a platform for public speaking. **b** a conductor's platform facing the orchestra. **c** a similar platform for other purposes, e.g. for supporting a film or television camera. **2** *Zool.* & *Bot.* a beak, stiff snout, or beaklike part, esp. of an insect or arachnid. **3** *Rom. Antiq.* the beak of a war-galley. □□ (all in sense 2) **rostrate** /-strət/ *adj.* **rostriferous** /-stríffərəss/ *adj.* **rostriform** *adj.* [L, = beak f. *rodere ros-* gnaw: orig. *rostra* (pl., in sense 1a) in the Roman forum adorned with beaks of captured galleys]

■ **1 a** platform, stage, dais, podium, stand.

rosy /rṓzi/ *adj.* (**rosier, rosiest**) **1** coloured like a pink or red rose (esp. of the complexion as indicating good health, of a blush, wine, the sky, light, etc.). **2** optimistic, hopeful, cheerful (*a rosy future*; *a rosy attitude to life*). □□ **rosily** *adv.* **rosiness** *n.*

■ **1** pink, rose-coloured, red, roseate, reddish, pinkish, cherry, cerise, ruddy, flushed, glowing, blushing, ruby, rubicund, florid, rose-red. **2** optimistic, promising, favourable, auspicious, hopeful, encouraging, sunny, bright, cheerful.

rot /rot/ *v.*, *n.*, & *int.* ● *v.* (**rotted, rotting**) **1** *intr.* **a** (of animal or vegetable matter) lose its original form by the chemical action of bacteria, fungi, etc.; decay. **b** (foll. by *off*, *away*) crumble or drop from a stem etc. through decomposition. **2** *intr.* **a** (of society, institutions, etc.) gradually perish from lack of vigour or use. **b** (of a prisoner etc.) waste away (*left to rot in prison*); (of a person) languish. **3** *tr.* cause to rot, make rotten. **4** *tr. Brit. sl.* tease, abuse, denigrate. **5** *intr. Brit. sl.* joke. ● *n.* **1** the process or state of rotting. **2** *sl.* nonsense; an absurd or foolish statement, argument, or proposal. **3** a sudden series of (usu. unaccountable) failures; a rapid decline in standards etc. (*a rot set in*; *we must try to stop the rot*). **4** (often prec. by *the*) a virulent liver-disease of sheep. ● *int.* expressing incredulity or ridicule. □ **rot-gut** *sl.* cheap harmful alcoholic liquor. [OE *rotian* (v.): (n.) ME, perh. f. Scand.: cf. Icel., Norw. *rot*]

■ *v.* **1 a** decay, decompose, fester, moulder (away); spoil, go bad *or* off, be tainted, mould. **b** corrode, disintegrate, deteriorate, crumble *or* go *or* fall to pieces.
2 a degenerate, decay, decline, atrophy, waste away, wither, disintegrate, crumble, fall apart, deteriorate.
b waste away, wither away, moulder (away), degenerate, decay; languish, die, decline, deteriorate, atrophy. **4** see TEASE *v.* **5** see JOKE *v.* 1. ● *n.* **1** decay, decomposition, putrefaction, putrescence, blight, corrosion, disintegration, deterioration; corruption. **2** (stuff and) nonsense, balderdash, rubbish, bunkum, twaddle, drivel,

claptrap, moonshine, *esp. US* trash *colloq.* hogwash, malarkey, tosh, *sl.* tommy-rot, bosh, eyewash, bunk, boloney, poppycock, bull, *Brit. sl.* codswallop, cobblers, a load of (old) cobblers. ● *int.* see *go on!* (GO[1]), FIDDLESTICK.

rota /rṓtə/ *n.* **1** esp. *Brit.* a list of persons acting, or duties to be done, in rotation; a roster. **2** (**Rota**) *RC Ch.* the supreme ecclesiastical and secular court. [L, = wheel]
■ **1** roster.

Rotarian /rōtáiriən/ *n.* & *adj.* ● *n.* a member of Rotary. ● *adj.* of Rotary. [ROTARY + -AN]

rotary /rṓtəri/ *adj.* & *n.* ● *adj.* acting by rotation (*rotary drill*; *rotary pump*). ● *n.* (*pl.* **-ies**) **1** a rotary machine. **2** *US* a traffic roundabout. **3** (**Rotary**) (in full **Rotary International**) a worldwide charitable society of businessmen, orig. named from members entertaining in rotation. □ **Rotary club** a local branch of Rotary. **rotary-wing** (of an aircraft) deriving lift from rotary aerofoils. [med.L *rotarius* (as ROTA)]
■ *adj.* rotating, rotatory, revolving, spinning. ● *n.* **2** see ROUNDABOUT *n.* 1.

rotate[1] /rōtáyt/ *v.* **1** *intr.* & *tr.* move round an axis or centre, revolve. **2 a** *tr.* take or arrange in rotation. **b** *intr.* act or take place in rotation (*the chairmanship will rotate*). □□ **rotatable** *adj.* **rotative** /rṓtətiv/ *adj.* **rotatory** /rṓtətəri, -táytəri/ *adj.* [L *rotare* f. *rota* wheel]
■ **1** revolve, go round, gyrate, pirouette, whirl, twirl, pivot, reel; turn, spin, whirl *or* twirl round, wheel round. **2** change, alternate, interchange, switch, swap; exchange; trade places, take turns.

rotate[2] /rṓtayt/ *adj. Bot.* wheel-shaped. [formed as ROTA]

rotation /rōtáysh'n/ *n.* **1** the act or an instance of rotating or being rotated. **2** a recurrence; a recurrent series or period; a regular succession of various members of a group in office etc. **3** a system of growing different crops in regular order to avoid exhausting the soil. □□ **rotational** *adj.* **rotationally** *adv.* [L *rotatio*]
■ **1** see REVOLUTION 3, 4.

rotator /rōtáytər/ *n.* **1** a machine or device for causing something to rotate. **2** *Anat.* a muscle that rotates a limb etc. **3** a revolving apparatus or part. [L (as ROTATE[1])]

Rotavator /rṓtəvaytər/ *n.* (also **Rotovator**) *propr.* a machine with a rotating blade for breaking up or tilling the soil. □□ **rotavate** *v.tr.* [ROTARY + CULTIVATOR]

rote /rōt/ *n.* (usu. prec. by *by*) mechanical or habitual repetition (with ref. to acquiring knowledge). [ME: orig. unkn.]
■ routine, ritual; (*by rote*) by heart, from memory; unthinkingly, automatically, mechanically.

rotenone /rṓtənōn/ *n.* a toxic crystalline substance obtained from the roots of derris and other plants, used as an insecticide. [Jap. *rotenon* f. *roten* derris]

rotifer /rṓtifər/ *n.* any minute aquatic animal of the phylum Rotifera, with rotatory organs used in swimming and feeding. [mod.L *rotiferus* f. L *rota* wheel + *-fer* bearing]

rotisserie /rōtíssəri/ *n.* **1** a restaurant etc. where meat is roasted or barbecued. **2** a cooking appliance with a rotating spit for roasting and barbecuing meat. [F *rôtisserie* (as ROAST)]

rotogravure /rṓtəgrəvyóor/ *n.* **1** a printing system using a rotary press with intaglio cylinders, usu. running at high speed. **2** a sheet etc. printed with this system. [G *Rotogravur* (name of a company) assim. to PHOTOGRAVURE]

rotor /rṓtər/ *n.* **1** a rotary part of a machine, esp. in the distributor of an internal-combustion engine. **2** a set of radiating aerofoils round a hub on a helicopter, providing lift when rotated. [irreg. for ROTATOR]

Rotovator var. of ROTAVATOR.

rotten /rótt'n/ *adj.* (**rottener**, **rottenest**) **1** rotting or rotted; falling to pieces or liable to break or tear from age or use. **2 a** morally, socially, or politically corrupt. **b** despicable, contemptible. **3** *sl.* **a** disagreeable, unpleasant (*had a rotten time*). **b** (of a plan etc.) ill-advised, unsatisfactory (*a rotten idea*). **c** disagreeably ill (*feel rotten today*). □ **rotten borough** *hist.* (before 1832) an English borough able to elect an MP though having very few voters. **rotten-stone** decomposed siliceous limestone used as a powder for polishing metals. □□ **rottenly** *adv.* **rottenness** *n.* [ME f. ON *rotinn*, rel. to ROT, RET]
■ **1** rotted, decayed, decomposed, rotting, decomposing, putrid, putrescent, putrescing, mouldy, mouldering, spoilt, spoiled, mildewy, tainted, festering, bad, off; corroded, deteriorating, disintegrating, crumbling, crumbly, friable; falling to pieces. **2 a** immoral, corrupt, dishonest, deceitful, venal, shameless, degenerate, villainous, heinous, iniquitous, evil, wicked, vile, debased, base, perverted, depraved, unscrupulous, unprincipled, amoral, warped, *sl.* bent. **b** base, despicable, wretched, miserable, horrific, nasty, contemptible, low-down, dirty-rotten, mean, low, filthy. **3 a** disagreeable, unpleasant, *colloq.* vile, awful, terrible, horrible, lousy, *sl.* stinking. **b** see UNSATISFACTORY. **c** ill, unwell, off colour, sick, *colloq.* rough, *Brit. colloq.* ropy.

rotter /róttər/ *n.* esp. *Brit. sl.* an objectionable, unpleasant, or reprehensible person. [ROT]
■ see WRETCH 2.

Rottweiler /rótvīlər, -wīlər/ *n.* **1** a dog of a tall black-and-tan breed. **2** this breed. [G f. *Rottweil* in SW Germany]

rotund /rōtúnd/ *adj.* **1 a** circular, round. **b** (of a person) large and plump, podgy. **2** (of speech, literary style, etc.) sonorous, grandiloquent. □□ **rotundity** *n.* **rotundly** *adv.* [L *rotundus* f. *rotare* ROTATE[1]]
■ **1 a** round(ed), circular, globular, spherical, *formal* orbicular. **b** chubby, plump, podgy, portly, tubby, heavy, fleshy, corpulent, stout, fat, obese, overweight, roly-poly, *colloq.* pudgy, *Austral. colloq.* poddy. **2** orotund; grandiloquent, imposing, grand; full, full-toned, deep, resonant, reverberant, reverberating, sonorous, rich, round, mellow; see also POMPOUS 2.

rotunda /rōtúndə/ *n.* **1** a building with a circular ground-plan, esp. one with a dome. **2** a circular hall or room. [earlier *rotonda* f. It. *rotonda* (*camera*) round (chamber), fem. of *rotondo* round (as ROTUND)]

rouble /róob'l/ *n.* (also **ruble**) the chief monetary unit of Russia, the USSR (*hist.*), and some other former republics of the USSR. [F f. Russ. *rubl'*]

roué /róo-ay/ *n.* a debauchee, esp. an elderly one; a rake. [F, past part. of *rouer* break on wheel, = one deserving this]
■ playboy, womanizer, rake, lecher, Lothario, Don Juan, Casanova, libertine, debauchee, flirt, lady-killer, gay dog, *sl.* wolf, dirty old man.

rouge /roozh/ *n.* & *v.* ● *n.* **1** a red powder or cream used for colouring the cheeks. **2** powdered ferric oxide etc. as a polishing agent esp. for metal. ● *v.* **1** *tr.* colour with rouge. **2** *intr.* **a** apply rouge to one's cheeks. **b** become red, blush. □ **rouge-et-noir** /róozhaynwaar/ a gambling game using a table with red and black marks, on which players place stakes. [F, = red, f. L *rubeus*, rel. to RED]

rough /ruf/ *adj.*, *adv.*, *n.*, & *v.* ● *adj.* **1 a** having an uneven or irregular surface, not smooth or level or polished. **b** *Tennis* applied to the side of a racket from which the twisted gut projects. **2** (of ground, country, etc.) having many bumps, obstacles, etc. **3 a** hairy, shaggy. **b** (of cloth) coarse in texture. **4 a** (of a person or behaviour) not mild or quiet or gentle; boisterous, unrestrained (*rough manners*; *rough play*). **b** (of language etc.) coarse, indelicate. **c** (of wine etc.) sharp or harsh in taste. **d** (of a sound, the voice) harsh, discordant; gruff, hoarse. **5** (of the sea, weather, etc.) violent, stormy. **6** disorderly, riotous (*a rough part of town*). **7** harsh, insensitive, inconsiderate (*rough words*; *rough treatment*). **8 a** unpleasant, severe, demanding (*had a rough time*). **b** unfortunate, unreasonable, undeserved (*had rough luck*). **c** (foll. by *on*) hard or unfair towards. **9** lacking finish, elaboration, comfort, etc. (*rough lodgings*; *a rough welcome*). **10** incomplete, rudimentary (*a rough attempt*; *a rough makeshift*). **11 a** inexact, approximate, preliminary (*a rough estimate*; *a rough sketch*). **b** (of stationery etc.) for use in writing rough notes etc. **12** *colloq.* **a** ill, unwell (*am feeling rough*). **b** depressed, dejected. ● *adv.* in a rough manner (*the land should be ploughed rough; play rough*). ● *n.* **1** (usu. prec. by *the*) a hard part or aspect of life; hardship (*take the rough with the smooth*). **2** rough ground (*over rough and smooth*). **3** a rough or violent person (*met a bunch of roughs*). **4** *Golf* rough ground off the fairway between tee and green. **5** an unfinished or provisional or natural state (*have written it in rough; shaped from the rough*); a rough draft or sketch. **6** (prec. by *the*) the general way or tendency (*is true in the rough*). ● *v.tr.* **1** (foll. by *up*) ruffle (feathers, hair, etc.) by rubbing against the grain. **2 a** (foll. by *out*) shape or plan roughly. **b** (foll. by *in*) sketch roughly. **3** give the first shaping to (a gun, lens, etc.). □ **rough-and-ready** rough or crude but effective; not elaborate or over-particular. **rough-and-tumble** *adj.* irregular, scrambling, disorderly. ● *n.* a haphazard fight; a scuffle. **rough breathing** see BREATHING. **rough coat** a first coat of plaster applied to a surface. **rough copy 1** a first or original draft. **2** a copy of a picture etc. showing only the essential features. **rough deal** hard or unfair treatment. **rough diamond 1** an uncut diamond. **2** a person of good nature but rough manners. **rough-dry** (**-dries, -dried**) dry (clothes) without ironing. **the rough edge** (or **side**) **of one's tongue** severe or harsh words. **rough-handle** treat or handle roughly. **rough-hew** (*past part.* **-hewed** or **-hewn**) shape out roughly; give crude form to. **rough-hewn** uncouth, unrefined. **rough house** *sl.* a disturbance or row; boisterous play. **rough-house** *v. sl.* **1** *tr.* handle (a person) roughly. **2** *intr.* make a disturbance; act violently. **rough it** do without basic comforts. **rough justice 1** treatment that is approximately fair. **2** treatment that is not at all fair. **rough passage 1** a crossing over rough sea. **2** a difficult time or experience. **rough ride** a difficult time or experience. **rough-rider** a person who breaks in or can ride unbroken horses. **rough stuff** *colloq.* boisterous or violent behaviour. **rough tongue** a habit of rudeness in speaking. **rough trade** *sl.* a tough or sadistic element among male homosexuals. **rough up** *sl.* treat (a person) with violence; attack violently. **rough work 1** preliminary or provisional work. **2** *colloq.* violence. **3** a task requiring the use of force. **sleep rough** sleep outdoors, or not in a proper bed. □□ **roughness** *n.* [OE *rūh* f. WG]

■ *adj.* **1 a** uneven, irregular, coarse, jagged, rugged, bumpy, lumpy. **2** uneven, rugged, broken; see also BUMPY 1. **3 a** see HAIRY 1. **b** see COARSE 1a. **4 a** brusque, bluff, curt, short, abrupt, unpleasant, churlish, discourteous, impolite, ungracious, surly, disrespectful, rude, uncouth, loutish, unrefined, uncivil, uncivilized, uncultured, vulgar, unladylike, ungentlemanly, coarse, ill-mannered, ill-bred; boisterous, unrestrained. **b** see COARSE 2. **d** harsh, grating, cacophonous, discordant, jarring, strident, raucous; rasping, gruff, husky, hoarse; unmusical, *esp. Mus.* inharmonious. **5** agitated, turbulent, choppy, stormy, storm-tossed, tempestuous, violent, roiled. **6** tough, rough-and-tumble, roughneck; rowdy, disorderly, riotous. **7** harsh, insensitive, inconsiderate, violent, unfeeling, unjust, severe, cruel, tough, hard, brutal, extreme, ungentle. **8 a** hard, tough, severe, demanding, difficult, arduous, laborious, unpleasant. **b** unfair, unjust, bad, tough; unlucky, unfortunate, unreasonable, undeserved. **9** see RUDE 2. **10** unfinished, incomplete, uncompleted, imperfect, undeveloped, unworked, unwrought, unprocessed, unrefined, unpolished, raw; rudimentary, rough-and-ready, rough-hewn, *colloq.* sketchy. **11 a** crude, general, estimated, approximate, inexact, cursory, quick, sketchy, vague, *US colloq.* ballpark; preliminary, roughcast, shapeless, formless, unformed. **12 a** see ROTTEN 3c. **b** see MELANCHOLY *adj.* ● *adv.* violently, savagely, brutally, brutishly; see also ROUGHLY 1. ● *n.* **3** rowdy, tough, hooligan, hoodlum, ruffian, thug, brawler, yahoo, *Austral.* larrikin, *esp. Sc. & Austral.* roughie, *colloq.* roughneck, *Brit. sl.* yob, *US sl.* mug. **5** sketch, (rough) draft, rough copy, mock-up, outline. ● *v.* **2** sketch, draft, mock up, outline, mark out; trace (out), block out. □ **rough-and-tumble** (*adj.*) see IRREGULAR *adj.* 4, DISORDERLY 1. (*n.*) see BRAWL *n.* **rough copy 1** rough, rough draft; see also DRAFT *n.* 1. **rough house** boisterousness, rowdiness, rowdyism, violence, brawling, disorderliness, disorderly conduct, ruffianism; see also FRACAS. **rough-house 2** see BRAWL *v.* **rough passage** rough ride, hard time; see also ORDEAL. **rough ride** rough passage, hard time; see also ORDEAL. **rough up** beat (up), thrash, attack, batter, assault, knock about, *colloq.* lambaste. **rough work 2** see VIOLENCE 1.

roughage /rúffij/ *n.* **1** coarse material with a high fibre content, the part of food which stimulates digestion. **2** coarse fodder. [ROUGH + -AGE 3]

roughcast /rúfkaast/ *n., adj., & v.* ● *n.* plaster of lime and gravel, used on outside walls. ● *adj.* **1** (of a wall etc.) coated with roughcast. **2** (of a plan etc.) roughly formed, preliminary. ● *v.tr.* (*past* and *past part.* **-cast**) **1** coat (a wall) with roughcast. **2** prepare (a plan, essay, etc.) in outline.

■ *adj.* **2** see ROUGH *adj.* 10, 11a.

roughen /rúff'n/ *v.tr.* & *intr.* make or become rough.

roughie /rúffi/ *n. sl.* **1** esp. *Sc. & Austral.* a rough; a hooligan. **2** *Austral.* **a** an outsider in a horse race etc. **b** an unfair or unreasonable act.

roughish /rúffish/ *adj.* somewhat rough.

roughly /rúfli/ *adv.* **1** in a rough manner. **2** approximately (*roughly 20 people attended*). □ **roughly speaking** in an approximate sense (*it is, roughly speaking, a square*).

■ **1** harshly, unkindly, severely, sternly, unsympathetically, brutally, violently, savagely, inhumanly, mercilessly, unmercifully, ruthlessly, pitilessly, cruelly, heartlessly; clumsily, rudely, crudely, awkwardly, primitively, inexpertly, amateurishly, maladroitly, heavy-handedly, ineptly, inefficiently, unskilfully. **2** around, (a)round about, about, nearly; see also *approximately* (APPROXIMATE).

roughneck /rúfnek/ *n. colloq.* **1** a rough or rowdy person. **2** a worker on an oil rig.

■ **1** see ROUGH *n.* 3.

roughshod /rúfshod/ *adj.* (of a horse) having shoes with nail-heads projecting to prevent slipping. □ **ride roughshod over** treat inconsiderately or arrogantly.

roughy /rúffi/ *n.* (*pl.* **-ies**) *Austral. & NZ* a fish, *Arripis georgianus*, of the perch family. [perh. f. ROUGH]

roulade /roolaád/ *n.* **1** a dish cooked or served in the shape of a roll, esp. a rolled piece of meat or sponge with a filling. **2** a florid passage of runs etc. in solo vocal music, usu. sung to one syllable. [F f. *rouler* to roll]

rouleau /rŏŏlō/ *n.* (*pl.* **rouleaux** or **rouleaus** /-lōz/) **1** a cylindrical packet of coins. **2** a coil or roll of ribbon etc., esp. as trimming. [F f. *rôle* ROLL *n.*]

roulette /roolét/ *n.* **1** a gambling game using a table in which a ball is dropped on to a revolving wheel with numbered compartments, players betting on the number at which the ball comes to rest. **2** *Math.* a curve generated by a point on a curve rolling on another. **3 a** a revolving toothed wheel used in engraving. **b** a similar wheel for making perforations between postage stamps in a sheet. □□ **rouletted** *adj.* (in sense 3b). [F, dimin. of *rouelle* f. LL *rotella* dimin. of L *rota* wheel]

round /rownd/ *adj., n., adv., prep., & v.* ● *adj.* **1** shaped like or approximately like a circle, sphere, or cylinder; having a convex or circular outline or surface; curved, not angular. **2** done with or involving circular motion. **3 a** entire, continuous, complete (*a round dozen*); fully expressed or developed; all together, not broken or defective or scanty. **b** (of a sum of money) considerable. **4** genuine, candid, outspoken; (of a statement etc.) categorical, unmistakable. **5** (usu. *attrib.*) (of a number) expressed for convenience or as an estimate in fewer significant numerals or with a fraction removed (*spent £297.32, or in round figures £300*). **6 a** (of a style) flowing. **b** (of a voice) not harsh. **7** *Phonet.* (of a vowel) pronounced with rounded lips. ● *n.* **1** a round object or form. **2 a** a revolving motion, a circular or recurring course (*the earth in its yearly round*). **b** a regular recurring series of activities or functions (*one's daily round*; *a continuous round of pleasure*). **c** a recurring succession or series of meetings for discussion etc. (*a new round of talks on disarmament*). **3 a** a fixed route on which things are regularly delivered (*milk round*). **b** a route or sequence by which people or things are regularly supervised or inspected (*a watchman's round*; *a doctor's rounds*). **4** an allowance of something distributed or measured out, esp.: **a** a single provision of drinks etc. to each member of a group. **b** ammunition to fire one shot; the act of firing this. **5 a** a slice across a loaf of bread. **b** a sandwich made from whole slices of bread. **c** a thick disc of beef cut from the haunch as a joint. **6** each of a set or series, a sequence of actions by each member of a group in turn, esp. **a** one spell of play in a game etc. **b** one stage in a competition. **7** *Golf* the playing of all the holes in a course once. **8** *Archery* a fixed number of arrows shot from a fixed distance. **9** (**the round**) a form of sculpture in which the figure stands clear of any ground (cf. RELIEF 6a). **10** *Mus.* a canon for three or more unaccompanied voices singing at the same pitch or in octaves. **11** (in *pl.*) *Mil.* **a** a watch that goes round inspecting sentries. **b** a circuit made by this. **12** a rung of a ladder. **13** (foll. by *of*) the circumference, bounds, or extent of (*in all the round of Nature*). ● *adv.* **1** with circular motion (*wheels go round*). **2** with return to the starting-point or an earlier state (*summer soon comes round*). **3 a** with rotation, or change to an opposite position (*he turned round to look*). **b** with change to an opposite opinion etc. (*they were angry but I soon won them round*). **4** to, at, or affecting all or many points of a circumference or an area or the members of a company etc. (*tea was then handed round*; *may I look round?*). **5** in every direction from a centre or within a radius (*spread destruction round*; *everyone for a mile round*). **6** by a circuitous way (*will you jump over or go round?*; *go a long way round*). **7 a** to a person's house etc. (*ask him round*; *will be round soon*). **b** to a more prominent or convenient position (*brought the car round*). **8** measuring a (specified distance) in girth. **9** from beginning to end; through the whole time or course (*all the year round*). ● *prep.* **1** so as to encircle or enclose (*tour round the world*; *has a blanket round him*). **2** at or to points on the circumference of (*sat round the table*). **3** with successive visits to (*hawks them round the cafés*). **4** in various directions from or with regard to (*towns round Birmingham*; *shells bursting round them*). **5** having as an axis of revolution or as a central point (*turns round its centre of gravity*; *write a book round an event*). **6 a** so as to double or pass in a curved course (*go round the corner*). **b** having passed in this way (*be round the corner*). **c** in the position that would result from this (*find them round the corner*). **7** so as to come close from various sides but not into contact. **8** at various places in or around (*had lots of clocks round the house to always know the time*). ● *v.* **1 a** *tr.* give a round shape to. **b** *intr.* assume a round shape. **2** *tr.* double or pass round (a corner, cape, etc.). **3** *tr.* express (a number) in a less exact but more convenient form (also foll. by *down* when the number is decreased and *up* when it is increased). **4** *tr.* pronounce (a vowel) with rounded lips. □ **go the round** (or **rounds**) (of news etc.) be passed on from person to person. **in the round 1** with all features shown; all things considered. **2** *Theatr.* with the audience round at least three sides of the stage. **3** (of sculpture) with all sides shown; not in relief. **make the round of** go round. **make** (or **go**) **one's rounds** take a customary route for inspection etc. **round about 1** in a ring (about); all round; on all sides (of). **2** with a change to an opposite position. **3** approximately (*cost round about £50*). **round and round** several times round. **round-arm** *Cricket* (of bowling) with the arm swung horizontally. **round the bend** see BEND[1]. **round brackets** brackets of the form (). **round dance 1** a dance in which couples move in circles round the ballroom. **2** a dance in which the dancers form one large circle. **round down** see sense 3 of *v.* **round off** (or **out**) **1** bring to a complete or symmetrical or well-ordered state. **2** smooth out; blunt the corners or angles of. **round on a person** make a sudden verbal attack on or unexpected retort to a person. **round out** = *round off* 1. **round peg in a square hole** = *square peg in a round hole* (see PEG). **round robin 1** a petition esp. with signatures written in a circle to conceal the order of writing. **2** *US* a tournament in which each competitor plays in turn against every other. **round-shouldered** with shoulders bent forward so that the back is rounded. **Round Table** (in allusion to that at which King Arthur and his knights sat so that none should have precedence) **1** an international charitable association which holds discussions, debates, etc., and undertakes community service. **2** (**round table**) an assembly for discussion, esp. at a conference (often *attrib.*: *round-table talks*). **round trip** a trip to one or more places and back again (esp. by a circular route). **round the twist** see TWIST. **round up** collect or bring together, esp. by going round (see also sense 3 of *v.*). **round-up** *n.* **1** a systematic rounding up of people or things. **2** a summary; a résumé of facts or events. □□ **roundish** *adj.* **roundness** *n.* [ME f. OF *ro(u)nd-* stem of *ro(o)nt*, *reont* f. L *rotundus* ROTUND]

■ *adj.* **1** circular, disc-shaped, discoid, disc-like; ring-shaped, annular, hoop-shaped, hoop-like; spherical, ball-shaped, ball-like, globular, spheroid, spheroidal, globe-shaped, globelike, orb-shaped, orb-like, *formal* orbicular; curved, curvilinear, rounded, arched. **2** circular, roundabout, circuitous, twisting, spiralling. **3 a** exact, precise, complete, entire, full, continuous. **b** see CONSIDERABLE 1, 2. **4** plain, honest, straightforward, direct, unvarnished, outspoken, candid, genuine, truthful, frank, open, blunt, *colloq.* upfront; categorical, unmistakable. **5** approximate, rough, *US colloq.* ballpark; rounded off. **6 a** see FLUENT 1a. **b** rounded, mellow, full, vibrant, reverberant, reverberating, sonorous, rich, mellifluous. ● *n.* **1** circle, disc; ring, hoop, *esp. Math.* & *Biol.* annulus; ball, sphere, globe, orb, bead. **2 a** see CYCLE *n.* 1a. **c** cycle, series, sequence, succession, bout, spell. **3** circuit, course; beat, tour, turn; see also ROUTE *n.* **4 b** bullet(s), cartridge(s), shell(s), shot(s). **6** heat, stage, level, turn, game, bout. **13** circumference, bounds, extent, scope, compass; see also RANGE *n.* 1a–c. ● *adv.* **3 a** around, about. **4** around, about. **5** about, around, in the neighbourhood *or* vicinity, in the area, on all sides. **6** around, in a circle *or* circuit, in *or* by a circular route *or* path, in *or* by a circuitous route *or* path, circuitously. **8** in perimeter *or* periphery, around. **9** through, throughout, from beginning to end, from start to finish. ● *prep.* **1** about, around, encircling, enclosing; orbiting. **2** about, around, near. **4** about, around, near, in the neighbourhood *or* vicinity of, in the area of. **8** here and there in, about, around, throughout, all over, everywhere in. ● *v.* **2** turn, go (a)round; orbit, go (a)round. □ **make the round of** go round, look in on; see also VISIT *v.* 1. **round about 1** see AROUND *adv.* 1, *prep.* 2. **3** see *approximately* (APPROXIMATE). **round off** *or* **out 1** complete, close, end, bring to an end *or* a close, finish. **round on a person** see ATTACK *v.* 3. **round up** gather, assemble, muster, draw *or* get *or* bring together, pull together, collect, herd, marshal, corral, *US* wrangle. **round-up 1** gathering, assembly, rally, collection, herding, corralling, *US* wrangling. **2** summary, synopsis, digest, outline, recapitulation, review, survey, *colloq.* recap.

roundabout /ráwndəbowt/ *n.* & *adj.* ● *n.* **1** *Brit.* a road junction at which traffic moves in one direction round a central island. **2** *Brit.* **a** a large revolving device in a playground, for children to ride on. **b** = MERRY-GO-ROUND 1. ● *adj.* circuitous, circumlocutory, indirect.

■ *n.* **1** *Brit.* mini-roundabout, *US* rotary, traffic circle. **2** merry-go-round, whirligig, *US* carousel. ● *adj.* circuitous, circular, indirect, long; circumlocutory, devious, evasive, oblique.

roundel /równd'l/ *n.* **1** a small disc, esp. a decorative medallion. **2** a circular identifying mark painted on military aircraft, esp. the red, white, and blue of the RAF. **3** a poem of eleven lines in three stanzas. [ME f. OF *rondel(le)* (as ROUND)]

roundelay /równdilay/ *n.* a short simple song with a refrain. [F *rondelet* (as RONDEL), with assim. to LAY³ or *virelay*]

rounder /równdər/ *n.* **1** (in *pl.*; treated as *sing.*) a game with a bat and ball in which players after hitting the ball run through a round of bases. **2** a complete run of a player through all the bases as a unit of scoring in rounders.

Roundhead /równdhed/ *n. hist.* a member of the Parliamentary party in the English Civil War. [f. their custom of wearing the hair cut short]

roundhouse /równdhowss/ *n.* **1** a circular repair-shed for railway locomotives, built round a turntable. **2** *sl.* **a** a blow given with a wide sweep of the arm. **b** *US Baseball* a pitch made with a sweeping sidearm motion. **3** *hist.* a prison; a place of detention. **4** *Naut.* a cabin or set of cabins on the after part of the quarterdeck, esp. on a sailing-ship.

roundly /równdli/ *adv.* **1** bluntly, in plain language, severely (*was roundly criticized*; *told them roundly that he refused*). **2** in a thoroughgoing manner (*go roundly to work*). **3** in a circular way (*swells out roundly*).

roundsman /równdzmən/ *n.* (*pl.* **-men**) **1** *Brit.* a tradesman's employee going round delivering and taking orders. **2** *US* a police officer in charge of a patrol. **3** *Austral.* a journalist covering a specified subject (*political roundsman*).

roundworm /równdwurm/ *n.* a worm, esp. a nematode, with a rounded body.

roup¹ /rowp/ *n.* & *v. Sc.* & *N.Engl.* ● *n.* an auction. ● *v.tr.* sell by auction. [ME 'to shout', of Scand. orig.]

roup² /ro͞op/ *n.* an infectious poultry-disease, esp. of the respiratory tract. ▫▫ **roupy** *adj.* [16th c.: orig. unkn.]

rouse /rowz/ *v.* **1 a** *tr.* (often foll. by *from*, *out of*) bring out of sleep, wake. **b** *intr.* (often foll. by *up*) cease to sleep, wake up. **2** (often foll. by *up*) **a** *tr.* stir up, make active or excited, startle out of inactivity or confidence or carelessness (*roused them from their complacency*; *was roused to protest*). **b** *intr.* become active. **3** *tr.* provoke to anger (*is terrible when roused*). **4** *tr.* evoke (feelings). **5** *tr.* (usu. foll. by *in*, *out*, *up*) *Naut.* haul vigorously. **6** *tr.* startle (game) from a lair or cover. **7** *tr.* stir (liquid, esp. beer while brewing). ▫ **rouse oneself** overcome one's indolence. ▫▫ **rousable** *adj.* **rouser** *n.* [orig. as a hawking and hunting term, so prob. f. AF: orig. unkn.]

■ **1** arouse; waken, awaken, wake (up), get up; *esp. archaic* & *poet.* arise. **2 a** stir (up), arouse, stimulate, inspirit, animate, invigorate, prod, prompt, electrify, galvanize, move, excite, fire. **b** see STIR¹ *v.* 2c, 3. **3** provoke, stir (up), goad, incite, work up, fire up. **4** see EVOKE 2.
▫ **rouse oneself** see STIR¹ *v.* 2c.

rouseabout /rówzəbowt/ *n. Austral.* & *NZ* an unskilled labourer or odd jobber, esp. on a farm.

rousing /rówzing/ *adj.* **1** exciting, stirring (*a rousing cheer*; *a rousing song*). **2** (of a fire) blazing strongly. ▫▫ **rousingly** *adv.*

■ **1** stimulating, inspiriting, animating, enlivening, energizing, inspiring, invigorating, vitalizing, electrifying, exciting, stirring.

roust /rowst/ *v.tr.* **1** (often foll. by *up*, *out*) **a** rouse, stir up. **b** root out. **2** *US sl.* jostle, harass, rough up. ▫ **roust around** rummage. [perh. alt. of ROUSE]

roustabout /rówstəbowt/ *n.* **1** a labourer on an oil rig. **2** an unskilled or casual labourer. **3** *US* a dock labourer or deck hand. **4** *Austral.* = ROUSEABOUT.

rout¹ /rowt/ *n.* & *v.* ● *n.* **1 a** a disorderly retreat of defeated troops. **b** a heavy defeat. **2 a** an assemblage or company esp. of revellers or rioters. **b** *Law* an assemblage of three or more persons who have made a move towards committing an illegal act. **3** riot, tumult, disturbance, clamour, fuss. **4** *Brit. archaic* a large evening party or reception. ● *v.tr.* put to rout. ▫ **put to rout** put to flight, defeat utterly. [ME f. AF *rute*, OF *route* ult. f. L *ruptus* broken]

■ *n.* **1 a** dispersal, withdrawal; see also RETREAT *n.* 1a.
b defeat, trouncing, overthrow, subjugation, *literary* vanquishment; débâcle, conquest, thrashing, beating; *colloq.* licking, *US sl.* shellacking. ● *v.* defeat, win out over, trounce, overthrow, bring down, subjugate, subdue, suppress, conquer, overwhelm, overpower, put to rout *or* flight, worst, beat, crush, destroy, put down, *colloq.* best, lick, wipe the floor with, walk (all) over, *literary* vanquish, *sl.* clobber, *US sl.* shellack, skunk.

rout² /rowt/ *v.* **1** *intr.* & *tr.* = ROOT². **2** *tr.* cut a groove, or any pattern not extending to the edges, in (a wooden or metal surface). ▫ **rout out** force or fetch out of bed or from a house or hiding-place. [var. of ROOT²]

route /ro͞ot, *Mil.* also rowt/ *n.* & *v.* ● *n.* **1** a way or course taken (esp. regularly) in getting from a starting-point to a destination. **2** *US* a round travelled in delivering, selling, or collecting goods. **3** *Mil. archaic* marching orders. ● *v.tr.* (**routeing**) send or forward or direct to be sent by a particular route. ▫ **route man** *US* = ROUNDSMAN 1. **route march** a training-march for troops. [ME f. OF *r(o)ute* road ult. f. L *ruptus* broken]

■ *n.* **1** way, itinerary, course, direction, path, road, avenue. ● *v.* direct, send; see also FORWARD *v.* 1.

router /rówtər/ *n.* a type of plane with two handles used in routing.

routine /ro͞oteen/ *n.*, *adj.*, & *v.* ● *n.* **1** a regular course or procedure, an unvarying performance of certain acts. **2** a set sequence in a performance, esp. a dance, comedy act, etc. **3** *Computing* a sequence of instructions for performing a task. ● *adj.* **1** performed as part of a routine; unvarying, mechanical (*routine duties*; *a routine job shelling peas*). **2** of a customary or standard kind. ● *v.tr.* organize according to a routine. ▫▫ **routinely** *adv.* [F (as ROUTE)]

■ *n.* **1** procedure, way, method; pattern, practice, drill, formula; ways, customs; programme, schedule, plan. **2** act, performance, number, part, *sl.* shtick. ● *adj.* **1** accustomed; regular, ordinary, run-of-the-mill, everyday, unvarying, unchanging, unvaried; programmed, assigned, designated, scheduled; boring, tedious, tiresome, unimaginative, uninteresting; hackneyed, trite, stereotypic(al), clichéd; monotonous, uneventful, automatic, mechanical, perfunctory. **2** customary, habitual, familiar, standard, conventional, usual. ● *v.* routinize.

routinism /ro͞oteeniz'm/ *n.* the prevalence of routine. ▫▫ **routinist** *n.* & *adj.*

routinize /ro͞oteenīz/ *v.tr.* (also **-ise**) subject to a routine; make into a matter of routine. ▫▫ **routinization** /-záysh'n/ *n.*

roux /ro͞o/ *n.* (*pl.* same) a mixture of fat (esp. butter) and flour used in making sauces etc. [F, = browned (butter): see RUSSET]

rove¹ /rōv/ *v.* & *n.* ● *v.* **1** *intr.* wander without a settled destination, roam, ramble. **2** *intr.* (of eyes) look in changing directions. **3** *tr.* wander over or through. ● *n.* an act of roving (*on the rove*). ▫ **rove-beetle** any long-bodied beetle of the family Staphylinidae, usu. found in decaying animal and vegetable matter. **roving commission** authority given to a person or persons conducting an inquiry to travel as may be necessary. **roving eye** a tendency to ogle or towards infidelity. [ME, orig. a term in archery = shoot at a casual mark with the range not determined, perh. f. dial. *rave* stray, prob. of Scand. orig.]

rove² *past* of REEVE².

rove³ /rōv/ *n.* & *v.* ● *n.* a sliver of cotton, wool, etc., drawn out and slightly twisted. ● *v.tr.* form into roves. [18th c.: orig. unkn.]

rove⁴ /rōv/ *n.* a small metal plate or ring for a rivet to pass through and be clenched over, esp. in boat-building. [ON *ró*, with excrescent *v*]

rover¹ /rṓvər/ *n.* **1** a roving person; a wanderer. **2** *Croquet* **a** a ball that has passed all the hoops but not pegged out. **b** a player whose ball is a rover. **3** *Archery* **a** a mark chosen at

undetermined range. **b** a mark for long-distance shooting. **4** (**Rover**) *Brit.* a senior Scout. ¶ Now called *Venture Scout*.
■ **1** wanderer, bird of passage, itinerant, traveller, rolling stone, nomad, gypsy, wayfarer, sojourner, drifter, tramp, gadabout, vagabond, vagrant, *US* hobo, *US sl.* bum.

rover[2] /rṓvər/ *n.* a sea robber, a pirate. [ME f. MLG, MDu. *rōver* f. *rōven* rob, rel. to REAVE]

rover[3] /rṓvər/ *n.* a person or machine that makes roves of fibre.

row[1] /rō/ *n.* **1** a number of persons or things in a more or less straight line. **2** a line of seats across a theatre etc. (*in the front row*). **3** a street with a continuous line of houses along one or each side. **4** a line of plants in a field or garden. **5** a horizontal line of entries in a table etc. □ **a hard row to hoe** a difficult task. **in a row 1** forming a row. **2** *colloq.* in succession (*two Sundays in a row*). **row-house** *US* a terrace house. [ME *raw*, *row*, f. OE f. Gmc]
■ **1, 4** line, file, column, rank, string. **2** see TIER. □ **in a row 2** consecutively, one after the other; see also *in succession* (SUCCESSION).

row[2] /rō/ *v.* & *n.* ● *v.* **1** *tr.* propel (a boat) with oars. **2** *tr.* convey (a passenger) in a boat in this way. **3** *intr.* propel a boat in this way. **4** *tr.* make (a stroke) or achieve (a rate of striking) in rowing. **5** *tr.* compete in (a race) by rowing. **6** *tr.* row a race with. ● *n.* **1** a spell of rowing. **2** an excursion in a rowing-boat. □ **row-boat** *US* = *rowing-boat*. **row down** overtake in a rowing, esp. bumping, race. **rowing-boat** *Brit.* a small boat propelled by oars. **rowing-machine** a device for exercising the muscles used in rowing. **row out** exhaust by rowing (*the crew were completely rowed out at the finish*). **row over** complete the course of a boat race with little effort, owing to the absence or inferiority of competitors. □□ **rower** *n.* [OE *rōwan* f. Gmc, rel. to RUDDER, L *remus* oar]

row[3] /row/ *n.* & *v. colloq.* ● *n.* **1** a loud noise or commotion. **2** a fierce quarrel or dispute. **3 a** a severe reprimand. **b** the condition of being reprimanded (*shall get into a row*). ● *v.* **1** *intr.* make or engage in a row. **2** *tr.* reprimand. □ **make** (or **kick up**) **a row 1** raise a noise. **2** make a vigorous protest. [18th-c. sl.: orig. unkn.]
■ *n.* **1** commotion, disturbance, clamour, hubbub, racket, din, tumult, uproar, brouhaha, fuss, stir, turmoil, hullabaloo, *esp. US* ruckus, *US colloq.* rumpus. **2** altercation, argument, dispute, quarrel, disagreement, squabble, tiff, conflict, fracas, slanging-match, falling-out, *colloq.* shouting match, scrap, *US colloq.* spat. ● *v.* **1** dispute, quarrel, argue, disagree, wrangle, cross swords, have words, bicker, tiff, fall out. **2** see REPRIMAND *v.* □ **make** (or **kick up**) **a row 2** see PROTEST *v.* 1.

rowan /rṓən, rów-/ *n.* (in full **rowan-tree**) **1** *Sc.* & *N.Engl.* the mountain ash. **2** *US* a similar tree, *Sorbus americana*, native to America. **3** (in full **rowan-berry**) the scarlet berry of either of these trees. [Scand., corresp. to Norw. *rogn*, *raun*, Icel. *reynir*]

rowdy /rówdi/ *adj.* & *n.* ● *adj.* (**rowdier**, **rowdiest**) noisy and disorderly. ● *n.* (*pl.* **-ies**) a rowdy person. □□ **rowdily** *adv.* **rowdiness** *n.* **rowdyism** *n.* [19th-c. US, orig. = lawless backwoodsman: orig. unkn.]
■ *adj.* boisterous, uproarious, disorderly, noisy, loud, obstreperous, unruly. ● *n.* ruffian, tough, hooligan, yahoo, brawler, lout, hoodlum, *colloq.* lager lout, *Brit. sl.* bovver boy. □□ **rowdyism** rowdiness, ruffianism, hooliganism, rough house, barbarism, troublemaking, brawling, unruliness, boisterousness, *Brit. sl.* aggro, bovver.

rowel /rówəl/ *n.* & *v.* ● *n.* **1** a spiked revolving disc at the end of a spur. **2** a circular piece of leather etc. with a hole in the centre inserted between a horse's skin and flesh to discharge an exudate. ● *v.tr.* (**rowelled**, **rowelling**; *US* **roweled**, **roweling**) **1** urge with a rowel. **2** insert a rowel in. [ME f. OF *roel(e)* f. LL *rotella* dimin. of L *rota* wheel]

rowen /rówən/ *n.* (in *sing.* or *pl.*) *US* a second growth of grass, an aftermath. [ME f. OF *regain* (as GAIN)]

rowlock /róllək, rúllək/ *n.* a device on a boat's gunwale, esp. a pair of thole-pins, serving as a fulcrum for an oar and keeping it in place. [alt. of earlier OARLOCK, after ROW[2]]

Rowton house /rówt'n/ *n. Brit. hist.* a type of lodging-house for poor men, providing better conditions than a common lodging-house. [Lord *Rowton*, English social reformer d. 1903]

royal /róyəl/ *adj.* & *n.* ● *adj.* **1** of or suited to or worthy of a king or queen. **2** in the service or under the patronage of a king or queen. **3** belonging to the king or queen (*the royal hands*; *the royal anger*). **4** of the family of a king or queen. **5** kingly, majestic, stately, splendid. **6** on a great scale, of exceptional size or quality, first-rate (*gave us royal entertainment*; *in royal spirits*; *had a royal time*). ● *n.* **1** *colloq.* a member of the royal family. **2** a royal sail or mast. **3** a royal stag. **4** a size of paper, about 620 x 500 mm (25 x 20 in.). **5** (**the Royals**) the Royal Marines. □ **Royal Air Force** the British air force. **royal assent** see ASSENT. **royal blue** *Brit.* a deep vivid blue. **Royal British Legion** a national association of ex-members of the armed forces, founded in 1921. **royal burgh** *hist.* (in Scotland) a burgh holding a charter from the Crown. **Royal Commission** see COMMISSION. **royal duke** see DUKE. **Royal Engineers** the engineering branch of the British army. **royal family** the family to which a sovereign belongs. **royal fern** a fern, *Osmunda regalis*, with huge spreading fronds. **royal flush** see FLUSH[3]. **royal icing** a hard white icing made from icing sugar and egg-whites. **Royal Institution** a British society founded in 1799 for the diffusion of scientific knowledge. **royal jelly** a substance secreted by honey-bee workers and fed by them to future queen bees. **Royal Marine** a British marine (see MARINE *n.* 2). **royal mast** a mast above a topgallant mast. **Royal Navy** the British navy. **royal oak** a sprig of oak worn on 29 May to commemorate the restoration of Charles II (1660), who hid in an oak after the battle of Worcester (1651). **royal plural** the first person plural 'we' used by a single person. **royal road to** way of attaining without trouble. **royal sail** a sail above a topgallant sail. **Royal Society** (in full **Royal Society of London**) a society founded in 1662 to promote scientific discussion. **royal stag** a stag with a head of 12 or more points. **royal standard** a banner bearing royal heraldic arms. **royal tennis** real tennis. **Royal Victorian Chain** (in the UK) an order founded by Edward VII in 1902 and conferred by the sovereign on special occasions. **Royal Victorian Order** (in the UK) an order founded by Queen Victoria in 1896 and conferred usu. for great service rendered to the sovereign. **royal warrant** a warrant authorizing a tradesperson to supply goods to a specified royal person. □□ **royally** *adv.* [ME f. OF *roial* f. L *regalis* REGAL]
■ *adj.* **1, 3** see SOVEREIGN *adj.* 4. **5** stately, queenly, kingly, queenlike, kinglike, regal, imperial, sovereign, princely; see also MAJESTIC. **6** grand, splendid, stately, impressive, august, imposing, superior, superb, magnificent, majestic; first-rate.

royalist /róyəlist/ *n.* **1 a** a supporter of monarchy. **b** *hist.* a supporter of the royal side in the English Civil War. **2** *US* a reactionary, esp. a reactionary business tycoon. □□ **royalism** *n.*

royalty /róyəlti/ *n.* (*pl.* **-ies**) **1** the office or dignity or power of a king or queen, sovereignty. **2 a** royal persons. **b** a member of a royal family. **3** a sum paid to a patentee for the use of a patent or to an author etc. for each copy of a book etc. sold or for each public performance of a work. **4 a** a royal right (now esp. over minerals) granted by the sovereign to an individual or corporation. **b** a payment made by a producer of minerals, oil, or natural gas to the owner of the site or of the mineral rights over it. [ME f. OF *roialté* (as ROYAL)]
■ **1** see *sovereignty* (SOVEREIGN). **3** percentage, commission, share, payment, compensation.

rozzer /rózzər/ *n. Brit. sl.* a policeman. [19th c.: orig. unkn.]
■ see *police officer*.

RP *abbr.* received pronunciation.

RPI *abbr.* retail price index.

r.p.m. *abbr.* **1** revolutions per minute. **2** resale price maintenance.
RPO *abbr.* Royal Philharmonic Orchestra.
RR *abbr. US* **1** railroad. **2** rural route.
RS *abbr.* **1** (in the UK) Royal Society. **2** *US* Received Standard. **3** (in the UK) Royal Scots.
Rs. *abbr.* rupee(s).
RSA *abbr.* **1** (in the UK) Royal Society of Arts. **2** Royal Scottish Academy. **3** Republic of South Africa.
RSC *abbr.* **1** (in the UK) Royal Shakespeare Company. **2** (in the UK) Royal Society of Chemistry.
RSFSR *abbr.* Russian Soviet Federative Socialist Republic.
RSI *abbr.* repetitive strain injury.
RSJ *abbr.* rolled steel joist.
RSM *abbr.* Regimental Sergeant-Major.
RSPB *abbr.* (in the UK) Royal Society for the Protection of Birds.
RSPCA *abbr.* (in the UK) Royal Society for the Prevention of Cruelty to Animals.
RSV *abbr.* Revised Standard Version (of the Bible).
RSVP *abbr.* (in an invitation etc.) please answer. [F *répondez s'il vous plaît*]
RT *abbr.* **1** radio telegraphy. **2** radio telephony.
rt. *abbr.* right.
Rt. Hon. *abbr. Brit.* Right Honourable.
Rt. Revd. *abbr.* (also **Rt. Rev.**) Right Reverend.
RU *abbr.* Rugby Union.
Ru *symb. Chem.* the element ruthenium.
rub[1] /rub/ *v.* & *n.* ● *v.* (**rubbed, rubbing**) **1** *tr.* move one's hand or another object with firm pressure over the surface of. **2** *tr.* (usu. foll. by *against, in, on, over*) apply (one's hand etc.) in this way. **3** *tr.* clean or polish or make dry or bare by rubbing. **4** *tr.* (often foll. by *over*) apply (polish, ointment, etc.) by rubbing. **5** *tr.* (foll. by *in, into, through*) use rubbing to make (a substance) go into or through something. **6** *tr.* (often foll. by *together*) move or slide (objects) against each other. **7** *intr.* (foll. by *against, on*) move with contact or friction. **8** *tr.* chafe or make sore by rubbing. **9** *intr.* (of cloth, skin, etc.) become frayed or worn or sore or bare with friction. **10** *tr.* reproduce the design of (a sepulchral brass or a stone) by rubbing paper laid on it with heelball or coloured chalk etc. **11** *tr.* (foll. by *to*) reduce to powder etc. by rubbing. **12** *intr. Bowls* (of a bowl) be slowed or diverted by the unevenness of the ground. ● *n.* **1** a spell or an instance of rubbing (*give it a rub*). **2 a** an impediment or difficulty (*there's the rub*). **b** *Bowls* an inequality of the ground impeding or diverting a bowl; the diversion or hindering of a bowl by this. □ **rub along** *colloq.* cope or manage without undue difficulty. **rub away** remove by rubbing. **rub down** dry or smooth or clean by rubbing. **rub-down** *n.* an instance of rubbing down. **rub elbows with** *US* = *rub shoulders with.* **rub one's hands** rub one's hands together usu. in sign of keen satisfaction, or for warmth. **rub it in** (or **rub a person's nose in it**) emphasize or repeat an embarrassing fact etc. **rub noses** rub one's nose against another's in greeting. **rub off 1** (usu. foll. by *on*) be transferred by contact, be transmitted (*some of his attitudes have rubbed off on me*). **2** remove by rubbing. **rub of** (or **on**) **the green** *Golf* an accidental interference with the course or position of a ball. **rub on** *colloq.* = *rub along.* **rub out 1** erase with a rubber. **2** esp. *US sl.* kill, eliminate. **rub shoulders with** associate or come into contact with (another person). **rub up 1** polish (a tarnished object). **2** brush up (a subject or one's memory). **3** mix (pigment etc.) into paste by rubbing. **rub-up** *n.* the act or an instance of rubbing up. **rub (up) the wrong way** irritate or repel as by stroking a cat against the lie of its fur. [ME *rubben*, perh. f. LG *rubben*, of unkn. orig.]
■ *v.* **1** massage, knead, smooth, stroke. **3** scour, scrub, clean; wipe, polish, shine, buff, burnish. **4** apply, smooth, smear, spread, put. **5** (*rub in* or *into* or *through*) smooth in *or* into, spread in *or* into *or* through. **8** see CHAFE *v.* 1. **9** wear (down), chafe, abrade, erode; see also FRAY[1]. ● *n.* **1** wipe, stroke, rubbing, rub-down, massage. **2 a** hindrance, obstacle, impediment, difficulty, problem, trouble; catch, hitch, snag. □ **rub along** see MANAGE *v.* 2, 3, 5a. **rub away** see ERODE. **rub down** clean, wash, sponge; dry; see SMOOTH *v.* 1. **rub it in** (or **rub a person's nose in it**) keep going on about it, make an issue of it, harp on it, dwell on it. **rub off 1** be passed on *or* along, be transferred, be transmitted *or* communicated *or* imparted; (*rub off on*) affect. **2** erase, remove, delete, eliminate, eradicate. **rub out 1** erase, efface, remove, *colloq.* scrub. **2** see KILL *v.* 1a. **rub shoulders with** associate with, socialize with, hobnob with, mix with, fraternize with, keep company with, consort with, *US* rub elbows with, *US colloq.* run *or* pal *or* chum around with. **rub up 1** see POLISH *v.* 1. **2** brush up, refresh; see also STUDY *v.* 1, 3. **rub (up) the wrong way** annoy, irritate, irk, provoke, anger, stroke a person (*or* a person's hair) the wrong way, *colloq.* get under a person's skin, peeve, *sl.* bug.
rub[2] /rub/ *n.* = RUBBER[2]. [abbr.]
rub-a-dub /rúbbədub/ *n.* & *v.* ● *n.* **1** the rolling sound of a drum. **2** (also **rub-a-dub-dub**) *Austral. rhyming sl.* a pub. ● *v.intr.* (**rub-a-dubbed, rub-a-dubbing**) make this sound. [imit.]
rubato /roobaátō/ *adj.* & *n. Mus.* ● *n.* (*pl.* **-os** or **rubati** /-ti/) the temporary disregarding of strict tempo. ● *adj.* performed with a flexible tempo. [It., = robbed]
rubber[1] /rúbbər/ *n.* **1** a tough elastic polymeric substance made from the latex of plants or synthetically. **2** esp. *Brit.* a piece of this or another substance for erasing pencil or ink marks. **3** *colloq.* a condom. **4** (in *pl.*) *US* galoshes. **5** a person who rubs; a masseur or masseuse. **6 a** an implement used for rubbing. **b** part of a machine operating by rubbing. □ **rubber band** a loop of rubber for holding papers etc. together. **rubber plant 1** an evergreen plant, *Ficus elastica*, with dark-green shiny leaves, often cultivated as a house-plant. **2** (also **rubber tree**) any of various tropical trees yielding latex, esp. *Hevea brasiliensis.* **rubber solution** a liquid drying to a rubber-like material, used esp. as an adhesive in mending rubber articles. **rubber stamp 1** a device for inking and imprinting on a surface. **2 a** a person who mechanically copies or agrees to others' actions. **b** an indication of such agreement. **rubber-stamp** *v.tr.* approve automatically without proper consideration. □□ **rubbery** *adj.* **rubberiness** *n.* [RUB[1] + -ER[1], from its early use to rub out pencil marks]
■ □□ **rubbery** see YIELDING 2. **rubberiness** see *elasticity* (ELASTIC).
rubber[2] /rúbbər/ *n.* **1** a match of three or five successive games between the same sides or persons at whist, bridge, cricket, lawn tennis, etc. **2** (prec. by *the*) **a** the act of winning two games in a rubber. **b** a third game when each side has won one. [orig. unkn.: used as a term in bowls from *c.*1600]
rubberize /rúbbərīz/ *v.tr.* (also **-ise**) treat or coat with rubber.
rubberneck /rúbbərnek/ *n.* & *v. colloq.* ● *n.* a person, esp. a tourist, who stares inquisitively or stupidly. ● *v.intr.* act in this way.
■ *n.* tourist, sightseer, rubbernecker, *US* out-of-towner. ● *v.* gape, stare, goggle, gawk.
rubbing /rúbbing/ *n.* **1** in senses of RUB[1] *v.* **2** an impression or copy made by rubbing (see RUB[1] *v.* 10).
■ **1** see FRICTION 1.
rubbish /rúbbish/ *n.* & *v.* ● *n.* esp. *Brit.* **1** waste material; debris, refuse, litter. **2** worthless material or articles; junk. **3** (often as *int.*) absurd ideas or suggestions; nonsense. ● *v.tr. colloq.* **1** criticize severely. **2** reject as worthless. □□ **rubbishy** *adj.* [ME f. AF *rubbous* etc., perh. f. RUBBLE]
■ *n.* **1** refuse, waste, litter, garbage, dross, sweepings, offal; debris, detritus, *Austral. or dial.* mullock, *esp. US* trash, *esp. US sl.* dreck. **2** junk, rejects, dregs, lees, scraps, fragments, leftovers, remnants, leavings, *esp. US* trash. **3** (stuff and) nonsense, balderdash, moonshine,

gibberish, bunkum, garbage, *esp. US* trash, *colloq.* gobbledegook, flapdoodle, piffle, malarkey, hogwash, tosh, gammon, *Sc. colloq.* havers, *sl.* tommy-rot, twaddle, rot, bosh, hooey, bunk, boloney, poppycock, eyewash, bilge-water, bull, *Brit. sl.* codswallop, cobblers, a load of (old) cobblers, *esp. US sl.* hokum. ● *v.* **1** criticize, attack, *US* bad-mouth, *colloq.* pan, jump on, *esp. US colloq.* trash, *sl.* clobber.

rubbity /rúbbiti/ *n.* (also **rubbity-dub**) = RUB-A-DUB *n.* 2.

rubble /rúbb'l/ *n.* **1** waste or rough fragments of stone or brick etc. **2** pieces of undressed stone used, esp. as filling-in, for walls. **3** *Geol.* loose angular stones etc. as the covering of some rocks. **4** water-worn stones. ▫▫ **rubbly** *adj.* [ME *robyl, rubel*, of uncert. orig.: cf. OF *robe* spoils]
■ **1** debris.

rube /rōōb/ *n. US colloq.* a country bumpkin. [abbr. of the name *Reuben*]
■ see PEASANT.

rubefy /rōōbifī/ *v.tr.* (also **rubify**) (**-ies, -ied**) **1** make red. **2** *Med.* (of a counterirritant) stimulate (the skin etc.) to redness. ▫▫ **rubefacient** /-fáysh'nt/ *adj.* & *n.* **rubefaction** /rōōbifáksh'n/ *n.* [ME f. OF *rubifier, rubefier* f. med.L *rubificare* f. L *rubefacere* f. *rubeus* red]

rubella /roobéllə/ *n. Med.* an acute infectious virus disease with a red rash; German measles. [mod.L, neut. pl. of L *rubellus* reddish]

rubellite /rōōbəlīt/ *n.* a red variety of tourmaline. [L *rubellus* reddish]

rubeola /roobeéələ/ *n. Med.* measles. [med.L f. L *rubeus* red]

Rubicon /rōōbikon/ *n.* **1** a boundary which once crossed betokens irrevocable commitment; a point of no return. **2** (**rubicon**) the act of winning a game in piquet before an opponent has scored 100. [the ancient name of a stream forming the boundary of Julius Caesar's province and crossed by him in 49 BC as the start of a war with Pompey]

rubicund /rōōbikund/ *adj.* (of a face, complexion, or person in these respects) ruddy, high-coloured. ▫▫ **rubicundity** /-kúnditi/ *n.* [F *rubicond* or L *rubicundus* f. *rubēre* be red]
■ see ROSY 1.

rubidium /roobíddiəm/ *n. Chem.* a soft silvery element occurring naturally in various minerals and as the radioactive isotope rubidium-87. ¶ Symb.: **Rb**. [L *rubidus* red (with ref. to its spectral lines)]

rubify var. of RUBEFY.

rubiginous /roobíjinəss/ *adj. formal* rust-coloured. [L *rubigo- inis* rust]

Rubik's cube /rōōbiks/ *n.* a puzzle in which the aim is to restore the faces of a composite cube to single colours by rotating layers of constituent smaller cubes. [E. *Rubik*, its Hung. inventor]

ruble var. of ROUBLE.

rubric /rōōbrik/ *n.* **1** a direction for the conduct of divine service inserted in a liturgical book. **2** a heading or passage in red or special lettering. **3** explanatory words. **4** an established custom. ▫▫ **rubrical** *adj.* [ME f. OF *rubrique, rubrice* or L *rubrica (terra)* red (earth or ochre) as writing-material, rel. to *rubeus* red]

rubricate /rōōbrikayt/ *v.tr.* **1** mark with red; print or write in red. **2** provide with rubrics. ▫▫ **rubrication** /-káysh'n/ *n.* **rubricator** *n.* [L *rubricare* f. *rubrica*: see RUBRIC]

ruby /rōōbi/ *n., adj., & v.* ● *n.* (*pl.* **-ies**) **1** a rare precious stone consisting of corundum with a colour varying from deep crimson or purple to pale rose. **2** a glowing purple-tinged red colour. ● *adj.* of this colour. ● *v.tr.* (**-ies, -ied**) dye or tinge ruby-colour. ▫ **ruby glass** glass coloured with oxides of copper, iron, lead, tin, etc. **ruby-tail** a wasp, *Chrysis ignita*, with a ruby-coloured hinder part. **ruby wedding** the fortieth anniversary of a wedding. [ME f. OF *rubi* f. med.L *rubinus (lapis)* red (stone), rel. to L *rubeus* red]

RUC *abbr.* Royal Ulster Constabulary.

ruche /rōōsh/ *n.* a frill or gathering of lace etc. as a trimming. ▫▫ **ruched** *adj.* **ruching** *n.* [F f. med.L *rusca* tree-bark, of Celt. orig.]
■ see RUFFLE *n.* 1.

ruck[1] /ruk/ *n.* **1** (prec. by *the*) the main body of competitors not likely to overtake the leaders. **2** an undistinguished crowd of persons or things. **3** *Rugby Football* a loose scrum with the ball on the ground. **4** *Austral. Rules* a group of three mobile players. [ME, = stack of fuel, heap, rick: app. Scand., = Norw. *ruka* in the same senses]

ruck[2] /ruk/ *v.* & *n.* ● *v.tr.* & *intr.* (often foll. by *up*) make or become creased or wrinkled. ● *n.* a crease or wrinkle. [ON *hrukka*]
■ *v.* see PUCKER *v.* ● *n.* see PUCKER *n.*

ruckle /rúkk'l/ *v.* & *n. Brit.* = RUCK[2].

rucksack /rúksak, rōōk-/ *n.* a bag slung by straps from both shoulders and resting on the back. [G f. *rucken* dial. var. of *Rücken* back + *Sack* SACK[1]]
■ pack, backpack, knapsack, haversack.

ruckus /rúkkəss/ *n.* esp. *US* a row or commotion. [cf. RUCTION, RUMPUS]
■ see ROW[3] *n.* 1.

ruction /rúksh'n/ *n. colloq.* **1** a disturbance or tumult. **2** (in *pl.*) unpleasant arguments or reactions. [19th c.: orig. unkn.]
■ **1** see DISTURBANCE 2. **2** (*ructions*) see TROUBLE *n.* 5, 6.

rudaceous /roodáyshəss/ *adj.* (of rock) composed of fragments of relatively large size. [L *rudus* rubble]

rudbeckia /rudbékkiə/ *n.* a composite garden plant of the genus *Rudbeckia*, native to N. America. [mod.L f. O. *Rudbeck*, Sw. botanist d. 1740]

rudd /rud/ *n.* (*pl.* same) a freshwater fish, *Scardinius erythrophthalmus*, resembling a roach and having red fins. [app. rel. to *rud* red colour f. OE *rudu*, rel. to RED]

rudder /rúddər/ *n.* **1 a** a flat piece hinged vertically to the stern of a ship for steering. **b** a vertical aerofoil pivoted from the tailplane of an aircraft, for controlling its horizontal movement. **2** a guiding principle etc. ▫▫ **rudderless** *adj.* [OE *rōther* f. WG *rōthra-* f. the stem of ROW[2]]

ruddle /rúdd'l/ *n.* & *v.* ● *n.* a red ochre, esp. of a kind used for marking sheep. ● *v.tr.* mark or colour with or as with ruddle. [rel. to obs. *rud*: see RUDD]

ruddock /rúddək/ *n. dial.* the robin redbreast. [OE *rudduc* (as RUDDLE)]

ruddy /rúddi/ *adj.* & *v.* ● *adj.* (**ruddier, ruddiest**) **1 a** (of a person or complexion) freshly or healthily red. **b** (of health, youth, etc.) marked by this. **2** reddish. **3** *Brit. colloq.* bloody, damnable. ● *v.tr.* & *intr.* (**-ies, -ied**) make or grow ruddy. ▫▫ **ruddily** *adv.* **ruddiness** *n.* [OE *rudig* (as RUDD)]
■ *adj.* **1a, 2** see ROSY 1.

rude /rōōd/ *adj.* **1** (of a person, remark, etc.) impolite or offensive. **2** roughly made or done; lacking subtlety or accuracy (*a rude plough*). **3** primitive or uneducated (*rude chaos; rude simplicity*). **4** abrupt, sudden, startling, violent (*a rude awakening; a rude reminder*). **5** *colloq.* indecent, lewd (*a rude joke*). **6** vigorous or hearty (*rude health*). ▫ **be rude to** speak impolitely to; insult. ▫▫ **rudely** *adv.* **rudeness** *n.* **rudery** *n.* **rudish** *adj.* [ME f. OF f. L *rudis* unwrought]
■ **1** impolite, impertinent, impudent, discourteous, unmannerly, ungentlemanly, unladylike, ungallant, ungracious, unceremonious; insulting, insolent, offensive, saucy, bold, disrespectful, uncivil, flippant, brusque, curt, gruff, tactless, outrageous, *colloq.* fresh; ill-mannered, bad-mannered, ill-bred, uncouth, rough, boorish, churlish, oafish, loutish. **2** crude, rough, clumsy, awkward, unskilful, unskilled, artless, inartistic, imperfect, unpolished, inaccurate, raw, inelegant, makeshift, homespun, primitive, unfinished, simple, basic, bare. **3** primitive, uneducated, coarse, unrefined, unpolished; uncivilized, uncultured; plain, unsophisticated. **4** sudden, startling, violent; see also ABRUPT 1. **5** naughty, unrefined, ribald, bawdy, indecent, indelicate, vulgar, obscene, dirty, filthy, lubricious, lewd, gross, smutty, taboo, pornographic. **6** see VIGOROUS 2.

ruderal /rōōdərəl/ *adj.* & *n.* ● *adj.* (of a plant) growing on or in rubbish or rubble. ● *n.* a ruderal plant. [mod.L *ruderalis* f. L *rudera* pl. of *rudus* rubble]

rudiment /rōōdimənt/ *n.* **1** (in *pl.*) the elements or first principles of a subject. **2** (in *pl.*) an imperfect beginning of something undeveloped or yet to develop. **3** a part or organ imperfectly developed as being vestigial or having no function (e.g. the breast in males). [F *rudiment* or L *rudimentum* (as RUDE, after *elementum* ELEMENT)]
▪ **1** (*rudiments*) basics, elements, essentials, fundamentals, first principles.

rudimentary /rōōdiméntəri/ *adj.* **1** involving basic principles; fundamental. **2** incompletely developed; vestigial. □□ **rudimentarily** /-méntərili/ *adv.* **rudimentariness** /-méntəriniss/ *n.*
▪ **1** basic, essential, elementary, fundamental, primary, introductory, first, elemental, primal. **2** unshaped, unfinished, imperfect, primitive, undeveloped, primordial, immature, embryonic; seminal, vestigial.

rue[1] /rōō/ *v.* & *n.* ● *v.tr.* (**rues, rued, rueing** or **ruing**) repent of; bitterly feel the consequences of; wish to be undone or non-existent (esp. *rue the day*). ● *n. archaic* **1** repentance; dejection at some occurrence. **2** compassion or pity. [OE *hrēow*, *hrēowan*]
▪ *v.* see REGRET *v.* ● *n.* **1** see REGRET *n.*

rue[2] /rōō/ *n.* a perennial evergreen shrub, *Ruta graveolens*, with bitter strong-scented leaves formerly used in medicine. [ME f. OF f. L *ruta* f. Gk *rhutē*]

rueful /rōōfōōl/ *adj.* expressing sorrow, genuine or humorously affected. □□ **ruefully** *adv.* **ruefulness** *n.* [ME, f. RUE[1]]
▪ see REGRETFUL. □□ **ruefully** see *sadly* (SAD). **ruefulness** see REGRET *n.*

rufescent /roofés'nt/ *adj. Zool.* etc. reddish. □□ **rufescence** *n.* [L *rufescere* f. *rufus* reddish]

ruff[1] /ruf/ *n.* **1** a projecting starched frill worn round the neck esp. in the 16th c. **2** a projecting or conspicuously coloured ring of feathers or hair round a bird's or animal's neck. **3** a domestic pigeon like a jacobin. **4** (*fem.* **reeve** /reev/) a wading bird, *Philomachus pugnax*, of which the male has a ruff and ear-tufts in the breeding season. □□ **rufflike** *adj.* [perh. f. *ruff* = ROUGH]
▪ **1** see RUFFLE *n.* 1.

ruff[2] /ruf/ *n.* (also **ruffe**) any of various fish, esp. a perch-like freshwater fish, *Gymnocephalus cernua*, found in European lakes and rivers. [ME, prob. f. ROUGH]

ruff[3] /ruf/ *v.* & *n.* ● *v.intr.* & *tr.* trump at cards. ● *n.* an act of ruffing. [orig. the name of a card-game: f. OF *roffle*, *rouffle*, = It. *ronfa* (perh. alt. of *trionfo* TRUMP[1])]

ruffian /rúffiən/ *n.* a violent lawless person. □□ **ruffianism** *n.* **ruffianly** *adv.* [F *ruf(f)ian* f. It. *ruffiano*, perh. f. dial. *rofia* scurf]
▪ see THUG.

ruffle /rúff'l/ *v.* & *n.* ● *v.* **1** *tr.* disturb the smoothness or tranquillity of. **2** *tr.* upset the calmness of (a person). **3** *tr.* gather (lace etc.) into a ruffle. **4** *tr.* (often foll. by *up*) (of a bird) erect (its feathers) in anger, display, etc. **5** *intr.* undergo ruffling. **6** *intr.* lose smoothness or calmness. ● *n.* **1** an ornamental gathered or goffered frill of lace etc. worn at the opening of a garment esp. round the wrist, breast, or neck. **2** perturbation, bustle. **3** a rippling effect on water. **4** the ruff of a bird etc. (see RUFF[1] 2). **5** *Mil.* a vibrating drum-beat. [ME: orig. unkn.]
▪ *v.* **1** see DISTURB 1. **2** agitate, disconcert, confuse, discompose, discomfit, upset, disturb, stir up, perturb, unsettle, disorient, unnerve, fluster, affect, bother, put out, vex, shake up, trouble, worry, *colloq.* rattle, throw, *US joc.* discombobulate, *esp. US sl.* get (a person) all shook up; (*ruffled*) unstrung. **6** see FRET[1] *v.* 1a. ● *n.* **1** trimming, flounce, frill, ruff, ruche, ruching. **2** perturbation, bustle, flurry; see also STIR[1] *n.* 2. **3** ripple, disturbance, undulation, *US* riffle.

rufous /rōōfəss/ *adj.* (esp. of animals) reddish-brown. [L *rufus* red, reddish]

rug /rug/ *n.* **1** a floor-mat of shaggy material or thick pile. **2** a thick woollen coverlet or wrap. □ **pull the rug from under** deprive of support; weaken, unsettle. [prob. f. Scand.: cf. Norw. dial. *rugga* coverlet, Sw. *rugg* ruffled hair: rel. to RAG[1]]

Rugby /rúgbi/ *n.* (in full **Rugby football**) a team game played with an oval ball that may be kicked, carried, and passed from hand to hand. □ **Rugby League** partly professional Rugby football with teams of 13. **Rugby Union** amateur Rugby football with teams of 15. [*Rugby* School in S. England, where it was first played]

rugged /rúggid/ *adj.* **1** (of ground or terrain) having a rough uneven surface. **2** (of features) strongly marked; irregular in outline. **3 a** unpolished; lacking gentleness or refinement (*rugged grandeur*). **b** harsh in sound. **c** austere, unbending (*rugged honesty*). **d** involving hardship (*a rugged life*). **4** (esp. of a machine) robust, sturdy. □□ **ruggedly** *adv.* **ruggedness** *n.* [ME, prob. f. Scand.: cf. RUG, and Sw. *rugga*, roughen]
▪ **1** rough, uneven, broken, irregular, bumpy, jagged. **2** craggy, strong; irregular. **3 a** rude, uncouth, uncultured, uncivilized, unrefined, unpolished, crude, ungraceful, churlish. **b** see STRIDENT. **c** austere, unbending; see also DOUR. **d** tough, rough, severe, hard, harsh, difficult, arduous, Spartan, austere, rigorous, onerous, stern, demanding, burdensome. **4** hardy, durable, strong, sturdy, hale, robust, tough, vigorous, hard, stalwart.

rugger /rúggər/ *n. Brit. colloq.* Rugby football.

rugose /rōōgōss, -gōz/ *adj.* esp. *Biol.* wrinkled, corrugated. □□ **rugosely** *adv.* **rugosity** /-góssiti/ *n.* [L *rugosus* f. *ruga* wrinkle]

ruin /rōō-in/ *n.* & *v.* ● *n.* **1** a destroyed or wrecked state (*after centuries of neglect, the palace fell to ruin*). **2 a** a person's or thing's downfall or elimination (*the ruin of my hopes*). **b** *archaic* a woman's loss of chastity by seduction or rape; dishonour resulting from this. **3 a** the complete loss of one's property or position (*bring to ruin*). **b** a person who has suffered ruin. **4** (in *sing.* or *pl.*) the remains of a building etc. that has suffered ruin (*an old ruin*; *ancient ruins*). **5** a cause of ruin; a destructive thing or influence (*will be the ruin of us*). ● *v.* **1** *tr.* **a** bring to ruin (*your extravagance has ruined me*). **b** utterly impair or wreck (*the rain ruined my hat*). **c** *archaic* seduce and abandon (a woman). **2** *tr.* (esp. as **ruined** *adj.*) reduce to ruins. **3** *intr. poet.* fall headlong or with a crash. □ **in ruins 1** in a state of ruin. **2** completely wrecked (*their hopes were in ruins*). [ME f. OF *ruine* f. L *ruina* f. *ruere* fall]
▪ *n.* **1** see DESTRUCTION 1. **2 a** downfall, destruction, collapse, fall, devastation, undoing, breakdown, breakup, débâcle, disintegration, ruination, dissolution, wiping out, failure, decay, end, defeat, overthrow; elimination, liquidation. **b** degradation, dishonour, debasement, defilement; seduction, violation, defloration. **3 a** bankruptcy, penury, insolvency; see also DOWNFALL. **4** wreck; (*ruins*) debris, fragments, rubble, remains. **5** nemesis, curse, end, bane. ● *v.* **1 a** bring to ruin, undo, reduce to nothing, crush, *archaic or literary* reduce to naught; pauperize, impoverish, reduce to penury *or* poverty *or* destitution. **b** spoil, damage, mess up, make a mess of, mar, destroy, wreck, damage, harm, hurt, impair *Austral.* euchre; poison, put the kibosh on, botch, *sl.* louse up, screw up, *Brit. sl.* scupper; disfigure, uglify. **c** violate, deflower, ravish, seduce, lead astray, defile, debase, *archaic* dishonour. **2** destroy, devastate, demolish, annihilate, wipe out, lay waste, raze, wreck, flatten, reduce to nothing, pulverize. □ **in ruins 1** see DILAPIDATED. **2** see UNDONE 3.

ruination /rōō-ináysh'n/ *n.* **1** the act of bringing to ruin. **2** the act of ruining or the state of being ruined. [obs. *ruinate* (as RUIN)]
▪ see RUIN *n.* 2a.

ruinous /rōō-inəss/ *adj.* **1** bringing ruin; disastrous (*at ruinous expense*). **2** in ruins; dilapidated. □□ **ruinously** *adv.* **ruinousness** *n.* [ME f. L *ruinosus* (as RUIN)]

■ **1** disastrous, destructive, catastrophic, calamitous, deleterious, pernicious, crippling, baleful, fatal, noxious, harmful, injurious, nasty, baneful. **2** see DILAPIDATED.

rule /rōōl/ *n.* & *v.* ● *n.* **1** a principle to which an action conforms or is required to conform. **2** a prevailing custom or standard; the normal state of things. **3** government or dominion (*under British rule*; *the rule of law*). **4** a graduated straight measure used in carpentry etc.; a ruler. **5** *Printing* **a** a thin strip of metal for separating headings, columns, etc. **b** a thin line or dash. **6** a code of discipline of a religious order. **7** *Law* an order made by a judge or court with reference to a particular case only. **8** (**Rules**) *Austral.* = *Australian Rules.* ● *v.* **1** *tr.* exercise decisive influence over; keep under control. **2** *tr.* & (often foll. by *over*) *intr.* have sovereign control of (*rules over a vast kingdom*). **3** *tr.* (often foll. by *that* + clause) pronounce authoritatively (*was ruled out of order*). **4** *tr.* **a** make parallel lines across (paper). **b** make (a straight line) with a ruler etc. **5** *intr.* (of prices or goods etc. in regard to price or quality etc.) have a specified general level; be for the most part (*the market ruled high*). **6** *tr.* (in *passive*; foll. by *by*) consent to follow (advice etc.); be guided by. □ **as a rule** usually; more often than not. **by rule** in a regulation manner; mechanically. **rule of the road** see ROAD[1]. **rule of three** a method of finding a number in the same ratio to one given as exists between two others given. **rule of thumb** a rule for general guidance, based on experience or practice rather than theory. **rule out** exclude; pronounce irrelevant or ineligible. **rule the roost** (or **roast**) be in control. **run the rule over** examine cursorily for correctness or adequacy. □□ **ruleless** *adj.* [ME f. OF *reule*, *reuler* f. LL *regulare* f. L *regula* straight stick]

■ *n.* **1** regulation, order, law, ordinance, ruling, decree, statute, principle, direction, guide, guideline, precept, ukase. **2** fact, standard, benchmark, custom, practice, form, routine, convention, policy, way things are. **3** dominion, authority, government, control, sovereignty, sway, command, ascendancy, direction, oversight, supervision, mastery. ● *v.* **1** direct, guide, manage, control, lead, head (up), preside over, superintend, oversee, supervise, regulate, govern, run. **2** run, control; govern, be in control (of *or* over), be in charge (of), be in command (of), reign (over), be in power (over), hold sway (over); wield the sceptre, wear the crown. **3** decide, resolve, judge, decree, find, declare, pronounce; hand down a judgement *or* decision, *formal* deem. □ **as a rule** generally, usually, normally, customarily, for the most part, mostly, ordinarily, mainly, in the main, chiefly, on the whole, commonly, more often than not. **by rule** mechanically, automatically; unthinkingly. **rule out** ban, bar, prohibit, exclude, eliminate, forbid, preclude, proscribe, dismiss, disregard. **rule the roost** (or **roast**) see DOMINATE 1.

ruler /rōōlər/ *n.* **1** a person exercising government or dominion. **2** a straight usu. graduated strip or cylinder of wood, metal, etc., used to draw lines or measure distance. □□ **rulership** *n.*

■ **1** see LEADER 1. **2** rule, measure.

ruling /rōōling/ *n.* & *adj.* ● *n.* an authoritative decision or announcement. ● *adj.* dominant; prevailing; currently in force (*ruling prices*). □ **ruling passion** a motive that habitually directs one's actions.

■ *n.* see DECISION 2, 3. ● *adj.* prevalent, dominating; see also DOMINANT *adj.*

rum[1] /rum/ *n.* **1** a spirit distilled from sugar-cane residues or molasses. **2** *US* intoxicating liquor. □ **rum baba** see BABA. [17th c.: perh. abbr. of contemporary forms *rumbullion*, *rumbustion*, of unkn. orig.]

rum[2] /rum/ *adj. Brit. colloq.* **1** odd, strange, queer. **2** difficult, dangerous. □ **rum go** (or **do** or **start**) *colloq.* a surprising occurrence or unforeseen turn of affairs. □□ **rumly** *adv.* **rumness** *n.* [16th-c. cant, orig. = fine, spirited, perh. var. of ROM]

■ **1** see STRANGE 1.

Rumanian var. of ROMANIAN.

Rumansh var. of ROMANSH.

rumba /rúmbə/ *n.* & *v.* (also **rhumba**) ● *n.* **1** an Afro-Cuban dance. **2 a** a ballroom dance imitative of this. **b** the music for it. ● *v.tr.* (**rumbas, rumbaed** /-bəd/ or **rumba'd, rumbaing** /-bəing/) dance the rumba. [Amer. Sp.]

rumble /rúmb'l/ *v.* & *n.* ● *v.* **1** *intr.* make a continuous deep resonant sound as of distant thunder. **2** *intr.* (foll. by *along*, *by*, *past*, etc.) (of a person or vehicle) move with a rumbling noise. **3** *tr.* (often foll. by *out*) utter or say with a rumbling sound. **4** *tr. Brit. sl.* find out about (esp. something illicit). ● *n.* **1** a rumbling sound. **2** *US sl.* a street-fight between gangs. □ **rumble seat** *US* an uncovered folding seat in the rear of a motor car. □□ **rumbler** *n.* [ME *romble*, prob. f. MDu. *rommelen*, *rummelen* (imit.)]

■ *v.* **1** see THUNDER *v.* 2. **4** see DISCOVER 1a, b. ● *n.* **1** see THUNDER *n.* 1, 2. **2** see FIGHT *n.* 1a.

rumbustious /rumbúss-chəss/ *adj. colloq.* boisterous, noisy, uproarious. □□ **rumbustiously** *adv.* **rumbustiousness** *n.* [prob. var. of *robustious* boisterous, ROBUST]

■ see BOISTEROUS 1.

rumen /rōōmen/ *n.* (*pl.* **rumens** or **rumina** /-minə/) the first stomach of a ruminant, in which food, esp. cellulose, is partly digested by bacteria. [L *rumen ruminis* throat]

ruminant /rōōminənt/ *n.* & *adj.* ● *n.* an animal that chews the cud regurgitated from its rumen. ● *adj.* **1** of or belonging to ruminants. **2** contemplative; given to or engaged in meditation. [L *ruminari ruminant-* (as RUMEN)]

ruminate /rōōminayt/ *v.* **1** *tr.* & (foll. by *over*, *on*, etc.) *intr.* meditate, ponder. **2** *intr.* (of ruminants) chew the cud. □□ **rumination** /-náysh'n/ *n.* **ruminative** /-nətiv/ *adj.* **ruminatively** /-nətivli/ *adv.* **ruminator** *n.*

■ **1** (*ruminate over, on*) see PONDER.

rummage /rúmmij/ *v.* & *n.* ● *v.* **1** *tr.* & (foll. by *in*, *through*, *among*) *intr.* search, esp. untidily and unsystematically. **2** *tr.* (foll. by *out*, *up*) find among other things. **3** *tr.* (foll. by *about*) disarrange; make untidy in searching. ● *n.* **1** an instance of rummaging. **2** things found by rummaging; a miscellaneous accumulation. □ **rummage sale** esp. *US* a jumble sale. □□ **rummager** *n.* [earlier as noun in obs. sense 'arranging of casks etc. in a hold': OF *arrumage* f. *arrumer* stow (as AD-, *run* ship's hold f. MDu. *ruim* ROOM)]

■ *v.* **1** search, comb, scour, *colloq.* turn inside out, turn upside down, *Austral* & *NZ colloq.* fossick about *or* around; (*rummage in, through, among*) search in *or* through *or* among, hunt in *or* through *or* among, comb through, scour through, scrabble about in, sift through. **2** (*rummage out* or *up*) search out, hunt out *or* up; see also LOCATE 1, 3. ● *n.* **2** jumble, miscellanea, knick-knacks, bits and pieces, odds and ends.

rummer /rúmmər/ *n.* a large drinking-glass. [rel. to Du. *roemer*, LG *römer* f. *roemen* praise, boast]

rummy[1] /rúmmi/ *n.* a card-game played usu. with two packs, in which the players try to form sets and sequences of cards. [20th c.: orig. unkn.]

rummy[2] /rúmmi/ *adj. Brit. colloq.* = RUM[2].

rumour /rōōmər/ *n.* & *v.* (*US* **rumor**) ● *n.* **1** general talk or hearsay of doubtful accuracy. **2** (often foll. by *of*, or *that* + clause) a current but unverified statement or assertion (*heard a rumour that you are leaving*). ● *v.tr.* (usu. in *passive*) report by way of rumour (*it is rumoured that you are leaving*; *you are rumoured to be leaving*). [ME f. OF *rumur*, *rumor* f. L *rumor -oris* noise]

■ *n.* **1** gossip, hearsay, chat, tittle-tattle, *colloq.* chit-chat, scuttlebutt, *US sl.* poop. **2** a piece of gossip *or* hearsay, *on dit*; see also WORD *n.* 7. ● *v.* bruit about *or* abroad, noise (abroad), intimate, breathe, suggest, whisper, leak, reveal, make known, put about, say, report, tell.

rump /rump/ *n.* **1** the hind part of a mammal, esp. the buttocks. **2 a** a small or contemptible remnant of a parliament or similar body. **b** (**the Rump**) *hist.* the remnant of the English Long Parliament 1648–53 or after its restoration in 1659. □ **rump steak** a cut of beef from the rump. □□ **rumpless** *adj.* [ME, prob. f. Scand.]

rumple /rúmp'l/ *v.tr.* & *intr.* make or become creased or ruffled. □□ **rumply** *adj.* [obs. *rumple* (n.) f. MDu. *rompel* f. *rompe* wrinkle]

▪ wrinkle, crumple, crush, crease, crinkle, ruffle, scrunch (up), pucker.

rumpus /rúmpəss/ *n. colloq.* a disturbance, brawl, row, or uproar. □ **rumpus room** *US* a room in the basement of a house for games and play. [18th c.: prob. fanciful]

▪ commotion, disturbance, fuss, confusion, uproar, tumult, to-do, brouhaha, stir, *literary* pother; affray, fracas, mêlée, brawl, *colloq.* row, *sl.* rough house.

run /run/ *v.* & *n.* ● *v.* (**running**; *past* **ran** /ran/; *past part.* **run**) **1** *intr.* go with quick steps on alternate feet, never having both or all feet on the ground at the same time. **2** *intr.* flee, abscond. **3** *intr.* go or travel hurriedly, briefly, etc. **4** *intr.* **a** advance by or as by rolling or on wheels, or smoothly or easily. **b** be in action or operation (*left the engine running*). **5** *intr.* be current or operative; have duration (*the lease runs for 99 years*). **6** *intr.* (of a bus, train, etc.) travel or be travelling on its route (*the train is running late*). **7** *intr.* (of a play, exhibition, etc.) be staged or presented (*is now running at the Apollo*). **8** *intr.* extend; have a course or order or tendency (*the road runs by the coast*; *prices are running high*). **9 a** *intr.* compete in a race. **b** *intr.* finish a race in a specified position. **c** *tr.* compete in (a race). **10** *intr.* (often foll. by *for*) seek election (*ran for president*). **11 a** *intr.* (of a liquid etc. or its container) flow or be wet; drip. **b** *tr.* flow with (a specified liquid) (*after the massacre, the rivers ran blood*). **12** *tr.* **a** cause (water etc.) to flow. **b** fill (a bath) with water. **13** *intr.* spread rapidly or beyond the proper place (*ink ran over the table*; *a shiver ran down my spine*). **14** *intr. Cricket* (of a batsman) run from one wicket to the other in scoring a run. **15** *tr.* traverse or make one's way through or over (a course, race, or distance). **16** *tr.* perform (an errand). **17** *tr.* publish (an article etc.) in a newspaper or magazine. **18 a** *tr.* cause (a machine or vehicle etc.) to operate. **b** *intr.* (of a mechanism or component etc.) move or work freely. **19** *tr.* direct or manage (a business, household, etc.). **20** *tr.* own and use (a vehicle) regularly. **21** *tr.* take (a person) for a journey in a vehicle (*shall I run you to the shops?*). **22** *tr.* cause to run or go in a specified way (*ran the car into a tree*). **23** *tr.* enter (a horse etc.) for a race. **24** *tr.* smuggle (guns etc.). **25** *tr.* chase or hunt. **26** *tr.* allow (an account) to accumulate for a time before paying. **27** *intr. Naut.* (of a ship etc.) go straight and fast. **28** *intr.* (of salmon) go up river from the sea. **29** *intr.* (of a colour in a fabric) spread from the dyed parts. **30 a** *intr.* (of a thought, the eye, the memory, etc.) pass in a transitory or cursory way (*ideas ran through my mind*). **b** *tr.* cause (one's eye) to look cursorily (*ran my eye down the page*). **c** *tr.* pass (a hand etc.) rapidly over (*ran his fingers down her spine*). **31** *intr.* (of hosiery) ladder. **32** *intr.* (of a candle) gutter. **33** *intr.* (of an orifice, esp. the eyes or nose) exude liquid matter. **34** *tr.* sew (fabric) loosely or hastily with running stitches. **35** *tr.* turn (cattle etc.) out to graze. ● *n.* **1** an act or spell of running. **2** a short trip or excursion, esp. for pleasure. **3** a distance travelled. **4** a general tendency of development or movement. **5** a rapid motion. **6** a regular route. **7 a** a continuous or long stretch or spell or course (*a metre's run of wiring*; *had a run of bad luck*). **b** a series or sequence, esp. of cards in a specified suit. **8** (often foll. by *on*) **a** a high general demand (for a commodity, currency, etc.) (*a run on the dollar*). **b** a sudden demand for repayment by a large number of customers of (a bank). **9** a quantity produced in one period of production (*a print run*). **10** a general or average type or class (*not typical of the general run*). **11 a** *Cricket* a point scored by the batsmen each running to the other's wicket, or an equivalent point awarded for some other reason. **b** *Baseball* a point scored usu. by the batter returning to the plate after touching the other bases. **12** (foll. by *of*) free use of or access to (*had the run of the house*). **13 a** an animal's regular track. **b** an enclosure for domestic animals or fowls. **c** a range of pasture. **14** a ladder in hosiery. **15** *Mus.* a rapid scale passage. **16** a class or line of goods. **17** a batch or drove of animals born or reared together. **18** a shoal of fish in motion. **19** a trough for water to run in. **20** *US* a small stream or brook. **21 a** a single journey, esp. by an aircraft. **b** (of an aircraft) a flight on a straight and even course at a constant speed before or while dropping bombs. **c** an offensive military operation. **22** a slope used for skiing or tobogganing. **23** (**the runs**) *colloq.* an attack of diarrhoea. □ **at a** (or **the**) **run** running. **on the run 1** escaping, running away. **2** hurrying about from place to place. **run about 1** bustle; hurry from one person or place to another. **2** (esp. of children) play or wander without restraint. **run across 1** happen to meet. **2** (foll. by *to*) make a brief journey or a flying visit (to a place). **run after 1** pursue with attentions; seek the society of. **2** give much time to (a pursuit etc.). **3** pursue at a run. **run against** happen to meet. **run along** *colloq.* depart. **run around 1** *Brit.* take from place to place by car etc. **2** deceive or evade repeatedly. **3** (often foll. by *with*) *sl.* engage in sexual relations (esp. casually or illicitly). **run-around** *n.* (esp. in phr. **give a person the run-around**) deceit or evasion. **run at** attack by charging or rushing. **run away 1** get away by running; flee, abscond. **2** elope. **3** (of a horse) bolt. **run away with 1** carry off (a person, stolen property, etc.). **2** win (a prize) easily. **3** accept (a notion) hastily. **4** (of expense etc.) consume (money etc.). **5** (of a horse) bolt with (a rider, a carriage or its occupants). **run a blockade** see BLOCKADE. **run down 1** knock down or collide with. **2** reduce the strength or numbers of (resources). **3** (of an unwound clock etc.) stop. **4** (of a person or a person's health) become feeble from overwork or underfeeding. **5** discover after a search. **6** disparage. **run-down** *n.* **1** a reduction in numbers. **2** a summary or brief analysis. ● *adj.* **1** decayed after prosperity. **2** enfeebled through overwork etc. **run dry** cease to flow, be exhausted. **run for it** seek safety by fleeing. **a run** (or **a good run**) **for one's money 1** vigorous competition. **2** pleasure or reward derived from an activity. **run foul of** collide or become entangled with (another vessel etc.). **run the gauntlet** see GAUNTLET². **run a person hard** (or **close**) press a person severely in a race or competition, or in comparative merit. **run high 1** (of the sea) have a strong current with a high tide. **2** (of feelings) be strong. **run in 1** run (a new engine or vehicle) carefully in the early stages. **2** *colloq.* arrest. **3** (of a combatant) rush to close quarters. **4** incur (a debt). **run-in** *n.* **1** the approach to an action or event. **2** a quarrel. **run in the family** (of a trait) be common in the members of a family. **run into 1** collide with. **2** encounter. **3** reach as many as (a specified figure). **4** fall into (a practice, absurdity, etc.). **5** be continuous or coalesce with. **run into the ground** *colloq.* bring (a person) to exhaustion etc. **run it fine** see FINE¹. **run its course** follow its natural progress; be left to itself. **run low** (or **short**) become depleted, have too little (*our tea ran short*; *we ran short of tea*). **run off 1** flee. **2** produce (copies etc.) on a machine. **3** decide (a race or other contest) after a series of heats or in the event of a tie. **4** flow or cause to flow away. **5** write or recite fluently. **6** digress suddenly. **run-off** *n.* **1** an additional competition, election, race, etc., after a tie. **2** an amount of rainfall that is carried off an area by streams and rivers. **3** *NZ* a separate area of land where young animals etc. are kept. **run off at the mouth** *US sl.* talk incessantly. **run off one's feet** very busy. **run-of-the-mill** ordinary, undistinguished. **run on 1** (of written characters) be joined together. **2** continue in operation. **3** elapse. **4** speak volubly. **5** talk incessantly. **6** *Printing* continue on the same line as the preceding matter. **run** (or **pass**) **one's eye over** see EYE. **run out 1** come to an end; become used up. **2** (foll. by *of*) exhaust one's stock of. **3** put down the wicket of (a batsman who is running). **4** escape from a containing vessel. **5** (of rope) pass out; be paid out. **6** jut out. **7** come out of a contest in a specified position etc. or complete a required score etc. (*they ran out worthy winners*). **8** complete (a race). **9** advance (a gun etc.) so as to project. **10** exhaust oneself by running. **run-out** *n.*

the dismissal of a batsman by being run out. **run out on** *colloq.* desert (a person). **run over 1** overflow; extend beyond. **2** study or repeat quickly. **3** (of a vehicle or its driver) pass over, knock down or crush. **4** touch (the notes of a piano etc.) in quick succession. **5** (often foll. by *to*) go quickly by a brief journey or for a flying visit. **run ragged** exhaust (a person). **run rings round** see RING[1]. **run riot** see RIOT. **run a** (or **the**) **risk** see RISK. **run the show** *colloq.* dominate in an undertaking etc. **run a temperature** be feverish. **run through 1** examine or rehearse briefly. **2** peruse. **3** deal successively with. **4** consume (an estate etc.) by reckless or quick spending. **5** traverse. **6** pervade. **7** pierce with a sword etc. **8** draw a line through (written words). **run-through** *n.* **1** a rehearsal. **2** a brief survey. **run to 1** have the money or ability for. **2** reach (an amount or number). **3** (of a person) show a tendency to (*runs to fat*). **4 a** be enough for (some expense or undertaking). **b** have the resources or capacity for. **5** fall into (ruin). **run to earth 1** *Hunting* chase to its lair. **2** discover after a long search. **run to meet** anticipate (one's troubles etc.). **run to seed** see SEED. **run up 1** accumulate (a debt etc.) quickly. **2** build or make hurriedly. **3** raise (a flag). **4** grow quickly. **5** rise in price. **6** (foll. by *to*) amount to. **7** force (a rival bidder) to bid higher. **8** add up (a column of figures). **9** (foll. by *to*) go quickly by a brief journey or for a flying visit. **run-up** *n.* **1** (often foll. by *to*) the period preceding an important event. **2** *Golf* a low approach shot. **run up against** meet with (a difficulty or difficulties). **run upon** (of a person's thoughts etc.) be engrossed by; dwell upon. **run wild** grow or stray unchecked or undisciplined or untrained. □□ **runnable** *adj.* [OE *rinnan*]

■ *v.* **1, 3** sprint, race, scamper, scurry, scud, dart, bolt, dash, flit, tear, scuttle, zip, whiz, gallop, hare, lope, *colloq.* scoot; rush, hurry, hasten, scramble, hustle, *archaic or poet.* hie; step lively, put on some speed, hotfoot (it), *colloq.* step on it, get a move on, leg it, get cracking, stir one's stumps, *US colloq.* step on the gas, *sl.* hoof it, hop (to) it, *esp. US sl.* get a wiggle on. **2** run away *or* off, flee, escape, take (to) flight, take to one's heels, bolt, decamp, abscond, beat a hasty retreat, make off *or* away, (make a) run for it, make a getaway, take off, take French leave, *colloq.* clear out, show a clean pair of heels, scram, skedaddle, skip (out), *sl.* cut and run, beat it, do a runner, take a powder, *Austral. sl.* go through, *Brit. sl.* scarper, do a bunk, *US sl.* go on the lam, vamoose, skiddoo. **4 a** see ADVANCE *v.* 1, 2. **b** see WORK *v.* 5. **5** be current *or* operative, last, be in effect, be in force, be effective *or* valid, have force *or* effect. **7** play, show, be on, be presented *or* screened. **8** extend, stretch, reach; amount, total up, mount up. **9 a** compete, take part, participate. **b** finish, come (in). **10** compete, be a candidate, vie, fight, stand; contend.**11a, 13** flow, pour, stream, flood, gush, spill, dribble, drip, spurt, trickle, seep, cascade, spout; issue, pass, move. **15** go, cover, sprint, race. **16** perform, do, fulfil, carry out. **17** print, publish, reproduce, issue, put out, release, carry. **18 b** operate, perform, function, work, tick, go. **19** operate, manage, direct, supervise, oversee, conduct, superintend, control, handle, manipulate, head, lead, regulate, take care of, look after, administer, be in charge of, coordinate; keep, maintain. **21** convey, transport, give (a person) a lift, drive, take, bring. **22** drive, steer, pilot; guide, navigate. **23** enter, put in, put down, register; enrol, enlist. **24** smuggle, bootleg, deal *or* traffic in. **25** see CHASE[1] *v.* 1, 4. **29** spread, flow, diffuse. **30 a** pass, meander, flow, float, drift, flit, fly, race. ● *n.* **1** sprint, dash, race, jog, trot. **2** trip, outing, excursion, jaunt, junket; *colloq.* spin, joyride. **3** way, journey; see also DISTANCE *n.* 2. **6** route, circuit, round; beat. **7 a** period, spate, spell, stretch, course, interval, time. **b** series, sequence, string, succession. **8 a** demand, call, request. **10** type, category, class, kind, sort. **12** freedom, liberty, free use of *or* access to. **13 b** pen, enclosure. **c** paddock, field; pound; see also PASTURE *n.* **15** roulade. **16** class, range; see also LINE[1] *n.* 22. **20** stream, brook, runnel, rill, rivulet, *N. Engl.* beck, *Sc.* burn, *esp. US* creek, *US dial.* kill. **21 a** journey, flight, crossing, passage. **22** trail, track, piste, path, slope. **23** (**the runs**) see DIARRHOEA. □ **on the run 1** on the loose, fleeing, escaping, in flight, running away, *US sl.* on the lam. **2** running *or* hurrying about, on the move, hastily, in haste, hurriedly, at speed, in a rush *or* a hurry, *colloq.* on the go. **run about 1** bustle, hurry; see also SCURRY *v.* **run across 1** meet (up with), run into *or* against, come across, find, stumble (up)on, hit (up)on, chance (up)on, happen (up)on, *colloq.* bump into. **run after 1** chase, pursue, go after, court, woo, set one's cap at. **run against** see *run across* above. **run along** go away, leave, *sl.* get lost; see also DEPART 1. **run around 3** philander, be unfaithful, *colloq.* gallivant, sleep around, play the field. **run away 1** see RUN *v.* 2 above. **run away with 1** see STEAL *v.* 1, ABDUCT. **run down 1** run over, knock over *or* down, collide with, strike, hit, smash *or* crash into, *sl.* slam into. **3** stop (working), play itself out; burn out, fail; see also PETER[1] *v.* **4** weaken, tire, become weary *or* exhausted *or* worn out *or* feeble, be out of shape *or* condition *or* below par. **5** trace, track *or* hunt (down), find, discover; see also LOCATE 1, 3. **6** criticize, decry, defame, vilify, disparage, deprecate, depreciate, denigrate, *colloq.* pan, *sl.* knock. **run-down** (*n.*) **2** run-through, synopsis, summary, survey, précis, résumé, (thumbnail) sketch, outline, rough idea, review, recapitulation. (*adj.*) **1** ramshackle, dilapidated, tumbledown, decrepit, rickety, broken-down. **2** weary, exhausted, debilitated, weak, worn out, peaked, fatigued, enervated, tired, drained, enfeebled, spent, burnt-out, *sl.* knackered; out of shape *or* condition, below par, in bad shape; unhealthy, sickly, ill. **run** (or **a good run**) **for one's money 2** return, satisfaction, reward, recompense, compensation, profit. **run in 2** arrest, take into custody, apprehend, take *or* bring in, pinch, collar, *colloq.* pull in, *esp. US colloq.* bust, *sl.* nab, *Brit. sl.* nick. **run-in** disagreement, argument, dispute, altercation, quarrel, confrontation, contretemps. **run into 1** see COLLIDE 1. **2** see *run across* above. **run off 1** see RUN *v.* 2 above. **2** duplicate, print, turn out, produce, make, do, churn out. **6** see DIGRESS. **run off one's feet** see BUSY *adj.* 1, 3. **run-of-the-mill** see ORDINARY *adj.* **run on 3** see ELAPSE. **run out 1** be exhausted, end, finish, go, be used up, peter out; expire, terminate, come to a close *or* end, draw to a close *or* end, cease. **2** (*run out of*) use up, consume, eat up, exhaust, be out of. **run out on** desert, abandon, leave high and dry, forsake, leave in the lurch, leave holding the baby. **run over 1** overflow, spill (over), brim over, slosh over, pour over; extend *or* reach *or* spread *or* stretch over *or* beyond, exceed, go beyond, overreach, overshoot. **2** rehearse, run through, repeat, practise, review, go over, study, learn. **3** see *run down* 1 above. **run the show** be in charge, *colloq.* be boss; see also *call the shots*. **run through 1** see *run over* 2 above. **2** peruse, scan, go over, look over, flip *or* leaf *or* thumb through, look at, skim (through), browse through, dip into, review. **4** squander, consume, use up, waste, fritter away, exhaust, spend, dissipate, throw away, *sl.* blow. **7** pierce, stab, transfix, stick, spit. **run-through 1** rehearsal, practice, trial, test. **2** see SURVEY *n.* **run to 2** see REACH *v.* 5. **3** see TEND[1] 1. **run to earth 2** see *run down* 5 above. **run up 1** accumulate. **2** see *knock up* 1. **5** see SOAR 2. **6** (*run up to*) see AMOUNT *v.* 1. **8** see ADD 2. **run up against** see ENCOUNTER *v.* 3. **run upon** see *dwell on*. **run wild** wander, rove, roam, meander, drift; see also *on the rampage* (RAMPAGE).

runabout /rúnnəbowt/ *n.* a light car or aircraft.

runaway /rúnnəway/ *n.* **1** a fugitive. **2** an animal or vehicle that is running out of control. **3** (*attrib.*) **a** that is running away or out of control (*runaway inflation*; *had a runaway success*). **b** done or performed after running away (*a runaway wedding*).

■ **1** fugitive, escapee, refugee, deserter, truant, absconder. **3 a** (*attrib.*) wild, uncontrolled, unchecked, rampant, unsuppressed; driverless, riderless; overwhelming; see also *out and out*.

runcible spoon /rúnsib'l/ *n.* a fork curved like a spoon, with three broad prongs, one edged. [nonsense word used by E. Lear, Engl. humorist d. 1888, perh. after *rouncival* large pea]

runcinate /rúnsinət/ *adj. Bot.* (of a leaf) saw-toothed, with lobes pointing towards the base. [mod.L *runcinatus* f. L *runcina* PLANE² (formerly taken to mean saw)]

rune /ro͞on/ *n.* **1** any of the letters of the earliest Germanic alphabet used by Scandinavians and Anglo-Saxons from about the 3rd c. and formed by modifying Roman or Greek characters to suit carving. **2** a similar mark of mysterious or magic significance. **3** a Finnish poem or a division of it. □ **rune-staff 1** a magic wand inscribed with runes. **2** a runic calendar. □□ **runic** *adj.* [ON *rún* (only in pl. *rúnar*) magic sign, rel. to OE *rūn*]

rung¹ /rung/ *n.* **1** each of the horizontal supports of a ladder. **2** a strengthening crosspiece in the structure of a chair etc. □□ **runged** *adj.* **rungless** *adj.* [OE *hrung*]

rung² *past part.* of RING².

runlet /rúnlit/ *n.* a small stream.

runnel /rúnn'l/ *n.* **1** a brook or rill. **2** a gutter. [later form (assim. to RUN) of *rinel* f. OE *rynel* (as RUN)]

runner /rúnnər/ *n.* **1** a person, horse, etc. that runs, esp. in a race. **2 a** a creeping plant-stem that can take root. **b** a twining plant. **3** a rod or groove or blade on which a thing slides. **4** a sliding ring on a rod etc. **5** a messenger, scout, collector, or agent for a bank etc.; a tout. **6** *hist.* a police officer. **7** a running bird. **8 a** a smuggler. **b** = *blockade-runner*. **9** a revolving millstone. **10** *Naut.* a rope in a single block with one end round a tackle-block and the other having a hook. **11** (in full **runner bean**) *Brit.* a twining bean plant, *Phaseolus coccineus*, with red flowers and long green seed pods. Also called *scarlet runner*. **12** each of the long pieces on the underside of a sledge etc. that forms the contact in sliding. **13** a roller for moving a heavy article. **14** a long narrow ornamental cloth or rug. □ **do a runner** *sl.* leave hastily; flee. **runner-up** (*pl.* **runners-up** or **runner-ups**) the competitor or team taking second place.
■ **1** sprinter, racer, jogger; *colloq.* miler. **2 b** creeper, twining plant. **5** messenger, courier, errand-boy, errand-girl, messenger-boy, messenger-girl, page, dispatch-bearer, dispatch-rider, *esp. US sl.* gofer; scout; collector, agent, tout. **6** see *police officer*. □ **do a runner** see FLEE 1.

running /rúnning/ *n.* & *adj.* ● *n.* **1** the action of runners in a race etc. **2** the way a race etc. proceeds. **3** management, control; operation ● *adj.* **1** continuing on an essentially continuous basis though changing in detail (*a running battle*). **2** consecutive; one after another (*three days running*). **3** done with a run (*a running jump*). □ **in** (or **out of**) **the running** (of a competitor) with a good (or poor) chance of winning. **make** (or **take up**) **the running** take the lead; set the pace. **running account** a current account. **running-board** a footboard on either side of a vehicle. **running commentary** an oral description of events as they occur. **running fire** successive shots from a line of troops etc. **running gear** the moving or running parts of a machine, esp. the wheels and suspension of a vehicle. **running hand** writing in which the pen etc. is not lifted after each letter. **running head** (or **headline**) a heading printed at the top of a number of consecutive pages of a book etc. **running knot** a knot that slips along the rope etc. and changes the size of a noose. **running light 1** = *navigation light*. **2** each of a small set of lights on a motor vehicle that remain illuminated while the vehicle is running. **running mate** *US* **1** a candidate for a secondary position in an election. **2** a horse entered in a race in order to set the pace for another horse from the same stable which is intended to win. **running repairs** minor or temporary repairs etc. to machinery while in use. **running rope** a rope that is freely movable through a pulley etc. **running sore** a suppurating sore. **running stitch 1** a line of small non-overlapping stitches for gathering etc. **2** one of these stitches. **running water** water flowing in a stream or from a tap etc. **take a running jump** (esp. as *int.*) *sl.* go away.
■ *n.* **3** see OPERATION 1, 2. ● *adj.* **1** continuous, on-going, perpetual, sustained, constant, uninterrupted, ceaseless, unceasing. **2** see SUCCESSIVE. □ **make** (or **take up**) **the running** take the lead, set the pace; see also LEAD¹ *v.* 5. **take a running jump** see *go away* (GO¹).

runny /rúnni/ *adj.* (**runnier, runniest**) **1** tending to run or flow. **2** excessively fluid.

runt /runt/ *n.* **1** a small pig, esp. the smallest in a litter. **2** a weakling; an undersized person. **3** a large domestic pigeon. **4** a small ox or cow, esp. of various Scottish Highland or Welsh breeds. □□ **runty** *adj.* [16th c.: orig. unkn.]
■ **2** dwarf, pygmy, midget; see also WEAKLING.

runway /rúnway/ *n.* **1** a specially prepared surface along which aircraft take off and land. **2** a trail to an animals' watering-place. **3** an incline down which logs are slid. **4** a raised gangway in a theatre, fashion display, etc.

rupee /ro͞opée/ *n.* the chief monetary unit of India, Pakistan, Sri Lanka, Nepal, Mauritius, and the Seychelles. [Hind. *rūpiyah* f. Skr. *rūpya* wrought silver]

rupiah /ro͞opéeə/ *n.* the chief monetary unit of Indonesia. [as RUPEE]

rupture /rúpchər/ *n.* & *v.* ● *n.* **1** the act or an instance of breaking; a breach. **2** a breach of harmonious relations; a disagreement and parting. **3** *Med.* an abdominal hernia. ● *v.* **1** *tr.* break or burst (a cell or membrane etc.). **2** *tr.* sever (a connection). **3** *intr.* undergo a rupture. **4** *tr.* & *intr.* affect with or suffer a hernia. □□ **rupturable** *adj.* [ME f. OF *rupture* or L *ruptura* f. *rumpere rupt-* break]
■ *n.* **1, 2** break-up, breach, disagreement, schism, breaking up, severance, division, separation, parting; break, breaking, rift, split, splitting; fissure, cleavage, bursting. ● *v.* **1** break, split. **2** sever, break, breach, *archaic or literary* sunder. **3** divide, separate.

rural /ro͝orəl/ *adj.* **1** in, of, or suggesting the country (opp. URBAN); pastoral or agricultural (*in rural seclusion*; *a rural constituency*). **2** often *derog.* characteristic of country people; rustic, plain, simple. □ **rural dean** see DEAN¹. **rural district** *Brit. hist.* a group of country parishes governed by an elected council. □□ **ruralism** *n.* **ruralist** *n.* **rurality** /-rálliti/ *n.* **ruralize** *v.* (also **-ise**). **ruralization** /-līzáysh'n/ *n.* **rurally** *adv.* [ME f. OF *rural* or LL *ruralis* f. *rus ruris* the country]
■ **1** country, pastoral, countrified, sylvan, bucolic, rustic, Arcadian, exurban, ruralist; agricultural, agrarian. **2** see RUSTIC *adj.* 2.

Ruritanian /ro͝oritáyniən/ *adj.* relating to or characteristic of romantic adventure or its setting. [*Ruritania*, an imaginary setting in SE Europe in the novels of Anthony Hope (d. 1933)]

rusa /ro͞ossə/ *n.* any of various E. Indian deer of the genus *Cervus*, esp. a sambur. [mod.L f. Malay]

ruse /ro͞oz/ *n.* a stratagem or trick. [ME f. OF f. *ruser* drive back, perh. ult. f. L *rursus* backwards: cf. RUSH¹]
■ trick, device, deception, manoeuvre, dodge, pretence, subterfuge, stratagem, wile, artifice, imposture, expedient, *colloq.* ploy.

rush¹ /rush/ *v.* & *n.* ● *v.* **1** *intr.* go, move, or act precipitately or with great speed. **2** *tr.* move or transport with great haste (*was rushed to hospital*). **3** *intr.* (foll. by *at*) **a** move suddenly and quickly towards. **b** begin impetuously. **4** *tr.* perform or deal with hurriedly (*don't rush your dinner*; *the bill was rushed through Parliament*). **5** *tr.* force (a person) to act hastily. **6** *tr.* attack or capture by sudden assault. **7** *tr. sl.* overcharge (a customer). **8** *tr. US* pay attentions to (a person) with a view to securing acceptance of a proposal. **9** *tr.* pass (an obstacle) with a rapid dash. **10** *intr.* flow, fall, spread, or roll impetuously or fast (*felt the blood rush to my face*; *the river rushes past*). ● *n.* **1** an act of rushing; a violent advance or attack. **2** a period of great activity; a commotion. **3** (*attrib.*) done with great haste or speed (*a rush job*). **4** a sudden migration of large numbers. **5** a surge of emotion, excitement, etc. **6** (foll. by *on*, *for*) a sudden strong demand for a commodity. **7** (in *pl.*) *colloq.* the first prints of a film after a period of shooting. **8** *Football* **a** a combined dash by several players with the ball. **b** *US* the act of carrying the ball. □ **rush one's fences** act with undue haste. **rush hour** a time each day when traffic is at its heaviest. □□ **rusher** *n.* **rushingly** *adv.* [ME f. AF *russher*, = OF *ruser*, *russer*: see RUSE]

■ *v.* **1** hurry (up), hasten, run, race, bustle, make haste, dash, speed, scurry, jump, sprint, scuttle, hustle, scramble, hotfoot (it), go like a bat out of hell, shake a leg, *colloq.* scoot, move (it), step on it, make it snappy, get moving, get cracking, look alive *or* lively, *US colloq.* hightail (it), step on the gas, *esp. US sl.* get a wiggle on. **3 a** run, race, dash, jump; see also TEAR[1] *v.* 5. **4** hurry, race, push. **6** attack, assault, charge, storm, *colloq.* blitz. **7** see FLEECE *v.* 1. **10** see SURGE *v.* 1. ● *n.* **1** hurry, haste, (hustle and) bustle; surge, charge, advance; see also ATTACK *n.* 1. **2** fuss, excitement, flurry, commotion, ferment, to-do, *literary* pother. **3** (*attrib.*) hasty, speedy, urgent, pressing, high-priority, top-priority, emergency. **5** surge, sensation, thrill.

rush[2] /rush/ *n.* **1 a** any marsh or waterside plant of the family Juncaceae, with naked slender tapering pith-filled stems (properly leaves) formerly used for strewing floors and still used for making chair-bottoms and plaiting baskets etc. **b** a stem of this. **c** (*collect.*) rushes as a material. **2** *archaic* a thing of no value (*not worth a rush*). □ **rush candle** a candle made by dipping the pith of a rush in tallow. □□ **rushlike** *adv.* **rushy** *adj.* [OE *rysc*, *rysce*, corresp. to MLG, MHG *rusch*]

rushlight /rúshlīt/ *n.* a rush candle.

rusk /rusk/ *n.* a slice of bread rebaked usu. as a light biscuit, esp. as food for babies. [Sp. or Port. *rosca* twist, coil, roll of bread]

russet /rússit/ *adj.* & *n.* ● *adj.* **1** reddish-brown. **2** *archaic* rustic, homely, simple. ● *n.* **1** a reddish-brown colour. **2** a kind of rough-skinned russet-coloured apple. **3** *hist.* a coarse homespun reddish-brown or grey cloth used for simple clothing. □□ **russety** *adj.* [ME f. AF f. OF *rosset*, *rousset*, dimin. of *roux* red f. Prov. *ros*, It. *rosso* f. L *russus* red]

Russia leather /rúshə/ *n.* a durable bookbinding leather from skins impregnated with birch-bark oil. [*Russia* in E. Europe]

Russian /rúsh'n/ *n.* & *adj.* ● *n.* **1 a** a native or national of Russia or the former Soviet Union. **b** a person of Russian descent. **2** the language of Russia and the official language of the former Soviet Union. ● *adj.* **1** of or relating to Russia. **2** of or in Russian. □ **Russian boot** a boot that loosely encloses the calf. **Russian olive** = OLEASTER. **Russian roulette 1** an act of daring in which one (usu. with others in turn) squeezes the trigger of a revolver held to one's head with one chamber loaded, having first spun the chamber. **2** a potentially dangerous enterprise. **Russian salad** a salad of mixed diced vegetables with mayonnaise. □□ **Russianize** *v.tr.* (also **-ise**). **Russianization** /-nīzáysh'n/ *n.* **Russianness** *n.* [med.L *Russianus*]

Russify /rússifī/ *v.tr.* (**-ies, -ied**) make Russian in character. □□ **Russification** /-fikáysh'n/ *n.*

Russki /rúski/ *n.* (also **Russky**) (*pl.* **Russkis** or **-ies**) often *offens.* a Russian or (formerly) a Soviet citizen. [RUSSIAN after Russ. surnames ending in *-ski*]

Russo- /rússō/ *comb. form* Russian; Russian and.

Russophile /rússōfīl/ *n.* a person who is fond of Russia or the Russians.

rust /rust/ *n.* & *v.* ● *n.* **1 a** a reddish or yellowish-brown coating formed on iron or steel by oxidation, esp. as a result of moisture. **b** a similar coating on other metals. **2 a** any of various plant-diseases with rust-coloured spots caused by fungi of the order *Uredinales*. **b** the fungus causing this. **3** an impaired state due to disuse or inactivity. ● *v.* **1** *tr.* & *intr.* affect or be affected with rust; undergo oxidation. **2** *intr.* (of bracken etc.) become rust-coloured. **3** *intr.* (of a plant) be attacked by rust. **4** *intr.* lose quality or efficiency by disuse or inactivity. □□ **rustless** *adj.* [OE *rūst* f. Gmc]

rustic /rústik/ *adj.* & *n.* ● *adj.* **1** having the characteristics of or associations with the country or country life. **2** unsophisticated, simple, unrefined. **3** of rude or country workmanship. **4** made of untrimmed branches or rough timber (*a rustic bench*). **5** (of lettering) freely formed. **6** *Archit.* with rough-hewn or roughened surface or with sunk joints. ● *n.* a person from or living in the country, esp. a simple unsophisticated one. □□ **rustically** *adv.* **rusticity** /-tíssiti/ *n.* [ME f. L *rusticus* f. *rus* the country]

■ *adj.* **1** see RURAL 1. **2** peasant, plain, simple, uncomplicated, unsophisticated, naïve, ingenuous, guileless, artless, unrefined, unpolished, countrified, uncultivated, uncultured, crude, rough, unmannerly, cloddish, lumpen, boorish, oafish, loutish, *colloq. often derog.* hill-billy. ● *n.* peasant, ryot, bumpkin, yokel, countryman, countrywoman, country boy *or* girl, *archaic* villain, *Austral.* & *NZ colloq.* bushy, *esp. US colloq.* hick, *US colloq.* hayseed, *US colloq. often derog.* hill-billy, *often derog.* country cousin, *sl.* clodhopper, clod, .

rusticate /rústikayt/ *v.* **1** *tr.* send down (a student) temporarily from university. **2** *intr.* retire to or live in the country. **3** *tr.* make rural. **4** *tr.* mark (masonry) with sunk joints or a roughened surface. □□ **rustication** /-káysh'n/ *n.* [L *rusticari* live in the country (as RUSTIC)]

rustle /rúss'l/ *v.* & *n.* ● *v.* **1** *intr.* & *tr.* make or cause to make a gentle sound as of dry leaves blown in a breeze. **2** *intr.* (often foll. by *along* etc.) move with a rustling sound. **3** *tr.* (also *absol.*) steal (cattle or horses). **4** *intr. US colloq.* hustle. ● *n.* a rustling sound or movement. □ **rustle up** *colloq.* produce quickly when needed. □□ **rustler** *n.* (esp. in sense 3 of *v.*). [ME *rustel* etc. (imit.): cf. obs. Flem. *ruysselen*, Du. *ritselen*]

■ *v.* **1** whisper, swish. ● *n.* whisper, whispering, rustling, swish, swishing, *literary* susurration.

rustproof /rústproo͞f/ *adj.* & *v.* ● *adj.* (of a metal) not susceptible to corrosion by rust. ● *v.tr.* make rustproof.

rustre /rústər/ *n. Heraldry* a lozenge with a round hole. [F]

rusty /rústi/ *adj.* (**rustier, rustiest**) **1** rusted or affected by rust. **2** stiff with age or disuse. **3** (of knowledge etc.) faded or impaired by neglect (*my French is a bit rusty*). **4** rust-coloured. **5** (of black clothes) discoloured by age. **6 a** of antiquated appearance. **b** antiquated or behind the times. **7** (of a voice) croaking or creaking. □□ **rustily** *adv.* **rustiness** *n.* [OE *rūstig* (as RUST)]

rut[1] /rut/ *n.* & *v.* ● *n.* **1** a deep track made by the passage of wheels. **2** an established (esp. tedious) mode of practice or procedure. ● *v.tr.* (**rutted, rutting**) mark with ruts. □ **in a rut** following a fixed (esp. tedious or dreary) pattern of behaviour that is difficult to change. □□ **rutty** *adj.* [prob. f. OF *rote* (as ROUTE)]

■ **1** groove, furrow, track. **2** routine, groove, grind, treadmill, dead end.

rut[2] /rut/ *n.* & *v.* ● *n.* the periodic sexual excitement of a male deer, goat, sheep, etc. ● *v.intr.* (**rutted, rutting**) be affected with rut. □□ **ruttish** *adj.* [ME f. OF *rut*, *ruit* f. L *rugitus* f. *rugire* roar]

rutabaga /roo͞təbáygə/ *n.* a swede. [Sw. dial. *rotabagge*]

ruthenium /roothéeniəm/ *n. Chem.* a rare hard white metallic transition element, occurring naturally in platinum ores, and used as a chemical catalyst and in certain alloys. ¶ Symb.: **Ru**. [med.L *Ruthenia* Russia (from its discovery in ores from the Urals)]

rutherfordium /rúthərfórdiəm/ *n. Chem.* an artificially made transuranic metallic element produced by bombarding an isotope of Californium. ¶ Symb.: **Rf**. Also called KURCHATOVIUM. [E. *Rutherford*, Engl. physicist d. 1937]

ruthless /roo͞thliss/ *adj.* having no pity or compassion. □□ **ruthlessly** *adv.* **ruthlessness** *n.* [ME, f. *ruth* compassion f. RUE[1]]

■ pitiless, unpitying, cruel, unsympathetic, merciless, unmerciful, harsh, fierce, remorseless, uncompassionate, vicious, savage, ferocious, hard-hearted, callous, unfeeling, tough, severe, heartless, inhuman, brutal, brutish, unrelenting, relentless, *US* mean.

rutile /rōōtīl/ *n.* a mineral form of titanium dioxide. [F *rutile* or G *Rutil* f. L *rutilus* reddish]

RV *abbr.* **1** Revised Version (of the Bible). **2** *US* recreational vehicle, as a motorized caravan.

Ry. *abbr.* Railway.

-ry /ri/ *suffix* = -ERY (*infantry*; *rivalry*). [shortened f. -ERY, or by analogy]

rye /rī/ *n.* **1 a** a cereal plant, *Secale cereale*, with spikes bearing florets which yield wheatlike grains. **b** the grain of this used for bread and fodder. **2** (in full **rye whisky**) whisky distilled from fermented rye. [OE *ryge* f. Gmc]

ryegrass /rígraass/ *n.* any forage or lawn grass of the genus *Lolium*, esp. *L. perenne*. [obs. *ray-grass*, of unkn. orig.]

ryokan /riókən/ *n.* a traditional Japanese inn. [Jap.]

ryot /ríət/ *n.* an Indian peasant. [Urdu *ra'īyat* f. Arab. *ra'īya* flock, subjects f. *ra'ā* to pasture]

Ss

S[1] /ess/ *n.* (also **s**) (*pl.* **Ss** or **S's** /éssiz/) **1** the nineteenth letter of the alphabet. **2** an S-shaped object or curve.

S[2] *abbr.* (also **S.**) **1** Saint. **2** siemens. **3** Society. **4** South, Southern.

S[3] *symb. Chem.* the element sulphur.

s. *abbr.* **1** second(s). **2** shilling(s). **3** singular. **4** son. **5** succeeded. [sense 2 orig. f. L *solidus*: see SOLIDUS]

-s' /ss; z after a vowel sound or voiced consonant/ *suffix* denoting the possessive case of plural nouns and sometimes of singular nouns ending in *s* (*the boys' shoes*; *Charles' book*). [as -'s[1]]

's- /ss, z/ *prefix archaic* (esp. in oaths) God's (*'sblood*; *'struth*). [abbr.]

's /ss; z after a vowel sound or voiced consonant/ *abbr.* **1** is, has (*he's*; *it's*; *John's*; *Charles's*). **2** us (*let's*). **3** *colloq.* does (*what's he say?*).

-s[1] /ss; z after a vowel sound or voiced consonant, e.g. *ways*, *bags*/ *suffix* denoting the plurals of nouns (cf. -ES[1]). [OE *-as* pl. ending]

-s[2] /ss; z after a vowel sound or voiced consonant, e.g. *ties*, *begs*/ *suffix* forming the 3rd person sing. present of verbs (cf. -ES[2]). [OE dial., prob. f. OE 2nd person sing. present ending *-es*, *-as*]

-s[3] /ss; z after a vowel sound or voiced consonant, e.g. *besides*/ *suffix* **1** forming adverbs (*afterwards*; *besides*; *mornings*). **2** forming possessive pronouns (*hers*; *ours*). [formed as -'s[1]]

-s[4] /ss; z after a vowel sound or voiced consonant/ *suffix* forming nicknames or pet names (*Fats*; *ducks*). [after -s[1]]

-'s[1] /ss; z after a vowel sound or voiced consonant/ *suffix* denoting the possessive case of singular nouns and of plural nouns not ending in *-s* (*John's book*; *the book's cover*; *the children's shoes*). [OE genit. sing. ending]

-'s[2] /ss; z after a vowel sound or voiced consonant/ *suffix* denoting the plural of a letter or symbol (*S's*; *8's*). [as -s[1]]

SA *abbr.* **1** Salvation Army. **2** sex appeal. **3 a** South Africa. **b** South America. **c** South Australia. **4** *hist.* *Sturmabteilung* (the paramilitary force of the Nazi party).

sabadilla /sábbədíllə/ *n.* **1** a Mexican plant, *Schoenocaulon officinale*, with seeds yielding veratrine. **2** a preparation of these seeds, used in medicine and agriculture. [Sp. *cebadilla* dimin. of *cebada* barley]

Sabaoth /sábbaa-oth, sabáa-oth/ *n.pl. Bibl.* heavenly hosts (see HOST[1] 2) (*Lord of Sabaoth*). [ME f. LL f. Gk *Sabaōth* f. Heb. *ṣᵉbāʼōṯ* pl. of *ṣābâ* host (of heaven)]

Sabbatarian /sábbətáiriən/ *n.* & *adj.* ● *n.* **1** a strict sabbath-keeping Jew. **2** a Christian who favours observing Sunday strictly as the sabbath. **3** a Christian who observes Saturday as the sabbath. ● *adj.* relating to or holding the tenets of Sabbatarians. □□ **Sabbatarianism** *n.* [LL *sabbatarius* f. L *sabbatum*: see SABBATH]

sabbath /sábbəth/ *n.* **1** (in full **sabbath day**) a day of rest and religious observance kept by Christians on Sunday, Jews on Saturday, and Muslims on Friday. **2** a period of rest. **3** (in full **witches' sabbath**) a supposed general midnight meeting of witches with the Devil. [OE *sabat*, L *sabbatum*, & OF *sabbat*, f. Gk *sabbaton* f. Heb. *šabbāṯ* f. *šāḇaṯ* to rest]

sabbatical /səbáttik'l/ *adj.* & *n.* ● *adj.* **1** of or appropriate to the sabbath. **2** (of leave) granted at intervals to a university teacher for study or travel, orig. every seventh year. ● *n.* a period of sabbatical leave. □ **sabbatical year 1** *Bibl.* every seventh year, prescribed by the Mosaic law to be observed as a 'sabbath', during which the land was allowed to rest. **2** a year's sabbatical leave. □□ **sabbatically** *adv.* [LL *sabbaticus* f. Gk *sabbatikos* of the sabbath]

■ *n.* see LEAVE[2] 2.

saber *US* var. of SABRE.

Sabian /sáybiən/ *adj.* & *n.* ● *adj.* of a sect classed in the Koran with Muslims, Jews, and Christians, as believers in the true God. ● *n.* a member of this sect. [Arab. *ṣābiʼ*]

sabicu /sábbikoo/ *n.* **1** a W. Indian tree, *Lysiloma latisiliqua*, grown for timber. **2** the mahogany-like wood of this tree. [Cuban Sp. *sabicú*]

Sabine /sábbīn/ *adj.* & *n.* ● *adj.* of or relating to a people of the central Apennines in ancient Italy. ● *n.* a member of this people. [L *Sabinus*]

Sabin vaccine /sáybin/ *n.* an oral vaccine giving immunity against poliomyelitis. [A. B. *Sabin*, US virologist b. 1906]

sable[1] /sáyb'l/ *n.* **1 a** a small brown-furred flesh-eating mammal, *Martes zibellina*, of N. Europe and parts of N. Asia, related to the marten. **b** its skin or fur. **2** a fine paintbrush made of sable fur. [ME f. OF f. med.L *sabelum* f. Slav.]

sable[2] /sáyb'l/ *n.* & *adj.* ● *n.* **1** esp. *poet.* black. **2** (in *pl.*) mourning garments. **3** (in full **sable antelope**) a large stout-horned African antelope, *Hippotragus niger*, the males of which are mostly black in old age. ● *adj.* **1** (usu. placed after noun) *Heraldry* black. **2** esp. *poet.* dark, gloomy. □□ **sabled** *adj.* **sably** *adv.* [ME f. OF (in Heraldry): gen. taken to be identical with SABLE[1], although sable fur is dark brown]

■ *n.* **2** (*sables*) see MOURNING 2. ● *adj.* **2** see *pitch-black* (PITCH[2]).

sabot /sábbō, sábbō/ *n.* **1** a kind of simple shoe hollowed out from a block of wood. **2** a wooden-soled shoe. **3** *Austral.* a small snub-nosed yacht. □□ **saboted** /sábbōd/ *adj.* [F, blend of *savate* shoe + *botte* boot]

sabotage /sábbətaazh/ *n.* & *v.* ● *n.* deliberate damage to productive capacity, esp. as a political act. ● *v.tr.* **1** commit sabotage on. **2** destroy, spoil; make useless (*sabotaged my plans*). [F f. *saboter* make a noise with sabots, bungle, wilfully destroy: see SABOT]

■ *n.* destruction, damage, wrecking, impairment; subversion, treachery, treason. ● *v.* damage, incapacitate, disable, cripple; destroy, wreck, spoil, ruin, disrupt; subvert, undermine; queer a person's pitch.

saboteur /sábbətőr/ *n.* a person who commits sabotage. [F]

■ see SUBVERSIVE *n.*

sabra /sábrə/ *n.* a Jew born in Israel. [mod. Heb. *sābrāh* opuntia fruit]

sabre /sáybər/ *n.* & *v.* (*US* **saber**) ● *n.* **1** a cavalry sword with a curved blade. **2** a cavalry soldier and horse. **3** a light fencing-sword with a tapering blade. ● *v.tr.* cut down or wound with a sabre. □ **sabre-bill** any S. American bird of the genus *Campylorhamphus* with a long curved bill.

sabre-cut 1 a blow with a sabre. **2** a wound made or a scar left by this. **sabre-rattling** a display or threat of military force. **sabre-toothed** designating any of various extinct mammals having long sabre-shaped upper canines. **sabre-wing** a S. American humming-bird, *Campylopterus falcatus*, with curved wings. [F, earlier *sable* f. G *Sabel*, *Säbel*, *Schabel* f. Pol. *szabla* or Magyar *szablya*]
▪ *n.* **1, 3** see BLADE 6.

sabretache /sábbərtash/ *n.* a flat satchel on long straps worn by some cavalry officers from the left of the waist-belt. [F f. G *Säbeltasche* (as SABRE, *Tasche* pocket)]

sabreur /sabrőr/ *n.* a user of the sabre, esp. a cavalryman. [F f. *sabrer* SABRE *v.*]

SAC *abbr.* (in the UK) Senior Aircraftman.

sac /sak/ *n.* **1** a baglike cavity, enclosed by a membrane, in an animal or plant. **2** the distended membrane surrounding a hernia, cyst, tumour, etc. [F *sac* or L *saccus* SACK[1]]

saccade /sakaád/ *n.* a brief rapid movement of the eye between fixation points. ▫▫ **saccadic** /səkáddik/ *adj.* [F, = violent pull, f. OF *saquer*, *sachier* pull]

saccate /sákkayt/ *adj. Bot.* **1** dilated into a bag. **2** contained in a sac.

saccharide /sákkərīd/ *n. Chem.* = SUGAR *n.* 2. [mod.L *saccharum* sugar + -IDE]

saccharimeter /sákkərímmitər/ *n.* any instrument, esp. a polarimeter, for measuring the sugar content of a solution. [F *saccharimètre* (as SACCHARIDE)]

saccharin /sákkərin/ *n.* a very sweet substance used as a non-fattening substitute for sugar. [G (as SACCHARIDE) + -IN]

saccharine /sákkəreen/ *adj.* **1** sugary. **2** of, containing, or like sugar. **3** unpleasantly over-polite, sentimental, etc.
▪ **3** see SENTIMENTAL.

saccharo- /sákkərō/ *comb. form* sugar; sugar and. [Gk *sakkharon* sugar]

saccharogenic /sákkərōjénnik/ *adj.* producing sugar.

saccharometer /sákkərómmitər/ *n.* any instrument, esp. a hydrometer, for measuring the sugar content of a solution.

saccharose /sákkərōss, -rōz/ *n.* sucrose. [mod.L *saccharum* sugar + -OSE[2]]

sacciform /sáksiform/ *adj.* sac-shaped. [L *saccus* sac + -FORM]

saccule /sákyo͞ol/ *n.* a small sac or cyst. ▫▫ **saccular** *adj.* [L *sacculus* (as SAC)]

sacerdotal /sákkərdőt'l/ *adj.* **1** of priests or the priestly office; priestly. **2** (of a doctrine etc.) ascribing sacrificial functions and supernatural powers to ordained priests; claiming excessive authority for the priesthood. ▫▫ **sacerdotalism** *n.* **sacerdotalist** *n.* **sacerdotally** *adv.* [ME f. OF *sacerdotal* or L *sacerdotalis* f. *sacerdos -dotis* priest]
▪ **1** see PRIESTLY.

sachem /sáychəm/ *n.* **1** the supreme chief of some American Indian tribes. **2** *US* a political leader. [Narragansett, = SAGAMORE]

sachet /sáshay/ *n.* **1** a small bag or packet containing a small portion of a substance, esp. shampoo. **2** a small perfumed bag. **3 a** dry perfume for laying among clothes etc. **b** a packet of this. [F, dimin. of *sac* f. L *saccus*]

sack[1] /sak/ *n.* & *v.* ● *n.* **1 a** a large strong bag, usu. made of hessian, paper, or plastic, for storing or conveying goods. **b** (usu. foll. by *of*) this with its contents (*a sack of potatoes*). **c** a quantity contained in a sack. **2** (prec. by *the*) *colloq.* dismissal from employment. **3** (prec. by *the*) *US sl.* bed. **4 a** a woman's short loose dress with a sacklike appearance. **b** *archaic* or *hist.* a woman's loose gown, or a silk train attached to the shoulders of this. **5** a man's or woman's loose-hanging coat not shaped to the back. ● *v.tr.* **1** put into a sack or sacks. **2** *colloq.* dismiss from employment. ▫ **sack race** a race between competitors in sacks up to the waist or neck. ▫▫ **sackful** *n.* (*pl.* **-fuls**). **sacklike** *adj.* [OE *sacc* f. L *saccus* f. Gk *sakkos*, of Semitic orig.]
▪ *n.* **1** bag, pouch, *dial.* poke. **2** one's marching orders, *colloq.* one's walking papers, the boot, the push, *US colloq.* the bounce, *Brit. sl.* the chop. ● *v.* **2** dismiss, discharge, lay off, axe, make *or* declare redundant, give a person his *or* her marching orders, *colloq.* give a person his *or* her walking papers, give a person the sack *or* boot *or* push, *Austral. colloq.* tramp, *US colloq.* bounce, *sl.* fire, *Brit. sl.* give a person the chop.

sack[2] /sak/ *v.* & *n.* ● *v.tr.* **1** plunder and destroy (a captured town etc.). **2** steal valuables from (a place). ● *n.* the sacking of a captured place. [orig. as noun, f. F *sac* in phr. *mettre à sac* put to sack, f. It. *sacco* SACK[1]]

sack[3] /sak/ *n. hist.* a white wine formerly imported into Britain from Spain and the Canaries (*sherry sack*). [16th-c. *wyne seck*, f. F *vin sec* dry wine]

sackbut /sákbut/ *n.* an early form of trombone. [F *saquebute*, earlier *saqueboute* hook for pulling a man off a horse f. *saquer* pull, *boute* (as BUTT[1])]

sackcloth /sák-kloth/ *n.* **1** a coarse fabric of flax or hemp. **2** clothing made of this, formerly worn as a penance or in mourning (esp. *sackcloth and ashes*).
▪ **2** see MOURNING 2.

sacking /sákking/ *n.* material for making sacks; sackcloth.

sacra *pl.* of SACRUM.

sacral /sáykrəl/ *adj.* **1** *Anat.* of or relating to the sacrum. **2** *Anthropol.* of or for sacred rites. [E or L *sacrum*: see SACRUM]

sacrament /sákrəmənt/ *n.* **1** a religious ceremony or act of the Christian Churches regarded as an outward and visible sign of inward and spiritual grace: applied by the Eastern, pre-Reformation Western, and Roman Catholic Churches to the seven rites of baptism, confirmation, the Eucharist, penance, extreme unction, ordination, and matrimony, but restricted by most Protestants to baptism and the Eucharist. **2** a thing of mysterious and sacred significance; a sacred influence, symbol, etc. **3** (also **Blessed** or **Holy Sacrament**) (prec. by *the*) **a** the Eucharist. **b** the consecrated elements, esp. the bread or Host. **4** an oath or solemn engagement taken. [ME f. OF *sacrement* f. L *sacramentum* solemn oath etc. f. *sacrare* hallow f. *sacer* SACRED, used in Christian L as transl. of Gk *mustērion* MYSTERY[1]]
▪ **3** see EUCHARIST.

sacramental /sákrəmént'l/ *adj.* & *n.* ● *adj.* **1** of or of the nature of a sacrament or the sacrament. **2** (of a doctrine etc.) attaching great importance to the sacraments. ● *n.* an observance analogous to but not reckoned among the sacraments, e.g. the use of holy water or the sign of the cross. ▫▫ **sacramentalism** *n.* **sacramentalist** *n.* **sacramentality** /-tálliti/ *n.* **sacramentally** *adv.* [ME f. F *sacramental* or LL *sacramentalis* (as SACRAMENT)]
▪ *adj.* **1** see SACRED 1b–c, 2a.

sacrarium /səkráiriəm/ *n.* (*pl.* **sacraria** /-riə/) **1** the sanctuary of a church. **2** *RC Ch.* a piscina. **3** *Rom. Antiq.* a shrine; the room (in a house) containing the penates. [L f. *sacer sacri* holy]

sacred /sáykrid/ *adj.* **1 a** (often foll. by *to*) exclusively dedicated or appropriated (to a god or to some religious purpose). **b** made holy by religious association. **c** connected with religion; used for a religious purpose (*sacred music*). **2 a** safeguarded or required by religion, reverence, or tradition. **b** sacrosanct. **3** (of writings etc.) embodying the laws or doctrines of a religion. ▫ **Sacred College** *RC Ch.* the body of cardinals. **sacred cow** *colloq.* an idea or institution unreasonably held to be above criticism (with ref. to the Hindus' respect for the cow as a holy animal). **Sacred Heart** *RC Ch.* the heart of Christ as an object of devotion. **sacred number** a number associated with religious symbolism, e.g. 7. ▫▫ **sacredly** *adv.* **sacredness** *n.* [ME, past part. of obs. *sacre* consecrate f. OF *sacrer* f. L *sacrare* f. *sacer sacri* holy]
▪ **1 a** dedicated, consecrated. **b** hallowed, holy, blessed, sanctified, revered, divine, venerable, venerated, *poet.* blest. **c** religious, spiritual; church, chapel, ecclesiastical; priestly, hieratic. **2 a** ritual, ceremonial, solemn,

sacramental, liturgical, votive. **b** inviolable, inviolate, untouchable, protected, sacrosanct.

sacrifice /sákrifīss/ *n.* & *v.* ● *n.* **1 a** the act of giving up something valued for the sake of something else more important or worthy. **b** a thing given up in this way. **c** the loss entailed in this. **2 a** the slaughter of an animal or person or the surrender of a possession as an offering to a deity. **b** an animal, person, or thing offered in this way. **3** an act of prayer, thanksgiving, or penitence as propitiation. **4** *Theol.* **a** Christ's offering of himself in the Crucifixion. **b** the Eucharist as either a propitiatory offering of the body and blood of Christ or an act of thanksgiving. **5** (in games) a loss incurred deliberately to avoid a greater loss or to obtain a compensating advantage. ● *v.* **1** *tr.* give up (a thing) as a sacrifice. **2** *tr.* (foll. by *to*) devote or give over to. **3** *tr.* (also *absol.*) offer or kill as a sacrifice. □□ **sacrificial** /-fish'l/ *adj.* **sacrificially** /-fishəli/ *adv.* [ME f. OF f. L *sacrificium* f. *sacrificus* (as SACRED)]

■ *n.* **1 a** forfeiture, forgoing, giving up, relinquishment, loss. **b** loss, forfeit; see also OFFERING. **2 a** immolation; surrender, forfeiture, forgoing, giving up, yielding up, offering (up). **b** (burnt) offering, holocaust, hecatomb; donation, gift, *Relig.* oblation. ● *v.* **1** give up, forgo, forfeit, relinquish, surrender, let go (of), lose, yield, renounce, forswear; cease, stop, refrain from, *literary* desist from, forbear (from). **2** devote to, give over *or* up to, offer up to, yield up to. **3** immolate, offer (up), yield (up), give up. □□ **sacrificial** sacrificed, immolated, surrendered; atoning, expiatory, propitiatory, conciliatory.

sacrilege /sákrilij/ *n.* the violation or misuse of what is regarded as sacred. □□ **sacrilegious** /-lijəss/ *adj.* **sacrilegiously** /-lijəsli/ *adv.* [ME f. OF f. L *sacrilegium* f. *sacrilegus* stealer of sacred things, f. *sacer sacri* sacred + *legere* take possession of]

■ desecration, profanation, debasement, violation, prostitution, dishonouring, vitiation, defilement, fouling, contamination, misuse, abuse, perversion, impiety, heresy, violation, profanity, blasphemy, irreverence, *poet.* befouling; outrage; impiousness, disrespect, maltreatment. □□ **sacrilegious** profane, impious, heretical, blasphemous, irreverent, disrespectful.

sacring /sáykring/ *n. archaic* **1** the consecration of the Eucharistic elements. **2** the ordination and consecration of a bishop, sovereign, etc. □ **sacring bell** a bell rung at the elevation of the elements in the Eucharist. [ME f. obs. *sacre*: see SACRED]

sacristan /sákristən/ *n.* **1** a person in charge of a sacristy and its contents. **2** *archaic* the sexton of a parish church. [ME f. med.L *sacristanus* (as SACRED)]

sacristy /sákristi/ *n.* (*pl.* **-ies**) a room in a church, where the vestments, sacred vessels, etc., are kept and the celebrant can prepare for a service. [F *sacristie* or It. *sacrestia* or med.L *sacristia* (as SACRED)]

sacro- /sáykrō/ *comb. form* denoting the sacrum (*sacro-iliac*).

sacrosanct /sákrōsangkt/ *adj.* (of a person, place, law, etc.) most sacred; inviolable. □□ **sacrosanctity** /-sángktiti/ *n.* [L *sacrosanctus* f. *sacro* ablat. of *sacrum* sacred rite (see SACRED) + *sanctus* (as SAINT)]

■ see SACRED 2b.

sacrum /sáykrəm/ *n.* (*pl.* **sacra** /-krə/ or **sacrums**) *Anat.* a triangular bone formed from fused vertebrae and situated between the two hip-bones of the pelvis. [L *os sacrum* transl. Gk *hieron osteon* sacred bone (from its sacrificial use)]

SACW *abbr.* (in the UK) Senior Aircraftwoman.

SAD *abbr.* seasonal affective disorder.

sad /sad/ *adj.* (**sadder, saddest**) **1** unhappy; feeling sorrow or regret. **2** causing or suggesting sorrow (*a sad story*). **3** regrettable. **4** shameful, deplorable (*is in a sad state*). **5** (of a colour) dull, neutral-tinted. **6** (of dough etc.) heavy, having failed to rise. □ **sad-iron** a solid flat-iron. **sad sack** *US colloq.* a very inept person. □□ **saddish** *adj.* **sadly** *adv.* **sadness** *n.* [OE *sæd* f. Gmc, rel. to L *satis*]

■ **1** unhappy, melancholy, downcast, dejected, depressed, low, sorrowful, gloomy, morose, glum, lugubrious, mournful, heartsick, crestfallen, chap-fallen, disheartened, downhearted, blue, despondent, broken-hearted, heartbroken, woebegone, miserable, wretched. **2** depressing, gloomy, disheartening, dreary, dismal, funereal, sombre, lugubrious, saddening, tearful, heartbreaking, bleak, distressing, dispiriting, calamitous. **3** see REGRETTABLE. **4** unfortunate, unsatisfactory, awful, bad, shabby, dirty, shameful, lamentable, miserable, sorry, wretched, pathetic, pitiful, pitiable, deplorable, terrible, *colloq.* lousy, *sl.* rotten. □□ **sadly** unhappily, gloomily, morosely, mournfully, despondently, miserably, wretchedly, dejectedly, dismally, sombrely, lugubriously; unfortunately, alas, unluckily, lamentably, regrettably, deplorably, sad to relate. **sadness** unhappiness, misery, sorrow, dispiritedness, grief, depression, dejection, dejectedness, sorrowfulness, despondency, melancholy, gloom, gloominess, *literary* dolour.

sadden /sádd'n/ *v.tr.* & *intr.* make or become sad.

■ depress, deject, sorrow, dishearten, distress, dispirit, discourage, grieve.

saddle /sádd'l/ *n.* & *v.* ● *n.* **1** a seat of leather etc., usu. raised at the front and rear, fastened on a horse etc. for riding. **2** a seat for the rider of a bicycle etc. **3** a joint of meat consisting of the two loins. **4** a ridge rising to a summit at each end. **5** the part of a draught-horse's harness to which the shafts are attached. **6** a part of an animal's back resembling a saddle in shape or marking. **7** the rear part of a male fowl's back. **8** a support for a cable or wire on top of a suspension-bridge, pier, or telegraph-pole. **9** a fireclay bar for supporting ceramic ware in a kiln. ● *v.tr.* **1** put a saddle on (a horse etc.). **2 a** (foll. by *with*) burden (a person) with a task, responsibility, etc. **b** (foll. by *on, upon*) impose (a burden) on a person. **3** (of a trainer) enter (a horse) for a race. □ **in the saddle 1** mounted. **2** in office or control. **saddle-bag 1** each of a pair of bags laid across a horse etc. behind the saddle. **2** a bag attached behind the saddle of a bicycle or motor cycle. **saddle-bow** the arched front or rear of a saddle. **saddle-cloth** a cloth laid on a horse's back under the saddle. **saddle-horse** a horse for riding. **saddle-sore** chafed by riding on a saddle. **saddle stitch** a stitch of thread or a wire staple passed through the centre of a magazine or booklet. **saddle-tree 1** the frame of a saddle. **2** a tulip-tree (with saddle-shaped leaves). □□ **saddleless** *adj.* [OE *sadol, sadul* f. Gmc]

■ *v.* **2** see BURDEN *v.* □ **saddle-horse** see HACK[2] *n.* 1.

saddleback /sádd'lbak/ *n.* **1** *Archit.* a tower-roof with two opposite gables. **2** a hill with a concave upper outline. **3** a black pig with a white stripe across the back. **4** any of various birds with a saddle-like marking esp. a New Zealand bird, *Philesturnus carunculatus.* □□ **saddlebacked** *adj.*

saddler /sádlər/ *n.* a maker of or dealer in saddles and other equipment for horses.

saddlery /sádləri/ *n.* (*pl.* **-ies**) **1** the saddles and other equipment of a saddler. **2** a saddler's business or premises.

■ **1** see TACK[2].

Sadducee /sádyoosee/ *n.* a member of a Jewish sect or party of the time of Christ that denied the resurrection of the dead, the existence of spirits, and the obligation of the traditional oral law (cf. PHARISEE, ESSENE). □□ **Sadducean** /-seéən/ *adj.* [OE *sadducēas* f. LL *Sadducaeus* f. Gk *Saddoukaios* f. Heb. *ṣᵉdûḳî*, prob. = descendant of Zadok (2 Sam. 8:17)]

sadhu /saádoo/ *n.* (in India) a holy man, sage, or ascetic. [Skr., = holy man]

sadism /sáydiz'm/ *n.* **1** a form of sexual perversion characterized by the enjoyment of inflicting pain or suffering on others (cf. MASOCHISM). **2** *colloq.* the enjoyment of cruelty to others. □□ **sadist** *n.* **sadistic** /sədístik/ *adj.* **sadistically** /sədístikəli/ *adv.* [F *sadisme* f. Count or 'Marquis' de *Sade*, Fr. writer d. 1814]

■ **2** see *brutality* (BRUTAL). □□ **sadist** brute, beast, savage, monster, devil. **sadistic** cruel, monstrous, brutal, brutish, beastly, ruthless, perverse, algolagnic.

sado-masochism /sáydōmássəkiz'm/ *n.* the combination of sadism and masochism in one person. □□ **sado-masochist** *n.* **sado-masochistic** /-kístik/ *adj.*

s.a.e. *abbr.* stamped addressed envelope.

safari /səfaári/ *n.* (*pl.* **safaris**) **1** a hunting or scientific expedition, esp. in E. Africa (*go on safari*). **2** a sightseeing trip to see African animals in their natural habitat. □ **safari park** an enclosed area where lions etc. are kept in the open and through which visitors may drive. **safari suit** a lightweight suit usu. with short sleeves and four pleated pockets in the jacket. [Swahili f. Arab. *safara* to travel]

safe /sayf/ *adj.* & *n.* ● *adj.* **1 a** free of danger or injury. **b** (often foll. by *from*) out of or not exposed to danger (*safe from their enemies*). **2** affording security or not involving danger or risk (*put it in a safe place*). **3** reliable, certain; that can be reckoned on (*a safe catch*; *a safe method*; *is safe to win*). **4** prevented from escaping or doing harm (*have got him safe*). **5** (also **safe and sound**) uninjured; with no harm done. **6** cautious and unenterprising; consistently moderate. ● *n.* **1** a strong lockable cabinet etc. for valuables. **2** = *meat safe.* □ **on the safe side** with a margin of security against risks. **safe bet** a bet that is certain to succeed. **safe-breaker** (or **-blower** or **-cracker**) a person who breaks open and robs safes. **safe conduct 1** a privilege of immunity from arrest or harm, esp. on a particular occasion. **2** a document securing this. **safe deposit** a building containing strong-rooms and safes let separately. **safe house** a place of refuge or rendezvous for spies etc. **safe keeping** preservation in a safe place. **safe light** *Photog.* a filtered light for use in a darkroom. **safe period** the time during and near the menstrual period when conception is least likely. **safe seat** a seat in Parliament etc. that is usually won with a large margin by a particular party. **safe sex** sexual activity in which precautions are taken to reduce the risk of spreading sexually transmitted diseases, esp. Aids. □□ **safely** *adv.* **safeness** *n.* [ME f. AF *saf*, OF *sauf* f. L *salvus* uninjured: (n.) orig. *save* f. SAVE[1]]

■ *adj.* **1 a** see HARMLESS 1. **2** secure, protected, secured, sheltered, shielded; see also IMPREGNABLE[1]. **3** certain, sure, secure, sound, risk-free, riskless, safe as the Bank of England, reliable, dependable, solid, tried and tested *or* true, as safe as houses. **5** unharmed, whole, uninjured, unhurt, sound, secure, out of harm's way, all right, *colloq.* OK. **6** cautious, conservative, moderate, tame; see also STEADY *adj.* 4, MODERATE *adj.* 1. ● *n.* **1** strongbox, safe-deposit box; coffer, chest. □ **on the safe side** secure, safe; see also SOUND[2] *adj.* 4. **safe house** see REFUGE 1, 2. **safe keeping** safety, preservation; see also PROTECTION 1a.

safeguard /sáyfgaard/ *n.* & *v.* ● *n.* **1** a proviso, stipulation, quality, or circumstance, that tends to prevent something undesirable. **2** a safe conduct. ● *v.tr.* guard or protect (rights etc.) by a precaution or stipulation. [ME f. AF *salve garde*, OF *sauve garde* (as SAFE, GUARD)]

■ *n.* **1** precaution, preventive measure, safety measure, countermeasure, preventive, preventative. ● *v.* protect, defend, conserve, save, keep, care for, look after, shield, keep safe, guard.

safety /sáyfti/ *n.* (*pl.* **-ies**) **1** the condition of being safe; freedom from danger or risks. **2** (*attrib.*) **a** designating any of various devices for preventing injury from machinery (*safety bar*; *safety lock*). **b** designating items of protective clothing (*safety helmet*). □ **safety-belt 1** = *seat-belt.* **2** a belt or strap securing a person to prevent injury. **safety-catch** a contrivance for locking a gun-trigger or preventing the accidental operation of machinery. **safety curtain** a fireproof curtain that can be lowered to cut off the auditorium in a theatre from the stage. **safety factor** (or **factor of safety**) **1** the ratio of a material's strength to an expected strain. **2** a margin of security against risks. **safety film** a cinematographic film on a slow-burning or non-flammable base. **safety first** a motto advising caution. **safety fuse 1** a fuse (see FUSE[2]) containing a slow-burning composition for firing detonators from a distance. **2** *Electr.* a protective fuse (see FUSE[1]). **safety glass** glass that will not splinter when broken. **safety harness** a system of belts or restraints to hold a person to prevent falling or injury. **safety lamp** a miner's lamp so protected as not to ignite firedamp. **safety match** a match igniting only on a specially prepared surface. **safety net** a net placed to catch an acrobat etc. in case of a fall. **safety pin** a pin with a point that is bent back to the head and is held in a guard when closed. **safety razor** a razor with a guard to reduce the risk of cutting the skin. **safety-valve 1** (in a steam boiler) a valve opening automatically to relieve excessive pressure. **2** a means of giving harmless vent to excitement etc. **safety zone** *US* an area of a road marked off for pedestrians etc. to wait safely. [ME *sauvete* f. OF *sauveté* f. med.L *salvitas -tatis* f. L *salvus* (as SAFE)]

■ **1** safeness, protection, shelter, security; aegis, cover, refuge, sanctuary; safe keeping.

safflower /sáflowr/ *n.* **1 a** a thistle-like plant, *Carthamus tinctorius*, yielding a red dye. **b** its dried petals. **2** a dye made from these, used in rouge etc. [Du. *saffloer* or G *Safflor* f. OF *saffleur* f. obs. It. *saffiore*, of unkn. orig.]

saffron /sáfrən/ *n.* & *adj.* ● *n.* **1** an orange flavouring and food colouring made from the dried stigmas of the crocus, *Crocus sativus*. **2** the colour of this. **3** = *meadow saffron.* ● *adj.* saffron-coloured. □□ **saffrony** *adj.* [ME f. OF *safran* f. Arab. *za'farān*]

safranine /sáfrəneen/ *n.* (also **safranin** /-nin/) any of a large group of mainly red dyes used in biological staining etc. [F *safranine* (as SAFFRON): orig. of dye from saffron]

sag /sag/ *v.* & *n.* ● *v.intr.* (**sagged, sagging**) **1** sink or subside under weight or pressure, esp. unevenly. **2** have a downward bulge or curve in the middle. **3 a** fall in price. **b** (of a price) fall. **4** (of a ship) drift from its course, esp. to leeward. ● *n.* **1 a** the amount that a rope etc. sags. **b** the distance from the middle of its curve to a straight line between its supports. **2** a sinking condition; subsidence. **3** a fall in price. **4** *Naut.* a tendency to leeward. □□ **saggy** *adj.* [ME f. MLG *sacken*, Du. *zakken* subside]

■ *v.* **1, 2** droop, sink, subside, slump, bend, dip; swag, bag. **3 a** drop, go *or* come down, fall, decrease, lessen. **b** drop, go *or* come down, fall, decline, slide, slip, weaken, slump, descend, diminish. ● *n.* **2** sagging, drop, droop, sinking, sinkage, subsidence, dip. **3** reduction, fall, decrease, drop, decline, slide, weakening, slump, flagging, faltering.

saga /saágə/ *n.* **1** a long story of heroic achievement, esp. a medieval Icelandic or Norwegian prose narrative. **2** a series of connected books giving the history of a family etc. **3** a long involved story. [ON, = narrative, rel. to SAW[3]]

■ **1** legend, epic, romance; Edda.

sagacious /səgáyshəss/ *adj.* **1** mentally penetrating; gifted with discernment; having practical wisdom. **2** acute-minded, shrewd. **3** (of a saying, plan, etc.) showing wisdom. **4** (of an animal) exceptionally intelligent; seeming to reason or deliberate. □□ **sagaciously** *adv.* **sagacity** /səgássiti/ *n.* [L *sagax sagacis*]

■ see ASTUTE 1. □□ **sagacity** see *astuteness* (ASTUTE).

sagamore /sággəmor/ *n.* = SACHEM 1. [Penobscot *sagamo*]

sage[1] /sayj/ *n.* **1** an aromatic herb, *Salvia officinalis*, with dull greyish-green leaves. **2** its leaves used in cookery. □ **sage and onion** (or **onions**) a stuffing used with poultry, pork, etc. **sage Derby** (or **cheese**) a cheese made with an infusion of sage which flavours and mottles it. **sage-green** the colour of sage-leaves. **sage tea** a medicinal infusion of sage-leaves. □□ **sagy** *adj.* [ME f. OF *sauge* f. L *salvia* healing plant f. *salvus* safe]

sage[2] /sayj/ *n.* & *adj.* ● *n.* **1** often *iron.* a profoundly wise man. **2** any of the ancients traditionally regarded as the wisest of their time. ● *adj.* **1** profoundly wise, esp. from experience. **2** of or indicating profound wisdom. **3** often *iron.* wise-looking; solemn-faced. ▫▫ **sagely** *adv.* **sageness** *n.* **sageship** *n.* [ME f. OF ult. f. L *sapere* be wise]

■ *n.* **1** wise man, guru, pundit, oracle, savant, expert, authority, elder, doyen *or* doyenne, Solomon. ● *adj.* **1** sensible, judicious, wise, prudent, commonsensical; common-sense. **2** wise, sagacious, perspicacious, profound, discerning, shrewd, intelligent, acute, penetrating.

sagebrush /sáyjbrush/ *n.* **1** a growth of shrubby aromatic plants of the genus *Artemisia*, esp. *A. tridentata*, found in some semi-arid regions of western N. America. **2** this plant.

saggar /sággər/ *n.* (also **sagger**) a protective fireclay box enclosing ceramic ware while it is being fired. [prob. contr. of SAFEGUARD]

sagittal /sájit'l/ *adj. Anat.* **1** of or relating to the suture between the parietal bones of the skull. **2** in the same plane as this, or in a parallel plane. [F f. med.L *sagittalis* f. *sagitta* arrow]

Sagittarius /sájitáiriəss/ *n.* **1** a constellation, traditionally regarded as contained in the figure of an archer. **2 a** the ninth sign of the zodiac (the Archer). **b** a person born when the sun is in this sign. ▫▫ **Sagittarian** *adj.* & *n.* [ME f. L, = archer, f. *sagitta* arrow]

sagittate /sájitayt/ *adj. Bot.* & *Zool.* shaped like an arrowhead.

sago /sáygō/ *n.* (*pl.* **-os**) **1** a kind of starch, made from the powdered pith of the sago palm and used in puddings etc. **2** (in full **sago palm**) any of several tropical palms and cycads, esp. *Cycas circinalis* and *Metroxylon sagu*, from which sago is made. [Malay *sāgū* (orig. through Port.)]

saguaro /sagwaárō/ *n.* (also **sahuaro** /sawaárō/) (*pl.* **-os**) a giant cactus, *Carnegiea gigantea*, of the SW United States and Mexico. [Mex. Sp.]

sahib /saab, saáhib/ *n.* **1** *hist.* (in India) a form of address, often placed after the name, to European men. **2** *colloq.* a gentleman (*pukka sahib*). [Urdu f. Arab. *ṣāḥīb* friend, lord]

said *past* and *past part.* of SAY.

saiga /sīgə, sáy-/ *n.* an antelope, *Saiga tatarica*, of the Asian steppes. [Russ.]

sail /sayl/ *n.* & *v.* ● *n.* **1** a piece of material (orig. canvas, now usu. nylon etc.) extended on rigging to catch the wind and propel a boat or ship. **2** a ship's sails collectively. **3 a** a voyage or excursion in a sailing-ship. **b** a voyage of specified duration. **4** a ship, esp. as discerned from its sails. **5** (*collect.*) ships in a squadron or company (*a fleet of twenty sail*). **6** (in *pl.*) *Naut.* **a** *sl.* a maker or repairer of sails. **b** *hist.* a chief petty officer in charge of rigging. **7** a wind-catching apparatus, usu. a set of boards, attached to the arm of a windmill. **8 a** the dorsal fin of a sailfish. **b** the tentacle of a nautilus. **c** the float of a Portuguese man-of-war. ● *v.* **1** *intr.* travel on water by the use of sails or engine-power. **2** *tr.* **a** navigate (a ship etc.). **b** travel on (a sea). **3** *tr.* set (a toy boat) afloat. **4** *intr.* glide or move smoothly or in a stately manner. **5** *intr.* (often foll. by *through*) *colloq.* succeed easily (*sailed through the exams*). ▫ **sail-arm** the arm of a windmill. **sail close to** (or **near**) **the wind 1** sail as nearly against the wind as possible. **2** *colloq.* come close to indecency or dishonesty; risk overstepping the mark. **sail-fluke** = MEGRIM². **sailing-boat** (or **-ship** or **-vessel**) a vessel driven by sails. **sailing-master** an officer navigating a ship, esp. *Brit.* a yacht. **sailing orders** instructions to a captain regarding departure, destination, etc. **sail into** *colloq.* attack physically or verbally with force. **take in sail 1** furl the sail or sails of a vessel. **2** moderate one's ambitions. **under sail** with sails set. ▫▫ **sailable** *adj.* **sailed** *adj.* (also in *comb.*). **sailless** *adj.* [OE *segel* f. Gmc]

■ *n.* **3** voyage, journey, trip, cruise; excursion. ● *v.* **1** go sailing *or* boating *or* yachting, cruise, set sail, put (out) to sea, travel. **2 a** navigate, pilot, steer. **4** drift, flow, waft, sweep, coast, float, scud, glide, slide, slip, skim; plane. **5** *colloq.* romp. ▫▫ **sail close to** (or **near**) **the wind 2** take risks, play with fire, take one's life in one's hands, stick one's neck out, *colloq.* skate on thin ice; *sl.* go for broke.

sailboard /sáylbord/ *n.* a board with a mast and sail, used in windsurfing. ▫▫ **sailboarder** *n.* **sailboarding** *n.*

sailboat /sáylbōt/ *n. US* a boat driven by sails.

■ see BOAT *n.*

sailcloth /sáylkloth/ *n.* **1** canvas for sails. **2** a canvas-like dress material.

sailer /sáylər/ *n.* a ship of specified sailing-power (*a good sailer*).

sailfish /sáylfish/ *n.* **1** any fish of the genus *Istiophorus*, with a large dorsal fin. **2** a basking shark.

sailor /sáylər/ *n.* **1** a seaman or mariner, esp. one below the rank of officer. **2** a person considered as liable or not liable to seasickness (*a good sailor*). ▫ **sailor hat 1** a straw hat with a straight narrow brim and flat top. **2** a hat with a turned-up brim in imitation of a sailor's, worn by women and children. ▫▫ **sailoring** *n.* **sailorless** *adj.* **sailorly** *adj.* [var. of SAILER]

■ **1** seaman, seafarer, seafaring man *or* woman, seagoing man *or* woman, mariner, (old) salt, sea dog, bluejacket, Jack Tar, *colloq.* tar, *sl.* shellback, gob; yachtsman, yachtswoman.

sailplane /sáylplayn/ *n.* a glider designed for sustained flight.

sainfoin /sáynfoyn, sán-/ *n.* a leguminous plant, *Onobrychis viciifolia*, grown for fodder and having pink flowers. [obs. F *saintfoin* f. mod.L *sanum foenum* wholesome hay (because of its medicinal properties)]

saint /saynt, before a name usu. sənt/ *n.* & *v.* ● *n.* (*abbr.* **St** or **S**; *pl.* **Sts** or **SS**) **1** a holy or (in some Churches) a canonized person regarded as having a place in heaven. **2** (**Saint or St**) the title of a saint or archangel, hence the name of a church etc. (*St Paul's*) or (often with the loss of the apostrophe) the name of a town etc. (*St Andrews*; *St Albans*). **3** a very virtuous person; a person of great real or affected holiness (*would try the patience of a saint*). **4** a member of the company of heaven (*with all the angels and saints*). **5** (*Bibl.*, *archaic*, and used by Puritans, Mormons, etc.) one of God's chosen people; a member of the Christian Church or one's own branch of it. ● *v.tr.* **1** canonize; admit to the calendar of saints. **2** call or regard as a saint. **3** (as **sainted** *adj.*) sacred; of a saintly life; worthy to be regarded as a saint. ▫ **my sainted aunt** see AUNT. **saint's day** a Church festival in memory of a saint. ▫▫ **saintdom** *n.* **sainthood** *n.* **saintlike** *adj.* **saintling** *n.* **saintship** *n.* [ME f. OF *seint*, *saint* f. L *sanctus* holy, past part. of *sancire* consecrate]

■ *v.* **3** (**sainted**) see SAINTLY. ▫▫ **saintlike** see HOLY 1, 2.

St Andrew's cross /ándrōōz/ *n.* an X-shaped cross.

St Anthony cross /ántəni/ *n.* (also **St Anthony's cross** /ántəniz/) a T-shaped cross.

St Anthony's fire /ántəniz/ *n.* erysipelas or ergotism.

St Bernard /bérnərd/ *n.* (in full **St Bernard dog**) **1** a very large dog of a breed orig. kept to rescue travellers by the monks of the Hospice on the Great St Bernard pass in the Alps. **2** this breed.

St Elmo's fire /élmōz/ *n.* a corposant.

St George's cross /jórjiz/ *n.* a +-shaped cross, red on a white background.

St John's wort /jonz/ *n.* any yellow-flowered plant of the genus *Hypericum*, esp. *H. androsaemum*.

St Leger /léjər/ *n.* a horse-race at Doncaster in England for three-year-olds. [f. the founder's name]

St Luke's summer /lōōks/ *n. Brit.* a period of fine weather expected about 18 Oct.

saintly /sáyntli/ *adj.* (**saintlier**, **saintliest**) very holy or virtuous. ▫▫ **saintliness** *n.*

■ holy, blessed, beatific, godly, sainted, angelic, seraphic, pure, righteous, virtuous, blameless, *poet.* blest.

St Martin's summer /maártinz/ *n. Brit.* a period of fine weather expected about 11 Nov.

saintpaulia /səntpáwliə/ *n.* any plant of the genus *Saintpaulia*, esp. the African violet. [Baron W. von *Saint Paul*, Ger. soldier d. 1910, its discoverer]

St Vitus's dance /vī́təsiz/ *n.* = *Sydenham's chorea* (see CHOREA).

saith /seth/ *archaic 3rd sing. present* of SAY.

saithe /sayth/ *n. Sc.* a codlike fish, *Pollachius virens*, with skin that soils fingers like wet coal. Also called COALFISH, COLEY, POLLACK. [ON *seithr*]

sake[1] /sayk/ *n.* □ **for Christ's** (or **God's** or **goodness'** or **Heaven's** or **Pete's** etc.) **sake** an expression of urgency, impatience, supplication, anger, etc. **for old times' sake** in memory of former times. **for the sake of** (or **for a person's sake**) **1** out of consideration for; in the interest of; because of; owing to (*for my own sake as well as yours*). **2** in order to please, honour, get, or keep (*for the sake of uniformity*). [OE *sacu* contention, charge, fault, sake f. Gmc]

■ □ **for Christ's** (or **God's** or **goodness'** or **Heaven's** or **Pete's** etc.) **sake** see GOD *int.* **for the sake of** out of consideration for, in the interest of, because of, owing to, for the benefit *or* well-being *or* good of. **for a person's sake** on a person's behalf *or* account.

sake[2] /saáki/ *n.* a Japanese alcoholic drink made from rice. [Jap.]

saker /sáykər/ *n.* **1** a large falcon, *Falco cherrug*, used in hawking, esp. the larger female bird. **2** *hist.* an old form of cannon. [ME f. OF *sacre* (in both senses), f. Arab. *ṣaḳr*]

saki /saáki/ *n.* (*pl.* **sakis**) any monkey of the genus *Pithecia* or *Chiropotes*, native to S. America, having coarse fur and a long non-prehensile tail. [F f. Tupi *çahy*]

Sakta /shaáktə/ *n.* a member of a Hindu sect worshipping the Sakti. [Skr. *śākta* relating to power or to the SAKTI]

Sakti /shákti/ *n.* (also **sakti**) (in Hinduism) the female principle, esp. when personified as the wife of a god. [Skr. *śakti* power, divine energy]

sal /saal/ *n.* a N. Indian tree, *Shorea robusta*, yielding teaklike timber and dammar resin. [Hindi *sāl*]

salaam /səlaám/ *n.* & *v.* ● *n.* **1** the oriental salutation 'Peace'. **2** an Indian obeisance, with or without the salutation, consisting of a low bow of the head and body with the right palm on the forehead. **3** (in *pl.*) respectful compliments. ● *v.* **1** *tr.* make a salaam to (a person). **2** *intr.* make a salaam . [Arab. *salām*]

■ *n.* **2** see BOW[2] *n.* ● *v.* **2** see BOW[2] *v.* 1.

salable var. of SALEABLE.

salacious /səláyshəss/ *adj.* **1** lustful; lecherous. **2** (of writings, pictures, talk, etc.) tending to cause sexual desire. □□ **salaciously** *adv.* **salaciousness** *n.* **salacity** /səlássiti/ *n.* [L *salax salacis* f. *salire* leap]

■ **1** see LECHEROUS. **2** see EROTIC. □□ **salaciousness** see RIBALDRY.

salad /sálləd/ *n.* **1** a cold dish of various mixtures of raw or cooked vegetables or herbs, usu. seasoned with oil, vinegar, etc. **2** a vegetable or herb suitable for eating raw. □ **salad cream** creamy salad-dressing. **salad days** a period of youthful inexperience. **salad-dressing** a mixture of oil, vinegar, etc., used with salad. [ME f. OF *salade* f. Prov. *salada* ult. f. L *sal* salt]

■ □ **salad days** see YOUTH 1.

salade var. of SALLET.

salamander /sálləmandər/ *n.* **1** *Zool.* any tailed newtlike amphibian of the order Urodela, esp. the genus *Salamandra*, once thought able to endure fire. **2** a mythical lizard-like creature credited with this property. **3** *US* = GOPHER[1] 1. **4** an elemental spirit living in fire. **5** a red-hot iron used for lighting pipes, gunpowder, etc. **6** a metal plate heated and placed over food to brown it. □□ **salamandrian** /-mándriən/ *adj.* **salamandrine** /-mándrin/ *adj.* **salamandroid** /-mándroyd/ *adj.* & *n.* (in sense 1). [ME f. OF *salamandre* f. L *salamandra* f. Gk *salamandra*]

salami /səlaámi/ *n.* (*pl.* **salamis**) a highly-seasoned orig. Italian sausage often flavoured with garlic. [It., pl. of *salame*, f. LL *salare* (unrecorded) to salt]

sal ammoniac /sál əmṓniak/ *n.* ammonium chloride, a white crystalline salt. [L *sal ammoniacus* 'salt of Ammon', associated with the Roman temple of Ammon in N. Africa]

salariat /səláiriət/ *n.* the salaried class. [F f. *salaire* (see SALARY), after *prolétariat*]

salary /sálləri/ *n.* & *v.* ● *n.* (*pl.* **-ies**) a fixed regular payment, usu. monthly or quarterly, made by an employer to an employee, esp. a professional or white-collar worker (cf. WAGE *n.* 1). ● *v.tr.* (**-ies, -ied**) (usu. as **salaried** *adj.*) pay a salary to. [ME f. AF *salarie*, OF *salaire* f. L *salarium* orig. soldier's salt-money f. *sal* salt]

■ *n.* income, pay, earnings, emolument, *US* compensation; wage(s).

sale /sayl/ *n.* **1** the exchange of a commodity for money etc.; an act or instance of selling. **2** the amount sold (*the sales were enormous*). **3** the rapid disposal of goods at reduced prices for a period esp. at the end of a season etc. **4 a** an event at which goods are sold. **b** a public auction. □ **on** (or **for** or **up for**) **sale** offered for purchase. **sale of work** an event where goods made by parishioners etc. are sold for charity. **sale or return** an arrangement by which a purchaser takes a quantity of goods with the right of returning surplus goods without payment. **sale-ring** a circle of buyers at an auction. **sales clerk** *US* a salesman or saleswoman in a shop. **sales department** etc. the section of a firm concerned with selling as opposed to manufacturing or dispatching goods. **sales engineer** a salesperson with technical knowledge of the goods and their market. **sales resistance** the opposition or apathy of a prospective customer etc. to be overcome by salesmanship. **sales talk** persuasive talk to promote the sale of goods or the acceptance of an idea etc. **sales tax** a tax on sales or on the receipts from sales. [OE *sala* f. ON]

■ **1** selling, vending, marketing, trafficking, trading, traffic, trade; exchange, transaction. □ **on** (or **for** or **up for**) **sale** on the market, on offer, *US* on the block.

saleable /sáyləb'l/ *adj.* (also **salable**) fit to be sold; finding purchasers. □□ **saleability** /-bílliti/ *n.*

■ popular, sought-after, commercial, marketable.

salep /sálləp/ *n.* a starchy preparation of the dried tubers of various orchids, used in cookery and formerly medicinally. [F f. Turk. *sālep* f. Arab. (*ḳuṣa-'l-*) *ta'lab* fox, fox's testicles]

saleratus /sálləráytəss/ *n.* *US* an ingredient of baking powder consisting mainly of potassium or sodium bicarbonate. [mod.L *sal aeratus* aerated salt]

saleroom /sáylrōōm, -rŏŏm/ *n.* esp. *Brit.* a room in which items are sold at auction.

salesgirl /sáylzgurl/ *n.* a saleswoman.

■ salesperson, cashier, *Brit.* shop assistant.

Salesian /səleézh'n/ *n.* & *adj.* ● *n.* a member of an educational religious order within the RC Church. ● *adj.* of or relating to this order. [St François de *Sales*, Fr. RC bishop d. 1622]

saleslady /sáylzlaydi/ *n.* (*pl.* **-ies**) a saleswoman.

■ salesperson, cashier, *Brit.* shop assistant.

salesman /sáylzmən/ *n.* (*pl.* **-men**; *fem.* **saleswoman**, *pl.* **-women**) **1** a person employed to sell goods in a shop, or as an agent between the producer and retailer. **2** *US* a commercial traveller.

■ **1** salesperson, cashier, *Brit.* shop assistant. **2** see REPRESENTATIVE *n.* 2b.

salesmanship /sáylzmənship/ *n.* **1** skill in selling. **2** the techniques used in selling.

salesperson /sáylzpers'n/ *n.* a salesman or saleswoman (used as a neutral alternative).

■ salesman, saleswoman, saleslady, salesgirl, *Brit.* shop assistant, *US* clerk, sales clerk.

salesroom /sáylzrōōm, -rŏŏm/ *n.* *US* = SALEROOM.

Salian /sáyliən/ *adj.* & *n.* ● *adj.* of or relating to the Salii, a 4th-c. Frankish people living near the River Ijssel, from which the Merovingians were descended. ● *n.* a member of this people. [LL *Salii*]

Salic /sállik, sáy-/ *adj.* = SALIAN. □ **Salic law** *hist.* **1** a law excluding females from dynastic succession, esp. as the alleged fundamental law of the French monarchy. **2** a

Frankish law-book extant in Merovingian and Carolingian times. [F *Salique* or med.L *Salicus* f. *Salii* (as SALIAN)]

salicet /sállisit/ *n.* an organ stop like a salicional but one octave higher. [as SALICIONAL]

salicin /sállisin/ *n.* (also **salicine** /-seen/) a bitter crystalline glucoside with analgesic properties, obtained from poplar and willow bark. [F *salicine* f. L *salix -icis* willow]

salicional /səlíshən'l/ *n.* an organ stop with a soft reedy tone like that of a willow-pipe. [G f. L *salix* as SALICIN]

salicylic acid /sállisíllik/ *n.* a bitter chemical used as a fungicide and in the manufacture of aspirin and dyestuffs. □□ **salicylate** /səlíssilayt/ *n.* [*salicyl* its radical f. F *salicyle* (as SALICIN)]

salient /sáyliənt/ *adj.* & *n.* ● *adj.* **1** jutting out; prominent; conspicuous, most noticeable. **2** (of an angle, esp. in fortification) pointing outwards (opp. RE-ENTRANT). **3** *Heraldry* (of a lion etc.) standing on its hind legs with the forepaws raised. **4** *archaic* **a** leaping or dancing. **b** (of water etc.) jetting forth. ● *n.* a salient angle or part of a work in fortification; an outward bulge in a line of military attack or defence. □ **salient point** *archaic* the initial stage, origin, or first beginning. □□ **salience** *n.* **saliency** *n.* **saliently** *adv.* [L *salire* leap]
■ *adj.* **1** conspicuous, outstanding, pronounced, noticeable, prominent, significant, important, marked, striking, remarkable, distinguishing, distinctive, eminent, noteworthy, notable, principal, chief, primary, *disp.* unique.

salientian /sáyliénsh'n/ *adj.* & *n.* = ANURAN. [mod.L *Salientia* (as SALIENT)]

saliferous /səlíffərəss/ *adj. Geol.* (of rock etc.) containing much salt. [L *sal* salt + -FEROUS]

salina /səlīnə/ *n.* a salt lake. [Sp. f. med.L, = salt pit (as SALINE)]

saline /sáylīn/ *adj.* & *n.* ● *adj.* **1** (of natural waters, springs, etc.) impregnated with or containing salt or salts. **2** (of food or drink etc.) tasting of salt. **3** of chemical salts. **4** of the nature of a salt. **5** (of medicine) containing a salt or salts of alkaline metals or magnesium. ● *n.* **1** a salt lake, spring, marsh, etc. **2** a salt-pan or salt-works. **3** a saline substance, esp. a medicine. **4** a solution of salt in water. □□ **salinity** /səlínniti/ *n.* **salinization** /sállinīzáysh'n/ *n.* **salinometer** /sállinómmitər/ *n.* [ME f. L *sal* salt]
■ *adj.* **1, 2** see SALT *adj.*

saliva /səlīvə/ *n.* liquid secreted into the mouth by glands to provide moisture and facilitate chewing and swallowing. □ **saliva test** a scientific test requiring a saliva sample. □□ **salivary** /səlīvəri, sálli-/ *adj.* [ME f. L]
■ see SPIT[1] *n.*

salivate /sállivayt/ *v.* **1** *intr.* secrete or discharge saliva esp. in excess or in greedy anticipation. **2** *tr.* produce an unusual secretion of saliva in (a person) usu. with mercury. □□ **salivation** /sállivàysh'n/ *n.* [L *salivare* (as SALIVA)]
■ **1** see SLAVER[2] *v.*

Salk vaccine /sawlk/ *n.* a vaccine developed against polio. [J. E. *Salk*, Amer. scientist b. 1914]

sallee /sállee/ *n.* (also **sally**) (*pl.* **-ees** or **-ies**) *Austral.* any of several eucalypts and acacias resembling the willow. [Aboriginal]

sallet /sállit/ *n.* (also **salade** /səlaád/) *hist.* a light helmet with an outward-curving rear part. [F *salade* ult. f. L *caelare* engrave f. *caelum* chisel]

sallow[1] /sállō/ *adj.* & *v.* ● *adj.* (**sallower**, **sallowest**) (of the skin or complexion, or of a person) of a sickly yellow or pale brown. ● *v.tr.* & *intr.* make or become sallow. □□ **sallowish** *adj.* **sallowness** *n.* [OE *salo* dusky f. Gmc]
■ *adj.* see PALE[1] *adj.* 1.

sallow[2] /sállō/ *n.* **1** a willow-tree, esp. one of a low-growing or shrubby kind. **2** the wood or a shoot of this. □□ **sallowy** *adj.* [OE *salh salg-* f. Gmc, rel. to OHG *salaha*, ON *selja*, L *salix*]

Sally /sálli/ *n.* (*pl.* **-ies**) *colloq.* **1** (usu. prec. by *the*) the Salvation Army. **2** a member of this. [abbr.]

sally[1] /sálli/ *n.* & *v.* (*pl.* **-ies**) ● *n.* **1** a sudden charge from a fortification upon its besiegers; a sortie. **2** a going forth; an excursion. **3** a witticism; a piece of banter; a lively remark esp. by way of attack upon a person or thing or of a diversion in argument. **4** a sudden start into activity; an outburst. **5** *archaic* an escapade. ● *v.intr.* (**-ies**, **-ied**) **1** (usu. foll. by *out*, *forth*) go for a walk, set out on a journey etc. **2** (usu. foll. by *out*) make a military sally. **3** *archaic* issue or come out suddenly. □ **sally-port** an opening in a fortification for making a sally from. [F *saillie* fem. past part. of *saillir* issue f. OF *salir* f. L *salire* leap]
■ *n.* **1** see CHARGE *n.* 4a. **3** see WITTICISM. ● *v.* **1** (*sally forth*) see *set forth* 1 (SET[1]). **3** see ISSUE *v.* 1.

sally[2] /sálli/ *n.* (*pl.* **-ies**) **1** the part of a bell-rope prepared with inwoven wool for holding. **2** **a** the first movement of a bell when set for ringing. **b** the bell's position when set. □ **sally-hole** the hole through which the bell-rope passes. [perh. f. SALLY[1] in sense 'leaping motion']

sally[3] var. of SALLEE.

Sally Lunn /sálli lún/ *n. Brit.* a sweet light teacake, properly served hot. [perh. f. the name of a woman selling them at Bath *c.*1800]

salmagundi /sálməgúndi/ *n.* (*pl.* **salmagundis**) **1** a dish of chopped meat, anchovies, eggs, onions, etc., and seasoning. **2** a general mixture; a miscellaneous collection of articles, subjects, qualities, etc. [F *salmigondis* of unkn. orig.]
■ **2** see MIXTURE 2.

salmanazar /sálmənáyzər/ *n.* a wine bottle of about 12 times the standard size. [*Shalmaneser* king of Assyria (2 Kings 17-18)]

salmi /sálmi/ *n.* (*pl.* **salmis**) a ragout or casserole esp. of partly roasted game-birds. [F, abbr. formed as SALMAGUNDI]

salmon /sámmən/ *n.* & *adj.* ● *n.* (*pl.* same or (esp. of types) **salmons**) **1** any anadromous fish of the family Salmonidae, esp. of the genus *Salmo*, much prized for its (often smoked) pink flesh. **2** *Austral.* & *NZ* the barramundi or a similar fish. ● *adj.* salmon-pink. □ **salmon-ladder** (or **-leap**) a series of steps or other arrangement incorporated in a dam to allow salmon to pass upstream. **salmon-pink** the colour of salmon flesh. **salmon trout** a large silver-coloured trout, *Salmo trutta*. □□ **salmonoid** *adj.* & *n.* (in sense 1). **salmony** *adj.* [ME f. AF *sa(u)moun*, OF *saumon* f. L *salmo -onis*]
■ *adj.* see PINK[1] *adj.* 1.

salmonella /sálmənéllə/ *n.* (*pl.* **salmonellae** /-lee/) **1** any bacterium of the genus *Salmonella*, esp. any of various serotypes causing food poisoning. **2** food poisoning caused by infection with salmonellae. □□ **salmonellosis** /-lṓsiss/ *n.* [mod.L f. D. E. *Salmon*, Amer. veterinary surgeon d. 1914]

salon /sállon, -LON/ *n.* **1** the reception room of a large, esp. French or continental, house. **2** a room or establishment where a hairdresser, beautician, etc., conducts trade. **3** *hist.* a meeting of eminent people in the reception room of a (esp. Parisian) lady of fashion. **4** (**Salon**) an annual exhibition in Paris of the work of living artists. □ **salon music** light music for the drawing-room etc. [F: see SALOON]
■ **1** see LOUNGE *n.* 1.

saloon /səlṓōn/ *n.* **1** **a** a large room or hall, esp. in a hotel or public building. **b** a public room or gallery for a specified purpose (*billiard-saloon*; *shooting-saloon*). **2** (in full **saloon car**) a motor car with a closed body and no partition behind the driver. **3** a public room on a ship. **4** *US* a drinking-bar. **5** (in full **saloon bar**) *Brit.* the more comfortable bar in a public house. **6** (in full **saloon car**) *Brit.* a luxurious railway carriage serving as a lounge etc. □ **saloon deck** a deck for passengers using the saloon. **saloon-keeper** *US* a publican or bartender. **saloon pistol** (or **rifle**) a pistol or rifle adapted for short-range practice in a shooting-saloon. [F *salon* f. It. *salone* augment. of *sala* hall]
■ **3** *US* sedan. **4, 5** see BAR[1] *n.* 4b, c.

Salopian /səlṓpiən/ *n.* & *adj.* ● *n.* a native or inhabitant of Shropshire. ● *adj.* of or relating to Shropshire. [AF *Salopesberia* f. ME f. OE *Scrobbesbyrig* Shrewsbury]

salpiglossis /sálpiglóssiss/ *n.* any solanaceous plant of the genus *Salpiglossis*, cultivated for its funnel-shaped flowers. [mod.L, irreg. f. Gk *salpigx* trumpet + *glōssa* tongue]

salping- /sálping/ *comb. form Med.* denoting the Fallopian tubes. [Gk *salpigx salpiggos*, lit. 'trumpet']

salpingectomy /sálpinjéktəmi/ *n.* (*pl.* **-ies**) *Med.* the surgical removal of the Fallopian tubes.

salpingitis /sálpinjī́tiss/ *n. Med.* inflammation of the Fallopian tubes.

salsa /sálsə/ *n.* **1** a kind of dance music of Latin American origin, incorporating jazz and rock elements. **2** a dance performed to this music. [Sp. (as SAUCE)]

salsify /sálsifi, -fī/ *n.* (*pl.* **-ies**) **1** a European plant, *Tragopogon porrifolius*, with long cylindrical fleshy roots. **2** this root used as a vegetable. □ **black salsify** scorzonera. [F *salsifis* f. obs. It. *salsefica*, of unkn. orig.]

SALT /sawlt, solt/ *abbr.* Strategic Arms Limitation Talks (or Treaty).

salt /sawlt, solt/ *n.*, *adj.*, & *v.* ● *n.* **1** (also **common salt**) sodium chloride; the substance that gives sea water its characteristic taste, got in crystalline form by mining from strata consisting of it or by the evaporation of sea water, and used for seasoning or preserving food, or for other purposes. **2** a chemical compound formed from the reaction of an acid with a base, with all or part of the hydrogen of the acid replaced by a metal or metal-like radical. **3** sting; piquancy; pungency; wit (*added salt to the conversation*). **4** (in *sing.* or *pl.*) **a** a substance resembling salt in taste, form, etc. (*bath salts*; *Epsom salts*; *smelling-salts*). **b** (esp. in *pl.*) this type of substance used as a laxative. **5** a marsh, esp. one flooded by the tide, often used as a pasture or for collecting water for salt-making. **6** (also **old salt**) an experienced sailor. **7** (in *pl.*) an exceptional rush of sea water up river. ● *adj.* **1** impregnated with, containing, or tasting of salt; cured or preserved or seasoned with salt. **2** (of a plant) growing in the sea or in salt marshes. **3** (of tears etc.) bitter. **4** (of wit) pungent. ● *v.tr.* **1** cure or preserve with salt or brine. **2** season with salt. **3** make (a narrative etc.) piquant. **4** sprinkle (the ground etc.) with salt esp. in order to melt snow etc. **5** treat with a solution of salt or mixture of salts. **6** (as **salted** *adj.*) (of a horse or person) hardened or proof against diseases etc. caused by the climate or by special conditions. □ **eat salt with** be a guest of. **in salt** sprinkled with salt or immersed in brine as a preservative. **not made of salt** not disconcerted by wet weather. **put salt on the tail of** capture (with ref. to jocular directions given to children for catching a bird). **salt an account** *sl.* set an extremely high or low price for articles. **salt-and-pepper** (of materials etc. and esp. of hair) with light and dark colours mixed together. **salt away** (or **down**) *sl.* put money etc. by. **salt the books** *sl.* show receipts as larger than they really have been. **salt-cat** a mass of salt mixed with gravel, urine, etc., to attract pigeons and keep them at home. **salt dome** a mass of salt forced up into sedimentary rocks. **salt fish** *W.Ind.* preserved cod. **salt-glaze** a hard stoneware glaze produced by throwing salt into a hot kiln containing the ware. **salt-grass** *US* grass growing in salt meadows or in alkaline regions. **salt horse** *Naut. sl.* **1** salt beef. **2** a naval officer with general duties. **salt lake** a lake of salt water. **salt-lick 1** a place where animals go to lick salt from the ground. **2** this salt. **salt-marsh** = sense 5 of *n.* **salt meadow** a meadow subject to flooding with salt water. **salt-mine** a mine yielding rock-salt. **salt a mine** *sl.* introduce extraneous ore, material, etc., to make the source seem rich. **the salt of the earth** a person or people of great worthiness, reliability, honesty, etc.; those whose qualities are a model for the rest (Matt. 5:13). **salt-pan** a vessel, or a depression near the sea, used for getting salt by evaporation. **salt-shaker** *US* a container of salt for sprinkling on food. **salt-spoon** a small spoon usu. with a short handle and a roundish deep bowl for taking table salt. **salt water 1** sea water. **2** *sl.* tears. **salt-water** *adj.* of or living in the sea. **salt-well** a bored well yielding brine. **salt-works** a place where salt is produced. **take with a pinch** (or **grain**) **of salt** regard as exaggerated; be incredulous about; believe only part of. **worth one's salt** efficient, capable. □□ **saltish** *adj.* **saltless** *adj.* **saltly** *adv.* **saltness** *n.* [OE *s(e)alt s(e)altan*, OS, ON, Goth. *salt*, OHG *salz* f. Gmc]

■ *n.* **1** sodium chloride; sea salt, rock-salt, table salt. **3** sting, piquancy, spice, spiciness, zest, zestiness, pungency, vigour, vitality, liveliness, pepper, poignancy, bite, seasoning, zip, *colloq.* pep, zing, punch; wit, Attic salt *or* wit. **6** see SAILOR. ● *adj.* **1** salty, saline, brackish, briny; pickled, kippered, soused; corned, cured. ● *v.* **1** cure, preserve, corn; pickle, souse. **2** season, flavour. **3** see SPICE *v.* 2. □ **in salt** cured, soused, in brine, in pickle. **salt away** (or **down**) save (up), hoard, put *or* lay by, put *or* lay *or* set aside, squirrel (away), store up, stockpile, amass, accumulate, pile up, *archaic* set by, *colloq.* stash away. **salt the books** *colloq.* cook the books. **salt-shaker** see SALT-CELLAR. **take with a pinch** (or **grain**) **of salt** see DISTRUST *v.* **worth one's salt** see CAPABLE 1.

saltarello /sáltərélló/ *n.* (*pl.* **-os** or **saltarelli** /-li/) an Italian and Spanish dance for one couple, with sudden skips. [It. *salterello*, Sp. *saltarelo*, rel. to It. *saltare* and Sp. *saltar* leap, dance f. L *saltare* (as SALTATION)]

saltation /saltáysh'n/ *n.* **1** the act or an instance of leaping or dancing; a jump. **2** a sudden transition or movement. □□ **saltatory** /sáltətəri/ *adj.* **saltatorial** /sáltətóriəl/ *adj.* [L *saltatio* f. *saltare* frequent. of *salire salt-* leap]

saltbush /sáwltbŏŏsh, sólt-/ *n.* = ORACHE.

salt-cellar /sáwltsellər, sólt-/ *n.* **1** a vessel holding salt for table use. **2** *colloq.* an unusually deep hollow above the collar-bone, esp. found in women. [SALT + obs. *saler* f. AF f. OF *salier* salt-box f. L (as SALARY), assim. to CELLAR]

■ **1** cruet, *US* salt-shaker.

salter /sáwltər, sól-/ *n.* **1** a manufacturer or dealer in salt. **2** a workman at a salt-works. **3** a person who salts fish etc. **4** = *dry-salter*. [OE *sealtere* (as SALT)]

saltern /sáwltərn, sól-/ *n.* **1** a salt-works. **2** a set of pools for the natural evaporation of sea water. [OE *sealtærn* (as SALT, *ærn* building)]

saltigrade /sáltigrayd/ *adj.* & *n. Zool.* ● *adj.* (of arthropods) moving by leaping or jumping. ● *n.* a saltigrade arthropod, e.g. a spider, sand-hopper, etc. [mod.L *Saltigradae* f. L *saltus* leap f. *salire salt-* + *-gradus* walking]

salting /sáwlting, sól-/ *n.* **1** in senses of SALT *v.* **2** (esp. in *pl.*) *Geol.* a salt marsh; a marsh overflowed by the sea.

saltire /sáwltīr/ *n. Heraldry* an ordinary formed by a bend and a bend sinister crossing like a St Andrew's cross. □ **in saltire** arranged in this way. □□ **saltirewise** *adv.* [ME f. OF *sau(l)toir* etc. stirrup-cord, stile, saltire, f. med.L *saltatorium* (as SALTATION)]

saltpetre /sóltpeétər, sáwlt-/ *n.* (*US* **saltpeter**) potassium nitrate, a white crystalline salty substance used in preserving meat and as a constituent of gunpowder. [ME f. OF *salpetre* f. med.L *salpetra* prob. for *sal petrae* (unrecorded) salt of rock (i.e. found as an incrustation): assim. to SALT]

saltus /sáltəss/ *n. literary* a sudden transition; a breach of continuity. [L, = leap]

saltwort /sáwltwurt, sólt-/ *n.* any plant of the genus *Salsola*; glasswort.

salty /sáwlti, sól-/ *adj.* (**saltier**, **saltiest**) **1** tasting of, containing, or preserved with salt. **2** racy, risqué. □□ **saltiness** *n.*

■ **2** see RACY 2.

salubrious /səlóŏbriəss, səlyóŏ-/ *adj.* **1** health-giving; healthy. **2** (of surroundings etc.) pleasant; agreeable. □□ **salubriously** *adv.* **salubriousness** *n.* **salubrity** *n.* [L *salubris* f. *salus* health]

■ **1** see WHOLESOME 1. **2** see PLEASANT.

saluki /səlóŏki/ *n.* (*pl.* **salukis**) **1** a tall swift slender dog of a silky-coated breed with large ears and a fringed tail and feet. **2** this breed. [Arab. *salūḳī*]

salutary /sályootəri, -tri/ *adj.* **1** producing good effects; beneficial. **2** *archaic* health-giving. [ME f. F *salutaire* or L *salutaris* f. *salus -utis* health]
■ see BENEFICIAL.

salutation /sályootáysh'n/ *n.* **1** a sign or expression of greeting or recognition of another's arrival or departure. **2** (usu. in *pl.*) words spoken or written to enquire about another's health or well-being. ▫▫ **salutational** *adj.* [ME f. OF *salutation* or L *salutatio* (as SALUTE)]
■ **1** greeting, glad hand.

salutatory /səlyóotətəri, səlóo-/ *adj.* & *n.* ● *adj.* of salutation. ● *n.* (*pl.* **-ies**) *US* an oration, esp. as given by a member of a graduating class, often the second-ranking member. ▫▫ **salutatorian** /-tóriən/ *n.* (in sense of n.). [L *salutatorius* (as SALUTE)]

salute /səlóot, -lyóot/ *n.* & *v.* ● *n.* **1** a gesture of respect, homage, or courteous recognition, esp. made to or by a person when arriving or departing. **2 a** *Mil.* & *Naut.* a prescribed or specified movement of the hand or of weapons or flags as a sign of respect or recognition. **b** (prec. by *the*) the attitude taken by an individual soldier, sailor, policeman, etc., in saluting. **3** the discharge of a gun or guns as a formal or ceremonial sign of respect or celebration. **4** *Fencing* the formal performance of certain guards etc. by fencers before engaging. ● *v.* **1 a** *tr.* make a salute to. **b** *intr.* (often foll. by *to*) perform a salute. **2** *tr.* greet; make a salutation to. **3** *tr.* (foll. by *with*) receive or greet with (a smile etc.). **4** *tr. archaic* hail as (king etc.). ▫ **take the salute 1** (of the highest officer present) acknowledge it by gesture as meant for him. **2** receive ceremonial salutes by members of a procession. ▫▫ **saluter** *n.* [ME f. L *salutare* f. *salus -utis* health]
■ *n.* **1** greeting, salutation. ● *v.* **2** greet, hail, accost; address. **4** hail as, acclaim, recognize *or* acknowledge as.

salvage /sálvij/ *n.* & *v.* ● *n.* **1** the rescue of a ship, its cargo, or other property, from loss at sea, destruction by fire, etc. **2** the property etc. saved in this way. **3 a** the saving and utilization of waste paper, scrap material, etc. **b** the materials salvaged. **4** payment made or due to a person who has saved a ship or its cargo. ● *v.tr.* **1** save from a wreck, fire, etc. **2** retrieve or preserve (something favourable) in adverse circumstances (*tried to salvage some dignity*). ▫▫ **salvageable** *adj.* **salvager** *n.* [F f. med.L *salvagium* f. L *salvare* SAVE[1]]
■ *n.* **1** recovery, rescue, retrieval, deliverance, reclamation, salvation. **3 a** reclamation, recycling, re-use, reutilization. ● *v.* **1** save, recover, rescue, deliver, retrieve, salve, reclaim. **2** preserve, retain, save, retrieve; see also RECOVER *v.* 1.

salvation /salváysh'n/ *n.* **1** the act of saving or being saved; preservation from loss, calamity, etc. **2** deliverance from sin and its consequences and admission to heaven, brought about by Christ. **3** a religious conversion. **4** a person or thing that saves (*was the salvation of*). ▫ **Salvation Army** a worldwide evangelical organization on quasi-military lines for the revival of Christianity and helping the poor. ▫▫ **salvationism** *n.* **salvationist** *n.* (both nouns esp. with ref. to the Salvation Army). [ME f. OF *sauvacion, salvacion,* f. eccl.L *salvatio -onis* f. *salvare* SAVE[1], transl. Gk *sōtēria*]
■ **1** see SALVAGE *n.* 1. **2** redemption, deliverance. **4** see SAVIOUR 1. ▫▫ **salvationist** *colloq.* Sally, *Austral. sl.* Salvo.

salve[1] /salv, saav/ *n.* & *v.* ● *n.* **1** a healing ointment. **2** (often foll. by *for*) a thing that is soothing or consoling for wounded feelings, an uneasy conscience, etc. **3** *archaic* a thing that explains away a discrepancy or palliates a fault. ● *v.tr.* **1** soothe (pride, self-love, conscience, etc.). **2** *archaic* anoint (a wound etc.). **3** *archaic* smooth over, make good, vindicate, harmonize, etc. [OE *s(e)alf(e), s(e)alfian* f. Gmc; senses 1 and 3 of v. partly f. L *salvare* SAVE[1]]
■ *n.* **1** balm, ointment, unguent, lotion; dressing; embrocation, liniment. **2** balm, palliative, opiate, narcotic, relief. ● *v.* **1** relieve, ease, alleviate, assuage, palliate, soothe, mollify, comfort, appease. **3** see *sort out* 4.

salve[2] /salv/ *v.tr.* **1** save (a ship or its cargo) from loss at sea. **2** save (property) from fire. ▫▫ **salvable** *adj.* [back-form. f. SALVAGE]
■ see SALVAGE *v.* 1.

salver /sálvər/ *n.* a tray usu. of gold, silver, brass, or electroplate, on which drinks, letters, etc., are offered. [F *salve* tray for presenting food to the king f. Sp. *salva* assaying of food f. *salvar* SAVE: assoc. with *platter*]
■ see PLATTER.

Salve Regina /sálvay rəjeénə/ *n.* **1** a Roman Catholic hymn or prayer said or sung after compline and after the Divine Office from Trinity Sunday to Advent. **2** the music for this. [f. the opening words *salve regina* hail (holy) queen]

salvia /sálviə/ *n.* any plant of the genus *Salvia*, esp. *S. splendens* with red or blue flowers. [L, = SAGE[1]]

Salvo /sálvō/ *n.* (*pl.* **-os**) *Austral. sl.* a member of the Salvation Army. [abbr.]

salvo[1] /sálvō/ *n.* (*pl.* **-oes** or **-os**) **1** the simultaneous firing of artillery or other guns esp. as a salute, or in a sea-fight. **2** a number of bombs released from aircraft at the same moment. **3** a round or volley of applause. [earlier *salve* f. F f. It. *salva* salutation (as SAVE[1])]
■ **1, 2** see VOLLEY *n.* 1. **3** see APPLAUSE 1.

salvo[2] /sálvō/ *n.* (*pl.* **-os**) **1** a saving clause; a reservation (*with an express salvo of their rights*). **2** a tacit reservation. **3** a quibbling evasion; a bad excuse. **4** an expedient for saving reputation or soothing pride or conscience. [L, ablat. of *salvus* SAFE as used in *salvo jure* without prejudice to the rights of (a person)]

sal volatile /sál volátili/ *n.* ammonium carbonate, esp. in the form of a flavoured solution in alcohol used as smelling-salts. [mod.L, = volatile salt]

salvor /sálvər/ *n.* a person or ship making or assisting in salvage. [SALVE[2]]

SAM *abbr.* surface-to-air missile.

Sam. *abbr.* Samuel (Old Testament).

samadhi /səmaádi/ *n.* *Buddhism* & *Hinduism* **1** a state of concentration induced by meditation. **2** a state into which a perfected holy man is said to pass at his apparent death. [Skr. *samādhi* contemplation]

samara /sámmərə, səmaá-/ *n. Bot.* a winged seed from the sycamore, ash, etc. [mod.L f. L, = elm-seed]

Samaritan /səmárrit'n/ *n.* & *adj.* ● *n.* **1** (in full **good Samaritan**) a charitable or helpful person (with ref. to Luke 10:33 etc.). **2** a member of an organization which counsels people in distress by telephone or face to face. **3** a native of Samaria in West Jordan. **4** the language of this people. **5** an adherent of the Samaritan religious system, accepting only the Samaritan Pentateuch. ● *adj.* of Samaria or the Samaritans. ▫ **Samaritan Pentateuch** a recension used by Samaritans of which the MSS are in archaic characters. ▫▫ **Samaritanism** *n.* [LL *Samaritanus* f. Gk *Samareitēs* f. *Samareia* Samaria]

samarium /səmáiriəm/ *n. Chem.* a hard silvery metallic element of the lanthanide series, occurring naturally in monazite etc. and used in making ferromagnetic alloys. ¶ Symb.: **Sm**. [*samarskite* the mineral in which its spectrum was first observed, f. *Samarski* name of a 19th-c. Russ. official]

samba /sámbə/ *n.* & *v.* ● *n.* **1** a Brazilian dance of African origin. **2** a ballroom dance imitative of this. **3** the music for this. ● *v.intr.* (**sambas, sambaed** /-bəd/ or **samba'd, sambaing** /-bəing/) dance the samba. [Port., of Afr. orig.]

sambar /sámbər/ *n.* (also **samba, sambhar**) either of two large deer, *Cervus unicolor* or *C. equinus*, native to S. Asia. [Hindi *sā(m)bar*]

Sambo /sámbō/ *n.* (*pl.* **-os** or **-oes**) **1** *sl. offens.* a Black person. **2** (**sambo**) *hist.* a person of mixed race esp. of Negro and Indian or Negro and European blood. [Sp. *zambo* perh. = *zambo* bandy-legged; sense 1 perh. a different word f. Foulah *sambo* uncle]

Sam Browne /sam brówn/ *n.* (in full **Sam Browne belt**) an army officer's belt and the strap supporting it. [Sir *Sam*uel J. *Browne*, Brit. military commander d. 1901]

same /saym/ *adj.*, *pron.*, & *adv.* ● *adj.* **1** (often prec. by *the*) identical; not different; unchanged (*everyone was looking in the same direction*; *the same car was used in another crime*; *saying the same thing over and over*). **2** unvarying, uniform, monotonous (*the same old story*). **3** (usu. prec. by *this*, *these*, *that*, *those*) (of a person or thing) previously alluded to; just mentioned; aforesaid (*this same man was later my husband*). ● *pron.* (prec. by *the*) **1** the same person or thing (*the others asked for the same*). **2** *Law* or *archaic* the person or thing just mentioned (*detected the youth breaking in and apprehended the same*). ● *adv.* (usu. prec. by *the*) similarly; in the same way (*we all feel the same*; *I want to go, the same as you do*). □ **all** (or **just**) **the same 1** emphatically the same. **2** in spite of changed conditions, adverse circumstances, etc. (*but you should offer, all the same*). **at the same time 1** simultaneously. **2** notwithstanding; in spite of circumstances etc. **be all** (or **just**) **the same to** an expression of indifference or impartiality (*it's all the same to me what we do*). **by the same token** see TOKEN. **same here** *colloq.* the same applies to me. **the same to you!** may you do, have, find, etc., the same thing; likewise. **the very same** emphatically the same. □□ **sameness** *n.* [ME f. ON *sami*, *sama*, with Gmc cognates]

■ *adj.* **1** identical, exactly *or* just the same; selfsame, very; unchanged, unaltered. **2** unchanging, changeless, unchanged, unmodified, unaltered, constant, uniform, unvaried, unvarying, monotonous. **3** aforesaid, aforementioned, aforestated, above-mentioned, above-stated, above-named. ● *pron.* **2** see SAME *adj.* 3 above. ● *adv.* (*the same*) similarly, in the same way; see also ALIKE *adv.* □ **all** (or **just**) **the same 2** at the same time, nevertheless, none the less, even so, yet, but, anyway, anyhow, in any case, in any event, at any rate, regardless, notwithstanding, still, for all that, *colloq.* still and all; that (having been) said, having said that, when all is said and done. **at the same time 1** see *at once* 2 (ONCE). **2** see NOTWITHSTANDING *adv.*, *conj.* □□ **sameness** see UNIFORMITY.

samey /sáymi/ *adj.* (**samier**, **samiest**) *colloq.* lacking in variety; monotonous. □□ **sameyness** *n.*

samfu /sámfōō/ *n.* a suit consisting of a jacket and trousers, worn by Chinese women and sometimes men. [Cantonese]

Samhain /sown, sówin/ *n. Brit.* 1 Nov., celebrated by the Celts as a festival marking the beginning of winter. [Ir. *Samhain*]

Samian /sáymiən/ *n.* & *adj.* ● *n.* a native or inhabitant of Samos, an island in the Aegean sea. ● *adj.* of Samos. □ **Samian ware** fine red pottery from various parts of the Roman Empire, esp. Gaulish pottery often found on Roman sites in Britain. [L *Samius* f. Gk *Samios* Samos]

samisen /sámmisin/ *n.* a long three-stringed Japanese guitar, played with a plectrum. [Jap. f. Chin. *san-hsien* f. *san* three + *hsien* string]

samite /sámmīt, sáy-/ *n. hist.* a rich medieval dress-fabric of silk occas. interwoven with gold. [ME f. OF *samit* f. med.L *examitum* f. med. Gk *hexamiton* f. Gk *hexa-* six + *mitos* thread]

samizdat /sámmizdát/ *n.* a system of clandestine publication of banned literature in the former USSR. [Russ., = self-publishing house]

Samnite /sámnīt/ *n.* & *adj.* ● *n.* **1** a member of a people of ancient Italy often at war with republican Rome. **2** the language of this people. ● *adj.* of this people or their language. [ME f. L *Samnites* (pl.), rel. to *Sabinus* SABINE]

Samoan /səmṓən/ *n.* & *adj.* ● *n.* **1** a native of Samoa, a group of islands in the Pacific. **2** the language of this people. ● *adj.* of or relating to Samoa or its people or language. [*Samoa*]

samosa /səmṓsə/ *n.* a triangular pastry fried in ghee or oil, containing spiced vegetables or meat. [Hind.]

samovar /sámməvaar/ *n.* a Russian urn for making tea, with an internal heating tube to keep water at boiling-point. [Russ., = self-boiler]

Samoyed /sámməyed/ *n.* **1** a member of a people of northern Siberia. **2** the language of this people. **3** (also **samoyed**) **a** a dog of a white Arctic breed. **b** this breed. [Russ. *samoed*]

Samoyedic /sámməyéddik/ *n.* & *adj.* ● *n.* the language of the Samoyeds. ● *adj.* of or relating to the Samoyeds.

samp /samp/ *n. US* **1** coarsely-ground maize. **2** porridge made of this. [Algonquian *nasamp* softened by water]

sampan /sámpan/ *n.* a small boat usu. with a stern-oar or stern-oars, used in the Far East. [Chin. *san-ban* f. *san* three + *ban* board]

samphire /sámfīr/ *n.* **1** an umbelliferous maritime rock plant, *Crithmum maritimum*, with aromatic fleshy leaves used in pickles. **2** the glasswort. [earlier *samp(i)ere* f. F (*herbe de*) *Saint Pierre* St Peter('s herb)]

sample /saámp'l/ *n.* & *v.* ● *n.* **1** (also *attrib.*) a small part or quantity intended to show what the whole is like. **2** a small amount of fabric, food, or other commodity, esp. given to a prospective customer. **3** a specimen, esp. one taken for scientific testing or analysis. **4** an illustrative or typical example. ● *v.tr.* **1** take or give samples of. **2** try the qualities of. **3** get a representative experience of. □ **sample bag** *Austral.* an (orig. free) bag of advertisers' samples. [ME f. AF *assample*, OF *essample* EXAMPLE]

■ *n.* **1** specimen, example, representative, representation, illustration, sampling, cross-section, *US* sampler; (*attrib.*) specimen, representative, illustrative, trial, test. **2** swatch; bite, nibble, taste. **3** specimen, *Biol.* section. **4** see ILLUSTRATION 2. ● *v.* test, taste, experience; see also TRY *v.* 3.

sampler[1] /saámplər/ *n.* a piece of embroidery worked in various stitches as a specimen of proficiency (often displayed on a wall etc.). [OF *essamplaire* (as EXEMPLAR)]

sampler[2] /saámplər/ *n.* **1** a person who samples. **2** *US* a collection of representative items etc.

■ **2** see SAMPLE *n.* 1.

sampling /saámpling/ *n.* a technique in electronic music involving digitally encoding a piece of sound and re-using it as part of a composition or recording.

samsara /səmsaárə/ *n. Ind. Philos.* the endless cycle of death and rebirth to which life in the material world is bound. □□ **samsaric** *adj.* [Skr. *saṃsāra* a wandering through]

samskara /səmskaárə/ *n. Ind. Philos.* **1** a purificatory ceremony or rite marking an event in one's life. **2** a mental impression, instinct, or memory. [Skr. *samskāra* a making perfect, preparation]

Samson /sáms'n/ *n.* a person of great strength or resembling Samson in some respect. □ **Samson-** (or **Samson's-**) **post** **1** a strong pillar passing through the hold of a ship or between decks. **2** a post in a whaleboat to which a harpoon rope is attached. [LL f. Gk *Sampsōn* f. Heb. *šimšôn* (Judg. 13–16)]

samurai /sámmoorī, -yoorī/ *n.* (*pl.* same) **1** a Japanese army officer. **2** *hist.* a military retainer; a member of a military caste in Japan. [Jap.]

san /san/ *n.* = SANATORIUM 2. [abbr.]

sanative /sánnətiv/ *adj.* **1** healing; curative. **2** of or tending to physical or moral health. [ME f. OF *sanatif* or LL *sanativus* f. L *sanare* cure]

■ **1** see MEDICINAL *adj.*

sanatorium /sánnətóriəm/ *n.* (*pl.* **sanatoriums** or **sanatoria** /-riə/) **1** an establishment for the treatment of invalids, esp. of convalescents and the chronically sick. **2** *Brit.* a room or building for sick people in a school etc. [mod.L (as SANATIVE)]

■ **1** rest-home, convalescent home, nursing home, health farm, *US* sanitarium. **2** infirmary, sickroom, sick bay.

sanctify /sángktifī/ *v.tr.* (**-ies**, **-ied**) **1** consecrate; set apart or observe as holy. **2** purify or free from sin. **3** make legitimate or binding by religious sanction; justify; give the colour of morality or innocence to. **4** make productive of or conducive to holiness. □□ **sanctification** /-fikáysh'n/ *n.* **sanctifier** *n.* [ME f. OF *saintifier* f. eccl.L *sanctificare* f. L *sanctus* holy]

■ **1** consecrate, hallow, make sacred *or* holy; glorify, exalt. **2** purify, cleanse; see also PURGE *v.* 1. **3** confirm, sanction, ratify, justify, legitimate, legitimatize, legitimize, legalize, license, canonize.

sanctimonious /sángktimṓniəss/ *adj.* making a show of sanctity or piety. □□ **sanctimoniously** *adv.* **sanctimoniousness** *n.* **sanctimony** /sángktiməni/ *n.* [L *sanctimonia* sanctity (as SAINT)]

■ hypocritical, self-righteous, canting, Pharisaical, pietistic, unctuous, *colloq.* holier-than-thou, goody-goody, smarmy, *Brit. sl.* pi.

sanction /sángksh'n/ *n.* & *v.* ● *n.* **1** approval or encouragement given to an action etc. by custom or tradition; express permission. **2** confirmation or ratification of a law etc. **3 a** a penalty for disobeying a law or rule, or a reward for obeying it. **b** a clause containing this. **4** *Ethics* a consideration operating to enforce obedience to any rule of conduct. **5** (esp. in *pl.*) military or esp. economic action by a State to coerce another to conform to an international agreement or norms of conduct. **6** *Law hist.* a law or decree. ● *v.tr.* **1** authorize, countenance, or agree to (an action etc.). **2** ratify; attach a penalty or reward to; make binding. □□ **sanctionable** *adj.* [F f. L *sanctio -onis* f. *sancire sanct-* make sacred]

■ *n.* **1** agreement, concurrence, acceptance, affirmation, assent, acquiescence, compliance, approval, permission, OK, encouragement, support, advocacy, backing, sponsorship, favour, countenance. **2** confirmation, ratification, authorization, legalization, legitimatization, legitimation, legitimization, validation, licence, certification, approval, permission, imprimatur, seal *or* stamp (of approval), signet. **3 a** see PENALTY 1, REWARD *n.* 1a. ● *v.* **1** authorize, countenance, agree to, approve, permit, allow, subscribe to, commission, consent to, support, encourage, advocate, back, sponsor, favour, *US* approbate. **2** confirm, ratify, second, authorize, legalize, legitimatize, legitimize, legitimate, validate, license, certify, *US* notarize.

sanctitude /sángktityōōd/ *n. archaic* saintliness. [ME f. L *sanctitudo* (as SAINT)]

■ see SANCTITY 1.

sanctity /sángktiti/ *n.* (*pl.* **-ies**) **1** holiness of life; saintliness. **2** sacredness; the state of being hallowed. **3** inviolability. **4** (in *pl.*) sacred obligations, feelings, etc. [ME f. OF *sain(c)tité* or L *sanctitas* (as SAINT)]

■ **1** piety, holiness, saintliness, divinity, grace, sacredness, godliness, *archaic* sanctitude. **2** sacredness, holiness. **3** unassailability, inviolability, indomitability.

sanctuary /sángktyoori/ *n.* (*pl.* **-ies**) **1** a holy place; a church, temple, etc. **2 a** the inmost recess or holiest part of a temple etc. **b** the part of the chancel containing the high altar. **3** a place where birds, wild animals, etc., are bred and protected. **4** a place of refuge, esp. for political refugees. **5 a** immunity from arrest. **b** the right to offer this. **6** *hist.* a sacred place where a fugitive from the law or a debtor was secured by medieval Church law against arrest or violence. □ **take sanctuary** resort to a place of refuge. [ME f. AF *sanctuarie*, OF *sanctuaire* f. L *sanctuarium* (as SAINT)]

■ **1** sanctum, shrine, chapel, temple, church, house of worship, house of God, holy place; synagogue, mosque, pagoda. **3** reserve, preserve, conservation area, national park. **4** asylum, refuge, retreat, shelter. **5 a** asylum, refuge, protection, shelter, safety. □ **take sanctuary** seek asylum.

sanctum /sángktəm/ *n.* (*pl.* **sanctums**) **1** a holy place. **2** *colloq.* a person's private room, study, or den. □ **sanctum sanctorum** /sangktórəm/ **1** the holy of holies in the Jewish temple. **2** = sense 2 of n. **3** an inner retreat. **4** an esoteric doctrine etc. [L, neut. of *sanctus* holy, past part. of *sancire* consecrate: *sanctorum* genit. pl. in transl. of Heb. *ḳōdeš hakḳ°dāšîm* holy of holies]

■ **1** sanctuary, holy place, shrine, chapel, temple. **2** sanctum sanctorum, den, study, retreat; hiding-place, hideaway, cubby(-hole), *colloq.* hide-out.

sanctus /sángktəss/ *n.* (also **Sanctus**) **1** the prayer or hymn beginning 'Holy, holy, holy' said or sung at the end of the Eucharistic preface. **2** the music for this. □ **sanctus bell** a handbell or the bell in the turret at the junction of the nave and the chancel, rung at the sanctus or at the elevation of the Eucharist. [ME f. L, = holy]

sand /sand/ *n.* & *v.* ● *n.* **1** a loose granular substance resulting from the wearing down of esp. siliceous rocks and found on the seashore, river-beds, deserts, etc. **2** (in *pl.*) grains of sand. **3** (in *pl.*) an expanse or tracts of sand. **4** a light yellow-brown colour like that of sand. **5** (in *pl.*) a sandbank. **6** *US colloq.* firmness of purpose; grit. ● *v.tr.* **1** smooth or polish with sandpaper or sand. **2** sprinkle or overlay with, or bury under, sand. **3** adulterate (sugar etc.) with sand. □ **sand bar** a sandbank at the mouth of a river or *US* on the coast. **sand-bath** a vessel of heated sand to provide uniform heating. **sand-bed** a stratum of sand. **sand-cloud** driving sand in a simoom. **sand-crack 1** a fissure in a horse's hoof. **2** a crack in the human foot from walking on hot sand. **3** a crack in brick due to imperfect mixing. **sand dollar** *US* any of various round flat sea urchins, esp. of the order Clypeasteroida. **sand-dune** (or **-hill**) a mound or ridge of sand formed by the wind. **sand eel** any eel-like fish of the family Ammodytidae or Hypotychidae: also called LAUNCE. **sand-flea** a chigoe or sand-hopper. **sand-glass** = HOURGLASS. **sand-groper** *Austral.* **1** a gold-rush pioneer. **2** *joc.* a Western Australian. **sand-hill** a dune. **sand-hopper** any of various small jumping crustaceans of the order Amphipoda, burrowing on the seashore. **sand-martin** a swallow-like bird, *Riparia riparia*, nesting in the side of a sandy bank etc. **the sands are running out** the allotted time is nearly at an end. **sand-shoe** a shoe with a canvas, rubber, hemp, etc., sole for use on sand. **sand-skipper** = *sand-hopper*. **sand-yacht** a boat on wheels propelled along a beach by wind. □□ **sander** *n.* **sandlike** *adj.* [OE *sand* f. Gmc]

■ *n.* **6** see GRIT *n.* ● *v.* **1** see SMOOTH *v.* 1. □ **sand bar** see SHALLOW *n.*

sandal[1] /sánd'l/ *n.* & *v.* ● *n.* **1** a light shoe with an openwork upper or no upper, attached to the foot usu. by straps. **2** a strap for fastening a low shoe, passing over the instep or around the ankle. ● *v.tr.* (**sandalled, sandalling**; *US* **sandaled, sandaling**) **1** (esp. as **sandalled** *adj.*) put sandals on (a person, a person's feet). **2** fasten or provide (a shoe) with a sandal. [ME f. L *sandalium* f. Gk *sandalion* dimin. of *sandalon* wooden shoe, prob. of Asiatic orig.]

sandal[2] /sánd'l/ *n.* = SANDALWOOD. □ **sandal-tree** any tree yielding sandalwood, esp. the white sandalwood, *Santalum album*, of India. [ME f. med.L *sandalum*, ult. f. Skr. *candana*]

sandalwood /sánd'lwŏŏd/ *n.* **1** the scented wood of a sandal-tree. **2** a perfume derived from this. □ **red sandalwood** the red wood from either of two SE Asian trees, *Adenanthera pavonina* and *Pterocarpus santalinus*, used as timber and to produce a red dye. **sandalwood oil** a yellow aromatic oil made from the sandal-tree.

sandarac /sándərak/ *n.* (also **sandarach**) **1** the gummy resin of a N. African conifer, *Tetraclinis articulata*, used in making varnish. **2** = REALGAR. [L *sandaraca* f. Gk *sandarakē*, of Asiatic orig.]

sandbag /sándbag/ *n.* & *v.* ● *n.* a bag filled with sand for use: **1** (in fortification) for making temporary defences or for the protection of a building etc. against blast and splinters or floodwaters. **2** as ballast esp. for a boat or balloon. **3** as a weapon to inflict a heavy blow without leaving a mark. **4** to stop a draught from a window or door. ● *v.tr.* (**-bagged, -bagging**) **1** barricade or defend. **2** place sandbags against (a window, chink, etc.). **3** fell with a blow from a sandbag. **4** *US* coerce by harsh means. □□ **sandbagger** *n.*

sandbank /sándbangk/ *n.* a deposit of sand forming a shallow place in the sea or a river.
■ see SHALLOW *n.*

sandblast /sándblaast/ *v.* & *n.* ● *v.tr.* roughen, treat, or clean with a jet of sand driven by compressed air or steam. ● *n.* this jet. □□ **sandblaster** *n.*

sandbox /sándboks/ *n.* **1** *Railways* a box of sand on a locomotive for sprinkling slippery rails. **2** *Golf* a container for sand used in teeing. **3** a sandpit enclosed in a box. **4** *hist.* a device for sprinkling sand to dry ink.

sandboy /sándboy/ *n.* □ **happy as a sandboy** extremely happy or carefree. [prob. = a boy hawking sand for sale]

sandcastle /sándkaass'l/ *n.* a shape like a castle made in sand, usu. by a child on the seashore.

sanderling /sándərling/ *n.* a small wading bird, *Calidris alba*, of the sandpiper family. [perh. f. an OE form *sandyrthling* (unrecorded, as SAND + *yrthling* ploughman, also the name of a bird)]

sanders /sándərz/ *n.* (also **saunders** /sáwn-/) sandalwood, esp. red sandalwood. [ME f. OF *sandre* var. of *sandle* SANDAL[2]]

sandfly /sándflī/ *n.* (*pl.* **-ies**) **1** any midge of the genus *Simulium*. **2** any biting fly of the genus *Phlebotomus* transmitting the viral disease leishmaniasis.

sandhi /sándi/ *n. Gram.* the process whereby the form of a word changes as a result of its position in an utterance (e.g. the change from *a* to *an* before a vowel). [Skr. *saṃdhi* putting together]

sandhog /sándhog/ *n. US* a person who works underwater laying foundations, constructing tunnels, etc.

sandiver /sándivər/ *n.* liquid scum formed in glass-making. [ME app. f. F *suin de verre* exhalation of glass f. *suer* to sweat]

sandlot /sándlot/ *n. US* a piece of unoccupied sandy land used for children's games.

sandman /sándman/ *n.* the personification of tiredness causing children's eyes to smart towards bedtime.

sandpaper /sándpaypər/ *n.* & *v.* ● *n.* paper with sand or another abrasive stuck to it for smoothing or polishing. ● *v.tr.* smooth with sandpaper.

sandpiper /sándpīpər/ *n.* any of various wading birds of the family Scolopacidae, frequenting moorland and coastal areas.

sandpit /sándpit/ *n.* a hollow partly filled with sand, usu. for children to play in.

sandsoap /sándsōp/ *n.* heavy-duty gritty soap.

sandstock /sándstok/ *n.* brick made with sand dusted on the surface.

sandstone /sándstōn/ *n.* **1** any clastic rock containing particles visible to the naked eye. **2** a sedimentary rock of consolidated sand commonly red, yellow, brown, grey, or white.

sandstorm /sándstorm/ *n.* a desert storm of wind with clouds of sand.
■ see STORM *n.* 1.

sandwich /sánwij, -wich/ *n.* & *v.* ● *n.* **1** two or more slices of usu. buttered bread with a filling of meat, cheese, etc., between them. **2** a cake of two or more layers with jam or cream between (*bake a sponge sandwich*). ● *v.tr.* **1** put (a thing, statement, etc.) between two of another character. **2** squeeze in between others (*sat sandwiched in the middle*). □ **sandwich-board** one of two advertisement boards carried by a sandwich-man. **sandwich course** a course of training with alternate periods of practical experience and theoretical instruction. **sandwich-man** (*pl.* **-men**) a man who walks the streets with sandwich-boards hanging before and behind. [4th Earl of *Sandwich*, Engl. nobleman d. 1792, said to have eaten food in this form so as not to leave the gaming-table]
■ *n.* **1** *N.Eng.* butty, *Brit. colloq.* sarnie.

sandwort /sándwurt/ *n.* any low-growing plant of the genus *Arenaria*, usu. bearing small white flowers.

sandy /sándi/ *adj.* (**sandier, sandiest**) **1** having the texture of sand. **2** having much sand. **3 a** (of hair) yellowish-red. **b** (of a person) having sandy hair. □ **sandy blight** *Austral.* conjunctivitis with sandlike grains in the eye. □□ **sandiness** *n.* **sandyish** *adj.* [OE *sandig* (as SAND)]
■ **1** gritty, grainy, granular. **3 a** see RED *adj.* 4.

sane /sayn/ *adj.* **1** of sound mind; not mad. **2** (of views etc.) moderate; sensible. □□ **sanely** *adv.* **saneness** *n.* [L *sanus* healthy]
■ **1** normal, of sound mind, rational, *compos (mentis)*, *colloq.* right in the head, all there. **2** sound, well-balanced, right-minded, level-headed, reasonable, moderate, sensible, judicious.

sang *past* of SING.

sangar /sánggər/ *n.* (also **sanga** /sánggə/) a stone breastwork round a hollow. [Pashto *sangar*]

sangaree /sánggərée/ *n.* a cold drink of wine diluted and spiced. [Sp. *sangría* SANGRIA]

sang-froid /sonfrwaá/ *n.* composure, coolness, etc., in danger or under agitating circumstances. [F, = cold blood]
■ cold-bloodedness, coolness, cool-headedness, indifference, composure, phlegm, self-possession, self-control, poise, imperturbability, equanimity, *colloq.* unflappability, *sl.* cool.

sangrail /sanggráyl/ *n.* = GRAIL. [ME f. OF *saint graal* (as SAINT, GRAIL)]

sangria /sanggréeə/ *n.* a Spanish drink of red wine with lemonade, fruit, etc. [Sp., = bleeding: cf. SANGAREE]

sanguinary /sánggwinəri/ *adj.* **1** accompanied by or delighting in bloodshed. **2** bloody; bloodthirsty. **3** (of laws) inflicting death freely. □□ **sanguinarily** *adv.* **sanguinariness** *n.* [L *sanguinarius* f. *sanguis -inis* blood]
■ **1** bloodthirsty, gory; slaughterous, murderous, homicidal; brutal, brutish, savage, barbarous. **2** bloody, bloodthirsty, sanguineous, *archaic* sanguine.

sanguine /sánggwin/ *adj.* & *n.* ● *adj.* **1** optimistic; confident. **2** (of the complexion) florid; bright; ruddy. **3** *hist.* of a ruddy complexion with a courageous and hopeful amorous disposition. **4** *hist.* of the temperament in which blood predominates over the other humours. **5** *Heraldry* or *literary* blood red. **6** *archaic* bloody; bloodthirsty. ● *n.* **1** a blood-red colour. **2** a crayon of chalk coloured red or flesh with iron oxide. □□ **sanguinely** *adv.* **sanguineness** *n.* (both in sense 1 of *n.*). [ME f. OF *sanguin -ine* blood-red f. L *sanguineus* (as SANGUINARY)]
■ *adj.* **1** optimistic, rosy, confident, hopeful. **2** florid, bright, ruddy; see also ROSY 1. **6** bloody, bloodthirsty; see also GORY.

sanguineous /sanggwinniəss/ *adj.* **1** sanguinary. **2** *Med.* of or relating to blood. **3** blood-red. **4** full-blooded; plethoric. [L *sanguineus* (as SANGUINE)]
■ **1** sanguinary, bloody.

Sanhedrin /sánnidrin/ *n.* (also **Sanhedrim** /-drim/) the highest court of justice and the supreme council in ancient Jerusalem with 71 members. [late Heb. *sanhedrîn* f. Gk *sunedrion* (as SYN-, *hedra* seat)]

sanicle /sánnik'l/ *n.* any umbelliferous plant of the genus *Sanicula*, esp. *S. europaea*, formerly believed to have healing properties. [ME ult. f. med.L *sanicula* perh. f. L *sanus* healthy]

sanify /sánnifī/ *v.tr.* (**-ies, -ied**) make healthy; improve the sanitary state of. [L *sanus* healthy]

sanitarium /sánnitáiriəm/ *n.* (*pl.* **sanitariums** or **sanitaria** /-riə/) *US* = SANATORIUM. [pseudo-L f. L *sanitas* health]

sanitary /sánnitəri, -tri/ *adj.* **1** of the conditions that affect health, esp. with regard to dirt and infection. **2** hygienic; free from or designed to kill germs, infection, etc. □ **sanitary engineer** a person dealing with systems needed to maintain public health. **sanitary towel** (*US* **napkin**) an absorbent pad used during menstruation. **sanitary ware** porcelain for lavatories etc. □□ **sanitarian** /-táiriən/ *n.* &

adj. **sanitarily** *adv.* **sanitariness** *n.* [F *sanitaire* f. L *sanitas*: see SANITY]
■ **2** clean, sterile, hygienic, antiseptic, disinfected, aseptic, germ-free, bacteria-free.

sanitation /sánnitáysh'n/ *n.* **1** sanitary conditions. **2** the maintenance or improving of these. **3** the disposal of sewage and refuse from houses etc. □□ **sanitate** /sánnitayt/ *v.tr.* & *intr.* **sanitationist** *n.* [irreg. f. SANITARY]

sanitize /sánnitīz/ *v.tr.* (also **-ise**) **1** make sanitary; disinfect. **2** render (information etc.) more acceptable by removing improper or disturbing material. □□ **sanitizer** *n.*
■ **1** see DISINFECT. □□ **sanitizer** see DISINFECTANT *n.*

sanity /sánniti/ *n.* **1 a** the state of being sane. **b** mental health. **2** the tendency to avoid extreme views. [ME f. L *sanitas* (as SANE)]
■ **1** saneness, reason, mental health *or* soundness, normality, rationality, stability, balance. **2** see SENSE *n.* 4, 5, STABILITY.

sank *past* of SINK.

sannyasi /sunyaási/ *n.* (also **sanyasi**) (*pl.* same) a Hindu religious mendicant. [Hindi & Urdu *sannyāsī* f. Skr. *saṃnyāsin* laying aside f. *saṃ* together, *ni* down, *as* throw]

sans /sanz, SON/ *prep. archaic* or *joc.* without. [ME f. OF *san(z)*, *sen(s)* ult. f. L *sine*, infl. by L *absentia* in the absence of]

sansculotte /sánzkyoolót, sónkyoo-/ *n.* **1** *hist.* a lower-class Parisian republican in the French Revolution. **2** an extreme republican or revolutionary. □□ **sansculottism** *n.* [F, lit. = without knee-breeches]
■ **2** see REVOLUTIONARY *n.*

sanserif /sansérrif/ *n.* & *adj.* (also **sans-serif**) *Printing* ● *n.* a form of type without serifs. ● *adj.* without serifs. [app. f. SANS + SERIF]

Sanskrit /sánskrit/ *n.* & *adj.* ● *n.* the ancient and sacred language of the Hindus in India. ● *adj.* of or in this language. □□ **Sanskritic** /-skríttik/ *adj.* **Sanskritist** *n.* [Skr. *saṃskṛta* composed, elaborated, f. *saṃ* together, *kṛ* make, *-ta* past part. ending]

Santa Claus /sántə klawz/ *n.* (also *colloq.* **Santa**) an imaginary person said to bring children presents on the night before Christmas. [orig. US f. Du. dial. *Sante Klaas* St Nicholas]

santolina /sántəleénə/ *n.* any aromatic shrub of the genus *Santolina*, with finely divided leaves and small usu. yellow flowers. [mod.L, var. of SANTONICA]

santonica /santónnikə/ *n.* **1** a shrubby wormwood plant, *Artemisia cina*, yielding santonin. **2** the dried flower-heads of this used as an anthelmintic. [L f. *Santones* an Aquitanian tribe]

santonin /sántənin/ *n.* a toxic drug extracted from santonica and other plants of the genus *Artemisia*, used as an anthelmintic. [SANTONICA + -IN]

sanyasi var. of SANNYASI.

sap[1] /sap/ *n.* & *v.* ● *n.* **1** the vital juice circulating in plants. **2** vigour; vitality. **3** = SAPWOOD. **4** *US sl.* a bludgeon (orig. one made from a sapling). ● *v.tr.* (**sapped**, **sapping**) **1** drain or dry (wood) of sap. **2** exhaust the vigour of (*my energy had been sapped by disappointment*). **3** remove the sapwood from (a log). **4** *US sl.* hit with a sap. □ **sap-green** *n.* **1** the pigment made from buckthorn berries. **2** the colour of this. ● *adj.* of this colour. □□ **sapful** *adj.* **sapless** *adj.* [OE *sæp* prob. f. Gmc]
■ *n.* **1** (vital) juice *or* fluid. **2** vigour, vitality, lifeblood, *poet.* ichor; see also LIFE 8. ● *v.* **2** bleed, drain, draw, rob, milk.

sap[2] /sap/ *n.* & *v.* ● *n.* **1** a tunnel or trench to conceal assailants' approach to a fortified place; a covered siege-trench. **2** an insidious or slow undermining of a belief, resolution, etc. ● *v.* (**sapped**, **sapping**) **1** *intr.* **a** dig a sap or saps. **b** approach by a sap. **2** *tr.* undermine; make insecure by removing the foundations. **3** *tr.* weaken or destroy insidiously. [ult. f. It. *zappa* spade, spadework, in part through F *sappe sap(p)er*, prob. of Arab. orig.]
■ *v.* **2** see UNDERCUT *v.* 4. **3** weaken, devitalize, deplete, drain, erode, enervate, debilitate; destroy, cripple, wreck; see also UNDERMINE 1, 2.

sap[3] /sap/ *n. sl.* a foolish person. [abbr. of *sapskull* f. SAP[1] = sapwood + SKULL]
■ fool, nincompoop, ninny, dunce, ass, simpleton, ignoramus, noddy, noodle, *colloq.* idiot, nitwit, dim-wit, chump, muggins, *Brit. sl.* (right) charlie, *esp. Brit. sl.* twit; dupe, gull, *colloq.* pushover, *sl.* sucker, fall guy, (easy) mark, *esp. US sl.* patsy, *US sl.* schnook.

sapanwood var. of SAPPANWOOD.

sapele /səpeéli/ *n.* **1** any of several large W. African hardwood trees of the genus *Entandrophragma*. **2** the reddish-brown mahogany-like timber of these trees. [W. Afr. name]

sapid /sáppid/ *adj. literary* **1** having (esp. an agreeable) flavour; savoury; palatable; not insipid. **2** *literary* (of talk, writing, etc.) not vapid or uninteresting. □□ **sapidity** /səpídditi/ *n.* [L *sapidus* f. *sapere* taste]
■ **1** see TASTY.

sapient /sáypiənt/ *adj. literary* **1** wise. **2** aping wisdom; of fancied sagacity. □□ **sapience** *n.* **sapiently** *adv.* [ME f. OF *sapient* or L part. stem of *sapere* be wise]
■ **1** see WISE *adj.* 1. □□ **sapience** see WISDOM 2, 3.

sapiential /sáypiénsh'l, sáp-/ *adj. literary* of or relating to wisdom. [ME f. F *sapiential* or eccl.L *sapientialis* f. L *sapientia* wisdom]

sapling /sápling/ *n.* **1** a young tree. **2** a youth. **3** a greyhound in its first year.

sapodilla /sáppədíllə/ *n.* a large evergreen tropical American tree, *Manilkara zapota*, with edible fruit and durable wood, and sap from which chicle is obtained. □ **sapodilla plum** the fruit of this tree. [Sp. *zapotillo* dimin. of *zapote* f. Aztec *tzápotl*]

saponaceous /sáppənáyshəss/ *adj.* **1** of, like, or containing soap; soapy. **2** *joc.* unctuous; flattering. [mod.L *saponaceus* f. L *sapo -onis* soap]
■ **2** see OILY 3.

saponify /səpónnifī/ *v.* (**-ies**, **-ied**) **1** *tr.* turn (fat or oil) into soap by reaction with an alkali. **2** *tr.* convert (an ester) to an acid and alcohol. **3** *intr.* become saponified. □□ **saponifiable** *adj.* **saponification** /-fikáysh'n/ *n.* [F *saponifier* (as SAPONACEOUS)]

saponin /sáppənin/ *n.* any of a group of plant glycosides, esp. those derived from the bark of the tree *Quillaja saponaria*, that foam when shaken with water and are used in detergents and fire extinguishers. [F *saponine* f. L *sapo -onis* soap]

sapor /sáypor/ *n.* **1** a quality perceptible by taste, e.g. sweetness. **2** the distinctive taste of a substance. **3** the sensation of taste. [ME f. L *sapere* taste]

sappanwood /sáppənwood/ *n.* (also **sapanwood**) the heart-wood of an E. Indian tree, *Caesalpinia sappan*, formerly used as a source of red dye. [Du. *sapan* f. Malay *sapang*, of S. Indian orig.]

sapper /sáppər/ *n.* **1** a person who digs saps. **2** *Brit.* a soldier of the Royal Engineers (esp. as the official term for a private).

Sapphic /sáffik/ *adj.* & *n.* ● *adj.* **1** of or relating to Sappho, poetess of Lesbos *c.*600 BC, or her poetry. **2** lesbian. ● *n.* (in *pl.*) (**sapphics**) verse in a metre associated with Sappho. [F *sa(p)phique* f. L *Sapphicus* f. Gk *Sapphikos* f. *Sapphō*]

sapphire /sáffīr/ *n.* & *adj.* ● *n.* **1** a transparent blue precious stone consisting of corundum. **2** precious transparent corundum of any colour. **3** the bright blue of a sapphire. **4** a humming-bird with bright blue colouring. ● *adj.* of sapphire blue. □ **sapphire wedding** a 45th wedding anniversary. □□ **sapphirine** /sáffirīn/ *adj.* [ME f. OF *safir* f. L *sapphirus* f. Gk *sappheiros* prob. = lapis lazuli]

sappy /sáppi/ *adj.* (**sappier**, **sappiest**) **1** full of sap. **2** young and vigorous. □□ **sappily** *adv.* **sappiness** *n.*

sapro- /sáprō/ *comb. form Biol.* rotten, putrefying. [Gk *sapros* putrid]

saprogenic /sáprəjénnik/ *adj.* causing or produced by putrefaction.

saprophagous /sapróffəgəss/ *adj.* feeding on decaying matter.

saprophile /sáprəfīl/ *n.* a bacterium inhabiting putrid matter. □□ **saprophilous** /-próffiləss/ *adj.*

saprophyte /sáprəfīt/ *n.* any plant or micro-organism living on dead or decayed organic matter. □□ **saprophytic** /-fittik/ *adj.*

sapwood /sápwŏŏd/ *n.* the soft outer layers of recently formed wood between the heartwood and the bark.

saraband /sárrəband/ *n.* **1** a stately old Spanish dance. **2** music for this or in its rhythm, usu. in triple time often with a long note on the second beat of the bar. [F *sarabande* f. Sp. & It. *zarabanda*]

Saracen /sárrəs'n/ *n.* & *adj. hist.* ● *n.* **1** an Arab or Muslim at the time of the Crusades. **2** a nomad of the Syrian and Arabian desert. ● *adj.* of the Saracens. □ **Saracen corn** *Brit. archaic* buckwheat. **Saracen's head** the head of a Saracen or Turk as a heraldic charge or inn-sign. □□ **Saracenic** /sárrəsénnik/ *adj.* [ME f. OF *sar(r)azin, sar(r)acin* f. LL *Saracenus* f. late Gk *Sarakēnos* perh. f. Arab. *šarḳī* eastern]

sarangi /səránggi/ *n.* (*pl.* **sarangis**) an Indian stringed instrument played with a bow. [Hindi *sāraṅgī*]

sarape var. of SERAPE.

sarcasm /saárkaz'm/ *n.* **1** a bitter or wounding remark. **2** a taunt, esp. one ironically worded. **3** language consisting of such remarks. **4** the use of or the faculty of using this. □□ **sarcastic** /saarkástik/ *adj.* **sarcastically** /saarkástikəli/ *adv.* [F *sarcasme* or f. LL *sarcasmus* f. late Gk *sarkasmos* f. Gk *sarkazō* tear flesh, in late Gk gnash the teeth, speak bitterly f. *sarx sarkos* flesh]

■ **1, 2** see TAUNT *n.*, DIG *n.* 3. **3** irony, contumely, satire. **4** irony, scorn, derision, ridicule, venom; sharpness, edge, trenchancy, mordancy. □□ **sarcastic** scornful, derisive, derisory, mocking, ridiculing, satiric(al), ironic, sardonic, scathing, caustic, cutting, trenchant, incisive, biting, acerbic, acid, acidic, acidulous, venomous, poisonous, *Brit. sl.* sarky.

sarcenet var. of SARSENET.

sarcoma /saarkṓmə/ *n.* (*pl.* **sarcomas** or **sarcomata** /-mətə/) a malignant tumour of connective or other non-epithelial tissue. □□ **sarcomatosis** /-mətṓsiss/ *n.* **sarcomatous** *adj.* [mod.L f. Gk *sarkōma* f. *sarkoō* become fleshy f. *sarx sarkos* flesh]

■ see TUMOUR.

sarcophagus /saarkóffəgəss/ *n.* (*pl.* **sarcophagi** /-gī, -jī/) a stone coffin, esp. one adorned with a sculpture or inscription. [L f. Gk *sarkophagos* flesh-consuming (as SARCOMA, *-phagos* -eating)]

■ coffin, *US* casket.

sarcoplasm /saárkəplaz'm/ *n. Anat.* the cytoplasm in which muscle fibrils are embedded. [Gk *sarx sarkos* flesh + PLASMA]

sarcous /saárkəss/ *adj.* consisting of flesh or muscle. [Gk *sarx sarkos* flesh]

sard /saard/ *n.* a yellow or orange-red cornelian. [ME f. F *sarde* or L *sarda* = LL *sardius* f. Gk *sardios* prob. f. *Sardō* Sardinia]

sardelle /saardél/ *n.* any of several fish resembling the sardine. [It. *sardella* dimin. of *sarda* f. L (as SARDINE[1])]

sardine[1] /saardeén/ *n.* a young pilchard or similar young or small herring-like marine fish. □ **like sardines** crowded close together (as sardines are in tins). [ME f. OF *sardine* = It. *sardina* f. L f. *sarda* f. Gk, perh. f. *Sardō* Sardinia]

sardine[2] /saárdīn/ *n.* a precious stone mentioned in Rev. 4:3. [ME f. LL *sardinus* f. Gk *sardinos* var. of *sardios* SARD]

sardius /saárdiəss/ *n. Bibl.* etc. a precious stone. [ME f. LL f. Gk *sardios* sard]

sardonic /saardónnik/ *adj.* **1** grimly jocular. **2** (of laughter etc.) bitterly mocking or cynical. □□ **sardonically** *adv.* **sardonicism** /-nisiz'm/ *n.* [F *sardonique*, earlier *sardonien* f. L *sardonius* f. Gk *sardonios* of Sardinia, alt. of *sardanios* Homeric epithet of bitter or scornful laughter]

■ **1** ironic, cynical, sarcastic; see also INCISIVE 3. **2** derisive, derisory, mocking, cynical, sarcastic, ironic.

sardonyx /saárdəniks/ *n.* onyx in which white layers alternate with sard. [ME f. L f. Gk *sardonux* (prob. as SARD, ONYX)]

saree var. of SARI.

sargasso /saargássō/ *n.* (also **sargassum**) (*pl.* **-os** or **-oes** or **sargassa**) any seaweed of the genus *Sargassum*, with berry-like air-vessels, found floating in island-like masses, esp. in the Sargasso Sea of the N. Atlantic. Also called GULFWEED. [Port. *sargaço*, of unkn. orig.]

sarge /saarj/ *n. sl.* sergeant. [abbr.]

sari /saáree/ *n.* (also **saree**) (*pl.* **saris** or **sarees**) a length of cotton or silk draped round the body, traditionally worn as a main garment by Indian women. [Hindi *sāṛ(h)ī*]

sark /saark/ *n. Sc.* & *N.Engl.* a shirt or chemise. [ME *serk* f. ON *serkr* f. Gmc]

sarking /saárking/ *n.* boarding between the rafters and the roof. [SARK + -ING[1]]

sarky /saárki/ *adj.* (**sarkier, sarkiest**) *Brit. sl.* sarcastic. □□ **sarkily** *adv.* **sarkiness** *n.* [abbr.]

sarmentose /saármantōss/ *adj.* (also **sarmentous** /-méntəss/) *Bot.* having long thin trailing shoots. [L *sarmentosus* f. *sarmenta* (pl.) twigs, brushwood, f. *sarpere* to prune]

sarnie /saárni/ *n. Brit. colloq.* a sandwich. [abbr.]

sarong /səróng/ *n.* **1** a Malay and Javanese garment consisting of a long strip of (often striped) cloth worn by both sexes tucked round the waist or under the armpits. **2** a woman's garment resembling this. [Malay, lit. 'sheath']

saros /saáross/ *n. Astron.* a period of about 18 years between repetitions of eclipses. [Gk f. Babylonian *šār(u)* 3,600 (years)]

sarrusophone /sərŏŏssəfōn/ *n.* a metal wind instrument played with a double reed like an oboe. [*Sarrus*, 19th-c. Fr. inventor]

sarsaparilla /saársəpərillə/ *n.* **1** a preparation of the dried roots of various plants, esp. smilax, used to flavour some drinks and medicines and formerly as a tonic. **2** any of the plants yielding this. [Sp. *zarzaparilla* f. *zarza* bramble, prob. + dimin. of *parra* vine]

sarsen /saárs'n/ *n. Geol.* a sandstone boulder carried by ice during a glacial period. [prob. var. of SARACEN]

sarsenet /saársənit/ *n.* (also **sarcenet**) a fine soft silk material used esp. for linings. [ME f. AF *sarzinett* perh. dimin. of *sarzin* SARACEN after OF *drap sarrasinois* Saracen cloth]

sartorial /saartóriəl/ *adj.* **1** of a tailor or tailoring. **2** of men's clothes. □□ **sartorially** *adv.* [L *sartor* tailor f. *sarcire sart-* patch]

sartorius /saartóriəss/ *n. Anat.* the long narrow muscle running across the front of each thigh. [mod.L f. L *sartor* tailor (the muscle being used in adopting a tailor's cross-legged posture)]

Sarum use /sáirəm/ *n. Eccl.* the order of divine service used in the diocese of Salisbury before the Reformation. [med.L *Sarum* Salisbury, perh. f. L *Sarisburia*]

SAS *abbr.* (in the UK) Special Air Service.

s.a.s.e. *abbr. US* self-addressed stamped envelope.

sash[1] /sash/ *n.* a long strip or loop of cloth etc. worn over one shoulder usu. as part of a uniform or insignia, or worn round the waist, usu. by a woman or child. □□ **sashed** *adj.* [earlier *shash* f. Arab. *šāš* muslin, turban]

■ see BELT *n.* 1.

sash[2] /sash/ *n.* **1** a frame holding the glass in a sash-window and usu. made to slide up and down in the grooves of a window aperture. **2** the glazed sliding light of a glasshouse or garden frame. □ **sash-cord** a strong cord attaching the sash-weights to a sash. **sash-tool** a glazier's or painter's brush for work on sash-windows. **sash-weight** a weight attached to each end of a sash to balance it at any height. **sash-window** a window with one or two sashes of which one or each can be slid vertically over the other to make an opening. ▫▫ **sashed** *adj.* [*sashes* corrupt. of CHASSIS, mistaken for pl.]

sashay /sáshay/ *v.intr.* esp. *US colloq.* walk or move ostentatiously, casually, or diagonally. [corrupt. of CHASSÉ]
■ see SWAGGER *v.* 1.

sashimi /sáshimi/ *n.* a Japanese dish of garnished raw fish in thin slices. [Jap.]

sasin /sássin/ *n.* = BLACKBUCK. [Nepali]

sasine /séssin/ *n. Sc. Law* **1** the possession of feudal property. **2** an act or document granting this. [var. of SEISIN]

Sask. *abbr.* Saskatchewan.

sasquatch /sáskwach/ *n.* a supposed yeti-like animal of NW America. [Amer. Ind.]

sass /sass/ *n.* & *v. US colloq.* ● *n.* impudence, cheek. ● *v.tr.* be impudent to, cheek. [var. of SAUCE]
■ *n.* see SAUCE *n.* 3.

sassaby /sássəbi/ *n.* (*pl.* **-ies**) a S. African antelope, *Damaliscus lunatus*, similar to the hartebeest. [Setswana *tsessébe*, *-ábi*]

sassafras /sássəfrass/ *n.* **1** a small tree, *Sassafras albidum*, native to N. America, with aromatic leaves and bark. **2** a preparation of oil extracted from the leaves or bark of this tree, used medicinally or in perfumery. [Sp. *sasafrás* or Port. *sassafraz*, of unkn. orig.]

Sassanian /sasáyniən/ *n.* & *adj.* (also **Sassanid** /sássənid/) ● *n.* a member of a Persian dynasty ruling 211-651. ● *adj.* of or relating to this dynasty. [*Sasan*, founder of the dynasty]

Sassenach /sássənakh, -nak/ *n.* & *adj. Sc.* & *Ir.* usu. *derog.* ● *n.* an English person. ● *adj.* English. [Gael. *Sasunnoch*, Ir. *Sasanach* f. L *Saxones* Saxons]

sassy /sássi/ *adj.* (**sassier, sassiest**) esp. *US colloq.* = SAUCY. ▫▫ **sassily** *adv.* **sassiness** *n.* [var. of SAUCY]

sastrugi /sastróogi/ *n.pl.* wavelike irregularities on the surface of hard polar snow, caused by winds. [Russ. *zastrugi* small ridges]

Sat. *abbr.* Saturday.

sat *past* and *past part.* of SIT.

Satan /sáyt'n/ *n.* the Devil; Lucifer. [OE f. LL f. Gk f. Heb. *śāṭān* lit. 'adversary' f. *śaṭan* oppose, plot against]
■ see DEVIL *n.* 1, 2.

satanic /sətánnik/ *adj.* **1** of, like, or befitting Satan. **2** diabolical, hellish. ▫▫ **satanically** *adv.*
■ diabolic, fiendish, devilish, Mephistophelian, demonic, demoniac(al), infernal, cacodemonic, ghoulish; hellish, diabolical, evil, wicked, iniquitous, corrupt, depraved, perverted, perverse, godless, ungodly, impious, unholy, sinister, dark, black, immoral, amoral; dire, monstrous, heinous, atrocious, hideous, horrible, horrendous, horrid, horrifying, loathsome, vile, abhorrent, unspeakable, damnable, despicable, abominable.

Satanism /sáytəniz'm/ *n.* **1** the worship of Satan, with a travesty of Christian forms. **2** the pursuit of evil for its own sake. **3** deliberate wickedness. ▫▫ **Satanist** *n.* **Satanize** *v.tr.* (also **-ise**).

Satanology /sáytənólləji/ *n.* **1** beliefs concerning the Devil. **2** a history or collection of these.

satay /sáttay/ *n.* (also **satai, saté**) an Indonesian and Malaysian dish consisting of small pieces of meat grilled on a skewer and usu. served with spiced sauce. [Malayan *satai sate*, Indonesian *sate*]

SATB *abbr. Mus.* soprano, alto, tenor, and bass (as a combination of voices).

satchel /sáchəl/ *n.* a small bag usu. of leather and hung from the shoulder with a strap, for carrying books etc. esp. to and from school. [ME f. OF *sachel* f. L *saccellus* (as SACK[1])]
■ see BAG *n.* 1, 2a.

sate /sayt/ *v.tr.* **1** gratify (desire, or a desirous person) to the full. **2** cloy, surfeit, weary with over-abundance (*sated with pleasure*). ▫▫ **sateless** *adj. poet.* [prob. f. dial. *sade*, OE *sadian* (as SAD), assim. to SATIATE]
■ **1** satiate, slake, satisfy, gratify, content, quench. **2** satiate, stuff, glut, gorge, cloy, surfeit, overfill, overstuff, pall, overindulge, saturate, deluge, flood, suffocate; weary, exhaust, bore, tire, jade.

sateen /satéen/ *n.* cotton fabric woven like satin with a glossy surface. [*satin* after *velveteen*]

satellite /sáttəlīt/ *n.* & *adj.* ● *n.* **1** a celestial body orbiting the earth or another planet. **2** an artificial body placed in orbit round the earth or another planet. **3** a follower; a hanger-on. **4** an underling; a member of an important person's staff or retinue. **5** (in full **satellite State**) a small country etc. nominally independent but controlled by or dependent on another. ● *adj.* **1** transmitted by satellite (*satellite communications*; *satellite television*). **2** esp. *Computing* secondary; dependent; minor (*networks of small satellite computers*). ▫ **satellite dish** a concave dish-shaped aerial for receiving broadcasting signals transmitted by satellite. **satellite town** a small town economically or otherwise dependent on a nearby larger town. ▫▫ **satellitic** /-líttik/ *adj.* **satellitism** *n.* [F *satellite* or L *satelles satellitis* attendant]
■ *n.* **1** moon, planet. **2** sputnik, spacecraft, rocket. **3** follower, disciple, shadow, hanger-on, parasite, sycophant, *derog.* minion. **4** underling, *derog.* minion; aide-de-camp, assistant, attendant, acolyte, *esp. US* aide, *hist.* retainer. ● *adj.* **2** secondary, dependent, minor, subsidiary, ancillary.

sati var. of SUTTEE.

satiate /sáyshiayt/ *adj.* & *v.* ● *adj. archaic* satiated. ● *v.tr.* = SATE. ▫▫ **satiable** /-shəb'l/ *adj. archaic.* **satiation** /-áysh'n/ *n.* [L *satiatus* past part. of *satiare* f. *satis* enough]

satiety /sətī́-iti/ *n.* **1** the state of being glutted or satiated. **2** the feeling of having too much of something. **3** (foll. by *of*) a cloyed dislike of. ▫ **to satiety** to an extent beyond what is desired. [obs. F *sacieté* f. L *satietas -tatis* f. *satis* enough]
■ **1** surfeit, glut, superabundance, overindulgence, saturation, excess, superfluity. **3** excess, surfeit; see also DISGUST *n.* 2.

satin /sáttin/ *n.*, *adj.*, & *v.* ● *n.* a fabric of silk or various man-made fibres, with a glossy surface on one side produced by a twill weave with the weft-threads almost hidden. ● *adj.* smooth as satin. ● *v.tr.* (**satined, satining**) give a glossy surface to (paper). ▫ **satin finish 1** a polish given to silver etc. with a metallic brush. **2** any effect resembling satin in texture produced on materials in various ways. **satin paper** fine glossy writing paper. **satin spar** a fibrous variety of gypsum. **satin stitch** a long straight embroidery stitch, giving the appearance of satin. **satin white** a white pigment of calcium sulphate and alumina. ▫▫ **satinized** *adj.* (also **-ised**). **satiny** *adj.* [ME f. OF f. Arab. *zaytūnī* of *Tseutung* in China]
■ ▫▫ **satiny** see SILKY 1.

satinette /sáttinét/ *n.* (also **satinet**) a satin-like fabric made partly or wholly of cotton or synthetic fibre.

satinflower /sáttinflowr/ *n.* **1** any plant of the genus *Clarkia*, with pink or lavender flowers. **2** = HONESTY 3.

satinwood /sáttinwŏŏd/ *n.* **1 a** (in full **Ceylon satinwood**) a tree, *Chloroxylon swietenia*, native to central and southern India and Ceylon. **b** (in full **West Indian satinwood**) a tree, *Fagara flava*, native to the West Indies, Bermuda, the Bahamas, and southern Florida. **2** the yellow glossy timber of either of these trees.

satire /sáttīr/ *n.* **1** the use of ridicule, irony, sarcasm, etc., to expose folly or vice or to lampoon an individual. **2** a work or composition in prose or verse using satire. **3** this branch of literature. **4** a thing that brings ridicule upon something else. **5** *Rom. Antiq.* a poetic medley, esp. a poem ridiculing prevalent vices or follies. [F *satire* or L *satira* later form of *satura* medley]
■ **1** ridicule, irony, sarcasm, mockery, caricature, *colloq.* spoofing. **2** burlesque, lampoon, parody, pasquinade, caricature, *colloq.* take-off, spoof, *Brit. colloq.* send-up.

satiric /sətírrik/ *adj.* **1** of satire or satires. **2** containing satire (*wrote a satiric review*). **3** writing satire (*a satiric poet*). [F *satirique* or LL *satiricus* (as SATIRE)]

■ see SATIRICAL.

satirical /sətírrik'l/ *adj.* **1** = SATIRIC. **2** given to the use of satire in speech or writing or to cynical observation of others; sarcastic; humorously critical. ◻◻ **satirically** *adv.*
■ **2** satiric, ironic, sarcastic, mocking, irreverent, derisive, scornful, flippant, ridiculing, chaffing, teasing, *colloq.* spoofing.

satirist /sáttərist/ *n.* **1** a writer of satires. **2** a satirical person.
■ see WIT[1] 3.

satirize /sáttirīz/ *v.tr.* (also **-ise**) **1** assail or ridicule with satire. **2** write a satire upon. **3** describe satirically. ◻◻ **satirization** /-záysh'n/ *n.* [F *satiriser* (as SATIRE)]
■ **1** poke fun at, ridicule, make fun *or* sport of, pillory, deride, mock. **2, 3** lampoon, burlesque, parody, caricature, travesty, *Brit. colloq.* send up; mimic, imitate, *colloq.* take off.

satisfaction /sáttisfáksh'n/ *n.* **1** the act or an instance of satisfying; the state of being satisfied (*heard this with great satisfaction*). **2** a thing that satisfies desire or gratifies feeling (*is a great satisfaction to me*). **3** a thing that settles an obligation or pays a debt. **4 a** (foll. by *for*) atonement; compensation (*demanded satisfaction*). **b** *Theol.* Christ's atonement for the sins of mankind. ◻ **to one's satisfaction** so that one is satisfied. [ME f. OF f. L *satisfactio -onis* (as SATISFY)]
■ **1** gratification, comfort, delight, joy, pleasure, happiness, fulfilment, contentment, enjoyment. **2** comfort, delight, joy, pleasure. **4 a** payment, requital, repayment, reparation, compensation, remuneration, recompense, restitution, indemnity, indemnification, damages; redress, atonement, expiation, amends, retribution.

satisfactory /sáttisfáktəri, -tri/ *adj.* **1** adequate; causing or giving satisfaction (*was a satisfactory pupil*). **2** satisfying expectations or needs; leaving no room for complaint (*a satisfactory result*). ◻◻ **satisfactorily** *adv.* **satisfactoriness** *n.* [F *satisfactoire* or med.L *satisfactorius* (as SATISFY)]
■ adequate, sufficient, acceptable, passable, good enough, fair, *colloq.* OK, *Austral.* & *NZ sl.* jake; all right, not bad, *colloq.* all-right.

satisfy /sáttisfī/ *v.* (**-ies, -ied**) **1** *tr.* **a** meet the expectations or desires of; comply with (a demand). **b** be accepted by (a person, his taste) as adequate; be equal to (a preconception etc.). **2** *tr.* put an end to (an appetite or want) by supplying what was required. **3** *tr.* rid (a person) of an appetite or want in a similar way. **4** *intr.* give satisfaction; leave nothing to be desired. **5** *tr.* pay (a debt or creditor). **6** *tr.* adequately meet, fulfil, or comply with (conditions, obligations, etc.) (*has satisfied all the legal conditions*). **7** *tr.* (often foll. by *of*, *that*) provide with adequate information or proof, convince (*satisfied the others that they were right*; *satisfy the court of their innocence*). **8** *tr. Math.* (of a quantity) make (an equation) true. **9** *tr.* (in *passive*) **a** (foll. by *with*) contented or pleased with. **b** (foll. by *to*) demand no more than or consider it enough to do. ◻ **satisfy the examiners** reach the standard required to pass an examination. **satisfy oneself** (often foll. by *that* + clause) be certain in one's own mind. ◻◻ **satisfiable** *adj.* **satisfiability** /-fīəbilliti/ *n.* **satisfiedly** *adv.* **satisfying** *adj.* **satisfyingly** *adv.* [ME f. OF *satisfier* f. L *satisfacere satisfact-* f. *satis* enough]
■ **1a, 6** meet, comply with; see also FULFIL 4, 5. **1 b** gratify, please, fulfil, comfort, content; placate, appease, pacify. **2, 3** slake, quench, sate, satiate; meet, fulfil, provide for, look after, serve, answer, gratify, indulge. **4** see SUIT *v.* 2. **5** pay, repay, make good, settle, liquidate. **7** convince, persuade, assure; reassure, content; put a person's mind at rest. **9** (*be satisfied*) be contented *or* pleased *or* happy. ◻◻ **satisfying** gratifying, satisfactory, fulfilling, filling, satiating; comforting, pleasing, pacifying, pleasurable.

satori /sətóri/ *n. Buddhism* sudden enlightenment. [Jap.]

satrap /sátrap/ *n.* **1** a provincial governor in the ancient Persian empire. **2** a subordinate ruler, colonial governor, etc. [ME f. OF *satrape* or L *satrapa* f. Gk *satrapēs* f. OPers. *xšathra-pāvan* country-protector]

satrapy /sátrəpi/ *n.* (*pl.* **-ies**) a province ruled over by a satrap.

satsuma /sátsoomə/ *n.* **1** /also satsóómə/ a variety of tangerine orig. grown in Japan. **2** (**Satsuma**) (in full **Satsuma ware**) cream-coloured Japanese pottery. [*Satsuma* a province in Japan]

saturate /sáchərayt, sátyoorayt/ *v.tr.* **1** fill with moisture; soak thoroughly. **2** (often foll. by *with*) fill to capacity. **3** cause (a substance, solution, vapour, metal, or air) to absorb, hold, or combine with the greatest possible amount of another substance, or of moisture, magnetism, electricity, etc. **4** cause (a substance) to combine with the maximum amount of another substance. **5** supply (a market) beyond the point at which the demand for a product is satisfied. **6** (foll. by *with*, *in*) imbue with or steep in (learning, tradition, prejudice, etc.). **7** overwhelm (enemy defences, a target area, etc.) by concentrated bombing. **8** (as **saturated** *adj.*) **a** (of colour) full; rich; free from an admixture of white. **b** (of fat molecules) containing the greatest number of hydrogen atoms. ◻◻ **saturate** /-rət/ *adj. literary.* **saturable** /-rəb'l/ *adj.* **saturant** /-rənt/ *n.* & *adj.* [L *saturare* f. *satur* full]
■ **1** soak, drench, waterlog. **2** steep, fill; see also IMPREGNATE *v.* 1, 2. **5** flood, glut; overload; see also SWAMP *v.* **6** (*saturate with* or *in*) imbue *or* suffuse *or* impregnate *or* permeate with, steep in.

saturation /sáchəráysh'n, sátyooráysh'n/ *n.* the act or an instance of saturating; the state of being saturated. ◻ **saturation point** the stage beyond which no more can be absorbed or accepted.
■ see GLUT *n.*

Saturday /sáttərday, -di/ *n.* & *adv.* ● *n.* the seventh day of the week, following Friday. ● *adv. colloq.* **1** on Saturday. **2** (**Saturdays**) on Saturdays; each Saturday. [OE *Sætern(es) dæg* transl. of L *Saturni dies* day of Saturn]

Saturn /sáttərn/ *n.* **1 a** the sixth planet from the sun, with a system of broad flat rings circling it, and the most distant of the five planets known in the ancient world. **b** *Astrol.* Saturn as a supposed astrological influence on those born under its sign, characterized by coldness and gloominess. **2** *Alchemy* the metal lead. ◻◻ **Saturnian** /satúrniən/ *adj.* [L *Saturnus*, Roman god of agriculture, identified with Kronos, father of Zeus, perh. f. Etruscan]

saturnalia /sáttərnáyliə/ *n.* (*pl.* same or **saturnalias**) **1** (usu. **Saturnalia**) *Rom.Hist.* the festival of Saturn in December, characterized by unrestrained merrymaking for all, the predecessor of Christmas. **2** (as *sing.* or *pl.*) a scene of wild revelry or tumult; an orgy. ◻◻ **saturnalian** *adj.* [L, neut. pl. of *Saturnalis* (as SATURN)]
■ **2** see ORGY 1. ◻◻ **saturnalian** see EPICUREAN *adj.* 2.

saturnic /sətúrnik/ *adj. Med.* affected with lead-poisoning. ◻◻ **saturnism** /sáttərniz'm/ [SATURN 2]

saturniid /satúrni-id/ *n.* any large moth of the family Saturniidae, including emperor moths. [mod.L]

saturnine /sáttərnīn/ *adj.* **1 a** of a sluggish gloomy temperament. **b** (of looks etc.) dark and brooding. **2** *archaic* **a** of the metal lead. **b** *Med.* of or affected by lead-poisoning. ◻◻ **saturninely** *adv.* [ME f. OF *saturnin* f. med.L *Saturninus* (as SATURN)]
■ **1 a** see GLOOMY 2.

satyagraha /sutyaágrəhaa/ *n. Ind.* **1** *hist.* a policy of passive resistance to British rule advocated by Gandhi. **2** passive resistance as a policy. [Skr. f. *satya* truth + *āgraha* obstinacy]

satyr /sáttər/ *n.* **1** (in Greek mythology) one of a class of Greek woodland gods with a horse's ears and tail, or (in Roman representations) with a goat's ears, tail, legs, and budding horns. **2** a lustful or sensual man. **3** = SATYRID. [ME f. OF *satyre* or L *satyrus* f. Gk *saturos*]

satyriasis /sáttirī́əsiss/ *n. Med.* excessive sexual desire in men. [LL f. Gk *saturiasis* (as SATYR)]

satyric /sətírrik/ *adj.* (in Greek mythology) of or relating to satyrs. ◻ **satyric drama** a kind of ancient Greek comic play with a chorus of satyrs. [L *satyricus* f. Gk *saturikos* (as SATYR)]

satyrid /sətírrid/ *n.* any butterfly of the family Satyridae, with distinctive eyelike markings on the wings. [mod.L *Satyridae* f. the genus-name *Satyrus* (as SATYR)]

sauce /sawss/ *n.* & *v.* ● *n.* **1** any of various liquid or semi-solid preparations taken as a relish with food; the liquid constituent of a dish (*mint sauce*; *tomato sauce*; *chicken in a lemon sauce*). **2** something adding piquancy or excitement. **3** *colloq.* impudence, impertinence, cheek. **4** *US* stewed fruit etc. eaten as dessert or used as a garnish. ● *v.tr.* **1** *colloq.* be impudent to; cheek. **2** *archaic* **a** season with sauce or condiments. **b** add excitement to. □ **sauce-boat** a kind of jug or dish used for serving sauces etc. **sauce for the goose** what is appropriate in one case (by implication appropriate in others). □□ **sauceless** *adj.* [ME f. OF ult. f. L *salsus* f. *salere sals-* to salt f. *sal* salt]

■ *n.* **1** gravy, condiment, relish, dressing. **2** see SPICE *n.* 3a. **3** impertinence, sauciness, impudence, audacity, insolence, brazenness, pertness, disrespect, disrespectfulness, cheek, cheekiness, *colloq.* lip, *Brit. colloq.* backchat, brass, nerve, crust, *esp. US colloq.* sassiness, *US colloq.* back talk, sass, *sl.* gall. ● *v.* **2 b** see ENLIVEN 1.

saucepan /sáwspən/ *n.* a usu. metal cooking pan, usu. round with a lid and a long handle at the side, used for boiling, stewing, etc., on top of a cooker. □□ **saucepanful** *n.* (*pl.* **-fuls**).

■ see PAN[1] *n.* 1.

saucer /sáwsər/ *n.* **1** a shallow circular dish used for standing a cup on and to catch drips. **2** any similar dish used to stand a plant pot etc. on. □□ **saucerful** *n.* (*pl.* **-fuls**). **saucerless** *adj.* [ME, = condiment-dish, f. OF *saussier(e)* sauce-boat, prob. f. LL *salsarium* (as SAUCE)]

saucy /sáwsi/ *adj.* (**saucier, sauciest**) **1** impudent, cheeky. **2** *colloq.* smart-looking (*a saucy hat*). **3** *colloq.* smutty, suggestive. □□ **saucily** *adv.* **sauciness** *n.* [earlier sense 'savoury', f. SAUCE]

■ **1** see IMPUDENT 1, 2. **2** jaunty, *colloq.* swish, natty, *sl.* snazzy. **3** see BAWDY *adj.* □□ **sauciness** see *impudence* (IMPUDENT).

Saudi /sówdi/ *n.* & *adj.* (also **Saudi Arabian**) ● *n.* (*pl.* **Saudis**) **1 a** a native or national of Saudi Arabia. **b** a person of Saudi descent. **2** a member of the dynasty founded by King Saud. ● *adj.* of or relating to Saudi Arabia or the Saudi dynasty. [A. Ibn-*Saud*, Arab. king d. 1953]

sauerkraut /sówərkrowt/ *n.* a German dish of chopped pickled cabbage. [G f. *sauer* SOUR + *Kraut* vegetable]

sauger /sáwgər/ *n.* *US* a small American pike-perch. [19th c.: orig. unkn.]

sauna /sáwnə/ *n.* **1** a Finnish-style steam bath. **2** a building used for this. [Finn.]

saunders var. of SANDERS.

saunter /sáwntər/ *v.* & *n.* ● *v.intr.* **1** walk slowly; amble, stroll. **2** proceed without hurry or effort. ● *n.* **1** a leisurely ramble. **2** a slow gait. □□ **saunterer** *n.* [ME, = muse: orig. unkn.]

■ *v.* walk, stroll, amble, ramble, wander, *colloq. or dial.* traipse, *sl.* mosey. ● *n.* **1** walk, ramble, stroll, amble, wander, *colloq. or dial.* traipse, *sl.* mosey. **2** see WALK *n.* 1, 2b.

saurian /sáwriən/ *adj.* of or like a lizard. [mod.L *Sauria* f. Gk *saura* lizard]

sauropod /sáwrōpod/ *n.* any of a group of plant-eating dinosaurs with a long neck and tail, and four thick limbs. [Gk *saura* lizard + *pous pod-* foot]

saury /sáwri/ *n.* (*pl.* **-ies**) a long-beaked marine fish, *Scomberesox saurus*, of temperate waters. [perh. f. LL f. Gk *sauros* horse-mackerel]

sausage /sóssij/ *n.* **1 a** minced pork, beef, or other meat seasoned and often mixed with other ingredients, encased in cylindrical form in a skin, for cooking and eating hot or cold. **b** a length of this. **2** a sausage-shaped object. □ **not a sausage** *colloq.* nothing at all. **sausage dog** *Brit. colloq.* a dachshund. **sausage machine 1** a sausage-making machine. **2** a relentlessly uniform process. **sausage meat** minced meat used in sausages or as a stuffing etc. **sausage roll** *Brit.* sausage meat enclosed in a pastry roll and baked. [ME f. ONF *saussiche* f. med.L *salsicia* f. L *salsus*: see SAUCE]

sauté /sṑtay/ *adj.*, *n.*, & *v.* ● *adj.* (esp. of potatoes etc.) quickly fried in a little hot fat. ● *n.* food cooked in this way. ● *v.tr.* (**sautéd** or **sautéed**) cook in this way. [F, past part. of *sauter* jump]

Sauternes /sōtérn/ *n.* a sweet white wine from Sauternes in the Bordeaux region of France.

savage /sávvij/ *adj.*, *n.*, & *v.* ● *adj.* **1** fierce; cruel (*savage persecution*; *a savage blow*). **2** wild; primitive (*savage tribes*; *a savage animal*). **3** *archaic* (of scenery etc.) uncultivated (*a savage scene*). **4** *colloq.* angry; bad-tempered (*in a savage mood*). **5** *Heraldry* (of the human figure) naked. ● *n.* **1** *Anthropol. derog.* a member of a primitive tribe. **2** a cruel or barbarous person. ● *v.tr.* **1** (esp. of a dog, wolf, etc.) attack and bite or trample. **2** (of a critic etc.) attack fiercely. □□ **savagedom** *n.* **savagely** *adv.* **savageness** *n.* **savagery** *n.* (*pl.* **-ies**). [ME f. OF *sauvage* wild f. L *silvaticus* f. *silva* a wood]

■ *adj.* **1** vicious, ferocious, fierce, beastly, bestial, brutish, bloodthirsty, brutal, cruel, ruthless, pitiless, merciless, harsh, bloody, unmerciful, barbarous, barbaric, murderous, demonic, demoniac, sadistic, *poet. or rhet.* fell. **2** primitive, uncivilized, bestial, inhuman, barbaric, barbarous, rude, wild; untamed, undomesticated, feral, unbroken. **4** angry, bad-tempered; see also NASTY 3. ● *n.* **1** wild man *or* woman. **2** see BEAST 2a. ● *v.* **2** see ATTACK *v.* 3.

savannah /səvánnə/ *n.* (also **savanna**) a grassy plain in tropical and subtropical regions, with few or no trees. [Sp. *zavana* perh. of Carib orig.]

■ see PLAIN[1] *n.*

savant /sávv'nt, savóN/ *n.* (*fem.* **savante** /sávv'nt or savóNt/) a learned person, esp. a distinguished scientist etc. [F, part. of *savoir* know (as SAPIENT)]

■ see SCHOLAR 1.

savate /səváat/ *n.* a form of boxing in which feet and fists are used. [F, orig. a kind of shoe: cf. SABOT]

save[1] /sayv/ *v.* & *n.* ● *v.* **1** *tr.* (often foll. by *from*) rescue, preserve, protect, or deliver from danger, harm, discredit, etc. (*saved my life*; *saved me from drowning*). **2** *tr.* (often foll. by *up*) keep for future use; reserve; refrain from spending (*saved up £150 for a new bike*; *likes to save plastic bags*). **3** *tr.* (often *refl.*) **a** relieve (another person or oneself) from spending (money, time, trouble, etc.); prevent exposure to (annoyance etc.) (*saved myself £50*; *a word processor saves time*). **b** obviate the need or likelihood of (*soaking saves scrubbing*). **4** *tr.* preserve from damnation; convert (*saved her soul*). **5** *tr.* & *refl.* husband or preserve (one's strength, health, etc.) (*saving himself for the last lap*; *save your energy*). **6** *intr.* (often foll. by *up*) save money for future use. **7** *tr.* **a** avoid losing (a game, match, etc.). **b** prevent an opponent from scoring (a goal etc.). **c** stop (a ball etc.) from entering the goal. ● *n.* **1** *Football* etc. the act of preventing an opponent's scoring etc. **2** *Bridge* a sacrifice-bid to prevent unnecessary losses. □ **save-all 1** a device to prevent waste. **2** *hist.* a pan with a spike for burning up candle-ends. **save appearances** present a prosperous, respectable, etc. appearance. **save-as-you-earn** *Brit.* a method of saving by regular deduction from earnings at source. **save one's breath** not waste time speaking to no effect. **save a person's face** see FACE. **save the situation** (or **day**) find or provide a solution to difficulty or disaster. **save one's skin** (or **neck** or **bacon**) avoid loss, injury, or death; escape from danger. **save the tide** get in or out (of port etc.) while it lasts. **save the trouble** avoid useless or pointless effort. □□ **savable** *adj.* (also **saveable**). [ME f. AF *sa(u)ver*, OF *salver*, *sauver* f. LL *salvare* f. L *salvus* SAFE]

■ *v.* **1** (come to a person's) rescue, deliver; (set) free, liberate, release, redeem, bail out; recover, salvage, retrieve; keep, preserve, guard, safeguard, protect, conserve, shelter, shield. **2** lay *or* put *or* set aside, lay *or* put by, lay *or* put away, keep; retain, reserve, preserve, conserve. **3 a** obviate, preclude, spare, prevent. **b** obviate, prevent, stop; see also PRECLUDE 2. **4** see REDEEM 4. **5** see CONSERVE *v.* 1. **6** scrimp, scrape; see also ECONOMIZE 1. □ **save the situation** (or **day**) come to the rescue.

save[2] /sayv/ *prep.* & *conj. archaic* or *poet.* ● *prep.* except; but (*all save him*). ● *conj.* (often foll. by *for*) unless; but; except (*happy save for one want*; *is well save that he has a cold*). [ME f. OF *sauf sauve* f. L *salvo*, *salva*, ablat. sing. of *salvus* SAFE]

saveloy /sávvəloy/ *n.* a seasoned red pork sausage, dried and smoked, and sold ready to eat. [corrupt. of F *cervelas*, *-at*, f. It. *cervellata* (*cervello* brain)]

saver /sáyvər/ *n.* **1** a person who saves esp. money. **2** (often in *comb.*) a device for economical use (of time etc.) (*found the short cut a time-saver*). **3** *Racing sl.* a hedging bet.

savin /sávvin/ *n.* (also **savine**) **1** a bushy juniper, *Juniperus sabina*, usu. spreading horizontally, and yielding oil formerly used in the treatment of amenorrhoea. **2** *US* = *red cedar*. [OE f. OF *savine* f. L *sabina* (*herba*) Sabine (herb)]

saving /sáyving/ *adj.*, *n.*, & *prep.* ● *adj.* (often in *comb.*) making economical use of (*labour-saving*). ● *n.* **1** anything that is saved. **2** an economy (*a saving in expenses*). **3** (usu. in *pl.*) money saved. ● *prep.* **1** with the exception of; except (*all saving that one*). **2** without offence to (*saving your presence*). □ **saving clause** *Law* a clause containing a stipulation of exemption etc. **saving grace 1** the redeeming grace of God. **2** a redeeming quality or characteristic. **savings account** a deposit account. **savings bank** a bank receiving small deposits at interest and returning the profits to the depositors. **savings certificate** *Brit.* an interest-bearing document issued by the Government for the benefit of savers. [ME f. SAVE[1]: prep. prob. f. SAVE[2] after *touching*]

■ *n.* **3** (*savings*) cache, nest egg; see also HOARD *n.* □ **saving grace 2** redeeming quality, good point; see also VIRTUE 4.

saviour /sáyvyər/ *n.* (*US* **savior**) **1** a person who saves or delivers from danger, destruction, etc. (*the saviour of the nation*). **2** (**Saviour**) (prec. by *the*, *our*) Christ. [ME f. OF *sauvëour* f. eccl.L *salvator -oris* (transl. Gk *sōtēr*) f. LL *salvare* SAVE[1]]

■ **1** rescuer, salvation, Good Samaritan, liberator, redeemer, deliverer, emancipator, champion, knight in shining armour. **2** (*the* or *our Saviour*) Christ, the Redeemer, Jesus, (the) Messiah, The Lamb (of God), Our Lord, the Son of God, the King of Kings, the Prince of Peace.

savoir faire /sávwaar fáir/ *n.* the ability to act suitably in any situation; tact. [F, = know how to do]

■ tact, tactfulness, discretion; sophistication, finesse, urbanity, knowledgeability, diplomacy, smoothness, polish, suavity, suaveness, poise, grace, style, skill, adroitness, knowledge, *sl.* savvy.

savoir vivre /sávwaar veévrə/ *n.* knowledge of the world and the ways of society; ability to conduct oneself well; sophistication. [F, = know how to live]

■ knowledge; breeding, upbringing, polish; see also *sophistication* (SOPHISTICATE).

savor *US* var. of SAVOUR.

savory[1] /sáyvəri/ *n.* (*pl.* **-ies**) any herb of the genus *Satureia*, esp. *S. hortensis* and *S. montana*, used esp. in cookery. [ME *saverey*, perh. f. OE *sætherie* f. L *satureia*]

savory[2] *US* var. of SAVOURY.

savour /sáyvər/ *n.* & *v.* (*US* **savor**) ● *n.* **1** a characteristic taste, flavour, relish, etc. **2** a quality suggestive of or containing a small amount of another. **3** *archaic* a characteristic smell. ● *v.* **1** *tr.* **a** appreciate and enjoy the taste of (food). **b** enjoy or appreciate (an experience etc.). **2** *intr.* (foll. by *of*) **a** suggest by taste, smell, etc. (*savours of mushrooms*). **b** imply or suggest a specified quality (*savours of impertinence*). □□ **savourless** *adj.* [ME f. OF f. L *sapor -oris* f. *sapere* to taste]

■ *n.* **1** taste, flavour, zest, tang, piquancy. **2** hint, suggestion, redolence, smack, breath, trace, quality, soupçon, dash. **3** odour, scent, fragrance, smell, perfume, redolence, bouquet, breath. ● *v.* **1** enjoy, relish, appreciate; smack one's lips over; indulge in, bask in, revel in, delight in, value, cherish, luxuriate in. **2 b** (*savour of*) see SUGGEST 2.

savoury /sáyvəri/ *adj.* & *n.* (*US* **savory**) ● *adj.* **1** having an appetizing taste or smell. **2** (of food) salty or piquant, not sweet (*a savoury omelette*). **3** pleasant; acceptable. ● *n.* (*pl.* **-ies**) *Brit.* a savoury dish served as an appetizer or at the end of dinner. □□ **savourily** *adv.* **savouriness** *n.* [ME f. OF *savouré* past part. (as SAVOUR)]

■ *adj.* **1** palatable, delicious, tasty, toothsome, appetizing, flavourful, flavorous, flavoursome, ambrosial, *colloq.* luscious, *literary* delectable. **3** acceptable, pleasant, honest, proper, decent, reputable, respectable, honourable, creditable, upright, decorous, seemly, wholesome. ● *n.* appetizer, hors-d'œuvre, starter.

savoy /səvóy/ *n.* a hardy variety of cabbage with wrinkled leaves. [*Savoy* in SE France]

Savoyard /səvóyaard, sávvoyaárd/ *n.* & *adj.* ● *n.* a native of Savoy in SE France. ● *adj.* of or relating to Savoy or its people etc. [F f. *Savoie* Savoy]

savvy /sávvi/ *v.*, *n.*, & *adj. sl.* ● *v.intr.* & *tr.* (**-ies**, **-ied**) know. ● *n.* knowingness; shrewdness; understanding. ● *adj.* (**savvier**, **savviest**) *US* knowing; wise. [orig. Black & Pidgin E after Sp. *sabe usted* you know]

■ *n.* see UNDERSTANDING *n.* 1. ● *adj.* see INTELLIGENT 2.

saw[1] /saw/ *n.* & *v.* ● *n.* **1 a** a hand tool having a toothed blade used to cut esp. wood with a to-and-fro movement. **b** any of several mechanical power-driven devices with a toothed rotating disk or moving band, for cutting. **2** *Zool.* etc. a serrated organ or part. ● *v.* (*past part.* **sawn** /sawn/ or **sawed**) **1** *tr.* **a** cut (wood etc.) with a saw. **b** make (boards etc.) with a saw. **2** *intr.* use a saw. **3 a** *intr.* move to and fro with a motion as of a saw or person sawing (*sawing away on his violin*). **b** *tr.* divide (the air etc.) with gesticulations. □ **saw-doctor** a machine for making the teeth of a saw. **saw-edged** with a jagged edge like a saw. **saw-frame** a frame in which a saw-blade is held taut. **saw-gate** = *saw-frame*. **saw-gin** = *cotton-gin*. **saw-horse** a rack supporting wood for sawing. **sawn-off** (*US* **sawed-off**) **1** (of a gun) having part of the barrel sawn off to make it easier to handle and give a wider field of fire. **2** *colloq.* (of a person) short. **saw-pit** a pit in which the lower of two men working a pit-saw stands. **saw-set** a tool for wrenching saw-teeth in alternate directions to allow the saw to work freely. **saw-wort** a composite plant, *Serratula tinctoria*, yielding a yellow dye from its serrated leaves. □□ **sawlike** *adj.* [OE *saga* f. Gmc]

saw[2] *past* of SEE[1].

saw[3] /saw/ *n.* a proverb; a maxim (*that's just an old saw*). [OE *sagu* f. Gmc, rel. to SAY: cf. SAGA]

■ proverb, maxim, saying, aphorism, apophthegm, axiom, adage, epigram, gnome, byword, slogan, motto, dictum.

sawbill /sáwbil/ *n.* a merganser.

sawbones /sáwbōnz/ *n. sl.* a doctor or surgeon.

■ see DOCTOR *n.* 1a.

sawbuck /sáwbuk/ *n.* *US* **1** a saw-horse. **2** *sl.* a $10 note.

sawdust /sáwdust/ *n.* powdery particles of wood produced in sawing.

sawfish /sáwfish/ *n.* any large marine fish of the family Pristidae, with a toothed flat snout used as a weapon.

sawfly /sáwflī/ *n.* (*pl.* **-flies**) any insect of the superfamily Tenthredinoidea, with a serrated ovipositor, the larvae of which are injurious to plants.

sawmill /sáwmil/ *n.* a factory in which wood is sawn mechanically into planks or boards.

sawn *past part.* of SAW[1].

sawtooth /sáwtōōth/ *adj.* **1** (also **sawtoothed** /-tōōtht/) (esp. of a roof, wave, etc.) shaped like the teeth of a saw with one steep and one slanting side. **2** (of a wave-form) showing a slow linear rise and rapid linear fall.

sawyer /sáwyər/ *n.* **1** a person who saws timber professionally. **2** *US* an uprooted tree held fast by one end in a river. **3** *NZ* a large wingless horned grasshopper whose grubs bore in wood. [ME, earlier *sawer*, f. SAW[1]]

sax[1] /saks/ *n. colloq.* **1** a saxophone. **2** a saxophone-player. □□ **saxist** *n.* [abbr.]

sax[2] /saks/ *n.* (also **zax** /zaks/) a slater's chopper, with a point for making nail-holes. [OE *seax* knife f. Gmc]

saxatile /sáksətīl, -til/ *adj.* living or growing on or among rocks. [F *saxatile* or L *saxatilis* f. *saxum* rock]

saxboard /sáksbord/ *n.* the uppermost strake of an open boat. [SAX[2] + BOARD]

saxe /saks/ *n.* (in full **saxe blue**) (often *attrib.*) a lightish blue colour with a greyish tinge. [F, = Saxony, the source of a dye of this colour]

saxhorn /sáks-horn/ *n.* any of a series of different-sized brass wind instruments with valves and a funnel-shaped mouthpiece, used mainly in military and brass bands. [*Sax*, name of its Belgian inventors, + HORN]

saxicoline /saksíkkəlīn/ *adj.* (also **saxicolous**) *Biol.* = SAXATILE. [mod.L *saxicolus* f. *saxum* rock + *colere* inhabit]

saxifrage /sáksifrayj/ *n.* any plant of the genus *Saxifraga*, growing on rocky or stony ground and usu. bearing small white, yellow, or red flowers. [ME f. OF *saxifrage* or LL *saxifraga* (*herba*) f. L *saxum* rock + *frangere* break]

Saxon /sáks'n/ *n.* & *adj.* ● *n.* **1** *hist.* **a** a member of the Germanic people that conquered parts of England in 5th–6th c. **b** (usu. **Old Saxon**) the language of the Saxons. **2** = ANGLO-SAXON. **3** a native of modern Saxony in Germany. **4** the Germanic (as opposed to Latin or Romance) elements of English. ● *adj.* **1** *hist.* of or concerning the Saxons. **2** belonging to or originating from the Saxon language or Old English. **3** of or concerning modern Saxony or Saxons. □ **Saxon architecture** the form of Romanesque architecture preceding the Norman in England. **Saxon blue** a solution of indigo in sulphuric acid as a dye. □□ **Saxondom** *n.* **Saxonism** *n.* **Saxonist** *n.* **Saxonize** /-nīz/ *v.tr.* & *intr.* (also **-ise**). [ME f. OF f. LL *Saxo -onis* f. Gk *Saxones* (pl.) f. WG: cf. OE *Seaxan, Seaxe* (pl.)]

saxony /sáksəni/ *n.* **1** a fine kind of wool. **2** cloth made from this. [*Saxony* in Germany f. LL *Saxonia* (as SAXON)]

saxophone /sáksəfōn/ *n.* **1** a keyed brass reed instrument in several sizes and registers, used esp. in jazz and dance music. **2** a saxophone-player. □□ **saxophonic** /-fónnik/ *adj.* **saxophonist** /-sóffənist, -səfōnist/ *n.* [*Sax* (as SAXHORN) + -PHONE]

say /say/ *v.* & *n.* ● *v.* (*3rd sing. present* **says** /sez/; *past* and *past part.* **said** /sed/) **1** *tr.* (often foll. by *that* + clause) **a** utter (specified words) in a speaking voice; remark (*said 'Damn!'*; *said that he was satisfied*). **b** put into words; express (*that was well said*; *cannot say what I feel*). **2** *tr.* (often foll. by *that* + clause) **a** state; promise or prophesy (*says that there will be war*). **b** have specified wording; indicate (*says here that he was killed*; *the clock says ten to six*). **3** *tr.* (in *passive*; usu. foll. by *to* + infin.) be asserted or described (*is said to be 93 years old*). **4** *tr.* (foll. by *to* + infin.) *colloq.* tell a person to do something (*he said to bring the car*). **5** *tr.* convey (information) (*spoke for an hour but said little*). **6** *tr.* put forward as an argument or excuse (*much to be said in favour of it*; *what have you to say for yourself?*). **7** *tr.* (often *absol.*) form and give an opinion or decision as to (*who did it I cannot say*; *do say which you prefer*). **8** *tr.* select, assume, or take as an example or (a specified number etc.) as near enough (*shall we say this one?*; *paid, say, £20*). **9** *tr.* **a** speak the words of (prayers, Mass, a grace, etc.). **b** repeat (a lesson etc.); recite (*can't say his tables*). **10** *tr. Art* etc. convey (inner meaning or intention) (*what is the director saying in this film?*). **11** *intr.* **a** speak; talk. **b** (in *imper.*) *poet.* tell me (*what is your name, say!*). **12** *tr.* (**the said**) *Law* or *joc.* the previously mentioned (*the said witness*). **13** *intr.* (as *int.*) *US* an exclamation of surprise, to attract attention, etc. ● *n.* **1 a** an opportunity for stating one's opinion etc. (*let him have his say*). **b** a stated opinion. **2** a share in a decision (*had no say in the matter*). □ **how say you?** *Law* how do you find? (addressed to the jury requesting its verdict). **I** etc. **cannot** (or **could not**) **say** I etc. do not know. **I'll say** *colloq.* yes indeed. **I say!** *Brit.* an exclamation expressing surprise, drawing attention, etc. **it is said** the rumour is that. **not to say** and indeed; or possibly even (*his language was rude not to say offensive*). **said he** (or **I** etc.) *colloq.* or *poet.* he etc. said. **say for oneself** say by way of conversation, oratory, etc. **say much** (or **something**) **for** indicate the high quality of. **say no** refuse or disagree. **say out** express fully or candidly. **says I** (or **he** etc.) *colloq.* I, he, etc., said (used in reporting conversation). **say-so 1** the power of decision. **2** mere assertion (*cannot proceed merely on his say-so*). **say something** make a short speech. **says you!** *colloq.* I disagree. **say when** *colloq.* indicate when enough drink or food has been given. **say the word 1** indicate that you agree or give permission. **2** give the order etc. **say yes** agree. **that is to say 1** in other words, more explicitly. **2** or at least. **they say** it is rumoured. **to say nothing of** = *not to mention* (see MENTION). **what do** (or **would**) **you say to?** would you like? **when all is said and done** after all, in the long run. **you can say that again!** (or **you said it!**) *colloq.* I agree emphatically. **you don't say so** *colloq.* an expression of amazement or disbelief. □□ **sayable** *adj.* **sayer** *n.* [OE *secgan* f. Gmc]

■ *v.* **1 a** remark, state, affirm, declare, utter, maintain, hold, assert, claim, asseverate, announce, *formal* aver. **b** tell, put, express, verbalize, communicate, explain, reveal, impart. **2 a** state; promise, prophesy, predict, prognosticate, foretell. **3** (*be said*) be described, be mentioned, be asserted, be suggested *or* hinted. **4** order *or* require *or* command a person, *archaic or literary* bid a person. **5** see COMMUNICATE 1a. **6** reply, respond, answer; see also STATE *v.* 1. **7** guess, estimate, conjecture, venture, imagine, believe, think, judge, decide; tell. **8** suppose, assume; for example, for instance, e.g.; approximately, about, roughly, *circa*, nearly. **9 a** deliver, utter, speak. **10** signify, denote, symbolize, communicate, indicate, convey, suggest, imply, mean, get across. **11 a** speak, talk, chat, declaim; see also SPEAK 1. **12** (*the said*) the aforementioned, the aforesaid; see also *preceding* (PRECEDE). ● *n.* **1 a** turn, chance, opportunity, moment. **2** voice, authority, influence, power, weight, sway, *colloq.* clout. □ **I** etc. **cannot** (or **could not**) **say** I etc. do not know, *colloq.* I etc. have no idea; see also *ask me another*. **I'll say** see ABSOLUTELY 6. **it is said** it is alleged *or* reported *or* rumoured *or* whispered *or* bruited about *or* put about *or* noised (abroad), they say, the rumour is, rumour has it. **say no** see DIFFER 2; (*say no to*) see REFUSE[1] 1. **say out** see EXPRESS[1] 1, 2. **say-so 1** authority, say; word; authorization. **say yes** see CONSENT *v.* **that is to say 1** see NAMELY. **they say** see *it is said* above. **when all is said and done** see EVENTUALLY. **you can say that again!** (or **you said it!**) see ABSOLUTELY 6. **you don't say so** well, I declare; well I never; *colloq.* well I'm damned, *sl.* well I'll be blowed.

SAYE *abbr. Brit.* save-as-you-earn.

saying /sáying/ *n.* **1** the act or an instance of saying. **2** a maxim, proverb, adage, etc. □ **as the saying goes** (or **is**) an expression used in introducing a proverb, cliché, etc. **go without saying** be too well known or obvious to need mention. **there is no saying** it is impossible to know.

■ **2** see MAXIM.

Sb *symb. Chem.* the element antimony. [L *stibium*]

SBN *abbr.* Standard Book Number (cf. ISBN).

S. by E. *abbr.* South by East.

S. by W. *abbr.* South by West.

SC *abbr.* **1** *US* South Carolina (also in official postal use). **2** special constable.

Sc *symb. Chem.* the element scandium.

sc. *abbr.* scilicet.

■ see NAMELY.

s.c. *abbr.* small capitals.

scab /skab/ *n.* & *v.* ● *n.* **1** a dry rough crust formed over a cut, sore, etc. in healing. **2** (often *attrib.*) *colloq. derog.* a person who refuses to strike or join a trade union, or who tries to break a strike by working; a blackleg. **3** the mange or a similar skin disease esp. in animals. **4** a fungous plant-disease causing scablike roughness. **5** a dislikeable person. ● *v.intr.* (**scabbed, scabbing**) **1** act as a scab. **2** (of a wound etc.) form a scab; heal over. □□ **scabbed** *adj.* **scabby** *adj.* (**scabbier, scabbiest**). **scabbiness** *n.* **scablike** *adj.* [ME f. ON *skabbr* (unrecorded), corresp. to OE *sceabb*]

■ *n.* **2** strikebreaker, *Brit. derog.* blackleg.

scabbard /skábbərd/ *n.* **1** *hist.* a sheath for a sword, bayonet, etc. **2** *US* a sheath for a revolver etc. □ **scabbard-fish** any of various silvery-white marine fish shaped like a sword-scabbard, esp. *Lepidopus caudatus.* [ME *sca(u)berc* etc. f. AF prob. f. Frank.]

scabies /skáybeez/ *n.* a contagious skin disease causing severe itching (cf. ITCH). [ME f. L f. *scabere* scratch]

scabious /skáybiəss/ *n.* & *adj.* ● *n.* any plant of the genus *Scabiosa, Knautia,* etc., with pink, white, or esp. blue pincushion-shaped flowers. ● *adj.* affected with mange; scabby. [ME f. med.L *scabiosa (herba)* formerly regarded as a cure for skin disease: see SCABIES]

scabrous /skáybrəss/ *adj.* **1** having a rough surface; bearing short stiff hairs, scales, etc.; scurfy. **2** (of a subject, situation, etc.) requiring tactful treatment; hard to handle with decency. **3 a** indecent, salacious. **b** behaving licentiously. □□ **scabrously** *adv.* **scabrousness** *n.* [F *scabreux* or LL *scabrosus* f. L *scaber* rough]

■ **2** see DELICATE 3a. **3 a** see INDECENT 1. **b** see LEWD 1.

scad /skad/ *n.* any fish of the family Carangidae native to tropical and subtropical seas, usu. having an elongated body and very large spiky scales. [17th c.: orig. unkn.]

scads /skadz/ *n.pl. US colloq.* large quantities. [19th c.: orig. unkn.]

■ see LOT *n.* 1.

scaffold /skáffōld, -f'ld/ *n.* & *v.* ● *n.* **1 a** *hist.* a raised wooden platform used for the execution of criminals. **b** a similar platform used for drying tobacco etc. **2** = SCAFFOLDING. **3** (prec. by *the*) death by execution. ● *v.tr.* attach scaffolding to (a building). □□ **scaffolder** *n.* [ME f. AF f. OF *(e)schaffaut,* earlier *escadafaut*: cf. CATAFALQUE]

scaffolding /skáffōlding, -fəlding/ *n.* **1 a** a temporary structure formed of poles, planks, etc., erected by workmen and used by them while building or repairing a house etc. **b** materials used for this. **2** a temporary conceptual framework used for constructing theories etc.

■ **2** see FRAME *n.* 6a.

scagliola /skalyṓlə/ *n.* imitation stone or plaster mixed with glue. [It. *scagliuola* dimin. of *scaglia* SCALE[1]]

scalable /skáyləb'l/ *adj.* capable of being scaled or climbed. □□ **scalability** /-billiti/ *n.*

scalar /skáylər/ *adj.* & *n. Math.* & *Physics* ● *adj.* (of a quantity) having only magnitude, not direction. ● *n.* a scalar quantity (cf. VECTOR). [L *scalaris* f. *scala* ladder; see SCALE[3]]

scalawag var. of SCALLYWAG.

scald[1] /skawld, skold/ *v.* & *n.* ● *v.tr.* **1** burn (the skin etc.) with hot liquid or steam. **2** heat (esp. milk) to near boiling-point. **3** (usu. foll. by *out*) clean (a pan etc.) by rinsing with boiling water. **4** treat (poultry etc.) with boiling water to remove feathers etc. ● *n.* **1** a burn etc. caused by scalding. **2** a skin disease caused esp. by air pollution etc. affecting the fruits of some plants. □ **like a scalded cat** moving unusually fast. **scalded cream** a dessert made from milk scalded and allowed to stand. **scalding tears** hot bitter tears of grief etc. □□ **scalder** *n.* [ME f. AF, ONF *escalder,* OF *eschalder* f. LL *excaldare* (as EX-[1], L *calidus* hot)]

scald[2] var. of SKALD.

scale[1] /skayl/ *n.* & *v.* ● *n.* **1** each of the small thin bony or horny overlapping plates protecting the skin of fish and reptiles. **2** something resembling a fish-scale, esp.: **a** a pod or husk. **b** a flake of skin; a scab. **c** a rudimentary leaf, feather, or bract. **d** each of the structures covering the wings of butterflies and moths. **e** *Bot.* a layer of a bulb. **3 a** a flake formed on the surface of rusty iron. **b** a thick white deposit formed in a kettle, boiler, etc. by the action of heat on water. **4** plaque formed on teeth. ● *v.* **1** *tr.* remove scale or scales from (fish, nuts, iron, etc.). **2** *tr.* remove plaque from (teeth) by scraping. **3** *intr.* **a** (of skin, metal, etc.) form, come off in, or drop, scales. **b** (usu. foll. by *off*) (of scales) come off. □ **scale-armour** *hist.* armour formed of metal scales attached to leather etc. **scale-board** very thin wood used for the back of a mirror, picture, etc. **scale-bug** = *scale insect.* **scale-fern** any of various spleenworts, esp. *Asplenium ceterach.* **scale insect** any of various insects, esp. of the family Coccidae, clinging to plants and secreting a shieldlike scale as covering. **scale-leaf** a modified leaf resembling a scale. **scale-moss** a type of liverwort with scalelike leaves. **scales fall from a person's eyes** a person is no longer deceived (cf. Acts 9:18). **scale-winged** lepidopterous. **scale-work** an overlapping arrangement. □□ **scaled** *adj.* (also in *comb.*). **scaleless** /skáyl-liss/ *adj.* **scaler** *n.* [ME f. OF *escale* f. Gmc, rel. to SCALE[2]]

■ *n.* **1** flake; plate, lamina, lamella, scute, scutum. **2 a** pod, husk, shell, skin, case, *US* shuck. **c** squama. **4** tartar, plaque. □ **scales fall from a person's eyes** be undeceived.

scale[2] /skayl/ *n.* & *v.* ● *n.* **1 a** (often in *pl.*) a weighing machine or device (*bathroom scales*). **b** (also **scale-pan**) each of the dishes on a simple scale balance. **2** (**the Scales**) the zodiacal sign or constellation Libra. ● *v.tr.* (of something weighed) show (a specified weight) in the scales. □ **pair of scales** a simple balance. **throw into the scale** cause to be a factor in a contest, debate, etc. **tip** (or **turn**) **the scales 1** (usu. foll. by *at*) outweigh the opposite scale-pan (at a specified weight); weigh. **2** (of a motive, circumstance, etc.) be decisive. [ME f. ON *skál* bowl f. Gmc]

■ *n.* **1 a** see BALANCE *n.* 1.

scale[3] /skayl/ *n.* & *v.* ● *n.* **1** a series of degrees; a graded classification system (*pay fees according to a prescribed scale; high on the social scale; seven points on the Richter scale*). **2 a** (often *attrib.*) *Geog.* & *Archit.* a ratio of size in a map, model, picture, etc. (*on a scale of one centimetre to the kilometre; a scale model*). **b** relative dimensions or degree (*generosity on a grand scale*). **3** *Mus.* an arrangement of all the notes in any system of music in ascending or descending order (*chromatic scale; major scale*). **4 a** a set of marks on a line used in measuring, reducing, enlarging, etc. **b** a rule determining the distances between these. **c** a piece of metal, apparatus, etc. on which these are marked. **5** (in full **scale of notation**) *Math.* the ratio between units in a numerical system (*decimal scale*). ● *v.* **1** *tr.* **a** (also *absol.*) climb (a wall, height, etc.) esp. with a ladder. **b** climb (the social scale, heights of ambition, etc.). **2** *tr.* represent in proportional dimensions; reduce to a common scale. **3** *intr.* (of quantities etc.) have a common scale; be commensurable. □ **economies of scale** proportionate savings gained by using larger quantities. **in scale** (of drawing etc.) in proportion to the surroundings etc. **play** (or **sing**) **scales** *Mus.* perform the notes of a scale as an exercise for the fingers or voice. **scale down** make smaller in proportion; reduce in size. **scale up** make larger in proportion; increase in size. **scaling-ladder** *hist.* a ladder used to climb esp. fortress walls, esp. to break a siege. **to scale** with a uniform reduction or enlargement. □□ **scaler** *n.* [(n.) ME (= ladder): (v.) ME f. OF *escaler* or med.L *scalare* f. L *scala* f. *scandere* climb]

■ *n.* **1** ranking, graduation, hierarchy, range, classification. **2 a** proportion, ratio. ● *v.* **1** climb, ascend, mount, clamber up, go up. **2** regulate, prorate, standardize.

□ **scale down** decrease, reduce, diminish. **scale up** see ENLARGE 1, 3.

scalene /skáyleen/ *adj.* & *n.* ● *adj.* (esp. of a triangle) having sides unequal in length. ● *n.* **1** (in full **scalene muscle**) = SCALENUS. **2** a scalene triangle. □ **scalene cone** (or **cylinder**) a cone (or cylinder) with the axis not perpendicular to the base. [LL *scalenus* f. Gk *skalēnos* unequal, rel. to *skolios* bent]

scalenus /skəleénəss/ *n.* (*pl.* **scaleni** /-nī/) any of several muscles extending from the neck to the first and second ribs. [mod.L: see SCALENE]

scallawag var. of SCALLYWAG.

scallion /skályən/ *n.* a shallot or spring onion; any long-necked onion with a small bulb. [ME f. AF *scal(o)un* = OF *escalo(i)gne* ult. f. L *Ascalonia* (*caepa*) (onion) of *Ascalon* in anc. Palestine]

scallop /skólləp, skól-/ *n.* & *v.* (also **scollop** /skól-/) ● *n.* **1** any of various bivalve molluscs of the family Pectinidae, esp. of the genus *Chlamys* or *Pecten*, much prized as food. **2** (in full **scallop shell**) **a** a single valve from the shell of a scallop, with grooves and ridges radiating from the middle of the hinge and edged with small rounded lobes, often used for cooking or serving food. **b** *hist.* a representation of this shell worn as a pilgrim's badge. **3** (in *pl.*) an ornamental edging cut in material in imitation of a scallop-edge. **4** a small pan or dish shaped like a scallop shell and used for baking or serving food. ● *v.tr.* (**scalloped, scalloping**) **1** cook in a scallop. **2** ornament (an edge or material) with scallops or scalloping. □□ **scalloper** *n.* **scalloping** *n.* (in sense 3 of *n.*). [ME f. OF *escalope* prob. f. Gmc]

■ *v.* **2** pink, serrate, notch.

scallywag /skálliwag/ *n.* (also **scalawag, scallawag** /skállə-/) a scamp; a rascal. [19th-c. US sl.: orig. unkn.]

■ see RASCAL.

scalp /skalp/ *n.* & *v.* ● *n.* **1** the skin covering the top of the head, with the hair etc. attached. **2 a** *hist.* the scalp of an enemy cut or torn away as a trophy by an American Indian. **b** a trophy or symbol of triumph, conquest, etc. **3** *Sc.* a bare rock projecting above water etc. ● *v.tr.* **1** *hist.* take the scalp of (an enemy). **2** criticize savagely. **3** *US* defeat; humiliate. **4** *US colloq.* resell (shares, tickets, etc.) at a high or quick profit. □□ **scalpless** *adj.* [ME, prob. of Scand. orig.]

scalpel /skálp'l/ *n.* a surgeon's small sharp knife shaped for holding like a pen. [F *scalpel* or L *scalpellum* dimin. of *scalprum* chisel f. *scalpere* scratch]

scalper /skálpər/ *n.* **1** a person or thing that scalps (esp. in sense 4 of *v.*). **2** (also **scauper** /skáwpər/, **scorper** /skáwrpər/) an engraver's tool for hollowing out woodcut or linocut designs. [SCALP + -ER[1]: sense 2 also f. L *scalper* cutting tool f. *scalpere* carve]

scaly /skáyli/ *adj.* (**scalier, scaliest**) covered in or having many scales or flakes. □□ **scaliness** *n.*

■ imbricated, lamellar, laminar, lamellate, scutate; squamous, squamose, scurfy, *Med.* furfuraceous.

scam /skam/ *n. US sl.* **1** a trick or swindle; a fraud. **2** a story or rumour. [20th c.: orig. unkn.]

■ **1** see TRICK *n.* 1.

scammony /skámməni/ *n.* (*pl.* **-ies**) an Asian plant, *Convolvulus scammonia*, bearing white or pink flowers, the dried roots of which are used as a purgative. [ME f. OF *scamonee, escamonie* or L *scammonia* f. Gk *skammōnia*]

scamp[1] /skamp/ *n. colloq.* a rascal; a rogue. □□ **scampish** *adj.* [*scamp* rob on highway, prob. f. MDu. *schampen* decamp f. OF *esc(h)amper* (as EX-[1], L *campus* field)]

■ see RASCAL. □□ **scampish** see WICKED 3.

scamp[2] /skamp/ *v.tr.* do (work etc.) in a perfunctory or inadequate way. [perh. formed as SCAMP[1]: cf. SKIMP]

scamper /skámpər/ *v.* & *n.* ● *v.intr.* (usu. foll. by *about, through*) run and skip impulsively or playfully. ● *n.* the act or an instance of scampering. [prob. formed as SCAMP[1]]

■ *v.* see SCURRY *v.*

scampi /skámpi/ *n.pl.* **1** Norway lobsters. **2** (often treated as *sing.*) a dish of these, usu. fried. [It.]

scan /skan/ *v.* & *n.* ● *v.* (**scanned, scanning**) **1** *tr.* look at intently or quickly (*scanned the horizon*; *rapidly scanned the speech for errors*). **2** *intr.* (of a verse etc.) be metrically correct; be capable of being recited etc. metrically (*this line doesn't scan*). **3** *tr.* **a** examine all parts of (a surface etc.) to detect radioactivity etc. **b** cause (a particular region) to be traversed by a radar etc. beam. **4** *tr.* resolve (a picture) into its elements of light and shade in a prearranged pattern for the purposes esp. of television transmission. **5** *tr.* test the metre of (a line of verse etc.) by reading with the emphasis on its rhythm, or by examining the number of feet etc. **6** *tr.* **a** make a scan of (the body or part of it). **b** examine (a patient etc.) with a scanner. ● *n.* **1** the act or an instance of scanning. **2** an image obtained by scanning or with a scanner. □□ **scannable** *adj.* [ME f. L *scandere* climb: in LL = scan verses (from the raising of one's foot in marking rhythm)]

■ *v.* **1** glance at *or* through, look at *or* over, pass *or* run one's eye over, skim, read over, peruse, flick *or* flip through, thumb *or* leaf through. ● *n.* **1** look, survey, inspection, examination, overview. **2** see IMAGE *n.* 3, 4.

scandal /skánd'l/ *n.* **1 a** a thing or a person causing general public outrage or indignation. **b** the outrage etc. so caused, esp. as a subject of common talk. **c** malicious gossip or backbiting. **2** *Law* a public affront, esp. an irrelevant abusive statement in court. □ **scandal sheet** *derog.* a newspaper etc. giving prominence to esp. malicious gossip. □□ **scandalous** *adj.* **scandalously** *adv.* **scandalousness** *n.* [ME f. OF *scandale* f. eccl.L *scandalum* f. Gk *skandalon* snare, stumbling-block]

■ **1 a** disgrace, embarrassment, dishonour, discredit; defilement, stigma; blemish, spot, smirch, black mark, blot (on one's escutcheon), skeleton in the cupboard, *Brit.* blot on one's copybook. **b** shame, sin, outrage, disgrace; discredit, damage, ignominy, obloquy, dishonour, degradation, disrepute, infamy. **c** slander, libel, calumny, abuse, dirt, defamation; gossip, rumour, backbiting. □ **scandalous** shocking, disgraceful, ignominious, improper, indecorous, unseemly, infamous, outrageous, shameful, immodest, dishonourable, disreputable, sordid, despicable, wicked, sinful, iniquitous, profligate, immoral, atrocious, heinous, disgusting, taboo, unmentionable, unspeakable; defamatory, libellous, slanderous, calumnious, calumniatory, aspersive, abusive, injurious, scurrilous.

scandalize /skándəlīz/ *v.tr.* (also **-ise**) offend the moral feelings, sensibilities, etc. of; shock. [ME in sense 'make a scandal of' f. F *scandaliser* or eccl.L *scandaliso* f. Gk *skandalizō* (as SCANDAL)]

■ appal, shock, outrage, affront, offend, horrify, upset, disturb.

scandalmonger /skánd'lmunggər/ *n.* a person who spreads malicious scandal.

■ see GOSSIP *n.* 3.

Scandinavian /skándináyviən/ *n.* & *adj.* ● *n.* **1 a** a native or inhabitant of Scandinavia (Denmark, Norway, Sweden, and Iceland). **b** a person of Scandinavian descent. **2** the family of languages of Scandinavia. ● *adj.* of or relating to Scandinavia or its people or languages. [L *Scandinavia*]

scandium /skándiəm/ *n. Chem.* a rare soft silver-white metallic element occurring naturally in lanthanide ores. ¶ Symb.: **Sc**. [mod.L f. *Scandia* Scandinavia (source of the minerals containing it)]

scannable see SCAN.

scanner /skánnər/ *n.* **1** a device for scanning or systematically examining all the parts of something. **2** a machine for measuring the intensity of radiation, ultrasound reflections, etc., from the body as a diagnostic aid. **3** a person who scans or examines critically. **4** a person who scans verse.

scansion /skánsh'n/ *n.* **1** the metrical scanning of verse. **2** the way a verse etc. scans. [L *scansio* (LL of metre) f. *scandere scans-* climb]

■ **1** prosody. **2** rhythm, metre.

scant /skant/ *adj.* & *v.* ● *adj.* barely sufficient; deficient (*with scant regard for the truth*; *scant of breath*). ● *v.tr. archaic* provide (a supply, material, a person, etc.) grudgingly; skimp; stint. □□ **scantly** *adv.* **scantness** *n.* [ME f. ON *skamt* neut. of *skammr* short]
■ *adj.* see INSUFFICIENT.

scantling /skántling/ *n.* **1 a** a timber beam of small cross-section. **b** a size to which a stone or timber is to be cut. **2** a set of standard dimensions for parts of a structure, esp. in shipbuilding. **3** (usu. foll. by *of*) *archaic* **a** a specimen or sample. **b** one's necessary supply; a modicum or small amount. [alt. after -LING[1] f. obs. *scantlon* f. OF *escantillon* sample]

scanty /skánti/ *adj.* (**scantier, scantiest**) **1** of small extent or amount. **2** barely sufficient. □□ **scantily** *adv.* **scantiness** *n.* [obs. *scant* scanty supply f. ON *skamt* neut. adj.: see SCANT]
■ scant, sparse, scarce, meagre, slight, skimpy, minimal, small, little; barely adequate *or* sufficient, limited, insufficient, restricted, *colloq.* measly; short, in short supply, thin on the ground.

scape /skayp/ *n.* **1** a long flower-stalk coming directly from the root. **2** the base of an insect's antenna. [L *scapus* f. Gk *skapos*, rel. to SCEPTRE]

-scape /skayp/ *comb. form* forming nouns denoting a view or a representation of a view (*moonscape*; *seascape*). [after LANDSCAPE]

scapegoat /skáypgōt/ *n.* & *v.* ● *n.* **1** a person bearing the blame for the sins, shortcomings, etc. of others, esp. as an expedient. **2** *Bibl.* a goat sent into the wilderness after the Jewish chief priest had symbolically laid the sins of the people upon it (Lev. 16). ● *v.tr.* make a scapegoat of. □□ **scapegoater** *n.* [*scape* (archaic, = escape) + GOAT, = the goat that escapes]
■ *n.* **1** victim, cat's-paw, whipping-boy, man of straw, Aunt Sally, *sl.* fall guy. ● *v.* see ACCUSE 2.

scapegrace /skáypgrayss/ *n.* a rascal; a scamp, esp. a young person or child. [*scape* (as SCAPEGOAT) + GRACE = one who escapes the grace of God]
■ see RASCAL.

scaphoid /skáffoyd/ *adj.* & *n. Anat.* = NAVICULAR. [mod.L *scaphoides* f. Gk *skaphoeidēs* f. *skaphos* boat]

scapula /skápyoolə/ *n.* (*pl.* **scapulae** /-lee/ or **scapulas**) the shoulder-blade. [LL, sing. of L *scapulae*]

scapular /skápyoolər/ *adj.* & *n.* ● *adj.* of or relating to the shoulder or shoulder-blade. ● *n.* **1 a** a monastic short cloak covering the shoulders. **b** a symbol of affiliation to an ecclesiastical order, consisting of two strips of cloth hanging down the breast and back and joined across the shoulders. **2** a bandage for or over the shoulders. **3** a scapular feather. □ **scapular feather** a feather growing near the insertion of the wing. [(adj.) f. SCAPULA: (n.) f. LL *scapulare* (as SCAPULA)]

scapulary /skápyooləri/ *n.* (*pl.* **-ies**) **1** = SCAPULAR *n.* 1. **2** = SCAPULAR *n.* 3. [ME f. OF *eschapeloyre* f. med.L *scapelorium*, *scapularium* (as SCAPULA)]

scar[1] /skaar/ *n.* & *v.* ● *n.* **1** a usu. permanent mark on the skin left after the healing of a wound, burn, or sore. **2** the lasting effect of grief etc. on a person's character or disposition. **3** a mark left by damage etc. (*the table bore many scars*). **4** a mark left on the stem etc. of a plant by the fall of a leaf etc. ● *v.* (**scarred, scarring**) **1** *tr.* (esp. as **scarred** *adj.*) mark with a scar or scars (*was scarred for life*). **2** *intr.* heal over; form a scar. **3** *tr.* form a scar on. □□ **scarless** *adj.* [ME f. OF *eschar(r)e* f. LL *eschara* f. Gk *eskhara* scab]
■ *n.* **1** blemish, mark, disfigurement, cicatrice. ● *v.* **1** blemish, mark, disfigure, mar, wound, injure, damage.

scar[2] /skaar/ *n.* (also **scaur** /skawr/) a steep craggy outcrop of a mountain or cliff. [ME f. ON *sker* low reef in the sea]

scarab /skárrəb/ *n.* **1 a** the sacred dung-beetle of ancient Egypt. **b** = SCARABAEID. **2** an ancient Egyptian gem cut in the form of a beetle and engraved with symbols on its flat side, used as a signet etc. [L *scarabaeus* f. Gk *skarabeios*]

scarabaeid /skárrəbee-id/ *n.* any beetle of the family Scarabaeidae, including the dung-beetle, cockchafer, etc. [mod.L *Scarabaeidae* (as SCARAB)]

scaramouch /skárrəmoosh/ *n. archaic* a boastful coward; a braggart. [It. *Scaramuccia* stock character in Italian farce f. *scaramuccia* = SKIRMISH, infl. by F form *Scaramouche*]
■ see BRAGGART *n.*

scarce /skairss/ *adj.* & *adv.* ● *adj.* **1** (usu. *predic.*) (esp. of food, money, etc.) insufficient for the demand; scanty. **2** hard to find; rare. ● *adv. archaic* or *literary* scarcely. □ **make oneself scarce** *colloq.* keep out of the way; surreptitiously disappear. □□ **scarceness** *n.* [ME f. AF & ONF *(e)scars*, OF *eschars* f. L *excerpere*: see EXCERPT]
■ *adj.* **1** scanty, scant, insufficient, inadequate, deficient, meagre, wanting, lacking. **2** at a premium, in short supply, hard to find *or* come by; rare, unusual, few and far between, thin on the ground, seldom met with. ● *adv.* see HARDLY 1, 2. □ **make oneself scarce** see BOLT[1] *v.* 4a.

scarcely /skáirsli/ *adv.* **1** hardly; barely; only just (*I scarcely know him*). **2** surely not (*he can scarcely have said so*). **3** a mild or apologetic or ironical substitute for 'not' (*I scarcely expected to be insulted*).
■ **1** hardly, barely; only just, not quite, almost not. **2** surely *or* certainly *or* definitely not, not at all, not in the least, by no means, on no account, under no circumstances, nowise, noway. **3** see HARDLY 1, 2.

scarcity /skáirsiti/ *n.* (*pl.* **-ies**) (often foll. by *of*) a lack or inadequacy, esp. of food.
■ lack, want, need, paucity, dearth, insufficiency, shortage, inadequacy.

scare /skair/ *v.* & *n.* ● *v.* **1** *tr.* frighten, esp. suddenly (*his expression scared us*). **2** *tr.* (as **scared** *adj.*) (usu. foll. by *of*, or *to* + infin.) frightened; terrified (*scared of his own shadow*). **3** *tr.* (usu. foll. by *away*, *off*, *up*, etc.) drive away by frightening. **4** *intr.* become scared (*they don't scare easily*). ● *n.* **1** a sudden attack of fright (*gave me a scare*). **2** a general, esp. baseless, fear of war, invasion, epidemic, etc. (*a measles scare*). **3** a financial panic causing share-selling etc. □ **scaredy-cat** /skáirdikat/ *colloq.* a timid person. **scare-heading** (or **-head**) a shockingly sensational newspaper headline. **scare up** (or **out**) esp. *US* **1** frighten (game etc.) out of cover. **2** *colloq.* manage to find; discover (*see if we can scare up a meal*). □□ **scarer** *n.* [ME *skerre* f. ON *skirra* frighten f. *skjarr* timid]
■ *v.* **1** frighten, alarm, startle, shock, give a person a shock *or* a fright, terrify, terrorize, horrify, make a person's hair stand on end, *colloq.* scarify, scare the pants off, scare the life *or* the living daylights *or* the hell out of, scare out of one's wits, make a person's flesh creep *or* crawl, give a person goose bumps *or* goose-pimples, *US sl.* spook. **2** (**scared**) alarmed, afraid, shocked, terrified, horrified, startled, frightened, *colloq.* scared out of one's wits, *US sl.* spooked. **3** (*scare off*) see SHOO *v.* **4** frighten, shock, *US sl.* spook. ● *n.* **1** fright, shock, surprise, start. □ **scaredy-cat** see COWARD *n.* **scare up** (or **out**) **2** scrape together *or* up, find, dig up, discover, get, come by, gather, collect, *colloq.* raise.

scarecrow /skáirkrō/ *n.* **1** a human figure dressed in old clothes and set up in a field to scare birds away. **2** *colloq.* a badly-dressed, grotesque-looking, or very thin person. **3** *archaic* an object of baseless fear.

scaremonger /skáirmunggər/ *n.* a person who spreads frightening reports or rumours. □□ **scaremongering** *n.*

scarf[1] /skaarf/ *n.* (*pl.* **scarves** /skaarvz/ or **scarfs**) a square, triangular, or esp. long narrow strip of material worn round the neck, over the shoulders, or tied round the head (of a woman), for warmth or ornament. □ **scarf-pin** (or **-ring**) *Brit.* an ornamental device for fastening a scarf. **scarf-skin** the outermost layer of the skin constantly scaling off, esp. that at the base of the nails. **scarf-wise** worn diagonally across the body from shoulder to hip. □□ **scarfed** *adj.*

[prob. alt. of *scarp* (infl. by SCARF[2]) f. ONF *escarpe* = OF *escherpe* sash]
■ see MUFFLER 1.

scarf[2] /skaarf/ *v.* & *n.* ● *v.tr.* join the ends of (pieces of esp. timber, metal, or leather) by bevelling or notching them to fit and then bolting, brazing, or sewing them together; cut the blubber of (a whale). ● *n.* **1** a joint made by scarfing. **2** a cut on a whale made by scarfing. [ME (earlier as noun) prob. f. OF *escarf* (unrecorded) perh. f. ON]

scarifier /skárrifīər, skáir-/ *n.* **1** a thing or person that scarifies. **2** a machine with prongs for loosening soil without turning it. **3** a spiked road-breaking machine.

scarify[1] /skárrifī, skáir-/ *v.tr.* (**-ies, -ied**) **1 a** make superficial incisions in. **b** cut off skin from. **2** hurt by severe criticism etc. **3** loosen (soil) with a scarifier. □□ **scarification** /-fikáysh'n/ *n.* [ME f. F *scarifier* f. LL *scarificare* f. L *scarifare* f. Gk *skariphaomai* f. *skariphos* stylus]

scarify[2] /skáirifī/ *v.tr.* & *intr.* (**-ies, -ied**) *colloq.* scare; terrify.

scarious /skáiriəss/ *adj.* (of a part of a plant etc.) having a dry membranous appearance; thin and brittle. [F *scarieux* or mod.L *scariosus*]

scarlatina /skaárlәteénә/ *n.* = *scarlet fever.* [mod.L f. It. *scarlattina* (*febbre* fever) dimin. of *scarlatto* SCARLET]

scarlet /skaárlit/ *n.* & *adj.* ● *n.* **1** a brilliant red colour tinged with orange. **2** clothes or material of this colour (*dressed in scarlet*). ● *adj.* of a scarlet colour. □ **scarlet fever** an infectious bacterial fever, affecting esp. children, with a scarlet rash. **scarlet hat** *RC Ch.* a cardinal's hat as a symbol of rank. **scarlet pimpernel** a small annual wild plant, *Anagallis arvensis*, with small esp. scarlet flowers closing in rainy or cloudy weather: also called *poor man's weather-glass*. **scarlet rash** = ROSEOLA 1. **scarlet runner 1** a runner bean. **2** a scarlet-flowered climber bearing this bean. **scarlet woman** *derog.* a notoriously promiscuous woman, a prostitute. [ME f. OF *escarlate*: ult. orig. unkn.]

scaroid /skárroyd, skáir-/ *n.* & *adj.* ● *n.* any colourful marine fish of the family Scaridae, native to tropical and temperate seas, including the scarus. ● *adj.* of or relating to this family.

scarp /skaarp/ *n.* & *v.* ● *n.* **1** the inner wall or slope of a ditch in a fortification (cf. COUNTERSCARP). **2** a steep slope. ● *v.tr.* **1** make (a slope) perpendicular or steep. **2** provide (a ditch) with a steep scarp and counterscarp. **3** (as **scarped** *adj.*) (of a hillside etc.) steep; precipitous. [It. *scarpa*]
■ *n.* **2** see SLOPE *n.* 1–3. ● *v.* **3** (**scarped**) see STEEP[1] *adj.* 1.

scarper /skaárpər/ *v.intr. Brit. sl.* run away; escape. [prob. f. It. *scappare* escape, infl. by rhyming sl. *Scapa Flow* = go]
■ see RUN *v.* 2.

scarus /skáirəss/ *n.* any fish of the genus *Scarus*, with brightly coloured scales, and teeth fused to form a parrot-like beak used for eating coral. Also called *parrot-fish*. [L f. Gk *skaros*]

scarves *pl.* of SCARF[1].

scary /skáiri/ *adj.* (**scarier, scariest**) *colloq.* scaring, frightening. □□ **scarily** *adv.*
■ frightening, scaring, eerie, terrifying, hair-raising, unnerving, blood-curdling, horrifying, spine-chilling, horrendous, horrid, horrible, *colloq.* creepy, crawly, spooky.

scat[1] /skat/ *v.* & *int. colloq.* ● *v.intr.* (**scatted, scatting**) depart quickly. ● *int.* go! [perh. abbr. of SCATTER]
■ *int.* see SHOO *int.*

scat[2] /skat/ *n.* & *v.* ● *n.* improvised jazz singing using sounds imitating instruments, instead of words. ● *v.intr.* (**scatted, scatting**) sing scat. [prob. imit.]
■ *n.* improvisation, extemporization. ● *v.* see IMPROVISE 1.

scathe /skayth/ *v.* & *n.* ● *v.tr.* **1** *poet.* injure esp. by blasting or withering. **2** (as **scathing** *adj.*) witheringly scornful (*scathing sarcasm*). **3** (with *neg.*) do the least harm to (*shall not be scathed*) (cf. UNSCATHED). ● *n.* (usu. with *neg.*) *archaic* harm; injury (*without scathe*). □□ **scatheless** *predic.adj.* **scathingly** *adv.* [(v.) ME f. ON *skatha* = OE *sceathian*: (n.) OE f. ON *skathi* = OE *sceatha* malefactor, injury, f. Gmc]
■ *v.* **2** (**scathing**) searing, withering, scornful, damaging, harmful, severe, harsh, nasty, biting, acrid, acrimonious, mordant, incisive, cutting, virulent, vitriolic, acid, burning, fierce, savage, ferocious, *colloq.* scorching.
□□ **scatheless** see UNSCATHED.

scatology /skatóllәji/ *n.* **1 a** a morbid interest in excrement. **b** a preoccupation with obscene literature, esp. that concerned with the excretory functions. **c** such literature. **2** the study of fossilized dung. **3** the study of excrement for esp. diagnosis. □□ **scatological** /-tәlójik'l/ *adj.* [Gk *skōr skatos* dung + -LOGY]
■ **1 a** coprophilia. □□ **scatological** see FOUL *adj.* 5.

scatophagous /skatóffәgәss/ *adj.* feeding on dung. [as SCATOLOGY + Gk *-phagos* -eating]

scatter /skáttər/ *v.* & *n.* ● *v.* **1** *tr.* **a** throw here and there; strew (*scattered gravel on the road*). **b** cover by scattering (*scattered the road with gravel*). **2** *tr.* & *intr.* **a** move or cause to move in flight etc.; disperse (*scattered to safety at the sound*). **b** disperse or cause (hopes, clouds, etc.) to disperse. **3** *tr.* (as **scattered** *adj.*) not clustered together; wide apart; sporadic (*scattered villages*). **4** *tr. Physics* deflect or diffuse (light, particles, etc.). **5 a** *intr.* (of esp. a shotgun) fire a charge of shot diffusely. **b** *tr.* fire (a charge) in this way. ● *n.* (also **scattering**) **1** the act or an instance of scattering. **2** a small amount scattered. **3** the extent of distribution of esp. shot. □ **scatter cushions** (or **rugs**, etc.) cushions, rugs, etc., placed here and there for effect. **scatter-shot** *n.* & *adj. US* firing at random. □□ **scatterer** *n.* [ME, prob. var. of SHATTER]
■ *v.* **1 a** shower, sprinkle, strew, spread. **b** shower, sprinkle, besprinkle, strew, bestrew, litter; blanket. **2** dispel, diffuse; dissipate, go off, disappear; see also DISPERSE 1, 2a. **3** (**scattered**) see DIFFUSE *adj.* 1, SPORADIC. ● *n.* **2** (**scattering**) smattering, sprinkling, bit; suggestion, hint, soupçon, suspicion; see also TOUCH *n.* 3.

scatterbrain /skáttərbrayn/ *n.* a person given to silly or disorganized thought with lack of concentration. □□ **scatterbrained** *adj.*
■ □□ **scatterbrained** dazed, wool-gathering, dizzy, *colloq.* dopey, *Brit. colloq.* scatty, *sl.* dippy.

scatty /skátti/ *adj.* (**scattier, scattiest**) *Brit. colloq.* scatterbrained; disorganized. □□ **scattily** *adv.* **scattiness** *n.* [abbr.]

scaup /skawp/ *n.* any diving duck of the genus *Aythya*. [*scaup* Sc. var. of *scalp* mussel-bed, which it frequents]

scauper var. of SCALPER 2.

scaur var. of SCAR[2].

scavenge /skávvinj/ *v.* **1** *tr.* & *intr.* (usu. foll. by *for*) search for and collect (discarded items). **2** *tr.* remove unwanted products from (an internal-combustion engine cylinder etc.). [back-form. f. SCAVENGER]

scavenger /skávvinjər/ *n.* **1** a person who seeks and collects discarded items. **2** an animal, esp. a beetle, feeding on carrion, refuse, etc. **3** *Brit. archaic* a person employed to clean the streets etc. □□ **scavengery** *n.* [ME *scavager* f. AF *scawager* f. *scawage* f. ONF *escauwer* inspect f. Flem. *scauwen*, rel. to SHOW: for *-n-* cf. MESSENGER]

scazon /skáyz'n, skáz-/ *n. Prosody* a Greek or Latin metre of limping character, esp. a trimeter of two iambuses and a spondee or trochee. [L f. Gk *skazōn* f. *skazō* limp]

Sc.D. *abbr.* Doctor of Science. [L *scientiae doctor*]

SCE *abbr.* Scottish Certificate of Education.

scena /sháynaa/ *n. Mus.* **1** a scene or part of an opera. **2** an elaborate dramatic solo usu. including recitative. [It. f. L: see SCENE]

scenario /sinaáriō, -náiriō/ *n.* (*pl.* **-os**) **1** an outline of the plot of a play, film, opera, etc., with details of the scenes, situations, etc. **2** a postulated sequence of future events. □□ **scenarist** *n.* (in sense 1). [It. (as SCENA)]

■ **1** synopsis, plot (summary), schema, sequence of events; scheme, framework, structure.

scend /send/ *n.* & *v. Naut.* ● *n.* **1** the impulse given by a wave or waves (*scend of the sea*). **2** a plunge of a vessel. ● *v.intr.* (of a vessel) plunge or pitch owing to the impulse of a wave. [alt. f. SEND OR DESCEND]

scene /seen/ *n.* **1** a place in which events in real life, drama, or fiction occur; the locality of an event etc. (*the scene was set in India*; *the scene of the disaster*). **2 a** an incident in real life, fiction, etc. (*distressing scenes occurred*). **b** a description or representation of an incident etc. (*scenes of clerical life*). **3** a public incident displaying emotion, temper, etc., esp. when embarrassing to others (*made a scene in the restaurant*). **4 a** a continuous portion of a play in a fixed setting and usu. without a change of personnel; a subdivision of an act. **b** a similar section of a film, book, etc. **5 a** any of the pieces of scenery used in a play. **b** these collectively. **6** a landscape or a view (*a desolate scene*). **7** *colloq.* **a** an area of action or interest (*not my scene*). **b** a way of life; a milieu (*well-known on the jazz scene*). **8** *archaic* the stage of a theatre. □ **behind the scenes 1** *Theatr.* among the actors, scenery, etc. offstage. **2** unknown to the public; secret(ly). **behind-the-scenes** (*attrib.*) secret, using secret information (*a behind-the-scenes investigation*). **change of scene** a variety of surroundings esp. through travel. **come on the scene** arrive. **quit the scene** die; leave. **scene-dock** a space for storing scenery near the stage. **scene-shifter** a person who moves scenery in a theatre. **scene-shifting** this activity. **set the scene 1** describe the location of events. **2** give preliminary information. [L *scena* f. Gk *skēnē* tent, stage]

■ **1** location, site, place, area, locale, spot, locality, setting. **2 a** see INCIDENT *n.* 1. **3** commotion, upset, brouhaha, disturbance, furore, tantrum, argument, altercation, episode, incident, *colloq.* row. **4 b** episode, part, chapter, section, segment. **5 a** *Theatr.* flat. **b** scenery, *Theatr. mise en scène.* **6** view, sight, landscape, panorama, vista, picture, prospect. **7 a** see SPECIALITY 1. **b** see SPHERE *n.* 4. □ **behind the scenes 2** secret(ly), private(ly), clandestine(ly), confidential(ly), surreptitious(ly), *colloq.* on the q.t. **behind-the-scenes** see SECRET *adj.* 1, 2. **come on the scene** see ARRIVE 1. **quit the scene** see DIE[1] 1, LEAVE[1] *v.* 1b, 3, 4.

scenery /séenəri/ *n.* **1** the general appearance of the natural features of a landscape, esp. when picturesque. **2** *Theatr.* the painted representations of landscape, rooms, etc., used as the background in a play etc. □ **change of scenery** = *change of scene* (see SCENE). [earlier *scenary* f. It. SCENARIO: assim. to -ERY]

■ **1** see LANDSCAPE *n.* **2** see SET[2] 18.

scenic /séenik/ *adj.* **1 a** picturesque; impressive or beautiful (*took the scenic route*). **b** of or concerning natural scenery (*flatness is the main scenic feature*). **2** (of a picture etc.) representing an incident. **3** *Theatr.* of or on the stage (*scenic performances*). □ **scenic railway 1** a miniature railway running through artificial scenery at funfairs etc. **2** = *big dipper* 1. □□ **scenically** *adv.* [L *scenicus* f. Gk *skēnikos* of the stage (as SCENE)]

■ **1 a** picturesque, pretty, beautiful, impressive, grand, striking, spectacular, breathtaking, awesome, awe-inspiring.

scent /sent/ *n.* & *v.* ● *n.* **1** a distinctive, esp. pleasant, smell (*the scent of hay*). **2 a** a scent trail left by an animal perceptible to hounds etc. **b** clues etc. that can be followed like a scent trail (*lost the scent in Paris*). **c** the power of detecting or distinguishing smells etc. or of discovering things (*some dogs have little scent*; *the scent for talent*). **3** *Brit.* = PERFUME 2. **4** a trail laid in a paper-chase. ● *v.* **1** *tr.* **a** discern by scent (*the dog scented game*). **b** sense the presence of (*scent treachery*). **2** *tr.* make fragrant or foul-smelling. **3** *tr.* (as **scented** *adj.*) having esp. a pleasant smell (*scented soap*). **4** *intr.* exercise the sense of smell (*goes scenting about*). **5** *tr.* apply the sense of smell to (*scented the air*). □ **false scent 1** a scent trail laid to deceive. **2** false clues etc. intended to deflect pursuers. **on the scent** having a clue. **put** (or **throw**) **off the scent** deceive by false clues etc. **scent-bag** a bag of aniseed etc. used to lay a trail in drag-hunting. **scent-gland** (or **-organ**) a gland in some animals secreting musk, civet, etc. **scent out** discover by smelling or searching. □□ **scentless** *adj.* [ME *sent* f. OF *sentir* perceive, smell, f. L *sentire*; *-c-* (17th c.) unexpl.]

■ *n.* **1** fragrance, aroma, perfume, redolence, smell, odour, bouquet, whiff. **2 a** trail, spoor, track, smell. ● *v.* **1 a** smell, sniff (out). **b** discern, perceive, detect, distinguish, recognize, sense, smell, sniff. **3** (**scented**) see FRAGRANT. **5** perfume. □ **false scent 2** see *misinformation* (MISINFORM). **scent out** smell *or* sniff out, detect; see also DISCOVER 1a, b.

scepsis /sképsiss/ *n.* (*US* **skepsis**) **1** philosophic doubt. **2** sceptical philosophy. [Gk *skepsis* inquiry, doubt f. *skeptomai* consider]

■ Pyrrhonism; see also *scepticism* (SCEPTIC).

scepter *US* var. of SCEPTRE.

sceptic /sképtik/ *n.* & *adj.* (*US* **skeptic**) ● *n.* **1** a person inclined to doubt all accepted opinions; a cynic. **2** a person who doubts the truth of Christianity and other religions. **3** *hist.* a person who accepts the philosophy of Pyrrhonism. ● *adj.* = SCEPTICAL. □□ **scepticism** /-tisiz'm/ *n.* [F *sceptique* or L *scepticus* f. Gk *skeptikos* (as SCEPSIS)]

■ *n.* **1** doubter, questioner, doubting Thomas, Pyrrhonist, scoffer, cynic. **2** disbeliever, nullifidian, agnostic, dissenter; see also INFIDEL *n.* □□ **scepticism** doubt, dubiousness, doubtfulness, scepsis, Pyrrhonism, disbelief, unbelief, incredulity, incredulousness, cynicism, mistrust, distrust, mistrustfulness, distrustfulness, *literary* dubiety; agnosticism.

sceptical /sképtik'l/ *adj.* (*US* **skeptical**) **1** inclined to question the truth or soundness of accepted ideas, facts, etc.; critical; incredulous. **2** *Philos.* of or accepting the philosophy of Pyrrhonism, denying the possibility of knowledge. □□ **sceptically** *adv.*

■ **1** doubting, dubious, doubtful, questioning, critical, incredulous, scoffing, cynical, mistrustful, distrustful, disbelieving; agnostic.

sceptre /séptər/ *n.* (*US* **scepter**) **1** a staff borne esp. at a coronation as a symbol of sovereignty. **2** royal or imperial authority. □□ **sceptred** *adj.* [ME f. OF (*s*)*ceptre* f. L *sceptrum* f. Gk *skēptron* f. *skēptō* lean on]

■ **1** see STAFF[1] *n.* 1a, b.

sch. *abbr.* **1** scholar. **2** school. **3** schooner.

schadenfreude /sha͞adənfroydə/ *n.* the malicious enjoyment of another's misfortunes. [G f. *Schaden* harm + *Freude* joy]

schappe /sháppə/ *n.* fabric or yarn made from waste silk. [G, = waste silk]

schedule /shédyool, skéd-/ *n.* & *v.* ● *n.* **1 a** a list or plan of intended events, times, etc. **b** a plan of work (*not on my schedule for next week*). **2** a list of rates or prices. **3** *US* a timetable. **4** a tabulated inventory etc. esp. as an appendix to a document. ● *v.tr.* **1** include in a schedule. **2** make a schedule of. **3** *Brit.* include (a building) in a list for preservation or protection. □ **according to schedule** (or **on schedule**) as planned; on time. **behind schedule** behind time. **scheduled flight** (or **service** etc.) a public flight, service, etc., according to a regular timetable. **scheduled territories** *hist.* = *sterling area.* □□ **scheduler** *n.* [ME f. OF *cedule* f. LL *schedula* slip of paper, dimin. of *scheda* f. Gk *skhedē* papyrus-leaf]

■ *n.* **1** programme, timetable, plan; calendar, agenda, outline, list, listing. **2** list, index. ● *v.* **1, 2** programme, organize, plan, timetable, arrange, book, time, appoint, assign, allot; list, record, register; outline, *US* slate. □ **according to schedule** (or **on schedule**) as planned; on time, on target. **behind schedule** behind time, behind target; see also OVERDUE.

scheelite /shéelīt/ *n. Mineral.* calcium tungstate in its mineral crystalline form. [K. W. *Scheele*, Sw. chemist d. 1786]

schema /skeémə/ *n.* (*pl.* **schemata** /-mətə/ or **schemas**) **1** a synopsis, outline, or diagram. **2** a proposed arrangement. **3** *Logic* a syllogistic figure. **4** (in Kantian philosophy) a conception of what is common to all members of a class; a general type or essential form. [Gk *skhēma -atos* form, figure]
■ **1, 2** see OUTLINE *n.* 1, 2.

schematic /skimáttik, skee-/ *adj.* & *n.* ● *adj.* **1** of or concerning a scheme or schema. **2** representing objects by symbols etc. ● *n.* a schematic diagram, esp. of an electronic circuit. ▫▫ **schematically** *adv.*
■ *adj.* **2** diagrammatical, representational; symbolic. ● *n.* diagram, schema; layout, design, plan, pattern, configuration.

schematism /skeémətiz'm/ *n.* a schematic arrangement or presentation. [mod.L *schematismus* f. Gk *skhēmatismos* (as SCHEMATIZE)]

schematize /skeémətīz/ *v.tr.* (also **-ise**) **1** put in a schematic form; arrange. **2** represent by a scheme or schema. ▫▫ **schematization** /-záysh'n/ *n.*

scheme /skeem/ *n.* & *v.* ● *n.* **1 a** a systematic plan or arrangement for work, action, etc. **b** a proposed or operational systematic arrangement (*a colour scheme*). **2** an artful or deceitful plot. **3** a timetable, outline, syllabus, etc. ● *v.* **1** *intr.* (often foll. by *for*, or *to* + infin.) plan esp. secretly or deceitfully; intrigue. **2** *tr.* plan to bring about, esp. artfully or deceitfully (*schemed their downfall*). ▫▫ **schemer** *n.* [L *schema* f. Gk (as SCHEMA)]
■ *n.* **1 a** plan, design, programme, system, course (of action), schema, projection, draft, outline, *US* game plan. **b** pattern, arrangement, layout, design, blueprint, chart, map, schematic, order, organization, schema. **2** plot, plan, manoeuvre, strategy, stratagem, tactic, machination, subterfuge, trick, device, dodge, wile, ruse, intrigue, *colloq.* ploy, *sl.* racket; (*schemes*) games, scheming. ● *v.* **1** plan, plot, conspire, manoeuvre, intrigue with, machinate, connive. **2** plan, plot, devise, contrive, concoct, *colloq.* cook up.

scheming /skeéming/ *adj.* & *n.* ● *adj.* artful, cunning, or deceitful. ● *n.* plots; intrigues. ▫▫ **schemingly** *adv.*
■ *adj.* conniving, plotting, crafty, cunning, artful, sly, wily, devious, machiavellian, intriguing, nefarious, treacherous, slick, calculating, tricky, foxy, slippery, underhand(ed), duplicitous, deceitful.

schemozzle var. of SHEMOZZLE.

scherzando /skairtsándō/ *adv.*, *adj.*, & *n.* *Mus.* ● *adv.* & *adj.* in a playful manner. ● *n.* (*pl.* **scherzandos** or **scherzandi** /-di/) a passage played in this way. [It., gerund of *scherzare* to jest (as SCHERZO)]

scherzo /skáirtsō/ *n.* (*pl.* **-os**) *Mus.* a vigorous, light, or playful composition, usu. as a movement in a symphony, sonata, etc. [It., lit. 'jest']

schilling /shilling/ *n.* **1** the chief monetary unit of Austria. **2** a coin equal to the value of one schilling. [G (as SHILLING)]

schipperke /skíppərki, ship-/ *n.* **1** a small black tailless dog of a breed with a ruff of fur round its neck. **2** this breed. [Du. dial., = little boatman, f. its use as a watchdog on barges]

schism /sízz'm, skíz-/ *n.* **1 a** the division of a group into opposing sections or parties. **b** any of the sections so formed. **2 a** the separation of a Church into two Churches or the secession of a group owing to doctrinal, disciplinary, etc., differences. **b** the offence of causing or promoting such a separation. [ME f. OF *s(c)isme* f. eccl.L *schisma* f. Gk *skhisma -atos* cleft f. *skhizō* to split]
■ **1 a** split, rift, break, breach; division, rupture, separation; disunion. **b** faction, cabal, splinter group, clique, wing, camarilla, camp, set, sect, coterie, circle.

schismatic /sizmáttik, skiz-/ *adj.* & *n.* (also **schismatical**) ● *adj.* inclining to, concerning, or guilty of, schism. ● *n.* **1** a holder of schismatic opinions. **2** a member of a schismatic faction or a seceded branch of a Church. ▫▫ **schismatically** *adv.* [ME f. OF *scismatique* f. eccl.L *schismaticus* f. eccl.Gk *skhismatikos* (as SCHISM)]
■ *adj.* separatist, divisive, dissident, heretical; breakaway. ● *n.* **1** separatist, dissident, dissenter, heretic; see also INFIDEL *n.*

schist /shist/ *n.* a foliated metamorphic rock composed of layers of different minerals and splitting into thin irregular plates. ▫▫ **schistose** *adj.* [F *schiste* f. L *schistos* f. Gk *skhistos* split (as SCHISM)]

schistosome /shístəsōm/ *n.* = BILHARZIA 1. [Gk *skhistos* divided (as SCHISM) + *sōma* body]

schistosomiasis /shístəsəmīəsiss/ *n.* = BILHARZIASIS. [mod.L *Schistosoma* (the genus-name, as SCHISTOSOME)]

schizanthus /skizánthəss/ *n.* any plant of the genus *Schizanthus*, with showy flowers in various colours, and finely-divided leaves. [mod.L f. Gk *skhizō* to split + *anthos* flower]

schizo /skítsō/ *adj.* & *n.* *colloq.* ● *adj.* schizophrenic. ● *n.* (*pl.* **-os**) a schizophrenic. [abbr.]

schizocarp /skízzəkaarp/ *n.* *Bot.* any of a group of dry fruits that split into single-seeded parts when ripe. ▫▫ **schizocarpic** /-kaárpik/ *adj.* **schizocarpous** /-kaárpəss/ *adj.* [Gk *skhizō* to split + *karpos* fruit]

schizoid /skítsoyd/ *adj.* & *n.* ● *adj.* (of a person or personality etc.) tending to or resembling schizophrenia or a schizophrenic, but usu. without delusions. ● *n.* a schizoid person.

schizomycete /skítsəmīseet/ *n.* a former name for a bacterium. [Gk *skhizō* to split + *mukēs -ētos* mushroom]

schizophrenia /skítsəfreéniə/ *n.* a mental disease marked by a breakdown in the relation between thoughts, feelings, and actions, frequently accompanied by delusions and retreat from social life. ▫▫ **schizophrenic** /-frénnik, -freénik/ *adj.* & *n.* [mod.L f. Gk *skhizō* to split + *phrēn* mind]

schizothymia /skítsōthīmiə, skíz-/ *n.* *Psychol.* an introvert condition with a tendency to schizophrenia. ▫▫ **schizothymic** *adj.* [mod.L (as SCHIZOPHRENIA + Gk *thumos* temper)]

schlemiel /shləmeél/ *n.* *US colloq.* a foolish or unlucky person. [Yiddish *shlumiel*]
■ see LOSER.

schlep /shlep/ *v.* & *n.* (also **schlepp**) *colloq.* ● *v.* (**schlepped, schlepping**) **1** *tr.* carry, drag. **2** *intr.* go or work tediously or effortfully. ● *n.* esp. *US* trouble or hard work. [Yiddish *shlepn* f. G *schleppen* drag]
■ *v.* **1** see CARRY *v.* 1, 2. ● *n.* see STRUGGLE *n.* 1, 3.

schlieren /shleérən/ *n.* **1** a visually discernible area or stratum of different density in a transparent medium. **2** *Geol.* an irregular streak of mineral in igneous rock. [G, pl. of *Schliere* streak]

schlock /shlok/ *n.* *US colloq.* inferior goods; trash. [Yiddish *shlak* a blow]

schmaltz /shmawlts, shmalts/ *n.* esp. *US colloq.* sentimentality, esp. in music, drama, etc. ▫▫ **schmaltzy** *adj.* (**schmaltzier, schmaltziest**). [Yiddish f. G *Schmalz* dripping, lard]
■ see *sentimentality* (SENTIMENTAL). ▫▫ **schmaltzy** see SENTIMENTAL.

schmuck /shmuk/ *n.* esp. *US sl.* a foolish or contemptible person. [Yiddish]
■ see FOOL[1] *n.* 1.

schnapps /shnaps/ *n.* any of various spirits drunk in N. Europe. [G, = dram of liquor f. LG & Du. *snaps* mouthful (as SNAP)]

schnauzer /shnówtsər, shnówzər/ *n.* **1** a dog of a German breed with a close wiry coat and heavy whiskers round the muzzle. **2** this breed. [G f. *Schnauze* muzzle, SNOUT]

schnitzel /shníts'l/ *n.* an escalope of veal. ▫ **Wiener** /veénər/ (or **Vienna** /vee-énnə/) schnitzel a breaded, fried, and garnished schnitzel. [G, = slice]

schnook /shnŏŏk/ *n.* *US sl.* A dupe, a sucker; a simpleton. [perh. f. G *Schnucke* a small sheep or Yiddish *shnuk* snout.]

schnorkel var. of SNORKEL.

schnorrer /shnórər/ *n.* esp. *US sl.* a beggar or scrounger; a layabout. [Yiddish f. G *Schnurrer*]

scholar /skóllər/ *n.* **1** a learned person, esp. in language, literature, etc.; an academic. **2** the holder of a scholarship. **3 a** a person with specified academic ability (*is a poor scholar*). **b** a person who learns (*am a scholar of life*). **4** *archaic colloq.* a person able to read and write. **5** *archaic* a schoolboy or schoolgirl. □ **scholar's mate** see MATE². □□ **scholarly** *adj.* **scholarliness** *n.* [ME f. OE *scol(i)ere* & OF *escol(i)er* f. LL *scholaris* f. L *schola* SCHOOL¹]
■ **1** authority, expert, pundit, savant, intellectual, longhair, *colloq.* highbrow, egghead, brain; bookman; man of letters; academic, professor, teacher, *archaic or derog.* pedagogue. **3 a** student, pupil, learner. **5** pupil, student, schoolboy, schoolgirl. □□ **scholarly** learned, erudite, lettered, scholastic, intellectual, academic, brainy, *colloq.* highbrow.

scholarship /skóllərship/ *n.* **1 a** academic achievement; learning of a high level. **b** the methods and standards characteristic of a good scholar (*shows great scholarship*). **2** payment from the funds of a school, university, local government, etc., to maintain a student in full-time education, awarded on the basis of scholarly achievement.
■ **1 a** learning, erudition, knowledge, know-how, expertise. **2** grant, endowment, award, fellowship, *Brit.* exhibition, bursarship, bursary.

scholastic /skəlástik/ *adj.* & *n.* ● *adj.* **1** of or concerning universities, schools, education, teachers, etc. **2** pedantic; formal (*shows scholastic precision*). **3** *Philos. hist.* of, resembling, or concerning the schoolmen, esp. in dealing with logical subtleties. ● *n.* **1** a student. **2** *Philos. hist.* a schoolman. **3** a theologian of scholastic tendencies. **4** *RC Ch.* a member of any of several religious orders, who is between the novitiate and the priesthood. □□ **scholastically** *adv.* **scholasticism** /-tisiz'm/ *n.* [L *scholasticus* f. Gk *skholastikos* studious f. *skholazō* be at leisure, formed as SCHOOL¹]
■ *adj.* **1** see ACADEMIC *adj.* 1.

scholiast /skṓliast/ *n. hist.* an ancient or medieval scholar, esp. a grammarian, who annotated ancient literary texts. □□ **scholiastic** /-ástik/ *adj.* [med.Gk *skholiastēs* f. *skholiazō* write scholia: see SCHOLIUM]

scholium /skṓliəm/ *n.* (*pl.* **scholia** /-liə/) a marginal note or explanatory comment, esp. by an ancient grammarian on a classical text. [mod.L f. Gk *skholion* f. *skholē* disputation: see SCHOOL¹]
■ see NOTE *n.* 2, 5.

school¹ /skōōl/ *n.* & *v.* ● *n.* **1 a** an institution for educating or giving instruction, esp. *Brit.* for children under 19 years, or *US* for any level of instruction including college or university. **b** (*attrib.*) associated with or for use in school (*a school bag; school dinners*). **2 a** the buildings used by such an institution. **b** the pupils, staff, etc. of a school. **c** the time during which teaching is done, or the teaching itself (*no school today*). **3 a** a branch of study with separate examinations at a university; a department or faculty (*the history school*). **b** *Brit.* the hall in which university examinations are held. **c** (in *pl.*) *Brit.* such examinations. **4 a** the disciples, imitators, or followers of a philosopher, artist, etc. (*the school of Epicurus*). **b** a group of artists etc. whose works share distinctive characteristics. **c** a group of people sharing a cause, principle, method, etc. (*school of thought*). **5** *Brit.* a group of gamblers or of persons drinking together (*a poker school*). **6** *colloq.* instructive or disciplinary circumstances, occupation, etc. (*the school of adversity; learnt in a hard school*). **7** *hist.* a medieval lecture-room. **8** *Mus.* (usu. foll. by *of*) a handbook or book of instruction (*school of counterpoint*). **9** (in *pl.*; prec. by *the*) *hist.* medieval universities, their teachers, disputations, etc. ● *v.tr.* **1** send to school; provide for the education of. **2** (often foll. by *to*) discipline; train; control. **3** (as **schooled** *adj.*) (foll. by *in*) educated or trained (*schooled in humility*). □ **at** (*US* **in**) **school** attending lessons etc. **go to school 1** begin one's education. **2** attend lessons. **leave school** finish one's education. **of the old school** according to former and esp. better tradition (*a gentleman of the old school*). **school age** the age-range in which children normally attend school. **school board** *US* or *hist.* a board or authority for local education. **school-days** the time of being at school, esp. in retrospect. **school-inspector** a government official reporting on the efficiency, teaching standards, etc. of schools. **school-leaver** *Brit.* a child leaving school esp. at the minimum specified age. **school-leaving age** the minimum age at which a schoolchild may leave school. **school-ma'm** (or **-marm**) *US colloq.* a schoolmistress. **school-marmish** *colloq.* prim and fussy. **school-ship** a training-ship. **school-time 1** lesson-time at school or at home. **2** school-days. **school year** = *academic year*. [ME f. OE *scōl*, *scolu*, & f. OF *escole* ult. f. L *schola* school f. Gk *skholē* leisure, disputation, philosophy, lecture-place]
■ *n.* **1a, 2a, b** (educational) institution; institute, college, university, seminary. **4 a** followers, devotees, adherents, votaries, disciples. **b** set, circle, group, coterie, clique, sect. **c** see PERSUASION 4. ● *v.* **1** see EDUCATE 1, 2. **2** discipline, control; train, teach, mould, shape, form. **3** (**schooled**) educated, drilled, indoctrinated, instructed, tutored, trained, disciplined, coached, prepared, primed, equipped. □ **school-marmish** prim, straight-laced, fussy, punctilious, *colloq.* schoolmistressy.

school² /skōōl/ *n.* & *v.* ● *n.* (often foll. by *of*) a shoal of fish, porpoises, whales, etc. ● *v.intr.* form schools. [ME f. MLG, MDu. *schōle* f. WG]

schoolable /skṓōləb'l/ *adj.* liable by age etc. to compulsory education.

schoolboy /skṓōlboy/ *n.* a boy attending school.
■ pupil, student.

schoolchild /skṓōlchīld/ *n.* a child attending school.
■ pupil, student.

schoolfellow /skṓōlfellō/ *n.* a past or esp. present member of the same school.

schoolgirl /skṓōlgurl/ *n.* a girl attending school.
■ pupil, student.

schoolhouse /skṓōlhowss/ *n. Brit.* **1** a building used as a school, esp. in a village. **2** a dwelling-house adjoining a school.

schoolie /skṓōli/ *n. Austral. sl.* & *dial.* a schoolteacher.
■ see TEACHER.

schooling /skṓōling/ *n.* **1** education, esp. at school. **2** training or discipline, esp. of an animal.
■ **1** education, teaching, instruction, tutelage, tuition, guidance, training, preparation, indoctrination.

schoolman /skṓōlmən/ *n.* (*pl.* **-men**) **1** *hist.* a teacher in a medieval European university. **2** *RC Ch. hist.* a theologian seeking to deal with religious doctrines by the rules of Aristotelian logic. **3** *US* a male teacher.

schoolmaster /skṓōlmaastər/ *n.* a head or assistant male teacher. □□ **schoolmasterly** *adj.*
■ see TEACHER.

schoolmastering /skṓōlmaastəring/ *n.* teaching as a profession.

schoolmate /skṓōlmayt/ *n.* = SCHOOLFELLOW.

schoolmistress /skṓōlmistriss/ *n.* a head or assistant female teacher.
■ see TEACHER.

schoolmistressy /skṓōlmistrisi/ *adj. colloq.* prim and fussy.
■ see *school-marmish* (SCHOOL¹).

schoolroom /skṓōlrōōm, -rŏŏm/ *n.* a room used for lessons in a school or esp. in a private house.

schoolteacher /skṓōlteechər/ *n.* a person who teaches in a school. □□ **schoolteaching** *n.*
■ see TEACHER.

schooner /skṓōnər/ *n.* **1** a fore-and-aft rigged ship with two or more masts, the foremast being smaller than the other masts. **2 a** *Brit.* a measure or glass for esp. sherry. **b** *US* & *Austral.* a tall beer-glass. **3** *US hist.* = *prairie schooner*. [18th c.: orig. uncert.]

schorl /shorl/ *n.* black tourmaline. [G *Schörl*]

schottische /shoteésh/ *n.* **1** a kind of slow polka. **2** the music for this. [G *der schottische Tanz* the Scottish dance]

Schottky effect /shótki/ *n. Electronics* the increase in thermionic emission from a solid surface due to the presence of an external electric field. [W. *Schottky*, Ger. physicist d. 1976]

Schrödinger equation /shrṓdingər/ *n. Physics* a differential equation used in quantum mechanics for the wave function of a particle. [E. *Schrödinger*, Austrian physicist d. 1961]

schuss /shŏŏss/ *n.* & *v.* ● *n.* a straight downhill run on skis. ● *v.intr.* make a schuss. [G, lit. 'shot']

schwa /shwaa, shvaa/ *n.* (also **sheva** /shəvaá/) *Phonet.* **1** the indistinct unstressed vowel sound as in *a* moment *ago*. **2** the symbol /ə/ representing this in the International Phonetic Alphabet. [G f. Heb. *šᵉwā*, app. f. *šāw'* emptiness]

sciagraphy /skīágrəfi/ *n.* (also **skiagraphy**) the art of shading in drawing etc. □□ **sciagram** /skī́əgram/ *n.* **sciagraph** /skī́əgraaf/ *n.* & *v.tr.* **sciagraphic** /skīəgráffik/ *adj.* [F *sciagraphie* f. L *sciagraphia* f. Gk *skiagraphia* f. *skia* shadow]

sciamachy /sīámməki/ *n.* (also **skiamachy** /skī-/) *formal* **1** fighting with shadows. **2** imaginary or futile combat. [Gk *skiamakhia* (as SCIAGRAPHY, *-makhia* -fighting)]

sciatic /sīáttik/ *adj.* **1** of the hip. **2** of or affecting the sciatic nerve. **3** suffering from or liable to sciatica. □ **sciatic nerve** the largest nerve in the human body, running from the pelvis to the thigh. □□ **sciatically** *adv.* [F *sciatique* f. LL *sciaticus* f. L *ischiadicus* f. Gk *iskhiadikos* subject to sciatica f. *iskhion* hip-joint]

sciatica /sīáttikə/ *n.* neuralgia of the hip and thigh; a pain in the sciatic nerve. [ME f. LL *sciatica* (*passio*) fem. of *sciaticus*: see SCIATIC]

science /sī́ənss/ *n.* **1** a branch of knowledge conducted on objective principles involving the systematized observation of and experiment with phenomena, esp. concerned with the material and functions of the physical universe (see also *natural science*). **2 a** systematic and formulated knowledge, esp. of a specified type or on a specified subject (*political science*). **b** the pursuit or principles of this. **3** an organized body of knowledge on a subject (*the science of philology*). **4** skilful technique rather than strength or natural ability. **5** *archaic* knowledge of any kind. □ **science fiction** fiction based on imagined future scientific discoveries or environmental changes, frequently dealing with space travel, life on other planets, etc. **science park** an area devoted to scientific research or the development of science-based industries. [ME f. OF f. L *scientia* f. *scire* know]
■ **3** body of knowledge *or* information, discipline, branch, field, area, subject, realm, sphere. **4** skill, art, technique, method, system.

scienter /sīéntər/ *adv. Law* intentionally; knowingly. [L f. *scire* know]

sciential /sīénsh'l/ *adj.* concerning or having knowledge. [LL *scientialis* (as SCIENCE)]

scientific /sīəntíffik/ *adj.* **1 a** (of an investigation etc.) according to rules laid down in exact science for performing observations and testing the soundness of conclusions. **b** systematic, accurate. **2** used in, engaged in, or relating to (esp. natural) science (*scientific discoveries*; *scientific terminology*). **3** assisted by expert knowledge. □□ **scientifically** *adv.* [F *scientifique* or LL *scientificus* (as SCIENCE)]
■ **1 b** (well-)organized, (well-)regulated, controlled, (well-)ordered, orderly, systematic, methodical, precise, accurate, meticulous, thorough. **3** see PROFESSIONAL *adj.*

scientism /sī́əntiz'm/ *n.* **1 a** a method or doctrine regarded as characteristic of scientists. **b** the use or practice of this. **2** often *derog.* an excessive belief in or application of scientific method. □□ **scientistic** /-tístik/ *adj.*

scientist /sī́əntist/ *n.* **1** a person with expert knowledge of a (usu. physical or natural) science. **2** a person using scientific methods.

Scientology /sīəntólləji/ *n.* a religious system based on self-improvement and promotion through grades of esp. self-knowledge. □□ **Scientologist** *n.* [L *scientia* knowledge + -LOGY]

sci-fi /sī́fī/ *n.* (often *attrib.*) *colloq.* science fiction. [abbr.: cf. HI-FI]

scilicet /sī́liset, skeéliket/ *adv.* to wit; that is to say; namely (introducing a word to be supplied or an explanation of an ambiguity). [ME f. L, = *scire licet* one is permitted to know]
■ see NAMELY.

scilla /síllə/ *n.* any liliaceous plant of the genus *Scilla*, related to the bluebell, usu. bearing small blue star-shaped or bell-shaped flowers and having long glossy straplike leaves. [L f. Gk *skilla*]

Scillonian /silṓniən/ *adj.* & *n.* ● *adj.* of or relating to the Scilly Isles off the coast of Cornwall. ● *n.* a native of the Scilly Isles. [*Scilly*, perh. after *Devonian*]

scimitar /símmitər/ *n.* an oriental curved sword usu. broadening towards the point. [F *cimeterre*, It. *scimitarra*, etc., of unkn. orig.]

scintigram /síntigram/ *n.* an image of an internal part of the body, produced by scintigraphy.

scintigraphy /sintígrəfi/ *n.* the use of a radioisotope and a scintillation counter to get an image or record of a bodily organ etc. [SCINTILLATION + -GRAPHY]

scintilla /sintíllə/ *n.* **1** a trace. **2** a spark. [L]
■ **1** see TRACE[1] *n.* 1b. **2** see SPARK[1] *n.* 2.

scintillate /síntilayt/ *v.intr.* **1** (esp. as **scintillating** *adj.*) talk cleverly or wittily; be brilliant. **2** sparkle; twinkle; emit sparks. **3** *Physics* fluoresce momentarily when struck by a charged particle etc. □□ **scintillant** *adj.* **scintillatingly** *adv.* [L *scintillare* (as SCINTILLA)]
■ **1** (**scintillating**) witty, clever; see also BRILLIANT *adj.* 2. **2** see TWINKLE *v.*

scintillation /síntiláysh'n/ *n.* **1** the process or state of scintillating. **2** the twinkling of a star. **3** a flash produced in a material by an ionizing particle etc. □ **scintillation counter** a device for detecting and recording scintillation.
■ **1, 2** see TWINKLE *n.*

scintiscan /síntiskan/ *n.* an image or other record showing the distribution of radioactive traces in parts of the body, used in the detection and diagnosis of various diseases. [SCINTILLATION + SCAN]

sciolist /sī́əlist/ *n.* a superficial pretender to knowledge. □□ **sciolism** /-liz'm/ *n.* **sciolistic** /-lístik/ *adj.* [LL *sciolus* smatterer f. L *scire* know]

scion /sī́ən/ *n.* **1** (*US* **cion**) a shoot of a plant etc., esp. one cut for grafting or planting. **2** a descendant; a younger member of (esp. a noble) family. [ME f. OF *ciun*, *cion*, *sion* shoot, twig, of unkn. orig.]
■ **1** see SHOOT *n.* **2** see DESCENDANT.

scire facias /sī́ri fáyshiass/ *n. Law* a writ to enforce or annul a judgement, patent, etc. [L, = let (him) know]

scirocco var. of SIROCCO.

scirrhus /sírrəss, skí-/ *n.* (*pl.* **scirrhi** /-rī/) a carcinoma which is hard to the touch. □□ **scirrhoid** *adj.* **scirrhosity** /sirróssiti/ *n.* **scirrhous** *adj.* [mod.L f. Gk *skir(r)os* f. *skiros* hard]

scissel /skíss'l/ *n.* waste clippings etc. of metal produced during coin manufacture. [F *cisaille* f. *cisailler* clip with shears]

scissile /síssīl/ *adj.* able to be cut or divided. [L *scissilis* f. *scindere sciss-* cut]
■ see SEPARABLE.

scission /sísh'n/ *n.* **1** the act or an instance of cutting; the state of being cut. **2** a division or split. [ME f. OF *scission* or LL *scissio* (as SCISSILE)]
■ see SEPARATION.

scissor /sízzər/ *v.tr.* **1** (usu. foll. by *off*, *up*, *into*, etc.) cut with scissors. **2** (usu. foll. by *out*) clip out (a newspaper cutting etc.).

scissors /sízzərz/ *n.pl.* **1** (also **pair of scissors** *sing.*) an instrument for cutting fabric, paper, hair, etc., having two pivoted blades with finger and thumb holes in the handles, operating by closing on the material to be cut. **2** (treated as *sing.*) **a** a method of high jump with a forward and backward movement of the legs. **b** a hold in wrestling in which the opponent's body or esp. head is gripped between the legs. □ **scissor-bill** = SKIMMER 4. **scissor-bird** (or **-tail**) a fork-tailed flycatcher, *Tyrannus forficatus*. **scissors and paste** a method of compiling a book, article, etc., from extracts from others or without independent research. □□ **scissorwise** *adv.* [ME *sisoures* f. OF *cisoires* f. LL *cisoria* pl. of *cisorium* cutting instrument (as CHISEL): assoc. with L *scindere sciss-* cut]

■ **1** see SNIP *n.* 4.

sciurine /sī́yoorīn/ *adj.* **1** of or relating to the family Sciuridae, including squirrels and chipmunks. **2** squirrel-like. □□ **sciuroid** *adj.* [L *sciurus* f. Gk *skiouros* squirrel f. *skia* shadow + *oura* tail]

sclera /skle͞erə/ *n.* the white of the eye; a white membrane coating the eyeball. □□ **scleral** *adj.* **scleritis** /skleerī́tiss/ *n.* **sclerotomy** /-róttəmi/ *n.* (*pl.* **-ies**). [mod.L f. fem. of Gk *sklēros* hard]

sclerenchyma /skleeréngkimə/ *n.* the woody tissue found in a plant, formed from lignified cells and usu. providing support. [mod.L f. Gk *sklēros* hard + *egkhuma* infusion, after *parenchyma*]

scleroid /skle͞eroyd/ *adj. Bot.* & *Zool.* having a hard texture; hardened. [Gk *sklēros* hard]

scleroma /skleerṓmə/ *n.* (*pl.* **scleromata** /-mətə/) an abnormal patch of hardened skin or mucous membrane. [mod.L f. Gk *sklērōma* (as SCLEROSIS)]

sclerometer /skleerómmitər/ *n.* an instrument for determining the hardness of materials. [Gk *sklēros* hard + -METER]

sclerophyll /skle͞erəfil/ *n.* any woody plant with leathery leaves retaining water. □□ **sclerophyllous** /-róffiləss/ *adj.* [Gk *sklēros* hard + *phullon* leaf]

scleroprotein /skle͞erōprṓteen/ *n. Biochem.* any insoluble structural protein. [Gk *sklēros* hard + PROTEIN]

sclerosed /skle͞erōst, -rōzd/ *adj.* affected by sclerosis.

sclerosis /skleerṓsiss/ *n.* **1** an abnormal hardening of body tissue (see also ARTERIOSCLEROSIS, ATHEROSCLEROSIS). **2** (in full **multiple** or **disseminated sclerosis**) a chronic and progressive disease of the nervous system resulting in symptoms including paralysis and speech defects. **3** *Bot.* the hardening of a cell-wall with lignified matter. [ME f. med.L f. Gk *sklērōsis* f. *sklēroō* harden]

sclerotic /skleeróttik/ *adj.* & *n.* ● *adj.* **1** of or having sclerosis. **2** of or relating to the sclera. ● *n.* = SCLERA. □□ **sclerotitis** /-rətī́tiss/ *n.* [med.L *sclerotica* (as SCLEROSIS)]

sclerous /skle͞erəss/ *adj. Physiol.* hardened; bony. [Gk *sklēros* hard]

SCM *abbr.* (in the UK) **1** State Certified Midwife. **2** Student Christian Movement.

scoff[1] /skof/ *v.* & *n.* ● *v.intr.* (usu. foll. by *at*) speak derisively, esp. of serious subjects; mock; be scornful. ● *n.* **1** mocking words; a taunt. **2** an object of ridicule. □□ **scoffer** *n.* **scoffingly** *adv.* [perh. f. Scand.: cf. early mod. Da. *skuf*, *skof* jest, mockery]

■ *v.* mock, chaff, tease, sneer (at), poke fun (at), jeer (at), hiss, *colloq.* kid; (*scoff at*) deride, belittle, dismiss, disparage, make light of, twit, ridicule, lampoon, *Brit.* rag, *colloq.* spoof, rib.

scoff[2] /skof/ *v.* & *n. colloq.* ● *v.tr.* & *intr.* eat greedily. ● *n.* food; a meal. [(n.) f. Afrik. *schoff* repr. Du. *schoft* quarter of a day (hence, meal): (v.) orig. var. of dial. *scaff*, assoc. with the noun]

■ *v.* devour, put away, wolf (down), bolt, gulp (down), ingurgitate, *colloq.* gollop; gorge oneself (on), stuff oneself (with), gobble (up *or* down), guzzle. ● *n.* food, victuals, edibles, provisions, *colloq.* grub, eats, *sl.* nosh, chow.

scold /skōld/ *v.* & *n.* ● *v.* **1** *tr.* rebuke (esp. a child, employee, or inferior). **2** *intr.* find fault noisily; complain; rail. ● *n.* *archaic* a nagging or grumbling woman. □□ **scolder** *n.* **scolding** *n.* [ME (earlier as noun), prob. f. ON *skáld* SKALD]

■ *v.* **1** reprimand, reprove, upbraid, criticize, censure, find fault with, rebuke, reproach, lecture, berate, rate, castigate, take to task, rap on *or* over the knuckles, give a person a piece of one's mind, give a person a tongue-lashing, haul over the coals, rip *or* tear into, *archaic or literary* chide, *colloq.* bawl out, dress down, give a person hell *or* what for, jump on, jump down a person's throat, give a person a (good) talking-to, tell *or* tick off, carpet, have a person on the carpet, light *or* lace *or* sail into, *US colloq.* chew out. **2** find fault, complain, rail, lecture, *archaic or literary* chide. ● *n.* nag, shrew, termagant, virago, fishwife, harridan, hell-cat, fury, tigress, Xanthippe, *archaic* beldam, *colloq.* battleaxe.

scolex /skṓleks/ *n.* (*pl.* **scoleces** /-le͞eseez/ or **scolices** /-liseez/) the head of a larval or adult tapeworm. [mod.L f. Gk *skōlēx* worm]

scoliosis /skólliṓsiss/ *n.* an abnormal lateral curvature of the spine. □□ **scoliotic** /-lióttik/ *adj.* [mod.L f. Gk f. *skolios* bent]

scollop var. of SCALLOP.

scolopendrium /skóllәpéndriәm/ *n.* any of various ferns, esp. hart's tongue. [mod.L f. Gk *skolopendrion* f. *skolopendra* millipede (because of the supposed resemblance)]

scomber /skómbər/ *n.* any marine fish of the family Scombridae, including mackerels, tunas, and bonitos. □□ **scombrid** *n.* **scombroid** *adj.* & *n.* [L f. Gk *skombros*]

sconce[1] /skonss/ *n.* **1** a flat candlestick with a handle. **2** a bracket candlestick to hang on a wall. [ME f. OF *esconse* lantern or med.L *sconsa* f. L *absconsa* fem. past part. of *abscondere* hide: see ABSCOND]

sconce[2] /skonss/ *n.* **1** a small fort or earthwork usu. defending a ford, pass, etc. **2** *archaic* a shelter or screen. [Du. *schans* brushwood f. MHG *schanze*]

scone /skon, skōn/ *n.* a small sweet or savoury cake of flour, fat, and milk, baked quickly in an oven. [orig. Sc., perh. f. MDu. *schoon(broot)*, MLG *schon(brot)* fine (bread)]

scoop /sko͞op/ *n.* & *v.* ● *n.* **1** any of various objects resembling a spoon, esp.: **a** a short-handled deep shovel used for transferring grain, sugar, coal, coins, etc. **b** a large long-handled ladle used for transferring liquids. **c** the excavating part of a digging-machine etc. **d** *Med.* a long-handled spoonlike instrument used for scraping parts of the body etc. **e** an instrument used for serving portions of mashed potato, ice-cream, etc. **2** a quantity taken up by a scoop. **3** a movement of or resembling scooping. **4** a piece of news published by a newspaper etc. in advance of its rivals. **5** a large profit made quickly or by anticipating one's competitors. **6** *Mus.* a singer's exaggerated portamento. **7** a scooped-out hollow etc. ● *v.tr.* **1** (usu. foll. by *out*) hollow out with or as if with a scoop. **2** (usu. foll. by *up*) lift with or as if with a scoop. **3** forestall (a rival newspaper, reporter, etc.) with a scoop. **4** secure (a large profit etc.) esp. suddenly. □ **scoop-neck** the rounded low-cut neck of a garment. **scoop-net** a net used for sweeping a river bottom, or for catching bait. □□ **scooper** *n.* **scoopful** *n.* (*pl.* **-fuls**). [ME f. MDu., MLG *schōpe* bucket etc., rel. to SHAPE]

■ *n.* **1 b** ladle, dipper, spoon, bailer. **c** bucket. **5** killing. ● *v.* **1** (*scoop out*) gouge out, spoon out, hollow out, cut, dig out, excavate. **2** (*scoop up*) pick up, gather (up), sweep up, take up *or* in.

scoot /sko͞ot/ *v.* & *n. colloq.* ● *v.intr.* run or dart away, esp. quickly. ● *n.* the act or an instance of scooting. [19th-c. US (earlier *scout*): orig. unkn.]

■ *v.* see SCURRY *v.*

scooter /sko͞otər/ *n.* & *v.* ● *n.* **1** a child's toy consisting of a footboard mounted on two wheels and a long steering-handle, propelled by resting one foot on the footboard and pushing the other against the ground. **2** (in full **motor scooter**) a light two-wheeled open motor vehicle with a shieldlike protective front. **3** *US* a sailboat able to travel on both water and ice. ● *v.intr.* travel or ride on a scooter. □□ **scooterist** *n.*

scopa /skṓpə/ *n.* (*pl.* **scopae** /-pee/) a small brushlike tuft of hairs, esp. on the leg of a bee for collecting pollen. [sing. of L *scopae* = twigs, broom]

scope[1] /skōp/ *n.* **1 a** the extent to which it is possible to range; the opportunity for action etc. (*this is beyond the scope of our research*). **b** the sweep or reach of mental activity, observation, or outlook (*an intellect limited in its scope*). **2** *Naut.* the length of cable extended when a ship rides at anchor. **3** *archaic* a purpose, end, or intention. [It. *scopo* aim f. Gk *skopos* target f. *skeptomai* look at]

■ **1** space, room, leeway, elbow-room, freedom, opportunity; range, reach, extent, compass, orbit, span, breadth, expanse, capacity, stretch, latitude, spread; sphere, field, area.

scope[2] /skōp/ *n. colloq.* a telescope, microscope, or other device ending in *-scope*. [abbr.]

-scope /skōp/ *comb. form* forming nouns denoting: **1** a device looked at or through (*kaleidoscope*; *telescope*). **2** an instrument for observing or showing (*gyroscope*; *oscilloscope*). □□ **-scopic** /skóppik/ *comb. form* forming adjectives. [from or after mod.L *-scopium* f. Gk *skopeō* look at]

scopolamine /skəpólləmin, -meen/ *n.* = HYOSCINE. [*Scopolia* genus-name of the plants yielding it, f. G. A. *Scopoli*, It. naturalist d. 1788 + AMINE]

scopula /skópyoolə/ *n.* (*pl.* **scopulae** /-lee/) any of various small brushlike structures, esp. on the legs of spiders. [LL, dimin. of L *scopa*: see SCOPA]

-scopy /skəpi/ *comb. form* indicating viewing or observation, usu. with an instrument ending in *-scope* (*microscopy*).

scorbutic /skorbyóótik/ *adj.* & *n.* ● *adj.* relating to, resembling, or affected with scurvy. ● *n.* a person affected with scurvy. □□ **scorbutically** *adv.* [mod.L *scorbuticus* f. med.L *scorbutus* scurvy, perh. f. MLG *schorbūk* f. *schoren* break + *būk* belly]

scorch /skorch/ *v.* & *n.* ● *v.* **1** *tr.* **a** burn the surface of with flame or heat so as to discolour, parch, injure, or hurt. **b** affect with the sensation of burning. **2** *intr.* become discoloured etc. with heat. **3** *tr.* (as **scorching** *adj.*) *colloq.* **a** (of the weather) very hot. **b** (of criticism etc.) stringent; harsh. **4** *intr. colloq.* (of a motorist etc.) go at excessive speed. ● *n.* **1** a mark made by scorching. **2** *colloq.* a spell of fast driving etc. □ **scorched earth policy** the burning of crops etc. and the removing or destroying of anything that might be of use to an enemy force occupying a country. □□ **scorchingly** *adv.* [ME, perh. rel. to *skorkle* in the same sense]

■ *v.* **1, 2** sear, burn, roast; singe, char, blacken. **3** (**scorching**) **a** hot, torrid, boiling, roasting, sweltering, searing, parching, shrivelling, tropical, hellish, sizzling, *esp. US* broiling. **b** stringent, critical, caustic, scathing, mordant, vituperative, harsh, acrimonious, bitter. **4** see SPEED *v.* 1.

scorcher /skórchər/ *n.* **1** a person or thing that scorches. **2** *colloq.* **a** a very hot day. **b** a fine specimen.

score /skor/ *n.* & *v.* ● *n.* **1 a** the number of points, goals, runs, etc., made by a player, side, etc., in some games. **b** the total number of points etc. at the end of a game (*the score was five–nil*). **c** the act of gaining esp. a goal (*a superb score there!*). **2** (*pl.* same or **scores**) twenty or a set of twenty. **3** (in *pl.*) a great many (*scores of people arrived*). **4 a** a reason or motive (*rejected on the score of absurdity*). **b** topic, subject (*no worries on that score*). **5** *Mus.* **a** a usu. printed copy of a composition showing all the vocal and instrumental parts arranged one below the other. **b** the music composed for a film or play, esp. for a musical. **6** *colloq.* **a** a piece of good fortune. **b** the act or an instance of scoring off another person. **7** *colloq.* the state of affairs; the present situation (*asked what the score was*). **8** a notch, line, etc. cut or scratched into a surface. **9 a** an amount due for payment. **b** a running account kept by marks against a customer's name. **10** *Naut.* a groove in a block or dead-eye to hold a rope. ● *v.* **1** *tr.* **a** win or gain (a goal, run, points, etc., or success etc.) (*scored a century*). **b** count for a score of (points in a game etc.) (*a bull's-eye scores most points*). **c** allot a score to (a competitor etc.). **d** make a record of (a point etc.). **2** *intr.* **a** make a score in a game (*failed to score*). **b** keep the tally of points, runs, etc. in a game. **3** *tr.* mark with notches, incisions, lines, etc.; slash; furrow (*scored his name on the desk*). **4** *intr.* secure an advantage by luck, cunning, etc. (*that is where he scores*). **5** *tr. Mus.* **a** orchestrate (a piece of music). **b** (usu. foll. by *for*) arrange for an instrument or instruments. **c** write the music for (a film, musical, etc.). **d** write out in a score. **6** *tr.* **a** (usu. foll. by *up*) mark (a total owed etc.) in a score (see sense 9b of *n.*). **b** (usu. foll. by *against*, *to*) enter (an item of debt to a customer). **7** *intr. sl.* **a** obtain drugs illegally. **b** (of a man) make a sexual conquest. **8** *tr.* (usu. foll. by *against*, *to*) mentally record (an offence etc.). **9** *tr. US* criticize (a person) severely. □ **keep score** (or **the score**) register the score as it is made. **know the score** *colloq.* be aware of the essential facts. **on the score of** for the reason that; because of. **on that score** so far as that is concerned. **score-book** (or **-card** or **-sheet**) a book etc. prepared for entering esp. cricket scores in. **score draw** a draw in football in which goals are scored. **score off** (or **score points off**) *colloq.* humiliate, esp. verbally in repartee etc. **score out** draw a line through (words etc.). **score under** underline. □□ **scorer** *n.* **scoring** *n. Mus.* [(n.) f. OE: sense 5 f. the line or bar drawn through all staves: (v.) partly f. ON *skora* f. ON *skor* notch, tally, twenty, f. Gmc: see SHEAR]

■ *n.* **1 a, b** number, tally, sum (total), total. **3** (*scores*) a great many, dozens, hundreds, (tens *or* hundreds of) thousands, millions, droves, hordes, multitudes, herds, legions, lots, masses, shoals, bevies, swarms, flocks, armies, crowds, throngs. **4 a** ground(s), basis, account, rationale, cause, reason, motive. **b** see SUBJECT *n.* 1a. **5 a** music, accompaniment; vocal score, *Mus.* full score. **7** state of affairs *or* things *or* play, situation, news, status quo, word, intelligence, latest, *US sl.* poop. **8** nick, groove, scratch, line, mark, stroke, notch, cut. **9 b** see TALLY *n.* 1. ● *v.* **1 a** see GAIN *v.* 1. **d** record, notch up; see also TALLY *v.* 2. **2 b** keep the tally, keep (the) score. **3** mark, line, incise, scratch, nick, notch, cut, groove, furrow, scrape, gouge, slash, *archaic* scotch. **4** succeed, be successful, triumph, win, make an impression, have an impact, make a hit. **5 c** write, orchestrate; see also COMPOSE *v.* 1a. **6 b** charge, chalk up, put on account, *Brit.* put on the slate. □ **keep score** (or **the score**) score, keep the tally. **know the score** be in the picture, *colloq.* be in the know, be switched-on. **on the score of** see *by reason of* (REASON). **score out** see DELETE. **score under** underline, underscore; highlight.

scoreboard /skórbord/ *n.* a large board for publicly displaying the score in a game or match.

scoria /skóriə/ *n.* (*pl.* **scoriae** /-ri-ee/) **1** cellular lava, or fragments of it. **2** the slag or dross of metals. □□ **scoriaceous** /-riáyshəss/ *adj.* [L f. Gk *skōria* refuse f. *skōr* dung]

scorify /skórifī/ *v.tr.* (**-ies, -ied**) **1** reduce to dross. **2** assay (precious metal) by treating a portion of its ore fused with lead and borax. □□ **scorification** /-fikáysh'n/ *n.* **scorifier** *n.*

scorn /skorn/ *n.* & *v.* ● *n.* **1** disdain, contempt, derision. **2** an object of contempt etc. (*the scorn of all onlookers*). ● *v.tr.* **1** hold in contempt or disdain. **2** (often foll. by *to* + infin.) abstain from or refuse to do as unworthy (*scorns lying*; *scorns to lie*). □ **think scorn of** despise. □□ **scorner** *n.* [ME f. OF *esc(h)arn(ir)* ult. f. Gmc: cf. OS *skern* MOCKERY]

■ *n.* **1** contumely, contempt, contemptuousness, disdain, deprecation, mockery, derision, derisiveness, sneering, ridicule, scoffing, jeering, taunting; dismissal. ● *v.* **1** reject, rebuff, disown, disavow, disregard, ignore, shun, snub, flout, treat with contempt, hold in contempt, have no use for, disdain, spurn, mock, deride, despise, curl one's lip at, sneer at, scoff at, jeer at, make fun of, laugh at, ridicule, look down on *or* upon, look down one's nose at, thumb one's nose at, pooh-pooh, *colloq.* turn up one's nose at, put down, *literary* contemn, *sl.* cock a snook at. **2** (*scorn to*) see REFRAIN[1]. □ **think scorn of** see DESPISE.

scornful /skórnfōōl/ *adj.* (often foll. by *of*) full of scorn; contemptuous. □□ **scornfully** *adv.* **scornfulness** *n.*
■ contemptuous, disdainful, disparaging, derisory, derisive, snide, contumelious, deprecative, supercilious, mocking, sneering, scoffing, haughty, high-handed, superior, *colloq.* snooty, snotty.

scorper var. of SCALPER 2.

Scorpio /skórpiō/ *n.* (*pl.* **-os**) **1** a constellation, traditionally regarded as contained in the figure of a scorpion. **2 a** the eighth sign of the zodiac (the Scorpion). **b** a person born when the sun is in this sign. □□ **Scorpian** *adj.* & *n.* [ME f. L (as SCORPION)]

scorpioid /skórpioyd/ *adj.* & *n.* ● *adj.* **1** *Zool.* of, relating to, or resembling a scorpion; of the scorpion order. **2** *Bot.* (of an inflorescence) curled up at the end, and uncurling as the flowers develop. ● *n.* this type of inflorescence. [Gk *skorpioeidēs* (as SCORPIO)]

scorpion /skórpiən/ *n.* **1** an arachnid of the order Scorpionida, with lobster-like pincers and a jointed tail that can be bent over to inflict a poisoned sting on prey held in its pincers. **2** (in full **false scorpion**) a similar arachnid of the order Pseudoscorpionida, smaller and without a tail. **3** (**the Scorpion**) the zodiacal sign or constellation Scorpio. **4** *Bibl.* a whip with metal points (1 Kings 12:11). □ **scorpion fish** any of various marine fish of the family Scorpaenidae, with venomous spines on the head and gills. **scorpion fly** any insect of the order Mecoptera, esp. of the family Panorpidae, the males of which have a swollen abdomen curved upwards like a scorpion's sting. **scorpion grass** = *forget-me-not.* [ME f. OF f. L *scorpio -onis* f. *scorpius* f. Gk *skorpios*]

scorzonera /skórzənéērə/ *n.* **1** a composite plant, *Scorzonera hispanica*, with long tapering purple-brown roots. **2** the root used as a vegetable. [It. f. *scorzone* venomous snake ult. f. med.L *curtio*]

Scot /skot/ *n.* **1 a** a native of Scotland. **b** a person of Scottish descent. **2** *hist.* a member of a Gaelic people that migrated from Ireland to Scotland around the 6th c. [OE *Scottas* (pl.) f. LL *Scottus*]

scot /skot/ *n. hist.* a payment corresponding to a modern tax, rate, etc. □ **pay scot and lot** share the financial burdens of a borough etc. (and so be allowed to vote). **scot-free** unharmed; unpunished; safe. [ME f. ON *skot* & f. OF *escot*, of Gmc orig.: cf. SHOT[1]]
■ see TAX *n.* 1.

Scotch /skoch/ *adj.* & *n.* ● *adj.* var. of SCOTTISH or SCOTS. ● *n.* **1** var. of SCOTTISH or SCOTS. **2** Scotch whisky. □ **Scotch broth** a soup made from beef or mutton with pearl barley etc. **Scotch cap** = BONNET *n.* 1b. **Scotch catch** *Mus.* a short note on the beat followed by a long one. **Scotch egg** a hard-boiled egg enclosed in sausage meat and fried. **Scotch fir** (or **pine**) a pine tree, *Pinus sylvestris*, native to Europe and Asia. **Scotch kale** a variety of kale with purplish leaves. **Scotch mist 1** a thick drizzly mist common in the Highlands. **2** a retort made to a person implying that he or she has imagined or failed to understand something. **Scotch pebble** agate, jasper, cairngorm, etc., found in Scotland. **Scotch pine** = *Scotch fir.* **Scotch snap** = *Scotch catch.* **Scotch terrier 1** a small terrier of a rough-haired short-legged breed. **2** this breed. **Scotch whisky** whisky distilled in Scotland, esp. from malted barley. ¶ *Scots* or *Scottish* is generally preferred in Scotland, except in the special compounds given above. [contr. of SCOTTISH]
■ *n.* **2** see WHISKY.

scotch[1] /skoch/ *v.* & *n.* ● *v.tr.* **1** put an end to; frustrate (*injury scotched his attempt*). **2** *archaic* **a** wound without killing; slightly disable. **b** make incisions in; score. ● *n.* **1** *archaic* a slash. **2** a line on the ground for hopscotch. [ME: orig. unkn.]

scotch[2] /skoch/ *n.* & *v.* ● *n.* a wedge or block placed against a wheel etc. to prevent its slipping. ● *v.tr.* hold back (a wheel, barrel, etc.) with a scotch. [17th c.: perh. = *scatch* stilt f. OF *escache*]

Scotchman /skóchmən/ *n.* (*pl.* **-men**; *fem.* **Scotchwoman**, *pl.* **-women**) = SCOTSMAN. ¶ *Scotsman* etc. are generally preferred in Scotland.

scoter /skṓtər/ *n.* (*pl.* same or **scoters**) a large marine duck of the genus *Melanitta.* [17th c.: orig. unkn.]

scotia /skṓshə/ *n.* a concave moulding, esp. at the base of a column. [L f. Gk *skotia* f. *skotos* darkness, with ref. to the shadow produced]

Scoticism var. of SCOTTICISM.

Scoticize var. of SCOTTICIZE.

Scotland Yard /skótlənd yaárd/ *n.* **1** the headquarters of the London Metropolitan Police. **2** its Criminal Investigation Department. [Great and New *Scotland Yard*, streets where it was successively situated until 1967]

scotoma /skotṓmə/ *n.* (*pl.* **scotomata** /-mətə/) a partial loss of vision or blind spot in an otherwise normal visual field. [LL f. Gk *skotōma* f. *skotoō* darken f. *skotos* darkness]

Scots /skots/ *adj.* & *n.* esp. *Sc.* ● *adj.* **1** = SCOTTISH *adj.* **2** in the dialect, accent, etc., of (esp. Lowlands) Scotland. ● *n.* **1** = SCOTTISH *n.* **2** the form of English spoken in (esp. Lowlands) Scotland. [ME orig. *Scottis*, north. var. of SCOTTISH]

Scotsman /skótsmən/ *n.* (*pl.* **-men**; *fem.* **Scotswoman**, *pl.* **-women**) **1** a native of Scotland. **2** a person of Scottish descent.

Scotticism /skóttisiz'm/ *n.* (also **Scoticism**) a Scottish phrase, word, or idiom. [LL *Scot(t)icus*]

Scotticize /skóttisīz/ *v.* (also **Scoticize, -ise**) **1** *tr.* imbue with or model on Scottish ways etc. **2** *intr.* imitate the Scottish in idiom or habits.

Scottie /skótti/ *n. colloq.* **1** (also **Scottie dog**) a Scotch terrier. **2** a Scot.

Scottish /skóttish/ *adj.* & *n.* ● *adj.* of or relating to Scotland or its inhabitants. ● *n.* (prec. by *the*; treated as *pl.*) the people of Scotland (see also SCOTS). □□ **Scottishness** *n.*

scoundrel /skówndrəl/ *n.* an unscrupulous villain; a rogue. □□ **scoundreldom** *n.* **scoundrelism** *n.* **scoundrelly** *adj.* [16th c.: orig. unkn.]
■ villain, rogue, wretch, good-for-nothing, scapegrace, blackguard, cur, cad, knave, *colloq.* scamp, heel, *colloq. or joc.* bounder, *often joc.* rascal, *sl.* louse, *Austral. sl.* dingo, *esp. Brit. sl.* rotter.

scour[1] /skowr/ *v.* & *n.* ● *v.tr.* **1 a** cleanse or brighten by rubbing, esp. with soap, chemicals, sand, etc. **b** (usu. foll. by *away*, *off*, etc.) clear (rust, stains, reputation, etc.) by rubbing, hard work, etc. (*scoured the slur from his name*). **2** (of water, or a person with water) clear out (a pipe, channel, etc.) by flushing through. **3** *hist.* purge (the bowels) drastically. ● *n.* **1** the act or an instance of scouring; the state of being scoured, esp. by a swift water current (*the scour of the tide*). **2** diarrhoea in cattle. **3** a substance used for scouring. □ **scouring-rush** any of various horsetail plants with a rough siliceous coating used for polishing wood etc. □□ **scourer** *n.* [ME f. MDu., MLG *schūren* f. F *escurer* f. LL *excurare* clean (off) (as EX-[1], CURE)]
■ *v.* **1 a** scrub, clean, wash, rub, polish, burnish, buff, shine, *usu. formal* cleanse. **b** clear; (*scour away, off, etc.*) scrub *or* clean *or* wash *or* rub off, scrub *or* clean *or* wash *or* rub away.

scour[2] /skowr/ *v.* **1** *tr.* hasten over (an area etc.) searching thoroughly (*scoured the streets for him*; *scoured the pages of the newspaper*). **2** *intr.* range hastily esp. in search or pursuit. [ME: orig. unkn.]
■ **1** rake, comb, search, hunt through.

scourge /skurj/ *n.* & *v.* ● *n.* **1** a whip used for punishment, esp. of people. **2** a person or thing seen as punishing, esp. on a large scale (*the scourge of famine*; *Genghis Khan, the scourge of Asia*). ● *v.tr.* **1** whip. **2** punish; afflict; oppress. □□ **scourger** *n.* [ME f. OF *escorge* (n.), *escorgier* (v.) (ult. as EX-[1], L *corrigia* thong, whip)]

■ *n.* **1** whip, lash, quirt, horsewhip, *hist.* cat-o'-nine-tails, knout. **2** curse, misfortune, bane, evil, affliction, plague, torment, misery, *archaic or literary* woe. ● *v.* **1** whip, flog, beat, lash, belt, flagellate, *esp. US colloq.* whale. **2** punish, castigate, chastise, discipline, afflict, oppress, torment.

Scouse /skowss/ *n.* & *adj. colloq.* ● *n.* **1** the dialect of Liverpool. **2** (also **Scouser** /skówsə/) a native of Liverpool. **3** (**scouse**) = LOBSCOUSE. ● *adj.* of or relating to Liverpool. [abbr. of LOBSCOUSE]

scout[1] /skowt/ *n.* & *v.* ● *n.* **1** a person, esp. a soldier, sent out to get information about the enemy's position, strength, etc. **2** the act of seeking (esp. military) information (*on the scout*). **3** = *talent-scout*. **4** (**Scout**) a member of the Scout Association, a boys' association intended to develop character esp. by open-air activities. **5** a domestic worker at a college, esp. at Oxford University. **6** *colloq.* a person; a fellow. **7** a ship or aircraft designed for reconnoitring, esp. a small fast aircraft. ● *v.* **1** *intr.* act as a scout. **2** *intr.* (foll. by *about*, *around*) make a search. **3** *tr.* (often foll. by *out*) *colloq.* explore to get information about (territory etc.). □ **Queen's** (or **King's**) **Scout** a Scout who has reached the highest standard of proficiency. □□ **scouter** *n.* **scouting** *n.* [ME f. OF *escouter* listen, earlier *ascolter* ult. f. L *auscultare*]
■ *n.* **6** person, *colloq.* fellow; see also GUY[1] *n.* 1. ● *v.* **1** spy, reconnoitre. **2, 3** search *or* look (about *or* around *or* round) (for), hunt (about *or* around) (for), cast around *or* about (for), check (about *or* around) (for); reconnoitre, investigate, explore.

scout[2] /skowt/ *v.tr.* reject (an idea etc.) with scorn. [Scand.: cf. ON *skúta*, *skúti* taunt]

Scouter /skówtər/ *n.* an adult member of the Scout Association.

Scoutmaster /skówtmaastər/ *n.* a person in charge of a group of Scouts.

scow /skow/ *n.* esp. *US* a flat-bottomed boat used as a lighter etc. [Du. *schouw* ferry-boat]

scowl /skowl/ *n.* & *v.* ● *n.* a severe frown producing a sullen, bad-tempered, or threatening look on a person's face. ● *v.intr.* make a scowl. □□ **scowler** *n.* [ME, prob. f. Scand.: cf. Da. *skule* look down or sidelong]
■ *n.* frown, grimace, glare, glower, lour, *colloq.* dirty look. ● *v.* glower, frown, grimace, glare, look daggers, lour.

SCPS *abbr.* (in the UK) Society of Civil and Public Servants.

SCR *abbr. Brit.* Senior Common (or Combination) Room.

scr. *abbr.* scruple(s) (of weight).

scrabble /skrább'l/ *v.* & *n.* ● *v.intr.* (often foll. by *about*, *at*) scratch or grope to find or collect or hold on to something. ● *n.* **1** an act of scrabbling. **2** (**Scrabble**) *propr.* a game in which players build up words from letter-blocks on a board. [MDu. *schrabbelen* frequent. of *schrabben* SCRAPE]

scrag /skrag/ *n.* & *v.* ● *n.* **1** (also **scrag-end**) the inferior end of a neck of mutton. **2** a skinny person or animal. **3** *colloq.* a person's neck. ● *v.tr.* (**scragged**, **scragging**) *sl.* **1** strangle, hang. **2** seize roughly by the neck. **3** handle roughly; beat up. [perh. alt. f. dial. *crag* neck, rel. to MDu. *crāghe*, MLG *krage*]

scraggly /skrágli/ *adj.* sparse and irregular.

scraggy /skrággi/ *adj.* (**scraggier**, **scraggiest**) thin and bony. □□ **scraggily** *adv.* **scragginess** *n.*
■ see THIN *adj.* 4.

scram /skram/ *v.intr.* (**scrammed**, **scramming**) (esp. in *imper.*) *colloq.* go away. [20th c.: perh. f. SCRAMBLE]
■ see BEAT IT.

scramble /skrámb'l/ *v.* & *n.* ● *v.* **1** *intr.* make one's way over rough ground, rocks, etc., by clambering, crawling, etc. **2** *intr.* (foll. by *for*, *at*) struggle with competitors (for a thing or share of it). **3** *intr.* move with difficulty or awkwardly. **4** *tr.* **a** mix together indiscriminately. **b** jumble or muddle. **5** *tr.* cook (eggs) by heating them when broken and well mixed with butter, milk, etc. **6** *tr.* change the speech frequency of (a broadcast transmission or telephone conversation) so as to make it unintelligible without a corresponding decoding device. **7** *intr.* move hastily. **8** *tr. colloq.* execute (an action etc.) awkwardly and inefficiently. **9** *intr.* (of fighter aircraft or their pilots) take off quickly in an emergency or for action. ● *n.* **1** an act of scrambling. **2** a difficult climb or walk. **3** (foll. by *for*) an eager struggle or competition. **4** *Brit.* a motor-cycle race over rough ground. **5** an emergency take-off by fighter aircraft. □ **scrambled egg** *colloq.* gold braid on a military officer's cap. [16th c. (imit.): cf. dial. synonyms *scamble*, *cramble*]
■ *v.* **1** climb, clamber, crawl, scrabble, struggle. **2** jostle, tussle, struggle, wrestle, grapple, fight, battle. **3** struggle, flounder, blunder. **4** mix up, confuse, shuffle, jumble (up), intermingle, mingle, *literary* commingle. **7** rush, hurry, scamper, run, hasten, race, scurry, scuttle, dash, hotfoot (it), hustle, *colloq.* scoot, skedaddle, *US colloq.* hightail. **8** see *knock up* 1. ● *n.* **1** scrabble, scrimmage, struggle, tussle. **2** struggle, pull, climb. **3** (*scramble for*) competition *or* contest for, race *or* rush for, commotion *or* riot *or* free-for-all over.

scrambler /skrámblər/ *n.* a device for scrambling telephone conversations.

scran /skran/ *n. sl.* **1** food, eatables. **2** remains of food. □ **bad scran** *Ir.* bad luck. [18th c.: orig. unkn.]

scrap[1] /skrap/ *n.* & *v.* ● *n.* **1** a small detached piece; a fragment or remnant. **2** rubbish or waste material. **3** an extract or cutting from something written or printed. **4** discarded metal for reprocessing (often *attrib.*: *scrap metal*). **5** (with *neg.*) the smallest piece or amount (*not a scrap of food left*). **6** (in *pl.*) **a** odds and ends. **b** bits of uneaten food. **7** (in *sing* or *pl.*) a residuum of melted fat or of fish with the oil expressed. ● *v.tr.* (**scrapped**, **scrapping**) discard as useless. □ **scrap heap 1** a pile of scrap materials. **2** a state of uselessness. **scrap merchant** a dealer in scrap. [ME f. ON *skrap*, rel. to *skrapa* SCRAPE]
■ *n.* **1** bit, piece, shred, remnant; see also FRAGMENT *n.* **2** waste, debris, junk; see also RUBBISH *n.* 1. **3** extract, cutting, excerpt, clipping. **5** mite, bit, shred, morsel, piece, fragment, particle, sliver, snippet, snip, crumb, whit, iota, jot, tittle, drop, grain, speck, molecule, atom, trace, scintilla, vestige, trace, *US* & *Austral. colloq.* skerrick. **6** (*scraps*) **a** remnants, leavings, remains; see also *odds and ends*. **b** leftovers, leavings, scrapings, crumbs. ● *v.* discard, throw away, reject, abandon, give up, consign to the scrap heap, get rid of, dispose of, dispense with, junk.

scrap[2] /skrap/ *n.* & *v. colloq.* ● *n.* a fight or rough quarrel, esp. a spontaneous one. ● *v.tr.* (**scrapped**, **scrapping**) (often foll. by *with*) have a scrap. □□ **scrapper** *n.* [perh. f. SCRAPE]
■ *n.* fight, brawl, fracas, fray, affray, scuffle, Donnybrook, battle (royal), *esp. US* ruckus, *colloq.* rumpus, dust-up; dispute, argument, quarrel, disagreement, wrangle, squabble, tiff, *colloq.* row, set-to, *US colloq.* spat. ● *v.* fight, brawl, scuffle, battle; row, wrangle, spar, argue, disagree, squabble, bicker.

scrapbook /skrápbŏŏk/ *n.* a book of blank pages for sticking cuttings, drawings, etc., in.
■ album, portfolio, collection.

scrape /skrayp/ *v.* & *n.* ● *v.* **1** *tr.* **a** move a hard or sharp edge across (a surface), esp. to make something smooth. **b** apply (a hard or sharp edge) in this way. **2** *tr.* (foll. by *away*, *off*, etc.) remove (a stain, projection, etc.) by scraping. **3** *tr.* **a** rub (a surface) harshly against another. **b** scratch or damage by scraping. **4** *tr.* make (a hollow) by scraping. **5 a** *tr.* draw or move with a sound of, or resembling, scraping. **b** *intr.* emit or produce such a sound. **c** *tr.* produce such a sound from. **6** *intr.* (often foll. by *along*, *by*, *through*, etc.) move or pass along while almost touching close or surrounding features, obstacles, etc. (*the car scraped through the narrow lane*). **7** *tr.* just manage to achieve (a living, an examination pass, etc.). **8** *intr.* (often foll. by *by*, *through*) **a** barely manage. **b** pass an examination etc. with difficulty. **9** *tr.* (foll. by *together*, *up*) contrive to bring or provide; amass with difficulty. **10** *intr.* be economical. **11** *intr.* draw back a foot in making a clumsy bow. **12** *tr.* clear (a ship's bottom) of barnacles etc. **13** *tr.* completely clear (a plate) of food. **14** *tr.* (foll. by *back*) draw (the hair) tightly back off the forehead. ● *n.* **1** the act or sound of scraping. **2** a scraped place (on the skin etc.). **3** a thinly applied layer of butter etc. on bread. **4** the scraping of a foot in bowing. **5** *colloq.* an awkward predicament, esp. resulting from an escapade. □ **scrape acquaintance with** contrive to get to know (a person). **scrape the barrel** *colloq.* be reduced to one's last resources. [ME f. ON *skrapa* or MDu. *schrapen*]

■ *v.* **2** (*scrape away, off, etc.*) rub off *or* away, scour off *or* away, scrub off *or* away, clean off *or* away, scratch off *or* away. **3 b** graze, scratch, abrade, bark, scuff, bruise, damage, injure. **4** gouge out, dig out; see also SCOOP *v.* 1. **6** squeeze. **7** eke out, manage. **8 a** get by, cope, (barely) manage, survive, scratch along. **b** just *or* barely pass, *colloq.* squeak by *or* through. **9** gather, garner, glean, get together, save (up), get hold of, marshal, amass, muster, aggregate, compile, accumulate, pile up, assemble; scratch together *or* up, rake together, dredge up. **10** skimp, scrimp, save, stint, be frugal *or* stingy *or* parsimonious *or* thrifty, pinch, economize. ● *n.* **2** abrasion, bruise, scratch, graze, scuff; injury. **5** predicament, difficulty, quandary, plight, pretty kettle of fish, muddle, mess, tight spot *or* place *or* corner, tough spot, *colloq.* pickle, fix, *disp.* dilemma. □ **scrape acquaintance with** see CULTIVATE 3b.

scraper /skráypər/ *n.* a device used for scraping, esp. for removing dirt etc. from a surface.

scraperboard /skráypərbord/ *n. Brit.* cardboard or board with a blackened surface which can be scraped off for making white-line drawings.

scrapie /skráypi/ *n.* a viral disease of sheep involving the central nervous system and characterized by lack of coordination causing affected animals to rub against trees etc. for support.

scraping /skráyping/ *n.* **1** in senses of SCRAPE *v.* & *n.* **2** (esp. in *pl.*) a fragment produced by this.

■ **1** see FRICTION 1, *grovelling* (GROVEL). **2** see SHRED *n.* 1, SCRAP[1] *n.* 6b.

scrappy /skráppi/ *adj.* (**scrappier, scrappiest**) **1** consisting of scraps. **2** incomplete; carelessly arranged or put together. □□ **scrappily** *adv.* **scrappiness** *n.*

■ **2** see INCOMPLETE.

scrapyard /skrápyaard/ *n.* a place where (esp. metal) scrap is collected.

scratch /skrach/ *v.*, *n.*, & *adj.* ● *v.* **1** *tr.* score or mark the surface of with a sharp or pointed object. **2** *tr.* **a** make a long narrow superficial wound in (the skin). **b** cause (a person or part of the body) to be scratched (*scratched himself on the table*). **3** *tr.* (also *absol.*) scrape without marking, esp. with the hand to relieve itching (*stood there scratching*). **4** *tr.* make or form by scratching. **5** *tr.* scribble; write hurriedly or awkwardly (*scratched a quick reply*; *scratched a large A*). **6** *tr.* (foll. by *together, up*, etc.) obtain (a thing) by scratching or with difficulty. **7** *tr.* (foll. by *out, off, through*) cancel or strike (out) with a pencil etc. **8** *tr.* (also *absol.*) withdraw (a competitor, candidate, etc.) from a race or competition. **9** *intr.* (often foll. by *about, around*, etc.) **a** scratch the ground etc. in search. **b** look around haphazardly (*they were scratching about for evidence*). ● *n.* **1** a mark or wound made by scratching. **2** a sound of scratching. **3** a spell of scratching oneself. **4** *colloq.* a superficial wound. **5** a line from which competitors in a race (esp. those not receiving a handicap) start. **6** (in *pl.*) a disease of horses in which the pastern appears scratched. **7** *sl.* money. ● *attrib.adj.* **1** collected by chance. **2** collected or made from whatever is available; heterogeneous (*a scratch crew*). **3** with no handicap given (*a scratch race*). □ **from scratch 1** from the beginning. **2** without help or advantage. **scratch along** make a living etc. with difficulty. **scratch one's head** be perplexed. **scratch my back and I will scratch yours 1** do me a favour and I will return it. **2** used in reference to mutual aid or flattery. **scratch pad 1** esp. *US* a pad of paper for scribbling. **2** *Computing* a small fast memory for the temporary storage of data. **scratch the surface** deal with a matter only superficially. **up to scratch** up to the required standard. □□ **scratcher** *n.* [ME, prob. f. synonymous ME *scrat* & *cratch*, both of uncert. orig.: cf. MLG *kratsen*, OHG *krazzōn*]

■ *v.* **1** score, mar, mark, gouge, claw. **2** gash, abrade, graze, scuff, bruise; damage, injure. **3** scrape, chafe, rub. **5** scribble, scrawl; see also WRITE 3, 4. **7** obliterate, cross out, delete, strike out *or* off, expunge. **8** withdraw, take out, eliminate, remove. **9 b** cast about *or* around, look round, search. ● *n.* **1** gouge; gash, abrasion, scrape, graze, scuff, bruise, injury, wound. **4** scrape, graze, scuff, bruise. **7** see MONEY 1. ● *attrib.adj.* **2** random, haphazard, casual, makeshift, extempore, stopgap; heterogeneous, composite, motley. □ **from scratch 1** from the start *or* beginning *or* outset, *colloq.* from the word go. **scratch along** see SCRAPE *v.* 8a. **up to scratch** up to standard *or* par, adequate, sufficient, good enough, competent, satisfactory, *colloq.* up to snuff.

scratchy /skráchi/ *adj.* (**scratchier, scratchiest**) **1** tending to make scratches or a scratching noise. **2** (esp. of a garment) tending to cause itchiness. **3** (of a drawing etc.) done in scratches or carelessly. □□ **scratchily** *adv.* **scratchiness** *n.*

■ **1** rough, hoarse, raw, grating, raspy; jagged, jaggy. **2** itchy, irritating, prickly. **3** see SKETCHY.

scrawl /skrawl/ *v.* & *n.* ● *v.* **1** *tr.* & *intr.* write in a hurried untidy way. **2** *tr.* (foll. by *out*) cross out by scrawling over. ● *n.* **1** a piece of hurried writing. **2** a scrawled note. □□ **scrawly** *adj.* [perh. f. obs. *scrawl* sprawl, alt. of CRAWL]

■ *v.* **1** scribble; scratch. ● *n.* **1** scribble, squiggle. □□ **scrawly** see SKETCHY.

scrawny /skráwni/ *adj.* (**scrawnier, scrawniest**) lean, scraggy. □□ **scrawniness** *n.* [var. of dial. *scranny*: cf. archaic *scrannel* (of sound) weak, feeble]

■ bony, skinny, spare, reedy, lean, lank(y), scraggy, gaunt, raw-boned, angular, emaciated, cadaverous; *colloq.* anorexic.

scream /skreem/ *n.* & *v.* ● *n.* **1** a loud high-pitched piercing cry expressing fear, pain, extreme fright, etc. **2** the act of emitting a scream. **3** *colloq.* an irresistibly funny occurrence or person. ● *v.* **1** *intr.* emit a scream. **2** *tr.* speak or sing (words etc.) in a screaming tone. **3** *intr.* make or move with a shrill sound like a scream. **4** *intr.* laugh uncontrollably. **5** *intr.* be blatantly obvious or conspicuous. **6** *intr. colloq.* turn informer. [OE or MDu.]

■ *n.* **1** shriek, screech, squeal, yowl, wail, caterwaul, howl, cry. **3** *colloq.* card, riot, hoot. ● *v.* **1, 2** shriek, screech, squeal, yowl, wail, caterwaul, howl, cry. **4** laugh, roar, howl, guffaw, *colloq.* hoot. **5** glare, stick out like a sore thumb, stick out a mile. **6** see INFORM 2.

screamer /skréemər/ *n.* **1** a person or thing that screams. **2** any S. American goose-like bird of the family Anhimidae, frequenting marshland and having a characteristic shrill cry. **3** *colloq.* a tale that raises screams of laughter. **4** *US colloq.* a sensational headline.

scree /skree/ *n.* (in *sing.* or *pl.*) **1** small loose stones. **2** a mountain slope covered with these. [prob. back-form. f. *screes* (pl.) ult. f. ON *skritha* landslip, rel. to *skrítha* glide]

screech /skreech/ *n.* & *v.* ● *n.* a harsh high-pitched scream. ● *v.tr.* & *intr.* utter with or make a screech. □ **screech-owl** any owl that screeches instead of hooting, esp. a barn-owl or a small American owl, *Otus asio*. □□ **screecher** *n.* **screechy** *adj.* (**screechier, screechiest**). [16th-c. var. of ME *scritch* (imit.)]

■ *n.* see SCREAM *n.* 1. ● *v.* see SCREAM *v.* 1, 2. □□ **screechy** see SHRILL *adj.*

screed /skreed/ *n.* **1** a long usu. tiresome piece of writing or speech. **2 a** a strip of plaster or other material placed on a surface as a guide to thickness. **b** a levelled layer of material (e.g. cement) applied to a floor or other surface. [ME, prob. var. of SHRED]

■ **1** see LECTURE *n.* 2.

screen /skreen/ *n.* & *v.* ● *n.* **1** a fixed or movable upright partition for separating, concealing, or sheltering from draughts or excessive heat or light. **2** a thing used as a shelter, esp. from observation. **3 a** a measure adopted for concealment. **b** the protection afforded by this (*under the screen of night*). **4 a** a blank usu. white or silver surface on which a photographic image is projected. **b** (prec. by *the*) the cinema industry. **5** the surface of a cathode-ray tube or similar electronic device, esp. of a television, VDU, etc., on which images appear. **6** = *sight-screen*. **7** = WINDSCREEN. **8** a frame with fine wire netting to keep out flies, mosquitoes, etc. **9** *Physics* a body intercepting light, heat, electric or magnetic induction, etc., in a physical apparatus. **10** *Photog.* a piece of ground glass in a camera for focusing. **11** a large sieve or riddle, esp. for sorting grain, coal, etc., into sizes. **12** a system of checking for the presence or absence of a disease, ability, attribute, etc. **13** *Printing* a transparent finely-ruled plate or film used in half-tone reproduction. **14** *Mil.* a body of troops, ships, etc., detached to warn of the presence of an enemy force. ● *v.tr.* **1** (often foll. by *from*) **a** afford shelter to; hide partly or completely. **b** protect from detection, censure, etc. **2** (foll. by *off*) shut off or hide behind a screen. **3 a** show (a film etc.) on a screen. **b** broadcast (a television programme). **4** prevent from causing, or protect from, electrical interference. **5 a** test (a person or group) for the presence or absence of a disease. **b** check on (a person) for the presence or absence of a quality, esp. reliability or loyalty. **6** pass (grain, coal, etc.) through a screen. □ **screen printing** a process like stencilling with ink forced through a prepared sheet of fine material (orig. silk). **screen test** an audition for a part in a cinema film. □□ **screenable** *adj.* **screener** *n.* [ME f. ONF *escren*, *escran*: cf. OHG *skrank* barrier]

■ *n.* **1** partition, divider, wall, shield. **2** shelter, shield, cover; see also VEIL *n.* 4. **3 b** protection, shelter, cover, concealment; camouflage, curtain, shroud, cloak. **4 b** cinema (industry), silver screen, *esp. US colloq.* movies. **11** sieve, strainer, filter, riddle, colander. **12** scan, survey; see also CHECK[1] *n.* 1 ● *v.* **1** shield, shelter, protect, guard, hide, conceal, cover, mask, veil. **2** partition (off), separate, divide, wall off, shut off. **3 b** see BROADCAST *v.* 1a. **5 b** check (on *or* out), test, evaluate, examine, investigate, inspect, look over, vet.

screenings /skréeningz/ *n.pl.* refuse separated by sifting.

screenplay /skréenplay/ *n.* the script of a film, with acting instructions, scene directions, etc.

■ see SCRIPT *n.* 4.

screenwriter /skréenrītər/ *n.* a person who writes a screenplay.

■ see DRAMATIST.

screw /skrōō/ *n.* & *v.* ● *n.* **1** a thin cylinder or cone with a spiral ridge or thread running round the outside (**male screw**) or the inside (**female screw**). **2** (in full **wood-screw**) a metal male screw with a slotted head and a sharp point for fastening things, esp. in carpentry, by being rotated to form a thread in wood etc. **3** (in full **screw-bolt**) a metal male screw with a blunt end on which a nut is threaded to bolt things together. **4** a wooden or metal straight screw used to exert pressure. **5** (in *sing.* or *pl.*) an instrument of torture acting in this way. **6** (in full **screw-propeller**) a form of propeller with twisted blades acting like a screw on the water or air. **7** one turn of a screw. **8** (foll. by *of*) *Brit.* a small twisted-up paper (of tobacco etc.). **9** *Brit.* (in billiards etc.) an oblique curling motion of the ball. **10** *sl.* a prison warder. **11** *Brit. sl.* an amount of salary or wages. **12** *coarse sl.* **a** an act of sexual intercourse. **b** a partner in this. ¶ Usually considered a taboo use. **13** *sl.* a mean or miserly person. **14** *sl.* a worn-out horse. ● *v.* **1** *tr.* fasten or tighten with a screw or screws. **2** *tr.* turn (a screw). **3** *intr.* twist or turn round like a screw. **4** *intr.* (of a ball etc.) swerve. **5** *tr.* **a** put psychological etc. pressure on to achieve an end. **b** oppress. **6** *tr.* (foll. by *out of*) extort (consent, money, etc.) from (a person). **7** *tr.* (also *absol.*) *coarse sl.* have sexual intercourse with. ¶ Usually considered a taboo use. **8** *intr.* (of a rolling ball, or of a person etc.) take a curling course; swerve. **9** *intr.* (often foll. by *up*) make tenser or more efficient. □ **have one's head screwed on the right way** *colloq.* have common sense. **have a screw loose** *colloq.* be slightly crazy. **put the screws on** *colloq.* exert pressure on, esp. to extort or intimidate. **screw cap** = *screw top*. **screw-coupling** a female screw with threads at both ends for joining lengths of pipes or rods. **screw eye** a screw with a loop for passing cord etc. through instead of a slotted head. **screw gear** an endless screw with a cog-wheel or pinion. **screw hook** a hook to hang things on, with a screw point for fastening it. **screw-jack** a vehicle jack (see JACK[1]) worked by a screw device. **screw pine** any plant of the genus *Pandanus*, with its leaves arranged spirally and resembling those of a pineapple. **screw-plate** a steel plate with threaded holes for making male screws. **screw-tap** a tool for making female screws. **screw top** (also (with hyphen) *attrib.*) a cap or lid that can be screwed on to a bottle, jar, etc. **screw up 1** contract or contort (one's face etc.). **2** contract and crush into a tight mass (a piece of paper etc.). **3** summon up (one's courage etc.). **4** *sl.* **a** bungle or mismanage. **b** spoil or ruin (an event, opportunity, etc.). **screw-up** *n. sl.* a bungle, muddle, or mess. **screw valve** a stopcock opened and shut by a screw. □□ **screwable** *adj.* **screwer** *n.* [ME f. OF *escroue* female screw, nut, f. L *scrofa* sow]

■ *n.* **3** bolt. **7** twist, turn, rotation, revolution, wind, coil. **13** see MISER. ● *v.* **2, 3** twist, turn, rotate. **5 a** see INDUCE 1. **b** see OPPRESS 1, 2. **6** (*screw out of*) extort *or* force from. **8** see SWERVE *v.* **9** see TIGHTEN. □ **have a screw loose** be crazy, be as mad as a hatter *or* March hare, have bats in the belfry. **put the screws on** pressure, influence, force, constrain, press, coerce, compel, apply pressure to, bring pressure to bear on *or* upon, pressurize, *colloq.* twist a person's arm, put the squeeze on. **screw up 1** contract, contort, twist. **2** crumple, scrumple. **3** raise, stretch, strain, summon (up), call up, call upon, tap, draw on *or* upon. **4** ruin, spoil, destroy, make a mess of, botch, bungle, muddle, mismanage, mishandle, *colloq.* make a hash of, *sl.* louse up, *Brit. sl.* scupper.

screwball /skrōōbawl/ *n.* & *adj.* *US sl.* ● *n.* a crazy or eccentric person. ● *adj.* crazy.

■ *n.* see MADMAN. ● *adj.* see CRAZY 1.

screwdriver /skrōōdrīvər/ *n.* a tool with a shaped tip to fit into the head of a screw to turn it.

screwed /skrōōd/ *adj.* **1** twisted. **2** *sl.* **a** ruined; rendered ineffective. **b** drunk.

screwy /skrōō-i/ *adj.* (**screwier**, **screwiest**) *sl.* **1** crazy or eccentric. **2** absurd. □□ **screwiness** *n.*

■ **1** see CRAZY 1. **2** see ABSURD.

scribble[1] /skríbb'l/ *v.* & *n.* ● *v.* **1** *tr.* & *intr.* write carelessly or hurriedly. **2** *intr.* often *derog.* be an author or writer. **3** *intr.* & *tr.* draw carelessly or meaninglessly. ● *n.* **1** a scrawl. **2** a hasty note etc. **3** careless handwriting. □□ **scribbler** *n.* **scribbly** *adj.* [ME f. med.L *scribillare* dimin. of L *scribere* write]

■ *v.* **1, 3** scrawl, scratch. □□ **scribbler** see WRITER 1.

scribble[2] /skríbb'l/ *v.tr.* card (wool, cotton, etc.) coarsely. [prob. f. LG: cf. G *schrubbeln* (in the same sense), frequent. f. LG *schrubben*: see SCRUB[1]]

scribe /skrīb/ *n.* & *v.* ● *n.* **1** a person who writes out documents, esp. an ancient or medieval copyist of manuscripts. **2** *Bibl.* an ancient Jewish record-keeper or professional theologian and jurist. **3** (in full **scribe-awl**) a pointed instrument for making marks on wood, bricks, etc., to guide a saw, or in sign-writing. **4** *US colloq.* a writer, esp. a journalist. ● *v.tr.* mark (wood etc.) with a scribe (see sense 3 of *n.*). □□ **scribal** *adj.* **scriber** *n.* [(n.) ME f. L *scriba* f. *scribere* write: (v.) perh. f. DESCRIBE]

■ *n.* **1** copyist, copier, transcriber, *hist.* scrivener; amanuensis, clerk, secretary. **4** writer, author, penman, wordsmith, hack, penny-a-liner, *often derog.* scribbler; columnist, journalist, gentleman *or* lady of the press, newspaperman, newspaperwoman, reporter, *Austral. colloq.* journo, *joc.* member of the fourth estate. ● *v.*

inscribe, incise, etch, engrave, mark, scratch, score, grave, scrimshaw, carve; chase, enchase.

scrim /skrim/ *n.* open-weave fabric for lining or upholstery etc. [18th c.: orig. unkn.]

scrimmage /skrímmij/ *n.* & *v.* • *n.* **1** a rough or confused struggle; a brawl. **2** *Amer. Football* a sequence of play beginning with the placing of the ball on the ground with its longest axis at right angles to the goal-line. • *v.* **1** *intr.* engage in a scrimmage. **2** *tr. Amer. Football* put (the ball) into a scrimmage. □□ **scrimmager** *n.* [var. of SKIRMISH]
▪ *n.* **1** skirmish, scuffle, fray, affray, disturbance, brouhaha, mêlée, riot, brawl, struggle, scramble, tussle, fracas, Donnybrook, battle, fight, free-for-all, *esp. US* ruckus, *colloq.* row, rumpus, set-to, dust-up, scrap, *Brit. sl.* (bit of) bovver. • *v.* **1** see BRAWL *v.*

scrimp /skrimp/ *v.* **1** *intr.* be sparing or parsimonious. **2** *tr.* use sparingly. □□ **scrimpy** *adj.* [18th c., orig. Sc.: perh. rel. to SHRIMP]
▪ **1** see ECONOMIZE 1. □□ **scrimpy** see MEAGRE 1.

scrimshank /skrímshangk/ *v.intr. Brit. sl.* esp. *Mil.* shirk duty. □□ **scrimshanker** *n.* [19th c.: orig. unkn.]
▪ see SLACK[1] *v.* 2. □□ **scrimshanker** see SLACKER.

scrimshaw /skrímshaw/ *v.* & *n.* • *v.tr.* (also *absol.*) adorn (shells, ivory, etc.) with carved or coloured designs (as sailors' pastime at sea). • *n.* work or a piece of work of this kind. [19th c.: perh. f. a surname]
▪ *v.* see SCRIBE *v.*

scrip /skrip/ *n.* **1** a provisional certificate of money subscribed to a bank or company etc. entitling the holder to a formal certificate and dividends. **2** (*collect.*) such certificates. **3** an extra share or shares instead of a dividend. [abbr. of *subscription receipt*]

script /skript/ *n.* & *v.* • *n.* **1** handwriting as distinct from print; written characters. **2** type imitating handwriting. **3** an alphabet or system of writing (*the Russian script*). **4** the text of a play, film, or broadcast. **5** an examinee's set of written answers. **6** *Law* an original document as distinct from a copy. • *v.tr.* write a script for (a film etc.). [ME, = thing written, f. OF *escri(p)t* f. L *scriptum*, neut. past part. of *scribere* write]
▪ *n.* **1** handwriting, (cursive) writing, calligraphy. **4** manuscript, text, book, play, screenplay, libretto.

scriptorium /skriptóriəm/ *n.* (*pl.* **scriptoria** /-riə/ or **scriptoriums**) a room set apart for writing, esp. in a monastery. □□ **scriptorial** *adj.* [med.L (as SCRIPT)]

scriptural /skrípchərəl, -choorəl/ *adj.* **1** of or relating to a scripture, esp. the Bible. **2** having the authority of a scripture. □□ **scripturally** *adv.* [LL *scripturalis* f. L *scriptura*: see SCRIPTURE]

scripture /skrípchər/ *n.* **1** sacred writings. **2** (**Scripture** or **the Scriptures**) **a** the Bible as a collection of sacred writings in Christianity. **b** the sacred writings of any other religion. [ME f. L *scriptura* (as SCRIPT)]
▪ **1** sacred writings, Holy Writ. **2** (**Scripture** *or* **the Scriptures**) **a** the Bible, the good book, Holy Writ *or* Scripture, the Word (of God), Gospel(s). **b** Shastra; Koran; Granth; Upanishads; Sutra.

scriptwriter /skríptrītər/ *n.* a person who writes a script for a film, broadcast, etc. □□ **scriptwriting** *n.*
▪ see DRAMATIST.

scrivener /skrívvənər/ *n. hist.* **1** a copyist or drafter of documents. **2** a notary. **3** a broker. **4** a moneylender. [ME f. obs. *scrivein* f. OF *escrivein* ult. f. L (as SCRIBE)]
▪ **1** see SCRIBE *n.* 1. **3** see BROKER 1.

scrobiculate /skrəbíkyoolət/ *adj. Bot.* & *Zool.* pitted, furrowed. [L *scrobiculus* f. *scrobis* trench]

scrod /skrod/ *n. US* a young cod or haddock, esp. as food. [19th c.: perh. rel. to SHRED]

scrofula /skrófyoolə/ *n. archaic* a disease with glandular swellings, prob. a form of tuberculosis. Also called *king's evil.* □□ **scrofulous** *adj.* [ME f. med.L (sing.) f. LL *scrofulae* (pl.) scrofulous swelling, dimin. of L *scrofa* a sow]

scroll /skrōl/ *n.* & *v.* • *n.* **1** a roll of parchment or paper esp. with writing on it. **2** a book in the ancient roll form. **3** an ornamental design or carving imitating a roll of parchment. • *v.* **1** *tr.* (often foll. by *down, up*) move (a display on a VDU screen) in order to view new material. **2** *tr.* inscribe in or like a scroll. **3** *intr.* curl up like paper. □ **scroll saw** a saw for cutting along curved lines in ornamental work. [ME *scrowle* alt. f. *rowle* ROLL, perh. after *scrow* (in the same sense), formed as ESCROW]
▪ *n.* **3** coil, spiral, whorl.

scrolled /skrōld/ *adj.* having a scroll ornament.

scrollwork /skrōlwurk/ decoration of spiral lines, esp. as cut by a scroll saw.

Scrooge /skrōōj/ *n.* a mean or miserly person. [a character in Dickens's *Christmas Carol*]
▪ see MISER.

scrotum /skrṓtəm/ *n.* (*pl.* **scrota** /-tə/ or **scrotums**) a pouch of skin containing the testicles. □□ **scrotal** *adj.* **scrotitis** /-tī́tiss/ *n.* [L]

scrounge /skrownj/ *v.* & *n. colloq.* • *v.* **1** *tr.* (also *absol.*) obtain (things) illicitly or by cadging. **2** *intr.* search about to find something at no cost. • *n.* an act of scrounging. □ **on the scrounge** engaged in scrounging. □□ **scrounger** *n.* [var. of dial. *scrunge* steal]
▪ *v.* **1** cadge, beg, sponge, *US sl.* bum. **2** sponge, *US sl.* freeload. □□ **scrounger** cadger, parasite, sponger, *US sl.* freeloader.

scrub[1] /skrub/ *v.* & *n.* • *v.* (**scrubbed, scrubbing**) **1** *tr.* rub hard so as to clean, esp. with a hard brush. **2** *intr.* use a brush in this way. **3** *intr.* (often foll. by *up*) (of a surgeon etc.) thoroughly clean the hands and arms by scrubbing, before operating. **4** *tr. colloq.* scrap or cancel (a plan, order, etc.). **5** *tr.* use water to remove impurities from (gas etc.). • *n.* the act or an instance of scrubbing; the process of being scrubbed. □ **scrubbing-brush** (*US* **scrub-brush**) a hard brush for scrubbing floors. **scrub round** *colloq.* circumvent, avoid. [ME prob. f. MLG, MDu. *schrobben, schrubben*]
▪ *v.* **1, 2** scour, rub, scrape, clean, *usu. formal* cleanse. **4** cancel, scrap, call off, abort, drop, terminate, give up, end, abandon, stop, cease, discontinue, do away with. □ **scrub round** circumvent, avoid; see also EVADE 1, 2.

scrub[2] /skrub/ *n.* **1 a** vegetation consisting mainly of brushwood or stunted forest growth. **b** an area of land covered with this. **2** (of livestock) of inferior breed or physique (often *attrib.*: *scrub horse*). **3** a small or dwarf variety (often *attrib.*: *scrub pine*). **4** *US Sport colloq.* a team or player not of the first class. □ **scrub turkey** a megapode. **scrub typhus** a rickettsial disease of the W. Pacific transmitted by mites. □□ **scrubby** *adj.* [ME, var. of SHRUB[1]]

scrubber /skrúbbər/ *n.* **1** an apparatus using water or a solution for purifying gases etc. **2** *sl. derog.* a sexually promiscuous woman.

scruff[1] /skruf/ *n.* the back of the neck as used to grasp and lift or drag an animal or person by (esp. *scruff of the neck*). [alt. of *scuff*, perh. f. ON *skoft* hair]

scruff[2] /skruf/ *n. colloq.* an untidy or scruffy person. [orig. = SCURF, later 'worthless thing', or back-form. f. SCRUFFY]

scruffy /skrúffi/ *adj.* (**scruffier, scruffiest**) *colloq.* shabby, slovenly, untidy. □□ **scruffily** *adv.* **scruffiness** *n.* [*scruff* var. of SCURF + -Y[1]]
▪ see SHABBY 1, 2.

scrum /skrum/ *n.* **1** *Rugby Football* an arrangement of the forwards of each team in two opposing groups, each with arms interlocked and heads down, with the ball thrown in between them to restart play. **2** *colloq.* a milling crowd. □ **scrum-half** a half-back who puts the ball into the scrum. [abbr. of SCRUMMAGE]

scrummage /skrúmmij/ *n. Rugby Football* = SCRUM 1. [as SCRIMMAGE]

scrummy /skrúmi/ *adj. colloq.* excellent; enjoyable; delicious. [SCRUMPTIOUS + -Y[1]]

scrump /skrump/ *v.tr. Brit. colloq.* steal (fruit) from an orchard or garden. [cf. SCRUMPY]

scrumple /skrúmp'l/ *v.tr.* crumple, wrinkle. [var. of CRUMPLE]

scrumptious /skrúmpshəss/ *adj. colloq.* **1** delicious. **2** pleasing, delightful. □□ **scrumptiously** *adv.* **scrumptiousness** *n.* [19th c.: orig. unkn.]
■ **1** see DELICIOUS.

scrumpy /skrúmpi/ *n. Brit. colloq.* rough cider, esp. as made in the West Country of England. [dial. *scrump* small apple]

scrunch /skrunch/ *v.* & *n.* ● *v.tr.* & *intr.* **1** (usu. foll. by *up*) make or become crushed or crumpled. **2** make or cause to make a crunching sound. ● *n.* the act or an instance of scrunching. [var. of CRUNCH]
■ *v.* **1** see RUMPLE. **2** see MUNCH.

scruple /skrōōp'l/ *n.* & *v.* ● *n.* **1** (in *sing.* or *pl.*) **a** regard to the morality or propriety of an action. **b** a feeling of doubt or hesitation caused by this. **2** *Brit. hist.* an apothecaries' weight of 20 grains. **3** *archaic* a very small quantity. ● *v.intr.* **1** (foll. by *to* + infin.; usu. with *neg.*) be reluctant because of scruples (*did not scruple to stop their allowance*). **2** feel or be influenced by scruples. [F *scrupule* or L *scrupulus* f. *scrupus* rough pebble, anxiety]
■ *n.* **1** qualm, misgiving, doubt, twinge of conscience. ● *v.* **1** (*scruple to*) baulk at, have (any) scruples about, hesitate to, have any doubts *or* compunction about, shrink from *or* at, have (any) misgivings *or* qualms about *or* over, think twice about, be loath *or* reluctant to. **2** hesitate, think twice, pause, falter, vacillate, demur, waver.

scrupulous /skrōōpyooləss/ *adj.* **1** conscientious or thorough even in small matters. **2** careful to avoid doing wrong. **3** punctilious; over-attentive to details. □□ **scrupulosity** /-lóssiti/ *n.* **scrupulously** *adv.* **scrupulousness** *n.* [ME f. F *scrupuleux* or L *scrupulosus* (as SCRUPLE)]
■ **1, 3** careful, cautious, meticulous, exacting, precise, nice, strict, rigid, rigorous, severe, critical, fastidious, neat, conscientious, painstaking, thorough; finicky, finical, fussy, punctilious. **2** ethical, honourable, upstanding, moral, righteous, principled, high-minded, just.

scrutineer /skrōōtinéer/ *n.* a person who scrutinizes or examines something, esp. the conduct and result of a ballot.

scrutinize /skrōōtinīz/ *v.tr.* (also **-ise**) look closely at; examine with close scrutiny. □□ **scrutinizer** *n.*
■ examine, analyse, dissect, investigate, probe, study, inspect, sift, go over *or* through, check.

scrutiny /skrōōtini/ *n.* (*pl.* **-ies**) **1** a critical gaze. **2** a close investigation or examination of details. **3** an official examination of ballot-papers to check their validity or accuracy of counting. [ME f. L *scrutinium* f. *scrutari* search f. *scruta* rubbish: orig. of rag-collectors]
■ **2** examination, analysis, investigation, probing, study, inspection, sifting, inquiry, enquiry, exploration; probe, check.

scry /skrī/ *v.intr.* (**-ies**, **-ied**) divine by crystal-gazing. □□ **scryer** *n.* [shortening f. DESCRY]

scuba /skōōbə, skyōō-/ *n.* (*pl.* **scubas**) an aqualung. [acronym f. *s*elf-*c*ontained *u*nderwater *b*reathing *a*pparatus]

scuba-diving /skōōbədīving, skyōō-/ *n.* swimming underwater using a scuba, esp. as a sport. □□ **scuba-dive** *v.intr.* **scuba-diver** *n.*

scud /skud/ *v.* & *n.* ● *v.intr.* (**scudded**, **scudding**) **1** fly or run straight, fast, and lightly; skim along. **2** *Naut.* run before the wind. ● *n.* **1** a spell of scudding. **2** a scudding motion. **3** vapoury driving clouds. **4** a driving shower; a gust. **5** wind-blown spray. **6** (**Scud**) a type of long-range surface-to-surface guided missile originally developed in the former Soviet Union. [perh. alt. of SCUT, as if to race like a hare]
■ *v.* **1** fly, skim, race, speed, shoot, *colloq.* scoot.

scuff /skuf/ *v.* & *n.* ● *v.* **1** *tr.* graze or brush against. **2** *tr.* mark or wear down (shoes) in this way. **3** *intr.* walk with dragging feet; shuffle. ● *n.* a mark of scuffing. [imit.]
■ *v.* **2** see SCRAPE *v.* 3b. **3** shuffle, stumble, drag one's feet. ● *n.* see SCRAPE *n.* 2.

scuffle /skúff'l/ *n.* & *v.* ● *n.* a confused struggle or disorderly fight at close quarters. ● *v.intr.* engage in a scuffle. [prob. f. Scand.: cf. Sw. *skuffa* to push, rel. to SHOVE]
■ *n.* see FIGHT *n.* 1a. ● *v.* see FIGHT *v.* 1a.

sculduggery var. of SKULDUGGERY.

scull /skul/ *n.* & *v.* ● *n.* **1** either of a pair of small oars used by a single rower. **2** an oar placed over the stern of a boat to propel it, usu. by a twisting motion. **3** (in *pl.*) a race between boats with single pairs of oars. ● *v.tr.* propel (a boat) with sculls. [ME: orig. unkn.]
■ *n.* **1, 2** oar, paddle, sweep. ● *v.* see PADDLE[1] *v.* 1, 2.

sculler /skúllər/ *n.* **1** a user of sculls. **2** a boat intended for sculling.
■ **1** see OAR 2.

scullery /skúlləri/ *n.* (*pl.* **-ies**) a small kitchen or room at the back of a house for washing dishes etc. [ME f. AF *squillerie*, OF *escuelerie* f. *escuele* dish f. L *scutella* salver dimin. of *scutra* wooden platter]
■ see KITCHEN.

scullion /skúlyən/ *n. archaic* **1** a cook's boy. **2** a person who washes dishes etc. [ME: orig. unkn.]
■ see SERVANT.

sculpin /skúlpin/ *n.* any of numerous fish of the family Cottidae, native to non-tropical regions, having large spiny heads. [perh. f. obs. *scorpene* f. L *scorpaena* f. Gk *skorpaina* a fish]

sculpt /skulpt/ *v.tr.* & *intr.* (also **sculp**) sculpture. [F *sculpter* f. *sculpteur* SCULPTOR: now regarded as an abbr.]
■ see SCULPTURE *v.*

sculptor /skúlptər/ *n.* (*fem.* **sculptress** /-triss/) an artist who makes sculptures. [L (as SCULPTURE)]

sculpture /skúlpchər/ *n.* & *v.* ● *n.* **1** the art of making forms, often representational, in the round or in relief by chiselling stone, carving wood, modelling clay, casting metal, etc. **2** a work or works of sculpture. **3** *Zool.* & *Bot.* raised or sunken markings on a shell etc. ● *v.* **1** *tr.* represent in or adorn with sculpture. **2** *intr.* practise sculpture. □□ **sculptural** *adj.* **sculpturally** *adv.* **sculpturesque** *adj.* [ME f. L *sculptura* f. *sculpere sculpt-* carve]
■ *n.* **2** statue, statuette, relief; (*sculptures*) marbles. ● *v.* **1** sculpt, model, chisel, carve, cast, form, fashion.

scum /skum/ *n.* & *v.* ● *n.* **1** a layer of dirt, froth, or impurities etc. forming at the top of liquid, esp. in boiling or fermentation. **2** (foll. by *of*) the most worthless part of something. **3** *colloq.* a worthless person or group. ● *v.* (**scummed**, **scumming**) **1** *tr.* remove scum from; skim. **2** *tr.* be or form a scum on. **3** *intr.* (of a liquid) develop scum. □□ **scummy** *adj.* (**scummier**, **scummiest**) *adj.* [ME f. MLG, MDu. *schūm*, OHG *scūm* f. Gmc]
■ *n.* **1** see DIRT 1. **3** see RIFF-RAFF. □□ **scummy** see FILTHY *adj.* 1.

scumbag /skúmbag/ *n. sl.* a worthless despicable person.
■ see WRETCH 2.

scumble /skúmb'l/ *v.* & *n.* ● *v.tr.* **1** modify (a painting) by applying a thin opaque coat of paint to give a softer or duller effect. **2** modify (a drawing) similarly with light pencilling etc. ● *n.* **1** material used in scumbling. **2** the effect produced by scumbling. [perh. frequent. of SCUM *v.tr.*]

scuncheon /skúnchən/ *n.* the inside face of a door-jamb, window-frame, etc. [ME f. OF *escoinson* (as EX-[1], COIN)]

scunge /skunj/ *n. Austral.* & *NZ colloq.* **1** dirt, scum. **2** a dirty or disagreeable person. □□ **scungy** *adj.* (**scungier**, **scungiest**). [perh. f. E dial. *scrunge* steal: cf. SCROUNGE]
■ **1** see DIRT 1.

scunner /skúnnər/ *v.* & *n. Sc.* ● *v.intr.* & *tr.* feel disgust; nauseate. ● *n.* **1** a strong dislike (esp. *take a scunner at* or *against*). **2** an object of loathing. [14th c.: orig. uncert.]

scup /skup/ *n.* an E. American fish, *Stenostomus chrysops*, a kind of porgy. [Narragansett *mishcup* thick-scaled f. *mishe* large + *cuppi* scale]

scupper[1] /skúppər/ *n.* a hole in a ship's side to carry off water from the deck. [ME (perh. f. AF) f. OF *escopir* f. Rmc *skuppire* (unrecorded) to spit: orig. imit.]

scupper[2] /skúppər/ *v.tr. Brit. sl.* **1** sink (a ship or its crew). **2** defeat or ruin (a plan etc.). **3** kill. [19th c.: orig. unkn.]
■ **2** see RUIN *v.* 1b.

scurf /skurf/ *n.* **1** flakes on the surface of the skin, cast off as fresh skin develops below, esp. those of the head; dandruff. **2** any scaly matter on a surface. □□ **scurfy** *adj.* [OE, prob. f. ON & earlier OE *sceorf*, rel. to *sceorfan* gnaw, *sceorfian* cut to shreds]
■ scaliness, flakiness, scales, flakes, particles, laminae; dandruff. □□ **scurfy** see SCALY.

scurrilous /skúrriləss/ *adj.* **1** (of a person or language) grossly or indecently abusive. **2** given to or expressed with low humour. □□ **scurrility** /-rílliti/ *n.* (*pl.* **-ies**). **scurrilously** *adv.* **scurrilousness** *n.* [F *scurrile* or L *scurrilus* f. *scurra* buffoon]
■ **1** foul-mouthed, gross, indecent, vulgar, obscene, licentious, foul, coarse, scabrous, low, vile; nasty, vituperative, defamatory, derogatory, disparaging, vilifying, calumnious, malign, aspersive, opprobrious, offensive, abusive, insulting. **2** see COARSE 2.

scurry /skúrri/ *v.* & *n.* ● *v.intr.* (**-ies, -ied**) run or move hurriedly, esp. with short quick steps; scamper. ● *n.* (*pl.* **-ies**) **1** the act or sound of scurrying. **2** bustle, haste. **3** a flurry of rain or snow. [abbr. of *hurry-scurry* redupl. of HURRY]
■ *v.* dash, scramble, dart, fly, race, sprint, scamper, scuttle, hurry, hasten, speed, hustle, rush, tear, zoom, zip, bolt, rip, scud, *colloq.* scoot. ● *n.* **2** haste, rush, hustle, bustle; see also FLURRY *n.* 3.

scurvy /skúrvi/ *n.* & *adj.* ● *n.* a disease caused by a deficiency of vitamin C, characterized by swollen bleeding gums and the opening of previously healed wounds, esp. formerly affecting sailors. ● *adj.* (**scurvier, scurviest**) paltry, low, mean, dishonourable, contemptible. □ **scurvy grass** any cresslike seaside plant of the genus *Cochlearia*, orig. taken as a cure for scurvy. □□ **scurvied** *adj.* **scurvily** *adv.* [SCURF + -Y[1]: noun sense by assoc. with F *scorbut* (cf. SCORBUTIC)]
■ *adj.* low, paltry, miserable, contemptible, vile, base, despicable, rotten, sorry, bad, ignoble, dishonourable, mean, worthless, shabby.

scut /skut/ *n.* a short tail, esp. of a hare, rabbit, or deer. [ME: orig. unkn.: cf. obs. *scut* short, shorten]
■ see TAIL[1] *n.* 1.

scuta *pl.* of SCUTUM.

scutage /skyóotij/ *n. hist.* money paid by a feudal landowner instead of personal service. [ME f. med.L *scutagium* f. L *scutum* shield]

scutch /skuch/ *v.tr.* dress (fibrous material, esp. retted flax) by beating. □□ **scutcher** *n.* [OF *escouche, escoucher* (dial.), *escousser*, ult. f. L *excutere excuss-* (as EX-[1], *quatere* shake)]

scutcheon /skúchən/ *n.* **1** = ESCUTCHEON. **2** an ornamented brass etc. plate round or over a keyhole. **3** a plate for a name or inscription. [ME f. ESCUTCHEON]

scute /skyoot/ *n. Zool.* = SCUTUM. [L (as SCUTUM)]

scutellum /skyootélləm/ *n.* (*pl.* **scutella** /-lə/) *Bot.* & *Zool.* a scale, plate, or any shieldlike formation on a plant, insect, bird, etc., esp. one of the horny scales on a bird's foot. □□ **scutellate** /skyóotələt/ *adj.* **scutellation** /skyóotəláysh'n/ *n.* [mod.L dimin. of L *scutum* shield]

scutter /skúttər/ *v.* & *n.* ● *v.intr. colloq.* scurry. ● *n.* the act or an instance of scuttering. [perh. alt. of SCUTTLE[2]]

scuttle[1] /skútt'l/ *n.* **1** a receptacle for carrying and holding a small supply of coal. **2** *Brit.* the part of a motor-car body between the windscreen and the bonnet. [ME f. ON *skutill*, OHG *scuzzila* f. L *scutella* dish]
■ **1** bucket, pail.

scuttle[2] /skútt'l/ *v.* & *n.* ● *v.intr.* **1** scurry; hurry along. **2** run away; flee from danger or difficulty. ● *n.* **1** a hurried gait. **2** a precipitate flight or departure. [cf. dial. *scuddle* frequent. of SCUD]
■ *v.* **1** see SCURRY *v.*

scuttle[3] /skútt'l/ *n.* & *v.* ● *n.* a hole with a lid in a ship's deck or side. ● *v.tr.* let water into (a ship) to sink it, esp. by opening the seacocks. [ME, perh. f. obs. F *escoutille* f. Sp. *escotilla* hatchway dimin. of *escota* cutting out cloth]
■ *v.* sink, *Brit. sl.* scupper.

scuttlebutt /skútt'lbut/ *n.* **1** a water-butt on the deck of a ship, for drinking from. **2** *colloq.* rumour, gossip.
■ **2** see RUMOUR *n.* 1.

scutum /skyóotəm/ *n.* (*pl.* **scuta** /-tə/) each of the shieldlike plates or scales forming the bony covering of a crocodile, sturgeon, turtle, armadillo, etc. □□ **scutal** *adj.* **scutate** *adj.* [L, = oblong shield]
■ see SCALE[1] *n.* 1.

scuzzy /skúzzi/ *adj. sl.* abhorrent or disgusting. [prob. f. DISGUSTING]

Scylla and Charybdis /síllə ənd kəríbdiss/ *n.pl.* two dangers such that avoidance of one increases the risk from the other. [the names of a sea-monster and whirlpool in Gk mythology]

scyphozoan /sífəzóən/ *n.* & *adj.* ● *n.* any marine jellyfish of the class Scyphozoa, with tentacles bearing stinging cells. ● *adj.* of or relating to this class. [as SCYPHUS + Gk *zōion* animal]

scyphus /sífəss/ *n.* (*pl.* **scyphi** /-fī/) **1** *Gk Antiq.* a footless drinking-cup with two handles below the level of the rim. **2** *Bot.* a cup-shaped part as in a narcissus flower or in lichens. □□ **scyphose** *adj.* [mod.L f. Gk *skuphos*]

scythe /sīth/ *n.* & *v.* ● *n.* a mowing and reaping implement with a long curved blade swung over the ground by a long pole with two short handles projecting from it. ● *v.tr.* cut with a scythe. [OE *sīthe* f. Gmc]
■ *v.* see MOW[1].

Scythian /síthiən/ *adj.* & *n.* ● *adj.* of or relating to ancient Scythia, a region north of the Black Sea. ● *n.* **1** an inhabitant of Scythia. **2** the language of this region. [L *Scythia* f. Gk *Skuthia* Scythia]

SD *abbr. US* South Dakota (in official postal use).

S.Dak. *abbr.* South Dakota.

SDI *abbr.* strategic defence initiative.

SDLP *abbr.* (in N. Ireland) Social Democratic and Labour Party.

SDP *abbr.* (in the UK) Social Democratic Party.

SDR *abbr.* special drawing right (from the International Monetary Fund).

SE *abbr.* **1** south-east. **2** south-eastern.

Se *symb. Chem.* the element selenium.

se- /sə, si/ *prefix* apart, without (*seclude*; *secure*). [L f. OL *se* (prep. & adv.)]

sea /see/ *n.* **1** the expanse of salt water that covers most of the earth's surface and surrounds its land masses. **2** any part of this as opposed to land or fresh water. **3** a particular (usu. named) tract of salt water partly or wholly enclosed by land (*the North Sea*; *the Dead Sea*). **4** a large inland lake (*the Sea of Galilee*). **5** the waves of the sea, esp. with reference to their local motion or state (*a choppy sea*). **6** (foll. by *of*) a vast quantity or expanse (*a sea of troubles*; *a sea of faces*). **7** (*attrib.*) living or used in, on, or near the sea (often prefixed to the name of a marine animal, plant, etc., having a superficial resemblance to what it is named after) (*sea lettuce*). □ **at sea 1** in a ship on the sea. **2** (also **all at sea**) perplexed, confused. **by sea** in a ship or ships. **go to sea** become a sailor. **on the sea 1** in a ship at sea. **2** situated on the coast. **put** (or **put out**) **to sea** leave land or port. **sea anchor** a device such as a heavy bag dragged in the water to retard the drifting of a ship. **sea anemone** any of various coelenterates of the order Actiniaria having a polypoid body bearing a ring of tentacles around the mouth. **sea-angel** an angel-fish. **sea bass** any of various marine fishes like the bass, esp. *Centropristis striatus*. **sea bird** a bird frequenting the sea or the land near the sea. **sea bream** = PORGY. **sea breeze** a breeze blowing towards the land from the sea, esp. during the day (cf. *land breeze*). **sea buckthorn** a maritime shrub, *Hippophaë rhamnoides* with orange berries. **sea change** a notable or unexpected transformation (with ref. to Shakesp. *Tempest* I. ii. 403). **sea-chest** a sailor's storage-chest. **sea coal** *archaic* mineral coal, as distinct from charcoal etc. **sea cow 1** a sirenian. **2** a walrus. **sea cucumber** a holothurian, esp. a *bêche-de-mer*. **sea dog** an old or experienced sailor. **sea eagle** any fish-eating eagle esp. of the genus *Haliaëtus*. **sea-ear** = ORMER. **sea elephant** any large seal of the genus *Mirounga*, the male of which has a proboscis: also called *elephant seal*. **sea fan** any colonial coral of the order Gorgonacea supported by a fanlike horny skeleton. **sea front** the part of a coastal town directly facing the sea. **sea-girt** *literary* surrounded by sea. **sea gooseberry** any marine animal of the phylum Ctenophora, with an ovoid body bearing numerous cilia. **sea-green** bluish-green (as of the sea). **sea hare** any of various marine molluscs of the order Anaspidea, having an internal shell and long extensions from its foot. **sea holly** a spiny-leaved blue-flowered evergreen plant, *Eryngium maritimum*. **sea horse 1** any of various small upright marine fish of the family Syngnathidae, esp. *Hippocampus hippocampus*, having a body suggestive of the head and neck of a horse. **2** a mythical creature with a horse's head and fish's tail. **sea-island cotton** a fine-quality long-stapled cotton grown on islands off the southern US. **sea lavender** any maritime plant of the genus *Limonium*, with small brightly-coloured funnel-shaped flowers. **sea legs** the ability to keep one's balance and avoid seasickness when at sea. **sea level** the mean level of the sea's surface, used in reckoning the height of hills etc. and as a barometric standard. **sea lily** any of various sessile echinoderms, esp. of the class Crinoidea, with long jointed stalks and feather-like arms for trapping food. **sea lion** any large, eared seal of the Pacific, esp. of the genus *Zalophus* or *Otaria*. **sea loch** = LOCH 2. **Sea Lord** (in the UK) a naval member of the Admiralty Board. **sea mile** = *nautical mile*. **sea mouse** any iridescent marine annelid of the genus *Aphrodite*. **sea onion** = SQUILL 2. **sea otter** a Pacific otter, *Enhydra lutris*, using a stone balanced on its abdomen to crack bivalve molluscs. **sea pink** a maritime plant, *Armeria maritima*, with bright pink flowers: also called THRIFT. **sea purse** the egg-case of a skate or shark. **sea room** clear space at sea for a ship to turn or manoeuvre in. **sea salt** salt produced by evaporating sea water. **Sea Scout** a member of the maritime branch of the Scout Association. **sea serpent** (or **snake**) **1** a snake of the family Hydrophidae, living in the sea. **2** an enormous legendary serpent-like sea monster. **sea shell** the shell of a salt-water mollusc. **sea snail 1** a small slimy fish of the family Liparididae, with a ventral sucker. **2** any spiral-shelled mollusc, e.g. a whelk. **sea squirt** any marine tunicate of the class Ascidiacea, consisting of a bag-like structure with apertures for the flow of water. **sea trout** = *salmon trout*. **sea urchin** a small marine echinoderm of the class Echinoidea, with a spherical or flattened spiny shell. **sea wall** a wall or embankment erected to prevent encroachment by the sea. **sea water** water in or taken from the sea. [OE *sǣ* f. Gmc]

■ **1** ocean, high sea(s), blue water, *archaic or poet.* main, *colloq.* the drink, *joc.* pond, *poet.* deep, *Brit. sl.* briny. **5** see WAVE *n.* 1, 2. **6** plethora, quantity, abundance, surfeit, profusion, flood, multitude, spate, legion, mass, mountain, *colloq.* lot, heap, pile, load. □ **at sea 2** confused, disoriented, bewildered, perplexed, baffled, mystified, lost; at sixes and sevens, adrift. **sea change** transformation, watershed, landmark, turning-point, crossroads. **sea dog** see SAILOR.

seabed /séebed/ *n.* the ground under the sea; the ocean floor.

seaboard /séebord/ *n.* **1** the seashore or coastal region. **2** the line of a coast.

■ see COAST *n.*

seaborne /séeborn/ *adj.* transported by sea.

seacock /séekok/ *n.* a valve below a ship's water-line for letting water in or out.

■ see TAP[1] *n.* 1.

seafarer /séefairər/ *n.* **1** a sailor. **2** a traveller by sea.

■ **1** see SAILOR.

seafaring /séefairing/ *adj.* & *n.* travelling by sea, esp. regularly.

■ *adj.* maritime, nautical, naval, marine.

seafood /séefo͞od/ *n.* edible sea fish or shellfish.

seagoing /séegōing/ *adj.* **1** (of ships) fit for crossing the sea. **2** (of a person) seafaring.

■ **2** seafaring, ocean-going.

seagull /séegul/ *n.* = GULL[1].

seakale /séekayl/ *n.* a cruciferous maritime plant, *Crambe maritima*, having coarsely-toothed leaves and used as a vegetable. □ **seakale beet** = CHARD.

seal[1] /seel/ *n.* & *v.* ● *n.* **1** a piece of wax, lead, paper, etc., with a stamped design, attached to a document as a guarantee of authenticity. **2** a similar material attached to a receptacle, envelope, etc., affording security by having to be broken to allow access to the contents. **3** an engraved piece of metal, gemstone, etc., for stamping a design on a seal. **4 a** a substance or device used to close an aperture or act as a fastening. **b** an amount of water standing in the trap of a drain to prevent foul air from rising. **5** an act or gesture or event regarded as a confirmation or guarantee (*gave her seal of approval to the venture*). **6** a significant or prophetic mark (*has the seal of death in his face*). **7** a decorative adhesive stamp. **8** esp. *Eccl.* a vow of secrecy; an obligation to silence. ● *v.tr.* **1** close securely or hermetically. **2** stamp or fasten with a seal. **3** fix a seal to. **4** certify as correct with a seal or stamp. **5** (often foll. by *up*) confine or fasten securely. **6** settle or decide (*their fate is sealed*). **7** (foll. by *off*) put barriers round (an area) to prevent entry and exit, esp. as a security measure. **8** apply a non-porous coating to (a surface) to make it impervious. □ **Great Seal** (in the UK) the seal in the charge of the Lord Chancellor or Lord Keeper used in sealing important State papers. **one's lips are sealed** one is obliged to keep a secret. **sealed-beam** (*attrib.*) designating a vehicle headlamp with a sealed unit consisting of the light source, reflector, and lens. **sealed book** see BOOK. **sealed orders** orders for procedure not to be opened before a specified time. **sealing-wax** a mixture of shellac and rosin with turpentine and pigment, softened by heating and used to make seals. **seal ring** a finger ring with a seal. **seals of office** (in the UK) those held during tenure esp. by the Lord Chancellor or a Secretary of State. **set one's seal to** (or **on**) authorize or confirm. □□ **sealable** *adj.* [ME f. AF *seal*, OF *seel* f. L *sigillum* dimin. of *signum* SIGN]

■ *n.* **5** authentication, confirmation, verification, validation, affirmation, attestation, ratification, corroboration, assurance, guarantee, guaranty, endorsement, substantiation, notification. **6** see SIGN *n.* 1. ● *v.* **1** seal up, close up, zip up, plug (up), stop (up), lock, bolt, secure, batten down, make airtight *or* waterproof; cork. **4** authenticate, confirm, verify, validate, affirm, attest, ratify, corroborate, guarantee, endorse. **7** close off, shut off, barricade, block.

seal[2] /seel/ *n.* & *v.* ● *n.* any fish-eating amphibious sea mammal of the family Phocidae or Otariidae, with flippers and webbed feet. ● *v.intr.* hunt for seals. [OE *seolh seol-* f. Gmc]

sealant /séelənt/ *n.* material for sealing, esp. to make something airtight or watertight.

sealer /séelər/ *n.* a ship or person engaged in hunting seals.

sealery /séeləri/ *n.* (*pl.* **-ies**) a place for hunting seals.

sealskin /séelskin/ *n.* **1** the skin or prepared fur of a seal. **2** (often *attrib.*) a garment made from this.

Sealyham /séeliəm/ *n.* (in full **Sealyham terrier**) **1** a terrier of a wire-haired short-legged breed. **2** this breed. [*Sealyham* in S. Wales]

seam /seem/ *n.* & *v.* ● *n.* **1** a line where two edges join, esp. of two pieces of cloth etc. turned back and stitched together, or of boards fitted edge to edge. **2** a fissure between parallel edges. **3** a wrinkle or scar. **4** a stratum of coal etc. ● *v.tr.* **1** join with a seam. **2** (esp. as **seamed** *adj.*) mark or score with or as with a seam. □ **bursting at the seams** full to overflowing. **seam bowler** *Cricket* a bowler who makes the ball deviate by bouncing off its seam. □□ **seamer** *n.* **seamless** *adj.* [OE *sēam* f. Gmc]

■ *n.* **1** junction, juncture, join, joint, commissure. **3** wrinkle, scar, cicatrice. **4** lode, vein, stratum, bed, layer. □ **bursting at the seams** see FULL[1] *adj.* 1.

seaman /seéman/ *n.* (*pl.* **-men**) **1** a sailor, esp. one below the rank of officer. **2** a person regarded in terms of skill in navigation (*a poor seaman*). □□ **seamanlike** *adj.* **seamanly** *adj.* [OE *sǣman* (as SEA, MAN)]

■ **1** see SAILOR. **2** see NAVIGATOR.

seamanship /seémanship/ *n.* skill in managing a ship or boat.

■ see NAVIGATION.

seamstress /sémstriss/ *n.* (also **sempstress**) a woman who sews, esp. professionally; a needlewoman. [OE *sēamestre* fem. f. *sēamere* tailor, formed as SEAM + -STER + -ESS[1]]

■ see DRESSMAKER.

seamy /seémi/ *adj.* (**seamier, seamiest**) **1** marked with or showing seams. **2** unpleasant, disreputable (esp. *the seamy side*). □□ **seaminess** *n.*

■ **2** sordid, nasty, dark, disreputable, unpleasant, shameful, unwholesome, unpalatable, unsavoury, distasteful, unseemly, squalid, low, depraved, degenerate, degraded, foul, vile, odious, abhorrent, contemptible, scurvy, rotten, unattractive, ugly, repulsive, repellent.

Seanad /shánnath/ *n.* the upper House of Parliament in the Republic of Ireland. [Ir., = senate]

seance /sáyonss/ *n.* (also **séance**) a meeting at which spiritualists attempt to make contact with the dead. [F *séance* f. OF *seoir* f. L *sedēre* sit]

seaplane /seéplayn/ *n.* an aircraft designed to take off from and land and float on water.

seaport /seéport/ *n.* a town with a harbour for seagoing ships.

■ port, harbour, haven.

SEAQ *abbr.* Stock Exchange Automated Quotations (computerized access to share information).

seaquake /seékwayk/ *n.* an earthquake under the sea.

sear /seer/ *v.* & *adj.* ● *v.tr.* **1 a** scorch, esp. with a hot iron; cauterize, brand. **b** (as **searing** *adj.*) scorching, burning (*searing pain*). **2** cause pain or great anguish to. **3** brown (meat) quickly at a high temperature so that it will retain its juices in cooking. **4** make (one's conscience, feelings, etc.) callous. **5** *archaic* blast, wither. ● *adj.* (also **sere**) *literary* (esp. of a plant etc.) withered, dried up. [OE *sēar* (adj.), *sēarian* (v.), f. Gmc]

■ *v.* **1 a** see SCORCH *v.* 1, 2. **b** (**searing**) see *scorching* (SCORCH *v.* 3). ● *adj.* withered, shrivelled (up), dry, parched.

search /serch/ *v.* & *n.* ● *v.* **1** *tr.* look through or go over thoroughly to find something. **2** *tr.* examine or feel over (a person) to find anything concealed. **3** *tr.* **a** probe or penetrate into. **b** examine or question (one's mind, conscience, etc.) thoroughly. **4** *intr.* (often foll. by *for*) make a search or investigation. **5** *intr.* (as **searching** *adj.*) (of an examination) thorough; leaving no loopholes. **6** *tr.* (foll. by *out*) look probingly for; seek out. ● *n.* **1** an act of searching. **2** an investigation. □ **in search of** trying to find. **right of search** a belligerent's right to stop a neutral vessel and search it for prohibited goods. **search me!** *colloq.* I do not know. **search-party** a group of people organized to look for a lost person or thing. **search warrant** an official authorization to enter and search a building. □□ **searchable** *adj.* **searcher** *n.* **searchingly** *adv.* [ME f. AF *sercher*, OF *cerchier* f. LL *circare* go round (as CIRCUS)]

■ *v.* **1, 3** search through, examine, scrutinize, check, comb (through), explore, go through, investigate, inspect, look at *or* into, probe, scour, sift through, hunt *or* rummage through, plough through; probe, penetrate, pry into; inquire *or* enquire of. **2** see FRISK *v.* 2. **4** look (about *or* around), cast about, seek. **5** (**searching**) see THOROUGH 2. **6** seek (out), scout out, look for, hunt for; track down, uncover, pinpoint. ● *n.* **1** hunt, pursuit; see also QUEST *n.* **2** analysis, investigation, exploration, examnation, scrutiny, probe, study, perusal, sifting, inspection, scouring, inquiry, enquiry. □ **search me!** see *ask me another*. □□ **searchingly** penetratingly, piercingly, intently, deeply.

searchlight /sérchlīt/ *n.* **1** a powerful outdoor electric light with a concentrated beam that can be turned in any direction. **2** the light or beam from this.

■ spotlight, arc light, spot; beam, ray, shaft.

seascape /seéskayp/ *n.* a picture or view of the sea.

■ see VIEW *n.* 2.

seashore /seéshor/ *n.* **1** land close to or bordering on the sea. **2** *Law* the area between high and low water marks.

■ **1** see COAST *n.*

seasick /seéssik/ *adj.* suffering from sickness or nausea from the motion of a ship at sea. □□ **seasickness** *n.*

■ see SICK[1] *adj.* 1. □□ **seasickness** *mal de mer.*

seaside /seéssīd/ *n.* the sea-coast, esp. as a holiday resort.

■ see COAST *n.*

season /seéz'n/ *n.* & *v.* ● *n.* **1** each of the four divisions of the year (spring, summer, autumn, and winter) associated with a type of weather and a stage of vegetation. **2** a time of year characterized by climatic or other features (*the dry season*). **3 a** the time of year when a plant is mature or flowering etc. **b** the time of year when an animal breeds or is hunted. **4** a proper or suitable time. **5** a time when something is plentiful or active or in vogue. **6** (usu. prec. by *the*) = *high season*. **7** the time of year regularly devoted to an activity (*the football season*). **8** the time of year dedicated to social life generally (*went up to London for the season*). **9** a period of indefinite or varying length. **10** *Brit. colloq.* = *season ticket*. ● *v.* **1** *tr.* flavour (food) with salt, herbs, etc. **2** *tr.* enhance with wit, excitement, etc. **3** *tr.* temper or moderate. **4** *tr.* & *intr.* **a** make or become suitable or in the desired condition, esp. by exposure to the air or weather; mature. **b** (usu. as **seasoned** *adj.*) make or become experienced or accustomed (*seasoned soldiers*). □ **in season 1** (of foodstuff) available in plenty and in good condition. **2** (of an animal) on heat. **3** timely. **season ticket** a ticket entitling the holder to any number of journeys, admittances, etc., in a given period. □□ **seasoner** *n.* [ME f. OF *seson* f. L *satio -onis* (in Rmc sense 'seed-time') f. *serere sat-* sow]

■ *n.* **1–3, 5** time, period. ● *v.* **1** spice, salt, flavour, *colloq.* pep up. **2** see ENLIVEN 1. **3** see MODERATE *v.* 1. **4 a** ripen, mature, age, condition, mellow. **b** (**seasoned**) experienced, long-standing, practised, well-versed, habituated, acclimatized, accustomed, familiarized, prepared, established, veteran, tempered, hardened, toughened, inured, *US* acclimated. □ **in season 1** ripe, ready, edible; seasoned, seasonable; available, plentiful. **3** see TIMELY.

seasonable /seézanab'l/ *adj.* **1** suitable to or usual in the season. **2** opportune. **3** meeting the needs of the occasion. □□ **seasonableness** *n.* **seasonably** *adv.*

■ **1** appropriate, suitable, apt, opportune, timely, fitting, well-timed, proper, fit. **2, 3** appropriate, suitable, apt, opportune, timely, fitting, well-timed, proper, fit, propitious, welcome, well-suited, providential, happy, lucky, fortunate, convenient, auspicious, favourable, advantageous, expedient.

seasonal /seézan'l/ *adj.* of, depending on, or varying with the season. □ **seasonal affective disorder** a depressive state associated with late autumn and winter and thought to be caused by a lack of light. □□ **seasonality** /-nálliti/ *n.* **seasonally** *adv.*

■ see INTERMITTENT.

seasoning /seézaning/ *n.* condiments added to food.

■ spice, flavouring, zest, relish, sauce; condiments.

seat /seet/ *n.* & *v.* ● *n.* **1** a thing made or used for sitting on; a chair, stool, saddle, etc. **2** the buttocks. **3** the part of the trousers etc. covering the buttocks. **4** the part of a chair etc. on which the sitter's weight directly rests. **5** a place for one person in a theatre, vehicle, etc. **6** the occupation of a seat. **7** esp. *Brit.* **a** the right to occupy a seat, esp. as a Member of the House of Commons. **b** a member's constituency. **8** the part of a machine that supports or guides another part. **9** a site or location of something specified (*a seat of learning; the seat of the emotions*). **10** a country mansion, esp. with large grounds. **11** the manner of sitting on a horse etc. ● *v.tr.* **1** cause to sit. **2 a** provide sitting accommodation for (*the cinema seats 500*). **b** provide with seats. **3** (as **seated** *adj.*) sitting. **4** put or fit in position. □ **be seated** sit down. **by the seat of one's pants** *colloq.* by instinct rather than logic or knowledge. **seat-belt** a belt securing a person in the seat of a car or aircraft. **take a** (or **one's**) **seat** sit down. □□ **seatless** *adj.* [ME f. ON *sæti* (= OE *gesete* f. Gmc)]

■ *n.* **1** place, chair; bench, sofa, settee, settle, stool, throne, saddle. **2** bottom, buttocks, posterior(s), rump, hindquarters, *colloq.* behind, behind, backside, rear, *colloq. euphem. derrière*, *joc.* fundament, *Brit. sl.* bum, *esp. US sl.* tush, butt, tail. **7 a** place, position; incumbency. **9** focus, base, centre, heart, hub, site, location, capital, cradle, headquarters, fountain-head. **10** (country) house, abode, residence, home, domicile, estate, mansion. ● *v.* **2** hold, accommodate, contain, have room *or* capacity *or* space for, sit, have seats *or* seating for. **3** (**seated**) sitting (down); sedentary. **4** locate, position, site, fit.

-seater /séetər/ *n.* (in *comb.*) having a specified number of seats (*a 16-seater bus*).

seating /séeting/ *n.* **1** seats collectively. **2** sitting accommodation.

■ accommodation, capacity, space, room.

SEATO /séetō/ *abbr.* South-East Asia Treaty Organization.

seaward /séeward/ *adv.*, *adj.*, & *n.* ● *adv.* (also **seawards**) towards the sea. ● *adj.* going or facing towards the sea. ● *n.* such a direction or position.

seaway /séeway/ *n.* **1** an inland waterway open to seagoing ships. **2** a ship's progress. **3** a ship's path across the sea.

seaweed /séeweed/ *n.* any of various algae growing in the sea or on the rocks on a shore.

seaworthy /séewurthi/ *adj.* (esp. of a ship) fit to put to sea. □□ **seaworthiness** *n.*

■ see NAVIGABLE 2, 3.

sebaceous /sibáyshəss/ *adj.* fatty; of or relating to tallow or fat. □ **sebaceous gland** (or **follicle** or **duct**) a gland etc. secreting or conveying oily matter to lubricate the skin and hair. [L *sebaceus* f. *sebum* tallow]

■ see FAT *adj.* 4.

seborrhoea /sébbəreéə/ *n.* (*US* **seborrhea**) excessive discharge of sebum from the sebaceous glands. □□ **seborrhoeic** *adj.* [SEBUM after *gonorrhoea* etc.]

sebum /séebəm/ *n.* the oily secretion of the sebaceous glands. [mod.L f. L *sebum* grease]

Sec. *abbr.* secretary.

sec[1] *abbr.* secant.

sec[2] /sek/ *n. colloq.* (in phrases) a second (of time). [abbr.]

■ see SECOND[2].

sec. *abbr.* second(s).

sec /sek/ *adj.* (of wine) dry. [F f. L *siccus*]

secant /séekənt, sék-/ *adj.* & *n. Math.* ● *adj.* cutting (*secant line*). ● *n.* **1** a line cutting a curve at one or more points. **2** the ratio of the hypotenuse to the shorter side adjacent to an acute angle (in a right-angled triangle). ¶ Abbr.: **sec.** [F *sécant(e)* f. L *secare secant-* cut]

secateurs /sékkətúrz/ *n.pl.* esp. *Brit.* a pair of pruning clippers for use with one hand. [F *sécateur* cutter, irreg. f. L *secare* cut]

secco /sékkō/ *n.* the technique of painting on dry plaster with pigments mixed in water. [It., = dry, f. L *siccus*]

secede /siséed/ *v.intr.* (usu. foll. by *from*) withdraw formally from membership of a political federation or a religious body. □□ **seceder** *n.* [L *secedere secess-* (as SE-, *cedere* go)]

■ withdraw, resign, retire, apostatize, break away, disaffiliate, defect, drop *or* pull out; (*secede from*) withdraw *or* resign *or* retire from, abandon, quit, leave, forsake, break with, break away from, drop *or* pull out of, turn one's back to *or* on, separate from, wash one's hands of, have nothing further to do with.

secession /siséshʼn/ *n.* **1** the act or an instance of seceding. **2** (**Secession**) *hist.* the withdrawal of eleven southern States from the US Union in 1860, leading to the Civil War. □□ **secessional** *adj.* **secessionism** *n.* **secessionist** *n.* [F *sécession* or L *secessio* (as SECEDE)]

■ **1** withdrawal, seceding, defection, break, breaking, disaffiliation, retirement, separation, splitting off *or* away, apostasy.

seclude /siklóod/ *v.tr.* (also *refl.*) **1** keep (a person or place) retired or away from company. **2** (esp. as **secluded** *adj.*) hide or screen from view. [ME f. L *secludere seclus-* (as SE-, *claudere* shut)]

■ **1** see SEGREGATE[1] 1. **2** (**secluded**) private, separated, isolated, lonely, cloistered, sequestered, segregated, detached, solitary, eremitic, monastic; off the beaten track, out of the way, remote, far-away, far-off.

seclusion /siklóozhʼn/ *n.* **1** a secluded state; retirement, privacy. **2** a secluded place. □□ **seclusionist** *n.* **seclusive** /-klóossiv/ *adj.* [med.L *seclusio* (as SECLUDE)]

■ **1** privacy, retirement, separation, isolation, loneliness, solitude. **2** see RETREAT *n.* 3.

second[1] /sékkənd/ *n.*, *adj.*, & *v.* ● *n.* **1** the position in a sequence corresponding to that of the number 2 in the sequence 1–2. **2** something occupying this position. **3** the second person etc. in a race or competition. **4** *Mus.* **a** an interval or chord spanning two consecutive notes in the diatonic scale (e.g. C to D). **b** a note separated from another by this interval. **5** = *second gear*. **6** another person or thing in addition to one previously mentioned or considered (*the policeman was then joined by a second*). **7** (in *pl.*) **a** goods of a second or inferior quality. **b** coarse flour, or bread made from it. **8** (in *pl.*) *colloq.* **a** a second helping of food at a meal. **b** the second course of a meal. **9** an attendant assisting a combatant in a duel, boxing-match, etc. **10 a** a place in the second class of an examination. **b** a person having this. ● *adj.* **1** that is the second; next after first. **2** additional, further; other besides one previously mentioned or considered (*ate a second cake*). **3** subordinate in position or importance etc.; inferior. **4** *Mus.* performing a lower or subordinate part (*second violins*). **5** such as to be comparable to; closely reminiscent of (*a second Callas*). ● *v.tr.* **1** supplement, support; back up. **2** formally support or endorse (a nomination or resolution etc., or its proposer). □ **at second hand** by hearsay, not direct observation etc. **in the second place** as a second consideration etc. **second advent** a supposed return of Christ to earth. **second ballot** a deciding ballot between candidates coming first (without an absolute majority) and second in a previous ballot. **second-best** *adj.* next after best. ● *n.* a less adequate or desirable alternative. **second cause** *Logic* a cause that is itself caused. **second chamber** the upper house of a bicameral parliament. **second class** the second-best group or category, esp. of hotel or train accommodation or (in the UK) of postal services. **second-class** *adj.* **1** of or belonging to the second class. **2** inferior in quality, status, etc. (*second-class citizens*). ● *adv.* by second-class post, train, etc. (*travelled second-class*). **second coming** *Theol.* the second advent of Christ on earth. **second cousin** see COUSIN. **second-degree** *Med.* denoting burns that cause blistering but not permanent scars. **second fiddle** see FIDDLE. **second floor** **1** *Brit.* the floor two levels above the ground floor. **2** *US* the floor above the ground floor. **second gear** the second (and next to lowest) in a sequence of gears. **second-generation** denoting the offspring of a first generation, esp. of immigrants. **second-guess** *colloq.* **1** anticipate or predict by guesswork. **2** judge or criticize with hindsight. **second honeymoon** a holiday like a honeymoon, taken by a couple after some years of marriage. **second in**

command the officer next in rank to the commanding or chief officer. **second lieutenant** an army officer next below lieutenant or *US* first lieutenant. **second name** a surname. **second nature** (often foll. by *to*) an acquired tendency that has become instinctive (*is second nature to him*). **second officer** an assistant mate on a merchant ship. **second person** *Gram.* see PERSON. **second-rate** of mediocre quality; inferior. **second-rater** a person or thing that is second-rate. **second reading** a second presentation of a bill to a legislative assembly, in the UK to approve its general principles and in the US to debate committee reports. **second self** a close friend or associate. **second sight** the supposed power of being able to perceive future or distant events. **second-sighted** having the gift of second sight. **second string** an alternative course of action, means of livelihood, etc., invoked if the main one is unsuccessful. **second teeth** the teeth that replace the milk teeth in a mammal. **second thoughts** a new opinion or resolution reached after further consideration. **second to none** surpassed by no other. **second wind 1** recovery of the power of normal breathing during exercise after initial breathlessness. **2** renewed energy to continue an effort. ▫▫ **seconder** *n.* (esp. in sense 2 of *v.*). [ME f. OF f. L *secundus* f. *sequi* follow]

▪ *n.* **7 a** (*seconds*) rejects, defective *or* imperfect merchandise *or* goods. ● *adj.* **2** additional, further, other, subsequent, later, following, next, more recent. **3** subordinate, next; inferior, second-best. **5** duplicate; reincarnate, reborn, redivivus. ● *v.* **1** supplement, support, back up, aid, help, assist, approve of, subscribe to, espouse, sponsor, patronize, favour, encourage, go along with. **2** support, back, endorse, approve, go along with.

second[2] /sékkənd/ *n.* **1** a sixtieth of a minute of time or angular distance. ¶ Symb.: ″. **2** the SI unit of time, based on the natural periodicity of the caesium atom. ¶ Abbr.: **s**. **3** *colloq.* a very short time (*wait a second*). ▫ **second-hand** an extra hand in some watches and clocks, recording seconds. [F f. med.L *secunda (minuta)* secondary (minute)]

▪ **3** moment, instant, flash, minute, split second, *colloq.* sec, jiffy, jiff, tick, (half a) mo; (*in a second*) in a twinkle *or* a twinkling *or* the twinkle of an eye, in two shakes (of a lamb's *or* dog's tail).

second[3] /sikónd/ *v.tr. Brit.* transfer (a military officer or other official or worker) temporarily to other employment or to another position. ▫▫ **secondment** *n.* [F *en second* in the second rank (of officers)]

▪ transfer, move, shift, relocate.

secondary /sékkəndəri, -dri/ *adj.* & *n.* ● *adj.* **1** coming after or next below what is primary. **2** derived from or depending on or supplementing what is primary. **3** (of education, a school, etc.) for those who have had primary education, usu. from 11 to 18 years. **4** *Electr.* **a** (of a cell or battery) having a reversible chemical reaction and therefore able to store energy. **b** denoting a device using electromagnetic induction, esp. a transformer. ● *n.* (*pl.* **-ies**) **1** a secondary thing. **2** a secondary device or current. ▫ **secondary colour** the result of mixing two primary colours. **secondary feather** a feather growing from the second joint of a bird's wing. **secondary picketing** the picketing of premises of a firm not otherwise involved in the dispute in question. **secondary planet** a satellite of a planet (cf. *primary planet*). **secondary sexual characteristics** those distinctive of one sex but not directly related to reproduction. ▫▫ **secondarily** *adv.* **secondariness** *n.* [ME f. L *secundarius* (as SECOND[1])]

▪ *adj.* **1** subsidiary, ancillary, subordinate, inferior, minor, unimportant, inessential, unessential, non-essential, non-critical. **2** derivative, derived, indirect, second-hand, unoriginal.

seconde /səkónd/ *n. Fencing* the second of eight parrying positions. [F, fem. of *second* SECOND[1]]

second-hand /sékkəndhánd/ *adj.* & *adv.* ● *adj.* **1 a** (of goods) having had a previous owner; not new. **b** (of a shop etc.) where such goods can be bought. **2** (of information etc.) accepted on another's authority and not from original investigation. ● *adv.* **1** on a second-hand basis. **2** at second hand; not directly.

▪ *adj.* **1 a** used, old, worn, *colloq.* hand-me-down.

secondly /sékkəndli/ *adv.* **1** furthermore; in the second place. **2** as a second item.

secondo /sikóndō/ *n.* (*pl.* **secondi** /-di/) *Mus.* the second or lower part in a duet etc. [It.]

secrecy /séekrisi/ *n.* **1** the keeping of secrets as a fact, habit, or faculty. **2** a state in which all information is withheld (*was done in great secrecy*). ▫ **sworn to secrecy** having promised to keep a secret. [ME f. *secretie* f. obs. *secre* (adj.) or SECRET *adj.*]

▪ mystery, concealment, confidentiality, stealth, secretiveness, surreptitiousness, privacy, furtiveness, covertness, clandestineness.

secret /séekrit/ *adj.* & *n.* ● *adj.* **1** kept or meant to be kept private, unknown, or hidden from all or all but a few. **2** acting or operating secretly. **3** fond of, prone to, or able to preserve secrecy. **4** (of a place) hidden, completely secluded. ● *n.* **1** a thing kept or meant to be kept secret. **2** a thing known only to a few. **3** a mystery. **4** a valid but not commonly known or recognized method of achieving or maintaining something (*what's their secret?*; *correct breathing is the secret of good health*). **5** *RC Ch.* a prayer concluding the offertory of the mass. ▫ **in secret** secretly. **in** (or **in on**) **the secret** among the number of those who know it. **keep a secret** not reveal it. **secret agent** a spy acting for a country. **secret ballot** a ballot in which votes are cast in secret. **secret police** a police force operating in secret for political purposes. **secret service** a government department concerned with espionage. **secret society** a society whose members are sworn to secrecy about it. ▫▫ **secretly** *adv.* [ME f. OF f. L *secretus* (adj.) separate, set apart f. *secernere secret-* (as SE-, *cernere* sift)]

▪ *adj.* **1** concealed, hidden, private, shrouded, under wraps, confidential, classified, quiet, undercover, *colloq.* hush-hush; unpublishable, unpublished; cryptographic, encrypted, encoded. **2** confidential, private, under cover, *colloq.* hush-hush. **3** private, clandestine, covert, secretive, arcane, mysterious, cryptic, *colloq.* hush-hush. **4** concealed, hidden, covert, secluded. ● *n.* **1, 2** private *or* confidential matter *or* affair. **3** see MYSTERY[1] 1. ▫ **in secret** see *secretly* below. **in** (or **in on**) **the secret** in the picture, *colloq.* in the know. ▫▫ **secretly** surreptitiously, quietly, privately, covertly, furtively, under cover, by stealth, stealthily, mysteriously, clandestinely, in secret, confidentially, on the sly, slyly, *sub rosa*, *colloq.* on the q.t.

secretaire /sékritáir/ *n.* an escritoire. [F (as SECRETARY)]

secretariat /sékritáiriət/ *n.* **1** a permanent administrative office or department, esp. a governmental one. **2** its members or premises. **3** the office of secretary. [F *secrétariat* f. med.L *secretariatus* (as SECRETARY)]

secretary /sékritəri, sékrətri, *disp.* sékkitairi/ *n.* (*pl.* **-ies**) **1** a person employed by an individual or in an office etc. to assist with correspondence, keep records, make appointments, etc. **2** an official appointed by a society etc. to conduct its correspondence, keep its records, etc. **3** (in the UK) the principal assistant of a government minister, ambassador, etc. ▫ **secretary bird** a long-legged snake-eating African bird, *Sagittarius serpentarius*, with a crest likened to a quill pen stuck over a writer's ear. **Secretary-General** the principal administrator of an organization. **Secretary of State 1** (in the UK) the head of a major government department. **2** (in the US) the chief government official responsible for foreign affairs. ▫▫ **secretarial** /-táiriəl/ *adj.* **secretaryship** *n.* [ME f. LL *secretarius* (as SECRET)]

▪ ▫▫ **secretarial** see CLERICAL 2.

secrete[1] /sikréet/ *v.tr. Biol.* (of a cell, organ, etc.) produce by secretion. ▫▫ **secretor** *n.* **secretory** *adj.* [back-form. f. SECRETION]

■ excrete, pass, generate, release, ooze, exude, discharge, leak, drip, drop, dribble, trickle, emit, give off, emanate, emit, extravasate.

secrete[2] /sikréet/ *v.tr.* conceal; put into hiding. [obs. *secret* (v.) f. SECRET]

■ hide, conceal, cache, bury, *colloq.* stash away.

secretion /sikréesh'n/ *n.* **1** *Biol.* **a** a process by which substances are produced and discharged from a cell for a function in the organism or for excretion. **b** the secreted substance. **2** the act or an instance of concealing (*the secretion of stolen goods*). [F *sécrétion* or L *secretio* separation (as SECRET)]

■ **1 a** secreting, release, oozing, seeping, seepage, discharge, discharging, leak, leaking, leakage, drip, dripping, drop, dropping, dribbling, trickling, trickle, running, drain, draining, emission, emitting, giving off, exudation, transudation, excretion, excreting, emanation, emanating, generation, extravasation. **b** discharge, excreta. **2** concealment, hiding.

secretive /séekritiv/ *adj.* inclined to make or keep secrets; uncommunicative. ▫▫ **secretively** *adv.* **secretiveness** *n.* [back-form. f. *secretiveness* after F *secrétivité* (as SECRET)]

■ cryptic, mysterious, enigmatic; conspiratorial, furtive; reticent, silent, close-mouthed, taciturn, uncommunicative, reserved, tight-lipped, close, *colloq.* mum.

sect /sekt/ *n.* **1 a** a body of people subscribing to religious doctrines usu. different from those of an established Church from which they have separated. **b** usu. *derog.* a nonconformist or other Church. **c** a party or faction in a religious body. **d** a religious denomination. **2** the followers of a particular philosopher or philosophy, or school of thought in politics etc. [ME f. OF *secte* or L *secta* f. the stem of *sequi secut-* follow]

■ **1** religious group *or* denomination *or* body *or* cult, persuasion. **2** school (of thought), faction, set, clique, cabal, *colloq. usu. derog.* ism.

sect. *abbr.* section.

sectarian /sektáiriən/ *adj.* & *n.* ● *adj.* **1** of or concerning a sect. **2** bigoted or narrow-minded in following the doctrines of one's sect. ● *n.* **1** a member of a sect. **2** a bigot. ▫▫ **sectarianism** *n.* **sectarianize** *v.tr.* (also **-ise**). [SECTARY]

■ *adj.* **1** partisan, factional, cliquish, *usu. derog.* clannish. **2** parochial, narrow, narrow-minded, limited, insular, provincial, rigid, fanatic(al), prejudicial, prejudiced, bigoted, partial, dogmatic, doctrinaire. ● *n.* **1** adherent, member, sectary, votary, cultist, partisan. **2** dogmatist, fanatic, bigot, zealot, extremist.

sectary /séktəri/ *n.* (*pl.* **-ies**) a member of a religious or political sect. [med.L *sectarius* adherent (as SECT)]

■ see SECTARIAN *n.* 1.

section /séksh'n/ *n.* & *v.* ● *n.* **1** a part cut off or separated from something. **2** each of the parts into which a thing is divided (actually or conceptually) or divisible or out of which a structure can be fitted together. **3** a distinct group or subdivision of a larger body of people (*the wind section of an orchestra*). **4** a subdivision of a book, document, statute, etc. **5** *US* **a** an area of land. **b** one square mile of land. **c** a particular district of a town (*residential section*). **6** a subdivision of an army platoon. **7** esp. *Surgery* a separation by cutting. **8** *Biol.* a thin slice of tissue etc., cut off for microscopic examination. **9 a** the cutting of a solid by or along a plane. **b** the resulting figure or the area of this. **10** a representation of the internal structure of something as if cut across along a vertical or horizontal plane. **11** *Biol.* a group, esp. a subgenus. ● *v.tr.* **1** arrange in or divide into sections. **2** *Brit.* cause (a person) to be compulsorily committed to a psychiatric hospital in accordance with a section of a mental health act. **3** *Biol.* cut into thin slices for microscopic examination. ▫ **section-mark** the sign (§) used as a reference mark to indicate the start of a section of a book etc. [F *section* or L *sectio* f. *secare sect-* cut]

■ *n.* **1** part, fraction, segment, portion, slice, sample, division. **2** part, segment, portion, fraction, division, slice; sample, cross-section; stage, stretch, lap. **3** part, division, department, branch, sector, group, segment, portion, subdivision, component, element. **4** part, subdivision; paragraph; chapter. **5 c** district, quarter; see also ZONE *n.* **8** sample, slice, cross-section. ● *v.* **1** cut (up), divide (up), segment, split, *literary* cleave.

sectional /sékshən'l/ *adj.* **1 a** relating to a section, esp. of a community. **b** partisan. **2** made in sections. **3** local rather than general. ▫▫ **sectionalism** *n.* **sectionalist** *n.* & *adj.* **sectionalize** *v.tr.* (also **-ise**). **sectionally** *adv.*

sector /séktər/ *n.* **1** a distinct part or branch of an enterprise, or of society, the economy, etc. **2** *Mil.* a subdivision of an area for military operations, controlled by one commander or headquarters. **3** the plane figure enclosed by two radii of a circle, ellipse, etc., and the arc between them. **4** a mathematical instrument consisting of two arms hinged at one end and marked with sines, tangents, etc., for making diagrams etc. ▫▫ **sectoral** *adj.* [LL, techn. use of L *sector* cutter (as SECTION)]

■ **1** see SECTION *n.* 3.

sectorial /sektóriəl/ *adj.* **1** of or like a sector or sectors. **2** = CARNASSIAL.

secular /sékyoolər/ *adj.* & *n.* ● *adj.* **1** concerned with the affairs of this world; not spiritual or sacred. **2** (of education etc.) not concerned with religion or religious belief. **3 a** not ecclesiastical or monastic. **b** (of clergy) not bound by a religious rule. **4** occurring once in an age or century. **5** lasting for or occurring over an indefinitely long time. ● *n.* a secular priest. ▫ **secular variation** *Astron.* variation compensated over a long period of time. ▫▫ **secularism** *n.* **secularist** *n.* **secularity** /-lárriti/ *n.* **secularize** *v.tr.* (also **-ise**). **secularization** /-rīzáysh'n/ *n.* **secularly** *adv.* [ME (in senses 1–3 f. OF *seculer*) f. L *saecularis* f. *saeculum* generation, age]

■ *adj.* **1** worldly, terrestrial, mundane, temporal, material, lay, laic(al), non-clerical, non-ecclesiastic(al), non-spiritual, non-religious.

secund /sikúnd/ *adj. Bot.* arranged on one side only (as the flowers of lily of the valley). ▫▫ **secundly** *adv.* [L *secundus* (as SECOND[1])]

secure /sikyóor/ *adj.* & *v.* ● *adj.* **1** untroubled by danger or fear. **2** safe against attack: impregnable. **3** reliable; certain not to fail (*the plan is secure*). **4** fixed or fastened so as not to give way or get loose or be lost (*made the door secure*). **5 a** (foll. by *of*) certain to achieve (*secure of victory*). **b** (foll. by *against, from*) safe, protected (*secure against attack*). ● *v.tr.* **1** make secure or safe; fortify. **2** fasten, close, or confine securely. **3** succeed in obtaining or achieving (*have secured front seats*). **4** guarantee against loss (*a loan secured by property*). **5** compress (a blood-vessel) to prevent bleeding. ▫ **secure arms** *Mil.* hold a rifle with the muzzle downward and the lock in the armpit to guard it from rain. ▫▫ **securable** *adj.* **securely** *adv.* **securement** *n.* [L *securus* (as SE-, *cura* care)]

■ *adj.* **1** untroubled, unthreatened, protected, sheltered, safe, shielded, unexposed, immune, snug, cosy. **2** safe, sheltered, shielded, protected, unexposed; impregnable. **3** reliable, safe, good, solid, healthy. **4** firm, steady, stable, fixed, fast, immovable, closed, shut, fastened, locked (up), tight, sound, solid, sturdy, strong; moored, anchored. **5 a** sure, certain, assured. **b** safe, sheltered, shielded, protected. ● *v.* **1** see FORTIFY 1. **2** fasten, close, make fast, fix, affix, attach, anchor; confine. **3** obtain, get (hold of), come by, acquire, procure, win, gain, get possession of, take possession of. **4** guarantee, underwrite.

security /sikyóoriti/ *n.* (*pl.* **-ies**) **1** a secure condition or feeling. **2** a thing that guards or guarantees. **3 a** the safety of a State, company, etc., against espionage, theft, or other danger. **b** an organization for ensuring this. **4** a thing deposited or pledged as a guarantee of the fulfilment of an undertaking or the payment of a loan, to be forfeited in case

of default. **5** (often in *pl.*) a certificate attesting credit or the ownership of stock, bonds, etc. □ **on security of** using as a guarantee. **security blanket 1** an official sanction on information in the interest of security. **2** a blanket or other familiar object given as a comfort to a child. **Security Council** a permanent body of the United Nations seeking to maintain peace and security. **security guard** a person employed to protect the security of buildings, vehicles, etc. **security risk** a person whose presence may threaten security. [ME f. OF *securité* or L *securitas* (as SECURE)]
■ **1** confidence, certainty, assurance, conviction, safety, protection, fastness. **2** refuge, sanctuary, asylum, shelter. **3 a** safeguarding, guarding, safe keeping, protection. **4** guarantee, collateral, deposit, gage, pledge, insurance.

sedan /sidán/ *n.* **1** (in full **sedan chair**) an enclosed chair for conveying one person, carried between horizontal poles by two porters, common in the 17th–18th c. **2** *US* an enclosed motor car for four or more people. [perh. alt. f. It. dial., ult. f. L *sella* saddle f. *sedēre* sit]
■ **1** see LITTER *n.* 4, 5. **2** saloon (car).

sedate[1] /sidáyt/ *adj.* tranquil and dignified; equable, serious. □□ **sedately** *adv.* **sedateness** *n.* [L *sedatus* past part. of *sedare* settle f. *sedēre* sit]
■ composed, serene, peaceful, calm, tranquil, cool, collected, even-tempered, equable, detached, imperturbable, unruffled, undisturbed, unperturbed, controlled, placid, grave, serious, sober, solemn, *colloq.* unflappable; dignified, decorous, formal, stiff, staid, proper, strait-laced, prudish, fussy, prim, conventional, old-fashioned.

sedate[2] /sidáyt/ *v.tr.* put under sedation. [back-form. f. SEDATION]

sedation /sidáysh'n/ *n.* a state of rest or sleep esp. produced by a sedative drug. [F *sédation* or L *sedatio* (as SEDATE[1])]

sedative /séddətiv/ *n.* & *adj.* ● *n.* a drug, influence, etc., that tends to calm or soothe. ● *adj.* calming, soothing; inducing sleep. [ME f. OF *sedatif* or med.L *sedativus* (as SEDATE[1])]
■ *n.* narcotic, tranquillizer, opiate, sleeping-pill, soporific, calmative, anodyne, depressant, hypnotic, barbiturate, *Med.* lenitive, *sl.* downer, Mickey Finn; knock-out drops. ● *adj.* narcotic, tranquillizing, relaxing, soothing, calming, opiate, soporific, sleep-inducing, calmative, anodyne, lenitive, depressing, hypnotic.

sedentary /séddəntəri, -tri/ *adj.* **1** sitting (*a sedentary posture*). **2** (of work etc.) characterized by much sitting and little physical exercise. **3** (of a person) spending much time seated. **4** *Zool.* not migratory, free-swimming, etc. □□ **sedentarily** *adv.* **sedentariness** *n.* [F *sédentaire* or L *sedentarius* f. *sedēre* sit]
■ **1** seated, sitting. **2, 3** stationary, immobile, unmoving, housebound, desk-bound; seated, sitting.

Seder /sáydər/ *n.* the ritual for the first night or first two nights of the Passover. [Heb. *sēder* order]

sederunt /sidáirənt/ *n. Sc.* a sitting of an ecclesiastical assembly or other body. [L, = (the following persons) sat f. *sedēre* sit]

sedge /sej/ *n.* **1** any grasslike plant of the genus *Carex* with triangular stems, usu. growing in wet areas. **2** an expanse of this plant. □ **sedge-warbler** (or **-wren**) a small warbler, *Acrocephalus schoenobaenus*, that breeds in sedge. □□ **sedgy** *adj.* [OE *secg* f. Gmc]

sedile /sidíli/ *n.* (*pl.* **sedilia** /-dílliə/) (usu. in *pl.*) *Eccl.* each of usu. three stone seats for priests in the south wall of a chancel, often canopied and decorated. [L, = seat f. *sedēre* sit]

sediment /séddimənt/ *n.* **1** matter that settles to the bottom of a liquid; dregs. **2** *Geol.* matter that is carried by water or wind and deposited on the surface of the land, and may in time become consolidated into rock. □□ **sedimentary** /-méntəri/ *adj.* **sedimentation** /-táysh'n/ *n.* [F *sédiment* or L *sedimentum* (as SEDILE)]
■ **1** lees, dregs, deposit, grounds, remains, residue, residuum, *Chem.* precipitate.

sedition /sidísh'n/ *n.* **1** conduct or speech inciting to rebellion or a breach of public order. **2** agitation against the authority of a State. □□ **seditious** *adj.* **seditiously** *adv.* [ME f. OF *sedition* or L *seditio* f. *sed-* = SE- + *ire it-* go]
■ **1** agitation, rabble-rousing, insubordination; fomentation, incitement, instigation, stirring *or* whipping up. **2** agitation, mutiny, insurrection, uprising, insurgency, insurgence, rebellion; treason, treachery. □□ **seditious** rebellious, mutinous, riotous, revolutionary, insurgent, insurrectionist, insurrectionary, refractory, subversive, dissenting, insubordinate, treacherous, dissident, disloyal, turncoat, unfaithful; inflammatory, rabble-rousing, unruly, restive, factious.

seduce /sidyōōss/ *v.tr.* **1** tempt or entice into sexual activity or into wrongdoing. **2** coax or lead astray; tempt (*seduced by the smell of coffee*). □□ **seducer** *n.* **seducible** *adj.* [L *seducere seduct-* (as SE-, *ducere* lead)]
■ **1** defile, debauch, deflower, violate, ravish; vamp; dishonour, ruin, corrupt, lead astray. **2** lure, entice, attract, allure, enthral, bewitch, tempt, mislead, beguile, inveigle, deceive, decoy, lead astray, draw on, charm, captivate, blandish, entrap, ensnare, trap, *colloq.* sweet-talk. □□ **seducer** rake, libertine, roué, debauchee, debaucher, Lothario, lecher, Casanova, playboy, Don Juan, philanderer, tempter, ravisher, ladies' man, *colloq.* lady-killer, *sl.* wolf; see also SEDUCTRESS.

seduction /sidúksh'n/ *n.* **1** the act or an instance of seducing; the process of being seduced. **2** something that tempts or allures. [F *séduction* or L *seductio* (as SEDUCE)]
■ see *enticement* (ENTICE).

seductive /sidúktiv/ *adj.* tending to seduce; alluring, enticing. □□ **seductively** *adv.* **seductiveness** *n.* [SEDUCTION after *inductive* etc.]
■ alluring, attractive, tempting, enticing, inviting, seducing, enchanting, entrancing, bewitching, fascinating, captivating, beguiling, provocative, tantalizing, irresistible, winning, winsome, appealing, prepossessing, ravishing, sexy; siren; flirtatious, coquettish.

seductress /sidúktriss/ *n.* a female seducer. [obs. *seductor* male seducer (as SEDUCE)]
■ temptress, siren, *femme fatale*, enchantress, Circe, coquette, Jezebel, *colloq.* vamp.

sedulous /sédyooləss/ *adj.* **1** persevering, diligent, assiduous. **2** (of an action etc.) deliberately and consciously continued; painstaking. □□ **sedulity** /sidyōōliti/ *n.* **sedulously** *adv.* **sedulousness** *n.* [L *sedulus* zealous]
■ **1** see DILIGENT. **2** see CAREFUL 1, 3. □□ **sedulity** see *exertion* (EXERT). **sedulously** see HARD *adv.* 1. **sedulousness** see *exertion* (EXERT).

sedum /seedəm/ *n.* any plant of the genus *Sedum*, with fleshy leaves and star-shaped yellow, pink, or white flowers, e.g. stonecrop. [L, = houseleek]

see[1] /see/ *v.* (*past* **saw** /saw/; *past part.* **seen** /seen/) **1** *tr.* discern by use of the eyes; observe; look at (*can you see that spider?*; *saw him fall over*). **2** *intr.* have or use the power of discerning objects with the eyes (*sees best at night*). **3** *tr.* discern mentally; understand (*I see what you mean*; *could not see the joke*). **4** *tr.* watch; be a spectator of (a film, game, etc.). **5** *tr.* ascertain or establish by inquiry or research or reflection (*I will see if the door is open*). **6** *tr.* consider; deduce from observation (*I see that you are a brave man*). **7** *tr.* contemplate; foresee mentally (*we saw that no good would come of it*; *can see myself doing this job indefinitely*). **8** *tr.* look at for information (usu. in *imper.* as a direction in or to a book: *see page 15*). **9** *tr.* meet or be near and recognize (*I saw your mother in town*). **10** *tr.* **a** meet socially (*sees her sister most weeks*). **b** meet regularly as a boyfriend or girlfriend; court (*is still seeing that tall man*). **11** *tr.* give an interview to (*the doctor will see you now*). **12** *tr.* visit to consult (*went to see the doctor*). **13** *tr.* find out or learn, esp.

from a visual source (*I see the match has been cancelled*). **14 a** *intr.* reflect; consider further; wait until one knows more (*we shall have to see*). **b** *tr.* (foll. by *whether* or *if* + clause) consider, decide (on). **15** *tr.* interpret or have an opinion of (*I see things differently now*). **16** *tr.* experience; have presented to one's attention (*I never thought I would see this day*). **17** *tr.* recognize as acceptable; foresee (*do you see your daughter marrying this man?*). **18** *tr.* observe without interfering (*stood by and saw them squander my money*). **19** *tr.* (usu. foll. by *in*) find attractive (*can't think what she sees in him*). **20** *intr.* (usu. foll. by *to*, or *that* + infin.) make provision for; ensure; attend to (*shall see to your request immediately*; *see that he gets home safely*) (cf. *see to it*). **21** *tr.* escort or conduct (to a place etc.) (*saw them home*). **22** *tr.* be a witness of (an event etc.) (*see the New Year in*). **23** *tr.* supervise (an action etc.) (*will stay and see the doors locked*). **24** *tr.* **a** (in gambling, esp. poker) equal (a bet). **b** equal the bet of (a player), esp. to see the player's cards. □ **as far as I can see** to the best of my understanding or belief. **as I see it** in my opinion. **do you see?** do you understand? **has seen better days** has declined from former prosperity, good condition, etc. **I'll be seeing you** *colloq.* an expression on parting. **I see** I understand (referring to an explanation etc.). **let me see** an appeal for time to think before speaking etc. **see about 1** attend to. **2** consider; look into. **see after 1** take care of. **2** = *see about*. **see the back of** *colloq.* be rid of (an unwanted person or thing). **see a person damned first** *colloq.* refuse categorically and with hostility to do what a person wants. **see eye to eye** see EYE. **see fit** see FIT[1]. **see here!** = *look here*. **see into** investigate. **see life** gain experience of the world, often by enjoying oneself. **see the light 1** realize one's mistakes etc. **2** suddenly see the way to proceed. **3** undergo religious conversion. **see the light of day** (usu. with *neg.*) come into existence. **see off 1** be present at the departure of (a person) (*saw them off at Heathrow*). **2** *colloq.* ward off, get the better of (*managed to see off an investigation into their working methods*). **see out 1** accompany out of a building etc. **2** finish (a project etc.) completely. **3** remain awake, alive, etc., until the end of (a period). **4** last longer than; outlive. **see over** inspect; tour and examine. **see reason** see REASON. **see red** become suddenly enraged. **see a person right** make sure that a person is rewarded, safe, etc. **see service** see SERVICE. **see stars** *colloq.* see lights before one's eyes as a result of a blow on the head. **see things** have hallucinations or false imaginings. **see through 1** not be deceived by; detect the true nature of. **2** penetrate visually. **see-through** *adj.* (esp. of clothing) translucent. **see a person through** support a person during a difficult time; assist financially. **see a thing through** persist with it until it is completed. **see to** = *see about*. **see to it** (foll. by *that* + clause) ensure (*see to it that I am not disturbed*) (cf. sense 20 of *v.*). **see one's way clear to** feel able or entitled to. **see the world** see WORLD. **see you** (or **see you later**) *colloq.* an expression on parting. **we shall see 1** let us await the outcome. **2** a formula for declining to act at once. **will see about it** a formula for declining to act at once. **you see 1** you understand. **2** you will understand when I explain. □□ **seeable** *adj.* [OE *sēon* f. Gmc]

■ **1** perceive, note, notice, mark, spot, watch, witness, discern, distinguish, observe, sight, catch sight of, spy, make out, view, glimpse, catch a glimpse of, *literary* behold, espy, descry, *sl.* get a load of. **3** understand, comprehend, apprehend, perceive, appreciate, fathom, grasp, take in, realize, know, be aware *or* conscious of, get the idea *or* meaning of, *colloq.* get, *sl.* dig, get the drift of, get the hang of. **4** attend, watch, look at, observe, view. **5** determine, ascertain, establish, find out, discover, learn; investigate, study, probe, look into, make enquiries, enquire about. **6** see PERCEIVE 2. **7, 17** contemplate, foresee, foretell, imagine, envisage, envision, visualize, picture, conceive (of). **10 a** socialize with, spend time with, keep company with, consort with, associate with. **b** court, woo, *colloq.* go out with, go steady with, *esp. US colloq.* date. **11** receive, meet (with), talk *or* speak to *or* with, have a word with, sit down with, (give an) interview (to); welcome, greet. **12** confer with, consult (with), talk *or* speak to *or* with, have a word with, visit, sit down with. **13** see LEARN 5. **14 a** think, reflect, decide, consider, make up one's mind; wait (and see). **b** think (about), decide (on), consider, mull over, ponder on *or* over, contemplate, reflect (on), meditate (on *or* over *or* about), ruminate (on *or* over), brood over. **15** see TAKE *v.* 18. **16** see MEET[1] *v.* 8, EXPERIENCE *v.* 1. **18** see WATCH *v.* 2b. **19** see LIKE[2] *v.* 1. **20** see to it, attend to, make provision for; ensure, assure, make sure *or* certain, mind. **21** accompany, escort, show, lead, conduct, usher, take, convoy, bring, walk, drive. □ **as I see it** see *to my mind* (MIND). **I'll be seeing you** see GOODBYE *int.* **I see** I comprehend, I understand, *colloq.* I get it, I get the drift, I twig. **see about 1** see to, attend to, look after, take care *or* charge of, look to, organize, manage, do, undertake, sort out. **2** consider, give some thought to, pay attention *or* heed to; investigate, study, probe, look into, make enquiries about, enquire about. **see after 1** take care of, look after; keep safe. **see the back of** see *be rid of* (RID). **see into** see INVESTIGATE. **see the light of day** see OCCUR 1. **see off 1** say *or* wave goodbye, wave (off), *archaic or literary* bid adieu *or bon voyage*. **2** see *ward off*. **see out 2** see COMPLETE *v.* 1. **3** last out *or* through, wait out, live through; endure. **4** see OUTLAST. **see over** see INSPECT. **see red** see *blow up* 6 (BLOW[1]). **see through 1** penetrate, detect, perceive, *colloq.* be *or* get wise to. **see-through** sheer, diaphanous, gauzy, transparent, translucent, gossamer, filmy, peekaboo. **see a person through** help, aid, guide, shepherd, assist, support; finance, pay a person's way, sponsor; last. **see a thing through** persevere *or* persist with; *colloq.* stick (out). **see you** (or **see you later**) see GOODBYE *int.*

see[2] /see/ *n.* **1** the area under the authority of a bishop or archbishop, a diocese (*the see of Norwich*). **2** the office or jurisdiction of a bishop or archbishop (*fill a vacant see*). □ **See of Rome** the papacy, the Holy See. [ME f. AF *se(d)* ult. f. L *sedes* seat f. *sedēre* sit]

seed /seed/ *n.* & *v.* ● *n.* **1 a** a flowering plant's unit of reproduction (esp. in the form of grain) capable of developing into another such plant. **b** seeds collectively, esp. as collected for sowing (*is full of seed*; *to be kept for seed*). **2 a** semen. **b** milt. **3** (foll. by *of*) prime cause, beginning, germ (*seeds of doubt*). **4** *archaic* offspring, progeny, descendants (*the seed of Abraham*). **5** *Sport* a seeded player. **6** a small seedlike container for the application of radium etc. **7** a seed crystal. ● *v.* **1** *tr.* **a** place seeds in. **b** sprinkle with or as with seed. **2** *intr.* sow seeds. **3** *intr.* produce or drop seed. **4** *tr.* remove seeds from (fruit etc.). **5** *tr.* place a crystal or crystalline substance in (a solution etc.) to cause crystallization or condensation (esp. in a cloud to produce rain). **6** *tr. Sport* **a** assign to (a strong competitor in a knockout competition) a position in an ordered list so that strong competitors do not meet each other in early rounds (*is seeded seventh*). **b** arrange (the order of play) in this way. **7** *intr.* go to seed. □ **go** (or **run**) **to seed 1** cease flowering as seed develops. **2** become degenerate, unkempt, ineffective, etc. **raise up seed** *archaic* beget children. **seed-bed 1** a bed of fine soil in which to sow seeds. **2** a place of development. **seed-cake** cake containing whole seeds esp. of caraway as flavouring. **seed-coat** the outer integument of a seed. **seed-corn 1** good quality corn kept for seed. **2** assets reused for future profit or benefit. **seed crystal** a crystal used to initiate crystallization. **seed-eater** a bird (esp. a finch) living mainly on seeds. **seed-fish** a fish that is ready to spawn. **seed-leaf** a cotyledon. **seed-lip** a basket for seed in sowing by hand. **seed money** money allocated to initiate a project. **seed-pearl** a very small pearl. **seed-plot** a place of development. **seed-potato** a potato kept for seed. **seed-time** the sowing season. **seed-vessel** a pericarp. □□ **seedless** *adj.* [OE *sǣd* f. Gmc, rel. to SOW[1]]

■ *n.* **1 a** grain, spore, kernel, bulb, ovum, ovule, germ, *Biol.* egg, *US* pit. **2** semen, spermatozoa, sperm; milt, (soft) roe. **3** germ, beginning, root, origin, cause; reason, basis, source; grounds. **4** offspring, children, progeny, young, descendants, heirs, successors, *Law* issue. ● *v.* **1** sow, plant. **4** stone, *US* pit. ▫ **go** (or **run**) **to seed** **2** become dilapidated *or* worn out *or* shabby *or* seedy *or* run down, decay, decline, degenerate, deteriorate, go to rack and ruin, *colloq.* go downhill, go to pot. **raise up seed** see REPRODUCE 3.

seeder /séedər/ *n.* **1** a person or thing that seeds. **2** a machine for sowing seed, esp. a drill. **3** an apparatus for seeding raisins etc. **4** *Brit.* a spawning fish.

seedling /séedling/ *n.* a young plant, esp. one raised from seed and not from a cutting etc.

seedsman /séedzmən/ *n.* (*pl.* **-men**) a dealer in seeds.

seedy /séedi/ *adj.* (**seedier, seediest**) **1** full of seed. **2** going to seed. **3** shabby-looking, in worn clothes. **4** *colloq.* unwell. ▫▫ **seedily** *adv.* **seediness** *n.*

■ **3** shabby, dilapidated, worn (out), mangy, grubby, scruffy, *colloq.* tatty; run-down, broken-down, decaying, squalid, sleazy, *colloq.* ratty. **4** unwell, out of sorts, poorly, *colloq.* under the weather; ailing, ill, sickly.

seeing /séeing/ *conj.* & *n.* ● *conj.* (usu. foll. by *that* + clause) considering that, inasmuch as, because (*seeing that you do not know it yourself*). ● *n. Astron.* the quality of observed images as determined by atmospheric conditions.

■ *conj.* in view of (the fact that), whereas, in the light of, inasmuch as, since, considering that, because, *US* in light of.

seek /seek/ *v.* (*past* and *past part.* **sought** /sawt/) **1 a** *tr.* make a search or inquiry for. **b** *intr.* (foll. by *for, after*) make a search or inquiry. **2** *tr.* **a** try or want to find or get. **b** ask for; request (*sought help from him; seeks my aid*). **3** *tr.* (foll. by *to* + infin.) endeavour or try. **4** *tr.* make for or resort to (a place or person, for advice, health, etc.) (*sought his bed; sought a fortune-teller; sought the shore*). **5** *tr. archaic* aim at, attempt. **6** *intr.* (foll. by *to*) *archaic* resort. ▫ **seek dead** an order to a retriever to find killed game. **seek out 1** search for and find. **2** single out for companionship, etc. **sought-after** much in demand; generally desired or courted. **to seek** (or **much to seek** or **far to seek**) deficient, lacking, or not yet found (*the reason is not far to seek; an efficient leader is yet to seek*). ▫▫ **seeker** *n.* (also in *comb.*). [OE *sēcan* f. Gmc]

■ **1a, 2a** look for, be after, search for, hunt (for), quest for *or* after, pursue. **2 b** ask for, request, beg, solicit, invite; demand. **3** attempt, try, endeavour, undertake, hope, aim, aspire. **4** see *take to* 5. **5** attempt, aim at, contrive, plot. ▫ **seek out 1** see DISCOVER 1a, b. **to seek** (or **much to seek** or **far to seek**) see ELUSIVE 1.

seel /seel/ *v.tr. archaic* close (a person's eyes). [obs. *sile* f. F *ciller, siller*, or med.L *ciliare* f. L *cilium* eyelid]

seem /seem/ *v.intr.* **1** give the impression or sensation of being (*seems ridiculous; seems certain to win*). **2** (foll. by *to* + infin.) appear or be perceived or ascertained (*he seems to be breathing; they seem to have left*). ▫ **can't seem to** *colloq.* seem unable to. **do not seem to** *colloq.* somehow do not (*I do not seem to like him*). **it seems** (or **would seem**) (often foll. by *that* + clause) it appears to be true or the fact (in a hesitant, guarded, or ironical statement). [ME f. ON *sœma* honour f. *sœmr* fitting]

■ **1** appear, look; sound, feel, have (all) the hallmarks *or* earmarks of, give every indication *or* appearance of (being). **2** appear, look; see also FEEL *v.* 7. ▫ **it seems** (or **would seem**) it appears, it would appear.

seeming[1] /séeming/ *adj.* **1** apparent but perhaps not real (*with seeming sincerity*). **2** apparent only; ostensible (*the seeming and the real; seeming-virtuous*). ▫▫ **seemingly** *adv.*

■ **1** see APPARENT 2, OUTWARD 1, 3. **2** apparent; ostensible, superficial, surface, assumed, feigned, pretended, false, so-called, specious, alleged, purported, professed. ▫ **seemingly** evidently; apparently, outwardly, ostensibly, superficially, falsely, allegedly, speciously, on the face of it, purportedly, professedly.

seeming[2] /séeming/ *n. literary* **1** appearance, aspect. **2** deceptive appearance.

seemly /séemli/ *adj.* (**seemlier, seemliest**) conforming to propriety or good taste; decorous, suitable. ▫▫ **seemliness** *n.* [ME f. ON *sœmiligr* (as SEEM)]

■ proper, fitting, appropriate, becoming, suitable, fit, befitting, apt, right, apropos, apposite, *archaic* meet; *comme il faut*; decent, decorous, dignified, genteel, gentlemanly, ladylike, diplomatic, discreet, prudent, sensible, reasonable, politic.

seen *past part.* of SEE[1].

seep /seep/ *v.* & *n.* ● *v.intr.* ooze out; percolate slowly. ● *n.* *US* a place where petroleum etc. oozes slowly out of the ground. [perh. dial. form of OE *sipian* to soak]

■ *v.* see OOZE[1] *v.*

seepage /séepij/ *n.* **1** the act of seeping. **2** the quantity that seeps out.

■ see LEAK *n.* 1b, c.

seer[1] /séeər, seer/ *n.* **1** a person who sees. **2** a prophet; a person who sees visions; a person of supposed supernatural insight esp. as regards the future. [ME f. SEE[1]]

■ **2** soothsayer, fortune-teller, oracle, augur, prophesier, clairvoyant, psychic, crystal-gazer, *usu. derog. or joc.* star-gazer, *formal* vaticinator; sibyl, prophetess; prophet.

seer[2] /seer/ *n.* an Indian (varying) measure of weight (about one kilogram) or liquid measure (about one litre). [Hindi *ser*]

seersucker /séersukkər/ *n.* material of linen, cotton, etc., with a puckered surface. [Pers. *šir o šakar*, lit. 'milk and sugar']

see-saw /sée-saw/ *n., v., adj.,* & *adv.* ● *n.* **1 a** a device consisting of a long plank balanced on a central support for children to sit on at each end and move up and down by pushing the ground with their feet. **b** a game played on this. **2** an up-and-down or to-and-fro motion. **3** a contest in which the advantage repeatedly changes from one side to the other. ● *v.intr.* **1** play on a see-saw. **2** move up and down as on a see-saw. **3** vacillate in policy, emotion, etc. ● *adj.* & *adv.* with up-and-down or backward-and-forward motion (*see-saw motion*). ▫ **go see-saw** vacillate or alternate. [redupl. of SAW[1]]

■ *v.* **3** teeter, totter, waver, vary, vacillate, oscillate, alternate, fluctuate, swing, switch. ▫ **go see-saw** vacillate, alternate; see also OSCILLATE.

seethe /seeth/ *v.* **1** *intr.* boil, bubble over. **2** *intr.* be very agitated, esp. with anger (*seething with discontent; I was seething inwardly*). **3** *tr.* & *intr. archaic* cook by boiling. ▫▫ **seethingly** *adv.* [OE *sēothan* f. Gmc]

■ **1** boil, simmer, foam, bubble (over). **2** foam at the mouth, fume, burn with anger, rage, rant (and rave), be furious *or* incensed *or* livid, get hot under the collar, get up steam, *colloq.* take on, get red in the face, get (all) steamed up, *Austral. sl.* spit chips; simmer, smoulder.

segment /ségmənt/ *n.* & *v.* ● *n.* **1** each of several parts into which a thing is or can be divided or marked off. **2** *Geom.* a part of a figure cut off by a line or plane intersecting it, esp.: **a** the part of a circle enclosed between an arc and a chord. **b** the part of a line included between two points. **c** the part of a sphere cut off by any plane not passing through the centre. **3** the smallest distinct part of a spoken utterance. **4** *Zool.* each of the longitudinal sections of the body of certain animals (e.g. worms). ● *v.* /usu. -mént/ **1** *intr.* & *tr.* divide into segments. **2** *intr. Biol.* (of a cell) undergo cleavage or divide into many cells. ▫▫ **segmental** /-mént'l/ *adj.* **segmentalize** /-méntəlīz/ *v.tr.* (also **-ise**). **segmentalization** /-mentəlīzáysh'n/ *n.* **segmentally** /-méntəli/ *adv.* **segmentary** *adj.* **segmentation** /-táysh'n/ *n.* [L *segmentum* f. *secare* cut]

■ *n.* **1** section, part, division, portion, piece, fraction, fragment, slice, wedge; component, element. ● *v.* **1** divide, separate, part, split, subdivide, fragment, *literary* cleave; partition, section.

sego /séegō/ *n.* (*pl.* **-os**) (in full **sego lily**) a N. American plant, *Calochortus nuttallii*, with green and white bell-shaped flowers. [Paiute]

segregate[1] /ségrigayt/ *v.* **1** *tr.* put apart from the rest; isolate. **2** *tr.* enforce racial segregation on (persons) or in (a community etc.). **3** *intr.* separate from a mass and collect together. **4** *intr. Biol.* (of alleles) separate into dominant and recessive groups. □□ **segregable** /-gəb'l/ *adj.* **segregative** *adj.* [L *segregare* (as SE-, *grex gregis* flock)]
■ **1** partition, seclude, sequester, set apart, compartmentalize, exclude, isolate, ostracize. **3** separate, segment; see also COLLECT[1] *v.* 1.

segregate[2] /ségrigət/ *adj.* **1** *Zool.* simple or solitary, not compound. **2** *archaic* set apart, separate. [L *segregatus* past part. (as SEGREGATE[1])]

segregation /ségrigáysh'n/ *n.* **1** enforced separation of racial groups in a community etc. **2** the act or an instance of segregating; the state of being segregated. □□ **segregational** *adj.* **segregationist** *n.* & *adj.* [LL *segregatio* (as SEGREGATE[1])]
■ **1** apartheid, *US* Jim Crowism. **2** separation, segmentation, partition, seclusion, isolation, sequestration, setting apart, compartmentalization, exclusion; ostracism.

segue /ségway/ *v.* & *n.* esp. *Mus.* ● *v.intr.* (**segues, segued, seguing**) (usu. foll. by *into*) go on without a pause. ● *n.* an uninterrupted transition from one song or melody to another. [It., = follows]

seguidilla /séggidílyə/ *n.* **1** a Spanish dance in triple time. **2** the music for this. [Sp. f. *seguida* following f. *seguir* follow]

Sehnsucht /záynzōōkht/ *n.* yearning, wistful longing. [G]
■ see LONGING *n.*

sei /say/ *n.* a small rorqual, *Balaenoptera borealis.* [Norw. *sejhval* sei whale]

seicento /saychéntō/ *n.* the style of Italian art and literature of the 17th c. □□ **seicentist** *n.* **seicentoist** *n.* [It., = 600, used with ref. to the years 1600–99]

seiche /saysh/ *n.* a fluctuation in the water-level of a lake etc., usu. caused by changes in barometric pressure. [Swiss F]

Seidlitz powder /sédlits/ *n.* (*US* **Seidlitz powders**) a laxative medicine of two powders mixed separately with water and then poured together to effervesce. [named with ref. to the mineral water of *Seidlitz* in Bohemia]

seif /seef, sayf/ *n.* (in full **seif dune**) a sand-dune in the form of a long narrow ridge. [Arab. *saif* sword (from its shape)]

seigneur /saynyṓr/ *n.* (also **seignior** /sáynyər/) a feudal lord; the lord of a manor. □ **grand seigneur** /groN/ a person of high rank or noble presence. □□ **seigneurial** *adj.* **seigniorial** /-nyóriəl/ *adj.* [ME f. OF *seigneur, seignor* f. L SENIOR]

seigniorage /sáynyərij/ *n.* (also **seignorage**) **1 a** a profit made by issuing currency, esp. by issuing coins rated above their intrinsic value. **b** *hist.* the Crown's right to a percentage on bullion brought to a mint for coining. **2** *hist.* something claimed by a sovereign or feudal superior as a prerogative. [ME f. OF *seignorage, seigneurage* (as SEIGNEUR)]

seigniory /sáynyəri/ *n.* (*pl.* **-ies**) **1** lordship, sovereign authority. **2** (also **seigneury**) a seigneur's domain. [ME f. OF *seignorie* (as SEIGNEUR)]

seine /sayn/ *n.* & *v.* ● *n.* (also **seine-net**) a fishing-net for encircling fish, with floats at the top and weights at the bottom edge, and usu. hauled ashore. ● *v.intr.* & *tr.* fish or catch with a seine. □□ **seiner** *n.* [ME f. OF *saïne*, & OE *segne* f. WG f. L *sagena* f. Gk *sagēnē*]

seise var. of SEIZE 9.

seisin /seézin/ *n.* (also **seizin**) *Law* **1** possession of land by freehold. **2** the act of taking such possession. **3** what is so held. [ME f. AF *sesine*, OF *seisine, saisine* (as SEIZE)]

seismic /sīzmik/ *adj.* of or relating to an earthquake or earthquakes. □□ **seismal** *adj.* **seismical** *adj.* **seismically** *adv.* [Gk *seismos* earthquake f. *seiō* shake]

seismo- /sīzmō/ *comb. form* earthquake. [Gk *seismos*]

seismogram /sīzməgram/ *n.* a record given by a seismograph.

seismograph /sīzməgraaf/ *n.* an instrument that records the force, direction, etc., of earthquakes. □□ **seismographic** /-gráffik/ *adj.* **seismographical** /-gráffik'l/ *adj.*

seismology /sīzmólləji/ *n.* the scientific study and recording of earthquakes and related phenomena. □□ **seismological** /-məlójik'l/ *adj.* **seismologically** /-məlójikəli/ *adv.* **seismologist** *n.*

seize /seez/ *v.* **1** *tr.* take hold of forcibly or suddenly. **2** *tr.* take possession of forcibly (*seized the fortress; seized power*). **3** *tr.* **a** take possession of (contraband goods, documents, etc.) by warrant or legal right, confiscate, impound. **b** arrest or apprehend (a person); take prisoner. **4** *tr.* affect suddenly (*panic seized us; was seized by apoplexy; was seized with remorse*). **5** *tr.* take advantage of (an opportunity). **6** *tr.* comprehend quickly or clearly. **7** *intr.* (usu. foll. by *on, upon*) **a** take hold forcibly or suddenly. **b** take advantage eagerly (*seized on a pretext*). **8** *intr.* (usu. foll. by *up*) (of a moving part in a machine) become stuck or jammed from undue heat, friction, etc. **9** *tr.* (also **seise**) (usu. foll. by *of*) *Law* put in possession of. **10** *tr. Naut.* fasten or attach by binding with turns of yarn etc. □ **seized** (or **seised**) **of 1** possessing legally. **2** aware or informed of. □□ **seizable** *adj.* **seizer** *n.* [ME f. OF *seizir, saisir* give seisin f. Frank. f. L *sacire* f. Gmc]
■ **1** grab, grasp, clutch, grip, snatch. **2** capture, take, appropriate, commandeer; see also GRAB *v.* 2. **3 a** confiscate, take (away), capture, take possession of, impound. **b** capture, catch, arrest, take into custody, apprehend, round up, collar, pick up, *esp. US colloq.* bust, *sl.* pinch, nab, *Brit. sl.* nick. **4** catch, transfix, stop, hold, possess, take possession of, afflict, beset, visit. **5** take advantage of, make the most of, make good use of, exploit. **6** see REALIZE 2. **8** jam, stop, lock (up), stick, freeze (up). □ **seized of 2** see AWARE 1.

seizin var. of SEISIN.

seizing /seézing/ *n. Naut.* a cord or cords used for seizing (see SEIZE 10).

seizure /seézhər/ *n.* **1** the act or an instance of seizing; the state of being seized. **2** a sudden attack of apoplexy etc., a stroke.
■ **1** seizing, confiscating, confiscation, impounding, capture, taking, possession; annexation, appropriation, commandeering, usurpation. **2** spasm, attack, fit, paroxysm, convulsion, *Med.* ictus; stroke.

sejant /seéjənt/ *adj.* (placed after noun) *Heraldry* (of an animal) sitting upright on its haunches. [properly *seiant* f. OF var. of *seant* sitting f. *seoir* f. L *sedēre* sit]

Sekt /zekt/ *n.* a German sparkling white wine. [G]

selachian /siláykiən/ *n.* & *adj.* ● *n.* any fish of the subclass Selachii, including sharks and dogfish. ● *adj.* of or relating to this subclass. [mod.L *Selachii* f. Gk *selakhos* shark]

seladang /səlaádang/ *n.* a Malayan gaur. [Malay]

selah /seélə/ *int.* often used at the end of a verse in Psalms and Habakkuk, supposed to be a musical direction. [Heb. *selāh*]

seldom /séldəm/ *adv.* & *adj.* ● *adv.* rarely, not often. ● *adj.* rare, uncommon. [OE *seldan* f. Gmc]
■ *adv.* rarely, infrequently, not often, hardly ever, very occasionally. ● *adj.* see RARE 1.

select /silékt/ *v.* & *adj.* ● *v.tr.* choose, esp. as the best or most suitable. ● *adj.* **1** chosen for excellence or suitability; choice. **2** (of a society etc.) exclusive, cautious in admitting members. □ **select committee** see COMMITTEE. □□ **selectable** *adj.* **selectness** *n.* [L *seligere select-* (as SE-, *legere* choose)]
■ *v.* choose, pick, show (a) preference for, prefer, opt for, single out, hand-pick. ● *adj.* **1** selected, chosen, hand-picked, choice, special, preferred, favoured, favourite, exceptional, excellent, first-rate, first-class, superior, supreme, prime, best, finest, *colloq.* tiptop. **2** privileged, élite, closed; see also EXCLUSIVE *adj.* 3, 4.

selectee /síllekteé/ *n. US* a conscript.

selection /siléksh'n/ *n.* **1** the act or an instance of selecting; the state of being selected. **2** a selected person or thing. **3** things from which a choice may be made. **4** *Biol.* the process in which environmental and genetic influences determine which types of organism thrive better than others, regarded as a factor in evolution. ▫▫ **selectional** *adj.* **selectionally** *adv.* [L *selectio* (as SELECT)]

■ **1** selecting, choosing, picking, singling out; electing, voting; election. **2** choice, pick, preference, option. **3** assortment, variety, collection, range, batch, number, set, series, group.

selective /siléktiv/ *adj.* **1** using or characterized by selection. **2** able to select, esp. (of a radio receiver) able to respond to a chosen frequency without interference from others. ▫ **selective service** *US hist.* service in the armed forces under conscription. ▫▫ **selectively** *adv.* **selectiveness** *n.* **selectivity** /síllektívviti, sél-, séel-/ *n.*

■ **1** particular, discerning, discriminative, discriminating, discriminatory, exacting, demanding, *colloq.* choosy, picky.

selector /siléktər/ *n.* **1** a person who selects, esp. one who selects a representative team in a sport. **2** a device that selects, esp. a device in a vehicle that selects the required gear.

selenite /séllinīt/ *n.* a form of gypsum occurring as transparent crystals or thin plates. ▫▫ **selenitic** /-nittik/ *adj.* [L *selenites* f. Gk *selēnitēs lithos* moonstone f. *selēnē* moon]

selenium /siléeniəm/ *n. Chem.* a non-metallic element occurring naturally in various metallic sulphide ores and characterized by the variation of its electrical resistivity with intensity of illumination. ¶ Symb.: **Se.** ▫ **selenium cell** a piece of this used as a photoelectric device. ▫▫ **selenate** /séllinayt/ *n.* **selenic** /siléenik/ *adj.* **selenious** *adj.* [mod.L f. Gk *selēnē* moon + -IUM]

seleno- /siléenō/ *comb. form* moon. [Gk *selēnē* moon]

selenography /séelinógrəfi/ *n.* the study or mapping of the moon. ▫▫ **selenographer** *n.* **selenographic** /-nəgráffik/ *adj.*

selenology /séelinólləji/ *n.* the scientific study of the moon. ▫▫ **selenologist** *n.*

self /self/ *n.* & *adj.* ● *n.* (*pl.* **selves** /selvz/) **1** a person's or thing's own individuality or essence (*showed his true self*). **2** a person or thing as the object of introspection or reflexive action (*the consciousness of self*). **3 a** one's own interests or pleasure (*cares for nothing but self*). **b** concentration on these (*self is a bad guide to happiness*). **4** *Commerce* or *colloq.* myself, yourself, himself, etc. (*cheque drawn to self*; *ticket admitting self and friend*). **5** used in phrases equivalent to *myself, yourself, himself*, etc. (*his very self*; *your good selves*). **6** (*pl.* **selfs**) a flower of uniform colour, or of the natural wild colour. ● *adj.* **1** of the same colour as the rest or throughout. **2** (of a flower) of the natural wild colour. **3** (of colour) uniform, the same throughout. ▫ **one's better self** one's nobler impulses. **one's former** (or **old**) **self** oneself as one formerly was. [OE f. Gmc]

■ *n.* **1** see IDENTITY 1.

self- /self/ *comb. form* expressing reflexive action: **1** of or directed towards oneself or itself (*self-respect*; *self-cleaning*). **2** by oneself or itself, esp. without external agency (*self-evident*). **3** on, in, for, or relating to oneself or itself (*self-absorbed*; *self-confident*).

self-abandon /sélfəbándən/ *n.* (also **self-abandonment**) the abandonment of oneself, esp. to passion or an impulse. ▫▫ **self-abandoned** *adj.*

self-abasement /sélfəbáysmənt/ *n.* the abasement of oneself; self-humiliation; cringing.

■ see HUMILITY 1.

self-abhorrence /sélfəbhórrənss/ *n.* the abhorrence of oneself; self-hatred.

self-abnegation /sélfábnigáysh'n/ *n.* the abnegation of oneself, one's interests, needs, etc.; self-sacrifice.

self-absorption /sélfəbzórpsh'n/ *n.* **1** absorption in oneself. **2** *Physics* the absorption, by a body, of radiation emitted within it. ▫▫ **self-absorbed** /-zórbd/ *adj.*

■ ▫▫ **self-absorbed** see *egoistic* (EGOISM).

self-abuse /sélfəbyóoss/ *n.* **1** the reviling or abuse of oneself. **2** *archaic* masturbation.

■ **1** self-deprecation, self-hatred; masochism. **2** see *masturbation* (MASTURBATE).

self-accusation /sélfákyoozáysh'n/ *n.* the accusing of oneself. ▫▫ **self-accusatory** /-əkyóozətəri/ *adj.*

self-acting /sélfákting/ *adj.* acting without external influence or control; automatic. ▫▫ **self-action** /-áksh'n/ *n.* **self-activity** /-aktívviti/ *n.*

■ see AUTOMATIC *adj.* 1.

self-addressed /sélfədrést/ *adj.* (of an envelope etc.) having one's own address on for return communication.

self-adhesive /sélfədhéessiv/ *adj.* (of an envelope, label, etc.) adhesive, esp. without being moistened.

self-adjusting /sélfəjústing/ *adj.* (of machinery etc.) adjusting itself. ▫▫ **self-adjustment** *n.*

self-admiration /sélfádmərάysh'n/ *n.* the admiration of oneself; pride; conceit.

■ see CONCEIT 1.

self-advancement /sélfədváansmənt/ *n.* the advancement of oneself.

self-advertisement /sélfədvértismənt/ *n.* the advertising or promotion of oneself. ▫▫ **self-advertiser** /-ádvərtīzər/ *n.*

self-affirmation /sélfáffərmáysh'n/ *n. Psychol.* the recognition and assertion of the existence of the conscious self.

self-aggrandizement /sélfəgrándizmənt/ *n.* the act or process of enriching oneself or making oneself powerful. ▫▫ **self-aggrandizing** /-grándīzing/ *adj.*

self-analysis /sélfənállisiss/ *n. Psychol.* the analysis of oneself, one's motives, character, etc. ▫▫ **self-analysing** /-ánnəlīzing/ *adj.*

self-appointed /sélfəpóyntid/ *adj.* designated so by oneself, not authorized by another (*a self-appointed guardian*).

■ see SELF-STYLED.

self-appreciation /sélfəpréeshiáysh'n/ *n.* a good opinion of oneself; conceit.

self-approbation /sélfáprəbáysh'n/ *n.* = SELF-APPRECIATION.

self-approval /sélfəpróov'l/ *n.* = SELF-APPRECIATION.

self-assembly /sélfəsémbli/ *n.* (often *attrib.*) construction (of furniture etc.) from materials sold in kit form.

self-assertion /sélfəsérsh'n/ *n.* the aggressive promotion of oneself, one's views, etc. ▫▫ **self-asserting** *adj.* **self-assertive** *adj.* **self-assertiveness** *n.*

■ see *arrogance* (ARROGANT). ▫▫ **self-assertive** see ARROGANT.

self-assurance /sélfəshóorənss/ *n.* confidence in one's own abilities etc. ▫▫ **self-assured** *adj.* **self-assuredly** *adv.*

■ confidence, self-confidence, self-respect, self-esteem, assurance, poise, aplomb, self-reliance, self-sufficiency. ▫▫ **self-assured** confident, self-confident, assured, poised, self-reliant, secure, positive, definite, assertive, independent; sure of oneself; self-collected.

self-aware /sélfəwáir/ *adj.* conscious of one's character, feelings, motives, etc. ▫▫ **self-awareness** *n.*

self-begotten /sélfbigótt'n/ *adj.* produced by oneself or itself; not made externally.

self-betrayal /sélfbitráyəl/ *n.* **1** the betrayal of oneself. **2** the inadvertent revelation of one's true thoughts etc.

self-binder /sélfbīndər/ *n.* a reaping machine with an automatic mechanism for binding the sheaves.

self-born /sélfbórn/ *adj.* produced by itself or oneself; not made externally.

self-catering /sélfkáytəring/ *adj.* (esp. of a holiday or holiday premises) providing rented accommodation with cooking facilities but without food.

self-censorship /sélfsénsərship/ *n.* the censoring of oneself.

self-centred /sélfséntərd/ *adj.* preoccupied with one's own personality or affairs. ▫▫ **self-centredly** *adv.* **self-centredness** *n.*

■ see SELFISH. ▫▫ **self-centredness** see SELF-ESTEEM 2.

self-certification /sélfsértifikáysh'n/ *n.* the practice by which an employee declares in writing that an absence from work was due to illness.

self-cleaning /sélfkleéning/ *adj.* (esp. of an oven) cleaning itself when heated etc.

self-closing /sélfklózing/ *adj.* (of a door etc.) closing automatically.

self-cocking /sélfkókking/ *adj.* (of a gun) with the hammer raised by the trigger, not by hand.

self-collected /sélfkəléktid/ *adj.* composed, serene, self-assured.

self-coloured /sélfkúllərd/ *adj.* **1 a** having the same colour throughout (*buttons and belt are self-coloured*). **b** (of material) natural; undyed. **2 a** (of a flower) of uniform colour. **b** having its colour unchanged by cultivation or hybridization.

self-command /sélfkəmaánd/ *n.* = SELF-CONTROL.

self-communion /sélfkəmyoóniən/ *n.* meditation upon one's own character, conduct, etc.

self-conceit /sélfkənseét/ *n.* = SELF-SATISFACTION. ▫▫ **self-conceited** *adj.*

self-condemnation /sélfkóndemnáysh'n/ *n.* **1** the blaming of oneself. **2** the inadvertent revelation of one's own sin, crime, etc. ▫▫ **self-condemned** /-kəndémd/ *adj.*

■ **1** self-reproach, self-accusation.

self-confessed /sélfkənfést/ *adj.* openly admitting oneself to be (*a self-confessed thief*).

self-confidence /sélfkónfid'nss/ *n.* = SELF-ASSURANCE. ▫▫ **self-confident** *adj.* **self-confidently** *adv.*

self-congratulation /sélfkənggrátyooláysh'n/ *n.* = SELF-SATISFACTION. ▫▫ **self-congratulatory** /-kəng grátyoolətəri/ *adj.*

self-conquest /sélfkóngkwest/ *n.* the overcoming of one's worst characteristics etc.

self-conscious /sélfkónshəss/ *adj.* **1** socially inept through embarrassment or shyness. **2** *Philos.* having knowledge of one's own existence; self-contemplating. ▫▫ **self-consciously** *adv.* **self-consciousness** *n.*

■ **1** embarrassed, coy, diffident, shy, self-effacing, sheepish, shrinking, retiring, unsure, apprehensive, reserved, insecure, affected, awkward, nervous, uncomfortable, hesitant, timid, timorous.

self-consistent /sélfkənsístənt/ *adj.* (of parts of the same whole etc.) consistent; not conflicting. ▫▫ **self-consistency** *n.*

self-constituted /sélfkónstityootid/ *adj.* (of a person, group, etc.) assuming a function without authorization or right; self-appointed.

self-contained /sélfkəntáynd/ *adj.* **1** (of a person) uncommunicative or reserved; independent, self-possessed. **2** *Brit.* (esp. of living-accommodation) complete in itself. ▫▫ **self-containment** *n.*

■ **1** uncommunicative, reserved, distant, aloof, withdrawn, reticent, standoffish; self-possessed, unemotional, self-controlled, self-collected, composed, serene, peaceful, calm, tranquil, cool, collected, even-tempered, detached, imperturbable, unruffled, undisturbed, unperturbed, controlled, placid, grave, serious, sober, solemn, *colloq.* unflappable; in control. **2** whole, entire, complete.

self-contempt /sélfkəntémpt/ *n.* contempt for oneself. ▫▫ **self-contemptuous** *adj.*

self-content /sélfkəntént/ *n.* satisfaction with oneself, one's life, achievements, etc. ▫▫ **self-contented** *adj.*

self-contradiction /sélfkóntrədíksh'n/ *n.* internal inconsistency. ▫▫ **self-contradictory** *adj.*

■ see PARADOX. ▫▫ **self-contradictory** see PARADOXICAL.

self-control /sélfkəntról/ *n.* the power of controlling one's external reactions, emotions, etc.; equanimity. ▫▫ **self-controlled** *adj.*

■ self-discipline, self-restraint, restraint, forbearance, self-denial, control, will-power, strength (of character *or* of mind *or* of will), mettle, fortitude, moral fibre, self-possession, determination, resoluteness, resolve, will; poise, balance, equilibrium, level-headedness, calmness, tranquillity, serenity, placidity, imperturbability, cool-headedness, coolness, patience, composure, aplomb, dignity, equanimity, forbearance, even temper.

self-convicted /sélfkənvíktid/ *adj.* = SELF-CONDEMNED (see SELF-CONDEMNATION).

self-correcting /sélfkərékting/ *adj.* correcting itself without external help.

self-created /sélfkriáytid/ *adj.* created by oneself or itself. ▫▫ **self-creation** /-áysh'n/ *n.*

self-critical /sélfkríttik'l/ *adj.* critical of oneself, one's abilities, etc. ▫▫ **self-criticism** /-tisiz'm/ *n.*

self-deception /sélfdisépsh'n/ *n.* deceiving oneself esp. concerning one's true feelings etc. ▫▫ **self-deceit** /-diseét/ *n.* **self-deceiver** /-diseévər/ *n.* **self-deceiving** /-diseéving/ *adj.* **self-deceptive** *adj.*

self-defeating /sélfdifeéting/ *adj.* (of an attempt, action, etc.) doomed to failure because of internal inconsistencies etc.

self-defence /sélfdifénss/ *n.* **1** an aggressive act, speech, etc., intended as defence (*had to hit him in self-defence*). **2** (usu. **the noble art of self-defence**) boxing. ▫▫ **self-defensive** *adj.*

self-delight /sélfdilít/ *n.* delight in oneself or one's existence.

self-delusion /sélfdilóozh'n, -lyóozh'n/ *n.* the act or an instance of deluding oneself.

self-denial /sélfdiníəl/ *n.* the negation of one's interests, needs, or wishes, esp. in favour of those of others; self-control, forbearance. ▫ **self-denying ordinance** *hist.* a resolution of the Long Parliament 1645 depriving Members of Parliament of civil and military office. ▫▫ **self-denying** *adj.*

■ self-sacrifice, self-abnegation, renunciation, selflessness, altruism, unselfishness, magnanimity, self-mortification, asceticism, privation, renunciation, temperance, sobriety, moderation, abstemiousness, abstinence, abstention, self-deprivation, refusal, giving up, desisting, *colloq.* swearing off; see also SELF-CONTROL.

self-dependence /sélfdipéndənss/ *adj.* dependence only on oneself or itself; independence. ▫▫ **self-dependent** *adj.*

self-deprecation /sélfdéprikáysh'n/ *n.* the act of disparaging or belittling oneself. ▫▫ **self-deprecating** /-déprikayting/ *adj.* **self-deprecatingly** /-déprikaytingli/ *adv.*

self-despair /sélfdispáir/ *n.* despair with oneself.

self-destroying /sélfdistróying/ *adj.* destroying oneself or itself.

self-destruct /sélfdistrúkt/ *v.* & *adj.* esp. *US* ● *v.intr.* (of a spacecraft, bomb, etc.) explode or disintegrate automatically, esp. when pre-set to do so. ● *attrib.adj.* enabling a thing to self-destruct (*a self-destruct device*).

self-destruction /sélfdistrúksh'n/ *n.* **1** the process or an act of destroying oneself or itself. **2** esp. *US* the process or an act of self-destructing. ▫▫ **self-destructive** *adj.* **self-destructively** *adv.*

self-determination /sélfditérmináysh'n/ *n.* **1** a nation's right to determine its own allegiance, government, etc. **2** the ability to act with free will, as opposed to fatalism etc. ▫▫ **self-determined** /-términd/ *adj.* **self-determining** /-términing/ *adj.*

■ **1** see SELF-GOVERNMENT.

self-development /sélfdivélləpmənt/ *n.* the development of oneself, one's abilities, etc.

self-devotion /sélfdivósh'n/ *n.* the devotion of oneself to a person or cause.

self-discipline /sélfdíssiplin/ *n.* the act of or ability to apply oneself, control one's feelings, etc.; self-control. ▫▫ **self-disciplined** *adj.*

■ see SELF-CONTROL.

self-discovery /sélfdiskúvvəri/ *n.* the process of acquiring insight into oneself, one's character, desires, etc.

self-disgust /sélfdisgúst/ *n.* disgust with oneself.

self-doubt /sélfdówt/ *n.* lack of confidence in oneself, one's abilities, etc.

self-drive /sélfdrī́v/ *adj.* (of a hired vehicle) driven by the hirer.

self-educated /sélfédyookaytid/ *adj.* educated by oneself by reading etc., without formal instruction. □□ **self-education** /-káysh'n/ *n.*

self-effacing /sélfifáysing/ *adj.* retiring; modest; timid. □□ **self-effacement** *n.* **self-effacingly** *adv.*
■ see RETIRING. □□ **self-effacement** see HUMILITY 1.

self-elective /sélfiléktiv/ *adj.* (of a committee etc.) proceeding esp. by co-opting members etc.

self-employed /sélfimplóyd/ *adj.* working for oneself, as a freelance or owner of a business etc.; not employed by an employer. □□ **self-employment** *n.*

self-esteem /sélfistéem/ *n.* **1** a good opinion of oneself; self-confidence. **2** an unduly high regard for oneself; conceit.
■ **1** see SELF-ASSURANCE. **2** conceit, vanity, egoism, narcissism, self-centredness, egotism, self-approbation, self-satisfaction, self-admiration, self-love, self-adulation, self-idolatry, smugness, self-importance, self-regard, *amour propre*.

self-evident /sélfévvid'nt/ *adj.* obvious; without the need of evidence or further explanation. □□ **self-evidence** *n.* **self-evidently** *adv.*
■ evident, obvious, patent, clear, incontrovertible, definite, distinct, clear-cut, apparent, unmistakable, undeniable, inescapable, incontestable, plain, axiomatic, proverbial, manifest, true, palpable, tangible; express.

self-examination /sélfigzámmináysh'n/ *n.* **1** the study of one's own conduct, reasons, etc. **2** the examining of one's body for signs of illness etc.

self-executing /sélféksikyōōting/ *adj. Law* (of a law, legal clause, etc.) not needing legislation etc. to be enforced; automatic.

self-existent /sélfigzístənt/ *adj.* existing without prior cause; independent.

self-explanatory /sélfiksplánnətəri, -tri/ *adj.* easily understood; not needing explanation.
■ see OBVIOUS.

self-expression /sélfikspré sh'n/ *n.* the expression of one's feelings, thoughts, etc., esp. in writing, painting, music, etc. □□ **self-expressive** *adj.*

self-faced /sélf-fáyst/ *adj.* (of stone) unhewn; undressed.

self-feeder /sélf-féedər/ *n.* **1** a furnace, machine, etc., that renews its own fuel or material automatically. **2** a device for supplying food to farm animals automatically. □□ **self-feeding** *adj.*

self-fertile /sélf-fértīl/ *adj.* (of a plant etc.) self-fertilizing. □□ **self-fertility** /-tílliti/ *n.*

self-fertilization /sélf-fértilīzáysh'n/ *n.* the fertilization of plants by their own pollen, not from others. □□ **self-fertilized** /-fértilīzd/ *adj.* **self-fertilizing** /-fértilīzing/ *adj.*

self-financing /sélf-fī́nansing/ *adj.* that finances itself, esp. (of a project or undertaking) that pays for its own implementation or continuation. □□ **self-finance** *v.tr.*

self-flattery /sélf-fláttəri/ *n.* = SELF-APPRECIATION. □□ **self-flattering** *adj.*

self-forgetful /sélf-fərgétfōōl/ *adj.* unselfish. □□ **self-forgetfulness** *n.*

self-fulfilling /sélf-fōōlfilling/ *adj.* (of a prophecy, forecast, etc.) bound to come true as a result of actions brought about by its being made.

self-fulfilment /sélf-fōōlfilmənt/ *n.* (*US* **-fulfillment**) the fulfilment of one's own hopes and ambitions.

self-generating /sélfjénnərayting/ *adj.* generated by itself or oneself, not externally.

self-glorification /sélfglórifikáysh'n/ *n.* the proclamation of oneself, one's abilities, etc.; self-satisfaction.

self-government /sélfgúvvərnmənt/ *n.* **1** (esp. of a former colony etc.) government by its own people. **2** = SELF-CONTROL. □□ **self-governed** *adj.* **self-governing** *adj.*
■ **1** self-rule, independence, self-determination, home rule, autonomy, freedom.

self-gratification /sélfgráttifikáysh'n/ *n.* **1** gratification or pleasing of oneself. **2** self-indulgence, dissipation. **3** masturbation. □□ **self-gratifying** *adj.*
■ **1, 2** see INDULGENCE 1, DISSIPATION 1. **3** see MASTURBATION. □□ **self-gratifying** see SELF-INDULGENT.

self-hate /sélfháyt/ *n.* = SELF-HATRED.

self-hatred /sélfháytrid/ *n.* hatred of oneself, esp. of one's actual self when contrasted with one's imagined self.

self-heal /sélfhéel/ *n.* any of several plants, esp. *Prunella vulgaris*, believed to have healing properties.

self-help /sélfhélp/ *n.* **1** the theory that individuals should provide for their own support and improvement in society. **2** the act or faculty of providing for or improving oneself.

selfhood /sélfhŏŏd/ *n.* personality, separate and conscious existence.

self-image /sélfimmij/ *n.* one's own idea or picture of oneself, esp. in relation to others.

self-importance /sélfimpórt'nss/ *n.* a high opinion of oneself; pompousness. □□ **self-important** *adj.* **self-importantly** *adv.*
■ see *arrogance* (ARROGANT), VANITY 1. □□ **self-important** conceited, self-centred, self-seeking, self-absorbed, vain, egotistic(al), self-satisfied, smug, pompous, arrogant, overweening, overbearing, self-glorifying, self-engrossed, presumptuous, snobbish, haughty, *colloq.* snooty, snotty, swollen-headed, big-headed, stuck-up, *literary* vainglorious.

self-imposed /sélfimpṓzd/ *adj.* (of a task or condition etc.) imposed on and by oneself, not externally (*self-imposed exile*).

self-improvement /sélfimprōōvmənt/ *n.* the improvement of one's own position or disposition by one's own efforts.

self-induced /sélfindyōōst/ *adj.* **1** induced by oneself or itself. **2** *Electr.* produced by self-induction.

self-inductance /selfindúktənss/ *n. Electr.* the property of an electric circuit that causes an electromotive force to be generated in it by a change in the current flowing through it (cf. *mutual inductance*).

self-induction /sélfindúksh'n/ *n. Electr.* the production of an electromotive force in a circuit when the current in that circuit is varied. □□ **self-inductive** *adj.*

self-indulgent /sélfindúljənt/ *adj.* indulging or tending to indulge oneself in pleasure, idleness, etc. □□ **self-indulgence** *n.* **self-indulgently** *adv.*
■ self-gratifying, selfish, extravagant, intemperate, overindulgent, immoderate, hedonistic, sybaritic, epicurean, pleasure-seeking; dissolute, dissipated, licentious, profligate, sensual; gluttonous, greedy, gormandizing.

self-inflicted /sélfinflíktid/ *adj.* (esp. of a wound, damage, etc.) inflicted by and on oneself, not externally.

self-interest /sélfintrəst, -trist/ *n.* one's personal interest or advantage. □□ **self-interested** *adj.*
■ □□ **self-interested** see SELFISH.

selfish /sélfish/ *adj.* **1** deficient in consideration for others; concerned chiefly with one's own personal profit or pleasure; actuated by self-interest. **2** (of a motive etc.) appealing to self-interest. □□ **selfishly** *adv.* **selfishness** *n.*
■ inconsiderate, thoughtless, ungenerous, illiberal, grudging, uncharitable; self-indulgent, self-aggrandizing, self-seeking, self-loving, self-centred, self-absorbed, self-interested, self-serving, egotistic(al), egoistic(al); greedy, acquisitive, covetous, grasping, avaricious, mercenary.

self-justification /sélfjústifikáysh'n/ *n.* the justification or excusing of oneself, one's actions, etc.

self-knowledge /sélfnóllij/ *n.* the understanding of oneself, one's motives, etc.

selfless /sélfliss/ *adj.* disregarding oneself or one's own interests; unselfish. □□ **selflessly** *adv.* **selflessness** *n.*

■ unselfish, charitable, self-denying, generous, altruistic, ungrudging, magnanimous, considerate, thoughtful; self-sacrificing.

self-loading /sélflṓding/ *adj.* (esp. of a gun) loading itself. □□ **self-loader** *n.*

self-locking /sélflókking/ *adj.* locking itself.

self-love /sélflúv/ *n.* **1** selfishness; self-indulgence. **2** *Philos.* regard for one's own well-being and happiness.
■ **1** selfishness, self-regard, self-indulgence, selfness; see also CONCEIT 1.

self-made /sélfmáyd/ *adj.* **1** successful or rich by one's own effort. **2** made by oneself.
■ **1** independent, self-reliant, entrepreneurial, self-sufficient.

self-mastery /sélfmaástəri/ *n.* = SELF-CONTROL.

selfmate /sélfmayt/ *n. Chess* checkmate in which a player forces the opponent to achieve checkmate.

self-mocking /sélfmókking/ *adj.* mocking oneself or itself.

self-motion /sélfmṓsh'n/ *n.* motion caused by oneself or itself, not externally. □□ **self-moving** /-mṑoving/ *adj.*

self-motivated /sélfmṓtivaytid/ *adj.* acting on one's own initiative without external pressure. □□ **self-motivation** /-váysh'n/ *n.*

self-murder /sélfmúrdər/ *n.* = SUICIDE. □□ **self-murderer** *n.*

self-neglect /sélfniglékt/ *n.* neglect of oneself.

selfness /sélfniss/ *n.* **1** individuality, personality, essence. **2** selfishness or self-regard.

self-opinionated /sélfəpínyənaytid/ *adj.* **1** stubbornly adhering to one's own opinions. **2** arrogant. □□ **self-opinion** *n.*

self-perpetuating /sélfpərpétyoo-ayting/ *adj.* perpetuating itself or oneself without external agency. □□ **self-perpetuation** /-áysh'n/ *n.*

self-pity /sélfpítti/ *n.* extreme sorrow for one's own troubles etc. □□ **self-pitying** *adj.* **self-pityingly** *adv.*

self-pollination /sélfpóllináysh'n/ *n.* the pollination of a flower by pollen from the same plant. □□ **self-pollinated** *adj.* **self-pollinating** *adj.* **self-pollinator** *n.*

self-portrait /sélfpórtrit/ *n.* a portrait or description of an artist, writer, etc., by himself or herself.

self-possessed /sélfpəzést/ *adj.* habitually exercising self-control; composed. □□ **self-possession** /-zésh'n/ *n.*
■ composed, cool, serene, placid, collected, self-assured, peaceful, calm, tranquil, even-tempered, detached, imperturbable, unruffled, undisturbed, unperturbed, (self-)controlled, dignified, refined, *colloq.* unflappable.

self-praise /sélfpráyz/ *n.* boasting; self-glorification.

self-preservation /sélfprézzərváysh'n/ *n.* **1** the preservation of one's own life, safety, etc. **2** this as a basic instinct of human beings and animals.

self-proclaimed /sélfprəkláymd/ *adj.* proclaimed by oneself or itself to be such.

self-propagating /sélfpróppəgayting/ *adj.* (esp. of a plant) able to propagate itself.

self-propelled /sélfprəpéld/ *adj.* (esp. of a motor vehicle etc.) moving or able to move without external propulsion. □□ **self-propelling** *adj.*

self-protection /sélfprətéksh'n/ *n.* protecting oneself or itself. □□ **self-protective** *adj.*

self-raising /sélfráyzing/ *adj. Brit.* (of flour) having a raising agent already added.
■ *US* self-rising.

self-realization /sélfreéəlīzáysh'n/ *n.* **1** the development of one's faculties, abilities, etc. **2** this as an ethical principle.

self-recording /sélfrikórding/ *adj.* (of a scientific instrument etc.) automatically recording its measurements.

self-regard /sélfrigaárd/ *n.* **1** a proper regard for oneself. **2 a** selfishness. **b** conceit.
■ **1** see SELF-RESPECT. **2 b** see SELF-ESTEEM 2.

self-registering /sélfréjistəring/ *adj.* (of a scientific instrument etc.) automatically registering its measurements.

self-regulating /sélfrégyoolayting/ *adj.* regulating oneself or itself without intervention. □□ **self-regulation** /-láysh'n/ *n.* **self-regulatory** /-lətəri/ *adj.*
■ see AUTOMATIC *adj.* 1.

self-reliance /sélfrilī́ənss/ *n.* reliance on one's own resources etc.; independence. □□ **self-reliant** *adj.* **self-reliantly** *adv.*
■ see INDEPENDENCE. □□ **self-reliant** see INDEPENDENT *adj.* 2a, 3.

self-renewal /sélfrinyṑoəl/ *n.* the act or process of renewing oneself or itself.

self-renunciation /sélfrinúnsiáysh'n/ *n.* **1** = SELF-SACRIFICE. **2** unselfishness.

self-reproach /sélfriprṓch/ *n.* reproach or blame directed at oneself. □□ **self-reproachful** *adj.*
■ self-condemnation, self-accusation.
□□ **self-reproachful** see PENITENT *adj.*

self-respect /sélfrispékt/ *n.* respect for oneself, a feeling that one is behaving with honour, dignity, etc. □□ **self-respecting** *adj.*
■ honour, dignity, integrity, self-regard, self-esteem, pride, *amour propre*, morale.

self-restraint /sélfristráynt/ *n.* = SELF-CONTROL. □□ **self-restrained** *adj.*

self-revealing /sélfriveéling/ *adj.* revealing one's character, motives, etc., esp. inadvertently. □□ **self-revelation** /-révvəláysh'n/ *n.*

self-righteous /sélfrī́chəss/ *adj.* excessively conscious of or insistent on one's rectitude, correctness, etc. □□ **self-righteously** *adv.* **self-righteousness** *n.*
■ Pharisaic(al), sanctimonious, pietistic, hypocritical, complacent, smug, self-satisfied, priggish, superior, canting, *colloq.* holier-than-thou, goody-goody, *Brit. sl.* pi.

self-righting /sélfrī́ting/ *adj.* (of a boat) righting itself when capsized.

self-rising /sélfrī́zing/ *adj. US* = SELF-RAISING.

self-rule /sélfrṑol/ *n.* = SELF-GOVERNMENT 1.

self-sacrifice /sélfsákrifiss/ *n.* the negation of one's own interests, wishes, etc., in favour of those of others. □□ **self-sacrificing** *adj.*
■ see SELF-DENIAL. □□ **self-sacrificing** see SELFLESS.

selfsame /sélfsaym/ *attrib.adj.* (prec. by *the*) the very same (*the selfsame village*).
■ see SAME *adj.* 1.

self-satisfaction /sélfsáttisfáksh'n/ *n.* excessive and unwarranted satisfaction with oneself, one's achievements, etc.; complacency. □□ **self-satisfied** /-sáttisfīd/ *adj.* **self-satisfiedly** /-sáttisfīdli/ *adv.*
■ see SELF-ESTEEM 2. □□ **self-satisfied** see SMUG.

self-sealing /sélfseéling/ *adj.* **1** (of a pneumatic tyre, fuel tank, etc.) automatically able to seal small punctures. **2** (of an envelope) self-adhesive.

self-seeking /sélfseéking/ *adj.* & *n.* seeking one's own welfare before that of others. □□ **self-seeker** *n.*
■ see SELFISH.

self-selection /sélfsiléksh'n/ *n.* the act of selecting oneself or itself. □□ **self-selecting** *adj.*

self-service /sélfsérviss/ *adj.* & *n.* ● *adj.* (often *attrib.*) **1** (of a shop, restaurant, garage, etc.) where customers serve themselves and pay at a checkout counter etc. **2** (of a machine) serving goods after the insertion of coins. ● *n. colloq.* a self-service store, garage, etc.

self-serving /sélfsérving/ *adj.* = SELF-SEEKING.

self-slaughter /sélfsláwtər/ *n.* = SUICIDE.

self-sown /sélfsṓn/ *adj.* grown from seed scattered naturally.

self-starter /sélfstaártər/ *n.* **1** an electric appliance for starting a motor vehicle engine without the use of a crank. **2** an ambitious person who needs no external motivation.

self-sterile /sélfstérrīl/ *adj. Biol.* not being self-fertile. □□ **self-sterility** /-stərílliti/ *n.*

self-styled /sélfstī́ld/ *adj.* called so by oneself; would-be; pretended (*a self-styled artist*).

■ would-be, *soi-disant*, professed, self-appointed, self-proclaimed, so-called, quasi-.

self-sufficient /sélfsəfísh'nt/ *adj.* **1 a** needing nothing; independent. **b** (of a person, nation, etc.) able to supply one's needs for a commodity, esp. food, from one's own resources. **2** content with one's own opinion; arrogant. □□ **self-sufficiency** *n.* **self-sufficiently** *adv.* **self-sufficing** /-səfísing/ *adj.*

■ **1** independent, self-reliant, self-supporting, self-sustaining. **2** see SELF-CONTAINED 1, ARROGANT.

self-suggestion /sélfsəjéss-chən/ *n.* = AUTO-SUGGESTION.

self-supporting /sélfsəpórting/ *adj.* **1** capable of maintaining oneself or itself financially. **2** staying up or standing without external aid. □□ **self-support** *n.*

■ **1** see SELF-SUFFICIENT 1.

self-surrender /sélfsəréndər/ *n.* the surrender of oneself or one's will etc. to an influence, emotion, or other person.

self-sustaining /sélfsəstáyning/ *adj.* sustaining oneself or itself. □□ **self-sustained** *adj.*

■ see SELF-SUFFICIENT 1. □□ **self-sustained** see UNATTACHED 1.

self-taught /sélftáwt/ *adj.* educated or trained by oneself, not externally.

self-torture /sélftórchər/ *n.* the inflicting of pain, esp. mental, on oneself.

self-willed /sélfwíld/ *adj.* obstinately pursuing one's own wishes. □□ **self-will** *n.*

■ headstrong, determined, refractory, stubborn, obstinate, bullish, mulish, pigheaded, wilful, ungovernable, uncontrollable, unruly, unmanageable, intractable, contrary, intransigent, uncooperative, contumacious, recalcitrant, stiff-necked, vexatious, restive, difficult, incorrigible, disobedient.

self-winding /sélfwínding/ *adj.* (of a watch etc.) having an automatic winding apparatus.

self-worth /sélfwúrth/ *n.* = SELF-ESTEEM 1.

Seljuk /séljōōk/ *n.* & *adj.* ● *n.* a member of any of the Turkish dynasties (11th–13th c.) of central and western Asia preceding Ottoman rule. ● *adj.* of or relating to the Seljuks. □□ **Seljukian** /-jōōkiən/ *adj.* & *n.* [Turk. *seljūq* (name of their reputed ancestor)]

sell /sel/ *v.* & *n.* ● *v.* (*past* and *past part.* **sold** /sōld/) **1** *tr.* make over or dispose of in exchange for money. **2** *tr.* keep a stock of for sale or be a dealer in (*do you sell candles?*). **3** *intr.* (of goods) be purchased (*will never sell; these are selling well*). **4** *intr.* (foll. by *at, for*) have a specified price (*sells at £5*). **5** *tr.* betray for money or other reward (*sell one's country*). **6** *tr.* offer dishonourably for money or other consideration; make a matter of corrupt bargaining (*sell justice; sell oneself; sell one's honour*). **7** *tr.* **a** advertise or publish the merits of. **b** give (a person) information on the value of something, inspire with a desire to buy or acquire or agree to something. **8** *tr.* cause to be sold (*the author's name alone will sell many copies*). **9** *tr. sl.* disappoint by not keeping an engagement etc., by failing in some way, or by trickery (*sold again!*). ● *n. colloq.* **1** a manner of selling (*soft sell*). **2** a deception or disappointment. □ **sell-by date** the latest recommended date of sale marked on the packaging of esp. perishable food. **sell down the river** see RIVER. **sell the** (or **a**) **dummy** see DUMMY. **selling-point** an advantageous feature. **selling-race** a horse-race after which the winning horse must be auctioned. **sell one's life dear** (or **dearly**) do great injury before being killed. **sell off** sell the remainder of (goods) at reduced prices. **sell out 1 a** sell all one's stock-in-trade, one's shares in a company, etc. **b** sell (all or some of one's stock, shares, etc.). **2 a** betray. **b** be treacherous or disloyal. **sell-out** *n.* **1** a commercial success, esp. the selling of all tickets for a show. **2** a betrayal. **sell the pass** see PASS[2]. **sell a pup** see PUP. **sell short** disparage, underestimate. **sell up** *Brit.* **1** sell one's business, house, etc. **2** sell the goods of (a debtor). **sold on** *colloq.* enthusiastic about. □□ **sellable** *adj.* [OE *sellan* f. Gmc]

■ *v.* **1** *Law* vend, *Brit. sl.* flog. **2** market, deal in, merchandise, trade in, traffic in, peddle, vend, hawk, handle, retail, carry, stock, offer, *Brit. sl.* flog; *colloq.* push. **3** go, be sold, move. **7** advertise, push; see also PROMOTE 3. **9** see *let down* 2 (LET[1]). □ **sell out 2** inform against, give away, *colloq.* rat on, tell on, sell down the river, blow the whistle on, *esp. Brit. sl.* shop, *Brit. sl.* grass on, tattle on; see also BETRAY 2. **sell-out 2** see *betrayal* (BETRAY). **sell short** see DISPARAGE 1, UNDERESTIMATE *v.* **sold on** enthusiastic *or* persuaded *or* convinced about, won over by.

seller /séllər/ *n.* **1** a person who sells. **2** a commodity that sells well or badly. □ **seller's** (or **sellers'**) **market** an economic position in which goods are scarce and expensive.

■ **1** dealer, vendor, merchant, retailer, shopkeeper, peddler, hawker, monger; salesperson, salesman, saleswoman, saleslady, *Brit.* shop assistant, *US* clerk, sales-clerk, shop-girl; sales agent, representative, traveller, commercial traveller, travelling salesman, *colloq.* rep, *esp. US colloq.* drummer.

Sellotape /séllətayp/ *n.* & *v.* ● *n. propr.* adhesive usu. transparent cellulose or plastic tape. ● *v.tr.* (**sellotape**) fix with Sellotape. [CELLULOSE + TAPE]

seltzer /séltsər/ *n.* (in full **seltzer water**) **1** medicinal mineral water from Nieder-Selters in Germany. **2** an artificial substitute for this; soda water. [G *Selterser* (adj.) f. *Selters*]

■ **2** soda (water), mineral water, tonic water.

selvage /sélvij/ *n.* (also **selvedge**) **1 a** an edging that prevents cloth from unravelling (either an edge along the warp or a specially woven edging). **b** a border of different material or finish intended to be removed or hidden. **2** *Geol.* an alteration zone at the edge of a rock mass. **3** the edge-plate of a lock with an opening for the bolt. [ME f. SELF + EDGE, after Du. *selfegghe*]

selves *pl.* of SELF.

semanteme /simánteem/ *n. Linguistics* a fundamental element expressing an image or idea. [F *sémantème* (as SEMANTIC)]

semantic /simántik/ *adj.* relating to meaning in language; relating to the connotations of words. □□ **semantically** *adv.* [F *sémantique* f. Gk *sēmantikos* significant f. *sēmainō* signify f. *sēma* sign]

semantics /simántiks/ *n.pl.* (usu. treated as *sing.*) the branch of linguistics concerned with meaning. □□ **semantician** /-tísh'n/ *n.* **semanticist** /-tisist/ *n.*

semaphore /sémməfor/ *n.* & *v.* ● *n.* **1** *Mil.* etc. a system of sending messages by holding the arms or two flags in certain positions according to an alphabetic code. **2** a signalling apparatus consisting of a post with a movable arm or arms, lanterns, etc., for use (esp. on railways) by day or night. ● *v.intr.* & *tr.* signal or send by semaphore. □□ **semaphoric** /-fórrik/ *adj.* **semaphorically** /-fórrikəli/ *adv.* [F *sémaphore*, irreg. f. Gk *sēma* sign + *-phoros* -PHORE]

semasiology /simáysióllәji/ *n.* semantics. □□ **semasiological** /-siəlójik'l/ *adj.* [G *Semasiologie* f. Gk *sēmasia* meaning f. *sēmainō* signify]

sematic /simáttik/ *adj. Zool.* (of colouring, markings, etc.) significant; serving to warn off enemies or attract attention. [Gk *sēma sēmatos* sign]

semblable /sémbləb'l/ *n.* & *adj.* ● *n.* a counterpart or equal. ● *adj. archaic* having the semblance of something, seeming. [ME f. OF (as SEMBLANCE)]

semblance /sémbləns/ *n.* **1** the outward or superficial appearance of something (*put on a semblance of anger*). **2** resemblance. [ME f. OF f. *sembler* f. L *similare, simulare* SIMULATE]

■ **1** appearance, image, bearing, aspect, air, look, exterior, mask, façade, front, face, show, veneer, guise, pretence, cloak, impression, affectation, *literary* mien. **2** see RESEMBLANCE.

semé /sémmi, sémmay/ *adj.* (also **semée**) *Heraldry* covered with small bearings of indefinite number (e.g. stars, fleurs-de-lis) arranged all over the field. [F, past part. of *semer* to sow]

sememe /sémmeem, seém-/ *n. Linguistics* the unit of meaning carried by a morpheme. [as SEMANTIC]
semen /seémən/ *n.* the reproductive fluid of male animals, containing spermatozoa in suspension. [ME f. L *semen seminis* seed f. *serere* to sow]
semester /siméstər/ *n.* a half-year course or term in (esp. German and US) universities. [G f. L *semestris* six-monthly f. *sex* six + *mensis* month]
■ term, session.
semi /sémmi/ *n.* (*pl.* **semis**) *colloq.* **1** *Brit.* a semi-detached house. **2** *US* a semi-trailer. [abbr.]
semi- /sémmi/ *prefix* **1** half (*semicircle*). **2** partly; in some degree or particular (*semi-official*; *semi-detached*). **3** almost (*a semi-smile*). **4** occurring or appearing twice in a specified period (*semi-annual*). [F, It., etc. or L, corresp. to Gk HEMI-, Skr. *sāmi*]
■ **1** demi-, hemi-.
semi-annual /sémmiányooəl/ *adj.* occurring, published, etc., twice a year. □□ **semi-annually** *adv.*
semi-automatic /sémmiáwtəmáttik/ *adj.* **1** partially automatic. **2** (of a firearm) having a mechanism for continuous loading but not for continuous firing.
semi-basement /sémmibáysmənt/ *n.* a storey partly below ground level.
semi-bold /sémmibṓld/ *adj. Printing* printed in a type darker than normal but not as dark as bold.
semibreve /sémmibreev/ *n. Mus.* the longest note now in common use, having the time value of two minims or four crotchets, and represented by a ring with no stem. Also called *whole note*.
semicircle /sémmisurk'l/ *n.* **1** half of a circle or of its circumference. **2** a set of objects ranged in, or an object forming, a semicircle. [L *semicirculus* (as SEMI-, CIRCLE)]
semicircular /sémmisúrkyoolər/ *adj.* **1** forming or shaped like a semicircle. **2** arranged as or in a semicircle. □ **semicircular canal** one of three fluid-filled channels in the ear giving information to the brain to help maintain balance. [LL *semicircularis* (as SEMICIRCLE)]
semi-civilized /sémmisívvilīzd/ *adj.* partially civilized.
semicolon /sémmikṓlən, -lon/ *n.* a punctuation mark (;) of intermediate value between a comma and full stop.
semiconducting /sémmikəndúkting/ *adj.* having the properties of a semiconductor.
semiconductor /sémmikəndúktər/ *n.* a solid substance that is a non-conductor when pure or at a low temperature but has a conductivity between that of insulators and that of most metals when containing a suitable impurity or at a higher temperature and is used in integrated circuits, transistors, diodes, etc.
semi-conscious /sémmikónshəss/ *adj.* partly or imperfectly conscious.
semicylinder /sémmisíllindər/ *n.* half of a cylinder cut longitudinally. □□ **semicylindrical** /-líndrik'l/ *adj.*
semidemisemiquaver /sémmidémmisémmikwayvər/ *n. Mus.* = HEMIDEMISEMIQUAVER. [SEMI- + DEMISEMIQUAVER]
semi-deponent /sémmidipṓnənt/ *adj. Gram.* (of a Latin verb) having active forms in present tenses and passive forms with active sense in perfect tenses.
semi-detached /sémmiditácht/ *adj.* & *n.* ● *adj.* (of a house) joined to another by a party-wall on one side only. ● *n.* a semi-detached house.
semidiameter /sémmidīámmitər/ *n.* half of a diameter. [LL (as SEMI-, DIAMETER)]
semi-documentary /sémmidókyooméntəri/ *adj.* & *n.* ● *adj.* (of a film) having a factual background and a fictitious story. ● *n.* (*pl.* **-ies**) a semi-documentary film.
semi-dome /sémmidōm/ *n.* **1** a half-dome formed by vertical section. **2** a part of a structure more or less resembling a dome.
semi-double /sémmidúbb'l/ *adj.* (of a flower) intermediate between single and double in having only the outer stamens converted to petals.
semifinal /sémmifīn'l/ *n.* a match or round immediately preceding the final.
semifinalist /sémmifīnəlist/ *n.* a competitor in a semifinal.
semi-finished /sémmifinnisht/ *adj.* prepared for the final stage of manufacture.
semi-fitted /sémmifittid/ *adj.* (of a garment) shaped to the body but not closely fitted.
semifluid /sémmiflóō-id/ *adj.* & *n.* ● *adj.* of a consistency between solid and liquid. ● *n.* a semifluid substance.
semi-infinite /sémmi-ínfinit/ *adj. Math.* limited in one direction and stretching to infinity in the other.
semi-invalid /sémmi-ínvəleed, -lid/ *n.* a person somewhat enfeebled or partially disabled.
semi-liquid /sémmilíkwid/ *adj.* & *n.* = SEMIFLUID.
semi-lunar /sémmilóōnər/ *adj.* shaped like a half moon or crescent. □ **semi-lunar bone** a bone of this shape in the carpus. **semi-lunar cartilage** a cartilage of this shape in the knee. **semi-lunar valve** a valve of this shape in the heart. [mod.L *semilunaris* (as SEMI-, LUNAR)]
semi-metal /sémmimétt'l/ *n.* a substance with some of the properties of metals. [mod.L *semimetallum* (as SEMI-, METAL)]
semi-monthly /sémmimúnthli/ *adj.* & *adv.* ● *adj.* occurring, published, etc., twice a month. ● *adv.* twice a month.
seminal /sémmin'l/ *adj.* **1** of or relating to seed, semen, or reproduction. **2** germinal. **3** rudimentary, undeveloped. **4** (of ideas etc.) providing the basis for future development. □ **seminal fluid** semen. □□ **seminally** *adv.* [ME f. OF *seminal* or L *seminalis* (as SEMEN)]
■ **2, 3** embryonic, germinal, rudimentary, potential, inchoate, unformed, undeveloped, incipient. **4** original, basic, creative, plastic, primary, prime, formative, innovative, new, unprecedented, landmark, important, influential.
seminar /sémminaar/ *n.* **1** a small class at a university etc. for discussion and research. **2** a short intensive course of study. **3** a conference of specialists. [G (as SEMINARY)]
■ **1** class; workshop. **2** course, lecture series. **3** see CONFERENCE 2.
seminary /sémminəri/ *n.* (*pl.* **-ies**) **1** a training-college for priests, rabbis, etc. **2** a place of education or development. □□ **seminarist** *n.* [ME f. L *seminarium* seed-plot, neut. of *seminarius* (adj.) (as SEMEN)]
■ **2** academy, school, institute, institution, college, university.
seminiferous /sémminíffərəss/ *adj.* **1** bearing seed. **2** conveying semen. [L *semin-* f. SEMEN + -FEROUS]
semi-official /sémmiəfish'l/ *adj.* **1** partly official; rather less than official. **2** (of communications to newspapers etc.) made by an official with the stipulation that the source should not be revealed. □□ **semi-officially** *adv.*
semiology /seémiólləji, sém-/ *n.* (also **semeiology**) = SEMIOTICS. □□ **semiological** /-miəlójik'l/ *adj.* **semiologist** *n.* [Gk *sēmeion* sign f. *sēma* mark]
semi-opaque /sémmiōpáyk/ *adj.* not fully transparent.
semiotics /seémióttiks, sém-/ *n.* (also **semeiotics**) **1** the study of signs and symbols in various fields, esp. language. **2** *Med.* symptomatology. □□ **semiotic** *adj.* **semiotical** *adj.* **semiotically** *adv.* **semiotician** /-tísh'n/ *n.* [Gk *sēmeiōtikos* of signs (as SEMIOLOGY)]
semi-permanent /sémmipérmənənt/ *adj.* rather less than permanent.
semi-permeable /sémmipérmiəb'l/ *adj.* (of a membrane etc.) allowing small molecules, but not large ones, to pass through.
semi-plume /sémmiplóōm/ *n.* a feather with a firm stem and a downy web.
semiprecious /sémmipréshəss/ *adj.* (of a gem) less valuable than a precious stone.
semi-pro /sémmiprṓ/ *adj.* & *n.* (*pl.* **-os**) *US colloq.* = SEMI-PROFESSIONAL.
semi-professional /sémmiprəféshən'l/ *adj.* & *n.* ● *adj.* **1** receiving payment for an activity but not relying on it for a

living. **2** involving semi-professionals. ● *n.* a semi-professional musician, sportsman, etc.

semiquaver /sémmikwayvər/ *n. Mus.* a note having the time value of half a quaver and represented by a large dot with a two-hooked stem. Also called *sixteenth note.*

semi-rigid /sémmiríjid/ *adj.* (of an airship) having a stiffened keel attached to a flexible gas container.

semi-skilled /sémmiskíld/ *adj.* (of work or a worker) having or needing some training but less than for a skilled worker.

semi-skimmed /sémmiskímd/ *adj.* (of milk) from which some cream has been skimmed.

semi-smile /sémmismīl/ *n.* an expression that is not quite a smile.

semi-solid /sémmisóllid/ *adj.* viscous, semifluid.
■ see STIFF *adj.* 1, 2.

semi-sweet /sémmisweét/ *adj.* (of biscuits etc.) slightly sweetened.

semi-synthetic /sémmisinthéttik/ *adj. Chem.* (of a substance) that is prepared synthetically but derives from a naturally occurring material.

Semite /seémīt, sém-/ *n.* a member of any of the peoples supposed to be descended from Shem, son of Noah (Gen. 10:21 ff.), including esp. the Jews, Arabs, Assyrians, and Phoenicians. □□ **Semitism** /sémmitiz'm/ *n.* **Semitist** /sémmitist/ *n.* **Semitize** /sémmitīz/ *v.tr.* (also **-ise**). **Semitization** /sémmitīzáysh'n/ *n.* [mod.L *Semita* f. LL f. Gk *Sēm* Shem]

Semitic /simíttik/ *adj.* **1** of or relating to the Semites, esp. the Jews. **2** of or relating to the languages of the family including Hebrew and Arabic. [mod.L *Semiticus* (as SEMITE)]

semitone /sémmitōn/ *n. Mus.* the smallest interval used in classical European music; half a tone.

semi-trailer /sémmitráylər/ *n.* a trailer having wheels at the back but supported at the front by a towing vehicle.

semi-transparent /sémmitránzpárrənt, sémmitraánz-, -páirənt/ *adj.* partially or imperfectly transparent.
■ translucent, semi-opaque.

semi-tropics /sémmitróppiks/ *n.pl.* = SUBTROPICS. □□ **semi-tropical** *adj.*

semi-vowel /sémmivowəl/ *n.* **1** a sound intermediate between a vowel and a consonant (e.g. *w, y*). **2** a letter representing this. [after L *semivocalis*]

semi-weekly /sémmiweékli/ *adj.* & *adv.* ● *adj.* occurring, published, etc., twice a week. ● *adv.* twice a week.

semmit /sémmit/ *n. Sc.* an undershirt. [ME: orig. unkn.]

semolina /sémməleénə/ *n.* **1** the hard grains left after the milling of flour, used in puddings etc. and in pasta. **2** a pudding etc. made of this. [It. *semolino* dimin. of *semola* bran f. L *simila* flour]

sempiternal /sémpitérn'l/ *adj. rhet.* eternal, everlasting. □□ **sempiternally** *adv.* **sempiternity** *n.* [ME f. OF *sempiternel* f. LL *sempiternalis* f. L *sempiternus* f. *semper* always + *aeternus* eternal]
■ see EVERLASTING *adj.* 1.

semplice /sémplichay, -chi/ *adv. Mus.* in a simple style of performance. [It., = SIMPLE]

sempre /sémpray, -ri/ *adv. Mus.* throughout, always (*sempre forte*). [It.]

sempstress var. of SEAMSTRESS.

Semtex /sémteks/ *n. propr.* a highly malleable, odourless plastic explosive. [prob. f. *Semtín*, a village in the Czech republic near the place of production]

SEN *abbr.* (in the UK) State Enrolled Nurse.

Sen. *abbr.* **1** Senior. **2** *US* **a** Senator. **b** Senate.

senarius /sináiriəss/ *n.* (*pl.* **senarii** /-i-ī/) *Prosody* a verse of six feet, esp. an iambic trimeter. [L: see SENARY]

senary /seénəri, sén-/ *adj.* of six, by sixes. [L *senarius* f. *seni* distrib. of *sex* six]

senate /sénnit/ *n.* **1** a legislative body, esp. the upper and smaller assembly in the US, France, and other countries, in the States of the US, etc. **2** the governing body of a university or (in the US) a college. **3** *Rom.Hist.* the State council of the republic and empire sharing legislative power with the popular assemblies, administration with the magistrates, and judicial power with the knights. [ME f. OF *senat* f. L *senatus* f. *senex* old man]
■ **1** see CHAMBER *n.* 1b, c.

senator /sénnətər/ *n.* **1** a member of a senate. **2** (in Scotland) a Lord of Session. □□ **senatorial** /-tóriəl/ *adj.* **senatorship** *n.* [ME f. OF *senateur* f. L *senator -oris* (as SENATE)]
■ **1** see POLITICIAN.

send /send/ *v.* (*past* and *past part.* **sent** /sent/) **1** *tr.* **a** order or cause to go or be conveyed (*send a message to headquarters; sent me a book; sends goods all over the world*). **b** propel; cause to move (*send a bullet; sent him flying*). **c** cause to go or become (*send into raptures; send to sleep*). **d** dismiss with or without force (*sent her away; sent him about his business*). **2** *intr.* send a message or letter (*he sent to warn me*). **3** *tr.* (of God, providence, etc.) grant or bestow or inflict; bring about; cause to be (*send rain; send a judgement; send her victorious!*). **4** *tr. sl.* affect emotionally, put into ecstasy. **5** *tr.* (freq. foll. by *forth* or *off*) emit, give out (light, heat, odour, etc.); utter or produce (sound); cause (a voice, cry, etc.) to carry, or travel. □ **send away for** send an order to a dealer for (goods). **send down** *Brit.* **1** rusticate or expel from a university. **2** sentence to imprisonment. **3** *Cricket* bowl (a ball or an over). **send for 1** summon. **2** order by post. **send in 1** cause to go in. **2** submit (an entry etc.) for a competition etc. **send off 1** get (a letter, parcel, etc.) dispatched. **2** attend the departure of (a person) as a sign of respect etc. **3** *Sport* (of a referee) order (a player) to leave the field and take no further part in the game. **send-off** *n.* a demonstration of goodwill etc. at the departure of a person, the start of a project, etc. **send off for** = *send away for.* **send on** transmit to a further destination or in advance of one's own arrival. **send a person to Coventry** see COVENTRY. **send up 1** cause to go up. **2** transmit to a higher authority. **3** *Brit. colloq.* satirize or ridicule, esp. by mimicking. **4** *US* sentence to imprisonment. **send-up** *n. Brit. colloq.* a satire or parody. **send word** send information. □□ **sendable** *adj.* **sender** *n.* [OE *sendan* f. Gmc]
■ **1 a** communicate, transmit, convey, deliver, consign, address to, mail, post, fax, remit, ship, forward; broadcast, telecast, televise, radio, telegraph. **b** release, discharge, shoot, propel, fire, fling, project, hurl; cast, throw, toss, let fly, *colloq.* sling, chuck. **d** dismiss, dispatch, commission, charge, depute, delegate, assign. **3** see BESTOW, INFLICT. **4** delight, please, charm, enrapture, stir, thrill, move, electrify, *colloq.* turn on, *sl.* blow a person's mind. **5** emit, radiate, discharge, pour out *or* forth, give out *or* off, exude, emanate; produce, yield, generate, propagate; utter, let out, issue. □ **send down 2** imprison, incarcerate, jail, *Brit.* gaol, *US* send up. **send for** call for, summon; order, request, ask for. **send in 2** see SUBMIT 2. **send off 3** dismiss, discharge, expel, send away, *colloq.* send packing, give a person his *or* her walking papers; order off, give a person his *or* her marching orders, *Football* show a person the red card. **send on** see FORWARD *v.* 1b. **send up 3** lampoon, satirize, burlesque, ridicule, parody, make fun of, *colloq.* take off, spoof, *sl.* take the mickey out of. **4** see *send down* above. **send-up** see PARODY *n.* 1.

sendal /sénd'l/ *n. hist.* **1** a thin rich silk material. **2** a garment of this. [ME f. OF *cendal*, ult. f. Gk *sindōn*]

senecio /sineéshiō/ *n.* any composite plant of the genus *Senecio*, including many cultivated species as well as groundsel and ragwort. [L *senecio* old man, groundsel, with ref. to the hairy fruits]

senesce /sinéss/ *v.intr.* grow old. □□ **senescence** *n.* **senescent** *adj.* [L *senescere* f. *senex* old]
■ □□ **senescence** see AGE *n.* 3. **senescent** see ELDERLY *adj.*

seneschal /sénnish'l/ *n.* **1** the steward or major-domo of a medieval great house. **2** a judge in Sark. [ME f. OF f. med.L *seniscalus* f. Gmc, = old servant]

■ **1** see SERVANT. **2** see JUDGE *n.* 1.

senhor /saynyór/ *n.* a title used of or to a Portuguese or Brazilian man. [Port. f. L *senior*: see SENIOR]

senhora /saynyórə/ *n.* a title used of or to a Portuguese woman or a Brazilian married woman. [Port., fem. of SENHOR]

senhorita /sáynyəreétə/ *n.* a title used of or to a Brazilian unmarried woman. [Port., dimin. of SENHORA]

senile /seénīl/ *adj.* & *n.* ● *adj.* **1** of or characteristic of old age (*senile apathy*; *senile decay*). **2** having the weaknesses or diseases of old age. ● *n.* a senile person. □ **senile dementia** a severe form of mental deterioration in old age, characterized by loss of memory and disorientation, and most often due to Alzheimer's desease. □□ **senility** /sinílliti/ *n.* [F *sénile* or L *senilis* f. *senex* old man]

■ *adj.* **2** senescent, decrepit, declining, failing, geriatric, in one's dotage, doddering, in one's second childhood, *colloq.* past it; simple, feeble-minded, *colloq.* dotty; forgetful. □□ **senility** old age, senescence; dotage, second childhood; decrepitude, decline; senile dementia, Alzheimer's disease.

senior /seéniər/ *adj.* & *n.* ● *adj.* **1** (often foll. by *to*) more or most advanced in age or standing. **2** of high or highest position. **3** (placed after a person's name) senior to another of the same name. **4** (of a school) having pupils in an older age-range (esp. over 11). **5** *US* of the final year at a university, high school, etc. ● *n.* **1** a person of advanced age or comparatively long service etc. **2** one's elder, or one's superior in length of service, membership, etc. (*is my senior*). **3** a senior student. □ **senior citizen** an elderly person, esp. an old-age pensioner. **senior college** *US* a college in which the last two years' work for a bachelor's degree is done. **senior common** (or **combination**) **room** *Brit.* a room for use by senior members of a college. **senior nursing officer** the person in charge of nursing services in a hospital. **senior officer** an officer to whom a junior is responsible. **senior partner** the head of a firm. **senior service** *Brit.* the Royal Navy as opposed to the Army. **senior tutor** *Brit.* a college tutor in charge of the teaching arrangements. □□ **seniority** /seéniórriti/ *n.* [ME f. L, = older, older man, compar. of *senex senis* old man, old]

■ *adj.* **1–3** elder, older, *Brit.* major; (higher-)ranking, superior; chief. **4** secondary, upper. □ **senior citizen** elderly person, retired person, (old-age) pensioner, retirer, *Brit.* OAP, *esp. US* retiree, *US* golden-ager, *sl. offens.* wrinkly; geriatric. □□ **seniority** see STATUS 2.

senna /sénnə/ *n.* **1** a cassia tree. **2** a laxative prepared from the dried pod of this. [med.L *sena* f. Arab. *sanā*]

sennet[1] /sénnit/ *n. hist.* a signal call on a trumpet or cornet (in the stage directions of Elizabethan plays). [perh. var. of SIGNET]

sennet[2] var. of SINNET.

sennight /sénnīt/ *n. archaic* a week. [OE *seofon nihta* seven nights]

sennit /sénnit/ *n.* **1** *hist.* plaited straw, palm leaves, etc., used for making hats. **2** = SINNET. [var. of SINNET]

señor /senyór/ *n.* (*pl.* **señores** /-rez/) a title used of or to a Spanish-speaking man. [Sp. f. L *senior*: see SENIOR]

señora /senyórə/ *n.* a title used of or to a Spanish-speaking married woman. [Sp., fem. of SEÑOR]

señorita /sényəreétə/ *n.* a title used of or to a Spanish-speaking unmarried woman. [Sp., dimin. of SEÑORA]

Senr. *abbr.* Senior.

sensate /sénsayt/ *adj.* perceived by the senses. [LL *sensatus* having senses (as SENSE)]

sensation /sensáysh'n/ *n.* **1** the consciousness of perceiving or seeming to perceive some state or condition of one's body or its parts or senses or of one's mind or its emotions; an instance of such consciousness (*lost all sensation in my left arm*; *had a sensation of giddiness*; *a sensation of pride*; *in search of a new sensation*). **2 a** a stirring of emotions or intense interest esp. among a large group of people (*the news caused a sensation*). **b** a person, event, etc., causing such interest. **3** the sensational use of literary etc. material. [med.L *sensatio* f. L *sensus* SENSE]

■ **1** feeling, sense, impression, awareness, perception, experience; foreboding, presentiment, prescience; (sneaking) suspicion, hunch, conjecture. **2 a** commotion, stir, thrill, furore, storm; excitement. **b** success, sell-out, *colloq.* hit, show-stopper, riot, *sl.* blockbuster.

sensational /sensáyshən'l/ *adj.* **1** causing or intended to cause great public excitement etc. **2** of or causing sensation. □□ **sensationalize** *v.tr.* **sensationally** *adv.*

■ **1** exciting, stimulating, electrifying, galvanizing, shocking, hair-raising, spine-tingling, thrilling, stirring, breathtaking, stupendous, amazing, astonishing, astounding, staggering, mind-boggling, unbelievable, incredible, spectacular, far-out, *sl.* mind-blowing; good, great, marvellous, wonderful, superior, superb, matchless, peerless, unequalled, nonpareil, extraordinary, terrific, phenomenal, splendid, *colloq.* fabulous, fantastic, super, smashing; lurid, vivid, overdone, overdrawn, extreme, melodramatic, exaggerated, dramatic, extravagant.

sensationalism /sensáyshənəliz'm/ *n.* **1** the use of or interest in the sensational in literature, political agitation, etc. **2** *Philos.* the theory that ideas are derived solely from sensation (opp. RATIONALISM). □□ **sensationalist** *n.* & *adj.* **sensationalistic** /-lístik/ *adj.*

■ □□ **sensationalistic** see *melodramatic* (MELODRAMA).

sense /senss/ *n.* & *v.* ● *n.* **1 a** any of the special bodily faculties by which sensation is roused (*has keen senses*; *has a dull sense of smell*). **b** sensitiveness of all or any of these. **2** the ability to perceive or feel or to be conscious of the presence or properties of things. **3** (foll. by *of*) consciousness; intuitive awareness (*sense of having done well*; *sense of one's own importance*). **4** (often foll. by *of*) **a** quick or accurate appreciation, understanding, or instinct regarding a specified matter (*sense of the ridiculous*; *road sense*; *the moral sense*). **b** the habit of basing one's conduct on such instinct. **5** practical wisdom or judgement, common sense; conformity to these (*has plenty of sense*; *what is the sense of talking like that?*; *has more sense than to do that*). **6 a** a meaning; the way in which a word etc. is to be understood (*the sense of the word is clear*; *I mean that in the literal sense*). **b** intelligibility or coherence or possession of a meaning. **7** the prevailing opinion among a number of people. **8** (in *pl.*) a person's sanity or normal state of mind (*taken leave of his senses*). **9** *Math.* etc. **a** a direction of movement. **b** that which distinguishes a pair of entities which differ only in that each is the reverse of the other. ● *v.tr.* **1** perceive by a sense or senses. **2** be vaguely aware of. **3** realize. **4** (of a machine etc.) detect. **5** *US* understand. □ **bring a person to his** or **her senses 1** cure a person of folly. **2** restore a person to consciousness. **come to one's senses 1** regain consciousness. **2** become sensible after acting foolishly. **the five senses** sight, hearing, smell, taste, and touch. **in a** (or **one**) **sense** if the statement is understood in a particular way (*what you say is true in a sense*). **in one's senses** sane. **make sense** be intelligible or practicable. **make sense of** show or find the meaning of. **man of sense** a sagacious man. **out of one's senses** in or into a state of madness (*is out of her senses*; *frightened him out of his senses*). **sense-datum** (*pl.* **-data**) *Philos.* an element of experience received through the senses. **sense of direction** the ability to know without guidance the direction in which one is or should be moving. **sense of humour** see HUMOUR. **sense-organ** a bodily organ conveying external stimuli to the sensory system. **take leave of one's senses** go mad. **take the sense of the meeting** ascertain the prevailing opinion. **under a sense of wrong** feeling wronged. [ME f. L *sensus* faculty of feeling, thought, meaning, f. *sentire sens-* feel]

■ *n.* **1** faculty; sight, vision, hearing, taste, smell, touch. **2, 3** see UNDERSTANDING *n.* 1. **4, 5** common sense, intelligence, perception, quick-wittedness, quickness, (mother) wit, judgement, reason, sanity, wisdom, sagacity, discrimination, discernment, brains, *colloq.*

nous. **6** meaning; intelligibility, coherence, drift, gist, import, purport, nuance, significance, message, substance. **7** consensus. **8** (*senses*) see SANITY 1. ● *v.* feel, perceive, detect, realize, divine, intuit, have a hunch *or* feeling, have *or* get the impression, suspect; see also UNDERSTAND 1, 2. □ **bring a person to his** or **her senses 1** see ENLIGHTEN 1a. **2** see WAKE[1] *v.* 1. **come to one's senses 1** see AWAKE *v.* 1. **in a** (or **one sense**) in a way, in a manner of speaking. **make sense** see *add up* 3. **take leave of one's senses** go mad, go out of one's head, go insane, *sl.* flip one's lid, lose one's marbles.

senseless /sénsliss/ *adj.* **1** unconscious. **2** wildly foolish. **3** without meaning or purpose. **4** incapable of sensation. □□ **senselessly** *adv.* **senselessness** *n.*

■ **1, 4** insensible, unconscious, (knocked) out (cold), stunned, insensate, comatose; unfeeling, benumbed, anaesthetized, dead, deadened, insentient. **2, 3** pointless, purposeless, ridiculous, ludicrous, unintelligent, illogical, irrational, incongruous, meaningless, absurd, wild, mad, demented, insane, asinine, nonsensical, simple-minded, fatuous, stupid, foolish, silly, dizzy, halfwitted, mindless, brainless, witless, empty-headed, hare-brained, muddle-headed, *colloq.* crazy, dotty, imbecilic, imbecile, idiotic, moronic, pea-brained, birdbrained, *esp. Brit. colloq.* daft, *sl.* daffy, nutty, nuts, batty, wacky, dippy. □□ **senselessness** see FOLLY 1, *emptiness* (EMPTY).

sensibility /sénsibílliti/ *n.* (*pl.* **-ies**) **1** capacity to feel (*little finger lost its sensibility*). **2 a** openness to emotional impressions, susceptibility, sensitiveness (*sensibility to kindness*). **b** an exceptional or excessive degree of this (*sense and sensibility*). **3** (in *pl.*) emotional capacities or feelings. [ME f. LL *sensibilitas* (as SENSIBLE)]

■ **1** see FEELING *n.* 1. **2 a** responsiveness, responsivity, openness, susceptibility, sensitivity, sensitiveness. **3** (*sensibilities*) feelings, emotions, sentiments, susceptibilities.

sensible /sénsib'l/ *adj.* **1** having or showing wisdom or common sense; reasonable, judicious (*a sensible person*; *a sensible compromise*). **2 a** perceptible by the senses (*sensible phenomena*). **b** great enough to be perceived; appreciable (*a sensible difference*). **3** (of clothing etc.) practical and functional. **4** (foll. by *of*) aware; not unmindful (*was sensible of his peril*). □ **sensible horizon** see HORIZON 1b. □□ **sensibleness** *n.* **sensibly** *adv.* [ME f. OF *sensible* or L *sensibilis* (as SENSE)]

■ **1, 3** reasonable, realistic, logical, commonsensical, rational, reasoned, sound, practical, prudent, judicious, discreet, intelligent, sage, wise, sane; down-to-earth, practical; well-thought-out; functional. **2** perceivable, perceptible, detectable, evident, discernible, recognizable, ascertainable, apprehensible, cognizable, manifest, palpable, physical, tangible, corporeal, material, visible, observable, seeable, *archaic* substantive; appreciable, significant, considerable, substantial, noticeable. **4** (*sensible of*) aware of, acquainted with, cognizant of, sensitive to, alive to, mindful of, understanding of, in touch with, observant of, awake to, alert to, *US colloq.* wise to, *sl.* hip to.

sensitive /sénsitiv/ *adj.* & *n.* ● *adj.* **1** (often foll. by *to*) very open to or acutely affected by external stimuli or mental impressions; having sensibility. **2** (of a person) easily offended or emotionally hurt. **3** (often foll. by *to*) (of an instrument etc.) responsive to or recording slight changes. **4** (often foll. by *to*) **a** (of photographic materials) prepared so as to respond (esp. rapidly) to the action of light. **b** (of any material) readily affected by or responsive to external action. **5** (of a topic etc.) subject to restriction of discussion to prevent embarrassment, ensure security, etc. **6** (of a market) liable to quick changes of price. ● *n.* a person who is sensitive (esp. to supposed occult influences). □ **sensitive plant 1** a plant whose leaves curve downwards and leaflets fold together when touched, esp. mimosa. **2** a sensitive person. □□ **sensitively** *adv.* **sensitiveness** *n.* [ME, = sensory, f. OF *sensitif -ive* or med.L *sensitivus*, irreg. f. L *sentire sens-* feel]

■ *adj.* **1** delicate, tender, sore, susceptible. **2** touchy, susceptible, susceptive, reactive, responsive, attuned, impressionable, emotional, thin-skinned, tender, vulnerable, supersensitive, hypersensitive, testy, irascible, quarrelsome, irritable, volatile, excitable, temperamental, petulant, hot-tempered, quick-tempered. **3, 4, 6** finely tuned, delicate, responsive, subtle, acute, reactive, receptive. **5** see DELICATE 3a.

sensitivity /sénsitívviti/ *n.* the quality or degree of being sensitive.

■ sensibility, sensitiveness, delicacy, touchiness, over-sensitivity, hypersensitivity, supersensitivity; soreness, irritability; awareness, consciousness, acuteness, perception, understanding, intuition, feeling, sense, receptivity, receptiveness, appreciation, appreciativeness, susceptibility, susceptibleness, susceptivity, susceptiveness; compassion, concern, sympathy, tenderness, tender-heartedness, kind-heartedness, kindliness, warmth.

sensitize /sénsitīz/ *v.tr.* (also **-ise**) **1** make sensitive. **2** *Photog.* make sensitive to light. **3** make (an organism etc.) abnormally sensitive to a foreign substance. □□ **sensitization** /-záysh'n/ *n.* **sensitizer** *n.*

sensitometer /sénsitómmitər/ *n. Photog.* a device for measuring sensitivity to light.

sensor /sénsər/ *n.* a device giving a signal for the detection or measurement of a physical property to which it responds. [SENSORY, after MOTOR]

■ probe, feeler.

sensorium /sensóriəm/ *n.* (*pl.* **sensoria** /-riə/ or **sensoriums**) **1** the seat of sensation, the brain, brain and spinal cord, or grey matter of these. **2** *Biol.* the whole sensory apparatus including the nerve-system. □□ **sensorial** *adj.* **sensorially** *adv.* [LL f. L *sentire sens-* feel]

sensory /sénsəri/ *adj.* of sensation or the senses. □□ **sensorily** *adv.* [as SENSORIUM]

sensual /sénsyooəl, sénshooəl/ *adj.* **1 a** of or depending on the senses only and not on the intellect or spirit; carnal, fleshly (*sensual pleasures*). **b** given to the pursuit of sensual pleasures or the gratification of the appetites; self-indulgent sexually or in regard to food and drink; voluptuous, licentious. **c** indicative of a sensual nature (*sensual lips*). **2** of sense or sensation, sensory. **3** *Philos.* of, according to, or holding the doctrine of, sensationalism. □□ **sensualism** *n.* **sensualist** *n.* **sensualize** *v.tr.* (also **-ise**). **sensually** *adv.* [ME f. LL *sensualis* (as SENSE)]

■ **1** physical, appetitive, voluptuous, carnal, bodily, fleshly; erotic, sexual, lustful, unchaste, abandoned, dissolute, profligate, dissipated, licentious, lewd, lascivious, lubricious, goatish, lecherous, libidinous, salacious, prurient, rakish, wanton, debauched, loose, dirty, randy. □□ **sensualist** lecher, profligate, wanton, debauchee, roué, rake, Romeo, Don Juan, Casanova, Lothario, libertine; voluptuary, hedonist, sybarite, *bon viveur*, *bon vivant*, epicure, epicurean, gourmet, gourmand, gastronome, pleasure-seeker.

sensuality /sénsyoo-álliti, sénshoo-/ *n.* gratification of the senses, self-indulgence. [ME f. F *sensualité* f. LL *sensualitas* (as SENSUAL)]

■ eroticism, sexuality, physicality, carnality.

sensum /sénsəm/ *n.* (*pl.* **sensa** /-sə/) *Philos.* a sense-datum. [mod.L, neut. past part. of L *sentire* feel]

sensuous /sénsyooəss/ *adj.* **1** of or derived from or affecting the senses, esp. aesthetically rather than sensually; aesthetically pleasing. **2** readily affected by the senses. □□ **sensuously** *adv.* **sensuousness** *n.* [L *sensus* sense]

■ **1** sensory, sensorial; sumptuous, luxurious, rich, affective, intense. **2** responsive, receptive; see also SENSITIVE *adj.* 2

sent *past* and *past part.* of SEND.

sentence /séntənss/ *n.* & *v.* ● *n.* **1 a** a set of words complete in itself as the expression of a thought, containing or implying a subject and predicate, and conveying a statement, question, exclamation, or command. **b** a piece of writing or speech between two full stops or equivalent pauses, often including several grammatical sentences (e.g. *I went*; *he came*). **2 a** a decision of a lawcourt, esp. the punishment allotted to a person convicted in a criminal trial. **b** the declaration of this. **3** *Logic* a series of signs or symbols expressing a proposition in an artificial or logical language. ● *v.tr.* **1** declare the sentence of (a convicted criminal etc.). **2** (foll. by *to*) declare (such a person) to be condemned to a specified punishment. □ **under sentence of** having been condemned to (*under sentence of death*). [ME f. OF f. L *sententia* opinion f. *sentire* be of opinion]
■ *n.* **2** judgement, decision, ruling, verdict, decree, determination; punishment.

sentential /senténsh'l/ *adj.* *Gram.* & *Logic* of a sentence. [L *sententialis* (as SENTENCE)]

sententious /senténshəss/ *adj.* **1** (of a person) fond of pompous moralizing. **2** (of a style) affectedly formal. **3** aphoristic, pithy, given to the use of maxims, affecting a concise impressive style. □□ **sententiously** *adv.* **sententiousness** *n.* [L *sententiosus* (as SENTENCE)]
■ **1** see *pedantic* (PEDANT). **2** see POMPOUS 2. **3** see *epigrammatic* (EPIGRAM).

sentient /sénsh'nt/ *adj.* having the power of perception by the senses. □□ **sentience** *n.* **sentiency** *n.* **sentiently** *adv.* [L *sentire* feel]

sentiment /séntimənt/ *n.* **1** a mental feeling (*the sentiment of pity*). **2 a** the sum of what one feels on some subject. **b** a verbal expression of this. **3** the expression of a view or desire esp. as formulated for a toast (*concluded his speech with a sentiment*). **4** an opinion as distinguished from the words meant to convey it (*the sentiment is good though the words are injudicious*). **5** a view or tendency based on or coloured with emotion (*animated by noble sentiments*). **6** such views collectively, esp. as an influence (*sentiment unchecked by reason is a bad guide*). **7** the tendency to be swayed by feeling rather than by reason. **8 a** mawkish tenderness. **b** the display of this. **9** an emotional feeling conveyed in literature or art. [ME f. OF *sentement* f. med.L *sentimentum* f. L *sentire* feel]
■ **1, 9** attitude, feeling, sensibility, emotion. **2, 5** thought; (*sentiments*) view, outlook, opinion, belief, position, judgement. **4** thought. **8** sentimentality, sentimentalism.

sentimental /séntimént'l/ *adj.* **1** of or characterized by sentiment. **2** showing or affected by emotion rather than reason. **3** appealing to sentiment. □ **sentimental value** the value of a thing to a particular person because of its associations. □□ **sentimentalism** *n.* **sentimentalist** *n.* **sentimentality** /-tálliti/ *n.* **sentimentalize** *v.intr.* & *tr.* (also **-ise**). **sentimentalization** /-līzáysh'n/ *n.* **sentimentally** *adv.*
■ emotional; sympathetic, compassionate, tender, warm-hearted, tender-hearted; romantic, nostalgic, maudlin, mawkish, over-emotional, tearful, sickening, nauseating, simpering, sweet, saccharine, sickly, mushy, gushy, *colloq.* weepy, sloppy, slushy, lovey-dovey, corny, icky, sick-making, *Brit. colloq.* soppy, *esp. US colloq.* schmaltzy, *sl.* gooey, drippy, yucky. □□ **sentimentality** romanticism, nostalgia, pathos, emotionalism, mawkishness, over-emotionalism, tenderness, tearfulness, sweetness, sickliness, mushiness, gushiness, *colloq.* sloppiness, weepiness, corniness, corn, *Brit. colloq.* soppiness, *esp. US colloq.* schmaltz, schmaltziness, *sl.* gooeyness,slushiness, drippiness, ickiness, yuckiness.

sentinel /séntin'l/ *n.* & *v.* ● *n.* a sentry or lookout. ● *v.tr.* (**sentinelled, sentinelling**; *US* **sentineled, sentineling**) **1** station sentinels at or in. **2** *poet.* keep guard over or in. [F *sentinelle* f. It. *sentinella*, of unkn. orig.]
■ *n.* sentry, guard, watchman, watch, lookout, patrol, *Mil.* picket.

sentry /séntri/ *n.* (*pl.* **-ies**) a soldier etc. stationed to keep guard. □ **sentry-box** a wooden cabin intended to shelter a standing sentry. **sentry-go** the duty of pacing up and down as a sentry. [perh. f. obs. *centrinel*, var. of SENTINEL]
■ see GUARD *n.* 2.

sepal /sépp'l, seé-/ *n.* *Bot.* each of the divisions or leaves of the calyx. [F *sépale*, mod.L *sepalum*, perh. formed as SEPARATE + PETAL]

separable /sépparəb'l/ *adj.* **1** able to be separated. **2** *Gram.* (of a prefix, or a verb in respect of a prefix) written as a separate word in some collocations. □□ **separability** /-bílliti/ *n.* **separableness** *n.* **separably** *adv.* [F *séparable* or L *separabilis* (as SEPARATE)]
■ **1** distinguishable; segregable, detachable, divisible, severable, removable, fissile, scissile.

separate *adj.*, *n.*, & *v.* ● *adj.* /sépparət/ (often foll. by *from*) forming a unit that is or may be regarded as apart or by itself; physically disconnected, distinct, or individual (*living in separate rooms*; *the two questions are essentially separate*). ● *n.* /sépparət/ **1** (in *pl.*) separate articles of clothing suitable for wearing together in various combinations. **2** an offprint. ● *v.* /sépparayt/ **1** *tr.* make separate, sever, disunite. **2** *tr.* prevent union or contact of. **3** *intr.* go different ways, disperse. **4** *intr.* cease to live together as a married couple. **5** *intr.* (foll. by *from*) secede. **6** *tr.* **a** divide or sort (milk, ore, fruit, light, etc.) into constituent parts or sizes. **b** (often foll. by *out*) extract or remove (an ingredient, waste product, etc.) by such a process for use or rejection. **7** *tr.* *US* discharge, dismiss. □□ **separately** *adv.* **separateness** *n.* **separative** /-rətiv/ *adj.* **separatory** /-rətəri/ *adj.* [L *separare separat-* (as SE-, *parare* make ready)]
■ *adj.* divided, separated, disjoined, disconnected, detached, isolated, discrete, distinct, individual, independent, solitary, different; unrelated, other; withdrawn, solitary, alone; shut *or* closed off *or* away, apart, removed, cloistered, secluded, sequestered. ● *v.* **1** sever, disjoin, pull *or* take *or* break apart, take *or* break to pieces, split *or* divide *or* break (up), split *or* break (off *or* away), disconnect, disengage, part, partition, uncouple, disarticulate, disassemble, unhook, detach, disunite, unyoke, disentangle, unravel. **3, 4** disperse, split (up), break up, part (company), divide (up), disband, divorce; fork, bifurcate, diverge, branch. **5** see SECEDE. **6 a** distinguish, discriminate, analyse, sort (out), break down, classify, segregate, single out, sequester, type, codify, organize, split up; group, collate. □□ **separately** individually, independently, singly, one by one, one at a time, personally, alone, severally.

separation /séppəráysh'n/ *n.* **1** the act or an instance of separating; the state of being separated. **2** (in full **judicial separation** or **legal separation**) an arrangement by which a husband and wife remain married but live apart. **3** any of three or more monochrome reproductions of a coloured picture which can combine to reproduce the full colour of the original. □ **separation order** an order of court for judicial separation. [ME f. OF f. L *separatio -onis* (as SEPARATE)]
■ **1, 2** partition, division, split, schism; dissociation, disassociation, severance; disintegration, shattering, break-up, fragmentation, disunion, dismemberment, taking *or* keeping apart, segregation, disjunction, fission, scission, rupture, fracture, break; rift, split, split-up, estrangement.

separatist /sépparətist/ *n.* a person who favours separation, esp. for political or ecclesiastical independence (opp. UNIONIST 2). □□ **separatism** *n.*

separator /sépparaytər/ *n.* a machine for separating, e.g. cream from milk.

Sephardi /sifaárdi/ *n.* (*pl.* **Sephardim** /-dim/) a Jew of Spanish or Portuguese descent (cf. ASHKENAZI). □□ **Sephardic** *adj.* [LHeb., f. sᵉp̄āraḏ, a country mentioned in Obad. 20 and taken to be Spain]

sepia /seépiə/ *n.* **1** a dark reddish-brown colour. **2 a** a brown pigment prepared from a black fluid secreted by cuttlefish, used in monochrome drawing and in water-colours. **b** a brown tint used in photography. **3** a drawing done in sepia. **4** the fluid secreted by cuttlefish. [L f. Gk *sēpia* cuttlefish]

sepoy /séepoy/ *n. hist.* a native Indian soldier under European, esp. British, discipline. [Urdu & Pers. *sipāhī* soldier f. *sipāh* army]

seppuku /sepóokoo/ *n.* hara-kiri. [Jap.]

sepsis /sépsiss/ *n.* **1** the state of being septic. **2** blood-poisoning. [mod.L f. Gk *sēpsis* f. *sēpō* make rotten]

Sept. *abbr.* **1** September. **2** Septuagint.

sept /sept/ *n.* a clan, esp. in Ireland. [prob. alt. of SECT]
■ see TRIBE.

sept- var. of SEPTI-.

septa *pl.* of SEPTUM.

septal[1] /séptəl/ *adj.* **1** of a septum or septa. **2** *Archaeol.* (of a stone or slab) separating compartments in a burial chamber. [SEPTUM]

septal[2] /séptəl/ *adj.* of a sept or septs.

septate /séptayt/ *adj. Bot., Zool., & Anat.* having a septum or septa; partitioned. □□ **septation** /-táysh'n/ *n.*

septcentenary /séptsentéenəri/ *n.* & *adj.* ● *n.* (*pl.* **-ies**) **1** a seven-hundredth anniversary. **2** a festival marking this. ● *adj.* of or concerning a septcentenary.

September /septémbər/ *n.* the ninth month of the year. [ME f. L *September* f. *septem* seven: orig. the seventh month of the Roman year]

septenarius /séptináiriəss/ *n.* (*pl.* **septenarii** /-ri-ī/) *Prosody* a verse of seven feet, esp. a trochaic or iambic tetrameter catalectic. [L f. *septeni* distributive of *septem* seven]

septenary /septéenəri, séptin-/ *adj.* & *n.* ● *adj.* of seven, by sevens, on the basis of seven. ● *n.* (*pl.* **-ies**) **1** a group or set of seven (esp. years). **2** a septenarius. [L *septenarius* (as SEPTENARIUS)]

septenate /séptinayt/ *adj. Bot.* **1** growing in sevens. **2** having seven divisions. [L *septeni* (as SEPTENARIUS)]

septennial /septénniəl/ *adj.* **1** lasting for seven years. **2** recurring every seven years. [LL *septennis* f. L *septem* seven + *annus* year]

septennium /septénniəm/ *n.* (*pl.* **septenniums** or **septennia** /-niə/) a period of seven years.

septet /septét/ *n.* (also **septette**) **1** *Mus.* **a** a composition for seven performers. **b** the performers of such a composition. **2** any group of seven. [G *Septett* f. L *septem* seven]

septfoil /sétfoyl/ *n.* **1** a seven-lobed ornamental figure. **2** *archaic* tormentil. [LL *septifolium* after CINQUEFOIL, TREFOIL]

septi- /sépti/ *comb. form* (also **sept-** before a vowel) seven. [L f. *septem* seven]

septic /séptik/ *adj.* contaminated with bacteria from a festering wound etc., putrefying. □ **septic tank** a tank in which the organic matter in sewage is disintegrated through bacterial activity. □□ **septically** *adv.* **septicity** /-tíssiti/ *n.* [L *septicus* f. Gk *sēptikos* f. *sēpō* make rotten]
■ see *ulcerous* (ULCER).

septicaemia /séptiséemiə/ *n.* (*US* **septicemia**) blood-poisoning. □□ **septicaemic** *adj.* [mod.L f. Gk *sēptikos* + *haima* blood]

septillion /septílyən/ *n.* (*pl.* same) a thousand raised to the eighth (or formerly, esp. *Brit.*, the fourteenth) power (10^{24} and 10^{42} respectively). [F f. *sept* seven, after *billion* etc.]

septimal /séptim'l/ *adj.* of the number seven. [L *septimus* seventh f. *septem* seven]

septime /sépteem/ *n. Fencing* the seventh of the eight parrying positions. [L *septimus* (as SEPTIMAL)]

septivalent /septívvələnt/ *adj.* (also **septavalent**) *Chem.* having a valency of seven.

septuagenarian /séptyooəjináiriən/ *n.* & *adj.* ● *n.* a person from 70 to 79 years old. ● *adj.* of this age. [L *septuagenarius* f. *septuageni* distributive of *septuaginta* seventy]

Septuagesima /séptyooəjéssimə/ *n.* (in full **Septuagesima Sunday**) the Sunday before Sexagesima. [ME f. L, = seventieth (day), formed as SEPTUAGINT, perh. after QUINQUAGESIMA or with ref. to the period of 70 days from Septuagesima to the Saturday after Easter]

Septuagint /séptyooəjint/ *n.* a Greek version of the Old Testament including the Apocrypha, said to have been made about 270 BC by seventy-two translators. [L *septuaginta* seventy]

septum /séptəm/ *n.* (*pl.* **septa** /-tə/) *Anat., Bot., & Zool.* a partition such as that between the nostrils or the chambers of a poppy-fruit or of a shell. [L *s(a)eptum* f. *saepire saept-* enclose f. *saepes* hedge]

septuple /séptyoop'l/ *adj., n.,* & *v.* ● *adj.* **1** sevenfold, having seven parts. **2** being seven times as many or as much. ● *n.* a sevenfold number or amount. ● *v.tr.* & *intr.* multiply by seven. [LL *septuplus* f. L *septem* seven]

septuplet /séptyooplit, septyóoplit/ *n.* **1** one of seven children born at one birth. **2** *Mus.* a group of seven notes to be played in the time of four or six. [as SEPTUPLE, after TRIPLET etc.]

sepulchral /sipúlkrəl/ *adj.* **1** of a tomb or interment (*sepulchral mound; sepulchral customs*). **2** suggestive of the tomb, funereal, gloomy, dismal (*sepulchral look*). □□ **sepulchrally** *adv.* [F *sépulchral* or L *sepulchralis* (as SEPULCHRE)]
■ **2** see FUNEREAL.

sepulchre /séppəlkər/ *n.* & *v.* (*US* **sepulcher**) ● *n.* a tomb esp. cut in rock or built of stone or brick, a burial vault or cave. ● *v.tr.* **1** lay in a sepulchre. **2** serve as a sepulchre for. □ **the Holy Sepulchre** the tomb in which Christ was laid. **whited sepulchre** a hypocrite (with ref. to Matt. 23:27). [ME f. OF f. L *sepulc(h)rum* f. *sepelire sepult-* bury]
■ *n.* tomb, mausoleum, burial vault, grave, crypt, pyramid, burial-place.

sepulture /séppəlchər/ *n. literary* the act or an instance of burying or putting in the grave. [ME f. OF f. L *sepultura* (as SEPULCHRE)]
■ see BURIAL 1.

seq. *abbr.* (*pl.* **seqq.**) the following. [L *sequens* etc.]

sequacious /sikwáyshəss/ *adj.* **1** (of reasoning or a reasoner) not inconsequent, coherent. **2** *archaic* inclined to follow, lacking independence or originality, servile. □□ **sequaciously** *adv.* **sequacity** /sikwássiti/ *n.* [L *sequax* f. *sequi* follow]

sequel /séekwəl/ *n.* **1** what follows (esp. as a result). **2** a novel, film, etc., that continues the story of an earlier one. □ **in the sequel** as things developed afterwards. [ME f. OF *sequelle* or L *sequel(l)a* f. *sequi* follow]
■ upshot, issue, result, consequence, development; follow-up, supplement.

sequela /sikwéelə/ *n.* (*pl.* **sequelae** /-lee/) *Med.* (esp. in *pl.*) a morbid condition or symptom following a disease. [L f. *sequi* follow]

sequence /séekwənss/ *n.* & *v.* ● *n.* **1** succession, coming after or next. **2** order of succession (*shall follow the sequence of events; give the facts in historical sequence*). **3** a set of things belonging next to one another on some principle of order; a series without gaps. **4** a part of a film dealing with one scene or topic. **5** a set of poems on one theme. **6** a set of three or more playing-cards next to one another in value. **7** *Mus.* repetition of a phrase or melody at a higher or lower pitch. **8** *Eccl.* a hymn said or sung after the Gradual or Alleluia that precedes the Gospel. **9** succession without implication of causality (opp. CONSEQUENCE). ● *v.tr.* **1** arrange in a definite order. **2** *Biochem.* ascertain the sequence of monomers in (esp. a polypeptide or nucleic acid). □ **sequence of tenses** *Gram.* the dependence of the tense of a subordinate verb on the tense of the principal verb, according to certain rules (e.g. *I think you* are, *thought you* were, *wrong*). [ME f. LL *sequentia* f. L *sequens* pres. part. of *sequi* follow]
■ *n.* **1–3** succession, progression, chronology, order, series, chain, string, course, cycle, arrangement, organization, train, line, set, run, concatenation; system.

sequencer /seékwənsər/ *n.* a programmable device for storing sequences of musical notes, chords, etc., and transmitting them when required to an electronic musical instrument.

sequent /seékwənt/ *adj.* **1** following as a sequence or consequence. **2** consecutive. ▫▫ **sequently** *adv.* [OF *sequent* or L *sequens* (as SEQUENCE)]

sequential /sikwénsh'l/ *adj.* forming a sequence or consequence or sequela. ▫▫ **sequentiality** /-shiálliti/ *n.* **sequentially** *adv.* [SEQUENCE, after CONSEQUENTIAL]
■ successive, ordered, orderly, serial, progressive, organized, systematic, continuous.

sequester /sikwéstər/ *v.tr.* **1** (esp. as **sequestered** *adj.*) seclude, isolate, set apart (*sequester oneself from the world*; *a sequestered life*; *a sequestered cottage*). **2** = SEQUESTRATE. **3** *Chem.* bind (a metal ion) so that it cannot react. [ME f. OF *sequestrer* or LL *sequestrare* commit for safe keeping f. L *sequester* trustee]
■ **1** see ISOLATE 1.

sequestrate /sikwéstrayt, seékwi-/ *v.tr.* **1** confiscate, appropriate. **2** *Law* take temporary possession of (a debtor's estate etc.). **3** *Eccl.* apply (the income of a benefice) to clearing the incumbent's debts or accumulating a fund for the next incumbent. ▫▫ **sequestrable** *adj.* **sequestration** /seékwistráysh'n/ *n.* **sequestrator** /seékwistraytər/ *n.* [LL *sequestrare* (as SEQUESTER)]
■ **1** see CONFISCATE. ▫▫ **sequestration** see FORFEIT *n.* 4.

sequestrum /sikwéstrəm/ *n.* (*pl.* **sequestra** /-trə/) a piece of dead bone or other tissue detached from the surrounding parts. ▫▫ **sequestral** *adj.* **sequestrotomy** /seékwistróttəmi/ *n.* (*pl.* **-ies**). [mod.L, neut. of L *sequester* standing apart]

sequin /seékwin/ *n.* **1** a circular spangle for attaching to clothing as an ornament. **2** *hist.* a Venetian gold coin. ▫▫ **sequinned** *adj.* (also **sequined**). [F f. It. *zecchino* f. *zecca* a mint f. Arab. *sikka* a die]

sequoia /sikwóyə/ *n.* a Californian evergreen coniferous tree, *Sequoia sempervirens*, of very great height. [mod.L genus-name, f. *Sequoiah*, the name of a Cherokee]

sera *pl.* of SERUM.

serac /serák/ *n.* one of the tower-shaped masses into which a glacier is divided at steep points by crevasses crossing it. [Swiss F *sérac*, orig. the name of a compact white cheese]

seraglio /seraáliō/ *n.* (*pl.* **-os**) **1** a harem. **2** *hist.* a Turkish palace, esp. that of the Sultan with government offices etc. at Constantinople. [It. *serraglio* f. Turk. f. Pers. *sarāy* palace: cf. SERAI]

serai /serī́/ *n.* a caravanserai. [Turk. f. Pers. (as SERAGLIO)]

serang /səráng/ *n.* *Anglo-Ind.* a native head of a Lascar crew. [Hindi f. Pers. *sarhang* commander]

serape /seraápay/ *n.* (also **sarape** /sa-/, **zarape** /za-/) a shawl or blanket worn as a cloak by Spanish Americans. [Mexican Sp.]
■ see WRAP *n.* 1.

seraph /sérrəf/ *n.* (*pl.* **seraphim** /-fim/ or **seraphs**) an angelic being, one of the highest order of the ninefold celestial hierarchy gifted esp. with love and associated with light, ardour, and purity. [back-form. f. *seraphim* (cf. CHERUB) (pl.) f. LL f. Gk *seraphim* f. Heb. *śᵉrāpīm*]

seraphic /səráffik/ *adj.* **1** of or like the seraphim. **2** ecstatically adoring, fervent, or serene. ▫▫ **seraphically** *adv.* [med.L *seraphicus* f. LL (as SERAPH)]
■ angelic, celestial, divine, heavenly, blissful, sublime, empyrean, Elysian, ethereal, holy, saintly, godly.

seraskier /sérrəskeéər/ *n.* *hist.* the Turkish Commander-in-Chief and minister of war. [Turk. f. Pers. *sar ʿaskar* head of army]

Serb /serb/ *n.* & *adj.* ● *n.* **1** a native of Serbia in the former Yugoslavia. **2** a person of Serbian descent. ● *adj.* = SERBIAN. [Serbian *Srb*]

Serbian /sérbiən/ *n.* & *adj.* ● *n.* **1** the dialect of the Serbs (cf. SERBO-CROAT). **2** = SERB. ● *adj.* of or relating to the Serbs or their dialect.

Serbo- /sérbō/ *comb. form* Serbian.

Serbo-Croat /sérbōkrṓ-at/ *n.* & *adj.* (also **Serbo-Croatian** /-krō-áysh'n/) ● *n.* the main official language of the former Yugoslavia, combining Serbian and Croatian dialects. ● *adj.* of or relating to this language.

SERC *abbr.* (in the UK) Science and Engineering Research Council.

sere[1] /seer/ *n.* a catch of a gunlock holding the hammer at half or full cock. [prob. f. OF *serre* lock, bolt, grasp, f. *serrer* (see SERRIED)]

sere[2] var. of SEAR *adj.*

sere[3] /seer/ *n.* *Ecol.* a sequence of animal or plant communities. [L *serere* join in a SERIES]

serein /sərán/ *n.* a fine rain falling in tropical climates from a cloudless sky. [F f. OF *serain* ult. f. L *serum* evening f. *serus* late]

serenade /sérrənáyd/ *n.* & *v.* ● *n.* **1** a piece of music sung or played at night, esp. by a lover under his lady's window, or suitable for this. **2** = SERENATA. ● *v.tr.* sing or play a serenade to. ▫▫ **serenader** *n.* [F *sérénade* f. It. *serenata* f. *sereno* SERENE]

serenata /sérrənaátə/ *n.* *Mus.* **1** a cantata with a pastoral subject. **2** a simple form of suite for orchestra or wind band. [It. (as SERENADE)]

serendipity /sérrəndíppiti/ *n.* the faculty of making happy and unexpected discoveries by accident. ▫▫ **serendipitous** *adj.* **serendipitously** *adv.* [coined by Horace Walpole (1754) after *The Three Princes of Serendip* (Sri Lanka), a fairy-tale]
■ see LUCK 3. ▫▫ **serendipitous** see ACCIDENTAL *adj.* 1. **serendipitously** see *at random* (RANDOM).

serene /sireén/ *adj.* & *n.* ● *adj.* (**serener**, **serenest**) **1 a** (of the sky, the air, etc.) clear and calm. **b** (of the sea etc.) unruffled. **2** placid, tranquil, unperturbed. ● *n.* *poet.* a serene expanse of sky, sea, etc. ▫ **all serene** *Brit. sl.* all right. **Serene Highness** a title used in addressing and referring to members of some European royal families (*His Serene Highness*; *Their Serene Highnesses*; *Your Serene Highness*). ▫▫ **serenely** *adv.* **sereneness** *n.* [L *serenus*]
■ *adj.* peaceful, tranquil, calm, pacific, peaceable, restful, halcyon, idyllic, bucolic, pastoral, undisturbed, unruffled, imperturbable, unperturbed, untroubled, quiet, still; cool, collected, placid, composed, self-possessed, poised, unexcitable, even-tempered, temperate, nonchalant, easygoing, cool-headed, easy, *colloq.* unflappable.

serenity /sirénniti/ *n.* (*pl.* **-ies**) **1** tranquillity, being serene. **2** (**Serenity**) a title used in addressing and referring to a reigning prince or similar dignitary (*your Serenity*). [F *sérénité* or L *serenitas* (as SERENE)]
■ **1** peacefulness, peace, tranquillity, calm, calmness, restfulness, quiet, stillness; peaceableness, unexcitability, composure, self-possession, poise, aplomb, even-temperedness, nonchalance, cool-headedness, placidity, *colloq.* unflappability.

serf /serf/ *n.* **1** *hist.* a labourer not allowed to leave the land on which he worked, a villein. **2** an oppressed person, a drudge. ▫▫ **serfage** *n.* **serfdom** *n.* **serfhood** *n.* [OF f. L *servus* slave]
■ **1** *hist.* vassal, villein. **2** see MENIAL *n.* 1. ▫▫ **serfdom** see SLAVERY 1.

serge /serj/ *n.* a durable twilled worsted etc. fabric. [ME f. OF *sarge*, *serge* ult. f. L *serica* (*lana*): see SILK]

sergeant /saárjənt/ *n.* **1** a non-commissioned Army or Air Force officer next below warrant officer. **2** a police officer ranking below (*Brit.*) inspector or (*US*) captain. ▫ **company sergeant-major** *Mil.* the highest non-commissioned officer of a company. **Sergeant Baker** *Austral.* a large brightly-coloured marine fish, *Aulopus purpurissatus*. **sergeant-fish** a marine fish, *Rachycentron canadum*, with lateral stripes suggesting a chevron. **sergeant-major** *Mil.* **1** (in full **regimental sergeant-major**) *Brit.* a warrant-officer assisting the adjutant of a regiment or battalion. **2**

US the highest-ranking non-commissioned officer. □□ **sergeancy** *n.* (*pl.* **-ies**). **sergeantship** *n.* [ME f. OF *sergent* f. L *serviens -entis* servant f. *servire* SERVE]

Sergt. *abbr.* Sergeant.

serial /séeriəl/ *n.* & *adj.* ● *n.* **1** a story, play, or film which is published, broadcast, or shown in regular instalments. **2** a periodical. ● *adj.* **1** of or in or forming a series. **2** (of a story etc.) in the form of a serial. **3** *Mus.* using transformations of a fixed series of notes (see SERIES). **4** (of a publication) appearing in successive parts published usu. at regular intervals; periodical. □ **serial killer** a person who murders continually with no apparent motive. **serial number** a number showing the position of an item in a series. **serial rights** the right to publish a story or book as a serial. □□ **seriality** /-riálliti/ *n.* **serially** *adv.* [SERIES + -AL]
■ *n.* **2** see PERIODICAL *n.* ● *adj.* **1** see SEQUENTIAL.

serialist /séeriəlist/ *n.* a composer or advocate of serial music. □□ **serialism** *n.*

serialize /séeriəlīz/ *v.tr.* (also **-ise**) **1** publish or produce in instalments. **2** arrange in a series. **3** *Mus.* compose according to a serial technique. □□ **serialization** /-záysh'n/ *n.*

seriate *adj.* & *v.* ● *adj.* /séeriət/ in the form of a series; in orderly sequence. ● *v.tr.* /séeriayt/ arrange in a seriate manner. □□ **seriation** /-áysh'n/ *n.*

seriatim /séeriáytim, sérri-/ *adv.* point by point; taking one subject etc. after another in regular order (*consider seriatim*). [med.L f. L *series*, after LITERATIM etc.]
■ see *singly* (SINGLE).

Seric /séerik/ *adj. archaic* Chinese. [L *sericus*; see SILK]

sericeous /siríshəss/ *adj. Bot.* & *Zool.* covered with silky hairs. [LL *sericeus* silken]
■ see SILKY 1.

sericulture /sérrikulchər/ *n.* **1** silkworm-breeding. **2** the production of raw silk. □□ **sericultural** /-kúlchərəl/ *adj.* **sericulturist** /-kúlchərist/ *n.* [F *sériciculture* f. LL *sericum*: see SILK, CULTURE]

seriema /sérri-éemə/ *n.* (also **cariama** /kárriaámə/) *Zool.* any S. American bird of the family Cariamidae, having a long neck and legs and a crest above the bill. [mod.L f. Tupi *siriema* etc. crested]

series /séereez, -riz/ *n.* (*pl.* same) **1** a number of things of which each is similar to the preceding or in which each successive pair are similarly related; a sequence, succession, order, row, or set. **2** a set of successive games between the same teams. **3** a set of programmes with the same actors etc. or on related subjects but each complete in itself. **4** a set of lectures by the same speaker or on the same subject. **5 a** a set of successive issues of a periodical, of articles on one subject or by one writer, etc., esp. when numbered separately from a preceding or following set (*second series*). **b** a set of independent books in a common format or under a common title or supervised by a common general editor. **6** *Philately* a set of stamps, coins, etc., of different denominations but issued at one time, in one reign, etc. **7** *Geol.* **a** a set of strata with a common characteristic. **b** the rocks deposited during a specific epoch. **8** *Mus.* an arrangement of the twelve notes of the chromatic scale as a basis for serial music. **9** *Electr.* **a** a set of circuits or components arranged so that the current passes through each successively. **b** a set of batteries etc. having the positive electrode of each connected with the negative electrode of the next. **10** *Chem.* a set of elements with common properties or of compounds related in composition or structure. **11** *Math.* a set of quantities constituting a progression or having the several values determined by a common relation. □ **arithmetical** (or **geometrical**) **series** a series in arithmetical (or geometrical) progression. **in series 1** in ordered succession. **2** *Electr.* (of a set of circuits or components) arranged so that the current passes through each successively. [L, = row, chain f. *serere* join, connect]
■ **1** see SEQUENCE *n.* **2–6** see SET² 1, 2.

serif /sérrif/ *n.* a slight projection finishing off a stroke of a letter as in T contrasted with T (cf. SANSERIF). □□ **seriffed** *adj.* [perh. f. Du. *schreef* dash, line f. Gmc]

serigraphy /sərígrəfi/ *n.* the art or process of printing designs by means of a silk screen. □□ **serigraph** /sérrigraaf/ *n.* **serigrapher** *n.* [irreg. f. L *sericum* SILK]

serin /sérrin/ *n.* any small yellow Mediterranean finch of the genus *Serinus*, esp. the wild canary *S. serinus*. [F, of uncert. orig.]

serinette /sérrinét/ *n.* an instrument for teaching cage-birds to sing. [F (as SERIN)]

seringa /səríngə/ *n.* **1** = SYRINGA. **2** any of various rubber-trees of the genus *Hevea*, native to Brazil. [F (as SYRINGA)]

serio-comic /séeriōkómmik/ *adj.* combining the serious and the comic, jocular in intention but simulating seriousness or vice versa. □□ **serio-comically** *adv.*

serious /séeriəss/ *adj.* **1** thoughtful, earnest, sober, sedate, responsible, not reckless or given to trifling (*has a serious air*; *a serious young person*). **2** important, demanding consideration (*this is a serious matter*). **3** not slight or negligible (*a serious injury*; *a serious offence*). **4** sincere, in earnest, not ironical or joking (*are you serious?*). **5** (of music and literature) not merely for amusement (opp. LIGHT² 5a). **6** not perfunctory (*serious thought*). **7** not to be trifled with (*a serious opponent*). **8** concerned with religion or ethics (*serious subjects*). □□ **seriousness** *n.* [ME f. OF *serieux* or LL *seriosus* f. L *serius*]
■ **1** grave, solemn, earnest, unsmiling, poker-faced, straight-faced, sedate, sober, pensive, thoughtful; responsible; humourless, sombre, grim, dour, severe. **2, 3, 7** grave, important, vital, weighty, significant, momentous, crucial, consequential, life-and-death, urgent, pressing; acute, critical, life-threatening, bad, dangerous, nasty, perilous, alarming, severe, precarious. **4** sincere, straightforward, genuine, (in) earnest, honest.

seriously /séeriəsli/ *adv.* **1** in a serious manner (esp. introducing a sentence, implying that irony etc. is now to cease). **2** to a serious extent. **3** *colloq.* (as an intensifier) very, really, substantially (*seriously rich*).
■ **1** soberly, earnestly, without a doubt, at face value; really, honestly, sincerely, truly, candidly, openly, joking aside *or* apart. **2** gravely, badly, severely, critically, grievously, dangerously, acutely. **3** see VERY *adv.*

serjeant /saárjənt/ *n.* **1** (in full **serjeant-at-law**, *pl.* **serjeants-at-law**) *hist.* a barrister of the highest rank. **2** *Brit.* (in official lists) a sergeant in the Army. □ **Common Serjeant** *Brit.* a circuit judge of the Central Criminal Court with duties in the City of London. **serjeant-at-arms** (*pl.* **serjeants-at-arms**) an official of a court or city or parliament, with ceremonial duties. □□ **serjeantship** *n.* [var. of SERGEANT]

sermon /sérmən/ *n.* **1** a spoken or written discourse on a religious or moral subject, esp. a discourse based on a text or passage of Scripture and delivered in a service by way of religious instruction or exhortation. **2** a piece of admonition or reproof, a lecture. **3** a moral reflection suggested by natural objects etc. (*sermons in stones*). □ **Sermon on the Mount** the discourse of Christ recorded in Matt. 5-7. [ME f. AF *sermun*, OF *sermon* f. L *sermo -onis* discourse, talk]
■ **1** homily, address, exhortation, lecture, speech, talk, *literary* discourse. **2** lecture, lesson, reprimand, reproach, admonition, reproof, rebuke, remonstration, remonstrance, scolding, harangue, *colloq.* talking-to, telling-off, ticking-off, dressing-down.

sermonette /sérmənét/ *n.* a short sermon.

sermonize /sérmənīz/ *v.* (also **-ise**) **1** *tr.* deliver a moral lecture to. **2** *intr.* deliver a moral lecture. □□ **sermonizer** *n.*
■ see LECTURE *v.* 1, 2.

serology /seeróllәji/ *n.* the scientific study of blood sera and their effects. □□ **serological** /-rəlójik'l/ *adj.* **serologist** *n.*

serosa /sərṓsə/ *n.* a serous membrane. [mod.L, fem. of med.L *serosus* SEROUS]

serotine /sérrətin/ *n.* a chestnut-coloured European bat, *Eptesicus serotinus*. [F *sérotine* f. L *serotinus* late, of the evening, f. *serus* late]

serotonin /sérrətṓnin/ *n. Biol.* a compound present in blood serum, which constricts the blood vessels and acts as a neurotransmitter. [SERUM + TONIC + -IN]

serous /séerəss/ *adj.* of or like or producing serum; watery. □ **serous gland** (or **membrane**) a gland or membrane with a serous secretion. □□ **serosity** /-róssiti/ *n.* [F *séreux* or med.L *serosus* (as SERUM)]

serpent /sérp'nt/ *n.* **1** usu. *literary* **a** a snake, esp. of a large kind. **b** a scaly limbless reptile. **2** a sly or treacherous person, esp. one who exploits a position of trust to betray it. **3** *Mus.* an old bass wind instrument made from leather-covered wood, roughly in the form of an S. **4** (**the Serpent**) *Bibl.* Satan (see Gen. 3, Rev. 20). [ME f. OF f. L *serpens -entis* part. of *serpere* creep]
■ **1 a** snake, ophidian. **2** see SNAKE *n.* 2.

serpentine /sérpəntīn/ *adj.*, *n.*, & *v.* ● *adj.* **1** of or like a serpent. **2** coiling, tortuous, sinuous, meandering, writhing (*the serpentine windings of the stream*). **3** cunning, subtle, treacherous. ● *n.* **1** a soft rock mainly of hydrated magnesium silicate, usu. dark green and sometimes mottled or spotted like a serpent's skin, taking a high polish and used as a decorative material. **2** *Skating* a figure of three circles in a line. ● *v.intr.* move sinuously, meander. □ **serpentine verse** a metrical line beginning and ending with the same word. [ME f. OF *serpentin* f. LL *serpentinus* (as SERPENT)]
■ *adj.* **2** twisting, winding, tortuous, coiling, writhing, snaking, snakelike, sinuous, anfractuous, roundabout, meandering, indirect, devious, crooked, labyrinthine, vermicular, vermiculate, complex, complicated, Byzantine. **3** evil, bad, diabolic(al), satanic, Mephistophelean, reptilian, devilish, wily, cunning, treacherous, conniving, sneaky, shrewd, artful, crafty, subtle, slick, sly, insidious, tricky, scheming, plotting, furtive, machiavellian, *colloq.* shifty; snakelike, vermicular.

serpiginous /serpíjinəss/ *adj.* (of a skin-disease etc.) creeping from one part to another. [med.L *serpigo -ginis* ringworm f. L *serpere* creep]

SERPS /serps/ *abbr.* (in the UK) State earnings-related pension scheme.

serpula /sérpyoolə/ *n.* (*pl.* **serpulae** /-lee/) any of various marine worms of the family Serpulidae, living in intricately twisted shell-like tubes. [LL, = small serpent, f. L *serpere* creep]

serra /sérrə/ *n.* (*pl.* **serrae** /-ree/) a serrated organ, structure, or edge. [L, = saw]

serradilla /sérrədíllə/ *n.* (*pl.* **serradillae** /-lee/) a clover, *Ornithopus sativus*, grown as fodder. [Port., dimin. of *serrado* serrated]

serran /sérrən/ *n.* any marine fish of the family Serranidae. [mod.L *serranus* f. L *serra* saw]

serrate *v.* & *adj.* ● *v.tr.* /seráyt/ (usu. as **serrated** *adj.*) provide with a sawlike edge. ● *adj.* /sérrayt/ esp. *Anat.*, *Bot.*, & *Zool.* notched like a saw. □□ **serration** *n.* [LL *serrare serrat-* f. L *serra* saw]
■ *v.* (**serrated**) sawlike, sawtooth(ed), crenellated, toothed, notched, zigzag, jagged, serrate, *esp. Anat.*, *Bot.*, & *Zool.* serrulate, *Bot.* & *Zool.* crenate(d), *Zool.* denticulate. □□ **serration** tooth, spike, point, prong; notch.

serried /sérrid/ *adj.* (of ranks of soldiers, rows of trees, etc.) pressed together; without gaps; close. [past part. of *serry* press close prob. f. F *serré* past part. of *serrer* close ult. f. L *sera* lock, or past part. of obs. *serr* f. OF *serrer*]
■ ranked, tiered, ranged, assembled, packed, close, tight, compacted, compact.

serrulate /sérroolayt/ *adj.* esp. *Anat.*, *Bot.*, & *Zool.* finely serrate; with a series of small notches. □□ **serrulation** /-láysh'n/ *n.* [mod.L *serrulatus* f. L *serrula* dimin. of *serra* saw]

serum /séerəm/ *n.* (*pl.* **sera** /-rə/ or **serums**) **1 a** an amber-coloured liquid that separates from a clot when blood coagulates. **b** whey. **2** *Med.* blood serum (usu. from a non-human mammal) as an antitoxin or therapeutic agent, esp. in inoculation. **3** a watery fluid in animal bodies. □ **serum sickness** a reaction to an injection of serum, characterized by skin eruption, fever, etc. [L, = whey]

serval /sérv'l/ *n.* a tawny black-spotted long-legged African feline, *Felis serval*. [F f. Port. *cerval* deerlike f. *cervo* deer f. L *cervus*]

servant /sérv'nt/ *n.* **1** a person who has undertaken (usu. in return for stipulated pay) to carry out the orders of an individual or corporate employer, esp. a person employed in a house on domestic duties or as a personal attendant. **2** a devoted follower, a person willing to serve another (*a servant of Jesus Christ*). □ **your humble servant** *Brit. archaic* a formula preceding a signature or expressing ironical courtesy. **your obedient servant** *Brit.* a formula preceding a signature, now used only in certain formal letters. [ME f. OF (as SERVE)]
■ **1** domestic, help, menial, lackey, drudge, amah, factotum, *archaic* servitor, *colloq.* dogsbody, *joc.* retainer; maid, housemaid, maidservant, chambermaid, lady's maid, boy, page, valet, man, gentleman's gentleman, manservant, *hist.* parlour-maid; housekeeper, major-domo, steward, seneschal, butler, houseman, houseboy, serving-man, footman, chauffeur, driver, coachman, postilion, attendant, groom, *Brit.* boots; governess, nurse, nursemaid, nanny, ayah, au pair (girl); cook, chef, waiter, waitress, stewardess, *sommelier*, *archaic* scullion; charwoman, charlady, cleaner, *Brit. colloq.* char, daily.

serve /serv/ *v.* & *n.* ● *v.* **1** *tr.* do a service for (a person, community, etc.). **2** *tr.* (also *absol.*) be a servant to. **3** *intr.* carry out duties (*served on six committees*). **4** *intr.* **a** (foll. by *in*) be employed in (an organization, esp. the armed forces, or a place, esp. a foreign country) (*served in the air force*). **b** be a member of the armed forces. **5 a** *tr.* be useful to or serviceable for; meet the needs of; do what is required for (*serve a purpose*; *one packet serves him for a week*). **b** *intr.* meet requirements; perform a function (*a sofa serving as a bed*). **c** *intr.* (foll. by *to* + infin.) avail, suffice (*his attempt served only to postpone the inevitable*; *it serves to show the folly of such action*). **d** *tr.* (of the memory) to prove reliable; to assist or prompt (*if memory serves*). **6** *tr.* go through a due period of (office, apprenticeship, a prison sentence, etc.). **7** *tr.* set out or present (food) for those about to eat it (*asparagus served with butter*; *dinner was then served*). **8** *intr.* (in full **serve at table**) act as a waiter. **9** *tr.* **a** attend to (a customer in a shop). **b** (foll. by *with*) supply with (goods) (*was serving a customer with apples*; *served the town with gas*). **10** *tr.* treat or act towards (a person) in a specified way (*has served me shamefully*; *you may serve me as you will*). **11** *tr.* **a** (often foll. by *on*) deliver (a writ etc.) to the person concerned in a legally formal manner (*served a warrant on him*). **b** (foll. by *with*) deliver a writ etc. to (a person) in this way (*served her with a summons*). **12** *tr. Tennis* etc. **a** (also *absol.*) deliver (a ball etc.) to begin or resume play. **b** produce (a fault etc.) by doing this. **13** *tr. Mil.* keep (a gun, battery, etc.) firing. **14** *tr.* (of an animal, esp. a stallion etc. hired for the purpose) copulate with (a female). **15** *tr.* distribute (*served the ammunition out*; *served the rations round*). **16** *tr.* render obedience to (a deity etc.). **17** *Eccl.* **a** *intr.* act as a server. **b** *tr.* act as a server at (a service). **18** *intr.* (of a tide) be suitable for a ship to leave harbour etc. **19** *tr. Naut.* bind (a rope etc.) with thin cord to strengthen it. **20** *tr.* play (a trick etc.) on. ● *n.* **1** *Tennis* etc. **a** the act or an instance of serving. **b** a manner of serving. **c** a person's turn to serve. **2** *Austral. sl.* a reprimand. □ **it will serve** it will be adequate. **serve one's needs** (or **need**) be adequate. **serve out** retaliate on. **serve the purpose of** take the place of, be used as. **serve a person right** be a person's deserved punishment or misfortune. **serve one's time 1** hold office for the normal period. **2** (also **serve time**) undergo imprisonment, apprenticeship, etc. **serve one's** (or **the**) **turn** be adequate. **serve up** offer for acceptance. [ME f. OF *servir* f. L *servire* f. *servus* slave]

■ *v.* **1, 2, 9a** attend (to *or* on), wait on *or* upon, minister to, look after, assist, help, be of assistance *or* help to, be at a person's service, oblige, accommodate, gratify; fight for; be obedient to. **3, 4** see WORK *v.* 2a. **5 a–c** fulfil, carry out, perform, discharge, work, do, suffice, be used *or* of use *or* useful, function, act, fill the bill, be serviceable, be available, answer, be sufficient *or* adequate *or* suitable, suit, be advantageous *or* of advantage (to), avail. **d** not fail, not play tricks (on), work *or* function (for), be accurate *or* correct. **6** go through, complete; survive. **7, 8, 15** distribute, deal out, dole out, give out, present, set out, provide, supply, offer, pass out *or* about *or* around, make available, dish up *or* out; wait. **9 b** see SUPPLY[1] *v.* 1, 2. **10** see TREAT *v.* 1. **11 a** deliver, hand over *or* out, give, present. **b** (*serve with*) deliver *or* give to, present with, hand over *or* out to. **16** see WORSHIP *v.* **18** be convenient *or* opportune *or* favourable *or* right. □ **serve up** see PROPOSE 1.

server /sérvər/ *n.* **1** a person who serves. **2** *Eccl.* a person assisting the celebrant at a service, esp. the Eucharist.

servery /sérvəri/ *n.* (*pl.* **-ies**) a room from which meals etc. are served and in which utensils are kept.

service[1] /sérviss/ *n.* & *v.* ● *n.* **1** the act of helping or doing work for another or for a community etc. **2** work done in this way. **3** assistance or benefit given to someone. **4** the provision or system of supplying a public need, e.g. transport, or (often in *pl.*) the supply of water, gas, electricity, telephone, etc. **5 a** the fact or status of being a servant. **b** employment or a position as a servant. **6** a state or period of employment doing work for an individual or organization (*resigned after 15 years' service*). **7 a** a public or Crown department or organization employing officials working for the State (*civil service; secret service*). **b** employment in this. **8** (in *pl.*) the armed forces. **9** (*attrib.*) of the kind issued to the armed forces (*a service revolver*). **10 a** a ceremony of worship according to prescribed forms. **b** a form of liturgy for this. **11 a** the provision of what is necessary for the installation and maintenance of a machine etc. or operation. **b** a periodic routine maintenance of a motor vehicle etc. **12** assistance or advice given to customers after the sale of goods. **13 a** the act or process of serving food, drinks, etc. **b** an extra charge nominally made for this. **14** a set of dishes, plates, etc., used for serving meals (*a dinner service*). **15** *Tennis* etc. **a** the act or an instance of serving. **b** a person's turn to serve. **c** the manner or quality of serving. **d** (in full **service game**) a game in which a particular player serves. ● *v.tr.* **1** provide service or services for, esp. maintain. **2** maintain or repair (a car, machine, etc.). **3** pay interest on (a debt). **4** supply with a service. □ **at a person's service** ready to serve or assist a person. **be of service** be available to assist. **in service 1** employed as a servant. **2** available for use. **on active service** serving in the armed forces in wartime. **out of service** not available for use. **see service 1** have experience of service, esp. in the armed forces. **2** (of a thing) be much used. **service area 1** an area beside a major road for the supply of petrol, refreshments, etc. **2** the area served by a broadcasting station. **service-book** a book of authorized forms of worship of a Church. **service bus** (or **car**) *Austral.* & *NZ* a motor coach. **service charge** an additional charge for service in a restaurant, hotel, etc. **service dress** ordinary military etc. uniform. **service flat** a flat in which domestic service and sometimes meals are provided by the management. **service industry** one providing services not goods. **service line** (in tennis etc.) a line marking the limit of the area into which the ball must be served. **service road** a road parallel to a main road, serving houses, shops, etc. **service station** an establishment beside a road selling petrol and oil etc. to motorists and often able to carry out maintenance. **take service with** become a servant to. [ME f. OF *service* or L *servitium* f. *servus* slave]

■ *n.* **1–3, 12** help, assistance, aid, backing, support; use, usefulness, utility, benefit, advantage; serving, care, attention; advice. **4** see SYSTEM 1, SUPPLY[1] *n.* 1. **5, 6** employment, employ; assignment, post, position, appointment. **8** (*services*) army, navy, air force, marines; forces, troops, armed forces *or* services, military; militia. **10** rite, ceremony, ritual, worship; liturgy. **11** maintenance, overhaul, servicing, checking, repair, mending. **15** serve. ● *v.* **1, 2** see MAINTAIN 4. □ **out of service** see DEFUNCT 1, 2.

service[2] /sérviss/ *n.* (in full **service tree**) a European tree of the genus *Sorbus*, esp. *S. domestica* with toothed leaves, cream-coloured flowers, and small round or pear-shaped fruit eaten when overripe. □ **service-berry 1** the fruit of the service tree. **2 a** any American shrub of the genus *Amelanchier*. **b** the edible fruit of this. [earlier *serves*, pl. of obs. *serve* f. OE *syrfe* f. Gmc *surbhjōn* ult. f. L *sorbus*]

serviceable /sérvisəb'l/ *adj.* **1** useful or usable. **2** able to render service. **3** durable; capable of withstanding difficult conditions. **4** suited for ordinary use rather than ornament. □□ **serviceability** /-bílliti/ *n.* **serviceableness** *n.* **serviceably** *adv.* [ME f. OF *servisable* (as SERVICE[1])]

■ **1, 2** workable, working, functional, functioning, usable, useful, operative. **3** hard-wearing, durable, long-lasting, tough, wear-resistant. **4** practical, functional, utilitarian.

serviceman /sérvismən/ *n.* (*pl.* **-men**) **1** a man serving in the armed forces. **2** a man providing service or maintenance.

■ **1** see SOLDIER *n.*

servicewoman /sérviswŏŏmmən/ *n.* (*pl.* **-women**) a woman serving in the armed forces.

■ see SOLDIER *n.*

serviette /sérvi-ét/ *n.* esp. *Brit.* a napkin for use at table. [ME f. OF f. *servir* SERVE]

servile /sérvīl/ *adj.* **1** of or being or like a slave or slaves. **2** slavish, fawning; completely dependent. □□ **servilely** *adv.* **servility** /-villiti/ *n.* [ME f. L *servilis* f. *servus* slave]

■ **2** submissive, subservient, menial, craven, acquiescent, abject, cringing, slavish, mean, fawning, deferential, ingratiating, grovelling, obsequious, toadying, toadyish, sycophantish, sycophantic, wheedling, unctuous, slimy, flattering, time-serving, *colloq.* smarmy, bootlicking, creepy. □□ **servility** submissiveness, submission, subservience, acquiescence, abjectness, abjection, cringing, slavishness, meanness, fawning, grovelling, obsequiousness, toadying, toadyism, sycophancy, truckling, wheedling, unctuousness, sliminess, flattery, *colloq.* smarminess, bootlicking.

serving /sérving/ *n.* a quantity of food served to one person.

■ see PORTION *n.* 2.

servitor /sérvitər/ *n.* **1** *archaic* **a** a servant. **b** an attendant. **2** *hist.* an Oxford undergraduate performing menial duties in exchange for assistance from college funds. □□ **servitorship** *n.* [ME f. OF f. LL (as SERVE)]

■ **1** see SERVANT.

servitude /sérvityōōd/ *n.* **1** slavery. **2** subjection (esp. involuntary); bondage. **3** *Law* the subjection of property to an easement. [ME f. OF f. L *servitudo -inis* f. *servus* slave]

■ **1, 2** bondage, slavery, serfdom, subjugation, enslavement, subjection, *hist.* vassalage, *literary* thrall, thraldom.

servo /sérvō/ *n.* (*pl.* **-os**) **1** (in full **servo-mechanism**) a powered mechanism producing motion or forces at a higher level of energy than the input level, e.g. in the brakes and steering of large motor vehicles, esp. where feedback is employed to make the control automatic. **2** (in full **servo-motor**) the motive element in a servo-mechanism. **3** (in *comb.*) of or involving a servo-mechanism (*servo-assisted*). [L *servus* slave]

sesame /séssəmi/ *n. Bot.* **1** an E. Indian herbaceous plant, *Sesamum indicum*, with seeds used as food and yielding an edible oil. **2** its seeds. □ **open sesame** a means of acquiring or achieving what is normally unattainable (from the magic words used in the *Arabian Nights' Entertainments*). [L *sesamum* f. Gk *sēsamon*, *sēsamē*]

sesamoid /séssəmoyd/ *adj.* & *n.* ● *adj.* shaped like a sesame seed; nodular (esp. of small independent bones developed in tendons passing over an angular structure such as the kneecap and the navicular bone). ● *n.* a sesamoid bone.

sesqui- /séskwi/ *comb. form* **1** denoting one and a half. **2** *Chem.* (of a compound) in which there are three equivalents of a named element or radical to two others. [L (as SEMI-, *-que* and)]

sesquicentenary /séskwisenteénəri/ *n.* (*pl.* **-ies**) a one-hundred-and-fiftieth anniversary.

sesquicentennial /séskwisenténniəl/ *n.* & *adj.* ● *n.* = SESQUICENTENARY. ● *adj.* of or relating to a sesquicentennial.

sess var. of CESS[1].

sessile /séssīl/ *adj.* **1** *Bot.* & *Zool.* (of a flower, leaf, eye, etc.) attached directly by its base without a stalk or peduncle. **2** fixed in one position; immobile. □ **sessile oak** = DURMAST. [L *sessilis* f. *sedēre sess-* sit]

session /sésh'n/ *n.* **1** the process of assembly of a deliberative or judicial body to conduct its business. **2** a single meeting for this purpose. **3** a period during which such meetings are regularly held. **4 a** an academic year. **b** the period during which a school etc. has classes. **5** a period devoted to an activity (*poker session*; *recording session*). **6** the governing body of a Presbyterian Church. □ **in session** assembled for business; not on vacation. **petty sessions 1** a meeting of two or more magistrates for the summary trial of certain offences. **2** = *quarter sessions.* □□ **sessional** *adj.* [ME f. OF *session* or L *sessio -onis* (as SESSILE)]

■ **1, 2** sitting, seating, assembly, conference, meeting, hearing, *Sc.* sederunt. **3, 5** see TIME *n.* 4, 6. **4 b** term, semester, *US* trimester.

sesterce /sésterss/ *n.* (also **sestertius** /sestérshəss/) (*pl.* **sesterces** /séstərseez/ or **sestertii** /-stérshi-i/) an ancient Roman coin and monetary unit equal to one quarter of a denarius. [L *sestertius* (*nummus* coin) = $2\frac{1}{2}$ f. *semis* half + *tertius* third]

sestet /sestét/ *n.* **1** the last six lines of a sonnet. **2** a sextet. [It. *sestetto* f. *sesto* f. L *sextus* a sixth]

sestina /sesteénə/ *n.* a form of rhymed or unrhymed poem with six stanzas of six lines and a final triplet, all stanzas having the same six words at the line-ends in six different sequences. [It. (as SESTET)]

set[1] /set/ *v.* (**setting**; *past* and *past part.* **set**) **1** *tr.* put, lay, or stand (a thing) in a certain position or location (*set it on the table*; *set it upright*). **2** *tr.* (foll. by *to*) apply (one thing) to (another) (*set pen to paper*). **3** *tr.* **a** fix ready or in position. **b** dispose suitably for use, action, or display. **4** *tr.* **a** adjust the hands of (a clock or watch) to show the right time. **b** adjust (an alarm clock) to sound at the required time. **5** *tr.* **a** fix, arrange, or mount. **b** insert (a jewel) in a ring, framework, etc. **6** *tr.* make (a device) ready to operate. **7** *tr.* lay (a table) for a meal. **8** *tr.* arrange (the hair) while damp so that it dries in the required style. **9** *tr.* (foll. by *with*) ornament or provide (a surface, esp. a precious item) (*gold set with gems*). **10** *tr.* bring by placing or arranging or other means into a specified state; cause to be (*set things in motion*; *set it on fire*). **11** *intr.* & *tr.* harden or solidify (*the jelly is set*; *the cement has set*). **12** *intr.* (of the sun, moon, etc.) appear to move towards and below the earth's horizon (as the earth rotates). **13** *tr.* represent (a story, play, scene, etc.) as happening in a certain time or place. **14** *tr.* **a** (foll. by *to* + infin.) cause or instruct (a person) to perform a specified activity (*set them to work*). **b** (foll. by pres. part.) start (a person or thing) doing something (*set him chatting*; *set the ball rolling*). **15** *tr.* present or impose as work to be done or a matter to be dealt with (*set them an essay*). **16** *tr.* exhibit as a type or model (*set a good example*). **17** *tr.* initiate; take the lead in (*set the fashion*; *set the pace*). **18** *tr.* establish (a record etc.). **19** *tr.* determine or decide (*the itinerary is set*). **20** *tr.* appoint or establish (*set them in authority*). **21** *tr.* join, attach, or fasten. **22** *tr.* **a** put parts of (a broken or dislocated bone, limb, etc.) into the correct position for healing. **b** deal with (a fracture or dislocation) in this way. **23** *tr.* (in full **set to music**) provide (words etc.) with music for singing. **24** *tr.* (often foll. by *up*) *Printing* **a** arrange or produce (type or film etc.) as required. **b** arrange the type or film etc. for (a book etc.). **25** *intr.* (of a tide, current, etc.) have a certain motion or direction. **26** *intr.* (of a face) assume a hard expression. **27** *tr.* **a** cause (a hen) to sit on eggs. **b** place (eggs) for a hen to sit on. **28** *tr.* put (a seed, plant, etc.) in the ground to grow. **29** *tr.* give the teeth of (a saw) an alternate outward inclination. **30** *tr.* esp. *US* start (a fire). **31** *intr.* (of eyes etc.) become motionless. **32** *intr.* feel or show a certain tendency (*opinion is setting against it*). **33** *intr.* **a** (of blossom) form into fruit. **b** (of fruit) develop from blossom. **c** (of a tree) develop fruit. **34** *intr.* (in full **set to partner**) (of a dancer) take a position facing one's partner. **35** *intr.* (of a hunting dog) take a rigid attitude indicating the presence of game. **36** *intr. dial.* or *sl.* sit. □ **set about 1** begin or take steps towards. **2** *colloq.* attack. **set a person** (or **thing**) **against** (**another**) **1** consider or reckon (a person or thing) as a counterpoise or compensation for. **2** cause to oppose. **set apart** separate, reserve, differentiate. **set aside** see ASIDE. **set back 1** place further back in place or time. **2** impede or reverse the progress of. **3** *colloq.* cost (a person) a specified amount. **set-back** *n.* **1** a reversal or arrest of progress. **2** a relapse. **set by** *archaic* save for future use. **set down 1** record in writing. **2** allow to alight from a vehicle. **3** (foll. by *to*) attribute to. **4** (foll. by *as*) explain or describe to oneself as. **set eyes on** see EYE. **set one's face against** see FACE. **set foot on** (or **in**) see FOOT. **set forth 1** begin a journey. **2** make known; expound. **set forward** begin to advance. **set free** release. **set one's hand to** see HAND. **set one's heart** (or **hopes**) **on** want or hope for eagerly. **set in 1** (of weather, a condition, etc.) begin (and seem likely to continue), become established. **2** insert (esp. a sleeve etc. into a garment). **set little by** consider to be of little value. **set a person's mind at rest** see MIND. **set much by** consider to be of much value. **set off 1** begin a journey. **2** detonate (a bomb etc.). **3** initiate, stimulate. **4** cause (a person) to start laughing, talking, etc. **5** serve as an adornment or foil to; enhance. **6** (foll. by *against*) use as a compensating item. **set-off** *n.* **1** a thing set off against another. **2** a thing of which the amount or effect may be deducted from that of another or opposite tendency. **3** a counterpoise. **4** a counter-claim. **5** a thing that embellishes; an adornment to something. **6** *Printing* = OFFSET 7. **set on** (or **upon**) **1** attack violently. **2** cause or urge to attack. **set out 1** begin a journey. **2** (foll. by *to* + infin.) aim or intend. **3** demonstrate, arrange, or exhibit. **4** mark out. **5** declare. **set sail 1** hoist the sails. **2** begin a voyage. **set the scene** see SCENE. **set store by** (or **on**) see STORE. **set one's teeth 1** clench them. **2** summon one's resolve. **set to** begin doing something vigorously, esp. fighting, arguing, or eating. **set-to** *n.* (*pl.* **-tos**) *colloq.* a fight or argument. **set up 1** place in position or view. **2** organize or start (a business etc.). **3** establish in some capacity. **4** supply the needs of. **5** begin making (a loud sound). **6** cause or make arrangements for (a condition or situation). **7** prepare (a task etc. for another). **8** restore or enhance the health of (a person). **9** establish (a record). **10** propound (a theory). **11** *colloq.* put (a person) in a dangerous or vulnerable position. **set-up** *n.* **1** an arrangement or organization. **2** the manner or structure or position of this. **3** *colloq.* a trick or conspiracy, esp. to make an innocent person appear guilty. **set oneself up as** make pretensions to being. [OE *settan* f. Gmc]

■ **1, 3, 5** set down, place, put, situate, locate, site, plant, position, station, stand, lay, install, insert, lodge, mount, park, deposit, plump, drop, plonk (down), *US* plunk (down); prepare, set up, concoct; arrange, fix, dispose, set out. **2** put, apply, place, lay, bring. **4, 6** adjust, regulate, turn, synchronize, fix, calibrate, coordinate. **7** arrange, lay, spread; prepare. **9** see ORNAMENT *v.* **11** stiffen, harden, freeze; gel, congeal, solidify, clot, coagulate, thicken, cake, *colloq.* jell. **12** go down, sink, decline. **13** see SITUATE *v.* **14 a** see CAUSE *v.* 2. **b** see INITIATE *v.* 1. **15** see ASSIGN *v.* 1a. **17** see INITIATE *v.* 1. **18–20** lay down, appoint, impose, stipulate, define, designate, specify, determine, decide, establish, introduce, set up; indicate, set *or* mark off, delineate; fix.

21, 22 see ATTACH 1, MEND *v.* 1. **26** stiffen, harden, freeze. **28** sow, plant. □ **set about 1** get *or* make ready, start, begin, get to work on, get under way, undertake, launch into, tackle, address oneself to, enter upon, *colloq.* get cracking on. **2** assail, assault, set on *or* upon, beat up, mug, *colloq.* lay into; see also ATTACK *v.* 1. **set a person** or **thing against** (**another**) **1** compare with, rate against, balance against, weigh (up) against, juxtapose with, contrast with. **2** antagonize, set at odds with, alienate *or* divide *or* disunite from. **set apart** distinguish, separate, differentiate; reserve, put *or* set aside, store, earmark, put away, lay away, save, keep back, *archaic* set by. **set back 2** put back, hinder, slow, hold up, retard, delay, impede, obstruct, thwart, frustrate, inhibit, *archaic or literary* stay. **set-back 1** hindrance, hitch, check, reverse, reversal, impediment, block, obstruction, defeat, hold-up, delay, check, obstacle, hiccup, snag. **2** see RELAPSE *n.* **set down 1** write (down), put in writing, put down, record, register, mark *or* jot down, make a note of, note, list. **2** put down, land, drop (off), let out. **3** ascribe, assign, attribute, impute. **set forth 1** set out *or* off, begin, start (out), get under way, go, embark, put out, sally forth, depart, leave, *formal* put forth. **2** make known, expound, express, voice, propose, propound, state, offer, submit, suggest, broach, move; set out, present, declare, describe, state, articulate, enunciate. **set free** see RELEASE *v.* 1. **set one's heart on** see WANT *v.* 1a. **set in 1** begin, start, get underway, become established, arrive, come, settle in. **set off 1** see *set forth* 1 above. **2** ignite, kindle, detonate, explode, blow up, light, touch off, trigger, trip. **3** see INITIATE *v.* 1. **4** start off *or* up, get going. **5** dramatize, enhance, highlight, throw into relief, show (off), display. **set on** (or **upon**) **1** attack, assault, pounce on *or* upon, fall on *or* upon, fly at; ambush, beat up, set about, mug. **set out 1** see *set forth* 1 above. **2** (*set out to*) see AIM *v.* 1, 4. **3** put out, lay out, arrange, dispose; display, exhibit, demonstrate. **5** see DECLARE 1, 2. **set-to** see FIGHT *n.* 1a, ARGUMENT 1. **set up 1** build, put up, erect, assemble, construct, raise, elevate, put together, arrange, prepare. **2, 3** start, begin, initiate, organize, establish, found. **4** finance, fund, invest in, back, subsidize; supply. **6** see ORGANIZE 2b. **7** see PREPARE *v.* 1. **9** see SET[1] 18–20 above. **10** see *set forth* 2 above. **11** trap, entrap, *sl.* frame. **set-up 1, 2** arrangement, system, organization, layout, regime, structure, make-up, composition, framework; conditions, circumstances. **3** trick, trap, ambush, *sl.* frame, put-up job, *US sl.* frame-up; conspiracy.

set[2] /set/ *n.* **1** a number of things or persons that belong together or resemble one another or are usually found together. **2** a collection or group. **3** a section of society consorting together or having similar interests etc. **4** a collection of implements, vessels, etc., regarded collectively and needed for a specified purpose (*cricket set*; *teaset*; *a set of teeth*). **5** a piece of electric or electronic apparatus, esp. a radio or television receiver. **6** (in tennis etc.) a group of games counting as a unit towards a match for the player or side that wins a defined number or proportion of the games. **7** *Math.* & *Logic* a collection of distinct entities, individually specified or satisfying specified conditions, forming a unit. **8** a group of pupils or students having the same average ability. **9 a** a slip, shoot, bulb, etc., for planting. **b** a young fruit just set. **10 a** a habitual posture or conformation; the way the head etc. is carried or a dress etc. flows. **b** (also **dead set**) a setter's pointing in the presence of game. **11** the way, drift, or tendency (of a current, public opinion, state of mind, etc.) (*the set of public feeling is against it*). **12** the way in which a machine, device, etc., is set or adjusted. **13** esp. *Austral.* & *NZ colloq.* a grudge. **14 a** the alternate outward deflection of the teeth of a saw. **b** the amount of this. **15** the last coat of plaster on a wall. **16** *Printing* **a** the amount of spacing in type controlling the distance between letters. **b** the width of a piece of type. **17** a warp or bend or displacement caused by continued pressure or a continued position. **18** a setting, including stage furniture etc., for a play or film etc. **19** a sequence of songs or pieces performed in jazz or popular music. **20** the setting of the hair when damp. **21** (also **sett**) a badger's burrow. **22** (also **sett**) a granite paving-block. **23** a predisposition or expectation influencing a response. **24** a number of people making up a square dance. □ **make a dead set at 1** make a determined attack on. **2** seek to win the affections of. **set point** *Tennis* etc. **1** the state of a game when one side needs only one more point to win the set. **2** this point. **set theory** the branch of mathematics concerned with the manipulation of sets. [sense 1 (and related senses) f. OF *sette* f. L *secta* SECT: other senses f. SET[1]]

■ **1, 2** collection, group, combination, number, grouping, assortment, selection, arrangement, series, unit; order, ordering, succession, array, disposition. **3** clique, coterie, company, circle, ring, crowd, faction, sect, gang, cabal, fraternity, league, lobby; see also GROUP *n.* 1, 3. **4, 5** kit, outfit, rig; equipment, apparatus, deck, console, system, machine, gadget; service, canteen. **8** band, stream; class. **10 a** drape, hang; carriage, bearing, gait; see also POSTURE *n.* 1. **18** setting, scene, mounting, scenery, *mise en scène*. **19** sequence, cycle, series.

set[3] /set/ *adj.* **1** in senses of SET[1]. **2** prescribed or determined in advance. **3** fixed, unchanging, unmoving. **4** (of a phrase or speech etc.) having invariable or predetermined wording; not extempore. **5** prepared for action. **6** (foll. by *on*, *upon*) determined to acquire or achieve etc. **7** (of a book etc.) specified for reading in preparation for an examination. **8** (of a meal) served according to a fixed menu. □ **set fair** (of the weather) fine without a sign of breaking. **set phrase** an invariable or usual arrangement of words. **set piece 1** a formal or elaborate arrangement, esp. in art or literature. **2** fireworks arranged on scaffolding etc. **set screw** a screw for adjusting or clamping parts of a machine. **set scrum** *Rugby Football* a scrum ordered by the referee. **set square** a right-angled triangular plate for drawing lines, esp. at 90°, 45°, 60°, or 30°. [past part. of SET[1]]

■ **2–4, 7, 8** fixed, established, determined, predetermined, arranged, prearranged, prescribed, decided, defined, scheduled; customary, usual, normal, regular, agreed, conventional, habitual, routine, standard, wonted; definite, firm, unvarying, unchanging, rigid, strict, settled; stereotyped, trite, hackneyed, traditional, unchanged, unvaried, invariable. **5** prepared, ready, fit, primed, ripe, equipped. **6** see INTENT *adj.* 1a.

seta /se̅etə/ *n.* (*pl.* **setae** /-tee/) *Bot.* & *Zool.* stiff hair; bristle. □□ **setaceous** /-táyshəss/ *adj.* [L, = bristle]

■ hair, bristle, whisker. □□ **setaceous** see PRICKLY 1.

setiferous /sitíffərəss/ *adj.* (also **setigerous** /sitíjərəss/) *Biol.* having bristles. [L *seta* bristle, *setiger* bristly + -FEROUS, -GEROUS]

■ see PRICKLY 1, HAIRY 1.

seton /se̅et'n/ *n.* *Surgery* a skein of cotton etc. passed below the skin and left with the ends protruding to promote drainage etc. [ME f. med.L *seto*, *seta* silk, app. f. L *seta* bristle]

setose /se̅etōz/ *adj.* *Biol.* bristly. [L *seta* bristle]

■ see PRICKLY 1, HAIRY 1.

Setswana var. of TSWANA (and the preferred form for the language).

sett var. of SET[2] 21, 22.

settee /setée/ *n.* a seat (usu. upholstered), with a back and usu. arms, for more than one person. [18th c.: perh. a fanciful var. of SETTLE[2]]

■ see SEAT *n.* 1.

setter /séttər/ *n.* **1 a** a dog of a large long-haired breed trained to stand rigid when scenting game (see SET[1] 35). **b** this breed. **2** a person or thing that sets.

setting /sétting/ *n.* **1** the position or manner in which a thing is set. **2** the immediate surroundings (of a house etc.). **3** the surroundings of any object regarded as its framework; the environment of a thing. **4** the place and time, scenery, etc., of a story, drama, etc. **5** a frame in which a jewel is set.

6 the music to which words of a poem, song, etc., are set. **7** a set of cutlery and other accessories for one person at a table. **8** the way in which or level at which a machine is set to operate. □ **setting lotion** lotion used to prepare the hair for being set.

■ **1–3** scenery, background, backdrop, locale, location, surroundings, situation, habitat, home, environs, environment, milieu, frame, context, site, placement, mounting; (stage) set, scene, *mise en scène*.

settle[1] /sétt'l/ *v.* **1** *tr.* & *intr.* (often foll. by *down*) establish or become established in a more or less permanent abode or way of life. **2** *intr.* & *tr.* (often foll. by *down*) **a** cease or cause to cease from wandering, disturbance, movement, etc. **b** adopt a regular or secure style of life. **c** (foll. by *to*) apply oneself (to work, an activity, a way of life, etc.) (*settled down to writing letters*). **3 a** *intr.* sit or come down to stay for some time. **b** *tr.* cause to do this. **4** *tr.* & *intr.* bring to or attain fixity, certainty, composure, or quietness. **5** *tr.* determine or decide or agree upon (*shall we settle a date?*). **6** *tr.* **a** resolve (a dispute etc.). **b** deal with (a matter) finally. **7** *tr.* terminate (a lawsuit) by mutual agreement. **8** *intr.* **a** (foll. by *for*) accept or agree to (esp. an alternative not one's first choice). **b** (foll. by *on*) decide on. **9** *tr.* (also *absol.*) pay (a debt, an account, etc.). **10** *intr.* (as **settled** *adj.*) not likely to change for a time (*settled weather*). **11** *tr.* **a** aid the digestion of (food). **b** remedy the disordered state of (nerves, the stomach, etc.). **12** *tr.* **a** colonize. **b** establish colonists in. **13** *intr.* subside; fall to the bottom or on to a surface (*the foundations have settled*; *wait till the sediment settles*; *the dust will settle*). **14** *intr.* (of a ship) begin to sink. **15** *tr.* get rid of the obstruction of (a person) by argument or conflict or killing. □ **settle one's affairs** make any necessary arrangements (e.g. write a will) when death is near. **settle a person's hash** see HASH[1]. **settle in** become established in a place. **settle up 1** (also *absol.*) pay (an account, debt, etc.). **2** finally arrange (a matter). **settle with 1** pay all or part of an amount due to (a creditor). **2** get revenge on. **settling day** the fortnightly pay-day on the Stock Exchange. □□ **settleable** *adj.* [OE *setlan* (as SETTLE[2]) f. Gmc]

■ **1, 2a, b** (*intr.*) take up residence, go, come, move, make one's home, set up home *or* house, put down roots, locate, *archaic* abide, *literary* dwell. **2 c** see APPLY 5. **3** light, alight, land, come down, sit down, put down, set down, (come to) rest, descend, perch. **4** calm down, subside, quiet (down), *Brit.* quieten (down); calm, soothe, tranquillize, relax; arrange, order, dispose, organize, straighten out, put in *or* into order, compose, sort out, classify, coordinate, resolve, set to rights; clarify, clear. **5–7, 8b** decide (on), establish, appoint, set, confirm, affirm, make sure *or* certain (of), determine, agree (upon *or* on), pick, choose, select; decide, reconcile, resolve, put an end to, clear up, patch up, negotiate, mediate, adjust. **8 a** see CONSENT *v.* **9** pay, square, dispose of, clear, defray, balance, liquidate, discharge; settle up. **12** populate, people, colonize, plant. **13** subside, sink, decline, fall; gravitate, precipitate (out). □ **settle up** see SETTLE[1] 9 above.

settle[2] /sétt'l/ *n.* a bench with a high back and arms and often with a box fitted below the seat. [OE *setl* place to sit f. Gmc]

settlement /sétt'lmənt/ *n.* **1** the act or an instance of settling; the process of being settled. **2 a** the colonization of a region. **b** a place or area occupied by settlers. **c** a small village. **3 a** a political or financial etc. agreement. **b** an arrangement ending a dispute. **4 a** the terms on which property is given to a person. **b** a deed stating these. **c** the amount or property given. **d** = *marriage settlement*. **5** the process of settling an account. **6** subsidence of a wall, house, soil, etc.

■ **1** settling, decision, conclusion, confirmation, affirmation, establishment, setting, stabilization, determination, agreement, choice, selection. **2 a** colonization, settling, populating, *hist.* plantation. **b, c** colony, outpost, post, camp, community, encampment, *hist.* plantation; village, hamlet. **3** agreement, *rapprochement*, resolution, adjustment, elimination, reconciliation, working-out, accommodation, arbitration, arrangement. **5** payment, defrayal, discharge, liquidation, satisfaction, settling, clearance, settling up. **6** see SAG *n.* 2.

settler /sétlər/ *n.* a person who goes to settle in a new country or place; an early colonist.

■ colonist, colonizer, frontiersman, pioneer, immigrant, *US hist.* homesteader.

settlor /sétlər/ *n. Law* a person who makes a settlement esp. of a property.

seven /sévv'n/ *n.* & *adj.* ● *n.* **1** one more than six, or three less than ten; the sum of four units and three units. **2** a symbol for this (7, vii, VII). **3** a size etc. denoted by seven. **4** a set or team of seven individuals. **5** the time of seven o'clock (*is it seven yet?*). **6** a card with seven pips. ● *adj.* that amount to seven. □ **the seven deadly sins** the sins of pride, covetousness, lust, anger, gluttony, envy, and sloth. **the seven seas** the oceans of the world: the Arctic, Antarctic, N. Pacific, S. Pacific, N. Atlantic, S. Atlantic, and Indian Oceans. **the seven wonders of the world** see WONDER. **seven year itch** a supposed tendency to infidelity after seven years of marriage. [OE *seofon* f. Gmc]

sevenfold /sévv'nfōld/ *adj.* & *adv.* **1** seven times as much or as many. **2** consisting of seven parts.

seventeen /sévv'ntéen/ *n.* & *adj.* ● *n.* **1** one more than sixteen, or seven more than ten. **2** a symbol for this (17, xvii, XVII). **3** a size etc. denoted by seventeen. ● *adj.* that amount to seventeen. □□ **seventeenth** *adj.* & *n.* [OE *seofontīene*]

seventh /sévv'nth/ *n.* & *adj.* ● *n.* **1** the position in a sequence corresponding to the number 7 in the sequence 1–7. **2** something occupying this position. **3** one of seven equal parts of a thing. **4** *Mus.* **a** an interval or chord spanning seven consecutive notes in the diatonic scale (e.g. C to B). **b** a note separated from another by this interval. ● *adj.* that is the seventh. □ **in seventh heaven** see HEAVEN. **Seventh-Day Adventists** a staunchly protestant branch of the Adventists with beliefs based rigidly on faith and the Scriptures and the imminent return of Christ to earth, and observing the sabbath on Saturday. □□ **seventhly** *adv.*

seventy /sévv'nti/ *n.* & *adj.* ● *n.* (*pl.* **-ies**) **1** the product of seven and ten. **2** a symbol for this (70, lxx, LXX). **3** (in *pl.*) the numbers from 70 to 79, esp. the years of a century or of a person's life. ● *adj.* that amount to seventy. □ **seventy-first, -second**, etc. the ordinal numbers between seventieth and eightieth. **seventy-one, -two**, etc. the cardinal numbers between seventy and eighty. □□ **seventieth** *adj.* & *n.* **seventyfold** *adj.* & *adv.* [OE *-seofontig*]

sever /sévvər/ *v.* **1** *tr.* & *intr.* (often foll. by *from*) divide, break, or make separate, esp. by cutting. **2** *tr.* & *intr.* break off or away; separate, part, divide (*severed our friendship*). **3** *tr.* end the employment contract of (a person). □□ **severable** *adj.* [ME f. AF *severer*, OF *sevrer* ult. f. L *separare* SEPARATE *v.*]

■ **1** cut (off *or* apart *or* in two), lop *or* chop *or* hack (off), hew *or* shear off, slice (off), dock, bob, dissever, split, break, separate, divide, disjoin, detach, disconnect, *literary* cleave. **2** separate, part, divide, disunite; dissolve, break off *or* up, terminate, end, cease, stop, discontinue, suspend, abandon, put an end to.

several /sévrəl/ *adj.* & *n.* ● *adj.* & *n.* more than two but not many. ● *adj.* **1** separate or respective; distinct (*all went their several ways*). **2** *Law* applied or regarded separately (opp. JOINT). □□ **severally** *adv.* [ME f. AF f. AL *separalis* f. L *separ* SEPARATE *adj.*]

■ *adj.* & *n.* some, a few, not too many, not very many, a handful *or* a sprinkling *or* a number (of). ● *adj.* **1** separate, various, sundry, diverse, different, respective, individual, distinct, disparate, particular, specific, discrete, dissimilar, *archaic or literary* divers.

severalty /sévrəlti/ *n.* **1** separateness. **2** the individual or unshared tenure of an estate etc. (esp. *in severalty*). [ME f. AF *severalte* (as SEVERAL)]

severance /sévvərənss/ *n.* **1** the act or an instance of severing. **2** a severed state. □ **severance pay** an amount paid to an employee on the early termination of a contract.
■ see SEPARATION.

severe /sivéer/ *adj.* **1** rigorous, strict, and harsh in attitude or treatment (*a severe critic; severe discipline*). **2** serious, critical (*a severe shortage*). **3** vehement or forceful (*a severe storm*). **4** extreme (in an unpleasant quality) (*a severe winter; severe cold*). **5** arduous or exacting; making great demands on energy, skill, etc. (*severe competition*). **6** unadorned; plain in style (*severe dress*). □□ **severely** *adv.* **severity** /-vérriti/ *n.* [F *sévère* or L *severus*]
■ **1, 5** strict, harsh, rigorous, austere, hard, stony, stony-hearted, hard-hearted, flinty, inexorable, oppressive, unbending, rigid, uncompromising, relentless, unyielding, obdurate, pitiless, merciless, unsympathetic, unfeeling, cruel, brutal, mean, savage, inhuman, beastly, ruthless, *Austral.* & *NZ colloq.* solid; despotic, dictatorial, tyrannical, autocratic; demanding, exacting, arduous, exigent, taxing; painstaking, fastidious; stringent, punishing, punitive, burdensome, tough, onerous, grievous, painful, Draconian; stern, forbidding, dour, glowering, grave, grim, stiff, strait-laced, serious, unsmiling, sober, cold, frigid, aloof. **2** serious, dangerous, critical, grave, terrible, dreadful, life-threatening, acute, dire, *colloq.* awful; mortal, fatal, terminal. **3, 4** harsh, bitter, cold, extreme, intense, fierce, inclement, keen, violent, vehement, forceful, stormy, turbulent; wicked. **6** stark, bare, plain, austere, Spartan, ascetic, primitive, simple, crude, sparse, spare, monastic, modest, unadorned, unembellished, unembroidered. □□ **severely** acutely, seriously, badly, dangerously, dreadfully, critically; strictly, harshly, rigorously, austerely, oppressively, relentlessly, mercilessly, cruelly, brutally, savagely, inhumanly, tyrannically; sternly, forbiddingly, dourly, gloweringly, gravely, grimly, unsmilingly, soberly, coldly, coolly; stringently, punitively, onerously, grievously, painfully, mortally, fatally, terminally; starkly, plainly, barely, modestly, ascetically, monastically, primitively, simply, crudely, sparsely, sparely. **severity** strictness, harshness, rigour, rigorousness, austerity, hardness, flintiness, inexorability, inexorableness, stringency, oppression, oppressiveness, rigidity, inflexibility, relentlessness, obduracy, obdurateness, pitilessness, mercilessness, cold-bloodedness, abusiveness, cruelty, brutality, meanness, savagery, inhumanity, beastliness, ruthlessness, despotism, tyranny; fastidiousness, exigency; coldness, aloofness, sternness, gravity, grimness, frigidity, solemnity; dangerousness, acuteness, seriousness, ferocity, fierceness, virulence, violence, intensity, extremeness; punitiveness, punishment, onerousness, grievousness, painfulness, burdensomeness; inclemency, storminess, fury, furiousness, tempestuousness; plainness, starkness, asceticism, bareness, modesty, simplicity, primitiveness, spareness, sparseness, monasticism, crudeness.

severy /sévvəri/ *n.* (*pl.* **-ies**) *Archit.* a space or compartment in a vaulted ceiling. [ME f. OF *civoire* (as CIBORIUM)]

Seville orange /sévvil/ *n.* a bitter orange used for marmalade. [*Seville* in Spain]

Sèvres /sáyvrə/ *n.* fine porcelain, often with elaborate decoration, made at Sèvres in the suburbs of Paris.

sew /sō/ *v.tr.* (*past part.* **sewn** /sōn/ or **sewed**) **1** (also *absol.*) fasten, join, etc., by making stitches with a needle and thread or a sewing-machine. **2** make (a garment etc.) by sewing. **3** (often foll. by *on, in,* etc.) attach by sewing (*shall I sew on your buttons?*). □ **sew up 1** join or enclose by sewing. **2** *colloq.* (esp. in *passive*) satisfactorily arrange or finish dealing with (a project etc.). **3** esp. *US* obtain exclusive use of. □□ **sewer** *n.* [OE *si(o)wan*]
■ **1, 3** sew up, stitch, darn, mend, repair; sew on, attach, fasten; tack, baste, hem. □ **sew up 1** see SEW above. **2** see CLINCH *v.* 1.

sewage /sóō-ij, syóō-/ *n.* waste matter, esp. excremental, conveyed in sewers. □ **sewage farm** (or **works**) a place where sewage is treated, esp. to produce manure.
■ see MUCK *n.* 1, 2.

sewen var. of SEWIN.

sewer /sóōər, syóō-/ *n.* a conduit, usu. underground, for carrying off drainage water and sewage. □ **sewer rat** the common brown rat. [ME f. AF *sever(e)*, ONF *se(u)wiere* channel to carry off the overflow from a fishpond, ult. f. L *ex-* out of + *aqua* water]
■ see DRAIN *n.* 1a.

sewerage /sóōərij, syóō-/ *n.* a system of or drainage by sewers.

sewin /syóō-in/ *n.* (also **sewen**) a salmon trout of Welsh etc. rivers. [16th c.: orig. unkn.]

sewing /sṓ-ing/ *n.* a piece of material or work to be sewn.

sewing-machine /sṓ-ingməsheen/ *n.* a machine for sewing or stitching.

sewn *past part.* of SEW.

sex /seks/ *n., adj.,* & *v.* ● *n.* **1** either of the main divisions (male and female) into which living things are placed on the basis of their reproductive functions. **2** the fact of belonging to one of these. **3** males or females collectively. **4** sexual instincts, desires, etc., or their manifestation. **5** *colloq.* sexual intercourse. ● *adj.* **1** of or relating to sex (*sex education*). **2** arising from a difference or consciousness of sex (*sex antagonism; sex urge*). ● *v.tr.* **1** determine the sex of. **2** (as **sexed** *adj.*) **a** having a sexual appetite (*highly sexed*). **b** having sexual characteristics. □ **sex act** (usu. prec. by *the*) the (or an) act of sexual intercourse. **sex appeal** sexual attractiveness. **sex change** an apparent change of sex by surgical means and hormone treatment. **sex chromosome** a chromosome concerned in determining the sex of an organism, which in most animals are of two kinds, the X-chromosome and the Y-chromosome. **sex hormone** a hormone affecting sexual development or behaviour. **sex kitten** *colloq.* a young woman who asserts her sex appeal. **sex life** a person's activity related to sexual instincts. **sex-linked** *Genetics* carried on or by a sex chromosome. **sex maniac** *colloq.* a person needing or seeking excessive gratification of the sexual instincts. **sex object** a person regarded mainly in terms of sexual attractiveness. **sex-starved** lacking sexual gratification. **sex symbol** a person widely noted for sex appeal. □□ **sexer** *n.* [ME f. OF *sexe* or L *sexus*]
■ *n.* **1, 2** gender. **5** see *sexual intercourse.* ● *adj.* see SEXUAL 1. □ **sex maniac** nymphomaniac, *colloq.* nympho; see also PLAYBOY.

sexagenarian /séksəjináiriən/ *n.* & *adj.* ● *n.* a person from 60 to 69 years old. ● *adj.* of this age. [L *sexagenarius* f. *sexageni* distrib. of *sexaginta* sixty]

Sexagesima /séksəjéssimə/ *n.* the Sunday before Quinquagesima. [ME f. eccl.L, = sixtieth (day), prob. named loosely as preceding QUINQUAGESIMA]

sexagesimal /séksəjéssim'l/ *adj.* & *n.* ● *adj.* **1** of sixtieths. **2** of sixty. **3** reckoning or reckoned by sixtieths. ● *n.* (in full **sexagesimal fraction**) a fraction with a denominator equal to a power of 60 as in the divisions of the degree and hour. □□ **sexagesimally** *adv.* [L *sexagesimus* (as SEXAGESIMA)]

sexcentenary /séksentéenəri/ *n.* & *adj.* ● *n.* (*pl.* **-ies**) **1** a six-hundredth anniversary. **2** a celebration of this. ● *adj.* **1** of or relating to a sexcentenary. **2** occurring every six hundred years.

sexennial /seksénniəl/ *adj.* **1** lasting six years. **2** recurring every six years. [SEXI- + L *annus* year]

sexfoil /séksfoyl/ *n.* a six-lobed ornamental figure. [SEXI-, after CINQUEFOIL, TREFOIL]

sexi- /séksi/ *comb. form* (also **sex-** before a vowel) six. [L *sex* six]

sexism /séksiz'm/ *n.* prejudice or discrimination, esp. against women, on the grounds of sex. ▫▫ **sexist** *adj.* & *n.*
■ see PREJUDICE *n.* 1c.

sexivalent /séksivaylənt/ *adj.* (also **sexvalent**) *Chem.* having a valency of six.

sexless /séksliss/ *adj.* **1** *Biol.* neither male nor female. **2** lacking in sexual desire or attractiveness. ▫▫ **sexlessly** *adv.* **sexlessness** *n.*
■ **1** see NEUTER *adj.* 2, 3.

sexology /seksólləji/ *n.* the study of sexual life or relationships, esp. in human beings. ▫▫ **sexological** /séksəlójik'l/ *adj.* **sexologist** *n.*

sexpartite /sekspaártīt/ *adj.* divided into six parts.

sexploitation /séksploytáysh'n/ *n. colloq.* the exploitation of sex, esp. commercially.

sexpot /séks-pot/ *n. colloq.* a sexy person (esp. a woman).
■ see TEMPTER 1.

sext /sekst/ *n. Eccl.* **1** the canonical hour of prayer appointed for the sixth daytime hour (i.e. noon). **2** the office of sext. [ME f. L *sexta hora* sixth hour f. *sextus* sixth]

sextant /sékstənt/ *n.* an instrument with a graduated arc of 60^0 used in navigation and surveying for measuring the angular distance of objects by means of mirrors. [L *sextans -ntis* sixth part f. *sextus* sixth]

sextet /sekstét/ *n.* (also **sextette**) **1** *Mus.* a composition for six voices or instruments. **2** the performers of such a piece. **3** any group of six. [alt. of SESTET after L *sex* six]

sextillion /sekstílyən/ *n.* (*pl.* same or **sextillions**) a thousand raised to the seventh (or formerly, esp. *Brit.*, the twelfth) power (10^{21} and 10^{36} respectively) (cf. BILLION). ▫▫ **sextillionth** [F f. L *sex* six, after *septillion* etc.]

sexto /séksto͞/ *n.* (*pl.* **-os**) **1** a size of book or page in which each leaf is one-sixth that of a printing-sheet. **2** a book or sheet of this size. [L *sextus* sixth, as QUARTO]

sextodecimo /séksto͞déssimo͞/ *n.* (*pl.* **-os**) **1** a size of book or page in which each leaf is one-sixteenth that of a printing-sheet. **2** a book or sheet of this size. [L *sextus decimus* 16th (as QUARTO)]

sexton /sékstən/ *n.* a person who looks after a church and churchyard, often acting as bell-ringer and gravedigger. ▫ **sexton beetle** any beetle of the genus *Necrophorus*, burying carrion to serve as a nidus for its eggs. [ME *segerstane* etc., f. AF, OF *segerstein, secrestein* f. med.L *sacristanus* SACRISTAN]

sextuple /sékstyoop'l/ *adj.*, *n.*, & *v.* • *adj.* **1** sixfold. **2** having six parts. **3** being six times as many or much. • *n.* a sixfold number or amount. • *v.tr.* & *intr.* multiply by six; increase sixfold. ▫▫ **sextuply** *adv.* [med.L *sextuplus*, irreg. f. L *sex* six, after LL *quintuplus* QUINTUPLE]

sextuplet /sékstyooplit, -tyo͝oplit/ *n.* **1** each of six children born at one birth. **2** *Mus.* a group of six notes to be played in the time of four. [SEXTUPLE, after *triplet* etc.]

sexual /séksyooəl, sékshooəl/ *adj.* **1** of or relating to sex, or to the sexes or the relations between them. **2** *Bot.* (of classification) based on the distinction of sexes in plants. **3** *Biol.* having a sex. ▫ **sexual intercourse** the insertion of a man's erect penis into a woman's vagina, usu. followed by the ejaculation of semen. ▫▫ **sexuality** /-yoo-álliti, -shoo-álliti/ *n.* **sexually** *adv.* [LL *sexualis* (as SEX)]
■ **1** sex, reproductive, genital, procreative, procreant, progenitive, propagative; erotic, carnal, fleshly, voluptuous, libidinous, earthy, bodily, physical, lustful, animal, sexy. ▫ **sexual intercourse** sexual intercourse, mating, copulation, sexual relations, (sexual) union, intimacy, lovemaking, making love, coupling, *Law* carnal knowledge, *Med.* coitus, coition, *colloq.* going to bed.

sexvalent var. of SEXIVALENT.

sexy /séksi/ *adj.* (**sexier**, **sexiest**) **1** sexually attractive or stimulating. **2** sexually aroused. **3** concerned with or engrossed in sex. ▫▫ **sexily** *adv.* **sexiness** *n.*
■ **1** erotic, arousing, exciting, sensual, sensuous, seductive, suggestive, provocative, inviting, alluring, flirtatious, appealing, fascinating, striking, tempting, captivating, enchanting, *colloq.* come-hither; bedroom. **2** randy, (sexually) aroused, lustful, lecherous, libidinous, hot, *formal* concupiscent, *sl.* horny. **3** blue, dirty, pornographic, obscene, filthy, smutty, lewd, foul, lascivious, indecent, explicit, gross, vulgar, rude, coarse, risqué, titillating, bawdy, ribald, lusty, immodest, indelicate, suggestive, unseemly, improper, indecorous, naughty, shameless, *US* off colour, *colloq.* raunchy.

sez /sez/ *sl.* says (*sez you*). [phonetic repr.]

SF *abbr.* science fiction.

sf *abbr. Mus.* sforzando.

SFA *abbr.* Scottish Football Association.

sforzando /sfortsándo͞/ *adj.*, *adv.*, & *n.* (also **sforzato** /-tsaáto͞/) • *adj.* & *adv. Mus.* with sudden emphasis. • *n.* (*pl.* **-os** or **sforzandi** /-di/) **1** a note or group of notes especially emphasized. **2** an increase in emphasis and loudness. [It., verbal noun and past part. of *sforzare* use force]

sfumato /sfoomaáto͞/ *adj.* & *n. Painting* • *adj.* with indistinct outlines. • *n.* the technique of allowing tones and colours to shade gradually into one another. [It., past part. of *sfumare* shade off f. *s-* = EX-[1] + *fumare* smoke]

sfz *abbr. Mus.* sforzando.

SG *abbr.* **1** *US* senior grade. **2** *Law* Solicitor-General. **3** specific gravity.

sgd. *abbr.* signed.

sgraffito /sgraafeéto͞/ *n.* (*pl.* **sgraffiti** /-ti/) a form of decoration made by scratching through wet plaster on a wall or through slip on ceramic ware, showing a different-coloured under-surface. [It., past part. of *sgraffire* scratch f. *s-* = EX-[1] + *graffio* scratch]

Sgt. *abbr.* Sergeant.

sh *int.* calling for silence. [var. of HUSH]

sh. *abbr. Brit. hist.* shilling(s).

shabby /shábbi/ *adj.* (**shabbier**, **shabbiest**) **1** in bad repair or condition; faded and worn, dingy, dilapidated. **2** dressed in old or worn clothes. **3** of poor quality. **4** contemptible, dishonourable (*a shabby trick*). ▫▫ **shabbily** *adv.* **shabbiness** *n.* **shabbyish** *adj.* [*shab* scab f. OE *sceabb* f. ON, rel. to SCAB]
■ **1, 2** worn (out), dingy, faded, threadbare, tattered, frayed, raggedy, ragged, scruffy, dilapidated, dirty, bedraggled, mangy, run-down, seedy, the worse for wear, down at heel, grubby, *colloq.* tatty, *esp. US colloq.* tacky; tumbledown, broken-down, shattered, battered, run-down, ramshackle, neglected, squalid, slummy, *colloq.* beat-up, crummy, *Austral. sl.* warby. **3** see POOR 3b, c. **4** unpleasant, nasty, disagreeable, mean, contemptible, demeaning, grudging, ungenerous, impolite, rude, unfriendly, unhelpful, shoddy, ungentlemanly, unladylike, dishonourable, unworthy, scurvy; stingy, niggardly, contemptible, low, lowly, base, mean-spirited, despicable, vile, uncouth, discreditable, disreputable, infamous, abominable, ignoble, atrocious, ignominious, odious, detestable, opprobrious, *sl.* rotten.

shabrack /shábrak/ *n. hist.* a cavalry saddle-cloth. [G *Schabracke* of E. European orig.: cf. Russ. *shabrak*]

shack /shak/ *n.* & *v.* • *n.* a roughly built hut or cabin. • *v.intr.* (foll. by *up*) *sl.* cohabit, esp. as lovers. [perh. f. Mex. *jacal*, Aztec *xacatli* wooden hut]
■ *n.* hut, hovel, shanty, cabin, lean-to. • *v.* (*shack up*) live together, cohabit, *colloq.* live in sin.

shackle /shákk'l/ *n.* & *v.* • *n.* **1** a metal loop or link, closed by a bolt, to connect chains etc. **2** a fetter enclosing the ankle or wrist. **3** (usu. in *pl.*) a restraint or impediment. • *v.tr.* fetter, impede, restrain. ▫ **shackle-bolt 1** a bolt for closing a shackle. **2** a bolt with a shackle at its end. [OE *sc(e)acul* fetter, corresp. to LG *shäkel* link, coupling, ON *skökull* wagon-pole f. Gmc]
■ *n.* **2** fetter(s), leg-iron, chain, irons, gyve(s), ball and chain, manacle, handcuff, trammel(s), *colloq.* cuffs, *hist.* bilboes, *sl.* bracelet(s), *Brit. sl.* darbies. **3** (*shackles*) restriction, restraint, trammels, deterrent, impediment,

check, obstacle, obstruction, barrier, hindrance, bar, encumbrance. ● *v.* chain, fetter, manacle, handcuff, bind, tie, trammel, secure, truss, pinion, tether; restrain, impede, hold back, check, deter, hinder, discourage, hobble, handicap, restrict, curb, rein, bridle, control, inhibit, limit.

shad /shad/ *n.* (*pl.* same or **shads**) *Zool.* any deep-bodied edible marine fish of the genus *Alosa*, spawning in fresh water. [OE *sceadd*, of unkn. orig.]

shaddock /sháddək/ *n. Bot.* **1** the largest citrus fruit, with a thick yellow skin and bitter pulp. Also called POMELO. **2** the tree, *Citrus grandis*, bearing these. [Capt. *Shaddock*, who introduced it to the W. Indies in the 17th c.]

shade /shayd/ *n.* & *v.* ● *n.* **1** comparative darkness (and usu. coolness) caused by shelter from direct light and heat. **2** a place or area sheltered from the sun. **3** a darker part of a picture etc. **4** a colour, esp. with regard to its depth or as distinguished from one nearly like it. **5** comparative obscurity. **6** a slight amount (*am a shade better today*). **7** a translucent cover for a lamp etc. **8** a screen excluding or moderating light. **9** an eye-shield. **10** (in *pl.*) esp. *US colloq.* sun-glasses. **11** a slightly differing variety (*all shades of opinion*). **12** *literary* **a** a ghost. **b** (in *pl.*) Hades. **13** (in *pl.*; foll. by *of*) suggesting reminiscence or unfavourable comparison (*shades of Dr Johnson!*). ● *v.* **1** *tr.* screen from light. **2** *tr.* cover, moderate, or exclude the light of. **3** *tr.* darken, esp. with parallel pencil lines to represent shadow etc. **4** *intr.* & *tr.* (often foll. by *away, off, into*) (cause to) pass or change by degrees; border on. □ **in the shade** in comparative obscurity. **put in** (or **into**) **the shade** eclipse, surpass; appear superior. □□ **shadeless** *adj.* [OE *sc(e)adu* f. Gmc]

■ *n.* **1, 2, 5** shadow, shadiness, dimness, duskiness, semi-darkness, gloominess, murkiness, dusk, gloom, murk, darkness, obscurity. **4** tint, tinge, tone, colour, hue; intensity. **6** hint, intimation, tinge, suggestion, modicum, sprinkling, soupçon, trace, suspicion, undertone, overtone, touch, speck, dash, nuance, atom, grain, scintilla, iota, jot, tittle, *US colloq.* tad; fraction, hair's breadth, bit, *colloq.* smidgen, whisker. **7, 8** lampshade; blind, window-blind, curtain, venetian blind; screen, cover, covering, protection, veil, awning, canopy, shield, shelter, umbrella, parasol, sunshade. **10** (*shades*) sun-glasses, *propr.* Polaroids. **11** variation, variety, difference, nuance, degree, modulation. **12 a** ghost, spectre, apparition, phantom, phantasm, spirit, wraith, vision, *colloq.* spook. ● *v.* **1, 2** screen, protect, shield, shelter, cover; dim, shadow, veil, blot out, cloud, conceal, hide, obscure, shroud; mask, camouflage, disguise. **3** darken, opaque, black out, blacken; shadow, hatch. **4** see MERGE, BORDER *v.* 3. □ **put in** (or **into**) **the shade** overshadow, exceed, surpass, outstrip, outclass, eclipse, outshine, better, beat, put to shame, outplay, outperform, outdo, *colloq.* run rings *or* circles around, show up.

shading /sháyding/ *n.* **1** the representation of light and shade, e.g. by pencilled lines, on a map or drawing. **2** the graduation of tones from light to dark to create a sense of depth.

shadoof /shədóof/ *n.* a pole with a bucket and counterpoise used esp. in Egypt for raising water. [Egypt. Arab. *šādūf*]

shadow /sháddō/ *n.* & *v.* ● *n.* **1** shade or a patch of shade. **2** a dark figure projected by a body intercepting rays of light, often regarded as an appendage. **3** an inseparable attendant or companion. **4** a person secretly following another. **5** the slightest trace (*not the shadow of a doubt*). **6** a weak or insubstantial remnant or thing (*a shadow of his former self*). **7** (*attrib.*) *Brit.* denoting members of a political party in opposition holding responsibilities parallel to those of the government (*shadow Home Secretary*; *shadow cabinet*). **8** the shaded part of a picture. **9** a substance used to colour the eyelids. **10** gloom or sadness. ● *v.tr.* **1** cast a shadow over. **2** secretly follow and watch the movements of. □ **shadow-boxing** boxing against an imaginary opponent as a form of training. □□ **shadower** *n.* **shadowless** *adj.* [repr. OE *scead(u)we*, oblique case of *sceadu* SHADE]

■ *n.* **1** shade, darkness, gloom, dimness, dusk, obscurity. **3** companion, alter ego, other half, comrade, crony, second self, *fidus Achates*, mate, *colloq.* sidekick, chum, (bosom) pal, *esp. US colloq.* (bosom) buddy. **4** *colloq.* tail. **5** hint, intimation, suggestion, suspicion, trace, vestige; remnant. **10** see GLOOM *n.* 2. ● *v.* **2** follow, trail, track, dog, stalk, pursue, trace, tail, *colloq.* keep tabs on.

shadowgraph /sháddōgraaf/ *n.* **1** an image or photograph made by means of X-rays; = RADIOGRAM 2. **2** a picture formed by a shadow cast on a lighted surface. **3** an image formed by light refracted differently by different densities of a fluid.

shadowy /sháddō-i/ *adj.* **1** like or having a shadow. **2** full of shadows. **3** vague, indistinct. **4 a** unreal, imaginary. **b** spectral, ghostly. □□ **shadowiness** *n.*

■ **1, 2** dark, shady, bowery, leafy, shaded, gloomy, dusky, dim, *literary* bosky. **3** vague, dim, dark, obscure, faint, indistinct, indefinite, hazy, ill-defined, unclear, indeterminate. **4 a** illusory, dreamlike, imaginary, visionary, chimerical, hallucinatory, unreal, unsubstantial, fleeting, impalpable, transitory, ethereal, immaterial. **b** spectral, ghostly, phantom, phantasmal, wraithlike, phantasmagoric(al).

shady /sháydi/ *adj.* (**shadier**, **shadiest**) **1** giving shade. **2** situated in shade. **3** (of a person or behaviour) disreputable; of doubtful honesty. □□ **shadily** *adv.* **shadiness** *n.*

■ **3** questionable, doubtful, uncertain, unreliable, suspicious, suspect, dubious, disreputable, devious, tricky, slippery, underhand(ed), unethical, unscrupulous, dishonourable, dishonest, *colloq.* shifty, crooked, dodgy, *sl.* fishy, bent.

shaft /shaaft/ *n.* & *v.* ● *n.* **1 a** an arrow or spear. **b** the long slender stem of these. **2** a remark intended to hurt or provoke (*a shaft of malice*; *shafts of wit*). **3** (foll. by *of*) **a** a ray (of light). **b** a bolt (of lightning). **4** the stem or handle of a tool, implement, etc. **5** a column, esp. between the base and capital. **6** a long narrow space, usu. vertical, for access to a mine, a lift in a building, for ventilation, etc. **7** a long and narrow part supporting or connecting or driving a part or parts of greater thickness etc. **8** each of the pair of poles between which a horse is harnessed to a vehicle. **9** the central stem of a feather. **10** *Mech.* a large axle or revolving bar transferring force by belts or cogs. **11** *US colloq.* harsh or unfair treatment. ● *v.tr.* **1** *US colloq.* treat unfairly. **2** *coarse sl.* (of a man) copulate with. [OE *scæft*, *sceaft* f. Gmc]

■ *n.* **1 a** arrow, spear; see also LANCE *n.* **2** thrust, barb, sting, dart, gibe, taunt, rebuff, affront, slap in the face, *colloq.* put-down. **3** beam, ray, gleam, streak, *Optics* pencil; bolt, flash, fulmination, *archaic* levin. **4, 7** pole, rod, staff, stick, stem, shank, handle, helve. **5** pillar, column, post, stanchion, upright. **6** mine-shaft, tunnel, adit, well, pit; air-shaft, duct, vent, flue; passage, entrance, access.

shafting /shaáfting/ *n. Mech.* **1** a system of connected shafts for transmitting motion. **2** material from which shafts are cut.

shag[1] /shag/ *n.* **1** a rough growth or mass of hair etc. **2** a coarse kind of cut tobacco. **3** a cormorant, esp. the crested cormorant, *Phalacrocorax aristotelis*. [OE *sceacga*, rel. to ON *skegg* beard, OE *sceaga* coppice]

■ **1** see PILE[3].

shag[2] /shag/ *v.* & *n. coarse sl.* ¶ Usually considered a taboo word. ● *v.tr.* (**shagged**, **shagging**) **1** have sexual intercourse with. **2** (usu. in *passive*; often foll. by *out*) exhaust; tire out. ● *n.* (an act of) sexual intercourse. [18th c.: orig. unkn.]

shaggy /shággi/ *adj.* (**shaggier**, **shaggiest**) **1** hairy, rough-haired. **2** unkempt. **3** (of the hair) coarse and abundant. **4** *Biol.* having a hairlike covering. □ **shaggy-dog story** a long rambling story amusing only by its being inconsequential. □□ **shaggily** *adv.* **shagginess** *n.*

■ **1, 2** hairy, woolly, unkempt, unshorn, uncut, hirsute, dishevelled, matted, untidy.

shagreen /shagréen/ *n.* **1** a kind of untanned leather with a rough granulated surface. **2** a sharkskin rough with natural denticles, used for rasping and polishing. [var. of CHAGRIN in the sense 'rough skin']

shah /shaa/ *n. hist.* a title of the former monarch of Iran. □□ **shahdom** *n.* [Pers. *šāh* f. OPers. *kšāyṯiya* king]

■ see SOVEREIGN *n.*

shaikh var. of SHEIKH.

shake /shayk/ *v.* & *n.* ● *v.* (*past* **shook** /shŏŏk/; *past part.* **shaken** /sháykən/) **1** *tr.* & *intr.* move forcefully or quickly up and down or to and fro. **2 a** *intr.* tremble or vibrate markedly. **b** *tr.* cause to do this. **3** *tr.* **a** agitate or shock. **b** *colloq.* upset the composure of. **4** *tr.* weaken or impair; make less convincing or firm or courageous (*shook his confidence*). **5** *intr.* (of a voice, note, etc.) make tremulous or rapidly alternating sounds; trill (*his voice shook with emotion*). **6** *tr.* brandish; make a threatening gesture with (one's fist, a stick, etc.). **7** *intr. colloq.* shake hands (*they shook on the deal*). **8** *tr.* esp. *US colloq.* = *shake off*. ● *n.* **1** the act or an instance of shaking; the process of being shaken. **2** a jerk or shock. **3** (in *pl.*; prec. by *the*) a fit of or tendency to trembling or shivering. **4** *Mus.* a trill. **5** = *milk shake*. □ **in two shakes** (**of a lamb's** or **dog's tail**) very quickly. **no great shakes** *colloq.* not very good or significant. **shake a person by the hand** = *shake hands*. **shake down 1** settle or cause to fall by shaking. **2** settle down. **3** become established; get into harmony with circumstances, surroundings, etc. **4** *US sl.* extort money from. **shake the dust off one's feet** depart indignantly or disdainfully. **shake hands** (often foll. by *with*) clasp right hands at meeting or parting, in reconciliation or congratulation, or over a concluded bargain. **shake one's head** move one's head from side to side in refusal, denial, disapproval, or concern. **shake in one's shoes** tremble with apprehension. **shake a leg 1** begin dancing. **2** make a start. **shake off 1** get rid of (something unwanted). **2** manage to evade (a person who is following or pestering one). **shake out 1** empty by shaking. **2** spread or open (a sail, flag, etc.) by shaking. **shake-out** *n.* = *shake-up*. **shake up 1** mix (ingredients) by shaking. **2** restore to shape by shaking. **3** disturb or make uncomfortable. **4** rouse from lethargy, apathy, conventionality, etc. **shake-up** *n.* an upheaval or drastic reorganization. □□ **shakeable** *adj.* (also **shakable**). [OE *sc(e)acan* f. Gmc]

■ *v.* **1, 2, 5** quiver, quake, shudder, rattle, waver, wobble, tremble, shiver; wriggle, squirm, shimmy, twitch, joggle, jiggle, rock, sway, swing, roll, bump, grind, vibrate, oscillate, pulsate, gyrate, *colloq.* waggle, wiggle. **3** agitate, stir (up), mix (up); upset, distress, frighten, scare, shock, disturb, unnerve, unsettle, disconcert, discomfit, worry, fluster, disquiet, confound, confuse, perplex, puzzle, *colloq.* rattle, get to, throw. **4** weaken, undermine, impair, harm, damage, discourage; disenchant, disappoint, disaffect. **6** wave, brandish, flourish; display, show (off). ● *n.* **1** rattle, quiver, quake, shudder, waver, wobble, tremble, shiver, wiggle, wriggle, twitch, joggle, jiggle, sway, swing, roll, gyration. **2** agitation, shaking, stirring (up), jolt, jar, shock, jounce; see also JERK *n.* 1, 2. **3** (*the shakes*) trembling, tremors, delirium tremens, D.T.('s), the horrors, *colloq.* the jitters, the jim-jams, the jumps, the willies, *sl.* the heebie-jeebies. □ **in two shakes** see SOON 1. **no great shakes** see UNDISTINGUISHED. **shake down 2** settle down; break in, condition, test, prove, *colloq.* debug. **4** blackmail, extort *or* extract *or* squeeze *or* wrest money from, squeeze, threaten. **shake a leg 2** see RUSH[1] *v.* 1. **shake off** get rid of, discard, dislodge, drop; brush off, elude, evade, lose, throw off, rid oneself of, give a person the slip, *esp. US colloq.* shake. **shake up 3** see DISTURB 2a. **4** see ROUSE 2a. **shake-up** reorganization, rearrangement, overhaul, revamp, restructuring, rehabilitation, realignment; upheaval.

shakedown /sháykdown/ *n.* **1** a makeshift bed. **2** *US sl.* a swindle; a piece of extortion. **3** (*attrib.*) *US colloq.* denoting a voyage, flight, etc., to test a new ship or aircraft and its crew.

■ **3** (*attrib.*) see MAIDEN 5.

shaken *past part.* of SHAKE.

shaker /sháykər/ *n.* **1** a person or thing that shakes. **2** a container for shaking together the ingredients of cocktails etc. **3** (**Shaker**) a member of an American religious sect living simply, in celibate mixed communities. □□ **Shakeress** *n.* (in sense 3). **Shakerism** *n.* (in sense 3). [ME, f. SHAKE: sense 3 from religious dances]

Shakespearian /shaykspéeriən/ *adj.* & *n.* (also **Shakespearean**) ● *adj.* **1** of or relating to William Shakespeare, English dramatist d. 1616. **2** in the style of Shakespeare. ● *n.* a student of Shakespeare's works etc.

shako /sháykō/ *n.* (*pl.* **-os**) a cylindrical peaked military hat with a plume. [F *schako* f. Magyar *csákó* (*süveg*) peaked (cap) f. *csák* peak f. G *Zacken* spike]

shakuhachi /shúkkoohúchi/ *n.* (*pl.* **shakuhachis**) a Japanese bamboo flute. [Jap. f. *shaku* a measure of length + *hachi* eight (tenths)]

shaky /sháyki/ *adj.* (**shakier, shakiest**) **1** unsteady; apt to shake; trembling. **2** unsound, infirm (*a shaky hand*). **3** unreliable, wavering (*a shaky promise*; *got off to a shaky start*). □□ **shakily** *adv.* **shakiness** *n.*

■ uncertain, wobbly, unstable, precarious, unsound, rickety, insecure, flimsy, weak, feeble, infirm, unsteady, tottering, teetering, unsupported, unsubstantiated, undependable, unreliable, wavering, tenuous, untrustworthy, dubious, questionable, doubtful, *colloq.* rocky, iffy, dodgy; dilapidated, unsound, ramshackle, on its last legs, decrepit, falling down *or* apart, unsubstantial, insubstantial.

shale /shayl/ *n.* soft finely stratified rock that splits easily, consisting of consolidated mud or clay. □ **shale oil** oil obtained from bituminous shale. □□ **shaly** *adj.* [prob. f. G *Schale* f. OE *sc(e)alu* rel. to ON *skál* (see SCALE[2])]

shall /shal, sh'l/ *v.aux.* (*3rd sing. present* **shall**; *archaic* 2nd sing. present **shalt** as below; *past* **should** /shŏŏd, shəd/) (foll. by infin. without *to*, or *absol.*; present and past only in use) **1** (in the 1st person) expressing the future tense (*I shall return soon*) or (with *shall* stressed) emphatic intention (*I shall have a party*). **2** (in the 2nd and 3rd persons) expressing a strong assertion or command rather than a wish (cf. WILL[1]) (*you shall not catch me again*; *they shall go to the party*). ¶ For the other persons in senses 1, 2 see WILL[1]. **3** expressing a command or duty (*thou shalt not steal*; *they shall obey*). **4** (in 2nd-person questions) expressing an enquiry, esp. to avoid the form of a request (cf. WILL[1]) (*shall you go to France?*). □ **shall I?** do you want me to? [OE *sceal* f. Gmc]

shallot /shəlót/ *n.* an onion-like plant, *Allium ascalonicum*, with a cluster of small bulbs. [*eschalot* f. F *eschalotte* alt. of OF *eschaloigne*: see SCALLION]

shallow /shállō/ *adj.*, *n.*, & *v.* ● *adj.* **1** of little depth. **2** superficial, trivial (*a shallow mind*). ● *n.* (often in *pl.*) a shallow place. ● *v.intr.* & *tr.* become or make shallow. □□ **shallowly** *adv.* **shallowness** *n.* [ME, prob. rel. to *schald*, OE *sceald* SHOAL[2]]

■ *adj.* surface, skin-deep, superficial, thin; empty, flimsy, trivial, unimportant, slight, frivolous, idle, foolish. ● *n.* shoal, sand bar, sandbank, bank, shelf.

shalom /shəlóm/ *n.* & *int.* a Jewish salutation at meeting or parting. [Heb. *šālôm* peace]

shalt /shalt/ *archaic 2nd person sing.* of SHALL.

sham /sham/ *v.*, *n.*, & *adj.* ● *v.* (**shammed, shamming**) **1** *intr.* feign, pretend. **2** *tr.* **a** pretend to be. **b** simulate (*is shamming sleep*). ● *n.* **1** imposture, pretence. **2** a person or thing pretending or pretended to be what he or she or it is not. ● *adj.* pretended, counterfeit. □□ **shammer** *n.* [perh. north. dial. var. of SHAME]

■ *v.* **1** feign, pretend, fake, dissemble. **2** simulate, feign, fake, affect, dissemble, make a pretence of. ● *n.* fake, fraud, counterfeit, imitation, hoax, humbug, pretence, forgery, copy, imposture, ersatz, charlatan, *colloq.* pseud, phoney. ● *adj.* fake, fraudulent, counterfeit, imitation, paste, simulated, pretend(ed), false, make-believe, fictitious, made-up, bogus, spurious, mock, ersatz, artificial, synthetic, pseudo, *colloq.* phoney.

shaman /shámmən/ *n.* a witch-doctor or priest claiming to communicate with gods etc. □□ **shamanism** *n.* **shamanist** *n.* & *adj.* **shamanistic** /-nístik/ *adj.* [G *Schamane* & Russ. *shaman* f. Tungusian *samán*]
■ see SORCERER. □□ **shamanism** see *sorcery* (SORCERER). **shamanistic** see MAGIC *adj.* 1.

shamateur /shámmətər/ *n. derog.* a sports player who makes money from sporting activities though classed as an amateur. □□ **shamateurism** *n.* [SHAM + AMATEUR]

shamble /shámb'l/ *v.* & *n.* ● *v.intr.* walk or run with a shuffling or awkward gait. ● *n.* a shambling gait. [prob. f. dial. *shamble* (adj.) ungainly, perh. f. *shamble legs* with ref. to straddling trestles: see SHAMBLES]
■ *v.* shuffle, scrape along; see also HOBBLE *v.* 1. ● *n.* see SHUFFLE *n.* 1.

shambles /shámb'lz/ *n.pl.* (usu. treated as *sing.*) **1** *colloq.* a mess or muddle (*the room was a shambles*). **2** a butcher's slaughterhouse. **3** a scene of carnage. [pl. of *shamble* stool, stall f. OE *sc(e)amul* f. WG f. L *scamellum* dimin. of *scamnum* bench]
■ **1** chaos, devastation, mess, disaster, pigsty, muddle, *US* pigpen.

shambolic /shambóllik/ *adj. colloq.* chaotic, unorganized. [SHAMBLES, prob. after SYMBOLIC]
■ see *chaotic* (CHAOS).

shame /shaym/ *n.* & *v.* ● *n.* **1** a feeling of distress or humiliation caused by consciousness of the guilt or folly of oneself or an associate. **2** a capacity for experiencing this feeling, esp. as imposing a restraint on behaviour (*has no sense of shame*). **3** a state of disgrace, discredit, or intense regret. **4 a** a person or thing that brings disgrace etc. **b** a thing or action that is wrong or regrettable. ● *v.tr.* **1** bring shame on; make ashamed; put to shame. **2** (foll. by *into*, *out of*) force by shame (*was shamed into confessing*). □ **for shame!** a reproof to a person for not showing shame. **put to shame** disgrace or humiliate by revealing superior qualities etc. **shame on you!** you should be ashamed. **what a shame!** how unfortunate! [OE *sc(e)amu*]
■ *n.* **1** embarrassment, humiliation, mortification, chagrin, ignominy, shamefacedness, loss of face, abashment, guilt. **2** humility, modesty, (sense of) decency *or* decorum *or* propriety, respectability, decorousness; diffidence, shyness, coyness, prudishness, timidity, shamefacedness. **3, 4** disgrace, ignominy, dishonour, disrepute, degradation, opprobrium, vilification, calumniation, infamy, obloquy, odium, contempt, scandal, denigration, loss of face, defamation, discredit, disesteem, disfavour, derogation, disparagement; pity, calamity, disaster, catastrophe; outrage. ● *v.* **1** embarrass, humiliate, mortify, humble, chagrin, disconcert, discountenance, put down, bring down, abash, chasten, take a person down a peg or two; disgrace, dishonour, degrade, debase, defame, discredit, stigmatize; blacken, stain, taint, besmirch, tarnish. **2** coerce, force, drive; embarrass, humiliate. □ **put to shame** surpass, eclipse, outclass, overshadow, put in the shade, outdo, outstrip, outshine, show up. **what a shame!** (what a) pity, how unfortunate.

shamefaced /sháymfáyst/ *adj.* **1** showing shame. **2** bashful, diffident. □□ **shamefacedly** /-fáystli, -fáysidli/ *adv.* **shamefacedness** *n.* [16th-c. alt. of *shamefast*, by assim. to FACE]
■ **1** ashamed, shamed, abashed, embarrassed, humiliated, dishonoured, mortified, humbled, chastened, chagrined, uncomfortable, discomfited, remorseful, red-faced, sheepish. **2** bashful, shy, modest, self-effacing, diffident, timid, meek, coy, sheepish, timorous.

shameful /sháymfŏŏl/ *adj.* **1** that causes or is worthy of shame. **2** disgraceful, scandalous. □□ **shamefully** *adv.* **shamefulness** *n.* [OE *sc(e)amful* (as SHAME, -FUL)]
■ disgraceful, dishonourable, base, low, mean, vile, degrading, indecent, inglorious, deplorable, discreditable, corrupt, disreputable, infamous, ignominious, humiliating, embarrassing, mortifying, humbling, chastening, discomfiting, shaming, blameworthy, scandalous, outrageous, unprincipled.

shameless /sháymliss/ *adj.* **1** having or showing no sense of shame. **2** impudent. □□ **shamelessly** *adv.* **shamelessness** *n.* [OE *sc(e)amlēas* (as SHAME, -LESS)]
■ wild, flagrant, unreserved, uncontrolled, immodest, wanton, indecorous, indecent, rude, improper, forward, bold, unblushing, audacious, brazen, brash, unabashed, unashamed, impudent, shocking, outrageous.

shammy /shámmi/ *n.* (*pl.* **-ies**) (in full **shammy leather**) *colloq.* = CHAMOIS 2. [repr. corrupted pronunc.]

shampoo /shampóó/ *n.* & *v.* ● *n.* **1** liquid or cream used to lather and wash the hair. **2** a similar substance for washing a car or carpet etc. **3** an act or instance of cleaning with shampoo. ● *v.tr.* (**shampoos, shampooed**) wash with shampoo. [Hind. *chhāmpo*, imper. of *chhāmpnā* to press]
■ *n.* **3** see WASH *n.* 1. ● *v.* see WASH *v.* 1, 3.

shamrock /shámrok/ *n.* any of various plants with trifoliate leaves, esp. *Trifolium repens* or *Medicago lupulina*, used as the national emblem of Ireland. [Ir. *seamróg* trefoil, dimin. of *seamar* clover + *og* young]

shamus /sháyməss/ *n. US sl.* a detective. [20th c.: orig. uncert.]
■ see SLEUTH *n.*

shandy /shándi/ *n.* (*pl.* **-ies**) a mixture of beer with lemonade or ginger beer. [19th c.: orig. unkn.]

shanghai /shanghī́/ *v.* & *n.* ● *v.tr.* (**shanghais, shanghaied, shanghaiing**) **1** force (a person) to be a sailor on a ship by using drugs or other trickery. **2** *colloq.* put into detention or an awkward situation by trickery. **3** *Austral.* & *NZ* shoot with a catapult. ● *n.* (*pl.* **shanghais**) *Austral.* & *NZ* a catapult. [*Shanghai* in China]

Shangri-La /shánggrilaá/ *n.* an imaginary paradise on earth. [the name of a hidden Tibetan valley in J. Hilton's *Lost Horizon* (1933)]
■ see PARADISE 2.

shank /shangk/ *n.* **1 a** the leg. **b** the lower part of the leg; the leg from knee to ankle. **c** the shin-bone. **2** the lower part of an animal's foreleg, esp. as a cut of meat. **3** a shaft or stem. **4 a** the long narrow part of a tool etc. joining the handle to the working end. **b** the stem of a key, spoon, anchor, etc. **c** the straight part of a nail or fish-hook. **5** the narrow middle of the sole of a shoe. □ **shanks's mare** (or **pony**) one's own legs as a means of conveyance. □□ **shanked** *adj.* (also in *comb.*). [OE *sceanca* f. WG]
■ **1** see LEG *n.* 1, 3. **2** see LEG *n.* 2. **3** see SHAFT *n.* 4, 7. **4 a** see TANG[1] 3.

shanny /shánni/ *n.* (*pl.* **-ies**) a long-bodied olive-green European marine fish, *Blennius pholis*. [19th c.: orig. unkn.: cf. 18th-c. *shan*]

shan't /shaant/ *contr.* shall not.

shantung /shantúng/ *n.* soft undressed Chinese silk, usu. undyed. [*Shantung*, Chinese province]

shanty[1] /shánti/ *n.* (*pl.* **-ies**) **1** a hut or cabin. **2** a crudely built shack. □ **shanty town** a poor or depressed area of a town, consisting of shanties. [19th c., orig. N.Amer.: perh. f. Can.F *chantier*]
■ **1** see HUT *n.* **2** see SHACK *n.* □ **shanty town** see SLUM *n.* 1.

shanty[2] /shánti/ *n.* (also **chanty**) (*pl.* **-ies**) (in full **sea shanty**) a song with alternating solo and chorus, of a kind orig. sung by sailors while hauling ropes etc. [prob. F *chantez*, imper. pl. of *chanter* sing: see CHANT]

SHAPE /shayp/ *abbr.* Supreme Headquarters Allied Powers Europe.

shape /shayp/ *n.* & *v.* ● *n.* **1** the total effect produced by the outlines of a thing. **2** the external form or appearance of a

shape /shayp/ *n.* & *v.* ● *n.* **1** the total effect produced by the outlines of a thing. **2** the external form or appearance of a person or thing. **3** a specific form or guise. **4** a description or sort or way (*not on offer in any shape or form*). **5** a definite or proper arrangement (*must get our ideas into shape*). **6 a** condition, as qualified in some way (*in good shape*; *in poor shape*). **b** (when unqualified) good condition (*back in shape*). **7** a person or thing as seen, esp. indistinctly or in the imagination (*a shape emerged from the mist*). **8** a mould or pattern. **9** a jelly etc. shaped in a mould. **10** a piece of material, paper, etc., made or cut in a particular form. ● *v.* **1** *tr.* give a certain shape or form to; fashion, create. **2** *tr.* (foll. by *to*) adapt or make conform. **3** *intr.* give signs of a future shape or development. **4** *tr.* frame mentally; imagine. **5** *intr.* assume or develop into a shape. **6** *tr.* direct (one's life, course, etc.). □ **lick** (or **knock** or **whip**) **into shape** make presentable or efficient. **shape up 1** take a (specified) form. **2** show promise; make good progress. **shape up well** be promising. □□ **shapable** *adj.* (also **shapeable**). **shaped** *adj.* (also in *comb.*). **shaper** *n.* [OE *gesceap* creation f. Gmc]

■ *n.* **1, 2** appearance, form, pattern, configuration, structure, aspect, figure, build, body, physique; line(s), profile, silhouette, outline, contour(s). **3** guise, disguise, form, appearance, likeness, image. **4** see DESCRIPTION 2. **5** see ORDER *n.* 1. **6** state, condition, fettle, status, (state of) health, order, trim. ● *v.* **1** form, fashion, mould, cast, make, create, model, sculpture, sculpt; cut, carve, hew, hack, trim; word, express, embody in words, put, formulate. **2** change, modify, remodel, accommodate, fit, adapt, adjust. **3** see *turn out* 9. **4** see IMAGINE 1. **6** determine, control, govern, affect, regulate, condition, influence, decree, frame, define, direct. □ **shape up 1** take form, take shape, develop, evolve, proceed. **2** improve, (make) progress, go *or* move *or* come along, show improvement *or* promise.

shapeless /sháypliss/ *adj.* lacking definite or attractive shape. □□ **shapelessly** *adv.* **shapelessness** *n.*

■ amorphous, formless, nebulous, unformed, indefinite, unstructured, vague; unshapely, deformed, misshapen, distorted, twisted, bent, battered, baggy.

shapely /sháypli/ *adj.* (**shapelier**, **shapeliest**) **1** well formed or proportioned. **2** of elegant or pleasing shape or appearance. □□ **shapeliness** *n.*

■ curvy, comely, well-proportioned, graceful, neat, well turned out, good-looking, pleasing, attractive, *colloq.* curvaceous; voluptuous, sexy.

shard /shaard/ *n.* **1** a broken piece of pottery or glass etc. **2** = POTSHERD. **3** a fragment of volcanic rock. **4** the wing-case of a beetle. [OE *sceard*: sense 3 f. *shard-borne* (Shakesp.) = born in a shard (dial., = cow-dung), wrongly taken as 'borne on shards']

■ **1** see FRAGMENT *n.*

share[1] /shair/ *n.* & *v.* ● *n.* **1** a portion that a person receives from or gives to a common amount. **2 a** a part contributed by an individual to an enterprise or commitment. **b** a part received by an individual from this (*got a large share of the credit*). **3** part-proprietorship of property held by joint owners, esp. any of the equal parts into which a company's capital is divided entitling its owner to a proportion of the profits. ● *v.* **1** *tr.* get or have or give a share of. **2** *tr.* use or benefit from jointly with others. **3** *intr.* have a share; be a sharer (*shall I share with you?*). **4** *intr.* (foll. by *in*) participate. **5** *tr.* (often foll. by *out*) **a** divide and distribute. **b** give away part of. □ **share and share alike** make an equal division. **share-farmer** *Austral.* & *NZ* a tenant farmer who receives a share of the profits from the owner. □□ **shareable** *adj.* (also **sharable**). **sharer** *n.* [ME f. OE *scearu* division, rel. to SHEAR]

■ *n.* **1** portion, allotment, division, apportionment, allocation, ration, appropriation, dispensation, allowance, part, due, percentage, interest, dividend, quota, helping, serving, *colloq.* cut. **2, 3** interest, piece, part, stake, equity, slice. ● *v.* **1, 2, 5** share out, divide up, allot, apportion, allocate, ration, appropriate, share in, split, partition, parcel *or* deal *or* dole out, pay out, *colloq.* divvy (up). **4** (*share in*) see PARTICIPATE.

share[2] /shair/ *n.* = PLOUGHSHARE. [OE *scear*, *scær* f. Gmc]

sharecropper /sháirkroppər/ *n.* esp. *US* a tenant farmer who gives a part of each crop as rent. □□ **sharecrop** *v.tr.* & *intr.* (**-cropped**, **-cropping**).

shareholder /sháirhōldər/ *n.* an owner of shares in a company.

shareware /sháirwair/ *n.* *Computing* software that is developed for sharing free of charge with other computer users rather than for sale.

shariah /shəreéə/ *n.* the Muslim code of religious law. [Arab. *šarī'a*]

sharif /shəreéf/ *n.* (also **shereef**, **sherif**) **1** a descendant of Muhammad through his daughter Fatima, entitled to wear a green turban or veil. **2** a Muslim leader. [Arab. *šarīf* noble f. *šarafa* be exalted]

shark[1] /shaark/ *n.* any of various large usu. voracious marine fish with a long body and prominent dorsal fin. [16th c.: orig. unkn.]

shark[2] /shaark/ *n.* *colloq.* a person who unscrupulously exploits or swindles others. [16th c.: orig. perh. f. G *Schurke* worthless rogue: infl. by SHARK[1]]

■ see *swindler* (SWINDLE).

sharkskin /shaárkskin/ *n.* **1** the skin of a shark. **2** a smooth dull-surfaced fabric.

sharp /shaarp/ *adj.*, *n.*, *adv.*, & *v.* ● *adj.* **1** having an edge or point able to cut or pierce. **2** tapering to a point or edge. **3** abrupt, steep, angular (*a sharp fall*; *a sharp turn*). **4** well-defined, clean-cut. **5 a** severe or intense (*has a sharp temper*). **b** (of food etc.) pungent, keen (*a sharp appetite*). **c** (of a frost) severe, hard. **6** (of a voice or sound) shrill and piercing. **7** (of sand etc.) composed of angular grains. **8** (of words etc.) harsh or acrimonious (*had a sharp tongue*). **9** (of a person) acute; quick to perceive or comprehend. **10** quick to take advantage; artful, unscrupulous, dishonest. **11** vigorous or brisk. **12** *Mus.* **a** above the normal pitch. **b** (of a key) having a sharp or sharps in the signature. **c** (**C**, **F**, etc., **sharp**) a semitone higher than C, F, etc. **13** *colloq.* stylish or flashy with regard to dress. ● *n.* **1** *Mus.* **a** a note raised a semitone above natural pitch. **b** the sign (♯) indicating this. **2** *colloq.* a swindler or cheat. **3** a fine sewing-needle. ● *adv.* **1** punctually (*at nine o'clock sharp*). **2** suddenly, abruptly, promptly (*pulled up sharp*). **3** at a sharp angle. **4** *Mus.* above the true pitch (*sings sharp*). ● *v.* **1** *intr.* *archaic* cheat or swindle at cards etc. **2** *tr.* *US Mus.* make sharp. □ **sharp end** *colloq.* **1** the bow of a ship. **2** the scene of direct action or decision. **sharp-eyed** having good sight; observant. **sharp practice** dishonest or barely honest dealings. **sharp-set 1** set with a sharp edge. **2** hungry. □□ **sharply** *adv.* **sharpness** *n.* [OE *sc(e)arp* f. Gmc]

■ *adj.* **1, 2** acute, keen; razor-sharp, knife-edged, sharpened; pointed. **3** abrupt, sudden, steep, precipitous, sheer, vertical, marked, angular, tight. **4** see DEFINITE 2. **5 a, c** hard, poignant, severe, cutting, intense, sudden, piercing, extreme, keen, acute, fierce. **b** hot, spicy, pungent, piquant, tangy, sour, tart. **6** high-pitched, shrill, penetrating, piercing, strident, harsh, ear-splitting, loud. **8** acid, acidulous, acerbic, harsh, vitriolic, acrimonious, cutting, piquant, biting, bitter, unkind, strict, hurtful, spiteful, virulent, sarcastic, sardonic, trenchant, severe, scathing, malicious, nasty, malignant, venomous, poisonous. **9** acute, keen, keen-witted, keen-minded, sharp-witted, shrewd, intelligent, smart, alert, bright, quick, agile, astute, clever, on the qui vive, penetrating, observant. **10** clever, shrewd, artful, crafty, sly, cunning, foxy, calculating, unscrupulous, dishonest, sneaky, *Brit. sl.* fly. **11** see VIGOROUS 1, 3, 4, BRISK *adj.* 1. **13** chic, dapper, spruce, stylish, smart, fashionable, *colloq.* snappy, natty, classy, nifty, swanky. ● *adv.* **1** precisely, exactly, punctually, on the dot, *esp. US sl.* on the button, on the nose. **2** sharply, abruptly, promptly; see also *suddenly* (SUDDEN). □ **sharp-eyed** keen-sighted, eagle-eyed, hawk-eyed, lynx-eyed; watchful, observant, alert. □□ **sharply** severely, sternly, harshly, cuttingly, acerbically, peremptorily, angrily, strictly, firmly; suddenly, quickly, abruptly, precipitously, precipitately; acutely, distinctly, definitely, definitively.

sharpen /sha'arp'n/ *v.tr.* & *intr.* make or become sharp. □□ **sharpener** *n.*
■ hone, grind, strop, whet; put an edge on.

sharper /sha'arpər/ *n.* a swindler, esp. at cards.
■ see *swindler* (SWINDLE).

sharpish /sha'arpish/ *adj.* & *adv. colloq.* ● *adj.* fairly sharp. ● *adv.* **1** fairly sharply. **2** quite quickly.

sharpshooter /sha'arpshōōtər/ *n.* a skilled marksman. □□ **sharpshooting** *n.* & *adj.*

sharp-witted /sha'arpwittid/ *adj.* keenly perceptive or intelligent. □□ **sharp-wittedly** *adv.* **sharp-wittedness** *n.*
■ see INTELLIGENT 2.

shashlik /sháshlik/ *n.* (in Asia and E. Europe) a kebab of mutton and garnishings. [Russ. *shashlyk*, ult. f. Turk. *šiš* spit, skewer: cf. SHISH KEBAB]

Shasta /shástə/ *n.* (in full **Shasta daisy**) a European plant, *Chrysanthemum maximum*, with large daisy-like flowers. [*Shasta* in California]

Shastra /sha'astrə/ *n.* Hindu sacred writings. [Hindi *śāstr*, Skr. *śāstra*]

shatter /sháttər/ *v.* **1** *tr.* & *intr.* break suddenly in pieces. **2** *tr.* severely damage or utterly destroy (*shattered hopes*). **3** *tr.* greatly upset or discompose. **4** *tr.* (usu. as **shattered** *adj.*) exhaust. □□ **shatterer** *n.* **shattering** *adj.* **shatteringly** *adv.* **shatter-proof** *adj.* [ME, rel. to SCATTER]
■ **1** disintegrate, burst, pulverize, shiver, smash, demolish, break (to smithereens), splinter, fragment, fracture, dash to pieces, disrupt. **2** destroy, ruin, devastate, wreck, dash, crush, demolish, torpedo, undermine, disrupt, blast. **3** upset, disturb, perturb, trouble, discompose, unnerve, overcome, overwhelm, crush, devastate, depress, deject, rattle, shake (up), unsettle, agitate, confound, confuse, stupefy, daze, stun, paralyse, *colloq.* throw. **4** (**shattered**) see *exhausted* (EXHAUST *v.* 2). □□ **shattering** see OVERWHELMING.

shave /shayv/ *v.* & *n.* ● *v.tr.* (*past part.* **shaved** or (as *adj.*) **shaven**) **1** remove (bristles or hair) from the face etc. with a razor. **2** (also *absol.*) remove bristles or hair with a razor from the face etc. of (a person) or (a part of the body). **3 a** reduce by a small amount. **b** take (a small amount) away from. **4** cut thin slices from the surface of (wood etc.) to shape it. **5** pass close to without touching; miss narrowly. ● *n.* **1** an act of shaving or the process of being shaved. **2** a close approach without contact. **3** a narrow miss or escape; = *close shave* (see CLOSE[1]). **4** a tool for shaving wood etc. [OE *sc(e)afan* (sense 4 of noun f. OE *sceafa*) f. Gmc]
■ *v.* **3** trim, clip, crop; pare; snip off. **4** pare (down *or* away), scrape, plane, whittle, shave off, trim.

shaveling /sháyvling/ *n. archaic* **1** a shaven person. **2** a monk, friar, or priest.

shaven see SHAVE.

shaver /sháyvər/ *n.* **1** a person or thing that shaves. **2** an electric razor. **3** *colloq.* a young lad.
■ **3** see LAD 1.

Shavian /sháyviən/ *adj.* & *n.* ● *adj.* of or in the manner of G. B. Shaw, Irish-born dramatist d. 1950, or his ideas. ● *n.* an admirer of Shaw. [*Shavius*, Latinized form of *Shaw*]

shaving /sháyving/ *n.* **1** a thin strip cut off the surface of wood etc. **2** (*attrib.*) used in shaving the face (*shaving-cream*).
■ **1** see SLIVER *n.*

Shavuoth /shəvōōəss, sha'avōō-ót/ *n.* (also **Shavuot**) the Jewish Pentecost. [Heb. *šābû'ôt*, = weeks, with ref. to the weeks between Passover and Pentecost]

shaw /shaw/ *n.* esp. *Brit.* the stalks and leaves of potatoes, turnips, etc. [perh. = SHOW *n.*]

shawl /shawl/ *n.* a piece of fabric, usu. rectangular and often folded into a triangle, worn over the shoulders or head or wrapped round a baby. □ **shawl collar** a rolled collar extended down the front of a garment without lapel notches. □□ **shawled** *adj.* [Urdu etc. f. Pers. *šāl*, prob. f. *Shāliāt* in India]
■ see WRAP *n.* 1.

shawm /shawm/ *n. Mus.* a medieval double-reed wind instrument with a sharp penetrating tone. [ME f. OF *chalemie*, *chalemel*, *chalemeaus* (pl.), ult. f. L *calamus* f. Gk *kalamos* reed]

shchi /shee/ *n.* a Russian cabbage soup. [Russ.]

she /shee/ *pron.* & *n.* ● *pron.* (*obj.* **her**; *poss.* **her**; *pl.* **they**) **1** the woman or girl or female animal previously named or in question. **2** a thing regarded as female, e.g. a vehicle or ship. **3** *Austral.* & *NZ colloq.* it; the state of affairs (*she'll be right*). ● *n.* **1** a female; a woman. **2** (in *comb.*) female (*she-goat*). □ **she-devil** a malicious or spiteful woman. [ME *scæ*, *sche*, etc., f. OE fem. demonstr. pron. & adj. *sīo*, *sēo*, acc. *sīe*]
■ □ **she-devil** see FURY 5.

s/he *pron.* a written representation of 'he or she' used to indicate both sexes.

shea /shee/ *n.* a W. African tree, *Vitellaria paradoxa*, bearing nuts containing a large amount of fat. □ **shea-butter** a butter made from this fat. [Mandingo *si*, *se*, *sye*]

sheading /sheéding/ *n.* each of the six administrative divisions of the Isle of Man. [SHED[1] + -ING[1]]

sheaf /sheef/ *n.* & *v.* ● *n.* (*pl.* **sheaves** /sheevz/) a group of things laid lengthways together and usu. tied, esp. a bundle of cornstalks tied after reaping, or a collection of papers. ● *v.tr.* make into sheaves. [OE *scēaf* f. Gmc (as SHOVE)]
■ *n.* see BUNDLE *n.* 1.

shealing var. of SHIELING.

shear /sheer/ *v.* & *n.* ● *v.* (*past* **sheared**, *archaic* except *Austral.* & *NZ* **shore** /shor/; *past part.* **shorn** /shorn/ or **sheared**) **1** *tr.* cut with scissors or shears etc. **2** *tr.* remove or take off by cutting. **3** *tr.* clip the wool off (a sheep etc.). **4** *tr.* (foll. by *of*) **a** strip bare. **b** deprive. **5** *tr.* & *intr.* (often foll. by *off*) distort or be distorted, or break, from a structural strain. ● *n.* **1** *Mech.* & *Geol.* a strain produced by pressure in the structure of a substance, when its layers are laterally shifted in relation to each other. **2** (in *pl.*) (also **pair of shears** *sing.*) a large clipping or cutting instrument shaped like scissors for use in gardens etc. □□ **shearer** *n.* [OE *sceran* f. Gmc]
■ *v.* **1–3** see CUT *v.* 3a. **4 a** see STRIP *v.* 1. ● *n.* **2** (*shears*) see SNIP *n.* 4.

shearling /sheérling/ *n.* **1** a sheep that has been shorn once. **2** wool from a shearling.

shearwater /sheérwawtər/ *n.* **1** any long-winged sea bird of the genus *Puffinus*, usu. flying near the surface of the water. **2** = SKIMMER 4.

sheatfish /sheétfish/ *n.* (*pl.* same or **sheatfishes**) a large freshwater catfish, *Silurus glanis*, native to European waters. [earlier *sheath-fish*, prob. after G *Scheid*]

sheath /sheeth/ *n.* (*pl.* **sheaths** /sheethz, sheeths/) **1** a close-fitting cover, esp. for the blade of a knife or sword. **2** a condom. **3** *Bot.*, *Anat.*, & *Zool.* an enclosing case or tissue. **4** the protective covering round an electric cable. **5** a woman's close-fitting dress. □ **sheath knife** a dagger-like knife carried in a sheath. □□ **sheathless** *adj.* [OE *scǣth*, *scēath*]

sheathe /sheeth/ *v.tr.* **1** put into a sheath. **2** encase; protect with a sheath. [ME f. SHEATH]
■ see COVER *v.* 3a.

sheathing /sheéthing/ *n.* a protective casing or covering.

sheave[1] /sheev/ *v.tr.* make into sheaves.

sheave[2] /sheev/ *n.* a grooved wheel in a pulley-block etc., for a rope to run on. [ME f. OE *scīfe* (unrecorded) f. Gmc]
■ see TACKLE *n.* 2.

sheaves *pl.* of SHEAF.

shebang /shibáng/ *n. US sl.* **1** a matter or affair (esp. *the whole shebang*). **2** a shed or hut. [19th c.: orig. unkn.]

shebeen /shibeén/ *n.* esp. *Ir.* an unlicensed house selling alcoholic liquor. [Anglo-Ir. *sībín* f. *séibe* mugful]

shed[1] /shed/ *n.* **1** a one-storeyed structure usu. of wood for storage or shelter for animals etc., or as a workshop. **2** a large roofed structure with one side open, for storing or maintaining machinery etc. **3** *Austral.* & *NZ* an open-sided building for shearing sheep or milking cattle. [app. var. of SHADE]
▪ **1** hut, shack, stall, booth, cote, hutch.

shed[2] /shed/ *v.tr.* (**shedding**; *past* and *past part.* **shed**) **1** let or cause to fall off (*trees shed their leaves*). **2** take off (clothes). **3** reduce (an electrical power load) by disconnection etc. **4** cause to fall or flow (*shed blood*; *shed tears*). **5** disperse, diffuse, radiate (*shed light*). □ **shed light on** see LIGHT[1]. [OE *sc(e)adan* f. Gmc]
▪ **1** let fall, drop, spill, scatter; moult, cast. **2** take off, remove, strip, cast, discard, divest oneself of, *literary* doff. **4** spill, drop, pour out *or* forth, discharge, emit, emanate. **5** disperse, diffuse, dissipate, radiate, spread; emanate, emit, send forth *or* out.

she'd /sheed, shid/ *contr.* **1** she had. **2** she would.

shedder /shéddər/ *n.* **1** a person or thing that sheds. **2** a female salmon after spawning.

shedhand /shédhand/ *n. Austral.* & *NZ* an unskilled assistant in a shearing shed.

sheen /sheen/ *n.* **1** a gloss or lustre on a surface. **2** radiance, brightness. □□ **sheeny** *adj.* [obs. *sheen* beautiful, resplendent f. OE *scēne*: sense assim. to SHINE]
▪ shine, gleam, polish, lustre, shininess, burnish, brightness, gloss, glow, glimmer, shimmer, radiance, glint, dazzle.

sheep /sheep/ *n.* (*pl.* same) **1** any ruminant mammal of the genus *Ovis* with a thick woolly coat, esp. kept in flocks for its wool or meat, and noted for its timidity. **2** a bashful, timid, or silly person. **3** (usu. in *pl.*) **a** a member of a minister's congregation. **b** a parishioner. □ **separate the sheep from the goats** divide into superior and inferior groups (cf. Matt. 25:33). **sheep-dip 1** a preparation for cleansing sheep of vermin or preserving their wool. **2** the place where sheep are dipped in this. **sheep-run** an extensive sheepwalk, esp. in Australia. **sheep's-bit** a plant, *Jasione montana*, resembling a scabious. □□ **sheeplike** *adj.* [OE *scēp*, *scǣp*, *scēap*]
▪ **1** *Austral. colloq.* jumbuck, *joc.* mutton.

sheepdog /sheépdog/ *n.* **1** a dog trained to guard and herd sheep. **2 a** a dog of various breeds suitable for this. **b** any of these breeds.

sheepfold /sheépfōld/ *n.* an enclosure for penning sheep.

sheepish /sheépish/ *adj.* **1** bashful, shy, reticent. **2** embarrassed through shame. □□ **sheepishly** *adv.* **sheepishness** *n.*
▪ **1** bashful, shy, reticent, timid, withdrawn, passive, docile, obedient, compliant, sheeplike, manipulable, tractable, pliable, meek, amenable. **2** see SHAMEFACED 1.

sheepshank /sheépshangk/ *n.* a knot used to shorten a rope temporarily.

sheepskin /sheépskin/ *n.* **1** a garment or rug of sheep's skin with the wool on. **2** leather from a sheep's skin used in bookbinding.

sheepwalk /sheépwawk/ *n. Brit.* a tract of land on which sheep are pastured.

sheer[1] /sheer/ *adj.* & *adv.* ● *adj.* **1** no more or less than; mere, unqualified, absolute (*sheer luck*; *sheer determination*). **2** (of a cliff or ascent etc.) perpendicular; very steep. **3** (of a textile) very thin; diaphanous. ● *adv.* **1** directly, outright. **2** perpendicularly. □□ **sheerly** *adv.* **sheerness** *n.* [ME *schere* prob. f. dial. *shire* pure, clear f. OE *scīr* f. Gmc]
▪ *adj.* **1** absolute, unmitigated, unqualified, downright, out-and-out, unalloyed, unadulterated, pure, unmixed, plain, simple, mere, rank, total, complete, arrant, thorough, thoroughgoing, utter. **2** steep, precipitous, abrupt, perpendicular, bluff, vertical. **3** transparent, see-through, thin, diaphanous, filmy, gauzy, gossamer, translucent, peekaboo.

sheer[2] /sheer/ *v.* & *n.* ● *v.intr.* **1** esp. *Naut.* swerve or change course. **2** (foll. by *away*, *off*) go away, esp. from a person or topic one dislikes or fears. ● *n. Naut.* a deviation from a course. [perh. f. MLG *scheren* = SHEAR *v.*]

sheer[3] /sheer/ *n.* the upward slope of a ship's lines towards the bow and stern. [prob. f. SHEAR *n.*]

sheerlegs /sheérlegz/ *n.pl.* (treated as *sing.*) a hoisting apparatus made from poles joined at or near the top and separated at the bottom for masting ships, installing engines, etc. [*sheer*, var. of SHEAR *n.* + LEG]

sheet[1] /sheet/ *n.* & *v.* ● *n.* **1** a large rectangular piece of cotton or other fabric, used esp. in pairs as inner bedclothes. **2 a** a broad usu. thin flat piece of material (e.g. paper or metal). **b** (*attrib.*) made in sheets (*sheet iron*). **3** a wide continuous surface or expanse of water, ice, flame, falling rain, etc. **4** a set of unseparated postage stamps. **5** *derog.* a newspaper, esp. a disreputable one. **6** a complete piece of paper of the size in which it was made, for printing and folding as part of a book. ● *v.* **1** *tr.* provide or cover with sheets. **2** *tr.* form into sheets. **3** *intr.* (of rain etc.) fall in sheets. □ **sheet lightning** a lightning flash with its brightness diffused by reflection. **sheet metal** metal formed into thin sheets by rolling, hammering, etc. **sheet music** music published in cut or folded sheets, not bound. [OE *scēte*, *scīete* f. Gmc]
▪ *n.* **2a, 3** pane, panel, plate, slab; lamina, lamination, layer, stratum, veneer, membrane; area, expanse, stretch, film, coat, coating, covering, blanket, cover, surface, skin. **5** newspaper, journal, paper, tabloid, gazette, daily, weekly, monthly, *derog.* rag. **6** leaf, folio, page.

sheet[2] /sheet/ *n.* **1** a rope or chain attached to the lower corner of a sail for securing or controlling it. **2** (in *pl.*) the space at the bow or stern of an open boat. □ **flowing sheets** sheets eased for free movement in the wind. **sheet anchor** **1** a second anchor for use in emergencies. **2** a person or thing depended on in the last resort. **sheet bend** a method of temporarily fastening one rope through the loop of another. [ME f. OE *scēata*, ON *skaut* (as SHEET[1])]

sheeting /sheéting/ *n.* material for making bed linen.

sheikh /shayk/ *n.* (also **shaikh**, **sheik**) **1** a chief or head of an Arab tribe, family, or village. **2** a Muslim leader. □□ **sheikhdom** *n.* [ult. f. Arab. *šayḵ* old man, sheikh, f. *šāḵa* be or grow old]

sheila /sheélə/ *n. Austral.* & *NZ sl.* a girl or young woman. [orig. *shaler* (of unkn. orig.): assim. to the name *Sheila*]
▪ see GIRL 2.

shekel /shékk'l/ *n.* **1** the chief monetary unit of modern Israel. **2** *hist.* a silver coin and unit of weight used in ancient Israel and the Middle East. **3** (in *pl.*) *colloq.* money; riches. [Heb. *šeḵel* f. *šāḵal* weigh]
▪ **3** (*shekels*) see MONEY 1, 3.

shelduck /shélduk/ *n.* (*pl.* same or **shelducks**; *masc.* **sheldrake**, *pl.* same or **sheldrakes**) any bright-plumaged coastal wild duck of the genus *Tadorna*, esp. *T. tadorna*. [ME prob. f. dial. *sheld* pied, rel. to MDu. *schillede* variegated, + DUCK[1], DRAKE]

shelf[1] /shelf/ *n.* (*pl.* **shelves** /shelvz/) **1 a** a thin flat piece of wood or metal etc. projecting from a wall, or as part of a unit, used to support books etc. **b** a flat-topped recess in a wall etc. used for supporting objects. **2 a** a projecting horizontal ledge in a cliff face etc. **b** a reef or sandbank under water. **c** = *continental shelf*. □ **on the shelf 1** (of a woman) past the age when she might expect to be married. **2** (esp. of a retired person) no longer active or of use. **shelf-life** the amount of time for which a stored item of food etc. remains usable. **shelf-mark** a notation on a book showing its place in a library. **shelf-room** available space on a shelf. □□ **shelved** /shelvd/ *adj.* **shelfful** *n.* (*pl.* **-fuls**). **shelflike** *adj.* [ME f. (M)LG *schelf*, rel. to OE *scylfe* partition, *scylf* crag]
▪ **1** see LEDGE. **2 a** see OVERHANG *n.* **b** see SHALLOW *n.*

shelf[2] /shelf/ *n.* & *v. Austral. sl.* ● *n.* an informer. ● *v.tr.* inform upon. [20th c.: orig. uncert.]

■ *n.* see INFORMER 1. ● *v.* see INFORM 2.

shell /shel/ *n.* & *v.* ● *n.* **1 a** the hard outer case of many marine molluscs (*cockle shell*). **b** the esp. hard but fragile outer covering of a bird's, reptile's, etc. egg. **c** the usu. hard outer case of a nut-kernel, seed, etc. **d** the carapace of a tortoise, turtle, etc. **e** the wing-case or pupa-case of many insects etc. **2 a** an explosive projectile or bomb for use in a big gun or mortar. **b** a hollow metal or paper case used as a container for fireworks, explosives, cartridges, etc. **c** *US* a cartridge. **3** a mere semblance or outer form without substance. **4** any of several things resembling a shell in being an outer case, esp.: **a** a light racing-boat. **b** a hollow pastry case. **c** the metal framework of a vehicle body etc. **d** the walls of an unfinished or gutted building, ship, etc. **e** an inner or roughly-made coffin. **f** a building shaped like a conch. **g** the handguard of a sword. **5** a group of electrons with almost equal energy in an atom. ● *v.* **1** *tr.* remove the shell or pod from. **2** *tr.* bombard (a town, troops, etc.) with shells. **3** *tr.* provide or cover with a shell or shells. **4** *intr.* (usu. foll. by *off*) (of metal etc.) come off in scales. **5** *intr.* (of a seed etc.) be released from a shell. □ **come out of one's shell** cease to be shy; become communicative. **shell-bit** a gouge-shaped boring bit. **shell company** an unimportant firm made the subject of a take-over bid because of its status on the Stock Exchange etc. **shell egg** an egg still in its shell, not dried etc. **shell-heap** (or **-mound**) *hist.* a kitchen midden. **shell-jacket** an army officer's tight-fitting undress jacket reaching to the waist. **shell-lime** fine quality lime produced by burning sea shells. **shell-money** shells used as a medium of exchange, e.g. wampum. **shell out** (also *absol.*) *colloq.* **1** pay (money). **2** hand over (a required sum). **shell-out** *n.* **1** the act of shelling out. **2** a game of snooker etc. played by three or more people. **shell-pink** a delicate pale pink. **shell-shock** a nervous breakdown resulting from exposure to battle. **shell-shocked** suffering from shell-shock. **shell suit** a track suit with a soft lining and a weatherproof nylon outer 'shell', used for leisure wear. **shell-work** ornamentation consisting of shells cemented on to wood etc. □□ **shelled** *adj.* **shell-less** *adj.* **shell-like** *adj.* **shellproof** *adj.* (in sense 2a of *n.*). **shelly** *adj.* [OE *sc(i)ell* f. Gmc: cf. SCALE[1]]

■ *n.* **1** case, cover, covering, shield; armour, carapace, integument, pellicle, wing-case, pupa-case, cocoon; shuck, husk, rind, crust, pod. **2** cartridge, projectile, shot, bomb; case, casing. **3** see FRONT *n.* 5b. **4 c, d** exterior, outside, façade, framework, frame, chassis, external(s), skeleton, hull. ● *v.* **1** husk, peel, hull, decorticate, *US* shuck. **2** fire on *or* upon, bombard, cannonade. □ **shell out** pay out, give out, disburse, spend, expend, lay out, *US* ante up, *Brit. colloq.* stump up, *sl.* fork out *or* up; hand over, hand out, *sl.* dish out.

she'll /sheel, shil/ *contr.* she will; she shall.

shellac /shəlák/ *n.* & *v.* ● *n.* lac resin melted into thin flakes and used for making varnish (cf. LAC[1]). ● *v.tr.* (**shellacked, shellacking**) **1** varnish with shellac. **2** *US sl.* defeat or thrash soundly. [SHELL + LAC, transl. F *laque en écailles* lac in thin plates]

■ *n.* see GLAZE *n.* ● *v.* **1** see GLAZE *v.* 6. **2** see BEAT *v.* 3a.

shellback /shélbak/ *n. sl.* an old sailor.

■ see SAILOR.

shellfish /shélfish/ *n.* **1** an aquatic shelled mollusc, e.g. an oyster, winkle, etc. **2** a crustacean, e.g. a crab, shrimp, etc.

Shelta /shéltə/ *n.* an ancient hybrid secret language used by Irish tinkers, gypsies, etc. [19th c.: orig. unkn.]

shelter /shéltər/ *n.* & *v.* ● *n.* **1** anything serving as a shield or protection from danger, bad weather, etc. **2 a** a place of refuge provided esp. for the homeless etc. **b** *US* an animal sanctuary. **3** a shielded condition; protection (*took shelter under a tree*). ● *v.* **1** *tr.* act or serve as shelter to; protect; conceal; defend (*sheltered them from the storm; had a sheltered upbringing*). **2** *intr.* & *refl.* find refuge; take cover (*sheltered under a tree; sheltered themselves behind the wall*). □ **shelter-belt** a line of trees etc. planted to protect crops from the wind. □□ **shelterer** *n.* **shelterless** *adj.* [16th c.: perh. f. obs. *sheltron* phalanx f. OE *scieldtruma* (as SHIELD, *truma* troop)]

■ *n.* **1, 3** protection, cover, shield, refuge, asylum, sanctuary, haven, safety, security; covering, concealment, screen, umbrella. **2 a** habitation, home, housing, accommodation, hostel, *formal* dwelling(-place), *Austral. sl.* kipsie. ● *v.* **1** protect, screen, shield, defend, safeguard, guard, keep, secure, harbour, conceal. **2** seek *or* take *or* find refuge *or* shelter *or* cover, lie low, *US colloq.* hole up.

sheltie /shélti/ *n.* (also **shelty**) (*pl.* **-ies**) a Shetland pony or sheepdog. [prob. repr. ON *Hjalti* Shetlander, as pronounced in Orkney]

shelve[1] /shelv/ *v.tr.* **1** put (books etc.) on a shelf. **2 a** abandon or defer (a plan etc.). **b** remove (a person) from active work etc. **3** fit (a cupboard etc.) with shelves. □□ **shelver** *n.* **shelving** *n.* [*shelves* pl. of SHELF]

■ **2 a** postpone, defer, put off *or* aside, pigeon-hole, table, lay aside, hold in abeyance, *colloq.* put on ice; abandon.

shelve[2] /shelv/ *v.intr.* (of ground etc.) slope in a specified direction (*land shelved away to the horizon*). [perh. f. *shelvy* (adj.) having underwater reefs f. *shelve* (n.) ledge, f. SHELVE[1]]

shelves *pl.* of SHELF.

shemozzle /shimózz'l/ *n.* (also **schemozzle**) *sl.* **1** a brawl or commotion. **2** a muddle. [Yiddish after LHeb. *šel-lō'-mazzāl* of no luck]

shenanigan /shinánnigən/ *n.* (esp. in *pl.*) *colloq.* **1** high-spirited behaviour; nonsense. **2** trickery; dubious manoeuvres. [19th c.: orig. unkn.]

■ **1** (*shenanigans*) see HANKY-PANKY 1.

Sheol /shée-ōl, -ol/ *n.* the Hebrew underworld abode of the dead. [Heb. *šᵉ'ôl*]

■ see HELL 1.

shepherd /shéppərd/ *n.* & *v.* ● *n.* **1** (*fem.* **shepherdess** /shéppədiss/) a person employed to tend sheep, esp. at pasture. **2** a member of the clergy etc. who cares for and guides a congregation. ● *v.tr.* **1 a** tend (sheep etc.) as a shepherd. **b** guide (followers etc.). **2** marshal or drive (a crowd etc.) like sheep. □ **the Good Shepherd** Christ. **shepherd dog** a sheepdog. **shepherd's crook** a staff with a hook at one end used by shepherds. **shepherd's needle** a white-flowered common plant, *Scandix pecten-veneris*, with spiny fruit. **shepherd's pie** a dish of minced meat under a layer of mashed potato. **shepherd's plaid 1** a small black and white check pattern. **2** woollen cloth with this pattern. **shepherd's purse** a white-flowered hairy cornfield plant, *Capsella bursa-pastoris*, with triangular or cordate pods. [OE *scēaphierde* (as SHEEP, HERD)]

■ *v.* **1** see TEND[2] 1. **1b, 2** lead, convoy, escort, conduct, guide, usher, marshal, drive, take, pursue.

sherardize /shérrərdīz/ *v.tr.* (also **-ise**) coat (iron or steel) with zinc by heating in contact with zinc dust. [*Sherard* Cowper-Coles, Engl. inventor d. 1936]

Sheraton /shérrət'n/ *n.* (often *attrib.*) a style of furniture introduced in England *c.*1790, with delicate and graceful forms. [T. *Sheraton*, Engl. furniture-maker d. 1806]

sherbet /shérbət/ *n.* **1 a** a flavoured sweet effervescent powder or drink. **b** *US* a water-ice. **2** a cooling drink of sweet diluted fruit-juices esp. in Arab countries. **3** *Austral. joc.* beer. [Turk. *şerbet*, Pers. *šerbet* f. Arab. *šarba* drink f. *šariba* to drink: cf. SHRUB[2], SYRUP]

sherd /sherd/ *n.* = POTSHERD. [var. of SHARD]

shereef (also **sherif**) var. of SHARIF.

sheriff /shérrif/ *n.* **1** *Brit.* **a** (also **High Sheriff**) the chief executive officer of the Crown in a county, administering justice etc. **b** an honorary officer elected annually in some towns. **2** *US* an elected officer in a county, responsible for keeping the peace. □ **sheriff court** *Sc.* a county court. **sheriff-depute** *Sc.* the chief judge of a county or district. □□ **sheriffalty** *n.* (*pl.* **-ies**). **sheriffdom** *n.* **sheriffhood** *n.* **sheriffship** *n.* [OE *scīr-gerēfa* (as SHIRE, REEVE[1])]

Sherpa /shérpə/ *n.* (*pl.* same or **Sherpas**) **1** a Himalayan people living on the borders of Nepal and Tibet, and skilled in mountaineering. **2** a member of this people. [native name]

sherry /shérri/ *n.* (*pl.* **-ies**) **1** a fortified wine orig. from S. Spain. **2** a glass of this. □ **sherry cobbler** see COBBLER 2. **sherry-glass** a small wineglass used for sherry. [earlier *sherris* f. Sp. (*vino de*) *Xeres* (now Jerez de la Frontera) in Andalusia]

she's /sheez, shiz/ *contr.* **1** she is. **2** she has.

Shetlander /shétləndər/ *n.* a native of the Shetland Islands, NNE of the mainland of Scotland.

Shetland lace /shétlənd/ *n.* openwork woollen trimming.

Shetland pony /shétlənd/ *n.* **1** a pony of a small hardy rough-coated breed. **2** this breed.

Shetland sheepdog /shétlənd/ *n.* **1** a small dog of a collie-like breed. **2** this breed.

Shetland wool /shétlənd/ *n.* a fine loosely twisted wool from Shetland sheep.

sheva var. of SCHWA.

shew *archaic* var. of SHOW.

shewbread /shṓbred/ *n.* twelve loaves that were displayed in a Jewish temple and renewed each sabbath.

Shiah /shée̋ə/ *n.* one of the two main branches of Islam, esp. in Iran, that rejects the first three Sunni Caliphs and regards Ali as Muhammad's first successor. [Arab. *šī'a* party (of Ali, Muhammad's cousin and son-in-law)]

shiatsu /shiátsoo/ *n.* a kind of therapy of Japanese origin, in which pressure is applied with the fingers to certain points of the body. [Jap., = finger pressure]

shibboleth /shíbbəleth/ *n.* a long-standing formula, doctrine, or phrase, etc., held to be true by a party or sect (*must abandon outdated shibboleths*). [ME f. Heb. *šibbōleṯ* ear of corn, used as a test of nationality for its difficult pronunciation (Judg. 12:6)]

■ byword, watchword, password, catchword, catch-phrase, buzz-word; *colloq.* sacred cow; see also FORMULA 3b, DOCTRINE 2.

shicer /shī́sər/ *n. Austral.* **1** *Mining* an unproductive claim or mine. **2** *sl.* **a** a swindler, welsher, or cheat. **b** a worthless thing; a failure. [G *Scheisser* contemptible person]

■ **2 a** see *swindler* (SWINDLE). **b** see *wash-out* 1.

shicker /shíkkər/ *adj.* (also **shickered** /shíkkərd/) *Austral.* & *NZ sl.* drunk. [Yiddish *shiker* f. Heb. *šikkôr* f. *šākar* be drunk]

■ see DRUNK *adj.* 1.

shield /sheeld/ *n.* & *v.* ● *n.* **1 a** esp. *hist.* a piece of armour of esp. metal, carried on the arm or in the hand to deflect blows from the head or body. **b** a thing serving to protect (*insurance is a shield against disaster*). **2** a thing resembling a shield, esp.: **a** a trophy in the form of a shield. **b** a protective plate or screen in machinery etc. **c** a shieldlike part of an animal, esp. a shell. **d** a similar part of a plant. **e** *Geol.* a large rigid area of the earth's crust, usu. of Precambrian rock, which has been unaffected by later orogenic episodes. **f** *US* a policeman's shield-shaped badge. **3** *Heraldry* a stylized representation of a shield used for displaying a coat of arms etc. ● *v.tr.* protect or screen, esp. from blame or lawful punishment. □ **shield fern 1** any common fern of the genus *Polystichum*, with shield-shaped indusia. **2** = BUCKLER 2. □□ **shieldless** *adj.* [OE *sc(i)eld* f. Gmc: prob. orig. = board, rel. to SCALE[1]]

■ *n.* **1 b** protection, guard, safeguard, defence, screen, bulwark, shelter. **2 c, d** see SHELL *n.* 1. ● *v.* protect, guard, safeguard, keep, defend, screen, shelter.

shieling /sheéling/ *n.* (also **shealing**) *Sc.* **1** a roughly constructed hut orig. esp. for pastoral use. **2** pasture for cattle. [Sc. *shiel* hut: ME, of unkn. orig.]

shier *compar.* of SHY[1].

shiest *superl.* of SHY[1].

shift /shift/ *v.* & *n.* ● *v.* **1** *intr.* & *tr.* change or move or cause to change or move from one position to another. **2** *tr.* remove, esp. with effort (*washing won't shift the stains*). **3** *sl.* **a** *intr.* hurry (*we'll have to shift!*). **b** *tr.* consume (food or drink) hastily or in bulk. **c** *tr.* sell (esp. dubious goods). **4** *intr.* contrive or manage as best one can. **5** *US* **a** *tr.* change (gear) in a vehicle. **b** *intr.* change gear. **6** *intr.* (of cargo) get shaken out of place. **7** *intr. archaic* be evasive or indirect. ● *n.* **1 a** the act or an instance of shifting. **b** the substitution of one thing for another; a rotation. **2 a** a relay of workers (*the night shift*). **b** the time for which they work (*an eight-hour shift*). **3 a** a device, stratagem, or expedient. **b** a dodge, trick, or evasion. **4 a** a woman's straight unwaisted dress. **b** *archaic* a loose-fitting undergarment. **5** a displacement of spectral lines (see also *red shift*). **6** (also **sound shift**) a systematic change in pronunciation as a language evolves. **7** a key on a keyboard used to switch between lower and upper case etc. **8** *Bridge* **a** a change of suit in bidding. **b** *US* a change of suit in play. **9** the positioning of successive rows of bricks so that their ends do not coincide. **10** *US* **a** a gear lever in a motor vehicle. **b** a mechanism for this. □ **make shift** manage or contrive; get along somehow (*made shift without it*). **shift for oneself** rely on one's own efforts. **shift one's ground** take up a new position in an argument etc. **shift off** get rid of (responsibility etc.) to another. □□ **shiftable** *adj.* **shifter** *n.* [OE *sciftan* arrange, divide, etc., f. Gmc]

■ *v.* **1** move, change position, switch; edge, budge; relocate, rearrange, transpose. **2** budge, get rid of; see also REMOVE *v.* 2b. **3 a** see HURRY *v.* 1. **b** see BOLT[1] *v.* 5, SWALLOW *v.* 1. **c** sell, market. **4** manage, make do, scrape by *or* through, *colloq.* get by. **7** see EQUIVOCATE. ● *n.* **1 a** change, movement, switch, transfer, deflection, swerve, veer. **b** see SUBSTITUTE *n.* 1a. **2 a** workforce, relay, crew, staff, squad, team, corps, group, gang; workers. **b** stint. **3 a** see STRATAGEM 1. **b** see TRICK *n.* 1, EVASION 2. **4 a** smock, muu-muu, caftan, *hist.* chemise. **b** *hist.* chemise. □ **make shift** see SHIFT *v.* 4 above. **shift for oneself** fend for oneself, look after oneself, make do (on one's own), take care of oneself, *colloq.* get by (on one's own). **shift one's ground** try another tack, change one's tack, wriggle.

shiftless /shíftliss/ *adj.* lacking resourcefulness; lazy; inefficient. □□ **shiftlessly** *adv.* **shiftlessness** *n.*

■ unambitious, lazy, indolent, idle, lackadaisical, aimless, slothful, unenterprising, inefficient, ineffective, ne'er-do-well, good-for-nothing, fainéant, inactive, uninspired, unmotivated, *archaic* otiose.

shifty /shífti/ *adj. colloq.* (**shiftier, shiftiest**) not straightforward; evasive; deceitful. □□ **shiftily** *adv.* **shiftiness** *n.*

■ tricky, artful, shrewd, canny, cunning, foxy, wily, sharp, devious, slick, evasive, slippery, scheming, designing, conniving, calculating, underhand(ed), conspiratorial, treacherous, traitorous, deceitful, deceiving, duplicitous, two-faced, dishonest, untrustworthy, *colloq.* crooked, *sl.* bent.

shigella /shigéllə/ *n.* any airborne bacterium of the genus *Shigella*, some of which cause dysentery. [mod.L f. K. *Shiga*, Jap. bacteriologist d. 1957 + dimin. suffix]

shih-tzu /sheetsóo/ *n.* **1** a dog of a breed with long silky erect hair and short legs. **2** this breed. [Chin. *shizi* lion]

Shiite /shée-īt/ *n.* & *adj.* ● *n.* an adherent of the Shiah branch of Islam. ● *adj.* of or relating to Shiah. □□ **Shiism** /shée-iz'm/ *n.*

shikar /shikaár/ *n. Ind.* hunting. [Urdu f. Pers. *šikār*]

shiksa /shíksə/ *n.* often *offens.* (used by Jews) a gentile girl or woman. [Yiddish *shikse* f. Heb. *šiqṣâ* f. *šeqeṣ* detested thing + *-â fem. suffix*]

shill /shil/ *n. US* a person employed to decoy or entice others into buying, gambling, etc. [prob. f. earlier *shillaber*, of unkn. orig.]

shillelagh /shiláylə, -li/ *n.* a thick stick of blackthorn or oak used in Ireland esp. as a weapon. [*Shillelagh* in Co. Wicklow, Ireland]

■ see STAFF[1] *n.* 1a, b.

shilling /shílling/ *n.* **1** *hist.* a former British coin and monetary unit worth one-twentieth of a pound or twelve pence. **2** a monetary unit in Kenya, Tanzania, and Uganda. □ **shilling-mark** *hist.* = SOLIDUS. **take the King's** (or

Queen's) shilling *hist.* enlist as a soldier (formerly a soldier was paid a shilling on enlisting). [OE *scilling*, f. Gmc]

shilly-shally /shíllishálli/ *v.*, *adj.*, & *n.* ● *v.intr.* (**-ies, -ied**) hesitate to act or choose; be undecided; vacillate. ● *adj.* vacillating. ● *n.* indecision; vacillation. ▫▫ **shilly-shallyer** *n.* (also **-shallier**). [orig. *shill I, shall I*, redupl. of *shall I?*]
■ *v.* hem and haw, hum and haw, hum and ha, see-saw, yo-yo, vacillate, waver, alternate, fluctuate, dither, falter, tergiversate, *Brit.* haver, *Sc.* swither, *colloq.* dilly-dally; delay, hesitate, dawdle. ● *n.* see INDECISION.

shily var. of SHYLY (see SHY[1]).

shim /shim/ *n.* & *v.* ● *n.* a thin strip of material used in machinery etc. to make parts fit. ● *v.tr.* (**shimmed, shimming**) fit or fill up with a shim. [18th c.: orig. unkn.]

shimmer /shímmər/ *v.* & *n.* ● *v.intr.* shine with a tremulous or faint diffused light. ● *n.* such a light. ▫▫ **shimmeringly** *adv.* **shimmery** *adj.* [OE *scymrian* f. Gmc: cf. SHINE]
■ *v.* shine, gleam, glow, glimmer, glint, glisten, ripple, flicker. ● *n.* shimmering, shine, gleam, glow, glimmer, glint, gloss, flicker, light.

shimmy /shímmi/ *n.* & *v.* ● *n.* (*pl.* **-ies**) **1** *hist.* a kind of ragtime dance in which the whole body is shaken. **2** *archaic colloq.* = CHEMISE. **3** *US* an abnormal vibration of esp. the front wheels of a motor vehicle. ● *v.intr.* (**-ies, -ied**) **1 a** *hist.* dance a shimmy. **b** move in a similar manner. **2** shake or vibrate abnormally. [20th c.: orig. uncert.]
■ *v.* **2** see SHAKE *v.* 1, 2, 5.

shin /shin/ *n.* & *v.* ● *n.* **1** the front of the leg below the knee. **2** a cut of beef from the lower foreleg. ● *v.tr.* & (usu. foll. by *up, down*) *intr.* (**shinned, shinning**) climb quickly by clinging with the arms and legs. ▫ **shin-bone** = TIBIA. **shin-pad** (or **-guard**) a protective pad for the shins, worn when playing football etc. [OE *sinu*]
■ *v.* climb, clamber, scramble, *US colloq.* shinny; (*shin up*) scale.

shindig /shíndig/ *n. colloq.* **1** a festive, esp. noisy, party. **2** = SHINDY 1. [prob. f. SHINDY]
■ **1** see PARTY[1] *n.* 1.

shindy /shíndi/ *n.* (*pl.* **-ies**) *colloq.* **1** a brawl, disturbance, or noise (*kicked up a shindy*). **2** = SHINDIG 1. [perh. alt. of SHINTY]

shine /shīn/ *v.* & *n.* ● *v.* (*past* and *past part.* **shone** /shon/ or **shined**) **1** *intr.* emit or reflect light; be bright; glow (*the lamp was shining; his face shone with gratitude*). **2** *intr.* (of the sun, a star, etc.) not be obscured by clouds etc.; be visible. **3** *tr.* cause (a lamp etc.) to shine. **4** *tr.* (*past* and *past part.* **shined**) make bright; polish (*shined his shoes*). **5** *intr.* be brilliant in some respect; excel (*does not shine in conversation; is a shining example*). ● *n.* **1** light; brightness, esp. reflected. **2** a high polish; lustre. **3** *US* the act or an instance of shining esp. shoes. ▫ **shine up to** *US* seek to ingratiate oneself with. **take the shine out of 1** spoil the brilliance or newness of. **2** throw into the shade by surpassing. **take a shine to** *colloq.* take a fancy to; like. ▫▫ **shiningly** *adv.* [OE *scīnan* f. Gmc]
■ *v.* **1** gleam, glow, shimmer, radiate, beam, glare, flare, glisten, glitter, coruscate, twinkle, sparkle, scintillate, glint, flash, flicker. **4** polish, burnish, rub, buff, brush, brighten. **5** excel, stand out, be brilliant *or* outstanding *or* pre-eminent *or* excellent. ● *n.* **1, 2** gleam, glow, shimmer, sparkle, brightness, radiance, light, gloss, lustre, sheen, glaze. ▫ **shine up to** see INGRATIATE. **take the shine out of 1** see MAR 1. **2** see ECLIPSE *v.* 3. **take a shine to** see LIKE[2] *v.* 1.

shiner /shīnər/ *n.* **1** a thing that shines. **2** *colloq.* a black eye. **3** *US* any of various small silvery freshwater fish, esp. of the genus *Notropis*. **4** (usu. in *pl.*) *sl.* **a** *archaic* money. **b** a jewel.

shingle[1] /shíngg'l/ *n.* (in *sing.* or *pl.*) small rounded pebbles, esp. on a sea-shore. ▫▫ **shingly** *adj.* [16th c.: orig. uncert.]
■ ▫▫ **shingly** see STONY 1.

shingle[2] /shíngg'l/ *n.* & *v.* ● *n.* **1** a rectangular wooden tile used on roofs, spires, or esp. walls. **2** *archaic* **a** shingled hair. **b** the act of shingling hair. **3** *US* a small signboard, esp. of a doctor, lawyer, etc. ● *v.tr.* **1** roof or clad with shingles. **2** *archaic* **a** cut (a woman's hair) very short. **b** cut the hair of (a person or head) in this way. [ME app. f. L *scindula*, earlier *scandula*]
■ *n.* **3** see SIGN *n.* 4.

shingles /shíngg'lz/ *n.pl.* (usu. treated as *sing.*) an acute painful viral inflammation of the nerve ganglia, with a skin eruption often forming a girdle around the middle of the body. [ME f. med.L *cingulus* f. L *cingulum* girdle f. *cingere* gird]

shinny /shínni/ *v.intr.* (**-ies, -ied**) (usu. foll. by *up, down*) *US colloq.* shin (up or down a tree etc.).
■ see SHIN *v.*

Shinto /shíntō/ *n.* the official religion of Japan incorporating the worship of ancestors and nature-spirits. ▫▫ **Shintoism** *n.* **Shintoist** *n.* [Jap. f. Chin. *shen dao* way of the gods]

shinty /shínti/ *n.* (*pl.* **-ies**) *Brit.* **1** a game like hockey played with a ball and curved sticks, and taller goalposts. **2** a stick or ball used in shinty. [earlier *shinny*, app. f. the cry used in the game *shin ye, shin you, shin t' ye*, of unkn. orig.]

shiny /shīni/ *adj.* (**shinier, shiniest**) **1** having a shine; glistening; polished; bright. **2** (of clothing, esp. the seat of trousers etc.) having the nap worn off. ▫▫ **shinily** *adv.* **shininess** *n.* [SHINE]
■ **1** gleaming, glowing, shimmering, glossy, shimmery, lustrous, radiant, bright, beaming, glistening, polished, burnished, glittering, dazzling, coruscating, twinkling, sparkling, scintillating, glinting, flashing, flickering, lambent, *pœt. or rhet.* fulgent.

ship /ship/ *n.* & *v.* ● *n.* **1 a** any large seagoing vessel (cf. BOAT). **b** a sailing-vessel with a bowsprit and three, four, or five square-rigged masts. **2** *US* an aircraft. **3** a spaceship. **4** *colloq.* a boat, esp. a racing-boat. ● *v.* (**shipped, shipping**) **1** *tr.* put, take, or send away (goods, passengers, sailors, etc.) on board ship. **2** *tr.* **a** take in (water) over the side of a ship, boat, etc. **b** take (oars) from the rowlocks and lay them inside a boat. **c** fix (a rudder etc.) in its place on a ship etc. **d** step (a mast). **3** *intr.* **a** take ship; embark. **b** (of a sailor) take service on a ship (*shipped for Africa*). **4** *tr.* deliver (goods) to a forwarding agent for conveyance. ▫ **ship-breaker** a contractor who breaks up old ships. **ship-broker** an agent in shipping goods and insuring ships. **ship burial** *Archaeol.* burial in a wooden ship under a mound. **ship-canal** a canal large enough for ships to pass inland. **ship** (or **ship's**) **chandler** see CHANDLER. **ship-fever** typhus. **ship-money** *hist.* a tax raised to provide ships for the navy in the 17th c. **ship of the desert** the camel. **ship off 1** send or transport by ship. **2** *colloq.* send (a person) away. **ship of the line** *hist.* a large battleship fighting in the front line of battle. **ship-rigged** square-rigged. **ship's articles** the terms on which seamen take service on a ship. **ship's biscuit** *hist.* a hard coarse kind of biscuit kept and eaten on board ship. **ship's boat** a small boat carried on board a ship. **ship's company** a ship's crew. **ship's corporal** see CORPORAL[1] 2. **ship a sea** be flooded by a wave. **ship's husband** an agent appointed by the owners to see to the provisioning of a ship in port. **ship's papers** documents establishing the ownership, nationality, nature of the cargo, etc., of a ship. **take ship** embark. **when a person's ship comes home** (or **in**) when a person's fortune is made. ▫▫ **shipless** *adj.* **shippable** *adj.* [OE *scip*, *scipian* f. Gmc]
■ *n.* **1 a** vessel. ● *v.* **1, 4** send, deliver, dispatch, freight, haul; ferry, transport, carry. **3 a** take ship, embark, set sail, leave, depart. ▫ **ship off 2** see *send off*. **take ship** see SHIP *v.* 3a.

-ship /ship/ *suffix* forming nouns denoting: **1** a quality or condition (*friendship; hardship*). **2** status, office, or honour (*authorship; lordship*). **3** a tenure of office (*chairmanship*). **4** a skill in a certain capacity (*workmanship*). **5** the collective individuals of a group (*membership*). [OE *-scipe* etc. f. Gmc]

shipboard /shípbord/ *n.* (usu. *attrib.*) used or occurring on board a ship (*a shipboard romance*). ▫ **on shipboard** on board ship.

shipbuilder /shípbildər/ *n.* a person, company, etc., that constructs ships. □□ **shipbuilding** *n.*

shiplap /shíplap/ *v.* & *n.* ● *v.tr.* fit (boards) together for cladding etc. so that each overlaps the one below. ● *n.* such cladding.

shipload /shíplōd/ *n.* a quantity of goods forming a cargo.
■ see CARGO.

shipmaster /shípmaastər/ *n.* a ship's captain.

shipmate /shípmayt/ *n.* a fellow member of a ship's crew.

shipment /shípmənt/ *n.* **1** an amount of goods shipped; a consignment. **2** the act or an instance of shipping goods etc.
■ **1** see LOAD *n.* 1. **2** see TRANSPORT *n.* 1a.

shipowner /shíppōnər/ *n.* a person owning a ship or ships or shares in ships.

shipper /shíppər/ *n.* a person or company that sends or receives goods by ship, or *US* by land or air. [OE *scipere* (as SHIP)]
■ see CARRIER 1, 2.

shipping /shípping/ *n.* **1** the act or an instance of shipping goods etc. **2** ships, esp. the ships of a country, port, etc. □ **shipping-agent** a person acting for a ship or ships at a port etc. **shipping-articles** = *ship's articles*. **shipping-bill** *Brit.* a manifest of goods shipped. **shipping-master** *Brit.* an official presiding at the signing of ship's articles, paying off of seamen, etc. **shipping-office** the office of a shipping-agent or -master.
■ **1** see TRANSPORT *n.* 1a.

shipshape /shípshayp/ *adv.* & *predic.adj.* in good order; trim and neat.
■ neat, trim, spotless, orderly, spick and span, tidy, *orig. Naut.* shipshape and Bristol fashion.

shipway /shípway/ *n.* a slope on which a ship is built and down which it slides to be launched.

shipworm /shípwurm/ *n.* = TEREDO.

shipwreck /shíprek/ *n.* & *v.* ● *n.* **1 a** the destruction of a ship by a storm, foundering, etc. **b** a ship so destroyed. **2** (often foll. by *of*) the destruction of hopes, dreams, etc. ● *v.* **1** *tr.* inflict shipwreck on (a ship, a person's hopes, etc.). **2** *intr.* suffer shipwreck.
■ *n.* **1 b** wreck, hulk, ruins. ● *v.* see WRECK *v.*

shipwright /shíprīt/ *n.* **1** a shipbuilder. **2** a ship's carpenter.

shipyard /shípyaard/ *n.* a place where ships are built, repaired, etc.

shiralee /shírrəlee/ *n. Austral.* a tramp's swag or bundle. [20th c.: orig. unkn.]

shire /shīr/ *n. Brit.* **1** a county. **2** (**the Shires**) **a** a group of English counties with names ending or formerly ending in *-shire*, extending NE from Hampshire and Devon. **b** the midland counties of England. **c** the fox-hunting district of mainly Leicestershire and Northants. **3** *Austral.* a rural area with its own elected council. □ **shire-horse** a heavy powerful type of draught-horse bred chiefly in the midland counties of England. [OE *scīr*, OHG *scīra* care, official charge: orig. unkn.]

-shire /shər, sheer/ *suffix* forming the names of counties (*Derbyshire*; *Hampshire*).

shirk /shurk/ *v.* & *n.* ● *v.tr.* (also *absol.*) shrink from; avoid; get out of (duty, work, responsibility, fighting, etc.). ● *n.* a person who shirks. □□ **shirker** *n.* [obs. *shirk* (n.) sponger, perh. f. G *Schurke* scoundrel]
■ *v.* avoid, evade, shun, dodge, get out of, shrink from, *colloq.* duck (out of), *Brit. sl.* skive. ● *n.* see TRUANT *n.* □□ **shirker** see TRUANT *n.*

shirr /shur/ *n.* & *v.* ● *n.* **1** two or more rows of esp. elastic gathered threads in a garment etc. forming smocking. **2** elastic webbing. ● *v.tr.* **1** gather (material) with parallel threads. **2** *US* bake (eggs) without shells. □□ **shirring** *n.* [19th c.: orig. unkn.]
■ *v.* **1** gather, ruffle, pucker.

shirt /shurt/ *n.* **1** a man's upper-body garment of cotton etc., having a collar, sleeves, and esp. buttons down the front, and often worn under a jacket or sweater. **2** a similar garment worn by a woman; a blouse. **3** = NIGHTSHIRT. □ **keep one's shirt on** *colloq.* keep one's temper. **put one's shirt on** *colloq.* bet all one has on; be sure of. **shirt blouse** = sense 2 of *n.* **shirt-dress** = SHIRTWAISTER. **shirt-front** the breast of a shirt, esp. of a stiffened evening shirt. **the shirt off one's back** *colloq.* one's last remaining possessions. **shirt-tail** the lower curved part of a shirt below the waist. □□ **shirted** *adj.* **shirting** *n.* **shirtless** *adj.* [OE *scyrte*, corresp. to ON *skyrta* (cf. SKIRT) f. Gmc: cf. SHORT]

shirtsleeve /shúrtsleev/ *n.* (usu. in *pl.*) the sleeve of a shirt. □ **in shirtsleeves** wearing a shirt with no jacket etc. over it.

shirtwaist /shúrtwayst/ *n.* esp. *US* a woman's blouse resembling a shirt.

shirtwaister /shúrtwaystər/ *n. US* a woman's dress with a bodice like a shirt. [SHIRT, WAIST]

shirty /shúrti/ *adj.* (**shirtier**, **shirtiest**) *colloq.* angry; annoyed. □□ **shirtily** *adv.* **shirtiness** *n.*
■ see CROSS *adj.* 1.

shish kebab /shísh kibáb/ *n.* a dish of pieces of marinated meat and vegetables cooked and served on skewers. [Turk. *şiş kebabı* f. *şiş* skewer, KEBAB roast meat]

shit /shit/ *v.*, *n.*, & *int. coarse sl.* ¶ Usually considered a taboo word. ● *v.* (**shitting**; *past* and *past part.* **shitted** or **shit**) *intr.* & *tr.* expel faeces from the body or cause (faeces etc.) to be expelled. ● *n.* **1** faeces. **2** an act of defecating. **3** a contemptible or worthless person or thing. **4** nonsense. **5** an intoxicating drug, esp. cannabis. ● *int.* an exclamation of disgust, anger, etc. [OE *scītan* (unrecorded) f. Gmc]

shitty /shítti/ *adj.* (**shittier**, **shittiest**) *coarse sl.* **1** disgusting, contemptible. **2** covered with excrement.

Shiva var. of SIVA.

shivaree esp. *US* var. of CHARIVARI.

shiver[1] /shívvər/ *v.* & *n.* ● *v.intr.* **1** tremble with cold, fear, etc. **2** suffer a quick trembling movement of the body; shudder. ● *n.* **1** a momentary shivering movement. **2** (in *pl.*) an attack of shivering, esp. from fear or horror (*got the shivers in the dark*). □□ **shiverer** *n.* **shiveringly** *adv.* **shivery** *adj.* [ME *chivere*, perh. f. *chavele* chatter (as JOWL[1])]
■ *v.* shake, quake, tremble, shudder, quiver, quaver, tremor, oscillate, vibrate. ● *n.* **1** shake, tremble, shudder, quiver, trembling, shivering, tremor, flutter. **2** (*shivers*) trembling, shivering; (*the shivers*) the shakes.

shiver[2] /shívvər/ *n.* & *v.* ● *n.* (esp. in *pl.*) each of the small pieces into which esp. glass is shattered when broken; a splinter. ● *v.tr.* & *intr.* break into shivers. □ **shiver my timbers** a reputed piratical curse. [ME *scifre*, rel. to OHG *scivaro* splinter f. Gmc]
■ *n.* splinter, fragment, piece, shard, chip, sliver. ● *v.* shatter, fragment, splinter, disintegrate, explode, implode, smash (to smithereens).

shivoo /shivóó/ *n. Austral. colloq.* a party or celebration.
■ see PARTY *n.* 1.

shoal[1] /shōl/ *n.* & *v.* ● *n.* **1** a great number of fish swimming together (cf. SCHOOL[2]). **2** a multitude; a crowd (*shoals of letters*). ● *v.intr.* (of fish) form shoals. [prob. re-adoption of MDu. *schōle* SCHOOL[2]]
■ *n.* see SWARM[1] *n.* 1–3.

shoal[2] /shōl/ *n.*, *v.*, & *adj.* ● *n.* **1 a** an area of shallow water. **b** a submerged sandbank visible at low water. **2** (esp. in *pl.*) hidden danger or difficulty. ● *v.* **1** *intr.* (of water) get shallower. **2** *tr.* (of a ship etc.) move into a shallower part of (water). ● *adj. archaic* (of water) shallow. □□ **shoaly** *adj.* [OE *sceald* f. Gmc, rel. to SHALLOW]
■ *n.* **1** see SHALLOW *n.*

shoat /shōt/ *n. US* a young pig, esp. newly weaned. [ME: cf. W.Flem. *schote*]

shock[1] /shok/ *n.* & *v.* ● *n.* **1** a violent collision, impact, tremor, etc. **2** a sudden and disturbing effect on the emotions, physical reactions, etc. (*the news was a great shock*). **3** an acute state of prostration following a wound, pain, etc., esp. when much blood is lost (*died of shock*). **4** = *electric shock*. **5** a disturbance in stability causing fluctuations in an organization, monetary system, etc. ● *v.* **1** *tr.* **a** affect with shock; horrify; outrage; disgust; sadden. **b** (*absol.*) cause shock. **2** *tr.* (esp. in *passive*) affect with an electric or pathological shock. **3** *intr.* experience shock (*I don't shock easily*). **4** *intr. archaic* collide violently. □ **shock absorber** a device on a vehicle etc. for absorbing shocks, vibrations, etc. **shock-brigade** (or **-workers**) a body of esp. voluntary workers in the former USSR engaged in an especially arduous task. **shock stall** excessive strain produced by air resistance on an aircraft approaching the speed of sound. **shock tactics 1** sudden and violent action. **2** *Mil.* a massed cavalry charge. **shock therapy** (or **treatment**) *Psychol.* a method of treating depressive patients by electric shock or drugs inducing coma and convulsions. **shock troops** troops specially trained for assault. **shock wave** a sharp change of pressure in a narrow region travelling through air etc. caused by explosion or by a body moving faster than sound. □□ **shockable** *adj.* **shockability** /shókkəbílliti/ *n.* [F *choc*, *choquer*, of unkn. orig.]

■ *n.* **1** jolt, tremor, collision; see also IMPACT *n.* 1. **2** surprise, thunderbolt, bolt from the blue, bombshell, revelation, jolt, *colloq.* shocker, eye-opener; trauma. ● *v.* **1** horrify, frighten, scare, petrify, traumatize, appal; outrage, disgust, nauseate, repel, revolt, sicken, upset, sadden, disquiet, disturb, perturb, discompose, unsettle, startle, surprise, stagger, jar, jolt, shake (up), astonish, astound; stun, numb, paralyse, daze, stupefy, dumbfound, *colloq.* bowl over, throw, flabbergast, give a person a turn. **3** scare, frighten.

shock[2] /shok/ *n.* & *v.* ● *n.* a group of usu. twelve corn-sheaves stood up with their heads together in a field. ● *v.tr.* arrange (corn) in shocks. [ME, perh. repr. OE *sc(e)oc* (unrecorded)]

shock[3] /shok/ *n.* an unkempt or shaggy mass of hair. [cf. obs. *shock(-dog)*, earlier *shough*, shaggy-haired poodle]

shocker /shókkər/ *n. colloq.* **1** a shocking, horrifying, unacceptable, etc. person or thing. **2** *hist.* a sordid or sensational novel etc. **3** a shock absorber.

■ **1** see TERROR 2, FRIGHT *n.* 2.

shocking /shókking/ *adj.* & *adv.* ● *adj.* **1** causing indignation or disgust. **2** *colloq.* very bad (*shocking weather*). ● *adv. colloq.* shockingly (*shocking bad manners*). □ **shocking pink** a vibrant shade of pink. □□ **shockingly** *adv.* **shockingness** *n.*

■ *adj.* **1** disgusting, revolting, nauseating, nauseous, sickening, repulsive, abominable, hideous, horrible, horrifying, horrific, horrid, foul, loathsome, abhorrent, ghastly, hideous, unspeakable, dreadful, distressing, outrageous, appalling, monstrous, scandalous. **2** see AWFUL 1a, b.

shockproof /shókproof/ *adj.* resistant to the effects of (esp. physical) shock.

shod *past* and *past part.* of SHOE.

shoddy /shóddi/ *adj.* & *n.* ● *adj.* (**shoddier, shoddiest**) **1** trashy; shabby; poorly made. **2** counterfeit. ● *n.* (*pl.* **-ies**) **1** **a** an inferior cloth made partly from the shredded fibre of old woollen cloth. **b** such fibre. **2** any thing of shoddy quality. □□ **shoddily** *adv.* **shoddiness** *n.* [19th c.: orig. dial.]

■ *adj.* **1** shabby, inferior, poor, cheapjack, rubbishy, cheap, pinchbeck, meretricious, tawdry, gaudy, Brummagem, plastic, plasticky, tinsel, tinselly, second-rate, trashy, *colloq.* tatty, *esp. US colloq.* tacky, *sl.* naff. **2** see COUNTERFEIT *adj.* 1.

shoe /shoo/ *n.* & *v.* ● *n.* **1** either of a pair of protective foot-coverings of leather, plastic, etc., having a sturdy sole and, in Britain, not reaching above the ankle. **2** a metal rim nailed to the hoof of a horse etc.; a horseshoe. **3** anything resembling a shoe in shape or use, esp.: **a** a drag for a wheel. **b** = *brake shoe* (see BRAKE[1]). **c** a socket. **d** a ferrule, esp. on a sledge-runner. **e** a mast-step. **f** a box from which cards are dealt in casinos at baccarat etc. ● *v.tr.* (**shoes, shoeing**; *past* and *past part.* **shod** /shod/) **1** fit (esp. a horse etc.) with a shoe or shoes. **2** protect (the end of a pole etc.) with a metal shoe. **3** (as **shod** *adj.*) (in *comb.*) having shoes etc. of a specified kind (*dry-shod*; *roughshod*). □ **be in a person's shoes** be in his or her situation, difficulty, etc. **dead men's shoes** property or a position etc. coveted by a prospective successor. **if the shoe fits** *US* = *if the cap fits* (see CAP). **shoe-bill** an African stork-like bird, *Balaeniceps rex*, with a large flattened bill for catching aquatic prey. **shoe-buckle** a buckle worn as ornament or as a fastening on a shoe. **shoe-leather** leather for shoes, esp. when worn through by walking. **shoe-tree** a shaped block for keeping a shoe in shape when not worn. **where the shoe pinches** where one's difficulty or trouble is. □□ **shoeless** *adj.* [OE *scōh*, *scōg(e)an* f. Gmc]

shoeblack /shooblak/ *n.* a person who cleans the shoes of passers-by for payment.

shoebox /shooboks/ *n.* **1** a box for packing shoes. **2** a very small space or dwelling.

shoehorn /shoohorn/ *n.* a curved piece of horn, metal, etc., for easing the heel into a shoe.

shoelace /shoolayss/ *n.* a cord for lacing up shoes.

■ see LACE *n.* 2.

shoemaker /shoomaykər/ *n.* a maker of boots and shoes. □□ **shoemaking** *n.*

shoeshine /shooshīn/ *n.* esp. *US* a polish given to shoes.

shoestring /shoostring/ *n.* **1** a shoelace. **2** *colloq.* a small esp. inadequate amount of money (*living on a shoestring*). **3** (*attrib.*) barely adequate; precarious (*a shoestring majority*).

■ **1** see LACE *n.* 2.

shofar /shṓfər/ *n.* (*pl.* **shofroth** /shṓfrōt/) a ram's-horn trumpet used by Jews in religious ceremonies and as an ancient battle-signal. [Heb. *šôpār*, pl. *šôpārôt*]

shogun /shṓgoon/ *n. hist.* any of a succession of Japanese hereditary Commanders-in-Chief and virtual rulers before 1868. □□ **shogunate** /-nət/ *n.* [Jap., = general, f. Chin. *jiang jun*]

shone *past* and *past part.* of SHINE.

shonky /shóngki/ *adj.* (**shonkier, shonkiest**) *Austral. sl.* unreliable, dishonest. [perh. E dial. *shonk* smart]

shoo /shoo/ *int.* & *v.* ● *int.* an exclamation used to frighten away birds, children, etc. ● *v.* (**shoos, shooed**) **1** *intr.* utter the word 'shoo!'. **2** *tr.* (usu. foll. by *away*) drive (birds etc.) away by shooing. □ **shoo-in** *US* something easy or certain to succeed. [imit.]

■ *int.* go away, go, away *or* be off (with you), *colloq.* scat, scram, *poet.* begone, *sl.* beat it, get lost. ● *v.* **2** (*shoo away*) scare off, frighten away, drive away, force to leave. □ **shoo-in** see BREEZE[1] *n.* 5.

shook[1] /shook/ *past* of SHAKE. ● *predic.adj. colloq.* **1** (foll. by *up*) emotionally or physically disturbed; upset. **2** (foll. by *on*) *Austral.* & *NZ* keen on; enthusiastic about (*not too shook on the English climate*).

shook[2] /shook/ *n. US* a set of staves and headings for a cask, ready for fitting together. [18th c.: orig. unkn.]

shoot /shoot/ *v.*, *n.*, & *int.* ● *v.* (*past* and *past part.* **shot** /shot/) **1** *tr.* **a** cause (a gun, bow, etc.) to fire. **b** discharge (a bullet, arrow, etc.) from a gun, bow, etc. **c** kill or wound (a person, animal, etc.) with a bullet, arrow, etc. from a gun, bow, etc. **2** *intr.* discharge a gun etc. esp. in a specified way (*shoots well*). **3** *tr.* send out, discharge, propel, etc., esp. violently or swiftly (*shot out the contents*; *shot a glance at his neighbour*). **4** *intr.* (often foll. by *out*, *along*, *forth*, etc.) come or go swiftly or vigorously. **5** *intr.* **a** (of a plant etc.) put forth buds etc. **b** (of a bud etc.) appear. **6** *intr.* **a** hunt game etc. with a gun. **b** (usu. foll. by *over*) shoot game over an estate etc. **7** *tr.* shoot game in or on (coverts, an estate, etc.). **8** *tr.* film or photograph (a scene, film, etc.). **9** *tr.* (also *absol.*) esp. *Football* **a** score (a goal). **b** take a shot at (the goal). **10** *tr.* (of a boat) sweep swiftly down or under (a bridge, rapids, falls, etc.). **11** *tr.* move (a door-bolt) to fasten or unfasten a door etc. **12** *tr.* let (rubbish, a load, etc.) fall or slide from a container, lorry, etc. **13** *intr.* **a** (usu. foll. by *through*, *up*, etc.) (of a pain) pass with a stabbing sensation. **b** (of part of the body) be intermittently painful. **14** *intr.* (often foll. by *out*) project abruptly (*the mountain shoots out against the sky*). **15** *tr.* (often foll. by *up*) *sl.* inject esp. oneself with (a drug). **16** *tr. US colloq.* **a** play a game of (craps, pool, etc.). **b** throw (a die or dice). **17** *tr. Golf colloq.* make (a specified score) for a round or hole. **18** *tr. colloq.* pass (traffic-lights at red). **19** *tr.* plane (the edge of a board) accurately. **20** *intr. Cricket* (of a ball) dart along the ground after pitching. ● *n.* **1** the act or an instance of shooting. **2 a** a young branch or sucker. **b** the new growth of a plant. **3** *Brit.* **a** a hunting party, expedition, etc. **b** land shot over for game. **4** = CHUTE[1]. **5** a rapid in a stream. ● *int. colloq.* **1** a demand for a reply, information, etc. **2** *US euphem.* an exclamation of disgust, anger, etc. (see SHIT). □ **shoot ahead** come quickly to the front of competitors etc. **shoot one's bolt** see BOLT[1]. **shoot down 1** kill (a person) by shooting. **2** cause (an aircraft, its pilot, etc.) to crash by shooting. **3** argue effectively against (a person, argument, etc.). **shoot it out** *sl.* engage in a decisive gun-battle. **shoot a line** *sl.* talk pretentiously. **shoot one's mouth off** *sl.* talk too much or indiscreetly. **shoot-out** *colloq.* a decisive gun battle. **shoot through** *Austral.* & *NZ sl.* depart; escape, abscond. **shoot up 1** grow rapidly, esp. (of a person) grow taller. **2** rise suddenly. **3** terrorize (a district) by indiscriminate shooting. **4** *sl.* = sense 15 of *v.* **the whole shoot** = *the whole shooting match* (see SHOOTING). □□ **shootable** *adj.* [OE *scēotan* f. Gmc: cf. SHEET[1], SHOT[1], SHUT]

■ *v.* **1 b** discharge, fire, let fly, launch, propel, project. **c** wound, hurt, harm, injure; kill, *literary or joc.* slay; gun (down), pot, *colloq.* blast, *sl.* plug. **3** see EJECT 1a, 5. **4** dart, whisk, speed, bolt, run, race, rush, flash, fly, dash, hurtle, streak, scuttle, bound, leap, spring, *colloq.* scoot, zip, whiz. **5** sprout, germinate; grow, spring up; mushroom, develop. **14** stand out, jut out; see also *stick out* (STICK[1]). ● *n.* **2** sprout, stem, bud, branch, offshoot, slip, scion, sucker. ● *int.* **1** *colloq.* spill the beans, spit it out, out with it. **2** damn, blast, *esp. Brit.* bother, *colloq.* hell, *euphem.* sugar. □ **shoot down 3** pull apart, take to pieces; see also ATTACK *v.* 3. **shoot one's mouth off** see PRATTLE *v.* **shoot through** see ESCAPE *v.* 1.

shooter /shōōtər/ *n.* **1** a person or thing that shoots. **2 a** (in *comb.*) a gun or other device for shooting (*peashooter*; *six-shooter*). **b** *sl.* a pistol etc. **3** a player who shoots or is able to shoot a goal in football, netball, etc. **4** *Cricket* a ball that shoots. **5** a person who throws a die or dice.

shooting /shōōting/ *n.* & *adj.* ● *n.* **1** the act or an instance of shooting. **2 a** the right of shooting over an area of land. **b** an estate etc. rented to shoot over. ● *adj.* moving, growing, etc. quickly (*a shooting pain in the arm*). □ **shooting-box** *Brit.* a lodge used by sportsmen in the shooting-season. **shooting-brake** (or **-break**) *Brit.* an estate car. **shooting-coat** (or **-jacket**) a coat designed to be worn when shooting game. **shooting-gallery** a place used for shooting at targets with rifles etc. **shooting-iron** esp. *US colloq.* a firearm. **shooting-range** a ground with butts for rifle practice. **shooting star** a small meteor moving rapidly and burning up on entering the earth's atmosphere. **shooting-stick** a walking-stick with a foldable seat. **shooting war** a war in which there is shooting (opp. *cold war*, *war of nerves* etc.). **the whole shooting match** *colloq.* everything.

■ *n.* **1** see DISCHARGE *n.* 4. ● *adj.* see ACUTE *adj.* 1b. □ **shooting-iron** see PISTOL *n.*

shop /shop/ *n.* & *v.* ● *n.* **1** a building, room, etc., for the retail sale of goods or services (*chemist's shop*; *betting-shop*). **2** a place in which manufacture or repairing is done; a workshop (*engineering-shop*). **3** a profession, trade, business, etc., esp. as a subject of conversation (*talk shop*). **4** *colloq.* an institution, establishment, place of business, etc. ● *v.* (**shopped, shopping**) **1** *intr.* **a** go to a shop or shops to buy goods. **b** *US* = *window-shop*. **2** *tr.* esp. *Brit. sl.* inform against (a criminal etc.). □ **all over the shop** *colloq.* **1** in disorder (*scattered all over the shop*). **2** in every place (*looked for it all over the shop*). **3** wildly (*hitting out all over the shop*). **set up shop** establish oneself in business etc. **shop around** look for the best bargain. **shop assistant** *Brit.* a person who serves customers in a shop. **shop-boy** (or **-girl**) an assistant in a shop. **shop-floor** workers in a factory etc. as distinct from management. **shop-soiled 1** (of an article) soiled or faded by display in a shop. **2** (of a person, idea, etc.) grubby; tarnished; no longer fresh or new. **shop steward** a person elected by workers in a factory etc. to represent them in dealings with management. **shop-window 1** a display window in a shop. **2** an opportunity for displaying skills, talents, etc. **shop-worn** = *shop-soiled*. □□ **shopless** *adj.* **shoppy** *adj.* [ME f. AF & OF *eschoppe* booth f. MLG *schoppe*, OHG *scopf* porch]

■ *n.* **1** boutique, *esp. US* store. **2** workshop, machine shop; see also FACTORY. **4** see ESTABLISHMENT 2a. ● *v.* **2** betray, inform on *or* against, give away, *colloq.* peach on, rat on, blow the whistle on, *sl.* snitch on, *Austral.* & *NZ sl.* put a person's pot on, *US sl.* fink on; see also INFORM 2. □ **all over the shop 1** see *chaotic* (CHAOS). **2** see EVERYWHERE. **shop-soiled 2** see MUSTY 3. **shop-window 2** see OPPORTUNITY.

shopkeeper /shópkeepər/ *n.* the owner and manager of a shop. □□ **shopkeeping** *n.*

■ see TRADESMAN.

shoplifter /shópliftər/ *n.* a person who steals goods while appearing to shop. □□ **shoplifting** *n.*

■ see THIEF. □□ **shoplifting** see THEFT.

shopman /shópmən/ *n.* (*pl.* **-men**) **1** *Brit.* a shopkeeper or shopkeeper's assistant. **2** a workman in a repair shop.

shopper /shóppər/ *n.* **1** a person who makes purchases in a shop. **2** a shopping bag or trolley. **3** *sl.* an informer.

■ **1** client, customer; patron. **3** see INFORMER 1.

shopping /shópping/ *n.* **1** (often *attrib.*) the purchase of goods etc. (*shopping expedition*). **2** goods purchased (*put the shopping on the table*). □ **shopping centre** an area or complex of shops, with associated facilities.

shopwalker /shópwawkər/ *n. Brit.* an attendant in a large shop who directs customers, supervises assistants, etc.

shoran /shóran/ *n.* a system of aircraft navigation using the return of two radar signals by two ground stations. [*sho*rt *ra*nge *n*avigation]

shore[1] /shor/ *n.* **1** the land that adjoins the sea or a large body of water. **2** (usu. in *pl.*) a country; a sea-coast (*often visits these shores*; *on a distant shore*). **3** *Law* land between ordinary high and low water marks. □ **in shore** on the water near or nearer to the shore (cf. INSHORE). **on shore** ashore. **shore-based** operating from a base on shore. **shore leave** *Naut.* **1** permission to go ashore. **2** a period of time ashore. □□ **shoreless** *adj.* **shoreward** *adj.* & *adv.* **shorewards** *adv.* [ME f. MDu., MLG *schōre*, perh. f. the root of SHEAR]

■ **1** see COAST *n.*

shore[2] /shor/ *v.* & *n.* ● *v.tr.* (often foll. by *up*) support with or as if with a shore or shores; hold up. ● *n.* a prop or beam set obliquely against a ship, wall, tree, etc., as a support. □□ **shoring** *n.* [ME f. MDu., MLG *schōre* prop, of unkn. orig.]

■ *v.* see SUPPORT *v.* 1, 2; 4, 6. ● *n.* see PROP[1] *n.* 1.

shore[3] see SHEAR.

shoreline /shórlīn/ *n.* the line along which a stretch of water, esp. a sea or lake, meets the shore.

shoreweed /shórweed/ *n.* a stoloniferous plant, *Littorella uniflora*, growing in shallow water.

shorn *past part.* of SHEAR.

short /short/ *adj.*, *adv.*, *n.*, & *v.* ● *adj.* **1 a** measuring little; not long from end to end (*a short distance*). **b** not long in duration; brief (*a short time ago*; *had a short life*). **c** seeming less than the stated amount (*a few short years of happiness*). **2** of small height; not tall (*a short square tower*; *was shorter than average*). **3 a** (usu. foll. by *of*, *on*) having a partial or total lack; deficient; scanty (*short of spoons*; *is rather short on sense*). **b** *colloq.* having little money. **c** not far-reaching; acting or being near at hand (*within short range*). **4 a** concise; brief (*kept his speech short*). **b** curt; uncivil (*was short with her*). **5** (of the memory) unable to remember distant events. **6** *Phonet.* & *Prosody* of a vowel or syllable: **a** having the lesser of the two recognized durations. **b** unstressed. **c** (of an English vowel) having a sound other than that called long (cf. LONG[1] *adj.* 8). **7 a** (of pastry) crumbling; not holding together. **b** (of clay) having poor plasticity. **8** esp. *Stock Exch.* **a** (of stocks, a stockbroker, crops, etc.) sold or selling when the amount is not in hand, with reliance on getting the deficit in time for delivery. **b** (of a bill of exchange) maturing at an early date. **9** *Cricket* **a** (of a ball) pitching relatively near the bowler. **b** (of a fielder or his position) relatively near the batsman. **10** (of a drink of spirits) undiluted. ● *adv.* **1** before the natural or expected time or place; abruptly (*pulled up short*; *cut short the celebrations*). **2** rudely; uncivilly (*spoke to him short*). ● *n.* **1** *colloq.* a short drink, esp. spirits. **2** a short circuit. **3** a short film. **4** *Stock Exch.* **a** a person who sells short. **b** (in *pl.*) short-dated stocks. **5** *Phonet.* **a** a short syllable or vowel. **b** a mark indicating that a vowel is short. **6** (in *pl.*) a mixture of bran and coarse flour. ● *v.tr.* & *intr.* short-circuit. □ **be caught** (or **taken**) **short 1** be put at a disadvantage. **2** *colloq.* urgently need to urinate or defecate. **bring up** (or **pull up**) **short** check or pause abruptly. **come short** be inadequate or disappointing. **come short of** fail to reach or amount to. **for short** as a short name (*Tom for short*). **get** (or **have**) **by the short hairs** *colloq.* be in complete control of (a person). **go short** (often foll. by *of*) not have enough. **in short** to use few words; briefly. **in short order** *US* immediately. **in the short run** over a short period of time. **in short supply** scarce. **in the short term** = *in the short run.* **make short work of** accomplish, dispose of, destroy, consume, etc. quickly. **short and sweet** esp. *iron.* brief and pleasant. **short-arm** (of a blow etc.) delivered with the arm not fully extended. **short back and sides** a haircut in which the hair is cut short at the back and the sides. **short change** insufficient money given as change. **short-change** *v.tr.* rob or cheat by giving short change. **short circuit** an electric circuit through small resistance, esp. instead of the resistance of a normal circuit. **short-circuit** *v.* **1** cause a short circuit or a short circuit in. **2** shorten or avoid (a journey, work, etc.) by taking a more direct route etc. **short commons** insufficient food. **short cut 1** a route shortening the distance travelled. **2** a quick way of accomplishing something. **short date** an early date for the maturing of a bill etc. **short-dated** due for early payment or redemption. **short-day** (of a plant) needing the period of light each day to fall below some limit to cause flowering. **short division** *Math.* division in which the quotient is written directly without being worked out in writing. **short drink** a strong alcoholic drink served in small measures. **short-eared owl** an owl, *Asio flammeus*, frequenting open country and hunting at dawn or dusk. **short for** an abbreviation for (*'Bob' is short for 'Robert'*). **short fuse** *colloq.* a quick temper. **short game** *Golf* approaching and putting. **short-handed** undermanned or understaffed. **short haul 1** the transport of goods over a short distance. **2** a short-term effort. **short head** *Racing* a distance less than the length of a horse's head. **short-head** *v.tr.* beat by a short head. **short hundredweight** see HUNDREDWEIGHT. **short list** *Brit.* a list of selected candidates from which a final choice is made. **short-list** *v.tr. Brit.* put on a short list. **short-lived** ephemeral; not long-lasting. **short mark** = BREVE 2. **short measure** less than the professed amount. **short metre** *Prosody* a hymn stanza of four lines with 6, 6, 8, and 6 syllables. **short notice** an insufficient length of warning time. **short odds** nearly equal stakes or chances in betting. **short of 1** see sense 3a of *adj.* **2** less than (*nothing short of a miracle*). **3** distant from (*two miles short of home*). **4** without going so far as; except (*did everything short of destroying it*). **short of breath** panting, short-winded. **short on** *colloq.* see sense 3a of *adj.* **short order** *US* an order in a restaurant for quickly cooked food. **short-pitched** *Cricket* (of a ball) pitching relatively near the bowler. **short-range 1** having a short range. **2** relating to a fairly immediate future time (*short-range possibilities*). **short rib** = *floating rib.* **short score** *Mus.* a score not giving all parts. **short shrift** curt or dismissive treatment. **short sight** the inability to focus except on comparatively near objects. **short-sleeved** with sleeves not reaching below the elbow. **short-staffed** having insufficient staff. **short story** a story with a fully developed theme but shorter than a novel. **short suit** a suit of less than four cards. **short temper** self-control soon or easily lost. **short-tempered** quick to lose one's temper; irascible. **short-term** occurring in or relating to a short period of time. **short time** the condition of working fewer than the regular hours per day or days per week. **short title** an abbreviated form of a title of a book etc. **short ton** see TON. **short view** a consideration of the present only, not the future. **short waist 1** a high or shallow waist of a dress. **2** a short upper body. **short wave** a radio wave of frequency greater than 3 MHz. **short weight** weight less than it is alleged to be. **short whist** whist with ten or five points to a game. **short wind** quickly exhausted breathing-power. **short-winded 1** having short wind. **2** incapable of sustained effort. □□ **shortish** *adj.* **shortness** *n.* [OE *sceort* f. Gmc: cf. SHIRT, SKIRT]

▪ *adj.* **1 b** quick, limited; short-lived; see also BRIEF *adj.* 1. **2** small, little, diminutive, elfin; midget, dwarfish, squat, runty, undersized, stubby, stunted, *colloq.* pint-sized, sawn-off. **3 a** (*short of* or *on*) deficient in, lacking in, needful of, wanting in, low on, *colloq.* shy. **b** impecunious, straitened, pinched, underfunded, deficient; see also BROKE. **c** close, near. **4 a** concise, compact, pocket, abbreviated, abridged, cut; laconic, terse, succinct, pithy, sententious, epigrammatic; direct, straight, straightforward, short and sweet; see also BRIEF *adj.* 2. **b** curt, terse, sharp, blunt, bluff, brusque, offhand, gruff, discourteous, uncivil, impolite; see also ABRUPT 2. ● *adv.* **1** abruptly, suddenly, peremptorily, without warning, instantly, unexpectedly, hurriedly, hastily. **2** bluntly, shortly, curtly, rudely, brusquely, sharply, abruptly, uncivilly, direct, straight ● *n.* **1** nip, short drink; see also SHOT[1] 11a. □ **be caught** (or **taken**) **short 1** be handicapped *or* constrained *or* trammelled *or* impeded, be out on a limb, be caught napping, *archaic* be on the hip. **bring up short** see CHECK[1] *v.* 2a. **come short of** fail, disappoint, be *or* prove inadequate *or* insufficient to. **get** (or **have**) **by the short hairs** have at one's beck and call, have under control; see also *twist around one's finger* (FINGER). **in short** briefly, in a word, to cut a long story short, in a nutshell. **in short order** see IMMEDIATELY *adv.* 1. **in the short run** in the short term. **in short supply** rare, scarce, unplentiful, thin on the ground, hard to come by, at a premium, limited, few and far between. **short-lived** ephemeral, evanescent, temporary, fleeting, transitory, transient, passing, *literary* fugacious. **short of 4** excepting, except for, leaving out, apart from, setting aside, excluding, exclusive of, barring. **short-staffed** undermanned, short-handed, understaffed. **short-tempered** testy, irascible, curt, abrupt, gruff, bluff, terse, brusque, crabbed, crabby, touchy, petulant, peevish, bearish, snappish, waspish, shrewish, curmudgeonly, crusty, surly, *colloq.* grouchy; see also IRRITABLE 1. **short-winded 1** short of *or* out of breath, winded, breathless, panting, huffing (and puffing), gasping (for air *or* for breath), *Med.* dyspnoeal.

shortage /shórtij/ *n.* (often foll. by *of*) a deficiency; an amount lacking (*a shortage of 100 tons*).

▪ deficit, deficiency, shortfall, dearth, scarcity, lack, want, paucity.

shortbread /shórtbred/ *n.* a crisp rich crumbly type of biscuit made with butter, flour, and sugar.

shortcake /shórtkayk/ *n.* **1** = SHORTBREAD. **2** a cake made of short pastry and filled with fruit and cream.

shortcoming /shórtkumming/ *n.* failure to come up to a standard; a defect.

▪ defect, deficiency, weakness, frailty, drawback, liability, imperfection, weak point, flaw, *formal* defalcation.

shortcrust /shórtkrust/ *n.* (in full **shortcrust pastry**) a type of crumbly pastry made with flour and fat.

shorten /shórt'n/ *v.* **1** *intr.* & *tr.* become or make shorter or short; curtail. **2** *tr. Naut.* reduce the amount of (sail spread). **3** *intr.* & *tr.* (with reference to gambling odds, prices, etc.) become or make shorter; decrease.
■ **1** cut, curtail, cut off *or* down *or* short, reduce, diminish, condense, abridge, abbreviate, digest, compress; trim.

shortening /shórt'ning/ *n.* fat used for making pastry, esp. for making short pastry.

shortfall /shórtfawl/ *n.* a deficit below what was expected.
■ see DEFICIT.

shorthand /shórt-hand/ *n.* **1** (often *attrib.*) a method of rapid writing in abbreviations and symbols esp. for taking dictation. **2** an abbreviated or symbolic mode of expression. □ **shorthand typist** *Brit.* a typist qualified to take and transcribe shorthand.
■ **1** stenography, tachygraphy, phonography.

shorthorn /shórt-horn/ *n.* **1** an animal of a breed of cattle with short horns. **2** this breed.

shortie var. of SHORTY.

shortly /shórtli/ *adv.* **1** (often foll. by *before*, *after*) before long; soon (*will arrive shortly*; *arrived shortly after him*). **2** in a few words; briefly. **3** curtly. [OE *scortlice* (as SHORT, -LY[2])]
■ **1** soon, presently, before long, in a (little) while, by and by, *archaic or literary* anon, *poet. or archaic* ere long. **3** abruptly, peremptorily, curtly, brusquely, bluntly, sharply, tersely, gruffly, rudely.

shorts /shorts/ *n.pl.* **1** trousers reaching only to the knees or higher. **2** *US* underpants.
■ **1** Bermudas, knee-breeches, lederhosen, trunks. **2** see BRIEF *n.* 1.

short-sighted /shórtsītid/ *adj.* **1** having short sight. **2** lacking imagination or foresight. □□ **short-sightedly** *adv.* **short-sightedness** *n.*
■ **1** myopic, dim-sighted, *esp. US* near-sighted. **2** unimaginative, unprogressive, improvident, imprudent, injudicious, rash, impolitic, limited, thoughtless, unmindful.

shortstop /shórtstop/ *n.* a baseball fielder between second and third base.

shorty /shórti/ *n.* (also **shortie**) (*pl.* **-ies**) *colloq.* **1** a person shorter than average. **2** a short garment, esp. a nightdress or raincoat.

shot[1] /shot/ *n.* **1** the act or an instance of firing a gun, cannon, etc. (*several shots were heard*). **2** an attempt to hit by shooting or throwing etc. (*took a shot at him*). **3 a** a single non-explosive missile for a cannon, gun, etc. **b** (*pl.* same or **shots**) a small lead pellet used in quantity in a single charge or cartridge in a shotgun. **c** (as *pl.*) these collectively. **4 a** a photograph. **b** a film sequence photographed continuously by one camera. **5 a** a stroke or a kick in a ball game. **b** *colloq.* an attempt to guess or do something (*let him have a shot at it*). **6** *colloq.* a person having a specified skill with a gun etc. (*is not a good shot*). **7** a heavy ball thrown by a shot-putter. **8** the launch of a space rocket (*a moonshot*). **9** the range, reach, or distance to or at which a thing will carry or act (*out of earshot*). **10** a remark aimed at a person. **11** *colloq.* **a** a drink of esp. spirits. **b** an injection of a drug, vaccine, etc. (*has had his shots*). □ **like a shot** *colloq.* without hesitation; willingly. **make a bad shot** guess wrong. **not a shot in one's** (or **the**) **locker** **1** no money left. **2** not a chance left. **shot-blasting** the cleaning of metal etc. by the impact of a stream of shot. **shot-firer** a person who fires a blasting-charge in a mine etc. **shot in the arm** *colloq.* **1** stimulus or encouragement. **2** an alcoholic drink. **shot in the dark** a mere guess. **shot-put** an athletic contest in which a shot is thrown a great distance. **shot-putter** an athlete who puts the shot. **shot-tower** *hist.* a tower in which shot was made from molten lead poured through sieves at the top and falling into water at the bottom. □□ **shotproof** *adj.* [OE *sc(e)ot*, *gesc(e)ot* f. Gmc: cf. SHOOT]
■ **1** blast. **3** bullet, ball, slug, cannon-ball, pellet, projectile, missile; buckshot. **4 a** photograph, print, snapshot, picture, snap, photo, *colloq.* pic. **5 a** see KICK *n.* 1. **b** attempt, try, opportunity, chance, endeavour, *colloq.* stab, crack, go, whirl, *sl.* bash. **6** marksman, shooter. **8** (space) launch *or* launching. **9** see RANGE *n.* 1a–c. **11 a** drink, jigger, tot, dram, nip, *esp. US* slug, *colloq.* swig, finger, spot, snort. **b** injection, inoculation, vaccination, *colloq.* jab. □ **like a shot** quickly, swiftly, rapidly, speedily, hurriedly, hastily, at once, like a flash, immediately, instantly, instantaneously, in two shakes of a lamb's tail, before you can say Jack Robinson, *colloq.* like greased lightning; without hesitation, without a murmur, uncomplainingly; see also *willingly* (WILLING). **not a shot in one's** (or **the**) **locker 1** (*not have a shot in one's* (or *the*) *locker*) see *not have a brass farthing* (BRASS). **2** see *not an earthly* (EARTHLY). **shot in the arm 1** stimulus, encouragement, incentive, inducement, provocation, motivation, *colloq.* boost. **2** see DRINK *n.* 2b. **shot in the dark** see GUESS *n.*

shot[2] /shot/ *past* and *past part.* of SHOOT. ● *adj.* **1** (of coloured material) woven so as to show different colours at different angles. **2** *colloq.* **a** exhausted; finished. **b** drunk. **3** (of a board-edge) accurately planed. □ **be** (or **get**) **shot of** *sl.* be (or get) rid of. **shot through** permeated or suffused. [past part. of SHOOT]

shot[3] /shot/ *n. colloq.* a reckoning, a bill, esp. at an inn etc. (*paid his shot*). [ME, = SHOT[1]: cf. OE *scēotan* shoot, pay, contribute, and SCOT]

shotgun /shótgun/ *n.* a smooth-bore gun for firing small shot at short range. □ **shotgun marriage** (or **wedding**) *colloq.* an enforced or hurried wedding, esp. because of the bride's pregnancy.

shotten herring /shótt'n/ *n.* **1** a herring that has spawned. **2** *archaic* a weakened or dispirited person. [ME, archaic past part. of SHOOT]

should /shŏŏd, shəd/ *v.aux.* (*3rd sing.* **should**) *past* of SHALL, used esp.: **1** in reported speech, esp. with the reported element in the 1st person (*I said I should be home by evening*). ¶ Cf. WILL[1], WOULD, now more common in this sense, esp. to avoid implications of sense 2. **2 a** to express a duty, obligation, or likelihood; = OUGHT[1] (*I should tell you*; *you should have been more careful*; *they should have arrived by now*). **b** (in the 1st person) to express a tentative suggestion (*I should like to say something*). **3 a** expressing the conditional mood in the 1st person (cf. WOULD) (*I should have been killed if I had gone*). **b** forming a conditional protasis or indefinite clause (*if you should see him*; *should they arrive, tell them where to go*). **4** expressing purpose = MAY, MIGHT[1] (*in order that we should not worry*).
■ **2 a** see MUST[1] *v.*

shoulder /shṓldər/ *n.* & *v.* ● *n.* **1 a** the part of the body at which the arm, foreleg, or wing is attached. **b** (in full **shoulder joint**) the end of the upper arm joining with the collar-bone and blade-bone. **c** either of the two projections below the neck from which the arms hang. **2** the upper foreleg and shoulder blade of a pig, lamb, etc. when butchered. **3** (often in *pl.*) **a** the upper part of the back and arms. **b** this part of the body regarded as capable of bearing a burden or blame, providing comfort, etc. (*needs a shoulder to cry on*). **4** a strip of land next to a metalled road (*pulled over on to the shoulder*). **5** a part of a garment covering the shoulder. **6** a part of anything resembling a shoulder in form or function, as in a bottle, mountain, tool, etc. ● *v.* **1 a** *tr.* push with the shoulder; jostle. **b** *intr.* make one's way by jostling (*shouldered through the crowd*). **2** *tr.* take (a burden etc.) on one's shoulders (*shouldered the family's problems*). □ **put** (or **set**) **one's shoulder to the wheel** make an effort. **shoulder arms** hold a rifle with the barrel against the shoulder and the butt in the hand. **shoulder-bag** a woman's handbag that can be hung from the shoulder. **shoulder-belt** a bandolier or other strap passing over one shoulder and under the opposite arm. **shoulder-blade** *Anat.* either of the large flat bones of the upper back; the scapula. **shoulder-high** up to or as high as the shoulders. **shoulder-holster** a gun holster worn in the armpit. **shoulder-knot** a knot of ribbon, metal, lace, etc. worn as part of a ceremonial dress. **shoulder-length** (of hair etc.) reaching to the shoulders. **shoulder loop** *US* the shoulder-strap of an army, air-force, or marines officer. **shoulder mark** *US* the shoulder-strap of a naval officer. **shoulder-note** *Printing* a marginal note at the top of a page. **shoulder-of-mutton sail** = *leg-of-mutton sail.* **shoulder-pad** a pad sewn into a garment to bulk out the shoulder. **shoulder-strap 1** a strip of fabric, leather, etc. suspending a bag or garment from the shoulder. **2** a strip of cloth from shoulder to collar on a military uniform bearing a symbol of rank etc. **3** a similar strip on a raincoat. **shoulder to shoulder 1** side by side. **2** with closed ranks or united effort. □□ **shouldered** *adj.* (also in *comb.*). [OE *sculdor* f. WG]

■ *n.* **4** side, edge, verge; *Brit.* hard shoulder. ● *v.* **1 a** push, shove, jostle, hustle, thrust, elbow, force. **2** support, carry, bear, take upon oneself, take on, accept, assume. □ **put** (or **set**) **one's shoulder to the wheel** make every effort, make an effort, strive, work hard, pitch in, apply oneself, roll up one's sleeves, set *or* get to work, knuckle down, buckle down, keep one's nose to the grindstone. **shoulder to shoulder** side by side, united, as one, cooperatively, jointly, together, arm in arm, hand in hand, in partnership.

shouldn't /sho͝odd'nt/ *contr.* should not.

shout /showt/ *v.* & *n.* ● *v.* **1** *intr.* make a loud cry or vocal sound; speak loudly (*shouted for attention*). **2** *tr.* say or express loudly; call out (*shouted that the coast was clear*). **3** *tr.* (also *absol.*) *Austral.* & *NZ colloq.* treat (another person) to drinks etc. ● *n.* **1** a loud cry expressing joy etc. or calling attention. **2** *colloq.* one's turn to order and pay for a round of drinks etc. (*your shout I think*). □ **all over bar** (or **but**) **the shouting** *colloq.* the contest is virtually decided. **shout at** speak loudly to etc. **shout down** reduce to silence by shouting. **shout for** call for by shouting. **shout-up** *colloq.* a noisy argument. □□ **shouter** *n.* [ME, perh. rel. to SHOOT: cf. ON *skúta* SCOUT]

■ *v.* **1, 2** bellow, bawl, roar (out), cry (out), call (out), yell, scream, *US colloq.* holler. **3** see TREAT *v.* 5. ● *n.* **1** yell, scream, bellow, howl, yelp, roar, cry, call, whoop, *US colloq.* holler. **2** round. □ **all over bar** (or **but**) **the shouting** almost over *or* finished, nearly over; *fait accompli.* **shout-up** see ARGUMENT 1.

shove /shuv/ *v.* & *n.* ● *v.* **1** *tr.* (also *absol.*) push vigorously; move by hard or rough pushing (*shoved him out of the way*). **2** *intr.* (usu. foll. by *along*, *past*, *through*, etc.) make one's way by pushing (*shoved through the crowd*). **3** *tr. colloq.* put somewhere (*shoved it in the drawer*). ● *n.* an act of shoving or of prompting a person into action. □ **shove-halfpenny** a form of shovelboard played with coins etc. on a table esp. in licensed premises. **shove off 1** start from the shore in a boat. **2** *sl.* depart; go away (*told him to shove off*). [OE *scūfan* f. Gmc]

■ *v.* **1** see PUSH *v.* 1. **2** thrust *or* elbow *or* force *or* jostle one's way; see also PUSH *v.* 6. **3** see STUFF *v.* 2. ● *n.* push, thrust, nudge. □ **shove off 1** push off. **2** see *push off.*

shovel /shúvv'l/ *n.* & *v.* ● *n.* **1 a** a spadelike tool for shifting quantities of coal, earth, etc., esp. having the sides curved upwards. **b** the amount contained in a shovel; a shovelful. **2** a machine or part of a machine having a similar form or function. ● *v.tr.* (**shovelled, shovelling**; *US* **shoveled, shoveling**) **1** shift or clear (coal etc.) with or as if with a shovel. **2** *colloq.* move (esp. food) in large quantities or roughly (*shovelled peas into his mouth*). □ **shovel hat** a broad-brimmed hat esp. worn by some clergymen. □□ **shovelful** *n.* (*pl.* **-fuls**). [OE *scofl* f. Gmc (see SHOVE)]

shovelboard /shúvv'lbord/ *n.* a game played esp. on a ship's deck by pushing discs with the hand or with a long-handled shovel over a marked surface. [earlier *shoveboard* f. SHOVE + BOARD]

shovelhead /shúvv'lhed/ *n.* a shark, *Sphyrna tiburo*, like the hammerhead but smaller. Also called BONNETHEAD.

shoveller /shúvvələr/ *n.* (also **shoveler**) **1** a person or thing that shovels. **2** a duck, *Anas clypeata*, with a broad shovel-like beak. [SHOVEL: sense 2 earlier *shovelard* f. -ARD, perh. after *mallard*]

show /shō/ *v.* & *n.* ● *v.* (*past part.* **shown** /shōn/ or **showed**) **1** *intr.* & *tr.* be, or allow or cause to be, visible; manifest; appear (*the buds are beginning to show*; *white shows the dirt*). **2** *tr.* (often foll. by *to*) offer, exhibit, or produce (a thing) for scrutiny etc. (*show your tickets please*; *showed him my poems*). **3** *tr.* **a** indicate (one's feelings) by one's behaviour etc. (*showed mercy to him*). **b** indicate (one's feelings to a person etc.) (*showed him particular favour*). **4** *intr.* (of feelings etc.) be manifest (*his dislike shows*). **5** *tr.* **a** demonstrate; point out; prove (*has shown it to be false*; *showed that he knew the answer*). **b** (usu. foll. by *how to* + infin.) cause (a person) to understand or be capable of doing (*showed them how to knit*). **6** *tr.* (*refl.*) exhibit oneself as being (*showed herself to be fair*). **7** *tr.* & *intr.* (with ref. to a film) be presented or cause to be presented. **8** *tr.* exhibit (a picture, animal, flower, etc.) in a show. **9** *tr.* (often foll. by *in*, *out*, *up*, etc.) conduct or lead (*showed them to their rooms*). **10** *intr.* = *show up* 3 (*waited but he didn't show*). **11** *intr. US* finish in the first three in a race. ● *n.* **1** the act or an instance of showing; the state of being shown. **2 a** a spectacle, display, exhibition, etc. (*a fine show of blossom*). **b** a collection of things etc. shown for public entertainment or in competition (*dog show*; *flower show*). **3 a** a play etc., esp. a musical. **b** a light entertainment programme on television etc. **c** any public entertainment or performance. **4 a** an outward appearance, semblance, or display (*made a show of agreeing*; *a show of strength*). **b** empty appearance; mere display (*did it for show*; *that's all show*). **5** *colloq.* an undertaking, business, etc. (*sold the whole show*). **6** *colloq.* an opportunity of acting, defending oneself, etc. (*gave him a fair show*; *made a good show of it*). **7** *Med.* a discharge of blood etc. from the vagina at the onset of childbirth. □ **get the show on the road** *colloq.* get started, begin an undertaking. **give the show** (or **whole show**) **away** demonstrate the inadequacies or reveal the truth. **good** (or **bad** or **poor**) **show!** *colloq.* **1** that was well (or badly) done. **2** that was lucky (or unlucky). **nothing to show for** no visible result of (effort etc.). **on show** being exhibited. **show business** *colloq.* the theatrical profession. **show-card** a card used for advertising. **show one's cards** = *show one's hand.* **show cause** *Law* allege with justification. **show a clean pair of heels** *colloq.* retreat speedily; run away. **show one's colours** make one's opinion clear. **show a person the door** dismiss or eject a person. **show one's face** make an appearance; let oneself be seen. **show fight** be persistent or belligerent. **show the flag** see FLAG[1]. **show forth** *archaic* exhibit; expound. **show one's hand 1** disclose one's plans. **2** reveal one's cards. **show house** (or **flat** etc.) a furnished and decorated house (or flat etc.) on a new estate shown to prospective buyers. **show in** see sense 9 of *v.* **show a leg** *colloq.* get out of bed. **show off 1** display to advantage. **2** *colloq.* act pretentiously; display one's wealth, knowledge, etc. **show-off** *n. colloq.* a person who shows off. **show of force** proof that one is prepared to use force. **show of hands** raised hands indicating a vote for or against, usu. without being counted. **show oneself 1** be seen in public. **2** see sense 6 of *v.* **show out** see sense 9 of *v.* **show-piece 1** an item of work presented for exhibition or display. **2** an outstanding example or specimen. **show-place** a house etc. that tourists go to see. **show round** take (a person) to places of interest; act as guide for (a person) in a building etc. **show-stopper** *colloq.* a performance receiving prolonged applause. **show one's teeth** reveal one's strength; be aggressive. **show through 1** be visible although supposedly concealed. **2** (of real feelings etc.) be revealed inadvertently. **show trial** esp. *hist.* a judicial trial designed by the State to terrorize or impress the public. **show up 1** make or be conspicuous or clearly visible. **2** expose (a fraud, impostor, inferiority, etc.). **3** *colloq.* appear; be present; arrive. **4** *colloq.* embarrass or humiliate (*don't show me up by wearing jeans*). **show the way 1** indicate what has to be done etc. by attempting it first. **2** show others which way to go etc. **show the white feather** appear cowardly (see also *white feather*). **show willing** display a willingness to help etc. **show-window** a window for exhibiting goods etc. [ME f. OE *scēawian* f. WG: cf. SHEEN]

■ *v.* **1** appear, become *or* be visible, peek through, be seen; represent, symbolize, depict, portray, picture, illustrate; see also DISPLAY *v.* 1. **2** display, present, exhibit. **3** demonstrate, indicate, register; (lay) bare, disclose, reveal, expose, betray, make known, divulge, express, make clear *or* plain *or* manifest; grant, accord, bestow. **4** be apparent *or* manifest, show through. **5 a** prove, demonstrate, point out, illustrate, confirm, corroborate, verify, substantiate, bear out, certify, authenticate; exhibit, reveal, indicate, display, register. **b** teach, instruct, tell, inform, give an idea of, give a lesson in. **7** present, put on, screen; play, be presented *or* played *or* screened. **9** escort, accompany, conduct, usher, lead, guide, direct. ● *n.* **2 a** see DISPLAY *n.* 2. **b** display, exhibition, exposition, fair, Expo. **3** production, presentation, play, musical, entertainment. **4 a** see SEMBLANCE 1. **b** display, appearance, pretence; see also OSTENTATION. **5** see UNDERTAKING 1. □ **give the show** (or **whole show**) **away** see *let on* 1 (LET[1]). **good show! 1** bravo, well done, good for you, congratulations. **on show** in the public eye, in the limelight, under the spotlight, high-profile. **show a clean pair of heels** see RUN *v.* 2. **show a person the door** see DISMISS *v.* 2. **show one's face** make *or* put in an appearance, show oneself, be seen, turn up; see also APPEAR 1. **show forth** see *set forth* 2 (SET[1]). **show one's hand** see *put one's cards on the table* (CARD[1]). **show a leg** get up, rise, greet the dawn, get out of bed, *colloq.* surface. **show off** make an exhibition *or* a spectacle of, flaunt, advertise, display, parade; pose, swagger, posture, boast, brag. **show-off** braggart, exhibitionist, swaggerer, egotist, boaster, *archaic* scaramouche, *colloq.* blowhard, *Austral. sl.* lair. **show-piece 2** masterpiece; see also MODEL *n.* 5a. **show up 1** stand out, be conspicuous, be noticeable, contrast; make visible, reveal, show. **2** expose, reveal; see also *give away* 3. **3** make *or* put in an appearance, appear, show, show one's face, arrive, come, turn up. **4** embarrass, (put to) shame, mortify, humiliate.

showbiz /shṓbiz/ *n. colloq.* = *show business.*

showboat /shṓbōt/ *n. US* a river steamer on which theatrical performances are given.

showcase /shṓkayss/ *n.* & *v.* ● *n.* **1** a glass case used for exhibiting goods etc. **2** a place or medium for presenting (esp. attractively) to general attention. ● *v.tr.* display in or as if in a showcase.

showdown /shṓdown/ *n.* **1** a final test or confrontation; a decisive situation. **2** the laying down face up of the players' cards in poker.

■ **1** confrontation, climax, moment of truth, final settlement, moment of decision, *colloq.* crunch.

shower /showr/ *n.* & *v.* ● *n.* **1** a brief fall of esp. rain, hail, sleet, or snow. **2 a** a brisk flurry of arrows, bullets, dust, stones, sparks, etc. **b** a similar flurry of gifts, letters, honours, praise, etc. **3** (in full **shower-bath**) **a** a cubicle, bath, etc. in which one stands under a spray of water. **b** the apparatus etc. used for this. **c** the act of bathing in a shower. **4** a group of particles initiated by a cosmic-ray particle in the earth's atmosphere. **5** *US* a party for giving presents to a prospective bride, etc. **6** *Brit. sl.* a contemptible or unpleasant person or group of people. ● *v.* **1** *tr.* **a** discharge (water, missiles, etc.) in a shower. **b** make wet with (or as if with) a shower. **2** *intr.* use a shower-bath. **3** *tr.* (usu. foll. by *on, upon*) lavishly bestow (gifts etc.). **4** *intr.* descend or come in a shower (*it showered on and off all day*). □□ **showery** *adj.* [OE *scūr* f. Gmc]

■ *n.* **1** sprinkle, sprinkling, fall, drizzle, precipitation. **2** flurry, deluge, torrent, flood, influx, stream, barrage, overflow, abundance, profusion. **3 b, c** douche. ● *v.* **1** sprinkle, rain, pour, spray, splash, hail. **2** douche. **3** lavish, bestow, heap. **4** fall, descend, hail, pelt; rain, sprinkle, pour, drizzle, mizzle. □□ **showery** see WET *adj.* 2.

showerproof /shówrproof/ *adj.* & *v.* ● *adj.* resistant to light rain. ● *v.tr.* render showerproof.

showgirl /shṓgurl/ *n.* an actress who sings and dances in musicals, variety shows, etc.

showing /shṓ-ing/ *n.* **1** the act or an instance of showing. **2** a usu. specified quality of performance (*made a poor showing*). **3** the presentation of a case; evidence (*on present showing it must be true*). [OE *scēawung* (as SHOW)]

■ **1** exhibition; see also DEMONSTRATION 3.

showjumping /shṓjumping/ *n.* the sport of riding horses over a course of fences and other obstacles, with penalty points for errors. □□ **showjump** *v.intr.* **showjumper** *n.*

showman /shṓmən/ *n.* (*pl.* **-men**) **1** the proprietor or manager of a circus etc. **2** a person skilled in self-advertisement or publicity. □□ **showmanship** *n.*

■ **1** producer, impresario, director, manager, regisseur. □□ **showmanship** éclat, pyrotechnics, show, staginess, *sl.* razzle-dazzle; see also VERVE.

shown *past part.* of SHOW.

showroom /shṓroom, -room/ *n.* a room in a factory, office building, etc. used to display goods for sale.

showy /shṓ-i/ *adj.* (**showier, showiest**) **1** brilliant; gaudy, esp. vulgarly so. **2** striking. □□ **showily** *adv.* **showiness** *n.*

■ flashy, garish, flamboyant, brilliant, conspicuous, striking, imposing, ostentatious, pretentious, grandiose, bravura, gaudy, lurid, loud, *colloq.* flash; elaborate, fancy, florid, flowery, ornate, fussy, intricate, baroque, rococo, Byzantine, arabesque.

s.h.p. *abbr.* shaft horsepower.

shrank *past* of SHRINK.

shrapnel /shrápn'l/ *n.* **1** fragments of a bomb etc. thrown out by an explosion. **2** a shell containing bullets or pieces of metal timed to burst short of impact. [Gen. H. *Shrapnel*, Brit. soldier d. 1842, inventor of the shell]

shred /shred/ *n.* & *v.* ● *n.* **1** a scrap, fragment, or strip of esp. cloth, paper, etc. **2** the least amount, remnant (*not a shred of evidence*). ● *v.tr.* (**shredded, shredding**) tear or cut into shreds. □ **tear to shreds** completely refute (an argument etc.). [OE *scrēad* (unrecorded) piece cut off, *scrēadian* f. WG: see SHROUD]

■ *n.* **1** scrap, fragment, bit, remnant, snippet, piece, tatter, strip, rag, sliver, chip. **2** atom, trace, whit, grain, jot (or tittle), tittle, scintilla, hint, suggestion, iota, speck, *US* & *Austral. colloq.* skerrick; see also FRAGMENT *n.* ● *v.* tear (up), rip (up), fragment, *archaic or rhet.* rend; destroy, demolish.

shredder /shréddər/ *n.* **1** a machine used to reduce documents to shreds. **2** any device used for shredding.

shrew /shroo/ *n.* **1** any small usu. insect-eating mouselike mammal of the family Soricidae, with a long pointed snout. **2** a bad-tempered or scolding woman. □□ **shrewish** *adj.* (in sense 2). **shrewishly** *adv.* **shrewishness** *n.* [OE *scrēawa*, *scrǣwa* shrew-mouse: cf. OHG *scrawaz* dwarf, MHG *schrawaz* etc. devil]

■ **2** harridan, virago, termagant, vixen, fishwife, nag, fury, spitfire, maenad, harpy, witch, hag, crone, hell-cat, dragon, Xanthippe, *Ir.* & *Sc.* banshee, *archaic* scold, beldam, *colloq.* battleaxe, *sl. offens.* bitch. □□ **shrewish** see *short-tempered.*

shrewd /shrood/ *adj.* **1 a** showing astute powers of judgement; clever and judicious (*a shrewd observer; made a shrewd guess*). **b** (of a face etc.) shrewd-looking. **2** *archaic* **a** (of pain, cold, etc.) sharp, biting. **b** (of a blow, thrust, etc.) severe, hard. **c** mischievous; malicious. □□ **shrewdly** *adv.* **shrewdness** *n.* [ME, = malignant, f. SHREW in sense 'evil person or thing', or past part. of obs. *shrew* to curse, f. SHREW]

■ **1 a** clever, smart, astute, cunning, canny, acute, sharp, keen-minded, keen, quick-witted, crafty, artful, manipulative, calculating, calculated, judicious, foxy, sly, wily, knowing, perceptive, percipient, perspicacious, discerning, wise, sage, sagacious, prudent, long-headed, far-sighted, far-seeing, intelligent, adroit, *colloq.* wide awake, *Brit. sl.* fly. □□ **shrewdness** see JUDGEMENT 1, 2.

shriek /shreek/ *v.* & *n.* ● *v.* **1** *intr.* **a** utter a shrill screeching sound or words esp. in pain or terror. **b** (foll. by *of*) provide a clear or blatant indication of. **2** *tr.* **a** utter (sounds or words) by shrieking (*shrieked his name*). **b** indicate clearly or blatantly. ● *n.* a high-pitched piercing cry or sound; a scream. □ **shriek out** say in shrill tones. **shriek with laughter** laugh uncontrollably. □□ **shrieker** *n.* [imit.: cf. dial. *screak*, ON *skrækja*, and SCREECH]

■ *v.* & *n.* scream, cry, screech, squeal, squawk, squall.

shrieval /shreév'l/ *adj.* of or relating to a sheriff. [*shrieve* obs. var. of SHERIFF]

shrievalty /shreév'lti/ *n.* (*pl.* **-ies**) **1** a sheriff's office or jurisdiction. **2** the tenure of this. [as SHRIEVAL + *-alty* as in mayoralty etc.]

shrift /shrift/ *n. archaic* **1** confession to a priest. **2** confession and absolution. □ **short shrift 1** curt treatment. **2** *archaic* little time between condemnation and execution or punishment. [OE *scrift* (verbal noun) f. SHRIVE]

■ **2** see FORGIVENESS 1.

shrike /shrīk/ *n.* any bird of the family Laniidae, with a strong hooked and toothed bill, that impales its prey of small birds and insects on thorns. Also called *butcher-bird*. [perh. rel. to OE *scric* thrush, MLG *schrīk* corncrake (imit.): cf. SHRIEK]

shrill /shril/ *adj.* & *v.* ● *adj.* **1** piercing and high-pitched in sound. **2** *derog.* (esp. of a protester) sharp, unrestrained, unreasoning. ● *v.* **1** *intr.* (of a cry etc.) sound shrilly. **2** *tr.* (of a person etc.) utter or send out (a song, complaint, etc.) shrilly. □□ **shrilly** *adv.* **shrillness** *n.* [ME, rel. to LG *schrell* sharp in tone or taste f. Gmc]

■ *adj.* **1** high-pitched, high, ear-splitting, piercing, ear-piercing, sharp, piping, screeching, screechy, penetrating.

shrimp /shrimp/ *n.* & *v.* ● *n.* **1** (*pl.* same or **shrimps**) any of various small (esp. marine) edible crustaceans, with ten legs, grey-green when alive and pink when boiled. **2** *colloq.* a very small slight person. ● *v.intr.* go catching shrimps. □ **shrimp plant** an evergreen shrub, *Justicia brandegeana*, bearing small white flowers in clusters of pinkish-brown bracts. □□ **shrimper** *n.* [ME, prob. rel. to MLG *schrempen* wrinkle, MHG *schrimpfen* contract, and SCRIMP]

shrine /shrīn/ *n.* & *v.* ● *n.* **1** esp. *RC Ch.* **a** a chapel, church, altar, etc., sacred to a saint, holy person, relic, etc. **b** the tomb of a saint etc. **c** a casket esp. containing sacred relics; a reliquary. **d** a niche containing a holy statue etc. **2** a place associated with or containing memorabilia of a particular person, event, etc. **3** a Shinto place of worship. ● *v.tr. poet.* enshrine. [OE *scrīn* f. Gmc f. L *scrinium* case for books etc.]

■ *n.* **1 a** see SANCTUARY 1.

shrink /shringk/ *v.* & *n.* ● *v.* (*past* **shrank** /shrangk/; *past part.* **shrunk** /shrungk/ or (esp. as *adj.*) **shrunken** /shrúngkən/) **1** *tr.* & *intr.* make or become smaller; contract, esp. by the action of moisture, heat, or cold. **2** *intr.* (usu. foll. by *from*) **a** retire; recoil; flinch; cower (*shrank from her touch*). **b** be averse from doing (*shrinks from meeting them*). **3** (as **shrunken** *adj.*) (esp. of a face, person, etc.) having grown smaller esp. because of age, illness, etc. ● *n.* **1** the act or an instance of shrinking; shrinkage. **2** *sl.* a psychiatrist (from 'head-shrinker'). □ **shrinking violet** an exaggeratedly shy person. **shrink into oneself** become withdrawn. **shrink on** slip (a metal tyre etc.) on while expanded with heat and allow to tighten. **shrink-resistant** (of textiles etc.) resistant to shrinkage when wet etc. **shrink-wrap** (**-wrapped**, **-wrapping**) enclose (an article) in (esp. transparent) film that shrinks tightly on to it. □□ **shrinkable** *adj.* **shrinker** *n.* **shrinkingly** *adv.* **shrink-proof** *adj.* [OE *scrincan*: cf. *skrynka* to wrinkle]

■ *v.* **1** wither, shrivel (up), contract, compress; diminish, dwindle, decrease; reduce. **2 a** withdraw, draw back, retire, recoil, back away *or* off, retreat, shy away; cower, cringe, flinch, wince. **b** (*shrink from*) see SCRUPLE *v.* 1. **3** (**shrunken**) see *emaciated* (EMACIATE). ● *n.* **2** see *therapist* (THERAPY).

shrinkage /shríngkij/ *n.* **1 a** the process or fact of shrinking. **b** the degree or amount of shrinking. **2** an allowance made for the reduction in takings due to wastage, theft, etc.

■ **1** erosion, depletion, waste, wastage; see also DECREASE *n.*

shrive /shrīv/ *v.tr.* (*past* **shrove** /shrōv/; *past part.* **shriven** /shrívv'n/) *RC Ch. archaic* **1** (of a priest) hear the confession of, assign penance to, and absolve. **2** (*refl.*) (of a penitent) submit oneself to a priest for confession etc. [OE *scrīfan* impose as penance, WG f. L *scribere* write]

shrivel /shrívv'l/ *v.tr.* & *intr.* (**shrivelled**, **shrivelling** or *US* **shriveled**, **shriveling**) contract or wither into a wrinkled, folded, rolled-up, contorted, or dried-up state. [perh. f. ON: cf. Sw. dial. *skryvla* to wrinkle]

■ shrivel up, shrink, wrinkle, pucker (up), curl (up), wizen, contract; wither, wilt, dry up, desiccate, dehydrate.

shriven *past part.* of SHRIVE.

shroud /shrowd/ *n.* & *v.* ● *n.* **1** a sheetlike garment for wrapping a corpse for burial. **2** anything that conceals like a shroud (*wrapped in a shroud of mystery*). **3** (in *pl.*) *Naut.* a set of ropes forming part of the standing rigging and supporting the mast or topmast. ● *v.tr.* **1** clothe (a body) for burial. **2** cover, conceal, or disguise (*hills shrouded in mist*). □ **shroud-laid** (of a rope) having four strands laid right-handed on a core. □□ **shroudless** *adj.* [OE *scrūd* f. Gmc: see SHRED]

■ *n.* **1** winding-sheet, grave-clothes, *hist.* cerecloth, *literary* cerement. **2** veil, cover, shield, cloak, blanket, mask, mantle, pall, screen, covering, cloud. ● *v.* **2** swathe, wrap, cover, clothe, protect; screen, veil, mask, disguise, camouflage, shield, cloak, blanket, mantle, shade, obscure, hide, conceal; see also ENVELOP.

shrove *past* of SHRIVE.

Shrovetide /shrṓvtīd/ *n.* Shrove Tuesday and the two days preceding it when it was formerly customary to be shriven. [ME *shrove* abnormally f. SHROVE]

Shrove Tuesday /shrōv/ *n.* the day before Ash Wednesday.

shrub[1] /shrub/ *n.* a woody plant smaller than a tree and having a very short stem with branches near the ground. □□ **shrubby** *adj.* [ME f. OE *scrubb*, *scrybb* shrubbery: cf. NFris. *skrobb* brushwood, WFlem. *schrobbe* vetch, Norw. *skrubba* dwarf cornel, and SCRUB[2]]

shrub[2] /shrub/ *n.* a cordial made of sweetened fruit-juice and spirits, esp. rum. [Arab. *šurb*, *šarāb* f. *šariba* to drink: cf. SHERBET, SYRUP]

shrubbery /shrúbbəri/ *n.* (*pl.* **-ies**) an area planted with shrubs.

■ shrubs, planting(s), hedge(s), hedging, hedgerow, thicket, brake, bracken, coppice, copse, undergrowth, *US* underbrush.

shrug /shrug/ *v.* & *n.* ● *v.* (**shrugged**, **shrugging**) **1** *intr.* slightly and momentarily raise the shoulders to express indifference, helplessness, contempt, etc. **2** *tr.* **a** raise (the shoulders) in this way. **b** shrug the shoulders to express (indifference etc.) (*shrugged his consent*). ● *n.* the act or an instance of shrugging. □ **shrug off** dismiss as unimportant etc. by or as if by shrugging. [ME: orig. unkn.]

■ □ **shrug off** see DISMISS 4.

shrunk (also **shrunken**) *past part.* of SHRINK.

shtick /shtik/ *n. sl.* a theatrical routine, gimmick, etc. [Yiddish f. G *Stück* piece]

■ see ACT *n.* 3a.

shuck /shuk/ *n.* & *v. US* ● *n.* **1** a husk or pod. **2** the shell of an oyster or clam. **3** (in *pl.*) *colloq.* an expression of contempt or regret or self-deprecation in response to praise. ● *v.tr.*

remove the shucks of; shell. ▫▫ **shucker** *n.* [17th c.: orig. unkn.]

■ *n.* **1, 2** see SHELL *n.* 1. ● *v.* see SHELL *v.* 1.

shudder /shúddər/ *v.* & *n.* ● *v.intr.* **1** shiver esp. convulsively from fear, cold, repugnance, etc. **2** feel strong repugnance etc. (*shudder to think what might happen*). **3** (of a machine etc.) vibrate or quiver. ● *n.* **1** the act or an instance of shuddering. **2** (in *pl.*; prec. by *the*) *colloq.* a state of shuddering. ▫▫ **shudderingly** *adv.* **shuddery** *adj.* [ME *shod(d)er* f. MDu. *schūderen*, MLG *schōderen* f. Gmc]

■ *v.* **1** quiver, shake, tremble, shiver, jerk, convulse, quaver, quake. **2** see DREAD *v.* **3** vibrate, rattle, quiver, shake, quake, quaver, *esp. Brit.* judder. ● *n.* **1** quiver, shake, tremble, tremor, twitch, shiver, convulsion, paroxysm, spasm, quaver; vibration, rattle, *esp. Brit.* judder. **2** (*the shudders*) see SHAKE *n.* 3.

shuffle /shúff'l/ *v.* & *n.* ● *v.* **1** *tr.* & *intr.* move with a scraping, sliding, or dragging motion (*shuffles along*; *shuffling his feet*). **2** *tr.* **a** (also *absol.*) rearrange (a pack of cards) by sliding them over each other quickly. **b** rearrange; intermingle; confuse (*shuffled the documents*). **3** *tr.* (usu. foll. by *on*, *off*, *into*) assume or remove (clothes, a burden, etc.) esp. clumsily or evasively (*shuffled on his clothes*; *shuffled off responsibility*). **4** *intr.* **a** equivocate; prevaricate. **b** continually shift one's position; fidget. **5** *intr.* (foll. by *out of*) escape evasively (*shuffled out of the blame*). ● *n.* **1** a shuffling movement. **2** the act or an instance of shuffling cards. **3** a general change of relative positions. **4** a piece of equivocation; sharp practice. **5** a quick scraping movement of the feet in dancing (see also *double shuffle*). ▫ **shuffle-board** = SHOVELBOARD. **shuffle the cards** change policy etc. ▫▫ **shuffler** *n.* [perh. f. LG *schuffeln* walk clumsily f. Gmc: cf. SHOVE]

■ *v.* **1** scuff *or* drag (one's feet), scrape along, shamble; see also HOBBLE *v.* 1. **2 b** mix (up), intermix, intermingle, disarrange, rearrange, interfile, intersperse, jumble, confuse, scramble; shift (about), mess up, turn topsy-turvy, scatter, disorganize. **4 a** equivocate, bumble, cavil, fence, be evasive, dodge, niggle, split hairs, quibble, prevaricate, hum and haw, hem and haw, *archaic* shift, *colloq.* be shifty, *esp. Brit. colloq.* waffle. **b** see FIDGET *v.* 1. **5** (*shuffle out of*) see EVADE 1, 2. ● *n.* **1** shamble, shambling, scuffing, scraping. **3** rearrangement, reorganization, reshuffle, shake-up. **4** sidestep, evasion, subterfuge, trick, dodge, shift, prevarication, quibble.

shufti /shŏŏfti/ *n.* (*pl.* **shuftis**) *Brit. colloq.* a look or glimpse. [Arab. *šaffa* try to see]

■ see GLANCE *n.* 1.

shun /shun/ *v.tr.* (**shunned, shunning**) avoid; keep clear of (*shuns human company*). [OE *scunian*, of unkn. orig.]

■ avoid, keep *or* shy away from, keep *or* steer clear of, shrink from, fight shy of, run *or* turn (away) from, flee *or* escape from, *literary* eschew; forgo, give up; disdain, spurn, rebuff, reject, cold-shoulder, give the cold shoulder to.

shunt /shunt/ *v.* & *n.* ● *v.* **1** *intr.* & *tr.* diverge or cause (a train) to be diverted esp. on to a siding. **2** *tr. Electr.* provide (a current) with a shunt. **3** *tr.* **a** postpone or evade. **b** divert (a decision etc.) on to another person etc. ● *n.* **1** the act or an instance of shunting on to a siding. **2** *Electr.* a conductor joining two points of a circuit, through which more or less of a current may be diverted. **3** *Surgery* an alternative path for the circulation of the blood. **4** *sl.* a motor accident, esp. a collision of vehicles travelling one close behind another. ▫▫ **shunter** *n.* [ME, perh. f. SHUN]

■ *v.* **1** sidetrack, divert. **3 a** see DEFER[1].

shush /shŏŏsh, shush/ *int.* & *v.* ● *int.* = HUSH *int.* ● *v.* **1** *intr.* **a** call for silence by saying *shush*. **b** be silent (*they shushed at once*). **2** *tr.* make or attempt to make silent. [imit.]

■ *v.* see SILENCE *v.*

shut /shut/ *v.* (**shutting**; *past* and *past part.* **shut**) **1** *tr.* **a** move (a door, window, lid, lips, etc.) into position so as to block an aperture (*shut the lid*). **b** close or seal (a room, window, box, eye, mouth, etc.) by moving a door etc. (*shut the box*). **2** *intr.* become or be capable of being closed or sealed (*the door shut with a bang*; *the lid shuts automatically*). **3** *intr.* & *tr.* become or make (a shop, business, etc.) closed for trade (*the shops shut at five*; *shuts his shop at five*). **4** *tr.* bring (a book, hand, telescope, etc.) into a folded-up or contracted state. **5** *tr.* (usu. foll. by *in*, *out*) keep (a person, sound, etc.) in or out of a room etc. by shutting a door etc. (*shut out the noise*; *shut them in*). **6** *tr.* (usu. foll. by *in*) catch (a finger, dress, etc.) by shutting something on it (*shut her finger in the door*). **7** *tr.* bar access to (a place etc.) (*this entrance is shut*). ▫ **be** (or **get**) **shut of** *sl.* be (or get) rid of (*were glad to get shut of him*). **shut the door on** refuse to consider; make impossible. **shut down 1** stop (a factory, nuclear reactor, etc.) from operating. **2** (of a factory etc.) stop operating. **3** push or pull (a window-sash etc.) down into a closed position. **shut-down** *n.* the closure of a factory etc. **shut-eye** *colloq.* sleep. **shut one's eyes** (or **ears** or **heart** or **mind**) **to** pretend not, or refuse, to see (or hear or feel sympathy for or think about). **shut in** (of hills, houses, etc.) encircle, prevent access etc. to or escape from (*were shut in by the sea on three sides*) (see also sense 5). **shut off 1** stop the flow of (water, gas, etc.) by shutting a valve. **2** separate from society etc. **shut-off** *n.* **1** something used for stopping an operation. **2** a cessation of flow, supply, or activity. **shut out 1** exclude (a person, light, etc.) from a place, situation, etc. **2** screen (landscape etc.) from view. **3** prevent (a possibility etc.). **4** block (a painful memory etc.) from the mind. **5** *US* prevent (an opponent) from scoring (see also sense 5). **shut-out bid** *Bridge* a pre-emptive bid. **shut to 1** close (a door etc.). **2** (of a door etc.) close as far as it will go. **shut up 1** close all doors and windows of (a house etc.); bolt and bar. **2** imprison (a person). **3** close (a box etc.) securely. **4** *colloq.* reduce to silence by rebuke etc. **5** put (a thing) away in a box etc. **6** (esp. in *imper.*) *colloq.* stop talking. **shut up shop 1** close a business, shop, etc. **2** cease business etc. permanently. **shut your face** (or **head** or **mouth** or **trap**)! *sl.* an impolite request to stop talking. [OE *scyttan* f. WG: cf. SHOOT]

■ **1, 2** close (up), fasten, shut up, secure, bolt, lock (up), seal (up); latch. **3, 4, 7** close. **5** (*shut in*) confine, seclude, keep in, secure; see also *shut up* 2 below; (*shut out*) see *shut out* 1 below. **6** catch, trap, jam, squash, crush. ▫ **shut down 1, 2** switch *or* turn *or* shut off, stop; close down, discontinue, cease, suspend, halt, leave off, shut up. **shut-eye** see NAP[1] *n.* **shut one's eyes to** see OVERLOOK 1. **shut in** see ENCLOSE 1, 6, SHUT *v.* 5 above. **shut off 1** switch *or* turn off; shut (down), kill, douse, close (off), cut (off), disconnect. **2** separate, isolate, seclude, segregate, sequester, bar, shut out, cut off, send to Coventry. **shut out 1** exclude, eliminate, bar, debar, lock out, ban, keep out *or* away; screen, block out, cut out. **2** screen, mask, hide, conceal, veil, cover. **3** see PRECLUDE. **4** block out, keep out, exclude, repress. **shut up 1, 3** see SHUT 1 above. **2** confine, shut in, coop (up), cage (in); imprison, jail, incarcerate, intern, immure. **4** silence, keep quiet, stifle, mute, gag, shush, *Brit.* quieten. **6** (*imper.*) see *wrap up* 3. **shut up shop** see *close down* (CLOSE[2]). **shut your face** (or **head** or **mouth** or **trap**)! see *wrap up* 3.

shutter /shúttər/ *n.* & *v.* ● *n.* **1** a person or thing that shuts. **2 a** each of a pair or set of panels fixed inside or outside a window for security or privacy or to keep the light in or out. **b** a structure of slats on rollers used for the same purpose. **3** a device that exposes the film in a photographic camera. **4** *Mus.* the blind of a swell-box in an organ used for controlling the sound-level. ● *v.tr.* **1** put up the shutters of. **2** provide with shutters. ▫ **put up the shutters 1** cease business for the day. **2** cease business etc. permanently. ▫▫ **shutterless** *adj.*

■ ▫ **put up the shutters 2** see *close down*.

shuttering /shúttəring/ *n.* **1** a temporary structure usu. of wood, used to hold concrete during setting. **2** material for making shutters.

shuttle /shútt'l/ *n.* & *v.* ● *n.* **1 a** a bobbin with two pointed ends used for carrying the weft-thread across between the warp-threads in weaving. **b** a bobbin carrying the lower thread in a sewing-machine. **2** a train, bus, etc., going to and fro over a short route continuously. **3** = SHUTTLECOCK. **4** = *space shuttle.* ● *v.* **1** *intr.* & *tr.* move or cause to move to and fro like a shuttle. **2** *intr.* travel in a shuttle. □ **shuttle armature** *Electr.* an armature with a single coil wound on an elongated iron bobbin. **shuttle diplomacy** negotiations conducted by a mediator who travels successively to several countries. **shuttle service** a train or bus etc. service operating to and fro over a short route. [OE *scytel* dart f. Gmc: cf. SHOOT]
■ *v.* **2** commute; alternate.

shuttlecock /shútt'lkok/ *n.* **1** a cork with a ring of feathers, or a similar device of plastic, used instead of a ball in badminton and in battledore and shuttlecock. **2** a thing passed repeatedly back and forth. [SHUTTLE + COCK[1], prob. f. the flying motion]

shy[1] /shī/ *adj.*, *v.*, & *n.* ● *adj.* (**shyer, shyest** or **shier, shiest**) **1 a** diffident or uneasy in company; timid. **b** (of an animal, bird, etc.) easily startled; timid. **2** (foll. by *of*) avoiding; chary of (*shy of his aunt*; *shy of going to meetings*). **3** (in *comb.*) showing fear of or distaste for (*gun-shy*; *work-shy*). **4** (often foll. by *of, on*) *colloq.* having lost; short of (*I'm shy three quid*; *shy of the price of admission*). ● *v.intr.* (**shies, shied**) **1** (usu. foll. by *at*) (esp. of a horse) start suddenly aside (at an object, noise, etc.) in fright. **2** (usu. foll. by *away from, at*) avoid accepting or becoming involved in (a proposal etc.) in alarm. ● *n.* a sudden startled movement. □□ **shyer** *n.* **shyly** *adv.* (also **shily**). **shyness** *n.* [OE *sceoh* f. Gmc]
■ *adj.* **1** diffident, coy, bashful, retiring, withdrawn, withdrawing, reserved, reticent, timid, quiet, meek, modest, sheepish, mousy, unconfident, self-conscious, introverted, nervous, apprehensive, timorous, uneasy. **2** cautious, wary, chary, guarded, afraid, fearful, frightened, anxious, worried, suspicious, distrustful, *sl.* leery. **4** missing, lacking, deficient in, short of. ● *v.* **1** see START *v.* 11. **2** (*shy (away) from*) see SHUN.

shy[2] /shī/ *v.* & *n.* ● *v.tr.* (**shies, shied**) (also *absol.*) fling or throw (a stone etc.). ● *n.* (*pl.* **shies**) the act or an instance of shying. □ **have a shy at** *colloq.* **1** try to hit with a stone etc. **2** make an attempt at. **3** jeer at. □□ **shyer** *n.* [18th c.: orig. unkn.]

Shylock /shīlok/ *n.* a hard-hearted money-lender; a miser. [character in Shakesp. *Merchant of Venice*]

shyster /shīstər/ *n.* esp. *US colloq.* a person, esp. a lawyer, who uses unscrupulous methods. [19th c.: orig. uncert.]
■ see TWISTER 1.

SI *abbr.* **1** (Order of the) Star of India. **2** the international system of units of measurement (F *Système International*).

Si *symb. Chem.* the element silicon.

si /see/ *n. Mus.* = TE. [F f. It., perh. f. the initials of *Sancte Iohannes*: see GAMUT]

sialogogue /sīələgog/ *n.* & *adj.* ● *n.* a medicine inducing the flow of saliva. ● *adj.* inducing such a flow. [F f. Gk *sialon* saliva + *agōgos* leading]

siamang /sīəmang, seeə-/ *n.* a large black gibbon, *Hylobates syndactylus*, native to Sumatra and the Malay peninsula. [Malay]

Siamese /sīəmeez/ *n.* & *adj.* ● *n.* (*pl.* same) **1 a** a native of Siam (now Thailand) in SE Asia. **b** the language of Siam. **2** (in full **Siamese cat**) **a** a cat of a cream-coloured short-haired breed with a brown face and ears and blue eyes. **b** this breed. ● *adj.* of or concerning Siam, its people, or language. □ **Siamese twins 1** twins joined at any part of the body and sometimes sharing organs etc. **2** any closely associated pair.

sib /sib/ *n.* & *adj.* ● *n.* **1** a brother or sister (cf. SIBLING). **2** a blood relative. **3** a group of people recognized by an individual as his or her kindred. ● *adj.* (usu. foll. by *to*) esp. *Sc.* related; akin. [OE *sib(b)*]

Siberian /sībeeriən/ *n.* & *adj.* ● *n.* **1** a native of Siberia in the north-eastern part of the Russian Federation. **2** a person of Siberian descent. ● *adj.* **1** of or relating to Siberia. **2** *colloq.* (esp. of weather) extremely cold.

sibilant /síbbilənt/ *adj.* & *n.* ● *adj.* **1** (of a letter or set of letters, as *s, sh*) sounded with a hiss. **2** hissing (*a sibilant whisper*). ● *n.* a sibilant letter or letters. □□ **sibilance** *n.* **sibilancy** *n.* [L *sibilare sibilant-* hiss]
■ □□ **sibilance** hiss, hissing; see also RUSTLE *n.*

sibilate /síbbilayt/ *v.tr.* & *intr.* pronounce with or utter a hissing sound. □□ **sibilation** /-láysh'n/ *n.*

sibling /síbling/ *n.* each of two or more children having one or both parents in common. [SIB + -LING[1]]
■ brother, sister, sib.

sibship /síbship/ *n.* **1** the state of belonging to a sib or the same sib. **2** a group of children having the same two parents.

sibyl /síbbil/ *n.* **1** any of the women in ancient times supposed to utter the oracles and prophecies of a god. **2** a prophetess, fortune-teller, or witch. [ME f. OF *Sibile* or med.L *Sibilla* f. L *Sibylla* f. Gk *Sibulla*]
■ see PROPHET 2a.

sibylline /síbbilīn/ *adj.* **1** of or from a sibyl. **2** oracular; prophetic. □ **the Sibylline books** a collection of oracles belonging to the ancient Roman State and used for guidance by magistrates etc. [L *Sibyllinus* (as SIBYL)]
■ **2** see PROPHETIC.

sic /sik/ *adv.* (usu. in brackets) used, spelt, etc., as written (confirming, or calling attention to, the form of quoted or copied words). [L, = so, thus]
■ see *to the letter* (LETTER).

siccative /síkkətiv/ *n.* & *adj.* ● *n.* a substance causing drying, esp. mixed with oil-paint etc. for quick drying. ● *adj.* having such properties. [LL *siccativus* f. *siccare* to dry]

sice[1] /sīss/ *n.* the six on dice. [ME f. OF *sis* f. L *sex* six]

sice[2] var. of SYCE.

Sicilian /sisílyən/ *n.* & *adj.* ● *n.* **1** a native of Sicily, an island off the S. coast of Italy. **2** a person of Sicilian descent. ● *adj.* of or relating to Sicily. [L *Sicilia* Sicily]

siciliano /sichilyáanō/ *n.* (*pl.* **-os**) (also **siciliana** /-nə/) a dance, song, or instrumental piece in 6/8 or 12/8 time, often in a minor key, and evoking a pastoral mood. [It., = Sicilian]

sick[1] /sik/ *adj.*, *n.*, & *v.* ● *adj.* **1** (often in *comb.*) esp. *Brit.* vomiting or tending to vomit (*I think I'm going to be sick*; *seasick*). **2** esp. *US* & *Austral.* ill; affected by illness (*has been sick for a week*; *a sick man*; *sick with measles*). **3 a** (often foll. by *at*) esp. mentally perturbed; disordered (*the product of a sick mind*; *sick at heart*). **b** (often foll. by *for*, or in *comb.*) pining; longing (*sick for a sight of home*; *lovesick*). **4** (often foll. by *of*) *colloq.* **a** disgusted; surfeited (*sick of chocolates*). **b** angry, esp. because of surfeit (*am sick of being teased*). **5** *colloq.* (of humour etc.) jeering at misfortune, illness, death, etc.; morbid (*sick joke*). **6** (of a ship) needing repair (esp. of a specified kind) (*paint-sick*). ● *n. Brit. colloq.* vomit. ● *v.tr.* (usu. foll. by *up*) *Brit. colloq.* vomit (*sicked up his dinner*). □ **go sick** report oneself as ill. **look sick** *colloq.* be unimpressive or embarrassed. **sick at** (or **to**) **one's stomach** *US* vomiting or tending to vomit. **sick-benefit** *Brit.* = *sickness benefit.* **sick building syndrome** a high incidence of illness in office workers, attributed to the immediate working surroundings. **sick-call 1** a visit by a doctor to a sick person etc. **2** *Mil.* a summons for sick men to attend. **sick-flag** a yellow flag indicating disease at a quarantine station or on ship. **sick headache** a migraine headache with vomiting. **sick-leave** leave of absence granted because of illness. **sick-list** a list of the sick, esp. in a regiment, ship, etc. **sick-making** *colloq.* sickening. **sick nurse** = NURSE. **sick-pay** pay given to an employee etc. on sick-leave. **take sick** *colloq.* be taken ill. □□ **sickish** *adj.* [OE *sēoc* f. Gmc]
■ *adj.* **1** nauseated, queasy, squeamish, qualmish, bilious; green about *or* around the gills, seasick, carsick, airsick, *US* sick to one's stomach. **2** ill, unwell, unhealthy, sickly,

poorly, indisposed, laid up, infirm, ailing, diseased, afflicted, on the sick-list, *colloq.* under the weather, not (feeling) up to snuff, *Austral.* & *NZ colloq.* crook, *Brit. colloq.* (a bit) off. **3 a** affected, troubled, perturbed, heartsick, wretched, miserable, burdened, weighed down, *archaic* stricken; mad, insane, deranged, disturbed, neurotic, unbalanced, psychoneurotic, psychotic, *colloq.* mental, crazy, *sl.* off one's trolley, off one's rocker. **4** sickened, put out, upset, appalled, disgusted, revolted, repulsed, offended, repelled, nauseated; annoyed, chagrined, irritated; surfeited, jaded; *colloq.* turned off; (*sick of*) (sick and) tired of, bored with, weary of, fed up with, glutted with, sated with. **5** peculiar, unconventional, far-out, strange, weird, odd, bizarre, grotesque, macabre, shocking, ghoulish, morbid, gruesome, stomach-turning, sadistic, masochistic, sado-masochistic, warped, perverted, *colloq.* kinky, *US colloq.* off, *sl.* bent; black. ● *n.* vomit, *Austral. sl.* chunder. ● *v.* see VOMIT *v.* 1. □ **sick-making** see DISGUSTING. **take sick** see SICKEN 2a.

sick[2] /sik/ *v.tr.* (usu. in *imper.*) (esp. to a dog) set upon (a rat etc.). [19th c., dial. var. of SEEK]

sickbay /síkbay/ *n.* **1** part of a ship used as a hospital. **2** any room etc. for sick people.

sickbed /síkbed/ *n.* **1** an invalid's bed. **2** the state of being an invalid.

sicken /síkkən/ *v.* **1** *tr.* affect with loathing or disgust. **2** *intr.* **a** (often foll. by *for*) show symptoms of illness (*is sickening for measles*). **b** (often foll. by *at*, or *to* + infin.) feel nausea or disgust (*he sickened at the sight*). **3** (as **sickening** *adj.*) **a** loathsome, disgusting. **b** *colloq.* very annoying. □□ **sickeningly** *adv.*

■ **1** make ill *or* sick, afflict, affect, disgust, nauseate, turn one's stomach, upset, appal, shock, repel, revolt, repulse, offend, make one's gorge rise; put off, *colloq.* turn off. **2 a** fall *or* take ill, take sick, fail, weaken; (*sicken for*) contract, catch, come down with, *archaic* be stricken by *or* with. **3** (**sickening**) **a** see DISGUSTING.

sickie /síkki/ *n. Austral.* & *NZ colloq.* a period of sick-leave, usu. taken with insufficient medical reason.

sickle /síkk'l/ *n.* **1** a short-handled farming tool with a semicircular blade, used for cutting corn, lopping, or trimming. **2** anything sickle-shaped, esp. the crescent moon. □ **sickle-bill** any of various curlews with a sickle-shaped bill. **sickle-cell** a sickle-shaped blood-cell, esp. as found in a type of severe hereditary anaemia. **sickle-feather** each of the long middle feathers of a cock's tail. [OE *sicol*, *sicel* f. L *secula* f. *secare* cut]

sickly /síkli/ *adj.* (**sicklier, sickliest**) **1 a** of weak health; apt to be ill. **b** (of a person's complexion, look, etc.) languid, faint, or pale, suggesting sickness (*a sickly smile*). **c** (of light or colour) faint, pale, feeble. **2** causing ill health (*a sickly climate*). **3** (of a book etc.) sentimental or mawkish. **4** inducing or connected with nausea (*a sickly taste*). **5** (of a colour etc.) of an unpleasant shade inducing nausea (*a sickly green*). □□ **sickliness** *n.* [ME, prob. after ON *sjukligr* (as SICK[1])]

■ **1 a** see SICK[1] *adj.* 2. **b** languid, ailing, feeble, delicate, wan, weak, faint, pallid, drawn, pasty, peaked, peaky, peakish; see also PALE *adj.* 1. **c** faint, feeble, weak, colourless, wishy-washy; see also PALE *adj.* 2. **2** see UNHEALTHY 2. **3** sentimental, mushy, mawkish, maudlin, cloying, syrupy, saccharine, treacly, insipid, weak, watery, sloppy, *Brit. colloq.* soppy. **4** nauseating, cloying; see also DISGUSTING. **5** *colloq.* icky, *sl.* yuk; see also REVOLTING. **sickliness** see *infirmity* (INFIRM).

sickness /síkniss/ *n.* **1** the state of being ill; disease. **2** a specified disease (*sleeping sickness*). **3** vomiting or a tendency to vomit. □ **sickness benefit** (in the UK) benefit paid by the State for sickness interrupting paid employment. [OE *sēocnesse* (as SICK[1], -NESS)]

■ **1, 2** see DISEASE.

sickroom /síkrōōm, -rŏŏm/ *n.* **1** a room occupied by a sick person. **2** a room adapted for sick people.

sidalcea /sidálsiə/ *n.* any mallow-like plant of the genus *Sidalcea*, bearing racemes of white, pink, or purple flowers. [mod.L f. *Sida* + *Alcea*, names of related genera]

side /sīd/ *n.* & *v.* ● *n.* **1 a** each of the more or less flat surfaces bounding an object (*a cube has six sides*; *this side up*). **b** a more or less vertical inner or outer plane or surface (*the side of a house*; *a mountainside*). **c** such a vertical lateral surface or plane as distinct from the top or bottom, front or back, or ends (*at the side of the house*). **2 a** the half of a person or animal that is on the right or the left, esp. of the torso (*has a pain in his right side*). **b** the left or right half or a specified part of a thing, area, building, etc. (*put the box on that side*). **c** (often in *comb.*) a position next to a person or thing (*grave-side*; *seaside*; *stood at my side*). **d** a specified direction relating to a person or thing (*on the north side of*; *came from all sides*). **e** half of a butchered carcass (*a side of bacon*). **3 a** either surface of a thing regarded as having two surfaces. **b** the amount of writing needed to fill one side of a sheet of paper (*write three sides*). **4** any of several aspects of a question, character, etc. (*many sides to his character*; *look on the bright side*). **5 a** each of two sets of opponents in war, politics, games, etc. (*the side that bats first*; *much to be said on both sides*). **b** a cause or philosophical position etc. regarded as being in conflict with another (*on the side of right*). **6 a** a part or region near the edge and remote from the centre (*at the side of the room*). **b** (*attrib.*) a subordinate, peripheral, or detached part (*a side-road*; *a side-table*). **7 a** each of the bounding lines of a plane rectilinear figure (*a hexagon has six sides*). **b** each of two quantities stated to be equal in an equation. **8** a position nearer or farther than, or right or left of, a dividing line (*on this side of the Alps*; *on the other side of the road*). **9** a line of hereditary descent through the father or the mother. **10** (in full **side spin**) *Brit.* a spinning motion given to a billiard-ball etc. by hitting it on one side, not centrally. **11** *Brit. sl.* boastfulness; swagger (*has no side about him*). **12** *Brit. colloq.* a television channel (*shall we try another side?*). ● *v.intr.* (usu. foll. by *with*) take part or be on the same side as a disputant etc. (*sided with his father*). □ **by the side of 1** close to. **2** compared with. **from side to side 1** right across. **2** alternately each way from a central line. **let the side down** fail one's colleagues, esp. by frustrating their efforts or embarrassing them. **on one side 1** not in the main or central position. **2** aside (*took him on one side to explain*). **on the . . . side** fairly, somewhat (qualifying an adjective: *on the high side*). **on the side 1** as a sideline; in addition to one's regular work etc. **2** secretly or illicitly. **3** *US* as a side dish. **on this side of the grave** in life. **side-arms** swords, bayonets, or pistols. **side-band** a range of frequencies near the carrier frequency of a radio wave, concerned in modulation. **side-bet** a bet between opponents, esp. in card-games, over and above the ordinary stakes. **side-bone** either of the small forked bones under the wings of poultry. **side by side** standing close together, esp. for mutual support. **side-car 1** a small car for a passenger or passengers attached to the side of a motor cycle. **2** a cocktail of orange liqueur, lemon juice, and brandy. **3** a jaunting car. **side-chapel** a chapel in the aisle or at the side of a church. **side dish** an extra dish subsidiary to the main course. **side-door 1** a door in or at the side of a building. **2** an indirect means of access. **side-drum** a small double-headed drum in a jazz or military band or in an orchestra (orig. hung at the drummer's side). **side-effect** a secondary, usu. undesirable, effect. **side-glance** a sideways or brief glance. **side-issue** a point that distracts attention from what is important. **side-note** a marginal note. **side-on** *adv.* from the side. ● *adj.* **1** from or towards one side. **2** (of a collision) involving the side of a vehicle. **side-road** a minor or subsidiary road, esp. joining or diverging from a main road. **side-saddle** *n.* a saddle for a woman rider with both feet on the same side of the horse. ● *adv.* sitting in this position on a horse. **side salad** a salad served as a side dish. **side-seat** a seat in a vehicle etc. in which the occupant has his back to the side of the vehicle. **side-slip** *n.* **1** a skid. **2** *Aeron.* a sideways movement instead of forward. ● *v.intr.*

1 skid. **2** *Aeron.* move sideways instead of forward. **side-splitting** causing violent laughter. **side-street** a minor or subsidiary street. **side-stroke 1** a stroke towards or from a side. **2** an incidental action. **3** a swimming stroke in which the swimmer lies on his or her side. **side-swipe** *n.* **1** a glancing blow along the side. **2** incidental criticism etc. ● *v.tr.* hit with or as if with a side-swipe. **side-table** a table placed at the side of a room or apart from the main table. **side-trip** a minor excursion during a voyage or trip; a detour. **side valve** a valve in a vehicle engine, operated from the side of the cylinder. **side-view 1** a view obtained sideways. **2** a profile. **side-wheeler** *US* a steamer with paddle-wheels. **side-whiskers** whiskers growing on the cheeks. **side wind 1** wind from the side. **2** an indirect agency or influence. **take sides** support one or other cause etc. □□ **sideless** *adj.* [OE *sīde* f. Gmc]

▪ *n.* **1 a** surface, face, plane; facet. **b** flank, edge, face, elevation. **4** see ASPECT 1a. **5 a** army; faction, interest, party, part, sect, camp; team, string, squad; *Soccer or Cricket* eleven, *Rugby Union* fifteen. **b** (point of) view, viewpoint, aspect, opinion, standpoint, stand, cause, angle, position, attitude, school, philosophy. **6 a** edge, margin, verge, bank, rim, brim, brink, border, boundary, limit; perimeter, periphery. **b** (*attrib.*) secondary, incidental, subordinate, tangential, subsidiary, auxiliary, indirect, ancillary, lesser, minor, unimportant, inconsequential, inconsiderable, insignificant, marginal, peripheral. **11** affectation, pretension, haughtiness, arrogance, insolence, boastfulness, pretentiousness, airs, swagger, *colloq.* swank. ● *v.* (*side with*) take sides with, show preference for, be partial to, show favouritism to *or* for, sympathize with, support, back, stand up for, stand by, favour, prefer, go in *or* along with, join ((up) with), ally with, be *or* become allied with, team up with, throw in one's lot with. □ **on the side 2** see *on the sly* (SLY). **side by side** together, jointly, cheek by jowl, shoulder to shoulder. **side-note** see NOTE *n.* 2, 5. **side-road** see *turn-off* 1. **side-splitting** see HILARIOUS 1. **side-trip** see EXCURSION 1. **side-view** profile, outline, contour, silhouette. **take sides** show preference, be partial, show favouritism; see also SIDE *v.* above. **side-whiskers** muttons, mutton-chop whiskers; sideburns, *Brit. colloq.* sideboards.

sideboard /sīdbord/ *n.* a table or esp. a flat-topped cupboard at the side of a dining-room for supporting and containing dishes, table linen, decanters, etc.

sideboards /sīdbordz/ *n.pl. Brit. colloq.* hair grown by a man down the sides of his face; side-whiskers.

sideburns /sīdburnz/ *n.pl.* = SIDEBOARDS. [*burnsides* pl. of *burnside* f. General *Burnside* d. 1881 who affected this style]

sided /sīdid/ *adj.* **1** having sides. **2** (in *comb.*) having a specified side or sides (*one-sided*). □□ **-sidedly** *adv.* **sidedness** *n.* (also in *comb.*).

sidehill /sīdhil/ *n. US* a hillside.

sidekick /sīdkik/ *n. colloq.* a close associate.

▪ see ACCOMPLICE.

sidelight /sīdlīt/ *n.* **1** a light from the side. **2** incidental information etc. **3** *Brit.* a light at the side of the front of a motor vehicle to warn of its presence. **4** *Naut.* the red port or green starboard light on a ship under way.

sideline /sīdlīn/ *n.* & *v.* ● *n.* **1** work etc. done in addition to one's main activity. **2** (usu. in *pl.*) **a** a line bounding the side of a hockey-pitch, tennis-court, etc. **b** the space next to these where spectators etc. sit. ● *v.tr. US* remove (a player) from a team through injury, suspension, etc. □ **on** (or **from**) **the sidelines** in (or from) a position removed from the main action.

▪ *n.* **1** see HOBBY[1] 1. □ **on the sidelines** in the wings, standing by, aside, alongside; see also *in reserve* (RESERVE).

sidelong /sīdlong/ *adj.* & *adv.* ● *adj.* inclining to one side; oblique (*a sidelong glance*). ● *adv.* obliquely (*moved sidelong*). [*sideling* (as SIDE, -LING[2]): see -LONG]

▪ *adj.* oblique, indirect, sideways, lateral, covert, surreptitious, sly. ● *adv.* see SIDEWAYS *adv.*

sidereal /sīdēeriəl/ *adj.* of or concerning the constellations or fixed stars. □ **sidereal clock** a clock showing sidereal time. **sidereal day** the time between successive meridional transits of a star or esp. of the first point of Aries, about four minutes shorter than the solar day. **sidereal time** time measured by the apparent diurnal motion of the stars. **sidereal year** a year longer than the solar year by 20 minutes 23 seconds because of precession. [L *sidereus* f. *sidus sideris* star]

▪ stellar, astral, star.

siderite /siddərīt/ *n.* **1** a mineral form of ferrous carbonate. **2** a meteorite consisting mainly of nickel and iron. [Gk *sidēros* iron]

siderostat /siddərəstat/ *n.* an instrument used for keeping the image of a celestial body in a fixed position. [L *sidus sideris* star, after *heliostat*]

sideshow /sīdshō/ *n.* **1** a minor show or attraction in an exhibition or entertainment. **2** a minor incident or issue.

sidesman /sīdzmən/ *n.* (*pl.* **-men**) an assistant churchwarden, who shows worshippers to their seats, takes the collection, etc.

sidestep /sīdstep/ *n.* & *v.* ● *n.* a step taken sideways. ● *v.tr.* (**-stepped, -stepping**) **1** esp. *Football* avoid (esp. a tackle) by stepping sideways. **2** evade. □□ **sidestepper** *n.*

▪ *v.* avoid, dodge, circumvent, skirt, bypass, evade, shun, steer clear of, shirk, get out of, *colloq.* duck.

sidetrack /sīdtrak/ *n.* & *v.* ● *n.* a railway siding. ● *v.tr.* **1** turn into a siding; shunt. **2 a** postpone, evade, or divert treatment or consideration of. **b** divert (a person) from considering etc.

▪ *n.* (railway) siding. ● *v.* **1** shunt, divert. **2** divert, deflect, draw off *or* away, distract, turn aside.

sidewalk /sīdwawk/ *n. US* a pedestrian path at the side of a road; a pavement.

▪ see PAVEMENT 1.

sideward /sīdwərd/ *adj.* & *adv.* ● *adj.* = SIDEWAYS. ● *adv.* (also **sidewards** /-wərdz/) = SIDEWAYS.

sideways /sīdwayz/ *adv.* & *adj.* ● *adv.* **1** to or from a side (*moved sideways*). **2** with one side facing forward (*sat sideways on the bus*). ● *adj.* to or from a side (*a sideways movement*). □□ **sidewise** *adv.* & *adj.*

▪ *adv.* obliquely, laterally, edgeways, edgewise, edge on, sidelong, crabwise; indirectly. ● *adj.* see SIDELONG *adj.*

sidewinder /sīdwīndər/ *n.* **1** a desert rattlesnake, *Crotalus cerastes*, native to N. America, moving with a lateral motion. **2** *US* a sideways blow.

siding /sīding/ *n.* **1** a short track at the side of and opening on to a railway line, used for shunting trains. **2** *US* cladding material for the outside of a building.

sidle /sīd'l/ *v.* & *n.* ● *v.intr.* (usu. foll. by *along*, *up*) walk in a timid, furtive, stealthy, or cringing manner. ● *n.* the act or an instance of sidling. [back-form. f. *sideling*, SIDELONG]

▪ *v.* edge, slink, steal; see also CREEP *v.* 2.

SIDS *abbr.* sudden infant death syndrome; = *cot-death* (see COT[1]).

siege /seej/ *n.* **1 a** a military operation in which an attacking force seeks to compel the surrender of a fortified place by surrounding it and cutting off supplies etc. **b** a similar operation by police etc. to force the surrender of an armed person. **c** the period during which a siege lasts. **2** a persistent attack or campaign of persuasion. □ **lay siege to** esp. *Mil.* conduct the siege of. **raise the siege of** abandon or cause the abandonment of an attempt to take (a place) by siege. **siege-gun** *hist.* a heavy gun used in sieges. **siege-train** artillery and other equipment for a siege, with vehicles etc. [ME f. OF *sege* seat f. *assegier* BESIEGE]

▪ **1** blockade, encirclement. □ **lay siege to** besiege, blockade, beleaguer, cordon off, encircle, box *or* pen *or* shut in, bottle up.

siemens /seémənz/ *n. Electr.* the SI unit of conductance, equal to one reciprocal ohm. ¶ Abbr.: **S**. [W. von *Siemens*, Ger. electrical engineer, d. 1892]

sienna /siénnə/ *n.* **1** a kind of ferruginous earth used as a pigment in paint. **2** its colour of yellowish-brown (**raw sienna**) or reddish-brown (**burnt sienna**). [It. (*terra di*) *Sienna* (earth of) Siena in Tuscany]

sierra /siérrə/ *n.* a long jagged mountain chain, esp. in Spain or Spanish America. [Sp. f. L *serra* saw]

siesta /siéstə/ *n.* an afternoon sleep or rest esp. in hot countries. [Sp. f. L *sexta* (*hora*) sixth hour]
■ see REST[1] *n.* 1.

sieve /siv/ *n.* & *v.* ● *n.* a utensil having a perforated or meshed bottom for separating solids or coarse material from liquids or fine particles, or for reducing a soft solid to a fine pulp. ● *v.tr.* **1** put through or sift with a sieve. **2** examine (evidence etc.) to select or separate. □ **head like a sieve** *colloq.* a memory that retains little. □□ **sievelike** *adj.* [OE *sife* f. WG]
■ *n.* see MESH *n.* 1–3a. ● *v.* **1** see SIFT 1–3. **2** see SIFT 4.

siffleur /seeflốr/ *n.* (*fem.* ***siffleuse*** /-flốz/) a professional whistler. [F f. *siffler* whistle]

sift /sift/ *v.* **1** *tr.* sieve (material) into finer and coarser parts. **2** *tr.* (usu. foll. by *from*, *out*) separate (finer or coarser parts) from material. **3** *tr.* sprinkle (esp. sugar) from a perforated container. **4** *tr.* examine (evidence, facts, etc.) in order to assess authenticity etc. **5** *intr.* (of snow, light, etc.) fall as if from a sieve. □ **sift through** examine by sifting. □□ **sifter** *n.* (also in *comb.*). [OE *siftan* f. WG]
■ **1** strain, sieve, riddle, filter, screen, bolt, winnow, *Austral.* yandy. **2** (*sift out*) winnow, separate, weed out, filter out, sort out; select, choose, pick. **3** sprinkle, dredge, sieve. **4** sift through, examine, analyse, study, probe, screen, scrutinize, investigate. □□ **sifter** riddle, sieve, colander.

Sig. *abbr.* Signor.

sigh /sī/ *v.* & *n.* ● *v.* **1** *intr.* emit a long deep audible breath expressive of sadness, weariness, longing, relief, etc. **2** *intr.* (foll. by *for*) yearn for (a lost person or thing). **3** *tr.* utter or express with sighs (*'Never!' he sighed*). **4** *intr.* (of the wind etc.) make a sound like sighing. ● *n.* **1** the act or an instance of sighing. **2** a sound made in sighing (*a sigh of relief*). [ME *sihen* etc., prob. back-form. f. *sihte* past of *sīhen* f. OE *sīcan*]
■ *v.* **1** breathe, sough; groan, moan. **2** (*sigh for*) yearn *or* long *or* pine for; bemoan, lament *or* mourn *or* grieve *or* weep for, bewail. **4** sough, moan. ● *n.* **1** exhalation. **2** murmur, sound.

sight /sīt/ *n.* & *v.* ● *n.* **1 a** the faculty of seeing with the eyes (*lost his sight*). **b** the act or an instance of seeing; the state of being seen. **2** a thing seen; a display, show, or spectacle (*not a pretty sight*; *a beautiful sight*). **3** a way of looking at or considering a thing (*in my sight he can do no wrong*). **4** a range of space within which a person etc. can see or an object be seen (*he's out of sight*; *they are just coming into sight*). **5** (usu. in *pl.*) noteworthy features of a town, area, etc. (*went to see the sights*). **6 a** a device on a gun or optical instrument used for assisting the precise aim or observation. **b** the aim or observation so gained (*got a sight of him*). **7** *colloq.* a person or thing having a ridiculous, repulsive, or dishevelled appearance (*looked a perfect sight*). **8** *colloq.* a great quantity (*will cost a sight of money*; *is a sight better than he was*). ● *v.tr.* **1** get sight of, esp. by approaching (*they sighted land*). **2** observe the presence of (esp. aircraft, animals, etc.) (*sighted buffalo*). **3** take observations of (a star etc.) with an instrument. **4 a** provide (a gun, quadrant, etc.) with sights. **b** adjust the sight of (a gun etc.). **c** aim (a gun etc.) with sights. □ **at first sight** on first glimpse or impression. **at** (or **on**) **sight** as soon as a person or a thing has been seen (*plays music at sight*; *liked him on sight*). **catch** (or **lose**) **sight of** begin (or cease) to see or be aware of. **get a sight of** manage to see; glimpse. **have lost sight of** no longer know the whereabouts of. **in sight 1** visible. **2** near at hand (*salvation is in sight*). **in** (or **within**) **sight of** so as to see or be seen from. **lower one's sights** become less ambitious. **out of my sight!** go at once! **out of sight 1** not visible. **2** *colloq.* excellent; delightful. **out of sight out of mind** we forget the absent. **put out of sight** hide, ignore. **set one's sights on** aim at (*set her sights on a directorship*). **sight for the gods** (or **sight for sore eyes**) a welcome person or thing, esp. a visitor. **sight-glass** a transparent device for observing the interior of apparatus etc. **sighting shot** an experimental shot to guide riflemen in adjusting their sights. **sight-line** a hypothetical line from a person's eye to what is seen. **sight-read** (*past* and *past part.* **-read** /-red/) read and perform (music) at sight. **sight-reader** a person who sight-reads. **sight-screen** *Cricket* a large white screen on wheels placed near the boundary in line with the wicket to help the batsman see the ball. **sight-sing** sing (music) at sight. **sight unseen** without previous inspection. □□ **sighter** *n.* [OE (*ge*)*sihth*]
■ *n.* **1 a** eyesight, vision, eyes, visual acuity. **b** glimpse, peep, peek, glance, look; see also VIEW *n.* 3. **2** spectacle, scene, display, show; rarity, marvel, wonder, phenomenon; pageant. **3** view, opinion, judgement. **4** field of view *or* vision, range of vision, ken, perception, view, eyeshot, gaze. **7** mess, disaster, eyesore, monstrosity, fright, *colloq.* atrocity. **8** see LOT *n.* 1. ● *v.* **1–3** spot, see, catch sight of, mark, observe, view, distinguish, discern, identify, note, notice, remark, glimpse, spy, *literary* behold, descry, espy. □ **catch** (or **lose**) **sight of** (*catch sight of*) spot, notice, spy, glance at, glimpse, catch a glimpse of, (get a) look *or* peep *or* peek at, *colloq.* get a look-see at, *sl.* take a gander at, get a load of; see also SIGHT *v.* 1–3 above; (*lose sight of*) see *lose track of* (TRACK[1]). **in sight 1** see OUT *adv.* 2a, b, 3a, 12. **2** see *at hand* (HAND). **out of sight 1** remote, distant, far-away, unseeable, imperceptible, invisible. **2** unusual, rare, extraordinary, outrageous, imaginative, awe-inspiring, incredible, shocking, moving, jolting, excellent, splendid, superb, delightful, far-out, *colloq.* out of this world, brilliant, *colloq.* brill, *esp. US sl.* cool, *US sl.* neat, *US* & *Austral. sl.* unreal. **set one's sights on** see AIM *v.* 1, 4. **sight for the gods** (or **sight for sore eyes**) vision, welcome sight, dream, picture.

sighted /sītid/ *adj.* **1** capable of seeing; not blind. **2** (in *comb.*) having a specified kind of sight (*long-sighted*).

sightless /sītliss/ *adj.* **1** blind. **2** *poet.* invisible. □□ **sightlessly** *adv.* **sightlessness** *n.*
■ **1** see BLIND *adj.* 1.

sightly /sītli/ *adj.* attractive to the sight; not unsightly. □□ **sightliness** *n.*

sightseer /sītseeər/ *n.* a person who visits places of interest; a tourist. □□ **sightsee** *v.intr.* & *tr.* **sightseeing** *n.*
■ tourist, traveller, globe-trotter, visitor, *esp. Brit.* holiday-maker, *Brit.* tripper, day-tripper, *colloq.* rubberneck. □□ **sightsee** see TRIP *v.* 4.

sightworthy /sītwurthi/ *adj.* worth seeing.

sigillate /síjilət/ *adj.* **1** (of pottery) having impressed patterns. **2** *Bot.* having seal-like marks. [L *sigillatus* f. *sigillum* seal dimin. of *signum* sign]

siglum /sígləm/ *n.* (*pl.* **sigla** /-lə/) a letter (esp. an initial) or other symbol used to denote a word in a book, esp. to refer to a particular text. [LL *sigla* (pl.), perh. f. *singula* neut. pl. of *singulus* single]

sigma /sígmə/ *n.* the eighteenth letter of the Greek alphabet (Σ, σ, or, when final, ς). [L f. Gk]

sigmate /sígmət/ *adj.* **1** sigma-shaped. **2** S-shaped.

sigmoid /sígmoyd/ *adj.* & *n.* ● *adj.* **1** curved like the uncial sigma (**C**); crescent-shaped. **2** S-shaped. ● *n.* (in full **sigmoid flexure**) *Anat.* the curved part of the intestine between the colon and the rectum. [Gk *sigmoeidēs* (as SIGMA)]

sign /sīn/ *n.* & *v.* ● *n.* **1 a** a thing indicating or suggesting a quality or state etc.; a thing perceived as indicating a future state or occurrence (*violence is a sign of weakness*; *shows all the signs of decay*). **b** a miracle evidencing supernatural power; a portent (*did signs and wonders*). **2 a** a mark, symbol, or device used to represent something or to distinguish the thing on which it is put (*marked the jar with a sign*). **b** a technical symbol used in algebra, music, etc. (*a minus sign*; *a repeat sign*). **3** a gesture or action used to convey information, an order, request, etc. (*gave him a sign to leave*; *conversed by signs*). **4** a publicly displayed board etc. giving information; a signboard or signpost. **5** any objective evidence of a disease, usu. specified (*Babinski's sign*). **6** a password (*advanced and gave the sign*). **7** any of the twelve divisions of the zodiac, named from the constellations formerly situated in them (*the sign of Cancer*). **8** *US* the trail of a wild animal. **9** *Math.* etc. the positiveness or negativeness of a quantity. **10** = *sign language*. ● *v.* **1** *tr.* **a** (also *absol.*) write (one's name, initials, etc.) on a document etc. indicating that one has authorized it. **b** write one's name etc. on (a document) as authorization. **2** *intr.* & *tr.* communicate by gesture (*signed to me to come*; *signed their assent*). **3** *tr.* & *intr.* engage or be engaged by signing a contract etc. (see also *sign on*, *sign up*). **4** *tr.* mark with a sign (esp. with the sign of the cross in baptism). □ **make no sign** seem unconscious; not protest. **sign and countersign** secret words etc. used as passwords. **sign away** convey (one's right, property, etc.) by signing a deed etc. **sign for** acknowledge receipt of by signing. **sign language** a system of communication by visual gestures, used esp. by the deaf. **sign of the cross** a Christian sign made in blessing or prayer, by tracing a cross from the forehead to the chest and to each shoulder, or in the air. **sign off 1** end work, broadcasting, a letter, etc., esp. by writing or speaking one's name. **2 a** end a period of employment, contract, etc. **b** end the period of employment or contract of (a person). **3** *Brit.* stop receiving unemployment benefit after finding work. **4** *Bridge* indicate by a conventional bid that one is seeking to end the bidding. **sign-off** *n. Bridge* such a bid. **sign of the times** a portent etc. showing a likely trend. **sign on 1** agree to a contract, employment, etc. **2** begin work, broadcasting, etc., esp. by writing or announcing one's name. **3** employ (a person). **4** *Brit.* register as unemployed. **sign-painter** (or **-writer**) a person who paints signboards etc. **sign up 1** engage or employ (a person). **2** enlist in the armed forces. **3 a** commit (another person or oneself) by signing etc. (*signed you up for dinner*). **b** enrol (*signed up for evening classes*). □□ **signable** *adj.* **signer** *n.* [ME f. OF *signe*, *signer* f. L *signum*, *signare*]

■ *n.* **1** token, symbol, indication, mark, signal, indicator; notice; trace, evidence, manifestation, proof, reminder, pointer, clue, hint, suggestion, vestige; omen, augury, warning, forewarning, portent, writing on the wall, prophecy, prognostication, foreshadowing. **2** device, mark, symbol, representation, emblem, trade mark, badge, insignia, brand, stamp, seal, ideogram, ideograph, phonogram, hieroglyph, rebus, logo(type), colophon, ensign, standard, banner, flag; monogram, initials, cipher, *Archaeol.* cartouche, *Linguistics* grapheme. **3** movement, gesture, motion, signal, cue, gesticulation; nod, wave. **4** signboard, advertisement, placard, poster, notice, announcement; *US* shingle; signpost. **5** see SYMPTOM. **6** password, watchword, countersign. **8** see TRAIL *n.* 1. ● *v.* **1** inscribe, mark, subscribe; sign on the dotted line; autograph, put one's signature on *or* to, countersign, endorse, witness, put *or* set one's hand to. **2** see SIGNAL[1] *v.* 1, 2a. □ **sign away** forgo, relinquish, give up, abandon (claim to), quit claim to, waive, release, surrender, dispose of, sacrifice, get rid of; sign over, assign, consign, transfer, make over, deliver, give, donate, present, dispose of, turn over. **sign off 1** close down, end (off), terminate *or* discontinue. **sign on 1** sign up, enrol, enlist, register, volunteer, join (up), contract. **3** sign up, enrol, enlist, hire, employ, put under contract, retain, engage, take on. **sign up 1** see *sign on* 3 above. **2, 3b** see *sign on* 1 above.

signal[1] /sígn'l/ *n.* & *v.* ● *n.* **1 a** a usu. prearranged sign conveying information, guidance, etc., esp. at a distance (*waved as a signal to begin*). **b** a message made up of such signs (*signals made with flags*). **2** an immediate occasion for or cause of movement, action, etc. (*the uprising was a signal for repression*). **3** *Electr.* **a** an electrical impulse or impulses or radio waves transmitted as a signal. **b** a sequence of these. **4** a light, semaphore, etc., on a railway giving instructions or warnings to train-drivers etc. **5** *Bridge* a prearranged mode of bidding or play to convey information to one's partner. ● *v.* (**signalled, signalling**; *US* **signaled, signaling**) **1** *intr.* make signals. **2** *tr.* **a** (often foll. by *to* + infin.) make signals to; direct. **b** transmit (an order, information, etc.) by signal; announce (*signalled her agreement*; *signalled that the town had been taken*). □ **signal-book** a list of signals arranged for sending esp. naval and military messages. **signal-box** *Brit.* a building beside a railway track from which signals are controlled. **signal of distress** esp. *Naut.* an appeal for help, esp. from a ship by firing guns. **signal-tower** *US* = *signal-box*. □□ **signaller** *n.* [ME f. OF f. Rmc & med.L *signale* neut. of LL *signalis* f. L *signum* SIGN]

■ *n.* **1** see SIGN *n.* 1, 3. **2** incitement, stimulus, spur, impetus, goad, *archaic* prick. ● *v.* **1, 2a** motion, indicate, gesture, gesticulate, whistle, wink, blink, nod, beckon, flag, semaphore, wave, sign; direct. **2 b** announce; see also COMMUNICATE 1a.

signal[2] /sígn'l/ *adj.* remarkably good or bad; noteworthy (*a signal victory*). □□ **signally** *adv.* [F *signalé* f. It. past part. *segnalato* distinguished f. *segnale* SIGNAL[1]]

■ remarkable, conspicuous, striking, extraordinary, unusual, unique, singular, special, noteworthy, notable, exceptional, significant, important, outstanding, momentous, consequential, weighty. □□ **signally** see *notably* (NOTABLE).

signalize /sígnəlīz/ *v.tr.* (also **-ise**) **1** make noteworthy or remarkable. **2** lend distinction or lustre to. **3** indicate.

signalman /sígn'lmən/ *n.* (*pl.* **-men**) **1** a railway employee responsible for operating signals and points. **2** a person who displays or receives naval etc. signals.

signary /sígnəri/ *n.* (*pl.* **-ies**) a list of signs constituting the syllabic or alphabetic symbols of a language. [L *signum* SIGN + -ARY[1], after *syllabary*]

signatory /sígnətəri, -tri/ *n.* & *adj.* ● *n.* (*pl.* **-ies**) a party or esp. a State that has signed an agreement or esp. a treaty. ● *adj.* having signed such an agreement etc. [L *signatorius* of sealing f. *signare signat-* mark]

■ *n.* see PARTY[1] *n.* 4.

signature /sígnəchər/ *n.* **1 a** a person's name, initials, or mark used in signing a letter, document, etc. **b** the act of signing a document etc. **2** *archaic* a distinctive action, characteristic, etc. **3** *Mus.* **a** = *key signature*. **b** = *time signature*. **4** *Printing* **a** a letter or figure placed at the foot of one or more pages of each sheet of a book as a guide for binding. **b** such a sheet after folding. **5** *US* directions given to a patient as part of a medical prescription. □ **signature tune** esp. *Brit.* a distinctive tune used to introduce a particular programme or performer on television or radio. [med.L *signatura* (LL = marking of sheep), as SIGNATORY]

■ **1 a** see STAMP *n.* 2, 4. **2** see TOUCH *n.* 5.

signboard /sīnbord/ *n.* a board with a name or symbol etc. displayed outside a shop or hotel etc.

■ see SIGN *n.* 4.

signet /sígnit/ *n.* **1** a seal used instead of or with a signature as authentication. **2** (prec. by *the*) the royal seal formerly used for special purposes in England and Scotland, and in Scotland later as the seal of the Court of Session. □ **signet-ring** a ring with a seal set in it. [ME f. OF *signet* or med.L *signetum* (as SIGN)]

■ **1** see SANCTION *n.* 2.

significance /signífikənss/ *n.* **1** importance; noteworthiness (*his opinion is of no significance*). **2** a concealed or real meaning (*what is the significance of his statement?*). **3** the state of being significant. **4** *Statistics* the extent to which a result deviates from a hypothesis such that the difference is due to more than errors in sampling. [OF *significance* or L *significantia* (as SIGNIFY)]

■ **1** importance, weight, weightiness, consequence, moment, relevance, noteworthiness, value, import. **2** meaning, sense, signification, denotation, message, idea, point, import, purport, implication, portent, content, pith, essence; gist, drift, vein, impression, connotation.

significant /signíffikənt/ *adj.* **1** having a meaning; indicative. **2** having an unstated or secret meaning; suggestive (*refused it with a significant gesture*). **3** noteworthy; important; consequential (*a significant figure in history*). **4** *Statistics* of or relating to the significance in the difference between an observed and calculated result. □ **significant figure** *Math.* a digit conveying information about a number containing it, and not a zero used simply to fill vacant space at the beginning or end. □□ **significantly** *adv.* [L *significare*: see SIGNIFY]

■ **1, 2** meaningful, informative, indicative; eloquent, pithy, expressive, telling, pregnant, suggestive, tell-tale. **3** important, weighty, momentous, consequential, critical, considerable, goodly, substantial, major, great, noteworthy, notable, valuable, valued, meritorious, outstanding, impressive, historic, relevant, signal, *archaic* substantive. □□ **significantly** see MATERIALLY.

signification /sígnifikáysh'n/ *n.* **1** the act of signifying. **2** (usu. foll. by *of*) exact meaning or sense, esp. of a word or phrase. [ME f. OF f. L *significatio -onis* (as SIGNIFY)]

■ **2** see MEANING *n.* 1, 2.

significative /signíffikətiv/ *adj.* **1** (esp. of a symbol etc.) signifying. **2** having a meaning. **3** (usu. foll. by *of*) serving as a sign or evidence. [ME f. OF *significatif -ive*, or LL *significativus* (as SIGNIFY)]

signify /sígnifī/ *v.* (**-ies, -ied**) **1** *tr.* be a sign or indication of (*a yawn signifies boredom*). **2** *tr.* mean; have as its meaning ('*Dr*' *signifies* '*doctor*'). **3** *tr.* communicate; make known (*signified their agreement*). **4** *intr.* be of importance; matter (*it signifies little*). □□ **signifier** *n.* [ME f. OF *signifier* f. L *significare* (as SIGN)]

■ **1, 2** indicate, be a sign of, symbolize, betoken, represent, express, denote, say, mean, stand for, specify, spell; imply, connote, intimate, suggest, reveal, disclose. **3** sign, signal, communicate, make known, convey, announce, tell, show, declare, express, intimate, indicate. **4** matter, count, be significant, be important, be consequential, be of significance, be of importance, be of consequence, carry weight, stand out, deserve *or* merit consideration.

signing /síning/ *n.* a person who has signed a contract, esp. to join a professional sports team.

signor /séenyor/ *n.* (*pl.* **signori** /-nyóree/) **1** a title or form of address used of or to an Italian-speaking man, corresponding to Mr or sir. **2** an Italian man. [It. f. L *senior*: see SENIOR]

signora /seenyórə/ *n.* **1** a title or form of address used of or to an Italian-speaking married woman, corresponding to Mrs or madam. **2** a married Italian woman. [It., fem. of SIGNOR]

signorina /séenyəréenə/ *n.* **1** a title or form of address used of or to an Italian-speaking unmarried woman. **2** an Italian unmarried woman. [It., dimin. of SIGNORA]

signory /séenyəri/ *n.* (*pl.* **-ies**) **1** = SEIGNIORY. **2** *hist.* the governing body of a medieval Italian republic. [ME f. OF *s(e)ignorie* (as SEIGNEUR)]

signpost /sínpōst/ *n.* & *v.* ● *n.* **1** a post erected at a crossroads with arms indicating the direction to and sometimes also the distance from various places. **2** a means of guidance; an indication. ● *v.tr.* **1** provide with a signpost or signposts. **2** indicate (a course of action, direction, etc.).

■ *n.* **1** see MARK[1] *n.* 6. **2** see CLUE *n.* 1, 2.

sika /séekə/ *n.* a small forest-dwelling deer, *Cervus nippon*, native to Japan. [Jap. *shika*]

Sikh /seek, sik/ *n.* a member of an Indian monotheistic faith founded in the 16th c. [Hindi, = disciple, f. Skr. *sishya*]

Sikhism /séekiz'm, sik-/ *n.* the religious tenets of the Sikhs.

silage /sīlij/ *n.* & *v.* ● *n.* **1** storage in a silo. **2** green fodder that has been stored in a silo. ● *v.tr.* put into a silo. [alt. of ENSILAGE after *silo*]

■ *n.* **2** see FEED *n.* 1.

sild /silt/ *n.* a small immature herring, esp. one caught in N. European seas. [Da. & Norw.]

silence /sīlənss/ *n.* & *v.* ● *n.* **1** absence of sound. **2** abstinence from speech or noise. **3** the avoidance of mentioning a thing, betraying a secret, etc. **4** oblivion; the state of not being mentioned. ● *v.tr.* make silent, esp. by coercion or superior argument. □ **in silence** without speech or other sound. **reduce** (or **put**) **to silence** refute in argument. [ME f. OF f. L *silentium* (as SILENT)]

■ *n.* **1** quiet, quietness, stillness, soundlessness, noiselessness, calm, calmness, hush, quietude, tranquillity, peace, peacefulness, serenity. **2, 3** speechlessness, muteness, dumbness; reticence, taciturnity, reserve, uncommunicativeness, secretiveness. ● *v.* quiet, mute, hush, still, shush, calm, tranquillize, soothe, *Brit.* quieten; mollify, take the sting out of, propitiate, pacify, blunt, suppress, repress, restrain, subdue, inhibit, put down, damp (down), squelch, quash, emasculate, muzzle, muffle, shut off, gag, stifle, smother, deaden (the effect of), *colloq.* shut up. □□ **in silence** see *quietly* (QUIET).

silencer /sīlənsər/ *n.* any of various devices for reducing the noise emitted by the exhaust of a motor vehicle, a gun, etc.

silent /sīlənt/ *adj.* **1** not speaking; not uttering or making or accompanied by any sound. **2** (of a letter) written but not pronounced, e.g. *b* in *doubt*. **3** (of a film) without a synchronized soundtrack. **4** (of a person) taciturn; speaking little. **5** (of an agreement) unspoken, unrecorded. **6** saying or recording nothing on some subject (*the records are silent on the incident*). **7** (of spirits) unflavoured. □ **silent majority** those of moderate opinions who rarely assert them. **silent partner** *US* = *sleeping partner* (see SLEEP). □□ **silently** *adv.* [L *silēre silent-* be silent]

■ **1** unspeaking, mute, dumb, speechless; quiet, still, soundless, noiseless, tranquil, hushed, shushed; calm, serene, placid, peaceful, pacific, unagitated, unruffled, untroubled, undisturbed, *poet.* stilly. **2** unpronounced, unuttered, unsounded. **4** uncommunicative, mute, close-mouthed, taciturn, reticent, reserved, tight-lipped, secretive, *colloq.* mum. **5** unspoken, unexpressed, unrecorded, tacit, understood, implicit, implied, unstated. □ **silent majority** see PEOPLE *n.* 2. □□ **silently** quietly, soundlessly, noiselessly, with catlike tread, as quiet(ly) as a mouse, stealthily; wordlessly, speechlessly, mutely.

silenus /sīléenəss/ *n.* (*pl.* **sileni** /-nī/) (in Greek mythology) a bearded old man like a satyr, sometimes with the tail and legs of a horse. [L f. Gk *seilēnos*]

silex /sīleks/ *n.* a kind of glass made of fused quartz. [L (as SILICA)]

silhouette /sílloo-ét/ *n.* & *v.* ● *n.* **1** a representation of a person or thing showing the outline only, usu. done in solid black on white or cut from paper. **2** the dark shadow or outline of a person or thing against a lighter background. ● *v.tr.* represent or (usu. in *passive*) show in silhouette. □ **in silhouette** seen or placed in outline. [Étienne de *Silhouette*, Fr. author and politician d. 1767]

■ *n.* outline, profile, contour, form, figure, shape, shadow, configuration, periphery, perimeter.

silica /síllikə/ *n.* silicon dioxide, occurring as quartz etc. and as a principal constituent of sandstone and other rocks. □ **silica gel** hydrated silica in a hard granular form used as a desiccant. □□ **siliceous** /-líshəss/ *adj.* (also **silicious**). **silicic** /-líssik/ *adj.* **silicify** /-líssifī/ *v.tr.* & *intr.* (**-ies, -ied**). **silicification** /-líssifikáysh'n/ *n.* [L *silex -icis* flint, after *alumina* etc.]

silicate /síllikayt/ *n.* any of the many insoluble compounds of a metal combined with silicon and oxygen, occurring widely in the rocks of the earth's crust.

silicon /síllikən/ *n. Chem.* a non-metallic element occurring widely in silica and silicates, and used in the manufacture of glass. ¶ Symb.: **Si.** □ **silicon chip** a silicon microchip. **silicon carbide** = CARBORUNDUM. **Silicon Valley** an area with a high concentration of electronics industries. [L *silex -icis* flint (after *carbon, boron*), alt. of earlier *silicium*]

silicone /síllikōn/ *n.* any of the many polymeric organic compounds of silicon and oxygen with high resistance to cold, heat, water, and the passage of electricity.

silicosis /síllikṓsiss/ *n.* lung fibrosis caused by the inhalation of dust containing silica. □□ **silicotic** /-kóttik/ *adj.*

siliqua /síllikwə/ *n.* (also **silique** /siléek/) (*pl.* **siliquae** /-kwee/ or **siliques** /siléeks/) the long narrow seed-pod of a cruciferous plant. □□ **siliquose** /-kwōss/ *adj.* **siliquous** /-kwəss/ *adj.* [L, = pod]

silk /silk/ *n.* **1** a fine strong soft lustrous fibre produced by silkworms in making cocoons. **2** a similar fibre spun by some spiders etc. **3 a** thread or cloth made from silk fibre. **b** a thread or fabric resembling silk. **4** (in *pl.*) kinds of silk cloth or garments made from it, esp. as worn by a jockey in a horse-owner's colours. **5** *Brit. colloq.* Queen's (or King's) Counsel, as having the right to wear a silk gown. **6** (*attrib.*) made of silk (*silk blouse*). **7** the silky styles of the female maize-flower. □ **silk cotton** kapok or a similar substance. **silk-fowl** a breed of fowl with a silky plumage. **silk-gland** a gland secreting the substance produced as silk. **silk hat** a tall cylindrical hat covered with silk plush. **silk moth** any of various large moths of the family Saturniidae, esp. *Hyalophora cecropia.* **silk-screen printing** = *screen printing.* **take silk** *Brit.* become a Queen's (or King's) Counsel. □□ **silklike** *adj.* [OE *sioloc, seolec* (cf. ON *silki*) f. LL *sericum* neut. of L *sericus* f. *seres* f. Gk *Sēres* an oriental people]

■ □□ **silklike** see SILKY 1.

silken /sílkən/ *adj.* **1** made of silk. **2** wearing silk. **3** soft or lustrous as silk. **4** (of a person's manner etc.) suave or insinuating. [OE *seolcen* (as SILK)]

■ **1, 3** see SILKY 1. **4** see SMOOTH *adj.* 9.

silkworm /sílkwurm/ *n.* the caterpillar of the moth *Bombyx mori*, which spins its cocoon of silk.

silky /sílki/ *adj.* (**silkier, silkiest**) **1** like silk in smoothness, softness, fineness, or lustre. **2** (of a person's manner etc.) suave, insinuating. □□ **silkily** *adv.* **silkiness** *n.*

■ **1** silken, silklike, delicate, fine, sleek, soft, smooth, satiny, shiny, glossy, lustrous, *Bot.* & *Zool.* sericeous. **2** see SMOOTH *adj.* 9.

sill /sil/ *n.* (also **cill**) **1** a shelf or slab of stone, wood, or metal at the foot of a window or doorway. **2** a horizontal timber at the bottom of a dock or lock entrance, against which the gates close. **3** *Geol.* a tabular sheet of igneous rock intruded between other rocks and parallel with their planar structure. [OE *syll, sylle*]

■ **1** see LEDGE.

sillabub var. of SYLLABUB.

sillimanite /síllimənīt/ *n.* an aluminium silicate occurring in orthorhombic crystals or fibrous masses. [B. *Silliman*, Amer. chemist d. 1864]

silly /sílli/ *adj.* & *n.* ● *adj.* (**sillier, silliest**) **1** lacking sense; foolish, imprudent, unwise. **2** weak-minded. **3** *Cricket* (of a fielder or position) very close to the batsman (*silly mid-off*). **4** *archaic* innocent, simple, helpless. **5** *colloq.* stunned (as) by a blow (*I was knocked silly*). ● *n.* (*pl.* **-ies**) *colloq.* a foolish person. □ **silly billy** *colloq.* a foolish person. **the silly season** high summer as the season when newspapers often publish trivial material for lack of important news. □□ **sillily** *adv.* **silliness** *n.* [later form of ME *sely* (dial. *seely*) happy, repr. OE *sǣlig* (recorded in *unsǣlig* unhappy) f. Gmc]

■ *adj.* **1** senseless, nonsensical, absurd, ridiculous, ludicrous, laughable, risible, farcical, asinine, apish, anserine, inane, preposterous, idiotic, childish, puerile, foolish, foolhardy, irresponsible, unreasonable, illogical, irrational, pointless, fatuous, stupid, unwise, imprudent, hare-brained, mad, insane, *colloq.* imbecilic, crazy, *esp. Brit. colloq.* daft. **2** see *halfwitted* (HALFWIT). **5** stunned, stupefied, dazed, giddy, dizzy, muzzy, benumbed. ● *n.* fool, nincompoop, dunce, clown, ninny, simpleton, numskull, booby, dolt, jackass, dodo, blockhead, ignoramus, *colloq.* idiot, dim-wit, nitwit, halfwit, dummy, thickhead, knucklehead, fat-head, chump, goose, muggins, drip, silly billy, *Brit. colloq.* clot, *sl.* bonehead, clod, twerp, goof, dope, jerk, *Austral. sl.* nong, dill, galah, *Austral.* & *NZ sl.* drongo, *esp. Brit. sl.* twit, mug, *esp. US sl.* nerd.

silo /sīlō/ *n.* & *v.* ● *n.* (*pl.* **-os**) **1** a pit or airtight structure in which green crops are pressed and kept for fodder, undergoing fermentation. **2** a pit or tower for the storage of grain, cement, etc. **3** an underground chamber in which a guided missile is kept ready for firing. ● *v.tr.* (**-oes, -oed**) make silage of. [Sp. f. L *sirus* f. Gk *siros* corn-pit]

silt /silt/ *n.* & *v.* ● *n.* sediment deposited by water in a channel, harbour, etc. ● *v.tr.* & *intr.* (often foll. by *up*) choke or be choked with silt. □□ **siltation** /-táysh'n/ *n.* **silty** *adj.* [ME, perh. rel. to Da., Norw. *sylt*, OLG *sulta*, OHG *sulza* salt marsh, formed as SALT]

■ *n.* deposit, sediment, alluvium, ooze, sludge, slime, mud. ● *v.* silt up *or* over; clog, choke, block, obstruct, dam, congest; become clogged *or* choked *or* blocked *or* obstructed *or* dammed *or* congested.

siltstone /síltstōn/ *n.* rock of consolidated silt.

Silurian /sīlyóoriən/ *adj.* & *n. Geol.* ● *adj.* of or relating to the third period of the Palaeozoic era with evidence of the first fish and land plants, and the formation of mountains and new land areas. ¶ Cf. Appendix VII. ● *n.* this period or system. [L *Silures*, a people of ancient SE Wales]

silva var. of SYLVA.

silvan var. of SYLVAN.

silver /sílvər/ *n., adj.,* & *v.* ● *n. Chem.* **1** a greyish-white lustrous malleable ductile precious metallic element, occurring naturally as the element and in mineral form, and used chiefly with an admixture of harder metals for coin, plate, and ornaments, as a subordinate monetary medium, and in compounds for photography etc. ¶ Symb.: **Ag. 2** the colour of silver. **3** silver or cupro-nickel coins. **4** esp. *Sc.* money. **5** silver vessels or implements, esp. cutlery. **6** household cutlery of any material. **7** = *silver medal.* ● *adj.* **1** made wholly or chiefly of silver. **2** coloured like silver. ● *v.* **1** *tr.* coat or plate with silver. **2** *tr.* provide (a mirror-glass) with a backing of tin amalgam etc. **3** *tr.* (of the moon or a white light) give a silvery appearance to. **4 a** *tr.* turn (the hair) grey or white. **b** *intr.* (of the hair) turn grey or white. □ **silver age** a period regarded as inferior to a golden age, e.g. that of post-classical Latin literature in the early Imperial period. **silver band** *Brit.* a band playing silver-plated instruments. **silver birch** a common birch, *Betula alba*, with silver-coloured bark. **silver fir** any fir of the genus *Abies*, with the under-sides of its leaves coloured silver. **silver fox 1** an American red fox at a time when its fur is black with white tips. **2** its fur. **silver gilt 1** gilded silver. **2** an imitation gilding of yellow lacquer over silver leaf. **silver-grey** a lustrous grey. **silver jubilee 1** the 25th anniversary of a sovereign's accession. **2** any other 25th anniversary. **silver Latin** literary Latin of the early Imperial period. **silver-leaf** a fungal disease of fruit trees. **silver lining** a consolation or hopeful feature in misfortune. **silver medal** a medal of silver, usu. awarded as second prize. **silver nitrate** a colourless solid that is soluble in water and was formerly used in photography. **silver paper 1** a fine white tissue-paper for wrapping silver. **2** aluminium or tin foil. **silver plate** vessels, spoons, etc., of copper etc. plated with silver. **silver salmon** a coho. **silver sand** a fine pure sand used in gardening. **silver screen** (usu. prec. by *the*) motion pictures collectively. **silver solder** solder containing silver. **silver spoon** a sign of future prosperity. **silver standard** a system by which the value of a currency is defined in terms of silver, for which the currency may be exchanged. **silver thaw** a glassy coating of ice formed on the ground or an exposed surface, caused by freezing rain or a sudden light frost. **silver tongue** eloquence. **silver**

wedding the 25th anniversary of a wedding. **silver weed** a plant with silvery leaves, esp. a potentilla, *Potentilla anserina*, with silver-coloured leaves. [OE *seolfor* f. Gmc]

■ *n.* **2** greyish, white, whitish-grey, greyish-white, silver-grey, grey. **4** see MONEY 1. **5, 6** silverware, sterling, (silver) plate; hollowware; cutlery, *US* flatware. ● *adj.* **2** silvery, shiny, shining, polished, burnished, lustrous, pearly, nacreous, bright, gleaming; silver-grey, whitish-grey, grey, greyish, greyish-white, white; *Heraldry* argent.

silverfish /sílvərfish/ *n.* (*pl.* same or **-fishes**) **1** any small silvery wingless insect of the order Thysanura, esp. *Lepisma saccharina* in houses and other buildings. **2** a silver-coloured fish, esp. a colourless variety of goldfish.

silvern /sílvərn/ *adj. archaic* or *poet.* = SILVER *adj.* [OE *seolfren, silfren* (as SILVER)]

silverside /sílvərsīd/ *n. Brit.* the upper side of a round of beef from the outside of the leg.

silversmith /sílvərsmith/ *n.* a worker in silver; a manufacturer of silver articles. ▫▫ **silversmithing** *n.*

silverware /sílvərwair/ *n.* articles made of or coated with silver.

■ see SILVER *n.* 5, 6.

silvery /sílvəri/ *adj.* **1** like silver in colour or appearance. **2** having a clear gentle ringing sound. **3** (of the hair) white and lustrous. ▫▫ **silveriness** *n.*

■ **1** see SILVER *adj.* **2** silver-toned, silver-tongued; see also MELODIOUS 2.

silviculture /sílvikulchər/ *n.* (also **sylviculture**) the growing and tending of trees as a branch of forestry. ▫▫ **silvicultural** /-kúlchərəl/ *adj.* **silviculturist** /-kúlchərist/ *n.* [F f. L *silva* a wood + F *culture* CULTURE]

simian /símmiən/ *adj.* & *n.* ● *adj.* **1** of or concerning the anthropoid apes. **2** like an ape or monkey (*a simian walk*). ● *n.* an ape or monkey. [L *simia* ape, perh. f. L *simus* f. Gk *simos* flat-nosed]

■ *n.* monkey, ape, primate.

similar /símmilər/ *adj.* **1** like, alike. **2** (often foll. by *to*) having a resemblance. **3** of the same kind, nature, or amount. **4** *Geom.* shaped alike. ▫▫ **similarity** /-lárriti/ *n.* (*pl.* **-ies**). **similarly** *adv.* [F *similaire* or med.L *similaris* f. L *similis* like]

■ **1, 3** like, almost identical, comparable, equivalent, nearly the same; alike, akin, kindred, related, of a piece, of the same sort *or* kind *or* type. **2** (*similar to*) resembling, like, corresponding to, comparable with, reminiscent of, redolent of, along the same lines as. ▫▫ **similarity** see LIKENESS 1, UNIFORMITY. **similarly** see ALIKE *adv.*

simile /símmili/ *n.* **1** a figure of speech involving the comparison of one thing with another of a different kind, as an illustration or ornament (e.g. *as brave as a lion*). **2** the use of such comparison. [ME f. L, neut. of *similis* like]

■ see METAPHOR.

similitude /simíllityōōd/ *n.* **1** the likeness, guise, or outward appearance of a thing or person. **2** a comparison or the expression of a comparison. **3** *archaic* a counterpart or facsimile. [ME f. OF *similitude* or L *similitudo* (as SIMILE)]

■ **1** see LIKENESS 1, 2.

simmer /símmər/ *v.* & *n.* ● *v.* **1** *intr.* & *tr.* be or keep bubbling or boiling gently. **2** *intr.* be in a state of suppressed anger or excitement. ● *n.* a simmering condition. ▫ **simmer down** become calm or less agitated. [alt. of ME (now dial.) *simper*, perh. imit.]

■ *v.* **1** stew, cook, boil, bubble, *archaic* seethe. **2** chafe, seethe, stew, steam, smoulder, fume, rage, burn. ▫ **simmer down** calm *or* cool down, cool off, calm oneself, become quiet, control oneself, get control of *or* over oneself, quiet down, *Brit.* quieten down, *sl.* cool it.

simnel cake /símn'l/ *n. Brit.* a rich fruit cake, usu. with a marzipan layer and decoration, eaten esp. at Easter or during Lent. [ME f. OF *simenel*, ult. f. L *simila* or Gk *semidalis* fine flour]

simon-pure /sīmənpyoor/ *adj.* real, genuine. [(*the real*) *Simon Pure*, a character in Centlivre's *Bold Stroke for a Wife* (1717)]

simony /sīməni, sím-/ *n.* the buying or selling of ecclesiastical privileges, e.g. pardons or benefices. ▫▫ **simoniac** /-mōniak/ *adj.* & *n.* **simoniacal** /-nīək'l/ *adj.* [ME f. OF *simonie* f. LL *simonia* f. *Simon* Magus (Acts 8:18)]

■ ▫▫ **simoniacal** see VENAL.

simoom /simōōm/ *n.* (also **simoon** /-mōōn/) a hot dry dust-laden wind blowing at intervals esp. in the Arabian desert. [Arab. *samūm* f. *samma* to poison]

■ see STORM *n.* 1.

simp /simp/ *n. US colloq.* a simpleton. [abbr.]

simpatico /simpáttikō/ *adj.* congenial, likeable. [It. & Sp. (as SYMPATHY)]

■ see LIKEABLE.

simper /símpər/ *v.* & *n.* ● *v.* **1** *intr.* smile in a silly or affected way. **2** *tr.* express by or with simpering. ● *n.* such a smile. ▫▫ **simperingly** *adv.* [16th c.: cf. Du. and Scand. *semper, simper*, G *zimp(f)er* elegant, delicate]

■ *v.* **1** see SMILE *v.* 1. **2** twitter, warble, trill, tweet, prattle, giggle, titter, snicker, snigger. ● *n.* grin, smile, smirk.

simple /símp'l/ *adj.* & *n.* ● *adj.* **1** easily understood or done; presenting no difficulty (*a simple explanation*; *a simple task*). **2** not complicated or elaborate; without luxury or sophistication. **3** not compound; consisting of or involving only one element or operation etc. **4** absolute, unqualified, straightforward (*the simple truth*; *a simple majority*). **5** foolish or ignorant; gullible, feeble-minded (*am not so simple as to agree to that*). **6** plain in appearance or manner; unsophisticated, ingenuous, artless. **7** of low rank; humble, insignificant (*simple people*). **8** *Bot.* **a** consisting of one part. **b** (of fruit) formed from one pistil. ● *n. archaic* **1** a herb used medicinally. **2** a medicine made from it. ▫ **simple eye** an eye of an insect, having only one lens. **simple fracture** a fracture of the bone only, without a skin wound. **simple harmonic motion** see HARMONIC. **simple interest** interest payable on a capital sum only (cf. *compound interest* (see COMPOUND)). **simple interval** *Mus.* an interval of one octave or less. **simple machine** any of the basic mechanical devices for applying a force (e.g. an inclined plane, wedge, or lever). **simple sentence** a sentence with a single subject and predicate. **Simple Simon** a foolish person (from the nursery-rhyme character). **simple time** *Mus.* a time with two, three, or four beats in a bar. ▫▫ **simpleness** *n.* [ME f. OF f. L *simplus*]

■ *adj.* **1** uncomplicated, plain, uninvolved, unsophisticated, understandable, intelligible, (easily) understood, comprehensible, clear, lucid, obvious, straightforward, easy, painless, effortless, elementary, basic, *esp. Computing* user-friendly. **2** uncomplicated; plain, unadorned, undecorated, unembellished, unadulterated, unsophisticated, basic, fundamental, elementary, elemental, mere, unostentatious, unassuming, unpretentious, modest, classic, uncluttered, stark, clean, severe, austere, Spartan, homely; unvarnished, naked, honest. **4** see PURE 8. **5** foolish, ignorant, naïve, green, gullible, credulous, slow, slow-witted, stupid, thick, simple-minded, feeble-minded, oafish, bovine, dense, obtuse, dull, dull-witted, witless, halfwitted, brainless, backward, *colloq.* imbecilic, imbecile, thickheaded, moronic, cretinous, *esp. US colloq.* dumb. **6** sincere, frank, candid, open, unaffected, uncomplicated, unpretentious, straightforward, above-board, simple-hearted, uncontrived, direct, upright, square, forthright, four-square, righteous, honest, naïve, guileless, artless, undesigning, childlike, ingenuous, unsophisticated, innocent. **7** lowly, humble, inferior, mean, base, subservient, common, subordinate, insignificant.

simple-minded /símp'lmīndid/ *adj.* **1** natural, unsophisticated. **2** feeble-minded. ▫▫ **simple-mindedly** *adv.* **simple-mindedness** *n.*

■ **1** see NAÏVE. **2** see FOOLISH. □□ **simple-mindedness** see *stupidity* (STUPID).

simpleton /símp'ltən/ *n.* a foolish, gullible, or halfwitted person. [SIMPLE after surnames f. place-names in *-ton*]
■ see FOOL[1] *n.* 1.

simplex /simpleks/ *adj.* & *n.* ● *adj.* **1** simple; not compounded. **2** *Computing* (of a circuit) allowing transmission of signals in one direction only. ● *n.* a simple or uncompounded thing, esp. a word. [L, = single, var. of *simplus* simple]

simplicity /simplíssiti/ *n.* the fact or condition of being simple. □ **be simplicity itself** be extremely easy. [OF *simplicité* or L *simplicitas* (as SIMPLEX)]
■ understandability, comprehensibility, lucidity, straightforwardness, clarity, intelligibility, decipherability; uncomplicatedness; plainness, cleanness, severity, starkness, austerity, asceticism, restraint, bareness, purity; stupidity, foolishness, slow-wittedness, simple-mindedness, feeble-mindedness, oafishness, cloddishness, obtuseness, dullness, dull-wittedness, witlessness, imbecility, brainlessness, *colloq.* thickheadedness, halfwittedness; sincerity, openness, artlessness, candour, guilelessness, frankness, unsophisticatedness, ingenuousness, forthrightness, unaffectedness, unpretentiousness, modesty, naïvety; directness, inelegance, rusticity, pastoralism.

simplify /símplifī/ *v.tr.* (**-ies, -ied**) make simple; make easy or easier to do or understand. □□ **simplification** /-fikáysh'n/ *n.* [F *simplifier* f. med.L *simplificare* (as SIMPLE)]
■ clarify, clear up, make easy, paraphrase, explain, explicate, disentangle, untangle, unravel, streamline. □□ **simplification** see *interpretation* (INTERPRET).

simplism /símpliz'm/ *n.* **1** affected simplicity. **2** the unjustifiable simplification of a problem etc.

simplistic /simplístik/ *adj.* **1** excessively or affectedly simple. **2** oversimplified so as to conceal or distort difficulties. □□ **simplistically** *adv.*
■ see LITERAL *adj.* 1, 2.

simply /símpli/ *adv.* **1** in a simple manner. **2** absolutely; without doubt (*simply astonishing*). **3** merely (*was simply trying to please*).
■ **1** distinctly, unambiguously, obviously, unmistakably; naïvely, artlessly, guilelessly, openly, innocently, ingenuously, unaffectedly, unpretentiously, plainly, naturally; modestly, starkly, severely, sparely, sparsely, austerely, ascetically. **2** totally, completely, absolutely, altogether, entirely, fully, wholly, just, plainly, obviously, really, unreservedly, unqualifiedly. **3** merely, purely, only, solely, just.

simulacrum /símyooláykrəm/ *n.* (*pl.* **simulacra** /-krə/) **1** an image of something. **2 a** a shadowy likeness; a deceptive substitute. **b** mere pretence. [L (as SIMULATE)]
■ **1** see IMAGE *n.* 3. **2 a** see IMAGE *n.* 5.

simulate /símyoolayt/ *v.tr.* **1 a** pretend to have or feel (an attribute or feeling). **b** pretend to be. **2** imitate or counterfeit. **3 a** imitate the conditions of (a situation etc.), e.g. for training. **b** produce a computer model of (a process). **4** (as **simulated** *adj.*) made to resemble the real thing but not genuinely such (*simulated fur*). **5** (of a word) take or have an altered form suggested by (a word wrongly taken to be its source, e.g. *amuck*). □□ **simulation** /-láysh'n/ *n.* **simulative** /-lətiv/ *adj.* [L *simulare* f. *similis* like]
■ **1** see FAKE[1] *v.* 2. **2, 3a** see IMITATE 3. **4** (**simulated**) see FALSE 2a. □□ **simulation** see IMITATION *n.*

simulator /símyoolaytər/ *n.* **1** a person or thing that simulates. **2** a device designed to simulate the operations of a complex system, used esp. in training.

simulcast /símməlkaast/ *n.* simultaneous transmission of the same programme on radio and television. [SIMULTANEOUS + BROADCAST]

simultaneous /símməltáyniəss/ *adj.* (often foll. by *with*) occurring or operating at the same time. □ **simultaneous equations** equations involving two or more unknowns that are to have the same values in each equation. □□ **simultaneity** /-tənáyiti/ *n.* **simultaneously** *adv.* **simultaneousness** *n.* [med.L *simultaneus* f. L *simul* at the same time, prob. after *instantaneus* etc.]
■ coincident, coinciding, concurrent, contemporaneous, synchronous; contemporary. □□ **simultaneity** see COINCIDENCE 1. **simultaneously** see *at once* 2 (ONCE).

simurg /simúrg/ *n.* a monstrous bird of Persian myth, with the power of reasoning and speech. [Pers. *sīmurġ* f. Pahlavi *sīn* eagle + *murġ* bird]

sin[1] /sin/ *n.* & *v.* ● *n.* **1 a** the breaking of divine or moral law, esp. by a conscious act. **b** such an act. **2** an offence against good taste or propriety etc. ● *v.* (**sinned, sinning**) **1** *intr.* commit a sin. **2** *intr.* (foll. by *against*) offend. **3** *tr. archaic* commit (a sin). □ **as sin** *colloq.* extremely (*ugly as sin*). **for one's sins** *joc.* as a judgement on one for something done. **like sin** *colloq.* vehemently or forcefully. **live in sin** *colloq.* live together without being married. **sin bin** *colloq.* **1** *Ice Hockey* a penalty box. **2** a place set aside for offenders of various kinds. □□ **sinless** *adj.* **sinlessly** *adv.* **sinlessness** *n.* [OE *syn(n)*]
■ *n.* **1** wickedness, sinfulness, vice, corruption, ungodliness, unrighteousness, badness, evil, wrongfulness, iniquity, iniquitousness, immorality, depravity, impiety, irreverence, impiousness, sacrilege; transgression, offence, wrong, misdeed, profanation, desecration, devilry, crime, infraction, dereliction, infringement, violation, misdemeanour, fault, foible, peccadillo, *archaic* trespass. **2** see SCANDAL 1b. ● *v.* **1** transgress, offend, fall (from grace), lapse, go wrong, stray, go astray, err, *literary or archaic* trespass. **2** (*sin against*) offend (against), err against, *literary or archaic* trespass against. □ **live in sin** live together, cohabit. □□ **sinless** see HOLY 1, 2. **sinlessness** see PURITY 2.

sin[2] /sīn/ *abbr.* sine.

Sinaitic /sīnayíttik/ *adj.* of or relating to Mount Sinai or of the Sinai peninsula. [var. of *Sinaic* f. *Sinai* f. Heb. *sīnay*, with *t* added for euphony]

sinanthropus /sinánthrəpəss/ *n.* an apelike human of the extinct genus *Sinanthropus*. [mod.L, as SINO- Chinese (remains having been found near Peking) + Gk *anthrōpos* man]

since /sinss/ *prep.*, *conj.*, & *adv.* ● *prep.* throughout, or at a point in, the period between (a specified time, event, etc.) and the time present or being considered (*must have happened since yesterday*; *has been going on since June*; *the greatest composer since Beethoven*). ● *conj.* **1** during or in the time after (*what have you been doing since we met?*; *has not spoken since the dog died*). **2** for the reason that, because; inasmuch as (*since you are drunk I will drive you home*). **3** (*ellipt.*) as being (*a more useful, since better designed, tool*). ● *adv.* **1** from that time or event until now or the time being considered (*have not seen them since*; *had been healthy ever since*; *has since been cut down*). **2** ago (*happened many years since*). [ME, reduced form of obs. *sithence* or f. dial. *sin* (f. *sithen*) f. OE *siththon*]

sincere /sinséer/ *adj.* (**sincerer, sincerest**) **1** free from pretence or deceit; the same in reality as in appearance. **2** genuine, honest, frank. □□ **sincereness** *n.* **sincerity** /-sérriti/ *n.* [L *sincerus* clean, pure]
■ honest, truthful, true, genuine, bona fide, heartfelt, earnest, true-hearted, wholehearted, undissembling, unfeigned, open, (open and) above-board, straightforward, direct, frank, candid, guileless, artless, *colloq.* upfront, on the level, *Austral.* & *NZ colloq.* dinkum, *esp. US colloq.* on the up and up, *formal* veracious. □□ **sincerity** honesty, truthfulness, straightforwardness, openness, forthrightness, frankness, candour, candidness, seriousness, genuineness, uprightness.

sincerely /sinséerli/ *adv.* in a sincere manner. □ **yours sincerely** a formula for ending an informal letter.

■ truly, honestly, really, wholeheartedly, candidly, frankly, unequivocally, seriously, earnestly, genuinely, deeply, fervently.

sinciput /sínsipoŏt/ *n. Anat.* the front of the skull from the forehead to the crown. ▫▫ **sincipital** /-síppit'l/ *adj.* [L f. *semi-* half + *caput* head]

sine /sīn/ *n. Math.* **1** the trigonometric function that is equal to the ratio of the side opposite a given angle (in a right-angled triangle) to the hypotenuse. **2** a function of the line drawn from one end of an arc perpendicularly to the radius through the other. ▫ **sine curve** (or **wave**) a curve representing periodic oscillations of constant amplitude as given by a sine function: also called SINUSOID. [L *sinus* curve, fold of a toga, used in med.L as transl. of Arab. *jayb* bosom, sine]

sinecure /sínikyoor, sín-/ *n.* a position that requires little or no work but usu. yields profit or honour. ▫▫ **sinecurism** *n.* **sinecurist** *n.* [L *sine cura* without care]

sine die /sīni dī-i, sínnay deeay/ *adv.* (of business adjourned indefinitely) with no appointed date. [L, = without day]

sine qua non /sinnay kwaa nōn/ *n.* an indispensable condition or qualification. [L, = without which not]

■ see PRECONDITION *n.*

sinew /sínyoo/ *n.* & *v.* ● *n.* **1** tough fibrous tissue uniting muscle to bone; a tendon. **2** (in *pl.*) muscles; bodily strength; wiriness. **3** (in *pl.*) that which forms the strength or framework of a plan, city, organization, etc. ● *v.tr. poet.* serve as the sinews of; sustain; hold together. ▫ **the sinews of war** money. ▫▫ **sinewless** *adj.* **sinewy** *adj.* [OE *sin(e)we* f. Gmc]

■ *n.* **1** ligament, tendon. **2** (*sinews*) muscles, strength, force, power, energy, brawn, vigour, might, stamina, vitality; wiriness. ▫▫ **sinewy** strong, powerful, muscular, mighty, stout, wiry, robust, tough, stringy; strapping, brawny, burly.

sinfonia /sínfəneeə, sinfōniə/ *n. Mus.* **1** a symphony. **2** (in Baroque music) an orchestral piece used as an introduction to an opera, cantata, or suite. **3** (**Sinfonia**; usu. in names) a small symphony orchestra. [It., = SYMPHONY]

sinfonietta /sínfənyéttə/ *n. Mus.* **1** a short or simple symphony. **2** (**Sinfonietta**; usu. in names) a small symphony orchestra. [It., dimin. of *sinfonia*: see SINFONIA]

sinful /sínfool/ *adj.* **1** (of a person) committing sin, esp. habitually. **2** (of an act) involving or characterized by sin. ▫▫ **sinfully** *adv.* **sinfulness** *n.* [OE *synfull* (as SIN, -FUL)]

■ corrupt, evil, wicked, bad, iniquitous, vile, base, profane, immoral, profligate, depraved, dissolute, criminal, sacrilegious, ungodly, unholy, unrighteous, godless, demonic, diabolic(al), irreligious, impious, irreverent, wrong, wrongful. ▫▫ **sinfulness** see SIN *n.* 1.

sing /sing/ *v.* & *n.* ● *v.* (*past* **sang** /sang/; *past part.* **sung** /sung/) **1** *intr.* utter musical sounds with the voice, esp. words with a set tune. **2** *tr.* utter or produce by singing (*sing another song*). **3** *intr.* (of the wind, a kettle, etc.) make inarticulate melodious or humming, buzzing, or whistling sounds. **4** *intr.* (of the ears) be affected as with a buzzing sound. **5** *intr. sl.* turn informer; confess. **6** *intr. archaic* compose poetry. **7** *tr.* & (foll. by *of*) *intr.* celebrate in verse. **8** *tr.* (foll. by *in*, *out*) usher (esp. the new or old year) in or out with singing. **9** *tr.* bring to a specified state by singing (*sang the child to sleep*). ● *n.* **1** an act or spell of singing. **2** *US* a meeting for amateur singing. ▫ **sing-along** a tune etc. to which one can sing in accompaniment. **singing hinny** see HINNY[2]. **singing saw** = *musical saw*. **sing out** call out loudly; shout. **sing the praises of** see PRAISE. **sing up** sing more loudly. ▫▫ **singable** *adj.* **singer** *n.* **singingly** *adv.* [OE *singan* f. Gmc]

■ *v.* **1, 2** chant, intone, carol, serenade, vocalize, trill, croon, pipe, chirp, warble; chorus; yodel. **3** whistle, peep, tootle, skirl; drone, hum, whir, purr, murmur; buzz. **5** tell, tattle, name names; confess; *colloq.* rat, blow the whistle, spill the beans, peach, *sl.* snitch, squeal. ▫▫ **singer** vocalist, soloist, songster, crooner, *chanteuse*, nightingale, minstrel, troubadour, balladeer, caroller, chorister, choirboy, choir girl, choir member, chorus-boy, chorus girl, chorus-member.

sing. *abbr.* singular.

singe /sinj/ *v.* & *n.* ● *v.* (**singeing**) **1** *tr.* & *intr.* burn superficially or lightly. **2** *tr.* burn the bristles or down off (the carcass of a pig or fowl) to prepare it for cooking. **3** *tr.* burn off the tips of (the hair) in hairdressing. ● *n.* a superficial burn. ▫ **singe one's wings** suffer some harm esp. in a risky attempt. [OE *sencgan* f. WG]

■ *v.* char, blacken, sear, scorch, burn.

Singh /sing/ *n.* **1** a title adopted by the warrior castes of N. India. **2** a surname adopted by male Sikhs. [Hind. *singh* f. Skr. *sinhá* lion]

Singhalese var. of SINHALESE.

single /síngg'l/ *adj.*, *n.*, & *v.* ● *adj.* **1** one only, not double or multiple. **2** united or undivided. **3 a** designed or suitable for one person (*single room*). **b** used or done by one person etc. or one set or pair. **4** one by itself; not one of several (*a single tree*). **5** regarded separately (*every single thing*). **6** not married. **7** *Brit.* (of a ticket) valid for an outward journey only, not for the return. **8** (with *neg.* or *interrog.*) even one; not to speak of more (*did not see a single person*). **9** (of a flower) having only one circle of petals. **10** lonely, unaided. **11** *archaic* free from duplicity, sincere, consistent, guileless, ingenuous. ● *n.* **1** a single thing, or item in a series. **2** *Brit.* a single ticket. **3** a short pop record with one piece of music etc. on each side. **4** *Cricket* a hit for one run. **5** (usu. *in pl.*) a game with one player on each side. **6** an unmarried person (*young singles*). **7** *sl. US* a one-dollar note. ● *v.tr.* (foll. by *out*) choose as an example or as distinguishable or to serve some purpose. ▫ **single acrostic** see ACROSTIC. **single-acting** (of an engine etc.) having pressure applied only to one side of the piston. **single-breasted** (of a coat etc.) having only one set of buttons and buttonholes, not overlapping. **single combat** a duel. **single cream** thin cream with a relatively low fat-content. **single cut** (of a file) with grooves cut in one direction only, not crossing. **single-decker** esp. *Brit.* a bus having only one deck. **single entry** a system of bookkeeping in which each transaction is entered in one account only. **single file** a line of people or things arranged one behind another. **single-handed** *adv.* **1** without help from another. **2** with one hand. ● *adj.* **1** done etc. single-handed. **2** for one hand. **single-handedly** in a single-handed way. **single-lens reflex** denoting a reflex camera in which a single lens serves the film and the viewfinder. **single-line** with movement of traffic in only one direction at a time. **single market** an association of countries trading without restrictions, esp. as a basis for the European Community. **single parent** a person bringing up a child or children without a partner. **singles bar** a bar for single people seeking company. **single-seater** a vehicle with one seat. **single stick 1** a basket-hilted stick of about a sword's length. **2** one-handed fencing with this. **single-tree** *US* = SWINGLETREE. ▫▫ **singleness** *n.* **singly** *adv.* [ME f. OF f. L *singulus*, rel. to *simplus* SIMPLE]

■ *adj.* **1, 4** one, only, sole, lone, unique, isolated, solitary; singular, individual, distinct. **5** separate, distinct, individual, solitary. **6** unmarried, unwed, unattached, free. **7** one-way. **10** alone, unaccompanied, unaided, unsupported; see also LONELY 1. ● *v.* (*single out*) select, choose, pick (out), separate, target, take aside *or* apart, put aside *or* apart, set aside *or* apart, earmark, distinguish, cull, segregate, fix *or* fasten on.
▫ **single-handed** (*adv.*) **1** single-handedly, by oneself, alone, solo, on one's own, independently. (*adj.*) **1** solo, lone, solitary, independent, unaided, unassisted. **single-handedly** see *single-handed* (*adv.*) above.
▫▫ **singleness** bachelorhood, spinsterhood, celibacy; see also UNITY 1. **singly** one at a time, separately, individually, one by one, successively, one after the other, seriatim.

single-minded /síngg'lmīndid/ *adj.* having or intent on only one purpose. ▫▫ **single-mindedly** *adv.* **single-mindedness** *n.*

■ dedicated, devoted, resolute, steadfast, persevering, firm, determined, dogged, unswerving, unwavering, tireless, purposeful. □□ **single-mindedness** see PURPOSE *n.* 3.

singlet /síngglit/ *n.* **1** *Brit.* a garment worn under or instead of a shirt; a vest. **2** a single unresolvable line in a spectrum. [SINGLE + -ET[1], after *doublet*, the garment being unlined]

singleton /síngg'ltən/ *n.* **1** one card only of a suit, esp. as dealt to a player. **2 a** a single person or thing. **b** an only child. **3** a single child or animal born, not a twin etc. [SINGLE, after *simpleton*]

singsong /síngsong/ *adj.*, *n.*, & *v.* ● *adj.* uttered with a monotonous rhythm or cadence. ● *n.* **1** a singsong manner. **2** *Brit.* an informal gathering for singing. ● *v.intr.* & *tr.* (*past* and *past part.* **singsonged**) speak or recite in a singsong manner.

■ *v.* see CHANT *v.* 1.

singular /síngyoolər/ *adj.* & *n.* ● *adj.* **1** unique; much beyond the average; extraordinary. **2** eccentric or strange. **3** *Gram.* (of a word or form) denoting or referring to a single person or thing. **4** *Math.* possessing unique properties. **5** single, individual. ● *n. Gram.* **1** a singular word or form. **2** the singular number. □□ **singularly** *adv.* [ME f. OF *singuler* f. L *singularis* (as SINGLE)]

■ *adj.* **1** unique, outstanding, prominent, eminent, pre-eminent, noteworthy, significant, important, conspicuous, particular, notable, signal, exceptional, superior, unparalleled, matchless, extraordinary, remarkable, special. **2** unusual, different, atypical, abnormal, eccentric, uncommon, strange, odd, peculiar, bizarre, outlandish, curious, queer, *outré*, offbeat, far-out. **5** lone, isolated, single, separate, uncommon, rare, unique, individual, distinct, one of a kind. □□ **singularly** see ESPECIALLY.

singularity /síngyoolárriti/ *n.* (*pl.* **-ies**) **1** the state or condition of being singular. **2** an odd trait or peculiarity. **3** *Physics* & *Math.* a point at which a function takes an infinite value, esp. in space-time when matter is infinitely dense. [ME f. OF *singularité* f. LL *singularitas* (as SINGULAR)]

■ **1** individuality, distinctiveness, uniqueness, strangeness, oddness, queerness, eccentricity, peculiarity, outlandishness, uncommonness. **2** idiosyncrasy, eccentricity, quirk, trait, foible, oddity, peculiarity, curiosity, kink.

singularize /síngyoolərīz/ *v.tr.* (also **-ise**) **1** distinguish, individualize. **2** make singular. □□ **singularization** /-záysh'n/ *n.*

sinh /shīn, sīnáych/ *abbr. Math.* hyperbolic sine. [*sine* + *h*yperbolic]

Sinhalese /sinhəléez, sínnə-/ *n.* & *adj.* (also **Singhalese** /sínggə-/) ● *n.* (*pl.* same) **1** a member of a people originally from N. India and now forming the majority of the population of Sri Lanka. **2** an Indic language spoken by this people. ● *adj.* of or relating to this people or language. [Skr. *siṅhalam* Sri Lanka (Ceylon) + -ESE]

sinister /sínnistər/ *adj.* **1** suggestive of evil; looking malignant or villainous. **2** wicked or criminal (*a sinister motive*). **3** of evil omen. **4** *Heraldry* of or on the left-hand side of a shield etc. (i.e. to the observer's right). **5** *archaic* left-hand. □□ **sinisterly** *adv.* **sinisterness** *n.* [ME f. OF *sinistre* or L *sinister* left]

■ **1, 3** dark, gloomy, black; alarming, disquieting, frightening; fateful, inauspicious, unfavourable, forbidding, threatening, menacing, minatory, portentous, ominous, unpropitious, disastrous. **2** evil, bad, corrupt, base, malevolent, malignant, malign, harmful, pernicious, treacherous, nefarious, wicked, criminal, devilish, diabolic(al), satanic, infernal, baleful, villainous, insidious, sneaky, furtive, underhand(ed).

sinistral /sínnistrəl/ *adj.* & *n.* ● *adj.* **1** left-handed. **2** of or on the left. **3** (of a flat-fish) with the left side uppermost. **4** (of a spiral shell) with whorls rising to the left and not (as usually) to the right. ● *n.* a left-handed person. □□ **sinistrality** /-trálliti/ *n.* **sinistrally** *adv.*

■ *adj.* **1** left-handed, *colloq.* southpaw, cack-handed. **2** see LEFT[1] *adj.*

sinistrorse /sínnistrorss/ *adj.* rising towards the left, esp. of the spiral stem of a plant. [L *sinistrorsus* f. *sinister* left + *vorsus* past part. of *vertere* turn]

sink /singk/ *v.* & *n.* ● *v.* (*past* **sank** /sangk/ or **sunk** /sungk/; *past part.* **sunk** or **sunken**) **1** *intr.* fall or come slowly downwards. **2** *intr.* disappear below the horizon (*the sun is sinking*). **3** *intr.* **a** go or penetrate below the surface esp. of a liquid. **b** (of a ship) go to the bottom of the sea etc. **4** *intr.* settle down comfortably (*sank into a chair*). **5** *intr.* **a** gradually lose strength or value or quality etc.; decline (*my heart sank*). **b** (of the voice) descend in pitch or volume. **c** (of a sick person) approach death. **6** *tr.* send (a ship) to the bottom of the sea etc. **7** *tr.* cause or allow to sink or penetrate (*sank its teeth into my leg*). **8** *tr.* cause the failure of (a plan etc.) or the discomfiture of (a person). **9** *tr.* dig (a well) or bore (a shaft). **10** *tr.* engrave (a die) or inlay (a design). **11** *tr.* **a** invest (money) (*sunk a large sum into the business*). **b** lose (money) by investment. **12** *tr.* **a** cause (a ball) to enter a pocket in billiards, a hole at golf, etc. **b** achieve this by (a stroke). **13** *tr.* overlook or forget; keep in the background (*sank their differences*). **14** *intr.* (of a price etc.) become lower. **15** *intr.* (of a storm or river) subside. **16** *intr.* (of ground) slope down, or reach a lower level by subsidence. **17** *intr.* (foll. by *on*, *upon*) (of darkness) descend (on a place). **18** *tr.* lower the level of. **19** *tr.* (usu. in *passive*; foll. by *in*) absorb; hold the attention of (*be sunk in thought*). ● *n.* **1** a fixed basin with a water-supply and outflow pipe. **2** a place where foul liquid collects. **3** a place of vice or corruption. **4** a pool or marsh in which a river's water disappears by evaporation or percolation. **5** *Physics* a body or process used to absorb or dissipate heat. **6** (in full **sink-hole**) *Geol.* a cavity in limestone etc. into which a stream etc. disappears. □ **sink in 1** penetrate or make its way in. **2** become gradually comprehended (*paused to let the words sink in*). **sinking feeling** a bodily sensation caused by hunger or apprehension. **sinking fund** money set aside for the gradual repayment of a debt. **sink or swim** even at the risk of complete failure (*determined to try, sink or swim*). **sunk fence** a fence formed by, or along the bottom of, a ditch. □□ **sinkable** *adj.* **sinkage** *n.* [OE *sincan* f. Gmc]

■ *v.* **1** descend, go down *or* downward(s), drop, fall, move down *or* downward(s), come down *or* downward(s); sag, droop, slump; settle, precipitate. **2** set, go down, go lower, descend, decline, drop; disappear, vanish, fade away, *poet.* droop. **3** become submerged, go down, go under, plunge, descend, be engulfed, dive; see also FOUNDER[2] *v.* 1a. **5 a, c** decline, weaken, worsen, degenerate, subside, deteriorate, dwindle, flag, ebb, wane, fail, diminish, slip, fade (away), waste (away), die, expire; languish; *colloq.* go downhill. **6** scupper, scuttle. **7** submerge, immerse, plunge, dig. **8** see WRECK *v.* 2, FOIL[1] *v.* 1. **9** bore, put down, drill, dig, excavate, drive. **11 a** invest, venture, risk, put. **12 a** pocket; hole. **15** see SUBSIDE 1, 4. **16** subside, cave in, collapse, settle, drop, fall in, go down, slip away. **19** see IMMERSE 2. ● *n.* **1** basin, wash-basin, wash-bowl, lavabo; *Ch.* font, stoup, piscina. **3** cesspool, cesspit, pit, hell-hole, den of iniquity, *colloq.* dive. **6** sink-hole, *Brit.* swallow-hole. □ **sink in 1** (*sink into*) seep in, soak in, permeate; see also PENETRATE 1b. **2** be absorbed, be understood, penetrate, register, make an impression, get through.

sinker /síngkər/ *n.* **1** a weight used to sink a fishing-line or sounding-line. **2** *US* a doughnut.

■ **1** see PLUMB[1] *n.*

sinner /sínnər/ *n.* a person who sins, esp. habitually.

■ transgressor, wrongdoer, miscreant, offender, evil-doer, malefactor, reprobate, *literary or archaic* trespasser.

sinnet /sínnit/ *n.* (also **sennit**) *Naut.* braided cordage made in flat or round or square form from 3 to 9 cords. [17th c.: orig. unkn.]

Sinn Fein /shin fáyn/ *n.* a political movement and party seeking a united republican Ireland, now linked to the IRA. □□ **Sinn Feiner** *n.* [Ir. *sinn féin* we ourselves]

Sino- /sī́nō/ *comb. form* Chinese; Chinese and (*Sino-American*). [Gk *Sinai* the Chinese]

sinologue /sī́nəlog, sín-/ *n.* an expert in sinology. [F, formed as SINO- + Gk *-logos* speaking]

sinology /sīnólləji, sin-/ *n.* the study of Chinese language, history, customs, etc. □□ **sinological** /-nəlójik'l/ *adj.* **sinologist** *n.*

sinter /síntər/ *n.* & *v.* ● *n.* **1** a siliceous or calcareous rock formed by deposition from springs. **2** a substance formed by sintering. ● *v.intr.* & *tr.* coalesce or cause to coalesce from powder into solid by heating. [G, = E *sinder* CINDER]

sinuate /sínyooət/ *adj.* esp. *Bot.* wavy-edged; with distinct inward and outward bends along the edge. [L *sinuatus* past part. of *sinuare* bend]

sinuosity /sínyoo-óssiti/ *n.* (*pl.* **-ies**) **1** the state of being sinuous. **2** a bend, esp. in a stream or road. [F *sinuosité* or med.L *sinuositas* (as SINUOUS)]
■ **2** see TURN *n.* 4.

sinuous /sínyooəss/ *adj.* with many curves; tortuous, undulating. □□ **sinuously** *adv.* **sinuousness** *n.* [F *sinueux* or L *sinuosus* (as SINUS)]
■ see TORTUOUS 1.

sinus /sī́nəss/ *n.* **1** a cavity of bone or tissue, esp. in the skull connecting with the nostrils. **2** *Med.* a fistula esp. to a deep abscess. **3** *Bot.* the curve between the lobes of a leaf. [L, = bosom, recess]

sinusitis /sī́nəsī́tiss/ *n.* inflammation of a nasal sinus.

sinusoid /sī́nəsoyd/ *n.* **1** a curve having the form of a sine wave. **2** a small irregular-shaped blood-vessel, esp. found in the liver. □□ **sinusoidal** /-sóyd'l/ *adj.* [F *sinusoïde* f. L *sinus*: see SINUS]

Sion var. of ZION.

-sion /sh'n, zh'n/ *suffix* forming nouns (see -ION) from Latin participial stems in *-s-* (*mansion*; *mission*; *persuasion*).

Sioux /sōō/ *n.* & *adj.* ● *n.* (*pl.* same) **1** a member of a group of N. American Indian peoples. **2** the language of this group. ● *adj.* of or relating to this people or language. □□ **Siouan** /sōōən/ *adj.* & *n.* [F f. a native name]

sip /sip/ *v.* & *n.* ● *v.tr.* & *intr.* (**sipped**, **sipping**) drink in one or more small amounts or by spoonfuls. ● *n.* **1** a small mouthful of liquid (*a sip of brandy*). **2** the act of taking this. □□ **sipper** *n.* [ME: perh. a modification of SUP^1]
■ *v.* taste, sample, sup. ● *n.* taste, sample, soupçon, drop, bit, mouthful, spoonful, thimbleful, nip, dram; sup, swallow, draught, drink, *colloq.* swig.

sipe /sīp/ *n.* a groove or channel in the tread of a tyre to improve its grip. [dial. *sipe* to ooze f. OE *sīpian*, MLG *sīpen*, of unkn. orig.]

siphon /sī́f'n/ *n.* & *v.* (also **syphon**) ● *n.* **1** a pipe or tube shaped like an inverted V or U with unequal legs to convey a liquid from a container to a lower level by atmospheric pressure. **2** (in full **siphon-bottle**) an aerated-water bottle from which liquid is forced out through a tube by the pressure of gas. **3** *Zool.* **a** a canal or conduit esp. in cephalopods. **b** the sucking-tube of some insects etc. ● *v.tr.* & *intr.* (often foll. by *off*) **1** conduct or flow through a siphon. **2** divert or set aside (funds etc.). □□ **siphonage** *n.* **siphonal** *adj.* **siphonic** /-fónnik/ *adj.* [F *siphon* or L *sipho -onis* f. Gk *siphōn* pipe]
■ *v.* **1** see PUMP^1 *v.* 1, 3a, 5. **2** see DIVERT 1a.

siphonophore /sīfónnəfor/ *n.* any usu. translucent marine hydrozoan of the order Siphonophora, e.g. the Portuguese man-of-war. [Gk *siphōno-* (as SIPHON, -PHORE)]

sippet /síppit/ *n.* **1** a small piece of bread etc. soaked in liquid. **2** a piece of toast or fried bread as a garnish. **3** a fragment. [app. dimin. of SOP]

sir /sur/ *n.* **1** a polite or respectful form of address or mode of reference to a man. **2** (**Sir**) a titular prefix to the forename of a knight or baronet. [ME, reduced form of SIRE]

sirdar /súrdaar/ *n.* *Ind.* etc. **1** a person of high political or military rank. **2** a Sikh. [Urdu *sardār* f. Pers. *sar* head + *dār* possessor]

sire /sīr/ *n.* & *v.* ● *n.* **1** the male parent of an animal, esp. a stallion kept for breeding. **2** *archaic* a respectful form of address, now esp. to a king. **3** *archaic poet.* a father or male ancestor. ● *v.tr.* (esp. of a stallion) beget. [ME f. OF ult. f. L *senior*: see SENIOR]
■ *n.* **1** father, progenitor. ● *v.* see FATHER *v.* 1.

siren /sī́rən/ *n.* **1 a** a device for making a loud prolonged signal or warning sound, esp. by revolving a perforated disc over a jet of compressed air or steam. **b** the sound made by this. **2** (in Greek mythology) each of a number of women or winged creatures whose singing lured unwary sailors on to rocks. **3** a sweet singer. **4 a** a dangerously fascinating woman; a temptress. **b** a tempting pursuit etc. **5** (*attrib.*) irresistibly tempting. **6** an eel-shaped tailed amphibian of the family Sirenidae. □ **siren suit** a one-piece garment for the whole body, easily put on or taken off, orig. for use in air-raid shelters. [ME f. OF *sereine*, *sirene* f. LL *Sirena* fem. f. L f. Gk *Seirēn*]
■ **1** whistle, wailer, horn, foghorn; signal, alarm, warning, alert, tocsin. **4 a** temptress, seductress, enchantress, charmer, sorceress, *femme fatale*, Circe, *colloq.* vamp.

sirenian /sīréeniən/ *adj.* & *n.* ● *adj.* of the order Sirenia of large aquatic plant-eating mammals, e.g. the manatee and dugong. ● *n.* any mammal of this order. [mod.L *Sirenia* (as SIREN)]

sirgang /súrgang/ *n.* an Asian magpie, *Kitta chinensis*, having mainly green plumage with red wings. [a name in the E. Indies]

sirloin /súrloyn/ *n.* the upper and choicer part of a loin of beef. [OF (as SUR-^{1}, LOIN)]

sirocco /sirókkō/ *n.* (also **scirocco**) (*pl.* **-os**) **1** a Saharan simoom reaching the northern shores of the Mediterranean. **2** a warm sultry rainy wind in S. Europe. [F f. It. *scirocco*, ult. f. Arab. *Sarūḳ* east wind]
■ **1** see STORM *n.* 1.

sirrah /sírrə/ *n.* *archaic* = SIR (as a form of address). [prob. f. ME *sīrĕ* SIR]

sirree /siréé/ *int.* *US colloq.* as an emphatic, esp. after *yes* or *no*. [SIR + emphatic suffix]

sirup *US* var. of SYRUP.

SIS *abbr.* Secret Intelligence Service.

sis /siss/ *n.* *colloq.* a sister. [abbr.]

sisal /sī́s'l/ *n.* **1** a Mexican plant, *Agave sisalana*, with large fleshy leaves. **2** the fibre made from this plant, used for cordage, ropes, etc. [*Sisal*, the port of Yucatan, Mexico]

siskin /sískin/ *n.* a dark-streaked yellowish-green songbird, *Carduelis spinus*, allied to the goldfinch. [MDu. *siseken* dimin., rel. to MLG *sīsek*, MHG *zīse*, *zīsec*, of Slav. origin]

sissy /síssi/ *n.* & *adj.* (also **cissy**) *colloq.* ● *n.* (*pl.* **-ies**) an effeminate or cowardly person. ● *adj.* (**sissier**, **sissiest**) effeminate; cowardly. □□ **sissified** *adj.* **sissiness** *n.* **sissyish** *adj.* [SIS + -Y^2]
■ *n.* milksop, namby-pamby, weakling, coward, baby, cry-baby, mollycoddle, *colloq.* softie, *Brit. colloq.* wet, mummy's boy, *Austral.* & *NZ sl. derog.* sook. ● *adj.* see EFFEMINATE, SOFT *adj.* 11b. □□ **sissified** see SOFT *adj.* 11b.

sister /sístər/ *n.* **1** a woman or girl in relation to sons and other daughters of her parents. **2 a** (often as a form of address) a close female friend or associate. **b** a female fellow member of a trade union, class, sect, or the human race. **3** a senior female nurse. **4** a member of a female religious order. **5** (*attrib.*) of the same type or design or origin etc. (*sister ship*; *prose, the younger sister of verse*). □ **sister german** see GERMAN. **sister-in-law** (*pl.* **sisters-in-law**) **1** the sister of one's wife or husband. **2** the wife of one's brother. **3** the wife of one's brother-in-law. **Sister of Mercy** a member of an educational or charitable order of women, esp. that founded in Dublin in 1827. **sister uterine** see UTERINE. □□ **sisterless** *adj.* **sisterly** *adj.* **sisterliness** *n.* [ME *sister* (f. ON), *suster* etc. (repr. OE *sweoster* f. Gmc)]
■ **2** see INTIMATE^1 *n.* **3** see NURSE *n.* **5** see ASSOCIATE *adj.* 2.

sisterhood /sístərhōōd/ *n.* **1 a** the relationship between sisters. **b** sisterly friendliness; companionship; mutual support. **2 a** a society or association of women, esp. when bound by monastic vows or devoting themselves to religious or charitable work or the feminist cause. **b** its members collectively.

■ **1** see LOVE *n.* 1. **2** see SOCIETY 8.

Sistine /sísteen, sístīn/ *adj.* of any of the Popes called Sixtus, esp. Sixtus IV. □ **Sistine Chapel** a chapel in the Vatican, with frescoes by Michelangelo and other painters. [It. *Sistino* f. *Sisto* Sixtus]

sistrum /sístrəm/ *n.* (*pl.* **sistra** /-trə/) a jingling metal instrument used by the ancient Egyptians esp. in the worship of Isis. [ME f. L f. Gk *seistron* f. *seiō* shake]

■ rattle, noise-maker.

Sisyphean /sízzifeéən/ *adj.* (of toil) endless and fruitless like that of Sisyphus in Greek mythology (whose task in Hades was to push uphill a stone that at once rolled down again).

■ see BOOTLESS.

sit /sit/ *v.* & *n.* ● *v.* (**sitting**; *past* and *past part.* **sat** /sat/) **1** *intr.* adopt or be in a position in which the body is supported more or less upright by the buttocks resting on the ground or a raised seat etc., with the thighs usu. horizontal. **2** *tr.* cause to sit; place in a sitting position. **3** *intr.* **a** (of a bird) perch. **b** (of an animal) rest with the hind legs bent and the body close to the ground. **4** *intr.* (of a bird) remain on its nest to hatch its eggs. **5** *intr.* **a** be engaged in an occupation in which the sitting position is usual. **b** (of a committee, legislative body, etc.) be engaged in business. **c** (of an individual) be entitled to hold some office or position (*sat as a magistrate*). **6** *intr.* (usu. foll. by *for*) pose in a sitting position (for a portrait). **7** *intr.* (foll. by *for*) be a Member of Parliament for (a constituency). **8** *tr.* & (foll. by *for*) *intr. Brit.* be a candidate for (an examination). **9** *intr.* be in a more or less permanent position or condition (esp. of inactivity or being out of use or out of place). **10** *intr.* (of clothes etc.) fit or hang in a certain way. **11** *tr.* keep or have one's seat on (a horse etc.). **12** *intr.* act as a babysitter. **13** *intr.* (often foll. by *before*) (of an army) take a position outside a city etc. to besiege it. **14** *tr.* = SEAT *v.* 2a. ● *n.* the way a dress etc. sits on a person. □ **be sitting pretty** be comfortably or advantageously placed. **make a person sit up** *colloq.* surprise or interest a person. **sit at a person's feet** be a person's pupil. **sit at home** be inactive. **sit back** relax one's efforts. **sit by** look on without interfering. **sit down 1** sit after standing. **2** cause to sit. **3** (foll. by *under*) submit tamely to (an insult etc.). **sit-down** *adj.* (of a meal) eaten sitting at a table. **sit-down strike** a strike in which workers refuse to leave their place of work. **sit heavy on the stomach** take a long time to be digested. **sit in 1** occupy a place as a protest. **2** (foll. by *for*) take the place of. **3** (foll. by *on*) be present as a guest or observer at (a meeting etc.). **sit-in** *n.* a protest involving sitting in. **sit in judgement** assume the right of judging others; be censorious. **sit loosely on** not be very binding. **sit on 1** be a member of (a committee etc.). **2** hold a session or inquiry concerning. **3** *colloq.* delay action about (*the government has been sitting on the report*). **4** *colloq.* repress or rebuke or snub (*felt rather sat on*). **sit on the fence** see FENCE. **sit on one's hands 1** take no action. **2** refuse to applaud. **sit out 1** take no part in (a dance etc.). **2** stay till the end of (esp. an ordeal). **3** sit outdoors. **4** outstay (other visitors). **sit tight** *colloq.* **1** remain firmly in one's place. **2** not be shaken off or move away or yield to distractions. **sit up 1** rise from a lying to a sitting position. **2** sit firmly upright. **3** go to bed later than the usual time. **4** *colloq.* become interested or aroused etc. **sit-up** *n.* a physical exercise in which a person sits up without raising the legs from the ground. **sit up and take notice** *colloq.* have one's interest aroused, esp. suddenly. **sit-upon** *colloq.* the buttocks. **sit well** have a good seat in riding. **sit well on** suit or fit. [OE *sittan* f. Gmc]

■ *v.* **1** be *or* get seated, settle, sit down, take a seat, rest, perch, *colloq.* take the weight off one's feet, squat. **2** seat, sit down, install, ensconce, place, put. **3 a** perch, nest, roost, rest. **4** brood, incubate. **5 b** hold a session, be in session, assemble, meet, convene; gather, get together, congregate. **6** pose, model. **9** remain, stay, lie, rest; relax, mark time, *archaic* abide, *literary* dwell. **10** fit, hang; seem, appear, look. □ **sit back** see RELAX *v.* 1c, 4. **sit-down strike** see STRIKE *n.* 2. **sit in 2** (*sit in for*) substitute for, fill in for, stand in for, double for, take the place of, cover for, deputize for, *colloq.* sub for. **3** (*sit in on*) observe, watch, be present at, attend; join in, participate in, take part in. **sit-in** see DEMONSTRATION 2. **sit on 1** have *or* hold *or* occupy a seat on, participate in, be a member of. **sit out 2** wait out, last through, live through. **4** outwait, outstay, outlast, outlive. **sit tight** wait, hang back, hold back, be patient, bide one's time, play a waiting game, take no action, delay, temporize, *colloq.* hold one's horses. **sit up 4** awaken, pay attention, notice, take notice, become alert *or* interested *or* concerned, *colloq.* sit up and take notice. **sit well on** sit well *or* right (with), suit, fit, befit, look good *or* well on, become, agree with, be agreeable to.

sitar /síttaar, sitaár/ *n.* a long-necked Indian lute with movable frets. □□ **sitarist** /sitaárist/ *n.* [Hindi *sitār*]

sitcom /sítkom/ *n. colloq.* a situation comedy. [abbr.]

site /sīt/ *n.* & *v.* ● *n.* **1** the ground chosen or used for a town or building. **2** a place where some activity is or has been conducted (*camping site*; *launching site*). ● *v.tr.* **1** locate or place. **2** provide with a site. [ME f. AF *site* or L *situs* local position]

■ *n.* location, place, plot, ground, spot, setting, locale, area, milieu, neighbourhood, locality, purlieus, placement, position; situation, orientation, *US* plat. ● *v.* locate, position, place, put, situate, install.

Sitka /sítkə/ *n.* (in full **Sitka spruce**) a fast-growing spruce, *Picea sitchensis*, native to N. America and yielding timber. [*Sitka* in Alaska]

sitrep /sítrep/ *n.* a report on the current military situation in an area. [*sit*uation *rep*ort]

sits vac /sits vák/ *abbr.* situations vacant.

sitter /síttər/ *n.* **1** a person who sits, esp. for a portrait. **2** = BABYSITTER (see BABYSIT). **3** *colloq.* **a** an easy catch or shot. **b** an easy task. **4** a sitting hen.

■ **1** model, subject, poser. **3** see BREEZE[1] *n.* 5.

sitting /sítting/ *n.* & *adj.* ● *n.* **1** a continuous period of being seated, esp. engaged in an activity (*finished the book in one sitting*). **2** a time during which an assembly is engaged in business. **3** a session in which a meal is served (*dinner will be served in two sittings*). **4** *Brit. Law* = TERM 5c. **5** a clutch of eggs. ● *adj.* **1** having sat down. **2** (of an animal or bird) not running or flying. **3** (of a hen) engaged in hatching. □ **sitting duck** (or **target**) *colloq.* a vulnerable person or thing. **sitting pretty** see PRETTY. **sitting-room 1** a room in a house for relaxed sitting in. **2** space enough to accommodate seated persons. **sitting tenant** a tenant already in occupation of premises.

■ *n.* **2** see SESSION 1, 2. ● *adj.* **1** sedentary, seated. □ **sitting-room 1** see PARLOUR.

situate *v.* & *adj.* ● *v.tr.* /sítyoo-ayt/ (usu. in *passive*) **1** put in a certain position or circumstances (*is situated at the top of a hill*; *how are you situated at the moment?*). **2** establish or indicate the place of; put in a context. ● *adj.* /sítyooət/ *Law* or *archaic* situated. [med.L *situare situat-* f. L *situs* site]

■ *v.* **1** place in a position *or* situation *or* location, place, position, locate, set, site, spot, put, install.

situation /sítyoo-áysh'n/ *n.* **1** a place and its surroundings (*the house stands in a fine situation*). **2** a set of circumstances; a position in which one finds oneself; a state of affairs (*came out of a difficult situation with credit*). **3** an employee's position or job. **4** a critical point or complication in a drama. □ **situation comedy** a comedy in which the humour derives from the situations the characters are placed in. **situations vacant** (or **wanted**) headings of lists of employment offered and sought. □□ **situational** *adj.* [ME f. F *situation* or med.L *situatio* (as SITUATE)]

■ **1** place, position, location, spot, site, locale, setting. **2** state (of affairs *or* things *or* play), condition, circumstances, case, status (quo), lie of the land, picture; plight, predicament, kettle of fish; *esp. US colloq.* ball game. **3** position, place, job, employment, post, *colloq.* berth, billet.

sitz-bath /sítsbaath/ *n.* a hip-bath. [partial transl. of G *Sitzbad* f. *sitzen* sit + *Bad* bath]
■ hip-bath, *propr.* Jacuzzi.

Siva /séevə, shéevə/ *n.* (also **Shiva** /shéevə/) a Hindu deity associated with the powers of reproduction and dissolution, regarded by some as the supreme being and by others as a member of the triad. ▫▫ **Sivaism** *n.* **Sivaite** *n.* & *adj.* [Skr. *Śiva*, lit. the auspicious one]

six /siks/ *n.* & *adj.* ● *n.* **1** one more than five, or four less than ten; the product of two units and three units. **2** a symbol for this (6, vi, VI). **3** a size etc. denoted by six. **4** a set or team of six individuals. **5** *Cricket* a hit scoring six runs by clearing the boundary without bouncing. **6** the time of six o'clock (*is it six yet?*). **7** a card etc. with six pips. ● *adj.* that amount to six. ▫ **at sixes and sevens** in confusion or disagreement. **knock for six** *colloq.* utterly surprise or overcome (a person). **the Six Counties** the counties of N. Ireland. **six-gun** = *six-shooter*. **six of one and half a dozen of the other** a situation of little real difference between the alternatives. **six-shooter** a revolver with six chambers. [OE *siex* etc. f. Gmc]
■ ▫ **at sixes and sevens** see *chaotic* (CHAOS). **six of one and half a dozen of the other** nothing to choose (between them), much of a muchness, a case of Tweedledum and Tweedledee.

sixain /síksayn/ *n.* a six-line stanza. [F f. *six* six]

sixer /síksər/ *n.* **1** the leader of a group of six Brownies or Cubs. **2** *Cricket* a hit for six runs.

sixfold /síksfōld/ *adj.* & *adv.* **1** six times as much or as many. **2** consisting of six parts.

sixpence /síkspənss/ *n. Brit.* **1** the sum of six pence, esp. before decimalization. **2** *hist.* a coin worth six old pence ($2\frac{1}{2}$p). ▫ **turn on a sixpence** *colloq.* make a sharp turn in a motor vehicle.

sixpenny /síkspəni/ *adj. Brit.* costing or worth six pence, esp. before decimalization.

sixte /sikst/ *n. Fencing* the sixth of the eight parrying positions. [F f. L *sextus* sixth]

sixteen /sìksteén/ *n.* & *adj.* ● *n.* **1** one more than fifteen, or six more than ten. **2** a symbol for this (16, xvi, XVI). **3** a size etc. denoted by sixteen. ● *adj.* that amount to sixteen. ▫ **sixteenth note** esp. *US Mus.* = SEMIQUAVER. ▫▫ **sixteenth** *adj.* & *n.* [OE *siextiene* (as SIX, -TEEN)]

sixteenmo /sìksteénmō/ *n.* (*pl.* **-os**) sextodecimo. [English reading of the symbol 16mo]

sixth /siksth/ *n.* & *adj.* ● *n.* **1** the position in a sequence corresponding to that of the number 6 in the sequence 1-6. **2** something occupying this position. **3** any of six equal parts of a thing. **4** *Mus.* **a** an interval or chord spanning six consecutive notes in the diatonic scale (e.g. C to A). **b** a note separated from another by this interval. ● *adj.* that is the sixth. ▫ **sixth form** *Brit.* a form in a secondary school for pupils over 16. **sixth-form college** *Brit.* a college for pupils over 16. **sixth-former** a pupil in the sixth form. **sixth sense 1** a supposed faculty giving intuitive or extrasensory knowledge. **2** such knowledge. ▫▫ **sixthly** *adv.* [SIX]
■ ▫ **sixth sense** see INTUITION.

Sixtine /síksteen, -tīn/ *adj.* = SISTINE. [mod.L *Sixtinus* f. *Sixtus*]

sixty /síksti/ *n.* & *adj.* ● *n.* (*pl.* **-ies**) **1** the product of six and ten. **2** a symbol for this (60, lx, LX). **3** (in *pl.*) the numbers from 60 to 69, esp. the years of a century or of a person's life. **4** a set of sixty persons or things. ● *adj.* that amount to sixty. ▫ **sixty-first, -second,** etc. the ordinal numbers between sixtieth and seventieth. **sixty-fourmo** /síkstifórmō/ (*pl.* **-os**) **1** a size of book in which each leaf is one-sixty-fourth of a printing-sheet. **2** a book of this size (*after* DUODECIMO etc.). **sixty-fourth note** esp. *US Mus.* = HEMIDEMISEMIQUAVER. **sixty-four thousand** (or **sixty-four**) **dollar question** a difficult and crucial question (from the top prize in a broadcast quiz show). **sixty-one, -two,** etc. the cardinal numbers between sixty and seventy. ▫▫ **sixtieth** *adj.* & *n.* **sixtyfold** *adj.* & *adv.* [OE *siextig* (as SIX, -TY[2])]

sizable var. of SIZEABLE.

sizar /sízər/ *n.* a student at Cambridge or at Trinity College, Dublin, paying reduced fees and formerly having certain menial duties. ▫▫ **sizarship** *n.* [SIZE[1] = ration]

size[1] /sīz/ *n.* & *v.* ● *n.* **1** the relative bigness or extent of a thing, dimensions, magnitude (*is of vast size; size matters less than quality*). **2** each of the classes, usu. numbered, into which things otherwise similar, esp. garments, are divided according to size (*is made in several sizes; takes size 7 in gloves; is three sizes too big*). ● *v.tr.* sort or group in sizes or according to size. ▫ **of a size** having the same size. **of some size** fairly large. **the size of** as big as. **the size of it** *colloq.* a true account of the matter (*that is the size of it*). **size-stick** a shoemaker's measure for taking the length of a foot. **size up 1** estimate the size of. **2** *colloq.* form a judgement of. **what size?** how big? ▫▫ **sized** *adj.* (also in *comb.*). **sizer** *n.* [ME f. OF *sise* f. *assise* ASSIZE, or f. ASSIZE]
■ *n.* **1** magnitude, largeness, bigness, bulk, extent, scope, range, dimensions, proportions, measurement(s), expanse, area, square footage, volume, capacity, mass, weight; breadth, width, length, height, depth; amount; hugeness, immensity, greatness, vastness, enormousness. ● *v.* see SORT *v.* ▫ **size up 1** see ESTIMATE *v.* 1–3. **2** assess, judge, evaluate, measure, take the measure of, appraise, assay, make an estimate of, estimate, value, gauge, rate.

size[2] /sīz/ *n.* & *v.* ● *n.* a gelatinous solution used in glazing paper, stiffening textiles, preparing plastered walls for decoration, etc. ● *v.tr.* glaze or stiffen or treat with size. [ME, perh. = SIZE[1]]

sizeable /sízəb'l/ *adj.* (also **sizable**) large or fairly large. ▫▫ **sizeably** *adv.*
■ see LARGE *adj.* 1, 2.

sizzle /sízz'l/ *v.* & *n.* ● *v.intr.* **1** make a sputtering or hissing sound as of frying. **2** *colloq.* be in a state of great heat or excitement or marked effectiveness. ● *n.* **1** a sizzling sound. **2** *colloq.* a state of great heat or excitement. ▫▫ **sizzler** *n.* **sizzling** *adj.* & *adv.* (*sizzling hot*). [imit.]
■ *v.* **1** see FIZZ *v.* 1. **2** see BOIL[1] *v.* 3b. ▫▫ **sizzling** (*adj.*) see HOT *adj.* 1.

SJ *abbr.* Society of Jesus.

SJAA *abbr.* (in the UK) St John Ambulance Association.

SJAB *abbr.* (in the UK) St John Ambulance Brigade.

sjambok /shámbok/ *n.* & *v.* ● *n.* (in S. Africa) a rhinoceros-hide whip. ● *v.tr.* flog with a sjambok. [Afrik. f. Malay *samboq, chambok* f. Urdu *chābuk*]

SJC *abbr.* (in the US) Supreme Judicial Court.

skald /skawld, skold/ *n.* (also **scald**) (in ancient Scandinavia) a composer and reciter of poems honouring heroes and their deeds. ▫▫ **skaldic** *adj.* [ON *skáld*, of unkn. orig.]
■ see MINSTREL.

skat /skaat/ *n.* a three-handed card-game with bidding. [G f. It. *scarto* a discard f. *scartare* discard]

skate[1] /skayt/ *n.* & *v.* ● *n.* **1** each of a pair of steel blades (or of boots with blades attached) for gliding on ice. **2** (in full **roller skate**) each of a pair of metal frames with small wheels, fitted to shoes for riding on a hard surface. **3** a device on which a heavy object moves. ● *v.* **1 a** *intr.* move on skates. **b** *tr.* perform (a specified figure) on skates. **2** *intr.* (foll. by *over*) refer fleetingly to, disregard. ▫ **get one's skates on** *Brit. sl.* make haste. **skate on thin ice** *colloq.* behave rashly, risk danger, esp. by dealing with a subject needing tactful treatment. **skating-rink** a piece of ice artificially made, or a floor used, for skating. ▫▫ **skater** *n.* [orig. *scates* (pl.) f. Du. *schaats* (sing.) f. ONF *escace*, OF *eschasse* stilt]

■ *v.* **1 a** see SLIDE *v.* 1, 2. □ **skate on thin ice** see *sail close to the wind.*

skate[2] /skayt/ *n.* (*pl.* same or **skates**) any cartilaginous marine fish of the family Rajidae, esp. *Raja batis*, a large flat rhomboidal fish used as food. [ME f. ON *skata*]

skate[3] /skayt/ *n. sl.* a contemptible, mean, or dishonest person (esp. *cheap skate*). [19th c.: orig. uncert.]

skateboard /skáytbord/ *n.* & *v.* ● *n.* a short narrow board on roller-skate wheels for riding on while standing. ● *v.intr.* ride on a skateboard. □□ **skateboarder** *n.*

skean /skeen, skeéən/ *n. hist.* a Gaelic dagger formerly used in Ireland and Scotland. □ **skean-dhu** /-do͞o/ *n.* a dagger worn in the stocking as part of Highland costume. [Gael. *sgian* knife, *dubh* black]

■ see DAGGER.

sked /sked/ *n.* & *v. colloq.* ● *n.* = SCHEDULE *n.* ● *v.tr.* (**skedded, skedding**) = SCHEDULE *v.* [abbr.]

skedaddle /skidádd'l/ *v.* & *n. colloq.* ● *v.intr.* run away, depart quickly, flee. ● *n.* a hurried departure or flight. [19th c.: orig. unkn.]

■ *v.* see FLEE 1.

skeet /skeet/ *n.* a shooting sport in which a clay target is thrown from a trap to simulate the flight of a bird. [ON *skjóta* SHOOT]

skeeter[1] /skeétər/ *n. US* & *Austral. sl.* a mosquito. [abbr.]

skeeter[2] var. of SKITTER.

skeg /skeg/ *n.* **1** a fin underneath the rear of a surfboard. **2** the after part of a vessel's keel or a projection from it. [ON *skeg* beard, perh. via Du. *scheg(ge)*]

skein /skayn/ *n.* **1** a loosely coiled bundle of yarn or thread. **2** a flock of wild geese etc. in flight. **3** a tangle or confusion. [ME f. OF *escaigne*, of unkn. orig.]

■ **2** see FLIGHT[1] *n.* 3a. **3** see TANGLE[1] *n.* 1.

skeleton /skéllit'n/ *n.* **1 a** a hard internal or external framework of bones, cartilage, shell, woody fibre, etc., supporting or containing the body of an animal or plant. **b** the dried bones of a human being or other animal fastened together in the same relative positions as in life. **2** the supporting framework or structure or essential part of a thing. **3** a very thin or emaciated person or animal. **4** the remaining part of anything after its life or usefulness is gone. **5** an outline sketch, an epitome or abstract. **6** (*attrib.*) having only the essential or minimum number of persons, parts, etc. (*skeleton plan; skeleton staff*). □ **skeleton at the feast** something that spoils one's pleasure; an intrusive worry. **skeleton in the cupboard** (*US* **closet**) a discreditable or embarrassing fact kept secret. **skeleton key** a key designed to fit many locks by having the interior of the bit hollowed. □□ **skeletal** *adj.* **skeletally** *adv.* **skeletonize** *v.tr.* (also **-ise**). [mod.L f. Gk, neut. of *skeletos* dried-up f. *skellō* dry up]

■ **1 a** see FRAME *n.* 4. **2** see FRAME *n.* 2. **5** see OUTLINE *n.* 1, 2. □ **skeleton in the cupboard** see SCANDAL 1a. **skeleton key** key, passkey, opener. □□ **skeletal** see *emaciated* (EMACIATE).

skep /skep/ *n.* **1 a** a wooden or wicker basket of any of various forms. **b** the quantity contained in this. **2** a straw or wicker beehive. [ME f. ON *skeppa*]

skepsis *US* var. of SCEPSIS.

skeptic *US* var. of SCEPTIC.

skeptical *US* var. of SCEPTICAL.

skerrick /skérrik/ *n.* (usu. with *neg.*) *US* & *Austral. colloq.* the smallest bit (*not a skerrick left*). [N.Engl. dial.; orig. uncert.]

■ see SCRAP[1] *n.* 5.

skerry /skérri/ *n.* (*pl.* **-ies**) *Sc.* a reef or rocky island. [Orkney dial. f. ON *sker*: cf. SCAR[2]]

sketch /skech/ *n.* & *v.* ● *n.* **1** a rough, slight, merely outlined, or unfinished drawing or painting, often made to assist in making a more finished picture. **2** a brief account without many details conveying a general idea of something, a rough draft or general outline. **3** a very short play, usu. humorous and limited to one scene. **4** a short descriptive piece of writing. **5** a musical composition of a single movement. **6** *colloq.* a comical person or thing. ● *v.* **1** *tr.* make or give a sketch of. **2** *intr.* draw sketches esp. of landscape (*went out sketching*). **3** *tr.* (often foll. by *in, out*) indicate briefly or in outline. □ **sketch-book** (or **-block**) a pad of drawing-paper for doing sketches on. **sketch-map** a roughly drawn map with few details. □□ **sketcher** *n.* [Du. *schets* or G *Skizze* f. It. *schizzo* f. *schizzare* make a sketch ult. f. Gk *skhēdios* extempore]

■ *n.* **1** see DRAWING. **2** see OUTLINE *n.* 1, 2. **3** see ACT *n.* 3a. **4, 5** see PIECE *n.* 3. ● *v.* **1** see ROUGH *v.* **2** see DRAW *v.* 10. **3** see OUTLINE *v.*

sketchy /skéchi/ *adj.* (**sketchier, sketchiest**) **1** giving only a slight or rough outline, like a sketch. **2** *colloq.* unsubstantial or imperfect esp. through haste. □□ **sketchily** *adv.* **sketchiness** *n.*

■ cursory, superficial, incomplete, patchy, unsubstantial, rough, perfunctory, skimpy, imperfect, crude, hasty, hurried, vague, ill-defined, fuzzy, indistinct, inexact, imprecise, unrefined, unpolished, rough-hewn, unfinished. □□ **sketchily** cursorily, superficially, incompletely, patchily, roughly, perfunctorily, skimpily, vaguely, imperfectly, crudely, hastily, hurriedly.

skeuomorph /skyo͞o-ōmorf/ *n.* **1** an object or feature copying the design of a similar artefact in another material. **2** an ornamental design resulting from the nature of the material used or the method of working it. □□ **skeuomorphic** /-mórfik/ *adj.* [Gk *skeuos* vessel, implement + *morphē* form]

skew /skyo͞o/ *adj.*, *n.*, & *v.* ● *adj.* **1** oblique, slanting, set askew. **2** *Math.* **a** lying in three dimensions (*skew curve*). **b** (of lines) not coplanar. **c** (of a statistical distribution) not symmetrical. ● *n.* **1** a slant. **2** *Statistics* skewness. ● *v.* **1** *tr.* make skew. **2** *tr.* distort. **3** *intr.* move obliquely. **4** *intr.* twist. □ **on the skew** askew. **skew arch** (or **bridge**) an arch (or bridge) with the line of the arch not at right angles to the abutment. **skew chisel** a chisel with an oblique edge. **skew-eyed** *Brit.* squinting. **skew gear** a gear consisting of two cog-wheels having non-parallel, non-intersecting axes. **skew-whiff** /skyo͞owíf/ *Brit. colloq.* askew. □□ **skewness** *n.* [ONF *eskiu(w)er* (v.) = OF *eschuer*: see ESCHEW]

■ *adj.* **1** see IRREGULAR *adj.* 1, 2. ● *n.* **1** see TWIST *n.* 4, SLOPE *n.* 1–3. **2** bias, skewness, distortion. ● *v.* **2** see BIAS *v.* **3** see SWERVE *v.*

skewback /skyo͞obak/ *n.* the sloping face of the abutment on which an extremity of an arch rests.

skewbald /skyo͞obawld/ *adj.* & *n.* ● *adj.* (of an animal) with irregular patches of white and another colour (properly not black) (cf. PIEBALD). ● *n.* a skewbald animal, esp. a horse. [ME *skued* (orig. uncert.), after PIEBALD]

■ *adj.* see SPOTTY 1.

skewer /skyo͞oər/ *n.* & *v.* ● *n.* a long pin designed for holding meat compactly together while cooking. ● *v.tr.* fasten together or pierce with or as with a skewer. [17th c., var. of dial. *skiver*: orig. unkn.]

■ *n.* see SPIKE[1] *n.* 1b. ● *v.* see PIERCE 1a, b.

ski /skee/ *n.* & *v.* ● *n.* (*pl.* **skis** or **ski**) **1** each of a pair of long narrow pieces of wood etc., usu. pointed and turned up at the front, fastened under the feet for travelling over snow. **2** a similar device under a vehicle or aircraft. **3** = WATER-SKI. **4** (*attrib.*) for wear when skiing (*ski boots*). ● *v.* (**skis, ski'd** or **skied** /skeed/; **skiing**) **1** *intr.* travel on skis. **2** *tr.* ski at (a place). □ **ski-bob** *n.* a machine like a bicycle with skis instead of wheels. ● *v.intr.* (**-bobbed, -bobbing**) ride a ski-bob. **ski-bobber** a person who ski-bobs. **ski-jump 1** a steep slope levelling off before a sharp drop to allow a skier to leap through the air. **2** a jump made from this. **ski-jumper** a person who takes part in ski-jumping. **ski-jumping** the sport of leaping off a ski-jump with marks awarded for style and distance attained. **ski-lift** a device for carrying skiers up a slope, usu. on seats hung from an overhead cable. **ski-plane** an aeroplane having its undercarriage fitted with skis for landing on snow or ice. **ski-run** a slope prepared for skiing. □□ **skiable** *adj.* [Norw. f. ON *skíth* billet, snow-shoe]

skiagraphy var. of SCIAGRAPHY.

skiamachy var. of SCIAMACHY.

skid /skid/ *v.* & *n.* ● *v.* (**skidded, skidding**) **1** *intr.* (of a vehicle, a wheel, or a driver) slide on slippery ground, esp. sideways or obliquely. **2** *tr.* cause (a vehicle etc.) to skid. **3** *intr.* slip, slide. **4** *intr. colloq.* fail or decline or err. **5** *tr.* support or move or protect or check with a skid. ● *n.* **1** the act or an instance of skidding. **2** a piece of wood etc. serving as a support, ship's fender, inclined plane, etc. **3** a braking device, esp. a wooden or metal shoe preventing a wheel from revolving or used as a drag. **4** a runner beneath an aircraft for use when landing. □ **hit the skids** *colloq.* enter a rapid decline or deterioration. **on the skids** *colloq.* **1** about to be discarded or defeated. **2** ready for launching. **put the skids under** *colloq.* **1** hasten the downfall or failure of. **2** cause to hasten. **skid-lid** *sl.* a crash-helmet. **skid-pan** *Brit.* **1** a slippery surface prepared for vehicle-drivers to practise control of skidding. **2** a braking device. **skid road** *US* **1** a road for hauling logs along. **2** *colloq.* a part of a town frequented by loggers or vagrants. **skid row** *US colloq.* a part of a town frequented by vagrants, alcoholics, etc. [17th c.: orig. unkn.]

■ *v.* **1–3** see SLIDE *v.* 1, 2. □ **on the skids 1** see *on the decline* (DECLINE). **skid row** see SLUM *n.* 1.

skiddoo /skidóō/ *v.intr.* (also **skidoo**) (**-oos, -ooed**) *US sl.* go away; depart. [perh. f. SKEDADDLE]

skier[1] /skéeər/ *n.* a person who skis.

skier[2] var. of SKYER.

skiff /skif/ *n.* a light rowing-boat or sculling-boat. [F *esquif* f. It. *schifo*, rel. to SHIP]

■ see BOAT *n.*

skiffle /skiff'l/ *n.* a kind of folk music played by a small group, mainly with a rhythmic accompaniment to a singing guitarist etc. [perh. imit.]

ski-joring /skéejoring, shee-yóring/ *n.* a winter sport in which a skier is towed by a horse or vehicle. □□ **ski-jorer** *n.* [Norw. *skikjøring* (as SKI, *kjøre* drive)]

skilful /skílfŏŏl/ *adj.* (*US* **skillful**) (often foll. by *at*, *in*) having or showing skill; practised, expert, adroit, ingenious. □□ **skilfully** *adv.* **skilfulness** *n.*

■ skilled, accomplished, adept, adroit, dexterous, expert, proficient, masterly, masterful, gifted, ingenious, brilliant, apt, able, clever, talented, capable, consummate, professional, trained, qualified, experienced, practised. □□ **skilfulness** see SKILL.

skill /skil/ *n.* (often foll. by *in*) expertness, practised ability, facility in an action; dexterity or tact. □□ **skill-less** *adj.* (*archaic* **skilless**). [ME f. ON *skil* distinction]

■ talent, ability, aptitude, expertness, expertise, facility, prowess, skilfulness, art, artistry, cleverness, adeptness, adroitness, mastery, dexterity, handiness, ingenuity, experience, proficiency, finesse, knack, quickness, deftness, technique; accomplishment, forte, strength, gift, capability, know-how, faculty.

skilled /skild/ *adj.* **1** (often foll. by *in*) having or showing skill; skilful. **2** (of a worker) highly trained or experienced. **3** (of work) requiring skill or special training.

■ **1** see SKILFUL. **2** see EXPERIENCED 2.

skillet /skíllit/ *n.* **1** *Brit.* a small metal cooking-pot with a long handle and usu. legs. **2** *US* a frying-pan. [ME, perh. f. OF *escuelete* dimin. of *escuele* platter f. LL *scutella*]

■ see PAN[1] *n.* 1.

skillful *US* var. of SKILFUL.

skilly /skílli/ *n. Brit.* **1** a thin broth or soup or gruel (usu. of oatmeal and water flavoured with meat). **2** an insipid beverage; tea or coffee. [abbr. f. *skilligalee*, prob. fanciful]

skim /skim/ *v.* & *n.* ● *v.* (**skimmed, skimming**) **1** *tr.* **a** take scum or cream or a floating layer from the surface of (a liquid). **b** take (cream etc.) from the surface of a liquid. **2** *tr.* **a** keep touching lightly or nearly touching (a surface) in passing over. **b** deal with or treat (a subject) superficially. **3** *intr.* **a** (often foll. by *over*, *along*) go lightly over a surface, glide along in the air. **b** (foll. by *over*) = sense 2b of *v.* **4 a** *tr.* read superficially, look over cursorily, gather the salient facts contained in. **b** *intr.* (usu. foll. by *through*) read or look over cursorily. **5** *tr. US sl.* conceal or divert (income) to avoid paying tax. ● *n.* **1** the act or an instance of skimming. **2** a thin covering on a liquid (*skim of ice*). □ **skim the cream off** take the best part of. **skim** (or **skimmed**) **milk** milk from which the cream has been skimmed. [ME, back-form. f. SKIMMER]

■ *v.* **1 a** cream (off). **b** skim off, separate, scoop *or* ladle off, take off, remove. **3 a** soar, glide, skate, slide, sail, scud, fly, plane, aquaplane, coast. **4** skim through *or* over, scan, flip *or* thumb *or* leaf through, skip through, glance at *or* through, dip into.

skimmer /skímmər/ *n.* **1** a device for skimming liquids. **2** a person who skims. **3** a flat hat, esp. a broad-brimmed straw hat. **4** any long-winged marine bird of the genus *Rynchops* that feeds by skimming over water with its knifelike lower mandible immersed. **5** a hydroplane, hydrofoil, hovercraft, or other vessel that has little or no displacement at speed. **6** *US* a sheath-like dress. [ME f. OF *escumoir* f. *escumer* f. *escume* SCUM]

skimmia /skímmiə/ *n.* any evergreen shrub of the genus *Skimmia*, native to E. Asia, with red berries. [mod.L f. Jap.]

skimp /skimp/ *v.*, *adj.*, & *n.* ● *v.* **1** *tr.* (often foll. by *in*) supply (a person etc.) meagrely with food, money, etc. **2** *tr.* use a meagre or insufficient amount of, stint (material, expenses, etc.). **3** *intr.* be parsimonious. ● *adj.* scanty. ● *n. colloq.* a small or scanty thing, esp. a skimpy garment. [18th c.: orig. unkn.: cf. SCRIMP]

■ *v.* see STINT *v.*

skimpy /skímpi/ *adj.* (**skimpier, skimpiest**) meagre; not ample or sufficient. □□ **skimpily** *adv.* **skimpiness** *n.*

■ see MEAGRE 1. □□ **skimpily** see POORLY.

skin /skin/ *n.* & *v.* ● *n.* **1** the flexible continuous covering of a human or other animal body. **2 a** the skin of a flayed animal with or without the hair etc. **b** a material prepared from skins esp. of smaller animals (opp. HIDE[2]). **3** a person's skin with reference to its colour or complexion (*has a fair skin*). **4** an outer layer or covering, esp. the coating of a plant, fruit, or sausage. **5** a film like skin on the surface of a liquid etc. **6** a container for liquid, made of an animal's whole skin. **7 a** the planking or plating of a ship or boat, inside or outside the ribs. **b** the outer covering of any craft or vehicle, esp. an aircraft or spacecraft. **8** *Brit. sl.* a skinhead. **9** *US Cards* a game in which each player has one card which he bets will not be the first to be matched by a card dealt from the pack. **10** = *gold-beater's skin*. **11** a duplicating stencil. ● *v.* (**skinned, skinning**) **1** *tr.* remove the skin from. **2** (often foll. by *over*) **a** *tr.* cover (a sore etc.) with or as with skin. **b** *intr.* (of a wound etc.) become covered with new skin. **3** *tr. sl.* fleece or swindle. □ **be skin and bone** be very thin. **by** (or **with**) **the skin of one's teeth** by a very narrow margin. **change one's skin** undergo an impossible change of character etc. **get under a person's skin** *colloq.* interest or annoy a person intensely. **have a thick** (or **thin**) **skin** be insensitive (or sensitive) to criticism etc. **no skin off one's nose** *colloq.* a matter of indifference or even benefit to one. **skin-deep** (of a wound, or of an emotion, an impression, beauty, etc.) superficial, not deep or lasting. **skin-diver** a person who swims underwater without a diving-suit, usu. in deep water with an aqualung and flippers. **skin-diving** such swimming. **skin effect** *Electr.* the tendency of a high-frequency alternating current to flow through the outer layer only of a conductor. **skin-flick** *sl.* an explicitly pornographic film. **skin-food** a cosmetic intended to improve the condition of the skin. **skin friction** friction at the surface of a solid and a fluid in relative motion. **skin game** *US sl.* a swindling game, a swindle. **skin-graft 1** the surgical transplanting of skin. **2** a piece of skin transferred in this way. **skin test** a test to determine whether an immune reaction is elicited when a substance is applied to or injected into the skin. **skin-tight** (of a garment) very close-fitting. **to the skin** through all one's clothing (*soaked to the skin*). **with a whole skin**

unwounded. □□ **skinless** *adj.* **skin-like** *adj.* **skinned** *adj.* (also in *comb.*). [OE *scin(n)* f. ON *skinn*]
■ *n.* **1, 3** epidermis, dermis. **2 a** hide, pelt, fleece, fell. **4** coat, film, coating, covering, casing, integument, crust, incrustation, husk, peel, rind, outside, shell, pellicle, veneer, outer layer, lamina, overlay. **5** membrane, sheet, pellicle; see also FILM *n.* 1. ● *v.* **1** flay, strip, decorticate, excoriate; peel, hull, husk, shell; abrade, scrape, graze, bark. **3** see FLEECE *v.* 1. □ **by** (or **with**) **the skin of one's teeth** see *narrowly* (NARROW). **get under a person's skin** see INTRIGUE *v.* 2, IRRITATE 1. **skin-deep** superficial, shallow, surface, slight, external, unimportant, trivial, unprofound, insubstantial. **skin game** see SWINDLE *n.* 1, 3.

skinflint /skínflint/ *n.* a miserly person.
■ see MISER.

skinful /skínfo͝ol/ *n.* (*pl.* **-fuls**) *colloq.* enough alcoholic liquor to make one drunk.

skinhead /skínhed/ *n.* **1** *Brit.* a youth with close-cropped hair, esp. one of an aggressive gang. **2** *US* a recruit in the Marines.
■ **1** see BARBARIAN *n.* 1.

skink /skingk/ *n.* any small lizard of the family Scincidae. [F *scinc* or L *scincus* f. Gk *skigkos*]

skinner /skínnər/ *n.* **1** a person who skins animals or prepares skins. **2** a dealer in skins, a furrier. **3** *Austral. Racing sl.* a result very profitable to bookmakers.

skinny /skínni/ *adj.* (**skinnier, skinniest**) **1** thin or emaciated. **2** (of clothing) tight-fitting. **3** made of or like skin. □ **skinny-dipping** esp. *US colloq.* bathing in the nude. □□ **skinniness** *n.*
■ **1** thin, underweight, gaunt, bony, scraggy, scrawny, rangy, lean, lank, lanky, gangly, gangling, raw-boned, meagre, spare, emaciated, half-starved, undernourished, pinched, hollow-cheeked, wasted, shrunken.

skint /skint/ *adj. Brit. sl.* having no money left. [= *skinned*, past part. of SKIN]
■ see BROKE.

skip[1] /skip/ *v.* & *n.* ● *v.* (**skipped, skipping**) **1** *intr.* **a** move along lightly, esp. by taking two steps with each foot in turn. **b** jump lightly from the ground, esp. so as to clear a skipping-rope. **c** jump about, gambol, caper, frisk. **2** *intr.* (often foll. by *from, off, to*) move quickly from one point, subject, or occupation to another; be desultory. **3** *tr.* (also *absol.*) omit in dealing with a series or in reading (*skip every tenth row*; *always skips the small print*). **4** *tr. colloq.* not participate in. **5** *tr. colloq.* depart quickly from; leave hurriedly. **6** *intr.* (often foll. by *out, off*) *colloq.* make off, disappear. **7** *tr.* make (a stone) ricochet on the surface of water. ● *n.* **1** a skipping movement or action. **2** *Computing* the action of passing over part of a sequence of data or instructions. **3** *US colloq.* a person who defaults or absconds. □ **skip it** *sl.* **1** abandon a topic etc. **2** make off, disappear. **skipping-rope** (*US* **skip-rope**) a length of rope revolved over the head and under the feet while jumping as a game or exercise. **skip zone** the annular region round a broadcasting station where neither direct nor reflected waves are received. [ME, prob. f. Scand.]
■ *v.* **1** leap, caper, gambol, frisk, prance, spring, jump, hop, romp, bound, dance, *sl.* cavort. **2** see FLIT *v.* 1. **3** omit, leave out, pass by, overlook, pass over, avoid, ignore, disregard, steer clear of, cut. **4** see AVOID 1. **5** see LEAVE[1] *v.* 1b, 3, 4. **6** see *make away*. ● *n.* **1** leap, caper, gambol, frisk, prance, jump, bound, dance, hop, romp. □ **skip it 2** see *make away*. **skipping rope** *US* jump-rope.

skip[2] /skip/ *n.* **1** a large container for builders' refuse etc. **2** a cage, bucket, etc., in which men or materials are lowered and raised in mines and quarries. **3** = SKEP. [var. of SKEP]

skip[3] /skip/ *n.* & *v.* ● *n.* the captain or director of a side at bowls or curling. ● *v.tr.* (**skipped, skipping**) be the skip of. [abbr. of SKIPPER[1]]

skipjack /skípjak/ *n.* **1** (in full **skipjack tuna**) a small striped Pacific tuna, *Katsuwonus pelamus*, used as food. **2** a click beetle. **3** a kind of sailing-boat used off the East coast of the US. [SKIP[1] + JACK[1]]

skipper[1] /skíppər/ *n.* & *v.* ● *n.* **1** a sea captain, esp. the master of a small trading or fishing vessel. **2** the captain of an aircraft. **3** the captain of a side in games. ● *v.tr.* act as captain of. [ME f. MDu., MLG *schipper* f. *schip* SHIP]
■ *n.* captain, master, commander; leader, chief, director, *colloq.* boss. ● *v.* see LEAD *v.* 6, 7a.

skipper[2] /skíppər/ *n.* **1** a person who skips. **2** any brown thick-bodied butterfly of the family Hesperiidae.

skippet /skíppit/ *n.* a small round wooden box to enclose and protect a seal attached to a document. [ME: orig. unkn.]

skirl /skurl/ *n.* & *v.* ● *n.* the shrill sound characteristic of bagpipes. ● *v.intr.* make a skirl. [prob. Scand.: ult. imit.]
■ *v.* pipe, tootle, whistle.

skirmish /skúrmish/ *n.* & *v.* ● *n.* **1** a piece of irregular or unpremeditated fighting esp. between small or outlying parts of armies or fleets, a slight engagement. **2** a short argument or contest of wit etc. ● *v.intr.* engage in a skirmish. □□ **skirmisher** *n.* [ME f. OF *eskirmir, escremir* f. Frank.]
■ *n.* **1** fight, encounter, fray, brush, clash, engagement, confrontation, showdown, combat, battle, conflict, struggle, contest, incident, scrimmage, fracas, tussle, mêlée, affray, *colloq.* scrap, dust-up, set-to. **2** see ARGUMENT 1. ● *v.* fight, clash, struggle, battle, tussle.

skirr /skur/ *v.intr.* move rapidly esp. with a whirring sound. [perh. rel. to SCOUR[1] or SCOUR[2]]

skirret /skírrit/ *n.* a perennial umbelliferous plant, *Sium sisarum*, formerly cultivated in Europe for its edible root. [ME *skirwhit(e)*, perh. formed as SHEER[1], WHITE]

skirt /skurt/ *n.* & *v.* ● *n.* **1** a woman's outer garment hanging from the waist. **2** the part of a coat etc. that hangs below the waist. **3** a hanging part round the base of a hovercraft. **4** (in *sing.* or *pl.*) an edge, border, or extreme part. **5** (also **bit of skirt**) *sl. offens.* a woman regarded as an object of sexual desire. **6** (in full **skirt of beef** etc.) **a** the diaphragm and other membranes as food. **b** *Brit.* a cut of meat from the lower flank. **7** a flap of a saddle. **8** a surface that conceals or protects the wheels or underside of a vehicle or aircraft. ● *v.* **1** *tr.* go along or round or past the edge of. **2** *tr.* be situated along. **3** *tr.* avoid dealing with (an issue etc.). **4** *intr.* (foll. by *along*) go along the coast, a wall, etc. □ **skirt-dance** a dance with graceful manipulation of a full skirt. □□ **skirted** *adj.* (also in *comb.*). **skirtless** *adj.* [ME f. ON *skyrta* shirt, corresp. to OE *scyrte*: see SHIRT]
■ *n.* **5** see *bit of fluff* (FLUFF). ● *v.* **1, 3** see BYPASS *v.*

skirting /skúrting/ *n.* (in full **skirting-board**) *Brit.* a narrow board etc. along the bottom of the wall of a room.

skit[1] /skit/ *n.* (often foll. by *on*) a light, usu. short, piece of satire or burlesque. [rel. to *skit* move lightly and rapidly, perh. f. ON (cf. *skjóta* SHOOT)]
■ see ACT *n.* 3a.

skit[2] /skit/ *n. colloq.* **1** a large number, a crowd. **2** (in *pl.*) heaps, lots. [20th c.: cf. SCADS]

skite /skīt/ *v.* & *n.* ● *v.intr. Austral.* & *NZ colloq.* boast, brag. ● *n.* **1** *Austral.* & *NZ colloq.* **a** a boaster. **b** boasting; boastfulness. **2** *Sc.* a drinking-bout; a spree (*on the skite*). [Sc. & N.Engl. dial., = a person regarded with contempt: cf. BLATHERSKITE]
■ *v.* see BOAST *v.* 1. ● *n.* **1 b** see BRAVADO. **2** see BENDER.

skitter /skíttər/ *v.intr.* (also **skeeter** /skéetər/) **1 a** (usu. foll. by *along, across*) move lightly or hastily. **b** (usu. foll. by *about, off*) hurry about, dart off. **2** fish by drawing bait jerkily across the surface of the water. [app. frequent. of dial. *skite*, perh. formed as SKIT[1]]
■ **1** see DASH *v.* 1. **2** see HURRY *v.* 1.

skittery /skíttəri/ *adj.* skittish, restless.

skittish /skíttish/ *adj.* **1** lively, playful. **2** (of a horse etc.) nervous, inclined to shy, fidgety. □□ **skittishly** *adv.* **skittishness** *n.* [ME, perh. formed as SKIT[1]]

■ **1** see LIVELY 1. **2** see NERVOUS 1–3, 5. ▫▫ **skittishness** playfulness, impishness, mischievousness; see also JUMP *n.* 2b.

skittle /skitt'l/ *n.* & *v.* ● *n.* **1** a pin used in the game of skittles. **2** (in *pl.*; usu. treated as *sing.*) **a** a game like ninepins played with usu. nine wooden pins set up at the end of an alley to be bowled down usu. with wooden balls or a wooden disc. **b** (in full **table skittles**) a game played with similar pins set up on a board to be knocked down by swinging a suspended ball. **c** *colloq.* chess not played seriously. ● *v.tr.* (often foll. by *out*) *Cricket* get (batsmen) out in rapid succession. [17th c. (also *kittle-pins*): orig. unkn.]

skive /skīv/ *v.* & *n.* ● *v.* **1** *tr.* split or pare (hides, leather, etc.). **2** *intr. Brit. sl.* **a** evade a duty, shirk. **b** (often foll. by *off*) avoid work by absenting oneself, play truant. ● *n. sl.* **1** an instance of shirking. **2** an easy option. ▫▫ **skiver** *n.* [ON *skifa*, rel. to ME *schīve* slice]

■ *v.* **2 a** see SLACK[1] *v.* 2. **b** see TRUANT *v.* ▫▫ **skiver** see TRUANT *n.*

skivvy /skivvi/ *n.* (*pl.* **-ies**) **1** *Brit. colloq. derog.* a female domestic servant. **2** *US* **a** a thin high-necked long-sleeved garment. **b** (in *pl.*) underwear of vest and underpants. [20th c.: orig. unkn.]

■ **1** see SLAVE *n.* 1. **2 b** (*skivvies*) see UNDERCLOTHES.

skol /skol, skōl/ *n.* (also ***skoal***) used as a toast in drinking. [Da. *skaal*, Sw. *skål*, f. ON *skál* bowl]

■ see *bottoms up!* (BOTTOM).

skua /skyoōə/ *n.* any large predatory sea bird of the family Stercorariidae which pursues other birds and makes them disgorge the fish they have caught. [mod.L f. Faroese *skúgvur*, ON *skúfr*]

skulduggery /skuldúggəri/ *n.* (also **sculduggery**, **skullduggery**) trickery; unscrupulous behaviour. [earlier *sculduddery*, orig. Sc. = unchastity (18th c.: orig. unkn.)]

■ see TRICKERY.

skulk /skulk/ *v.* & *n.* ● *v.intr.* **1** move stealthily, lurk, or keep oneself concealed, esp. in a cowardly or sinister way. **2** stay or sneak away in time of danger. **3** shirk duty. ● *n.* **1** a person who skulks. **2** a company of foxes. ▫▫ **skulker** *n.* [ME f. Scand.: cf. Norw. *skulka* lurk, Da. *skulke*, Sw. *skolka* shirk]

■ *v.* **1** see LURK *v.* 1, 2. **2** see SNEAK *v.* 1.

skull /skul/ *n.* **1** the bony case of the brain of a vertebrate. **2** **a** the part of the skeleton corresponding to the head. **b** this with the skin and soft internal parts removed. **c** a representation of this. **3** the head as the seat of intelligence. ▫ **out of one's skull** *sl.* out of one's mind, crazy. **skull and crossbones** a representation of a skull with two thigh-bones crossed below it as an emblem of piracy or death. **skull session** *US sl.* a discussion or conference. ▫▫ **skulled** *adj.* (also in *comb.*). [ME *scolle*: orig. unkn.]

■ **3** see HEAD *n.* 1, 2.

skullcap /skúlkap/ *n.* **1** a small close-fitting peakless cap. **2** the top part of the skull. **3** any plant of the genus *Scutellaria*, with helmet-shaped bilabiate flowers.

skunk /skungk/ *n.* & *v.* ● *n.* **1 a** any of various cat-sized flesh-eating mammals of the family Mustelidae, esp. *Mephitis mephitis* having a distinctive black and white striped fur and able to emit a powerful stench from a liquid secreted by its anal glands as a defence. **b** its fur. **2** *colloq.* a thoroughly contemptible person. ● *v.tr.* **1** *US sl.* defeat. **2** fail to pay (a bill etc.). ▫ **skunk-bear** *US* a wolverine. **skunk-cabbage** *US* a herbaceous plant, *Lysichiton americanum*, with an offensive-smelling spathe. [Amer. Ind. *segankw*, *segongw*]

■ *n.* **2** see STINKER. ● *v.* **1** see BEAT *v.* 3a.

sky /skī/ *n.* & *v.* ● *n.* (*pl.* **skies**) (in *sing.* or *pl.*) **1** the region of the atmosphere and outer space seen from the earth. **2** the weather or climate evidenced by this. ● *v.tr.* (**skies**, **skied**) **1** *Cricket* etc. hit (a ball) high into the air. **2** hang (a picture) high on a wall. ▫ **sky-blue** *adj.* & *n.* a bright clear blue. **sky-blue pink** an imaginary colour. **sky-clad** *sl.* naked (esp. in witchcraft). **sky cloth** *Theatr.* a backcloth painted or coloured to represent the sky. **sky-high** *adv.* & *adj.* as if reaching the sky, very high. **the sky is the limit** there is practically no limit. **sky pilot** *sl.* a clergyman. **sky-rocket** *n.* a rocket exploding high in the air. ● *v.intr.* (**-rocketed**, **-rocketing**) (esp. of prices etc.) rise very steeply or rapidly. **sky-shouting** the sending of messages from an aircraft to the ground by means of a loudspeaker. **sky-sign** an advertisement on the roof of a building. **sky wave** a radio wave reflected from the ionosphere. **sky-writing** legible smoke-trails made by an aeroplane esp. for advertising. **to the skies** very highly; without reserve (*praised to the skies*). **under the open sky** out of doors. ▫▫ **skyey** *adj.* **skyless** *adj.* [ME *ski(es)* cloud(s) f. ON *ský*]

■ *n.* **1** heaven(s), skies, arch *or* vault of heaven, (wild) blue (yonder), ether, atmosphere, space, empyrean, *literary* firmament, *poet.* welkin, azure. ▫ **sky-high** see *towering* (TOWER *v.* 3a). **sky pilot** see MINISTER *n.* 2. **sky-rocket** (*v.*) see SOAR 2. **to the skies** excessively, extravagantly, unreservedly, fulsomely, profusely, inordinately, highly, *esp. US* & *Sc.* overly.

skydiving /skídīving/ *n.* the sport of performing acrobatic manoeuvres under free fall with a parachute. ▫▫ **skydive** *v.intr.* **skydiver** *n.*

skyer /skíər/ *n.* (also **skier**) *Cricket* a high hit.

Skye terrier /skī/ *n.* a small long-bodied short-legged long-haired slate or fawn coloured variety of Scotch terrier. [*Skye*, an island of the Inner Hebrides]

skyjack /skíjak/ *v.* & *n. sl.* ● *v.tr.* hijack (an aircraft). ● *n.* an act of skyjacking. ▫▫ **skyjacker** *n.* [SKY + HIJACK]

skylark /skílaark/ *n.* & *v.* ● *n.* a lark, *Alauda arvensis* of Eurasia and N. Africa, that sings while hovering in flight. ● *v.intr.* play tricks or practical jokes, indulge in horseplay, frolic. [SKY + LARK[1]: (v.) with pun on LARK[2]]

■ *v.* see FROLIC *v.*

skylight /skílīt/ *n.* a window set in the plane of a roof or ceiling.

skyline /skílīn/ *n.* the outline of hills, buildings, etc., defined against the sky; the visible horizon.

skysail /skísayl, -s'l/ *n.* a light sail above the royal in a square-rigged ship.

skyscape /skískayp/ *n.* **1** a picture chiefly representing the sky. **2** a view of the sky.

skyscraper /skískraypər/ *n.* a very tall building of many storeys.

skyward /skíwərd/ *adv.* & *adj.* ● *adv.* (also **skywards**) towards the sky. ● *adj.* moving skyward.

skywatch /skíwoch/ *n.* the activity of watching the sky for aircraft etc.

skyway /skíway/ *n.* **1** a route used by aircraft. **2** the sky as a medium of transport.

slab /slab/ *n.* & *v.* ● *n.* **1** a flat broad fairly thick usu. square or rectangular piece of solid material, esp. stone. **2** a large flat piece of cake, chocolate, etc. **3** (of timber) an outer piece sawn from a log. **4** *Brit.* a mortuary table. ● *v.tr.* (**slabbed**, **slabbing**) remove slabs from (a log or tree) to prepare it for sawing into planks. [ME: orig. unkn.]

■ *n.* **1, 2** slice, wedge, piece, hunk, chunk, tranche, block, brick, cake, tablet, *Brit. colloq.* wodge.

slack[1] /slak/ *adj.*, *n.*, *v.*, & *adv.* ● *adj.* **1** (of rope etc.) not taut. **2** inactive or sluggish. **3** negligent or remiss. **4** (of tide etc.) neither ebbing nor flowing. **5** (of trade or business or a market) with little happening. **6** loose. **7** *Phonet.* lax. **8** relaxed, languid. ● *n.* **1** the slack part of a rope (*haul in the slack*). **2** a slack time in trade etc. **3** *colloq.* a spell of inactivity or laziness. **4** (in *pl.*) full-length loosely cut trousers for informal wear. ● *v.* **1 a** *tr.* & *intr.* slacken. **b** *tr.* loosen (rope etc.). **2** *intr. colloq.* take a rest, be lazy. **3** *tr.* slake (lime). ● *adv.* **1** slackly. **2** slowly or insufficiently (*dry slack*; *bake slack*). ▫ **slack hand** lack of full control in riding or governing. **slack lime** slaked lime. **slack off 1** loosen. **2** lose or cause to lose vigour. **slack rein** = *slack hand*. **slack suit** *US* casual clothes of slacks and a jacket or shirt. **slack up** reduce the speed of a train etc. before stopping. **slack water** a time near the turn of the tide, esp. at

low tide. **take up the slack** use up a surplus or make up a deficiency; avoid an undesirable lull. □□ **slackly** *adv.* **slackness** *n.* [OE *slæc* f. Gmc]
■ *adj.* **1** loose, limp, lax. **2** indolent, lazy, idle, slothful, inactive, sluggish, lethargic, laggard, shiftless, fainéant, *archaic* otiose. **3** remiss, careless, negligent, lax, neglectful, delinquent, inattentive, dilatory, tardy, easygoing, do-nothing, *colloq.* asleep at the wheel *or* on the job. **5** inactive, slow, flat, quiet, sluggish. **6** loose, flabby, flaccid, soft, limp, baggy, droopy, saggy, floppy. ● *n.* **2** lull, pause, inactivity, cut-back, lessening, reduction, abatement, drop-off, downturn, diminution, decline, fall-off, decrease, dwindling. ● *v.* **1** slack off *or* up, slacken (off *or* up), relax, ease (out *or* off), let up (on); slow (down *or* up), delay, reduce speed, tire, decline, decrease, diminish, moderate, abate, weaken; loose, loosen, let go, let run, let loose, release. **2** shirk, skulk, *sl.* goof around *or* off, *Brit. sl.* skive (off); relax, rest. □ **slack off 1** see SLACK[1] *v.* 1 above. **slack up** see SLACK[1] *v.* 1 above. □□ **slackness** looseness, play, give, leeway; see also NEGLECT *n.* 1.

slack[2] /slak/ *n.* coal-dust or small pieces of coal. [ME prob. f. LG or Du.]

slacken /slákkən/ *v.tr.* & *intr.* make or become slack. □ **slacken off** = *slack off* (see SLACK[1]).
■ see LOOSE *v.* 2–4.

slacker /slákkər/ *n.* a shirker; an indolent person.
■ shirker, loafer, idler, skulker, *Brit. sl.* skiver, *Brit. sl. esp. Mil.* scrimshanker, *US sl.* gold brick.

slag /slag/ *n.* & *v.* ● *n.* **1** vitreous refuse left after ore has been smelted, dross separated in a fused state in the reduction of ore, clinkers. **2** volcanic scoria. **3** *sl. derog.* **a** a prostitute or promiscuous woman. **b** a worthless or insignificant person. ● *v.* (**slagged**, **slagging**) **1** *intr.* **a** form slag. **b** cohere into a mass like slag. **2** *tr.* (often foll. by *off*) *sl.* criticize, insult. □ **slag-heap** a hill of refuse from a mine etc. **slag-wool** = *mineral wool.* □□ **slaggy** *adj.* (**slaggier**, **slaggiest**). [MLG *slagge*, perh. f. *slagen* strike, with ref. to fragments formed by hammering]
■ *n.* **3 a** see PROSTITUTE *n.* 1a. **b** see WRETCH 2. ● *v.* **2** see INSULT *v.* 1.

slain *past part.* of SLAY[1].

slainte /slaánchə/ *int.* a Gaelic toast: good health! [Gael. *sláinte*, lit. 'health']

slake /slayk/ *v.tr.* **1** assuage or satisfy (thirst, revenge, etc.). **2** disintegrate (quicklime) by chemical combination with water. [OE *slacian* f. *slæc* SLACK[1]]
■ **1** satisfy, quench, gratify, satiate, sate, allay, assuage, ease, relieve.

slalom /slaáləm/ *n.* **1** a ski-race down a zigzag course defined by artificial obstacles. **2** an obstacle race in canoes or cars or on skateboards or water-skis. [Norw., lit. 'sloping track']

slam[1] /slam/ *v.* & *n.* ● *v.* (**slammed**, **slamming**) **1** *tr.* & *intr.* shut forcefully and loudly. **2** *tr.* put down (an object) with a similar sound. **3** *intr.* move violently (*he slammed out of the room*). **4** *tr.* & *intr.* put or come into sudden action (*slam the brakes on*). **5** *tr. sl.* criticize severely. **6** *tr. sl.* hit. **7** *tr. sl.* gain an easy victory over. ● *n.* **1** a sound of or as of a slammed door. **2** the shutting of a door etc. with a loud bang. **3** (usu. prec. by *the*) *US sl.* prison. [prob. f. Scand.: cf. ON *slam(b)ra*]
■ *v.* **1** shut, fling closed, bang; go bang. **4** jam, ram. **5** criticize, attack, vilify, pillory, run down, disparage, denigrate, denounce, put down, flay, pounce on *or* upon, shoot down, *colloq.* pan, *Brit. colloq.* slate. **6** hit, slap, bang, smack; smash, crash, ram. ● *n.* **1** see IMPACT *n.* 1. **3** see JAIL *n.* 1.

slam[2] /slam/ *n. Cards* the winning of every trick in a game. □ **grand slam 1** *Bridge* the winning of 13 tricks. **2** the winning of all of a group of championships or matches in a sport. **small** (or **little**) **slam** *Bridge* the winning of 12 tricks. [orig. name of a card-game: perh. f. obs. *slampant* trickery]

slambang /slámbáng/ *adv.* & *adj.* ● *adv.* with the sound of a slam. ● *adj. colloq.* impressive, exciting, or energetic.

slammer /slámmər/ *n.* (usu. prec. by *the*) *sl.* prison.
■ see PRISON *n.* 1.

slander /slaándər/ *n.* & *v.* ● *n.* **1** a malicious, false, and injurious statement spoken about a person. **2** the uttering of such statements; calumny. **3** *Law* false oral defamation (cf. LIBEL). ● *v.tr.* utter slander about; defame falsely. □□ **slanderer** *n.* **slanderous** *adj.* **slanderously** *adv.* [ME *sclaundre* f. AF *esclaundre*, OF *esclandre* alt. f. *escandle* f. LL *scandalum*: see SCANDAL]
■ *n.* defamation (of character), calumny, obloquy, misrepresentation, vilification, denigration, traducement; slur, smear. ● *v.* defame, calumniate, calumny, disparage, discredit, traduce, malign, smear, vilify, decry, *archaic or US* slur. □□ **slanderous** defamatory, calumnious, calumniatory, disparaging, smear, injurious, scandalous, malicious, vituperative, deprecatory, depreciative, discrediting, decrying.

slang /slang/ *n.* & *v.* ● *n.* words, phrases, and uses that are regarded as very informal and are often restricted to special contexts or are peculiar to a specified profession, class, etc. (*racing slang*; *schoolboy slang*). ● *v.* **1** *tr.* use abusive language to. **2** *intr.* use such language. □ **slanging-match** a prolonged exchange of insults. [18th-c. cant: orig. unkn.]
■ *n.* see DIALECT 2. □ **slanging-match** see ROW[3] *n.* 2.

slangy /slángi/ *adj.* (**slangier**, **slangiest**) **1** of the character of slang. **2** fond of using slang. □□ **slangily** *adv.* **slanginess** *n.*

slant /slaant/ *v.*, *n.*, & *adj.* ● *v.* **1** *intr.* slope; diverge from a line; lie or go obliquely to a vertical or horizontal line. **2** *tr.* cause to do this. **3** *tr.* (often as **slanted** *adj.*) present (information) from a particular angle esp. in a biased or unfair way. ● *n.* **1** a slope; an oblique position. **2** a way of regarding a thing; a point of view, esp. a biased one. ● *adj.* sloping, oblique. □ **on a** (or **the**) **slant** aslant. **slant-eyed** having slanting eyes. **slant height** the height of a cone from the vertex to the periphery of the base. [aphetic form of ASLANT: (v.) rel. to ME *slent* f. ON *sletta* dash, throw]
■ *v.* **1, 2** tilt, angle, incline, pitch, cant, slope, bend, lean, list, tip, bevel, shelve. **3** bend, distort, deviate, twist, warp, colour, weight, bias. ● *n.* **1** slope, incline, tilt, ramp, gradient, pitch, lean, leaning, deflection, angle, rake, cant, camber. **2** angle, viewpoint, (point of) view, standpoint, approach, twist, idea, aspect, attitude, position; bias, prejudice, partiality, one-sidedness, turn, bent. ● *adj.* see OBLIQUE 1.

slantwise /slaántwīz/ *adv.* aslant.

slap /slap/ *v.*, *n.*, & *adv.* ● *v.* (**slapped**, **slapping**) **1** *tr.* & *intr.* strike with the palm of the hand or a flat object, or so as to make a similar noise. **2** *tr.* lay forcefully (*slapped the money on the table*; *slapped a writ on the offender*). **3** *tr.* put hastily or carelessly (*slap some paint on the walls*). **4** *tr.* (often foll. by *down*) *colloq.* reprimand or snub. ● *n.* **1** a blow with the palm of the hand or a flat object. **2** a slapping sound. ● *adv.* **1** with the suddenness or effectiveness or true aim of a blow, suddenly, fully, directly (*ran slap into him*; *hit me slap in the eye*). **2** = *slap-bang.* □ **slap and tickle** *Brit. colloq.* light-hearted amorous amusement. **slap-bang** violently, noisily, headlong. **slap-happy** *colloq.* **1** cheerfully casual or flippant. **2** punch-drunk. **slap in the face** a rebuff or affront. **slap on the back** *n.* congratulations. ● *v.tr.* congratulate. **slap on the wrist** *n. colloq.* a mild reprimand or rebuke. ● *v.tr. colloq.* reprimand. **slap-up** esp. *Brit. colloq.* excellent, lavish; done regardless of expense (*slap-up meal*). [LG *slapp* (imit.)]
■ *v.* **1** smack, cuff, rap, *colloq.* whack; spank; clout, *sl.* wallop; flap, whip, beat, bat; see also HIT *v.* 1a. **3** fling, toss, splash, hurl, throw, sling. ● *n.* **1** smack, blow, cuff, whack, rap, clout, *sl.* wallop. ● *adv.* **1** exactly, directly, precisely, straight, point-blank, right, squarely, plumb, fully, smack, *colloq.* bang, *US colloq.* spang. □ **slap-bang** violently, noisily; headlong; see also PELL-MELL *adv.* 1. **slap in the face** reprimand, reproof, rebuff, criticism,

censure, rebuke, attack, insult, offence, *colloq.* put-down, smack in the eye. **slap on the back** (*v.*) congratulate, felicitate, compliment. **slap-up** see LUXURIOUS 1, PLUSH.

slapdash /slápdash/ *adj.* & *adv.* ● *adj.* hasty and careless. ● *adv.* in a slapdash manner.
■ *adj.* see CARELESS 1. ● *adv.* see PELL-MELL *adv.*

slapjack /slápjak/ *n.* *US* a kind of pancake cooked on a griddle. [SLAP + JACK[1]]

slapstick /slápstik/ *n.* **1** boisterous knockabout comedy. **2** a flexible divided lath used by a clown. [SLAP + STICK[1]]

slash /slash/ *v.* & *n.* ● *v.* **1** *intr.* make a sweeping or random cut or cuts with a knife, sword, whip, etc. **2** *tr.* make such a cut or cuts at. **3** *tr.* make a long narrow gash or gashes in. **4** *tr.* reduce (prices etc.) drastically. **5** *tr.* censure vigorously. **6** *tr.* make (one's way) by slashing. **7** *tr.* **a** lash (a person etc.) with a whip. **b** crack (a whip). ● *n.* **1 a** a slashing cut or stroke. **b** a wound or slit made by this. **2** an oblique stroke; a solidus. **3** *Brit. sl.* an act of urinating. **4** *US* debris resulting from the felling or destruction of trees. □ **slash-and-burn** (of cultivation) in which vegetation is cut down, allowed to dry, and then burned off before seeds are planted. □□ **slasher** *n.* [ME perh. f. OF *esclachier* break in pieces]
■ *v.* **2, 3** cut, gash, hack, score, slit, slice, knife, lacerate; wound; scar. **4** cut, reduce, decrease, drop, mark down, trim, lower. **6** cut, hack. **7 a** lash, whip, scourge, flog, beat, horsewhip, flail, flagellate, flay, lambaste, thrash. ● *n.* **1** cut, gash, incision, slit, slice, gouge, rent, rip, score, laceration; wound. **2** solidus, stroke, oblique.

slashed /slasht/ *adj.* (of a sleeve etc.) having slits to show a lining or puffing of other material.

slashing /sláshing/ *adj.* vigorously incisive or effective.

slat /slat/ *n.* a thin narrow piece of wood or plastic or metal, esp. used in an overlapping series as in a fence or Venetian blind. [ME *s(c)lat* f. OF *esclat* splinter etc. f. *esclater* split f. Rmc]
■ see STRIP[2] *n.*

slate /slayt/ *n.*, *v.*, & *adj.* ● *n.* **1** a fine-grained grey, green, or bluish-purple metamorphic rock easily split into flat smooth plates. **2** a piece of such a plate used as roofing-material. **3** a piece of such a plate used for writing on, usu. framed in wood. **4** the colour of slate. **5** *US* a list of nominees for office etc. ● *v.tr.* **1** cover with slates esp. as roofing. **2** *Brit. colloq.* criticize severely; scold. **3** *US* make arrangements for (an event etc.). **4** *US* propose or nominate for office etc. ● *adj.* made of slate. □ **on the slate** *Brit.* recorded as a debt to be paid. **slate-blue** (or **-black**) a shade of blue (or black) occurring in slate. **slate-colour** a dark bluish or greenish grey. **slate-coloured** of this colour. **slate-grey** a shade of grey occurring in slate. **slate-pencil** a small rod of soft slate used for writing on slate. **wipe the slate clean** forgive or cancel the record of past offences. □□ **slating** *n.* **slaty** *adj.* [ME *s(c)late* f. OF *esclate*, fem. form of *esclat* SLAT]
■ *n.* **5** see LIST[1] *n.* ● *v.* **2** see CRITICIZE *v.* 1. **3** see SCHEDULE *v.* □□ **slating** see REPRIMAND *n.*

slater /sláytər/ *n.* **1** a person who slates roofs etc. **2** a woodlouse or similar crustacean.

slather /sláthər/ *n.* & *v.* ● *n.* **1** (usu. in *pl.*) *US colloq.* a large amount. **2** (often **open slather**) *Austral.* & *NZ sl.* unrestricted scope for action. ● *v.tr.* *US colloq.* **1** spread thickly. **2** squander. [19th c.: orig. unkn.]

slatted /sláttid/ *adj.* having slats.

slattern /sláttərn/ *n.* a slovenly woman. □□ **slatternly** *adj.* **slatternliness** *n.* [17th c.: rel. to *slattering* slovenly, f. dial. *slatter* to spill, slop, waste, frequent. of *slat* strike]
■ see SLUT. □□ **slatternly** see UNTIDY.

slaughter /sláwtər/ *n.* & *v.* ● *n.* **1** the killing of an animal or animals for food. **2** the killing of many persons or animals at once or continuously; carnage, massacre. ● *v.tr.* **1** kill (people) in a ruthless manner or on a great scale. **2** kill for food, butcher. **3** *colloq.* defeat utterly. □□ **slaughterer** *n.* **slaughterous** *adj.* [ME *slahter* ult. f. ON *slátr* butcher's meat, rel. to SLAY[1]]
■ *n.* **1** butchery, butchering. **2** massacre, killing, bloodshed, blood bath, murder, homicide, manslaughter, carnage, extermination, execution, liquidation, slaying, butchery, pogrom, genocide, mass murder *or* execution *or* extermination, holocaust, sacrifice, hecatomb, *joc.* blood-letting. ● *v.* **1** butcher, kill, murder, execute, exterminate, massacre, put to the sword, put to death, liquidate, destroy, *literary or joc.* slay. **2** butcher, kill. **3** defeat, beat, win (out) over, overcome, overwhelm, smash, crush, thrash, destroy, rout, upset, trounce, *US* whitewash, *literary* vanquish, *sl.* clobber. □□ **slaughterer** see BUTCHER *n.* **slaughterous** see SANGUINARY.

slaughterhouse /sláwtərhowss/ *n.* **1** a place for the slaughter of animals as food. **2** a place of carnage.
■ **1** abattoir.

Slav /slaav/ *n.* & *adj.* ● *n.* a member of a group of peoples in Central and Eastern Europe speaking Slavonic languages. ● *adj.* **1** of or relating to the Slavs. **2** Slavonic. □□ **Slavism** *n.* [ME *Sclave* f. med.L *Sclavus*, late Gk *Sklabos*, & f. med.L *Slavus*]

slave /slayv/ *n.* & *v.* ● *n.* **1** a person who is the legal property of another or others and is bound to absolute obedience, a human chattel. **2** a drudge, a person working very hard. **3** (foll. by *of*, *to*) a helpless victim of some dominating influence (*slave of fashion*; *slave to duty*). **4** a machine, or part of one, directly controlled by another. ● *v.* **1** *intr.* (often foll. by *at*, *over*) work very hard. **2** *tr.* (foll. by *to*) subject (a device) to control by another. □ **slave-bangle** a bangle of gold, glass, etc., worn by a woman usu. above the elbow. **slave-born** born in slavery, born of slave parents. **slave-bracelet** = *slave-bangle*. **slave-drive** (*past* **-drove**; *past part.* **-driven**) work (a person) hard, esp. excessively. **slave-driver 1** an overseer of slaves at work. **2** a person who works others hard. **slave labour** forced labour. **slave ship** *hist.* a ship transporting slaves, esp. from Africa. **Slave State** *hist.* any of the southern States of the US in which slavery was legal before the Civil War. **slave-trade** *hist.* the procuring, transporting, and selling of human beings, esp. African Blacks, as slaves. **slave-trader** *hist.* a person engaged in the slave-trade. [ME f. OF *esclave* = med.L *sclavus*, *sclava* Slav (captive): see SLAV]
■ *n.* **1** lackey, bondsman, *archaic* scullion, *colloq.* slavey, *Brit. colloq. derog.* skivvy, *hist.* serf, helot, odalisque, vassal, blackbird, *literary* thrall. **2** drudge, workhorse, hack, grind, toiler, labourer, serf, *Brit.* fag, *colloq.* dogsbody, slavey, *esp. US sl.* gofer. ● *v.* **1** labour, toil, grind, grub, drudge, sweat, burn the midnight oil, work one's fingers to the bone, work like a Trojan, *archaic* moil, *Austral. colloq.* bullock, *literary* lucubrate. □ **slave-driver 1** see MASTER *n.* 1. **2** see *oppressor* (OPPRESS). **slave ship** see SLAVER[1]. **slave-trade** slavery, White slavery, *hist.* blackbirding. **slave-trader** see SLAVER[1].

slaver[1] /sláyvər/ *n.* *hist.* a ship or person engaged in the slave-trade.
■ slave ship; slave-trader, White slaver, pimp, pander, *hist.* blackbirder.

slaver[2] /slávvər/ *n.* & *v.* ● *n.* **1** saliva running from the mouth. **2 a** fulsome or servile flattery. **b** drivel, nonsense. ● *v.intr.* **1** let saliva run from the mouth, dribble. **2** (foll. by *over*) show excessive sentimentality over, or desire for. [ME prob. f. LG or Du.: cf. SLOBBER]
■ *n.* **1** drool, saliva, drivel, dribble, spit, spittle. **2 a** see FLATTERY. **b** nonsense, drivel, rubbish, twaddle, *colloq.* piffle; see also FLANNEL *n.* 3. ● *v.* dribble, drivel, spit; drool, salivate, slobber.

slavery /sláyvəri/ *n.* **1** the condition of a slave. **2** exhausting labour; drudgery. **3** the custom of having slaves.
■ **1** enslavement, bondage, enthralment, servitude, serfdom, vassalage, yoke, *literary* thraldom, thrall; subjugation, captivity. **2** toil, drudgery, grind, strain,

(hard) labour, *archaic* moil, *literary* travail, *Austral. sl.* (hard) yakka.

slavey /sláyvi/ *n.* (*pl.* **-eys**) *colloq.* a maidservant, esp. a hard-worked one.

■ see SLAVE *n.* 2.

Slavic /slaávik/ *adj.* & *n.* = SLAVONIC.

slavish /sláyvish/ *adj.* **1** of, like, or as of slaves. **2** showing no attempt at originality or development. **3** abject, servile, base. ▫▫ **slavishly** *adv.* **slavishness** *n.*

■ **3** see SERVILE. ▫▫ **slavishness** see *servility* (SERVILE).

Slavonic /sləvónnik/ *adj.* & *n.* ● *adj.* **1** of or relating to the group of Indo-European languages including Russian, Polish, and Czech. **2** of or relating to the Slavs. ● *n.* the Slavonic language-group. ▫ **Old Church Slavonic** the earliest written Slavonic language, surviving as a liturgical language in the Orthodox Church. [med.L *S(c)lavonicus* f. *S(c)lavonia* country of Slavs f. *Sclavus* SLAV]

slaw /slaw/ *n.* coleslaw. [Du. *sla*, shortened f. *salade* SALAD]

slay[1] /slay/ *v.tr.* (*past* **slew** /sloō/; *past part.* **slain** /slayn/) **1** *literary* or *joc.* kill. **2** *sl.* overwhelm with delight; convulse with laughter. ▫▫ **slayer** *n.* [OE *slēan* f. Gmc]

■ **1** see KILL *v.* 1a. ▫▫ **slayer** see KILLER 1.

slay[2] var. of SLEY.

SLBM *abbr.* submarine-launched ballistic missile.

SLD *abbr.* (in the UK) Social and Liberal Democrats. ¶ In 1989 officially replaced by *Liberal Democrats*.

sleaze /sleez/ *n.* & *v. colloq.* ● *n.* **1** sleaziness. **2** a person of low moral standards. ● *v.intr.* move in a sleazy fashion. [back-form. f. SLEAZY]

sleazy /sleézi/ *adj.* (**sleazier, sleaziest**) **1** squalid, tawdry. **2** slatternly. **3** (of textiles etc.) flimsy. ▫▫ **sleazily** *adv.* **sleaziness** *n.* [17th c.: orig. unkn.]

■ **1** disreputable, low-class, low-grade, squalid, dirty, filthy, shabby, mangy, seedy, sordid, base, contemptible, run-down, slummy, dilapidated, ramshackle, rickety, gimcrack, jerry-built, slipshod, mean, cheap, poor, tawdry, trashy, worthless, chintzy, *colloq.* crummy, tatty, *esp. US colloq.* tacky, *sl.* cheesy. **2** slovenly, slatternly, shabby, dirty, untidy, sloppy. **3** unsubstantial, insubstantial, flimsy, thin, slight.

sled /sled/ *n.* & *v. US* ● *n.* a sledge. ● *v.intr.* (**sledded, sledding**) ride on a sledge. [MLG *sledde*, rel. to SLIDE]

sledge[1] /slej/ *n.* & *v.* ● *n.* **1** a vehicle on runners for conveying loads or passengers esp. over snow, drawn by horses, dogs, or reindeer or pushed or pulled by one or more persons. **2** a toboggan. ● *v.intr.* & *tr.* travel or convey by sledge. [MDu. *sleedse*, rel. to SLED]

■ toboggan, *US* sled.

sledge[2] /slej/ *n.* = SLEDGEHAMMER.

sledgehammer /sléjhammər/ *n.* **1** a large heavy hammer used to break stone etc. **2** (*attrib.*) heavy or powerful (*a sledgehammer blow*). [OE *slecg*, rel. to SLAY[1]]

sleek /sleek/ *adj.* & *v.* ● *adj.* **1** (of hair, fur, or skin, or an animal or person with such hair etc.) smooth and glossy. **2** looking well-fed and comfortable. **3** ingratiating. **4** (of a thing) smooth and polished. ● *v.tr.* make sleek, esp. by stroking or pressing down. ▫▫ **sleekly** *adv.* **sleekness** *n.* **sleeky** *adj.* [later var. of SLICK]

■ *adj.* **1** smooth, velvety, lustrous, shiny, shining, glossy, silky, silken, *colloq.* slick. **2** well-fed, contented, complacent, comfortable, thriving. **3** suave, unctuous, slimy, fawning, oily, specious, hypocritical, smooth, *colloq.* slick, smarmy. **4** polished, glossy, lustrous, shining, shiny, smooth; graceful, trim, streamlined.

sleep /sleep/ *n.* & *v.* ● *n.* **1** a condition of body and mind such as that which normally recurs for several hours every night, in which the nervous system is inactive, the eyes closed, the postural muscles relaxed, and consciousness practically suspended. **2** a period of sleep (*shall try to get a sleep*). **3** a state like sleep, such as rest, quiet, negligence, or death. **4** the prolonged inert condition of hibernating animals. **5** a substance found in the corners of the eyes after sleep. ● *v.* (*past* and *past part.* **slept** /slept/) **1** *intr.* **a** be in a state of sleep. **b** fall asleep. **2** *intr.* (foll. by *at*, *in*, etc.) spend the night. **3** *tr.* provide sleeping accommodation for (*the house sleeps six*). **4** *intr.* (foll. by *with*, *together*) have sexual intercourse, esp. in bed. **5** *intr.* (foll. by *on*, *over*) not decide (a question) until the next day. **6** *intr.* (foll. by *through*) fail to be woken by. **7** *intr.* be inactive or dormant. **8** *intr.* be dead; lie in the grave. **9** *tr.* **a** (foll. by *off*) remedy by sleeping (*slept off his hangover*). **b** (foll. by *away*) spend in sleeping (*sleep the hours away*). **10** *intr.* (of a top) spin so steadily as to seem motionless. ▫ **get to sleep** manage to fall asleep. **go to sleep 1** enter a state of sleep. **2** (of a limb) become numbed by pressure. **in one's sleep** while asleep. **last sleep** death. **let sleeping dogs lie** avoid stirring up trouble. **put to sleep 1** anaesthetize. **2** kill (an animal) painlessly. **sleep around** *colloq.* be sexually promiscuous. **sleep in 1** remain asleep later than usual in the morning. **2** sleep by night at one's place of work. **sleeping-bag** a lined or padded bag to sleep in esp. when camping etc. **Sleeping Beauty** a fairy-tale heroine who slept for 100 years. **sleeping-car** (or **-carriage**) a railway coach provided with beds or berths. **sleeping-draught** a drink to induce sleep. **sleeping partner** a partner not sharing in the actual work of a firm. **sleeping-pill** a pill to induce sleep. **sleeping policeman** a ramp etc. in the road intended to cause traffic to reduce speed. **sleeping sickness** any of several tropical diseases with extreme lethargy caused by a trypanosome transmitted by a tsetse-fly bite. **sleeping-suit** a child's one-piece night-garment. **sleep-learning** learning by hearing while asleep. **sleep like a log** (or **top**) sleep soundly. **the sleep of the just** sound sleep. **sleep out** sleep by night out of doors, or not at one's place of work. **sleep-out** *Austral.* & *NZ* a veranda, porch, or outbuilding providing sleeping accommodation. [OE *slēp*, *slǣp* (n.), *slēpan*, *slǣpan* (v.) f. Gmc]

■ *n.* **2** nap, doze, rest, siesta, beauty sleep, catnap, *colloq.* forty winks, snooze, zizz, shut-eye, *poet. rhet.* slumber, *Brit. sl.* kip. **4** hibernation, dormancy. ● *v.* **1** doze, (take a) nap, (have a) catnap, rest, repose, drowse, be in the land of Nod, snore, *colloq.* snooze, drop *or* nod off, (take *or* have a) zizz, catch forty winks, *poet. rhet.* slumber, *Brit. sl.* kip. ▫ **put to sleep 2** see *put down* 7 (PUT[1]). **sleeping partner** inactive partner, non-participating partner, passive partner, quiescent partner, *US* silent partner. **sleeping-pill** see SEDATIVE *n.*

sleeper /sleépər/ *n.* **1** a person or animal that sleeps. **2** *Brit.* a wooden or concrete beam laid horizontally as a support, esp. for railway track. **3 a** a sleeping-car. **b** a berth in this. **4** *Brit.* a ring worn in a pierced ear to keep the hole from closing. **5** a thing that is suddenly successful after being undistinguished. **6** a sleeping-suit. **7** a spy or saboteur etc. who remains inactive while establishing a secure position.

■ **2** (railway) tie.

sleepless /sleépliss/ *adj.* **1** characterized by lack of sleep (*a sleepless night*). **2** unable to sleep. **3** continually active or moving. ▫▫ **sleeplessly** *adv.* **sleeplessness** *n.*

■ **1, 2** restless, wakeful; disturbed; insomniac, alert, watchful, vigilant, unsleeping, awake.

sleepwalk /sleépwawk/ *v.intr.* walk or perform other actions while asleep. ▫▫ **sleepwalker** *n.* **sleepwalking** *n.*

■ ▫▫ **sleepwalker** somnambulist, noctambulist. **sleepwalking** somnambulism, noctambulism.

sleepy /sleépi/ *adj.* (**sleepier, sleepiest**) **1** drowsy; ready for sleep; about to fall asleep. **2** lacking activity or bustle (*a sleepy little town*). **3** habitually indolent, unobservant, etc. ▫ **sleepy sickness** encephalitis lethargica, an infection of the brain with drowsiness and sometimes a coma. ▫▫ **sleepily** *adv.* **sleepiness** *n.*

■ **1** drowsy, somnolent, tired, nodding, dozy, lethargic, torpid, comatose, sluggish, *poet.* & *rhet.* slumberous; weary, fatigued, exhausted, *colloq.* dead on one's feet, knocked out, fagged (out), dopey, *US colloq.* pooped, *sl.* beat. **2** boring, inactive, dull, quiet, soporific, slow, sluggish, dormant; gentle, relaxed, *colloq.* laid-back.

sleepyhead /sleépihed/ *n.* (esp. as a form of address) a sleepy or inattentive person.

sleet /sleet/ *n.* & *v.* ● *n.* **1** a mixture of snow and rain falling together. **2** hail or snow melting as it falls. **3** *US* a thin coating of ice. ● *v.intr.* (prec. by *it* as subject) sleet falls (*it is sleeting*; *if it sleets*). □□ **sleety** *adj.* [ME prob. f. OE: rel. to MLG *slōten* (pl.) hail, MHG *slōz(e)* f. Gmc]

■ *n.* **1, 2** see PRECIPITATION *n.* 3a. ● *v.* see STORM *v.* 4.

sleeve /sleev/ *n.* **1** the part of a garment that wholly or partly covers an arm. **2** the cover of a gramophone record. **3** a tube enclosing a rod or smaller tube. **4 a** a wind-sock. **b** a drogue towed by an aircraft. □ **roll up one's sleeves** prepare to fight or work. **sleeve-board** a small ironing-board for pressing sleeves. **sleeve-coupling** a tube for connecting shafts or pipes. **sleeve-link** a cuff-link. **sleeve-note** a descriptive note on a record-sleeve. **sleeve-nut** a long nut with right-hand and left-hand screw-threads for drawing together pipes or shafts conversely threaded. **sleeve-valve** a valve in the form of a cylinder with a sliding movement. **up one's sleeve** concealed but ready for use, in reserve. □□ **sleeved** *adj.* (also in *comb.*). **sleeveless** *adj.* [OE *slēfe, slīefe, slȳf*]

sleeving /sleéving/ *n.* tubular covering for electric cable etc.

sleigh /slay/ *n.* & *v.* ● *n.* a sledge, esp. one for riding on. ● *v.intr.* travel on a sleigh. □ **sleigh-bell** any of a number of tinkling bells attached to the harness of a sleigh-horse etc. [orig. US, f. Du. *slee*, rel. to SLED]

sleight /slīt/ *n. archaic* **1** a deceptive trick or device or movement. **2** dexterity. **3** cunning. □ **sleight of hand 1** dexterity esp. in conjuring or fencing. **2** a display of dexterity, esp. a conjuring trick. [ME *sleghth* f. ON *slœgth* f. *slœgr* SLY]

■ □ **sleight of hand 1** see DEXTERITY 1. **2** see TRICK *n.* 4.

slender /sléndər/ *adj.* (**slenderer, slenderest**) **1 a** of small girth or breadth (*a slender pillar*). **b** gracefully thin (*a slender waist*). **2** relatively small or scanty; slight, meagre, inadequate (*slender hopes*; *slender resources*). □ **slender loris** see LORIS. □□ **slenderly** *adv.* **slenderness** *n.* [ME: orig. unkn.]

■ **1** slim, lean, willowy, sylphlike, svelte, lissom, lithe, graceful, thin, spare, slight, lanky, fine; attenuated, tenuous. **2** slim, slight, small, little, scanty; narrow, unlikely, remote; meagre, poor, weak, feeble; limited, inadequate, insufficient, insignificant, trifling.

slenderize /sléndərīz/ *v.* (also **-ise**) **1** *tr.* **a** make (a thing) slender. **b** make (one's figure) appear slender. **2** *intr.* make oneself slender; slim.

■ see SLIM *v.*

slept *past* and *past part.* of SLEEP.

sleuth /sloōth/ *n.* & *v. colloq.* ● *n.* a detective. ● *v.* **1** *intr.* act as a detective. **2** *tr.* investigate. □ **sleuth-hound 1** a bloodhound. **2** *colloq.* a detective, an investigator. [orig. in *sleuth-hound*: ME f. *sleuth* f. ON *slóth* track, trail: cf. SLOT[2]]

■ *n.* (private) detective, (private) investigator, *colloq.* private eye, sleuth-hound, snoop, tec, *sl.* dick, *US sl.* shamus, gumshoe.

slew[1] /sloō/ *v.* & *n.* (also **slue**) ● *v.tr.* & *intr.* (often foll. by *round*) turn or swing forcibly or with effort out of the forward or ordinary position. ● *n.* such a change of position. [18th-c. Naut.: orig. unkn.]

■ *v.* see WIND[2] *v.* 1.

slew[2] *past* of SLAY[1].

slew[3] /sloō/ *n.* esp. *US colloq.* a large number or quantity. [Ir. *sluagh*]

■ see HEAP *n.* 2.

sley /slay/ *n.* (also **slay**) a weaver's reed. [OE *slege*, rel. to SLAY[1]]

slice /slīss/ *n.* & *v.* ● *n.* **1** a thin broad piece or wedge cut off or out esp. from meat or bread or a cake, pie, or large fruit. **2** a share; a part taken or allotted or gained (*a slice of territory*; *a slice of the profits*). **3** an implement with a broad flat blade for serving fish etc. or for scraping or chipping. **4** *Golf* & *Lawn Tennis* a slicing stroke. ● *v.* **1** *tr.* (often foll. by *up*) cut into slices. **2** *tr.* (foll. by *off*) cut (a piece) off. **3** *intr.* (foll. by *into, through*) cut with or like a knife. **4** *tr.* (also *absol.*) **a** *Golf* strike (the ball) so that it deviates away from the striker. **b** (in other sports) propel (the ball) forward at an angle. **5** *tr.* go through (air etc.) with a cutting motion. □ **slice of life** a realistic representation of everyday experience. □□ **sliceable** *adj.* **slicer** *n.* (also in *comb.*). [ME f. OF *esclice, esclicier* splinter f. Frank. *slītjan*, rel. to SLIT]

■ *n.* **1** piece, portion, segment, slab, wedge, sliver, helping; rasher, collop, escalope, shaving, layer. **2** share, helping, cut, portion, piece, part. **3** spatula; slicer, fish-slice. ● *v.* **1–3** divide, cut, *Biol.* section; shear; carve.

slick /slik/ *adj.*, *n.*, & *v.* ● *adj. colloq.* **1 a** (of a person or action) skilful or efficient; dexterous (*gave a slick performance*). **b** superficially or pretentiously smooth and dexterous. **c** glib. **2 a** sleek, smooth. **b** slippery. ● *n.* **1** a smooth patch of oil etc., esp. on the sea. **2** *Motor Racing* a smooth tyre. **3** *US* a glossy magazine. **4** *US sl.* a slick person. ● *v.tr. colloq.* **1** make sleek or smart. **2** (usu. foll. by *down*) flatten (one's hair etc.). □□ **slickly** *adv.* **slickness** *n.* [ME *slike(n)*, prob. f. OE: cf. SLEEK]

■ *adj.* **1 a** smooth, clever, skilful, adroit, dexterous, efficient, professional, ingenious, imaginative, inventive, creative, neat. **b** superficial, shallow, meretricious, specious, glib. **c** smooth, urbane, suave, smooth-spoken, glib, smug, plausible; disingenuous, artful, wily, cunning, *colloq.* shifty; sycophantic, unctuous, oily, *colloq.* smarmy. **2 a** smooth, sleek, glossy, silky, silken, shiny, shining. **b** slippery, glassy, greasy, oily, *colloq.* slippy. ● *v.* **2** slick down, smooth, flatten, plaster down, grease, oil.

slicker /slíkkər/ *n. US* **1** *colloq.* **a** a plausible rogue. **b** a smart and sophisticated city-dweller (cf. *city slicker*). **2** a raincoat of smooth material.

■ **1 a** confidence man, cheat, swindler, mountebank, *sl.* con man. **b** city-dweller, *usu. derog.* city slicker, *derog.* townee. **2** raincoat, oilskin, mackintosh.

slide /slīd/ *v.* & *n.* ● *v.* (*past* and *past part.* **slid** /slid/) **1 a** *intr.* move along a smooth surface with continuous contact on the same part of the thing moving (cf. ROLL). **b** *tr.* cause to do this (*slide the drawer into place*). **2** *intr.* move quietly; glide; go smoothly along. **3** *intr.* pass gradually or imperceptibly. **4** *intr.* glide over ice on one or both feet without skates (under gravity or with momentum got by running). **5** *intr.* (foll. by *over*) barely touch upon (a delicate subject etc.). **6** *intr.* & *tr.* (often foll. by *into*) move or cause to move quietly or unobtrusively (*slid his hand into mine*). **7** *intr.* take its own course (*let it slide*). **8** *intr.* decline (*shares slid to a new low*). ● *n.* **1 a** the act or an instance of sliding. **b** a rapid decline. **2** an inclined plane down which children, goods, etc., slide; a chute. **3 a** a track made by or for sliding, esp. on ice. **b** a slope prepared with snow or ice for tobogganing. **4** a part of a machine or instrument that slides, esp. a slide-valve. **5 a** a thing slid into place, esp. a piece of glass holding an object for a microscope. **b** a mounted transparency usu. placed in a projector for viewing on a screen. **6** *Brit.* = *hair-slide*. **7** a part or parts of a machine on or between which a sliding part works. □ **let things slide** be negligent; allow deterioration. **slide fastener** *US* a zip-fastener. **slide-rule** a ruler with a sliding central strip, graduated logarithmically for making rapid calculations, esp. multiplication and division. **slide-valve** a sliding piece that opens and closes an aperture by sliding across it. **sliding door** a door drawn across an aperture on a slide, not turning on hinges. **sliding keel** *Naut.* a centreboard. **sliding roof** a part of a roof (esp. in a motor car) made able to slide and so form an aperture. **sliding scale** a scale of fees, taxes, wages, etc., that varies as a whole in accordance with variation of some standard. **sliding seat** a seat able to slide to and fro on runners etc., esp. in a racing-boat to adjust the length of a stroke. □□ **slidable** *adj.* **slidably** *adv.* **slider** *n.* [OE *slīdan*]

■ *v.* **1, 2** glide, slip; coast, skim, glissade, skate, plane, skid, toboggan, slither. **6** creep, steal, slip, slink, move. **7** (*let slide*) forget, ignore, neglect, gloss *or* pass over, pay no heed *or* mind to. **8** decline, decrease, drop, fall. ● *n.* **1 b** see DECLINE *n.* 1, 4. **2** see CHUTE 1, 2.

slideway /slī́dway/ *n.* = SLIDE *n.* 7.

slight /slīt/ *adj.*, *v.*, & *n.* ● *adj.* **1 a** inconsiderable; of little significance (*has a slight cold; the damage is very slight*). **b** barely perceptible (*a slight smell of gas*). **c** not much or great or thorough, inadequate, scanty (*a conclusion based on very slight observation; paid him slight attention*). **2** slender, frail-looking (*saw a slight figure approaching; supported by a slight framework*). **3** (in *superl.*, with *neg.* or *interrog.*) any whatever (*paid not the slightest attention*). ● *v.tr.* **1** treat or speak of (a person etc.) as not worth attention, fail in courtesy or respect towards, markedly neglect. **2** *hist.* make militarily useless, raze (a fortification etc.). ● *n.* a marked piece of neglect, a failure to show due respect. □ **not in the slightest** not at all. **put a slight upon** = sense 1 of *v.* □□ **slightingly** *adv.* **slightish** *adj.* **slightly** *adv.* **slightness** *n.* [ME *slyght*, *sleght* f. ON *sléttr* level, smooth f. Gmc]

■ *adj.* **1 a** small, little, minor, negligible, insignificant, inconsequential, inconsiderable. **b** trifling, tiny, slender, minute, infinitesimal. **c** see SCANTY, SLENDER 2. **2** slender, slim, thin, small, short, petite, diminutive, tiny, miniature, bantam, wee, *colloq.* pint-sized; insubstantial, unsubstantial, weak, feeble, delicate, dainty, frail, unstable, fragile, flimsy, lightly made *or* built, precarious, inadequate, rickety, insecure. ● *v.* **1** disregard, ignore, disdain, scorn, snub, rebuff, cut, cold-shoulder; insult, offend, affront, mortify, diminish, minimize, depreciate, disparage, put a slight upon. ● *n.* snub, insult, affront, slur, indignity, outrage, offence, disrespect. □□ **slightly** a little, somewhat, to a certain extent *or* degree *or* measure, to a slight extent *or* degree *or* measure, to a minor extent *or* degree *or* measure, marginally; moderately, rather.

slily var. of SLYLY (see SLY).

slim /slim/ *adj.*, *v.*, & *n.* ● *adj.* (**slimmer, slimmest**) **1 a** of small girth or thickness, of long narrow shape. **b** gracefully thin, slenderly built. **c** not fat or overweight. **2** small, insufficient (*a slim chance of success*). **3** clever, artful, crafty, unscrupulous. ● *v.* (**slimmed, slimming**) **1** *intr.* make oneself slimmer by dieting, exercise, etc. **2** *tr.* make slim or slimmer. ● *n.* a course of slimming. □□ **slimly** *adv.* **slimmer** *n.* **slimming** *n.* & *adj.* **slimmish** *adj.* **slimness** *n.* [LG or Du. f. Gmc]

■ *adj.* **1** see SLENDER 1. **2** see SLENDER 2. ● *v.* **1** reduce, lose *or* shed weight, diet, slenderize.

slime /slīm/ *n.* & *v.* ● *n.* thick slippery mud or a substance of similar consistency, e.g. liquid bitumen or a mucus exuded by fish etc. ● *v.tr.* cover with slime. □ **slime mould** a spore-bearing micro-organism secreting slime. [OE *slīm* f. Gmc, rel. to L *limus* mud, Gk *limnē* marsh]

■ *n.* see MUD 1.

slimline /slímlīn/ *adj.* of slender design.

slimy /slī́mi/ *adj.* (**slimier, slimiest**) **1** of the consistency of slime. **2** covered, smeared with, or full of slime. **3** disgustingly dishonest, meek, or flattering. **4** slippery, hard to hold. □□ **slimily** *adv.* **sliminess** *n.*

■ **1, 2** oozy, slippery, mucky, squashy, squishy, viscous, sticky, gluey, mucilaginous, glutinous, mucous, clammy, mushy, *Bot.* uliginose, *colloq.* squidgy, *sl.* gooey, gunky. **3** slippery, unctuous, oily, slick, obsequious, sycophantic, toadying, servile, creeping, crawling, fawning, grovelling, abject, *colloq.* smarmy. **4** see SLIPPERY 1, 2.

sling[1] /sling/ *n.* & *v.* ● *n.* **1** a strap, belt, etc., used to support or raise a hanging weight, e.g. a rifle, a ship's boat, or goods being transferred. **2** a bandage looped round the neck to support an injured arm. **3** a strap or string used with the hand to give impetus to a small missile, esp. a stone. **4** *Austral. sl.* a tip or bribe. ● *v.tr.* (*past* and *past part.* **slung** /slung/) **1** (also *absol.*) hurl (a stone etc.) from a sling. **2** *colloq.* throw. **3** suspend with a sling, allow to swing suspended, arrange so as to be supported from above, hoist or transfer with a sling. □ **sling-back 1** a shoe held in place by a strap above the heel. **2** (in full **sling-back chair**) a chair with a fabric seat suspended from a rigid frame. **sling-bag** a bag with a long strap which may be hung from the shoulder. **sling one's hook** see HOOK. **sling off at** *Austral.* & *NZ sl.* disparage; mock; make fun of. **slung shot** a metal ball attached by a thong etc. to the wrist and used esp. by criminals as a weapon. [ME, prob. f. ON *slyngva* (v.)]

■ *n.* **1, 2** support, strap, band; belt. **3** catapult, *Austral.* & *NZ* shanghai, *US* slingshot, *hist.* trebuchet. **4** see BRIBE *n.* ● *v.* **1, 2** catapult, propel, hurl, shy, fling, fire, shoot, let fly, launch; toss, throw, cast, pitch, heave, lob; *Austral.* & *NZ* shanghai, *colloq.* chuck. **3** suspend, hang, dangle, swing, drape, string. □ **sling off at** see MOCK *v.* 1, 3.

sling[2] /sling/ *n.* a sweetened drink of spirits (esp. gin) and water. [18th c.: orig. unkn.]

slinger /slíngər/ *n.* a person who slings, esp. the user of a sling.

slingshot /slíngshot/ *n. US* a catapult.

■ see SLING[1] *n.* 3.

slink[1] /slingk/ *v.intr.* (*past* and *past part.* **slunk** /slungk/) (often foll. by *off*, *away*, *by*) move in a stealthy or guilty or sneaking manner. [OE *slincan* crawl]

■ sneak, creep, steal, prowl, skulk, slip.

slink[2] /slingk/ *v.* & *n.* ● *v.tr.* (also *absol.*) (of an animal) produce (young) prematurely. ● *n.* **1** an animal, esp. a calf, so born. **2** its flesh. [app. f. SLINK[1]]

slinky /slíngki/ *adj.* (**slinkier, slinkiest**) **1** stealthy. **2** (of a garment) close-fitting and flowing, sinuous. **3** gracefully slender. □□ **slinkily** *adv.* **slinkiness** *n.*

slip[1] /slip/ *v.* & *n.* ● *v.* (**slipped, slipping**) **1** *intr.* slide unintentionally esp. for a short distance; lose one's footing or balance or place by unintended sliding. **2** *intr.* go or move with a sliding motion (*as the door closes the catch slips into place; slipped into her nightdress*). **3** *intr.* escape restraint or capture by being slippery or hard to hold or by not being grasped (*the eel slipped through his fingers*). **4** *intr.* **a** make one's or its way unobserved or quietly or quickly (*just slip across to the baker's; errors will slip in*). **b** (foll. by *by*) (of time) go by rapidly or unnoticed. **5** *intr.* **a** make a careless or casual mistake. **b** fall below the normal standard, deteriorate, lapse. **6** *tr.* insert or transfer stealthily or casually or with a sliding motion (*slipped a coin into his hand; slipped the papers into his pocket*). **7** *tr.* **a** release from restraint (*slipped the greyhounds from the leash*). **b** detach (an anchor) from a ship. **c** *Brit.* detach (a carriage) from a moving train. **d** release (the clutch of a motor vehicle) for a moment. **e** (of an animal) produce (young) prematurely. **8** *tr.* move (a stitch) to the other needle without knitting it. **9** *tr.* (foll. by *on*, *off*) pull (a garment) hastily on or off. **10** *tr.* escape from; give the slip to (*the dog slipped its collar; point slipped my mind*). ● *n.* **1** the act or an instance of slipping. **2** an accidental or slight error. **3** a loose covering or garment, esp. a petticoat or pillowcase. **4 a** a reduction in the movement of a pulley etc. due to slipping of the belt. **b** a reduction in the distance travelled by a ship or aircraft arising from the nature of the medium in which its propeller revolves. **5** (in *sing.* or *pl.*) **a** an artificial slope of stone etc. on which boats are landed. **b** an inclined structure on which ships are built or repaired. **6** *Cricket* **a** a fielder stationed for balls glancing off the bat to the off side. **b** (in *sing.* or *pl.*) the position of such a fielder (*caught in the slips; caught at slip*). **7** a leash to slip dogs. □ **give a person the slip** escape from or evade him or her. **let slip 1** release accidentally or deliberately, esp. from a leash. **2** miss (an opportunity). **3** utter inadvertently. **let slip the dogs of war** *poet.* open hostilities. **let slip through one's fingers 1** lose hold of. **2** miss the opportunity of having. **slip away** depart without leave-taking etc. **slip-carriage** *Brit.* a railway carriage on an express for detaching at a station where the rest of the train does not stop. **slip-case** a close-fitting case for a book. **slip-coach** *Brit.* = *slip-carriage*. **slip-cover 1 a** a calico etc. cover for furniture out of use. **b** *US* = *loose cover*. **2** a jacket or slip-case for a book. **slip form** a mould in which a structure of uniform cross-section is cast by filling it with concrete and continually moving and refilling it. **slip-hook** a hook with a contrivance for releasing it readily when necessary. **slip-knot 1** a knot that can be undone by a pull. **2** a running knot. **slip off** depart without leave-taking etc. **slip of the pen** (or **tongue**) a small mistake in which something is written (or said) unintentionally. **slip-on** *adj.* (of shoes or clothes) that can be easily slipped on and off. ● *n.* a slip-on shoe or garment. **slip-over** (of a garment) to be slipped on over the head. **slipped disc** a disc between vertebrae that has become displaced and causes lumbar pain. **slip-ring** a ring for sliding contact in a dynamo or electric motor. **slip-road** *Brit.* a road for entering or leaving a motorway etc. **slip-rope** *Naut.* a rope with both ends on board so that casting loose either end frees the ship from her moorings. **slip sheet** *Printing* a sheet of paper placed between newly printed sheets to prevent set-off or smudging. **slip something over on** *colloq.* outwit. **slip-stitch** *n.* **1** a loose stitch joining layers of fabric and not visible externally. **2** a stitch moved to the other needle without being knitted. ● *v.tr.* sew with slip-stitch. **slip up** *colloq.* make a mistake. **slip-up** *n. colloq.* a mistake, a blunder. **there's many a slip 'twixt cup and lip** nothing is certain till it has happened. [ME prob. f. MLG *slippen*: cf. SLIPPERY]

■ *v.* **1** slide, skid, glide, aquaplane, slither; stumble, lose one's footing *or* balance, miss one's footing, trip; fall, tumble. **4 a** sneak, slink, steal, creep, edge, skulk; (*slip in*) enter, get in, sneak in. **b** (*slip by*) pass, elapse, vanish, go by. **5 a** see *slip up* (SLIP[1]) below. **b** see DETERIORATE. ● *n.* **2** blunder, error, mistake, fault, oversight, slip of the tongue *or* pen, Freudian slip, *lapsus linguae*, gaffe, inadvertence, indiscretion, impropriety, transgression, peccadillo, *faux pas*, *colloq.* slip-up, *esp. US colloq.* blooper, *sl.* bloomer, booboo, fluff, *Brit. sl.* boob. □ **give a person the slip** see ELUDE 1. **let slip 2** see MISS[1] *v.* 8. **3** reveal, divulge, blurt out, leak, let out, disclose, expose, come out with, blab. **slip away, slip off** slip out, escape, disappear, leave, vanish, steal away, go away *or* off *or* out, run away *or* off *or* out, break away, get away, sneak away *or* off *or* out. **slip of the pen** (or **tongue**) see SLIP[1] *n.* above. **slip-road** see *turn-off* 1. **slip something over on** see OUTSMART. **slip up** slip, err, blunder, make a mistake, miscalculate, botch (up), *sl.* screw up, goof. **slip-up** see SLIP[1] *n.* above.

slip[2] /slip/ *n.* **1 a** a small piece of paper esp. for writing on. **b** a long narrow strip of thin wood, paper, etc. **c** a printer's proof on such paper; a galley proof. **2** a cutting taken from a plant for grafting or planting, a scion. □ **slip of a** small and slim (*a slip of a girl*). [ME, prob. f. MDu., MLG *slippe* cut, strip, etc.]

■ **1** paper, note, chit; permit, permission, pass, document; piece, scrap, strip, sliver. **2** shoot, scion, cutting, set, sprig, twig, sprout, runner, offshoot.

slip[3] /slip/ *n.* clay in a creamy mixture with water, used mainly for decorating earthenware. □ **slip casting** the manufacture of ceramic ware by allowing slip to solidify in a mould. **slip-ware** ware decorated with slip. [OE *slipa*, *slyppe* slime: cf. COWSLIP]

slipover /slípōvər/ *n.* a pullover, usu. without sleeves.

slippage /slíppij/ *n.* **1** the act or an instance of slipping. **2 a** a decline, esp. in popularity or value. **b** failure to meet a deadline or fulfil a promise; delay.

slipper /slíppər/ *n.* & *v.* ● *n.* **1** a light loose comfortable indoor shoe. **2** a light slip-on shoe for dancing etc. ● *v.tr.* beat or strike with a slipper. □ **slipper bath** *Brit.* a bath shaped like a slipper, with a covered end. □□ **slippered** *adj.*

slipperwort /slíppərwurt/ *n.* calceolaria.

slippery /slíppəri/ *adj.* **1** difficult to hold firmly because of smoothness, wetness, sliminess, or elusive motion. **2** (of a surface) difficult to stand on, causing slips by its smoothness or muddiness. **3** unreliable, unscrupulous, shifty. **4** (of a subject) requiring tactful handling. □ **slippery elm 1** the N. American red elm, *Ulmus fulva*. **2** the medicinal inner bark of this. **slippery slope** a course leading to disaster. □□ **slipperily** *adv.* **slipperiness** *n.* [prob. coined by Coverdale (1535) after Luther's *schlipfferig*, MHG *slipferig* f. *slipfern*, *slipfen* f. Gmc: partly f. *slipper* slippery (now dial.) f. OE *slipor* f. Gmc]

■ **1, 2** slick, sleek, slimy, icy, glassy, smooth, slithery, greasy, oily, lubricated, *colloq.* slippy. **3** evasive, devious, unreliable, undependable, questionable, untrustworthy, dishonest, treacherous, disloyal, perfidious, slick, crafty, sly, foxy, cunning, tricky, sneaky, false, reptilian, faithless, shady, *colloq.* shifty.

slippy /slíppi/ *adj.* (**slippier, slippiest**) *colloq.* slippery. □ **look** (or **be**) **slippy** *Brit.* look sharp; make haste. □□ **slippiness** *n.*

slipshod /slípshod/ *adj.* **1** (of speech or writing, a speaker or writer, a method of work, etc.) careless, unsystematic; loose in arrangement. **2** slovenly. **3** having shoes down at heel.

■ **1, 2** careless, slapdash, haphazard, messy, untidy, disorganized, lax, unorganized, unmethodical, unsystematic, slovenly, sloppy, shoddy.

slipstream /slípstreem/ *n.* & *v.* ● *n.* **1** a current of air or water driven back by a revolving propeller or a moving vehicle. **2** an assisting force regarded as drawing something along with or behind something else. ● *v.tr.* **1** follow closely behind (another vehicle). **2** pass after travelling in another's slipstream.

slipway /slípway/ *n.* a slip for building ships or landing boats.

slit /slit/ *n.* & *v.* ● *n.* **1** a long straight narrow incision. **2** a long narrow opening comparable to a cut. ● *v.tr.* (**slitting**; *past* and *past part.* **slit**) **1** make a slit in; cut or tear lengthwise. **2** cut into strips. □ **slit-eyed** having long narrow eyes. **slit-pocket** a pocket with a vertical opening giving access to the pocket or to a garment beneath. **slit trench** a narrow trench for a soldier or a weapon. □□ **slitter** *n.* [ME *slitte*, rel. to OE *slītan*, f. Gmc]

■ *n.* split, cut, gash, incision, fissure, groove, slash, rift, crack, cleft, vent, aperture, opening. ● *v.* **1** split, cut, slash, gash, slice, tear, rip, *literary* cleave.

slither /slí*th*ər/ *v.* & *n.* ● *v.intr.* slide unsteadily; go with an irregular slipping motion. ● *n.* an instance of slithering. □□ **slithery** *adj.* [ME var. of *slidder* (now dial.) f. OE *slid(e)rian* frequent. f. *slid-*, weak grade of *slīdan* SLIDE]

■ *v.* slide, worm, snake, slip, slink, glide, skitter, creep, crawl.

slitty /slítti/ *adj.* (**slittier, slittiest**) (of the eyes) long and narrow.

sliver /slívvər, slīvər/ *n.* & *v.* ● *n.* **1** a long thin piece cut or split off. **2** a piece of wood torn from a tree or from timber. **3** a splinter, esp. from an exploded shell. **4** a strip of loose textile fibres after carding. ● *v.tr.* & *intr.* **1** break off as a sliver. **2** break up into slivers. **3** form into slivers. [ME, rel. to *slive* cleave (now dial.) f. OE]

■ *n.* **1–3** fragment, piece, shard, shred, splinter, slip, shaving, paring, flake, chip, bit, scrap, strip, slice, snippet, snip.

slivovitz /slívvəvits/ *n.* a plum brandy made esp. in Romania and the former Yugoslavia. [Serbo-Croat *šljivovica* f. *šljiva* plum]

Sloane /slōn/ *n.* (in full **Sloane Ranger**) *Brit. sl.* a fashionable and conventional upper-class young woman, esp. living in London. □□ **Sloaney** *adj.* [*Sloane* Square, London + Lone *Ranger*, a cowboy hero]

slob /slob/ *n.* **1** *colloq.* a stupid, careless, coarse, or fat person. **2** *Ir.* muddy land. □□ **slobbish** *adj.* [Ir. *slab* mud f. E *slab* ooze, sludge, prob. f. Scand.]

■ **1** oaf, boor, lout, churl, yahoo, barbarian, *colloq.* pig, galoot, *Brit. sl.* yob, yobbo.

slobber /slóbbər/ *v.* & *n.* ● *v.intr.* **1** slaver. **2** (foll. by *over*) show excessive sentiment. ● *n.* saliva running from the mouth; slaver. □□ **slobbery** *adj.* [ME, = Du. *slobbern*, of imit. orig.]

■ *v.* **1** see SLAVER² *v.*

sloe /slō/ *n.* **1** = BLACKTHORN. **2** its small bluish-black fruit with a sharp sour taste. □ **sloe-eyed 1** having eyes of this colour. **2** slant-eyed. **sloe-gin** a liqueur of sloes steeped in gin. [OE *slā(h)* f. Gmc]
■ □ **sloe-eyed 2** slit-eyed, slant-eyed.

slog /slog/ *v.* & *n.* ● *v.* (**slogged, slogging**) **1** *intr.* & *tr.* hit hard and usu. wildly esp. in boxing or at cricket. **2** *intr.* (often foll. by *away, on*) walk or work doggedly. ● *n.* **1** a hard random hit. **2 a** hard steady work or walking. **b** a spell of this. □□ **slogger** *n.* [19th c.: orig. unkn.: cf. SLUG²]
■ *v.* **1** see STRIKE *v.* 1. **2** see WALK *v.* 1, 2. ● *n.* **2** see *drudgery* (DRUDGE), WALK *n.* 2.

slogan /slṓgən/ *n.* **1** a short catchy phrase used in advertising etc. **2** a party cry; a watchword or motto. **3** *hist.* a Scottish Highland war-cry. [Gael. *sluagh-ghairm* f. *sluagh* army + *gairm* shout]
■ catchword, watchword, byword, catch-phrase; motto, jingle, saying; war-cry, battle-cry, rallying cry.

sloop /slo͞op/ *n.* **1** a small one-masted fore-and-aft-rigged vessel with mainsail and jib. **2** (in full **sloop of war**) *Brit. hist.* a small warship with guns on the upper deck only. □ **sloop-rigged** rigged like a sloop. [Du. *sloep(e)*, of unkn. orig.]

sloosh /slo͞osh/ *n.* & *v. colloq.* ● *n.* a pouring or pouring sound of water. ● *v.intr.* **1** flow with a rush. **2** make a heavy splashing or rushing noise. [imit.]

sloot /slo͞ot/ *n.* (also **sluit**) *S.Afr.* a deep gully formed by heavy rain. [Afrik. f. Du. *sloot* ditch]

slop¹ /slop/ *v.* & *n.* ● *v.* (**slopped, slopping**) **1** (often foll. by *over*) **a** *intr.* spill or flow over the edge of a vessel. **b** *tr.* allow to do this. **2** *tr.* make (the floor, clothes, etc.) wet or messy by slopping, spill or splash liquid on. **3** *intr.* (usu. foll. by *over*) gush; be effusive or maudlin. ● *n.* **1** a quantity of liquid spilled or splashed. **2** weakly sentimental language. **3** (in *pl.*) waste liquid, esp. dirty water or the waste contents of kitchen, bedroom, or prison vessels. **4** (in *sing.* or *pl.*) unappetizing weak liquid food. **5** *Naut.* a choppy sea. □ **slop about** move about in a slovenly manner. **slop-basin** *Brit.* a basin for the dregs of cups at table. **slop out** carry slops out (in prison etc.). **slop-pail** a pail for removing bedroom or kitchen slops. [earlier sense 'slush', prob. rel. to *slyppe*: cf. COWSLIP]
■ *v.* **1** see SPILL¹ *v.* 1. ● *n.* **3** (*slops*) see GARBAGE 1a.

slop² /slop/ *n.* **1** a workman's loose outer garment. **2** (in *pl.*) ready-made or cheap clothing. **3** (in *pl.*) clothes and bedding supplied to sailors in the navy. **4** (in *pl.*) *archaic* wide baggy trousers esp. as worn by sailors. [ME: cf. OE *oferslop* surplice f. Gmc]

slope /slōp/ *n.* & *v.* ● *n.* **1** an inclined position or direction; a state in which one end or side is at a higher level than another; a position in a line neither parallel nor perpendicular to level ground or to a line serving as a standard. **2** a piece of rising or falling ground. **3 a** a difference in level between the two ends or sides of a thing (*a slope of 5 metres*). **b** the rate at which this increases with distance etc. **4** a place for skiing on the side of a hill or mountain. **5** (prec. by *the*) the position of a rifle when sloped. ● *v.* **1** *intr.* have or take a slope; slant esp. up or down; lie or tend obliquely, esp. to ground level. **2** *tr.* place or arrange or make in or at a slope. □ **slope arms** place one's rifle in a sloping position against one's shoulder. **slope off** *sl.* go away, esp. to evade work etc. [shortening of ASLOPE]
■ *n.* **1–3** incline, decline, ascent, descent, acclivity, declivity, rise, fall, ramp, dip, sink, drop, angle, slant, pitch, tilt, rake, tip, camber, cant, bevel, hill, bank, scarp, gradient, grade, *US* upgrade, downgrade. **4** trail, track, piste. ● *v.* **1** incline, decline, ascend, descend, rise, fall, dip, sink, drop (off), angle, slant, cant, pitch, tilt, tip, lean, list. **2** slant, angle, bevel, cant, grade, incline, tilt, lean, tip. □ **slope off** see *beat it*.

sloppy /slóppi/ *adj.* (**sloppier, sloppiest**) **1 a** (of the ground) wet with rain; full of puddles. **b** (of food etc.) watery and disagreeable. **c** (of a floor, table, etc.) wet with slops, having water etc. spilt on it. **2** unsystematic, careless, not thorough. **3** (of a garment) ill-fitting or untidy; (of a person) wearing such garments. **4** (of sentiment or talk) weakly emotional, maudlin. **5** *colloq.* (of the sea) choppy. □□ **sloppily** *adv.* **sloppiness** *n.*
■ **1 a, c** wet, slushy, soggy, soppy, sopping, sodden, sloshy, muddy, rainy. **b** watery, thin, runny, liquid, messy, slushy, *sl.* gooey. **2** slovenly, careless, slipshod, shoddy, slapdash, lax, unsystematic, untidy, messy, disordered, disorderly. **3** ill-fitting; shabby, dirty, untidy, messy, dowdy, frumpy, frumpish; draggle-tailed, bedraggled, dishevelled, unkempt, *colloq.* scruffy. **4** sentimental, gushy, gushing, mawkish, maudlin, mushy, over-emotional, romantic, sloshy, *colloq.* slushy, *Brit. colloq.* wet, soppy.

slosh /slosh/ *v.* & *n.* ● *v.* **1** *intr.* (often foll. by *about*) splash or flounder about, move with a splashing sound. **2** *tr. Brit. sl.* hit esp. heavily. **3** *tr. colloq.* **a** pour (liquid) clumsily. **b** pour liquid on. ● *n.* **1** slush. **2 a** an instance of splashing. **b** the sound of this. **3** *Brit. sl.* a heavy blow. **4** a quantity of liquid. [var. of SLUSH]
■ *v.* **1** see SPLASH *v.* 3. **2** see HIT *v.* 1a. ● *n.* **2** see SPLASH *n.* 2. **3** see BLOW² 1.

sloshed /slosht/ *adj. Brit. sl.* drunk.
■ see DRUNK *adj.* 1.

sloshy /slóshi/ *adj.* (**sloshier, sloshiest**) **1** slushy. **2** sloppy, sentimental.
■ **1** see SLOPPY 1a, c. **2** see SLOPPY 4.

slot¹ /slot/ *n.* & *v.* ● *n.* **1** a slit or other aperture in a machine etc. for something (esp. a coin) to be inserted. **2** a slit, groove, channel, or long aperture into which something fits or in which something works. **3** an allotted place in an arrangement or scheme, esp. in a broadcasting schedule. ● *v.* (**slotted, slotting**) **1** *tr.* & *intr.* place or be placed into or as if into a slot. **2** *tr.* provide with a slot or slots. □ **slot-machine** a machine worked by the insertion of a coin, esp.: **1** one for automatic retail of small articles. **2** one allowing a spell of play at a pin-table etc. **3** *US* = *fruit machine*. [ME, = hollow of the breast, f. OF *esclot*, of unkn. orig.]
■ *n.* **1, 2** groove, fissure, notch, slit, opening, hollow, depression, channel, track, *Anat.* sulcus. **3** opening, position, vacancy, job, place, assignment, niche, space, spot, pigeon-hole, time. ● *v.* **1** assign, schedule, place, position, pigeon-hole, fit. **2** groove, fissure, notch, slit, hollow out.

slot² /slot/ *n.* **1** the track of a deer etc. esp. as shown by footprints. **2** a deer's foot. [OF *esclot* hoof-print of a horse, prob. f. ON *slóth* trail: cf. SLEUTH]

sloth /slōth/ *n.* **1** laziness or indolence; reluctance to make an effort. **2** any slow-moving nocturnal mammal of the family Bradypodidae or Megalonychidae of S. America, having long limbs and hooked claws for hanging upside down from branches of trees. □ **sloth bear** a large-lipped black shaggy bear, *Melursus ursinus*, of India. [ME f. SLOW + -TH²]
■ **1** idleness, laziness, indolence, slothfulness, inertia, apathy, indifference, accidie, torpor, torpidity, sluggishness, languor, languidness, lethargy, phlegm, *literary* hebetude.

slothful /slṓthfo͝ol/ *adj.* lazy; characterized by sloth. □□ **slothfully** *adv.* **slothfulness** *n.*
■ idle, lazy, indolent, apathetic, indifferent, torpid, inert, slack, lax, shiftless, fainéant, inactive, supine, do-nothing, sluggish, sluggardly, slow, laggard, languorous, languid, lethargic, lackadaisical, phlegmatic.

slouch /slowch/ *v.* & *n.* ● *v.* **1** *intr.* stand or move or sit in a drooping ungainly fashion. **2** *tr.* bend one side of the brim of (a hat) downwards (opp. COCK¹). **3** *intr.* droop, hang down loosely. ● *n.* **1** a slouching posture or movement, a stoop. **2** a downward bend of a hat-brim (opp. COCK¹). **3** *sl.* an incompetent or slovenly worker or operator or performance (*he's no slouch*). □ **slouch hat** a hat with a wide flexible brim. □□ **slouchy** *adj.* (**slouchier, slouchiest**). [16th c.: orig. unkn.]

■ *v.* **1** droop, sag, stoop, loll, slump; hunch. ● *n.* **1** stoop, sag, droop, slump; hunch. **3** sloven, loafer, sluggard, laggard, idler, malingerer, *colloq.* lazybones.

slough[1] /slow/ *n.* a swamp; a miry place; a quagmire. □ **Slough of Despond** a state of hopeless depression (with ref. to Bunyan's *Pilgrim's Progress*). □□ **sloughy** *adj.* [OE *slōh, slō(g)*]
■ see SWAMP *n.*

slough[2] /sluf/ *n.* & *v.* ● *n.* **1** a part that an animal casts or moults, esp. a snake's cast skin. **2** dead tissue that drops off from living flesh etc. **3** a habit etc. that has been abandoned. ● *v.* **1** *tr.* cast off as a slough. **2** *intr.* (often foll. by *off*) drop off as a slough. **3** *intr.* cast off a slough. **4** *intr.* (often foll. by *away, down*) (of soil, rock, etc.) collapse or slide into a hole or depression. □□ **sloughy** *adj.* [ME, perh. rel. to LG *slu(we)* husk]

Slovak /slṓvak/ *n.* & *adj.* ● *n.* **1** a member of a Slavonic people inhabiting Slovakia in central Europe, formerly part of Czechoslovakia and now an independent republic. **2** the West Slavonic language of this people. ● *adj.* of or relating to this people or language. [Slovak etc. *Slovák*, rel. to SLOVENE]

sloven /slúvv'n/ *n.* a person who is habitually untidy or careless. [ME perh. f. Flem. *sloef* dirty or Du. *slof* careless]
■ see SLOUCH *n.* 3.

Slovene /slṓveen, sləveén/ (also **Slovenian** /-veéniən/) *n.* & *adj.* ● *n.* **1** a member of a Slavonic people in Slovenia in the former Yugoslavia. **2** the language of this people. ● *adj.* of or relating to Slovenia or its people or language. [G *Slowene* f. Styrian etc. *Slovenec* f. OSlav. *Slov-*, perh. rel. to *slovo* word]

slovenly /slúvvənli/ *adj.* & *adv.* ● *adj.* careless and untidy; unmethodical. ● *adv.* in a slovenly manner. □□ **slovenliness** *n.*
■ *adj.* see UNTIDY.

slow /slō/ *adj., adv.,* & *v.* ● *adj.* **1 a** taking a relatively long time to do a thing or cover a distance (also foll. by *of*: *slow of speech*). **b** not quick; acting or moving or done without speed. **2** gradual; obtained over a length of time (*slow growth*). **3** not producing, allowing, or conducive to speed (*in the slow lane*). **4** (of a clock etc.) showing a time earlier than is the case. **5** (of a person) not understanding readily; not learning easily. **6** dull; uninteresting; tedious. **7** slack or sluggish (*business is slow*). **8** (of a fire or oven) giving little heat. **9** *Photog.* **a** (of a film) needing long exposure. **b** (of a lens) having a small aperture. **10 a** reluctant; tardy (*not slow to defend himself*). **b** not hasty or easily moved (*slow to take offence*). **11** (of a cricket-pitch, tennis-court, putting-green, etc.) on which the ball bounces or runs slowly. ● *adv.* **1** at a slow pace; slowly. **2** (in *comb.*) (*slow-moving traffic*). ● *v.* (usu. foll. by *down, up*) **1** *intr.* & *tr.* reduce one's speed or the speed of (a vehicle etc.). **2** *intr.* reduce one's pace of life; live or work less intensely. □ **slow and sure** of the attitude that haste is risky. **slow but sure** achieving the required result eventually. **slow-down** the action of slowing down; a go-slow. **slow handclap** slow clapping by an audience as a sign of displeasure or boredom. **slow loris** see LORIS. **slow march** the marching time adopted by troops in a funeral procession etc. **slow-match** a slow-burning match for lighting explosives etc. **slow motion 1** the operation or speed of a film using slower projection or more rapid exposure so that actions etc. appear much slower than usual. **2** the simulation of this in real action. **slow neutron** a neutron with low kinetic energy esp. after moderation (cf. *fast neutron* (see FAST[1])). **slow poison** a poison eventually causing death by repeated doses. **slow puncture** a puncture causing only slow deflation of the tyre. **slow reactor** *Physics* a nuclear reactor using mainly slow neutrons (cf. *fast reactor* (see FAST[1])). **slow virus** a progressive disease caused by a virus or virus-like organism that multiplies slowly in the host organism and has a long incubation period, such as scrapie or BSE. **slow-witted** stupid. □□ **slowish** *adj.* **slowly** *adv.* **slowness** *n.* [OE *slāw* f. Gmc]
■ *adj.* **1** lagging, laggard, dawdling, sluggish, sluggardly, slow-moving, leaden, ponderous, unhurried, plodding, snail-like, tortoise-like, torpid, leaden-footed, creeping, crawling; dilatory, deliberate, slow-paced, leisurely, gradual, easy, relaxed, lax, lackadaisical, lazy, *US sl.* lallygagging; see also LATE *adj.* 1. **2** gradual, progressive, moderate, perceptible, almost imperceptible, measurable. **4** behindhand, unpunctual, behind time. **5** dense, dull, slow-witted, dull-witted, obtuse, backward, retarded, bovine, dim, dim-witted, stupid, unresponsive, blockish, cloddish, unintelligent, doltish, simple, stolid, unimaginative, *colloq.* slow on the uptake, not with it, thick, *esp. US colloq.* dumb. **6** boring, dull, tiresome, tedious, sleepy, somnolent, torpid, soporific, wearisome, dry as dust, uninteresting, monotonous, tame, uneventful, humdrum, dead, *Brit.* dead-and-alive. **7** slack, inactive, quiet, sluggish; unproductive. **10** reluctant, unwilling, hesitant, disinclined, averse, loath, indisposed; not quick, not hasty, tardy, dilatory. ● *adv.* **1** slowly, unhurriedly, cautiously, carefully, circumspectly; easy, leisurely, easily; tardily, unpunctually, late, behindhand. ● *v.* (*slow down* or *up*) **1** slack *or* slacken off, reduce speed, decelerate, go slower, hold back, put on the brakes, take it easy; see also RETARD *v.* **2** relax, take it easy, ease up, let up. □ **slow-down** work-to-rule, *Brit.* go-slow; *Brit.* industrial action. □□ **slowly** see *gradually* (GRADUAL), SLOW *adv.* above.

slowcoach /slṓkōch/ *n. Brit.* **1** a slow or lazy person. **2** a dull-witted person. **3** a person behind the times in opinions etc.
■ **1** see LAGGARD *n.*

slowpoke /slṓpōk/ *n. US* = SLOWCOACH.

slow-worm /slṓwurm/ *n.* a small European legless lizard, *Anguis fragilis*, giving birth to live young. Also called BLINDWORM. [OE *slā-wyrm*: first element of uncert. orig., assim. to SLOW]

SLR *abbr.* **1** *Photog.* single-lens reflex. **2** self-loading rifle.

slub[1] /slub/ *n.* & *adj.* ● *n.* **1** a lump or thick place in yarn or thread. **2** fabric woven from thread etc. with slubs. ● *adj.* (of material etc.) with an irregular appearance caused by uneven thickness of the warp. [19th c.: orig. unkn.]

slub[2] /slub/ *n.* & *v.* ● *n.* wool slightly twisted in preparation for spinning. ● *v.tr.* (**slubbed, slubbing**) twist (wool) in this way. [18th c.: orig. unkn.]

sludge /sluj/ *n.* **1** thick greasy mud. **2** muddy or slushy sediment. **3** sewage. **4** *Mech.* an accumulation of dirty oil, esp. in the sump of an internal-combustion engine. **5** *Geol.* sea-ice newly formed in small pieces. **6** (usu. *attrib.*) a muddy colour (*sludge green*). □□ **sludgy** *adj.* [cf. SLUSH]
■ **1, 2** mire, ooze, mud, slime, dregs, silt, residue, precipitate, slush, goo, *colloq.* muck, *sl.* gunk.

slue var. of SLEW[1].

slug[1] /slug/ *n.* **1** a small shell-less mollusc of the class Gastropoda often destructive to plants. **2 a** a bullet esp. of irregular shape. **b** a missile for an airgun. **3** *Printing* **a** a metal bar used in spacing. **b** a line of type in Linotype printing. **4** esp. *US* a tot of liquor. **5** a unit of mass, given an acceleration of 1 foot per second per second by a force of 1 lb. **6** a roundish lump of metal. [ME *slugg(e)* sluggard, prob. f. Scand.]
■ **2** see SHOT[1] 3. **4** see DRINK *n.* 1b.

slug[2] /slug/ *v.* & *n. US* ● *v.tr.* (**slugged, slugging**) strike with a hard blow. ● *n.* a hard blow. □ **slug it out 1** fight it out. **2** endure; stick it out. □□ **slugger** *n.* [19th c.: orig. unkn.]
■ *v.* see PUNCH[1] *v.* 1. ● *n.* see PUNCH[1] *n.* 1. □□ **slugger** see PUGILIST.

slugabed /slúggəbed/ *n. archaic* a lazy person who lies late in bed. [*slug* (v.) (see SLUGGARD) + ABED]
■ see IDLER.

sluggard /slúggərd/ *n.* a lazy sluggish person. □□ **sluggardly** *adj.* **sluggardliness** *n.* [ME f. *slug* (v.) be slothful (prob. f. Scand.: cf. SLUG[1]) + -ARD]

■ see IDLER.

sluggish /slúggish/ *adj.* inert; inactive; slow-moving; torpid; indolent (*a sluggish circulation*; *a sluggish stream*). ▫▫ **sluggishly** *adv.* **sluggishness** *n.* [ME f. SLUG[1] or *slug* (v.): see SLUGGARD]
■ see TORPID 1. ▫▫ **sluggishness** sloth, laziness, slothfulness, indolence, idleness, languor, lassitude, lethargy, languidness, laggardness, torpor, phlegm, lifelessness, stagnation, inactivity, inertia, shiftlessness, fainéancy, accidie, *literary* hebetude.

sluice /slo͞oss/ *n.* & *v.* ● *n.* **1** (also **sluice-gate, sluice-valve**) a sliding gate or other contrivance for controlling the volume or flow of water. **2** (also **sluice-way**) an artificial water-channel esp. for washing ore. **3** a place for rinsing. **4** the act or an instance of rinsing. **5** the water above or below or issuing through a floodgate. ● *v.* **1** *tr.* provide or wash with a sluice or sluices. **2** *tr.* rinse, pour or throw water freely upon. **3** *tr.* (foll. by *out, away*) wash out or away with a flow of water. **4** *tr.* flood with water from a sluice. **5** *intr.* (of water) rush out from a sluice, or as if from a sluice. [ME f. OF *escluse* ult. f. L *excludere* EXCLUDE]
■ *n.* **1** lock. **2** see CHANNEL[1] *n.* 5a, 6.

sluit var. of SLOOT.

slum /slum/ *n.* & *v.* ● *n.* **1** an overcrowded and squalid back street, district, etc., usu. in a city and inhabited by very poor people. **2** a house or building unfit for human habitation. ● *v.intr.* (**slummed, slumming**) **1** live in slumlike conditions. **2** go about the slums through curiosity, to examine the condition of the inhabitants, or for charitable purposes. ▫ **slum clearance** the demolition of slums and rehousing of their inhabitants. **slum it** *colloq.* put up with conditions less comfortable than usual. ▫▫ **slummy** *adj.* (**slummier, slummiest**). **slumminess** *n.* [19th c.: orig. cant]
■ *n.* **1** slums, ghetto, warren, shanty town, *US colloq.* skid row *or* road. **2** see HOLE *n.* 4a. ▫▫ **slummy** see SHABBY 1, 2.

slumber /slúmbər/ *v.* & *n. poet. rhet.* ● *v.intr.* **1** sleep, esp. in a specified manner. **2** be idle, drowsy, or inactive. ● *n.* a sleep, esp. of a specified kind (*fell into a fitful slumber*). ▫ **slumber away** spend (time) in slumber. **slumber-wear** nightclothes. ▫▫ **slumberer** *n.* **slumberous** *adj.* **slumbrous** *adj.* [ME *slūmere* etc. f. *slūmen* (v.) or *slūme* (n.) f. OE *slūma*: *-b-* as in *number*]
■ *v.* **1** see SLEEP *v.* ● *n.* see SLEEP *n.* 2. ▫▫ **slumberous** see SLEEPY 1.

slump /slump/ *n.* & *v.* ● *n.* **1** a sudden severe or prolonged fall in prices or values of commodities or securities. **2** a sharp or sudden decline in trade or business usu. bringing widespread unemployment. **3** a lessening of interest or commitment in a subject or undertaking. ● *v.intr.* **1** undergo a slump; fail; fall in price. **2** sit or fall heavily or limply (*slumped into a chair*). **3** lean or subside. [17th c., orig. 'sink in a bog': imit.]
■ *n.* **1, 2** dip, trough, depreciation, decline, downturn, recession, depression, falling-off, fall-off, fall, drop, plunge, descent, crash, collapse, failure; nosedive, tailspin. ● *v.* **1** decline, slip, recede, fall (off), drop, plunge, descend, sink, crash, collapse, fail, tumble, dive, plummet, take a nosedive *or* tailspin, go into a nosedive *or* tailspin. **2** fall, sink, flop, drop, collapse, tumble, crash. **3** lean, subside, sink; see also SLOUCH *v.*

slung *past* and *past part.* of SLING[1].

slunk *past* and *past part.* of SLINK[1].

slur /slur/ *v.* & *n.* ● *v.* (**slurred, slurring**) **1** *tr.* & *intr.* pronounce or write indistinctly so that the sounds or letters run into one another. **2** *tr. Mus.* **a** perform (a group of two or more notes) legato. **b** mark (notes) with a slur. **3** *tr. archaic* or *US* put a slur on (a person or a person's character); make insinuations against. **4** *tr.* (usu. foll. by *over*) pass over (a fact, fault, etc.) lightly; conceal or minimize. ● *n.* **1** an imputation of wrongdoing; blame; stigma (*a slur on my reputation*). **2** the act or an instance of slurring in pronunciation, singing, or writing. **3** *Mus.* a curved line to show that two or more notes are to be sung to one syllable or played or sung legato. [17th c.: orig. unkn.]
■ *v.* **1** mumble, garble, stutter, lisp. **3** see SLANDER *v.* **4** (*slur over*) gloss over, pass over, disregard, overlook, give short shrift to, ignore, conceal, minimize. ● *n.* **1** smear, insult, calumny, aspersion, affront, stigma, stain, blot, spot, (black) mark, discredit, insinuation, innuendo, imputation, slander, libel, slight, *colloq.* put-down.

slurp /slurp/ *v.* & *n.* ● *v.tr.* eat or drink noisily. ● *n.* the sound of this; a slurping gulp. [Du. *slurpen, slorpen*]

slurry /slúrri/ *n.* (*pl.* **-ies**) **1** a semi-liquid mixture of fine particles and water; thin mud. **2** thin liquid cement. **3** a fluid form of manure. **4** a residue of water and particles of coal left at pit-head washing plants. [ME, rel. to dial. *slur* thin mud]

slush /slush/ *n.* **1** watery mud or thawing snow. **2** silly sentiment. ▫ **slush fund** reserve funding esp. as used for political bribery. [17th c., also *sludge* and *slutch*: orig. unkn.]
■ **1** see SLUDGE.

slushy /slúshi/ *adj.* (**slushier, slushiest**) **1** like slush; watery. **2** *colloq.* weakly sentimental; insipid. ▫▫ **slushiness** *n.*
■ **1** see SLOPPY 1b. **2** see SENTIMENTAL.

slut /slut/ *n. derog.* a slovenly woman; a slattern; a hussy. ▫▫ **sluttish** *adj.* **sluttishness** *n.* [ME: orig. unkn.]
■ sloven, slattern, trollop; whore, prostitute, streetwalker, lady of the evening, woman of ill repute, loose *or* fallen woman, call-girl, *archaic* harlot, trull, *derog.* jade, hussy, *literary* wanton, *sl.* tart, hooker, hustler, *Austral. sl.* bike, *esp. US sl. derog.* tramp.

sly /slī/ *adj.* (**slyer, slyest**) **1** cunning; crafty; wily. **2 a** (of a person) practising secrecy or stealth. **b** (of an action etc.) done etc. in secret. **3** hypocritical; ironical. **4** knowing; arch; bantering; insinuating. **5** *Austral.* & *NZ sl.* (esp. of liquor) illicit. ▫ **on the sly** privately; covertly; without publicity (*smuggled some through on the sly*). **sly dog** *colloq.* a person who is discreet about mistakes or pleasures. ▫▫ **slyly** *adv.* (also **slily**). **slyness** *n.* [ME *sleh* etc. f. ON *slœgr* cunning, orig. 'able to strike' f. *slóg-* past stem of *slá* strike: cf. SLEIGHT]
■ **1** cunning, artful, crafty, clever, wily, guileful, underhand(ed), deceitful, treacherous, foxy, scheming, plotting, designing, conniving, furtive, shrewd, sneaky, insidious, devious, disingenuous, tricky, sharp, canny, shady, *colloq.* shifty. **2** see STEALTHY. **3** see INSINCERE. **4** knowing, impish, elfish, roguish, mischievous, puckish, devilish, scampish, naughty, arch, waggish. **5** see ILLEGAL 2. ▫ **on the sly** slyly, quietly, surreptitiously, privately, covertly, stealthily, furtively, sneakily, underhandedly, clandestinely, secretly, by stealth, on the side, on the quiet, *colloq.* on the q.t. ▫▫ **slyly** see *on the sly* (SLY) above. **slyness** see STEALTH.

slyboots /slībo͞ots/ *n. colloq.* a sly person.
■ see DEVIL *n.* 3b.

slype /slīp/ *n.* a covered way or passage between a cathedral etc. transept and the chapter house or deanery. [perh. = *slipe* a long narrow piece of ground, = SLIP[2] 1]

SM *abbr.* **1** sadomasochism. **2** Sergeant-Major.

Sm *symb. Chem.* the element samarium.

smack[1] /smak/ *n.*, *v.*, & *adv.* ● *n.* **1** a sharp slap or blow esp. with the palm of the hand or a flat object. **2** a hard hit at cricket etc. **3** a loud kiss (*gave her a hearty smack*). **4** a loud sharp sound (*heard the smack as it hit the floor*). ● *v.* **1** *tr.* strike with the open hand etc. **2** *tr.* part (one's lips) noisily in eager anticipation or enjoyment of food or another delight. **3** *tr.* crack (a whip). **4** *tr.* & *intr.* move, hit, etc., with a smack. ● *adv. colloq.* **1** with a smack. **2** suddenly; directly; violently (*landed smack on my desk*). **3** exactly (*hit it smack in the centre*). ▫ **have a smack at** *colloq.* make an attempt, attack, etc., at. **a smack in the eye** (or **face**) *colloq.* a rebuff; a set-back. [MDu. *smack(en)* of imit. orig.]

■ *n.* **1** see SLAP *n.* **2** see HIT *n.* 1a. **3** see KISS *n.* ● *v.* **1** see SLAP *v.* 1. **4** see HIT *v.* 1a. ● *adv.* **2, 3** see SLAP *adv.* □ **smack in the eye** (or **face**) see *slap in the face.*

smack[2] /smak/ *v.* & *n.* (foll. by *of*) ● *v.intr.* **1** have a flavour of; taste of (*smacked of garlic*). **2** suggest the presence or effects of (*it smacks of nepotism*). ● *n.* **1** a flavour; a taste that suggests the presence of something. **2** (in a person's character etc.) a barely discernible quality (*just a smack of superciliousness*). **3** (in food etc.) a very small amount (*add a smack of ginger*). [OE *smæc*]

■ *v.* **1** taste, savour, have a *or* the flavour. **2** see SUGGEST 2. ● *n.* **1** see TASTE *n.* 1a. **2, 3** see TOUCH *n.* 3.

smack[3] /smak/ *n.* a single-masted sailing-boat for coasting or fishing. [Du. *smak* f. earlier *smacke*; orig. unkn.]

smack[4] /smak/ *n. sl.* a hard drug, esp. heroin, sold or used illegally. [prob. alt. of Yiddish *schmeck* sniff]

smacker /smákkər/ *n. sl.* **1** a loud kiss. **2** a resounding blow. **3 a** *Brit.* £1. **b** *US* $1.

■ **1** see KISS *n.*

small /smawl/ *adj.*, *n.*, & *adv.* ● *adj.* **1** not large or big. **2** slender; thin. **3** not great in importance, amount, number, strength, or power. **4** not much; trifling (*a small token; paid small attention*). **5** insignificant; unimportant (*a small matter; from small beginnings*). **6** consisting of small particles (*small gravel; small shot*). **7** doing something on a small scale (*a small farmer*). **8** socially undistinguished; poor or humble. **9** petty; mean; ungenerous; paltry (*a small spiteful nature*). **10** lacking in imagination (*they have such small minds*). **11** young; not fully grown or developed (*a small child*). ● *n.* **1** the slenderest part of something (esp. *small of the back*). **2** (in *pl.*) *Brit. colloq.* small items of laundry, esp. underwear. ● *adv.* into small pieces (*chop it small*). □ **feel** (or **look**) **small** be humiliated; appear mean or humiliated. **in a small way** unambitiously; on a small scale. **no small** considerable; a good deal of (*no small excitement about it*). **small arms** portable firearms, esp. rifles, pistols, light machine-guns, sub-machine-guns, etc. **small beer 1** a trifling matter; something unimportant. **2** weak beer. **small-bore** (of a firearm) with a narrow bore, in international and Olympic shooting usu. .22 inch calibre (5.6 millimetre bore). **small capital** a capital letter which is of the same dimensions as the lower-case letters in the same typeface minus ascenders and descenders, as THIS. **small change 1** money in the form of coins as opposed to notes. **2** trivial remarks. **small circle** see CIRCLE. **small claims court** *Brit.* a local tribunal in which claims for small amounts can be heard and decided quickly and cheaply without legal representation. **small craft** a general term for small boats and fishing vessels. **small fry 1** young children or the young of various species. **2** small or insignificant things or people. **small hours** the early hours of the morning after midnight. **small intestine** see INTESTINE. **small letter** (in printed material) a lower-case letter. **small mercy** a minor concession, benefit, etc. (*be grateful for small mercies*). **small potatoes** an insignificant person or thing. **small print 1** printed matter in small type. **2** inconspicuous and usu. unfavourable limitations etc. in a contract. **small profits and quick returns** the policy of a cheap shop etc. relying on large trade. **small-scale** made or occurring in small amounts or to a lesser degree. **small screen** television. **small slam** see SLAM[2]. **small-sword** a light tapering thrusting-sword, esp. *hist.* for duelling. **small talk** light social conversation. **small-time** *colloq.* unimportant or petty. **small-timer** *colloq.* a small-time operator; an insignificant person. **small-town** relating to or characteristic of a small town; unsophisticated; provincial. **small wonder** not very surprising. □□ **smallish** *adj.* **smallness** *n.* [OE *smæl* f. Gmc]

■ *adj.* **1** little, tiny, short, diminutive, petite, elfin, lilliputian, midget, miniature, minute, minuscule, baby, pygmy, dwarf, pocket(-sized), mini-, undersized, stunted; poky, compact; *esp. Sc.* wee, *archaic* piccaninny, *colloq.* teeny, teeny-weeny, weeny, pint-sized. **2** see THIN *adj.* 4. **3–5** slight, secondary, insignificant, trivial, inconsequential, lesser, puny, negligible, minor, trifling, nugatory, unimportant, paltry, tiny, little; diminished, limited, reduced. **7, 8** small-scale, small-time, minor; humble, modest, poor, unpretentious, insignificant, undistinguished. **9** skimpy, niggardly, stingy, uncharitable, ungenerous, scanty, meagre, cheap, petty, parsimonious, grudging, stinting, selfish, mean, miserly, tight, tight-fisted, close-fisted, close; paltry, poor, insignificant, inadequate, insufficient, unsatisfactory, negligible, trifling, *colloq.* piddling, measly. **10** unimaginitive, shallow, unoriginal, mundane, everyday, limited, unprofound, uninspired, commonplace, matter-of-fact, flat, two-dimensional. **11** young, immature, under age, baby, undeveloped. ● *n.* **2** (*smalls*) see UNDERCLOTHES. □ **feel** (or **look**) **small** feel embarrassed *or* ashamed *or* shamed *or* humiliated *or* foolish, feel discomfited *or* disconcerted *or* uncomfortable, feel mortified *or* chagrined, *colloq.* feel put down. **small change 1** coins, coppers, silver, cash, specie. **small craft** see BOAT *n.* **small fry 1** see YOUNG *n.* **small potatoes** peanuts, chicken-feed, nothing; see also *triviality* (TRIVIAL). **small print 2** see CONDITION *n.* 1, CATCH *n.* 3b. **small-scale** see LITTLE *adj.* 1, 2, 6, 7. **small talk** see CHAT[1] *n.* 1. **small-time** small, small-scale, unimportant, petty, piddling, minor, insignificant, trifling, trivial. **small-town** see PROVINCIAL *adj.* 2.

smallgoods /smáwlgŏŏdz/ *n. Austral.* delicatessen meats.

smallholder /smáwlhōldər/ *n. Brit.* a person who farms a smallholding.

■ farmer, *Brit. esp hist.* yeoman.

smallholding /smáwlhōlding/ *n. Brit.* an agricultural holding smaller than a farm.

small-minded /smáwlmīndid/ *adj.* petty; of rigid opinions or narrow outlook. □□ **small-mindedly** *adv.* **small-mindedness** *n.*

■ small, petty, selfish, stingy, grudging, niggardly, ungenerous, mean, narrow-minded, close-minded, narrow, uncharitable, hidebound, rigid, intolerant, bigoted, illiberal, prejudiced, unimaginative, short-sighted, myopic, *esp. US* near-sighted.

smallpox /smáwlpoks/ *n. hist.* an acute contagious viral disease, with fever and pustules, usu. leaving permanent scars.

smalt /smolt, smawlt/ *n.* **1** glass coloured blue with cobalt. **2** a pigment made by pulverizing this. [F f. It. *smalto* f. Gmc, rel. to SMELT[1]]

smarm /smaarm/ *v.tr. colloq.* **1** (often foll. by *down*) smooth, plaster down (hair etc.) usu. with cream or oil. **2** flatter fulsomely. [orig. dial. (also *smalm*), of uncert. orig.]

smarmy /smaármi/ *adj.* (**smarmier**, **smarmiest**) *colloq.* ingratiating; flattering; obsequious. □□ **smarmily** *adv.* **smarminess** *n.*

■ see OBSEQUIOUS. □□ **smarminess** see *servility* (SERVILE).

smart /smaart/ *adj.*, *v.*, *n.*, & *adv.* ● *adj.* **1 a** clever; ingenious; quickwitted (*a smart talker; gave a smart answer*). **b** keen in bargaining; quick to take advantage. **c** (of transactions etc.) unscrupulous to the point of dishonesty. **2** well-groomed; neat; bright and fresh in appearance (*a smart suit*). **3** in good repair; showing bright colours, new paint, etc. (*a smart red bicycle*). **4** stylish; fashionable; prominent in society (*in all the smart restaurants; the smart set*). **5** quick; brisk (*set a smart pace*). **6** painfully severe; sharp; vigorous (*a smart blow*). ● *v.intr.* **1** (of a person or a part of the body) feel or give acute pain or distress (*my eye smarts; smarting from the insult*). **2** (of an insult, grievance, etc.) rankle. **3** (foll. by *for*) suffer the consequences of (*you will smart for this*). ● *n.* a bodily or mental sharp pain; a stinging sensation. ● *adv.* smartly; in a smart manner. □ **look smart** make haste. **smart-arse** (or **-ass**) *sl.* = SMART ALEC. **smart-money 1** money paid or exacted as a penalty or compensation. **2** money invested by persons with expert knowledge. □□ **smartingly** *adv.* **smartish** *adj.* & *adv.* **smartly** *adv.* **smartness** *n.* [OE *smeart*, *smeortan*]

■ *adj.* **1 a** intelligent, clever, bright, brilliant, quick-witted, sharp, acute, astute, capable, able, adept, apt, quick, ingenious; pert, pointed, saucy, witty, nimble-witted, poignant, trenchant, effective; canny, perspicacious, perceptive, percipient, discerning, knowledgeable, *au fait*, well-educated, well-read, erudite, learned, well-versed, aware, shrewd, *esp. US* streetwise, *sl.* hip, tuned in, *US sl.* savvy. **2** well-groomed, trim, neat, dapper, spruce, *soigné(e)*, elegant, chic, stylish, *colloq.* snappy, natty, swagger. **3** spick and span, bright, gleaming, shipshape, spotless, shiny. **4** see STYLISH 1, PROMINENT 3. **5** brisk, vigorous, animated, active, energetic, spirited, lively; quick, swift, alert, jaunty, perky, breezy, fast, speedy, spanking, rattling, *colloq.* snappy, *sl.* cracking. **6** severe, stiff, smarting, stinging, sharp, vigorous. ● *v.* **1** sting, hurt, pinch, pain, ache, tingle, prickle, burn, throb, stab, pierce. ● *n.* injury, harm, pain, pang, twinge, affliction, suffering. □ **look smart** see HURRY *v.* 1. □□ **smartness** see INGENUITY, PANACHE.

smart alec /állik/ *n.* (also **aleck, alick**) *colloq.* a person displaying ostentatious or smug cleverness. □□ **smart-alecky** *adj.* [SMART + *Alec*, dimin. of the name *Alexander*]
■ see *wise guy* (WISE[1]).

smarten /smaart'n/ *v.tr.* & *intr.* (usu. foll. by *up*) make or become smart or smarter.
■ see SPRUCE[1] *v.*

smarty /smaarti/ *n.* (*pl.* **-ies**) *colloq.* **1** a know-all; a smart alec. **2** a smartly-dressed person; a member of a smart set. □ **smarty-boots** (or **-pants**) = SMARTY 1. [SMART]
■ **1** see *wise guy.*

smash /smash/ *v., n., & adv.* ● *v.* **1** *tr.* & *intr.* (often foll. by *up*) **a** break into pieces; shatter. **b** bring or come to sudden or complete destruction, defeat, or disaster. **2** *tr.* (foll. by *into, through*) (of a vehicle etc.) move with great force and impact. **3** *tr.* & *intr.* (foll. by *in*) break in with a crushing blow (*smashed in the window*). **4** *tr.* (in tennis, squash, etc.) hit (a ball etc.) with great force, esp. downwards (*smashed it back over the net*). **5** *intr.* (of a business etc.) go bankrupt, come to grief. **6** *tr.* (as **smashed** *adj.*) *sl.* intoxicated. ● *n.* **1** the act or an instance of smashing; a violent fall, collision, or disaster. **2** the sound of this. **3** (in full **smash hit**) a very successful play, song, performer, etc. **4** a stroke in tennis, squash, etc., in which the ball is hit esp. downwards with great force. **5** a violent blow with a fist etc. **6** bankruptcy; a series of commercial failures. **7** a mixture of spirits (usu. brandy) with flavoured water and ice. ● *adv.* with a smash (*fell smash on the floor*). □ **go to smash** be ruined etc. **smash-and-grab** (of a robbery etc.) in which the thief smashes a shop-window and seizes goods. **smash-up** *colloq.* a violent collision; a complete smash. [18th c., prob. imit. after *smack, smite* and *bash, mash*, etc.]
■ *v.* **1a, 3** see SHATTER 1. **1 b** see DESTROY 1, 2. **2** see BUMP *v.* 1, 2. **5** go bankrupt, go under, go to the wall, crash, flounder, collapse, fail, *US colloq.* go belly up. **6** (**smashed**) see DRUNK *adj.* 1. ● *n.* **1** see COLLISION 1. **2** see CRASH[1] *n.* 1a. **3** see HIT *n.* 3. **5** see BLOW[2] 1. □ **smash-up** see COLLISION 1.

smasher /smáshər/ *n.* **1** *colloq.* a very beautiful or pleasing person or thing. **2** a person or thing that smashes.

smashing /smáshing/ *adj. colloq.* superlative; excellent; wonderful; beautiful. □□ **smashingly** *adv.*
■ see EXCELLENT. □□ **smashingly** see *beautifully* (BEAUTIFUL).

smatter /smáttər/ *n.* (also **smattering**) **1** a slight superficial knowledge of a language or subject. **2** esp. *US colloq.* a small quantity; a scattering. □□ **smatterer** *n.* [ME *smatter* talk ignorantly, prate: orig. unkn.]
■ **2** see TOUCH *n.* 3.

smear /smeer/ *v.* & *n.* ● *v.tr.* **1** daub or mark with a greasy or sticky substance or with something that stains. **2** blot; smudge; obscure the outline of (writing, artwork, etc.). **3** defame the character of; slander; attempt to or succeed in discrediting (a person or his name) publicly. ● *n.* **1** the act or an instance of smearing. **2** *Med.* **a** material smeared on a microscopic slide etc. for examination. **b** a specimen of this. □ **smear test** = *cervical smear*. □□ **smearer** *n.* **smeary** *adj.* [OE *smierwan* f. Gmc]
■ *v.* **1** daub, rub, anoint, spread, cover, coat, wipe, plaster, bedaub, dab; besmirch, dirty, smudge, stain, soil, begrime. **2** blot, smudge, blur. **3** blacken, besmirch, smirch, soil, sully, calumniate, slander, discredit, defame, denigrate, tarnish, defile, vilify, scandalize, stigmatize. ● *n.* **1** smudge, daub, stain, blot, taint, spot, blotch, streak, *colloq.* splodge, splotch; slander, scandal, libel, vilification, defamation, calumny, aspersion, reflection.

smegma /smégmə/ *n.* a sebaceous secretion in the folds of the skin, esp. of the foreskin. □□ **smegmatic** /-máttik/ *adj.* [L f. Gk *smēgma -atos* detergent f. *smēkhō* cleanse]

smell /smel/ *n.* & *v.* ● *n.* **1** the faculty of perceiving odours or scents (*has a fine sense of smell*). **2** the quality in substances that is perceived by this (*the smell of thyme; this rose has no smell*). **3** an unpleasant odour. **4** the act of inhaling to ascertain smell. ● *v.* (*past* and *past part.* **smelt** /smelt/ or **smelled**) **1** *tr.* perceive the smell of; examine by smell (*thought I could smell gas*). **2** *intr.* emit odour. **3** *intr.* seem by smell to be (*this milk smells sour*). **4** *intr.* (foll. by *of*) **a** be redolent of (*smells of fish*). **b** be suggestive of (*smells of dishonesty*). **5** *intr.* stink; be rank. **6** *tr.* perceive as if by smell; detect, discern, suspect (*smell a bargain; smell blood*). **7** *intr.* have or use a sense of smell. **8** *intr.* (foll. by *about*) sniff or search about. **9** *intr.* (foll. by *at*) inhale the smell of. □ **smelling-bottle** a small bottle of smelling-salts. **smelling-salts** ammonium carbonate mixed with scent to be sniffed as a restorative in faintness etc. **smell out 1** detect by smell; find out by investigation. **2** (of a dog etc.) hunt out by smell. **smell a rat** begin to suspect trickery etc. □□ **smellable** *adj.* **smeller** *n.* **smell-less** *adj.* [ME *smel(le)*, prob. f. OE]
■ *n.* **2** odour, scent, aroma, perfume, fragrance, bouquet, breath, whiff, redolence. **3** stink, stench, fetor, fetidness, mephitis, effluvium, *Brit. colloq.* pong, hum. ● *v.* **1** scent, sniff, nose (out), get a whiff of, get wind of. **4** (*smell of*) **a** savour of, be redolent of. **b** smack of, savour of, suggest, imply. **5** stink, reek, *Brit. colloq.* pong, hum. **6** see DETECT. □ **smell out** see *track down*. **smell a rat** mistrust, doubt, be suspicious, suspect, have misgivings, have *or* harbour suspicions.

smelly /smélli/ *adj.* (**smellier, smelliest**) having a strong or unpleasant smell. □□ **smelliness** *n.*
■ malodorous, evil-smelling, foul-smelling, foul, mephitic, fetid, putrid, reeky, stinking, rank, offensive, odoriferous, rancid, strong, high, gamy, *archaic* miasmic, miasmatic, miasmal, *colloq.* whiffy, *Brit. colloq.* pongy, *literary* noisome, *Austral. sl.* on the nose.

smelt[1] /smelt/ *v.tr.* **1** extract metal from (ore) by melting. **2** extract (metal) from ore by melting. □□ **smelter** *n.* **smeltery** *n.* (*pl.* **-ies**). [MDu., MLG *smelten*, rel. to MELT]

smelt[2] *past* and *past part.* of SMELL.

smelt[3] /smelt/ *n.* (*pl.* same or **smelts**) any small green and silver fish of the genus *Osmerus* etc. allied to salmon and used as food. [OE, of uncert. orig.: cf. SMOLT]

smew /smyoo/ *n.* a small merganser, *Mergus albellus*. [17th c., rel. to *smeath, smee* = smew, widgeon, etc.]

smidgen /smijən/ *n.* (also **smidgin**) *colloq.* a small bit or amount. [perh. f. *smitch* in the same sense: cf. dial. *smitch* wood-smoke]
■ see BIT[1] 1.

smilax /smīlaks/ *n.* **1** any climbing shrub of the genus *Smilax*, the roots of some species of which yield sarsaparilla. **2** a climbing kind of asparagus, *Asparagus medeoloides*, used decoratively by florists. [L f. Gk, = bindweed]

smile /smīl/ *v.* & *n.* ● *v.* **1** *intr.* relax the features into a pleased or kind or gently sceptical expression or a forced imitation of these, usu. with the lips parted and the corners of the mouth turned up. **2** *tr.* express by smiling (*smiled*

their consent). **3** *tr.* give (a smile) of a specified kind (*smiled a sardonic smile*). **4** *intr.* (foll. by *on, upon*) adopt a favourable attitude towards; encourage (*fortune smiled on me*). **5** *intr.* have a bright or favourable aspect (*the smiling countryside*). **6** *tr.* (foll. by *away*) drive (a person's anger etc.) away (*smiled their tears away*). **7** *intr.* (foll. by *at*) **a** ridicule or show indifference to (*smiled at my feeble attempts*). **b** favour; smile on. **8** *tr.* (foll. by *into, out of*) bring (a person) into or out of a specified mood etc. by smiling (*smiled them into agreement*). ● *n.* **1** the act or an instance of smiling. **2** a smiling expression or aspect. □ **come up smiling** *colloq.* recover from adversity and cheerfully face what is to come. □□ **smileless** *adj.* **smiler** *n.* **smiley** *adj.* **smilingly** *adv.* [ME perh. f. Scand., rel. to SMIRK: cf. OHG *smīlenter*]
■ *v.* **1** grin, beam; smirk, simper, sneer. **4** (*smile on* or *upon*) see FAVOUR *v.* 3b. ● *n.* grin; smirk, simper, sneer.

smirch /smurch/ *v.* & *n.* ● *v.tr.* mark, soil, or smear (a thing, a person's reputation, etc.). ● *n.* **1** a spot or stain. **2** a blot (on one's character etc.). [ME: orig. unkn.]
■ *v.* see MUDDY *v.*, STAIN *v.* 2. ● *n.* **1** see STAIN *n.* 1. **2** see STAIN *n.* 2.

smirk /smurk/ *n.* & *v.* ● *n.* an affected, conceited, or silly smile. ● *v.intr.* put on or wear a smirk. □□ **smirker** *n.* **smirkingly** *adv.* **smirky** *adj.* **smirkily** *adv.* [OE *sme(a)rcian*]
■ *n.* leer, sneer, grin, grimace, simper, simpering smile. ● *v.* sneer, grin, grimace, leer, simper.

smit /smit/ *archaic past part.* of SMITE.

smite /smīt/ *v.* & *n.* ● *v.* (*past* **smote** /smōt/; *past part.* **smitten** /smítt'n/) *archaic* or *literary* **1** *tr.* strike or hit. **2** *tr.* chastise; defeat. **3** *tr.* (in *passive*) **a** have a sudden strong effect on (*was smitten by his conscience*). **b** infatuate, fascinate (*was smitten by her beauty*). **4** *intr.* (foll. by *on, upon*) come forcibly or abruptly upon. ● *n.* a blow or stroke. □□ **smiter** *n.* [OE *smītan* smear f. Gmc]
■ *v.* **1** see HIT *v.* 1a. **3** (*smitten*) **a** affected, afflicted, beset, troubled, distressed, burdened, crushed, plagued, haunted, worried, bothered, vexed, *archaic* stricken. **b** captivated, fascinated, enthralled, struck, bewitched, enchanted, beguiled, charmed, enraptured, infatuated, enamoured, swept off one's feet, besotted, *colloq.* bowled over, *sl.* gaga.

smith /smith/ *n.* & *v.* ● *n.* **1** (esp. in *comb.*) a worker in metal (*goldsmith*; *tinsmith*). **2** a person who forges iron; a blacksmith. **3** a craftsman (*wordsmith*). ● *v.tr.* make or treat by forging. [OE f. Gmc]

smithereens /smíthəreénz/ *n.pl.* (also **smithers** /smíthərz/) small fragments (*smash into smithereens*). [19th c.: orig. unkn.]
■ see FRAGMENT *n.*

smithery /smíthəri/ *n.* (*pl.* **-ies**) **1** a smith's work. **2** (esp. in naval dockyards) a smithy.

smithy /smíthi/ *n.* (*pl.* **-ies**) a blacksmith's workshop; a forge. [ME f. ON *smithja*]

smitten *past part.* of SMITE.

smock /smok/ *n.* & *v.* ● *n.* **1** a loose shirtlike garment with the upper part closely gathered in smocking. **2** (also **smock-frock**) a loose overall, esp. *hist.* a field-labourer's outer linen garment. ● *v.tr.* adorn with smocking. [OE *smoc*, prob. rel. to OE *smūgan* creep, ON *smjúga* put on a garment]
■ *n.* see SHIFT *n.* 4a.

smocking /smókking/ *n.* an ornamental effect on cloth made by gathering the material tightly into pleats, often with stitches in a honeycomb pattern.

smog /smog/ *n.* fog intensified by smoke. □□ **smoggy** *adj.* (**smoggier, smoggiest**). [portmanteau word]
■ see FOG *n.* 1. □□ **smoggy** see THICK *adj.* 6.

smoke /smōk/ *n.* & *v.* ● *n.* **1** a visible suspension of carbon etc. in air, emitted from a burning substance. **2** an act or period of smoking tobacco (*had a quiet smoke*). **3** *colloq.* a cigarette or cigar (*got a smoke?*). **4** (**the Smoke**) *Brit.* & *Austral. colloq.* a big city, esp. London. ● *v.* **1** *intr.* **a** emit smoke or visible vapour (*smoking ruins*). **b** (of a lamp etc.) burn badly with the emission of smoke. **c** (of a chimney or fire) discharge smoke into the room. **2 a** *intr.* inhale and exhale the smoke of a cigarette or cigar or pipe. **b** *intr.* do this habitually. **c** *tr.* use (a cigarette etc.) in this way. **3** *tr.* darken or preserve by the action of smoke (*smoked salmon*). **4** *tr.* spoil the taste of in cooking. **5** *tr.* **a** rid of insects etc. by the action of smoke. **b** subdue (insects, esp. bees) in this way. **6** *tr. archaic* make fun of. **7** *tr.* bring (oneself) into a specified state by smoking. □ **go up in smoke** *colloq.* **1** be destroyed by fire. **2** (of a plan etc.) come to nothing. **no smoke without fire** rumours are not entirely baseless. **smoke-ball 1** a puff-ball. **2** a projectile filled with material emitting dense smoke, used to conceal military operations etc. **smoke bomb** a bomb that emits dense smoke on exploding. **smoke-bush** = *smoke-plant*. **smoked glass** glass darkened with smoke. **smoke-dried** cured in smoke. **smoke-ho** *Austral.* & *NZ colloq.* = SMOKO. **smoke out 1** drive out by means of smoke. **2** drive out of hiding or secrecy etc. **smoke-plant** (or **-tree**) any ornamental shrub of the genus *Cotinus*, with feathery smokelike fruit-stalks. **smoke-ring** smoke from a cigarette etc. exhaled in the shape of a ring. **smoke-room** *Brit.* = SMOKING-ROOM. **smoke-stone** cairngorm. **smoke-tunnel** a form of wind-tunnel using smoke filaments to show the motion of air. □□ **smokable** *adj.* (also **smokeable**). [OE *smoca* f. weak grade of the stem of *smēocan* emit smoke]
■ *n.* **1** see FUME *n.* 1. **3** see CIGARETTE 1. **4** see TOWN 1. ● *v.* **1** see FUME *v.* 1. **2** see PUFF *v.* 2. **3** see PRESERVE *v.* 4a. **6** see JEER *v.* 2. □ **smoke out 2** see LOCATE 1, 3.

smokeless /smṓkliss/ *adj.* having or producing little or no smoke. □ **smokeless zone** a district in which it is illegal to create smoke and where only smokeless fuel may be used.

smoker /smṓkər/ *n.* **1** a person or thing that smokes, esp. a person who habitually smokes tobacco. **2** a compartment on a train, in which smoking is allowed. **3** esp. *US* an informal social gathering of men. □ **smoker's cough** an ailment caused by excessive smoking.

smokescreen /smṓkskreen/ *n.* **1** a cloud of smoke diffused to conceal (esp. military) operations. **2** a device or ruse for disguising one's activities.
■ **2** see COVER *n.* 4.

smokestack /smṓkstak/ *n.* **1** a chimney or funnel for discharging the smoke of a locomotive or steamer. **2** a tall chimney.
■ stack, chimney, chimney-stack, funnel.

smoking-jacket /smṓkingjakkit/ *n.* an ornamental jacket formerly worn by men while smoking.

smoking-room /smṓkingrōōm, -rŏŏm/ *n.* a room in a hotel or house, kept for smoking in.

smoko /smṓkō/ *n.* (*pl.* **-os**) *Austral.* & *NZ colloq.* **1** a stoppage of work for a rest and a smoke. **2** a tea break.

smoky /smṓki/ *adj.* (**smokier, smokiest**) **1** emitting, veiled or filled with, or obscured by, smoke (*smoky fire*; *smoky room*). **2** stained with or coloured like smoke (*smoky glass*). **3** having the taste or flavour of smoked food (*smoky bacon*). □□ **smokily** *adv.* **smokiness** *n.*
■ **1** see THICK *adj.* 6. **2** see GREY *adj.* 1.

smolder *US* var. of SMOULDER.

smolt /smōlt/ *n.* a young salmon migrating to the sea for the first time. [ME (orig. Sc. & N.Engl.): orig. unkn.]

smooch /smōōch/ *n.* & *v. colloq.* ● *n.* **1** *Brit.* a period of slow dancing close together. **2** a spell of kissing and caressing. ● *v.intr.* engage in a smooch. □□ **smoocher** *n.* **smoochy** *adj.* (**smoochier, smoochiest**). [dial. *smouch* imit.]
■ *n.* **2** see KISS *n.* ● *v.* see KISS *v.* 3.

smoodge /smōōj/ *v.intr.* (also **smooge**) *Austral.* & *NZ* **1** behave in a fawning or ingratiating manner. **2** behave amorously. [prob. var. of dial. *smudge* kiss, sidle up to, beg in a sneaking way]
■ **1** see TRUCKLE *v.* **2** see PET[1] *v.* 2.

smooth /smōōth/ *adj.*, *v.*, *n.*, & *adv.* ● *adj.* **1** having a relatively even and regular surface; free from perceptible projections, lumps, indentations, and roughness. **2** not wrinkled, pitted, scored, or hairy (*smooth skin*). **3** that can be traversed without check. **4** (of liquids) of even consistency; without lumps (*mix to a smooth paste*). **5** (of the sea etc.) without waves or undulations. **6** (of a journey, passage, progress, etc.) untroubled by difficulties or adverse conditions. **7** having an easy flow or correct rhythm (*smooth breathing*; *a smooth metre*). **8 a** not harsh in sound or taste. **b** (of wine etc.) not astringent. **9** (of a person, his or her manner, etc.) suave, conciliatory, flattering, unruffled, or polite (*a smooth talker*; *he's very smooth*). **10** (of movement etc.) not suddenly varying; not jerky. ● *v.* **1** *tr.* & *intr.* (often foll. by *out, down*) make or become smooth. **2** (often foll. by *out, down, over, away*) **a** *tr.* reduce or get rid of (differences, faults, difficulties, etc.) in fact or appearance. **b** *intr.* (of difficulties etc.) diminish, become less obtrusive (*it will all smooth over*). **3** *tr.* modify (a graph, curve, etc.) so as to lessen irregularities. **4** *tr.* free from impediments or discomfort (*smooth the way*; *smooth the declining years*). ● *n.* **1** a smoothing touch or stroke (*gave his hair a smooth*). **2** the easy part of life (*take the rough with the smooth*). ● *adv.* smoothly (*the course of true love never did run smooth*). □ **in smooth water** having passed obstacles or difficulties. **smooth-bore** a gun with an unrifled barrel. **smooth-faced** hypocritically friendly. **smoothing-iron** *hist.* a flat-iron. **smoothing-plane** a small plane for finishing the planing of wood. **smooth muscle** a muscle without striations, usu. occurring in hollow organs and performing involuntary functions. **smooth talk** *colloq.* bland specious language. **smooth-talk** *v.tr.* address or persuade with this. **smooth-tongued** insincerely flattering. □□ **smoothable** *adj.* **smoother** *n.* **smoothish** *adj.* **smoothly** *adv.* **smoothness** *n.* [OE *smōth*]

■ *adj.* **1** regular, even, flush, flat, level, plane; unbroken. **2** unwrinkled, uniform, slick, sleek, shiny, glossy, glassy, mirror-like, polished, burnished; silky, silken, velvety, satiny; hairless, bald, bare, naked, clean-shaven, smooth-shaven, smooth-skinned, depilated, glabrous. **4** creamy, flowing. **5** calm, serene, tranquil, peaceful, glassy, flat, still, unruffled, unbroken, undisturbed. **6** unobstructed, easy, effortless, free, uncluttered, even, steady, orderly, well-ordered, uneventful, flowing, unconstrained, uninterrupted. **8 a** sweet, dulcet, mellow, well-modulated, silver-tongued. **b** mellow, pleasant, mild, suave. **9** suave, slippery, unctuous, silken, silky, glib, urbane, *soigné*, agreeable, winning, facile, nonchalant, unruffled, courtly, eloquent, smooth-spoken, smooth-tongued, persuasive, flattering, oily, slimy, syrupy, conciliatory; scheming, conniving, crafty, shrewd, cunning, tricky, sly, foxy, machiavellian, sophistic(al), plausible, credible, believable, *colloq.* slick, shifty, smarmy. **10** see GRACEFUL. ● *v.* **1** flatten, even, level, iron, press, calender, *esp. Brit. hist.* mangle; sand, plane, polish, buff, burnish. **2 a** assuage, allay, calm, gloss over, minimize, mitigate, lessen, soothe, reduce, temper, mollify, soften, palliate, appease, *formal* ameliorate. **4** prepare, lay, pave, ease, ready, clear, open, prime, lubricate, facilitate. □ **smooth-tongued** see SMOOTH *adj.* 9 above. □□ **smoothly** see EASILY 1. **smoothness** see FLUENCY, SAVOIR FAIRE.

smoothie /smōōthi/ *n. colloq.* a person who is smooth (see SMOOTH *adj.* 9). [SMOOTH]

■ see *charmer* (CHARM).

smorgasbord /smórgəsbord/ *n.* open sandwiches served with delicacies as hors-d'œuvres or a buffet. [Sw. f. *smör* butter + *gås* goose, lump of butter + *bord* table]

■ see HORS-D'ŒUVRE.

smorzando /smortsándō/ *adj., adv.,* & *n. Mus.* ● *adj.* & *adv.* dying away. ● *n.* (*pl.* **-os** or **smorzandi** /-di/) a smorzando passage. [It., gerund of *smorzare* extinguish]

smote *past* of SMITE.

smother /smúthər/ *v.* & *n.* ● *v.* **1** *tr.* suffocate; stifle; kill by stopping the breath of or excluding air from. **2** *tr.* (foll. by *with*) overwhelm with (kisses, gifts, kindness, etc.) (*smothered with affection*). **3** *tr.* (foll. by *in, with*) cover entirely in or with (*chicken smothered in mayonnaise*). **4** *tr.* extinguish or deaden (a fire or flame) by covering it or heaping it with ashes etc. **5** *intr.* **a** die of suffocation. **b** have difficulty breathing. **6** *tr.* (often foll. by *up*) suppress or conceal; keep from notice or publicity. **7** *tr. US* defeat rapidly or utterly. ● *n.* **1** a cloud of dust or smoke. **2** obscurity caused by this. □ **smothered mate** *Chess* checkmate in which the king, having no vacant square to move to, is checkmated by a knight. [ME *smorther* f. the stem of OE *smorian* suffocate]

■ *v.* **1** suffocate, stifle, choke, asphyxiate. **2, 3** overwhelm, overcome, blanket, inundate, shower, drench; cover, envelop, wrap, surround, *literary* enshroud. **4** extinguish, put out, snuff out, quench, deaden. **5 a** suffocate, be suffocated *or* stifled *or* asphyxiated, be choked. **6** repress, subdue, suppress, conceal, hide, keep *or* hold back, cover up, mask, choke back *or* down, check; stifle, muffle, blanket, blank out; silence.

smothery /smúthəri/ *adj.* tending to smother; stifling.

smoulder /smṓldər/ *v.* & *n.* (*US* **smolder**) ● *v.intr.* **1** burn slowly with smoke but without a flame; slowly burn internally or invisibly. **2** (of emotions etc.) exist in a suppressed or concealed state. **3** (of a person) show silent or suppressed anger, hatred, etc. ● *n.* a smouldering or slow-burning fire. [ME, rel. to LG *smöln*, MDu. *smölen*]

■ *v.* **1** burn, smoke. **2, 3** burn, seethe, simmer, chafe, rage, fume, foam, boil, stew, fester; get hot under the collar, see red, *colloq.* get (all) steamed up, *US sl.* get (all) burned up.

smriti /smrítti/ *n.* Hindu traditional teachings on religion etc. [Skr. *smṛti* remembrance]

smudge[1] /smuj/ *n.* & *v.* ● *n.* **1** a blurred or smeared line or mark; a blot; a smear of dirt. **2** a stain or blot on a person's character etc. ● *v.* **1** *tr.* make a smudge on. **2** *intr.* become smeared or blurred (*smudges easily*). **3** *tr.* smear or blur the lines of (writing, drawing, etc.) (*smudge the outline*). **4** *tr.* defile, sully, stain, or disgrace (a person's name, character, etc.). □□ **smudgeless** *adj.* [ME: orig. unkn.]

■ *n.* **1** see BLOT *n.* 1. **2** see STAIN *n.* 2. ● *v.* **1–3** see SMEAR *v.* 1, 2.

smudge[2] /smuj/ *n. US* an outdoor fire with dense smoke made to keep off insects, protect plants against frost, etc. □ **smudge-pot** a container holding burning material that produces a smudge. [*smudge* (v.) cure (herring) by smoking (16th c.: orig. unkn.)]

smudgy /smúji/ *adj.* (**smudgier, smudgiest**) **1** smudged. **2** likely to produce smudges. □□ **smudgily** *adv.* **smudginess** *n.*

smug /smug/ *adj.* (**smugger, smuggest**) self-satisfied; complacent. □□ **smugly** *adv.* **smugness** *n.* [16th c., orig. 'neat' f. LG *smuk* pretty]

■ self-satisfied, complacent, holier-than-thou, self-important, self-righteous, overconfident, conceited, *colloq.* slick. □□ **smugness** see PRIDE *n.* 2.

smuggle /smúgg'l/ *v.tr.* **1** (also *absol.*) import or export (goods) illegally esp. without payment of customs duties. **2** (foll. by *in, out*) convey secretly. **3** (foll. by *away*) put into concealment. □□ **smuggler** *n.* **smuggling** *n.* [17th c. (also *smuckle*) f. LG *smukkeln smuggelen*]

■ **1, 2** see RUN *v.* 24.

smut /smut/ *n.* & *v.* ● *n.* **1** a small flake of soot etc. **2** a spot or smudge made by this. **3** obscene or lascivious talk, pictures, or stories. **4 a** a fungous disease of cereals in which parts of the ear change to black powder. **b** any fungus of the order Ustilaginales causing this. ● *v.* (**smutted, smutting**) **1** *tr.* mark with smuts. **2** *tr.* infect (a plant) with smut. **3** *intr.* (of a plant) contract smut. □ **smut-ball** *Agriculture* grain affected by smut. **smut-mill** a machine for freeing grain from smut. □□ **smutty** *adj.* (**smuttier, smuttiest**) (esp. in sense 3 of *n.*). **smuttily** *adv.* **smuttiness** *n.* [rel. to LG *smutt*, MHG *smutz(en)* etc.: cf. OE *smitt(ian)* smear, and SMUDGE[1]]

■ *n.* **3** see DIRT 3. **4** see MOULD[2]. □□ **smutty** see OBSCENE 1. **smuttiness** see RIBALDRY.

Sn *symb. Chem.* the element tin.

snack /snak/ *n.* & *v.* ● *n.* **1** a light, casual, or hurried meal. **2** a small amount of food eaten between meals. **3** *Austral. sl.* something easy to accomplish. ● *v.intr.* eat a snack. □ **snack bar** a place where snacks are sold. [ME, orig. a snap or bite, f. MDu. *snac(k)* f. *snacken* (v.), var. of *snappen*]

■ *n.* **1, 2** bite, nibble, morsel, titbit, refreshment(s), *Ind.* tiffin, *Brit. colloq.* elevenses, tuck, *US sl.* nosh. **3** see PUSHOVER 1. ● *v.* nibble, pick, *US sl.* nosh.

snaffle /snáff'l/ *n.* & *v.* ● *n.* (in full **snaffle-bit**) a simple bridle-bit without a curb and usu. with a single rein. ● *v.tr.* **1** put a snaffle on. **2** *colloq.* steal; seize; appropriate. [prob. f. LG or Du.: cf. MLG, MDu. *snavel* beak, mouth]

■ *v.* **2** see APPROPRIATE *v.* 1.

snafu /snafóo/ *adj.* & *n. sl.* ● *adj.* in utter confusion or chaos. ● *n.* this state. [acronym for '*s*ituation *n*ormal: *a*ll *f*ouled (or *f*ucked) *u*p']

■ *adj.* see *confused* (CONFUSE 5). ● *n.* see CHAOS *n.* 1a.

snag[1] /snag/ *n.* & *v.* ● *n.* **1** an unexpected or hidden obstacle or drawback. **2** a jagged or projecting point or broken stump. **3** a tear in material etc. **4** a short tine of an antler. ● *v.tr.* (**snagged, snagging**) **1** catch or tear on a snag. **2** clear (land, a waterway, a tree-trunk, etc.) of snags. **3** *US* catch or obtain by quick action. □□ **snagged** *adj.* **snaggy** *adj.* [prob. f. Scand.: cf. Norw. dial. *snag(e)* sharp point]

■ *n.* **1** hitch, catch, problem, (stumbling-)block, stricture, bottleneck, complication, obstacle, impediment, obstruction, hindrance, difficulty, drawback, *sl.* hang-up. ● *v.* **1** catch, tear, rip.

snag[2] /snag/ *n.* (usu. in *pl.*) *Austral. sl.* a sausage. [20th c.: orig. unkn.]

snaggle-tooth /snágg'l/ *n.* (*pl.* **snaggle-teeth**) an irregular or projecting tooth. □□ **snaggle-toothed** *adj.* [SNAG[1] + -LE[2]]

snail /snayl/ *n.* **1** any slow-moving gastropod mollusc with a spiral shell able to enclose the whole body. **2** a slow or lazy person; a dawdler. □ **snail's pace** a very slow movement. □□ **snail-like** *adj.* [OE *snæg(e)l* f. Gmc]

■ **2** see LAGGARD *n.* □□ **snail-like** see SLOW *adj.* 1.

snake /snayk/ *n.* & *v.* ● *n.* **1 a** any long limbless reptile of the suborder Ophidia, including boas, pythons, and poisonous forms such as cobras and vipers. **b** a limbless lizard or amphibian. **2** (also **snake in the grass**) a treacherous person or secret enemy. **3** (prec. by *the*) a system of interconnected exchange rates for the EC currencies. ● *v.intr.* move or twist like a snake. □ **snake bird** a fish-eating bird, *Anhinga anhinga*, with a long slender neck. **snake-charmer** a person appearing to make snakes move by music etc. **snake-pit 1** a pit containing snakes. **2** a scene of vicious behaviour. **snakes and ladders** a game with counters moved along a board with advances up 'ladders' or returns down 'snakes' depicted on the board. **snake's head** a bulbous plant, *Fritillaria meleagris*, with bell-shaped pendent flowers. □□ **snakelike** *adj.* [OE *snaca*]

■ *n.* **1a** reptile, ophidian, viper, cobra, boa, python, *usu. literary* serpent. **2** viper, serpent, traitor, turncoat, Judas, quisling, betrayer, double-crosser, informer, rat, *esp. US sl.* ratfink, *US sl.* fink. ● *v.* slither, glide, creep, crawl, worm, wriggle; twist, wind, curve, bend, turn, zigzag, wander, loop, coil, crook, meander. □□ **snakelike** see SERPENTINE *adj.* 2.

snakeroot /snáykroot/ *n.* any of various N. American plants, esp. *Cimicifuga racemosa*, with roots reputed to contain an antidote to snake's poison.

snaky /snáyki/ *adj.* **1** of or like a snake. **2** winding; sinuous. **3** showing coldness, ingratitude, venom, or guile. **4 a** infested with snakes. **b** (esp. of the hair of the Furies) composed of snakes. **5** *Austral. sl.* angry; irritable. □□ **snakily** *adv.* **snakiness** *n.*

snap /snap/ *v.*, *n.*, *adv.*, & *adj.* ● *v.* (**snapped, snapping**) **1** *intr.* & *tr.* break suddenly or with a snap. **2** *intr.* & *tr.* emit or cause to emit a sudden sharp sound or crack. **3** *intr.* & *tr.* open or close with a snapping sound (*the bag snapped shut*). **4 a** *intr.* (often foll. by *at*) speak irritably or spitefully (to a person) (*did not mean to snap at you*). **b** *tr.* say irritably or spitefully. **5** *intr.* (often foll. by *at*) (esp. of a dog etc.) make a sudden audible bite. **6** *tr.* & *intr.* move quickly (*snap into action*). **7** *tr.* take a snapshot of. **8** *tr. Amer. Football* put (the ball) into play on the ground by a quick backward movement. ● *n.* **1** an act or sound of snapping. **2** a crisp biscuit or cake (*brandy snap*; *ginger snap*). **3** a snapshot. **4** (in full **cold snap**) a sudden brief spell of cold weather. **5** *Brit.* **a** a card-game in which players call 'snap' when two similar cards are exposed. **b** (as *int.*) on noticing the (often unexpected) similarity of two things. **6** crispness of style; fresh vigour or liveliness in action; zest; dash; spring. **7** *US sl.* an easy task (*it was a snap*). ● *adv.* with the sound of a snap (*heard it go snap*). ● *adj.* done or taken on the spur of the moment, unexpectedly, or without notice (*snap decision*). □ **snap at** accept (bait, a chance, etc.) eagerly (see also senses 4a and 5 of *v.*). **snap bean** *US* a bean grown for its pods which are broken into pieces and eaten. **snap-bolt** (or **-lock**) a bolt etc. which locks automatically when a door or window closes. **snap-brim** (of a hat) with a brim that can be turned up and down at opposite sides. **snap-fastener** = *press-stud* (see PRESS[1]). **snap one's fingers 1** make an audible fillip, esp. in rhythm to music etc. **2** (often foll. by *at*) defy; show contempt for. **snap-hook** (or **-link**) a hook or link with a spring allowing the entrance but barring the escape of a cord, link, etc. **snap off** break off or bite off. **snap off a person's head** address a person angrily or rudely. **snap out** say irritably. **snap out of** *sl.* get rid of (a mood, habit, etc.) by a sudden effort. **snapping turtle** any large American freshwater turtle of the family Chelydridae which seizes prey with a snap of its jaws. **snap up 1** accept (an offer, a bargain) quickly or eagerly. **2** pick up or catch hastily or smartly. **3** interrupt (another person) before he or she has finished speaking. □□ **snappable** *adj.* **snappingly** *adv.* [prob. f. MDu. or MLG *snappen*, partly imit.]

■ *v.* **1** break (off), separate, crack; split, fracture, give way, part, *literary* cleave. **2, 3** click; pop; crack. **4** (*snap at*) **a** attack, lunge at, lash out at, snarl at, growl at, bark at, be brusque *or* short *or* curt with, snap off a person's head, *colloq.* jump down a person's throat, fly off the handle at. **5** (*snap at*) bite at, nip, gnash at, snatch at. **6** jump, leap; see also SPRING *v.* 1. **7** shoot, photograph, catch. ● *n.* **1** crack, crackle, pop, click. **3** snapshot, photograph, photo, picture. **4** spell, period, interval, wave. **6** energy, vigour, animation, liveliness, vitality, bounce, spring, alertness, sprightliness, *élan*, dash, sparkle, verve, zip, zest, *colloq.* zing, get-up-and-go, pep, *sl.* pizazz. **7** easy job, *colloq.* cinch, pushover, picnic, *esp. US colloq.* breeze, *sl.* snip, *Austral. sl.* snack. ● *adj.* abrupt, sudden, precipitate, hurried, hasty, incautious, rash, unpremeditated, unplanned, not well-thought-out, quick, instantaneous, instant. □ **snap at** see *snap up* below. **snap-fastener** press-stud, fastener, fastening, clasp. **snap one's fingers 2** (*snap one's fingers at*) disdain, scorn, flout, dismiss, disregard, ignore, defy, mock, deride, thumb one's nose at, *literary* contemn, *sl.* cock a snook at. **snap off a person's head** see SNAP *v.* 4 above. **snap out of** get rid of, shake off; (*snap out of it*) recover, come round *or* around, revive, awaken, wake up, perk up, liven up, cheer up, rally; get a grip on *or* of oneself, get (a) hold on *or* of oneself, pull oneself together, (re)gain control of oneself. **snap up 1, 2** accept, snap at, grab (up), snatch (up), seize, pluck, pounce on *or* upon, make off with, take (away), capture, catch, get, secure.

snapdragon /snápdraggən/ *n.* a plant, *Antirrhinum majus*, with a bag-shaped flower like a dragon's mouth.

snapper /snáppər/ *n.* **1** a person or thing that snaps. **2** any of several fish of the family Lutjanidae, used as food. **3** a snapping turtle. **4** *US* a cracker (as a toy).

snappish /snáppish/ *adj.* **1** (of a person's manner or a remark) curt; ill-tempered; sharp. **2** (of a dog etc.) inclined to snap. □□ **snappishly** *adv.* **snappishness** *n.*
■ **1** curt, short, abrupt, brusque, curmudgeonly, cantankerous, sharp, cross, grouchy, gruff, crusty, crabby, crabbed, acid, tart, acerbic, churlish, dyspeptic, choleric, splenetic, ill-humoured, ill-tempered, temperamental, moody, short-tempered, testy, petulant, peevish, irritable, prickly, touchy, irascible, quick to anger, quick-tempered, hot-tempered, waspish, *esp. US* cranky, *colloq.* snappy.

snappy /snáppi/ *adj.* (**snappier**, **snappiest**) *colloq.* **1** brisk, full of zest. **2** neat and elegant (*a snappy dresser*). **3** snappish. □ **make it snappy** be quick about it. □□ **snappily** *adv.* **snappiness** *n.*
■ **1** quick, sharp, brisk, smart, crisp, rapid, speedy, lively, energetic, vigorous. **2** fashionable, chic, sharp, smart, stylish, dapper, modish, *colloq.* natty, *colloq. often derog.* trendy. **3** see SNAPPISH.

snapshot /snápshot/ *n.* a casual photograph taken quickly with a small hand-camera.
■ see PHOTOGRAPH *n.*

snare /snair/ *n.* & *v.* ● *n.* **1** a trap for catching birds or animals, esp. with a noose of wire or cord. **2** a thing that acts as a temptation. **3** a device for tempting an enemy etc. to expose himself or herself to danger, failure, loss, capture, defeat, etc. **4** (in *sing.* or *pl.*) *Mus.* twisted strings of gut, hide, or wire stretched across the lower head of a side-drum to produce a rattling sound. **5** (in full **snare drum**) a drum fitted with snares. **6** *Surgery* a wire loop for extracting polyps etc. ● *v.tr.* **1** catch (a bird etc.) in a snare. **2** ensnare; lure or trap (a person) with a snare. □□ **snarer** *n.* (also in *comb.*). [OE *sneare* f. ON *snara*: senses 4 & 5 prob. f. MLG or MDu.]
■ *n.* **1** trap, net, springe, noose, gin, booby trap, pitfall, *US* deadfall. **2** see TEMPTATION 2. ● *v.* trap, catch, entrap, seize, capture, ensnare; net, bag, hook; lure, decoy.

snark /snaark/ *n.* a fabulous animal, orig. the subject of a nonsense poem. [*The Hunting of the Snark* (1876) by Lewis Carroll]

snarl[1] /snaarl/ *v.* & *n.* ● *v.* **1** *intr.* (of a dog) make an angry growl with bared teeth. **2** *intr.* (of a person) speak cynically; make bad-tempered complaints or criticisms. **3** *tr.* (often foll. by *out*) **a** utter in a snarling tone. **b** express (discontent etc.) by snarling. ● *n.* the act or sound of snarling. □□ **snarler** *n.* **snarlingly** *adv.* **snarly** *adj.* (**snarlier**, **snarliest**). [earlier *snar* f. (M)LG, MHG *snarren*]
■ *v.* **1, 3** growl; snap. **2** see COMPLAIN 1, 2b, CARP[2]. ● *n.* growl.

snarl[2] /snaarl/ *v.* & *n.* ● *v.* **1** *tr.* (often foll. by *up*) twist; entangle; confuse and hamper the movement of (traffic etc.). **2** *intr.* (often foll. by *up*) become entangled, congested, or confused. **3** *tr.* adorn the exterior of (a narrow metal vessel) with raised work. ● *n.* a knot or tangle. □ **snarling iron** an implement used for snarling metal. **snarl-up** *colloq.* a traffic jam; a muddle; a mistake. [ME f. *snare* (n. & v.): sense 3 perh. f. noun in dial. sense 'knot in wood']
■ *v.* **1** tangle, entangle, complicate, confuse; impede, hinder, hamper, obstruct; scramble, muddle, twist, mix *or* mess up, *sl.* screw up. **2** tangle, entangle, knot, twist, ravel, jam, kink. ● *n.* knot, tangle, entanglement, snag, jungle, maze, labyrinth. □ **snarl-up** jam, hold-up, hitch, blockage; complexity, snag, problem, difficulty, complication, muddle, mess, predicament, fix, quandary, tight spot, *disp.* dilemma; mix-up, mistake, bungle; *colloq.* pickle.

snatch /snach/ *v.* & *n.* ● *v.tr.* **1** seize quickly, eagerly, or unexpectedly, esp. with outstretched hands. **2** steal (a wallet, handbag, etc.); kidnap. **3** secure with difficulty (*snatched an hour's rest*). **4** (foll. by *away*, *from*) take away or from esp. suddenly (*snatched away my hand*). **5** (foll. by *from*) rescue narrowly (*snatched from the jaws of death*). **6** (foll. by *at*) **a** try to seize by stretching or grasping suddenly. **b** take (an offer etc.) eagerly. ● *n.* **1** an act of snatching (*made a snatch at it*). **2** a fragment of a song or talk etc. (*caught a snatch of their conversation*). **3** *US sl.* a kidnapping. **4** (in weight-lifting) the rapid raising of a weight from the floor to above the head. **5** a short spell of activity etc. □ **in** (or **by**) **snatches** in fits and starts. □□ **snatcher** *n.* (esp. in sense 3 of *n.*). **snatchy** *adj.* [ME *snecchen*, *sna(c)che*, perh. rel. to SNACK]
■ *v.* **1, 3** grab, grasp, seize, clasp, clutch, pluck, take (hold of), catch, lay hold of, wrest, latch on to, capture, snap up, win, get, lay *or* get one's hands on. **2** see PILFER, KIDNAP. **5** save, rescue, deliver; remove. **6 b** see *jump at*. ● *n.* **1** grab, clutch, grasp. **2** scrap, bit, fragment, snippet, segment, morsel; specimen, sample.

snavel /snávv'l/ *v.tr.* (also **snavle**, **snavvle**) *Austral. sl.* catch; take; steal. [E dial. (as SNAFFLE)]

snazzy /snázzi/ *adj.* (**snazzier**, **snazziest**) *sl.* smart or attractive esp. in an ostentatious way. □□ **snazzily** *adv.* **snazziness** *n.* [20th c.: orig. unkn.]
■ see STYLISH 1.

sneak /sneek/ *v.*, *n.*, & *adj.* ● *v.* **1** *intr.* & *tr.* (foll. by *in*, *out*, *past*, *away*, etc.) go or convey furtively; slink. **2** *tr. sl.* steal unobserved; make off with. **3** *intr. Brit. school sl.* tell tales; turn informer. **4** *intr.* (as **sneaking** *adj.*) **a** furtive; undisclosed (*have a sneaking affection for him*). **b** persistent in one's mind; nagging (*a sneaking feeling that it is not right*). ● *n.* **1** a mean-spirited cowardly underhand person. **2** *Brit. school sl.* a tell-tale. ● *adj.* acting or done without warning; secret (*a sneak attack*). □ **sneak-thief** a thief who steals without breaking in; a pickpocket. □□ **sneakingly** *adv.* [16th c., prob. dial.: perh. rel. to ME *snike*, OE *snīcan* creep]
■ *v.* **1** lurk, slink, steal, creep, skulk, cower, pad, prowl, sidle, slip, pussyfoot, tiptoe; smuggle. **2** see STEAL *v.* 1. **3** see INFORM 2. **4** (**sneaking**) **a** innate, intuitive, inherent, private, secret, furtive, suppressed, hidden, unexpressed, undeclared, unvoiced, unavowed, unconfessed, unrevealed, unadmitted, undivulged, undisclosed, covert. **b** persistent, lingering, lurking, nagging, worrying, worrisome, niggling, intuitive, deep-rooted, deep-seated, gut. ● *n.* **2** informer, tell-tale, talebearer, stool-pigeon, *US* tattle-tale, *sl.* snitch, *Brit. sl.* grass, nark, *esp. US sl.* ratfink, *US sl.* fink, stoolie, *US* & *Austral. sl.* dog.

sneaker /sneékər/ *n. sl.* each of a pair of soft-soled canvas etc. shoes.
■ see PLIMSOLL.

sneaky /sneéki/ *adj.* (**sneakier**, **sneakiest**) given to or characterized by sneaking; furtive, mean. □□ **sneakily** *adv.* **sneakiness** *n.*
■ underhand(ed), devious, furtive, sly, slippery, stealthy, disingenuous, deceitful, dishonest, unscrupulous, treacherous, crafty, mean, low-down, *colloq.* shifty. □□ **sneakily** see *in private* (PRIVATE). **sneakiness** see STEALTH.

sneck /snek/ *n.* & *v. Sc.* & *N.Engl.* ● *n.* a latch. ● *v.tr.* latch (a door etc.); close or fasten with a sneck. [ME, rel. to SNATCH]

sneer /sneer/ *n.* & *v.* ● *n.* a derisive smile or remark. ● *v.* **1** *intr.* (often foll. by *at*) smile derisively. **2** *tr.* say sneeringly. **3** *intr.* (often foll. by *at*) speak derisively esp. covertly or ironically (*sneered at his attempts*). □□ **sneerer** *n.* **sneeringly** *adv.* [16th c.: orig. unkn.]
■ *n.* jeer, scoff, boo, hiss, hoot, gibe, taunt. ● *v.* **1** smirk, curl one's lip. **3** (*sneer at*) scorn, disdain, despise, sniff at, scoff at, jeer at, laugh at, deride, mock, ridicule; underrate, pooh-pooh, *literary* contemn; *colloq.* turn up one's nose at, *sl.* knock.

sneeze /sneez/ *n.* & *v.* ● *n.* **1** a sudden involuntary expulsion of air from the nose and mouth caused by irritation of the nostrils. **2** the sound of this. ● *v.intr.* make a sneeze. □ **not to be sneezed at** *colloq.* not contemptible; considerable; notable. □□ **sneezer** *n.* **sneezy** *adj.* [ME *snese*, app. alt. of obs. *fnese* f. OE *-fnēsan*, ON *fnýsa* & replacing earlier and less expressive *nese*]

sneezewort /snéezwurt/ *n.* a kind of yarrow, *Achillea ptarmica*, whose dried leaves are used to induce sneezing.

Snell's law /snelz/ *n. Physics* the law that the ratio of the sines of the angles of incidence and refraction of a wave are constant when it passes between two given media. [W. *Snell*, Du. mathematician d. 1626]

snib /snib/ *v.* & *n. Sc.* & *Ir.* • *v.tr.* (**snibbed, snibbing**) bolt, fasten, or lock (a door etc.). • *n.* a lock, catch, or fastening for a door or window. [19th c.: orig. uncert.]

snick /snik/ *v.* & *n.* • *v.tr.* **1** cut a small notch in. **2** make a small incision in. **3** *Cricket* deflect (the ball) slightly with the bat. • *n.* **1** a small notch or cut. **2** *Cricket* a slight deflection of the ball by the bat. [18th c.: prob. f. *snick-a-snee* fight with knives]

snicker /sníkkər/ *v.* & *n.* • *v.intr.* **1** = SNIGGER *v.* **2** whinny, neigh. • *n.* **1** = SNIGGER *n.* **2** a whinny, a neigh. □□ **snickeringly** *adv.* [imit.]

▪ *v.* **2** whinny, neigh, bray. • *n.* **2** whinny, neigh, bray.

snicket /sníkkit/ *n. dial.* a narrow passage between houses; an alleyway. [orig. unkn.]

snide /snīd/ *adj.* & *n.* • *adj.* **1** sneering; slyly derogatory; insinuating. **2** counterfeit; bogus. **3** *US* mean; underhand. • *n.* a snide person or remark. □□ **snidely** *adv.* **snideness** *n.* [19th-c. colloq.: orig. unkn.]

▪ *adj.* **1** see SCORNFUL. **3** see SLY 1.

sniff /snif/ *v.* & *n.* • *v.* **1** *intr.* draw up air audibly through the nose to stop it running or to detect a smell or as an expression of contempt. **2** *tr.* (often foll. by *up*) draw in (a scent, drug, liquid, or air) through the nose. **3** *tr.* draw in the scent of (food, drink, flowers, etc.) through the nose. • *n.* **1** an act or sound of sniffing. **2** the amount of air etc. sniffed up. □ **sniff at 1** try the smell of; show interest in. **2** show contempt for or discontent with. **sniff out** detect; discover by investigation. □□ **sniffingly** *adv.* [ME, imit.]

▪ *v.* **1** snivel, sniffle, snuffle. **2** snuff, draw in, breathe in, inhale, *sl.* snort. **3** smell, scent, nose (out). • *n.* **1** sniffle, snuffle. **2** whiff, breath, odour, scent. □ **sniff at 2** see SNEER *v.* 3. **sniff out** see DETECT *v.*

sniffer /sníffər/ *n.* **1** a person who sniffs, esp. one who sniffs a drug or toxic substances (often in *comb.*: *glue-sniffer*). **2** *sl.* the nose. **3** *colloq.* any device for detecting gas, radiation, etc. □ **sniffer-dog** *colloq.* a dog trained to sniff out drugs or explosives.

sniffle /sníff'l/ *v.* & *n.* • *v.intr.* sniff slightly or repeatedly. • *n.* **1** the act of sniffling. **2** (in *sing.* or *pl.*) a cold in the head causing a running nose and sniffling. □□ **sniffler** *n.* **sniffly** *adj.* [imit.: cf. SNIVEL]

▪ *v.* sniff, snivel, snuffle. • *n.* **1** sniff, snuffle.

sniffy /sníffi/ *adj. colloq.* (**sniffier, sniffiest**) **1** inclined to sniff. **2** disdainful; contemptuous. □□ **sniffily** *adv.* **sniffiness** *n.*

snifter /sníftər/ *n.* **1** *sl.* a small drink of alcohol. **2** *US* a balloon glass for brandy. □ **snifter-valve** a valve in a steam engine to allow air in or out. [dial. *snift* sniff, perh. f. Scand.: imit.]

▪ **1** see DRINK *n.* 2b.

snig /snig/ *v.tr.* (**snigged, snigging**) *Austral.* & *NZ* drag with a jerk. □ **snigging chain** a chain used to move logs. [E dial.]

snigger /sníggər/ *n.* & *v.* • *n.* a half-suppressed secretive laugh. • *v.intr.* utter such a laugh. □□ **sniggerer** *n.* **sniggeringly** *adv.* [var. of SNICKER]

▪ *n.* snicker, chuckle, giggle, tee-hee, titter; laugh. • *v.* snicker, chuckle, giggle, titter, laugh up one's sleeve, tee-hee.

sniggle /snígg'l/ *v.intr.* fish (for eels) by pushing bait into a hole. [ME *snig* small eel, of unkn. orig.]

snip /snip/ *v.* & *n.* • *v.tr.* (**snipped, snipping**) (also *absol.*) cut (cloth, a hole, etc.) with scissors or shears, esp. in small quick strokes. • *n.* **1** an act of snipping. **2** a piece of material etc. snipped off. **3** *sl.* **a** something easily achieved. **b** *Brit.* a bargain; something cheaply acquired. **4** (in *pl.*) hand-shears for metal cutting. □ **snip at** make snipping strokes at. □□ **snipping** *n.* [LG & Du. *snippen* imit.]

▪ *v.* nip, clip, crop, cut, lop, prune, dock, trim. • *n.* **1** cut, slit, gash, slash, incision, nick. **2** bit, scrap, shred, snippet, fragment, sliver, patch, cutting, clipping, sample, remnant, morsel. **3 a** see BREEZE[1] *n.* 5. **b** see BARGAIN *n.* 2. **4** (*snips*) scissors, shears, hand-shears, tinsnips, clippers.

snipe /snīp/ *n.* & *v.* • *n.* (*pl.* same or **snipes**) any of various wading birds, esp. of the genus *Gallinago*, with a long straight bill and frequenting marshes. • *v.* **1** *intr.* fire shots from hiding usu. at long range. **2** *tr.* kill by sniping. **3** *intr.* (foll. by *at*) make a sly critical attack. **4** *intr.* go snipe-shooting. □ **snipe eel** any eel of the family Nemichthyidae, having a long slender snout. **snipe fish** any marine fish of the family Macrorhamphosidae, with a long slender snout. □□ **sniper** *n.* [ME, prob. f. Scand.: cf. Icel. *mýrisnípa*, & MDu., MLG *snippe*, OHG *snepfa*]

▪ *v.* **1** shoot, fire. **3** (*snipe at*) attack, criticize, deride, find fault with, carp at, pick apart. □□ **sniper** see SHOT[1] 6.

snippet /snípit/ *n.* **1** a small piece cut off. **2** (usu. in *pl.*; often foll. by *of*) **a** a scrap or fragment of information, knowledge, etc. **b** a short extract from a book, newspaper, etc. □□ **snippety** *adj.*

▪ **1, 2a** see FRAGMENT *n.* **2 b** see CLIP[2] *n.* 3.

snippy /snípi/ *adj.* (**snippier, snippiest**) *colloq.* fault-finding, snappish, sharp. □□ **snippily** *adv.* **snippiness** *n.*

snit /snit/ *n. US* a rage; a sulk (esp. *in a snit*). [20th c.: orig. unkn.]

snitch /snich/ *v.* & *n. sl.* • *v.* **1** *tr.* steal. **2** *intr.* (often foll. by *on*) inform on a person. • *n.* an informer. [17th c.: orig. unkn.]

▪ *v.* **1** see STEAL *v.* 1. **2** see INFORM 2. • *n.* see INFORMER 1.

snivel /snívv'l/ *v.* & *n.* • *v.intr.* (**snivelled, snivelling**; *US* **sniveled, sniveling**) **1** weep with sniffling. **2** run at the nose; make a repeated sniffing sound. **3** show weak or tearful sentiment. • *n.* **1** running mucus. **2** hypocritical talk; cant. □□ **sniveller** *n.* **snivelling** *adj.* **snivellingly** *adv.* [ME f. OE *snyflan* (unrecorded) f. *snofl* mucus: cf. SNUFFLE]

▪ *v.* **1, 2** sniffle, snuffle, sniff; blubber, whimper, whine, mewl; cry, weep, *colloq.* whinge, *literary* pule.
□□ **snivelling** see TEARFUL 1, *grovelling* (GROVEL).

snob /snob/ *n.* **1 a** a person with an exaggerated respect for social position or wealth and who despises socially inferior connections. **b** (*attrib.*) related to or characteristic of this attitude. **2** a person who behaves with servility to social superiors. **3** a person who despises others whose (usu. specified) tastes or attainments are considered inferior (*an intellectual snob*; *a wine snob*). □□ **snobbery** *n.* (*pl.* **-ies**). **snobbish** *adj.* **snobbishly** *adv.* **snobbishness** *n.* **snobby** *adj.* (**snobbier, snobbiest**). [18th c. (now dial.) 'cobbler': orig. unkn.]

▪ □□ **snobbery, snobbishness** pretentiousness, pretension, hauteur, haughtiness, superciliousness, condescension, loftiness, contemptuousness, presumptuousness, lordliness, disdainfulness, disdain, pompousness, pomposity, affectation, inflatedness, self-importance, conceit, arrogance; vainness, vanity, narcissism, self-admiration, self-centredness, egotism; smugness, *colloq.* snootiness, *esp. Brit. colloq.* uppishness, *sl.* snottiness. **snobbish** condescending, superior, patronizing, arrogant, haughty, lordly, lofty, putting on airs, disdainful, supercilious, contemptuous, pretentious, smug, scornful, self-important, affected, conceited, egotistic(al), vain, self-satisfied, complacent, pompous, hoity-toity, *colloq.* snooty, highfalutin, on one's high horse, uppity, high and mighty, high-hat, stuck-up, *esp. Brit. colloq.* uppish, *sl.* snotty, *esp. Brit. sl.* toffee-nosed.

snoek /snōōk/ *n. S.Afr.* a barracouta. [Afrik. f. Du., = PIKE[1], f. MLG *snōk*, prob. rel. to SNACK]

snog /snog/ *v.* & *n. Brit. sl.* • *v.intr.* (**snogged, snogging**) engage in kissing and caressing. • *n.* a spell of snogging. [20th c.: orig. unkn.]

snood /snōōd/ *n.* **1** an ornamental hairnet usu. worn at the back of the head. **2** a ring of woollen etc. material worn as a hood. **3** a short line attaching a hook to a main line in sea fishing. **4** *hist.* a ribbon or band worn by unmarried women in Scotland to confine their hair. [OE *snōd*]

snook[1] /snōōk/ *n. sl.* a contemptuous gesture with the thumb to the nose and the fingers spread out. □ **cock a snook** (often foll. by *at*) **1** make this gesture. **2** register one's contempt (for a person, establishment, etc.). [19th c.: orig. unkn.]

■ □ **cock a snook** (*cock a snook at*) **2** scoff at, deride, jeer at, mock, dismiss, scorn, flout, be contemptuous of, show contempt for, exhibit defiance for, be defiant of, *literary* contemn.

snook[2] /snōōk/ *n.* a marine fish, *Centropomus undecimalis*, used as food. [Du. *snoek*: see SNOEK]

snooker /snōōkər/ *n.* & *v.* ● *n.* **1** a game played with cues on a rectangular baize-covered table in which the players use a cue-ball (white) to pocket the other balls (15 red and 6 coloured) in a set order. **2** a position in this game in which a direct shot at a permitted ball is impossible. ● *v.tr.* **1** (also *refl.*) subject (oneself or another player) to a snooker. **2** (esp. as **snookered** *adj.*) *sl.* defeat; thwart. [19th c.: orig. unkn.]

■ *v.* **2** see BEAT *v.* 3a.

snoop /snōōp/ *v.* & *n. colloq.* ● *v.intr.* **1** pry into matters one need not be concerned with. **2** (often foll. by *about*, *around*) investigate in order to find out transgressions of the law etc. ● *n.* **1** an act of snooping. **2** a person who snoops; a detective. □□ **snooper** *n.* **snoopy** *adj.* [Du. *snœpen* eat on the sly]

■ *v.* **1** pry, spy, interfere, meddle, intrude, nose around *or* about, butt in, *colloq.* be nosy, stick *or* poke one's nose in, *Austral.* & *NZ sl.* stickybeak. ● *n.* **2** busybody, meddler, spy, intruder, snooper; private detective *or* investigator, *colloq.* private eye, sleuth, *esp. Brit. colloq.* Nosy Parker, *Austral.* & *NZ sl.* stickybeak, *US sl.* peeper, shamus. □□ **snoopy** see NOSY.

snooperscope /snōōpərskōp/ *n. US* a device which converts infrared radiation into a visible image, esp. used for seeing in the dark.

snoot /snōōt/ *n. sl.* the nose. [var. of SNOUT]

snooty /snōōti/ *adj.* (**snootier**, **snootiest**) *colloq.* supercilious; conceited. □□ **snootily** *adv.* **snootiness** *n.* [20th c.: orig. unkn.]

■ see SUPERCILIOUS. □□ **snootiness** see *snobbery* (SNOB).

snooze /snōōz/ *n.* & *v. colloq.* ● *n.* a short sleep, esp. in the daytime. ● *v.intr.* take a snooze. □□ **snoozer** *n.* **snoozy** *adj.* (**snoozier**, **snooziest**). [18th-c. sl.: orig. unkn.]

■ *n.* see SLEEP *n.* 2. ● *v.* see SLEEP *v.*

snore /snor/ *n.* & *v.* ● *n.* a snorting or grunting sound in breathing during sleep. ● *v.intr.* make this sound. □ **snore away** pass (time) sleeping or snoring. □□ **snorer** *n.* **snoringly** *adv.* [ME, prob. imit.: cf. SNORT]

snorkel /snórk'l/ *n.* & *v.* (also **schnorkel** /shnór-/) ● *n.* **1** a breathing-tube for an underwater swimmer. **2** a device for supplying air to a submerged submarine. ● *v.intr.* (**snorkelled**, **snorkelling**; *US* **snorkeled**, **snorkeling**) use a snorkel. □□ **snorkeller** *n.* [G *Schnorchel*]

snort /snort/ *n.* & *v.* ● *n.* **1** an explosive sound made by the sudden forcing of breath through the nose, esp. expressing indignation or incredulity. **2** a similar sound made by an engine etc. **3** *colloq.* a small drink of liquor. **4** *sl.* an inhaled dose of a (usu. illegal) powdered drug. ● *v.* **1** *intr.* make a snort. **2** *intr.* (of an engine etc.) make a sound resembling this. **3** *tr.* (also *absol.*) *sl.* inhale (a usu. illegal narcotic drug, esp. cocaine or heroin). **4** *tr.* express (defiance etc.) by snorting. □ **snort out** express (words, emotions, etc.) by snorting. [ME, prob. imit.: cf. SNORE]

■ *n.* **1** see GASP *n.* **3** see DRINK *n.* 2b. ● *v.* **3** see SNIFF *v.* 2.

snorter /snórtər/ *n. colloq.* **1** something very impressive or difficult. **2** something vigorous or violent.

snot /snot/ *n. sl.* **1** nasal mucus. **2** a term of contempt for a person. □ **snot-rag** a handkerchief. [prob. f. MDu., MLG *snotte*, MHG *snuz*, rel. to SNOUT]

■ **2** see STINKER.

snotty /snótti/ *adj.* (**snottier**, **snottiest**) *sl.* **1** running or foul with nasal mucus. **2** *colloq.* contemptible. **3** *colloq.* supercilious, conceited. □□ **snottily** *adv.* **snottiness** *n.*

■ **3** see CONCEITED. □□ **snottiness** see *snobbery* (SNOB).

snout /snowt/ *n.* **1** the projecting nose and mouth of an animal. **2** *derog.* a person's nose. **3** the pointed front of a thing; a nozzle. **4** *Brit. sl.* tobacco or a cigarette. □ **snout-beetle** a weevil. □□ **snouted** *adj.* (also in *comb.*). **snoutlike** *adj.* **snouty** *adj.* [ME f. MDu., MLG *snūt*]

■ **1** muzzle, trunk, proboscis; see also MOUTH *n.* 1. **2** nose, *Sc.* & *N.Engl.* neb, *sl.* conk, snoot, hooter, beak.

snow /snō/ *n.* & *v.* ● *n.* **1** atmospheric vapour frozen into ice crystals and falling to earth in light white flakes. **2** a fall of this, or a layer of it on the ground. **3** a thing resembling snow in whiteness or texture etc. **4** a mass of flickering white spots on a television or radar screen, caused by interference or a poor signal. **5** *sl.* cocaine. **6** a dessert or other dish resembling snow. **7** frozen carbon dioxide. ● *v.* **1** *intr.* (prec. by *it* as subject) snow falls (*it is snowing*; *if it snows*). **2** *tr.* (foll. by *in*, *over*, *up*, etc.) confine or block with large quantities of snow. **3** *tr.* & *intr.* sprinkle or scatter or fall as or like snow. **4** *intr.* come in large numbers or quantities. **5** *tr. US sl.* deceive or charm with plausible words. □ **be snowed under** be overwhelmed, esp. with work. **snow-blind** temporarily blinded by the glare of light reflected by large expanses of snow. **snow-blindness** this blindness. **snow-blink** the reflection in the sky of snow or ice fields. **snow boot** an overboot of rubber and cloth. **snow-broth** melted or melting snow. **snow bunting** a mainly white finch, *Plectrophenax nivalis*. **snow goose** a white Arctic goose, *Anser caerulescens*, with black-tipped wings. **snow-ice** opaque white ice formed from melted snow. **snow job** esp. *US sl.* an attempt at flattery or deception. **snow-job** *v.tr.* esp. *US sl.* do a snow job on (a person). **snow leopard** = OUNCE[2]. **snow owl** = *snowy owl*. **snow partridge** a mainly white partridge, *Lerwa lerwa*. **snow-slip** an avalanche. **snow-white** pure white. □□ **snowless** *adj.* **snowlike** *adj.* [OE *snāw* f. Gmc]

■ *n.* **1, 2** see PRECIPITATION 3a. **4** see INTERFERENCE 2. ● *v.* **1** see STORM *v.* 4. **5** see FOOL[1] *v.* 1, 3. □ **snow-white** see WHITE *adj.* 1.

snowball /snṓbawl/ *n.* & *v.* ● *n.* **1** snow pressed together into a ball, esp. for throwing in play. **2** anything that grows or increases rapidly like a snowball rolled on snow. ● *v.* **1** *intr.* & *tr.* throw or pelt with snowballs. **2** *intr.* increase rapidly. □ **snowball-tree** a guelder rose.

■ *v.* **2** see INCREASE *v.* 1.

snowberry /snṓbəri/ *n.* (*pl.* **-ies**) any shrub of the genus *Symphoricarpos*, with white berries.

snowblower /snṓblōər/ *n.* a machine that clears snow by blowing it to the side of the road etc.

snowbound /snṓbownd/ *adj.* prevented by snow from going out or travelling.

snowcap /snṓkap/ *n.* **1** the tip of a mountain when covered with snow. **2** a white-crowned humming-bird, *Microchera albocoronata*, native to Central America. □□ **snowcapped** *adj.*

snowdrift /snṓdrift/ *n.* a bank of snow heaped up by the action of the wind.

snowdrop /snṓdrop/ *n.* a bulbous plant, *Galanthus nivalis*, with white drooping flowers in the early spring.

snowfall /snṓfawl/ *n.* **1** a fall of snow. **2** *Meteorol.* the amount of snow that falls on one occasion or on a given area within a given time.

■ see PRECIPITATION 3a.

snowfield /snṓfeeld/ *n.* a permanent wide expanse of snow in mountainous or polar regions.

snowflake /snṓflayk/ *n.* **1** each of the small collections of crystals in which snow falls. **2 a** any bulbous plant of the

genus *Leucojum*, with snowdrop-like flowers. **b** the white flower of this plant.
■ **1** flake.

snowline /snṓlīn/ *n*. the level above which snow never melts entirely.

snowman /snṓman/ *n*. (*pl*. **-men**) a figure resembling a man, made of compressed snow.

snowmobile /snṓməbeel/ *n*. a motor vehicle, esp. with runners or Caterpillar tracks, for travelling over snow.

snowplough /snṓplow/ *n*. (*US* **snowplow**) a device, or a vehicle equipped with one, for clearing roads of thick snow.

snowshoe /snṓshoo/ *n*. & *v*. ● *n*. a flat device like a racket attached to a boot for walking on snow without sinking in. ● *v.intr*. travel on snowshoes. □□ **snowshoer** *n*.

snowstorm /snṓstorm/ *n*. a heavy fall of snow, esp. with a high wind.
■ see STORM *n*. 1.

snowy /snṓ-i/ *adj*. (**snowier, snowiest**) **1** of or like snow. **2** (of the weather etc.) with much snow. □ **snowy owl** a large white owl, *Nyctea scandiaca*, native to the Arctic. □□ **snowily** *adv*. **snowiness** *n*.
■ **1** see WHITE *adj*. 1. **2** see WINTRY 1.

SNP *abbr*. Scottish National Party.

Snr. *abbr*. Senior.

snub /snub/ *v*., *n*., & *adj*. ● *v.tr*. (**snubbed, snubbing**) **1** rebuff or humiliate with sharp words or a marked lack of cordiality. **2** check the movement of (a boat, horse, etc.) esp. by a rope wound round a post etc. ● *n*. an act of snubbing; a rebuff. ● *adj*. short and blunt in shape. □ **snub nose** a short turned-up nose. **snub-nosed** having a snub nose. □□ **snubber** *n*. **snubbingly** *adv*. [ME f. ON *snubba* chide, check the growth of]
■ *v*. **1** see REBUFF *v*. ● *n*. see REBUFF *n*.

snuff[1] /snuf/ *n*. & *v*. ● *n*. the charred part of a candle-wick. ● *v.tr*. trim the snuff from (a candle). □ **snuff it** *Brit*. *sl*. die. **snuff out 1** extinguish by snuffing. **2** kill; put an end to. [ME *snoffe*, *snuffe*: orig. unkn.]
■ □ **snuff it** see DIE[1] 1. **snuff out 1** see QUENCH 2. **2** see KILL[1] *v*. 1a.

snuff[2] /snuf/ *n*. & *v*. ● *n*. powdered tobacco or medicine taken by sniffing it up the nostrils. ● *v.intr*. take snuff. □ **snuff-coloured** dark yellowish-brown. **up to snuff** *colloq*. **1** *Brit*. knowing; not easily deceived. **2** up to standard. [Du. *snuf* (*tabak* tobacco) f. MDu. *snuffen* snuffle]
■ *v*. see SNIFF *v*. 2. □ **up to snuff 2** see *up to scratch* (SCRATCH).

snuffbox /snúfboks/ *n*. a small usu. ornamental box for holding snuff.

snuffer /snúffər/ *n*. **1** a small hollow cone with a handle used to extinguish a candle. **2** (in *pl*.) an implement like scissors used to extinguish a candle or trim its wick.

snuffle /snúff'l/ *v*. & *n*. ● *v*. **1** *intr*. make sniffing sounds. **2 a** *intr*. speak nasally, whiningly, or like one with a cold. **b** *tr*. (often foll. by *out*) say in this way. **3** *intr*. breathe noisily as through a partially blocked nose. **4** *intr*. sniff. ● *n*. **1** a snuffling sound or tone. **2** (in *pl*.) a partial blockage of the nose causing snuffling. **3** a sniff. □□ **snuffler** *n*. **snuffly** *adj*. [prob. f. LG & Du. *snuffelen* (as SNUFF[2]): cf. SNIVEL]
■ *v*. **1, 4** sniff, snivel, sniffle. ● *n*. **1, 3** sniffle, snuffle.

snuffy[1] /snúffi/ *adj*. (**snuffier, snuffiest**) **1** annoyed. **2** irritable. **3** supercilious or contemptuous. [SNUFF[1] + -Y[1]]

snuffy[2] /snúffi/ *adj*. like snuff in colour or substance. [SNUFF[2] + -Y[2]]

snug /snug/ *adj*. & *n*. ● *adj*. (**snugger, snuggest**) **1 a** cosy, comfortable, sheltered; well enclosed or placed or arranged. **b** cosily protected from the weather or cold. **c** close-fitting. **2** (of an income etc.) allowing comfort and comparative ease. ● *n*. *Brit*. a small room in a pub or inn. □□ **snugly** *adv*. **snugness** *n*. [16th c. (orig. Naut.): prob. of LG or Du. orig.]
■ *adj*. **1a, b** cosy, comfortable, intimate, relaxing, restful, warm, sheltered, secure, friendly, easy, homely, casual, *colloq*. comfy. **c** see TIGHT *adj*. 1, 2a.

snuggery /snúggəri/ *n*. (*pl*. **-ies**) **1** a snug place, esp. a person's private room or den. **2** *Brit*. = SNUG *n*.
■ **1** see NEST *n*. 2, 3.

snuggle /snúgg'l/ *v.intr*. & *tr*. (usu. foll. by *down*, *up*, *together*) settle or draw into a warm comfortable position. [SNUG + -LE[4]]
■ cuddle, nestle, nuzzle.

So. *abbr*. South.

so[1] /sō/ *adv*. & *conj*. ● *adv*. **1** (often foll. by *that* + clause) to such an extent, or to the extent implied (*why are you so angry?*; *do stop complaining so*; *they were so pleased that they gave us a bonus*). **2** (with *neg*.; often foll. by *as* + clause) to the extent to which ... is or does etc., or to the extent implied (*was not so late as I expected*; *am not so eager as you*). ¶ In positive constructions *as* ... *as* ... is used: see AS[1]. **3** (foll. by *that* or *as* + clause) to the degree or in the manner implied (*so expensive that few can afford it*; *so small as to be invisible*; *am not so foolish as to agree to that*). **4** (adding emphasis) to that extent; in that or a similar manner (*I want to leave and so does she*; *you said it was good, and so it is*). **5** to a great or notable degree (*I am so glad*). **6** (with verbs of state) in the way described (*am not very fond of it but may become so*). **7** (with verb of saying or thinking etc.) as previously mentioned or described (*I think so*; *so he said*; *so I should hope*). ● *conj*. (often foll. by *that* + clause) **1** with the result that (*there was none left, so we had to go without*). **2** in order that (*came home early so that I could see you*). **3** and then; as the next step (*so then the car broke down*; *and so to bed*). **4 a** (introducing a question) then; after that (*so what did you tell them?*). **b** (*absol*.) = *so what?* □ **and so on** (or **forth**) **1** and others of the same kind. **2** and in other similar ways. **so as** (foll. by *to* + infin.) in order to (*did it so as to get it finished*). **so be it** an expression of acceptance or resignation. **so-called** commonly designated or known as, often incorrectly. **so far** see FAR. **so far as** see FAR. **so far so good** see FAR. **so long!** *colloq*. goodbye till we meet again. **so long as** see LONG[1]. **so much 1** a certain amount (of). **2** a great deal of (*is so much nonsense*). **3** (with *neg*.) **a** less than; to a lesser extent (*not so much forgotten as ignored*). **b** not even (*didn't give me so much as a penny*). **so much for** that is all that need be done or said about. **so so** *adj*. (usu. *predic*.) indifferent; not very good. ● *adv*. indifferently; only moderately well. **so to say** (or **speak**) an expression of reserve or apology for an exaggeration or neologism etc. **so what?** *colloq*. why should that be considered significant? [OE *swā* etc.]
■ *conj*. **1** see CONSEQUENTLY. **2** see *in order that* (ORDER). □ **so-called** self-styled, *soi-disant*, professed, alleged, pretended, supposed, ostensible; misnamed, misdesignated; suspect. **so long!** see GOODBYE *int*. **so so** (*adj*.) mediocre, all right, average, undistinguished, passable, not (too) bad *or* good, adequate, fair (to middling), middling, indifferent, ordinary, tolerable, *comme ci, comme ça*, modest, *colloq*. OK. **so to say** (or **speak**) as it were, in a manner of speaking, figuratively *or* metaphorically (speaking); see also *in effect* (EFFECT). **so what?** *colloq*. big deal, so?, I couldn't (*US* could) care less.

so[2] var. of SOH.

-so /sō/ *comb. form* = -SOEVER.

soak /sōk/ *v*. & *n*. ● *v*. **1** *tr*. & *intr*. make or become thoroughly wet through saturation with or in liquid. **2** *tr*. (of rain etc.) drench. **3** *tr*. (foll. by *in*, *up*) **a** absorb (liquid). **b** acquire (knowledge etc.) copiously. **4** *refl*. (often foll. by *in*) steep (oneself) in a subject of study etc. **5** *intr*. (foll. by *in*, *into*, *through*) (of liquid) make its way or penetrate by saturation. **6** *tr*. *colloq*. extract money from by an extortionate charge, taxation, etc. (*soak the rich*). **7** *intr*. *colloq*. drink persistently, booze. **8** *tr*. (as **soaked** *adj*.) very drunk. ● *n*. **1** the act of soaking or the state of being soaked. **2** a drinking-bout. **3** *colloq*. a hard drinker. □□ **soakage** *n*. **soaker** *n*. **soaking** *n*. & *adj*. [OE *socian* rel. to *soc* sucking at the breast, *sūcan* SUCK]

■ *v.* **1** drench, saturate, wet; immerse, submerge, souse, douse, sop, bathe, steep, inundate, flood, ret; macerate; marinate. **2** drench, saturate, wet. **3** (*soak up*) **a** absorb, take in *or* up, sponge up, sop up. **b** acquire, absorb, take in, assimilate, learn. **4** see *steep in* (STEEP²). **5** see IMPREGNATE *v.* 1, 2. **6** see STING *v.* 4. **8** (**soaked**) see DRUNK *adj.* 1. ● *n.* **2** see BENDER. **3** alcoholic, drunkard, drunk, dipsomaniac, drinker, tippler, sot, *archaic or literary* toper, *colloq.* sponge, souse, boozer, *esp. US sl.* lush, *US sl.* juicer. □□ **soaking** (*n.*) drenching, wetting, dousing, immersing, saturating. (*adj.*) wet, sopping, drenched, dripping, saturated, soaked, wringing wet, streaming, sodden, waterlogged.

soakaway /sṓkəway/ *n.* an arrangement for disposing of waste water by letting it percolate through the soil.

so-and-so /sṓəndsō/ *n.* (*pl.* **so-and-so's**) **1** a particular person or thing not needing to be specified (*told me to do so-and-so*). **2** *colloq.* a person disliked or regarded with disfavour (*the so-and-so left me behind*).

■ **1** such-and-such, something or other. **2** see STINKER.

soap /sōp/ *n.* & *v.* ● *n.* **1** a cleansing agent that is a compound of fatty acid with soda or potash or (**insoluble soap**) with another metallic oxide, of which the soluble kinds when rubbed in water yield a lather used in washing. **2** *colloq.* = *soap opera.* ● *v.tr.* **1** apply soap to. **2** scrub or rub with soap. □ **soap flakes** soap in the form of thin flakes, for washing clothes etc. **soap opera** a broadcast drama, usu. serialized in many episodes, dealing with sentimental domestic themes (so called because orig. sponsored in the US by soap manufacturers). **soap powder** powdered soap esp. with additives. □□ **soapless** *adj.* **soaplike** *adj.* [OE *sāpe* f. WG]

■ *n.* **1** see DETERGENT *n.* ● *v.* see WASH *v.* 1, 3. □ **soap powder** see DETERGENT *n.*

soapbark /sṓpbaark/ *n.* an American tree, *Quillaja saponaria*, with bark yielding saponin.

soapberry /sṓpberri/ *n.* (*pl.* **-ies**) any of various tropical American shrubs, esp. of the genus *Sapindus*, with fruits yielding saponin.

soapbox /sṓpboks/ *n.* **1** a box for holding soap. **2** a makeshift stand for a public speaker.

soapstone /sṓpstōn/ *n.* steatite.

soapsuds /sṓpsudz/ *n.pl.* = SUDS 1.

soapwort /sṓpwurt/ *n.* a European plant, *Saponaria officinalis*, with pink or white flowers and leaves yielding a soapy substance.

soapy /sṓpi/ *adj.* (**soapier, soapiest**) **1** of or like soap. **2** containing or smeared with soap. **3** (of a person or manner) unctuous or flattering. □□ **soapily** *adv.* **soapiness** *n.*

■ **1, 2** see OILY 1, 2. **3** see OILY 3.

soar /sor/ *v.intr.* **1** fly or rise high. **2** reach a high level or standard (*prices soared*). **3** maintain height in the air without flapping the wings or using power. □□ **soarer** *n.* **soaringly** *adv.* [ME f. OF *essorer* ult. f. L (as EX-¹, *aura* breeze)]

■ **1** rise, ascend, fly. **2** rise, increase, escalate, climb, mount, spiral upwards, shoot up *or* upwards, rocket, sky-rocket. **3** fly, hover, float, hang, glide.

S.O.B. *abbr.* esp. *US sl.* = *son of a bitch.*

sob /sob/ *v.* & *n.* ● *v.* (**sobbed, sobbing**) **1** *intr.* draw breath in convulsive gasps usu. with weeping under mental distress or physical exhaustion. **2** *tr.* (usu. foll. by *out*) utter with sobs. **3** *tr.* bring (oneself) to a specified state by sobbing (*sobbed themselves to sleep*). ● *n.* a convulsive drawing of breath, esp. in weeping. □ **sob story** a story or explanation appealing mainly to the emotions. **sob-stuff** *colloq.* sentimental talk or writing. □□ **sobber** *n.* **sobbingly** *adv.* [ME *sobbe* (prob. imit.)]

■ *v.* cry, shed tears, weep, blubber, snivel, whimper, sniff, snuffle, wail, moan, mewl, bawl, howl, yowl, *literary* pule. ● *n.* cry, snivel, whimper, sniff, snuffle, wail, moan, howl, yowl.

sober /sṓbər/ *adj.* & *v.* ● *adj.* (**soberer, soberest**) **1** not affected by alcohol. **2** not given to excessive drinking of alcohol. **3** moderate, well-balanced, tranquil, sedate. **4** not fanciful or exaggerated (*the sober truth*). **5** (of a colour etc.) quiet and inconspicuous. ● *v.tr.* & *intr.* (often foll. by *down, up*) make or become sober or less wild, reckless, enthusiastic, visionary, etc. (*a sobering thought*). □ **as sober as a judge** completely sober. □□ **soberingly** *adv.* **soberly** *adv.* [ME f. OF *sobre* f. L *sobrius*]

■ *adj.* **1** clear-headed, lucid, rational, sensible, in control, steady, composed, collected, calm. **2** temperate, abstemious; teetotal, *sl.* on the (water-)wagon. **3** serious, solemn, earnest, dispassionate, unruffled, unflustered, unexcited, unperturbed, steady, sedate, staid, composed, dignified, cool, calm, serene, tranquil, collected, cool-headed, level-headed, sane, balanced, moderate, practical, realistic, rational, clear-headed, *colloq.* together. **4** see MATTER-OF-FACT 1. **5** sedate, sombre, plain, simple, subdued, quiet, inconspicuous, dreary, dark, drab, colourless, neutral. ● *v.* detoxify, recover, dry out.

sobriety /səbrī́-iti/ *n.* the state of being sober. [ME f. OF *sobrieté* or L *sobrietas* (as SOBER)]

■ abstemiousness, temperance, teetotalism, abstention, abstinence, non-indulgence; seriousness, solemnity, staidness, gravity, temperateness, sedateness, formality, dignity.

sobriquet /sṓbrikay/ *n.* (also **soubriquet** /sṓō-/) **1** a nickname. **2** an assumed name. [F, orig. = 'tap under the chin']

■ see NICKNAME *n.*

Soc. *abbr.* **1** Socialist. **2** Society.

socage /sókkij/ *n.* (also **soccage**) a feudal tenure of land involving payment of rent or other non-military service to a superior. [ME f. AF *socage* f. *soc* f. OE *sōcn* SOKE]

soccer /sókkər/ *n.* Association football. [Assoc. + -ER³]

sociable /sṓshəb'l/ *adj.* & *n.* ● *adj.* **1** fitted for or liking the society of other people; ready and willing to talk and act with others. **2** (of a person's manner or behaviour etc.) friendly. **3** (of a meeting etc.) marked by friendliness, not stiff or formal. ● *n.* **1** an open carriage with facing side seats. **2** an S-shaped couch for two occupants partly facing each other. **3** *US* a social. □□ **sociability** /-bílliti/ *n.* **sociableness** *n.* **sociably** *adv.* [F *sociable* or L *sociabilis* f. *sociare* to unite f. *socius* companion]

■ *adj.* **1, 2** social, gregarious, outgoing, extrovert(ed), companionable, accessible, approachable, friendly, affable, amiable, genial, congenial, convivial, warm, cosy, cordial, neighbourly, hospitable, welcoming, hail-fellow-well-met, *colloq.* chummy. □□ **sociability, sociableness** see FRIENDSHIP 2.

social /sṓsh'l/ *adj.* & *n.* ● *adj.* **1** of or relating to society or its organization. **2** concerned with the mutual relations of human beings or of classes of human beings. **3** living in organized communities; unfitted for a solitary life (*man is a social animal*). **4 a** needing companionship; gregarious, interdependent. **b** cooperative; practising the division of labour. **5** existing only as a member of a compound organism. **6 a** (of insects) living together in organized communities. **b** (of birds) nesting near each other in communities. **7** (of plants) growing thickly together and monopolizing the ground they grow on. ● *n.* **1** a social gathering, esp. one organized by a club, congregation, etc. **2** *colloq.* = *Social Security.* □ **social anthropology** the comparative study of peoples through their culture and kinship systems. **social climber** *derog.* a person anxious to gain a higher social status. **social contract** (or **compact**) an agreement to cooperate for social benefits, e.g. by sacrificing some individual freedom for State protection. **social credit** the economic theory that the profits of industry should be distributed to the general public. **social democracy** a socialist system achieved by democratic means. **social democrat** a person who advocates social democracy. **social order** the network of human relationships in society. **social realism** the expression of social or political views in art. **social science a** the scientific study of human society and social relationships. **b** a branch of this (e.g. politics or economics). **social scientist** a student of or expert in the social sciences. **social secretary** a person who makes arrangements for the social activities of a person or organization. **social security** State assistance to those lacking in economic security and welfare, e.g. the aged and the unemployed. **social service** philanthropic activity. **social services** services provided by the State for the community, esp. education, health, and housing. **social war** *hist.* a war fought between allies. **social work** work of benefit to those in need of help or welfare, esp. done by specially trained personnel. **social worker** a person trained to do social work. □□ **sociality** /sōshiálliti/ *n.* **socially** *adv.* [F *social* or L *socialis* allied f. *socius* friend]

■ *adj.* **1, 2** communal, community, common, collective, group, public, popular, societal. **4 a** see SOCIABLE. **b** cooperative, collective, collaborative. ● *n.* see DANCE *n.*, RECEPTION 3. □ **social climber** see PARVENU *n.*

socialism /sṓshəliz'm/ *n.* **1** a political and economic theory of social organization which advocates that the community as a whole should own and control the means of production, distribution, and exchange. **2** policy or practice based on this theory. □□ **socialist** *n.* & *adj.* **socialistic** /-lístik/ *adj.* **socialistically** /-lístikəli/ *adv.* [F *socialisme* (as SOCIAL)]

■ □□ **socialist** (*n.*) see *left-winger* (LEFT[1]). (*adj.*) see PINK[1] *adj.* 2.

socialite /sṓshəlīt/ *n.* a person prominent in fashionable society.

socialize /sṓshəlīz/ *v.* (also **-ise**) **1** *intr.* act in a sociable manner. **2** *tr.* make social. **3** *tr.* organize on socialistic principles. □ **socialized medicine** *US* often *derog.* the provision of medical services for all from public funds. □□ **socialization** /-záysh'n/ *n.*

■ **1** mix, get together, fraternize, keep company, go out, get out; associate, hobnob, rub shoulders *or US* elbows.

society /səsī́əti/ *n.* (*pl.* **-ies**) **1** the sum of human conditions and activity regarded as a whole functioning interdependently. **2** a social community (*all societies must have firm laws*). **3 a** a social mode of life. **b** the customs and organization of an ordered community. **4** *Ecol.* a plant community. **5 a** the socially advantaged or prominent members of a community (*society would not approve*). **b** this, or a part of it, qualified in some way (*is not done in polite society*). **6** participation in hospitality; other people's homes or company (*avoids society*). **7** companionship, company (*avoids the society of such people*). **8** an association of persons united by a common aim or interest or principle (*formed a music society*). □ **Society of Friends** see QUAKER. **Society of Jesus** see JESUIT. □□ **societal** *adj.* (esp. in sense 1). **societally** *adv.* [F *société* f. L *societas -tatis* f. *socius* companion]

■ **2, 3** culture, civilization, community, way of life, world; organization, system. **5 a** high society, *haut monde*, beau monde, upper classes, polite society, élite, gentry, *colloq.* upper crust. **b** circles, company, spheres, set. **6** company, people. **7** companionship, company, camaraderie, friendship, fellowship, association, intercourse. **8** organization, club, association, circle, league, institute, academy, alliance, guild, group, fraternity, sorority, confraternity, brotherhood, sisterhood, fellowship, union, sodality. □□ **societal** see PUBLIC *adj.* 1.

socio- /sṓsiō, sṓshiō/ *comb. form* **1** of society (and). **2** of or relating to sociology (and). [L *socius* companion]

sociobiology /sṓsiōbīólləji, sṓshiō-/ *n.* the scientific study of the biological aspects of social behaviour. □□ **sociobiological** /-bīəlójik'l/ *adj.* **sociobiologically** /-bīəlójikəli/ *adv.* **sociobiologist** *n.*

sociocultural /sṓsiōkúlchərəl, sṓshiō-/ *adj.* combining social and cultural factors. □□ **socioculturally** *adv.*

socio-economic /sṓsiō-éékənómmik, sṓshiō-/ *adj.* relating to or concerned with the interaction of social and economic factors. □□ **socio-economically** *adv.*

sociolinguistic /sṓsiōlinggwístik, sṓshiō-/ *adj.* relating to or concerned with language in its social aspects. □□ **sociolinguist** *n.* **sociolinguistically** *adv.*

sociolinguistics /sṓsiōlinggwístiks, sṓshiō-/ *n.* the study of language in relation to social factors.

sociology /sṓsiólləji, sṓshi-/ *n.* **1** the study of the development, structure, and functioning of human society. **2** the study of social problems. □□ **sociological** /-əlójik'l/ *adj.* **sociologically** /-əlójikəli/ *adv.* **sociologist** *n.* [F *sociologie* (as SOCIO-, -LOGY)]

sociometry /sṓsiómmitri, sṓshi-/ *n.* the study of relationships within a group of people. □□ **sociometric** /-əmétrik/ *adj.* **sociometrically** /-əmétrikəli/ *adv.* **sociometrist** *n.*

sock[1] /sok/ *n.* (*pl.* **socks** or *colloq.* & *Commerce* **sox** /soks/) **1** a short knitted covering for the foot, usu. not reaching the knee. **2** a removable inner sole put into a shoe for warmth etc. **3** an ancient Greek or Roman comic actor's light shoe. **4** comic drama. □ **pull one's socks up** *Brit. colloq.* make an effort to improve. **put a sock in it** *Brit. sl.* be quiet. [OE *socc* f. L *soccus* comic actor's shoe, light low-heeled slipper, f. Gk *sukkhos*]

sock[2] /sok/ *v.* & *n. colloq.* ● *v.tr.* hit (esp. a person) forcefully. ● *n.* **1** a hard blow. **2** *US* the power to deliver a blow. □ **sock it to** attack or address (a person) vigorously. [*c.*1700 (cant): orig. unkn.]

■ *v.* see HIT *v.* 1a. ● *n.* **1** see HIT *n.* 1a.

socket /sókkit/ *n.* & *v.* ● *n.* **1** a natural or artificial hollow for something to fit into or stand firm or revolve in. **2** *Electr.* a device receiving a plug, light-bulb, etc., to make a connection. **3** *Golf* the part of an iron club into which the shaft is fitted. ● *v.tr.* (**socketed, socketing**) **1** place in or fit with a socket. **2** *Golf* hit (a ball) with the socket of a club. [ME f. AF, dimin. of OF *soc* ploughshare, prob. of Celt. orig.]

sockeye /sókkī/ *n.* a blue-backed salmon of Alaska etc., *Oncorhynchus nerka*. [Salish *sukai* fish of fishes]

socking /sókking/ *adv.* & *adj.* ● *adv. colloq.* exceedingly, very (*a socking great diamond ring*). ● *adj. sl.* confounded, bloody.

socle /sṓk'l/ *n. Archit.* a plain low block or plinth serving as a support for a column, urn, statue, etc., or as the foundation of a wall. [F f. It. *zoccolo* orig. 'wooden shoe' f. L *socculus* f. *soccus* SOCK[1]]

■ see PEDESTAL *n.*

Socratic /səkráttik/ *adj.* & *n.* ● *adj.* of or relating to the Greek philosopher Socrates (d. 399 BC) or his philosophy, esp. the method associated with him of seeking the truth by a series of questions and answers. ● *n.* a follower of Socrates. □ **Socratic irony** a pose of ignorance assumed in order to entice others into making statements that can then be challenged. □□ **Socratically** *adv.* [L *Socraticus* f. Gk *Sōkratikos* f. *Sōkratēs*]

sod[1] /sod/ *n.* & *v.* ● *n.* **1** turf or a piece of turf. **2** the surface of the ground. ● *v.tr.* (**sodded, sodding**) cover (the ground) with sods. □ **under the sod** in the grave. [ME f. MDu., MLG *sode*, of unkn. orig.]

■ *n.* **1** see TURF *n.* 1. **2** see EARTH *n.* 2b.

sod[2] /sod/ *n.* & *v.* esp. *Brit. coarse sl.* ¶ Often considered a taboo word. ● *n.* **1** an unpleasant or awkward person or thing. **2** a person of a specified kind; a fellow (*the lucky sod*). ● *v.tr.* (**sodded, sodding**) **1** (often *absol.* or as *int.*) an exclamation of annoyance (*sod them, I don't care!*). **2** (as **sodding** *adj.*) a general term of contempt. □ **sod off** go away. **Sod's Law** = MURPHY'S LAW. [abbr. of SODOMITE]

soda /sṓdə/ *n.* **1** any of various compounds of sodium in common use, e.g. washing soda, caustic soda. **2** (in full **soda water**) water made effervescent by impregnation with carbon dioxide under pressure and used alone or with spirits etc. as a drink (orig. made with sodium bicarbonate). **3** esp. *US* a sweet effervescent drink. □ **soda bread** bread leavened with baking-soda. **soda fountain 1** a device supplying soda water. **2** a shop or counter equipped with this. **soda lime** a mixture of calcium oxide and sodium hydroxide. [med.L, perh. f. *sodanum* glasswort (used as a remedy for headaches) f. *soda* headache f. Arab. *ṣudā'* f. *ṣada'a* split]

■ **2** see WATER *n.* **3** pop, fizzy drink.

sodality /sōdálliti/ *n.* (*pl.* **-ies**) a confraternity or association, esp. a Roman Catholic religious guild or brotherhood. [F *sodalité* or L *sodalitas* f. *sodalis* comrade]
■ fraternity, brotherhood.

sodden /sódd'n/ *adj.* & *v.* ● *adj.* **1** saturated with liquid; soaked through. **2** rendered stupid or dull etc. with drunkenness. **3** (of bread etc.) doughy; heavy and moist. ● *v.intr.* & *tr.* become or make sodden. ▫▫ **soddenly** *adv.* **soddenness** *n.* [archaic past part. of SEETHE]
■ *adj.* **1** see *soaking* (SOAK).

sodium /sṓdiəm/ *n. Chem.* a soft silver-white reactive metallic element, occurring naturally in soda, salt, etc., that is important in industry and is an essential element in living organisms. ¶ Symb.: **Na**. ▫ **sodium bicarbonate** a white soluble powder used in the manufacture of fire extinguishers and effervescent drinks. **sodium carbonate** a white powder with many commercial applications including the manufacture of soap and glass. **sodium chloride** a colourless crystalline compound occurring naturally in sea water and halite; common salt. **sodium hydroxide** a deliquescent compound which is strongly alkaline and used in the manufacture of soap and paper: also called *caustic soda.* **sodium nitrate** a white powdery compound used mainly in the manufacture of fertilizers. **sodium-vapour lamp** (or **sodium lamp**) a lamp using an electrical discharge in sodium vapour and giving a yellow light. ▫▫ **sodic** *adj.* [SODA + -IUM]
■ ▫ **sodium chloride** salt, sea salt, rock-salt.

Sodom /sóddəm/ *n.* a wicked or depraved place. [*Sodom* in ancient Palestine, destroyed for its wickedness (Gen. 18–19)]

sodomite /sóddəmīt/ *n.* a person who practises sodomy. [ME f. OF f. LL *Sodomita* f. Gk *Sodomitēs* inhabitant of Sodom f. *Sodoma* Sodom]

sodomy /sóddəmi/ *n.* = BUGGERY. ▫▫ **sodomize** *v.tr.* (also **-ise**). [ME f. med.L *sodomia* f. LL *peccatum Sodomiticum* sin of Sodom: see SODOM]

soever /sō-évvər/ *adv. literary* of any kind; to any extent (*how great soever it may be*).

-soever /sō-évvər/ *comb. form* (added to relative pronouns, adverbs, and adjectives) of any kind; to any extent (*whatsoever; howsoever*).

sofa /sṓfə/ *n.* a long upholstered seat with a back and arms, for two or more people. ▫ **sofa bed** a sofa that can be converted into a temporary bed. [F, ult. f. Arab. *ṣuffa*]
■ see COUCH[1] *n.*

soffit /sóffit/ *n.* the under-surface of an architrave, arch, balcony, etc. [F *soffite* or It. *soffitta, -itto* ult. f. L *suffixus* (as SUFFIX)]

S. of S. *abbr.* Song of Songs (Old Testament).

soft /soft/ *adj., adv.,* & *n.* ● *adj.* **1** (of a substance, material, etc.) lacking hardness or firmness; yielding to pressure; easily cut. **2** (of cloth etc.) having a smooth surface or texture; not rough or coarse. **3** (of air etc.) mellow, mild, balmy; not noticeably cold or hot. **4** (of water) free from mineral salts and therefore good for lathering. **5** (of a light or colour etc.) not brilliant or glaring. **6** (of a voice or sounds) gentle and pleasing. **7** *Phonet.* **a** (of a consonant) sibilant or palatal (as *c* in *ice*, *g* in *age*). **b** voiced or unaspirated. **8** (of an outline etc.) not sharply defined. **9** (of an action or manner etc.) gentle, conciliatory, complimentary, amorous. **10** (of the heart or feelings etc.) compassionate, sympathetic. **11** (of a person) **a** feeble, lenient, silly, sentimental. **b** weak; not robust. **12** *colloq.* (of a job etc.) easy. **13** (of drugs) mild; not likely to cause addiction. **14** (of radiation) having little penetrating power. **15** (also **soft-core**) (of pornography) suggestive or erotic but not explicit. **16** *Stock Exch.* (of currency, prices, etc.) likely to fall in value. **17** *Polit.* moderate; willing to compromise (*the soft left*). **18** peaceful (*soft slumbers*). **19** *Brit.* (of the weather etc.) rainy or moist or thawing. ● *adv.* softly (*play soft*). ● *n.* a silly weak person. ▫ **be soft on** *colloq.* **1** be lenient towards. **2** be infatuated with. **have a soft spot for** be fond of or affectionate towards (a person). **soft answer** a good-tempered answer to abuse or an accusation. **soft-boiled** (of an egg) lightly boiled with the yolk soft or liquid. **soft-centred** (of a person) soft-hearted, sentimental. **soft coal** bituminous coal. **soft detergent** a biodegradable detergent. **soft drink** a non-alcoholic drink. **soft focus** *Photog.* the slight deliberate blurring of a picture. **soft fruit** *Brit.* small stoneless fruit (strawberry, currant, etc.). **soft furnishings** *Brit.* curtains, rugs, etc. **soft goods** *Brit.* textiles. **soft-headed** feeble-minded. **soft-headedness** feeble-mindedness. **soft in the head** feeble-minded. **soft-land** make a soft landing. **soft landing** a landing by a spacecraft without its suffering major damage. **soft option** the easier alternative. **soft palate** the rear part of the palate. **soft-paste** denoting an 'artificial' porcelain containing glassy materials and fired at a comparatively low temperature. **soft pedal** a pedal on a piano that makes the tone softer. **soft-pedal** *v.tr.* & (often foll. by *on*) *intr.* (**-pedalled, -pedalling**; *US* **-pedaled, -pedaling**) **1** refrain from emphasizing; be restrained (about). **2** play with the soft pedal down. **soft roe** see ROE[1]. **soft sell** restrained or subtly persuasive salesmanship. **soft-sell** *v.tr.* (*past* and *past part.* **-sold**) sell by this method. **soft soap 1** a semifluid soap made with potash. **2** *colloq.* persuasive flattery. **soft-soap** *v.tr. colloq.* persuade (a person) with flattery. **soft-spoken** speaking with a gentle voice. **soft sugar** granulated or powdered sugar. **soft tack** bread or other good food (opp. *hard tack*). **soft tissues** tissues of the body that are not bony or cartilaginous. **soft touch** *colloq.* a gullible person, esp. over money. **soft wicket** a wicket with moist or sodden turf. ▫▫ **softish** *adj.* **softness** *n.* [OE *sōfte* agreeable, earlier *sēfte* f. WG]
■ *adj.* **1** yielding, cushiony, plushy, spongy, flabby, squeezable, compressible, squashy, squashable, flexible, plastic, pliable, pliant, malleable, supple, springy, unstarched, *archaic* flexile. **2** downy, silky, silken, satiny, furry, fluffy, feathery, fleecy, fuzzy, velvety, smooth (as a baby's bottom). **3** gentle, mild, balmy, mellow, pleasant, moderate, warm, halcyon, springlike, summery, restful, tranquil, relaxing, lazy. **5** pastel, pale, faint, delicate, fine, subdued, light, matt, quiet, muted, toned down, diffuse(d), soothing, gentle. **6** subdued, toned *or* turned down, muted, low, quiet, melodious, mellifluous, mellifluent, mellow, gentle, faint, softened, soothing, smooth. **8** fuzzy, woolly, blurred, blurry, foggy, hazy, indistinct, diffuse(d). **9** gentle, good-tempered, mild, conciliatory, soothing, complimentary, pacific; amorous. **10** compassionate, tender-hearted, sympathetic, understanding, caring, humane, benign, merciful, kind-hearted, kind. **11 a** easygoing, tolerant, gentle, merciful, lenient, indulgent, permissive, liberal, lax, easy, docile, tame, submissive, deferential; soft in the head, feeble-minded, foolish, silly, simple, sentimental, *esp. Brit. colloq.* daft. **b** weak, feeble, frail, effete, delicate, non-physical, non-muscular, puny, flabby, out of training *or* condition *or* shape, pampered; namby-pamby, effeminate, unmanly, unmanful, *colloq.* sissified, sissy. **12** easy, comfortable, undemanding, *colloq.* cushy. **13** harmless, mild, non-addictive. ▫ **have a soft spot for** favour, be partial *or* predisposed to, be fond of, have a weakness *or* liking for, feel an attraction to *or* towards, *disp.* feel an affinity to *or* for. **soft drink** pop, fizzy drink, squash, crush, juice, *esp. US* soda. **soft-headed, soft in the head** see *weak-minded* 1. **soft-pedal 1** see SOFTEN 1. **2** see MUTE *v.* **soft sell** see *promotion* (PROMOTE), PERSUASION 1. **soft soap 2** see FLANNEL *n.* 3. **soft-soap** see FLATTER 1. **soft touch** see PUSHOVER 2.

softa /sóftə/ *n.* a Muslim student of sacred law and theology. [Turk. f. Pers. *sūḵta* burnt, afire]

softball /sóftbawl/ *n.* **1** a ball like a baseball but softer and larger. **2** a modified form of baseball using this.

soften /sóff'n/ *v.* **1** *tr.* & *intr.* make or become soft or softer. **2** *tr.* (often foll. by *up*) **a** reduce the strength of (defences) by bombing or some other preliminary attack. **b** reduce the resistance of (a person). □ **softening of the brain** a morbid degeneration of the brain, esp. in old age. □□ **softener** *n.*

■ **1** muffle, deaden, damp, soft-pedal, lower, still, quiet, tone down, subdue, lessen, diminish, lighten, turn down, quell, mitigate, assuage, moderate, reduce, cushion, buffer, weaken, allay, alleviate, ease, abate, temper, relieve, *Brit.* quieten. **2 b** soften up, melt, affect, mollify, mellow, palliate, soothe, relax, appease.

soft-hearted /sóft-ha̋artid/ *adj.* tender, compassionate; easily moved. □□ **soft-heartedness** *n.*

■ tender-hearted, compassionate, tender, warm-hearted, sentimental, charitable, generous, giving, sympathetic, indulgent, merciful, forgiving, soft, kind, kind-hearted, responsive. □□ **soft-heartedness** see MERCY 1, 2.

softie /sófti/ *n.* (also **softy**) *colloq.* a weak or silly or soft-hearted person.

■ see WEAKLING.

softly /sóftli/ *adv.* in a soft, gentle, or quiet manner. □ **softly softly** (of an approach or strategy) cautious; discreet and cunning.

■ see *quietly* (QUIET).

software /sóftwair/ *n.* the programs and other operating information used by a computer (opp. HARDWARE 3).

softwood /sóftwo͝od/ *n.* the wood of pine, spruce, or other conifers, easily sawn.

softy var. of SOFTIE.

SOGAT /sṓgat/ *abbr.* (in the UK) Society of Graphical and Allied Trades. ¶ From 1982 officially called SOGAT 82.

soggy /sóggi/ *adj.* (**soggier**, **soggiest**) sodden, saturated, dank. □□ **soggily** *adv.* **sogginess** *n.* [dial. *sog* a swamp]

■ see WET *adj.* 1.

soh /sō/ *n.* (also **so**, **sol** /sol/) *Mus.* **1** (in tonic sol-fa) the fifth note of a major scale. **2** the note G in the fixed-doh system. [*sol* f. ME *sol* f. L *solve*: see GAMUT]

soi-disant /swa̋adeezóɴ/ *adj.* self-styled or pretended. [F f. *soi* oneself + *disant* saying]

■ see SELF-STYLED.

soigné /swa̋anyay/ *adj.* (*fem.* ***soignée*** *pronunc.* same) carefully finished or arranged; well-groomed. [past part. of F *soigner* take care of f. *soin* care]

■ see ELEGANT 1, 2.

soil[1] /soyl/ *n.* **1** the upper layer of earth in which plants grow, consisting of disintegrated rock usu. with an admixture of organic remains (*alluvial soil*; *rich soil*). **2** ground belonging to a nation; territory (*on British soil*). □ **soil mechanics** the study of the properties of soil as affecting its use in civil engineering. **soil science** pedology. □□ **soilless** *adj.* **soily** *adj.* [ME f. AF, perh. f. L *solium* seat, taken in sense of L *solum* ground]

■ **1** earth, loam, dirt, ground, turf, humus; clay, marl. **2** ground, territory, land.

soil[2] /soyl/ *v.* & *n.* ● *v.tr.* **1** make dirty; smear or stain with dirt (*soiled linen*). **2** tarnish, defile; bring discredit to (*would not soil my hands with it*). ● *n.* **1** a dirty mark; a stain, smear, or defilement. **2** filth; refuse matter. □ **soil pipe** the discharge-pipe of a lavatory. [ME f. OF *suiller*, *soiller*, etc., ult. f. L *sucula* dimin. of *sus* pig]

■ *v.* **1** dirty, stain, begrime, muddy, smear, spot. **2** pollute, contaminate, sully, defile, foul, tarnish, besmirch, disgrace, muddy, smear, blacken, *poet.* befoul; blot. ● *n.* **2** dirt, filth, muck, mire, mud, sludge, dregs, refuse; excrement, waste (matter), sewage.

soil[3] /soyl/ *v.tr.* feed (cattle) on fresh-cut green fodder (orig. for purging). [perh. f. SOIL[2]]

soirée /swa̋aray/ *n.* an evening party, usu. in a private house, for conversation or music. [F f. *soir* evening]

■ see PARTY[1] *n.* 1.

soixante-neuf /swaasoɴtnṓf/ *n. sl.* sexual activity between two people involving mutual oral stimulation of the genitals. [F, = sixty-nine, from the position of the couple]

sojourn /sójurn/ *n.* & *v.* ● *n.* a temporary stay. ● *v.intr.* stay temporarily. □□ **sojourner** *n.* [ME f. OF *sojorn* etc. f. LL SUB- + *diurnum* day]

■ *n.* stay, stop, stopover, visit, rest, holiday, vacation. ● *v.* stay, stop (over), visit, rest, holiday, vacation, *archaic or literary* tarry.

soke /sōk/ *n. Brit. hist.* **1** a right of local jurisdiction. **2** a district under a particular jurisdiction and administration. [ME f. AL *sōca* f. OE *sōcn* prosecution f. Gmc]

Sol /sol/ *n.* (in Roman mythology) the sun, esp. as a personification. [ME f. L]

sol[1] var. of SOH.

sol[2] /sol/ *n. Chem.* a liquid suspension of a colloid. [abbr. of SOLUTION]

sola[1] /sṓlə/ *n.* a pithy-stemmed E. Indian swamp plant, *Aeschynomene indica.* □ **sola topi** an Indian sun-helmet made from its pith. [Urdu & Bengali *solā*, Hindi *sholā*]

sola[2] *fem.* of SOLUS.

solace /sólləss/ *n.* & *v.* ● *n.* comfort in distress, disappointment, or tedium. ● *v.tr.* give solace to. □ **solace oneself with** find compensation or relief in. [ME f. OF *solas* f. L *solatium* f. *solari* CONSOLE[1]]

■ *n.* comfort, consolation, condolence, relief, balm, support, help, succour; reassurance, cheer. ● *v.* comfort, console, condole, support, help, succour, soothe, allay, alleviate, mitigate, assuage, relieve, *formal* ameliorate; cheer (up), reassure, hearten.

solan /sṓlən/ *n.* (in full **solan goose**) a gannet, *Sula bassana.* [prob. f. ON *súla* gannet + *önd*, *and-* duck]

solanaceous /sóllənáyshəss/ *adj.* of or relating to the plant family Solanaceae, including potatoes, nightshades, and tobacco. [mod.L *solanaceae* f. L *sōlānum* nightshade]

solar /sṓlər/ *adj.* & *n.* ● *adj.* of, relating to, or reckoned by the sun (*solar eclipse*; *solar time*). ● *n.* **1** a solarium. **2** an upper chamber in a medieval house. □ **solar battery** (or **cell**) a device converting solar radiation into electricity. **solar constant** the quantity of heat reaching the earth from the sun. **solar day** the interval between successive meridian transits of the sun at a place. **solar month** one-twelfth of the solar year. **solar myth** a tale explained as symbolizing solar phenomena. **solar panel** a panel designed to absorb the sun's rays as a source of energy for operating electricity or heating. **solar plexus** a complex of radiating nerves at the pit of the stomach. **solar system** the sun and the celestial bodies whose motion it governs. **solar wind** the continuous flow of charged particles from the sun. **solar year** the time taken for the earth to travel once round the sun, equal to 365 days, 5 hours, 48 minutes, and 46 seconds. [ME f. L *solaris* f. *sol* sun]

solarium /səláiriəm/ *n.* (*pl.* **solaria** /-riə/) a room equipped with sun-lamps or fitted with extensive areas of glass for exposure to the sun. [L, = sundial, sunning-place (as SOLAR)]

solarize /sṓlərīz/ *v.intr.* & *tr.* (also **-ise**) *Photog.* undergo or cause to undergo change in the relative darkness of parts of an image by long exposure. □□ **solarization** /-záysh'n/ *n.*

solatium /səláyshiəm/ *n.* (*pl.* **solatia** /-shiə/) a thing given as a compensation or consolation. [L, = SOLACE]

sold *past* and *past part.* of SELL.

soldanella /sóldənéllə/ *n.* any dwarf Alpine plant of the genus *Soldanella*, having bell-shaped flowers with fringed petals. [mod.L f. It.]

solder /sṓldər, sól-/ *n.* & *v.* ● *n.* **1** a fusible alloy used to join less fusible metals or wires etc. **2** a cementing or joining agency. ● *v.tr.* join with solder. □ **soldering iron** a tool used for applying solder. □□ **solderable** *n.* **solderer** *n.* [ME f. OF *soudure* f. *souder* f. L *solidare* fasten f. *solidus* SOLID]

■ *n.* see CEMENT *n.* 2. ● *v.* see JOIN *v.* 1, 2.

soldier /sṓljər/ *n.* & *v.* ● *n.* **1** a person serving in or having served in an army. **2** (in full **common soldier**) a private or NCO in an army. **3** a military commander of specified ability (*a great soldier*). **4** (in full **soldier ant**) a wingless ant or termite with a large head and jaws for fighting in defence of its colony. **5** (in full **soldier beetle**) a reddish-coloured beetle, *Rhagonycha fulva*, with flesh-eating larvae. ● *v.intr.* serve as a soldier (*was off soldiering*). □ **soldier of Christ** an active or proselytizing Christian. **soldier of fortune** an adventurous person ready to take service under any State or person; a mercenary. **soldier on** *colloq.* persevere doggedly. □□ **soldierly** *adj.* **soldiership** *n.* [ME *souder* etc. f. OF *soudier, soldier* f. *soulde* (soldier's) pay f. L *solidus*: see SOLIDUS]

■ *n.* **1, 2** serviceman, servicewoman, regular (soldier), GI, recruit, conscript, fighter, infantryman, foot-soldier, trooper, warrior, military man, *US* GI, enlisted man, *archaic* man-at-arms, *colloq.* Tommy (Atkins), *US colloq.* doughboy, *Brit. sl.* squaddie; mercenary; private (soldier), NCO, non-commissioned officer. ● *v.* serve (in the army). □ **soldier of fortune** mercenary, *usu. derog.* hireling; see also ADVENTURER 1. **soldier on** continue, persist, persevere, battle on, struggle on, endure, keep going, keep on, grind away. □□ **soldierly** see MARTIAL.

soldiery /sṓljəri/ *n.* (*pl.* **-ies**) **1** soldiers, esp. of a specified character. **2** a group of soldiers.

■ **1** see MILITARY *n.*

sole[1] /sōl/ *n.* & *v.* ● *n.* **1** the under-surface of the foot. **2** the part of a shoe, sock, etc., corresponding to this (esp. excluding the heel). **3** the lower surface or base of an implement, e.g. a plough, golf-club head, etc. **4** the floor of a ship's cabin. ● *v.tr.* provide (a shoe etc.) with a sole. □ **sole-plate** the bedplate of an engine etc. □□ **-soled** *adj.* (in *comb.*). [OF ult. f. L *solea* sandal, sill: cf. OE unrecorded *solu* or *sola* f. *solum* bottom, pavement, sole]

sole[2] /sōl/ *n.* any flatfish of the family Soleidae, esp. *Solea solea* used as food. [ME f. OF f. Prov. *sola* ult. f. L *solea* (as SOLE[1], named from its shape)]

sole[3] /sōl/ *adj.* **1** (*attrib.*) one and only; single, exclusive (*the sole reason; has the sole right*). **2** *archaic* or *Law* (esp. of a woman) unmarried. **3** *archaic* alone, unaccompanied. □□ **solely** *adv.* [ME f. OF *soule* f. L *sola* fem. of *solus* alone]

■ **1** lone, (one and) only, single, singular, unique, solitary; particular, exclusive, individual, personal.

solecism /sóllisiz'm/ *n.* **1** a mistake of grammar or idiom; a blunder in the manner of speaking or writing. **2** a piece of bad manners or incorrect behaviour. □□ **solecist** *n.* **solecistic** /-sístik/ *adj.* [F *solécisme* or L *soloecismus* f. Gk *soloikismos* f. *soloikos* speaking incorrectly]

■ catachresis; error, slip, impropriety, fault, breach, violation, lapse, mistake, misusage, incongruity, inconsistency, barbarism, blunder, gaffe, bungle, fumble, gaucherie, *faux pas*, botch, *esp. US colloq.* blooper, *US colloq.* flub, *sl.* booboo, boner, bloomer, *Brit. sl.* boob.

solemn /sólləm/ *adj.* **1** serious and dignified (*a solemn occasion*). **2** formal; accompanied by ceremony (*a solemn oath*). **3** mysteriously impressive. **4** (of a person) serious or cheerless in manner (*looks rather solemn*). **5** full of importance; weighty (*a solemn warning*). **6** grave, sober, deliberate; slow in movement or action (*a solemn promise; solemn music*). □ **solemn mass** = *high mass* (see MASS[2]). □□ **solemnly** *adv.* **solemness** *n.* [ME f. OF *solemne* f. L *sol(l)emnis* customary, celebrated at a fixed date f. *sollus* entire]

■ **1** serious, dignified, ceremonial, ceremonious, ritual, formal, stately, grand, august, imposing, impressive, awe-inspiring, awesome, important, momentous. **2** formal, ceremonial, sacramental, ritual, ritualistic, liturgical, religious, official. **3** imposing, impressive, awe-inspiring, awesome. **4** serious, sober, reserved, grave, earnest, sedate, staid, taciturn; morose, mirthless, cheerless, sad, unsmiling, gloomy, funereal, sombre, grim; glum, long-faced, po-faced, saturnine. **5** important, weighty, grave, serious. **6** grave, sober, deliberate, earnest, measured. □□ **solemness** see SOLEMNITY 1.

solemnity /səlémniti/ *n.* (*pl.* **-ies**) **1** the state of being solemn; a solemn character or feeling; solemn behaviour. **2** a rite or celebration; a piece of ceremony. [ME f. OF *solem(p)nité* f. L *sollemnitas -tatis* (as SOLEMN)]

■ **1** solemness, gravity, seriousness, soberness, reserve, sedateness, taciturnity, staidness, earnestness, impressiveness, grandeur, importance, momentousness, consequence. **2** see RITE.

solemnize /sólləmnīz/ *v.tr.* (also **-ise**) **1** duly perform (a ceremony esp. of marriage). **2** celebrate (a festival etc.). **3** make solemn. □□ **solemnization** /-záysh'n/ *n.* [ME f. OF *solem(p)niser* f. med.L *solemnizare* (as SOLEMN)]

■ **1, 2** see CELEBRATE *v.* 1, 2. □□ **solemnization** see *celebration* (CELEBRATE).

solen /sṓlən/ *n.* any razor-shell of the genus *Solen*. [L f. Gk *sōlēn* tube, shellfish]

solenoid /sṓlənoyd, sól-/ *n.* a cylindrical coil of wire acting as a magnet when carrying electric current. □□ **solenoidal** /-nóyd'l/ *adj.* [F *solénoïde* (as SOLEN)]

sol-fa /sólfaa/ *n.* & *v.* ● *n.* = SOLMIZATION; (cf. *tonic sol-fa*). ● *v.tr.* (**-fas, -faed**) sing (a tune) with sol-fa syllables. [SOL[1] + FA]

solfatara /sólfətaárə/ *n.* a volcanic vent emitting only sulphurous and other vapours. [name of a volcano near Naples, f. It. *solfo* sulphur]

solfeggio /solféjiō/ *n.* (*pl.* **solfeggi** /-ji/) *Mus.* **1** an exercise in singing using sol-fa syllables. **2** solmization. [It. (as SOL-FA)]

soli *pl.* of SOLO.

solicit /səlíssit/ *v.* (**solicited, soliciting**) **1** *tr.* & (foll. by *for*) *intr.* ask repeatedly or earnestly for or seek or invite (business etc.). **2** *tr.* (often foll. by *for*) make a request or petition to (a person). **3** *tr.* accost (a person) and offer one's services as a prostitute. □□ **solicitation** /-táysh'n/ *n.* [ME f. OF *solliciter* f. L *sollicitare* agitate f. *sollicitus* anxious f. *sollus* entire + *citus* past part., = set in motion]

■ **1, 2** entreat, beseech, ask (for), implore, petition (for), importune, appeal for *or* to, call on *or* upon, beg, supplicate, pray (for), request; crave, seek. **3** accost, approach, entice, lure, *colloq.* proposition, *sl.* hustle.

solicitor /səlíssitər/ *n.* **1** *Brit.* a member of the legal profession qualified to deal with conveyancing, draw up wills, etc., and to advise clients and instruct barristers. **2** a person who solicits. **3** *US* a canvasser. **4** *US* the chief law officer of a city etc. □ **Solicitor-General 1** (in the UK) the Crown law officer below the Attorney-General or (in Scotland) below the Lord Advocate. **2** (in the US) the law officer below the Attorney-General. [ME f. OF *solliciteur* (as SOLICIT)]

■ **1** lawyer, legal practitioner, conveyancer, *US* attorney.

solicitous /səlíssitəss/ *adj.* **1** (often foll. by *of, about*, etc.) showing interest or concern. **2** (foll. by *to* + infin.) eager, anxious. □□ **solicitously** *adv.* **solicitousness** *n.* [L *sollicitus* (as SOLICIT)]

■ **1** concerned, caring, considerate, thoughtful, tender, attentive, uneasy, troubled, anxious, apprehensive, worried. **2** eager, earnest, keen, anxious, desirous, ardent, avid. □□ **solicitousness** see SOLICITUDE, SYMPATHY 2.

solicitude /səlíssityood/ *n.* **1** the state of being solicitous; solicitous behaviour. **2** anxiety or concern. [ME f. OF *sollicitude* f. L *sollicitudo* (as SOLICITOUS)]

■ concern, consideration, regard, solicitousness, disquiet, disquietude, uneasiness, anxiety, apprehension, worry, nervousness, fear, fearfulness, alarm.

solid /sóllid/ *adj.* & *n.* ● *adj.* (**solider, solidest**) **1** firm and stable in shape; not liquid or fluid (*solid food; water becomes solid at 0°C*). **2** of such material throughout, not hollow or containing cavities (*a solid sphere*). **3** of the same substance throughout (*solid silver*). **4** of strong material or construction or build, not flimsy or slender etc. **5 a** having three dimensions. **b** concerned with solids (*solid geometry*). **6 a** sound and reliable; genuine (*solid arguments*). **b** staunch and dependable (*a solid Tory*). **7** sound but without any special flair etc. (*a solid piece of work*). **8** financially sound. **9** (of time) uninterrupted, continuous (*spend four solid hours on it*). **10 a** unanimous, undivided (*support has been pretty solid so far*). **b** (foll. by *for*) united in favour of. **11** (of printing) without spaces between the lines etc. **12** (of a tyre) without a central air space. **13** (foll. by *with*) *US colloq.* on good terms. **14** *Austral.* & *NZ colloq.* severe, unreasonable. ● *n.* **1** a solid substance or body. **2** (in *pl.*) solid food. **3** *Geom.* a body or magnitude having three dimensions. □ **solid angle** an angle formed by planes etc. meeting at a point. **solid colour** colour covering the whole of an object, without a pattern etc. **solid-drawn** (of a tube etc.) pressed or drawn out from a solid bar of metal. **solid solution** solid material containing one substance uniformly distributed in another. **solid state** the state of matter that retains its boundaries without support. **solid-state** *adj.* using the electronic properties of solids (e.g. a semiconductor) to replace those of valves. □□ **solidly** *adv.* **solidness** *n.* [ME f. OF *solide* f. L *solidus*, rel. to *salvus* safe, *sollus* entire]

■ *adj.* **1** firm, hard, compact, stable, rigid. **2** see DENSE 1. **3** consistent, homogeneous, uniform, unalloyed, unmixed, pure, continuous, unbroken, real, authentic, true, genuine, 24-carat, unadulterated, *colloq.* honest-to-God. **4** stable, sturdy, strong, substantial, sound, firm, well-built, well-constructed, well-made, tough, durable, robust, rugged, stout. **5** three-dimensional, cubic. **6 a** cogent, sound, concrete, weighty, proved, proven, provable, valid, reasonable, sensible, rational, sober, well-founded, authoritative, indisputable, incontrovertible, irrefutable, incontestable, reliable, genuine, good, strong, powerful, potent, forceful, telling, convincing, persuasive. **b** staunch, dependable, reliable, steady, steadfast, unshakeable, stalwart, sober, straight, estimable, sure, trustworthy, true-blue, loyal, worthy, law-abiding, upstanding, upright, decent, stout, *archaic or joc.* trusty. **8** see SOLVENT *adj.* **9** continuous, uninterrupted, undivided, unbroken, unrelieved. **10** see UNITED 3. □□ **solidly** see *firmly* (FIRM[1]), SURELY 3.

solidarity /sóllidárriti/ *n.* **1** unity or agreement of feeling or action, esp. among individuals with a common interest. **2** mutual dependence. [F *solidarité* f. *solidaire* f. *solide* SOLID]

■ **1** unity, unanimity, accord, concord, concordance, harmony, concurrence, like-mindedness, agreement, single-mindedness, singleness (of purpose), community of interest, *esprit de corps*, camaraderie, comradeship.

solidi *pl.* of SOLIDUS.

solidify /səlíddifī/ *v.tr.* & *intr.* (**-ies, -ied**) make or become solid. □□ **solidification** /-fikáysh'n/ *n.* **solidifier** *n.*

■ harden, freeze, set, firm up, thicken, cake, clot, congeal, coagulate, sinter, consolidate, crystallize, *Chem.* sublimate, sublime; compact, compress, *literary* inspissate; gel, *colloq.* jell.

solidity /səlídditi/ *n.* the state of being solid; firmness.

■ see STABILITY.

solidus /sóllidəss/ *n.* (*pl.* **solidi** /-dī/) **1** an oblique stroke (/) used in writing fractions (3/4), to separate other figures and letters, or to denote alternatives (*and/or*) and ratios (*miles/day*). **2** (in full **solidus curve**) a curve in a graph of the temperature and composition of a mixture, below which the substance is entirely solid. **3** *hist.* a gold coin of the later Roman Empire. [ME (in sense 3) f. L: see SOLID]

■ **1** see LINE[1] *n.* 1.

solifluction /sōliflúksh'n, sól-/ *n.* the gradual movement of wet soil etc. down a slope. [L *solum* soil + L *fluctio* flowing f. *fluere fluct-* flow]

soliloquy /səlílləkwi/ *n.* (*pl.* **-ies**) **1** the act of talking when alone or regardless of any hearers, esp. in drama. **2** part of a play involving this. □□ **soliloquist** *n.* **soliloquize** *v.intr.* (also **-ise**). [LL *soliloquium* f. L *solus* alone + *loqui* speak]

soliped /sólliped/ *adj.* & *n.* ● *adj.* (of an animal) solid-hoofed. ● *n.* a solid-hoofed animal. [F *solipède* or mod.L *solipes -pedis* f. L *solidipes* f. *solidus* solid + *pes* foot]

solipsism /sóllipsiz'm/ *n. Philos.* the view that the self is all that exists or can be known. □□ **solipsist** *n.* **solipsistic** /-sístik/ *adj.* **solipsistically** /-sístikəli/ *adv.* [L *solus* alone + *ipse* self]

solitaire /sóllitáir/ *n.* **1** a diamond or other gem set by itself. **2** a ring having a single gem. **3** a game for one player played by removing pegs etc. one at a time from a board by jumping others over them until only one is left. **4** *US* = PATIENCE 4. **5** any of various extinct dodo-like flightless birds of the family Raphidae. **6** any American thrush of the genus *Myadestes*. [F f. L *solitarius* (as SOLITARY)]

solitary /sóllitəri, -tri/ *adj.* & *n.* ● *adj.* **1** living alone; not gregarious; without companions; lonely (*a solitary existence*). **2** (of a place) secluded or unfrequented. **3** single or sole (*a solitary instance*). **4** (of an insect) not living in communities. **5** *Bot.* growing singly, not in a cluster. ● *n.* (*pl.* **-ies**) **1** a recluse or anchorite. **2** *colloq.* = *solitary confinement*. □ **solitary confinement** isolation of a prisoner in a separate cell as a punishment. □□ **solitarily** *adv.* **solitariness** *n.* [ME f. L *solitarius* f. *solus* alone]

■ *adj.* **1** alone, single; unattended, solo, companionless, friendless, lonesome, lonely, unsocial, cloistered, secluded, reclusive, separate, eremitic(al), hermitic(al), remote, withdrawn, distant, *literary* unfriended. **2** secluded, remote, distant, out-of-the-way, unfrequented, lonely, desolate. **3** single, lone, sole, individual, isolated; unique. ● *n.* **1** see HERMIT. □ **solitary confinement** isolation, separation, *colloq.* solitary; see also SEGREGATION. □□ **solitarily** see SOLO *adv.* **solitariness** see SOLITUDE 1.

solitude /sóllityōōd/ *n.* **1** the state of being solitary. **2** a lonely place. [ME f. OF *solitude* or L *solitudo* f. *solus* alone]

■ **1** solitariness, aloneness, isolation, seclusion, privacy; loneliness, remoteness. **2** emptiness, wilderness; desert island.

solmization /sólmizáysh'n/ *n. Mus.* a system of associating each note of a scale with a particular syllable, now usu. *doh ray me fah soh lah te*, with doh as C in the fixed-doh system and as the keynote in the movable-doh or tonic sol-fa system. □□ **solmizate** /sólmizayt/ *v.intr.* & *tr.* [F *solmisation* (as SOL[1], MI)]

solo /sōlō/ *n.*, *v.*, & *adv.* ● *n.* (*pl.* **-os**) **1** (*pl.* **-os** or **soli** /-li/) **a** a vocal or instrumental piece or passage, or a dance, performed by one person with or without accompaniment. **b** (*attrib.*) performed or performing as a solo (*solo passage*; *solo violin*). **2 a** an unaccompanied flight by a pilot in an aircraft. **b** anything done by one person unaccompanied. **c** (*attrib.*) unaccompanied, alone. **3** (in full **solo whist**) **a** a card-game like whist in which one player may oppose the others. **b** a declaration or the act of playing to win five tricks at this. ● *v.* (**-oes, -oed**) **1** *intr.* perform a solo, esp. a solo flight. **2** *tr.* perform or achieve as a solo. ● *adv.* unaccompanied, alone (*flew solo for the first time*). □ **solo stop** an organ stop especially suitable for imitating a solo performance on another instrument. [It. f. L *solus* alone]

■ *n.* **1b, 2c** (*attrib.*) unaccompanied, individual, solitary; single-handed, unaided. ● *adv.* alone, unaccompanied, solus, on one's own, single-handed(ly).

soloist /sōlō-ist/ *n.* a performer of a solo, esp. in music.

Solomon /sólləmən/ *n.* a very wise person. □ **Solomon's seal 1** a figure like the Star of David. **2** any liliaceous plant of the genus *Polygonatum*, with arching stems and drooping green and white flowers. □□ **Solomonic** /sólləmónnik/ *adj.* [*Solomon*, king of Israel in the 10th c. BC, famed for his wisdom]

■ see SAGE[2] *n.* 1.

solstice /sólstiss/ *n.* **1** either of the times when the sun is furthest from the equator. **2** the point in its ecliptic reached by the sun at a solstice. □ **summer solstice** the time at which the sun is furthest north from the equator, about 21 June in the northern hemisphere. **winter solstice** the time at which the sun is furthest south from the equator, about 22 Dec. in the northern hemisphere. □□ **solstitial** /solstísh'l/ *adj.* [ME f. OF f. L *solstitium* f. *sol* sun + *sistere stit-* make stand]

solubilize /sólyoobilīz/ *v.tr.* (also **-ise**) make soluble or more soluble. ▫▫ **solubilization** /-záysh'n/ *n.*

soluble /sólyoob'l/ *adj.* **1** that can be dissolved, esp. in water. **2** that can be solved. ▫ **soluble glass** = *water-glass.* ▫▫ **solubility** /-bílliti/ *n.* [ME f. OF f. LL *solubilis* (as SOLVE)]

solus /sṓləss/ *predic.adj.* (*fem.* **sola** /-lə/) (esp. in a stage direction) alone, unaccompanied. [L]

solute /sólyo͞ot/ *n.* a dissolved substance. [L *solutum*, neut. of *solutus*: see SOLVE]

solution /səló͞osh'n, -lyó͞osh'n/ *n.* **1 a** the act or a means of solving a problem or difficulty. **b** an explanation, answer, or decision. **2 a** the conversion of a solid or gas into a liquid by mixture with a liquid solvent. **b** a liquid mixture produced by this. **c** the state resulting from this (*held in solution*). **3** the act of dissolving or the state of being dissolved. **4** the act of separating or breaking. **5** = *rubber solution* (see RUBBER[1]). ▫ **solution set** *Math.* the set of all the solutions of an equation or condition. [ME f. OF f. L *solutio -onis* (as SOLVE)]

■ **1** solving, working *or* figuring out, unravelling, explication, decipherment, elucidation, clarification, explanation; answer, decision, key; settlement, resolution, result. **2a, 3** dissolving, mixing, blending. **2b** mixture, blend, compound, infusion; liquid, fluid; emulsion, suspension, *Chem.* colloid, colloidal solution, colloidal suspension.

Solutrean /səló͞otriən/ *adj.* & *n.* (also **Solutrian**) ● *adj.* of the palaeolithic period in Europe following the Aurignacian and preceding the Magdalenian. ● *n.* the culture of this period. [*Solutré* in E. France, where remains of it were found]

solvate /sólvayt/ *v.intr.* & *tr.* enter or cause to enter combination with a solvent. ▫▫ **solvation** /-váysh'n/ *n.*

solve /solv/ *v.tr.* find an answer to, or an action or course that removes or effectively deals with (a problem or difficulty). ▫▫ **solvable** *adj.* **solver** *n.* [ME, = loosen, f. L *solvere solut-* unfasten, release]

■ work *or* figure out, unravel, disentangle, untangle, sort out, clarify, clear up, make plain *or* clear, interpret, explicate, decipher, explain, elucidate, reveal, answer, resolve, *colloq.* crack, *Brit. sl.* suss out.

solvent /sólv'nt/ *adj.* & *n.* ● *adj.* **1** able to dissolve or form a solution with something. **2** having enough money to meet one's liabilities. ● *n.* **1** a solvent liquid etc. **2** a dissolving or weakening agent. ▫▫ **solvency** *n.* (in sense 2).

■ *adj.* **2** creditworthy, (financially) sound, solid, reliable; debt-free; profitable.

Som. *abbr.* Somerset.

soma[1] /sṓmə/ *n.* **1** the body as distinct from the soul. **2** the body of an organism as distinct from its reproductive cells. [Gk *sōma -atos* body]

soma[2] /sṓmə/ *n.* **1** an intoxicating drink used in Vedic ritual. **2** a plant yielding this. [Skr. *sōma*]

Somali /səmáali/ *n.* & *adj.* ● *n.* **1** (*pl.* same or **Somalis**) a member of a Hamitic Muslim people of Somalia in NE Africa. **2** the Cushitic language of this people. ● *adj.* of or relating to this people or language. ▫▫ **Somalian** *adj.* [native name]

somatic /səmáttik/ *adj.* of or relating to the body, esp. as distinct from the mind. ▫ **somatic cell** any cell of a living organism except the reproductive cells. ▫▫ **somatically** *adv.* [Gk *sōmatikos* (as SOMA[1])]

■ see PHYSICAL *adj.* 2.

somato- /sṓmətō/ *comb. form* the human body. [Gk *sōma -atos* body]

somatogenic /sṓmətōjénnik/ *adj.* originating in the body.

somatology /sṓmətólləji/ *n.* the science of living bodies physically considered.

somatotonic /sṓmətōtónnik/ *adj.* like a mesomorph in temperament, with predominantly physical interests.

somatotrophin /sṓmətōtrṓfin/ *n.* a growth hormone secreted by the pituitary gland. [as SOMATO-, TROPHIC]

somatotype /sṓmətōtīp/ *n.* physique expressed in relation to various extreme types.

sombre /sómbər/ *adj.* (also *US* **somber**) **1** dark, gloomy (*a sombre sky*). **2** oppressively solemn or sober. **3** dismal, foreboding (*a sombre prospect*). ▫▫ **sombrely** *adv.* **sombreness** *n.* [F *sombre* f. OF *sombre* (n.) ult. f. L SUB- + *umbra* shade]

■ **1** dark, shadowy, murky, leaden, grey, black, overcast, louring, dusky, dim, dingy, dull, *formal* subfusc, *poet.* darkling; gloomy, foreboding, bleak, depressing, dismal, dreary, cheerless. **2** gloomy, morose, lugubrious, funereal, morbid, louring, melancholy, sad, dismal, unhappy, cheerless, joyless, serious, sober, staid, sedate, solemn, doleful, mournful, depressed, depressing, grave, grim, grim-faced, melancholic, *literary* grim-visaged, *literary or joc.* dolorous, *poet.* darksome. **3** gloomy, foreboding, bleak, depressing, dismal, dreary, cheerless. ▫▫ **sombrely** see *sadly* (SAD). **sombreness** see GRAVITY 3b.

sombrero /sombráirō/ *n.* (*pl.* **-os**) a broad-brimmed felt or straw hat worn esp. in Mexico and the south-west US. [Sp. f. *sombra* shade (as SOMBRE)]

some /sum/ *adj.*, *pron.*, & *adv.* ● *adj.* **1** an unspecified amount or number of (*some water*; *some apples*; *some of them*). **2** that is unknown or unnamed (*will return some day*; *some fool has locked the door*; *to some extent*). **3** denoting an approximate number (*waited some twenty minutes*). **4** a considerable amount or number of (*went to some trouble*). **5** (usu. stressed) **a** at least a small amount of (*do have some consideration*). **b** such to a certain extent (*that is some help*). **c** *colloq.* notably such (*I call that some story*). ● *pron.* some people or things, some number or amount (*I have some already*; *would you like some more?*). ● *adv. colloq.* to some extent (*we talked some*; *do it some more*). ▫ **and then some** *sl.* and plenty more than that. **some few** see FEW. [OE *sum* f. Gmc]

■ *adj.* **1** see SEVERAL *adj.*

-some[1] /səm/ *suffix* forming adjectives meaning: **1** adapted to; productive of (*cuddlesome*; *fearsome*). **2** characterized by being (*fulsome*; *lithesome*). **3** apt to (*tiresome*; *meddlesome*). [OE *-sum*]

-some[2] /səm/ *suffix* forming nouns from numerals, meaning 'a group of (so many)' (*foursome*). [OE *sum* SOME, used after numerals in genit. pl.]

-some[3] /sōm/ *comb. form* denoting a portion of a body, esp. of a cell (*chromosome*; *ribosome*). [Gk *sōma* body]

somebody /súmbədi/ *pron.* & *n.* ● *pron.* some person. ● *n.* (*pl.* **-ies**) a person of importance (*is really somebody now*).

■ *pron.* one, someone, some person. ● *n.* personage, celebrity, dignitary, VIP, luminary, notable, star, superstar, megastar, *colloq.* bigwig, big shot, big noise, big pot, hot stuff, heavyweight, *esp. US colloq.* hotshot, *sl.* big gun, big bug, big-timer, Big Chief *or* Daddy, (big) cheese, *US sl.* big wheel, Mr Big.

someday /súmday/ *adv.* at some time in the future.

■ see SOMETIME *adv.* 1.

somehow /súmhow/ *adv.* **1** for some reason or other (*somehow I never liked them*). **2** in some unspecified or unknown way (*he somehow dropped behind*). **3** no matter how (*must get it finished somehow*).

■ **2, 3** (in) one way or another, in some way, somehow or other, no matter how, by hook or by crook, by fair means or foul, come hell or high water.

someone /súmwun/ *n.* & *pron.* = SOMEBODY.

someplace /súmplayss/ *adv. US colloq.* = SOMEWHERE.

somersault /súmmərsolt/ *n.* & *v.* (also **summersault**) ● *n.* an acrobatic movement in which a person turns head over heels in the air or on the ground and lands on the feet. ● *v.intr.* perform a somersault. [OF *sombresault* alt. f. *sobresault* ult. f. L *supra* above + *saltus* leap f. *salire* to leap]

■ *n.* tumble, roll.

something /súmthing/ *n.*, *pron.*, & *adv.* ● *n.* & *pron.* **1 a** some unspecified or unknown thing (*have something to tell* *you; something has happened*). **b** (in full **something or other**) as a substitute for an unknown or forgotten description (*a student of something or other*). **2** a known or understood but unexpressed quantity, quality, or extent (*there is something about it I do not like; is something of a fool*). **3** *colloq.* an important or notable person or thing (*the party was quite something*). ● *adv. archaic* in some degree. □ **or something** or some unspecified alternative possibility (*must have run away or something*). **see something of** encounter (a person) briefly or occasionally. **something else 1** something different. **2** *colloq.* something exceptional. **something like 1** an amount in the region of (*left something like a million pounds*). **2** somewhat like (*shaped something like a cigar*). **3** *colloq.* impressive; a fine specimen of. **something of** to some extent; in some sense (*is something of an expert*). [OE *sum thing* (as SOME, THING)]

sometime /súmtīm/ *adv.* & *adj.* ● *adv.* **1** at some unspecified time. **2** formerly. ● *attrib.adj.* former (*the sometime mayor*).
■ *adv.* **1** at some time or other, someday, one day, any time, on a future occasion, when *or* if the opportunity arises, soon, by and by, one of these days, sooner or later, in (due) time, in the fullness of time, in due course, in the long run, one fine day, eventually, when all is said and done, before long, before you know it. **2** see FORMERLY. ● *adj.* former, erstwhile, past, recent, one-time, quondam, late, ex-.

sometimes /súmtīmz/ *adv.* at some times; occasionally.
■ occasionally, on occasion, (every) now and then, now and again, off and on, on and off, at (some) times, from time to time, every so often, (every) once in a while.

somewhat /súmwot/ *adv.*, *n.*, & *pron.* ● *adv.* to some extent (*behaviour that was somewhat strange; answered somewhat hastily*). ● *n.* & *pron. archaic* something (*loses somewhat of its force*). □ **more than somewhat** *colloq.* very (*was more than somewhat perplexed*).
■ *adv.* rather, quite, relatively, more or less, moderately, pretty, fairly, to some extent *or* degree *or* measure, to a certain extent *or* degree *or* measure, slightly, a bit, a little, *colloq.* sort of, kind of.

somewhen /súmwen/ *adv. colloq.* at some time.

somewhere /súmwair/ *adv.* & *pron.* ● *adv.* in or to some place. ● *pron.* some unspecified place. □ **get somewhere** *colloq.* achieve success. **somewhere about** approximately.

somite /sṓmīt/ *n.* each body-division of a metamerically segmented animal. □□ **somitic** /sōmíttik/ *adj.* [Gk *sōma* body + -ITE[1]]

sommelier /sómməlyay/ *n.* a wine waiter. [F, = butler, f. *somme* pack (as SUMPTER)]
■ see WAITER.

somnambulism /somnámbyooliz'm/ *n.* **1** sleepwalking. **2** a condition of the brain inducing this. □□ **somnambulant** *adj.* **somnambulantly** *adv.* **somnambulist** *n.* **somnambulistic** /-lístik/ *adj.* **somnambulistically** /-lístikəli/ *adv.* [L *somnus* sleep + *ambulare* walk]
■ **1** sleepwalking, noctambulism.

somniferous /somníffərəss/ *adj.* inducing sleep; soporific. [L *somnifer* f. *somnium* dream]

somnolent /sómnələnt/ *adj.* **1** sleepy, drowsy. **2** inducing drowsiness. **3** *Med.* in a state between sleeping and waking. □□ **somnolence** *n.* **somnolency** *n.* **somnolently** *adv.* [ME f. OF *sompnolent* or L *somnolentus* f. *somnus* sleep]
■ **1** see SLEEPY 1. **2** see NARCOTIC *adj.* □□ **somnolence** see TORPOR.

son /sun/ *n.* **1** a boy or man in relation to either or both of his parents. **2 a** a male descendant. **b** (foll. by *of*) a male member of a family, nation, etc. **3** a person regarded as inheriting an occupation, quality, etc., or associated with a particular attribute (*sons of freedom; sons of the soil*). **4** (in full **my son**) a form of address esp. to a boy. **5** (**the Son**) (in Christian belief) the second person of the Trinity. □ **son-in-law** (*pl.* **sons-in-law**) the husband of one's daughter. **son of a bitch** *sl.* a general term of contempt. **son of a gun** *colloq.* a jocular or affectionate form of address or reference. □□ **sonless** *adj.* **sonship** *n.* [OE *sunu* f. Gmc]
■ □ **son of a bitch** see STINKER, WRETCH 2.

sonant /sṓnənt/ *adj.* & *n. Phonet.* ● *adj.* (of a sound) voiced and syllabic. ● *n.* a voiced sound, esp. other than a vowel and capable of forming a syllable, e.g. *l, m, n, ng, r.* □□ **sonancy** *n.* [L *sonare sonant-* sound]

sonar /sṓnər/ *n.* **1** a system for the underwater detection of objects by reflected or emitted sound. **2** an apparatus for this. [*so*und *na*vigation and *r*anging, after *radar*]

sonata /sənaátə/ *n.* a composition for one instrument or two (one usu. being a piano accompaniment), usu. in several movements with one (esp. the first) or more in sonata form. □ **sonata form** a type of composition in three sections (exposition, development, and recapitulation) in which two themes (or subjects) are explored according to set key relationships. [It., = sounded (orig. as distinct from sung): fem. past part. of *sonare* sound]

sonatina /sónnəteénə/ *n.* a simple or short sonata. [It., dimin. of SONATA]

sonde /sond/ *n.* a device sent up to obtain information about atmospheric conditions, esp. = RADIOSONDE. [F, = sounding(-line)]

sone /sōn/ *n.* a unit of subjective loudness, equal to 40 phons. [L *sonus* sound]

son et lumière /són ay lóomyair/ *n.* an entertainment by night at a historic monument, building, etc., using lighting effects and recorded sound to give a dramatic narrative of its history. [F, = sound and light]

song /song/ *n.* **1** a short poem or other set of words set to music or meant to be sung. **2** singing or vocal music (*burst into song*). **3** a musical composition suggestive of a song. **4** the musical cry of some birds. **5** a short poem in rhymed stanzas. **6** *archaic* poetry or verse. □ **for a song** *colloq.* very cheaply. **on song** *Brit. colloq.* performing exceptionally well. **song and dance** *colloq.* a fuss or commotion. **song cycle** a set of musically linked songs on a romantic theme. **Song of Songs** (or **of Solomon**) a poetic Old Testament book traditionally attributed to Solomon. **song sparrow** a N. American sparrow, *Melospiza melodia*, with a characteristic musical song. **song thrush** a thrush, *Turdus philomelos*, of Europe and W. Asia, with a song partly mimicked from other birds. □□ **songless** *adj.* [OE *sang* f. Gmc (as SING)]
■ **1** tune, air, melody, strain, ditty, number; chant, lay, ballad, madrigal, serenade, shanty, jingle; hymn, carol, anthem. □ **for a song** cheaply, inexpensively, at a bargain price, on the cheap. **song and dance** fuss, to-do, commotion, bother, ado, palaver, *colloq.* flap, performance, *esp. Brit. colloq.* kerfuffle.

songbird /sóngburd/ *n.* a bird with a musical call.

songbook /sóngbŏŏk/ *n.* a collection of songs with music.

songsmith /sóngsmith/ *n.* a writer of songs.

songster /sóngstər/ *n.* (*fem.* **songstress** /-striss/) **1** a singer, esp. a fluent and skilful one. **2** a songbird. **3** a poet. **4** *US* a songbook. [OE *sangestre* (as SONG, -STER)]
■ **1** see *singer* (SING).

songwriter /sóngrītər/ *n.* a writer of songs or the music for them.

sonic /sónnik/ *adj.* of or relating to or using sound or sound waves. □ **sonic bang** (or **boom**) a loud explosive noise caused by the shock wave from an aircraft when it passes the speed of sound. **sonic barrier** = *sound barrier* (see SOUND[1]). **sonic mine** a mine exploded by the sound of a passing ship. □□ **sonically** *adv.* [L *sonus* sound]

sonnet /sónnit/ *n.* & *v.* ● *n.* a poem of 14 lines (usu. pentameters) using any of a number of formal rhyme schemes, in English usu. having ten syllables per line. ● *v.* (**sonneted, sonneting**) **1** *intr.* write sonnets. **2** *tr.* address sonnets to. [F *sonnet* or It. *sonetto* dimin. of *suono* SOUND[1]]

sonneteer /sónniteér/ *n.* usu. *derog.* a writer of sonnets.
■ see POET.

sonny /súnni/ *n. colloq.* a familiar form of address to a young boy.

sonobuoy /sṓnəboy/ *n.* a buoy for detecting underwater sounds and transmitting them by radio. [L *sonus* sound + BUOY]

sonometer /sənómmitər/ *n.* **1** an instrument for measuring the vibration frequency of a string etc. **2** an audiometer. [L *sonus* sound + -METER]

sonorous /sónnərəss, sənórəss/ *adj.* **1** having a loud, full, or deep sound; resonant. **2** (of a speech, style, etc.) imposing, grand. □□ **sonority** /sənórriti/ *n.* **sonorously** *adv.* **sonorousness** *n.* [L *sonorus* f. *sonor* sound]

■ **1** see DEEP *adj.* 5. **2** see ROTUND 2. □□ **sonority, sonorousness** see TONE *n.* 2.

sonsy /sónsi/ *adj.* (also **sonsie**) (**sonsier, sonsiest**) *Sc.* **1** plump, buxom. **2** of a cheerful disposition. **3** bringing good fortune. [ult. f. Ir. & Gael. *sonas* good fortune f. *sona* fortunate]

■ **1** see BUXOM. **2** see GENIAL[1] 1.

sook /sŏŏk/ *n. Austral.* & *NZ sl.* **1** *derog.* a timid bashful person; a coward or sissy. **2** a hand-reared calf. [E dial. *suck*, call-word for a calf]

■ **1** see SISSY *n.*

sool /sōōl/ *v.tr. Austral.* & *NZ sl.* **1** (of a dog) attack or worry (an animal). **2** (often foll. by *on*) urge or goad. □□ **sooler** *n.* [var. of 17th-c. (now dial.) *sowl* seize roughly, of unkn. orig.]

soon /sōōn/ *adv.* **1** after no long interval of time (*shall soon know the result*). **2** relatively early (*must you go so soon?*). **3** (prec. by *how*) early (with relative rather than distinctive sense) (*how soon will it be ready?*). **4** readily or willingly (in expressing choice or preference: *which would you sooner do?*; *would as soon stay behind*). □ **as** (or **so**) **soon as** (implying a causal or temporal connection) at the moment that; not later than; as early as (*came as soon as I heard about it*; *disappears as soon as it's time to pay*). **no sooner . . . than** at the very moment that (*we no sooner arrived than the rain stopped*). **sooner or later** at some future time; eventually. □□ **soonish** *adv.* [OE *sōna* f. WG]

■ **1** before long, presently, in the near future, any minute (now), before you know it, in good time, in a little while, in a minute, in a moment, shortly, quickly, speedily, swiftly, at once, promptly, immediately, directly, without delay, straight away, right away, forthwith, at the double, in a second, in two shakes (of a lamb's *or* dog's tail), in a wink, *tout de suite*, *US* in short order, momentarily, *archaic or literary* anon, *colloq.* in a jiffy, pronto, lickety-split, *poet. or archaic* ere long. **2, 3** early, fast; quickly, swiftly, speedily. **4** willingly, gladly, happily, readily, *archaic* lief. □ **as soon as** as quickly as, as speedily as, as swiftly as, as promptly as, as early as; see also IMMEDIATELY *conj.* **sooner or later** at some time or other, some time, one day, in time, in due course, eventually, ultimately, in the end, at the end of the day, in the long run, when all is said and done, in the last *or* final analysis.

soot /sŏŏt/ *n.* & *v.* ● *n.* a black carbonaceous substance rising in fine flakes in the smoke of wood, coal, oil, etc., and deposited on the sides of a chimney etc. ● *v.tr.* cover with soot. [OE *sōt* f. Gmc]

■ *n.* see DIRT 1.

sooth /sōōth/ *n. archaic* truth, fact. □ **in sooth** really, truly. [OE *sōth* (orig. adj., = true) f. Gmc]

soothe /sōōth/ *v.tr.* **1** calm (a person or feelings). **2** soften or mitigate (pain). **3** *archaic* flatter or humour. □□ **soother** *n.* **soothing** *adj.* **soothingly** *adv.* [OE *sōthian* verify f. *sōth* true: see SOOTH]

■ **1** see CALM *v.* **2** see MITIGATE. **3** see FLATTER 1, HUMOUR *v.* □□ **soothing** relaxing, restful, serene, peaceful, pacifying, sedative, calm, calming, quiet, soft, quieting; mollifying, comforting, palliative, balsamic, emollient, lenitive, demulcent.

soothsayer /sōōthsayər/ *n.* a diviner or seer. [ME, = one who says the truth: see SOOTH]

■ see SEER.

sooty /sŏŏtti/ *adj.* (**sootier, sootiest**) **1** covered with or full of soot. **2** (esp. of an animal or bird) black or brownish-black. □ **sooty albatross** an albatross, *Diomedia chrysostoma*, with grey-brown plumage. □□ **sootily** *adv.* **sootiness** *n.*

■ **1** see DIRTY *adj.* 1. **2** see BLACK *adj.* 1.

sop /sop/ *n.* & *v.* ● *n.* **1** a piece of bread etc. dipped in gravy etc. **2** a thing given or done to pacify or bribe. ● *v.* (**sopped, sopping**) **1** *intr.* be drenched (*came home sopping*). **2** *tr.* (foll. by *up*) absorb (liquid) in a towel etc. **3** *tr.* wet thoroughly; soak. [OE *sopp*, corresp. to MLG *soppe*, OHG *sopfa* bread and milk, prob. f. a weak grade of the base of OE *sūpan*: see SUP[1]]

sophism /sóffiz'm/ *n.* a false argument, esp. one intended to deceive. [ME f. OF *sophime* f. L f. Gk *sophisma* clever device f. *sophizomai* become wise f. *sophos* wise]

■ see QUIBBLE *n.* 3.

sophist /sóffist/ *n.* **1** one who reasons with clever but fallacious arguments. **2** *Gk Antiq.* a paid teacher of philosophy and rhetoric, esp. one associated with moral scepticism and specious reasoning. □□ **sophistic** /-fístik/ *adj.* **sophistical** /səfístik'l/ *adj.* **sophistically** /səfístikəli/ *adv.* [L *sophistes* f. Gk *sophistēs* f. *sophizomai*: see SOPHISM]

■ □□ **sophistic, sophistical** specious, fallacious, deceptive, deceitful, misleading, meretricious, hypocritical, false, unsound, baseless, groundless, casuistic(al), captious, bogus, sham, untenable, *often offens.* Jesuitic(al).

sophisticate *v.*, *adj.*, & *n.* ● *v.* /səfístikayt/ **1** *tr.* make (a person etc.) educated, cultured, or refined. **2** *tr.* make (equipment or techniques etc.) highly developed or complex. **3** *tr.* **a** involve (a subject) in sophistry. **b** mislead (a person) by sophistry. **4** *tr.* deprive (a person or thing) of its natural simplicity, make artificial by worldly experience etc. **5** *tr.* tamper with (a text etc.) for purposes of argument etc. **6** *tr.* adulterate (wine etc.). **7** *intr.* use sophistry. ● *adj.* /səfístikət/ sophisticated. ● *n.* /səfístikət/ a sophisticated person. □□ **sophistication** /-káysh'n/ *n.* [med.L *sophisticare* tamper with f. *sophisticus* (as SOPHISM)]

■ □□ **sophistication** worldliness, urbanity, culture, refinement, knowledge, knowledgeability, cosmopolitanism, polish, elegance, poise, suavity, *savoir faire*, *savoir vivre*, finesse, discrimination, discernment, awareness, taste, tastefulness, style; complexity, intricacy, subtlety, refinement.

sophisticated /səfístikaytid/ *adj.* **1** (of a person) educated and refined; discriminating in taste and judgement. **2** (of a thing, idea, etc.) highly developed and complex. □□ **sophisticatedly** *adv.*

■ **1** cultivated, cultured, refined, educated, experienced, worldly, cosmopolitan, discriminating, polished, elegant, urbane, worldly-wise, knowledgeable, knowing, suave, *soigné(e)*, blasé, chichi, *colloq.* slick, with it, *sl.* hip, hep, cool. **2** advanced, complex, complicated, intricate, elaborate, subtle, refined, multifaceted.

sophistry /sóffistri/ *n.* (*pl.* **-ies**) **1** the use of sophisms. **2** a sophism.

■ **1** see EVASION 2.

sophomore /sóffəmor/ *n. US* a second-year university or high-school student. □□ **sophomoric** /-mórrik/ *adj.* [earlier *sophumer* f. *sophum*, obs. var. of SOPHISM]

Sophy /sṓfi/ *n.* (*pl.* **-ies**) *hist.* a ruler of Persia in the 16th–17th c. [Pers. *ṣafī* surname of the dynasty, f. Arab. *ṣafī-ud-dīn* pure of religion, title of the founder's ancestor]

soporific /sóppəríffik/ *adj.* & *n.* ● *adj.* tending to produce sleep. ● *n.* a soporific drug or influence. □□ **soporiferous** *adj.* **soporifically** *adv.* [L *sopor* sleep + -FIC]

■ *adj.* see TIRESOME 1. ● *n.* see SEDATIVE *n.*

sopping /sópping/ *adj.* (also **sopping wet**) soaked with liquid; wet through. [pres. part. of SOP *v.*]

■ see WET *adj.* 1.

soppy /sóppi/ *adj.* (**soppier, soppiest**) **1** *Brit. colloq.* **a** silly or foolish in a feeble or self-indulgent way. **b** mawkishly sentimental. **2** *Brit. colloq.* (foll. by *on*) foolishly infatuated with. **3** soaked with water. □□ **soppily** *adv.* **soppiness** *n.* [SOP + -Y[1]]

■ **1 b** see SENTIMENTAL. **2** (*soppy on*) see INFATUATED. **3** see WET *adj.* 1. □□ **soppiness** see *sentimentality* (SENTIMENTAL).

sopranino /sóprəneénō/ *n.* (*pl.* **-os**) *Mus.* an instrument higher than soprano, esp. a recorder or saxophone. [It., dimin. of SOPRANO]

soprano /səpraánō/ *n.* (*pl.* **-os** or **soprani** /-ni/) **1 a** the highest singing-voice. **b** a female or boy singer with this voice. **c** a part written for it. **2 a** an instrument of a high or the highest pitch in its family. **b** its player. □ **soprano-clef** an obsolete clef placing middle C on the lowest line of the staff. [It. f. *sopra* above f. L *supra*]

sora /sórə/ *n.* (in full **sora rail**) a bird, *Porzana carolina*, frequenting the marshes of N. and S. Carolina etc. in the autumn and used as food. [prob. a native name]

sorb /sorb/ *n.* **1** = *service tree* (see SERVICE²). **2** (in full **sorb-apple**) its fruit. [F *sorbe* or L *sorbus* service tree, *sorbum* service-berry]

sorbefacient /sórbifáysh'nt/ *adj.* & *n.* *Med.* ● *adj.* causing absorption. ● *n.* a sorbefacient drug etc. [L *sorbēre* suck in + -FACIENT]

sorbet /sórbay, -bit/ *n.* **1** a water-ice. **2** sherbet. [F f. It. *sorbetto* f. Turk. *şerbet* f. Arab. *šarba* to drink: cf. SHERBET]

Sorbo /sórbō/ *n.* *Brit.* *propr.* (in full **Sorbo rubber**) a spongy rubber. [ABSORB + -O]

sorcerer /sórsərər/ *n.* (*fem.* **sorceress** /-riss/) a person who claims to use magic powers; a magician or wizard. □□ **sorcerous** *adj.* **sorcery** *n.* (*pl.* **-ies**). [obs. *sorcer* f. OF *sorcier* ult. f. L *sors sortis* lot]

■ magus, necromancer, wizard, enchanter, magician, thaumaturgist, thaumaturge, shaman, witch-doctor, medicine man, *archaic* warlock; (*sorceress*) witch, enchantress, *Sc.* spaewife. □□ **sorcery** witchcraft, enchantment, sortilege, necromancy, wizardry, (black *or* white) magic, shamanism, black art, diabolism, the occult.

sordid /sórdid/ *adj.* **1** dirty or squalid. **2** ignoble, mean, or mercenary. **3** mean or niggardly. **4** dull-coloured. □□ **sordidly** *adv.* **sordidness** *n.* [F *sordide* or L *sordidus* f. *sordēre* be dirty]

■ **1** dirty, foul, filthy, squalid, unclean, untidy, mean, slummy, seamy, seedy, unsanitary, insanitary, offensive, defiled, polluted, fetid, feculent, mucky, maggoty, putrid, fly-blown, slimy; wretched, miserable, poor, poverty-stricken, down-and-out, impoverished, ramshackle, hovel-like, tumbledown, dingy, deteriorated, sleazy. **2** base, vile, corrupt, low, ignoble, debased, degraded, abased, mean, mercenary, ignominious, dishonourable, despicable, disreputable, shabby, shameful, scurvy, rotten, execrable. **3** avaricious, greedy, grasping, mercenary, mean, piggish, hoggish, selfish, rapacious, penny-pinching, stingy, parsimonious, niggardly, *colloq.* money-grubbing. □□ **sordidness** see MISERY 1.

sordino /sordeénō/ *n.* (*pl.* **sordini** /-ni/) *Mus.* a mute for a bowed or wind instrument. [It. f. *sordo* mute f. L *surdus*]

sore /sor/ *adj.*, *n.*, & *adv.* ● *adj.* **1** (of a part of the body) painful from injury or disease (*has a sore arm*). **2** (of a person) suffering pain. **3** (often foll. by *about*, *at*) aggrieved or vexed. **4** *archaic* grievous or severe (*in sore need*). ● *n.* **1** a sore place on the body. **2** a source of distress or annoyance (*reopen old sores*). ● *adv.* *archaic* grievously, severely. □ **sore point** a subject causing distress or annoyance. **sore throat** an inflammation of the lining membrane at the back of the mouth etc. □□ **soreness** *n.* [OE *sār* (n. & adj.), *sāre* (adv.), f. Gmc]

■ *adj.* **1** painful, sensitive, tender, raw, angry, burning, stinging, smarting, aching, hurting; irritated, inflamed, chafed. **3** angry, angered, aggrieved, annoyed, irritated, vexed, irked, upset, *colloq.* peeved. **4** dire, serious, grievous, severe, acute, extreme, critical, urgent, pressing, desperate; painful, troublesome, distressing, distressful, harrowing, agonizing, bitter, fierce, burdensome, onerous, heavy, oppressive. ● *n.* **1** swelling, rawness, infection, inflammation, bruise, abrasion, cut, laceration, scrape, burn, canker, ulcer.

sorehead /sórhed/ *n.* *US* a touchy or disgruntled person.

sorel /sórrəl/ *n.* *Brit.* a male fallow deer in its third year. [var. of SORREL²]

sorely /sórli/ *adv.* **1** extremely, badly (*am sorely tempted*; *sorely in need of repair*). **2** severely (*am sorely vexed*). [OE *sārlīce* (as SORE, -LY²)]

sorghum /sórgəm/ *n.* any tropical cereal grass of the genus *Sorghum*, e.g. durra. [mod.L f. It. *sorgo*, perh. f. unrecorded Rmc *syricum* (*gramen*) Syrian (grass)]

sori *pl.* of SORUS.

soroptimist /səróptimist/ *n.* a member of an international association of clubs for professional and business women. [L *soror* sister + OPTIMIST (as OPTIMISM)]

sorority /sərórriti/ *n.* (*pl.* **-ies**) *US* a female students' society in a university or college. [med.L *sororitas* or L *soror* sister, after *fraternity*]

sorosis /sərṓsiss/ *n.* (*pl.* **soroses** /-seez/) *Bot.* a fleshy compound fruit, e.g. a pineapple or mulberry. [mod.L f. Gk *sōros* heap]

sorption /sórpsh'n/ *n.* absorption or adsorption happening jointly or separately. [back-form. f. *absorption*, *adsorption*]

sorrel¹ /sórrəl/ *n.* any acid-leaved herb of the genus *Rumex*, used in salads and for flavouring. [ME f. OF *surele*, *sorele* f. Gmc]

sorrel² /sórrəl/ *adj.* & *n.* ● *adj.* of a light reddish-brown colour. ● *n.* **1** this colour. **2** a sorrel animal, esp. a horse. **3** *Brit.* a sorel. [ME f. OF *sorel* f. *sor* yellowish f. Frank.]

sorrow /sórrō/ *n.* & *v.* ● *n.* **1** mental distress caused by loss or disappointment etc. **2** a cause of sorrow. **3** lamentation. ● *v.intr.* **1** feel sorrow. **2** mourn. □□ **sorrower** *n.* **sorrowing** *adj.* [OE *sorh*, *sorg*]

■ *n.* **1** sadness, heartbreak, grief, unhappiness, melancholy, misery, anguish, distress, suffering, torment, agony, wretchedness, heartache, desolation, desolateness, *archaic or literary* woe, *literary* dolour. **2** affliction, trouble, trial, tribulation, misfortune, hardship, adversity, bad *or* hard luck, cares, pressure, strain, *literary* travail. ● *v.* grieve, lament, mourn, weep, keen, agonize, moan, wail; (*sorrow for* or *over*) regret, bemoan, bewail.

sorrowful /sórrōfōōl/ *adj.* **1** feeling or showing sorrow. **2** distressing, lamentable. □□ **sorrowfully** *adv.* **sorrowfulness** *n.* [OE *sorhful* (as SORROW, -FUL)]

■ **1** sad, unhappy, regretful, sorry, depressed, dejected, crestfallen, chap-fallen, gloomy, downcast, blue, dispirited, melancholy, in the doldrums, wretched, woebegone, miserable, heartsick, disheartened, piteous, heavy-hearted, broken-hearted, heartbroken, rueful, woeful, tearful, disconsolate, inconsolable, grief-stricken, *colloq.* down in the mouth, in the dumps. **2** distressing, lamentable, doleful, unfortunate, bitter, distressful, grievous, unlucky, hapless, afflictive, *archaic or literary* troublous. □□ **sorrowfulness** see *penitence* (PENITENT), *sadness* (SAD).

sorry /sórri/ *adj.* (**sorrier**, **sorriest**) **1** (*predic.*) pained or regretful or penitent (*were sorry for what they had done*; *am sorry that you have to go*). **2** (*predic.*; foll. by *for*) feeling pity or sympathy for (a person). **3** as an expression of apology. **4** wretched; in a poor state (*a sorry sight*). □ **sorry for oneself** dejected. □□ **sorrily** *adv.* **sorriness** *n.* [OE *sārig* f. WG (as SORE, -Y²)]

■ **1** regretful, penitent, remorseful, contrite, conscience-stricken, guilt-ridden, repentant, apologetic, penitential; see also SORROWFUL 1. **2** (*feel sorry for*) see PITY *v.* **4** abject, miserable, depressing, wretched, woeful, pitiful, pitiable, lamentable, pathetic, deplorable, stark, grim, sordid, dismal, base; ill-starred, *archaic* star-crossed.

sort /sort/ *n.* & *v.* ● *n.* **1** a group of things etc. with common attributes; a class or kind. **2** (foll. by *of*) roughly of the kind specified (*is some sort of doctor*). **3** *colloq.* a person of a specified character or kind (*a good sort*). **4** *Printing* a letter or piece in a fount of type. **5** *Computing* the arrangement of data in a prescribed sequence. **6** *archaic* a manner or way. ● *v.tr.* (often foll. by *out, over*) arrange systematically or according to type, class, etc. □ **after a sort** after a fashion. **in some sort** to a certain extent. **of a sort** (or **of sorts**) *colloq.* not fully deserving the name (*a holiday of sorts*). **out of sorts 1** slightly unwell. **2** in low spirits; irritable. **sort of** *colloq.* as it were; to some extent (*I sort of expected it*). **sort out 1** separate into sorts. **2** select (things of one or more sorts) from a miscellaneous group. **3** disentangle or put into order. **4** resolve (a problem or difficulty). **5** *colloq.* deal with or reprimand (a person). □□ **sortable** *adj.* **sorter** *n.* **sorting** *n.* [ME f. OF *sorte* ult. f. L *sors sortis* lot, condition]

■ *n.* **1** kind, variety, type, class, classification, group, category, brand, make, mark, stamp, description, mould, stripe, kidney, character, nature, *colloq. disp.* ilk; manner; species, genus, family, phylum, subgenus, subspecies, race, breed, strain, stock. **2** kind, type, *archaic* manner. **3** person, individual, type. ● *v.* assort, classify, file, order, rank, grade, class, size, categorize, separate, divide, combine, merge, arrange, organize, systemize, systematize, catalogue, group, *esp. Biol.* & *Med.* type; describe, characterize. □ **out of sorts 1** not oneself, unwell, ailing, indisposed, (slightly) ill, low, poorly, *colloq.* under the weather, *Brit. colloq.* not up to snuff. **2** see MOODY *adj.* **sort of** see SOMEWHAT *adv.* **sort out 1** see SORT *v.* above. **2** choose, select, pick out; separate. **3** disentangle, untangle, unravel, set *or* put straight, straighten out, tidy (up), clear up. **4** resolve, solve, straighten out, clarify, clear up, rectify, put right *or* straight, fix, settle.

sortie /sórti/ *n.* & *v.* ● *n.* **1** a sally, esp. from a besieged garrison. **2** an operational flight by a single military aircraft. ● *v.intr.* (**sorties, sortied, sortieing**) make a sortie; sally. [F, fem. past part. of *sortir* go out]

■ *n.* **1** see CHARGE *n.* 4a.

sortilege /sórtilij/ *n.* divination by lots. [ME f. OF f. med.L *sortilegium* sorcery f. L *sortilegus* sorcerer (as SORT, *legere* choose)]

■ see *sorcery* (SORCERER).

sorus /sórəss/ *n.* (*pl.* **sori** /-rī/) *Bot.* a heap or cluster, esp. of spore-cases on the under-surface of a fern-leaf, or in a fungus or lichen. [mod.L f. Gk *sōros* heap]

SOS /éssō-éss/ *n.* (*pl.* **SOSs**) **1** an international code-signal of extreme distress, used esp. by ships at sea. **2** an urgent appeal for help. **3** *Brit.* a message broadcast to an untraceable person in an emergency. [chosen as being easily transmitted and recognized in Morse code]

sostenuto /sóstənōōtō/ *adv., adj.,* & *n. Mus.* ● *adv.* & *adj.* in a sustained or prolonged manner. ● *n.* (*pl.* **-os**) a passage to be played in this way. [It., past part. of *sostenere* SUSTAIN]

sot /sot/ *n.* & *v.* ● *n.* a habitual drunkard. ● *v.intr.* (**sotted, sotting**) tipple. □□ **sottish** *adj.* [OE *sott* & OF *sot* foolish, f. med.L *sottus*, of unkn. orig.]

■ *n.* see DRUNK *n.* 1. ● *v.* see DRINK *v.* 2.

soteriology /soteériólləji/ *n. Theol.* the doctrine of salvation. [Gk *sōtēria* salvation + -LOGY]

Sothic /sṓthik/ *adj.* of or relating to the dog-star, esp. with ref. to the ancient Egyptian year fixed by its heliacal rising. [Gk *Sōthis* f. the Egypt. name of the dog-star]

sotto voce /sóttō vṓchi/ *adv.* in an undertone or aside. [It. *sotto* under + *voce* voice]

sou /sōō/ *n.* **1** *hist.* a former French coin of low value. **2** (usu. with *neg.*) *colloq.* a very small amount of money (*hasn't a sou*). [F, orig. pl. *sous* f. OF *sout* f. L SOLIDUS]

soubrette /soobrét/ *n.* **1** a pert maidservant or similar female character in a comedy. **2** an actress taking this part. [F f. Prov. *soubreto* fem. of *soubret* coy f. *sobrar* f. L *superare* be above]

soubriquet var. of SOBRIQUET.

souchong /sōōshong/ *n.* a fine black kind of China tea. [Chin. *xiao* small + *zhong* sort]

souffle /sōōf'l/ *n. Med.* a low murmur heard in the auscultation of various organs etc. [F f. *souffler* blow f. L *sufflare*]

soufflé /sōōflay/ *n.* & *adj.* ● *n.* **1** a light spongy dish usu. made with flavoured egg yolks added to stiffly beaten whites of eggs and baked (*cheese soufflé*). **2** any of various light sweet or savoury dishes made with beaten egg whites. ● *adj.* **1** light and frothy or spongy (*omelette soufflé*). **2** (of ceramics) decorated with small spots. [F past part. (as SOUFFLE)]

sough /sow, suf/ *v.* & *n.* ● *v.intr.* make a moaning, whistling, or rushing sound as of the wind in trees etc. ● *n.* this sound. [OE *swōgan* resound]

■ *v.* sigh, groan, moan.

sought *past* and *past part.* of SEEK.

souk /sōōk/ *n.* (also **suk, sukh, suq**) a market-place in Muslim countries. [Arab. *sūḳ*]

■ bazaar.

soul /sōl/ *n.* **1** the spiritual or immaterial part of a human being, often regarded as immortal. **2** the moral or emotional or intellectual nature of a person or animal. **3** the personification or pattern of something (*the very soul of discretion*). **4** an individual (*not a soul in sight*). **5 a** a person regarded with familiarity or pity etc. (*the poor soul was utterly confused*). **b** a person regarded as embodying moral or intellectual qualities (*left that to meaner souls*). **6** a person regarded as the animating or essential part of something (*the life and soul of the party*). **7** emotional or intellectual energy or intensity, esp. as revealed in a work of art (*pictures that lack soul*). **8** Black American culture or music etc. □ **soul-destroying** (of an activity etc.) deadeningly monotonous. **soul food** the traditional food of American Blacks. **soul mate** a person ideally suited to another. **soul music** a kind of music incorporating elements of rhythm and blues and gospel music, popularized by American Blacks. **the soul of honour** a person incapable of dishonourable conduct. **soul-searching** *n.* the examination of one's emotions and motives. ● *adj.* characterized by this. **upon my soul** an exclamation of surprise. □□ **-souled** *adj.* (in *comb.*). [OE *sāwol, sāwel, sāwl*, f. Gmc]

■ **1, 2** (vital) spirit *or* force, being, (inner *or* true) self, essence, psyche, heart, mind, intellect, reason, *Psychol.* anima. **3** incarnation, embodiment, epitome, personification, typification, essence, quintessence, example, model, pattern. **4** person, individual, man, woman, mortal, (human) being. **7** emotion, feeling, sentiment, sincerity, fervour, ardour, warmth, dynamism, vivacity, energy, spirit, vitality, force. □ **soul-destroying** see TEDIOUS. **upon my soul** see GRACIOUS *int.*

soulful /sṓlfŏŏl/ *adj.* **1** having or expressing or evoking deep feeling. **2** *colloq.* over-emotional. □□ **soulfully** *adv.* **soulfulness** *n.*

■ **1** sincere, deep, profound, heartfelt, moving, emotional, warm, ardent, intense, fervent, expressive, eloquent.

soulless /sṓl-liss/ *adj.* **1** lacking sensitivity or noble qualities. **2** having no soul. **3** undistinguished or uninteresting. □□ **soullessly** *adv.* **soullessness** *n.*

sound[1] /sownd/ *n.* & *v.* ● *n.* **1** a sensation caused in the ear by the vibration of the surrounding air or other medium. **2 a** vibrations causing this sensation. **b** similar vibrations whether audible or not. **3** what is or may be heard. **4** an idea or impression conveyed by words (*don't like the sound of that*). **5** mere words (*sound and fury*). **6** (in full **musical sound**) sound produced by continuous and regular vibrations (opp. NOISE *n.* 3). **7** any of a series of articulate utterances (*vowel and consonant sounds*). **8** music, speech, etc., accompanying a film or other visual presentation. **9** (often *attrib.*) broadcasting by radio as distinct from television. ● *v.* **1** *intr.* & *tr.* emit or cause to emit sound. **2** *tr.* utter or pronounce (*sound a note of alarm*). **3** *intr.* convey an impression when heard (*you sound worried*). **4** *tr.* give an audible signal for (an alarm etc.). **5** *tr.* test (the lungs etc.) by noting the sound produced. **6** *tr.* cause to resound; make known (*sound their praises*). □ **sound barrier** the high resistance of air to objects moving at speeds near that of sound. **sound bite** a short extract from a recorded interview, chosen for its pungency or appropriateness. **sound effect** a sound other than speech or music made artificially for use in a play, film, etc. **sound engineer** an engineer dealing with acoustics etc. **sound-hole** an aperture in the belly of some stringed instruments. **sound off** talk loudly or express one's opinions forcefully. **sound-post** a small prop between the belly and back of some stringed instruments. **sound shift** see SHIFT *n.* 6. **sound spectrograph** an instrument for analysing sound into its frequency components. **sound wave** a wave of compression and rarefaction, by which sound is propagated in an elastic medium, e.g. air. ▫▫ **soundless** *adj.* **soundlessly** *adv.* **soundlessness** *n.* [ME f. AF *soun*, OF *son* (n.), AF *suner*, OF *soner* (v.) f. L *sonus*]

■ *n.* **1** tone, noise, din, cacophony, report. **4** ring, tone, idea, quality, effect, aspect, look, feel. **8** soundtrack, voice-over, narration. ● *v.* **1** resound, reverberate, echo, resonate; see also BLARE *v.*, RING[2] *v.* 1. **2** articulate, pronounce, enunciate, utter; voice, vocalize. **3** seem, appear; strike a person as, give a person the impression *or* feeling *or* sense that. **4** ring, activate, set *or* touch off, signal. **6** shout (out), cry out, yell (out); make known, proclaim. ▫ **sound off** vituperate, complain, bluster, grumble, *colloq.* bitch; go on. ▫▫ **soundless** see NOISELESS. **soundlessly** see *silently* (SILENT). **soundlessness** see SILENCE *n.* 1.

sound[2] /sownd/ *adj.* & *adv.* ● *adj.* **1** healthy; not diseased or injured. **2** undamaged; in good condition. **3** (of an opinion or policy etc.) correct, orthodox, well-founded, judicious. **4** financially secure (*a sound investment*). **5** undisturbed (*a sound sleep*). **6** severe, hard (*a sound blow*). ● *adv.* soundly (*sound asleep*). ▫▫ **soundly** *adv.* **soundness** *n.* [ME *sund*, *isund* f. OE *gesund* f. WG]

■ *adj.* **1** healthy, hale (and hearty), fit (as a fiddle), in good condition *or* shape, robust, vigorous, blooming, rosy, ruddy; undiseased, uninjured. **2** undamaged, whole, unmarred, intact, unimpaired, unscathed; in good condition, firm, solid, substantial, strong, sturdy, dependable. **3** correct, orthodox, well-founded, valid, good, judicious, reliable, useful; sane, balanced, normal, rational, wholesome, reasoning, reasonable, clear-headed, lucid, right-minded, responsible, practical, prudent, politic, wise, sensible, logical, common-sense, commonsensical, astute, far-sighted, perceptive, perspicacious, percipient. **4** safe, secure, good, conservative, non-speculative, solid, riskless; profitable. **5** unbroken, uninterrupted, continuous, undisturbed, untroubled, peaceful, deep, heavy. ▫▫ **soundly** see FAST[1] *adv.* 2. **soundness** see STRENGTH 1.

sound[3] /sownd/ *v.* & *n.* ● *v.tr.* & *intr.* **1** *tr.* test the depth or quality of the bottom of (the sea or a river etc.). **2** *tr.* (often foll. by *out*) inquire (esp. cautiously or discreetly) into the opinions or feelings of (a person). **3** *tr.* find the depth of water in (a ship's hold). **4** *tr.* get records of temperature, humidity, pressure, etc. from (the upper atmosphere). **5** *tr.* examine (a person's bladder etc.) with a probe. **6** *intr.* (of a whale or fish) dive to the bottom. ● *n.* a surgeon's probe. ▫▫ **sounder** *n.* [ME f. OF *sonder* ult. f. L SUB- + *unda* wave]

■ *v.* **1** plumb, probe, fathom, test. **2** plumb, probe, test, check (into), inquire of, enquire of, question, poll, canvass, investigate, examine, survey, *US* check out. **6** see DIVE *v.* 1, 2.

sound[4] /sownd/ *n.* **1 a** a narrow passage of water connecting two seas or a sea with a lake etc. **b** an arm of the sea. **2** a fish's swim-bladder. [OE *sund*, = ON *sund* swimming, strait, f. Gmc (as SWIM)]

■ **1** strait(s), inlet, fiord, firth, arm of the sea, cove, *Sc.* (sea) loch.

soundboard /sówndbord/ *n.* a thin sheet of wood over which the strings of a piano etc. pass to increase the sound produced.

soundbox /sówndboks/ *n.* the hollow chamber providing resonance and forming the body of a stringed musical instrument.

sounding[1] /sównding/ *n.* **1 a** the action or process of measuring the depth of water, now usu. by means of echo. **b** an instance of this (*took a sounding*). **2** (in *pl.*) **a** a region close to the shore of the right depth for sounding. **b** *Naut.* measurements taken by sounding. **c** cautious investigation (*made soundings as to his suitability*). **3 a** the determination of any physical property at a depth in the sea or at a height in the atmosphere. **b** an instance of this. ▫ **sounding-balloon** a balloon used to obtain information about the upper atmosphere. **sounding-line** a line used in sounding the depth of water. **sounding-rod** a rod used in finding the depth of water in a ship's hold (see SOUND[3]).

sounding[2] /sównding/ *adj.* **1** giving forth (esp. loud or resonant) sound (*sounding brass*). **2** emptily boastful, resonant, or imposing (*sounding promises*).

sounding-board /sówndingbord/ *n.* **1** a canopy over a pulpit etc. to direct sound towards the congregation. **2** = SOUNDBOARD. **3 a** a means of causing opinions etc. to be more widely known (*used his students as a sounding-board*). **b** a person etc. used as a trial audience.

soundproof /sówndproof/ *adj.* & *v.* ● *adj.* impervious to sound. ● *v.tr.* make soundproof.

soundtrack /sówndtrak/ *n.* **1** the recorded sound element of a film. **2** this recorded on the edge of a film in optical or magnetic form.

soup /soop/ *n.* & *v.* ● *n.* **1** a usu. savoury liquid dish made by boiling meat, fish, or vegetables etc. in stock or water. **2** *US sl.* nitroglycerine or gelignite, esp. for safe-breaking. **3** *sl.* the chemicals in which film is developed. **4** *colloq.* fog; thick cloud. ● *v.tr.* (usu. foll. by *up*) *colloq.* **1** increase the power and efficiency of (an engine). **2** increase the power or impact of (writing, music, etc.). ▫ **in the soup** *colloq.* in difficulties. **soup and fish** *colloq.* evening dress. **soup-kitchen** a place dispensing soup etc. to the poor. **soup-plate** a deep wide-rimmed plate for serving soup. **soup-spoon** a large round-bowled spoon for drinking soup. [F *soupe* sop, broth, f. LL *suppa* f. Gmc: cf. SOP, SUP[1]]

■ *n.* **1** see BROTH.

soupçon /soopson/ *n.* a very small quantity; a dash. [F f. OF *sou(s)peçon* f. med.L *suspectio -onis*: see SUSPICION]

■ see DASH *n.* 7.

soupy /soopi/ *adj.* (**soupier**, **soupiest**) **1** of or resembling soup. **2** *colloq.* sentimental; mawkish. ▫▫ **soupily** *adv.* **soupiness** *n.*

■ **1** see THICK *adj.* 6. **2** see MAUDLIN *adj.*

sour /sowr/ *adj.*, *n.*, & *v.* ● *adj.* **1** having an acid taste like lemon or vinegar, esp. because of unripeness (*sour apples*). **2 a** (of food, esp. milk or bread) bad because of fermentation. **b** smelling or tasting rancid or unpleasant. **3** (of a person, temper, etc.) harsh; morose; bitter. **4** (of a thing) unpleasant; distasteful. **5** (of the soil) deficient in lime and usually dank. ● *n.* **1** *US* a drink with lemon- or lime-juice (*whisky sour*). **2** an acid solution used in bleaching etc. ● *v.tr.* & *intr.* make or become sour (*soured the cream*; *soured by misfortune*). ▫ **go** (or **turn**) **sour 1** (of food etc.) become sour. **2** turn out badly (*the job went sour on him*). **3** lose one's keenness. **sour cream** cream deliberately fermented by adding bacteria. **sour grapes** resentful disparagement of something one cannot personally acquire. **sour mash** *US* a brewing- or distilling-mash made acid to promote fermentation. ▫▫ **sourish** *adj.* **sourly** *adv.* **sourness** *n.* [OE *sūr* f. Gmc]

■ *adj.* **1** acid, acidic, tart, vinegary, lemony, sharp, acidulous, acidulated, acerbic. **2** turned, bad, (gone) off, fermented, curdled, rancid, spoilt. **3** acrimonious, bitter, embittered, harsh, unpleasant, churlish, ill-natured, ill-tempered, bad-tempered, crusty, curmudgeonly, crabbed, crabby, cross, testy, petulant, impatient, abrupt, nasty, curt, caustic, brusque, peevish, snappish, edgy, sullen, morose, gloomy, glum, discontented, *esp. US* cranky, *colloq.* grouchy. **4** disagreeable, unpleasant, distasteful, bad, nasty, bitter. ● *v.* turn, spoil, curdle, go bad *or* off, ferment; embitter, disenchant, exasperate, vex, *colloq.* peeve.

source /sorss/ *n.* & *v.* ● *n.* **1** a spring or fountain-head from which a stream issues (*the sources of the Nile*). **2** a place, person, or thing from which something originates (*the source of all our troubles*). **3** a person or document etc. providing evidence (*reliable sources of information*; *historical source material*). **4 a** a body emitting radiation etc. **b** *Physics* a place from which a fluid or current flows. **c** *Electronics* a part of a transistor from which carriers flow into the interelectrode channel. ● *v.tr.* obtain (esp. components) from a specified source. □ **at source** at the point of origin or issue. **source-criticism** the evaluation of different, esp. successive, literary or historical sources. [ME f. OF *sors*, *sourse*, past part. of *sourdre* rise f. L *surgere*]

■ *n.* **1** (fountain-)head, well-head, (well-)spring, origin; provenance, inception, start, beginning, root(s), rise, *US* provenience, *formal* commencement. **2** originator, initiator, author, creator, begetter, cause, origin, root. **3** authority, documentation; informant, horse's mouth.

sourcebook /sórsbŏŏk/ *n.* a collection of documentary sources for the study of a subject.

sourdough /sówrdō/ *n. US* **1** fermenting dough, esp. that left over from a previous baking, used as leaven. **2** an old-timer in Alaska etc. [dial., = leaven, in allusion to piece of sour dough for raising bread baked in winter]

sourpuss /sówrpŏŏss/ *n. colloq.* a sour-tempered person. [SOUR + PUSS = face]

■ see MISERY 3.

soursop /sówrsop/ *n.* **1** a W. Indian evergreen tree, *Annona muricata*. **2** the large succulent fruit of this tree.

sous- /sōōz/ *prefix* (in words adopted from French) subordinate, under (*sous-chef*). [F]

sousaphone /sṓōzəfōn/ *n.* a large brass bass wind instrument encircling the player's body. □□ **sousaphonist** *n.* [J. P. *Sousa*, Amer. bandmaster d. 1932, after *saxophone*]

souse /sowss/ *v.* & *n.* ● *v.* **1** *tr.* put (gherkins, fish, etc.) in pickle. **2** *tr.* & *intr.* plunge into liquid. **3** *tr.* (as **soused** *adj.*) *colloq.* drunk. **4** *tr.* (usu. foll. by *in*) soak (a thing) in liquid. **5** *tr.* (usu. foll. by *over*) throw (liquid) over a thing. ● *n.* **1 a** pickle made with salt. **b** *US* food, esp. a pig's head etc., in pickle. **2** a dip, plunge, or drenching in water. **3** *colloq.* **a** a drinking-bout. **b** a drunkard. [ME f. OF *sous*, *souz* pickle f. OS *sultia*, OHG *sulza* brine f. Gmc: cf. SALT]

■ *v.* **1** see SALT *v.* 1. **2, 4** see SOAK *v.* 1. **3** (**soused**) see DRUNK *adj.* 1. ● *n.* **3 a** see JAG[2] 1. **b** see DRUNK *n.* 1.

soutache /sōōtásh/ *n.* a narrow flat ornamental braid used to trim garments. [F f. Magyar *sujtás*]

■ see BRAID *n.* 1.

soutane /sōōtaán/ *n. RC Ch.* a cassock worn by a priest. [F f. It. *sottana* f. *sotto* under f. L *subtus*]

souteneur /sṓōtənṓr/ *n.* a pimp. [F, = protector]

souter /sṓōtər/ *n. Sc.* & *N.Engl.* a shoemaker; a cobbler. [OE *sūtere* f. L *sutor* f. *suere sut-* sew]

souterrain /sṓōtərayn/ *n.* esp. *Archaeol.* an underground chamber or passage. [F f. *sous* under + *terre* earth]

south /sowth/ *n.*, *adj.*, *adv.*, & *v.* ● *n.* **1** the point of the horizon 90° clockwise from east. **2** the compass point corresponding to this. **3** the direction in which this lies. **4** (usu. **the South**) **a** the part of the world or a country or a town lying to the south. **b** the Southern States of the US. **5** *Bridge* a player occupying the position designated 'south'. ● *adj.* **1** towards, at, near, or facing the south (*a south wall*; *south country*). **2** coming from the south (*south wind*). ● *adv.* **1** towards, at, or near the south (*they travelled south*). **2** (foll. by *of*) further south than. ● *v.intr.* **1** move towards the south. **2** (of a celestial body) cross the meridian. □ **South African** *adj.* of or relating to the republic of South Africa. ● *n.* **1** a native or national of South Africa. **2** a person of South African descent. **South American** *adj.* of or relating to South America. ● *n.* a native or citizen of South America. **south by east** (or **west**) between south and south-south-east (or south-south-west). **south-east** *n.* **1** the point of the horizon midway between south and east. **2** the compass point corresponding to this. **3** the direction in which this lies. ● *adj.* of, towards, or coming from the south-east. ● *adv.* towards, at, or near the south-east. **South-East** the part of a country or town lying to the south-east. **south-easterly** *adj.* & *adv.* = *south-east*. **south-eastern** lying on the south-east side. **south pole** see POLE[2]. **South Sea** the southern Pacific Ocean. **South Sea Bubble** *hist.* a scheme for trading in the southern hemisphere to repay the British national debt, which started and collapsed in 1720. **south-south-east** the point or direction midway between south and south-east. **south-south-west** the point or direction midway between south and south-west. **south-west** *n.* **1** the point of the horizon midway between south and west. **2** the compass point corresponding to this. **3** the direction in which this lies. ● *adj.* of, towards, or coming from the south-west. ● *adv.* towards, at, or near the south-west. **South-West** the part of a country or town lying to the south-west. **south-westerly** *adj.* & *adv.* = *south-west*. **south-western** lying on the south-west side. **south wind** a wind blowing from the south. **to the south** (often foll. by *of*) in a southerly direction. [OE *sūth*]

southbound /sówthbownd/ *adj.* travelling or leading southwards.

Southdown /sówthdown/ *n.* **1** a sheep of a breed raised esp. for mutton, orig. on the South Downs of Hampshire and Sussex. **2** this breed.

southeaster /sówtheéstər/ *n.* a south-east wind.

souther /sówthər/ *n.* a south wind.

southerly /súthərli/ *adj.*, *adv.*, & *n.* ● *adj.* & *adv.* **1** in a southern position or direction. **2** (of a wind) blowing from the south. ● *n.* (*pl.* **-ies**) a southerly wind.

southern /súthərn/ *adj.* esp. *Geog.* **1** of or in the south; inhabiting the south. **2** lying or directed towards the south (*at the southern end*). □ **Southern Cross** a southern constellation in the shape of a cross. **Southern hemisphere** the half of the earth below the equator. **southern lights** the aurora australis. **Southern States** the States in the south, esp. the south-east, of the US. □□ **southernmost** *adj.* [OE *sūtherne* (as SOUTH, -ERN)]

southerner /súthərnər/ *n.* a native or inhabitant of the south.

southernwood /súthərnwŏŏd/ *n.* a bushy kind of wormwood, *Artemisia abrotanum*.

southing /sówthing/ *n.* **1** a southern movement. **2** *Naut.* the distance travelled or measured southward. **3** *Astron.* the angular distance of a star etc. south of the celestial equator.

southpaw /sówthpaw/ *n.* & *adj. colloq.* ● *n.* a left-handed person, esp. in boxing. ● *adj.* left-handed.

southward /sówthwərd/ *adj.*, *adv.*, & *n.* ● *adj.* & *adv.* (also **southwards**) towards the south. ● *n.* a southward direction or region.

southwester /sówthwéstər/ *n.* a south-west wind.

souvenir /sṓōvəneér/ *n.* & *v.* ● *n.* (often foll. by *of*) a memento of an occasion, place, etc. ● *v.tr. sl.* take as a 'souvenir'; pilfer, steal. [F f. *souvenir* remember f. L *subvenire* occur to the mind (as SUB-, *venire* come)]

■ *n.* see MEMENTO. ● *v.* see STEAL *v.* 1.

souvlaki /soovlaáki/ *n.* (*pl.* ***souvlakia*** /-kiə/) a Greek dish of pieces of meat grilled on a skewer. [mod. Gk]

sou'wester /sow-wéstər/ *n.* **1** = SOUTHWESTER. **2** a waterproof hat with a broad flap covering the neck.

sov. /sov/ *abbr. Brit.* sovereign.

sovereign /sóvrin/ *n.* & *adj.* ● *n.* **1** a supreme ruler, esp. a monarch. **2** *Brit. hist.* a gold coin nominally worth £1. ● *adj.* **1 a** supreme (*sovereign power*). **b** unmitigated (*sovereign contempt*). **2** excellent; effective (*a sovereign remedy*). **3** possessing sovereign power (*a sovereign State*). **4** royal (*our sovereign lord*). □ **the sovereign good** the greatest good, esp. for a State, its people, etc. **sovereign pontiff** see

PONTIFF. □□ **sovereignly** *adv.* **sovereignty** *n.* (*pl.* **-ies**). [ME f. OF *so(u)verain* f. L: *-g-* by assoc. with *reign*]

■ *n.* **1** monarch, ruler, emperor, empress, tsar, king, queen, prince, princess, Elector, grand duke *or* duchess, potentate, supremo, chief, master, mistress, emir, sheikh, sultan, *hist.* shah. ● *adj.* **1** supreme, paramount, highest, principal, foremost, greatest, predominant, dominant, ranking, leading, chief, superior, pre-eminent, ruling, regnant, reigning, governing, all-powerful, absolute, unlimited, unmitigated, unqualified. **3** see INDEPENDENT *adj.* 1b. **4** royal, regal, majestic, noble, lordly, aristocratic, kingly, queenly. □□ **sovereignty** suzerainty, hegemony, dominion, rule, reign, pre-eminence, power, jurisdiction, authority, leadership, command, sway, supremacy, ascendancy, primacy; kingship, queenship.

soviet /sṓviət, sóv-/ *n.* & *adj. hist.* ● *n.* **1** an elected local, district, or national council in the former USSR. **2** (**Soviet**) a citizen of the former USSR. **3** a revolutionary council of workers, peasants, etc. before 1917. ● *adj.* (usu. **Soviet**) of or concerning the former Soviet Union. □□ **Sovietize** *v.tr.* (also **-ise**). **Sovietization** /-tīzáysh'n/ *n.* [Russ. *sovet* council]

sovietologist /sṓviətólləjist, sóv-/ *n.* a person who studies the former Soviet Union.

sow[1] /sō/ *v.tr.* (*past* **sowed** /sōd/; *past part.* **sown** /sōn/ or **sowed**) **1** (also *absol.*) **a** scatter or put (seed) on or in the earth. **b** (often foll. by *with*) plant (a field etc.) with seed. **2** initiate; arouse (*sowed doubt in her mind*). **3** (foll. by *with*) cover thickly with. □ **sow the seed** (or **seeds**) **of** first give rise to; implant (an idea etc.). □□ **sower** *n.* **sowing** *n.* [OE *sāwan* f. Gmc]

■ **1** plant, strew, scatter, spread; broadcast; seed. **2** see PLANT *v.* 6.

sow[2] /sow/ *n.* **1 a** a female adult pig, esp. after farrowing. **b** a female guinea-pig. **c** the female of some other species. **2 a** the main trough through which molten iron runs into side-channels to form pigs. **b** a large block of iron so formed. **3** (in full **sow bug**) esp. *US* a woodlouse. [OE *sugu*]

sowback /sówbak/ *n.* a low ridge of sand etc.

sowbread /sówbred/ *n.* a tuberous plant, *Cyclamen hederifolium*, with solitary nodding flowers.

sown *past part.* of SOW[1].

sowthistle /sówthiss'l/ *n.* any plant of the genus *Sonchus* with thistle-like leaves and milky juice.

sox *colloq.* or *Commerce pl.* of SOCK[1].

soy /soy/ *n.* (also **soya** /sóyə/) **1** (also **soy sauce**) a sauce made in Japan and China from pickled soya beans. **2** (in full **soy bean**) = *soya bean.* [Jap. *shō-yu* f. Chin. *shi-you* f. *shi* salted beans + *you* oil]

soya /sóyə/ *n.* (in full **soya bean**) **1 a** a leguminous plant, *Glycine soja*, orig. of SE Asia, cultivated for the edible oil and flour it yields, and used as a replacement for animal protein in certain foods. **b** the seed of this. **2** (also **soya sauce**) = SOY 1. [Du. *soja* f. Malay *soi* (as SOY)]

sozzled /sózz'ld/ *adj. colloq.* very drunk. [past part. of dial. *sozzle* mix sloppily (prob. imit.)]

■ see DRUNK *adj.* 1.

SP *abbr.* starting price.

spa /spaa/ *n.* **1** a curative mineral spring. **2** a place or resort with this. [*Spa* in Belgium]

■ **1** see SPRING *n.* 6.

space /spayss/ *n.* & *v.* ● *n.* **1 a** a continuous unlimited area or expanse which may or may not contain objects etc. **b** an interval between one, two, or three-dimensional points or objects (*a space of 10 metres*). **c** an empty area; room (*clear a space in the corner*; *occupies too much space*). **2** a large unoccupied region (*the wide open spaces*). **3** = *outer space.* **4** an interval of time (*in the space of an hour*). **5** the amount of paper used in writing etc. (*hadn't the space to discuss it*). **6 a** a blank between printed, typed, or written words, etc. **b** a piece of metal providing this. **7** *Mus.* each of the blanks between the lines of a staff. ● *v.tr.* **1** set or arrange at intervals. **2** put spaces between (esp. words, letters, lines, etc. in printing, typing, or writing). **3** (as **spaced** *adj.*) (often foll. by *out*) *sl.* in a state of euphoria, esp. from taking drugs. □ **space age** the era when space travel has become possible. **space-bar** a long key in a typewriter (or on a similar keyboard) for making a space between words etc. **space flight 1** a journey through space. **2** = *space travel.* **space out** put more or wider spaces or intervals between. **space probe** = PROBE *n.* 4. **space rocket** a rocket used to launch a spacecraft. **space-saving** occupying little space. **space shuttle** a rocket for repeated use esp. between the earth and a space station. **space station** an artificial satellite used as a base for operations in space. **space-time** (or **space-time continuum**) the fusion of the concepts of space and time, esp. as a four-dimensional continuum. **space travel** travel through outer space. **space traveller** a traveller in outer space; an astronaut. **space vehicle** = SPACECRAFT. **space walk** any physical activity by an astronaut in space outside a spacecraft. □□ **spacer** *n.* **spacing** *n.* (esp. in sense 2 of *v.*). [ME f. OF *espace* f. L *spatium*]

■ *n.* **1 a** expanse, area, extent, compass, tract. **b** interval, interspace, interstice, gap, opening, lacuna, hiatus, window, daylight, clearance. **c** place, area, capacity, room, elbow-room, leeway, margin, latitude, clearance, play. **4** interval, lapse, period, time, hiatus, lacuna, span, while, duration, extent, spell, stretch, pause, wait, intermission, gap, break, interruption. **6** blank, gap. ● *v.* **1** arrange, organize, array, set out, align, range, order, rank, lay out, measure (out). **3** (*spaced out*) see HIGH *adj.* 8b.

spacecraft /spáyskraaft/ *n.* a vehicle used for travelling in space.

■ see CRAFT *n.* 3.

spaceman /spáysman/ *n.* (*pl.* **-men**; *fem.* **spacewoman**, *pl.* **-women**) = *space traveller.*

spaceship /spáyss-ship/ *n.* a spacecraft, esp. one controlled by its crew.

■ see CRAFT *n.* 3.

spacesuit /spáyss-sōōt, -syōōt/ *n.* a garment designed to allow an astronaut to survive in space.

spacial var. of SPATIAL.

spacious /spáyshəss/ *adj.* having ample space; covering a large area; roomy. □□ **spaciously** *adv.* **spaciousness** *n.* [ME f. OF *spacios* or L *spatiosus* (as SPACE)]

■ vast, large, extensive, enormous, wide, broad, commodious, ample, expansive, roomy, huge, sizeable, capacious, great, immense, outsized, voluminous, oversize(d).

spade[1] /spayd/ *n.* & *v.* ● *n.* **1** a tool used for digging or cutting the ground etc., with a sharp-edged metal blade and a long handle. **2** a tool of a similar shape for various purposes, e.g. for removing the blubber from a whale. **3** anything resembling a spade. ● *v.tr.* dig over (ground) with a spade. □ **call a spade a spade** speak plainly or bluntly. **spade beard** an oblong-shaped beard. **spade foot** a square spadelike enlargement at the end of a chair-leg. □□ **spadeful** *n.* (*pl.* **-fuls**). [OE *spadu*, *spada*]

■ □ **call a spade a spade** talk straight, not mince (one's) words.

spade[2] /spayd/ *n.* **1 a** a playing-card of a suit denoted by black inverted heart-shaped figures with small stalks. **b** (in *pl.*) this suit. **2** *sl. offens.* a Black. □ **in spades** *sl.* to a high degree, with great force. **spade guinea** *hist.* a guinea of George III's reign with a spade-shaped shield on the reverse. [It. *spade* pl. of *spada* sword f. L *spatha* f. Gk *spathē*, rel. to SPADE[1]: assoc. with the shape of a pointed spade]

spadework /spáydwurk/ *n.* hard or routine preparatory work.

■ see PREPARATION 1.

spadille /spədíl/ *n.* **1** the ace of spades in ombre and quadrille. **2** the highest trump, esp. the ace of spades. [F f. Sp. *espadilla* dimin. of *espada* sword (as SPADE[2])]

spadix /spáydiks/ *n.* (*pl.* **spadices** /-seez/) *Bot.* a spike of flowers closely arranged round a fleshy axis and usu. enclosed in a spathe. □□ **spadiceous** /-dishəss/ *adj.* [L f. Gk, = palm-branch]

spae /spay/ *v.intr.* & *tr. Sc.* foretell; prophesy. [ME f. ON *spá*]

spaewife /spáywīf/ *n. Sc.* a female fortune-teller or witch.

spaghetti /spəgétti/ *n.* pasta made in solid strings, between macaroni and vermicelli in thickness. □ **spaghetti Bolognese** /bóllənáyz/ spaghetti served with a sauce of minced beef, tomato, onion, etc. **spaghetti junction** a multi-level road junction, esp. on a motorway. **spaghetti western** a western film made cheaply in Italy. [It., pl. of dimin. of *spago* string: *Bolognese* It., = of Bologna]

spahi /spaáhee/ *n. hist.* **1** a member of the Turkish irregular cavalry. **2** a member of the Algerian cavalry in French service. [Turk. *sipāhī* formed as SEPOY]

spake /spayk/ *archaic past* of SPEAK.

spall /spawl/ *n.* & *v.* ● *n.* a splinter or chip, esp. of rock. ● *v.intr.* & *tr.* break up or cause (ore) to break up in preparation for sorting. [ME (also *spale*): orig. unkn.]

spallation /spawláysh'n/ *n. Physics* the breakup of a bombarded nucleus into several parts.

spalpeen /spalpeén/ *n. Ir.* **1** a rascal; a villain. **2** a youngster. [Ir. *spailpín*, of unkn. orig.]

Spam /spam/ *n. propr.* a tinned meat product made mainly from ham. [*sp*iced h*am*]

span[1] /span/ *n.* & *v.* ● *n.* **1** the full extent from end to end in space or time (*the span of a bridge*; *the whole span of history*). **2** each arch or part of a bridge between piers or supports. **3** the maximum lateral extent of an aeroplane, its wing, a bird's wing, etc. **4 a** the maximum distance between the tips of the thumb and little finger. **b** this as a measurement, equal to 9 inches. **5** a short distance or time (*our life is but a span*). ● *v.* (**spanned, spanning**) **1** *tr.* **a** (of a bridge, arch, etc.) stretch from side to side of; extend across (*the bridge spanned the river*). **b** (of a builder etc.) bridge (a river etc.). **2** *tr.* extend across (space or a period of time etc.). **3** *tr.* measure or cover the extent of (a thing) with one's hand with the fingers stretched (*spanned a tenth on the piano*). **4** *intr. US* move in distinct stretches like the span-worm. □ **span roof** a roof with two inclined sides (opp. PENTHOUSE 2, *lean-to* (see LEAN[1])). **span-worm** *US* the caterpillar of the geometer moth. [OE *span(n)* or OF *espan*]

■ *n.* **1** extent, reach, spread, sweep, breadth, width; course, interval, stretch, duration, period, time. **5** see SPELL[3] *n.* 1. ● *v.* **1, 2** cross, stretch over *or* across, reach over *or* across, extend over *or* across, go over *or* across, bridge, straddle.

span[2] /span/ *n.* **1** *Naut.* a rope with both ends fastened to take purchase in a loop. **2** *US* a matched pair of horses, mules, etc. **3** *S.Afr.* a team of two or more pairs of oxen. [LG & Du. *span* f. *spannen* unite]

span[3] see SPICK AND SPAN.

span[4] /span/ *archaic past* of SPIN.

spandrel /spándril/ *n. Archit.* **1** the almost triangular space between one side of the outer curve of an arch, a wall, and the ceiling or framework. **2** the space between the shoulders of adjoining arches and the ceiling or moulding above. □ **spandrel wall** a wall built on the curve of an arch, filling in the spandrel. [perh. f. AF *spaund(e)re*, or f. *espaundre* EXPAND]

spang /spang/ *adv. US colloq.* exactly; completely (*spang in the middle*). [20th c.: orig. unkn.]

■ see SLAP *adv.*

spangle /spángg'l/ *n.* & *v.* ● *n.* **1** a small thin piece of glittering material esp. used in quantity to ornament a dress etc.; a sequin. **2** a small sparkling object. **3** (in full **spangle gall**) a spongy excrescence on oak-leaves. ● *v.tr.* (esp. as **spangled** *adj.*) cover with or as with spangles (*star-spangled*; *spangled costume*). □□ **spangly** /spánggli/ *adj.* [ME f. *spang* f. MDu. *spange*, OHG *spanga*, ON *spöng* brooch f. Gmc]

Spaniard /spányərd/ *n.* **1 a** a native or national of Spain in southern Europe. **b** a person of Spanish descent. **2** *NZ* a spear grass. [ME f. OF *Espaignart* f. *Espaigne* Spain]

spaniel /spányəl/ *n.* **1 a** a dog of any of various breeds with a long silky coat and drooping ears. **b** any of these breeds. **2** an obsequious or fawning person. [ME f. OF *espaigneul* Spanish (dog) f. Rmc *Hispaniolus* (unrecorded) f. *Hispania* Spain]

■ **2** see *yes-man*.

Spanish /spánnish/ *adj.* & *n.* ● *adj.* of or relating to Spain or its people or language. ● *n.* **1** the language of Spain and Spanish America. **2** (prec. by *the*; treated as *pl.*) the people of Spain. □ **Spanish America** those parts of America orig. settled by Spaniards, including Central and South America and part of the West Indies. **Spanish Armada** *hist.* the Spanish war fleet sent against England in 1588. **Spanish bayonet** a yucca, *Yucca aloifolia*, with stiff sharp-pointed leaves. **Spanish chestnut** = CHESTNUT *n.* 1b. **Spanish fly** a bright green beetle, *Lytta vesicatoria*, formerly dried and used for raising blisters, as a supposed aphrodisiac, etc. **Spanish goat** a goat, *Capra pyrenaica*, inhabiting the Pyrenees. **Spanish guitar** the standard six-stringed acoustic guitar, used esp. for classical and folk music. **Spanish mackerel** any of various large mackerels, esp. *Scomber colias* or *S. maculatus*. **Spanish Main** *hist.* the NE coast of South America between the Orinoco river and Panama, and adjoining parts of the Caribbean Sea. **Spanish omelette** an omelette containing chopped vegetables and often not folded. **Spanish onion** a large mild-flavoured onion. **Spanish windlass** the use of a stick as a lever for tightening ropes etc. [ME f. *Spain*, with shortening of the first element]

spank /spangk/ *v.* & *n.* ● *v.* **1** *tr.* slap esp. on the buttocks with the open hand, a slipper, etc. **2** *intr.* (of a horse etc.) move briskly, esp. between a trot and a gallop. ● *n.* a slap esp. with the open hand on the buttocks. [perh. imit.]

■ *v.* **1** slap, smack, put *or* take over one's knee, thrash, hit, paddle, *colloq.* whack, give a person a (good) licking *or* hiding, *sl.* wallop, tan (a person's hide). ● *n.* see SLAP *n.*

spanker /spángkər/ *n.* **1** a person or thing that spanks. **2** *Naut.* a fore-and-aft sail set on the after side of the mizen-mast. **3** a fast horse. **4** *colloq.* a person or thing of notable size or quality.

spanking /spángking/ *adj.*, *adv.*, & *n.* ● *adj.* **1** (esp. of a horse) moving quickly; lively; brisk (*at a spanking trot*). **2** *colloq.* striking; excellent. ● *adv. colloq.* very, exceedingly (*spanking clean*). ● *n.* the act or an instance of slapping, esp. on the buttocks as a punishment for children.

■ *adj.* **1** quick, rapid, swift, lively, fast, smart, energetic, vigorous, brisk, *colloq.* snappy; crisp, bracing, fresh, freshening, rattling, strong, stiff. **2** see EXCELLENT. ● *adv.* see EXCEEDINGLY 1. ● *n.* see WHIPPING 1.

spanner /spánnər/ *n.* **1** *Brit.* an instrument for turning or gripping a nut on a screw etc. (cf. WRENCH). **2** the cross-brace of a bridge etc. □ **a spanner in the works** *Brit. colloq.* a drawback or impediment. [G *spannen* draw tight: see SPAN[2]]

spar[1] /spaar/ *n.* **1** a stout pole esp. used for the mast, yard, etc. of a ship. **2** the main longitudinal beam of an aeroplane wing. □ **spar-buoy** a buoy made of a spar with one end moored so that the other stands up. **spar-deck** the light upper deck of a vessel. [ME *sparre*, *sperre* f. OF *esparre* or ON *sperra* or direct f. Gmc: cf. MDu., MLG *sparre*, OS, OHG *sparro*]

■ **1** mast, yard, yard-arm, boom, gaff, jigger, mizen, pole, *Naut. sl.* stick.

spar[2] /spaar/ *v.* & *n.* ● *v.intr.* (**sparred, sparring**) **1** (often foll. by *at*) make the motions of boxing without landing heavy blows. **2** engage in argument (*they are always sparring*). **3** (of a gamecock) fight with the feet or spurs. ● *n.* **1 a** a sparring motion. **b** a boxing-match. **2** a cock-fight. **3** an argument or dispute. □ **sparring partner 1** a boxer employed to engage in sparring with another as training. **2** a person with whom one enjoys arguing. [ME f. OE *sperran*, *spyrran*, of unkn. orig.: cf. ON *sperrask* kick out]

■ *v.* **1** fight, box, exchange blows; shadow-box. **2** dispute, argue, quarrel, bicker, squabble, wrangle, bandy words, have words; fight, *colloq.* scrap. ● *n.* **3** see ARGUMENT 1.

spar[3] /spaar/ *n.* any crystalline, easily cleavable and non-lustrous mineral, e.g. calcite or fluorspar. □□ **sparry** *adj.* [MLG, rel. to OE *spæren* of plaster, *spærstān* gypsum]

sparable /spárrəb'l/ *n.* a headless nail used for the soles and heels of shoes. [contr. of *sparrow-bill*, also used in this sense]

sparaxis /spəráksiss/ *n.* any S. African iridaceous plant of the genus *Sparaxis*, with showy flowers and jagged spathes. [mod.L f. Gk, = laceration, f. *sparassō* tear]

spare /spair/ *adj.*, *n.*, & *v.* ● *adj.* **1 a** not required for ordinary use; extra (*have no spare cash*; *spare time*). **b** reserved for emergency or occasional use (*slept in the spare room*). **2** lean; thin. **3** scanty; frugal; not copious (*a spare diet*; *a spare prose style*). **4** *colloq.* not wanted or used by others (*a spare seat in the front row*). ● *n.* **1** *Brit.* a spare part; a duplicate. **2** *Bowling* the knocking-down of all the pins with the first two balls. ● *v.* **1** *tr.* afford to give or do without; dispense with (*cannot spare him just now*; *can spare you a couple*). **2** *tr.* **a** abstain from killing, hurting, wounding, etc. (*spared his feelings*; *spared her life*). **b** abstain from inflicting or causing; relieve from (*spare me this talk*; *spare my blushes*). **3** *tr.* be frugal or grudging of (*no expense spared*). **4** *intr. archaic* be frugal. □ **go spare** *colloq.* **1** *Brit.* become extremely angry or distraught. **2** be unwanted by others. **not spare oneself** exert one's utmost efforts. **spare part** a duplicate part to replace a lost or damaged part of a machine etc. **spare tyre 1** an extra tyre carried in a motor vehicle for emergencies. **2** *Brit. colloq.* a roll of fat round the waist. **to spare** left over; additional (*an hour to spare*). □□ **sparely** *adv.* **spareness** *n.* **sparer** *n.* [OE *spær*, *sparian* f. Gmc]

■ *adj.* **1** extra, surplus, excess, supernumerary, auxiliary, supplementary, additional; odd, left over; unoccupied, leisure, free; in reserve, in addition. **2** thin, lean, skinny, scrawny, cadaverous, gaunt, raw-boned, meagre, gangling, lank(y), wiry, slim, slender; all skin and bones. **3** meagre, small, skimpy, modest, scanty; frugal, economical, mean, sparing; plain, sparse, stark, austere, clean. **4** unoccupied, free, unused, unwanted, unneeded, not spoken for. ● *v.* **1** allow, relinquish, let go (of), give, award, bestow, afford, let a person have, donate, part with, yield, dispense with, manage *or* do without, forgo, forsake, surrender, give up, sacrifice. **2 a** pardon, let go, release, have mercy on, let off, free, liberate. **b** save from, rescue from, deliver from, redeem from; relieve from, exempt from. □ **spare tyre 2** see STOMACH *n.* 2b. □□ **sparely** see SIMPLY 1. **spareness** plainness, cleanness, severity, starkness, austerity.

spare-rib /spáir-ríb/ *n.* closely-trimmed ribs of esp. pork. [prob. f. MLG *ribbesper*, by transposition and assoc. with SPARE]

sparge /spaarj/ *v.tr.* moisten by sprinkling, esp. in brewing. □□ **sparger** *n.* [app. f. L *spargere* sprinkle]

sparing /spáiring/ *adj.* **1** inclined to save; economical. **2** restrained; limited. □□ **sparingly** *adv.* **sparingness** *n.*

■ **1** thrifty, saving, frugal, spare, careful, prudent, parsimonious, economical; penurious, mean, penny-pinching, stingy, niggardly, miserly, close, close-fisted, cheap, *colloq.* tight, tight-fisted, *Brit. colloq.* mingy. **2** sparse, meagre, scant, little, limited, restrained, inappreciable, not much, insignificant. □□ **sparingness** see THRIFT.

spark[1] /spaark/ *n.* & *v.* ● *n.* **1** a fiery particle thrown off from a fire, or alight in ashes, or produced by a flint, match, etc. **2** (often foll. by *of*) a particle of a quality etc. (*not a spark of life*; *a spark of interest*). **3** *Electr.* **a** a light produced by a sudden disruptive discharge through the air etc. **b** such a discharge serving to ignite the explosive mixture in an internal-combustion engine. **4 a** a flash of wit etc. **b** anything causing interest, excitement, etc. **c** (also **bright spark**) a witty or lively person. **5** a small bright object or point, e.g. in a gem. **6** (**Sparks**) a nickname for a radio operator or an electrician. ● *v.* **1** *intr.* emit sparks of fire or electricity. **2** *tr.* (often foll. by *off*) stir into activity; initiate (a process) suddenly. **3** *intr. Electr.* produce sparks at the point where a circuit is interrupted. □ **spark chamber** an apparatus designed to show ionizing particles. **spark-gap** the space between electric terminals where sparks occur. **sparking-plug** *Brit.* = *spark-plug*. **spark-plug** a device for firing the explosive mixture in an internal-combustion engine. □□ **sparkless** *adj.* **sparky** *adj.* [ME f. OE *spærca*, *spearca*]

■ *n.* **2** scintilla, flicker, glimmer, glint, sparkle, speck, hint, suggestion, vestige, atom, particle, whit, jot (or tittle), iota. **3** see FLASH *n.* 1. ● *v.* **1** see FLASH *v.* 2. **2** set *or* touch off, ignite, kindle, electrify, animate, trigger, energize, galvanize, activate, excite, inspire, inspirit, stimulate, *literary* enkindle; set in motion, bring about, start (up), begin, initiate, provoke, precipitate.

spark[2] /spaark/ *n.* & *v.* ● *n.* **1** a lively young fellow. **2** a gallant, a beau. ● *v.intr.* play the gallant. □□ **sparkish** *adj.* [prob. a fig. use of SPARK[1]]

sparkle /spaárk'l/ *v.* & *n.* ● *v.intr.* **1 a** emit or seem to emit sparks; glitter; glisten (*her eyes sparkled*). **b** be witty; scintillate (*sparkling repartee*). **2** (of wine etc.) effervesce (cf. STILL[1] *adj.* 4). ● *n.* **1** a gleam, spark. **2** vivacity, liveliness. □□ **sparkly** *adj.* [ME f. SPARK[1] + -LE[4]]

■ *v.* **1 a** glitter, glisten, scintillate, glint, gleam, flicker, shine, twinkle, wink, blink, glimmer, flash, coruscate, blaze, burn, flame. **b** scintillate, dazzle. **2** effervesce, fizz, bubble. ● *n.* **1** glitter, scintillation, twinkle, coruscation, dazzle, spark, gleam, brightness, brilliance, radiance. **2** vivacity, liveliness, fire, brightness, wittiness, effervescence, ebullience, excitement, animation, vigour, energy, spirit, cheer, joy, light-heartedness, *élan*, zeal, zip, gusto, dash, life, gaiety, cheer, cheerfulness, *colloq.* vim, zing, *sl.* pizazz, oomph.

sparkler /spaárklər/ *n.* **1** a person or thing that sparkles. **2** a hand-held sparkling firework. **3** *colloq.* a diamond or other gem.

■ **3** see JEWEL *n.* 1a.

sparling /spaárling/ *n.* a European smelt, *Osmerus eperlanus*. [ME f. OF *esperlinge*, of Gmc orig.]

sparoid /spárroyd/ *n.* & *adj.* ● *n.* any marine fish of the family Sparidae, e.g. a porgy. ● *adj.* of or concerning the Sparidae. [mod.L *Sparoides* f. L *sparus* f. Gk *sparos* sea-bream]

sparrow /spárrō/ *n.* **1** any small brownish-grey bird of the genus *Passer*, esp. the house sparrow and tree sparrow. **2** any of various birds of similar appearance such as the hedge sparrow. □ **sparrow-grass** *dial.* or *colloq.* asparagus. [OE *spearwa* f. Gmc]

sparrowhawk /spárrōhawk/ *n.* a small hawk, *Accipiter nisus*, preying on small birds.

sparse /spaarss/ *adj.* thinly dispersed or scattered; not dense (*sparse population*; *sparse greying hair*). □□ **sparsely** *adv.* **sparseness** *n.* **sparsity** *n.* [L *sparsus* past part. of *spargere* scatter]

■ thin (on the ground), few (and far between), meagre, scanty, (thinly *or* widely) dispersed, (thinly *or* widely) scattered, spread out, in short supply, scarce. □□ **sparseness, sparsity** see DEARTH.

Spartan /spaárt'n/ *adj.* & *n.* ● *adj.* **1** of or relating to Sparta in ancient Greece. **2 a** possessing the qualities of courage, endurance, stern frugality, etc., associated with Sparta. **b** (of a regime, conditions, etc.) lacking comfort; austere. ● *n.* a citizen of Sparta. [ME f. L *Spartanus* f. *Sparta* f. Gk *Sparta*, *-tē*]

■ *adj.* **2** austere, strict, severe, harsh, hard, stern, rigorous, rigid, simple, plain, frugal, ascetic, stringent, controlled, disciplined, self-denying, abstinent, abstemious.

spartina /spaarteénə/ *n.* any grass of the genus *Spartina*, with rhizomatous roots and growing in wet or marshy ground. [Gk *spartinē* rope]

spasm /spázz'm/ *n.* **1** a sudden involuntary muscular contraction. **2** a sudden convulsive movement or emotion etc. (*a spasm of coughing*). **3** (usu. foll. by *of*) *colloq.* a brief spell of an activity. [ME f. OF *spasme* or L *spasmus* f. Gk *spasmos, spasma* f. *spaō* pull]
■ **1** convulsion, throe, fit, twitch, tic, paroxysm, shudder. **2** fit, seizure, convulsion, paroxysm, outburst, attack. **3** spell, burst, eruption, spurt.

spasmodic /spazmóddik/ *adj.* **1** of, caused by, or subject to, a spasm or spasms (*a spasmodic jerk; spasmodic asthma*). **2** occurring or done by fits and starts (*spasmodic efforts*). □□ **spasmodically** *adv.* [mod.L *spasmodicus* f. Gk *spasmōdēs* (as SPASM)]
■ **1** paroxysmal, convulsive, jerky, jerking, sudden, *Med.* spastic. **2** fitful, irregular, intermittent, random, interrupted, sporadic, erratic, occasional, periodic, unsustained, discontinuous, pulsating, cyclic(al), broken. □□ **spasmodically** see *by fits and starts* (FIT[2]).

spastic /spástik/ *adj.* & *n.* ● *adj.* **1** *Med.* suffering from cerebral palsy with spasm of the muscles. **2** *sl. offens.* weak, feeble, incompetent. **3** spasmodic. ● *n. Med.* a person suffering from cerebral palsy. □□ **spastically** *adv.* **spasticity** /-tissiti/ *n.* [L *spasticus* f. Gk *spastikos* pulling f. *spaō* pull]
■ *adj.* **3** see SPASMODIC 1.

spat[1] *past* and *past part.* of SPIT[1].

spat[2] /spat/ *n.* **1** (usu. in *pl.*) *hist.* a short cloth gaiter protecting the shoe from mud etc. **2** a cover for an aircraft wheel. [abbr. of SPATTERDASH]

spat[3] /spat/ *n.* & *v. US colloq.* ● *n.* **1** a petty quarrel. **2** a slight amount. ● *v.intr.* (**spatted, spatting**) quarrel pettily. [prob. imit.]
■ *n.* **1** see QUARREL[1] *n.* 1. ● *v.* see ARGUE 1.

spat[4] /spat/ *n.* & *v.* ● *n.* the spawn of shellfish, esp. the oyster. ● *v.* (**spatted, spatting**) **1** *intr.* (of an oyster) spawn. **2** *tr.* shed (spawn). [AF, of unkn. orig.]

spatchcock /spáchkok/ *n.* & *v.* ● *n.* a chicken or esp. game bird split open and grilled. ● *v.tr.* **1** treat (poultry) in this way. **2** *colloq.* insert or interpolate (a phrase, sentence, story, etc.) esp. incongruously. [orig. in Ir. use, expl. by Grose (1785) as f. *dispatch-cock*, but cf. SPITCHCOCK]

spate /spayt/ *n.* **1** a river-flood (*the river is in spate*). **2** a large or excessive amount (*a spate of enquiries*). [ME, Sc. & N.Engl.: orig. unkn.]
■ **1** flood, inundation, deluge, torrent. **2** flood, inundation, onrush, rush, deluge, torrent.

spathe /spayth/ *n. Bot.* a large bract or pair of bracts enveloping a spadix or flower-cluster. □□ **spathaceous** /spətháyshəss/ *adj.* [L f. Gk *spathē* broad blade etc.]

spathic /spáthik/ *adj.* (of a mineral) like spar (see SPAR[3]), esp. in cleavage. □ **spathic iron ore** = SIDERITE. □□ **spathose** *adj.* [*spath* spar f. G *Spath*]

spatial /spáysh'l/ *adj.* (also **spacial**) of or concerning space (*spatial extent*). □□ **spatiality** /-shiálliti/ *n.* **spatialize** *v.tr.* (also **-ise**). **spatially** *adv.* [L *spatium* space]

spatio-temporal /spáyshiōtémpərəl/ *adj. Physics* & *Philos.* belonging to both space and time or to space-time. □□ **spatio-temporally** *adv.* [formed as SPATIAL + TEMPORAL]

spatter /spáttər/ *v.* & *n.* ● *v.* **1** *tr.* **a** (often foll. by *with*) splash (a person etc.) (*spattered him with mud*). **b** scatter or splash (liquid, mud, etc.) here and there. **2** *intr.* (of rain etc.) fall here and there (*glass spattered down*). **3** *tr.* slander (a person's honour etc.). ● *n.* **1** (usu. foll. by *of*) a splash (*a spatter of mud*). **2** a quick pattering sound. [frequent. f. base as in Du., LG *spatten* burst, spout]
■ *v.* **1 a** splash, speckle, pepper, bespatter, spray, shower, scatter, dabble, daub, bedaub, sprinkle, besprinkle, *US* splatter, *colloq.* splodge, splotch. **b** splash, bespatter, spray, shower, scatter, daub, sprinkle, *US* splatter. **2** see FALL *v.* 1. ● *n.* **1** see SPLASH *n.* 2, 3. **2** see PATTER[1] *n.*

spatterdash /spáttərdash/ *n.* **1** (usu. in *pl.*) *hist.* a cloth or other legging to protect the stockings etc. from mud etc. **2** *US* = ROUGHCAST.

spatula /spátyoolə/ *n.* **1** a broad-bladed knife-like implement used for spreading, stirring, mixing (paints), etc. **2** a doctor's instrument for pressing the tongue down or to one side. [L, var. of *spathula*, dimin. of *spatha* SPATHE]

spatulate /spátyoolət/ *adj.* **1** spatula-shaped. **2** (esp. of a leaf) having a broad rounded end. [SPATULA]

spavin /spávvin/ *n. Vet.* a disease of a horse's hock with a hard bony tumour or excrescence. □ **blood** (or **bog**) **spavin** a distension of the joint by effusion of lymph or fluid. **bone spavin** a deposit of bony substance uniting the bones. □□ **spavined** *adj.* [ME f. OF *espavin*, var. of *esparvain* f. Gmc]

spawn /spawn/ *v.* & *n.* ● *v.* **1 a** *tr.* (also *absol.*) (of a fish, frog, mollusc, or crustacean) produce (eggs). **b** *intr.* be produced as eggs or young. **2** *tr. derog.* (of people) produce (offspring). **3** *tr.* produce or generate, esp. in large numbers. ● *n.* **1** the eggs of fish, frogs, etc. **2** *derog.* human or other offspring. **3** a white fibrous matter from which fungi are produced; mycelium. □□ **spawner** *n.* [ME f. AF *espaundre* shed roe, OF *espandre* EXPAND]
■ *v.* **1a** produce, yield, bear. **2** give birth to, bring forth, breed, create, father, sire, *literary* beget. **3** generate, give rise to, bring about, produce, cause, give birth to, bring forth, breed, beget, create, father, sire, *archaic* engender, *literary* beget. ● *n.* **2** see ISSUE *n.* 5.

spay /spay/ *v.tr.* sterilize (a female animal) by removing the ovaries. [ME f. AF *espeier*, OF *espeer* cut with a sword f. *espee* sword f. L *spatha*: see SPATHE]
■ see STERILIZE 2.

SPCK *abbr.* Society for Promoting Christian Knowledge.

speak /speek/ *v.* (*past* **spoke** /spōk/; *past part.* **spoken** /spṓkən/) **1** *intr.* make articulate verbal utterances in an ordinary (not singing) voice. **2** *tr.* **a** utter (words). **b** make known or communicate (one's opinion, the truth, etc.) in this way (*never speaks sense*). **3** *intr.* **a** (foll. by *to, with*) hold a conversation (*spoke to him for an hour; spoke with them about their work*). **b** (foll. by *of*) mention in writing etc. (*speaks of it in his novel*). **c** (foll. by *for*) articulate the feelings of (another person etc.) in speech or writing (*speaks for our generation*). **4** *intr.* (foll. by *to*) **a** address; converse with (a person etc.). **b** speak in confirmation of or with reference to (*spoke to the resolution; can speak to his innocence*). **c** *colloq.* reprove (*spoke to them about their lateness*). **5** *intr.* make a speech before an audience etc. (*spoke for an hour on the topic; has a good speaking voice*). **6** *tr.* use or be able to use (a specified language) (*cannot speak French*). **7** *intr.* (of a gun, a musical instrument, etc.) make a sound. **8** *intr.* (usu. foll. by *to*) *poet.* communicate feeling etc., affect, touch (*the sunset spoke to her*). **9** *intr.* (of a hound) bark. **10** *tr.* hail and hold communication with (a ship). **11** *tr. archaic* **a** (of conduct etc.) show (a person) to be (*his conduct speaks him generous*). **b** be evidence of (*the loud laugh speaks the vacant mind*). □ **not** (or **nothing**) **to speak of** not (or nothing) worth mentioning; practically not (or nothing). **speak for itself** need no supporting evidence. **speak for oneself 1** give one's own opinions. **2** not presume to speak for others. **speak one's mind** speak bluntly or frankly. **speak out** speak loudly or freely, give one's opinion. **speak up** = *speak out*. **speak volumes** (of a fact etc.) be very significant. **speak volumes** (or **well** etc.) **for 1** be abundant evidence of. **2** place in a favourable light. □□ **speakable** *adj.* [OE *sprecan*, later *specan*]
■ **1** talk, converse, discourse, vocalize. **2** express, utter, talk, say, state, tell, pronounce, enunciate, voice, vocalize, mouth; articulate, make known, communicate, reveal, indicate, verbalize. **3 a** (*speak to* or *with*) talk to *or* with, converse *or* discourse with, communicate with, address, say something to, chat to *or* with. **b** (*speak of*) mention, allude to, refer to, make reference to, comment on, speak *or* talk about, *literary* advert to. **c** (*speak for*) act on *or US* in behalf of, act for, represent, act as agent for. **4** (*speak to*) **a** accost, address, talk to; apostrophize. **b** see SPEAK 5 below, VOUCH. **c** reprove, scold, talk to, reprimand, rebuke, admonish, warn, lecture. **5** (*speak on* or *about*) discuss, address, discourse upon *or* on, lecture

on, talk about, treat (of), deal with, examine, touch upon *or* on. **6** talk, communicate in, discourse in, converse in, utter in, articulate in, use. **8** (*speak to*) be meaningful to, appeal to, influence, affect, touch. **11 b** bespeak, show to be; symbolize, betoken, signify, communicate, convey, indicate. □ **speak for itself** be self-evident, be obvious, be significant. **speak one's mind** talk freely *or* unreservedly, express one's opinion, speak out *or* up, declare, pipe up, come out with it, state one's position, voice one's thoughts, take a stand. **speak out, speak up** talk (more) loudly *or* clearly, make oneself heard, raise one's voice; see also *speak one's mind* above.

speakeasy /spéekeezi/ *n.* (*pl.* **-ies**) *US hist. sl.* an illicit liquor shop or drinking club during Prohibition.

speaker /spéekər/ *n.* **1** a person who speaks, esp. in public. **2** a person who speaks a specified language (esp. in *comb.*: *a French-speaker*). **3** (**Speaker**) the presiding officer in a legislative assembly, esp. the House of Commons. **4** = LOUDSPEAKER. □□ **speakership** *n.*

■ **1** orator, lecturer, speech-maker, talker, preacher; spokesperson, spokesman, spokeswoman; rabble-rouser, demagogue, *colloq.* tub-thumper, *esp. US sl.* spieler.

speaking /spéeking/ *n.* & *adj.* ● *n.* the act or an instance of uttering words etc. ● *adj.* **1** that speaks; capable of articulate speech. **2** (of a portrait) lifelike; true to its subject (*a speaking likeness*). **3** (in *comb.*) speaking or capable of speaking a specified foreign language (*French-speaking*). **4** with a reference or from a point of view specified (*roughly speaking*; *professionally speaking*). □ **on speaking terms** (foll. by *with*) **1** slightly acquainted. **2** on friendly terms. **speaking acquaintance 1** a person one knows slightly. **2** this degree of familiarity. **speaking clock** *Brit.* a telephone service giving the correct time in words. **speaking-trumpet** *hist.* an instrument for making the voice carry. **speaking-tube** a tube for conveying the voice from one room, building, etc., to another.

■ *n.* see SPEECH 1. □ **on speaking terms 1** (*be on speaking terms with*) see *be acquainted with* (ACQUAINT).

spear /speer/ *n.* & *v.* ● *n.* **1** a thrusting or throwing weapon with a pointed usu. steel tip and a long shaft. **2** a similar barbed instrument used for catching fish etc. **3** *archaic* a spearman. **4** a pointed stem of asparagus etc. ● *v.tr.* pierce or strike with or as if with a spear (*speared an olive*). □ **spear gun** a gun used to propel a spear in underwater fishing. **spear side** the male side of a family. [OE *spere*]

■ *n.* **1, 2** see LANCE *n.* ● *v.* see PIERCE 1a, b.

spearhead /spéerhed/ *n.* & *v.* ● *n.* **1** the point of a spear. **2** an individual or group chosen to lead a thrust or attack. ● *v.tr.* act as the spearhead of (an attack etc.).

■ *n.* **2** vanguard, advance guard, van, forefront, front line, cutting edge, leader(s), pioneer(s), trail-blazer(s). ● *v.* **1** launch, initiate, lead (the way in), take the initiative in, pioneer, blaze the trail for, take the lead in, be in the van *or* vanguard *or* forefront of.

spearman /spéermən/ *n.* (*pl.* **-men**) *archaic* a person, esp. a soldier, who uses a spear.

spearmint /spéermint/ *n.* a common garden mint, *Mentha spicata*, used in cookery and to flavour chewing-gum.

spearwort /spéerwurt/ *n.* an aquatic plant, *Ranunculus lingua*, with thick hollow stems, long narrow spear-shaped leaves, and yellow flowers.

spec[1] /spek/ *n. colloq.* a commercial speculation or venture. □ **on spec** in the hope of success; as a gamble, on the off chance. [abbr. of SPECULATION]

spec[2] /spek/ *n. colloq.* a detailed working description; a specification. [abbr. of SPECIFICATION]

special /spésh'l/ *adj.* & *n.* ● *adj.* **1 a** particularly good; exceptional; out of the ordinary (*bought them a special present*; *today is a special day*; *took special trouble*). **b** peculiar; specific; not general (*lacks the special qualities required*; *the word has a special sense*). **2** for a particular purpose (*sent on a special assignment*). **3** in which a person specializes (*statistics is his special field*). **4** denoting education for children with particular needs, e.g. the handicapped. ● *n.* a special person or thing, e.g. a special constable, train, examination, edition of a newspaper, dish on a menu, etc. □ **special area** *Brit.* a district for which special economic provision is made in legislation. **Special Branch** (in the UK) a police department dealing with political security. **special case 1** a written statement of fact presented by litigants to a court. **2** an exceptional or unusual case. **special constable** *Brit.* a policeman sworn in to assist in times of emergency etc. **special correspondent** a journalist writing for a newspaper on special events or a special area of interest. **special delivery** a delivery of mail in advance of the regular delivery. **special drawing rights** the right to purchase extra foreign currency from the International Monetary Fund. **special edition** an extra edition of a newspaper including later news than the ordinary edition. **special effects** scenic illusions created by props and camera-work. **special intention** see INTENTION. **special jury** a jury with members of a particular social standing (cf. *common jury*). **special licence** *Brit.* a marriage licence allowing immediate marriage without banns, or at an unusual time or place. **special pleading 1** *Law* pleading with reference to new facts in a case. **2** (in general use) a specious or unfair argument favouring the speaker's point of view. **special verdict** *Law* a verdict stating the facts as proved but leaving the court to draw conclusions from them. □□ **specially** *adv.* **specialness** *n.* [ME f. OF *especial* ESPECIAL or L *specialis* (as SPECIES)]

■ *adj.* **1 a** exceptional, uncommon, especial, rare, unusual, out of the ordinary, extraordinary, remarkable, inimitable; distinguished, notable, noteworthy, particularly good; significant, important, momentous, earth-shaking, memorable, red-letter; gala, festive, celebratory; particular, extra, pointed, concerted, deliberate, determined. **b** specific, particular, different, unorthodox, unconventional, unique, precise, individual, singular, distinctive, specialized, certain, idiosyncratic, curious, peculiar, odd, strange, bizarre, weird, one of a kind. **2** exclusive, express, individual, tailor-made, specialized, specific. ● *n.* extra, *colloq.* one-off; see also SPECIALITY 1. □□ **specially** especially, particularly, custom-, expressly, exclusively, specifically.

specialist /spéshəlist/ *n.* (usu. foll. by *in*) **1** a person who is trained in a particular branch of a profession, esp. medicine (*a specialist in dermatology*). **2** a person who specially or exclusively studies a subject or a particular branch of a subject. □□ **specialism** /-liz'm/ *n.* **specialistic** /-lístik/ *adj.*

■ **1** consultant, expert. **2** expert, authority, professional, master, connoisseur, maestro, artiste, artist, adept.

speciality /spéshiálliti/ *n.* (*pl.* **-ies**) **1** a special pursuit, product, operation, etc., to which a company or a person gives special attention. **2** a special feature, characteristic, or skill. [ME f. OF *especialité* or LL *specialitas* (as SPECIAL)]

■ **1** *pièce de résistance*, special, *esp. US* specialty; sphere, field, area, line, subject, concentration, specialization, *métier*, baby, *colloq.* thing, cup of tea, claim to fame, *sl.* bag. **2** expertise, talent, genius, gift, skill, aptitude, trade, craft, accomplishment, ability, strength, forte, strong point, art, *esp. US* specialty.

specialize /spéshəlīz/ *v.* (also **-ise**) **1** *intr.* (often foll. by *in*) **a** be or become a specialist (*specializes in optics*). **b** devote oneself to an area of interest, skill, etc. (*specializes in insulting people*). **2** *Biol.* **a** *tr.* (esp. in *passive*) adapt or set apart (an organ etc.) for a particular purpose. **b** *intr.* (of an organ etc.) become adapted etc. in this way. **3** *tr.* make specific or individual. **4** *tr.* modify or limit (an idea, statement, etc.). □□ **specialization** /-záysh'n/ *n.* [F *spécialiser* (as SPECIAL)]

■ **2, 4** see DIFFERENTIATE 3. □□ **specialization** see FIELD *n.* 8.

specialty /spésh'lti/ *n.* (*pl.* **-ies**) **1** esp. *US* = SPECIALITY. **2** *Law* an instrument under seal; a sealed contract. [ME f. OF (*e*)*specialté* (as SPECIAL)]

speciation /spéessiáysh'n, spéesh-/ *n. Biol.* the formation of a new species in the course of evolution.

specie /spéeshee, -shi/ *n.* coin money as opposed to paper money. [L, ablat. of SPECIES in phrase *in specie*]
▪ see COIN *n.*

species /spéeshiz, -sheez, spées-/ *n.* (*pl.* same) **1** a class of things having some common characteristics. **2** *Biol.* a category in the system of classification of living organisms consisting of similar individuals capable of exchanging genes or interbreeding. **3** a kind or sort. **4** *Logic* a group subordinate to a genus and containing individuals agreeing in some common attribute(s) and called by a common name. **5** *Law* a form or shape given to materials. **6** *Eccl.* the visible form of each of the elements of consecrated bread and wine in the Eucharist. [L, = appearance, kind, beauty, f. *specere* look]
▪ **2** breed, stock, strain. **3** see SORT *n.* 1.

specific /spisíffik/ *adj.* & *n.* ● *adj.* **1** clearly defined; definite (*has no specific name; told me so in specific terms*). **2** relating to a particular subject; peculiar (*a style specific to that*). **3 a** of or concerning a species (*the specific name for a plant*). **b** possessing, or concerned with, the properties that characterize a species (*the specific forms of animals*). **4** (of a duty or a tax) assessed by quantity or amount, not by the value of goods. ● *n.* **1** *archaic* a specific medicine or remedy. **2** a specific aspect or factor (*shall we discuss specifics?*). □ **specific cause** the cause of a particular form of a disease. **specific difference** a factor that differentiates a species. **specific disease** a disease caused by one identifiable agent. **specific gravity** = *relative density*. **specific heat capacity** the heat required to raise the temperature of the unit mass of a given substance by a given amount (usu. one degree). **specific medicine** a medicine having a distinct effect in curing a certain disease. **specific performance** *Law* the performance of a contractual duty, as ordered in cases where damages would not be adequate remedy. □□ **specifically** *adv.* **specificity** /spéssifissiti/ *n.* **specificness** *n.* [LL *specificus* (as SPECIES)]
▪ *adj.* **1** definite, precise, exact, particular, explicit, express, unambiguous, definitive, clear-cut, unequivocal, categorical, (well-)defined, determined, specified, certain, limited, indicated, predetermined, established, spelt out, delineated, set, distinct, fixed, circumscribed, restricted. **2** unique (to), typical (of), characteristic (of), peculiar (to), personal (to), discrete, distinctive (to), special (to), individual, *sui generis*, proper to, relating to, identified with, associated with. ● *n.* **1** see REMEDY *n.* 1. **2** see DETAIL *n.* 1.

specification /spéssifikáysh'n/ *n.* **1** the act or an instance of specifying; the state of being specified. **2** (esp. in *pl.*) a detailed description of the construction, workmanship, materials, etc., of work done or to be done, prepared by an architect, engineer, etc. **3** a description by an applicant for a patent of the construction and use of his invention. **4** *Law* the conversion of materials into a new product not held to be the property of the owner of the materials. [med.L *specificatio* (as SPECIFY)]
▪ **1** identification, description, particularization, naming; requirement, qualification, stipulation, condition, restriction, consideration. **2** (*specifications*) itemization, list, listing, check-list, inventory, list of particulars, detail(s), enumeration, description.

specify /spéssifī/ *v.tr.* (**-ies, -ied**) **1** (also *absol.*) name or mention expressly (*specified the type he needed*). **2** (usu. foll. by *that* + clause) name as a condition (*specified that he must be paid at once*). **3** include in specifications (*a French window was not specified*). □□ **specifiable** *adj.* **specifier** *n.* [ME f. OF *specifier* or LL *specificare* (as SPECIFIC)]
▪ particularize, enumerate, itemize, name, denominate, be specific about, list, indicate, mention, identify, cite, define, detail, stipulate, spell out, set out *or* forth, individualize, disambiguate, delineate, determine, establish.

specimen /spéssimən/ *n.* **1** an individual or part taken as an example of a class or whole, esp. when used for investigation or scientific examination (*specimens of copper ore; a specimen of your handwriting*). **2** *Med.* a sample of urine for testing. **3** *colloq.* usu. *derog.* a person of a specified sort. [L f. *specere* look]
▪ **1** sample, example, instance, exemplar, representative, representation; illustration, case (in point), type, model, pattern.

speciology /spéessióllәji/ *n.* the scientific study of species or of their origin etc. □□ **speciological** /-siәlójik'l/ *adj.*

specious /spéeshәss/ *adj.* **1** superficially plausible but actually wrong (*a specious argument*). **2** misleadingly attractive in appearance. □□ **speciosity** /-shióssiti/ *n.* **speciously** *adv.* **speciousness** *n.* [ME, = beautiful, f. L *speciosus* (as SPECIES)]
▪ **1** deceptive, superficial, casuistic, ostensible, misleading, fallacious, sophistic(al), plausible, likely. □□ **speciously** see *seemingly* (SEEMING[1]).

speck /spek/ *n.* & *v.* ● *n.* **1** a small spot, dot, or stain. **2** (foll. by *of*) a particle (*speck of dirt*). **3** a rotten spot in fruit. ● *v.tr.* (esp. as **specked** *adj.*) marked with specks. □□ **speckless** *adj.* [OE *specca*: cf. SPECKLE]
▪ *n.* **1** see SPOT *n.* 1a, b. **2** spot, dot, fleck, mote, speckle, mark, bit, particle; crumb, iota, jot (or tittle), whit, atom, molecule, touch, hint, suggestion, suspicion, tinge, trace, modicum, amount, grain, *colloq.* smidgen. ● *v.* (**specked**) see *speckled* (SPECKLE *v.*).

speckle /spékk'l/ *n.* & *v.* ● *n.* a small spot, mark, or stain, esp. in quantity on the skin, a bird's egg, etc. ● *v.tr.* (esp. as **speckled** *adj.*) mark with speckles or patches. [ME f. MDu. *spekkel*]
▪ *n.* see SPOT *n.* 1a, b. ● *v.* (**speckled**) spotted, mottled, dotted, sprinkled, flecked, specked, stippled, dapple, freckled, brindled; discoloured, spattered, bespattered, spotty.

specs /speks/ *n.pl. colloq.* a pair of spectacles. [abbr.]
▪ see SPECTACLES.

spectacle /spéktәk'l/ *n.* **1** a public show, ceremony, etc. **2** anything attracting public attention (*a charming spectacle; a disgusting spectacle*). □ **make a spectacle of oneself** make oneself an object of ridicule. [ME f. OF f. L *spectaculum* f. *spectare* frequent. of *specere* look]
▪ **1** show, display, performance, event, presentation, exhibition, exposition, demonstration, extravaganza, spectacular, ceremony. **2** sight, exhibit, exhibition, marvel, wonder, sensation, curiosity. □ **make a spectacle of oneself** make a fool *or* a laughing-stock *or* an exhibition of oneself.

spectacled /spéktәk'ld/ *adj.* **1** wearing spectacles. **2** (of an animal) having facial markings resembling spectacles. □ **spectacled bear** a S. American bear, *Tremarctos ornatus*. **spectacled cobra** the Indian cobra.

spectacles /spéktәk'lz/ *n.pl.* (also **pair of spectacles** *sing.*) a pair of lenses in a frame resting on the nose and ears, used to correct defective eyesight or protect the eyes.
▪ eyeglasses, glasses, *colloq.* specs; bifocals, trifocals.

spectacular /spektákyoolәr/ *adj.* & *n.* ● *adj.* **1** of or like a public show; striking, amazing, lavish. **2** strikingly large or obvious (*a spectacular increase in output*). ● *n.* an event intended to be spectacular, esp. a musical film or play. □□ **spectacularly** *adv.* [SPECTACLE, after *oracular* etc.]
▪ *adj.* **1** see SENSATIONAL. ● *n.* see EXTRAVAGANZA 2. □□ **spectacularly** see FAMOUSLY 1.

spectate /spektáyt/ *v.intr.* be a spectator, esp. at a sporting event. [back-form. f. SPECTATOR]

spectator /spektáytәr/ *n.* a person who looks on at a show, game, incident, etc. □ **spectator sport** a sport attracting spectators rather than participants. □□ **spectatorial** /-tәtóriәl/ *adj.* [F *spectateur* or L *spectator* f. *spectare*: see SPECTACLE]

■ witness, eyewitness, observer, viewer, onlooker, looker-on, watcher, beholder, bystander.

spectra *pl.* of SPECTRUM.

spectral /spéktrəl/ *adj.* **1 a** of or relating to spectres or ghosts. **b** ghostlike. **2** of or concerning spectra or the spectrum (*spectral colours; spectral analysis*). ▫▫ **spectrally** *adv.*

■ **1** ghostly, ghostlike, phantom, eerie, wraithlike, incorporeal, disembodied, unearthly, supernatural, weird, *colloq.* spooky.

spectre /spéktər/ *n.* (*US* **specter**) **1** a ghost. **2** a haunting presentiment or preoccupation (*the spectre of war*). **3** (in *comb.*) used in the names of some animals because of their thinness, transparency, etc. (*spectre-bat; spectre-crab*). ▫ **Spectre of the Brocken** a huge shadowy image of the observer projected on mists about a mountain-top (observed on the Brocken in Germany). [F *spectre* or L *spectrum*: see SPECTRUM]

■ **1** ghost, phantom, wraith, apparition, vision, spirit, revenant, *Doppelgänger*, chimera, bogeyman, poltergeist, *colloq.* spook, *literary* shade. **2** shadow, image, vision, (mental) picture; presentiment.

spectro- /spéktrō/ *comb. form* a spectrum.

spectrochemistry /spéktrōkémmistri/ *n.* chemistry based on the study of the spectra of substances.

spectrogram /spéktrōgram/ *n.* a record obtained with a spectrograph.

spectrograph /spéktrōgraaf/ *n.* an apparatus for photographing or otherwise recording spectra. ▫▫ **spectrographic** /-gráffik/ *adj.* **spectrographically** /-gráffikəli/ *adv.* **spectrography** /spektrógrəfi/ *n.*

spectroheliograph /spéktrōhéeliəgraaf/ *n.* an instrument for taking photographs of the sun in the light of one wavelength only.

spectrohelioscope /spéktrōhéeliəskōp/ *n.* a device similar to a spectroheliograph, for visual observation.

spectrometer /spektrómmitər/ *n.* an instrument used for the measurement of observed spectra. ▫▫ **spectrometric** /spéktrəmétrik/ *adj.* **spectrometry** *n.* [G *Spektrometer* or F *spectromètre* (as SPECTRO-, -METER)]

spectrophotometer /spéktrōfōtómmitər/ *n.* an instrument for measuring and recording the intensity of light in various parts of the spectrum. ▫▫ **spectrophotometric** /-təmétrik/ *adj.* **spectrophotometry** *n.*

spectroscope /spéktrəskōp/ *n.* an instrument for producing and recording spectra for examination. ▫▫ **spectroscopic** /-skóppik/ *adj.* **spectroscopical** /-skóppik'l/ *adj.* **spectroscopist** /-tróskəpist/ *n.* **spectroscopy** /-tróskəpi/ *n.* [G *Spektroskop* or F *spectroscope* (as SPECTRO-, -SCOPE)]

spectrum /spéktrəm/ *n.* (*pl.* **spectra** /-trə/) **1** the band of colours, as seen in a rainbow etc., arranged in a progressive series according to their refrangibility or wavelength. **2** the entire range of wavelengths of electromagnetic radiation. **3 a** an image or distribution of parts of electromagnetic radiation arranged in a progressive series according to wavelength. **b** this as characteristic of a body or substance when emitting or absorbing radiation. **4** a similar image or distribution of energy, mass, etc., arranged according to frequency, charge, etc. **5** the entire range or a wide range of anything arranged by degree or quality etc. **6** (in full **ocular spectrum**) an after-image. ▫ **spectrum** (or **spectral**) **analysis** chemical analysis by means of a spectroscope. [L, = image, apparition f. *specere* look]

■ **5** see GAMUT.

specula *pl.* of SPECULUM.

specular /spékyoolər/ *adj.* **1** of or having the nature of a speculum. **2** reflecting. ▫ **specular iron ore** lustrous haematite. [L *specularis* (as SPECULUM)]

speculate /spékyoolayt/ *v.* **1** *intr.* (usu. foll. by *on, upon, about*) form a theory or conjecture, esp. without a firm factual basis; meditate (*speculated on their prospects*). **2** *tr.* (foll. by *that, how*, etc. + clause) conjecture, consider (*speculated how he might achieve it*). **3** *intr.* **a** invest in stocks etc. in the hope of gain but with the possibility of loss. **b** gamble recklessly. ▫▫ **speculator** *n.* [L *speculari* spy out, observe f. *specula* watch-tower f. *specere* look]

■ **1, 2** reflect, meditate, cogitate, think, mull (over), chew on *or* over, ruminate, wonder, deliberate, surmise, theorize, conjecture, postulate, hypothesize, *literary* muse; ponder, contemplate; consider, weigh, judge. **3** gamble, wager, play the market, take a chance *or* risk, *colloq.* plunge, *Brit. sl.* have a flutter. ▫▫ **speculator** see PUNTER 1.

speculation /spékyooláysh'n/ *n.* **1** the act or an instance of speculating; a theory or conjecture (*made no speculation as to her age; is given to speculation*). **2 a** a speculative investment or enterprise (*bought it as a speculation*). **b** the practice of business speculating. **3** a game in which trump cards are bought or sold. [ME f. OF *speculation* or LL *speculatio* (as SPECULATE)]

■ **1** thinking, rumination, cogitation, reflection, meditation, contemplation, consideration, cerebration, pondering, wondering, deliberation, evaluation; conjecture, guess, hypothesis, theory, guesswork, postulation, surmise, supposition, opinion. **2** gamble, wager, flutter; gambling, wagering, taking a chance *or* risk, chance-taking, risk-taking.

speculative /spékyoolətiv/ *adj.* **1** of, based on, engaged in, or inclined to speculation. **2** (of a business investment) involving the risk of loss (*a speculative builder*). ▫▫ **speculatively** *adv.* **speculativeness** *n.* [ME f. OF *speculatif -ive* or LL *speculativus* (as SPECULATE)]

■ **1** intellectual, ideational, abstract, cogitative, notional, theoretical, hypothetical, conjectural, suppositional, supposititious, suppositious, suppositive, rational, ratiocinative, ideal, idealized, idealistic, unrealistic, unpractical, impractical, analytical; groundless, unfounded. **2** risky, hazardous, uncertain, unreliable, untrustworthy, doubtful, dubious, untested, unproven, unproved, chancy, *colloq.* iffy, dodgy, *sl.* dicey.

speculum /spékyooləm/ *n.* (*pl.* **specula** /-lə/) **1** *Surgery* an instrument for dilating the cavities of the human body for inspection. **2** a mirror, usu. of polished metal, esp. in a reflecting telescope. **3** *Ornithol.* a lustrous coloured area on the wing of some birds, esp. ducks. ▫ **speculum-metal** an alloy of copper and tin used as a mirror, esp. in a telescope. [L, = mirror, f. *specere* look]

■ **2** see MIRROR *n.* 1.

sped *past* and *past part.* of SPEED.

speech /speech/ *n.* **1** the faculty or act of speaking. **2** a usu. formal address or discourse delivered to an audience or assembly. **3** a manner of speaking (*a man of blunt speech*). **4** a remark (*after this speech he was silent*). **5** the language of a nation, region, group, etc. **6** *Mus.* the act of sounding in an organ-pipe etc. ▫ **the Queen's** (or **King's**) **Speech** a statement including the Government's proposed measures read by the sovereign at the opening of Parliament. **speech day** *Brit.* an annual prize-giving day in many schools, usu. marked by speeches etc. **speech-reading** lip-reading. **speech therapist** a person who practises speech therapy. **speech therapy** treatment to improve defective speech. **speech-writer** a person employed to write speeches for a politician etc. to deliver. ▫▫ **speechful** *adj.* [OE *sprǣc*, later *spēc* f. WG, rel. to SPEAK]

■ **1** communication, speaking, talking, language, articulation. **2** oration, address, lecture, talk, disquisition, sermon, homily, *literary* discourse; monologue, soliloquy; tirade, harangue, philippic; *colloq.* blast, song and dance, line, (sales) pitch; *sl.* spiel. **3** articulation, diction, expression, enunciation, elocution, speech pattern, speaking, talking. **5** dialect, idiolect, jargon, parlance, idiom, language, tongue, *colloq.* lingo.

speechify /spéechifī/ *v.intr.* (**-ies, -ied**) *joc.* or *derog.* make esp. boring or long speeches. ▫▫ **speechification** /-fikáysh'n/ *n.* **speechifier** *n.*

▪ see *hold forth* 2 (HOLD[1]).

speechless /spéechliss/ *adj.* **1** temporarily unable to speak because of emotion etc. (*speechless with rage*). **2** dumb. ▫▫ **speechlessly** *adv.* **speechlessness** *n.* [OE *spǣclēas* (as SPEECH, -LESS)]

▪ **1** dumbfounded, dumbstruck, wordless, silent, struck dumb, tongue-tied, thunderstruck, shocked, dazed, inarticulate, paralysed, nonplussed, *sl.* gobsmacked. **2** mute, dumb, voiceless. ▫▫ **speechlessly** see *silently* (SILENT). **speechlessness** see SILENCE *n.* 2, 3.

speed /speed/ *n.* & *v.* ● *n.* **1** rapidity of movement (*with all speed; at full speed*). **2** a rate of progress or motion over a distance in time (*attains a high speed*). **3 a** a gear appropriate to a range of speeds of a bicycle. **b** esp. *US* or *archaic* such a gear in a motor vehicle. **4** *Photog.* **a** the sensitivity of film to light. **b** the light-gathering power of a lens. **c** the duration of an exposure. **5** *sl.* an amphetamine drug, esp. methamphetamine. **6** *archaic* success, prosperity (*send me good speed*). ● *v.* (*past* and *past part.* **sped** /sped/) **1** *intr.* go fast (*sped down the street*). **2** (*past* and *past part.* **speeded**) **a** *intr.* (of a motorist etc.) travel at an illegal or dangerous speed. **b** *tr.* regulate the speed of (an engine etc.). **c** *tr.* cause (an engine etc.) to go at a fixed speed. **3** *tr.* send fast or on its way (*speed an arrow from the bow*). **4** *intr.* & *tr.* *archaic* be or make prosperous or successful (*how have you sped?; God speed you!*). ▫ **at speed** moving quickly. **speed bump** (or **hump**) a transverse ridge in the road to control the speed of vehicles. **speed limit** the maximum speed at which a road vehicle may legally be driven in a particular area etc. **speed merchant** *colloq.* a motorist who enjoys driving fast. **speed up** move or work at greater speed. **speed-up** *n.* an increase in the speed or rate of working. ▫▫ **speeder** *n.* [OE *spēd*, *spēdan* f. Gmc]

▪ *n.* **1** rapidity, quickness, speediness, swiftness, velocity, dispatch, hurry, hurriedness, haste, hastiness, alacrity, expeditiousness, expedition, briskness, promptness, timeliness, *archaic or literary* celerity, *poet. or literary* fleetness; suddenness, precipitousness, abruptness. **2** see PACE *n.* 2. ● *v.* **1** hasten, make haste, hurry, rush, charge, dart, bolt, shoot, run, race, sprint, fly, streak, scurry, tear, hustle, scramble, scamper, career, bowl along, rattle along, zip, zoom, go *or* fly like the wind, *colloq.* go hell for leather, go like a bat out of hell, step on it, step on the gas, put one's foot down, skedaddle, go like a shot, go like greased lightning, make tracks, *Austral. colloq.* give it the herbs, *US colloq.* hightail it, *sl.* belt along, *Brit. sl.* go like the clappers. ▫ **speed bump** (or **hump**) sleeping policeman, *Brit.* ramp. **speed up** accelerate, hurry up, quicken, pick up speed, *colloq.* get a move on.

speedball /spéedbawl/ *n. sl.* a mixture of cocaine with heroin or morphine.

speedboat /spéedbōt/ *n.* a motor boat designed for high speed.

▪ motor boat, powerboat.

speedo /spéedō/ *n.* (*pl.* **-os**) *colloq.* = SPEEDOMETER. [abbr.]

speedometer /speedómmitər/ *n.* an instrument on a motor vehicle etc. indicating its speed to the driver. [SPEED + METER[1]]

speedway /spéedway/ *n.* **1 a** motor-cycle racing. **b** a stadium or track used for this. **2** *US* a road or track used for fast motor traffic.

speedwell /spéedwel/ *n.* any small herb of the genus *Veronica*, with a creeping or ascending stem and tiny blue or pink flowers. [app. f. SPEED + WELL[1]]

speedy /spéedi/ *adj.* (**speedier**, **speediest**) **1** moving quickly; rapid. **2** done without delay; prompt (*a speedy answer*). ▫▫ **speedily** *adv.* **speediness** *n.*

▪ **1** nimble, wing-footed, winged, fast, quick, rapid, swift, brisk, *poet. or literary* fleet. **2** prompt, immediate, expeditious, quick, swift, rapid, hasty, precipitate, precipitous, hurried, summary, *colloq.* snappy. ▫▫ **speedily** see *promptly* (PROMPT), *quickly* (QUICK). **speediness** see SPEED *n.* 1.

speiss /spīss/ *n.* a compound of arsenic, iron, etc., formed in smelting certain lead ores. [G *Speise* food, amalgam]

speleology /spéeliólləji, spél-/ *n.* **1** the scientific study of caves. **2** the exploration of caves. ▫▫ **speleological** /-liəlójik'l/ *adj.* **speleologist** *n.* [F *spéléologie* f. L *spelaeum* f. Gk *spēlaion* cave]

▪ **2** see CAVING.

spell[1] /spel/ *v.tr.* (*past* and *past part.* **spelt** or **spelled**) **1** (also *absol.*) write or name the letters that form (a word etc.) in correct sequence (*spell 'exaggerate'; cannot spell properly*). **2 a** (of letters) make up or form (a word etc.). **b** (of circumstances, a scheme, etc.) result in; involve (*spell ruin*). ▫ **spell out 1** make out (words, writing, etc.) letter by letter. **2** explain in detail (*spelled out what the change would mean*). ▫▫ **spellable** *adj.* [ME f. OF *espel(l)er*, f. Frank. (as SPELL[2])]

▪ **2 b** augur, portend, presage, promise, hold promise of, signify, point to, indicate, omen, bode, look like, amount to, mean, involve, result in. ▫ **spell out 2** specify, delineate, make clear *or* plain *or* explicit, clarify, elucidate, explain.

spell[2] /spel/ *n.* **1** a form of words used as a magical charm or incantation. **2** an attraction or fascination exercised by a person, activity, quality, etc. ▫ **under a spell** mastered by or as if by a spell. [OE *spel(l)* f. Gmc]

▪ **1** incantation, formula, charm, conjuration. **2** attraction, lure, allure, appeal, draw, pull, magnetism, influence, mesmerism, hypnotic effect, enchantment, fascination, captivation, enthralment, charm, magic, witchcraft, witchery.

spell[3] /spel/ *n.* & *v.* ● *n.* **1** a short or fairly short period (*a cold spell in April*). **2** a turn of work (*did a spell of woodwork*). **3** *Austral.* a period of rest from work. ● *v.* **1** *tr.* **a** relieve or take the place of (a person) in work etc. **b** allow to rest briefly. **2** *intr.* *Austral.* take a brief rest. [earlier as verb: later form of dial. *spele* take place of f. OE *spelian*, of unkn. orig.]

▪ *n.* **1** period, interval, time, term, season; snap. **2** stint, turn, run, course, shift, tour (of duty), watch, round, stretch. **3** see BREAK[1] *n.* 2. ● *v.* **1** relieve, replace, substitute for, take over for *or* from.

spell[4] /spel/ *n.* a splinter of wood etc. [perh. f. obs. *speld*]

spellbind /spélbīnd/ *v.tr.* (*past* and *past part.* **spellbound**) **1** bind with or as if with a spell; entrance. **2** (as **spellbound** *adj.*) entranced, fascinated, esp. by a speaker, activity, quality, etc. ▫▫ **spellbinder** *n.* **spellbindingly** *adv.*

▪ **1** bewitch, cast a spell on *or* over, charm, entrance, mesmerize, hypnotize; captivate, fascinate, enthral, enchant, enrapture, overpower. **2** (**spellbound**) see RAPT 1. ▫▫ **spellbinder** see *talker* (TALK).

speller /spéllər/ *n.* **1** a person who spells esp. in a specified way (*is a poor speller*). **2** a book on spelling.

spellican var. of SPILLIKIN.

spelling /spélling/ *n.* **1** the process or activity of writing or naming the letters of a word etc. **2** the way a word is spelled. **3** the ability to spell (*his spelling is weak*). ▫ **spelling-bee** a spelling competition.

spelt[1] *past* and *past part.* of SPELL[1].

spelt[2] /spelt/ *n.* a species of wheat, *Triticum aestivum*. [OE f. OS *spelta* (OHG *spelza*), ME f. MLG, MDu. *spelte*]

spelter /spéltər/ *n.* impure zinc, esp. for commercial purposes. [corresp. to OF *espeautre*, MDu. *speauter*, G *Spialter*, rel. to PEWTER]

spelunker /spilúngkər/ *n.* *US* a person who explores caves, esp. as a hobby. ▫▫ **spelunking** *n.* [obs. *spelunk* cave f. L *spelunca*]

spence /spenss/ *n.* *archaic* a buttery or larder. [ME f. OF *despense* f. L *dispensa* fem. past part. of *dispendere*: see DISPENSE]

spencer[1] /spénsər/ *n.* **1** a short close-fitting jacket. **2** a woman's thin usu. woollen under-bodice worn for extra warmth in winter. [prob. f. the 2nd Earl *Spencer*, Engl. politician d. 1834]

spencer[2] /spénsər/ *n. Naut.* a trysail. [perh. f. K. *Spencer* (early 19th c.)]

spend /spend/ *v.tr.* (*past* and *past part.* **spent** /spent/) **1** (usu. foll. by *on*) **a** (also *absol.*) pay out (money) in making a purchase etc. (*spent £5 on a new pen*). **b** pay out (money) for a particular person's benefit or for the improvement of a thing (*had to spend £200 on the car*). **2 a** use or consume (time or energy) (*shall spend no more effort; how do you spend your Sundays?*). **b** (also *refl.*) use up; exhaust; wear out (*their ammunition was all spent; his anger was soon spent; spent herself campaigning for justice*). **3** *tr.* (as **spent** *adj.*) having lost its original force or strength; exhausted (*the storm is spent; spent bullets*). □ **spending money** pocket money. **spend a penny** *Brit. colloq.* urinate or defecate (from the coin-operated locks of public lavatories). □□ **spendable** *adj.* **spender** *n.* [OE *spendan* f. L *expendere* (see EXPEND): in ME perh. also f. obs. *dispend* f. OF *despendre* expend f. L *dispendere*: see DISPENSE]

■ **1** pay out, disburse, expend, lay out, squander, throw away, fritter away, waste, lavish, dissipate, *colloq.* go through, shell out, splash out, splurge, *sl.* fork out, dish out, cough up, blow, blue, *Austral.* & *NZ sl.* knock down. **2 a** use, consume, devote, allot, assign, invest, put in, pass, occupy, fill, while away, fritter away. **b** use up, consume, expend, drain, deplete; exhaust, tire, fatigue, weary, prostrate, fag out, wear out, *esp. US* burn out, *colloq.* do in, *Brit. sl.* knacker. **3** (**spent**) exhausted, used (up), emptied, gone, expended, finished, played out, consumed, depleted; drained, prostrate, tired (out), fatigued, weary, wearied, worn out, dog-tired, *esp. US* burnt-out, *colloq.* done in *or* up *or* for, all in, fagged (out), *US colloq.* pooped, *sl.* (dead) beat, *Austral.* & *NZ sl.* stonkered, *Brit. sl.* knackered. □□ **spender** see SPENDTHRIFT *n.*

spendthrift /spéndthrift/ *n.* & *adj.* ● *n.* an extravagant person; a prodigal. ● *adj.* extravagant; prodigal.

■ *n.* profligate, wastrel, waster, (big) spender, squanderer, prodigal. ● *adj.* wasteful, free-spending, prodigal, profligate, squandering, extravagant, improvident.

Spenserian /spenséeriən/ *adj.* of, relating to, or in the style of Edmund Spenser, Engl. poet d. 1599. □ **Spenserian stanza** the stanza used by Spenser in the *Faerie Queene*, with eight iambic pentameters and an alexandrine, rhyming ababbcbcc. [E. *Spenser*]

spent *past* and *past part.* of SPEND.

sperm /sperm/ *n.* (*pl.* same or **sperms**) **1** = SPERMATOZOON. **2** the male reproductive fluid containing spermatozoa; semen. **3** = *sperm whale*. **4** = SPERMACETI. **5** = *sperm oil*. □ **sperm bank** a supply of semen stored for use in artificial insemination. **sperm count** the number of spermatozoa in one ejaculation or a measured amount of semen. **sperm oil** an oil obtained from the head of a sperm whale, and used as a lubricant. **sperm whale** a large whale, *Physeter macrocephalus*, hunted for the spermaceti and sperm oil contained in its bulbous head, and for the ambergris found in its intestines: also called CACHALOT. [ME f. LL *sperma* f. Gk *sperma -atos* seed f. *speirō* sow: in *sperm whale* an abbr. of SPERMACETI]

spermaceti /spérməsétti/ *n.* a white waxy substance produced by the sperm whale to aid buoyancy, and used in the manufacture of candles, ointments, etc. □□ **spermacetic** *adj.* [ME f. med.L f. LL *sperma* sperm + *ceti* genit. of *cetus* f. Gk *kētos* whale, from the belief that it was whale-spawn]

spermary /spérməri/ *n.* (*pl.* **-ies**) an organ in which human or animal sperms are generated. [mod.L *spermarium* (as SPERM)]

spermatic /spermáttik/ *adj.* of or relating to a sperm or spermary. □ **spermatic cord** a bundle of nerves, ducts, and blood vessels passing to the testicles. [LL *spermaticus* f. Gk *spermatikos* (as SPERM)]

spermatid /spérmətid/ *n. Biol.* an immature male sex cell formed from a spermatocyte, which may develop into a spermatozoon. □□ **spermatidal** /-tīd'l/ *adj.*

spermato- /spérmətō/ *comb. form Biol.* a sperm or seed.

spermatocyte /spérmətōsīt/ *n.* a cell produced from a spermatogonium and which may divide by meiosis into spermatids.

spermatogenesis /spérmətōjénnisiss/ *n.* the production or development of mature spermatozoa. □□ **spermatogenetic** /-jinéttik/ *adj.*

spermatogonium /spérmətōgṓniəm/ *n.* (*pl.* **spermatogonia** /-niə/) a cell produced at an early stage in the formation of spermatozoa, from which spermatocytes develop. [SPERM + mod.L *gonium* f. Gk *gonos* offspring, seed]

spermatophore /spérmətōfor/ *n.* an albuminous capsule containing spermatozoa found in various invertebrates. □□ **spermatophoric** /-fórik/ *adj.*

spermatophyte /spérmətōfīt/ *n.* any seed-bearing plant.

spermatozoid /spérmətōzṓ-id/ *n.* the mature motile male sex cell of some plants.

spermatozoon /spérmətōzṓ-on/ *n.* (*pl.* **spermatozoa** /-zṓə/) the mature motile sex cell in animals. □□ **spermatozoal** *adj.* **spermatozoan** *adj.* **spermatozoic** *adj.* [SPERM + Gk *zōion* animal]

spermicide /spérmisīd/ *n.* a substance able to kill spermatozoa. □□ **spermicidal** /-sī́d'l/ *adj.*

spermo- /spérmō/ *comb. form* = SPERMATO-.

spew /spyōō/ *v.* (also **spue**) **1** *tr.* & *intr.* vomit. **2** (often foll. by *out*) **a** *tr.* expel (contents) rapidly and forcibly. **b** *intr.* (of contents) be expelled in this way. □□ **spewer** *n.* [OE *spīwan*, *spēowan* f. Gmc]

■ **1** see VOMIT *v.* 1. **2** spew forth *or* out *or* up, belch (up *or* out *or* forth), spout, discharge, gush, pour forth, spurt; vomit (up *or* forth), throw up *or* out, spit up *or* out, expectorate, expel, emit, eject, disgorge, send forth.

sp. gr. *abbr.* specific gravity.

sphagnum /sfágnəm/ *n.* (*pl.* **sphagna** /-nə/) (in full **sphagnum moss**) any moss of the genus *Sphagnum*, growing in bogs and peat, and used as packing esp. for plants, as fertilizer, etc. [mod.L f. Gk *sphagnos* a moss]

sphalerite /sfállərīt/ *n.* = BLENDE. [Gk *sphaleros* deceptive: cf. BLENDE]

spheno- /sféenō/ *comb. form Anat.* the sphenoid bone. [Gk f. *sphēn* wedge]

sphenoid /sféenoyd/ *adj.* & *n.* ● *adj.* **1** wedge-shaped. **2** of or relating to the sphenoid bone. ● *n.* (in full **sphenoid bone**) a large compound bone forming the base of the cranium behind the eyes. □□ **sphenoidal** /-nóyd'l/ *adj.* [mod.L *sphenoides* f. Gk *sphēnoeidēs* f. *sphēn* wedge]

sphere /sfeer/ *n.* & *v.* ● *n.* **1** a solid figure, or its surface, with every point on its surface equidistant from its centre. **2** an object having this shape; a ball or globe. **3 a** any celestial body. **b** a globe representing the earth. **c** *poet.* the heavens; the sky. **d** the sky perceived as a vault upon or in which celestial bodies are represented as lying. **e** *hist.* each of a series of revolving concentrically arranged spherical shells in which celestial bodies were formerly thought to be set in a fixed relationship. **4 a** a field of action, influence, or existence (*have done much within their own sphere*). **b** a (usu. specified) stratum of society or social class (*moves in quite another sphere*). ● *v.tr. archaic* or *poet.* **1** enclose in or as in a sphere. **2** form into a sphere. □ **music** (or **harmony**) **of the spheres** the natural harmonic tones supposedly produced by the movement of the celestial spheres (see sense 3e of *n.*) or the bodies fixed in them. **oblique** (or **parallel** or **right**) **sphere** the sphere of the apparent heavens at a place where there is an oblique, zero, or right angle between the equator and the horizon. **sphere of influence** the claimed or recognized area of a State's interests, an individual's control, etc. □□ **spheral** *adj.* [ME *sper(e)* f. OF *espere* f. LL *sphera*, L f. Gk *sphaira* ball]

■ *n.* **1, 2** globe, orb, ball, globule, spherule; bubble; spheroid. **4 a** area, field, province, territory, subject, discipline, range, speciality, forte, *colloq.* department, thing, *joc.* bailiwick, *sl.* bag. **b** society, class, level, caste, rank, domain, milieu, world, circle, walk of life, station, stratum, position.

-sphere /sfeer/ *comb. form* **1** having the form of a sphere (*bathysphere*). **2** a region round the earth (*atmosphere*).

spheric /sféerik/ *adj.* = SPHERICAL. ▫▫ **sphericity** /-rissiti/ *n.*

spherical /sférrik'l/ *adj.* **1** shaped like a sphere; globular. **2 a** of or relating to the properties of spheres (*spherical geometry*). **b** formed inside or on the surface of a sphere (*spherical triangle*). ▫ **spherical aberration** a loss of definition in the image produced by a spherically curved mirror or lens. **spherical angle** an angle formed by the intersection of two great circles of a sphere. ▫▫ **spherically** *adv.* [LL *sphaericus* f. Gk *sphairikos* (as SPHERE)]

▪ **1** spheric, spheral, globular, round, ball-shaped, ball-like, globelike, globe-shaped, globose, globulous, globoid, spherelike, spheroidal.

spheroid /sféeroyd/ *n.* **1** a spherelike but not perfectly spherical body. **2** a solid generated by a half-revolution of an ellipse about its major axis (**prolate spheroid**) or minor axis (**oblate spheroid**). ▫▫ **spheroidal** /sfeeróyd'l/ *adj.* **spheroidicity** /-dissiti/ *n.*

▪ ▫▫ **spheroidal** see SPHERICAL.

spherometer /sfeerómmitər/ *n.* an instrument for finding the radius of a sphere and for the exact measurement of the thickness of small bodies. [F *sphéromètre* (as SPHERE, -METER)]

spherule /sférrool/ *n.* a small sphere. ▫▫ **spherular** *adj.* [LL *sphaerula* dimin. of L *sphaera* (as SPHERE)]

▪ see SPHERE *n.* 1, 2.

spherulite /sférrəlīt/ *n.* a vitreous globule as a constituent of volcanic rocks. ▫▫ **spherulitic** /-líttik/ *adj.*

sphincter /sfíngktər/ *n. Anat.* a ring of muscle surrounding and serving to guard or close an opening or tube, esp. the anus. ▫▫ **sphincteral** *adj.* **sphinctered** *adj.* **sphincterial** /-teeriəl/ *adj.* **sphincteric** /-térrik/ *adj.* [L f. Gk *sphigktēr* f. *sphiggō* bind tight]

sphingid /sfínggid/ *n.* any hawk moth of the family Sphingidae. [as SPHINX + -ID[3]]

sphinx /sfingks/ *n.* **1** (**Sphinx**) (in Greek mythology) the winged monster of Thebes, having a woman's head and a lion's body, whose riddle Oedipus guessed and who consequently killed herself. **2** *Antiq.* **a** any of several ancient Egyptian stone figures having a lion's body and a human or animal head. **b** (**the Sphinx**) the huge sphinx near the Pyramids at Giza. **3** an enigmatic or inscrutable person. **4 a** a hawk moth. **b** a species of baboon, *Papio sphinx*. [L f. Gk *Sphigx*, app. f. *sphiggō* draw tight]

sphragistics /sfrəjístiks/ *n.pl.* (also treated as *sing.*) the study of engraved seals. [F *sphragistique* (n. & adj.) f. Gk *sphragistikos* f. *sphragis* seal]

sphygmo- /sfígmō/ *comb. form Physiol.* a pulse or pulsation. [Gk *sphugmo-* f. *sphugmos* pulse f. *sphuzō* to throb]

sphygmogram /sfígmōgram/ *n.* a record produced by a sphygmograph.

sphygmograph /sfígmōgraaf/ *n.* an instrument for showing the character of a pulse in a series of curves. ▫▫ **sphygmographic** /-gráffik/ *adj.* **sphygmographically** /-gráffikəli/ *adv.* **sphygmography** /-mógrəfi/ *n.*

sphygmology /sfigmólləji/ *n.* the scientific study of the pulse. ▫▫ **sphygmological** /-məlójik'l/ *adj.*

sphygmomanometer /sfígmōmənómmitər/ *n.* an instrument for measuring blood pressure. ▫▫ **sphygmomanometric** /-nəmétrik/ *adj.*

spica /spíkə/ *n.* **1** *Bot.* a spike or spikelike form. **2** *Surgery* a spiral bandage with reversed turns, suggesting an ear of corn. ▫▫ **spicate** /-kayt/ *adj.* **spicated** /-káytid/ *adj.* [L, = spike, ear of corn, rel. to *spina* SPINE: in sense 2 after Gk *stakhus*]

spiccato /spikaátō/ *n., adj., & adv. Mus.* ● *n.* (*pl.* **-os**) **1** a style of staccato playing on stringed instruments involving bouncing the bow on the strings. **2** a passage in this style. ● *adj.* performed or to be performed in this style. ● *adv.* in this style. [It., = detailed, distinct]

spice /spīss/ *n. & v.* ● *n.* **1** an aromatic or pungent vegetable substance used to flavour food, e.g. cloves, pepper, or mace. **2** spices collectively (*a dealer in spice*). **3 a** an interesting or piquant quality. **b** (foll. by *of*) a slight flavour or suggestion (*a spice of malice*). ● *v.tr.* **1** flavour with spice. **2** add an interesting or piquant quality to (*a book spiced with humour*). [ME f. OF *espice(r)* f. L *species* specific kind: in LL pl. = merchandise]

▪ *n.* **1** condiment, relish, seasoning, flavour(ing); herb. **3 a** zest, spiciness, piquancy, tang, pungency, bite, sharpness, poignancy, salt, seasoning, ginger, gusto, excitement, dash, *élan*, colour, life, vigour, zip, interest, stimulation, stimulant, spirit, *colloq.* vim, pep, kick, punch, *sl.* pizazz. **b** see TOUCH *n.* 3. ● *v.* **1** season, flavour. **2** spice up, enliven, inspirit, stimulate, invigorate.

spicebush /spísbōōsh/ *n.* any aromatic shrub of the genus *Lindera* or *Calycanthus*, native to America.

spick and span /spík ənd spán/ *adj.* **1** smart and new. **2** neat and clean. [16th-c. *spick and span new*, emphatic extension of ME *span new* f. ON *spán-nýr* f. *spánn* chip + *nýr* new]

▪ **1** see SMART *adj.* 3. **2** see NEAT[1] 1.

spicknel /spíkn'l/ *n.* = BALDMONEY. [var. of SPIGNEL]

spicule /spíkyool/ *n.* **1** any small sharp-pointed body. **2** *Zool.* a small hard calcareous or siliceous body, esp. in the framework of a sponge. **3** *Bot.* a small or secondary spike. **4** *Astron.* a spikelike prominence, esp. one appearing as a jet of gas in the sun's corona. ▫▫ **spicular** *adj.* **spiculate** /-lət/ *adj.* [mod.L *spicula*, *spiculum*, dimins. of SPICA]

▪ **1–3** see SPINE 2. ▫▫ **spiculate** see PRICKLY 1.

spicy /spísi/ *adj.* (**spicier**, **spiciest**) **1** of, flavoured with, or fragrant with spice. **2** piquant, pungent; sensational or improper (*a spicy story*). ▫▫ **spicily** *adv.* **spiciness** *n.*

▪ **1** zesty, zestful, piquant, tangy, (well-)spiced, (well-)seasoned, hot, peppery, sharp, pungent, biting, full-bodied, aromatic, savoury, flavoursome, flavourful. **2** piquant, pungent; indelicate, suggestive, risqué, improper, indecent, indecorous, ribald, racy, bawdy, unseemly, offensive, titillating, sexy, *US* off colour; scandalous, sensational, outrageous, notorious, revealing, revelatory, intimate, *colloq.* juicy. ▫▫ **spiciness** see SPICE *n.* 3a.

spider /spídər/ *n. & v.* ● *n.* **1 a** any eight-legged arthropod of the order Araneae with a round unsegmented body, many of which spin webs for the capture of insects as food. **b** any of various similar or related arachnids, e.g. a red spider. **2** any object comparable to a spider, esp. as having numerous or prominent legs or radiating spokes. **3** *Brit.* a radiating series of elastic ties used to hold a load in place on a vehicle etc. ● *v.intr.* **1** move in a scuttling manner suggestive of a spider (*fingers spidered across the map*). **2** cause to move or appear in this way. **3** (as **spidering** *adj.*) spiderlike in form, manner, or movement (*spidering streets*). ▫ **spider crab** any of various crabs of the family Majidae with a pear-shaped body and long thin legs. **spider monkey** any S. American monkey of the genus *Ateles*, with long limbs and a prehensile tail. **spider plant** any of various house plants with long narrow striped leaves. ▫▫ **spiderish** *adj.* [OE *spīthra* (as SPIN)]

spiderman /spídərman/ *n.* (*pl.* **-men**) *Brit. colloq.* a person who works at great heights in building construction.

spiderwort /spídərwurt/ *n.* any plant of the genus *Tradescantia*, esp. *T. virginiana*, having flowers with long hairy stamens.

spidery /spídəri/ *adj.* elongated and thin (*spidery handwriting*).

spiegeleisen /speeg'līz'n/ *n.* an alloy of iron and manganese, used in steel-making. [G f. *Spiegel* mirror + *Eisen* iron]

spiel /shpeel/ *n.* & *v. sl.* ● *n.* a glib speech or story, esp. a salesman's patter. ● *v.* **1** *intr.* speak glibly; hold forth. **2** *tr.* reel off (patter etc.). [G, = play, game]
■ *n.* see SPEECH 2. ● *v.* **1** see LECTURE *v.* 1.

spieler /shpeélər/ *n. sl.* **1** esp. *US* a person who spiels. **2** *Austral.* a gambler; a swindler. [G (as SPIEL)]
■ **1** see SPEAKER. **2** see CHEAT *n.* 1.

spiffing /spíffing/ *adj. Brit. archaic sl.* **1** excellent. **2** smart, handsome. [19th c.: orig. unkn.]

spiffy /spíffi/ *adj.* (**spiffier, spiffiest**) esp. *US sl.* = SPIFFING. □□ **spiffily** *adv.*

spiflicate /spíflikayt/ *v.tr.* (also **spifflicate**) esp. *joc.* **1** destroy. **2** beat (in a fight etc.). [18th c.: fanciful]

spignel /spígn'l/ *n.* = BALDMONEY. [perh. f. ME *spigurnel* plant-name, f. med.L *spigurnellus*, of unkn. orig.]

spigot /spíggət/ *n.* **1** a small peg or plug, esp. for insertion into the vent-hole of a cask. **2 a** *US* a tap. **b** a device for controlling the flow of liquid in a tap. **3** the plain end of a pipe-section fitting into the socket of the next one. [ME, perh. f. Prov. *espigou(n)* f. L *spiculum* dimin. of *spicum* = SPICA]
■ **1** see STOPPER *n.* **2** see TAP[1] *n.* 1.

spike[1] /spīk/ *n.* & *v.* ● *n.* **1 a** a sharp point. **b** a pointed piece of metal, esp. the top of an iron railing etc. **2 a** any of several metal points set into the sole of a running-shoe to prevent slipping. **b** (in *pl.*) a pair of running-shoes with spikes. **3 a** a pointed metal rod standing on a base and used for filing news items etc. esp. when rejected for publication. **b** a similar spike used for bills etc. **4** a large stout nail esp. as used for railways. **5** *sl.* a hypodermic needle. **6** *Brit. sl.* a doss-house. **7** *Electronics* a pulse of very short duration in which a rapid increase in voltage is followed by a rapid decrease. ● *v.tr.* **1 a** fasten or provide with spikes. **b** fix on or pierce with spikes. **2** (of a newspaper editor etc.) reject (a story) by filing it on a spike. **3** *colloq.* **a** lace (a drink) with alcohol, a drug, etc. **b** contaminate (a substance) with something added. **4** make useless, put an end to, thwart (an idea etc.). **5** *hist.* plug up the vent of (a gun) with a spike. □ **spike a person's guns** spoil his or her plans. **spike heel** a high tapering heel of a shoe. [ME perh. f. MLG, MDu. *spiker*, rel. to SPOKE[1]]
■ *n.* **1 a** see POINT *n.* 1. **b** skewer, spit, stake, prong, tine, treenail, nail, peg, picket, pin, spine, barb, *hist.* pike. ● *v.* **1** impale, transfix, stab, stick, skewer, spear, pierce, spit, lance, pin, rivet. **3 a** lace, strengthen, *sl.* slip a Mickey Finn into; drug, poison, *colloq.* doctor. **4** disable, thwart, stymie, nullify, disarm, block, frustrate, foil, void, baulk, check, cancel, annul, put an end to.

spike[2] /spīk/ *n. Bot.* **1** a flower-cluster formed of many flower-heads attached closely on a long stem. **2** a separate sprig of any plant in which flowers form a spikelike cluster. □□ **spikelet** *n.* [ME, = ear of corn, f. L SPICA]

spikenard /spíknaard/ *n.* **1** *Bot.* an Indian plant, *Nardostachys grandiflora*. **2** *hist.* a costly perfumed ointment made from this. [ME ult. f. med.L *spica nardi* (as SPIKE[2], NARD) after Gk *nardostakhus*]

spiky[1] /spíki/ *adj.* (**spikier, spikiest**) **1** like a spike; having many spikes. **2** *colloq.* easily offended; prickly. □□ **spikily** *adv.* **spikiness** *n.*
■ **1** see PRICKLY 1. **2** see PRICKLY 2a.

spiky[2] /spíki/ *adj. Bot.* having spikes or ears.

spile /spīl/ *n.* & *v.* ● *n.* **1** a wooden peg or spigot. **2** a large timber or pile for driving into the ground. **3** *US* a small spout for tapping the sap from a sugar-maple etc. ● *v.tr.* broach (a cask etc.) with a spile in order to draw off liquid. [MDu., MLG, = wooden peg etc.: in sense 'pile' app. alt. of PILE[2]]
■ *n.* **1** see STOPPER *n.* 1.

spill[1] /spil/ *v.* & *n.* ● *v.* (*past* and *past part.* **spilt** or **spilled**) **1** *intr.* & *tr.* fall or run or cause (a liquid, powder, etc.) to fall or run out of a vessel, esp. unintentionally. **2 a** *tr.* & *intr.* throw (a person etc.) from a vehicle, saddle, etc. **b** *intr.* (esp. of a crowd) tumble out quickly from a place etc. (*the fans spilled into the street*). **3** *tr. sl.* disclose (information etc.). **4** *tr. Naut.* **a** empty (a sail) of wind. **b** lose (wind) from a sail. ● *n.* **1 a** the act or an instance of spilling or being spilt. **b** a quantity spilt. **2** a tumble or fall, esp. from a horse etc. (*had a nasty spill*). **3** *Austral.* the vacating of all or several posts of a parliamentary party to allow reorganization. □ **spill the beans** *colloq.* divulge information etc., esp. unintentionally or indiscreetly. **spill blood** be guilty of bloodshed. **spill the blood of** kill or injure (a person). **spill over 1** overflow. **2** (of a surplus population) be forced to move (cf. OVERSPILL). □□ **spillage** /spíllij/ *n.* **spiller** *n.* [OE *spillan* kill, rel. to OE *spildan* destroy: orig. unkn.]
■ *v.* **1** pour (out *or* over), overflow, slop *or* run *or* brim over; leak, escape; see also UPSET *v.* 1a. **2 a** dislodge, throw, unseat, unhorse; shed, discharge, tip. **b** see STREAM *v.* 1. **3** see DISCLOSE 1. ● *n.* **1** spillage, spilth, outpouring, flood, leak, leakage. **2** fall, tumble, accident, *colloq.* header, *sl.* cropper. **3** reshuffle, shuffle, rearrangement. □ **spill the beans** reveal all *or* everything, tell all *or* everything, disclose all *or* everything, divulge all *or* everything, blab, tattle, let the cat out of the bag, give the show away, confess, be a stool-pigeon, *sl.* squeal, sing (like a canary), *Brit. sl.* blow the gaff, *US sl.* be a stoolie. □□ **spillage** see SPILL *n.*[1] 1 above.

spill[2] /spil/ *n.* a thin strip of wood, folded or twisted paper, etc., used for lighting a fire, candles, a pipe, etc. [ME, rel. to SPILE]

spillikin /spíllikin/ *n.* (also **spellican** /spéllikən/) **1** a splinter of wood, bone, etc. **2** (in *pl.*) a game in which a heap of spillikins is to be removed one at a time without moving the others. [SPILL[2] + -KIN]

spillover /spíllōvər/ *n.* **1 a** the process or an instance of spilling over. **b** a thing that spills over. **2** a consequence, repercussion, or by-product.

spillway /spílway/ *n.* a passage for surplus water from a dam.

spilt *past* and *past part.* of SPILL[1].

spilth /spilth/ *n.* **1** material that is spilled. **2** the act or an instance of spilling. **3** an excess or surplus.

spin /spin/ *v.* & *n.* ● *v.* (**spinning**; *past* and *past part.* **spun** /spun/) **1** *intr.* & *tr.* turn or cause (a person or thing) to turn or whirl round quickly. **2** *tr.* (also *absol.*) **a** draw out and twist (wool, cotton, etc.) into threads. **b** make (yarn) in this way. **c** make a similar type of thread from (a synthetic substance etc.). **3** *tr.* (of a spider, silkworm, etc.) make (a web, gossamer, a cocoon, etc.) by extruding a fine viscous thread. **4** *tr.* tell or write (a story, essay, article, etc.) (*spins a good tale*). **5** *tr.* impart spin to (a ball). **6** *intr.* (of a person's head etc.) be dizzy through excitement, astonishment, etc. **7** *tr.* shape (metal) on a mould in a lathe etc. **8** *intr.* esp. *Cricket* (of a ball) move through the air with spin. **9** *tr.* (as **spun** *adj.*) converted into threads (*spun glass*; *spun gold*; *spun sugar*). **10** *tr.* fish in (a stream, pool, etc.) with a spinner. **11** *tr.* toss (a coin). **12** *tr.* = *spin-dry*. ● *n.* **1** a spinning motion; a whirl. **2** an aircraft's diving descent combined with rotation. **3 a** a revolving motion through the air, esp. in a rifle bullet or in a billiard, tennis, or table tennis ball struck aslant. **b** *Cricket* a twisting motion given to the ball in bowling. **4** *colloq.* a brief drive in a motor vehicle, aeroplane, etc., esp. for pleasure. **5** *Physics* the intrinsic angular momentum of an elementary particle. **6** *Austral.* & *NZ sl.* a piece of good or bad luck. □ **spin bowler** *Cricket* an expert at bowling with spin. **spin doctor** *US* a political pundit who is employed to promote a favourable interpretation of political developments to the media. **spin-drier** a machine for drying wet clothes etc. centrifugally in a revolving drum. **spin-dry** (**-dries, -dried**) dry (clothes etc.) in this way. **spin off** throw off by centrifugal force in spinning. **spin-off** *n.* an incidental result or results esp. as a side benefit from industrial technology. **spin out 1** prolong (a discussion etc.). **2** make (a story, money, etc.) last as long as possible. **3** spend or consume (time, one's life, etc., by discussion or in an occupation etc.). **4** *Cricket* dismiss (a batsman or side) by spin bowling. **spin a yarn** *orig. Naut.* tell a story. **spun silk** a cheap material made of short-fibred and waste silk. **spun yarn** *Naut.* a line formed of rope-yarns twisted together. [OE *spinnan*]

▪ *v.* **1** revolve, turn, rotate, wheel, gyrate, twirl, swirl, twist, reel, pirouette, pivot, swivel. **4** invent, concoct, make up, devise, produce, fabricate; weave, relate, retail, recount, narrate, tell, write, unfold. **6** be dizzy, suffer vertigo, swim, whirl, reel, be giddy. ● *n.* **1, 3** whirl, twirl, turn, gyration, reel, pirouette, revolution, rotation. **4** drive, whirl, ride, tour, excursion, outing, jaunt, *colloq.* joyride. □ **spin off** throw off, separate. **spin-off** see OFFSHOOT 2. **spin out 1, 2** prolong, protract, drag *or* draw out, stretch *or* string out, perpetuate, continue, extend, keep alive, keep going; pad out, lengthen.

spina bifida /spī́nə bíffidə/ *n.* a congenital defect of the spine, in which part of the spinal cord and its meninges are exposed through a gap in the backbone. [mod.L (as SPINE, BIFID)]

spinach /spínnij, -ich/ *n.* **1** a green garden vegetable, *Spinacia oleracea*, with succulent leaves. **2** the leaves of this plant used as food. □ **spinach beet** a variety of beetroot cultivated for its edible leaves. □□ **spinaceous** /-náyshəss/ *adj.* **spinachy** *adj.* [prob. MDu. *spinaetse*, *spinag(i)e*, f. OF *espinage*, *espinache* f. med.L *spinac(h)ia* etc. f. Arab. *'isfānāk* f. Pers. *ispānāk*: perh. assim. to L *spina* SPINE, with ref. to its prickly seeds]

spinal /spī́n'l/ *adj.* of or relating to the spine (*spinal curvature*; *spinal disease*). □ **spinal canal** a cavity through the vertebrae containing the spinal cord. **spinal column** the spine. **spinal cord** a cylindrical structure of the central nervous system enclosed in the spine, connecting all parts of the body with the brain. □□ **spinally** *adv.* [LL *spinalis* (as SPINE)]

▪ □ **spinal column** backbone, spine, vertebrae.

spindle /spínd'l/ *n.* & *v.* ● *n.* **1 a** a pin in a spinning-wheel used for twisting and winding the thread. **b** a small bar with tapered ends used for the same purpose in hand-spinning. **c** a pin bearing the bobbin of a spinning-machine. **2** a pin or axis that revolves or on which something revolves. **3** a turned piece of wood used as a banister, chair leg, etc. **4** *Biol.* a spindle-shaped mass of microtubules formed when a cell divides. **5** a varying measure of length for yarn. **6** a slender person or thing. ● *v.intr.* have, or grow into, a long slender form. □ **spindle berry** the fruit of the spindle tree. **spindle-shanked** having long thin legs. **spindle-shanks** a person with such legs. **spindle-shaped** having a circular cross-section and tapering towards each end. **spindle side** = *distaff side*. **spindle tree** any shrub or small tree of the genus *Euonymus*, esp. *E. europaeus* with greenish-white flowers, pink or red berries, and hard wood used for spindles. [OE *spinel* (as SPIN)]

▪ *n.* **2** see PIVOT *n.* 1. **3** leg, cabriole.

spindly /spíndli/ *adj.* (**spindlier**, **spindliest**) long or tall and thin; thin and weak.

▪ see THIN *adj.* 4.

spindrift /spíndrift/ *n.* spray blown along the surface of the sea. [Sc. var. of *spoondrift* f. *spoon* run before wind or sea + DRIFT]

▪ see SPRAY[1] *n.* 1.

spine /spīn/ *n.* **1** a series of vertebrae extending from the skull to the small of the back, enclosing the spinal cord and providing support for the thorax and abdomen; the backbone. **2** *Zool.* & *Bot.* any hard pointed process or structure. **3** a sharp ridge or projection, esp. of a mountain range or slope. **4** a central feature, main support, or source of strength. **5** the part of a book's jacket or cover that encloses the page-fastening part and usu. faces outwards on a shelf. □ **spine-chiller** a frightening story, film, etc. **spine-chilling** (esp. of a story etc.) frightening. **spine-tingling** thrilling, pleasurably exciting. □□ **spined** *adj.* [ME f. OF *espine* or L *spina* thorn, backbone]

▪ **1** backbone, spinal column, vertebrae. **2** thorn, needle, barb, spike, spur, prong, quill, ray, barbel, bristle, prickle, barbule, spicule. **3** see CREST *n.* 2, RIDGE. **4** see BACKBONE 2, 3. □ **spine-chilling** see SCARY. **spine-tingling** see *thrilling* (THRILL).

spinel /spinél/ *n.* **1** any of a group of hard crystalline minerals of various colours, consisting chiefly of oxides of magnesium and aluminium. **2** any substance of similar composition or properties. □ **spinel ruby** a deep-red variety of spinel used as a gem. [F *spinelle* f. It. *spinella*, dimin. of *spina*: see SPINE]

spineless /spī́nliss/ *adj.* **1 a** having no spine; invertebrate. **b** (of a fish) having no fin-spines. **2** (of a person) lacking energy or resolution; weak and purposeless. □□ **spinelessly** *adv.* **spinelessness** *n.*

▪ **1 a** invertebrate. **2** weak, feeble, flabby, irresolute, weak-willed, weak-kneed, indecisive, ineffectual, ineffective, impotent, powerless, purposeless, invertebrate; cowardly, dastardly, pusillanimous, timorous, lily-livered, craven, fearful, timid, spiritless, squeamish, chicken-hearted, *colloq.* yellow, chicken, yellow-bellied, wimpish, gutless, *Brit. colloq.* wet.

spinet /spinét, spínnit/ *n.* *Mus. hist.* a small harpsichord with oblique strings. [obs. F *espinette* f. It. *spinetta* virginal, spinet, dimin. of *spina* thorn etc. (as SPINE), with ref. to the plucked strings]

spinifex /spínnifeks/ *n.* any Australian grass of the genus *Spinifex*, with coarse, spiny leaves. [mod.L f. L *spina* SPINE + *-fex* maker f. *facere* make]

spinnaker /spínnəkər/ *n.* a large triangular sail carried opposite the mainsail of a racing-yacht running before the wind. [fanciful f. *Sphinx*, name of yacht first using it, perh. after *spanker*]

spinner /spínnər/ *n.* **1** a person or thing that spins. **2** *Cricket* **a** a spin bowler. **b** a spun ball. **3** a spin-drier. **4 a** a real or artificial fly for esp. trout-fishing. **b** revolving bait. **5** a manufacturer or merchant engaged in (esp. cotton-) spinning. **6** = SPINNERET. **7** *archaic* a spider.

spinneret /spínnəret/ *n.* **1** the spinning-organ in a spider, silkworm, etc. **2** a device for forming filaments of synthetic fibre.

spinney /spínni/ *n.* (*pl.* **-eys**) *Brit.* a small wood; a thicket. [OF *espinei* f. L *spinetum* thicket f. *spina* thorn]

▪ see THICKET.

spinning /spínning/ *n.* the act or an instance of spinning. □ **spinning-jenny** *hist.* a machine for spinning with more than one spindle at a time. **spinning-machine** a machine that spins fibres continuously. **spinning-top** = TOP[2]. **spinning-wheel** a household machine for spinning yarn or thread with a spindle driven by a wheel attached to a crank or treadle.

▪ see TWIRL *n.* 1.

spinose /spī́nōss/ *adj.* (also **spinous** /-nəss/) *Bot.* (of a plant) having many spines.

▪ see THORNY 1.

Spinozism /spinṓziz'm/ *n.* *Philos.* the doctrine of Spinoza that there is one infinite substance of which extension and thought are attributes and human beings are changing forms. □□ **Spinozist** *n.* **Spinozistic** /-zístik/ *adj.* [B. de *Spinoza*, Du. philosopher d. 1677]

spinster /spínstər/ *n.* **1** an unmarried woman. **2** a woman, esp. elderly, thought unlikely to marry. □□ **spinsterhood** *n.* **spinsterish** *adj.* **spinsterishness** *n.* [ME, orig. = woman who spins]

▪ celibate, *derog.* old maid.

spinthariscope /spinthárriskōp/ *n.* an instrument with a fluorescent screen showing the incidence of alpha particles by flashes. [irreg. f. Gk *spintharis* spark + -SCOPE]

spinule /spínyool/ *n.* *Bot.* & *Zool.* a small spine. □□ **spinulose** *adj.* **spinulous** *adj.* [L *spinula* dimin. of *spina* SPINE]

▪ □□ **spinulose, spinulous** see THORNY 1.

spiny /spī́ni/ *adj.* (**spinier**, **spiniest**) **1** full of spines; prickly. **2** perplexing, troublesome, thorny. □ **spiny anteater** =

ECHIDNA. **spiny lobster** any of various large edible crustaceans of the family Palinuridae, esp. *Palinuris vulgaris*, with a spiny shell and no large anterior claws. ▫▫ **spininess** *n.*
■ **1** see THORNY 1. **2** see THORNY 2.

spiracle /spīrək'l/ *n.* (also **spiraculum** /spīrákyooləm/) (*pl.* **spiracles** or **spiracula** /-lə/) an external respiratory opening in insects, whales, and some fish. ▫▫ **spiracular** /-rákyoolər/ *adj.* [L *spiraculum* f. *spirare* breathe]
■ see VENT[1] *n.* 1.

spiraea /spīreeə/ *n.* (*US* **spirea**) any rosaceous shrub of the genus *Spiraea*, with clusters of small white or pink flowers. [L f. Gk *speiraia* f. *speira* coil]

spiral /spīrəl/ *adj.*, *n.*, & *v.* ● *adj.* **1** winding about a centre in an enlarging or decreasing continuous circular motion, either on a flat plane or rising in a cone; coiled. **2** winding continuously along or as if along a cylinder, like the thread of a screw. ● *n.* **1** a plane or three-dimensional spiral curve. **2** a spiral spring. **3** a spiral formation in a shell etc. **4** a spiral galaxy. **5** a progressive rise or fall of prices, wages, etc., each responding to an upward or downward stimulus provided by the other (*a spiral of rising prices and wages*). ● *v.* (**spiralled**, **spiralling**; *US* **spiraled**, **spiraling**) **1** *intr.* move in a spiral course, esp. upwards or downwards. **2** *tr.* make spiral. **3** *intr.* esp. *Econ.* (of prices, wages, etc.) rise or fall, esp. rapidly (cf. sense 5 of *n.*). ▫ **spiral balance** a device for measuring weight by the torsion of a spiral spring. **spiral galaxy** a galaxy in which the matter is concentrated mainly in one or more spiral arms. **spiral staircase** a staircase rising in a spiral round a central axis. ▫▫ **spirality** /-rálliti/ *n.* **spirally** *adv.* [F *spiral* or med.L *spiralis* (as SPIRE[2])]
■ *adj.* helical, coiled, screw, corkscrew, cochlear; scrolled, volute(d), whorled. ● *n.* **1** helix, coil, corkscrew, screw, scroll; whorl, volute, turn, curl. ● *v.* **1** see TWIRL *v.* **3** (*spiral downwards*) see DROP *v.* 8a; (*spiral upwards*) see SOAR 2.

spirant /spīrənt/ *adj.* & *n. Phonet.* ● *adj.* (of a consonant) uttered with a continuous expulsion of breath, esp. fricative. ● *n.* such a consonant. [L *spirare spirant-* breathe]

spire[1] /spīr/ *n.* & *v.* ● *n.* **1** a tapering cone- or pyramid-shaped structure built esp. on a church tower (cf. STEEPLE). **2** the continuation of a tree trunk above the point where branching begins. **3** any tapering thing, e.g. the spike of a flower. ● *v.tr.* provide with a spire. ▫▫ **spiry** /spīri/ *adj.* [OE *spīr*]
■ *n.* **1** pinnacle, *flèche*; column, belfry; steeple. **3** top, pinnacle, apex, peak, summit, acme, tip, crest, crown, vertex.

spire[2] /spīr/ *n.* **1 a** a spiral; a coil. **b** a single twist of this. **2** the upper part of a spiral shell. [F f. L *spira* f. Gk *speira* coil]

spirea *US* var. of SPIRAEA.

spirillum /spīrilləm/ *n.* (*pl.* **spirilla** /-lə/) **1** any bacterium of the genus *Spirillum*, characterized by a rigid spiral structure. **2** any bacterium with a similar shape. [mod.L, irreg. dimin. of L *spira* SPIRE[2]]

spirit /spírrit/ *n.* & *v.* ● *n.* **1 a** the vital animating essence of a person or animal (*was sadly broken in spirit*). **b** the intelligent non-physical part of a person; the soul. **2 a** a rational or intelligent being without a material body. **b** a supernatural being such as a ghost, fairy, etc. (*haunted by spirits*). **3** a prevailing mental or moral condition or attitude; a mood; a tendency (*public spirit*; *took it in the wrong spirit*). **4 a** (usu. in *pl.*) strong distilled liquor, e.g. brandy, whisky, gin, rum. **b** a distilled volatile liquid (*wood spirit*). **c** purified alcohol (*methylated spirit*). **d** a solution of a volatile principle in alcohol; a tincture (*spirit of ammonia*). **5 a** a person's mental or moral nature or qualities, usu. specified (*has an unbending spirit*). **b** a person viewed as possessing these (*is an ardent spirit*). **c** (in full **high spirit**) courage, energy, vivacity, dash (*played with spirit*; *infused him with spirit*). **6** the real meaning as opposed to lip-service or verbal expression (*the spirit of the law*). **7** *archaic* an immaterial principle thought to govern vital phenomena (*animal spirits*). ● *v.tr.* (**spirited**, **spiriting**) (usu. foll. by *away*, *off*, etc.) convey rapidly and secretly by or as if by spirits. ▫ **in** (or **in the**) **spirit** inwardly (*shall be with you in spirit*). **spirit duplicator** a duplicator using an alcoholic solution to reproduce copies from a master sheet. **spirit gum** a quick-drying solution of gum used esp. for attaching false hair. **spirit-lamp** a lamp burning methylated or other volatile spirits instead of oil. **spirit-level** a bent glass tube nearly filled with alcohol used to test horizontality by the position of an air-bubble. **the spirit moves a person** he or she feels inclined (to do something) (orig. in Quaker use). **spirit** (or **spirits**) **of wine** *archaic* purified alcohol. **spirits of salt** *archaic* hydrochloric acid. **spirit up** animate or cheer (a person). [ME f. AF *(e)spirit*, OF *esp(e)rit*, f. L *spiritus* breath, spirit f. *spirare* breathe]
■ *n.* **1** breath, life, vitality, vital spirit, soul, consciousness, psyche, self, heart, essence, *Psychol.* anima. **2 b** see SPECTRE 1. **3** attitude, principle, thought, idea, inspiration, notion, feeling, inclination, tendency, impulse; atmosphere, mood; temper, sentiment, cheer, humour, frame of mind; morale, *esprit de corps*, team spirit. **4 a** (*spirits*) alcohol, liquor, strong drink, *colloq.* booze, fire-water, *US colloq.* hooch. **5 a** character, temperament, temper, nature, persona, disposition, heart, mind, will, will-power, attitude, bent, inclination. **b** character, soul. **c** bravery, courage, grit, backbone, valour, pluck, daring, mettle, stout-heartedness, manfulness, manliness, gameness, resoluteness, resolution, resolve, will, will-power; energy, ardour, desire, impetus, drive, urge, eagerness, enthusiasm, motivation, intention, enterprise; zest, zeal, zealousness, fire, passion, pungency, piquancy, warmth, animation, life, liveliness, vivacity, vivaciousness, panache, *élan*, dash, spice, *colloq.* sauce; vim, spunk, get-up-and-go, (right) stuff, guts, *US colloq.* sand. **6** meaning, sense, tenor, signification, purport, intent, intention, purpose, aim, implication, message, essence, quintessence, core, heart, meat, pith, substance, marrow. ● *v.* (*spirit away* or *off*) abduct, make off *or* away with, carry off, transport, take away, kidnap, steal (off *or* away with), whisk away, abscond with; make disappear.

spirited /spírritid/ *adj.* **1** full of spirit; animated, lively, brisk, or courageous (*a spirited attack*; *a spirited translation*). **2** having a spirit or spirits of a specified kind (*high-spirited*; *mean-spirited*). ▫▫ **spiritedly** *adv.* **spiritedness** *n.*
■ **1** lively, sprightly, energetic, vigorous, racy, animated, brisk, sparkling, dynamic, buoyant, effervescent, vivacious; frisky, playful, sportive; ardent, fervent, impassioned; plucky, mettlesome, venturesome, courageous; *colloq.* spunky. ▫▫ **spiritedly** see *vigorously* (VIGOROUS). **spiritedness** see ANIMATION.

spiritless /spírritliss/ *adj.* lacking courage, vigour, or vivacity. ▫▫ **spiritlessly** *adv.* **spiritlessness** *n.*
■ see LIFELESS 3.

spiritual /spírrityooəl/ *adj.* & *n.* ● *adj.* **1** of or concerning the spirit as opposed to matter. **2** concerned with sacred or religious things; holy; divine; inspired (*the spiritual life*; *spiritual songs*). **3** (of the mind etc.) refined, sensitive; not concerned with the material. **4** (of a relationship etc.) concerned with the soul or spirit etc., not with external reality (*his spiritual home*). ● *n.* = *Negro spiritual*. ▫ **spiritual courts** ecclesiastical courts. ▫▫ **spirituality** /-yoo-álliti/ *n.* **spiritually** *adv.* **spiritualness** *n.* [ME f. OF *spirituel* f. L *spiritualis* (as SPIRIT)]
■ *adj.* **1, 4** non-material, incorporeal, psychic(al), mental, psychological, inner. **2** sacred, ecclesiastic(al), churchly, clerical, priestly, devotional, holy, divine, sacerdotal, religious, non-secular; inspired. ▫▫ **spirituality** see DEVOTION 2c.

spiritualism /spírrityooəliz'm/ *n.* **1 a** the belief that the spirits of the dead can communicate with the living, esp. through mediums. **b** the practice of this. **2** *Philos.* the doctrine that the spirit exists as distinct from matter, or that spirit is the only reality (cf. MATERIALISM). ▫▫ **spiritualist** *n.* **spiritualistic** /-listik/ *adj.*

■ ▫▫ **spiritualist** see PSYCHIC *n.* **spiritualistic** see PSYCHIC *adj.* 1b.

spiritualize /spírrityooəlīz/ *v.tr.* (also **-ise**) **1** make (a person or a person's character, thoughts, etc.) spiritual; elevate. **2** attach a spiritual as opposed to a literal meaning to. ▫▫ **spiritualization** /-záysh'n/ *n.*

spirituel /spírrityoo-él/ *adj.* (also **spirituelle**) (of the mind) refined and yet spirited; witty. [F *spirituel*, fem. *-elle* (as SPIRITUAL)]

spirituous /spírrityooəss/ *adj.* **1** containing much alcohol. **2** distilled, as whisky, rum, etc. (*spirituous liquor*). ▫▫ **spirituousness** *n.* [L *spiritus* spirit, or F *spiritueux*]
■ **1** hard, potent; see also STRONG *adj.* 14.

spiro-[1] /spī́rō/ *comb. form* a coil. [L *spira*, Gk *speira* coil]

spiro-[2] /spī́rō/ *comb. form* breath. [irreg. f. L *spirare* breathe]

spirochaete /spī́rōkeet/ *n.* (*US* **spirochete**) any of various flexible spiral-shaped bacteria. [SPIRO-[1] + Gk *khaitē* long hair]

spirograph /spī́rəgraaf/ *n.* an instrument for recording breathing movements. ▫▫ **spirographic** /-gráffik/ *adj.* **spirographically** /-gráffikəli/ *adv.*

spirogyra /spī́rōjī́rə/ *n.* any freshwater alga of the genus *Spirogyra*, with cells containing spiral bands of chlorophyll. [mod.L f. SPIRO-[1] + Gk *guros gura* round]

spirometer /spīrómmitər/ *n.* an instrument for measuring the air capacity of the lungs.

spirt var. of SPURT.

spit[1] /spit/ *v.* & *n.* ● *v.* (**spitting**; *past* and *past part.* **spat** /spat/ or **spit**) **1** *intr.* **a** eject saliva from the mouth. **b** do this as a sign of hatred or contempt (*spat at him*). **2** *tr.* (usu. foll. by *out*) **a** eject (saliva, blood, food, etc.) from the mouth (*spat the meat out*). **b** utter (oaths, threats, etc.) vehemently (*'Damn you!' he spat*). **3** *intr.* (of a fire, pen, pan, etc.) send out sparks, ink, hot fat, etc. **4** *intr.* (of rain) fall lightly (*it's only spitting*). **5** *intr.* (esp. of a cat) make a spitting or hissing noise in anger or hostility. ● *n.* **1** spittle. **2** the act or an instance of spitting. **3** the foamy liquid secretion of some insects used to protect their young. ▫ **the spit** (or **very spit**) **of** *colloq.* the exact double of (cf. *spitting image*). **spit and polish 1** the cleaning and polishing duties of a soldier etc. **2** exaggerated neatness and smartness. **spit chips** *Austral. sl.* **1** feel extreme thirst. **2** be angry or frustrated. **spit it out** *colloq.* say what is on one's mind. **spitting cobra** the African black-necked cobra, *Naja nigricollis*, that ejects venom by spitting, not striking. **spitting distance** a very short distance. **spitting image** (foll. by *of*) *colloq.* the exact double of (another person or thing). ▫▫ **spitter** *n.* [OE *spittan*, of imit. orig.: cf. SPEW]
■ *v.* **1 a** expectorate; dribble, salivate, drool, slaver. **2 a** expectorate, discharge, spew (forth), eject. **2b, 3** hiss, sputter, splutter; fizz. ● *n.* **1** spittle, saliva, drool, sputum, slaver. ▫ **spit chips 2** see SEETHE 2. **spitting image** twin, duplicate, double, clone, image, counterpart, likeness, look-alike, copy, *colloq.* (very) spit, *esp. US sl.* (dead) ringer.

spit[2] /spit/ *n.* & *v.* ● *n.* **1** a slender rod on which meat is skewered before being roasted on a fire etc.; a skewer. **2 a** a small point of land projecting into the sea. **b** a long narrow underwater bank. ● *v.tr.* (**spitted, spitting**) **1** thrust a spit through (meat etc.). **2** pierce or transfix with a sword etc. ▫ **spit-roast** cook on a spit. ▫▫ **spitty** *adj.* [OE *spitu* f. WG]

spit[3] /spit/ *n.* (*pl.* same or **spits**) a spade-depth of earth (*dig it two spit deep*). [MDu. & MLG, = OE *spittan* dig with spade, prob. rel. to SPIT[2]]

spitball /spítbawl/ *n.* & *v.* ● *n. US* **1** a ball of chewed paper etc. used as a missile. **2** a baseball moistened by the pitcher to impart spin. ● *v.intr.* throw out suggestions for discussion. ▫▫ **spitballer** *n.*

spitchcock /spíchkok/ *n.* & *v.* ● *n.* an eel split and grilled or fried. ● *v.tr.* prepare (an eel, fish, bird, etc.) in this way. [16th c.: orig. unkn.: cf. SPATCHCOCK]

spite /spīt/ *n.* & *v.* ● *n.* **1** ill will, malice towards a person (*did it from spite*). **2** a grudge. ● *v.tr.* thwart, mortify, annoy (*does it to spite me*). ▫ **in spite of** notwithstanding. **in spite of oneself** etc. though one would rather have done otherwise. [ME f. OF *despit* DESPITE]
■ *n.* **1** spitefulness, maliciousness, malice, malevolence, malignity, ill will, venom, spleen, rancour, animosity, gall (and wormwood), resentment, bitterness, hostility, antagonism, hatred, hate, *sl.* bitchiness. **2** grudge, grievance, resentment. ● *v.* annoy, irritate, vex, upset, disconcert, offend, provoke, discomfit, pique, put out, hurt, injure, wound, mortify, thwart, *colloq.* peeve, get under a person's skin, needle. ▫ **in spite of** despite, notwithstanding, regardless of, ignoring, in defiance of.

spiteful /spī́tfŏŏl/ *adj.* motivated by spite; malevolent. ▫▫ **spitefully** *adv.* **spitefulness** *n.*
■ malevolent, malicious, malignant, venomous, vindictive, hateful, invidious, hostile, antagonistic, unfriendly, unforgiving, retaliative, retaliatory, punitive, retributive, retributory, *sl.* bitchy. ▫▫ **spitefulness** see SPITE *n.* 1.

spitfire /spítfīr/ *n.* a person of fiery temper.
■ see SHREW.

spittle /spítt'l/ *n.* saliva, esp. as ejected from the mouth. ▫▫ **spittly** *adj.* [alt. of ME (now dial.) *spattle* = OE *spātl* f. *spǣtan* to spit, after SPIT[1]]
■ see SPIT[1] *n.*

spittoon /spitŏŏn/ *n.* a metal or earthenware pot with esp. a funnel-shaped top, used for spitting into.

spitz /spits/ *n.* **1** a small type of dog with a pointed muzzle, esp. a Pomeranian. **2** this breed. [G *Spitz(hund)* f. *spitz* pointed + *Hund* dog]

spiv /spiv/ *n. Brit. colloq.* a man, often characterized by flashy dress, who makes a living by illicit or unscrupulous dealings. ▫▫ **spivvish** *adj.* **spivvy** *adj.* [20th c.: orig. unkn.]

splanchnic /splángknik/ *adj.* of or relating to the viscera; intestinal. [mod.L *splanchnicus* f. Gk *splagkhnikos* f. *splagkhna* entrails]

splash /splash/ *v.* & *n.* ● *v.* **1** *intr.* & *tr.* spatter or cause (liquid) to spatter in small drops. **2** *tr.* cause (a person) to be spattered with liquid etc. (*splashed them with mud*). **3** *intr.* **a** (of a person) cause liquid to spatter (*was splashing about in the bath*). **b** (usu. foll. by *across*, *along*, etc.) move while spattering liquid etc. (*splashed across the carpet in his boots*). **c** step, fall, or plunge etc. into a liquid etc. so as to cause a splash (*splashed into the sea*). **d** (foll. by *down*) (of a spacecraft) alight on the sea after flight. **4** *tr.* display (news) prominently. **5** *tr.* decorate with scattered colour. **6** *tr.* spend (money) ostentatiously. ● *n.* **1** the act or an instance of splashing. **2 a** a quantity of liquid splashed. **b** the resulting noise (*heard a splash*). **3** a spot of dirt etc. splashed on to a thing. **4** a prominent news feature etc. **5** a daub or patch of colour, esp. on an animal's coat. **6** *Brit. colloq.* a small quantity of liquid, esp. of soda water etc. to dilute spirits. ▫ **make a splash** attract much attention, esp. by extravagance. **splash out** *colloq.* spend money freely. ▫▫ **splashy** *adj.* (**splashier, splashiest**). [alt. of PLASH[1]]
■ *v.* **1** spatter, bespatter, spray, shower, scatter, daub, sprinkle, *US* splatter, *colloq.* slosh. **2** spatter, speckle, bespatter, spray, shower, scatter, dabble, daub, bedaub, sprinkle, besprinkle, *US* splatter, *colloq.* slosh, splodge, splotch. **3** splatter, slosh, plash, wade, dabble, paddle, *colloq.* splurge, splosh. **4** blazon, display, spread, plaster. ● *n.* **2** splatter, spatter, slosh, *colloq.* splosh. **3** spatter, spray, sprinkle, spot, stain, smear, smudge, blotch, *colloq.* splodge, splotch. **5** patch, daub, blotch, *colloq.* splodge, splotch. **6** see DASH *n.* 7. ▫ **make a splash** make an impression *or* impact, cause a sensation *or* brouhaha *or* to-do *or* commotion, cause an uproar. **splash out** see SPLURGE *v.*

splashback /spláshbak/ *n.* a panel behind a sink etc. to protect the wall from splashes.

splashdown /spláshdown/ *n.* the alighting of a spacecraft on the sea.

splat[1] /splat/ *n.* a flat piece of thin wood in the centre of a chair-back. [*splat* (v.) split up, rel. to SPLIT]

splat[2] /splat/ *n.*, *adv.*, & *v. colloq.* ● *n.* a sharp cracking or slapping sound (*hit the wall with a splat*). ● *adv.* with a splat (*fell splat on his head*). ● *v.intr.* & *tr.* (**splatted, splatting**) fall or hit with a splat. [abbr. of SPLATTER]

splatter /spláttər/ *v.* & *n.* ● *v.* **1** *tr.* & *intr.* splash esp. with a continuous noisy action. **2** *tr.* (often foll. by *with*) *US* make wet or dirty by splashing. ● *n.* a noisy splashing sound. [imit.]
■ *v.* see SPLASH *v.* 1–3. ● *n.* see SPLASH *n.* 2.

splay /splay/ *v.*, *n.*, & *adj.* ● *v.* **1** *tr.* (usu. foll. by *out*) spread (the elbows, feet, etc.) out. **2** *intr.* (of an aperture or its sides) diverge in shape or position. **3** *tr.* construct (a window, doorway, aperture, etc.) so that it diverges or is wider at one side of the wall than the other. ● *n.* a surface making an oblique angle with another, e.g. the splayed side of a window or embrasure. ● *adj.* **1** wide and flat. **2** turned outward. □ **splay-foot** a broad flat foot turned outward. **splay-footed** having such feet. [ME f. DISPLAY]

spleen /spleen/ *n.* **1** an abdominal organ involved in maintaining the proper condition of blood in most vertebrates. **2** lowness of spirits; moroseness, ill temper, spite (from the earlier belief that the spleen was the seat of such feelings) (*a fit of spleen*; *vented their spleen*). □□ **spleenful** *adj.* **spleeny** *adj.* [ME f. OF *esplen* f. L *splen* f. Gk *splēn*]
■ **2** see SPITE *n.* 1.

spleenwort /spléenwurt/ *n.* any fern of the genus *Asplenium*, formerly used as a remedy for disorders of the spleen.

splen- /spleen/ *comb. form Anat.* the spleen. [Gk (as SPLEEN)]

splendent /spléndənt/ *adj. formal* **1** shining; lustrous. **2** illustrious. [ME f. L *splendēre* to shine]

splendid /spléndid/ *adj.* **1** magnificent, gorgeous, brilliant, sumptuous (*a splendid palace*; *a splendid achievement*). **2** dignified; impressive (*splendid isolation*). **3** excellent; fine (*a splendid chance*). □□ **splendidly** *adv.* **splendidness** *n.* [F *splendide* or L *splendidus* (as SPLENDENT)]
■ **1** magnificent, resplendent, dazzling, gorgeous, showy, dashing, marvellous, spectacular, grand, glorious, lavish, ornate, sumptuous, majestic, brilliant, extraordinary, exceptional, superb, supreme, imposing, impressive, awe-inspiring, awesome, lush, plush, rich, luxurious, swanky, *colloq.* posh, ritzy, *esp. US colloq.* swank, *colloq. or joc.* splendiferous; eminent, prominent, superior, noteworthy, notable, celebrated, illustrious, famous, distinguished, dignified, exemplary, remarkable, admirable, conspicuous, outstanding, sublime, striking, successful, meritorious, creditable, *formal* splendent. **3** excellent, superior, pre-eminent, fine, marvellous, extraordinary, exceptional, unbelievable, incredible, far-out, first-class, unequalled, unsurpassed, stupendous, peerless, matchless, nonpareil, superlative, praiseworthy, admirable, laudable, *colloq.* great, colossal, fabulous, fab, fantastic, terrific, super, smashing, A1, tiptop, capital, way-out, out of sight, keen, brilliant, brill, *esp. US colloq.* dandy, *esp. US sl.* cool, *US sl.* neat. □□ **splendidness** see SPLENDOUR 2.

splendiferous /splendíffərəss/ *adj. colloq.* or *joc.* splendid. □□ **splendiferously** *adv.* **splendiferousness** *n.* [irreg. f. SPLENDOUR]
■ see SPLENDID 1.

splendour /spléndər/ *n.* (*US* **splendor**) **1** great or dazzling brightness. **2** magnificence; grandeur. [ME f. AF *splendeur* or L *splendor* (as SPLENDENT)]
■ **1** brilliance, shine, lustre, light, brightness, glitter, dazzle, luminosity, luminousness, gloss, *literary* effulgence, refulgence. **2** magnificence, grandeur, brilliance, display, radiance, resplendence, sumptuousness, stateliness, majesty, panoply, spectacle, show, glory, pomp, gorgeousness, dazzle, beauty, splendidness, exquisiteness, luxuriousness, richness, lavishness, luxury, swankiness, *colloq.* poshness, swank, ritziness, *colloq. or joc.* splendiferousness, *literary* refulgence.

splenectomy /spleenéktəmi/ *n.* (*pl.* **-ies**) the surgical excision of the spleen.

splenetic /splinéttik/ *adj.* & *n.* ● *adj.* **1** ill-tempered; peevish. **2** of or concerning the spleen. ● *n.* a splenetic person. □□ **splenetically** *adv.* [LL *spleneticus* (as SPLEEN)]
■ *adj.* **1** see PEEVISH.

splenic /splénnik, spléē-/ *adj.* of or in the spleen. □ **splenic fever** anthrax. □□ **splenoid** /spléenoyd/ *adj.* [F *splénique* or L *splenicus* f. Gk *splēnikos* (as SPLEEN)]

splenitis /spleenītiss/ *n.* inflammation of the spleen.

splenius /spléeniəss/ *n.* (*pl.* **splenii** /-ni-ī/) *Anat.* either section of muscle on each side of the neck and back serving to draw back the head. □□ **splenial** *adj.* [mod.L f. Gk *splēnion* bandage]

splenology /spleenólləji/ *n.* the scientific study of the spleen.

splenomegaly /spléenəméggəli/ *n.* a pathological enlargement of the spleen. [SPLEN- + *megaly* (as MEGALO-)]

splenotomy /spleenóttəmi/ *n.* (*pl.* **-ies**) a surgical incision into or dissection of the spleen.

splice /splīss/ *v.* & *n.* ● *v.tr.* **1** join the ends of (ropes) by interweaving strands. **2** join (pieces of timber, magnetic tape, film, etc.) in an overlapping position. **3** (esp. as **spliced** *adj.*) *colloq.* join in marriage. ● *n.* a joint consisting of two ropes, pieces of wood, film, etc., made by splicing, e.g. the handle and blade of a cricket bat. □ **splice the main brace** *Naut. hist.* issue an extra tot of rum. □□ **splicer** *n.* [prob. f. MDu. *splissen*, of uncert. orig.]
■ *v.* **1** entwine, intertwine, braid, plait, twist, interlace, interweave, knit. **2** dovetail, mesh, fit (together), knit, interlock, engage. **3** join, unite, marry, bind, conjoin. ● *n.* union, joint, connection, tie, bond, binding, fastening, linkage.

spliff /splif/ *n.* (also **splif**) *sl.* a cannabis cigarette. [20th c.: orig. unkn.]

spline /splīn/ *n.* & *v.* ● *n.* **1** a rectangular key fitting into grooves in the hub and shaft of a wheel and allowing longitudinal play. **2** a slat. **3** a flexible wood or rubber strip used esp. in drawing large curves. ● *v.tr.* fit with a spline (sense 1). [orig. E. Anglian dial., perh. rel. to SPLINTER]

splint /splint/ *n.* & *v.* ● *n.* **1 a** a strip of rigid material used for holding a broken bone etc. when set. **b** a rigid or flexible strip of esp. wood used in basketwork etc. **2** a tumour or bony excrescence on the inside of a horse's leg. **3** a thin strip of wood etc. used to light a fire, pipe, etc. **4** = *splint-bone*. ● *v.tr.* secure (a broken limb etc.) with a splint or splints. □ **splint-bone 1** either of two small bones in a horse's foreleg lying behind and close to the cannon-bone. **2** the human fibula. **splint-coal** hard bituminous laminated coal burning with great heat. [ME *splent(e)* f. MDu. *splinte* or MLG *splinte*, *splente* metal plate or pin, rel. to SPLINTER]

splinter /splíntər/ *v.* & *n.* ● *v.tr.* & *intr.* break into fragments. ● *n.* a small thin sharp-edged piece broken off from wood, stone, etc. □ **splinter-bar** *Brit.* a crossbar in a vehicle to which traces are attached; a swingletree. **splinter group** (or **party**) a group or party that has broken away from a larger one. **splinter-proof** proof against splinters e.g. from bursting shells or bombs. □□ **splintery** *adj.* [ME f. MDu. (= LG) *splinter*, *splenter*, rel. to SPLINT]
■ *v.* shatter, break, fragment, split, disintegrate, shiver, smash to smithereens. ● *n.* sliver, shiver, fragment, piece; scrap, shard, shred, chip.

split /split/ *v.* & *n.* ● *v.* (**splitting**; *past* and *past part.* **split**) **1** *intr.* & *tr.* **a** break or cause to break forcibly into parts, esp. with the grain or into halves. **b** (often foll. by *up*) divide into parts (*split into groups*; *split up the money equally*). **2** *tr.* & *intr.* (often foll. by *off*, *away*) remove or be removed by breaking, separating, or dividing (*split the top off the bottle*; *split away from the main group*). **3** *intr.* & *tr.* **a** (usu. foll. by *up*, *on*, *over*, etc.) separate esp. through discord (*split up after ten years*; *they were split on the question of picketing*). **b** (foll. by *with*) quarrel or cease association with (another person etc.). **4** *tr.* cause the fission of (an atom). **5** *intr.* & *tr. sl.* leave, esp. suddenly. **6** *intr.* (usu. foll. by *on*) *colloq.* betray secrets; inform (*split on them to the police*). **7** *intr.* **a** (as **splitting** *adj.*) (esp. of a headache) very painful; acute. **b** (of the head) suffer great pain from a headache, noise, etc. **8** *intr.* (of a ship) be wrecked. **9** *tr. US colloq.* dilute (whisky etc.) with water. ● *n.* **1** the act or an instance of splitting; the state of being split. **2** a fissure, vent, crack, cleft, etc. **3** a separation into parties; a schism. **4** (in *pl.*) *Brit.* the athletic feat of leaping in the air or sitting down with the legs at right angles to the body in front and behind, or at the sides with the trunk facing forwards. **5** a split osier etc. used for parts of basketwork. **6** each strip of steel, cane, etc., of the reed in a loom. **7** a single thickness of split hide. **8** the turning up of two cards of equal value in faro, so that the stakes are divided. **9 a** half a bottle of mineral water. **b** half a glass of liquor. **10** *colloq.* a division of money, esp. the proceeds of crime. □ **split the difference** take the average of two proposed amounts. **split gear** (or **pulley** or **wheel**) a gear etc. made in halves for removal from a shaft. **split hairs** make small and insignificant distinctions. **split infinitive** a phrase consisting of an infinitive with an adverb etc. inserted between *to* and the verb, e.g. *seems to really like it.* **split-level** (of a building) having a room or rooms a fraction of a storey higher than other parts. **split mind** = SCHIZOPHRENIA. **split pea** a pea dried and split in half for cooking. **split personality** the alteration or dissociation of personality occurring in some mental illnesses, esp. schizophrenia and hysteria. **split pin** a metal cotter passed through a hole and held by the pressing back of the two ends. **split ring** a small steel ring with two spiral turns, such as a key-ring. **split-screen** a screen on which two or more separate images are displayed. **split second** a very brief moment of time. **split shift** a shift comprising two or more separate periods of duty. **split shot** (or **stroke**) *Croquet* a stroke driving two touching balls in different directions. **split one's sides** be convulsed with laughter. **split the ticket** (or **one's vote**) *US* vote for candidates of more than one party. **split the vote** *Brit.* (of a candidate or minority party) attract votes from another so that both are defeated by a third. □□ **splitter** *n.* [orig. Naut. f. MDu. *splitten*, rel. to *spletten*, *splīten*, MHG *splīzen*]

▪ *v.* **1 a** split up *or* apart, divide, separate, cut *or* chop apart, cut *or* chop in two, pull *or* tear apart, break *or* snap apart, break *or* snap in two, break up, fracture, come apart, fall apart, rupture, partition, detach, become detached, *archaic or rhet.* rend, *literary* cleave; bisect, dichotomize, halve; burst, *colloq.* bust. **b** divide (up), apportion, deal out, dole out, distribute, allot, allocate, share *or* parcel out, carve up; branch, fork, bifurcate, diverge, separate. **3 a** (*split up*) divorce, separate, go separate ways, break up, part company, *colloq.* bust up. **5** see LEAVE[1] *v.* 1b, 3, 4. **6** see INFORM 2. **7 a** (**splitting**) severe, bad, acute, *colloq.* awful, thumping. **9** see DILUTE *v.* ● *n.* **1** see SEPARATION. **2** crack, cleft, fissure, chink, cranny, slit, slot, crevice, cleavage, groove, furrow, channel; gap, hiatus, lacuna, opening, separation, division, chasm; rift, break, rupture, fracture; slash, gash, tear, rip, rent, vent; *Anat.* sulcus. **3** division, dichotomy, schism, breach, rupture, partition, disunion, dissociation, discord; break, separation, divorce. □ **split hairs** see QUIBBLE *v.* **split second** see SECOND[2]. **split one's sides** see LAUGH *v.* 1.

splodge /sploj/ *n.* & *v. colloq.* ● *n.* a daub, blot, or smear. ● *v.tr.* make a large, esp. irregular, spot or patch on. □□ **splodgy** *adj.* [imit., or alt. of SPLOTCH]

▪ *n.* see BLOT *n.* 1. ● *v.* see SPLASH *v.* 2.

splosh /splosh/ *v.* & *n. colloq.* ● *v.tr.* & *intr.* move with a splashing sound. ● *n.* **1** a splashing sound. **2** a splash of water etc. **3** *sl.* money. [imit.]

splotch /sploch/ *n.* & *v.tr.* = SPLODGE. □□ **splotchy** *adj.* [perh. f. SPOT + obs. *plotch* BLOTCH]

splurge /splurj/ *n.* & *v. colloq.* ● *n.* **1** an ostentatious display or effort. **2** an instance of sudden great extravagance. ● *v.intr.* **1** (usu. foll. by *on*) spend effort or esp. large sums of money (*splurged on new furniture*). **2** splash heavily. [19th-c. US: prob. imit.]

▪ *n.* **1** display, show, ostentatiousness, ostentation, splash, burst, outburst, access. **2** extravagance, indulgence, fling, *colloq.* spree. ● *v.* **1** squander *or* dissipate *or* waste money, burn (up) money, throw away money, show off one's money, flaunt one's money, lash out, *colloq.* splash out, *sl.* blow one's money.

splutter /splúttər/ *v.* & *n.* ● *v.* **1** *intr.* **a** speak in a hurried, vehement, or choking manner. **b** emit particles from the mouth, sparks, hot oil, etc., with spitting sounds. **2** *tr.* **a** speak or utter (words, threats, a language, etc.) rapidly or incoherently. **b** emit (food, sparks, hot oil, etc.) with a spitting sound. ● *n.* spluttering speech. □□ **splutterer** *n.* **splutteringly** *adv.* [SPUTTER by assoc. with *splash*]

▪ *v.* **1b, 2b** see SPIT[1]*v.* 2b, 3.

Spode /spōd/ *n.* a type of fine pottery or porcelain. [J. *Spode*, Engl. maker of china d. 1827]

spoil /spoyl/ *v.* & *n.* ● *v.* (*past* and *past part.* **spoilt** or **spoiled**) **1** *tr.* **a** damage; diminish the value of (*was spoilt by the rain; will spoil all the fun*). **b** reduce a person's enjoyment etc. of (*the news spoiled his dinner*). **2** *tr.* injure the character of (esp. a child, pet, etc.) by excessive indulgence. **3** *intr.* **a** (of food) go bad, decay; become unfit for eating. **b** (usu. in *neg.*) (of a joke, secret, etc.) become stale through long keeping. **4** *tr.* render (a ballot paper) invalid by improper marking. **5** *tr.* (foll. by *of*) *archaic* or *literary* plunder or deprive (a person of a thing) by force or stealth (*spoiled him of all his possessions*). ● *n.* **1** (usu. in *pl.*) **a** plunder taken from an enemy in war, or seized by force. **b** esp. *joc.* profit or advantages gained by succeeding to public office, high position, etc. **2** earth etc. thrown up in excavating, dredging, etc. □ **be spoiling for** aggressively seek (a fight etc.). **spoils system** *US* the practice of giving public office to the adherents of a successful party. **spoilt for choice** having so many choices that it is difficult to choose. [ME f. OF *espoillier*, *espoille* f. L *spoliare* f. *spolium* spoil, plunder, or f. DESPOIL]

▪ *v.* **1** ruin, destroy, wreck, blight, queer, mess up, bungle, botch, upset, demolish, sabotage, undermine, harm, damage, vitiate, mar, injure, debase, deface, disfigure, mutilate, scar, blemish, kill, *colloq.* make a hash of, fluff, *sl.* blow, *Austral. sl.* cruel. **2** baby, mollycoddle, coddle, cosset, indulge, overindulge, pamper, dote on, spoonfeed. **3 a** turn, go off, go bad, deteriorate, curdle, moulder, decay, decompose, perish, become addle(d), rot, putrefy, mildew. ● *n.* **1** (*spoils*) **a** loot, booty, plunder, pillage, prizes, pickings, takings, *esp. US* take, *sl.* swag, boodle. **b** benefits, advantages, perquisites, *Brit. colloq.* perks. □ **be spoiling for** itch for *or* after, yearn for, be eager for, be keen for, look for, be bent on, be desirous of, crave, be after. **spoilt for choice** (*be spoilt for choice*) have an *embarras de choix* or *richesse(s)*.

spoilage /spóylij/ *n.* **1** paper spoilt in printing. **2** the spoiling of food etc. by decay.

spoiler /spóylər/ *n.* **1** a person or thing that spoils. **2 a** a device on an aircraft to retard its speed by interrupting the air flow. **b** a similar device on a vehicle to improve its road-holding at speed.

spoilsman /spóylzmən/ *n.* (*pl.* **-men**) *US* esp. *Polit.* **1** an advocate of the spoils system. **2** a person who seeks to profit by it.

spoilsport /spóylsport/ *n.* a person who spoils others' pleasure or enjoyment.

▪ killjoy, damper, dog in the manger, *colloq.* wet blanket, *Austral. sl.* wowser, *esp. US sl.* party pooper.

spoilt *past* and *past part.* of SPOIL.

spoke[1] /spōk/ *n.* & *v.* ● *n.* **1** each of the bars running from the hub to the rim of a wheel. **2** a rung of a ladder. **3** each radial handle of the wheel of a ship etc. ● *v.tr.* **1** provide with spokes. **2** obstruct (a wheel etc.) by thrusting a spoke in. □ **put a spoke in a person's wheel** *Brit.* thwart or hinder a person. **spoke-bone** the radius of the forearm. □□ **spokewise** *adv.* [OE *spāca* f. WG]

■ □ **put a spoke in a person's wheel** see FOIL[1] *v.* 1.

spoke[2] *past* of SPEAK.

spoken /spṓkən/ *past part.* of SPEAK. ● *adj.* (in *comb.*) speaking in a specified way (*smooth-spoken*; *well-spoken*). □ **spoken for** claimed, requisitioned (*this seat is spoken for*).

■ *adj.* speaking. □ **spoken for** reserved, bespoke, set aside, accounted for, chosen, selected, claimed, requisitioned, engaged, betrothed, attached.

spokeshave /spṓkshayv/ *n.* a blade set between two handles, used for shaping spokes and other esp. curved work where an ordinary plane is not suitable.

spokesman /spṓksmən/ *n.* (*pl.* **-men**; *fem.* **spokeswoman**, *pl.* **-women**) **1** a person who speaks on behalf of others, esp. in the course of public relations. **2** a person deputed to express the views of a group etc. [irreg. f. SPOKE[2] after *craftsman* etc.]

spokesperson /spṓkspers'n/ *n.* (*pl.* **-persons** or **-people**) a spokesman or spokeswoman.

spoliation /spṓliáysh'n/ *n.* **1 a** plunder or pillage, esp. of neutral vessels in war. **b** extortion. **2** *Eccl.* the taking of the fruits of a benefice under a pretended title etc. **3** *Law* the destruction, mutilation, or alteration, of a document to prevent its being used as evidence. □□ **spoliator** /spṓliaytər/ *n.* **spoliatory** /spṓliətəri/ *adj.* [ME f. L *spoliatio* (as SPOIL)]

spondaic /spondáyik/ *adj.* **1** of or concerning spondees. **2** (of a hexameter) having a spondee as a fifth foot. [F *spondaïque* or LL *spondaicus* = LL *spondiacus* f. Gk *spondeiakos* (as SPONDEE)]

spondee /spóndee/ *n.* *Prosody* a foot consisting of two long (or stressed) syllables. [ME f. OF *spondee* or L *spondeus* f. Gk *spondeios* (*pous* foot) f. *spondē* libation, as being characteristic of music accompanying libations]

spondulicks /spondyṓōliks/ *n.pl. sl.* money. [19th c.: orig. unkn.]

■ see MONEY 1.

spondylitis /spóndilī́tiss/ *n.* inflammation of the vertebrae. [L *spondylus* vertebra f. Gk *spondulos* + -ITIS]

sponge /spunj/ *n.* & *v.* ● *n.* **1** any aquatic animal of the phylum Porifera, with pores in its body wall and a rigid internal skeleton. **2 a** the skeleton of a sponge, esp. the soft light elastic absorbent kind used in bathing, cleansing surfaces, etc. **b** a piece of porous rubber or plastic etc. used similarly. **3** a thing of spongelike absorbency or consistency, e.g. a sponge pudding, cake, porous metal, etc. (*lemon sponge*). **4** = SPONGER. **5** *colloq.* a person who drinks heavily. **6** cleansing with or as with a sponge (*had a quick sponge this morning*). ● *v.* **1** *tr.* wipe or cleanse with a sponge. **2** *tr.* (also *absol.*; often foll. by *down*, *over*) sluice water over (the body, a car, etc.). **3** *tr.* (often foll. by *out*, *away*, etc.) wipe off or efface (writing, a memory, etc.) with or as with a sponge. **4** *tr.* (often foll. by *up*) absorb with or as with a sponge. **5** *intr.* (often foll. by *on*, *off*) live as a parasite; be meanly dependent upon (another person). **6** *tr.* obtain (drink etc.) by sponging. **7** *intr.* gather sponges. **8** *tr.* apply paint with a sponge to (walls, furniture, etc.). □ **sponge bag** a waterproof bag for toilet articles. **sponge cake** a very light cake with a spongelike consistency. **sponge cloth 1** soft, lightly-woven cloth with a slightly wrinkled surface. **2** a thin spongy material used for cleaning. **sponge pudding** *Brit.* a steamed or baked pudding of fat, flour, and eggs with a usu. specified flavour. **sponge rubber** liquid rubber latex processed into a spongelike substance. **sponge tree** a spiny tropical acacia, *Acacia farnesiana*, with globose heads of fragrant yellow flowers yielding a perfume: also called OPOPANAX. □□ **spongeable** *adj.* **spongelike** *adj.* **spongiform** *adj.* (esp. in senses 1, 2). [OE f. L *spongia* f. Gk *spoggia*, *spoggos*]

■ *n.* **5** see DRUNK *n.* 1. ● *v.* **1, 2** see CLEAN *v.* 1. **3** see ERASE. **4** (*sponge up*) see SOAK *v.* 3a. **5** (*sponge off*) *US. sl.* bum off. **6** see BUM[2] *v.* 2. □□ **spongelike** see POROUS 1, 2.

sponger /spúnjər/ *n.* a person who contrives to live at another's expense.

■ see PARASITE.

spongy /spúnji/ *adj.* (**spongier**, **spongiest**) **1** like a sponge, esp. in being porous, compressible, elastic, or absorbent. **2** (of metal) finely divided and loosely coherent. □□ **spongily** *adv.* **sponginess** *n.*

■ **1** see POROUS 1, 2, SOFT *adj.* 1.

sponsion /spónsh'n/ *n.* **1** being a surety for another. **2** a pledge or promise made on behalf of the State by an agent not authorized to do so. [L *sponsio* f. *spondēre spons-* promise solemnly]

sponson /spóns'n/ *n.* **1** a projection from the side of a warship or tank to enable a gun to be trained forward and aft. **2** a short subsidiary wing to stabilize a seaplane. **3** a triangular platform supporting the wheel on a paddle-steamer. [19th c.: orig. unkn.]

sponsor /spónsər/ *n.* & *v.* ● *n.* **1** a person who supports an activity done for charity by pledging money in advance. **2 a** a person or organization that promotes or supports an artistic or sporting activity etc. **b** esp. *US* a business organization that promotes a broadcast programme in return for advertising time. **3** an organization lending support to an election candidate. **4** a person who introduces a proposal for legislation. **5** a godparent at baptism or esp. *RC Ch.* a person who presents a candidate for confirmation. **6** a person who makes himself or herself responsible for another. ● *v.tr.* be a sponsor for. □□ **sponsorial** /sponsóriəl/ *adj.* **sponsorship** *n.* [L (as SPONSION)]

■ *n.* **1, 2a, 3** backer, supporter, promoter, patron, Maecenas, benefactor, subsidizer, *sl.* angel. **2 b** (radio *or* television) advertiser. ● *v.* back, support, promote, fund, patronize, subsidize, finance, underwrite. □□ **sponsorship** see BACKING 1a, b.

spontaneous /spontáyniəss/ *adj.* **1** acting or done or occurring without external cause. **2** voluntary, without external incitement (*made a spontaneous offer of his services*). **3** *Biol.* (of structural changes in plants and muscular activity esp. in young animals) instinctive, automatic, prompted by no motive. **4** (of bodily movement, literary style, etc.) gracefully natural and unconstrained. **5** (of sudden movement etc.) involuntary, not due to conscious volition. **6** growing naturally without cultivation. □ **spontaneous combustion** the ignition of a mineral or vegetable substance (e.g. a heap of rags soaked with oil, a mass of wet coal) from heat engendered within itself, usu. by rapid oxidation. **spontaneous generation** the supposed production of living from non-living matter as inferred from the appearance of life (due in fact to bacteria etc.) in some infusions; abiogenesis. **spontaneous suggestion** suggestion from association of ideas without conscious volition. □□ **spontaneity** /spóntəneé-iti, -náyiti/ *n.* **spontaneously** *adv.* **spontaneousness** *n.* [LL *spontaneus* f. *sponte* of one's own accord]

■ **2** see VOLUNTARY *adj.* 1. **4** unconstrained, unforced, natural, unstudied, unaffected. **5** involuntary, instinctive, instinctual, unconscious, reflex, automatic, mechanical, immediate, offhand, unguarded, unthinking, unwitting, impetuous, impulsive, knee-jerk. □□ **spontaneously** see *automatically* (AUTOMATIC), *voluntarily* (VOLUNTARY).

spoof /spōōf/ *n.* & *v.* *colloq.* ● *n.* **1** a parody. **2** a hoax or swindle. ● *v.tr.* **1** parody. **2** hoax, swindle. □□ **spoofer** *n.* **spoofery** *n.* [invented by A. Roberts, English comedian d. 1933]

■ *n.* **1** see PARODY *n.* 1. ● *v.* **1** see PARODY *v.*

spook /spōōk/ *n.* & *v.* ● *n.* **1** *colloq.* a ghost. **2** *US sl.* a spy. ● *v. US sl.* **1** *tr.* frighten, unnerve, alarm. **2** *intr.* take fright, become alarmed. [Du., = MLG *spōk*, of unkn. orig.]

■ *n.* **1** see GHOST *n.* 1. **2** see AGENT 1b. ● *v.* **1** see SCARE *v.* 1. **2** scare, frighten, *US sl.* spook.

spooky /spṓōki/ *adj.* (**spookier**, **spookiest**) **1** *colloq.* ghostly, eerie. **2** *US sl.* nervous; easily frightened. **3** *US sl.* of spies or espionage. □□ **spookily** *adv.* **spookiness** *n.*

■ **1** see GHOSTLY. **2** see JUMPY 1.

spool /spōōl/ *n.* & *v.* ● *n.* **1 a** a reel for winding magnetic tape, photographic film, etc., on. **b** a reel for winding yarn or *US* thread on. **c** a quantity of tape, yarn, etc., wound on a spool. **2** the revolving cylinder of an angler's reel. ● *v.tr.* wind on a spool. [ME f. OF *espole* or f. MLG *spōle*, MDu. *spoele*, OHG *spuolo*, of unkn. orig.]

■ *n.* **1 c** see ROLL *n.* 5a, TAPE *n.* 4b. ● *v.* reel, wind.

spoon /spo͞on/ *n.* & *v.* ● *n.* **1 a** a utensil consisting of an oval or round bowl and a handle for conveying food (esp. liquid) to the mouth, for stirring, etc. **b** a spoonful, esp. of sugar. **c** (in *pl.*) *Mus.* a pair of spoons held in the hand and beaten together rhythmically. **2** a spoon-shaped thing, esp.: **a** (in full **spoon-bait**) a bright revolving piece of metal used as a lure in fishing. **b** an oar with a broad curved blade. **c** a wooden-headed golf club. **3** *colloq.* **a** a silly or demonstratively fond lover. **b** a simpleton. ● *v.* **1** *tr.* (often foll. by *up*, *out*) take (liquid etc.) with a spoon. **2** *tr.* hit (a ball) feebly upwards. **3** *colloq.* **a** *intr.* behave in an amorous way, esp. foolishly. **b** *tr. archaic* woo in a silly or sentimental way. **4** *intr.* fish with a spoon-bait. □ **born with a silver spoon in one's mouth** born in affluence. **spoon-bread** *US* soft maize bread. □□ **spooner** *n.* **spoonful** *n.* (*pl.* **-fuls**). [OE *spōn* chip of wood f. Gmc]

■ *n.* **1 a** see SCOOP *n.* 1b. ● *v.* **1** (*spoon out*) see SCOOP *v.* 1. **3 a** see KISS *v.* 3. □□ **spoonful** see MOUTHFUL 1.

spoonbill /spo͞onbil/ *n.* **1** any large wading bird of the subfamily Plataleidae, having a bill with a very broad flat tip. **2** a shoveller duck.

spoonerism /spo͞onəriz'm/ *n.* a transposition, usu. accidental, of the initial letters etc. of two or more words, e.g. *you have hissed the mystery lectures*. [Revd W. A. *Spooner*, English scholar d. 1930, reputed to make such errors in speaking]

spoonfeed /spo͞onfeed/ *v.tr.* (*past* and *past part.* **-fed**) **1** feed (a baby etc.) with a spoon. **2** provide help, information, etc., to (a person) without requiring any effort on the recipient's part. **3** artificially encourage (an industry) by subsidies or import duties.

■ **2** see SPOIL *v.* 2.

spoony /spo͞oni/ *adj.* & *n. colloq. archaic* ● *adj.* (**spoonier**, **spooniest**) **1** (often foll. by *on*) sentimental, amorous. **2** foolish, silly. ● *n.* (*pl.* **-ies**) a simpleton. □□ **spoonily** *adv.* **spooniness** *n.*

spoor /spoor/ *n.* & *v.* ● *n.* the track or scent of an animal. ● *v.tr.* & *intr.* follow by the spoor. □□ **spoorer** *n.* [Afrik. f. MDu. *spo(o)r* f. Gmc]

■ *n.* see TRACK[1] *n.* 1. ● *v.* see TRACK *v.* 1.

sporadic /spəráddik/ *adj.* occurring only here and there or occasionally, separate, scattered. □□ **sporadically** *adv.* [med.L *sporadicus* f. Gk *sporadikos* f. *sporas -ados* scattered: cf. *speirō* to sow]

■ occasional, intermittent, random, casual, odd, irregular, patchy, spotty, scattered, uneven, erratic, chance, unexpected; spasmodic(al), fitful, periodic(al); separate. □□ **sporadically** see *occasionally* (OCCASIONAL).

sporangium /spəránjiəm/ *n.* (*pl.* **sporangia** /-jiə/) *Bot.* a receptacle in which spores are found. □□ **sporangial** *adj.* [mod.L f. Gk *spora* SPORE + *aggeion* vessel]

spore /spor/ *n.* **1** a specialized reproductive cell of many plants and micro-organisms. **2** these collectively. [mod.L *spora* f. Gk *spora* sowing, seed f. *speirō* sow]

■ **1** see SEED *n.* 1a.

sporo- /spórō/ *comb. form Biol.* a spore. [Gk *spora* (as SPORE)]

sporogenesis /spórəjénnisiss/ *n.* the process of spore formation.

sporogenous /spərójinəss/ *adj.* producing spores.

sporophyte /spórəfīt/ *n.* a spore-producing form of plant with alternating sexual and asexual generations. □□ **sporophytic** /-fittik/ *adj.* **sporophytically** /-fittikəli/ *adv.*

sporran /spórrən/ *n.* a pouch, usu. of leather or sealskin covered with fur etc., worn by a Highlander in front of the kilt. [Gael. *sporan* f. med.L *bursa* PURSE]

sport /sport/ *n.* & *v.* ● *n.* **1 a** a game or competitive activity, esp. an outdoor one involving physical exertion, e.g. cricket, football, racing, hunting. **b** such activities collectively (*the world of sport*). **2** (in *pl.*) *Brit.* **a** a meeting for competing in sports, esp. athletics (*school sports*). **b** athletics. **3** amusement, diversion, fun. **4** *colloq.* **a** a fair or generous person. **b** a person behaving in a specified way, esp. regarding games, rules, etc. (*a bad sport at tennis*). **c** *Austral.* a form of address, esp. between males. **d** *US* a playboy. **5** *Biol.* an animal or plant deviating suddenly or strikingly from the normal type. **6** a plaything or butt (*was the sport of Fortune*). ● *v.* **1** *intr.* **a** divert oneself, take part in a pastime. **b** frolic, gambol. **2** *tr.* wear, exhibit, or produce, esp. ostentatiously (*sported a gold tie-pin*). **3** *intr. Biol.* become or produce a sport. □ **have good sport** be successful in shooting, fishing, etc. **in sport** jestingly. **make sport of** make fun of, ridicule. **the sport of kings** horse-racing (less often war, hunting, or surfing). **sports car** an open, low-built fast car. **sports coat** (or **jacket**) a man's jacket for informal wear. **sports writer** a person who writes (esp. as a journalist) on sports. □□ **sporter** *n.* [ME f. DISPORT]

■ *n.* **1 a** game, activity, pastime, recreation. **b** games, recreation, play. **3** recreation, diversion, amusement, entertainment, play, distraction, relaxation, divertissement, pleasure, enjoyment, fun, dalliance. **4 a, b** sportsman, sportswoman. ● *v.* **1** amuse oneself, divert oneself; frolic, gambol, romp, caper, play, frisk, rollick, skip about, *colloq.* lark, *literary* wanton, *sl.* cavort. **2** show off, exhibit, flaunt, display, wear, parade, flourish. □ **in sport** in jest, jestingly, jokingly, in fun, teasingly, playfully. **make sport of** make fun of, tease, deride, make a laughing-stock of, (hold up to) ridicule, make a fool of, *sl.* take the mickey out of.

sporting /spórting/ *adj.* **1** interested in sport (*a sporting man*). **2** sportsmanlike, generous (*a sporting offer*). **3** concerned in sport (*a sporting dog*; *sporting news*). □ **a sporting chance** some possibility of success. **sporting house** *US* a brothel. □□ **sportingly** *adv.*

■ **2** see LAVISH *adj.* 2. □ **sporting house** see BROTHEL.

sportive /spórtiv/ *adj.* playful. □□ **sportively** *adv.* **sportiveness** *n.*

■ frisky, gambolling, frolicking, romping, capering, rollicking, sprightly, coltish, skittish, spirited, frolicsome, buoyant, gamesome, gay, kittenish, merry, playful, gleeful, light-hearted, mischievous, puckish, impish, prankish, waggish, *poet.* blithe, *sl.* cavorting.

sportscast /spórtskaast/ *n. US* a broadcast of a sports event or information about sport. □□ **sportscaster** *n.*

sportsman /spórtsmən/ *n.* (*pl.* **-men**; *fem.* **sportswoman**, *pl.* **-women**) **1** a person who takes part in much sport, esp. professionally. **2** a person who behaves fairly and generously. □□ **sportsmanlike** *adj.* **sportsmanly** *adj.* **sportsmanship** *n.*

■ **1** see PLAYER 1a. **2** *colloq.* sport. □□ **sportsmanship** fair play, fairness, honourableness, honesty, honour, probity, scrupulousness, integrity, uprightness, justice, justness.

sportswear /spórtswair/ *n.* clothes worn for sport or for casual outdoor use.

sporty /spórti/ *adj.* (**sportier**, **sportiest**) *colloq.* **1** fond of sport. **2** rakish, showy. □□ **sportily** *adv.* **sportiness** *n.*

■ **2** informal, casual; stylish, chic, smart, fashionable, modish, à la mode, up to date, showy, rakish, swanky, loud, flashy, *colloq.* classy, sharp, swell, *esp. US colloq.* swank, *colloq. often derog.* trendy, *sl.* snazzy, *esp. US sl.* spiffy.

sporule /spórōol/ *n.* a small spore or a single spore. □□ **sporular** *adj.* [F *sporule* or mod.L *sporula* (as SPORE)]

spot /spot/ *n.* & *v.* ● *n.* **1 a** a small part of the surface of a thing distinguished by colour, texture, etc., usu. round or less elongated than a streak or stripe (*a blue tie with pink spots*). **b** a small mark or stain. **c** a pimple. **d** a small circle or other shape used in various numbers to distinguish faces of dice, playing-cards in a suit, etc. **e** a moral blemish or stain (*without a spot on his reputation*). **2 a** a particular place; a definite locality (*dropped it on this precise spot*; *the spot where William III landed*). **b** a place used for a particular activity (often in *comb.*: *nightspot*). **c** (prec. by *the*) *Football* the place from which a penalty kick is taken. **3** a particular part of one's body or aspect of one's character. **4 a** *colloq.* one's esp. regular position in an organization, programme of events, etc. **b** a place or position in a performance or show (*did the spot before the interval*). **5** *Brit.* **a** *colloq.* a small quantity of anything (*a spot of lunch*; *a spot of trouble*). **b** a drop (*a spot of rain*). **c** *colloq.* a drink. **6** = SPOTLIGHT. **7** *colloq.* an awkward or difficult situation (esp. in *in a* (*tight* etc.) *spot*). **8** (usu. *attrib.*) money paid or goods delivered immediately after a sale (*spot cash*; *spot silver*). **9** *Billiards* etc. **a** a small round black patch to mark the position where a ball is placed at certain times. **b** (in full **spot-ball**) the white ball distinguished from the other by two black spots. ● *v.* (**spotted, spotting**) **1** *tr.* **a** *colloq.* single out beforehand (the winner of a race etc.). **b** *colloq.* recognize the identity, nationality, etc., of (*spotted him at once as the murderer*). **c** watch for and take note of (trains, talent, etc.). **d** *colloq.* catch sight of. **e** *Mil.* locate (an enemy's position), esp. from the air. **2 a** *tr.* & *intr.* mark or become marked with spots. **b** *tr.* stain, soil (a person's character etc.). **3** *intr.* make spots, rain slightly (*it was spotting with rain*). **4** *tr.* *Billiards* place (a ball) on a spot. □ **on the spot 1** at the scene of an action or event. **2** *colloq.* in a position such that response or action is required. **3** without delay or change of place, then and there. **4** (of a person) wide awake, equal to the situation, in good form at a game etc. **put on the spot** *US sl.* decide to murder. **running on the spot** raising the feet alternately as in running but without moving forwards or backwards. **spot check** a test made on the spot or on a randomly-selected subject. **spot height 1** the altitude of a point. **2** a figure on a map showing this. **spot on** *Brit. colloq. adj.* precise; on target. ● *adv.* precisely. **spot weld** a weld made in spot welding. **spot-weld** *v.tr.* join by spot welding. **spot welder** a person or device that spot-welds. **spot welding** welding two surfaces together in a series of discrete points. [ME, perh. f. MDu. *spotte*, LG *spot*, ON *spotti* small piece]

■ *n.* **1 a, b** mark, patch, dot, speck, blot, blotch, blemish, speckle, fleck, particle, mote, macula, smudge, stain, stigma, discoloration, splotch. **c** eruption, pimple, pustule, blackhead, whitehead; boil, blain, wen; pock-mark; *Med.* comedo, *colloq.* splodge, *esp. US sl.* zit; (*spots*) acne. **d** pip. **e** stain, blemish, blot (on the escutcheon); see also STIGMA 1. **2 a, b** site, place, locale, location, position, locality, scene, setting, section, area, neighbourhood, quarter. **4** see SLOT[1] *n.* 3. **5 a** bit, bite, morsel, *colloq.* smidgen; see also MODICUM. **b** drop, blob, bead. **7** predicament, tricky *or* difficult situation, quandary, mess, trouble, straits, *colloq.* pickle, jam, fix. ● *v.* **1** identify, pick out, distinguish, single out, detect, locate, recognize, discern, see, catch sight of, sight, glimpse, make out, *literary* descry. **2** mark, stain, fleck, speckle, spray, splash, spatter, bespatter, soil, dirty, taint, besmirch, smudge, *poet.* sully. □ **on the spot 3** see *on the nail* (NAIL). **spot on** (*adj.*) see ACCURATE. (*adv.*) precisely, exactly; *Brit. colloq.* bang on, *US sl.* on the nose.

spotless /spótliss/ *adj.* immaculate; absolutely clean or pure. □□ **spotlessly** *adv.* **spotlessness** *n.*

■ immaculate, clean, gleaming, shiny, polished, unspotted, spick and span; pure, unsullied, flawless, faultless, impeccable, untarnished, unassailable, blameless, irreproachable.

spotlight /spótlīt/ *n.* & *v.* ● *n.* **1** a beam of light directed on a small area, esp. on a particular part of a theatre stage or of the road in front of a vehicle. **2** a lamp projecting this. **3** full attention or publicity. ● *v.tr.* (*past* and *past part.* **-lighted** or **-lit**) **1** direct a spotlight on. **2** make conspicuous, draw attention to.

■ *n.* **1, 2** arc light, searchlight, spot. **3** focus (of attention), limelight, public eye. ● *v.* light (up), illuminate, focus light upon *or* on, shine light upon *or* on, shed light upon *or* on, throw light upon *or* on, cast light upon *or* on; emphasize, highlight, make conspicuous, draw attention to, focus upon *or* on, feature, give prominence to, stress, accentuate, accent, point up, underscore, underline.

spotted /spóttid/ *adj.* marked or decorated with spots. □ **spotted dick** (or **dog**) **1** *Brit.* a suet pudding containing currants. **2** a Dalmatian dog. **spotted fever 1** cerebrospinal meningitis. **2** typhus. □□ **spottedness** *n.*

■ see SPOTTY 1.

spotter /spóttər/ *n.* **1** (often in *comb.*) a person who spots people or things (*train-spotter*). **2** an aviator or aircraft employed in locating enemy positions etc.

spotty /spótti/ *adj.* (**spottier, spottiest**) **1** marked with spots. **2** patchy, irregular. □□ **spottily** *adv.* **spottiness** *n.*

■ **1** spotted, dotted, speckled, freckled, flecked, blotched, blotchy, stained, marked, pied, piebald, brindle(d), skewbald, mottled, motley, dapple(d), macular, foxed; soiled, dirty; *colloq.* splodgy, splodged, splotchy, splotched; pimply, pimpled, acned, pock-marked, pocky, bad. **2** patchy, uneven, erratic, sporadic, capricious, fitful; see also IRREGULAR 4.

spouse /spowz, spowss/ *n.* a husband or wife. [ME *spūs(e)* f. OF *sp(o)us* (masc.), *sp(o)use* (fem.), vars. of *espous(e)* f. L *sponsus sponsa* past part. of *spondēre* betroth]

■ see MATE[1] *n.* 3b.

spout /spowt/ *n.* & *v.* ● *n.* **1 a** a projecting tube or lip through which a liquid etc. is poured from a teapot, kettle, jug, etc., or issues from a fountain, pump, etc. **b** a sloping trough down which a thing may be shot into a receptacle. **c** *hist.* a lift serving a pawnbroker's storeroom. **2** a jet or column of liquid, grain, etc. **3** (in full **spout-hole**) a whale's blow-hole. ● *v.tr.* & *intr.* **1** discharge or issue forcibly in a jet. **2** utter (verses etc.) or speak in a declamatory manner, speechify. □ **up the spout** *sl.* **1** useless, ruined, hopeless. **2** pawned. **3** pregnant. □□ **spouter** *n.* **spoutless** *adj.* [ME f. MDu. *spouten*, orig. imit.]

■ *n.* **1 a** waterspout, lip, gargoyle, duct, drain, outlet, conduit, *Brit.* downpipe, *US* downspout. **2** see GUSH *n.* 1. ● *v.* **1** discharge, squirt, spurt, spit, shoot, gush, pour (out *or* forth), spew (up *or* out *or* forth), disgorge; emit, eject, vomit (up *or* forth); flow, issue, stream, jet, erupt. **2** ramble on, rant, rave, carry on, pontificate, declaim, hold forth, maunder (on), expatiate, talk, *colloq.* go on, witter on, *Brit. colloq.* rabbit on, *esp. joc. or derog.* orate, *joc. or derog.* speechify. □ **up the spout 1** gone, lost, destroyed, ruined, hopeless, useless, beyond hope *or* recovery, to be written off *or* abandoned, *colloq.* down the drain. **2** *esp. US colloq.* hocked, in hock. **3** see PREGNANT 1.

SPQR *abbr.* **1** *hist.* the Senate and people of Rome. **2** small profits and quick returns. [sense 1 f. L *Senatus Populusque Romanus*]

Spr. *abbr.* (in the UK) Sapper.

sprag /sprag/ *n.* **1** a thick piece of wood or similar device used as a brake. **2** a support-prop in a coal mine. [19th c.: orig. unkn.]

sprain /sprayn/ *v.* & *n.* ● *v.tr.* wrench (an ankle, wrist, etc.) violently so as to cause pain and swelling but not dislocation. ● *n.* **1** such a wrench. **2** the resulting inflammation and swelling. [17th c.: orig. unkn.]

■ *v.* see WRENCH *v.* 1b. ● *n.* **1** see STRAIN[1] *n.* 2.

sprang *past* of SPRING.

sprat /sprat/ *n.* & *v.* ● *n.* **1** a small European herring-like fish, *Sprattus sprattus*, much used as food. **2** a similar fish, e.g. a sand eel or a young herring. ● *v.intr.* (**spratted, spratting**) fish for sprats. □ **a sprat to catch a mackerel** a small risk to gain much. □□ **spratter** *n.* **spratting** *n.* [OE *sprot*]

sprauncy /spráwnsi/ *adj.* (**sprauncier, sprauncier**) *Brit. sl.* smart or showy. [20th c.: perh. rel. to dial. *sprouncey* cheerful]

sprawl /sprawl/ *v.* & *n.* ● *v.* **1 a** *intr.* sit or lie or fall with limbs flung out or in an ungainly way. **b** *tr.* spread (one's limbs) in this way. **2** *intr.* (of handwriting, a plant, a town, etc.) be of irregular or straggling form. ● *n.* **1** a sprawling movement or attitude. **2** a straggling group or mass. **3** the straggling expansion of an urban or industrial area. ▫▫ **sprawlingly** *adv.* [OE *spreawlian*]

■ *v.* **1 a** spread out, stretch out, loll, lounge, slouch, slump, recline, lie about *or* around. **2** spread (out), stretch (out), ramble, meander, wander, straggle, branch out. ● *n.* **3** spread, stretch, expansion, extension.

spray[1] /spray/ *n.* & *v.* ● *n.* **1** water or other liquid flying in small drops from the force of the wind, the dashing of waves, or the action of an atomizer etc. **2** a liquid preparation to be applied in this form with an atomizer etc., esp. for medical purposes. **3** an instrument or apparatus for such application. ● *v.tr.* (also *absol.*) **1** throw (liquid) in the form of spray. **2** sprinkle (an object) with small drops or particles, esp. (a plant) with an insecticide. **3** (*absol.*) (of a tom-cat) mark its environment with the smell of its urine, as an attraction to females. ▫ **spray-dry** (**-dries**, **-dried**) dry (milk etc.) by spraying into hot air etc. **spray-gun** a gunlike device for spraying paint etc. **spray-paint** paint (a surface) by means of a spray. ▫▫ **sprayable** *adj.* **sprayer** *n.* [earlier *spry*, perh. rel. to MDu. *spra(e)yen*, MHG *spræjen* sprinkle]

■ *n.* **1** shower, sprinkling, drizzle, mist, sprinkle, spindrift. **3** atomizer, sprayer, sprinkler, vaporizer, aerosol, spray-gun. ● *v.* **1** sprinkle, shower, spatter, scatter, disperse, diffuse, spread. **2** sprinkle, shower, spatter, besprinkle; see also WATER *v.* 1. ▫▫ **sprayer** see SPRAY[1] *n.* 3 above.

spray[2] /spray/ *n.* **1** a sprig of flowers or leaves, or a branch of a tree with branchlets or flowers, esp. a slender or graceful one. **2** an ornament in a similar form (*a spray of diamonds*). ▫▫ **sprayey** /spráyi/ *adj.* [ME f. OE *spræg* (unrecorded)]

■ **1** flower *or* floral arrangement, nosegay, posy, bouquet, sprig; branch, bough.

spread /spred/ *v.* & *n.* ● *v.* (*past* and *past part.* **spread**) **1** *tr.* (often foll. by *out*) **a** open or extend the surface of. **b** cause to cover a larger surface (*spread butter on bread*). **c** display to the eye or the mind (*the view was spread out before us*). **2** *intr.* (often foll. by *out*) have a wide or specified or increasing extent (*on every side spread a vast desert*; *spreading trees*). **3** *intr.* & *tr.* become or make widely known, felt, etc. (*rumours are spreading*; *spread a little happiness*). **4** *tr.* **a** cover the surface of (*spread the wall with paint*; *a meadow spread with daisies*). **b** lay (a table). ● *n.* **1** the act or an instance of spreading. **2** capability of expanding (*has a large spread*). **3** diffusion (*spread of learning*). **4** breadth, compass (*arches of equal spread*). **5** an aircraft's wing-span. **6** increased bodily girth (*middle-aged spread*). **7** the difference between two rates, prices, etc. **8** *colloq.* an elaborate meal. **9** a sweet or savoury paste for spreading on bread etc. **10** a bedspread. **11** printed matter spread across two facing pages or across more than one column. **12** *US* a ranch with extensive land. ▫ **spread eagle 1** a representation of an eagle with legs and wings extended as an emblem. **2** *hist.* a person secured with arms and legs spread out, esp. to be flogged. **spread-eagle** *v.tr.* (usu. as **spread-eagled** *adj.*) **1** place (a person) in this position. **2** defeat utterly. **3** spread out. ● *adj.* *US* bombastic, esp. noisily patriotic. **spread oneself** be lavish or discursive. **spread one's wings** see WING. ▫▫ **spreadable** *adj.* **spreader** *n.* [OE *-sprǣdan* f. WG]

■ *v.* **1 a** unfold, draw out, display, stretch out, open out, extend, lay out, fan out, unroll, unfurl. **b** smear, apply, smooth, put, rub, cover, layer, plaster, paint; diffuse, distribute, disperse, disseminate, broadcast, sow, scatter, strew. **c** lay out, unfurl, unfold. **2** grow, develop, increase, broaden, expand, extend, widen, enlarge, mushroom, proliferate, sprawl, branch out, *Physiol.* metastasize. **3** spread about *or* around, broadcast, publicize, make known, bruit about, air, televise, circulate, publish, distribute, disseminate, trumpet, announce, pronounce, promulgate, advertise, make public, tell the world, repeat, recite. **4 a** cover, smear, rub, plaster, plate, layer, coat, suffuse, wash, glaze, paint, varnish, overlay, overspread; strew; cloak, mantle, swaddle, swathe, wrap, blanket. **b** set, lay, arrange. ● *n.* **1** extension, expansion, enlargement, development, increase, proliferation, broadening, growth, widening, mushrooming, dispersion, dispersal, dissemination, distribution, dispensation. **3** see CIRCULATION 2a. **4** extent, expanse, area, span, sweep, vastness, stretch, reach, breadth, depth, size, dimensions, compass, scope, limits, bounds, boundary, boundaries. **7** range, extent, scope, span, difference. **8** feast, banquet, meal, dinner, barbecue, *formal* repast; table; *colloq.* feed. **9** butter, margarine, jam, jelly, preserve, conserve, paste, pâté, *US* oleomargarine. **10** bedspread, counterpane, coverlet, bed-cover, cover, quilt, eiderdown, duvet, afghan, *US* comforter, throw. **12** ranch, landholding, holding, property, place, plantation, farm, homestead, *Austral.* & *NZ* station. ▫ **spread-eagled 1, 3** see FLAT[1] *adv.* 1.

spreadsheet /sprédsheet/ *n.* a computer program allowing manipulation and flexible retrieval of esp. tabulated numerical data.

Sprechgesang /shprékhgəzaang/ *n.* *Mus.* a style of dramatic vocalization between speech and song. [G, lit. 'speech song']

spree /spree/ *n.* & *v.* *colloq.* ● *n.* **1** a lively extravagant outing (*shopping spree*). **2** a bout of fun or drinking etc. ● *v.intr.* (**sprees**, **spreed**) have a spree. ▫ **on the spree** engaged in a spree. [19th c.: orig. unkn.]

■ *n.* **1** outing, trip, jaunt, fling, blow-out, *colloq.* splurge. **2** frolic, romp, escapade, revel, wild party, fling, debauch, orgy, bacchanal, bacchanalia, saturnalia, *Austral.* jamberoo, *colloq.* lark, *Austral. colloq.* jollo; drinking-bout, carousal, carouse, blow-out, *sl.* bender, binge, jag, tear. ● *v.* see REVEL *v.* 1.

sprig[1] /sprig/ *n.* & *v.* ● *n.* **1** a small branch or shoot. **2** an ornament resembling this, esp. on fabric. **3** usu. *derog.* a youth or young man (*a sprig of the nobility*). ● *v.tr.* (**sprigged**, **sprigging**) **1** ornament with sprigs (*a dress of sprigged muslin*). **2** (usu. as **sprigging** *n.*) decorate (ceramic ware) with ornaments in applied relief. ▫▫ **spriggy** *adj.* [ME f. or rel. to LG *sprick*]

■ *n.* **1** see TWIG[1].

sprig[2] /sprig/ *n.* a small tapering headless tack. [ME: orig. unkn.]

sprightly /sprítli/ *adj.* (**sprightlier**, **sprightliest**) vivacious, lively, brisk. ▫▫ **sprightliness** *n.* [*spright* var. of SPRITE + -LY[1]]

■ lively, spry, vivacious, cheerful, gay, brisk, animated, sportive, active, alert, nimble, agile, energetic, vigorous, jaunty, perky, playful, spirited, *esp. US colloq.* chipper. ▫▫ **sprightliness** see LIFE 8.

spring /spring/ *v.* & *n.* ● *v.* (*past* **sprang** /sprang/ or *US* **sprung** /sprung/; *past part.* **sprung**) **1** *intr.* jump; move rapidly or suddenly (*sprang from his seat*; *sprang through the gap*; *sprang to their assistance*). **2** *intr.* move rapidly as from a constrained position or by the action of a spring (*the branch sprang back*; *the door sprang to*). **3** *intr.* (usu. foll. by *from*) originate or arise (*springs from an old family*; *their actions spring from a false conviction*). **4** *intr.* (usu. foll. by *up*) come into being; appear, esp. suddenly (*a breeze sprang up*; *the belief has sprung up*). **5** *tr.* cause to act suddenly, esp. by means of a spring (*spring a trap*). **6** *tr.* (often foll. by *on*) produce or develop or make known suddenly or unexpectedly (*has sprung a new theory*; *loves to spring surprises*). **7** *tr. sl.* contrive the escape or release of. **8** *tr.* rouse (game) from earth or covert. **9 a** *intr.* become warped or split. **b** *tr.* split, crack (wood or a wooden implement). **10** *tr.* (usu. as **sprung** *adj.*) provide (a motor vehicle etc.) with springs. **11 a** *tr. colloq.* spend (money). **b** *intr.* (usu. foll. by *for*) *US* & *Austral. sl.* pay for a treat. **12** *tr.* cause (a mine) to explode. ● *n.* **1** a jump (*took a spring*; *rose with a spring*). **2** a backward movement from a constrained position; a recoil, e.g. of a bow. **3** elasticity; ability to spring back strongly (*a mattress with plenty of spring*). **4** a resilient device usu. of bent or coiled metal used esp. to drive clockwork or for cushioning in furniture or vehicles. **5 a** the season in which vegetation begins to appear, the first season of the year, in the N. hemisphere from March to May and in the S. hemisphere from September to November. **b** *Astron.* the period from the vernal equinox to the summer solstice. **c** (often foll. by *of*) the early stage of life etc. **d** = *spring tide*. **6** a place where water, oil, etc., wells up from the earth; the basin or flow so formed (*hot springs*; *mineral springs*). **7** the motive for or origin of an action, custom, etc. (*the springs of human action*). **8** *sl.* an escape or release from prison. **9** the upward curve of a beam etc. from a horizontal line. **10** the splitting or yielding of a plank etc. under strain. □ **spring balance** a balance that measures weight by the tension of a spring. **spring bed** a bed with a spring mattress. **spring chicken 1** a young fowl for eating (orig. available only in spring). **2** (esp. with *neg.*) a young person (*she's no spring chicken*). **spring-clean** *n.* a thorough cleaning of a house or room, esp. in spring. ● *v.tr.* clean (a house or room) in this way. **spring fever** a restless or lethargic feeling sometimes associated with spring. **spring greens** the leaves of young cabbage plants. **spring a leak** develop a leak (orig. *Naut.*, from timbers springing out of position). **spring-loaded** containing a compressed or stretched spring pressing one part against another. **spring mattress** a mattress containing or consisting of springs. **spring onion** an onion taken from the ground before the bulb has formed, and eaten raw in salad. **spring roll** a Chinese snack consisting of a pancake filled with vegetables etc. and fried. **spring tide** a tide just after new and full moon when there is the greatest difference between high and low water. **spring water** water from a spring, as opposed to river or rain water. **sprung rhythm** a poetic metre approximating to speech, each foot having one stressed syllable followed by a varying number of unstressed. □□ **springless** *adj.* **springlet** *n.* **springlike** *adj.* [OE *springan* f. Gmc]

■ *v.* **1** leap, bound, jump, hop, vault, dart, fly, bounce, start. **3** originate, begin, start, arise, evolve; proceed, stem, issue, descend, derive, come, develop. **4** arise, appear, grow, develop, come up, rise, come into being *or* existence, be born, emerge, sprout, shoot up, burst forth, start up. **6** produce suddenly *or* unexpectedly, develop suddenly *or* unexpectedly, broach, pop, introduce suddenly *or* unexpectedly, divulge suddenly *or* unexpectedly, reveal suddenly *or* unexpectedly, disclose suddenly *or* unexpectedly. **11 b** (*spring for*) pay for, foot the bill for, treat a person to, *Austral.* & *NZ colloq.* shout a person to. ● *n.* **1** leap, bound, jump, hop, vault, bounce, skip. **3** bounciness, bounce, resiliency, resilience, springiness, buoyancy, elasticity, give, sprightliness, airiness, flexibility. **5 a–c** springtime, Eastertide, Maytime, *poet.* springtide; (*attrib.*) vernal. **6** source, fountain, fountain-head, well-spring, well, spa, geyser, origin, beginning, root, *poet.* fount. □□ **springlike** see SOFT *adj.* 3.

springboard /springbord/ *n.* **1** a springy board giving impetus in leaping, diving, etc. **2** a source of impetus in any activity. **3** *US* & *Austral.* a platform inserted in the side of a tree, on which a lumberjack stands to chop at some height from the ground.

springbok /springbok/ *n.* **1** a southern African gazelle, *Antidorcas marsupialis*, with the ability to run with high springing jumps. **2** (**Springbok**) a South African, esp. one who has played for South Africa in international sporting competitions. [Afrik. f. Du. *springen* SPRING + *bok* antelope]

springe /sprinj/ *n.* a noose or snare for catching small game. [ME, rel. to obs. *sprenge*, and SPRING]

■ see SNARE *n.* 1.

springer /springər/ *n.* **1** a person or thing that springs. **2 a** a small spaniel of a breed used to spring game. **b** this breed. **3** *Archit.* **a** the part of an arch where the curve begins. **b** the lowest stone of this. **c** the bottom stone of the coping of a gable. **d** a rib of a groined roof or vault. **4** a springbok.

springtail /springtayl/ *n.* any wingless insect of the order Collembola, leaping by means of a springlike caudal part.

springtide /springtīd/ *n. poet.* = SPRINGTIME.

springtime /springtīm/ *n.* **1** the season of spring. **2** a time compared to this.

■ **1** see SPRING *n.* 5a–c. **2** see PRIME[1] *n.* 1.

springy /springi/ *adj.* (**springier, springiest**) **1** springing back quickly when squeezed or stretched, elastic. **2** (of movements) as of a springy substance. □□ **springily** *adv.* **springiness** *n.*

■ see ELASTIC *adj.* 1, 2. □□ **springiness** see *elasticity* (ELASTIC).

sprinkle /springk'l/ *v.* & *n.* ● *v.tr.* **1** scatter (liquid, ashes, crumbs, etc.) in small drops or particles. **2** (often foll. by *with*) subject (the ground or an object) to sprinkling with liquid etc. **3** (of liquid etc.) fall on in this way. **4** distribute in small amounts. ● *n.* (usu. foll. by *of*) **1** a light shower. **2** = SPRINKLING. [ME, perh. f. MDu. *sprenkelen*]

■ *v.* **1, 4** see SCATTER *v.* 1a. ● *n.* **1** see SHOWER *n.* 1.

sprinkler /springklər/ *n.* a person or thing that sprinkles, esp. a device for sprinkling water on a lawn or to extinguish fires.

■ see SPRAY[1] *n.* 3.

sprinkling /springkling/ *n.* (usu. foll. by *of*) a small thinly distributed number or amount.

■ see HANDFUL 2.

sprint /sprint/ *v.* & *n.* ● *v.* **1** *intr.* run a short distance at full speed. **2** *tr.* run (a specified distance) in this way. ● *n.* **1** such a run. **2** a similar short spell of maximum effort in cycling, swimming, motor racing, etc. □□ **sprinter** *n.* [ON *sprinta* (unrecorded), of unkn. orig.]

■ *v.* **1** see RUN *v.* 1, 3. **2** see RUN *v.* 15. ● *n.* **1** see RUN *n.* 1. □□ **sprinter** see RUNNER 1.

sprit /sprit/ *n.* a small spar reaching diagonally from the mast to the upper outer corner of the sail. [OE *sprēot* pole, rel. to SPROUT]

sprite /sprīt/ *n.* an elf, fairy, or goblin. [ME f. *sprit* var. of SPIRIT]

■ see IMP *n.* 2.

spritsail /sprits'l, -sayl/ *n.* **1** a sail extended by a sprit. **2** *hist.* a sail extended by a yard set under the bowsprit.

spritz /sprits/ *v.* & *n.* *US* ● *v.tr.* sprinkle, squirt, or spray. ● *n.* the act or an instance of spritzing. [G *spritzen* to squirt]

spritzer /spritsər/ *n.* a mixture of wine and soda water. [G *Spritzer* a splash]

sprocket /sprokkit/ *n.* **1** each of several teeth on a wheel engaging with links of a chain, e.g. on a bicycle, or with holes in film or tape or paper. **2** (also **sprocket-wheel**) a wheel with sprockets. [16th c.: orig. unkn.]

■ **1** cog, tooth, gear-tooth.

sprog /sprog/ *n. sl.* a child; a baby. [orig. services' sl., = new recruit: perh. f. obs. *sprag* lively young man]

■ see CHILD 1b.

sprout /sprowt/ *v.* & *n.* ● *v.* **1** *tr.* put forth, produce (shoots, hair, etc.) (*has sprouted a moustache*). **2** *intr.* begin to grow, put forth shoots. **3** *intr.* spring up, grow to a height. ● *n.* **1** a shoot of a plant. **2** = BRUSSELS SPROUT. [OE *sprūtan* (unrecorded) f. WG]

■ *v.* **1** grow, put forth. **2** bud, germinate, come up, arise, begin, *literary* burgeon. **3** spring up, shoot up, grow, develop. ● *n.* **1** see SHOOT *n.*

spruce[1] /sproōss/ *adj.* & *v.* ● *adj.* neat in dress and appearance; trim, smart. ● *v.tr.* & *intr.* (also *refl.*; usu. foll. by *up*) make or become smart. □□ **sprucely** *adv.* **spruceness** *n.* [perh. f. SPRUCE[2] in obs. sense 'Prussian', in the collocation *spruce (leather) jerkin*]

■ *adj.* neat, dapper, smart, trim, tidy, well turned out, well-groomed, elegant, *colloq.* natty. ● *v.* tidy (up), neaten (up), primp, preen, clean (up), straighten out *or* up, smarten (up), *colloq.* titivate.

spruce[2] /sproōss/ *n.* **1** any coniferous tree of the genus *Picea*, with dense foliage growing in a distinctive conical shape. **2**

the wood of this tree used as timber. □ **spruce beer** a fermented beverage using spruce twigs and needles as flavouring. [alt. of obs. *Pruce* Prussia: cf. PRUSSIAN]

spruce[3] /sprōōss/ *v. Brit. sl.* **1** *tr.* deceive. **2** *intr.* lie, practise deception. **3** *intr.* evade a duty, malinger. □□ **sprucer** *n.* [20th c.: orig. unkn.]

sprue[1] /sprōō/ *n.* **1** a channel through which metal or plastic is poured into a mould. **2** a piece of metal or plastic which has filled a sprue and solidified there. [19th c.: orig. unkn.]

sprue[2] /sprōō/ *n.* a tropical disease with ulceration of the mucous membrane of the mouth and chronic enteritis. [Du. *spruw* THRUSH[2]; cf. Flem. *spruwen* sprinkle]

spruik /sprōōk/ *v.intr. Austral. & NZ sl.* speak in public, esp. as a showman. □□ **spruiker** *n.* [20th c.: orig. unkn.]

spruit /sprayt/ *n. S.Afr.* a small watercourse, usu. dry except during the rainy season. [Du., rel. to SPROUT]

sprung see SPRING.

spry /sprī/ *adj.* (**spryer, spryest**) active, lively. □□ **spryly** *adv.* **spryness** *n.* [18th c., dial. & US: orig. unkn.]
■ see LIVELY 1.

spud /spud/ *n.* & *v.* ● *n.* **1** *sl.* a potato. **2** a small narrow spade for cutting the roots of weeds etc. ● *v.tr.* (**spudded, spudding**) **1** (foll. by *up, out*) remove (weeds) with a spud. **2** (also *absol.*; often foll. by *in*) make the initial drilling for (an oil well). □ **spud-bashing** *Brit. sl.* a lengthy spell of peeling potatoes. [ME: orig. unkn.]

spue var. of SPEW.

spumante /spoománti/ *n.* an Italian sparkling white wine (cf. ASTI). [It., = 'sparkling']

spume /spyōōm/ *n.* & *v.intr.* froth, foam. □□ **spumous** *adj.* **spumy** *adj.* (**spumier, spumiest**). [ME f. OF (*e*)*spume* or L *spuma*]
■ *n.* see FROTH *n.* 1a. ● *v.* see FROTH *v.* 1.

spumoni /spoomṓni/ *n. US* a kind of ice-cream dessert. [It. *spumone* f. *spuma* SPUME]

spun *past* and *past part.* of SPIN.

spunk /spungk/ *n.* **1** touchwood. **2** *colloq.* courage, mettle, spirit. **3** *coarse sl.* semen. ¶ Usually considered a taboo use. [16th c.: orig. unkn.: cf. PUNK]
■ **2** nerve, courage, pluck, spirit, gameness, resolve, resolution, mettle, heart, grit, backbone, marrow, *colloq.* guts, gumption, *US colloq.* sand, *Brit. sl.* bottle.

spunky /spúngki/ *adj.* (**spunkier, spunkiest**) *colloq.* brave, spirited. □□ **spunkily** *adv.*
■ see SPIRITED.

spur /spur/ *n.* & *v.* ● *n.* **1** a device with a small spike or a spiked wheel worn on a rider's heel for urging a horse forward. **2** a stimulus or incentive. **3** a spur-shaped thing, esp.: **a** a projection from a mountain or mountain range. **b** a branch road or railway. **c** a hard projection on a cock's leg. **d** a steel point fastened to the leg of a gamecock. **e** a climbing-iron. **f** a small support for ceramic ware in a kiln. **4** *Bot.* **a** a slender hollow projection from part of a flower. **b** a short fruit-bearing shoot. ● *v.* (**spurred, spurring**) **1** *tr.* prick (a horse) with spurs. **2** *tr.* **a** (often foll. by *on*) incite (a person) (*spurred him on to greater efforts; spurred her to try again*). **b** stimulate (interest etc.). **3** *intr.* (often foll. by *on, forward*) ride a horse hard. **4** *tr.* (esp. as **spurred** *adj.*) provide (a person, boots, a gamecock) with spurs. □ **on the spur of the moment** on a momentary impulse; impromptu. **put** (or **set**) **spurs to 1** spur (a horse). **2** stimulate (resolution etc.). **spur-gear** = *spur-wheel.* **spur-of-the-moment** *adj.* unpremeditated; impromptu. **spur royal** *hist.* a 15-shilling coin of James I bearing a spurlike sun with rays. **spur-wheel** a cog-wheel with radial teeth. □□ **spurless** *adj.* [OE *spora, spura* f. Gmc, rel. to SPURN]
■ *n.* **2** goad, prod, impulse, impetus, incitement, instigation, pressure, stimulus, stimulation, incentive, provocation, inducement, enticement, encouragement, motive, motivation. **3** projection, prong, spike, spine, gaff, barb, quill, tine, barbel, barbule, *Anat.*, *Zool.*, & *Bot.* process. ● *v.* **2** goad, prod, urge, egg on, impel, incite, prompt, press, push, pressure, pressurize, drive, motivate; stimulate, provoke, induce, encourage, excite, animate, inspire. □ **on the spur of the moment** impetuously, impulsively, unthinkingly, unpremeditatedly, impromptu, offhand, on the spot; rashly, thoughtlessly, recklessly, hastily, brashly, incautiously, unexpectedly, suddenly.

spurge /spurj/ *n.* any plant of the genus *Euphorbia*, exuding an acrid milky juice once used medicinally as a purgative. □ **spurge laurel** any shrub of the genus *Daphne*, esp. *D. laureola*, with small yellow flowers. [ME f. OF *espurge* f. *espurgier* f. L *expurgare* (as EX-[1], PURGE)]

spurious /spyóoriəss/ *adj.* **1** not genuine, not being what it purports to be, not proceeding from the pretended source (*a spurious excuse*). **2** having an outward similarity of form or function only. **3** (of offspring) illegitimate. □□ **spuriously** *adv.* **spuriousness** *n.* [L *spurius* false]
■ **1** false, counterfeit, sham, fake, fraudulent, bogus, mock, imitation, simulated, unauthentic, ungenuine, forged, feigned, pretended, deceitful, meretricious, contrived, factitious, artificial, ersatz, synthetic, pseudo, *colloq.* phoney. □□ **spuriousness** see *falsity* (FALSE).

spurn /spurn/ *v.* & *n.* ● *v.* **1** reject with disdain; treat with contempt. **2** repel or thrust back with one's foot. ● *n.* an act of spurning. □□ **spurner** *n.* [OE *spurnan, spornan*, rel. to SPUR]
■ *v.* **1** reject, disdain, scorn, despise, rebuff, repudiate, refuse, sneer at, snub, cold-shoulder, brush off, turn down, turn one's back on *or* upon, look down on *or* upon, *colloq.* turn up one's nose at, *literary* contemn.

spurrier /spúrriər/ *n.* a spur-maker.

spurry /spúrri/ *n.* (also **spurrey**) (*pl.* **-ies** or **-eys**) a slender plant of the genus *Spergula*, esp. the corn-spurry, a white-flowered weed in cornfields etc. [Du. *spurrie*, prob. rel. to med.L *spergula*]

spurt /spurt/ *v.* & *n.* ● *v.* **1** (also **spirt**) **a** *intr.* gush out in a jet or stream. **b** *tr.* cause (liquid etc.) to do this. **2** *intr.* make a sudden effort. ● *n.* **1** (also **spirt**) a sudden gushing out, a jet. **2** a short sudden effort or increase of pace esp. in racing. [16th c.: orig. unkn.]
■ *v.* **1 a** gush, spew, squirt, shoot, spout, stream, spray, jet, erupt, burst, surge. **b** spew, squirt, shoot, spout, stream, spray. ● *n.* **1** see GUSH *n.* 1. **2** burst, access, effort, outbreak; increase, advance, acceleration, rise, improvement; see also DASH *n.* 1.

sputnik /spóotnik, spút-/ *n.* each of a series of Russian artificial satellites launched from 1957. [Russ., = fellow-traveller]
■ satellite, spaceship, spacecraft, rocket.

sputter /spúttər/ *v.* & *n.* ● *v.* **1** *intr.* emit spitting sounds, esp. when being heated. **2** *intr.* (often foll. by *at*) speak in a hurried or vehement fashion. **3** *tr.* emit with a spitting sound. **4** *tr.* speak or utter (words, threats, a language, etc.) rapidly or incoherently. **5** *tr. Physics* deposit (metal) by using fast ions etc. to eject particles of it from a target. ● *n.* a sputtering sound, esp. sputtering speech. □□ **sputterer** *n.* [Du. *sputteren* (imit.)]
■ *v.* **1, 3** see SPIT[1] *v.* 2b, 3.

sputum /spyóotəm/ *n.* (*pl.* **sputa** /-tə/) **1** saliva, spittle. **2** a mixture of saliva and mucus expectorated from the respiratory tract, usu. a sign of disease. [L, neut. past part. of *spuere* spit]
■ **1** see SPIT[1] *n.*

spy /spī/ *n.* & *v.* ● *n.* (*pl.* **spies**) **1** a person who secretly collects and reports information on the activities, movements, etc., of an enemy, competitor, etc. **2** a person who keeps watch on others, esp. furtively. ● *v.* (**spies, spied**) **1** *tr.* discern or make out, esp. by careful observation (*spied a house in the distance*). **2** *intr.* (often foll. by *on*) act as a spy, keep a close and secret watch. **3** *intr.* (often foll. by *into*) pry. □ **I-spy** a children's game of guessing a visible object from the initial letter of its name. **spy-master** *colloq.* the head of an organization of spies. **spy out** explore or discover, esp. secretly. □□ **spying** *n.* [ME f. OF *espie* espying, *espier* espy f. Gmc]

■ *n.* double agent, foreign agent, secret(-service) agent, intelligence agent, undercover agent, fifth-columnist, CIA man *or* woman *or* agent, MI5 man *or* woman *or* agent, MI6 man *or* woman *or* agent; informer, informant, stool-pigeon, *colloq.* mole, snoop, snooper, fink, *esp. US sl.* ratfink, *US sl.* stoolie. ● *v.* **1** glimpse, spot, catch sight of, sight, catch a glimpse of, make out, note, notice, see, discern, *literary* espy, descry. **2** (*spy on*) follow, shadow, trail, watch, observe, reconnoitre, keep under surveillance, *US* check out, *colloq.* tail, *sl.* case. **3** see SNOOP *v.* □□ **spying** espionage, undercover work, intelligence, surveillance.

spyglass /spīglaass/ *n.* a small telescope.

■ see TELESCOPE *n.*

spyhole /spīhōl/ *n.* a peep-hole.

sq. *abbr.* square.

Sqn. Ldr. *abbr.* Squadron Leader.

squab /skwob/ *n.* & *adj.* ● *n.* **1** a short fat person. **2** a young esp. unfledged pigeon or other bird. **3 a** a stuffed cushion. **b** *Brit.* the padded back or side of a car-seat. **4** a sofa or ottoman. ● *adj.* short and fat, squat. □ **squab-chick** an unfledged bird. **squab pie 1** pigeon pie. **2** a pie of mutton, pork, onions, and apples. [17th c.: orig. unkn.: cf. obs. *quab* shapeless thing, Sw. dial. *sqvabba* fat woman]

squabble /skwóbb'l/ *n.* & *v.* ● *n.* a petty or noisy quarrel. ● *v.intr.* engage in a squabble. □□ **squabbler** *n.* [prob. imit.: cf. Sw. dial. *sqvabbel* a dispute]

■ *n.* see QUARREL *n.* 1. ● *v.* see QUARREL *v.* 2.

squabby /skwóbbi/ *adj.* (**squabbier**, **squabbiest**) short and fat; squat.

squad /skwod/ *n.* **1** a small group of people sharing a task etc. **2** *Mil.* a small number of men assembled for drill etc. **3** *Sport* a group of players forming a team. **4 a** (often in *comb.*) a specialized unit within a police force (*drug squad*). **b** = *flying squad.* **5** a group or class of people of a specified kind (*the awkward squad*). □ **squad car** a police car having a radio link with headquarters. [F *escouade* var. of *escadre* f. It. *squadra* SQUARE]

■ unit, team, band, company, crew, force, troop, cohort, corps, detail, detachment, cadre, squadron, platoon, party, gang, section, group.

squaddie /skwóddi/ *n.* (also **squaddy**) (*pl.* **-ies**) *Brit. Mil. sl.* **1** a recruit. **2** a private.

■ see SOLDIER *n.*

squadron /skwódrən/ *n.* **1** an organized body of persons. **2** a principal division of a cavalry regiment or armoured formation, consisting of two troops. **3** a detachment of warships employed on a particular duty. **4** a unit of the Royal Air Force with 10 to 18 aircraft. □ **Squadron Leader** the commander of a squadron of the Royal Air Force, the officer next below Wing Commander. [It. *squadrone* (as SQUAD)]

■ see SQUAD.

squail /skwayl/ *n.* **1** (in *pl.*) a game with small wooden discs propelled across a table or board. **2** each of these discs. □ **squail-board** a board used in squails. [19th c.: orig. unkn.: cf. dial. *kayles* skittles]

squalid /skwóllid/ *adj.* **1** filthy, repulsively dirty. **2** mean or poor in appearance. **3** wretched, sordid. □□ **squalidity** *n.* /-lídditi/ **squalidly** *adv.* **squalidness** *n.* [L *squalidus* f. *squalēre* be rough or dirty]

■ **1** see FILTHY *adj.* 1. **2, 3** see MEAN[2] 3, 4, SORDID 1.

squall /skwawl/ *n.* & *v.* ● *n.* **1** a sudden or violent gust or storm of wind, esp. with rain or snow or sleet. **2** a discordant cry; a scream (esp. of a baby). **3** (esp. in *pl.*) trouble, difficulty. ● *v.* **1** *intr.* utter a squall; scream, cry out violently as in fear or pain. **2** *tr.* utter in a screaming or discordant voice. □□ **squally** *adj.* [prob. f. SQUEAL after BAWL]

■ *n.* **1** see TEMPEST 1. **2** see SHRIEK *n.* ● *v.* see SHRIEK *v.* □□ **squally** see INCLEMENT.

squalor /skwóllər/ *n.* the state of being filthy or squalid. [L, as SQUALID]

■ see MISERY 1, IMPURITY 1.

squama /skwáymə/ *n.* (*pl.* **squamae** /-mee/) **1** a scale on an animal or plant. **2** a thin scalelike plate of bone. **3** a scalelike feather. □□ **squamate** /-mayt/ *adj.* **squamose** *adj.* **squamous** *adj.* **squamule** *n.* [L *squama*]

■ **1, 3** scale, flake, feather, tuft, flock. □□ **squamose, squamous** see SCALY.

squander /skwóndər/ *v.tr.* **1** spend (money, time, etc.) wastefully. **2** dissipate (a fortune etc.) wastefully. □□ **squanderer** *n.* [16th c.: orig. unkn.]

■ see WASTE *v.* 1. □□ **squanderer** see PROFLIGATE *n.*

square /skwair/ *n.*, *adj.*, *adv.*, & *v.* ● *n.* **1** an equilateral rectangle. **2 a** an object of this shape or approximately this shape. **b** a small square area on a game-board. **c** a square scarf. **d** an academic cap with a stiff square top; a mortarboard. **3 a** an open (usu. four-sided) area surrounded by buildings, esp. one planted with trees etc. and surrounded by houses. **b** an open area at the meeting of streets. **c** *Cricket* a closer-cut area at the centre of a ground, any strip of which may be prepared as a wicket. **d** an area within barracks etc. for drill. **e** *US* a block of buildings bounded by four streets. **4** the product of a number multiplied by itself (*81 is the square of 9*). **5** an L-shaped or T-shaped instrument for obtaining or testing right angles. **6** *sl.* a conventional or old-fashioned person, one ignorant of or opposed to current trends. **7** a square arrangement of letters, figures, etc. **8** a body of infantry drawn up in rectangular form. **9** a unit of 100 sq. ft. as a measure of flooring etc. **10** *US* a square meal (*three squares a day*). ● *adj.* **1** having the shape of a square. **2** having or in the form of a right angle (*table with square corners*). **3** angular and not round; of square section (*has a square jaw*). **4** designating a unit of measure equal to the area of a square whose side is one of the unit specified (*square metre*). **5** (often foll. by *with*) **a** level, parallel. **b** on a proper footing; even, quits. **6 a** (usu. foll. by *to*) at right angles. **b** *Cricket* on a line through the stumps at right angles to the wicket. **7** having the breadth more nearly equal to the length or height than is usual (*a man of square frame*). **8** properly arranged; in good order, settled (*get things square*). **9** (also **all square**) **a** not in debt, with no money owed. **b** having equal scores, esp. *Golf* having won the same number of holes as one's opponent. **c** (of scores) equal. **10** fair and honest (*his dealings are not always quite square*). **11** uncompromising, direct, thorough (*was met with a square refusal*). **12** *sl.* conventional or old-fashioned, unsophisticated, conservative (cf. sense 6 of *n.*). **13** *Mus.* (of rhythm) simple, straightforward. ● *adv.* **1** squarely (*sat square on his seat*). **2** fairly, honestly (*play square*). ● *v.* **1** *tr.* make square or rectangular, give a rectangular cross-section to (timber etc.). **2** *tr.* multiply (a number) by itself (*3 squared is 9*). **3** *tr.* & *intr.* (usu. foll. by *to*, *with*) adjust; make or be suitable or consistent; reconcile (*the results do not square with your conclusions*). **4** *tr.* mark out in squares. **5** *tr.* settle or pay (a bill etc.). **6** *tr.* place (one's shoulders etc.) squarely facing forwards. **7** *tr. colloq.* **a** pay or bribe. **b** secure the acquiescence etc. of (a person) in this way. **8** *tr.* (also *absol.*) make the scores of (a match etc.) all square. **9** *intr.* assume the attitude of a boxer. **10** *tr. Naut.* **a** lay (yards) at right angles with the keel making them at the same time horizontal. **b** get (dead-eyes) horizontal. **c** get (ratlines) horizontal and parallel to one another. □ **back to square one** *colloq.* back to the starting-point with no progress made. **get square with** pay or compound with (a creditor). **on the square** *adj.* **1** *colloq.* honest, fair. **2** having membership of the Freemasons. ● *adv. colloq.* honestly, fairly (*can be trusted to act on the square*). **out of square** not at right angles. **perfect square** = *square number.* **square accounts with** see ACCOUNT. **square away** *US* tidy up. **square-bashing** *Brit. Mil. sl.* drill on a barrack-square.

square brackets brackets of the form []. **square-built** of comparatively broad shape. **square the circle 1** construct a square equal in area to a given circle (a problem incapable of a purely geometrical solution). **2** do what is impossible. **square dance** a dance with usu. four couples facing inwards from four sides. **square deal** a fair bargain, fair treatment. **squared paper** paper marked out in squares, esp. for plotting graphs. **square-eyed** *joc.* affected by or given to excessive viewing of television. **square leg** *Cricket* **1** the fielding position at some distance on the batsman's leg side and nearly opposite the stumps. **2** a fielder in this position. **square meal** a substantial and satisfying meal. **square measure** measure expressed in square units. **square number** the square of an integer e.g. 1, 4, 9, 16. **square off 1** *US* assume the attitude of a boxer. **2** *Austral.* placate or conciliate. **3** mark out in squares. **square peg in a round hole** see PEG. **square piano** an early type of piano, small and oblong in shape. **square-rigged** with the principal sails at right angles to the length of the ship and extended by horizontal yards slung to the mast by the middle (opp. *fore-and-aft rigged*). **square root** the number that multiplied by itself gives a specified number (*3 is the square root of 9*). **square sail** a four-cornered sail extended on a yard slung to the mast by the middle. **square-shouldered** with broad and not sloping shoulders (cf. *round-shouldered*). **square-toed 1** (of shoes or boots) having square toes. **2** wearing such shoes or boots. **3** formal, prim. **square up** settle an account etc. **square up to 1** move towards (a person) in a fighting attitude. **2** face and tackle (a difficulty etc.) resolutely. **square wave** *Physics* a wave with periodic sudden alternations between only two values of quantity. □□ **squarely** *adv.* **squareness** *n.* **squarer** *n.* **squarish** *adj.* [ME f. OF *esquare, esquarré, esquarrer*, ult. f. EX-[1] + L *quadra* square]

▪ *n.* **3 a** plaza, piazza, place, park, (village) green, market-place, market (square), quadrangle. **d** parade-ground, parade, ground. **6** conservative, conformist, traditionalist, bourgeois, (old) fogy, die-hard; *colloq.* straight, stuffed shirt, stick-in-the-mud, *sl.* fuddy-duddy, *esp. US sl.* nerd, *US sl.* dweeb. ● *adj.* **1** equilateral, quadrangular, rectangular, quadrilateral, four-sided, boxy. **2** right-angled. **5** equal, on a par, even, level, parallel; on equal *or* even terms, quits, settled, balanced. **8** straight, straightened out, settled, in order, organized, arranged. **9 b, c** equal, even, level, drawn, tied, neck and neck, *Brit.* level pegging. **10** honourable, upright, honest, straightforward, fair (and square), decent, ethical, open, (open and) above-board, right, (right and) proper, clean, just, equitable, *colloq.* on the level, *esp. US colloq.* on the up and up. **12** conservative, conventional, unsophisticated, provincial, old-fashioned, behind the times, conformist, strait-laced, bourgeois, unimaginative, predictable, stuffy, *colloq.* antediluvian, not with it, not in the know, straight, *US colloq.* uptight, *sl.* not hip *or* hep, unhip. ● *adv.* **1** see FULL[1] *adv.* 3. **2** see HONESTLY 1. ● *v.* **3** adapt, adjust, change, modify, harmonize, accommodate, arrange, fit; (*square with*) meet, match (with), conform to *or* with, comply with, obey, correspond to *or* with, tally with, line up with, make *or* be consistent with, accord with, agree with, reconcile with *or* to. **5** see SETTLE[1] 9. **6** stiffen, throw back, straighten (up), tense. **7** see BRIBE *v.* □ **square off 2** see CALM *v.* □□ **squarely** see FULL[1] *adv.* 3.

squarrose /skwórrōss/ *adj. Bot.* & *Zool.* rough with scalelike projections. [L *squarrosus* scurfy, scabby]

squash[1] /skwosh/ *v.* & *n.* ● *v.* **1** *tr.* crush or squeeze flat or into pulp. **2** *intr.* (often foll. by *into*) make one's way by squeezing. **3** *tr.* pack tight, crowd. **4** *tr.* **a** silence (a person) with a crushing retort etc. **b** dismiss (a proposal etc.). **c** quash (a rebellion). ● *n.* **1** a crowd; a crowded assembly. **2** a sound of or as of something being squashed, or of a soft body falling. **3** *Brit.* a concentrated drink made of crushed fruit etc., diluted with water. **4** (in full **squash rackets**) a game played with rackets and a small fairly soft ball against the walls of a closed court. **5** a squashed thing or mass. □ **squash tennis** *US* a game similar to squash, played with a lawn-tennis ball. □□ **squashy** *adj.* (**squashier, squashiest**). **squashily** *adv.* **squashiness** *n.* [alt. of QUASH]

▪ *v.* **1** see SQUEEZE *v.* 1. **3** see SQUEEZE *v.* 3a, b. **4 c** see WHIP *v.* 5b. ● *n.* **1** see SQUEEZE *n.* 3. □□ **squashy** see *mushy* (MUSH[1]).

squash[2] /skwosh/ *n.* (*pl.* same or **squashes**) **1** any of various trailing plants of the genus *Cucurbita*, esp. *C. maxima*, *C. moschata*, and *C. melopepo*, having pumpkin-like fruits. **2** the fruit of these cooked and eaten as a vegetable. [obs. *(i)squoutersquash* f. Narragansett *asquutasquash* f. *asq* uncooked + *squash* green]

squat /skwot/ *v.*, *adj.*, & *n.* ● *v.* (**squatted, squatting**) **1** *intr.* **a** crouch with the hams resting on the backs of the heels. **b** sit on the ground etc. with the knees drawn up and the heels close to or touching the hams. **2** *tr.* put (a person) into a squatting position. **3** *intr. colloq.* sit down. **4 a** *intr.* act as a squatter. **b** *tr.* occupy (a building) as a squatter. **5** *intr.* (of an animal) crouch close to the ground. ● *adj.* (**squatter, squattest**) **1** (of a person etc.) short and thick, dumpy. **2** in a squatting posture. ● *n.* **1** a squatting posture. **2 a** a place occupied by a squatter or squatters. **b** being a squatter. □□ **squatly** *adv.* **squatness** *n.* [ME f. OF *esquatir* flatten f. *es-* EX-[1] + *quatir* press down, crouch ult. f. L *coactus* past part. of *cogere* compel: see COGENT]

▪ *v.* **1, 5** see CROUCH *v.* ● *adj.* **1** see DUMPY. ● *n.* **1** crouch, stoop, hunch.

squatter /skwóttər/ *n.* **1** a person who takes unauthorized possession of unoccupied premises. **2** *Austral.* **a** a sheep-farmer esp. on a large scale. **b** *hist.* a person who gets the right of pasturage from the government on easy terms. **3** a person who settles on new esp. public land without title. **4** a person who squats.

▪ **1, 3** see INTRUDER.

squaw /skwaw/ *n.* a N. American Indian woman or wife. □ **squaw-man** a White married to a squaw. **squaw winter** (in N. America) a brief wintry spell before an Indian Summer. [Narragansett *squaws*, Massachusetts *squaw* woman]

squawk /skwawk/ *n.* & *v.* ● *n.* **1** a loud harsh cry esp. of a bird. **2** a complaint. ● *v.tr.* & *intr.* utter with or make a squawk. □ **squawk-box** *colloq.* a loudspeaker or intercom. □□ **squawker** *n.* [imit.]

▪ *n.* **1** screech, shriek, yell, yowl, whoop, hoot, scream, call, cry, wail, squall, cackle. **2** complaint, grumble, whine, protest, objection, *colloq.* gripe, grouse, grouch, whinge, *sl.* beef. ● *v.* screech, shriek, yell, yowl, whoop, hoot, scream, call, cry, wail, squall, cackle; complain, grumble, whine, protest, object, kick, (make a) fuss, kick up (a fuss), *colloq.* bitch, gripe, grouse, grouch, whinge, yap, *sl.* bellyache, beef.

squeak /skweek/ *n.* & *v.* ● *n.* **1 a** a short shrill cry as of a mouse. **b** a slight high-pitched sound as of an unoiled hinge. **2** (also **narrow squeak**) a narrow escape, a success barely attained. ● *v.* **1** *intr.* make a squeak. **2** *tr.* utter (words) shrilly. **3** *intr.* (foll. by *by*, *through*) *colloq.* pass narrowly. **4** *intr. sl.* turn informer. [ME, imit.: cf. SQUEAL, SHRIEK, and Sw. *skväka* croak]

▪ *n.* **1 a** see PEEP[2] *n.* 1. **2** see *near miss*. ● *v.* **1, 2** see PEEP[2] *v.*, SING *v.* 1, 2. **3** (*squeak by, through*) see SCRAPE *v.* 8b. **4** see INFORM 2.

squeaker /skweékər/ *n.* **1** a person or thing that squeaks. **2** a young bird, esp. a pigeon.

▪ **1** see GRASS *n.* 6.

squeaky /skweéki/ *adj.* (**squeakier, squeakiest**) making a squeaking sound. □ **squeaky clean 1** completely clean. **2** above criticism; beyond reproach. □□ **squeakily** *adv.* **squeakiness** *n.*

▪ see HIGH *adj.* 9.

squeal /skweel/ *n.* & *v.* ● *n.* a prolonged shrill sound, esp. a cry of a child or a pig. ● *v.* **1** *intr.* make a squeal. **2** *tr.* utter (words) with a squeal. **3** *intr. sl.* turn informer. **4** *intr. sl.* protest loudly or excitedly. □□ **squealer** *n.* [ME, imit.]

■ *n.* see SHRIEK *n.* ● *v.* **1, 2** see SHRIEK *v.* **3** see INFORM 2. □□ **squealer** see INFORMER 1.

squeamish /skwéemish/ *adj.* **1** easily nauseated or disgusted. **2** fastidious or overscrupulous in questions of propriety, honesty, etc. □□ **squeamishly** *adv.* **squeamishness** *n.* [ME var. of *squeamous* (now dial.), f. AF *escoymos*, of unkn. orig.]

■ **1** qualmish, queasy, easily disgusted *or* revolted *or* nauseated. **2** dainty, delicate, prudish, qualmish, punctilious, demanding, critical, exacting, difficult, fussy, overscrupulous, scrupulous, fastidious, meticulous, painstaking, finicky, finical, *colloq.* pernickety, *sl.* fuddy-duddy. □□ **squeamishness** see *prudery* (PRUDE).

squeegee /skwéejee/ *n.* & *v.* ● *n.* **1** a rubber-edged implement set on a long handle and used for cleaning windows, etc. **2** a small similar instrument or roller used in photography. ● *v.tr.* (**squeegees, squeegeed**) treat with a squeegee. [*squeege*, strengthened form of SQUEEZE]

squeeze /skweez/ *v.* & *n.* ● *v.* **1** *tr.* **a** exert pressure on from opposite or all sides, esp. in order to extract moisture or reduce size. **b** compress with one's hand or between two bodies. **c** reduce the size of or alter the shape of by squeezing. **2** *tr.* (often foll. by *out*) extract (moisture) by squeezing. **3 a** *tr.* force (a person or thing) into or through a small or narrow space. **b** *intr.* make one's way by squeezing. **c** *tr.* make (one's way) by squeezing. **4** *tr.* **a** harass by exactions; extort money etc. from. **b** constrain; bring pressure to bear on. **c** (usu. foll. by *out of*) obtain (money etc.) by extortion, entreaty, etc. **d** *Bridge* subject (a player) to a squeeze. **5** *tr.* press or hold closely as a sign of sympathy, affection, etc. **6** *tr.* (often foll. by *out*) produce with effort (*squeezed out a tear*). ● *n.* **1** an instance of squeezing; the state of being squeezed. **2 a** *Brit.* a close embrace. **b** esp. *US sl.* a man's close female friend, esp. a girlfriend. **3** a crowd or crowded state; a crush. **4** a small quantity produced by squeezing (*a squeeze of lemon*). **5** a sum of money extorted or exacted, esp. an illicit commission. **6** *Econ.* a restriction on borrowing, investment, etc., in a financial crisis. **7** an impression of a coin etc. taken by pressing damp paper, wax, etc., against it. **8** (in full **squeeze play**) **a** *Bridge* leading winning cards until an opponent is forced to discard an important card. **b** *Baseball* hitting a ball short to the infield to enable a runner on third base to start for home as soon as the ball is pitched. **9** *colloq.* a difficult situation, an emergency. □ **put the squeeze on** *colloq.* coerce or pressure (a person). **squeeze bottle** a flexible container whose contents are extracted by squeezing it. **squeeze-box** *sl.* an accordion or concertina. □□ **squeezable** *adj.* **squeezer** *n.* [earlier *squise*, intensive of obs. *queise*, of unkn. orig.]

■ *v.* **1** press, compress, compact, constrict, crush, squash, wring, pinch, nip, grip, tweak. **2** see EXPRESS[1] 4. **3 a, b** ram, jam, pack, squash, stuff, cram, crowd, force, press, wedge. **c** inch, force, push, drive, thrust, propel; (*squeeze one's way*) see THREAD *v.* 4. **4 a** milk, bleed, screw, *colloq.* lean on, put the screws on, put the squeeze on, twist a person's arm, *Austral. sl.* put the acid on, *US sl.* shake down. **c** extract, wrest, exact, extort, screw, wrench, tear, *US* pry. **5** clasp, clench, hold, clutch, grip, clip; embrace, hug, enfold, *poet.* fold. ● *n.* **1** pinch, nip, tweak, grip. **2 a** clasp, embrace, hug, clutch, grasp, grip, *colloq.* clinch. **b** see GIRL 3. **3** crush, jam, crowd, squash, press. **6** pressure, restrictions. **9** see DILEMMA 3, EMERGENCY 1. □ **put the squeeze on** press, bring pressure to bear on, put the screws on, twist a person's arm, coerce, urge, influence, pressurize, pressure.

squelch /skwelch/ *v.* & *n.* ● *v.* **1** *intr.* **a** make a sucking sound as of treading in thick mud. **b** move with a squelching sound. **2** *tr.* **a** disconcert, silence. **b** stamp on, crush flat, put an end to. ● *n.* an instance of squelching. □□ **squelcher** *n.* **squelchy** *adj.* [imit.]

■ *v.* **2 a** suppress, subdue, silence, put down, quell, quash, defeat, overcome, humiliate, disconcert, shoot down, take a person down a peg or two, take the wind out of a person's sails, *colloq.* slap down, settle a person's hash. **b** stamp on, suppress, squash, crush, quash, quell, put an end to.

squib /skwib/ *n.* & *v.* ● *n.* **1** a small firework burning with a hissing sound and usu. with a final explosion. **2** a short satirical composition, a lampoon. ● *v.* (**squibbed, squibbing**) **1** *tr. US Football* kick (the ball) a comparatively short distance on a kick-off; execute (a kick) in this way. **2** *archaic* **a** *intr.* write lampoons. **b** *tr.* lampoon. [16th c.: orig. unkn.: perh. imit.]

■ *n.* **2** see LAMPOON *n.* ● *v.* **2b** see LAMPOON *v.*

squid /skwid/ *n.* & *v.* ● *n.* **1** any of various ten-armed cephalopods, esp. of the genus *Loligo*, used as bait or food. **2** artificial bait for fish imitating a squid in form. ● *v.intr.* (**squidded, squidding**) fish with squid as bait. [17th c.: orig. unkn.]

squidgy /skwíji/ *adj.* (**squidgier, squidgiest**) *colloq.* squashy, soggy. [imit.]

■ see *mushy* (MUSH[1]).

squiffed /skwift/ *adj. sl.* = SQUIFFY.

squiffy /skwíffi/ *adj.* (**squiffier, squiffiest**) esp. *Brit. sl.* slightly drunk. [19th c.: orig. unkn.]

■ see DRUNK *adj.* 1.

squiggle /skwigg'l/ *n.* & *v.* ● *n.* a short curly line, esp. in handwriting or doodling. ● *v.* **1** *tr.* write in a squiggly manner; scrawl. **2** *intr.* wriggle, squirm. □□ **squiggly** *adj.* [imit.]

■ *n.* zigzag, curly *or* wavy *or* squiggly line, doodle, scrawl, scribble. ● *v.* **1** doodle, scrawl, scribble. **2** see WRIGGLE *v.*

squill /skwil/ *n.* **1** any bulbous plant of the genus *Scilla*, esp. *S. autumnalis*. **2** a seashore plant, *Urginea maritima*, having bulbs used in diuretic and purgative preparations. Also called *sea onion*. **3** any crustacean of the genus *Squilla*. [ME f. L *squilla*, *scilla* f. Gk *skilla*]

squinch /skwinch/ *n.* a straight or arched structure across an interior angle of a square tower to carry a superstructure, e.g. a dome. [var. of obs. *scunch*, abbr. of SCUNCHEON]

squint /skwint/ *v.*, *n.*, & *adj.* ● *v.* **1** *intr.* have the eyes turned in different directions, have a squint. **2** *intr.* (often foll. by *at*) look obliquely or with half-closed eyes. **3** *tr.* close (one's eyes) quickly, hold (one's eyes) half-shut. ● *n.* **1** = STRABISMUS. **2** a stealthy or sidelong glance. **3** *colloq.* a glance or look (*had a squint at it*). **4** an oblique opening through the wall of a church affording a view of the altar. **5** a leaning or inclination towards a particular object or aim. ● *adj.* **1** squinting. **2** looking different ways. □ **squint-eyed** **1** squinting. **2** malignant, ill-willed. □□ **squinter** *n.* **squinty** *adj.* [ASQUINT: (adj.) perh. f. *squint-eyed* f. obs. *squint* (adv.) f. ASQUINT]

■ *v.* **2** see PEEP[1] *v.* ● *n.* **2, 3** see PEEP[1] *n.*

squire /skwīr/ *n.* & *v.* ● *n.* **1** a country gentleman, esp. the chief landowner in a country district. **2** *hist.* a knight's attendant. **3** *Brit. colloq.* a jocular form of address to a man. **4** *US* a magistrate or lawyer. **5** *Austral.* a young snapper fish. ● *v.tr.* (of a man) attend upon or escort (a woman). □□ **squiredom** *n.* **squirehood** *n.* **squirelet** *n.* **squireling** *n.* **squirely** *adj.* **squireship** *n.* [ME f. OF *esquier* ESQUIRE]

■ *n.* **1** gentleman, landowner, landholder, landed proprietor, *archaic* esquire. ● *v.* attend upon, escort, accompany, conduct, go with.

squirearch /skwīraark/ *n.* a member of the squirearchy. □□ **squirearchical** /-aárkik'l/ *adj.* (also **squirarchical**). [back-form. f. SQUIREARCHY, after MONARCH]

squirearchy /skwīraarki/ *n.* (also **squirarchy**) (*pl.* **-ies**) landowners collectively, esp. as a class having political or social influence; a class or body of squires. [SQUIRE, after HIERARCHY etc.]

■ see GENTRY 1.

squireen /skwīréen/ *n. Brit.* the owner of a small landed property esp. in Ireland.

squirl /skwurl/ *n. colloq.* a flourish or twirl, esp. in handwriting. [perh. f. SQUIGGLE + TWIRL or WHIRL]

squirm /skwurm/ *v.* & *n.* ● *v.intr.* **1** wriggle, writhe. **2** show or feel embarrassment or discomfiture. ● *n.* a squirming movement. ▫▫ **squirmer** *n.* **squirmy** *adj.* (**squirmier, squirmiest**). [imit., prob. assoc. with WORM]
▪ *v.* **1** wriggle, writhe, twist, flounder, shift, fidget. **2** be (very) embarrassed *or* uncomfortable, agonize, sweat. ● *n.* see WRIGGLE *n.*

squirrel /skwírrəl/ *n.* & *v.* ● *n.* **1** any rodent of the family Sciuridae, e.g. the red squirrel, grey squirrel, etc., often of arboreal habits, with a bushy tail arching over its back, and pointed ears. **2** the fur of this animal. **3** a person who hoards objects, food, etc. ● *v.* (**squirrelled, squirrelling**; *US* **squirreled, squirreling**) **1** *tr.* (often foll. by *away*) hoard (objects, food, time, etc.) (*squirrelled it away in the cupboard*). **2** *intr.* (often foll. by *around*) bustle about. ▫ **squirrel cage 1** a small cage containing a revolving cylinder like a treadmill, on which a captive squirrel may exercise. **2** a form of rotor used in small electric motors, resembling the cylinder of a squirrel cage. **3** a monotonous or repetitive way of life. **squirrel** (or **squirrel-tail**) **grass** a grass, *Hordeum jubatum*, with bushy spikelets. **squirrel-monkey** a small yellow-haired monkey, *Saimiri sciureus*, native to S. America. [ME f. AF *esquirel*, OF *esquireul*, ult. f. L *sciurus* f. Gk *skiouros* f. *skia* shade + *oura* tail]
▪ *v.* **1** (*squirrel away*) see HOARD *v.* 1.

squirrelly /skwírrəli/ *adj.* **1** like a squirrel. **2 a** inclined to bustle about. **b** (of a person) unpredictable, nervous, demented.

squirt /skwurt/ *v.* & *n.* ● *v.* **1** *tr.* eject (liquid or powder) in a jet as from a syringe. **2** *intr.* (of liquid or powder) be discharged in this way. **3** *tr.* splash with liquid or powder ejected by squirting. ● *n.* **1 a** a jet of water etc. **b** a small quantity produced by squirting. **2 a** a syringe. **b** (in full **squirt-gun**) a kind of toy syringe. **3** *colloq.* an insignificant but presumptuous person. ▫▫ **squirter** *n.* [ME, imit.]
▪ *v.* **1** see SPURT *v.* 1b. **2** see SPURT *v.* 1a.

squish /skwish/ *n.* & *v.* ● *n.* a slight squelching sound. ● *v.* **1** *intr.* move with a squish. **2** *tr. colloq.* squash, squeeze. ▫▫ **squishy** *adj.* (**squishier, squishiest**). [imit.]
▪ *v.* **2** see TRAMPLE *v.* 2. ▫▫ **squishy** see *mushy* (MUSH[1]).

squit /skwit/ *n. Brit.* **1** *sl.* a small or insignificant person. **2** *dial.* nonsense. [cf. dial. *squirt* insignificant person, and *squit* to squirt]

squitch /skwich/ *n.* couch grass. [alt. f. QUITCH]

squiz /skwiz/ *n. Austral.* & *NZ sl.* a look or glance. [prob. f. QUIZ[2]]
▪ see GLANCE[1] *n.* 1.

Sr *symb. Chem.* the element strontium.

Sr. *abbr.* **1** Senior. **2** Señor. **3** Signor. **4** *Eccl.* Sister.

sr *abbr.* steradian(s).

SRC *abbr.* (in the UK) Science Research Council.

Sri Lankan /shree lángkən, sri/ *n.* & *adj.* ● *n.* **1** a native or national of Sri Lanka (formerly Ceylon), an island in the Indian Ocean. **2** a person of Sri Lankan descent. ● *adj.* of or relating to Sri Lanka or its people.

SRN *abbr.* (in the UK) State Registered Nurse.

SRO *abbr.* standing room only.

SS *abbr.* **1** Saints. **2** steamship. **3** *hist.* Nazi special police force. [sense 3 f. G *Schutz-Staffel*]

SSAFA *abbr.* (in the UK) Soldiers', Sailors', and Airmen's Families Association.

SSC *abbr.* (in Scotland) Solicitor to the Supreme Court.

SSE *abbr.* south-south-east.

SSP *abbr.* (in the UK) statutory sick pay.

SSRC *abbr.* (in the UK) Social Science Research Council.

SSSI *abbr.* (in the UK) Site of Special Scientific Interest.

SST *abbr.* supersonic transport.

SSW *abbr.* south-south-west.

St *abbr.* **1** Saint. **2** stokes.

St. *abbr.* Street.

st. *abbr.* **1** stone (in weight). **2** *Cricket* stumped by.

-st var. of -EST[2].

Sta. *abbr.* Station.

stab /stab/ *v.* & *n.* ● *v.* (**stabbed, stabbing**) **1** *tr.* pierce or wound with a (usu. short) pointed tool or weapon e.g. a knife or dagger. **2** *intr.* (often foll. by *at*) aim a blow with such a weapon. **3** *intr.* cause a sensation like being stabbed (*stabbing pain*). **4** *tr.* hurt or distress (a person, feelings, conscience, etc.). **5** *intr.* (foll. by *at*) aim a blow at a person's reputation, etc. ● *n.* **1 a** an instance of stabbing. **b** a blow or thrust with a knife etc. **2** a wound made in this way. **3** a sharply painful (physical or mental) sensation; a blow inflicted on a person's feelings. **4** *colloq.* an attempt, a try. ▫ **stab in the back** *n.* a treacherous or slanderous attack. ● *v.tr.* slander or betray. ▫▫ **stabber** *n.* [ME: cf. dial. *stob* in sense 1 of *v.*]
▪ *v.* **1** stick, puncture, prick, lance, jab, pierce, run through, impale, gore, transfix, knife, bayonet, skewer, spike, spit, spear, pin. **2** lunge, poke, thrust. **3** see SMART *v.* ● *n.* **1, 2** thrust, jab; prick, puncture, (stab-)wound. **3** pang, twinge, sting, pain, ache, hurt, stitch. **4** attempt, try, *formal* essay; guess, conjecture; *colloq.* crack, go, shot. ▫ **stab in the back** (*n.*) treachery, betrayal, double-cross, kiss of death, duplicity. (*v.*) harm, sell out, double-cross, play false with; see also DISPARAGE 2, BETRAY 2.

Stabat Mater /staábat maátər/ *n.* **1** a Latin hymn on the suffering of the Virgin Mary at the Crucifixion. **2** a musical setting for this. [the opening words, L *Stabat mater dolorosa* 'Stood the mother, full of grief']

stabile /stáybīl, -bil/ *n.* a rigid, free-standing abstract sculpture or structure of wire, sheet metal, etc. [L *stabilis* STABLE[1], after MOBILE]

stability /stəbílliti/ *n.* the quality or state of being stable. [ME f. OF *stableté* f. L *stabilitas* f. *stabilis* STABLE[1]]
▪ steadiness, solidity, firmness, soundness, sturdiness, strength; steadfastness, constancy, dependability, reliability, tenacity, resolve, resoluteness, perseverance, determination, persistence, durability, lasting quality, permanence.

stabilize /stáybilīz/ *v.tr.* & *intr.* (also **-ise**) make or become stable. ▫▫ **stabilization** /-záysh'n/ *n.*
▪ see STEADY *v.* ▫▫ **stabilization** see SETTLEMENT 1.

stabilizer /stáybilīzər/ *n.* (also **-iser**) a device or substance used to keep something stable, esp.: **1** a gyroscope device to prevent rolling of a ship. **2** *US* the horizontal tailplane of an aircraft. **3** (in *pl.*) a pair of small wheels fitted to the rear wheel of a child's bicycle.
▪ see ANCHOR *n.* 2.

stable[1] /stáyb'l/ *adj.* (**stabler, stablest**) **1** firmly fixed or established; not easily adjusted, destroyed, or altered (*a stable structure; a stable government*). **2 a** firm, resolute; not wavering or fickle (*a stable and steadfast friend*). **b** (of a person) well-adjusted, sane, sensible. **3** *Chem.* (of a compound) not readily decomposing. **4** *Physics* (of an isotope) not subject to radioactive decay. ▫ **stable equilibrium** a state in which a body when disturbed tends to return to equilibrium. ▫▫ **stableness** *n.* **stably** *adv.* [ME f. AF *stable*, OF *estable* f. L *stabilis* f. *stare* stand]
▪ **1** steady, solid, firm, sound, sturdy, strong, durable, well-founded, fast, fixed, sure, established, deep-rooted, stout. **2 a** lasting, enduring, long-lasting, long-standing, secure, steadfast, steady, strong, unchanging, unchanged, changeless, unchangeable, unalterable, fixed, invariable, firm, resolute, unwavering, immutable, permanent, constant. **b** sane, (well-)balanced, responsible, reasonable, sensible, well-adjusted; competent, accountable.

stable[2] /stáyb'l/ *n.* & *v.* ● *n.* **1** a building set apart and adapted for keeping horses. **2** an establishment where racehorses are kept and trained. **3** the racehorses of a particular stable. **4** persons, products, etc., having a common origin or affiliation. **5** such an origin or affiliation. ● *v.tr.* put or keep (a horse) in a stable. ▫ **stable-boy** a boy employed in a stable. **stable-companion** (or **-mate**) **1** a horse of the same stable. **2** a member of the same organization. **stable-girl** a girl employed in a stable. **stable-lad** a person employed in a stable. □□ **stableful** *n.* (*pl.* **-fuls**). [ME f. OF *estable* f. L *stabulum* f. *stare* stand]

stableman /stáyb'lmən/ *n.* (*pl.* **-men**) a person employed in a stable.
■ see GROOM *n.*

stabling /stáybling/ *n.* accommodation for horses.

stablish /stáblish/ *v.tr. archaic* fix firmly; establish; set up. [var. of ESTABLISH]

staccato /stəkaátō/ *adv.*, *adj.*, & *n.* esp. *Mus.* ● *adv.* & *adj.* with each sound or note sharply detached or separated from the others (cf. LEGATO, TENUTO). ● *n.* (*pl.* **-os**) **1** a staccato passage in music etc. **2** staccato delivery or presentation. □ **staccato mark** a dot or stroke above or below a note, indicating that it is to be played staccato. [It., past part. of *staccare* = *distaccare* DETACH]

stack /stak/ *n.* & *v.* ● *n.* **1** a pile or heap, esp. in orderly arrangement. **2** a circular or rectangular pile of hay, straw, etc., or of grain in sheaf, often with a sloping thatched top, a rick. **3** *colloq.* a large quantity (*a stack of work*; *has stacks of money*). **4 a** = *chimney-stack*. **b** = SMOKESTACK. **c** a tall factory chimney. **5** a stacked group of aircraft. **6** (also **stack-room**) a part of a library where books are compactly stored, esp. one to which the public does not have direct access. **7** *Brit.* a high detached rock esp. off the coast of Scotland and the Orkneys. **8** a pyramidal group of rifles, a pile. **9** *Computing* a set of storage locations which store data in such a way that the most recently stored item is the first to be retrieved. **10** *Brit.* a measure for a pile of wood of 108 cu. ft. (30.1 cubic metres). ● *v.tr.* **1** pile in a stack or stacks. **2 a** arrange (cards) secretly for cheating. **b** manipulate (circumstances etc.) to one's advantage. **3** cause (aircraft) to fly round the same point at different levels while waiting to land at an airport. □ **stack arms** *hist.* = *pile arms*. **stack up** *US colloq.* present oneself, measure up. **stack-yard** an enclosure for stacks of hay, straw, etc. □□ **stackable** *adj.* **stacker** *n.* [ME f. ON *stakkr* haystack f. Gmc]
■ *n.* **1** pile, heap, mound, mass, accumulation, hill, mountain, store, stock, bank, deposit, supply, stockpile, hoard, load, bundle, bale, *colloq.* stash. **2** haystack, cock, haycock, rick, hayrick, clamp. **3** collection, aggregation, accumulation, mass, load, lot, pile, pack, abundance, plenty, profusion, sea, throng, multitude, swarm, host. **4** smokestack, chimney, chimney-stack, funnel, stalk. ● *v.* **1** stack up, pile (up), heap, accumulate, amass, store, stock, stockpile, hoard, collect, gather, aggregate, agglomerate, squirrel away, *colloq.* stash (away). □ **stack up** present oneself, measure up; (*stack up to* or *with*) compare with, hold a candle to, be on a par with, be as good as.

stacte /stáktee/ *n.* a sweet spice used by the ancient Jews in making incense. [ME f. L f. Gk *staktē* f. *stazō* drip]

staddle /stádd'l/ *n.* a platform or framework supporting a rick etc. □ **staddle-stone** a stone supporting a staddle or rick etc. [OE *stathol* base f. Gmc, rel. to STAND]

stadium /stáydiəm/ *n.* (*pl.* **stadiums**) **1** an athletic or sports ground with tiers of seats for spectators. **2** (*pl.* **stadiums** or **stadia** /-diə/) *Antiq.* **a** a course for a foot-race or chariot-race. **b** a measure of length, about 185 metres. **3** a stage or period of development etc. [ME f. L f. Gk *stadion*]
■ **1** arena, (sports *or* athletic) ground, amphitheatre, hippodrome, colosseum, *Rom. Antiq.* circus.

stadtholder /staádhōldər, staát-/ *n.* (also **stadholder**) *hist.* **1** the chief magistrate of the United Provinces of the Netherlands. **2** the viceroy or governor of a province or town in the Netherlands. □□ **stadtholdership** *n.* [Du. *stadhouder* deputy f. *stad* STEAD + *houder* HOLDER, after med.L LOCUM TENENS]

staff[1] /staaf/ *n.* & *v.* ● *n.* **1 a** a stick or pole for use in walking or climbing or as a weapon. **b** a stick or pole as a sign of office or authority. **c** a person or thing that supports or sustains. **d** a flagstaff. **e** *Surveying* a rod for measuring distances, heights, etc. **f** a token given to an engine-driver on a single-track railway as authority to proceed over a given section of line. **g** a spindle in a watch. **2 a** a body of persons employed in a business etc. (*editorial staff of a newspaper*). **b** those in authority within an organization, esp. the teachers in a school. **c** *Mil.* etc. a body of officers assisting an officer in high command and concerned with an army, regiment, fleet, or air force as a whole (*general staff*). **d** (usu. **Staff**) *Mil.* = *staff sergeant*. **3** (*pl.* **staffs** or **staves** /stayvz/) *Mus.* a set of usu. five parallel lines on any one or between any adjacent two of which a note is placed to indicate its pitch. ● *v.tr.* provide (an institution etc.) with staff. □ **staff college** *Brit. Mil.* etc. a college at which officers are trained for staff duties. **staff notation** *Mus.* notation by means of a staff, esp. as distinct from tonic sol-fa. **staff nurse** *Brit.* a nurse ranking just below a sister. **staff officer** *Mil.* an officer serving on the staff of an army etc. **staff sergeant 1** *Brit.* the senior sergeant of a non-infantry company. **2** *US* a non-commissioned officer ranking just above sergeant. □□ **staffed** *adj.* (also in *comb.*). [OE *stæf* f. Gmc]
■ *n.* **1 a, b** stick, pole, standard, baton, rod, pikestaff, pike, stake, cane, stave, shaft, alpenstock, shillelagh, club, truncheon, mace, crook, crozier, sceptre, wand, verge, caduceus. **d** flagstaff, flag-pole, pole. **2** personnel, employees, help, workforce, crew, team, organization. ● *v.* man, people, crew.

staff[2] /staaf/ *n.* a mixture of plaster of Paris, cement, etc., as a temporary building-material. [19th c.: orig. unkn.]

staffage /stəfaázh/ *n.* accessory items in a painting, esp. figures or animals in a landscape picture. [G f. *staffieren* decorate, perh. f. OF *estoffer*: see STUFF]

staffer /staáfər/ *n. US* a member of a staff, esp. of a newspaper.
■ see JOURNALIST.

Staffs. *abbr.* Staffordshire.

stag /stag/ *n.* & *v.* ● *n.* **1** an adult male deer, esp. one with a set of antlers. **2** *Brit. Stock Exch.* a person who applies for shares of a new issue with a view to selling at once for a profit. **3** a man who attends a social gathering unaccompanied by a woman. ● *v.tr.* (**stagged**, **stagging**) *Brit. Stock Exch.* deal in (shares) as a stag. □ **stag beetle** any beetle of the family Lucanidae, the male of which has large branched mandibles resembling a stag's antlers. **stag-** (or **stag's-**) **horn 1** the horn of a stag, used to make knife-handles, snuff-boxes, etc. **2** any of various ferns, esp. of the genus *Platycerium*, having fronds like antlers. **stag-night** (or **-party**) an all-male celebration, esp. in honour of a man about to marry. [ME f. OE *stacga*, *stagga* (unrecorded): cf. *docga* dog, *frogga* frog, etc., and ON *steggr*, *steggi* male bird]

stage /stayj/ *n.* & *v.* ● *n.* **1** a point or period in a process or development (*reached a critical stage*; *is in the larval stage*). **2 a** a raised floor or platform, esp. one on which plays etc. are performed before an audience. **b** (prec. by *the*) the acting or theatrical profession, dramatic art or literature. **c** the scene of action (*the stage of politics*). **d** = *landing-stage*. **3 a** a regular stopping-place on a route. **b** the distance between two stopping-places. **c** *Brit.* = *fare-stage*. **4** *Astronaut.* a section of a rocket with a separate engine, jettisoned when its propellant is exhausted. **5** *Geol.* a range of strata forming a subdivision of a series. **6** *Electronics* a single amplifying transistor or valve with the associated equipment. **7** the surface on which an object is placed for inspection through a microscope. ● *v.tr.* **1** present (a play etc.) on stage. **2** arrange the occurrence of (*staged a demonstration*; *staged a comeback*). □ **go on the stage** become an actor. **hold the stage** dominate a conversation etc. **stage direction** an instruction in the text of a play as to the movement, position, tone, etc., of an actor, or sound effects etc. **stage door** an actors' and workmen's entrance from the street to a theatre behind the stage. **stage effect 1** an effect produced in acting or on the stage. **2** an artificial or theatrical effect produced in real life. **stage fright** nervousness on facing an audience esp. for the first time. **stage-hand** a person handling scenery etc. during a performance on stage. **stage left** (or **right**) on the left (or right) side of the stage, facing the audience. **stage-manage 1** be the stage-manager of. **2** arrange and control for effect. **stage-management** the job or craft of a stage-manager. **stage-manager** the person responsible for lighting and other mechanical arrangements for a play etc. **stage name** a name assumed for professional purposes by an actor. **stage play** a play performed on stage rather than broadcast etc. **stage rights** exclusive rights to perform a particular play. **stage-struck** filled with an inordinate desire to go on the stage. **stage whisper 1** an aside. **2** a loud whisper meant to be heard by others than the person addressed. ▫▫ **stageable** *adj.* **stageability** /stáyjəbílliti/ *n.* **stager** *n.* [ME f. OF *estage* dwelling ult. f. L *stare* stand]

▪ *n.* **1** position, situation, grade, level, step, station, place, point, spot, juncture, period, division, phase, lap; status, condition. **2 a** platform, dais, podium; rostrum. **b** (*the stage*) show business, the theatre, the boards, the footlights, the West End; acting, Thespianism; *colloq.* showbiz. **3 b** see SECTION *n.* 2. ● *v.* **1** put on, produce, present, mount, exhibit. **2** put on, contrive, organize, arrange, originate, devise, make up, concoct, fake, trump up, stage-manage, manipulate. ▫ **stage-manage 2** see STAGE *v.* 2 above. **stage name** see PSEUDONYM. **stage play** see DRAMA 1.

stagecoach /stáyjkōch/ *n. hist.* a large closed horse-drawn coach running regularly by stages between two places.

stagecraft /stáyjkraaft/ *n.* skill or experience in writing or staging plays.

▪ see THEATRE 2a.

stagey var. of STAGY.

stagflation /stagfláysh'n/ *n. Econ.* a state of inflation without a corresponding increase of demand and employment. [STAGNATION (as STAGNATE) + INFLATION]

stagger /stággər/ *v.* & *n.* ● *v.* **1 a** *intr.* walk unsteadily, totter. **b** *tr.* cause to totter (*was staggered by the blow*). **2 a** *tr.* shock, confuse; cause to hesitate or waver (*the question staggered them; they were staggered at the suggestion*). **b** *intr.* hesitate; waver in purpose. **3** *tr.* arrange (events, hours of work, etc.) so that they do not coincide. **4** *tr.* arrange (objects) so that they are not in line, esp.: **a** arrange (a road-crossing) so that the side-roads are not in line. **b** set (the spokes of a wheel) to incline alternately to right and left. ● *n.* **1** a tottering movement. **2** (in *pl.*) **a** a disease of the brain and spinal cord esp. in horses and cattle, causing staggering. **b** giddiness. **3** an overhanging or slantwise or zigzag arrangement of like parts in a structure etc. ▫▫ **staggerer** *n.* [alt. of ME *stacker* (now dial.) f. ON *stakra* frequent. of *staka* push, stagger]

▪ *v.* **1 a** totter, dodder, reel, lurch, teeter, sway, walk unsteadily *or* shakily, stumble, falter, waver, pitch, rock, wobble. **2 a** surprise, amaze, astound, astonish, overwhelm, overcome, dumbfound, shock, stupefy, stun, nonplus, confound, confuse, bewilder, startle, jolt, shake (up), take a person's breath away, make a person's head swim, take aback, throw off balance, tax, burden, *colloq.* flabbergast, flummox, bowl over, floor, *sl.* blow a person's mind. **3, 4** alternate, space (out), vary, rearrange.

staggering /stággəring/ *adj.* **1** astonishing, bewildering. **2** that staggers. ▫▫ **staggeringly** *adv.*

▪ **1** see *amazing* (AMAZE).

staghound /stág-hownd/ *n.* **1** any large dog of a breed used for hunting deer by sight or scent. **2** this breed.

staging /stáyjing/ *n.* **1** the presentation of a play etc. **2 a** a platform or support or scaffolding, esp. temporary. **b** shelves for plants in a greenhouse. ▫ **staging area** an intermediate assembly point for troops in transit. **staging post** a regular stopping-place, esp. on an air route.

▪ **1** see PRODUCTION 1. **2 a** see SUPPORT *n.* 2.

stagnant /stágnənt/ *adj.* **1** (of liquid) motionless, having no current; stale or foul due to this. **2** (of life, action, the mind, business, a person) showing no activity, dull, sluggish. ▫▫ **stagnancy** *n.* **stagnantly** *adv.* [L *stagnare stagnant-* f. *stagnum* pool]

▪ **1** motionless, standing, still, quiet, sluggish, unmoving, immobile, flat; stale, foul, putrid, putrescent, putrefied, polluted, dirty, contaminated, filthy. **2** see INACTIVE 1, 2.

stagnate /stagnáyt/ *v.intr.* be or become stagnant. ▫▫ **stagnation** *n.*

▪ languish, idle, vegetate, deteriorate, degenerate, decline, decay, rust, moulder, decompose, spoil, rot, *colloq.* go to seed *or* pot.

stagy /stáyji/ *adj.* (also **stagey**) (**stagier**, **stagiest**) theatrical, artificial, exaggerated. ▫▫ **stagily** *adv.* **staginess** *n.*

▪ see THEATRICAL *adj.* ▫▫ **staginess** see THEATRE 2c, PRETENCE 4.

staid /stayd/ *adj.* of quiet and steady character; sedate. ▫▫ **staidly** *adv.* **staidness** *n.* [= *stayed*, past part. of STAY[1]]

▪ sedate, rigid, stiff, prim, dignified, sober, calm, composed, quiet, restrained, steady, solemn, serious, serious-minded, grave. ▫▫ **staidness** see SOBRIETY.

stain /stayn/ *v.* & *n.* ● *v.* **1** *tr.* & *intr.* discolour or be discoloured by the action of liquid sinking in. **2** *tr.* sully, blemish, spoil, damage (a reputation, character, etc.). **3** *tr.* colour (wood, glass, etc.) by a process other than painting or covering the surface. **4** *tr.* impregnate (a specimen) for microscopic examination with colouring matter that makes the structure visible by being deposited in some parts more than in others. **5** *tr.* print colours on (wallpaper). ● *n.* **1** a discoloration, a spot or mark caused esp. by contact with foreign matter and not easily removed (*a cloth covered with tea-stains*). **2 a** a blot or blemish. **b** damage to a reputation etc. (*a stain on one's character*). **3** a substance used in staining. ▫ **stained glass** dyed or coloured glass, esp. in a lead framework in a window (also (with hyphen) *attrib.*: *stained-glass window*). ▫▫ **stainable** *adj.* **stainer** *n.* [ME f. *distain* f. OF *desteindre desteign-* (as DIS-, TINGE)]

▪ *v.* **1** blot, mark, spot, discolour, blotch, speckle, dye, spatter, splatter, tinge, smudge, splash. **2** spoil, defile, ruin, smirch, besmirch, taint, tarnish, stigmatize, shame, disgrace, sully, contaminate, soil, corrupt, blemish, damage. ● *n.* **1** blot, mark, spot, discoloration, blotch, smirch, speck, *colloq.* splodge, splotch. **2** mark, blot (on the escutcheon), stigma, blemish, damage, smirch, smudge, blot on one's copybook. **3** dye, colour, colouring, colourant, tint, tinge, pigment.

stainless /stáynliss/ *adj.* **1** (esp. of a reputation) without stains. **2** not liable to stain. ▫ **stainless steel** chrome steel not liable to rust or tarnish under ordinary conditions.

▪ **1** see IMMACULATE 1, 3.

stair /stair/ *n.* **1** each of a set of fixed indoor steps (*on the top stair but one*). **2** (usu. in *pl.*) a set of indoor steps (*passed him on the stairs; down a winding stair*). **3** (in *pl.*) a landing-stage. ▫ **stair-rod** a rod for securing a carpet in the angle between two steps. [OE *stǣger* f. Gmc]

▪ **1, 2** see STEP *n.* 4a.

staircase /stáirkayss/ *n.* **1** a flight of stairs and the supporting structure. **2** a part of a building containing a staircase.

stairhead /stáirhed/ *n.* a level space at the top of stairs.

stairway /stáirway/ *n.* **1** a flight of stairs, a staircase. **2** the way up this.

stairwell /stáirwel/ *n.* the shaft in which a staircase is built.

staithe /stayth/ *n. Brit.* a wharf, esp. a waterside coal depot equipped for loading vessels. [ME f. ON *stöth* landing-stage f. Gmc, rel. to STAND]

stake[1] /stayk/ *n.* & *v.* ● *n.* **1** a stout stick or post sharpened at one end and driven into the ground as a support, boundary mark, etc. **2** *hist.* **a** the post to which a person was tied to be burnt alive. **b** (prec. by *the*) death by burning as a punishment (*was condemned to the stake*). **3** a long vertical rod in basket-making. **4** a metalworker's small anvil fixed on a bench by a pointed prop. ● *v.tr.* **1** fasten, secure, or support with a stake or stakes. **2** (foll. by *off*, *out*) mark off (an area) with stakes. **3** state or establish (a claim). ▫

pull (or **pull up**) **stakes** depart; go to live elsewhere. **stake-boat** a boat anchored to mark the course for a boat race etc. **stake-body** (*pl.* **-ies**) *US* a body for a lorry etc. having a flat open platform with removable posts along the sides. **stake-net** a fishing-net hung on stakes. **stake out** *colloq.* **1** place under surveillance. **2** place (a person) to maintain surveillance. **stake-out** *n.* esp. *US colloq.* a period of surveillance. [OE *staca* f. WG, rel. to STICK²]

■ *n.* **1** stick, post, spike, picket, paling, pale, pole, pike, stave; palisade, upright, pillar, column. ● *v.* **1** tether, tie (up), secure, fasten, picket, lash, leash, hitch, chain; support. **2** (*stake off* or *out*) mark off *or* out, define, delimit, outline, demarcate, delineate, circumscribe; fence (in *or* off), enclose, close in *or* off, wall in. □ **pull** (or **pull up**) **stakes** move (house), resettle, move on, migrate, emigrate, leave, depart, *colloq.* clear off *or* out.

stake² /stayk/ *n.* & *v.* ● *n.* **1** a sum of money etc. wagered on an event, esp. deposited with a stakeholder. **2** (often foll. by *in*) an interest or concern, esp. financial. **3** (in *pl.*) **a** money offered as a prize esp. in a horse-race. **b** such a race (*maiden stakes; trial stakes*). ● *v.tr.* **1 a** wager (*staked £5 on the next race*). **b** risk (*staked everything on convincing him*). **2** *US colloq.* give financial or other support to. □ **at stake 1** risked, to be won or lost (*life itself is at stake*). **2** at issue, in question. □□ **staker** *n.* [16th c.: perh. f. STAKE¹]

■ *n.* **1** bet, wager, punt, ante, risk, hazard. **2** investment, interest, share, involvement, concern. **3 a** (*stakes*) see PRIZE¹ *n.* 2. ● *v.* **1** wager, bet, gamble, put, *colloq.* punt; risk, venture, chance, hazard. □ **at stake 1** at hazard, hazarded, at risk, risked, on the table, in jeopardy, jeopardized. **2** at issue, in question, concerned, involved, to be decided *or* resolved.

stakeholder /stáyk-hōldər/ *n.* an independent party with whom each of those who make a wager deposits the money etc. wagered.

Stakhanovite /stəkaánəvīt/ *n.* a worker (esp. in the former USSR) who increases his or her output to an exceptional extent, and so gains special awards. □□ **Stakhanovism** /-viz'm/ *n.* **Stakhanovist** /-vist/ *n.* & *adj.* [A. G. *Stakhanov*, Russian coal-miner d. 1977]

stalactite /stálləktīt, stəlák-/ *n.* a deposit of calcium carbonate having the shape of a large icicle, formed by the trickling of water from the roof of a cave, cliff overhang, etc. □□ **stalactic** /-láktik/ *adj.* **stalactiform** /-láktiform/ *adj.* **stalactitic** /-títtik/ *adj.* [mod.L *stalactites* f. Gk *stalaktos* dripping f. *stalassō* drip]

Stalag /stállag/ *n. hist.* a German prison camp, esp. for non-commissioned officers and privates. [G f. *Stamm* base, main stock, *Lager* camp]

stalagmite /stálləgmīt/ *n.* a deposit of calcium carbonate formed by the dripping of water into the shape of a large inverted icicle rising from the floor of a cave etc., often uniting with a stalactite. □□ **stalagmitic** /-míttik/ *adj.* [mod.L *stalagmites* f. Gk *stalagma* a drop f. *stalassō* (as STALACTITE)]

stale¹ /stayl/ *adj.* & *v.* ● *adj.* (**staler**, **stalest**) **1 a** not fresh, not quite new (*stale bread is best for toast*). **b** musty, insipid, or otherwise the worse for age or use. **2** trite or unoriginal (*a stale joke; stale news*). **3** (of an athlete or other performer) having ability impaired by excessive exertion or practice. **4** *Law* (esp. of a claim) having been left dormant for an unreasonably long time. ● *v.tr.* & *intr.* make or become stale. □□ **stalely** *adv.* **staleness** *n.* [ME, prob. f. AF & OF f. *estaler* halt: cf. STALL¹]

■ *adj.* **1** old, past its prime, dry, dried-out, hardened, limp, wilted, withered, flat, sour, rank, rancid, turned, (gone) off, mouldy, musty, spoiled, rotten. **2** old, banal, overused, antiquated, old-fashioned, threadbare, trite, clichéd, unoriginal, hackneyed, stereotyped, ready-made, tired, weary, boring, tiresome, shop-worn, familiar, stock, well-known, hand-me-down, reach-me-down, warmed-up.

stale² /stayl/ *n.* & *v.* ● *n.* the urine of horses and cattle. ● *v.intr.* (esp. of horses and cattle) urinate. [ME, perh. f. OF *estaler* adopt a position (cf. STALE¹)]

stalemate /stáylmayt/ *n.* & *v.* ● *n.* **1** *Chess* a position counting as a draw, in which a player is not in check but cannot move except into check. **2** a deadlock or drawn contest. ● *v.tr.* **1** *Chess* bring (a player) to a stalemate. **2** bring to a standstill. [obs. *stale* (f. AF *estale* f. *estaler* be placed: cf. STALE¹) + MATE²]

■ *n.* **2** impasse, deadlock, standstill, (dead *or* full) stop, tie, draw, checkmate, *US* stand-off.

Stalinism /staáliniz'm/ *n.* **1** the policies followed by Stalin in the government of the former USSR, esp. centralization, totalitarianism, and the pursuit of socialism. **2** any rigid centralized authoritarian form of socialism. □□ **Stalinist** *n.* [J. V. *Stalin* (Dzhugashvili), Soviet statesman d. 1953]

■ **2** totalitarianism.

stalk¹ /stawk/ *n.* **1** the main stem of a herbaceous plant. **2** the slender attachment or support of a leaf, flower, fruit, etc. **3** a similar support for an organ etc. in an animal. **4** a slender support or linking shaft in a machine, object, etc., e.g. the stem of a wineglass. **5** the tall chimney of a factory etc. □ **stalk-eyed** (of crabs, snails, etc.) having the eyes mounted on stalks. □□ **stalked** *adj.* (also in *comb.*). **stalkless** *adj.* **stalklet** *n.* **stalklike** *adj.* **stalky** *adj.* [ME *stalke*, prob. dimin. of (now dial.) *stale* rung of a ladder, long handle, f. OE *stalu*]

■ **1** stem, trunk, cane, main axis, shaft. **2** leaf-stalk, stem, shaft, spike, shoot, bine, *Bot.* petiole, pedicel, peduncle. **3** *Zool.* peduncle, pedicel.

stalk² /stawk/ *v.* & *n.* ● *v.* **1 a** *tr.* pursue or approach (game or an enemy) stealthily. **b** *intr.* steal up to game under cover. **2** *intr.* stride, walk in a stately or haughty manner. ● *n.* **1** the stalking of game. **2** an imposing gait. □ **stalking-horse 1** a horse behind which a hunter is concealed. **2** a pretext concealing one's real intentions or actions. □□ **stalker** *n.* (also in *comb.*). [OE f. Gmc, rel. to STEAL]

■ *v.* **1 a** follow, dog, haunt, shadow, trail, track (down), hunt (down), prey on, pursue, hound, chase, *colloq.* tail. **2** see WALK *v.* 1, 2. □□ **stalker** see HUNTER 1a.

stall¹ /stawl/ *n.* & *v.* ● *n.* **1 a** a trader's stand or booth in a market etc., or out of doors. **b** a compartment in a building for the sale of goods. **c** a table in this on which goods are exposed. **2 a** a stable or cowhouse. **b** a compartment for one animal in this. **3 a** a fixed seat in the choir or chancel of a church, more or less enclosed at the back and sides and often canopied, esp. one appropriated to a clergyman (*canon's stall; dean's stall*). **b** the office or dignity of a canon etc. **4** (usu. in *pl.*) *Brit.* each of a set of seats in a theatre, usu. on the ground floor. **5 a** a compartment for one person in a shower-bath, lavatory, etc. **b** a compartment for one horse at the start of a race. **6 a** the stalling of an engine or aircraft. **b** the condition resulting from this. **7** a receptacle for one object (*finger-stall*). ● *v.* **1 a** *intr.* (of a motor vehicle or its engine) stop because of an overload on the engine or an inadequate supply of fuel to it. **b** *intr.* (of an aircraft or its pilot) reach a condition where the speed is too low to allow effective operation of the controls. **c** *tr.* cause (an engine or vehicle or aircraft) to stall. **2** *tr.* **a** put or keep (cattle etc.) in a stall or stalls esp. for fattening (*a stalled ox*). **b** furnish (a stable etc.) with stalls. **3** *intr.* **a** (of a horse or cart) stick fast as in mud or snow. **b** *US* be snowbound. □ **stall-feed** fatten (cattle) in a stall. [OE *steall* f. Gmc, rel. to STAND: partly f. OF *estal* f. Frank.]

■ *n.* **1** stand, booth, cubicle, kiosk; compartment, alcove, section, space, area, slot, enclosure, quarters; counter, table. **2** shed, pen, cote, fold, coop, sty, enclosure, cowshed, byre, barn, stable, *US* corral. ● *v.* **1 a** stop, halt, die, shut down, fail, cease operating, come to a standstill, *US* quit, *colloq.* conk out.

stall² /stawl/ *v.* & *n.* ● *v.* **1** *intr.* play for time when being questioned etc. **2** *tr.* delay, obstruct, block. ● *n.* the act or an instance of stalling. □ **stall off** evade or deceive. [*stall* pickpocket's confederate, orig. 'decoy' f. AF *estal(e)*, prob. rel. to STALL[1]]

■ *v.* **1** delay, dawdle, dally, temporize, equivocate, hesitate, prevaricate, play for time, waste time, stonewall, be obstructive, put a person *or* thing off; vacillate, dither, hedge, procrastinate; beat about the bush, drag one's feet, give a person the run-around, *Brit.* haver, *colloq.* dilly-dally. **2** see OBSTRUCT 2. ● *n.* delay, hedge, pretext, subterfuge, wile, trick, ruse, artifice, stratagem, manoeuvre, move, run-around, stalling, stonewalling, obstructionism, playing for time, procrastination, beating about the bush.

stallage /stáwlij/ *n. Brit.* **1** space for a stall or stalls in a market etc. **2** the rent for such a stall. **3** the right to erect such a stall. [ME f. OF *estalage* f. *estal* STALL[1]]

stallholder /stáwlhōldər/ *n.* a person in charge of a stall at a market etc.

stallion /stályən/ *n.* an uncastrated adult male horse, esp. one kept for breeding. [ME f. OF *estalon* ult. f. a Gmc root rel. to STALL[1]]

stalwart /stáwlwərt/ *adj.* & *n.* ● *adj.* **1** strongly built, sturdy. **2** courageous, resolute, determined (*stalwart supporters*). ● *n.* a stalwart person, esp. a loyal uncompromising partisan. ▫▫ **stalwartly** *adv.* **stalwartness** *n.* [Sc. var. of obs. *stalworth* f. OE *stǣlwierthe* f. *stǣl* place, WORTH]

■ *adj.* **1** robust, stout, strong, mighty, powerful, rugged, staunch, hardy, sturdy, vigorous, lusty, indomitable, solid, able-bodied, brawny, husky, hefty, beefy, sinewy, muscular, fit, healthy, hale, (hale and) hearty. **2** brave, courageous, daring, intrepid, valiant, heroic, manly, manful, fearless, indomitable, stout-hearted, bold, audacious, game, red-blooded, plucky, mettlesome, lion-hearted, spirited; redoubtable, undaunted, resolute, firm, determined, unbending, steadfast, staunch, tenacious, unswerving, unwavering, unfaltering, unflinching, uncompromising, unyielding, persevering, persistent, unflagging, relentless, tireless, untiring, indefatigable. ● *n.* supporter, upholder, sustainer, partisan, loyalist, (party) faithful, trouper; hero, heroine. ▫▫ **stalwartly** see *vigorously* (VIGOROUS). **stalwartness** see BRAVERY, STAMINA.

stamen /stáymən/ *n.* the male fertilizing organ of a flowering plant, including the anther containing pollen. ▫▫ **staminiferous** /stámminífførəss/ *adj.* [L *stamen staminis* warp in an upright loom, thread]

stamina /stámminə/ *n.* the ability to endure prolonged physical or mental strain; staying power, power of endurance. [L, pl. of STAMEN in sense 'warp, threads spun by the Fates']

■ ruggedness, vigour, vigorousness, fortitude, robustness, indefatigability, staying power, endurance, energy, power, might, mettle, (inner) strength, staunchness, stalwartness, courage, indomitability, *colloq.* grit, guts, *US colloq.* sand, *Brit. sl.* bottle.

staminate /stámminət/ *adj.* (of a plant) having stamens, esp. stamens but not pistils.

stammer /stámmər/ *v.* & *n.* ● *v.* **1** *intr.* speak (habitually, or on occasion from embarrassment etc.) with halting articulation, esp. with pauses or rapid repetitions of the same syllable. **2** *tr.* (often foll. by *out*) utter (words) in this way (*stammered out an excuse*). ● *n.* **1** a tendency to stammer. **2** an instance of stammering. ▫▫ **stammerer** *n.* **stammeringly** *adv.* [OE *stamerian* f. WG]

■ *v.* **1** stutter, hesitate, hem and haw, hum and haw, stumble, falter, pause. ● *n.* stutter.

stamp /stamp/ *v.* & *n.* ● *v.* **1** **a** *tr.* bring down (one's foot) heavily on the ground etc. **b** *tr.* crush, flatten, or bring into a specified state in this way (*stamped down the earth round the plant*). **c** *intr.* bring down one's foot heavily; walk with heavy steps. **2** *tr.* **a** impress (a pattern, mark, etc.) on metal, paper, butter, etc., with a die or similar instrument of metal, wood, rubber, etc. **b** impress (a surface) with a pattern etc. in this way. **3** *tr.* affix a postage or other stamp to (an envelope or document). **4** *tr.* assign a specific character to; characterize; mark out (*stamps the story an invention*). **5** *tr.* crush or pulverize (ore etc.). ● *n.* **1** an instrument for stamping a pattern or mark. **2** **a** a mark or pattern made by this. **b** the impression of an official mark required to be made for revenue purposes on deeds, bills of exchange, etc., as evidence of payment of tax. **3** a small adhesive piece of paper indicating that a price, fee, or tax has been paid, esp. a postage stamp. **4** a mark impressed on or label etc. affixed to a commodity as evidence of quality etc. **5** **a** a heavy downward blow with the foot. **b** the sound of this. **6** **a** a characteristic mark or impress (*bears the stamp of genius*). **b** character, kind (*avoid people of that stamp*). **7** the block that crushes ore in a stamp-mill. ▫ **Stamp Act** an act concerned with stamp-duty, esp. that imposing the duty on the American colonies in 1765 and repealed in 1766. **stamp-collecting** the collecting of postage stamps as objects of interest or value. **stamp-collector** a person engaged in stamp-collecting. **stamp-duty** a duty imposed on certain kinds of legal document. **stamp-hinge** see HINGE. **stamping-ground** a favourite haunt or place of action. **stamp-machine** a coin-operated machine for selling postage stamps. **stamp-mill** a mill for crushing ore etc. **stamp-office** an office for the issue of government stamps and the receipt of stamp-duty etc. **stamp on** **1** impress (an idea etc.) on (the memory etc.). **2** suppress. **stamp out** **1** produce by cutting out with a die etc. **2** put an end to, crush, destroy. **stamp-paper** **1** paper with the government revenue stamp. **2** the gummed marginal paper of a sheet of postage stamps. ▫▫ **stamper** *n.* [prob. f. OE *stampian* (v.) (unrecorded) f. Gmc: infl. by OF *estamper* (v.) and F *estampe* (n.) also f. Gmc]

■ *v.* **1 b** trample, tramp, crush, flatten, squash, press, tread on, *colloq.* squish. **c** tramp, stomp, thump; tread *or* step heavily. **2** impress, mark, imprint, print, brand; engrave, emboss, inscribe. **4** brand, label, mark, tag, term, name, style, identify, categorize, classify, characterize, designate, denominate, show to be. ● *n.* **1** die, block, punch, seal, matrix, plate, die-stamp, stereotype; rubber stamp, signet(-ring). **2, 4** seal, (trade) mark, brand, logotype, symbol, representation, colophon, imprint, emblem, insignia, label, monogram, sign, crest, coat of arms, escutcheon, signature, initials, *Archit.* & *Archaeol.* cartouche, *colloq.* logo. **6 a** mark, sign, impress, hallmark, earmark, trait(s), feature(s), characteristic(s). **b** character, kind, sort, make, fashion, type, cast, mould, grade, style, cut, genre, class, level, kidney, classification, species, genus, variety, description, *US* stripe.
▫ **stamp-collecting** philately. **stamp-collector** philatelist. **stamping-ground** see HAUNT *n.* **stamp on** **1** impress on, imprint on, etch on, engrave on, inscribe on, print on, record in, document in, register in, log in. **2** see SQUELCH *v.* 2b. **stamp out** **2** eliminate, eradicate, abolish, get rid of, annihilate, exterminate, kill, snuff out, terminate, end, put an end to, destroy, put down, put out, extinguish, extirpate; crush, quell, subdue, suppress, squelch, repress.

stampede /stampéed/ *n.* & *v.* ● *n.* **1** a sudden flight and scattering of a number of horses, cattle, etc. **2** a sudden flight or hurried movement of people due to interest or panic. **3** *US* the spontaneous response of many persons to a common impulse. ● *v.* **1** *intr.* take part in a stampede. **2** *tr.* cause to do this. **3** *tr.* cause to act hurriedly or unreasoningly. ▫▫ **stampeder** *n.* [Sp. *estampida* crash, uproar, ult. f. Gmc, rel. to STAMP]

■ *n.* **1, 2** rout, flight, scattering, panic, rush, dash. ● *v.* **1** rush, run, race, charge, take to one's heels, dash, flee, take flight. **2** panic, frighten, rush, scatter, rout, put to flight. **3** see RAILROAD *v.*

stance /staanss, stanss/ *n.* **1** an attitude or position of the body esp. when hitting a ball etc. **2** a standpoint; an attitude of mind. **3** *Sc.* a site for a market, taxi rank, etc. [F f. It. *stanza*: see STANZA]

■ **1** position, posture, attitude, stand, carriage, bearing, deportment. **2** standpoint, viewpoint, point of view, attitude, stand; see also POSITION *n.* 5.

stanch[1] /staanch, stawnch/ *v.tr.* (also **staunch**) **1** restrain the flow of (esp. blood). **2** restrain the flow from (esp. a wound). [ME f. OF *estanchier* f. Rmc]
■ **1** stem, halt, check, arrest, end, cease, prevent, *archaic or literary* stay; see also STOP *v.* 1b.

stanch[2] var. of STAUNCH[1].

stanchion /staánsh'n/ *n.* & *v.* ● *n.* **1** a post or pillar, an upright support, a vertical strut. **2** an upright bar, pair of bars, or frame, for confining cattle in a stall. ● *v.tr.* **1** supply with a stanchion. **2** fasten (cattle) to a stanchion. [ME f. AF *stanchon*, OF *estanchon* f. *estance* prob. ult. f. L *stare* stand]
■ *n.* **1** see POST[1] *n.*

stand /stand/ *v.* & *n.* ● *v.* (*past* and *past part.* **stood** /sto͝od/) **1** *intr.* have or take or maintain an upright position, esp. on the feet or a base. **2** *intr.* be situated or located (*here once stood a village*). **3** *intr.* be of a specified height (*stands six foot three*). **4** *intr.* be in a specified condition (*stands accused*; *the thermometer stood at 90°*; *the matter stands as follows*; *stood in awe of them*). **5** *tr.* place or set in an upright or specified position (*stood it against the wall*). **6** *intr.* **a** move to and remain in a specified position (*stand aside*). **b** take a specified attitude (*stand aloof*). **7** *intr.* maintain a position; avoid falling or moving or being moved (*the house will stand for another century*; *stood for hours arguing*). **8** *intr.* assume a stationary position; cease to move (*now stand still*). **9** *intr.* remain valid or unaltered; hold good (*the former conditions must stand*). **10** *intr. Naut.* hold a specified course (*stand in for the shore*; *you are standing into danger*). **11** *tr.* endure without yielding or complaining; tolerate (*cannot stand the pain*; *how can you stand him?*). **12** *tr.* provide for another or others at one's own expense (*stood him a drink*). **13** *intr.* (often foll. by *for*) *Brit.* be a candidate (for an office, legislature, or constituency) (*stood for Parliament*; *stood for Finchley*). **14** *intr.* act in a specified capacity (*stood proxy*). **15** *tr.* undergo (trial). **16** *intr. Cricket* act as umpire. **17** *intr.* (of a dog) point, set. **18** *intr.* (in full **stand at stud**) (of a stallion) be available for breeding. ● *n.* **1** a cessation from motion or progress, a stoppage (*was brought to a stand*). **2 a** a halt made, or a stationary condition assumed, for the purpose of resistance. **b** resistance to attack or compulsion (esp. *make a stand*). **c** *Cricket* a prolonged period at the wicket by two batsmen. **3 a** a position taken up (*took his stand near the door*). **b** an attitude adopted. **4** a rack, set of shelves, table, etc., on or in which things may be placed (*music stand*; *hatstand*). **5 a** a small open-fronted structure for a trader outdoors or in a market etc. **b** a structure occupied by a participating organization at an exhibition. **6** a standing-place for vehicles (*cab-stand*). **7 a** a raised structure for persons to sit or stand on. **b** *US* a witness-box (*take the stand*). **8** *Theatr.* etc. each halt made on a tour to give one or more performances. **9** a group of growing plants (*stand of trees*; *stand of clover*). □ **as it stands 1** in its present condition, unaltered. **2** in the present circumstances. **be at a stand** *archaic* be unable to proceed, be in perplexity. **it stands to reason** see REASON. **stand alone** be unequalled. **stand and deliver!** *hist.* a highwayman's order to hand over valuables etc. **stand at bay** see BAY[5]. **stand back 1** withdraw; take up a position further from the front. **2** withdraw psychologically in order to take an objective view. **stand by 1** stand nearby; look on without interfering (*will not stand by and see him ill-treated*). **2** uphold, support, side with (a person). **3** adhere to, abide by (terms or promises). **4** *Naut.* stand ready to take hold of or operate (an anchor etc.). **stand-by** *n.* (*pl.* **-bys**) **1** a person or thing ready if needed in an emergency etc. **2** readiness for duty (*on stand-by*). ● *adj.* **1** ready for immediate use. **2** (of air travel) not booked in advance but allocated on the basis of earliest availability. **stand camera** a camera for use on a tripod, not hand-held. **stand a chance** see CHANCE. **stand corrected** accept correction. **stand down 1** withdraw (a person) or retire from a team, witness-box, or similar position. **2** *Brit.* cease to be a candidate etc. **3** *Brit. Mil.* go off duty. **stand easy!** see EASY. **stand for 1** represent, signify, imply (*'US' stands for 'United States'*; *democracy stands for a great deal more than that*). **2** (often with *neg.*) *colloq.* endure, tolerate, acquiesce in. **3** espouse the cause of. **stand one's ground** maintain one's position, not yield. **stand high** be high in status, price, etc. **stand in** (usu. foll. by *for*) deputize; act in place of another. **stand-in** *n.* a deputy or substitute, esp. for an actor when the latter's acting ability is not needed. **stand in the breach** see BREACH. **stand in good stead** see STEAD. **stand in with** be in league with. **stand of arms** *Brit. Mil.* a complete set of weapons for one man. **stand of colours** *Brit. Mil.* a regiment's flags. **stand off 1** move or keep away, keep one's distance. **2** *Brit.* temporarily dispense with the services of (an employee). **stand-off** *n.* **1** *US* a deadlock. **2** = *stand-off half*. **stand-off half** *Rugby Football* a half-back who forms a link between the scrum-half and the three-quarters. **stand on 1** insist on, observe scrupulously (*stand on ceremony*; *stand on one's dignity*). **2** *Naut.* continue on the same course. **stand on me** *sl.* rely on me; believe me. **stand on one's own feet** (or **legs**) be self-reliant or independent. **stand out 1** be prominent or conspicuous or outstanding. **2** (usu. foll. by *against*, *for*) hold out; persist in opposition or support or endurance. **stand over 1** stand close to (a person) to watch, control, threaten, etc. **2** be postponed, be left for later settlement etc. **stand pat** see PAT[2]. **stand to 1** *Mil.* stand ready for an attack (esp. before dawn or after dark). **2** abide by, adhere to (terms or promises). **3** be likely or certain to (*stands to lose everything*). **4** uphold, support, or side with (a person). **stand treat** bear the expense of entertainment etc. **stand up 1 a** rise to one's feet from a sitting or other position. **b** come to or remain in or place in a standing position. **2** (of an argument etc.) be valid. **3** *colloq.* fail to keep an appointment with. **stand-up** *attrib.adj.* **1** (of a meal) eaten standing. **2** (of a fight) violent, thorough, or fair and square. **3** (of a collar) upright, not turned down. **4** (of a comedian) performing by standing before an audience and telling jokes. **stand up for** support, side with, maintain (a person or cause). **stand upon** = *stand on*. **stand up to 1** meet or face (an opponent) courageously. **2** be resistant to the harmful effects of (wear, use, etc.). **stand well** (usu. foll. by *with*) be on good terms or in good repute. **take one's stand on** base one's argument etc. on, rely on. □□ **stander** *n.* [OE *standan* f. Gmc]
■ *v.* **1** stand up, rise, get up, be upstanding, be upright, *esp. archaic* & *poet.* arise; stay, remain (standing). **2** be, be located *or* situated *or* positioned, exist, lie. **5** stand up, set, place (upright), position, put, move; up-end. **8** stop, remain, halt, *archaic or literary* stay. **9** continue, remain, persist, be *or* remain in effect, be *or* remain in force, prevail, obtain, apply, hold good, exist. **11** endure, survive, tolerate, countenance, face, confront, last through, abide, allow, accept, take, suffer, bear, withstand, undergo, experience, cope with, brave, stand *or* bear up under, stand for, stomach, weather, handle, put up with, *literary* brook. **12** treat to, buy, *Austral.* & *NZ colloq.* shout. **13** campaign, run, be a candidate, present oneself as a candidate, seek election. **15** see UNDERGO. ● *n.* **1** see STANDSTILL. **2 b** defence, resistance, effort. **3 a** position, place. **b** position, attitude, stance, posture, policy, philosophy, point of view, viewpoint, standpoint, belief, opinion, sentiment, feeling, line. **4** rack, frame, bracket; hatstand, coat-rack; easel; tripod. **5** counter, booth, stall, kiosk, table; wagon, barrow, cart. **6** *Brit.* rank, *esp. US* lot. **7 a** platform, dais, stage, staging, rostrum, bandstand. **b** witness-box, *US* witness-stand. **8** stop, stopover, halt, stay; performance, show. **9** copse, grove, wood, thicket, brake, coppice, *Brit.* spinney. □ **stand by 1** wait (in the wings), stand *or* wait *or* stay *or* remain on the sidelines, stand back, stand aside *or* alongside, be *or* stand ready, be *or* stand available, be *or* stand accessible, be *or* stand in readiness. **2** support, defend, back, stand up for, stick up for, stand behind, stand alongside, be *or* remain loyal to, be *or* remain faithful to, uphold, take the side of, side with, stand to,

sympathize with. **3** stick to, adhere to, support, maintain, persist in, affirm, reaffirm, confirm, abide by, stand to. **stand-by** (*n.*) **1** substitute, surrogate, replacement, reserve, backup, understudy, second, deputy, stand-in, *esp. US* alternate; resource, support. **2** (*on stand-by*) see standing by, ready, available, on call, on hand, in reserve, in readiness, able to cover. **stand down 1, 2** lay off, suspend, *Brit.* stand off; resign, quit, step aside, step down, withdraw, pull out, retire. **stand for 1** symbolize, betoken, represent, signify, mean, be emblematic of, be short for, exemplify, epitomize, illustrate, typify, refer to, allude to, imply. **2** see STAND *v.* 11 above. **3** support, advocate, favour, sponsor, promote, espouse (the cause of), subscribe to, back, champion, lend support to, lend one's name to, second. **stand in** (*stand in for*) substitute for, understudy for, replace, relieve, double for, cover for, deputize for, take the place of. **stand-in** double, substitute, stunt man; surrogate, replacement, stand-by, backup, understudy, second, deputy, *esp. US* alternate, *US* pinch-hitter. **stand off 2** stand down, lay off, suspend. **stand-off 1** see STALEMATE *n.* **stand out 1** be prominent, be conspicuous, be noticeable, be notable, be noteworthy, be outstanding; protrude, project, stick out, jut out, bulge, obtrude, beetle, overhang, extend. **stand to 2** see *stand by* 3 above. **4** see *stand by* 2 above. **stand up 1 a** stand, rise, get to one's feet, get up, be upstanding, *esp. archaic* & *poet.* arise. **b** see STAND *v.* 1 above. **2** see *hold good* (HOLD[1]). **3** jilt, break an appointment with, fail to keep an appointment with. **stand up for** support, defend, take the side of, side with, champion, uphold, maintain, stick up for, stand by. **stand up to 1** confront, face (up to), brave, stick up to, challenge, dispute, question, tackle, oppose, resist, defy, withstand. **2** resist, defy, withstand, endure, outlast, last through, survive, suffer.

standalone /stándəlōn/ *adj.* (of a computer) operating independently of a network or other system.

standard /stándərd/ *n.* & *adj.* ● *n.* **1** an object or quality or measure serving as a basis or example or principle to which others conform or should conform or by which the accuracy or quality of others is judged (*by present-day standards*). **2 a** the degree of excellence etc. required for a particular purpose (*not up to standard*). **b** average quality (*of a low standard*). **3** the ordinary procedure, or quality or design of a product, without added or novel features. **4** a distinctive flag, esp. the flag of a cavalry regiment as distinct from the *colours* of an infantry regiment. **5 a** an upright support. **b** an upright water or gas pipe. **6 a** a tree or shrub that grows on an erect stem of full height and stands alone without support. **b** a shrub grafted on an upright stem and trained in tree form (*standard rose*). **7** a document specifying nationally or internationally agreed properties for manufactured goods etc. (*British Standard*). **8** a thing recognized as a model for imitation etc. **9** a tune or song of established popularity. **10 a** a system by which the value of a currency is defined in terms of gold or silver or both. **b** the prescribed proportion of the weight of fine metal in gold or silver coins. **11** a measure for timber, equivalent to 165 cu. ft. (4.7 cubic metres). **12** *Brit. hist.* a grade of classification in elementary schools. ● *adj.* **1** serving or used as a standard (*a standard size*). **2** of a normal or prescribed quality or size etc. **3** having recognized and permanent value; authoritative (*the standard book on the subject*). **4** (of language) conforming to established educated usage (*Standard English*). □ **multiple standard** a standard of value obtained by averaging the prices of a number of products. **raise a standard** take up arms; rally support (*raised the standard of revolt*). **standard-bearer 1** a soldier who carries a standard. **2** a prominent leader in a cause. **standard deviation** see DEVIATION. **standard lamp** *Brit.* a lamp set on a tall upright with its base standing on the floor. **standard of living** the degree of material comfort available to a person or class or community. **standard time** a uniform time for places in approximately the same longitude, established in a country or region by law or custom. [ME f. AF *estaundart*, OF *estendart* f. *estendre*, as EXTEND: in senses 5 and 6 of *n.* affected by association with STAND]
▪ *n.* **1, 8** model, pattern, archetype, paradigm, paragon, exemplar, example, sample, type, ideal, *beau idéal*; criterion, measure, benchmark, touchstone, yardstick, gauge, guide, guideline, rule, canon, law, requirement, precept, principle. **2** quality, grade, level, rating. **3** mean, average, norm, par, usual. **4** flag, banner, ensign, jack, emblem, pennant, burgee, insignia, guidon, gonfalon, labarum. **5 a** upright, pole, post, stanchion, lamppost, column, pillar, support, pedestal, pier, footing, (upright) bar *or* rod *or* timber. ● *adj.* **2–4** recognized, prevailing, prevalent, usual, customary, habitual, orthodox, set, established, prescribed, defined, required, regular, familiar, ordinary, traditional, accepted, approved, recognized, classic, textbook, definitive, authoritative, official, regulative, regulatory. □ **standard-bearer 2** see PROTAGONIST 3.

Standardbred /stándərdbred/ *n. US* **1** a horse of a breed able to attain a specified speed, developed esp. for trotting. **2** this breed.

standardize /stándərdīz/ *v.tr.* (also **-ise**) **1** cause to conform to a standard. **2** determine the properties of by comparison with a standard. □□ **standardizable** *adj.* **standardization** /-záysh'n/ *n.* **standardizer** *n.*
▪ **1** regiment, systematize, codify, normalize, regularize, homogenize, equalize.

standee /standée/ *n. colloq.* a person who stands, esp. when all seats are occupied.

standing /stánding/ *n.* & *adj.* ● *n.* **1** esteem or repute, esp. high; status, position (*people of high standing*; *is of no standing*). **2** duration (*a dispute of long standing*). **3** length of service, membership, etc. ● *adj.* **1** that stands, upright. **2 a** established, permanent (*a standing rule*). **b** not made, raised, etc., for the occasion (*a standing army*). **3** (of a jump, start, race, etc.) performed from rest or from a standing position. **4** (of water) stagnant. **5** (of corn) unreaped. **6** (of a stallion) that stands at stud. **7** *Printing* (formerly, of type) not yet distributed after use. □ **all standing 1** *Naut.* without time to lower the sails. **2** taken by surprise. **in good standing** fully paid-up as a member etc. **leave a person standing** make far more rapid progress than he or she. **standing committee** see COMMITTEE. **standing joke** an object of permanent ridicule. **standing order** an instruction to a banker to make regular payments, or to a newsagent etc. for a regular supply of a periodical etc. **standing orders** the rules governing the manner in which all business shall be conducted in a parliament, council, society, etc. **standing ovation** see OVATION. **standing rigging** rigging which is fixed in position. **standing-room** space to stand in. **standing wave** *Physics* the vibration of a system in which some particular points remain fixed while others between them vibrate with the maximum amplitude (cf. *travelling wave*).
▪ *n.* **1** eminence, prominence, esteem, repute, reputation; status, rank, station, footing, position, place, grade, order, level, stratum. **2** duration; endurance, longevity. **3** experience, seniority. ● *adj.* **1** erect, upright, on one's feet, vertical, unseated. **2 a** established, set, standard, conventional, customary, usual, normal, regular, fixed, permanent, continued, continuing, continuous, ongoing, perpetual, unbroken. **b** permanent, regular, established. **4** stagnant, motionless, unmoving, stationary, still, static.

standoffish /stándóffish/ *adj.* cold or distant in manner. □□ **standoffishly** *adv.* **standoffishness** *n.*
▪ aloof, haughty, unsocial, reserved, cool, cold, frosty, frigid, withdrawn, remote, removed, distant, detached, unapproachable, inaccessible, uncongenial, unfriendly, unsociable; Olympian, lordly, pompous, *colloq.* highfalutin, snooty. □□ **standoffishness** see RESERVE *n.* 3.

standout /stándowt/ *n. US* a remarkable person or thing.

standpipe /stándpīp/ *n.* a vertical pipe extending from a water supply, esp. one connecting a temporary tap to the mains.

standpoint /stándpoynt/ *n.* **1** the position from which a thing is viewed. **2** a mental attitude.
■ viewpoint, point of view, vantage point, position, stance, perspective, angle, aspect, slant; view, outlook, attitude, opinion.

standstill /stándstil/ *n.* a stoppage; an inability to proceed.
■ (dead *or* full) stop, halt, stand, stoppage, deadlock, stalemate, impasse.

stanhope /stánhōp/ *n.* a light open carriage for one with two or four wheels. [Fitzroy *Stanhope*, Engl. clergyman d. 1864, for whom the first one was made]

staniel /stányəl/ *n.* a kestrel. [OE *stāngella* 'stone-yeller' f. *stān* stone + *gellan* yell]

stank *past* of STINK.

stannary /stánnəri/ *n.* (*pl.* **-ies**) *Brit.* **1** a tin-mine. **2** (usu. in *pl.*) a tin-mining district in Cornwall and Devon. □ **stannary court** a legal body for the regulation of tin-miners in the stannaries. [med.L *stannaria* (pl.) f. LL *stannum* tin]

stannic /stánnik/ *adj. Chem.* of or relating to tetravalent tin (*stannic acid*; *stannic chloride*). [LL *stannum* tin]

stannous /stánnəss/ *adj. Chem.* of or relating to bivalent tin (*stannous salts*; *stannous chloride*).

stanza /stánzə/ *n.* **1** the basic metrical unit in a poem or verse consisting of a recurring group of lines (often four lines and usu. not more than twelve) which may or may not rhyme. **2** a group of four lines in some Greek and Latin metres. □□ **stanza'd** *adj.* (also **stanzaed**) (also in *comb.*). **stanzaic** /-záyik/ *adj.* [It., = standing-place, chamber, stanza, ult. f. L *stare* stand]
■ see PASSAGE[1] 6.

stapelia /stəpeéliə/ *n.* any S. African plant of the genus *Stapelia*, with flowers having an unpleasant smell. [mod.L f. J. B. von *Stapel*, Du. botanist d. 1636]

stapes /stáypeez/ *n.* (*pl.* same) a small stirrup-shaped bone in the ear of a mammal. [mod.L f. med.L *stapes* stirrup]

staphylococcus /stáffiləkókkəss/ *n.* (*pl.* **staphylococci** /-kī/) any bacterium of the genus *Staphylococcus*, occurring in grapelike clusters, and sometimes causing pus formation usu. in the skin and mucous membranes of animals. □□ **staphylococcal** *adj.* [mod.L f. Gk *staphulē* bunch of grapes + *kokkos* berry]

staple[1] /stáyp'l/ *n.* & *v.* ● *n.* a U-shaped metal bar or piece of wire with pointed ends for driving into, securing, or fastening together various materials or for driving through and clenching papers, netting, electric wire, etc. ● *v.tr.* provide or fasten with a staple. □ **staple gun** a hand-held device for driving in staples. □□ **stapler** *n.* [OE *stapol* f. Gmc]

staple[2] /stáyp'l/ *n.*, *adj.*, & *v.* ● *n.* **1** the principal or an important article of commerce (*the staples of British industry*). **2** the chief element or a main component, e.g. of a diet. **3** a raw material. **4** the fibre of cotton or wool etc. as determining its quality (*cotton of fine staple*). ● *adj.* **1** main or principal (*staple commodities*). **2** important as a product or an export. ● *v.tr.* sort or classify (wool etc.) according to fibre. [ME f. OF *estaple* market f. MLG, MDu. *stapel* market (as STAPLE[1])]
■ *n.* **1, 2** necessity, essential, basic, fundamental. ● *adj.* **1** basic, elementary, essential, necessary, requisite, required, vital, indispensable, critical, fundamental, primary, principal, main, chief; standard, usual, habitual, ordinary, customary, prevailing, normal, conventional, universal.

star /staar/ *n.* & *v.* ● *n.* **1** a celestial body appearing as a luminous point in the night sky. **2** (in full **fixed star**) such a body so far from the earth as to appear motionless (cf. PLANET, COMET). **3** a large naturally luminous gaseous body such as the sun is. **4** a celestial body regarded as influencing a person's fortunes etc. (*born under a lucky star*). **5** a thing resembling a star in shape or appearance. **6** a star-shaped mark, esp. a white mark on a horse's forehead. **7** a figure or object with radiating points esp. as the insignia of an order, as a decoration or mark of rank, or showing a category of excellence (*a five-star hotel*; *was awarded a gold star*). **8 a** a famous or brilliant person; the principal or most prominent performer in a play, film, etc. (*the star of the show*). **b** (*attrib.*) outstanding; particularly brilliant (*star pupil*). **9** (in full **star connection**) *Electr.* a Y-shaped arrangement of three-phase windings. **10** = *star prisoner*. ● *v.* (**starred, starring**) **1 a** *tr.* (of a film etc.) feature as a principal performer. **b** *intr.* (of a performer) be featured in a film etc. **2** (esp. as **starred** *adj.*) **a** mark, set, or adorn with a star or stars. **b** put an asterisk or star beside (a name, an item in a list, etc.). □ **my stars!** *colloq.* an expression of surprise. **star-apple** an edible purple apple-like fruit (with a starlike cross-section) of a tropical evergreen tree, *Chrysophyllum cainito*. **Star Chamber** *Brit. Law* **1** *hist.* a court of civil and criminal jurisdiction noted for its arbitrary procedure, and abolished in 1640. **2** any arbitrary or oppressive tribunal. **star-crossed** *archaic* ill-fated. **star fruit** = CARAMBOLA. **star-gaze 1** gaze at or study the stars. **2** gaze intently. **star-gazer 1** *colloq.* usu. *derog.* or *joc.* an astronomer or astrologer. **2** *Austral. sl.* a horse that turns its head when galloping. **star of Bethlehem** any of various plants with starlike flowers esp. *Ornithogalum umbellatum* with white star-shaped flowers striped with green on the outside (see Matt. 2:9). **Star of David** a figure consisting of two interlaced equilateral triangles used as a Jewish and Israeli symbol. **star prisoner** *Brit. sl.* a convict serving a first prison sentence. **star route** *US* a postal delivery route served by private contractors. **Stars and Bars** the flag of the Confederate States of the US. **Stars and Stripes** the national flag of the US. **star sapphire** a cabochon sapphire reflecting a star-like image due to its regular internal structure. **star shell** an explosive projectile designed to burst in the air and light up the enemy's position. **star-spangled** (esp. of the US national flag) covered or glittering with stars. **star stream** a systematic drift of stars. **star-studded** containing or covered with many stars, esp. featuring many famous performers. **star turn** the principal item in an entertainment or performance. **Star Wars** *colloq.* the strategic defence initiative. □□ **stardom** *n.* **starless** *adj.* **starlike** *adj.* [OE *steorra* f. Gmc]
■ *n.* **1** celestial body, heavenly body; fixed star, evening star, morning star, falling star, shooting star, comet, lodestar, pole star; nova, supernova. **5** asterisk, pentagram. **8 a** celebrity, personage, dignitary, VIP, name, somebody, luminary, leading light, leading man, leading woman *or* lady, lead, principal, diva, prima donna, hero, heroine, idol, superstar, megastar, big name, (big) draw, pin-up, *US* headliner, *colloq.* bigwig, big noise *or* shot *or US* wheel, celeb, *sl.* big-timer. **b** principal, major, leading, important, celebrated, famous, famed, prominent, eminent, pre-eminent, outstanding, distinguished, brilliant, illustrious, unequalled, peerless, matchless, incomparable, unrivalled, inimitable, unmatched, unparalleled, top, foremost. ● *v.* **1 a** feature. **b** be featured; play *or* perform *or* act *or* take the lead *or* leading part *or* leading role. □ **Star Chamber 2** interrogation, third degree, grilling, *usu derog.* inquisition; *esp. hist.* show trial. **star-crossed** see *doomed* (DOOM *v.* 2). **star-gazer 1** astronomer, astrologer; see also *fortune-teller*. □□ **stardom** see FAME 1, 2. **starless** see BLACK *adj.* 2.

starboard /staárbərd/ *n.* & *v. Naut.* & *Aeron.* ● *n.* the right-hand side (looking forward) of a ship, boat, or aircraft (cf. PORT[3]). ● *v.tr.* (also *absol.*) turn (the helm) to starboard. □ **starboard tack** see TACK[1] 4. **starboard watch** see WATCH *n.* 3b. [OE *stēorbord* = rudder side (see STEER, BOARD), early Teutonic ships being steered with a paddle over the right side]
■ *n.* right (side *or* hand).

starch /staarch/ *n.* & *v.* ● *n.* **1** an odourless tasteless polysaccharide occurring widely in plants and obtained chiefly from cereals and potatoes, forming an important constitutent of the human diet. **2** a preparation of this for stiffening fabric before ironing. **3** stiffness of manner; formality. • *v.tr.* stiffen (clothing) with starch. □ **starch-reduced** (esp. of food) containing less than the normal proportion of starch. □□ **starcher** *n.* [earlier as verb: ME *sterche* f. OE *stercan* (unrecorded) stiffen f. Gmc: cf. STARK]

starchy /staárchi/ *adj.* (**starchier, starchiest**) **1 a** of or like starch. **b** containing much starch. **2** (of a person) precise, prim. □□ **starchily** *adv.* **starchiness** *n.*
▪ **2** see STIFF *adj.* 5.

stardust /staárdust/ *n.* **1** a twinkling mass. **2** a romantic mystical look or sensation. **3** a multitude of stars looking like dust.

stare /stair/ *v.* & *n.* • *v.* **1** *intr.* (usu. foll. by *at*) look fixedly with eyes open, esp. as the result of curiosity, surprise, bewilderment, admiration, horror, etc. (*sat staring at the door*; *stared in amazement*). **2** *intr.* (of eyes) be wide open and fixed. **3** *intr.* be unpleasantly prominent or striking. **4** *tr.* (foll. by *into*) reduce (a person) to a specified condition by staring (*stared me into silence*). • *n.* a staring gaze. □ **stare down** (or **out**) outstare. **stare a person in the face** be evident or imminent. □□ **starer** *n.* [OE *starian* f. Gmc]
▪ *v.* **1** gaze, gape, goggle, watch, peer, glare; ogle; *archaic* quiz, *colloq.* gawk, rubberneck, *Brit. colloq.* gawp. • *n.* (fixed *or* blank) look; goggle, gaze, glare.

starfish /staárfish/ *n.* an echinoderm of the class Asteroidea with five or more radiating arms.

stark /staark/ *adj.* & *adv.* • *adj.* **1** desolate, bare (*a stark landscape*). **2** sharply evident; brutally simple. (*in stark contrast, the stark reality*). **3** downright, sheer (*stark madness*). **4** completely naked. **5** *archaic* strong, stiff, rigid. • *adv.* completely, wholly (*stark mad*; *stark naked*). □□ **starkly** *adv.* **starkness** *n.* [OE *stearc* f. Gmc: stark naked f. earlier *start-naked* f. obs. *start* tail: cf. REDSTART]
▪ *adj.* **1** harsh, severe, bleak, barren, desolate, dreary, grey, cold, cheerless, depressing, grim, ravaged, empty, vacant, austere, bare, plain, simple, Spartan, unembellished, unadorned, *colloq.* spooky, *poet.* drear. **2** clear, plain, evident, obvious, patent, manifest, overt, conspicuous, flagrant, blatant, gross, rank; bare, blunt, unadorned, unembellished, harsh, hard, grim. **3** sheer, complete, utter, absolute, perfect, pure, thorough, thoroughgoing, arrant, unmitigated, out and out, downright, outright, total, unconditional, unqualified. **4** see NAKED 1. • *adv.* completely, utterly, unqualifiedly, wholly, absolutely, entirely, quite, totally, fully, altogether, plainly, obviously, clearly. □□ **starkly** see *clearly* (CLEAR), *severely* (SEVERE). **starkness** see *severity* (SEVERE).

Stark effect /staark/ *n. Physics* the splitting of a spectrum line into several components by the application of an electric field. [J. *Stark*, Ger. physicist d. 1957]

starkers /staárkərz/ *adj. Brit. sl.* stark naked.
▪ see NAKED 1.

starlet /staárlit/ *n.* **1** a promising young performer, esp. a woman. **2** a little star.

starlight /staárlīt/ *n.* **1** the light of the stars (*walked home by starlight*). **2** (*attrib.*) = STARLIT (*a starlight night*).

starling[1] /staárling/ *n.* **1** a small gregarious partly migratory bird, *Sturnus vulgaris*, with blackish-brown speckled lustrous plumage, chiefly inhabiting cultivated areas. **2** any similar bird of the family Sturnidae. [OE *stærlinc* f. *stær* starling f. Gmc: cf. -LING[1]]

starling[2] /staárling/ *n.* piles built around or upstream of a bridge or pier to protect it from floating rubbish etc. [perh. corrupt. of (now dial.) *staddling* STADDLE]

starlit /staárlit/ *adj.* **1** lighted by stars. **2** with stars visible.

starry /staári/ *adj.* (**starrier, starriest**) **1** covered with stars. **2** resembling a star. □ **starry-eyed** *colloq.* **1** visionary; enthusiastic but impractical. **2** euphoric. □□ **starrily** *adv.* **starriness** *n.*
▪ □ **starry-eyed** see *idealistic* (IDEALISM).

START /staart/ *abbr.* Strategic Arms Reduction Treaty (or Talks).

start /staart/ *v.* & *n.* • *v.* **1** *tr.* & *intr.* begin; commence (*started work*; *started crying*; *started to shout*; *the play starts at eight*). **2** *tr.* set (proceedings, an event, etc.) in motion (*start the meeting*; *started a fire*). **3** *intr.* (often foll. by *on*) make a beginning (*started on a new project*). **4** *intr.* (often foll. by *after, for*) set oneself in motion or action (*'wait!' he shouted, and started after her*). **5** *intr.* set out; begin a journey etc. (*we start at 6 a.m.*). **6** (often foll. by *up*) **a** *intr.* (of a machine) begin operating (*the car wouldn't start*). **b** *tr.* cause (a machine etc.) to begin operating (*tried to start the engine*). **7** *tr.* **a** cause or enable (a person) to make a beginning (with something) (*started me in business with £10,000*). **b** (foll. by pres. part.) cause (a person) to begin (doing something) (*the smoke started me coughing*). **c** *Brit. colloq.* complain or be critical (*don't you start*). **8** *tr.* (often foll. by *up*) found or establish; originate. **9** *intr.* (foll. by *at, with*) have as the first of a series of items, e.g. in a meal (*we started with soup*). **10** *tr.* give a signal to (competitors) to start in a race. **11** *intr.* (often foll. by *up, from,* etc.) make a sudden movement from surprise, pain, etc. (*started at the sound of my voice*). **12** *intr.* (foll. by *out, up, from,* etc.) spring out, up, etc. (*started up from the chair*). **13** *tr.* conceive (a baby). **14** *tr.* rouse (game etc.) from its lair. **15 a** *intr.* (of timbers etc.) spring from their proper position; give way. **b** *tr.* cause or experience (timbers etc.) to do this. **16** *intr.* (foll. by *out, to,* etc.) (of a thing) move or appear suddenly (*tears started to his eyes*). **17** *intr.* (foll. by *from*) (of eyes, usu. with exaggeration) burst forward (from their sockets etc.). **18** *tr.* pour out (liquor) from a cask. • *n.* **1** a beginning of an event, action, journey, etc. (*missed the start*; *an early start tomorrow*; *made a fresh start*). **2** the place from which a race etc. begins. **3** an advantage given at the beginning of a race etc. (*a 15-second start*). **4** an advantageous initial position in life, business, etc. (*a good start in life*). **5** a sudden movement of surprise, pain, etc. (*you gave me a start*). **6** an intermittent or spasmodic effort or movement (esp. *in* or *by fits and starts*). **7** *colloq.* a surprising occurrence (*a queer start*; *a rum start*). □ **for a start** *colloq.* as a beginning; in the first place. **get the start of** gain an advantage over. **start a hare** see HARE. **start in** *colloq.* **1** begin. **2** (foll. by *on*) *US* make a beginning on. **start off 1** begin; commence (*started off on a lengthy monologue*). **2** begin to move (*it's time we started off*). **start out 1** begin a journey. **2** *colloq.* (foll. by *to* + infin.) proceed as intending (to do something). **start over** *US* begin again. **start school** attend school for the first time. **start something** *colloq.* cause trouble. **start up** arise; occur. **to start with 1** in the first place; before anything else is considered (*should never have been there to start with*). **2** at the beginning (*had six members to start with*). [OE (orig. in sense 11) f. Gmc]
▪ *v.* **1, 2** start off *or* up, begin, get going, get under way, open, set in motion, activate, trigger (off), get *or* start the ball rolling, *colloq.* get off the ground, kick off, start in, *formal* commence. **3** (*start on*) embark on, enter upon, begin on, take up, strike out on, *US colloq.* start in on. **4, 5** start off *or* up *or* out, go, leave, depart, get going, move (off *or* out *or* on), make a move, get under way, be on one's way, set off *or* out *or* forth, *colloq.* start in, get the show on the road, *sl.* hit the road, *US sl.* hit the trail. **6 b** start up, turn on, switch on, crank up, activate, set in motion. **8** establish, found, begin, set up, launch, introduce, inaugurate, initiate, instigate, institute, originate, create, pioneer, father, give birth to, *archaic* engender, *literary* beget. **9** begin, open, *formal* commence. **11** jump, flinch, blench, quail, shy, recoil, wince, shrink, draw back. **12** see SPRING *v.* 1. **14** rouse, cause to spring *or* leap *or* dart *or* jump *or* bound. **16** see WELL[2] *v.* **17** bulge, protrude, stick out. • *n.* **1** beginning(s), opening, outset, onset, inception, initiation, rise, genesis, creation, emergence, origin, inauguration, launch, founding, foundation,

introduction, institution, establishment, *formal* commencement, *rhet.* birth; dawn, threshold, brink, verge, start-up; *colloq.* kick-off. **2** starting-line, starting-gate, starting post; starting-point. **3** head start, advantage, lead, edge, *colloq.* jump, drop. **4** advantage, head start, opportunity, chance, beginning, opening, *colloq.* break. **5** see JUMP *n.* 2a, TURN *n.* 13. □ **start in** **1** see START *v.* 1, 2 above. **2** (*start in on*) see START *v.* 3 above. **start off** **1** see START *v.* 1, 2 above; (*start off on*) see START *v.* 3 above. **2** see START *v.* 4, 5 above. **start out** **1** see START *v.* 4, 5 above. **start up** start (off *or* in), arise, occur, come up, come to be, come into being, emerge, crop up, develop, begin, get under way, originate, *formal* commence. **to start with** see FIRST *adv.* 1.

starter /staártər/ *n.* **1** a person or thing that starts. **2** an esp. automatic device for starting the engine of a motor vehicle etc. **3** a person giving the signal for the start of a race. **4** a horse or competitor starting in a race (*a list of probable starters*). **5** the first course of a meal. **6** the initial action etc. □ **for starters** *sl.* to start with. **under starter's orders** (of racehorses etc.) in a position to start a race and awaiting the starting-signal.

■ **1** see APPRENTICE *n.* **5** see HORS-D'ŒUVRE.

starting /staárting/ *n.* in senses of START *v.* □ **starting-block** a shaped rigid block for bracing the feet of a runner at the start of a race. **starting-gate** a movable barrier for securing a fair start in horse-races. **starting-handle** *Brit. Mech.* a crank for starting a motor engine. **starting pistol** a pistol used to give the signal for the start of a race. **starting-point** the point from which a journey, process, argument, etc. begins. **starting post** the post from which competitors start in a race. **starting price** the odds ruling at the start of a horse-race. **starting stall** a compartment for one horse at the start of a race.

■ □ **starting-point** see BASE[1] *n.* 2, 3.

startle /staárt'l/ *v.tr.* give a shock or surprise to; cause (a person etc.) to start with surprise or sudden alarm. □□ **startler** *n.* [OE *steartlian* (as START, -LE[4])]

■ frighten, alarm, surprise, scare, disturb, unsettle, upset, discompose, catch unawares, make a person jump, jolt, jar, dismay, perturb, stun, take aback, take by surprise, shock, astound, astonish, shake up, give a person a start, *colloq.* give a person a turn, *US joc.* discombobulate.

startling /staártling/ *adj.* **1** surprising. **2** alarming (*startling news*). □□ **startlingly** *adv.*

■ surprising, amazing, astounding, astonishing, awesome, staggering, shocking, unexpected, unforeseen, jarring, disturbing, unsettling, upsetting, alarming, terrifying, frightening.

starve /staarv/ *v.* **1** *intr.* die of hunger; suffer from malnourishment. **2** *tr.* cause to die of hunger or suffer from lack of food. **3** *intr.* suffer from extreme poverty. **4** *intr. colloq.* (esp. as **starved** or **starving** *adjs.*) feel very hungry (*I'm starving*). **5** *intr.* **a** suffer from mental or spiritual want. **b** (foll. by *for*) feel a strong craving for (sympathy, amusement, knowledge, etc.). **6** *tr.* **a** (foll. by *of*) deprive of; keep scantily supplied with (*starved of affection*). **b** cause to suffer from mental or spiritual want. **7** *tr.* **a** (foll. by *into*) compel by starving (*starved into submission*). **b** (foll. by *out*) compel to surrender etc. by starving (*starved them out*). **8** *intr. archaic* or *dial.* perish with or suffer from cold. □□ **starvation** /-váysh'n/ *n.* [OE *steorfan* die]

■ **4** (**starved** or **starving**) (extremely) hungry, famished, ravenous. **5 b** (*starve for*) yearn for, hanker for, hunger for, pine for, long for, crave (for), thirst for *or* after, desire, ache for; (*be starving for*) be dying for, be hungry for, be burning for, be desirous of. **6** (*starve of*) deprive of; (*be starved of*) be in need *or* want of, be lacking, be bereft of. □□ **starvation** hunger, deprivation, undernourishment, malnutrition, malnourishment, *archaic* famine.

starveling /staárvling/ *n.* & *adj. archaic* ● *n.* a starving or ill-fed person or animal. ● *adj.* **1** starving. **2** meagre.

starwort /staárwurt/ *n.* a plant of the genus *Stellaria* with star-like flowers.

stash /stash/ *v.* & *n. colloq.* ● *v.tr.* (often foll. by *away*) **1** conceal; put in a safe or hidden place. **2** hoard, stow, store. ● *n.* **1** a hiding-place or hide-out. **2** a thing hidden; a cache. [18th c.: orig. unkn.]

■ *v.* see CACHE *v.* ● *n.* **1** see CACHE *n.* 1. **2** see CACHE *n.* 2.

stasis /stáysiss, stássiss/ *n.* (*pl.* **stases** /-seez/) **1** inactivity; stagnation; a state of equilibrium. **2** a stoppage of circulation of any of the body fluids. [mod.L f. Gk f. *sta-* STAND]

-stasis /stássiss, stáysiss/ *comb. form* (*pl.* **-stases** /-seez/) *Physiol.* forming nouns denoting a slowing or stopping (*haemostasis*). □□ **-static** *comb. form* forming adjectives.

-stat /stat/ *comb. form* forming nouns with ref. to keeping fixed or stationary (*rheostat*). [Gk *statos* stationary]

state /stayt/ *n.* & *v.* ● *n.* **1** the existing condition or position of a person or thing (*in a bad state of repair*; *in a precarious state of health*). **2** *colloq.* **a** an excited, anxious, or agitated mental condition (esp. *in a state*). **b** an untidy condition. **3** (usu. **State**) **a** an organized political community under one government; a commonwealth; a nation. **b** such a community forming part of a federal republic, esp. the United States of America. **c** (**the States**) the US. **4** (usu. **State**) (*attrib.*) **a** of, for, or concerned with the State (*State documents*). **b** reserved for or done on occasions of ceremony (*State apartments*; *State visit*). **c** involving ceremony (*State opening of Parliament*). **5** (usu. **State**) civil government (*Church and State*; *Secretary of State*). **6 a** pomp, rank, dignity (*as befits their state*). **b** imposing display; ceremony, splendour (*arrive in state*). **7** (**the States**) the legislative body in Jersey, Guernsey, and Alderney. **8** *Bibliog.* one of two or more variant forms of a single edition of a book. **9 a** an etched or engraved plate at a particular stage of its progress. **b** an impression taken from this. ● *v.tr.* **1** express, esp. fully or clearly, in speech or writing (*have stated my opinion*; *must state full particulars*). **2** fix, specify (*at stated intervals*). **3** *Law* specify the facts of (a case) for consideration. **4** *Mus.* play (a theme etc.) so as to make it known to the listener. □ **in state** with all due ceremony. **of State** concerning politics or government. **State capitalism** a system of State control and use of capital. **State Department** (in the US) the department of foreign affairs. **State-house** *US* the building where the legislature of a State meets. **State house** *NZ* a private house built at the government's expense. **state of the art** **1** the current stage of development of a practical or technological subject. **2** (usu. **state-of-the-art**) (*attrib.*) using the latest techniques or equipment (*state-of-the-art weaponry*). **state of grace** the condition of being free from grave sin. **state of life** rank and occupation. **state of things** (or **affairs** or **play**) the circumstances; the current situation. **state of war** the situation when war has been declared or is in progress. **State prisoner** see PRISONER. **State school** a school managed and funded by the public authorities. **State's evidence** see EVIDENCE. **States General** *hist.* the legislative body in the Netherlands, and in France before 1789. **State socialism** a system of State control of industries and services. **States' rights** *US* the rights and powers not assumed by the United States but reserved to its individual States. **State trial** prosecution by the State. **State university** *US* a university managed by the public authorities of a State. □□ **statable** *adj.* **statedly** *adv.* **statehood** *n.* [ME: partly f. ESTATE, partly f. L STATUS]

■ *n.* **1** condition(s), circumstance(s), situation, state of affairs, status, position; shape, structure, form, constitution, phase, stage; trim, order, repair, fettle; see also *frame of mind* (FRAME *n.* 7). **2 a** see STEW *n.* 2. **b** see SHAMBLES. **3 a** nation, country, land, commonwealth, body politic, domain, *formal esp. Law* realm. **4** (*attrib.*) **a** governmental, government, national, federal. **b, c** ceremonial, formal, dignified, stately, solemn, official; royal, regal, imperial, majestic. **5** government, administration. **6 b** grandeur, pomp, style, ceremony, splendour, magnificence, glory, brilliance. ● *v.* **1** assert, asseverate, declare, affirm, express, report, articulate, formulate, enunciate, voice, communicate, announce, proclaim, specify, delineate, claim, maintain, allege, submit, confirm, *formal* aver; say, testify, hold, have it that. **2** fix, specify, define, delineate, designate, determine, set. □ **state of things** (or **affairs** or **play**) see SITUATION 2. **State school** government school, *US*, *Austral.*, & *Sc. etc.* public school.

statecraft /stáytkraaft/ *n.* the art of conducting affairs of State.
▪ see POLITICS 1.

stateless /stáytliss/ *adj.* **1** (of a person) having no nationality or citizenship. **2** without a State. □□ **statelessness** *n.*

stately /stáytli/ *adj.* (**statelier, stateliest**) dignified; imposing; grand. □ **stately home** *Brit.* a large magnificent house, esp. one open to the public. □□ **stateliness** *n.*
▪ dignified, august, solemn, distinguished, impressive, striking, imposing, awesome, grand, lofty, elevated, noble, majestic, regal, royal, imperial. □ **stately home** see RESIDENCE 2c. □□ **stateliness** see DIGNITY 1.

statement /stáytmənt/ *n.* **1** the act or an instance of stating or being stated; expression in words. **2** a thing stated; a declaration (*that statement is unfounded*). **3** a formal account of facts, esp. to the police or in a court of law (*make a statement*). **4** a record of transactions in a bank account etc. **5** a formal notification of the amount due to a tradesman etc.
▪ **1–3** assertion, allegation, declaration, affirmation, asseveration, averment, announcement, annunciation, proclamation, profession, utterance, expression, disclosure, communication; communiqué, proposition, report, account, testimony, *Law* deposition, affidavit, *sl.* verbal. **5** account, bill, invoice.

stater /stáytər/ *n.* an ancient Greek gold or silver coin. [ME f. LL f. Gk *statēr*]

stateroom /stáytrōōm, -rŏŏm/ *n.* **1** a state apartment in a palace, hotel, etc. **2** a private compartment in a passenger ship or *US* train.

Stateside /stáytsīd/ *adj. US colloq.* of, in, or towards the United States.

statesman /stáytsmən/ *n.* (*pl.* **-men**; *fem.* **stateswoman**, *pl.* **-women**) **1** a person skilled in affairs of State, esp. one taking an active part in politics. **2** a distinguished and capable politician. □□ **statesmanlike** *adj.* **statesmanly** *adj.* **statesmanship** *n.* [= *state's man* after F *homme d'état*]
▪ see POLITICIAN. □□ **statesmanship** see POLITICS 1.

statewide /stáytwīd/ *adj. US* so as to include or cover a whole State.

static /státtik/ *adj.* & *n.* ● *adj.* **1** stationary; not acting or changing; passive. **2** *Physics* **a** concerned with bodies at rest or forces in equilibrium (opp. DYNAMIC). **b** acting as weight but not moving (*static pressure*). **c** of statics. ● *n.* **1** static electricity. **2** atmospherics. **3** orig. *US sl.* aggravation, fuss; criticism. □ **static electricity** electricity not flowing as a current. **static line** a length of cord attached to an aircraft etc. which releases a parachute without the use of a ripcord. [mod.L *staticus* f. Gk *statikos* f. *sta-* stand]
▪ *adj.* **1** immovable, immobile, unmoving, motionless, stationary, fixed, stagnant, inert, still, passive, unchanging, unchanged, changeless, unvarying, invariable, constant, steady. ● *n.* **2** interference, noise, atmospherics. **3** difficulty, trouble, problem(s), aggravation, fuss, confusion, interference, *colloq.* hassle; flak, criticism.

statical /státtik'l/ *adj.* = STATIC. □□ **statically** *adv.*

statice /státtisi/ *n.* **1** sea lavender. **2** sea pink. [L f. Gk, fem. of *statikos* STATIC (with ref. to stanching of blood)]

statics /státtiks/ *n.pl.* (usu. treated as *sing.*) **1** the science of bodies at rest or of forces in equilibrium (opp. DYNAMICS). **2** = STATIC. [STATIC *n.* in the same senses + -ICS]

station /stáysh'n/ *n.* & *v.* ● *n.* **1 a** a regular stopping place on a public transport route, esp. one on a railway line with a platform and usu. administrative buildings. **b** these buildings (see also *bus station*, *coach station*). **2** a place or building etc. where a person or thing stands or is placed, esp. habitually or for a definite purpose. **3 a** a designated point or establishment where a particular service or activity is based or organized (*police station*; *polling station*). **b** *US* a subsidiary post office. **4** an establishment involved in radio or television broadcasting. **5 a** a military or naval base esp. *hist.* in India. **b** the inhabitants of this. **6** position in life; rank or status (*ideas above your station*). **7** *Austral.* & *NZ* a large sheep or cattle farm. **8** *Bot.* a particular place where an unusual species etc. grows. ● *v.tr.* **1** assign a station to. **2** put in position. □ **station-bill** *Naut.* a list showing the prescribed stations of a ship's crew for various drills or in an emergency. **station break** *US* a pause between broadcast programmes for an announcement of the identity of the station transmitting them. **station hand** *Austral.* a worker on a large sheep or cattle farm. **station house** *US* a police station. **station-keeping** the maintenance of one's proper relative position in a moving body of ships etc. **station of the cross** *RC Ch.* **a** each of a series of usu. 14 images or pictures representing the events in Christ's passion before which devotions are performed in some churches. **b** each of these devotions. **station pointer** *Naut.* a ship's navigational instrument, often a three-armed protractor, for fixing one's place on a chart from the angle in the horizontal plane between two land- or sea-marks. **station sergeant** *Brit.* the sergeant in charge of a police station. **station-wagon** an estate car. [ME, = standing, f. OF f. L *statio -onis* f. *stare* stand]
▪ *n.* **1** railway station, train station, passenger station; stopping place, stop, stage; terminus, terminal; bus station, coach station, *US* depot. **2** place, position, spot, point, post, site, location, situation. **3 a** base, headquarters, centre, depot, office. **4** broadcaster, transmitter; channel. **5 a** see BASE[1] *n.* 3. **6** position, place, status, rank, caste, standing, class, level. ● *v.* **1** assign, appoint, post, install, garrison, billet, quarter. **2** position, place, spot, post, site, situate, locate, install, put, set, stand.

stationary /stáyshənəri, -shənri/ *adj.* **1** remaining in one place, not moving (*hit a stationary car*). **2** not meant to be moved; not portable (*stationary troops*; *stationary engine*). **3** not changing in magnitude, number, quality, efficiency, etc. (*stationary temperature*). **4** (of a planet) having no apparent motion in longitude. □ **stationary air** air remaining in the lungs during ordinary respiration. **stationary bicycle** a fixed exercise-machine resembling a bicycle. **stationary point** *Math.* a point on a curve where the gradient is zero. **stationary wave** = *standing wave*. □□ **stationariness** *n.* [ME f. L *stationarius* (as STATION)]
▪ **1, 3** see STATIC *adj.* **2** see IMMOVABLE *adj.* 1.

stationer /stáyshənər/ *n.* a person who sells writing materials etc. □ **Stationers' Hall** *Brit.* the hall of the Stationers' Company in London, at which a book was formerly registered for purposes of copyright. [ME, = bookseller (as STATIONARY in med.L sense 'shopkeeper', esp. bookseller, as opposed to pedlar)]

stationery /stáyshənəri, -shənri/ *n.* writing materials etc. sold by a stationer. □ **Stationery Office** (in the UK) the Government's publishing house which also provides stationery for Government offices.
▪ writing-paper, letterhead(s), paper and envelopes, writing materials *or* implements *or* supplies; office supplies *or* equipment.

stationmaster /stáysh'nmaastər/ *n.* the official in charge of a railway station.

statism /stáytiz'm/ *n.* centralized State administration and control of social and economic affairs.

statist /stáytist, státtist/ *n.* **1** a statistician. **2** a supporter of statism. [orig. 'politician' f. It. *statista* (as STATE)]

statistic /stətistik/ *n.* & *adj.* ● *n.* a statistical fact or item. ● *adj.* = STATISTICAL. [G *statistisch*, *Statistik* f. *Statist* (as STATIST)]

statistical /stətístik'l/ *adj.* of or relating to statistics. □ **statistical physics** physics as it is concerned with large numbers of particles to which statistics can be applied. **statistical significance** = SIGNIFICANCE 4. □□ **statistically** *adv.*

statistics /stətístiks/ *n.pl.* **1** (usu. treated as *sing.*) the science of collecting and analysing numerical data, esp. in or for large quantities, and usu. inferring proportions in a whole from proportions in a representative sample. **2** any systematic collection or presentation of such facts. □□ **statistician** /státtistísh'n/ *n.*
■ **2** see DATA.

stator /stáytər/ *n. Electr.* the stationary part of a machine, esp. of an electric motor or generator. [STATIONARY, after ROTOR]

statoscope /státtəskōp/ *n.* an aneroid barometer used to show minute variations of pressure, esp. to indicate the altitude of an aircraft. [Gk *statos* fixed f. *sta-* stand + -SCOPE]

statuary /státyoori/ *adj.* & *n.* ● *adj.* of or for statues (*statuary art*). ● *n.* (*pl.* **-ies**) **1** statues collectively. **2** the art of making statues. **3** a sculptor. □ **statuary marble** fine-grained white marble. [L *statuarius* (as STATUE)]

statue /státyoo, stáchoo/ *n.* a sculptured, cast, carved, or moulded figure of a person or animal, esp. life-size or larger (cf. STATUETTE). □□ **statued** *adj.* [ME f. OF f. L *statua* f. *stare* stand]
■ sculpture, figure, figurine, statuette, carving, casting, model, bronze, image, icon, effigy, representation, likeness; bust, colossus, figurehead, *Archit.* caryatid, *Bibl.* graven image.

statuesque /státyoo-ésk, stáchoo-ésk/ *adj.* like, or having the dignity or beauty of, a statue. □□ **statuesquely** *adv.* **statuesqueness** *n.* [STATUE + -ESQUE, after *picturesque*]
■ imposing, impressive, majestic, regal, stately, magnificent, noble, dignified, august, grand, well-proportioned, comely, handsome, queenly.

statuette /státyoo-ét, stáchoo-ét/ *n.* a small statue; a statue less than life-size. [F, dimin. of *statue*]
■ see STATUE.

stature /stáchər/ *n.* **1** the height of a (esp. human) body. **2** a degree of eminence, social standing, or advancement (*recruit someone of his stature*). □□ **statured** *adj.* (also in *comb.*). [ME f. OF f. L *statura* f. *stare stat-* stand]
■ **2** see STATUS 2.

status /stáytəss/ *n.* **1** rank, social position, relation to others, relative importance (*not sure of their status in the hierarchy*). **2** a superior social etc. position (*considering your status in the business*). **3** *Law* a person's legal standing which determines his or her rights and duties, e.g. citizen, alien, commoner, civilian, etc. **4** the position of affairs (*let me know if the status changes*). □ **status symbol** a possession etc. taken to indicate a person's high status. [L, = standing f. *stare* stand]
■ **1** see STANDING *n.* 1. **2** eminence, prominence, pre-eminence, standing, stature, importance, significance, repute, reputation, prestige, rank, station. **4** see SITUATION 2.

status quo /stáytəss kwō/ *n.* the existing state of affairs. [L, = the state in which]
■ see SCORE *n.* 7.

statutable /státyootəb'l/ *adj.* = STATUTORY, esp. in amount or value. □□ **statutably** *adv.*

statute /státyoot/ *n.* **1** a written law passed by a legislative body, e.g. an Act of Parliament. **2** a rule of a corporation, founder, etc., intended to be permanent (*against the University Statutes*). **3** divine law (*kept thy statutes*). □ **statute-barred** (of a case etc.) no longer legally enforceable by reason of the lapse of time. **statute-book 1** a book or books containing the statute law. **2** the body of a country's statutes. **statute law 1** (*collect.*) the body of principles and rules of law laid down in statutes as distinct from rules formulated in practical application (cf. *common law*, *case-law* (see CASE[1])). **2** a statute. **statute mile** see MILE 1. **statute-roll 1** the rolls in the Public Records Office containing the statutes of the Parliament of England. **2** = *statute-book*. **statutes at large** the statutes as originally enacted, regardless of later modifications. [ME f. OF *statut* f. LL *statutum* neut. past part. of L *statuere* set up f. *status*: see STATUS]
■ **1** see LAW 1b. **2** see RULE *n.* 1.

statutory /státyootəri, -tri/ *adj.* **1** required, permitted, or enacted by statute (*statutory minimum*; *statutory provisions*). **2** (of a criminal offence) carrying a penalty prescribed by statute. □ **statutory rape** *US* the offence of sexual intercourse with a minor. □□ **statutorily** *adv.*
■ **1** legal, constitutional, statutable.

staunch[1] /stawnch, staanch/ *adj.* (also **stanch**) **1** trustworthy, loyal (*my staunch friend and supporter*). **2** (of a ship, joint, etc.) strong, watertight, airtight, etc. □□ **staunchly** *adv.* **staunchness** *n.* [ME f. OF *estanche* fem. of *estanc* f. Rmc: see STANCH[1]]
■ **1** steadfast, loyal, firm, unflinching, steady, unshrinking, unswerving, dependable, reliable, stalwart, (tried and) true, devoted, constant, true-blue, trustworthy, trusted, faithful, unfaltering, undeviating, unwavering, *archaic or joc.* trusty. **2** strong, solid, sturdy, sound, well-built, stout, substantial, well-constructed, well-made, tough, rugged, long-lasting; watertight, seaworthy; airtight. □□ **staunchly** see *firmly* (FIRM[1]). **staunchness** see *tenacity* (TENACIOUS).

staunch[2] var. of STANCH[1].

stave /stayv/ *n.* & *v.* ● *n.* **1** each of the curved pieces of wood forming the sides of a cask, pail, etc. **2** = STAFF[1] *n.* 3. **3** a stanza or verse. **4** the rung of a ladder. ● *v.tr.* (*past* and *past part.* **stove** /stōv/ or **staved**) **1** break a hole in. **2** crush or knock out of shape. **3** fit or furnish (a cask etc.) with staves. □ **stave in** crush by forcing inwards. **stave off** avert or defer (danger or misfortune). **stave rhyme** alliteration, esp. in old Germanic poetry. [ME, back-form. f. *staves*, pl. of STAFF[1]]
■ □ **stave off** see PREVENT 1.

staves *pl.* of STAFF[1] *n.* 3.

stavesacre /stáyvzaykər/ *n.* a larkspur, *Delphinium staphisagria*, yielding seeds used as poison for vermin. [ME f. L *staphisagria* f. Gk *staphis agria* wild raisin]

stay[1] /stay/ *v.* & *n.* ● *v.* **1** *intr.* continue to be in the same place or condition; not depart or change (*stay here until I come back*). **2** *intr.* **a** (often foll. by *at*, *in*, *with*) have temporary residence as a visitor etc. (*stayed with them for Christmas*). **b** *Sc.* & *S.Afr.* dwell permanently. **3** *archaic* or *literary* **a** *tr.* stop or check (progress, the inroads of a disease, etc.). **b** *intr.* (esp. in *imper.*) pause in movement, action, speech, etc. (*Stay! You forget one thing*). **4** *tr.* postpone (judgement, decision, etc.). **5** *tr.* assuage (hunger etc.) esp. for a short time. **6 a** *intr.* show endurance. **b** *tr.* show endurance to the end of (a race etc.). **7** *tr.* (often foll. by *up*) *literary* support, prop up (as or with a buttress etc.). **8** *intr.* (foll. by *for*, *to*) wait long enough to share or join in an activity etc. (*stay to supper*; *stay for the film*). ● *n.* **1 a** the act or an instance of staying or dwelling in one place. **b** the duration of this (*just a ten-minute stay*; *a long stay in London*). **2** a suspension or postponement of a sentence, judgement, etc. (*was granted a stay of execution*). **3** *archaic* or *literary* a check or restraint (*will endure no stay*; *a stay upon his activity*). **4** endurance, staying power. **5** a prop or support. **6** (in *pl.*) *hist.* a corset esp. with whalebone etc. stiffening, and laced. □ **has come** (or **is here**) **to stay** *colloq.* must be regarded as permanent. **stay-at-home** *adj.* remaining habitually at home. ● *n.* a person who does this. **stay-bar** (or **-rod**) a support used in building or in machinery. **stay the course** pursue a course of action or endure a struggle etc. to the end. **stay one's hand** see HAND. **stay in** remain indoors or at home, esp. in school after hours as a punishment. **staying power** endurance, stamina. **stay-in strike** = *sit-down strike*. **stay the night** remain until the next day. **stay put** *colloq.* remain where it is placed or where one is. **stay up** not go to bed (until late at night). □□ **stayer** *n.* [AF *estai-* stem of OF *ester* f. L *stare* stand: sense 5 f. OF *estaye(r)* prop, formed as STAY[2]]

■ *v.* **1** remain, stop, wait, linger, loiter, hang about *or* around, *archaic or literary* tarry; stand, freeze; continue (to be), keep; *archaic or dial.* bide. **2** remain, stop, sojourn, visit; lodge, reside, live, *archaic* abide, *literary* dwell. **3 a** stop, arrest, thwart, prevent, put an end to, halt, interrupt, discontinue, block, check; stanch, stem, curb, retard, slow, delay, impede, foil, obstruct, hamper, hinder, discourage, deter. **4** delay, put off, defer, prorogue; see also POSTPONE. **6 a** see LAST[2]. **7** see PROP[1] *v.* **8** remain, linger, wait, hang about *or* around, *archaic or literary* tarry. ● *n.* **1** stopover, sojourn, visit, stop, stopoff, layover. **2** suspension, delay, postponement, deferment, deferral, reprieve; moratorium. **3** see CHECK[1] *n.* 2c. **4** see ENDURANCE 2. **5** see SUPPORT *n.* 2. □ **staying power** see ENDURANCE 2. **stay put** see REMAIN 2.

stay[2] /stay/ *n.* & *v.* ● *n.* **1** *Naut.* a rope or guy supporting a mast, spar, flagstaff, etc. **2** a tie-piece in an aircraft etc. ● *v.tr.* **1** support (a mast etc.) by stays. **2** put (a ship) on another tack. □ **be in stays** (of a sailing ship) be head to the wind while tacking. **miss stays** fail to be in stays. [OE *stæg* be firm, f. Gmc]

■ *n.* **1** guy, line, rope, cable, chain, support, brace, reinforcement; *Naut.* (running) backstay, forestay, mainstay, mizen-stay. ● *v.* **1** support, strengthen, secure, reinforce, brace, buttress, shore (up), *literary* gird.

staysail /stáysayl, stáys'l/ *n.* a triangular fore-and-aft sail extended on a stay.

STD *abbr.* **1** subscriber trunk dialling. **2** Doctor of Sacred Theology. [sense 2 f. L *Sanctae Theologiae Doctor*]

stead /sted/ *n.* □ **in a person's** or **thing's stead** as a substitute; instead of him or her or it. **stand a person in good stead** be advantageous or serviceable to him or her. [OE *stede* f. Gmc]

■ □ **in a person's** or **thing's stead** see INSTEAD 1.

steadfast /stédfaast/ *adj.* constant, firm, unwavering. □□ **steadfastly** *adv.* **steadfastness** *n.* [OE *stedefæst* (as STEAD, FAST[1])]

■ resolute, determined, persevering, resolved, single-minded, steady, unflinching, unfaltering, unwavering, unswerving, indefatigable, dependable, immovable, immutable, stable, firm, fixed, constant, persistent, unflagging, tireless, enduring, dedicated, deep-rooted, faithful, true, loyal, staunch. □□ **steadfastness** see PERSEVERANCE.

steading /stédding/ *n. Brit.* a farmstead.

■ see FARM *n.* 1.

steady /stéddi/ *adj.*, *v.*, *adv.*, *int.*, & *n.* ● *adj.* (**steadier**, **steadiest**) **1** firmly fixed or supported or standing or balanced; not tottering, rocking, or wavering. **2** done or operating or happening in a uniform and regular manner (*a steady pace*; *a steady increase*). **3 a** constant in mind or conduct; not changeable. **b** persistent. **4** (of a person) serious and dependable in behaviour; of industrious and temperate habits; safe; cautious. **5** regular, established (*a steady girlfriend*). **6** accurately directed; not faltering, controlled (*a steady hand*; *a steady eye*; *steady nerves*). **7** (of a ship) on course and upright. ● *v.tr.* & *intr.* (**-ies**, **-ied**) make or become steady (*steady the boat*). ● *adv.* steadily (*hold it steady*). ● *int.* as a command or warning to take care. ● *n.* (*pl.* **-ies**) *colloq.* a regular boyfriend or girlfriend. □ **go steady** (often foll. by *with*) *colloq.* have as a regular boyfriend or girlfriend. **steady down** become steady. **steady-going** staid; sober. **steady on!** a call to take care. **steady state** an unvarying condition, esp. in a physical process, e.g. of the universe having no beginning and no end. □□ **steadier** *n.* **steadily** *adv.* **steadiness** *n.* [STEAD = place, + -Y[1]]

■ *adj.* **1** stable, balanced, poised, settled, firm, fast, secure, solid. **2** even, regular, uniform, invariable, unvarying, unfluctuating, unwavering, undeviating, changeless, unchanging, continuous, constant; perpetual, non-stop, round the clock, persistent, uninterrupted, unbroken, unrelieved, unceasing, ceaseless, incessant, relentless, unremitting, sustained, never-ending, unending, endless. **3** see STEADFAST. **4** staid, sedate, sober, temperate, moderate, dignified, poised, sensible, down-to-earth, settled, serious, level-headed, reliable, dependable, industrious, diligent, conscientious, safe, cautious, careful, *colloq.* unflappable. **5** regular, established, devoted, firm, staunch, faithful, loyal, constant, long-standing, inveterate, consistent, confirmed, serious, persistent. **6** unflinching, unblinking, fixed, constant, continuous, unfaltering, accurate, direct; controlled, calm, cool, balanced, equable. ● *v.* stabilize, balance, hold fast; brace, secure, support. ● *adv.* firmly, fast, immovably, solidly, securely; steadily. ● *n.* (regular) boyfriend *or* girlfriend, sweetheart, woman, *colloq.* (regular) fellow *or* girl, man, guy, *sl.* gal. □ **go steady** keep company, consort, *colloq.* date regularly. □□ **steadily** see SURELY 3. **steadiness** see *regularity* (REGULAR), STABILITY.

steak /stayk/ *n.* **1** a thick slice of meat (esp. beef) or fish, often cut for grilling, frying, etc. **2** beef cut for stewing or braising. □ **steak-house** a restaurant specializing in serving beefsteaks. **steak-knife** a knife with a serrated steel blade for eating steak. [ME f. ON *steik* rel. to *steikja* roast on spit, *stikna* be roasted]

steal /steel/ *v.* & *n.* ● *v.* (*past* **stole** /stōl/; *past part.* **stolen** /stṓlən/) **1** *tr.* (also *absol.*) **a** take (another person's property) illegally. **b** take (property etc.) without right or permission, esp. in secret with the intention of not returning it. **2** *tr.* obtain surreptitiously or by surprise (*stole a kiss*). **3** *tr.* **a** gain insidiously or artfully. **b** (often foll. by *away*) win or get possession of (a person's affections etc.), esp. insidiously (*stole her heart away*). **4** *intr.* (foll. by *in*, *out*, *away*, *up*, etc.) **a** move, esp. silently or stealthily (*stole out of the room*). **b** (of a sound etc.) become gradually perceptible. **5** *tr.* **a** (in various sports) gain (a run, the ball, etc.) surreptitiously or by luck. **b** *Baseball* run to (a base) while the pitcher is in the act of delivery. ● *n.* **1** *US colloq.* the act or an instance of stealing or theft. **2** *colloq.* an unexpectedly easy task or good bargain. □ **steal a march on** get an advantage over by surreptitious means; anticipate. **steal the show** outshine other performers, esp. unexpectedly. **steal a person's thunder** use another person's words, ideas, etc., without permission and without giving credit. □□ **stealer** *n.* (also in *comb.*). **stealing** *n.* [OE *stelan* f. Gmc]

■ *v.* **1** take (away), appropriate, filch, thieve, shoplift, pilfer, plunder, make off with, walk off *or* away with, get away with; embezzle, misappropriate, peculate; hijack, usurp; plagiarize, pirate, borrow, poach, copy, imitate; *colloq.* lift, swipe, *formal or joc.* purloin, *sl.* pinch, snitch, sneak, knock off, hook, liberate, souvenir, *Austral. sl.* duff, snavel, *Brit. sl.* nick, *US sl.* heist. **4 a** sneak, creep, slip, slink, tiptoe, prowl, lurk, skulk, pussyfoot. ● *n.* **2** bargain, (good) buy, *colloq.* give-away, *Brit. sl.* snip. □ **steal a march on** see OUTSMART. □□ **stealer** see THIEF. **stealing** see THEFT.

stealth /stelth/ *n.* secrecy, a secret procedure. □ **by stealth** surreptitiously. [ME f. OE (as STEAL, -TH[2])]

■ stealthiness, furtiveness, secrecy, clandestinity, clandestineness, surreptitiousness, sneakiness, slyness, underhandedness. □ **by stealth** see *on the sly* (SLY).

stealthy /stélthi/ *adj.* (**stealthier**, **stealthiest**) **1** (of an action) done with stealth; proceeding imperceptibly. **2** (of a person or thing) acting or moving with stealth. □□ **stealthily** *adv.* **stealthiness** *n.*

■ furtive, secret, sly, clandestine, hugger-mugger, surreptitious, stealthful, insidious, sneaky, sneaking, undercover, underground, underhand(ed), covert, closet, backstairs; secretive, skulking. □□ **stealthily** see *on the sly* (SLY). **stealthiness** see STEALTH.

steam /steem/ *n.* & *v.* ● *n.* **1 a** the gas into which water is changed by boiling, used as a source of power by virtue of its expansion of volume. **b** a mist of liquid particles of water produced by the condensation of this gas. **2** any similar vapour. **3 a** energy or power provided by a steam engine or other machine. **b** *colloq.* power or energy generally. ● *v.* **1** *tr.* **a** cook (food) in steam. **b** soften or make pliable (timber etc.) or otherwise treat with steam. **2** *intr.* give off steam or other vapour, esp. visibly. **3** *intr.* **a** move under steam power (*the ship steamed down the river*). **b** (foll. by *ahead, away*, etc.) *colloq.* proceed or travel fast or with vigour. **4** *tr.* & *intr.* (usu. foll. by *up*) **a** cover or become covered with condensed steam. **b** (as **steamed up** *adj.*) *colloq.* angry or excited. **5** *tr.* (foll. by *open* etc.) apply steam to the gum of (a sealed envelope) to get it open. □ **get up steam 1** generate enough power to work a steam engine. **2** work oneself into an energetic or angry state. **let off steam** relieve one's pent up feelings or energy. **run out of steam** lose one's impetus or energy. **steam age** the era when trains were drawn by steam locomotives. **steam bath** a room etc. filled with steam for bathing in. **steam boiler** a vessel (in a steam engine etc.) in which water is boiled to generate steam. **steam engine 1** an engine which uses the expansion or rapid condensation of steam to generate power. **2** a locomotive powered by this. **steam gauge** a pressure gauge attached to a steam boiler. **steam hammer** a forging-hammer powered by steam. **steam-heat** the warmth given out by steam-heated radiators etc. **steam iron** an electric iron that emits steam from its flat surface, to improve its pressing ability. **steam-jacket** a casing for steam round a cylinder, for heating its contents. **steam organ** a fairground pipe-organ driven by a steam engine and played by means of a keyboard or a system of punched cards. **steam power** the force of steam applied to machinery etc. **steam shovel** an excavator powered by steam. **steam-tight** impervious to steam. **steam train** a train driven by a steam engine. **steam tug** a steamer for towing ships etc. **steam turbine** a turbine in which a high-velocity jet of steam rotates a bladed disc or drum. **under one's own steam** without assistance; unaided. [OE *stēam* f. Gmc]

■ *n.* **1** vapour, mist, fog, cloud, haze. ● *v.* **2** see REEK *v.* 3. **4 a** (*steam up*) see MIST *v.* **b** (**steamed up**) see ANGRY 1. □ **steam organ** *US* calliope.

steamboat /steémbōt/ *n.* a boat propelled by a steam engine.

steamer /steémər/ *n.* **1** a person or thing that steams. **2** a vessel propelled by steam, esp. a ship. **3** a vessel in which things are steamed, esp. cooked by steam. □ **steamer rug** *US* a travelling-rug.

steamroller /steémrōlər/ *n.* & *v.* ● *n.* **1** a heavy slow-moving vehicle with a roller, used to flatten new-made roads. **2** a crushing power or force. ● *v.tr.* **1** crush forcibly or indiscriminately. **2** (foll. by *through*) force (a measure etc.) through a legislature by overriding opposition.

steamship /steémship/ *n.* a ship propelled by a steam engine.

steamy /steémi/ *adj.* (**steamier, steamiest**) **1** like or full of steam. **2** *colloq.* erotic, salacious. □□ **steamily** *adv.* **steaminess** *n.*

■ **1** humid, steaming, damp, moist, muggy, sticky, dank, sweaty, sweltering, sodden, sultry, boiling, wet; steamed (up), fogged (up), befogged, misty, misted, hazy, clouded, cloudy, beclouded, dim, blurred. **2** erotic, passionate, (sexually) exciting, salacious, arousing, hot, torrid, sexy, *colloq.* raunchy.

stearic /steérik/ *adj.* derived from stearin. □ **stearic acid** a solid saturated fatty acid obtained from animal or vegetable fats. □□ **stearate** /-rayt/ *n.* [F *stéarique* f. Gk *stear steatos* tallow]

stearin /steérin/ *n.* **1** a glyceryl ester of stearic acid, esp. in the form of a white crystalline constituent of tallow etc. **2** a mixture of fatty acids used in candle-making. [F *stéarine* f. Gk *stear steatos* tallow]

steatite /steéətīt/ *n.* a soapstone or other impure form of talc. □□ **steatitic** /-títtik/ *adj.* [L *steatitis* f. Gk *steatītēs* f. *stear steatos* tallow]

steatopygia /steéətōpíjiə/ *n.* an excess of fat on the buttocks. □□ **steatopygous** /-pīgəss, -tóppigəss/ *adj.* [mod.L (as STEATITE + Gk *pugē* rump)]

steed /steed/ *n. archaic* or *poet.* a horse, esp. a fast powerful one. [OE *stēda* stallion, rel. to STUD[2]]

■ see MOUNT[1] *n.* 3a.

steel /steel/ *n., adj.,* & *v.* ● *n.* **1** any of various alloys of iron and carbon with other elements increasing strength and malleability, much used for making tools, weapons, etc., and capable of being tempered to many different degrees of hardness. **2** hardness of character; strength, firmness (*nerves of steel*). **3 a** a rod of steel, usu. roughened and tapering, on which knives are sharpened. **b** a strip of steel for expanding a skirt or stiffening a corset. **4** (not in *pl.*) *literary* a sword, lance, etc. (*foemen worthy of their steel*). ● *adj.* **1** made of steel. **2** like or having the characteristics of steel. ● *v.tr.* & *refl.* harden or make resolute (*steeled myself for a shock*). □ **cold steel** cutting or thrusting weapons. **pressed steel** steel moulded under pressure. **steel band** a group of usu. W. Indian musicians with percussion instruments made from oil drums. **steel-clad** wearing armour. **steel engraving** the process of engraving on or an impression taken from a steel-coated copper plate. **steel wool** an abrasive substance consisting of a mass of fine steel shavings. [OE *stȳle, stēli* f. Gmc, rel. to STAY[2]]

■ *n.* **4** sword, dagger, knife, dirk, stiletto, lance, *poet.* blade. ● *adj.* **2** see STEELY. ● *v.* inure, insulate, protect; brace, nerve, stiffen, strengthen, fortify, prepare; (*steel oneself*) grit one's teeth, bear up, screw up one's courage; *sl.* bite the bullet.

steelhead /steélhed/ *n.* a large N. American rainbow trout.

steelwork /steélwurk/ *n.* articles of steel.

steelworks /steélwurks/ *n.pl.* (usu. treated as *sing.*) a place where steel is manufactured. □□ **steelworker** *n.*

steely /steéli/ *adj.* (**steelier, steeliest**) **1** of, or hard as, steel. **2** inflexibly severe; cold; ruthless (*steely composure; steely-eyed glance*). □□ **steeliness** *n.*

■ **1** steel; greyish, grey; hard, iron, tough, strong, unyielding, inflexible. **2** iron, tough, severe, obdurate, adamant, adamantine, hard, strong, rugged, unyielding, unimpressionable, flinty, sturdy; ruthless; see also STONY 2.

steelyard /steélyaard/ *n.* a kind of balance with a short arm to take the item to be weighed and a long graduated arm along which a weight is moved until it balances.

steenbok /stáynbok, steén-/ *n.* an African dwarf-antelope, *Raphicerus campestris.* [Du. f. *steen* STONE + *bok* BUCK[1]]

steep[1] /steep/ *adj.* & *n.* ● *adj.* **1** sloping sharply; almost perpendicular (*a steep hill; steep stairs*). **2** (of a rise or fall) rapid (*a steep drop in share prices*). **3** (*predic.*) *colloq.* **a** (of a demand, price, etc.) exorbitant; unreasonable (esp. *a bit steep*). **b** (of a story etc.) exaggerated; incredible. ● *n.* a steep slope; a precipice. □□ **steepen** *v.intr.* & *tr.* **steepish** *adj.* **steeply** *adv.* **steepness** *n.* [OE *stēap* f. WG, rel. to STOOP[1]]

■ *adj.* **1** sheer, abrupt, precipitous, scarped, bluff, sharp, nearly vertical *or* perpendicular *or* upright, high-pitched. **2** sharp, rapid, abrupt, sudden. **3 a** dear, high, exorbitant, excessive, extravagant, extortionate, over the odds, *colloq.* stiff; unreasonable, outrageous, *colloq.* over-the-top. **b** see TALL 4.

steep[2] /steep/ *v.* & *n.* ● *v.tr.* soak or bathe in liquid. ● *n.* **1** the act or process of steeping. **2** the liquid for steeping. □ **steep in 1** pervade or imbue with (*steeped in misery*). **2** make deeply acquainted with (a subject etc.) (*steeped in the classics*). [ME f. OE f. Gmc (as STOUP)]

■ *v.* soak, submerge, souse, drench, immerse, bathe, saturate, douse, wet, ret; pickle, marinate. □ **steep in** imbue with, fill with, impregnate with, pervade with, saturate with, immerse in, inundate with, soak in; bury in.

steeple /steép'l/ *n.* a tall tower, esp. one surmounted by a spire, above the roof of a church. □ **steeple-crowned** (of a hat) with a tall pointed crown. □□ **steepled** *adj.* [OE *stēpel stȳpel* f. Gmc (as STEEP[1])]

■ see SPIRE[1] *n.* 1.

steeplechase /stéep'lchayss/ *n.* **1** a horse-race (orig. with a steeple as the goal) across the countryside or on a racecourse with ditches, hedges, etc., to jump. **2** a cross-country foot-race. □□ **steeplechaser** *n.* **steeplechasing** *n.*

steeplejack /stéep'ljak/ *n.* a person who climbs tall chimneys, steeples, etc., to do repairs etc.

steer[1] /steer/ *v.* & *n.* ● *v.* **1** *tr.* **a** guide (a vehicle, aircraft, etc.) by a wheel etc. **b** guide (a vessel) by a rudder or helm. **2** *intr.* guide a vessel or vehicle in a specified direction (*tried to steer left*). **3** *tr.* direct (one's course). **4** *intr.* direct one's course in a specified direction (*steered for the railway station*). **5** *tr.* guide the movement or trend of (*steered them into the garden; steered the conversation away from that subject*). ● *n. US* steering; guidance. □ **steer clear of** take care to avoid. **steering-column** the shaft or column which connects the steering-wheel, handlebars, etc. of a vehicle to the rest of the steering-gear. **steering committee** a committee deciding the order of dealing with business, or priorities and the general course of operations. **steering-wheel** a wheel by which a vehicle etc. is steered. □□ **steerable** *adj.* **steerer** *n.* **steering** *n.* (esp. in senses 1, 2 of *v.*). [OE *stieran* f. Gmc]

■ *v.* **1** guide, pilot, direct, navigate; manage, control. **4** see HEAD *v.* 4a. **5** see GUIDE *v.* 1, 3. ● *n.* steering; guidance, advice, tip, suggestion, hint, information. □ **steer clear of** avoid, dodge, keep away from, shun, circumvent, give a wide berth to, fight shy of. □□ **steerable** see NAVIGABLE 2, 3. **steering** see NAVIGATION.

steer[2] /steer/ *n.* a young male bovine animal, esp. one castrated and raised for beef. [OE *stēor* f. Gmc]

steerage /stéerij/ *n.* **1** the act of steering. **2** the effect of the helm on a ship. **3** *archaic* the part of a ship allotted to passengers travelling at the cheapest rate. **4** *hist.* (in a warship) quarters assigned to midshipmen etc. just forward of the wardroom. □ **steerage-way** the amount of headway required by a vessel to enable her to be controlled by the helm.

steersman /stéerzmən/ *n.* (*pl.* **-men**) a person who steers a vessel.

■ see NAVIGATOR.

steeve[1] /steev/ *n.* & *v. Naut.* ● *n.* the angle of the bowsprit in relation to the horizontal. ● *v.* **1** *intr.* (of a bowsprit) make an angle with the horizontal. **2** *tr.* cause (the bowsprit) to do this. [17th c.: orig. unkn.]

steeve[2] /steev/ *n.* & *v. Naut.* ● *n.* a long spar used in stowing cargo. ● *v.tr.* stow with a steeve. [ME f. OF *estiver* or Sp. *estivar* f. L *stipare* pack tight]

stegosaurus /stéggəsáwrəss/ *n.* any of a group of plant-eating dinosaurs with a double row of large bony plates along the spine. [mod. L f. Gk *stegē* covering + *sauros* lizard]

stein /stīn/ *n.* a large earthenware mug, esp. for beer. [G, lit. 'stone']

■ see MUG[1] *n.* 1.

steinbock /stīnbok/ *n.* **1** an ibex native to the Alps. **2** = STEENBOK. [G f. *Stein* STONE + *Bock* BUCK[1]]

stela /stéelə/ *n.* (*pl.* **stelae** /-lee/) *Archaeol.* an upright slab or pillar usu. with an inscription and sculpture, esp. as a gravestone. [L f. Gk (as STELE)]

stele /steel, stéeli/ *n.* **1** *Bot.* the axial cylinder of vascular tissue in the stem and roots of most plants. **2** *Archaeol.* = STELA. □□ **stelar** *adj.* [Gk *stēlē* standing block]

stellar /stéllər/ *adj.* **1** of or relating to a star or stars. **2** esp *US* having the quality of a star entertainer or performer; leading, outstanding. □□ **stelliform** *adj.* [LL *stellaris* f. L *stella* star]

■ **1** astral, sidereal, star. **2** chief, starring, principal, leading, main, headlining.

stellate /stéllayt/ *adj.* (also **stellated** /steláytid/) **1** arranged like a star; radiating. **2** *Bot.* (of leaves) surrounding the stem in a whorl. [L *stellatus* f. *stella* star]

stellular /stélyoolər/ *adj.* shaped like, or set with, small stars. [LL *stellula* dimin. of L *stella* star]

stem[1] /stem/ *n.* & *v.* ● *n.* **1** the main body or stalk of a plant or shrub, usu. rising into light, but occasionally subterranean. **2** the stalk supporting a fruit, flower, or leaf, and attaching it to a larger branch, twig, or stalk. **3** a stem-shaped part of an object: **a** the slender part of a wineglass between the body and the foot. **b** the tube of a tobacco-pipe. **c** a vertical stroke in a letter or musical note. **d** the winding-shaft of a watch. **4** *Gram.* the root or main part of a noun, verb, etc., to which inflections are added; the part that appears unchanged throughout the cases and derivatives of a noun, persons of a tense, etc. **5** *Naut.* the main upright timber or metal piece at the bow of a ship to which the ship's sides are joined at the fore end (*from stem to stern*). **6** a line of ancestry, branch of a family, etc. (*descended from an ancient stem*). **7** (in full **drill stem**) a rotating rod, cylinder, etc., used in drilling. ● *v.* (**stemmed, stemming**) **1** *intr.* (foll. by *from*) spring or originate from (*stems from a desire to win*). **2** *tr.* remove the stem or stems from (fruit, tobacco, etc.). **3** *tr.* (of a vessel etc.) hold its own or make headway against (the tide etc.). □ **stem cell** *Biol.* an undifferentiated cell from which specialized cells develop. **stem stitch** an embroidery stitch used for narrow stems etc. **stem-winder** *US* a watch wound by turning a head on the end of a stem rather than by a key. □□ **stemless** *adj.* **stemlet** *n.* **stemlike** *adj.* **stemmed** *adj.* (also in *comb.*). [OE *stemn, stefn* f. Gmc, rel. to STAND]

■ *n.* **1** trunk, stalk, cane, stock; *Bot.* peduncle. **2** stalk, shoot, bine, twig, *Bot.* peduncle, pedicel, petiole. **3** shaft, shank, stalk, support, upright. **4** see BASE[1] *n.* 12. **5** *Naut.* bow(s), prow, stem-post. ● *v.* **1** come, arise, develop, derive, issue, flow, generate, originate, spring, emanate, sprout, grow, descend, result, proceed. **3** resist, withstand, make headway *or* progress against, go *or* advance against, hold its own against, prevail over *or* against.

stem[2] /stem/ *v.* & *n.* ● *v.* (**stemmed, stemming**) **1** *tr.* check or stop. **2** *tr.* dam up (a stream etc.). **3** *intr.* slide the tail of one ski or both skis outwards usu. in order to turn or slow down. ● *n.* an act of stemming on skis. □ **stem-turn** a turn on skis made by stemming with one ski. [ON *stemma* f. Gmc: cf. STAMMER]

■ *v.* **1** check, stop, halt, stanch, staunch, arrest, curb, control, quell, suppress, *archaic or literary* stay; retard, slow, lessen, diminish, reduce, cut, cut back (on). **2** dam up, block, obstruct, hold back, restrain, stop.

stemma /stémmə/ *n.* (*pl.* **stemmata** /stémmətə/) **1** a family tree; a pedigree. **2** the line of descent e.g. of variant texts of a work. **3** *Zool.* a simple eye; a facet of a compound eye. [L f. Gk *stemma* wreath f. *stephō* wreathe]

stemple /stémp'l/ *n.* each of several crossbars in a mineshaft serving as supports or steps. [17th c.: orig. uncert.: cf. MHG *stempfel*]

stemware /stémwair/ *n. US* glasses with stems.

stench /stench/ *n.* an offensive or foul smell. □ **stench trap** a trap in a sewer etc. to prevent the upward passage of gas. [OE *stenc* smell f. Gmc, rel. to STINK]

■ stink, reek, mephitis, fetor, foul odour, effluvium, *Brit. colloq.* pong, hum, *literary* noisomeness.

stencil /sténsil/ *n.* & *v.* ● *n.* **1** (in full **stencil-plate**) a thin sheet of plastic, metal, card, etc., in which a pattern or lettering is cut, used to produce a corresponding pattern on the surface beneath it by applying ink, paint, etc. **2** the pattern, lettering, etc., produced by a stencil-plate. **3** a waxed sheet etc. from which a stencil is made by means of a typewriter. ● *v.tr.* (**stencilled, stencilling**; *US* **stenciled, stenciling**) **1** (often foll. by *on*) produce (a pattern) with a stencil. **2** decorate or mark (a surface) in this way. [ME f. OF *estanceler* sparkle, cover with stars, f. *estencele* spark ult. f. L *scintilla*]

■ *n.* **1** see PATTERN *n.* 3.

Sten gun /sten/ *n.* a type of lightweight sub-machine-gun. [*S* and *T* (the initials of the inventors' surnames, Shepherd and Turpin) + *-en* after BREN]

steno /sténnō/ *n.* (*pl.* **-os**) *US colloq.* a stenographer. [abbr.]

stenography /stenógrəfi/ *n.* shorthand or the art of writing this. □□ **stenographer** *n.* **stenographic** /sténnəgráffik/ *adj.* [Gk *stenos* narrow + -GRAPHY]

■ shorthand, tachygraphy, phonography, speedwriting. □□ **stenographer** secretary, amanuensis, stenotypist, tachygrapher, phonographer, *US colloq.* steno.

stenosis /stinṓsiss/ *n. Med.* the abnormal narrowing of a passage in the body. □□ **stenotic** /-nóttik/ *adj.* [mod.L f. Gk *stenōsis* narrowing f. *stenoō* make narrow f. *stenos* narrow]

stenotype /sténnətīp/ *n.* **1** a machine like a typewriter for recording speech in syllables or phonemes. **2** a symbol or the symbols used in this process. □□ **stenotypist** *n.* [STENOGRAPHY + TYPE]

Stentor /sténtər/ *n.* (also **stentor**) a person with a powerful voice. □□ **stentorian** /-tóriən/ *adj.* [Gk *Stentōr*, herald in the Trojan War (Homer, *Iliad* v. 785)]

■ □□ **stentorian** see LOUD *adj.* 1.

step /step/ *n.* & *v.* ● *n.* **1 a** the complete movement of one leg in walking or running (*took a step forward*). **b** the distance covered by this. **c** (in *pl.*) the course followed by a person in walking etc. **2** a unit of movement in dancing. **3** a measure taken, esp. one of several in a course of action (*took steps to prevent it*; *considered it a wise step*). **4 a** a surface on which a foot is placed on ascending or descending a stair or tread. **b** a block of stone or other platform before a door, altar, etc. **c** the rung of a ladder. **d** a notch cut for a foot in ice-climbing. **e** a platform etc. in a vehicle provided for stepping up or down. **5** a short distance (*only a step from my door*). **6** the sound or mark made by a foot in walking etc. (*heard a step on the stairs*). **7** the manner of walking etc. as seen or heard (*know her by her step*). **8 a** a degree in the scale of promotion, advancement, or precedence. **b** one of a series of fixed points on a payscale etc. **9 a** stepping (or not stepping) in time with others or music (esp. *in* or *out of step*). **b** the state of conforming to what others are doing (*refuses to keep step with the team*). **10** (in *pl.*) (also **pair of steps** *sing.*) = STEPLADDER. **11** esp. *US Mus.* a melodic interval of one degree of the scale, i.e. a tone or semitone. **12** *Naut.* a block, socket, or platform supporting a mast. ● *v.* (**stepped, stepping**) **1** *intr.* lift and set down one's foot or alternate feet in walking. **2** *intr.* come or go in a specified direction by stepping. **3** *intr.* make progress in a specified way (*stepped into a new job*). **4** *tr.* (foll. by *off, out*) measure (distance) by stepping. **5** *tr.* perform (a dance). **6** *tr. Naut.* set up (a mast) in a step. □ **in a person's steps** following a person's example. **mind** (or **watch**) **one's step** be careful. **step by step** gradually; cautiously; by stages or degrees. **step-cut** (of a gem) cut in straight facets round the centre. **step down 1** resign from a position etc. **2** *Electr.* decrease (voltage) by using a transformer. **step in 1** enter a room, house, etc. **2 a** intervene to help or hinder. **b** act as a substitute for an indisposed colleague etc. **step-in** *attrib.adj.* (of a garment) put on by being stepped into without unfastening. ● *n.* such a garment. **step it** dance. **step on it** (or **on the gas**) *colloq.* **1** accelerate a motor vehicle. **2** hurry up. **step out 1** leave a room, house, etc. **2** be active socially. **3** take large steps. **stepping-stone 1** a raised stone, usu. one of a set in a stream, muddy place, etc., to help in crossing. **2** a means or stage of progress to an end. **step this way** a deferential formula meaning 'follow me'. **step up 1** increase, intensify (*must step up production*). **2** *Electr.* increase (voltage) using a transformer. **take a step** (or **steps**) implement a course of action leading to a specific result; proceed. **turn one's steps** go in a specified direction. □□ **steplike** *adj.* **stepped** *adj.* **stepwise** *adv.* & *adj.* [OE *stæpe, stepe* (n.), *stæppan, steppan* (v.), f. Gmc]

■ *n.* **1a, b, 5** pace, footstep, stride. **1 c** (*steps*) course, way, route, direction, path, movement, passage; journey, journeying, travels, travelling. **2** movement, move. **3** action, initiative, measure, activity, procedure, move, motion; *démarche*. **4 a** stair, tread, tread-board; (*steps*) stairs, stair, stairway, staircase, *US* stoop. **b** doorstep, ledge, sill. **6** footfall, footstep, tread; footprint, trace, spoor, track, mark, impression; imprint. **7** see WALK *n.* 1. **8** see NOTCH *n.* 3. **9** (*in step*) in time, in line, in keeping, in harmony, in agreement, in accord, in conformity, in tune; harmonious, agreeable, according, concordant, attuned, consonant, consistent, conforming, appropriate, fitting; conventional, traditional, routine; (*out of step*) not in time, out of *or* not in keeping, out of *or* not in line, out of *or* not in harmony, out of *or* not in agreement, out of *or* not in tune, not harmonious, not agreeable, not according, discordant, not concordant, not attuned, not consonant, inconsistent, nonconforming, inappropriate, not fitting; offbeat, unconventional, eccentric, kinky. **10** (*steps*) see STEPLADDER. ● *v.* **1, 2** tread, move; pace, stride; see also WALK *v.* 1, 2. **4** pace, measure. □ **mind** (or **watch**) **one's step** tread carefully *or* cautiously, be cautious, be careful, exercise care *or* caution, be wary, be discreet, be on the qui vive, be *or* remain alert, be on one's guard, have *or* keep one's wits about one, watch it, watch oneself, take care *or* heed, pussyfoot (about *or* around). **step by step** gradually, a step at a time, by stages, by degrees, slowly, steadily, stealthily, cautiously. **step down 1** resign, abdicate, quit, bow out, retire. **2** decrease, diminish, reduce. **step in 1** enter, go in, come in. **2 a** intervene, interfere, intercede, become involved. **b** (*step in for*) see SUBSTITUTE *v.* 1. **step on it** (or **on the gas**) **1** accelerate, speed up, *colloq.* put one's foot down, *Austral. colloq.* give it the herbs. **2** hurry (up), make haste, hasten, speed up, get a move on. **step out 1** go outside, go out of doors, leave. **2** go out, socialize. **3** pace, stride. **step up** increase, raise, intensify, strengthen, escalate, up, augment, *colloq.* boost. **take a step** (or **steps**) proceed, move, begin *or* start to act *or* to take action, do something, *formal* commence to act. **turn one's steps** see HEAD *v.* 4a.

step- /step/ *comb. form* denoting a relationship like the one specified but resulting from a parent's remarriage. [OE *stēop-* orphan-]

stepbrother /stépbruthər/ *n.* a son of a step-parent by a marriage other than with one's father or mother.

stepchild /stépchīld/ *n.* a child of one's husband or wife by a previous marriage. [OE *stēopcīld* (as STEP-, CHILD)]

stepdaughter /stépdawtər/ *n.* a female stepchild. [OE *stēopdohtor* (as STEP-, DAUGHTER)]

stepfather /stépfaathər/ *n.* a male step-parent. [OE *stēopfæder* (as STEP-, FATHER)]

■ see PARENT *n.* 2.

stephanotis /stéffənṓtiss/ *n.* any climbing tropical plant of the genus *Stephanotis*, cultivated for its fragrant waxy usu. white flowers. [mod.L f. Gk, = fit for a wreath f. *stephanos* wreath]

stepladder /stépladdər/ *n.* a short ladder with flat steps and a folding prop, used without being leant against a surface.

■ (pair of) steps, ladder.

stepmother /stépmuthər/ *n.* a female step-parent. [OE *stēopmōdor* (as STEP-, MOTHER)]

■ see PARENT *n.* 2.

step-parent /stép-pairənt/ *n.* a mother's or father's later husband or wife.

■ see PARENT *n.* 2.

steppe /step/ *n.* a level grassy unforested plain, esp. in SE Europe and Siberia. [Russ *step'*]

■ see PLAIN[1] *n.*

stepsister /stépsistər/ *n.* a daughter of a step-parent by a marriage other than with one's father or mother.

stepson /stépsun/ *n.* a male stepchild. [OE *stēopsunu* (as STEP-, SON)]

-ster /stər/ *suffix* denoting a person engaged in or associated with a particular activity or thing (*brewster*; *gangster*; *youngster*). [OE *-estre* etc. f. Gmc]

steradian /stəráydiən/ *n.* the SI unit of solid angle, equal to the angle at the centre of a sphere subtended by a part of the surface equal in area to the square of the radius. ¶ Abbr.: **sr.** [Gk *stereos* solid + RADIAN]

stercoraceous /stérkəráyshəss/ *adj.* **1** consisting of or resembling dung or faeces. **2** living in dung. [L *stercus -oris* dung]

stere /steer/ *n.* a unit of volume equal to one cubic metre. [F *stère* f. Gk *stereos* solid]

stereo /stérriō, stéeriō/ *n.* & *adj.* ● *n.* (*pl.* **-os**) **1 a** a stereophonic record-player, tape recorder, etc. **b** = STEREOPHONY (see STEREOPHONIC). **2** = STEREOSCOPE. ● *adj.* **1** = STEREOPHONIC. **2** = STEREOSCOPIC (see stereoscope). [abbr.]

stereo- /stérriō, stéeriō/ *comb. form* solid; having three dimensions. [Gk *stereos* solid]

stereobate /stérriəbayt, stéeriə-/ *n. Archit.* a solid mass of masonry as a foundation for a building. [F *stéréobate* f. L *stereobata* f. Gk *stereobatēs* (as STEREO-, *bainō* walk)]

stereochemistry /stérriōkémmistri, stéeriō-/ *n.* the branch of chemistry dealing with the three-dimensional arrangement of atoms in molecules.

stereography /stérriógrəfi, stéeri-/ *n.* the art of depicting solid bodies in a plane.

stereoisomer /stérriō-ísəmər, stéeriō/ *n. Chem.* any of two or more compounds differing only in their spatial arrangement of atoms.

stereometry /stérriómmitri, stéeri-/ *n.* the measurement of solid bodies.

stereophonic /stérriōfónnik, stéeriō-/ *adj.* (of sound reproduction) using two or more channels so that the sound has the effect of being distributed and of coming from more than one source. □□ **stereophonically** *adv.* **stereophony** /-rióffəni/ *n.*

stereoscope /stérriəskōp, stéeriə-/ *n.* a device by which two photographs of the same object taken at slightly different angles are viewed together, giving an impression of depth and solidity as in ordinary human vision. □□ **stereoscopic** /-skóppik/ *adj.* **stereoscopically** /-skóppikəli/ *adv.* **stereoscopy** /-rióskəpi/ *n.*

stereotype /stérriōtīp, stéeriō/ *n.* & *v.* ● *n.* **1 a** a person or thing that conforms to an unjustifiably fixed, usu. standardized, mental picture. **b** such an impression or attitude. **2** a printing-plate cast from a mould of composed type. ● *v.tr.* **1** (esp. as **stereotyped** *adj.*) formalize, standardize; cause to conform to a type. **2 a** print from a stereotype. **b** make a stereotype of. □□ **stereotypic** /-típpik/ *adj.* **stereotypical** /-típpik'l/ *adj.* **stereotypically** /-típpikəli/ *adv.* **stereotypy** *n.* [F *stéréotype* (adj.) (as STEREO-, TYPE)]

■ *n.* **1** see CLICHÉ. **2** see STAMP *n.* 1. ● *v.* **1** (**stereotyped**) see STOCK *adj.* 2. □□ **stereotypical** see BANAL.

steric /stéerik/ *adj. Chem.* relating to the spatial arrangement of atoms in a molecule. □ **steric hindrance** the inhibiting of a chemical reaction by the obstruction of reacting atoms. [irreg. f. Gk *stereos* solid]

sterile /stérrīl/ *adj.* **1** not able to produce crop or fruit or (of an animal) young; barren. **2** unfruitful, unproductive (*sterile discussions*). **3** free from living micro-organisms etc. **4** lacking originality or emotive force; mentally barren. □□ **sterilely** *adv.* **sterility** /stərílliti/ *n.* [F *stérile* or L *sterilis*]

■ **1** barren, fruitless, unfruitful, childless, unproductive, lifeless, arid, infertile. **2** barren, unfruitful, unproductive, fruitless, unprofitable, ineffectual, useless, abortive, *archaic* bootless. **3** pure, aseptic, uninfected, unpolluted, uncontaminated, disinfected, sanitary, sterilized, germ-free, hygienic, antiseptic, clean. **4** barren, unproductive, stale, unoriginal, unimaginative, dull, uninspired, uninspiring, effete.

sterilize /stérrilīz/ *v.tr.* (also **-ise**) **1** make sterile. **2** deprive of the power of reproduction. □□ **sterilizable** *adj.* **sterilization** /-záysh'n/ *n.* **sterilizer** *n.*

■ **1** purify, disinfect, clean, fumigate, depurate, pasteurize, decontaminate, *usu. formal* cleanse. **2** castrate, emasculate, hysterectomize, vasectomize; geld, spay, desex, neuter, caponize, fix, cut, *US* & *Austral.* alter, *colloq.* doctor. □□ **sterilizer** see DISINFECTANT *n.*

sterlet /stérlit/ *n.* a small sturgeon, *Acipenser ruthenus*, found in the Caspian Sea area and yielding fine caviare. [Russ. *sterlyad'*]

sterling /stérling/ *adj.* & *n.* ● *adj.* **1** of or in British money (*pound sterling*). **2** (of a coin or precious metal) genuine; of standard value or purity. **3** (of a person or qualities etc.) of solid worth; genuine, reliable (*sterling work*). ● *n.* British money (*paid in sterling*). □ **sterling area** a group of countries with currencies tied to British sterling and holding reserves mainly in sterling. **sterling silver** silver of 92½% purity. □□ **sterlingness** *n.* [prob. f. late OE *steorling* (unrecorded) f. *steorra* star + -LING[1] (because some early Norman pennies bore a small star): recorded earlier in OF *esterlin*]

■ *adj.* **2** genuine, authentic, real, true, pure. **3** excellent, superior, superb, superlative, first-class, exceptional, matchless, peerless, unequalled, nonpareil, incomparable, fine, very good, worthy, worthwhile, estimable, admirable; solid, reliable, genuine.

stern[1] /stern/ *adj.* severe, grim, strict; enforcing discipline or submission (*a stern expression*; *stern treatment*). □ **the sterner sex** men. □□ **sternly** *adv.* **sternness** *n.* [OE *styrne*, prob. f. a Gmc root = be rigid]

■ severe, serious, frowning, grim, forbidding, grave, gloomy, dour, sombre, saturnine, lugubrious, gruff, taciturn, crabby, crabbed, crusty, churlish, sour; austere, Spartan, strict, stringent, demanding, critical, rigid, rigorous, flinty, steely, authoritarian, uncompromising, hard, tough, inflexible, firm, immovable, unmoved, unrelenting, unremitting, steadfast, resolute, determined, unyielding, adamant, adamantine, obdurate, hard-hearted, stony, stony-hearted, unsparing, unforgiving, unsympathetic, harsh. □□ **sternly** see ROUGHLY 1, *severely* (SEVERE). **sternness** see *severity* (SEVERE).

stern[2] /stern/ *n.* **1** the rear part of a ship or boat. **2** any rear part. □ **stern foremost** moving backwards. **stern on** with the stern presented. **stern-post** the central upright support at the stern, usu. bearing the rudder. □□ **sterned** *adj.* (also in *comb.*). **sternmost** *adj.* **sternward** *adj.* & *adv.* **sternwards** *adv.* [ME prob. f. ON *stjórn* steering f. *stýra* STEER[1]]

sternal /stérn'l/ *adj.* of or relating to the sternum. □ **sternal rib** = *true rib.*

sternum /stérnəm/ *n.* (*pl.* **sternums** or **sterna** /-nə/) the breastbone. [mod.L f. Gk *sternon* chest]

sternutation /stérnyootáysh'n/ *n. Med.* or *joc.* a sneeze or attack of sneezing. [L *sternutatio* f. *sternutare* frequent. of *sternuere* sneeze]

sternutator /stérnyootaytər/ *n.* a substance, esp. poison gas, that causes nasal irritation, violent coughing, etc. □□ **sternutatory** /-nyóotətəri/ *adj.* & *n.* (*pl.* **-ies**).

sternway /stérnway/ *n. Naut.* a backward motion or impetus of a ship.

steroid /stéeroyd, stérroyd/ *n. Biochem.* any of a group of organic compounds with a characteristic structure of four rings of carbon atoms, including many hormones, alkaloids, and vitamins. □□ **steroidal** /-róyd'l/ *adj.* [STEROL + -OID]

sterol /stérrol/ *n. Chem.* any of a group of naturally occurring steroid alcohols. [CHOLESTEROL, ERGOSTEROL, etc.]

stertorous /stértərəss/ *adj.* (of breathing etc.) laboured and noisy; sounding like snoring. □□ **stertorously** *adv.* **stertorousness** *n.* [*stertor*, mod.L f. L *stertere* snore]

stet /stet/ *v.* (**stetted, stetting**) **1** *intr.* (usu. as an instruction written on a proof-sheet etc.) ignore or cancel the correction or alteration; let the original form stand. **2** *tr.* write 'stet' against; cancel the correction of. [L, = let it stand, f. *stare* stand]

stethoscope /stéthəskōp/ *n.* an instrument used in listening to the action of the heart, lungs, etc., usu. consisting of a circular piece placed against the chest, with tubes leading to earpieces. □□ **stethoscopic** /-skóppik/ *adj.* **stethoscopically** /-skóppikəli/ *adv.* **stethoscopist** /stethóskəpist/ *n.* **stethoscopy** /stethóskəpi/ *n.* [F *stéthoscope* f. Gk *stēthos* breast: see -SCOPE]

stetson /stéts'n/ *n.* a slouch hat with a very wide brim and a high crown. [J. B. *Stetson*, Amer. hat-maker d. 1906]

stevedore /steévədor/ *n.* a person employed in loading and unloading ships. [Sp. *estivador* f. *estivar* stow a cargo f. L *stipare*: see STEEVE[2]]
■ see DOCKER.

stevengraph /steév'ngraaf/ *n.* a colourful woven silk picture. [T. *Stevens*, Engl. weaver d. 1888, whose firm made them]

stew[1] /styoo/ *v.* & *n.* ● *v.* **1** *tr.* & *intr.* cook by long simmering in a closed vessel with liquid. **2** *intr. colloq.* be oppressed by heat or humidity, esp. in a confined space. **3** *intr. colloq.* **a** suffer prolonged embarrassment, anxiety, etc. **b** (foll. by *over*) fret or be anxious. **4** *tr.* make (tea) bitter or strong with prolonged brewing. **5** *tr.* (as **stewed** *adj.*) *colloq.* drunk. **6** *intr.* (often foll. by *over*) *colloq.* study hard. ● *n.* **1** a dish of stewed meat etc. **2** *colloq.* an agitated or angry state (*be in a stew*). **3** *archaic* **a** a hot bath. **b** (in *pl.*) a brothel. □ **stew in one's own juice** be left to suffer the consequences of one's own actions. [ME f. OF *estuve*, *estuver* prob. ult. f. EX-[1] + Gk *tuphos* smoke, steam]
■ *v.* **1** casserole, braise, boil, simmer, jug. **2** roast, swelter, *colloq.* boil. **3** agonize, fret, dither, chafe, burn, smoulder, simmer, seethe, be anxious, sweat, *colloq.* get steamed up, work oneself (up) into a sweat *or* lather *or* state. **5** (**stewed**) see DRUNK *adj.* 1. **6** study, cram, burn the midnight oil, *Brit. colloq.* swot, *sl.* mug. ● *n.* **1** casserole, fricassee, cassoulet, ragout, hotpot, hotchpotch, goulash, olla podrida, olio. **2** state of excitement *or* alarm *or* anxiety, bother, lather, *colloq.* sweat, tizzy, dither, state, *literary* pother. **3 b** (*stews*) see BROTHEL.

stew[2] /styoo/ *n. Brit.* **1** an artificial oyster-bed. **2** a pond or large tank for keeping fish for eating. [ME f. F *estui* f. *estoier* confine ult. f. L *studium*: see STUDY]

steward /styoo͝ərd/ *n.* & *v.* ● *n.* **1** a passengers' attendant on a ship or aircraft or train. **2** an official appointed to keep order or supervise arrangements at a meeting or show or demonstration etc. **3** = *shop steward.* **4** a person responsible for supplies of food etc. for a college or club etc. **5** a person employed to manage another's property. **6** *Brit.* the title of several officers of State or the royal household (*Lord High Steward*). ● *v.tr.* act as a steward of (*will steward the meeting*). □□ **stewardship** *n.* [OE *stīweard* f. *stig* prob. = house, hall + *weard* WARD]
■ *n.* **1** see ATTENDANT *n.* □□ **stewardship** see MANAGEMENT 1.

stewardess /styoo͝ərdéss, styoo͝ərdiss/ *n.* a female steward, esp. on a ship or aircraft.
■ see ATTENDANT *n.*

stg. *abbr.* sterling.

Sth. *abbr.* South.

sthenic /sthénnik/ *adj. Med.* (of a disease etc.) with a morbid increase of vital action esp. of the heart and arteries. [Gk *sthenos* strength, after *asthenic*]

stick[1] /stik/ *n.* **1 a** a short slender branch or length of wood broken or cut from a tree. **b** this trimmed for use as a support or weapon. **2** a thin rod or spike of wood etc. for a particular purpose (*cocktail stick*). **3 a** an implement used to propel the ball in hockey or polo etc. **b** (in *pl.*) the raising of the stick above the shoulder in hockey. **4** a gear lever. **5** a conductor's baton. **6 a** a slender piece of a thing, e.g. celery, dynamite, deodorant, etc. **b** a number of bombs or paratroops released rapidly from aircraft. **7** (often prec. by *the*) punishment, esp. by beating. **8** *colloq.* adverse criticism; censure, reproof (*took a lot of stick*). **9** *colloq.* a piece of wood as part of a house or furniture (*a few sticks of furniture*). **10** *colloq.* a person, esp. one who is dull or unsociable (*a funny old stick*). **11** (in *pl.*; prec. by *the*) *colloq.* remote rural areas. **12** (in *pl.*) *Austral. sl.* goalposts. **13** *Naut. sl.* a mast or spar. □ **stick insect** any usu. wingless female insect of the family Phasmidae with a twiglike body. **up sticks** *colloq.* go to live elsewhere. □□ **stickless** *adj.* **sticklike** *adj.* [OE *sticca* f. WG]
■ **1 a** branch, twig, stalk, switch. **b** stake, pole, pike, rod, mace, wand, staff, cane, walking-stick, crook; club, cudgel, truncheon, bludgeon, *Austral.* & *NZ* waddy. **7** see PUNISHMENT 1, 2. **10** person, man, woman, *colloq.* fellow, chap, guy, bird, codger, *sl.* geezer, *Brit. sl.* bloke. **11** (*the sticks*) the country, the provinces, the countryside, the backwoods, the back of beyond, the hinterland, *esp. Austral.* the outback, *esp. Austral.* & *Afr.* the bush, *Austral.* & *NZ* the backblocks, *Austral.* & *NZ sl.* Woop Woop, *US sl.* the boondocks, the boonies.

stick[2] /stik/ *v.* (*past* and *past part.* **stuck** /stuk/) **1** *tr.* (foll. by *in*, *into*, *through*) insert or thrust (a thing or its point) (*stuck a finger in my eye*; *stick a pin through it*). **2** *tr.* insert a pointed thing into; stab. **3** *tr.* & *intr.* (foll. by *in*, *into*, *on*, etc.) **a** fix or be fixed on a pointed thing. **b** fix or be fixed by or as by a pointed end. **4** *tr.* & *intr.* fix or become or remain fixed by or as by adhesive etc. (*stick a label on it*; *the label won't stick*). **5** *intr.* endure; make a continued impression (*the scene stuck in my mind*; *the name stuck*). **6** *intr.* lose or be deprived of the power of motion or action through adhesion or jamming or other impediment. **7** *colloq.* **a** *tr.* put in a specified position or place, esp. quickly or haphazardly (*stick them down anywhere*). **b** *intr.* remain in a place (*stuck indoors*). **8** *colloq.* **a** *intr.* (of an accusation etc.) be convincing or regarded as valid (*could not make the charges stick*). **b** *tr.* (foll. by *on*) place the blame for (a thing) on (a person). **9** *tr. colloq.* endure, tolerate (*could not stick it any longer*). **10** *tr.* (foll. by *at*) *colloq.* persevere with. □ **be stuck for** be at a loss for or in need of. **be stuck on** *colloq.* be infatuated with. **be stuck with** *colloq.* be unable to get rid of or escape from; be permanently involved with. **get stuck in** (or **into**) *sl.* begin in earnest. **stick around** *colloq.* linger; remain at the same place. **stick at it** *colloq.* persevere. **stick at nothing** allow nothing, esp. no scruples, to deter one. **stick by** (or **with**) stay loyal or close to. **stick 'em up!** *colloq.* hands up! **stick fast** adhere or become firmly fixed or trapped in a position or place. **stick in one's gizzard** see GIZZARD. **sticking-plaster** an adhesive plaster for wounds etc. **sticking-point** the limit of progress, agreement, etc. **stick-in-the-mud** *colloq.* an unprogressive or old-fashioned person. **stick in one's throat** be against one's principles. **stick it on** *sl.* **1** make high charges. **2** tell an exaggerated story. **stick it out** *colloq.* put up with or persevere with a burden etc. to the end. **stick one's neck** (or **chin**) **out** expose oneself to censure etc. by acting or speaking boldly. **stick out** protrude or cause to protrude or project (*stuck his tongue out*; *stick out your chest*). **stick out for** persist in demanding. **stick out a mile** (or **like a sore thumb**) *colloq.* be very obvious or incongruous. **stick pigs** engage in pigsticking. **stick to 1** remain close to or fixed on or to. **2** remain faithful to. **3** keep to (a subject etc.) (*stick to the point*). **stick to a person's fingers** *colloq.* (of money) be embezzled by a person. **stick together** *colloq.* become or remain united or mutually loyal. **stick to one's guns** see GUN. **stick to it** persevere. **stick to one's last** see LAST[3]. **stick up 1** be or make erect or protruding upwards. **2** fasten to an upright surface. **3** *colloq.* rob or threaten with a gun. **stick-up** *n. colloq.* an armed robbery. **stick up for** support or defend or champion (a person or cause). **stick up to** be assertive in the face of; offer resistance to. **stick with** *colloq.* remain in touch with or faithful to; persevere with. **stuck-up** *colloq.* affectedly superior and aloof, snobbish. □□ **stickability** /stíkkəbílliti/ *n.* [OE *stician* f. Gmc]
■ **1** put, poke, push, thrust, prod, dig, jab; insert. **2** pierce, stab, transfix, pin, spike, impale, spear, skewer, spit, run through, poke, gore, jab, prick, puncture, punch, penetrate, drill, bore, riddle, perforate. **3** attach, fasten, affix, fix, nail, pin, tack. **4** fix, affix, attach, fasten, glue,

cement, paste, gum, weld, solder, bind, tie, tape, wire; bond, melt, fuse, unite, join; cohere, adhere, stay *or* remain *or* cling together, *literary* cleave together. **5** endure, linger, remain (fixed), continue, stay, *literary* dwell. **6** become lodged *or* embedded, be jammed, be wedged, be trapped, become fixed *or* fast, become entangled, become bogged down; catch, wedge, jam, lodge, remain (fixed), stay. **7 a** put, drop, place, deposit, plop, plonk, *US* plunk, *colloq.* shove, *Brit. sl.* bung. **b** remain, stay, linger. **8 a** hold, go through, be upheld, be *or* remain effective. **9** stand, abide, tolerate, endure, bear, put up with, suffer, *colloq.* lump. **10** (*stick at*) see PERSEVERE. □ **be stuck for** be at a loss for, be stumped for; be in need *or* want of, need. **be stuck on** be infatuated with, be in love with, be taken with, be enamoured of, be fond of, be keen on, be mad about, *colloq.* be sweet on, have a thing about, be wild *or* nuts *or* crazy about, *sl.* be batty about. **be stuck with** be burdened *or* encumbered *or* saddled *or* charged with, be weighed down with. **get stuck in** (or **into**) see *get a move on* 2 (MOVE). **stick around** wait, linger, stay, stand by, remain, hang around *or* about, *archaic or literary* tarry, *colloq.* hang on. **stick at it** see PERSEVERE. **stick at nothing** stop *or* hesitate *or* pause *or* baulk at nothing. **stick by** (or **with**) stick to, support, be loyal *or* faithful to, stand by, stick up for. **stick-in-the-mud** (old) fogy, conservative, anachronism, dodo, *colloq.* fossil, *derog.* museum piece, troglodyte, *sl.* fuddy-duddy, square, back number. **stick in one's throat** see SCANDALIZE. **stick it on 2** see EXAGGERATE 1. **stick it out** persevere, persist, stand fast, bear it, be resolute, hold one's ground, grin and bear it, see it through, weather it, *colloq.* stick it, tough it out, soldier on. **stick one's neck** (or **chin**) **out** see *sail close to the wind* 2. **stick out** protrude, jut (out), extend, project, poke (out); bulge, obtrude, stand out, overhang, beetle. **stick to 2** see *stick by* above. **3** see KEEP *v.* 7a. **stick together** be *or* remain united, be *or* remain loyal, be as one, hang together, work together, cooperate; unite, unify, join (forces), consolidate, merge, confederate, amalgamate. **stick to it** see PERSEVERE. **stick up 1** stand up *or* out, poke out *or* up, protrude, jut, extend, project, obtrude. **2** put up, post, affix, display. **3** rob, mug, hold up, *Austral.* & *NZ* bail up, *US sl.* heist. **stick-up** see *hold-up* 2 (HOLD[1]). **stick up for** rally to the support of, support, stand by, stand up for, defend, champion, speak for, speak on *or US* in behalf of, take up the cudgels for. **stick up to** see *stand up to* 1. **stick with** stick by *or* to, stand by, support, be loyal *or* faithful to, stay *or* remain *or* continue with; persevere with, persist in, stay *or* remain *or* continue with, not change one's mind about. **stuck-up** see *snobbish* (SNOB).

sticker /stíkkər/ *n.* **1** an adhesive label or notice etc. **2** a person or thing that sticks. **3** a persistent person.
■ **1** see LABEL *n.* 1.

stickleback /stíkk'lbak/ *n.* any small fish of the family Gasterosteidae, esp. *Gasterosteus aculeatus*, with sharp spines along the back. [ME f. OE *sticel* thorn, sting + *bæc* BACK]

stickler /stíklər/ *n.* (foll. by *for*) a person who insists on something (*a stickler for accuracy*). [obs. *stickle* be umpire, ME *stightle* control, frequent. of *stight* f. OE *stiht(i)an* set in order]
■ see *perfectionist* (PERFECTIONISM).

stickpin /stíkpin/ *n.* *US* an ornamental tie-pin.
■ see PIN *n.* 1c, d.

stickweed /stíkweed/ *n.* *US* = RAGWEED 2.

sticky /stíkki/ *adj.* & *n.* ● *adj.* (**stickier, stickiest**) **1** tending or intended to stick or adhere. **2** glutinous, viscous. **3** (of the weather) humid. **4** *colloq.* awkward or uncooperative; intransigent (*was very sticky about giving me leave*). **5** *colloq.* difficult, awkward (*a sticky problem*). **6** *colloq.* very unpleasant or painful (*came to a sticky end*). ● *n.* *colloq.* glue. □ **sticky wicket 1** *Cricket* a pitch that has been drying after rain and is difficult for the batsman. **2** *colloq.* difficult or awkward circumstances. □□ **stickily** *adv.* **stickiness** *n.*
■ *adj.* **1** adhesive, gummed, glued; clinging. **2** gluey, gummy, viscous, tacky, glutinous, viscid, mucilaginous, *sl.* gooey. **3** humid, clammy, dank, damp, muggy, close, sultry, oppressive, sweltering, steamy. **5** awkward, ticklish, tricky, difficult, sensitive, delicate, uncomfortable, discomfiting, discomforting, embarrassing, *sl.* hairy. ● *n.* see GLUE *n.* □□ **stickiness** see *tenacity* (TENACIOUS).

stickybeak /stíkkibeek/ *n.* & *v.* *Austral.* & *NZ sl.* ● *n.* an inquisitive person. ● *v.intr.* pry.

stiff /stif/ *adj.* & *n.* ● *adj.* **1** rigid; not flexible. **2** hard to bend or move or turn etc.; not working freely. **3** hard to cope with; needing strength or effort (*a stiff test*; *a stiff climb*). **4** severe or strong (*a stiff breeze*; *a stiff penalty*; *stiff opposition*). **5** (of a person or manner) formal, constrained; lacking spontaneity. **6** (of a muscle or limb etc., or a person affected by these) aching when used, owing to previous exertion, injury, etc. **7** (of an alcoholic or medicinal drink) strong. **8** (*predic.*) *colloq.* to an extreme degree (*bored stiff*; *scared stiff*). **9** (foll. by *with*) *colloq.* abounding in (*a place stiff with tourists*). **10** *colloq.* (of a price, demand, etc.) unusually high, excessive. ● *n.* *sl.* **1** a corpse. **2** a foolish or useless person (*you big stiff*). □ **stiff neck** a rheumatic condition in which the head cannot be turned without pain. **stiff-necked** obstinate or haughty. **stiff upper lip** firmness, fortitude. □□ **stiffish** *adj.* **stiffly** *adv.* **stiffness** *n.* [OE *stīf* f. Gmc]
■ *adj.* **1, 2** firm, rigid, inelastic, unbending, inflexible, hard, unbendable, tough, solid, solidified, stiffened, unyielding, brittle; semi-solid, semifluid, viscous, heavy, thick, dense, compact. **3** difficult, hard, steep, uphill, laborious, arduous, onerous, tiring, fatiguing, exhausting, harrowing, toilsome, rigorous, challenging, demanding, exacting, rough, tough. **4** strong, steady, powerful, fresh, brisk, gusty, forceful, howling; severe, harsh, punitive, hurtful, punishing, abusive, torturous, distressing, afflictive, painful, overwhelming, unbearable, tormenting, merciless, strict, stringent, tough, excruciating, cruel, drastic; vigorous, energetic, staunch, dogged, tenacious, resolute, resolved, determined, stubborn, obstinate, unyielding, indomitable, relentless. **5** cool, haughty, rigid, wooden, stuffy, aloof, tense, intense, unrelaxed, starchy, forced, pompous, pedantic, turgid, stilted, constrained, artificial, laboured, mannered, ceremonious, austere, formal, prim, chilly, cold, frigid, unfriendly, standoffish, reserved, snobbish, *colloq.* snooty, *US colloq.* uptight. **7** strong, potent, powerful, overpowering, alcoholic. **10** excessive, exorbitant, high, *colloq.* steep; unreasonable, extortionate. ● *n.* **1** corpse, body, *esp. Med.* cadaver. □ **stiff-necked** see SELF-WILLED. □□ **stiffish** see THICK *adj.* 5a.

stiffen /stíff'n/ *v.tr.* & *intr.* make or become stiff. □□ **stiffener** *n.* **stiffening** *n.*
■ thicken, coagulate, clot, harden, set, solidify, congeal, crystallize, *colloq.* jell; brace, reinforce, tauten, tighten, rigidify, toughen, strengthen. □□ **stiffener** thickener, hardener; see also BRACE *n.* 1b.

stifle[1] /stīf'l/ *v.* **1** *tr.* smother, suppress (*stifled a yawn*). **2** *intr.* & *tr.* experience or cause to experience constraint of breathing (*stifling heat*). **3** *tr.* kill by suffocating. □□ **stifler** /stīflər/ *n.* **stiflingly** *adv.* [perh. alt. of ME *stuffe*, *stuffle* f. OF *estouffer*]
■ **1** smother, choke back, keep *or* hold back, withhold, repress, suppress, hold in, restrain, prevent, curb, check, cover up, control, silence, muffle, stop, destroy, crush, demolish, extinguish, dampen, stamp out, kill, quash. **2, 3** suffocate, smother, choke, strangle, throttle, asphyxiate.

stifle[2] /stīf'l/ *n.* (in full **stifle-joint**) a joint in the legs of horses, dogs, etc., equivalent to the knee in humans. □

stifle-bone the bone in front of this joint. [ME: orig. unkn.]

stigma /stígmə/ *n.* (*pl.* **stigmas** or esp. in sense 4 **stigmata** /-mətə, -maátə/) **1** a mark or sign of disgrace or discredit. **2** (foll. by *of*) a distinguishing mark or characteristic. **3** the part of a pistil that receives the pollen in pollination. **4** (in *pl.*) *Eccl.* (in Christian belief) marks corresponding to those left on Christ's body by the Crucifixion, said to have been impressed on the bodies of St Francis of Assisi and others. **5** a mark or spot on the skin or on a butterfly-wing. **6** *Med.* a visible sign or characteristic of a disease. **7** an insect's spiracle. [L f. Gk *stigma -atos* a mark made by a pointed instrument, a brand, a dot: rel. to STICK[1]]

■ **1** brand, (bad) mark, blot, smirch, stain, spot, taint, blemish, demerit, blot on the escutcheon, blot in one's copybook. **2** see MARK[1] *n.* 2a, 3, 4a.

stigmatic /stigmáttik/ *adj.* & *n.* ● *adj.* **1** of or relating to a stigma or stigmas. **2** = ANASTIGMATIC. ● *n. Eccl.* a person bearing stigmata. □□ **stigmatically** *adv.*

stigmatist /stígmətist/ *n. Eccl.* = STIGMATIC *n.*

stigmatize /stígmətīz/ *v.tr.* (also **-ise**) **1** (often foll. by *as*) describe as unworthy or disgraceful. **2** *Eccl.* produce stigmata on. □□ **stigmatization** /-záysh'n/ *n.* [F *stigmatiser* or med.L *stigmatizo* f. Gk *stigmatizō* (as STIGMA)]

■ **1** brand, disparage, depreciate, discredit, denounce, condemn, calumniate, defame, pillory, slander, vilify.

stilb /stilb/ *n.* a unit of luminance equal to one candela per square centimetre. [F f. Gk *stilbō* glitter]

stilbene /stílbeen/ *n. Chem.* an aromatic hydrocarbon forming phosphorescent crystals. [as STILB + -ENE]

stilboestrol /stilbeéstrol/ *n.* (*US* **stilbestrol**) a powerful synthetic oestrogen derived from stilbene. [STILBENE + OESTRUS]

stile[1] /stīl/ *n.* an arrangement of steps allowing people but not animals to climb over a fence or wall. [OE *stigel* f. a Gmc root *stig-* (unrecorded) climb]

stile[2] /stīl/ *n.* a vertical piece in the frame of a panelled door, wainscot, etc. (cf. RAIL[1] *n.* 5). [prob. f. Du. *stijl* pillar, doorpost]

stiletto /stiléttō/ *n.* (*pl.* **-os**) **1** a short dagger with a thick blade. **2** a pointed instrument for making eyelets etc. **3** (in full **stiletto heel**) **a** a long tapering heel of a shoe. **b** a shoe with such a heel. [It., dimin. of *stilo* dagger (as STYLUS)]

■ **1** see DAGGER.

still[1] /stil/ *adj., n., adv.,* & *v.* ● *adj.* **1** not or hardly moving. **2** with little or no sound; calm and tranquil (*a still evening*). **3** (of sounds) hushed, stilled. **4** (of a drink) not effervescing. ● *n.* **1** deep silence (*in the still of the night*). **2** an ordinary static photograph (as opposed to a motion picture), esp. a single shot from a cinema film. ● *adv.* **1** without moving (*stand still*). **2** even now or at a particular time (*they still did not understand; why are you still here?*). **3** nevertheless; all the same. **4** (with *compar.* etc.) even, yet, increasingly (*still greater efforts; still another explanation*). ● *v.tr.* & *intr.* make or become still; quieten. □ **still and all** *colloq.* nevertheless. **still life** (*pl.* **still lifes**) **1** a painting or drawing of inanimate objects such as fruit or flowers. **2** this genre of painting. **still waters run deep** a quiet manner conceals depths of feeling or knowledge or cunning. □□ **stillness** *n.* [OE *stille* (adj. & adv.), *stillan* (v.), f. WG]

■ *adj.* **1** quiet, serene, placid, calm, tranquil, motionless, unmoving, immobile, peaceful, pacific, at rest, quiescent, inert, inactive, even, flat, smooth, undisturbed, unruffled, stationary, static, standing, stagnant. **2** silent, quiet, noiseless, soundless; calm, tranquil, hushed, restful, *poet.* stilly. **3** hushed, stilled, quiet. **4** see FLAT[1] *adj.* 4. ● *n.* **1** stillness, hush, quiet, silence, tranquillity, quietness, quietude, noiselessness, soundlessness, peace, peacefulness, serenity, calm. ● *adv.* **1** motionlessly, quietly, silently, stock-still. **2** even now *or* then, to this *or* that time, till this *or* that time, until this *or* that time, (up) till *or* until now *or* then, yet. **3** notwithstanding, yet, all the same, even then *or* so, *colloq.* still and all; see also NEVERTHELESS. ● *v.* calm, allay, assuage, alleviate, relieve, pacify, tranquillize, soothe, mollify, appease, subdue, suppress; silence, lull, quiet, hush, *Brit.* quieten. □ **still and all** see YET *adv.* 6. □□ **stillness** see STILL[1] *n.* above.

still[2] /stil/ *n.* an apparatus for distilling spirituous liquors etc. □ **still-room** *Brit.* **1** a room for distilling. **2** a housekeeper's storeroom in a large house. [obs. *still* (v.), ME f. DISTILL]

stillage /stíllij/ *n.* a bench, frame, etc., for keeping articles off the floor while draining, drying, waiting to be packed, etc. [app. f. Du. *stellagie* scaffold f. *stellen* to place + F *-age*]

stillbirth /stílburth/ *n.* the birth of a dead child.

stillborn /stílborn/ *adj.* **1** (of a child) born dead. **2** (of an idea, plan, etc.) abortive; not able to succeed.

Stillson /stíls'n/ *n.* (in full **Stillson wrench**) a large wrench with jaws that tighten as pressure is increased. [D. C. *Stillson*, its inventor d. 1899]

stilly /stílli/ *adv.* & *adj.* ● *adv.* in a still manner. ● *adj. poet.* still, quiet. [(adv.) OE *stillīce*: (adj.) f. STILL[1]]

stilt /stilt/ *n.* **1** either of a pair of poles with supports for the feet enabling the user to walk at a distance above the ground. **2** each of a set of piles or posts supporting a building etc. **3 a** any wading bird of the genus *Himantopus* with long legs. **b** (in *comb.*) denoting a long-legged kind of bird (*stilt-petrel*). **4** a three-legged support for ceramic ware in a kiln. □ **on stilts 1** supported by stilts. **2** bombastic, stilted. □□ **stiltless** *adj.* [ME & LG *stilte* f. Gmc]

stilted /stíltid/ *adj.* **1** (of a literary style etc.) stiff and unnatural; bombastic. **2** standing on stilts. **3** *Archit.* (of an arch) with pieces of upright masonry between the imposts and the springers. □□ **stiltedly** *adv.* **stiltedness** *n.*

■ **1** awkward, ungraceful, graceless, clumsy, wooden, stiff, turgid, affected, artificial, unnatural, mannered, forced, laboured; pretentious, formal, pompous, lofty, bombastic, grandiloquent, high-flown, inflated.

Stilton /stílt'n/ *n. propr.* a kind of strong rich cheese, often with blue veins, orig. sold in Stilton in East Anglia.

stimulant /stímyoolənt/ *adj.* & *n.* ● *adj.* that stimulates, esp. bodily or mental activity. ● *n.* **1** a stimulant substance, esp. a drug or alcoholic drink. **2** a stimulating influence. [L *stimulare stimulant-* urge, goad]

■ *adj.* see TONIC *adj.* ● *n.* **1** energizer, antidepressant, tonic, restorative, analeptic, pick-me-up, *colloq.* bracer, shot in the arm, pep pill, *sl.* upper, speed. **2** stimulus, incentive, provocation, spur, prompt, goad, urge, prod, fillip, impetus, incitement, drive, impulse, push, pull, draw, *colloq.* boost.

stimulate /stímyoolayt/ *v.tr.* **1** apply or act as a stimulus to. **2** animate, excite, arouse. **3** be a stimulant to. □□ **stimulating** *adj.* **stimulatingly** *adv.* **stimulation** /-láysh'n/ *n.* **stimulative** /-lətiv/ *adj.* **stimulator** *n.*

■ rouse, arouse, waken, awaken, wake up, excite, incite, inspire, encourage, spur, sting, quicken, animate, inflame, foment, fire, kindle, fuel, nourish, whet, activate, whip *or* stir up, goad, galvanize, energize, jog, jolt, fillip, inspirit, impassion, work up, *literary* enkindle; increase, encourage, prompt, provoke, quicken; see also VITALIZE. □□ **stimulating** exciting, inspirational, inspiring, arousing, rousing, stirring, animating, invigorating, tonic, exhilarating, thrilling, provocative, thought-provoking, challenging. **stimulation** see SPUR *n.* 2, THRILL *n.* 1.

stimulus /stímyooləss/ *n.* (*pl.* **stimuli** /-lī/) **1** a thing that rouses to activity or energy. **2** a stimulating or rousing effect. **3** a thing that evokes a specific functional reaction in an organ or tissue. [L, = goad, spur, incentive]

■ **1** see *incitement* (INCITE). **2** see INSPIRATION 1a.

stimy var. of STYMIE.

sting /sting/ *n.* & *v.* ● *n.* **1** a sharp often poisonous wounding organ of an insect, snake, nettle, etc. **2 a** the act of inflicting a wound with this. **b** the wound itself or the pain caused by it. **3** a wounding or painful quality or effect (*the sting of* *hunger*; *stings of remorse*). **4** pungency, sharpness, vigour (*a sting in the voice*). **5** *sl.* a swindle or robbery. ● *v.* (*past* and *past part.* **stung** /stung/) **1 a** *tr.* wound or pierce with a sting. **b** *intr.* be able to sting; have a sting. **2** *intr.* & *tr.* feel or cause to feel a tingling physical or sharp mental pain. **3** *tr.* (foll. by *into*) incite by a strong or painful mental effect (*was stung into replying*). **4** *tr. sl.* swindle or charge exorbitantly. □ **stinging-nettle** a nettle, *Urtica dioica*, having stinging hairs. **sting in the tail** unexpected pain or difficulty at the end. □□ **stingingly** *adv.* **stingless** *adj.* **stinglike** *adj.* [OE *sting* (n.), *stingan* (v.), f. Gmc]

■ *n.* **2 b** pain, tingle; see also PRICK *n.* 3. ● *v.* **1 a** prick, stab, pierce, stick, wound; bite, nip. **2** hurt, ache, smart; wound, pain, injure, distress, nettle, pique, prick, cut to the quick. **3** see STIMULATE. **4** cheat, overcharge, swindle, fleece, rook, defraud, *colloq.* rip off, take for a ride, diddle, *colloq.* rob, soak, *sl.* chisel, gyp.

stingaree /stínggəree/ *n. US* & *Austral.* = STINGRAY.

stinger /stíngər/ *n.* **1** a stinging insect, snake, nettle, etc. **2** a sharp painful blow.

stingray /stíngray/ *n.* any of various broad flat-fish esp. of the family Dasyatidae, having a long poisonous serrated spine at the base of its tail.

stingy /stínji/ *adj.* (**stingier**, **stingiest**) niggardly, mean. □□ **stingily** *adv.* **stinginess** *n.* [perh. f. dial. *stinge* STING]

■ see MEAN[2] 1. □□ **stinginess** see THRIFT.

stink /stingk/ *v.* & *n.* ● *v.* (*past* **stank** /stangk/ or **stunk** /stungk/; *past part.* **stunk**) **1** *intr.* emit a strong offensive smell. **2** *tr.* (often foll. by *out*) fill (a place) with a stink. **3** *tr.* (foll. by *out* etc.) drive (a person) out etc. by a stink. **4** *intr. colloq.* be or seem very unpleasant, contemptible, or scandalous. **5** *intr.* (foll. by *of*) *colloq.* have plenty of (esp. money). ● *n.* **1** a strong or offensive smell; a stench. **2** *colloq.* a row or fuss (*the affair caused quite a stink*). □ **like stink** *colloq.* intensely; extremely hard or fast etc. (*working like stink*). **stink bomb** a device emitting a stink when exploded. [OE *stincan* ult. f. WG: cf. STENCH]

■ *v.* **1** see SMELL *v.* 5. ● *n.* **1** see SMELL *n.* 3. **2** see FUSS *n.* 1, 2a. □ **like stink** intensely; like a bat out of hell, like a demon, at a rate of knots, *colloq.* like a bomb, like greased lightning, like nobody's business, *sl.* like billy-oh, like blazes, *Brit. sl.* like the clappers; see also *quickly* (QUICK).

stinker /stíngkər/ *n.* **1** a person or thing that stinks. **2** *sl.* an objectionable person or thing. **3** *sl.* **a** a difficult task. **b** a letter etc. conveying strong disapproval.

■ **2** wretch, villain, scoundrel, cad, beast, cur, viper, snake in the grass, blackguard, rogue, knave, *archaic* dastard, whoreson, *archaic or joc.* varlet, *colloq.* rat, skunk, swine, nasty piece of work, so-and-so, heel, *colloq. or joc.* bounder, *Brit. colloq.* blighter, *poet. or archaic* (base) caitiff, *sl.* louse, creep, stinkpot, ratbag, (rotten) bastard, son of a bitch, *esp. Brit. sl.* rotter, toerag, *esp. US sl.* S.O.B., bum.

stinkhorn /stíngk-horn/ *n.* any foul-smelling fungus of the order Phallales.

stinking /stíngking/ *adj.* & *adv.* ● *adj.* **1** that stinks. **2** *sl.* very objectionable. ● *adv. sl.* extremely and usu. objectionably (*stinking rich*). □ **stinking badger** a teledu. □□ **stinkingly** *adv.*

■ *adj.* **1** foul-smelling, evil-smelling, smelly, fetid, mephitic, rank, malodorous, reeky, reeking, putrid, rancid, gamy, high, off, *archaic* miasmal, miasmatic, miasmatical, miasmic, *colloq.* whiffy, *Brit. colloq.* pongy, *literary* noisome, *Austral. sl.* on the nose. **2** wretched, villainous, beastly, vile, contemptible, objectionable, low, despicable, mean, nasty, disgusting, dastardly, *colloq.* terrible, awful, lousy, *sl.* rotten. ● *adv. colloq.* horribly, disgustingly; see also *extremely* (EXTREME).

stinko /stíngkō/ *adj. sl.* drunk.

■ see DRUNK *adj.* 1.

stinkpot /stíngkpot/ *n. sl.* **1** a term of contempt for a person. **2** a vehicle or boat that emits foul exhaust fumes.

■ **1** see STINKER.

stinkweed /stíngkweed/ *n.* = *wall-rocket* (see ROCKET[2]).

stinkwood /stíngkwŏŏd/ *n.* an African tree, *Ocotea bullata*, with foul-smelling timber.

stint /stint/ *v.* & *n.* ● *v.* **1 a** *tr.* supply (food or aid etc.) in a niggardly amount or grudgingly. **b** *intr.* (foll. by *on*) be grudging or mean about. **2** (often *refl.*) supply (a person etc.) in this way. ● *n.* **1** a limitation of supply or effort (*without stint*). **2** a fixed or allotted amount of work (*do one's stint*). **3** a small sandpiper, esp. a dunlin. □□ **stinter** *n.* **stintless** *adj.* [OE *styntan* to blunt, dull, f. Gmc, rel. to STUNT[1]]

■ *v.* **1** skimp, scrimp, hold back (on), withhold; be stingy, be mean, be cheap, be niggardly, be penurious, be parsimonious, be sparing, be frugal, economize, pinch (pennies), cut corners, *Brit. colloq.* be mingy. **2** control, curb, limit, restrict. ● *n.* **1** control, curb, limit, limitation, restriction, check, restraint, constraint, condition, qualification, reservation. **2** share, quota, allotment, assignment, stretch, shift, term, time, spell, bout, turn, tour, *colloq.* bit, *sl.* whack.

stipe /stīp/ *n. Bot.* & *Zool.* a stalk or stem, esp. the support of a carpel, the stalk of a frond, the stem of a fungus, or an eye-stalk. □□ **stipiform** *adj.* **stipitate** /stíppitayt/ *adj.* **stipitiform** /stipíttiform/ *adj.* [F f. L *stipes*: see STIPES]

stipel /stī́p'l/ *n. Bot.* a secondary stipule at the base of the leaflets of a compound leaf. □□ **stipellate** /stīpéllayt/ *adj.* [F *stipelle* f. mod.L *stipella* dimin. (as STIPULE)]

stipend /stī́pend/ *n.* a fixed regular allowance or salary, esp. paid to a clergyman. [ME f. OF *stipend(i)e* or L *stipendium* f. *stips* wages + *pendere* to pay]

■ pay, salary, wage, payment, remuneration, remittance, recompense, compensation, reward, emolument, fee, earnings, income; grant, subvention, scholarship, subsidy, allowance, allotment, (financial) support.

stipendiary /stīpéndyəri/ *adj.* & *n.* ● *adj.* **1** receiving a stipend. **2** working for pay, not voluntarily. ● *n.* (*pl.* **-ies**) a person receiving a stipend. □ **stipendiary magistrate** a paid professional magistrate. [L *stipendiarius* (as STIPEND)]

stipes /stī́peez/ *n.* (*pl.* **stipites** /stíppiteez/) = STIPE. [L, = log, tree-trunk]

stipple /stípp'l/ *v.* & *n.* ● *v.* **1** *tr.* & *intr.* draw or paint or engrave etc. with dots instead of lines. **2** *tr.* roughen the surface of (paint, cement, etc.). ● *n.* **1** the process or technique of stippling. **2** the effect of stippling. □□ **stippler** *n.* **stippling** *n.* [Du. *stippelen* frequent. of *stippen* to prick f. *stip* point]

stipulate[1] /stípyoolayt/ *v.tr.* **1** demand or specify as part of a bargain or agreement. **2** (foll. by *for*) mention or insist upon as an essential condition. **3** (as **stipulated** *adj.*) laid down in the terms of an agreement. □□ **stipulation** /-láysh'n/ *n.* **stipulator** *n.* [L *stipulari*]

■ **1** specify, demand, require, covenant, set forth, prescribe, lay down, agree (to), provide (for), guarantee, warrant, promise, insist upon *or* on; call for. □□ **stipulation** condition, demand, essential, given, requirement, requisite, prerequisite, precondition, qualification, specification, undertaking, obligation, covenant, clause, proviso, term, agreement, provision, guarantee, warranty, promise.

stipulate[2] /stípyoolət/ *adj. Bot.* having stipules. [L *stipula* (as STIPULE)]

stipule /stípyŏŏl/ *n.* a small leaflike appendage to a leaf, usu. at the base of a leaf-stem. □□ **stipular** *adj.* [F *stipule* or L *stipula* straw]

stir[1] /stur/ *v.* & *n.* ● *v.* (**stirred**, **stirring**) **1** *tr.* move a spoon or other implement round and round in (a liquid etc.) to mix the ingredients or constituents. **2 a** *tr.* cause to move or be disturbed, esp. slightly (*a breeze stirred the lake*). **b** *intr.* be or begin to be in motion (*not a creature was stirring*). **c** *refl.* rouse (oneself), esp. from a lethargic state. **3** *intr.* rise from sleep (*is still not stirring*). **4** *intr.* (foll. by *out of*) leave; go out of (esp. one's house). **5** *tr.* arouse or inspire or excite (the emotions etc., or a person as regards these) (*was stirred to anger*; *it stirred the imagination*). **6** *esp. Austral. colloq.* **a** *tr.* annoy; tease. **b** *intr.* cause trouble. ● *n.* **1** an act of stirring (*give it a good stir*). **2** commotion or excitement; public attention (*caused quite a stir*). **3** the slightest movement (*not a stir*). □ **not stir a finger** make no effort to help. **stir the blood** inspire enthusiasm etc. **stir in** mix (an added ingredient) with a substance by stirring. **stir one's stumps** *colloq.* **1** begin to move. **2** become active. **stir up 1** mix thoroughly by stirring. **2** incite (trouble etc.) (*loved stirring things up*). **3** stimulate, excite, arouse (*stirred up their curiosity*). □□ **stirless** *adj.* [OE *styrian* f. Gmc]

■ *v.* **1** stir up, agitate, mix (up), scramble, amalgamate, mingle, intermingle, merge, blend, fold (in), churn (up), beat, whip (up), whisk, *literary* commingle. **2 a** disturb, ruffle, shake (up). **b** see MOVE *v.* 1, 4. **c** (*stir oneself*) rouse oneself, bestir oneself, get up, get moving, *colloq.* get a move on, shake a leg, look *or* step lively, look alive, stir one's stumps, *exp. US sl.* get a wiggle on. **3** rise, get up, wake up, waken, awaken, *esp. archaic* & *poet.* arise; start *or* begin the day, be up and about, *colloq.* turn out. **5** arouse, rouse, inspire, excite, affect, stimulate, energize, galvanize, electrify, animate, provoke, activate. **6 a** see ANNOY 1, TEASE *v.* 1. **b** see *make difficulties* (DIFFICULTY). ● *n.* **1** beat, whisk, whip, mix, blend, shake. **2** bustle, activity, movement, stirring, action, commotion, flurry, confusion, tumult, ado, to-do, fuss, disturbance, excitement, hubbub, *esp. Brit. colloq.* kerfuffle. **3** movement, stirring, move, flicker. □ **stir one's stumps** see STIR[1] *v.* 2c above. **stir up 1** see STIR[1] *v.* 1 above. **2** incite, whip up, provoke, inspire, foment, instigate; motivate, move, encourage, spur, prod, induce; (*stir up trouble*) make *or* cause trouble. **3** stimulate, energize, galvanize, electrify, animate, quicken, excite, inspire, provoke, rouse, arouse, awaken; revive, resuscitate.

stir[2] /stur/ *n. sl.* a prison (esp. *in stir*). □ **stir-crazy** deranged from long imprisonment. [19th c.: orig. unkn.]

■ see PRISON *n.* 1. □ **stir-crazy** see *deranged* (DERANGE 2).

stir-fry /stúrfrī/ *v.* & *n.* ● *v.tr.* (**-ies, -ied**) fry rapidly while stirring and tossing. ● *n.* a dish consisting of stir-fried meat, vegetables, etc.

stirk /sturk/ *n. Brit. dial.* a yearling bullock or heifer. [OE *stirc*, perh. dimin. of *stēor* STEER[2]: see -OCK]

stirps /sturps/ *n.* (*pl.* **stirpes** /-peez/) **1** *Biol.* a classificatory group. **2** *Law* **a** a branch of a family. **b** its progenitor. [L, = stock]

stirrer /stúrər/ *n.* **1** a thing or a person that stirs. **2** *colloq.* a troublemaker; an agitator.

stirring /stúring/ *adj.* **1** stimulating, exciting, rousing. **2** actively occupied (*lead a stirring life*). □□ **stirringly** *adv.* [OE *styrende* (as STIR[1])]

■ **1** moving, telling, emotional, emotive, emotion-charged, impassioned, rousing, stimulating, inspiring, affecting, gripping, evocative, exciting, thrilling, melodramatic, dramatic, heady, intoxicating, spirited, inspiriting, exhilarating, awe-inspiring. **2** see BUSY *adj.* 2.

stirrup /stírrəp/ *n.* **1** each of a pair of devices attached to each side of a horse's saddle, in the form of a loop with a flat base to support the rider's foot. **2** (*attrib.*) having the shape of a stirrup. **3** (in full **stirrup bone**) = STAPES. □ **stirrup-cup** a cup of wine etc. offered to a person about to depart, orig. on horseback. **stirrup-iron** the metal loop of a stirrup. **stirrup-leather** (or **-strap**) the strap attaching a stirrup to a saddle. **stirrup-pump** a hand-operated water-pump with a foot-rest, used to extinguish small fires. [OE *stigrāp* f. *stigan* climb (as STILE[1]) + ROPE]

■ □ **stirrup-cup** see DRINK *n.* 2b.

stitch /stich/ *n.* & *v.* ● *n.* **1 a** (in sewing or knitting or crocheting etc.) a single pass of a needle or the thread or loop etc. resulting from this. **b** a particular method of sewing or knitting etc. (*am learning a new stitch*). **2** (usu. in *pl.*) *Surgery* each of the loops of material used in sewing up a wound. **3** the least bit of clothing (*hadn't a stitch on*). **4** an acute pain in the side of the body induced by running etc. ● *v.tr.* **1** sew; make stitches (in). **2** join or close with stitches. □ **in stitches** *colloq.* laughing uncontrollably. **a stitch in time** a timely remedy. **stitch up 1** join or mend by sewing or stitching. **2** *sl.* betray or cheat. □□ **stitcher** *n.* **stitchery** *n.* **stitchless** *adj.* [OE *stice* f. Gmc, rel. to STICK[2]]

■ *n.* **1 a** tack, basting (stitch). **4** see TWINGE *n.* ● *v.* see SEW. □ **stitch up 2** see CHEAT *v.* 1a.

stitchwort /stíchwurt/ *n.* any plant of the genus *Stellaria*, esp. *S. media* with an erect stem and white starry flowers, once thought to cure a stitch in the side.

stiver /stī́vər/ *n.* the smallest quantity or amount (*don't care a stiver*). [Du. *stuiver* a small coin, prob. rel. to STUB]

stoa /stṓə/ *n.* (*pl.* **stoas**) **1** a portico or roofed colonnade in ancient Greek architecture. **2** (**the Stoa**) the Stoic school of philosophy. [Gk: cf. STOIC]

stoat /stōt/ *n.* a flesh-eating mammal, *Mustela erminea*, of the weasel family, having brown fur in the summer turning mainly white in the winter. Also called ERMINE. [ME: orig. unkn.]

stochastic /stəkástik/ *adj.* **1** determined by a random distribution of probabilities. **2** (of a process) characterized by a sequence of random variables. **3** governed by the laws of probability. □□ **stochastically** *adv.* [Gk *stokhastikos* f. *stokhazomai* aim at, guess f. *stokhos* aim]

stock /stok/ *n.*, *adj.*, & *v.* ● *n.* **1** a store of goods etc. ready for sale or distribution etc. **2** a supply or quantity of anything for use (*lay in winter stocks of fuel*; *a great stock of information*). **3** equipment or raw material for manufacture or trade etc. (*rolling-stock*; *paper stock*). **4 a** farm animals or equipment. **b** = FATSTOCK. **5 a** the capital of a business company. **b** shares in this. **6** one's reputation or popularity (*his stock is rising*). **7 a** money lent to a government at fixed interest. **b** the right to receive such interest. **8** a line of ancestry; family origins (*comes of Cornish stock*). **9** liquid made by stewing bones, vegetables, fish, etc., as a basis for soup, gravy, sauce, etc. **10** any of various fragrant-flowered cruciferous plants of the genus *Matthiola* or *Malcolmia* (orig. *stock-gillyflower*, so-called because it had a stronger stem than the clove gillyflower). **11** a plant into which a graft is inserted. **12** the main trunk of a tree etc. **13** (in *pl.*) *hist.* a timber frame with holes for the feet and occas. the hands and head, in which offenders were locked as a public punishment. **14** *US* **a** = *stock company*. **b** the repertory of this. **15 a** a base or support or handle for an implement or machine. **b** the crossbar of an anchor. **16** the butt of a rifle etc. **17 a** = HEADSTOCK. **b** = TAILSTOCK. **18** (in *pl.*) the supports for a ship during building. **19** a band of material worn round the neck esp. in horse-riding or below a clerical collar. **20** hard solid brick pressed in a mould. ● *adj.* **1** kept in stock and so regularly available (*stock sizes*). **2** perpetually repeated; hackneyed, conventional (*a stock answer*). ● *v.tr.* **1** have or keep (goods) in stock. **2 a** provide (a shop or a farm etc.) with goods, equipment, or livestock. **b** fill with items needed (*shelves well-stocked with books*). **3** fit (a gun etc.) with a stock. □ **in stock** available immediately for sale etc. **on the stocks** in construction or preparation. **out of stock** not immediately available for sale. **stock-book** a book showing amounts of goods acquired and disposed of. **stock-car 1** a specially strengthened production car for use in racing in which collision occurs. **2** *US* a railway truck for transporting livestock. **stock company** *US* a repertory company performing mainly at a particular theatre. **stock dove** a European wild pigeon, *Columba oenas*, with a shorter tail and squarer head than a wood pigeon and breeding in tree-trunks. **Stock Exchange 1** a place where stocks and shares are bought and sold. **2** the dealers working there. **stock-in-trade 1** goods kept on sale by a retailer, dealer, etc. **2** all the requisites of a trade or profession. **3** a ready supply of characteristic phrases, attitudes, etc. **stock market 1** = *Stock Exchange*. **2** transactions on this. **stock-still** without moving. **stock up 1** provide with or get stocks or supplies. **2** (foll. by *with*, *on*) get in or gather a stock of (food, fuel, etc.). **take stock 1** make an inventory of one's stock. **2** (often foll. by *of*) make a review or estimate of (a situation etc.). **3** (foll. by *in*) concern oneself with. □□ **stocker** *n.* **stockless** *adj.* [OE *stoc, stocc* f. Gmc]

■ *n.* **1, 2** supply, store, inventory, stockpile, reserve, reservoir, cache, hoard, accumulation, quantity; wares, merchandise, goods, commodities, resources. **4** livestock, (domestic *or* farm) animals, cattle, beasts; horses, cows, oxen, sheep, goats. **5** capital, funds; property, assets. **6** see REPUTATION 2. **8** pedigree, bloodline, blood, house, dynasty, (line of) descent, extraction, roots, origins, lineage, family, ancestry, parentage, breeding, heritage. **9** see BROTH. **12** see TRUNK 1. **16** butt, handle. ● *adj.* **1** standard, ordinary, regular, routine, staple. **2** routine, stereotyped, banal, clichéd, unoriginal, commonplace, usual, hackneyed, ordinary, stale, staple, ready-made, run-of-the-mill, tired, old, everyday, customary, set, standard, predictable, traditional, conventional, trite, worn out, *colloq.* corny. ● *v.* **1** carry, have, have *or* make available, handle, deal in, market, sell, supply, furnish, provide, offer, trade in, keep. **2 a** see OUTFIT *v.* **b** fill, supply, provide, furnish. □ **in stock** available, on the shelf, for sale. **out of stock** unavailable, sold out. **Stock Exchange 1** see EXCHANGE *n.* 4. **stock-in-trade 1** see WARE[1]. **stock market 1** see EXCHANGE *n.* 4. **stock-still** see STILL[1] *adv.* 1. **stock up 2** (*stock up with* or *on*) accumulate, amass, pile up, stockpile, gather, garner, hoard, store (up), cache, lay in, get in, buy in. **take stock 2** (*take stock of*) weigh (up), estimate, review, appraise, look at, *colloq.* size up.

stockade /stokáyd/ *n.* & *v.* ● *n.* a line or enclosure of upright stakes. ● *v.tr.* fortify with a stockade. [obs. F *estocade*, alt. of *estacade* f. Sp. *estacada*: rel. to STAKE[1]]

■ *n.* see WALL *n.* 1.

stockbreeder /stókbreedər/ *n.* a farmer who raises livestock. □□ **stockbreeding** *n.*

stockbroker /stókbrōkər/ *n.* = BROKER 2. □ **stockbroker belt** *Brit.* an affluent residential area, esp. near a business centre such as London. □□ **stockbrokerage** *n.* **stockbroking** *n.*

stockfish /stókfish/ *n.* cod or a similar fish split and dried in the open air without salt.

stockholder /stók-hōldər/ *n.* an owner of stocks or shares. □□ **stockholding** *n.*

stockinet /stókkinét/ *n.* (also **stockinette**) an elastic knitted material. [prob. f. *stocking-net*]

stocking /stókking/ *n.* **1 a** either of a pair of long separate coverings for the legs and feet, usu. close-woven in wool or nylon and worn esp. by women and girls. **b** esp. *US* = SOCK[1]. **2** any close-fitting garment resembling a stocking (*bodystocking*). **3** a differently-coloured, usu. white, lower part of the leg of a horse etc. □ **in one's stocking** (or **stockinged**) **feet** without shoes (esp. while being measured). **stocking cap** a knitted usu. conical cap. **stocking-filler** *Brit.* a small present suitable for a Christmas stocking. **stocking-stitch** *Knitting* a stitch of alternate rows of plain and purl, making an even pattern. □□ **stockinged** *adj.* (also in *comb.*). **stockingless** *adj.* [STOCK in (now dial.) sense 'stocking' + -ING[1]]

stockist /stókkist/ *n. Brit.* a dealer who stocks goods of a particular type for sale.

■ see DEALER.

stockjobber /stókjobbər/ *n.* **1** *Brit.* = JOBBER 1. **2** *US* = JOBBER 2b. □□ **stockjobbing** *n.*

stocklist /stóklist/ *n. Brit.* a regular publication stating a dealer's stock of goods with current prices etc.

stockman /stókmən/ *n.* (*pl.* **-men**) **1 a** *Austral.* a man in charge of livestock. **b** *US* an owner of livestock. **2** *US* a person in charge of a stock of goods in a warehouse etc.

stockpile /stókpīl/ *n.* & *v.* ● *n.* an accumulated stock of goods, materials, weapons, etc., held in reserve. ● *v.tr.* accumulate a stockpile of. □□ **stockpiler** *n.*

■ *n.* see ACCUMULATION 2. ● *v.* see ACCUMULATE 1.

stockpot /stókpot/ *n.* a pot for cooking stock for soup etc.

stockroom /stókrōōm, -rōōm/ *n.* a room for storing goods in stock.

■ see WAREHOUSE.

stocktaking /stóktayking/ *n.* **1** the process of making an inventory of stock in a shop etc. **2** a review of one's position and resources.

stocky /stókki/ *adj.* (**stockier, stockiest**) (of a person, plant, or animal) short and strongly built; thickset. □□ **stockily** *adv.* **stockiness** *n.*

■ thickset, sturdy, chunky, dumpy, solid, stumpy, burly, beefy, heavy-set, squat, mesomorphic, *Anthropol.* pyknic.

stockyard /stókyaard/ *n.* an enclosure with pens etc. for the sorting or temporary keeping of cattle.

stodge /stoj/ *n.* & *v. colloq.* ● *n.* **1** food esp. of a thick heavy kind. **2** an unimaginative person or idea. ● *v.tr.* stuff with food etc. [earlier as verb: imit., after *stuff* and *podge*]

stodgy /stóji/ *adj.* (**stodgier, stodgiest**) **1** (of food) heavy and indigestible. **2** dull and uninteresting. **3** (of a literary style etc.) turgid and dull. □□ **stodgily** *adv.* **stodginess** *n.*

■ **1** heavy, indigestible, solid, filling. **2, 3** stuffy, dull, heavy, ponderous, boring, tedious, humdrum, tiresome, turgid, uninteresting, unimaginative, dreary, bland, *colloq.* deadly.

stoep /stōōp/ *n. S.Afr.* a terraced veranda in front of a house. [Du., rel. to STEP]

stogy /stṓgi/ *n.* (also **stogie**) (*pl.* **-ies**) *US* **1** a long narrow roughly-made cigar. **2** a rough heavy boot. [orig. *stoga*, short for *Conestoga* in Pennsylvania]

Stoic /stṓ-ik/ *n.* & *adj.* ● *n.* **1** a member of the ancient Greek school of philosophy founded at Athens by Zeno *c.*308 BC, which sought virtue as the greatest good and taught control of one's feelings and passions. **2** (**stoic**) a stoical person. ● *adj.* **1** of or like the Stoics. **2** (**stoic**) = STOICAL. [ME f. L *stoicus* f. Gk *stōikos* f. STOA (with ref. to Zeno's teaching in the *Stoa Poikilē* or Painted Porch at Athens)]

stoical /stṓ-ik'l/ *adj.* having or showing great self-control in adversity. □□ **stoically** *adv.*

■ stoic, impassive, resigned, cool, unemotional, emotionless, imperturbable, calm, philosophical, dispassionate, indifferent, phlegmatic, long-suffering, patient, stolid, disciplined, self-possessed, (self-)controlled, *colloq.* unflappable.

stoichiometry /stóykiómmitri/ *n.* (also **stoichometry** /stoykómmitri/) *Chem.* **1** the fixed, usu. rational numerical relationship between the relative quantities of substances in a reaction or compound. **2** the determination or measurement of these quantities. □□ **stoichiometric** /-kiəmétrik/ *adj.* [Gk *stoikheion* element + -METRY]

Stoicism /stṓ-isiz'm/ *n.* **1** the philosophy of the Stoics. **2** (**stoicism**) a stoical attitude.

■ **2** (**stoicism**) self-possession, austerity, self-control, fortitude, calmness, calm, coolness, imperturbability, forbearance, patience, fatalism, resignation, philosophy, *colloq.* unflappability.

stoke /stōk/ *v.* (often foll. by *up*) **1 a** *tr.* feed and tend (a fire or furnace etc.). **b** *intr.* act as a stoker. **2** *intr. colloq.* consume food, esp. steadily and in large quantities. [back-form. f. STOKER]

stokehold /stṓk-hōld/ *n.* a compartment in a steamship, containing its boilers and furnace.

stokehole /stṓk-hōl/ *n.* a space for stokers in front of a furnace.

stoker /stṓkər/ *n.* a person who tends to the furnace on a steamship. [Du. f. *stoken* stoke f. MDu. *stoken* push, rel. to STICK[1]]

stokes /stōks/ *n.* (*pl.* same) the cgs unit of kinematic viscosity, corresponding to a dynamic viscosity of 1 poise and a density of 1 gram per cubic centimetre, equivalent to 10^{-4} square metres per second. [Sir G. G. *Stokes*, Brit. physicist d. 1903]

STOL *abbr. Aeron.* short take-off and landing.

stole[1] /stōl/ *n.* **1** a woman's long garment like a scarf, worn over the shoulders. **2** a strip of silk etc. worn similarly as a vestment by a priest. [OE *stol, stole* (orig. a long robe) f. L *stola* f. Gk *stolē* equipment, clothing]
■ **1** tippet, scarf, boa, shawl, wrap, cape.

stole[2] *past* of STEAL.

stolen *past part.* of STEAL.

stolid /stóllid/ *adj.* **1** lacking or concealing emotion or animation. **2** not easily excited or moved. □□ **stolidity** /-lídditi/ *n.* **stolidly** *adv.* **stolidness** *n.* [obs. F *stolide* or L *stolidus*]
■ impassive, exanimate, phlegmatic, unemotional, stoical; vegetating, lethargic, apathetic, indifferent, uninterested; wooden, slow, lumpish. □□ **stolidity** see INDIFFERENCE 1.

stolon /stṓlon/ *n.* **1** *Bot.* a horizontal stem or branch that takes root at points along its length, forming new plants. **2** *Zool.* a branched stemlike structure in some invertebrates such as corals. □□ **stolonate** /-nayt/ *adj.* **stoloniferous** /-nífferəss/ *adj.* [L *stolo -onis*]

stoma /stṓmə/ *n.* (*pl.* **stomas** or **stomata** /-mətə/) **1** *Bot.* a minute pore in the epidermis of a leaf. **2 a** *Zool.* a small mouthlike opening in some lower animals. **b** *Surgery* a similar artificial orifice made in the stomach. □□ **stomal** *adj.* [mod.L f. Gk *stoma -atos* mouth]
■ **1** see PORE[1].

stomach /stúmmək/ *n.* & *v.* ● *n.* **1 a** the internal organ in which the first part of digestion occurs, being in man a pear-shaped enlargement of the alimentary canal linking the oesophagus to the small intestine. **b** any of several such organs in animals, esp. ruminants, in which there are four (cf. RUMEN, RETICULUM, OMASUM, ABOMASUM). **2 a** the belly, abdomen, or lower front of the body (*pit of the stomach*). **b** a protuberant belly (*what a stomach he has got!*). **3** (usu. foll. by *for*) **a** an appetite (for food). **b** liking, readiness, or inclination (for controversy, conflict, danger, or an undertaking) (*had no stomach for the fight*). ● *v.tr.* **1** find sufficiently palatable to swallow or keep down. **2** submit to or endure (an affront etc.) (usu. with *neg.*: *cannot stomach it*). □ **muscular stomach** any organ that grinds or squeezes to aid digestion, such as a gizzard. **on an empty stomach** not having eaten recently. **on a full stomach** soon after a large meal. **stomach-ache** a pain in the belly or bowels. **stomach-pump** a syringe for forcing liquid etc. into or out of the stomach. **stomach-tube** a tube introduced into the stomach via the gullet for cleansing or emptying it. **stomach upset** (or **upset stomach**) a temporary slight disorder of the digestive system. □□ **stomachful** *n.* (*pl.* **-fuls**). **stomachless** *adj.* [ME *stomak* f. OF *stomaque, estomac* f. L *stomachus* f. Gk *stomakhos* gullet f. *stoma* mouth]
■ *n.* **2 a** abdomen, belly, gut, paunch, *colloq.* tummy, insides, guts, *Austral. colloq.* bingie, *sl.* bread basket. **b** pot-belly, pot, paunch, beer-gut, *Brit. colloq.* spare tyre, *joc.* corporation. **3 b** tolerance; taste, appetite, desire, hunger, thirst, craving, need; inclination, relish; see also LIKING 2. ● *v.* **1** swallow, keep down, digest, eat. **2** abide, tolerate, endure, stand, bear, suffer, take, accept, swallow, resign *or* reconcile oneself to, put up with, submit to, countenance, *colloq.* stick, *literary* brook.
□ **stomach-ache** see INDIGESTION.

stomacher /stúmməkər/ *n. hist.* **1** a pointed front-piece of a woman's dress covering the breast and pit of the stomach, often jewelled or embroidered. **2** an ornament worn on the front of a bodice. [ME, prob. f. OF *estomachier* (as STOMACH)]

stomachic /stəmákkik/ *adj.* & *n.* ● *adj.* **1** of or relating to the stomach. **2** promoting the appetite or assisting digestion. ● *n.* a medicine or stimulant for the stomach. [F *stomachique* or L *stomachicus* f. Gk *stomakhikos* (as STOMACH)]

stomata *pl.* of STOMA.

stomatitis /stṓmətī́tiss/ *n. Med.* inflammation of the mucous membrane of the mouth.

stomatology /stṓmətólləji/ *n.* the scientific study of the mouth or its diseases. □□ **stomatological** /-təlójik'l/ *adj.* **stomatologist** *n.*

stomp /stomp/ *v.* & *n.* ● *v.intr.* tread or stamp heavily. ● *n.* a lively jazz dance with heavy stamping. □□ **stomper** *n.* [US dial. var. of STAMP]
■ *v.* see STAMP *v.* 1c.

stone /stōn/ *n.* & *v.* ● *n.* **1 a** solid non-metallic mineral matter, of which rock is made. **b** a piece of this, esp. a small piece. **2** *Building* **a** = LIMESTONE (*Portland stone*). **b** = SANDSTONE (*Bath stone*). **3** *Mineral.* = *precious stone.* **4** a stony meteorite, an aerolite. **5** (often in *comb.*) a piece of stone of a definite shape or for a particular purpose (*tombstone*; *stepping-stone*). **6 a** a thing resembling stone in hardness or form, e.g. the hard case of the kernel in some fruits. **b** *Med.* (often in *pl.*) a hard morbid concretion in the body esp. in the kidney or gall-bladder (*gallstones*). **7** (*pl.* same) *Brit.* a unit of weight equal to 14 lb. (6.35 kg). **8** (*attrib.*) **a** made of stone. **b** of the colour of stone. ● *v.tr.* **1** pelt with stones. **2** remove the stones from (fruit). **3** face or pave etc. with stone. □ **cast** (or **throw**) **stones** (or **the first stone**) make aspersions on a person's character etc. **leave no stone unturned** try all possible means. **Stone Age** a prehistoric period when weapons and tools were made of stone. **stone-coal** anthracite. **stone-cold** completely cold. **stone-cold sober** completely sober. **stone the crows** *Brit. sl.* an exclamation of surprise or disgust. **stone curlew** any mottled brown and grey wader of the family Burhinidae, esp. *Burhinus oedicnemus*, inhabiting esp. stony open country. **stone-dead** completely dead. **stone-deaf** completely deaf. **stone-fruit** a fruit with flesh or pulp enclosing a stone. **stone parsley** an umbelliferous hedge-plant, *Sison amomum*, with aromatic seeds. **stone pine** a S. European pine-tree, *Pinus pinea*, with branches at the top spreading like an umbrella. **stone-pit** a quarry. **a stone's throw** a short distance. □□ **stoned** *adj.* (also in *comb.*). **stoneless** *adj.* **stoner** *n.* [OE *stān* f. Gmc]
■ *n.* **1 b** see ROCK[1] 4. **5** see TABLET 3. **6 a** pip, seed, *US* pit.
□ **stone-cold** see COLD *adj.* 1. **stone the crows** *sl.* well blow me down, well knock me down with a feather; see also *well I'll be damned* (DAMN). **stone-deaf** deaf, hard of hearing.

stonechat /stṓnchat/ *n.* any small brown bird of the thrush family with black and white markings, esp. *Saxicola torquata* with a call like stones being knocked together.

stonecrop /stṓnkrop/ *n.* any succulent plant of the genus *Sedum*, usu. having yellow or white flowers and growing amongst rocks or in walls.

stonecutter /stṓnkuttər/ *n.* a person or machine that cuts or carves stone.

stoned /stōnd/ *adj. sl.* under the influence of alcohol or drugs.
■ see DRUNK *adj.* 1, HIGH *adj.* 8b.

stonefish /stṓnfish/ *n.* (*pl.* same) a venomous tropical fish, *Synanceia verrucosa*, with poison glands underlying its erect dorsal spines. Also called DEVILFISH.

stonefly /stṓnflī/ *n.* (*pl.* **-flies**) any insect of the order Plecoptera, with aquatic larvae found under stones.

stoneground /stṓngrownd/ *adj.* (of flour) ground with millstones.

stonehatch /stṓnhach/ *n.* a ringed plover.

stonemason /stṓnmays'n/ *n.* a person who cuts, prepares, and builds with stone. □□ **stonemasonry** *n.*

stonewall /stṓnwawl/ *v.* **1** *tr.* & *intr.* obstruct (discussion or investigation) or be obstructive with evasive answers or denials etc. **2** *intr. Cricket* bat with excessive caution. □□ **stonewaller** *n.* **stonewalling** *n.*
■ **1** see STALL[2] *v.* 1.

stoneware /stṓnwair/ *n.* ceramic ware which is impermeable and partly vitrified but opaque.

■ see POTTERY.

stonewashed /stŏnwosht/ *adj.* (of a garment or fabric, esp. denim) washed with abrasives to produce a worn or faded appearance.

stoneweed /stŏnweed/ *n.* = GROMWELL.

stonework /stŏnwurk/ *n.* **1** masonry. **2** the parts of a building made of stone. □□ **stoneworker** *n.*

stonewort /stŏnwurt/ *n.* **1** = *stone parsley*. **2** any plant of the genus *Chara*, with a calcareous deposit on the stem.

stonkered /stóngkərd/ *adj. Austral.* & *NZ sl.* utterly defeated or exhausted. [20th c.: orig. unkn.]
■ see BEAT *adj.*

stony /stŏni/ *adj.* (**stonier, stoniest**) **1** full of or covered with stones (*stony soil*; *a stony road*). **2 a** hard, rigid. **b** cold, unfeeling, uncompromising (*a stony stare*; *a stony silence*). □ **stony-broke** *Brit. sl.* entirely without money. **stony-hearted** unfeeling, obdurate. □□ **stonily** *adv.* **stoniness** *n.* [OE *stānig* (as STONE)]
■ **1** rocky, pebbly, shingly, shingled, gravelly; rough, rugged. **2** hard, obdurate, adamant, adamantine, heartless, stony-hearted, hard-hearted, indifferent, unsympathetic, implacable, intractable, insensitive, insensible, unfeeling, unresponsive, unsentimental, merciless, pitiless, cold, cold-hearted, chilly, frigid, icy, tough, hard-boiled, callous, steely, rigid, inflexible, uncompromising. □ **stony-broke** bankrupt, penniless, indigent, penurious, poverty-stricken, poor, *colloq.* broke, *Brit. sl.* skint. **stony-hearted** see STONY 2 above.

stood *past* and *past part.* of STAND.

stooge /stōōj/ *n.* & *v. colloq.* ● *n.* **1** a butt or foil, esp. for a comedian. **2** an assistant or subordinate, esp. for routine or unpleasant work. **3** a compliant person; a puppet. ● *v.intr.* **1** (foll. by *for*) act as a stooge for. **2** (foll. by *about*, *around*, etc.) move about aimlessly. [20th c.: orig. unkn.]
■ *n.* **1** see FOOL *n.* 3. **2** see INFERIOR *n.* 1. **3** see PUPPET.

stook /stōōk, stŏŏk/ *n.* & *v.* ● *n.* a group of sheaves of grain stood on end in a field. ● *v.tr.* arrange in stooks. [ME *stouk*, from or rel. to MLG *stūke*]

stool /stōōl/ *n.* & *v.* ● *n.* **1** a seat without a back or arms, usu. for one person and consisting of a wooden slab on three or four short legs. **2 a** = FOOTSTOOL. **b** a low bench for kneeling on. **3** (usu. in *pl.*) = FAECES. **4** the root or stump of a tree or plant from which the shoots spring. **5** *US* a decoy-bird in hunting. ● *v.intr.* (of a plant) throw up shoots from the root. □ **fall between two stools** fail from vacillation between two courses etc. **stool-pigeon 1** a person acting as a decoy (orig. a decoy of a pigeon fixed to a stool). **2** a police informer. [OE *stōl* f. Gmc, rel. to STAND]
■ *n.* **1** see SEAT *n.* 1. □ **stool-pigeon 1** see DECOY *n.* **2** see INFORMER 1.

stoolball /stōōlbawl/ *n.* a team-game played in the UK, with a bat and ball and pairs of batters scoring runs between bases.

stoolie /stōōli/ *n. US sl.* a person acting as a stool-pigeon.
■ see INFORMER 1.

stoop[1] /stōōp/ *v.* & *n.* ● *v.* **1** *tr.* bend (one's head or body) forwards and downwards. **2** *intr.* carry one's head and shoulders bowed forward. **3** *intr.* (often foll. by *down*) lower the body by bending forward, sometimes also bending at the knee. **4** *intr.* (foll. by *to* + infin.) deign or condescend. **5** *intr.* (foll. by *to*) descend or lower oneself to (some conduct) (*has stooped to crime*). **6** *intr.* (of a hawk etc.) swoop on its prey. ● *n.* **1** a stooping posture. **2** the downward swoop of a hawk etc. [OE *stūpian* f. Gmc, rel. to STEEP[1]]
■ *v.* **1** bend, bow, duck, lean, hunch, double up. **3** stoop down, bend (down), bow, duck (down), lean (down), crouch (down), squat, scrunch down, *US* hunch (down). **4, 5** condescend, deign, lower *or* abase *or* degrade oneself, sink, descend, humble oneself. **6** see SWOOP *v.* 1. ● *n.* **1** hunch, slouch, crouch, *Med.* kyphosis, curvature of the spine. **2** see SWOOP *n.*

stoop[2] /stōōp/ *n. US* a porch or small veranda or set of steps in front of a house. [Du. *stoep*: see STOEP]

stoop[3] var. of STOUP.

stop /stop/ *v.* & *n.* ● *v.* (**stopped, stopping**) **1** *tr.* **a** put an end to (motion etc.); completely check the progress or motion or operation of. **b** effectively hinder or prevent (*stopped them playing so loudly*). **c** discontinue (an action or sequence of actions) (*stopped playing*; *stopped my visits*). **2** *intr.* come to an end; cease (*supplies suddenly stopped*). **3** *intr.* cease from motion or speaking or action; make a halt or pause (*the car stopped at the lights*; *he stopped in the middle of a sentence*; *my watch has stopped*). **4** *tr.* cause to cease action; defeat. **5** *tr. sl.* receive (a blow etc.). **6** *intr.* remain; stay for a short time. **7** *tr.* (often foll. by *up*) block or close up (a hole or leak etc.). **8** *tr.* not permit or supply as usual; discontinue or withhold (*shall stop their wages*). **9** *tr.* (in full **stop payment of** or **on**) instruct a bank to withhold payment on (a cheque). **10** *tr. Brit.* put a filling in (a tooth). **11** *tr.* obtain the required pitch from (the string of a violin etc.) by pressing at the appropriate point with the finger. **12** *tr.* plug the upper end of (an organ-pipe), giving a note an octave lower. **13** *tr. Bridge* be able to prevent opponents from taking all the tricks in (a suit). **14** *tr.* make (a sound) inaudible. **15** *tr. Boxing* **a** parry (a blow). **b** knock out (an opponent). **16** *tr. Hort.* pinch back (a plant). **17** *tr.* make (a clock, factory, etc.) cease working. **18** *tr. Brit.* provide with punctuation. **19** *tr. Naut.* make fast; stopper (a cable etc.). ● *n.* **1** the act or an instance of stopping; the state of being stopped (*put a stop to*; *the vehicle was brought to a stop*). **2** a place designated for a bus or train etc. to stop. **3** a punctuation mark, esp. = *full stop* (see FULL[1]). **4** a device for stopping motion at a particular point. **5** a change of pitch effected by stopping a string. **6 a** (in an organ) a row of pipes of one character. **b** a knob etc. operating these. **7** a manner of speech adopted to produce a particular effect. **8** *Optics* & *Photog.* = DIAPHRAGM 3. **9 a** the effective diameter of a lens. **b** a device for reducing this. **c** a unit of change of relative aperture or exposure (with a reduction of one stop equivalent to halving it). **10** (of sound) = PLOSIVE. **11** (in telegrams etc.) a full stop (see FULL[1]). **12** *Bridge* a card or cards stopping a suit. **13** *Naut.* a small line used as a lashing. □ **put a stop to** cause to end, esp. abruptly. **stop at nothing** be ruthless. **stop by** (also *absol.*) call at (a place). **stop dead** (or **short**) cease abruptly. **stop down** *Photog.* reduce the aperture of (a lens) with a diaphragm. **stop-drill** a drill with a shoulder limiting the depth of penetration. **stop one's ears 1** put one's fingers in one's ears to avoid hearing. **2** refuse to listen. **stop a gap** serve to meet a temporary need. **stop-go 1** alternate stopping and restarting of progress. **2** *Brit.* the alternate restriction and stimulation of economic demand. **stop in** *US* pay a brief visit. **stop-knob** a knob controlling an organ stop. **stop lamp** a light on the rear of a vehicle showing when the brakes are applied. **stop light 1** a red traffic-light. **2** = *stop lamp*. **stop a person's mouth** induce a person by bribery or other means to keep silence about something. **stop off** (or **over**) break one's journey. **stop out 1** stay out. **2** cover (part of an area) to prevent printing, etching, etc. **stop payment** declare oneself insolvent. **stop press** *Brit.* **1** (often *attrib.*) late news inserted in a newspaper after printing has begun. **2** a column in a newspaper reserved for this. **stop valve** a valve closing a pipe against the passage of liquid. **stop-volley** (esp. in lawn tennis) a checked volley close to the net, dropping the ball dead on the other side. **with all the stops out** exerting extreme effort. □□ **stopless** *adj.* **stoppable** *adj.* [ME f. OE *-stoppian* f. LL *stuppare* STUFF: see ESTOP]
■ *v.* **1 a** put an end to, put a stop to, bring to a stop *or* halt *or* close *or* standstill, immobilize, paralyse, freeze, deactivate, bring to an end, shut down, check, arrest, nip in the bud; see also ABOLISH. **b** curb, restrain, thwart, frustrate, put a stopper on; block, bar, obstruct, intercept, dam, keep *or* hold back, prevent, preclude, hinder, hamper, delay; slow, impede, stem, stanch,

staunch. **c** discontinue, halt, terminate, cease, break off, cut off, interrupt, suspend, give up, quit, leave off, finish, end, conclude, refrain from, abstain from, abandon, drop, *colloq.* cut (out), lay off, knock off, pack in *or* up, *literary* desist (from). **2** draw to a close, be over, come to a stop *or* halt *or* close, come to an end, expire, cease, end, finish, halt, cut out, peter out, run out. **3** halt, pause, pull up, draw up, come to a stop *or* halt *or* standstill, come to rest, cut out, end up, turn up, arrive; pull in *or* over; *esp. Austral.* prop. **4** see DEFEAT *v.* 2. **6** pause, break, take a break, *archaic or literary* tarry; sojourn, rest, remain, stay, put up, lodge, visit, stop off *or* over. **7** obstruct, block (up), jam (up), plug (up), bung (up), clog (up), choke (up), stuff (up), fill (up), caulk, occlude, seal, close (up *or* off). **8** discontinue, terminate, suspend, withhold, keep *or* hold back. **10** fill. ● *n.* **1** stop off, stopover, halt, end, finish, cessation, termination, ban, prohibition; close, standstill, conclusion; stoppage; see also *interruption* (INTERRUPT). **2** stopping-place, station, terminal, stage, terminus, *US* depot. **3** point, full stop, *esp. US* period. □ **put a stop to** see STOP *v.* 1a above. **stop at nothing** see PERSEVERE. **stop by** see VISIT *v.* 1. **stop dead** see FREEZE *v.* 6a. **stop-go 1** see INTERMITTENT. **stop in** see VISIT *v.* 1. **stop off** (or **over**) see STOP *v.* 6 above.

stopbank /stópbangk/ *n. Austral.* & *NZ* an embankment built to prevent river-flooding.

stopcock /stópkok/ *n.* an externally operated valve regulating the flow of a liquid or gas through a pipe etc.
■ see TAP[1] *n.* 1.

stope /stōp/ *n.* a steplike part of a mine where ore etc. is being extracted. [app. rel. to STEP *n.*]

stopgap /stópgap/ *n.* (often *attrib.*) a temporary substitute.
■ improvisation; (*often attrib.*) makeshift, substitute, stand-in, stand-by, temporary, emergency; (*attrib.*) improvised, impromptu, provisional, *Naut.* jury-rigged.

stopoff /stóppof/ *n.* a break in one's journey.

stopover /stóppōvər/ *n.* = STOPOFF.

stoppage /stóppij/ *n.* **1** the condition of being blocked or stopped. **2** a stopping (of pay). **3** a stopping or interruption of work in a factory etc.
■ **1** blockage, blocking, obstruction, block. **3** see *interruption* (INTERRUPT).

stopper /stóppər/ *n.* & *v.* ● *n.* **1** a plug for closing a bottle etc. **2** a person or thing that stops something. **3** *Naut.* a rope or clamp etc. for checking and holding a rope cable or chain cable. ● *v.tr.* close or secure with a stopper. □ **put a stopper on 1** put an end to (a thing). **2** keep (a person) quiet.
■ *n.* **1** stopple, cork, plug, bung, peg, spigot, spile. ● *v.* see PLUG *v.* 1. □ **put a stopper on 1** see END *v.* 1, 2. **2** see GAG *v.* 2.

stopping /stópping/ *n. Brit.* a filling for a tooth.

stopple /stópp'l/ *n.* & *v.* ● *n.* a stopper or plug. ● *v.tr.* close with a stopple. [ME: partly f. STOP + -LE[1], partly f. ESTOPPEL]
■ *n.* see STOPPER *n.* ● *v.* see PLUG *v.* 1.

stopwatch /stópwoch/ *n.* a watch with a mechanism for recording elapsed time, used to time races etc.

storage /stórij/ *n.* **1 a** the storing of goods etc. **b** a particular method of storing or the space available for it. **2** the cost of storing. **3** the electronic retention of data in a computer etc. □ **storage battery** (or **cell**) a battery (or cell) for storing electricity. **storage heater** *Brit.* an electric heater accumulating heat outside peak hours for later release.

storax /stóraks/ *n.* **1 a** a fragrant resin, obtained from the tree *Styrax officinalis* and formerly used in perfume. **b** this tree. **2** (in full **Levant** or **liquid storax**) a balsam obtained from the tree *Liquidambar orientalis.* [L f. Gk, var. of STYRAX]

store /stor/ *n.* & *v.* ● *n.* **1** a quantity of something kept available for use (*a store of wine*; *a store of wit*). **2** (in *pl.*) **a** articles for a particular purpose accumulated for use (*naval stores*). **b** a supply of these or the place where they are kept. **3 a** = *department store.* **b** esp. *US* any retail outlet or shop. **c** (often in *pl.*) a shop selling basic necessities (*general stores*). **4** a warehouse for the temporary keeping of furniture etc. **5** a device in a computer for storing retrievable data; a memory. ● *v.tr.* **1** put (furniture etc.) in store. **2** (often foll. by *up*, *away*) accumulate (stores, energy, electricity, etc.) for future use. **3** stock or provide with something useful (*a mind stored with facts*). **4** (of a receptacle) have storage capacity for. **5** enter or retain (data) for retrieval. □ **in store 1** kept in readiness. **2** coming in the future. **3** (foll. by *for*) destined or intended. **set** (or **lay** or **put**) **store by** (or **on**) consider important or valuable. □□ **storable** *adj.* **storer** *n.* [ME f. obs. *astore* (n. & v.) f. OF *estore*, *estorer* f. L *instaurare* renew: cf. RESTORE]
■ *n.* **1** supply, inventory, collection, accumulation, stock, stockpile, reservoir, reserve, hoard, cache, fund, quantity, wealth, mine. **2** (*stores*) **a** see PROVISION *n.* 2. **b** see STOREHOUSE. **3 a** department store, emporium. **b** shop, market, retailer, outlet, cooperative (store), supermarket, *esp. Brit.* warehouse, *Brit.* hypermarket, *Brit. colloq.* co-op. **4** see WAREHOUSE *n.* ● *v.* **1** keep, hold, stow (away), preserve, warehouse, house. **2** stock, collect, accumulate, put by, lay away, set aside, pile (up), stockpile, aggregate, amass, cumulate; hoard. **3** stock, supply, provide, fill. □ **in store 1** see *in reserve* (RESERVE). **2** see *impending* (IMPEND). **set** (or **lay** or **put**) **store by** (or **on**) give credence to, believe (in), have faith *or* trust in, trust (in), bank *or* rely on, depend (up)on, count on, value.

storefront /stórfrunt/ *n.* esp. *US* **1** the side of a shop facing the street. **2** a room at the front of a shop.

storehouse /stórhowss/ *n.* a place where things are stored.
■ warehouse, depository, repository, storeroom, bank, store(s), depot, godown; treasury; arsenal, magazine, armoury.

storekeeper /stórkeepər/ *n.* **1** a storeman. **2** *US* a shopkeeper.
■ **2** see DEALER.

storeman /stórmən/ *n.* (*pl.* **-men**) a person responsible for stored goods.

storeroom /stór-rōōm, -rŏŏm/ *n.* a room in which items are stored.
■ see WAREHOUSE *n.*

storey /stóri/ *n.* (also **story**) (*pl.* **-eys** or **-ies**) **1** any of the parts into which a building is divided horizontally; the whole of the rooms etc. having a continuous floor (*a third-storey window*; *a house of five storeys*). **2** a thing forming a horizontal division. □□ **-storeyed** (in *comb.*) (also **-storied**). [ME f. AL *historia* HISTORY (perh. orig. meaning a tier of painted windows or sculpture)]
■ **1** floor, level, tier.

storiated /stóriaytid/ *adj.* decorated with historical, legendary, or emblematic designs. □□ **storiation** /-áysh'n/ *n.* [shortening of HISTORIATED]

storied /stórid/ *adj. literary* celebrated in or associated with stories or legends.

stork /stork/ *n.* **1** any long-legged large wading bird of the family Ciconiidae, esp. *Ciconia ciconia* with white plumage, black wing-tips, a long reddish beak, and red feet, nesting esp. on tall buildings. **2** this bird as the pretended bringer of babies. □ **stork's-bill** a plant of the genus *Pelargonium* or *Erodium.* [OE *storc*, prob. rel. to STARK (from its rigid posture)]

storm /storm/ *n.* & *v.* ● *n.* **1** a violent disturbance of the atmosphere with strong winds and usu. with thunder and rain or snow etc. **2** *Meteorol.* a wind intermediate between gale and hurricane, esp. (on the Beaufort scale) of 55–72 m.p.h. **3** a violent disturbance of the established order in human affairs. **4** (foll. by *of*) **a** a violent shower of missiles or blows. **b** an outbreak of applause, indignation, hisses, etc. (*they were greeted by a storm of abuse*). **5 a** a direct assault by troops on a fortified place. **b** the capture of a place by such an assault. ● *v.* **1** *intr.* (often foll. by *at*, *away*) talk violently, rage, bluster. **2** *intr.* (usu. foll. by *in*, *out of*, etc.) move violently or angrily (*stormed out of the meeting*). **3** *tr.* attack or capture by storm. **4** *intr.* (of wind, rain, etc.) rage; be violent. □ **storm-bird** = *storm petrel.* **storm centre 1** the point to which the wind blows spirally inward in a cyclonic storm. **2** a subject etc. upon which agitation or disturbance is concentrated. **storm cloud 1** a heavy rain-cloud. **2** a threatening state of affairs. **storm-cock** a mistle-thrush. **storm-collar** a high coat-collar that can be turned up and fastened. **storm cone** *Brit.* a tarred-canvas cone hoisted as a warning of high wind, upright for the north and inverted for the south. **storm-door** an additional outer door for protection in bad weather or winter. **storm-finch** *Brit.* = *storm petrel.* **storm-glass** a sealed tube containing a solution of which the clarity is thought to change when storms approach. **storming-party** a detachment of troops ordered to begin an assault. **storm in a teacup** *Brit.* great excitement over a trivial matter. **storm-lantern** *Brit.* a hurricane lamp. **storm petrel 1** a small petrel, *Hydrobates pelagicus*, of the North Atlantic, with black and white plumage. **2** a person causing unrest. **storm-sail** a sail of smaller size and stouter canvas than the corresponding one used in ordinary weather. **storm-signal** a device warning of an approaching storm. **storm trooper 1** *hist.* a member of the Nazi political militia. **2** a member of the shock troops. **storm troops 1** = *shock troops* (see SHOCK[1]). **2** *hist.* the Nazi political militia. **storm window** an additional outer sash-window used like a storm-door. **take by storm 1** capture by direct assault. **2** rapidly captivate (a person, audience, etc.). □□ **stormless** *adj.* **stormproof** *adj.* [OE f. Gmc]

■ *n.* **1** tempest, disturbance, turbulence; mistral, gale, whirlwind, hurricane, tornado, typhoon, cyclone; shower, cloudburst, downpour, rainstorm, deluge, monsoon, thunder-shower, thunderstorm, electrical storm; dust-storm, sandstorm, harmattan, khamsin, sirocco; snowstorm, blizzard; hailstorm; *Austral.* willy-willy. **3** disturbance, stir, commotion, agitation, uproar, furore, to-do, tumult, *colloq.* rumpus; turbulence, strife, turmoil, disorder. **4** shower, torrent, flood, deluge, hail, volley, barrage, bombardment; outburst, outbreak, outcry, explosion, eruption, outpouring. ● *v.* **1** rage, rant, rave, bluster, fume, explode, thunder, roar, *colloq.* raise the roof, raise hell, raise Cain, raise the devil, fly off the handle, blow one's top, *US colloq.* blow one's stack. **2** charge, stamp, stomp, ramp, march, fling, stride. **3** attack, assault, assail, raid, rush, charge, take *or* capture by storm, take over, *colloq.* blitz. **4** blow, rage, bluster, howl. □ **take by storm 1** see STORM *v.* 3 above.

stormbound /stórmbownd/ *adj.* prevented by storms from leaving port or continuing a voyage.

stormy /stórmi/ *adj.* (**stormier, stormiest**) **1** of or affected by storms. **2** (of a wind etc.) violent, raging, vehement. **3** full of angry feeling or outbursts; lively, boisterous (*a stormy meeting*). □ **stormy petrel** = *storm petrel.* □□ **stormily** *adv.* **storminess** *n.*

■ **1** foul, nasty, bad, inclement, wild, rough, squally, blustery, choppy, gusty, windy, thundery, boisterous. **2** violent, tempestuous, blustery, turbulent, wild, vehement, howling, raging, roaring. **3** violent, tempestuous, turbulent, fierce, fiery, frantic, frenetic, nerve-racking, frenzied, feverish, raving, wild, boisterous, noisy, impassioned, *joc.* lively. □□ **storminess** see *severity* (SEVERE).

story[1] /stóri/ *n.* (*pl.* **-ies**) **1** an account of imaginary or past events; a narrative, tale, or anecdote. **2** the past course of the life of a person or institution etc. (*my story is a strange one*). **3** (in full **story-line**) the narrative or plot of a novel or play etc. **4** facts or experiences that deserve narration. **5** *colloq.* a fib or lie. **6** a narrative or descriptive item of news. □ **the old** (or **same old**) **story** the familiar or predictable course of events. **story-book 1** a book of stories for children. **2** (*attrib.*) unreal, romantic (*a story-book ending*). **the story goes** it is said. **to cut** (or **make**) **a long story short** a formula excusing the omission of details. [ME *storie* f. AF *estorie* (OF *estoire*) f. L *historia* (as HISTORY)]

■ **1** narrative, tale, recounting, anecdote, yarn; account, recital, chronicle, record, history; legend, myth, fairy tale *or* story, novel, novelette, romance, fable, fabliau; epic, saga, Edda; allegory, parable; article, piece, composition; joke, gag; mystery, detective story, thriller, horror story, *colloq.* whodunit; testimony, version, statement, representation, description, contention, assertion, allegation. **2, 4** biography, curriculum vitae, life (story); tale, yarn, saga. **3** story-line, plot, scenario, (plot) outline, thread, summary, narrative. **5** fib, lie, excuse, untruth, falsehood, fabrication, *disp.* alibi; tall tale, *Austral. sl.* furphy. **6** article, piece, item, report, dispatch, news, release, information, copy, feature, *literary* tidings; scoop, exclusive. □ **story-book 2** (*attrib.*) see FABULOUS 3.

story[2] var. of STOREY.

storyboard /stóribord/ *n.* a displayed sequence of pictures etc. outlining the plan of a film, television advertisement, etc.

storyteller /stóritellər/ *n.* **1** a person who tells stories. **2** *colloq.* a liar. □□ **storytelling** *n.* & *adj.*

■ **1** see RACONTEUR. **2** see LIAR. □□ **storytelling** (*adj.*) see NARRATIVE *adj.*

stoup /stoop/ *n.* (also **stoop**) **1** a holy-water basin. **2** *archaic* a flagon, beaker, or drinking-vessel. [ME f. ON *staup* (= OE *stēap*) f. Gmc, rel. to STEEP[2]]

■ **1** see SINK *n.* 1. **2** see MUG[1] *n.* 1.

stoush /stowsh/ *v.* & *n.* *Austral.* & *NZ sl.* ● *v.tr.* **1** hit; fight with. **2** attack verbally. ● *n.* a fight; a beating. [19th c.: orig. uncert.]

stout /stowt/ *adj.* & *n.* ● *adj.* **1** rather fat; corpulent; bulky. **2** of considerable thickness or strength (*a stout stick*). **3** brave, resolute, vigorous (*a stout fellow; put up stout resistance*). ● *n.* a strong dark beer brewed with roasted malt or barley. □ **a stout heart** courage, resolve. **stout-hearted** courageous. **stout-heartedly** courageously. **stout-heartedness** courage. □□ **stoutish** *adj.* **stoutly** *adv.* **stoutness** *n.* [ME f. AF & dial. OF *stout* f. WG, perh. rel. to STILT]

■ *adj.* **1** fat, obese, tubby, overweight, thickset, heavy-set, stocky, big, bulky, burly, corpulent, fleshy, heavy, plump, portly, rotund, *colloq.* hulking; brawny, beefy, husky, sturdy. **2** thick, fat, solid, sturdy, strong, robust, substantial. **3** valiant, brave, undaunted, dauntless, hardy, courageous, gallant, plucky, valorous, staunch, resolute, determined, steadfast, stalwart, vigorous, bold, *archaic or joc.* doughty. □ **stout-hearted** see BRAVE *adj.* 1. **stout-heartedness** see PLUCK *n.* □□ **stoutness** see *fatness* (FAT), STRENGTH 1.

stove[1] /stōv/ *n.* & *v.* ● *n.* **1** a closed apparatus burning fuel or electricity for heating or cooking. **2** *Brit. Hort.* a hothouse with artificial heat. ● *v.tr. Brit.* force or raise (plants) in a stove. □ **stove-enamel** a heatproof enamel produced by the treatment of enamelled objects in a stove. **stove-pipe** a pipe conducting smoke and gases from a stove to a chimney. **stove-pipe hat** *colloq.* a tall silk hat. [ME = sweating-room, f. MDu., MLG *stove*, OHG *stuba* f. Gmc, perh. rel. to STEW[1]]

■ *n.* **1** see RANGE *n.* 6b.

stove[2] *past* and *past part.* of STAVE *v.*

stow /stō/ *v.tr.* **1** pack (goods etc.) tidily and compactly. **2** *Naut.* place (a cargo or provisions) in its proper place and order. **3** fill (a receptacle) with articles compactly arranged. **4** (usu. in *imper.*) *sl.* abstain or cease from (*stow the noise!*). □ **stow away 1** place (a thing) where it will not cause an obstruction. **2** be a stowaway on a ship etc. [ME, f. BESTOW: in Naut. use perh. infl. by Du. *stouwen*]

■ **1, 2** pack, store, load, deposit, put (away), place, tuck away, *colloq.* stash (away). **3** fill, pack, load, jam, cram. **4** see REFRAIN[1].

stowage /stṓ-ij/ *n.* **1** the act or an instance of stowing. **2** a place for this.

stowaway /stṓəway/ *n.* a person who hides on board a ship or aircraft etc. to get free passage.

STP *abbr.* **1** Professor of Sacred Theology. **2** standard temperature and pressure.

str. *abbr.* **1** strait. **2** stroke (of an oar).

strabismus /strəbízməss/ *n. Med.* the abnormal condition of one or both eyes not correctly aligned in direction; a squint. ▫▫ **strabismal** *adj.* **strabismic** *adj.* [mod.L f. Gk *strabismos* f. *strabizō* squint f. *strabos* squinting]

Strad /strad/ *n. colloq.* a Stradivarius. [abbr.]

straddle /strádd'l/ *v.* & *n.* ● *v.* **1** *tr.* **a** sit or stand across (a thing) with the legs wide apart. **b** be situated across or on both sides of (*the town straddles the border*). **2** *intr.* **a** sit or stand in this way. **b** (of the legs) be wide apart. **3** *tr.* part (one's legs) widely. **4** *tr.* drop shots or bombs short of and beyond (a target). **5** *tr.* vacillate between two policies etc. regarding (an issue). ● *n.* **1** the act or an instance of straddling. **2** *Stock Exch.* an option giving the holder the right of either calling for or delivering stock at a fixed price. ▫▫ **straddler** *n.* [alt. of *striddle*, back-form. f. *striddlings* astride f. *strid-* = STRIDE]

■ *v.* **1 b** see SPAN *v.* 1, 2.

Stradivarius /stráddiváiriəss/ *n.* a violin or other stringed instrument made by Antonio Stradivari of Cremona (d. 1737) or his followers. [Latinized f. *Stradivari*]

strafe /straaf, strayf/ *v.* & *n.* ● *v.tr.* **1** bombard; harass with gunfire. **2** reprimand. **3** abuse. **4** thrash. ● *n.* an act of strafing. [joc. adaptation of G catchword (1914) *Gott strafe England* may God punish England]

■ *v.* **1** see PELT[1] *v.* 1. **2** see CASTIGATE. **3** see ABUSE *v.* 3. **4** see BEAT *v.* 1.

straggle /strágg'l/ *v.* & *n.* ● *v.intr.* **1** lack or lose compactness or tidiness. **2** be or become dispersed or sporadic. **3** trail behind others in a march or race etc. **4** (of a plant, beard, etc.) grow long and loose. ● *n.* a body or group of straggling or scattered persons or things. ▫▫ **straggler** *n.* **straggly** *adj.* (**stragglier, straggliest**). [ME, perh. rel. to dial. *strake* go, rel. to STRETCH]

■ *v.* **1** see SPRAWL *v.* 2. **2** (be) spread (out), disperse, scatter, thin out. **3** stray, ramble, rove, prowl, range, drift, wander, meander, *sl.* mosey; see also TRAIL *v.* 4. ▫▫ **straggler** stray; see also LAGGARD *n.* **straggly** unkempt, untidy, loose, lank, *colloq.* ratty; see also RAMBLING 3.

straight /strayt/ *adj.*, *n.*, & *adv.* ● *adj.* **1 a** extending uniformly in the same direction; without a curve or bend etc. **b** *Geom.* (of a line) lying on the shortest path between any two of its points. **2** successive, uninterrupted (*three straight wins*). **3** in proper order or place or condition; duly arranged; level, symmetrical (*is the picture straight?*; *put things straight*). **4** honest, candid; not evasive (*a straight answer*). **5** (of thinking etc.) logical, unemotional. **6** (of drama etc.) serious as opposed to popular or comic; employing the conventional techniques of its art form. **7 a** unmodified. **b** (of a drink) undiluted. **8** *colloq.* (of music) classical. **9** *colloq.* **a** (of a person etc.) conventional or respectable. **b** heterosexual. **10** (of an arch) flat-topped. **11** (of a person's back) not bowed. **12** (of the hair) not curly or wavy. **13** (of a knee) not bent. **14** (of the legs) not bandy or knock-kneed. **15** (of a garment) not flared. **16** coming direct from its source. **17** (of an aim, look, blow, or course) going direct to the mark. ● *n.* **1** the straight part of something, esp. the concluding stretch of a racecourse. **2** a straight condition. **3** a sequence of five cards in poker. **4** *colloq.* **a** a conventional person. **b** a heterosexual. ● *adv.* **1** in a straight line; direct; without deviation or hesitation or circumlocution (*came straight from Paris*; *I told them straight*). **2** in the right direction, with a good aim (*shoot straight*). **3** correctly (*can't see straight*). **4** *archaic* at once or immediately. ▫ **go straight** live an honest life after being a criminal. **the straight and narrow** morally correct behaviour. **straight angle** an angle of 180°. **straight away** at once; immediately. **straight-bred** not cross-bred. **straight-cut** (of tobacco) cut lengthwise into long silky fibres. **straight-edge** a bar with one edge accurately straight, used for testing. **straight-eight 1** an internal-combustion engine with eight cylinders in line. **2** a vehicle having this. **straight eye** the ability to detect deviation from the straight. **straight face** an intentionally expressionless face, esp. avoiding a smile though amused. **straight-faced** having a straight face. **straight fight** *Brit. Polit.* a direct contest between two candidates. **straight flush** see FLUSH[3]. **straight from the shoulder 1** (of a blow) well delivered. **2** (of a verbal attack) delivered in a frank or direct manner. **straight man** a comedian's stooge. **straight off** *colloq.* without hesitation, deliberation, etc. (*cannot tell you straight off*). **straight-out** *US* **1** uncompromising. **2** straightforward, genuine. **straight razor** *US* a cutthroat razor. **straight-up** *US colloq.* **1** truthfully, honestly. **2** (of food, drink, etc.) without admixture or dilution. ▫▫ **straightish** *adj.* **straightly** *adv.* **straightness** *n.* [ME, past part. of STRETCH]

■ *adj.* **1** direct, unbending, undeviating, unswerving, uncurved, regular, linear. **2** see SUCCESSIVE. **3** shipshape, orderly, neat, tidy, in order, arranged, organized, sorted out, straightened out; even, square, true, right, flat, smooth, horizontal, level; vertical, upright, perpendicular, plumb; symmetrical. **4** honest, frank, candid, straightforward, direct, downright, forthright, legitimate, (fair and) square, fair, equitable, just, above-board, upright, upstanding, respectable, decent, trustworthy, honourable, dependable, reliable; unequivocal, unambiguous, plain, simple, explicit, blunt, unembellished, unelaborated, unqualified, outright, accurate, point-blank, straight from the shoulder, no-nonsense, *colloq.* upfront. **5** see LOGICAL 2, 3. **7** undiluted, neat, unmixed, pure, unadulterated, uncut, unmodified, unaltered, unalloyed, *US colloq.* straight-up. **9 a** see CONSERVATIVE *adj.* 1, RESPECTABLE 3a, b. **b** heterosexual, *colloq.* hetero. **11** erect, vertical, upright, perpendicular, plumb. **16** see DIRECT *adj.* 3. **17** direct, unswerving, undeviating. ● *n.* **1** home straight, *US* home stretch. **4 a** see SQUARE *n.* 6. **b** heterosexual, *colloq.* hetero. ● *adv.* **1** directly, right, undeviatingly, unswervingly; as the crow flies, in a beeline; (straight) ahead; unequivocally, unambiguously, forthrightly, straightforwardly, point-blank, candidly, frankly, plainly, simply, in plain *or* simple English, straight from the shoulder, explicitly, outright, honestly, *US* straight-out, *US colloq.* straight-up. **2** accurately, precisely. **3** properly, correctly. **4** see *straight away* below. ▫ **go straight** reform, mend one's ways, turn over a new leaf. **straight away** immediately, at once, without delay, instantly, post-haste, summarily, directly, right (away *or* off), promptly, *US* right off the bat, *archaic* straight, straightway, *colloq.* p.d.q. **straight-faced** sober, staid, sedate, serious, unsmiling, unemotional, impassive, emotionless, taciturn, composed. **straight from the shoulder 2** directly, straightforwardly, candidly, frankly, honestly, openly, unabashedly, unashamedly, unambiguously, unequivocally, plainly, bluntly, man to man, (with) no holds barred, outright, without beating about the bush, without pulling (any) punches, *US colloq.* straight-up. **straight off** see *straight away* above. **straight-up 1** see STRAIGHT *adv.* 1, *straight from the shoulder* above. **2** neat, without ice, undiluted, pure, straight.

straightaway /stráytəway/ *adj. US* **1** (of a course etc.) straight. **2** straightforward.

straighten /stráyt'n/ *v.tr.* & *intr.* **1** (often foll. by *out*) make or become straight. **2** (foll. by *up*) stand erect after bending. ▫▫ **straightener** *n.*

■ **1** uncurl, untangle, disentangle, unsnarl, unravel, unkink, unbend, untwist; straighten up, tidy (up), arrange, rearrange, neaten, spruce up, put in order, clean (up); (*straighten out*) clear (up), settle, resolve, patch up, sort out, set *or* put straight, set *or* put right, set *or* put to rights, correct, adjust, rectify; reform, rehabilitate, organize, reorganize.

straightforward /stráytfórwərd/ *adj.* **1** honest or frank. **2** (of a task etc.) uncomplicated. ▫▫ **straightforwardly** *adv.* **straightforwardness** *n.*

■ **1** see HONEST *adj.* 2. **2** see EASY *adj.* 1. ▫▫ **straightforwardly** see HONESTLY 1. **straightforwardness** see HONESTY 2.

straightway /stráytway/ *adv. archaic* = *straight away.*

strain[1] /strayn/ *v.* & *n.* ● *v.* **1** *tr.* & *intr.* stretch tightly; make or become taut or tense. **2** *tr.* exercise (oneself, one's senses, a thing, etc.) intensely or excessively, press to extremes. **3 a** *intr.* make an intensive effort. **b** *intr.* (foll. by *after*) strive intensely for (*straining after perfection*). **4** *intr.* (foll. by *at*) tug, pull (*the dog strained at the leash*). **5** *intr.* hold out with difficulty under pressure (*straining under the load*). **6** *tr.* **a** distort from the true intention or meaning. **b** apply (authority, laws, etc.) beyond their province or in violation of their true intention. **7** *tr.* overtask or injure by overuse or excessive demands (*strain a muscle; strained their loyalty*). **8 a** *tr.* clear (a liquid) of solid matter by passing it through a sieve etc. **b** *tr.* (foll. by *out*) filter (solids) out from a liquid. **c** *intr.* (of a liquid) percolate. **9** *tr.* hug or squeeze tightly. **10** *tr.* use (one's ears, eyes, voice, etc.) to the best of one's power. ● *n.* **1 a** the act or an instance of straining. **b** the force exerted in this. **2** an injury caused by straining a muscle etc. **3 a** a severe demand on physical strength or resources. **b** the exertion needed to meet this (*is suffering from strain*). **4** (in *sing.* or *pl.*) a snatch or spell of music or poetry. **5** a tone or tendency in speech or writing (*more in the same strain*). **6** *Physics* **a** the condition of a body subjected to stress; molecular displacement. **b** a quantity measuring this, equal to the amount of deformation usu. divided by the original dimension. ▫ **at strain** (or **full strain**) exerted to the utmost. **strain every nerve** make every possible effort. **strain oneself 1** injure oneself by effort. **2** make undue efforts. ▫▫ **strainable** *adj.* [ME f. OF *estreindre estreign-* f. L *stringere strict-* draw tight]

■ *v.* **1** stretch, crane, tense, tauten, tension; see also TIGHTEN. **2** see TAX *v.* 3. **3** try (hard), struggle, strive, labour, toil, push, make an effort, exert oneself. **4** push, pull, tug, heave, stretch, twist, wrench, struggle. **6** see STRETCH *v.* 6. **7** injure, hurt, harm, impair, damage, pull, tear, twist, sprain, rick, wrench; stretch, force, tax, overtax, burden, overburden, overwork, overtask, overextend, push. **8 a, b** filter, sift, drain, screen, sieve, riddle; leach, winnow, separate. **c** percolate, seep, filter, drain. ● *n.* **1 a** see *exertion* (EXERT). **2** sprain, rick, injury, damage, harm, wrench, pull. **3 a** tax, demand, burden, stress, pressure, obligation. **b** stress, tension, pressure, overexertion, overwork; anxiety, worry. **4** air, melody, tune, song, sound, music, phrase, cadence. **5** tenor, tone, drift, inclination, tendency, quality, spirit, mood, humour, character, complexion, cast, impression, thread, vein, theme. ▫ **strain every nerve** move mountains, strain oneself, go all out, give it one's all, give it all one has, *colloq.* bust a gut, *Austral. sl.* go for the doctor.

strain[2] /strayn/ *n.* **1** a breed or stock of animals, plants, etc. **2** a moral tendency as part of a person's character (*a strain of aggression*). [ME, = progeny, f. OE *strēon* (recorded in *ġestrēonan* beget), rel. to L *struere* build]

■ **1** family, stock, ancestry, roots, extraction, derivation, background, heritage, descent, parentage, lineage, pedigree, bloodline, race, line, breed, variety. **2** trace, hint, suggestion, suspicion, soupçon, streak, trait, tendency, mark, indication, vestige, evidence, sign.

strained /straynd/ *adj.* **1** constrained, forced, artificial. **2** (of a relationship) mutually distrustful or tense. **3** (of an interpretation) involving an unreasonable assumption; far-fetched, laboured.

■ **1** laboured, forced, artificial, false, constrained, stiff, self-conscious, unnatural, insincere, put-on. **2** tense, awkward, uneasy, uncomfortable, difficult, fraught, tension-ridden. **3** see *far-fetched.*

strainer /stráynər/ *n.* a device for straining liquids, vegetables, etc.

strait /strayt/ *n.* & *adj.* ● *n.* **1** (in *sing.* or *pl.*) a narrow passage of water connecting two seas or large bodies of water. **2** (usu. in *pl.*) difficulty, trouble, or distress (usu. *in dire* or *desperate straits*). ● *adj. archaic* **1** narrow, limited; confined or confining. **2** strict or rigorous. ▫ **strait-laced** severely virtuous; morally scrupulous; puritanical. ▫▫ **straitly** *adv.* **straitness** *n.* [ME *streit* f. OF *estreit* tight, narrow f. L *strictus* STRICT]

■ *n.* **1** narrows, channel, sound, neck. **2** (*dire* or *desperate* or *sore straits*) bad *or* poor state, bad *or* poor condition, trouble, difficulty, distress, need, predicament, plight, mess, tight spot, *colloq.* hot water, bind, pickle, jam, fix, scrape, pretty *or* fine kettle of fish, *disp.* dilemma. ● *adj.* **1** narrow, tight, constricted, constricting, confining, confined, restricting, restricted, limited, limiting, rigorous, demanding, exacting; difficult, straitened. **2** see STRICT 1. ▫ **strait-laced** priggish, prim, conservative, old-fashioned, Victorian, old-maidish, proper, prudish, puritanical, moralistic, stuffy, strict, narrow-minded, (over-)scrupulous, fussy, *colloq.* goody-goody, pernickety, *sl.* square.

straiten /stráyt'n/ *v.* **1** *tr.* restrict in range or scope. **2** *tr.* (as **straitened** *adj.*) (esp. of circumstances) characterized by poverty. **3** *tr.* & *intr. archaic* make or become narrow.

■ **1** restrict, confine, limit. **2** (**straitened**) reduced; poverty-stricken, impoverished.

strait-jacket /stráytjakkit/ *n.* & *v.* ● *n.* **1** a strong garment with long arms for confining the arms of a violent prisoner, mental patient, etc. **2** restrictive measures. ● *v.tr.* (**-jacketed, -jacketing**) **1** restrain with a strait-jacket. **2** severely restrict.

strake /strayk/ *n.* **1** a continuous line of planking or plates from the stem to the stern of a ship. **2** a section of the iron rim of a wheel. [ME: prob. rel. to OE *streccan* STRETCH]

stramonium /strəmṓniəm/ *n.* **1** datura. **2** the dried leaves of this plant used in the treatment of asthma. [mod.L, perh. f. Tartar *turman* horse-medicine]

strand[1] /strand/ *v.* & *n.* ● *v.* **1** *tr.* & *intr.* run aground. **2** *tr.* (as **stranded** *adj.*) in difficulties, esp. without money or means of transport. ● *n. rhet.* or *poet.* the margin of a sea, lake, or river, esp. the foreshore. [OE]

■ *v.* **1** see BEACH *v.* 2. **2** (**stranded**) see *deserted* (DESERT[1] 5). ● *n.* see BEACH *n.* 1.

strand[2] /strand/ *n.* & *v.* ● *n.* **1** each of the threads or wires twisted round each other to make a rope or cable. **2 a** a single thread or strip of fibre. **b** a constituent filament. **3** a lock of hair. **4** an element or strain in any composite whole. ● *v.tr.* **1** break a strand in (a rope). **2** arrange in strands. [ME: orig. unkn.]

■ *n.* **1, 2** see THREAD *n.* 1. **3** see LOCK[2] 1a. **4** thread, element, strain; aspect.

strange /straynj/ *adj.* **1** unusual, peculiar, surprising, eccentric, novel. **2 a** (often foll. by *to*) unfamiliar, alien, foreign (*lost in a strange land*). **b** not one's own (*strange gods*). **3** (foll. by *to*) unaccustomed. **4** not at ease; out of one's element (*felt strange in such company*). ▫ **feel strange** be unwell. **strange particle** *Physics* an elementary particle classified as having a non-zero value for strangeness. **strange to say** it is surprising or unusual (that). ▫▫ **strangely** *adv.* [ME f. OF *estrange* f. L *extraneus* EXTRANEOUS]

■ **1** odd, peculiar, bizarre, weird, curious, uncommon, unusual, unwonted, rare, singular, exceptional, eccentric, funny, quaint, fantastic, out of the ordinary, extraordinary, out-of-the-way, far-out, offbeat, unconventional, queer, outlandish, unheard-of, grotesque, abnormal, atypical, remarkable, surprising, inexplicable, unaccountable, uncanny, novel, new, different, *colloq.* way-out, kinky, *Brit. colloq.* rum, *sl.* kooky. **2** unknown, alien, foreign, exotic, new; see also UNFAMILIAR. **3** see UNACCUSTOMED 1. **4** ill at ease, uneasy, uncomfortable, awkward, out of one's element, out of place, like a fish out of water, lost, not at home. □ **feel strange** feel sick *or* ill *or* unwell *or* queasy *or* poorly, *colloq.* feel under the weather. □□ **strangely** see *notably* (NOTABLE).

strangeness /stráynjniss/ *n.* **1** the state or fact of being strange or unfamiliar etc. **2** *Physics* a property of certain elementary particles that is conserved in strong interactions.
■ **1** see ODDITY 3.

stranger /stráynjər/ *n.* **1** a person who does not know or is not known in a particular place or company. **2** (often foll. by *to*) a person one does not know (*was a complete stranger to me*). **3** (foll. by *to*) a person entirely unaccustomed to (a feeling, experience, etc.) (*no stranger to controversy*). **4** a floating tea-leaf etc. held to foretell the arrival of a visitor. **5** *Parl.* a person who is not a member or official of the House of Commons. [ME f. OF *estrangier* ult. f. L (as STRANGE)]
■ **1** foreigner, outlander, outsider, alien, newcomer, visitor.

strangle /stránggʼl/ *v.tr.* **1** squeeze the windpipe or neck of, esp. so as to kill. **2** hamper or suppress (a movement, impulse, cry, etc.). □□ **strangler** *n.* [ME f. OF *estrangler* f. L *strangulare* f. Gk *straggalaō* f. *straggalē* halter: cf. *straggos* twisted]
■ **1** throttle, choke, garrotte. **2** see SUPPRESS.

stranglehold /strángg'lhōld/ *n.* **1** a wrestling hold that throttles an opponent. **2** a deadly grip. **3** complete and exclusive control.

strangles /strángg'lz/ *n.pl.* (usu. treated as *sing.*) an infectious streptococcal fever, esp. affecting the respiratory tract, in a horse, ass, etc. [pl. of *strangle* (n.) f. STRANGLE]

strangulate /strángyoolayt/ *v.tr. Surgery* **1** prevent circulation through (a vein, intestine, etc.) by compression. **2** remove (a tumour etc.) by binding with a cord. □ **strangulated hernia** *Med.* a hernia in which the protruding part is constricted, preventing circulation. [L *strangulare strangulat-* (as STRANGLE)]

strangulation /strángyooláysh'n/ *n.* **1** the act of strangling or the state of being strangled. **2** the act of strangulating. [L *strangulatio* (as STRANGULATE)]

strangury /stránggyoori/ *n.* a condition in which urine is passed painfully and in drops. □□ **strangurious** /-gyóoriəss/ *adj.* [ME f. L *stranguria* f. Gk *straggouria* f. *stragx -ggos* drop squeezed out + *ouron* urine]

strap /strap/ *n.* & *v.* ● *n.* **1** a strip of leather or other flexible material, often with a buckle or other fastening for holding things together etc. **2** a thing like this for keeping a garment in place. **3** a loop for grasping to steady oneself in a moving vehicle. **4 a** a strip of metal used to secure or connect. **b** a leaf of a hinge. **5** *Bot.* a tongue-shaped part in a floret. **6** (prec. by *the*) punishment by beating with a strap. ● *v.tr.* (**strapped, strapping**) **1** (often foll. by *down*, *up*, etc.) secure or bind with a strap. **2** beat with a strap. **3** (esp. as **strapped** *adj.*) *colloq.* subject to a shortage. **4** (often foll. by *up*) close (a wound) or bind (a part) with adhesive plaster. □ **strap-work** ornamentation imitating plaited straps. □□ **strapper** *n.* **strappy** *adj.* [dial. form of STROP]
■ *n.* **1, 2** see TAPE *n.* 1. **3** see TAB[1] *n.* 1. ● *v.* **1** see CONNECT 1a, b. **2** see FLOG 1a. **3** (**strapped**) see *straitened* (STRAITEN 2).

straphanger /stráp-hangər/ *n. sl.* a standing passenger in a bus or train. □□ **straphang** *v.intr.*

strapless /strápliss/ *adj.* (of a garment) without straps, esp. shoulder-straps.

strappado /strəpaádō/ *n.* (*pl.* **-os**) *hist.* a form of torture in which the victim is secured to a rope and made to fall from a height almost to the ground then stopped with a jerk; an application of this; the instrument used. [F (*e*)*strapade* f. It. *strappata* f. *strappare* snatch]

strapping /strápping/ *adj.* (esp. of a person) large and sturdy.
■ see STURDY *adj.* 1.

strata *pl.* of STRATUM.

stratagem /stráttəjəm/ *n.* **1** a cunning plan or scheme, esp. for deceiving an enemy. **2** trickery. [ME f. F *stratagème* f. L *stratagema* f. Gk *stratēgēma* f. *stratēgeō* be a general (*stratēgos*) f. *stratos* army + *agō* lead]
■ **1** trick, artifice, device, dodge, subterfuge, lure, wile, ruse, deceit, deception, plan, scheme, plot, intrigue, manoeuvre, tactic, *colloq.* ploy. **2** see TRICKERY.

stratal see STRATUM.

strategic /strəteéjik/ *adj.* **1** of or serving the ends of strategy; useful or important with regard to strategy (*strategic considerations, strategic move*). **2** (of materials) essential in fighting a war. **3** (of bombing or weapons) done or for use against an enemy's home territory as a longer-term military objective (opp. TACTICAL). □ **strategic defence initiative** a projected US system of defence against nuclear weapons using satellites. □□ **strategical** *adj.* **strategically** *adv.* **strategics** *n.pl.* (usu. treated as *sing.*). [F *stratégique* f. Gk *stratēgikos* (as STRATAGEM)]
■ **1** calculated, planned, deliberate, politic, tactical, well-thought-out, well-considered, prudent, judicious, wise, clever.

strategy /stráttiji/ *n.* (*pl.* **-ies**) **1** the art of war. **2 a** the management of an army or armies in a campaign. **b** the art of moving troops, ships, aircraft, etc. into favourable positions (cf. TACTICS). **c** an instance of this or a plan formed according to it. **3** a plan of action or policy in business or politics etc. (*economic strategy*). □□ **strategist** *n.* [F *stratégie* f. Gk *stratēgia* generalship f. *stratēgos*: see STRATAGEM]
■ **1** generalship, military science. **2c, 3** plan, tactic(s), design, policy, procedure, approach, manoeuvre, scheme, blueprint, scenario, master plan, *esp. US* game plan. □□ **strategist** see *tactician* (TACTICS).

strath /strath/ *n. Sc.* a broad mountain valley. [Gael. *srath*]
■ see VALLEY.

strathspey /strathspáy/ *n.* **1** a slow Scottish dance. **2** the music for this. [*Strathspey*, valley of the river Spey]

strati *pl.* of STRATUS.

straticulate /strətíkyoolət/ *adj. Geol.* (of rock-formations) arranged in thin strata. [STRATUM, after *vermiculate* etc.]

stratify /stráttifī/ *v.tr.* (**-ies, -ied**) **1** (esp. as **stratified** *adj.*) arrange in strata. **2** construct in layers, social grades, etc. □□ **stratification** /-fikáysh'n/ *n.* [F *stratifier* (as STRATUM)]
■ □□ **stratification** see STRATUM 1–3.

stratigraphy /strətigrəfi/ *n. Geol.* & *Archaeol.* **1** the order and relative position of strata. **2** the study of this as a means of historical interpretation. □□ **stratigraphic** /stráttigráffik/ *adj.* **stratigraphical** /stráttigráffik'l/ *adj.* [STRATUM + -GRAPHY]

strato- /stráttō/ *comb. form* stratus.

stratocirrus /stráttōsírrəss/ *n.* clouds combining stratus and cirrus features.

stratocracy /strətókrəsi/ *n.* (*pl.* **-ies**) **1** a military government. **2** domination by soldiers. [Gk *stratos* army + -CRACY]

stratocumulus /stráttōkyóomyooləss/ *n.* clouds combining cumulus and stratus features.

stratopause /stráttōpawz/ *n.* the interface between the stratosphere and the ionosphere.

stratosphere /stráttəsfeer/ *n.* a layer of atmospheric air above the troposphere extending to about 50 km above the earth's surface, in which the lower part changes little in temperature and the upper part increases in temperature with height (cf. IONOSPHERE). □□ **stratospheric** /-sférrik/ *adj.* [STRATUM + SPHERE after *atmosphere*]

stratum /straátəm, stráy-/ *n.* (*pl.* **strata** /-tə/) **1** esp. *Geol.* a layer or set of successive layers of any deposited substance. **2** an atmospheric layer. **3** a layer of tissue etc. **4 a** a social grade, class, etc. (*the various strata of society*). **b** *Statistics* each of the groups into which a population is divided in stratified sampling. □□ **stratal** *adj.* [L, = something spread or laid down, neut. past part. of *sternere* strew]
■ **1–3** layer, level, stratification; lamina, sheet, thickness, vein, seam; table, plane. **4 a** level, caste, class, rank, echelon, station, status, standing, bracket, group, *archaic or literary* estate.

stratus /stráytəss, straá-/ *n.* (*pl.* **strati** /-tī/) a continuous horizontal sheet of cloud. [L, past part. of *sternere*: see STRATUM]

straw /straw/ *n.* **1** dry cut stalks of grain for use as fodder or as material for thatching, packing, making hats, etc. **2** a single stalk or piece of straw. **3** a thin hollow paper or plastic tube for sucking drink from a glass etc. **4** an insignificant thing (*not worth a straw*). **5** the pale yellow colour of straw. **6** a straw hat. □ **catch** (or **grasp**) **at a straw** resort to an utterly inadequate expedient in desperation, like a person drowning. **straw boss** *US* an assistant foreman. **straw-colour** pale yellow. **straw-coloured** of pale yellow. **straw in the wind** a slight hint of future developments. **straw vote** (or **poll**) an unofficial ballot as a test of opinion. **straw-worm** a caddis-worm. □□ **strawy** *adj.* [OE *strēaw* f. Gmc, rel. to STREW]

■ **4** see *PIN n.* 3. □ **straw boss** see FOREMAN.

strawberry /stráwbəri/ *n.* (*pl.* **-ies**) **1 a** any plant of the genus *Fragaria*, esp. any of various cultivated varieties, with white flowers, trifoliate leaves, and runners. **b** the pulpy red edible fruit of this, having a seed-studded surface. **2** a deep pinkish-red colour. □ **strawberry blonde 1** pinkish-blonde hair. **2** a woman with such hair. **strawberry mark** a soft reddish birthmark. **strawberry pear 1** a W. Indian cactaceous plant, *Hylocereus undatus*. **2** the fruit of this. **strawberry roan** see ROAN[1]. **strawberry-tree** an evergreen tree, *Arbutus unedo*, bearing strawberry-like fruit. [OE *strēa(w)berige*, *strēowberige* (as STRAW, BERRY): reason for the name unkn.]

strawboard /stráwbord/ *n.* a coarse cardboard made of straw pulp.

stray /stray/ *v.*, *n.*, & *adj.* ● *v.intr.* **1 a** wander from the right place; become separated from one's companions etc.; go astray. **b** (often foll. by *from*, *off*) digress. **2** deviate morally. **3** (as **strayed** *adj.*) that has gone astray. ● *n.* **1** a person or thing that has strayed, esp. a domestic animal. **2** (esp. in *pl.*) electrical phenomena interfering with radio reception. ● *adj.* **1** strayed or lost. **2** isolated; found or occurring occasionally (*a stray customer or two*; *hit by a stray bullet*). **3** *Physics* wasted or unwanted (*eliminate stray magnetic fields*). □□ **strayer** *n.* [ME f. AF & OF *estrayer* (v.), AF *strey* (n. & adj.) f. OF *estraié* (as ASTRAY)]

■ *v.* **1** wander, roam, rove, range, straggle, drift, meander, go astray; deviate, diverge, digress, ramble, get *or* go off the track, get *or* go off the subject, go off on *or* at a tangent, get sidetracked, *literary* divagate. **2** see SIN[1] *v.* 1. **3** (**strayed**) see STRAY *adj.* 1 below. ● *n.* **1** straggler, vagrant, *US* dogie. ● *adj.* **1** strayed, vagrant, lost, roving, roaming, wandering, homeless. **2** isolated, separate(d), lone, odd, single; random, casual, chance, accidental, haphazard, singular, freak, unexpected.

streak /streek/ *n.* & *v.* ● *n.* **1** a long thin usu. irregular line or band, esp. distinguished by colour (*black with red streaks*; *a streak of light above the horizon*). **2** a strain or element in a person's character (*has a streak of mischief*). **3** a spell or series (*a winning streak*). **4** a line of bacteria etc. placed on a culture medium. ● *v.* **1** *tr.* mark with streaks. **2** *intr.* move very rapidly. **3** *intr. colloq.* run naked in a public place as a stunt. □ **streak of lightning** a sudden prominent flash of lightning. □□ **streaker** *n.* **streaking** *n.* [OE *strica* pen-stroke f. Gmc: rel. to STRIKE]

■ *n.* **1** stripe, strip, stroke, bar, band, line, mark, smear, slash, dash, touch, daub, fleck, trace; vein, layer, seam, stratum, *Anat.*, *Bot.*, & *Zool.* striation. **2** see VEIN 6. **3** spell, period, stretch, run, spate, series, *colloq.* patch; (*winning streak*) *Austral. colloq.* purple passage *or* patch, *Austral.* & *NZ sl.* spin. ● *v.* **1** stripe, line, bar, mark, smear, daub, slash, *Anat.*, *Bot.*, & *Zool.* striate. **2** race, run, rush, dash, sprint, dart, hurtle, fly, flit, speed, hasten, hurry, whistle, zip, zoom, *colloq.* whiz, tear, scoot. □ **streak of lightning** flash *or* bolt *or* shaft of lightning.

streaky /streéki/ *adj.* (**streakier**, **streakiest**) **1** full of streaks. **2** (of bacon) with alternate streaks of fat and lean. □□ **streakily** *adv.* **streakiness** *n.*

■ **1** see *mottled* (MOTTLE *v.*).

stream /streem/ *n.* & *v.* ● *n.* **1** a flowing body of water, esp. a small river. **2 a** the flow of a fluid or of a mass of people (*a stream of lava*). **b** (in *sing.* or *pl.*) a large quantity of something that flows or moves along. **3** a current or direction in which things are moving or tending (*against the stream*). **4** *Brit.* a group of schoolchildren taught together as being of similar ability for a given age. ● *v.* **1** *intr.* flow or move as a stream. **2** *intr.* run with liquid (*my eyes were streaming*). **3** *intr.* (of a banner or hair etc.) float or wave in the wind. **4** *tr.* emit a stream of (blood etc.). **5** *tr. Brit.* arrange (schoolchildren) in streams. □ **go with the stream** do as others do. **on stream** (of a factory etc.) in operation. **stream-anchor** an anchor intermediate in size between a bower and a kedge, esp. for use in warping. **stream of consciousness 1** *Psychol.* a person's thoughts and conscious reactions to events perceived as a continuous flow. **2** a literary style depicting events in such a flow in the mind of a character. □□ **streamless** *adj.* **streamlet** *n.* [OE *strēam* f. Gmc]

■ *n.* **1** brook, brooklet, streamlet, rivulet, river, tributary, branch, freshet, run, watercourse, waterway, channel, runlet, rill, runnel, *esp. Austral.* anabranch, *N.Engl.* beck, *Sc.* burn, *US*, *Austral.* & *NZ* creek, *US dial.* kill. **2** flow, current, outpouring, effluence, efflux, effusion, rush, spurt, surge, fountain, geyser, gush, torrent, flood, deluge, shower, cataract, cascade; swarm, tide, spate, succession, series, row, line, string, chain, barrage, *esp. Brit.* queue. **3** current, course, direction, tide, mainstream; see also TREND *n.* ● *v.* **1** run, flow, course, glide, rush, slide, slip, surge; pour, issue, emanate, gush, flood, spout, well up *or* out *or* forth, squirt, spurt, shoot, jet, cascade, spill; teem, swarm; file, proceed, march, walk, move. **3** float, flutter, flap, waft, blow; see also WAVE *v.* 2.

streamer /streémər/ *n.* **1** a long narrow flag. **2** a long narrow strip of ribbon or paper, esp. in a coil that unrolls when thrown. **3** a banner headline. **4** (in *pl.*) the aurora borealis or australis.

■ **1** pennant, banner, pennon, flag, banderole, gonfalon, jack, ensign, burgee.

streamline /streémlīn/ *v.* & *n.* ● *v.tr.* **1** give (a vehicle etc.) the form which presents the least resistance to motion. **2** make (an organization, process, etc.) simple or more efficient or better organized. **3** (as **streamlined** *adj.*) **a** having a smooth, slender, or elongated form; aerodynamic. **b** having a simplified and more efficient structure or organization. ● *n.* **1** the natural course of water or air currents. **2** (often *attrib.*) the shape of an aircraft, car, etc., calculated to cause the least air resistance.

■ *v.* **3** (**streamlined**) **a** aerodynamic, curved, curvilinear; smooth, flowing, sleek. **b** modernized, up to date, modernistic, time-saving, labour-saving, (well-)organized, efficient, automated, well-run, smooth, efficient, automated, simplified.

street /street/ *n.* **1 a** a public road in a city, town, or village. **b** this with the houses or other buildings on each side. **2** the persons who live or work on a particular street. □ **in the street 1** in the area outside the houses. **2** (of Stock Exchange business) done after closing-time. **not in the same street with** *colloq.* utterly inferior to in ability etc. **on the streets 1** living by prostitution. **2** homeless. **street Arab** often *offens.* **1** a homeless child. **2** an urchin. **street credibility** (or *colloq.* **cred**) familiarity with a fashionable urban subculture. **street cries** *Brit.* the cries of street hawkers. **street door** a main outer house-door opening on the street. **street jewellery** enamel advertising plates as collectors' items. **streets ahead** (often foll. by *of*) *colloq.* much superior (to). **street value** the value of drugs sold illicitly. **take to the streets** gather outdoors in order to protest etc. **up** (or **right up**) **a person's street** (or **alley**) *colloq.* **1** within a person's range of interest or knowledge. **2** to a person's liking. □□ **streeted** *adj.* (also in *comb.*). **streetward** *adj.* & *adv.* [OE *strǣt* f. LL *strāta* (*via*) paved (way), fem. past part. of *sternere* lay down]

■ **1** thoroughfare, way, road, roadway, high road, avenue, concourse, boulevard, lane, drive, terrace, crescent, cul-de-sac, row, passage, alley, byway, side-street. □ **on the streets 2** see HOMELESS *adj.* **up** (or **right up**) **a person's street** (or **alley**) suiting a person to a T, *colloq.* one's cup of tea, *joc.* in a person's bailiwick.

streetcar /stréetkaar/ *n. US* a tram.

■ see TRAM[1].

streetwalker /stréetwawkər/ *n.* a prostitute seeking customers in the street. □□ **streetwalking** *n.* & *adj.*

■ see PROSTITUTE *n.* 1a.

streetwise /stréetwīz/ *n.* esp. *US* familiar with the ways of modern urban life.

■ see SMART *adj.* 1a.

strength /strength, *disp.* strengkth/ *n.* **1** the state of being strong; the degree or respect in which a person or thing is strong. **2 a** a person or thing affording strength or support. **b** an attribute making for strength of character (*patience is your great strength*). **3** the number of persons present or available. **4** a full complement (*below strength*). □ **from strength** from a strong position. **from strength to strength** with ever-increasing success. **in strength** in large numbers. **on the strength of** relying on; on the basis of. **the strength of** the essence or main features of. □□ **strengthless** *adj.* [OE *strengthu* f. Gmc (as STRONG)]

■ **1** power, might, force, mightiness, robustness, toughness, stoutness, sturdiness, brawn, brawniness, muscle, sinew, vigour, energy; durability, reliability, resistance, solidity, stamina, ruggedness, endurance; fortitude, backbone, tenacity, tenaciousness, will-power, perseverance, persistence, resoluteness, resolution, pertinacity, nerve, pluck, determination, gameness, intrepidity, firmness, stability; concentration, intensity, potency; efficacy, persuasiveness, cogency, weight, convincingness, incisiveness, soundness; *colloq.* guts, grit, gutsiness, spunk. **2 a** see PILLAR 2. **b** talent, ability, aptitude, endowment, gift, strong point *or* suit, forte, asset, long suit. □ **on the strength of** on the basis of, according to, by *or* in virtue of. **the strength of** see ESSENCE 1.

strengthen /stréngthən, *disp.* stréngkthən/ *v.tr.* & *intr.* make or become stronger. □ **strengthen a person's hand** (or **hands**) encourage a person to vigorous action. □□ **strengthener** *n.*

■ reinforce, renew, bolster, fortify, toughen, stiffen, support, brace (up), buttress; confirm, consolidate, back up, corroborate, substantiate; step up, increase, intensify, heighten, enhance; encourage, hearten, invigorate, rejuvenate, nourish, energize, vitalize, steel, *colloq.* boost.

strenuous /strényooəss/ *adj.* **1** requiring or using great effort. **2** energetic or unrelaxing. □□ **strenuously** *adv.* **strenuousness** *n.* [L *strenuus* brisk]

■ **1** demanding, taxing, tough, arduous, laborious, toilsome, burdensome, tiring, exhausting, gruelling, punishing, difficult, hard, uphill. **2** energetic, active, vigorous, enthusiastic, zealous, earnest, dynamic, intense, indefatigable, tireless, unremitting, persistent, dogged, determined, tenacious, pertinacious, resolute, sincere, eager. □□ **strenuously** see HARD *adv.* 1.

strep /strep/ *n. colloq.* = STREPTOCOCCUS. [abbr.]

streptococcus /stréptəkókkəss/ *n.* (*pl.* **streptococci** /-kókkī/) any bacterium of the genus *Streptococcus*, usu. occurring in chains, some of which cause infectious diseases. □□ **streptococcal** *adj.* [Gk *streptos* twisted f. *strephō* turn + COCCUS]

streptomycin /stréptōmīsin/ *n.* an antibiotic produced by the bacterium *Streptomyces griseus*, effective against many disease-producing bacteria. [Gk *streptos* (as STREPTOCOCCUS) + *mukēs* fungus]

stress /stress/ *n.* & *v.* ● *n.* **1 a** pressure or tension exerted on a material object. **b** a quantity measuring this. **2 a** demand on physical or mental energy. **b** distress caused by this (*suffering from stress*). **3 a** emphasis (*the stress was on the need for success*). **b** accentuation; emphasis laid on a syllable or word. **c** an accent, esp. the principal one in a word (*the stress is on the first syllable*). **4** *Mech.* force per unit area exerted between contiguous bodies or parts of a body. ● *v.tr.* **1** lay stress on; emphasize. **2** subject to mechanical or physical or mental stress. □ **lay stress on** indicate as important. **stress disease** a disease resulting from continuous mental stress. □□ **stressless** *adj.* [ME f. DISTRESS, or partly f. OF *estresse* narrowness, oppression, ult. f. L *strictus* STRICT]

■ *n.* **1** see PRESSURE *n.* 1a, b, TENSION *n.* 1. **2** (stress and) strain, burden, anxiety, worry, distress, pain, grief, suffering, anguish, pressure, tenseness, tension. **3 a** emphasis, importance, weight, force, insistence. **b, c** emphasis, force, forcefulness, accentuation, accent, prominence, *Prosody* ictus. ● *v.* **1** emphasize, accent, accentuate, lay stress *or* emphasis on, underscore, underline, mark, note, make a point of, bring home, dwell on, insist on, focus on, bring into prominence, spotlight, feature, highlight. **2** strain, put under strain *or* stress, upset, disturb, burden, worry, distress, pressurize, pressure.

stressful /strésfŏŏl/ *adj.* causing stress; mentally tiring (*had a stressful day*). □□ **stressfully** *adv.* **stressfulness** *n.*

■ see TRYING.

stretch /strech/ *v.* & *n.* ● *v.* **1** *tr.* & *intr.* draw or be drawn or admit of being drawn out into greater length or size. **2** *tr.* & *intr.* make or become taut. **3** *tr.* & *intr.* place or lie at full length or spread out (*with a canopy stretched over them*). **4** *tr.* (also *absol.*) **a** extend (an arm, leg, etc.). **b** (often *refl.*) thrust out one's limbs and tighten one's muscles after being relaxed. **5** *intr.* have a specified length or extension; extend (*farmland stretches for many miles*). **6** *tr.* strain or exert extremely or excessively; exaggerate (*stretch the truth*). **7** *intr.* (as **stretched** *adj.*) elongated or extended. ● *n.* **1** a continuous extent or expanse or period (*a stretch of open road*). **2** the act or an instance of stretching; the state of being stretched. **3** (*attrib.*) able to stretch; elastic (*stretch fabric*). **4 a** *colloq.* a period of imprisonment. **b** a period of service. **5** *US* the straight side of a racetrack. **6** *Naut.* the distance covered on one tack. □ **at full stretch** working to capacity. **at a stretch 1** in one continuous period (*slept for two hours at a stretch*). **2** with much effort. **stretch one's legs** exercise oneself by walking. **stretch marks** marks on the skin resulting from a gain of weight, or on the abdomen after pregnancy. **stretch out 1** *tr.* extend (a hand or foot etc.). **2** *intr.* & *tr.* last for a longer period; prolong. **3** *tr.* make (money etc.) last for a sufficient time. **stretch a point** agree to something not normally allowed. **stretch one's wings** see WING. □□ **stretchable** *adj.* **stretchability** /stréchəbílliti/ *n.* **stretchy** *adj.* **stretchiness** *n.* [OE *streccan* f. WG: cf. STRAIGHT]

■ *v.* **1** distend, lengthen, elongate, widen, broaden, swell, draw *or* pull out, balloon, inflate, enlarge, expand, extend, increase, dilate, blow up. **2** see TENSE *v.* **3** see SPREAD *v.* 1a. **5** extend, reach, continue; span, spread. **6** overtax, overextend, overburden, tax; warp, strain, distort, bend, break; exaggerate, overstate. ● *n.* **1** extent, reach, span, distance, length, spread, expanse, sweep, range, area, tract, *US* section; see also PERIOD *n.* 1. **3** (*attrib.*) see ELASTIC *adj.* 1, 2. **4** stint, period, spell, term; *colloq.* time; tour (of duty), *US sl.* hitch. **5** straight. □ **stretch one's legs** (take *or* go for a) walk, (take *or* get some) exercise. **stretch out 1** see REACH *v.* 1, 2. **2** see PROLONG 1. □□ **stretchable, stretchy** see ELASTIC 1, 2. **stretchability, stretchiness** see *elasticity* (ELASTIC).

stretcher /stréchər/ *n.* & *v.* ● *n.* **1** a framework of two poles with canvas etc. between, for carrying sick, injured, or dead persons in a lying position. **2** a brick or stone laid with its long side along the face of a wall (cf. HEADER). **3** a board in a boat against which a rower presses the feet. **4** a rod or bar as a tie between chair-legs etc. **5** a wooden frame over which a canvas is stretched ready for painting. **6** *archaic sl.* an exaggeration or lie. ● *v.tr.* (often foll. by *off*) convey (a sick or injured person) on a stretcher. □ **stretcher-bearer** a person who helps to carry a stretcher, esp. in war or at a major accident.

■ *n.* **1** see LITTER *n.* 4, 5.

stretto /stréttō/ *adv. Mus.* in quicker time. [It., = narrow]

strew /stroo/ *v.tr.* (*past part.* **strewn** or **strewed**) **1** scatter or spread about over a surface. **2** (usu. foll. by *with*) spread (a surface) with scattered things. □□ **strewer** *n.* [OE *stre(o)wian*]

■ scatter, bestrew, sprinkle, spread, litter; disperse, toss, distribute.

'strewth var. of 'STRUTH.

stria /strī́ə/ *n.* (*pl.* **-ae** /strī́ee/) **1** *Anat.*, *Zool.*, *Bot.*, & *Geol.* **a** a linear mark on a surface. **b** a slight ridge, furrow, or score. **2** *Archit.* a fillet between the flutes of a column. [L]

■ see GROOVE *n.* 1a.

striate *adj.* & *v. Anat.*, *Zool.*, *Bot.*, & *Geol.* ● *adj.* /strī́ət/ (also **striated** /strī́aytid/) marked with striae. ● *v.tr.* /strī́ayt/ mark with striae. □□ **striation** /strīáysh'n/ *n.*

■ *adj.* (**striated**) see STRIPED. ● *v.* see STREAK *v.* 1. □□ **striation** see STRIPE 1.

stricken /stríkkən/ *adj.* **1** affected or overcome with illness or misfortune etc. (*stricken with measles*; *grief-stricken*). **2** levelled with a strickle. **3** (often foll. by *from* etc.) *US Law* deleted. □ **stricken in years** *archaic* enfeebled by age. [archaic past part. of STRIKE]

■ **1** broken, crushed, demoralized, broken-hearted, grief-stricken; (*stricken by* or *with*) struck (down) by, hit by, laid low by *or* with, affected by *or* with, afflicted with, racked by *or* with, overwhelmed by *or* with, overcome by *or* with, plagued by *or* with, tormented by, troubled by, *archaic or literary* smitten by. □ **stricken in years** enfeebled, infirm, doddering, doddery, faltering, shaky, frail; see also AGED 2.

strickle /stríkk'l/ *n.* **1** a rod used in strike-measure. **2** a whetting tool. [OE *stricel*, rel. to STRIKE]

strict /strikt/ *adj.* **1** precisely limited or defined; without exception or deviation (*lives in strict seclusion*). **2 a** (of a person) severe; rigorous in upholding standards of conscience or morality. **b** requiring complete compliance or exact performance; enforced rigidly (*gave strict orders*). □□ **strictness** *n.* [L *strictus* past part. of *stringere* tighten]

■ **1** rigorous, narrow, close, undeviating, confining, constricting, constrictive, rigid, defined, precise, accurate, exact, exacting, stringent, meticulous, compulsive, punctilious, finicky, finical, scrupulous, attentive, conscientious, faithful, literal, thorough, complete, *archaic* strait. **2 a** severe, austere, authoritarian, autocratic, stern, firm, hard, tough, uncompromising, inflexible, cold-blooded, tyrannical, harsh, ruthless, pitiless, unsympathetic **b** rigid, set, unalterable, invariable, hard and fast, tight, binding, stringent. □□ **strictness** see PRECISION 1, *severity* (SEVERE).

strictly /stríktli/ *adv.* **1** in a strict manner. **2** (also **strictly speaking**) applying words in their strict sense (*he is, strictly, an absconder*). **3** esp. *US colloq.* definitely.

stricture /stríkchər/ *n.* **1** (usu. in *pl.*; often foll. by *on*, *upon*) a critical or censorious remark. **2** *Med.* a morbid narrowing of a canal or duct in the body. □□ **strictured** *adj.* [ME f. L *strictura* (as STRICT)]

■ **1** criticism, censure, condemnation. **2** constriction, narrowing.

stride /strīd/ *v.* & *n.* ● *v.* (*past* **strode** /strōd/; *past part.* **stridden** /strídd'n/) **1** *intr.* & *tr.* walk with long firm steps. **2** *tr.* cross with one step. **3** *tr.* bestride; straddle. ● *n.* **1 a** a single long step. **b** the length of this. **2** a person's gait as determined by the length of stride. **3** (usu. in *pl.*) progress (*has made great strides*). **4** a settled rate of progress (*get into one's stride*; *be thrown out of one's stride*). **5** (in *pl.*) *sl.* trousers. **6** the distance between the feet parted either laterally or as in walking. □ **take in one's stride 1** clear (an obstacle) without changing one's gait to jump. **2** manage without difficulty. □□ **strider** *n.* [OE *strīdan*]

■ *v.* **1** see WALK *v.* 1, 2. ● *n.* **1** see STEP *n.* 1a, b, 5. **2** see WALK *n.* 1. **3** (*strides*) progress, advances, steps.

strident /strī́d'nt/ *adj.* loud and harsh. □□ **stridency** *n.* **stridently** *adv.* [L *stridere strident-* creak]

■ shrill, raucous, harsh, loud, clamorous, noisy, grating, stridulant, scraping, scratching, scratchy, screeching, grinding, hoarse, rough, guttural, gravelly, rasping, jarring, discordant, inconsonant, unharmonious, unmelodious, unmusical, cacophonous, croaking, creaking.

stridulate /strídyoolayt/ *v.intr.* (of insects, esp. the cicada and grasshopper) make a shrill sound by rubbing esp. the legs or wing-cases together. □□ **stridulant** *adj.* **stridulation** /-láysh'n/ *n.* [F *striduler* f. L *stridulus* creaking (as STRIDENT)]

strife /strīf/ *n.* **1** conflict; struggle between opposed persons or things. **2** *Austral. colloq.* trouble of any kind. [ME f. OF *estrif*: cf. OF *estriver* STRIVE]

■ **1** discord, disharmony, disagreement, difference, conflict, rivalry, competition, contention, dispute, dissension, struggle, squabbling, bickering, arguing, quarrelling; animosity, friction, hard feelings, bad feeling(s), bad blood, antagonism, ill will, hatred, enmity, hostility, unfriendliness. **2** see TROUBLE *n.* 1.

strigil /stríjil/ *n.* **1** *Gk* & *Rom. Antiq.* a skin-scraper used by bathers after exercise. **2** a structure on the leg of an insect used to clean its antennae etc. [L *strigilis* f. *stringere* graze]

strigose /strī́gōss/ *adj.* **1** (of leaves etc.) having short stiff hairs or scales. **2** (of an insect etc.) streaked, striped, or ridged. [L *striga* swath, furrow]

■ **1** see HAIRY 1.

strike /strīk/ *v.* & *n.* ● *v.* (*past* **struck** /struk/; *past part.* **struck** or *archaic* **stricken** /stríkkən/) **1 a** *tr.* subject to an impact. **b** *tr.* deliver (a blow) or inflict a blow on. **2** *tr.* come or bring sharply into contact with (*the ship struck a rock*). **3** *tr.* propel or divert with a blow (*struck the ball into the pond*). **4** *intr.* (foll. by *at*) try to hit. **5** *tr.* cause to penetrate (*struck terror into him*). **6** *tr.* ignite (a match) or produce (sparks etc.) by rubbing. **7** *tr.* make (a coin) by stamping. **8** *tr.* produce (a musical note) by striking. **9 a** *tr.* (also *absol.*) (of a clock) indicate (the time) by the sounding of a chime etc. **b** *intr.* (of time) be indicated in this way. **10** *tr.* **a** attack or affect suddenly (*was struck with sudden terror*). **b** (of a disease) afflict. **11** *tr.* cause to become suddenly (*was struck dumb*). **12** *tr.* reach or achieve (*strike a balance*). **13** *tr.* agree on (a bargain). **14** *tr.* assume (an attitude) suddenly and dramatically. **15** *tr.* **a** discover or come across. **b** find (oil etc.) by drilling. **c** encounter (an unusual thing etc.). **16** come to the attention of or appear to (*it strikes me as silly*; *an idea suddenly struck me*). **17 a** *intr.* (of employees) engage in a strike; cease work as a protest. **b** *tr. US* act in this way against (an employer). **18 a** *tr.* lower or take down (a flag or tent etc.). **b** *intr.* signify surrender by striking a flag; surrender. **19** *intr.* take a specified direction (*struck east*). **20** *tr.* (also *absol.*) secure a hook in the mouth of (a fish) by jerking the tackle. **21** *tr.* (of a snake) wound with its fangs. **22** *intr.* (of oysters) attach themselves to a bed. **23 a** *tr.* insert (the cutting of a plant) in soil to take root. **b** *tr.* (also *absol.*) (of a plant or cutting etc.) put forth (roots). **24** *tr.* level (grain etc. or the measure) in strike-measure. **25** *tr.* **a** ascertain (a balance) by deducting credit or debit from the other. **b** arrive at (an average, state of balance) by equalizing all items. **26** compose (a jury) esp. by allowing both sides to reject the same number. ● *n.* **1** the act or an instance of striking. **2 a** the organized refusal by employees to work until some grievance is remedied. **b** a similar refusal to participate in some other expected activity. **3** a sudden find or success (*a lucky strike*). **4** an attack, esp. from the air. **5** *Baseball* a batter's unsuccessful attempt to hit a pitched ball, or another event counting equivalently against a batter.

6 the act of knocking down all the pins with the first ball in bowling. **7** horizontal direction in a geological structure. **8** a strickle. □ **on strike** taking part in an industrial etc. strike. **strike at the root** (or **roots**) **of** see ROOT[1]. **strike back 1** strike or attack in return. **2** (of a gas-burner) burn from an internal point before the gas has become mixed with air. **strike down 1** knock down. **2** bring low; afflict (*struck down by a virus*). **strike home 1** deal an effective blow. **2** have an intended effect (*my words struck home*). **strike in 1** intervene in a conversation etc. **2** (of a disease) attack the interior of the body from the surface. **strike it rich** *colloq.* find a source of abundance or success. **strike a light 1** produce a light by striking a match. **2** *Brit. sl.* an expression of surprise, disgust, etc. **strike lucky** have a lucky success. **strike-measure** measurement by passing a rod across the top of a heaped vessel to ensure that it is exactly full. **strike off 1** remove with a stroke. **2** delete (a name etc.) from a list. **3** produce (copies of a document). **strike oil 1** find petroleum by sinking a shaft. **2** attain prosperity or success. **strike out 1** hit out. **2** act vigorously. **3** delete (an item or name etc.). **4** set off or begin (*struck out eastwards*). **5** use the arms and legs in swimming. **6** forge or devise (a plan etc.). **7** *Baseball* **a** dismiss (a batter) by means of three strikes. **b** be dismissed in this way. **strike pay** an allowance paid to strikers by their trade union. **strike through** delete (a word etc.) with a stroke of one's pen. **strike up 1** start (an acquaintance, conversation, etc.) esp. casually. **2** (also *absol.*) begin playing (a tune etc.). **strike upon 1** have (an idea etc.) luckily occur to one. **2** (of light) illuminate. **strike while the iron is hot** act promptly at a good opportunity. **struck on** *colloq.* infatuated with. □□ **strikable** *adj.* [OE *strīcan* go, stroke f. WG]

■ *v.* **1** hit, deal a blow to, knock, smack, thump, trounce, crown, cuff, punch, slog, slap, spank, bash, clout; beat, hammer, belabour, batter, pummel, pommel, pelt, buffet, thrash; cudgel, bludgeon, club, whip, horsewhip, scourge, lash, cane, flog, birch, *US* slug, *archaic or literary* smite, *colloq.* whack, thwack, sock, lambaste, bop, swipe, *Austral.* & *NZ colloq.* dong, *sl.* belt, clobber, wallop, conk, *Austral. sl.* quilt, *Austral.* & *NZ sl.* stoush; deliver, deal, administer, inflict, aim, direct. **2** hit, collide with, land on *or* in *or* against, smash *or* bump *or* bang *or* knock *or* ram *or* crash *or* dash into, go *or* run into. **3** see HIT *v.* 9a. **4** see SWIPE *v.* 1. **5** instil, implant, induce. **6** light, ignite. **7** impress, print, stamp, punch, mint, make. **9 a** see CHIME[1] *v.* 1. **10 a** seize, beset, overcome, attack, afflict, infect, assail; penetrate, affect, get to *or* at, hit; see also CONSUME 3. **b** afflict, affect, attack, hit, *archaic or literary* smite; see also *strike down* 2 below. **12** reach, arrive at, attain, achieve; see also REALIZE 4. **13** make, reach, attain, conclude; agree *or* settle (on), ratify, confirm. **14** assume, adopt, put on, display, affect, take on, feign. **15** encounter, come *or* happen *or* hit upon, come across, chance upon, discover, stumble on, find. **16** occur *or* come to, dawn on *or* upon, hit, register with. **17 a** walk out (of the job), go on strike, stop *or* cease work, *Brit.* come out, take industrial action, *colloq.* down tools. **18 a** remove, take away, take apart, dismantle, knock down; take *or* pull *or* haul down, lower. ● *n.* **1** see HIT *n.* 1a. **2** walk-out, sit-down (strike), stoppage, *Brit.* industrial action. **3** see WINDFALL. **4** see ASSAULT *n.* 1, 5. □ **strike back 1** see RETALIATE 1. **strike down 1** see *knock down* 1. **2** afflict, attack, bring low, indispose, incapacitate, disable, cripple, invalid. **strike home 2** hit home. **strike in 1** see INTERVENE. **strike it rich** see *go places* (PLACE). **strike a light 2** see *stone the crows*. **strike off 1, 2** cross off *or* out, cancel, scratch, obliterate, expunge, erase, eradicate, remove, blot out, delete, eliminate, rub out, wipe out. **strike out 3** see *strike off* above. **4** see START *v.* 4, 5. **strike up 1** begin, start, *formal* commence. **strike upon 1** dream up, devise, conjure up, improvise, work out, invent, contrive, come up with, hit on *or* upon, arrive at. **strike while the iron is hot** take the opportunity, seize the day, make hay while the sun shines. **struck on** infatuated with, enamoured of, besotted by, impressed with, *archaic or literary* smitten by, *colloq.* bowled over by, stuck on.

strikebound /strīkbownd/ *adj.* immobilized or closed by a strike.

strikebreaker /strīkbraykər/ *n.* a person working or employed in place of others who are on strike. □□ **strikebreak** *v.intr.*

■ see BLACKLEG *n.*

striker /strīkər/ *n.* **1** a person or thing that strikes. **2** an employee on strike. **3** *Sport* the player who is to strike, or who is to be the next to strike, the ball. **4** *Football* an attacking player positioned well forward in order to score goals. **5** a device striking the primer in a gun.

■ **2** see PICKET *n.* 1. **4** forward.

striking /strīking/ *adj.* & *n.* ● *adj.* **1** impressive; attracting attention. **2** (of a clock) making a chime to indicate the hours etc. ● *n.* the act or an instance of striking. □ **striking-circle** (in hockey) an elongated semicircle in front of the goal, from within which the ball must be hit in order to score. **striking-force** a military body ready to attack at short notice. **within striking distance** near enough to hit or achieve. □□ **strikingly** *adv.* **strikingness** *n.*

■ *adj.* **1** remarkable, astounding, astonishing, amazing, awe-inspiring, awesome, impressive, imposing, great, grand, out of the ordinary, unusual, rare, exceptional, marvellous, extraordinary, magnificent, superb, splendid, stupendous; conspicuous, noticeable, prominent, salient, pronounced, marked, arresting, telling; *colloq.* smashing, fabulous, stunning, ripsnorting, *Brit. colloq.* top-hole, *poet.* wondrous, *Brit. archaic sl.* ripping, topping. ● *n.* see TOLL[2] *n.* □□ **strikingly** see ESPECIALLY.

Strine /strīn/ *n.* **1** a comic transliteration of Australian speech, e.g. *Emma Chissitt* = 'How much is it?'. **2** (esp. uneducated) Australian English. [= *Australian* in Strine]

string /string/ *n.* & *v.* ● *n.* **1** twine or narrow cord. **2** a piece of this or of similar material used for tying or holding together, pulling, etc. **3** a length of catgut or wire etc. on a musical instrument, producing a note by vibration. **4 a** (in *pl.*) the stringed instruments in an orchestra etc. **b** (*attrib.*) relating to or consisting of stringed instruments (*string quartet*). **5** (in *pl.*) an awkward condition or complication (*the offer has no strings*). **6** a set of things strung together; a series or line of persons or things (*a string of beads*; *a string of oaths*). **7** a group of racehorses trained at one stable. **8** a tough piece connecting the two halves of a bean-pod etc. **9** a piece of catgut etc. interwoven with others to form the head of a tennis etc. racket. **10** = STRINGBOARD. ● *v.* (*past* and *past part.* **strung** /strung/) **1** *tr.* supply with a string or strings. **2** *tr.* tie with string. **3** *tr.* thread (beads etc.) on a string. **4** *tr.* arrange in or as a string. **5** *tr.* remove the strings from (a bean). **6** *tr.* place a string ready for use on (a bow). **7** *tr. colloq.* hoax. **8** *intr.* (of glue etc.) become stringy. **9** *intr. Billiards* make the preliminary strokes that decide which player begins. □ **on a string** under one's control or influence. **string along** *colloq.* **1** deceive, esp. by appearing to comply with (a person). **2** (often foll. by *with*) keep company (with). **string bass** *Mus.* a double-bass. **string bean 1** any of various beans eaten in their fibrous pods, esp. runner beans or French beans. **2** *colloq.* a tall thin person. **string-course** a raised horizontal band or course of bricks etc. on a building. **string out** extend; prolong (esp. unduly). **string-piece** a long timber supporting and connecting the parts of a framework. **string tie** a very narrow necktie. **string up 1** hang up on strings etc. **2** kill by hanging. **3** make tense. **string vest** a vest with large meshes. □□ **stringless** *adj.* **stringlike** *adj.* [OE *streng* f. Gmc: cf. STRONG]

■ *n.* **1** line, cord, thread, twine, fibre, rope, cable, strand, filament. **2** tie, lace, cord, line; leash, lead, leader. **5** (*strings*) conditions, stipulations, provisos, qualifications, requirements, prerequisites, terms, obligations, limitations, provisions, catches, complications, *colloq.* musts. **6** line, row, series, sequence, succession, chain, concatenation, procession, stream, run, train, file, column, *esp. Brit.* queue. ● *v.* **2** tie, join, lace. **4** line up, align, array, connect, link, join, chain together, concatenate, loop. **7** see CHEAT *v.* 1a. ▫ **string along 1** fool, deceive, bluff, dupe, cheat, trick, hoax; keep dangling, keep on tenterhooks, play fast and loose with. **2** (*string along with*) accompany, go *or* tag along with, keep company with, associate with, hang around with, go *or* be with. **string out** stretch, extend; prolong, drag out, protract, spin out. **string up 1** festoon, loop, drape, suspend, sling, hang, array. **2** hang, lynch. **3** see TENSE[1] *v.* ▫▫ **stringlike** see THIN *adj.* 2.

stringboard /stríngbord/ *n.* a supporting timber or skirting in which the ends of a staircase steps are set.

stringed /stringd/ *adj.* (of musical instruments) having strings (also in *comb.*: *twelve-stringed guitar*).

stringendo /strinjéndō/ *adj.* & *adv. Mus.* with increasing speed. [It. f. *stringere* press: see STRINGENT]

stringent /strínjənt/ *adj.* **1** (of rules etc.) strict, precise; requiring exact performance; leaving no loophole or discretion. **2** (of a money market etc.) tight; hampered by scarcity; unaccommodating; hard to operate in. ▫▫ **stringency** *n.* **stringently** *adv.* [L *stringere* draw tight]
■ **1** see STRICT 1. ▫▫ **stringency** see *severity* (SEVERE). **stringently** see *severely* (SEVERE).

stringer /stríngər/ *n.* **1** a longitudinal structural member in a framework, esp. of a ship or aircraft. **2** *colloq.* a newspaper correspondent not on the regular staff. **3** = STRINGBOARD.
■ **2** see CORRESPONDENT *n.*

stringhalt /stríng-holt/ *n.* spasmodic movement of a horse's hind leg.

stringy /stríngi/ *adj.* (**stringier, stringiest**) **1** (of food etc.) fibrous, tough. **2** of or like string. **3** (of a person) tall, wiry, and thin. **4** (of a liquid) viscous; forming strings. ▫ **stringy-bark** *Austral.* any of various eucalyptus trees with tough fibrous bark. ▫▫ **stringily** *adv.* **stringiness** *n.*
■ **1** fibrous, chewy, sinewy, gristly, leathery, tough. **2** stringlike, ropy, threadlike, fibrous, filamentous. **3** gangling, rangy, leggy, long-legged, wiry; see also LANKY.

strip[1] /strip/ *v.* & *n.* ● *v.* (**stripped, stripping**) **1** *tr.* (often foll. by *of*) remove the clothes or covering from (a person or thing). **2** *intr.* (often foll. by *off*) undress oneself. **3** *tr.* (often foll. by *of*) deprive (a person) of property or titles. **4** *tr.* leave bare of accessories or fittings. **5** *tr.* remove bark and branches from (a tree). **6** *tr.* (often foll. by *down*) remove the accessory fittings of or take apart (a machine etc.) to inspect or adjust it. **7** *tr.* milk (a cow) to the last drop. **8** *tr.* remove the old hair from (a dog). **9** *tr.* remove the stems from (tobacco). **10** *tr.* tear the thread from (a screw). **11** *tr.* tear the teeth from (a gearwheel). **12** *tr.* remove (paint) or remove paint from (a surface) with solvent. **13** *tr.* (often foll. by *from*) pull or tear (a covering or property etc.) off (*stripped the masks from their faces*). **14** *intr.* (of a screw) lose its thread. **15** *intr.* (of a bullet) issue from a rifled gun without spin owing to a loss of surface. ● *n.* **1** an act of stripping, esp. of undressing in striptease. **2** *colloq.* the identifying outfit worn by the members of a sports team while playing. ▫ **strip club** a club at which striptease performances are given. **strip mine** *US* a mine worked by removing the material that overlies the ore etc. **strip-search** *n.* a search of a person involving the removal of all clothes. ● *v.tr.* search in this way. [ME f. OE *bestrīepan* plunder f. Gmc]
■ *v.* **1** disrobe, undress, strip to the skin, divest a person of clothes, *joc.* strip a person to his *or* her birthday suit; peel, skin, bare, uncover, expose, denude, lay bare, flay, excoriate; fleece, shear, pluck; defoliate. **2** get undressed, undress (oneself), unclothe (oneself), shed *or* remove one's clothes, take off one's clothes, get naked, strip down to nothing, peel off one's clothes, divest oneself of one's clothes, *colloq.* strip to the buff, *joc.* strip to one's birthday suit, *literary* doff one's clothes; (do a) striptease. **3** see DEPRIVE 1. **4** clear; gut, clean out, clear out, empty. **5** decorticate, debark, denude; lop. **6** dismantle, take apart. **13** take off, peel off, remove. ● *n.* **1** striptease.

strip[2] /strip/ *n.* **1** a long narrow piece (*a strip of land*). **2** a narrow flat bar of iron or steel. **3** (in full **strip cartoon**) = *comic strip*. ▫ **strip light** a tubular fluorescent lamp. **strip mill** a mill in which steel slabs are rolled into strips. **tear a person off a strip** *colloq.* angrily rebuke a person. [ME, from or rel. to MLG *strippe* strap, thong, prob. rel. to STRIPE]
■ **1** band, ribbon, fillet, belt, swathe, stripe, slat, lath, sliver, shred. ▫ **tear a person off a strip** see REBUKE *v.*

stripe /strīp/ *n.* **1** a long narrow band or strip differing in colour or texture from the surface on either side of it (*black with a red stripe*). **2** *Mil.* a chevron etc. denoting military rank. **3** *US* a category of character, opinion, etc. (*a man of that stripe*). **4** (usu. in *pl.*) *archaic* a blow with a scourge or lash. **5** (in *pl.*, treated as *sing.*) *colloq.* a tiger. [perh. back-form. f. *striped*: cf. MDu., MLG *strīpe*, MHG *strīfe*]
■ **1** band, bar, striation, strip, streak, vein, thread, line, stroke, slash, length, *Anat.* & *Zool.* striation. **3** style, kind, sort, class, category, type, complexion, character, nature, description, persuasion, kidney. **4** see LASH *n.* 1a.

striped /strīpt/ *adj.* marked with stripes (also in *comb.*: *red-striped*).
■ stripy, streaked, lined, banded, *Anat.* & *Zool.* striated.

stripling /strípling/ *n.* a youth not yet fully grown. [ME, prob. f. STRIP[2] + -LING[1], in the sense of having a figure not yet filled out]
■ lad, boy, adolescent, juvenile, minor, schoolboy, youngster, teenager, youth, young fellow *or* man, fledgling, *Ir.* gossoon, *colloq.* hobbledehoy, young 'un.

stripper /strípər/ *n.* **1** a person or thing that strips something. **2** a device or solvent for removing paint etc. **3** a striptease performer.

striptease /strípteez/ *n.* & *v.* ● *n.* an entertainment in which the performer gradually undresses before the audience. ● *v.intr.* perform a striptease. ▫▫ **stripteaser** *n.*

stripy /strīpi/ *adj.* (**stripier, stripiest**) striped; having many stripes.

strive /strīv/ *v.intr.* (*past* **strove** /strōv/; *past part.* **striven** /strívv'n/) **1** (often foll. by *for*, or *to* + infin.) try hard, make efforts (*strive to succeed*). **2** (often foll. by *with, against*) struggle or contend. ▫▫ **striver** *n.* [ME f. OF *estriver*, rel. to *estrif* STRIFE]
■ **1** endeavour, strain, struggle, make an *or* every effort, take pains, attempt, work, try (hard), aim, do one's best *or* utmost; exert oneself, work at, give (it) one's all, go all out. **2** compete, contend, fight, struggle, battle.

strobe /strōb/ *n. colloq.* **1** a stroboscope. **2** a stroboscopic lamp. [abbr.]

strobila /strəbīlə/ *n.* (*pl.* **strobilae** /-lī/) **1** a chain of proglottids in a tapeworm. **2** a sessile polyp-like form which divides horizontally to produce jellyfish larvae. [mod.L f. Gk *strobilē* twisted lint-plug f. *strephō* twist]

strobile /strṓbīl/ *n.* **1** the cone of a pine etc. **2** the layered flower of the hop. [F *strobile* or LL *strobilus* f. Gk *strobilos* f. *strephō* twist]

strobilus /strṓbiləss/ *n.* (*pl.* **strobili** /-lī/) *Bot.* = STROBILE 1. [LL (as STROBILE)]

stroboscope /strṓbəskōp/ *n.* **1** *Physics* an instrument for determining speeds of rotation etc. by shining a bright light at intervals so that a rotating object appears stationary. **2** a lamp made to flash intermittently, esp. for this purpose. ▫▫ **stroboscopic** /-skóppik/ *adj.* **stroboscopical** /-skóppik'l/ *adj.* **stroboscopically** /-skóppikəli/ *adv.* [Gk *strobos* whirling + -SCOPE]

strode *past* of STRIDE.

Stroganoff /stróggənof/ *adj.* (of meat) cut into strips and cooked in sour-cream sauce (*beef Stroganoff*). [P. *Stroganoff*, 19th-c. Russ. diplomat]

stroke /strōk/ *n.* & *v.* ● *n.* **1** the act or an instance of striking; a blow or hit (*with a single stroke*; *a stroke of* *lightning*). **2** a sudden disabling attack or loss of consciousness caused by an interruption in the flow of blood to the brain, esp. through thrombosis; apoplexy. **3 a** an action or movement esp. as one of a series. **b** the time or way in which such movements are done. **c** the slightest such action (*has not done a stroke of work*). **4** the whole of the motion (of a wing, oar, etc.) until the starting-position is regained. **5** (in rowing) the mode or action of moving the oar (*row a fast stroke*). **6** the whole motion (of a piston) in either direction. **7** *Golf* the action of hitting (or hitting at) a ball with a club, as a unit of scoring. **8** a mode of moving the arms and legs in swimming. **9** a method of striking with the bat etc. in games etc. (*played some unorthodox strokes*). **10** a specially successful or skilful effort (*a stroke of diplomacy*). **11 a** a mark made by the movement in one direction of a pen or pencil or paintbrush. **b** a similar mark printed. **12** a detail contributing to the general effect in a description. **13** the sound made by a striking clock. **14** (in full **stroke oar**) the oar or oarsman nearest the stern, setting the time of the stroke. **15** the act or a spell of stroking. ● *v.tr.* **1** pass one's hand gently along the surface of (hair or fur etc.); caress lightly. **2** act as the stroke of (a boat or crew). □ **at a stroke** by a single action. **finishing stroke** a *coup de grâce*; a final and fatal stroke. **off one's stroke** not performing as well as usual. **on the stroke** punctually. **on the stroke of nine** etc. with the clock about to strike nine etc. **stroke a person down** appease a person's anger. **stroke of business** a profitable transaction. **stroke of genius** an original or strikingly successful idea. **stroke of luck** (or **good luck**) an unforeseen opportune occurrence. **stroke play** *Golf* play in which the score is reckoned by counting the number of strokes taken for the round (cf. *match play* (see MATCH[1])). **stroke a person** (or **a person's hair**) **the wrong way** irritate a person. [OE *strācian* f. Gmc, rel. to STRIKE]

■ *n.* **1** blow, rap, tap, thump, knock, hit, lash, smack, slam, strike, drive, *colloq.* whack, swipe, *sl.* wallop. **2** attack, seizure, fit, apoplexy, apoplectic fit, spasm, paralytic attack *or* fit; *Med.* embolism, thrombosis, cerebrovascular accident, aneurysm, ictus. **3 a** action, motion, go, move, movement, feat, achievement. **c** bit, jot (or tittle), scrap, iota, touch, stitch. **10** achievement, accomplishment; feat, act, action, work; example; touch. **11** flourish, movement, gesture; mark, dash, sweep. **15** pat, touch, caress, rub, massage. ● *v.* **1** caress, pet, pat, fondle; massage, rub, soothe. □ **at a stroke** see *at once* 1 (ONCE). **finishing stroke** see CLINCHER. **off one's stroke** not up to par. **stroke of luck** (or **good luck**) see FLUKE[1] *n.* **stroke a person** (or **a person's hair**) **the wrong way** see *rub up the wrong way* (RUB[1]).

stroll /strōl/ *v.* & *n.* ● *v.intr.* saunter or walk in a leisurely way. ● *n.* a short leisurely walk (*go for a stroll*). □ **strolling players** actors etc. going from place to place to give performances. [orig. of a vagrant, prob. f. G *strollen*, *strolchen* f. *Strolch* vagabond, of unkn. orig.]

■ *v.* amble, saunter, ramble, walk, wander, promenade, meander, *sl.* mosey. ● *n.* amble, ramble, saunter, walk, wander, promenade, meander, constitutional.

stroller /strṓlər/ *n.* **1** a person who strolls. **2** *US* a pushchair.

■ **1** see PEDESTRIAN *n.*

stroma /strṓmə/ *n.* (*pl.* **stromata** /-mətə/) *Biol.* **1** the framework of an organ or cell. **2** a fungous tissue containing spore-producing bodies. □□ **stromatic** /-máttik/ *adj.* [mod.L f. LL f. Gk *strōma* coverlet]

strong /strong/ *adj.* & *adv.* ● *adj.* (**stronger** /strónggər/; **strongest** /strónggist/) **1** having the power of resistance; able to withstand great force or opposition; not easily damaged or overcome (*strong material*; *strong faith*; *a strong character*). **2** (of a person's constitution) able to overcome, or not liable to, disease. **3** (of a person's nerves) proof against fright, irritation, etc. **4** (of a patient) restored to health. **5** (of an economy) stable and prosperous; (of a market) having steadily high or rising prices. **6** capable of exerting great force or of doing much; muscular, powerful. **7** forceful or powerful in effect (*a strong wind*; *a strong protest*). **8** decided or firmly held (*a strong suspicion*; *strong views*). **9** (of an argument etc.) convincing or striking. **10** powerfully affecting the senses or emotions (*a strong light*; *strong acting*). **11** powerful in terms of size or numbers or quality (*a strong army*). **12** capable of doing much when united (*a strong combination*). **13 a** formidable; likely to succeed (*a strong candidate*). **b** tending to assert or dominate (*a strong personality*). **14** (of a solution or drink etc.) containing a large proportion of a substance in water or another solvent (*strong tea*). **15** *Chem.* (of an acid or base) fully ionized into cations and anions in aqueous solution. **16** (of a group) having a specified number (*200 strong*). **17** (of a voice) loud or penetrating. **18** (of food or its flavour) pungent. **19** (esp. of a person's breath) ill-smelling. **20** (of a literary style) vivid and terse. **21** (of a measure) drastic. **22** *Gram.* in Germanic languages: **a** (of a verb) forming inflections by change of vowel within the stem rather than by the addition of a suffix (e.g. *swim, swam*). **b** (of a noun or adjective) belonging to a declension in which the stem originally ended otherwise than in *-n* (opp. WEAK 9). **23** having validity or credence (*a stong possibility*; *a strong chance*). **24** unmistakable, noticeable (*a strong resemblance*; *a strong accent*). ● *adv.* strongly (*the tide is running strong*). □ **come it strong** *colloq.* go to great lengths; use exaggeration. **going strong** *colloq.* continuing action vigorously; in good health or trim. **strong-arm** using force (*strong-arm tactics*). **strong drink** see DRINK. **strong grade** the stressed ablaut-form. **strong interaction** *Physics* interaction between certain elementary particles that is very strong but is effective only at short distances. **strong language** forceful language; swearing. **strong meat** a doctrine or action acceptable only to vigorous or instructed minds. **strong-minded** having determination. **strong-mindedness** determination. **strong point 1** a thing at which one excels. **2** a specially fortified defensive position. **strong stomach** a stomach not easily affected by nausea. **strong suit 1** a suit at cards in which one can take tricks. **2** a thing at which one excels. □□ **strongish** *adj.* **strongly** *adv.* [OE f. Gmc: cf. STRING]

■ *adj.* **1** solid, sturdy, substantial, stout, tough, sound, well-built, reinforced, heavy-duty, durable, indestructible, unbreakable, hard-wearing. **4** see HEALTHY 1. **5** steady, stable, firm, balanced, sound, solvent, resilient, buoyant; prosperous, flourishing, thriving. **6** powerful, muscular, mighty, brawny, strapping, robust, sturdy, stalwart, burly, stout, sinewy, wiry, beefy, hefty, husky. **7** vigorous, forceful, powerful, heavy; urgent, strongly-worded, emphatic, assertive; effective, efficacious, effectual, formidable. **8** firm, decided, definite, unshakeable, unwavering; deep-felt, deep-seated, deep-rooted, basic, intense, fervent, fierce, passionate, deep, earnest, keen. **9** well-supported, irrefutable, well-substantiated, cogent, forceful, powerful, potent, substantial, weighty, solid, convincing, persuasive, influential, compelling, telling, striking, conclusive. **10** dazzling, glaring, bright, garish, brilliant, vivid, bold, blinding; affecting, impressive, powerful, compelling. **11** large, considerable, great, sizeable, numerous; redoubtable, substantial, powerful, mighty, formidable; invincible, unconquerable; well-established, well-founded. **13 a** formidable, likely; competent, talented, able, experienced, efficient, capable. **b** forthright, positive, wilful, forceful, impressive, dominating, assertive; self-willed, opinionated, doctinaire, stubborn, obstinate, dogmatic. **14** concentrated, undiluted, potent, intensified; fortified, stiff, alcoholic. **16** numerically, in number, in strength. **17** see *penetrating* (PENETRATE 5b). **18** powerful, concentrated, intense, pungent, potent, sharp, piquant, acrid, heady, aromatic, fragrant, hot, spicy. **19** smelly, odoriferous, malodorous, stinking, foul, ill-smelling, evil-smelling, mephitic, putrid, putrescent, rotten, *archaic* miasmic, *Brit. colloq.* pongy, *literary* noisome, *Austral. sl.* on the nose. **20** pithy, forceful, racy, vigorous, sharp, trenchant, incisive, terse, vivid.

21 drastic, extreme, Draconian, high-handed, severe, forceful, rigorous, harsh, stringent, aggressive, strenuous, stiff, tough, *colloq.* hard-nosed. **23** likely, substantial, good, reasonable, better than average. **24** definite, clear-cut, clear, pronounced, distinct, striking, marked, decided, unmistakable, noticeable, obvious. □ **come it strong** see EXAGGERATE. **going strong** on good form, up to par. **strong-arm** threatening, menacing, bullying, high-pressure, thuggish, violent, brutal, brutish, aggressive, terrorist, intimidating. **strong language** cursing, swearing, bad language, profanity. **strong-minded** strong-willed, obstinate, firm, determined, tenacious, uncompromising, resolute, resolved, independent. **strong-mindedness** see *tenacity* (TENACIOUS). **strong point 1** see FORTE[1]. **strong suit 2** see FORTE[1]. □□ **strongly** see *deeply* (DEEP), *vigorously* (VIGOROUS).

strongbox /stróngboks/ *n.* a strongly made small chest for valuables.
■ see SAFE *n.*

stronghold /stróng-hōld/ *n.* **1** a fortified place. **2** a secure refuge. **3** a centre of support for a cause etc.
■ **1** fortress, bulwark, bastion, fastness, fortification, fort, citadel, garrison, castle. **2** see REFUGE 1, 2. **3** bastion, fortress, bulwark.

strongroom /stróngroom, -room/ *n.* a room designed to protect valuables against fire and theft.

strontia /strónshə/ *n. Chem.* strontium oxide. [*strontian* native strontium carbonate f. Strontian in the Highland Region of Scotland, where it was discovered]

strontium /stróntiəm/ *n. Chem.* a soft silver-white metallic element occurring naturally in various minerals. ¶ Symb.: **Sr.** □ **strontium-90** a radioactive isotope of strontium concentrated selectively in bones and teeth when taken into the body. **strontium oxide** a white compound used in the manufacture of fireworks. [STRONTIA + -IUM]

strop /strop/ *n.* & *v.* ● *n.* **1** a device, esp. a strip of leather, for sharpening razors. **2** *Naut.* a collar of leather or spliced rope or iron used for handling cargo. ● *v.tr.* (**stropped, stropping**) sharpen on or with a strop. [ME f. MDu., MLG *strop*, OHG *strupf*, WG f. L *stroppus*]
■ *v.* see SHARPEN.

strophanthin /strəfánthin/ *n.* a white crystalline poisonous glucoside extracted from various tropical plants of the genus *Strophanthus* and used as a heart-tonic. [mod.L *strophanthus* f. Gk *strophos* twisted cord + *anthos* flower]

strophe /strṓfi/ *n.* **1 a** a turn in dancing made by an ancient Greek chorus. **b** lines recited during this. **c** the first section of an ancient Greek choral ode or of one division of it. **2** a group of lines forming a section of a lyric poem. □□ **strophic** *adj.* [Gk *strophē*, lit. turning, f. *strephō* turn]

stroppy /stróppi/ *adj.* (**stroppier, stroppiest**) *Brit. colloq.* bad-tempered; awkward to deal with. □□ **stroppily** *adv.* **stroppiness** *n.* [20th c.: perh. abbr. of OBSTREPEROUS]
■ awkward, difficult; see also PERVERSE 3.

strove *past* of STRIVE.

strow /strō/ *v.tr.* (*past part.* **strown** /strōn/ or **strowed**) *archaic* = STREW. [var. of STREW]

struck *past* and *past part.* of STRIKE.

structural /strúkchərəl/ *adj.* of, concerning, or having a structure. □ **structural engineering** the branch of civil engineering concerned with large modern buildings etc. **structural formula** *Chem.* a formula showing the arrangement of atoms in the molecule of a compound. **structural linguistics** the study of language as a system of interrelated elements. **structural psychology** the study of the arrangement and composition of mental states and conscious experiences. **structural steel** strong mild steel in shapes suited to construction work. □□ **structurally** *adv.*
■ see ORGANIC 5.

structuralism /strúkchərəliz'm/ *n.* **1** the doctrine that structure rather than function is important. **2** structural linguistics. **3** structural psychology. □□ **structuralist** *n.* & *adj.*

structure /strúkchər/ *n.* & *v.* ● *n.* **1 a** a whole constructed unit, esp. a building. **b** the way in which a building etc. is constructed (*has a flimsy structure*). **2** a set of interconnecting parts of any complex thing; a framework (*the structure of a sentence; a new wages structure*). ● *v.tr.* give structure to; organize; frame. □□ **structured** *adj.* (also in *comb.*). **structureless** *adj.* [ME f. OF *structure* or L *structura* f. *struere struct-* build]
■ *n.* **1 a** building, edifice, house, construction. **b** construction, fabric, framework, design. **2** form, shape, configuration, construction, organization, arrangement, make-up, fabric, composition, constitution, framework, layout, order, design, formation; system, set-up, mechanism, nature, character. ● *v.* construct, build, frame, organize, design, form, shape, arrange, systematize. □□ **structured** see ORGANIC 6.

strudel /stroōd'l/ *n.* a confection of thin pastry rolled up round a filling and baked (*apple strudel*). [G]

struggle /strúgg'l/ *v.* & *n.* ● *v.intr.* **1** make forceful or violent efforts to get free of restraint or constriction. **2** (often foll. by *for*, or *to* + infin.) make violent or determined efforts under difficulties; strive hard (*struggled for supremacy; struggled to get the words out*). **3** (foll. by *with, against*) contend; fight strenuously (*struggled with the disease; struggled against superior numbers*). **4** (foll. by *along, up*, etc.) make one's way with difficulty (*struggled to my feet*). **5** (esp. as **struggling** *adj.*) have difficulty in gaining recognition or a living (*a struggling artist*). ● *n.* **1** the act or a spell of struggling. **2** a hard or confused contest. **3** a determined effort under difficulties. □ **the struggle for existence** (or **life**) the competition between organisms esp. as an element in natural selection, or between persons seeking a livelihood. □□ **struggler** *n.* [ME *strugle* frequent. of uncert. orig. (perh. imit.)]
■ *v.* **1, 2** strive, strain, expend energy, exert oneself, schlep, labour, toil, wrestle, endeavour, try, attempt; wriggle, squirm, writhe, twist, worm, *colloq.* wiggle. **3** contend, fight, wrestle, battle, war, grapple; tussle, scuffle. **4** see FLOUNDER[1] *v.*, SCRAMBLE *v.* 1. ● *n.* **1, 3** effort, exertion, strain, endeavour; toil, work, labour, drudgery, *esp. US* schlep, *literary* travail; trial, *colloq.* grind. **2** contention, competition, contest, battle, fight, combat, tussle, scrimmage, scuffle, match, conflict, clash, encounter.

strum /strum/ *v.* & *n.* ● *v.tr.* (**strummed, strumming**) **1** play on (a stringed or keyboard instrument), esp. carelessly or unskilfully. **2** play (a tune etc.) in this way. ● *n.* the sound made by strumming. □□ **strummer** *n.* [imit.: cf. THRUM[1]]

struma /stroōmə/ *n.* (*pl.* **strumae** /-mee/) **1** *Med.* **a** = SCROFULA. **b** = GOITRE. **2** *Bot.* a cushion-like swelling of an organ. □□ **strumose** *adj.* **strumous** *adj.* [L, = scrofulous tumour]

strumpet /strúmpit/ *n. archaic* or *rhet.* a prostitute. [ME: orig. unkn.]
■ see PROSTITUTE *n.* 1a.

strung *past* and *past part.* of STRING.

strut /strut/ *n.* & *v.* ● *n.* **1** a bar forming part of a framework and designed to resist compression. **2** a strutting gait. ● *v.* (**strutted, strutting**) **1** *intr.* walk with a pompous or affected stiff erect gait. **2** *tr.* brace with a strut or struts. □□ **strutter** *n.* **struttingly** *adv.* [ME 'bulge, swell, strive', earlier *stroute* f. OE *strūtian* be rigid (?)]
■ *n.* **1** see BRACE *n.* 1b. **2** prance, swagger. ● *v.* **1** swagger, parade, promenade, prance. **2** see BRACE *v.* 2.

'struth /stroōth/ *int.* (also **'strewth**) *colloq.* a mild oath. [*God's truth*]

struthious /stroōthiəss/ *adj.* of or like an ostrich. [L *struthio* ostrich]

strychnine /strikneen/ *n.* a vegetable alkaloid obtained from plants of the genus *Strychnos* (esp. nux vomica), bitter and highly poisonous, used as a stimulant and (in small amounts) a tonic. □□ **strychnic** *adj.* [F f. L *strychnos* f. Gk *strukhnos* a kind of nightshade]

Sts *abbr.* Saints.

Stuart /styo͞oərt/ *adj.* & *n.* ● *adj.* of or relating to the royal family ruling Scotland 1371–1714 and England 1603–1649 and 1660–1714. ● *n.* a member of this family.

stub /stub/ *n.* & *v.* ● *n.* **1** the remnant of a pencil or cigarette etc. after use. **2** the counterfoil of a cheque or receipt etc. **3** a stunted tail etc. **4** the stump of a tree, tooth, etc. **5** (*attrib.*) going only part of the way through (*stub-mortise*; *stub-tenon*). ● *v.tr.* (**stubbed, stubbing**) **1** strike (one's toe) against something. **2** (usu. foll. by *out*) extinguish (a lighted cigarette) by pressing the lighted end against something. **3** (foll. by *up*) grub up by the roots. **4** clear (land) of stubs. □ **stub-axle** an axle supporting only one wheel of a pair. [OE *stub*, *stubb* f. Gmc]

■ *n.* **1, 4** butt(-end), end, stump, tail(-end), remnant, *Brit. sl.* fag-end. **2** counterfoil, butt; tally, receipt, *esp. US* check. ● *v.* **1** bump, knock, hit, strike. **2** (*stub out*) extinguish, put out.

stubble /stúbb'l/ *n.* **1** the cut stalks of cereal plants left sticking up after the harvest. **2 a** cropped hair or a cropped beard. **b** a short growth of unshaven hair. □□ **stubbled** *adj.* **stubbly** *adj.* [ME f. AF *stuble*, OF *estuble* f. L *stupla*, *stupula* var. of *stipula* straw]

stubborn /stúbbərn/ *adj.* **1** unreasonably obstinate. **2** unyielding, obdurate, inflexible. **3** refractory, intractable. □□ **stubbornly** *adj.* **stubbornness** *n.* [ME *stiborn*, *stoburn*, etc., of unkn. orig.]

■ obstinate, unyielding, inflexible, obdurate, intransigent, intractable, uncompromising, mulish, pigheaded, adamant, bull-headed, headstrong, persistent, tenacious, pertinacious, unrelenting, dogged, determined, refractory, wayward, perverse, defiant, recalcitrant, disobedient. □□ **stubbornness** see *obstinacy* (OBSTINATE).

stubby /stúbbi/ *adj.* & *n.* ● *adj.* (**stubbier, stubbiest**) short and thick. ● *n.* (*pl.* **-ies**) *Austral. colloq.* a small squat bottle of beer. □□ **stubbily** *adv.* **stubbiness** *n.*

■ *adj.* see SHORT *adj.* 2. ● *n.* see JAR[1] 2.

stucco /stúkkō/ *n.* & *v.* ● *n.* (*pl.* **-oes**) plaster or cement used for coating wall surfaces or moulding into architectural decorations. ● *v.tr.* (**-oes, -oed**) coat with stucco. [It., of Gmc orig.]

stuck *past* and *past part.* of STICK[2].

stuck-up see STICK[2].

stud[1] /stud/ *n.* & *v.* ● *n.* **1** a large-headed nail, boss, or knob, projecting from a surface esp. for ornament. **2** a double button esp. for use with two buttonholes in a shirt-front. **3** a small object projecting slightly from a road-surface as a marker etc. **4** a rivet or crosspiece in each link of a chain-cable. **5 a** a post to which laths are nailed. **b** *US* the height of a room as indicated by the length of this. ● *v.tr.* (**studded, studding**) **1** set with or as with studs. **2** (as **studded** *adj.*) (foll. by *with*) thickly set or strewn (*studded with diamonds*). **3** be scattered over or about (a surface). [OE *studu*, *stuthu* post, prop, rel. to G *stützen* to prop]

■ **1** see KNOB *n.* 1a. **5 a** see BEAM *n.* 1.

stud[2] /stud/ *n.* **1 a** a number of horses kept for breeding etc. **b** a place where these are kept. **2** (in full **stud-horse**) a stallion. **3** *colloq.* a young man (esp. one noted for sexual prowess). **4** (in full **stud poker**) a form of poker with betting after the dealing of successive rounds of cards face up. □ **at stud** (of a male horse) publicly available for breeding on payment of a fee. **stud-book** a book containing the pedigrees of horses. **stud-farm** a place where horses are bred. [OE *stōd* f. Gmc: rel. to STAND]

■ **3** see *philanderer* (PHILANDER).

studding /stúdding/ *n.* the woodwork of a lath-and-plaster wall.

studding-sail /stúns'l/ *n.* a sail set on a small extra yard and boom beyond the leech of a square sail in light winds. [16th c.: orig. uncert.: perh. f. MLG, MDu. *stōtinge* a thrusting]

student /styo͞od'nt/ *n.* **1** a person who is studying, esp. at university or another place of higher education. **2** (*attrib.*) studying in order to become (*a student nurse*). **3** a person of studious habits. **4** *Brit.* a graduate recipient of a stipend from the foundation of a college, esp. a fellow of Christ Church, Oxford. □□ **studentship** *n.* [ME f. L *studēre* f. *studium* STUDY]

■ **1** pupil, learner, undergraduate, postgraduate, schoolboy, schoolgirl, schoolchild, trainee, apprentice, disciple, protégé, *archaic* scholar. **3** *Brit. colloq.* swot, *US colloq.* grind.

studio /styo͞odiō/ *n.* (*pl.* **-os**) **1** the workroom of a painter or photographer etc. **2** a place where cinema films or recordings are made or where television or radio programmes are made or produced. □ **studio couch** a couch that can be converted into a bed. **studio flat** a flat containing a room suitable as an artist's studio, or only one main room. [It. f. L (as STUDY)]

■ **1** see STUDY *n.* 3.

studious /styo͞odiəss/ *adj.* **1** devoted to or assiduous in study or reading. **2** studied, deliberate, painstaking (*with studious care*). **3** (foll. by *to* + infin. or *in* + verbal noun) showing care or attention. **4** (foll. by *of* + verbal noun) anxiously desirous. □□ **studiously** *adv.* **studiousness** *n.* [ME f. L *studiosus* (as STUDY)]

■ **1** scholarly, bookish, academic. **2, 3** assiduous, sedulous, diligent, industrious, attentive, careful, painstaking, thorough, deliberate, tireless; see also *studied* (STUDY *v.* 6). □□ **studiously** see *intently* (INTENT).

study /stúddi/ *n.* & *v.* ● *n.* (*pl.* **-ies**) **1** the devotion of time and attention to acquiring information or knowledge, esp. from books. **2** (in *pl.*) the pursuit of academic knowledge (*continued their studies abroad*). **3** a room used for reading, writing, etc. **4** a piece of work, esp. a drawing, done for practice or as an experiment (*a study of a head*). **5** the portrayal in literature or another art form of an aspect of behaviour or character etc. **6** a musical composition designed to develop a player's skill. **7** a thing worth observing closely (*your face was a study*). **8** a thing that has been or deserves to be investigated. **9** *Theatr.* **a** the act of memorizing a role. **b** a person who memorizes a role. **10** *archaic* a thing to be secured by pains or attention. ● *v.* (**-ies, -ied**) **1** *tr.* make a study of; investigate or examine (a subject) (*study law*). **2** *intr.* (often foll. by *for*) apply oneself to study. **3** *tr.* scrutinize or earnestly contemplate (*studied their faces*; *studying the problem*). **4** *tr.* try to learn (the words of one's role etc.). **5** *tr.* take pains to achieve (a result) or pay regard to (a subject or principle etc.). **6** *tr.* (as **studied** *adj.*) deliberate, intentional, affected (*with studied politeness*). **7** *tr.* read (a book) attentively. **8** *tr.* (foll. by *to* + infin.) *archaic* **a** be on the watch. **b** try constantly to manage. □ **in a brown study** in a reverie; absorbed in one's thoughts. **make a study of** investigate carefully. **study group** a group of people meeting from time to time to study a particular subject or topic. □□ **studiedly** *adv.* **studiedness** *n.* [ME f. OF *estudie* f. L *studium* zeal, study]

■ *n.* **1, 2** learning, lessons, schooling, education, training, instruction, bookwork, work, reading, contemplation, investigation, research, cramming, *colloq.* boning up, *Brit. colloq.* swotting. **3** library, reading-room, writing-room, haunt, studio, retreat, den, workroom, office, *colloq.* sanctum. **4, 5** see PORTRAIT 1, 2. **8** project, programme; analysis, review, examination, survey, enquiry, investigation, research, exploration. ● *v.* **1, 3** make a study of, look into *or* over *or* at, go into *or* over, scan, examine, analyse, inspect, investigate, scrutinize, survey, monitor, observe, contemplate; learn (about), read; consider, reflect on, think over *or* about, ruminate on, chew over, turn over, weigh, ponder, deliberate over *or* on *or* about, mull over, meditate on *or* about *or* over, *literary* muse about *or* on. **2** burn the midnight oil, cram, *colloq.* bone up, *Brit. colloq.* swot, *literary* lucubrate. **4** memorize, practise, rehearse, go over, run through, learn (by heart), *archaic* con; *colloq.* bone up on, *Brit. colloq.* swot (up), *Brit. sl.* mug up. **5** pay *or* give regard *or* attention to, give thought to, consider.

6 (**studied**) premeditated, deliberate, calculated, measured, planned, intentional, wilful, well-thought-out, conscious, contrived, feigned, affected, forced, laboured. **7** see EXAMINE 1, 2. □ **in a brown study** see PENSIVE 1. **make a study of** see STUDY *v.* 1, 3 above.

stuff /stuf/ *n.* & *v.* ● *n.* **1** the material that a thing is made of; material that may be used for some purpose. **2** a substance or things or belongings of an indeterminate kind or a quality not needing to be specified (*there's a lot of stuff about it in the newspapers*). **3** a particular knowledge or activity (*know one's stuff*). **4** woollen fabric (esp. as distinct from silk, cotton, and linen). **5** valueless matter, trash, refuse, nonsense (*take that stuff away*). **6** (prec. by *the*) **a** *colloq.* an available supply of something, esp. drink or drugs. **b** *sl.* money. ● *v.* **1** *tr.* pack (a receptacle) tightly (*stuff a cushion with feathers; a head stuffed with weird notions*). **2** *tr.* (foll. by *in, into*) force or cram (a thing) (*stuffed the socks in the drawer*). **3** *tr.* fill out the skin of (an animal or bird etc.) with material to restore the original shape (*a stuffed owl*). **4** *tr.* fill (poultry etc.) with a savoury or sweet mixture, esp. before cooking. **5 a** *tr.* & *refl.* fill (a person or oneself) with food. **b** *tr.* & *intr.* eat greedily. **6** *tr.* push, esp. hastily or clumsily (*stuffed the note behind the cushion*). **7** *tr.* (usu. in *passive*; foll. by *up*) block up (a person's nose etc.). **8** *tr. sl.* (esp. as an expression of contemptuous dismissal) dispose of as unwanted (*you can stuff the job*). **9** *tr. US* place bogus votes in (a ballot-box). **10** *tr. coarse sl. offens.* have sexual intercourse with (a woman). □ **bit of stuff** *sl. offens.* a woman regarded as an object of sexual desire. **do one's stuff** *colloq.* do what one has to. **get stuffed** *sl.* an exclamation of dismissal, contempt, etc. **stuff and nonsense** an exclamation of incredulity or ridicule. **stuffed shirt** *colloq.* a pompous person. **stuff gown** *Brit.* a gown worn by a barrister who has not taken silk. **stuff it** *sl.* an expression of rejection or disdain. **that's the stuff** *colloq.* that is what is wanted. □□ **stuffer** *n.* (also in *comb.*). [ME *stoffe* f. OF *estoffe* (n.), *estoffer* (v.) equip, furnish f. Gk *stuphō* draw together]

■ *n.* **1** substance, material, matter, fabric, ingredients, constituents, essence, essentials, fundamentals, building blocks, makings. **2** matter, substance, material; things, articles, objects, creations, accomplishments, works; bits and pieces, goods, gear, equipment, materials, trappings, kit, tackle, accessories, paraphernalia, accoutrements, effects, belongings, possessions, impedimenta, baggage, property, chattels, lumber, junk, *esp. Brit.* rubbish, *colloq.* traps, *Brit. sl.* clobber. **5** refuse, *esp. Brit.* rubbish, junk; garbage; trash; nonsense, stuff and nonsense, twaddle, humbug, bunkum, balderdash, claptrap, drivel, *colloq.* tripe, malarkey, hogwash, piffle, flapdoodle, *sl.* poppycock, bunk, boloney, bosh, bull, rot, tommy-rot, *Brit. sl.* codswallop. **6 b** see MONEY 1. ● *v.* **1, 3, 4** line, fill, pack, pad. **2** jam, ram, cram, crowd, compress, pack, press, squeeze, squash, shove, thrust, force. **5 a** fill, overfeed, satiate, glut, surfeit, pall; (*stuff oneself*) overeat, gorge, overindulge, gormandize, gluttonize, make a pig *or* hog of oneself. **b** see DEVOUR 1. **6** push, shove, thrust, *colloq.* stick, stash, *Brit. colloq.* bung. **7** (*stuff up*) clog (up), congest, block (up), bung up; choke, plug (up), obstruct, stop up. □ **bit of stuff** see *bit of fluff* (FLUFF). **get stuffed** *colloq.* shut up, *sl.* go take a running jump, get knotted. **stuffed shirt** see PRIG.

stuffing /stúffing/ *n.* **1** padding used to stuff cushions etc. **2** a mixture used to stuff poultry etc., esp. before cooking. □ **knock** (or **take**) **the stuffing out of** *colloq.* make feeble or weak; defeat. **stuffing-box** a box packed with material, to allow the working of an axle while remaining airtight.

■ **1** see PAD[1] *n.* 1.

stuffy /stúffi/ *adj.* (**stuffier, stuffiest**) **1** (of a room or the atmosphere in it) lacking fresh air or ventilation; close. **2** dull or uninteresting. **3** (of a person's nose etc.) stuffed up. **4** (of a person) dull and conventional. □□ **stuffily** *adv.* **stuffiness** *n.*

■ **1** close, airless, unventilated, oppressive, stifling, suffocating, stale, musty, fusty, mouldy, mildewy, muggy, fetid, frowzy, *Brit.* frowsty, *colloq.* fuggy. **2** dull, dreary, uninteresting; see also BORING. **3** stuffed up, blocked up, congested, clogged up. **4** pompous, pedantic, narrow-minded, self-important, self-centred, stodgy, dull, old-fogyish, old-fashioned, strait-laced, staid, conventional, prim (and proper), priggish, niminy-piminy, stilted, stiff, rigid, formal, *US colloq.* uptight, *sl.* fuddy-duddy, square.

stultify /stúltifī/ *v.tr.* (**-ies, -ied**) **1** make ineffective, useless, or futile, esp. as a result of tedious routine (*stultifying boredom*). **2** cause to appear foolish or absurd. **3** negate or neutralize. □□ **stultification** /-fikáysh'n/ *n.* **stultifier** *n.* [LL *stultificare* f. L *stultus* foolish]

stum /stum/ *n.* & *v.* ● *n.* unfermented grape-juice; must. ● *v.tr.* (**stummed, stumming**) **1** prevent from fermenting, or secure (wine) against further fermentation in a cask, by the use of sulphur etc. **2** renew the fermentation of (wine) by adding stum. [Du. *stommen* (v.), *stom* (n.) f. *stom* (adj.) dumb]

stumble /stúmb'l/ *v.* & *n.* ● *v.* **1** *intr.* lurch forward or have a partial fall from catching or striking or misplacing one's foot. **2** *intr.* (often foll. by *along*) walk with repeated stumbles. **3** *intr.* make a mistake or repeated mistakes in speaking etc. **4** *intr.* (foll. by *on, upon, across*) find or encounter by chance (*stumbled on a disused well*). ● *n.* an act of stumbling. □ **stumbling-block** an obstacle or circumstance causing difficulty or hesitation. □□ **stumbler** *n.* **stumblingly** *adv.* [ME *stumble* (with euphonic *b*) corresp. to Norw. *stumla*: rel. to STAMMER]

■ *v.* **1** miss one's footing, slip, trip, stagger, lurch, flounder, totter, tumble, fall, falter. **2** see HOBBLE *v.* 1. **3** pause, hesitate, stammer, stutter, blunder. **4** (*stumble on* or *upon* or *across*) chance *or* come *or* happen (up)on, hit *or* light (up)on, come *or* run across, find, discover, encounter, *colloq.* bump into. ● *n.* see TRIP *n.* 2. □ **stumbling-block** impediment, obstacle, bar, block, obstruction, hurdle, hindrance, baulk, barrier, difficulty, snag.

stumblebum /stúmb'lbum/ *n. US colloq.* a clumsy or inept person.

stumer /styóomər/ *n. Brit. sl.* **1** a worthless cheque; a counterfeit coin or note. **2** a sham or fraud. **3** a failure. [19th c.: orig. unkn.]

stump /stump/ *n.* & *v.* ● *n.* **1** the projecting remnant of a cut or fallen tree. **2** the similar remnant of anything else (e.g. a branch or limb) cut off or worn down. **3** *Cricket* each of the three uprights of a wicket. **4** (in *pl.*) *joc.* the legs. **5** the stump of a tree, or other place, used by an orator to address a meeting. **6** a cylinder of rolled paper or other material with conical ends for softening pencil-marks and other uses in drawing. ● *v.* **1** *tr.* (of a question etc.) be too hard for; puzzle. **2** *tr.* (as **stumped** *adj.*) at a loss; baffled. **3** *tr. Cricket* (esp. of a wicket-keeper) put (a batsman) out by touching the stumps with the ball while the batsman is out of the crease. **4** *intr.* walk stiffly or noisily as on a wooden leg. **5** *tr.* (also *absol.*) *US* traverse (a district) making political speeches. **6** *tr.* use a stump on (a drawing, line, etc.). □ **on the stump** *colloq.* engaged in political speech-making or agitation. **stump up** *Brit. colloq.* pay or produce (the money required). **up a stump** *US* in difficulties. [ME *stompe* f. MDu. *stomp*, OHG *stumpf*]

■ *n.* **1, 2** stub, butt, end, remnant. **4** (*stumps*) see LEG *n.* 1, 3. ● *v.* **1** be beyond, mystify, confuse, perplex, bewilder, foil, puzzle, baffle, confound, dumbfound, stop, stymie, nonplus, bring up short, catch out, *colloq.* flummox, throw. **2** (**stumped**) see *confused* (CONFUSE 4b). **5** campaign, electioneer, canvass, *US* barnstorm. □ **stump up** pay up *or* out, contribute, donate, *colloq.* chip in, shell out, *sl.* cough up, fork out *or* up. **up a stump** see *in trouble* 1 (TROUBLE).

stumper /stúmpər/ *n. colloq.* **1** a puzzling question. **2** a wicket-keeper.

stumpy /stúmpi/ *adj.* (**stumpier**, **stumpiest**) short and thick. ▫▫ **stumpily** *adv.* **stumpiness** *n.*
■ see STOCKY.

stun /stun/ *v.tr.* (**stunned**, **stunning**) **1** knock senseless; stupefy. **2** bewilder or shock. **3** (of a sound) deafen temporarily. [ME f. OF *estoner* ASTONISH]
■ **1** daze, numb, benumb, knock out; stupefy, paralyse. **2** astonish, daze, paralyse, stagger, stupefy, transfix, overcome, overwhelm, astound, jar, shock, jolt, strike dumb, dumbfound, amaze, confound, bewilder, disconcert, take a person's breath away, shake up, *colloq.* bowl over, flabbergast, *US joc.* discombobulate.

stung *past* and *past part.* of STING.

stunk *past* and *past part.* of STINK.

stunner /stúnnər/ *n. colloq.* a stunning person or thing.
■ see KNOCKOUT 4.

stunning /stúnning/ *adj. colloq.* extremely impressive or attractive. ▫▫ **stunningly** *adv.*
■ beautiful, dazzling, brilliant, spectacular, ravishing, sensational, extraordinary, impressive, prodigious, remarkable, marvellous, stupendous, wonderful, superb, grand, sublime, lovely, exquisite, glorious, astonishing, astounding, amazing, striking, splendid, phenomenal, staggering, overpowering, earth-shattering, earth-shaking, magnificent, *colloq.* fabulous, fantastic, mind-boggling, gorgeous, divine, heavenly, super. ▫▫ **stunningly** see *notably* (NOTABLE).

stunsail /stúns'l/ *n.* (also **stuns'l**) = STUDDING-SAIL.

stunt[1] /stunt/ *v.tr.* **1** retard the growth or development of. **2** dwarf, cramp. ▫▫ **stuntedness** *n.* [*stunt* foolish (now dial.), MHG *stunz*, ON *stuttr* short f. Gmc, perh. rel. to STUMP]
■ **1** impede, hamper, hinder, inhibit, slow (down), retard. **2** dwarf, cramp, limit, delimit, restrict, check, curb, stop, arrest, put an end to, end.

stunt[2] /stunt/ *n.* & *v.* • *n.* **1** something unusual done to attract attention. **2** a trick or daring manoeuvre. **3** a display of concentrated energy. • *v.intr.* perform stunts, esp. aerobatics. ▫ **stunt man** a man employed to take an actor's place in performing dangerous stunts. [orig. unkn.: first used in 19th-c. US college athletics]
■ *n.* **1, 2** feat, act, deed, *tour de force*, exploit, trick.

stupa /stóopə/ *n.* a round usu. domed building erected as a Buddhist shrine. [Skr. *stūpa*]

stupe[1] /styoop/ *n.* & *v.* • *n.* a flannel etc. soaked in hot water, wrung out, and applied as a fomentation. • *v.tr.* treat with this. [ME f. L f. Gk *stupē* tow]

stupe[2] /styoop/ *n. sl.* a foolish or stupid person.

stupefy /styóopifī/ *v.tr.* (**-ies**, **-ied**) **1** make stupid or insensible (*stupefied with drink*). **2** stun with astonishment (*the news was stupefying*). ▫▫ **stupefacient** /-fáysh'nt/ *adj.* & *n.* **stupefaction** /-fáksh'n/ *n.* **stupefactive** *adj.* **stupefier** *n.* **stupefying** *adj.* **stupefyingly** *adv.* [F *stupéfier* f. L *stupefacere* f. *stupēre* be amazed]
■ **1** see DRUG *v.* 2b. **2** see STUN 2. ▫▫ **stupefacient** (*adj.*) see NARCOTIC *adj.* (*n.*) see NARCOTIC *n.* **stupefaction** see *astonishment* (ASTONISH). **stupefactive** see NARCOTIC *adj.* **stupefying** see NARCOTIC *adj.*, OVERWHELMING.

stupendous /styoopéndəss/ *adj.* amazing or prodigious, esp. in terms of size or degree (*a stupendous achievement*). ▫▫ **stupendously** *adv.* **stupendousness** *n.* [L *stupendus* gerundive of *stupēre* be amazed at]
■ see *amazing* (AMAZE).

stupid /styóopid/ *adj.* & *n.* (**stupider**, **stupidest**) • *adj.* **1** unintelligent, slow-witted, foolish (*a stupid fellow*). **2** typical of stupid persons (*put it in a stupid place*). **3** uninteresting or boring. **4** in a state of stupor or lethargy. **5** obtuse; lacking in sensibility. • *n. colloq.* a stupid person. ▫▫ **stupidity** /-pídditi/ *n.* (*pl.* **-ies**). **stupidly** *adv.* [F *stupide* or L *stupidus* (as STUPENDOUS)]
■ *adj.* **1, 5** unintelligent, fatuous, foolish, obtuse, bovine, dull, lumpish, doltish, cloddish, simple, simple-minded, *colloq.* moronic, imbecilic, cretinous; subnormal, feeble-minded, weak-minded, stolid, dull-witted, thick-witted, thick-skulled, slow-witted, witless, brainless, mindless, empty-headed, feather-brained, feather-headed, ox-like, addle-brained, addled, imbecile, *colloq.* dopey, dim, dim-witted, halfwitted, thick, thickheaded, dense, pinheaded, birdbrained, *esp. Brit. colloq.* gormless, *Brit. colloq.* dozy, *esp. US colloq.* dumb, *sl.* boneheaded, *Austral. sl.* dilly. **2** foolish, silly, frivolous, asinine, hare-brained, insane, mad, scatterbrained, absurd, inane, idiotic, lunatic, ridiculous, risible, laughable, ludicrous, nonsensical, senseless, irresponsible, irrational, ill-advised, imprudent, unwise, foolhardy, half-baked, *colloq.* crazy, crack-brained, cock-eyed, *esp. Brit. colloq.* daft, *sl.* cuckoo, *esp. Brit. sl.* barmy. **3** insipid, dull, tedious, boring, tiresome, humdrum, prosaic, monotonous, unimaginative, uninspired, uninteresting, vapid, vacuous, *colloq.* ho-hum. **4** stupefied, stunned, dazed, senseless, insensible, unconscious, semi-conscious, sluggish, lethargic. ▫▫ **stupidity** fatuity, fatuousness, obtuseness, dullness, denseness, lumpishness, doltishness, simplicity, simple-mindedness, feeble-mindedness, weak-mindedness, stolidity, dull-wittedness, thick-wittedness, slow-wittedness, witlessness, brainlessness, mindlessness, empty-headedness, feather-headedness, *archaic* bootlessness, *colloq.* dimness, dim-wittedness, halfwittedness, thickheadedness, dopiness, imbecility, cretinism, *Brit. colloq.* doziness, *sl.* boneheadedness; foolishness, folly, asininity, insanity, madness, absurdity, absurdness, inanity, idiocy, silliness, ridiculousness, risibility, ludicrousness, nonsense, senselessness, irresponsibility, irrationality, foolhardiness, *colloq.* craziness. **stupidly** see MADLY 1.

stupor /styóopər/ *n.* a dazed, torpid, or helplessly amazed state. ▫▫ **stuporous** *adj.* [ME f. L (as STUPENDOUS)]
■ insensibility, stupefaction, torpor, torpidity, lethargy, listlessness, languor, laziness, lassitude, lifelessness, supineness, inertia; inertness, coma, trance, daze, unconsciousness, numbness. ▫▫ **stuporous** see LETHARGIC 1.

sturdy /stúrdi/ *adj.* & *n.* • *adj.* (**sturdier**, **sturdiest**) **1** robust; strongly built. **2** vigorous and determined (*sturdy resistance*). • *n.* vertigo in sheep caused by a tapeworm larva encysted in the brain. ▫▫ **sturdied** *adj.* (in sense of *n.*). **sturdily** *adv.* **sturdiness** *n.* [ME 'reckless, violent', f. OF *esturdi*, *estourdi* past part. of *estourdir* stun, daze ult. f. L *ex* EX-[1] + *turdus* thrush (taken as a type of drunkenness)]
■ *adj.* **1** strong, solid, stout, rugged, tough, well-built, substantial, well-made; sound, durable; strapping, muscular, powerful, brawny, burly, robust, well-muscled, athletic, hardy, husky, hefty, stocky. **2** stalwart, staunch, steadfast, resolute, firm, vigorous, determined, uncompromising, unyielding, unwavering, unswerving, unfaltering, enduring, indomitable. • *n.* see VERTIGO. ▫▫ **sturdiness** see BACKBONE 3, STRENGTH 1.

sturgeon /stúrjən/ *n.* any large mailed sharklike fish of the family Acipenseridae etc. swimming up river to spawn, used as food and a source of caviare and isinglass. [ME f. AF *sturgeon*, OF *esturgeon* ult. f. Gmc]

Sturm und Drang /shtoorm oont dráng/ *n.* a literary and artistic movement in Germany in the late 18th c., characterized by the expression of emotional unrest and strong feeling. [G, = storm and stress]

stutter /stúttər/ *v.* & *n.* • *v.* **1** *intr.* stammer, esp. by involuntarily repeating the first consonants of words. **2** *tr.* (often foll. by *out*) utter (words) in this way. • *n.* **1** the act or habit of stuttering. **2** an instance of stuttering. ▫▫ **stutterer** *n.* **stutteringly** *adv.* [frequent. of ME (now dial.) *stut* f. Gmc]
■ *v.* see STAMMER *v.* • *n.* see STAMMER *n.*

sty[1] /stī/ *n.* & *v.* • *n.* (*pl.* **sties**) **1** a pen or enclosure for pigs. **2** a filthy room or dwelling. **3** a place of debauchery. • *v.tr.* & *intr.* (**sties**, **stied**) lodge in a sty. [OE *stī*, prob. = *stig* hall (cf. STEWARD), f. Gmc]

■ *n.* **1** see ENCLOSURE 2. **2** slum, *colloq.* dump, hole, hell-hole.

sty[2] /stī/ *n.* (also **stye**) (*pl.* **sties** or **styes**) an inflamed swelling on the edge of an eyelid. [*styany* (now dial.) = *styan eye* f. OE *stīgend* sty, lit. 'riser' f. *stīgan* rise + EYE, shortened as if = *sty on eye*]

Stygian /stíjiən/ *adj.* **1** (in Greek mythology) of or relating to the Styx, a river in Hades. **2** *literary* dark, gloomy, indistinct. [L *stugius* f. Gk *stugios* f. *Stux -ugos* Styx f. *stugnos* hateful, gloomy]
■ **2** see GLOOMY 1.

style /stīl/ *n.* & *v.* ● *n.* **1** a kind or sort, esp. in regard to appearance and form (*an elegant style of house*). **2** a manner of writing or speaking or performing (*written in a florid style*; *started off in fine style*). **3** the distinctive manner of a person or school or period, esp. in relation to painting, architecture, furniture, dress, etc. **4** the correct way of designating a person or thing. **5 a** a superior quality or manner (*do it in style*). **b** = FORM *n.* 9 (*bad style*). **6** a particular make, shape, or pattern (*in all sizes and styles*). **7** a method of reckoning dates (*old style*; *new style*). **8 a** an ancient writing-implement, a small rod with a pointed end for scratching letters on wax-covered tablets and a blunt end for obliterating them. **b** a thing of a similar shape esp. for engraving, tracing, etc. **9** the gnomon of a sundial. **10** *Bot.* the narrow extension of the ovary supporting the stigma. **11** (in *comb.*) = -WISE. ● *v.tr.* **1** design or make etc. in a particular (esp. fashionable) style. **2** designate in a specified way. □□ **styleless** *adj.* **stylelessness** *n.* **styler** *n.* [ME f. OF *stile*, *style* f. L *stilus*: spelling *style* due to assoc. with Gk *stulos* column]
■ *n.* **1, 6** type, kind, variety, category, genre, sort, manner, mode, make, design, fashion, look, pattern, configuration, line, cut, shape, form, version. **2, 3** quality, character, approach, treatment, vein, colouring, spirit, mood, form, technique, way, manner, method; tenor, tone, wording, phraseology, phrasing, mode of expression, language, vocabulary, word choice, diction, sentence structure; presentation; fashion, trend, vogue, mode, look, rage, craze, fad, *colloq.* (latest) thing. **4** see NAME *n.* 1, 2. **5 a** chic, stylishness, taste, smartness, flair, dash, *élan*, panache, cachet, tastefulness, fashionableness, elegance, refinement, finesse, polish, sophistication, sophisticatedness, cosmopolitanism; luxury, high style, comfort, opulence, splendour; *colloq.* class, ritziness, *sl.* pizazz. **8, 9** stylus. ● *v.* **1** fashion, design, arrange, set, do, cut, tailor, shape, form. **2** characterize, designate, denominate, call, name, term, label, tag, brand, title, *archaic* entitle.

stylet /stīlit/ *n.* **1** a slender pointed instrument; a stiletto. **2** *Med.* the stiffening wire of a catheter; a probe. [F *stilet* f. It. STILETTO]

styli *pl.* of STYLUS.

stylish /stīlish/ *adj.* **1** fashionable; elegant. **2** having a superior quality, manner, etc. □□ **stylishly** *adv.* **stylishness** *n.*
■ **1** chic, fashionable, smart, à la mode, modish, in style *or* fashion *or* vogue, elegant, neat, dapper; chichi, in, *colloq.* with it, classy, swanky, swell, natty, swagger, *colloq. often derog.* trendy, *sl.* snazzy, *esp. US sl.* spiffy. **2** see POSH *adj.* 1. □□ **stylishness** see STYLE *n.* 5a.

stylist /stīlist/ *n.* **1 a** a designer of fashionable styles etc. **b** a hairdresser. **2 a** a writer noted for or aspiring to good literary style. **b** (in sport or music) a person who performs with style.

stylistic /stīlistik/ *adj.* of or concerning esp. literary style. □□ **stylistically** *adv.* [STYLIST + -IC, after G *stilistisch*]
■ see RHETORICAL 2, 3.

stylistics /stīlistiks/ *n.* the study of literary style.

stylite /stīlīt/ *n. Eccl. hist.* an ancient or medieval ascetic living on top of a pillar. [eccl.Gk *stulitēs* f. *stulos* pillar]

stylize /stīlīz/ *v.tr.* (also **-ise**) (esp. as **stylized** *adj.*) paint, draw, etc. (a subject) in a conventional non-realistic style. □□ **stylization** /-záysh'n/ *n.* [STYLE + -IZE, after G *stilisieren*]

stylo /stīlō/ *n.* (*pl.* **-os**) *colloq.* = STYLOGRAPH. [abbr.]

stylobate /stīləbayt/ *n. Archit.* a continuous base supporting a row of columns. [L *stylobata* f. Gk *stulobatēs* f. *stulos* pillar, *bainō* walk]

stylograph /stīləgraaf/ *n.* a kind of fountain pen having a point instead of a split nib. □□ **stylographic** /-gráffik/ *adj.* [STYLUS + -GRAPH]

styloid /stīloyd/ *adj.* & *n.* ● *adj.* resembling a stylus or pen. ● *n.* (in full **styloid process**) a spine of bone, esp. that projecting from the base of the temporal bone. [mod.L *styloides* f. Gk *stuloeidēs* f. *stulos* pillar]

stylus /stīləss/ *n.* (*pl.* **-li** /-lī/ or **-luses**) **1 a** a hard, esp. diamond or sapphire, point following a groove in a gramophone record and transmitting the recorded sound for reproduction. **b** a similar point producing such a groove when recording sound. **2** = STYLE *n.* 8, 9. [erron. spelling of L *stilus*: cf. STYLE]

stymie /stīmi/ *n.* & *v.* (also **stimy**) ● *n.* (*pl.* **-ies**) **1** *Golf* a situation where an opponent's ball lies between the player and the hole, forming a possible obstruction to play (*lay a stymie*). **2** a difficult situation. ● *v.tr.* (**stymies**, **stymied**, **stymying** or **stymieing**) **1** obstruct; thwart. **2** *Golf* block (an opponent, his ball, or oneself) with a stymie. [19th c.: orig. unkn.]
■ *n.* **2** see DILEMMA 3. ● *v.* **1** thwart, obstruct, block, frustrate, defeat, spike, ruin, foil, confound, stump, nonplus, hinder, impede, *colloq.* flummox, *sl.* snooker.

styptic /stíptik/ *adj.* & *n.* ● *adj.* (of a drug etc.) that checks bleeding. ● *n.* a styptic drug or substance. [ME f. L *stypticus* f. Gk *stuptikos* f. *stuphō* contract]

styrax /stīraks/ *n.* **1** storax resin. **2** any tree or shrub of the genus *Styrax*, e.g. the storax-tree. [L f. Gk *sturax*: cf. STORAX]

styrene /stīreen/ *n. Chem.* a liquid hydrocarbon easily polymerized and used in making plastics etc. [STYRAX + -ENE]

suable /sóōəb'l, syóō-/ *adj.* capable of being sued. □□ **suability** /-bílliti/ *n.*

suasion /swáyzh'n/ *n. formal* persuasion as opposed to force (*moral suasion*). □□ **suasive** /swáysiv/ *adj.* [ME f. OF *suasion* or L *suasio* f. *suadēre suas-* urge]

suave /swaav/ *adj.* **1** (of a person, esp. a man) smooth; polite; sophisticated. **2** (of a wine etc.) bland, smooth. □□ **suavely** *adv.* **suaveness** *n.* **suavity** /-viti/ *n.* (*pl.* **-ies**). [F *suave* or L *suavis* agreeable: cf. SWEET]
■ **1** debonair, sophisticated, urbane, cosmopolitan, worldly, smooth, gracious, nonchalant, civilized, cultivated, well-bred, courteous, diplomatic, polite, charming, agreeable, affable, bland. **2** see SMOOTH *adj.* 8b. □□ **suaveness, suavity** see REFINEMENT 3.

sub /sub/ *n.* & *v. colloq.* ● *n.* **1** a submarine. **2** a subscription. **3** a substitute. **4** a sub-editor. **5** *Mil.* a subaltern. **6** *Brit.* an advance or loan against expected income. ● *v.* (**subbed**, **subbing**) **1** *intr.* (usu. foll. by *for*) act as a substitute for a person. **2** *tr. Brit. colloq.* lend or advance (a sum) to (a person) against expected income. **3** *tr.* sub-edit. [abbr.]
■ *n.* **2** see SUBSCRIPTION 2. **3** see SUBSTITUTE *n.* 1a. **6** see LOAN[1] *n.* ● *v.* **1** see SUBSTITUTE *v.* **2** see LEND 1, 2.

sub- /sub, səb/ *prefix* (also **suc-** before *c*, **suf-** before *f*, **sug-** before *g*, **sup-** before *p*, **sur-** before *r*, **sus-** before *c*, *p*, *t*) **1** at or to or from a lower position (*subordinate*; *submerge*; *subtract*; *subsoil*). **2** secondary or inferior in rank or position (*subclass*; *subcommittee*; *sub-lieutenant*; *subtotal*). **3** somewhat, nearly; more or less (*subacid*; *subarctic*; *subaquatic*). **4** (forming verbs) denoting secondary action (*subdivide*; *sublet*). **5** denoting support (*subvention*). **6** *Chem.* (of a salt) basic (*subacetate*). [from or after L *sub-* f. *sub* under, close to, towards]

subabdominal /súbbabdómmin'l/ *adj.* below the abdomen.

subacid /súbássid/ *adj.* moderately acid or tart (*subacid fruit*; *a subacid remark*). □□ **subacidity** /súbbəsídditi/ *n.* [L *subacidus* (as SUB-, ACID)]

subacute /súbbəkyóót/ *adj. Med.* (of a condition) between acute and chronic.

subagency /súbáyjənsi/ *n.* (*pl.* **-ies**) a secondary or subordinate agency. □□ **subagent** *n.*

subalpine /súbálpīn/ *adj.* of or situated in the higher slopes of mountains just below the timberline.

subaltern /súbbəltərn/ *n.* & *adj.* ● *n. Brit. Mil.* an officer below the rank of captain, esp. a second lieutenant. ● *adj.* **1** of inferior rank. **2** *Logic* (of a proposition) particular, not universal. [LL *subalternus* f. *alternus* ALTERNATE *adj.*]

■ *n.* see SUBORDINATE *n.*

subantarctic /súbbantaárktik/ *adj.* of or like regions immediately north of the Antarctic Circle.

sub-aqua /súbákwə/ *adj.* of or concerning underwater swimming or diving.

subaquatic /súbbəkwáttik/ *adj.* **1** of more or less aquatic habits or kind. **2** underwater.

subaqueous /súbáykwiəss/ *adj.* **1** existing, formed, or taking place under water. **2** lacking in substance or strength; wishy-washy.

subarctic /súbaárktik/ *adj.* of or like regions immediately south of the Arctic Circle.

subastral /súbástrəl/ *adj.* terrestrial.

■ see TERRESTRIAL *adj.* 1, 4.

subatomic /súbbətómmik/ *adj.* occurring in or smaller than an atom.

subaudition /súbbawdísh'n/ *n.* **1** the act of mentally supplying an omitted word or words in speech. **2** the act or process of understanding the unexpressed; reading between the lines. [LL *subauditio* f. *subaudire* understand (as SUB-, AUDITION)]

subaxillary /súbbakzílləri/ *adj.* **1** *Bot.* in or growing beneath the axil. **2** beneath the armpit.

sub-basement /súb-baysmənt/ *n.* a storey below a basement.

sub-branch /súb-braanch/ *n.* a secondary or subordinate branch.

sub-breed /súb-breed/ *n.* a secondary or inferior breed.

subcategory /súbkattigəri/ *n.* (*pl.* **-ies**) a secondary or subordinate category. □□ **subcategorize** *v.tr.* (also **-ise**). **subcategorization** /-rīzáysh'n/ *n.*

subcaudal /súbkáwd'l/ *adj.* of or concerning the region under the tail or the back part of the body.

subclass /súbklaass/ *n.* **1** a secondary or subordinate class. **2** *Biol.* a taxonomic category below a class.

sub-clause /súbklawz/ *n.* **1** esp. *Law* a subsidiary section of a clause. **2** *Gram.* a subordinate clause.

subclavian /súbkláyviən/ *adj.* & *n.* ● *adj.* (of an artery etc.) lying or extending under the collar-bone. ● *n.* such an artery. [mod.L *subclavius* (as SUB-, *clavis* key): cf. CLAVICLE]

subclinical /súbklínnik'l/ *adj. Med.* (of a disease) not yet presenting definite symptoms.

subcommissioner /súbkəmishənər/ *n.* a deputy commissioner.

subcommittee /súbkəmiti/ *n.* a secondary committee.

subconical /súbkónnik'l/ *adj.* approximately conical.

subconscious /súbkónshəss/ *adj.* & *n.* ● *adj.* of or concerning the part of the mind which is not fully conscious but influences actions etc. ● *n.* this part of the mind. □□ **subconsciously** *adv.* **subconsciousness** *n.*

■ *adj.* subliminal, unconscious, suppressed, preconscious, hidden, latent, repressed, inner, innermost, underlying, deep-rooted; intuitive, instinctive; *Psychol.* Freudian. ● *n.* unconscious, inner self, psyche, id; heart. □□ **subconsciously** see *vaguely* (VAGUE).

subcontinent /súbkóntinənt/ *n.* **1** a large land mass, smaller than a continent. **2** a large geographically or politically independent part of a continent. □□ **subcontinental** /-nént'l/ *adj.*

subcontract *v.* & *n.* ● *v.* /súbkəntrákt/ **1** *tr.* employ a firm etc. to do (work) as part of a larger project. **2** *intr.* make or carry out a subcontract. ● *n.* /subkóntrakt/ a secondary contract, esp. to supply materials, labour, etc. □□ **subcontractor** /-tráktər/ *n.*

■ *v.* **1** see LET[1] *v.* 5.

subcontrary /súbkóntrəri/ *adj.* & *n. Logic* ● *adj.* (of a proposition) incapable of being false at the same time as another. ● *n.* (*pl.* **-ies**) such a proposition. [LL *subcontrarius* (as SUB-, CONTRARY), transl. Gk *hupenantios*]

subcordate /súbkórdayt/ *adj.* approximately heart-shaped.

subcortical /súbkórtik'l/ *adj. Anat.* below the cortex.

subcostal /súbkóst'l/ *adj. Anat.* below the ribs.

subcranial /súbkráyniəl/ *adj. Anat.* below the cranium.

subcritical /súbkríttik'l/ *adj. Physics* of less than critical mass etc.

subculture /súbkulchər/ *n.* a cultural group within a larger culture, often having beliefs or interests at variance with those of the larger culture. □□ **subcultural** /-kúlchərəl/ *adj.*

subcutaneous /súbkyootáyniəss/ *adj.* under the skin. □□ **subcutaneously** *adv.*

subdeacon /súbdeékən/ *n. Eccl.* a minister of the order next below a deacon. □□ **subdiaconate** /-dīákkənayt, -dīákkənət/ *n.*

subdean /súbdeén/ *n.* an official ranking next below, or acting as a deputy for, a dean. □□ **subdeanery** *n.* (*pl.* **-ies**). **subdecanal** /-dikáyn'l/ *adj.*

subdelirious /súbdilírriəss/ *adj.* capable of becoming delirious; mildly delirious. □□ **subdelirium** *n.*

subdivide /súbdivíd/ *v.tr.* & *intr.* divide again after a first division. [ME f. L *subdividere* (as SUB-, DIVIDE)]

■ see DIVIDE *v.* 1, 3a.

subdivision /súbdivízh'n/ *n.* **1** the act or an instance of subdividing. **2** a secondary or subordinate division. **3** *US* & *Austral.* an area of land divided into plots for sale.

■ **2** see SECTION *n.* 3, 4.

subdominant /súbdómminənt/ *n. Mus.* the fourth note of the diatonic scale of any key.

subdue /səbdyóó/ *v.tr.* (**subdues, subdued, subduing**) **1** conquer, subjugate, or tame (an enemy, nature, one's emotions, etc.). **2** (as **subdued** *adj.*) softened; lacking in intensity; toned down (*subdued light*; *in a subdued mood*). □□ **subduable** *adj.* **subdual** *n.* [ME *sodewe* f. OF *so(u)duire* f. L *subducere* (as SUB-, *ducere* lead, bring) used with the sense of *subdere* conquer (as SUB-, *-dere* put)]

■ **1** put down, beat down, quell, repress, suppress, quash, crush, control, master, overpower, conquer, defeat, overcome, gain mastery *or* control over, gain the upper hand over, get the better of, dominate, subjugate, subject, triumph over, hold *or* keep in check, restrain, check, curb, bridle, tame, chasten, *literary* vanquish. **2** (**subdued**) quiet, mellow(ed), toned down, moderate(d), tempered, hushed, muted, softened, soft; low-key, unenthusiastic, repressed, restrained, peaceful, tranquil, placid, calm(ed), temperate, reserved; chastened, sober, sobered, solemn, saddened, dejected, sad, crestfallen, downcast, grave, serious, *colloq.* down in the mouth.

sub-editor /súbbédditər/ *n.* **1** an assistant editor. **2** *Brit.* a person who edits material for printing in a book, newspaper, etc. □□ **sub-edit** *v.tr.* (**-edited, -editing**). **sub-editorial** /-tóriəl/ *adj.*

■ **2** copy-editor, copyreader.

suberect /súbbirékt/ *adj.* (of an animal, plant, etc.) almost erect.

subereous /syoobeériəss/ *adj.* (also **suberic** /syoobérrik/, **suberose** /syóóbərōss/) **1** of or concerning cork. **2** corky. [L *suber* cork, cork-oak]

subfamily /súbfammili/ *n.* (*pl.* **-ies**) **1** *Biol.* a taxonomic category below a family. **2** any subdivision of a group.

subfloor /súbflor/ *n.* a foundation for a floor in a building.

subform /súbform/ *n.* a subordinate or secondary form.

subfusc /súbfusk/ *adj.* & *n.* ● *adj. formal* dull; dusky; gloomy. ● *n.* formal clothing at some universities. [L *subfuscus* f. *fuscus* dark brown]

■ *adj.* see DARK *adj.* 1.

subgenus /súbjeenəss/ *n.* (*pl.* **subgenera** /-jénnərə/) *Biol.* a taxonomic category below a genus. □□ **subgeneric** /-jinérrik/ *adj.*

subglacial /súbgláysh'l, -gláysiəl/ *adj.* next to or at the bottom of a glacier.

subgroup /súbgroop/ *n. Math.* etc. a subset of a group.

subhead /súbhed/ *n.* (also **subheading**) **1** a subordinate heading or title in a chapter, article, etc. **2** a subordinate division in a classification.
■ **1** see TITLE *n.* 2.

subhuman /súbhyoomən/ *adj.* **1** (of an animal) closely related to man. **2** (of behaviour, intelligence, etc.) less than human.
■ **2** see ANIMAL *adj* 3.

subjacent /súbjáys'nt/ *adj.* underlying; situated below. [L *subjacēre* (as SUB-, *jacēre* lie)]

subject *n.*, *adj.*, *adv.*, & *v.* ● *n.* /súbjikt/ **1 a** a matter, theme, etc. to be discussed, described, represented, dealt with, etc. **b** (foll. by *for*) a person, circumstance, etc., giving rise to specified feeling, action, etc. (*a subject for congratulation*). **2** a department or field of study (*his best subject is geography*). **3** *Gram.* a noun or its equivalent about which a sentence is predicated and with which the verb agrees. **4 a** any person except a monarch living under a monarchy or any other form of government (*the ruler and his subjects*). **b** any person owing obedience to another. **5** *Philos.* **a** a thinking or feeling entity; the conscious mind; the ego, esp. as opposed to anything external to the mind. **b** the central substance or core of a thing as opposed to its attributes. **6** *Mus.* a theme of a fugue or sonata; a leading phrase or motif. **7** a person of specified mental or physical tendencies (*a hysterical subject*). **8** *Logic* the part of a proposition about which a statement is made. **9 a** a person or animal undergoing treatment, examination, or experimentation. **b** a dead body for dissection. ● *adj.* /súbjikt/ **1** (often foll. by *to*) owing obedience to a government, colonizing power, force, etc.; in subjection. **2** (foll. by *to*) liable, exposed, or prone to (*is subject to infection*). **3** (foll. by *to*) conditional upon; on the assumption of (*the arrangement is subject to your approval*). ● *adv.* /súbjikt/ (foll. by *to*) conditionally upon (*subject to your consent, I propose to try again*). ● *v.tr.* /səbjékt/ **1** (foll. by *to*) make liable; expose; treat (*subjected us to hours of waiting*). **2** (usu. foll. by *to*) subdue (a nation, person, etc.) to one's sway etc. □ **on the subject of** concerning, about. **subject and object** *Psychol.* the ego or self and the non-ego; consciousness and that of which it is or may be conscious. **subject catalogue** a catalogue, esp. in a library, arranged according to the subjects treated. **subject-heading** a heading in an index collecting references to a subject. **subject-matter** the matter treated of in a book, lawsuit, etc. □□ **subjection** /səbjéksh'n/ *n.* **subjectless** /súbjiktliss/ *adj.* [ME *soget* etc. f. OF *suget* etc. f. L *subjectus* past part. of *subjicere* (as SUB-, *jacere* throw)]
■ *n.* **1 a** (subject-)matter, topic; issue, theme, thesis, gist, substance, business, affair, concern, point. **b** cause, ground(s), motive, reason, basis, source, rationale; excuse. **2** course (of study), field, area, discipline, department, branch of knowledge. **4** citizen, national; taxpayer, voter; subordinate, servant, *hist.* liegeman, vassal. **6** see MOTIF. **9 a** participant, case, patient, guinea-pig, testee. ● *adj.* **1** dependent, subjugated, enslaved, captive; under someone's thumb; (*subject to*) answerable to, accountable to, amenable to, responsible to, bound by, obedient to, subservient to, submissive to, controlled by, under the control of. **2** (*subject to*) exposed to, open to, vulnerable to, susceptible to, prone to, disposed to, at the mercy of, liable to (suffer *or* undergo). **3** (*subject to*) dependent (up)on, conditional (up)on, contingent (up)on. ● *v.* **1** (*subject to*) expose to, lay open to, submit to, treat to, put through, impose on, cause to undergo, make liable to. **2** conquer, subjugate, dominate, subdue, enslave, enthral, crush, humble. □ **on the subject of** see REGARDING. **subject-matter** see CONTENT[2] 3. □□ **subjection** subordination, domination, conquest, subjugation, enslavement, servitude, bondage, enthralment, humbling, humiliation, *hist.* vassalage.

subjective /səbjéktiv/ *adj.* & *n.* ● *adj.* **1** (of art, literature, written history, a person's views, etc.) proceeding from personal idiosyncrasy or individuality; not impartial or literal. **2** esp. *Philos.* proceeding from or belonging to the individual consciousness or perception; imaginary, partial, or distorted. **3** *Gram.* of or concerning the subject. ● *n. Gram.* the subjective case. □ **subjective case** *Gram.* the nominative. □□ **subjectively** *adv.* **subjectiveness** *n.* **subjectivity** /súbjektívviti/ *n.* [ME f. L *subjectivus* (as SUBJECT)]
■ *adj.* **1, 2** personal, individual, idiosyncratic; prejudiced, biased, partial, distorted; self-centred, egoistic, egocentric, selfish, self-serving. ● *n.* subjective case, nominative.

subjectivism /səbjéktiviz'm/ *n. Philos.* the doctrine that knowledge is merely subjective and that there is no external or objective truth. □□ **subjectivist** *n.*

subjoin /súbjóyn/ *v.tr.* add or append (an illustration, anecdote, etc.) at the end. [obs. F *subjoindre* f. L *subjungere* (as SUB-, *jungere junct-* join)]
■ see SUFFIX *v.*

subjoint /súbjoynt/ *n.* a secondary joint (in an insect's leg etc.).

sub judice /sub joodisi, soob joodikay/ *adj. Law* under judicial consideration and therefore prohibited from public discussion elsewhere. [L, = under a judge]

subjugate /súbjoogayt/ *v.tr.* bring into subjection; subdue; vanquish. □□ **subjugable** /-gəb'l/ *adj.* **subjugation** /-gáysh'n/ *n.* **subjugator** *n.* [ME f. LL *subjugare* bring under the yoke (as SUB-, *jugum* yoke)]
■ dominate, subordinate, enslave, enthral, crush, humble, subject, oppress, suppress, put down, tyrannize, subdue, reduce, quell, overcome, overpower, conquer, make subservient *or* subordinate *or* submissive, humiliate, *literary* vanquish. □□ **subjugation** see *subjection* (SUBJECT).

subjunctive /səbjúngktiv/ *adj.* & *n. Gram.* ● *adj.* (of a mood) denoting what is imagined or wished or possible (e.g. *if I were you, God help you, be that as it may*). ● *n.* **1** the subjunctive mood. **2** a verb in this mood. □□ **subjunctively** *adv.* [F *subjonctif -ive* or LL *subjunctivus* f. L (as SUBJOIN), transl. Gk *hupotaktikos*, as being used in subjoined clauses]

subkingdom /súbkingdəm/ *n. Biol.* a taxonomic category below a kingdom.

sublease *n.* & *v.* ● *n.* /súbleess/ a lease of a property by a tenant to a subtenant. ● *v.tr.* /súbleess/ lease (a property) to a subtenant.

sublessee /súblesee/ *n.* a person who holds a sublease.

sublessor /súblesór/ *n.* a person who grants a sublease.

sublet *n.* & *v.* ● *n.* /súblet/ = SUBLEASE *n.* ● *v.tr.* /súblét/ (**-letting**; *past* and *past part.* **-let**) = SUBLEASE *v.*

sub-lieutenant /súblefténnənt/ *n. Brit.* a naval officer ranking next below lieutenant.

sublimate *v.*, *adj.*, & *n.* ● *v.* /súblimayt/ **1** *tr.* & *intr.* divert (the energy of a primitive impulse, esp. sexual) into a culturally higher activity. **2** *tr.* & *intr. Chem.* convert (a substance) from the solid state directly to its vapour by heat, and usu. allow it to solidify again. **3** *tr.* refine; purify; idealize. ● *adj.* /súblimət/ **1** *Chem.* (of a substance) sublimated. **2** purified, refined. ● *n.* /súblimət/ *Chem.* **1** a sublimated substance. **2** = *corrosive sublimate*. □□ **sublimation** /-máysh'n/ *n.* [L *sublimare sublimat-* SUBLIME *v.*]
■ *v.* **1** transmute, alter, transform; channel, divert, redirect. **3** sublime, refine, purify, rarefy; idealize, elevate.

sublime /səblīm/ *adj.* & *v.* ● *adj.* (**sublimer**, **sublimest**) **1** of the most exalted, grand, or noble kind; awe-inspiring (*sublime genius*). **2** (of indifference, impudence, etc.) arrogantly unruffled; extreme (*sublime ignorance*). ● *v.* **1** *tr.* &

intr. Chem. = SUBLIMATE *v.* 2. **2** *tr.* purify or elevate by or as if by sublimation; make sublime. **3** *intr.* become pure by or as if by sublimation. □ **Sublime Porte** see PORTE. □□ **sublimely** *adv.* **sublimity** /-límmiti/ *n.* [L *sublimis* (as SUB-, second element perh. rel. to *limen* threshold, *limus* oblique)]

■ *adj.* **1** lofty, high, supreme, exalted, elevated, empyrean, empyreal, heavenly, noble, glorious, grand, high-minded; honourable, ennobled, eminent, glorified, canonized, sanctified, *RC Ch.* beatified; great, magnificent, majestic, splendid, transcendent; awesome, overwhelming, inspiring, overpowering, humbling, awe-inspiring, *colloq.* mind-boggling. **2** extreme, lofty, supreme, utmost. ● *v.* **2** see SUBLIMATE *v.* 3. □□ **sublimely** see PERFECTLY 3. **sublimity** see NOBILITY 1.

subliminal /səblímmin'l/ *adj. Psychol.* (of a stimulus etc.) below the threshold of sensation or consciousness. □ **subliminal advertising** the use of subliminal images in advertising on television etc. to influence the viewer at an unconscious level. **subliminal self** the part of one's personality outside conscious awareness. □□ **subliminally** *adv.* [SUB- + L *limen -inis* threshold]

■ subconscious, unconscious, vague, indefinable. □□ **subliminally** see *vaguely* (VAGUE).

sublingual /súblínggwəl/ *adj.* under the tongue. [SUB- + L *lingua* tongue]

sublittoral /súblíttərəl/ *adj.* **1** (of plants, animals, deposits, etc.) living or found on the seashore just below the low-water mark. **2** of or concerning the seashore.

Sub-Lt. *abbr. Brit.* Sub-Lieutenant.

sublunary /súbloonəri, -lyoonəri/ *adj.* **1** beneath the moon. **2** *Astron.* **a** within the moon's orbit. **b** subject to the moon's influence. **3** of this world; earthly. [LL *sublunaris* (as SUB-, LUNAR)]

■ **3** see TERRESTRIAL *adj* 1, 4.

sub-machine-gun /súbməsheengun/ *n.* a hand-held lightweight machine-gun.

subman /súbman/ *n.* (*pl.* **-men**) *derog.* an inferior, brutal, or stupid man.

submarginal /súbmaarjin'l/ *adj.* **1** esp. *Econ.* not reaching minimum requirements. **2** (of land) that cannot be farmed profitably.

submarine /súbməreen/ *n.* & *adj.* ● *n.* a vessel, esp. a warship, capable of operating under water and usu. equipped with torpedoes, missiles, and a periscope. ● *adj.* existing, occurring, done, or used under the surface of the sea (*submarine cable*). □□ **submariner** /-márrinər/ *n.*

submaster /súbmaastər/ *n.* an assistant master or assistant headmaster in a school.

submaxillary /súbmaksílləri/ *adj.* beneath the lower jaw.

submediant /súbmeediənt/ *n. Mus.* the sixth note of the diatonic scale of any key.

submental /súbmént'l/ *adj.* under the chin.

submerge /səbmérj/ *v.* **1** *tr.* **a** place under water; flood; inundate. **b** flood or inundate with work, problems, etc. **2** *intr.* (of a submarine, its crew, a diver, etc.) dive below the surface of water. □ **the submerged tenth** the supposed fraction of the population permanently living in poverty. □□ **submergence** *n.* **submergible** *adj.* **submersion** /-mérsh'n/ *n.* [L *submergere* (as SUB-, *mergere mers-* dip)]

■ **1** flood, immerse, inundate, swamp, engulf, ingurgitate, overwhelm, deluge, drown, bury; plunge, submerse, dip, wash, soak, drench, saturate, wet, douse, souse, dunk, steep. **2** dive, plunge, go down, descend, sink, sound, plummet. □□ **submersion** see PLUNGE *n.*

submersible /səbmérsib'l/ *n.* & *adj.* ● *n.* a submarine operating under water for short periods. ● *adj.* capable of being submerged. [*submerse* (v.) = SUBMERGE]

submicroscopic /súbmīkrəsköppik/ *adj.* too small to be seen by an ordinary microscope.

subminiature /súbminnichər/ *adj.* **1** of greatly reduced size. **2** (of a camera) very small and using 16-mm film.

submission /səbmísh'n/ *n.* **1** **a** the act or an instance of submitting; the state of being submitted. **b** anything that is submitted. **2** humility, meekness, obedience, submissiveness (*showed great submission of spirit*). **3** *Law* a theory etc. submitted by counsel to a judge or jury. **4** (in wrestling) the surrender of a participant yielding to the pain of a hold. [ME f. OF *submission* or L *submissio* (as SUBMIT)]

■ **1** **a** concession, acquiescence, capitulation, surrender, yielding, giving in. **b** offering, tender, proposal, proposition, suggestion, contribution, entry. **2** obedience, compliance, deference, resignation, submissiveness, tractability; humility, meekness, docility, passivity, timidity, unassertiveness. **3** theory, proposition, proposal, contention, claim, suggestion. **4** surrender, capitulation, giving in.

submissive /səbmíssiv/ *adj.* **1** humble; obedient. **2** yielding to power or authority; willing to submit. □□ **submissively** *adv.* **submissiveness** *n.* [SUBMISSION after *remissive* etc.]

■ humble, obedient, deferential, biddable, compliant, yielding, acquiescent, tractable, amenable, agreeable, accommodating, passive, unresisting, pliant, flexible, manageable, unassertive, docile, meek, timid, resigned, uncomplaining; obsequious, abject, subservient, servile, slavish, ingratiating, truckling, sycophantic, toadying, *colloq.* bootlicking. □□ **submissively** see *cap in hand.* **submissiveness** see HUMILITY 1.

submit /səbmít/ *v.* (**submitted**, **submitting**) **1** (usu. foll. by *to*) **a** *intr.* cease resistance; give way; yield (*had to submit to defeat; will never submit*). **b** *refl.* surrender (oneself) to the control of another etc. **2** *tr.* present for consideration or decision. **3** *tr.* (usu. foll. by *to*) subject (a person or thing) to an operation, process, treatment, etc. (*submitted it to the flames*). **4** *tr.* esp. *Law* urge or represent esp. deferentially (*that, I submit, is a misrepresentation*). □□ **submitter** *n.* [ME f. L *submittere* (as SUB-, *mittere miss-* send)]

■ **1** **a** surrender, yield, capitulate, give in *or* up *or* way, throw in the towel, throw up *or* in the sponge; bow *or* bend, succumb, truckle, knuckle under; agree, concede, consent, accede, defer; (*submit to*) respect, accept, comply with, resign oneself to, be *or* become resigned to, put up with. **2** offer, proffer, tender, put in, advance, put forward, enter, propose, propound, present, deliver; hand *or* give in. **3** (*submit to*) see SUBJECT *v.* 1. **4** suggest, urge, represent, exhort, plead, supplicate.

submultiple /súbmúltip'l/ *n.* & *adj.* ● *n.* a number that can be divided exactly into a specified number. ● *adj.* being such a number.

subnormal /súbnórm'l/ *adj.* **1** (esp. as regards intelligence) below normal. **2** less than normal. □□ **subnormality** /-málliti/ *n.*

■ **1** see DEFECTIVE *adj.* 2.

subnuclear /súbnyookliər/ *adj. Physics* occurring in or smaller than an atomic nucleus.

subocular /súbbókyoolər/ *adj.* situated below or under the eyes.

suborbital /súbbórbit'l/ *adj.* **1** situated below the orbit of the eye. **2** (of a spaceship etc.) not completing a full orbit of the earth.

suborder /súbbordər/ *n.* a taxonomic category between an order and a family. □□ **subordinal** /-órdin'l/ *adj.*

subordinary /súbbórdinəri/ *n.* (*pl.* **-ies**) *Heraldry* a device or bearing that is common but less so than ordinaries.

subordinate *adj.*, *n.*, & *v.* ● *adj.* /səbórdinət/ (usu. foll. by *to*) of inferior importance or rank; secondary, subservient. ● *n.* /səbórdinət/ a person working under another's control or orders. ● *v.tr.* /səbórdinayt/ (usu. foll. by *to*) **1** make subordinate; treat or regard as of minor importance. **2** make subservient. □ **subordinate clause** a clause serving as an adjective, adverb, or noun in a main sentence because of its position or a preceding conjunction. □□ **subordinately** /səbórdinətli/ *adv.* **subordination** /-náysh'n/ *n.* **subordinative** /səbórdinətiv/ *adj.* [med.L *subordinare*, *subordinat-* (as SUB-, L *ordinare* ordain)]

■ *adj.* minor; inferior, lower, lesser, secondary, second, junior, subsidiary, subservient; (*subordinate to*) next to, below, beneath, under. ● *n.* assistant, aide, junior, staff member; inferior, servant, slave; *Brit. Mil.* subaltern, *US* staffer; *hist. or rhet.* vassal; *usu. derog.* flunkey, lackey, menial, hireling, underling. ● *v.* **1** see REDUCE 6. **2** see SUBJUGATE. □□ **subordination** see *subjection* (SUBJECT).

suborn /səbórn/ *v.tr.* induce by bribery etc. to commit perjury or any other unlawful act. □□ **subornation** /súbbornáysh'n/ *n.* **suborner** *n.* [L *subornare* incite secretly (as SUB-, *ornare* equip)]
■ see BRIBE *v.*

suboxide /súbbóksīd/ *n. Chem.* an oxide containing the smallest proportion of oxygen.

subphylum /súbfīləm/ *n.* (*pl.* **subphyla** /-lə/) *Biol.* a taxonomic category below a phylum.

sub-plot /súbplot/ *n.* a subordinate plot in a play etc.

subpoena /səpeenə, səpeenə/ *n.* & *v.* ● *n.* a writ ordering a person to attend a lawcourt. ● *v.tr.* (*past* and *past part.* **subpoenaed** or **subpoena'd**) serve a subpoena on. [ME f. L *sub poena* under penalty (the first words of the writ)]
■ *n.* see WARRANT *n.* 2. ● *v.* see INDICT.

subregion /súbreejən/ *n.* a division of a region, esp. with regard to natural life. □□ **subregional** /-reejən'l/ *adj.*

subreption /səbrépsh'n/ *n. formal* the obtaining of a thing by surprise or misrepresentation. [L *subreptio* purloining f. *subripere* (as SUB-, *rapere* snatch)]
■ see DECEIT 2.

subrogation /súbrəgáysh'n/ *n. Law* the substitution of one party for another as creditor, with the transfer of rights and duties. □□ **subrogate** /súbrəgayt/ *v.tr.* [LL *subrogatio* f. *subrogare* choose as substitute (as SUB-, *rogare* ask)]

sub rosa /sub rṓzə/ *adj.* & *adv.* (of communication, consultation, etc.) in secrecy or confidence. [L, lit. 'under the rose', as emblem of secrecy]
■ see *secretly* (SECRET).

subroutine /súbrōōteen/ *n. Computing* a routine designed to perform a frequently used operation within a program.

subscribe /səbskrīb/ *v.* **1** (usu. foll. by *to, for*) **a** *tr.* & *intr.* contribute (a specified sum) or make or promise a contribution to a fund, project, charity, etc., esp. regularly. **b** *intr.* enter one's name in a list of contributors to a charity etc. **c** *tr.* raise or guarantee raising (a sum) by so subscribing. **2** *intr.* (usu. foll. by *to*) express one's agreement with an opinion, resolution, etc. (*cannot subscribe to that*). **3** *tr.* **a** write (esp. one's name) at the foot of a document etc. (*subscribed a motto*). **b** write one's name at the foot of, sign (a document, picture, etc.). □ **subscribe for** agree to take a copy or copies of (a book) before publication. **subscribe oneself** sign one's name as. **subscribe to** arrange to receive (a periodical etc.) regularly. [ME f. L *subscribere* (as SUB-, *scribere script-* write)]
■ **1** (*subscribe to*) contribute to, support, give to, donate to, pledge to, promise to, sign (up) for, *colloq.* chip in to *or* for. **2** (*subscribe to*) endorse, support, underwrite, advocate, back (up), approve of, agree with *or* to, accept, consent to, assent to, sanction, countenance, tolerate, condone, go along with, hold with, allow, permit, *literary* brook. **3 a** append, tack on. **b** see SIGN *v.* 1.

subscriber /səbskrībər/ *n.* **1** a person who subscribes. **2** a person paying for the hire of a telephone line. □ **subscriber trunk dialling** *Brit.* the automatic connection of trunk calls by dialling without the assistance of an operator.
■ **1** see PROPONENT *n.*

subscript /súbskript/ *adj.* & *n.* ● *adj.* written or printed below the line, esp. *Math.* (of a symbol) written below and to the right of another symbol. ● *n.* a subscript number or symbol. [L *subscriptus* (as SUBSCRIBE)]

subscription /səbskrípsh'n/ *n.* **1 a** the act or an instance of subscribing. **b** money subscribed. **2** *Brit.* a fee for the membership of a society etc., esp. paid regularly. **3 a** an agreement to take and pay for usu. a specified number of issues of a newspaper, magazine, etc. **b** the money paid by this. **4** a signature on a document etc. **5** the offer of a reduced price to those ordering a book before publication. □ **subscription concert** etc. each of a series of concerts etc. for which tickets are sold in advance. [ME f. L *subscriptio* (as SUBSCRIBE)]
■ **1 a** obligation, pledge, promise, commitment, underwriting. **b** payment, remittance, investment; contribution. **2** dues, fee, contribution, *colloq.* sub. **3 b** fee, payment, remittance, price, cost.

subsection /súbseksh'n/ *n.* a division of a section.
■ see BRANCH *n.* 2, 3.

subsellium /səbsélliəm/ *n.* (*pl.* **subsellia** /-liə/) = MISERICORD 1. [L f. *sella* seat]

subsequence /súbsikwənss/ *n.* a subsequent incident; a consequence.

sub-sequence /súbseekwənss/ *n.* a sequence forming part of a larger one.

subsequent /súbsikwənt/ *adj.* (usu. foll. by *to*) following a specified event etc. in time, esp. as a consequence. □□ **subsequently** *adv.* [ME f. OF *subsequent* or L *subsequi* (as SUB-, *sequi* follow)]
■ succeeding, following, ensuing, next, future, later, posterior, successive; resultant, resulting, consequent; (*subsequent to*) after, following, succeeding, in the wake *or* aftermath of. □□ **subsequently** later (on), afterwards, *US* afterward.

subserve /səbsérv/ *v.tr.* serve as a means in furthering (a purpose, action, etc.). [L *subservire* (as SUB-, SERVE)]

subservient /səbsérviənt/ *adj.* **1** cringing; obsequious. **2** (usu. foll. by *to*) serving as a means; instrumental. **3** (usu. foll. by *to*) subordinate. □□ **subservience** *n.* **subserviency** *n.* **subserviently** *adv.* [L *subserviens subservient-* (as SUBSERVE)]
■ **1** see OBSEQUIOUS. **2** see INSTRUMENTAL *adj.* **3** see SUBORDINATE *adj.* □□ **subservience** see *servility* (SERVILE). **subserviently** see *cap in hand.*

subset /súbset/ *n.* **1** a secondary part of a set. **2** *Math.* a set all the elements of which are contained in another set.

subshrub /súbshrub/ *n.* a low-growing or small shrub.

subside /səbsīd/ *v.intr.* **1** cease from agitation; become tranquil; abate (*excitement subsided*). **2** (of water, suspended matter, etc.) sink. **3** (of the ground) cave in; sink. **4** (of a building, ship, etc.) sink lower in the ground or water. **5** (of a swelling etc.) become less. **6** usu. *joc.* (of a person) sink into a sitting, kneeling, or lying posture. □□ **subsidence** /-sīd'nss, súbsid'nss/ *n.* [L *subsidere* (as SUB-, *sidere* settle rel. to *sedēre* sit)]
■ **1** abate, quiet *or Brit.* quieten (down), calm (down), moderate, let up, decrease, diminish, lessen, slacken, die (down *or* off *or* out), ebb, pass (away), wear off, wane. **2** sink (down), drop (down), go down, recede, descend, decline; settle, *Chem. or Physics* precipitate. **3** cave in, collapse, fall in, sink, drop, settle. **4** sink (down), drop (down), go down, settle. **5** go down, lessen, decrease, reduce, abate. **6** sink, collapse, flop, drop, slump, settle. □□ **subsidence** see SAG *n.* 2, WANE *n.*

subsidiarity /səbsíddiárriti/ *n.* (*pl.* **-ies**) **1** the quality of being subsidiary. **2** the principle that a central authority should perform only tasks which cannot be performed effectively at a local level.

subsidiary /səbsíddiəri/ *adj.* & *n.* ● *adj.* **1** serving to assist or supplement; auxiliary. **2** (of a company) controlled by another. **3** (of troops): **a** paid for by subsidy. **b** hired by another nation. ● *n.* (*pl.* **-ies**) **1** a subsidiary thing or person; an accessory. **2** a subsidiary company. □□ **subsidiarily** *adv.* [L *subsidiarius* (as SUBSIDY)]
■ *adj.* **1** ancillary, auxiliary, additional, supplementary, supplemental, complementary, accessory, adjuvant, secondary, lesser, minor, subordinate. ● *n.* **1** accessory, auxiliary, extra, assistant, adjuvant, subordinate; adjunct, supplement.

subsidize /súbsidīz/ *v.tr.* (also **-ise**) **1** pay a subsidy to. **2** reduce the cost of by subsidy (*subsidized lunches*). □□ **subsidization** /-záysh'n/ *n.* **subsidizer** *n.*
■ **1** fund, finance, support, aid, sponsor, maintain, underwrite; capitalize, *US colloq.* bankroll.

subsidy /súbsidi/ *n.* (*pl.* **-ies**) **1 a** money granted by the State or a public body etc. to keep down the price of commodities etc. (*housing subsidy*). **b** money granted to a charity or other undertaking held to be in the public interest. **c** any grant or contribution of money. **2** money paid by one State to another in return for military, naval, or other aid. **3** *hist.* **a** a parliamentary grant to the sovereign for State needs. **b** a tax levied on a particular occasion. [ME f. AF *subsidie*, OF *subside* f. L *subsidium* assistance]
■ **1** funding, sponsorship, assistance, aid, contribution, support, grant, bounty, endowment, subvention, maintenance, backing, capitalization.

subsist /səbsíst/ *v.* **1** *intr.* (often foll. by *on*) keep oneself alive; be kept alive (*subsists on vegetables*). **2** *intr.* remain in being; exist. **3** *intr.* (foll. by *in*) be attributable to (*its excellence subsists in its freshness*). **4** *tr. archaic* provide sustenance for. □□ **subsistent** *adj.* [L *subsistere* stand firm (as SUB-, *sistere* set, stand)]
■ **1, 2** see EXIST 5.

subsistence /səbsístənss/ *n.* **1** the state or an instance of subsisting. **2 a** the means of supporting life; a livelihood. **b** a minimal level of existence or the income providing this (*a bare subsistence*). □ **subsistence allowance** (or **money**) esp. *Brit.* an allowance or advance on pay granted esp. as travelling expenses. **subsistence farming** farming which directly supports the farmer's household without producing a significant surplus for trade. **subsistence level** (or **wage**) a standard of living (or wage) providing only the bare necessities of life.
■ **1** existence, living, survival, subsisting, being. **2** see MAINTENANCE 2a.

subsoil /súbsoyl/ *n.* soil lying immediately under the surface soil (opp. TOPSOIL).

subsonic /súbsónnik/ *adj.* relating to speeds less than that of sound. □□ **subsonically** *adv.*

subspecies /súbspeesheez, -shiz/ *n.* (*pl.* same) *Biol.* a taxonomic category below a species, usu. a fairly permanent geographically isolated variety. □□ **subspecific** /-spəsíffik/ *adj.*

substance /súbstənss/ *n.* **1 a** the essential material, esp. solid, forming a thing (*the substance was transparent*). **b** a particular kind of material having uniform properties (*this substance is salt*). **2 a** reality; solidity (*ghosts have no substance*). **b** seriousness or steadiness of character (*there is no substance in him*). **3** the theme or subject of esp. a work of art, argument, etc. (*prefer the substance to the style*). **4** the real meaning or essence of a thing. **5** wealth and possessions (*a woman of substance*). **6** *Philos.* the essential nature underlying phenomena, which is subject to changes and accidents. □ **in substance** generally; apart from details. [ME f. OF f. L *substantia* (as SUB-, *stare* stand)]
■ **1** material, matter, stuff; fabric; composition, make-up. **2 a** reality, corporeality, solidity, actuality, concreteness. **3** theme, subject, gist, thrust, burden, point, content. **4** meaning, import, significance, purport, signification, point; essence, quintessence, pith, heart, core, meat, kernel, nub, crux, gravamen; sum total; *Philos.* quiddity, haecceity. **5** means, wealth, property, possessions, riches, resources, affluence, assets. □ **in substance** see *substantially* (SUBSTANTIAL).

substandard /súbstándərd/ *adj.* **1** of less than the required or normal quality or size; inferior. **2** (of language) not conforming to standard usage.
■ **1** see INFERIOR *adj.* 2.

substantial /səbstánsh'l/ *adj.* **1 a** of real importance, value, or validity (*made a substantial contribution*). **b** of large size or amount (*awarded substantial damages*). **2** of solid material or structure; stout (*a man of substantial build*; *a substantial house*). **3** commercially successful; wealthy. **4** essential; true in large part (*substantial truth*). **5** having substance; real. □□ **substantiality** /-shiálliti/ *n.* **substantially** *adv.* [ME f. OF *substantiel* or LL *substantialis* (as SUBSTANCE)]
■ **1 a** material, considerable, significant, great, worthwhile, consequential, important, valuable; well-founded, sound, weighty, solid, well-established, telling, good, valid, actual. **b** ample, goodly, respectable, abundant, generous, big, large, sizeable, major, *colloq.* tidy, healthy. **2** strong, solid, well-built, durable, sound, stout, sturdy, hefty; big, large, massive, huge, sizeable, impressive, vast. **3** wealthy, well-to-do, rich, affluent, prosperous, profitable, successful; landed, propertied. **4, 6** basic, fundamental; virtual; see also ESSENTIAL *adj.* 2. **5** see MATERIAL *adj.* 1. □□ **substantially** essentially, at bottom, fundamentally, basically, in essence, intrinsically, in reality, at heart, truly, actually, veritably, indeed, in fact, as a matter of fact, *literary* in truth; in substance; largely, to a large extent, in large measure, materially, practically, in the main, for the most part, mostly, virtually, to all intents and purposes; *archaic* verily.

substantialism /səbstánshəliz'm/ *n.* *Philos.* the doctrine that behind phenomena there are substantial realities. □□ **substantialist** *n.*

substantialize /səbstánshəlīz/ *v.tr.* & *intr.* (also **-ise**) invest with or acquire substance or actual existence.

substantiate /səbstánshiayt/ *v.tr.* prove the truth of (a charge, statement, claim, etc.); give good grounds for. □□ **substantiation** /-áysh'n/ *n.* [med.L *substantiare* give substance to (as SUBSTANCE)]
■ confirm, affirm, attest, corroborate, support, sustain, back up, bear out, authenticate, show (clearly), prove, document, verify, certify, validate, give substance to. □□ **substantiation** see PROOF *n.* 1.

substantive /súbstəntiv/ *adj.* & *n.* ● *adj.* /also səbstántiv/ **1** having separate and independent existence. **2** *Law* relating to rights and duties. **3** (of an enactment, motion, resolution, etc.) made in due form as such; not amended. **4** *Gram.* expressing existence. **5** (of a dye) not needing a mordant. **6** *Mil.* (of a rank etc.) permanent, not acting or temporary. **7** *archaic* denoting a substance. ● *n.* *Gram.* = NOUN. □ **the substantive verb** the verb 'to be'. □□ **substantival** /-tīv'l/ *adj.* **substantively** *adv.* esp. *Gram.* [ME f. OF *substantif* -*ive*, or LL *substantivus* (as SUBSTANCE)]
■ *adj.* **1** see INDEPENDENT *adj.* 1a, 5.

substation /súbstaysh'n/ *n.* a subordinate station, esp. one reducing the high voltage of electric power transmission to that suitable for supply to consumers.

substituent /səbstítyooənt/ *adj.* & *n.* *Chem.* ● *adj.* (of a group of atoms) replacing another atom or group in a compound. ● *n.* such a group. [L *substituere substituent-* (as SUBSTITUTE)]

substitute /súbstityoot/ *n.* & *v.* ● *n.* **1 a** (also *attrib.*) a person or thing acting or serving in place of another. **b** an artificial alternative to a natural substance (*butter substitute*). **2** *Sc. Law* a deputy. ● *v.* **1** *intr.* & *tr.* (often foll. by *for*) act or cause to act as a substitute; put or serve in exchange (*substituted for her mother*; *substituted it for the broken one*). **2** *tr.* (usu. foll. by *by*, *with*) *colloq.* replace (a person or thing) with another. **3** *tr.* *Chem.* replace (an atom or group in a molecule) with another. □□ **substitutable** *adj.* **substitutability** /-təbílliti/ *n.* **substitution** /-tyóosh'n/ *n.* **substitutional** /-tyóoshən'l/ *adj.* **substitutionary** /-tyóoshənəri/ *adj.* **substitutive** *adj.* [ME f. L *substitutus* past part. of *substituere* (as SUB-, *statuere* set up)]
■ *n.* **1 a** substitution, replacement, alternative, relief, supply, representative, proxy, deputy, delegate, stand-in, stand-by, stopgap, reserve, surrogate, succedaneum, locum tenens, *esp. Theatr.* understudy, *esp. US* alternate, *US* pinch-hitter, *colloq.* locum, sub. **b** alternative, replacement, ersatz, imitation. ● *v.* **1** *Austral.* & *NZ sl.* ring in; (*substitute for*) take the place of, stand in for, step in for, fill in for, double for, deputize for, cover for, relieve, *colloq.* sub for; replace; supersede, displace,

supplant. **2, 3** replace. ◻◻ **substitution** see SUBSTITUTE *n.* 1a above, CHANGE *n.* 4.

substrate /súbstrayt/ *n.* **1** = SUBSTRATUM. **2** a surface to be painted, printed, etc., on. **3** *Biol.* **a** the substance upon which an enzyme acts. **b** the surface or material on which any particular organism grows. [Anglicized f. SUBSTRATUM]

substratum /súbstraatəm, -straytəm/ *n.* (*pl.* **substrata** /-tə/) **1** an underlying layer or substance. **2** a layer of rock or soil beneath the surface. **3** a foundation or basis (*there is a substratum of truth in it*). [mod.L, past part. of L *substernere* (as SUB-, *sternere* strew): cf. STRATUM]
■ substrate, foundation, basis, base, substructure, groundwork.

substructure /súbstrukchər/ *n.* an underlying or supporting structure. ◻◻ **substructural** *adj.*
■ see SUPPORT *n.* 2.

subsume /səbsyóōm/ *v.tr.* (usu. foll. by *under*) include (an instance, idea, category, etc.) in a rule, class, category, etc. ◻◻ **subsumable** *adj.* **subsumption** /-súmpsh'n/ *n.* [med.L *subsumere* (as SUB-, *sumere sumpt-* take)]
■ see INCLUDE 1.

subtenant /súbtennənt/ *n.* a person who leases a property from a tenant. ◻◻ **subtenancy** *n.*

subtend /səbténd/ *v.tr.* **1 a** (usu. foll. by *at*) (of a line, arc, figure, etc.) form (an angle) at a particular point when its extremities are joined at that point. **b** (of an angle or chord) have bounding lines or points that meet or coincide with those of (a line or arc). **2** *Bot.* (of a bract etc.) extend under so as to embrace or enfold. [L *subtendere* (as SUB-, *tendere* stretch)]

subterfuge /súbtərfyōōj/ *n.* **1 a** an attempt to avoid blame or defeat esp. by lying or deceit. **b** a statement etc. resorted to for such a purpose. **2** this as a practice or policy. [F *subterfuge* or LL *subterfugium* f. L *subterfugere* escape secretly f. *subter* beneath + *fugere* flee]
■ **1** artifice, trick, device, stratagem, manoeuvre, scheme, evasion, deception, dodge, feint, shift, excuse, expedient, ruse, wile, contrivance, intrigue, *colloq.* ploy, *Austral. sl.* lurk. **2** see DECEIT 1.

subterminal /súbtérmin'l/ *adj.* nearly at the end.

subterranean /súbtəráyniən/ *adj.* **1** existing, occurring, or done under the earth's surface. **2** secret, underground, concealed. ◻◻ **subterraneously** *adv.* [L *subterraneus* (as SUB-, *terra* earth)]
■ **1** see UNDERGROUND *adj.* 1.

subtext /súbtekst/ *n.* an underlying often distinct theme in a piece of writing or conversation.

subtilize /súttilīz/ *v.* (also **-ise**) **1** *tr.* **a** make subtle. **b** elevate; refine. **2** *intr.* (usu. foll. by *upon*) argue or reason subtly. ◻◻ **subtilization** /-záysh'n/ *n.* [F *subtiliser* or med.L *subtilizare* (as SUBTLE)]
■ **1 b** see REFINE 3.

subtitle /súbtīt'l/ *n.* & *v.* ● *n.* **1** a secondary or additional title of a book etc. **2** a printed caption at the bottom of a film etc., esp. translating dialogue. ● *v.tr.* provide with a subtitle or subtitles.
■ *n.* **1** see TITLE *n.* 2.

subtle /sútt'l/ *adj.* (**subtler**, **subtlest**) **1** evasive or mysterious; hard to grasp (*subtle charm*; *a subtle distinction*). **2** (of scent, colour, etc.) faint, delicate, elusive (*subtle perfume*). **3 a** capable of making fine distinctions; perceptive; acute (*subtle intellect*; *subtle senses*). **b** ingenious; elaborate; clever (*a subtle device*). **4** *archaic* crafty, cunning. ◻◻ **subtleness** *n.* **subtly** *adv.* [ME f. OF *sotil* f. L *subtilis*]
■ **1** abstruse, arcane, recondite, remote, deep, profound, concealed, hidden, shadowy, nebulous, vague, obscure, veiled, thin, airy, insubstantial, elusive, evasive, mysterious, faint; sophistic(al); refined, fine, nice. **2** delicate, fine, refined, exquisite, nice; faint, elusive. **3 a** see ACUTE *adj.* 2. **b** see SOPHISTICATED 2. **4** tricky, shrewd, cunning, wily, sly, devious, crafty, smart, clever, foxy, artful, scheming, designing, underhand(ed), deceptive, machiavellian, ingenious, skilful, strategic, insidious, casuistic, slimy, *colloq.* shifty, slick, smarmy, *often offens.* Jesuitical. ◻◻ **subtleness** see SUBTLETY 1.

subtlety /sútt'lti/ *n.* (*pl.* **-ies**) **1** something subtle; the quality of being subtle. **2** a fine distinction; an instance of hair-splitting. [ME f. OF *s(o)utilté* f. L *subtilitas -tatis* (as SUBTLE)]
■ **1** treachery, guile, insidiousness, casuistry, cunning, artfulness, craftiness, deviousness, slyness, deceptiveness, subtleness; refinement, nicety, delicacy, exquisiteness, intricacy, fineness, acuteness, elegance, sophistication. **2** see REFINEMENT 6.

subtonic /súbtónnik/ *n.* *Mus.* the note below the tonic, the seventh note of the diatonic scale of any key.

subtopia /súbtōpiə/ *n.* *Brit. derog.* unsightly and sprawling suburban development. ◻◻ **subtopian** *adj.* [SUBURB, UTOPIA]

subtotal /súbtōt'l/ *n.* the total of one part of a group of figures to be added.

subtract /səbtrákt/ *v.tr.* (often foll. by *from*) deduct (a part, quantity, or number) from another. ◻◻ **subtracter** *n.* (cf. SUBTRACTOR). **subtraction** /-tráksh'n/ *n.* **subtractive** *adj.* [L *subtrahere subtract-* (as SUB-, *trahere* draw)]
■ deduct, take away *or* off; (*subtract from*) take from. ◻◻ **subtraction** see DEDUCTION 1a.

subtractor /səbtráktər/ *n.* *Electronics* a circuit or device that produces an output dependent on the difference of two inputs.

subtrahend /súbtrəhend/ *n.* *Math.* a quantity or number to be subtracted. [L *subtrahendus* gerundive of *subtrahere*: see SUBTRACT]

subtropics /súbtróppiks/ *n.pl.* the regions adjacent to or bordering on the tropics. ◻◻ **subtropical** *adj.*

subulate /súbyoolət/ *adj.* *Bot.* & *Zool.* slender and tapering. [L *subula* awl]

suburb /súbburb/ *n.* an outlying district of a city, esp. residential. [ME f. OF *suburbe* or L *suburbium* (as SUB-, *urbs urbis* city)]
■ see MUNICIPALITY.

suburban /səbúrb'n/ *adj.* **1** of or characteristic of suburbs. **2** *derog.* provincial, uncultured, or naïve. ◻◻ **suburbanite** *n.* **suburbanize** *v.tr.* (also **-ise**). **suburbanization** /-nīzáysh'n/ *n.* [L *suburbanus* (as SUBURB)]

suburbia /səbúrbiə/ *n.* often *derog.* the suburbs, their inhabitants, and their way of life.

subvention /səbvénsh'n/ *n.* a grant of money from a government etc.; a subsidy. [ME f. OF f. LL *subventio -onis* f. L *subvenire subvent-* assist (as SUB-, *venire* come)]
■ see GRANT *n.*

subversive /səbvérsiv/ *adj.* & *n.* ● *adj.* (of a person, organization, activity, etc.) seeking to subvert (esp. a government). ● *n.* a subversive person; a revolutionary. ◻◻ **subversion** /-vérsh'n/ *n.* **subversively** *adv.* **subversiveness** *n.* [med.L *subversivus* (as SUBVERT)]
■ *adj.* seditious, treasonous, treacherous, traitorous, mutinous, revolutionary, insurrectionary; undermining, destabilizing. ● *n.* traitor, insurgent, subverter, saboteur, fifth-columnist, collaborator, collaborationist, quisling, radical, revolutionary, insurrectionist; dissident, defector. ◻◻ **subversion** overthrow, ruin, destruction, undermining, destabilization, upheaval, displacement; see also MUTINY *n.*

subvert /səbvért/ *v.tr.* esp. *Polit.* overturn, overthrow, or upset (religion, government, the monarchy, morality, etc.). ◻◻ **subverter** *n.* [ME f. OF *subvertir* or L *subvertere* (as SUB-, *vertere vers-* turn)]
■ overthrow, overturn, ruin, destroy, undermine, destabilize, topple, upset, disrupt, demolish, wreck, sabotage, corrupt, pervert.

subway /súbway/ *n.* **1 a** a tunnel beneath a road etc. for pedestrians. **b** an underground passage for pipes, cables, etc. **2** esp. *US* an underground railway.

■ **1** tunnel, underpass. **2** underground (railway), metro, *colloq.* (the) tube.

subzero /súbzeérō/ *adj.* (esp. of temperature) lower than zero.

suc- /suk, sək/ *prefix* assim. form of SUB- before *c.*

succedaneum /súksidáyniəm/ *n.* (*pl.* **succedanea** /-niə/) a substitute, esp. for a medicine or drug. □□ **succedaneous** *adj.* [mod.L, neut. of L *succedaneus* (as SUCCEED)]

■ see SUBSTITUTE *n.* 1a.

succeed /səkseéd/ *v.* **1** *intr.* **a** (often foll. by *in*) accomplish one's purpose; have success; prosper (*succeeded in his ambition*). **b** (of a plan etc.) be successful. **2 a** *tr.* follow in order; come next after (*night succeeded day*). **b** *intr.* (foll. by *to*) come next, be subsequent. **3** *intr.* (often foll. by *to*) come by an inheritance, office, title, or property (*succeeded to the throne*). **4** *tr.* take over an office, property, inheritance, etc. from (*succeeded his father*; *succeeded the manager*). □ **nothing succeeds like success** one success leads to others. □□ **succeeder** *n.* [ME f. OF *succeder* or L *succedere* (as SUB-, *cedere cess-* go)]

■ **1 a** make good, thrive, prosper, flourish, be a success, be successful, progress, advance, get ahead *or* on, attain *or* gain *or* achieve success, win, triumph, be victorious, prevail, *esp. Theatr.* top one's part, *colloq.* make it, arrive, come *or* get to the top, get there. **b** be successful *or* effective, work, bear fruit. **2** follow, come (next) after, be subsequent to. **3** (*succeed to*) see INHERIT 1. **4** be successor to, follow, be heir to, replace, take the place of, inherit from, take over from.

succentor /səkséntər/ *n. Eccl.* a precentor's deputy in some cathedrals. □□ **succentorship** *n.* [LL f. L *succinere* (as SUB-, *canere* sing)]

succès de scandale /sŏŏksáy də skondaál/ *n.* a book, play, etc. having great success because of its scandalous nature or associations. [F]

success /səksés/ *n.* **1** the accomplishment of an aim; a favourable outcome (*their efforts met with success*). **2** the attainment of wealth, fame, or position (*spoilt by success*). **3** a thing or person that turns out well. **4** *archaic* a usu. specified outcome of an undertaking (*ill success*). □ **success story** a person's rise from poverty to wealth etc.; also, a person whose life has been a success story. [L *successus* (as SUCCEED)]

■ **1** good *or* happy result, good *or* happy outcome, good fortune, achievement, triumph, victory, attainment, ascendancy, prosperity. **3** star, superstar, megastar, success story celebrity, (big) name, *US* headliner; sensation, *colloq.* winner, hit.

successful /səksésfŏŏl/ *adj.* having success; prosperous. □□ **successfully** *adv.* **successfulness** *n.*

■ victorious, triumphant, first, winning; famous, well-known, famed, celebrated, renowned, eminent; prominent, pre-eminent, popular, leading, top, best-selling; effective; lucrative, booming, profitable, fruitful, moneymaking, remunerative; wealthy, rich, prosperous, fortunate, lucky, flourishing, thriving, well-to-do, affluent, *colloq.* well-heeled, flush, in the money, *sl.* loaded. □ **successfully** see SWIMMINGLY.

succession /səksésh'n/ *n.* **1 a** the process of following in order; succeeding. **b** a series of things or people in succession. **2 a** the right of succeeding to the throne, an office, inheritance, etc. **b** the act or process of so succeeding. **c** those having such a right. **3** *Biol.* the order of development of a species or community; = SERE[3]. □ **in quick succession** following one another at short intervals. **in succession** one after another, without intervention. **in succession to** as the successor of. **law of succession** the law regulating inheritance. **settle the succession** determine who shall succeed. **Succession State** a State resulting from the partition of a previously existing country. □□ **successional** *adj.* [ME f. OF *succession* or L *successio* (as SUCCEED)]

■ **1** sequence, progression, order, series, course, flow, run, chain, train, string, line, procession, round, cycle, *esp. Brit.* queue. **2 a** birthright, privilege. **b** accession, assumption, attainment, elevation, promotion; inheritance; passing (on), handing down *or* on, descent, transmittal, transmission, transfer, transferral, shift, conveyance. **c** lineage, descent, dynasty, ancestry, descendants, bloodline. □ **in succession** one after *or* behind the other, at intervals, successively, consecutively, in a row, running, without interruption, uninterruptedly, in order, in line, in turn.

successive /səksésiv/ *adj.* following one after another; running, consecutive. □□ **successively** *adv.* **successiveness** *n.* [ME f. med.L *successivus* (as SUCCEED)]

■ uninterrupted, continuous, unbroken, consecutive, straight, succeeding, following, running. □□ **successively** see *in succession* (SUCCESSION).

successor /səksésər/ *n.* (often foll. by *to*) a person or thing that succeeds another. [ME f. OF *successor* f. L *successor* (as SUCCEED)]

■ see HEIR.

succinct /səksíngkt/ *adj.* briefly expressed; terse, concise. □□ **succinctly** *adv.* **succinctness** *n.* [ME f. L *succinctus* past part. of *succingere* tuck up (as SUB-, *cingere* gird)]

■ compact, brief, concise, pithy, terse, short, compressed, condensed, epigrammatic. □□ **succinctly** see *in brief* (BRIEF). **succinctness** see BREVITY.

succinic acid /suksínnik/ *n. Chem.* a crystalline dibasic acid derived from amber etc. □□ **succinate** /súksinayt/ *n.* [F *succinique* f. L *succinum* amber]

succor *US* var. of SUCCOUR.

succory /súkkəri/ *n.* = CHICORY 1. [alt. f. *cicoree* etc., early forms of CHICORY]

succotash /súkkətash/ *n. US* a dish of green maize and beans boiled together. [Narragansett *msiquatash*]

Succoth /sŏŏkōt, súkkəth/ *n.* the Jewish autumn thanksgiving festival commemorating the sheltering in the wilderness. [Heb. *sukkôṯ* pl. of *sukkāh* thicket, hut]

succour /súkər/ *n.* & *v.* (*US* **succor**) ● *n.* **1** aid; assistance, esp. in time of need. **2** (in *pl.*) *archaic* reinforcements of troops. ● *v.tr.* assist or aid (esp. a person in danger or distress). □□ **succourless** *adj.* [ME f. OF *socours* f. med.L *succursus* f. L *succurrere* (as SUB-, *currere curs-* run)]

■ *n.* **1** see AID *n.* 1. ● *v.* see AID *v.* 1.

succubus /súkyoobəss/ *n.* (*pl.* **succubi** /-bī/) a female demon believed to have sexual intercourse with sleeping men. [LL *succuba* prostitute, med.L *succubus* f. *succubare* (as SUB-, *cubare* lie)]

succulent /súkyoolənt/ *adj.* & *n.* ● *adj.* **1** juicy; palatable. **2** *colloq.* desirable. **3** *Bot.* (of a plant, its leaves, or stems) thick and fleshy. ● *n. Bot.* a succulent plant, esp. a cactus. □□ **succulence** *n.* **succulently** *adv.* [L *succulentus* f. *succus* juice]

■ *adj.* **1** juicy, rich, luscious, mouth-watering, toothsome, palatable, tasty. **2** desirable, tempting, tantalizing, attractive, enticing, inviting. **3** fleshy; lush.

succumb /səkúm/ *v.intr.* (usu. foll. by *to*) **1** be forced to give way; be overcome (*succumbed to temptation*). **2** be overcome by death (*succumbed to his injuries*). [ME f. OF *succomber* or L *succumbere* (as SUB-, *cumbere* lie)]

■ **1** yield, give in, give up, give way, surrender, accede, submit, capitulate, fall, bow, cave in.

succursal /səkúrs'l/ *adj. Eccl.* (of a chapel etc.) subsidiary. [F *succursale* f. med.L *succursus* (as SUCCOUR)]

such /such/ *adj.* & *pron.* ● *adj.* **1** (often foll. by *as*) of the kind or degree in question or under consideration (*such a person*; *such people*; *people such as these*). **2** (usu. foll. by *as to* + infin. or *that* + clause) so great; in such high degree (*not such a fool as to believe them*; *had such a fright that he fainted*). **3** of a more than normal kind or degree (*we had such an enjoyable evening*; *such horrid language*). **4** of the kind or degree already indicated, or implied by the context (*there are no such things*; *such is life*). **5** *Law* or *formal* the aforesaid; of the aforesaid kind. ● *pron.* **1** the thing or action in question or referred to (*such were his words*; *such was not my intention*). **2 a** *Commerce* or *colloq.* the aforesaid thing or things; it, they, or them (*those without tickets should*

purchase such). **b** similar things; suchlike (*brought sandwiches and such*). □ **as such** as being what has been indicated or named (*a stranger is welcomed as such; there is no theatre as such*). **such-and-such** ● *adj.* of a particular kind but not needing to be specified. ● *n.* a person or thing of this kind. **such-and-such a person** someone; so-and-so. **such as 1** of a kind that; like (*a person such as we all admire*). **2** for example (*insects, such as moths and bees*). **3** those who (*such as don't need help*). **such as it is** despite its shortcomings (*you are welcome to it, such as it is*). **such a one 1** (usu. foll. by *as*) such a person or such a thing. **2** *archaic* some person or thing unspecified. [OE *swilc, swylc* f. Gmc: cf. LIKE[1]]
■ □ **such as 1, 2** see LIKE[1] *adj.* 1b.

suchlike /súchlīk/ *adj.* & *n. colloq.* ● *adj.* of such a kind. ● *n.* things, people, etc. of such a kind.

suck /suk/ *v.* & *n.* ● *v.* **1** *tr.* draw (a fluid) into the mouth by making a partial vacuum. **2** *tr.* (also *absol.*) **a** draw milk or other fluid from or through (the breast etc. or a container). **b** extract juice from (a fruit) by sucking. **3** *tr.* **a** draw sustenance, knowledge, or advantage from (a book etc.). **b** imbibe or gain (knowledge, advantage, etc.) as if by sucking. **4** *tr.* roll the tongue round (a sweet, teeth, one's thumb, etc.). **5** *intr.* make a sucking action or sound (*sucking at his pipe*). **6** *intr.* (of a pump etc.) make a gurgling or drawing sound. **7** *tr.* (usu. foll. by *down, in*) engulf, smother, or drown in a sucking movement. **8** *intr. US sl.* be or seem very unpleasant, contemptible, or scandalous. ● *n.* **1** the act or an instance of sucking, esp. the breast. **2** the drawing action or sound of a whirlpool etc. **3** (often foll. by *of*) a small draught of liquor. **4** (in *pl.*; esp. as *int.*) *colloq.* **a** an expression of disappointment. **b** an expression of derision or amusement at another's discomfiture. □ **give suck** *archaic* (of a mother, dam, etc.) suckle. **suck dry 1** exhaust the contents of (a bottle, the breast, etc.) by sucking. **2** exhaust (a person's sympathy, resources, etc.) as if by sucking. **suck in 1** absorb. **2** = sense 7 of *v.* **3** involve (a person) in an activity etc. esp. against his or her will. **suck up 1** (often foll. by *to*) *colloq.* behave obsequiously esp. for one's own advantage. **2** absorb. [OE *sūcan*, = L *sugere*]
■ □ **suck in 3** see *lead on* 1 (LEAD[1]). **suck up 1** (*suck up to*) see FLATTER 1.

sucker /súkkər/ *n.* & *v.* ● *n.* **1 a** a person or thing that sucks. **b** a sucking-pig, newborn whale, etc. **2** *sl.* **a** a gullible or easily deceived person. **b** (foll. by *for*) a person especially susceptible to. **3 a** a rubber cup etc. that adheres to a surface by suction. **b** an organ enabling an organism to cling to a surface by suction. **4** *Bot.* a shoot springing from the rooted part of a stem, from the root at a distance from the main stem, from an axil, or occasionally from a branch. **5** any of various fish that has a mouth capable of or seeming to be capable of adhering by suction. **6 a** the piston of a suction-pump. **b** a pipe through which liquid is drawn by suction. **7** *US colloq.* a lollipop. ● *v. Bot.* **1** *tr.* remove suckers from. **2** *intr.* produce suckers.
■ *n.* **2** dupe, pigeon, victim, butt, cat's-paw, fool, greenhorn, easy *or* fair game, *colloq.* goat, chump, pushover, soft touch, *sl.* (easy) mark, sap, fall guy, *Brit. sl.* mug, *esp. US sl.* patsy. **4** see OFFSHOOT 1a.

sucking /súkking/ *adj.* **1** (of a child, animal, etc.) not yet weaned. **2** *Zool.* unfledged (*sucking dove*). □ **sucking-disc** an organ used for adhering to a surface. **sucking-fish** = REMORA.

suckle /súk'l/ *v.* **1** *tr.* **a** feed (young) from the breast or udder. **b** nourish (*suckled his talent*). **2** *intr.* feed by sucking the breast etc. □□ **suckler** *n.* [ME, prob. back-form. f. SUCKLING]
■ **1 a** see NURSE *v.* 2.

suckling /súkling/ *n.* an unweaned child or animal.

sucrose /sóōkrōz, syóō-/ *n. Chem.* sugar, a disaccharide obtained from sugar cane, sugar beet, etc. [F *sucre* SUGAR]

suction /súksh'n/ *n.* **1** the act or an instance of sucking. **2 a** the production of a partial vacuum by the removal of air etc. in order to force in liquid etc. or procure adhesion. **b** the force produced by this process (*suction keeps the lid on*). □ **suction-pump** a pump for drawing liquid through a pipe into a chamber emptied by a piston. [LL *suctio* f. L *sugere suct-* SUCK]

suctorial /suktóriəl/ *adj. Zool.* **1** adapted for or capable of sucking. **2** having a sucker for feeding or adhering. □□ **suctorian** *n.* [mod.L *suctorius* (as SUCTION)]

Sudanese /sóōdənéez/ *adj.* & *n.* ● *adj.* of or relating to Sudan, a republic in NE Africa, or the Sudan region south of the Sahara. ● *n.* (*pl.* same) **1** a native, national, or inhabitant of Sudan. **2** a person of Sudanese descent.

sudarium /syoodáiriəm, sóō-/ *n.* (*pl.* **sudaria** /-riə/) **1** a cloth for wiping the face. **2** *RC Ch.* = VERONICA 2. [L, = napkin f. *sudor* sweat]

sudatorium /syóōdətóriəm, sóō-/ *n.* (*pl.* **sudatoria** /-riə/) esp. *Rom. Antiq.* **1** a hot-air or steam bath. **2** a room where such a bath is taken. [L, neut. of *sudatorius*: see SUDATORY]

sudatory /syóōdətəri, sóō-/ *adj.* & *n.* ● *adj.* promoting perspiration. ● *n.* (*pl.* **-ies**) **1** a sudatory drug. **2** = SUDATORIUM. [L *sudatorius* f. *sudare* sweat]

sudd /sud/ *n.* floating vegetation impeding the navigation of the White Nile. [Arab., = obstruction]

sudden /súdd'n/ *adj.* & *n.* ● *adj.* occurring or done unexpectedly or without warning; abrupt, hurried, hasty (*a sudden storm; a sudden departure*). ● *n. archaic* a hasty or abrupt occurrence. □ **all of a sudden** unexpectedly; hurriedly; suddenly. **on a sudden** *archaic* suddenly. **sudden death** *colloq.* a decision in a tied game etc. dependent on one move, card, toss of a coin, etc. **sudden infant death syndrome** *Med.* = *cot-death* (see COT[1]). □□ **suddenly** *adv.* **suddenness** *n.* [ME f. AF *sodein, sudein*, OF *soudain* f. LL *subitanus* f. L *subitaneus* f. *subitus* sudden]
■ *adj.* unexpected, unannounced, unanticipated, unforeseen; surprising, startling; precipitate, abrupt, quick, immediate, rapid, swift, brisk, hurried, whirlwind; impetuous, hasty, rash, impulsive, snap. □ **all of a sudden** see *suddenly* (SUDDEN) below. □□ **suddenly** in a flash, in a moment, in a split second, all at once, instantly, instantaneously, fleetingly, in the twinkling of an eye, in a trice, *US* momentarily; quickly, abruptly, swiftly, speedily, rapidly; all of a sudden, out of the blue, unexpectedly, without warning, on the spur of the moment, hastily, hurriedly, feverishly, *archaic* on a sudden. **suddenness** see SPEED *n.* 1.

sudoriferous /syóōdəríffərəss, sóō-/ *adj.* (of a gland etc.) secreting sweat. [LL *sudorifer* f. L *sudor* sweat]

sudorific /syóōdəríffik, sóō-/ *adj.* & *n.* ● *adj.* (of a drug) causing sweating. ● *n.* a sudorific drug. [mod.L *sudorificus* f. L *sudor* sweat]

Sudra /sóōdrə/ *n.* a member of the lowest of the four great Hindu castes. [Skr. *śūdra*]

suds /sudz/ *n.* & *v.* ● *n.pl.* **1** froth of soap and water. **2** *US colloq.* beer. ● *v.* **1** *intr.* form suds. **2** *tr.* lather, cover, or wash in soapy water. □□ **sudsy** *adj.* [orig. = fen waters etc., of uncert. orig.: cf. MDu., MLG *sudde*, MDu. *sudse* marsh, bog, prob. rel. to SEETHE]
■ *n.* **1** see FROTH *n.* 1a. ● *v.* **1** see FOAM *v.*

sue /sóō, syóō/ *v.* (**sues, sued, suing**) **1** *tr.* (also *absol.*) *Law* institute legal proceedings against (a person). **2** *tr.* (also *absol.*) entreat (a person). **3** *intr.* (often foll. by *to, for*) *Law* make application to a lawcourt for redress. **4** *intr.* (often foll. by *to, for*) make entreaty to a person for a favour. **5** *tr.* (often foll. by *out*) make a petition in a lawcourt for and obtain (a writ, pardon, etc.). □□ **suer** *n.* [ME f. AF *suer, siwer*, etc. f. OF *siu-* etc. stem of *sivre* f. L *sequi* follow]
■ **1** proceed *or* move *or* act (against), take (legal) action (against), bring suit (against), prefer charges (against), prosecute; summon(s), charge, accuse. **2, 4** petition, beg, plead (with), entreat, pray, request, solicit, beseech, implore, supplicate; apply (to), appeal (to). □□ **suer** see LITIGANT *n.*

suede /swayd/ *n.* (often *attrib.*) **1** leather, esp. kidskin, with the flesh side rubbed to make a velvety nap. **2** (also

suede-cloth) a woven fabric resembling suede. [F (*gants de*) *Suède* (gloves of) Sweden]

suet /sóō-it, syóō-it/ *n.* the hard white fat on the kidneys or loins of oxen, sheep, etc., used to make dough etc. □ **suet pudding** a pudding of suet etc., usu. boiled or steamed. □□ **suety** *adj.* [ME f. AF f. OF *seu* f. L *sebum* tallow]

suf- /suf, səf/ *prefix* assim. form of SUB- before *f*.

suffer /súffər/ *v.* **1** *intr.* **a** undergo pain, grief, etc. (*suffers acutely*; *suffers from neglect*). **b** be damaged, decline (*your reputation will suffer*). **2** *tr.* undergo, experience, or be subjected to (pain, loss, grief, defeat, change, etc.) (*suffered banishment*). **3** *tr.* put up with; tolerate (*does not suffer fools gladly*). **4** *intr.* undergo martyrdom. **5** *tr.* (foll. by *to* + infin.) *archaic* allow. □□ **sufferable** *adj.* **sufferer** *n.* **suffering** *n.* [ME f. AF *suffrir*, *soeffrir*, OF *sof(f)rir* f. L *sufferre* (as SUB-, *ferre* bear)]
■ **1 a** agonize, smart, hurt, writhe, sweat, ache. **b** decline, deteriorate, diminish, go down, fall off, be reduced *or* diminished; pay (dearly). **2** endure, undergo, experience, feel, bear, live *or* go through, withstand, sustain, take, submit to. **3** tolerate, take, abide, put up with, bear, stand, indulge. **5** allow, permit, let. □□ **sufferable** see *supportable* (SUPPORT). **sufferer** see INVALID[1] *n.* 1, VICTIM 1, 2. **suffering** pain, agony, anguish, distress, misery, grief, sorrow, affliction, hardship, hurt, torment, torture, tribulation, trials, *archaic or literary* woe.

sufferance /súffərənss/ *n.* **1** tacit consent, abstinence from objection. **2** *archaic* submissiveness. □ **on sufferance** with toleration implied by lack of consent or objection. [ME f. AF, OF *suffraunce* f. LL *sufferentia* (as SUFFER)]
■ **1** see TOLERANCE 1.

suffice /səfíss/ *v.* **1** *intr.* (often foll. by *for*, or *to* + infin.) be enough or adequate (*that will suffice for our purpose*; *suffices to prove it*). **2** *tr.* meet the needs of; satisfy (*six sufficed him*). □ **suffice it to say** I shall content myself with saying. [ME f. OF *suffire* (*suffis-*) f. L *sufficere* (as SUB-, *facere* make)]
■ **1** serve, do, be sufficient *or* enough *or* adequate, answer, *colloq.* do the trick. **2** satisfy, sate, satiate, do, serve, meet the needs of.

sufficiency /səfíshənsi/ *n.* (*pl.* **-ies**) **1** (often foll. by *of*) an adequate amount or adequate resources. **2** *archaic* being sufficient; ability; efficiency. [LL *sufficientia* (as SUFFICIENT)]
■ **1** see ENOUGH *n.*

sufficient /səfísh'nt/ *adj.* **1** sufficing, adequate, enough (*is sufficient for a family*; *didn't have sufficient funds*). **2** = SELF-SUFFICIENT. **3** *archaic* competent; of adequate ability, resources, etc. □□ **sufficiently** *adv.* [ME f. OF *sufficient* or L *sufficiens* (as SUFFICE)]
■ **1** adequate, enough; ample. **3** see *up to scratch* (SCRATCH). □□ **sufficiently** see ENOUGH *adv.* 1, 2.

suffix /súffiks/ *n.* & *v.* ● *n.* **1** a verbal element added at the end of a word to form a derivative (e.g. *-ation*, *-fy*, *-ing*, *-itis*). **2** *Math.* = SUBSCRIPT. ● *v.tr.* /also səfíks/ append, esp. as a suffix. □□ **suffixation** /-sáysh'n/ *n.* [*suffixum*, *suffixus* past part. of L *suffigere* (as SUB-, *figere fix-* fasten)]
■ *n.* **1** ending, termination, addition; *Gram.* affix. ● *v.* add (on), join, fasten to, subjoin, append, tack on.

suffocate /súffəkayt/ *v.* **1** *tr.* choke or kill by stopping breathing, esp. by pressure, fumes, etc. **2** *tr.* (often foll. by *by*, *with*) produce a choking or breathless sensation in, esp. by excitement, terror, etc. **3** *intr.* be or feel suffocated or breathless. □□ **suffocating** *adj.* **suffocatingly** *adv.* **suffocation** /-káysh'n/ *n.* [L *suffocare* (as SUB-, *fauces* throat)]
■ **1** see CHOKE[1] *v.* 1. □□ **suffocating** see STUFFY 1.

Suffolk /súffək/ *n.* **1** a sheep of a black-faced breed. **2** this breed. [*Suffolk* in S. England]

Suffolk punch see PUNCH[4] 2.

suffragan /súfrəgən/ *n.* (in full **suffragan bishop** or **bishop suffragan**) **1** a bishop appointed to help a diocesan bishop in the administration of a diocese. **2** a bishop in relation to his archbishop or metropolitan. □ **suffragan see** the see of a suffragan bishop. □□ **suffraganship** *n.* [ME f. AF & OF, repr. med.L *suffraganeus* assistant (bishop) f. L *suffragium* (see SUFFRAGE): orig. of a bishop summoned to vote in synod]

suffrage /súfrij/ *n.* **1 a** the right of voting in political elections (*full adult suffrage*). **b** a view expressed by voting; a vote (*gave their suffrages for and against*). **c** opinion in support of a proposal etc. **2** (esp. in *pl.*) *Eccl.* **a** a prayer made by a priest in the liturgy. **b** a short prayer made by a congregation esp. in response to a priest. **c** *archaic* an intercessory prayer. [ME f. L *suffragium*, partly through F *suffrage*]
■ **1** (right to) vote, voting right(s), franchise, voice, say, ballot, option, choice.

suffragette /súfrəjét/ *n. hist.* a woman seeking the right to vote through organized protest. [SUFFRAGE + -ETTE]

suffragist /súfrəjist/ *n.* esp. *hist.* a person who advocates the extension of the suffrage, esp. to women. □□ **suffragism** *n.*

suffuse /səfyóōz/ *v.tr.* **1** (of colour, moisture, etc.) spread from within to colour or moisten (*a blush suffused her cheeks*). **2** cover with colour etc. □□ **suffusion** /-fyóōzh'n/ *n.* [L *suffundere suffus-* (as SUB-, *fundere* pour)]
■ overspread, imbue, spread through *or* over, permeate, pervade, flood, flush, charge, penetrate, saturate, mantle, infuse, transfuse, cover, bathe, pour over, *literary* imbrue.

Sufi /sóōfi/ *n.* (*pl.* **Sufis**) a Muslim ascetic and mystic. □□ **Sufic** *adj.* **Sufism** *n.* [Arab. *ṣūfī*, perh. f. *ṣūf* wool (from the woollen garment worn)]

sug- /sug, səg/ *prefix* assim. form of SUB- before *g*.

sugar /shóōggər/ *n.*, *v.*, & *int.* ● *n.* **1** a sweet crystalline substance obtained from various plants, esp. the sugar cane and sugar beet, used in cookery, confectionery, brewing, etc.; sucrose. **2** *Chem.* any of a group of soluble usu. sweet-tasting crystalline carbohydrates found esp. in plants, e.g. glucose. **3** esp. *US colloq.* darling, dear (used as a term of address). **4** sweet words; flattery. **5** anything comparable to sugar encasing a pill in reconciling a person to what is unpalatable. **6** *sl.* a narcotic drug, esp. heroin or LSD (taken on a lump of sugar). ● *v.tr.* **1** sweeten with sugar. **2** make (one's words, meaning, etc.) more pleasant or welcome. **3** coat with sugar (*sugared almond*). **4** spread a sugar mixture on (a tree) to catch moths. ● *int. euphem.* = SHIT *int.* □ **sugar beet** a beet, *Beta vulgaris*, from which sugar is extracted. **sugar-candy** see CANDY 1. **sugar cane** *Bot.* any perennial tropical grass of the genus *Saccharum*, esp. *S. officinarum*, with tall stout jointed stems from which sugar is made. **sugar-coated 1** (of food) enclosed in sugar. **2** made superficially attractive. **sugar-daddy** (*pl.* **-ies**) *sl.* an elderly man who lavishes gifts on a young woman. **sugar-gum** *Bot.* an Australian eucalyptus, *Eucalyptus cladocalyx*, with sweet foliage eaten by cattle. **sugar loaf** a conical moulded mass of sugar. **sugar-maple** any of various trees, esp. *Acer saccharum*, from the sap of which sugar is made. **sugar of lead** *Chem.* = *lead acetate* (see LEAD[2]). **sugar-pea** a variety of pea eaten whole including the pod. **sugar the pill** see PILL. **sugar soap** an alkaline compound for cleaning or removing paint. □□ **sugarless** *adj.* [ME f. OF *çukre*, *sukere* f. It. *zucchero* prob. f. med.L *succarum* f. Arab. *sūkkar*]
■ *n.* **4** cajolery, sweet words, flattery, *colloq.* sweet talk, soft soap, *Brit. sl.* flannel. **6** see JUNK[1] *n.* 3. ● *v.* **1** sweeten, sugar-coat.

sugarplum /shóōggərplum/ *n. archaic* a small round sweet of flavoured boiled sugar.

sugary /shóōggəri/ *adj.* **1** containing or resembling sugar. **2** excessively sweet or esp. sentimental. **3** falsely sweet or pleasant (*sugary compliments*). □□ **sugariness** *n.*
■ **1** see SWEET *adj.* 1. **2** see ROMANTIC *adj.* 1. **3** see *flattering* (FLATTER).

suggest /səjést/ *v.tr.* **1** (often foll. by *that* + clause) propose (a theory, plan, or hypothesis) (*suggested to them that they should wait*; *suggested a different plan*). **2 a** cause (an idea, memory, association, etc.) to present itself; evoke (*this poem suggests peace*). **b** hint at (*his behaviour suggests guilt*). □

suggest itself (of an idea etc.) come into the mind. ▫▫ **suggester** *n.* [L *suggerere suggest-* (as SUB-, *gerere* bring)]
■ **1** propose, advance, propound, recommend, endorse, commend, urge, advise, advocate, offer, proffer, put *or* set forward, present, mention, introduce. **2** call to mind, evoke, bring up, hint (at), imply, insinuate, intimate, make a person think of, lead a person to believe, indicate, communicate.

suggestible /səjéstib'l/ *adj.* **1** capable of being suggested. **2** open to suggestion; easily swayed. ▫▫ **suggestibility** /-bílliti/ *n.*
■ **2** impressionable, susceptible, receptive, impressible, susceptive, open (to suggestion), mouldable.
▫▫ **suggestibility** susceptibility, impressionability, receptiveness, vulnerability, frailty.

suggestion /səjéss-chən/ *n.* **1** the act or an instance of suggesting; the state of being suggested. **2** a theory, plan, etc., suggested (*made a helpful suggestion*). **3** a slight trace; a hint (*a suggestion of garlic*). **4** *Psychol.* **a** the insinuation of a belief etc. into the mind. **b** such a belief etc. [ME f. OF f. L *suggestio -onis* (as SUGGEST)]
■ **1** counselling, prompting, urging, inducement.
2 proposal, proposition, recommendation, plan, advice, counsel, exhortation, tip, idea, notion, opinion, theory.
3 indication, trace, whisper, hint, soupçon, touch, tinge, suspicion, breath; iota, jot (or tittle).

suggestive /səjéstiv/ *adj.* **1** (usu. foll. by *of*) conveying a suggestion; evocative. **2** (esp. of a remark, joke, etc.) indecent; improper. ▫▫ **suggestively** *adv.* **suggestiveness** *n.*
■ **1** reminiscent, redolent, evocative, indicative, symptomatic, expressive; pregnant, significant, meaningful, eloquent. **2** provocative, risqué, ribald, racy, bawdy, earthy, lusty, rude, indelicate, unseemly, immodest, improper, indecent, obscene, prurient, blue, offensive, vulgar, smutty, dirty, pornographic, lewd, salacious, sexy, spicy, *US* off colour, *colloq.* raunchy, *colloq. joc.* naughty. ▫▫ **suggestiveness** see IMPROPRIETY 1.

suicidal /sóo-isíd'l, syóo-/ *adj.* **1** inclined to commit suicide. **2** of or concerning suicide. **3** self-destructive; fatally or disastrously rash. ▫▫ **suicidally** *adv.*

suicide /sóo-isīd, syóo-/ *n.* & *v.* ● *n.* **1 a** the intentional killing of oneself. **b** a person who commits suicide. **2** a self-destructive action or course (*political suicide*). **3** (*attrib.*) *Mil.* designating a highly dangerous or deliberately suicidal operation etc. (*a suicide mission*). ● *v.intr.* commit suicide. ▫ **suicide pact** an agreement between two or more people to commit suicide together. [mod.L *suicida*, *suicidium* f. L *sui* of oneself]

sui generis /syóo-ī jénnəriss, sóo-i gén-/ *adj.* of its own kind; unique. [L]
■ see UNIQUE *adj.* 1.

sui juris /syóo-ī jóoriss, sóo-i yóoriss/ *adj.* *Law* of age; independent. [L]

suilline /sóo-ilīn/ *adj.* of the pig family Suidae. [L *suillus* f. *sus* pig]

suint /swint/ *n.* the natural grease in sheep's wool. [F f. *suer* sweat]

suit /soot, syoot/ *n.* & *v.* ● *n.* **1 a** a set of outer clothes of matching material for men, consisting usu. of a jacket, trousers, and sometimes a waistcoat. **b** a similar set of clothes for women usu. having a skirt instead of trousers. **c** (esp. in *comb.*) a set of clothes for a special occasion, occupation, etc. (*play-suit*; *swimsuit*). **2 a** any of the four sets (spades, hearts, diamonds, clubs) into which a pack of cards is divided. **b** a player's holding in a suit (*his strong suit was clubs*). **c** *Bridge* one of the suits as proposed trumps in bidding, frequently as opposed to no trumps. **3** (in full **suit at law**) a lawsuit (*criminal suit*). **4 a** a petition esp. to a person in authority. **b** the process of courting a woman (*paid suit to her*). **5** (usu. foll. by *of*) a set of sails, armour, etc. ● *v.* **1** *tr.* go well with (a person's figure, features, character, etc.); become. **2** *tr.* (also *absol.*) meet the demands or requirements of; satisfy; agree with (*does not suit all tastes*; *that date will suit*). **3** *tr.* make fitting or appropriate; accommodate; adapt (*suited his style to his audience*). **4** *tr.* (as **suited** *adj.*) appropriate; well-fitted (*not suited to be an engineer*). **5** *intr.* (usu. foll. by *with*) go well with the appearance etc. of a person (*red hair suits with her complexion*). ▫ **suit the action to the word** carry out a promise or threat at once. **suit oneself 1** do as one chooses. **2** find something that satisfies one. [ME f. AF *siute*, OF *si(e)ute* f. fem. past part. of Rmc *sequere* (unrecorded) follow: see SUE]
■ *n.* **1** costume, outfit, two-piece, ensemble; uniform, habit; garb, clothing, clothes, livery. **3** lawsuit, action, case, proceeding, process, cause, trial; litigation.
4 a petition, plea, request, entreaty, prayer, solicitation, application, appeal, supplication. **b** courtship, wooing; court, attentions, addresses. ● *v.* **1** go well with; become, befit, look good on, be appropriate *or* suitable for. **2** please, satisfy, fill *or* meet *or* answer a person's needs, gratify, be acceptable (to *or* for), be suitable (to *or* for), be convenient (to *or* for), befit; conform (to), agree with, fit in (with). **3** adapt, accommodate, fit, adjust, tailor, gear, make appropriate *or* suitable. **4** (**suited**) see APPROPRIATE *adj.*, *tailor-made* 2.

suitable /sóotəb'l, syóot-/ *adj.* (usu. foll. by *to*, *for*) well fitted for the purpose; appropriate. ▫▫ **suitability** /-bílliti/ *n.* **suitableness** *n.* **suitably** *adv.* [SUIT + -ABLE, after *agreeable*]
■ appropriate, apt, apposite, fit, fitting, befitting, becoming, right, proper, correct, acceptable, satisfactory, applicable, qualified, eligible, seemly; pertinent, relevant, apropos; timely, opportune, convenient, *archaic* meet.
▫▫ **suitability, suitableness** see *fitness* (FIT[1]). **suitably** see *appropriately* (APPROPRIATE).

suitcase /sóotkayss, syóot-/ *n.* a usu. oblong case for carrying clothes etc., having a handle and a flat hinged lid. ▫▫ **suitcaseful** *n.* (*pl.* **-fuls**).
■ bag, case, trunk, overnight bag, travelling bag, portmanteau, *Austral.* port, *US* valise.

suite /sweet/ *n.* **1** a set of things belonging together, esp.: **a** a set of rooms in a hotel etc. **b** a sofa, armchairs, etc., of the same design. **2** *Mus.* **a** a set of instrumental compositions, orig. in dance style, to be played in succession. **b** a set of selected pieces from an opera, musical, etc., arranged to be played as one instrumental work. **3** a set of people in attendance; a retinue. [F (as SUIT)]
■ **1** set, series, collection, number; arrangement.
3 following, retinue, entourage, train, cortège, convoy, escort; followers, attendants, *hist.* retainers.

suiting /sóoting, syóot-/ *n.* cloth used for making suits.

suitor /sóotər, syóot-/ *n.* **1** a man seeking to marry a specified woman; a wooer. **2** a plaintiff or petitioner in a lawsuit. [ME f. AF *seutor*, *suitour*, etc., f. L *secutor -oris* f. *sequi secut-* follow]
■ **1** admirer, wooer, *US* beau; boyfriend, lover, inamorato, escort, *archaic or derog.* paramour, *poet.* swain. **2** see LITIGANT *n.*

suk (also **sukh**) var. of SOUK.

sukiyaki /sóokkiyáaki/ *n.* a Japanese dish of sliced meat simmered with vegetables and sauce. [Jap.]

sulcate /súlkayt/ *adj.* grooved, fluted, channelled. [L *sulcatus*, past part. of *sulcare* furrow (as SULCUS)]

sulcus /súlkəss/ *n.* (*pl.* **sulci** /-sī/) *Anat.* a groove or furrow, esp. on the surface of the brain. [L]
■ see FURROW *n.*

sulfa *US* var. of SULPHA.

sulfanilamide *US* var. of SULPHANILAMIDE.

sulfate etc. *US* var. of SULPHATE etc.

sulfur etc. *US* var. of SULPHUR etc.

sulk /sulk/ *v.* & *n.* ● *v.intr.* indulge in a sulk, be sulky. ● *n.* (also in *pl.*, prec. by *the*) a period of sullen esp. resentful silence (*having a sulk*; *got the sulks*). ▫▫ **sulker** *n.* [perh. back-form. f. SULKY]

■ *v.* mope, brood, pout, lour, be sullen *or* moody *or* ill-humoured.

sulky /súlki/ *adj.* & *n.* ● *adj.* (**sulkier, sulkiest**) **1** sullen, morose, or silent, esp. from resentment or ill temper. **2** sluggish. ● *n.* (*pl.* **-ies**) a light two-wheeled horse-drawn vehicle for one, esp. used in trotting-races. ▫▫ **sulkily** *adv.* **sulkiness** *n.* [perh. f. obs. *sulke* hard to dispose of]

■ *adj.* **1** see SULLEN *adj.* 1.

sullage /súllij/ *n.* filth, refuse, sewage. [perh. f. AF *suillage* f. *souiller* SOIL[2]]

■ see FILTH 1.

sullen /súllən/ *adj.* & *n.* ● *adj.* **1** morose, resentful, sulky, unforgiving, unsociable. **2 a** (of a thing) slow-moving. **b** dismal, melancholy (*a sullen sky*). ● *n.* (in *pl.*, usu. prec. by *the*) *archaic* a sullen frame of mind; depression. ▫▫ **sullenly** *adv.* **sullenness** *n.* [16th-c. alt. of ME *solein* f. AF f. *sol* SOLE[3]]

■ *adj.* **1** sulky, sulking, morose, brooding, broody, pouting, gloomy, moody, temperamental, dour, lugubrious, funereal, dismal, dreary, grim, depressed, churlish, ill-humoured, glum, grumpy, sombre, out of humour, antisocial, unsociable, resentful, cross, petulant, perverse, crusty, crotchety, choleric, crabby, ill-natured, ill-tempered, bad-tempered, splenetic, peevish, dyspeptic, out of sorts, *esp. US* cranky. **2 b** see LEADEN 4.

sully /súlli/ *v.tr.* (**-ies, -ied**) **1** disgrace or tarnish (a person's reputation or character, a victory, etc.). **2** *poet.* dirty; soil. [perh. f. F *souiller* (as SOIL[2])]

■ besmirch, stain, smirch, blemish, mar, defile, soil, disgrace, dirty, tarnish, pollute, contaminate, spoil.

sulpha /súlfə/ *n.* (*US* **sulfa**) any drug derived from sulphanilamide (often *attrib.*: *sulpha drug*). [abbr.]

sulphamic acid /sulfámmik/ *n.* (*US* **sulfamic**) a strong acid used in weed-killer, an amide of sulphuric acid. ▫▫ **sulphamate** /súlfəmayt/ *n.* [SULPHUR + AMIDE]

sulphanilamide /súlfənílləmīd/ *n.* (*US* **sulfanilamide**) a colourless sulphonamide drug with anti-bacterial properties. [*sulphanilic* (SULPHUR, ANILINE) + AMIDE]

sulphate /súlfayt/ *n.* (*US* **sulfate**) a salt or ester of sulphuric acid. [F *sulfate* f. L *sulphur*]

sulphide /súlfīd/ *n.* (*US* **sulfide**) *Chem.* a binary compound of sulphur.

sulphite /súlfīt/ *n.* (*US* **sulfite**) *Chem.* a salt or ester of sulphurous acid. [F *sulfite* alt. of *sulfate* SULPHATE]

sulphonamide /sulfónnəmīd/ *n.* (*US* **sulfonamide**) a substance derived from an amide of a sulphonic acid, able to prevent the multiplication of some pathogenic bacteria. [SULPHONE + AMIDE]

sulphonate /súlfənayt/ *n.* & *v.* (*US sulfonate*) *Chem.* ● *n.* a salt or ester of sulphonic acid. ● *v.tr.* convert into a sulphonate by reaction with sulphuric acid.

sulphone /súlfōn/ *n.* (*US* **sulfone**) an organic compound containing the SO_2 group united directly to two carbon atoms. ▫▫ **sulphonic** /-fónnik/ *adj.* [G *Sulfon* (as SULPHUR)]

sulphur /súlfər/ *n.* & *v.* (*US* **sulfur**) ● *n.* **1 a** a pale-yellow non-metallic element having crystalline and amorphous forms, burning with a blue flame and a suffocating smell, and used in making gunpowder, matches, and sulphuric acid, in the vulcanizing of rubber, and in the treatment of skin diseases. ¶ Symb.: **S. b** (*attrib.*) like or containing sulphur. **2** the material of which hell-fire and lightning were believed to consist. **3** any yellow butterfly of the family Pieridae. **4** a pale greenish yellow colour. ● *v.tr.* **1** treat with sulphur. **2** fumigate with sulphur. ▫ **sulphur candle** a candle burnt to produce sulphur dioxide for fumigating. **sulphur dioxide** a colourless pungent gas formed by burning sulphur in air and used as a food preservative. **sulphur spring** a spring impregnated with sulphur or its compounds. ▫▫ **sulphury** *adj.* [ME f. AF *sulf(e)re*, OF *soufre* f. L *sulfur*, *sulp(h)ur*]

■ *n.* **1, 2** *archaic* brimstone.

sulphurate /súlfyoorayt/ *v.tr.* (*US* **sulfurate**) impregnate, fumigate, or treat with sulphur, esp. in bleaching. ▫▫ **sulphuration** /-ráysh'n/ *n.* **sulphurator** *n.*

sulphureous /sulfyóoriəss/ *adj.* (*US* **sulfureous**) **1** of, like, or suggesting sulphur. **2** sulphur-coloured; yellow. [L *sulphureus* f. SULPHUR]

sulphuretted /súlfyoorettid/ *adj.* (*US* **sulfureted**) *archaic* containing sulphur in combination. ▫ **sulphuretted hydrogen** hydrogen sulphide. [*sulphuret* sulphide f. mod.L *sulphuretum*]

sulphuric /sulfyóorik/ *adj.* (*US* **sulfuric**) *Chem.* containing sexivalent sulphur. ▫ **sulphuric acid** a dense oily colourless highly acid and corrosive fluid much used in the chemical industry. ¶ Chem. formula: H_2SO_4. [F *sulfurique* (as SULPHUR)]

sulphurize /súlfyoorīz/ *v.tr.* (also **-ise**, *US* **sulfurize**) = SULPHURATE. ▫▫ **sulphurization** /-záysh'n/ *n.* [F *sulfuriser* (as SULPHUR)]

sulphurous /súlfərəss/ *adj.* (*US* **sulfurous**) **1** relating to or suggestive of sulphur, esp. in colour. **2** *Chem.* containing quadrivalent sulphur. ▫ **sulphurous acid** an unstable weak acid used as a reducing and bleaching acid. [L *sulphurosus* f. SULPHUR]

sultan /súlt'n/ *n.* **1 a** a Muslim sovereign. **b** (**the Sultan**) *hist.* the sultan of Turkey. **2** a variety of white domestic fowl from Turkey. ▫▫ **sultanate** /-nayt/ *n.* [F *sultan* or med.L *sultanus* f. Arab. *sulṭān* power, ruler f. *saluṭa* rule]

■ **1** see SOVEREIGN *n.*

sultana /sultaánə/ *n.* **1 a** a seedless raisin used in puddings, cakes, etc. **b** the small pale yellow grape producing this. **2** the mother, wife, concubine, or daughter of a sultan. [It., fem. of *sultano* = SULTAN]

sultry /súltri/ *adj.* (**sultrier, sultriest**) **1** (of the atmosphere or the weather) hot or oppressive; close. **2** (of a person, character, etc.) passionate; sensual. ▫▫ **sultrily** *adv.* **sultriness** *n.* [obs. *sulter* SWELTER]

■ **1** hot, humid, sticky, stuffy, stifling, oppressive, close, muggy, steamy, steaming, moist, damp, sweltering, suffocating. **2** lusty, lustful, passionate, erotic, seductive, voluptuous, provocative, sensual, sexy, hot.

sum /sum/ *n.* & *v.* ● *n.* **1** the total amount resulting from the addition of two or more items, facts, ideas, feelings, etc. (*the sum of two and three is five*; *the sum of their objections is this*). **2** a particular amount of money (*paid a large sum for it*). **3 a** an arithmetical problem (*could not work out the sum*). **b** (esp. *pl.*) *colloq.* arithmetic work, esp. at an elementary level (*was good at sums*). ● *v.tr.* (**summed, summing**) find the sum of. ▫ **in sum** in brief. **summing-up 1** a review of evidence and a direction given by a judge to a jury. **2** a recapitulation of the main points of an argument, case, etc. **sum total** = sense 1 of *n.* **sum up 1** (esp. of a judge) recapitulate or review the evidence in a case etc. **2** form or express an idea of the character of (a person, situation, etc.). **3** collect into or express as a total or whole. [ME f. OF *summe*, *somme* f. L *summa* main part, fem. of *summus* highest]

■ *n.* **1** total, aggregate, grand total, sum total, whole, totality; result, tally, score. **2** amount, figure, quantity. **3 a** problem, question. **b** (*sums*) arithmetic, figures, numbers, calculation, computation; mathematics, *Brit. colloq.* maths, *US colloq.* math. ● *v.* see ADD 2. ▫ **in sum** see *in brief* (BRIEF). **summing-up** review, recapitulation, summarization, summary, summation, synopsis, run-down. **sum up 1** recapitulate, summarize, encapsulate, synopsize, digest, abridge, condense, consolidate, epitomize, review. **2** estimate, evaluate, assess, size up, measure (up), take the measure of. **3** reckon, add up, calculate, total, tot up, sum.

sumac /sóomak, shóo-, syóo-/ *n.* (also **sumach**) **1** any shrub or tree of the genus *Rhus*, having reddish cone-shaped fruits used as a spice in cooking. **2** the dried and ground leaves of this used in tanning and dyeing. [ME f. OF *sumac* or med.L *sumac(h)* f. Arab. *summāk*]

Sumerian /soomeériən, syoo-/ *adj.* & *n.* ● *adj.* of or relating to the early and non-Semitic element in the civilization of ancient Babylonia. ● *n.* **1** a member of the early non-Semitic people of ancient Babylonia. **2** the Sumerian language. [F *sumérien* f. *Sumer* in Babylonia]

summa /súmmə/ *n.* (*pl.* **summae** /-mee/) a summary of what is known of a subject. [ME f. L: see SUM]

summa cum laude /sŏŏmmə kŏŏm lówday/ *adv.* & *adj.* esp. *US* (of a degree, diploma, etc.) of the highest standard; with the highest distinction. [L, = with highest praise]

summarize /súmmərīz/ *v.tr.* (also **-ise**) make or be a summary of; sum up. □□ **summarist** *n.* **summarizable** *adj.* **summarization** /-záysh'n/ *n.* **summarizer** *n.*

■ see *sum up* 1. □□ **summarization** see SUMMARY *n.*

summary /súmməri/ *n.* & *adj.* ● *n.* (*pl.* **-ies**) a brief account; an abridgement. ● *adj.* **1** dispensing with needless details or formalities; brief (*a summary account*). **2** *Law* (of a trial etc.) without the customary legal formalities (*summary justice*). □ **summary conviction** a conviction made by a judge or magistrates without a jury. **summary jurisdiction** the authority of a court to use summary proceedings and arrive at a judgement. **summary offence** an offence within the scope of a summary court. □□ **summarily** *adv.* **summariness** *n.* [ME f. L *summarium* f. L *summa* SUM]

■ *n.* summarization, recapitulation, encapsulation, compendium, synopsis, abstract, digest, abridgement, condensation, shortening, consolidation, epitome, epitomization, review, distillate, conspectus, outline, précis, résumé, *Law* brief. ● *adj.* **1** abrupt, sudden, short, quick, brief, laconic, perfunctory, curt, terse, concise, succinct. **2** peremptory; see also SPEEDY 2. □□ **summarily** immediately, at once, straight away, directly, quickly, without delay, unhesitatingly, without hesitation, forthwith, promptly, swiftly, speedily, expeditiously, instantly; suddenly, without warning, abruptly, peremptorily, precipitately; *colloq.* p.d.q. (= 'pretty damn quick').

summation /səmáysh'n/ *n.* **1** the finding of a total or sum; an addition. **2** a summing-up. □□ **summational** *adj.*

summer[1] /súmmər/ *n.* & *v.* ● *n.* **1** the warmest season of the year, in the N. hemisphere from June to August and in the S. hemisphere from December to February. **2** *Astron.* the period from the summer solstice to the autumnal equinox. **3** the hot weather typical of summer. **4** (often foll. by *of*) the mature stage of life; the height of achievement, powers, etc. **5** (esp. in *pl.*) *poet.* a year (esp. of a person's age) (*a child of ten summers*). **6** (*attrib.*) characteristic of or suitable for summer (*summer clothes*). ● *v.* **1** *intr.* (usu. foll. by *at*, *in*) pass the summer. **2** *tr.* (often foll. by *at*, *in*) pasture (cattle). □ **summer-house** a light building in a garden etc. used for sitting in in fine weather. **summer lightning** sheet lightning without thunder, resulting from a distant storm. **summer pudding** *Brit.* a pudding of soft summer fruit encased in bread or sponge. **summer school** a course of lectures etc. held during the summer vacation, esp. at a university. **summer solstice** see SOLSTICE. **summer time** *Brit.* the period between March and October during which the clocks are advanced an hour (cf. SUMMERTIME). **summer-weight** (of clothes) suitable for use in summer, esp. because of their light weight. □□ **summerless** *adj.* **summerly** *adv.* **summery** *adj.* [OE *sumor*]

■ □□ **summery** see SOFT *adj.* 3.

summer[2] /súmmər/ *n.* (in full **summer-tree**) a horizontal bearing beam, esp. one supporting joists or rafters. [ME f. AF *sumer*, *somer* packhorse, beam, OF *somier* f. LL *sagmarius* f. *sagma* f. Gk *sagma* pack-saddle]

summersault var. of SOMERSAULT.

summertime /súmmərtīm/ *n.* the season or period of summer (cf. *summer time*).

summit /súmmit/ *n.* **1** the highest point, esp. of a mountain; the apex. **2** the highest degree of power, ambition, etc. **3** (in full **summit meeting, talks**, etc.) a discussion, esp. on disarmament etc., between heads of government. □□ **summitless** *adj.* [ME f. OF *somet*, *som(m)ete* f. *som* top f. L *summum* neut. of *summus*]

■ **1, 2** peak, top, apex, acme, pinnacle, zenith, crown, height; culmination, apogee, climax.

summon /súmmən/ *v.tr.* **1** call upon to appear, esp. as a defendant or witness in a lawcourt. **2** (usu. foll. by *to* + infin.) call upon (*summoned her to assist*). **3** call together for a meeting or some other purpose (*summoned the members to attend*). □ **summon up** (often foll. by *to*, *for*) gather (courage, spirits, resources, etc.) (*summoned up her strength for the task*). □□ **summonable** *adj.* **summoner** *n.* [ME f. OF *somondre* f. L *summonēre* (as SUB-, *monēre* warn)]

■ **1, 2** subpoena, summons; call upon, send for, command, order. **3** call, assemble, convene, send for, invite, muster, get *or* gather together, rally, arouse, rouse, *formal* convoke. □ **summon up** call *or* draw (up)on, draw up, mobilize, muster (up), work up, whip up, gather, invoke.

summons /súmmənz/ *n.* & *v.* ● *n.* (*pl.* **summonses**) **1** an authoritative or urgent call to attend on some occasion or do something. **2 a** a call to appear before a judge or magistrate. **b** the writ containing such a summons. ● *v.tr.* esp. *Law* serve with a summons. [ME f. OF *somonce*, *sumunse* f. L *summonita* fem. past part. of *summonēre*: see SUMMON]

■ *n.* **1, 2a** see CALL *n.* 5. **2 b** see WARRANT *n.* 2. ● *v.* see INDICT.

summum bonum /sŏŏmməm bónnəm, bō-/ *n.* the highest good, esp. as the end or determining principle in an ethical system. [L]

sumo /sŏŏmō/ *n.* (*pl.* **-os**) **1** a style of Japanese wrestling, in which a participant is defeated by touching the ground with any part of the body except the soles of the feet or by moving outside the marked area. **2** a sumo wrestler. [Jap.]

sump /sump/ *n.* **1** a pit, well, hole, etc. in which superfluous liquid collects in mines, machines, etc. **2** a cesspool. [ME, = marsh f. MDu., MLG *sump*, or (mining) G *Sumpf*, rel. to SWAMP]

sumpter /súmptər/ *n.* *archaic* **1** a packhorse. **2** any pack-animal (*sumpter-mule*). [ME f. OF *som(m)etier* f. LL f. Gk *sagma -atos* pack-saddle: cf. SUMMER[2]]

sumptuary /súmptyoori/ *adj.* **1** regulating expenditure. **2** (of a law or edict etc.) limiting private expenditure in the interests of the State. [L *sumptuarius* f. *sumptus* cost f. *sumere sumpt-* take]

sumptuous /súmptyooəss/ *adj.* rich, lavish, costly (*a sumptuous setting*). □□ **sumptuosity** /-yoo-óssiti/ *n.* **sumptuously** *adv.* **sumptuousness** *n.* [ME f. OF *somptueux* f. L *sumptuosus* (as SUMPTUARY)]

■ expensive, costly, extravagant, exorbitant, dear, rich; lavish, luxurious, de luxe, opulent, palatial, royal, majestic, regal, magnificent, dazzling, splendid, gorgeous, grand, showy, plush, *colloq.* posh, plushy, ritzy. □□ **sumptuously** see RICHLY 1. **sumptuousness** see LUXURY 1.

Sun. *abbr.* Sunday.

sun /sun/ *n.* & *v.* ● *n.* **1 a** the star round which the earth orbits and from which it receives light and warmth. **b** any similar star in the universe with or without planets. **2** the light or warmth received from the sun (*pull down the blinds and keep out the sun*). **3** *poet.* a day or a year. **4** *poet.* a person or thing regarded as a source of glory, radiance, etc. ● *v.* (**sunned, sunning**) **1** *refl.* bask in the sun. **2** *tr.* expose to the sun. **3** *intr.* sun oneself. □ **against the sun** anticlockwise. **beneath** (or **under**) **the sun** anywhere in the world. **in the sun** exposed to the sun's rays. **on which the sun never sets** (of an empire etc.) worldwide. **sun and planet** a system of gearing cog wheels. **sun-baked** dried or hardened or baked from the heat of the sun. **sun-bath** a period of exposing the body to the sun. **sun bear** a small black bear, *Helarctos malayanus*, of SE Asia, with a light-coloured mark on its chest. **sun-blind** *Brit.* a window awning. **sun-bonnet** a bonnet of cotton etc. covering the neck and shading the face, esp. for children. **sun-bow** a spectrum of colours like a rainbow produced by the sun shining on spray etc. **sun-dance** a dance of N. American Indians in honour of the sun. **sun-deck** the upper deck of a steamer. **sun-disc** a winged disc, emblematic of the sun-god. **sun-dog** = PARHELION. **sun-dress** a dress without sleeves and with a low neck. **sun-dried** dried by the sun, not by artificial heat. **sun-glasses** glasses tinted to protect the eyes from sunlight or glare. **sun-god** the sun worshipped as a deity. **sun-hat** a hat designed to protect the head from the sun. **sun-helmet** a helmet of cork etc. formerly worn by White people in the tropics. **sun in splendour** *Heraldry* the sun with rays and a human face. **one's sun is set** the time of one's prosperity is over. **sun-kissed** warmed or affected by the sun. **sun-lamp 1** a lamp giving ultraviolet rays for an artificial suntan, therapy, etc. **2** *Cinematog.* a large lamp with a parabolic reflector used in film-making. **sun lounge** a room with large windows, designed to receive sunlight. **sun parlor** *US* = *sun lounge*. **sun-rays 1** sunbeams. **2** ultraviolet rays used therapeutically. **sun-roof** a sliding roof on a car. **sun-stone** a cat's eye gem, esp. feldspar with embedded flecks of haematite etc. **sun-suit** a play-suit, esp. for children, suitable for sunbathing. **sun-up** esp. *US* sunrise. **sun visor** a fixed or movable shield at the top of a vehicle windscreen to shield the eyes from the sun. **take** (or **shoot**) **the sun** *Naut.* ascertain the altitude of the sun with a sextant in order to fix the latitude. **with the sun** clockwise. □□ **sunless** *adj.* **sunlessness** *n.* **sunlike** *adj.* **sunproof** *adj.* **sunward** *adj.* & *adv.* **sunwards** *adv.* [OE *sunne, sunna*]

■ *n.* **2** sunshine, sunlight. ● *v.* **1, 3** bask, bake, sun oneself; tan, suntan, sunbathe, brown, bronze. **2** tan, bake, brown, bronze. □ **beneath** (or **under**) **the sun** see BELOW *adv.* 5. **sun-glasses** *esp. US colloq.* shades. **sun-up** see DAWN *n.* 1. □□ **sunless** dark, dull, grim, cheerless, unhappy, joyless, funereal, depressing, dreary, sombre, gloomy, overcast, grey, black, pitchy, inky, shadowy, unlit, unlighted, dusky, *formal* subfusc, *literary* tenebrous, Stygian, *poet.* darkling, drear.

sunbathe /súnbayth/ *v.intr.* bask in the sun, esp. to tan the body. □□ **sunbather** *n.*

■ see SUN *v.* 1, 3.

sunbeam /súnbeem/ *n.* a ray of sunlight.

sunbed /súnbed/ *n.* **1** a lightweight, usu. folding, chair with a seat long enough to support the legs, used for sunbathing. **2** a bed for lying on under a sun-lamp.

sunbelt /súnbelt/ *n.* a strip of territory receiving a high amount of sunshine, esp. the region in the southern US stretching from California to Florida.

sunbird /súnburd/ *n.* any small bright-plumaged Old World bird of the family Nectariniidae, resembling a humming-bird.

sunblock /súnblok/ *n.* a cream or lotion for protecting the skin from the sun.

sunburn /súnburn/ *n.* & *v.* ● *n.* tanning and inflammation of the skin caused by over-exposure to the sun. ● *v.intr.* **1** suffer from sunburn. **2** (as **sunburnt** or **sunburned** *adj.*) suffering from sunburn; brown or tanned.

sunburst /súnburst/ *n.* **1** something resembling the sun and its rays, esp.: **a** an ornament, brooch, etc. **b** a firework. **2** the sun shining suddenly from behind clouds.

sundae /súnday, -di/ *n.* a dish of ice-cream with fruit, nuts, syrup, etc. [perh. f. SUNDAY]

Sunday /súnday, -di/ *n.* & *adv.* ● *n.* **1** the first day of the week, a Christian holiday and day of worship. **2** a newspaper published on a Sunday. ● *adv. colloq.* **1** on Sunday. **2** (**Sundays**) on Sundays; each Sunday. □ **Sunday best** *joc.* a person's best clothes, kept for Sunday use. **Sunday letter** = *dominical letter*. **Sunday painter** an amateur painter, esp. one with little training. **Sunday school** a school for the religious instruction of children on Sundays. [OE *sunnandæg*, transl. of L *dies solis*, Gk *hēmera hēliou* day of the sun]

■ □ **Sunday best** see FINERY[1].

sunder /súndər/ *v.tr.* & *intr. archaic* or *literary* separate, sever. □ **in sunder** apart. [OE *sundrian*, f. *āsundrian* etc.: *in sunder* f. ME f. *o(n)sunder* ASUNDER]

■ see DIVIDE *v.* 1, 3a.

sundew /súndyoo/ *n.* any small insect-consuming bog-plant of the family Droseraceae, esp. of the genus *Drosera* with hairs secreting drops of moisture.

sundial /súndīəl/ *n.* an instrument showing the time by the shadow of a pointer cast by the sun on to a graduated disc.

sundown /súndown/ *n.* sunset.

■ see EVENING *n.* 1.

sundowner /súndownər/ *n.* **1** *Austral.* a tramp who arrives at a sheep station etc. in the evening for food and shelter. **2** *Brit. colloq.* an alcoholic drink taken at sunset.

■ **1** see TRAMP *n.* 1. **2** see DRINK *n.* 2b.

sundry /súndri/ *adj.* & *n.* ● *adj.* various; several (*sundry items*). ● *n.* (*pl.* **-ies**) **1** (in *pl.*) items or oddments not mentioned individually. **2** *Austral. Cricket* = EXTRA *n.* 5. [OE *syndrig* separate, rel. to SUNDER]

■ *adj.* various, varied, miscellaneous, assorted, different, mixed, diversified, diverse, several, *archaic* or *literary* divers. ● *n.* **1** (*sundries*) miscellanea, oddments, et ceteras.

sunfast /súnfaast/ *adj. US* (of dye) not subject to fading by sunlight.

sunfish /súnfish/ *n.* any of various almost spherical fish, esp. a large ocean fish, *Mola mola*.

sunflower /súnflowr/ *n.* any very tall plant of the genus *Helianthus*, esp. *H. annus* with very large showy golden-rayed flowers, grown also for its seeds which yield an edible oil.

sung *past part.* of SING.

sunk *past* and *past part.* of SINK.

sunken /súngkən/ *adj.* **1** that has been sunk. **2** beneath the surface; submerged. **3** (of the eyes, cheeks, etc.) hollow, depressed. □ **sunken garden** a garden placed below the general level of its surroundings. [past part. of SINK]

■ **1** buried, underground, in-ground, below-ground, settled, lowered. **2** submerged, undersea, underwater. **3** hollow, hollowed-out, depressed; haggard, drawn.

sunlight /súnlīt/ *n.* light from the sun.

■ see LIGHT[1] *n.* 2.

sunlit /súnlit/ *adj.* illuminated by sunlight.

■ see SUNNY 1.

sunn /sun/ *n.* (in full **sunn hemp**) an E. Indian hemplike fibre. [Urdu & Hindi *san* f. Skr. *śāṇá* hempen]

Sunna /súnnə/ *n.* a traditional portion of Muslim law based on Muhammad's words or acts, accepted by Muslims as authoritative. [Arab., = form, way, course, rule]

Sunni /súnni/ *n.* & *adj.* ● *n.* (*pl.* same or **Sunnis**) **1** one of the two main branches of Islam, regarding the Sunna as equal in authority to the Koran (cf. SHIAH). **2** an adherent of this branch of Islam. ● *adj.* (also **Sunnite**) of or relating to Sunni.

sunny /súnni/ *adj.* (**sunnier, sunniest**) **1 a** bright with sunlight. **b** exposed to or warmed by the sun. **2** cheery and bright in temperament. □ **the sunny side 1** the side of a house, street, etc. that gets most sun. **2** the more cheerful aspect of circumstances etc. (*always looks on the sunny side*). □□ **sunnily** *adv.* **sunniness** *n.*

■ **1** sunlit, sunshiny, brilliant, bright, radiant, fair, fine, cloudless, clear, unclouded. **2** cheerful, cheery, bright, happy, joyous, joyful, light-hearted, smiling, beaming, buoyant, gay, mirthful, jolly, bubbly, ebullient, genial, warm, friendly, outgoing, *poet.* blithe.

sunrise /súnrīz/ *n.* **1** the sun's rising at dawn. **2** the coloured sky associated with this. **3** the time at which sunrise occurs. □ **sunrise industry** any newly established industry, esp. in

electronics and telecommunications, regarded as signalling prosperity.
■ **1, 3** see DAWN *n.* 1.

sunset /súnset/ *n.* **1** the sun's setting in the evening. **2** the coloured sky associated with this. **3** the time at which sunset occurs. **4** the declining period of life.
■ **1, 3** see DUSK *n.* 1.

sunshade /súnshayd/ *n.* **1** a parasol. **2** an awning.

sunshine /súnshīn/ *n.* **1 a** the light of the sun. **b** an area lit by the sun. **2** fine weather. **3** cheerfulness; joy (*brought sunshine into her life*). **4** *Brit. colloq.* a form of address. □ **sunshine roof** = *sun-roof.* □□ **sunshiny** *adj.*
■ **1 a** see DAYLIGHT 1. **3** see JOY *n.* 1.

sunspot /súnspot/ *n.* one of the dark patches, changing in shape and size and lasting for varying periods, observed on the sun's surface.

sunstar /súnstaar/ *n.* any starfish of the genus *Solaster*, with many rays.

sunstroke /súnstrōk/ *n.* acute prostration or collapse from the excessive heat of the sun.

suntan /súntan/ *n.* & *v.* ● *n.* the brownish colouring of skin caused by exposure to the sun. ● *v.intr.* (**-tanned, -tanning**) colour the skin with a suntan.
■ *v.* see SUN *v.* 1, 3.

suntrap /súntrap/ *n.* a place sheltered from the wind and suitable for catching the sunshine.

sup[1] /sup/ *v.* & *n.* ● *v.tr.* (**supped, supping**) **1** take (soup, tea, etc.) by sips or spoonfuls. **2** esp. *N.Engl. colloq.* drink (alcohol). ● *n.* a sip of liquid. [OE *sūpan*]
■ *v.* **1** see SIP *v.* **2** see DRINK *v.* 2. ● *n.* see SIP *n.*

sup[2] /sup/ *v.intr.* (**supped, supping**) (usu. foll. by *off, on*) *archaic* take supper. [OF *super, soper*]
■ see DINE.

sup- /sup, səp/ *prefix* assim. form of SUB- before *p*.

super /sōōpər, syōō-/ *adj.* & *n.* ● *adj.* **1** (also **super-duper** /-dōōpər/) *colloq.* (also as *int.*) exceptional; splendid. **2** *Commerce* superfine. **3** *Commerce* (of a measure) superficial, in square (not lineal or solid) measure (*120 super ft.*; *120 ft. super*). ● *n. colloq.* **1** *Theatr.* a supernumerary actor. **2** a superintendent. **3** superphosphate. **4** an extra, unwanted, or unimportant person; a supernumerary. **5** *Commerce* superfine cloth or manufacture. [abbr.]
■ *adj.* **1** see SUPERB. ● *n.* **1** see EXTRA *n.* 3. **2** see SUPERINTENDENT *n.* 1.

super- /sōōpər, syōō-/ *comb. form* forming nouns, adjectives, and verbs, meaning: **1** above, beyond, or over in place or time or conceptually (*superstructure*; *supernormal*; *superimpose*). **2** to a great or extreme degree (*superabundant*; *superhuman*). **3** extra good or large of its kind (*supertanker*). **4** of a higher kind, esp. in names of classificatory divisions (*superclass*). [from or after L *super-* f. *super* above, beyond]

superable /sōōpərəb'l, syōō-/ *adj.* able to be overcome. [L *superabilis* f. *superare* overcome]

superabound /sōōpərəbównd, syōō-/ *v.intr.* be very or too abundant. [LL *superabundare* (as SUPER-, ABOUND)]

superabundant /sōōpərəbúndənt, syōō-/ *adj.* abounding beyond what is normal or right. □□ **superabundance** *n.* **superabundantly** *adv.* [ME f. LL *superabundare*: see SUPERABOUND]
■ see ABUNDANT 1. □□ **superabundance** see ABUNDANCE 1.

superadd /sōōpərád, syōō-/ *v.tr.* add over and above. □□ **superaddition** /-ədísh'n/ *n.* [ME f. L *superaddere* (as SUPER-, ADD)]

superaltar /sōōpərawltər, syōō-, -oltər/ *n. Eccl.* a portable slab of stone consecrated for use on an unconsecrated altar etc. [ME f. med.L *superaltare* (as SUPER-, ALTAR)]

superannuate /sōōpərányoo-ayt, syōō-/ *v.tr.* **1** retire (a person) with a pension. **2** dismiss or discard as too old for use, work, etc. **3** (as **superannuated** *adj.*) too old for work or use; obsolete. □□ **superannuable** *adj.* [back-form. f. *superannuated* f. med.L *superannuatus* f. L SUPER- + *annus* year]
■ **1** see *pension off* (PENSION[1]). **3** (**superannuated**) see OBSOLETE.

superannuation /sōōpərányoo-áysh'n, syōō-/ *n.* **1** a pension paid to a retired person. **2** a regular payment made towards this by an employed person. **3** the process or an instance of superannuating.
■ **1** see PENSION[1] *n.* 1.

superaqueous /sōōpəráykwiəss, syōō-/ *adj.* above water.

superb /soopérb, syoo-/ *adj.* **1** of the most impressive, splendid, grand, or majestic kind (*superb courage*; *a superb specimen*). **2** *colloq.* excellent; fine. □□ **superbly** *adv.* **superbness** *n.* [F *superbe* or L *superbus* proud]
■ wonderful, marvellous, excellent, superior, gorgeous, glorious, grand, majestic, magnificent, outstanding, exquisite, fine, splendid, unequalled, sensational, noteworthy, great, impressive, admirable, peerless, matchless, unrivalled, first-rate, superlative, perfect, classic, exceptional, extraordinary, striking, brilliant, dazzling, miraculous, incredible, unbelievable, stupendous, staggering, breathtaking, *colloq.* far-out, smashing, magic, terrific, fantastic, fabulous, out of sight, out of this world, divine, mind-boggling, super, super-duper, top-notch, crack, *Austral. sl.* grouse, *US* & *Austral. sl.* unreal, *esp. US sl.* cool, bad. □□ **superbly** see *beautifully* (BEAUTIFUL).

supercalender /sōōpərkállindər, syōō-/ *v.tr.* give a highly glazed finish to (paper) by extra calendering.

supercargo /sōōpərkaargō, syōō-/ *n.* (*pl.* **-oes**) an officer in a merchant ship managing sales etc. of cargo. [earlier *supracargo* f. Sp. *sobrecargo* f. *sobre* over + *cargo* CARGO]

supercelestial /sōōpərsiléstiəl, syōō-/ *adj.* **1** above the heavens. **2** more than heavenly. [LL *supercaelestis* (as SUPER-, CELESTIAL)]

supercharge /sōōpərchaarj, syōō-/ *v.tr.* **1** (usu. foll. by *with*) charge (the atmosphere etc.) with energy, emotion, etc. **2** use a supercharger on (an internal-combustion engine).

supercharger /sōōpərchaarjər, syōō-/ *n.* a device supplying air or fuel to an internal-combustion engine at above normal pressure to increase efficiency.

superciliary /sōōpərsílliəri, syōō-/ *adj. Anat.* of or concerning the eyebrow; over the eye. [L *supercilium* eyebrow (as SUPER-, *cilium* eyelid)]

supercilious /sōōpərsílliəss, syōō-/ *adj.* assuming an air of contemptuous indifference or superiority. □□ **superciliously** *adv.* **superciliousness** *n.* [L *superciliosus* (as SUPERCILIARY)]
■ haughty, contemptuous, superior, snobbish, disdainful, arrogant, condescending, patronizing, overbearing, scornful, lordly, high and mighty, pompous, lofty, pretentious, hoity-toity, *colloq.* highfalutin, uppity, snooty, stuck-up, la-di-da, *esp. Brit. colloq.* uppish, *esp. Brit. sl.* toffee-nosed. □□ **superciliousness** see *snobbery* (SNOB).

superclass /sōōpərklaass, syōō-/ *n.* a taxonomic category between class and phylum.

supercolumnar /sōōpərkəlúmnər, syōō-/ *adj. Archit.* having one order or set of columns above another. □□ **supercolumniation** /-niáysh'n/ *n.*

supercomputer /sōōpərkəmpyōōtər, syōō-/ *n.* a powerful computer capable of dealing with complex problems. □□ **supercomputing** *n.*

superconductivity /sōōpərkónduktívviti, syōō-/ *n. Physics* the property of zero electrical resistance in some substances at very low absolute temperatures. □□ **superconducting** /-kəndúkting/ *adj.* **superconductive** /-kəndúktiv/ *adj.*

superconductor /sōōpərkəndúktər, syōō-/ *n. Physics* a substance having superconductivity.

superconscious /sōōpərkónshəss, syōō-/ *adj.* transcending human consciousness. □□ **superconsciously** *adv.* **superconsciousness** *n.*

supercool /sōōpərkōōl, syōō-/ *v.* & *adj.* ● *v. Chem.* **1** *tr.* cool (a liquid) below its freezing-point without solidification or crystallization. **2** *intr.* (of a liquid) be cooled in this way. ● *adj. sl.* very cool, relaxed, fine, etc.

supercritical /sōōpərkríttik'l, syōō-/ *adj. Physics* of more than critical mass etc.

super-duper var. of SUPER *adj.* 1.

superego /sōōpəreégō, -éggō, syōō-/ *n.* (*pl.* **-os**) *Psychol.* the part of the mind that acts as a conscience and responds to social rules.

superelevation /sōōpərélliváysh'n, syōō-/ *n.* the amount by which the outer edge of a curve on a road or railway is above the inner edge.

supereminent /sōōpərémminənt, syōō-/ *adj.* supremely eminent, exalted, or remarkable. □□ **supereminence** *n.* **supereminently** *adv.* [L *supereminēre* rise above (as SUPER-, EMINENT)]

supererogation /sōōpərérrəgáysh'n, syōō-/ *n.* the performance of more than duty requires. □ **works of supererogation** *RC Ch.* actions believed to form a reserve fund of merit that can be drawn on by prayer in favour of sinners. □□ **supererogatory** /-iróggətəri/ *adj.* [LL *supererogatio* f. *supererogare* pay in addition (as SUPER-, *erogare* pay out)]
■ see EXCESS *n.* 1. □□ **supererogatory** see SUPERFLUOUS.

superexcellent /sōōpəréksələnt, syōō-/ *adj.* very or supremely excellent. □□ **superexcellence** *n.* **superexcellently** *adv.* [LL *superexcellens* (as SUPER-, EXCELLENT)]

superfamily /sōōpərfammili, syōō-/ *n.* (*pl.* **-ies**) a taxonomic category between family and order.

superfatted /sōōpərfáttid, syōō-/ *adj.* (of soap) containing extra fat.

superfecundation /sōōpərfeékəndáysh'n, syōō-/ *n.* = SUPERFETATION 1.

superfetation /sōōpərfeetáysh'n, syōō-/ *n.* **1** *Med. & Zool.* a second conception during pregnancy giving rise to embryos of different ages in the uterus. **2** *Bot.* the fertilization of the same ovule by different kinds of pollen. **3** the accretion of one thing on another. [F *superfétation* or f. mod.L *superfetatio* f. L *superfetare* (as SUPER-, *fetus* FOETUS)]

superficial /sōōpərfish'l, syōō-/ *adj.* **1** of or on the surface; lacking depth (*a superficial knowledge*; *superficial wounds*). **2** swift or cursory (*a superficial examination*). **3** apparent but not real (*a superficial resemblance*). **4** (esp. of a person) having no depth of character or knowlege; trivial; shallow. **5** *Commerce* (of a measure) square (cf. SUPER *adj.* 3). □□ **superficiality** /-shiálliti/ *n.* (*pl.* **-ies**). **superficially** *adv.* **superficialness** *n.* [LL *superficialis* f. L (as SUPERFICIES)]
■ **1** surface, external, exterior, shallow, skin-deep, slight, outside. **2** cursory, slapdash, quick, swift, hurried, hasty, perfunctory, passing. **3** surface, slight, external, apparent, skin-deep, outward, insignificant, passing, unimportant, empty, insubstantial, nominal, token, meaningless; paying lip-service, for appearances' sake, cosmetic. **4** trivial, frivolous, shallow, empty-headed, hollow, mindless. □□ **superficially** see *outwardly* (OUTWARD).

superficies /sōōpərfisheez, syōō-/ *n.* (*pl.* same) *Geom.* a surface. [L (as SUPER-, *facies* face)]
■ (outer) surface, façade, face, externals, outside.

superfine /sōōpərfīn, syōō-/ *adj.* **1** *Commerce* of extra quality. **2** pretending great refinement. [med.L *superfinus* (as SUPER-, FINE[1])]

superfluity /sōōpərflōō-iti, syōō-/ *n.* (*pl.* **-ies**) **1** the state of being superfluous. **2** a superfluous amount or thing. [ME f. OF *superfluité* f. LL *superfluitas -tatis* f. L *superfluus*: see SUPERFLUOUS]
■ **1** excess, superabundance, over-abundance, surplus, surfeit, glut, superfluousness, profusion, plethora, oversupply, supersaturation. **2** excess, surplus, leftovers, overflow.

superfluous /soopérflōōəss, syoo-/ *adj.* more than enough, redundant, needless. □□ **superfluously** *adv.* **superfluousness** *n.* [ME f. L *superfluus* (as SUPER-, *fluere* to flow)]
■ excessive, excess, superabundant, over-abundant, supererogatory, surplus, unneeded, uncalled-for, unnecessary, redundant, extra, non-essential; needless, dispensable, gratuitous. □□ **superfluousness** see SUPERFLUITY 1.

supergiant /sōōpərjīənt, syōō-/ *n.* a star of very great luminosity and size.

superglue /sōōpərglōō, syōō-/ *n.* any of various adhesives with an exceptional bonding capability.

supergrass /sōōpərgraass, syōō-/ *n. colloq.* a police informer who implicates a large number of people.

superheat /sōōpərheét, syōō-/ *v.tr. Physics* **1** heat (a liquid) above its boiling-point without vaporization. **2** heat (a vapour) above its boiling-point (*superheated steam*). □□ **superheater** *n.*

superhet /sōōpərhét, syōō-/ *n. colloq.* = SUPERHETERODYNE.

superheterodyne /sōōpərhéttərōdīn, syōō-/ *adj. & n.* ● *adj.* denoting or characteristic of a system of radio reception in which a local variable oscillator is tuned to beat at a constant ultrasonic frequency with carrier-wave frequencies, making it unnecessary to vary the amplifier tuning and securing greater selectivity. ● *n.* a superheterodyne receiver. [SUPERSONIC + HETERODYNE]

superhighway /sōōpərhīway, syōō-/ *n. US* a broad main road for fast traffic.
■ see ROAD[1] 1.

superhuman /sōōpərhyōōmən, syōō-/ *adj.* **1** beyond normal human capability. **2** higher than man. □□ **superhumanly** *adv.* [LL *superhumanus* (as SUPER-, HUMAN)]
■ **1** heroic, Herculean, godlike, legendary, valiant, courageous, brave, daring, dangerous, death-defying, extraordinary, miraculous, phenomenal, incredible, fabulous, fantastic, unbelievable, amazing, prodigious. **2** see DIVINE *adj.* 2a.

superhumeral /sōōpərhyōōmərəl, syōō-/ *n. Eccl.* a vestment worn over the shoulders, e.g. an amice, ephod, or pallium. [LL *superhumerale* (as SUPER-, HUMERAL)]

superimpose /sōōpərimpṓz, syōō-/ *v.tr.* (usu. foll. by *on*) lay (a thing) on something else. □□ **superimposition** /-pəzish'n/ *n.*
■ see LAY[1] *v.* 1.

superincumbent /sōōpərinkúmb'nt, syōō-/ *adj.* lying on something else.

superinduce /sōōpərindyōōss, syōō-/ *v.tr.* introduce or induce in addition. [L *superinducere* cover over, bring from outside (as SUPER-, INDUCE)]

superintend /sōōpərintén d, syōō-/ *v.tr. & intr.* be responsible for the management or arrangement of (an activity etc.); supervise and inspect. □□ **superintendence** *n.* **superintendency** *n.* [eccl.L *superintendere* (as SUPER-, INTEND), transl. Gk *episkopō*]
■ see SUPERVISE. □□ **superintendence** see MANAGEMENT 1.

superintendent /sōōpərinténdənt, syōō-/ *n. & adj.* ● *n.* **1 a** a person who superintends. **b** a director of an institution etc. **2 a** *Brit.* a police officer above the rank of inspector. **b** *US* the head of a police department. **3** *US* the caretaker of a building. ● *adj.* superintending. [eccl.L *superintendent-* part. stem of *superintendere*: see SUPERINTEND]
■ *n.* **1** supervisor, foreman, overseer, manager, administrator, chief, head; governor, controller, director, conductor; *colloq.* boss, super, *Brit. colloq.* gaffer. **3** see PORTER[2].

superior /soopeériər, syoo-/ *adj. & n.* ● *adj.* **1** in a higher position; of higher rank (*a superior officer*; *a superior court*). **2 a** above the average in quality etc. (*made of superior leather*). **b** having or showing a high opinion of oneself; supercilious (*had a superior air*). **3** (often foll. by *to*) **a** better or greater in some respect (*superior to its rivals in speed*). **b** above yielding, making concessions, paying attention, etc. (*is superior to bribery*; *superior to temptation*). **4** further above or out; higher, esp.: **a** *Astron.* (of a planet) having an orbit further from the sun than the earth's. **b** *Zool.* (of an insect's wings) folding over others. **c** *Printing* (of figures or letters) placed above the line. **d** *Bot.* (of the calyx) above the ovary. **e** *Bot.* (of the ovary) above the calyx. ● *n.* **1** a person superior to another in rank, character, etc. (*is deferential to his superiors; is his superior in courage*). **2** (*fem.* **superioress** /-riss/) *Eccl.* the head of a monastery or other religious institution (*Mother Superior; Father Superior*). **3** *Printing* a superior letter or figure. □ **superior numbers** esp. *Mil.* more men etc. or their strength (*overcome by superior numbers*). **superior persons** esp. *iron.* the better educated or élite; prigs. □□ **superiorly** *adv.* [ME f. OF *superiour* f. L *superior -oris*, compar. of *superus* that is above f. *super* above]

■ *adj.* **1** higher, upper, loftier, higher-ranking, higher-level, higher-class, higher-calibre, upper-level, upper-class, nobler, senior; of a higher order *or* status *or* standing, greater. **2 a** high-class, elevated, first-rate, distinguished, exceptional, excellent, better, preferred, choice, select, élitist, outstanding, superlative, matchless, unequalled, peerless, nonpareil, sterling, supreme, fine, noteworthy, notable, worthy, estimable, *colloq.* classier, *US colloq.* tonier. **b** see SUPERCILIOUS. **3 b** (*superior to*) see ABOVE *prep.* 4b. ● *n.* **1** better, senior, elder; see also *supervisor* (SUPERVISE).

superiority /soopeeriórriti, syoo-/ *n.* the state of being superior. □ **superiority complex** *Psychol.* an undue conviction of one's own superiority to others.

■ ascendancy, pre-eminence, supremacy, leadership, lead, dominance, predominance, primacy, precedence, advantage, hegemony; excellence, greatness, peerlessness, matchlessness, inimitability, superlativeness, prominence, eminence, importance, distinction, prestige, renown.

superjacent /sōōpərjáys'nt, syōō-/ *adj.* overlying; superincumbent. [L *superjacēre* (as SUPER-, *jacēre* lie)]

superlative /soopérlətiv, syoo-/ *adj.* & *n.* ● *adj.* **1** of the highest quality or degree (*superlative wisdom*). **2** *Gram.* (of an adjective or adverb) expressing the highest or a very high degree of a quality (e.g. *bravest, most fiercely*) (cf. POSITIVE, COMPARATIVE). ● *n.* **1** *Gram.* **a** the superlative expression or form of an adjective or adverb. **b** a word in the superlative. **2** something embodying excellence; the highest form of a thing. □□ **superlatively** *adv.* **superlativeness** *n.* [ME f. OF *superlatif -ive* f. LL *superlativus* f. L *superlatus* (as SUPER-, *latus* past part. of *ferre* take)]

■ *adj.* **1** unsurpassed, paramount, supreme, consummate, superior, best, choicest, finest, matchless, peerless, unequalled, unrivalled, unbeatable, singular, unique, incomparable, excellent, superb, dazzling, first-rate, first-class, exceptional, extraordinary, marvellous, spectacular, *colloq.* tiptop, capital, super, smashing, great, terrific, fantastic, crack, *sl.* ace. □□ **superlatively** see PERFECTLY 3. **superlativeness** see SUPERIORITY.

superlunary /sōōpərlōōnəri, syōō-, -lyōōnəri/ *adj.* **1** situated beyond the moon. **2** belonging to a higher world, celestial. [med.L *superlunaris* (as SUPER-, LUNAR)]

superman /sōōpərman, syōō-/ *n.* (*pl.* **-men**) **1** esp. *Philos.* the ideal superior man of the future. **2** *colloq.* a man of exceptional strength or ability. [SUPER- + MAN, formed by G. B. Shaw after Nietzsche's G *Übermensch*]

■ **2** hero, Hercules, Titan.

supermarket /sōōpərmaarkit, syōō-/ *n.* a large self-service store selling foods, household goods, etc.

■ see STORE *n.* 3b.

supermundane /sōōpərmúndayn, syōō-/ *adj.* superior to earthly things.

■ see PSYCHIC *adj.* 1b.

supernal /soopérn'l, syoo-/ *adj.* esp. *poet.* **1** heavenly; divine. **2** of or concerning the sky. **3** lofty. □□ **supernally** *adv.* [ME f. OF *supernal* or med.L *supernalis* f. L *supernus* f. *super* above]

■ **1** see HEAVENLY 1.

supernatant /sōōpərnáyt'nt, syōō-/ *adj.* & *n.* esp. *Chem.* ● *adj.* floating on the surface of a liquid. ● *n.* a supernatant substance. [SUPER- + *natant* swimming (as NATATION)]

supernatural /sōōpərnáchərəl, syōō-/ *adj.* & *n.* ● *adj.* attributed to or thought to reveal some force above the laws of nature; magical; mystical. ● *n.* (prec. by *the*) supernatural, occult, or magical forces, effects, etc. □□ **supernaturalism** *n.* **supernaturalist** *n.* **supernaturalize** *v.tr.* (also **-ise**). **supernaturally** *adv.* **supernaturalness** *n.*

■ *adj.* preternatural, unusual, extraordinary, exceptional, unnatural, miraculous, remarkable, fabulous, preterhuman, ghostly, spectral, abnormal, supernormal, inexplicable, unexplainable; metaphysical, hyperphysical, superphysical, other-worldly, unearthly, ultramundane, supramundane, extramundane, divine, occult, mystic(al), paranormal, psychic, uncanny, weird, mysterious, arcane, unreal, magical, dark. ● *n.* see *the occult* (OCCULT). □□ **supernaturalism** see MYSTIQUE 1.

supernormal /sōōpərnórm'l, syōō-/ *adj.* beyond what is normal or natural. □□ **supernormality** /-málliti/ *n.*

supernova /sōōpərnṓvə, syōō-/ *n.* (*pl.* **-novae** /-vee/ or **-novas**) *Astron.* a star that suddenly increases very greatly in brightness because of an explosion ejecting most of its mass.

■ see STAR *n.* 1.

supernumerary /sōōpərnyōōmərəri, syōō-/ *adj.* & *n.* ● *adj.* **1** in excess of the normal number; extra. **2** (of a person) engaged for extra work. **3** (of an actor) appearing on stage but not speaking. ● *n.* (*pl.* **-ies**) **1** an extra or unwanted person or thing. **2** a supernumerary actor. **3** a person engaged for extra work. [LL *supernumerarius* (soldier) added to a legion already complete, f. L *super numerum* beyond the number]

■ *adj.* **1** see SPARE *adj.* 1. ● *n.* **1** see UNNECESSARY *n.* **2** see THESPIAN *n.*

superorder /sōōpərordər, syōō-/ *n. Biol.* a taxonomic category between order and class. □□ **superordinal** /-órdin'l/ *adj.*

superordinate /sōōpərórdinət, syōō-/ *adj.* (usu. foll. by *to*) of superior importance or rank. [SUPER-, after *subordinate*]

superphosphate /sōōpərfósfayt, syōō-/ *n.* a fertilizer made by treating phosphate rock with sulphuric or phosphoric acid.

superphysical /sōōpərfízzik'l, syōō-/ *adj.* **1** unexplainable by physical causes; supernatural. **2** beyond what is physical.

superpose /sōōpərpṓz, syōō-/ *v.tr.* (usu. foll. by *on*) esp. *Geom.* place (a thing or a geometric figure) on or above something else, esp. so as to coincide. □□ **superposition** /-pəzísh'n/ *n.* [F *superposer* (as SUPER-, POSE[1])]

■ superimpose, place; see also LAY[1] *v.* 1.

superpower /sōōpərpowr, syōō-/ *n.* a State of supreme power and influence, esp. the US and the former USSR.

supersaturate /sōōpəsáchərayt, syōō-, -tyoorayt/ *v.tr.* add to (esp. a solution) beyond saturation point. □□ **supersaturation** /-ráysh'n/ *n.*

■ □□ **supersaturation** see SUPERFLUITY 1.

superscribe /sōōpərskrī́b, syōō-/ *v.tr.* **1** write (an inscription) at the top of or on the outside of a document etc. **2** write an inscription over or on (a thing). □□ **superscription** /-skrípsh'n/ *n.* [L *superscribere* (as SUPER-, *scribere script-* write)]

superscript /sōōpərskript, syōō-/ *adj.* & *n.* ● *adj.* written or printed above the line, esp. *Math.* (of a symbol) written above and to the right of another. ● *n.* a superscript number or symbol. [L *superscriptus* past part. of *superscribere*: see SUPERSCRIBE]

supersede /sōōpərseed, syōō-/ *v.tr.* **1 a** adopt or appoint another person or thing in place of. **b** set aside; cease to employ. **2** (of a person or thing) take the place of. □□ **supersedence** *n.* **supersedure** /-seejər/ *n.* **supersession** /-sésh'n/ *n.* [OF *superseder* f. L *supersedēre* be superior to (as SUPER-, *sedēre sess-* sit)]

■ **1** replace, put in place of, change. **2** replace, succeed, displace, supplant, oust, take the place of, take over from, substitute for.

supersonic /sóōpərsónnik, syóō-/ *adj.* designating or having a speed greater than that of sound. □□ **supersonically** *adv.*

supersonics /sóōpərsónniks, syóō-/ *n.pl.* (treated as *sing.*) =ULTRASONICS.

superstar /sóōpərstaar, syóō-/ *n.* an extremely famous or renowned actor, film star, musician, etc. □□ **superstardom** *n.*

■ see CELEBRITY 1.

superstition /sóōpərstísh'n, syóō-/ *n.* **1** credulity regarding the supernatural. **2** an irrational fear of the unknown or mysterious. **3** misdirected reverence. **4** a practice, opinion, or religion based on these tendencies. **5** a widely held but unjustified idea of the effects or nature of a thing. □□ **superstitious** *adj.* **superstitiously** *adv.* **superstitiousness** *n.* [ME f. OF *superstition* or L *superstitio* (as SUPER-, *stare stat-* stand)]

superstore /sóōpərstor, syóō-/ *n.* a large supermarket selling a wide range of goods.

■ see STORE *n.* 3b.

superstratum /sóōpərstraatəm, syóō-/ *n.* (*pl.* **-strata** /-tə/) an overlying stratum.

superstructure /sóōpərstrukchər, syóō-/ *n.* **1** the part of a building above its foundations. **2** a structure built on top of something else. **3** a concept or idea based on others. □□ **superstructural** *adj.*

supersubtle /sóōpərsútt'l, syóō-/ *adj.* extremely or excessively subtle. □□ **supersubtlety** *n.*

supertanker /sóōpərtangkər, syóō-/ *n.* a very large tanker ship.

supertax /sóōpərtaks, syóō-/ *n.* a tax on incomes above a certain level, esp. a surtax.

superterrestrial /sóōpərtəréstriəl, syóō-/ *adj.* **1** in or belonging to a region above the earth. **2** celestial.

supertonic /sóōpərtónnik, syóō-/ *n. Mus.* the note above the tonic, the second note of the diatonic scale of any key.

supervene /sóōpərvéen, syóō-/ *v.intr.* occur as an interruption in or a change from some state. □□ **supervenient** *adj.* **supervention** /-vénsh'n/ *n.* [L *supervenire supervent-* (as SUPER-, *venire* come)]

■ see SUCCEED 2. □□ **supervenient** see SUPPLEMENTARY.

supervise /sóōpərvīz, syóō-/ *v.tr.* **1** superintend, oversee the execution of (a task etc.). **2** oversee the actions or work of (a person). □□ **supervision** /-vízh'n/ *n.* **supervisor** *n.* **supervisory** *adj.* [med.L *supervidēre supervis-* (as SUPER-, *vidēre* see)]

■ oversee, overlook, watch (over), manage, run, control, superintend, govern, direct, head, be in *or* have charge of, handle, keep an eye on, administer. □□ **supervision** see *leadership* (LEADER). **supervisor** overseer, foreman, manager, controller, superintendent, superior, director, chief, head, administrator; invigilator; *colloq.* boss, super, *Brit. colloq.* gaffer, *sl.* governor. **supervisory** managerial, administrative, executive.

superwoman /sóōpərwŏŏmmən, syóō-/ *n.* (*pl.* **-women**) *colloq.* a woman of exceptional strength or ability.

supinate /sóōpinayt, syóō-/ *v.tr.* put (a hand or foreleg etc.) into a supine position (cf. PRONATE). □□ **supination** /-náysh'n/ *n.* [back-form. f. *supination* f. L *supinatio* f. *supinare* f. *supinus*: see SUPINE]

supinator /sóōpinaytər, syóō-/ *n. Anat.* a muscle in the forearm effecting supination.

supine /sóōpīn, syóō-/ *adj.* & *n.* ● *adj.* **1** lying face upwards (cf. PRONE). **2** having the front or ventral part upwards; (of the hand) with the palm upwards. **3** inert, indolent; morally or mentally inactive. ● *n.* a Latin verbal noun used only in the accusative and ablative cases, esp. to denote purpose (e.g. *mirabile dictu* wonderful to relate). □□ **supinely** *adv.* **supineness** *n.* [L *supinus*, rel. to *super*: (n.) f. LL *supinum* neut. (reason unkn.)]

■ *adj.* **1** face upwards, flat (on one's back); lying (down), recumbent, *Bot.* & *Zool.* decumbent. **3** indolent, lazy, lethargic, idle, listless, indifferent, apathetic, unconcerned, uninterested, torpid, languid, languorous, sluggish, slothful, phlegmatic, lymphatic, lackadaisical, inert, inactive, passive, motionless, inanimate, spiritless, abject. □□ **supineness** see STUPOR.

supper /súppər/ *n.* a light evening meal. □ **sing for one's supper** do something in return for a benefit. □□ **supperless** *adj.* [ME f. OF *soper*, *super*]

■ see MEAL[1].

supplant /səplaánt/ *v.tr.* dispossess and take the place of, esp. by underhand means. □□ **supplanter** *n.* [ME f. OF *supplanter* or L *supplantare* trip up (as SUB-, *planta* sole)]

■ replace, displace, oust, turn out, eject, remove, expel, dismiss, unseat, supersede, take the place of, substitute for.

supple /súpp'l/ *adj.* & *v.* ● *adj.* (**suppler**, **supplest**) **1** flexible, pliant; easily bent. **2** compliant; avoiding overt resistance; artfully or servilely submissive. ● *v.tr.* & *intr.* make or become supple. □□ **suppleness** *n.* [ME f. OF *souple* ult. f. L *supplex supplicis* submissive]

■ *adj.* **1** flexible, pliant, bendable, elastic, resilient, pliable; willowy, lithe, limber, nimble, lissom, graceful, athletic, *archaic* flexile. **2** tractable, compliant, yielding, accommodating, obliging, complaisant, acquiescent, submissive, unresistant, unresisting, servile, obsequious, ingratiating, fawning, toadying. □□ **suppleness** see *flexibility* (FLEXIBLE).

supplejack /súpp'ljak/ *n.* any of various strong twining tropical shrubs, esp. *Berchemia scandens.* [SUPPLE + JACK[1]]

supplely var. of SUPPLY[2].

supplement *n.* & *v.* ● *n.* /súplimənt/ **1** a thing or part added to remedy deficiencies (*dietary supplement*). **2** a part added to a book etc. to provide further information. **3** a separate section, esp. a colour magazine, added to a newspaper or periodical. **4** *Geom.* the amount by which an angle is less than 180° (cf. COMPLEMENT). ● *v.tr.* also /súpliment/ provide a supplement for. □□ **supplemental** /-mént'l/ *adj.* **supplementally** /-méntəli/ *adv.* **supplementation** /-táysh'n/ *n.* [ME f. L *supplementum* (as SUB-, *plēre* fill)]

■ *n.* **1** addition, extension, appendage, adjunct, appurtenance, accessory, prosthetic; surcharge, extra; supplementation, suppletion. **2** addendum, addition, appendix, epilogue, end-piece, postscript, codicil, rider, insert, extension, continuation, annexe. **3** insert, appendix, extra; (colour) magazine, *Brit.* colour supplement. ● *v.* add to, extend, augment, *colloq.* boost; complement, *esp. Brit.* top up. □□ **supplemental** see SUPPLEMENTARY.

supplementary /súpliméntəri, -tri/ *adj.* forming or serving as a supplement; additional. □ **supplementary benefit** *hist.* (in the UK) a weekly allowance paid by the State to those not in full-time employment and with an income below a certain level (replaced by *income support*). □□ **supplementarily** *adv.*

■ additional, added, annexed, adjunct, new; supplemental, supportive, contributory, ancillary, secondary, subordinate, attached, appended, subsidiary, auxiliary, accessory; extraneous, adventitious, supervenient, extra, excess, further; *Linguistics* suppletive.

suppletion /səpléesh'n/ *n.* the act or an instance of supplementing, esp. *Linguistics* the occurrence of unrelated forms to supply gaps in conjugation (e.g. *went* as the past of *go*). □□ **suppletive** *adj.* [ME f. OF f. med.L *suppletio -onis* (as SUPPLY[1])]

■ see SUPPLEMENT *n.* 1. □□ **suppletive** see SUPPLEMENTARY.

suppliant /súpliənt/ *adj.* & *n.* ● *adj.* **1** supplicating. **2** expressing supplication. ● *n.* a supplicating person. □□ **suppliantly** *adv.* [ME f. F *supplier* beseech f. L (as SUPPLICATE)]

■ *adj.* see *supplicant adj.* (SUPPLICATE). ● *n.* see *supplicant n.* (SUPPLICATE).

supplicate /súplikayt/ *v.* **1** *tr.* petition humbly to (a person) or for (a thing). **2** *intr.* (foll. by *to*, *for*) make a petition. □□ **supplicant** *adj.* & *n.* **supplication** /-káysh'n/ *n.* **supplicatory** *adj.* [ME f. L *supplicare* (as SUB-, *plicare* bend)]

■ **1** see PETITION *v.* 2. □□ **supplicant** (*adj.*) supplicatory, suppliant, imploring, solicitous, importunate, mendicant. (*n.*) applicant, suppliant, petitioner, beseecher, suitor, aspirant, beggar, mendicant; *Law* pleader, appellant, plaintiff. **supplication** entreaty, petition, prayer, appeal, pleading, plea, request, suit, solicitation, obsecration.

supply[1] /səplī́/ *v.* & *n.* ● *v.tr.* (**-ies, -ied**) **1** provide or furnish (a thing needed). **2** (often foll. by *with*) provide (a person etc. with a thing needed). **3** meet or make up for (a deficiency or need etc.). **4** fill (a vacancy, place, etc.) as a substitute. ● *n.* (*pl.* **-ies**) **1** the act or an instance of providing what is needed. **2** a stock, store, amount, etc., of something provided or obtainable (*a large supply of water*; *the gas-supply*). **3** (in *pl.*) **a** the collected provisions and equipment for an army, expedition, etc. **b** a grant of money by Parliament for the costs of government. **c** a money allowance to a person. **4** (often *attrib.*) a person, esp. a schoolteacher or clergyman, acting as a temporary substitute for another. **5** (*attrib.*) providing supplies or a supply (*supply officer*). □ **in short supply** available in limited quantity. **on supply** (of a schoolteacher etc.) acting as a supply. **supply and demand** *Econ.* quantities available and required as factors regulating the price of commodities. **supply-side** *Econ.* denoting a policy of low taxation and other incentives to produce goods and invest. □□ **supplier** *n.* [ME f. OF *so(u)pleer* etc. f. L *supplēre* (as SUB-, *plēre* fill)]

■ *v.* **1, 2** furnish, provide, give, endow, donate, present, purvey, deliver, come up with, yield, contribute, distribute, sell; stock, accommodate, afford, equip, outfit, gear (up), rig (out), fit (out), provision, kit out *or* up, minister (with); victual. **3** satisfy, fulfil, meet, replenish, fill. ● *n.* **1** provision, purveyance, distribution, delivery. **2** stock, stockpile, store, inventory, quantity, reservoir, reserve, cache, hoard, accumulation, fund. **3** (*supplies*) **a** see KIT[1] *n.* 1, PROVISION *n.* 2. **4** see SUBSTITUTE *n.* 1a. □ **in short supply** see LIMITED 1. □□ **supplier** see DEALER, DONOR.

supply[2] /súpli/ *adv.* (also **supplely** /súppəli/) in a supple manner .

support /səpórt/ *v.* & *n.* ● *v.tr.* **1** carry all or part of the weight of. **2** keep from falling or sinking or failing. **3** provide with a home and the necessities of life (*has a family to support*). **4** enable to last out; give strength to; encourage. **5** bear out; tend to substantiate or corroborate (a statement, charge, theory, etc.). **6** give help or countenance to, back up; second, further. **7** speak in favour of (a resolution etc.). **8** be actively interested in (a particular team or sport). **9** take a part that is secondary to (a principal actor etc.). **10** assist (a lecturer etc.) by one's presence. **11** endure, tolerate (*can no longer support the noise*). **12** maintain or represent (a part or character) adequately. **13** subscribe to the funds of (an institution). ● *n.* **1** the act or an instance of supporting; the process of being supported. **2** a person or thing that supports. □ **in support of** in order to support. **supporting film** (or **picture** etc.) a less important film in a cinema programme. **support price** a minimum price guaranteed to a farmer for agricultural produce and maintained by subsidy etc. □□ **supportable** *adj.* **supportability** /-təbílliti/ *n.* **supportably** *adv.* **supportingly** *adv.* **supportless** *adj.* [ME f. OF *supporter* f. L *supportare* (as SUB-, *portare* carry)]

■ *v.* **1, 2** carry, bear, take, hold up, sustain; brace, prop (up); strengthen, shore up, reinforce, fortify, buttress, bolster, underpin. **3** maintain, keep, provide for; pay for, fund, finance. **4, 6** back (up), stand by, stick by, help, assist, aid, bolster, uphold, brace, strengthen, fortify, buttress, prop (up), shore up, reinforce, encourage, sustain, *colloq.* boost; champion, take up the cudgels for, back (up), promote, forward, further, second, advance, advocate, stand up for, be supportive (of *or* in), stick up for. **5** verify, corroborate, authenticate, vouch for, endorse, confirm, affirm, bear out, attest to, certify, substantiate, validate, ratify. **7** speak *or* plead *or* argue for, speak *or* plead *or* argue in favour of, recommend, advocate, favour. **11** tolerate, bear, stand (for), suffer, submit to, undergo, stomach, endure, abide, countenance, face, weather, put up with, *colloq.* stick, *literary* brook. **13** give to, contribute to, donate to, finance, fund, subsidize, underwrite, patronize, sponsor, *US colloq.* bankroll. ● *n.* **1** help, backing, backup, reinforcement, encouragement, assistance, aid, succour, sustenance; contribution, allegiance, patronage, sponsorship. **2** brace, prop, stay, frame, foundation, underpinning, substructure, shoring, staging, truss, beam, joist, column, pillar, stilt, post, stanchion, strut, guy, guy wire, mainstay, crutch, bracket, buttress, bolster, reinforcement; sustenance, (living) expenses, keep, maintenance, subsistence, upkeep; finances, funding; see also SUPPORTER. □ **in support of** see *in favour* (FAVOUR). □□ **supportable** tolerable, bearable, endurable, acceptable, sufferable; defensible, confirmable, verifiable, demonstrable, tenable, believable.

supporter /səpórtər/ *n.* **1** a person or thing that supports, esp. a person supporting a team or sport. **2** *Heraldry* the representation of an animal etc., usu. one of a pair, holding up or standing beside an escutcheon.

■ **1** enthusiast, champion, promoter, fan, aficionado, devotee, admirer, backer, follower, support, advocate, defender, seconder, exponent, adherent, aid, assistant, ally, helper, benefactor, patron.

supportive /səpórtiv/ *adj.* providing support or encouragement. □□ **supportively** *adv.* **supportiveness** *n.*

■ helpful, sustaining, supporting, encouraging, sympathetic, understanding, reassuring.

suppose /səpṓz/ *v.tr.* (often foll. by *that* + clause) **1** assume, esp. in default of knowledge; be inclined to think (*I suppose they will return*; *what do you suppose he meant?*). **2** take as a possibility or hypothesis (*let us suppose you are right*). **3** (in *imper.*) as a formula of proposal (*suppose we go to the party*). **4** (of a theory or result etc.) require as a condition (*design in creation supposes a creator*). **5** (in *imper.* or *pres. part.* forming a question) in the circumstances that; if (*suppose he won't let you*; *supposing we stay*). **6** (as **supposed** *adj.*) generally accepted as being so; believed (*his supposed brother*; *generally supposed to be wealthy*). **7** (in *passive*; foll. by *to* + infin.) **a** be expected or required (*was supposed to write to you*). **b** (with *neg.*) not have to; not be allowed to (*you are not supposed to go in there*). □ **I suppose so** an expression of hesitant agreement. □□ **supposable** *adj.* [ME f. OF *supposer* (as SUB-, POSE[1])]

■ **1** assume, presume, presuppose, surmise, take, take as given, take as read, take for granted; believe, think, fancy, imagine; take it. **2** hypothesize, theorize, postulate, posit, assume. **4** require, presuppose, assume; see also INVOLVE 2. **5** (*supposing*) if, even if, *disp.* in the event that. **6** (**supposed**) alleged, assumed, putative, reputed, presumed; hypothetical, theoretical, theorized, suppositious, supposititious; believed, purported, thought, imagined. **7 a** (*be supposed*) be obliged, be expected, be required; be meant, be intended.

supposedly /səpṓzidli/ *adv.* as is generally supposed.

■ allegedly, reputedly, theoretically, hypothetically, presumably; (as) rumour has it.

supposition /súppəzísh'n/ *n.* **1** a fact or idea etc. supposed. **2** the act or an instance of supposing. □□ **suppositional** *adj.*

■ **1, 2** assumption, presumption, surmise, inference, conjecture, speculation; belief, thought, fancy, idea, guess, theory, hypothesis, postulate, proposal, proposition; postulation, guesswork, inference, conjecture, surmise, speculation. □□ **suppositional** see HYPOTHETICAL.

suppositious /súppəzíshəss/ *adj.* hypothetical, assumed. □□ **suppositiously** *adv.* **suppositiousness** *n.* [partly f. SUPPOSITITIOUS, partly f. SUPPOSITION + -OUS]

■ see HYPOTHETICAL.

suppositious /səpózzitíshəss/ *adj.* spurious; substituted for the real. □□ **suppositiously** *adv.* **suppositiousness** *n.* [L *suppositius*, *-icius* f. *supponere supposit-* substitute (as SUB- *ponere* place)]

suppository /səpózzitəri, -tri/ *n.* (*pl.* **-ies**) a medical preparation in the form of a cone, cylinder, etc., to be inserted into the rectum or vagina to melt. [ME f. med.L *suppositorium*, neut. of LL *suppositorius* placed underneath (as SUPPOSITITIOUS)]

suppress /səpréss/ *v.tr.* **1** end the activity or existence of, esp. forcibly. **2** prevent (information, feelings, a reaction, etc.) from being seen, heard, or known (*tried to suppress the report*; *suppressed a yawn*). **3 a** partly or wholly eliminate (electrical interference etc.). **b** equip (a device) to reduce such interference due to it. **4** *Psychol.* keep out of one's consciousness. □□ **suppressible** *adj.* **suppression** *n.* **suppressive** *adj.* **suppressor** *n.* [ME f. L *supprimere suppress-* (as SUB-, *premere* press)]

■ **1** end, discontinue, cut off, cease, stop, terminate, put an end to, halt, prohibit, preclude, prevent, repress, forbid, interdict, block, obstruct, stifle, inhibit, hinder, arrest; put down, quell, crush, squelch, quash, overcome, overpower, subdue, check, stamp out, snuff out, smother, extinguish, quench, *colloq.* crack down on. **2** keep down, control, keep under control, keep *or* hold in check, restrain, hold in *or* back, bottle up, swallow, stifle, repress, cover up, censor, conceal, hide, keep quiet *or* secret, mute, muffle, quiet, silence, *Brit.* quieten. □□ **suppression** end, discontinuation, cut-off, cessation, stop, termination, halt, prohibition, preclusion, prevention, repression, censorship, forbiddance, interdiction, obstruction, *literary* surcease; check, extinction, elimination, *colloq.* crack-down; control, restraint, concealment. **suppressive** see PROHIBITIVE 1, *repressive* (REPRESS).

suppressant /səpréss'nt/ *n.* a suppressing or restraining agent, esp. a drug that suppresses the appetite.

suppurate /súpyərayt/ *v.intr.* **1** form pus. **2** fester. □□ **suppuration** /-ráysh'n/ *n.* **suppurative** /-rətiv/ *adj.* [L *suppurare* (as SUB-, *purare* as PUS)]

■ **2** see FESTER 1. □□ **suppuration** see DISCHARGE *n.* 5. **suppurative** see *ulcerous* (ULCER).

supra /sóoprə, syóo-/ *adv.* above or earlier on (in a book etc.). [L, = above]

supra- /sóoprə, syóo-/ *prefix* **1** above. **2** beyond, transcending (*supranational*). [from or after L *supra-* f. *supra* above, beyond, before in time]

supramaxillary /sóoprəmaksílləri, syóo-/ *adj.* of or relating to the upper jaw.

supramundane /sóoprəmúndayn, syóo-/ *adj.* above or superior to the world.

■ see SUPERNATURAL *adj.*

supranational /sóoprənáshən'l, syóo-/ *adj.* transcending national limits. □□ **supranationalism** *n.* **supranationality** /-nálliti/ *n.*

■ see INTERNATIONAL *adj.*

supraorbital /sóoprəórbit'l, syóo-/ *adj.* situated above the orbit of the eye.

suprarenal /sóoprəreén'l, syóo-/ *adj.* situated above the kidneys.

supremacist /sooprémməsist, syoo-/ *n.* & *adj.* ● *n.* an advocate of the supremacy of a particular group, esp. determined by race or sex. ● *adj.* relating to or advocating such supremacy. □□ **supremacism** *n.*

■ *n.* bigot, racist, racialist, dogmatist, zealot, fanatic, chauvinist.

supremacy /sooprémməsi, syoo-/ *n.* (*pl.* **-ies**) **1** the state of being supreme. **2** supreme authority. □ **Act of Supremacy** an act securing ecclesiastical supremacy to the Crown and excluding the authority of the Pope.

■ **1** transcendency, pre-eminence, supremeness, superiority, ascendancy, predominance, excellence, primacy, peerlessness, matchlessness, incomparability, inimitability. **2** sovereignty, dominion, sway, mastery, control, dominance, (supreme *or* absolute) rule, (supreme *or* absolute) authority, autarchy, omnipotence, hegemony.

supreme /soopreém, syoo-/ *adj.* & *n.* ● *adj.* **1** highest in authority or rank. **2** greatest; most important. **3** (of a penalty or sacrifice etc.) involving death. ● *n.* **1** a rich cream sauce. **2** a dish served in this. □ **the Supreme Being** a name for God. **Supreme Court** the highest judicial court in a State etc. **supreme pontiff** see PONTIFF. **Supreme Soviet** the governing council of the former USSR or one of its constituent republics. □□ **supremely** *adv.* **supremeness** *n.* [L *supremus*, superl. of *superus* that is above f. *super* above]

■ *adj.* **1** highest, loftiest, topmost, greatest, first, foremost, principal, unsurpassed, top, uppermost, chief, paramount, sovereign. **2** best, greatest, first, outstanding, pre-eminent, first-rate, prime, primary, unexcelled, leading, crowning, consummate; superlative, matchless, peerless, incomparable, unparalleled, surpassing, transcendent, inimitable, sublime. **3** greatest, maximum, extreme, uttermost, utmost, ultimate. □□ **supremely** very, extremely, exceedingly, completely, perfectly, superlatively, sublimely, transcendently; see also *pre-eminently* (PRE-EMINENT). **supremeness** see SUPREMACY 1.

suprême /sooprém/ *n.* = SUPREME *n.* [F]

supremo /soopreémō, syoo-/ *n.* (*pl.* **-os**) **1** a supreme leader or ruler. **2** a person in overall charge. [Sp., = SUPREME]

■ see CHIEF *n.*

Supt. *abbr.* Superintendent.

sur-[1] /sur, sər/ *prefix* = SUPER- (*surcharge*; *surrealism*). [OF]

sur-[2] /sur, sər/ *prefix* assim. form of SUB- before *r*.

sura /sóorə/ *n.* (also **surah**) a chapter or section of the Koran. [Arab. *sūra*]

surah /syóorə/ *n.* a soft twilled silk for scarves etc. [F pronunc. of *Surat* in India, where it was orig. made]

sural /syóorəl/ *adj.* of or relating to the calf of the leg (*sural artery*). [mod.L *suralis* f. L *sura* calf]

surcease /surseéss/ *n.* & *v. literary* ● *n.* a cessation. ● *v.intr.* & *tr.* cease. [ME f. OF *sursis*, *-ise* (cf. AF *sursise* omission), past part. of OF *surseoir* refrain, delay f. L (as SUPERSEDE), with assim. to CEASE]

■ *n.* see *interruption* (INTERRUPT).

surcharge *n.* & *v.* ● *n.* /súrchaarj/ **1** an additional charge or payment. **2** a charge made by assessors as a penalty for false returns of taxable property. **3** a mark printed on a postage stamp changing its value. **4** an additional or excessive load. **5** *Brit.* an amount in an official account not passed by the auditor and having to be refunded by the person responsible. **6** the showing of an omission in an account for which credit should have been given. ● *v.tr.* /súrchaarj, -chaárj/ **1** exact a surcharge from. **2** exact (a sum) as a surcharge. **3** mark (a postage stamp) with a surcharge. **4** overload. **5** fill or saturate to excess. [ME f. OF *surcharger* (as SUR-[1], CHARGE)]

■ *n.* **1** see EXTRA *n.* 2. **2** see TRIBUTE 2. **4** see OVERLOAD *n.*

surcingle /súrsingg'l/ *n.* a band round a horse's body usu. to keep a pack etc. in place. [ME f. OF *surcengle* (as SUR-[1], *cengle* girth f. L *cingula* f. *cingere* gird)]

surcoat /súrkōt/ *n.* **1** *hist.* a loose robe worn over armour. **2** a similar sleeveless garment worn as part of the insignia of an order of knighthood. **3** *hist.* an outer coat of rich material. [ME f. OF *surcot* (as SUR-[1], *cot* coat)]

surculose /súrkyoolōss/ *adj. Bot.* producing suckers. [L *surculosus* f. *surculus* twig]

surd /surd/ *adj.* & *n.* ● *adj.* **1** *Math.* (of a number) irrational. **2** *Phonet.* (of a sound) uttered with the breath and not the voice (e.g. *f, k, p, s, t*). ● *n.* **1** *Math.* a surd number, esp. the root of an integer. **2** *Phonet.* a surd sound. [L *surdus* deaf, mute: sense 1 by mistransl. into L of Gk *alogos* irrational, speechless, through Arab. *jaḏr aṣamm* deaf root]

sure /shoor, shor/ *adj.* & *adv.* ● *adj.* **1** having or seeming to have adequate reason for a belief or assertion. **2** (often foll. by *of*, or *that* + clause) convinced. **3** (foll. by *of*) having a certain prospect or confident anticipation or satisfactory knowledge of. **4** reliable or unfailing (*there is one sure way to find out*). **5** (foll. by *to* + infin.) certain. **6** undoubtedly true or truthful. ● *adv. colloq.* certainly. □ **as sure as eggs is eggs** see EGG[1]. **as sure as fate** quite certain. **be sure** (in *imper.* or *infin.*; foll. by *that* + clause or *to* + infin.) take care to; not fail to (*be sure to turn the lights out*). **for sure** *colloq.* without doubt. **make sure 1** make or become certain; ensure. **2** (foll. by *of*) establish the truth or ensure the existence or happening of. **sure enough** *colloq.* **1** in fact; certainly. **2** with near certainty (*they will come sure enough*). **sure-fire** *colloq.* certain to succeed. **sure-footed** never stumbling or making a mistake. **sure-footedly** in a sure-footed way. **sure-footedness** being sure-footed. **sure thing** *n.* a certainty. ● *int.* esp. *US colloq.* certainly. **to be sure 1** it is undeniable or admitted. **2** it must be admitted. □□ **sureness** *n.* [ME f. OF *sur sure* (earlier *sëur*) f. L *securus* SECURE]

■ *adj.* **1, 2** certain, assured, convinced, persuaded, positive, definite; unwavering, unswerving, unflinching, steadfast, steady, unshakeable, undeviating, unfaltering. **3** confident, satisfied, certain. **4** accurate, reliable, dependable, tried and true, unfailing, unerring, infallible, foolproof, effective; established, firm, solid, stable, steadfast, steady, faithful, secure, safe, trustworthy; certain, inevitable, indubitable, unavoidable, ineluctable, inescapable, guaranteed, *colloq.* sure-fire. **5** see CERTAIN *adj.* 2. **6** see CERTAIN *adj.* 1b. ● *adv.* see SURELY 1. □ **for sure** see SURELY 1. **make sure 1** see ENSURE 1. **2** see ASSURE 2. **sure-fire** see SURE *adj.* 4 above. **sure thing** (*n.*) certainty, *colloq.* cinch. (*int.*) see ABSOLUTELY 6. **to be sure** see DEFINITELY *adv.* 2. □□ **sureness** see CONVICTION 2a.

surely /shŏŏrli, shór-/ *adv.* **1** with certainty (*the time approaches slowly but surely*). **2** as an appeal to likelihood or reason (*surely that can't be right*). **3** with safety; securely (*the goat plants its feet surely*).

■ **1** certainly, to be sure, positively, absolutely, definitely, undoubtedly, indubitably, unquestionably, beyond the shadow of a doubt, beyond question, doubtless, doubtlessly, assuredly, *colloq.* sure, for sure. **3** firmly, solidly, confidently, unfalteringly, steadily, unswervingly, unhesitatingly, determinedly, doggedly, securely.

surety /shŏŏriti, shŏŏrti/ *n.* (*pl.* **-ies**) **1** a person who takes responsibility for another's performance of an undertaking, e.g. to appear in court, or payment of a debt. **2** *archaic* a certainty. □ **of** (or **for**) **a surety** *archaic* certainly. **stand surety** become a surety, go bail. □□ **suretyship** *n.* [ME f. OF *surté*, *sëurté* f. L *securitas -tatis* SECURITY]

■ **1** see PLEDGE *n.* 2. **2** see CERTAINTY 1a.

surf /surf/ *n.* & *v.* ● *n.* **1** the swell of the sea breaking on the shore or reefs. **2** the foam produced by this. ● *v.intr.* go surf-riding. □ **surf-casting** fishing by casting a line into the sea from the shore. **surf-riding** the sport of being carried over the surf to the shore on a surfboard. □□ **surfer** *n.* **surfy** *adj.* [app. f. obs. *suff*, perh. assim. to *surge*: orig. applied to the Indian coast]

surface /súrfiss/ *n.* & *v.* ● *n.* **1 a** the outside of a material body. **b** the area of this. **2** any of the limits terminating a solid. **3** the upper boundary of a liquid or of the ground etc. **4** the outward aspect of anything; what is apparent on a casual view or consideration (*presents a large surface to view*; *all is quiet on the surface*). **5** *Geom.* a set of points that has length and breadth but no thickness. **6** (*attrib.*) **a** of or on the surface (*surface area*). **b** superficial (*surface politeness*). ● *v.* **1** *tr.* give the required surface to (a road, paper, etc.). **2** *intr.* & *tr.* rise or bring to the surface. **3** *intr.* become visible or known. **4** *intr. colloq.* become conscious; wake up. □ **come to the surface** become perceptible after being hidden. **surface-active** (of a substance, e.g. a detergent) able to affect the wetting properties of a liquid. **surface mail** mail carried over land and by sea, and not by air. **surface noise** extraneous noise in playing a gramophone record, caused by imperfections in the grooves. **surface tension** the tension of the surface-film of a liquid, tending to minimize its surface area. □□ **surfaced** *adj.* (usu. in *comb.*). **surfacer** *n.* [F (as SUR-[1], FACE)]

■ *n.* **1** exterior, covering, outside, top, skin, integument, façade, face, boundary. **2** side, face; boundary, limit, *Geom.* superficies, *esp. Physics* interface. **3** top; surface film; *Physics* meniscus. **4** exterior, outside, top, skin, façade, face; (*on the surface*) superficially, to all appearances, at first glance, outwardly, to the casual observer, extrinsically, ostensibly. **5** plane, *Geom.* superficies. **6** (*attrib.*) **a** see SUPERFICIAL 1. **b** see SUPERFICIAL 3. ● *v.* **1** coat, finish, top; pave, concrete, tar, tarmac. **2, 3** appear, show up, rise, come up, pop up, crop up, emerge, arise, *colloq.* materialize. **4** see AWAKE *v.* 1a.

surfactant /surfáktənt/ *n.* a substance which reduces surface tension. [*surf*ace-*act*ive]

■ see DETERGENT *n.*

surfboard /súrfbord/ *n.* a long narrow board used in surf-riding.

surfeit /súrfit/ *n.* & *v.* ● *n.* **1** an excess esp. in eating or drinking. **2** a feeling of satiety or disgust resulting from this. ● *v.* (**surfeited**, **surfeiting**) **1** *tr.* overfeed. **2** *intr.* overeat. **3** *intr.* & *tr.* (foll. by *with*) be or cause to be wearied through excess. [ME f. OF *sorfe(i)t*, *surfe(i)t* (as SUPER-, L *facere fact-* do)]

■ *n.* **1** over-abundance, superabundance, plethora, glut, excess, surplus, oversupply, overdose, satiety, overindulgence, overflow, flood, deluge, superfluity. **2** satiety, nausea, sickness, disgust. ● *v.* **1** overfeed, gorge, satiate, sate, stuff. **2** see OVEREAT. **3** sate, satiate, cloy, glut, pall.

surficial /surfish'l/ *adj. Geol.* of or relating to the earth's surface. □□ **surficially** *adv.* [SURFACE after *superficial*]

surge /surj/ *n.* & *v.* ● *n.* **1** a sudden or impetuous onset (*a surge of anger*). **2** the swell of the waves at sea. **3** a heavy forward or upward motion. **4** a rapid increase in price, activity, etc. over a short period. **5** a sudden marked increase in voltage of an electric current. ● *v.intr.* **1** (of waves, the sea, etc.) rise and fall or move heavily forward. **2** (of a crowd etc.) move suddenly and powerfully forwards in large numbers. **3** (of an electric current etc.) increase suddenly. **4** *Naut.* (of a rope, chain, or windlass) slip back with a jerk. □ **surge chamber** (or **tank**) a chamber designed to neutralize sudden changes of pressure in a flow of liquid. [OF *sourdre sourge-*, or *sorgir* f. Cat., f. L *surgere* rise]

■ *n.* **1** see OUTBURST. **2** swell, surf, upsurge, eddy, rush, gush, flood, stream, flow; see also WAVE *n.* 6a. **4** see SWELL *n.* 1. ● *v.* **1** swell, billow, bulge, heave, roll, undulate, well forth *or* up, rise and fall, ebb and flow, pulsate, rush, gush, pour, flood, stream, flow. **2** rush, pour, flood, stream, flow.

surgeon /súrjən/ *n.* **1** a medical practitioner qualified to practise surgery. **2** a medical officer in a navy or army or military hospital. □ **surgeon fish** any tropical marine fish of the genus *Acanthurus* with movable lancet-shaped spines on each side of the tail. **surgeon general** (*pl.* **surgeons general**) *US* the head of a public health service or of an army etc. medical service. **surgeon's knot** a reef-knot with a double twist. [ME f. AF *surgien* f. OF *serurgien* (as SURGERY)]

■ see PHYSICIAN.

surgery /súrjəri/ *n.* (*pl.* **-ies**) **1** the branch of medicine concerned with treatment of injuries or disorders of the body by incision, manipulation or alteration of organs etc., with the hands or with instruments. **2** *Brit.* **a** a place where a doctor, dentist, etc., treats patients. **b** the occasion of this (*the doctor will see you after surgery*). **3** *Brit.* **a** a place where

an MP, lawyer, or other professional person gives advice. **b** the occasion of this. [ME f. OF *surgerie* f. L *chirurgia* f. Gk *kheirourgia* handiwork, surgery f. *kheir* hand + *erg-* work]
■ **2 a** see INFIRMARY 2.

surgical /súrjik'l/ *adj.* **1** of or relating to or done by surgeons or surgery. **2** resulting from surgery (*surgical fever*). **3 a** used in surgery. **b** (of a special garment etc.) worn to correct a deformity etc. □ **surgical spirit** methylated spirit used in surgery for cleansing etc. □□ **surgically** *adv.* [earlier *chirurgical* f. *chirurgy* f. OF *sirurgie*: see SURGEON]

suricate /sŏŏrikayt/ *n.* a South African burrowing mongoose, *Suricata suricatta*, with grey and black stripes. [F f. S.Afr. native name]

Surinam toad /sŏŏrinám/ *n.* = PIPA. [*Surinam* in S. America]

surly /súrli/ *adj.* (**surlier, surliest**) bad-tempered and unfriendly; churlish. □□ **surlily** *adv.* **surliness** *n.* [alt. spelling of obs. *sirly* haughty f. SIR + -LY[1]]
■ unpleasant, unfriendly, rude, crusty, cantankerous, curmudgeonly, churlish, crabby, crabbed, choleric, splenetic, dyspeptic, bilious, temperamental, cross, crotchety, irritable, grumpy, bearish, gruff, sullen, testy, touchy, tetchy, short-tempered, ill-tempered, bad-tempered, ill-natured, bad-natured, ill-humoured, peevish, quarrelsome, argumentative, obnoxious, uncivil, rough, obstreperous, *colloq.* grouchy. □□ **surliness** see TEMPER *n.* 3.

surmise /sərmíz/ *n.* & *v.* ● *n.* a conjecture or suspicion about the existence or truth of something. ● *v.* **1** *tr.* (often foll. by *that* + clause) infer doubtfully; make a surmise about. **2** *tr.* suspect the existence of. **3** *intr.* make a guess. [ME f. AF & OF fem. past part. of *surmettre* accuse f. LL *supermittere supermiss-* (as SUPER-, *mittere* send)]
■ *n.* guess, conjecture, speculation, notion, hypothesis, theory, supposition, assumption, presumption, conclusion, understanding, fancy, suspicion, feeling, sense. ● *v.* **1** imagine, guess, conjecture, speculate, suppose, hypothesize, theorize, assume, presume, conclude, gather, infer, deduce, understand, fancy, suspect, feel, sense. **3** guess, conjecture, speculate.

surmount /sərmównt/ *v.tr.* **1** overcome or get over (a difficulty or obstacle). **2** (usu. in *passive*) cap or crown (*peaks surmounted with snow*). □□ **surmountable** *adj.* [ME f. OF *surmonter* (as SUR-[1], MOUNT[1])]
■ **1** see *get over* 2. **2** see CROWN *v.* 4.

surmullet /surmúllit/ *n.* the red mullet. [F *surmulet* f. OF *sor* red + *mulet* MULLET]

surname /súrnaym/ *n.* & *v.* ● *n.* **1** a hereditary name common to all members of a family, as distinct from a Christian or first name. **2** *archaic* an additional descriptive or allusive name attached to a person, sometimes becoming hereditary. ● *v.tr.* **1** give a surname to. **2** give (a person a surname). **3** (as **surnamed** *adj.*) having as a family name. [ME, alt. of *surnoun* f. AF (as SUR-[1], NOUN name)]
■ *n.* **1** family name, last name.

surpass /sərpaáss/ *v.tr.* **1** outdo, be greater or better than. **2** (as **surpassing** *adj.*) pre-eminent, matchless (*of surpassing intelligence*). □□ **surpassingly** *adv.* [F *surpasser* (as SUR-[1], PASS[1])]
■ **1** exceed, excel, go *or* pass beyond, outdo, beat, worst, better, outstrip, outdistance, outperform, outclass, outshine, eclipse, overshadow, top, cap, transcend, prevail over, leave behind, *colloq.* best. **2** (**surpassing**) excessive, extraordinary, great, enormous, pre-eminent, incomparable, unrivalled, unparalleled, matchless, peerless, unmatched, unequalled, unsurpassed. □□ **surpassingly** exceedingly, extraordinarily, incomparably.

surplice /súrpliss/ *n.* a loose white linen vestment reaching the knees, worn over a cassock by clergy and choristers at services. □□ **surpliced** *adj.* [ME f. AF *surplis*, OF *sourpelis*, f. med.L *superpellicium* (as SUPER-, *pellicia* PELISSE)]

surplus /súrpləss/ *n.* & *adj.* ● *n.* **1** an amount left over when requirements have been met. **2 a** an excess of revenue over expenditure in a given period, esp. a financial year (opp. DEFICIT). **b** the excess value of a company's assets over the face value of its stock. ● *adj.* exceeding what is needed or used. □ **surplus value** *Econ.* the difference between the value of work done and wages paid. [ME f. AF *surplus*, OF *s(o)urplus* f. med.L *superplus* (as SUPER-, + *plus* more)]
■ *n.* **1** overage, excess, superfluity, surfeit, over-abundance, oversupply, overdose, glut; leftovers, remainder, residue, balance. ● *adj.* excess, leftover, extra, spare, over-abundant, superfluous, unused, redundant.

surprise /sərpríz/ *n.* & *v.* ● *n.* **1** an unexpected or astonishing event or circumstance. **2** the emotion caused by this. **3** the act of catching a person etc. unawares, or the process of being caught unawares. **4** (*attrib.*) unexpected; made or done etc. without warning (*a surprise visit*). ● *v.tr.* **1** affect with surprise; turn out contrary to the expectations of (*your answer surprised me*; *I surprised her by arriving early*). **2** (usu. in *passive*; foll. by *at*) shock, scandalize (*I am surprised at you*). **3** capture or attack by surprise. **4** come upon (a person) unawares (*surprised him taking a biscuit*). **5** (foll. by *into*) startle (a person) by surprise into an action etc. (*surprised them into consenting*). □ **take by surprise** affect with surprise, esp. by an unexpected encounter or statement. □□ **surprisedly** /-prízidli/ *adv.* **surprising** *adj.* **surprisingly** *adv.* **surprisingness** *n.* [OF, fem. past part. of *surprendre* (as SUR-[1], *prendre* f. L *praehendere* seize)]
■ *n.* **1** blow, jolt, bolt from *or* out of the blue, bombshell, *colloq.* shocker, eye-opener. **2** shock, astonishment, amazement, stupefaction, wonder, incredulity. **4** (*attrib.*) see UNFORESEEN. ● *v.* **1** shock, astound, astonish, amaze, take by surprise, disconcert, nonplus, dumbfound, confound, stagger, startle, stupefy, stun, take aback, strike, *colloq.* floor, bowl over, flabbergast, knock for six. **2** shock, scandalize, appal, dismay, horrify, outrage. **3, 4** ambush, ambuscade, pounce on, swoop on, startle; take *or* catch unawares, take by surprise, catch red-handed, catch in the act, catch *in flagrante delicto*, catch out, catch napping, catch off guard, discover, detect, come upon, *colloq.* catch someone with his *or* her pants down. □□ **surprising** see *amazing* (AMAZE). **surprisingly** see PARTICULARLY 1.

surra /sŏŏrə, súrrə/ *n.* a febrile disease transmitted by bites of flies and affecting horses and cattle in the tropics. [Marathi]

surreal /səréeəl/ *adj.* **1** having the qualities of surrealism. **2** strange, bizarre. □□ **surreality** /-ree-álliti/ *n.* **surreally** *adv.* [back-form. f. SURREALISM etc.]
■ **2** see *dreamlike* (DREAM).

surrealism /səréeəliz'm/ *n.* a 20th-c. movement in art and literature aiming at expressing the subconscious mind, e.g. by the irrational juxtaposition of images. □□ **surrealist** *n.* & *adj.* **surrealistic** /-lístik/ *adj.* **surrealistically** /-lístikəli/ *adv.* [F *surréalisme* (as SUR-[1], REALISM)]

surrebutter /súrribúttər/ *n.* *Law* the plaintiff's reply to the defendant's rebutter. [SUR-[1] + REBUTTER, after SURREJOINDER]
■ see ANSWER *n.* 1.

surrejoinder /súrrijóyndər/ *n.* *Law* the plaintiff's reply to the defendant's rejoinder. [SUR-[1] + REJOINDER]
■ see ANSWER *n.* 1.

surrender /səréndər/ *v.* & *n.* ● *v.* **1** *tr.* hand over; relinquish possession of, esp. on compulsion or demand; give into another's power or control. **2** *intr.* **a** accept an enemy's demand for submission. **b** give oneself up; cease from resistance; submit. **3** *intr.* & *refl.* (foll. by *to*) give oneself over to a habit, emotion, influence, etc. **4** *tr.* give up rights under (a life-insurance policy) in return for a smaller sum received immediately. **5** *tr.* give up (a lease) before its expiry. **6** *tr.* abandon (hope etc.). ● *n.* the act or an instance of surrendering. □ **surrender to bail** duly appear in a lawcourt after release on bail. **surrender value** the amount payable to one who surrenders a life-insurance policy. [ME f. AF f. OF *surrendre* (as SUR-[1], RENDER)]

■ *v.* **1** give up, yield, let go (of), relinquish, deliver (up), hand over, forgo, forsake, turn over, turn in, part with, cede, concede. **2** give (oneself) up, yield, quit, cry quits, capitulate, throw up *or* in the sponge, throw in the towel, raise the white flag, throw up one's hands, succumb, submit, give way, acquiesce, comply, give in, concede, crumble, cave in. **6** abandon, give up. ● *n.* submission, capitulation, yielding, renunciation, relinquishment, forfeiture; transferral, transfer, transference, hand-over, conveyancing, ceding, cession, concession.

surreptitious /súrrəptíshəss/ *adj.* **1** covert; kept secret. **2** done by stealth; clandestine. ▫▫ **surreptitiously** *adv.* **surreptitiousness** *n.* [ME f. L *surrepticius -itius* f. *surripere surrept-* (as SUR-[1], *rapere* seize)]

■ furtive, secret, clandestine, stealthy, underhand(ed), devious, covert, sly, secretive, private, concealed, hidden, veiled, sneaky. ▫▫ **surreptitiously** see *secretly* (SECRET). **surreptitiousness** see SECRECY.

surrey /súrri/ *n.* (*pl.* **surreys**) *US* a light four-wheeled carriage with two seats facing forwards. [orig. of an adaptation of the *Surrey cart*, orig. made in *Surrey* in England]

surrogate /súrrəgət/ *n.* **1** a substitute, esp. for a person in a specific role or office. **2** *Brit.* a deputy, esp. of a bishop in granting marriage licences. **3** *US* a judge in charge of probate, inheritance, and guardianship. ▫ **surrogate mother 1** a person acting the role of mother. **2** a woman who bears a child on behalf of another woman, from her own egg fertilized by the other woman's partner. ▫▫ **surrogacy** *n.* **surrogateship** *n.* [L *surrogatus* past part. of *surrogare* elect as a substitute (as SUR-[1], *rogare* ask)]

■ **1** see SUBSTITUTE *n.* 1a. **2** see DEPUTY. **3** see JUDGE *n.* 1.

surround /sərównd/ *v.* & *n.* ● *v.tr.* **1** come or be all round; encircle, enclose. **2** (in *passive*; foll. by *by, with*) have on all sides (*the house is surrounded by trees*). ● *n.* **1** *Brit.* **a** a border or edging, esp. an area between the walls and carpet of a room. **b** a floor-covering for this. **2** an area or substance surrounding something. ▫▫ **surrounding** *adj.* [ME = overflow, f. AF *sur(o)under*, OF *s(o)uronder* f. LL *superundare* (as SUPER-, *undare* flow f. *unda* wave)]

■ *v.* encompass, encircle, envelop, enclose, hem in, hedge in, fence in, box in, ring, circle, skirt; cover, coat, encase; beset, besiege. ● *n.* **2** environs, environment, surroundings, atmosphere, ambience, setting. ▫▫ **surrounding** nearby, neighbouring, local, adjoining, neighbourhood, adjacent, bordering, abutting, circumambient, circumjacent.

surroundings /sərówndingz/ *n.pl.* the things in the neighbourhood of, or the conditions affecting, a person or thing.

■ see ENVIRONMENT 1, 2.

surtax /súrtaks/ *n.* & *v.* ● *n.* an additional tax, esp. levied on incomes above a certain level. ● *v.tr.* impose a surtax on. [F *surtaxe* (as SUR-[1], TAX)]

surtitle /súrtīt'l/ *n.* (esp. in opera) each of a sequence of captions projected above the stage, translating the text being sung.

surtout /surtōō, -tōōt/ *n. hist.* a greatcoat or frock-coat. [F f. *sur* over + *tout* everything]

surveillance /surváylənss, *disp.* səváy-yənss/ *n.* close observation, esp. of a suspected person. [F f. *surveiller* (as SUR-[1], *veiller* f. L *vigilare* keep watch)]

■ watch, scrutiny, reconnaissance; see also OBSERVATION 1, 2, 4.

survey *v.* & *n.* ● *v.tr.* /sərváy/ **1** take or present a general view of. **2** examine the condition of (a building etc.). **3** determine the boundaries, extent, ownership, etc., of (a district etc.). ● *n.* /súrvay/ **1** a general view or consideration of something. **2 a** the act of surveying property. **b** the result or findings of this, esp. in a written report. **3** an inspection or investigation. **4** a map or plan made by surveying an area. **5** a department carrying out the surveying of land. [ME f. AF *survei(e)r*, OF *so(u)rveeir* (pres. stem *survey-*) f. med.L *supervidēre* (as SUPER-, *vidēre* see)]

■ *v.* **1, 2** view, look at, get a bird's-eye view of, contemplate, scan, observe; consider, review; examine, appraise, evaluate, inspect, study, scrutinize, assess, investigate, look into *or* over. **3** measure, size up, take the measure of; plot, map (out), triangulate; explore, reconnoitre. ● *n.* **1, 3** view, observation, sight, contemplation, consideration; examination, appraisal, evaluation, assessment, review, measure, study, scan, scrutiny, inquiry, enquiry, measurement, investigation, probe, inspection; canvass, poll, census.

surveyor /sərváyər/ *n.* **1** a person who surveys land and buildings, esp. professionally. **2** *Brit.* an official inspector, esp. for measurement and valuation. **3** a person who carries out surveys. ▫▫ **surveyorship** *n.* (esp. in sense 2). [ME f. AF & OF *surve(i)our* (as SURVEY)]

survival /sərvīv'l/ *n.* **1** the process or an instance of surviving. **2** a person, thing, or practice that has remained from a former time. ▫ **survival kit** emergency rations etc., esp. carried by servicemen. **survival of the fittest** the process or result of natural selection.

■ **1** see ENDURANCE 3, SUBSISTENCE 1. **2** hangover.

survivalism /sərvīvəliz'm/ *n.* the practising of outdoor survival skills as a sport or hobby. ▫▫ **survivalist** *adj.* & *n.*

survive /sərvīv/ *v.* **1** *intr.* continue to live or exist; be still alive or existent. **2** *tr.* live or exist longer than. **3** *tr.* remain alive after going through, or continue to exist in spite of (a danger, accident, etc.). [ME f. AF *survivre*, OF *sourvivre* f. L *supervivere* (as SUPER, *vivere* live)]

■ **1** continue, last, live (on), carry on, persist, subsist, exist, pull through, endure, keep going, remain. **2** outlast, outlive. **3** see WEATHER *v.*

survivor /sərvīvər/ *n.* **1** a person who survives or has survived. **2** *Law* a joint tenant who has the right to the whole estate on the other's death.

Sus. *abbr.* Susanna (Apocrypha).

sus var. of SUSS.

sus- /suss, səss/ *prefix* assim. form of SUB- before *c, p, t*.

susceptibility /səséptibílliti/ *n.* (*pl.* **-ies**) **1** the state of being susceptible. **2** (in *pl.*) a person's sensitive feelings. **3** *Physics* the ratio of magnetization to a magnetizing force.

■ **1** see SENSITIVITY. **2** (*susceptibilities*) see SENSIBILITY 3.

susceptible /səséptib'l/ *adj.* **1** impressionable, sensitive; easily moved by emotion. **2** (*predic.*) **a** (foll. by *to*) likely to be affected by; liable or vulnerable to (*susceptible to pain*). **b** (foll. by *of*) allowing; admitting of (*facts not susceptible of proof*). ▫▫ **susceptibly** *adv.* [LL *susceptibilis* f. L *suscipere suscept-* (as SUB-, *capere* take)]

■ **1** impressionable, influenceable, vulnerable, reachable, accessible, credulous, suggestible, gullible, naïve; sensitive, susceptive; emotional. **2 a** (*susceptible to*) open to, liable to, prone to, subject to, disposed to, predisposed to, receptive to, affected by, vulnerable to, responsive to. **b** (*susceptible of*) allowing, permitting; admitting of, capable of.

susceptive /səséptiv/ *adj.* **1** concerned with the receiving of emotional impressions or ideas. **2** receptive. **3** = SUSCEPTIBLE. [LL *susceptivus* (as SUSCEPTIBLE)]

■ **1** see SENSITIVE *adj.* 2. **2** see RECEPTIVE.

sushi /sōōshi/ *n.* a Japanese dish of balls of cold rice flavoured and garnished. [Jap.]

suslik /súslik/ *n.* an E. European and Asian ground squirrel, *Citellus citellus*. [Russ.]

suspect *v.*, *n.*, & *adj.* ● *v.tr.* /səspékt/ **1** have an impression of the existence or presence of (*suspects poisoning*). **2** (foll. by *to be*) believe tentatively, without clear ground. **3** (foll. by *that* + clause) be inclined to think. **4** (often foll. by *of*) be inclined to mentally accuse; doubt the innocence of (*suspect him of complicity*). **5** doubt the genuineness or truth of. ● *n.* /súspekt/ a suspected person. ● *adj.* /súspekt/ subject to or deserving suspicion or distrust; not sound or trustworthy. [ME f. L *suspicere suspect-* (as SUB-, *specere* look)]

■ *v.* **3** feel, think, believe, sense, have a feeling, fancy, imagine, theorize, guess, surmise, suppose, have a sneaking suspicion, think it likely *or* probable, *colloq.* expect. **4, 5** disbelieve, doubt, mistrust, distrust, harbour suspicions about *or* of, have suspicions about *or* of, have misgivings about, be suspicious of, *Brit. sl.* suss. ● *n.* *Brit. sl.* suss. ● *adj.* suspicious, questionable, open to question *or* suspicion, doubtful, dubious, unreliable, untrustworthy, shady; suspected; *sl.* fishy.

suspend /səspénd/ *v.tr.* **1** hang up. **2** keep inoperative or undecided for a time; defer. **3** debar temporarily from a function, office, privilege, etc. **4** (as **suspended** *adj.*) (of solid particles or a body in a fluid medium) sustained somewhere between top and bottom. □ **suspended animation** a temporary cessation of the vital functions without death. **suspended sentence** a judicial sentence left unenforced subject to good behaviour during a specified period. **suspend payment** (of a company) fail to meet its financial engagements; admit insolvency. □□ **suspensible** *adj.* [ME f. OF *suspendre* or L *suspendere suspens-* (as SUB-, *pendere* hang)]

■ **1** hang (up), attach, fasten, dangle, swing, sling. **2** hold up *or* off (on), withhold, put off, put in *or* into abeyance, hold *or* keep in abeyance, shelve, postpone, delay, defer, interrupt, intermit, stop *or* check *or* cease *or* discontinue temporarily, table. **3** debar, exclude, eliminate, reject, expel, eject, evict; blackball; see also *lay off* 1 (LAY[1]).

suspender /səspéndər/ *n.* **1** an attachment to hold up a stocking or sock by its top. **2** (in *pl.*) *US* a pair of braces. □ **suspender belt** a woman's undergarment with suspenders.

suspense /səspénss/ *n.* **1** a state of anxious uncertainty or expectation. **2** *Law* a suspension; the temporary cessation of a right etc. □ **keep in suspense** delay informing (a person) of urgent information. **suspense account** an account in which items are entered temporarily before allocation to the right account. □□ **suspenseful** *adj.* [ME f. AF & OF *suspens* f. past part. of L *suspendere* SUSPEND]

■ **1** anxiety, tension, apprehension, nervousness, agitation, anxiousness, anticipation, expectation, excitement; uncertainty, indefiniteness, insecurity, incertitude, doubt, irresolution, expectancy, indecision, not knowing. **2** see SUSPENSION.

suspension /səspénsh'n/ *n.* **1** the act of suspending or the condition of being suspended. **2** the means by which a vehicle is supported on its axles. **3** a substance consisting of particles suspended in a medium. **4** *Mus.* the prolongation of a note of a chord to form a discord with the following chord. □ **suspension bridge** a bridge with a roadway suspended from cables supported by structures at each end. [F *suspension* or L *suspensio* (as SUSPEND)]

■ **1** intermission, moratorium, deferral, deferment, hold-up, delay, interruption, break, postponement, discontinuation, stay; debarment, exclusion, elimination, rejection, expulsion, ejection, eviction; disbarment; *Law* suspense.

suspensive /səspénsiv/ *adj.* **1** having the power or tendency to suspend or postpone. **2** causing suspense. □□ **suspensively** *adv.* **suspensiveness** *n.* [F *suspensif -ive* or med.L *suspensivus* (as SUSPEND)]

suspensory /səspénsəri/ *adj.* (of a ligament, muscle, bandage, etc.) holding an organ etc. suspended. [F *suspensoire* (as SUSPENSION)]

suspicion /səspísh'n/ *n.* **1** the feeling or thought of a person who suspects. **2** the act or an instance of suspecting; the state of being suspected. **3** (foll. by *of*) a slight trace of. □ **above suspicion** too obviously good etc. to be suspected. **under suspicion** suspected. [ME f. AF *suspeciun* (OF *sospeçon*) f. med.L *suspectio -onis* f. L *suspicere* (as SUSPECT): assim. to F *suspicion* & L *suspicio*]

■ **1** (funny) feeling, hunch, guess, presentiment, premonition, intuition, idea, notion, impression; qualm, doubt, misgiving; dubiousness, mistrust, distrust, scepticism, wariness, apprehension, apprehensiveness, cautiousness, hesitation, second thoughts, uncertainty, *literary* dubiety; *colloq.* bad vibes, *sl.* leeriness, *Brit. sl.* suss. **3** inkling, suggestion, hint, trace, vestige, flavour, soupçon, taste, dash, glimmer, tinge, touch, shadow, shade, whisper, scintilla, speck, *US colloq.* tad. □ **above suspicion** see IRREPROACHABLE. **under suspicion** see SUSPICIOUS 3.

suspicious /səspíshəss/ *adj.* **1** prone to or feeling suspicion. **2** indicating suspicion (*a suspicious glance*). **3** inviting or justifying suspicion (*a suspicious lack of surprise*). □□ **suspiciously** *adv.* **suspiciousness** *n.* [ME f. AF & OF f. L *suspiciosus* (as SUSPICION)]

■ **1, 2** mistrustful, distrustful, doubtful, in doubt, sceptical, suspecting, disbelieving, unbelieving, incredulous, doubting, questioning, apprehensive, wary, chary, uncertain, uneasy, *sl.* leery. **3** doubtful, in doubt, dubious, questionable, debatable, suspect, suspected, under suspicion, untrustworthy, open to doubt *or* question *or* misconstruction, shady, *sl.* fishy. □□ **suspiciously** see *jealously* (JEALOUS).

suss /suss/ *v.* & *n.* (also **sus**) *Brit. sl.* ● *v.tr.* (**sussed**, **sussing**) **1** suspect of a crime. **2** (usu. foll. by *out*) **a** investigate, inspect (*go and suss out the restaurants*). **b** work out; grasp, understand, realize (*he had the market sussed*). ● *n.* **1** a suspect. **2** a suspicion; suspicious behaviour. □ **on suss** on suspicion (of having committed a crime). [abbr. of SUSPECT, SUSPICION]

■ *v.* **2 a** see INSPECT. **b** see *find out* 4. ● *n.* **2** see SUSPICION 1.

Sussex /sússiks/ *n.* **1** a speckled or red domestic fowl of an English breed. **2** this breed. [*Sussex* in S. England]

sustain /səstáyn/ *v.tr.* **1** support, bear the weight of, esp. for a long period. **2** give strength to; encourage, support. **3** (of food) give nourishment to. **4** endure, stand; bear up against. **5** undergo or suffer (defeat or injury etc.). **6** (of a court etc.) uphold or decide in favour of (an objection etc.). **7** substantiate or corroborate (a statement or charge). **8 a** maintain or keep (a sound, effort, etc.) going continuously. **b** (as **sustained** *adj.*) maintained continuously over a long period. **9** continue to represent (a part, character, etc.) adequately. □□ **sustainable** *adj.* **sustainedly** /-stáynidli/ *adv.* **sustainer** *n.* **sustainment** *n.* [ME f. AF *sustein-*, OF *so(u)stein-* stressed stem of *so(u)stenir* f. L *sustinēre sustent-* (as SUB-, *tenēre* hold)]

■ **1** bear, carry, support, take, hold. **2** support, carry, bear, bolster, buoy (up), reinforce, keep a person going, encourage, strengthen, shore up, underpin, prop up, buttress. **3** nourish, feed, support, keep (alive), maintain. **4, 5** endure, stand, withstand, bear up under *or* against, put up with, suffer, undergo, experience, tolerate, weather, brave. **6** uphold, recognize, allow, admit, approve, ratify, sanction, authorize, endorse, validate. **7** see SUBSTANTIATE. **8a, 9** uphold, support, keep up, maintain, continue, keep going, keep alive, preserve; prolong, persist in. **8 b** (**sustained**) continued, continuous, continual, prolonged, *Mus.* sostenuto; steady, even, level. □□ **sustainable** see VIABLE. **sustainer** see STALWART *n.*

sustenance /sústinənss/ *n.* **1 a** nourishment, food. **b** the process of nourishing. **2** a means of support; a livelihood. [ME f. AF *sustenaunce*, OF *so(u)stenance* (as SUSTAIN)]

■ **1 a** nutriment, nourishment, food (and drink), daily bread, rations, victuals, provisions, groceries, edibles, eatables, foodstuff(s), *archaic* meat, *colloq.* grub, eats, scoff, *formal* aliment, viands, *joc.* provender, *sl.* chow, nosh. **2** livelihood, (means of) support, maintenance, upkeep, keep, (means of) subsistence, daily bread, living.

sustentation /sústəntáysh'n/ *n. formal* **1** the support of life. **2** maintenance. [ME f. OF *sustentation* or L *sustentatio* f. *sustentare* frequent. of *sustinēre* SUSTAIN]

■ see MAINTENANCE 1.

susurration /syŏŏssəráysh'n, sŏŏ-/ *n.* (also **susurrus** /syoosúrrəss, soo-/) *literary* a sound of whispering or rustling. [ME f. LL *susurratio* f. L *susurrare*]

■ see RUSTLE *n.*

sutler /sútlər/ *n. hist.* a person following an army and selling provisions etc. to the soldiers. [obs. Du. *soeteler* f. *soetelen* befoul, perform mean duties, f. Gmc]

Sutra /sōōtrə/ *n.* **1** an aphorism or set of aphorisms in Hindu literature. **2** a narrative part of Buddhist literature. **3** Jainist scripture. [Skr. *sūtra* thread, rule, f. *siv* SEW]

suttee /suteé, sútti/ *n.* (also **sati**) (*pl.* **suttees** or **satis**) esp. *hist.* **1** the Hindu practice of a widow immolating herself on her husband's funeral pyre. **2** a widow who undergoes or has undergone this. [Hindi & Urdu f. Skr. *satī* faithful wife f. *sat* good]

suture /sōōchər/ *n.* & *v.* ● *n.* **1** *Surgery* **a** the joining of the edges of a wound or incision by stitching. **b** the thread or wire used for this. **2** the seamlike junction of two bones, esp. in the skull. **3** *Bot.* & *Zool.* a similar junction of parts. ● *v.tr. Surgery* stitch up (a wound or incision) with a suture. □□ **sutural** *adj.* **sutured** *adj.* [F *suture* or L *sutura* f. *suere sut-* sew]

■ **2, 3** see JUNCTION 1.

suzerain /sōōzərən/ *n.* **1** a feudal overlord. **2** a sovereign or State having some control over another State that is internally autonomous. □□ **suzerainty** *n.* [F, app. f. *sus* above f. L *su(r)sum* upward, after *souverain* SOVEREIGN]

■ □□ **suzerainty** see *sovereignty* (SOVEREIGN).

s.v. *abbr.* **1** a side valve. **2** (in a reference) under the word or heading given. [sense 2 f. L *sub voce* (or *verbo*)]

svelte /svelt/ *adj.* slender, lissom, graceful. [F f. It. *svelto*]

■ see SLENDER 1.

SW *abbr.* **1** south-west. **2** south-western.

swab /swob/ *n.* & *v.* (also **swob**) ● *n.* **1** a mop or other absorbent device for cleaning or mopping up. **2 a** an absorbent pad used in surgery. **b** a specimen of a possibly morbid secretion taken with a swab for examination. **3** *sl.* a term of contempt for a person. ● *v.tr.* (**swabbed, swabbing**) **1** clean with a swab. **2** (foll. by *up*) absorb (moisture) with a swab. [back-form. f. *swabber* f. early mod.Du. *zwabber* f. a Gmc base = 'splash, sway']

■ *v.* see WIPE *v.* 1.

swaddle /swódd'l/ *v.tr.* swathe (esp. an infant) in garments or bandages etc. □ **swaddling-clothes** narrow bandages formerly wrapped round a newborn child to restrain its movements and quieten it. [ME f. SWATHE + -LE[4]]

■ see SWATHE *v.*

swag /swag/ *n.* & *v.* ● *n.* **1** *sl.* **a** the booty carried off by burglars etc. **b** illicit gains. **2 a** an ornamental festoon of flowers etc. **b** a carved etc. representation of this. **c** drapery of similar appearance. **3** *Austral.* & *NZ* a traveller's or miner's bundle of personal belongings. ● *v.* (**swagged, swagging**) **1** *tr.* arrange (a curtain etc.) in swags. **2** *intr.* **a** hang heavily. **b** sway from side to side. **3** *tr.* cause to sway or sag. [16th c.: prob. f. Scand.]

■ *n.* **1 a** see BOOTY 1. ● *v.* **2 a** see SAG *v.* 1, 2.

swage /swayj/ *n.* & *v.* ● *n.* **1** a die or stamp for shaping wrought iron etc. by hammering or pressure. **2** a tool for bending metal etc. ● *v.tr.* shape with a swage. □ **swage-block** a block with various perforations, grooves, etc., for shaping metal. [F *s(o)uage* decorative groove, of unkn. orig.]

swagger /swággər/ *v.*, *n.*, & *adj.* ● *v.intr.* **1** walk arrogantly or self-importantly. **2** behave arrogantly; be domineering. ● *n.* **1** a swaggering gait or manner. **2** swaggering behaviour. **3** a dashing or confident air or way of doing something. **4** smartness. ● *adj.* **1** *colloq.* smart or fashionable. **2** (of a coat) cut with a loose flare from the shoulders. □ **swagger stick** a short cane carried by a military officer. □□ **swaggerer** *n.* **swaggeringly** *adv.* [app. f. SWAG *v.* + -ER[4]]

■ *v.* **1** strut, prance, parade, *archaic* swash, *esp. US colloq.* sashay. **2** boast, brag, crow, *colloq.* show off, swank, *literary* vaunt; see also *lord it over*. ● *n.* **1** strut, prance, caper. **2** show, display, ostentation, braggadocio, arrogance, bravado, bluster, boastfulness, *colloq.* showing off. **3, 4** see PANACHE. ● *adj.* **1** see STYLISH 1. □□ **swaggerer** see BRAGGART *n.*

swagman /swágman/ *n.* (*pl.* **-men**) *Austral.* & *NZ* a tramp carrying a swag (see SWAG *n.* 3).

■ see TRAMP *n.* 1.

Swahili /swəheéli/ *n.* (*pl.* same) **1** a member of a Bantu people of Zanzibar and adjacent coasts. **2** their language, used widely as a lingua franca in E. Africa. [Arab. *sawāḥil* pl. of *sāḥil* coast]

swain /swayn/ *n.* **1** *archaic* a country youth. **2** *poet.* a young lover or suitor. [ME *swein* f. ON *sveinn* lad = OE *swān* swineherd, f. Gmc]

■ **1** see PEASANT. **2** see SUITOR 1.

swallow[1] /swóllō/ *v.* & *n.* ● *v.* **1** *tr.* cause or allow (food etc.) to pass down the throat. **2** *intr.* perform the muscular movement of the oesophagus required to do this. **3** *tr.* **a** accept meekly; put up with (an affront etc.). **b** accept credulously (an unlikely assertion etc.). **4** *tr.* repress; resist the expression of (a feeling etc.) (*swallow one's pride*). **5** *tr.* articulate (words etc.) indistinctly. **6** *tr.* (often foll. by *up*) engulf or absorb; exhaust; cause to disappear. ● *n.* **1** the act of swallowing. **2** an amount swallowed in one action. □ **swallow-hole** *Brit.* = *sink-hole* (see SINK *n.* 6). □□ **swallowable** *adj.* **swallower** *n.* [OE *swelg* (n.), *swelgan* (v.) f. Gmc]

■ *v.* **1** eat, consume, devour, ingest, dispatch; guzzle, gobble, bolt, wolf; drink, imbibe, gulp, swill, lap up, put away, *colloq.* down, swig, *literary* quaff. **3 a** see TOLERATE. **b** accept, allow, credit, believe, take, *colloq.* fall for, *sl.* buy. **4** keep back *or* down, choke back *or* down, repress, suppress, hold in, control, stifle, smother, overcome, conquer. **5** see MUMBLE *v.* **6** absorb, make disappear, swamp, engulf, envelop, enfold, consume, assimilate. ● *n.* drink, gulp, guzzle, sip, sup, *colloq.* swig; bite, nibble, morsel, mouthful, nip, draught, dram, tot. □ **swallow-hole** *Geol.* sink(-hole).

swallow[2] /swóllō/ *n.* any of various migratory swift-flying insect-eating birds of the family Hirundinidae, esp. *Hirundo rustica*, with a forked tail and long pointed wings. □ **one swallow does not make a summer** a warning against a hasty inference from one instance. **swallow-dive** a dive with the arms outspread until close to the water. **swallow-tail 1** a deeply forked tail. **2** anything resembling this shape. **3** any butterfly of the family Papilionidae with wings extended at the back to this shape. **swallow-tailed** having a swallow-tail. [OE *swealwe* f. Gmc]

swam *past* of SWIM.

swami /swaámi/ *n.* (*pl.* **swamis**) a Hindu male religious teacher. [Hindi *swāmī* master, prince, f. Skr. *svāmin*]

■ see MASTER *n.* 2.

swamp /swomp/ *n.* & *v.* ● *n.* a piece of waterlogged ground; a bog or marsh. ● *v.* **1 a** *tr.* overwhelm, flood, or soak with water. **b** *intr.* become swamped. **2** *tr.* overwhelm or make invisible etc. with an excess or large amount of something. □□ **swampy** *adj.* (**swampier, swampiest**). [17th c., = dial. *swamp* sunk (14th c.), prob. of Gmc orig.]

■ *n.* **1** bog, fen, marsh, quagmire, mire, slough; marshland, wetlands; *Sc.* & *N.Engl.* moss, *US* moor *literary* morass. ● *v.* overwhelm, flood, inundate, submerge, immerse, deluge; soak, drench, engulf, swallow up; overcome, overload, overtax, overburden, snow under. □□ **swampy** see MUDDY *adj.* 2.

swan /swon/ *n.* & *v.* ● *n.* **1** a large water-bird of the genus *Cygnus* etc., having a long flexible neck, webbed feet, and in most species snow-white plumage. **2** *literary* a poet. ● *v.intr.* (**swanned, swanning**) (usu. foll. by *about*, *off*, etc.) *colloq.* move or go aimlessly or casually or with a superior air. □ **swan-dive** *US* = *swallow-dive* (see SWALLOW[2]). **swan-neck** a curved structure shaped like a swan's neck. **Swan of Avon** *literary* Shakespeare. **swan-upping** *Brit.* the annual taking up and marking of Thames swans. □□ **swanlike** *adj.* & *adv.* [OE f. Gmc]

■ *v.* see MEANDER *v.*

swank /swangk/ *n.*, *v.*, & *adj. colloq.* ● *n.* ostentation, swagger, bluff. ● *v.intr.* behave with swank; show off. ● *adj.* esp. *US* = SWANKY. [19th c.: orig. uncert.]

■ *n.* see SPLENDOUR 2. ● *v.* see SWAGGER *v.* 2.

swankpot /swángkpot/ *n. Brit. colloq.* a person behaving with swank.

swanky /swángki/ *adj.* (**swankier**, **swankiest**) **1** marked by swank; ostentatiously smart or showy. **2** (of a person) inclined to swank; boastful. ▫▫ **swankily** *adv.* **swankiness** *n.*

■ **1** smart, stylish, fashionable, chic, chichi, fancy, showy, luxurious, grand, elegant, plush, *colloq.* nifty, plushy, posh, ritzy, swish, swell, swagger, *esp. US colloq.* swank, *sl.* snazzy, *US sl.* neat. **2** see BOASTFUL. ▫▫ **swankiness** see SPLENDOUR 2.

swannery /swónnəri/ *n.* (*pl.* **-ies**) a place where swans are bred.

swansdown /swónzdown/ *n.* **1** the fine down of a swan, used in trimmings and esp. in powder-puffs. **2** a kind of thick cotton cloth with a soft nap on one side.

swansong /swónsong/ *n.* **1** a person's last work or act before death or retirement etc. **2** a song like that fabled to be sung by a dying swan.

swap /swop/ *v.* & *n.* (also **swop**) ● *v.tr.* & *intr.* (**swapped**, **swapping**) exchange or barter (one thing for another). ● *n.* **1** an act of swapping. **2** a thing suitable for swapping. **3** a thing swapped. ▫▫ **swapper** *n.* [ME, orig. = 'hit': prob. imit.]

■ *v.* see EXCHANGE *v.* ● *n.* **1** see EXCHANGE *n.* 1.

SWAPO /swáapō/ *abbr.* South West Africa People's Organization.

Swaraj /swəráaj/ *n. hist.* self-government or independence for India. ▫▫ **Swarajist** *n.* [Skr., = self-ruling: cf. RAJ]

sward /swawrd/ *n. literary* **1** an expanse of short grass. **2** turf. ▫▫ **swarded** *adj.* [OE *sweard* skin]

■ see TURF *n.* 1.

sware /swair/ *archaic past* of SWEAR.

swarf /swawrf/ *n.* **1** fine chips or filings of stone, metal, etc. **2** wax etc. removed in cutting a gramophone record. [ON *svarf* file-dust]

swarm[1] /swawrm/ *n.* & *v.* ● *n.* **1** a cluster of bees leaving the hive with the queen to establish a new colony. **2** a large number of insects or birds moving in a cluster. **3** a large group of people, esp. moving over or filling a large area. **4** (in *pl.*; foll. by *of*) great numbers. **5** a group of zoospores. ● *v.intr.* **1** move in or form a swarm. **2** gather or move in large numbers. **3** (foll. by *with*) (of a place) be overrun, crowded, or infested (*was swarming with tourists*). [OE *swearm* f. Gmc]

■ *n.* **1–3** throng, horde, army, host, multitude, hive, herd, mob, mass, drove, flood, stream, cloud, flock, pack, shoal, bunch. **4** (*swarms*) see SCORE *n.* 3. ● *v.* **1, 2** throng, mass, crowd, congregate, cluster, flock, herd, gather, mob; flood, stream, flow, pour, surge. **3** (*swarm with*) crawl with, abound in *or* with, throng with, teem with, burst with, bristle with, be alive with, be crowded with, be overrun with, be infested with.

swarm[2] /swawrm/ *v.intr.* (foll. by *up*) & *tr.* climb (a rope or tree etc.), esp. in a rush, by clasping or clinging with the hands and knees etc. [16th c.: orig. unkn.]

swart /swawrt/ *adj. archaic* swarthy, dark-hued. [OE *sweart* f. Gmc]

■ see SWARTHY.

swarthy /swáwrthi/ *adj.* (**swarthier**, **swarthiest**) dark, dark-complexioned. ▫▫ **swarthily** *adv.* **swarthiness** *n.* [var. of obs. *swarty* (as SWART)]

■ dark, dusky, brown, tanned, weather-beaten, *archaic* swart.

swash[1] /swosh/ *v.* & *n.* ● *v.* **1** *intr.* (of water etc.) wash about; make the sound of washing or rising and falling. **2** *tr. archaic* strike violently. **3** *intr. archaic* swagger. ● *n.* the motion or sound of swashing water. [imit.]

■ *v.* **3** see SWAGGER *v.* 1.

swash[2] /swosh/ *adj.* **1** inclined obliquely. **2** (of a letter) having a flourished stroke or strokes. ▫ **swash-plate** an inclined disc revolving on an axle and giving reciprocating motion to a part in contact with it. [17th c.: orig. unkn.]

swashbuckler /swóshbuklər/ *n.* a swaggering bully or ruffian. ▫▫ **swashbuckling** *adj.* & *n.* [SWASH[1] + BUCKLER]

■ see ADVENTURER 1, BULLY[1] *n.* ▫▫ **swashbuckling** (*adj.*) adventurous, daring, daredevil, swaggering, roisterous, bold, dashing, flamboyant, macho.

swastika /swóstikə/ *n.* **1** an ancient symbol formed by an equal-armed cross with each arm continued at a right angle. **2** this with clockwise continuations as the symbol of Nazi Germany. [Skr. *svastika* f. *svastí* well-being f. *sú* good + *astí* being]

■ hakenkreuz.

swat /swot/ *v.* & *n.* ● *v.tr.* (**swatted**, **swatting**) **1** crush (a fly etc.) with a sharp blow. **2** hit hard and abruptly. ● *n.* a swatting blow. [17th c. in the sense 'sit down': N.Engl. dial. & US var. of SQUAT]

■ *v.* see HIT *v.* 1a. ● *n.* see HIT *n.* 1a.

swatch /swoch/ *n.* **1** a sample, esp. of cloth or fabric. **2** a collection of samples. [17th c.: orig. unkn.]

swath /swawth/ *n.* (also **swathe** /swayth/) (*pl.* **swaths** /swawths, swawthz/ or **swathes**) **1** a ridge of grass or corn etc. lying after being cut. **2** a space left clear after the passage of a mower etc. **3** a broad strip. ▫ **cut a wide swath** be effective in destruction. [OE *swæth*, *swathu*]

■ ridge, path, belt, strip, ribbon.

swathe /swayth/ *v.* & *n.* ● *v.tr.* bind or enclose in bandages or garments etc. ● *n.* a bandage or wrapping. [OE *swathian*]

■ *v.* tie, bind, bandage, wrap, swaddle, bundle (up), envelop, shroud, muffle (up), *literary* enwrap. ● *n.* bandage, wrapping, covering, wrapper, cover.

swatter /swóttər/ *n.* an implement for swatting flies.

sway /sway/ *v.* & *n.* ● *v.* **1** *intr.* & *tr.* lean or cause to lean unsteadily in different directions alternately. **2** *intr.* oscillate irregularly; waver. **3** *tr.* **a** control the motion or direction of. **b** have influence or rule over. ● *n.* **1** rule, influence, or government (*hold sway*). **2** a swaying motion or position. ▫ **sway-back** an abnormally hollowed back (esp. of a horse); lordosis. **sway-backed** (esp. of a horse) having a sway-back. [ME: cf. LG *swājen* be blown to and fro, Du. *zwaaien* swing, wave]

■ *v.* **1** bend, lean, roll, rock, swing (to and fro *or* back and forth *or* from side to side *or* backwards and forwards), move to and fro *or* back and forth *or* from side to side *or* backwards and forwards, wave, fluctuate, undulate, reel, totter, lurch. **2** see OSCILLATE. **3 a** move, incline, divert, veer, tilt, lean, slant, bias, swing. **b** influence, persuade, impress, win over, bring round, convince, talk into; move, incline, affect, bias, swing. ● *n.* **1** influence, control, power, command, authority, jurisdiction, dominion, rule, government, sovereignty, leadership, mastery, domination; grip, clutches, grasp; *colloq.* clout. **2** sweep, wave, swing, (period of) oscillation, libration.

swear /swair/ *v.* & *n.* ● *v.* (*past* **swore** /swor/; *past part.* **sworn** /sworn/) **1** *tr.* **a** (often foll. by *to* + infin. or *that* + clause) state or promise solemnly or on oath. **b** take (an oath). **2** *tr. colloq.* say emphatically; insist (*swore he had not seen it*). **3** *tr.* cause to take an oath (*swore them to secrecy*). **4** *intr.* (often foll. by *at*) use profane or indecent language, esp. as an expletive or from anger. **5** *tr.* (often foll. by *against*) make a sworn affirmation of (an offence) (*swear treason against*). **6** *intr.* (foll. by *by*) **a** appeal to as a witness in taking an oath (*swear by Almighty God*). **b** *colloq.* have or express great confidence in (*swears by yoga*). **7** *intr.* (foll. by *to*; usu. in *neg.*) admit the certainty of (*could not swear to it*). **8** *intr.* (foll. by *at*) *colloq.* (of colours etc.) fail to harmonize with. ● *n.* a spell of swearing. ▫ **swear blind** *colloq.* affirm emphatically. **swear in** induct into office etc. by administering an oath. **swear off** *colloq.* promise to abstain from (drink etc.). **swear-word** a profane or indecent word, esp. uttered as an expletive. □□ **swearer** *n.* [OE *swerian* f. Gmc, rel. to ANSWER]

■ *v.* **1a, 2** asseverate, declare, insist, assert, solemnly affirm *or* state, testify, promise, take an oath, state under *or* on oath, undertake, vow, avow, warrant, pledge, give one's word, agree, *Law* depose, *formal* aver. **4** curse, blaspheme, imprecate, use profanity, utter profanities, *colloq.* cuss. **6 b** (*swear by*) trust (in), believe in, rely on, have confidence in, count on. **7** (*swear to*) see PROVE 1. **8** (*swear at*) see CLASH *v.* 3b. □ **swear in** see INDUCT 1. **swear off** forswear, renounce, abjure, go off, forgo, shun, avoid, give up, forsake, throw over, *literary* eschew. **swear-word** see EXPLETIVE *n.*

sweat /swet/ *n.* & *v.* ● *n.* **1** moisture exuded through the pores of the skin, esp. from heat or nervousness. **2** a state or period of sweating. **3** *colloq.* a state of anxiety (*was in a sweat about it*). **4** *colloq.* **a** drudgery, effort. **b** a laborious task or undertaking. **5** condensed moisture on a surface. ● *v.* (*past* and *past part.* **sweated** or *US* **sweat**) **1** *intr.* exude sweat; perspire. **2** *intr.* be terrified, suffering, etc. **3** *intr.* (of a wall etc.) exhibit surface moisture. **4** *intr.* drudge, toil. **5** *tr.* heat (meat or vegetables) slowly in fat or water to extract the juices. **6** *tr.* emit (blood, gum, etc.) like sweat. **7** *tr.* make (a horse, athlete, etc.) sweat by exercise. **8** *tr.* **a** cause to drudge or toil. **b** (as **sweated** *adj.*) (of goods, workers, or labour) produced by or subjected to long hours under poor conditions. **9** *tr.* subject (hides or tobacco) to fermentation in manufacturing. □ **by the sweat of one's brow** by one's own hard work. **no sweat** *colloq.* there is no need to worry. **sweat-band** a band of absorbent material inside a hat or round a wrist etc. to soak up sweat. **sweat blood** *colloq.* **1** work strenuously. **2** be extremely anxious. **sweat gland** *Anat.* a spiral tubular gland below the skin secreting sweat. **sweating-sickness** an epidemic fever with sweating prevalent in England in the 15th–16th c. **sweat it out** *colloq.* endure a difficult experience to the end. [ME *swet(e)*, alt. (after *swete* v. f. OE *swǣtan* OHG *sweizzen* roast) of *swote* f. OE *swāt* f. Gmc]

■ *n.* **1, 2** perspiration, lather, *Med.* diaphoresis. **3** state of confusion *or* upset *or* excitement *or* distraction *or* agitation *or* anxiety *or* distress *or* worry; lather, bother, *colloq.* dither, tizzy, stew, flap, *literary* pother; (*in a sweat*) see NERVOUS 1–3, 5. **4 a** (hard) work, labour, effort, exertion, laboriousness, toil, drudgery, *archaic* moil, *colloq.* grind, *Brit. colloq.* swot, *Austral. sl.* (hard) yakka. **b** slog, labour, chore, *colloq.* grind. ● *v.* **1** perspire, glow. **2** worry, be anxious, agonize, anguish, bite one's nails, be on pins and needles, fret, fuss, torture *or* torment oneself, lose sleep, *colloq.* sweat blood, stew, be in a tizzy *or* stew. **4** slave (away), labour, drudge, grind, toil, slog, work like a Trojan, *archaic* toil and moil, *Brit. colloq.* swot. **6** ooze, exude, squeeze out, transude, emit. □ **no sweat** don't worry, everything is taken care of, all is well, that presents no difficulty, *colloq.* no problem(s), no worries, not to worry. **sweat it out** see ENDURE 1.

sweater /swéttər/ *n.* **1** a jersey or pullover of a kind worn before, during, or after exercise, or as an informal garment. **2** an employer who works employees hard in poor conditions for low pay.

sweatshirt /swétshurt/ *n.* a sleeved cotton sweater of a kind worn by athletes before and after exercise.

sweatshop /swétshop/ *n.* a workshop where sweated labour is used.

sweatsuit /swétsōōt, -syōōt/ *n.* a suit of a sweatshirt and loose trousers, as worn by athletes etc.

sweaty /swétti/ *adj.* (**sweatier**, **sweatiest**) **1** sweating; covered with sweat. **2** causing sweat. □□ **sweatily** *adv.* **sweatiness** *n.*

■ **2** see STEAMY 1.

Swede /sweed/ *n.* **1 a** a native or national of Sweden. **b** a person of Swedish descent. **2** (**swede**) (in full **swede turnip**) a large yellow-fleshed turnip, *Brassica napus*, orig. from Sweden. [MLG & MDu. *Swēde*, prob. f. ON *Svíthjóth* f. *Svíar* Swedes + *thjóth* people]

Swedish /sweédish/ *adj.* & *n.* ● *adj.* of or relating to Sweden or its people or language. ● *n.* the language of Sweden.

Sweeney /sweéni/ *n.* (prec. by *the*) *Brit. sl.* the members of a flying squad. [rhyming sl. f. *Sweeney* Todd, a barber who murdered his customers]

sweep /sweep/ *v.* & *n.* ● *v.* (*past* and *past part.* **swept** /swept/) **1** *tr.* clean or clear (a room or area etc.) with or as with a broom. **2** *intr.* (often foll. by *up*) clean a room etc. in this way. **3** *tr.* (often foll. by *up*) collect or remove (dirt or litter etc.) by sweeping. **4** *tr.* (foll. by *aside*, *away*, etc.) **a** push with or as with a broom. **b** dismiss or reject abruptly (*their objections were swept aside*). **5** *tr.* (foll. by *along*, *down*, etc.) carry or drive along with force. **6** *tr.* (foll. by *off*, *away*, etc.) remove or clear forcefully. **7** *tr.* traverse swiftly or lightly (*the wind swept the hillside*). **8** *tr.* impart a sweeping motion to (*swept his hand across*). **9** *tr.* swiftly cover or affect (*a new fashion swept the country*). **10** *intr.* **a** glide swiftly; speed along with unchecked motion. **b** go majestically. **11** *intr.* (of geographical features etc.) have continuous extent. **12** *tr.* drag (a river-bottom etc.) to search for something. **13** *tr.* (of artillery etc.) include in the line of fire; cover the whole of. **14** *tr.* propel (a barge etc.) with sweeps. ● *n.* **1** the act or motion or an instance of sweeping. **2** a curve in the road, a sweeping line of a hill, etc. **3** range or scope (*beyond the sweep of the human mind*). **4** = *chimney-sweep*. **5** a sortie by aircraft. **6** *colloq.* = SWEEPSTAKE. **7** a long oar worked from a barge etc. **8** the sail of a windmill. **9** a long pole mounted as a lever for raising buckets from a well. **10** *Electronics* the movement of a beam across the screen of a cathode-ray tube. □ **make a clean sweep of 1** completely abolish or expel. **2** win all the prizes etc. in (a competition etc.). **sweep away 1** abolish swiftly. **2** (usu. in *passive*) powerfully affect, esp. emotionally. **sweep the board 1** win all the money in a gambling-game. **2** win all possible prizes etc. **sweep second-hand** a second hand on a clock or watch, moving on the same dial as the other hands. **sweep under the carpet** see CARPET. **swept-back** (of an aircraft wing) fixed at an acute angle to the fuselage, inclining outwards towards the rear. **swept-up** (of hair) = UPSWEPT. **swept-wing** (of an aircraft) having swept-back wings. [ME *swepe* (earlier *swōpe*) f. OE *swāpan*]

■ *v.* **1** brush, clean, dust, clear, tidy up. **4 b** (*sweep aside*) see REJECT *v.* 1, 3. **6** remove, clear, wash away; expel, eliminate, get rid of, dispose of. **10 a** glide, sail; swoop, skim, dash, charge, fly, speed, rush, zoom, *colloq.* tear. **b** sail, glide, flounce, march, parade. **11** curve, arc, arch, bend, bow, circle, turn. ● *n.* **1** see WHISK *n.* 1. **2** curve, arc, arch, bow, bend, turn, curvature, flexure. **3** range, extent, compass, reach, stretch, scope, swing, span. **7** see PADDLE[1] *n.* □ **make a clean sweep of 1** see ABOLISH. **sweep away 1** see ABOLISH. **2** see INSPIRE 1, 2.

sweepback /sweépbak/ *n.* the angle at which an aircraft's wing is set back from a position at right angles to the body.

sweeper /sweépər/ *n.* **1** a person who cleans by sweeping. **2** a device for sweeping carpets etc. **3** *Football* a defensive player positioned close to the goalkeeper.

sweeping /sweéping/ *adj.* & *n.* ● *adj.* **1** wide in range or effect (*sweeping changes*). **2** taking no account of particular cases or exceptions (*a sweeping statement*). ● *n.* (in *pl.*) dirt etc. collected by sweeping. □□ **sweepingly** *adv.* **sweepingness** *n.*

■ *adj.* **1** comprehensive, (all-)inclusive, general, extensive, universal, all-embracing, broad, widespread, wide(-ranging), far-ranging, blanket, umbrella, catholic, exhaustive, radical, thorough(-going), out and out, across the board, wholesale, complete, total, overwhelming, *colloq.* wall-to-wall. **2** broad, generalized, unspecific, non-specific, imprecise, inexact, unqualified, oversimplified, general. ● *n.* (*sweepings*) see DIRT 6.

sweepstake /sweépstayk/ *n.* **1** a form of gambling on horse-races etc. in which all competitors' stakes are paid to the winners. **2** a race with betting of this kind. **3** a prize or prizes won in a sweepstake.

■ see LOTTERY.

sweet /sweet/ *adj.* & *n.* ● *adj.* **1** having the pleasant taste characteristic of sugar. **2** smelling pleasant like roses or perfume etc.; fragrant. **3** (of sound etc.) melodious or harmonious. **4 a** not salt, sour, or bitter. **b** fresh, with flavour unimpaired by rottenness. **c** (of water) fresh and readily drinkable. **5** (of wine) having a sweet taste (opp. DRY). **6** highly gratifying or attractive. **7** amiable, pleasant (*has a sweet nature*). **8** *colloq.* (of a person or thing) pretty, charming, endearing. **9** (foll. by *on*) *colloq.* fond of; in love with. ● *n.* **1** *Brit.* a small shaped piece of confectionery usu. made with sugar or sweet chocolate. **2** *Brit.* a sweet dish forming a course of a meal. **3** a sweet part of something; sweetness. **4** (in *pl.*) delights, gratification. **5** (esp. as a form of address) sweetheart etc. □ **she's sweet** *Austral. sl.* all is well. **sweet-and-sour** cooked in a sauce containing sugar and vinegar or lemon etc. **sweet basil** see BASIL. **sweet bay** = BAY[2]. **sweet-brier** see BRIER[1]. **sweet chestnut** see CHESTNUT. **sweet cicely** a white-flowered aromatic plant, *Myrrhis odorata*. **sweet corn 1** a kind of maize with kernels having a high sugar content. **2** these kernels, eaten as a vegetable when young. **sweet flag** = *sweet rush*. **sweet-gale** see GALE[2]. **sweet pea** any climbing plant of the genus *Lathyrus*, esp. *L. odoratus* with fragrant flowers in many colours. **sweet pepper** see PEPPER. **sweet potato 1** a tropical climbing plant, *Ipomoea batatas*, with sweet tuberous roots used for food. **2** the root of this. **sweet rocket** see ROCKET[2]. **sweet rush** (or **sedge**) a kind of sedge with a thick creeping aromatic rootstock used in medicine and confectionery. **sweet sultan** a sweet-scented plant, *Centaurea moschata* or *C. suaveolens*. **sweet talk** *colloq.* flattery, blandishment. **sweet-talk** *v.tr. colloq.* flatter in order to persuade. **sweet-tempered** amiable. **sweet tooth** a liking for sweet-tasting things. **sweet violet** a sweet-scented violet, *Viola odorata*. **sweet william** a plant, *Dianthus barbatus*, with clusters of vivid fragrant flowers. □□ **sweetish** *adj.* **sweetly** *adv.* [OE *swēte* f. Gmc]

■ *adj.* **1** sugary, honey-like, honeyed, sweetened; luscious, saccharine, cloying, sickly, treacly, syrupy. **2** fragrant, perfumed, scented, aromatic, ambrosial, sweet-smelling, sweet-scented, balmy, redolent. **3** harmonious, melodious, sweet-sounding, euphonious, dulcet, musical, tuneful, euphonic, mellifluous, mellow, lyric, silvery, bell-like, golden. **4 c** drinkable, potable, fresh, clean. **6** gratifying, satisfying, pleasant, nice, attractive; dear, beloved, precious, prized, treasured, wonderful, marvellous, splendid, *colloq.* great. **7** gentle, amiable, agreeable, genial, warm, friendly, nice, pleasant, unassuming, easygoing; considerate, attentive, solicitous, thoughtful, sympathetic, compassionate, kind, kind-hearted, generous, gracious, accommodating. **8** attractive, appealing, charming, endearing, winning, pleasant, pleasing, lovely; pretty, *esp. US colloq.* cute; dear, nice. **9** (*sweet on*) fond of, taken with, keen on, devoted to, enamoured of, infatuated with, (head over heels) in love with, mad about, *colloq.* wild *or* crazy about, nuts about *or* on *or* over, stuck on, *esp. Brit. colloq.* daft about, *sl.* gone on, batty about. ● *n.* **1** bon-bon, chocolate, confection, sweetmeat, fondant, toffee, *US* candy, *archaic* comfit, *Austral. colloq.* lolly. **2** dessert, *Brit.* pudding, *Brit. colloq.* afters, pud; (*sweets*) confectionery, *US* candy. **5** see DEAR *n.* □ **she's sweet** *Austral. colloq.* she's right, she'll be right, *esp. US colloq.* everything's hunky-dory, *Austral. sl.* she's apple(s), *Austral.* & *NZ sl.* she's jake. **sweet talk** see *cajolery* (CAJOLE). **sweet-talk** flatter, *colloq.* soft-soap; see also CAJOLE.

sweetbread /swe͞etbred/ *n.* the pancreas or thymus of an animal, esp. as food.

sweeten /swe͞et'n/ *v.tr.* & *intr.* **1** make or become sweet or sweeter. **2** make agreeable or less painful. □ **sweeten the pill** see PILL. □□ **sweetening** *n.*

■ **1** sugar, sugar-coat. **2** dress up, make more attractive *or* agreeable, sugar-coat, embellish, embroider; make less painful, mitigate, alleviate, assuage, lighten, soften, palliate, mollify, ease, allay, moderate, mellow, temper.

sweetener /swe͞etnər/ *n.* **1** a substance used to sweeten food or drink. **2** *colloq.* a bribe or inducement.

sweetheart /swe͞et-hart/ *n.* **1** a lover or darling. **2** a term of endearment (esp. as a form of address). □ **sweetheart agreement** (or **deal**) *colloq.* an industrial agreement reached privately by employers and trade unions in their own interests.

■ **1** girlfriend, boyfriend, friend, admirer, darling, dear, love, beloved, lover, inamorato, inamorata, lady-love, betrothed, fiancé(e), *esp. US* beau, *archaic* sweeting, *archaic or derog.* paramour, *archaic or poet.* mistress, *colloq.* intended, heartthrob, flame, steady, *poet.* swain. **2** see DEAR *n.*

sweetie /swe͞eti/ *n. colloq.* **1** *Brit.* a sweet. **2** (also **sweetie-pie**) a term of endearment (esp. as a form of address).

■ **2** see DEAR *n.*

sweeting /swe͞eting/ *n.* **1** a sweet-flavoured variety of apple. **2** *archaic* darling.

sweetmeal /swe͞etmeel/ *n.* **1** sweetened wholemeal. **2** a sweetmeal biscuit.

sweetmeat /swe͞etmeet/ *n.* **1** a sweet (see SWEET *n.* 1). **2** a small fancy cake.

■ **1** see SWEET *n.* 1. **2** see DELICACY 4.

sweetness /swe͞etniss/ *n.* the quality of being sweet; fragrance, melodiousness, etc. □ **sweetness and light** a display of (esp. uncharacteristic) mildness and reason.

■ see MELODY 4, *sentimentality* (SENTIMENTAL).

sweetshop /swe͞etshop/ *n. Brit.* a shop selling sweets as its main item.

sweetsop /swe͞etsop/ *n.* **1** a tropical American evergreen shrub, *Annona squamosa*. **2** the fruit of this, having a green rind and a sweet pulp.

swell /swel/ *v.*, *n.*, & *adj.* ● *v.* (*past part.* **swollen** /swṓlən/ or **swelled**) **1** *intr.* & *tr.* grow or cause to grow bigger or louder or more intense; expand; increase in force or intensity. **2** *intr.* (often foll. by *up*) & *tr.* rise or raise up from the surrounding surface. **3** *intr.* (foll. by *out*) bulge. **4** *intr.* (of the heart as the seat of emotion) feel full of joy, pride, relief, etc. **5** *intr.* (foll. by *with*) be hardly able to restrain (pride etc.). **6** (as **swollen** *adj.*) distended or bulging. ● *n.* **1** an act or the state of swelling. **2** the heaving of the sea with waves that do not break, e.g. after a storm. **3 a** a crescendo. **b** a mechanism in an organ etc. for obtaining a crescendo or diminuendo. **4** *colloq.* a person of distinction or of dashing or fashionable appearance. **5** a protuberant part. ● *adj.* **1** esp. *US colloq.* fine, splendid, excellent. **2** *colloq.* smart, fashionable. □ **swell-box** *Mus.* a box in which organ-pipes are enclosed, with a shutter for controlling the sound-level. **swelled** (or **swollen**) **head** *colloq.* conceit. **swell-organ** *Mus.* a section of an organ with pipes in a swell-box. □□ **swellish** *adj.* [OE *swellan* f. Gmc]

■ *v.* **1** grow, increase, enlarge, expand, blow up *or* out, dilate, wax, extend; mushroom, snowball, multiply, accumulate, mount, rise, escalate; raise, augment, step up, build up, intensify, heighten, *colloq.* boost. **3** bloat, bulge, billow, belly, balloon, fatten, puff up *or* out, blow up *or* out, distend, inflate, tumefy. **5** (*swell with*) be filled with, be full of, be bursting with, brim with, overflow with. **6** (**swollen**) distended, enlarged, bulging, bulbous, tumid, tumescent. ● *n.* **1** enlargement, broadening, increase, extension, spread, swelling, inflation, expansion, growth, rise, surge, upsurge. **2** surge, waves, rollers, billows. **4** fop, dandy, coxcomb, *colloq.* clothes-horse, lounge lizard, *colloq. usu. archaic* gay blade, *hist.* macaroni, *Austral. sl.* lair, *Brit. sl.* nob, toff, *US sl.* dude. ● *adj.* **1** marvellous, thrilling, splendid, spectacular, first-rate, excellent, fine, *colloq.* great, super, terrific. **2** smart, chic, stylish, fashionable, modish, dapper; grand, luxurious, de luxe, elegant, first-rate, first-class, top-grade, swanky, *colloq.* posh, ritzy, *esp. US colloq.* swank.

swelling /swélling/ *n.* an abnormal protuberance on or in the body.

■ enlargement, distension, tumescence, protuberance, bump, prominence, bulge, lump, excrescence, protrusion, tumour, node, nodule; boil, blister, bunion.

swelter /swéltər/ *v.* & *n.* ● *v.intr.* (usu. as **sweltering** *adj.*) be uncomfortably hot. ● *n.* a sweltering atmosphere or condition. ▫▫ **swelteringly** *adv.* [base of (now dial.) *swelt* f. OE *sweltan* perish f. Gmc]

■ *v.* (**sweltering**) hot, torrid, steamy, sultry, stifling, sticky, suffocating, roasting, blistering, burning, tropical, close, *colloq.* baking, boiling, scorching.

swept *past* and *past part.* of SWEEP.

swerve /swerv/ *v.* & *n.* ● *v.intr.* & *tr.* change or cause to change direction, esp. abruptly. ● *n.* **1** a swerving movement. **2** divergence from a course. ▫▫ **swerveless** *adj.* **swerver** *n.* [ME, repr. OE *sweorfan* SCOUR[1]]

■ *v.* veer, career, swing, diverge, deviate, dodge, sheer off, skew, stray, turn (aside), *US* careen.

SWG *abbr.* standard wire gauge.

swift /swift/ *adj.*, *adv.*, & *n.* ● *adj.* **1** quick, rapid; soon coming or passing. **2** speedy, prompt (*a swift response*; *was swift to act*). ● *adv.* (*archaic* except in *comb.*) swiftly (*swift-moving*). ● *n.* **1** any swift-flying insect-eating bird of the family Apodidae, with long wings and a superficial resemblance to a swallow. **2** a revolving frame for winding yarn etc. from. ▫▫ **swiftly** *adv.* **swiftness** *n.* [OE, rel. to *swīfan* move in a course]

■ *adj.* fast, rapid, speedy, hasty, quick, *poet. or literary* fleet; lively, nimble, *poet. or literary* fleet-footed; brisk, sudden, abrupt; meteoric, whirlwind, express; prompt, expeditious. ▫▫ **swiftly** fast, quick(ly), speedily, rapidly, expeditiously, *literary* apace; briskly, hurriedly, hastily, post-haste, suddenly, abruptly, in a flash, in a trice, in the wink of an eye, in an instant, in no time, like the wind, precipitately, unexpectedly, *colloq.* like a bat out of hell, before you can say Jack Robinson, before you can say knife, like a shot, like greased lightning, lickety-split, in a jiff(y), pronto, p.d.q., *joc.* in less than no time. **swiftness** see SPEED *n.* 1.

swiftie /swífti/ *n. Austral. sl.* **1** a deceptive trick. **2** a person who acts or thinks quickly.

swiftlet /swíftlit/ *n.* a small swift of the genus *Collocalia*.

swig /swig/ *v.* & *n. colloq.* ● *v.tr.* & *intr.* (**swigged**, **swigging**) drink in large draughts. ● *n.* a swallow of drink, esp. a large amount. ▫▫ **swigger** *n.* [16th c., orig. as noun in obs. sense 'liquor': orig. unkn.]

■ *v.* see DRINK *v.* 1. ● *n.* see DRINK *n.* 1b.

swill /swil/ *v.* & *n.* ● *v.* **1** *tr.* (often foll. by *out*) rinse or flush; pour water over or through. **2** *tr.* & *intr.* drink greedily. ● *n.* **1** an act of rinsing. **2** mainly liquid refuse as pig-food. **3** inferior liquor. **4** worthless matter, rubbish. ▫▫ **swiller** *n.* [OE *swillan*, *swilian*, of unkn. orig.]

■ *v.* **1** see FLUSH[1] *v.* 3a. **2** drink, guzzle, swallow, toss off, polish off, *colloq.* swig, *literary* quaff, *Brit. sl.* knock back. ● *n.* **1** rinse, clean, wash. **2, 4** hogwash, pigswill, refuse, pigwash, slop(s), garbage, waste, rubbish.

swim /swim/ *v.* & *n.* ● *v.* (**swimming**; *past* **swam** /swam/; *past part.* **swum** /swum/) **1** *intr.* propel the body through water by working the arms and legs, or (of a fish) the fins and tail. **2** *tr.* **a** traverse (a stretch of water or its distance) by swimming. **b** compete in (a race) by swimming. **c** use (a particular stroke) in swimming. **3** *intr.* float on or at the surface of a liquid (*bubbles swimming on the surface*). **4** *intr.* appear to undulate or reel or whirl. **5** *intr.* have a dizzy effect or sensation (*my head swam*). **6** *intr.* (foll. by *in*, *with*) be flooded. ● *n.* **1** a spell or the act of swimming. **2** a deep pool frequented by fish in a river. ▫ **in the swim** involved in or acquainted with what is going on. **swim-bladder** a gas-filled sac in fishes used to maintain buoyancy. **swimming-bath** (or **-pool**) an artificial indoor or outdoor pool for swimming. **swimming-costume** *Brit.* a garment worn for swimming. ▫▫ **swimmable** *adj.* **swimmer** *n.* [OE *swimman* f. Gmc]

■ *v.* **3** see FLOAT *v.* 2. **5** see SPIN *v.* 6. ● *n.* **1** see DIP *n.* 3. ▫ **in the swim** see SWINGING. **swimming-costume** swimsuit, bathing-costume, bathing-suit, costume.

swimmeret /swímmərət/ *n.* a swimming-foot in crustaceans.

swimmingly /swímmingli/ *adv.* with easy and unobstructed progress.

■ smoothly, easily, effortlessly, well, successfully, without a hitch *or* problem, like clockwork, like a house on fire, without difficulty, readily, *colloq.* like a dream.

swimsuit /swímsōōt, -syōōt/ *n.* a one-piece swimming-costume worn by women. ▫▫ **swimsuited** *adj.*

swimwear /swímwair/ *n.* clothing worn for swimming.

swindle /swínd'l/ *v.* & *n.* ● *v.tr.* (often foll. by *out of*) **1** cheat (a person) of money, possessions, etc. (*was swindled out of all his savings*). **2** cheat a person of (money etc.) (*swindled all his savings out of him*). ● *n.* **1** an act of swindling. **2** a person or thing represented as what it is not. **3** a fraudulent scheme. ▫▫ **swindler** *n.* [back-form. f. *swindler* f. G *Schwindler* extravagant maker of schemes, swindler, f. *schwindeln* be dizzy]

■ *v.* **1** cheat, defraud, deceive, double-cross, hoodwink, take in, flimflam, fleece, pluck, rook, dupe, fool, mulct, gull, make a fool (out) of, victimize, exploit, trick, hoax, euchre, screw, *colloq.* bamboozle, diddle, pull a fast one on, take for a ride, rip off, *Brit. colloq.* twist, *literary* cozen, *sl.* con, fiddle, chisel, bilk, sting, gyp, *Austral. sl.* pull a swiftie on, *Brit. sl.* ramp, *US sl.* buffalo, bunco. ● *n.* **1, 3** fraud, confidence trick, deception, racket, trick, chicane; *US* confidence game, *colloq.* fiddle, rip-off, *Brit. colloq.* swizzle, swizz, *sl.* con, gyp, *Austral. sl.* rort, *Brit. sl.* ramp, *US sl.* scam, skin game, bunco; double-dealing, trickery, sharp practice, thimblerigging, chicanery, knavery. **2** see DECEIT 2. ▫▫ **swindler** cheat, confidence man, hoaxer, mountebank, charlatan, knave, scoundrel, sharper, racketeer, fraud, trickster, thimblerigger, villain, flimflam man, *US* four-flusher, *colloq.* sharp, shark, *Brit. colloq.* twister, *formal* defalcator, *sl.* con man, *Austral. sl.* shicer, magsman, illywhacker, *US sl.* bunco-artist.

swine /swīn/ *n.* (*pl.* same) **1** *formal* or *US* a pig. **2** *colloq.* (*pl.* **swine** or **swines**) **a** a term of contempt or disgust for a person. **b** a very unpleasant or difficult thing. ▫ **swine fever** an intestinal virus disease of pigs. ▫▫ **swinish** *adj.* (esp. in sense 2). **swinishly** *adv.* **swinishness** *n.* [OE *swīn* f. Gmc]

■ **2 a** see WRETCH 2.

swineherd /swīnherd/ *n.* a person who tends pigs.

swing /swing/ *v.* & *n.* ● *v.* (*past* and *past part.* **swung** /swung/) **1** *intr.* & *tr.* move or cause to move with a to-and-fro or curving motion, as of an object attached at one end and hanging free at the other. **2** *intr.* & *tr.* **a** sway. **b** hang so as to be free to sway. **c** oscillate or cause to oscillate. **3** *intr.* & *tr.* revolve or cause to revolve. **4** *intr.* move by gripping something and leaping etc. (*swung from tree to tree*). **5** *intr.* go with a swinging gait (*swung out of the room*). **6** *intr.* (foll. by *round*) move round to the opposite direction. **7** *intr.* change from one opinion or mood to another. **8** *intr.* (foll. by *at*) attempt to hit or punch. **9 a** *intr.* (also **swing it**) play music with a swing rhythm. **b** *tr.* play (a tune) with swing. **10** *intr. colloq.* **a** be lively or up to date; enjoy oneself. **b** be promiscuous. **11** *intr. colloq.* (of a party etc.) be lively, successful, etc. **12** *tr.* have a decisive influence on (esp. voting etc.). **13** *tr. colloq.* deal with or achieve; manage. **14** *intr. colloq.* be executed by hanging. **15** *Cricket* **a** *intr.* (of the ball) deviate from a straight course in the air. **b** *tr.* cause (the ball) to do this. ● *n.* **1** the act or an instance of swinging. **2** the motion of swinging. **3** the extent of swinging. **4** a swinging or smooth gait or rhythm or action. **5 a** a seat slung by ropes or chains etc. for swinging on or in. **b** a spell of swinging on this. **6** an easy but vigorous continued action. **7 a** jazz or dance music with an easy flowing rhythm. **b** the rhythmic feeling or drive of this music. **8** a discernible change in opinion, esp. the amount by which votes or points scored etc. change from one side to another. **9** *colloq.* the regular procedure or course of events (*get into the swing of things*). □ **swing-boat** a boat-shaped swing at fairs. **swing-bridge** a bridge that can be swung to one side to allow the passage of ships. **swing-door** a door able to open in either direction and close itself when released. **swing the lead** *Brit. colloq.* malinger; shirk one's duty. **swings and roundabouts** a situation affording no eventual gain or loss (from the phr. *lose on the swings what you make on the roundabouts*). **swing shift** *US* a work shift from afternoon to late evening. **swing-wing** an aircraft wing that can move from a right-angled to a swept-back position. **swung dash** a dash (~) with alternate curves. □□ **swinger** *n.* (esp. in sense 10 of *v.*). [OE *swingan* to beat f. Gmc]

■ *v.* **1, 2a, c** sway, move *or* go to and fro, move *or* go back and forth, move *or* go backwards and forwards, come and go, rock, wave, flourish, flap, fluctuate, oscillate, vibrate, waver, zigzag, wobble, *colloq.* waggle, wigwag. **2 b** hang, dangle, sling, suspend; be suspended. **6** see WHEEL *v.* 2. **7** see OSCILLATE. **8** swipe, lash out. **12** see SWAY *v.* 3. **13** see ACCOMPLISH, WANGLE *v.* 1. **14** hang, be hanged, be strung up. ● *n.* **1, 2** sway, toing and froing, fluctuation, flap, oscillation, vibration, libration, waver, wobble, zigzag, flourish, *colloq.* waggle, wigwag; stroke, *colloq.* swipe. **3** sweep, scope, range, extent, compass, limit(s). **8** change, switch, shift, movement, trend, fluctuation, variation, oscillation. **9** pace, pattern, routine, groove.

swinge /swinj/ *v.tr.* (**swingeing**) *archaic* strike hard; beat. [alt. f. ME *swenge* f. OE *swengan* shake, shatter, f. Gmc]

swingeing /swínjing/ *adj.* esp. *Brit.* **1** (of a blow) forcible. **2** huge or far-reaching, esp. in severity (*swingeing economies*). □□ **swingeingly** *adv.*

■ **2** huge, immense, enormous, considerable, drastic, far-reaching, violent, forcible, severe, harsh, stringent, punishing, punitive, devastating, painful, excruciating, major, daunting, Draconian, oppressive, exorbitant, excessive, *colloq.* thumping, *sl.* whopping, walloping.

swinging /swínging/ *adj.* **1** (of gait, melody, etc.) vigorously rhythmical. **2** *colloq.* **a** lively; up to date; excellent. **b** promiscuous. □□ **swingingly** *adv.*

■ **2 a** fashionable, chic, up to date, modern, lively, in the swim, *colloq.* with it, *colloq. often derog.* trendy, *sl.* hip, groovy, in the groove.

swingle /swíngg'l/ *n.* & *v.* ● *n.* **1** a wooden instrument for beating flax and removing the woody parts from it. **2** the swinging part of a flail. ● *v.tr.* clean (flax) with a swingle. [ME f. MDu. *swinghel* (as SWING, -LE[1])]

swingletree /swíngg'ltree/ *n.* a crossbar pivoted in the middle, to which the traces are attached in a cart, plough, etc.

swingy /swíngi/ *adj.* (**swingier, swingiest**) **1** (of music) characterized by swing (see SWING *n.* 7). **2** (of a skirt or dress) designed to swing with body movement.

swipe /swīp/ *v.* & *n. colloq.* ● *v.* **1** *tr.* & (often foll. by *at*) *intr.* hit hard and recklessly. **2** *tr.* steal. ● *n.* a reckless hard hit or attempted hit. □□ **swiper** *n.* [perh. var. of SWEEP]

■ *v.* **1** strike, hit, *sl.* belt, wallop; (*swipe at*) lash out at, swing at. **2** steal, filch, pilfer, snatch, *colloq.* lift, snaffle, *formal or joc.* purloin, *sl.* pinch, snitch, *Brit. sl.* nick, whip. ● *n.* swing, strike, hit, stroke, clip.

swipple /swípp'l/ *n.* the swingle of a flail. [ME, prob. formed as SWEEP + -LE[1]]

swirl /swurl/ *v.* & *n.* ● *v.intr.* & *tr.* move or flow or carry along with a whirling motion. ● *n.* **1** a swirling motion of or in water, air, etc. **2** the act of swirling. **3** a twist or curl, esp. as part of a pattern or design. □□ **swirly** *adj.* [ME (orig. as noun): orig. Sc., perh. of LG or Du. orig.]

■ *v.* whirl, spin, eddy, churn, circulate, gyrate, surge, boil, seethe; twist, curl, roll, furl, curve, spiral, twirl, wind (round). ● *n.* twist, whirl, curl, roll, twirl, spiral; see also EDDY *n.*

swish /swish/ *v.*, *n.*, & *adj.* ● *v.* **1** *tr.* swing (a scythe or stick etc.) audibly through the air, grass, etc. **2** *intr.* move with or make a swishing sound. **3** *tr.* (foll. by *off*) cut (a flower etc.) in this way. ● *n.* a swishing action or sound. ● *adj. colloq.* smart, fashionable. □□ **swishy** *adj.* [imit.]

■ *v.* **2** hiss, whisk, rustle, whoosh, swoosh, whisper. ● *n.* hiss, hissing sound, whoosh, swoosh, rustle, whistle. ● *adj.* elegant, fashionable, stylish, *de rigueur*, smart, plush, swanky, *colloq.* posh, plushy, ritzy, swell, swagger, *esp. US colloq.* swank, *sl.* snazzy.

Swiss /swiss/ *adj.* & *n.* ● *adj.* of or relating to Switzerland in Western Europe or its people. ● *n.* (*pl.* same) **1** a native or national of Switzerland. **2** a person of Swiss descent. □ **Swiss chard** = CHARD. **Swiss cheese plant** a climbing house-plant, *Monstera deliciosa*, with aerial roots and holes in the leaves (as in some Swiss cheeses). **Swiss roll** a cylindrical cake with a spiral cross-section, made from a flat piece of sponge cake spread with jam etc. and rolled up. [F *Suisse* f. MHG *Swīz*]

switch /swich/ *n.* & *v.* ● *n.* **1** a device for making and breaking the connection in an electric circuit. **2 a** a transfer, change-over, or deviation. **b** an exchange. **3** a slender flexible shoot cut from a tree. **4** a light tapering rod. **5** *US* a device at the junction of railway tracks for transferring a train from one track to another; = POINT *n.* 17. **6** a tress of false or detached hair tied at one end used in hairdressing. ● *v.* **1** *tr.* (foll. by *on*, *off*) turn (an electrical device) on or off. **2** *intr.* change or transfer position, subject, etc. **3** *tr.* change or transfer. **4** *tr.* reverse the positions of; exchange (*switched chairs*). **5** *tr.* swing or snatch (a thing) suddenly (*switched it out of my hand*). **6** *tr.* beat or flick with a switch. □ **switch-blade** a pocket knife with the blade released by a spring. **switched-on** *colloq.* **1** up to date; aware of what is going on. **2** excited; under the influence of drugs. **switch off** *colloq.* cease to pay attention. **switch over** change or exchange. **switch-over** *n.* a change or exchange. □□ **switcher** *n.* [earlier *swits*, *switz*, prob. f. LG]

■ *n.* **1** circuit-breaker. **2 a** change, alteration, shift, change-over, transfer, reversal, deflection, deviation. **b** trade, swap; see also EXCHANGE *n.* 1. **3, 4** twitch, lash, whip, rod, birch(-rod), scourge. ● *v.* **1** (*switch on*) see *turn on* 1; (*switch off*) see *turn off* 1. **2** change, chop and change, deviate, shift, see-saw. **3** change, shift, transfer, divert, turn, rechannel, redirect, direct. **4** change, shift, swap, reverse, replace, substitute, exchange, switch over. **5** swing, swish; whisk, whip, snatch. **6** lash, whip, birch, beat, strike, thrash, scourge, flog; flick. □ **switch-blade** flick-knife. **switched-on 1** see AWARE 2. **2** see HIGH *adj.* 8b.

switchback /swíchbak/ *n.* **1** *Brit.* a railway at a fair etc., in which the train's ascents are effected by the momentum of its previous descents. **2** (often *attrib.*) a railway or road with alternate sharp ascents and descents.

switchboard /swíchbord/ *n.* an apparatus for varying connections between electric circuits, esp. in telephony.

swither /swíthər/ *v.* & *n. Sc.* ● *v.intr.* hesitate; be uncertain. ● *n.* doubt or uncertainty. [16th c.: orig. unkn.]

■ *v.* see SHILLY-SHALLY *v.*

swivel /swívv'l/ *n.* & *v.* ● *n.* a coupling between two parts enabling one to revolve without turning the other. ● *v.tr.* & *intr.* (**swivelled, swivelling**; *US* **swiveled, swiveling**) turn on or as on a swivel. □ **swivel chair** a chair with a seat able to be turned horizontally. [ME f. weak grade *swif-* of OE *swīfan* sweep + -LE[1]: cf. SWIFT]

■ *n.* pivot, elbow-joint, gimbals, ball-and-socket joint. ● *v.* pivot, turn, rotate, spin, revolve, wheel, twirl, pirouette, gyrate, move freely.

swizz /swiz/ *n.* (also **swiz**) (*pl.* **swizzes**) *Brit. colloq.* **1** something unfair or disappointing. **2** a swindle. [abbr. of SWIZZLE[2]]

■ **2** see SWINDLE *n.* 1, 3.

swizzle[1] /swízz'l/ *n.* & *v. colloq.* ● *n.* a mixed alcoholic drink esp. of rum or gin and bitters made frothy. ● *v.tr.* stir with a swizzle-stick. □ **swizzle-stick** a stick used for frothing or flattening drinks. [19th c.: orig. unkn.]

swizzle[2] /swízz'l/ *n. Brit. colloq.* = SWIZZ. [20th c.: prob. alt. of SWINDLE]

swob var. of SWAB.
swollen *past part.* of SWELL.
swoon /swo͞on/ *v.* & *n. literary* ● *v.intr.* faint; fall into a fainting-fit. ● *n.* an occurrence of fainting. [ME *swoune* perh. back-form. f. *swogning* (n.) f. *iswogen* f. OE *geswogen* overcome]
▪ *v.* see FAINT *v.* 1. ● *n.* see FAINT *n.*
swoop /swo͞op/ *v.* & *n.* ● *v.* **1** *intr.* (often foll. by *down*) descend rapidly like a bird of prey. **2** *intr.* (often foll. by *on*) make a sudden attack from a distance. **3** *tr.* (often foll. by *up*) *colloq.* snatch the whole of at one swoop. ● *n.* a swooping or snatching movement or action. □ **at** (or **in**) **one fell swoop** see FELL[4]. [perh. dial. var. of obs. *swōpe* f. OE *swāpan*: see SWEEP]
▪ *v.* **1** descend, dive, sweep down, pounce, stoop, plunge, plummet, nosedive. **2** see RAID *v.* 1. **3** (*swoop on*) scoop up, sweep up; see also SNATCH *v.* 1, 3. ● *n.* descent, dive, sweep, pounce, stoop, stroke, blow, rush.
swoosh /swo͝osh/ *n.* & *v.* ● *n.* the noise of a sudden rush of liquid, air, etc. ● *v.intr.* move with this noise. [imit.]
▪ *n.* see SWISH *n.* ● *v.* see SWISH *v.*
swop var. of SWAP.
sword /sord/ *n.* **1** a weapon usu. of metal with a long blade and hilt with a handguard, used esp. for thrusting or striking, and often worn as part of ceremonial dress. **2** (prec. by *the*) **a** war. **b** military power. □ **put to the sword** kill, esp. in war. **sword-bearer** an official carrying the sovereign's etc. sword on a formal occasion. **sword dance** a dance in which the performers brandish swords or step about swords laid on the ground. **sword grass** a grass, *Scirpus americanus*, with swordlike leaves. **sword knot** a ribbon or tassel attached to a sword-hilt orig. for securing it to the wrist. **sword lily** = GLADIOLUS. **sword of Damocles** /dámməkleez/ an imminent danger (from *Damokles*, flatterer of Dionysius of Syracuse (4th c. BC) made to feast while a sword hung by a hair over him). **the sword of justice** judicial authority. **Sword of State** a sword borne before the sovereign on State occasions. **sword-swallower** a person ostensibly or actually swallowing sword blades as entertainment. □□ **swordlike** *adj.* [OE *sw(e)ord* f. Gmc]
▪ **1** see BLADE 6.
swordbill /sórdbil/ *n.* a long-billed humming-bird, *Ensifera ensifera*.
swordfish /sórdfish/ *n.* a large marine fish, *Xiphias gladius*, with an extended swordlike upper jaw.
swordplay /sórdplay/ *n.* **1** fencing. **2** repartee; cut-and-thrust argument.
swordsman /sórdzmən/ *n.* (*pl.* **-men**) a person of (usu. specified) skill with a sword. □□ **swordsmanship** *n.*
swordstick /sórdstik/ *n.* a hollow walking-stick containing a blade that can be used as a sword.
swordtail /sórdtayl/ *n.* **1** a tropical fish, *Xiphophorus helleri*, with a long tail. **2** = *horseshoe crab*.
swore *past* of SWEAR.
sworn /sworn/ **1** *past part.* of SWEAR. **2** *adj.* bound by or as by an oath (*sworn enemies*).
▪ **2** see PROFESSED 1.
swot /swot/ *v.* & *n. Brit. colloq.* ● *v.* (**swotted, swotting**) **1** *intr.* study assiduously. **2** *tr.* (often foll. by *up*) study (a subject) hard or hurriedly. ● *n.* **1** a person who swots. **2 a** hard study. **b** a thing that requires this. [dial. var. of SWEAT]
▪ *v.* **1** see STUDY *v.* 2. ● *n.* **1** see STUDENT 1. **2 a** see LABOUR *n.* 1.
swum *past part.* of SWIM.
swung *past* and *past part.* of SWING.
swy /swī/ *n. Austral.* two-up. [G *zwei* two]
SY *abbr.* steam yacht.
sybarite /síbbərīt/ *n.* & *adj.* ● *n.* a person who is self-indulgent or devoted to sensuous luxury. ● *adj.* fond of luxury or sensuousness. □□ **sybaritic** /-ríttik/ *adj.* **sybaritical** /-ríttik'l/ *adj.* **sybaritically** /-ríttikəli/ *adv.* **sybaritism** *n.* [orig. an inhabitant of Sybaris in S. Italy, noted for luxury, f. L *sybarita* f. Gk *subaritēs*]
▪ *n.* epicure, epicurean, hedonist, voluptuary, sensualist, aesthete, gastronome, gourmet, *bon vivant*, *bon viveur*, pleasure-seeker, playboy, *colloq.* jet-setter. ● *adj.* see *epicurean* (EPICUREAN *adj.* 2). □□ **sybaritic, sybaritical** see *epicurean* (EPICUREAN *adj.* 2). **sybaritism** see LUXURY 1.
sycamine /síkkəmīn, -min/ *n. Bibl.* the black mulberry tree, *Morus nigra* (see Luke 17:6; in modern versions translated as 'mulberry tree'). [L *sycaminus* f. Gk *sukaminos* mulberry-tree f. Heb. *šiḳmāh* sycamore, assim. to Gk *sukon* fig]
sycamore /síkkəmor/ *n.* **1** (in full **sycamore maple**) **a** a large maple, *Acer pseudoplatanus*, with winged seeds, grown for its shade and timber. **b** its wood. **2** *US* the plane-tree or its wood. **3** *Bibl.* a fig-tree, *Ficus sycomorus*, growing in Egypt, Syria, etc. [var. of SYCOMORE]
syce /sīss/ *n.* (also **sice**) *Anglo-Ind.* a groom. [Hind. f. Arab. *sā'is, sāyis*]
sycomore /síkkəmor/ *n. Bot.* = SYCAMORE 3. [ME f. OF *sic(h)amor* f. L *sycomorus* f. Gk *sukomoros* f. *sukon* fig + *moron* mulberry]
syconium /sīkṓniəm/ *n.* (*pl.* **syconia**) *Bot.* a fleshy hollow receptacle developing into a multiple fruit as in the fig. [mod.L f. Gk *sukon* fig]
sycophant /síkkəfant/ *n.* a servile flatterer; a toady. □□ **sycophancy** *n.* **sycophantic** /-fántik/ *adj.* **sycophantically** /-fántikəli/ *adv.* [F *sycophante* or L *sycophanta* f. Gk *sukophantēs* informer f. *sukon* fig + *phainō* show: the reason for the name is uncert., and association with informing against the illegal exportation of figs from ancient Athens (recorded by Plutarch) cannot be substantiated]
▪ see *flatterer* (FLATTER). □□ **sycophancy** see *servility* (SERVILE). **sycophantic** see OBSEQUIOUS.
sycosis /sīkṓsiss/ *n.* a skin-disease of the bearded part of the face with inflammation of the hair-follicles. [mod.L f. Gk *sukōsis* f. *sukon* fig: orig. of a figlike ulcer]
syenite /sī́ənīt/ *n.* a grey crystalline rock of feldspar and hornblende with or without quartz. □□ **syenitic** /-níttik/ *adj.* [F *syénite* f. L *Syenites* (*lapis*) (stone) of *Syene* in Egypt]
syl- /sil/ *prefix* assim. form of SYN- before *l*.
syllabary /sílləbəri/ *n.* (*pl.* **-ies**) a list of characters representing syllables and (in some languages or stages of writing) serving the purpose of an alphabet. [mod.L *syllabarium* (as SYLLABLE)]
syllabi *pl.* of SYLLABUS.
syllabic /silábbik/ *adj.* **1** of, relating to, or based on syllables. **2** *Prosody* based on the number of syllables. **3** (of a symbol) representing a whole syllable. **4** articulated in syllables. □□ **syllabically** *adv.* **syllabicity** /-bissiti/ *n.* [F *syllabique* or LL *syllabicus* f. Gk *sullabikos* (as SYLLABLE)]
syllabication /sìllabikáysh'n/ *n.* (also **syllabification**) (/-bifikáysh'n/) division into or articulation by syllables. □□ **syllabify** *v.tr.* (**-ies, -ied**). [med.L *syllabicatio* f. *syllabicare* f. L *syllaba*: see SYLLABLE]
syllabize /sílləbīz/ *v.tr.* (also **-ise**) divide into or articulate by syllables. [med.L *syllabizare* f. Gk *sullabizō* (as SYLLABLE)]
syllable /sílləb'l/ *n.* & *v.* ● *n.* **1** a unit of pronunciation uttered without interruption, forming the whole or a part of a word and usu. having one vowel sound often with a consonant or consonants before or after: there are two syllables in *water* and three in *inferno*. **2** a character or characters representing a syllable. **3** (usu. with *neg.*) the least amount of speech or writing (*did not utter a syllable*). ● *v.tr.* pronounce by syllables; articulate distinctly. □ **in words of one syllable** expressed plainly or bluntly. □□ **syllabled** *adj.* (also in *comb.*). [ME f. AF *sillable* f. OF *sillabe* f. L *syllaba* f. Gk *sullabē* (as SYN-, *lambanō* take)]
syllabub /sílləbub/ *n.* (also **sillabub**) a dessert made of cream or milk flavoured, sweetened, and whipped to thicken it. [16th c.: orig. unkn.]
syllabus /sílləbəss/ *n.* (*pl.* **syllabuses** or **syllabi** /-bī/) **1 a** the programme or outline of a course of study, teaching, etc. **b** a statement of the requirements for a particular examination. **2** *RC Ch.* a summary of points decided by

papal decree regarding heretical doctrines or practices. [mod.L, orig. a misreading of L *sittybas* accus. pl. of *sittyba* f. Gk *sittuba* title-slip or label]
■ **1** see PROGRAMME *n.* 4. **2** see EPITOME 3.

syllepsis /silépsiss/ *n.* (*pl.* **syllepses** /-seez/) a figure of speech in which a word is applied to two others in different senses (e.g. *caught the train and a bad cold*) or to two others of which it grammatically suits one only (e.g. *neither they nor it is working*) (cf. ZEUGMA). □□ **sylleptic** *adj.* **sylleptically** *adv.* [LL f. Gk *sullēpsis* taking together f. *sullambanō*: see SYLLABLE]

syllogism /sílləjiz'm/ *n.* **1** a form of reasoning in which a conclusion is drawn from two given or assumed propositions (premisses): a common or middle term is present in the two premisses but not in the conclusion, which may be invalid (e.g. *all trains are long*; *some buses are long*; *therefore some buses are trains*: the common term is *long*). **2** deductive reasoning as distinct from induction. □□ **syllogistic** /-jístik/ *adj.* **syllogistically** /-jístikəli/ *adv.* [ME f. OF *silogisme* or L *syllogismus* f. Gk *sullogismos* f. *sullogizomai* (as SYN-, *logizomai* to reason f. *logos* reason)]
■ □□ **syllogistic** see LOGICAL 1.

syllogize /sílləjīz/ *v.* (also **-ise**) **1** *intr.* use syllogisms. **2** *tr.* put (facts or an argument) in the form of syllogism. [ME f. OF *sillogiser* or LL *syllogizare* f. Gk *sullogizomai* (as SYLLOGISM)]

sylph /silf/ *n.* **1** an elemental spirit of the air. **2** a slender graceful woman or girl. **3** any humming-bird of the genus *Aglaiocercus* with a long forked tail. □□ **sylphlike** *adj.* [mod.L *sylphes*, G *Sylphen* (pl.), perh. based on L *sylvestris* of the woods + *nympha* nymph]
■ □□ **sylphlike** see SLENDER 1.

sylva /sílvə/ *n.* (also **silva**) (*pl.* **sylvae** /-vee/ or **sylvas**) **1** the trees of a region, epoch, or environment. **2** a treatise on or a list of such trees. [L *silva* a wood]

sylvan /sílv'n/ *adj.* (also **silvan**) **1 a** of the woods. **b** having woods; wooded. **2** rural. [F *sylvain* (obs. *silvain*) or L *Silvanus* woodland deity f. *silva* a wood]
■ **1 b** see WOODED. **2** see RURAL 1.

sylviculture var. of SILVICULTURE.

sym- /sim/ *prefix* assim. form of SYN- before *b*, *m*, *p*.

symbiont /símbiənt/ *n.* an organism living in symbiosis. [Gk *sumbiōn -ountos* part. of *sumbioō* live together (as SYMBIOSIS)]

symbiosis /símbī-ṓsiss, símbi-/ *n.* (*pl.* **symbioses** /-seez/) **1 a** an interaction between two different organisms living in close physical association, usu. to the advantage of both (cf. ANTIBIOSIS). **b** an instance of this. **2 a** a mutually advantageous association or relationship between persons. **b** an instance of this. □□ **symbiotic** /-bīóttik/ *adj.* **symbiotically** /-bīóttikəli/ *adv.* [mod.L f. Gk *sumbiōsis* a living together f. *sumbioō* live together, *sumbios* companion (as SYN-, *bios* life)]

symbol /símb'l/ *n.* & *v.* ● *n.* **1** a thing conventionally regarded as typifying, representing, or recalling something, esp. an idea or quality (*white is a symbol of purity*). **2** a mark or character taken as the conventional sign of some object, idea, function, or process, e.g. the letters standing for the chemical elements or the characters in musical notation. ● *v.tr.* (**symbolled, symbolling**; *US* **symboled, symboling**) symbolize. □□ **symbology** /-bóləji/ *n.* [ME f. L *symbolum* f. Gk *sumbolon* mark, token (as SYN-, *ballō* throw)]
■ *n.* representation, figure, metaphor, allegory, token, sign, image, emblem; insignia, badge, logotype, mark, hallmark, stamp, trade mark, colophon, brand, code, abbreviation, character, phonogram, logogram, pictogram, pictograph, ideogram, ideograph, initialism, cryptogram, acronym, monogram, password, shibboleth, watchword, code word; arms, bearing, armorial bearing, crest, escutcheon, coat of arms, banner, flag, pennant, standard, *colloq.* logo. ● *v.* see SYMBOLIZE.

symbolic /simbóllik/ *adj.* (also **symbolical** /-bóllik'l/) **1** of or serving as a symbol. **2** involving the use of symbols or symbolism. □ **symbolic logic** the use of symbols to denote propositions etc. in order to assist reasoning. □□ **symbolically** *adv.* [F *symbolique* or LL *symbolicus* f. Gk *sumbolikos*]
■ symbolical, figurative, allegoric(al), metaphoric(al); emblematic, typical, representative, token, symptomatic, characteristic, allusive, denotative, connotative, suggestive, mnemonic.

symbolism /símbəliz'm/ *n.* **1 a** the use of symbols to represent ideas. **b** symbols collectively. **2** an artistic and poetic movement or style using symbols and indirect suggestion to express ideas, emotions, etc. □□ **symbolist** *n.* **symbolistic** /-lístik/ *adj.*
■ **1 a** see IMAGERY 1.

symbolize /símbəlīz/ *v.tr.* (also **-ise**) **1** be a symbol of. **2** represent by means of symbols. □□ **symbolization** /-záysh'n/ *n.* [F *symboliser* f. *symbole* SYMBOL]
■ **1** represent, stand for, denote, connote, suggest, express, imply, signify, mean, indicate, typify, exemplify, betoken, illustrate, embody, epitomize, symbol.

symmetry /símmitri/ *n.* (*pl.* **-ies**) **1 a** correct proportion of the parts of a thing; balance, harmony. **b** beauty resulting from this. **2 a** a structure that allows an object to be divided into parts of an equal shape and size and similar position to the point or line or plane of division. **b** the possession of such a structure. **c** approximation to such a structure. **3** the repetition of exactly similar parts facing each other or a centre. **4** *Bot.* the possession by a flower of sepals and petals and stamens and pistils in the same number or multiples of the same number. □□ **symmetric** /simétrik/ *adj.* **symmetrical** /-métrik'l/ *adj.* **symmetrically** /-métrikəli/ *adv.* **symmetrize** *v.tr.* (also **-ise**). [obs. F *symmétrie* or L *summetria* f. Gk (as SYN-, *metron* measure)]
■ **1, 3** balance, proportion, evenness, order, orderliness, regularity, uniformity, congruity, congruousness, correspondence, agreement, harmony, consistency, equality. □□ **symmetric, symmetrical** (well-)balanced, proportionate, proportional, well-proportioned, orderly, (well-)ordered, in proportion, even, regular, congruous, congruent, uniform, harmonious; equal, mirror-image, mirror-like.

sympathectomy /símpəthéktəmi/ *n.* (*pl.* **-ies**) the surgical removal of a sympathetic ganglion etc.

sympathetic /símpəthéttik/ *adj.* & *n.* ● *adj.* **1** of, showing, or expressing sympathy. **2** due to sympathy. **3** likeable or capable of evoking sympathy. **4** (of a person) friendly and cooperative. **5** (foll. by *to*) inclined to favour (a proposal etc.) (*was most sympathetic to the idea*). **6** (of a landscape etc.) that touches the feelings by association etc. **7** (of a pain etc.) caused by a pain or injury to someone else or in another part of the body. **8** (of a sound, resonance, or string) sounding by a vibration communicated from another vibrating object. **9 a** designating the part of the nervous system consisting of nerves leaving the thoracic and lumbar regions of the spinal cord and connecting with the nerve cells in or near the viscera (see PARASYMPATHETIC). **b** (of a nerve or ganglion) belonging to this system. ● *n.* **1** a sympathetic nerve. **2** the sympathetic system. □ **sympathetic magic** a type of magic that seeks to achieve an effect by performing an associated action or using an associated thing. □□ **sympathetically** *adv.* [SYMPATHY, after *pathetic*]
■ *adj.* **1** compassionate, commiserative, understanding, supportive, caring, concerned, interested, solicitous, warm-hearted, kind-hearted, kindly, soft-hearted, tender-hearted, merciful, responsive, well-meaning, well-intentioned, good-natured, considerate, empathetic, empathic; like-minded; comforting, consoling. **3** likeable, appealing, congenial, agreeable, attractive, pleasant, *simpatico*. **4** friendly, cooperative, responsive, congenial; see also CONSIDERATE. **5** (*sympathetic to*) well-disposed to, favourably disposed to, supportive of, approving of, agreeable to. □□ **sympathetically** compassionately,

kindly, benignantly, considerately, supportively, empathetically; see also *favourably* (FAVOURABLE).

sympathize /símpəthīz/ *v.intr.* (also **-ise**) (often foll. by *with*) **1** feel or express sympathy; share a feeling or opinion. **2** agree with a sentiment or opinion. ▫▫ **sympathizer** *n.* [F *sympathiser* (as SYMPATHY)]

■ **1** (*sympathize with*) suffer *or* grieve *or* mourn with, feel (sorry) for, have pity for, condole with, commiserate with, offer condolences to; empathize with, harmonize with, get along with, relate to, identify with, see eye to eye with, side with, understand, be *en rapport* with, be in sympathy with, have (a) rapport with, *colloq.* be on the same wavelength with *or* as. **2** (*sympathize with*) agree with, go along with, favour, support, understand, appreciate, relate to, identify with, *sl.* dig. ▫▫ **sympathizer** condoner, approver, conspirator, co-conspirator, collaborator, accomplice, accessory, supporter, ally, fellow-traveller, *Polit.* comrade; see also PATRON 1.

sympathy /símpəthi/ *n.* (*pl.* **-ies**) **1 a** the state of being simultaneously affected with the same feeling as another. **b** the capacity for this. **2** (often foll. by *with*) **a** the act of sharing or tendency to share (with a person etc.) in an emotion or sensation or condition of another person or thing. **b** (in *sing.* or *pl.*) compassion or commiseration; condolences. **3** (often foll. by *for*) a favourable attitude; approval. **4** (in *sing.* or *pl.*; often foll. by *with*) agreement (with a person etc.) in opinion or desire. **5** (*attrib.*) in support of another cause (*sympathy strike*). ▫ **in sympathy** (often foll. by *with*) **1** having or showing or resulting from sympathy (with another). **2** by way of sympathetic action (*working to rule in sympathy*). [L *sympathia* f. Gk *sumpatheia* (as SYN-, *pathēs* f. *pathos* feeling)]

■ **2** compassion, commiseration, pity, concern, feeling, fellow-feeling, tenderness, empathy, understanding, solicitousness, warmth, tender-heartedness, warm-heartedness; condolences. **3** see PATRONAGE 1, AGREEMENT 1, 2. **4** agreement, harmony, compatibility, rapport, concord, accord, affinity, closeness, unity, unanimity; fellow-feeling, congeniality, communion, fellowship, camaraderie. ▫ **in sympathy 1** in agreement, in accord, agreed, united, unanimous.

sympetalous /simpéttələss/ *adj. Bot.* having the petals united.

symphonic /simfónnik/ *adj.* (of music) relating to or having the form or character of a symphony. ▫ **symphonic poem** an extended orchestral piece, usu. in one movement, on a descriptive or rhapsodic theme. ▫▫ **symphonically** *adv.*

■ ▫ **symphonic poem** tone poem.

symphonist /símfənist/ *n.* a composer of symphonies.

symphony /símfəni/ *n.* (*pl.* **-ies**) **1** an elaborate composition usu. for full orchestra, and in several movements with one or more in sonata form. **2** an interlude for orchestra alone in a large-scale vocal work. **3** = *symphony orchestra*. ▫ **symphony orchestra** a large orchestra suitable for playing symphonies etc. [ME, = harmony of sound, f. OF *symphonie* f. L *symphonia* f. Gk *sumphōnia* (as SYN-, *-phōnos* f. *phōnē* sound)]

symphyllous /simfílləss/ *adj. Bot.* having the leaves united. [SYN- + Gk *phullon* leaf]

symphysis /símfisiss/ *n.* (*pl.* **symphyses** /-seez/) **1** the process of growing together. **2 a** a union between two bones esp. in the median plane of the body. **b** the place or line of this. ▫▫ **symphyseal** /-fízziəl/ *adj.* **symphysial** /-fízziəl/ *adj.* [mod.L f. Gk *sumphusis* (as SYN-, *phusis* growth)]

sympodium /simpṓdiəm/ *n.* (*pl.* **sympodia** /-diə/) *Bot.* the apparent main axis or stem of a vine etc., made up of successive secondary axes. ▫▫ **sympodial** *adj.* [mod.L (as SYN-, Gk *pous podos* foot)]

symposium /simpṓziəm/ *n.* (*pl.* **symposia** /-ziə/) **1 a** a conference or meeting to discuss a particular subject. **b** a collection of essays or papers for this purpose. **2** a philosophical or other friendly discussion. **3** a drinking-party, esp. of the ancient Greeks with conversation etc. after a banquet. [L f. Gk *sumposion* in sense 3 (as SYN-, *-potēs* drinker)]

■ **1 a** see CONFERENCE 2.

symptom /símptəm/ *n.* **1** *Med.* a change in the physical or mental condition of a person, regarded as evidence of a disorder (cf. SIGN 5). **2** a sign of the existence of something. [ME *synthoma* f. med.L *sinthoma*, & f. LL *symptoma* f. Gk *sumptōma -atos* chance, symptom, f. *sumpiptō* happen (as SYN-, *piptō* fall)]

■ manifestation, evidence, mark, token, indication, indicator, cue, clue, (warning) sign, characteristic, trait, feature, earmark, marker, *colloq.* pointer.

symptomatic /símptəmáttik/ *adj.* serving as a symptom. ▫▫ **symptomatically** *adv.*

■ indicative, representative, suggestive, characteristic, emblematic, symbolic, typical.

symptomatology /símptəmətólləji/ *n.* the branch of medicine concerned with the study and interpretation of symptoms.

syn- /sin/ *prefix* with, together, alike. [from or after Gk *sun-* f. *sun* with]

synaeresis /sineérisiss/ *n.* (*US* **syneresis**) (*pl.* **synaereses** /-seez/) the contraction of two vowels into a diphthong or single vowel. [LL f. Gk *sunairesis* (as SYN-, *hairesis* f. *haireō* take)]

synaesthesia /sínnees-theéziə/ *n.* (*US* **synesthesia**) **1** *Psychol.* the production of a mental sense-impression relating to one sense by the stimulation of another sense. **2** a sensation produced in a part of the body by stimulation of another part. ▫▫ **synaesthetic** /-théttik/ *adj.* [mod.L f. SYN- after *anaesthesia*]

synagogue /sínnəgog/ *n.* **1** the building where a Jewish assembly or congregation meets for religious observance and instruction. **2** the assembly itself. ▫▫ **synagogal** /-gógg'l/ *adj.* **synagogical** /-gójik'l/ *adj.* [ME f. OF *sinagoge* f. LL *synagoga* f. Gk *sunagōgē* meeting (as SYN-, *agō* bring)]

■ **1** see TEMPLE[1].

synallagmatic /sínnəlagmáttik/ *adj.* (of a treaty or contract) imposing reciprocal obligations. [SYN- + Gk *allassō* exchange]

synapse /sínaps, sín-/ *n. Anat.* a junction of two nerve-cells. [Gk *synapsis* (as SYN-, *hapsis* f. *haptō* join)]

synapsis /sinápsiss/ *n.* (*pl.* **synapses** /-seez/) **1** *Anat.* = SYNAPSE. **2** *Biol.* the fusion of chromosome-pairs at the start of meiosis. ▫▫ **synaptic** /-náptik/ *adj.* **synaptically** /-náptikəli/ *adv.*

synarthrosis /sínnaarthrṓsiss/ *n.* (*pl.* **synarthroses** /-seez/) *Anat.* an immovably fixed bone-joint, e.g. the sutures of the skull. [SYN- + Gk *arthrōsis* jointing f. *arthron* joint]

sync /singk/ *n.* & *v.* (also **synch**) *colloq.* ● *n.* synchronization. ● *v.tr.* & *intr.* synchronize. ▫ **in** (or **out of**) **sync** (often foll. by *with*) according or agreeing well (or badly). [abbr.]

■ ▫ **out of sync** see WRONG *adj.* 4.

syncarp /sínkaarp/ *n.* a compound fruit from a flower with several carpels, e.g. a blackberry. [SYN- + Gk *karpos* fruit]

syncarpous /sinkaárpəss/ *adj.* (of a flower or fruit) having the carpels united (opp. APOCARPOUS). [SYN- + Gk *karpos* fruit]

synch var. of SYNC.

synchondrosis /síngkondrṓsiss/ *n.* (*pl.* **synchondroses** /-seez/) *Anat.* an almost immovable bone-joint bound by a layer of cartilage, as in the spinal vertebrae. [SYN- + Gk *khondros* cartilage]

synchro- /síngkrō/ *comb. form* synchronized, synchronous.

synchrocyclotron /síngkrōsíklətron/ *n.* a cyclotron able to achieve higher energies by decreasing the frequency of the accelerating electric field as the particles increase in energy and mass.

synchromesh /síngkrōmesh/ *n.* & *adj.* ● *n.* a system of gear-changing, esp. in motor vehicles, in which the driving and driven gearwheels are made to revolve at the same speed during engagement by means of a set of friction clutches, thereby easing the change. • *adj.* relating to or using this system. [abbr. of *synchronized mesh*]

synchronic /singkrónnik/ *adj.* describing a subject (esp. a language) as it exists at one point in time (opp. DIACHRONIC). □□ **synchronically** *adv.* [LL *synchronus*: see SYNCHRONOUS]
■ see CONTEMPORARY *adj.* 1.

synchronism /síngkrəniz'm/ *n.* **1** = SYNCHRONY. **2** the process of synchronizing sound and picture in cinematography, television, etc. □□ **synchronistic** /-nístik/ *adj.* **synchronistically** /-nístikəli/ *adv.* [Gk *sugkhronismos* (as SYNCHRONOUS)]

synchronize /síngkrənīz/ *v.* (also **-ise**) **1** *intr.* (often foll. by *with*) occur at the same time; be simultaneous. **2** *tr.* cause to occur at the same time. **3** *tr.* carry out the synchronism of (a film). **4** *tr.* ascertain or set forth the correspondence in the date of (events). **5 a** *tr.* cause (clocks etc.) to show a standard or uniform time. **b** *intr.* (of clocks etc.) be synchronized. □ **synchronized swimming** a form of swimming in which participants make coordinated leg and arm movements in time to music. □□ **synchronization** /-záysh'n/ *n.* **synchronizer** *n.*
■ **1** see COINCIDE 1, 2. **2, 5a** see COORDINATE *v.* 1.

synchronous /síngkrənəss/ *adj.* (often foll. by *with*) existing or occurring at the same time. □ **synchronous motor** *Electr.* a motor having a speed exactly proportional to the current frequency. □□ **synchronously** *adv.* [LL *synchronus* f. Gk *sugkhronos* (as SYN-, *khronos* time)]
■ see SIMULTANEOUS.

synchrony /síngkrəni/ *n.* **1** the state of being synchronic or synchronous. **2** the treatment of events etc. as being synchronous. [Gk *sugkhronos*: see SYNCHRONOUS]
■ **1** see COINCIDENCE 1.

synchrotron /síngkrətron/ *n. Physics* a cyclotron in which the magnetic field strength increases with the energy of the particles to keep their orbital radius constant.

syncline /síngklīn/ *n.* a rock-bed forming a trough. □□ **synclinal** /-klīn'l/ *adj.* [*synclinal* (as SYN-, Gk *klinō* lean)]

syncopate /síngkəpayt/ *v.tr.* **1** *Mus.* displace the beats or accents in (a passage) so that strong beats become weak and vice versa. **2** shorten (a word) by dropping interior sounds or letters, as *symbology* for *symbolology*, *Gloster* for *Gloucester*. □□ **syncopation** /-páysh'n/ *n.* **syncopator** *n.* [LL *syncopare* swoon (as SYNCOPE)]

syncope /síngkəpi/ *n.* **1** *Gram.* the omission of interior sounds or letters in a word (see SYNCOPATE 2). **2** *Med.* a temporary loss of consciousness caused by a fall in blood pressure. □□ **syncopal** *adj.* [ME f. LL *syncopē* f. Gk *sugkopē* (as SYN-, *koptō* strike, cut off)]
■ **2** see FAINT *n.*

syncretism /síngkrətiz'm/ *n.* **1** *Philos.* & *Theol.* the process or an instance of syncretizing (see SYNCRETIZE). **2** *Philol.* the merging of different inflectional varieties in the development of a language. □□ **syncretic** /-kréttik/ *adj.* **syncretist** *n.* **syncretistic** /-tistik/ *adj.* [mod.L *syncretismus* f. Gk *sugkrētismos* f. *sugkrētizō* (of two parties) combine against a third f. *krēs* Cretan (orig. of ancient Cretan communities)]

syncretize /síngkrətīz/ *v.tr.* (also **-ise**) *Philos.* & *Theol.* attempt, esp. inconsistently, to unify or reconcile differing schools of thought.

syncytium /sinsíttiəm/ *n.* (*pl.* **syncytia** /-tiə/) *Biol.* a mass of cytoplasm with several nuclei, not divided into separate cells. □□ **syncytial** *adj.* [formed as SYN- + -CYTE + -IUM]

syndactyl /sindáktil/ *adj.* (of an animal) having digits united as in webbed feet etc. □□ **syndactylism** *n.* **syndactylous** *adj.*

syndesis /síndisiss/ *n.* (*pl.* **syndeses** /-seez/) *Biol.* = SYNAPSIS 2. [mod.L f. Gk *syndesis* binding together f. *sundeō* bind together]

syndesmosis /síndezmṓsiss/ *n.* the union and articulation of bones by means of ligaments. [mod.L f. Gk *sundesmos* binding, fastening + -OSIS]

syndetic /sindéttik/ *adj. Gram.* of or using conjunctions. [Gk *sundetikos* (as SYNDESIS)]

syndic /síndik/ *n.* **1** a government official in various countries. **2** *Brit.* a business agent of certain universities and corporations, esp. (at Cambridge University) a member of a committee of the senate. □□ **syndical** *adj.* [F f. LL *syndicus* f. Gk *sundikos* (as SYN-, *-dikos* f. *dikē* justice)]

syndicalism /síndikəliz'm/ *n. hist.* a movement for transferring the ownership and control of the means of production and distribution to workers' unions. □□ **syndicalist** *n.* [F *syndicalisme* f. *syndical* (as SYNDIC)]

syndicate *n.* & *v.* • *n.* /síndikət/ **1** a combination of individuals or commercial firms to promote some common interest. **2** an association or agency supplying material simultaneously to a number of newspapers or periodicals. **3** a group of people who combine to buy or rent property, gamble, organize crime, etc. **4** a committee of syndics. • *v.tr.* /síndikayt/ **1** form into a syndicate. **2** publish (material) through a syndicate. □□ **syndication** /-káysh'n/ *n.* [F *syndicat* f. med.L *syndicatus* f. LL *syndicus*: see SYNDIC]
■ *n.* **1, 3** trust, monopoly, pool, bloc, cartel, syndication, group, association, alliance, combine, consortium, cooperative, collective, federation, confederation, coalition, league, union; Cosa Nostra, mafia. • *v.* **1** ally, associate, amalgamate, consolidate, league, confederate, synthesize, combine.

syndrome /síndrōm/ *n.* **1** a group of concurrent symptoms of a disease. **2** a characteristic combination of opinions, emotions, behaviour, etc. □□ **syndromic** /-drómmik/ *adj.* [mod.L f. Gk *sundromē* (as SYN-, *dromē* f. *dramein* to run)]

syne /sīn/ *adv.*, *conj.*, & *prep. Sc.* since. [contr. f. ME *sithen* SINCE]

synecdoche /sinékdəki/ *n.* a figure of speech in which a part is made to represent the whole or vice versa (e.g. *new faces at the meeting*; *England lost by six wickets*). □□ **synecdochic** /-dókkik/ *adj.* [ME f. L f. Gk *sunekdokhē* (as SYN-, *ekdokhē* f. *ekdekhomai* take up)]

synecology /sínnikólləji/ *n.* the ecological study of plant or animal communities. □□ **synecological** /sínneekəlójik'l/ *adj.* **synecologist** *n.*

syneresis *US* var. of SYNAERESIS.

synergism /sínnərjiz'm/ *n.* (also **synergy** /sínnərji/) the combined effect of drugs, organs, etc., that exceeds the sum of their individual effects. □□ **synergetic** /-jéttik/ *adj.* **synergic** /-nérjik/ *adj.* **synergistic** /-jístik/ *adj.* **synergistically** /-jístikəli/ *adv.* [Gk *sunergos* working together (as SYN-, *ergon* work)]
■ □□ **synergetic, synergistic** see UNITED 2a.

synergist /sínnərjist/ *n.* a medicine or a bodily organ (e.g. a muscle) that cooperates with another or others.

synesthesia *US* var. of SYNAESTHESIA.

syngamy /sínggəmi/ *n. Biol.* the fusion of gametes or nuclei in reproduction. □□ **syngamous** *adj.* [SYN- + Gk *gamos* marriage]

syngenesis /sinjénnisiss/ *n.* sexual reproduction from combined male and female elements.

synod /sínnəd/ *n.* **1** a Church council attended by delegated clergy and sometimes laity (see also *General Synod*). **2** a Presbyterian ecclesiastical court above the presbyteries and subject to the General Assembly. **3** any meeting for debate. [ME f. LL *synodus* f. Gk *sunodos* meeting (as SYN-, *hodos* way)]
■ **1, 3** see ASSEMBLY 1, 2a.

synodic /sinóddik/ *adj. Astron.* relating to or involving the conjunction of stars, planets, etc. □ **synodic period** the time between the successive conjunctions of a planet with the sun. [LL *synodicus* f. Gk *sunodikos* (as SYNOD)]

synodical /sinóddik'l/ *adj.* **1** (also **synodal** /sínnəd'l/) of, relating to, or constituted as a synod. **2** = SYNODIC.

synoecious /sinéeshəss/ *adj. Bot.* having male and female organs in the same flower or receptacle. [SYN- after *dioecious* etc.]

synonym /sínnənim/ *n.* **1** a word or phrase that means exactly or nearly the same as another in the same language (e.g. *shut* and *close*). **2** a word denoting the same thing as another but suitable to a different context (e.g. *serpent* for *snake*, *Hellene* for *Greek*). **3** a word equivalent to another in some but not all senses (e.g. *ship* and *vessel*). ▫▫ **synonymic** /-nímmik/ *adj.* **synonymity** /-nímmiti/ *n.* [ME f. L *synonymum* f. Gk *sunōnumon* neut. of *sunōnumos* (as SYN-, *onoma* name): cf. ANONYMOUS]

synonymous /sinónniməss/ *adj.* (often foll. by *with*) **1** having the same meaning; being a synonym (of). **2** (of a name, idea, etc.) suggestive of or associated with another (*excessive drinking regarded as synonymous with violence*). ▫▫ **synonymously** *adv.* **synonymousness** *n.*
■ **1** (*synonymous with*) equal to, equivalent to; tantamount to; transposable with, exchangeable with, identical to *or* with, interchangeable with, the same as. **2** (*synonymous with*) identified with, associated with, suggestive of, corresponding to *or* with.

synonymy /sinónnimi/ *n.* (*pl.* **-ies**) **1** the state of being synonymous. **2** the collocation of synonyms for emphasis (e.g. *in any shape or form*). **3 a** a system or collection of synonyms. **b** a treatise on synonyms. [LL *synonymia* f. Gk *sunōnumia* (as SYNONYM)]
■ **3 a** see THESAURUS 1b.

synopsis /sinópsiss/ *n.* (*pl.* **synopses** /-seez/) **1** a summary or outline. **2** a brief general survey. ▫▫ **synopsize** *v.tr.* (also **-ise**). [LL f. Gk (as SYN-, *opsis* seeing)]
■ **1** summary, condensation, abridgement, epitomization, outline, abstract, digest, précis, epitome, compendium, conspectus, *aperçu*, résumé, round-up. **2** survey, run-through, review, conspectus, *aperçu*. ▫▫ **synopsize** see *sum up* 1.

synoptic /sinóptik/ *adj.* & *n.* ● *adj.* **1** of, forming, or giving a synopsis. **2** taking or affording a comprehensive mental view. **3** of the Synoptic Gospels. **4** giving a general view of weather conditions. ● *n.* **1** a Synoptic Gospel. **2** the writer of a Synoptic Gospel. ▫ **Synoptic Gospels** the Gospels of Matthew, Mark, and Luke, describing events from a similar point of view. ▫▫ **synoptical** *adj.* **synoptically** *adv.* [Gk *sunoptikos* (as SYNOPSIS)]

synoptist /sinóptist/ *n.* the writer of a Synoptic Gospel.

synostosis /sinnostṓsiss/ *n.* the joining of bones by ankylosis etc. [SYN- + Gk *osteon* bone + -OSIS]

synovia /sīnṓviə, sin-/ *n.* *Physiol.* a viscous fluid lubricating joints and tendon sheaths. ▫ **synovial membrane** a dense membrane of connective tissue secreting synovia. ▫▫ **synovial** *adj.* [mod.L, formed prob. arbitrarily by Paracelsus]

synovitis /sī́nōvī́tiss, sin-/ *n.* inflammation of the synovial membrane.

syntactic /sintáktik/ *adj.* of or according to syntax. ▫▫ **syntactical** *adj.* **syntactically** *adv.* [Gk *suntaktikos* (as SYNTAX)]

syntagma /sintágmə/ *n.* (*pl.* **syntagmas** or **syntagmata** /-mətə/) **1** a word or phrase forming a syntactic unit. **2** a systematic collection of statements. ▫▫ **syntagmatic** /-máttik/ *adj.* **syntagmic** *adj.* [LL f. Gk *suntagma* (as SYNTAX)]

syntax /síntaks/ *n.* **1** the grammatical arrangement of words, showing their connection and relation. **2** a set of rules for or an analysis of this. [F *syntaxe* or LL *syntaxis* f. Gk *suntaxis* (as SYN-, *taxis* f. *tassō* arrange)]

synth /sinth/ *n. colloq.* = SYNTHESIZER.

synthesis /sínthisiss/ *n.* (*pl.* **syntheses** /-seez/) **1** the process or result of building up separate elements, esp. ideas, into a connected whole, esp. into a theory or system. **2** a combination or composition. **3** *Chem.* the artificial production of compounds from their constituents as distinct from extraction from plants etc. **4** *Gram.* **a** the process of making compound and derivative words. **b** the tendency in a language to use inflected forms rather than groups of words, prepositions, etc. **5** the joining of divided parts in surgery. ▫▫ **synthesist** *n.* [L f. Gk *sunthesis* (as SYN-, THESIS)]
■ **1, 2** combination, composition, union, amalgamation, coalescence, integration, fusion, unification, mix; compounding, combining, blending, merging, integrating, mixing, fusing, unifying, synthesizing; blend, compound, amalgam, merger, composite, mixture, concoction. **3** manufacture, production, making.

synthesize /sínthisīz/ *v.tr.* (also **synthetize** /-tīz/, **-ise**) **1** make a synthesis of. **2** combine into a coherent whole.
■ see COMBINE *v.* 3.

synthesizer /sínthisīzər/ *n.* an electronic musical instrument, esp. operated by a keyboard, producing a wide variety of sounds by generating and combining signals of different frequencies.

synthetic /sinthéttik/ *adj.* & *n.* ● *adj.* **1** made by chemical synthesis, esp. to imitate a natural product (*synthetic rubber*). **2** (of emotions etc.) affected, insincere. **3** *Logic* (of a proposition) having truth or falsity determinable by recourse to experience (cf. ANALYTIC 3). **4** *Philol.* using combinations of simple words or elements in compounded or complex words (cf. ANALYTICAL). ● *n. Chem.* a synthetic substance. ▫ **synthetic resin** *Chem.* see RESIN *n.* 2. ▫▫ **synthetical** *adj.* **synthetically** *adv.* [F *synthétique* or mod.L *syntheticus* f. Gk *sunthetikos* f. *sunthetos* f. *suntithēmi* (as SYN-, *tithēmi* put)]
■ *adj.* **1** artificial, man-made, manufactured, ersatz; fake, false, counterfeit, sham, bogus, spurious, mock, imitation, pseudo, plastic, *colloq.* phoney. **2** see ARTIFICIAL 3.

syphilis /síffiliss/ *n.* a contagious venereal disease progressing from infection of the genitals via the skin and mucous membrane to the bones, muscles, and brain. ▫▫ **syphilitic** /-líttik/ *adj.* **syphilize** /-līz/ *v.tr.* (also **-ise**). **syphiloid** /-loyd/ *adj.* [mod.L f. title (*Syphilis, sive Morbus Gallicus*) of a Latin poem (1530), f. *Syphilus*, a character in it, the supposed first sufferer from the disease]
■ ▫▫ **syphilitic** see VENEREAL 2.

syphon var. of SIPHON.

Syriac /sírriak/ *n.* & *adj.* ● *n.* the language of ancient Syria, western Aramaic. ● *adj.* in or relating to this language. [L *Syriacus* f. Gk *Suriakos* f. *Suria* Syria]

Syrian /sírriən/ *n.* & *adj.* ● *n.* **1** a native or national of the modern State of Syria in the Middle East; a person of Syrian descent. **2** a native or inhabitant of the region of Syria in antiquity or later. ● *adj.* of or relating to the region or State of Syria.

syringa /siríngə/ *n. Bot.* **1** = *mock orange*. **2** any plant of the genus *Syringa*, esp. the lilac. [mod.L, formed as SYRINX (with ref. to the use of its stems as pipe-stems)]

syringe /sirínj/ *n.* & *v.* ● *n.* **1** *Med.* **a** a tube with a nozzle and piston or bulb for sucking in and ejecting liquid in a fine stream, used in surgery. **b** (in full **hypodermic syringe**) a similar device with a hollow needle for insertion under the skin. **2** any similar device used in gardening, cooking, etc. ● *v.tr.* sluice or spray (the ear, a plant, etc.) with a syringe. [ME f. med.L *syringa* (as SYRINX)]

syrinx /sírringks/ *n.* (*pl.* **syrinxes** or **syringes** /sirínjeez/) **1** a set of pan-pipes. **2** *Archaeol.* a narrow gallery cut in rock in an ancient Egyptian tomb. **3** the lower larynx or song-organ of birds. ▫▫ **syringeal** /sirínjiəl/ *adj.* [L *syrinx -ngis* f. Gk *surigx suriggos* pipe, channel]

Syro- /sī́rō/ *comb. form* Syrian; Syrian and (*Syro-Phoenician*). [Gk *Suro-* f. *Suros* a Syrian]

syrup /sírrəp/ *n.* (*US* **sirup**) **1 a** a sweet sauce made by dissolving sugar in boiling water, often used for preserving fruit etc. **b** a similar sauce of a specified flavour as a drink, medicine, etc. (*rose-hip syrup*). **2** condensed sugar-cane juice; part of this remaining uncrystallized at various stages of refining; molasses, treacle. **3** excessive sweetness of style or manner. ▫▫ **syrupy** *adj.* [ME f. OF *sirop* or med.L *siropus* f. Arab. *šarāb* beverage: cf. SHERBET, SHRUB[2]]

■ □□ **syrupy** see SWEET *adj*. 1.

syssarcosis /sissaarkṓsiss/ *n*. (*pl*. **syssarcoses** /-seez/) *Anat*. a connection between bones formed by intervening muscle. [mod.L f. Gk *sussarkōsis* (as SYN-, *sarx*, *sarkos* flesh)]

systaltic /sistáltik/ *adj*. (esp. of the heart) contracting and dilating rhythmically; pulsatory (cf. SYSTOLE, DIASTOLE). [LL *systalticus* f. Gk *sustaltikos* (as SYN-, *staltos* f. *stellō* put)]

system /sístəm/ *n*. **1 a** a complex whole; a set of connected things or parts; an organized body of material or immaterial things. **b** the composition such a body; arrangement, set-up. **2** a set of devices (e.g. pulleys) functioning together. **3** *Physiol*. **a** a set of organs in the body with a common structure or function (*the digestive system*). **b** the human or animal body as a whole. **4 a** method; considered principles of procedure or classification. **b** classification. **5** orderliness. **6 a** a body of theory or practice relating to or prescribing a particular form of government, religion, etc. **b** (prec. by *the*) the prevailing political or social order, esp. regarded as oppressive and intransigent. **7** a method of choosing one's procedure in gambling etc. **8** *Computing* a group of related hardware units or programs or both, esp. when dedicated to a single application. **9** one of seven general types of crystal structure. **10** a major group of geological strata (*the Devonian system*). **11** *Physics* a group of associated bodies moving under mutual gravitation etc. **12** *Mus*. the braced staves of a score. □ **get a thing out of one's system** *colloq*. be rid of a preoccupation or anxiety. **systems analysis** the analysis of a complex process or operation in order to improve its efficiency, esp. by applying a computer system. □□ **systemless** *adj*. [F *système* or LL *systema* f. Gk *sustēma* -*atos* (as SYN-, *histēmi* set up)]

■ **1** organized whole, organization, set, group, combination, network; structure, arrangement, set-up; see also FRAME *n*. 6. **4 a** scheme, method, approach, *modus operandi*, way, procedure, methodology, technique, plan, process, practice, routine; logic, principles, rules. **b** classification, organization, categorization, codification, arrangement, grouping, division, ordering, taxonomy. **5** see ORDER *n*. 1. **6 a** see CODE *n*. 5. **b** regime, government, bureaucracy, (prevailing) order, status quo, Establishment, powers that be, *archaic* regimen.

systematic /sístəmáttik/ *adj*. **1** methodical; done or conceived according to a plan or system. **2** regular, deliberate (*a systematic liar*). □ **systematic theology** a form of theology in which the aim is to arrange religious truths in a self-consistent whole. □□ **systematically** *adv*. **systematism** /sístəmətiz'm/ *n*. **systematist** /sístəmətist/ *n*. [F *systématique* f. LL *systematicus* f. late Gk *sustēmatikos* (as SYSTEM)]

■ **1** organized, systematized, planned, methodical, businesslike, orderly, well-organized, well-ordered, regular, routine, standardized, standard. **2** deliberate, regular, habitual, inveterate, persistent, *colloq. disp.* chronic.

systematics /sístəmáttiks/ *n.pl.* (usu. treated as *sing*.) the study or a system of classification; taxonomy.

systematize /sístəmətīz/ *v.tr.* (also **-ise**) **1** make systematic. **2** devise a system for. □□ **systematization** /-záysh'n/ *n*. **systematizer** *n*.

■ see ORGANIZE 1. □□ **systematization** see ORGANIZATION 1.

systemic /sistémmik/ *adj*. **1** *Physiol*. **a** of or concerning the whole body, not confined to a particular part (*systemic infection*). **b** (of blood circulation) other than pulmonary. **2** *Hort*. (of an insecticide, fungicide, etc.) entering the plant via the roots or shoots and passing through the tissues. □□ **systemically** *adv*. [irreg. f. SYSTEM]

systemize /sístəmīz/ *v.tr.* = SYSTEMATIZE. □□ **systemization** /-záysh'n/ *n*. **systemizer** *n*.

systole /sístəli/ *n*. *Physiol*. the contraction of the heart, when blood is pumped into the arteries (cf. DIASTOLE). □□ **systolic** /sistóllik/ *adj*. [LL f. Gk *sustolē* f. *sustellō* contract (as SYSTALTIC)]

syzygy /sízziji/ *n*. (*pl*. **-ies**) **1** *Astron*. conjunction or opposition, esp. of the moon with the sun. **2** a pair of connected or correlated things. [LL *syzygia* f. Gk *suzugia* f. *suzugos* yoked, paired (as SYN-, *zugon* yoke)]

Tt

T[1] /tee/ *n.* (also **t**) (*pl.* **Ts** or **T's**) **1** the twentieth letter of the alphabet. **2** a T-shaped thing (esp. *attrib.*: *T-joint*). □ **to a T** exactly; to a nicety.

■ □ **to a T** see EXACTLY 1.

T[2] *abbr.* **1** tera-. **2** tesla.

T[3] *symb. Chem.* the isotope tritium.

t. *abbr.* **1** ton(s). **2** tonne(s).

't *pron. contr.* of IT[1] (*'tis*).

-t[1] /t/ *suffix* = -ED[1] (*crept*; *sent*).

-t[2] /t/ *suffix* = -EST[2] (*shalt*).

TA *abbr.* (in the UK) Territorial Army.

Ta *symb. Chem.* the element tantalum.

ta /taa/ *int. Brit. colloq.* thank you. [infantile form]

Taal /taal/ *n.* (prec. by *the*) *hist.* an early form of Afrikaans. [Du., = language, rel. to TALE]

TAB *abbr.* **1** typhoid-paratyphoid A and B vaccine. **2** *Austral.* Totalizator Agency Board.

tab[1] /tab/ *n.* & *v.* ● *n.* **1 a** a small flap or strip of material attached for grasping, fastening, or hanging up, or for identification. **b** a similar object as part of a garment etc. **2** *US colloq.* a bill or price (*picked up the tab*). **3** *Brit. Mil.* a marking on the collar distinguishing a staff officer. **4 a** a stage-curtain. **b** a loop for suspending this. ● *v.tr.* (**tabbed**, **tabbing**) provide with a tab or tabs. □ **keep tabs** (or **a tab**) **on** *colloq.* **1** keep account of. **2** have under observation or in check. [prob. f. dial.: cf. TAG[1]]

■ *n.* **1** flap, tag, loop, ticket, sticker, label, flag, lappet, strap, handle. **2** charge, bill, account, reckoning, *US* check. ● *v.* see TAG[1] *v.* 1.

tab[2] /tab/ *n.* **1** = TABULATOR 2. **2** = TABULATOR 3. [abbr.]

tabard /tábbərd/ *n.* **1** a herald's official coat emblazoned with the arms of the sovereign. **2** a woman's or girl's sleeveless jerkin. **3** *hist.* a knight's short emblazoned garment worn over armour. [ME f. OF *tabart*, of unkn. orig.]

tabaret /tábbərit/ *n.* an upholstery fabric of alternate satin and plain stripes. [prob. f. TABBY]

tabasco /təbáskō/ *n.* **1** a pungent pepper made from the fruit of *Capsicum frutescens*. **2** (**Tabasco**) *propr.* a sauce made from this used to flavour food. [*Tabasco* in Mexico]

tabbouleh /təbo͞olay/ *n.* an Arabic vegetable salad made with cracked wheat. [Arab. *tabbūla*]

tabby /tábbi/ *n.* (*pl.* **-ies**) **1** (in full **tabby cat**) **a** a grey or brownish cat mottled or streaked with dark stripes. **b** any domestic cat, esp. female. **2** a kind of watered silk. **3** a plain weave. [F *tabis* (in sense 2) f. Arab. *al-'attabiya* the quarter of Baghdad where tabby was manufactured: connection of other senses uncert.]

tabernacle /tábbərnakk'l/ *n.* **1** *hist.* a tent used as a sanctuary for the Ark of the Covenant by the Israelites during the Exodus. **2** *Eccl.* a canopied niche or receptacle esp. for the Eucharistic elements. **3** a place of worship in nonconformist creeds. **4** *Bibl.* a fixed or movable habitation usu. of light construction. **5** *Naut.* a socket or double post for a hinged mast that can be lowered to pass under low bridges. □ **feast of Tabernacles** = SUCCOTH. □□ **tabernacled** *adj.* [ME f. OF *tabernacle* or L *tabernaculum* tent, dimin. of *taberna* hut]

tabes /táybeez/ *n. Med.* **1** emaciation. **2** locomotor ataxy; a form of neurosyphilis. □□ **tabetic** /təbéttik/ *adj.* [L, = wasting away]

tabla /táblə, taá-/ *n. Ind. Mus.* a pair of small drums played with the hands. [Hind. f. Arab. *ṭabla* drum]

tablature /tábləchər/ *n. Mus.* an early form of notation indicating fingering (esp. in playing the lute), rhythm, and features other than notes. [F f. It. *tavolatura* f. *tavolare* set to music]

table /táyb'l/ *n.* & *v.* ● *n.* **1** a piece of furniture with a flat top and one or more legs, providing a level surface for eating, writing, or working at, playing games on, etc. **2** a flat surface serving a specified purpose (*altar table*; *bird table*). **3 a** food provided in a household (*keeps a good table*). **b** a group seated at table for dinner etc. **4 a** a set of facts or figures systematically displayed, esp. in columns (*a table of contents*). **b** matter contained in this. **c** = *multiplication table*. **5** a flat surface for working on or for machinery to operate on. **6 a** a slab of wood or stone etc. for bearing an inscription. **b** matter inscribed on this. **7** = TABLELAND. **8** *Archit.* **a** a flat usu. rectangular vertical surface. **b** a horizontal moulding, esp. a cornice. **9 a** a flat surface of a gem. **b** a cut gem with two flat faces. **10** each half or quarter of a folding board for backgammon. **11** (prec. by *the*) *Bridge* the dummy hand. ● *v.tr.* **1** bring forward for discussion or consideration at a meeting. **2** postpone consideration of (a matter). **3** *Naut.* strengthen (a sail) with a wide hem. □ **at table** taking a meal at a table. **lay on the table 1** submit for discussion. **2** postpone indefinitely. **on the table** offered for discussion. **table knife** a knife for use at meals, esp. in eating a main course. **table licence** a licence to serve alcoholic drinks only with meals. **table linen** tablecloths, napkins, etc. **table manners** decorum or correct behaviour while eating at table. **table-mat** a mat for protecting a tabletop from hot dishes, etc. **table salt** salt that is powdered or easy to powder for use at meals. **table talk** miscellaneous informal talk at table. **table tennis** an indoor game based on lawn tennis, played with small bats and a ball bounced on a table divided by a net. **table wine** ordinary wine for drinking with a meal. **turn the tables** (often foll. by *on*) reverse one's relations (with), esp. by turning an inferior into a superior position (orig. in backgammon). **under the table** *colloq.* drunken after a meal. □□ **tableful** *n.* (*pl.* **-fuls**). **tabling** *n.* [ME f. OF f. L *tabula* plank, tablet, list]

■ *n.* **3 a** food, victuals, edibles, eatables, fare, provisions, *archaic* board, *formal or joc.* comestibles, *joc.* provender. **4 a** list, listing, register, record, tabulation, chart, catalogue, index, inventory, itemization, précis; table of contents. **5** counter, bench. **6 a** see TABLET 3. **7** tableland, plateau. ● *v.* **1** submit, present, offer, proffer, bring forward, lay on the table, bring up, propose. **2** shelve, postpone, defer, suspend, put off, stay, pigeon-hole, mothball, *colloq.* put on ice. □ **table linen** tablecloths, napkins, *Sc. or archaic* napery. **table tennis** ping-pong. **under the table** see DRUNK *adj.* 1.

tableau /táblō/ *n.* (*pl.* **tableaux** /-lōz/) **1** a picturesque presentation. **2** = TABLEAU VIVANT. **3** a dramatic or effective situation suddenly brought about. □ **tableau curtains**

Theatr. a pair of curtains drawn open by a diagonal cord. [F, = picture, dimin. of *table*: see TABLE]
■ **1** scene, sight, spectacle, picture, image, presentation, representation, view. **2** composition, arrangement, grouping, *Theatr. tableau vivant.*

tableau vivant /táblō veévoN/ *n.* (*pl.* ***tableaux vivants*** *pronunc.* same) *Theatr.* a silent and motionless group of people arranged to represent a scene. [F, lit. 'living picture']

tablecloth /táyb'lkloth/ *n.* a cloth spread over the top of a table, esp. for meals.

table d'hôte /taáb'l dṓt/ *n.* a meal consisting of a set menu at a fixed price, esp. in a hotel (cf. À LA CARTE). [F, = host's table]

tableland /táyb'l-land/ *n.* an extensive elevated region with a level surface; a plateau.

tablespoon /táyb'lspōōn/ *n.* **1** a large spoon for serving food. **2** an amount held by this. ▫▫ **tablespoonful** *n.* (*pl.* **-fuls**).

tablet /táblit/ *n.* **1** a small measured and compressed amount of a substance, esp. of a medicine or drug. **2** a small flat piece of soap etc. **3** a flat slab of stone or wood, esp. for display or an inscription. **4** *Archit.* = TABLE 8. **5** *US* a writing-pad. [ME f. OF *tablete* f. Rmc, dimin. of L *tabula* TABLE]
■ **1** pill, capsule, troche, pellet, pastille, drop, lozenge, bolus. **2** block, bar, cake, slab, chunk, piece. **3** slab, plaque, plate, panel, table, plaquette; stone, gravestone, headstone, tombstone, memorial. **5** (scribbling *or* writing- *or* note- *or* memo) pad, (spiral(-bound)) notebook, jotter, *esp. US* scratch pad.

tabletop /táyb'ltop/ *n.* **1** the top or surface of a table. **2** (*attrib.*) that can be placed or used on a tabletop.

tableware /táyb'lwair/ *n.* dishes, plates, implements, etc., for use at meals.

tablier /tábliay/ *n. hist.* an apron-like part of a woman's dress. [F]

tabloid /táblоyd/ *n.* **1** a newspaper, usu. popular in style with bold headlines and large photographs, having pages of half size. **2** anything in a compressed or concentrated form. [orig. the propr. name of a medicine sold in tablets]

taboo /təbṓō/ *n.*, *adj.*, & *v.* (also **tabu**) ● *n.* (*pl.* **taboos** or **tabus**) **1** a system or the act of setting a person or thing apart as sacred or accursed. **2** a prohibition or restriction imposed by social custom. ● *adj.* **1** avoided or prohibited, esp. by social custom (*taboo words*). **2** designated as sacred and prohibited. ● *v.tr.* (**taboos, tabooed** or **tabus, tabued**) **1** put (a thing, practice, etc.) under taboo. **2** exclude or prohibit by authority or social influence. [Tongan *tabu*]
■ *n.* **1** anathema, excommunication, curse; consecration, sanctification. **2** interdict, interdiction, proscription, ban, prohibition, restriction; see also BOYCOTT *n.* ● *adj.* anathema, forbidden, interdicted, off limits, out of bounds, *verboten*, proscribed, banned, prohibited, restricted, unmentionable, unspeakable; censored, censorable, unacceptable, rude, impolite, indecorous, dirty, explicit; outlawed, illegal, illicit, unlawful. ● *v.* forbid, interdict, proscribe, ban, prohibit, exclude.

tabor /táybər/ *n. hist.* a small drum, esp. one used to accompany a pipe. [ME f. OF *tabour*, *tabur*: cf. TABLA, Pers. *tabīra* drum]

tabouret /tábbərit/ *n.* (*US* **taboret**) a low seat usu. without arms or a back. [F, = stool, dimin. as TABOR]

tabu var. of TABOO.

tabular /tábyoolər/ *adj.* **1** of or arranged in tables or lists. **2** broad and flat like a table. **3** (of a crystal) having two broad flat faces. **4** formed in thin plates. ▫▫ **tabularly** *adv.* [L *tabularis* (as TABLE)]

tabula rasa /tábyoolə raázə/ *n.* **1** an erased tablet. **2** the human mind (esp. at birth) viewed as having no innate ideas. [L, = scraped tablet]

tabulate /tábyoolayt/ *v.tr.* arrange (figures or facts) in tabular form. ▫▫ **tabulation** /-láysh'n/ *n.* [LL *tabulare tabulat-* f. *tabula* table]
■ systematize, organize, order, group, list, arrange, classify, categorize, rate, grade, catalogue, codify, pigeon-hole, sort, assort, index, itemize; record, note. ▫▫ **tabulation** see TABLE *n.* 4a.

tabulator /tábyoolaytər/ *n.* **1** a person or thing that tabulates. **2** a device on a typewriter for advancing to a sequence of set positions in tabular work. **3** *Computing* a machine that produces lists or tables from a data storage medium such as punched cards.

tacamahac /tákkəməhak/ *n.* **1** a resinous gum obtained from certain tropical trees esp. of the genus *Calophyllum*. **2** **a** the balsam poplar. **b** the resin of this. [obs. Sp. *tacamahaca* f. Aztec *tecomahiyac*]

tac-au-tac /tákkōtak/ *n. Fencing* a parry combined with a riposte. [F: imit.]

tacet /tássit, táy-/ *v.intr. Mus.* an instruction for a particular voice or instrument to be silent. [L, = is silent]

tachism /táshiz'm/ *n.* (also **tachisme**) a form of action painting with dabs of colour arranged randomly to evoke a subconscious feeling. [F *tachisme* f. *tache* stain]

tachistoscope /təkístəskōp/ *n.* an instrument for very brief measured exposure of objects to the eye. ▫▫ **tachistoscopic** /-skóppik/ *adj.* [Gk *takhistos* swiftest + -SCOPE]

tacho /tákkō/ *n.* (*pl.* **-os**) *colloq.* = TACHOMETER. [abbr.]

tacho- /tákkō/ *comb. form* speed. [Gk *takhos* speed]

tachograph /tákkəgraaf/ *n.* a device used esp. in heavy goods vehicles and coaches etc. for automatically recording speed and travel time.

tachometer /təkómmitər/ *n.* an instrument for measuring the rate of rotation of a shaft and hence the speed or velocity of a vehicle.

tachy- /tákki/ *comb. form* swift. [Gk *takhus* swift]

tachycardia /tákkikaárdiə/ *n. Med.* an abnormally rapid heart rate. [TACHY- + Gk *kardia* heart]

tachygraphy /təkígrəfi/ *n.* **1** stenography, esp. that of the ancient Greeks and Romans. **2** the abbreviated medieval writing of Greek and Latin. ▫▫ **tachygrapher** *n.* **tachygraphic** /tákkigráffik/ *adj.* **tachygraphical** /tákkigráffik'l/ *adj.*

tachymeter /təkímmitər/ *n.* **1** *Surveying* an instrument used to locate points rapidly. **2** a speed-indicator.

tacit /tássit/ *adj.* understood or implied without being stated (*tacit consent*). ▫▫ **tacitly** *adv.* [L *tacitus* silent f. *tacēre* be silent]
■ unspoken, undeclared, unsaid, unstated, unvoiced, unuttered, silent, mute, understood, unexpressed, implied, implicit.

taciturn /tássiturn/ *adj.* reserved in speech; saying little; uncommunicative. ▫▫ **taciturnity** /-túrniti/ *n.* **taciturnly** *adv.* [F *taciturne* or L *taciturnus* (as TACIT)]
■ silent, uncommunicative, mute, reticent, reserved, unforthcoming, tight-lipped, close-mouthed, untalkative, quiet, secretive. ▫▫ **taciturnity** see SILENCE *n.* 2, 3.

tack[1] /tak/ *n.* & *v.* ● *n.* **1** a small sharp broad-headed nail. **2** *US* a drawing-pin. **3** a long stitch used in fastening fabrics etc. lightly or temporarily together. **4** **a** the direction in which a ship moves as determined by the position of its sails and regarded in terms of the direction of the wind (*starboard tack*). **b** a temporary change of direction in sailing to take advantage of a side wind etc. **5** a course of action or policy (*try another tack*). **6** *Naut.* **a** a rope for securing the corner of some sails. **b** the corner to which this is fastened. **7** a sticky condition of varnish etc. **8** *Brit.* an extraneous clause appended to a bill in Parliament. ● *v.* **1** *tr.* (often foll. by *down* etc.) fasten with tacks. **2** *tr.* stitch (pieces of cloth etc.) lightly together. **3** *tr.* (foll. by *to*, *on*) annex (a thing). **4** *intr.* (often foll. by *about*) **a** change a ship's course by turning its head to the wind (cf. WEAR[2]). **b** make a series of tacks. **5** *intr.* change one's conduct or policy etc. **6** *tr.*

Brit. append (a clause) to a bill. ▫▫ **tacker** *n.* [ME *tak* etc., of uncert. orig.: cf. Bibl. *tache* clasp, link f. OF *tache*]
■ *n.* **1** nail. **2** pin, tin-tack, *Brit.* drawing-pin, *esp. US* thumbtack. **3** fastening, stitch, baste. **4** direction, bearing, heading, course. **5** approach, way, path, direction, course, policy, procedure, method, technique, attack, line, angle. ● *v.* **1** pin, attach, fasten, secure, join, couple, unite, combine, stick, fix, affix, staple, nail, skewer, peg, screw, bolt, rivet. **2** baste, stitch, sew, bind. **3** (*tack on*) add (on), append, annex, attach, join on, tag on. **4** change direction *or* heading *or* course; zigzag; veer off *or* away, *Naut.* go about, beat.

tack[2] /tak/ *n.* the saddle, bridle, etc., of a horse. [shortened f. TACKLE]
■ harness, saddlery, bridle, tackle, gear, equipment, equipage, fittings, fitments, kit, outfit, rig, rigging, accoutrements.

tack[3] /tak/ *n. colloq.* cheap or shoddy material; tat, kitsch. [back-form. f. TACKY[2]]

tacker /tákkər/ *n. Austral.* & *dial.* a small boy.
■ see LAD 1.

tackle /tákk'l/ *n.* & *v.* ● *n.* **1** equipment for a task or sport (*fishing-tackle*). **2** a mechanism, esp. of ropes, pulley-blocks, hooks, etc., for lifting weights, managing sails, etc. (*block and tackle*). **3** a windlass with its ropes and hooks. **4** an act of tackling in football etc. **5** *Amer. Football* **a** the position next to the end of the forward line. **b** the player in this position. ● *v.tr.* **1** try to deal with (a problem or difficulty). **2** grapple with or try to overcome (an opponent). **3** enter into discussion with. **4** obstruct, intercept, or seize and stop (a player running with the ball). **5** secure by means of tackle. ▫ **tackle-block** a pulley over which a rope runs. **tackle-fall** a rope for applying force to the blocks of a tackle. ▫▫ **tackler** *n.* **tackling** *n.* [ME, prob. f. MLG *takel* f. *taken* lay hold of]
■ *n.* **1** gear, rig, fittings, equipment, things, equipage, rig(ging), paraphernalia, kit, outfit, tools, implements, apparatus, trappings, accoutrements, *Brit. sl.* clobber. **2** block (and tackle), hoisting gear, pulley, hoist, fall, sheave. **3** windlass. ● *v.* **1** come *or* get to grips with, grapple with, approach, take on, try to solve, (try to) deal *or* cope with, stand *or* face up to, face, confront, address (oneself to), attend to, set about, pursue, have a go at, *colloq.* have a crack at. **2, 4** grapple with, take on, attack, contend with, challenge; intercept, obstruct, block, stop, seize.

tacky[1] /tákki/ *adj.* (**tackier**, **tackiest**) (of glue or paint etc.) still slightly sticky after application. ▫▫ **tackiness** *n.* [TACK[1] + -Y[1]]
■ sticky, gluey, gummy, adhesive, ropy, viscous, viscid, glutinous, *sl.* gooey.

tacky[2] /tákki/ *adj.* (**tackier**, **tackiest**) esp. *US colloq.* **1** showing poor taste or style. **2** tatty or seedy. ▫▫ **tackily** *adv.* **tackiness** *n.* [19th c.: orig. unkn.]
■ **1** tawdry, cheap, Brummagem, gaudy, chintzy, tasteless, vulgar, flashy, kitsch(y), *colloq.* flash, *sl.* naff. **2** shabby, sleazy, shoddy, seedy, dowdy, *colloq.* tatty.

taco /taákō/ *n.* (*pl.* **-os**) a Mexican dish of meat etc. in a folded or rolled tortilla. [Mex. Sp.]

tact /takt/ *n.* **1** adroitness in dealing with others or with difficulties arising from personal feeling. **2** intuitive perception of the right thing to do or say. [F f. L *tactus* touch, sense of touch f. *tangere tact-* touch]
■ tactfulness, discretion, diplomacy, sensitivity, *savoir faire*, judgement, *politesse*, delicacy, finesse, cleverness, prudence, care, carefulness, dexterity, dexterousness, discernment, judiciousness, adroitness, skill, acumen, acuteness, perception, understanding, consideration, thoughtfulness, politeness, courtesy.

tactful /táktfōōl/ *adj.* having or showing tact. ▫▫ **tactfully** *adv.* **tactfulness** *n.*
■ discreet, diplomatic, sensitive, politic, judicious, delicate, clever, prudent, careful, dexterous, discerning, adroit, skilful, acute, perceptive, understanding, considerate, thoughtful, polite, courteous. ▫▫ **tactfulness** see TACT.

tactic /táktik/ *n.* **1** a tactical manoeuvre. **2** = TACTICS. [mod.L *tactica* f. Gk *taktikē* (*tekhnē* art): see TACTICS]
■ **1** move, manoeuvre, caper, plan, strategy, stratagem, policy, line, tack, device, ruse, plot, scheme, design, *colloq.* ploy.

tactical /táktik'l/ *adj.* **1** of, relating to, or constituting tactics (*a tactical retreat*). **2** (of bombing or weapons) done or for use in immediate support of military or naval operations (opp. STRATEGIC). **3** adroitly planning or planned. **4** (of voting) aimed at preventing the strongest candidate from winning by supporting the next strongest. ▫▫ **tactically** *adv.* [Gk *taktikos* (as TACTICS)]
■ **1, 3** artful, clever, cunning, shrewd, adroit, strategic, planned, calculated, skilful, adept, politic, smart, tactful.

tactics /táktiks/ *n.pl.* **1** (also treated as *sing.*) the art of disposing armed forces esp. in contact with an enemy (cf. STRATEGY). **2 a** the plans and means adopted in carrying out a scheme or achieving some end. **b** a skilful device or devices. ▫▫ **tactician** /taktísh'n/ *n.* [mod.L *tactica* f. Gk *taktika* neut.pl. f. *taktos* ordered f. *tassō* arrange]
■ **1** military science, military operation(s), generalship, manoeuvring. **2 a** manoeuvres, strategy, plans, campaign, orchestration, engineering, masterminding, approach, *esp. US* game plan. **b** device(s), ruse(s), plot(s), scheme(s), stratagem(s), trick(s), dodge(s), *colloq.* ploy(s). ▫▫ **tactician** strategist, campaigner, mastermind, intriguer, plotter, planner, schemer, manipulator, manoeuvrer, orchestrator, *colloq.* operator.

tactile /táktīl/ *adj.* **1** of or connected with the sense of touch. **2** perceived by touch. **3** tangible. **4** *Art* (in painting) producing or concerning the effect of three-dimensional solidity. ▫▫ **tactual** /táktyooəl/ *adj.* (in senses 1, 2). **tactility** /-tílliti/ *n.* [L *tactilis* f. *tangere tact-* touch]

tactless /táktliss/ *adj.* having or showing no tact. ▫▫ **tactlessly** *adv.* **tactlessness** *n.*
■ coarse, boorish, uncivilized, unsophisticated, rough, rude, uncouth, discourteous, ungentlemanly, unladylike, crude, gruff, bluff, abrupt, blunt, brusque, impertinent, disrespectful, uncivil, impolite, insensitive, awkward, bungling, clumsy, maladroit, inept, undiplomatic, thoughtless, unthinking, gauche, unskilful, impolitic, imprudent, inconsiderate, injudicious, indiscreet, unwise. ▫▫ **tactlessness** see INCIVILITY, *impudence* (IMPUDENT).

tad /tad/ *n. US colloq.* a small amount (often used adverbially: *a tad too salty*). [19th c.: orig. unkn.]
■ see DASH *n.* 7.

tadpole /tádpōl/ *n.* a larva of an amphibian, esp. a frog, toad, or newt in its aquatic stage and breathing through gills. [ME *taddepolle* (as TOAD, POLL[1] from the size of its head)]

taedium vitae /teédiəm veétī, vītee/ *n.* weariness of life (often as a pathological state, with a tendency to suicide). [L]

taenia /teéniə/ *n.* (*US* **tenia**) (*pl.* **taeniae** /-ni-ee/ or **taenias**) **1** *Archit.* a fillet between a Doric architrave and frieze. **2** *Anat.* any flat ribbon-like structure, esp. the muscles of the colon. **3** any large tapeworm of the genus *Taenia*, esp. *T. saginata* and *T. soleum*, parasitic on humans. **4** *Gk Antiq.* a fillet or headband. ▫▫ **taenioid** *adj.* [L f. Gk *tainia* ribbon]

taffeta /táffitə/ *n.* a fine lustrous silk or silklike fabric. [ME f. OF *taffetas* or med.L *taffata*, ult. f. Pers. *tāfta* past part. of *tāftan* twist]

taffrail /táfrayl/ *n. Naut.* a rail round a ship's stern. [earlier *tafferel* f. Du. *taffereel* panel, dimin. of *tafel* (as TABLE): assim. to RAIL[1]]

Taffy /táffi/ *n.* (*pl.* **-ies**) *colloq.* often *offens.* a Welshman. [supposed Welsh pronunc. of *Davy* = *David* (Welsh *Dafydd*)]

taffy /táffi/ *n.* (*pl.* **-ies**) *US* **1** a confection like toffee. **2** insincere flattery. [19th c.: orig. unkn.]

tafia /táffiə/ *n. W.Ind.* rum distilled from molasses etc. [18th c.: orig. uncert.]

tag[1] /tag/ *n.* & *v.* ● *n.* **1 a** a label, esp. one for tying on an object to show its address, price, etc. **b** *colloq.* an epithet or popular name serving to identify a person or thing. **c** *sl.* the signature or identifying mark of a graffiti artist. **2** a metal or plastic point at the end of a lace etc. to assist insertion. **3** a loop at the back of a boot used in pulling it on. **4** *US* a licence plate of a motor vehicle. **5** a loose or ragged end of anything. **6** a ragged lock of wool on a sheep. **7** *Theatr.* a closing speech addressed to the audience. **8** a trite quotation or stock phrase. **9 a** the refrain of a song. **b** a musical phrase added to the end of a piece. **10** an animal's tail, or its tip. ● *v.tr.* (**tagged**, **tagging**) **1** provide with a tag or tags. **2** (often foll. by *on*, *on to*) join or attach. **3** *colloq.* follow closely or trail behind. **4** *Computing* identify (an item of data) by its type for later retrieval. **5** label radioactively (see LABEL *v.* 3). **6 a** find rhymes for (verses). **b** string (rhymes) together. **7** shear away tags from (sheep). □ **tag along** (often foll. by *with*) go along or accompany passively. **tag end** esp. *US* the last remnant of something. [ME: orig. unkn.]

■ *n.* **1 a** label, name *or* price tag, mark, marker, tab, tally, ticket, sticker, stub, docket. **b** name, epithet, label, designation, title, nickname, byname, *colloq.* handle, *formal* appellation, *sl.* moniker. **9 a** see REFRAIN[2]. **10** see TAIL[1] *n.* 1. ● *v.* **1** label, mark, ticket, identify, earmark, tab; name, call, dub, nickname, style, christen, baptize, *archaic* entitle. **2** (*tag on*) see TACK[1] *v.* 3. **3** follow, trail behind *or* after, shadow, *colloq.* tail. □ **tag along** go along; (*tag along with*) accompany, attend, escort; trail (along) after. **tag end** see REAR[1] *n.* 1.

tag[2] /tag/ *n.* & *v.* ● *n.* **1** a children's game in which one chases the rest, and anyone who is caught then becomes the pursuer. **2** *Baseball* the act of tagging a runner. ● *v.tr.* (**tagged**, **tagging**) **1** touch in a game of tag. **2** (often foll. by *out*) put (a runner) out by touching with the ball or with the hand holding the ball. [18th c.: orig. unkn.]

Tagalog /təgáalog/ *n.* & *adj.* ● *n.* **1** a member of the principal people of the Philippine Islands. **2** the language of this people. ● *adj.* of or relating to this people or language. [Tagalog f. *taga* native + *ilog* river]

tagetes /təjéeteez/ *n.* any plant of the genus *Tagetes*, esp. any of various marigolds with bright orange or yellow flowers. [mod.L f. L *Tages* an Etruscan god]

tagliatelle /tályətélli/ *n.* a form of pasta in narrow ribbons. [It.]

Tahitian /təhéesh'n/ *n.* & *adj.* ● *n.* **1** a native or national of Tahiti in the S. Pacific. **2** the language of Tahiti. ● *adj.* of or relating to Tahiti or its people or language.

tahr /taar/ *n.* any goatlike mammal of the genus *Hemitragus*, esp. *H. jemlahicus* of the Himalayas. [native name in Nepal]

tahsil /taaséel/ *n.* an administrative area in parts of India. [Urdu *taḥsīl* f. Arab., = collection]

t'ai chi ch'uan /tī chee chwáan/ *n.* (also **t'ai chi**) a Chinese martial art and system of callisthenics consisting of sequences of very slow controlled movements. [Chin., = great ultimate boxing]

Taig /tayg/ *n. sl. offens.* (in Northern Ireland) a Protestant name for a Catholic. [var. of *Teague*, Anglicized spelling of the Irish name *Tadhg*, a nickname for an Irishman]

taiga /tīgə/ *n.* coniferous forest lying between tundra and steppe, esp. in Siberia. [Russ.]

tail[1] /tayl/ *n.* & *v.* ● *n.* **1** the hindmost part of an animal, esp. when prolonged beyond the rest of the body. **2 a** a thing like a tail in form or position, esp. something extending downwards or outwards at an extremity. **b** the rear end of anything, e.g. of a procession. **c** a long train or line of people, vehicles, etc. **3 a** the rear part of an aeroplane, with the tailplane and rudder, or of a rocket. **b** the rear part of a motor vehicle. **4** the luminous trail of particles following a comet. **5 a** the inferior or weaker part of anything, esp. in a sequence. **b** *Cricket* the end of the batting order, with the weakest batsmen. **6 a** the part of a shirt below the waist. **b** the hanging part of the back of a coat. **7** (in *pl.*) *colloq.* **a** a tailcoat. **b** evening dress including this. **8** (in *pl.*) the reverse of a coin as a choice when tossing. **9** *colloq.* a person following or shadowing another. **10** an extra strip attached to the lower end of a kite. **11** the stem of a note in music. **12** the part of a letter (e.g. *y*) below the line. **13 a** the exposed end of a slate or tile in a roof. **b** the unexposed end of a brick or stone in a wall. **14** the slender backward prolongation of a butterfly's wing. **15** a comparative calm at the end of a gale. **16** a calm stretch following rough water in a stream. ● *v.* **1** *tr.* remove the stalks of (fruit). **2** *tr.* & (foll. by *after*) *intr. colloq.* shadow or follow closely. **3** *tr.* provide with a tail. **4** *tr.* dock the tail of (a lamb etc.). **5** *tr.* (often foll. by *on to*) join (one thing to another). □ **on a person's tail** closely following a person. **tail back** (of traffic) form a tailback. **tail covert** any of the feathers covering the base of a bird's tail feathers. **tail-end 1** the hindmost or lowest or last part. **2** (sense 5 of the *n.*). **tail-ender** a person at the tail-end of something, esp. in cricket and athletic races. **tail in** fasten (timber) by one end into a wall etc. **tail-light** (or **-lamp**) *US* a light at the rear of a train, motor vehicle, or bicycle. **tail off** (or **away**) **1** become fewer, smaller, or slighter. **2** fall behind or away in a scattered line. **tail-off** *n.* a decline or gradual reduction, esp. in demand. **tail-race** the part of a mill-race below the water-wheel. **tail-skid** a support for the tail of an aircraft when on the ground. **tail wind** a wind blowing in the direction of travel of a vehicle or aircraft etc. **with one's tail between one's legs** in a state of dejection or humiliation. **with one's tail up** in good spirits; cheerful. □□ **tailed** *adj.* (also in *comb.*). **tailless** *adj.* [OE *tægl*, *tægel* f. Gmc]

■ *n.* **1** appendage, brush (*of a fox*), scut (*of a hare, rabbit*, or *deer*), dock, caudal fin (*of a fish*), uropygium (*of a bird*), parson's nose, tailpiece, tag; tail-end, buttocks, seat, croup, rump, posterior(s), *colloq.* backside, bottom, behind, rear (end), *Brit. sl.* bum. **2 b** see REAR[1] *n.* 1. **c** see QUEUE *n.* 1. **3** rear, back. **5** tail-end, bottom, *esp. US* tag end, *Brit. sl.* fag-end. **8** (*tails*) reverse. ● *v.* **2** dog, follow, pursue, trail, stalk, shadow, track. □ **tail-end 1** see REAR[1] *n.* 1. **tail off** (or **away**) **1** see DECLINE *v.* 1, 7. **tail-off** see DECREASE *n.*

tail[2] /tayl/ *n.* & *adj. Law* ● *n.* limitation of ownership, esp. of an estate limited to a person and that person's heirs. ● *adj.* so limited (*estate tail*; *fee tail*). □ **in tail** under such a limitation. [ME f. OF *taille* notch, cut, tax, f. *taillier* cut ult. f. L *talea* twig]

tailback /táylbak/ *n. Brit.* a long line of traffic extending back from an obstruction.

tailboard /táylbord/ *n.* a hinged or removable flap at the rear of a lorry etc.

tailcoat /táylkōt/ *n.* a man's morning or evening coat with a long skirt divided at the back into tails and cut away in front, worn as part of formal dress.

tailgate /táylgayt/ *n.* & *v.* ● *n.* **1** esp. *US* **a** = TAILBOARD. **b** the tail door of an estate car or hatchback. **2** the lower end of a canal lock. ● *v. US colloq.* **1** *intr.* drive too closely behind another vehicle. **2** *tr.* follow (a vehicle) too closely. □□ **tailgater** *n.*

tailie /táyli/ *n. Austral.* & *NZ* in two-up, one who bets on the coins falling tail upwards.

tailing /táyling/ *n.* **1** (in *pl.*) the refuse or inferior part of grain or ore etc. **2** the part of a beam or projecting brick etc. embedded in a wall.

tailor /táylər/ *n.* & *v.* ● *n.* a maker of clothes, esp. one who makes men's outer garments to measure. ● *v.* **1** *tr.* make (clothes) as a tailor. **2** *tr.* make or adapt for a special purpose. **3** *intr.* work as or be a tailor. **4** *tr.* (esp. as **tailored** *adj.*) make clothes for (*he was immaculately tailored*). **5** *tr.* (as **tailored** *adj.*) = *tailor-made*. □ **tailor-bird** any small Asian etc. bird of the genus *Orthotomus* that stitches leaves together to form a nest. **tailor-made** *adj.* **1** (of clothing) made to order by a tailor. **2** made or suited for a particular purpose (*a job tailor-made for me*). ● *n.* a tailor-made garment. **tailor's chair** a chair without legs for sitting cross-legged like a tailor at work. **tailor's twist** a fine strong silk thread used by tailors. □□ **tailoring** *n.* [ME & AF *taillour*, OF *tailleur* cutter, formed as TAIL[2]]

■ *n.* couturier, couturière, clothier, garment-maker, outfitter, costumier, costumer, seamstress, dressmaker, modiste. ● *v.* **2** fit, adapt, suit, adjust, alter, accommodate, gear, modify, change, convert, cut, fashion, mould, stretch. □ **tailor-made** (*adj.*) **1** fitted, tailored, custom-made, made to measure, made to order, bespoke. **2** ideal, perfect, customized, made to order, custom-made, suited, suitable, (just) right, *colloq.* (right) up one's street *or* alley.

tailored /táylərd/ *adj.* (of clothing) well or closely fitted.

tailpiece /táylpeess/ *n.* **1** an appendage at the rear of anything. **2** the final part of a thing. **3** a decoration in a blank space at the end of a chapter etc. in a book. **4** a piece of wood to which the strings of some musical instruments are attached at their lower ends.

tailpipe /táylpīp/ *n.* the rear section of the exhaust pipe of a motor vehicle.

tailplane /táylplayn/ *n.* a horizontal aerofoil at the tail of an aircraft.

tailspin /táylspin/ *n.* & *v.* ● *n.* **1** a spin (see SPIN *n.* 2) by an aircraft with the tail spiralling. **2** a state of chaos or panic. ● *v.intr.* (**-spinning**; *past* and *past part.* **-spun**) perform a tailspin.

tailstock /táylstok/ *n.* the adjustable part of a lathe holding the fixed spindle.

taint /taynt/ *n.* & *v.* ● *n.* **1** a spot or trace of decay, infection, or some bad quality. **2** a corrupt condition or infection. ● *v.* **1** *tr.* affect with a taint. **2** *tr.* (foll. by *with*) affect slightly. **3** *intr.* become tainted. □□ **taintless** *adj.* [ME, partly f. OF *teint(e)* f. L *tinctus* f. *tingere* dye, partly f. ATTAINT]

■ *n.* stain, blot, blemish, slur, tarnish, tinge, tincture, (black *or* bad) mark, stigma, imperfection, flaw, scar, defect; discredit, dishonour. ● *v.* **1** sully, tarnish, stain, stigmatize, smear, harm, hurt, damage, debase, vitiate, blacken, foul, contaminate, pollute, adulterate, dirty, muddy, smirch, besmirch, blemish, soil, corrupt, spoil, defile, ruin, destroy, infect, poison. **2** see TINT *v.*

taipan[1] /tīpan/ *n.* the head of a foreign business in China. [Chin.]

taipan[2] /tīpan/ *n.* a large venomous Australian snake, *Oxyuranus microlepidotus.* [Aboriginal]

taj /taaj/ *n.* a tall conical cap worn by a dervish. [Arab. *tāj*]

takahe /taákəhi/ *n.* = NOTORNIS. [Maori]

take /tayk/ *v.* & *n.* ● *v.* (**took** /tŏŏk/; **taken** /táykən/) **1** *tr.* lay hold of; get into one's hands. **2** *tr.* acquire, get possession of, capture, earn, or win. **3** *tr.* get the use of by purchase or formal agreement (*take lodgings*). **4** *tr.* (in a recipe) avail oneself of; use. **5** *tr.* use as a means of transport (*took a taxi*). **6** *tr.* regularly buy or subscribe to (a particular newspaper or periodical etc.). **7** *tr.* obtain after fulfilling the required conditions (*take a degree*). **8** *tr.* occupy (*take a chair*). **9** *tr.* make use of (*take precautions*). **10** *tr.* consume as food or medicine (*took tea; took the pills*). **11** *intr.* **a** be successful or effective (*the inoculation did not take*). **b** (of a plant, seed, etc.) begin to grow. **12** *tr.* **a** require or use up (*will only take a minute; these things take time*). **b** accommodate, have room for (*the lift takes three people*). **13** *tr.* cause to come or go with one; convey (*take the book home; the bus will take you all the way*). **14** *tr.* **a** remove; dispossess a person of (*someone has taken my pen*). **b** destroy, annihilate (*took her own life*). **c** (often foll. by *for*) *sl.* defraud, swindle. **15** *tr.* catch or be infected with (fire or fever etc.). **16** *tr.* **a** experience or be affected by (*take fright; take pleasure*). **b** give play to (*take comfort*). **c** exert (*take courage; take no notice*). **d** exact, get (*take revenge*). **17** *tr.* find out and note (a name and address; a person's temperature etc.) by enquiry or measurement. **18** *tr.* grasp mentally; understand (*I take your point; I took you to mean yes*). **19** *tr.* treat or regard in a specified way (*took the news calmly; took it badly*). **20** *tr.* (foll. by *for* or *to be*) regard as being (*do you take me for an idiot?*). **21** *tr.* **a** accept (*take the offer*). **b** submit to (*take a joke; take no nonsense; took a risk*). **22** *tr.* choose or assume (*took a different view; took a job; took the initiative; took responsibility*). **23** *tr.* derive (*takes its name from the inventor*). **24** *tr.* (foll. by *from*) subtract (*take 3 from 9*). **25** *tr.* execute, make, or undertake; perform or effect (*take notes; take an oath; take a decision; take a look*). **26** *tr.* occupy or engage oneself in; indulge in; enjoy (*take a rest; take exercise; take a holiday*). **27** *tr.* conduct (*took the school assembly*). **28** *tr.* deal with in a certain way (*took the corner too fast*). **29** *tr.* **a** teach or be taught (a subject). **b** be examined in (a subject). **30** *tr.* make (a photograph) with a camera; photograph (a person or thing). **31** *tr.* use as an instance (*let us take Napoleon*). **32** *tr. Gram.* have or require as part of the appropriate construction (*this verb takes an object*). **33** *tr.* have sexual intercourse with (a woman). **34** *tr.* (in *passive*; foll. by *by*, *with*) be attracted or charmed by. ● *n.* **1** an amount taken or caught in one session or attempt etc. **2** a scene or sequence of film photographed continuously at one time. **3** esp. *US* takings, esp. money received at a theatre for seats. **4** *Printing* the amount of copy set up at one time. □ **be taken ill** become ill, esp. suddenly. **have what it takes** *colloq.* have the necessary qualities etc. for success. **take account of** see ACCOUNT. **take action** see ACTION. **take advantage of** see ADVANTAGE. **take advice** see ADVICE. **take after** resemble (esp. a parent or ancestor). **take against** begin to dislike, esp. impulsively. **take aim** see AIM. **take apart 1** dismantle. **2** *colloq.* beat or defeat. **take aside** see ASIDE. **take as read** accept without reading or discussing. **take away 1** remove or carry elsewhere. **2** subtract. **3** *Brit.* buy (food etc.) at a shop or restaurant for eating elsewhere. **take-away** *Brit. attrib.adj.* (of food) bought at a shop or restaurant for eating elsewhere. ● *n.* **1** an establishment selling this. **2** the food itself (*let's get a take-away*). **take back 1** retract (a statement). **2** convey (a person or thing) to his or her or its original position. **3** carry (a person) in thought to a past time. **4** *Printing* transfer to the previous line. **take the biscuit** (or **bun** or **cake**) *colloq.* be the most remarkable. **take a bow** see BOW[2]. **take care of** see CARE. **take a chance** etc. see CHANCE. **take down 1** write down (spoken words). **2** remove (a structure) by separating it into pieces. **3** humiliate. **take effect** see EFFECT. **take for granted** see GRANT. **take fright** see FRIGHT. **take from** diminish; weaken; detract from. **take heart** be encouraged. **take hold** see HOLD[1]. **take home** earn. **take-home pay** the pay received by an employee after the deduction of tax etc. **take ill** (*US* **sick**) *colloq.* be taken ill. **take in 1** receive as a lodger etc. **2** undertake (work) at home. **3** make (a garment etc.) smaller. **4** understand (*did you take that in?*). **5** cheat (*managed to take them all in*). **6** include or comprise. **7** *colloq.* visit (a place) on the way to another (*shall we take in Avebury?*). **8** furl (a sail). **9** *Brit.* regularly buy (a newspaper etc.). **take-in** *n.* a deception. **take in hand 1** undertake; start doing or dealing with. **2** undertake the control or reform of (a person). **take into account** see ACCOUNT. **take it 1** (often foll. by *that* + clause) assume (*I take it that you have finished*). **2** see TAKE *v.* 19. **take it easy** see EASY. **take it from me** (or **take my word for it**) I can assure you. **take it ill** resent it. **take it into one's head** see HEAD. **take it on one** (or **oneself**) (foll. by *to* + infin.) venture or presume. **take it or leave it** (esp. in *imper.*) an expression of indifference or impatience about another's decision after making an offer. **take it out of 1** exhaust the strength of. **2** have revenge on. **take it out on** relieve one's frustration by attacking or treating harshly. **take one's leave of** see LEAVE[2]. **take a lot of** (or **some**) **doing** be hard to do. **take a person's name in vain** see VAIN. **take off 1 a** remove (clothing) from one's or another's body. **b** remove or lead away. **2** deduct (part of an amount). **3** depart, esp. hastily (*took off in a fast car*). **4** *colloq.* mimic humorously. **5** jump from the ground. **6** become airborne. **7** (of a scheme, enterprise, etc.) become successful or popular. **8** have (a period) away from work. **take-off 1** the act of becoming airborne. **2** *colloq.* an act of mimicking. **3** a place from which one jumps. **take oneself off** go away. **take on 1** undertake (work, a responsibility, etc.). **2** engage (an employee). **3** be willing or ready to meet (an adversary in sport, argument, etc., esp. a stronger one). **4** acquire (a new meaning etc.). **5** *colloq.* show strong emotion. **take orders** see ORDER. **take out 1** remove from within a place; extract. **2** escort on an outing. **3** get (a licence or summons etc.) issued. **4** *US* = *take away* 3. **5** *Bridge* remove (a partner or a partner's call) from a suit by bidding a different one or no trumps. **6** murder or destroy. **take a person out of himself** or **herself** make a person forget his or her worries. **take over 1** succeed to the management or ownership of. **2** take control. **3** *Printing* transfer to the next line. **take-over** *n.* the assumption of control (esp. of a business); the buying-out of one company by another. **take part** see PART. **take place** see PLACE. **take a person's point** see POINT. **take shape** assume a distinct form; develop into something definite. **take sides** see SIDE. **take stock** see STOCK. **take the sun** see SUN. **take that!** an exclamation accompanying a blow etc. **take one's time** not hurry. **take to 1** begin or fall into the habit of (*took to smoking*). **2** have recourse to. **3** adapt oneself to. **4** form a liking for. **5** make for (*took to the hills*). **take to heart** see HEART. **take to one's heels** see HEEL[1]. **take to pieces** see PIECE. **take the trouble** see TROUBLE. **take up 1** become interested or engaged in (a pursuit, a cause, etc.). **2** adopt as a protégé. **3** occupy (time or space). **4** begin (residence etc.). **5** resume after an interruption. **6** interrupt or question (a speaker). **7** accept (an offer etc.). **8** shorten (a garment). **9** lift up. **10** absorb (*sponges take up water*). **11** take (a person) into a vehicle. **12** pursue (a matter etc.) further. **take a person up on** accept (a person's offer etc.). **take up with** begin to associate with. □□ **takable** *adj.* (also **takeable**). [OE *tacan* f. ON *taka*]

■ *v.* **1** grip, seize, grasp, clasp, get, get *or* take hold of, hold, grab, snatch, clutch, pluck, lay hold of, lay hands on, *sl.* nab. **2** obtain, procure, acquire, get, gain (possession of), take possession of, lay one's hands on, carry off, capture, catch, abduct; earn, secure, win. **3** reserve, book, engage, get the use of; hire, rent, lease, borrow. **5** catch, use, travel by; get on(to) *or* in(to), board. **6** buy, subscribe to, get, *Brit.* take in. **9** use, employ, make use of, establish, put in(to) place, adopt, put into effect, apply; resort to, have recourse to, turn to. **10** swallow, eat, consume, ingest, devour, gulp down, gobble up *or* down, wolf, bolt; drink, imbibe, *literary* quaff; inhale. **11 a** prove *or* be effective, prove *or* be efficacious, take effect, take hold, operate, function, work, *colloq.* do the trick. **b** strike, take root, germinate. **12 a** require, demand, need, necessitate, call for; use up, consume. **b** hold, contain, accommodate, have room for, accept, fit in. **13** conduct, escort, lead, convoy, guide, accompany; carry, convey, bear, transport, run, bring, deliver, ferry, haul, cart. **14 a** appropriate, carry off *or* away, steal, pilfer, filch, palm, pocket, remove, walk off *or* away with, run off *or* away with, make off *or* away with, help oneself to, dispossess a person of; embezzle, misappropriate, peculate; plagiarize, pirate; *colloq.* lift, swipe, rip off, bag, snaffle, *euphem.* abstract, *formal or joc.* purloin, *sl.* knock off, hook, pinch, liberate, souvenir, snitch, nab, *Brit. sl.* nick. **b** end, terminate, annihilate, wipe out. **c** cheat, swindle, defraud, *sl.* bilk, con, fiddle. **16 a** experience, entertain, feel, be affected by; get, derive. **d** exact, extract, get. **18** understand, gather, interpret, perceive, apprehend, deduce, conclude, construe, infer, judge, assume, suppose, imagine, see, *formal* deem. **19** bear, accept, receive; treat, regard. **20** believe, think, judge, hold, feel, *formal* deem; (*take for*) assess as, consider (as), regard as, view as. **21 a** accept, take up, jump at. **b** accept, bear, withstand, stand, endure, weather, tolerate, abide, brave, go through, undergo, suffer, submit to, swallow, put up with, stomach, *colloq.* stick, *literary* brook. **22** pick, select, choose, opt for, settle *or* decide *or* fasten (up)on; assume, bear, undertake, adopt, arrogate (to oneself); acknowledge, accept. **23** acquire, get, adopt; derive, obtain, draw, receive, inherit. **24** subtract, deduct, remove, take away *or* off. **26** occupy *or* engage oneself in, partake of, have, experience, indulge in, enjoy. **27** conduct, lead, direct, preside over, chair. **28** clear, get over *or* past *or* round *or* through, go over *or* past *or* round *or* through; negotiate. **29 a** teach; take up, study, be involved in *or* with, be occupied in *or* with, apply oneself to, learn, have lessons in; read, tackle. **30** see PHOTOGRAPH *v.* **34** (*be taken*) be captivated, be entranced, be enchanted, be attracted, be charmed, be bewitched, be infatuated. ● *n.* **3** revenue, takings, yield, return, receipts, proceeds, gain, profit(s); gate(-money). □ **take after** resemble, look like, be the spitting image *or* spit and image of, favour, remind a person of. **take apart 1** see *knock down* 5. **take as read** see SUPPOSE 1. **take away 1** see CONFISCATE, REMOVE *v.* 2a. **2** see SUBTRACT. **take back 1** retract, withdraw, recant, disavow, repudiate, rescind. **2** see RETURN *v.* 2. **take down 1** note, make a note *or* memo *or* memorandum of, write down, record, put *or* set down, put in writing, document, transcribe, chronicle. **2** see *knock down* 5. **3** debase, deflate, lower, diminish, belittle, depreciate, deprecate, humble, humiliate, shame, disparage, degrade, disgrace. **take from** see DETRACT. **take home** see EARN 1. **take-home pay** see PAY[1] *n.* **take ill** see SICKEN 2a. **take in 1** accommodate, receive, let in, quarter, billet, board, lodge, house, put up. **4** see COMPREHEND 1. **5** deceive, fool, trick, impose upon, overcharge, cheat, mulct, defraud, dupe, gull, mislead, hoax, hoodwink, swindle, pull the wool over a person's eyes, *colloq.* bamboozle, *literary* cozen, *sl.* bilk, con, do. **6** include, subsume, embrace, comprise, cover, encompass, contain, incorporate. **7** see VISIT *v.* 1. **9** see TAKE *v.* 6 above. **take it 1** see SUPPOSE 1. **take it out of 1** see EXHAUST *v.* 2. **take off 1 a** remove, strip *or* peel off, discard, shed, divest (oneself) of, *literary* doff. **2** see DEDUCT. **3** depart, leave, go (away), decamp, flee; *colloq.* skedaddle, make oneself scarce, scram, *sl.* beat it, split, hit the road *or US* trail. **4** satirize, lampoon, caricature, mock, parody, travesty, burlesque, mimic, imitate, *colloq.* spoof, *Brit. colloq.* send up. **6** fly (off), become airborne, take to the air, take wing, lift off, blast off. **take-off 1** launch, lift-off, blast-off, taking off, departure, leaving, going; flight, flying. **2** satire, lampoon, caricature, mockery, parody, travesty, burlesque, imitation, *colloq.* spoof, *Brit. colloq.* send-up. **take on 1** assume, accept, undertake, tackle; shoulder, carry. **2** hire, engage, employ, enrol, enlist, sign up, retain, appoint, recruit. **3** challenge, face, contend with, oppose, match *or* pit oneself against, vie with, fight. **5** see SEETHE 2. **take out 1** see EXTRACT *v.* 1. **2** entertain, escort, invite out; court, woo. **6** see MURDER *v.* 1. **take over 1** seize, arrogate (to oneself), assume, assume control *or* possession *or* command of, take control *or* possession *or* command of, usurp control *or* possession *or* command of, take, usurp, gain control *or* possession *or* command of. **take-over** buy-out, *esp. US* leveraged buyout; see also OCCUPATION 4a. **take shape** see JELL 1. **take one's time** dawdle, dilly-dally, delay, linger, loiter. **take to 2** see RESORT *v.* 1. **4** like, find pleasant *or* pleasing, feel affection *or* liking for, find suitable, *disp.* feel affinity for. **5** leave for, depart for, take off for, run for, head for, flee to, make for. **take up 1** become interested *or* involved *or* engaged in; embark on, start, begin, *formal* commence; espouse, embrace, support, sponsor, advocate. **3** occupy, cover, use (up), consume, fill (up), eat up. **5** resume, carry on, continue, go on with, follow on with, pick up. **7** accept, agree to, acquiesce to, accede to. **9** raise (up), lift (up), pick up. **12** pursue, deal with, treat, consider, discuss, bring up, raise. **take up with** see FRATERNIZE.

taker /táykər/ *n.* **1** a person who takes a bet. **2** a person who accepts an offer.

takin /taákin/ *n.* a large Tibetan horned ruminant, *Budorcas taxicolor.* [Mishmi]

taking /táyking/ *adj.* & *n.* ● *adj.* **1** attractive or captivating. **2** catching or infectious. ● *n.* (in *pl.*) an amount of money taken in business. ▫▫ **takingly** *adv.* **takingness** *n.*
■ *adj.* **1** attractive, alluring, engaging, captivating, winning, winsome, charming, entrancing, enchanting, bewitching, fetching, fascinating, delightful, irresistible, compelling, intriguing, prepossessing. **2** see INFECTIOUS 2, 3. ● *n.* (*takings*) see REVENUE.

tala /taálə/ *n.* any of the traditional rhythmic patterns of Indian music. [Skr.]

talapoin /tálləpoyn/ *n.* **1** a Buddhist monk or priest. **2** a small West African monkey, *Miopithecus talapoin.* [Port. *talapão* f. Talaing *tala pói* my lord]

talaria /təláiriə/ *n.pl.* (in Roman mythology) winged sandals as an attribute of Mercury, Iris, and others. [L, neut. pl. of *talaris* f. *talus* ankle]

talc /talk/ *n.* & *v.* ● *n.* **1** talcum powder. **2** any crystalline form of magnesium silicate that occurs in soft flat plates, usu. white or pale green in colour and used as a lubricator etc. ● *v.tr.* (**talcked, talcking**) treat (a surface) with talc to lubricate or dry it. ▫▫ **talcose** *adj.* **talcous** *adj.* **talcy** *adj.* (in sense 1). [F *talc* or med.L *talcum*, f. Arab. *ṭalḳ* f. Pers. *ṭalḳ*]

talcum /tálkəm/ *n.* **1** = TALC. **2** (in full **talcum powder**) powdered talc for toilet and cosmetic use, usu. perfumed. [med.L: see TALC]

tale /tayl/ *n.* **1** a narrative or story, esp. fictitious and imaginatively treated. **2** a report of an alleged fact, often malicious or in breach of confidence (*all sorts of tales will get about*). **3** *archaic* or *literary* a number or total (*the tale is complete*). ▫ **tale of a tub** an idle fiction. [OE *talu* f. Gmc: cf. TELL[1]]
■ **1** story, narrative, report, account, record, chronicle, history, saga, narration, recital, anecdote, myth, legend, romance, fable; fiction, fabrication, fairy story *or* tale, tale of a tub, shaggy-dog story, cock-and-bull story, *colloq.* yarn, tall tale *or* story, *sl.* fishy story, *Austral. sl.* furphy. **2** rumour, gossip, slander, allegation, tittle-tattle, libel, story, *colloq.* scuttlebutt, *Austral. sl.* furphy; see also LIE[2] *n.*

talebearer /táylbairər/ *n.* a person who maliciously gossips or reveals secrets. ▫▫ **talebearing** *n.* & *adj.*
■ gossip, rumour-monger, gossip-monger, taleteller, scandalmonger, newsmonger, tell-tale, tattler, informer, stool-pigeon, rat, blabbermouth, *US* tattle-tale, *archaic* quidnunc, *colloq.* big-mouth, *sl.* squealer, *Brit. sl.* nark, *Brit. school sl.* sneak, *esp. US sl.* ratfink, *US sl.* fink, stoolie.

talent /tállənt/ *n.* **1** a special aptitude or faculty (*a talent for music*; *has real talent*). **2** high mental ability. **3 a** a person or persons of talent (*is a real talent*; *plenty of local talent*). **b** *colloq.* members of the opposite sex regarded in terms of sexual promise. **4** an ancient weight and unit of currency, esp. among the Greeks. ▫ **talent-scout** (or **-spotter**) a person looking for talented performers, esp. in sport and entertainment. ▫▫ **talented** *adj.* **talentless** *adj.* [OE *talente* & OF *talent* f. L *talentum* inclination of mind f. Gk *talanton* balance, weight, sum of money]
■ **1** ability, power, gift, faculty, flair, genius, brilliance, facility, aptitude, capacity, knack, ingenuity, expertise, forte, strength; endowment; see also BENT[1] *n.* 2. **3 a** see VIRTUOSO 1a. ▫▫ **talented** gifted, accomplished, brilliant, skilled, skilful, masterful, expert, adept, adroit, dexterous, deft, clever, good, polished, proficient, first-rate, excellent, *colloq.* crack, top-notch, top-drawer, *sl.* ace, *sl. esp. Brit.* wizard, *US sl.* crackerjack.

tales /táyleez/ *n. Law* **1** a writ for summoning jurors to supply a deficiency. **2** a list of persons who may be summoned. [ME f. L *tales* (*de circumstantibus*) such (of the bystanders), the first words of the writ]

talesman /táyleezmən, táylz-/ *n.* (*pl.* **-men**) *Law* a person summoned by a *tales.*

taleteller /táyltellər/ *n.* **1** a person who tells stories. **2** a person who spreads malicious reports.

tali *pl.* of TALUS[1].

talion /tálliən/ *n.* = LEX TALIONIS. [ME f. OF f. L *talio -onis* f. *talis* such]

talipes /tállipeez/ *n. Med.* = *club-foot.* [mod.L f. L *talus* ankle + *pes* foot]

talipot /tállipot/ *n.* a tall S. Indian palm, *Corypha umbraculifera*, with very large fan-shaped leaves that are used as sunshades etc. [Malayalam *tālipat*, Hindi *tālpāt* f. Skr. *tālapattra* f. *tāla* palm + *pattra* leaf]

talisman /tállizmən/ *n.* (*pl.* **talismans**) **1** an object, esp. an inscribed ring or stone, supposed to be endowed with magic powers esp. of averting evil from or bringing good luck to its holder. **2** a charm or amulet; a thing supposed capable of working wonders. ▫▫ **talismanic** /-mánnik/ *adj.* [F & Sp., = It. *talismano*, f. med.Gk *telesmon*, Gk *telesma* completion, religious rite f. *teleō* complete f. *telos* end]
■ amulet, charm, fetish, ju-ju, periapt, mascot; wishbone, rabbit's foot, *esp. Brit.* merry thought, *NZ* tiki.

talk /tawk/ *v.* & *n.* ● *v.* **1** *intr.* (often foll. by *to*, *with*) converse or communicate ideas by spoken words. **2** *intr.* have the power of speech. **3** *intr.* (foll. by *about*) **a** have as the subject of discussion. **b** (in *imper.*) *colloq.* as an emphatic statement (*talk about expense! It cost me £50*). **4** *tr.* express or utter in words; discuss (*you are talking nonsense*; *talked cricket all day*). **5** *tr.* use (a language) in speech (*is talking Spanish*). **6** *intr.* (foll. by *at*) address pompously. **7** *tr.* (usu. foll. by *into*, *out of*) bring into a specified condition etc. by talking (*talked himself hoarse*; *how did you talk them into it?*; *talked them out of the difficulty*). **8** *intr.* reveal (esp. secret) information; betray secrets. **9** *intr.* gossip (*people are beginning to talk*). **10** *intr.* have influence (*money talks*). **11** *intr.* communicate by radio. ● *n.* **1** conversation or talking. **2** a particular mode of speech (*baby-talk*). **3** an informal address or lecture. **4 a** rumour or gossip (*there is talk of a merger*). **b** its theme (*their success was the talk of the town*). **c** empty words, verbiage (*mere talk*). **5** (often in *pl.*) extended discussions or negotiations. ▫ **know what one is talking about** be expert or authoritative. **now you're talking** *colloq.* I like what you say, suggest, etc. **talk away 1** consume (time) in talking. **2** carry on talking (*talk away! I'm listening*). **talk back 1** reply defiantly. **2** respond on a two-way radio system. **talk big** *colloq.* talk boastfully. **talk down** denigrate, belittle. **talk down to** speak patronizingly or condescendingly to. **talk a person down 1** silence a person by greater loudness or persistence. **2** bring (a pilot or aircraft) to landing by radio instructions from the ground. **talk the hind leg off a donkey** talk incessantly. **talk nineteen to the dozen** see DOZEN. **talk of 1** discuss or mention. **2** (often foll. by verbal noun) express some intention of (*talked of moving to London*). **talk of the town** what is being talked about generally. **talk out** *Brit.* block the course of (a bill in Parliament) by prolonging discussion to the time of adjournment. **talk over** discuss at length. **talk a person over** (or **round**) gain agreement or compliance from a person by talking. **talk shop** talk, esp. tediously or inopportunely, about one's occupation, business, etc. **talk show** = *chat show* (see CHAT[1]). **talk tall** boast. **talk through one's hat** (or **neck**) *colloq.* **1** exaggerate. **2** bluff. **3** talk wildly or nonsensically. **talk to** reprove or scold (a person). **talk to oneself** soliloquize. **talk turkey** see TURKEY. **talk up** discuss (a subject) in order to arouse interest in it. **you can't** (or **can**) **talk** *colloq.* a reproof that the person addressed is just as culpable etc. in the matter at issue. ▫▫ **talker** *n.* [ME *talken* frequent. verb f. TALE or TELL[1]]
■ *v.* **1, 3a** speak, give *or* deliver a speech, give *or* deliver a talk, give *or* deliver an address, lecture; converse, communicate, confer, consult, parley, negotiate, have a (little) talk, (have a) chat, confabulate; chatter, prate, prattle, jabber, blather, blether, gibber, gabble, cackle, babble, patter, rattle on, gossip, palaver, *Austral.* & *NZ colloq.* yabber; *US* have a bull session, *colloq.* confab, gab, gas, jaw, natter, go on, witter (on), *Brit. colloq.* rabbit (on), *sl.* rap, chin-wag, chew the fat *or* rag.

2 speak, communicate, vocalize. **4** see DISCUSS 1, SPEAK 2. **5** talk in, speak in, use, communicate in, converse in, express oneself in, discourse in. **7** (*talk into*) convince that, bring round to, persuade to, argue into, prevail (up)on to; (*talk out of*) discourage from, dissuade from, deter from, put off from, divert from, argue out of. **8** confess, give the game away, tell, *colloq.* come clean, spill the beans, rat, *sl.* squeal, sing, *Brit. sl.* grass. **9** see GOSSIP *v.* ● *n.* **1** conversation, conference, discussion, meeting, consultation, dialogue, colloquy, parley, chat, tête-à-tête, powwow, confabulation, *literary* discourse; palaver, gossip, claptrap, patter, prattle, prattling, chatter, verbiage, cackle; *colloq.* confab, chit-chat, *Austral.* & *NZ colloq.* yabber, *sl.* chin-wag, rap session. **2** dialect, speech, way *or* manner of speaking, language, jargon, argot, cant, patois, accent, *colloq.* lingo. **3** oration, lecture, address, presentation, speech, report, disquisition, dissertation, *literary* discourse; sermon; harangue, tirade, *sl.* spiel. **4 a** gossip, rumour, hearsay, news, report. **b** subject *or* topic of conversation, subject *or* topic of gossip, subject *or* topic of rumour, information, news, *colloq.* info, *sl.* dope, *Brit. sl.* gen. **c** empty words, palaver, gossip, claptrap, prattle, prattling, chatter, verbiage, cackle, bunkum, nonsense, rubbish, balderdash, stuff and nonsense, twaddle, *colloq.* malarkey, piffle, tosh, tripe, hogwash, *sl.* bunk, bilge(-water), bull, guff, hot air, bosh, poppycock, hooey, *esp. US sl.* hokum. **5** see *negotiation* (NEGOTIATE). □ **talk back 1** answer back. **talk big** boast, brag, crow, bluster, exaggerate, blow one's own trumpet, *colloq.* swank, show off, *Austral.* & *NZ colloq.* skite, *US* & *Austral. colloq.* blow, *literary* vaunt. **talk down** depreciate, deprecate, denigrate, disparage, belittle, minimize, diminish, criticize, *colloq.* knock, pan, put down. **talk down to** condescend to, patronize. **talk of 1** see DISCUSS 1, MENTION *v.* 1, 2. **talk over** see DISCUSS 1. **talk a person over** (or **round**) see *win over*. **talk to** see SPEAK 4c. **talk up** promote, support, sponsor, advertise, publicize, push, *colloq.* plug, *sl.* hype. □□ **talker** speaker, lecturer, orator, speech-maker, spellbinder, rabble-rouser, demagogue, haranguer, ranter; blusterer, blatherskite, swaggerer, show-off, *colloq.* tub-thumper, windbag, blowhard, *sl.* gasbag, lot of hot air, *esp. US sl.* spieler.

talkathon /táwkəthon/ *n. colloq.* a prolonged session of talking or discussion. [TALK + MARATHON]

talkative /táwkətiv/ *adj.* fond of or given to talking. □□ **talkatively** *adv.* **talkativeness** *n.*
■ garrulous, loquacious, verbose, long-winded, voluble, prolix, wordy, chatty, gossipy, effusive, expansive, communicative, forthcoming, logorrhoeic, *colloq.* gabby, windy.

talkback /táwkbak/ *n.* **1** (often *attrib.*) a system of two-way communication by loudspeaker. **2** *Austral.* & *NZ* = *phone-in* (see PHONE[1]).

talkie /táwki/ *n.* esp. *US colloq.* a film with a soundtrack, as distinct from a silent film. [TALK + -IE, after *movie*]

talking /táwking/ *adj.* & *n.* ● *adj.* **1** that talks. **2** having the power of speech (*a talking parrot*). **3** expressive (*talking eyes*). ● *n.* in senses of TALK *v.* □ **talking book** a recorded reading of a book, esp. for the blind. **talking film** (or **picture**) a film with a soundtrack. **talking head** *colloq.* a presenter etc. on television, speaking to the camera and viewed in close-up. **talking of** while we are discussing (*talking of food, what time is lunch?*). **talking-point** a topic for discussion or argument. **talking-shop** *derog.* an institution regarded as a place of argument rather than action. **talking-to** *colloq.* a reproof or reprimand (*gave them a good talking-to*).

tall /tawl/ *adj.* & *adv.* ● *adj.* **1** of more than average height. **2** of a specified height (*looks about six feet tall*). **3** higher than the surrounding objects (*a tall building*). **4** *colloq.* extravagant or excessive (*a tall story*; *tall talk*). ● *adv.* as if tall; proudly; in a tall or extravagant way (*sit tall*). □ **tall drink** a drink served in a tall glass. **tall hat** = *top hat* (see TOP[1]). **tall order** an exorbitant or unreasonable demand. **tall ship** a sailing ship with a high mast. □□ **tallish** *adj.* **tallness** *n.* [ME, repr. OE *getæl* swift, prompt]
■ *adj.* **1** lanky, gangling, rangy, leggy, long-legged, *colloq.* long; big, giant, huge, gigantic, large. **3** high, towering, big, soaring, giant, gigantic, *literary* lofty; multi-storey. **4** exaggerated, overblown, far-fetched, improbable, unbelievable, incredible, preposterous, outrageous, extravagant, excessive, overdone, absurd, *colloq.* steep. □□ **tallness** height, size.

tallage /tállij/ *n. hist.* **1** a form of taxation on towns etc., abolished in the 14th c. **2** a tax on feudal dependants etc. [ME f. OF *taillage* f. *tailler* cut: see TAIL[2]]

tallboy /táwlboy/ *n.* a tall chest of drawers sometimes in lower and upper sections or mounted on legs.
■ see *chest of drawers*.

tallith /tállith/ *n.* a scarf worn by Jewish men esp. at prayer. [Rabbinical Heb. *ṭallīt* f. *ṭillel* to cover]

tallow /tállō/ *n.* & *v.* ● *n.* the harder kinds of (esp. animal) fat melted down for use in making candles, soap, etc. ● *v.tr.* grease with tallow. □ **tallow-tree** any of various trees, esp. *Sapium sebiferum* of China, yielding vegetable tallow. **vegetable tallow** a vegetable fat used as tallow. □□ **tallowish** *adj.* **tallowy** *adj.* [ME *talg*, *talug*, f. MLG *talg*, *talch*, of unkn. orig.]

tally /tálli/ *n.* & *v.* ● *n.* (*pl.* **-ies**) **1** the reckoning of a debt or score. **2** a total score or amount. **3 a** a mark registering a fixed number of objects delivered or received. **b** such a number as a unit. **4** *hist.* **a** a piece of wood scored across with notches for the items of an account and then split into halves, each party keeping one. **b** an account kept in this way. **5** a ticket or label for identification. **6** a corresponding thing, counterpart, or duplicate. ● *v.* (**-ies**, **-ied**) (often foll. by *with*) **1** *intr.* agree or correspond. **2** *tr.* record or reckon by tally. □ **tally clerk** an official who keeps a tally of goods, esp. those loaded or unloaded in docks. **tally sheet** a paper on which a tally is kept. **tally system** a system of sale on short credit or instalments with an account kept by tally. □□ **tallier** *n.* [ME f. AF *tallie*, AL *tallia*, *talia* f. L *talea*: cf. TAIL[2]]
■ *n.* **1** reckoning, count, enumeration, record, account, register, addition, tabulation, itemization, listing, calculation, computation. **2** total, sum, score. **5** ticket, label, mark, marker, tag, tab. **6** counterfoil, stub, counterpart, duplicate, mate. ● *v.* **1** agree, coincide, accord, correspond, fit, compare, match (up), square, conform, concur, harmonize, *US colloq.* jibe. **2** tally up, count (up *or* out), enumerate, record, register, reckon, add (up), total (up), tot (up), tabulate, itemize, list, calculate, compute.

tally-ho /tállihṓ/ *int.*, *n.*, & *v.* ● *int.* a huntsman's cry to the hounds on sighting a fox. ● *n.* (*pl.* **-hos**) an utterance of this. ● *v.* (**-hoes**, **-hoed**) **1** *intr.* utter a cry of 'tally-ho'. **2** *tr.* indicate (a fox) or urge (hounds) with this cry. [cf. F *taïaut*]

tallyman /tállimən/ *n.* (*pl.* **-men**) **1** a person who keeps a tally. **2** a person who sells goods on credit, esp. from door to door.

Talmud /tálmo͝od, -məd/ *n.* the body of Jewish civil and ceremonial law and legend comprising the Mishnah and the Gemara. □□ **Talmudic** /-mo͝oddik/ *adj.* **Talmudical** /-mo͝oddik'l/ *adj.* **Talmudist** *n.* [late Heb. *talmûḏ* instruction f. Heb. *lāmaḏ* learn]

talon /tállən/ *n.* **1** a claw, esp. of a bird of prey. **2** the cards left after the deal in a card-game. **3** the last part of a dividend-coupon sheet, entitling the holder to a new sheet on presentation. **4** the shoulder of a bolt against which the key presses in shooting it in a lock. **5** an ogee moulding. □□ **taloned** *adj.* (also in *comb.*). [ME f. OF, = heel, ult. f. L *talus*: see TALUS[1]]

talus[1] /táyləss/ *n.* (*pl.* **tali** /-lī/) *Anat.* the ankle-bone supporting the tibia. Also called ASTRAGALUS. [L, = ankle, heel]

talus[2] /táylǝss/ *n.* (*pl.* **taluses**) **1** the slope of a wall that tapers to the top or rests against a bank. **2** *Geol.* a sloping mass of fragments at the foot of a cliff. [F: orig. unkn.]

TAM *abbr.* television audience measurement.

tam /tam/ *n.* a tam-o'-shanter. [abbr.]

tamable var. of TAMEABLE.

tamale /tǝmaáli/ *n.* a Mexican food of seasoned meat and maize flour steamed or baked in maize husks. [Mex. Sp. *tamal*, pl. *tamales*]

tamandua /tǝmándyooǝ/ *n.* any small Central and S. American arboreal anteater of the genus *Tamandua*, with a prehensile tail used in climbing . [Port. f. Tupi *tamanduà*]

tamarack /támmǝrak/ *n.* **1** an American larch, *Larix laricina*. **2** the wood from this. [Amer. Ind.]

tamarillo /támmǝríllō/ *n.* (*pl.* **-os**) esp. *Austral.* & *NZ* = *tree tomato*. [arbitrary marketing name: cf. Sp. *tomatillo* dimin. of *tomate* TOMATO]

tamarin /támmǝrin/ *n.* any S. American usu. insect-eating monkey of the genus *Saguinus*, having hairy crests and moustaches. [F f. Carib]

tamarind /támmǝrind/ *n.* **1** a tropical evergreen tree, *Tamarindus indica*. **2** the fruit of this, containing an acid pulp used as food and in making drinks. [med.L *tamarindus* f. Arab. *tamr-hindī* Indian date]

tamarisk /támmǝrisk/ *n.* any shrub of the genus *Tamarix*, usu. with long slender branches and small pink or white flowers, that thrives by the sea. [ME f. LL *tamariscus*, L *tamarix*]

tambour /támboor/ *n.* & *v.* ● *n.* **1** a drum. **2 a** a circular frame for holding fabric taut while it is being embroidered. **b** material embroidered in this way. **3** *Archit.* each of a sequence of cylindrical stones forming the shaft of a column. **4** *Archit.* the circular part of various structures. **5** *Archit.* a lobby with a ceiling and folding doors in a church porch etc. to obviate draughts. **6** a sloping buttress or projection in a fives-court etc. ● *v.tr.* (also *absol.*) decorate or embroider on a tambour. [F f. *tabour* TABOR]

tamboura /tambóorǝ/ *n. Mus.* an Indian stringed instrument used as a drone. [Arab. *ṭanbūra*]

tambourin /támbǝrin/ *n.* **1** a long narrow drum used in Provence. **2 a** a dance accompanied by a tambourin. **b** the music for this. [F, dimin. of TAMBOUR]

tambourine /támbǝréen/ *n.* a percussion instrument consisting of a hoop with a parchment stretched over one side and jingling discs in slots round the hoop. □□ **tambourinist** *n.* [F, dimin. of TAMBOUR]

tame /taym/ *adj.* & *v.* ● *adj.* **1** (of an animal) domesticated; not wild or shy. **2** insipid; lacking spirit or interest; dull (*tame acquiescence*). **3** (of a person) amenable and available. **4** *US* **a** (of land) cultivated. **b** (of a plant) produced by cultivation. ● *v.tr.* **1** make tame; domesticate; break in. **2** subdue, curb, humble; break the spirit of. □□ **tamely** *adv.* **tameness** *n.* **tamer** *n.* (also in *comb.*). [OE *tam* f. Gmc]

■ *adj.* **1** tamed, docile, disciplined, obedient, domesticated, house-broken, trained, broken, house-trained; mild, gentle, fearless, unafraid. **2** boring, tedious, tiresome, dull, insipid, bland, lifeless, flat, vapid, prosaic, humdrum, bland, unexciting, uninspired, uninspiring, run-of-the-mill, ordinary, uninteresting, dead, wishy-washy, *Brit.* dead-and-alive. **3** tractable, amenable, pliant, compliant, meek, submissive, passive, mild, under a person's control *or* thumb, subdued, suppressed; unassertive, ineffectual. ● *v.* **1** break, domesticate, train, gentle, master, subdue, subjugate. **2** calm, subdue, control, mollify, humble, pacify, mute, temper, soften, curb, tone down, moderate, mitigate, tranquillize.

tameable /táymǝb'l/ *adj.* (also **tamable**) capable of being tamed. □□ **tameability** /-bílliti/ *n.* **tameableness** *n.*

Tamil /támmil/ *n.* & *adj.* ● *n.* **1** a member of a Dravidian people inhabiting South India and Sri Lanka. **2** the language of this people. ● *adj.* of this people or their language. □□ **Tamilian** /-míllian/ *adj.* [native name *Tamiḻ*, rel. to DRAVIDIAN]

Tammany /támmǝni/ *n.* (also **Tammany Hall**) *US* **1** a corrupt political organization or group. **2** corrupt political activities. □□ **Tammanyism** *n.* [orig. the name of a benevolent society in New York with headquarters at Tammany Hall, which later became the headquarters of the Democratic Party in New York]

tammy /támmi/ *n.* (*pl.* **-ies**) = TAM-O'-SHANTER.

tam-o'-shanter /támmǝshántǝr/ *n.* a round woollen or cloth cap of Scottish origin fitting closely round the brows but large and full above. [the hero of Burns's *Tam o' Shanter*]

tamp /tamp/ *v.tr.* **1** pack (a blast-hole) full of clay etc. to get the full force of an explosion. **2** ram down (road material etc.). □□ **tamper** *n.* **tamping** *n.* (in sense 1). [perh. back-form. f. F *tampin* (var. of TAMPION, taken as = *tamping*]

tamper /támpǝr/ *v.intr.* (foll. by *with*) **1** meddle with or make unauthorized changes in. **2** exert a secret or corrupt influence upon; bribe. □□ **tamperer** *n.* **tamper-proof** *adj.* [var. of TEMPER]

■ **1** interfere, meddle, tinker, mess (about *or* around), fiddle *or* fool (about *or* around), monkey (around), *Brit. colloq.* muck (about); see also JUGGLE *v.* 3b.

tampion /támpiǝn/ *n.* (also **tompion** /tóm-/) **1** a wooden stopper for the muzzle of a gun. **2** a plug e.g. for the top of an organ-pipe. [ME f. F *tampon*, nasalized var. of *tapon*, rel. to TAP[1]]

tampon /támpon/ *n.* & *v.* ● *n.* a plug of soft material used to stop a wound or absorb secretions, esp. one inserted into the vagina. ● *v.tr.* (**tamponed**, **tamponing**) plug with a tampon. [F: see TAMPION]

tamponade /támpǝnáyd/ *n.* compression of the heart by an accumulation of fluid in the pericardial sac.

tamponage /támpǝnij/ *n.* = TAMPONADE.

tam-tam /támtam/ *n.* a large metal gong. [Hindi: see TOM-TOM]

tan[1] /tan/ *n.*, *adj.*, & *v.* ● *n.* **1** a brown skin colour resulting from exposure to ultraviolet light. **2** a yellowish-brown colour. **3** bark, esp. of oak, bruised and used to tan hides. **4** (in full **spent tan**) tan from which the tannic acid has been extracted, used for covering roads etc. ● *adj.* yellowish-brown. ● *v.* (**tanned**, **tanning**) **1** *tr.* & *intr.* make or become brown by exposure to ultraviolet light. **2** *tr.* convert (raw hide) into leather by soaking in a liquid containing tannic acid or by the use of mineral salts etc. **3** *tr. sl.* beat, thrash. □□ **tannable** *adj.* **tanning** *n.* **tannish** *adj.* [OE *tannian*, prob. f. med.L *tanare*, *tannare*, perh. f. Celtic]

■ *v.* **1** see SUN *v.* 2. **3** see BEAT *v.* 1. □□ **tanning** see *thrashing* (THRASH).

tan[2] /tan/ *abbr.* tangent.

tanager /tánnǝjǝr/ *n.* any small American bird of the subfamily Thraupinae, the male usu. having brightly-coloured plumage. [mod.L *tanagra* f. Tupi *tangara*]

tanbark /tánbaark/ *n.* the bark of oak and other trees, used to obtain tannin.

tandem /tándǝm/ *n.* & *adv.* ● *n.* **1** a bicycle or tricycle with two or more seats one behind another. **2** a group of two persons or machines etc. with one behind or following the other. **3** a carriage driven tandem. ● *adv.* with two or more horses harnessed one behind another (*drive tandem*). □ **in tandem** one behind another. [L, = at length (of time), used punningly]

tandoor /tándoor/ *n.* a clay oven. [Hind.]

tandoori /tandóori/ *n.* food cooked over charcoal in a tandoor (often *attrib.*: *tandoori chicken*). [Hind.]

Tang /tang/ *n.* **1** a dynasty ruling China 618–*c.*906. **2** (*attrib.*) designating art and artefacts of this period. [Chin. *táng*]

tang[1] /tang/ *n.* **1** a strong taste or flavour or smell. **2 a** a characteristic quality. **b** a trace; a slight hint of some quality, ingredient, etc. **3** the projection on the blade of a tool, esp. a knife, by which the blade is held firm in the handle. [ME f. ON *tange* point, tang of a knife]

■ **1** pungency, piquancy, bite, zest, zestiness, sharpness, poignancy, spiciness, nip, edge, spice, taste, flavour, savour, aroma, smell, odour, *colloq.* kick. **2 a** flavour, quality, character, feel, essence, smack, touch, taste. **b** tinge, hint, suggestion, suspicion, soupçon, trace, dab, smack, touch, smattering. **3** tab, projection, tongue, strip, shank, pin, spike.

tang[2] /tang/ *v.* & *n.* ● *v.tr.* & *intr.* ring, clang; sound loudly. ● *n.* a tanging sound. [imit.]

tanga /tánggə/ *n.* a skimpy bikini of small panels connected with strings. [Port.]

tangelo /tánjəlō/ *n.* (*pl.* **-os**) a hybrid of the tangerine and grapefruit. [TANGERINE + POMELO]

tangent /tánjənt/ *n.* & *adj.* ● *n.* **1** a straight line, curve, or surface that meets another curve or curved surface at a point, but if extended does not intersect it at that point. **2** the ratio of the sides opposite and adjacent to an angle in a right-angled triangle. ● *adj.* **1** (of a line or surface) that is a tangent. **2** touching. □ **at a tangent** diverging from a previous course of action or thought etc. (*go off at a tangent*). **tangent galvanometer** a galvanometer with a coil through which the current to be measured is passed, its strength being proportional to the tangent of the angle of deflection. □□ **tangency** *n.* [L *tangere tangent-* touch]

tangential /tanjénsh'l/ *adj.* **1** of or along a tangent. **2** divergent. **3** peripheral. □□ **tangentially** *adv.*

■ **2** divergent. **3** digressive, off *or* beside the point, peripheral, irrelevant, extraneous, unrelated.

tangerine /tánjərēen/ *n.* **1** a small sweet orange-coloured citrus fruit with a thin skin; a mandarin. **2** a deep orange-yellow colour. [*Tangier* in Morocco]

tangible /tánjib'l/ *adj.* **1** perceptible by touch. **2** definite; clearly intelligible; not elusive or visionary (*tangible proof*). □□ **tangibility** /-bílliti/ *n.* **tangibleness** *n.* **tangibly** /-bli/ *adv.* [F *tangible* or LL *tangibilis* f. *tangere* touch]

■ **1** touchable, tactile, palpable. **2** definite, material, real, physical, corporeal, solid, concrete, manifest, palpable, evident, actual, substantial, visible, seeable, discernible, intelligible, perceptible, objective, ostensive, *literary* ponderable.

tangle[1] /tángg'l/ *v.* & *n.* ● *v.* **1 a** *tr.* intertwine (threads or hairs etc.) in a confused mass; entangle. **b** *intr.* become tangled. **2** *intr.* (foll. by *with*) *colloq.* become involved (esp. in conflict or argument) with (*don't tangle with me*). **3** *tr.* complicate (*a tangled affair*). ● *n.* **1** a confused mass of intertwined threads etc. **2** a confused or complicated state (*be in a tangle; a love tangle*). [ME var. of obs. *tagle*, of uncert. orig.]

■ *v.* **1** confuse, knot, entangle, intertwist, interweave, entwine, jumble, mess up, scramble, shuffle, muddle; tangle up, mesh, snarl, twist, kink, ravel, jam, snag, intertwine, interlace. **2** (*tangle with*) wrangle with, contend with, fight with *or* against, (come into) conflict with, come *or* go up against, lock horns with, dispute with, cross swords with, disagree with, become involved with. **3** see COMPLICATE. ● *n.* **1** confusion, knot, mesh, snarl, twist, kink, entanglement, jam, snag, jumble, mess, skein, web, coil. **2** muddle, jumble, puzzle, scramble, mishmash, mix-up, hotchpotch, hodgepodge, disorder, jungle, morass, maze, labyrinth.

tangle[2] /tángg'l/ *n.* any of various seaweeds, esp. of the genus *Laminaria* or *Fucus*. [prob. f. Norw. *taangel* f. ON *thöngull*]

tangly /tánggli/ *adj.* (**tanglier, tangliest**) tangled.

tango[1] /tánggō/ *n.* & *v.* ● *n.* (*pl.* **-os**) **1** a slow S. American ballroom dance. **2** the music for this. ● *v.intr.* (**-oes, -oed**) dance the tango. [Amer. Sp.]

tango[2] /tánggō/ *n.* a tangerine colour. [abbr. after TANGO[1]]

tangram /tánggram/ *n.* a Chinese puzzle square cut into seven pieces to be combined into various figures. [19th c.: orig. unkn.]

tangy /tángi/ *adj.* (**tangier, tangiest**) having a strong usu. spicy tang. □□ **tanginess** *n.*

■ see SPICY 1.

tanh /than, tansh, tanáych/ *abbr.* hyperbolic tangent.

tanist /tánnist/ *n. hist.* the heir apparent to a Celtic chief, usu. his most vigorous adult relation, chosen by election. □□ **tanistry** *n.* [Ir. & Gael. *tánaiste* heir]

tank /tangk/ *n.* & *v.* ● *n.* **1** a large receptacle or storage chamber usu. for liquid or gas. **2** a heavy armoured fighting vehicle carrying guns and moving on a tracked carriage. **3** a container for the fuel supply in a motor vehicle. **4** the part of a locomotive tender containing water for the boiler. **5 a** *Ind.* & *Austral.* a reservoir. **b** *dial.* esp. *US* a pond. ● *v.* (usu. foll. by *up*) esp. *Brit.* **1** *tr.* fill the tank of (a vehicle etc.) with fuel. **2** *intr.* & *colloq. tr.* (in *passive*) drink heavily; become drunk. □ **tank engine** a railway engine carrying fuel and water receptacles in its own frame, not in a tender. **tank-farming** the practice of growing plants in tanks of water without soil. **tank top** a sleeveless, close-fitting upper garment with a scoop-neck. □□ **tankful** *n.* (*pl.* **-fuls**). **tankless** *adj.* [Gujurati *tānkh* etc., perh. f. Skr. *tadāga* pond]

tanka /tángkə/ *n.* a Japanese poem in five lines and thirty-one syllables giving a complete picture of an event or mood. [Jap.]

tankage /tángkij/ *n.* **1 a** storage in tanks. **b** a charge made for this. **2** the cubic content of a tank. **3** a kind of fertilizer obtained from refuse bones etc.

tankard /tángkərd/ *n.* **1** a tall mug with a handle and sometimes a hinged lid, esp. of silver or pewter for beer. **2** the contents of or an amount held by a tankard (*drank a tankard of ale*). [ME: orig. unkn.: cf. MDu. *tanckaert*]

tanker /tángkər/ *n.* a ship, aircraft, or road vehicle for carrying liquids, esp. mineral oils, in bulk.

tanner[1] /tánnər/ *n.* a person who tans hides.

tanner[2] /tánnər/ *n. Brit. hist. sl.* a sixpence. [19th c.: orig. unkn.]

tannery /tánnəri/ *n.* (*pl.* **-ies**) a place where hides are tanned.

tannic /tánnik/ *adj.* of or produced from tan. □ **tannic acid** a complex natural organic compound of a yellowish colour used as a mordant and astringent. □□ **tannate** /-nayt/ *n.* [F *tannique* (as TANNIN)]

tannin /tánnin/ *n.* any of a group of complex organic compounds found in certain tree-barks and oak-galls, used in leather production and ink manufacture. [F *tanin* (as TAN[1], -IN)]

tannish see TAN[1].

Tannoy /tánnoy/ *n. propr.* a type of public-address system. [20th c.: orig. uncert.]

tanrec var. of TENREC.

tansy /tánzi/ *n.* (*pl.* **-ies**) any plant of the genus *Tanacetum*, esp. *T. vulgare* with yellow button-like flowers and aromatic leaves, formerly used in medicines and cookery. [ME f. OF *tanesie* f. med.L *athanasia* immortality f. Gk]

tantalite /tántəlīt/ *n.* a rare dense black mineral, the principal source of the element tantalum. [G & Sw. *tantalit* (as TANTALUM)]

tantalize /tántəlīz/ *v.tr.* (also **-ise**) **1** torment or tease by the sight or promise of what is unobtainable. **2** raise and then dash the hopes of; torment with disappointment. □□ **tantalization** /-záysh'n/ *n.* **tantalizer** *n.* **tantalizingly** *adv.* [Gk *Tantalos* mythical king of Phrygia condemned to stand in water that receded when he tried to drink it and under branches that drew back when he tried to pick the fruit]

■ tease, taunt, provoke, torment, torture, bait, tempt, lead on, flirt with, plague, frustrate.

tantalum /tántələm/ *n. Chem.* a rare hard white metallic element occurring naturally in tantalite, resistant to heat and the action of acids, and used in surgery and for electronic components. ¶ Symb.: **Ta**. □□ **tantalic** *adj.* [formed as TANTALUS with ref. to its non-absorbent quality]

tantalus /tántələss/ *n.* **1** a stand in which spirit-decanters may be locked up but visible. **2** a wood ibis, *Mycteria americana*. [see TANTALIZE]

tantamount /tántəmownt/ *predic.adj.* (foll. by *to*) equivalent to (*was tantamount to a denial*). [f. obs. verb f. It. *tanto montare* amount to so much]
■ (*tantamount to*) amounting to, as good as, virtually the same as, (pretty) much the same as, equal to, equivalent to, like, comparable to, commensurate with.

tantivy /tantívvi/ *n.* & *adj. archaic* ● *n.* (*pl.* **-ies**) **1** a hunting cry. **2** a swift movement; a gallop or rush. ● *adj.* swift. [17th c.: perh. an imit. of hoof-beats]

tant mieux /toN myö̃/ *int.* so much the better. [F]

tant pis /toN peé/ *int.* so much the worse. [F]

tantra /tántrə/ *n.* any of a class of Hindu or Buddhist mystical and magical writings. ▫▫ **tantric** *adj.* **tantrism** *n.* **tantrist** *n.* [Skr., = loom, groundwork, doctrine f. *tan* stretch]

tantrum /tántrəm/ *n.* an outburst of bad temper or petulance (*threw a tantrum*). [18th c.: orig. unkn.]
■ fit (of anger *or* passion *or* temper), outburst, eruption, explosion, flare-up, storm, rage, fury, *colloq.* blow-up, *Brit. colloq.* paddy, *sl.* wax.

Taoiseach /teéshəkh/ *n.* the Prime Minister of the Irish Republic. [Ir., = chief, leader]

Taoism /tówiz'm, taáō-/ *n.* a Chinese philosophy based on the writings of Laoze (*c.*500 BC), advocating humility and religious piety. ▫▫ **Taoist** /-ist/ *n.* **Taoistic** /-ístik/ *adj.* [Chin. *dao* (right) way]

tap[1] /tap/ *n.* & *v.* ● *n.* **1** a device by which a flow of liquid or gas from a pipe or vessel can be controlled. **2** an act of tapping a telephone etc.; also, the device used for this. **3** *Brit.* a taproom. **4** an instrument for cutting the thread of a female screw. ● *v.tr.* (**tapped, tapping**) **1 a** provide (a cask) with a tap. **b** let out (a liquid) by means of, or as if by means of, a tap. **2** draw sap from (a tree) by cutting into it. **3 a** obtain information or supplies or resources from. **b** establish communication or trade with. **4** connect a listening device to (a telephone or telegraph line etc.) to listen to a call or transmission. **5** cut a female screw-thread in. ▫ **on tap 1** ready to be drawn off by tap. **2** *colloq.* ready for immediate use; freely available. **tap root** a tapering root growing vertically downwards. **tap water** water from a piped supply. ▫▫ **tapless** *adj.* **tappable** *adj.* [OE *tæppian* (v.), *tæppa* (n.) f. Gmc]
■ *n.* **1** cock, stopcock, seacock, spout, valve, bung, stopper, cork, spile, plug, stopple, peg, *esp. US* faucet, *US* spigot. **2** wire-tapping, bugging, electronic eavesdropping; wire-tap, bug, listening device, electronic eavesdropper. ● *v.* **1 b** drain, draw (off), siphon off *or* out, extract, withdraw, broach. **2** sap, milk. **3 a** sap, bleed, milk, mine, use, utilize, make use of, put to use, draw on *or* upon, exploit, turn to account. **4** eavesdrop on, listen in to *or* on, wire-tap, *sl.* bug. ▫ **on tap 1** on draught, out of the barrel *or* keg. **2** ready, available, on *or* at hand, waiting, in reserve, on call. **tap root** see ROOT[1] *n.* 1a. **tap water** see WATER *n.*

tap[2] /tap/ *v.* & *n.* ● *v.* (**tapped, tapping**) **1** *intr.* (foll. by *at*, *on*) strike a gentle but audible blow. **2** *tr.* strike lightly (*tapped me on the shoulder*). **3** *tr.* (foll. by *against* etc.) cause (a thing) to strike lightly (*tapped a stick against the window*). **4** *intr.* = TAP-DANCE *v.* (*can you tap?*). ● *n.* **1 a** a light blow; a rap. **b** the sound of this (*heard a tap at the door*). **2 a** = TAP-DANCE *n.* (*goes to tap classes*). **b** a piece of metal attached to the toe and heel of a tap-dancer's shoe to make the tapping sound. **3** (in *pl.*, usu. treated as *sing.*) *US* **a** a bugle call for lights to be put out in army quarters. **b** a similar signal at a military funeral. ▫ **tap-tap** a repeated tap; a series of taps. ▫▫ **tapper** *n.* [ME *tappe* (imit.), perh. through F *taper*]
■ *v.* **1, 2** rap, knock, dab, pat, strike, hit, peck; drum, beat. **3** knock, beat, rap, drum. ● *n.* **1** rap, knock, dab, strike, peck, pat; tapping, tap-tap, rapping, knocking, pecking, beat, beating, patter, pattering.

tapa /taápə/ *n.* **1** the bark of a paper-mulberry tree. **2** cloth made from this, used in the Pacific islands. [Polynesian]

tap-dance /tápdaanss/ *n.* & *v.* ● *n.* a form of display dance performed wearing shoes fitted with metal taps, with rhythmical tapping of the toes and heels. ● *v.intr.* perform a tap-dance. ▫▫ **tap-dancer** *n.* **tap-dancing** *n.*

tape /tayp/ *n.* & *v.* ● *n.* **1** a narrow strip of woven material for tying up, fastening, etc. **2 a** a strip of material stretched across the finishing line of a race. **b** a similar strip for marking off an area or forming a notional barrier. **3** (in full **adhesive tape**) a strip of opaque or transparent paper or plastic etc., esp. coated with adhesive for fastening, sticking, masking, insulating, etc. **4 a** = *magnetic tape*. **b** a tape recording or tape cassette. **5** = *tape-measure*. ● *v.tr.* **1 a** tie up or join etc. with tape. **b** apply tape to. **2** (foll. by *off*) seal or mark off an area or thing with tape. **3** record on magnetic tape. **4** measure with tape. ▫ **breast the tape** win a race. **have** (or **get**) **a person** or **thing taped** *Brit. colloq.* understand a person or thing fully. **on tape** recorded on magnetic tape. **tape deck** a platform with capstans for using magnetic tape. **tape machine** a machine for receiving and recording telegraph messages. **tape-measure** a strip of tape or thin flexible metal marked for measuring lengths. **tape-record** record (sounds) on magnetic tape. **tape recorder** apparatus for recording sounds on magnetic tape and afterwards reproducing them. **tape recording** a recording on magnetic tape. ▫▫ **tapeable** *adj.* (esp. in sense 3 of *v.*). **tapeless** *adj.* **tapelike** *adj.* [OE *tæppa*, *tæppe*, of unkn. orig.]
■ *n.* **1** strip, band, fillet, stripe, strap, binding, belt, ribbon, braid. **4 b** (tape) recording, reel, spool, cassette, video, videotape. ● *v.* **1** strap, band, bind; fasten, fix, join, seal, stick, sellotape. **3** record, tape-record, video, videotape.

taper /táypər/ *n.* & *v.* ● *n.* **1** a wick coated with wax etc. for conveying a flame. **2** a slender candle. ● *v.* (often foll. by *off*) **1** *intr.* & *tr.* diminish or reduce in thickness towards one end. **2** *tr.* & *intr.* make or become gradually less. [OE *tapur*, *-or*, *-er* wax candle, f. L PAPYRUS, whose pith was used for candle-wicks]
■ *n.* **1** see LIGHT[1] *n.* 7. ● *v.* **1** narrow (down), thin, diminish, attenuate. **2** taper off, diminish, reduce, thin out, wind down, decrease, fade, lessen, peter out, tail off, wane, subside, let up, slacken, die away *or* down *or* off *or* out, decline, slow (down *or* up), weaken, abate, ebb, slump, drop (off), fall (off), plummet.

tapestry /táppistri/ *n.* (*pl.* **-ies**) **1 a** a thick textile fabric in which coloured weft threads are woven to form pictures or designs. **b** embroidery imitating this, usu. in wools on canvas. **c** a piece of such embroidery. **2** events or circumstances etc. compared with a tapestry in being intricate, interwoven, etc. (*life's rich tapestry*). ▫▫ **tapestried** *adj.* [ME, alt. f. *tapissery* f. OF *tapisserie* f. *tapissier* tapestry-worker or *tapisser* to carpet, f. *tapis*: see TAPIS]

tapetum /təpeétəm/ *n.* a light-reflecting part of the choroid membrane in the eyes of certain mammals, e.g. cats. [LL f. L *tapete* carpet]

tapeworm /táypwurm/ *n.* any flatworm of the class Cestoda, with a body like segmented tape, living as a parasite in the intestines.

tapioca /táppiṓkə/ *n.* a starchy substance in hard white grains obtained from cassava and used for puddings etc. [Tupi-Guarani *tipioca* f. *tipi* dregs + *og*, *ok* squeeze out]

tapir /táypər, -peer/ *n.* any nocturnal hoofed mammal of the genus *Tapirus*, native to Central and S. America and Malaysia, having a short flexible protruding snout used for feeding on vegetation. ▫▫ **tapiroid** *adj.* & *n.* [Tupi *tapira*]

tapis /táppee/ *n.* a covering or tapestry. ▫ **on the tapis** (of a subject) under consideration or discussion. [ME, a kind of cloth, f. OF *tapiz* f. LL *tapetium* f. Gk *tapētion* dimin. of *tapēs tapētos* tapestry]

tapotement /təpṓtmənt/ *n. Med.* rapid and repeated striking of the body as massage treatment. [F f. *tapoter* tap]

tapper see TAP[2].

tappet /táppit/ *n.* a lever or projecting part used in machinery to give intermittent motion, often in conjunction with a cam. [app. f. TAP[2] + -ET[1]]

taproom /táprōōm, -rŏŏm/ *n.* a room in which alcoholic drinks are available on tap.

tapster /tápstər/ *n.* a person who draws and serves alcoholic drinks at a bar. [OE *tæppestre* orig. fem. (as TAP[1], -STER)]

tapu /taápōō/ *n.* & *adj. NZ* = TABOO. [Maori]

tar[1] /taar/ *n.* & *v.* ● *n.* **1** a dark thick inflammable liquid distilled from wood or coal etc. and used as a preservative of wood and iron, in making roads, as an antiseptic, etc. **2** a similar substance formed in the combustion of tobacco etc. ● *v.tr.* (**tarred, tarring**) cover with tar. □ **tar and feather** smear with tar and then cover with feathers as a punishment. **tar-brush** a brush for applying tar. **tarred with the same brush** having the same faults. [OE *te(o)ru* f. Gmc, rel. to TREE]

tar[2] /taar/ *n. colloq.* a sailor. [abbr. of TARPAULIN]

taradiddle /tárrədidd'l/ *n.* (also **tarradiddle**) *colloq.* **1** a petty lie. **2** pretentious nonsense. [18th c.: cf. DIDDLE]
■ **2** see NONSENSE.

taramasalata /tárrəməsəlaátə/ *n.* (also **tarama**) a pinkish pâté made from the roe of mullet or other fish with olive oil, seasoning, etc. [mod.Gk *taramas* roe (f. Turk. *tarama*) + *salata* SALAD]

tarantass /tárrəntáss/ *n.* a springless four-wheeled Russian vehicle. [Russ. *tarantas*]

tarantella /tárrəntéllə/ *n.* (also **tarantelle** /-tél/) **1** a rapid whirling S. Italian dance. **2** the music for this. [It., f. *Taranto* in Italy (because the dance was once thought to be a cure for a tarantula bite): cf. TARANTISM]

tarantism /tárrəntiz'm/ *n. hist.* dancing mania, esp. that originating in S. Italy among those who had (actually or supposedly) been bitten by a tarantula. [mod.L *tarantismus*, It. *tarantismo* f. *Taranto* in S. Italy f. L *Tarentum*]

tarantula /təràntyoolə/ *n.* **1** any large hairy tropical spider of the family Theraphosidae. **2** a large black S. European spider, *Lycosa tarentula*, whose bite was formerly held to cause tarantism. [med.L f. It. *tarantola* (as TARANTISM)]

taraxacum /təráksəkəm/ *n.* **1** any composite plant of the genus *Taraxacum*, including the dandelion. **2** a tonic etc. prepared from the dried roots of this. [med.L f. Arab. *ṭarakšakūk* f. Pers. *talḵ* bitter + *chakūk* purslane]

tarboosh /taarbóōsh/ *n.* a cap like a fez, sometimes worn as part of a turban. [Egypt. Arab. *ṭarbūš*, ult. f. Pers. *sar-būš* head-cover]

Tardenoisian /taárdinóyziən/ *n.* & *adj. Archaeol.* ● *n.* a mesolithic culture using small flint implements. ● *adj.* of or relating to this culture. [*Tardenois* in NE France, where remains of it were found]

tardigrade /taárdigrayd/ *n.* & *adj.* ● *n.* any minute freshwater animal of the phylum Tardigrada, having a short plump body and four pairs of short legs. Also called *water bear*. ● *adj.* of or relating to this phylum. [F *tardigrade* f. L *tardigradus* f. *tardus* slow + *gradi* walk]

tardy /taárdi/ *adj.* (**tardier, tardiest**) **1** slow to act or come or happen. **2** delaying or delayed beyond the right or expected time. □□ **tardily** *adv.* **tardiness** *n.* [F *tardif*, *tardive* ult. f. L *tardus* slow]
■ **1** slow, dilatory, belated, slack, retarded, sluggish, reluctant, indolent, lackadaisical, listless, phlegmatic, slothful, lethargic, languid. **2** late, unpunctual, delayed, behind schedule, overdue, behindhand; belated.
□□ **tardily** see SLOW *adv.*

tare[1] /tair/ *n.* **1** vetch, esp. as corn-weed or fodder. **2** (in *pl.*) *Bibl.* an injurious corn-weed (Matt. 13:24-30). [ME: orig. unkn.]

tare[2] /tair/ *n.* **1** an allowance made for the weight of the packing or wrapping around goods. **2** the weight of a motor vehicle without its fuel or load. □ **tare and tret** the arithmetical rule for computing a tare. [ME f. F, = deficiency, tare, f. med.L *tara* f. Arab. *ṭarḥa* what is rejected f. *ṭaraḥa* reject]

targe /taarj/ *n. archaic* = TARGET *n.* 5. [ME f. OF]

target /taárgit/ *n.* & *v.* ● *n.* **1** a mark or point fired or aimed at, esp. a round or rectangular object marked with concentric circles. **2** a person or thing aimed at, or exposed to gunfire etc. (*they were an easy target*). **3** (also *attrib.*) an objective or result aimed at (*our export targets; target date*). **4** a person or thing against whom criticism, abuse, etc., is or may be directed. **5** *archaic* a shield or buckler, esp. a small round one. ● *v.tr.* (**targeted, targeting**) **1** identify or single out (a person or thing) as an object of attention or attack. **2** aim or direct (*missiles targeted on major cities; should target our efforts where needed*). □□ **targetable** *adj.* [ME, dimin. of ME and OF *targe* shield]
■ *n.* **1, 3** goal, mark, object, objective, aim, end. **4** butt, quarry, prey, victim, object. ● *v.* **1** see SINGLE *v.* **2** see DIRECT *v.* 4.

tariff /tárrif/ *n.* & *v.* ● *n.* **1** a table of fixed charges (*a hotel tariff*). **2 a** a duty on a particular class of imports or exports. **b** a list of duties or customs to be paid. **3** standard charges agreed between insurers etc. ● *v.tr.* subject (goods) to a tariff. [F *tarif* f. It. *tariffa* f. Turk. *tarife* f. Arab. *ta'rīf(a)* f. *'arrafa* notify]
■ *n.* **1** schedule (of charges), price-list. **2 a** tax, assessment, duty, excise, levy, impost, toll. ● *v.* tax, impose *or* levy a tax on.

tarlatan /taárlət'n/ *n.* a thin stiff open-weave muslin. [F *tarlatane*, prob. of Ind. orig.]

Tarmac /taármak/ *n.* & *v.* ● *n. propr.* **1** = TARMACADAM. **2** a surface made of this, e.g. a runway. ● *v.tr.* (**tarmac**) (**tarmacked, tarmacking**) apply tarmacadam to. [abbr.]

tarmacadam /taármakáddəm/ *n.* a material of stone or slag bound with tar, used in paving roads etc. [TAR[1] + MACADAM]

tarn /taarn/ *n.* a small mountain lake. [ME *terne*, *tarne* f. ON]

tarnation /taarnáysh'n/ *int.* esp. *US sl.* damn, blast. [alt. of DAMNATION, *darnation*]
■ see BOTHER *int.*

tarnish /taárnish/ *v.* & *n.* ● *v.* **1** *tr.* lessen or destroy the lustre of (metal etc.). **2** *tr.* impair (one's reputation etc.). **3** *intr.* (of metal etc.) lose lustre. ● *n.* **1 a** a loss of lustre. **b** a film of colour formed on an exposed surface of a mineral or metal. **2** a blemish; a stain. □□ **tarnishable** *adj.* [F *ternir* f. *terne* dark]
■ *v.* **1, 3** dull, blacken, stain, discolour. **2** sully, disgrace, taint, blacken, blemish, stain, blot, soil, spot, smirch, besmirch, dirty, contaminate, defame, injure, spoil, ruin, mar, damage, harm, hurt, stigmatize, debase, degrade, denigrate, dishonour. ● *n.* **2** see DISCREDIT *n.* 1.

taro /taárō/ *n.* (*pl.* **-os**) a tropical aroid plant, *Colocasia esculenta*, with tuberous roots used as food. Also called EDDO. [Polynesian]

tarot /tárrō/ *n.* **1** (in *sing.* or *pl.*) **a** any of several games played with a pack of cards having five suits, the last of which is a set of permanent trumps. **b** a similar pack used in fortune-telling. **2 a** any of the trump cards. **b** any of the cards from a fortune-telling pack. [F *tarot*, It. *tarocchi*, of unkn. orig.]

tarp /taarp/ *n. US* & *Austral. colloq.* tarpaulin. [abbr.]

tarpan /taárpan/ *n.* an extinct N. European primitive wild horse. [Kirghiz Tartar]

tarpaulin /taarpáwlin/ *n.* **1** heavy-duty waterproof cloth esp. of tarred canvas. **2** a sheet or covering of this. **3 a** a sailor's tarred or oilskin hat. **b** *archaic* a sailor. [prob. f. TAR[1] + PALL[1] + -ING[1]]

tarpon /taárpon/ *n.* **1** a large silvery fish, *Tarpon atlanticus*, common in the tropical Atlantic. **2** a similar fish, *Megalops cyprinoides*, of the Pacific ocean. [Du. *tarpoen*, of unkn. orig.]

tarradiddle var. of TARADIDDLE.

tarragon /tárrəgən/ *n.* a bushy herb, *Artemisia dracunculus*, with leaves used to flavour salads, stuffings, vinegar, etc. [= med.L *tarchon* f. med. Gk *tarkhōn*, perh. through Arab. f. Gk *drakōn* dragon]

tarras var. of TRASS.

tarry[1] /taári/ *adj.* (**tarrier, tarriest**) of or like or smeared with tar. □□ **tarriness** *n.*

tarry[2] /tárri/ *v.intr.* (**-ies**, **-ied**) *archaic* or *literary* **1** defer coming or going. **2** linger, stay, wait. **3** be tardy. □□ **tarrier** *n.* [ME: orig. uncert.]

■ **1** delay, pause, wait, linger, loiter, stall, procrastinate, dawdle, dally, temporize, hang back *or* about *or* (a)round, *colloq.* hang on, dilly-dally. **2** remain, sojourn, stay, stop, rest, linger, wait, bide one's time, settle, *archaic or dial.* bide.

tarsal /taárs'l/ *adj.* & *n.* ● *adj.* of or relating to the bones in the ankle. ● *n.* a tarsal bone. [TARSUS + -AL]

tarsi *pl.* of TARSUS.

tarsi- /taársi/ *comb. form* (also **tarso-** /taársō/) tarsus.

tarsia /taársiə/ *n.* = INTARSIA. [It.]

tarsier /taársiər/ *n.* any small large-eyed arboreal nocturnal primate of the genus *Tarsius*, native to Borneo, the Philippines, etc., with a long tail and long hind legs used for leaping from tree to tree. [F (as TARSUS), from the structure of its foot]

tarso- *comb. form* var. of TARSI-.

tarsus /taársəss/ *n.* (*pl.* **tarsi** /-sī/) **1 a** the group of bones forming the ankle and upper foot. **b** the shank of a bird's leg. **c** the terminal segment of a limb in insects. **2** the fibrous connective tissue of the eyelid. [mod.L f. Gk *tarsos* flat of the foot, rim of the eyelid]

tart[1] /taart/ *n.* **1** an open pastry case containing jam etc. **2** esp. *Brit.* a pie with a fruit or sweet filling. □□ **tartlet** *n.* [ME f. OF *tarte* = med.L *tarta*, of unkn. orig.]

■ **1** tartlet, pastry, flan, quiche. **2** pie, turnover, patty, pasty.

tart[2] /taart/ *n.* & *v.* ● *n. sl.* **1** a prostitute; a promiscuous woman. **2** *sl. offens.* a girl or woman. ● *v.* (foll. by *up*) esp. *Brit. colloq.* **1** *tr.* (usu. *refl.*) smarten (oneself or a thing) up, esp. flashily or gaudily. **2** *intr.* dress up gaudily. [prob. abbr. of SWEETHEART]

■ *n.* **1** streetwalker, prostitute, fallen woman, trollop, *fille de joie*, call-girl, loose woman, drab, *demi-mondaine*, woman of ill repute, lady of the night, lady of easy virtue, *archaic* trull, demirep, harlot, *archaic or rhet.* strumpet, *colloq.* floozie, vamp, *derog.* hussy, whore, slut, jade, *literary* doxy, wanton, courtesan, *sl.* hooker, working girl, *sl. derog.* slag, scrubber, *Austral. sl.* bike, *esp. US sl. derog.* tramp. ● *v.* **1** see DECORATE 1; (*tart oneself up*) see PRIMP 2. **2** see PRIMP 2.

tart[3] /taart/ *adj.* **1** sharp or acid in taste. **2** (of a remark etc.) cutting, bitter. □□ **tartly** *adv.* **tartness** *n.* [OE *teart*, of unkn. orig.]

■ **1** sour, acidic, acidulous, acidulated, lemony, citrous, vinegary, acetic, acetous; sharp, tangy, astringent, acerb, acerbic, acrid, bitter, pungent, piquant, harsh. **2** biting, bitter, caustic, acid, corrosive, mordant, astringent, acrimonious, trenchant, harsh, scathing, stinging, acerbic, incisive, cutting, keen, sharp, barbed, nasty, curmudgeonly, testy, crusty, abusive, virulent, sarcastic, sardonic, satiric(al), vicious, cynical.

tartan[1] /taárt'n/ *n.* **1** a pattern of coloured stripes crossing at right angles, esp. the distinctive plaid worn by the Scottish Highlanders to denote their clan. **2** woollen cloth woven in this pattern (often *attrib.*: *a tartan scarf*). [perh. f. OF *tertaine, tiretaine*]

tartan[2] /taárt'n/ *n.* a lateen-sailed single-masted ship used in the Mediterranean. [F *tartane* f. It. *tartana*, perh. f. Arab. *ṭarīda*]

Tartar /taártər/ *n.* & *adj.* (also **Tatar** except in sense 2 of *n.*) ● *n.* **1 a** a member of a group of Central Asian peoples including Mongols and Turks. **b** the Turkic language of these peoples. **2** (**tartar**) a violent-tempered or intractable person. ● *adj.* **1** of or relating to the Tartars. **2** of or relating to Central Asia E. of the Caspian Sea. □ **tartar sauce** a sauce of mayonnaise and chopped gherkins, capers, etc. □□ **Tartarian** /-táiriən/ *adj.* [ME *tartre* f. OF *Tartare* or med.L *Tartarus*]

tartar /taártər/ *n.* **1** a hard deposit of saliva, calcium phosphate, etc., that forms on the teeth. **2** a deposit of acid potassium tartrate that forms a hard crust on the inside of a cask during the fermentation of wine. □ **tartar emetic** potassium antimony tartrate used as a mordant and in medicine (formerly as an emetic). □□ **tartarize** *v.tr.* (also **-ise**). [ME f. med.L f. med.Gk *tartaron*]

tartare /taartaár/ *adj.* (in full **sauce tartare**) = *tartar sauce* (see TARTAR). [F, = tartar]

tartaric /taartárrik/ *adj. Chem.* of or produced from tartar. □ **tartaric acid** a natural carboxylic acid found esp. in unripe grapes, used in baking powders and as a food additive. [F *tartarique* f. med.L *tartarum*: see TARTAR]

Tartarus /taártərəss/ *n.* (in Greek mythology): **1** an abyss below Hades where the Titans were confined. **2** a place of punishment in Hades. □□ **Tartarean** /-táiriən/ *adj.* [L f. Gk *Tartaros*]

tartrate /taártrayt/ *n. Chem.* any salt or ester of tartaric acid. [F (as TARTAR, -ATE[1])]

tartrazine /taártrəzeen/ *n. Chem.* a brilliant yellow dye derived from tartaric acid and used to colour food, drugs, and cosmetics. [as TARTAR + AZO- + -INE[4]]

tarty /taárti/ *adj. colloq.* (**tartier**, **tartiest**) (esp. of a woman) vulgar, gaudy; promiscuous. □□ **tartily** *adv.* **tartiness** *n.* [TART[2] + -Y[1]]

Tarzan /taárz'n/ *n.* a man of great agility and powerful physique. [name of the hero of stories by E. R. Burroughs, Amer. writer d. 1950]

Tas. *abbr.* Tasmania.

Tashi lama /táshi laámə/ *n.* = PANCHEN LAMA.

task /taask/ *n.* & *v.* ● *n.* a piece of work to be done or undertaken. ● *v.tr.* **1** make great demands on (a person's powers etc.). **2** assign a task to. □ **take to task** rebuke, scold. **task force** (or **group**) **1** *Mil.* an armed force organized for a special operation. **2** a unit specially organized for a task. [ME f. ONF *tasque* = OF *tasche* f. med.L *tasca*, perh. f. *taxa* f. L *taxare* TAX]

■ *n.* duty, assignment, business, job, charge, function, role, office, stint, mission, (piece of) work, chore, commission, errand, undertaking; (major) effort, test (of strength), struggle, strain. ● *v.* **1** see TAX *v.* 3. □ **take to task** scold, reprimand, call to account, blame, censure, reproach, reprove, rebuke, castigate, criticize, lecture, upbraid, reprehend, *archaic or literary* chide, *colloq.* tell off. **task force 1** see FLEET[1].

taskmaster /taáskmaastər/ *n.* (*fem.* **taskmistress** /-mistriss/) a person who imposes a task or burden, esp. regularly or severely.

■ see DISCIPLINARIAN.

Tasmanian /tazmáyniən/ *n.* & *adj.* ● *n.* **1** a native of Tasmania, an island State of Australia. **2** a person of Tasmanian descent. ● *adj.* of or relating to Tasmania. □ **Tasmanian devil** a badger-like nocturnal flesh-eating marsupial, *Sarcophilus harrisii*, now found only in Tasmania. [*Tasmania* f. A. J. *Tasman*, Du. navigator d. 1659, who discovered the island]

Tass /tass/ *n. hist.* the official news agency of the former Soviet Union. [the initials of Russ. *Telegrafnoe agentstvo Sovetskogo Soyuza* Telegraphic Agency of the Soviet Union]

tass /tass/ *n. Sc.* **1** a cup or small goblet. **2** a small draught of brandy etc. [ME f. OF *tasse* cup f. Arab. *ṭāsa* basin f. Pers. *tast*]

tassel[1] /táss'l/ *n.* & *v.* ● *n.* **1** a tuft of loosely hanging threads or cords etc. attached for decoration to a cushion, scarf, cap, etc. **2** a tassel-like head of some plants, esp. a flower-head with prominent stamens at the top of a maize stalk. ● *v.* (**tasselled, tasselling**; *US* **tasseled, tasseling**) **1** *tr.* provide with a tassel or tassels. **2** *intr. US* (of maize etc.) form tassels. [ME f. OF *tas(s)el* clasp, of unkn. orig.]

tassel[2] /táss'l/ *n.* (also **torsel** /tór-/) a small piece of stone, wood, etc., supporting the end of a beam or joist. [OF ult. f. L *taxillus* small die, and *tessella*: see TESSELLATE]

tassie /tássi/ *n. Sc.* a small cup.

taste /tayst/ *n.* & *v.* ● *n.* **1 a** the sensation characteristic of a soluble substance caused in the mouth and throat by contact with that substance (*disliked the taste of garlic*). **b** the faculty of perceiving this sensation (*was bitter to the taste*). **2 a** a small portion of food or drink taken as a sample. **b** a hint or touch of some ingredient or quality. **3** a slight experience (*a taste of success*). **4** (often foll. by *for*) a liking or predilection (*has expensive tastes*; *is not to my taste*). **5 a** aesthetic discernment in art, literature, conduct, etc., esp. of a specified kind (*a person of taste*; *dresses in poor taste*). **b** a style or manner based on this (*a table in the French taste*). ● *v.* **1** *tr.* sample or test the flavour of (food etc.) by taking it into the mouth. **2** *tr.* (also *absol.*) perceive the flavour of (*could taste the lemon*; *cannot taste with a cold*). **3** *tr.* (esp. with *neg.*) eat or drink a small portion of (*had not tasted food for days*). **4** *tr.* have experience of (*had never tasted failure*). **5** *intr.* (often foll. by *of*) have a specified flavour (*tastes bitter*; *tastes of onions*). □ **a bad** (or **bitter** etc.) **taste** *colloq.* a strong feeling of regret or unease. **taste blood** see BLOOD. **taste bud** any of the cells or nerve-endings on the surface of the tongue by which things are tasted. **to taste** in the amount needed for a pleasing result (*add salt and pepper to taste*). □□ **tasteable** *adj.* [ME, = touch, taste, f. OF *tast*, *taster* touch, try, taste, ult. perh. f. L *tangere* touch + *gustare* taste]

■ *n.* **1 a** flavour, savour, relish, smack, tang. **2 a** sample, taster, morsel, mouthful, bite, nibble, titbit, *US* tidbit; sip, sup, nip, swallow. **b** drop, soupçon, suspicion, dash, pinch, smack, touch, hint, suggestion, grain, trace, bit. **3** sample, experience. **4** palate, desire, inclination, leaning, partiality, disposition, penchant, liking, fancy, preference, predilection, fondness, appetite, relish, stomach, tolerance. **5 a** discernment, discrimination, perception, judgement, cultivation, refinement, stylishness, style, grace, polish, finesse, elegance; decorum, discretion, tactfulness, delicacy, *politesse*, politeness, correctness, propriety, tastefulness. **b** style, mode, fashion, manner, form, design. ● *v.* **1** savour, sample, examine, try, test. **3** sup, sip, nibble; see also TOUCH *v.* 6c. **4** experience, sample, know, have knowledge of, undergo, encounter, meet (with), come up against. **5** (*taste of*) smack of, savour of, have the flavour of.

tasteful /táystfŏŏl/ *adj.* having, or done in, good taste. □□ **tastefully** *adv.* **tastefulness** *n.*

■ in good taste, decorous, refined, finished, tactful, polite, polished, restrained, correct, harmonious, fitting, fit, proper, discriminating, aesthetic, attractive, discriminative, fastidious, cultivated, *comme il faut*, elegant, stylish, graceful, charming. □□ **tastefulness** see GRACE *n.* 2.

tasteless /táystliss/ *adj.* **1** lacking flavour. **2** having, or done in, bad taste. □□ **tastelessly** *adv.* **tastelessness** *n.*

■ **1** insipid, bland, dull, flat, watery, weak, vapid, flavourless, wishy-washy. **2** in bad *or* poor taste, garish, gaudy, loud, kitsch(y), tawdry, meretricious, cheap, flashy, unrefined, inelegant, unaesthetic, *colloq.* tarty; improper, wrong, indecorous, indelicate, unseemly, uncultivated, uncouth, uncultured, gauche, boorish, maladroit, distasteful, unsavoury, coarse, crude, gross, vulgar, base, low, *esp. US colloq.* tacky.

taster /táystər/ *n.* **1** a person employed to test food or drink by tasting it, esp. for quality or *hist.* to detect poisoning. **2** a small cup used by a wine-taster. **3** an instrument for extracting a small sample from within a cheese. **4** a sample of food etc. [ME f. AF *tastour*, OF *tasteur* f. *taster*: see TASTE]

tasting /táysting/ *n.* a gathering at which food or drink (esp. wine) is tasted and evaluated.

tasty /táysti/ *adj.* (**tastier**, **tastiest**) (of food) pleasing in flavour; appetizing. □□ **tastily** *adv.* **tastiness** *n.*

■ delicious, luscious, flavorous, flavoursome, flavourful, piquant, savoury, toothsome, palatable, appetizing, mouth-watering, ambrosial, *colloq.* yummy, scrumptious, *literary* delectable, sapid. □□ **tastiness** see FLAVOUR *n.* 1.

tat[1] /tat/ *n. colloq.* **1 a** tatty or tasteless clothes; worthless goods. **b** rubbish, junk. **2** a shabby person. [back-form. f. TATTY]

tat[2] /tat/ *v.* (**tatted**, **tatting**) **1** *intr.* do tatting. **2** *tr.* make by tatting. [19th c.: orig. unkn.]

tat[3] see TIT[2].

ta-ta /tatáa/ *int. Brit. colloq.* goodbye (said esp. to or by a child). [19th c.: orig. unkn.]

■ see GOODBYE *int.*

Tatar var. of TARTAR.

tater /táytər/ *n.* (also **tatie** /-ti/, **tato** /-tō/) *sl.* = POTATO. [abbr.]

tatler *archaic* var. of TATTLER.

tats /tats/ *n.pl.* esp. *Austral. sl.* teeth. [f. *tats* = dice]

tatter /táttər/ *n.* (usu. in *pl.*) a rag; an irregularly torn piece of cloth or paper etc. □ **in tatters** *colloq.* (of a negotiation, argument, etc.) ruined, demolished. □□ **tattery** *adj.* [ME f. ON *tötrar* rags: cf. Icel. *töturr*]

■ (*tatters*) scraps, rags, shreds, bits, pieces. □ **in tatters** in ruins, in shreds, in pieces, destroyed, ruined, shattered, in disarray, demolished.

tattered /táttərd/ *adj.* in tatters; ragged.

■ ragged, torn, shredded, rent, ripped, frayed, threadbare, worn out, holey, in holes, in tatters, shabby, *colloq.* tatty.

tattersall /táttərsawl/ *n.* (in full **tattersall check**) a fabric with a pattern of coloured lines forming squares like a tartan. [R. *Tattersall*, Engl. horseman d. 1795: from the traditional design of horse blankets]

tatting /tátting/ *n.* **1** a kind of knotted lace made by hand with a small shuttle and used for trimming etc. **2** the process of making this. [19th c.: orig. unkn.]

tattle /tátt'l/ *v.* & *n.* ● *v.* **1** *intr.* prattle, chatter; gossip idly, speak indiscreetly. **2** *tr.* utter (words) idly, reveal (secrets). ● *n.* gossip; idle or trivial talk. □ **tattle-tale** *US* a tell-tale, esp. a child. [ME f. MFlem. *tatelen*, *tateren* (imit.)]

■ *v.* **1** gossip, prattle, prate, babble, chatter, jabber, blather, blether, *colloq.* natter, witter, *sl. derog.* yack; blab, tittle-tattle, tell, reveal *or* divulge *or* give away secrets, *sl.* squeal. **2** see BLURT. ● *n.* talk, small talk; see also CHATTER *n.* □ **tattle-tale** see TALEBEARER.

tattler /tátlər/ *n.* a prattler; a gossip.

tattoo[1] /tətóō/ *n.* (*pl.* **tattoos**) **1** an evening drum or bugle signal recalling soldiers to their quarters. **2** an elaboration of this with music and marching, presented as an entertainment. **3** a rhythmic tapping or drumming. [17th-c. *tap-too* f. Du. *taptoe*, lit. 'close the tap' (of the cask)]

■ see PATTER[1] *n.*

tattoo[2] /tətóō/ *v.* & *n.* ● *v.tr.* (**tattoos**, **tattooed**) **1** mark (the skin) with an indelible design by puncturing it and inserting pigment. **2** make (a design) in this way. ● *n.* (*pl.* **tattoos**) a design made by tattooing. □□ **tattooer** *n.* **tattooist** *n.* [Polynesian]

tatty /tátti/ *adj.* (**tattier**, **tattiest**) *colloq.* **1** tattered; worn and shabby. **2** inferior. **3** tawdry. □□ **tattily** *adv.* **tattiness** *n.* [orig. Sc., = shaggy, app. rel. to OE *tættec* rag, TATTER]

■ **1** see SHABBY 1, 2. **2** see INFERIOR *adj.* 2. **3** see TAWDRY *adj.*

tau /tow, taw/ *n.* the nineteenth letter of the Greek alphabet (T, τ). □ **tau cross** a T-shaped cross. **tau particle** *Physics* an unstable, heavy, and charged elementary particle of the lepton class. [ME f. Gk]

taught *past* and *past part.* of TEACH.

taunt /tawnt/ *n.* & *v.* ● *n.* a thing said in order to anger or wound a person. ● *v.tr.* **1** assail with taunts. **2** reproach (a person) contemptuously. □□ **taunter** *n.* **tauntingly** *adv.* [16th c., in phr. *taunt for taunt* f. F *tant pour tant* tit for tat, hence a smart rejoinder]

■ *n.* jeer, gibe, brickbat, insult, scoff, sneer, slap (in the face), *colloq.* dig. ● *v.* tease, jeer (at), twit, mock, torment, annoy, make fun *or* sport of, poke fun at, deride, heckle, sneer at, scoff at, insult, ridicule, burlesque, lampoon, guy, *Austral.* & *NZ* chiack, *US* ride, *colloq.* kid, rib, needle, put down, hassle, *sl.* bug, rag.

taupe /tōp/ *n.* a grey with a tinge of another colour, usu. brown. [F, = MOLE[1]]

taurine /táwreen, -rīn/ *adj.* of or like a bull; bullish. [L *taurinus* f. *taurus* bull]

tauromachy /tawrómmәki/ *n.* (*pl.* **-ies**) *archaic* **1** a bullfight. **2** bullfighting. [Gk *tauromakhia* f. *tauros* bull + *makhē* fight]

Taurus /táwrәss/ *n.* **1** a constellation. **2 a** the second sign of the zodiac (the Bull). **b** a person born when the sun is in this sign. ▫▫ **Taurean** *adj.* & *n.* [ME f. L, = bull]

taut /tawt/ *adj.* **1** (of a rope, muscles, etc.) tight; not slack. **2** (of nerves) tense. **3** (of a ship etc.) in good order or condition. ▫▫ **tauten** *v.tr.* & *intr.* **tautly** *adv.* **tautness** *n.* [ME *touht, togt*, perh. = TOUGH, infl. by *tog-* past part. stem of obs. *tee* (OE *tēon*) pull]

▪ **1** tight, tense, strained, stretched, rigid, stiff. **2** tense, strained. **3** neat, tidy, shipshape, spruce, (in) trim, smart, orderly, well-organized; well-disciplined, *orig. Naut.* Bristol fashion. ▫▫ **tauten** see TENSE[1] *v.* **tautness** see TENSION 1, 2.

tauto- /táwtō/ *comb. form* the same. [Gk, f. *tauto, to auto* the same]

tautog /tawtóg/ *n.* a fish, *Tautoga onitis*, found off the Atlantic coast of N. America, used as food. [Narragansett *tautauog* (pl.)]

tautology /tawtóllәji/ *n.* (*pl.* **-ies**) **1** the saying of the same thing twice over in different words, esp. as a fault of style (e.g. *arrived one after the other in succession*). **2** a statement that is necessarily true. ▫▫ **tautologic** /-tәlójik/ *adj.* **tautological** /-tәlójik'l/ *adj.* **tautologically** /-tәlójikәli/ *adv.* **tautologist** *n.* **tautologize** /-jīz/ *v.intr.* (also **-ise**). **tautologous** /-lәgәss/ *adj.* [LL *tautologia* f. Gk (as TAUTO-, -LOGY)]

▪ **1** repetition, redundancy, pleonasm, iteration, duplication; repetitiousness, repetitiveness, wordiness, prolixity, verbiage, verbosity, long-windedness. ▫▫ **tautological, tautologous** see REPETITIOUS.

tautomer /táwtәmәr/ *n. Chem.* a substance that exists as two mutually convertible isomers in equilibrium. ▫▫ **tautomeric** /-mérrik/ *adj.* **tautomerism** /-tómmәriz'm/ *n.* [TAUTO- + -MER]

tautophony /tawtóffәni/ *n.* repetition of the same sound. [TAUTO- + Gk *phōnē* sound]

tavern /távvәrn/ *n. literary* an inn or public house. [ME f. OF *taverne* f. L *taberna* hut, tavern]

taverna /tәvérnә/ *n.* a Greek eating house. [mod. Gk (as TAVERN)]

TAVR *abbr.* (in the UK) Territorial and Army Volunteer Reserve. ¶ The name in use 1967–79: now **TA**.

taw[1] /taw/ *v.tr.* make (hide) into leather without the use of tannin, esp. by soaking in a solution of alum and salt. ▫▫ **tawer** *n.* [OE *tawian* f. Gmc]

taw[2] /taw/ *n.* **1** a large marble. **2** a game of marbles. **3** a line from which players throw marbles. [18th c.: orig. unkn.]

tawdry /táwdri/ *adj.* & *n.* ● *adj.* (**tawdrier, tawdriest**) **1** showy but worthless. **2** over-ornamented, gaudy, vulgar. ● *n.* cheap or gaudy finery. ▫▫ **tawdrily** *adv.* **tawdriness** *n.* [earlier as noun: short for *tawdry lace*, orig. *St Audrey's lace* f. *Audrey* = *Etheldrida*, patron saint of Ely]

▪ *adj.* gaudy, cheap, worthless, flashy, Brummagem, showy, meretricious, garish, loud, vulgar, tasteless, tinsel, tinselly, plastic, tinny, shabby, cheapjack, *colloq.* tatty, *esp. US colloq.* tacky. ▫▫ **tawdriness** see GLARE[1] *n.* 3.

tawny /táwni/ *adj.* (**tawnier, tawniest**) of an orange- or yellow-brown colour. ▫ **tawny eagle** a brownish African or Asian eagle, *Aquila rapax*. **tawny owl** a reddish-brown European owl, *Strix aluco*. ▫▫ **tawniness** *n.* [ME f. AF *tauné*, OF *tané* f. *tan* TAN[1]]

taws /tawz/ *n.* (also **tawse**) *Sc. hist.* a thong with a slit end formerly used in schools for punishing children. [app. pl. of obs. *taw* tawed leather, f. TAW[1]]

tax /taks/ *n.* & *v.* ● *n.* **1** a contribution to State revenue compulsorily levied on individuals, property, or businesses (often foll. by *on*: *a tax on luxury goods*). **2** (usu. foll. by *on, upon*) a strain or heavy demand; an oppressive or burdensome obligation. ● *v.tr.* **1** impose a tax on (persons or goods etc.). **2** deduct tax from (income etc.). **3** make heavy demands on (a person's powers or resources etc.) (*you really tax my patience*). **4** (foll. by *with*) confront (a person) with a wrongdoing etc. **5** call to account. **6** *Law* examine and assess (costs etc.). ▫ **tax avoidance** the arrangement of financial affairs to minimize payment of tax. **tax-deductible** (of expenditure) that may be paid out of income before the deduction of income tax. **tax disc** *Brit.* a paper disc displayed on the windscreen of a motor vehicle, certifying payment of excise duty. **tax evasion** the illegal non-payment or underpayment of income tax. **tax-free** exempt from taxes. **tax haven** a country etc. where income tax is low. **tax return** a declaration of income for taxation purposes. **tax shelter** a means of organizing business affairs to minimize payment of tax. **tax year** see *financial year*. ▫▫ **taxable** *adj.* **taxer** *n.* **taxless** *adj.* [ME f. OF *taxer* f. L *taxare* censure, charge, compute, perh. f. Gk *tassō* fix]

▪ *n.* **1** levy, impost, duty, tariff, assessment, tribute, toll, excise, customs, dues, charge, contribution, octroi, tithe, *hist.* scot, *Brit.* rate(s), *Sc., Ir.,* & *Ind. etc.* cess. **2** onus, burden, weight, load, encumbrance, imposition, drain, strain, pressure, demand, obligation. ● *v.* **1** assess, exact *or* demand a tax from, charge, impose *or* levy a tax on, mulct, tithe. **3** burden, strain, put a strain on, try, task; load, overload, overwork, stretch, exhaust, tire, drain; encumber, weigh down, saddle, pressurize, pressure.

taxa *pl.* of TAXON.

taxation /taksáysh'n/ *n.* the imposition or payment of tax. [ME f. AF *taxacioun*, OF *taxation* f. L *taxatio -onis* f. *taxare*: see TAX]

taxi /táksi/ *n.* & *v.* ● *n.* (*pl.* **taxis**) **1** (in full **taxi-cab**) a motor car licensed to ply for hire and usu. fitted with a taximeter. **2** a boat etc. similarly used. ● *v.* (**taxis, taxied, taxiing** or **taxying**) **1 a** *intr.* (of an aircraft or pilot) move along the ground under the machine's own power before take-off or after landing. **b** *tr.* cause (an aircraft) to taxi. **2** *intr.* & *tr.* go or convey in a taxi. ▫ **taxi dancer** a dancing partner available for hire. **taxi-driver** a driver of a taxi. **taxi rank** (*US* **stand**) a place where taxis wait to be hired. [abbr. of *taximeter cab*]

▪ *n.* **1** taxi-cab, cab, hackney carriage, *Brit.* minicab, *US* hack. ● *v.* **2** drive, chauffeur; take a taxi *or* cab.

taxidermy /táksidermi/ *n.* the art of preparing, stuffing, and mounting the skins of animals with lifelike effect. ▫▫ **taxidermal** /-dérm'l/ *adj.* **taxidermic** /-dérmik/ *adj.* **taxidermist** *n.* [Gk *taxis* arrangement + *derma* skin]

taximeter /táksimeetәr/ *n.* an automatic device fitted to a taxi, recording the distance travelled and the fare payable. [F *taximètre* f. *taxe* tariff, TAX + -METER]

taxis /táksiss/ *n.* **1** *Surgery* the restoration of displaced bones or organs by manual pressure. **2** *Biol.* the movement of a cell or organism in response to an external stimulus. **3** *Gram.* order or arrangement of words. [Gk f. *tassō* arrange]

taxman /táksman/ *n. colloq.* (*pl.* **-men**) an inspector or collector of taxes.

taxon /táks'n/ *n.* (*pl.* **taxa** /táksә/) any taxonomic group. [back-form. f. TAXONOMY]

taxonomy /taksónnәmi/ *n.* **1** the science of the classification of living and extinct organisms. **2** the practice of this. ▫▫ **taxonomic** /-sәnómmik/ *adj.* **taxonomical** /-sәnómmik'l/ *adj.* **taxonomically** /-sәnómmikәli/ *adv.* **taxonomist** *n.* [F *taxonomie* (as TAXIS, Gk *-nomia* distribution)]

taxpayer /tákspayәr/ *n.* a person who pays taxes.

tayberry /táybәri/ *n.* (*pl.* **-ies**) a dark red soft fruit produced by crossing the blackberry and raspberry. [*Tay* in Scotland (where introduced in 1977)]

tazza /taátsə/ *n.* a saucer-shaped cup, esp. one mounted on a foot. [It.]

TB *abbr.* **1 a** tubercle bacillus. **b** tuberculosis. **2** torpedo boat.

Tb *symb. Chem.* the element terbium.

T-bone /teébōn/ *n.* a T-shaped bone, esp. in steak from the thin end of a loin.

tbsp. *abbr.* tablespoonful.

Tc *symb. Chem.* the element technetium.

TCD *abbr.* Trinity College, Dublin.

TCP *abbr. propr.* a disinfectant and germicide. [*tri*-*c*hloro*p*henylmethyliodasalicyl]

TD *abbr.* **1** (in the UK) Territorial (Officer's) Decoration. **2** *Ir.* Teachta Dála, Member of the Dáil.

Te *symb. Chem.* the element tellurium.

te /tee/ *n.* (also **ti**) **1** (in tonic sol-fa) the seventh note of a major scale. **2** the note B in the fixed-doh system. [earlier *si*: F f. It., perh. f. *S*ancte *I*ohannes: see GAMUT]

tea /tee/ *n.* & *v.* ● *n.* **1 a** (in full **tea plant**) an evergreen shrub or small tree, *Camellia sinensis*, of India, China, etc. **b** its dried leaves. **2** a drink made by infusing tea-leaves in boiling water. **3** a similar drink made from the leaves of other plants or from another substance (*camomile tea*; *beef tea*). **4 a** a light afternoon meal consisting of tea, bread, cakes, etc. **b** *Brit.* a cooked evening meal. ● *v.* (**teaed** or **tea'd** /teed/) **1** *intr.* take tea. **2** *tr.* give tea to (a person). □ **tea and sympathy** *colloq.* hospitable behaviour towards a troubled person. **tea bag** a small perforated bag of tea for infusion. **tea-ball** esp. *US* a ball of perforated metal to hold tea for infusion. **tea-bread** light or sweet bread for eating at tea. **tea break** *Brit.* a pause in work etc. to drink tea. **tea caddy** a container for tea. **tea ceremony** an elaborate Japanese ritual of serving and drinking tea, as an expression of Zen Buddhist philosophy. **tea chest** a light metal-lined wooden box in which tea is transported. **tea cloth** = *tea towel*. **tea cosy** a cover to keep a teapot warm. **tea dance** an afternoon tea with dancing. **tea garden** a garden in which afternoon tea is served to the public. **tea lady** a woman employed to make tea in offices etc. **tea-leaf 1** a dried leaf of tea, used to make a drink of tea. **2** (esp. in *pl.*) these after infusion or as dregs. **3** *rhyming sl.* a thief. **tea party** a party at teatime. **tea-planter** a proprietor or cultivator of a tea plantation. **tea rose** a hybrid shrub, *Rosa odorata*, with a scent resembling that of tea. **tea towel** a towel for drying washed crockery etc. **tea-tree** *Austral.* & *NZ* an aromatic evergreen flowering shrub, *Leptospermum scoparium*, the manuka. **tea trolley** (*US* **wagon**) a small wheeled trolley from which tea is served. [17th-c. *tay*, *tey*, prob. f. Du. *tee* f. Chin. (Amoy dial.) *te*, = Mandarin dial. *cha*]

teacake /teékayk/ *n. Brit.* a light yeast-based usu. sweet bun eaten at tea, often toasted.

teach /teech/ *v.tr.* (*past* and *past part.* **taught** /tawt/) **1 a** give systematic information to (a person) or about (a subject or skill). **b** (*absol.*) practise this professionally. **c** enable (a person) to do something by instruction and training (*taught me to swim*; *taught me how to dance*). **2** advocate as a moral etc. principle (*my parents taught me tolerance*). **3** (foll. by *to* + infin.) **a** induce (a person) by example or punishment to do or not to do a thing (*that will teach you to sit still*; *that will teach you not to laugh*). **b** *colloq.* make (a person) disinclined to do a thing (*I will teach you to interfere*). □ **teach-in 1** an informal lecture and discussion on a subject of public interest. **2** a series of these. **teach a person a lesson** see LESSON. **teach school** *US* be a teacher in a school. [OE *tǣcan* f. a Gmc root = 'show']

■ **1** show, inform about, familiarize *or* acquaint with; instruct, drill, discipline, educate, school, give a person lessons, guide, train, tutor, coach, enlighten, edify, indoctrinate; communicate, demonstrate, inculcate, instil, give lessons in; *US* teach school. **2** instil (in), din (into), inculcate (in), preach (to); imbue (with), indoctrinate (with).

teachable /teéchəb'l/ *adj.* **1** apt at learning. **2** (of a subject) that can be taught. □□ **teachability** /-billiti/ *n.* **teachableness** *n.*

teacher /teéchər/ *n.* a person who teaches, esp. in a school. □□ **teacherly** *adj.*

■ schoolteacher, educator, instructor, professor, tutor, fellow, lecturer, reader, preceptor, master, mistress, schoolmaster, schoolmistress, coach, trainer, guide, mentor, guru, cicerone, counsellor, governess, educationalist, educationist; rabbi; don, *Sc.* dominie, *archaic* doctor, *archaic or derog.* pedagogue, *Austral. colloq.* chalkie, *US colloq.* schoolma'm, *Austral. sl.* & *dial.* schoolie, *Brit. sl.* beak.

teaching /teéching/ *n.* **1** the profession of a teacher. **2** (often in *pl.*) what is taught; a doctrine. □ **teaching hospital** a hospital where medical students are taught. **teaching machine** any of various devices for giving instruction according to a programme measuring pupils' responses.

■ **1** see EDUCATION 1a. **2** see DOCTRINE.

teacup /teékup/ *n.* **1** a cup from which tea is drunk. **2** an amount held by this, about 150 ml. □□ **teacupful** *n.* (*pl.* **-fuls**).

teak /teek/ *n.* **1** a large deciduous tree, *Tectona grandis*, native to India and SE Asia. **2** its hard durable timber, much used in shipbuilding and furniture. [Port. *teca* f. Malayalam *tēkka*]

teal /teel/ *n.* (*pl.* same) **1** any of various small freshwater ducks of the genus *Anas*, esp. *A. crecca*. **2** a dark greenish-blue colour. [rel. to MDu. *tēling*, of unkn. orig.]

team /teem/ *n.* & *v.* ● *n.* **1** a set of players forming one side in a game (*a cricket team*). **2** two or more persons working together. **3 a** a set of draught animals. **b** one animal or more in harness with a vehicle. ● *v.* **1** *intr.* & *tr.* (usu. foll. by *up*) join in a team or in common action (*decided to team up with them*). **2** *tr.* harness (horses etc.) in a team. **3** *tr.* (foll. by *with*) match or coordinate (clothes). □ **team-mate** a fellow-member of a team or group. **team spirit** willingness to act as a member of a group rather than as an individual. **team-teaching** teaching by a team of teachers working together. [OE *tēam* offspring f. a Gmc root = 'pull', rel. to TOW[1]]

■ *n.* **1** side, line-up, club, squad. **2** pair, group, partnership, band, gang, alliance, body, corps, crew, cadre, squad, party, troupe. **3** pair, yoke, span, duo, set, rig, tandem. ● *v.* **1** join (up *or* together), band *or* club *or* get *or* work together, join forces, unite, ally, combine, link (up), cooperate, collaborate; conspire. **3** match, pair, mate, put together, coordinate, complement.
□ **team-mate** see COLLEAGUE. **team spirit** *esprit de corps*, unity, morale.

teamster /teémstər/ *n.* **1** *US* a lorry-driver. **2** a driver of a team of animals.

teamwork /teémwurk/ *n.* the combined action of a team, group, etc., esp. when effective and efficient.

■ see COOPERATION.

teapot /teépot/ *n.* a pot with a handle, spout, and lid, in which tea is brewed and from which it is poured.

teapoy /teépoy/ *n.* a small three- or four-legged table esp. for tea. [Hindi *tīn*, *tir*- three + Pers. *pāī* foot: sense and spelling infl. by TEA]

tear[1] /tair/ *v.* & *n.* ● *v.* (*past* **tore** /tor/; *past part.* **torn** /torn/) **1** *tr.* (often foll. by *up*) pull apart or to pieces with some force (*tear it in half*; *tore up the letter*). **2** *tr.* **a** make a hole or rent in by tearing (*have torn my coat*). **b** make (a hole or rent). **3** *tr.* (foll. by *away*, *off*, etc.) pull violently or with some force (*tore the book away from me*; *tore off the cover*; *tore a page out*; *tore down the notice*). **4** *tr.* violently disrupt or divide (*the country was torn by civil war*; *torn by conflicting emotions*). **5** *intr. colloq.* go or travel hurriedly or impetuously (*tore across the road*). **6** *intr.* undergo tearing (*the curtain tore down the middle*). **7** *intr.* (foll. by *at* etc.) pull violently or with some force. ● *n.* **1** a hole or other damage caused by tearing. **2** a torn part of cloth etc. **3** *sl.* a spree; a drinking-bout. □ **be torn between** have difficulty in choosing between. **tear apart 1** search (a place) exhaustively. **2** criticize forcefully. **tear one's hair out** behave with extreme desperation or anger. **tear into 1** attack verbally; reprimand. **2** make a vigorous start on (an activity). **tear oneself away** leave despite a strong desire to stay. **tear sheet** a page that can be removed from a newspaper or magazine etc. for use separately. **tear to shreds** *colloq.* refute or criticize thoroughly. **that's torn it** *Brit. colloq.* that has spoiled things, caused a problem, etc. □□ **tearable** *adj.* **tearer** *n.* [OE *teran* f. Gmc]

■ *v.* **1** rip, rupture, pull apart, shred, mutilate, mangle, claw, split, divide, separate, sever, *archaic or poet.* rive, *archaic or rhet.* rend. **2 a** rip, gash, lacerate, pierce, split, slit, snag. **b** rip, pierce. **3** pull, rip, snatch, seize, wrench. **4** disrupt, divide, split, disunite, *archaic or poet.* rive, *archaic or rhet.* rend. **5** dash, fly, run, gallop, race, rush, shoot, sprint, speed, bolt, dart, flit, scurry, scuttle, career, zoom, hurry, hasten, hurtle, spurt, zip, *colloq.* whiz, scoot. ● *n.* **1** rip, rent, rupture, hole, split, slash, gore, cut, score, slit, gash, fissure, rift, laceration. **3** see BENDER. □ **tear apart 1** see SCOUR². **tear one's hair out** see FRET¹ 1a. **tear into 1** see *pitch into* (PITCH¹).

tear² /teer/ *n.* **1** a drop of clear salty liquid secreted by glands, that serves to moisten and wash the eye and is shed from it in grief or other strong emotions. **2** a tearlike thing; a drop. □ **in tears** crying; shedding tears. **tear-drop** a single tear. **tear-duct** a drain for carrying tears to the eye or from the eye to the nose. **tear-gas** gas that disables by causing severe irritation to the eyes. **tear-jerker** *colloq.* a story, film, etc., calculated to evoke sadness or sympathy. **without tears** presented so as to be learned or done easily. □□ **tearlike** *adj.* [OE *tēar*]

tearaway /táirəway/ *n. Brit.* **1** an impetuous or reckless young person. **2** a hooligan.

tearful /teérfŏŏl/ *adj.* **1** crying or inclined to cry. **2** causing or accompanied with tears; sad (*a tearful event*). □□ **tearfully** *adv.* **tearfulness** *n.*

■ **1** weeping, crying, in tears, sobbing, whimpering, dewy-eyed, blubbering, snivelling, maudlin, *colloq.* weepy, *formal* lachrymose. **2** see SAD 2, SENTIMENTAL. □□ **tearfulness** see *sentimentality* (SENTIMENTAL).

tearing /táiring/ *adj.* extreme, overwhelming, violent (*in a tearing hurry*).

tearless /teérliss/ *adj.* not shedding tears. □□ **tearlessly** *adv.* **tearlessness** *n.*

tearoom /teé-rŏŏm, -rŏŏm/ *n.* a small restaurant or café where tea is served.

tease /teez/ *v.* & *n.* ● *v.tr.* (also *absol.*) **1 a** make fun of (a person or animal) playfully or unkindly or annoyingly. **b** tempt or allure, esp. sexually, while refusing to satisfy the desire aroused. **2** pick (wool, hair, etc.) into separate fibres. **3** dress (cloth) esp. with teasels. ● *n.* **1** *colloq.* a person fond of teasing. **2** an instance of teasing (*it was only a tease*). □ **tease out 1** separate (strands etc.) by disentangling. **2** search out, elicit (information etc.). □□ **teasingly** *adv.* [OE *tǣsan* f. WG]

■ *v.* **1** bait, taunt, torment, harass, bedevil, bother, nettle, plague, chaff, pester, annoy, irritate, goad, badger, provoke, vex, twit, tantalize, frustrate, pick on, drive mad *or* crazy, guy, make fun of, deride, laugh at, mock, gibe at, pull a person's leg, *colloq.* needle, rib, have on, drive up the wall, *esp. Austral. colloq.* stir, *disp.* aggravate, *sl.* take the mickey out of, rag, *Austral.* & *NZ sl.* sling off at, poke borak at; see also FLIRT *v.* 1. ● *n.* **1** see NUISANCE, FLIRT *n.* □ **tease out 2** elicit, search out, coax *or* worry *or* winkle *or* work out. □□ **teasingly** see *in fun* (FUN).

teasel /teéz'l/ *n.* & *v.* (also **teazel, teazle**) ● *n.* **1** any plant of the genus *Dipsacus*, with large prickly heads that are dried and used to raise the nap on woven cloth. **2** a device used as a substitute for teasels. ● *v.tr.* dress (cloth) with teasels. □□ **teaseler** *n.* [OE *tǣs(e)l*, = OHG *zeisala* (as TEASE)]

teaser /teézər/ *n.* **1** *colloq.* a hard question or task. **2** a teasing person. **3** esp. *US* a short introductory advertisement etc.

teaset /teésset/ *n.* a set of crockery for serving tea.

teashop /teéshop/ *n.* esp. *Brit.* = TEAROOM.

teaspoon /teéspōōn/ *n.* **1** a small spoon for stirring tea. **2** an amount held by this. □□ **teaspoonful** *n.* (*pl.* **-fuls**).

teat /teet/ *n.* **1** a mammary nipple, esp. of an animal. **2** a thing resembling this, esp. a device of rubber etc. for sucking milk from a bottle. [ME f. OF *tete*, prob. of Gmc orig., replacing TIT³]

teatime /teétīm/ *n.* the time in the afternoon when tea is served.

teazel (also **teazle**) var. of TEASEL.

tec /tek/ *n. colloq.* a detective. [abbr.]

tech /tek/ *n.* (also **tec**) *colloq.* a technical college. [abbr.]

technetium /tekneéshəm/ *n. Chem.* an artificially produced radioactive metallic element occurring in the fission products of uranium. ¶ Symb.: **Tc**. [mod.L f. Gk *tekhnētos* artificial f. *tekhnē* art]

technic /téknik/ *n.* **1** (usu. in *pl.*) **a** technology. **b** technical terms, details, methods, etc. **2** technique. □□ **technicist** /-nisist/ *n.* [L *technicus* f. Gk *tekhnikos* f. *tekhnē* art]

technical /téknik'l/ *adj.* **1** of or involving or concerned with the mechanical arts and applied sciences (*technical college*; *a technical education*). **2** of or relating to a particular subject or craft etc. or its techniques (*technical terms*; *technical merit*). **3** (of a book or discourse etc.) using technical language; requiring special knowledge to be understood. **4** due to mechanical failure (*a technical hitch*). **5** legally such; such in strict interpretation (*technical assault*; *lost on a technical point*). □ **technical hitch** a temporary breakdown or problem in machinery etc. **technical knockout** *Boxing* a termination of a fight by the referee on the grounds of a contestant's inability to continue, the opponent being declared the winner. □□ **technically** *adv.* **technicalness** *n.*

■ **1** mechanical, applied, industrial, polytechnic, technological. **2, 3** complex, complicated, detailed, intricate, esoteric, specialized. **4** mechanical.

technicality /téknikálliti/ *n.* (*pl.* **-ies**) **1** the state of being technical. **2** a technical expression. **3** a technical point or detail (*was acquitted on a technicality*).

■ **3** see DETAIL *n.* 1, *triviality* (TRIVIAL).

technician /tekníśh'n/ *n.* **1** an expert in the practical application of a science. **2** a person skilled in the technique of an art or craft. **3** a person employed to look after technical equipment and do practical work in a laboratory etc.

Technicolor /téknikullər/ *n.* (often *attrib.*) **1** *propr.* a process of colour cinematography using synchronized monochrome films, each of a different colour, to produce a colour print. **2** (usu. **technicolor**) *colloq.* **a** vivid colour. **b** artificial brilliance. □□ **technicolored** *adj.* [TECHNICAL + COLOR]

technique /tekneék/ *n.* **1** mechanical skill in an art. **2** a means of achieving one's purpose, esp. skilfully. **3** a manner of artistic execution in music, painting, etc. [F (as TECHNIC)]

■ **1** technic, art, craftsmanship, artistry, craft, knack, touch, skill, skilfulness, adroitness, adeptness, dexterousness, facility, competence, faculty, ability, aptitude, performance, proficiency, talent, gift, genius, expertise. **2** technic, method, approach, manner, mode, means, fashion, style, procedure, system, way, knack, tack, line, *modus operandi*, m.o., standard operating procedure.

technobabble /téknōbább'l/ *n. colloq.* incomprehensible technical jargon.

technocracy /teknókrəsi/ *n.* (*pl.* **-ies**) **1** the government or control of society or industry by technical experts. **2** an instance or application of this. [Gk *tekhnē* art + -CRACY]

technocrat /téknəkrat/ *n.* an exponent or advocate of technocracy. □□ **technocratic** /-kráttik/ *adj.* **technocratically** /-kráttikəli/ *adv.*

technological /téknəlójik'l/ *adj.* of or using technology. □□ **technologically** *adv.*

technology /teknóllәji/ *n.* (*pl.* **-ies**) **1** the study or use of the mechanical arts and applied sciences. **2** these subjects collectively. □□ **technologist** *n.* [Gk *tekhnologia* systematic treatment f. *tekhnē* art]

techy var. of TETCHY.

tectonic /tektónnik/ *adj.* **1** of or relating to building or construction. **2** *Geol.* relating to the deformation of the earth's crust or to the structural changes caused by this (see *plate tectonics*). □□ **tectonically** *adv.* [LL *tectonicus* f. Gk *tektonikos* f. *tektōn -onos* carpenter]

tectonics /tektónniks/ *n.pl.* (usu. treated as *sing.*) **1** *Archit.* the art and process of producing practical and aesthetically pleasing buildings. **2** *Geol.* the study of large-scale structural features (cf. *plate tectonics*).

tectorial /tektóriәl/ *adj. Anat.* **1** forming a covering. **2** (in full **tectorial membrane**) the membrane covering the organ of Corti (see CORTI) in the inner ear. [L *tectorium* a cover (as TECTRIX)]

tectrix /téktriks/ *n.* (*pl.* **tectrices** /-triseez, -trīseez/) = COVERT *n.* 2. [mod.L f. L *tegere tect-* cover]

Ted /ted/ *n.* (also **ted**) *Brit. colloq.* a Teddy boy. [abbr.]

ted /ted/ *v.tr.* (**tedded, tedding**) turn over and spread out (grass, hay, or straw) to dry or for a bedding etc. □□ **tedder** *n.* [ME f. ON *tethja* spread manure f. *tad* dung, *toddi* small piece]

teddy /téddi/ *n.* (also **Teddy**) (*pl.* **-ies**) (in full **teddy bear**) a soft toy bear. [*Teddy*, pet-name of *Theodore* Roosevelt, US president d. 1919, famous as a bear-hunter]

Teddy boy /téddi/ *n. Brit. colloq.* **1** a youth, esp. of the 1950s, affecting an Edwardian style of dress and appearance. **2** a young rowdy male. [*Teddy*, pet-form of *Edward*]

Te Deum /tee dée-әm, tay dáyәm/ **1 a** a hymn beginning *Te Deum laudamus*, 'We praise Thee, O God'. **b** the music for this. **2** an expression of thanksgiving or exultation. [L]

tedious /téediәss/ *adj.* tiresomely long; wearisome. □□ **tediously** *adv.* **tediousness** *n.* [ME f. OF *tedieus* or LL *taediosus* (as TEDIUM)]

■ over-long, long-drawn-out, prolonged, endless, unending, monotonous, unchanging, changeless, unvarying, laborious, long-winded, wearing, wearying, wearisome, tiring, exhausting, fatiguing, tiresome, boring, dreary, dull, dead, dry as dust, drab, colourless, vapid, insipid, flat, uninteresting, banal, unexciting, prosaic, prosy, soporific, humdrum, routine, repetitious, repetitive, mechanical, soul-destroying, automaton-like, automatic. □□ **tediousness** see TEDIUM.

tedium /téediәm/ *n.* the state of being tedious; boredom. [L *taedium* f. *taedēre* to weary]

■ tediousness, monotony, changelessness, invariability, long-windedness, wearisomeness, tiresomeness, boredom, ennui, dreariness, dullness, drabness, colourlessness, vapidity, insipidity, insipidness, vapidness, banality, routine, repetitiousness.

tee[1] /tee/ *n.* = T[1]. [phonet. spelling]

tee[2] /tee/ *n.* & *v.* ● *n.* **1** *Golf* **a** a cleared space from which a golf ball is struck at the beginning of play for each hole. **b** a small support of wood or plastic from which a ball is struck at a tee. **2** a mark aimed at in bowls, quoits, curling, etc. ● *v.tr.* (**tees, teed**) (often foll. by *up*) *Golf* place (a ball) on a tee ready to strike it. □ **tee off 1** *Golf* play a ball from a tee. **2** *colloq.* start, begin. [earlier (17th-c.) *teaz*, of unkn. orig.: in sense 2 perh. = TEE[1]]

tee-hee /teehée/ *n.* & *v.* (also **te-hee**) ● *n.* **1** a titter. **2** a restrained or contemptuous laugh. ● *v.intr.* (**tee-hees, tee-heed**) titter or laugh in this way. [imit.]

teem[1] /teem/ *v.intr.* **1** be abundant (*fish teem in these waters*). **2** (foll. by *with*) be full of or swarming with (*teeming with fish*; *teeming with ideas*). [OE *tēman* etc. give birth to f. Gmc, rel. to TEAM]

■ **1** proliferate, be prolific, abound, be abundant. **2** (*teem with*) be prolific in, abound in *or* with, be abundant in, swarm with, be alive with, crawl with, bristle with, overflow with, be overrun with, be full of, brim with, *colloq.* be lousy with.

teem[2] /teem/ *v.intr.* (often foll. by *down*) (of water etc.) flow copiously; pour (*it was teeming with rain*). [ME *tēmen* f. ON *tœma* f. *tómr* (adj.) empty]

■ pour, rain, stream (down), pelt (down), come down (in buckets), *colloq.* bucket down, rain cats and dogs.

teen /teen/ *adj.* & *n.* ● *adj.* = TEENAGE. ● *n.* = TEENAGER. [abbr. of TEENAGE, TEENAGER]

-teen /teen/ *suffix* forming the names of numerals from 13 to 19. [OE inflected form of TEN]

teenage /téenayj/ *adj.* relating to or characteristic of teenagers. □□ **teenaged** *adj.*

■ see ADOLESCENT *adj.*

teenager /téenayjәr/ *n.* a person from 13 to 19 years of age.

■ teen, adolescent, youth, boy, girl, young man, young lady *or* woman, stripling, juvenile, minor, *colloq.* kid.

teens /teenz/ *n.pl.* the years of one's age from 13 to 19 (*in one's teens*).

teensy /téenzi/ *adj.* (**teensier, teensiest**) *colloq.* = TEENY. □ **teensy-weensy** = *teeny-weeny*.

teeny /téeni/ *adj.* (**teenier, teeniest**) *colloq.* tiny. □ **teeny-weeny** very tiny. [var. of TINY]

■ see TINY .

teeny-bopper /téenibopper/ *n. colloq.* a young teenager, usu. a girl, who keenly follows the latest fashions in clothes, pop music, etc.

teepee var. of TEPEE.

teeshirt var. of T-SHIRT.

teeter /téetәr/ *v.intr.* **1** totter; stand or move unsteadily. **2** hesitate; be indecisive. □ **teeter on the brink** (or **edge**) be in imminent danger (of disaster etc.). [var. of dial. *titter*]

■ **1** wobble, rock, sway, totter, waver, tremble, stagger. **2** see SEE-SAW *v.*

teeth *pl.* of TOOTH.

teethe /teeth/ *v.intr.* grow or cut teeth, esp. milk teeth. □ **teething-ring** a small ring for an infant to bite on while teething. **teething troubles** initial difficulties in an enterprise etc., regarded as temporary. □□ **teething** *n.*

teetotal /teetṓt'l/ *adj.* advocating or characterized by total abstinence from alcoholic drink. □□ **teetotalism** *n.* [redupl. of TOTAL]

■ see SOBER *adj.* 2. □□ **teetotalism** see TEMPERANCE 2a.

teetotaller /teetṓtәlәr/ *n.* (*US* **teetotaler**) a person advocating or practising abstinence from alcoholic drink.

teetotum /teetṓtәm/ *n.* **1** a spinning-top with four sides lettered to determine whether the spinner has won or lost. **2** any top spun with the fingers. [*T* (the letter on one side) + L *totum* the whole (stakes), for which *T* stood]

teff /tef/ *n.* an African cereal, *Eragrostis tef.* [Amharic *ṭêf*]

TEFL /téff'l/ *abbr.* teaching of English as a foreign language.

Teflon /téflon/ *n. propr.* polytetrafluoroethylene, esp. used as a non-stick coating for kitchen utensils. [*te*tra- + *fluor-* + *-on*]

teg /teg/ *n.* a sheep in its second year. [ME *tegge* (recorded in place-names), repr. OE (unrecorded) *tegga* ewe]

tegular /tégyoolәr/ *adj.* **1** of or like tiles. **2** arranged like tiles. □□ **tegularly** *adv.* [L *tegula* tile f. *tegere* cover]

tegument /tégyoomәnt/ *n.* the natural covering of an animal's body or part of its body. □□ **tegumental** /-mént'l/ *adj.* **tegumentary** /-méntәri/ *adj.* [L *tegumentum* f. *tegere* cover]

te-hee var. of TEE-HEE.

tektite /téktīt/ *n. Geol.* a small roundish glassy body of unknown origin occurring in various parts of the earth. [G *Tektit* f. Gk *tēktos* molten f. *tēkō* melt]

Tel. *abbr.* **1** Telephone. **2 a** Telegraph. **b** Telegraphic.

telaesthesia /téllis-theéziә/ *n.* (*US* **telesthesia**) *Psychol.* the supposed perception of distant occurrences or objects otherwise than by the recognized senses. □□ **telaesthetic** /-théttik/ *adj.* [mod.L, formed as TELE- + Gk *aisthēsis* perception]

telamon /téllәmōn/ *n.* (*pl.* **telamones** /-mṓneez/) *Archit.* a male figure used as a pillar to support an entablature. [L *telamones* f. Gk *telamōnes* pl. of *Telamōn*, name of a mythical hero]

tele- /télli/ *comb. form* **1** at or to a distance (*telekinesis*). **2** forming names of instruments for operating over long distances (*telescope*). **3** television (*telecast*). **4** done by means of the telephone (*telesales*). [Gk *tēle-* f. *tēle* far off: sense 3 f. TELEVISION: sense 4 f. TELEPHONE]

tele-ad /télliad/ *n.* an advertisement placed in a newspaper etc. by telephone.

telecamera /téllikamrә, -mәrә/ *n.* **1** a television camera. **2** a telephotographic camera.

telecast /téllikaast/ *n.* & *v.* ● *n.* a television broadcast. ● *v.tr.* transmit by television. ▫▫ **telecaster** *n.* [TELE- + BROADCAST]

■ *n.* see BROADCAST *n.* ● *v.* see BROADCAST *v.* 1a.

telecine /téllisinni/ *n.* **1** the broadcasting of cinema film on television. **2** equipment for doing this. [TELE- + CINE]

telecommunication /téllikәmyōōnikáysh'n/ *n.* **1** communication over a distance by cable, telegraph, telephone, or broadcasting. **2** (usu. in *pl.*) the branch of technology concerned with this. [F *télécommunication* (as TELE-, COMMUNICATION)]

teleconference /téllikónfәrәnss/ *n.* a conference with participants in different locations linked by telecommunication devices. ▫▫ **teleconferencing** *n.*

teledu /téllidōō/ *n.* a badger, *Mydaus javanensis*, of Java and Sumatra, that secretes a foul-smelling liquid when attacked. [Jav.]

telefacsimile /téllifaksímmili/ *n.* facsimile transmission (see FACSIMILE *n.* 2).

Telefax /téllifaks/ *n. propr.* = TELEFACSIMILE. [abbr.]

telefilm /téllifilm/ *n.* = TELECINE.

telegenic /téllijénnik/ *adj.* having an appearance or manner that looks pleasing on television. [TELEVISION + *-genic* in PHOTOGENIC]

telegony /tiléggәni/ *n. Biol.* the supposed influence of a previous sire on the offspring of a dam with other sires. ▫▫ **telegonic** /télligónnik/ *adj.* [TELE- + Gk *-gonia* begetting]

telegram /télligram/ *n.* a message sent by telegraph and then usu. delivered in written form. ¶ In UK official use since 1981 only for international messages. [TELE- + -GRAM, after TELEGRAPH]

■ cable, cablegram, radiogram, radio-telegram, telex, *Brit.* telemessage, *esp. US colloq.* wire, *US trade mark* Mailgram.

telegraph /télligraaf, -graf/ *n.* & *v.* ● *n.* **1 a** a system of or device for transmitting messages or signals to a distance esp. by making and breaking an electrical connection. **b** (*attrib.*) used in this system (*telegraph pole*; *telegraph wire*). **2** (in full **telegraph board**) a board displaying scores or other information at a match, race meeting, etc. ● *v.* **1** *tr.* send a message by telegraph to. **2** *tr.* send by telegraph. **3** *tr.* give an advance indication of. **4** *intr.* make signals (*telegraphed to me to come up*). ▫ **telegraph key** a device for making and breaking the electric circuit of a telegraph system. **telegraph plant** an E. Indian plant, *Desmodium gyrans*, whose leaves have a spontaneous jerking motion. ▫▫ **telegrapher** /télligraafәr, tilégrәfәr/ *n.* [F *télégraphe* (as TELE-, -GRAPH)]

■ *v.* **1, 2** see TRANSMIT 1a. **4** see SIGNAL *v.* 1, 2a.

telegraphese /télligrәféez/ *n. colloq.* or *joc.* an abbreviated style usual in telegrams.

telegraphic /télligráffik/ *adj.* **1** of or by telegraphs or telegrams. **2** economically worded. ▫ **telegraphic address** an abbreviated or other registered address for use in telegrams. ▫▫ **telegraphically** *adv.*

telegraphist /tilégrәfist/ *n.* a person skilled or employed in telegraphy.

telegraphy /tilégrәfi/ *n.* the science or practice of using or constructing communication systems for the reproduction of information.

Telegu var. of TELUGU.

telekinesis /téllikīnéessis, -kinéessiss/ *n. Psychol.* movement of objects at a distance supposedly by paranormal means. ▫▫ **telekinetic** /-néttik/ *adj.* [mod.L (as TELE-, Gk *kinēsis* motion f. *kineō* move)]

■ ▫▫ **telekinetic** see PSYCHIC *adj.* 1b.

telemark /téllimaark/ *n.* & *v. Skiing* ● *n.* a swing turn with one ski advanced and the knee bent, used to change direction or stop short. ● *v.intr.* perform this turn. [*Telemark* in Norway]

telemarketing /téllimaarkiting/ *n.* the marketing of goods etc. by means of usu. unsolicited telephone calls. ▫▫ **telemarketer** *n.*

telemessage /téllimessij/ *n.* a message sent by telephone or telex and delivered in written form. ¶ In UK official use since 1981 for inland messages, replacing *telegram*.

■ see TELEGRAM.

telemeter /téllimeetәr, tilémmitәr/ *n.* & *v.* ● *n.* an apparatus for recording the readings of an instrument and transmitting them by radio. ● *v.* **1** *intr.* record readings in this way. **2** *tr.* transmit (readings etc.) to a distant receiving set or station. ▫▫ **telemetric** /-métrik/ *adj.* **telemetry** /tilémmәtri/ *n.*

teleology /télliólləji, teé-/ *n.* (*pl.* **-ies**) *Philos.* **1** the explanation of phenomena by the purpose they serve rather than by postulated causes. **2** *Theol.* the doctrine of design and purpose in the material world. ▫▫ **teleologic** /-liәlójik/ *adj.* **teleological** /-liәlójik'l/ *adj.* **teleologically** /-liәlójikәli/ *adv.* **teleologism** *n.* **teleologist** *n.* [mod.L *teleologia* f. Gk *telos teleos* end + -LOGY]

teleost /télliost/ *n.* any fish of the subclass Teleostei of bony fish, including eels, plaice, salmon, etc. [Gk *teleo-* complete + *osteon* bone]

telepath /téllipath/ *n.* a telepathic person. [back-form. f. TELEPATHY]

telepathy /tiléppәthi/ *n.* the supposed communication of thoughts or ideas otherwise than by the known senses. ▫▫ **telepathic** /téllipáthik/ *adj.* **telepathically** /téllipáthikәli/ *adv.* **telepathist** *n.* **telepathize** *v.tr.* & *intr.* (also **-ise**).

■ ▫▫ **telepathic** clairvoyant, magical; see also PSYCHIC *adj.* 1b.

telephone /téllifōn/ *n.* & *v.* ● *n.* **1** an apparatus for transmitting sound (esp. speech) to a distance by wire or cord or radio, esp. by converting acoustic vibrations to electrical signals. **2** a transmitting and receiving instrument used in this. **3** a system of communication using a network of telephones. ● *v.* **1** *tr.* speak to (a person) by telephone. **2** *tr.* send (a message) by telephone. **3** *intr.* make a telephone call. ▫ **on the telephone 1** having a telephone. **2** by use of or using the telephone. **over the telephone** by use of or using the telephone. **telephone book** = *telephone directory*. **telephone box** *Brit.* = *telephone booth*. **telephone booth** (or **kiosk**) a public booth or enclosure from which telephone calls can be made. **telephone call** = CALL *n.* 4. **telephone directory** a book listing telephone subscribers and numbers in a particular area. **telephone exchange** = EXCHANGE *n.* 3. **telephone number** a number assigned to a particular telephone and used in making connections to it. **telephone operator** esp. *US* an operator in a telephone exchange. ▫▫ **telephoner** *n.* **telephonic** /-fónnik/ *adj.* **telephonically** /-fónnikәli/ *adv.*

■ *n.* **1, 2** handset, *colloq.* phone, blower, *esp. US colloq.* horn. ● *v.* **1, 3** call (up), *Brit.* ring (up), *colloq.* phone, give a person a ring *or* call *or* bell, get a person on the blower, *Brit. colloq.* give a person a tinkle, *esp. US colloq.* get a person on the horn, *sl.* buzz, give a person a buzz. **2** see TRANSMIT 1a.

telephonist /tiléffәnist/ *n. Brit.* an operator in a telephone exchange or at a switchboard.

telephony /tiléffәni/ *n.* the use or a system of telephones.

telephoto /téllifōtō/ *n.* (*pl.* **-os**) (in full **telephoto lens**) a lens used in telephotography.

telephotographic /téllifōtәgráffik/ *adj.* of or for or using telephotography. ▫▫ **telephotographically** *adv.*

telephotography /téllifətógrəfi/ *n.* the photographing of distant objects with a system of lenses giving a large image.

teleport /télliport/ *v.tr. Psychol.* move by telekinesis. ▫▫ **teleportation** /-táysh'n/ *n.* [TELE- + PORT[4] 3]

teleprinter /télliprintər/ *n.* a device for transmitting telegraph messages as they are keyed, and for printing messages received.

teleprompter /télliprompter/ *n.* a device beside a television or cinema camera that slowly unrolls a speaker's script out of sight of the audience (cf. AUTOCUE).

telerecord /téllirikord/ *v.tr.* record for television broadcasting.

telerecording /téllirikording/ *n.* a recorded television broadcast.

telesales /téllisaylz/ *n.pl.* selling by means of the telephone.

telescope /tèlliskōp/ *n.* & *v.* ● *n.* **1** an optical instrument using lenses or mirrors or both to make distant objects appear nearer and larger. **2** = *radio telescope.* ● *v.* **1** *tr.* press or drive (sections of a tube, colliding vehicles, etc.) together so that one slides into another like the sections of a folding telescope. **2** *intr.* close or be driven or be capable of closing in this way. **3** *tr.* compress so as to occupy less space or time. [It. *telescopio* or mod.L *telescopium* (as TELE-, -SCOPE)]

■ *n.* **1** spyglass, glass; refracting telescope, reflecting telescope. ● *v.* **1** concertina, squash, crush. **3** shorten, compress, compact, abbreviate, contract, condense, summarize, précis, digest, tighten (up), boil down, abridge, abstract.

telescopic /télliskóppik/ *adj.* **1 a** of, relating to, or made with a telescope (*telescopic observations*). **b** visible only through a telescope (*telescopic stars*). **2** (esp. of a lens) able to focus on and magnify distant objects. **3** consisting of sections that telescope. ▫ **telescopic sight** a telescope used for sighting on a rifle etc. ▫▫ **telescopically** *adv.*

telesoftware /téllisóftwair/ *n.* software transmitted or broadcast to receiving terminals.

telesthesia *US* var. of TELAESTHESIA.

Teletex /tèlliteks/ *n. propr.* an electronic text transmission system.

teletext /téllitekst/ *n.* a news and information service, in the form of text and graphics, from a computer source transmitted to televisions with appropriate receivers (cf. CEEFAX, ORACLE).

telethon /téllithon/ *n.* esp. *US* an exceptionally long television programme, esp. to raise money for a charity. [TELE- + *-thon* in MARATHON]

Teletype /téllitīp/ *n.* & *v.* ● *n. propr.* a kind of teleprinter. ● *v.* (**teletype**) **1** *intr.* operate a teleprinter. **2** *tr.* send by means of a teleprinter.

teletypewriter /téllitīprītər/ *n.* esp. *US* = TELEPRINTER.

televangelist /téllivánjəlist/ *n.* esp. *US* an evangelical preacher who appears regularly on television to promote beliefs and appeal for funds.

televiewer /téllivyōōər/ *v.tr.* a person who watches television. ▫▫ **televiewing** *adj.*

televise /tèllivīz/ *v.tr.* transmit by television. ▫▫ **televisable** *adj.* [back-form. f. TELEVISION]

■ see BROADCAST *v.* 1a.

television /téllivízh'n/ *n.* **1** a system for reproducing on a screen visual images transmitted (usu. with sound) by radio signals. **2** (in full **television set**) a device with a screen for receiving these signals. **3** the medium, art form, or occupation of broadcasting on television; the content of television programmes.

■ **2, 3** TV, receiver, video (receiver), small screen, *colloq.* box, idiot box, *esp. Brit. colloq.* telly, *Brit. colloq.* goggle-box, *US colloq.* tube, *US sl.* boob tube.

televisual /téllivízhooəl, -vízyooəl/ *adj.* relating to or suitable for television. ▫▫ **televisually** *adv.*

telex /télleks/ *n.* & *v.* (also **Telex**) ● *n.* an international system of telegraphy with printed messages transmitted and received by teleprinters using the public telecommunications network. ● *v.tr.* send or communicate with by telex. [TELEPRINTER + EXCHANGE]

■ *v.* see TRANSMIT 1a.

tell[1] /tel/ *v.* (*past* and *past part.* **told** /tōld/) **1** *tr.* relate or narrate in speech or writing; give an account of (*tell me a story*). **2** *tr.* make known; express in words; divulge (*tell me your name; tell me what you want*). **3** *tr.* reveal or signify to (a person) (*your face tells me everything*). **4** *tr.* **a** utter (*don't tell lies*). **b** warn (*I told you so*). **5** *intr.* **a** (often foll. by *of*, *about*) divulge information or a description; reveal a secret (*I told of the plan; promise you won't tell*). **b** (foll. by *on*) *colloq.* inform against (a person). **6** *tr.* (foll. by *to* + infin.) give (a person) a direction or order (*tell them to wait; do as you are told*). **7** *tr.* assure (*it's true, I tell you*). **8** *tr.* explain in writing; instruct (*this book tells you how to cook*). **9** *tr.* decide, predict, determine, distinguish (*cannot tell what might happen; how do you tell one from the other?*). **10** *intr.* **a** (often foll. by *on*) produce a noticeable effect (*every disappointment tells; the strain was beginning to tell on me*). **b** reveal the truth (*time will tell*). **c** have an influence (*the evidence tells against you*). **11** *tr.* (often *absol.*) count (votes) at a meeting, election, etc. ▫ **as far as one can tell** judging from the available information. **tell apart** distinguish between (usu. with *neg.* or *interrog.*: *could not tell them apart*). **tell me another** *colloq.* an expression of incredulity. **tell off 1** *colloq.* reprimand, scold. **2** count off or detach for duty. **tell a tale** (or **its own tale**) be significant or revealing. **tell tales** report a discreditable fact about another. **tell that to the marines** see MARINE. **tell the time** determine the time from the face of a clock or watch. **there is no telling** it is impossible to know (*there's no telling what may happen*). **you're telling me** *colloq.* I agree wholeheartedly. ▫▫ **tellable** *adj.* [OE *tellan* f. Gmc, rel. to TALE]

■ **1** relate, narrate, recount, recite, report, chronicle. **2** say, mention, utter, state, declare, proclaim, announce, publish, broadcast, communicate, make known, report, impart, indicate, advertise, trumpet, herald, intimate, hint at, refer to, touch on, acknowledge, confess, apprise, advise, inform, let a person know, notify, acquaint a person with a thing; recount, describe, delineate, outline, portray, depict, express, put, word, explain; disclose, divulge, release, break, let a thing be known, bring to light, leak, admit, betray, blab, tattle, let out, let slip, *colloq.* get a thing off one's chest. **3** reveal, express, show, convey, communicate, signify, impart, indicate. **4 a** see SPEAK 2. **b** warn, advise, counsel, caution, forewarn, alert, inform, apprise. **5 a** unbosom oneself, unburden *or* disburden oneself, blab, tattle, talk, let the cat out of the bag, give the (whole) show away, *colloq.* spill the beans, *Brit. sl.* blow the gaff. **b** (*tell on*) denounce, tattle on, inform against, betray, report (on), sell, *archaic* delate, *colloq.* blow the whistle on, rat on, peach on *or* against, split on, *sl.* squeal on, squeak on, *Austral. sl.* dob on, shelf, pool, *esp. Brit. sl.* shop, *Brit. sl.* grass on, *Brit. school sl.* sneak on. **6** order, command, require, charge, direct, instruct, *archaic or literary* bid. **7** assure, swear to, promise. **8** recount, describe, delineate, detail, outline, depict; inform, instruct, explain, teach. **9** ascertain, determine, decide, perceive, understand, know; predict, prophesy, forecast, foretell, foresee; say, confirm, know for sure *or* certain, be sure *or* certain *or* positive; make out, discern, identify, recognize, distinguish, discriminate, differentiate. **10 a** be effective, have (an) effect, be noticeable, register. **b** show, reveal the truth. **c** carry weight, be influential. ▫ **as far as one can tell** see EVIDENTLY 2. **tell apart** see DISTINGUISH 1. **tell off 1** scold, reprimand, berate, castigate, censure, take to task, upbraid, admonish, rebuke, lecture, reproach, reprove, give a person a tongue-lashing, haul over the coals, give a person a piece of one's mind, *archaic or literary* chide, *colloq.* carpet, tick off, tear a strip off, *Austral.* & *NZ colloq.* go crook on, *US colloq.* chew out.

tell tales tattle, tittle-tattle, gossip, blab, *colloq.* name names.

tell[2] /tel/ *n. Archaeol.* an artificial mound in the Middle East etc. formed by the accumulated remains of ancient settlements. [Arab. *tall* hillock]

■ tumulus, mound, barrow, hillock.

teller /téllər/ *n.* **1** a person employed to receive and pay out money in a bank etc. **2** a person who counts (votes). **3** a person who tells esp. stories (*a teller of tales*). □□ **tellership** *n.*

telling /télling/ *adj.* **1** having a marked effect; striking. **2** significant. □□ **tellingly** *adv.*

■ effective, effectual, influential, weighty, important, powerful, forceful, potent, strong, compelling, significant, considerable, striking.

telling-off /téllingóf/ *n.* (*pl.* **tellings-off**) *colloq.* a reproof or reprimand.

■ see REPRIMAND *n.*

tell-tale /téltayl/ *n.* **1** a person who reveals (esp. discreditable) information about another's private affairs or behaviour. **2** (*attrib.*) that reveals or betrays (*a tell-tale smile*). **3** a device for automatic monitoring or registering of a process etc.

■ **2** (*attrib.*) see MEANINGFUL.

tellurian /telyoóriən/ *adj.* & *n.* ● *adj.* of or inhabiting the earth. ● *n.* an inhabitant of the earth. [L *tellus -uris* earth]

telluric /telyoórik/ *adj.* **1** of the earth as a planet. **2** of the soil. **3** *Chem.* of tellurium, esp. in its higher valency. □□ **tellurate** /télyoorət/ *n.* [L *tellus -uris* earth: sense 3 f. TELLURIUM]

tellurium /telyoóriəm/ *n. Chem.* a rare brittle lustrous silver-white element occurring naturally in ores of gold and silver, used in semiconductors. ¶ Symb.: **Te.** □□ **telluride** /télyoorīd/ *n.* **tellurite** /télyoorīt/ *n.* **tellurous** *adj.* [L *tellus -uris* earth, prob. named in contrast to *uranium*]

telly /télli/ *n.* (*pl.* **-ies**) esp. *Brit. colloq.* **1** television. **2** a television set. [abbr.]

telpher /télfər/ *n.* a system for transporting goods etc. by electrically driven trucks or cable-cars. □□ **telpherage** *n.* [TELE- + -PHORE]

telson /téls'n/ *n.* the last segment in the abdomen of Crustacea etc. [Gk, = limit]

Telugu /télləgoo/ *n.* (also **Telegu**) (*pl.* same or **Telegus**) **1** a member of a Dravidian people in SE India. **2** the language of this people. [Telugu]

temerarious /témməráiriəss/ *adj. literary* reckless, rash. [L *temerarius* f. *temere* rashly]

■ see FOOLHARDY .

temerity /timérriti/ *n.* **1** rashness. **2** audacity, impudence. [L *temeritas* f. *temere* rashly]

■ **2** see EFFRONTERY.

temp /temp/ *n.* & *v. colloq.* ● *n.* a temporary employee, esp. a secretary. ● *v.intr.* work as a temp. [abbr.]

temp.[1] /temp/ *abbr.* temperature.

temp.[2] /temp/ *abbr.* in the time of (*temp. Henry I*). [L *tempore* ablat. of *tempus* time]

temper /témpər/ *n.* & *v.* ● *n.* **1** habitual or temporary disposition of mind esp. as regards composure (*a person of a placid temper*). **2 a** irritation or anger (*in a fit of temper*). **b** an instance of this (*flew into a temper*). **3** a tendency to have fits of anger (*have a temper*). **4** composure or calmness (*keep one's temper*; *lose one's temper*). **5** the condition of metal as regards hardness and elasticity. ● *v.tr.* **1** bring (metal or clay) to a proper hardness or consistency. **2** (often foll. by *with*) moderate or mitigate (*temper justice with mercy*). **3** tune or modulate (a piano etc.) so as to distance intervals correctly. □ **in a bad temper** angry, peevish. **in a good temper** in an amiable mood. **out of temper** angry, peevish. **show temper** be petulant. □□ **temperable** *adj.* **temperative** /-pərətiv/ *adj.* **tempered** *adj.* **temperedly** *adv.* **temperer** *n.* [OE *temprian* (v.) f. L *temperare* mingle: infl. by OF *temprer*, *tremper*]

■ *n.* **1** disposition, temperament, character, personality, nature, make-up, constitution; mood, humour, state *or* frame of mind. **2 a** anger, irritation, passion, rage. **b** (temper) tantrum, fury, fit (of pique), rage, *Brit. colloq.* paddy, *literary* ire, *sl.* wax. **3** ill humour, ill temper, foul temper, irascibility, irritability, petulance, volatility, peevishness, huffiness, surliness, churlishness, hot temper, hotheadedness, hot-bloodedness. **4** composure, self-control, self-possession, calmness, equanimity, balance, sang-froid, coolness, *sl.* cool. ● *v.* **1** anneal, toughen, strengthen, harden. **2** modify, moderate, assuage, mollify, soften, cushion, tone down, allay, soothe, mitigate, palliate, reduce, relax, slacken, lighten, appease. **3** see MODULATE. □ **in a bad temper, out of temper** see ANGRY 1. □□ **tempered** see *subdued* (SUBDUE 2).

tempera /témpərə/ *n.* a method of painting using an emulsion e.g. of pigment with egg, esp. in fine art on canvas. [It.: cf. DISTEMPER[1]]

temperament /témprəmənt/ *n.* **1** a person's distinct nature and character, esp. as determined by physical constitution and permanently affecting behaviour (*a nervous temperament*; *the artistic temperament*). **2** a creative or spirited personality (*was full of temperament*). **3 a** an adjustment of intervals in tuning a piano etc. so as to fit the scale for use in all keys. **b** (**equal temperament**) an adjustment in which the 12 semitones are at equal intervals. [ME f. L *temperamentum* (as TEMPER)]

■ **1** see DISPOSITION 1.

temperamental /témprəmént'l/ *adj.* **1** of or having temperament. **2 a** (of a person) liable to erratic or moody behaviour. **b** (of a thing, e.g. a machine) working unpredictably; unreliable. □□ **temperamentally** *adv.*

■ **2 a** moody, erratic, sensitive, touchy, hypersensitive, volatile, mercurial, changeable, irascible, petulant, testy, short-tempered, hot-tempered, hotheaded, hot-blooded, excitable, explosive, capricious, impatient, ill-humoured, *colloq.* on a short fuse; see also IRRITABLE 1. **b** erratic, unreliable, inconsistent, undependable, unpredictable, capricious.

temperance /témpərənss/ *n.* **1** moderation or self-restraint esp. in eating and drinking. **2 a** total or partial abstinence from alcoholic drink. **b** (*attrib.*) advocating or concerned with abstinence. [ME f. AF *temperaunce* f. L *temperantia* (as TEMPER)]

■ **1** (self-)restraint, moderation, abstemiousness, (self-)control, forbearance, (self-)discipline, continence. **2 a** teetotalism, abstinence, sobriety, non-indulgence; prohibition.

temperate /témpərət/ *adj.* **1** avoiding excess; self-restrained. **2** moderate. **3** (of a region or climate) characterized by mild temperatures. **4** abstemious. □ **temperate zone** the belt of the earth between the frigid and the torrid zones. □□ **temperately** *adv.* **temperateness** *n.* [ME f. L *temperatus* past part. of *temperare*: see TEMPER]

■ **1, 2** moderate, reasonable, (self-)restrained, disciplined, controlled, forbearing, reasonable, sensible, sane, rational, not excessive, composed, steady, stable, even-tempered, equable, sober, sober-minded, mild, dispassionate, unimpassioned, cool, cool-headed, unexcited, calm, unruffled, tranquil, imperturbable, unperturbed, self-possessed, quiet, serene. **3** see MILD 3. **4** abstemious, teetotal, abstinent, continent, moderate, sober, self-restrained; chaste, celibate, austere, ascetic, self-denying, puritanical. □□ **temperately** see EASY *adv.* **temperateness** see SOBRIETY.

temperature /témprichər/ *n.* **1** the degree or intensity of heat of a body in relation to others, esp. as shown by a thermometer or perceived by touch etc. **2** *Med.* the degree of internal heat of the body. **3** *colloq.* a body temperature above the normal (*have a temperature*). **4** the degree of excitement in a discussion etc. □ **take a person's temperature** ascertain a person's body temperature, esp. as a diagnostic aid. **temperature-humidity index** a quantity giving the measure of discomfort due to the combined effects of the temperature and humidity of the air. [F *température* or L *temperatura* (as TEMPER)]

-tempered /témpərd/ *comb.form* having a specified temper or disposition (*bad-tempered*; *hot-tempered*). □□ **-temperedly** *adv.* **-temperedness** *n.*

tempest /témpist/ *n.* **1** a violent windy storm. **2** violent agitation or tumult. [ME f. OF *tempest(e)* ult. f. L *tempestas* season, storm, f. *tempus* time]

■ **1** storm, hailstorm, rainstorm, hurricane, typhoon, tornado, cyclone, squall, thunderstorm, *Naut.* gale. **2** storm, commotion, disturbance, upheaval, disruption, furore, turbulence, ferment, tumult, agitation, perturbation, hurly-burly, disorder, outbreak, unrest, riot, chaos, uproar, brouhaha, *sl.* hoo-ha.

tempestuous /tempéstyooəss/ *adj.* **1** stormy. **2** (of a person, emotion, etc.) turbulent, violent, passionate. □□ **tempestuously** *adv.* **tempestuousness** *n.* [LL *tempestuosus* (as TEMPEST)]

■ **1** see STORMY 1, 2. **2** stormy, wild, uncontrolled, uncontrollable, disrupting, disruptive, turbulent, tumultuous, riotous, chaotic, uproarious, boisterous, frantic, frenzied, frenetic, furious, vehement, violent, fiery, impassioned, passionate, fierce, *literary* wrathful. □□ **tempestuousness** see FURY 2.

tempi *pl.* of TEMPO.

Templar /támplər/ *n.* **1** a lawyer or law student with chambers in the Temple, London. **2** (in full **Knight Templar**) *hist.* a member of a religious and military order for the protection of pilgrims to the Holy Land, suppressed in 1312. [ME f. AF *templer*, OF *templier*, med.L *templarius* (as TEMPLE[1])]

template /témplit, -playt/ *n.* (also **templet**) **1 a** a pattern or gauge, usu. a piece of thin board or metal plate, used as a guide in cutting or drilling metal, stone, wood, etc. **b** a flat card or plastic pattern esp. for cutting cloth for patchwork etc. **2** a timber or plate used to distribute the weight in a wall or under a beam etc. **3** *Biochem.* the molecular pattern governing the assembly of a protein etc. [orig. *templet*: prob. f. TEMPLE[3] + -ET[1], alt. after *plate*]

■ **1** pattern, mould, guide, model, die.

temple[1] /témp'l/ *n.* **1** a building devoted to the worship, or regarded as the dwelling-place, of a god or gods or other objects of religious reverence. **2** *hist.* any of three successive religious buildings of the Jews in Jerusalem. **3** *US* a synagogue. **4** a place of Christian public worship, esp. a Protestant church in France. **5** a place in which God is regarded as residing, esp. a Christian's person or body. □ **temple block** a percussion instrument consisting of a hollow block of wood which is struck with a stick. [OE *temp(e)l*, reinforced in ME by OF *temple*, f. L *templum* open or consecrated space]

■ **1** place *or* house of worship, holy place, house of God, church, synagogue, mosque, pagoda, stupa, tope, gurdwara, cathedral, sanctuary, chapel, tabernacle, shrine.

temple[2] /témp'l/ *n.* the flat part of either side of the head between the forehead and the ear. [ME f. OF ult. f. L *tempora* pl. of *tempus*]

temple[3] /témp'l/ *n.* a device in a loom for keeping the cloth stretched. [ME f. OF, orig. the same word as TEMPLE[2]]

templet var. of TEMPLATE.

tempo /témpō/ *n.* (*pl.* **-os** or **tempi** /-pee/) **1** *Mus.* the speed at which music is or should be played, esp. as characteristic (*waltz tempo*). **2** the rate of motion or activity (*the tempo of the war is quickening*). [It. f. L *tempus* time]

■ **1** cadence, rhythm, beat, time, pulse, metre, measure. **2** pace, speed, rate.

temporal /témpərəl/ *adj.* **1** of worldly as opposed to spiritual affairs; of this life; secular. **2** of or relating to time. **3** *Gram.* relating to or denoting time or tense (*temporal conjunction*). **4** of the temples of the head (*temporal artery*; *temporal bone*). □ **temporal power** the power of an ecclesiastic, esp. the Pope, in temporal matters. □□ **temporally** *adv.* [ME f. OF *temporel* or f. L *temporalis* f. *tempus -oris* time]

■ **1** earthly, terrestrial, terrene, mundane, worldly, non-spiritual, non-clerical, lay, laic(al), secular, non-religious, non-ecclesiastic(al), material, civil, profane, fleshly, mortal.

temporality /témpərálliti/ *n.* (*pl.* **-ies**) **1** temporariness. **2** (usu. in *pl.*) a secular possession, esp. the properties and revenues of a religious corporation or an ecclesiastic. [ME f. LL *temporalitas* (as TEMPORAL)]

temporary /témpərəri/ *adj.* & *n.* ● *adj.* lasting or meant to last only for a limited time (*temporary buildings*; *temporary relief*). ● *n.* (*pl.* **-ies**) a person employed temporarily (cf. TEMP). □□ **temporarily** /témpərərili *disp.* tempəráir-/ *adv.* **temporariness** *n.* [L *temporarius* f. *tempus -oris* time]

■ *adj.* impermanent, makeshift, stopgap, stand-by, provisional, acting, interim; *pro tempore*, *ad interim*, transitory, transient, fleeting, fugitive, passing, ephemeral, evanescent, brief, short-lived, momentary, *colloq.* pro tem. ● *n.* stopgap, stand-in, *colloq.* temp. □□ **temporarily** for the time being, in the interim, *ad interim*, *pro tempore*, (in *or* for the) meantime, (in *or* for the) meanwhile, for now; briefly, fleetingly, for a (short *or* little) while, for a (short *or* little) time, for the moment, *colloq.* pro tem.

temporize /témpərīz/ *v.intr.* (also **-ise**) **1** avoid committing oneself so as to gain time; employ delaying tactics. **2** comply temporarily with the requirements of the occasion, adopt a time-serving policy. □□ **temporization** /-záysh'n/ *n.* **temporizer** *n.* [F *temporiser* bide one's time f. med. L *temporizare* delay f. *tempus -oris* time]

■ **1** see PROCRASTINATE .

tempt /tempt/ *v.tr.* **1** entice or incite (a person) to do a wrong or forbidden thing (*tempted him to steal it*). **2** allure, attract. **3** risk provoking (esp. an abstract force or power) (*would be tempting fate to try it*). **4** *archaic* make trial of; try the resolution of (*God did tempt Abraham*). □ **be tempted to** be strongly disposed to (*I am tempted to question this*). □□ **temptable** *adj.* **temptability** /témptəbílliti/ *n.* [ME f. OF *tenter*, *tempter* test f. L *temptare* handle, test, try]

■ **1** lead, induce, entice, incite, persuade, prompt, move, incline, dispose, coax, cajole, inveigle. **2** attract, entice, lure, allure, draw (in), invite, lead on, whet a person's appetite, seduce, captivate. **3** provoke, dare, (put to the) test. **4** try, test, *archaic* prove.

temptation /temptáysh'n/ *n.* **1 a** the act or an instance of tempting; the state of being tempted; incitement esp. to wrongdoing. **b** (**the Temptation**) the tempting of Christ by the Devil (see Matt. 4). **2** an attractive thing or course of action. **3** *archaic* putting to the test. [ME f. OF *tentacion*, *temptacion* f. L *temptatio -onis* (as TEMPT)]

■ **1 a** enticement, leading on, seduction, captivation, persuasion, coaxing, cajoling, incitement. **2** enticement, allurement, invitation, attraction, draw, lure, inducement, incentive, snare, pull, bait, *sl.* come-on.

tempter /témptər/ *n.* (*fem.* **temptress** /-triss/) **1** a person who tempts. **2** (**the Tempter**) the Devil. [ME f. OF *tempteur* f. eccl.L *temptator -oris* (as TEMPT)]

■ **1** charmer, seducer, enchanter; (*temptress*) seductress, siren, *femme fatale*, coquette, flirt, enchantress, Circe, *colloq.* sexpot, vamp, *US sl.* foxy lady, fox. **2** see DEVIL *n.* 1, 2.

tempting /témpting/ *adj.* **1** attractive, inviting. **2** enticing to evil. □□ **temptingly** *adv.*

■ **1** seductive, enticing, inviting, alluring, captivating, attractive, tantalizing, titillating, exciting, appealing, irresistible; (*of food*) appetizing, mouth-watering, delicious, savoury, succulent, luscious, toothsome, *literary* delectable.

tempura /témpoorə/ *n.* a Japanese dish of fish, shellfish, or vegetables, fried in batter. [Jap.]

ten /ten/ *n.* & *adj.* ● *n.* **1** one more than nine. **2** a symbol for this (10, x, X). **3** a size etc. denoted by ten. **4** the time of ten o'clock (*is it ten yet?*). **5** a card with ten pips. **6** a set of ten. ● *adj.* **1** that amount to ten. **2** (as a round number) several (*ten times as easy*). □ **the Ten Commandments** see COMMANDMENT. **ten-gallon hat** a cowboy's large broad-brimmed hat. **ten-week stock** a variety of stock, *Matthiola incana*, said to bloom ten weeks after the sowing of the seed . [OE *tīen*, *tēn* f. Gmc]

ten. *abbr.* tenuto.

tenable /ténnəb'l/ *adj.* **1** that can be maintained or defended against attack or objection (*a tenable position*; *a tenable theory*). **2** (foll. by *for*, *by*) (of an office etc.) that can be held for (a specified period) or by (a specified class of person). □□ **tenability** /-bílliti/ *n.* **tenableness** *n.* [F f. *tenir* hold f. L *tenēre*]

■ **1** defensible, supportable, justifiable, maintainable, sustainable, workable, viable, defendable, plausible, reasonable, rational, arguable, believable, credible, creditable, imaginable, conceivable, possible.

tenace /ténnəss/ *n.* **1** two cards, one ranking next above, and the other next below, a card held by an opponent. **2** the holding of such cards. [F f. Sp. *tenaza*, lit. 'pincers']

tenacious /tináyshəss/ *adj.* **1** (often foll. by *of*) keeping a firm hold of property, principles, life, etc.; not readily relinquishing. **2** (of memory) retentive. **3** holding fast. **4** strongly cohesive. **5** persistent, resolute. **6** adhesive, sticky. □□ **tenaciously** *adv.* **tenaciousness** *n.* **tenacity** /tinássiti/ *n.* [L *tenax -acis* f. *tenēre* hold]

■ **1** (*tenacious of*) clinging to, grasping, maintaining, keeping (up), staying with, retentive of, persisting *or* persistent in, retaining. **2** retentive, good. **3** firm, strong, sturdy, rigid, fast, secure, tight. **4** cohesive, strong, tough. **5** persistent, dogged, unfaltering, pertinacious, unswerving, determined, diligent, resolute, staunch, stalwart, steadfast, strong, sturdy, unwavering, strong-willed, strong-minded, unshaken, unshakeable, obstinate, intransigent, stubborn, adamant, obdurate, refractory, immovable, inflexible, rigid, firm, unyielding, uncompromising. **6** adhesive, sticky, clinging; gummy, gluey, mucilaginous, glutinous, viscous, viscid. □□ **tenaciousness, tenacity** persistence, doggedness, perseverance, pertinacity, determination, grit, diligence, resoluteness, resolution, purposefulness, resolve, staunchness, steadfastness, stamina, assiduity, sedulousness, strength, strong-mindedness, unshakeability, obstinacy, intransigence, stubbornness, obduracy, inflexibility, rigidity, firmness, uncompromisingness, *US colloq.* sand; cohesiveness, power, toughness, resilience; adhesiveness, stickiness, clinginess, gumminess, glueyness, mucilaginousness, glutinousness, viscousness, viscosity, viscidity.

tenaculum /tinákyooləm/ *n.* (*pl.* **tenacula** /-lə/) a surgeon's sharp hook for picking up arteries etc. [L, = holding instrument, f. *tenēre* hold]

tenancy /ténnənsi/ *n.* (*pl.* **-ies**) **1** the status of a tenant; possession as a tenant. **2** the duration or period of this.

■ occupancy, occupation, possession, holding, tenure, residence, residency.

tenant /ténnənt/ *n.* & *v.* ● *n.* **1** a person who rents land or property from a landlord. **2** (often foll. by *of*) the occupant of a place. **3** *Law* a person holding real property by private ownership. ● *v.tr.* occupy as a tenant. □ **tenant farmer** a person who farms rented land. **tenant right** *Brit.* the right of a tenant to continue a tenancy at the termination of the lease. □□ **tenantable** *adj.* **tenantless** *adj.* [ME f. OF, pres. part. of *tenir* hold f. L *tenēre*]

■ *n.* **1** lessee, renter, leaseholder. **2** occupant, resident, inhabitant, *Brit.* occupier, *poet.* denizen. ● *v.* see OCCUPY 1. □□ **tenantless** see UNINHABITED.

tenantry /ténnəntri/ *n.* the tenants of an estate etc.

tench /tench/ *n.* (*pl.* same) a European freshwater fish, *Tinca tinca*, of the carp family. [ME f. OF *tenche* f. LL *tinca*]

tend[1] /tend/ *v.intr.* **1** (usu. foll. by *to*) be apt or inclined (*tends to lose his temper*). **2** serve, conduce. **3** be moving; be directed; hold a course (*tends in our direction*; *tends downwards*; *tends to the same conclusion*). [ME f. OF *tendre* stretch f. L *tendere tens-* or *tent-*]

■ **1** be inclined *or* disposed *or* prone, be apt *or* likely, have *or* show *or* exhibit *or* demonstrate a tendency, *disp.* be liable. **3** incline, lean, verge, gravitate, trend, be biased; (*tend to*) favour.

tend[2] /tend/ *v.* **1** *tr.* take care of, look after (a person esp. an invalid, animals esp. sheep, a machine). **2** *intr.* (foll. by *on*, *upon*) wait on. **3** *intr.* (foll. by *to*) esp. *US* give attention to. □□ **tendance** *n. archaic.* [ME f. ATTEND]

■ **1** care for, take care of, look after, look out for, watch over, mind, attend to, see to, keep an eye on, cater for, minister to, nurse, nurture, cherish, protect. **2** (*tend on*) attend on, wait on, serve, minister to. **3** (*tend to*) attend to, see to, turn to, deal with, take care of, handle.

tendency /téndənsi/ *n.* (*pl.* **-ies**) **1** (often foll. by *to*, *towards*) a leaning or inclination, a way of tending. **2** a group within a larger political party or movement. [med.L *tendentia* (as TEND[1])]

■ **1** inclination, bent, leaning, disposition, propensity, instinct, predisposition, proclivity, predilection, penchant, susceptibility, proneness, readiness, partiality, affinity, bias, drift, direction, course, trend, movement.

tendentious /tendénshəss/ *adj. derog.* (of writing etc.) calculated to promote a particular cause or viewpoint; having an underlying purpose. □□ **tendentiously** *adv.* **tendentiousness** *n.* [as TENDENCY + -OUS]

■ see PARTISAN *adj.* 2. □□ **tendentiousness** see BIAS *n.* 1.

tender[1] /téndər/ *adj.* (**tenderer**, **tenderest**) **1** easily cut or chewed, not tough (*tender steak*). **2** easily touched or wounded, susceptible to pain or grief (*a tender heart*; *a tender conscience*). **3** easily hurt, sensitive (*tender skin*; *a tender place*). **4 a** delicate, fragile (*a tender plant*). **b** gentle, soft (*a tender touch*). **5** loving, affectionate, fond (*tender parents*; *wrote tender verses*). **6** requiring tact or careful handling, ticklish (*a tender subject*). **7** (of age) early, immature (*of tender years*). **8** (usu. foll. by *of*) solicitous, concerned (*tender of his honour*). □ **tender-eyed 1** having gentle eyes. **2** weak-eyed. **tender-hearted** having a tender heart, easily moved by pity etc. **tender-heartedness** being tender-hearted. **tender mercies** *iron.* attention or treatment which is not in the best interests of its recipient. **tender spot** a subject on which a person is touchy. □□ **tenderly** *adv.* **tenderness** *n.* [ME f. OF *tendre* f. L *tener*]

■ **1** chewable, edible, eatable, soft. **2** see SENSITIVE 2. **3** sore, raw, painful, sensitive, inflamed; smarting, burning, hurting, aching. **4 a** sensitive, delicate, fragile, frail, infirm, unstable, shaky, weak, feeble, unwell, sickly, ailing, unsound. **b** gentle, soft, delicate, light, sensitive, soothing. **5** loving, affectionate, fond, kind, kind-hearted, gentle, mild, compassionate, considerate, humane, benevolent, sympathetic, feeling, thoughtful, soft-hearted, warm, caring, merciful, solicitous, tender-hearted, warm-hearted, good-natured; touching, emotional, moving, stirring, soul-stirring, heart-rending, heartfelt, passionate, impassioned, poignant, sentimental, mawkish, maudlin; amatory, amorous, adoring, romantic. **6** sensitive, touchy, ticklish, troublesome, provocative, difficult, tricky, controversial. **7** young, youthful, immature, juvenile, inexperienced, impressionable, vulnerable, green, new, raw, undeveloped, untrained, uninitiated, callow. **8** solicitous, concerned, thoughtful, mindful, heedful, caring. □ **tender-hearted** see SYMPATHETIC *adj.* 1. **tender-heartedness** see MERCY 1, 2. □□ **tenderly** see *warmly* (WARM). **tenderness** see FEELING *n.* 3.

tender[2] /téndər/ *v.* & *n.* ● *v.* **1** *tr.* **a** offer, present (one's services, apologies, resignation, etc.). **b** offer (money etc.) as payment. **2** *intr.* (often foll. by *for*) make a tender for the supply of a thing or the execution of work. ● *n.* an offer, esp. an offer in writing to execute work or supply goods at a fixed price. □ **legal tender** see LEGAL. **plea of tender** *Law* a plea that the defendant has always been ready to satisfy the plaintiff's claim and now brings the sum into court. **put**

out to tender seek tenders in respect of (work etc.). □□ **tenderer** *n.* [OF *tendre*: see TEND[1]]

■ *v.* **1** offer, proffer, present, propose, put forward, extend, hold out, submit, advance, put up, set before, hand in, give. **2** bid, put in a bid, quote. ● *n.* offer, bid, presentation, proposal, proposition, submission, quotation, *colloq.* quote.

tender[3] /téndər/ *n.* **1** a person who looks after people or things. **2** a vessel attending a larger one to supply stores, convey passengers or orders, etc. **3** a special truck closely coupled to a steam locomotive to carry fuel, water, etc. [ME f. TEND[2] or f. ATTENDER (as ATTEND)]

■ **2** dinghy, gig, skiff, launch, boat, jolly (boat), *Brit.* rowing-boat, *US* row-boat.

tenderfoot /téndərfŏŏt/ *n.* a newcomer or novice, esp. in the bush or in the Scouts or Guides.

■ see NOVICE.

tenderize /téndərīz/ *v.tr.* (also **-ise**) make tender, esp. make (meat) tender by beating etc. □□ **tenderizer** *n.*

tenderloin /téndərloyn/ *n.* **1 a** *Brit.* the middle part of a pork loin. **b** *US* the undercut of a sirloin. **2** *US sl.* a district of a city where vice and corruption are prominent.

tendon /téndən/ *n.* **1** a cord or strand of strong tissue attaching a muscle to a bone etc. **2** (in a quadruped) = HAMSTRING. □□ **tendinitis** /téndinītiss/ *n.* **tendinous** /-dinəss/ *adj.* [F *tendon* or med.L *tendo -dinis* f. Gk *tenōn* sinew f. *teinō* stretch]

tendril /téndril/ *n.* **1** each of the slender leafless shoots by which some climbing plants cling for support. **2** a slender curl of hair etc. [prob. f. obs. F *tendrillon* dimin. of obs. *tendron* young shoot ult. f. L *tener* TENDER[1]]

■ see LOCK[2] 1a.

Tenebrae /ténnəbray/ *n.pl.* **1** *RC Ch. hist.* matins and lauds for the last three days of Holy Week, at which candles are successively extinguished. **2** this office set to music. [L, = darkness]

tenebrous /ténnibrəss/ *adj. literary* dark, gloomy. [ME f. OF *tenebrus* f. L *tenebrosus* (as TENEBRAE)]

■ see DARK *adj.* 1.

tenement /ténnimənt/ *n.* **1** a room or a set of rooms forming a separate residence within a house or block of flats. **2** *US* & *Sc.* a house divided into and let in tenements. **3** a dwelling-place. **4 a** a piece of land held by an owner. **b** *Law* any kind of permanent property, e.g. lands or rents, held from a superior. □ **tenement-house** *US* & *Sc.* = sense 2. □□ **tenemental** /-mént'l/ *adj.* **tenementary** /-méntəri/ *adj.* [ME f. OF f. med.L *tenementum* f. *tenēre* hold]

tenesmus /tinézməss/ *n. Med.* a continual inclination to evacuate the bowels or bladder accompanied by painful straining. [med.L f. Gk *teinesmos* straining f. *teinō* stretch]

tenet /ténnit, teénet/ *n.* a doctrine, dogma, or principle held by a group or person. [L, = he etc. holds f. *tenēre* hold]

■ belief, credo, creed, article of faith, ideology, precept, conviction, principle, dogma, idea, opinion, position, view, viewpoint, maxim, axiom, canon, teaching, doctrine.

tenfold /ténfōld/ *adj.* & *adv.* **1** ten times as much or as many. **2** consisting of ten parts.

tenia *US* var. of TAENIA.

Tenn. *abbr.* Tennessee.

tenné /ténni/ *n.* & (usu. placed after noun) *adj.* (also **tenny**) *Heraldry* orange-brown. [obs. F, var. of *tanné* TAWNY]

tenner /ténnər/ *n. colloq.* a ten-pound or ten-dollar note. [TEN]

tennis /ténniss/ *n.* either of two games (lawn tennis and real tennis) in which two or four players strike a ball with rackets over a net stretched across a court. □ **tennis-ball** a ball used in playing tennis. **tennis-court** a court used in playing tennis. **tennis elbow** a sprain caused by or as by playing tennis. **tennis-racket** a racket used in playing tennis. **tennis shoe** a light canvas or leather soft-soled shoe suitable for tennis or general casual wear. [ME *tenetz*, *tenes*, etc., app. f. OF *tenez* 'take, receive', called by the server to an opponent, imper. of *tenir* take]

tenno /ténnō/ *n.* (*pl.* **-os**) the Emperor of Japan viewed as a divinity. [Jap.]

tenny var. of TENNÉ.

Tennysonian /ténnisṓniən/ *adj.* relating to or in the style of Alfred (Lord) Tennyson, Engl. poet d. 1892.

tenon /ténnən/ *n.* & *v.* ● *n.* a projecting piece of wood made for insertion into a corresponding cavity (esp. a mortise) in another piece. ● *v.tr.* **1** cut as a tenon. **2** join by means of a tenon. □ **tenon-saw** a small saw with a strong brass or steel back for fine work. □□ **tenoner** *n.* [ME f. F f. *tenir* hold f. L *tenēre*]

tenor /ténnər/ *n.* **1 a** a singing-voice between baritone and alto or counter-tenor, the highest of the ordinary adult male range. **b** a singer with this voice. **c** a part written for it. **2 a** an instrument, esp. a viola, recorder, or saxophone, of which the range is roughly that of a tenor voice. **b** (in full **tenor bell**) the largest bell of a peal or set. **3** (usu. foll. by *of*) the general purport or drift of a document or speech. **4** (usu. foll. by *of*) a settled or prevailing course or direction, esp. the course of a person's life or habits. **5** *Law* **a** the actual wording of a document. **b** an exact copy. **6** the subject to which a metaphor refers (opp. VEHICLE 4). □ **tenor clef** *Mus.* a clef placing middle C on the second highest line of the staff. [ME f. AF *tenur*, OF *tenour* f. L *tenor -oris* f. *tenēre* hold]

■ **3** drift, tone, spirit, essence, character, gist, bias, import, substance, effect, significance, meaning, sense, connotation, theme, thread, implication, intent, purpose, tendency, purport, direction. **4** course, direction, tendency, inclination, trend.

tenosynovitis /ténnōsīnōvītiss/ *n.* inflammation and swelling of a tendon, usu. in the wrist, often caused by repetitive movements such as typing. [Gk *tenōn* tendon + SYNOVITIS]

tenotomy /tənóttəmi/ *n.* (*pl.* **-ies**) the surgical cutting of a tendon, esp. as a remedy for a club-foot. [F *ténotomie*, irreg. f. Gk *tenōn -ontos* tendon]

tenpin /ténpin/ *n.* **1** a pin used in tenpin bowling. **2** (in *pl.*) *US* = *tenpin bowling*. □ **tenpin bowling** a game developed from ninepins in which ten pins are set up at the end of an alley and bowled at to be knocked down.

tenrec /ténrek/ *n.* (also **tanrec** /tán-/) any hedgehog-like tailless insect-eating mammal of the family Tenrecidae, esp. *Tenrec ecaudatus* native to Madagascar. [F *tanrec*, f. Malagasy *tàndraka*]

tense[1] /tenss/ *adj.* & *v.* ● *adj.* **1** stretched tight, strained (*tense cord*; *tense muscle*; *tense nerves*; *tense emotion*). **2** causing tenseness (*a tense moment*). **3** *Phonet.* pronounced with the vocal muscles tense. ● *v.tr.* & *intr.* make or become tense. □ **tense up** become tense. □□ **tensely** *adv.* **tenseness** *n.* **tensity** *n.* [L *tensus* past part. of *tendere* stretch]

■ *adj.* **1** taut, strained, stretched, tight, stiff, under tension, rigid; intense, nervous, anxious, under (a) strain, highly-strung, high-strung, on edge, wrought up, keyed up, worked up, on tenterhooks, apprehensive, distressed, upset, disturbed, worried, edgy, on pins and needles, jumpy, fidgety, uneasy, overwrought, strung up, *colloq.* wound up, jittery, having a case of the jitters, uptight, *US colloq.* antsy. **2** nervous, anxious, worrying, worrisome, distressing, disturbing, stressful, nerve-racking, fraught, disquieting. ● *v.* tense up; tighten, stretch, strain, tauten, tension, stiffen; string up. □□ **tensely** see *tightly* (TIGHT). **tenseness** see TENSION *n.* 1, 2, STRESS *n.* 2.

tense[2] /tenss/ *n. Gram.* **1** a form taken by a verb to indicate the time (also the continuance or completeness) of the action etc. (*present tense*; *imperfect tense*). **2** a set of such forms for the various persons and numbers. □□ **tenseless** *adj.* [ME f. OF *tens* f. L *tempus* time]

tensile /ténsīl/ *adj.* **1** of or relating to tension. **2** capable of being drawn out or stretched. □ **tensile strength** resistance to breaking under tension. □□ **tensility** /tensílliti/ *n.* [med.L *tensilis* (as TENSE[1])]

■ **2** see FLEXIBLE 1.

tensimeter /tensímmitər/ *n.* **1** an instrument for measuring vapour pressure. **2** a manometer. [TENSION + -METER]

tension /ténsh'n/ *n.* & *v.* ● *n.* **1** the act or an instance of stretching; the state of being stretched; tenseness. **2** mental strain or excitement. **3** a strained (political, social, etc.) state or relationship. **4** *Mech.* the stress by which a bar, cord, etc. is pulled when it is part of a system in equilibrium or motion. **5** electromagnetic force (*high tension*; *low tension*). ● *v.tr.* subject to tension. □□ **tensional** *adj.* **tensionally** *adv.* **tensionless** *adj.* [F *tension* or L *tensio* (as TEND[1])]

■ *n.* **1** stress, tightness, tautness, strain, pull, traction, pressure, tenseness, force. **2** nervousness, anxiety, anxiousness, strain, edginess, apprehension, suspense, stress, tautness, distress, upset, worry, jumpiness, fidgetiness, *colloq.* jitteriness, (a case of) the jitters; see also *excitement* (EXCITE). **3** strain, stress, pressure. ● *v.* see TENSE[1] *v.*

tenson /téns'n/ *n.* (also **tenzon** /teénz'n/) **1** a contest in verse-making between troubadours. **2** a piece of verse composed for this. [F *tenson*, = Prov. *tenso* (as TENSION)]

tensor /ténsər/ *n.* **1** *Anat.* a muscle that tightens or stretches a part. **2** *Math.* a generalized form of vector involving an arbitrary number of indices. □□ **tensorial** /-sóriəl/ *adj.* [mod.L (as TEND[1])]

tent[1] /tent/ *n.* & *v.* ● *n.* **1** a portable shelter or dwelling of canvas, cloth, etc., supported by a pole or poles and stretched by cords attached to pegs driven into the ground. **2** *Med.* a tentlike enclosure for control of the air supply to a patient. ● *v.* **1** *tr.* cover with or as with a tent. **2** *intr.* **a** encamp in a tent. **b** dwell temporarily. □ **tent-bed** a bed with a tentlike canopy, or for a patient in a tent. **tent coat** (or **dress**) a coat (or dress) cut very full. **tent-fly** (*pl.* **-flies**) **1** a flap at the entrance to a tent. **2** a piece of canvas stretched over the ridge-pole of a tent leaving an open space but keeping off sun and rain. **tent-peg** any of the pegs to which the cords of a tent are attached. **tent-pegging** a sport in which a rider tries at full gallop to carry off on the point of a lance a tent-peg fixed in the ground. **tent-stitch** **1** a series of parallel diagonal stitches. **2** such a stitch. [ME f. OF *tente* ult. f. L *tendere* stretch: *tent-stitch* may be f. another word]

tent[2] /tent/ *n.* a deep-red sweet wine chiefly from Spain, used esp. as sacramental wine. [Sp. *tinto* deep-coloured f. L *tinctus* past part.: see TINGE]

tent[3] /tent/ *n. Surgery* a piece (esp. a roll) of lint, linen, etc., inserted into a wound or natural opening to keep it open. [ME f. OF *tente* f. *tenter* probe (as TEMPT)]

tentacle /téntək'l/ *n.* **1** a long slender flexible appendage of an (esp. invertebrate) animal, used for feeling, grasping, or moving. **2** a thing used like a tentacle as a feeler etc. **3** *Bot.* a sensitive hair or filament. □□ **tentacled** *adj.* (also in *comb.*). **tentacular** /-tákyoolər/ *adj.* **tentaculate** /-tákyoolət/ *adj.* [mod.L *tentaculum* f. L *tentare* = *temptare* (see TEMPT) + *-culum* -CULE]

■ **1** feeler, antenna, palp. **2** see FEELER 3.

tentative /téntətiv/ *adj.* & *n.* ● *adj.* **1** done by way of trial, experimental. **2** hesitant, not definite (*tentative suggestion*; *tentative acceptance*). ● *n.* an experimental proposal or theory. □□ **tentatively** *adv.* **tentativeness** *n.* [med.L *tentativus* (as TENTACLE)]

■ *adj.* **1** experimental, speculative, exploratory, trial, provisional. **2** unsure, hesitant, uncertain, indecisive, noncommittal, indefinite, cautious, timid, shy, diffident, uneasy, apprehensive. □□ **tentatively** see GINGERLY *adv.*

tenter[1] /téntər/ *n.* **1** a machine for stretching cloth to dry in shape. **2** = TENTERHOOK. [ME ult. f. med.L *tentorium* (as TEND[1])]

tenter[2] /téntər/ *n. Brit.* **1** a person in charge of something, esp. of machinery in a factory. **2** a workman's unskilled assistant. [*tent* (now Sc.) pay attention, perh. f. *tent* attention f. INTENT or obs. *attent* (as ATTEND)]

tenterhook /téntərhook/ *n.* any of the hooks to which cloth is fastened on a tenter. □ **on tenterhooks** in a state of suspense or mental agitation due to uncertainty.

■ □ **on tenterhooks** see TENSE[1] *adj.* 1.

tenth /tenth/ *n.* & *adj.* ● *n.* **1** the position in a sequence corresponding to the number 10 in the sequence 1-10. **2** something occupying this position. **3** one of ten equal parts of a thing. **4** *Mus.* **a** an interval or chord spanning an octave and a third in the diatonic scale. **b** a note separated from another by this interval. ● *adj.* that is the tenth. □ **tenth-rate** of extremely poor quality. □□ **tenthly** *adv.* [ME *tenthe*, alt. of OE *teogotha*]

tenuis /ténnyoo-iss/ *n.* (*pl.* **tenues** /-yoo-eez/) *Phonet.* a voiceless stop, e.g. *k*, *p*, *t*. [L, = thin, transl. Gk *psilos* smooth]

tenuity /tinyóo-iti/ *n.* **1** slenderness. **2** (of a fluid, esp. air) rarity, thinness. [L *tenuitas* (as TENUIS)]

tenuous /ténnyooəss/ *adj.* **1** slight, of little substance (*tenuous connection*). **2** (of a distinction etc.) oversubtle. **3** thin, slender, small. **4** rarefied. □□ **tenuously** *adv.* **tenuousness** *n.* [L *tenuis*]

■ **1** flimsy, slight, slender, insubstantial, unsubstantial, paltry, weak, feeble, frail, shaky, meagre, vague, negligible, insignificant, trifling, sketchy, hazy, nebulous. **2** overfine, oversubtle, over-nice, hair-splitting, quibbling, dubious, doubtful, *colloq.* nit-picking. **3** thin, slender, slight, small, fine, attenuated, delicate, gossamer, diaphanous, fragile. **4** see *rarefied* (RAREFY 1).

tenure /ténnyər/ *n.* **1** a condition, or form of right or title, under which (esp. real) property is held. **2** (often foll. by *of*) **a** the holding or possession of an office or property. **b** the period of this (*during his tenure of office*). **3** guaranteed permanent employment, esp. as a teacher or lecturer after a probationary period. [ME f. OF f. *tenir* hold f. L *tenēre*]

■ **1, 2** right, title, possession, holding, ownership, occupancy, incumbency. **3** (job) security, permanence, permanency.

tenured /ténnyərd/ *adj.* **1** (of an official position) carrying a guarantee of permanent employment. **2** (of a teacher, lecturer, etc.) having guaranteed tenure of office.

tenurial /tenyóoriəl/ *adj.* of the tenure of land. □□ **tenurially** *adv.* [med.L *tenūra* TENURE]

tenuto /tənóotō/ *adv.*, *adj.*, & *n. Mus.* ● *adv.* & *adj.* (of a note etc.) sustained, given its full time-value (cf. LEGATO, STACCATO). ● *n.* (*pl.* **-os**) a note or chord played tenuto. [It., = held]

tenzon var. of TENSON.

teocalli /teéəkálli/ *n.* (*pl.* **teocallis**) a temple of the Aztecs or other Mexican peoples, usu. on a truncated pyramid. [Nahuatl f. *teotl* god + *calli* house]

tepee /teépee/ *n.* (also **teepee**) a N. American Indian's conical tent, made of skins, cloth, or canvas on a frame of poles. [Sioux or Dakota Indian *tīpī*]

tephra /téfrə/ *n.* fragmented rock etc. ejected by a volcanic eruption. [Gk, = ash]

tepid /téppid/ *adj.* **1** slightly warm. **2** unenthusiastic. □□ **tepidity** /tipídditi/ *n.* **tepidly** *adv.* **tepidness** *n.* [L *tepidus* f. *tepēre* be lukewarm]

■ **1** lukewarm, warmish. **2** lukewarm, unenthusiastic, cool, indifferent, apathetic, uninterested, unconcerned, nonchalant, uncaring, neutral, half-hearted, blasé.

tequila /tekeélə/ *n.* a Mexican liquor made from an agave. [*Tequila* in Mexico]

ter- /ter/ *comb. form* three; threefold (*tercentenary*; *tervalent*). [L *ter* thrice]

tera- /térrə/ *comb. form* denoting a factor of 10^{12}. [Gk *teras* monster]

terai /tərī/ *n.* (in full **terai hat**) a wide-brimmed felt hat, often with a double crown, worn by travellers etc. in subtropical regions. [*Terai*, belt of marshy jungle between Himalayan foothills and plains, f. Hindi *tarāī* moist (land)]

terametre /térrəmeetər/ *n.* a unit of length equal to 10^{12} metres.

teraph /térrəf/ *n.* (*pl.* **teraphim**, also used as *sing.*) a small image as a domestic deity or oracle of the ancient Hebrews. [ME f. LL *theraphim*, Gk *theraphin* f. Heb. *tᵉrāpîm*]

terato- /térrətō/ *comb. form* monster. [Gk *teras -atos* monster]

teratogen /tərátəjən/ *n. Med.* an agent or factor causing malformation of an embryo. □□ **teratogenic** /térrətəjénnik/ *adj.* **teratogeny** /térrətójəni/ *n.*

teratology /térrətólləji/ *n.* **1** *Biol.* the scientific study of animal or vegetable monstrosities. **2** mythology relating to fantastic creatures, monsters, etc. □□ **teratological** /-təlójik'l/ *adj.* **teratologist** *n.*

teratoma /térrətṓmə/ *n. Med.* a tumour of heterogeneous tissues, esp. of the gonads.

terbium /térbiəm/ *n. Chem.* a silvery metallic element of the lanthanide series. ¶ Symb.: **Tb**. [mod.L f. *Ytterby* in Sweden]

terce /terss/ *n. Eccl.* **1** the office of the canonical hour of prayer appointed for the third daytime hour (i.e. 9 a.m.). **2** this hour. [var. of TIERCE]

tercel /térs'l/ *n.* (also **tiercel** /teérs'l/) *Falconry* the male of the hawk, esp. a peregrine or goshawk. [ME f. OF *tercel*, ult. a dimin. of L *tertius* third, perh. from a belief that the third egg of a clutch produced a male bird, or that the male was one-third smaller than the female]

tercentenary /társenteénəri, -ténnəri, terséntinəri/ *n.* & *adj.* ● *n.* (*pl.* **-ies**) **1** a three-hundredth anniversary. **2** a celebration of this. ● *adj.* of this anniversary.

tercentennial /térsenténniəl/ *adj.* & *n.* ● *adj.* **1** occurring every three hundred years. **2** lasting three hundred years. ● *n.* a tercentenary.

tercet /tércit/ *n.* (also **tiercet** /teér-/) *Prosody* a set or group of three lines rhyming together or connected by rhyme with an adjacent triplet. [F f. It. *terzetto* dimin. of *terzo* third f. L *tertius*]

terebene /térribeen/ *n.* a mixture of terpenes prepared by treating oil of turpentine with sulphuric acid, used as an expectorant etc. [TEREBINTH + -ENE]

terebinth /térribinth/ *n.* a small Southern European tree, *Pistacia terebinthus*, yielding turpentine. [ME f. OF *terebinte* or L *terebinthus* f. Gk *terebinthos*]

terebinthine /térribinthīn/ *adj.* **1** of the terebinth. **2** of turpentine. [L *terebinthinus* f. Gk *terebinthinos* (as TEREBINTH)]

teredo /təreédō/ *n.* (*pl.* **-os**) any bivalve mollusc of the genus *Teredo*, esp. *T. navalis*, that bores into wooden ships etc. Also called SHIPWORM. [L f. Gk *terēdōn* f. *teirō* rub hard, wear away, bore]

terete /təreét/ *adj. Biol.* smooth and rounded; cylindrical. [L *teres -etis*]

tergal /térg'l/ *adj.* of or relating to the back; dorsal. [L *tergum* back]

tergiversate /térjiversayt/ *v.intr.* **1** be apostate; change one's party or principles. **2** equivocate; make conflicting or evasive statements. **3** turn one's back on something. □□ **tergiversation** /-sáysh'n/ *n.* **tergiversator** *n.* [L *tergiversari* turn one's back f. *tergum* back + *vertere vers-* turn]

■ **1** recant, apostatize; see also DEFECT *v.* **2** see EQUIVOCATE. **3** see SECEDE. □□ **tergiversator** see TURNCOAT.

-teria /teériə/ *suffix* denoting self-service establishments (*washeteria*). [after CAFETERIA]

term /term/ *n.* & *v.* ● *n.* **1** a word used to express a definite concept, esp. in a particular branch of study etc. (*a technical term*). **2** (in *pl.*) language used; mode of expression (*answered in no uncertain terms*). **3** (in *pl.*) a relation or footing (*we are on familiar terms*). **4** (in *pl.*) **a** conditions or stipulations (*cannot accept your terms*; *do it on your own terms*). **b** charge or price (*his terms are £20 a lesson*). **5 a** a limited period of some state or activity (*for a term of five years*). **b** a period over which operations are conducted or results contemplated (*in the short term*). **c** a period of some weeks, alternating with holiday or vacation, during which instruction is given in a school, college, or university, or *Brit.* during which a lawcourt holds sessions. **d** a period of imprisonment. **e** a period of tenure. **6** *Logic* a word or words that may be the subject or predicate of a proposition. **7** *Math.* **a** each of the two quantities in a ratio. **b** each quantity in a series. **c** a part of an expression joined to the rest by + or – (e.g. *a*, *b*, *c* in $a + b - c$). **8** the completion of a normal length of pregnancy. **9** an appointed day, esp. a Scottish quarter day. **10** (in full *Brit.* term of years or *US* term for years) *Law* an interest in land for a fixed period. **11** = TERMINUS 6. **12** *archaic* a boundary or limit, esp. of time. ● *v.tr.* denominate, call; assign a term to (*the music termed classical*). □ **bring to terms** cause to accept conditions. **come to terms** yield, give way. **come to terms with 1** reconcile oneself to (a difficulty etc.). **2** conclude an agreement with. **in set terms** in definite terms. **in terms** explicitly. **in terms of 1** in the language peculiar to, using as a basis of expression or thought. **2** by way of. **make terms** conclude an agreement. **on terms** on terms of friendship or equality. **term paper** *US* an essay or dissertation representative of the work done during a term. **terms of reference** *Brit.* points referred to an individual or body of persons for decision or report; the scope of an inquiry etc.; a definition of this. **terms of trade** *Brit.* the ratio between prices paid for imports and those received for exports. □□ **termless** *adj.* **termly** *adj.* & *adv.* [ME f. OF *terme* f. L TERMINUS]

■ *n.* **1** name, title, designation, denomination, label, *formal* appellation; word, expression, locution, phrase. **2** (*terms*) language, words, phrases. **3** (*terms*) standing, position, basis, relationship, relation, relations, footing. **4** (*terms*) **a** conditions, provisions, articles, clauses, provisos; stipulations, qualifications, assumptions, basis. **b** payment, schedule, charges, prices, rates. **5 a, b** time, period (of time), interval, length of time, span (of time), duration, spell, stint, course, while. **c** semester, *US* trimester; sitting, session. **d** stretch. **e** incumbency, administration. ● *v.* call, name, label, designate, denominate, title, style, dub, *archaic* entitle; nickname. □ **come to terms** agree, yield, give way, assent, come to *or* reach an agreement, come to *or* reach an arrangement, come to *or* reach an understanding, be reconciled, settle, compromise. **come to terms with 1** accept, reconcile *or* resign oneself to, adjust to, cope with, face up to. **2** agree with, come to *or* reach an agreement with, come to *or* reach an arrangement with, come to *or* reach an understanding with, settle with. **in terms of 2** by way of, as, in the way of, as regards, concerning, regarding, with regard to, in the matter of. □□ **termly** terminal(ly).

termagant /térməgənt/ *n.* & *adj.* ● *n.* **1** an overbearing or brawling woman; a virago or shrew. **2** (**Termagant**) *hist.* an imaginary deity of violent and turbulent character, often appearing in morality plays. ● *adj.* violent, turbulent, shrewish. [ME *Tervagant* f. OF *Tervagan* f. It. *Trivigante*]

■ *n.* **1** see SHREW.

terminable /términəb'l/ *adj.* **1** that may be terminated. **2** coming to an end after a certain time (*terminable annuity*). □□ **terminableness** *n.*

terminal /términ'l/ *adj.* & *n.* ● *adj.* **1 a** (of a disease) ending in death, fatal. **b** (of a patient) in the last stage of a fatal disease. **c** (of a morbid condition) forming the last stage of a fatal disease. **d** *colloq.* ruinous, disastrous, very great (*terminal laziness*). **2** of or forming a limit or terminus (*terminal station*). **3 a** *Zool.* etc. ending a series (*terminal joints*). **b** *Bot.* borne at the end of a stem etc. **4** of or done etc. each term (*terminal accounts*; *terminal examinations*). ● *n.* **1** a terminating thing; an extremity. **2** a terminus for trains or long-distance buses. **3** a departure and arrival building for air passengers. **4** a point of connection for closing an electric circuit. **5** an apparatus for transmission of messages between a user and a computer, communications system, etc. **6** (in full **terminal figure**) = TERMINUS 6. **7** an installation where oil is stored at the end of a pipeline or at a port. **8** a patient suffering from a terminal illness. □ **terminal velocity** a velocity of a falling body such that the resistance of the air etc. prevents further increase of speed under gravity. □□ **terminally** *adv.* [L *terminalis* (as TERMINUS)]

■ *adj.* **1 a** deadly, mortal, fatal, lethal, incurable. **b** dying. **c** final, last. **2** closing, concluding, terminating, ending, final, ultimate, extreme. **4** termly. ● *n.* **1** see TIP[1] *n.* 1. **2** terminus, (terminal) station, end of the line, depot. **4** connection, wire, connector, coupler, coupling, conductor. **5** keyboard, monitor, position, (work) station, visual display unit, (personal) computer, VDU, PC, module, CRT, screen, (control) panel. □□ **terminally** see *severely* (SEVERE).

terminate /términayt/ *v.* **1** *tr.* & *intr.* bring or come to an end. **2** *intr.* (foll. by *in*) (of a word) end in (a specified letter or syllable etc.). **3** *tr.* end (a pregnancy) before term by artificial means. **4** *tr.* bound, limit. [L *terminare* (as TERMINUS)]

■ **1, 2** stop, end, finish, cease, conclude; put an end to, complete, discontinue, drop, bring to an end *or* close, wind up *or* down, cut off; come to an end, expire, sign off. **3** abort.

termination /términáysh'n/ *n.* **1** the act or an instance of terminating; the state of being terminated. **2** *Med.* an induced abortion. **3** an ending or result of a specified kind (*a happy termination*). **4** a word's final syllable or letters or letter esp. as an element in inflection or derivation. □ **put a termination to** (or **bring to a termination**) make an end of. □□ **terminational** *adj.* [ME f. OF *termination* or L *terminatio* (as TERMINATE)]

■ **1, 3** end, ending, stop, stoppage, cessation, discontinuation, cancellation, expiration, wind-up, close, dissolution, finish, conclusion, completion. **2** abortion. **4** suffix, ending.

terminator /términaytər/ *n.* **1** a person or thing that terminates. **2** the dividing line between the light and dark part of a planetary body.

terminer see OYER AND TERMINER.

termini *pl.* of TERMINUS.

terminism /términiz'm/ *n.* **1** the doctrine that everyone has a limited time for repentance. **2** = NOMINALISM. □□ **terminist** *n.* [L]

terminological /términəlójik'l/ *adj.* of terminology. □ **terminological inexactitude** *joc.* a lie. □□ **terminologically** *adv.*

terminology /términólləji/ *n.* (*pl.* **-ies**) **1** the system of terms used in a particular subject. **2** the science of the proper use of terms. □□ **terminologist** *n.* [G *Terminologie* f. med.L TERMINUS term]

■ **1** nomenclature, vocabulary, language, words, locutions, wording, terms, phraseology, phrasing, jargon, argot, cant, *colloq.* lingo, *often derog.* -ese.

terminus /términəss/ *n.* (*pl.* **termini** /-nī/ or **terminuses**) **1** a station at the end of a railway or bus route. **2** a point at the end of a pipeline etc. **3** a final point, a goal. **4** a starting-point. **5** *Math.* the end-point of a vector etc. **6** *Archit.* a figure of a human bust or an animal ending in a square pillar from which it appears to spring, orig. as a boundary-marker. □ ***terminus ad quem*** /ad kwém/ the finishing-point of an argument, policy, period, etc. ***terminus ante quem*** /ánti kwém/ the finishing-point of a period. ***terminus a quo*** /aa kwō/ the starting-point of an argument, policy, period, etc. ***terminus post quem*** /pōst kwém/ the starting-point of a period. [L, = end, limit, boundary]

■ **1** see TERMINAL *n.* 2. **3** see DESTINATION.

termitary /términitəri/ *n.* (*pl.* **-ies**) a nest of termites, usu. a large mound of earth.

termite /términīt/ *n.* a small antlike social insect of the order Isoptera, chiefly tropical and destructive to timber. [LL *termes -mitis*, alt. of L *tarmes* after *terere* rub]

termor /términər/ *n.* *Law* a person who holds lands etc. for a term of years, or for life. [ME f. AF *termer* (as TERM)]

tern[1] /tern/ *n.* any marine bird of the subfamily Sterninae, like a gull but usu. smaller and with a long forked tail. [of Scand. orig.: cf. Da. *terne*, Sw. *tärna* f. ON *therna*]

tern[2] /tern/ *n.* **1** a set of three, esp. three lottery numbers that when drawn together win a large prize. **2** such a prize. [F *terne* f. L *terni* three each]

ternary /térnəri/ *adj.* **1** composed of three parts. **2** *Math.* using three as a base (*ternary scale*). □ **ternary form** *Mus.* the form of a movement in which the first subject is repeated after an interposed second subject in a related key. [ME f. L *ternarius* f. *terni* three each]

ternate /térnayt/ *adj.* **1** arranged in threes. **2** *Bot.* (of a leaf): **a** having three leaflets. **b** whorled in threes. □□ **ternately** *adv.* [mod.L *ternatus* (as TERNARY)]

terne /tern/ *n.* (in full **terne-plate**) inferior tin-plate alloyed with much lead. [prob. f. F *terne* dull: cf. TARNISH]

terotechnology /térrōteknólləji, téer-/ *n.* the branch of technology and engineering concerned with the installation and maintenance of equipment. [Gk *tēreō* take care of + TECHNOLOGY]

terpene /térpeen/ *n.* *Chem.* any of a large group of unsaturated cyclic hydrocarbons found in the essential oils of plants, esp. conifers and oranges. [*terpentin* obs. var. of TURPENTINE]

Terpsichorean /térpsikəréeən/ *adj.* of or relating to dancing. [*Terpsichore* Muse of dancing]

terra alba /térrə álbə/ *n.* a white mineral, esp. pipeclay or pulverized gypsum. [L, = white earth]

terrace /térrəss, -riss/ *n.* & *v.* ● *n.* **1** each of a series of flat areas formed on a slope and used for cultivation. **2** a level paved area next to a house. **3 a** a row of houses on a raised level or along the top or face of a slope. **b** a row of houses built in one block of uniform style. **4** a flight of wide shallow steps as for spectators at a sports ground. **5** *Geol.* a raised beach, or a similar formation beside a river etc. ● *v.tr.* form into or provide with a terrace or terraces. □ **terraced house** *Brit.* = *terrace house*. **terraced roof** a flat roof esp. of an Indian or Eastern house. **terrace house** *Brit.* any of a row of houses joined by party-walls. [OF ult. f. L *terra* earth]

terracotta /térrəkóttə/ *n.* **1 a** unglazed usu. brownish-red earthenware used chiefly as an ornamental building-material and in modelling. **b** a statuette of this. **2** its colour. [It. *terra cotta* baked earth]

terra firma /térrə fúrmə/ *n.* dry land, firm ground. [L, = firm land]

■ see LAND *n.* 1.

terrain /teráyn/ *n.* a tract of land as regarded by the physical geographer or the military tactician. [F, ult. f. L *terrenum* neut. of *terrenus* TERRENE]

■ topography, landscape, ground, land, country, territory, zone.

terra incognita /térrə ingkógnitə, ínkognéetə/ *n.* an unknown or unexplored region. [L, = unknown land]

terramara /térrəmaárə/ *n.* (*pl.* **terramare** /-ray/) = TERRAMARE. [It. dial.: see TERRAMARE]

terramare /térrəmaári, -máir/ *n.* **1** an ammoniacal earthy deposit found in mounds in prehistoric lake-dwellings or settlements esp. in Italy. **2** such a dwelling or settlement. [F f. It. dial. *terra mara* f. *marna* marl]

terrapin /térrəpin/ *n.* **1** any of various N. American edible freshwater turtles of the family Emydidae. **2** (**Terrapin**) *propr.* a type of prefabricated one-storey building. [Algonquian]

terrarium /teráiriəm/ *n.* (*pl.* **terrariums** or **terraria** /-riə/) **1** a vivarium for small land animals. **2** a sealed transparent globe etc. containing growing plants. [mod.L f. L *terra* earth, after AQUARIUM]

terra sigillata /térrə sijiláytə/ *n.* **1** astringent clay from Lemnos or Samos. **2** Samian ware. [med.L, = sealed earth]

terrazzo /terátsō/ *n.* (*pl.* **-os**) a flooring-material of stone chips set in concrete and given a smooth surface. [It., = terrace]

terrene /teréen/ *adj.* **1** of the earth; earthly, worldly. **2** of earth, earthy. **3** of dry land; terrestrial. [ME f. AF f. L *terrenus* f. *terra* earth]

■ **1** see EARTHLY 1. **3** terrestrial, earthbound, telluric.

terreplein /táirplayn/ *n.* a level space where a battery of guns is mounted. [orig. a sloping bank behind a rampart f. F *terre-plein* f. It. *terrapieno* f. *terrapienare* fill with earth f. *terra* earth + *pieno* f. L *plenus* full]

terrestrial /təréstriəl/ *adj.* & *n.* ● *adj.* **1** of or on or relating to the earth; earthly. **2 a** of or on dry land. **b** *Zool.* living on or in the ground (opp. AQUATIC, ARBOREAL, AERIAL). **c** *Bot.* growing in the soil (opp. AQUATIC, EPIPHYTIC). **3** *Astron.* (of a planet) similar in size or composition to the earth. **4** of this world, worldly (*terrestrial sins*; *terrestrial interests*). ● *n.* an inhabitant of the earth. □ **terrestrial globe** a globe representing the earth. **the terrestrial globe** the earth. **terrestrial magnetism** the magnetic properties of the earth as a whole. **terrestrial telescope** a telescope giving an erect image for observation of terrestrial objects. □□ **terrestrially** *adv.* [ME f. L *terrestris* f. *terra* earth]

■ *adj.* **1** earthly, earthbound, terrene, tellurian, telluric, global, sublunary, subastral. **2** earthbound, terrene, telluric, terricolous. **4** worldly, terrene, mundane, temporal, secular. ● *n.* earth-man, earth-woman, earth-person, earthling, tellurian, mortal, human.

terret /térrit/ *n.* (also **territ**) each of the loops or rings on a harness-pad for the driving-reins to pass through. [ME, var. of *toret* (now dial.) f. OF *to(u)ret* dimin. of TOUR]

terre-verte /tairváirt/ *n.* a soft green earth used as a pigment. [F, = green earth]

terrible /térrib'l/ *adj.* **1** *colloq.* very great or bad (*a terrible bore*). **2** *colloq.* very incompetent (*terrible at tennis*). **3** causing terror; fit to cause terror; awful, dreadful, formidable. **4** (*predic.*; usu. foll. by *about*) *colloq.* full of remorse, sorry (*I felt terrible about it*). □□ **terribleness** *n.* [ME f. F f. L *terribilis* f. *terrēre* frighten]

■ **1** bad, serious, grave, severe, acute, distressing, nasty, foul, unbearable, loathsome, hideous, intolerable, egregious, atrocious; unhappy, unpleasant, disagreeable, miserable, woeful, joyless, lamentable, wretched, unfortunate; *colloq.* awful, dreadful, vile, ghastly, lousy, beastly, abysmal, *sl.* rotten. **2** see INCOMPETENT *adj.* 2. **3** gruesome, grisly, macabre, gory, grotesque, brutal, savage, horrible, horrendous, terrifying, terrific, harrowing, horrid, horrifying, horrific, ghastly, frightening, frightful, fearsome, formidable, redoubtable, awesome, awe-inspiring, unspeakable, monstrous, wicked, grievous, dread, appalling, shocking, alarming, awful, dreadful, foul, disgusting, revolting, nauseating, nauseous, offensive, vomit-provoking, obnoxious, stomach-turning, abominable, noxious, loathsome, hideous, evil, vile, rotten, *literary* noisome. **4** remorseful, regretful, rueful, sorry, contrite, ashamed, conscience-stricken, guilty, distressed.

terribly /térribli/ *adv.* **1** *colloq.* very, extremely (*he was terribly nice about it*). **2** in a terrible manner.

■ **1** very, extremely, exceedingly, thoroughly, decidedly, really, unbelievably, incredibly, monumentally, outrageously, awfully, fabulously, *colloq.* frightfully. **2** dreadfully, fearfully, awfully, frightfully; see also BADLY 1.

terricolous /teríkkələss/ *adj.* living on or in the earth. [L *terricola* earth-dweller f. *terra* earth + *colere* inhabit]

terrier[1] /térriər/ *n.* **1 a** a small dog of various breeds originally used for turning out foxes etc. from their earths. **b** any of these breeds. **2** an eager or tenacious person or animal. **3** (**Terrier**) *Brit. colloq.* a member of the Territorial Army etc. [ME f. OF (*chien*) *terrier* f. med.L *terrarius* f. L *terra* earth]

terrier[2] /térriər/ *n. hist.* **1** a book recording the site, boundaries, etc., of the land of private persons or corporations. **2** a rent-roll. **3** a collection of acknowledgements of vassals or tenants of a lordship. [ME f. OF *terrier* (adj.) = med.L *terrarius liber* (as TERRIER[1])]

terrific /təríffik/ *adj.* **1** *colloq.* **a** of great size or intensity. **b** excellent (*did a terrific job*). **c** excessive (*making a terrific noise*). **2** causing terror. □□ **terrifically** *adv.* [L *terrificus* f. *terrēre* frighten]

■ **1 a** see HUGE 1, INTENSE 1, 3. **b** wonderful, marvellous, splendid, breathtaking, extraordinary, outstanding, magnificent, exceptional, unbelievable, stupendous, sensational, superb, excellent, first-class, superior, *colloq.* great, fantastic, fabulous, mind-boggling, incredible, smashing, super, *sl.* ace, awesome. **c** see EXCESSIVE. **2** see TERRIBLE 3.

terrify /térrifī/ *v.tr.* (**-ies, -ied**) fill with terror; frighten severely (*terrified them into submission*; *is terrified of dogs*). □□ **terrifier** *n.* **terrifying** *adj.* **terrifyingly** *adv.* [L *terrificare* (as TERRIFIC)]

■ alarm, frighten, scare, terrorize, shock, make one's flesh crawl *or* creep, horrify, make one's blood run cold, make a person's hair stand on end, stun, paralyse, petrify; see also SCARE *v.* 1. □□ **terrifying** alarming, frightening, shocking, horrifying, paralysing, petrifying, *colloq.* scary.

terrigenous /teríjinəss/ *adj.* produced by the earth or the land (*terrigenous deposits*). [L *terrigenus* earth-born]

terrine /təreén/ *n.* **1** pâté or similar food. **2** an earthenware vessel, esp. one in which such food is cooked or sold. [orig. form of TUREEN]

territ var. of TERRET.

territorial /térritóriəl/ *adj.* & *n.* ● *adj.* **1** of territory (*territorial possessions*). **2** limited to a district (*the right was strictly territorial*). **3** (of a person or animal etc.) tending to defend an area of territory. **4** (usu. **Territorial**) of any of the Territories of the US or Canada. ● *n.* (**Territorial**) (in the UK) a member of the Territorial Army. □ **Territorial Army** (in the UK) a volunteer force locally organized to provide a reserve of trained and disciplined manpower for use in an emergency (known as *Territorial and Army Volunteer Reserve* 1967–79). **territorial waters** the waters under the jurisdiction of a State, esp. the part of the sea within a stated distance of the shore (traditionally three miles from low-water mark). □□ **territoriality** /-riálliti/ *n.* **territorialize** *v.tr.* (also **-ise**). **territorialization** /-līzáysh'n/ *n.* **territorially** *adv.* [LL *territorialis* (as TERRITORY)]

territory /térritəri, -tri/ *n.* (*pl.* **-ies**) **1** the extent of the land under the jurisdiction of a ruler, State, city, etc. **2** (**Territory**) an organized division of a country, esp. one not yet admitted to the full rights of a State. **3** a sphere of action or thought; a province. **4** the area over which a commercial traveller or goods-distributor operates. **5** *Zool.* an area defended by an animal or animals against others of the same species. **6** an area defended by a team or player in a game. **7** a large tract of land. [ME f. L *territorium* f. *terra* land]

■ **1, 7** area, region, district, neighbourhood, zone, sector, tract, land, terrain, country, precinct, quarter, domain, demesne, vicinage, vicinity, purlieu, enclave. **3** area, domain, sphere, province, preserve, haunt, stamping-ground, *colloq.* patch, *joc.* bailiwick, *sl.* turf. **5** area, domain, stamping-ground.

terror /térrər/ *n.* **1** extreme fear. **2 a** a person or thing that causes terror. **b** (also **holy terror**) *colloq.* a formidable person; a troublesome person or thing (*the twins are little terrors*). **3** the use of organized intimidation; terrorism. □ **reign of terror** a period of remorseless repression or bloodshed, esp. a period of the French Revolution 1793–4. **terror-stricken** (or **-struck**) affected with terror. [ME f. OF *terrour* f. L *terror -oris* f. *terrēre* frighten]

■ **1** fright, dread, fear, horror, panic, shock, alarm, anxiety, dismay, consternation, trepidation, intimidation, awe. **2** scourge, demon, brute, monster, fiend, devil, horror, dread. □ **terror-stricken** (or **-struck**) see *panic-stricken* (PANIC[1]).

terrorist /térrərist/ *n.* (also *attrib.*) a person who uses or favours violent and intimidating methods of coercing a government or community. □□ **terrorism** *n.* **terroristic** /-rístik/ *adj.* **terroristically** /-rístikəli/ *adv.* [F *terroriste* (as TERROR)]

■ subversive, radical, insurgent, revolutionary, freedom fighter, anarchist, nihilist; bomber, arsonist, incendiary; hijacker; desperado, gunman, thug, felon, criminal. □□ **terroristic** see *strong-arm*.

terrorize /térrərīz/ *v.tr.* (also **-ise**) **1** fill with terror. **2** use terrorism against. □□ **terrorization** /-záysh'n/ *n.* **terrorizer** *n.*

■ **1** see INTIMIDATE.

terry /térri/ *n.* & *adj.* ● *n.* (*pl.* **-ies**) a pile fabric with the loops uncut, used esp. for towels. ● *adj.* of this fabric. [18th c.: orig. unkn.]

terse /terss/ *adj.* (**terser, tersest**) **1** (of language) brief, concise, to the point. **2** curt, abrupt. □□ **tersely** *adv.* **terseness** *n.* [L *tersus* past part. of *tergēre* wipe, polish]

■ **1** concise, brief, short, compact, pithy, succinct, summary, laconic, short and sweet, to the point, sententious, crisp, epigrammatic, aphoristic; distilled, condensed, compendious, abbreviated, abridged, shortened, concentrated. **2** abrupt, curt, short, brusque, blunt, gruff, bluff, ungracious, petulant, tart, rude. □□ **terseness** see ECONOMY 3.

tertian /térsh'n/ *adj.* (of a fever) recurring every third day by inclusive counting. [ME (*fever*) *tersiane* f. L (*febris*) *tertiana* (as TERTIARY)]

tertiary /térshəri/ *adj.* & *n.* ● *adj.* **1** third in order or rank etc. **2** (**Tertiary**) *Geol.* of or relating to the first period in the Cenozoic era with evidence of the development of mammals and flowering plants (cf. PALAEOCENE, EOCENE, OLIGOCENE, MIOCENE, PLIOCENE). ¶ Cf. Appendix VII. ● *n.* **1** *Geol.* this period or system. **2** a member of the third order of a monastic body. □ **tertiary education** education, esp. in a college or university, that follows secondary education. [L *tertiarius* f. *tertius* third]

tertium quid /térshiəm kwíd, tértyəm/ *n.* a third something, esp. intermediate between mind and matter or between opposite things. [L, app. transl. Gk *triton ti*]

tervalent /térvələnt, -váylənt/ *adj. Chem.* having a valency of three. [TER- + *valent-* part. stem (as VALENCE[1])]

Terylene /térrileen/ *n. propr.* a synthetic polyester used as a textile fibre. [*terephthalic* acid (f. *terebic* f. TEREBINTH + PHTHALIC ACID) + ETHYLENE]

terza rima /táirtsə réemə/ *n. Prosody* an arrangement of (esp. iambic pentameter) triplets rhyming *aba bcb cdc* etc. as in Dante's *Divina Commedia*. [It., = third rhyme]

terzetto /tairtséttō, tert-/ *n.* (*pl.* **-os** or **terzetti** /-tee/) *Mus.* a vocal or instrumental trio. [It.: see TERCET]

TESL /téss'l/ *abbr.* teaching of English as a second language.

tesla /téslə/ *n.* the SI unit of magnetic flux density. □ **Tesla coil** a form of induction coil for producing high-frequency alternating currents. [N. *Tesla*, Croatian-born Amer. scientist d. 1943]

TESOL /téssol/ *abbr.* teaching of English to speakers of other languages.

TESSA /téssə/ *n.* (also **Tessa**) (in the UK) tax exempt special savings account.

tessellate /téssəlayt/ *v.tr.* **1** make from tesserae. **2** *Math.* cover (a plane surface) by repeated use of a single shape. [L *tessellare* f. *tessella* dimin. of TESSERA]

tessellated /téssəlaytid/ *adj.* **1** of or resembling mosaic. **2** *Bot.* & *Zool.* regularly chequered. [L *tessellatus* or It. *tessellato* (as TESSELLATE)]

tessellation /téssəláysh'n/ *n.* **1** the act or an instance of tessellating; the state of being tessellated. **2** an arrangement of polygons without gaps or overlapping, esp. in a repeated pattern.

tessera /téssərə/ *n.* (*pl.* **tesserae** /-ree/) **1** a small square block used in mosaic. **2** *Gk* & *Rom. Antiq.* a small square of bone etc. used as a token, ticket, etc. □□ **tesseral** *adj.* [L f. Gk, neut. of *tesseres, tessares* four]

tessitura /téssitoórə/ *n. Mus.* the range within which most tones of a voice-part fall. [It., = TEXTURE]

test[1] /test/ *n.* & *v.* ● *n.* **1** a critical examination or trial of a person's or thing's qualities. **2** the means of so examining; a standard for comparison or trial; circumstances suitable for this (*success is not a fair test*). **3** a minor examination, esp. in school (*spelling test*). **4** *colloq.* a test match. **5** a ground of admission or rejection (*is excluded by our test*). **6** *Chem.* a reagent or a procedure employed to reveal the presence of another in a compound. **7** *Brit.* a movable hearth in a reverberating furnace with a cupel used in separating gold or silver from lead. **8** (*attrib.*) done or performed in order to test (*a test run*). ● *v.tr.* **1** put to the test; make trial of (a person or thing or quality). **2** try severely; tax a person's powers of endurance etc. **3** *Chem.* examine by means of a reagent. **4** *Brit.* refine or assay (metal). □ **put to the test** cause to undergo a test. **Test Act** *hist.* **1** an act in force 1672–1828, requiring all persons before holding office in Britain to take oaths of supremacy and allegiance or an equivalent test. **2** an act of 1871 relaxing conditions for university degrees. **test bed** equipment for testing aircraft engines before acceptance for general use. **test card** a still television picture transmitted outside normal programme hours and designed for use in judging the quality and position of the image. **test case** *Law* a case setting a precedent for other cases involving the same question of law. **test drive** a drive taken to determine the qualities of a motor vehicle with a view to its regular use. **test-drive** *v.tr.* (*past* **-drove**; *past part.* **-driven**) drive (a vehicle) for this purpose. **test flight** a flight during which the performance of an aircraft is tested. **test-fly** *v.tr.* (**-flies**; *past* **-flew**; *past part.* **-flown**) fly (an aircraft) for this purpose. **test match** a cricket or Rugby match between teams of certain countries, usu. each of a series in a tour. **test meal** a meal of specified quantity and composition, eaten to assist tests of gastric secretion. **test out** put (a theory etc.) to a practical test. **test paper 1** a minor examination paper. **2** *Chem.* a paper impregnated with a substance changing colour under known conditions. **test pilot** a pilot who test-flies aircraft. **test-tube** a thin glass tube closed at one end used for chemical tests etc. **test-tube baby** *colloq.* a baby conceived by *in vitro* fertilization. □□ **testable** *adj.* **testability** /téstəbílliti/ *n.* **testee** /testée/ *n.* [ME f. OF f. L *testu(m)* earthen pot, collateral form of *testa* TEST[2]]

■ *n.* **1** trial, examination, exam, try-out, experiment, evaluation, check, check-up, investigation, inspection, appraisal, assessment, study, analysis. **2** see PROOF *n.* 4. **3** examination, exam, trial. **6** assay, analysis. ● *v.* **1** try (out), check (up) (on), examine, question, quiz, evaluate, appraise, assess, prove, put to the test, probe, sound out, vet, inspect, screen, audition, sample, experiment with, *US* check out. **2** see TAX *v.* 3. **3, 4** assay, analyse. □ **put to the test** see TEST[1] *v.* 1 above. □□ **testee** examinee, candidate.

test[2] /test/ *n.* the shell of some invertebrates, esp. foraminiferans and tunicates. [L *testa* tile, jug, shell, etc.: cf. TEST[1]]

testa /téstə/ *n.* (*pl.* **testae** /-tee/) *Bot.* a seed-coat. [L (as TEST[2])]

testaceous /testáyshəss/ *adj.* **1** *Biol.* having a hard continuous outer covering. **2** *Bot.* & *Zool.* of a brick-red colour. [L *testaceus* (as TEST[2])]

testament /téstəmənt/ *n.* **1** a will (esp. *last will and testament*). **2** (usu. foll. by *to*) evidence, proof (*is testament to his loyalty*). **3** *Bibl.* **a** a covenant or dispensation. **b** (**Testament**) a division of the Christian Bible (see *Old Testament, New Testament*). **c** (**Testament**) a copy of the New Testament. [ME f. L *testamentum* will (as TESTATE): in early Christian L rendering Gk *diathēkē* covenant]

■ **1** will, (last will and) testament, last wishes. **2** see MONUMENT 4, PROOF *n.* 3.

testamentary /téstəméntəri/ *adj.* of or by or in a will. [L *testamentarius* (as TESTAMENT)]

testate /téstayt/ *adj.* & *n.* ● *adj.* having left a valid will at death. ● *n.* a testate person. □□ **testacy** *n.* (*pl.* **-ies**). [L *testatus* past part. of *testari* testify, make a will, f. *testis* witness]

testator /testáytər/ *n.* (*fem.* **testatrix** /testáytriks/) a person who has made a will, esp. one who dies testate. [ME f. AF *testatour* f. L *testator* (as TESTATE)]

tester[1] /téstər/ *n.* **1** a person or thing that tests. **2** a sample of a cosmetic etc., allowing customers to try it before purchase.

tester[2] /téstər/ *n.* a canopy, esp. over a four-poster bed. [ME f. med.L *testerium, testrum, testura*, ult. f. L *testa* tile]

testes *pl.* of TESTIS.

testicle /téstik'l/ *n.* a male organ that produces spermatozoa etc., esp. one of a pair enclosed in the scrotum behind the penis of a man and most mammals. □□ **testicular** /-stíkyoolər/ *adj.* [ME f. L *testiculus* dimin. of *testis* witness (of virility)]

testiculate /testíkyoolət/ *adj.* **1** having or shaped like testicles. **2** *Bot.* (esp. of an orchid) having pairs of tubers so shaped. [LL *testiculatus* (as TESTICLE)]

testify /téstifī/ *v.* (**-ies, -ied**) **1** *intr.* (of a person or thing) bear witness (*testified to the facts*). **2** *intr. Law* give evidence. **3** *tr.* affirm or declare (*testified his regret; testified that she had been present*). **4** *tr.* (of a thing) be evidence of, evince. □□ **testifier** *n.* [ME f. L *testificari* f. *testis* witness]
■ **1** attest, (bear) witness. **2** give evidence *or* testimony. **3** state, assert, attest, swear, say, affirm, declare, avow, proclaim, announce, *formal* aver, vouchsafe. **4** see EVIDENCE *v.* □□ **testifier** see WITNESS *n.* 2.

testimonial /téstimṓniəl/ *n.* **1** a certificate of character, conduct, or qualifications. **2** a gift presented to a person (esp. in public) as a mark of esteem, in acknowledgement of services, etc. [ME f. OF *testimoignal* (adj.) f. *tesmoin* or LL *testimonialis* (as TESTIMONY)]
■ **1** endorsement, certification, commendation, (letter of) recommendation, reference, blurb. **2** see TRIBUTE 1.

testimony /téstiməni/ *n.* (*pl.* **-ies**) **1** *Law* an oral or written statement under oath or affirmation. **2** declaration or statement of fact. **3** evidence, demonstration (*called him in testimony; produce testimony*). **4** *Bibl.* the Ten Commandments. **5** *archaic* a solemn protest or confession. [ME f. L *testimonium* f. *testis* witness]
■ **1, 2** evidence, attestation, affirmation, avowal, deposition, statement, affidavit, declaration, assertion, claim, averment, asseveration; confirmation, verification, authentication, corroboration. **3** see DEMONSTRATION 4. **5** profession, admission, confession, protest, declaration, avowal, announcement.

testis /téstiss/ *n.* (*pl.* **testes** /-teez/) *Anat.* & *Zool.* a testicle. [L, = witness: cf. TESTICLE]

testosterone /testóstərōn/ *n.* a steroid androgen formed in the testicles. [TESTIS + STEROL + -ONE]

testudinal /testyoódin'l/ *adj.* of or shaped like a tortoise. [as TESTUDO]

testudo /testyoódō, testoó-/ *n.* (*pl.* **-os** or **testudines** /-dineez/) *Rom.Hist.* **1** a screen formed by a body of troops in close array with overlapping shields. **2** a movable screen to protect besieging troops. [L *testudo -dinis*, lit. 'tortoise' (as TEST[2])]

testy /tésti/ *adj.* (**testier, testiest**) irritable, touchy. □□ **testily** *adv.* **testiness** *n.* [ME f. AF *testif* f. OF *teste* head (as TEST[2])]
■ irritable, bad-tempered, irascible, short-tempered, petulant, touchy, tetchy, querulous, peevish, hot-tempered, crusty, cross, grumpy, bearish, crabby, crabbed, fretful, captious, waspish, snappish, prickly, quarrelsome, fractious, contentious, choleric, splenetic, ill-humoured, disagreeable, ill-tempered, edgy, on edge, quick-tempered, crotchety, cantankerous, *esp. US* cranky, *colloq.* grouchy, shirty, *Brit. colloq.* stroppy, *US colloq.* ornery, *Austral. sl.* snaky. □□ **testily** see SHORTLY 3.

tetanic /titánnik/ *adj.* of or such as occurs in tetanus. □□ **tetanically** *adv.* [L *tetanicus* f. Gk *tetanikos* (as TETANUS)]

tetanus /téttənəss/ *n.* **1** a bacterial disease affecting the nervous system and marked by tonic spasm of the voluntary muscles. **2** *Physiol.* the prolonged contraction of a muscle caused by rapidly repeated stimuli. □□ **tetanize** *v.tr.* (also **-ise**). **tetanoid** *adj.* [ME f. L f. Gk *tetanos* muscular spasm f. *teinō* stretch]

tetany /téttəni/ *n.* a disease with intermittent muscular spasms caused by malfunction of the parathyroid glands and a consequent deficiency of calcium. [F *tétanie* (as TETANUS)]

tetchy /téchi/ *adj.* (also **techy**) (**-ier, -iest**) peevish, irritable. □□ **tetchily** *adv.* **tetchiness** *n.* [prob. f. *tecche, tache* blemish, fault f. OF *teche, tache*]
■ see PEEVISH.

tête-à-tête /táytaatáyt/ *n.*, *adv.*, & *adj.* • *n.* **1** a private conversation or interview usu. between two persons. **2** an S-shaped sofa for two people to sit face to face. • *adv.* together in private (*dined tête-à-tête*). • *adj.* **1** private, confidential. **2** concerning only two persons. [F, lit. 'head-to-head']
■ *n.* **1** (cosy *or* personal) chat, dialogue, *causerie*, heart-to-heart, private talk *or* word *or* conversation, parley, interview, *colloq.* confab, *US colloq.* one-on-one. **2** see COUCH[1] *n.* • *adv.* intimately, privately, in private, face to face, heart to heart, confidentially, secretly, *à deux*, in secret, *US colloq.* one-on-one. • *adj.* **1** intimate, private, heart-to-heart, cosy.

tête-bêche /taytbésh/ *adj.* (of a postage stamp) printed upside down or sideways relative to another. [F f. *tête* head + *béchevet* double bed-head]

tether /té*th*ər/ *n.* & *v.* • *n.* **1** a rope etc. by which an animal is tied to confine it to the spot. **2** the extent of one's knowledge, authority, etc.; scope, limit. • *v.tr.* tie (an animal) with a tether. □ **at the end of one's tether** having reached the limit of one's patience, resources, abilities, etc. [ME f. ON *tjóthr* f. Gmc]
■ *n.* **1** lead, leash, rope, cord, fetter, restraint, halter, tie, chain. • *v.* tie (up *or* down), restrain, fetter, chain (up *or* down), leash, rope, manacle, secure, shackle, fasten, picket, stake. □ **at the end of one's tether** see DESPERATE 1.

tetra- /tétrə/ *comb. form* (also **tetr-** before a vowel) **1** four (*tetrapod*). **2** *Chem.* (forming names of compounds) containing four atoms or groups of a specified kind (*tetroxide*). [Gk f. *tettares* four]

tetrachord /tétrəkord/ *n. Mus.* **1** a scale-pattern of four notes, the interval between the first and last being a perfect fourth. **2** a musical instrument with four strings.

tetracyclic /tétrəsíklik/ *adj.* **1** *Bot.* having four circles or whorls. **2** *Chem.* (of a compound) having a molecular structure of four fused hydrocarbon rings.

tetracycline /tétrəsī́kleen/ *n.* an antibiotic with a molecule of four rings. [TETRACYCLIC + -INE[4]]

tetrad /tétrad/ *n.* **1** a group of four. **2** the number four. [Gk *tetras -ados* (as TETRA-)]

tetradactyl /tétrədáktil/ *n. Zool.* an animal with four toes on each foot. □□ **tetradactylous** *adj.*

tetraethyl lead /tétrəeéthīl/ *n.* a liquid added to petrol as an antiknock agent.

tetragon /tétrəgon/ *n.* a plane figure with four angles and four sides. [Gk *tetragōnon* quadrangle (as TETRA-, -GON)]

tetragonal /titrággən'l/ *adj.* **1** of or like a tetragon. **2** *Crystallog.* (of a crystal) having three axes at right angles, two of them equal. □□ **tetragonally** *adv.*

tetragram /tétrəgram/ *n.* a word of four letters.

Tetragrammaton /tétrəgrámmәton/ *n.* the Hebrew name of God written in four letters, articulated as *Yahweh* etc. [Gk (as TETRA-, *gramma*, *-atos* letter)]

tetragynous /titrájinəss/ *adj. Bot.* having four pistils.

tetrahedron /tétrəheédrən/ *n.* (*pl.* **tetrahedra** /-drə/ or **tetrahedrons**) a four-sided solid; a triangular pyramid. □□ **tetrahedral** *adj.* [late Gk *tetraedron* neut. of *tetraedros* four-sided (as TETRA-, -HEDRON)]

tetralogy /titrálləji/ *n.* (*pl.* **-ies**) **1** a group of four related literary or operatic works. **2** *Gk Antiq.* a trilogy of tragedies with a satyric drama.

tetramerous /titrámmərəss/ *adj.* having four parts.

tetrameter /titrámmitər/ *n. Prosody* a verse of four measures. [LL *tetrametrus* f. Gk *tetrametros* (as TETRA-, *metron* measure)]

tetrandrous /titrándrəss/ *adj. Bot.* having four stamens.

tetraplegia /tétrəpleéjiə, -jə/ *n. Med.* = QUADRIPLEGIA. ▫▫ **tetraplegic** *adj.* & *n.* [mod.L (as TETRA-, Gk *plēgē* blow, strike)]

tetraploid /tétrəployd/ *adj.* & *n. Biol.* • *adj.* (of an organism or cell) having four times the haploid set of chromosomes. • *n.* a tetraploid organism or cell.

tetrapod /tétrəpod/ *n.* **1** *Zool.* an animal with four feet. **2** a structure supported by four feet radiating from a centre. ▫▫ **tetrapodous** /titráppədəss/ *adj.* [mod.L *tetrapodus* f. Gk *tetrapous* (as TETRA-, *pous podos* foot)]

tetrapterous /titráptərəss/ *adj. Zool.* having four wings. [mod.L *tetrapterus* f. Gk *tetrapteros* (as TETRA-, *pteron* wing)]

tetrarch /tétraark/ *n.* **1** *Rom.Hist.* **a** the governor of a fourth part of a country or province. **b** a subordinate ruler. **2** one of four joint rulers. ▫▫ **tetrarchate** /-kayt/ *n.* **tetrarchical** /-ráarkik'l/ *adj.* **tetrarchy** *n.* (*pl.* **-ies**). [ME f. LL *tetrarcha* f. L *tetrarches* f. Gk *tetrarkhēs* (as TETRA-, *arkhō* rule)]

tetrastich /tétrəstik/ *n. Prosody* a group of four lines of verse. [L *tetrastichon* f. Gk (as TETRA-, *stikhon* line)]

tetrastyle /tétrəstīl/ *n.* & *adj.* • *n.* a building with four pillars esp. forming a portico in front or supporting a ceiling. • *adj.* (of a building) built in this way. [L *tetrastylos* f. Gk *tetrastulos* (as TETRA-, STYLE)]

tetrasyllable /tétrəsilləb'l/ *n.* a word of four syllables. ▫▫ **tetrasyllabic** /-lábbik/ *adj.*

tetrathlon /tetráthlən/ *n.* a contest comprising four events, esp. riding, shooting, swimming, and running. [TETRA- + Gk *athlon* contest, after PENTATHLON]

tetratomic /tétrətómmik/ *adj. Chem.* having four atoms (of a specified kind) in the molecule.

tetravalent /tétrəváylənt/ *adj. Chem.* having a valency of four; quadrivalent.

tetrode /tétrōd/ *n.* a thermionic valve having four electrodes. [TETRA- + Gk *hodos* way]

tetter /téttər/ *n. archaic* or *dial.* a pustular skin-eruption, e.g. eczema. [OE *teter*: cf. OHG *zittaroh*, G dial. *Zitteroch*, Skr. *dadru*]

Teut. *abbr.* Teutonic.

Teuto- /tyōōtō/ *comb. form* = TEUTON.

Teuton /tyōōt'n/ *n.* **1** a member of a Teutonic nation, esp. a German. **2** *hist.* a member of a N. European tribe which attacked the Roman republic *c.* 110 BC. [L *Teutones*, *Teutoni*, f. an IE base meaning 'people' or 'country']

Teutonic /tyootónnik/ *adj.* & *n.* • *adj.* **1** relating to or characteristic of the Germanic peoples or their languages. **2** German. • *n.* the early language usu. called Germanic. ▫▫ **Teutonicism** /-nisiz'm/ *n.* [F *teutonique* f. L *Teutonicus* (as TEUTON)]

Tex. *abbr.* Texas.

Texan /téks'n/ *n.* & *adj.* • *n.* a native of Texas in the US. • *adj.* of or relating to Texas.

text /tekst/ *n.* **1** the main body of a book as distinct from notes, appendices, pictures, etc. **2** the original words of an author or document, esp. as distinct from a paraphrase of or commentary on them. **3** a passage quoted from Scripture, esp. as the subject of a sermon. **4** a subject or theme. **5** (in *pl.*) books prescribed for study. **6** *US* a textbook. **7** (in full **text-hand**) a fine large kind of handwriting esp. for manuscripts. ▫ **text editor** *Computing* a system or program allowing the user to enter and edit text. **text processing** *Computing* the manipulation of text, esp. transforming it from one format to another. ▫▫ **textless** *adj.* [ME f. ONF *tixte*, *texte* f. L *textus* tissue, literary style (in med.L = Gospel) f. L *texere text-* weave]

▪ **1** wording, words, content, (subject-)matter; printed matter, (main) body (text), contents. **2** wording, words, script, transcript. **3** extract, abstract, section, quotation, part, paragraph, passage, verse, line; lesson. **4** subject(-matter), topic, theme, motif, issue, focus. **5** (*texts*) (set) books, works, writings, literary texts, literature. **6** textbook, school-book, reader, manual, handbook, primer, workbook, exercise book.

textbook /tékstbŏŏk/ *n.* & *adj.* • *n.* a book for use in studying, esp. a standard account of a subject. • *attrib.adj.* **1** exemplary, accurate (cf. COPYBOOK). **2** instructively typical. ▫▫ **textbookish** *adj.*

textile /tékstīl/ *n.* & *adj.* • *n.* **1** any woven material. **2** any cloth. • *adj.* **1** of weaving or cloth (*textile industry*). **2** woven (*textile fabrics*). **3** suitable for weaving (*textile materials*). [L *textilis* (as TEXT)]

▪ *n.* & *adj.* cloth, fabric, material.

textual /tékstyooəl/ *adj.* of, in, or concerning a text (*textual errors*). ▫ **textual criticism** the process of attempting to ascertain the correct reading of a text. ▫▫ **textually** *adv.* [ME f. med.L *textualis* (as TEXT)]

textualist /tékstyooəlist/ *n.* a person who adheres strictly to the letter of the text. ▫▫ **textualism** *n.*

texture /téks-chər/ *n.* & *v.* • *n.* **1** the feel or appearance of a surface or substance. **2** the arrangement of threads etc. in textile fabric. **3** the arrangement of small constituent parts. **4** *Art* the representation of the structure and detail of objects. **5** *Mus.* the quality of sound formed by combining parts. **6** the quality of a piece of writing, esp. with reference to imagery, alliteration, etc. **7** quality or style resulting from composition (*the texture of her life*). • *v.tr.* (usu. as **textured** *adj.*) provide with a texture. ▫▫ **textural** *adj.* **texturally** *adv.* **textureless** *adj.* [ME f. L *textura* weaving (as TEXT)]

▪ *n.* **1, 2** feel, surface, finish, nap, character, grain, features, consistency, weave, appearance. **3** configuration, composition, constitution, structure. **4–7** nature, structure, fabric, constitution, substance, quality, style.

texturize /téks-chərīz/ *v.tr.* (also **-ise**) (usu. as **texturized** *adj.*) impart a particular texture to (fabrics or food).

TG *abbr.* transformational grammar.

TGWU *abbr.* (in the UK) Transport and General Workers' Union.

Th *symb. Chem.* the element thorium.

Th. *abbr.* Thursday.

-th[1] /th/ *suffix* (also **-eth** /ith/) forming ordinal and fractional numbers from *four* onwards (*fourth*; *thirtieth*). [OE *-tha*, *-the*, *-otha*, *-othe*]

-th[2] /th/ *suffix* forming nouns denoting an action or process: **1** from verbs (*birth*; *growth*). **2** from adjectives (*breadth*; *filth*; *length*). [OE *-thu*, *-tho*, *-th*]

-th[3] var. of -ETH[2].

Thai /tī/ *n.* & *adj.* • *n.* (*pl.* same or **Thais**) **1 a** a native or national of Thailand in SE Asia; a member of the largest ethnic group in Thailand. **b** a person of Thai descent. **2** the language of Thailand. • *adj.* of or relating to Thailand or its people or language. [Thai, = free]

thalamus /thálləməss/ *n.* (*pl.* **thalami** /-mī/) **1** *Anat.* either of two masses of grey matter in the forebrain, serving as relay stations for sensory tracts. **2** *Bot.* the receptacle of a flower. **3** *Gk Antiq.* an inner room or women's apartment. ▫▫ **thalamic** /thəlámmik, thálləmik/ *adj.* (in senses 1 and 2). [L f. Gk *thalamos*]

thalassic /thəlássik/ *adj.* of the sea or seas, esp. small or inland seas. [F *thalassique* f. Gk *thalassa* sea]

▪ see MARINE *adj.* 1.

thaler /taalər/ *n. hist.* a German silver coin. [G *T(h)aler*: see DOLLAR]

thalidomide /thəlíddəmīd/ *n.* a drug formerly used as a sedative but found in 1961 to cause foetal malformation when taken by a mother early in pregnancy. ▫ **thalidomide baby** (or **child**) a baby or child born deformed from the effects of thalidomide. [ph*thali*mido*glutarimide*]

thalli *pl.* of THALLUS.

thallium /thálliəm/ *n. Chem.* a rare soft white metallic element, occurring naturally in zinc blende and some iron ores. □□ **thallic** *adj.* **thallous** *adj.* [formed as THALLUS, from the green line in its spectrum]

thallophyte /thálləfīt/ *n. Bot.* a plant having a thallus, e.g. alga, fungus, or lichen. [mod.L *Thallophyta* (as THALLUS) + -PHYTE]

thallus /thálləss/ *n.* (*pl.* **thalli** /-lī/) a plant-body without vascular tissue and not differentiated into root, stem, and leaves. □□ **thalloid** *adj.* [L f. Gk *thallos* green shoot f. *thallō* bloom]

thalweg /taálveg/ *n.* **1** *Geog.* a line where opposite slopes meet at the bottom of a valley, river, or lake. **2** *Law* a boundary between States along the centre of a river etc. [G f. *Thal* valley + *Weg* way]

than /thən, than/ *conj.* **1** introducing the second element in a comparison (*you are older than he is*; *you are older than he*). ¶ It is also possible to say *you are older than him*, with *than* treated as a preposition, esp. in less formal contexts. **2** introducing the second element in a statement of difference (*anyone other than me*). [OE *thanne* etc., orig. the same word as THEN]

thanage /tháynij/ *n. hist.* **1** the rank of thane. **2** the land granted to a thane. [ME f. AF *thanage* (as THANE)]

thanatology /thánnətólləji/ *n.* the scientific study of death and its associated phenomena and practices. [Gk *thanatos* death + -LOGY]

thane /thayn/ *n. hist.* **1** a man who held land from an English king or other superior by military service, ranking between ordinary freemen and hereditary nobles. **2** a man who held land from a Scottish king and ranked with an earl's son; the chief of a clan. □□ **thanedom** *n.* [OE *theg(e)n* servant, soldier f. Gmc]

thank /thangk/ *v.* & *n.* ● *v.tr.* **1** express gratitude to (*thanked him for the present*). **2** hold responsible (*you can thank yourself for that*). ● *n.* (in *pl.*) **1** gratitude (*expressed his heartfelt thanks*). **2** an expression of gratitude (*give thanks to Heaven*). **3** (as a formula) thank you (*thanks for your help*; *thanks very much*). □ **give thanks** say grace at a meal. **I will thank you** a polite formula, now usu. *iron.* implying reproach (*I will thank you to go away*). **no** (or **small**) **thanks to** despite. **thank goodness** (or **God** or **heavens** etc.) **1** *colloq.* an expression of relief or pleasure. **2** an expression of pious gratitude. **thank-offering** an offering made as an act of thanksgiving. **thanks to** as the (good or bad) result of (*thanks to my foresight*; *thanks to your obstinacy*). **thank you** a polite formula acknowledging a gift or service or an offer accepted or refused. **thank-you** *n. colloq.* an instance of expressing thanks. [OE *thancian*, *thanc* f. Gmc, rel. to THINK]

■ *v.* **1** express *or* show (one's) gratitude to, express *or* show (one's) thanks to, express *or* show (one's) appreciation to, say thank you *or* thanks to, give *or* offer *or* tender thanks to. **2** blame, hold responsible, credit, acknowledge. ● *n.* (*thanks*) **1** gratitude, appreciation, gratefulness, acknowledgement, recognition. **2** thanksgiving. □ **thanks to** owing to, because of, as a result of, in consequence of, as a consequence of, by reason of, through, by virtue of, by dint of, on account of, *disp.* due to.

thankful /thángkfŏŏl/ *adj.* **1** grateful, pleased. **2** (of words or acts) expressive of thanks. □□ **thankfulness** *n.* [OE *thancful* (as THANK, -FUL)]

■ **1** grateful, appreciative, indebted, pleased, glad, obliged, obligated, under (an) obligation, beholden. **2** grateful, appreciative. □□ **thankfulness** see GRATITUDE.

thankfully /thángkfŏŏli/ *adv.* **1** in a thankful manner. **2** *disp.* let us be thankful; fortunately (*thankfully, nobody was hurt*). [OE *thancfullice* (as THANKFUL, -LY[2])]

■ **2** see *happily* (HAPPY).

thankless /thángkliss/ *adj.* **1** not expressing or feeling gratitude. **2** (of a task etc.) giving no pleasure or profit. **3** not deserving thanks. □□ **thanklessly** *adv.* **thanklessness** *n.*

■ **1** ungrateful, unappreciative, unthankful. **2** unappreciated, unacknowledged, unrecognized, unrewarded, useless, unrewarding, fruitless, unprofitable, profitless, vain, futile, *archaic* bootless. □□ **thanklessness** see INGRATITUDE.

thanksgiving /thángksgívving/ *n.* **1 a** the expression of gratitude, esp. to God. **b** a form of words for this. **2** (**Thanksgiving** or **Thanksgiving Day**) a national holiday for giving thanks to God, the fourth Thursday in November in the US, usu. the second Monday in October in Canada. □ **General Thanksgiving** a form of thanksgiving in the Book of Common Prayer or the Alternative Service Book.

■ **1 a** see GRATITUDE.

thar var. of TAHR.

that /that/ *pron.*, *adj.*, *adv.*, & *conj.* ● *demons.pron.* (*pl.* **those** /thōz/) **1** the person or thing indicated, named, or understood, esp. when observed by the speaker or when familiar to the person addressed (*I heard that*; *who is that in the garden?*; *I knew all that before*; *that is not fair*). **2** (contrasted with *this*) the further or less immediate or obvious etc. of two (*this bag is much heavier than that*). **3** the action, behaviour, or circumstances just observed or mentioned (*don't do that again*). **4** *Brit.* (on the telephone etc.) the person spoken to (*who is that?*). **5** *colloq.* referring to a strong feeling just mentioned (*'Are you glad?' 'I am that'*). **6** (esp. in relative constructions) the one, the person, etc., described or specified in some way (*those who have cars can take the luggage*; *those unfit for use*; *a table like that described above*). **7** /thət/ (*pl.* **that**) used instead of *which* or *whom* to introduce a defining clause, esp. one essential to identification (*the book that you sent me*; *there is nothing here that matters*). ¶ As a relative *that* usually specifies, whereas *who* or *which* need not: compare *the book that you sent me is lost* with *the book, which I gave you, is lost*. ● *demons.adj.* (*pl.* **those** /thōz/) **1** designating the person or thing indicated, named, understood, etc. (cf. sense 1 of *pron.*) (*look at that dog*; *what was that noise?*; *things were easier in those days*). **2** contrasted with *this* (cf. sense 2 of *pron.*) (*this bag is heavier than that one*). **3** expressing strong feeling (*shall not easily forget that day*). ● *adv.* **1** to such a degree; so (*have done that much*; *will go that far*). **2** *Brit. colloq.* very (*not that good*). **3** /thət/ at which, on which, etc. (*at the speed that he was going he could not stop*; *the day that I first met her*). ¶ Often omitted in this sense: *the day I first met her*. ● *conj.* /thət except when stressed/ introducing a subordinate clause indicating: **1** a statement or hypothesis (*they say that he is better*; *there is no doubt that he meant it*; *the result was that the handle fell off*). **2** a purpose (*we live that we may eat*). **3** a result (*am so sleepy that I cannot keep my eyes open*). **4** a reason or cause (*it is rather that he lacks the time*). **5** a wish (*Oh, that summer were here!*). ¶ Often omitted in senses 1, 3: *they say he is better*. □ **all that** very (*not all that good*). **and all that** (or **and that** *colloq.*) and all or various things associated with or similar to what has been mentioned; and so forth. **like that 1** of that kind (*is fond of books like that*). **2** in that manner, as you are doing, as he has been doing, etc. (*wish they would not talk like that*). **3** *colloq.* without effort (*did the job like that*). **4** of that character (*he would not accept any payment — he is like that*). **that is** (or **that is to say**) a formula introducing or following an explanation of a preceding word or words. **that's** *colloq.* you are (by virtue of present or future obedience etc.) (*that's a good boy*). **that's more like it** an acknowledgement of improvement. **that's right** an expression of approval or *colloq.* assent. **that's that** a formula concluding a narrative or discussion or indicating completion of a task. **that there** *sl.* = sense 1 of *adj.* **that will do** no more is needed or desirable. [OE *thæt*, nom. & acc. sing. neut. of demons. pron. & adj. *se*, *sēo*, *thæt* f. Gmc; *those* f. OE *thās* pl. of *thes* THIS]

■ □ **that is** (**to say**) see NAMELY, LIKE[1] *adj.* 1b.

thatch /thach/ *n.* & *v.* ● *n.* **1** a roof-covering of straw, reeds, palm-leaves, or similar material. **2** *colloq.* the hair of the head. ● *v.tr.* (also *absol.*) cover (a roof or a building) with thatch. □□ **thatcher** *n.* [n. late collateral form of *thack* (now dial.) f. OE *thæc*, after v. f. OE *theccan* f. Gmc, assim. to *thack*]

thaumatrope /tháwmətrōp/ *n. hist.* **1** a disc or card with two different pictures on its two sides, which combine into one by the persistence of visual impressions when the disc is rapidly rotated. **2** a zoetrope. [irreg. f. Gk *thauma* marvel + *-tropos* -turning]

thaumaturge /tháwmətur j/ *n.* a worker of miracles; a wonder-worker. □□ **thaumaturgic** /-túrjik/ *adj.* **thaumaturgical** /-túrjik'l/ *adj.* **thaumaturgist** *n.* **thaumaturgy** *n.* [med.L *thaumaturgus* f. Gk *thaumatourgos* (adj.) f. *thauma -matos* marvel + *-ergos* -working]

thaw /thaw/ *v.* & *n.* ● *v.* **1** *intr.* (often foll. by *out*) (of ice or snow or a frozen thing) pass into a liquid or unfrozen state. **2** *intr.* (usu. prec. by *it* as subject) (of the weather) become warm enough to melt ice etc. (*it began to thaw*). **3** *intr.* become warm enough to lose numbness etc. **4** *intr.* become less cold or stiff in manner; become genial. **5** *tr.* (often foll. by *out*) cause to thaw. **6** *tr.* make cordial or animated. ● *n.* **1** the act or an instance of thawing. **2** the warmth of weather that thaws (*a thaw has set in*). **3** *Polit.* a relaxation of control or restriction. □□ **thawless** *adj.* [OE *thawian* f. WG; orig. unkn.]

■ *v.* **1, 5** melt, defrost, warm (up), heat (up), unfreeze, *Chem.* liquefy. **2, 3** warm (up), heat (up). **4, 6** soften, warm, melt, become (more) cordial *or* friendly, relax, yield, relent, unbend, let oneself go. ● *n.* **1** thawing, unfreezing, defrosting, melting, warming up, heating up.

the /before a vowel thi, before a consonant thə, when stressed thee/ *adj.* & *adv.* ● *adj.* (called the definite article) **1** denoting one or more persons or things already mentioned, under discussion, implied, or familiar (*gave the man a wave*; *shall let the matter drop*; *hurt myself in the arm*; *went to the theatre*). **2** serving to describe as unique (*the Queen*; *the Thames*). **3 a** (foll. by defining adj.) which is, who are, etc. (*ignored the embarrassed Mr Smith*; *Edward the Seventh*). **b** (foll. by adj. used *absol.*) denoting a class described (*from the sublime to the ridiculous*). **4** best known or best entitled to the name (with *the* stressed: *no relation to the Kipling*; *this is the book on this subject*). **5** used to indicate a following defining clause or phrase (*the book that you borrowed*; *the best I can do for you*; *the bottom of a well*). **6 a** used to indicate that a singular noun represents a species, class, etc. (*the cat loves comfort*; *has the novel a future?*; *plays the harp well*). **b** used with a noun which figuratively represents an occupation, pursuit, etc. (*went on the stage*; *too fond of the bottle*). **c** (foll. by the name of a unit) a, per (*5p in the pound*; *£5 the square metre*; *allow 8 minutes to the mile*). **d** *colloq.* or *archaic* designating a disease, affliction, etc. (*the measles*; *the toothache*; *the blues*). **7** (foll. by a unit of time) the present, the current (*man of the moment*; *questions of the day*; *book of the month*). **8** *Brit. colloq.* my, our (*the dog*; *the fridge*). **9** used before the surname of the chief of a Scottish or Irish clan (*the Macnab*). **10** *dial.* (esp. in Wales) used with a noun characterizing the occupation of the person whose name precedes (*Jones the Bread*). ● *adv.* (preceding comparatives in expressions of proportional variation) in or by that (or such a) degree; on that account (*the more the merrier*; *the more he gets the more he wants*). □ **all the** in the full degree to be expected (*that makes it all the worse*). **so much the** (tautologically) so much, in that degree (*so much the worse for him*). [(adj.) OE, replacing *se, sēo, thæt* (= THAT), f. Gmc: (adv.) f. OE *thȳ, thē*, instrumental case]

theandric /thee-ándrik/ *adj.* of the union, or by the joint agency, of the divine and human natures in Christ. [eccl.Gk *theandrikos* f. *theos* god + *anēr andros* man]

theanthropic /thée-anthróppik/ *adj.* **1** both divine and human. **2** tending to embody deity in human form. [eccl.Gk *theanthrōpos* god-man f. *theos* god + *anthrōpos* human being]

thearchy /thée-aarki/ *n.* (*pl.* **-ies**) **1** government by a god or gods. **2** a system or order of gods (*the Olympian thearchy*). [eccl.Gk *thearkhia* godhead f. *theos* god + *-arkhia* f. *arkhō* rule]

theatre /théətər/ *n.* (*US* **theater**) **1 a** a building or outdoor area for dramatic performances. **b** a cinema. **2 a** the writing and production of plays. **b** effective material for the stage (*makes good theatre*). **c** action with a dramatic quality; dramatic character or effect. **3** a room or hall for lectures etc. with seats in tiers. **4** *Brit.* an operating theatre. **5 a** a scene or field of action (*the theatre of war*). **b** (*attrib.*) designating weapons intermediate between tactical and strategic (*theatre nuclear missiles*). **6** a natural land-formation in a gradually rising part-circle like ancient Greek and Roman theatres. □ **theatre-goer** a frequenter of theatres. **theatre-going** frequenting theatres. **theatre-in-the-round** a dramatic performance on a stage surrounded by spectators. **theatre sister** a nurse supervising the nursing team in an operating theatre. [ME f. OF *t(h)eatre* or f. L *theatrum* f. Gk *theatron* f. *theaomai* behold]

■ **1 a** playhouse, (opera) house, (music-)hall, auditorium, amphitheatre, theatre-in-the-round, colosseum, hippodrome, arena (theatre). **b** see CINEMA 1. **2 a** drama, stagecraft, dramaturgy, melodrama, theatrics, histrionics, acting, performing, performance; the stage, dramatic *or* Thespian *or* histrionic art(s), the boards, show business, *colloq.* showbiz. **b** drama, entertainment. **c** drama, melodrama, staginess, theatricalism, theatrics, histrionics; (dramatic) effect. **5 a** area, arena, scene, sphere *or* place *or* field of action, setting, site.

theatric /thiátrik/ *adj.* & *n.* ● *adj.* = THEATRICAL. ● *n.* (in *pl.*) theatrical actions.

■ *n.* (*theatrics*) see DRAMA 4.

theatrical /thiátrik'l/ *adj.* & *n.* ● *adj.* **1** of or for the theatre; of acting or actors. **2** (of a manner, speech, gesture, or person) calculated for effect; showy, artificial, affected. ● *n.* (in *pl.*) **1** dramatic performances (*amateur theatricals*). **2** theatrical actions. □□ **theatricalism** *n.* **theatricality** /-kálliti/ *n.* **theatricalize** *v.tr.* (also **-ise**). **theatricalization** /-kəlīzáysh'n/ *n.* **theatrically** *adv.* [LL *theatricus* f. Gk *theatrikos* f. *theatron* THEATRE]

■ *adj.* **1** theatric, dramatic, stage, histrionic, Thespian; repertory. **2** stagy, overdone, melodramatic, histrionic, overwrought, exaggerated, forced, overacted, sensational, sensationalistic, mannered, affected, unnatural, artificial, fake, false, showy, ostentatious, spectacular, extravagant, *colloq.* phoney, camp, campy, hammy, *sl.* ham. ● *n.* **2** (*theatricals*) see DRAMA 3. □□ **theatricalism, theatricality** see DRAMA 4.

Theban /théeb'n/ *adj.* & *n.* ● *adj.* of or relating to Thebes in ancient Egypt or ancient Greece. ● *n.* a native or inhabitant of Thebes. [ME f. L *Thebanus* f. *Thebae* Thebes f. Gk *Thēbai*]

theca /théekə/ *n.* (*pl.* **thecae** /théessee/) **1** *Bot.* a part of a plant serving as a receptacle. **2** *Zool.* a case or sheath enclosing an organ or organism. □□ **thecate** *adj.* [L f. Gk *thēkē* case]

thé dansant /táy donsón/ *n.* = *tea dance*. [F]

thee /thee/ *pron. objective case* of THOU[1]. [OE]

theft /theft/ *n.* **1** the act or an instance of stealing. **2** *Law* dishonest appropriation of another's property with intent to deprive him or her of it permanently. [OE *thīefth, thēofth*, later *thēoft*, f. Gmc (as THIEF)]

■ **1** robbery, stealing, larceny, pilferage, pilfering, filching, shoplifting, thievery, thieving, embezzlement, peculation, hijacking, burglary, appropriation, misappropriation, fraud, pocketing, *colloq.* lifting, swiping, rip-off, ripping off, *formal or joc.* purloining, *sl.* pinching, snitching, knocking off, souveniring, *Austral. sl.* duffing, *Brit. sl.* nicking, *US sl.* heist.

thegn /thayn/ *n. hist.* an English thane. [OE: see THANE]

theine /thée-in, thée-een/ *n.* = CAFFEINE. [mod.L *thea* tea + -INE[4]]

their /thair/ *poss.pron.* (*attrib.*) **1** of or belonging to them or themselves (*their house*; *their own business*). **2** (**Their**) (in titles) that they are (*Their Majesties*). **3** *disp.* as a third person sing. indefinite meaning 'his or her' (*has anyone lost their purse?*). [ME f. ON *their(r)a* of them, genit. pl. of *sá* THE, THAT]

theirs /thairz/ *poss.pron.* the one or ones belonging to or associated with them (*it is theirs; theirs are over here*). □ **of theirs** of or belonging to them (*a friend of theirs*). [ME f. THEIR]

theism /thée-iz'm/ *n.* belief in the existence of gods or a god, esp. a God supernaturally revealed to man (cf. DEISM) and sustaining a personal relation to his creatures. □□ **theist** *n.* **theistic** /-ístik/ *adj.* **theistical** /-ístik'l/ *adj.* **theistically** /-ístikəli/ *adv.* [Gk *theos* god + -ISM]

them /thəm, or, when stressed, them/ *pron.* & *adj.* ● *pron.* **1** *objective case* of THEY (*I saw them*). **2** *colloq.* they (*it's them again; is older than them*). **3** *archaic* themselves (*they fell and hurt them*). ● *adj. sl.* or *dial.* those (*them bones*). [ME *theim* f. ON: see THEY]

thematic /thimáttik/ *adj.* **1** of or relating to subjects or topics (*thematic philately; the arrangement of the anthology is thematic*). **2** *Mus.* of melodic subjects (*thematic treatment*). **3** *Gram.* **a** of or belonging to a theme (*thematic vowel; thematic form*). **b** (of a form of a verb) having a thematic vowel. □ **thematic catalogue** *Mus.* a catalogue giving the opening themes of works as well as their names and other details. □□ **thematically** *adv.* [Gk *thematikos* (as THEME)]

theme /theem/ *n.* **1** a subject or topic on which a person speaks, writes, or thinks. **2** *Mus.* a prominent or frequently recurring melody or group of notes in a composition. **3** *US* a school exercise, esp. an essay, on a given subject. **4** *Gram.* the stem of a noun or verb; the part to which inflections are added, esp. composed of the root and an added vowel. **5** *hist.* any of the 29 provinces in the Byzantine empire. □ **theme park** an amusement park organized round a unifying idea. **theme song** (or **tune**) **1** a recurrent melody in a musical play or film. **2** a signature tune. [ME *teme* ult. f. Gk *thema -matos* f. *tithēmi* set, place]

■ **1** subject(-matter), topic, idea, notion, concept, thesis, text, thread, keynote, gist, core, substance, point, essence, argument, question, issue. **2** see MOTIF. **3** essay, paper, composition, review, article, story, piece, exposition, study, exercise, tract, thesis, dissertation, disquisition. **4** see BASE[1] *n.* 12.

themselves /thəmsélvz/ *pron.* **1 a** *emphat. form* of THEY or THEM. **b** *refl. form* of THEM; (cf. HERSELF). **2** in their normal state of body or mind (*are quite themselves again*). □ **be themselves** act in their normal, unconstrained manner.

■ **2** see NORMAL *adj.* 2.

then /then/ *adv., adj.,* & *n.* ● *adv.* **1** at that time; at the time in question (*was then too busy; then comes the trouble; the then existing laws*). **2 a** next, afterwards; after that (*then he told me to come in*). **b** and also (*then, there are the children to consider*). **c** after all (*it is a problem, but then that is what we are here for*). **3 a** in that case; therefore; it follows that (*then you should have said so*). **b** if what you say is true (*but then why did you take it?*). **c** (implying grudging or impatient concession) if you must have it so (*all right then, have it your own way*). **d** used parenthetically to resume a narrative etc. (*the policeman, then, knocked on the door*). ● *adj.* that or who was such at the time in question (*the then Duke*). ● *n.* that time (*until then*). □ **then and there** immediately and on the spot. [OE *thanne, thonne*, etc., f. Gmc, rel. to THAT, THE]

■ *adv.* **2 b** see FURTHER *adv.* **c** see YET *adv.* 6. **3 a, b** see THUS 2. □ **then and there** see IMMEDIATELY *adv.* 1.

thenar /théenər/ *n. Anat.* the ball of muscle at the base of the thumb. [earlier = palm of the hand: mod.L f. Gk]

thence /thenss/ *adv.* (also **from thence**) *archaic* or *literary* **1** from that place or source. **2** for that reason. [ME *thannes, thennes* f. *thanne, thenne* f. OE *thanon(e)* etc. f. WG]

■ **2** see THEREFORE.

thenceforth /thénsfórth/ *adv.* (also **from thenceforth**) *archaic* or *literary* from that time onward.

thenceforward /thénsfórwərd/ *adv. archaic* or *literary* thenceforth.

theo- /thée-ō/ *comb. form* God or gods. [Gk f. *theos* god]

theobromine /théeəbrṓmin, -meen/ *n.* a bitter white alkaloid obtained from cacao seeds, related to caffeine. [*Theobroma* cacao genus: mod.L f. Gk *theos* god + *brōma* food, + -INE[4]]

theocentric /théeəséntrik/ *adj.* having God as its centre.

theocracy /thiókrəsi/ *n.* (*pl.* **-ies**) **1** a form of government by God or a god directly or through a priestly order etc. **2** (**the Theocracy**) the Jewish commonwealth from Moses to the monarchy. □□ **theocrat** /théeəkrat/ *n.* **theocratic** /théeəkráttik/ *adj.* **theocratically** /théeəkráttikəli/ *adv.*

theocrasy /théeəkraysi, thiókrəsi/ *n.* **1** the mingling of deities into one personality. **2** the union of the soul with God through contemplation (among Neoplatonists etc.). [THEO- + Gk *krasis* mingling]

theodicy /thióddisi/ *n.* (*pl.* **-ies**) **1** the vindication of divine providence in view of the existence of evil. **2** an instance of this. □□ **theodicean** /-séeən/ *adj.* [THEO- + Gk *dikē* justice]

theodolite /thióddəlīt/ *n.* a surveying-instrument for measuring horizontal and vertical angles with a rotating telescope. □□ **theodolitic** /-líttik/ *adj.* [16th c. *theodelitus*, of unkn. orig.]

theogony /thióggəni/ *n.* (*pl.* **-ies**) **1** the genealogy of the gods. **2** an account of this. [THEO- + Gk *-gonia* begetting]

theologian /théeəlṓjiən, -jən/ *n.* a person trained in theology. [ME f. OF *theologien* (as THEOLOGY)]

theological /théeəlójik'l/ *adj.* of theology. □ **theological virtues** faith, hope, and charity. □□ **theologically** *adv.* [med.L *theologicalis* f. L *theologicus* f. Gk *theologikos* (as THEOLOGY)]

theology /thiólləji/ *n.* (*pl.* **-ies**) **1 a** the study of theistic (esp. Christian) religion. **b** a system of theistic (esp. Christian) religion. **c** the rational analysis of a religious faith. **2** a system of theoretical principles, esp. an impractical or rigid ideology. □□ **theologist** *n.* **theologize** *v.tr.* & *intr.* (also **-ise**). [ME f. OF *theologie* f. L *theologia* f. Gk (as THEO-, -LOGY)]

theomachy /thiómməki/ *n.* (*pl.* **-ies**) strife among or against the gods. [THEO- + Gk *makhē* fight]

theophany /thióffəni/ *n.* (*pl.* **-ies**) a visible manifestation of God or a god to man.

theophoric /théeəfórrik/ *adj.* bearing the name of a god.

theophylline /théeəfíllin, -leen/ *n.* an alkaloid similar to theobromine, found in tea-leaves. [irreg. f. mod.L *thea* tea + Gk *phullon* leaf + -INE[4]]

theorbo /thiórbō/ *n.* (*pl.* **-os**) a two-necked musical instrument of the lute class much used in the seventeenth century. □□ **theorbist** *n.* [It. *tiorba*, of unkn. orig.]

theorem /théerəm/ *n.* esp. *Math.* **1** a general proposition not self-evident but proved by a chain of reasoning; a truth established by means of accepted truths (cf. PROBLEM). **2** a rule in algebra etc., esp. one expressed by symbols or formulae (*binomial theorem*). □□ **theorematic** /-máttik/ *adj.* [F *théorème* or LL *theōrema* f. Gk *theōrēma* speculation, proposition f. *theōreō* look at]

■ **1** hypothesis, proposition, assumption, conjecture, statement, deduction, thesis, postulate. **2** rule, formula, principle.

theoretic /theeréttik/ *adj.* & *n.* ● *adj.* = THEORETICAL. ● *n.* (in *sing.* or *pl.*) the theoretical part of a science etc. [LL *theoreticus* f. Gk *theōrētikos* (as THEORY)]

theoretical /theeréttik'l/ *adj.* **1** concerned with knowledge but not with its practical application. **2** based on theory rather than experience or practice. □□ **theoretically** *adv.*

■ **1** impractical, unrealistic, pure, ideal, abstract, academic, theoretic. **2** hypothetical, conjectural, speculative, assumed, untested, unproved, unproven, moot, putative, debatable, tentative, unsubstantiated, supposititious, suppositional, theoretic. □□ **theoretically** see *ideally* (IDEAL).

theoretician /théeritísh'n/ *n.* a person concerned with the theoretical aspects of a subject.

theorist /théerist/ *n.* a holder or inventor of a theory or theories.
■ theoretician, speculator, hypothesizer, theorizer, philosopher, dreamer.

theorize /théerīz/ *v.intr.* (also **-ise**) evolve or indulge in theories. □□ **theorizer** *n.*
■ hypothesize, conjecture, speculate, surmise, guess.
□□ **theorizer** see THEORIST.

theory /théeri/ *n.* (*pl.* **-ies**) **1** a supposition or system of ideas explaining something, esp. one based on general principles independent of the particular things to be explained (cf. HYPOTHESIS) (*atomic theory; theory of evolution*). **2** a speculative (esp. fanciful) view (*one of my pet theories*). **3** the sphere of abstract knowledge or speculative thought (*this is all very well in theory, but how will it work in practice?*). **4** the exposition of the principles of a science etc. (*the theory of music*). **5** *Math.* a collection of propositions to illustrate the principles of a subject (*probability theory; theory of equations*). [LL *theoria* f. Gk *theōria* f. *theōros* spectator f. *theōreō* look at]
■ **1** see DOCTRINE 2. **2** see VIEW *n.* 5, FEELING 4a. **4** see LAW 11.

theosophy /thiόssəfi/ *n.* (*pl.* **-ies**) any of various philosophies professing to achieve a knowledge of God by spiritual ecstasy, direct intuition, or special individual relations, esp. a modern movement following Hindu and Buddhist teachings and seeking universal brotherhood. □□ **theosopher** *n.* **theosophic** /théeəsóffik/ *adj.* **theosophical** /théeəsóffik'l/ *adj.* **theosophically** /théeəsóffikəli/ *adv.* **theosophist** *n.* [med.L *theosophia* f. late Gk *theosophia* f. *theosophos* wise concerning God (as THEO-, *sophos* wise)]

therapeutic /thérrəpyóotik/ *adj.* **1** of, for, or contributing to the cure of disease. **2** contributing to general, esp. mental, well-being (*finds walking therapeutic*). □□ **therapeutical** *adj.* **therapeutically** *adv.* **therapeutist** *n.* [attrib. use of *therapeutic*, orig. form of THERAPEUTICS]
■ **1** therapeutical, healing, curative, remedial, restorative, corrective, medical, medicinal. **2** therapeutical, health-giving, healthy, beneficial, salubrious, *archaic* salutary. □□ **therapeutist** see *therapist* (THERAPY).

therapeutics /thérrəpyóotiks/ *n.pl.* (usu. treated as *sing.*) the branch of medicine concerned with the treatment of disease and the action of remedial agents. [F *thérapeutique* or LL *therapeutica* (pl.) f. Gk *therapeutika* neut. pl. of *therapeutikos* f. *therapeuō* wait on, cure]

therapy /thérrəpi/ *n.* (*pl.* **-ies**) **1** the treatment of physical or mental disorders, other than by surgery. **2 a** a particular type of such treatment. **b** psychotherapy. □□ **therapist** *n.* [mod.L *therapia* f. Gk *therapeia* healing]
■ **1** treatment, healing, cure. **2 a** technique, treatment, remedy, remedial programme. **b** psychotherapy, psychoanalysis, analysis, counselling, group therapy. □□ **therapist** healer, practitioner, therapeutist; psychotherapist, psychologist, analyst, psychiatrist, psychoanalyst, counsellor, adviser, *sl.* shrink.

Theravada /thérrəvaádə/ *n.* a more conservative form of Buddhism, practised in Burma (now Myanmar), Thailand, etc. [Pali *theravāda* f. *thera* elder, old + *vāda* speech, doctrine]

there /thair/ *adv.*; *n.*, & *int.* ● *adv.* **1** in, at, or to that place or position (*lived there for some years; goes there every day*). **2** at that point (in speech, performance, writing, etc.) (*there he stopped*). **3** in that respect (*I agree with you there*). **4** used for emphasis in calling attention (*you there!; there goes the bell*). **5** used to indicate the fact or existence of something (*there is a house on the corner*). ● *n.* that place (*lives somewhere near there*). ● *int.* **1** expressing confirmation, triumph, dismay, etc. (*there! what did I tell you?*). **2** used to soothe a child etc. (*there, there, never mind*). □ **have been there before** *sl.* know all about it. **so there** *colloq.* that is my final decision (whether you like it or not). **there and then** immediately and on the spot. **there it is 1** that is the trouble. **2** nothing can be done about it. **there's** *colloq.* you are (by virtue of present or future obedience etc.) (*there's a dear*). **there you are** (or **go**) *colloq.* **1** this is what you wanted etc. **2** expressing confirmation, triumph, resignation, etc. [OE *thǣr*, *thēr* f. Gmc, rel. to THAT, THE]
■ □ **there and then** see IMMEDIATELY *adv.* 1.

thereabouts /tháirəbówts/ *adv.* (also **thereabout**) **1** near that place (*ought to be somewhere thereabouts*). **2** near that number, quantity, etc. (*two litres or thereabouts*).

thereafter /tháiraáftər/ *adv. formal* after that.

thereanent /tháirənént/ *adv. Sc.* about that matter.

thereat /tháirát/ *adv. archaic* **1** at that place. **2** on that account. **3** after that.

thereby /tháirbī/ *adv.* by that means, as a result of that. □ **thereby hangs a tale** much could be said about that.

therefor /tháirfór/ *adv. archaic* for that object or purpose.

therefore /tháirfor/ *adv.* for that reason; accordingly, consequently.
■ consequently, so, as a result *or* consequence, hence, *ergo*, for that reason, accordingly, then, that being so *or* the case, *archaic* wherefore, *archaic or literary* thence, *formal* thus.

therefrom /tháirfróm/ *adv. archaic* from that or it.

therein /tháirín/ *adv. formal* **1** in that place etc. **2** in that respect.

thereinafter /tháirinaáftər/ *adv. formal* later in the same document etc.

thereinbefore /tháirinbifór/ *adv. formal* earlier in the same document etc.

thereinto /tháiríntoo/ *adv. archaic* into that place.

thereof /tháiróv/ *adv. formal* of that or it.

thereon /tháirón/ *adv. archaic* on that or it (of motion or position).

thereout /tháirówt/ *adv. archaic* out of that, from that source.

therethrough /tháirthróo/ *adv. archaic* through that.

thereto /tháirtóo/ *adv. formal* **1** to that or it. **2** in addition, to boot.

theretofore /tháirtoofór/ *adv. formal* before that time.
■ see *previously* (PREVIOUS).

thereunto /tháirúntoo/ *adv. archaic* to that or it.

thereupon /tháirəpón/ *adv.* **1** in consequence of that. **2** soon or immediately after that. **3** *archaic* upon that (of motion or position).

therewith /tháirwith/ *adv. archaic* **1** with that. **2** soon or immediately after that.

therewithal /tháirwitháwl/ *adv. archaic* in addition, besides.

theriac /théeriak/ *n. archaic* an antidote to the bites of poisonous animals, esp. snakes. [L *theriaca* f. Gk *thēriakē* antidote, fem. of *thēriakos* f. *thēr* wild beast]

therianthropic /théerianthróppik/ *adj.* of or worshipping beings represented in combined human and animal forms. [Gk *thērion* dimin. of *thēr* wild beast + *anthrōpos* human being]

theriomorphic /théeriəmórfik/ *adj.* (esp. of a deity) having an animal form. [as THERIANTHROPIC + Gk *morphē* form]

therm /therm/ *n.* a unit of heat, esp. as the former statutory unit of gas supplied in the UK equivalent to 100,000 British thermal units or 1.055 x 10^8 joules. [Gk *thermē* heat]

thermae /thérmee/ *n.pl. Gk & Rom. Antiq.* public baths. [L f. Gk *thermai* (pl.) (as THERM)]

thermal /thérm'l/ *adj.* & *n.* ● *adj.* **1** of, for, or producing heat. **2** promoting the retention of heat (*thermal underwear*). ● *n.* a rising current of heated air (used by gliders, balloons, and birds to gain height). □ **British thermal unit** the amount of heat needed to raise 1 lb. of water at maximum density through one degree Fahrenheit, equivalent to 1.055 x 10^3 joules. **thermal capacity** the number of heat units needed to raise the temperature of a body by one degree. **thermal neutron** a neutron in thermal equilibrium with its surroundings. **thermal reactor** a nuclear reactor using thermal neutrons. **thermal springs** springs of naturally hot water. **thermal unit** a unit for measuring heat. □□

thermalize *v.tr.* & *intr.* (also **-ise**). **thermalization** /-līzáysh'n/ *n.* **thermally** *adv.* [F (as THERM)]

thermic /thérmik/ *adj.* of or relating to heat.

thermidor see LOBSTER.

thermion /thérmion/ *n.* an ion or electron emitted by a substance at high temperature. [THERMO- + ION]

thermionic /thérmiónnik/ *adj.* of or relating to electrons emitted from a substance at very high temperature. □ **thermionic emission** the emission of electrons from a heated source. **thermionic valve** (*US* **tube**) a device giving a flow of thermionic electrons in one direction, used esp. in the rectification of a current and in radio reception.

thermionics /thérmiónniks/ *n.pl.* (treated as *sing.*) the branch of science and technology concerned with thermionic emission.

thermistor /thermístər/ *n. Electr.* a resistor whose resistance is greatly reduced by heating, used for measurement and control. [*thermal resistor*]

thermite /thérmīt/ *n.* (also **thermit** /-mit/) a mixture of finely powdered aluminium and iron oxide that produces a very high temperature on combustion (used in welding and for incendiary bombs). [G *Thermit* (as THERMO-, -ITE[1])]

thermo- /thérmō/ *comb. form* denoting heat. [Gk f. *thermos* hot, *thermē* heat]

thermochemistry /thérmōkémmistri/ *n.* the branch of chemistry dealing with the quantities of heat evolved or absorbed during chemical reactions. □□ **thermochemical** *adj.*

thermocouple /thérmōkupp'l/ *n.* a pair of different metals in contact at a point, generating a thermoelectric voltage that can serve as a measure of temperature at this point relative to their other parts.

thermodynamics /thérmōdīnámmiks/ *n.pl.* (usu. treated as *sing.*) the science of the relations between heat and other (mechanical, electrical, etc.) forms of energy. □□ **thermodynamic** *adj.* **thermodynamical** *adj.* **thermodynamically** *adv.* **thermodynamicist** /-misist/ *n.*

thermoelectric /thérmō-iléktrik/ *adj.* producing electricity by a difference of temperatures. □□ **thermoelectrically** *adv.* **thermoelectricity** /-ilektríssiti/ *n.*

thermogenesis /thérmōjénnisiss/ *n.* the production of heat, esp. in a human or animal body.

thermogram /thérməgram/ *n.* a record made by a thermograph.

thermograph /thérməgraaf/ *n.* **1** an instrument that gives a continuous record of temperature. **2** an apparatus used to obtain an image produced by infrared radiation from a human or animal body. □□ **thermographic** /-gráffik/ *adj.*

thermography /thermógrəfi/ *n. Med.* the taking or use of infrared thermograms, esp. to detect tumours.

thermolabile /thérmōláybīl, -bil/ *adj.* (of a substance) unstable when heated.

thermoluminescence /thérmōlōōminéss'nss/ *n.* the property of becoming luminescent when pretreated and subjected to high temperatures, used as a means of dating ancient artefacts. □□ **thermoluminescent** *adj.*

thermolysis /thermóllisiss/ *n.* decomposition by the action of heat. □□ **thermolytic** /-məlíttik/ *adj.*

thermometer /thərmómmitər/ *n.* an instrument for measuring temperature, esp. a graduated glass tube with a small bore containing mercury or alcohol which expands when heated. □□ **thermometric** /thérməmétrik/ *adj.* **thermometrical** /thérməmétrik'l/ *adj.* **thermometry** *n.* [F *thermomètre* or mod.L *thermometrum* (as THERMO-, -METER)]

thermonuclear /thérmōnyōōkliər/ *adj.* **1** relating to or using nuclear reactions that occur only at very high temperatures. **2** relating to or characterized by weapons using thermonuclear reactions.

thermophile /thérmōfīl/ *n.* & *adj.* (also **thermophil** /-fil/) ● *n.* a bacterium etc. growing optimally at high temperatures. ● *adj.* of or being a thermophile. □□ **thermophilic** /-fíllik/ *adj.*

thermopile /thérmōpīl/ *n.* a set of thermocouples esp. arranged for measuring small quantities of radiant heat.

thermoplastic /thérmōplástik/ *adj.* & *n.* ● *adj.* (of a substance) that becomes plastic on heating and hardens on cooling, and is able to repeat these processes. ● *n.* a thermoplastic substance.

Thermos /thérməss/ *n.* (in full **Thermos flask**) *propr.* a vacuum flask. [Gk (as THERMO-)]

thermosetting /thérmōsétting/ *adj.* (of plastics) setting permanently when heated. □□ **thermoset** *adj.*

thermosphere /thérməsfeer/ *n.* the region of the atmosphere beyond the mesosphere.

thermostable /thérmōstáyb'l/ *adj.* (of a substance) stable when heated.

thermostat /thérməstat/ *n.* a device that automatically regulates temperature, or that activates a device when the temperature reaches a certain point. □□ **thermostatic** /-státtik/ *adj.* **thermostatically** /-státtikəli/ *adv.* [THERMO- + Gk *statos* standing]

thermotaxis /thérmōtáksiss/ *n.* **1** the regulation of heat or temperature esp. in warm-blooded animals. **2** movement or stimulation in a living organism caused by heat. □□ **thermotactic** *adj.* **thermotaxic** *adj.*

thermotropism /thermótrəpiz'm/ *n.* the growing or bending of a plant towards or away from a source of heat. □□ **thermotropic** /thérmōtróppik/ *adj.*

thesaurus /thisáwrəss/ *n.* (*pl.* **thesauri** /-rī/ or **thesauruses**) **1 a** a collection of concepts or words arranged according to sense. **b** a book of synonyms and antonyms. **2** a dictionary or encyclopedia. [L f. Gk *thēsauros* treasure]

■ **1 b** synonym dictionary, synonymy. **2** dictionary, lexicon, encyclopedia, wordfinder.

these *pl.* of THIS.

thesis /theéssiss/ *n.* (*pl.* **theses** /-seez/) **1** a proposition to be maintained or proved. **2** a dissertation, esp. by a candidate for a degree. **3** /also théssiss/ an unstressed syllable or part of a metrical foot in Greek or Latin verse (opp. ARSIS). [ME f. LL f. Gk, = putting, placing, a proposition etc. f. *the-* root of *tithēmi* place]

■ **1** argument, theory, proposition, point, contention, belief, idea, premiss, assumption, view, assertion, precept, opinion, notion, theorem, axiom, postulate, hypothesis. **2** dissertation, disquisition, treatise, tract, monograph, paper, essay, *literary* discourse.

Thespian /théspiən/ *adj.* & *n.* ● *adj.* of or relating to tragedy or drama. ● *n.* an actor or actress. [Gk *Thespis* the traditional originator of Greek tragedy]

■ *adj.* dramatic, theatric(al), histrionic, acting, performing; *colloq.* hammy, *sl.* ham. ● *n.* actor, actress, performer, trouper, player; supernumerary, extra; matinée idol, star; *sl.* ham.

Thess. *abbr.* Thessalonians (New Testament).

theta /theétə/ *n.* the eighth letter of the Greek alphabet (Θ, θ). [Gk]

theurgy /theé-urji/ *n.* **1 a** supernatural or divine agency esp. in human affairs. **b** the art of securing this. **2** the magical science of the Neoplatonists. □□ **theurgic** /-úrjik/ *adj.* **theurgical** /-úrjik'l/ *adj.* **theurgist** *n.* [LL *theurgia* f. Gk *theourgia* f. *theos* god + *-ergos* working]

thew /thyōō/ *n.* (often in *pl.*) *literary* **1** muscular strength. **2** mental or moral vigour. [OE *thēaw* usage, conduct, of unkn. orig.]

they /thay/ *pron.* (*obj.* **them**; *poss.* **their**, **theirs**) **1** the people, animals, or things previously named or in question (*pl.* of HE, SHE, IT[1]). **2** people in general (*they say we are wrong*). **3** those in authority (*they have raised the fees*). **4** *disp.* as a third person sing. indefinite pronoun meaning 'he or she' (*anyone can come if they want to*). [ME *thei*, obj. *theim*, f. ON *their* nom. pl. masc., *theim* dat. pl. of *sá* THE that]

they'd /thayd/ *contr.* **1** they had. **2** they would.

they'll /thayl/ *contr.* **1** they will. **2** they shall.

they're /thair/ *contr.* they are.

they've /thayv/ *contr.* they have.

THI *abbr.* temperature-humidity index.

thiamine /thī́əmin, -meen/ *n.* (also **thiamin**) a vitamin of the B complex, found in unrefined cereals, beans, and liver, a deficiency of which causes beriberi. Also called *vitamin* B_1, or ANEURIN. [THIO- + *amin* from VITAMIN]

thick /thik/ *adj.*, *n.*, & *adv.* ● *adj.* **1 a** of great or specified extent between opposite surfaces (*a thick wall*; *a wall two metres thick*). **b** of large diameter (*a thick rope*). **2 a** (of a line etc.) broad; not fine. **b** (of script or type, etc.) consisting of thick lines. **3 a** arranged closely; crowded together; dense. **b** numerous (*fell thick as peas*). **c** bushy, luxuriant (*thick hair*; *thick growth*). **4** (usu. foll. by *with*) densely covered or filled (*air thick with snow*). **5 a** firm in consistency; containing much solid matter; viscous (*a thick paste*; *thick soup*). **b** made of thick material (*a thick coat*). **6** muddy, cloudy; impenetrable by sight (*thick darkness*). **7** *colloq.* (of a person) stupid, dull. **8 a** (of a voice) indistinct. **b** (of an accent) pronounced, exaggerated. **9** *colloq.* intimate or very friendly (esp. *thick as thieves*). ● *n.* a thick part of anything. ● *adv.* thickly (*snow was falling thick*; *blows rained down thick and fast*). □ **a bit thick** *Brit. colloq.* unreasonable or intolerable. **in the thick of 1** at the busiest part of. **2** heavily occupied with. **thick ear** *Brit. sl.* the external ear swollen as a result of a blow (esp. *give a person a thick ear*). **thick-skinned** not sensitive to reproach or criticism. **thick-skulled** (or **-witted**) stupid, dull; slow to learn. **through thick and thin** under all conditions; in spite of all difficulties. □□ **thickish** *adj.* **thickly** *adv.* [OE *thicce* (adj. & adv.) f. Gmc]

■ *adj.* **1 a** broad, wide, solid, thickset, burly, ample, bulky, fat, substantial, beamy, chunky, stout, broad-beamed. **2** broad, fat, wide. **3 a** compact, condensed, compressed, choking, packed, solid, impenetrable, impassable, dense, close, thickset, serried. **b** abundant, plentiful, numerous. **c** abundant, plentiful, bushy, luxuriant, lush. **4** dense, solid, packed, close-packed, crowded, choked, filled, full, deep, clotted, covered, chock-full, chock-a-block, teeming, swarming, alive, bristling, crawling, bursting, crammed, jammed, brimming, *colloq.* lousy. **5 a** dense, viscid, viscous, gelatinous, mucilaginous, gluey, glutinous, ropy, condensed, concentrated, coagulated, clotted, congealed, jelled, jellied, stiffish; stiff, firm, rigid, solid, *literary* inspissated. **b** heavy, bulky, chunky. **6** soupy, murky, misty, foggy, smoggy, smoky, opaque, impenetrable, obscure, obscuring, hazy, muddy, cloudy. **7** thickheaded, thick-witted, thick-skulled, dense, stupid, slow, slow-witted, dull, dull-witted, stolid, obtuse, fat-headed, addle-brained, halfwitted, blockheaded, doltish, imbecilic; insensitive, thick-skinned; *colloq.* moronic, cretinous, dim-witted, dopey, pinheaded, wooden-headed, *esp. Brit. colloq.* gormless, *esp. US colloq.* dumb, *sl.* boneheaded. **8 a** guttural, hoarse, throaty, raspy, rasping, rough, husky, grating, gravelly, indistinct, distorted, inarticulate; gruff, raucous. **b** marked, pronounced, exaggerated, strong, broad, decided, obvious, noticeable. **9** close, friendly, inseparable, devoted, hand in glove, on good terms, on the best (of) terms, intimate, matey, *colloq.* chummy, pally, like that, (as) thick as thieves, *Brit. colloq.* well in, *US colloq.* palsy-walsy. ● *n.* core, heart, centre, middle, focus, midst. □ **in the thick of 1** see AMID. **thick-skinned** insensitive, insensate, dull, obtuse, stolid, callous, numb(ed), steeled, hardened, toughened, tough, unsusceptible, inured, unfeeling, case-hardened, impervious, pachydermatous, *colloq.* hard-boiled. **thick-skulled** (or **-witted**) see THICK *adj.* 7 above.

thicken /thíkkən/ *v.* **1** *tr.* & *intr.* make or become thick or thicker. **2** *intr.* become more complicated (*the plot thickens*). □□ **thickener** *n.*

■ **1** coagulate, clot, congeal, gel, set, solidify, stiffen, harden, firm up, cake, *colloq.* jell, *literary* inspissate.

thickening /thíkkəning/ *n.* **1** the process of becoming thick or thicker. **2** a substance used to thicken liquid. **3** a thickened part.

thicket /thíkkit/ *n.* a tangle of shrubs or trees. [OE *thiccet* (as THICK, -ET[1])]

■ copse, brake, grove, coppice, thickset, covert, wood, *Brit.* spinney, *esp. US* & *Austral.* brush.

thickhead /thík-hed/ *n.* **1** *colloq.* a stupid person; a blockhead. **2** *Austral.* any bird of the genus *Pachycephala*; a whistler. □□ **thickheaded** /-héddid/ *adj.* **thickheadedness** /-héddidniss/ *n.*

■ **1** see FOOL *n.* 1. □□ **thickheaded** see STUPID *adj.* 1, 5. **thickheadedness** see *stupidity* (STUPID).

thickness /thíkniss/ *n.* **1** the state of being thick. **2** the extent to which a thing is thick. **3** a layer of material of a certain thickness (*three thicknesses of cardboard*). **4** a part that is thick or lies between opposite surfaces (*steps cut in the thickness of the wall*). [OE *thicness* (as THICK, -NESS)]

■ **1** see BODY *n.* 8, *stupidity* (STUPID). **2** see BREADTH 1. **3** see PLY[1] 1.

thickset /thíksét/ *adj.* & *n.* ● *adj.* **1** heavily or solidly built. **2** set or growing close together. ● *n.* a thicket.

■ *adj.* **1** see STOCKY. **2** see THICK *adj.* 3a. ● *n.* see THICKET.

thief /theef/ *n.* (*pl.* **thieves** /theevz/) a person who steals esp. secretly and without violence. [OE *thēof* f. Gmc]

■ robber, burglar, cat burglar, housebreaker, picklock, sneak-thief, safe-cracker, pilferer, shoplifter, stealer, kleptomaniac, *formal or joc.* purloiner; embezzler, peculator; pickpocket, purse-snatcher, mugger, highwayman, footpad, brigand, bandit, thug, dacoit, outlaw, plunderer, looter; poacher; pirate, (sea) rover, picaroon, corsair, freebooter, buccaneer, marauder; cheat, swindler, confidence man, mountebank, charlatan, sharper, trickster, thimblerigger, *archaic* cutpurse, *Austral. hist.* bush-ranger, *sl.* cracksman, dip, con man, con artist, *US sl.* highbinder.

thieve /theev/ *v.* **1** *intr.* be a thief. **2** *tr.* steal (a thing). [OE *thēofian* (as THIEF)]

■ **2** see STEAL *v.* 1.

thievery /theévəri/ *n.* the act or practice of stealing.

■ see THEFT.

thieves *pl.* of THIEF.

thievish /theévish/ *adj.* given to stealing. □□ **thievishly** *adv.* **thievishness** *n.*

thigh /thī/ *n.* **1** the part of the human leg between the hip and the knee. **2** a corresponding part in other animals. □ **thigh-bone** = FEMUR. **thigh-slapper** *colloq.* an exceptionally funny joke, etc. □□ **-thighed** *adj.* (in *comb.*). [OE *thēh*, *thēoh*, *thīoh*, OHG *dioh*, ON *thjó* f. Gmc]

thill /thil/ *n.* a shaft of a cart or carriage, esp. one of a pair. [ME: orig. unkn.]

thill-horse /thílhorss/ *n.* (also **thiller** /thíllər/) a horse put between thills.

thimble /thímb'l/ *n.* **1** a metal or plastic cap, usu. with a closed end, worn to protect the finger and push the needle in sewing. **2** *Mech.* a short metal tube or ferrule etc. **3** *Naut.* a metal ring concave on the outside and fitting in a loop of spliced rope to prevent chafing. [OE *thȳmel* (as THUMB, -LE[1])]

thimbleful /thímb'lfŏŏl/ *n.* (*pl.* **-fuls**) a small quantity, esp. of liquid to drink.

■ see DROP *n.* 1b, SIP *n.*

thimblerig /thímb'lrig/ *n.* a game often involving sleight of hand, in which three inverted thimbles or cups are moved about, contestants having to spot which is the one with a pea or other object beneath. □□ **thimblerigger** *n.* [THIMBLE + RIG[2] in sense 'trick, dodge']

thin /thin/ *adj.*, *adv.*, & *v.* ● *adj.* (**thinner**, **thinnest**) **1** having the opposite surfaces close together; of small thickness or diameter. **2 a** (of a line) narrow or fine. **b** (of a script or type etc.) consisting of thin lines. **3** made of thin material (*a thin dress*). **4** lean; not plump. **5 a** not dense or copious (*thin hair*; *a thin haze*). **b** not full or closely packed (*a thin audience*). **6** of slight consistency (*a thin paste*). **7** weak; lacking an important ingredient (*thin blood*; *a thin voice*). **8** (of an excuse, argument, disguise, etc.) flimsy or transparent.

● *adv.* thinly (*cut the bread very thin*). ● *v.* (**thinned, thinning**) **1** *tr.* & *intr.* make or become thin or thinner. **2** *tr.* & *intr.* (often foll. by *out*) reduce; make or become less dense or crowded or numerous. **3** *tr.* (often foll. by *out*) remove some of a crop of (seedlings, saplings, etc.) or some young fruit from (a vine or tree) to improve the growth of the rest. □ **have a thin time** *colloq.* have a wretched or uncomfortable time. **on thin ice** see ICE. **thin air** a state of invisibility or non-existence (*vanished into thin air*). **thin end of the wedge** see WEDGE[1]. **thin on the ground** see GROUND[1]. **thin on top** balding. **thin-skinned** sensitive to reproach or criticism; easily upset. □□ **thinly** *adv.* **thinness** *n.* **thinnish** *adj.* [OE *thynne* f. Gmc]

■ *adj.* **1** slim, slender, spindly, skinny. **2** attenuated, threadlike, stringlike, pencil-thin, fine; narrow. **3** airy, filmy, diaphanous, gossamer, sheer, light, delicate, chiffon, silky, silken, gauzy, flimsy, fine, translucent, see-through, transparent. **4** slim, slender, lean, spare, slight, small, lanky, spindly, skinny, thin as a rail *or* reed *or* rake, wispy, willowy, twiggy, wiry, skeletal, gaunt, gangling, bony, emaciated, cadaverous, meagre, scrawny, all skin and bones, raw-boned, scraggy, thinnish, undernourished, underfed, underweight, undersized, puny, sparse, hollow-cheeked, (half-)starved, pinched, withered, shrunken, shrivelled (up). **5** sparse, unsubstantial, poor, scant, scanty, insufficient, inadequate, slight, worthless, deficient, skimpy, unplentiful, meagre, paltry. **6** watery, runny, watered down, dilute(d), weak, unsatisfying. **8** flimsy, weak, feeble, slight, unsubstantial, insubstantial, tenuous, threadbare, transparent, fragile, frail, poor, lame; unbelievable, unconvincing. ● *v.* **1** thin down, draw out, attenuate, reduce, trim, cut down, prune; sharpen, taper. **2** thin down *or* out, dilute, water (down), weaken, decrease, reduce, diminish. □ **thin-skinned** see SENSITIVE *adj.* 2.

thine /th̲ī̲n/ *poss.pron. archaic* or *dial.* **1** (*predic.* or *absol.*) of or belonging to thee. **2** (*attrib.* before a vowel) = THY. [OE *thīn* f. Gmc]

thing /thing/ *n.* **1** a material or non-material entity, idea, action, etc., that is or may be thought about or perceived. **2** an inanimate material object (*take that thing away*). **3** an unspecified object or item (*have a few things to buy*). **4** an act, idea, or utterance (*a silly thing to do*). **5** an event (*an unfortunate thing to happen*). **6** a quality (*patience is a useful thing*). **7** (with ref. to a person) expressing pity, contempt, or affection (*poor thing!*; *a dear old thing*). **8** a specimen or type of something (*quarks are an important thing in physics*). **9** *colloq.* **a** one's special interest or concern (*not my thing at all*). **b** an obsession, fear, or prejudice (*spiders are a thing of mine*). **10** *colloq.* something remarkable (*now there's a thing!*). **11** (prec. by *the*) *colloq.* **a** what is conventionally proper or fashionable. **b** what is needed or required (*your suggestion was just the thing*). **c** what is to be considered (*the thing is, shall we go or not?*). **d** what is important (*the thing about them is their reliability*). **12** (in *pl.*) personal belongings or clothing (*where have I left my things?*). **13** (in *pl.*) equipment (*painting things*). **14** (in *pl.*) affairs in general (*not in the nature of things*). **15** (in *pl.*) circumstances or conditions (*things look good*). **16** (in *pl.* with a following adjective) all that is so describable (*all things Greek*). **17** (in *pl.*) *Law* property. □ **do one's own thing** *colloq.* pursue one's own interests or inclinations. **do things to** *colloq.* affect remarkably. **have a thing about** *colloq.* be obsessed, fearful, or prejudiced about. **make a thing of** *colloq.* **1** regard as essential. **2** cause a fuss about. **one** (or **just one**) **of those things** *colloq.* something unavoidable or to be accepted. [OE f. Gmc]

■ **2, 3** device, item, gadget, (inanimate) object, entity, article, possession, commodity, mechanism, contrivance, apparatus, instrument, utensil; whatnot, doodah, *US* doodad, *colloq.* whatchamacallit, what-d'you-call-it, what's-its-name, whatsit, thingummy, thingy, thingumajig, thingumabob, affair, *sl.* gismo. **4** act, action, deed, activity, proceeding; chore, task, job, responsibility, matter; idea, statement; item, subject, matter, detail, feature, aspect, affair, constituent, element, factor, point, particular. **5** event, happening, circumstance, occurrence, incident, phenomenon. **6** quality, attribute, property. **7** soul, dear. **9 a** interest, concern, fancy, love, passion, mania, fetish; see also BAG *n.* 9. **b** obsession, fixation, fetish, *idée fixe*; fear, phobia, terror, loathing, horror, detestation, dislike, aversion, *sl.* hang-up; prejudice, bias. **11 a** fad, trend, fashion, mode, rage. **12** (*things*) belongings, luggage, baggage, impedimenta, possessions, paraphernalia, effects, clothes, clothing, goods, chattels, stuff, junk, bits and pieces *or* bobs, *colloq.* gear, traps, *Brit. sl.* clobber. **13** (*things*) equipment, tools, utensils, implements, apparatus, stuff, paraphernalia, gear, outfit, tackle, kit. **14** (*things*) affairs, matters, business, concerns. **15** (*things*) circumstances, events, happenings, conditions, life. □ **have a thing about** have a feeling about *or* towards, have a reaction to, have an attitude to *or* towards, have an emotional attachment to; be preoccupied *or* obsessed with, be fixated on, like, be passionate about *or* partial to, *colloq.* fancy, love; fear, be afraid of, shudder at, recoil from, *sl.* be hung up on; hate, loathe, detest, abominate, execrate.

thingummy /thíngəmi/ *n.* (*pl.* **-ies**) (also **thingamy, thingumabob** /-məbob/, **thingumajig** /-məjig/) *colloq.* a person or thing whose name one has forgotten or does not know or does not wish to mention. [THING + meaningless suffix]

■ see THING 2, 3.

thingy /thíngi/ *n.* (*pl.* **-ies**) = THINGUMMY.

think /thingk/ *v.* & *n.* ● *v.* (*past* and *past part.* **thought** /thawt/) **1** *tr.* (foll. by *that* + clause) be of the opinion (*we think that they will come*). **2** *tr.* (foll. by *that* + clause or *to* + infin.) judge or consider (*is thought to be a fraud*). **3** *intr.* exercise the mind positively with one's ideas etc. (*let me think for a moment*). **4** *tr.* (foll. by *of* or *about*) **a** consider; be or become mentally aware of (*think of you constantly*). **b** form or entertain the idea of; imagine to oneself (*couldn't think of such a thing*). **c** choose mentally; hit upon (*think of a number*). **d** form or have an opinion of (*what do you think of them?*). **5** *tr.* have a half-formed intention (*I think I'll stay*). **6** *tr.* form a conception of (*cannot think how you do it*). **7** *tr.* reduce to a specified condition by thinking (*cannot think away a toothache*). **8** *tr.* recognize the presence or existence of (*the child thought no harm*). **9** *tr.* (foll. by *to* + infin.) intend or expect (*thinks to deceive us*). **10** *tr.* (foll. by *to* + infin.) remember (*did not think to lock the door*). ● *n. colloq.* an act of thinking (*must have a think about that*). □ **think again** revise one's plans or opinions. **think aloud** utter one's thoughts as soon as they occur. **think back to** recall (a past event or time). **think better of** change one's mind about (an intention) after reconsideration. **think big** see BIG. **think fit** see FIT[1]. **think for oneself** have an independent mind or attitude. **think little** (or **nothing**) **of** consider to be insignificant or unremarkable. **think much** (or **highly**) **of** have a high opinion of. **think on** (or **upon**) *archaic* think of or about. **think out 1** consider carefully. **2** produce (an idea etc.) by thinking. **think over** reflect upon in order to reach a decision. **think through** reflect fully upon (a problem etc.). **think twice** use careful consideration, avoid hasty action, etc. **think up** *colloq.* devise; produce by thought. □□ **thinkable** *adj.* [OE *thencan thōhte gethōht* f. Gmc]

■ *v.* **1** see BELIEVE 2. **2** judge, reckon, consider, regard as, characterize as, view as, believe, assume, *formal* deem. **3** contemplate, cogitate, ruminate, reflect, meditate, ponder, deliberate, reason, concentrate, cudgel *or* rack one's brains, use one's head, *literary* muse. **4** (*think of* or *about*) **a** see CONSIDER 4. **b** consider, ponder, weigh, contemplate, imagine, mull over, entertain the idea *or* notion of, have in mind, propose, *literary* muse over. **c** see *hit on*. **d** see VIEW *v.* 3. **5** believe, imagine, expect, dream, fancy, fantasize, suppose. **6** see CONCEIVE 3.

9 intend, have in mind, mean, design, purpose, plan, propose, expect. □ **think back to** recall, remember, recollect, call *or* bring to mind. **think better of** reconsider, think twice about, change one's mind about. **think little** (or **nothing**) **of** see UNDERESTIMATE *v.* **think much** (or **highly**) **of** see RESPECT *v.* 1. **think over** contemplate, consider, cogitate on *or* over *or* about, ruminate over *or* about, ponder (over *or* on), reflect on, meditate on *or* over *or* about, deliberate on *or* over *or* about, mull over, chew over, think about *or* of, *literary* muse on *or* over *or* about. **think through** see PUZZLE *v.* 4. **think twice** see SCRUPLE *v.* 2; (*think twice about*) see SCRUPLE *v.* 1. **think up** think of, devise, concoct, contrive, come up with, invent, conceive (of), dream up, create, make up, improvise, mastermind. □□ **thinkable** conceivable, possible, imaginable, feasible, reasonable, tenable, not unlikely, plausible, believable, credible.

thinker /thíngkər/ *n.* **1** a person who thinks, esp. in a specified way (*an original thinker*). **2** a person with a skilled or powerful mind.
■ **2** sage, wise man, savant, savante, Solomon, pundit, mastermind, philosopher, scholar, intellectual, learned person, mentor, expert.

thinking /thíngking/ *adj.* & *n.* ● *adj.* using thought or rational judgement. ● *n.* **1** opinion or judgement. **2** thought; train of thought. □ **put on one's thinking cap** *colloq.* meditate on a problem.
■ *adj.* rational, sensible, intelligent, reasoning, reasonable; meditative, contemplative, reflective, philosophical, cogitative, pensive, thoughtful, intellectual, *literary* ratiocinative. ● *n.* **1** opinion, judgement, belief, thought, point of view, viewpoint, assessment, evaluation, theory, reasoning, conclusion, idea, philosophy, outlook.

think-tank /thíngktangk/ *n.* a body of experts providing advice and ideas on specific national and commercial problems.

thinner /thínnər/ *n.* a volatile liquid used to dilute paint etc.

thio- /thī́-ō/ *comb. form* sulphur, esp. replacing oxygen in compounds (*thio-acid*). [Gk *theion* sulphur]

thiol /thī́ol/ *n. Chem.* any organic compound containing an alcohol-like group but with sulphur in place of oxygen. [THIO- + -OL[1]]

thiosulphate /thī́-ōsúlfayt/ *n.* a sulphate in which one oxygen atom is replaced by sulphur.

thiourea /thī́-ō-yoóriə/ *n.* a crystalline compound used in photography and the manufacture of synthetic resins.

third /thurd/ *n.* & *adj.* ● *n.* **1** the position in a sequence corresponding to that of the number 3 in the sequence 1–3. **2** something occupying this position. **3** each of three equal parts of a thing. **4** = *third gear.* **5** *Mus.* **a** an interval or chord spanning three consecutive notes in the diatonic scale (e.g. C to E). **b** a note separated from another by this interval. **6 a** a place in the third class in an examination. **b** a person having this. ● *adj.* that is the third. □ **third-best** *adj.* of third quality. ● *n.* a thing in this category. **third class** the third-best group or category, esp. of hotel and train accommodation. **third-class** *adj.* **1** belonging to or travelling by the third class. **2** of lower quality; inferior. ● *adv.* by the third class (*travels third-class*). **third degree** long and severe questioning esp. by police to obtain information or a confession. **third-degree** *Med.* denoting burns of the most severe kind, affecting lower layers of tissue. **third eye 1** *Hinduism* & *Buddhism* the 'eye of insight' in the forehead of an image of a deity, esp. the god Siva. **2** the faculty of intuitive insight. **third force** a political group or party acting as a check on conflict between two opposing parties. **third gear** the third (and often next to highest) in a sequence of gears. **third man** *Cricket* **1** a fielder positioned near the boundary behind the slips. **2** this position. **third part** each of three equal parts into which a thing is or might be divided. **third party 1** another party besides the two principals. **2** a bystander etc. **third-party** *adj.* (of insurance) covering damage or injury suffered by a person other than the insured. **third person 1** = *third party.* **2** *Gram.* see PERSON. **third-rate** inferior; very poor in quality. **third reading** a third presentation of a bill to a legislative assembly, in the UK to debate committee reports and in the US to consider it for the last time. **Third Reich** see REICH. **Third World** (usu. prec. by *the*) the developing countries of Asia, Africa, and Latin America. □□ **thirdly** *adv.* [OE *third(d)a, thridda* f. Gmc]

thirst /thurst/ *n.* & *v.* ● *n.* **1** a physical need to drink liquid, or the feeling of discomfort caused by this. **2** a strong desire or craving (*a thirst for power*). ● *v.intr.* (often foll. by *for* or *after*) **1** feel thirst. **2** have a strong desire. [OE *thurst, thyrstan* f. WG]
■ *n.* **1** thirstiness, dryness. **2** craving, desire, appetite, hunger, eagerness, avidity, ravenousness, voracity, voraciousness, lust, passion, enthusiasm, fancy, hankering, longing, yearning, itch, *colloq.* yen. ● *v.* **2** (*thirst for* or *after*) crave, desire, want, hunger for *or* after, lust for *or* after, fancy, hanker for *or* after, pant for, long for, yearn for, wish for.

thirsty /thúrsti/ *adj.* (**thirstier, thirstiest**) **1** feeling thirst. **2** (of land, a season, etc.) dry or parched. **3** (often foll. by *for* or *after*) eager. **4** *colloq.* causing thirst (*thirsty work*). □□ **thirstily** *adv.* **thirstiness** *n.* [OE *thurstig, thyrstig* (as THIRST, -Y[1])]
■ **1** parched, dry, dehydrated. **2** parched, dry, arid. **3** desirous, hungry, avid, eager, ravenous, voracious, burning, greedy, hankering, yearning, longing, craving, itching.

thirteen /thúrteén/ *n.* & *adj.* ● *n.* **1** one more than twelve, or three more than ten. **2** a symbol for this (13, xiii, XIII). **3** a size etc. denoted by thirteen. ● *adj.* that amount to thirteen. □□ **thirteenth** *adj.* & *n.* [OE *thrēotīene* (as THREE, -TEEN)]

thirty /thúrti/ *n.* & *adj.* ● *n.* (*pl.* **-ies**) **1** the product of three and ten. **2** a symbol for this (30, xxx, XXX). **3** (in *pl.*) the numbers from 30 to 39, esp. the years of a century or of a person's life. ● *adj.* that amount to thirty. □ **thirty-first, -second**, etc. the ordinal numbers between thirtieth and fortieth. **Thirty-nine Articles** the points of doctrine assented to by those taking orders in the Church of England. **thirty-one, -two**, etc. the cardinal numbers between thirty and forty. **thirty-second note** esp. *US Mus.* = DEMISEMIQUAVER. **thirty-two-mo** a book with 32 leaves to the printing-sheet. □□ **thirtieth** *adj.* & *n.* **thirtyfold** *adj.* & *adv.* [OE *thrītig* (as THREE, -TY[2])]

this /<u>th</u>iss/ *pron.*, *adj.*, & *adv.* ● *demons.pron.* (*pl.* **these** /<u>th</u>eez/) **1** the person or thing close at hand or indicated or already named or understood (*can you see this?*; *this is my cousin*). **2** (contrasted with *that*) the person or thing nearer to hand or more immediately in mind. **3** the action, behaviour, or circumstances under consideration (*this won't do at all*; *what do you think of this?*). **4** (on the telephone): **a** *Brit.* the person speaking. **b** *US* the person spoken to. ● *demons.adj.* (*pl.* **these** /<u>th</u>eez/) **1** designating the person or thing close at hand etc. (cf. senses 1, 2 of *pron.*). **2** (of time): **a** the present or current (*am busy all this week*). **b** relating to today (*this morning*). **c** just past or to come (*have been asking for it these three weeks*). **3** *colloq.* (in narrative) designating a person or thing previously unspecified (*then up came this policeman*). ● *adv.* to this degree or extent (*knew him when he was this high*; *did not reach this far*). □ **this and that** *colloq.* various unspecified examples of things (esp. trivial). **this here** *sl.* this particular (person or thing). **this much** the amount or extent about to be stated (*I know this much, that he was not there*). **this world** mortal life. [OE, neut. of *thes*]

thistle /thiss'l/ *n.* **1** any of various prickly composite herbaceous plants of the genus *Cirsium, Carlina*, or *Carduus* etc., usu. with globular heads of purple flowers. **2** this as the Scottish national emblem. [OE *thistel* f. Gmc]

thistledown /thíss'ldown/ *n.* a light fluffy stuff attached to thistle-seeds and blown about in the wind.

thistly /thísli/ *adj.* overgrown with thistles.

thither /thíthər/ *adv. archaic* or *formal* to or towards that place. [OE *thider*, alt. (after HITHER) of *thæder*]

thixotropy /thiksótrəpi/ *n.* the property of becoming temporarily liquid when shaken or stirred etc., and returning to a gel on standing. ▫▫ **thixotropic** /thíksətróppik/ *adj.* [Gk *thixis* touching + *tropē* turning]

tho' var. of THOUGH.

thole[1] /thōl/ *n.* (in full **thole-pin**) **1** a pin in the gunwale of a boat as the fulcrum for an oar. **2** each of two such pins forming a rowlock. [OE *thol* fir-tree, peg]

thole[2] /thōl/ *v.tr. Sc.* or *archaic* **1** undergo or suffer (pain, grief, etc.). **2** permit or admit of. [OE *tholian* f. Gmc]

tholos /thólloss/ *n.* (*pl.* **tholoi** /-loy/) *Gk Antiq.* a dome-shaped tomb, esp. of the Mycenaean period. [Gk]

Thomism /tṓmiz'm/ *n.* the doctrine of Thomas Aquinas, Italian scholastic philosopher and theologian d. 1274, or of his followers. ▫▫ **Thomist** *n.* **Thomistic** /-místik/ *adj.* **Thomistical** /-místik'l/ *adj.*

thong /thong/ *n.* & *v.* ● *n.* **1** a narrow strip of hide or leather used as the lash of a whip, as a halter or rein, etc. **2** *Austral.*, *NZ*, & *US* = FLIP-FLOP. ● *v.tr.* **1** provide with a thong. **2** strike with a thong. [OE *thwang*, *thwong* f. Gmc]

thorax /thóraks/ *n.* (*pl.* **thoraces** /thórəseez/ or **thoraxes**) **1** *Anat.* & *Zool.* the part of the trunk between the neck and the abdomen. **2** *Gk Antiq.* a breastplate or cuirass. ▫▫ **thoracal** /thórək'l/ *adj.* **thoracic** /thorássik/ *adj.* [L f. Gk *thōrax -akos*]

thoria /thóriə/ *n.* the oxide of thorium.

thorium /thóriəm/ *n. Chem.* a radioactive metallic element occurring naturally in monazite, the oxide of which is used in gas-mantles. ¶ Symb.: **Th.** [*Thor*, Scand. god of thunder]

thorn /thorn/ *n.* **1** a stiff sharp-pointed projection on a plant. **2** a thorn-bearing shrub or tree. **3** the name of an Old English and Icelandic runic letter, = th. ▫ **on thorns** continuously uneasy esp. in fear of being detected. **thorn-apple 1** a poisonous plant of the nightshade family, *Datura stramonium*. **2** the prickly fruit of this. **a thorn in one's flesh** (or **side**) a constant annoyance. ▫▫ **thornless** *adj.* **thornproof** *adj.* [OE f. Gmc]

■ **1** barb, spine, spike, prickle, bristle, brier, bur, point, bramble. ▫ **a thorn in one's flesh** (or **side**) bother, irritation, annoyance, nuisance, vexation, torment, torture, trial, scourge, plague, pest, affliction, irritant, bane, bur, *colloq.* headache, pain in the neck, *esp. US sl.* pain in the butt.

thornback /thórnbak/ *n.* a ray, *Raja clavata*, with spines on the back and tail.

thornbill /thórnbil/ *n.* **1** any Australian warbler of the genus *Acanthiza*. **2** any of various South American humming-birds, esp. of the genus *Chalcostigma*.

thorntail /thórntayl/ *n.* any S. American humming-bird of the genus *Popelairia*.

thorny /thórni/ *adj.* (**thornier**, **thorniest**) **1** having many thorns. **2** (of a subject) hard to handle without offence; problematic. ▫▫ **thornily** *adv.* **thorniness** *n.*

■ **1** prickly, barbed, spiny, spiked, brambly, *Bot.* spinous, spicular, spinose, spiculate, *Bot.* & *Zool.* setaceous, setiferous, setigerous, setose, spinulose, spinulous. **2** difficult, hard, tough, prickly, nettlesome, painful, ticklish, delicate, intricate, critical, complex, complicated, problematic, vexatious, knotty, tangled, involved, tricky, troublesome, controversial, nasty, worrying, *colloq.* sticky, *sl.* hairy.

thorough /thúrrə/ *adj.* **1** complete and unqualified; not superficial (*needs a thorough change*). **2** acting or done with great care and completeness (*the report is most thorough*). **3** absolute (*a thorough nuisance*). ▫ **thorough bass** a bass part for a keyboard player with numerals and symbols below to indicate the harmony. **thorough-paced 1** (of a horse) trained to all paces. **2** complete or unqualified. ▫▫ **thoroughly** *adv.* **thoroughness** *n.* [orig. as adv. and prep. in the senses of *through*, f. OE *thuruh* var. of *thurh* THROUGH]

■ **1** extensive, exhaustive, detailed, in-depth, comprehensive, full, complete, all-inclusive, unqualified, total, all-embracing, encyclopedic, universal, A-to-Z, all-out, thoroughgoing, profound. **2** exhaustive, extensive, searching, painstaking, meticulous, assiduous, careful, scrupulous, particular, conscientious, methodical, intensive. **3** thoroughgoing, complete, downright, perfect, total, real, unmitigated, undiluted, unmixed, unalloyed, out-and-out, unqualified, sheer, utter, arrant, absolute, ingrained, *colloq.* positive, proper, *colloq. or archaic* right. ▫▫ **thoroughly** carefully, painstakingly, exhaustively, extensively, assiduously, sedulously, methodically, conscientiously, scrupulously, meticulously, intensively, comprehensively, throughout, from top to bottom, from stem to stern, backwards and forwards, in every nook and cranny; completely, downright, perfectly, totally, unqualifiedly, utterly, absolutely, entirely, extremely, profoundly, unreservedly, wholly, fully, positively, definitely, quite.

thoroughbred /thúrrəbred/ *adj.* & *n.* ● *adj.* **1** of pure breed. **2** high-spirited. ● *n.* **1** a thoroughbred animal, esp. a horse. **2** (**Thoroughbred**) **a** a breed of racehorses originating from English mares and Arab stallions. **b** a horse of this breed.

thoroughfare /thúrrəfair/ *n.* a road or path open at both ends, esp. for traffic.

■ see ROAD[1] 1, PATH 1, PASSAGEWAY.

thoroughgoing /thúrrəgōing/ *adj.* **1** uncompromising; not superficial. **2** (usu. *attrib.*) extreme; out and out.

■ **1** see EXHAUSTIVE . **2** see *out and out* 1.

thorp /thorp/ *n.* (also **thorpe**) *archaic* a village or hamlet. ¶ Now usually only in place-names. [OE *thorp*, *throp*, f. Gmc]

Thos. *abbr.* Thomas.

those *pl.* of THAT.

thou[1] /thow/ *pron.* (*obj.* **thee** /thee/; *poss.* **thy** or **thine**; *pl.* **ye** or **you**) second person singular pronoun, now replaced by *you* except in some formal, liturgical, dialect, and poetic uses. [OE *thu* f. Gmc]

thou[2] /thow/ *n.* (*pl.* same or **thous**) *colloq.* **1** a thousand. **2** one thousandth. [abbr.]

though /thō/ *conj.* & *adv.* (also **tho'**) ● *conj.* **1** despite the fact that (*though it was early we went to bed*; *though annoyed, I agreed*). **2** (introducing a possibility) even if (*ask him though he may refuse*; *would not attend though the Queen herself were there*). **3** and yet; nevertheless (*she read on, though not to the very end*). **4** in spite of being (*ready though unwilling*). ● *adv. colloq.* however; all the same (*I wish you had told me, though*). [ME *thoh* etc. f. ON *thó* etc., corresp. to OE *thēah*, f. Gmc]

■ *conj.* **1** although, even though, while, in spite of *or* despite the fact that, notwithstanding that, granted, granting *or* conceding that, allowing *or* admitting that, *esp. Brit.* whilst, *archaic* whiles. **2** even if, supposing, although, even though. **4** although, in spite of *or* despite being, *literary* albeit. ● *adv.* however, nonetheless, nevertheless, yet, but, still, even so, be that as it may, all the same, notwithstanding, for all that, *Austral.*, *NZ*, & *Sc.* but, *colloq.* still and all.

thought[1] /thawt/ *n.* **1** the process or power of thinking; the faculty of reason. **2** a way of thinking characteristic of or associated with a particular time, people, group, etc. (*medieval European thought*). **3 a** sober reflection or consideration (*gave it much thought*). **b** care, regard, concern (*had no thought for others*). **4** an idea or piece of reasoning produced by thinking (*many good thoughts came out of the discussion*). **5** (foll. by *of* + verbal noun or *to* + infin.) a partly formed intention or hope (*gave up all thoughts of winning*; *had no thought to go*). **6** (usu. in *pl.*) what one is thinking; one's opinion (*have you any thoughts on this?*). **7** the subject of one's thinking (*my one thought was to get away*). **8** (prec. by *a*) somewhat (*seems to me a thought arrogant*). ▫ **give thought to** consider; think about. **in thought** thinking, meditating. **take thought** consider matters. **thought-provoking** stimulating serious thought.

thought-reader a person supposedly able to perceive another's thoughts. **thought-reading** the supposed perception of what another is thinking. **thought transference** telepathy. **thought-wave** an undulation of the supposed medium of thought transference. ▫▫ **-thoughted** *adj.* (in *comb.*). [OE *thōht* (as THINK)]

■ **1** thinking, intellect, intelligence, reasoning, rationality, reason, *literary* ratiocination. **2** see THINKING *n.* **3 a** reflection, meditation, contemplation, cogitation, musing, pondering, rumination, brooding, mental activity, mentation, introspection; brainwork, cerebration, concentration, deliberation, consideration, *literary* lucubration. **3 b** thoughtfulness, consideration, care, kindliness, kind-heartedness, concern, compassion, tenderness, kindness, sympathy, attention, attentiveness, regard, solicitude. **4** idea, notion, observation, conclusion, conjecture, concept, conception, *US* brainstorm, *colloq.* brainwave. **5** consideration, contemplation, planning, plan, scheme, design, intention, objective, expectation, hope, prospect, anticipation, dream, vision. **6** see OPINION 1, 3. **7** notion, idea, concept, concern. **8** bit, trifle, touch, little, *US colloq.* tad. ▫ **give thought to** see NOTE *v.* 1. **thought-provoking** see *stimulating* (STIMULATE).

thought[2] *past* and *past part.* of THINK.

thoughtful /tháwtfo͝ol/ *adj.* **1** engaged in or given to meditation. **2** (of a book, writer, remark, etc.) giving signs of serious thought. **3** (often foll. by *of*) (of a person or conduct) considerate; not haphazard or unfeeling. ▫▫ **thoughtfully** *adv.* **thoughtfulness** *n.*

■ **1** contemplative, pensive, reflective, musing, in a brown study, pondering, meditative, cogitative, engrossed, absorbed, introspective, rapt, wistful, brooding, broody, wool-gathering, day-dreaming. **2** see THINKING *adj.* **3** considerate, kind, kindly, kind-hearted, compassionate, caring, tender, sympathetic, attentive, solicitous, concerned, helpful, obliging, charitable; prudent, wary, cautious, mindful, heedful, thinking, circumspect, careful. ▫▫ **thoughtfully** see KINDLY 1. **thoughtfulness** see CONSIDERATION 2.

thoughtless /tháwtliss/ *adj.* **1** careless of consequences or of others' feelings. **2** due to lack of thought. ▫▫ **thoughtlessly** *adv.* **thoughtlessness** *n.*

■ **1** unthinking, inconsiderate, rude, impolite, insensitive, tactless, undiplomatic, untactful, indiscreet, uncaring, unfeeling; rash, imprudent, negligent, neglectful, reckless, heedless, careless; remiss, unreflective, absent-minded, forgetful, inattentive. **2** rash, imprudent, negligent, neglectful, reckless, heedless, careless; foolish, stupid, silly, ill-considered, inadvertent. ▫▫ **thoughtlessly** see *blindly* (BLIND). **thoughtlessness** see *imprudence* (IMPRUDENT).

thousand /thówz'nd/ *n.* & *adj.* ● *n.* (*pl.* **thousands** or (in sense 1) **thousand**) (in *sing.* prec. by *a* or *one*) **1** the product of a hundred and ten. **2** a symbol for this (1,000, m, M). **3** a set of a thousand things. **4** (in *sing.* or *pl.*) *colloq.* a large number. ● *adj.* that amount to a thousand. ▫▫ **thousandfold** *adj.* & *adv.* **thousandth** *adj.* & *n.* [OE *thūsend* f. Gmc]

■ *n.* **4** (*thousands*) see SCORE *n.* 3.

thrall /thrawl/ *n. literary* **1** (often foll. by *of*, *to*) a slave (of a person, or a power or influence). **2** bondage; a state of slavery or servitude (*in thrall*). ▫▫ **thraldom** *n.* (also **thralldom**). [OE *thrǣl* f. ON *thrǣll*, perh. f. a Gmc root =run]

thrash /thrash/ *v.* & *n.* ● *v.* **1** *tr.* beat severely, esp. with a stick or whip. **2** *tr.* defeat thoroughly in a contest. **3** *intr.* (of a paddle wheel, branch, etc.) act like a flail; deliver repeated blows. **4** *intr.* (foll. by *about*, *around*) move or fling the limbs about violently or in panic. **5** *intr.* (of a ship) keep striking the waves; make way against the wind or tide (*thrash to windward*). **6** *tr.* = THRESH 1. ● *n.* **1** an act of thrashing. **2** *colloq.* a party, esp. a lavish one. ▫ **thrash out** discuss to a conclusion. ▫▫ **thrashing** *n.* [OE *therscan*, later *threscan*, f. Gmc]

■ *v.* **1** see BEAT *v.* 1. **2** see DEFEAT *v.* 1. **4** (*thrash about* or *around*) see FLAP *v.* 1. ● *n.* **1** see *thrashing* (THRASH) below. ▫ **thrash out** see DEBATE *v.*, RESOLVE *v.* 1. ▫▫ **thrashing** beating, drubbing, whipping, flogging, caning, belting, mauling, lashing, trouncing, basting, battering, pounding, thrash, assault; punishment, chastisement, disciplining, discipline, castigation, *colloq.* hiding, lambasting, hammering, *sl.* tanning, pasting, walloping.

thrasher[1] /tháshər/ *n.* **1** a person or thing that thrashes. **2** = THRESHER.

thrasher[2] /tháshər/ *n.* any of various long-tailed N. American thrushlike birds of the family Mimidae. [perh. f. E dial. *thrusher* = THRUSH[1]]

thrawn /thrawn/ *adj. Sc.* **1** perverse or ill-tempered. **2** misshapen, crooked. [Sc. form of *thrown* in obs. senses]

thread /thred/ *n.* & *v.* ● *n.* **1 a** a spun-out filament of cotton, silk, or glass etc.; yarn. **b** a length of this. **2** a thin cord of twisted yarns used esp. in sewing and weaving. **3** anything regarded as threadlike with reference to its continuity or connectedness (*the thread of life*; *lost the thread of his argument*). **4** the spiral ridge of a screw. **5** (in *pl.*) *sl.* clothes. **6** a thin seam or vein of ore. ● *v.tr.* **1** pass a thread through the eye of (a needle). **2** put (beads) on a thread. **3** arrange (material in a strip form, e.g. film or magnetic tape) in the proper position on equipment. **4** make (one's way) carefully through a crowded place, over a difficult route, etc. **5** streak (hair etc.) as with threads. **6** form a screw-thread on. ▫ **hang by a thread** be in a precarious state, position, etc. **thread mark** a mark in the form of a thin line made in banknote paper with highly coloured silk fibres to prevent photographic counterfeiting. ▫▫ **threader** *n.* **threadlike** *adj.* [OE *thrǣd* f. Gmc]

■ *n.* **1** fibre, filament, strand, (piece of) yarn; cotton, silk, wool. **2** string, line, cord, twine; cotton, silk, wool. **3** theme, plot, story-line, subject, motif, thesis, course, drift, direction, tenor, train (of thought), sequence *or* train *or* chain of events. **5** (*threads*) see CLOTHES. **6** see VEIN 5. ● *v.* **2** string, lace. **4** (*thread one's way*) file, weave, wind (one's way), pass, squeeze, pick *or* make one's way, inch *or* ease (one's way). ▫▫ **threadlike** see FINE[1] *adj.* 7c.

threadbare /thrédbair/ *adj.* **1** (of cloth) so worn that the nap is lost and the thread visible. **2** (of a person) wearing such clothes. **3 a** hackneyed. **b** feeble or insubstantial (*a threadbare excuse*).

■ **1** frayed, worn (out), ragged, moth-eaten, tattered, tatty, shabby, torn, *colloq.* worn to a frazzle. **2** ragged, scruffy, shabby, seedy, wretched, sorry, slovenly. **3 a** trite, hackneyed, overused, overworked, reworked, stale, tired, time-worn, stereotyped, commonplace, clichéd, cliché-ridden, banal, prosaic, dull, monotonous, tedious, tiresome, boring, played out, *colloq.* old hat. **b** see THIN *adj.* 8.

threadfin /thrédfin/ *n.* any small tropical fish of the family Polynemidae, with long streamers from its pectoral fins.

threadworm /thrédwurm/ *n.* any of various esp. parasitic threadlike nematode worms, e.g. the pinworm.

thready /thréddi/ *adj.* (**threadier, threadiest**) **1** of or like a thread. **2** (of a person's pulse) scarcely perceptible.

threat /thret/ *n.* **1 a** a declaration of an intention to punish or hurt. **b** *Law* a menace of bodily hurt or injury, such as may restrain a person's freedom of action. **2** an indication of something undesirable coming (*the threat of war*). **3** a person or thing as a likely cause of harm etc. [OE *thrēat* affliction etc. f. Gmc]

■ **1 a** intimidation, menace, commination, sword of Damocles, warning, duress. **2** omen, presage, portent, foreboding, forewarning, warning, intimation. **3** menace, danger, hazard, peril.

threaten /thrétt'n/ *v.tr.* **1 a** make a threat or threats against. **b** constitute a threat to; be likely to harm; put into danger.

2 be a sign or indication of (something undesirable). **3** (foll. by *to* + infin.) announce one's intention to do an undesirable or unexpected thing (*threatened to resign*). **4** (also *absol.*) give warning of the infliction of (harm etc.) (*the clouds were threatening rain*). □□ **threatener** *n.* **threatening** *adj.* **threateningly** *adv.* [OE *thrēatnian* (as THREAT)]

■ **1 a** intimidate, menace, terrorize, daunt, cow, bully, browbeat, warn, caution. **b** imperil, put at risk, endanger, jeopardize, put in jeopardy. **4** augur, portend, presage, forebode, forewarn of, warn of; impend, loom, lour. □ **threatening** intimidating, menacing, minatory, comminatory; ominous, portentous, sinister, looming, inauspicious, foreboding, imminent, impending.

three /three/ *n.* & *adj.* ● *n.* **1 a** one more than two, or seven less than ten. **b** a symbol for this (3, iii, III). **2** a size etc. denoted by three. **3** the time of three o'clock. **4** a set of three. **5** a card with three pips. ● *adj.* that amount to three. □ **three-card trick** a game in which bets are made on which is the queen among three cards lying face downwards. **three cheers** see CHEER. **three-colour process** a process of reproducing natural colours by combining photographic images in the three primary colours. **three-cornered 1** triangular. **2** (of a contest etc.) between three parties as individuals. **three-decker 1** a warship with three gun-decks. **2** a novel in three volumes. **3** a sandwich with three slices of bread. **three-dimensional** having or appearing to have length, breadth, and depth. **three-handed 1** having or using three hands. **2** involving three players. **three-legged race** a running-race between pairs, one member of each pair having the left leg tied to the right leg of the other. **three-line whip** a written notice, underlined three times to denote urgency, to members of a political party to attend a parliamentary vote. **three parts** three quarters. **three-phase** see PHASE. **three-piece** consisting of three items (esp. of a suit of clothes or a suite of furniture). **three-ply** *adj.* of three strands, webs, or thicknesses. ● *n.* **1** three-ply wool. **2** three-ply wood made by gluing together three layers with the grain in different directions. **three-point landing** *Aeron.* the landing of an aircraft on the two main wheels and the tail wheel or skid simultaneously. **three-point turn** a method of turning a vehicle round in a narrow space by moving forwards, backwards, and forwards again in a sequence of arcs. **three-quarter** *n.* (also **three-quarter back**) *Rugby Football* any of three or four players just behind the half-backs. ● *adj.* **1** consisting of three-fourths of something. **2** (of a portrait) going down to the hips or showing three-fourths of the face (between full face and profile). **three-quarters** three parts out of four. **three-ring circus** esp. *US* **1** a circus with three rings for simultaneous performances. **2** an extravagant display. **the three Rs** reading, writing, and arithmetic, regarded as the fundamentals of learning. **three-way** involving three ways or participants. **three-wheeler** a vehicle with three wheels. [OE *thrī* f. Gmc]

■ *n.* **4** see TRIO.

threefold /threéfōld/ *adj.* & *adv.* **1** three times as much or as many. **2** consisting of three parts.

threepence /thréppənss, thrŏŏppənss/ *n. Brit.* the sum of three pence, esp. before decimalization.

threepenny /thríppəni, thrŏŏppəni/ *adj. Brit.* costing three pence, esp. before decimalization. □ **threepenny bit** *hist.* a former coin worth three old pence.

threescore /threéskór/ *n. archaic* sixty.

threesome /threéssəm/ *n.* **1** a group of three persons. **2** a game etc. for three, esp. *Golf* of one against two.

■ **1** see TRIO.

thremmatology /thrémmətóllәji/ *n.* the science of breeding animals and plants. [Gk *thremma -matos* nursling + -LOGY]

threnody /thrénnədi/ *n.* (also **threnode** /thrénnōd/) (*pl.* **-ies** or **threnodes**) **1** a lamentation, esp. on a person's death. **2** a song of lamentation. □□ **threnodial** /-nōdiəl/ *adj.* **threnodic** /-nóddik/ *adj.* **threnodist** /thrénnədist/ *n.* [Gk *thrēnōidia* f. *thrēnos* wailing + *ōidē* ODE]

threonine /threéəneen, -nin/ *n. Biochem.* an amino acid, considered essential for growth. [*threose* (name of a tetrose sugar) ult. f. Gk *eruthros* red + -INE[4]]

thresh /thresh/ *v.* **1** *tr.* beat out or separate grain from (corn etc.). **2** *intr.* = THRASH *v.* 4. **3** *tr.* (foll. by *over*) analyse (a problem etc.) in search of a solution. □ **threshing-floor** a hard level floor for threshing esp. with flails. **threshing-machine** a power-driven machine for separating the grain from the straw or husk. **thresh out** = *thrash out.* [var. of THRASH]

■ **3** (*thresh over*) see CONSIDER 1.

thresher /thréshər/ *n.* **1** a person or machine that threshes. **2** a shark, *Alopias vulpinus*, with a long upper lobe to its tail, that it can lash about.

threshold /thréshōld, thrésh-hōld/ *n.* **1** a strip of wood or stone forming the bottom of a doorway and crossed in entering a house or room etc. **2** a point of entry or beginning (*on the threshold of a new century*). **3** *Physiol.* & *Psychol.* a limit below which a stimulus causes no reaction (*pain threshold*). **4** *Physics* a limit below which no reaction occurs, esp. a minimum dose of radiation producing a specified effect. **5** (often *attrib.*) a step in a scale of wages or taxation, usu. operative in specified conditions. [OE *therscold*, *threscold*, etc., rel. to THRASH in the sense 'tread']

■ **1** sill, door-sill, doorstep; doorway, entrance. **2** brink, verge, edge, beginning, inception, outset, start, dawn, *formal* commencement.

threw *past* of THROW.

thrice /thrīss/ *adv. archaic* or *literary* **1** three times. **2** (esp. in *comb.*) highly (*thrice-blessed*). [ME *thries* f. *thrie* (adv.) f. OE *thrīwa*, *thrīga* (as THREE, -S[3])]

thrift /thrift/ *n.* **1** frugality; economical management. **2** a plant of the genus *Armeria*, esp. the sea pink. □ **thrift shop** (or **store**) a shop selling second-hand items usu. for charity. [ME f. ON (as THRIVE)]

■ **1** economy, husbandry, care, carefulness, prudence, providence, parsimony, frugality, thriftiness, sparingness, scrimping, skimping; penuriousness, close-fistedness, tight-fistedness, niggardliness, stinginess, miserliness.

thriftless /thríftliss/ *adj.* wasteful, improvident. □□ **thriftlessly** *adv.* **thriftlessness** *n.*

■ see IMPROVIDENT 2.

thrifty /thrífti/ *adj.* (**thriftier**, **thriftiest**) **1** economical, frugal. **2** thriving, prosperous. □□ **thriftily** *adv.* **thriftiness** *n.*

■ **1** economical, careful, prudent, parsimonious, frugal, sparing, scrimping, skimping; penurious, close-fisted, tight-fisted, niggardly, stingy, miserly, penny-pinching, cheap. **2** see SUCCESSFUL. □□ **thriftiness** see THRIFT.

thrill /thril/ *n.* & *v.* ● *n.* **1 a** a wave or nervous tremor of emotion or sensation (*a thrill of joy*; *a thrill of recognition*). **b** a thrilling experience (*seeking new thrills*). **2** a throb or pulsation. **3** *Med.* a vibratory movement or resonance heard in auscultation. ● *v.* **1** *intr.* & *tr.* feel or cause to feel a thrill (*thrilled to the sound*; *a voice that thrilled millions*). **2** *intr.* quiver or throb with or as with emotion. **3** *intr.* (foll. by *through*, *over*, *along*) (of an emotion etc.) pass with a thrill through etc. (*fear thrilled through my veins*). □ **thrills and spills** the excitement of potentially dangerous activities. □□ **thrilling** *adj.* **thrillingly** *adv.* [*thirl* (now dial.) f. OE *thyrlian* pierce f. *thyrel* hole f. *thurh* THROUGH]

■ *n.* **1a** excitement, titillation, *frisson*, shiver, tingle, tingling (sensation), stimulation, tremor, quiver, shudder, tremble, flutter, *colloq.* kick, *sl.* buzz. **2** tremor, quiver, shudder, tremble, flutter, throb, pulsation, vibration. ● *v.* **1** (*tr.*) excite, stimulate, animate, electrify, galvanize, enliven, stir, titillate, touch, strike, move, impassion, arouse, rouse, *colloq.* give a person a kick, *sl.* send. □□ **thrilling** exciting, stimulating, animating, electrifying, galvanizing, enlivening, stirring, titillating, striking, moving, arousing, rousing, gripping, wild, sensational, riveting, spine-tingling, soul-stirring.

thriller /thríllər/ *n.* an exciting or sensational story or play etc., esp. one involving crime or espionage.

thrips /thrips/ *n.* (*pl.* same) any insect of the order Thysanoptera, esp. a pest injurious to plants. [L f. Gk, = woodworm]

thrive /thrīv/ *v.intr.* (*past* **throve** /thrōv/ or **thrived**; *past part.* **thriven** /thrívv'n/ or **thrived**) **1** prosper or flourish. **2** grow rich. **3** (of a child, animal, or plant) grow vigorously. [ME f. ON *thrifask* refl. of *thrifa* grasp]

■ **1** succeed, prosper, boom, advance, flourish, do well. **3** grow, flourish, bloom, blossom, develop, wax, increase, fructify, ripen, *literary* burgeon.

thro' var. of THROUGH.

throat /thrōt/ *n.* **1 a** the windpipe or gullet. **b** the front part of the neck containing this. **2** *literary* **a** a voice, esp. of a songbird. **b** a thing compared to a throat, esp. a narrow passage, entrance, or exit. **3** *Naut.* the forward upper corner of a fore-and-aft sail. □ **cut one's own throat** bring about one's own downfall. **ram** (or **thrust**) **down a person's throat** force (a thing) on a person's attention. □□ **-throated** *adj.* (in *comb.*). [OE *throte*, *throtu* f. Gmc]

throaty /thrṓti/ *adj.* (**throatier, throatiest**) **1** (of a voice) deficient in clarity; hoarsely resonant. **2** guttural; uttered in the throat. **3** having a prominent or capacious throat. □□ **throatily** *adv.* **throatiness** *n.*

■ **1, 2** see GRUFF 1a, THICK *adj.* 8a.

throb /throb/ *v.* & *n.* ● *v.intr.* (**throbbed, throbbing**) **1** palpitate or pulsate, esp. with more than the usual force or rapidity. **2** vibrate or quiver with a persistent rhythm or with emotion. ● *n.* **1** a throbbing. **2** a palpitation or (esp. violent) pulsation. [ME, app. imit.]

■ *v.* see PULSATE, ACHE *v.* 1, VIBRATE 1, 2, 4; 3. ● *n.* see PULSE[1] *n.* 5, 6, THRILL *n.* 2.

throe /thrō/ *n.* (usu. in *pl.*) **1** a violent pang, esp. of childbirth or death. **2** anguish. □ **in the throes of** struggling with the task of. [ME *throwe* perh. f. OE *thrēa*, *thrawu* calamity, alt. perh. by assoc. with *woe*]

■ **1** pang, agony, pain, paroxysm, spasm; fit, seizure, convulsion, *Med.* ictus. **2** (*throes*) anguish, struggle, turmoil, tumult; see also AGONY 1.

thrombi *pl.* of THROMBUS.

thrombin /thrómbin/ *n.* an enzyme promoting the clotting of blood. [as THROMBUS + -IN]

thrombocyte /thrómbəsīt/ *n.* a blood platelet, a small plate of protoplasm concerned in the coagulation of blood. [as THROMBUS + -CYTE]

thrombose /thrombṓz/ *v.tr.* & *intr.* affect with or undergo thrombosis. [back-form. f. THROMBOSIS]

thrombosis /thrombṓsiss/ *n.* (*pl.* **thromboses** /-seez/) the coagulation of the blood in a blood-vessel or organ. □□ **thrombotic** /-bóttik/ *adj.* [mod.L f. Gk *thrombōsis* curdling (as THROMBUS)]

thrombus /thrómbəss/ *n.* (*pl.* **thrombi** /-bī/) a blood-clot formed in the vascular system and impeding blood flow. [mod.L f. Gk *thrombos* lump, blood-clot]

throne /thrōn/ *n.* & *v.* ● *n.* **1** a chair of State for a sovereign or bishop etc. **2** sovereign power (*came to the throne*). **3** (in *pl.*) the third order of the ninefold celestial hierarchy. **4** *colloq.* a lavatory seat and bowl. ● *v.tr.* place on a throne. □□ **throneless** *adj.* [ME f. OF *trone* f. L *thronus* f. Gk *thronos* high seat]

throng /throng/ *n.* & *v.* ● *n.* **1** a crowd of people. **2** (often foll. by *of*) a multitude, esp. in a small space. ● *v.* **1** *intr.* come in great numbers (*crowds thronged to the stadium*). **2** *tr.* flock into or crowd round; fill with or as with a crowd (*crowds thronged the streets*). [ME *thrang*, *throng*, OE *gethrang*, f. verbal stem *thring- thrang-*]

■ *n.* horde, crowd, host, assemblage, assembly, gathering, mass, crush, jam, multitude, congregation, rabble, army, press, swarm, herd, flock, mob, pack, bevy, drove. ● *v.* **1** crowd, swarm, flock; assemble, gather, mass, congregate. **2** crowd into *or* round, fill, pack (into), cram (into), crush into, jam into, pour into, press into *or* round, swarm into *or* round, herd into *or* round, flock into *or* to *or* round; assemble in *or* at *or* round, gather in *or* at *or* round, mass in *or* at *or* round, congregate in *or* at *or* round.

throstle /thróss'l/ *n.* **1** a song thrush. **2** (in full **throstle-frame**) a machine for continuously spinning wool or cotton etc. [OE f. Gmc: rel. to THRUSH[1]]

throttle /thrótt'l/ *n.* & *v.* ● *n.* **1 a** (in full **throttle-valve**) a valve controlling the flow of fuel or steam etc. in an engine. **b** (in full **throttle-lever**) a lever or pedal operating this valve. **2** the throat, gullet, or windpipe. ● *v.tr.* **1** choke or strangle. **2** prevent the utterance etc. of. **3** control (an engine or steam etc.) with a throttle. □ **throttle back** (or **down**) reduce the speed of (an engine or vehicle) by throttling. □□ **throttler** *n.* [ME *throtel* (v.), perh. f. THROAT + -LE[4]: (n.) perh. a dimin. of THROAT]

■ *v.* **1** see CHOKE[1] *v.* 1. **2** see GAG *v.* 2.

through /thro͞o/ *prep.*, *adv.*, & *adj.* (also **thro'**, *US* **thru**) ● *prep.* **1 a** from end to end or from side to side of. **b** going in one side or end and out the other of. **2** between or among (*swam through the waves*). **3** from beginning to end of (*read through the letter*; *went through many difficulties*; *through the years*). **4** because of; by the agency, means, or fault of (*lost it through carelessness*). **5** *US* up to and including (*Monday through Friday*). ● *adv.* **1** through a thing; from side to side, end to end, or beginning to end; completely, thoroughly (*went through to the garden*; *would not let us through*). **2** having completed (esp. successfully) (*are through their exams*). **3** so as to be connected by telephone (*will put you through*). ● *attrib.adj.* **1** (of a journey, route, etc.) done without a change of line or vehicle etc. or with one ticket. **2** (of traffic) going through a place to its destination. □ **be through** *colloq.* **1** (often foll. by *with*) have finished. **2** (often foll. by *with*) cease to have dealings. **3** have no further prospects (*is through as a politician*). **no through road** no thoroughfare. **through and through 1** thoroughly, completely. **2** through again and again. [OE *thurh* f. WG]

■ *prep.* **1** see OVER *prep.* 3, 4. **3** during, throughout, in *or* during the course of. **4** because of, on account of, owing to, as a consequence *or* result of, by virtue of, via, by means of, by way of, with the aid *or* help of, under the aegis *or* auspices of, *disp.* due to. ● *adv.* **1** by, past; entirely, through and through, completely, thoroughly, totally, wholly, utterly, fully, to the core, from head to foot *or* toe, from top to toe, from top to bottom, from stem to stern, from one end to the other, in every way, in all respects. ● *adj.* **1** direct, unbroken, nonstop. □ **be through 1** have done *or* finished. **2** (*be through with*) have finished with, be at the end of one's tether with, have washed *or* be washing one's hands of. **3** be finished, be played out, *esp. US sl.* be washed up. **through and through 1** see THROUGH *adv.* above.

throughout *prep.* & *adv.* ● *prep.* /thro͞o-ówt/ right through; from end to end of (*throughout the town*; *throughout the 18th century*). ● *adv.* /thro͞o-ówt/ in every part or respect (*the timber was rotten throughout*).

■ *prep.* during, all (the way) through, from the beginning to the end of; everywhere in, all over, in every part of, in every nook and cranny of, from one end to the other of. ● *adv.* all (the way) through, through and through, everywhere, from one end to the other, from top to bottom, in every part, wholly, entirely, completely, fully.

throughput /thro͞opo͝ot/ *n.* the amount of material put through a process, esp. in manufacturing or computing.

throughway /thro͞o-way/ *n.* (also **thruway**) *US* a thoroughfare, esp. a motorway.

■ see ROAD[1] 1.

throve *past* of THRIVE.

throw /thrō/ *v.* & *n.* ● *v.tr.* (*past* **threw** /thro͞o/; *past part.* **thrown** /thrōn/) **1** propel with some force through the air or in a particular direction. **2** force violently into a specified position or state (*the ship was thrown on the rocks*; *threw themselves down*). **3** compel suddenly to be in a specified condition (*was thrown out of work*). **4** turn or move (part of the body) quickly or suddenly (*threw an arm out*). **5** project or cast (light, a shadow, a spell, etc.). **6 a** bring to the ground in wrestling. **b** (of a horse) unseat (its rider). **7** *colloq.* disconcert (*the question threw me for a moment*). **8** (foll. by *on*, *off*, etc.) put (clothes etc.) hastily on or off etc. **9 a** cause (dice) to fall on a table. **b** obtain (a specified number) by throwing dice. **10** cause to pass or extend suddenly to another state or position (*threw in the army*; *threw a bridge across the river*). **11** move (a switch or lever) so as to operate it. **12 a** form (ceramic ware) on a potter's wheel. **b** turn (wood etc.) on a lathe. **13** have (a fit or tantrum etc.). **14** give (a party). **15** *colloq.* lose (a contest or race etc.) intentionally. **16** *Cricket* bowl (a ball) with an illegitimate sudden straightening of the elbow. **17** (of a snake) cast (its skin). **18** (of an animal) give birth to (young). **19** twist (silk etc.) into thread or yarn. **20** (often foll. by *into*) put into another form or language etc. ● *n.* **1** an act of throwing. **2** the distance a thing is or may be thrown (*a record throw with the hammer*). **3** the act of being thrown in wrestling. **4** *Geol.* & *Mining* **a** a fault in strata. **b** the amount of vertical displacement caused by this. **5** a machine or device giving rapid rotary motion. **6 a** the movement of a crank or cam etc. **b** the extent of this. **7** the distance moved by the pointer of an instrument etc. **8** (in full **throw rug**) *US* **a** a light cover for furniture. **b** a light rug. **c** a shawl or stole. **9** (prec. by *a*) *sl.* each; per item (*sold at £10 a throw*). □ **throw about** (or **around**) **1** throw in various directions. **2** spend (one's money) ostentatiously. **throw away 1** discard as useless or unwanted. **2** waste or fail to make use of (an opportunity etc.). **3** discard (a card). **4** *Theatr.* speak (lines) with deliberate underemphasis. **5** (in *passive*; often foll. by *on*) be wasted (*the advice was thrown away on him*). **throw-away** *adj.* **1** meant to be thrown away after (one) use. **2** (of lines etc.) deliberately underemphasized. ● *n.* a thing to be thrown away after (one) use. **throw back 1** revert to ancestral character. **2** (usu. in *passive*; foll. by *on*) compel to rely on (*was thrown back on his savings*). **throw-back** *n.* **1** reversion to ancestral character. **2** an instance of this. **throw cold water on** see COLD. **throw down** cause to fall. **throw down the gauntlet** (or **glove**) issue a challenge. **throw dust in a person's eyes** mislead a person by misrepresentation or distraction. **throw good money after bad** incur further loss in a hopeless attempt to recoup a previous loss. **throw one's hand in 1** abandon one's chances in a card game, esp. poker. **2** give up; withdraw from a contest. **throw in 1** interpose (a word or remark). **2** include at no extra cost. **3** throw (a football) from the edge of the pitch where it has gone out of play. **4** *Cricket* return (the ball) from the outfield. **5** *Cards* give (a player) the lead, to the player's disadvantage. **throw-in** *n.* the throwing in of a football during play. **throw in one's lot with** see LOT. **throw in the towel** admit defeat. **throw light on** see LIGHT[1]. **throw off 1** discard; contrive to get rid of. **2** write or utter in an offhand manner. **3** (of hounds or a hunt) begin hunting; make a start. **throw-off** the start in a hunt or race. **throw oneself at** seek blatantly as a spouse or sexual partner. **throw oneself into** engage vigorously in. **throw oneself on** (or **upon**) **1** rely completely on. **2** attack. **throw open** (often foll. by *to*) **1** cause to be suddenly or widely open. **2** make accessible. **throw out 1** put out forcibly or suddenly. **2** discard as unwanted. **3** expel (a troublemaker etc.). **4** build (a wing of a house, a pier, or a projecting or prominent thing). **5** put forward tentatively. **6** reject (a proposal or bill in Parliament). **7** confuse or distract (a person speaking, thinking, or acting) from the matter in hand. **8** *Cricket* & *Baseball* put out (an opponent) by throwing the ball to the wicket or base. **throw over** desert or abandon. **throw stones** cast aspersions. **throw together 1** assemble hastily. **2** bring into casual contact. **throw up 1** abandon. **2** resign from. **3** *colloq.* vomit. **4** erect hastily. **5** bring to notice. **6** lift (a sash-window) quickly. **throw up** (or **in**) **the sponge 1** (of a boxer or his attendant) throw the sponge used between rounds into the air as a token of defeat. **2** abandon a contest; admit defeat. **throw one's weight about** (or **around**) *colloq.* act with unpleasant self-assertiveness. □□ **throwable** *adj.* **thrower** *n.* (also in *comb.*). [OE *thrāwan* twist, turn f. WG]

■ *v.* **1, 2** toss, cast, hurl, fling, pitch, dash, propel, project, shy, bowl, send, precipitate, launch, lob, put, *colloq.* chuck, heave, sling, *Austral. sl.* hoy, *Brit. sl.* bung. **3** hurl, fling, cast. **4** fling. **5** cast, shed, project, emit. **6 b** unseat, unhorse, dislodge, buck off. **7** dismay, confound, confuse, dumbfound, baffle, disconcert, unnerve, throw off *or* out, unsettle, put off, put a person off his *or* her stride *or* pace *or* stroke, *colloq.* rattle, faze, *US joc.* discombobulate. ● *n.* **1** toss, lob, pitch, heave, shy, fling, hurl, launch, put, delivery. **8 a, b** see SPREAD *n.* 10. □ **throw away 1** discard, cast off, dispose of, jettison, get rid of, scrap, junk, throw out, toss away *or* out, dispense with, dump, *colloq.* chuck out, *esp. US colloq.* trash, *sl.* ditch. **2** waste, squander, lose, forgo, fritter away, fail to exploit *or* take advantage of, *sl.* blow. **throw-away 1** see DISPOSABLE *adj.* 1. **throw down** bring down, floor, fell, knock down *or* over, overthrow, upset, overturn, topple. **throw down the gauntlet** challenge a person, enter the lists. **throw dust in a person's eyes** see HOODWINK. **throw in 1** interpose, put in, interpolate, cut in with. **throw in the towel** see SURRENDER *v.* 2. **throw off 1** shake off, rid *or* free oneself of, get rid of, discard, reject, renounce, repudiate. **throw oneself on** (or **upon**) **2** see ATTACK *v.* 1. **throw out 1** see *cast out*. **2** see *throw away* 1 above. **3** expel, eject, force out, evict, turn *or* toss *or* boot out, *esp. Brit. colloq.* turf out, *sl.* bounce, kick out. **6** reject, say no to, veto, turn down; see also QUASH 1. **7** distract, divert, bewilder, confound, confuse, *colloq.* flummox, faze; see also THROW *v.* 7 above. **throw over** jilt, leave, abandon, desert, forsake, break *or* split up with, walk out on, *colloq.* chuck, drop, dump, *sl.* ditch. **throw together 1** see *throw up* 4 below. **2** see LUMP[1] *v.* **throw up 1, 2** abandon, quit, leave, throw over, give up, relinquish, resign (from), renounce, *colloq.* chuck. **3** vomit, spit up, spew (up), be sick; regurgitate, disgorge, *Brit. colloq.* sick up, *sl.* puke, barf, *Austral. sl.* chunder. **4** throw *or* slap *or* knock together. **5** reveal, bring out *or* up, bring to the surface *or* top, bring forward *or* forth, bring to light *or* notice. **throw up** (or **in**) **the sponge** see SURRENDER *v.* 2.

throwster /thrṓstər/ *n.* a person who throws silk.

thru *US* var. of THROUGH.

thrum[1] /thrum/ *v.* & *n.* ● *v.* (**thrummed, thrumming**) **1** *tr.* play (a stringed instrument) monotonously or unskilfully. **2** *intr.* (often foll. by *on*) beat or drum idly or monotonously. ● *n.* **1** such playing. **2** the resulting sound. [imit.]

■ *v.* **1** strum, pluck, *esp. US* pick, *usu. derog.* twang. **2** see PULSATE. ● *n.* **1** strumming. **2** see PATTER[1] *n.*

thrum[2] /thrum/ *n.* & *v.* ● *n.* **1** the unwoven end of a warp-thread, or the whole of such ends, left when the finished web is cut away. **2** any short loose thread. ● *v.tr.* (**thrummed, thrumming**) make of or cover with thrums. □□ **thrummer** *n.* **thrummy** *adj.* [OE f. Gmc]

thrush[1] /thrush/ *n.* any small or medium-sized songbird of the family Turdidae, esp. a song thrush or mistle thrush (see MISTLE THRUSH, *song thrush*). [OE *thrysce* f. Gmc: cf. THROSTLE]

thrush[2] /thrush/ *n.* **1 a** a disease, esp. of children, marked by whitish fungous vesicles in the mouth and throat. **b** a similar disease of the vagina. **2** inflammation affecting the frog of a horse's foot. [17th c.: orig. unkn.]

thrust /thrust/ *v.* & *n.* ● *v.* (*past* and *past part.* **thrust**) **1** *tr.* push with a sudden impulse or with force (*thrust the letter into my pocket*). **2** *tr.* (foll. by *on*) impose (a thing) forcibly; enforce acceptance of (a thing) (*had it thrust on me*). **3** *intr.* (foll. by *at*, *through*) pierce or stab; make a sudden lunge. **4** *tr.* make (one's way) forcibly. **5** *intr.* (foll. by *through*, *past*, etc.) force oneself (*thrust past me abruptly*). ● *n.* **1** a sudden or forcible push or lunge. **2** the propulsive force developed by a jet or rocket engine. **3** a strong attempt to penetrate an enemy's line or territory. **4** a remark aimed at a person. **5**

the stress between the parts of an arch etc. **6** (often foll. by *of*) the chief theme or gist of remarks etc. **7** an attack with the point of a weapon. **8** (in full **thrust fault**) *Geol.* a low-angle reverse fault, with older strata displaced horizontally over newer. □ **thrust-block** a casting or frame carrying or containing the bearings on which the collars of a propeller shaft press. **thrust oneself** (or **one's nose**) **in** obtrude, interfere. **thrust stage** a stage extending into the audience. [ME *thruste* etc. f. ON *thrýsta*]

■ *v.* **1** push, shove, drive, force, stuff, wedge, stick, jam, impel, ram, propel, urge, press. **2** press, impose, force, urge, foist, intrude. **3** stab, jab, poke, pierce, prod; lunge. **4** push, shove, drive, force, propel, urge, press, elbow, butt, jostle. **5** shoulder, jostle, elbow; push, shove, force oneself, press. ● *n.* **1, 7** shove, push, drive, lunge, poke, prod, stab, jab. **2** propulsion, force, power, energy, impetus, drive. **4** see GIBE *n.* **6** see IMPORT *n.* 3. □ **thrust oneself** (or **one's nose**) **in** see OBTRUDE, INTERFERE 2.

thruster /thrústər/ *n.* **1** a person or thing that thrusts. **2** a small rocket engine used to provide extra or correcting thrust on a spacecraft.

thruway *US* var. of THROUGHWAY.

thud /thud/ *n.* & *v.* ● *n.* a low dull sound as of a blow on a non-resonant surface. ● *v.intr.* (**thudded**, **thudding**) make or fall with a thud. □□ **thuddingly** *adv.* [prob. f. OE *thyddan* thrust]

■ *n.* clunk, thump, clonk, bump, *colloq.* wham. ● *v.* clunk, clonk, thump, bump, plump, clump, clomp.

thug /thug/ *n.* **1** a vicious or brutal ruffian. **2** (**Thug**) *hist.* a member of a religious organization of robbers and assassins in India. □□ **thuggery** *n.* **thuggish** *adj.* **thuggishly** *adv.* **thuggishness** *n.* [Hindi & Marathi *ṭhag* swindler]

■ **1** hooligan, gangster, desperado, gunman, hoodlum, ruffian, apache, tough, rough, mugger, *Austral.* larrikin, *colloq.* heavy, bruiser, *sl.* mobster, *Brit. sl.* yob, *esp. US sl.* goon, *US sl.* hood, mug. □□ **thuggish** see *strong-arm*.

thuggee /thugée/ *n. hist.* murder practised by the Thugs. □□ **thuggism** *n.* [Hindi *ṭhagī* (as THUG)]

thuja /thóōyə/ *n.* (also **thuya**) any evergreen coniferous tree of the genus *Thuja*, with small leaves closely pressed to the branches; arbor vitae. [mod.L f. Gk *thuia*, an Afr. tree]

thulium /thyóōliəm/ *n. Chem.* a soft metallic element of the lanthanide series, occurring naturally in apatite. ¶ Symb.: **Tm**. [mod.L f. L *Thule* name of a region in the remote north]

thumb /thum/ *n.* & *v.* ● *n.* **1 a** a short thick terminal projection on the human hand, set lower and apart from the other four and opposable to them. **b** a digit of other animals corresponding to this. **2** part of a glove etc. for a thumb. ● *v.* **1** *tr.* wear or soil (pages etc.) with a thumb (*a well-thumbed book*). **2** *intr.* turn over pages with or as with a thumb (*thumbed through the directory*). **3** *tr.* request or obtain (a lift in a passing vehicle) by signalling with a raised thumb. **4** *tr.* gesture at (a person) with the thumb. □ **be all thumbs** be clumsy with one's hands. **thumb index** *n.* a set of lettered grooves cut down the side of a diary, dictionary, etc. for easy reference. ● *v.tr.* provide (a book etc.) with these. **thumb one's nose** = *cock a snook* (see SNOOK[1]). **thumb-nut** a nut shaped for turning with the thumb and forefinger. **thumbs down** an indication of rejection or failure. **thumbs up** an indication of satisfaction or approval. **under a person's thumb** completely dominated by a person. □□ **thumbed** *adj.* (also in *comb.*). **thumbless** *adj.* [OE *thūma* f. a WG root = swell]

■ *n.* **1** pollex. ● *v.* **2** leaf, flick, flip, riffle, skim, browse. **3** *colloq.* hitch. □ **be all thumbs** be awkward, be clumsy, be maladroit, *colloq.* be a butter-fingers, be ham-fisted, be cack-handed. **thumbs down** see VETO *n.* **thumbs up** see APPROVAL. **under a person's thumb** under a person's control, wrapped round a person's little finger, in the palm of a person's hand, eating out of a person's hand, at a person's beck and call.

thumbnail /thúmnayl/ *n.* **1** the nail of a thumb. **2** (*attrib.*) denoting conciseness (*a thumbnail sketch*).

■ **2** (*attrib.*) rough, undetailed, cursory, sketchy, superficial; brief, short, quick; compact, concise, pithy, succinct.

thumbprint /thúmprint/ *n.* an impression of a thumb esp. as used for identification.

thumbscrew /thúmskrōō/ *n.* **1** an instrument of torture for crushing the thumbs. **2** a screw with a flattened head for turning with the thumb and forefinger.

thumbtack /thúmtak/ *n.* esp. *US* a drawing-pin.

thump /thump/ *v.* & *n.* ● *v.* **1** *tr.* beat or strike heavily esp. with the fist (*threatened to thump me*). **2** *intr.* throb or pulsate strongly (*my heart was thumping*). **3** *intr.* (foll. by *at*, *on*, etc.) deliver blows, esp. to attract attention (*thumped on the door*). **4** *tr.* (often foll. by *out*) play (a tune on a piano etc.) with a heavy touch. **5** *intr.* tread heavily. ● *n.* **1** a heavy blow. **2** the sound of this. □□ **thumper** *n.* [imit.]

■ *v.* **1** see BEAT *v.* 1. **2** see PULSATE. **3** see KNOCK *v.* 1. ● *n.* see KNOCK *n.*

thumping /thúmping/ *adj. colloq.* big, prominent (*a thumping majority*; *a thumping lie*).

■ great, huge, colossal, stupendous, gigantic, enormous, immense, monumental, massive, titanic, elephantine, gargantuan, mammoth, hefty, *colloq.* thundering, jumbo, *sl.* whopping, walloping; complete, utter, unmitigated, 24-carat, perfect.

thunder /thúndər/ *n.* & *v.* ● *n.* **1** a loud rumbling or crashing noise heard after a lightning flash and due to the expansion of rapidly heated air. **2** a resounding loud deep noise (*thunders of applause*). **3** strong censure or denunciation. ● *v.* **1** *intr.* (prec. by *it* as subject) thunder sounds (*it is thundering*; *if it thunders*). **2** *intr.* make or proceed with a noise suggestive of thunder (*the applause thundered in my ears*; *the traffic thundered past*). **3** *tr.* utter or communicate (approval, disapproval, etc.) loudly or impressively. **4** *intr.* (foll. by *against* etc.) **a** make violent threats etc. against. **b** criticize violently. □ **steal a person's thunder** spoil the effect of another's idea, action, etc. by expressing or doing it first. **thunder-box** *colloq.* a primitive lavatory. □□ **thunderer** *n.* **thunderless** *adj.* **thundery** *adj.* [OE *thunor* f. Gmc]

■ *n.* **1, 2** rumble, rumbling, roll, reverberation, boom, booming, roar, roaring, peal; crash, crashing, crack, cracking, explosion, blast. ● *v.* **2** roll, reverberate, boom, roar, rumble, resound; explode, crash, crack, blast. **3** shout, yell, scream, bellow, bark, bawl, roar. **4** (*thunder against* or *at*) **a** threaten, intimidate, menace; denounce, fulminate against, swear at, rail against *or* at, curse at, execrate.

thunderbolt /thúndərbōlt/ *n.* **1 a** a flash of lightning with a simultaneous crash of thunder. **b** a stone etc. imagined to be a destructive bolt. **2** a sudden or unexpected occurrence or item of news. **3** a supposed bolt or shaft as a destructive agent, esp. as an attribute of a god.

■ **2** see SHOCK[1] *n.* 2.

thunderclap /thúndərklap/ *n.* **1** a crash of thunder. **2** something startling or unexpected.

thundercloud /thúndərklowd/ *n.* a cumulus cloud with a tall diffuse top, charged with electricity and producing thunder and lightning.

thunderhead /thúndərhed/ *n.* esp. *US* a rounded cumulus cloud projecting upwards and heralding thunder.

thundering /thúndəring/ *adj. colloq.* very big or great (*a thundering nuisance*). □□ **thunderingly** *adv.*

■ see THUMPING .

thunderous /thúndərəs/ *adj.* **1** like thunder. **2** very loud. □□ **thunderously** *adv.* **thunderousness** *n.*

■ roaring, booming, thundering, tumultuous, noisy, loud, ear-splitting, deafening.

thunderstorm /thúndərstorm/ *n.* a storm with thunder and lightning and usu. heavy rain or hail.

thunderstruck /thúndərstruk/ *adj.* amazed; overwhelmingly surprised or startled.

■ dumbfounded, astonished, astounded, awestruck, awed, speechless, struck dumb, dumbstruck, amazed, taken aback, staggered, stunned, shocked, dazed, numb, paralysed, aghast, open-mouthed, nonplussed, *colloq.* flabbergasted, floored, bowled over, knocked for six.

Thur. *abbr.* Thursday.

thurible /thyŏŏrib'l/ *n.* a censer. [ME f. OF *thurible* or L *t(h)uribulum* f. *thus thur-* incense (as THURIFER)]

thurifer /thyŏŏrifər/ *n.* an acolyte carrying a censer. [LL f. *thus thuris* incense f. Gk *thuos* sacrifice + *-fer* -bearing]

Thurs. *abbr.* Thursday.

Thursday /thúrzday, -di/ *n.* & *adv.* ● *n.* the fifth day of the week, following Wednesday. ● *adv. colloq.* **1** on Thursday. **2** (**Thursdays**) on Thursdays; each Thursday. [OE *thunresdæg, thur(e)sdæg*, day of thunder, representing LL *Jovis dies* day of Jupiter]

thus /t͟huss/ *adv. formal* **1 a** in this way. **b** as indicated. **2 a** accordingly. **b** as a result or inference. **3** to this extent; so (*thus far*; *thus much*). ▫▫ **thusly** *adv. colloq.* [OE (= OS *thus*), of unkn. orig.]

■ **1** so, in this manner *or* way *or* fashion, as follows, as indicated, *archaic* in this wise, *colloq.* like so, thusly. **2** therefore, *ergo*, consequently, as a consequence, as a result, accordingly, (and) so, then, for this *or* that reason, hence, in which case *or* event, that being the case, that being so.

thuya var. of THUJA.

thwack /thwak/ *v.* & *n. colloq.* ● *v.tr.* hit with a heavy blow; whack. ● *n.* a heavy blow. [imit.]

■ *v.* see HIT *v.* 1a. ● *n.* see HIT *n.* 1a.

thwaite /thwayt/ *n. Brit. dial.* a piece of wild land made arable. ¶ Now usually only in place-names. [ON *thveit(i)* paddock, rel. to OE *thwītan* to cut]

thwart /thwawrt/ *v.*, *n.*, *prep.*, & *adv.* ● *v.tr.* frustrate or foil (a person or purpose etc.). ● *n.* a rower's seat placed across a boat. ● *prep.* & *adv. archaic* across, athwart. [ME *thwert* (adv.) f. ON *thvert* neut. of *thverr* transverse = OE *thwe(o)rh* f. Gmc]

■ *v.* frustrate, impede, check, stymie, baffle, stop, foil, hinder, obstruct, baulk, block, stand in the way of, oppose, negate, nullify, short-circuit, *Austral.* cruel, *Brit. sl.* scupper. ● *n.* brace; (rowing-)seat, bench.

thy /t͟hī/ *poss.pron.* (*attrib.*) (also **thine** /t͟hīn/ before a vowel) of or belonging to thee: now replaced by *your* except in some formal, liturgical, dialect, and poetic uses. [ME *thī*, reduced f. *thīn* THINE]

thyme /tīm/ *n.* any herb or shrub of the genus *Thymus* with aromatic leaves, esp. *T. vulgaris* grown for culinary use. ▫▫ **thymy** *adj.* [ME f. OF *thym* f. L *thymum* f. Gk *thumon* f. *thuō* burn a sacrifice]

thymi *pl.* of THYMUS.

thymine /thīmeen/ *n. Biochem.* a pyrimidine derivative found in all living tissue as a component base of DNA. [*thymic* (as THYMUS) + -INE[4]]

thymol /thīmol/ *n. Chem.* a white crystalline phenol obtained from oil of thyme and used as an antiseptic. [as THYME + -OL[1]]

thymus /thīməss/ *n.* (*pl.* **thymi** /-mī/) (in full **thymus gland**) *Anat.* a lymphoid organ situated in the neck of vertebrates (in humans becoming much smaller at the approach of puberty) producing lymphocytes for the immune response. [mod.L f. Gk *thumos*]

thyristor /thīristər/ *n. Electronics* a semiconductor rectifier in which the current between two electrodes is controlled by a signal applied to a third electrode. [Gk *thura* gate + TRANSISTOR]

thyro- /thīrō/ *comb. form* (also **thyreo-** /-riō/) thyroid.

thyroid /thīroyd/ *n.* & *adj.* ● *n.* (in full **thyroid gland**) **1** a large ductless gland in the neck of vertebrates secreting a hormone which regulates growth and development through the rate of metabolism. **2** an extract prepared from the thyroid gland of animals and used in treating goitre and cretinism etc. ● *adj. Anat.* & *Zool.* **1** connected with the thyroid cartilage (*thyroid artery*). **2** shield-shaped. ▫ **thyroid cartilage** a large cartilage of the larynx, the projection of which in man forms the Adam's apple. [obs.F *thyroide* or mod.L *thyroides*, irreg. f. Gk *thureoeidēs* f. *thureos* oblong shield]

thyroxine /thīróksin/ *n.* the main hormone produced by the thyroid gland, involved in controlling the rate of metabolic processes. [THYROID + OX- + -INE[4]]

thyrsus /thúrsəss/ *n.* (*pl.* **thyrsi** /-sī/) **1** *Gk* & *Rom. Antiq.* a staff tipped with an ornament like a pine-cone, an attribute of Bacchus. **2** *Bot.* an inflorescence as in lilac, with the primary axis racemose and the secondary axis cymose. [L f. Gk *thursos*]

thyself /t͟hīsélf/ *pron. archaic* emphat. & refl. form of THOU[1], THEE.

Ti *symb. Chem.* the element titanium.

ti[1] /tee/ *n.* any woody liliaceous plant of the genus *Cordyline*, esp. *C. terminalis* with edible roots. [Tahitian, Maori, etc.]

ti[2] var. of TE.

tiara /tiaárə/ *n.* **1** a jewelled ornamental band worn on the front of a woman's hair. **2** a three-crowned diadem worn by a pope. **3** *hist.* a turban worn by ancient Persian kings. ▫▫ **tiaraed** *adj.* (also **tiara'd**). [L f. Gk, of unkn. orig.]

Tibetan /tibétt'n/ *n.* & *adj.* ● *n.* **1 a** a native of Tibet. **b** a person of Tibetan descent. **2** the language of Tibet. ● *adj.* of or relating to Tibet or its language.

tibia /tíbbiə/ *n.* (*pl.* **tibiae** /-bi-ee/) **1** *Anat.* the inner and usu. larger of two bones extending from the knee to the ankle. **2** the tibiotarsus of a bird. **3** the fourth segment of the leg in insects. ▫▫ **tibial** *adj.* [L, = shin-bone]

tibiotarsus /tíbbiōtaársəss/ *n.* (*pl.* **tibiotarsi** /-sī/) the bone in a bird corresponding to the tibia fused at the lower end with some bones of the tarsus. [TIBIA + TARSUS]

tic /tik/ *n.* a habitual spasmodic contraction of the muscles esp. of the face. ▫ **tic douloureux** /dŏŏlərŏŏ, -rō/ trigeminal neuralgia. [F f. It. *ticchio*: *douloureux* F, = painful]

tice /tīss/ *n.* **1** *Cricket* = YORKER. **2** *Croquet* a stroke tempting an opponent to aim at one's ball. [*tice* (now dial.), = ENTICE]

tick[1] /tik/ *n.* & *v.* ● *n.* **1** a slight recurring click esp. that of a watch or clock. **2** esp. *Brit. colloq.* a moment; an instant. **3** a mark (✓) to denote correctness, check items in a list, etc. ● *v.* **1** *intr.* **a** (of a clock etc.) make ticks. **b** (foll. by *away*) (of time etc.) pass. **2** *intr.* (of a mechanism) work, function (*take it apart to see how it ticks*). **3** *tr.* **a** mark (a written answer etc.) with a tick. **b** (often foll. by *off*) mark (an item in a list etc.) with a tick in checking. ▫ **in two ticks** *Brit. colloq.* in a very short time. **tick off 1** *colloq.* reprimand. **2** *US sl.* annoy, anger; dispirit. **tick over 1** (of an engine etc.) idle. **2** (of a person, project, etc.) be working or functioning at a basic or minimum level. **tick-tack** (or **tic-tac**) *Brit.* a kind of manual semaphore signalling used by racecourse bookmakers to exchange information. **tick-tack-toe** *US* noughts and crosses. **tick-tock** the ticking of a large clock etc. **what makes a person tick** *colloq.* a person's motivation. ▫▫ **tickless** *adj.* [ME: cf. Du. *tik*, LG *tikk* touch, tick]

■ *n.* **2** see MOMENT 1, 2. **3** *US* check. ● *v.* **1b** (*tick away*) see GO[1] *v.* 9. **2** see WORK *v.* 5. **3** check off, mark. ▫ **tick off 1** see REPRIMAND *v.* **2** see ANNOY 1.

tick[2] /tik/ *n.* **1** any of various arachnids of the order Acarina, parasitic on the skin of dogs and cattle etc. **2** any of various insects of the family Hippoboscidae, parasitic on sheep and birds etc. **3** *colloq.* an unpleasant or despicable person. ▫ **tick-bird** = *ox-pecker*. **tick fever** a bacterial or rickettsial fever transmitted by the bite of a tick. [OE *ticca* (recorded as *ticia*); ME *teke, tyke*: cf. MDu., MLG *tēke*, OHG *zēcho*]

tick[3] /tik/ *n. colloq.* credit (*buy goods on tick*). [app. an abbr. of TICKET in phr. *on the ticket*]

tick[4] /tik/ *n.* **1** the cover of a mattress or pillow. **2** = TICKING. [ME *tikke, tēke* f. WG f. L *theca* f. Gk *thēkē* case]

ticker /tíkkər/ *n. colloq.* **1** the heart. **2** a watch. **3** *US* a tape machine. ▫ **ticker-tape 1** a paper strip from a tape machine. **2** this or similar material thrown from windows etc. to greet a celebrity.

ticket /tíkkit/ *n.* & *v.* ● *n.* **1** a written or printed piece of paper or card entitling the holder to enter a place, participate in an event, travel by public transport, use a public amenity, etc. **2** an official notification of a traffic offence etc. (*parking ticket*). **3** *Brit.* a certificate of discharge from the army. **4** a certificate of qualification as a ship's master, pilot, etc. **5** a label attached to a thing and giving its price or other details. **6** esp. *US* **a** a list of candidates put forward by one group esp. a political party. **b** the principles of a party. **7** (prec. by *the*) *colloq.* what is correct or needed. ● *v.tr.* (**ticketed, ticketing**) attach a ticket to. □ **have tickets on oneself** *Austral. colloq.* be conceited. **ticket-day** *Brit. Stock Exch.* the day before settling day, when the names of actual purchasers are handed to stockbrokers. **ticket office** an office or kiosk where tickets are sold for transport, entertainment, etc. **ticket-of-leave man** *Brit. hist.* a prisoner or convict who had served part of his time and was granted certain concessions, esp. leave. □□ **ticketed** *adj.* **ticketless** *adj.* [obs.F *étiquet* f. OF *estiquet(te)* f. *estiquier, estechier* fix f. MDu. *steken*]

■ *n.* **5** see TAG[1] *n.* 1a. **6 b** see POLICY[1] *n.* 1. ● *v.* see TAG[1] *v.* 1. □ **ticket-of-leave man** see PRISONER.

tickety-boo /tíkkətibōō/ *adj. Brit. colloq.* all right; in order. [20th c.: orig. uncert.]

■ see OK[1] *adj.*

ticking /tíkking/ *n.* a stout usu. striped material used to cover mattresses etc. [TICK[4] + -ING[1]]

tickle /tíkk'l/ *v.* & *n.* ● *v.* **1 a** *tr.* apply light touches or strokes to (a person or part of a person's body) so as to excite the nerves and usu. produce laughter and spasmodic movement. **b** *intr.* feel this sensation (*my foot tickles*). **2** *tr.* excite agreeably; amuse or divert (a person, a sense of humour, vanity, etc.) (*was highly tickled at the idea; this will tickle your fancy*). **3** *tr.* catch (a trout etc.) by rubbing it so that it moves backwards into the hand. ● *n.* **1** an act of tickling. **2** a tickling sensation. □ **tickled pink** (or **to death**) *colloq.* extremely amused or pleased. □□ **tickler** *n.* **tickly** *adj.* [ME, prob. frequent. of TICK[1]]

■ *v.* **1 a** titillate. **2** titillate, delight, please, gratify, amuse, entertain, divert, captivate, thrill, excite, *colloq.* tickle pink *or* to death. ● *n.* **2** see ITCH *n.* 1. □ **tickled pink** (or **to death**) see GLAD[1] *adj.* 1.

ticklish /tíklish/ *adj.* **1** sensitive to tickling. **2** (of a matter or person to be dealt with) difficult; requiring careful handling. □□ **ticklishly** *adv.* **ticklishness** *n.*

■ **2** uncertain, unsteady, unsure, unstable, unsettled, fickle, touch-and-go; delicate, precarious, risky, hazardous, dangerous, critical, thorny, fragile, awkward, difficult, tricky; sensitive, over-sensitive, hypersensitive, touchy, prickly. □□ **ticklishness** see DELICACY 3.

tic-tac var. of *tick-tack* (see TICK[1]).

tidal /tī́d'l/ *adj.* relating to, like, or affected by tides (*tidal basin; tidal river*). □ **tidal bore** a large wave or bore caused by constriction of the spring tide as it enters a long narrow shallow inlet. **tidal flow** the regulated movement of traffic in opposite directions on the same stretch of road at different times of the day. **tidal wave 1** *Geog.* an exceptionally large ocean wave esp. one caused by an underwater earthquake or volcanic eruption. **2** a widespread manifestation of feeling etc. □□ **tidally** *adv.*

■ □ **tidal wave 2** see FLOOD *n.* 2b.

tidbit *US* var. of TITBIT.

tiddledy-wink *US* var. of TIDDLY-WINK.

tiddler /tídlər/ *n. Brit. colloq.* **1** a small fish, esp. a stickleback or minnow. **2** an unusually small thing or person. [perh. rel. to TIDDLY[2] and *tittlebat*, a childish form of *stickleback*]

tiddly[1] /tídli/ *adj.* (**tiddlier, tiddliest**) esp. *Brit. colloq.* slightly drunk. [19th c., earlier = a drink: orig. unkn.]

■ see TIGHT *adj.* 6.

tiddly[2] /tídli/ *adj.* (**tiddlier, tiddliest**) *Brit. colloq.* little.

■ see LITTLE *adj.* 1, 2a.

tiddly-wink /tídliwingk/ *n.* (*US* **tiddledy-** /tídd'ldi-/) **1** a counter flicked with another into a cup etc. **2** (in *pl.*) this game. [19th c.: perh. rel. to TIDDLY[1]]

tide /tīd/ *n.* & *v.* ● *n.* **1 a** the periodic rise and fall of the sea due to the attraction of the moon and sun (see EBB *n.* 1, FLOOD *n.* 3). **b** the water as affected by this. **2** a time or season (usu. in *comb.*: *Whitsuntide*). **3** a marked trend of opinion, fortune, or events. ● *v.intr.* drift with the tide, esp. work in or out of harbour with the help of the tide. □ **tide-mill** a mill with a water-wheel driven by the tide. **tide over** enable or help (a person) to deal with an awkward situation, difficult period, etc. (*the money will tide me over until Friday*). **tide-rip** (or **-rips**) rough water caused by opposing tides. **work double tides** work twice the normal time, or extra hard. □□ **tideless** *adj.* [OE *tīd* f. Gmc, rel. to TIME]

■ *n.* **3** see WAVE *n.* 6a, TREND *n.*

tideland /tī́dland/ *n. US* land that is submerged at high tide.

tidemark /tī́dmaark/ *n.* **1** a mark made by the tide at high water. **2** esp. *Brit.* **a** a mark left round a bath at the level of the water in it. **b** a line on a person's body, garment, etc. marking the extent to which it has been washed.

tidetable /tī́dtayb'l/ *n.* a table indicating the times of high and low tides at a place.

tidewaiter /tī́dwaytər/ *n. hist.* a customs officer who boarded ships on their arrival to enforce the customs regulations.

tidewater /tī́dwawtər/ *n.* **1** water brought by or affected by tides. **2** (*attrib.*) *US* affected by tides (*tidewater region*).

tidewave /tī́dwayv/ *n.* an undulation of water passing round the earth and causing high and low tides.

tideway /tī́dway/ *n.* **1** a channel in which a tide runs, esp. the tidal part of a river. **2** the ebb or flow in a tidal channel.

tidings /tī́dingz/ *n.* (as *sing.* or *pl.*) *literary* news, information. [OE *tīdung*, prob. f. ON *títhindi* events f. *títhr* occurring]

■ see NEWS 1, 3.

tidy /tī́di/ *adj.*, *n.*, & *v.* ● *adj.* (**tidier, tidiest**) **1** neat, orderly; methodically arranged. **2** (of a person) methodically inclined. **3** *colloq.* considerable (*it cost a tidy sum*). ● *n.* (*pl.* **-ies**) **1** a receptacle for holding small objects or waste scraps, esp. in a kitchen sink. **2** an act or spell of tidying. **3** esp. *US* a detachable ornamental cover for a chair-back etc. ● *v.tr.* (**-ies, -ied**) (also *absol.*; often foll. by *up*) put in good order; make (oneself, a room, etc.) tidy. □□ **tidily** *adv.* **tidiness** *n.* [ME, = timely etc., f. TIDE + -Y[1]]

■ *adj.* **1** neat, orderly, trim, shipshape, spruce, spick and span, clean, smart, well-kept, well-groomed; well-organized, organized, well-ordered, methodical, systematic. **2** well-organized, organized, methodical, meticulous, systematic. **3** respectable, sizeable, significant, considerable, substantial, appreciable, good, goodly, good-sized, handsome, ample, large, big, fair, generous, not insignificant; *colloq.* not to be sneezed at. ● *v.* tidy up, neaten (up), straighten (out *or* up), clean (up), clear up, put in order, fix (up), spruce up, organize, reorganize, arrange, rearrange, *US* square away; see also GROOM *v.* 1. □□ **tidiness** see ORDER *n.* 1.

tie /tī/ *v.* & *n.* ● *v.* (**tying**) **1** *tr.* **a** attach or fasten with string or cord etc. (*tie the dog to the gate; tie his hands together; tied on a label*). **b** link conceptually. **2** *tr.* **a** form (a string, ribbon, shoelace, necktie, etc.) into a knot or bow. **b** form (a knot or bow) in this way. **3** *tr.* restrict or limit (a person) as to conditions, occupation, place, etc. (*is tied to his family*). **4** *intr.* (often foll. by *with*) achieve the same score or place as another competitor (*they tied at ten games each; tied with her for first place*). **5** *tr.* hold (rafters etc.) together by a crosspiece etc. **6** *tr. Mus.* **a** unite (written notes) by a tie. **b** perform (two notes) as one unbroken note. ● *n.* **1** a cord or chain etc. used for fastening. **2** a strip of material worn round the collar and tied in a knot at the front with the ends hanging down. **3** a thing that unites or restricts persons; a bond or obligation (*family ties; ties of friendship; children are a real tie*). **4** a draw, dead heat, or equality of score among competitors. **5** *Brit.* a match between any pair from a group of competing players or teams. **6** (also **tie-beam** etc.) a rod or beam holding parts of a structure together. **7** *Mus.* a curved line above or below two notes of the same pitch indicating that they are to be played for the combined duration of their time values. **8** *US* a railway sleeper. **9** *US* a shoe tied with a lace. □ **fit to be tied** *colloq.* very angry. **tie-break** (or **-breaker**) a means of deciding a winner from competitors who have tied. **tie down** = TIE *v.* 3 above. **tie-dye** (or **tie and dye**) a method of producing dyed patterns by tying string etc. to protect parts of the fabric from the dye. **tie in** (foll. by *with*) bring into or have a close association or agreement. **tie-in** *n.* **1** a connection or association. **2** (often *attrib.*) esp. *US* a form of sale or advertising that offers or requires more than a single purchase. **3** the joint promotion of related commodities etc. (e.g. a book and a film). **tie the knot** *colloq.* get married. **tie-line** a transmission line connecting parts of a system, esp. a telephone line connecting two private branch exchanges. **tie-pin** (or **-clip**) an ornamental pin or clip for holding a tie in place. **tie up 1** bind or fasten securely with cord etc. **2** invest or reserve (capital etc.) so that it is not immediately available for use. **3** moor (a boat). **4** secure (an animal). **5** obstruct; prevent from acting freely. **6** secure or complete (an undertaking etc.). **7** (often foll. by *with*) = *tie in*. **8** (usu. in *passive*) fully occupy (a person). □□ **tieless** *adj.* [OE *tīgan*, *tēgan* (v.), *tēah*, *tēg* (n.) f. Gmc]

■ *v.* **1 a** bind, fasten, make fast, tie up, lash, secure, truss (up), pinion, attach, hitch, tether, rope, chain, moor; connect, join, knot, link, couple, splice, unite. **b** connect, associate, unite, join, link, bind (up), affiliate, ally, league, team (up). **3** restrict, confine, restrain; limit, tie down, constrain, curtail, curb, cramp, hamper, hinder. **4** (*tie with*) equal, even, be equal *or* even with, match, be neck and neck with, draw with. ● *n.* **1** string, cord, lace, rope, thong, ribbon, band, ligature, shoelace, line, leash, lead, chain, stop. **2** cravat, bow-tie, string tie, *esp. US* necktie. **3** link, fastening, bond, band, connection, tie-in, relationship, affiliation, liaison, involvement, entanglement. **4** equality, dead heat, deadlock, draw, stalemate. **7** ligature. **8** sleeper, *US* railway tie. **9** lace-up. □ **fit to be tied** see ANGRY 1. **tie in** relate, connect, link, associate, coordinate; be consistent, make sense, correspond, coincide, fit (in), tie up, be logical, coordinate. **tie-in 1** relationship, relation, association, connection, link, linkage. **tie up 1, 3** see TIE *v.* 1a above. **2** commit, invest, sink, *US* obligate. **4** see TETHER *v.* **5** stop, halt, bring to a standstill; see also OBSTRUCT 2. **6** clinch, secure, confirm, complete, wrap up, nail down. **8** occupy, engage, (keep) busy, engross.

tied /tīd/ *adj. Brit.* **1** (of a house) occupied subject to the tenant's working for its owner. **2** (of a public house etc.) bound to supply the products of a particular brewery only.

tier /teer/ *n.* **1** a row or rank or unit of a structure, as one of several placed one above another (*tiers of seats*). **2** *Naut.* **a** a circle of coiled cable. **b** a place for a coiled cable. □□ **tiered** *adj.* (also in *comb.*). [earlier *tire* f. F f. *tirer* draw, elongate f. Rmc]

■ **1** row, line, level, order, range, course, series, stratum, layer, echelon, file, rank, storey. □□ **tiered** see SERRIED.

tierce /teerss/ *n.* **1** *Eccl.* = TERCE. **2** *Mus.* an interval of two octaves and a major third. **3** a sequence of three cards. **4** *Fencing* **a** the third of eight parrying positions. **b** the corresponding thrust. **5** *archaic* **a** a former wine-measure of one-third of a pipe. **b** a cask containing a certain quantity (varying with the goods) esp. of provisions. [ME f. OF *t(i)erce* f. L *tertia* fem. of *tertius* third]

tierced /teerst/ *adj. Heraldry* divided into three parts of different tinctures.

tiercel var. of TERCEL.

tiercet var. of TERCET.

tiff /tif/ *n.* & *v.* ● *n.* **1** a slight or petty quarrel. **2** a fit of peevishness. ● *v.intr.* have a petty quarrel; bicker. [18th c.: orig. unkn.]

■ *n.* **1** (petty) quarrel, disagreement, misunderstanding, dispute, argument, difference (of opinion), altercation, squabble, wrangle, *colloq.* row, *Brit. colloq.* barney, *US colloq.* spat. ● *v.* see BICKER.

tiffany /tíffəni/ *n.* (*pl.* **-ies**) thin gauze muslin. [orig. dress worn on Twelfth Night, f. OF *tifanie* f. eccl.L *theophania* f. Gk *theophaneia* Epiphany]

tiffin /tíffin/ *n.* & *v. Ind.* ● *n.* a light meal, esp. lunch. ● *v.intr.* (**tiffined, tiffining**) take lunch etc. [app. f. *tiffing* sipping]

■ *n.* lunch, light meal, collation, snack, *formal* luncheon, light repast. ● *v.* see EAT 1b.

tig /tig/ *n.* = TAG². [var. of TICK¹]

tiger /tī́gər/ *n.* **1** a large Asian feline, *Panthera tigris*, having a yellow-brown coat with black stripes. **2** a fierce, energetic, or formidable person. □ **tiger beetle** any flesh-eating beetle of the family Cicindelidae, with spotted or striped wing-covers. **tiger-cat 1** any moderate-sized feline resembling the tiger, e.g. the ocelot, serval, or margay. **2** *Austral.* any of various flesh-eating marsupials of the genus *Dasyurus*, including the Tasmanian devil. **tiger-eye** (or **tiger's-eye**) **1** a yellow-brown striped gem of brilliant lustre. **2** *US* a pottery-glaze of similar appearance. **tiger lily** a tall garden lily, *Lilium tigrinum*, with flowers of dull orange spotted with black or purple. **tiger moth** any moth of the family Arctiidae, esp. *Arctia caja*, having richly spotted and streaked wings suggesting a tiger's skin. **tiger-wood** a striped or streaked wood used for cabinet-making. □□ **tigerish** *adj.* **tigerishly** *adv.* [ME f. OF *tigre* f. L *tigris* f. Gk *tigris*]

tight /tīt/ *adj.*, *n.*, & *adv.* ● *adj.* **1** closely held, drawn, fastened, fitting, etc. (*a tight hold*; *a tight skirt*). **2 a** closely and firmly put together (*a tight joint*). **b** close, evenly matched (*a tight finish*). **3** (of clothes etc.) too closely fitting (*my shoes are rather tight*). **4** impermeable, impervious, esp. (in *comb.*) to a specified thing (*watertight*). **5** tense; stretched so as to leave no slack (*a tight bowstring*). **6** *colloq.* drunk. **7** *colloq.* (of a person) mean, stingy. **8 a** (of money or materials) not easily obtainable. **b** (of a money market) in which money is tight. **9 a** (of precautions, a programme, etc.) stringent, demanding. **b** presenting difficulties (*a tight situation*). **c** (of an organization, group, or member) strict, disciplined. **10** produced by or requiring great exertion or pressure (*a tight squeeze*). **11** (of control etc.) strictly imposed. ● *adv.* tightly (*hold tight!*). □ **tight corner** (or **place** or **spot**) a difficult situation. **tight-fisted** stingy. **tight-fitting** (of a garment) fitting (often too) close to the body. **tight-lipped** with or as with the lips compressed to restrain emotion or speech. □□ **tightly** *adv.* **tightness** *n.* [prob. alt. of *thight* f. ON *théttr* watertight, of close texture]

■ *adj.* **1, 2a** secure, firm, fast, fixed, secured, close-fitting, tight-fitting, snug. **2 b** close, (almost) even, (highly) competitive, evenly matched, ding-dong. **3** constricting, (too) small, ill-fitting, tight-fitting. **4** sealed, hermetically sealed, leak-proof, hermetic, impervious, impenetrable, impermeable, airtight, watertight, waterproof. **5** taut, stretched, tense. **6** tipsy, drunk, intoxicated, *colloq.* high, woozy, under the influence, *esp. Brit. colloq.* tiddly; see also DRUNK *adj.* 1. **7** stingy, niggardly, mean, penurious, miserly, parsimonious, penny-pinching, tight-fisted, close-fisted, *Brit. colloq.* mingy. **8 a** scarce, scanty, hard to find *or* come by, rare; dear, expensive. **9 a** strict, binding, restrictive, stringent, severe, tough, uncompromising, unyielding, rigorous, stern, austere, autocratic, harsh, hard and fast, inflexible; demanding, exacting. **b** difficult, trying, dangerous, perilous, risky, hazardous, touchy, problematic, tricky, ticklish, precarious, touch-and-go, *colloq.* sticky, *sl.* hairy. **c** (well-)disciplined, orderly, well-organized, strict. **11** see sense 9a above. ● *adv.* tightly, securely, firmly, fast; compactly, densely, solidly, closely. □ **tight corner** (or **place** or **spot**) see BIND *n.* 1b. **tight-fisted** see TIGHT *adj.* 7 above. **tight-lipped** close-mouthed, silent, quiet, mute, close-lipped, noncommittal, reticent, secretive, taciturn, unforthcoming, uncommunicative, reserved, *colloq.* mum. □□ **tightly** closely, tensely, vigorously, rigorously; compactly, densely, solidly; securely, firmly, fast, tight. **tightness** see TENSION *n.* 1.

tighten /tī́t'n/ *v.tr.* & *intr.* (also foll. by *up*) make or become tight or tighter. □ **tighten one's belt** see BELT.
■ make *or* become tighter *or* tenser *or* stronger, strengthen; tauten, stiffen, tense, close; anchor, fasten, fix, secure; make *or* become more rigorous *or* strict *or* stringent *or* severe *or* restrictive, close gaps in.

tightrope /tī́t-rōp/ *n.* a rope stretched tightly high above the ground, on which acrobats perform.

tights /tīts/ *n.pl.* **1** a thin close-fitting wool or nylon etc. garment covering the legs and the lower part of the torso, worn by women in place of stockings. **2** a similar garment worn by a dancer, acrobat, etc.
■ **1** pantihose, *US* panty hose.

tigon /tī́gən/ *n.* the offspring of a tiger and a lioness (cf. LIGER). [portmanteau word f. TIGER + LION]

tigress /tī́griss/ *n.* **1** a female tiger. **2** a fierce or passionate woman.

tike var. of TYKE.

tiki /tíkki/ *n.* (*pl.* **tikis**) *NZ* a large wooden or small ornamental greenstone image representing a human figure. [Maori]

tilbury /tílbəri/ *n.* (*pl.* **-ies**) *hist.* a light open two-wheeled carriage. [after the inventor's name]

tilde /tíldə/ *n.* a mark (˜), put over a letter, e.g. over a Spanish *n* when pronounced *ny* (as in *señor*) or a Portuguese *a* or *o* when nasalized (as in *São Paulo*). [Sp., ult. f. L *titulus* TITLE]

tile /tīl/ *n.* & *v.* ● *n.* **1** a thin slab of concrete or baked clay etc. used in series for covering a roof or pavement etc. **2** a similar slab of glazed pottery, cork, linoleum, etc., for covering a floor, wall, etc. **3** a thin flat piece used in a game (esp. mah-jong). ● *v.tr.* cover with tiles. □ **on the tiles** *colloq.* having a spree. [OE *tigule*, *-ele*, f. L *tegula*]

tiler /tī́lər/ *n.* **1** a person who makes or lays tiles. **2** the doorkeeper of a Freemasons' lodge.

tiling /tī́ling/ *n.* **1** the process of fixing tiles. **2** an area of tiles.

till[1] /til/ *prep.* & *conj.* ● *prep.* **1** up to or as late as (*wait till six o'clock*; *did not return till night*). **2** up to the time of (*faithful till death*; *waited till the end*). ● *conj.* **1** up to the time when (*wait till I return*). **2** so long that (*laughed till I cried*). ¶ *Until* is more usual when beginning a sentence. [OE & ON *til* to, rel. to TILL[3]]

till[2] /til/ *n.* a drawer for money in a shop or bank etc., esp. with a device recording the amount of each purchase. [ME: orig. unkn.]
■ money *or* cash-drawer, cash-box, cash register.

till[3] /til/ *v.tr.* prepare and cultivate (land) for crops. □□ **tillable** *adj.* **tiller** *n.* [OE *tilian* strive for, cultivate, f. Gmc]
■ plough, cultivate, farm, work, dig, hoe, harrow, manure, *poet.* delve.

till[4] /til/ *n.* stiff clay containing boulders, sand, etc. deposited by melting glaciers and ice-sheets. [17th c. (Sc.): orig. unkn.]

tillage /tíllij/ *n.* **1** the preparation of land for crop-bearing. **2** tilled land.

tiller[1] /tíllər/ *n.* a horizontal bar fitted to the head of a boat's rudder to turn it in steering. [ME f. AF *telier* weaver's beam f. med.L *telarium* f. L *tela* web]

tiller[2] /tíllər/ *n.* & *v.* ● *n.* **1** a shoot of a plant springing from the bottom of the original stalk. **2** a sapling. **3** a sucker. ● *v.intr.* put forth tillers. [app. repr. OE *telgor* extended f. *telga* bough]

tilt /tilt/ *v.* & *n.* ● *v.* **1** *intr.* & *tr.* assume or cause to assume a sloping position; heel over. **2** *intr.* (foll. by *at*) strike, thrust, or run at, with a weapon, esp. in jousting. **3** *intr.* (foll. by *with*) engage in a contest. **4** *tr.* forge or work (steel etc.) with a tilt-hammer. ● *n.* **1** the act or an instance of tilting. **2** a sloping position. **3** (of medieval knights etc.) the act of charging with a lance against an opponent or at a mark, done for exercise or as a sport. **4** an encounter between opponents; an attack esp. with argument or satire (*have a tilt at*). **5** = *tilt-hammer*. □ **full** (or **at full**) **tilt 1** at full speed. **2** with full force. **tilt-hammer** a heavy pivoted hammer used in forging. **tilt-yard** *hist.* a place where tilts (see sense 3 of *n.*) took place. □□ **tilter** *n.* [ME *tilte* perh. f. an OE form rel. to *tealt* unsteady f. Gmc: weapon senses of unkn. orig.]
■ *v.* **1** lean, slant, incline, slope, angle, tip, heel over, pitch, list, cant, careen. **2** (*tilt at*) strike at, thrust at, run at, lunge at, attack, *hist.* joust with. **3** (*tilt with*) compete with, battle with *or* against, contend with, spar with, cross swords with, attack, *hist.* joust with. ● *n.* **2** lean, slant, incline, slope, angle, tip, heel, list, pitch, cant, inclination. **3, 4** tourney, tournament, meeting, tilting, engagement, encounter, match, contest, test, trial, fight, combat, *hist.* joust; dispute, argument, difference, quarrel, altercation, squabble, tiff, attack, *colloq.* set-to, *US colloq.* spat. □ **full** (or **at full**) **tilt 1** see *post-haste* (POST[2]). **2** see *at full blast* (BLAST).

tilth /tilth/ *n.* **1** tillage, cultivation. **2** the condition of tilled soil (*in good tilth*). [OE *tilth(e)* (as TILL[3])]

Tim. *abbr.* Timothy (New Testament).

timbal /tímb'l/ *n.* *archaic* a kettledrum. [F *timbale*, earlier *tamballe* f. Sp. *atabal* f. Arab. *aṭ-ṭabl* the drum]

timbale /toNbaál/ *n.* a drum-shaped dish of minced meat or fish in a pastry shell. [F: see TIMBAL]

timber /tímbər/ *n.* **1** wood prepared for building, carpentry, etc. **2** a piece of wood or beam, esp. as the rib of a vessel. **3** large standing trees suitable for timber; woods or forest. **4** (esp. as *int.*) a warning cry that a tree is about to fall. □ **timber hitch** a knot used in attaching a rope to a log or spar. **timber wolf** a type of large N. American grey wolf. □□ **timbering** *n.* [OE, = building, f. Gmc]
■ **1** wood, beams, boards, planks, *US* lumber. **3** see WOOD 2.

timbered /tímbərd/ *adj.* **1** (esp. of a building) made wholly or partly of timber. **2** (of country) wooded.

timberland /tímbərland/ *n.* *US* land covered with forest yielding timber.

timberline /tímbərlīn/ *n.* (on a mountain) the line or level above which no trees grow.

timbre /támbər, táNbrə/ *n.* the distinctive character of a musical sound or voice apart from its pitch and intensity. [F f. Rmc f. med.Gk *timbanon* f. Gk *tumpanon* drum]
■ tone (colour *or* quality), tonality, colour, resonance.

timbrel /tímbrəl/ *n.* *archaic* a tambourine or similar instrument. [dimin. of ME *timbre* f. OF (as TIMBRE, -LE[2])]

Timbuctoo /tímbuktóó/ *n.* any distant or remote place. [*Timbuktu* in W. Africa]

time /tīm/ *n.* & *v.* ● *n.* **1** the indefinite continued progress of existence, events, etc., in past, present, and future regarded as a whole. **2 a** the progress of this as affecting persons or things (*stood the test of time*). **b** (**Time**) (in full **Father Time**) the personification of time, esp. as an old man with a scythe and hourglass. **3** a more or less definite portion of time belonging to particular events or circumstances (*the time of the Plague*; *prehistoric times*; *the scientists of the time*). **4** an allotted, available, or measurable portion of time; the period of time at one's disposal (*am wasting my time*; *had no time to visit*; *how much time do you need?*). **5** a point of time esp. in hours and minutes (*the time is 7.30*; *what time is it?*). **6** (prec. by *a*) an indefinite period (*waited for a time*). **7** time or an amount of time as reckoned by a conventional standard (*the time allowed is one hour*; *ran the mile in record time*; *eight o'clock New York time*). **8 a** an occasion (*last time I saw you*). **b** an event or occasion qualified in some way (*had a good time*). **9** a moment or definite portion of time destined or suitable for a purpose etc. (*now is the time to act*; *shall we fix a time?*). **10** (in *pl.*) expressing multiplication (*is four times as old*; *five times six is thirty*). **11** a lifetime (*will last my time*). **12** (in *sing.* or *pl.*) **a** the conditions of life or of a period (*hard times*; *times have changed*). **b** (prec. by *the*) the present age, or that being considered. **13** *colloq.* a prison sentence (*is doing time*). **14** an apprenticeship (*served his* *time*). **15** a period of gestation. **16** the date or expected date of childbirth (*is near her time*) or of death (*my time is drawing near*). **17** measured time spent in work (*put them on short time*). **18 a** any of several rhythmic patterns of music (*in waltz time*). **b** the duration of a note as indicated by a crotchet, minim, etc. **19** *Brit.* the moment at which the opening hours of a public house end. ● *v.tr.* **1** choose the time or occasion for (*time your remarks carefully*). **2** do at a chosen or correct time. **3** arrange the time of arrival of. **4** ascertain the time taken by (a process or activity, or a person doing it). **5** regulate the duration or interval of; set times for (*trains are timed to arrive every hour*). □ **against time** with utmost speed, so as to finish by a specified time (*working against time*). **ahead of time** earlier than expected. **ahead of one's time** having ideas too enlightened or advanced to be accepted by one's contemporaries. **all the time 1** during the whole of the time referred to (often despite some contrary expectation etc.) (*we never noticed, but he was there all the time*). **2** constantly (*nags all the time*). **3** at all times (*leaves a light on all the time*). **at one time 1** in or during a known but unspecified past period. **2** simultaneously (*ran three businesses at one time*). **at the same time 1** simultaneously; at a time that is the same for all. **2** nevertheless (*at the same time, I do not want to offend you*). **at a time** separately in the specified groups or numbers (*came three at a time*). **at times** occasionally, intermittently. **before time** (usu. prec. by *not*) before the due or expected time. **before one's time** prematurely (*old before his time*). **for the time being** for the present; until some other arrangement is made. **half the time** *colloq.* as often as not. **have no time for 1** be unable or unwilling to spend time on. **2** dislike. **have the time 1** be able to spend the time needed. **2** know from a watch etc. what time it is. **have a time of it** undergo trouble or difficulty. **in no** (or **less than no**) **time 1** very soon. **2** very quickly. **in one's own good time** at a time and a rate decided by oneself. **in one's own time** outside working hours. **in time 1** not late, punctual (*was in time to catch the bus*). **2** eventually (*in time you may agree*). **3** in accordance with a given rhythm or tempo, esp. of music. **in one's time** at or during some previous period of one's life (*in his time he was a great hurdler*). **keep good** (or **bad**) **time 1** (of a clock etc.) record time accurately (or inaccurately). **2** be habitually punctual (or not punctual). **keep time** move or sing etc. in time. **know the time of day** be well informed. **lose no time** (often foll. by *in* + verbal noun) act immediately (*lost no time in cashing the cheque*). **not before time** not too soon; timely. **on time** see ON. **no time** *colloq.* a very short interval (*it was no time before they came*). **out of time** unseasonable; unseasonably. **pass the time of day** *colloq.* exchange a greeting or casual remarks. **time after time 1** repeatedly, on many occasions. **2** in many instances. **time and** (or **time and time**) **again** on many occasions. **time and a half** a rate of payment for work at one and a half times the normal rate. **time-and-motion** (usu. *attrib.*) concerned with measuring the efficiency of industrial and other operations. **time bomb** a bomb designed to explode at a pre-set time. **time capsule** a box etc. containing objects typical of the present time, buried for discovery in the future. **time clock 1** a clock with a device for recording workers' hours of work. **2** a switch mechanism activated at pre-set times by a built-in clock. **time-consuming** using much or too much time. **time exposure** the exposure of photographic film for longer than the maximum normal shutter setting. **time factor** the passage of time as a limitation on what can be achieved. **time-fuse** a fuse calculated to burn for or explode at a given time. **time-honoured** esteemed by tradition or through custom. **time immemorial** (or **out of mind**) a longer time than anyone can remember or trace. **time-lag** an interval of time between an event, a cause, etc. and its effect. **time-lapse** (of photography) using frames taken at long intervals to photograph a slow process, and shown continuously as if at normal speed. **time-limit** the limit of time within which a task must be done. **the time of day** the hour by the clock. **time off** time for rest or recreation etc. **the time of one's life** a period or occasion of exceptional enjoyment. **time out** esp. *US* **1** a brief intermission in a game etc. **2** = *time off*. **time-scale** the time allowed for or taken by a sequence of events in relation to a broader period of time. **time-served** having completed a period of apprenticeship or training. **time-server** a person who changes his or her view to suit the prevailing circumstances, fashion, etc. **time-serving** self-seeking or obsequious. **time-share** a share in a property under a time-sharing scheme. **time-sharing 1** the operation of a computer system by several users for different operations at one time. **2** the use of a holiday home at agreed different times by several joint owners. **time sheet** a sheet of paper for recording hours of work etc. **time signal** an audible (esp. broadcast) signal or announcement of the exact time of day. **time signature** *Mus.* an indication of tempo following a clef, expressed as a fraction with the numerator giving the number of beats in each bar and the denominator giving the duration of each beat. **time switch** a switch acting automatically at a pre-set time. **time warp** an imaginary distortion of space in relation to time, whereby persons or objects of one age can be moved to another. **time was** there was a time (*time was when I could do that*). **time-work** work paid for by the time it takes. **time-worn** impaired by age. **time zone** a range of longitudes where a common standard time is used. [OE *tīma* f. Gmc]

■ *n.* **3** age, period, epoch, era, lifetime, heyday, day(s). **4, 6** period, interval, stretch, spell, patch, while, span, space, phase, season, term, session, duration. **5, 9** hour; point, moment, instant, juncture, date. **8 a** opportunity, chance, occasion. **b** experience. **11** see LIFE 3. **12 a** life, things, circumstances, conditions, everything, culture, mores, habits, values. **18 a** tempo, beat, rhythm, metre, measure. ● *v.* **2, 3** schedule, timetable, programme, set, organize, adjust, fix, arrange. **4** *colloq.* clock. **5** schedule, timetable, set, regulate, control. □ **ahead of time** (bright and) early, prematurely, beforehand, in good time. **all the time 2** always, ever, constantly, continuously, continually, perpetually, everlastingly, unceasingly, *literary* without surcease. **3** at all times, continuously, constantly, always, permanently, perpetually. **at one time 1** once, once upon a time, on one occasion, previously, formerly, in the (good) old days, *formal* heretofore, *literary* in days of yore. **2** simultaneously, (all) at once, at the same time, together, all together, in unison. **at the same time 1** see *at one time* 2 (TIME) above. **2** all the same, none the less, yet, even so, but, however, be that as it may, nevertheless, notwithstanding, just the same. **at times** from time to time, occasionally, (every) now and then, once in a while, on occasion, every so often, at intervals, intermittently, sometimes. **for the time being** for now, for the present, for the moment, meanwhile, temporarily, for the nonce, *pro tempore*, *colloq.* pro tem. **in no** (or **less than no**) **time 1** at once, forthwith, straight away, immediately, (very) soon, promptly, without delay, before you know it, right away. **2** quickly, speedily, swiftly, expeditiously, rapidly, in a flash *or* trice *or* moment, in an instant. **in one's own good time** at one's ease, at one's leisure, at one's (own) convenience. **in time 1** punctually, in timely fashion, early, in good time, in the nick of time. **2** soon, one of these days, sometime, someday, one day, eventually, sooner or later, *archaic or literary* anon. **time and** (or **time and time**) **again** again (and again), repeatedly, (over and) over again, time after time, frequently, often, many times, on many occasions. **time-consuming** see LONG[1] *adj.* 1–3, 5–7. **time-honoured** established, traditional, traditionary, habitual, customary, rooted, conventional, age-old, set, fixed; venerable, venerated, respected, revered, honoured. **time off** see BREAK[1] *n.* 2. **time-server** see *yes-man*. **time-serving** self-seeking, self-serving, selfish, self-indulgent, ambitious, mercenary, venal, greedy, opportunistic, hypocritical; obsequious, sycophantic, toadying, toadyish, subservient, cringing, grovelling, *colloq.* bootlicking, crawling, smarmy, on the make. **time was** see FORMERLY. **time-worn** ageing, old, tired, worn, time-scarred, decrepit, dilapidated, tumbledown, ramshackle, run-down, dog-eared, ragged, moth-eaten, threadbare, seedy, shabby, archaic, antique, well-worn, worn out, *passé*, broken-down, old-fashioned, outdated, dated, antiquated, ancient, obsolescent, obsolete, stereotyped, stereotypic(al), hackneyed, clichéd, stale, trite, overused, *colloq.* old hat.

timekeeper /tīmkeepər/ *n.* **1** a person who records time, esp. of workers or in a game. **2 a** a watch or clock as regards accuracy (*a good timekeeper*). **b** a person as regards punctuality. ▫▫ **timekeeping** *n.*

timeless /tīmliss/ *adj.* not affected by the passage of time; eternal. ▫▫ **timelessly** *adv.* **timelessness** *n.*

■ eternal, everlasting, immortal, undying, endless, unending, ceaseless, abiding, deathless, ageless, changeless, unchanged, immutable, unchanging, perpetual, permanent, indestructible, *rhet.* sempiternal. ▫▫ **timelessness** see ETERNITY 1, 3.

timely /tīmli/ *adj.* (**timelier, timeliest**) opportune; coming at the right time. ▫▫ **timeliness** *n.*

■ well-timed, propitious, opportune, seasonable, convenient, favourable, auspicious.

timepiece /tīmpeess/ *n.* an instrument, such as a clock or watch, for measuring time.

timer /tīmər/ *n.* **1** a person or device that measures or records time taken. **2** an automatic mechanism for activating a device etc. at a pre-set time.

timetable /tīmtayb'l/ *n.* & *v.* ● *n.* a list of times at which events are scheduled to take place, esp. the arrival and departure of buses or trains etc., or a sequence of lessons in a school or college. ● *v.tr.* include in or arrange to a timetable; schedule.

■ *n.* schedule, calendar, curriculum, programme, agenda, plan, diary. ● *v.* see SCHEDULE *v.*

timid /timmid/ *adj.* (**timider, timidest**) easily frightened; apprehensive, shy. ▫▫ **timidity** /-midditi/ *n.* **timidly** *adv.* **timidness** *n.* [F *timide* or L *timidus* f. *timēre* fear]

■ shy, retiring, modest, coy, bashful, diffident, timorous, fearful, apprehensive, faint-hearted, mousy, scared, frightened, nervous, cowardly, pusillanimous, craven, chicken-hearted, chicken-livered, lily-livered, *colloq.* yellow, yellow-bellied, chicken, gutless. ▫▫ **timidity, timidness** see COWARDICE. **timidly** see *fearfully* (FEARFUL).

timing /tīming/ *n.* **1** the way an action or process is timed, esp. in relation to others. **2** the regulation of the opening and closing of valves in an internal-combustion engine.

timocracy /timókrəsi/ *n.* (*pl.* **-ies**) **1** a form of government in which possession of property is required in order to hold office. **2** a form of government in which rulers are motivated by love of honour. ▫▫ **timocratic** /tímməkráttik/ *adj.* [OF *timocracie* f. med.L *timocratia* f. Gk *timokratia* f. *timē* honour, worth + *kratia* -CRACY]

timorous /timmərəss/ *adj.* **1** timid; easily alarmed. **2** frightened. ▫▫ **timorously** *adv.* **timorousness** *n.* [ME f. OF *temoreus* f. med.L *timorosus* f. L *timor* f. *timēre* fear]

■ **1** see TIMID. **2** see AFRAID. ▫▫ **timorously** see *fearfully* (FEARFUL), GINGERLY *adv.* **timorousness** see COWARDICE, HUMILITY 1.

timothy /tímməthi/ *n.* (in full **timothy grass**) a fodder grass, *Phleum pratense.* [*Timothy* Hanson, who introduced it in Carolina *c.*1720]

timothy[2] /tímməthi/ *n. Austral. sl.* a brothel. [20th c.: orig. unkn.]

■ see BROTHEL.

timpani /tímpəni/ *n.pl.* (also **tympani**) kettledrums. ▫▫ **timpanist** *n.* [It., pl. of *timpano* = TYMPANUM]

tin /tin/ *n.* & *v.* ● *n.* **1** *Chem.* a silvery-white malleable metallic element resisting corrosion, occurring naturally in cassiterite and other ores, and used esp. in alloys and for plating thin iron or steel sheets to form tin plate. ¶ Symb.: Sn. **2 a** a vessel or container made of tin or tinned iron. **b** *Brit.* an airtight sealed container made of tin plate or aluminium for preserving food. **3** = *tin plate.* **4** *Brit. sl.* money. ● *v.tr.* (**tinned, tinning**) **1** seal (food) in an airtight tin for preservation. **2** cover or coat with tin. ▫ **put the tin lid on** see LID. **tin can** a tin container (see sense 2 of *n.*), esp. an empty one. **tin foil** foil made of tin, aluminium, or tin alloy, used for wrapping food for cooking or storing. **tin-glaze** a glaze made white and opaque by the addition of tin oxide. **tin god 1** an object of unjustified veneration. **2** a self-important person. **tin hat** *colloq.* a military steel helmet. **tin Lizzie** *colloq.* an old or decrepit car. **tin-opener** a tool for opening tins. **tin-pan alley** the world of composers and publishers of popular music. **tin plate** sheet iron or sheet steel coated with tin. **tin-plate** *v.tr.* coat with tin. **tin soldier** a toy soldier made of metal. **tin-tack** an iron tack. **tin whistle** = *penny whistle.* [OE f. Gmc]

tinamou /tínnəmōō/ *n.* any South American bird of the family Tinamidae, resembling a grouse but related to the rhea . [F f. Galibi *tinamu*]

tinctorial /tingktóriəl/ *adj.* **1** of or relating to colour or dyeing. **2** producing colour. [L *tinctorius* f. *tinctor* dyer: see TINGE]

tincture /tíngkchər/ *n.* & *v.* ● *n.* (often foll. by *of*) **1** a slight flavour or trace. **2** a tinge (of a colour). **3** a medicinal solution (of a drug) in alcohol (*tincture of quinine*). **4** *Heraldry* an inclusive term for the metals, colours, and furs used in coats of arms. **5** *colloq.* an alcoholic drink. ● *v.tr.* **1** colour slightly; tinge, flavour. **2** (often foll. by *with*) affect slightly (with a quality). [ME f. L *tinctura* dyeing (as TINGE)]

■ *n.* **1, 2** see TINT *n.* 1, 2.

tinder /tíndər/ *n.* a dry substance such as wood that readily catches fire from a spark. ▫ **tinder-box** *hist.* a box containing tinder, flint, and steel, formerly used for kindling fires. ▫▫ **tindery** *adj.* [OE *tynder, tyndre* f. Gmc]

tine /tīn/ *n.* a prong or tooth or point of a fork, comb, antler, etc. ▫▫ **tined** *adj.* (also in *comb.*). [OE *tind*]

tinea /tínniə/ *n. Med.* ringworm. [L, = moth, worm]

ting /ting/ *n.* & *v.* ● *n.* a tinkling sound as of a bell. ● *v.intr.* & *tr.* emit or cause to emit this sound. [imit.]

tinge /tinj/ *v.* & *n.* ● *v.tr.* (also **tingeing**) (often foll. by *with*; often in *passive*) **1** colour slightly (*is tinged with red*). **2** affect slightly (*regret tinged with satisfaction*). ● *n.* **1** a tendency towards or trace of some colour. **2** a slight admixture of a feeling or quality. [ME f. L *tingere tinct-* dye, stain]

■ *v.* **1** see COLOUR *v.* 1. **2** see TINT *v.* ● *n.* **1** see TINT *n.* 1. **2** see SHADE *n.* 6.

tingle /tíngg'l/ *v.* & *n.* ● *v.* **1** *intr.* **a** feel a slight prickling, stinging, or throbbing sensation. **b** cause this (*the reply tingled in my ears*). **2** *tr.* make (the ear etc.) tingle. ● *n.* a tingling sensation. [ME, perh. var. of TINKLE]

■ *v.* **1** see PRICKLE *v.* ● *n.* see PRICKLE *n.* 3.

tingly /tíngli/ *adj.* (**tinglier, tingliest**) causing or characterized by tingling.

tinhorn /tínhorn/ *n.* & *adj. US sl.* ● *n.* a pretentious but unimpressive person. ● *adj.* cheap, pretentious.

tinker /tíngkər/ *n.* & *v.* ● *n.* **1** an itinerant mender of kettles and pans etc. **2** *Sc.* & *Ir.* a gypsy. **3** *colloq.* a mischievous person or animal. **4** a spell of tinkering. **5** a rough-and-ready worker. ● *v.* **1** *intr.* (foll. by *at, with*) work in an amateurish or desultory way, esp. to adjust or mend machinery etc. **2 a** *intr.* work as a tinker. **b** *tr.* repair (pots and pans). ▫▫ **tinkerer** *n.* [ME: orig. unkn.]

■ *v.* **1** trifle, dabble, meddle, tamper, mess (around *or* about), toy, fool (around *or* about), play (around *or* about), fiddle (about *or* around), monkey about *or* around, potter (about *or* around), *US* putter (about *or* around), *Brit. colloq.* muck (about *or* around).

tinkle /tíngk'l/ *v.* & *n.* ● *v.* **1** *intr.* & *tr.* make or cause to make a succession of short light ringing sounds. **2** *intr. colloq.* urinate. ● *n.* **1** a tinkling sound. **2** *Brit. colloq.* a telephone call (*will give you a tinkle on Monday*). **3** *colloq.* an act of urinating. [ME f. obs. *tink* to chink (imit.)]

■ *v.* **1** see RING² *v.* 1. **2** see URINATE. ● *n.* **1** see RING² *n.* 1. **2** see RING² *n.* 3. **3** *colloq.* piddle, pee, *sl.* leak, *esp. Brit. sl.* wee, *Brit. sl.* slash, wee-wee.

tinner /tínnər/ *n.* **1** a tin-miner. **2** a tinsmith.

tinnitus /tinítəss/ *n. Med.* a ringing in the ears. [L f. *tinnire tinnit-* ring, tinkle, of imit. orig.]

tinny /tínni/ *adj.* & *n.* ● *adj.* (**tinnier**, **tinniest**) **1** of or like tin. **2** (of a metal object) flimsy, insubstantial; of poor quality. **3 a** sounding like struck tin. **b** (of reproduced sound) thin and metallic, lacking low frequencies. **4** *Austral. sl.* lucky. ● *n.* (also **tinnie**) (*pl.* **-ies**) *Austral. sl.* a can of beer. □□ **tinnily** *adv.* **tinniness** *n.*

■ *adj.* **2** shabby, flimsy, flimsily *or* poorly made, shoddy, inferior, cheap, tawdry, insubstantial, *Brit.* tinpot. **3 b** metallic, harsh, twangy, thin. **4** see LUCKY 1.

tinpot /tínpot/ *adj. Brit.* cheap, inferior.

■ see CHEAP *adj.* 3.

tinsel /tíns'l/ *n.* & *v.* ● *n.* **1** glittering metallic strips, threads, etc., used as decoration to give a sparkling effect. **2** a fabric adorned with tinsel. **3** superficial brilliance or splendour. **4** (*attrib.*) showy, gaudy, flashy. ● *v.tr.* (**tinselled, tinselling**) adorn with or as with tinsel. □□ **tinselled** *adj.* **tinselly** *adj.* [OF *estincele* spark f. L *scintilla*]

tinsmith /tínsmith/ *n.* a worker in tin and tin plate.

tinsnips /tínsnips/ *n.* a pair of clippers for cutting sheet metal.

tinstone /tínstōn/ *n. Geol.* = CASSITERITE.

tint /tint/ *n.* & *v.* ● *n.* **1** a variety of a colour, esp. one made lighter by adding white. **2** a tendency towards or admixture of a different colour (*red with a blue tint*). **3** a faint colour spread over a surface, esp. as a background for printing on. **4** a set of parallel engraved lines to give uniform shading. ● *v.tr.* apply a tint to; colour. □□ **tinter** *n.* [alt. of earlier *tinct* f. L *tinctus* dyeing (as TINGE), perh. infl. by It. *tinto*]

■ *n.* **1** hue, colour, cast, shade, tone. **2** tincture, tinge, touch, hint, trace, dash, colouring, suggestion, nuance. **3** dye, rinse, wash, stain, tincture, colourant, colouring. ● *v.* dye, stain, colour, tinge; influence, affect, taint.

tintinnabulation /tíntinábyooláysh'n/ *n.* a ringing or tinkling of bells. [as L *tintinnabulum* tinkling bell f. *tintinnare* redupl. form of *tinnire* ring]

tinware /tínwair/ *n.* articles made of tin or tin plate.

tiny /tīni/ *adj.* (**tinier**, **tiniest**) very small or slight. □□ **tinily** *adv.* **tininess** *n.* [obs. *tine*, *tyne* (adj. & n.) small, a little: ME, of unkn. orig.]

■ microscopic, infinitesimal, minute, minuscule, ultramicroscopic, diminutive, small, little, miniature, micro-, mini-, pocket, pocket-sized, bantam, pygmy, midget, lilliputian, petite, delicate, dainty, elfin, slight, insignificant, imperceptible, negligible, trifling, paltry, inconsequential, puny, *archaic* piccaninny, *colloq.* pint-sized, wee, weeny, teeny, teeny-weeny, teensy-weensy, titchy, *colloq. usu. derog.* itty-bitty, itsy-bitsy.

-tion /sh'n/ *suffix* forming nouns of action, condition, etc. (see -ION, -ATION, -ITION, -UTION). [from or after F *-tion* or L *-tio -tionis*]

tip¹ /tip/ *n.* & *v.* ● *n.* **1** an extremity or end, esp. of a small or tapering thing (*tips of the fingers*). **2** a small piece or part attached to the end of a thing, e.g. a ferrule on a stick. **3** a leaf-bud of tea. ● *v.tr.* (**tipped**, **tipping**) **1** provide with a tip. **2** (foll. by *in*) attach (a loose sheet) to a page at the inside edge. □ **on the tip of one's tongue** about to be said, esp. after difficulty in recalling to mind. **the tip of the iceberg** a small evident part of something much larger or more significant. □□ **tipless** *adj.* **tippy** *adj.* (in sense 3). [ME f. ON *typpi* (n.), *typpa* (v.), *typptr* tipped f. Gmc (rel. to TOP¹): prob. reinforced by MDu. & MLG *tip*]

■ *n.* **1** end, extremity, peak, apex, summit, vertex, cap, top, pinnacle, crown, head, terminal, nib, point, *Archit.* finial, *Sc.* & *N.Engl.* neb, *colloq.* tiptop. **2** cap, ferrule, nib. ● *v.* **1** top, cap, crown, surmount.

tip² /tip/ *v.* & *n.* ● *v.* (**tipped**, **tipping**) **1 a** *intr.* lean or slant. **b** *tr.* cause to do this. **2** *tr.* (foll. by *into* etc.) **a** overturn or cause to overbalance (*was tipped into the pond*). **b** discharge the contents of (a container etc.) in this way. ● *n.* **1 a** a slight push or tilt. **b** a light stroke, esp. in baseball. **2** *Brit.* a place where material (esp. refuse) is tipped. □ **tip the balance** make the critical difference. **tip the scales** see SCALE². **tip-up** able to be tipped, e.g. of a seat in a theatre to allow passage past. [17th c.: orig. uncert.]

■ *v.* **1** slant, lean, incline, list, heel over, tilt, cant, careen. **2 a** tip over, upset, overthrow, knock *or* cast *or* throw down, up-end, knock over, overturn, topple (over), capsize. **b** empty, unload, dump, deposit, discharge, spill, pour out, *sl.* ditch. ● *n.* **1 a** see LIST² *n.* **2** (rubbish *or US* garbage) dump, rubbish *or* refuse *or* trash heap, dumping-ground.

tip³ /tip/ *v.* & *n.* ● *v.* (**tipped**, **tipping**) (often foll. by *over*, *up*) **1** *tr.* make a small present of money to, esp. for a service given (*have you tipped the porter?*). **2** *tr.* name as the likely winner of a race or contest etc. **3** *tr.* strike or touch lightly. **4** *tr. sl.* give, hand, pass (esp. in *tip the wink* below). ● *n.* **1** a small money present, esp. for a service given. **2** a piece of private or special information, esp. regarding betting or investment. **3** a small or casual piece of advice. □ **tip off 1** give (a person) a hint or piece of special information or warning, esp. discreetly or confidentially. **2** *Basketball* start play by throwing the ball up between two opponents. **tip-off** a hint or warning etc. given discreetly or confidentially. **tip a person the wink** give a person private information. □□ **tipper** *n.* [ME: orig. uncert.]

■ *v.* **1** reward, remunerate. ● *n.* **1** gratuity, baksheesh, *pourboire*, present, gift, *colloq.* little something, sweetener, *Austral. sl.* sling. **2** tip-off, bit of (inside) information, warning, piece of advice, suggestion, clue, hint, forecast, prediction, *colloq.* pointer, *Austral. sl.* drum, *Brit. sl.* bit of gen. **3** suggestion, hint, clue, piece of information, piece of advice, warning, recommendation, *colloq.* pointer. □ **tip off 1** advise, warn, caution, alert, forewarn, notify, let a person know, let a person in on. **tip-off** see TIP³ *n.* 2 above.

tipcat /típkat/ *n.* **1** a game with a short piece of wood tapering at the ends and struck with a stick. **2** this piece of wood.

tipper /típpər/ *n.* (often *attrib.*) a road haulage vehicle that tips at the back to discharge its load.

tippet /típpit/ *n.* **1** a covering of fur etc. for the shoulders formerly worn by women. **2** a similar garment worn as part of some official costumes, esp. by the clergy. **3** *hist.* a long narrow strip of cloth as part of or an attachment to a hood etc. [ME, prob. f. TIP¹]

tipple /típp'l/ *v.* & *n.* ● *v.* **1** *intr.* drink intoxicating liquor habitually. **2** *tr.* drink (liquor) repeatedly in small amounts. ● *n. colloq.* a drink, esp. a strong one. □□ **tippler** *n.* [ME, back-form. f. *tippler*, of unkn. orig.]

■ *v.* **1** see DRINK *v.* 2. ● *n.* see DRINK *n.* 2b.

tipstaff /típstaaf/ *n.* **1** a sheriff's officer. **2** a metal-tipped staff carried as a symbol of office. [contr. of *tipped staff*, i.e. tipped with metal]

tipster /típstər/ *n.* a person who gives tips, esp. about betting at horse-races.

■ tout, barker, touter.

tipsy /típsi/ *adj.* (**tipsier**, **tipsiest**) **1** slightly intoxicated. **2** caused by or showing intoxication (*a tipsy leer*). □ **tipsy-cake** *Brit.* a sponge cake soaked in wine or spirits and served with custard. □□ **tipsily** *adv.* **tipsiness** *n.* [prob. f. TIP² = inclined to lean, unsteady: for *-sy* cf. FLIMSY, TRICKSY]

■ see TIGHT *adj.* 6.

tiptoe /típtō/ *n.*, *v.*, & *adv.* ● *n.* the tips of the toes. ● *v.intr.* (**tiptoes**, **tiptoed**, **tiptoeing**) walk on tiptoe, or very stealthily. ● *adv.* (also **on tiptoe**) with the heels off the ground and the weight on the balls of the feet.

■ *v.* see STEAL *v.* 4a.

tiptop /típtóp/ *adj., adv.,* & *n. colloq.* ● *adj.* & *adv.* highest in excellence; very best. ● *n.* the highest point of excellence.
■ *adj.* see EXCELLENT.

TIR *abbr.* international road transport (esp. with ref. to EC regulations). [F, = *transport international routier*]

tirade /tīráyd, ti-/ *n.* a long vehement denunciation or declamation. [F, = long speech, f. It. *tirata* volley f. *tirare* pull f. Rmc]
■ declamation, harangue, diatribe, philippic, outburst, onslaught, screed, jeremiad, denunciation, rant, stream of abuse, invective.

tirailleur /teéraayőr, tírrəlőr/ *n.* **1** a sharpshooter. **2** a skirmisher. [F f. *tirailler* shoot independently f. *tirer* shoot, draw, f. Rmc]

tire[1] /tīr/ *v.* **1** *tr.* & *intr.* make or grow weary. **2** *tr.* exhaust the patience or interest of; bore. **3** *tr.* (in *passive*; foll. by *of*) have had enough of; be fed up with (*was tired of arguing*). [OE *tēorian*, of unkn. orig.]
■ **1** weary, tire out, fatigue, exhaust, wear out, drain, sap, enervate, debilitate, weaken, take it out of, fag (out). **2** bore, exasperate, weary, irk, irritate, annoy, bother. **3** (*be tired of*) be weary of, have had enough of, be bored with, be exasperated by, be irked *or* irritated *or* annoyed *or* bothered by, be fed up (to here) with, *colloq.* be sick (and tired) of.

tire[2] /tīr/ *n.* **1** a band of metal placed round the rim of a wheel to strengthen it. **2** *US* var. of TYRE. [ME, perh. = archaic *tire* head-dress]

tired /tīrd/ *adj.* **1** weary, exhausted; ready for sleep. **2** (of an idea etc.) hackneyed. ▫▫ **tiredly** *adv.* **tiredness** *n.*
■ **1** exhausted, tired out, worn out, weary, fatigued, enervated, lethargic, sleepy, drowsy, spent, drained, jaded, dog-tired, ready to drop, dead tired, *colloq.* fagged (out), knocked out, all in, done in, *esp. Brit. colloq.* whacked, *US colloq.* bushed, pooped, (dead) beat, tuckered out, *sl.* wiped out, *Austral.* & *NZ sl.* stonkered, *Brit. sl.* knackered. **2** overworked, overused, clichéd, stereotyped, stereotypic(al), hackneyed, unimaginative, trite, stale, worn out, unoriginal, commonplace.
▫▫ **tiredness** see FATIGUE *n.* 1.

tireless /tīrliss/ *adj.* having inexhaustible energy. ▫▫ **tirelessly** *adv.* **tirelessness** *n.*
■ energetic, vital, vigorous, dynamic, spirited, lively, indefatigable, hard-working, industrious, untiring, unflagging, unfaltering, unfailing, persistent, dogged, tenacious, pertinacious, persevering, staunch, sedulous, diligent, unwavering, unswerving, undeviating, steady, steadfast, resolute, determined. ▫▫ **tirelessly** see NON-STOP *adv.* **tirelessness** see PERSEVERANCE.

tiresome /tīrsəm/ *adj.* **1** wearisome, tedious. **2** *colloq.* annoying (*how tiresome of you!*). ▫▫ **tiresomely** *adv.* **tiresomeness** *n.*
■ **1** boring, dull, fatiguing, humdrum, monotonous, flat, tedious, wearisome, tiring, uninteresting, insipid, bland, dry as dust, fatiguing, soporific, hypnotic, *colloq.* deadly. **2** irritating, irksome, vexing, vexatious, annoying, bothersome, exasperating, trying, disagreeable, troublesome, unpleasant, *colloq.* infernal.
▫▫ **tiresomeness** see TEDIUM.

tiro /tīrō/ *n.* (also **tyro**) (*pl.* **-os**) a beginner or novice. [L *tiro*, med.L *tyro*, recruit]

'tis /tiz/ *archaic* it is. [contr.]

tisane /tizán/ *n.* an infusion of dried herbs etc. [F: see PTISAN]

tissue /tíshōō, tíssyōō/ *n.* **1** any of the coherent collections of specialized cells of which animals or plants are made (*muscular tissue*; *nervous tissue*). **2** = *tissue-paper*. **3** a disposable piece of thin soft absorbent paper for wiping, drying, etc. **4** fine woven esp. gauzy fabric. **5** (foll. by *of*) a connected series (*a tissue of lies*). ▫ **tissue-paper** thin soft unsized paper for wrapping or protecting fragile or delicate articles. [ME f. OF *tissu* rich material, past part. of *tistre* f. L *texere* weave]
■ **5** fabric, network, web, interweaving, combination, chain, series, accumulation, conglomeration, concatenation, pile, mass, pack.

Tit. *abbr.* Titus (New Testament).

tit[1] /tit/ *n.* any of various small birds esp. of the family Paridae. [prob. f. Scand.]

tit[2] /tit/ *n.* ▫ **tit for tat** /tat/ blow for blow; retaliation. [= earlier *tip* (TIP[2]) *for tap*]

tit[3] /tit/ *n.* **1** *colloq.* a nipple. **2** *coarse sl.* a woman's breast. ¶ Usually considered a taboo word in sense 2. ▫ **get on a person's tits** *coarse sl.* annoy, irritate. [OE: cf. MLG *titte*]

tit[4] /tit/ *n. coarse sl.* a term of contempt for a person. [20th c.: perh. f. TIT[3]]

Titan /tīt'n/ *n.* **1** (often **titan**) a person of very great strength, intellect, or importance. **2** (in Greek mythology) a member of a family of early gigantic gods, the offspring of Heaven and Earth. [ME f. L f. Gk]

titanic[1] /tītánnik/ *adj.* **1** of or like the Titans. **2** gigantic, colossal. ▫▫ **titanically** *adv.* [Gk *titanikos* (as TITAN)]
■ **2** see GIGANTIC.

titanic[2] /tītánnik, ti-/ *adj. Chem.* of titanium, esp. in quadrivalent form. ▫▫ **titanate** /tītənayt, tít-/ *n.*

titanium /tītáyniəm, ti-/ *n. Chem.* a grey metallic element occurring naturally in many clays etc., and used to make strong light alloys that are resistant to corrosion. ¶ Symb.: **Ti**. ▫ **titanium dioxide** (or **oxide**) a white oxide occurring naturally and used as a white pigment. [Gk (as TITAN) + -IUM, after *uranium*]

titbit /títbit/ *n.* (*US* **tidbit** /tíd-/) **1** a dainty morsel. **2** a piquant item of news etc. [perh. f. dial. *tid* tender + BIT[1]]
■ **1** delicacy, (dainty) morsel, treat, choice item, *bonne bouche*, goody, *US* tidbit.

titch /tich/ *n.* (also **tich**) *colloq.* a small person. [*Tich*, stage name of Harry Relph (d. 1928), Engl. music-hall comedian]

titchy /tíchi/ *adj.* (**titchier**, **titchiest**) *colloq.* very small.
■ see TINY.

titer *US* var. of TITRE.

titfer /títfər/ *n. Brit. sl.* a hat. [abbr. of *tit for tat*, rhyming sl.]

tithe /tīth/ *n.* & *v.* ● *n.* **1** one tenth of the annual produce of land or labour, formerly taken as a tax for the support of the Church and clergy. **2** a tenth part. ● *v.* **1** *tr.* subject to tithes. **2** *intr.* pay tithes. ▫ **tithe barn** a barn built to hold tithes paid in kind. ▫▫ **tithable** *adj.* [OE *teogotha* tenth]

tithing /tīthing/ *n.* **1** the practice of taking or paying a tithe. **2** *hist.* **a** ten householders living near together and collectively responsible for each other's behaviour. **b** the area occupied by them. [OE *tīgething* (as TITHE, -ING[1])]

titi /teétee/ *n.* (*pl.* **titis**) any South American monkey of the genus *Callicebus*. [Tupi]

Titian /tísh'n/ *adj.* (in full **Titian red**) (of hair) bright golden auburn. [name of *Tiziano* Vecelli, It. painter d. 1576]

titillate /títtilayt/ *v.tr.* **1** excite pleasantly. **2** tickle. ▫▫ **titillatingly** *adv.* **titillation** /-láysh'n/ *n.* [L *titillare titillat-*]
■ **1** see EXCITE 1c. ▫▫ **titillation** see THRILL *n.* 1.

titivate /títtivayt/ *v.tr.* (also **tittivate**) *colloq.* **1** adorn, smarten. **2** (often *refl.*) put the finishing touches to. ▫▫ **titivation** /-váysh'n/ *n.* [earlier *tidivate*, perh. f. TIDY after *cultivate*]
■ see BEAUTIFY, SPRUCE[1] *v.*

titlark /títlaark/ *n.* a pipit, esp. the meadow pipit.

title /tīt'l/ *n.* & *v.* ● *n.* **1** the name of a book, work of art, piece of music, etc. **2** the heading of a chapter, poem, document, etc. **3** **a** the contents of the title-page of a book. **b** a book regarded in terms of its title (*published 20 new titles*). **4** a caption or credit in a film, broadcast, etc. **5** a form of nomenclature indicating a person's status (e.g. *professor*, *queen*) or used as a form of address or reference (e.g. *Lord*, *Mr*, *Your Grace*). **6** a championship in sport. **7**

Law **a** the right to ownership of property with or without possession. **b** the facts constituting this. **c** (foll. by *to*) a just or recognized claim. **8** *Eccl.* **a** a fixed sphere of work and source of income as a condition for ordination. **b** a parish church in Rome under a cardinal. ● *v.tr.* give a title to. □ **title-deed** a legal instrument as evidence of a right, esp. to property. **title-page** a page at the beginning of a book giving the title and particulars of authorship etc. **title role** the part in a play etc. that gives it its name (e.g. Othello). [ME f. OF f. L *titulus* placard, title]

■ *n.* **1** name. **2** caption, inscription, headline, head, heading, subtitle, legend, subhead, subheading, rubric. **4** caption, credit. **5** designation, epithet, form of address; office, position, status, rank, *formal* appellation. **6** championship, crown. **7 a** right, interest, privilege, entitlement, ownership, possession, tenure. **b** (title-)deed, documentation of ownership. **c** (*title to*) claim *or* right to. ● *v.* name, call, designate, style, label, term, christen, baptize, nickname, denominate, tag, dub, *archaic* entitle. □ **title-deed** see DEED *n.* 4. **title role** see PROTAGONIST 1, 2.

titled /tī́t'ld/ *adj.* having a title of nobility or rank.

titling[1] /tī́tling/ *n.* the impressing of a title in gold leaf etc. on the cover of a book.

titling[2] /títling/ *n.* **1** a titlark. **2** a titmouse.

titmouse /títmowss/ *n.* (*pl.* **titmice** /-mīss/) any of various small tits, esp. of the genus *Parus.* [ME *titmōse* f. TIT[1] + OE *māse* titmouse, assim. to MOUSE]

titrate /tī́trayt, tít-/ *v.tr. Chem.* ascertain the amount of a constituent in (a solution) by measuring the volume of a known concentration of reagent required to complete the reaction. □□ **titratable** *adj.* **titration** /-tráysh'n/ *n.*

titre /tī́tər/ *n.* (*US* **titer**) *Chem.* the strength of a solution or the quantity of a constituent as determined by titration. [F, =TITLE]

titter /títtər/ *v.* & *n.* ● *v.intr.* laugh in a furtive or restrained way; giggle. ● *n.* a furtive or restrained laugh. □□ **titterer** *n.* **titteringly** *adv.* [imit.]

■ *v.* chuckle, snicker, chortle, giggle, snigger; laugh. ● *n.* chuckle, snicker, giggle, (suppressed) laugh *or* laughter, chortle, snigger.

tittivate var. of TITIVATE.

tittle /títt'l/ *n.* **1** a small written or printed stroke or dot. **2** a particle; a whit (esp. in *not one jot or tittle*). [ME f. L (as TITLE)]

tittlebat /títt'lbat/ *n. Brit.* a stickleback. [fanciful var.]

tittle-tattle /títt'ltatt'l/ *n.* & *v.* ● *n.* petty gossip. ● *v.intr.* gossip, chatter. [redupl. of TATTLE]

■ *n.* talk, small talk; see also CHATTER *n.* ● *v.* see BABBLE *v.* 1a, b.

tittup /títtəp/ *v.* & *n.* ● *v.intr.* (**tittuped, tittuping** or **tittupped, tittupping**) go about friskily or jerkily; bob up and down; canter. ● *n.* such a gait or movement. [perh. imit. of hoof-beats]

titty /títti/ *n.* (*pl.* **-ies**) *sl.* = TIT[3] (esp. as a child's term).

titubation /tityoobáysh'n/ *n. Med.* unsteadiness esp. as caused by nervous disease. [L *titubatio* f. *titubare* totter]

titular /tityoolər/ *adj.* & *n.* ● *adj.* **1** of or relating to a title (*the book's titular hero*). **2** existing, or being what is specified, in name or title only (*titular ruler; titular sovereignty*). ● *n.* **1** the holder of an office etc. esp. a benefice, without the corresponding functions or obligations. **2** a titular saint. □ **titular bishop** a bishop, esp. in a non-Christian country, with a see named after a Christian see no longer in existence. **titular saint** the patron saint of a particular church. □□ **titularly** *adv.* [F *titulaire* or mod.L *titularis* f. *titulus* TITLE]

■ *adj.* **2** nominal, so-called, token, putative, theoretical.

tizzy /tízzi/ *n.* (*pl.* **-ies**) (also **tizz, tiz**) *colloq.* a state of nervous agitation (*in a tizzy*). [20th c.: orig. unkn.]

■ see STEW[1] *n.* 2, FLAP *n.* 3.

T-junction /teéjungksh'n/ *n.* a road junction at which one road joins another at right angles without crossing it.

TKO *abbr. Boxing* technical knockout.

Tl *symb. Chem.* the element thallium.

TLC *abbr. colloq.* tender loving care.

TLS *abbr. Times Literary Supplement.*

TM *abbr.* Transcendental Meditation.

Tm *symb. Chem.* the element thulium.

tmesis /tmeéssiss/ *n.* (*pl.* **tmeses** /-seez/) *Gram.* the separation of parts of a compound word by an intervening word or words (esp. in colloq. speech, e.g. *can't find it any-blooming-where*). [Gk *tmēsis* cutting f. *temnō* cut]

TN *abbr. US* Tennessee (in official postal use).

tn *abbr.* **1** *US* ton(s). **2** town.

TNT *abbr.* trinitrotoluene, a high explosive formed from toluene by substitution of three hydrogen atoms with nitro groups.

to /tə, *before a vowel* tŏŏ, *emphat.* tōō/ *prep.* & *adv.* ● *prep.* **1** introducing a noun: **a** expressing what is reached, approached, or touched (*fell to the ground; went to Paris; put her face to the window; five minutes to six*). **b** expressing what is aimed at: often introducing the indirect object of a verb (*throw it to me; explained the problem to them*). **c** as far as; up to (*went on to the end; have to stay from Tuesday to Friday*). **d** to the extent of (*were all drunk to a man; was starved to death*). **e** expressing what is followed (*according to instructions; made to order*). **f** expressing what is considered or affected (*am used to that; that is nothing to me*). **g** expressing what is caused or produced (*turn to stone; tear to shreds*). **h** expressing what is compared (*nothing to what it once was; comparable to any other; equal to the occasion; won by three goals to two*). **i** expressing what is increased (*add it to mine*). **j** expressing what is involved or composed as specified (*there is nothing to it; more to him than meets the eye*). **k** expressing the substance of a debit entry in accounting (*to four chairs, sixty pounds*). **l** *archaic* for; by way of (*took her to wife*). **2** introducing the infinitive: **a** as a verbal noun (*to get there is the priority*). **b** expressing purpose, consequence, or cause (*we eat to live; left him to starve; am sorry to hear that*). **c** as a substitute for *to* + infinitive (*wanted to come but was unable to*). ● *adv.* **1** in the normal or required position or condition (*come to; heave to*). **2** (of a door) in a nearly closed position. □ **to and fro 1** backwards and forwards. **2** repeatedly between the same points. [OE *tō* (adv. & prep.) f. WG]

toad /tōd/ *n.* **1** any froglike amphibian of the family Bufonidae, esp. of the genus *Bufo*, breeding in water but living chiefly on land. **2** any of various similar amphibians including the Surinam toad. **3** a repulsive or detestable person. □ **toad-eater** *archaic* a toady. **toad-in-the-hole** *Brit.* sausages or other meat baked in batter. □□ **toadish** *adj.* [OE *tādige, tādde, tāda*, of unkn. orig.]

toadfish /tṓdfish/ *n.* any marine fish of the family Batrachoididae, with a large head and wide mouth, making grunting noises by vibrating the walls of its swim-bladder.

toadflax /tṓdflaks/ *n.* **1** any plant of the genus *Linaria* or *Chaenorrhinum*, with flaxlike leaves and spurred yellow or purple flowers. **2** a related plant, *Cymbalaria muralis*, with lilac flowers and ivy-shaped leaves.

toadstone /tṓdstōn/ *n.* a stone, sometimes precious, supposed to resemble or to have been formed in the body of a toad, formerly used as an amulet etc.

toadstool /tṓdstōōl/ *n.* the spore-bearing structure of various fungi, usu. poisonous, with a round top and slender stalk.

toady /tṓdi/ *n.* & *v.* ● *n.* (*pl.* **-ies**) a sycophant; an obsequious hanger-on. ● *v.tr.* & (foll. by *to*) *intr.* (**-ies, -ied**) behave servilely to; fawn upon. □□ **toadyish** *adj.* **toadyism** *n.* [contr. of *toad-eater*, a charlatan's attendant who ate toads (regarded as poisonous)]

■ *n.* see FLUNKEY 2. ● *v.* see TRUCKLE *v.* □□ **toadyish** see OBSEQUIOUS, SERVILE. **toadyism** see *servility* (SERVILE).

toast /tōst/ *n.* & *v.* ● *n.* **1** bread in slices browned on both sides by radiant heat. **2 a** a person (orig. esp. a woman) or thing in whose honour a company is requested to drink. **b** a call to drink or an instance of drinking in this way. ● *v.* **1** *tr.* cook or brown (bread, a teacake, cheese, etc.) by radiant heat. **2** *intr.* (of bread etc.) become brown in this way. **3** *tr.* warm (one's feet, oneself, etc.) at a fire etc. **4** *tr.* drink to the health or in honour of (a person or thing). □ **have a person on toast** *colloq.* be in a position to deal with a person as one wishes. **toasting-fork** a long-handled fork for making toast before a fire. **toast rack** a rack for holding slices of toast at table. [ME (orig. as verb) f. OF *toster* roast, ult. f. L *torrēre tost-* parch: sense 2 of the noun reflects the notion that a woman's name flavours the drink as spiced toast would]

■ *n.* **2 a** heroine, hero, favourite, darling, idol. **b** health, pledge. ● *v.* **1** brown, grill. **4** pay tribute to, salute, drink (a toast) to, drink the health of, raise one's glass to, pledge.

toaster /tṓstər/ *n.* an electrical device for making toast.

toastmaster /tṓstmaastər/ *n.* (*fem.* **toastmistress** /-mistriss/) an official responsible for announcing toasts at a public occasion.

tobacco /təbákkō/ *n.* (*pl.* **-os**) **1** (in full **tobacco-plant**) any plant of the genus *Nicotiana*, of American origin, with narcotic leaves used for smoking, chewing, or snuff. **2** its leaves, esp. as prepared for smoking. □ **tobacco mosaic virus** a virus that causes mosaic disease in tobacco, much used in biochemical research. **tobacco-pipe** see PIPE *n.* 2. **tobacco-stopper** an instrument for pressing down the tobacco in a pipe. [Sp. *tabaco*, of Amer. Ind. orig.]

tobacconist /təbákkənist/ *n.* a retail dealer in tobacco and cigarettes etc.

toboggan /təbóggən/ *n.* & *v.* ● *n.* a long light narrow sledge for sliding downhill esp. over compacted snow or ice. ● *v.intr.* ride on a toboggan. □□ **tobogganer** *n.* **tobogganing** *n.* **tobogganist** *n.* [Can. F *tabaganne* f. Algonquian]

toby jug /tṓbi/ *n.* a jug or mug for ale etc., usu. in the form of a stout old man wearing a three-cornered hat. [familiar form of the name *Tobias*]

toccata /təkaátə/ *n.* a musical composition for a keyboard instrument designed to exhibit the performer's touch and technique. [It., fem. past part. of *toccare* touch]

Toc H /tokáych/ *n. Brit.* a society, orig. of ex-servicemen and -women, founded after the war of 1914–18 for promoting Christian fellowship and social service. [*toc* (former telegraphy code for *T*) + *H*, for *T*albot *H*ouse, a soldier's club established in Belgium in 1915]

Tocharian /təkáiriən/ *n.* & *adj.* ● *n.* **1** an extinct Indo-European language of a central Asian people in the first millennium AD. **2** a member of the people speaking this language. ● *adj.* of or in this language. [F *tocharien* f. L *Tochari* f. Gk *Tokharoi* a Scythian tribe]

tocopherol /tŏkŏfeerol/ *n.* any of several closely related vitamins, found in wheat-germ oil, egg yolk, and leafy vegetables, and important in the stabilization of cell membranes etc. Also called *vitamin E.* [Gk *tokos* offspring + *pherō* bear + -OL[1]]

tocsin /tóksin/ *n.* an alarm bell or signal. [F f. OF *touquesain*, *toquassen* f. Prov. *tocasenh* f. *tocar* TOUCH + *senh* signal-bell]

■ see ALARM *n.* 2a.

tod /tod/ *n. Brit. sl.* □ **on one's tod** alone; on one's own. [20th c.: perh. f. rhyming sl. *on one's Tod Sloan* (name of a jockey)]

today /tədáy/ *adv.* & *n.* ● *adv.* **1** on or in the course of this present day (*shall we go today?*). **2** nowadays, in modern times. ● *n.* **1** this present day (*today is my birthday*). **2** modern times. □ **today week** (or **fortnight** etc.) a week (or fortnight etc.) from today. [OE *tō dæg* on (this) day (as TO, DAY)]

■ *adv.* **2** see NOW *adv.* 1, 4.

toddle /tódd'l/ *v.* & *n.* ● *v.intr.* **1** walk with short unsteady steps like those of a small child. **2** *colloq.* **a** (often foll. by *round*, *to*, etc.) take a casual or leisurely walk. **b** (usu. foll. by *off*) depart. ● *n.* **1** a toddling walk. **2** *colloq.* a stroll or short walk. [16th-c. *todle* (Sc. & N.Engl.), of unkn. orig.]

■ *v.* **1** see WADDLE *v.* **2 a** see STROLL *v.* **b** see DEPART 1. ● *n.* **2** see STROLL *n.*

toddler /tódlər/ *n.* a child who is just beginning to walk. □□ **toddlerhood** *n.*

■ see TOT[1] 1.

toddy /tóddi/ *n.* (*pl.* **-ies**) **1** a drink of spirits with hot water and sugar or spices. **2** the sap of some kinds of palm, fermented to produce arrack. [Hind. *tāṛī* f. *tār* palm f. Skr. *tâla* palmyra]

to-do /tədōō/ *n.* a commotion or fuss. [*to do* as in *what's to do* (= to be done)]

■ see FUSS *n.* 1, 2a.

tody /tṓdi/ *n.* (*pl.* **-ies**) any small insect-eating West Indian bird of the genus *Todus*, related to the kingfisher. [F *todier* f. L *todus*, a small bird]

toe /tō/ *n.* & *v.* ● *n.* **1** any of the five terminal projections of the foot. **2** the corresponding part of an animal. **3** the part of an item of footwear that covers the toes. **4** the lower end or tip of an implement etc. **5** *Archit.* a projection from the foot of a buttress etc. to give stability. **6** *Austral.* & *NZ sl.* speed, energy. ● *v.* (**toes, toed, toeing**) **1** *tr.* touch (a starting-line etc.) with the toes before starting a race. **2** *tr.* **a** mend the toe of (a sock etc.). **b** provide with a toe. **3** *intr.* (foll. by *in, out*) **a** walk with the toes pointed in (or out). **b** (of a pair of wheels) converge (or diverge) slightly at the front. **4** *tr. Golf* strike (the ball) with a part of the club too near the toe. □ **on one's toes** alert, eager. **toe-clip** a clip on a bicycle-pedal to prevent the foot from slipping. **toe-hold** **1** a small foothold. **2** a small beginning or advantage. **toe the line** conform to a general policy or principle, esp. unwillingly or under pressure. **turn up one's toes** *colloq.* die. □□ **toed** *adj.* (also in *comb.*). **toeless** *adj.* [OE *tā* f. Gmc]

■ *n.* **6** see ENERGY 1, PACE[1] *n.* 2. □ **on one's toes** see ALERT *adj.* 1. **toe-hold 2** see OPENING *n.* 2. **turn up one's toes** see DIE[1] 1.

toecap /tṓkap/ *n.* the (usu. strengthened) outer covering of the toe of a boot or shoe.

toenail /tṓnayl/ *n.* **1** the nail at the tip of each toe. **2** a nail driven obliquely through the end of a board etc.

toerag /tṓrag/ *n. Brit. sl.* a term of contempt for a person. [earlier = tramp, vagrant, f. the rag wrapped round the foot in place of a sock]

■ see STINKER.

toey /tṓ-i/ *adj. Austral. sl.* restless, nervous, touchy.

toff /tof/ *n.* & *v. Brit. sl.* ● *n.* a distinguished or well-dressed person; a dandy. ● *v.tr.* (foll. by *up*) dress up smartly. [perh. a perversion of *tuft* = titled undergraduate (from the gold tassel formerly worn on the cap)]

■ *n.* see DANDY *n.*

toffee /tóffi/ *n.* (also **toffy**) (*pl.* **toffees** or **toffies**) **1** a kind of firm or hard sweet softening when sucked or chewed, made by boiling sugar, butter, etc. **2** *Brit.* a small piece of this. □ **for toffee** *sl.* (prec. by *can't* etc.) (denoting incompetence) at all (*they couldn't sing for toffee*). **toffee-apple** an apple with a thin coating of toffee. **toffee-nosed** esp. *Brit. sl.* snobbish, pretentious. [earlier TAFFY]

■ □ **toffee-nosed** see *snobbish* (SNOB).

toft /toft/ *n. Brit.* **1** a homestead. **2** land once occupied by this. [OE f. ON *topt*]

tofu /tṓfōō/ *n.* (esp. in China and Japan) a curd made from mashed soya beans. [Jap. *tōfu* f. Chin., = rotten beans]

tog[1] /tog/ *n.* & *v. colloq.* ● *n.* (usu. in *pl.*) **1** an item of clothing. **2** *Austral.* & *NZ colloq.* a swimming costume. ● *v.tr.* & *intr.* (**togged, togging**) (foll. by *out, up*) dress, esp. elaborately. [app. abbr. of 16th-c. cant *togeman(s)*, *togman*, f. F *toge* or L *toga*: see TOGA]

■ *n.* **1** (*togs*) see CLOTHES. ● *v.* see CLOTHE 1.

tog[2] /tog/ *n.* a unit of thermal resistance used to express the insulating properties of clothes and quilts. [arbitrary, prob. f. TOG[1]]

toga /tṓgə/ *n. hist.* an ancient Roman citizen's loose flowing outer garment. ▫▫ **togaed** *adj.* (also **toga'd**). [L, rel. to *tegere* cover]

together /təgéthər/ *adv.* & *adj.* ● *adv.* **1** in company or conjunction (*walking together; built it together; were at school together*). **2** simultaneously; at the same time (*both shouted together*). **3** one with another (*were talking together*). **4** into conjunction; so as to unite (*tied them together; put two and two together*). **5** into company or companionship (*came together in friendship*). **6** uninterruptedly (*could talk for hours together*). ● *adj. colloq.* well organized or controlled. ▫ **together with** as well as; and also. [OE *tōgædere* f. TO + *gædre* together: cf. GATHER]

■ *adv.* **2** see *at once* 2 (ONCE), *at one time* 2 (TIME). ● *adj.* see POISED 1. ▫ **together with** see PLUS *prep.*

togetherness /təgéthərniss/ *n.* **1** the condition of being together. **2** a feeling of comfort from being together.

toggery /tóggəri/ *n. colloq.* clothes, togs.

toggle /tógg'l/ *n.* & *v.* ● *n.* **1** a device for fastening (esp. a garment), consisting of a crosspiece which can pass through a hole or loop in one position but not in another. **2** a pin or other crosspiece put through the eye of a rope, a link of a chain, etc., to keep it in place. **3** a pivoted barb on a harpoon. **4** *Computing* a switch action that is operated the same way but with opposite effect on successive occasions. ● *v.tr.* provide or fasten with a toggle. ▫ **toggle joint** a device for exerting pressure along two jointed rods by applying a transverse force at the joint. **toggle switch** an electric switch with a projecting lever to be moved usu. up and down. [18th-c. Naut.: orig. unkn.]

Togolese /tṓgəléez/ *adj.* & *n.* ● *adj.* of or relating to Togo in W. Africa. ● *n.* (*pl.* same) **1** a native or national of Togo. **2** a person of Togolese descent.

toil /toyl/ *v.* & *n.* ● *v.intr.* **1** work laboriously or incessantly. **2** make slow painful progress (*toiled along the path*). ● *n.* prolonged or intensive labour; drudgery. ▫ **toil-worn** worn or worn out by toil. ▫▫ **toiler** *n.* [ME f. AF *toiler* (v.), *toil* (n.), dispute, OF *tooilier*, *tooil*, f. L *tudiculare* stir about f. *tudicula* machine for bruising olives, rel. to *tundere* beat]

■ *v.* **1** see LABOUR *v.* 1, 2. **2** see LABOUR *v.* 5. ● *n.* see LABOUR *n.* 1. ▫ **toil-worn** see HAGGARD *adj.*

toile /twaal/ *n.* **1** cloth esp. for garments. **2** a garment reproduced in muslin or other cheap material for fitting or for making copies. [F *toile* cloth f. L *tela* web]

toilet /tóylit/ *n.* **1** = LAVATORY. **2** the process of washing oneself, dressing, etc. (*make one's toilet*). **3** the cleansing of part of the body after an operation or at the time of childbirth. ▫ **toilet paper** (or **tissue**) paper for cleaning oneself after excreting. **toilet roll** a roll of toilet paper. **toilet set** a set of hairbrushes, combs, etc. **toilet soap** soap for washing oneself. **toilet table** a dressing-table usu. with a mirror. **toilet-train** cause (a young child) to undergo toilet-training. **toilet-training** the training of a young child to use the lavatory. **toilet water** a dilute form of perfume used after washing. [F *toilette* cloth, wrapper, dimin. f. *toile*: see TOILE]

■ **1** lavatory, (water-)closet, WC, men's (room), ladies' room, powder-room, (public) convenience, facility *or* facilities, ablutions, urinal, *pissoir*; *esp. Mil.* latrine, *Naut.* head, *Brit.* the Ladies('), *esp. US* bathroom, rest room, *US* washroom, outhouse, *US or archaic* privy, *Brit. colloq.* loo, the Gents, *Brit. euphem.* cloakroom, *Austral. sl.* toot, *esp. Austral.* & *NZ sl.* dunny, *Brit. sl.* bog, *US sl.* john, can. **2** grooming, dressing, making up, toilette. ▫ **toilet water** see PERFUME *n.* 2.

toiletry /tóylitri/ *n.* (*pl.* **-ies**) (usu. in *pl.*) any of various articles or cosmetics used in washing, dressing, etc.

toilette /twaalét/ *n.* = TOILET 2. [F: see TOILET]

toils /toylz/ *n.pl.* a net or snare. [pl. of *toil* f. OF *toile* cloth f. L *tela* web]

toilsome /tóylsəm/ *adj.* involving toil; laborious. ▫▫ **toilsomely** *adv.* **toilsomeness** *n.*

■ arduous, laborious, tough, hard, difficult, strenuous, stiff, burdensome, onerous, back-breaking, exhausting, fatiguing, tiring, enervating, wearying, draining.

toing and froing /tóoing ənd frṓing/ *n.* constant movement to and fro; bustle; dispersed activity. [TO *adv.* + FRO + -ING[1]]

■ see ACTIVITY 1.

Tokay /təkáy/ *n.* **1** a sweet aromatic wine made near Tokaj in Hungary. **2** a similar wine produced elsewhere.

token /tṓkən/ *n.* **1** a thing serving as a symbol, reminder, or distinctive mark of something (*as a token of affection; in token of my esteem*). **2** a thing serving as evidence of authenticity or as a guarantee. **3** a voucher exchangeable for goods (often of a specified kind), given as a gift. **4** anything used to represent something else, esp. a metal disc etc. used instead of money in coin-operated machines etc. **5** (*attrib.*) **a** nominal or perfunctory (*token effort*). **b** conducted briefly to demonstrate strength of feeling (*token resistance; token strike*). **c** serving to acknowledge a principle only (*token payment*). **d** chosen by way of tokenism to represent a particular group (*the token woman on the committee*). ▫ **by this** (or **the same**) **token 1** similarly. **2** moreover. **token money** coins having a higher face value than their worth as metal. **token vote** a parliamentary vote of money, the stipulated amount of which is not meant to be binding. [OE *tāc(e)n* f. Gmc, rel. to TEACH]

■ **1, 2** symbol, sign, mark, marker, badge, emblem, indication, proof, evidence; souvenir, memento, keepsake, reminder, remembrance. **3** voucher, coupon. **4** coin, disc, counter. **5** (*attrib.*) **a, b** superficial, cosmetic, surface, perfunctory, minimal, slight, nominal. **d** symbolic, emblematic, representative.

tokenism /tṓkəniz'm/ *n.* **1** esp. *Polit.* the principle or practice of granting minimum concessions, esp. to appease radical demands etc. (cf. TOKEN 5d). **2** making only a token effort.

tolbooth var. of TOLLBOOTH.

told *past* and *past part.* of TELL[1].

Toledo /təléedō/ *n.* (*pl.* **-os**) a fine sword or sword-blade made in Toledo in Spain.

tolerable /tóllərəb'l/ *adj.* **1** able to be endured. **2** fairly good; mediocre. ▫▫ **tolerability** /-billiti/ *n.* **tolerableness** *n.* **tolerably** *adv.* [ME f. OF f. L *tolerabilis* (as TOLERATE)]

■ **1** bearable, supportable, allowable, endurable, permissible, acceptable, sufferable. **2** acceptable, unexceptional, common, fair, fair to middling, middling, *comme ci, comme ça*, ordinary, average, so so, mediocre, adequate, run-of-the-mill, passable, indifferent, fairly good, *colloq.* common or garden, OK, okay, not (too) bad, pretty good. ▫▫ **tolerably** see FAIRLY 2.

tolerance /tóllərənss/ *n.* **1** a willingness or ability to tolerate; forbearance. **2** the capacity to tolerate. **3** an allowable variation in any measurable property. **4** the ability to tolerate the effects of a drug etc. after continued use. [ME f. OF f. L *tolerantia* (as TOLERATE)]

■ **1** open-mindedness, toleration, forbearance, broad-mindedness, permissiveness, magnanimity, lenience, indulgence, sufferance, acceptance, patience, freedom from bigotry *or* prejudice, understanding. **3** play, clearance, allowance, variation. **4** toleration, resistance, endurance, imperviousness; immunity, insensitivity.

tolerant /tóllərənt/ *adj.* **1** disposed or accustomed to tolerate others or their acts or opinions. **2** (foll. by *of*) enduring or patient. ▫▫ **tolerantly** *adv.* [F *tolérant* f. L *tolerare* (as TOLERATE)]

■ **1** open-minded, objective, forbearing, forgiving, unprejudiced, unbigoted, dispassionate, broad-minded, indulgent, lenient, magnanimous, patient, generous, charitable, catholic, latitudinarian, permissive, liberal, easygoing, big-hearted, fair, even-handed, understanding, considerate.

tolerate /tóllərayt/ *v.tr.* **1** allow the existence or occurrence of without authoritative interference. **2** leave unmolested. **3**

endure or permit, esp. with forbearance. **4** sustain or endure (suffering etc.). **5** be capable of continued subjection to (a drug, radiation, etc.) without harm. **6** find or treat as endurable. ▫▫ **tolerator** *n.* [L *tolerare tolerat-* endure]

▪ **1, 3, 6** stand (for), allow, permit, bear, endure, suffer, countenance, accept, abide, admit, sanction, condone, swallow, stomach, turn a blind eye to, put up with, *colloq.* stick, lump, *Brit. colloq.* wear, *literary* brook, *sl.* hack. **4, 5** bear, stand, submit to, sustain, endure, weather, take, accept, put up with, undergo.

toleration /tóllәráysh'n/ *n.* the process or practice of tolerating, esp. the allowing of differences in religious opinion without discrimination. [F *tolération* f. L *toleratio* (as TOLERATE)]

▪ see TOLERANCE 1, 4.

toll[1] /tōl/ *n.* **1** a charge payable for permission to pass a barrier or use a bridge or road etc. **2** the cost or damage caused by a disaster, battle, etc., or incurred in an achievement (*death toll*). **3** *US* a charge for a long distance telephone call. ▫ **take its toll** be accompanied by loss or injury etc. **toll-bridge** a bridge at which a toll is charged. **toll-gate** a gate preventing passage until a toll is paid. **toll-house** a house at a toll-gate or -bridge, used by a toll-collector. **toll-road** a road maintained by the tolls collected on it. [OE f. med.L *toloneum* f. LL *teloneum* f. Gk *telōnion* toll-house f. *telos* tax]

▪ **1** charge, fee, dues, assessment, tariff; excise, duty, impost, levy, tribute, tax. **2** loss, penalty, cost, damage(s); exaction.

toll[2] /tōl/ *v.* & *n.* ● *v.* **1 a** *intr.* (of a bell) sound with a slow uniform succession of strokes. **b** *tr.* ring (a bell) in this way. **c** *tr.* (of a bell) announce or mark (a death etc.) in this way. **2** *tr.* strike (the hour). ● *n.* **1** the act of tolling. **2** a stroke of a bell. [ME, special use of (now dial.) *toll* entice, pull, f. an OE root *-tyllan* (recorded in *fortyllan* seduce)]

▪ *v.* ring, peal, chime, strike, sound, knell. ● *n.* ring, peal, chime, striking, sound, knell.

tollbooth /tṓlbōōth, -bōōth/ *n.* (also **tolbooth**) **1** a booth at the roadside from which tolls are collected. **2** *Sc. archaic* a town hall. **3** *Sc. archaic* a town jail.

Toltec /tóltek/ *n.* **1** a member of an American Indian people that flourished in Mexico before the Aztecs. **2** the language of this people. ▫▫ **Toltecan** *adj.* [Amer. Ind.]

tolu /tәlṓō, tṓlōō/ *n.* a fragrant brown balsam obtained from either of two South American trees, *Myroxylon balsamum* or *M. toluifera*, and used in perfumery and medicine. [Santiago de *Tolu* in Colombia]

toluene /tólyoo-een/ *n.* a colourless aromatic liquid hydrocarbon derivative of benzene, orig. obtained from tolu, used in the manufacture of explosives etc. Also called *methyl benzene*. ▫▫ **toluic** *adj.* **toluol** *n.* [TOLU + -ENE]

tom /tom/ *n.* a male of various animals, esp. (in full **tom-cat**) a male cat. [abbr. of the name *Thomas*]

tomahawk /tómmәhawk/ *n.* & *v.* ● *n.* **1** a N. American Indian war-axe with a stone or iron head. **2** *Austral.* a hatchet. ● *v.tr.* strike, cut, or kill with a tomahawk. [Renape *tämähāk* f. *tämäham* he etc. cuts]

tomato /tәmaátō/ *n.* (*pl.* **-oes**) **1** a glossy red or yellow pulpy edible fruit. **2** a solanaceous plant, *Lycopersicon esculentum*, bearing this. ▫▫ **tomatoey** *adj.* [17th-c. *tomate*, = F or Sp. & Port., f. Mex. *tomatl*]

tomb /tōōm/ *n.* **1** a large esp. underground vault for the burial of the dead. **2** an enclosure cut in the earth or in rock to receive a dead body. **3** a sepulchral monument. **4** (prec. by *the*) the state of death. [ME *t(o)umbe* f. AF *tumbe*, OF *tombe* f. LL *tumba* f. Gk *tumbos*]

▪ **1, 2** sepulchre, crypt, vault, grave, catacomb, burial-chamber, charnel-house, final *or* last resting-place. **3** monument, mausoleum, pyramid, dolmen, cromlech.

tombac /tómbak/ *n.* an alloy of copper and zinc used esp. as material for cheap jewellery. [F f. Malay *tambāga* copper]

tombola /tombṓlә/ *n. Brit.* a kind of lottery with tickets usu. drawn from a turning drum-shaped container, esp. at a fête or fair. [F *tombola* or It. f. *tombolare* tumble]

tombolo /tómbәlō/ *n.* (*pl.* **-os**) a spit joining an island to the mainland. [It., = sand-dune]

tomboy /tómboy/ *n.* a girl who behaves in a rough boyish way. ▫▫ **tomboyish** *adj.* **tomboyishness** *n.*

tombstone /tṓōmstōn/ *n.* a stone standing or laid over a grave, usu. with an epitaph.

▪ gravestone, headstone, tablet, marker, monument, cenotaph.

Tom Collins /tom kóllinz/ *n.* an iced cocktail of gin with soda, lemon or lime juice, and sugar. [20th c.: orig. unkn.]

Tom, Dick, and Harry /tóm dik әnd hárri/ *n.* (usu. prec. by *any*, *every*) usu. *derog.* ordinary people taken at random.

tome /tōm/ *n.* a large heavy book or volume. [F f. L *tomus* f. Gk *tomos* section, volume f. *temnō* cut]

▪ see BOOK *n.* 1.

-tome /tōm/ *comb. form* forming nouns meaning: **1** an instrument for cutting (*microtome*). **2** a section or segment. [Gk *tomē* a cutting, *-tomos* -cutting, f. *temnō* cut]

tomentum /tәméntәm/ *n.* (*pl.* **tomenta** /-tә/) **1** *Bot.* matted woolly down on stems and leaves. **2** *Anat.* the tufted inner surface of the pia mater in the brain. ▫▫ **tomentose** /tәméntōss/ *adj.* **tomentous** *adj.* [L, = cushion-stuffing]

tomfool /tómfṓōl/ *n.* **1** a foolish person. **2** (*attrib.*) silly, foolish (*a tomfool idea*).

tomfoolery /tómfṓōlәri/ *n.* (*pl.* **-ies**) **1** foolish behaviour; nonsense. **2** an instance of this.

▪ see NONSENSE.

Tommy /tómmi/ *n.* (*pl.* **-ies**) *colloq.* a British private soldier. [*Tommy* (*Thomas*) *Atkins*, a name used in specimens of completed official forms]

tommy-bar /tómmibaar/ *n.* a short bar for use with a box spanner.

tommy-gun /tómmigun/ *n.* a type of sub-machine-gun. [J. T. *Thompson*, US Army officer d. 1940, its co-inventor]

tommy-rot /tómmirot/ *n. sl.* nonsense.

▪ see RUBBISH *n.* 3.

tomogram /tómmәgram/ *n.* a record obtained by tomography.

tomography /tәmógrәfi/ *n.* a method of radiography displaying details in a selected plane within the body. [Gk *tomē* a cutting + -GRAPHY]

tomorrow /tәmórrō/ *adv.* & *n.* ● *adv.* **1** on the day after today. **2** at some future time. ● *n.* **1** the day after today. **2** the near future. ▫ **tomorrow morning** (or **afternoon** etc.) in the morning (or afternoon etc.) of tomorrow. **tomorrow week** a week from tomorrow. [TO + MORROW: cf. TODAY]

▪ *n.* **2** future, days *or* time to come.

tompion var. of TAMPION.

Tom Thumb /tom thúm/ *n.* **1** a dwarf or midget. **2** a dwarf variety of various plants. [the name of a tiny person in fairy stories]

tomtit /tómtit/ *n.* a tit, esp. a blue tit.

tom-tom /tómtom/ *n.* **1** a primitive drum beaten with the hands. **2** a tall drum beaten with the hands and used in jazz bands etc. [Hindi *tamtam*, imit.]

-tomy /tәmi/ *comb. form* forming nouns denoting cutting, esp. in surgery (*laparotomy*). [Gk *-tomia* cutting f. *temnō* cut]

ton[1] /tun/ *n.* **1** (in full **long ton**) a unit of weight equal to 2,240 lb. avoirdupois (1016.05 kg). **2** (in full **short ton**) a unit of weight equal to 2,000 lb. avoirdupois (907.19 kg). **3** (in full **metric ton**) = TONNE. **4 a** (in full **displacement ton**) a unit of measurement of a ship's weight or volume in terms of its displacement of water with the loadline just immersed, equal to 2,240 lb. or 35 cu. ft. (0.99 cubic metres). **b** (in full **freight ton**) a unit of weight or volume of cargo, equal to a metric ton (1,000 kg) or 40 cu. ft. **5 a** (in full **gross ton**) a unit of gross internal capacity, equal to 100 cu. ft. (2.83 cubic metres). **b** (in full **net** or **register ton**) an equivalent unit of net internal capacity. **6** a unit of

refrigerating power able to freeze 2,000 lb. of ice at 0°C in 24 hours. **7** a measure of capacity for various materials, esp. 40 cu. ft. of timber. **8** (usu. in *pl.*) *colloq.* a large number or amount (*tons of money*). **9** esp. *Brit. sl.* **a** a speed of 100 m.p.h. **b** a sum of £100. **c** a score of 100. □ **ton-mile** one ton of goods carried one mile, as a unit of traffic. **ton-up** *Brit. sl. n.* a speed of 100 m.p.h. ● *attrib.adj.* **1** (of a motor cyclist) achieving this, esp. habitually and recklessly (*ton-up kid*). **2** fond or capable of travelling at high speed. **weigh a ton** *colloq.* be very heavy. [orig. the same word as TUN: differentiated in the 17th c.]
■ **8** see HEAP *n.* 2, MANY *n.* 1.

ton[2] /toN/ *n.* **1** a prevailing mode or fashion. **2** fashionable society. [F]

tonal /tṓn'l/ *adj.* **1** of or relating to tone or tonality. **2** (of a fugue etc.) having repetitions of the subject at different pitches in the same key. □□ **tonally** *adv.* [med.L *tonalis* (as TONE)]

tonality /tənálliti/ *n.* (*pl.* **-ies**) **1** *Mus.* **a** the relationship between the tones of a musical scale. **b** the observance of a single tonic key as the basis of a composition. **2** the tone or colour scheme of a picture. **3** *Linguistics* the differentiation of words, syllables, etc. by a change of vocal pitch.

tondo /tóndō/ *n.* (*pl.* **tondi** /-di/) a circular painting or relief. [It., = round (plate), f. *rotondo* f. L *rotundus* round]

tone /tōn/ *n.* & *v.* ● *n.* **1** a musical or vocal sound, esp. with reference to its pitch, quality, and strength. **2** (often in *pl.*) modulation of the voice expressing a particular feeling or mood (*a cheerful tone*; *suspicious tones*). **3** a manner of expression in writing. **4** *Mus.* **a** a musical sound, esp. of a definite pitch and character. **b** an interval of a major second, e.g. C–D. **5 a** the general effect of colour or of light and shade in a picture. **b** the tint or shade of a colour. **6 a** the prevailing character of the morals and sentiments etc. in a group. **b** an attitude or sentiment expressed esp. in a letter etc. **7** the proper firmness of bodily organs. **8** a state of good or specified health or quality. **9** *Phonet.* **a** an accent on one syllable of a word. **b** a way of pronouncing a word to distinguish it from others of a similar sound (*Mandarin Chinese has four tones*). ● *v.* **1** *tr.* give the desired tone to. **2** *tr.* modify the tone of. **3** *intr.* (often foll. by *to*) attune. **4** *intr.* (foll. by *with*) be in harmony (esp. of colour) (*does not tone with the wallpaper*). **5** *tr. Photog.* give (a monochrome picture) an altered colour in finishing by means of a chemical solution. **6** *intr.* undergo a change in colour by toning. □ **tone-arm** the movable arm supporting the pick-up of a record-player. **tone control** a switch for varying the proportion of high and low frequencies in reproduced sound. **tone-deaf** unable to perceive differences of musical pitch accurately. **tone-deafness** the condition of being tone-deaf. **tone down 1** make or become softer in tone of sound or colour. **2** make (a statement etc.) less harsh or emphatic. **tone poem** = *symphonic poem.* **tone-row** = SERIES 8. **tone up 1** make or become stronger in tone of sound or colour. **2** make (a statement etc.) more emphatic. **3** make (muscles) firm by exercise etc.; make or become fitter. **whole-tone scale** see WHOLE. □□ **toneless** *adj.* **tonelessly** *adv.* **toner** *n.* [ME f. OF *ton* or L *tonus* f. Gk *tonos* tension, tone f. *teinō* stretch]
■ *n.* **1** sound, note. **2** stress, emphasis, force, accent, intonation, modulation, phrasing, inflection, pitch, tonality, timbre, sound (colour), tone colour *or* quality, colour *or* colouring, resonance, sonorousness, sonority, fullness, richness, expression, note, tone of voice. **3** manner, style, approach, mode of expression. **5** tint, tinge, shade, hue, colour, colouring, cast. **6 b** attitude, feeling, sentiment, air, atmosphere, mood, aspect, character, note, tenor, drift, temper, vein, spirit. ● *v.* **4** go with, be harmonious with, match. □ **tone down 1** temper, modify, reduce, moderate, modulate, soften, quiet, lower, dampen, dull, subdue, mute, soft-pedal, *Brit.* quieten. **2** see MITIGATE. **tone up 1, 2** see INTENSIFY. **3** (re)invigorate, tune (up), firm (up), brighten (up), (re)vitalize, freshen (up), limber up, get into condition *or* shape. □□ **toneless** muffled, dull, flat, low; see also NEUTRAL *adj.* 3, 5.

toneburst /tṓnburst/ *n.* an audio signal used in testing the transient response of audio components.

toneme /tṓneem/ *n.* a phoneme distinguished from another only by its tone. □□ **tonemic** /-néemik/ *adj.* [TONE after *phoneme*]

tong /tong/ *n.* a Chinese guild, association, or secret society. [Chin. *tang* meeting-place]

tonga /tónggə/ *n.* a light horse-drawn two-wheeled vehicle used in India. [Hindi *tāngā*]

tongs /tongz/ *n.pl.* (also **pair of tongs** *sing.*) an instrument with two hinged or sprung arms for grasping and holding. [pl. of *tong* f. OE *tang*(*e*) f. Gmc]

tongue /tung/ *n.* & *v.* ● *n.* **1** the fleshy muscular organ in the mouth used in tasting, licking, and swallowing, and (in man) for speech. **2** the tongue of an ox etc. as food. **3** the faculty of or a tendency in speech (*a sharp tongue*). **4** a particular language (*the German tongue*). **5** a thing like a tongue in shape or position, esp.: **a** a long low promontory. **b** a strip of leather etc., attached at one end only, under the laces in a shoe. **c** the clapper of a bell. **d** the pin of a buckle. **e** the projecting strip on a wooden etc. board fitting into the groove of another. **f** a vibrating slip in the reed of some musical instruments. **g** a jet of flame. ● *v.* (**tongues, tongued, tonguing**) **1** *tr.* produce staccato etc. effects with (a flute etc.) by means of tonguing. **2** *intr.* use the tongue in this way. □ **find** (or **lose**) **one's tongue** be able (or unable) to express oneself after a shock etc. **the gift of tongues** the power of speaking in unknown languages, regarded as one of the gifts of the Holy Spirit (Acts 2). **keep a civil tongue in one's head** avoid rudeness. **tongue-and-groove** applied to boards in which a tongue along one edge fits into a groove along the edge of the next, each board having a tongue on one edge and a groove on the other. **tongue-in-cheek** *adj.* ironic; slyly humorous. ● *adv.* insincerely or ironically. **tongue-lashing** a severe scolding or reprimand. **tongue-tie** a speech impediment due to a malformation of the tongue. **tongue-tied 1** too shy or embarrassed to speak. **2** having a tongue-tie. **tongue-twister** a sequence of words difficult to pronounce quickly and correctly. **with one's tongue hanging out** eagerly or expectantly. **with one's tongue in one's cheek** insincerely or ironically. □□ **tongued** *adj.* (also in *comb.*). **tongueless** *adj.* [OE *tunge* f. Gmc, rel. to L *lingua*]
■ *n.* **4** language, speech; dialect, patois, Creole, idiom, parlance, argot, talk, vernacular. □ **tongue-in-cheek** (*adj.*) see PLAYFUL 2. **tongue-lashing** scolding, berating, reproof, rebuke, reprimand, lecture; (verbal) abuse, castigation, chastisement, vituperation, revilement, *colloq.* dressing-down, telling-off, talking-to, ticking-off, wigging, *Brit. colloq.* slating. **tongue-tied 1** speechless, at a loss for words, struck dumb, dumbfounded, mute, inarticulate. **with one's tongue in one's cheek** tongue-in-cheek, facetiously, whimsically, ironically, jocularly, jokingly, teasingly, not seriously, in jest, jestingly, in fun, to be funny, insincerely, *colloq.* kiddingly.

tonguing /túnging/ *n. Mus.* the technique of playing a wind instrument using the tongue to articulate certain notes.

tonic /tónnik/ *n.* & *adj.* ● *n.* **1** an invigorating medicine. **2** anything serving to invigorate. **3** = *tonic water.* **4** *Mus.* the first degree of a scale, forming the keynote of a piece (see KEYNOTE 3). ● *adj.* **1** serving as a tonic; invigorating. **2** *Mus.* denoting the first degree of a scale. **3 a** producing tension, esp. of the muscles. **b** restoring normal tone to organs. □ **tonic accent** an accent marked by a change of pitch within a syllable. **tonic sol-fa** *Mus.* a system of notation used esp. in teaching singing, with doh as the keynote of all major keys and lah as the keynote of all minor keys. **tonic spasm** continuous muscular contraction (cf. CLONUS). **tonic water** a carbonated mineral water containing quinine. □□ **tonically** *adv.* [F *tonique* f. Gk *tonikos* (as TONE)]

■ *n.* **1, 2** stimulant, restorative, pick-me-up, refresher, *colloq.* boost, shot in the arm; ptisan, tisane, analeptic, *Med.* roborant, *colloq.* bracer, pick-up, *US colloq.* picker-upper. ● *adj.* **1** stimulant, stimulating, restorative, invigorating, fortifying, bracing, strengthening, reviving, enlivening, refreshing, analeptic, *Med.* roborant.

tonicity /tənissiti/ *n.* **1** the state of being tonic. **2** a healthy elasticity of muscles etc. **3** *Linguistics* phonetic emphasis at a certain place in an intonation pattern.

tonight /tənīt/ *adv.* & *n.* ● *adv.* on the present or approaching evening or night. ● *n.* the evening or night of the present day. [TO + NIGHT: cf. TODAY]

tonka bean /tóngkə/ *n.* the black fragrant seed of a South American tree, *Dipteryx odorata*, used in perfumery etc. [*tonka*, its name in Guyana, + BEAN]

tonnage /túnnij/ *n.* **1** a ship's internal cubic capacity or freight-carrying capacity measured in tons. **2** the total carrying capacity esp. of a country's mercantile marine. **3** a charge per ton on freight or cargo. [orig. in sense 'duty on a tun of wine': OF *tonnage* f. *tonne* TUN: later f. TON[1]]

tonne /tun/ *n.* a metric ton equal to 1,000 kg. [F: see TUN]

tonneau /tónnō/ *n.* the part of a motor car occupied by the back seats, esp. in an open car. □ **tonneau cover** a removable flexible cover for the passenger seats in an open car, boat, etc., when they are not in use. [F, lit. cask, tun]

tonometer /tənómmitər/ *n.* **1** a tuning-fork or other instrument for measuring the pitch of tones. **2** an instrument for measuring the pressure of fluid. [formed as TONE + -METER]

tonsil /tóns'l, -sil/ *n.* either of two small masses of lymphoid tissue on each side of the root of the tongue. □□ **tonsillar** *adj.* [F *tonsilles* or L *tonsillae* (pl.)]

tonsillectomy /tónsiléktəmi/ *n.* (*pl.* **-ies**) the surgical removal of the tonsils.

tonsillitis /tónsilītiss/ *n.* inflammation of the tonsils.

tonsorial /tonsóriəl/ *adj.* usu. *joc.* of or relating to a hairdresser or hairdressing. [L *tonsorius* f. *tonsor* barber f. *tondēre tons-* shave]

tonsure /tónsyər, tónshər/ *n.* & *v.* ● *n.* **1** the shaving of the crown of the head or the entire head, esp. of a person entering a priesthood or monastic order. **2** a bare patch made in this way. ● *v.tr.* give a tonsure to. [ME f. OF *tonsure* or L *tonsura* (as TONSORIAL)]

tontine /tontéen/ *n.* an annuity shared by subscribers to a loan, the shares increasing as subscribers die until the last survivor gets all, or until a specified date when the remaining survivors share the proceeds. [F, f. the name of Lorenzo *Tonti* of Naples, originator of tontines in France *c.* 1653]

tony /tōni/ *adj.* (**tonier, toniest**) *US colloq.* having 'tone'; stylish, fashionable.

too /tōō/ *adv.* **1** to a greater extent than is desirable, permissible, or possible for a specified or understood purpose (*too colourful for my taste; too large to fit*). **2** *colloq.* extremely (*you're too kind*). **3** in addition (*are they coming too?*). **4** moreover (*we must consider, too, the time of year*). □ **none too 1** rather less than (*feeling none too good*). **2** barely. **too bad** see BAD. **too much, too much for** see MUCH. **too right** see RIGHT. **too-too** *adj.* & *adv.* *colloq.* extreme, excessive(ly). [stressed form of TO, f. 16th-c. spelling *too*]

■ **1** see OVERLY. **2** see VERY *adv.* **3** see *in addition* (ADDITION). **4** see MOREOVER.

toodle-oo /tōōd'lōō/ *int.* (also **toodle-pip**) *colloq.* goodbye. [20th c.: orig. unkn.: perh. alt. of F *à tout à l'heure* see you soon]

■ see GOODBYE.

took *past* of TAKE.

tool /tōōl/ *n.* & *v.* ● *n.* **1** any device or implement used to carry out mechanical functions whether manually or by a machine. **2** a thing used in an occupation or pursuit (*the tools of one's trade; literary tools*). **3** a person used as a mere instrument by another. **4** *coarse sl.* the penis. ¶ Usually considered a taboo use. **5 a** a distinct figure in the tooling of a book. **b** a small stamp or roller used to make this. ● *v.tr.* **1** dress (stone) with a chisel. **2** impress a design on (a leather book-cover). **3** (foll. by *along*, *around*, etc.) *sl.* drive or ride, esp. in a casual or leisurely manner. **4** (often foll. by *up*) equip with tools. □ **tool-box** a box or container for keeping tools in. **tool-pusher** a worker directing the drilling on an oil rig. **tool up 1** *sl.* arm oneself. **2** equip oneself. □□ **tooler** *n.* [OE *tōl* f. Gmc]

■ *n.* **1** utensil, implement, instrument, device, apparatus, appliance, contrivance, aid, machine, mechanism, gadget; *colloq.* gimmick, *often derog. or joc.* contraption, *sl.* gismo; (*tools*) hardware, kit, gear. **2** instrument, gadget; (*tools*) kit, gear, tackle, paraphernalia; technique, method, methodology, agency, medium, vehicle. **3** puppet, cat's-paw, pawn, instrument, dupe, *colloq.* stooge, *sl.* sucker. ● *v.* **1** work, carve, cut, dress, shape. **2** embellish, decorate, ornament. **3** see DRIVE *v.* 3b.

tooling /tōōling/ *n.* **1** the process of dressing stone with a chisel. **2** the ornamentation of a book-cover with designs impressed by heated tools.

toolmaker /tōōlmaykər/ *n.* a person who makes precision tools, esp. tools used in a press. □□ **toolmaking** *n.*

toot[1] /tōōt/ *n.* & *v.* ● *n.* **1** a short sharp sound as made by a horn, trumpet, or whistle. **2** *US sl.* cocaine or a snort (see SNORT *n.* 4) of cocaine. **3** *sl.* a drinking session; a binge, a spree. ● *v.* **1** *tr.* sound (a horn etc.) with a short sharp sound. **2** *intr.* give out such a sound. □□ **tooter** *n.* [prob. f. MLG *tūten*, or imit.]

■ *n.* **3** see CAROUSE *n.*

toot[2] /tōōt/ *n.* *Austral. sl.* a lavatory. [20th c.: orig. unkn.]

■ see LAVATORY.

tooth /tōōth/ *n.* & *v.* ● *n.* (*pl.* **teeth** /teeth/) **1** each of a set of hard bony enamel-coated structures in the jaws of most vertebrates, used for biting and chewing. **2** a toothlike part or projection, e.g. the cog of a gearwheel, the point of a saw or comb, etc. **3** (often foll. by *for*) one's sense of taste; an appetite or liking. **4** (in *pl.*) force or effectiveness (*the penalties give the contract teeth*). ● *v.* **1** *tr.* provide with teeth. **2** *intr.* (of cog-wheels) engage, interlock. □ **armed to the teeth** completely and elaborately armed or equipped. **fight tooth and nail** fight very fiercely. **get one's teeth into** devote oneself seriously to. **in the teeth of 1** in spite of (opposition or difficulty etc.). **2** contrary to (instructions etc.). **3** directly against (the wind etc.). **set a person's teeth on edge** see EDGE. **tooth-billed** (of a bird) having toothlike projections on the cutting edges of the bill. **tooth-comb** = *fine-tooth comb* (see FINE[1]). **tooth powder** powder for cleaning the teeth. **tooth shell** = *tusk shell*. □□ **toothed** *adj.* (also in *comb.*). **toothless** *adj.* **toothlike** *adj.* [OE *tōth* (pl. *tēth*) f. Gmc]

■ □ **in the teeth of 1** see DESPITE *prep.*

toothache /tōōthayk/ *n.* a (usu. prolonged) pain in a tooth or teeth.

toothbrush /tōōthbrush/ *n.* a brush for cleaning the teeth.

toothing /tōōthing/ *n.* projecting bricks or stones left at the end of a wall to allow its continuation.

toothpaste /tōōthpayst/ *n.* a paste for cleaning the teeth.

toothpick /tōōthpik/ *n.* a small sharp instrument for removing small pieces of food lodged between the teeth.

toothsome /tōōthsəm/ *adj.* (of food) delicious, appetizing. □□ **toothsomely** *adv.* **toothsomeness** *n.*

■ see DELICIOUS.

toothwort /tōōthwurt/ *n.* a parasitic plant, *Lathraea squamaria*, with toothlike root scales.

toothy /tōōthi/ *adj.* (**toothier, toothiest**) having or showing large, numerous, or prominent teeth (*a toothy grin*). □□ **toothily** *adv.*

tootle /tōōt'l/ *v.intr.* **1** toot gently or repeatedly. **2** (usu. foll. by *along*, *around*, etc.) *colloq.* move casually or aimlessly. □□ **tootler** *n.*

■ **1** pipe, skirl, whistle. **2** see STROLL *v.*

tootsy /tōōtsi/ *n.* (also **tootsie**) (*pl.* **-ies**) *sl.* usu. *joc.* a foot. [E joc. dimin.: cf. FOOTSIE]

top[1] /top/ *n., adj.,* & *v.* ● *n.* **1** the highest point or part (*the top of the house*). **2 a** the highest rank or place (*at the top of the school*). **b** a person occupying this (*was top in maths*). **c** the upper end or head (*the top of the table*). **3** the upper surface of a thing, esp. of the ground, a table, etc. **4** the upper part of a thing, esp.: **a** a blouse, jumper, etc. for wearing with a skirt or trousers. **b** the upper part of a shoe or boot. **c** the stopper of a bottle. **d** the lid of a jar, saucepan, etc. **e** the creamy part of milk. **f** the folding roof of a car, pram, or carriage. **g** the upper edge or edges of a page or pages in a book (*gilt top*). **5** the utmost degree; height (*called at the top of his voice*). **6** (in *pl.*) *colloq.* a person or thing of the best quality (*he's tops at cricket*). **7** (esp. in *pl.*) the leaves etc. of a plant grown esp. for its root (*turnip-tops*). **8** (usu. in *pl.*) a bundle of long wool fibres prepared for spinning. **9** *Naut.* a platform round the head of the lower mast, serving to extend the topmost rigging or carry guns. **10** (in *pl.*) esp. *Bridge* the two or three highest cards of a suit. **11** *Brit.* = *top gear* (*climbed the hill in top*). **12** = TOPSPIN. ● *adj.* **1** highest in position (*the top shelf*). **2** highest in degree or importance (*at top speed; the top job*). ● *v.tr.* (**topped, topping**) **1** provide with a top, cap, etc. (*cake topped with icing*). **2** remove the top of (a plant, fruit, etc.), esp. to improve growth, prepare for cooking, etc. **3** be higher or better than; surpass; be at the top of (*topped the list*). **4** *sl.* **a** execute esp. by hanging, kill. **b** (*refl.*) commit suicide. **5** reach the top of (a hill etc.). **6** *Golf* **a** hit (a ball) above the centre. **b** make (a stroke) in this way. □ **at the top** (or **at the top of the tree**) in the highest rank of a profession etc. **come to the top** *colloq.* win distinction. **from top to toe** from head to foot; completely. **off the top of one's head** see HEAD. **on top 1** in a superior position; above. **2** on the upper part of the head (*bald on top*). **on top of 1** fully in command of. **2** in close proximity to. **3** in addition to. **4** above, over. **on top of the world** *colloq.* exuberant. **over the top 1** over the parapet of a trench (and into battle). **2** into a final or decisive state. **3** to excess, beyond reasonable limits (*that joke was over the top*). **top banana 1** *Theatr. sl.* a comedian who tops the bill of a show. **2** *US sl.* a leader; the head of an organization etc. **top-boot** esp. *hist.* a boot with a high top esp. of a different material or colour. **top brass** esp. *Mil. colloq.* the highest-ranking officers, heads of industries, etc. **top copy** the uppermost typed copy (cf. *carbon copy*). **top dog** *colloq.* a victor or master. **top drawer 1** the uppermost drawer in a chest etc. **2** *colloq.* high social position or origin. **top-drawer** *colloq.* of high social standing; of the highest level or quality. **top-dress** apply manure or fertilizer on the top of (earth) instead of ploughing it in. **top-dressing 1** this process. **2** manure so applied. **3** a superficial show. **top-flight** in the highest rank of achievement. **top fruit** *Brit.* fruit grown on trees, not bushes. **top gear** *Brit.* the highest gear in a motor vehicle or bicycle. **top-hamper** an encumbrance on top, esp. the upper sails and rigging of a ship. **top hat** a man's tall silk hat. **top-hole** *Brit. colloq.* first-rate. **top-level** of the highest level of importance, prestige, etc. **top-notch** *colloq.* first-rate. **top-notcher** *colloq.* a first-rate person or thing. **top off** (or **up**) put an end or the finishing touch to (a thing). **top out** put the highest stone on (a building). **top one's part** esp. *Theatr.* act or discharge one's part to perfection. **top-sawyer 1** a sawyer in the upper position in a saw-pit. **2** a person who holds a superior position; a distinguished person. **top secret** of the highest secrecy. **top ten** (or **twenty** etc.) the first ten (or twenty etc.) gramophone records in the charts. **top up** esp. *Brit.* **1 a** complete (an amount or number). **b** fill up (a glass or other partly full container). **2** top up something for (a person) (*may I top you up with sherry?*). **top-up** *n.* an addition; something that serves to top up (esp. a partly full glass). □□ **topmost** *adj.* [OE *topp*]

■ *n.* **1** summit, apex, peak, acme, crest, head, pinnacle, tip, vertex, zenith, meridian, crown, culmination, high point, height, apogee. **4 c, d** stopper, cork, bung; lid, cover, cap, covering. **6** (*tops*) see *high-class.* ● *adj.* **1** uppermost, topmost, highest. **2** greatest, highest, maximum, topmost; best, foremost, leading, pre-eminent, topping, eminent, first, first-rate, principal, prime, premier, finest, choicest; excellent, superior, superb, top-grade, top-level, supreme, peerless, unequalled, incomparable, top-flight, *colloq.* crack, A1, top-drawer, top-notch, *Brit. colloq.* top-hole, *sl.* ace. ● *v.* **1** surmount, cover, cap, crown, tip; finish, complete, garnish. **2** trim, crop, lop *or* cut off, clip, prune, nip, pinch (back). **3** surpass, better, best, outstrip, exceed, outdo, excel, beat, cap, transcend. **4 a** see HANG *v.* 7a. **5** scale, climb, ascend, surmount. □ **from top to toe** see THROUGH *adv.* **on top 1** above, overhead, on high, aloft; upstairs. **on top of 3** see *in addition to* (ADDITION). **4** see OVER *prep.* 1. **on top of the world** ecstatic, delighted, elated, happy, exultant, exuberant, overjoyed, rapturous, over the moon, in seventh heaven; *colloq.* on cloud nine *or* seven. **top banana 2** see HEAD *n.* 6a. **top dog** see MASTER *n.* 1, VICTOR. **top-drawer** see *high-class.* **top-flight** see GIFTED. **top-hole** see BRILLIANT *adj.* 4. **top-level** see IMPORTANT 2. **top-notch** see *first-rate adj.* **top off** (or **up**) see COMPLEMENT *v.* 1. **top up 1 b** fill (up), refresh, refill, replenish, *US* freshen (up). □□ **topmost** see TOP[1] *adj.* above, UPPERMOST *adj.* 1.

top[2] /top/ *n.* a wooden or metal toy, usu. conical, spherical, or pear-shaped, spinning on a point when set in motion by hand, string, etc. [OE, of uncert. orig.]

topaz /tṓpaz/ *n.* **1** a transparent or translucent aluminium silicate mineral, usu. yellow, used as a gem. **2** any South American humming-bird of the genus *Topaza.* [ME f. OF *topace, topaze* f. L *topazus* f. Gk *topazos*]

topazolite /təpázzəlīt/ *n.* a yellow or green kind of garnet. [TOPAZ + -LITE]

topcoat /tópkōt/ *n.* **1** an overcoat. **2** an outer coat of paint etc.

tope[1] /tōp/ *v.intr. archaic* or *literary* drink alcohol to excess, esp. habitually. □□ **toper** *n.* [perh. f. obs. *top* quaff]

tope[2] /tōp/ *n. Ind.* a grove, esp. of mangoes. [Telugu *tōpu*, Tamil *tōppu*]

tope[3] /tōp/ *n.* = STUPA. [Punjab *tōp* f. Prakrit & Pali *thūpo* f. Skr. STUPA]

tope[4] /tōp/ *n.* a small shark, *Galeorhinus galeus.* [perh. f. Corn.]

topee var. of TOPI.

topgallant /topgállənt, təgállənt/ *n. Naut.* the mast, sail, yard, or rigging immediately above the topmast and topsail.

top-heavy /tóphévvi/ *adj.* **1** disproportionately heavy at the top so as to be in danger of toppling. **2 a** (of an organization, business, etc.) having a disproportionately large number of people in senior administrative positions. **b** overcapitalized. **3** *colloq.* (of a woman) having a disproportionately large bust. □□ **top-heavily** *adv.* **top-heaviness** *n.*

Tophet /tṓfit/ *n. Bibl.* hell. [name of a place in the Valley of Hinnom near Jerusalem used for idolatrous worship and later for burning refuse: f. Heb. *tōpet*]

tophus /tṓfəss/ *n.* (*pl.* **tophi** /-fī/) **1** *Med.* a gouty deposit of crystalline uric acid and other substances at the surface of joints. **2** *Geol.* = TUFA. [L, name of loose porous stones]

topi /tṓpi/ *n.* (also **topee**) (*pl.* **topis** or **topees**) *Anglo-Ind.* a hat, esp. a sola topi. [Hindi *ṭopī*]

topiary /tṓpiəri/ *adj.* & *n.* ● *adj.* concerned with or formed by clipping shrubs, trees, etc. into ornamental shapes. ● *n.* (*pl.* **-ies**) **1** topiary art. **2** an example of this. □□ **topiarian** /-piáiriən/ *adj.* **topiarist** *n.* [F *topiaire* f. L *topiarius* landscape-gardener f. *topia opera* fancy gardening f. Gk *topia* pl. dimin. of *topos* place]

topic /tóppik/ *n.* **1** a theme for a book, discourse, essay, sermon, etc. **2** the subject of a conversation or argument. [L *topica* f. Gk (*ta*) *topika* topics, as title of a treatise by Aristotle f. *topos* a place, a commonplace]

■ subject(-matter), matter, issue, question, point, talking-point, thesis, theme, text, keynote, field *or* area of study, field *or* area of inquiry.

topical /tóppik'l/ *adj.* **1** dealing with the news, current affairs, etc. (*a topical song*). **2** dealing with a place; local. **3** *Med.* (of an ailment, medicine, etc.) affecting a part of the body. **4** of or concerning topics. ▫▫ **topicality** /-kálliti/ *n.* **topically** *adv.*
▪ **1** contemporary, current, up to date, timely. **3** local, localized.

topknot /tópnot/ *n.* a knot, tuft, crest, or bow of ribbon, worn or growing on the head.

topless /tópliss/ *adj.* **1** without or seeming to be without a top. **2 a** (of clothes) having no upper part. **b** (of a person) wearing such clothes; bare-breasted. **c** (of a place, esp. a beach) where women go topless. ▫▫ **toplessness** *n.*

toplofty /tóplófti/ *adj. US colloq.* haughty.

topman /tópmən/ *n.* (*pl.* **-men**) **1** a top-sawyer. **2** *Naut.* a man doing duty in a top.

topmast /tópmaast/ *n. Naut.* the mast next above the lower mast.

topography /təpógrəfi/ *n.* **1 a** a detailed description, representation on a map, etc., of the natural and artificial features of a town, district, etc. **b** such features. **2** *Anat.* the mapping of the surface of the body with reference to the parts beneath. ▫▫ **topographer** *n.* **topographic** /tóppəgráffik/ *adj.* **topographical** /tóppəgráffik'l/ *adj.* **topographically** /tóppəgráffikəli/ *adv.* [ME f. LL *topographia* f. Gk. *topos* place]

topoi *pl.* of TOPOS.

topology /təpólləji/ *n. Math.* the study of geometrical properties and spatial relations unaffected by the continuous change of shape or size of figures. ▫▫ **topological** /tóppəlójik'l/ *adj.* **topologically** /tóppəlójikəli/ *adv.* **topologist** *n.* [G *Topologie* f. Gk *topos* place]

toponym /tóppənim/ *n.* **1** a place-name. **2** a descriptive place-name, usu. derived from a topographical feature of the place. [TOPONYMY]

toponymy /təpónnimi/ *n.* the study of the place-names of a region. ▫▫ **toponymic** /tóppənímmik/ *adj.* [Gk *topos* place + *onoma* name]

topos /tóppos/ *n.* (*pl.* **topoi** /tóppoy/) a stock theme in literature etc. [Gk, = commonplace]

topper /tóppər/ *n.* **1** a thing that tops. **2** *colloq.* = *top hat* (see TOP[1]). **3** *colloq.* a good fellow; a good sort.

topping /tópping/ *adj.* & *n.* ● *adj.* **1** pre-eminent in position, rank, etc. **2** *Brit. archaic sl.* excellent. ● *n.* anything that tops something else, esp. icing etc. on a cake.
▪ *adj.* **2** see EXCELLENT.

topple /tópp'l/ *v.intr.* & *tr.* (usu. foll. by *over, down*) **1 a** fall or cause to fall as if top-heavy. **b** fall or cause to fall from power. **2** totter or cause to totter and fall. [TOP[1] + -LE[4]]
▪ **1 a** fall (over *or* down), drop, collapse, founder, overbalance, keel over, tumble down; upset, up-end, knock down *or* over, fell, capsize. **b** bring *or* throw down, overthrow, defeat, overcome, overturn, subvert, unseat, oust, *literary* vanquish. **2** see TOTTER *v.*

topsail /tópsayl, -s'l/ *n.* a square sail next above the lowest fore-and-aft sail on a gaff.

topside /tópsīd/ *n.* **1** *Brit.* the outer side of a round of beef. **2** the side of a ship above the water-line.

topsoil /tópsoyl/ *n.* the top layer of soil (opp. SUBSOIL).

topspin /tópspin/ *n.* a fast forward spinning motion imparted to a ball in tennis etc. by hitting it forward and upward.

topsy-turvy /tópsitúrvi/ *adv., adj.,* & *n.* ● *adv.* & *adj.* **1** upside down. **2** in utter confusion. ● *n.* utter confusion. ▫▫ **topsy-turvily** *adv.* **topsy-turviness** *n.* [app. f. TOP[1] + obs. *terve* overturn]
▪ *adj.* **1** upside down, wrong side up, head over heels, inverted, reversed, backwards, vice versa. **2** chaotic, muddled, jumbled, disorderly, disordered, disorganized, confused, mixed-up, messy, untidy, in a muddle, higgledy-piggledy, *US colloq.* every which way.

toque /tōk/ *n.* **1** a woman's small brimless hat. **2** *hist.* a small cap or bonnet for a man or woman. [F, app. = It. *tocca*, Sp. *toca*, of unkn. orig.]

toquilla /təkéeyə/ *n.* **1** a palmlike tree, *Carludovica palmata*, native to S. America. **2** a fibre produced from the leaves of this. [Sp., = small gauze head-dress, dimin. of *toca* toque]

tor /tor/ *n.* a hill or rocky peak, esp. in Devon or Cornwall. [OE *torr*: cf. Gael. *tòrr* bulging hill]

Torah /tórə/ *n.* **1** (usu. prec. by *the*) **a** the Pentateuch. **b** a scroll containing this. **2** the will of God as revealed in Mosaic law. [Heb. *tōrāh* instruction]

torc var. of TORQUE 1.

torch /torch/ *n.* & *v.* ● *n.* **1** (also **electric torch**) *Brit.* a portable battery-powered electric lamp. **2 a** a piece of wood, cloth, etc., soaked in tallow and lighted for illumination. **b** any similar lamp, e.g. an oil-lamp on a pole. **3** a source of heat, illumination, or enlightenment (*bore aloft the torch of freedom*). **4** esp. *US* a blowlamp. **5** *US sl.* an arsonist. ● *v.tr.* esp. *US sl.* set alight with or as with a torch. ▫ **carry a torch for** suffer from unrequited love for. **put to the torch** destroy by burning. **torch-fishing** catching fish by torchlight at night. **torch-race** *Gk Antiq.* a festival performance of runners handing lighted torches to others in relays. **torch singer** a woman who sings torch songs. **torch song** a popular song of unrequited love. **torch-thistle** any tall cactus of the genus *Cereus*, with funnel-shaped flowers which open at night. [ME f. OF *torche* f. L *torqua* f. *torquēre* twist]
▪ *n.* **1** *US* flashlight. **2** flambeau, lamp, light, *hist.* link, *poet.* brand.

torchère /torsháir/ *n.* a tall stand with a small table for a candlestick etc. [F (as TORCH)]

torchlight /tórchlīt/ *n.* the light of a torch or torches.

torchon /tórsh'n, -SHON/ *n.* (in full **torchon lace**) coarse bobbin lace with geometrical designs. [F, = duster, dishcloth f. *torcher* wipe]

tore[1] *past* of TEAR[1].

tore[2] /tor/ *n.* = TORUS 1, 4. [F f. L *torus*: see TORUS]

toreador /tórriədor/ *n.* a bullfighter, esp. on horseback. ▫ **toreador pants** close-fitting calf-length women's trousers. [Sp. f. *torear* fight bulls f. *toro* bull f. L *taurus*]

torero /toráirō/ *n.* (*pl.* **-os**) a bullfighter. [Sp. f. *toro*: see TOREADOR]

toreutic /tərо́otik/ *adj.* & *n.* ● *adj.* of or concerning the chasing, carving, and embossing of esp. metal. ● *n.* (in *pl.*) the art or practice of this. [Gk *toreutikos* f. *toreuō* work in relief]

torgoch /tórgokh/ *n.* a kind of red-bellied char found in some Welsh lakes. [Welsh f. *tor* belly + *coch* red]

tori *pl.* of TORUS.

toric /tórrik/ *adj. Geom.* having the form of a torus or part of a torus.

torii /tóri-i/ *n.* (*pl.* same) the gateway of a Shinto shrine, with two uprights and two crosspieces. [Jap.]

torment *n.* & *v.* ● *n.* /tórment/ **1** severe physical or mental suffering (*was in torment*). **2** a cause of this. **3** *archaic* **a** torture. **b** an instrument of torture. ● *v.tr.* /tormént/ **1** subject to torment (*tormented with worry*). **2** tease or worry excessively (*enjoyed tormenting the teacher*). ▫▫ **tormentedly** *adv.* **tormentingly** *adv.* **tormentor** /-méntər/ *n.* [ME f. OF *torment, tormenter* f. L *tormentum* missile-engine f. *torquēre* to twist]
▪ *n.* **1** agony, wretchedness, anguish, distress, misery, pain, painfulness, torture, suffering, hell, *archaic or literary* woe. **2** worry, vexation, annoyance, harassment, ordeal, persecution, nuisance, bane, irritation, bother, affliction, curse, plague, scourge, torture, *colloq.* needling. ● *v.* **1** torture, abuse, maltreat, mistreat, molest, distress, agonize, excruciate, crucify, harrow, rack, pain. **2** worry, trouble, plague, annoy, bedevil, vex, harry, badger, hector, harass, pester, nag, persecute, victimize, bully, nettle, irk, irritate, bother, torture, afflict, chivvy; tease, taunt, bait, chaff, *colloq.* needle, *sl.* rag. ▫▫ **tormentor** see *oppressor* (OPPRESS).

tormentil /tórməntil/ *n.* a low-growing plant, *Potentilla erecta*, with bright yellow flowers and a highly astringent rootstock used in medicine. [ME f. OF *tormentille* f. med.L *tormentilla*, of unkn. orig.]

torn *past part.* of TEAR[1].

tornado /tornáydō/ *n.* (*pl.* **-oes**) **1** a violent storm of small extent with whirling winds, esp.: **a** in West Africa at the beginning and end of the rainy season. **b** in the US etc. over a narrow path often accompanied by a funnel-shaped cloud. **2** an outburst or volley of cheers, hisses, missiles, etc. □□ **tornadic** /-náddik/ *adj.* [app. assim. of Sp. *tronada* thunderstorm (f. *tronar* to thunder) to Sp. *tornar* to turn]

toroid /tóroyd/ *n.* a figure of toroidal shape.

toroidal /toróyd'l/ *adj. Geom.* of or resembling a torus. □□ **toroidally** *adv.*

torose /tórōss/ *adj.* **1** *Bot.* (of plants, esp. their stalks) cylindrical with bulges at intervals. **2** *Zool.* knobby. [L *torosus* f. *torus*: see TORUS]

torpedo /torpeédō/ *n.* & *v.* ● *n.* (*pl.* **-oes**) **1 a** a cigar-shaped self-propelled underwater missile that explodes on impact with a ship. **b** (in full **aerial torpedo**) a similar device dropped from an aircraft. **2** *Zool.* an electric ray. **3** *US* an explosive device or firework. ● *v.tr.* (**-oes, -oed**) **1** destroy or attack with a torpedo. **2** make (a policy, institution, plan, etc.) ineffective or inoperative; destroy. □ **torpedo-boat** a small fast lightly armed warship for carrying or discharging torpedoes. **torpedo-net** (or **-netting**) netting of steel wire hung round a ship to intercept torpedoes. **torpedo-tube** a tube from which torpedoes are fired. □□ **torpedo-like** *adj.* [L, = numbness, electric ray f. *torpēre* be numb]

torpefy /tórpifī/ *v.tr.* (**-ies, -ied**) make numb or torpid. [L *torpefacere* f. *torpēre* be numb]

torpid /tórpid/ *adj.* **1** sluggish, inactive, dull, apathetic. **2** numb. **3** (of a hibernating animal) dormant. □□ **torpidity** /-pídditi/ *n.* **torpidly** *adv.* **torpidness** *n.* [L *torpidus* (as TORPOR)]

■ **1** sluggish, slow, slow-moving, slow-paced, tortoise-like, lethargic, apathetic, indolent, passive, slothful, dull, stupefied, sleepy, somnolent, inactive, inert, languid, languorous, phlegmatic, spiritless, lifeless, listless, fainéant, lackadaisical, indifferent, uncaring, unconcerned, insouciant. **2** see INSENSIBLE 1. **3** see DORMANT 1. □□ **torpidity, torpidness** see TORPOR.

torpor /tórpər/ *n.* torpidity. □□ **torporific** /-pəríffik/ *adj.* [L f. *torpēre* be sluggish]

■ torpidity, torpidness, sluggishness, sloth, lethargy, apathy, indolence, passivity, slothfulness, dullness, stupefaction, drowsiness, sleepiness, somnolence, inactivity, inertia, inertness, languor, laziness, phlegm, lifelessness, listlessness, idleness, fainéancy, accidie, indifference, unconcern.

torquate /tórkwayt/ *adj. Zool.* (of an animal) with a ring of distinctive colour or texture of hair or plumage round the neck. [L *torquatus* (as TORQUE)]

torque /tork/ *n.* **1** (also **torc**) *hist.* a necklace of twisted metal, esp. of the ancient Gauls and Britons. **2** *Mech.* the moment of a system of forces tending to cause rotation. □ **torque converter** a device to transmit the correct torque from the engine to the axle in a motor vehicle. [(sense 1 F f. L *torques*) f. L *torquēre* to twist]

torr /tor/ *n.* (*pl.* same) a unit of pressure used in measuring partial vacuums, equal to 133.32 pascals. [E. *Torricelli*, It. physicist d. 1647]

torrefy /tórrifī/ *v.tr.* (**-ies, -ied**) **1** roast or dry (metallic ore, a drug, etc.). **2** parch or scorch with heat. □□ **torrefaction** /-fáksh'n/ *n.* [F *torréfiér* f. L *torrefacere* f. *torrēre* scorch]

torrent /tórrənt/ *n.* **1** a rushing stream of water, lava, etc. **2** (usu. in *pl.*) a great downpour of rain (*came down in torrents*). **3** (usu. foll. by *of*) a violent or copious flow (*uttered a torrent of abuse*). □□ **torrential** /tərénsh'l/ *adj.* **torrentially** /tərénshəli/ *adv.* [F f. It. *torrente* f. L *torrens -entis* scorching, boiling, roaring f. *torrēre* scorch]

■ **1, 3** stream, rush, flood, deluge, effusion, gushing, outburst, outpouring, spate, inundation, flow, overflow, tide, cascade. **2** see DOWNPOUR. □□ **torrential** rushing, streaming, copious, profuse, teeming, relentless, violent; fierce, vehement, vociferous, ferocious.

Torricellian vacuum /tórichélliən, -sélliən/ *n.* a vacuum formed when mercury in a long tube closed at one end is inverted with the open end in a reservoir of mercury (the principle on which a barometer is made). [*Torricelli*: see TORR]

torrid /tórrid/ *adj.* **1 a** (of the weather) very hot and dry. **b** (of land etc.) parched by such weather. **2** (of language or actions) emotionally charged; passionate, intense. □ **torrid zone** the central belt of the earth between the Tropics of Cancer and Capricorn. □□ **torridity** /-ríddity/ *n.* **torridly** *adv.* **torridness** *n.* [F *torride* or L *torridus* f. *torrēre* parch]

■ **1 a** hot, fiery, sultry, stifling, sweltering, sizzling, roasting, blazing, burning, baking, cooking, boiling, blistering, scorching, parching, *esp. US* broiling; tropical. **b** scorched, parched, arid, dry, hot. **2** fervent, fervid, passionate, intense, ardent, inflamed, impassioned, lustful, amorous, erotic, sexy, hot. □□ **torridity, torridness** see HEAT *n.* 1a, b.

torse /torss/ *n. Heraldry* a wreath. [obs. F *torse, torce* wreath ult. f. L *torta* fem. past part. (as TORT)]

torsel var. of TASSEL[2].

torsion /tórsh'n/ *n.* **1** twisting, esp. of one end of a body while the other is held fixed. **2** *Math.* the extent to which a curve departs from being planar. **3** *Bot.* the state of being twisted into a spiral. **4** *Med.* the twisting of the cut end of an artery after surgery etc. to impede bleeding. □ **torsion balance** an instrument for measuring very weak forces by their effect upon a system of fine twisted wire. **torsion bar** a bar forming part of a vehicle suspension, twisting in response to the motion of the wheels, and absorbing their vertical movement. **torsion pendulum** a pendulum working by rotation rather than by swinging. □□ **torsional** *adj.* **torsionally** *adv.* **torsionless** *adj.* [ME f. OF f. LL *torsio -onis* f. L *tortio* (as TORT)]

torsk /torsk/ *n.* a fish of the cod family, *Brosmius brosme*, abundant in northern waters and often dried for food. [Norw. *to(r)sk* f. ON *tho(r)skr* prob. rel. to *thurr* dry]

torso /tórsō/ *n.* (*pl.* **-os**) **1** the trunk of the human body. **2** a statue of a human consisting of the trunk alone, without head or limbs. **3** an unfinished or mutilated work (esp. of art, literature, etc.). [It., = stalk, stump, torso, f. L *thyrsus*]

tort /tort/ *n. Law* a breach of duty (other than under contract) leading to liability for damages. [ME f. OF f. med.L *tortum* wrong, neut. past part. of L *torquēre tort-* twist]

torte /tórtə/ *n.* (*pl.* **torten** /tórt'n/ or **tortes**) an elaborate sweet cake or tart. [G]

tortfeasor /tórtfeezər/ *n. Law* a person guilty of tort. [OF *tort-fesor, tort-faiseur*, etc. f. *tort* wrong, *-fesor, faiseur* doer]

torticollis /tórtikólliss/ *n. Med.* a rheumatic etc. disease of the muscles of the neck, causing twisting and stiffness. [mod.L f. L *tortus* crooked + *collum* neck]

tortilla /torteéyə, -teélyə/ *n.* a thin flat orig. Mexican maize cake eaten hot or cold with or without a filling. [Sp. dimin. of *torta* cake f. LL]

tortious /tórshəss/ *adj. Law* constituting a tort; wrongful. □□ **tortiously** *adv.* [AF *torcious* f. *torcion* extortion f. LL *tortio* torture: see TORSION]

tortoise /tórtəss/ *n.* **1** any slow-moving land or freshwater reptile of the family Testudinidae, encased in a scaly or leathery domed shell, and having a retractile head and elephantine legs. **2** *Rom. Antiq.* = TESTUDO. □□ **tortoise-like** *adj.* & *adv.* [ME *tortuce*, OF *tortue*, f. med.L *tortuca*, of uncert. orig.]

tortoiseshell /tórtəss-shel/ *n.* & *adj.* ● *n.* **1** the yellowish-brown mottled or clouded outer shell of some turtles, used for decorative hair-combs, jewellery, etc. **2 a** = *tortoiseshell cat.* **b** = *tortoiseshell butterfly.* ● *adj.* having the colouring or appearance of tortoiseshell. □ **tortoiseshell butterfly** any of various butterflies, esp. of the genus *Aglais* or

Nymphalis, with wings mottled like tortoiseshell. **tortoiseshell cat** a domestic cat with markings resembling tortoiseshell.

tortrix /tórtriks/ *n.* any moth of the family Tortricidae, esp. *Tortrix viridana*, the larvae of which live inside rolled leaves. [mod.L, fem. of L *tortor* twister: see TORT]

tortuous /tórtyooəss/ *adj.* **1** full of twists and turns (*followed a tortuous route*). **2** devious, circuitous, crooked (*has a tortuous mind*). □□ **tortuosity** /-yoo-óssiti/ *n.* (*pl.* **-ies**). **tortuously** *adv.* **tortuousness** *n.* [ME f. OF f. L *tortuosus* f. *tortus* a twist (as TORT)]

■ **1** twisted, twisting, winding, wandering, serpentine, meandering, turning, crooked, sinuous, bent, curled, curling, curving, curved, curvy, curviform, curvilinear, flexuous, anfractuous, convoluted, involuted, zigzag, maze-like, mazy, labyrinthine. **2** roundabout, indirect, devious, intricate, involved, involuted, unstraightforward, complicated, ambiguous, circuitous, convoluted, warped, crooked, tricky, misleading, deceptive. □□ **tortuosity** see MEANDER *n.*

torture /tórchər/ *n.* & *v.* ● *n.* **1** the infliction of severe bodily pain esp. as a punishment or a means of persuasion. **2** severe physical or mental suffering (*the torture of defeat*). ● *v.tr.* **1** subject to torture (*tortured by guilt*). **2** force out of a natural position or state; deform; pervert. □□ **torturable** *adj.* **torturer** *n.* **torturous** *adj.* **torturously** *adv.* [F f. LL *tortura* twisting (as TORT)]

■ *n.* **1** see PERSECUTION. **2** see TORMENT *n.* 1. ● *v.* **1** see PERSECUTE, TORMENT *v.* **2** see DISTORT.

torula /tórroolə/ *n.* (*pl.* **torulae** /-lee/) **1** a yeast, *Candida utilis*, used medicinally as a food additive. **2** any yeast-like fungus of the genus *Torula*, growing on dead vegetation. [mod.L, dimin. of *torus*: see TORUS]

torus /tórəss/ *n.* (*pl.* **tori** /-rī/) **1** *Archit.* a large convex bun-shaped moulding esp. as the lowest part of the base of a column. **2** *Bot.* the receptacle of a flower. **3** *Anat.* a smooth ridge of bone or muscle. **4** *Geom.* a surface or solid formed by rotating a closed curve, esp. a circle, about a line in its plane but not intersecting it. [L, = swelling, bulge, cushion, etc.]

Tory /tóri/ *n.* & *adj.* ● *n.* (*pl.* **-ies**) **1** *colloq.* = CONSERVATIVE *n.* 2. **2** *hist.* a member of the party that opposed the exclusion of James II and later supported the established religious and political order and gave rise to the Conservative party (opp. WHIG). **3** *US hist.* a loyal colonist during the American Revolution. ● *adj. colloq.* = CONSERVATIVE *adj.* 3. □□ **Toryism** *n.* [orig. = Irish outlaw, prob. f. Ir. f. *tóir* pursue]

tosh /tosh/ *n. colloq.* rubbish, nonsense. [19th c.: orig. unkn.]

■ see RUBBISH *n.* 3.

toss /toss/ *v.* & *n.* ● *v.* **1** *tr.* throw up (a ball etc.) esp. with the hand. **2** *tr.* & *intr.* roll about, throw, or be thrown, restlessly or from side to side (*the ship tossed on the ocean; was tossing and turning all night; tossed her head angrily*). **3** *tr.* (usu. foll. by *to*, *away*, *aside*, *out*, etc.) throw (a thing) lightly or carelessly (*tossed the letter away*). **4** *tr.* **a** throw (a coin) into the air to decide a choice etc. by the side on which it lands. **b** (also *absol.*; often foll. by *for*) settle a question or dispute with (a person) in this way (*tossed him for the armchair; tossed for it*). **5** *tr.* **a** (of a bull etc.) throw (a person etc.) up with the horns. **b** (of a horse etc.) throw (a rider) off its back. **6** *tr.* coat (food) with dressing etc. by shaking. **7** *tr.* bandy about in debate; discuss (*tossed the question back and forth*). ● *n.* **1** the act or an instance of tossing (a coin, the head, etc.). **2** *Brit.* a fall, esp. from a horse. □ **toss one's head** throw it back esp. in anger, impatience, etc. **tossing the caber** the Scottish sport of throwing a tree-trunk. **toss oars** raise oars to an upright position in salute. **toss off 1** drink off at a draught. **2** dispatch (work) rapidly or without effort (*tossed off an omelette*). **3** *Brit. coarse sl.* masturbate. ¶ Usually considered a taboo use in sense 3. **toss a pancake** throw it up so that it flips on to the other side in the frying-pan. **toss up** toss a coin to decide a choice etc. **toss-up** *n.* **1** a doubtful matter; a close thing (*it's a toss-up whether he wins*). **2** the tossing of a coin. [16th c.: orig. unkn.]

■ *v.* **1, 5** throw, cast, lob, pitch, fling, hurl, heave, shy, launch, send, let fly, propel, catapult, sling, bowl, *colloq.* chuck. **2** pitch, yaw, roll, welter, lurch, bob, undulate, plunge; shake (up), jerk, stir (up), agitate, fling, throw, jiggle, tumble, joggle; wave, lash; writhe, wriggle, squirm, toss and turn, thrash. **4 a** flip, spin, flick. ● *n.* **1** throw, lob, pitch, heave, shy, fling, hurl, launch. □ **toss off 1** see DRINK *v.* 1.

tosser /tóssər/ *n.* **1** *Brit. coarse sl.* an unpleasant or contemptible person. **2** a person or thing that tosses.

tot[1] /tot/ *n.* **1** a small child (*a tiny tot*). **2** a dram of liquor. [18th c., of dial. orig.]

■ **1** child, toddler, infant, baby. **2** see NIP[2] *n.*

tot[2] /tot/ *v.* & *n.* ● *v.* (**totted, totting**) **1** *tr.* (usu. foll. by *up*) add (figures etc.). **2** *intr.* (foll. by *up*) (of items) mount up. ● *n. Brit. archaic* a set of figures to be added. □ **totting-up 1** the adding of separate items. **2** *Brit.* the adding of convictions for driving offences to cause disqualification. **tot up to** amount to. [abbr. of TOTAL or of L *totum* the whole]

tot[3] /tot/ *v.* & *n. Brit. sl.* ● *v.intr.* (**totted, totting**) collect saleable items from refuse as an occupation. ● *n.* an article collected from refuse. [19th c.: orig. unkn.]

total /tṓt'l/ *adj.*, *n.*, & *v.* ● *adj.* **1** complete, comprising the whole (*the total number of people*). **2** absolute, unqualified (*in total ignorance; total abstinence*). ● *n.* a total number or amount. ● *v.* (**totalled, totalling**; *US* **totaled, totaling**) **1** *tr.* **a** amount in number to (*they totalled 131*). **b** find the total of (things, a set of figures, etc.). **2** *intr.* (foll. by *to*, *up to*) amount to, mount up to. **3** *tr. US sl.* wreck completely. □ **total abstinence** abstaining completely from alcohol. **total eclipse** an eclipse in which the whole disc (of the sun, moon, etc.) is obscured. **total internal reflection** reflection without refraction of a light-ray meeting the interface between two media at more than a certain critical angle to the normal. **total recall** the ability to remember every detail of one's experience clearly. **total war** a war in which all available weapons and resources are employed. □□ **totally** *adv.* [ME f. OF f. med.L *totalis* f. *totus* entire]

■ *adj.* **1** whole, entire, complete, full, gross, overall, comprehensive. **2** complete, unalloyed, unmitigated, unqualified, unconditional, utter, out-and-out, thorough, thoroughgoing, perfect, outright, downright, all-out, absolute, *colloq.* blithering. ● *n.* sum (total), totality, aggregate, whole, amount, total number. ● *v.* **1 b** add (up), tot up, sum (up), reckon, compute. **2** (*total up to*) amount to, add up to, come to, mount up to, tot up to, make. **3** see TRASH *v.* 1. □□ **totally** completely, utterly, entirely, fully, unqualifiedly, unconditionally, perfectly, absolutely, thoroughly, wholly, consummately.

totalitarian /tōtállitáiriən/ *adj.* & *n.* ● *adj.* of or relating to a centralized dictatorial form of government requiring complete subservience to the State. ● *n.* a person advocating such a system. □□ **totalitarianism** *n.*

■ *adj.* absolute, absolutist, arbitrary, authoritarian, autocratic, dictatorial, Fascist(ic), undemocratic, illiberal, monolithic, Nazi, oppressive, despotic, tyrannical. ● *n.* absolutist, authoritarian, Fascist, Nazi. □□ **totalitarianism** see DESPOTISM.

totality /tōtálliti/ *n.* **1** the complete amount or sum. **2** *Astron.* the time during which an eclipse is total.

■ **1** total, aggregate, sum (total), whole, entirety, beginning and end, alpha and omega, be-all and end-all.

totalizator /tṓtəlīzaytər/ *n.* (also **totalisator**) **1** a device showing the number and amount of bets staked on a race, to facilitate the division of the total among those backing the winner. **2** a system of betting based on this.

totalize /tṓtəlīz/ *v.tr.* (also **-ise**) collect into a total; find the total of. □□ **totalization** /-záysh'n/ *n.*

totalizer /tṓtəlīzər/ *n.* = TOTALIZATOR.

tote[1] /tōt/ *n. sl.* **1** a totalizator. **2** a lottery. [abbr.]

tote[2] /tōt/ *v.tr.* esp. *US colloq.* carry, convey, esp. a heavy load (*toting a gun*). □ **tote bag** a woman's large bag for shopping etc. **tote box** *US* a small container for goods. □□ **toter** *n.* (also in *comb.*). [17th-c. US, prob. of dial. orig.]
■ see CARRY *v.* 1, 2.

totem /tṓtəm/ *n.* **1** a natural object, esp. an animal, adopted by North American Indians as an emblem of a clan or an individual. **2** an image of this. □ **totem-pole 1** a pole on which totems are carved or hung. **2** a hierarchy. □□ **totemic** /-témmik/ *adj.* **totemism** *n.* **totemist** *n.* **totemistic** /-təmístik/ *adj.* [Algonquian]

tother /tú*th*ər/ *adj.* & *pron.* (also **t'other**) *dial.* or *joc.* the other. □ **tell tother from which** *joc.* tell one from the other. [ME *the tother*, for earlier *thet other* 'that other'; now understood as = *the other*]

totter /tóttər/ *v.* & *n.* ● *v.intr.* **1** stand or walk unsteadily or feebly (*tottered out of the pub*). **2 a** (of a building etc.) shake or rock as if about to collapse. **b** (of a system of government etc.) be about to fall. ● *n.* an unsteady or shaky movement or gait. □□ **totterer** *n.* **tottery** *adj.* [ME f. MDu. *touteren* to swing]
■ *v.* dodder, falter, stagger, stumble, shiver; waver, topple, tremble, teeter, sway, rock, reel, wobble, quiver, shake, quake.

toucan /tṓōkən/ *n.* any tropical American fruit-eating bird of the family Ramphastidae, with an immense beak and brightly coloured plumage. [Tupi *tucana*, Guarani *tucã*]

touch /tuch/ *v.* & *n.* ● *v.* **1** *tr.* come into or be in physical contact with (another thing) at one or more points. **2** *tr.* (often foll. by *with*) bring the hand etc. into contact with (*touched her arm*). **3 a** *intr.* (of two things etc.) be in or come into contact with one another (*the balls were touching*). **b** *tr.* bring (two things) into mutual contact (*they touched hands*). **4** *tr.* rouse tender or painful feelings in (*was touched by his appeal*). **5** *tr.* strike lightly (*just touched the wall with the back bumper*). **6** *tr.* (usu. with *neg.*) **a** disturb or harm (*don't touch my things*). **b** have any dealings with (*won't touch bricklaying*). **c** consume; use up; make use of (*dare not touch alcohol; has not touched her breakfast; need not touch your savings*). **d** cope with; affect; manage (*soap won't touch this dirt*). **7** *tr.* **a** deal with (a subject) lightly or in passing (*touched the matter of their expenses*). **b** concern (*it touches you closely*). **8** *tr.* **a** reach or rise as far as, esp. momentarily (*the thermometer touched 90°*). **b** (usu. with *neg.*) approach in excellence etc. (*can't touch him for style*). **9** *tr.* affect slightly; modify (*pity touched with fear*). **10** *tr.* (as **touched** *adj.*) slightly mad. **11** *tr.* (often foll. by *in*) esp. *Art* mark lightly, put in (features etc.) with a brush, pencil, etc. **12** *tr.* **a** strike (the keys, strings, etc. of a musical instrument). **b** strike the keys or strings of (a piano etc.). **13** *tr.* (usu. foll. by *for*) *sl.* ask for and get money etc. from (a person) as a loan or gift (*touched him for £5*). **14** *tr.* injure slightly (*blossom touched by frost*). **15** *tr. Geom.* be tangent to (a curve). ● *n.* **1** the act or an instance of touching, esp. with the body or hand (*felt a touch on my arm*). **2 a** the faculty of perception through physical contact, esp. with the fingers (*has no sense of touch in her right arm*). **b** the qualities of an object etc. as perceived in this way (*the soft touch of silk*). **3** a small amount; a slight trace (*a touch of salt; a touch of irony*). **4 a** a musician's manner of playing keys or strings. **b** the manner in which the keys or strings respond to touch. **c** an artist's or writer's style of workmanship, writing, etc. (*has a delicate touch*). **5** a distinguishing quality or trait (*a professional touch*). **6** (esp. in *pl.*) **a** a light stroke with a pen, pencil, etc. **b** a slight alteration or improvement (*speech needs a few touches*). **7** = TAG[2]. **8** (prec. by *a*) slightly (*is a touch too arrogant*). **9** *sl.* **a** the act of asking for and getting money etc. from a person. **b** a person from whom money etc. is so obtained. **10** *Football* the part of the field outside the side limits. **11** *archaic* a test with or as if with a touchstone (*put it to the touch*). □ **at a touch** if touched, however lightly (*opened at a touch*). **easy touch** *sl.* a person who readily parts with money. **finishing touch** (or **touches**) the final details completing and enhancing a piece of work etc. **get** (or **put**) **in** (or **into**) **touch with** come or cause to come into communication with; contact. **in touch** (often foll. by *with*) **1** in communication (*we're still in touch after all these years*). **2** up to date, esp. regarding news etc. (*keeps in touch with events*). **3** aware, conscious, empathetic (*not in touch with her own feelings*). **keep in touch** (often foll. by *with*) **1** remain informed (*kept in touch with the latest developments*). **2** continue correspondence, a friendship, etc. **lose touch** (often foll. by *with*) **1** cease to be informed. **2** cease to correspond with or be in contact with another person. **lose one's touch** not show one's customary skill. **the Nelson touch** a masterly or sympathetic approach to a problem (from Horatio Nelson, Admiral at Trafalgar). **out of touch** (often foll. by *with*) **1** not in correspondence. **2** not up to date or modern. **3** lacking in awareness or sympathy (*out of touch with his son's beliefs*). **personal touch** a characteristic or individual approach to a situation. **soft touch** = *easy touch* (see TOUCH). **to the touch** when touched (*was cold to the touch*). **touch-and-go** uncertain regarding a result; risky (*it was touch-and-go whether we'd catch the train*). **touch at** (of a ship) call at (a port etc.). **touch bottom 1** reach the bottom of water with one's feet. **2** be at the lowest or worst point. **3** be in possession of the full facts. **touch down 1** *Rugby Football* & *Amer. Football* touch the ground with the ball behind one's own or the opponent's goal. **2** (of an aircraft) make contact with the ground in landing. **touch football** *US* football with touching in place of tackling. **touch-hole** a small hole in a gun for igniting the charge. **touch-in-goal** *Football* each of the four corners enclosed by continuations of the touch-lines and goal-lines. **touch-judge** *Rugby Football* a linesman. **touch-line** (in various sports) either of the lines marking the side boundaries of the pitch. **touch-mark** the maker's mark on pewter. **touch-me-not** any of various plants of the genus *Impatiens*, with ripe seed-capsules jerking open when touched. **touch-needle** a needle of gold or silver alloy of known composition used as a standard in testing other alloys on a touchstone. **touch off 1** represent exactly (in a portrait etc.). **2** explode by touching with a match etc. **3** initiate (a process) suddenly (*touched off a run on the pound*). **touch of nature 1** a natural trait. **2** *colloq.* an exhibition of human feeling with which others sympathize (from a misinterpretation of Shakesp. *Troilus and Cressida* III. iii. 169). **touch of the sun 1** a slight attack of sunstroke. **2** a little sunlight. **touch on** (or **upon**) **1** treat (a subject) briefly, refer to or mention casually. **2** verge on (*that touches on impudence*). **touch-paper** paper impregnated with nitre, for firing gunpowder, fireworks, etc. **touch the spot** *colloq.* find out or do exactly what was needed. **touch-type** type without looking at the keys. **touch-typing** this skill. **touch-typist** a person who touch-types. **touch up 1** give finishing touches to or retouch (a picture, writing, etc.). **2** *Brit. sl.* **a** caress so as to excite sexually. **b** sexually molest. **3** strike (a horse) lightly with a whip. **touch wood** touch something wooden with the hand to avert ill luck. **would not touch with a bargepole** see BARGEPOLE. □□ **touchable** *adj.* [ME f. OF *tochier*, *tuchier* (v.), *touche* (n.): prob. imit., imitating a knock]
■ *v.* **1** be in contact with, border, adjoin, meet, come into contact with, come up against, be (up) against, butt against, push *or* press *or* lean (up) against, brush *or* rub (up) against, abut. **2** put one's hand on, feel, handle; lay a hand *or* finger on; see also FONDLE. **3 a** be in contact, come *or* be together, meet. **b** bring into contact, place *or* put *or* bring together. **4** affect, impress, influence, disturb, move, stir, arouse, excite, impassion, stimulate, strike, *colloq.* get (to). **5** brush, graze, tap, knock. **6 a** lay a hand *or* finger on; disturb, harm, meddle with, have to do with, interfere with, tamper with; come near, approach. **b** have to do with, have dealings with, handle. **c** drink, eat, consume, partake of, take, taste, have to do with; have access to, access, use, employ, make use of, put to use, avail oneself of, get, take advantage of. **7 a** see *touch on* 1 below. **b** see CONCERN *v.* 1a. **8 a** reach, attain,

rise to. **b** rival, match, equal, compare with, come up to, be on a par with, be a match for, be in the same league as *or* with, be in the same class as *or* with, be on an equal footing with, reach, come *or* get near *or* close to, hold a candle to, measure up to *or* against, *US colloq.* stack up to. **10** (**touched**) see MAD *adj.* 1. **13** (*touch for*) see BORROW 1. ● *n.* **1** pat, tap, dab, blow, hit, stroke, brush, caress. **2 a** feel, feeling. **b** feeling, feel, texture. **3** dash, hint, intimation, suggestion, soupçon, bit, pinch, jot, spot, trace, tinge, taste, suspicion, smattering, colouring, smack, speck, dab, drop, whiff, odour, scent, smell. **4 a, c** approach, style, manner, technique, execution, method; feel, feeling, sensitivity; see also INSTINCT *n.* 2. **b** response, feel, responsiveness, feeling, movement, operation, performance level. **5** trade mark, characteristic, quality, feature, trait, influence, *archaic* signature. □ **easy touch** see MUG[1] *n.* 3. **get** (or **put**) **in** (or **into**) **touch with** see CONTACT *v.* **in touch 2** see INFORMED 1. **3** (*in touch with*) see SENSIBLE 4. **touch-and-go** see PRECARIOUS. **touch down 2** land, alight, come to earth. **touch off 2** detonate, spark (off), set alight, set off, ignite, light, fire, put a match to. **3** instigate, initiate, begin, start, set in motion, ignite, set off, trigger, provoke, foment, cause, give rise to. **touch on** (or **upon**) **1** touch, refer to, have reference to, pertain to, relate to, have a bearing on, regard, mention, allude to, speak *or* write of, tell of, bring up *or* in, raise, broach, deal with, cover. **2** verge on *or* upon, border on, approach, resemble. **touch up 1** retouch, patch up; edit, polish; beautify, enhance, titivate, renovate, restore, spruce up. **touch wood** keep one's fingers crossed, cross one's fingers, *US* knock (on) wood. □□ **touchable** tangible, tactile, palpable.

touchdown /túchdown/ *n.* **1** the act or an instance of an aircraft making contact with the ground during landing. **2** *Rugby Football* & *Amer. Football* the act or an instance of touching down.
■ **1** see LANDING 1a, b.

touché /tōōsháy/ *int.* **1** the acknowledgement of a hit by a fencing-opponent. **2** the acknowledgement of a justified accusation, a witticism, or a point made in reply to one's own. [F, past part. of *toucher* TOUCH]

toucher /túchər/ *n.* **1** a person or thing that touches. **2** *Bowls* a wood that touches the jack.

touching /túching/ *adj.* & *prep.* ● *adj.* moving; pathetic (*a touching incident*; *touching confidence*). ● *prep. literary* concerning; about. □□ **touchingly** *adv.* **touchingness** *n.* [ME f. TOUCH: (prep.) f. OF *touchant* pres. part. (as TOUCH)]
■ *adj.* moving, stirring, emotional, tender, heart-warming, poignant, pathetic, soul-stirring, heart-rending, heart-breaking, sad, pitiful, distressing, distressful. ● *prep.* see ABOUT *prep.* 1a, b, d.

touchstone /túchstōn/ *n.* **1** a fine-grained dark schist or jasper used for testing alloys of gold etc. by marking it with them and observing the colour of the mark. **2** a standard or criterion.
■ **2** standard, yardstick, criterion, reference, benchmark, test, norm, measure.

touchwood /túchwŏŏd/ *n.* readily inflammable wood, esp. when made soft by fungi, used as tinder.

touchy /túchi/ *adj.* (**touchier, touchiest**) **1** apt to take offence; over-sensitive. **2** not to be touched without danger; ticklish, risky, awkward. □□ **touchily** *adv.* **touchiness** *n.* [perh. alt. of TETCHY after TOUCH]
■ **1** (over-)sensitive, supersensitive, hypersensitive, high(ly)-strung, tense, thin-skinned, crabby, crabbed, testy, irascible, irritable, tetchy, prickly, edgy, temperamental, peevish, querulous, petulant, pettish, splenetic, captious, bad-tempered, short-tempered, hot-tempered, quick-tempered, crusty, cross, curmudgeonly, cantankerous, choleric, dyspeptic, waspish, bearish, snarling, snappish, snappy, argumentative, disputatious, contentious, *colloq.* grouchy, *esp. US* cranky. **2** critical, touch-and-go, sensitive, ticklish, risky, precarious, hazardous, chancy, unsure, uncertain, close, hairbreadth, dangerous, hair-raising, frightening, terrifying, nerve-racking, *archaic or joc.* parlous, *sl.* hairy; see also AWKWARD 4. □□ **touchiness** see SENSITIVITY.

tough /tuf/ *adj.* & *n.* ● *adj.* **1** hard to break, cut, tear, or chew; durable; strong. **2** (of a person) able to endure hardship; hardy. **3** unyielding, stubborn, difficult (*it was a tough job*; *a tough customer*). **4** *colloq.* **a** acting sternly; hard (*get tough with*). **b** (of circumstances, luck, etc.) severe, unpleasant, hard, unjust. **5** *colloq.* criminal or violent (*tough guys*). ● *n.* a tough person, esp. a ruffian or criminal. □ **tough guy** *colloq.* **1** a hard unyielding person. **2** a violent aggressive person. **tough it** (or **tough it out**) *colloq.* endure or withstand difficult conditions. **tough-minded** realistic, not sentimental. **tough-mindedness** being tough-minded. □□ **toughen** *v.tr.* & *intr.* **toughener** *n.* **toughish** *adj.* **toughly** *adv.* **toughness** *n.* [OE *tōh*]
■ *adj.* **1** hard, firm, durable, long-lasting, wear-resistant, hard-wearing, serviceable, heavy-duty, substantial, strong, stout, rugged, sturdy, sound, well-built, solid, indestructible, unbreakable, resilient; stiff, leathery, inflexible, chewy, fibrous, cartilaginous, cartilaginoid, gristly, sinewy, ropy, wiry, stringy. **2** strong, stalwart, brawny, burly, beefy, muscular, powerful, virile, manly, sturdy, intrepid, stout, rough, vigorous, robust, strapping, athletic, hardy, *archaic or joc.* doughty. **3** difficult, demanding, exacting, hard, troublesome; laborious, arduous, taxing, strenuous; baffling, thorny, puzzling, perplexing, mystifying, tricky, knotty, irksome; stubborn, obstinate, obdurate, inflexible, refractory, intractable, adamant, resolute, unyielding. **4 a** hardened, inured, hard, harsh, severe, stern, strict, inflexible, adamant, unyielding, ungiving, rigid, unbending, uncompromising, unsentimental, unfeeling, unsympathetic, merciless, ruthless, callous, hard-boiled, uncaring, cold, cool, icy, stony, *colloq.* hard-nosed. **b** see SEVERE 1, 5. ● *n.* hooligan, bully(-boy), rowdy, thug, ruffian, rough, *colloq.* roughneck, bruiser, tough guy, toughie, *sl.* trog, *US sl.* hood. □ **tough guy 2** see TOUGH *n.* above. **tough it out** see *stick it out* (STICK[2]). **tough-minded** see REALISTIC 2. □□ **toughen** see STRENGTHEN. **toughness** see STRENGTH 1.

toughie /túffi/ *n. colloq.* a tough person or problem.

toupee /tōōpay/ *n.* (also **toupet** /tōōpáy/) a wig or artificial hairpiece to cover a bald spot. [F *toupet* hair-tuft dimin. of OF *toup* tuft (as TOP[1])]

tour /toor/ *n.* & *v.* ● *n.* **1 a** a journey from place to place as a holiday. **b** an excursion, ramble, or walk (*made a tour of the garden*). **2 a** a spell of duty on military or diplomatic service. **b** the time to be spent at a particular post. **3** a series of performances, matches, etc., at different places on a route through a country etc. ● *v.* **1** *intr.* (usu. foll. by *through*) make a tour (*toured through India*). **2** *tr.* make a tour of (a country etc.). □ **on tour** (esp. of a team, theatre company, etc.) touring. **touring-car** a car with room for passengers and much luggage. **tour operator** a travel agent specializing in package holidays. [ME f. OF *to(u)r* f. L *tornus* f. Gk *tornos* lathe]
■ *n.* **1 a** journey, trip, excursion, outing, expedition, voyage, trek, jaunt, junket, *archaic or joc.* peregrination. **b** stroll, perambulation, walkabout, ramble, walk, drive, ride, excursion; round, circuit, ambit. **2** spell, shift, stint, assignment, turn, stretch, *Mil.* period of service *or* enlistment. ● *v.* **1** journey, travel, voyage, trip, trek, sightsee, cruise; *colloq.* globe-trot. **2** visit, see, sightsee, explore, go round, *colloq.* take in, do.

touraco var. of TURACO.

tour de force /to͝or də fórss/ *n.* a feat of strength or skill. [F]
■ see FEAT.

tourer /to͝orər/ *n.* a vehicle, esp. a car, for touring. [TOUR]

tourism /to͝oriz'm/ *n.* the organization and operation of (esp. foreign) holidays, esp. as a commercial enterprise.

■ tourist *or* leisure industry, travel trade; see also TRAVEL *n.* 1a.

tourist /tóorist/ *n.* a person making a visit or tour as a holiday; a traveller, esp. abroad (often *attrib.*: *tourist accommodation*). □ **tourist class** the lowest class of passenger accommodation in a ship, aircraft, etc. □□ **touristic** /-rístik/ *adj.* **touristically** /-rístikəli/ *adv.*
■ traveller, voyager, visitor, sightseer, day-tripper, *esp. Brit.* holiday-maker, *Brit.* tripper, *US* vacationer, vacationist, *colloq.* rubberneck, out-of-towner.

touristy /tóoristi/ *adj.* usu. *derog.* appealing to or visited by many tourists.

tourmaline /tóormәlin, -leen/ *n.* a boron aluminium silicate mineral of various colours, possessing unusual electrical properties, and used in electrical and optical instruments and as a gemstone. [F f. Sinh. *toramalli* porcelain]

tournament /tóornәmәnt/ *n.* **1** any contest of skill between a number of competitors, esp. played in heats (*chess tournament*; *tennis tournament*). **2** a display of military exercises etc. (*Royal Tournament*). **3** *hist.* **a** a pageant in which jousting with blunted weapons took place. **b** a meeting for jousting between single knights for a prize etc. [ME f. OF *torneiement* f. *torneier* TOURNEY]
■ **1** tourney, competition, contest, championship, match, meeting, event, meet. **3** tilt, *hist.* joust.

tournedos /tóornәdō/ *n.* (*pl.* same /-dōz/) a small round thick cut from a fillet of beef. [F]

tourney /tóorni/ *n.* & *v.* ● *n.* (*pl.* **-eys**) a tournament. ● *v.intr.* (**-eys, -eyed**) take part in a tournament. [ME f. OF *tornei* (n.), *torneier* (v.), ult. f. L *tornus* a turn]
■ *n.* see TOURNAMENT 1.

tourniquet /tóornikay/ *n.* a device for stopping the flow of blood through an artery by twisting a bar etc. in a ligature or bandage. [F prob. f. OF *tournicle* coat of mail, TUNICLE, infl. by *tourner* TURN]

tousle /tówz'l/ *v.tr.* **1** make (esp. the hair) untidy; rumple. **2** handle roughly or rudely. [frequent. of (now dial.) *touse*, ME f. OE rel. to OHG *-zuson*]
■ **1** dishevel, disorder, ruffle, disarrange, tangle (up), mess (up), rumple, disarray, *US colloq.* muss (up).

tous-les-mois /tōōlaymwaá/ *n.* **1** food starch obtained from tubers of a canna, *Canna indica*. **2** this plant. [F, lit. = every month, prob. corrupt. of W.Ind. *toloman*]

tout /towt/ *v.* & *n.* ● *v.* **1** *intr.* (usu. foll. by *for*) solicit custom persistently; pester customers (*touting for business*). **2** *tr.* solicit the custom of (a person) or for (a thing). **3** *intr.* **a** *Brit.* spy out the movements and condition of racehorses in training. **b** *US* offer racing tips for a share of the resulting profit. ● *n.* a person employed in touting. □□ **touter** *n.* [ME *tūte* look out = ME (now dial.) *toot* (OE *tōtian*) f. Gmc]
■ *v.* **2** (*tout (a thing)*) hawk, peddle, sell, promote, talk up, push, *colloq.* plug. ● *n.* barker, tipster, touter.

tout court /tōō kóor/ *adv.* without addition; simply (*called James tout court*). [F, lit. very short]

tout de suite /tōō dә sweet/ *adv.* at once, immediately. [F]
■ see IMMEDIATELY *adv.* 1.

tovarish /tәvaárish/ *n.* (also **tovarich**) (in the former USSR) comrade (esp. as a form of address). [Russ. *tovarishch*]

tow[1] /tō/ *v.* & *n.* ● *v.tr.* **1** (of a motor vehicle, horse, or person controlling it) pull (a boat, another motor vehicle, a caravan, etc.) along by a rope, tow-bar, etc. **2** pull (a person or thing) along behind one. ● *n.* the act or an instance of towing; the state of being towed. □ **have in** (or **on**) **tow 1** be towing. **2** be accompanied by and often in charge of (a person). **tow-bar** a bar for towing esp. a trailer or caravan. **tow-** (or **towing-**) **line** (or **rope**) a line etc. used in towing. **tow-** (or **towing-**) **net** a net used for dragging through water to collect specimens. **tow-** (or **towing-**) **path** a path beside a river or canal used for towing a boat by horse. □□ **towable** *adj.* **towage** /tṓ-ij/ *n.* [OE *togian* f. Gmc, rel. to TUG]
■ *v.* pull, drag, draw, haul, lug, trail, tug, trawl. ● *n.* pull, drag, haul, lug, tug, trawl.

tow[2] /tō/ *n.* **1** the coarse and broken part of flax or hemp prepared for spinning. **2** a loose bunch of rayon etc. strands. □ **tow-coloured** (of hair) very light. **tow-head** tow-coloured or unkempt hair. **tow-headed** having very light or unkempt hair. □□ **towy** /tṓ-i/ *adj.* [ME f. MLG *touw* f. OS *tou*, rel. to ON *tó* wool: cf. TOOL]

toward *prep.* & *adj.* ● *prep.* /tәwáwrd, twawrd, tawrd/ = TOWARDS. ● *adj.* /tṓәrd/ *archaic* **1** about to take place; in process. **2** docile, apt. **3** promising, auspicious. □□ **towardness** /tṓәrdniss/ *n.* (in sense of *adj.*).

towards /tәwáwrdz, twawrdz, tawrdz/ *prep.* **1** in the direction of (*set out towards town*). **2** as regards; in relation to (*his attitude towards death*). **3** as a contribution to; for (*put this towards your expenses*). **4** near (*towards the end of our journey*). [OE *tōweard* (adj.) future (as TO, -WARD)]
■ **1** toward, in the direction of, to; for, so as to approach *or* near, on the way *or* road to. **2** toward, as regards, in *or* with regard to, in relation to, concerning, about, regarding, with respect to. **3** toward, to, for, as a help to, supporting, promoting, assisting. **4** toward, near, nearing, close to, approaching, shortly before.

towel /tówәl/ *n.* & *v.* ● *n.* **1 a** a piece of rough-surfaced absorbent cloth used for drying oneself or a thing after washing. **b** absorbent paper used for this. **c** a cloth used for drying plates, dishes, etc.; a tea towel. **2** *Brit.* = *sanitary towel*. ● *v.* (**towelled, towelling**; *US* **toweled, toweling**) **1** *tr.* (often *refl.*) wipe or dry with a towel. **2** *intr.* wipe or dry oneself with a towel. **3** *tr. sl.* thrash. □ **towel-horse** (or **-rail**) a frame for hanging towels on. □□ **towelling** *n.* [ME f. OF *toail(l)e* f. Gmc]

tower /towr/ *n.* & *v.* ● *n.* **1 a** a tall esp. square or circular structure, often part of a church, castle, etc. **b** a fortress etc. comprising or including a tower. **c** a tall structure housing machinery, apparatus, operators, etc. (*cooling tower*; *control tower*). **2** a place of defence; a protection. ● *v.intr.* **1** (usu. foll. by *above*, *high*) reach or be high or above; be superior. **2** (of a bird) soar or hover. **3** (as **towering** *adj.*) **a** high, lofty (*towering intellect*). **b** violent (*towering rage*). □ **tower block** a tall building containing offices or flats. **tower of silence** a tall open-topped structure on which Parsees place their dead. **tower of strength** a person who gives strong and reliable support. □□ **towered** /tówәrd/ *adj.* **towery** *adj.* [OE *torr*, & ME *tūr*, AF & OF *tur* etc., f. L *turris* f. Gk]
■ *n.* **1 a** bell-tower, campanile, minaret, pagoda, obelisk; belfry, turret, steeple, *flèche*. **b** fortress, citadel, stronghold, castle, fastness; prison, *archaic* dungeon, *hist.* keep. **2** see PROTECTION 1b, c. ● *v.* **1** loom, soar, rise, ascend, rear; (*tower above*) see OVERSHADOW 1. **2** soar, rise, hover. **3** (**towering**) **a** tall, high, soaring, outstanding, elevated, sky-scraping, sky-high, *literary* lofty; great, impressive, imposing, huge, gigantic, mighty, supreme, superior, paramount, extraordinary, unmatched, unequalled, unrivalled, unparalleled, unsurpassed. **b** violent, fiery, burning, passionate, excessive, vehement, intense, consuming, mighty, overwhelming, unrestrained, immoderate, inordinate, intemperate, extreme, colossal, enormous.

town /town/ *n.* **1 a** a large urban area with a name, defined boundaries, and local government, being larger than a village and usu. not created a city. **b** any densely populated area, esp. as opposed to the country or suburbs. **c** the people of a town (*the whole town knows of it*). **2 a** *Brit.* London or the chief city or town in one's neighbourhood (*went up to town*). **b** the central business or shopping area in a neighbourhood (*just going into town*). **3** the permanent residents of a university town as distinct from the members of the university (cf. GOWN). **4** *US* = TOWNSHIP 2. □ **go to town** *colloq.* act or work with energy or enthusiasm. **on the town** *colloq.* enjoying the entertainments, esp. the night-life, of a town; celebrating. **town clerk 1** *US* & *hist.* the officer of the corporation of a town in charge of records etc. **2** *Brit. hist.* the secretary and legal adviser of a town corporation until 1974. **town council** the elective governing body in a municipality. **town councillor** an elected member of this. **town crier** see CRIER. **town gas** manufactured gas for domestic and commercial use. **town hall** a building for the administration of local government, having public meeting rooms etc. **town house 1** a town residence, esp. of a person with a house in the country. **2** a terrace house, esp. of a stylish modern type. **3** a house in a planned group in a town. **4** *Brit.* a town hall. **town-major** *hist.* the chief executive officer in a garrison town or fortress. **town mayor** *Brit.* the chairman of a town council. **town meeting** *US* a meeting of the voters of a town for the transaction of public business. **town planning** the planning of the construction and growth of towns. □□ **townish** *adj.* **townless** *adj.* **townlet** *n.* **townward** *adj.* & *adv.* **townwards** *adv.* [OE *tūn* enclosure f. Gmc]

■ **1** community, townlet; municipality, city, metropolis, borough, *Austral.* & *NZ* township, *hist.* burgh, *Brit. sl.* big smoke. **2 b** central business district, town *or* city centre, *US* downtown.

townee /townée/ *n.* (also **townie** /tówni/) *derog.* a person living in a town, esp. as opposed to a countryman or (in a university town) a student etc.

townscape /tównskayp/ *n.* **1** the visual appearance of a town or towns. **2** a picture of a town.

townsfolk /tównzfōk/ *n.* the inhabitants of a particular town or towns.

township /tównship/ *n.* **1** *S.Afr.* **a** an urban area set aside for Black (usu. African) occupation. **b** a White urban area (esp. if new or about to be developed). **2** *US* & *Can.* **a** a division of a county with some corporate powers. **b** a district six miles square. **3** *Brit. hist.* **a** a community inhabiting a manor, parish, etc. **b** a manor or parish as a territorial division. **c** a small town or village forming part of a large parish. **4** *Austral.* & *NZ* a small town; a town-site. [OE *tūnscipe* (as TOWN, -SHIP)]

■ **4** see TOWN 1.

townsman /tównzmən/ *n.* (*pl.* **-men**; *fem.* **townswoman**, *pl.* **-women**) an inhabitant of a town; a fellow citizen.

■ see CITIZEN 2a.

townspeople /tównzpeep'l/ *n.pl.* the people of a town.

towy see TOW[2].

toxaemia /tokseémiə/ *n.* (*US* **toxemia**) **1** blood-poisoning. **2** a condition in pregnancy characterized by increased blood pressure. □□ **toxaemic** *adj.* [as TOXI- + -AEMIA]

toxi- /tóksi/ *comb. form* (also **toxico-** /tóksikō/, **toxo-** /tóksō/) poison; poisonous, toxic.

toxic /tóksik/ *adj.* **1** of or relating to poison (*toxic symptoms*). **2** poisonous (*toxic gas*). **3** caused by poison (*toxic anaemia*). □□ **toxically** *adv.* **toxicity** /-síssiti/ *n.* [med.L *toxicus* poisoned f. L *toxicum* f. Gk *toxikon* (*pharmakon*) (poison for) arrows f. *toxon* bow, *toxa* arrows]

■ **2** see *poisonous* (POISON). □□ **toxicity** see *virulence* (VIRULENT).

toxicology /tóksikólləji/ *n.* the scientific study of poisons. □□ **toxicological** /-kəlójik'l/ *adj.* **toxicologist** *n.*

toxin /tóksin/ *n.* a poison produced by a living organism, esp. one formed in the body and stimulating the production of antibodies. [TOXIC + -IN]

■ see POISON *n.* 1.

toxocara /tóksōkaárə/ *n.* any nematode worm of the genus *Toxocara*, parasitic in the alimentary canal of dogs and cats. □□ **toxocariasis** /-kərīəsiss/ *n.* [*toxo-* (see TOXI-) + Gk *kara* head]

toxophilite /toksóffilīt/ *n.* & *adj.* ● *n.* a student or lover of archery. ● *adj.* of or concerning archery. □□ **toxophily** *n.* [Ascham's *Toxophilus* (1545) f. Gk *toxon* bow + *-philos* -PHILE]

toy /toy/ *n.* & *v.* ● *n.* **1 a** a plaything, esp. for a child. **b** (often *attrib.*) a model or miniature replica of a thing, esp. as a plaything (*toy gun*). **2 a** a thing, esp. a gadget or instrument, regarded as providing amusement or pleasure. **b** a task or undertaking regarded in an unserious way. **3** (usu. *attrib.*) a diminutive breed or variety of dog etc. ● *v.intr.* (usu. foll. by *with*) **1** trifle, amuse oneself, esp. with a person's affections; flirt (*toyed with the idea of going to Africa*). **2 a** move a material object idly (*toyed with her necklace*). **b** nibble at food etc. unenthusiastically (*toyed with a peach*). □ **toy-box** a usu. wooden box for keeping toys in. **toy boy** *colloq.* a woman's much younger male lover. **toy soldier 1** a miniature figure of a soldier. **2** *sl.* a soldier in a peacetime army. [16th c.: earlier = dallying, fun, jest, whim, trifle: orig. unkn.]

■ *n.* **1 a** plaything. **b** (*attrib.*) imitation, fake, simulated, artificial, *colloq.* phoney; see also LITTLE *adj.* 1, 2a. **2** trifle, trinket, bauble, gewgaw, gimcrack, knick-knack, bagatelle, bit of frippery, kickshaw. **3** miniature, tiny, diminutive, small, dwarf. ● *v.* **1** (*toy with*) flirt with, dally with, play with, deal with carelessly, amuse oneself with, *colloq.* dilly-dally with. **2 a** (*toy with*) trifle with, dally with, play with, sport with, fool with, fiddle with, tinker with, finger, twiddle (with).

Tpr. *abbr.* Trooper.

trabeation /tráybiáysh'n/ *n.* the use of beams instead of arches or vaulting in construction. □□ **trabeate** /tráybiət/ *adj.* [L *trabs trabis* beam]

trabecula /trəbékyoolə/ *n.* (*pl.* **trabeculae** /-lee/) **1** *Anat.* a supporting band or bar of connective or bony tissue, esp. dividing an organ into chambers. **2** *Bot.* a beamlike projection or process within a hollow structure. □□ **trabecular** *adj.* **trabeculate** /-lət/ *adj.* [L, dimin. of *trabs* beam]

tracasserie /trəkássəri/ *n.* **1** a state of annoyance. **2** a fuss; a petty quarrel. [F f. *tracasser* bustle]

trace[1] /trayss/ *v.* & *n.* ● *v.tr.* **1 a** observe, discover, or find vestiges or signs of by investigation. **b** (often foll. by *along*, *through*, *to*, etc.) follow or mark the track or position of (*traced their footprints in the mud*; *traced the outlines of a wall*). **c** (often foll. by *back*) follow to its origins (*can trace my family to the 12th century*; *the report has been traced back to you*). **2** (often foll. by *over*) copy (a drawing etc.) by drawing over its lines on a superimposed piece of translucent paper, or by using carbon paper. **3** (often foll. by *out*) mark out, delineate, sketch, or write esp. laboriously (*traced out a plan of the district*; *traced out his vision of the future*). **4** pursue one's way along (a path etc.). ● *n.* **1 a** a sign or mark or other indication of something having existed; a vestige (*no trace remains of the castle*; *has the traces of a vanished beauty*). **b** a very small quantity. **c** an amount of rainfall etc. too small to be measured. **2** a track or footprint left by a person or animal. **3** a track left by the moving pen of an instrument etc. **4** a line on the screen of a cathode-ray tube showing the path of a moving spot. **5** a curve's projection on or intersection with a plane etc. **6** a change in the brain caused by learning processes. □ **trace element 1** a chemical element occurring in minute amounts. **2** a chemical element required only in minute amounts by living organisms for normal growth. **trace fossil** a fossil that represents a burrow, footprint, etc., of an organism. □□ **traceable** *adj.* **traceability** /tráysəbílliti/ *n.* **traceless** *adj.* [ME f. OF *trace* (n.), *tracier* (v.) f. L *tractus* drawing: see TRACT[1]]

■ *v.* **1 a, c** investigate, discover, ascertain, detect, determine, find, seek, search for, hunt down *or* up, unearth, track, follow, observe. **b** dog, pursue, follow (in the footsteps of), stalk, track (down), locate, shadow, trail, *colloq.* tail. **2** copy, reproduce, go over, mark out, draw over. **3** delineate, outline, describe, draw, map, chart, mark (out), record, sketch. ● *n.* **1 a** hint, intimation, sign, token, suggestion, vestige, relic, remains, remnant, indication, mark, record, evidence, clue. **b** bit, spot, speck, streak, grain, jot, drop, dash, touch, suspicion, remnant, fragment, shred, tinge, taste, soupçon, iota, whiff, flicker, gleam, ray, shadow, suggestion, trifle, *US* & *Austral. colloq.* skerrick. **2** track(s), trail, spoor, footprint(s), print(s), footmark(s).

trace[2] /trayss/ *n.* each of the two side-straps, chains, or ropes by which a horse draws a vehicle. □ **kick over the traces** become insubordinate or reckless. **trace-horse** a horse that draws in traces or by a single trace, esp. one hitched on to help uphill etc. [ME f. OF *trais*, pl. of TRAIT]

tracer /tráysər/ *n.* **1** a person or thing that traces. **2** *Mil.* a bullet etc. that is visible in flight because of flames etc. emitted. **3** an artificially produced radioactive isotope capable of being followed through the body by the radiation it produces.

tracery /tráysəri/ *n.* (*pl.* **-ies**) **1** ornamental stone openwork esp. in the upper part of a Gothic window. **2** a fine decorative pattern. **3** a natural object finely patterned. □□ **traceried** *adj.*

trachea /trəkéeə, tráykiə/ *n.* (*pl.* **tracheae** /-kée-ee/) **1** the passage reinforced by rings of cartilage, through which air reaches the bronchial tubes from the larynx; the windpipe. **2** each of the air passages in the body of an insect etc. **3** any duct or vessel in a plant. □□ **tracheal** /tráykiəl/ *adj.* **tracheate** /tráykiayt/ *adj.* [ME f. med.L, = LL *trachia* f. Gk *trakheia* (*artēria*) rough (artery), f. *trakhus* rough]

tracheo- /tráykiō/ *comb. form.*

tracheotomy /trákkióttəmi/ *n.* (also **tracheostomy** /-óstəmi/) (*pl.* **-ies**) an incision made in the trachea to relieve an obstruction to breathing. □ **tracheotomy tube** a breathing-tube inserted into this incision.

trachoma /trəkṓmə/ *n.* a contagious disease of the eye with inflamed granulation on the inner surface of the lids. □□ **trachomatous** /-kṓmətəss, -kómmətəss/ *adj.* [mod.L f. Gk *trakhōma* f. *trakhus* rough]

trachyte /tráykīt, trák-/ *n.* a light-coloured volcanic rock rough to the touch. □□ **trachytic** /trəkíttik/ *adj.* [F f. Gk *trakhutēs* roughness (as TRACHOMA)]

tracing /tráysing/ *n.* **1** a copy of a drawing etc. made by tracing. **2** = TRACE[1] *n.* 3. **3** the act or an instance of tracing. □ **tracing-paper** translucent paper used for making tracings.

track[1] /trak/ *n.* & *v.* ● *n.* **1 a** a mark or marks left by a person, animal, or thing in passing. **b** (in *pl.*) such marks esp. footprints. **2** a rough path, esp. one beaten by use. **3** a continuous railway line (*laid three miles of track*). **4 a** a racecourse for horses, dogs, etc. **b** a prepared course for runners etc. **5 a** a groove on a gramophone record. **b** a section of a gramophone record containing one song etc. (*this side has six tracks*). **c** a lengthwise strip of magnetic tape containing one sequence of signals. **6 a** a line of travel, passage, or motion (*followed the track of the hurricane*; *America followed in the same track*). **b** the path travelled by a ship, aircraft, etc. (cf. COURSE *n.* 2c). **7** a continuous band round the wheels of a tank, tractor, etc. **8** the transverse distance between a vehicle's wheels. **9** = SOUNDTRACK. **10** a line of reasoning or thought (*this track proved fruitless*). ● *v.* **1** *tr.* follow the track of (an animal, person, spacecraft, etc.). **2** *tr.* make out (a course, development, etc.); trace by vestiges. **3** *intr.* (often foll. by *back*, *in*, etc.) (of a film or television camera) move in relation to the subject being filmed. **4** *intr.* (of wheels) run so that the back ones are exactly in the track of the front ones. **5** *intr.* (of a gramophone stylus) follow a groove. **6** *tr.* *US* **a** make a track with (dirt etc.) from the feet. **b** leave such a track on (a floor etc.). □ **in one's tracks** *colloq.* where one stands, there and then (*stopped him in his tracks*). **keep** (or **lose**) **track of** follow (or fail to follow) the course or development of. **make tracks** *colloq.* go or run away. **make tracks for** *colloq.* go in pursuit of or towards. **off the track** away from the subject. **on a person's track 1** in pursuit of him or her. **2** in possession of a clue to a person's conduct, plans, etc. **on the wrong side of** (or **across**) **the tracks** *colloq.* in an inferior or dubious part of town. **on the wrong** (or **right**) **track** following the wrong (or right) line of inquiry. **track down** reach or capture by tracking. **track events** running-races as opposed to jumping etc. (cf. *field events*). **tracking station** an establishment set up to track objects in the sky. **track-laying** (of a vehicle) having a caterpillar tread. **track record** a person's past performance or achievements. **track shoe** a spiked shoe worn by a runner. **track suit** a loose warm suit worn by an athlete etc. for exercising or jogging. **track system** *US* streaming in education. **track with** *Austral. sl.* associate with, court. □□ **trackage** *US n.* [ME f. OF *trac*, perh. f. LG or Du. *tre(c)k* draught etc.]

■ *n.* **1** spoor, trail, footprint(s), print(s), trace(s), mark(s), footmark(s), scent, slot, wake. **2** path, trail, route, footpath, course, road, street, alley. **3** line, rail(s), way, railway, *esp. US* railroad. **4** racecourse, course, racetrack, *Brit.* circuit. **6** see COURSE *n.* 2. **10** see LINE[1] 19. ● *v.* **1** follow, dog, pursue, trace, stalk, shadow, trail, spoor, hunt down, chase, *colloq.* tail. **2** see *keep track of* (TRACK[1]) below. □ **keep track of** trace, track, keep an eye on, follow, pursue, monitor, supervise, oversee, keep up with *or* on, watch, keep a record of *or* on, record. **lose track of** lose, misplace, mislay, lose sight of, forget. **make tracks** see *make away*. **track down** find, discover, seek out, ferret out, hunt down, trace, catch, apprehend, capture, recover, smell *or* sniff out, run to earth *or* ground, run down. **track record** see RECORD *n.* 5.

track[2] /trak/ *v.* **1** *tr.* tow (a boat) by rope etc. from a bank. **2** *intr.* travel by being towed. [app. f. Du. *trekken* to draw etc., assim. to TRACK[1]]

tracker /trákkər/ *n.* **1** a person or thing that tracks. **2** a police dog tracking by scent. **3** a wooden connecting-rod in the mechanism of an organ. **4** = *black tracker*.

tracking /trákking/ *n.* *Electr.* the formation of a conducting path over the surface of an insulating material.

tracklayer /tráklayər/ *n.* **1** *US* = TRACKMAN. **2** a tractor or other vehicle equipped with continuous tracks (see TRACK[1] *n.* 7).

tracklement /trákk'lmənt/ *n.* an item of food, esp. a jelly, served with meat. [20th c.: orig. unkn.]

trackless /trákliss/ *adj.* **1** without a track or tracks; untrodden. **2** leaving no track or trace. **3** not running on a track. □ **trackless trolley** *US* a trolleybus.

■ **1** empty, pathless, untrodden, unexplored, uncharted, virgin.

trackman /trákmən/ *n.* (*pl.* **-men**) a platelayer.

trackway /trákway/ *n.* a beaten path; an ancient roadway.

tract[1] /trakt/ *n.* **1** a region or area of indefinite, esp. large, extent (*pathless desert tracts*). **2** *Anat.* an area of an organ or system (*respiratory tract*). **3** *Brit. archaic* a period of time etc. [L *tractus* drawing f. *trahere tract-* draw, pull]

■ **1** region, area, stretch, territory, expanse, zone, portion, section, sector, quarter, district; patch, plot, parcel, *esp. US* lot.

tract[2] /trakt/ *n.* a short treatise in pamphlet form esp. on a religious subject. [app. abbr. of L *tractatus* TRACTATE]

■ treatise, monograph, essay, article, paper, dissertation, disquisition, homily, sermon; pamphlet, booklet, brochure, leaflet.

tract[3] /trakt/ *n.* *RC Ch.* & *Mus.* an anthem replacing the alleluia in some masses. [med.L *tractus* (*cantus*) drawn-out (song), past part. of L *trahere* draw]

tractable /tráktəb'l/ *adj.* **1** (of a person) easily handled; manageable; docile. **2** (of material etc.) pliant, malleable. □□ **tractability** /-bílliti/ *n.* **tractableness** *n.* **tractably** *adv.* [L *tractabilis* f. *tractare* handle, frequent. of *trahere tract-* draw]

■ **1** docile, amenable, tame, manageable, biddable, persuadable, persuasible, compliant, easygoing, willing, submissive, obedient, governable, yielding. **2** manageable, handleable, workable, adaptable, malleable, pliable, pliant, flexible, plastic, ductile. □□ **tractability, tractableness** see *flexibility* (FLEXIBLE).

Tractarianism /traktáiriəniz'm/ *n. hist.* = OXFORD MOVEMENT. □□ **Tractarian** *adj.* & *n.* [after *Tracts for the Times*, published in Oxford 1833–41 and outlining the movement's principles]

tractate /tráktayt/ *n.* a treatise. [L *tractatus* f. *tractare*: see TRACTABLE]

traction /tráksh'n/ *n.* **1** the act of drawing or pulling a thing over a surface, esp. a road or track (*steam traction*). **2 a** a sustained pulling on a limb, muscle, etc., by means of pulleys, weights, etc. **b** contraction, e.g. of a muscle. **3** the grip of a tyre on a road, a wheel on a rail, etc. **4** *US* the public transport service. □ **traction-engine** a steam or diesel engine for drawing heavy loads on roads, fields, etc. **traction-wheel** the driving-wheel of a locomotive etc. □□ **tractional** *adj.* **tractive** /tráktiv/ *adj.* [F *traction* or med.L *tractio* f. L *trahere tract-* draw]

■ **2 a** see TENSION *n.* 1. **3** grip, gripping power, drag, purchase, friction, adhesion.

tractor /tráktər/ *n.* **1** a motor vehicle used for hauling esp. farm machinery, heavy loads, etc. **2** a traction-engine. [LL *tractor* (as TRACTION)]

trad /trad/ *n.* & *adj.* esp. *Brit. colloq.* ● *n.* traditional jazz. ● *adj.* traditional. [abbr.]

trade /trayd/ *n.* & *v.* ● *n.* **1 a** buying and selling. **b** buying and selling conducted between nations etc. **c** business conducted for profit (esp. as distinct from a profession) (*a butcher by trade*). **d** business of a specified nature or time (*Christmas trade*; *tourist trade*). **2** a skilled handicraft esp. requiring an apprenticeship (*learnt a trade*; *his trade is plumbing*). **3** (usu. prec. by *the*) **a** the people engaged in a specific trade (*the trade will never agree to it*; *trade enquiries only*). **b** *Brit. colloq.* licensed victuallers. **c** *colloq.* the submarine service. **4** *US* a transaction, esp. a swap. **5** (usu. in *pl.*) a trade wind. ● *v.* **1** *intr.* (often foll. by *in*, *with*) engage in trade; buy and sell (*trades in plastic novelties*; *we trade with Japan*). **2** *tr.* **a** exchange in commerce; barter (goods). **b** exchange (insults, blows, etc.). **3** *intr.* (usu. foll. by *with*, *for*) have a transaction with a person for a thing. **4** *intr.* (usu. foll. by *to*) carry goods to a place. □ **be in trade** esp. *derog.* be in commerce, esp. keep a shop. **foreign trade** international trade. **Trade Board** *Brit. hist.* a statutory body for settling disputes etc. in certain industries. **trade book** a book published by a commercial publisher and intended for general readership. **trade cycle** *Brit.* recurring periods of boom and recession. **trade gap** the extent by which a country's imports exceed its exports. **trade in** (often foll. by *for*) exchange (esp. a used car etc.) in esp. part payment for another. **trade-in** *n.* a thing, esp. a car, exchanged in this way. **trade journal** a periodical containing news etc. concerning a particular trade. **trade-last** *US* a compliment from a third person which is reported to the person complimented in exchange for one to the reporter. **trade mark 1** a device, word, or words, secured by legal registration or established by use as representing a company, product, etc. **2** a distinctive characteristic etc. **trade name 1** a name by which a thing is called in a trade. **2** a name given to a product. **3** a name under which a business trades. **trade off** exchange, esp. as a compromise. **trade-off** *n.* such an exchange. **trade on** take advantage of (a person's credulity, one's reputation, etc.). **trade paper** = *trade journal*. **trade plates** number-plates used by a car-dealer etc. on unlicensed cars. **trade price** a wholesale price charged to the dealer before goods are retailed. **trade secret 1** a secret device or technique used esp. in a trade. **2** *joc.* any secret. **Trades Union Congress** *Brit.* the official representative body of British trade unions, meeting annually. **trade** (or **trades**) **union** an organized association of workers in a trade, group of trades, or a profession, formed to protect and further their rights and interests. **trade-** (or **trades-**) **unionism** this system of association. **trade-** (or **trades-**) **unionist** a member of a trade union. **trade wind** a wind blowing continually towards the equator and deflected westward, f. obs. *blow trade* = blow regularly. □□ **tradable** *adj.* **tradeable** *adj.* [ME f. MLG *trade* track f. OS *trada*, OHG *trata*: cf. TREAD]

■ *n.* **1 a, b** commerce, business, traffic, exchange, barter, dealing(s), buying and selling, merchandising, marketing, truck. **d** business; customers, clientele, custom, patrons, following, patronage, shoppers. **2** calling, occupation, pursuit, work, business, employment, line (of work), *métier*, job, vocation, craft, handicraft, career, profession. **4** swap, exchange, interchange, barter, transaction, *colloq.* deal. ● *v.* **1** transact *or* do business, buy, sell, deal, traffic, merchandise, have dealings. **2** exchange, swap, interchange, switch, barter; return. □ **trade in** see REDEEM 3. **trade mark 1** see BRAND *n.* 1b. **2** see HALLMARK *n.* 2. **trade name 2, 3** see BRAND *n.* 1b. **trade on** see *play on*.

trader /tráydər/ *n.* **1** a person engaged in trade. **2** a merchant ship.

■ **1** dealer, merchant, businessman, businesswoman, business person, broker, merchandiser, distributor, seller, salesman, saleswoman, salesperson, vendor, buyer, purchaser, shopkeeper, supplier, retailer, wholesaler, *Brit.* stockist; tradesman, tradeswoman; trafficker.

tradescantia /tráddiskántiə/ *n.* any usu. trailing plant of the genus *Tradescantia*, with large blue, white, or pink flowers. [mod.L f. J. *Tradescant*, Engl. naturalist d. 1638]

tradesman /tráydzmən/ *n.* (*pl.* **-men**; *fem.* **tradeswoman**, *pl.* **-women**) a person engaged in trading or a trade, esp. a shopkeeper or skilled craftsman.

■ merchant, dealer, shopkeeper, retailer, vendor, seller, trader; artisan, craftsman, journeyman, handicraftsman, *Brit.* roundsman.

tradespeople /tráydzpeep'l/ *n.pl.* people engaged in trade and their families.

trading /tráyding/ *n.* the act of engaging in trade. □ **trading estate** esp. *Brit.* a specially-designed industrial and commercial area. **trading post** a store etc. established in a remote or unsettled region. **trading-stamp** a stamp given to customers by some stores which is exchangeable in large numbers for various articles.

tradition /trədísh'n/ *n.* **1 a** a custom, opinion, or belief handed down to posterity esp. orally or by practice. **b** this process of handing down. **2** esp. *joc.* an established practice or custom (*it's a tradition to complain about the weather*). **3** artistic, literary, etc. principles based on experience and practice; any one of these (*stage tradition*; *traditions of the Dutch School*). **4** *Theol.* doctrine or a particular doctrine etc. claimed to have divine authority without documentary evidence, esp.: **a** the oral teaching of Christ and the Apostles. **b** the laws held by the Pharisees to have been delivered by God to Moses. **c** the words and deeds of Muhammad not in the Koran. **5** *Law* the formal delivery of property etc. □□ **traditionary** *adj.* **traditionist** *n.* **traditionless** *adj.* [ME f. OF *tradicion* or L *traditio* f. *tradere* hand on, betray (as TRANS-, *dare* give)]

■ **1, 2** custom, practice, habit, usage, convention, ritual, rite, unwritten law, institution, form, praxis, belief, lore, folklore.

traditional /trədíshən'l/ *adj.* **1** of, based on, or obtained by tradition. **2** (of jazz) in the style of the early 20th c. □□ **traditionally** *adv.*

■ **1** customary, usual, routine, habitual, standard, household, stock, time-honoured, traditionary, classical, established, well-known, conventional, orthodox, ritual, unwritten, accustomed, historic, old, ancestral.

traditionalism /trədíshənəliz'm/ *n.* **1** respect, esp. excessive, for tradition, esp. in religion. **2** a philosophical system referring all religious knowledge to divine revelation and tradition. □□ **traditionalist** *n.* **traditionalistic** /-lístik/ *adj.*

■ □□ **traditionalistic** see REACTIONARY *adj.*, ORTHODOX.

traditor /trádditər/ *n.* (*pl.* **traditors** or **traditores** /-tóreez/) *hist.* an early Christian who surrendered copies of Scripture or Church property to his or her persecutors to save his or her life. [L: see TRAITOR]

traduce /trədyóoss/ *v.tr.* speak ill of; misrepresent. □□ **traducement** *n.* **traducer** *n.* [L *traducere* disgrace (as TRANS-, *ducere duct-* lead)]

■ see DISPARAGE.

traffic /tráffik/ *n.* & *v.* ● *n.* **1** (often *attrib.*) **a** vehicles moving in a public highway, esp. of a specified kind, density, etc. (*heavy traffic on the M1*; *traffic warden*). **b** such movement in the air or at sea. **2** (usu. foll. by *in*) trade, esp. illegal (*the* *traffic in drugs*). **3 a** the transportation of goods, the coming and going of people or goods by road, rail, air, sea, etc. **b** the persons or goods so transported. **4** dealings or communication between people etc. (*had no traffic with them*). **5** the messages, signals, etc., transmitted through a communications system; the flow or volume of such business. ● *v.* (**trafficked, trafficking**) **1** *intr.* (usu. foll. by *in*) deal in something, esp. illegally (*trafficked in narcotics*; *traffics in innuendo*). **2** *tr.* deal in; barter. □ **traffic circle** *US* a roundabout. **traffic cop** esp. *US colloq.* a traffic policeman. **traffic island** a paved or grassed area in a road to divert traffic and provide a refuge for pedestrians. **traffic jam** traffic at a standstill because of roadworks, an accident, etc. **traffic-light** (or **-lights** or **-signal**) a usu. automatic signal controlling road traffic esp. at junctions by coloured lights. **traffic sign** a sign conveying information, a warning, etc., to vehicle-drivers. **traffic warden** *Brit.* a uniformed official employed to help control road traffic and esp. parking. □□ **trafficker** *n.* **trafficless** *adj.* [F *traf(f)ique*, Sp. *tráfico*, It. *traffico*, of unkn. orig.]

■ *n.* **2** see TRADE *n.* 1a, b. **3** movement, conveyance, shipping, transport, freight, transportation. **4** see DEALINGS. ● *v.* (*traffic in*) see DEAL[1] *v.* 2. □ **traffic circle** see ROUNDABOUT *n.* 1. **traffic jam** jam, gridlock, delay, congestion, stoppage, *esp. Brit.* traffic queue, *Brit.* tailback, *US* backup, *colloq.* snarl-up.

trafficator /tráffikaytər/ *n. Brit. hist.* a signal raised automatically to indicate a change of direction in a motor vehicle. [TRAFFIC + INDICATOR]

tragacanth /trággəkanth/ *n.* a white or reddish gum from a plant, *Astragalus gummifer*, used in pharmacy, calico-printing, etc., as a vehicle for drugs, dye, etc. [F *tragacante* f. L *tragacantha* f. Gk *tragakantha*, name of a shrub, f. *tragos* goat + *akantha* thorn]

tragedian /trəjeédiən/ *n.* **1** a writer of tragedies. **2** an actor in tragedy. [ME f. OF *tragediane* (as TRAGEDY)]

tragedienne /trəjeédi-én/ *n.* an actress in tragedy. [F fem. (as TRAGEDIAN)]

tragedy /trájidi/ *n.* (*pl.* **-ies**) **1** a serious accident, crime, or natural catastrophe. **2** a sad event; a calamity (*the team's defeat is a tragedy*). **3 a** a play in verse or prose dealing with tragic events and with an unhappy ending, esp. concerning the downfall of the protagonist. **b** tragic plays as a genre (cf. COMEDY). [ME f. OF *tragedie* f. L *tragoedia* f. Gk *tragōidia* app. goat-song f. *tragos* goat + *ōidē* song]

■ **1, 2** catastrophe, calamity, disaster, misfortune, adversity, blow.

tragic /trájik/ *adj.* **1** (also **tragical** /-k'l/) sad; calamitous; greatly distressing (*a tragic tale*). **2** of, or in the style of, tragedy (*tragic drama*; *a tragic actor*). □ **tragic irony** a device, orig. in Greek tragedy, by which words carry a tragic, esp. prophetic, meaning to the audience, unknown to the character speaking. □□ **tragically** *adv.* [F *tragique* f. L *tragicus* f. Gk *tragikos* f. *tragos* goat: see TRAGEDY]

■ **1** sad, depressing, lamentable, unhappy, funereal, forlorn, melancholy, cheerless, mournful, grievous, morose, lugubrious, dismal, piteous, pitiable, pitiful, pathetic(al), appalling, wretched, dreadful, awful, terrible, horrible, deplorable, miserable, distressing, heart-rending, disturbing, upsetting, shocking, unlucky, unfortunate, hapless, ill-fated, inauspicious, ill-omened, ill-starred, calamitous, catastrophic, crushing, disastrous, *archaic* star-crossed, *formal* lachrymose, *literary or joc.* dolorous; tragical.

tragicomedy /trájikómmidi/ *n.* (*pl.* **-ies**) **1 a** a play having a mixture of comedy and tragedy. **b** plays of this kind as a genre. **2** an event etc. having tragic and comic elements. □□ **tragicomic** *adj.* **tragicomically** *adv.* [F *tragicomédie* or It. *tragicomedia* f. LL *tragicomoedia* f. L *tragico-comoedia* (as TRAGIC, COMEDY)]

tragopan /trággəpan/ *n.* any Asian pheasant of the genus *Tragopan*, with erect fleshy horns on its head. [L f. Gk f. *tragos* goat + *Pan* the god Pan]

trahison des clercs /traá-izóɴ day kláir/ *n.* the betrayal of standards, scholarship, etc., by intellectuals. [F, title of a book by J. Benda (1927)]

trail /trayl/ *n.* & *v.* ● *n.* **1 a** a track left by a thing, person, etc., moving over a surface (*left a trail of wreckage*; *a slug's slimy trail*). **b** a track or scent followed in hunting, seeking, etc. (*he's on the trail*). **2** a beaten path or track, esp. through a wild region. **3** a part dragging behind a thing or person; an appendage (*a trail of smoke*; *a condensation trail*). **4** the rear end of a gun-carriage stock. ● *v.* **1** *tr.* & *intr.* draw or be drawn along behind, esp. on the ground. **2** *intr.* (often foll. by *behind*) walk wearily; lag; straggle. **3** *tr.* follow the trail of; pursue (*trailed him to his home*). **4** *intr.* be losing in a game or other contest (*trailing by three points*). **5** *intr.* (usu. foll. by *away*, *off*) peter out; tail off. **6** *intr.* **a** (of a plant etc.) grow or hang over a wall, along the ground etc. **b** (of a garment etc.) hang loosely. **7** *tr.* (often *refl.*) drag (oneself, one's limbs, etc.) along wearily etc. **8** *tr.* advertise (a film, a radio or television programme, etc.) in advance by showing extracts etc. **9** *tr.* apply (slip) through a nozzle or spout to decorate ceramic ware. □ **at the trail** *Mil.* with arms trailed. **trail arms** *Mil.* let a rifle etc. hang balanced in one hand and, *Brit.*, parallel to the ground. **trail bike** a light motor cycle for use in rough terrain. **trail-blazer 1** a person who marks a new track through wild country. **2** a pioneer; an innovator. **trail-blazing** *n.* the act or process of blazing a trail. ● *attrib.adj.* that blazes a trail; pioneering. **trail one's coat** deliberately provoke a quarrel, fight, etc. **trailing edge 1** the rear edge of an aircraft's wing etc. **2** *Electronics* the part of a pulse in which the amplitude diminishes (opp. *leading edge* (see LEADING[1])). **trailing wheel** a wheel not given direct motive power. **trail-net** a drag-net. [ME (earlier as verb) f. OF *traillier* to tow, or f. MLG *treilen* haul f. L *tragula* drag-net]

■ *n.* **1** track, spoor, scent, smell, trace, footsteps, footprints, path, wake, *US* sign. **2** (beaten) path, way, pathway, footpath, route, track, course. ● *v.* **1** tow, draw, drag (along), haul, pull, tag along, trawl, bring along (behind), carry along (behind); move, be drawn, stream, sweep, dangle. **2** lag (behind), dawdle, loiter, linger, follow, straggle, bring up the rear, hang back, fall *or* drop behind. **3** follow, pursue, dog, trace, shadow, stalk, track, chase, hunt, *colloq.* tail. **4** lag (behind), be losing, fall *or* drop behind, *Brit.* be down. **5** (*trail off* or *away*) diminish, decrease, fade away *or* out, disappear, dwindle, lessen, die out *or* away, peter out, subside, taper off, tail off, weaken, grow faint *or* dim. □ **trail-blazer 1** see PIONEER *n.* 2. **2** see PIONEER *n.* 1.

trailer /tráylər/ *n.* **1** a person or thing that trails. **2** a series of brief extracts from a film etc., used to advertise it in advance. **3** a vehicle towed by another, esp.: **a** the rear section of an articulated lorry. **b** an open cart. **c** a platform for transporting a boat etc. **d** *US* a caravan. **4** a trailing plant.

train /trayn/ *v.* & *n.* ● *v.* **1 a** *tr.* (often foll. by *to* + infin.) teach (a person, animal, oneself, etc.) a specified skill esp. by practice (*trained the dog to beg*; *was trained in midwifery*). **b** *intr.* undergo this process (*trained as a teacher*). **2** *tr.* & *intr.* bring or come into a state of physical efficiency by exercise, diet, etc.; undergo physical exercise, esp. for a specific purpose (*trained me for the high jump*; *the team trains every evening*). **3** *tr.* cause (a plant) to grow in a required shape (*trained the peach tree up the wall*). **4** (usu. as **trained** *adj.*) make (the mind, eye, etc.) sharp or discerning as a result of instruction, practice, etc. **5** *tr.* (often foll. by *on*) point or aim (a gun, camera, etc.) at an object etc. **6** *colloq.* **a** *intr.* go by train. **b** *tr.* (foll. by *it* as object) make a journey by train (*trained it to Aberdeen*). **7** *tr.* (usu. foll. by *away*) *archaic* entice, lure. ● *n.* **1** a series of railway carriages or trucks drawn by an engine. **2** something dragged along behind or forming the back part of a dress, robe, etc. (*wore a dress with a long train*; *the train of the peacock*). **3** a succession or series of people, things, events, etc. (*a long train of camels*; *interrupted my train of thought*; *a* *train of ideas*). **4** a body of followers; a retinue (*a train of admirers*). **5** a succession of military vehicles etc., including artillery, supplies, etc. (*baggage train*). **6** a line of gunpowder etc. to fire an explosive charge. **7** a series of connected wheels or parts in machinery. □ **in train** properly arranged or directed. **in a person's train** following behind a person. **in the train of** as a sequel of. **train-bearer** a person employed to hold up the train of a robe etc. **train down** train with exercise or diet to lower one's weight. **train-ferry** (*pl.* **-ies**) a ship that conveys a railway train across water. **train-mile** one mile travelled by one train, as a unit of traffic. **train-spotter** a person who collects locomotive numbers as a hobby. **train-spotting** this hobby. □□ **trainable** *adj.* **trainability** /tráynəbílliti/ *n.* **trainee** /-neé/ *n.* **trainless** *adj.* [ME f. OF *traïner*, *trahiner*, ult. f. L *trahere* draw]

■ *v.* **1 a** discipline, exercise, tutor, teach, coach, drill, school, instruct, prepare, fit, educate, edify, guide, bring up, indoctrinate, condition, rear, raise. **2** work out, exercise, practise. **4** (**trained**) see EXPERIENCED 2, SHARP *adj.* 9. **5** see AIM *v.* 2. ● *n.* **1** *colloq.* (*esp. as a child's word*) choo-choo. **3, 5** line, procession, succession, string, set, series, sequence, chain, concatenation, progression, stream, caravan, cavalcade, parade, column, file, row, *esp. Brit.* queue. **4** retinue, entourage, cortège, suite, following, escort, guard, attendants, followers, *hist.* retainers; staff, court, household,. □□ **trainable** see MANAGEABLE. **trainee** see NOVICE.

trainband /tráynband/ *n. hist.* any of several divisions of London citizen soldiers, esp. in the Stuart period.

trainer /tráynər/ *n.* **1** a person who trains. **2** a person who trains horses, athletes, footballers, etc., as a profession. **3** an aircraft or device simulating it used to train pilots. **4** *Brit.* a soft running shoe of leather, canvas, etc.

■ **2** see TEACHER.

training /tráyning/ *n.* the act or process of teaching or learning a skill, discipline, etc. (*physical training*). □ **go into training** begin physical training. **in training 1** undergoing physical training. **2** physically fit as a result of this. **out of training 1** no longer training. **2** physically unfit. **training-college** a college or school for training esp. prospective teachers. **training-ship** a ship on which young people are taught seamanship etc.

■ warming up, exercise, working-out; drilling, practice, preparation, rehearsal; see also EDUCATION 1a.

trainman /tráynman/ *n.* (*pl.* **-men**) a railway employee working on trains.

train-oil /tráynoyl/ *n.* oil obtained from the blubber of a whale (esp. of a right whale). [obs. *train*, *trane* train-oil f. MLG *trān*, MDu. *traen*, app. = TEAR²]

trainsick /tráynsik/ *adj.* affected with nausea by the motion of a train. □□ **trainsickness** *n.*

traipse /trayps/ *v.* & *n.* (also **trapes**) *colloq.* or *dial.* ● *v.intr.* **1** tramp or trudge wearily. **2** (often foll. by *about*) go on errands. ● *n.* **1** a tedious journey on foot. **2** *archaic* a slattern. [16th-c. *trapes* (v.), of unkn. orig.]

■ *v.* **1** see TRAMP *v.* 1a.

trait /tray, *disp.* trayt/ *n.* a distinguishing feature or characteristic esp. of a person. [F f. L *tractus* (as TRACT¹)]

■ feature, characteristic, attribute, quality, peculiarity, idiosyncrasy, quirk, lineament, mark, property, hallmark.

traitor /tráytər/ *n.* (*fem.* **traitress** /-triss/) (often foll. by *to*) a person who is treacherous or disloyal, esp. to his country. □□ **traitorous** *adj.* **traitorously** *adv.* [ME f. OF *traït(o)ur* f. L *traditor -oris* f. *tradere*: see TRADITION]

■ turncoat, Judas, quisling, betrayer, informer, renegade, fifth-columnist, double-crosser, snake (in the grass), viper in one's bosom, double-dealer, collaborator, *colloq.* two-timer, *hist.* traditor, *US* & *Austral. sl.* dog. □□ **traitorous** treacherous, perfidious, seditious, subversive, insurrectionist, insurrectionary, renegade, insurgent, disloyal, deceitful, untrue, unfaithful, faithless; treasonable, double-crossing, double-dealing, *colloq.* two-timing. **traitorously** treacherously, perfidiously, seditiously, subversively, disloyally, deceitfully, insidiously, behind a person's back.

trajectory /trəjéktəri, trájik-/ *n.* (*pl.* **-ies**) **1** the path described by a projectile flying or an object moving under the action of given forces. **2** *Geom.* a curve or surface cutting a system of curves or surfaces at a constant angle. [(orig. adj.) f. med.L *trajectorius* f. L *traicere traject-* (as TRANS-, *jacere* throw)]

■ **1** flight path, course, track.

tra-la /traalaá/ *int.* an expression of joy or gaiety. [imit. of song]

tram¹ /tram/ *n.* **1** *Brit.* an electrically-powered passenger vehicle running on rails laid in a public road. **2** a four-wheeled vehicle used in coal-mines. □ **tram-road** *hist.* a road with wooden, stone, or metal wheel-tracks. [MLG & MDu. *trame* balk, beam, barrow-shaft]

■ **1** *Brit.* tramcar, trolley bus, *US* streetcar, trolley(-car).

tram² /tram/ *n.* (in full **tram silk**) double silk thread used for the weft of some velvets and silks. [F *trame* f. L *trama* weft]

tramcar /trámkaar/ *n. Brit.* = TRAM¹ 1.

tramlines /trámlīnz/ *n.pl.* **1** rails for a tramcar. **2** *colloq.* **a** either pair of two sets of long parallel lines at the sides of a lawn-tennis court. **b** similar lines at the side or back of a badminton court. **3** inflexible principles or courses of action etc.

trammel /trámm'l/ *n.* & *v.* ● *n.* **1** (usu. in *pl.*) an impediment to free movement; a hindrance (*the trammels of domesticity*). **2** a triple drag-net for fish, which are trapped in a pocket formed when they attempt to swim through. **3** an instrument for drawing ellipses etc. with a bar sliding in upright grooves. **4** a beam-compass. **5** *US* a hook in a fireplace for a kettle etc. ● *v.tr.* (**trammelled, trammelling**; *US* **trammeled, trammeling**) confine or hamper with or as if with trammels. [in sense 'net' ME f. OF *tramail* f. med.L *tramaculum*, *tremaculum*, perh. formed as TRI- + *macula* (MAIL²): later history uncert.]

■ *n.* **1** impediment(s), hindrance(s), shackle(s), handicap(s), check(s), restriction(s), restraint(s), curb(s), deterrent(s), constraint(s), hitch(es), snag(s), (stumbling) block(s), obstacle(s). ● *v.* impede, hinder, handicap, check, restrain, curb, deter, constrain, block, obstruct, fetter, confine.

trammie /trámmi/ *n.* esp. *Austral.* & *NZ colloq.* the conductor or driver of a tram.

tramontana /traámontaánə/ *n.* a cold north wind in the Adriatic. [It.: see TRAMONTANE]

tramontane /trəmóntayn/ *adj.* & *n.* ● *adj.* **1** situated or living on the other side of mountains, esp. the Alps as seen from Italy. **2** (from the Italian point of view) foreign; barbarous. ● *n.* **1** a tramontane person. **2** = TRAMONTANA. [ME f. It. *tramontano* f. L *transmontanus* beyond the mountains (as TRANS-, *mons montis* mountain)]

■ *adj.* **1** transalpine, transmontane.

tramp /tramp/ *v.* & *n.* ● *v.* **1** *intr.* **a** walk heavily and firmly (*tramping about upstairs*). **b** go on foot, esp. a distance. **2** *tr.* **a** cross on foot, esp. wearily or reluctantly. **b** cover (a distance) in this way (*tramped forty miles*). **3** *tr.* (often foll. by *down*) tread on; trample; stamp on. **4** *tr. Austral. colloq.* dismiss from employment, sack. **5** *intr.* live as a tramp. ● *n.* **1** an itinerant vagrant or beggar. **2** the sound of a person, or esp. people, walking, marching, etc., or of horses' hooves. **3** a journey on foot, esp. protracted. **4 a** an iron plate protecting the sole of a boot used for digging. **b** the part of a spade that it strikes. **5** esp. *US sl. derog.* a promiscuous woman. **6** = *ocean tramp*. □□ **tramper** *n.* **trampish** *adj.* [ME *trampe* f. Gmc]

■ *v.* **1 a** plod, stamp, stomp, stump, clump, clomp, trudge, lumber, *colloq.* galumph, *colloq. or dial.* traipse. **b** march, hike, trudge, plod, slog, footslog, plough, tread, trek, walk, *US* mush. **2** see TRAVERSE *v.* 1, WALK *v.* 1, 2. **3** see TRAMPLE *v.* 1. **4** see DISMISS 2. ● *n.* **1** derelict, vagabond, vagrant, drifter, beachcomber, down-and-out, *Austral.*

traveller, sundowner, bagman, *Austral.* & *NZ* swagman, *US* hobo, down-and-outer, *colloq.* knight of the road, *Austral. sl.* whaler, *Austral.* & *NZ sl.* overlander, *Brit. sl.* dosser, *US sl.* bum. **2** step, tread, footfall, footstep. **3** march, trudge, plod, slog, footslog, trek, hike, walk, *colloq. or dial.* traipse. **5** see SLUT.

trample /trámp'l/ *v.* & *n.* ● *v.tr.* **1** tread underfoot. **2** press down or crush in this way. ● *n.* the sound or act of trampling. □ **trample on, trample underfoot 1** tread heavily on. **2** treat roughly or with contempt; disregard (a person's feelings etc.). □□ **trampler** *n.* [ME f. TRAMP + -LE[4]]

■ *v.* **1** trample on, tramp (down *or* on *or* upon), stamp (on), stomp (on *or* upon), tread (down *or* on), step on. **2** crush, press, squash, flatten, *colloq.* squish; stamp out, extinguish, put out, destroy, rout, defeat. □ **trample on, trample underfoot 2** trample upon, violate, damage, harm, hurt, infringe *or* encroach on, ride roughshod over, set at naught, scorn, disdain, defy, disregard, ignore, fly in the face of, fling *or* cast *or* throw to the winds, *literary* contemn.

trampoline /trámpəleen/ *n.* & *v.* ● *n.* a strong fabric sheet connected by springs to a horizontal frame, used by gymnasts etc. for somersaults, as a springboard, etc. ● *v.intr.* use a trampoline. □□ **trampolinist** *n.* [It. *trampolino* f. *trampoli* stilts]

tramway /trámway/ *n.* **1** = *tram-road* (see TRAM[1]). **2 a** rails for a tramcar. **b** a tramcar system.

trance /traanss/ *n.* & *v.* ● *n.* **1 a** a sleeplike or half-conscious state without response to stimuli. **b** a hypnotic or cataleptic state. **2** such a state as entered into by a medium. **3** a state of extreme exaltation or rapture; ecstasy. ● *v.tr. poet.* = ENTRANCE[2]. □□ **trancelike** *adj.* [ME f. OF *transe* f. *transir* depart, fall into trance f. L *transire*: see TRANSIT]

■ *n.* **1, 2** daze, stupor, semi-conscious *or* half-conscious *or* hypnotic *or* cataleptic *or* sleeplike *or* dream state, state of semi-consciousness *or* half-consciousness *or* catalepsy *or* suspended animation *or* stupefaction *or* abstraction *or* (complete) absorption; brown study, reverie. **3** exaltation, rapture; see also ECSTASY. □□ **trancelike** see GLASSY *adj.* 2.

tranche /traansh/ *n.* a portion, esp. of income, or of a block of shares. [F, = slice (as TRENCH)]

■ see PORTION *n.* 1, SLAB *n.*

tranny /tránni/ *n.* (*pl.* **-ies**) esp. *Brit. colloq.* a transistor radio. [abbr.]

tranquil /trángkwil/ *adj.* calm, serene, unruffled. □□ **tranquillity** /-kwílliti/ *n.* **tranquilly** *adv.* [F *tranquille* or L *tranquillus*]

■ calm, serene, placid, quiet, peaceful, still, smooth, unagitated, halcyon, relaxed, restful; unruffled, sedate, steady, regular, even, dispassionate, self-possessed, cool, self-controlled, collected, composed, cool-headed, unexcited, undisturbed, untroubled, unperturbed. □□ **tranquillity** see CALM *n.* 1. **tranquilly** see EASY *adv.*

tranquillize /trángkwilīz/ *v.tr.* (*US* **tranquilize, -ise**) make tranquil, esp. by a drug etc.

■ calm, soothe, pacify, still, quiet, relax, lull, compose, settle, sedate, *Brit.* quieten.

tranquillizer /trángkwilīzər/ *n.* (*US* **tranquilizer, -iser**) a drug used to diminish anxiety.

■ barbiturate, opiate, sedative, anti-psychotic, anti-anxiety drug, *Med.* calmative, palliative, lenitive, *Pharm.* bromide, *sl.* downer.

trans- /transs, traanss, tranz, traanz/ *prefix* **1** across, beyond (*transcontinental*; *transgress*). **2** on or to the other side of (*transatlantic*) (opp. CIS-). **3** through (*transonic*). **4** into another state or place (*transform*; *transcribe*). **5** surpassing, transcending (*transfinite*). **6** *Chem.* **a** (of an isomer) having the same atom or group on opposite sides of a given plane in the molecule (cf. CIS- 4). **b** having a higher atomic number than (*transuranic*). [from or after L *trans* across]

transact /tranzákt, traanz-/ *v.tr.* perform or carry through (business). □□ **transactor** *n.* [L *transigere transact-* (as TRANS-, *agere* do)]

■ do, carry on *or* out, conduct, manage, handle, negotiate, administer, discharge, perform, enact, settle, conclude, complete, finish.

transaction /tranzáksh'n, traanz-/ *n.* **1 a** a piece of esp. commercial business done; a deal (*a profitable transaction*). **b** the management of business etc. **2** (in *pl.*) published reports of discussions, papers read, etc., at the meetings of a learned society. □□ **transactional** *adj.* **transactionally** *adv.* [ME f. LL *transactio* (as TRANSACT)]

■ **1 a** deal, dealing, negotiation, matter, affair, business, action, proceeding, agreement, arrangement, bargain. **2** (*transactions*) proceedings, record(s), acts, minutes, annals, report(s).

transalpine /tránzálpīn, traánz-/ *adj.* beyond the Alps, esp. from the Italian point of view. [L *transalpinus* (as TRANS-, *alpinus* ALPINE)]

■ see TRAMONTANE *adj.*

transatlantic /tránzətlántik, traánz-/ *adj.* **1** beyond the Atlantic, esp.: **a** *Brit.* American. **b** *US* European. **2** crossing the Atlantic (*a transatlantic flight*).

transceiver /transeévər, traan-/ *n.* a combined radio transmitter and receiver.

transcend /transénd, traan-/ *v.tr.* **1** be beyond the range or grasp of (human experience, reason, belief, etc.). **2** excel; surpass. [ME f. OF *transcendre* or L *transcendere* (as TRANS-, *scandere* climb)]

■ **1** go beyond, lie outside, exceed. **2** surpass, outstrip, exceed, outdistance, outdo, excel, overshadow, top, rise above, outshine, eclipse, beat.

transcendent /transéndənt, traan-/ *adj.* & *n.* ● *adj.* **1** excelling, surpassing (*transcendent merit*). **2** transcending human experience. **3** *Philos.* **a** higher than or not included in any of Aristotle's ten categories in scholastic philosophy. **b** not realizable in experience in Kantian philosophy. **4** (esp. of the supreme being) existing apart from, not subject to the limitations of, the material universe (opp. IMMANENT). ● *n. Philos.* a transcendent thing. □□ **transcendence** *n.* **transcendency** *n.* **transcendently** *adv.*

■ *adj.* **1** peerless, incomparable, unequalled, matchless, unrivalled, unparalleled, unique, consummate, paramount, superior, surpassing, supreme, pre-eminent, sublime, excelling, superb, magnificent, marvellous; transcendental. □□ **transcendence, transcendency** see *predominance* (PREDOMINANT). **transcendently** see *supremely* (SUPREME).

transcendental /tránsendént'l, traán-/ *adj.* & *n.* ● *adj.* **1** = TRANSCENDENT. **2 a** (in Kantian philosophy) presupposed in and necessary to experience; a priori. **b** (in Schelling's philosophy) explaining matter and objective things as products of the subjective mind. **c** (esp. in Emerson's philosophy) regarding the divine as the guiding principle in man. **3 a** visionary, abstract. **b** vague, obscure. **4** *Math.* (of a function) not capable of being produced by the algebraical operations of addition, multiplication, and involution, or the inverse operations. ● *n.* a transcendental term, conception, etc. □ **transcendental cognition** a priori knowledge. **Transcendental Meditation** a method of detaching oneself from problems, anxiety, etc., by silent meditation and repetition of a mantra. **transcendental object** a real (unknown and unknowable) object. **transcendental unity** unity brought about by cognition. □□ **transcendentally** *adv.* [med.L *transcendentalis* (as TRANSCENDENT)]

■ *adj.* **3 a** see OCCULT *adj.* 1, 3. **b** see OCCULT *adj.* 2.

transcendentalism /tránsendéntəliz'm, traán-/ *n.* **1** transcendental philosophy. **2** exalted or visionary language. □□ **transcendentalist** *n.* **transcendentalize** *v.tr.* (also **-ise**).

transcode /tranzkṓd, traanz-/ *v.tr.* & *intr.* convert from one form of coded representation to another.

transcontinental /tránzkontinént'l, traánz-/ *adj.* & *n.* ● *adj.* (of a railway etc.) extending across a continent. ● *n.* a transcontinental railway or train. ▫▫ **transcontinentally** *adv.*

transcribe /transkrī́b, traan-/ *v.tr.* **1** make a copy of, esp. in writing. **2** transliterate. **3** write out (shorthand, notes, etc.) in ordinary characters or continuous prose. **4 a** record for subsequent reproduction. **b** broadcast in this form. **5** arrange (music) for a different instrument etc. ▫▫ **transcriber** *n.* **transcription** /-skrípsh'n/ *n.* **transcriptional** /-skrípshən'l/ *adj.* **transcriptive** /-skríptiv/ *adj.* [L *transcribere transcript-* (as TRANS-, *scribere* write)]

■ **1** copy, reproduce, replicate, duplicate, record. **2, 3** translate, transliterate, write out, render, represent, show, interpret. **4 a** see RECORD *v.* ▫▫ **transcriber** see SCRIBE *n.* 1. **transcription** see TRANSCRIPT 1.

transcript /tránskript, traán-/ *n.* **1** a written or recorded copy. **2** any copy. [ME f. OF *transcrit* f. L *transcriptum* neut. past part.: see TRANSCRIBE]

■ **1** transcription, record, copy, transliteration. **2** (carbon *or* machine *or* photostatic *or* xerographic) copy, carbon, duplicate, photocopy, facsimile, fax, reproduction, *propr.* Xerox, Photostat.

transducer /tranzdyóossər, traanz-/ *n.* any device for converting a non-electrical signal into an electrical one e.g. pressure into voltage. [L *transducere* lead across (as TRANS-, *ducere* lead)]

transect /transékt, traan-/ *v.tr.* cut across or transversely. ▫▫ **transection** *n.* [TRANS- + L *secare sect-* cut]

transept /tránsept, traán-/ *n.* **1** either arm of the part of a cross-shaped church at right angles to the nave (*north transept; south transept*). **2** this part as a whole. ▫▫ **transeptal** /-séptəl/ *adj.* [mod.L *transeptum* (as TRANS-, SEPTUM)]

transexual var. of TRANSSEXUAL.

transfer *v.* & *n.* ● *v.* /transfér, traans-/ (**transferred, transferring**) **1** *tr.* (often foll. by *to*) **a** convey, remove, or hand over (a thing etc.) (*transferred the bag from the car to the station*). **b** make over the possession of (property, a ticket, rights, etc.) to a person (*transferred his membership to his son*). **2** *tr.* & *intr.* change or move to another group, club, department, etc. **3** *intr.* change from one station, route, etc., to another on a journey. **4** *tr.* **a** convey (a drawing etc.) from one surface to another, esp. to a lithographic stone by means of transfer-paper. **b** remove (a picture) from one surface to another, esp. from wood or a wall to canvas. **5** *tr.* change (the sense of a word etc.) by extension or metaphor. ● *n.* /tránsfer, traáns-/ **1** the act or an instance of transferring or being transferred. **2 a** a design etc. conveyed or to be conveyed from one surface to another. **b** a small usu. coloured picture or design on paper, which is transferable to another surface. **3** a football player etc. who is or is to be transferred. **4 a** the conveyance of property, a right, etc. **b** a document effecting this. **5** *US* a ticket allowing a journey to be continued on another route etc. ▫ **transfer-book** a register of transfers of property, shares, etc. **transfer company** *US* a company conveying passengers or luggage between stations. **transfer fee** a fee paid for the transfer of esp. a professional footballer. **transfer ink** ink used for making designs on a lithographic stone or transfer-paper. **transfer list** a list of footballers available for transfer. **transfer-paper** specially coated paper to receive the impression of transfer ink and transfer it to stone. **transfer RNA** RNA conveying an amino-acid molecule from the cytoplasm to a ribosome for use in protein synthesis etc. ▫▫ **transferee** /-reé/ *n.* **transferor** /-férər/ esp. *Law n.* **transferrer** /-férər/ *n.* [ME f. F *transférer* or L *transferre* (as TRANS-, *ferre lat-* bear)]

■ *v.* **1 a** move, transport, translocate, convey, remove, carry, take, deliver, bring, transmit, cart, haul, shift, hand (on *or* over), turn over, give, pass (on *or* along *or* over). **b** see *make over* 1. **2** change, switch; see also TRANSPLANT *v.* 1, MOVE *v.* 7. **3** change, switch. ● *n.* **1** move, conveyance, transmittal, transmission, delivery, change, transferral, transference.

transferable /tránsférəb'l, traáns-/ *adj.* capable of being transferred. ▫ **transferable vote** a vote that can be transferred to another candidate if the first choice is eliminated. ▫▫ **transferability** /-bílliti/ *n.*

■ see MOVABLE *adj.*

transference /tránsfərənss, traáns-/ *n.* **1** the act or an instance of transferring; the state of being transferred. **2** *Psychol.* the redirection of childhood emotions to a new object, esp. to a psychoanalyst.

■ **1** see DISPOSITION 4a, SURRENDER *n.*, TRANSMISSION 1, TRANSIT *n.* 1.

transferral /transférəl, traans-/ *n.* = TRANSFER *n.* 1.

transferrin /transférin, traans-/ *n.* a protein transporting iron in the blood serum. [TRANS- + L *ferrum* iron]

transfiguration /tránsfigyooráysh'n, traáns-/ *n.* **1** a change of form or appearance. **2 a** Christ's appearance in radiant glory to three of his disciples (Matt. 17:2, Mark 9:2–3). **b** (**Transfiguration**) the festival of Christ's transfiguration, 6 Aug. [ME f. OF *transfiguration* or L *transfiguratio* (as TRANSFIGURE)]

■ **1** see TRANSFORMATION.

transfigure /transfíggər, traans-/ *v.tr.* change in form or appearance, esp. so as to elevate or idealize. [ME f. OF *transfigurer* or L *transfigurare* (as TRANS-, FIGURE)]

■ see TRANSFORM *v.*

transfinite /tránsfínīt, traáns-/ *adj.* **1** beyond or surpassing the finite. **2** *Math.* (of a number) exceeding all finite numbers.

transfix /transfíks, traans-/ *v.tr.* **1** pierce with a sharp implement or weapon. **2** root (a person) to the spot with horror or astonishment; paralyse the faculties of. ▫▫ **transfixion** /-fíksh'n/ *n.* [L *transfigere transfix-* (as TRANS-, FIX)]

■ **1** pin, fix, impale, skewer, nail, pierce, transpierce, spear, spike, spit, stick, stab. **2** enrapture, hypnotize, mesmerize, rivet, fascinate, bewitch, enchant, engross, root to the spot, stun, paralyse, freeze, stop dead, *colloq.* stop a person in his or her tracks.

transform *v.* & *n.* ● *v.* /transfórm, traans-/ **1 a** *tr.* make a thorough or dramatic change in the form, outward appearance, character, etc., of. **b** *intr.* (often foll. by *into, to*) undergo such a change. **2** *tr. Electr.* change the voltage etc. of (a current). **3** *tr. Math.* change (a mathematical entity) by transformation. ● *n.* /tránsform, traáns-/ *Math.* & *Linguistics* the product of a transformation. ▫▫ **transformable** *adj.* **transformative** *adj.* [ME f. OF *transformer* or L *transformare* (as TRANS-, FORM)]

■ *v.* **1** change, modify, transfigure, alter, transmute, metamorphose, turn into, convert, mutate, permute, revolutionize, *joc.* transmogrify. ▫▫ **transformable** see CHANGEABLE 2.

transformation /tránsfərmáysh'n, traáns-/ *n.* **1** the act or an instance of transforming; the state of being transformed. **2** *Zool.* a change of form at metamorphosis, esp. of insects, amphibia, etc. **3** the induced or spontaneous change of one element into another. **4** *Math.* a change from one geometrical figure, expression, or function to another of the same value, magnitude, etc. **5** *Biol.* the modification of a eukaryotic cell from its normal state to a malignant state. **6** *Linguistics* a process, with reference to particular rules, by which one grammatical pattern of sentence structure can be converted into another, or the underlying meaning of a sentence can be converted into a statement of syntax. **7** *archaic* a woman's wig. **8** a sudden dramatic change of scene on stage. [ME f. OF *transformation* or LL *transformatio* (as TRANSFORM)]

■ **1–3** change, modification, transfiguration, alteration, transmutation, metamorphosis, conversion, mutation, permutation, revolution, *joc.* transmogrification.

transformational /tránsfərmáyshən'l, traáns-/ *adj.* relating to or involving transformation. ▫ **transformational grammar** *Linguistics* a grammar that describes a language by means of transformation (see TRANSFORMATION 6). ▫▫ **transformationally** *adv.*

transformer /transfórmər, traans-/ *n.* **1** an apparatus for reducing or increasing the voltage of an alternating current. **2** a person or thing that transforms.

transfuse /transfyóoz, traans-/ *v.tr.* **1 a** permeate (*purple dye transfused the water*). **b** instil (an influence, quality, etc.) into (*transfused enthusiasm into everyone*). **2 a** transfer (blood) from one person or animal to another. **b** inject (liquid) into a blood-vessel to replace lost fluid. **3** cause (fluid etc.) to pass from one vessel etc. to another. □□ **transfusion** /-fyóozh'n/ *n.* [ME f. L *transfundere transfus-* (as TRANS-, *fundere* pour)]

■ **1 a** infuse, permeate, suffuse, imbue, percolate through. **b** instil, transmit, transfer, inject.

transgenic /tranzjénnik, traanz-/ *adj. Biol.* (of an animal or plant) having genetic material introduced from another species.

transgress /tranzgréss, traanz-/ *v.tr.* (also *absol.*) **1** go beyond the bounds or limits set by (a commandment, law, etc.); violate; infringe. **2** *Geol.* (of the sea) to spread over (the land). □□ **transgression** /-grésh'n/ *n.* **transgressive** *adj.* **transgressor** *n.* [F *transgresser* or L *transgredi transgress-* (as TRANS-, *gradi* go)]

■ **1** sin, offend, err, lapse, fall from grace, misbehave, go wrong *or* astray, do wrong, *literary or archaic* trespass; (*transgress the law*) break *or* violate *or* contravene *or* go beyond *or* exceed *or* overstep *or* infringe *or* breach *or* defy *or* disobey the law. □□ **transgression** sin, offence, error, lapse, fall from grace, disobedience, misbehaviour, wrong, violation, fault, misdeed, misdemeanour, crime, wrongdoing, infraction, peccadillo, *archaic* trespass. **transgressor** sinner, offender, criminal, felon, culprit, lawbreaker, wrongdoer, evil-doer, reprobate, villain, miscreant, malefactor, delinquent, *archaic* trespasser.

tranship var. of TRANSSHIP.

transhumance /tranz-hyóoməns, traanz-/ *n.* the seasonal moving of livestock to a different region. [F f. *transhumer* f. L TRANS- + *humus* ground]

transient /tránziənt, tráanz-/ *adj.* & *n.* ● *adj.* **1** of short duration; momentary; passing; impermanent (*life is transient*; *of transient interest*). **2** *Mus.* serving only to connect; inessential (*a transient chord*). ● *n.* **1** a temporary visitor, worker, etc. **2** *Electr.* a brief current etc. □□ **transience** *n.* **transiency** *n.* **transiently** *adv.* [L *transire* (as TRANS-, *ire* go)]

■ *adj.* **1** transitory, temporary, brief, fleeting, momentary, passing, ephemeral, fugitive, evanescent, short-lived, short-term, impermanent, fly-by-night, volatile, *literary* fugacious. ● *n.* **1** see MIGRANT *n.*

transilluminate /tránzilóominayt, tráanz-/ *v.tr.* pass a strong light through for inspection, esp. for medical diagnosis. □□ **transillumination** /-náysh'n/ *n.*

transire /transīri/ *n. Brit.* a customs permit for the passage of goods. [L *transire* go across (as TRANSIENT)]

transistor /tranzístər, traan-/ *n.* **1** a semiconductor device with three connections, capable of amplification in addition to rectification. **2** (in full **transistor radio**) a portable radio with transistors. [portmanteau word, f. TRANSFER + RESISTOR]

■ **2** see RADIO *n.*

transistorize /tranzístərīz, traan-/ *v.tr.* (also **-ise**) design or equip with, or convert to, transistors rather than valves. □□ **transistorization** /-záysh'n/ *n.*

transit /tránzit, tráanz-/ *n.* & *v.* ● *n.* **1** the act or process of going, conveying, or being conveyed, esp. over a distance (*transit by rail*; *made a transit of the lake*). **2** a passage or route (*the overland transit*). **3 a** the apparent passage of a celestial body across the meridian of a place. **b** such an apparent passage across the sun or a planet. **4** *US* the local conveyance of passengers on public routes. ● *v.* (**transited, transiting**) **1** *tr.* make a transit across. **2** *intr.* make a transit. □ **in transit** while going or being conveyed. **transit camp** a camp for the temporary accommodation of soldiers, refugees, etc. **transit-circle** (or **-instrument**) an instrument for observing the transit of a celestial body across the meridian. **transit-compass** (or **-theodolite**) a surveyor's instrument for measuring a horizontal angle. **transit-duty** duty paid on goods passing through a country. **transit lounge** a lounge at an airport for passengers waiting between flights. **transit visa** a visa allowing only passage through a country. [ME f. L *transitus* f. *transire* (as TRANSIENT)]

■ *n.* **1** moving, movement, travel, travelling, motion, passing, progress, progression, transition; passage, traverse, traversal, traversing; transport, transportation, carriage, haulage, cartage, conveyance, transfer, transference, transferral, transmittal. **2** passage, route. ● *v.* **1** cross, traverse, go across *or* over *or* through, move across *or* over *or* through, pass across *or* over *or* through, travel across *or* over *or* through. □ **in transit** see *on the move* 2 (MOVE).

transition /tranzísh'n, traan-/ *n.* **1** a passing or change from one place, state, condition, etc., to another (*an age of transition*; *a transition from plain to hills*). **2** *Mus.* a momentary modulation. **3** *Art* a change from one style to another, esp. *Archit.* from Norman to Early English. **4** *Physics* a change in an atomic nucleus or orbital electron with emission or absorption of radiation. □ **transition element** *Chem.* any of a set of elements in the periodic table characterized by partly filled *d* or *f* orbitals and the ability to form coloured complexes. **transition point** *Physics* the point at which different phases of the same substance can be in equilibrium. □□ **transitional** *adj.* **transitionally** *adv.* **transitionary** *adj.* [F *transition* or L *transitio* (as TRANSIT)]

■ **1** change, alteration, metamorphosis, change-over, transformation, transmutation, mutation, development, evolution, conversion, modification, *Physiol.* metastasis; movement, motion, passing, progress, progression, transit, passage. □□ **transitional, transitionary** see INTERMEDIATE *adj.*

transitive /tránzitiv, tráanz-/ *adj.* **1** *Gram.* (of a verb or sense of a verb) that takes a direct object (whether expressed or implied), e.g. *saw* in *saw the donkey*, *saw that she was ill* (opp. INTRANSITIVE). **2** *Logic* (of a relation) such as to be valid for any two members of a sequence if it is valid for every pair of successive members. □□ **transitively** *adv.* **transitiveness** *n.* **transitivity** /-tívviti/ *n.* [LL *transitivus* (as TRANSIT)]

transitory /tránzitəri, tráanz-/ *adj.* not permanent, brief, transient. □ **transitory action** *Law* an action that can be brought in any country irrespective of where the transaction etc. started. □□ **transitorily** *adv.* **transitoriness** *n.* [ME f. AF *transitorie*, OF *transitoire* f. L *transitorius* (as TRANSIT)]

■ see BRIEF *adj.* 1, TRANSIENT *adj.*

translate /tranzláyt, traanz-/ *v.* **1** *tr.* (also *absol.*) **a** (often foll. by *into*) express the sense of (a word, sentence, speech, book, etc.) in another language. **b** do this as a profession etc. (*translates for the UN*). **2** *intr.* (of a literary work etc.) be translatable, bear translation (*does not translate well*). **3** *tr.* express (an idea, book, etc.) in another, esp. simpler, form. **4** *tr.* interpret the significance of; infer as (*translated his silence as dissent*). **5** *tr.* move or change, esp. from one person, place, or condition, to another (*was translated by joy*). **6** *intr.* (foll. by *into*) result in; be converted into; manifest itself as. **7** *tr. Eccl.* **a** remove (a bishop) to another see. **b** remove (a saint's relics etc.) to another place. **8** *tr. Bibl.* convey to heaven without death; transform. **9** *tr. Mech.* **a** cause (a body) to move so that all its parts travel in the same direction. **b** impart motion without rotation to. □□ **translatable** *adj.* **translatability** /-laytəbílliti/ *n.* [ME f. L *translatus*, past part. of *transferre*: see TRANSFER]

■ **1** convert (into), paraphrase (in), change (into), rewrite (in), interpret (in), transcribe (into); render in, turn into; decode, decipher, metaphrase. **3** interpret, rewrite, explain, rephrase, reword, metaphrase, elucidate, spell out. **4** interpret, construe, take, understand, read; infer as. **5** transform, convert, change, mutate, turn, transmute, metamorphose, alter, *joc.* transmogrify; transfer, convey, carry, move, transport, send.

translation /tranzláysh'n, traanz-/ *n.* **1** the act or an instance of translating. **2** a written or spoken expression of the meaning of a word, speech, book, etc. in another language. □□ **translational** *adj.* **translationally** *adv.*
■ **1** interpretation, rewriting, rewrite, explanation, rewording, metaphrase, elucidation; metamorphosis, change, alteration, transmutation, transfiguration, transformation, conversion, *joc.* transmogrification; transfer, transference, transferral, conveyance, movement, transportation, transport, transmittal, transmission. **2** conversion, paraphrase, interpretation, transcription, transliteration, rendering, rendition, version, rewrite, rewriting, rewording, rephrasing, metaphrase, gloss, decipherment, decoding, explanation, elucidation.

translator /tranzláytər, traanz-/ *n.* **1** a person who translates from one language into another. **2** a television relay transmitter. **3** a program that translates from one (esp. programming) language into another.

transliterate /tranzlíttərayt, traanz-/ *v.tr.* represent (a word etc.) in the closest corresponding letters or characters of a different alphabet or language. □□ **transliteration** /-ráysh'n/ *n.* **transliterator** *n.* [TRANS- + L *littera* letter]
■ see TRANSCRIBE 2, 3. □□ **transliteration** see TRANSCRIPT *n.* 1, TRANSLATION 2.

translocate /tránzlōkáyt, traánz-/ *v.tr.* **1** move from one place to another. **2** (usu. in *passive*) *Bot.* move (substances in a plant) from one part to another. □□ **translocation** *n.*

translucent /tranzlóoss'nt, traanz-/ *adj.* **1** allowing light to pass through diffusely; semi-transparent. **2** transparent. □□ **translucence** *n.* **translucency** *n.* **translucently** *adv.* [L *translucēre* (as TRANS-, *lucēre* shine)]
■ see CLEAR *adj.* 3a, *see-through* (SEE[1]).

translunar /tránzlóonər, traánz-/ *adj.* **1** lying beyond the moon. **2** of or relating to space travel or a trajectory towards the moon.

transmarine /tránzməréen, traánz-/ *adj.* situated or going beyond the sea. [L *transmarinus* f. *marinus* MARINE]

transmigrant /tranzmígrənt, traanz-/ *adj.* & *n.* ● *adj.* passing through, esp. a country on the way to another. ● *n.* a migrant or alien passing through a country etc. [L *transmigrant-*, part. stem of *transmigrare* (as TRANSMIGRATE)]

transmigrate /tránzmīgráyt, traánz-/ *v.intr.* **1** (of the soul) pass into a different body; undergo metempsychosis. **2** migrate. □□ **transmigration** /-gráysh'n/ *n.* **transmigrator** *n.* **transmigratory** /-mígrətəri/ *adj.* [ME f. L *transmigrare* (as TRANS-, MIGRATE)]

transmission /tranzmísh'n, traanz-/ *n.* **1** the act or an instance of transmitting; the state of being transmitted. **2** a broadcast radio or television programme. **3** the mechanism by which power is transmitted from an engine to the axle in a motor vehicle. □ **transmission line** a conductor or conductors carrying electricity over large distances with minimum losses. [L *transmissio* (as TRANS-, MISSION)]
■ **1** transfer, transference, transferral, conveyance, carriage, movement, transportation, transport, forwarding, shipping, shipment, transmittal, dispatch; broadcasting, dissemination, communication, telecasting. **2** broadcast, telecast, programme, show.

transmit /tranzmít, traanz-/ *v.tr.* (**transmitted, transmitting**) **1 a** pass or hand on; transfer (*transmitted the message; how diseases are transmitted*). **b** communicate (ideas, emotions, etc.). **2 a** allow (heat, light, sound, electricity, etc.) to pass through; be a medium for. **b** be a medium for (ideas, emotions, etc.) (*his message transmits hope*). **3** broadcast (a radio or television programme). □□ **transmissible** /-míssəb'l/ *adj.* **transmissive** /-míssiv/ *adj.* **transmittable** *adj.* **transmittal** *n.* [ME f. L *transmittere* (as TRANS-, *mittere miss-* send)]
■ **1 a** send, transfer, convey, communicate, pass *or* hand on, relay, deliver, forward, dispatch; post, ship, cable, radio, telegraph, fax, telex, telephone, *esp. US* mail, *colloq.* phone, *esp. US colloq.* wire. **b** see COMMUNICATE 1a. **2** pass on, send, direct, conduct, channel. **3** see BROADCAST *v.* 1a. □□ **transmissible** see CATCHING 1a. **transmittal** see TRANSMISSION 1.

transmitter /tranzmíttər, traanz-/ *n.* **1** a person or thing that transmits. **2** a set of equipment used to generate and transmit electromagnetic waves carrying messages, signals, etc., esp. those of radio or television. **3** = NEUROTRANSMITTER.

transmogrify /tranzmógrifī, traanz-/ *v.tr.* (**-ies, -ied**) *joc.* transform, esp. in a magical or surprising manner. □□ **transmogrification** /-fikáysh'n/ *n.* [17th c.: orig. unkn.]
■ see TRANSFORM *v.* □□ **transmogrification** see TRANSFORMATION.

transmontane /tránzmóntáyn, traánz-/ *adj.* = TRAMONTANE. [L *transmontanus*: see TRAMONTANE]
■ see TRAMONTANE *adj.*

transmutation /tránzmyootáysh'n, traánz-/ *n.* **1** the act or an instance of transmuting or changing into another form etc. **2** *Alchemy hist.* the supposed process of changing base metals into gold. **3** *Physics* the changing of one element into another by nuclear bombardment etc. **4** *Geom.* the changing of a figure or body into another of the same area or volume. **5** *Biol.* Lamarck's theory of the change of one species into another. □□ **transmutational** *adj.* **transmutationist** *n.* [ME f. OF *transmutation* or LL *transmutatio* (as TRANSMUTE)]
■ **1** see TRANSFORMATION.

transmute /tranzmyóot, traanz-/ *v.tr.* **1** change the form, nature, or substance of. **2** *Alchemy hist.* subject (base metals) to transmutation. □□ **transmutable** *adj.* **transmutability** /-myóotəbílliti/ *n.* **transmutative** /-myóotətiv/ *adj.* **transmuter** *n.* [ME f. L *transmutare* (as TRANS-, *mutare* change)]
■ see TRANSFORM *v.*

transnational /tránznáshən'l, traánz-/ *adj.* extending beyond national boundaries.

transoceanic /tránzōshiánnik, traánz-/ *adj.* **1** situated beyond the ocean. **2** concerned with crossing the ocean (*transoceanic flight*).

transom /tránsəm/ *n.* **1** a horizontal bar of wood or stone across a window or the top of a door (cf. MULLION). **2** each of several beams fixed across the stern-post of a ship. **3** a beam across a saw-pit to support a log. **4** a strengthening crossbar. **5** *US* = *transom window*. □ **transom window 1** a window divided by a transom. **2** a window placed above the transom of a door or larger window; a fanlight. □□ **transomed** *adj.* [ME *traversayn*, *transyn*, *-ing*, f. OF *traversin* f. *traverse* TRAVERSE]

transonic /transónnik, traan-/ *adj.* (also **trans-sonic**) relating to speeds close to that of sound. [TRANS- + SONIC, after *supersonic* etc.]

transpacific /tránzpəsíffik, traánz-/ *adj.* **1** beyond the Pacific. **2** crossing the Pacific.

transparence /tranzpárrənss, traanz-, -páirənss/ *n.* = TRANSPARENCY 1.

transparency /tranzpárrənsi, traanz-, -páirənsi/ *n.* (*pl.* **-ies**) **1** the condition of being transparent. **2** *Photog.* a positive transparent photograph on glass or in a frame to be viewed using a slide projector etc. **3** a picture, inscription, etc., made visible by a light behind it. [med.L *transparentia* (as TRANSPARENT)]
■ **1** see CLARITY. **2** slide.

transparent /tranzpárrənt, traanz-, -páirənt/ *adj.* **1** allowing light to pass through so that bodies can be distinctly seen (cf. TRANSLUCENT). **2 a** (of a disguise, pretext, etc.) easily seen through. **b** (of a motive, quality, etc.) easily discerned; evident; obvious. **3** (of a person etc.) easily understood; frank; open. **4** *Physics* transmitting heat or other electromagnetic rays without distortion. □□ **transparently** *adv.* **transparentness** *n.* [ME f. OF f. med.L *transparens* f. L *transparēre* shine through (as TRANS-, *parēre* appear)]
■ **1** (crystal) clear, pellucid, diaphanous, see-through, limpid, crystalline, sheer. **2** plain, apparent, obvious, evident, unambiguous, patent, manifest, unmistakable,

(crystal) clear, as plain as day, as plain as the nose on one's face, undisguised, recognizable, understandable. **3** candid, open, frank, plain-spoken, direct, unambiguous, unequivocal, straightforward, ingenuous, forthright, above-board, artless, guileless, simple, naïve, undissembling, *colloq.* on the level, upfront.

transpierce /tranzpeérss, traanz-/ *v.tr.* pierce through.

transpire /transpír, traan-/ *v.* **1** *intr.* (of a secret or something unknown) leak out; come to be known. **2** *intr. disp.* **a** (prec. by *it* as subject) turn out; prove to be the case (*it transpired he knew nothing about it*). **b** occur; happen. **3** *tr.* & *intr.* emit (vapour, sweat, etc.), or be emitted, through the skin or lungs; perspire. **4** *intr.* (of a plant or leaf) release water vapour. □□ **transpirable** *adj.* **transpiration** /-spiráysh'n/ *n.* **transpiratory** /-spírətəri/ *adj.* [F *transpirer* or med.L *transpirare* (as TRANS-, L *spirare* breathe)]

■ **1** become known, be rumoured, be revealed, come to light, leak out, come out, get out, emerge. **2 a** turn out, emerge, be revealed. **b** happen, occur, take place, come about, come to pass, materialize, arise.

transplant *v.* & *n.* ● *v.tr.* /tranzplaánt, traanz-/ **1 a** plant in another place (*transplanted the daffodils*). **b** move to another place (*whole nations were transplanted*). **2** *Surgery* transfer (living tissue or an organ) and implant in another part of the body or in another body. ● *n.* /tránzplaant, traánz-/ **1** *Surgery* **a** the transplanting of an organ or tissue. **b** such an organ etc. **2** a thing, esp. a plant, transplanted. □□ **transplantable** /-plaántəb'l/ *adj.* **transplantation** /-plaantáysh'n/ *n.* **transplanter** /-plaántər/ *n.* [ME f. LL *transplantare* (as TRANS-, PLANT)]

■ *v.* **1** displace, move, relocate, shift, uproot, resettle, transfer, *formal* remove. **2** graft. ● *n.* **1 a** transplantation, implantation. **b** implant, graft.

transponder /tranzpóndər, traanz-/ *n.* a device for receiving a radio signal and automatically transmitting a different signal. [TRANSMIT + RESPOND]

transpontine /tránzpóntīn, traánz-/ *adj.* on the other side of a bridge, esp. on the south side of the Thames. [TRANS- + L *pons pontis* bridge]

transport *v.* & *n.* ● *v.tr.* /tranzpórt, traanz-/ **1** take or carry (a person, goods, troops, baggage, etc.) from one place to another. **2** *hist.* take (a criminal) to a penal colony; deport. **3** (as **transported** *adj.*) (usu. foll. by *with*) affected with strong emotion. ● *n.* /tránzport, traánz-/ **1 a** a system of conveying people, goods, etc., from place to place. **b** the means of this (*our transport has arrived*). **2** a ship, aircraft, etc. used to carry soldiers, stores, etc. **3** (esp. in *pl.*) vehement emotion (*transports of joy*). **4** *hist.* a transported convict. □ **transport café** *Brit.* a roadside café for (esp. commercial) drivers. [ME f. OF *transporter* or L *transportare* (as TRANS-, *portare* carry)]

■ *v.* **1** carry, bear, convey, move, remove, transfer, ferry, deliver, fetch, bring, get, take, ship, haul, cart, transmit, send, forward, freight. **2** exile, banish, deport, send away. **3** (**transported**) carried away, enraptured, captivated, delighted, charmed, spellbound, bewitched, fascinated, enchanted, entranced, enthralled, hypnotized, mesmerized, electrified, ravished; rapt, overjoyed, ecstatic, elated. ● *n.* **1 a** transportation, conveyance, shipping, transfer, transferral, shipment, haulage, cartage, carriage, moving. **b** carrier, conveyance, transporter, *esp. US* transportation. **3** rapture, ecstasy.

transportable /tranzpórtəb'l, traanz-/ *adj.* **1** capable of being transported. **2** *hist.* (of an offender or an offence) punishable by transportation. □□ **transportability** /-bílliti/ *n.*

■ **1** see PORTABLE *adj.*

transportation /tránzportáysh'n, traánz-/ *n.* **1** the act of conveying or the process of being conveyed. **2 a** a system of conveying. **b** esp. *US* the means of this. **3** *hist.* removal to a penal colony.

■ **1, 2** see TRANSIT *n.* 1. **3** see EXILE *n.* 1.

transporter /tranzpórtər, traanz-/ *n.* **1** a person or device that transports. **2** a vehicle used to transport other vehicles or large pieces of machinery etc. by road. □ **transporter bridge** a bridge carrying vehicles etc. across water on a suspended moving platform.

■ **1** see CARRIER 1, 2.

transpose /tranzpṓz, traanz-/ *v.tr.* **1 a** cause (two or more things) to change places. **b** change the position of (a thing) in a series. **2** change the order or position of (words or a word) in a sentence. **3** *Mus.* write or play in a different key. **4** *Algebra* transfer (a term) with a changed sign to the other side of an equation. □ **transposing instrument** *Mus.* an instrument producing notes different in pitch from the written notes. **transposing piano** etc. *Mus.* a piano etc. on which a transposition may be effected mechanically. □□ **transposable** *adj.* **transposal** *n.* **transposer** *n.* [ME, = transform f. OF *transposer* (as TRANS-, L *ponere* put)]

■ **1, 2** exchange, interchange, rearrange, reverse, switch, swap, trade, commute, transfer.

transposition /tránzpəzísh'n, traánz-/ *n.* the act or an instance of transposing; the state of being transposed. □□ **transpositional** *adj.* **transpositive** /-pózzitiv/ *adj.* [F *transposition* or LL *transpositio* (as TRANS-, POSITION)]

transputer /tranzpyṓōtər, traanz-/ *n.* a microprocessor with integral memory designed for parallel processing. [TRANSISTOR + COMPUTER]

transsexual /tránzséksyooəl, traánz-, -sékshooəl/ *adj.* & *n.* (also **transexual**) ● *adj.* having the physical characteristics of one sex and the supposed psychological characteristics of the other. ● *n.* **1** a transsexual person. **2** a person whose sex has been changed by surgery. □□ **transsexualism** *n.*

transship /tranz-shíp, traanz-/ *v.tr.* (also **tranship**) *intr.* (**-shipped, -shipping**) transfer from one ship or form of transport to another. □□ **transshipment** *n.*

trans-sonic var. of TRANSONIC.

transubstantiation /tránsəbstánshiáysh'n, traán-/ *n. Theol.* & *RC Ch.* the conversion of the Eucharistic elements wholly into the body and blood of Christ, only the appearance of bread and wine still remaining. [med.L (as TRANS-, SUBSTANCE)]

transude /transyṓōd, traan-/ *v.intr.* (of a fluid) pass through the pores or interstices of a membrane etc. □□ **transudation** /-dáysh'n/ *n.* **transudatory** /-dətəri/ *adj.* [F *transsuder* f. OF *tressuer* (as TRANS-, L *sudare* sweat)]

■ see PERCOLATE 1. □□ **transudation** see SECRETION[1] 1a.

transuranic /tránzyooránnik, traánz-/ *adj. Chem.* (of an element) having a higher atomic number than uranium.

transversal /tranzvérs'l, traanz-/ *adj.* & *n.* ● *adj.* (of a line) cutting a system of lines. ● *n.* a transversal line. □□ **transversality** /-sálliti/ *n.* **transversally** *adv.* [ME f. med.L *transversalis* (as TRANSVERSE)]

transverse /tránzvérss, traánz-/ *adj.* situated, arranged, or acting in a crosswise direction. □ **transverse magnet** a magnet with poles at the sides and not the ends. **transverse wave** *Physics* a wave in which the medium vibrates at right angles to the direction of its propagation. □□ **transversely** *adv.* [L *transvertere transvers-* turn across (as TRANS-, *vertere* turn)]

transvestism /tranzvéstiz'm, traanz-/ *n.* the practice of wearing the clothes of the opposite sex, esp. as a sexual stimulus. □□ **transvestist** *n.* [G *Transvestismus* f. TRANS- + L *vestire* clothe]

transvestite /tranzvéstīt, traanz-/ *n.* a person given to transvestism.

trap[1] /trap/ *n.* & *v.* ● *n.* **1 a** an enclosure or device, often baited, for catching animals, usu. by affording a way in but not a way out. **b** a device with bait for killing vermin, esp. = MOUSETRAP. **2** a trick betraying a person into speech or an act (*is this question a trap?*). **3** an arrangement to catch an unsuspecting person, e.g. a speeding motorist. **4** a device for hurling an object such as a clay pigeon into the air to be shot at. **5** a compartment from which a greyhound is released at the start of a race. **6** a shoe-shaped wooden device with a pivoted bar that sends a ball from its heel into the air on being struck at the other end with a bat. **7 a** a curve in a downpipe etc. that fills with liquid and forms a seal against the upward passage of gases. **b** a device for preventing the passage of steam etc. **8** *Golf* a bunker. **9** a device allowing pigeons to enter but not leave a loft. **10** a two-wheeled carriage (*a pony and trap*). **11** = TRAPDOOR. **12** *sl.* the mouth (esp. *shut one's trap*). **13** (esp. in *pl.*) *colloq.* a percussion instrument esp. in a jazz band. ● *v.tr.* (**trapped, trapping**) **1** catch (an animal) in a trap. **2** catch or catch out (a person) by means of a trick, plan, etc. **3** stop and retain in or as in a trap. **4** provide (a place) with traps. □ **trap-ball** a game played with a trap (see sense 6 of *n.*). **trap-shooter** a person who practises trap-shooting. **trap-shooting** the sport of shooting at objects released from a trap. □□ **traplike** *adj.* [OE *treppe*, *træppe*, rel. to MDu. *trappe*, med.L *trappa*, of uncert. orig.]

■ *n.* **1** snare, pitfall, gin, springe, *US* deadfall. **2** trick, subterfuge, wile, ruse, stratagem, deception, artifice, *colloq.* ploy. **3** ambush, device, snare, pitfall, mantrap, booby trap, set-up. **12** mouth, *esp. Brit. sl.* gob, *US sl.* yap. ● *v.* **1** snare, ensnare, entrap, catch, capture, net, corner, ambush. **2** trick, deceive, fool, dupe, beguile, inveigle, catch, catch out. **3** imprison, confine, lock, hold, keep, pin down.

trap[2] /trap/ *v.tr.* (**trapped, trapping**) (often foll. by *out*) **1** provide with trappings. **2** adorn. [obs. *trap* (n.): ME f. OF *drap*: see DRAPE]

trap[3] /trap/ *n.* (in full **trap-rock**) any dark-coloured igneous rock, fine-grained and columnar in structure, esp. basalt. [Sw. *trapp* f. *trappa* stair, f. the often stairlike appearance of its outcroppings]

trapdoor /trápdór/ *n.* a door or hatch in a floor, ceiling, or roof, usu. made flush with the surface. □ **trapdoor spider** any of various spiders, esp. of the family Ctenizidae, that make a hinged trapdoor at the top of their nest.

trapes var. of TRAIPSE.

trapeze /trəpéez/ *n.* a crossbar or set of crossbars suspended by ropes used as a swing for acrobatics etc. [F *trapèze* f. LL *trapezium*: see TRAPEZIUM]

trapezium /trəpéeziəm/ *n.* (*pl.* **trapezia** /-ziə/ or **trapeziums**) **1** *Brit.* a quadrilateral with only one pair of sides parallel. **2** *US* = TRAPEZOID 1. [LL f. Gk *trapezion* f. *trapeza* table]

trapezoid /tráppizoyd/ *n.* **1** *Brit.* a quadrilateral with no two sides parallel. **2** *US* = TRAPEZIUM 1. □□ **trapezoidal** *adj.* [mod.L *trapezoides* f. Gk *trapezoeidēs* (as TRAPEZIUM)]

trapper /tráppər/ *n.* a person who traps wild animals esp. to obtain furs.

trappings /tráppingz/ *n.pl.* **1** ornamental accessories, esp. as an indication of status (*the trappings of office*). **2** the harness of a horse esp. when ornamental. [ME (as TRAP[2])]

■ **1** accoutrements, panoply, caparison, equipage, apparatus, equipment, accompaniments, paraphernalia, appointments, furniture, gear, rig, decoration(s), embellishment(s), accessories, frippery, fripperies, adornment(s), ornaments, trimmings, fittings, finery, *archaic* raiment.

Trappist /tráppist/ *n.* & *adj.* ● *n.* a member of a branch of the Cistercian order founded in 1664 at La Trappe in Normandy and noted for an austere rule including a vow of silence. ● *adj.* of or relating to this order. [F *trappiste* f. *La Trappe*]

traps /traps/ *n.pl. colloq.* personal belongings; baggage. [perh. contr. f. TRAPPINGS]

trash /trash/ *n.* & *v.* ● *n.* **1** esp. *US* **a** worthless or poor quality stuff, esp. literature. **b** rubbish, refuse. **c** absurd talk or ideas; nonsense. **2** a worthless person or persons. **3** a thing of poor workmanship or material. **4** (in full **cane-trash**) *W.Ind.* the refuse of crushed sugar canes and dried stripped leaves and tops of sugar cane used as fuel. ● *v.tr.* **1** esp. *US colloq.* wreck. **2** strip (sugar canes) of their outer leaves to speed up the ripening process. **3** esp. *US colloq.* expose the worthless nature of; disparage. **4** esp. *US colloq.* throw away, discard. □ **trash can** *US* a dustbin. **trash-ice** (on a sea, lake, etc.) broken ice mixed with water. [16th c.: orig. unkn.]

■ *n.* **1 a** junk, knick-knacks, gewgaws, trifles, bric-à-brac, frippery, fripperies, bits and pieces, odds and ends, lumber, trinkets, tinsel, *Brit. colloq.* Brummagem goods; rubbish, garbage. **b** rubbish, litter, garbage, waste, refuse, debris, rubble, scrap, dregs, dross, scoria, slag, dirt, sweepings. **c** rubbish, (stuff and) nonsense, balderdash, moonshine, gibberish, bunkum, garbage, twaddle, *Sc.* havers, *colloq.* gobbledegook, gammon, flapdoodle, piffle, malarkey, hogwash, tosh, *sl.* tommy-rot, rot, bunk, bosh, hooey, poppycock, boloney, eyewash, bilge-water, bull, *Brit. sl.* codswallop, (a load of (old)) cobblers, *esp. US sl.* hokum. **2** see RABBLE[1] 2, 3. ● *v.* **1** destroy, ruin, wreck, vandalize, deface, *US sl.* total. **3** see PAN[1] *v.* 1. **4** see DISCARD *v.*

trashy /tráshi/ *adj.* (**trashier, trashiest**) worthless; poorly made. □□ **trashily** *adv.* **trashiness** *n.*

■ see WORTHLESS.

trass /trass/ *n.* (also **tarras** /tərás/) a light-coloured tuff used as cement-material. [Du. *trass*, earlier *terras*, *tiras* f. Rmc: cf. TERRACE]

trattoria /tráttəréeə/ *n.* an Italian restaurant. [It.]

trauma /tráwmə, trów-/ *n.* (*pl.* **traumata** /-mətə/ or **traumas**) **1** any physical wound or injury. **2** physical shock following this, characterized by a drop in body temperature, mental confusion, etc. **3** *Psychol.* emotional shock following a stressful event, sometimes leading to long-term neurosis. □□ **traumatize** *v.tr.* (also **-ise**). **traumatization** /-mətīzáysh'n/ *n.* [Gk *trauma traumatos* wound]

■ **1** see WOUND[1] *n.* 1. **2** shock. □□ **traumatize** see WOUND[1] *v.*, SHOCK[1] *v.* 1.

traumatic /trawmáttik, trow-/ *adj.* **1** of or causing trauma. **2** *colloq.* (in general use) distressing; emotionally disturbing (*a traumatic experience*). **3** of or for wounds. □□ **traumatically** *adv.* [LL *traumaticus* f. Gk *traumatikos* (as TRAUMA)]

■ **1, 2** shocking, upsetting, disturbing, painful, agonizing, distressing, harmful, hurtful, injurious, damaging, wounding, harrowing, traumatizing.

traumatism /tráwmətiz'm, trów-/ *n.* **1** the action of a trauma. **2** a condition produced by this.

travail /trávvayl/ *n.* & *v. literary* ● *n.* **1** painful or laborious effort. **2** the pangs of childbirth. ● *v.intr.* undergo a painful effort, esp. in childbirth. [ME f. OF *travail*, *travaillier* ult. f. med.L *trepalium* instrument of torture f. L *tres* three + *palus* stake]

■ *n.* **1** see LABOUR *n.* 1. **2** see LABOUR *n.* 3. ● *v.* see LABOUR *v.* 1, 2.

travel /trávv'l/ *v.* & *n.* ● *v.intr.* & *tr.* (**travelled, travelling**; *US* **traveled, traveling**) **1** *intr.* go from one place to another; make a journey esp. of some length or abroad. **2** *tr.* **a** journey along or through (a country). **b** cover (a distance) in travelling. **3** *intr. colloq.* withstand a long journey (*wines that do not travel*). **4** *intr.* go from place to place as a salesman. **5** *intr.* move or proceed in a specified manner or at a specified rate (*light travels faster than sound*). **6** *intr. colloq.* move quickly. **7** *intr.* pass esp. in a deliberate or systematic manner from point to point (*the photographer's eye travelled over the scene*). **8** *intr.* (of a machine or part) move or operate in a specified way. **9** *intr.* (of deer etc.) move onwards in feeding. ● *n.* **1 a** the act of travelling, esp. in foreign countries. **b** (often in *pl.*) a spell of this (*have returned from their travels*). **2** the range, rate, or mode of motion of a part in machinery. □ **travel agency** (or **bureau**) an agency that makes the necessary arrangements for travellers. **travel agent** a person or firm acting as a travel agency. **travelling crane** a crane able to move on rails, esp. along an overhead support. **travelling-rug** a rug used for warmth on a journey. **travelling salesman** = TRAVELLER 2. **travelling wave** *Physics* a wave in which the medium moves in the direction of propagation. **travel-sick** suffering from nausea caused by motion in travelling. **travel-sickness** the condition of being travel-sick. □□ **travelling** *adj.* [ME, orig. = TRAVAIL]

■ *v.* **1** journey, go, move, proceed, roam, rove, tour, take *or* make a trip, take *or* make a tour, take *or* make an excursion, take *or* make a junket, take *or* make a journey, commute, trek, voyage, *archaic or joc.* peregrinate. **2** see TRAVERSE *v.* 1. **5** proceed, move, advance, progress, go. **7** pass, move, go, roam, rove, range, wander. ● *n.* **1 a** travelling, tourism, touring, globe-trotting. **b** trip(s), expedition(s), journey(s), excursion(s), tour(s), voyage(s), touring, trek(s), trekking, travelling, wandering(s), junket(s), pilgrimage(s), *archaic or joc.* peregrination(s). □□ **travelling** itinerant, wandering, peripatetic, roving, mobile, nomadic, touring, wayfaring, migratory, restless.

travelled /trávv'ld/ *adj.* experienced in travelling (also in *comb.*: *much-travelled*).

traveller /trávvələr/ *n.* (*US* **traveler**) **1** a person who travels or is travelling. **2** a travelling salesman. **3** a Gypsy. **4** *Austral.* an itinerant workman; a swagman. **5** a moving mechanism, esp. a travelling crane. □ **traveller's cheque** (*US* **check**) a cheque for a fixed amount that may be cashed on signature, usu. internationally. **traveller's joy** a wild clematis, *Clematis vitalba*. **traveller's tale** an incredible and probably untrue story.

■ **1** tourist, voyager, sightseer, globe-trotter, wanderer, hiker, rover, wayfarer, bird of passage, day-tripper, commuter, passenger, *esp. Brit.* holiday-maker, *Brit.* tripper, *colloq.* rubberneck, jet-setter. **2** see SELLER.

travelogue /trávvəlog/ *n.* a film or illustrated lecture about travel. [TRAVEL after *monologue* etc.]

traverse /trávvərss, trəvérss/ *v.* & *n.* ● *v.* **1** *tr.* travel or lie across (*traversed the country*; *a pit traversed by a beam*). **2** *tr.* consider or discuss the whole extent of (a subject). **3** *tr.* turn (a large gun) horizontally. **4** *tr. Law* deny (an allegation) in pleading. **5** *tr.* thwart, frustrate, or oppose (a plan or opinion). **6** *intr.* (of the needle of a compass etc.) turn on or as on a pivot. **7** *intr.* (of a horse) walk obliquely. **8** *intr.* make a traverse in climbing. ● *n.* **1** a sideways movement. **2** an act of traversing. **3** a thing, esp. part of a structure, that crosses another. **4** a gallery extending from side to side of a church or other building. **5 a** a single line of survey, usu. plotted from compass bearings and chained or paced distances between angular points. **b** a tract surveyed in this way. **6** *Naut.* a zigzag line taken by a ship because of contrary winds or currents. **7** a skier's similar movement on a slope. **8** the sideways movement of a part in a machine. **9 a** a sideways motion across a rock-face from one practicable line of ascent or descent to another. **b** a place where this is necessary. **10** *Mil.* a pair of right-angle bends in a trench to avoid enfilading fire. **11** *Law* a denial, esp. of an allegation of a matter of fact. **12** the act of turning a large gun horizontally to the required direction. □□ **traversable** *adj.* **traversal** *n.* **traverser** *n.* [OF *traverser* f. LL *traversare*, *transversare* (as TRANSVERSE)]

■ *v.* **1** cross, criss-cross, pass over *or* through, move over *or* through, walk, cover, travel (over *or* through), roam, wander, range, tramp, tour; go across, lie across *or* athwart, extend across *or* athwart, bridge, span, intersect. **2** examine, look into, scrutinize, inspect, investigate, review, study, look at, consider, contemplate, scan, look over, check, survey, reconnoitre, observe. **5** oppose, cross, thwart, frustrate, go *or* act against, go *or* act in opposition to, go *or* act counter to, conflict (with), controvert, contravene, counter, obstruct, contradict, deny, *archaic or literary* gainsay. ● *n.* **2** see TRANSIT *n.* 1. □□ **traversable** see NAVIGABLE 1. **traversal** see PASSAGE[1] 1.

travertine /trávvərteen/ *n.* a white or light-coloured calcareous rock deposited from springs. [It. *travertino*, *tivertino* f. L *tiburtinus* of Tibur (Tivoli) near Rome]

travesty /trávvisti/ *n.* & *v.* ● *n.* (*pl.* **-ies**) a grotesque misrepresentation or imitation (*a travesty of justice*). ● *v.tr.* (**-ies**, **-ied**) make or be a travesty of. [(orig. adj.) f. F *travesti* past part. of *travestir* disguise, change the clothes of, f. It. *travestire* (as TRANS-, *vestire* clothe)]

■ *n.* see PARODY *n.* 2, MOCKERY 1b, 2. ● *v.* see MOCK *v.* 2.

travois /trəvóy/ *n.* (*pl.* same /-vóyz/) a N. American Indian vehicle of two joined poles pulled by a horse etc. for carrying a burden. [earlier *travail* f. F, perh. the same word as TRAVAIL]

trawl /trawl/ *v.* & *n.* ● *v.* **1** *intr.* **a** fish with a trawl or seine. **b** seek a suitable candidate etc. by sifting through a large number. **2** *tr.* **a** catch by trawling. **b** seek a suitable candidate etc. from (a certain area or group etc.) (*trawled the schools for new trainees*). ● *n.* **1** an act of trawling. **2** (in full **trawl-net**) a large wide-mouthed fishing-net dragged by a boat along the bottom. **3** (in full **trawl-line**) *US* a long sea-fishing line buoyed and supporting short lines with baited hooks. [prob. f. MDu. *traghelen* to drag (cf. *traghel* drag-net), perh. f. L *tragula*]

trawler /tráwlər/ *n.* **1** a boat used for trawling. **2** a person who trawls.

tray /tray/ *n.* **1** a flat shallow vessel usu. with a raised rim for carrying dishes etc. or containing small articles, papers, etc. **2** a shallow lidless box forming a compartment of a trunk. □□ **trayful** *n.* (*pl.* **-fuls**). [OE *trīg* f. Gmc, rel. to TREE]

treacherous /tréchərəss/ *adj.* **1** guilty of or involving treachery. **2** (of the weather, ice, the memory, etc.) not to be relied on; likely to fail or give way. □□ **treacherously** *adv.* **treacherousness** *n.* [ME f. OF *trecherous* f. *trecheor* a cheat f. *trechier*, *trichier*: see TRICK]

■ **1** see *perfidious* (PERFIDY), *traitorous* (TRAITOR). **2** see DANGEROUS. □□ **treacherously** see *behind a person's back*.

treachery /tréchəri/ *n.* (*pl.* **-ies**) **1** violation of faith or trust; betrayal. **2** an instance of this.

■ see *betrayal* (BETRAY).

treacle /tréek'l/ *n.* **1** esp. *Brit.* **a** a syrup produced in refining sugar. **b** molasses. **2** cloying sentimentality or flattery. □□ **treacly** *adj.* [ME *triacle* f. OF f. L *theriaca* f. Gk *thēriakē* antidote against venom, fem. of *thēriakos* (adj.) f. *thērion* wild beast]

tread /tred/ *v.* & *n.* ● *v.* (**trod** /trod/; **trodden** /tródd'n/ or **trod**) **1** *intr.* (often foll. by *on*) **a** set down one's foot; walk or step (*do not tread on the grass*; *trod on a snail*). **b** (of the foot) be set down. **2** *tr.* **a** walk on. **b** (often foll. by *down*) press or crush with the feet. **3** *tr.* perform (steps etc.) by walking (*trod a few paces*). **4** *tr.* make (a hole etc.) by treading. **5** *intr.* (foll. by *on*) suppress; subdue mercilessly. **6** *tr.* make a track with (dirt etc.) from the feet. **7** *tr.* (often foll. by *in*, *into*) press down into the ground with the feet (*trod dirt into the carpet*). **8** *tr.* (also *absol.*) (of a male bird) copulate with (a hen). ● *n.* **1** a manner or sound of walking (*recognized the heavy tread*). **2** (in full **tread-board**) the top surface of a step or stair. **3** the thick moulded part of a vehicle tyre for gripping the road. **4 a** the part of a wheel that touches the ground or rail. **b** the part of a rail that the wheels touch. **5** the part of the sole of a shoe that rests on the ground. **6** (of a male bird) copulation. □ **tread the boards** (or **stage**) be or become an actor; appear on the stage. **tread on air** see AIR. **tread on a person's toes** offend a person or encroach on a person's privileges etc. **tread out 1** stamp out (a fire etc.). **2** press out (wine or grain) with the feet. **tread water** maintain an upright position in the water by moving the feet with a walking movement and the hands with a downward circular motion. **tread-wheel** a treadmill or similar appliance. □□ **treader** *n.* [OE *tredan* f. WG]

■ *v.* **1, 3** see WALK *v.* 1, 2. **2** see TRAMPLE *v.* 1. ● *n.* **1** step, footstep, footfall. □ **tread on a person's toes** see OFFEND 1, 2.

treadle /trédd'l/ *n.* & *v.* ● *n.* a lever worked by the foot and imparting motion to a machine. ● *v.intr.* work a treadle. [OE *tredel* stair (as TREAD)]

treadmill /trédmil/ *n.* **1** a device for producing motion by the weight of persons or animals stepping on movable steps on the inner surface of a revolving upright wheel. **2** monotonous routine work.

■ **2** see RUT 2, LABOUR *n.* 1.

treadwheel /trédweel/ *n.* = TREADMILL 1.

treason /treéz'n/ *n.* **1** (in full **high treason**: see note below) violation by a subject of allegiance to the sovereign or to the State, esp. by attempting to kill or overthrow the sovereign or to overthrow the government. **2** (in full **petty treason**) *hist.* murder of one's master or husband, regarded as a form of treason. ¶ The crime of *petty treason* was abolished in 1828; the term *high treason*, originally distinguished from *petty treason*, now has the same meaning as *treason.* □□ **treasonous** *adj.* [ME f. AF *treisoun* etc., OF *traïson*, f. L *traditio* handing over (as TRADITION)]
■ **1** see PERFIDY.

treasonable /treézənəb'l/ *adj.* involving or guilty of treason. □□ **treasonably** *adv.*
■ see *perfidious* (PERFIDY), *traitorous* (TRAITOR).

treasure /trézhər/ *n.* & *v.* ● *n.* **1 a** precious metals or gems. **b** a hoard of these. **c** accumulated wealth. **2** a thing valued for its rarity, workmanship, associations, etc. (*art treasures*). **3** *colloq.* a much loved or highly valued person. ● *v.tr.* **1** (often foll. by *up*) store up as valuable. **2** value (esp. a long-kept possession) highly. □ **treasure hunt 1** a search for treasure. **2** a game in which players seek a hidden object from a series of clues. **treasure trove 1** *Law* treasure of unknown ownership found hidden. **2** a hidden store of valuables. [ME f. OF *tresor*, ult. f. Gk *thēsauros*: see THESAURUS]
■ *n.* **1** wealth, riches, money, fortune, valuables, cash, cache, hoard, trove, treasure trove. **3** pride (and joy), delight, joy, darling, ideal, apple of one's eye, jewel, gem, pearl, prize, find, catch. ● *v.* **2** hold dear, cherish, value, prize, esteem, rate *or* value highly, appreciate.

treasurer /trézhərər/ *n.* **1** a person appointed to administer the funds of a society or municipality etc. **2** an officer authorized to receive and disburse public revenues. □□ **treasurership** *n.* [ME f. AF *tresorer*, OF *tresorier* f. *tresor* (see TREASURE) after LL *thesaurarius*]

treasury /trézhəri/ *n.* (*pl.* **-ies**) **1** a place or building where treasure is stored. **2** the funds or revenue of a State, institution, or society. **3** (**Treasury**) **a** the department managing the public revenue of a country. **b** the offices and officers of this. **c** the place where the public revenues are kept. □ **Treasury bench** (in the UK) the front bench in the House of Commons occupied by the Prime Minister, Chancellor of the Exchequer, etc. **treasury bill** a bill of exchange issued by the government to raise money for temporary needs. **treasury note** *US* & *hist.* a note issued by the Treasury for use as currency. [ME f. OF *tresorie* (as TREASURE)]
■ **1** store, storehouse, repository, mine, treasure trove, hoard, cache; bank, coffers. **2** exchequer, purse, resources, funds, finances, money(s), revenue, *Rom. Hist.* fisc, *Sc.* fisk. **3** exchequer.

treat /treet/ *v.* & *n.* ● *v.* **1** *tr.* act or behave towards or deal with (a person or thing) in a certain way (*treated me kindly*; *treat it as a joke*). **2** *tr.* deal with or apply a process to; act upon to obtain a particular result (*treat it with acid*). **3** *tr.* apply medical care or attention to. **4** *tr.* present or deal with (a subject) in literature or art. **5** *tr.* (often foll. by *to*) provide with food or drink or entertainment, esp. at one's own expense (*treated us to dinner*). **6** *intr.* (often foll. by *with*) negotiate terms (with a person). **7** *intr.* (often foll. by *of*) give a spoken or written exposition. ● *n.* **1** an event or circumstance (esp. when unexpected or unusual) that gives great pleasure. **2** a meal, entertainment, etc., provided by one person for the enjoyment of another or others. **3** (prec. by *a*) extremely good or well (*they looked a treat*; *has come on a treat*). □□ **treatable** *adj.* **treater** *n.* **treating** *n.* [ME f. AF *treter*, OF *traitier* f. L *tractare* handle, frequent. of *trahere tract-* draw, pull]
■ *v.* **1** handle, manage, behave *or* act toward(s), deal with; use; consider, regard, look upon, view. **2** process, prepare, make, produce. **3** nurse, doctor, attend, care for, look after, tend, prescribe for, dose, medicate, vet. **4** handle, deal with, discuss, touch on *or* upon, present, consider, take up, study, examine, explore, investigate, scrutinize, analyse, go into, probe, survey, expound (on), criticize, review, critique. **5** take out, pay (the bill) for, buy for, regale, entertain, play host to; wine and dine; stand, *Austral.* & *NZ colloq.* shout, *US* & *Austral. sl.* spring for. **7** (*treat of*) see SPEAK 5. ● *n.* **1** see LUXURY 2, JOY *n.* 2. **2** favour, gift, present, boon, bonus, premium, *colloq.* shout, *esp. US colloq.* freebie.

treatise /treétiss, -iz/ *n.* a written work dealing formally and systematically with a subject. [ME f. AF *tretis* f. OF *traitier* TREAT]
■ see PAPER *n.* 8.

treatment /treétmənt/ *n.* **1** a process or manner of behaving towards or dealing with a person or thing (*received rough treatment*). **2** the application of medical care or attention to a patient. **3** a manner of treating a subject in literature or art. **4** (prec. by *the*) *colloq.* the customary way of dealing with a person, situation, etc. (*got the full treatment*).
■ **1** behaviour, conduct, action, handling, care, management, dealing(s), manipulation, reception; usage, use. **2** therapy, care, curing, remedying, healing; remedy, cure, medication.

treaty /treéti/ *n.* (*pl.* **-ies**) **1** a formally concluded and ratified agreement between States. **2** an agreement between individuals or parties, esp. for the purchase of property. □ **treaty port** *hist.* a port that a country was bound by treaty to keep open to foreign trade. [ME f. AF *treté* f. L *tractatus* TRACTATE]
■ pact, agreement, alliance, concordat, entente, covenant, convention, contract, compact, accord, *colloq.* deal.

treble /trébb'l/ *adj.*, *n.*, & *v.* ● *adj.* **1 a** threefold. **b** triple. **c** three times as much or many (*treble the amount*). **2** (of a voice) high-pitched. **3** *Mus.* = SOPRANO (esp. of an instrument or with ref. to a boy's voice). ● *n.* **1** a treble quantity or thing. **2** *Darts* a hit on the narrow ring enclosed by the two middle circles of a dartboard, scoring treble. **3 a** *Mus.* = SOPRANO (esp. a boy's voice or part, or an instrument). **b** a high-pitched voice. **4** the high-frequency output of a radio, record-player, etc., corresponding to the treble in music. **5** a system of betting in which the winnings and stake from the first bet are transferred to a second and then (if successful) to a third. **6** *Sport* three victories or championships in the same game, sport, etc. ● *v.* **1** *tr.* & *intr.* make or become three times as much or many; increase threefold; multiply by three. **2** *tr.* amount to three times as much as. □ **treble chance** a method of competing in a football pool in which the chances of winning depend on the number of draws and home and away wins predicted by the competitors. **treble clef** a clef placing G above middle C on the second lowest line of the staff. **treble rhyme** a rhyme including three syllables. □□ **trebly** *adv.* (in sense 1 of *adj.*). [ME f. OF f. L *triplus* TRIPLE]
■ *adj.* **2** see HIGH *adj.* 9.

trebuchet /trébyooshet/ *n.* (also **trebucket** /trébbukit, treé-/) *hist.* **1** a military machine used in siege warfare for throwing stones etc. **2** a tilting balance for accurately weighing light articles. [ME f. OF f. *trebucher* overthrow, ult. f. Frank.]

trecento /traychéntō/ *n.* the style of Italian art and literature of the 14th c. □□ **trecentist** *n.* [It., = 300 used with reference to the years 1300-99]

tree /tree/ *n.* & *v.* ● *n.* **1 a** a perennial plant with a woody self-supporting main stem or trunk when mature and usu. unbranched for some distance above the ground (cf. SHRUB[1]). **b** any similar plant having a tall erect usu. single stem, e.g. palm tree. **2** a piece or frame of wood etc. for various purposes (*shoe-tree*). **3** *archaic* or *poet.* **a** a gibbet. **b** a cross, esp. the one used for Christ's crucifixion. **4** (in full **tree diagram**) *Math.* a diagram with a structure of branching 1fpconnecting lines. **5** = *family tree.* ● *v.tr.* **1** force to take refuge in a tree. **2** esp. *US* put into a difficult position. **3** stretch on a shoe-tree. □ **grow on trees** (usu. with *neg.*) be plentiful. **tree agate** agate with treelike markings. **tree calf** a calf binding for books stained with a treelike design.

tree-fern a large fern, esp. of the family Cyatheaceae, with an upright trunklike stem. **tree frog** any arboreal tailless amphibian, esp. of the family Hylidae, climbing by means of adhesive discs on its digits. **tree hopper** any insect of the family Membracidae, living in trees. **tree house** a structure in a tree for children to play in. **tree line** = TIMBERLINE. **tree of heaven** an ornamental Asian tree, *Ailanthus altissima*, with evil-smelling flowers. **tree of knowledge** the branches of knowledge as a whole. **tree of life** = ARBOR VITAE. **tree ring** a ring in a cross section of a tree, from one year's growth. **tree shrew** any small insect-eating arboreal mammal of the family Tupaiidae having a pointed nose and bushy tail. **tree sparrow 1** *Brit.* a sparrow, *Passer montanus*, inhabiting woodland areas. **2** *US* a N. American finch, *Spizella arborea*, inhabiting grassland areas. **tree surgeon** a person who treats decayed trees in order to preserve them. **tree surgery** the art or practice of such treatment. **tree toad** = *tree frog*. **tree tomato** a South American shrub, *Cyphomandra betacea*, with egg-shaped red fruit. **tree-trunk** the trunk of a tree. **up a tree** esp. *US* cornered; nonplussed. □□ **treeless** *adj.* **treelessness** *n.* **tree-like** *adj.* [OE *trēow* f. Gmc]

treecreeper /tréekreepər/ *n.* any small creeping bird, esp. of the family Certhiidae, feeding on insects in the bark of trees.

treen /treen/ *n.* (treated as *pl.*) small domestic wooden objects, esp. antiques. [*treen* (adj.) wooden f. OE *trēowen* (as TREE)]

treenail /tréenayl/ *n.* (also **trenail**) a hard wooden pin for securing timbers etc.

treetop /tréetop/ *n.* the topmost part of a tree.

trefa /tráyfə/ *adj.* (also **tref** /trayf/ and other variants) not kosher. [Heb. *ṭ^{e}rēpāh* the flesh of an animal torn f. *ṭārap̱* rend]

trefoil /tréffoyl, trée-/ *n.* & *adj.* ● *n.* **1** any leguminous plant of the genus *Trifolium*, with leaves of three leaflets and flowers of various colours, esp. clover. **2** any plant with similar leaves. **3** a three-lobed ornamentation, esp. in tracery windows. **4** a thing arranged in or with three lobes. ● *adj.* of or concerning a three-lobed plant, window tracery, etc. □□ **trefoiled** *adj.* (also in *comb.*). [ME f. AF *trifoil* f. L *trifolium* (as TRI-, *folium* leaf)]

trek /trek/ *v.* & *n.* orig. *S.Afr.* ● *v.intr.* (**trekked, trekking**) **1** travel or make one's way arduously (*trekking through the forest*). **2** esp. *hist.* migrate or journey with one's belongings by ox-wagon. **3** (of an ox) draw a vehicle or pull a load. ● *n.* **1 a** a journey or walk made by trekking (*it was a trek to the nearest launderette*). **b** each stage of such a journey. **2** an organized migration of a body of persons. □□ **trekker** *n.* [S.Afr. Du. *trek* (n.), *trekken* (v.) draw, travel]
■ *v.* **1** see TRAVEL *v.* 1, TRAMP *v.* 1b. ● *n.* **1** see TRAMP *n.* 3.

trellis /trélliss/ *n.* & *v.* ● *n.* (in full **trellis-work**) a lattice or grating of light wooden or metal bars used esp. as a support for fruit-trees or creepers and often fastened against a wall. ● *v.tr.* (**trellised, trellising**) **1** provide with a trellis. **2** support (a vine etc.) with a trellis. [ME f. OF *trelis, trelice* ult. f. L *trilix* three-ply (as TRI-, *licium* warp-thread)]

trematode /trémmətōd/ *n.* any parasitic flatworm of the class Trematoda, esp. a fluke, equipped with hooks or suckers, e.g. a liver fluke. [mod.L *Trematoda* f. Gk *trēmatōdēs* perforated f. *trēma* hole]

tremble /trémb'l/ *v.* & *n.* ● *v.intr.* **1** shake involuntarily from fear, excitement, weakness, etc. **2** be in a state of extreme apprehension (*trembled at the very thought of it*). **3** move in a quivering manner (*leaves trembled in the breeze*). ● *n.* **1** a trembling state or movement; a quiver (*couldn't speak without a tremble*). **2** (in *pl.*) a disease (esp. of cattle) marked by trembling. □ **all of a tremble** *colloq.* **1** trembling all over. **2** extremely agitated. **trembling poplar** an aspen. □□ **tremblingly** *adv.* [ME f. OF *trembler* f. med.L *tremulare* f. L *tremulus* TREMULOUS]
■ *v.* quiver, shake, quake, shiver, shudder, tremor, quaver; vibrate, rock, dodder. ● *n.* **1** quiver, shake, quake, shiver, shudder, quaver, tremor; vibration. □ **all of a tremble 1** see TREMULOUS 1.

trembler /trémblər/ *n.* an automatic vibrator for making and breaking an electrical circuit.

trembly /trémbli/ *adj.* (**tremblier, trembliest**) *colloq.* trembling; agitated.
■ see TREMULOUS 1.

tremendous /triméndəss/ *adj.* **1** awe-inspiring, fearful, overpowering. **2** *colloq.* remarkable, considerable, excellent (*a tremendous explosion*; *gave a tremendous performance*). □□ **tremendously** *adv.* **tremendousness** *n.* [L *tremendus*, gerundive of *tremere* tremble]
■ **1** see OVERWHELMING. **2** see EXCELLENT, GREAT *adj.* 1a. □□ **tremendously** see *extremely* (EXTREME).

tremolo /trémmələ̄/ *n.* *Mus.* **1** a tremulous effect in playing stringed and keyboard instruments or singing, esp. by rapid reiteration of a note; in other instruments, by rapid alternation between two notes (cf. VIBRATO). **2** a device in an organ producing a tremulous effect. [It. (as TREMULOUS)]

tremor /trémmər/ *n.* & *v.* ● *n.* **1** a shaking or quivering. **2** a thrill (of fear or exultation etc.). **3** (in full **earth tremor**) a slight earthquake. ● *v.intr.* undergo a tremor or tremors. [ME f. OF *tremour* & L *tremor* f. *tremere* tremble]
■ *n.* **1** see QUIVER[1] *n.* **2** see THRILL *n.* 1. **3** earthquake, quake. ● *v.* see QUIVER[1] *v.*

tremulous /trémyooləss/ *adj.* **1** trembling or quivering (*in a tremulous voice*). **2** (of a line etc.) drawn by a tremulous hand. **3** timid or vacillating. □□ **tremulously** *adv.* **tremulousness** *n.* [L *tremulus* f. *tremere* tremble]
■ **1** trembling, a-tremble, quivering, shaking, quaking, shivering, shuddering, quavering, shaky, palpitating, *colloq.* trembly, all of a tremble. **3** timid, shy, bashful, anxious, worried, timorous, fearful, afraid, frightened, scared, nervous, jumpy; hesitant, vacillating, wavering, unsure, unsteady, faltering, doubtful; *colloq.* jittery.

trenail var. of TREENAIL.

trench /trench/ *n.* & *v.* ● *n.* **1** a long narrow usu. deep depression or ditch. **2** *Mil.* **a** this dug by troops to stand in and be sheltered from enemy fire. **b** (in *pl.*) a defensive system of these. **3** a long narrow deep depression in the ocean bed. ● *v.* **1** *tr.* dig a trench or trenches in (the ground). **2** *tr.* turn over the earth of (a field, garden, etc.) by digging a succession of adjoining ditches. **3** *intr.* (foll. by *on, upon*) *archaic* **a** encroach. **b** verge or border closely. □ **trench coat 1** a soldier's lined or padded waterproof coat. **2** a loose belted raincoat. **trench fever** a highly infectious disease transmitted by lice, that infested soldiers in the trenches in the war of 1914–18. **trench mortar** a light simple mortar throwing a bomb from one's own into the enemy trenches. **trench warfare** hostilities carried on from more or less permanent trenches. [ME f. OF *trenche* (n.) *trenchier* (v.), ult. f. L *truncare* TRUNCATE]
■ *n.* **1** see FURROW *n.*

trenchant /trénchənt/ *adj.* **1** (of a style or language etc.) incisive, terse, vigorous. **2** *archaic* or *poet.* sharp, keen. □□ **trenchancy** *n.* **trenchantly** *adv.* [ME f. OF, part. of *trenchier*: see TRENCH]
■ **1** cutting, keen, acute, sharp, pointed, poignant, penetrating, incisive, biting, mordant, sarcastic, bitter, acerbic, acid, vitriolic, tart, acrid, acrimonious, acidulous, corrosive, caustic; terse, epigrammatic, vigorous.

trencher /trénchər/ *n.* **1** *hist.* a wooden or earthenware platter for serving food. **2** (in full **trencher cap**) a stiff square academic cap; a mortarboard. [ME f. AF *trenchour*, OF *trencheoir* f. *trenchier*: see TRENCH]

trencherman /trénchərmən/ *n.* (*pl.* **-men**) a person who eats well, or in a specified manner (*a good trencherman*).

trend /trend/ *n.* & *v.* ● *n.* a general direction and tendency (esp. of events, fashion, or opinion etc.). ● *v.intr.* **1** bend or turn away in a specified direction. **2** be chiefly directed; have a general and continued tendency. □ **trend-setter** a person who leads the way in fashion etc. **trend-setting** establishing trends or fashions. [ME 'revolve' etc. f. OE *trendan* f. Gmc: cf. TRUNDLE]

■ *n.* tendency, leaning, bias, bent, drift, course, inclination, direction; fashion, style, vogue, mode, look, rage, craze, fad, *colloq.* thing. ● *v.* **1** lean, bend, incline, veer, turn, swing, shift, drift, head. **2** tend, be directed, be biased, head. □ **trend-setter** see PIONEER *n.* 1.

trendy /tréndi/ *adj.* & *n. colloq.* ● *adj.* (**trendier, trendiest**) often *derog.* fashionable; following fashionable trends. ● *n.* (*pl.* **-ies**) a fashionable person. □□ **trendily** *adv.* **trendiness** *n.*

■ *adj.* fashionable, stylish, à la mode, modern, latest, up to date, up to the minute, in vogue, voguish, in, all the rage, *colloq.* with it, flash, swinging, hot, *sl.* groovy, in the groove. ● *n.* coxcomb, exhibitionist, *colloq.* show-off, clothes-horse, pseud. □□ **trendiness** see *popularity* (POPULAR).

trente-et-quarante /tróntaykarónt/ *n.* = *rouge-et-noir.* [F, = thirty and forty]

trepan /tripán/ *n.* & *v.* ● *n.* **1** a cylindrical saw formerly used by surgeons for removing part of the bone of the skull. **2** a borer for sinking shafts. ● *v.tr.* (**trepanned, trepanning**) perforate (the skull) with a trepan. □□ **trepanation** /tréppənáysh'n/ *n.* **trepanning** *n.* [ME f. med.L *trepanum* f. Gk *trupanon* f. *trupaō* bore f. *trupē* hole]

trepang /tripáng/ *n.* = BÊCHE-DE-MER 1. [Malay *trīpang*]

trephine /trifín, -féen/ *n.* & *v.* ● *n.* an improved form of trepan with a guiding centre-pin. ● *v.tr.* operate on with this. □□ **trephination** /tréffináysh'n/ *n.* [orig. *trafine*, f. L *tres fines* three ends, app. formed after TREPAN]

trepidation /tréppidáysh'n/ *n.* **1** a feeling of fear or alarm; perturbation of the mind. **2** tremulous agitation. **3** the trembling of limbs, e.g. in paralysis. [L *trepidatio* f. *trepidare* be agitated, tremble, f. *trepidus* alarmed]

■ **1** see ALARM *n.* 3.

trespass /tréspəss/ *v.* & *n.* ● *v.intr.* **1** (usu. foll. by *on*, *upon*) make an unlawful or unwarrantable intrusion (esp. on land or property). **2** (foll. by *on*) make unwarrantable claims (*shall not trespass on your hospitality*). **3** (foll. by *against*) *literary* or *archaic* offend. ● *n.* **1** *Law* a voluntary wrongful act against the person or property of another, esp. unlawful entry to a person's land or property. **2** *archaic* a sin or offence. □ **trespass on a person's preserves** meddle in another person's affairs. □□ **trespasser** *n.* [ME f. OF *trespasser* pass over, trespass, *trespas* (n.), f. med.L *trans-passare* (as TRANS-, PASS[1])]

■ *v.* **1, 2** see ENCROACH 1. **3** see SIN[1] *v.* 2. ● *n.* **2** see SIN[1] *n.* 1. □□ **trespasser** see INTRUDER, SINNER.

tress /tress/ *n.* & *v.* ● *n.* **1** a long lock of human (esp. female) hair. **2** (in *pl.*) a woman's or girl's head of hair. ● *v.tr.* arrange (hair) in tresses. □□ **tressed** *adj.* (also in *comb.*). **tressy** *adj.* [ME f. OF *tresse*, perh. ult. f. Gk *trikha* threefold]

■ *n.* **1** see LOCK[2] 1a. **2** (*tresses*) hair, locks, *colloq.* mane.

tressure /tréshər/ *n. Heraldry* a narrow orle. [ME, orig. = hair-ribbon, f. OF *tressour* etc. (as TRESS)]

trestle /tréss'l/ *n.* **1** a supporting structure for a table etc., consisting of two frames fixed at an angle or hinged or of a bar supported by two divergent pairs of legs. **2** (in full **trestle-table**) a table consisting of a board or boards laid on trestles or other supports. **3** (in full **trestle-work**) an open braced framework to support a bridge etc. **4** (in full **trestle-tree**) *Naut.* each of a pair of horizontal pieces on a lower mast supporting the topmast etc. [ME f. OF *trestel* ult. f. L *transtrum*]

tret /tret/ *n. hist.* an allowance of extra weight formerly made to purchasers of some goods for waste in transportation. [ME f. AF & OF, var. of *trait* draught: see TRAIT]

trevally /triválli/ *n.* (*pl.* **-ies**) any Australian fish of the genus *Caranx*, used as food. [prob. alt. f. *cavally*, a kind of fish, f. Sp. *caballo* horse f. L (as CAVALRY)]

trews /trōōz/ *n.pl.* esp. *Brit.* trousers, esp. close-fitting tartan trousers worn by women. [Ir. *trius*, Gael. *triubhas* (sing.): cf. TROUSERS]

trey /tray/ *n.* (*pl.* **treys**) the three on dice or cards. [ME f. OF *trei*, *treis* three f. L *tres*]

TRH *abbr.* Their Royal Highnesses.

tri- /trī/ *comb. form* forming nouns and adjectives meaning: **1** three or three times. **2** *Chem.* (forming the names of compounds) containing three atoms or groups of a specified kind (*triacetate*). [L & Gk f. L *tres*, Gk *treis* three]

triable /tríəb'l/ *adj.* **1** liable to a judicial trial. **2** that may be tried or attempted. [ME f. AF (as TRY)]

triacetate /triássitayt/ *n.* a cellulose derivative containing three acetate groups, esp. as a base for man-made fibres.

triad /tríad/ *n.* **1** a group of three (esp. notes in a chord). **2** the number three. **3** a Chinese secret society, usu. criminal. **4** a Welsh form of literary composition with an arrangement in groups of three. □□ **triadic** /-áddik/ *adj.* **triadically** /-áddikəli/ *adv.* [F *triade* or LL *trias triad-* f. Gk *trias -ados* f. *treis* three]

■ **1** see TRIO.

triadelphous /trīədélfəss/ *adj. Bot.* having stamens united in three bundles. [TRI- + Gk *adelphos* brother]

triage /trí-ij/ *n.* **1** the act of sorting according to quality. **2** the assignment of degrees of urgency to decide the order of treatment of wounds, illnesses, etc. [F f. *trier*: cf. TRY]

trial /tríəl/ *n.* **1** a judicial examination and determination of issues between parties by a judge with or without a jury (*stood trial for murder*). **2** **a** a process or mode of testing qualities. **b** experimental treatment. **c** a test (*will give you a trial*). **d** an attempt. **e** (*attrib.*) experimental. **3** a trying thing or experience or person, esp. hardship or trouble (*the trials of old age*). **4** a sports match to test the ability of players eligible for selection to a team. **5** a test of individual ability on a motor cycle over rough ground or on a road. **6** any of various contests involving performance by horses, dogs, or other animals. □ **on trial 1** being tried in a court of law. **2** being tested; to be chosen or retained only if suitable. **trial and error** repeated (usu. varied and unsystematic) attempts or experiments continued until successful. **trial balance** (of a ledger in double-entry bookkeeping), a comparison of the totals on either side, the inequality of which reveals errors in posting. **trial jury** = *petty jury.* **trial run** a preliminary test of a vehicle, vessel, machine, etc. [AF *trial*, *triel* f. *trier* TRY]

■ **1** hearing, enquiry, inquiry, examination, inquisition, litigation, judicial proceeding, lawsuit, contest. **2 a–c** test, testing, experiment, proof, try-out, trying out, trial run, dummy run, examination, check, checking, *colloq.* dry run. **d** try, attempt, endeavour, effort, venture, go, fling, *colloq.* shot, stab, whirl, crack, *formal* essay, *sl.* whack. **e** sample, experimental, exploratory, provisional, probationary, tentative, conditional, pilot. **3** trouble, affliction, tribulation, hardship, adversity, suffering, grief, misery, distress, bad *or* hard luck, misfortune, hard times, ordeal, *archaic or literary* woe; nuisance, irritation, bother, bane, annoyance, pest, irritant, thorn in one's flesh *or* side, *colloq.* plague, hassle, pain (in the neck), headache, *esp. US sl.* pain in the butt. **4, 6** see MATCH[1] *n.* 1, HEAT *n.* 6. □ **trial run** see TRIAL 2a–c above.

trialist /tríəlist/ *n.* **1** a person who takes part in a sports trial, motor-cycle trial, etc. **2** a person involved in a judicial trial.

triandrous /triándrəss/ *adj. Bot.* having three stamens.

triangle /tríangg'l/ *n.* **1** a plane figure with three sides and angles. **2** any three things not in a straight line, with imaginary lines joining them. **3** an implement of this shape. **4** a musical instrument consisting of a steel rod bent into a triangle and sounded by striking it with a small steel rod. **5** a situation, esp. an emotional relationship, involving three people. **6** a right-angled triangle of wood etc. as a drawing-implement. **7** *Naut.* a device of three spars for raising weights. **8** *hist.* a frame of three halberds joined at the top to which a soldier was bound for flogging. □ **triangle of forces** a triangle whose sides represent in magnitude and direction three forces in equilibrium. [ME f. OF *triangle* or

L *triangulum* neut. of *triangulus* three-cornered (as TRI-, ANGLE[1])]

triangular /trīángyoolər/ *adj.* **1** triangle-shaped, three-cornered. **2** (of a contest or treaty etc.) between three persons or parties. **3** (of a pyramid) having a three-sided base. □□ **triangularity** /-lárriti/ *n.* **triangularly** *adv.* [LL *triangularis* (as TRIANGLE)]

triangulate *v.* & *adj.* ● *v.tr.* /trīángyoolayt/ **1** divide (an area) into triangles for surveying purposes. **2 a** measure and map (an area) by the use of triangles with a known base length and base angles. **b** determine (a height, distance, etc.) in this way. ● *adj.* /trīángyoolət/ *Zool.* marked with triangles. □□ **triangulately** /-lətli/ *adv.* **triangulation** /-láysh'n/ *n.* [L *triangulatus* triangular (as TRIANGLE)]

Triassic /trīássik/ *adj.* & *n.* *Geol.* ● *adj.* of or relating to the earliest period of the Mesozoic era with evidence of an abundance of reptiles (including the earliest dinosaurs) and the emergence of mammals. ¶ Cf. Appendix VII. ● *n.* this period or system. [LL *trias* (as TRIAD), because the strata are divisible into three groups]

triathlon /trīáthlon/ *n.* an athletic contest consisting of three different events. □□ **triathlete** *n.* [TRI- after DECATHLON]

triatomic /trīətómmik/ *adj.* *Chem.* **1** having three atoms (of a specified kind) in the molecule. **2** having three replacement atoms or radicals.

triaxial /trīáksiəl/ *adj.* having three axes.

tribade /tribbaad/ *n.* a woman who takes part in a simulation of sexual intercourse with another woman. □□ **tribadism** *n.* [F *tribade* or L *tribas* f. Gk f. *tribō* rub]

tribal /trīb'l/ *adj.* of, relating to, or characteristic of a tribe or tribes. □□ **tribally** *adv.*

tribalism /trībəliz'm/ *n.* tribal organization. □□ **tribalist** *n.* **tribalistic** /-lístik/ *adj.*

tribasic /trībáysik/ *adj.* *Chem.* (of an acid) having three replaceable hydrogen atoms.

tribe /trīb/ *n.* **1** a group of (esp. primitive) families or communities, linked by social, economic, religious, or blood ties, and usu. having a common culture and dialect, and a recognized leader. **2** any similar natural or political division. **3** *Rom.Hist.* each of the political divisions of the Roman people. **4** each of the 12 divisions of the Israelites. **5** usu. *derog.* a set or number of persons esp. of one profession etc. or family (*the whole tribe of actors*). **6** *Biol.* a group of organisms usu. ranking between genus and the subfamily. **7** (in *pl.*) large numbers. [ME, orig. in pl. form *tribuz*, *tribus* f. OF or L *tribus* (sing. & pl.)]

■ **1, 2** race, stock, strain, nation, breed, people, (ethnic) group, clan, blood, pedigree, family, sept, dynasty, house, *archaic* seed; caste, class; *Anthropol.* gens.

tribesman /trībzmən/ *n.* (*pl.* **-men**) a member of a tribe or of one's own tribe.

triblet /tríblit/ *n.* a mandrel used in making tubes, rings, etc. [F *triboulet*, of unkn. orig.]

tribo- /tríbbō, trī-/ *comb. form* rubbing, friction. [Gk *tribos* rubbing]

triboelectricity /tríbbō-íllektríssiti, trī-/ *n.* the generation of an electric charge by friction.

tribology /trībólləji/ *n.* the study of friction, wear, lubrication, and the design of bearings; the science of interacting surfaces in relative motion. □□ **tribologist** *n.*

triboluminescence /tríbbōlóōminéss'nss, trī-/ *n.* the emission of light from a substance when rubbed, scratched, etc. □□ **triboluminescent** *adj.*

tribometer /trībómmitər/ *n.* an instrument for measuring friction in sliding.

tribrach /trībrak, trí-/ *n.* *Prosody* a foot of three short or unstressed syllables. □□ **tribrachic** /-brákkik/ *adj.* [L *tribrachys* f. Gk *tribrakhus* (as TRI-, *brakhus* short)]

tribulation /tríbyooláysh'n/ *n.* **1** great affliction or oppression. **2** a cause of this (*was a real tribulation to me*). [ME f. OF f. eccl.L *tribulatio* *-onis* f. L *tribulare* press, oppress, f. *tribulum* sledge for threshing, f. *terere trit-* rub]

■ **1** see AFFLICTION 1. **2** see AFFLICTION 2.

tribunal /trībyóōn'l, tri-/ *n.* **1** *Brit.* a board appointed to adjudicate in some matter, esp. one appointed by the government to investigate a matter of public concern. **2** a court of justice. **3** a seat or bench for a judge or judges. **4 a** a place of judgement. **b** judicial authority (*the tribunal of public opinion*). [F *tribunal* or L *tribunus* (as TRIBUNE[2])]

■ **1** see BOARD *n.* 4. **2** court (of justice), lawcourt, bar, bench, judiciary.

tribune[1] /tríbyoōn/ *n.* **1** a popular leader or demagogue. **2** (in full **tribune of the people**) an official in ancient Rome chosen by the people to protect their interests. **3** (in full **military tribune**) a Roman legionary officer. □□ **tribunate** /-nət/ *n.* **tribuneship** *n.* [ME f. L *tribunus*, prob. f. *tribus* tribe]

tribune[2] /tríbyoōn/ *n.* **1 a** a bishop's throne in a basilica. **b** an apse containing this. **2** a dais or rostrum. **3** a raised area with seats. [F f. It. f. med.L *tribuna* TRIBUNAL]

tributary /tríbyootəri, -tri/ *n.* & *adj.* ● *n.* (*pl.* **-ies**) **1** a river or stream flowing into a larger river or lake. **2** *hist.* a person or State paying or subject to tribute. ● *adj.* **1** (of a river etc.) that is a tributary. **2** *hist.* **a** paying tribute. **b** serving as tribute. □□ **tributarily** *adv.* **tributariness** *n.* [ME f. L *tributarius* (as TRIBUTE)]

■ *n.* **1** branch, offshoot, streamlet, feeder, brook, brooklet, rivulet, run, rill, runnel, runlet, *Sc.* burn, *N.Engl.* beck, *esp. US* creek.

tribute /tríbyoōt/ *n.* **1** a thing said or done or given as a mark of respect or affection etc. (*paid tribute to their achievements*; *floral tributes*). **2** *hist.* **a** a payment made periodically by one State or ruler to another, esp. as a sign of dependence. **b** an obligation to pay this (*was laid under tribute*). **3** (foll. by *to*) an indication of (some praiseworthy quality) (*their success is a tribute to their perseverance*). **4** a proportion of ore or its equivalent paid to a miner for his work, or to the owner of a mine. [ME f. L *tributum* neut. past part. of *tribuere tribut-* assign, orig. divide between tribes (*tribus*)]

■ **1** honour, homage, recognition, celebration, respect, esteem, testimonial, compliment, encomium, acknowledgement, acclaim, acclamation, commendation, praise, accolade, panegyric, eulogy, glorification, exaltation, *colloq.* kudos, *formal* laudation. **2** tax, exaction, impost, duty, excise, levy, dues, assessment, tariff, charge, surcharge, payment, contribution, offering, gift; ransom; tithe, *RC Ch.* Peter's pence.

tricar /trīkaar/ *n.* *Brit.* a three-wheeled motor car.

trice /trīss/ *n.* □ **in a trice** in a moment; instantly. [ME *trice* (v.) pull, haul f. MDu. *trīsen*, MLG *trīssen*, rel. to MDu. *trīse* windlass, pulley]

■ □ **in a trice** see *at once* 1 (ONCE).

tricentenary /trīsenteénəri/ *n.* (*pl.* **-ies**) = TERCENTENARY.

triceps /trīseps/ *adj.* & *n.* ● *adj.* (of a muscle) having three heads or points of attachment. ● *n.* any triceps muscle, esp. the large muscle at the back of the upper arm. [L, = three-headed (as TRI-, *-ceps* f. *caput* head)]

triceratops /trīsérrətops/ *n.* a plant-eating dinosaur with three sharp horns on the forehead and a wavy-edged collar round the neck. [mod.L f. Gk *trikeratos* three-horned + *ōps* face]

trichiasis /trikīəsiss/ *n.* *Med.* ingrowth or introversion of the eyelashes. [LL f. Gk *trikhiasis* f. *trikhiaō* be hairy]

trichina /trikīnə/ *n.* (*pl.* **trichinae** /-nee/) any hairlike parasitic nematode worm of the genus *Trichinella*, esp. *T. spiralis*, the adults of which live in the small intestine, and whose larvae become encysted in the muscle tissue of humans and flesh-eating animals. □□ **trichinous** *adj.* [mod.L f. Gk *trikhinos* of hair: see TRICHO-]

trichinosis /tríkkinōsiss/ *n.* a disease caused by trichinae, usu. ingested in meat, and characterized by digestive disturbance, fever, and muscular rigidity.

tricho- /tríkkō/ *comb. form* hair. [Gk *thrix trikhos* hair]

trichogenous /trikójənəss/ *adj.* causing or promoting the growth of hair.

trichology /trikólləji, trī-/ *n.* the study of the structure, functions, and diseases of the hair. □□ **trichologist** *n.*

trichome /tríkōm/ *n. Bot.* a hair, scale, prickle, or other outgrowth from the epidermis of a plant. [Gk *trikhōma* f. *trikhoō* cover with hair (as TRICHO-)]

trichomonad /tríkkəmónnad/ *n.* any flagellate protozoan of the genus *Trichomonas*, parasitic in humans, cattle, and fowls.

trichomoniasis /tríkkəmənī́əsiss/ *n.* any of various infections caused by trichomonads parasitic on the urinary tract, vagina, or digestive system.

trichopathy /trikóppəthi/ *n.* the treatment of diseases of the hair. □□ **trichopathic** /tríkkəpáthik/ *adj.*

trichotomy /trīkóttəmi/ *n.* (*pl.* **-ies**) a division (esp. sharply defined) into three categories, esp. of human nature into body, soul, and spirit. □□ **trichotomic** /-kətómmik/ *adj.* [Gk *trikha* threefold f. *treis* three, after DICHOTOMY]

trichroic /trīkrṓ-ik/ *adj.* (esp. of a crystal viewed in different directions) showing three colours. □□ **trichroism** /trī́krō-iz'm/ *n.* [Gk *trikhroos* (as TRI-, *khrōs* colour)]

trichromatic /trī́krəmáttik/ *adj.* **1** having or using three colours. **2** (of vision) having the normal three colour-sensations, i.e. red, green, and purple. □□ **trichromatism** /-krṓmətiz'm/ *n.*

trick /trik/ *n.* & *v.* ● *n.* **1** an action or scheme undertaken to fool, outwit, or deceive. **2** an optical or other illusion (*a trick of the light*). **3** a special technique; a knack or special way of doing something. **4 a** a feat of skill or dexterity. **b** an unusual action (e.g. begging) learned by an animal. **5** a mischievous, foolish, or discreditable act; a practical joke (*a mean trick to play*). **6** a peculiar or characteristic habit or mannerism (*has a trick of repeating himself*). **7 a** the cards played in a single round of a card-game, usu. one from each player. **b** such a round. **c** a point gained as a result of this. **8** (*attrib.*) done to deceive or mystify or to create an illusion (*trick photography*; *trick question*). **9** *Naut.* a sailor's turn at the helm, usu. two hours. ● *v.tr.* **1** deceive by a trick; outwit. **2** (often foll. by *out of*, or *into* + verbal noun) cheat; treat deceitfully so as to deprive (*were tricked into agreeing*; *were tricked out of their savings*). **3** (of a thing) foil or baffle; take by surprise; disappoint the calculations of. □ **do the trick** *colloq.* accomplish one's purpose; achieve the required result. **how's tricks?** *colloq.* how are you? **not miss a trick** see MISS[1]. **trick cyclist 1** a cyclist who performs tricks, esp. in a circus. **2** *sl.* a psychiatrist. **trick of the trade** a special usu. ingenious technique or method of achieving a result in an industry or profession etc. **trick or treat** esp. *US* a children's custom of calling at houses at Hallowe'en with the threat of pranks if they are not given a small gift. **trick out** (or **up**) dress, decorate, or deck out esp. showily. **up to one's tricks** *colloq.* misbehaving. **up to a person's tricks** aware of what a person is likely to do by way of mischief. □□ **tricker** *n.* **trickish** *adj.* **trickless** *adj.* [ME f. OF dial. *trique*, OF *triche* f. *trichier* deceive, of unkn. orig.]

■ *n.* **1** ruse, artifice, device, stratagem, wile, deception, manoeuvre, deceit, fraud, hoax, imposture, intrigue, machination, conspiracy, subterfuge, dodge, confidence trick, sham, *US* confidence game, *colloq.* put-on, *Austral. colloq.* lurk, *sl.* con, *Austral. sl.* rort. **2** illusion, deception. **3** art, knack, technique, skill, secret, gift, ability, *colloq.* hang. **4** feat, accomplishment, deed; legerdemain, magic, stunt, *archaic* sleight of hand. **5** prank, frolic, antic, (practical) joke, hoax, gag, tomfoolery, antic, caper, jape; sport, horseplay, mischief; *Sc.* cantrip, *colloq.* leg-pull, shenanigans, *US colloq.* dido. **6** trait, characteristic, peculiarity, idiosyncrasy, eccentricity, quirk, practice, habit, mannerism, crotchet, weakness, foible. ● *v.* **1,2** fool, hoodwink, dupe, mislead, outwit, outmanoeuvre, deceive, misguide, misinform, gull, cheat, defraud, take in, swindle, humbug, rook, pull a person's leg, pull the wool over a person's eyes, *US* put a thing over a person, *colloq.* bamboozle, take for a ride, gammon, outfox, *literary* cozen, *sl.* bilk, *Brit. sl.* have. □ **do the trick** work, answer, fulfil the need, suffice, be effective, solve *or* take care of the problem, fill *or* fit the bill, *colloq.* do the needful *or* necessary. **trick out** (or **up**) see EMBELLISH 1.

trickery /tríkkəri/ *n.* (*pl.* **-ies**) **1** the practice or an instance of deception. **2** the use of tricks.

■ chicanery, deception, deceit, guile, beguilement, shrewdness, craftiness, trickiness, slyness, shiftiness, evasiveness, artfulness, artifice, craft, imposture, swindling, knavery, duplicity, double-dealing, fraud, cheating, skulduggery, hocus-pocus, legerdemain, stratagem, *archaic* sleight of hand, *colloq.* monkey business, *Brit. colloq.* jiggery-pokery, *sl.* funny business, hanky-panky.

trickle /tríkk'l/ *v.* & *n.* ● *v.* **1** *intr.* & *tr.* flow or cause to flow in drops or a small stream (*water trickled through the crack*). **2** *intr.* come or go slowly or gradually (*information trickles out*). ● *n.* a trickling flow. □ **trickle charger** an electrical charger for batteries that works at a steady slow rate from the mains. [ME *trekel*, *trikle*, prob. imit.]

■ *v.* **1** drip, drop, dribble, drizzle, run, flow, spill; ooze, seep, leak, exude, percolate. ● *n.* drip, seepage, spill, dribble, runnel, runlet, rivulet.

trickster /tríkstər/ *n.* a deceiver or rogue.

■ see ROGUE *n.* 1.

tricksy /tríksi/ *adj.* (**tricksier**, **tricksiest**) full of tricks; playful. □□ **tricksily** *adv.* **tricksiness** *n.* [TRICK: for *-sy* cf. FLIMSY, TIPSY]

tricky /tríkki/ *adj.* (**trickier**, **trickiest**) **1** difficult or intricate; requiring care and adroitness (*a tricky job*). **2** crafty or deceitful. **3** resourceful or adroit. □□ **trickily** *adv.* **trickiness** *n.*

■ **1** ticklish, risky, hazardous, sensitive, delicate, touch-and-go, thorny, difficult, awkward, complex, complicated, intricate, knotty, uncertain, *colloq.* iffy, sticky, *sl.* dicey. **2** deceitful, shady, deceptive, dodgy, artful, guileful, crafty, duplicitous, shrewd, cunning, dishonest, devious, sly, wily, slippery, foxy, double-dealing, cheating, *colloq.* shifty; unsportsmanlike, unfair. **3** see SHREWD. □□ **trickiness** see ARTIFICE 2a.

triclinic /trīklínnik/ *adj.* **1** (of a mineral) having three unequal oblique axes. **2** denoting the system classifying triclinic crystalline substances. [Gk TRI- + *klinō* incline]

triclinium /trīklínniəm, tri-/ *n.* (*pl.* **triclinia** /-niə/) *Rom. Antiq.* **1** a dining-table with couches along three sides. **2** a room containing this. [L f. Gk *triklinion* (as TRI-, *klinē* couch)]

tricolour /tríkkələr, trī́kullər/ *n.* & *adj.* (*US* **tricolor**) ● *n.* a flag of three colours, esp. the French national flag of blue, white, and red. ● *adj.* (also **tricoloured**) having three colours. [F *tricolore* f. LL *tricolor* (as TRI-, COLOUR)]

tricorn /trī́korn/ *adj.* & *n.* (also **tricorne**) ● *adj.* **1** having three horns. **2** (of a hat) having a brim turned up on three sides. ● *n.* **1** an imaginary animal with three horns. **2** a tricorn hat. [F *tricorne* or L *tricornis* (as TRI-, *cornu* horn)]

tricot /tríkkō, trée-/ *n.* **1 a** a hand-knitted woollen fabric. **b** an imitation of this. **2** a ribbed woollen cloth. [F, = knitting f. *tricoter* knit, of unkn. orig.]

tricrotic /trīkróttik/ *adj.* (of the pulse) having a triple beat. [TRI- after DICROTIC]

tricuspid /trīkúspid/ *n.* & *adj.* ● *n.* **1** a tooth with three cusps or points. **2** a heart-valve formed of three triangular segments. ● *adj.* (of a tooth) having three cusps or points.

tricycle /trī́sik'l/ *n.* & *v.* ● *n.* **1** a vehicle having three wheels, two on an axle at the back and one at the front, driven by pedals in the same way as a bicycle. **2** a three-wheeled motor vehicle for a disabled driver. ● *v.intr.* ride on a tricycle. □□ **tricyclist** *n.*

tridactyl /trīdáktil/ *adj.* (also **tridactylous** /-dáktiləss/) having three fingers or toes.

trident /trī́d'nt/ *n.* **1** a three-pronged spear, esp. as an attribute of Poseidon (Neptune) or Britannia. **2** (**Trident**) a US type of submarine-launched ballistic missile. [L *tridens trident-* (as TRI-, *dens* tooth)]

tridentate /trīdéntayt/ *adj.* having three teeth or prongs. [TRI- + L *dentatus* toothed]

Tridentine /trīdéntīn, tri-/ *adj.* & *n.* ● *adj.* of or relating to the Council of Trent, held at Trento in Italy 1545–63, esp. as the basis of Roman Catholic doctrine. ● *n.* a Roman Catholic adhering to this traditional doctrine. □ **Tridentine mass** the eucharistic liturgy used by the Roman Catholic Church from 1570 to 1964. [med.L *Tridentinus* f. *Tridentum* Trent]

triduum /trídyooəm/ *n.* *RC Ch.* esp. *hist.* three days' prayer in preparation for a saint's day or other religious occasion. [L (as TRI-, *dies* day)]

tridymite /tríddimīt/ *n.* a crystallized form of silica, occurring in cavities of volcanic rocks. [G *Tridymit* f. Gk *tridumos* threefold (as TRI-, *didumos* twin), from its occurrence in groups of three crystals]

tried *past* and *past part.* of TRY.

triennial /trī-énniəl/ *adj.* & *n.* ● *adj.* **1** lasting three years. **2** recurring every three years. ● *n.* a visitation of an Anglican diocese by its bishop every three years. □□ **triennially** *adv.* [LL *triennis* (as TRI-, L *annus* year)]

triennium /trī-énniəm/ *n.* (*pl.* **trienniums** or **triennia** /-niə/) a period of three years. [L (as TRIENNIAL)]

trier /trī́ər/ *n.* **1** a person who perseveres (*is a real trier*). **2** a tester, esp. of foodstuffs. **3** a person appointed to decide whether a challenge to a juror is well-founded.

trifacial nerve /trīfáysh'l/ *n.* = TRIGEMINAL NERVE.

trifecta /trīféktə/ *n.* *US*, *Austral.*, & *NZ* a form of betting in which the first three places in a race must be predicted in the correct order. [TRI- + PERFECTA]

trifid /trī́fid/ *adj.* esp. *Biol.* partly or wholly split into three divisions or lobes. [L *trifidus* (as TRI-, *findere fid-* split)]

trifle /trī́f'l/ *n.* & *v.* ● *n.* **1** a thing of slight value or importance. **2 a** a small amount esp. of money (*was sold for a trifle*). **b** (prec. by *a*) somewhat (*seems a trifle annoyed*). **3** *Brit.* a confection of sponge cake with custard, jelly, fruit, cream, etc. ● *v.* **1** *intr.* talk or act frivolously. **2** *intr.* (foll. by *with*) **a** treat or deal with frivolously or derisively; flirt heartlessly with. **b** refuse to take seriously. **3** *tr.* (foll. by *away*) waste (time, energies, money, etc.) frivolously. □□ **trifler** *n.* [ME f. OF *truf(f)le* by-form of *trufe* deceit, of unkn. orig.]

■ *n.* **1** knick-knack, trinket, bauble, bagatelle, toy, gewgaw, nothing, plaything, *bêtise*, triviality, doodah, *US* doodad. **2 b** little, bit, drop, iota, scintilla, suggestion, dash, dab, pinch, whiff, mite, whit, jot, tittle, *colloq.* smidgen, *US colloq.* tad. ● *v.* **2** (*trifle with*) dally with, flirt with, mess about with, toy with, *literary* wanton with; play with, dabble in *or* at, fiddle with, dandle, tinker with, fidget with. **3** (*trifle away*) see FRITTER[1]. □□ **trifler** see DILETTANTE *n.*

trifling /trī́fling/ *adj.* **1** unimportant, petty. **2** frivolous. □□ **triflingly** *adv.*

■ **1** trivial, insignificant, unimportant, puny, minor, paltry, slight, petty, inconsequential, frivolous, superficial, incidental, negligible, commonplace, inconsiderable, shallow, valueless, worthless, *US* picayune, *colloq.* piddling, piffling. **2** see IDLE *adj.* 5, 6.

trifocal /trīfṓk'l/ *adj.* & *n.* ● *adj.* having three focuses, esp. of a lens with different focal lengths. ● *n.* (in *pl.*) trifocal spectacles.

trifoliate /trīfṓliət/ *adj.* **1** (of a compound leaf) having three leaflets. **2** (of a plant) having such leaves.

triforium /trīfóriəm/ *n.* (*pl.* **triforia** /-riə/) a gallery or arcade above the arches of the nave, choir, and transepts of a church. [AL, of unkn. orig.]

triform /trī́form/ *adj.* (also **triformed**) **1** formed of three parts. **2** having three forms or bodies.

trifurcate *v.* & *adj.* ● *v.tr.* & *intr.* /trī́fərkayt/ divide into three branches. ● *adj.* /trifúrkət/ divided into three branches.

trig[1] /trig/ *n. colloq.* trigonometry. [abbr.]

trig[2] /trig/ *adj.* & *v.* *archaic* or *dial.* ● *adj.* trim or spruce. ● *v.tr.* (**trigged, trigging**) make trim; smarten. [ME, = trusty, f. ON *tryggr*, rel. to TRUE]

trigamous /tríggəməss/ *adj.* **1 a** three times married. **b** having three wives or husbands at once. **2** *Bot.* having male, female, and hermaphrodite flowers in the same head. □□ **trigamist** *n.* **trigamy** *n.* [Gk *trigamos* (as TRI-, *gamos* marriage)]

trigeminal nerve /trījémmin'l/ *n.* *Anat.* the largest cranial nerve which divides into the ophthalmic, maxillary, and mandibular nerves. □ **trigeminal neuralgia** *Med.* neuralgia involving one or more of these branches, and often causing severe pain. [as TRIGEMINUS]

■ trifacial nerve, trigeminus.

trigeminus /trījémminəss/ *n.* (*pl.* **trigemini** /-nī/) the trigeminal nerve. [L, = born as a triplet (as TRI-, *geminus* born at the same birth)]

trigger /tríggər/ *n.* & *v.* ● *n.* **1** a movable device for releasing a spring or catch and so setting off a mechanism (esp. that of a gun). **2** an event, occurrence, etc., that sets off a chain reaction. ● *v.tr.* **1** (often foll. by *off*) set (an action or process) in motion; initiate, precipitate. **2** fire (a gun) by the use of a trigger. □ **quick on the trigger** quick to respond. **trigger fish** any usu. tropical marine fish of the family Balistidae with a first dorsal fin-spine which can be depressed by pressing on the second. **trigger-happy** apt to shoot without or with slight provocation. □□ **triggered** *adj.* [17th-c. *tricker* f. Du. *trekker* f. *trekken* pull: cf. TREK]

■ *v.* **1** see INITIATE *v.* 1.

triglyph /trī́glif/ *n.* *Archit.* each of a series of tablets with three vertical grooves, alternating with metopes in a Doric frieze. □□ **triglyphic** /-glíffik/ *adj.* **triglyphical** /-glíffik'l/ *adj.* [L *triglyphus* f. Gk *trigluphos* (as TRI-, *gluphē* carving)]

trigon /trī́gon/ *n.* **1** a triangle. **2** an ancient triangular lyre or harp. **3** the cutting region of an upper molar tooth. [L *trigonum* f. Gk *trigōnon* neuter of *trigōnos* three-cornered (as TRI-, -GON)]

trigonal /tríggən'l/ *adj.* **1** triangular; of or relating to a triangle. **2** *Biol.* triangular in cross-section. **3** (of a crystal etc.) having an axis with threefold symmetry. □□ **trigonally** *adv.* [med.L *trigonalis* (as TRIGON)]

trigonometry /trìggənómmitri/ *n.* the branch of mathematics dealing with the relations of the sides and angles of triangles and with the relevant functions of any angles. □□ **trigonometric** /-nəmétrik/ *adj.* **trigonometrical** /-nəmétrik'l/ *adj.* [mod.L *trigonometria* (as TRIGON, -METRY)]

trigraph /trī́graaf/ *n.* (also **trigram** /-gram/) **1** a group of three letters representing one sound. **2** a figure of three lines.

trigynous /tríjinəss/ *adj.* *Bot.* having three pistils.

trihedral /trīhéedrəl/ *adj.* having three surfaces.

trihedron /trīhéedrən/ *n.* a figure of three intersecting planes.

trihydric /trīhī́drik/ *adj.* *Chem.* containing three hydroxyl groups.

trike /trīk/ *n.* & *v.intr.* *colloq.* tricycle. [abbr.]

trilabiate /trīláybiət/ *adj.* *Bot.* & *Zool.* three-lipped.

trilateral /trīláttərəl/ *adj.* & *n.* ● *adj.* **1** of, on, or with three sides. **2** shared by or involving three parties, countries, etc. (*trilateral negotiations*). ● *n.* a figure having three sides.

trilby /trílbi/ *n.* (*pl.* **-ies**) *Brit.* a soft felt hat with a narrow brim and indented crown. □□ **trilbied** *adj.* [name of the heroine in G. du Maurier's novel *Trilby* (1894), in the stage version of which such a hat was worn]

trilinear /trīlínniər/ *adj.* of or having three lines.

trilingual /trīlínggwəl/ *adj.* **1** able to speak three languages, esp. fluently. **2** spoken or written in three languages. □□ **trilingualism** *n.*

triliteral /trīlíttərəl/ *adj.* **1** of three letters. **2** (of a Semitic language) having (most) roots with three consonants.

trilith /trīlith/ *n.* (also **trilithon** /-lithən/) a monument consisting of three stones, esp. of two uprights and a lintel. ▫▫ **trilithic** /-líthik/ *adj.* [Gk *trilithon* (as TRI-, *lithos* stone)]

trill /tril/ *n.* & *v.* ● *n.* **1** a quavering or vibratory sound, esp. a rapid alternation of sung or played notes. **2** a bird's warbling sound. **3** the pronunciation of *r* with a vibration of the tongue. ● *v.* **1** *intr.* produce a trill. **2** *tr.* warble (a song) or pronounce (*r* etc.) with a trill. [It. *trillo* (n.), *trillare* (v.)]
▪ *n.* **2** see CHIRP *n.* ● *v.* see CHIRP *v.*

trillion /trílyən/ *n.* (*pl.* same or (in sense 3) **trillions**) **1** a million million (1,000,000,000,000 or 10^{12}). **2** (formerly, esp. *Brit.*) a million million million (1,000,000,000,000,000,000 or 10^{18}). **3** (in *pl.*) *colloq.* a very large number (*trillions of times*). ¶ Senses 1–2 correspond to the change in sense of *billion*. ▫▫ **trillionth** *adj.* & *n.* [F *trillion* or It. *trilione* (as TRI-, MILLION), after *billion*]
▪ **3** (*trillions*) see UMPTEEN *adj.*

trilobite /trīləbīt/ *n.* any fossil marine arthropod of the class Trilobita of Palaeozoic times, characterized by a three-lobed body. [mod.L *Trilobites* (as TRI-, Gk *lobos* lobe)]

trilogy /tríllәji/ *n.* (*pl.* **-ies**) **1** a group of three related literary or operatic works. **2** *Gk Antiq.* a set of three tragedies performed as a group. [Gk *trilogia* (as TRI-, -LOGY)]

trim /trim/ *v.*, *n.*, & *adj.* ● *v.* (**trimmed, trimming**) **1** *tr.* **a** set in good order. **b** make neat or of the required size or form, esp. by cutting away irregular or unwanted parts. **2** *tr.* (foll. by *off*, *away*) remove by cutting off (such parts). **3** *tr.* **a** (often foll. by *up*) make (a person) neat in dress and appearance. **b** ornament or decorate (esp. clothing, a hat, etc. by adding ribbons, lace, etc.). **4** *tr.* adjust the balance of (a ship or aircraft) by the arrangement of its cargo etc. **5** *tr.* arrange (sails) to suit the wind. **6** *intr.* **a** associate oneself with currently prevailing views, esp. to advance oneself. **b** hold a middle course in politics or opinion. **7** *tr. colloq.* **a** rebuke sharply. **b** thrash. **c** get the better of in a bargain etc. ● *n.* **1** the state or degree of readiness or fitness (*found everything in perfect trim*). **2** ornament or decorative material. **3** dress or equipment. **4** the act of trimming a person's hair. **5** the inclination of an aircraft to the horizontal. ● *adj.* **1** neat, slim, or spruce. **2** in good condition or order; well arranged or equipped. ▫ **in trim 1** looking smart, healthy, etc. **2** *Naut.* in good order. ▫▫ **trimly** *adv.* **trimness** *n.* [perh. f. OE *trymman*, *trymian* make firm, arrange: but there is no connecting evidence between OE and 1500]
▪ *v.* **1 b** curtail, shorten, abbreviate, abridge, reduce, prune, pare, lop, crop, bob, clip, cut, whittle, shave, shear, mow, dock; barber; neaten, shape, tidy. **2** cut (off), snip (off), prune, pare, lop (off), crop, clip, shave, shear. **3 a** see NEATEN. **b** decorate, embellish, dress up, embroider, adorn, ornament, deck out, caparison, beautify. ● *n.* **1** condition, state, fettle, health, form, order, fitness, repair, shape. **2** trimming, edging, piping, purfling, ricrac, embroidery, border, hem, frill, fringe, ornament, ornamentation, decoration, embellishment, adornment. ● *adj.* **1** neat, tidy, orderly, well-ordered, well-groomed, well turned out, well-kept, smart, crisp, dapper, spick and span, spruce, shipshape (and Bristol fashion), *archaic or dial.* trig, *archaic sl.* spiffing, *colloq.* natty, *esp. US sl.* spiffy; slim, slender, clean-cut, shapely, streamlined, compact. **2** in good *or* fine fettle, fit (as a fiddle), in good shape *or* condition *or* order, athletic, *colloq.* as right as a trivet; neat, tidy, orderly, well-ordered, well-organized, organized, well-equipped, streamlined.

trimaran /trīmәran/ *n.* a vessel like a catamaran, with three hulls side by side. [TRI- + CATAMARAN]

trimer /trīmәr/ *n. Chem.* a polymer comprising three monomer units. ▫▫ **trimeric** /-mérrik/ *adj.* [TRI- + -MER]

trimerous /trīmәrәss, trím-/ *adj.* having three parts.

trimester /trīméstәr/ *n.* a period of three months, esp. of human gestation or *US* as a university term. ▫▫ **trimestral** *adj.* **trimestrial** *adj.* [F *trimestre* f. L *trimestris* (as TRI-, *-mestris* f. *mensis* month)]

trimeter /trímmitәr/ *n. Prosody* a verse of three measures. ▫▫ **trimetric** /trīmétrik/ *adj.* **trimetrical** /trīmétrik'l/ *adj.* [L *trimetrus* f. Gk *trimetros* (as TRI-, *metron* measure)]

trimmer /trímmәr/ *n.* **1** a person who trims articles of dress. **2** a person who trims in politics etc.; a time-server. **3** an instrument for clipping etc. **4** *Archit.* a short piece of timber across an opening (e.g. for a hearth) to carry the ends of truncated joists. **5** a small capacitor etc. used to tune a radio set. **6** *Austral. colloq.* a striking or outstanding person or thing.
▪ **6** see KILLER 2a.

trimming /trímming/ *n.* **1** ornamentation or decoration, esp. for clothing. **2** (in *pl.*) *colloq.* the usual accompaniments, esp. of the main course of a meal. **3** (in *pl.*) pieces cut off in trimming.
▪ **1** see ORNAMENT *n.* 1, 2. **2** (*trimmings*) see TRAPPINGS.

trimorphism /trīmórfiz'm/ *n. Bot.*, *Zool.*, & *Crystallog.* existence in three distinct forms. ▫▫ **trimorphic** *adj.* **trimorphous** *adj.*

trine /trīn/ *adj.* & *n.* ● *adj.* **1** threefold, triple; made up of three parts. **2** *Astrol.* denoting the aspect of two heavenly bodies 120° (one-third of the zodiac) apart. ● *n. Astrol.* a trine aspect. ▫▫ **trinal** *adj.* [ME f. OF *trin trine* f. L *trinus* threefold f. *tres* three]

Trinitarian /trínnitáiriәn/ *n.* & *adj.* ● *n.* a person who believes in the doctrine of the Trinity. ● *adj.* of or relating to this belief. ▫▫ **Trinitarianism** *n.*

trinitrotoluene /trīnītrәtólyoo-een/ *n.* (also **trinitrotoluol** /-tólyoo-ol/) = TNT.

trinity /trínniti/ *n.* (*pl.* **-ies**) **1** the state of being three. **2** a group of three. **3** (**the Trinity** or **Holy Trinity**) *Theol.* the three persons of the Christian Godhead (Father, Son, and Holy Spirit). ▫ **Trinity Brethren** the members of Trinity House. **Trinity House** *Brit.* an association concerned with the licensing of pilots, the erection and maintenance of buoys, lighthouses, etc., in England, Wales, etc. **Trinity Sunday** the next Sunday after Whit Sunday. **Trinity term** *Brit.* the university and law term beginning after Easter. [ME f. OF *trinité* f. L *trinitas -tatis* triad (as TRINE)]
▪ **2** see TRIO.

trinket /tríngkit/ *n.* a trifling ornament, jewel, etc., esp. one worn on the person. ▫▫ **trinketry** *n.* [16th c.: orig. unkn.]
▪ see BAUBLE.

trinomial /trīnōmiәl/ *adj.* & *n.* ● *adj.* consisting of three terms. ● *n.* a scientific name or algebraic expression of three terms. [TRI- after BINOMIAL]

trio /trée-ō/ *n.* (*pl.* **-os**) **1** a set or group of three. **2** *Mus.* **a** a composition for three performers. **b** a group of three performers. **c** the central, usu. contrastive, section of a minuet, scherzo, or march. **3** (in piquet) three aces, kings, queens, or jacks in one hand. [F & It. f. L *tres* three, after *duo*]
▪ **1** threesome, trilogy, triad, triple, troika, triptych, triumvirate, triplet, trinity, triunity, three.

triode /trī-ōd/ *n.* **1** a thermionic valve having three electrodes. **2** a semiconductor rectifier having three connections. [TRI- + ELECTRODE]

trioecious /trī-éeshәss/ *adj. Bot.* having male, female, and hermaphrodite organs each on separate plants. [TRI- + Gk *oikos* house]

triolet /trée̓әlit, trīә-/ *n.* a poem of eight (usu. eight-syllabled) lines rhyming *abaaabab*, the first line recurring as the fourth and seventh and the second as the eighth. [F (as TRIO)]

trioxide /trīóksīd/ *n. Chem.* an oxide containing three oxygen atoms.

trip /trip/ *v.* & *n.* ● *v.intr.* & *tr.* (**tripped, tripping**) **1** *intr.* **a** walk or dance with quick light steps. **b** (of a rhythm etc.) run lightly. **2 a** *intr.* & *tr.* (often foll. by *up*) stumble or cause to stumble, esp. by catching or entangling the feet. **b** *intr.* & *tr.* (foll. by *up*) make or cause to make a slip or blunder. **3** *tr.* detect (a person) in a blunder. **4** *intr.* make an excursion to a place. **5** *tr.* release (part of a machine) suddenly by knocking aside a catch etc. **6 a** release and raise (an anchor) from the bottom by means of a cable. **b** turn (a yard etc.) from a horizontal to a vertical position for lowering. **7** *intr. colloq.* have a hallucinatory experience caused by a drug. ● *n.* **1** a journey or excursion, esp. for pleasure. **2 a** a stumble or blunder. **b** the act of tripping or the state of being tripped up. **3** a nimble step. **4** *colloq.* a hallucinatory experience caused by a drug. **5** a contrivance for a tripping mechanism etc. □ **trip-hammer** a large tilt-hammer operated by tripping. **trip the light fantastic** (toe) *joc.* dance. **trip-wire** a wire stretched close to the ground, operating an alarm etc. when disturbed. [ME f. OF *triper, tripper*, f. MDu. *trippen* skip, hop]

■ *v.* **1** dance, caper, skip, gambol, frolic, frisk, hop, spring, scamper, *sl.* cavort. **2 a** stumble, slip, blunder, misstep, fall (down), tumble, topple, dive, plunge, sprawl, lurch, flounder, stagger, falter. **b** (*trip up*) blunder, slip, err, *colloq.* slip up; trap, trick, catch out, unsettle, throw off, disconcert. **3** catch out. **4** journey, travel, voyage, visit, tour, trek, sightsee, cruise; *colloq.* globe-trot. **5** detonate, set off, trigger, operate, activate, release, explode, spark off. **7** hallucinate, *colloq.* freak out, turn on. ● *n.* **1** tour, journey, excursion, outing, expedition, voyage, passage, trek, pilgrimage, jaunt, junket, drive, *archaic or joc.* peregrination. **2** stumble, slip, blunder, false step, misstep, fall; *faux pas*, error, mistake, indiscretion, lapse, slip of the tongue, *lapsus linguae*, erratum, oversight; Freudian slip; *colloq.* slip-up, *Brit. sl.* boob. □ **trip the light fantastic** (**toe**) see DANCE *v.* 1.

tripartite /trīpaártīt/ *adj.* **1** consisting of three parts. **2** shared by or involving three parties. **3** *Bot.* (of a leaf) divided into three segments almost to the base. □□ **tripartitely** *adv.* **tripartition** /-tísh'n/ *n.* [ME f. L *tripartitus* (as TRI-, *partitus* past part. of *partiri* divide)]

tripe /trīp/ *n.* **1** the first or second stomach of a ruminant, esp. an ox, as food. **2** *colloq.* nonsense, rubbish (*don't talk such tripe*). [ME f. OF, of unkn. orig.]

■ **2** see RUBBISH *n.* 3.

triphibious /trīfíbbiəss/ *adj.* (of military operations) on land, on sea, and in the air. [irreg. f. TRI- after *amphibious*]

triphthong /tríf-thong/ *n.* **1** a union of three vowels (letters or sounds) pronounced in one syllable (as in *fire*). **2** three vowel characters representing the sound of a single vowel (as in *beau*). □□ **triphthongal** /-thóngg'l/ *adj.* [F *triphtongue* (as TRI-, DIPHTHONG)]

triplane /trīplayn/ *n.* an early type of aeroplane having three sets of wings, one above the other.

triple /trípp'l/ *adj., n.,* & *v.* ● *adj.* **1** consisting of three usu. equal parts or things; threefold. **2** involving three parties. **3** three times as much or many (*triple the amount; triple thickness*). ● *n.* **1** a threefold number or amount. **2** a set of three. **3** (in *pl.*) a peal of changes on seven bells. ● *v.tr.* & *intr.* multiply or increase by three. □ **triple crown 1** *RC Ch.* the pope's tiara. **2** the act of winning all three of a group of important events in horse-racing, rugby football, etc. **triple jump** an athletic exercise or contest comprising a hop, a step, and a jump. **triple play** *Baseball* the act of putting out three runners in a row. **triple rhyme** a rhyme including three syllables. **triple time** *Mus.* that with three beats to the bar; waltz time. □□ **triply** *adv.* [OF *triple* or L *triplus* f. Gk *triplous*]

■ *n.* **2** see TRIO.

triplet /tríplit/ *n.* **1** each of three children or animals born at one birth. **2** a set of three things, esp. of equal notes played in the time of two or of verses rhyming together. [TRIPLE + -ET[1], after *doublet*]

■ **2** see TRIO.

triplex /trípleks/ *adj.* & *n.* ● *adj.* triple or threefold. ● *n.* (**Triplex**) *Brit. propr.* toughened or laminated safety glass for car windows etc. [L *triplex -plicis* (as TRI-, *plic-* fold)]

triplicate *adj., n.,* & *v.* ● *adj.* /tríplikət/ **1** existing in three examples or copies. **2** having three corresponding parts. **3** tripled. ● *n.* /tríplikət/ each of a set of three copies or corresponding parts. ● *v.tr.* /tríplikayt/ **1** make in three copies. **2** multiply by three. □ **in triplicate** consisting of three exact copies. □□ **triplication** /-káysh'n/ *n.* [ME f. L *triplicatus* past part. of *triplicare* (as TRIPLEX)]

triplicity /triplíssiti/ *n.* (*pl.* **-ies**) **1** the state of being triple. **2** a group of three things. **3** *Astrol.* a set of three zodiacal signs. [ME f. LL *triplicitas* f. L TRIPLEX]

triploid /tríployd/ *n.* & *adj. Biol.* ● *n.* an organism or cell having three times the haploid set of chromosomes. ● *adj.* of or being a triploid. [mod.L *triploides* f. Gk (as TRIPLE)]

triploidy /tríployd i/ *n.* the condition of being triploid.

tripmeter /trípmeetər/ *n.* a vehicle instrument that can be set to record the distance of individual journeys.

tripod /trīpod/ *n.* **1** a three-legged stand for supporting a camera etc. **2** a stool, table, or utensil resting on three feet or legs. **3** *Gk Antiq.* a bronze altar at Delphi on which a priestess sat to utter oracles. □□ **tripodal** /tríppəd'l/ *adj.* [L *tripus tripodis* f. Gk *tripous* (as TRI-, *pous podos* foot)]

tripoli /tríppəli/ *n.* = *rotten-stone*. [F f. *Tripoli* in N. Africa or in Syria]

tripos /trīposs/ *n. Brit.* (at Cambridge University) the honours examination for the BA degree. [as TRIPOD, with ref. to the stool on which graduates sat to deliver a satirical speech at the degree ceremony]

tripper /tríppər/ *n.* **1** *Brit.* a person who goes on a pleasure trip or excursion. **2** *colloq.* a person experiencing hallucinatory effects of a drug.

triptych /tríptik/ *n.* **1 a** a picture or relief carving on three panels, usu. hinged vertically together and often used as an altarpiece. **b** a set of three associated pictures placed in this way. **2** a set of three writing-tablets hinged or tied together. **3** a set of three artistic works. [TRI-, after DIPTYCH]

triptyque /tripteék/ *n.* a customs permit serving as a passport for a motor vehicle. [F, as TRIPTYCH (orig. having three sections)]

triquetra /trīkwétrə/ *n.* (*pl.* **triquetrae** /-tree/) a symmetrical ornament of three interlaced arcs. [L, fem. of *triquetrus* three-cornered]

trireme /trīreem/ *n.* an ancient Greek warship, with three files of oarsmen on each side. [F *trirème* or L *triremis* (as TRI-, *remus* oar)]

trisaccharide /trīsákkərīd/ *n. Chem.* a sugar consisting of three linked monosaccharides.

Trisagion /trisággiən/ *n.* a hymn, esp. in the Eastern Churches, with a triple invocation of God as holy. [ME f. Gk, neut. of *trisagios* f. *tris* thrice + *hagios* holy]

trisect /trīsékt/ *v.tr.* cut or divide into three (usu. equal) parts. □□ **trisection** *n.* **trisector** *n.* [TRI- + L *secare sect-* cut]

trishaw /trīshaw/ *n.* a light three-wheeled pedalled vehicle used in the Far East. [TRI- + RICKSHAW]

triskelion /triskélliən/ *n.* a symbolic figure of three legs or lines from a common centre. [Gk TRI- + *skelos* leg]

trismus /trízməss/ *n. Med.* a variety of tetanus with tonic spasm of the jaw muscles causing the mouth to remain tightly closed. [mod.L f. Gk *trismos* = *trigmos* a scream, grinding]

triste /treest/ *adj.* sad, melancholy, dreary. [F f. L *tristis*]

trisyllable /trīsílləb'l, tri-/ *n.* a word or metrical foot of three syllables. □□ **trisyllabic** /-silábbik/ *adj.*

tritagonist /trītággənist, tri-/ *n.* the third actor in a Greek play (cf. DEUTERAGONIST). [Gk *tritagōnistēs* (as TRITO-, *agōnistēs* actor)]

trite /trīt/ *adj.* (of a phrase, opinion, etc.) hackneyed, worn out by constant repetition. □□ **tritely** *adv.* **triteness** *n.* [L *tritus* past part. of *terere* rub]

■ see BANAL.

tritiate /tríttiayt/ *v.tr.* replace the ordinary hydrogen in (a substance) by tritium. □□ **tritiation** /-áysh'n/ *n.*

tritium /tríttiəm/ *n. Chem.* a radioactive isotope of hydrogen with a mass about three times that of ordinary hydrogen. ¶ Symb.: **T**. [mod.L f. Gk *tritos* third]

trito- /trī́tō, tríttō/ *comb. form* third. [Gk *tritos* third]

Triton /trī́t'n/ *n.* **1** (in Greek mythology) a minor sea-god usu. represented as a man with a fish's tail and carrying a trident and shell-trumpet. **2** (**triton**) any marine gastropod mollusc of the family Cymatiidae, with a long conical shell. **3** (**triton**) a newt. [L f. Gk *Tritōn*]

triton /trī́t'n/ *n.* a nucleus of a tritium atom, consisting of a proton and two neutrons.

tritone /trī́tōn/ *n. Mus.* an interval of an augmented fourth, comprising three tones.

triturate /trítyoorayt/ *v.tr.* **1** grind to a fine powder. **2** masticate thoroughly. ▫▫ **triturable** *adj.* **trituration** /-ráysh'n/ *n.* **triturator** *n.* [L *triturare* thresh corn f. *tritura* rubbing (as TRITE)]

triumph /trī́əmf, -umf/ *n.* & *v.* ● *n.* **1 a** the state of being victorious or successful (*returned home in triumph*). **b** a great success or achievement. **2** a supreme example (*a triumph of engineering*). **3** joy at success; exultation (*could see triumph in her face*). **4** the processional entry of a victorious general into ancient Rome. ● *v.intr.* **1** (often foll. by *over*) gain a victory; be successful; prevail. **2** ride in triumph. **3** (often foll. by *over*) exult. [ME f. OF *triumphe* (n.), *triumpher* (v.), f. L *triump(h)us* prob. f. Gk *thriambos* hymn to Bacchus]

▪ *n.* **1 a** victory, success, ascendancy. **b** success, victory, conquest, win, achievement, accomplishment, attainment, coup, smash (hit), winner, *colloq.* knockout, hit. **3** exultation, rejoicing, exulting, elation, delight, rapture, exhilaration, jubilation, happiness, joy, celebration, glory. ● *v.* **1** win, succeed, carry the day, be victorious *or* successful, gain a victory, take the honours, thrive, dominate, prevail; (*triumph over*) defeat, beat, rout, best, conquer, overcome, overwhelm, subdue, *literary* vanquish. **3** see EXULT.

triumphal /trīúmfəl/ *adj.* of or used in or celebrating a triumph. [ME f. OF *triumphal* or L *triumphalis* (as TRIUMPH)]

▪ celebratory, rapturous, jubilant, joyful, glorious, exultant; commemorative.

triumphant /trīúmf'nt/ *adj.* **1** victorious or successful. **2** exultant. ▫▫ **triumphantly** *adv.* [ME f. OF *triumphant* or L *triumphare* (as TRIUMPH)]

▪ **1** victorious, successful, conquering, winning; undefeated. **2** see *exultant* (EXULT).

triumvir /trī́əmveer, -úmvər/ *n.* (*pl.* **triumvirs** or **triumviri** /-rī/) **1** each of three men holding a joint office. **2** a member of a triumvirate. ▫▫ **triumviral** *adj.* [L, orig. in pl. *triumviri*, back-form. f. *trium virorum* genit. of *tres viri* three men]

triumvirate /trīúmvirət/ *n.* **1** a board or ruling group of three men, esp. in ancient Rome. **2** the office of triumvir.

triune /trī́yoon/ *adj.* three in one, esp. with ref. to the Trinity. ▫▫ **triunity** /-yóoniti/ *n.* (*pl.* **-ies**). [TRI- + L *unus* one]

trivalent /trīváylənt/ *adj. Chem.* having a valency of three; tervalent. ▫▫ **trivalency** *n.*

trivet /trívvit/ *n.* **1** an iron tripod or bracket for a cooking pot or kettle to stand on. **2** an iron bracket designed to hook on to bars of a grate for a similar purpose. ▫ **as right as a trivet** *colloq.* in a perfectly good state, esp. healthy. **trivet table** a table with three feet. [ME *trevet*, app. f. L *tripes* (as TRI-, *pes pedis* foot)]

trivia /trívviə/ *n.pl.* trifles or trivialities. [mod.L, pl. of TRIVIUM, infl. by TRIVIAL]

▪ see FROTH *n.* 2.

trivial /trívviəl/ *adj.* **1** of small value or importance; trifling (*raised trivial objections*). **2** (of a person) concerned only with trivial things. **3** *archaic* commonplace or humdrum (*the trivial round of daily life*). **4** *Biol.* & *Chem.* of a name: **a** popular; not scientific. **b** specific, as opposed to generic. **5** *Math.* giving rise to no difficulty or interest. ▫▫ **triviality** /-viálliti/ *n.* (*pl.* **-ies**). **trivially** *adv.* **trivialness** *n.* [L *trivialis* commonplace f. *trivium*: see TRIVIUM]

▪ **1** see TRIFLING 1. **3** see BANAL. ▫▫ **triviality, trivialness** smallness, unimportance, insignificance, meaninglessness, inconsequentiality, inconsequentialness, inconsequence, pettiness, paltriness; trifle, technicality, non-essential, small matter, unimportant *or* insignificant *or* inconsequential *or* petty detail, *bêtise*.

trivialize /trívviəlīz/ *v.tr.* (also **-ise**) make trivial or apparently trivial; minimize. ▫▫ **trivialization** /-záysh'n/ *n.*

▪ belittle, denigrate, lessen, minimize, undervalue, depreciate, underestimate, underrate, make light of, laugh off, underplay, dismiss, disparage, deprecate, slight, scoff at, scorn, run down, decry, play down, pooh-pooh, *colloq.* put down, *literary* misprize.

trivium /trívviəm/ *n. hist.* a medieval university course of grammar, rhetoric, and logic. [L, = place where three roads meet (as TRI-, *via* road)]

tri-weekly /trīwéekli/ *adj.* produced or occurring three times a week or every three weeks.

-trix /triks/ *suffix* (*pl.* **-trices** /trisiz, trī́seez/ or **-trixes**) forming feminine agent nouns corresponding to masculine nouns in *-tor*, esp. in Law (*executrix*). [L *-trix -tricis*]

tRNA *abbr.* transfer RNA.

trocar /trṓkaar/ *n.* an instrument used for withdrawing fluid from a body cavity, esp. in oedema etc. [F *trois-quarts*, *trocart* f. *trois* three + *carre* side, face of an instrument, after its triangular form]

trochaic /trəkáyik/ *adj.* & *n. Prosody* ● *adj.* of or using trochees. ● *n.* (usu. in *pl.*) trochaic verse. [L *trochaicus* f. Gk *trokhaikos* (as TROCHEE)]

trochal /trṓk'l/ *adj. Zool.* wheel-shaped. ▫ **trochal disc** *Zool.* the retractable disc on the head of a rotifer bearing a crown of cilia, used for drawing in food or for propulsion. [Gk *trokhos* wheel]

trochanter /trəkántər/ *n.* **1** *Anat.* any of several bony protuberances by which muscles are attached to the upper part of the thigh-bone. **2** *Zool.* the second segment of the leg in insects. [F f. Gk *trokhantēr* f. *trekhō* run]

troche /trōsh/ *n.* a small usu. circular medicated tablet or lozenge. [obs. *trochisk* f. OF *trochisque* f. LL *trochiscus* f. Gk *trokhiskos* dimin. of *trokhos* wheel]

trochee /trṓkee, -ki/ *n. Prosody* a foot consisting of one long or stressed syllable followed by one short or unstressed syllable. [L *trochaeus* f. Gk *trokhaios* (*pous*) running (foot) f. *trekhō* run]

trochlea /tróklıə/ *n.* (*pl.* **trochleae** /-li-ee/) *Anat.* a pulley-like structure or arrangement of parts, e.g. the groove at the lower end of the humerus. ▫▫ **trochlear** *adj.* [L, = pulley f. Gk *trokhilia*]

trochoid /trṓkoyd/ *adj.* & *n.* ● *adj.* **1** *Anat.* rotating on its own axis. **2** *Geom.* (of a curve) traced by a point on a radius of a circle rotating along a straight line or another circle. ● *n.* a trochoid joint or curve. ▫▫ **trochoidal** /-kóyd'l/ *adj.* [Gk *trokhoeidēs* wheel-like f. *trokhos* wheel]

trod *past* and *past part.* of TREAD.

trodden *past part.* of TREAD.

trog /trog/ *n. sl.* a term of contempt for a person; a lout or hooligan. [abbr. of TROGLODYTE]

troglodyte /tróglədīt/ *n.* **1** a cave-dweller, esp. of prehistoric times. **2** a hermit. **3** *derog.* a wilfully obscurantist or old-fashioned person. ▫▫ **troglodytic** /-díttik/ *adj.* **troglodytical** /-díttik'l/ *adj.* **troglodytism** *n.* [L *troglodyta* f. Gk *trōglodutēs* f. the name of an Ethiopian people, after *trōglē* hole]

trogon /trṓgon/ *n.* any tropical bird of the family Trogonidae, with a long tail and brilliantly coloured plumage. [mod.L f. Gk *trōgōn* f. *trōgō* gnaw]

troika /tróykə/ *n.* **1 a** a Russian vehicle with a team of three horses abreast. **b** this team. **2** a group of three people, esp. as an administrative council. [Russ. f. *troe* three]

▪ **2** see TRIO.

troilism /tróyliz'm/ *n.* sexual activity involving three participants. [perh. f. F *trois* three]

Trojan /trṓjən/ *adj.* & *n.* ● *adj.* of or relating to ancient Troy in Asia Minor. ● *n.* **1** a native or inhabitant of Troy. **2** a person who works, fights, etc. courageously (*works like a Trojan*). □ **Trojan Horse 1** a hollow wooden horse said to have been used by the Greeks to enter Troy. **2** a person or device planted to bring about an enemy's downfall. [ME f. L *Troianus* f. *Troia* Troy]

troll[1] /trōl/ *n.* (in Scandinavian folklore) a fabulous being, esp. a giant or dwarf dwelling in a cave. [ON & Sw. *troll*, Da. *trold*]

troll[2] /trōl/ *v.* & *n.* ● *v.* **1** *intr.* sing out in a carefree jovial manner. **2** *tr.* & *intr.* fish by drawing bait along in the water. **3** *intr.* esp. *Brit.* walk, stroll. ● *n.* **1** the act of trolling for fish. **2** a line or bait used in this. □□ **troller** *n.* [ME 'stroll, roll': cf. OF *troller* quest, MHG *trollen* stroll]

trolley /trólli/ *n.* (*pl.* **-eys**) **1** esp. *Brit.* a table, stand, or basket on wheels or castors for serving food, transporting luggage or shopping, gathering purchases in a supermarket, etc. **2** esp. *Brit.* a low truck running on rails. **3** (in full **trolley-wheel**) a wheel attached to a pole etc. used for collecting current from an overhead electric wire to drive a vehicle. **4 a** *US* = *trolley-car*. **b** *Brit.* = *trolley bus*. □ **off one's trolley** *sl.* crazy. **trolley bus** *Brit.* an electric bus running on the road and using a trolley-wheel. **trolley-car** *US* an electric tram using a trolley-wheel. [of dial. orig., perh. f. TROLL[2]]

■ □ **off one's trolley** see CRAZY 1.

trollop /tróllәp/ *n.* **1** a disreputable girl or woman. **2** a prostitute. □□ **trollopish** *adj.* **trollopy** *adj.* [17th c.: perh. rel. to TRULL]

■ see TART[2] *n.*

trombone /trombṓn/ *n.* **1 a** a large brass wind instrument with a sliding tube. **b** its player. **2** an organ stop with the quality of a trombone. □□ **trombonist** *n.* [F or It. f. It. *tromba* TRUMPET]

trommel /trómm'l/ *n.* *Mining* a revolving cylindrical sieve for cleaning ore. [G, = drum]

tromometer /trәmómmitәr/ *n.* an instrument for measuring very slight earthquake shocks. [Gk *tromos* trembling + -METER]

trompe /tromp/ *n.* an apparatus for producing a blast in a furnace by using falling water to displace air. [F, = trumpet: see TRUMP[1]]

trompe-l'œil /troNplṓi/ *n.* a still-life painting etc. designed to give an illusion of reality. [F, lit. 'deceives the eye']

-tron /tron/ *suffix* *Physics* forming nouns denoting: **1** an elementary particle (*positron*). **2** a particle accelerator. **3** a thermionic valve. [after ELECTRON]

troop /troop/ *n.* & *v.* ● *n.* **1** an assembled company; an assemblage of people or animals. **2** (in *pl.*) soldiers or armed forces. **3** a cavalry unit commanded by a captain. **4** a unit of artillery and armoured formation. **5** a grouping of three or more Scout patrols. ● *v.* **1** *intr.* (foll. by *in*, *out*, *off*, etc.) come together or move in large numbers. **2** *tr.* form (a regiment) into troops. □ **troop the colour** esp. *Brit.* transfer a flag ceremonially at a public mounting of garrison guards. **troop-ship** a ship used for transporting troops. [F *troupe*, back-form. f. *troupeau* dimin. of med.L *troppus* flock, prob. of Gmc orig.]

■ *n.* **1** see FLOCK[1] *n.* 2. **2** (*troops*) see SERVICE *n.* 8. ● *v.* **1** see FILE[2] *v.*

trooper /troopәr/ *n.* **1** a private soldier in a cavalry or armoured unit. **2** *Austral.* & *US* a mounted or motor-borne policeman. **3** a cavalry horse. **4** esp. *Brit.* a troop-ship. □ **swear like a trooper** swear extensively or forcefully.

tropaeolum /trәpēәlәm/ *n.* a trailing or climbing plant of the genus *Tropaeolum*, with trumpet-shaped yellow, orange, or red flowers. [mod.L f. L *tropaeum* trophy, with ref. to the likeness of the flower and leaf to a helmet and shield]

trope /trōp/ *n.* a figurative (e.g. metaphorical or ironical) use of a word. [L *tropus* f. Gk *tropos* turn, way, trope f. *trepō* turn]

trophic /tróffik/ *adj.* of or concerned with nutrition (*trophic nerves*). [Gk *trophikos* f. *trophē* nourishment f. *trephō* nourish]

-trophic /tróffik/ *comb. form* relating to nutrition.

tropho- /tróffō/ *comb. form* nourishment. [Gk *trophē*: see TROPHIC]

trophoblast /tróffōblast/ *n.* a layer of tissue on the outside of a mammalian blastula, providing nourishment to an embryo.

trophy /trṓfi/ *n.* (*pl.* **-ies**) **1** a cup or other decorative object awarded as a prize or memento of victory or success in a contest etc. **2** a memento or souvenir, e.g. a deer's antlers, taken in hunting. **3** *Gk* & *Rom. Antiq.* the weapons etc. of a defeated army set up as a memorial of victory. **4** an ornamental group of symbolic or typical objects arranged for display. □□ **trophied** *adj.* (also in *comb.*). [F *trophée* f. L *trophaeum* f. Gk *tropaion* f. *tropē* rout f. *trepō* turn]

■ **1** prize, laurel(s), wreath, cup, award, reward, honour(s), medal, citation, palm, bays; gold (medal), silver (medal), bronze (medal), *colloq.* silverware. **2** memento, souvenir, token, record, reminder, remembrance, keepsake; booty, spoils.

tropic /tróppik/ *n.* & *adj.* ● *n.* **1** the parallel of latitude 23°27′ north (**tropic of Cancer**) or south (**tropic of Capricorn**) of the Equator. **2** each of two corresponding circles on the celestial sphere where the sun appears to turn after reaching its greatest declination. **3** (**the Tropics**) the region between the tropics of Cancer and Capricorn. ● *adj.* **1** = TROPICAL 1. **2** of tropism. □ **tropic bird** any sea bird of the family Phaethontidae, with very long central tail-feathers. [ME f. L *tropicus* f. Gk *tropikos* f. *tropē* turning f. *trepō* turn]

-tropic /tróppik/ *comb. form* **1** = -TROPHIC. **2** turning towards (*heliotropic*).

tropical /tróppik'l/ *adj.* **1** of, peculiar to, or suggesting the Tropics (*tropical fish*; *tropical diseases*). **2** very hot; passionate, luxuriant. **3** of or by way of a trope. □ **tropical year** see YEAR 1. □□ **tropically** *adv.*

■ **2** see *sweltering* (SWELTER *v.*)

tropism /trṓpiz'm/ *n.* *Biol.* the turning of all or part of an organism in a particular direction in response to an external stimulus. [Gk *tropos* turning f. *trepō* turn]

tropology /trәpóllәji/ *n.* **1** the figurative use of words. **2** figurative interpretation, esp. of the Scriptures. □□ **tropological** /tróppәlójik'l/ *adj.* [LL *tropologia* f. Gk *tropologia* (as TROPE)]

tropopause /tróppәpawz, trṓ-/ *n.* the interface between the troposphere and the stratosphere. [TROPOSPHERE + PAUSE]

troposphere /tróppәsfeer, trṓ-/ *n.* a layer of atmospheric air extending from about 6–10 km upwards from the earth's surface, in which the temperature falls with increasing height (cf. STRATOSPHERE, IONOSPHERE). □□ **tropospheric** /-sférrik/ *adj.* [Gk *tropos* turning + SPHERE]

troppo[1] /tróppō/ *adv.* *Mus.* too much (qualifying a tempo indication). □ **ma non troppo** but not too much so. [It.]

troppo[2] /tróppō/ *adj.* *Austral. sl.* mentally ill from exposure to a tropical climate.

Trot /trot/ *n.* *colloq.* usu. *derog.* a Trotskyist. [abbr.]

trot /trot/ *v.* & *n.* ● *v.* (**trotted**, **trotting**) **1** *intr.* (of a person) run at a moderate pace esp. with short strides. **2** *intr.* (of a horse) proceed at a steady pace faster than a walk lifting each diagonal pair of legs alternately. **3** *intr.* *colloq.* walk or go. **4** *tr.* cause (a horse or person) to trot. **5** *tr.* traverse (a distance) at a trot. ● *n.* **1** the action or exercise of trotting (*proceed at a trot*; *went for a trot*). **2** (**the trots**) *sl.* an attack of diarrhoea. **3** a brisk steady movement or occupation. **4** (in *pl.*) *Austral. colloq.* **a** trotting-races. **b** a meeting for these. **5** *US sl.* a literal translation of a text used by students; a crib. □ **on the trot** *colloq.* **1** continually busy (*kept them on the trot*). **2** in succession (*five weeks on the trot*). **trot out 1** cause (a horse) to trot to show his paces. **2** produce or introduce (as if) for inspection and approval, esp. tediously or repeatedly. [ME f. OF *troter* f. Rmc & med.L *trottare*, of Gmc orig.]

■ *v.* **1** jog, run; bustle, hustle, hurry, hasten, scamper, *colloq.* scoot, skedaddle. ● *n.* **1** jog, jogtrot, lope; run. **5** translation, gloss, *colloq.* crib. □ **on the trot 1** see ACTIVE *adj.* 1a. **trot out 2** bring out, show, display, exhibit, flaunt, come out with, produce; dredge up, drag out; recite, repeat.

troth /trōth/ *n. archaic* **1** faith, loyalty. **2** truth. □ **pledge** (or **plight**) **one's troth** pledge one's word esp. in marriage or betrothal. [ME *trowthe*, for OE *trēowth* TRUTH]

Trotskyism /trótski-iz'm/ *n.* the political or economic principles of L. Trotsky, Russian politician d. 1940, esp. as urging worldwide socialist revolution. □□ **Trotskyist** *n.* **Trotskyite** *n. derog.*

trotter /tróttər/ *n.* **1** a horse bred or trained for trotting. **2** (usu. in *pl.*) **a** an animal's foot as food (*pig's trotters*). **b** *joc.* a human foot.

trotting /trótting/ *n.* racing for trotting horses pulling a two-wheeled vehicle and driver.

troubadour /tro͞obədor/ *n.* **1** any of a number of French medieval lyric poets composing and singing in Provençal in the 11th–13th c. on the theme of courtly love. **2** a singer or poet. [F f. Prov. *trobador* f. *trobar* find, invent, compose in verse]

■ see MINSTREL.

trouble /trúbb'l/ *n.* & *v.* ● *n.* **1** difficulty or distress; vexation, affliction (*am having trouble with my car*). **2 a** inconvenience; unpleasant exertion; bother (*went to a lot of trouble*). **b** a cause of this (*the child was no trouble*). **3** a cause of annoyance or concern (*the trouble with you is that you can't say no*). **4** a faulty condition or operation (*kidney trouble*; *engine trouble*). **5 a** fighting, disturbance (*crowd trouble*; *don't want any trouble*). **b** (in *pl.*) political or social unrest, public disturbances. **6** disagreement, strife (*is having trouble at home*). ● *v.* **1** *tr.* cause distress or anxiety to; disturb (*were much troubled by their debts*). **2** *intr.* be disturbed or worried (*don't trouble about it*). **3** *tr.* afflict; cause pain etc. to (*am troubled with arthritis*). **4** *tr.* & *intr.* (often *refl.*) subject or be subjected to inconvenience or unpleasant exertion (*sorry to trouble you*; *don't trouble yourself*; *don't trouble to explain*). □ **ask** (or **look**) **for trouble** *colloq.* invite trouble or difficulty by one's actions, behaviour, etc.; behave rashly or indiscreetly. **be no trouble** cause no inconvenience etc. **go to the trouble** (or **some trouble** etc.) exert oneself to do something. **in trouble 1** involved in a matter likely to bring censure or punishment. **2** *colloq.* pregnant while unmarried. **take trouble** (or **the trouble**) exert oneself to do something. **trouble and strife** *rhyming sl.* wife. **trouble spot** a place where difficulties regularly occur. □□ **troubler** *n.* [ME f. OF *truble* (n.), *trubler*, *turbler* (v.) ult. f. L *turbidus* TURBID]

■ *n.* **1** distress, worry, concern, difficulty, discomfort, unpleasantness, inconvenience, vexation, grief, affliction, disquiet, suffering, tribulation, adversity, misfortune, hardship, anxiety, torment, anguish, *archaic or literary* woe, *colloq.* hassle, *Austral. colloq.* strife. **2 a** inconvenience, bother, effort, pains, exertion, care. **b** annoyance, bother, torment, irritation, nuisance, burden, problem, pest. **3** see HEADACHE. **4** affliction, defect, fault, malfunction, disability, disease, ailment, illness, sickness, disorder, complaint, problem. **5, 6** disorder, agitation, disturbance, turbulence, tumult, upset, dissatisfaction, unrest, discord, dispute, disagreement, unpleasantness, turmoil, rebellion, revolt, uprising, outbreak, fighting, fight, skirmishing, skirmish, fracas, fuss, *colloq.* row, *esp. Brit. colloq.* kerfuffle. ● *v.* **1, 3** bother, upset, anguish, alarm, worry, afflict, agitate, disquiet, discomfit, make uncomfortable, grieve, distress, disturb, perturb, discommode, inconvenience, discompose, discountenance, put out, burden, encumber, weigh down, oppress; annoy, irritate, irk, vex, plague, pester, torment, harass, hector, harry, provoke, nettle, exasperate, ruffle, get *or* grate on a person's nerves, *archaic* ail, *colloq.* hassle, get under a person's skin, *sl.* bug. **4** discommode, incommode, impose on, inconvenience, put out; care, be concerned, take the trouble *or* time, go *or* take to the trouble, bother, exert oneself, concern oneself, take pains. □ **in trouble 1** in deep trouble, in a mess, in a predicament, in dire straits, in strife, in a bad way, in a corner, *colloq.* in a pickle, in hot water, in the soup, in a jam, on the spot, in a scrape, in a (tight) spot, up a gum tree, *sl.* up the creek. **2** unmarried and pregnant *or* expecting *or archaic* in a delicate condition *or colloq.* in a family way. **trouble and strife** see WIFE.

troubled /trúbb'ld/ *adj.* showing, experiencing, or reflecting trouble, anxiety, etc. (*a troubled mind*; *a troubled childhood*).

■ see ANXIOUS 1, DIFFICULT 3.

troublemaker /trúbb'lmaykər/ *n.* a person who habitually causes trouble. □□ **troublemaking** *n.*

■ mischief-maker, rabble-rouser, gadfly, firebrand, *agent provocateur*, stormy petrel, incendiary, gossip-monger, scandalmonger, malcontent, instigator, ringleader, meddler, agitator, busybody, troubler, *colloq.* stirrer; see also DELINQUENT *n.* □□ **troublemaking** see *rowdyism* (ROWDY).

troubleshooter /trúbb'lsho͞otər/ *n.* **1** a mediator in industrial or diplomatic etc. disputes. **2** a person who traces and corrects faults in machinery etc. □□ **troubleshooting** *n.*

troublesome /trúbb'lsəm/ *adj.* **1** causing trouble. **2** vexing, annoying. □□ **troublesomely** *adv.* **troublesomeness** *n.*

■ **1** difficult, awkward, inconvenient, burdensome, onerous, problematical, niggling, trying, tough; uncooperative, unruly, unmanageable, refractory. **2** worrisome, worrying, annoying, irksome, irritating, vexatious, vexing, bothersome, wearisome, tiresome, distressing, pestiferous, pestilential, *esp. US colloq.* pesky. □□ **troublesomeness** see INCONVENIENCE *n.* 1.

troublous /trúbləss/ *adj. archaic* or *literary* full of troubles; agitated, disturbed (*troublous times*). [ME f. OF *troubleus* (as TROUBLE)]

trough /trof/ *n.* **1** a long narrow open receptacle for water, animal feed, etc. **2** a channel for conveying a liquid. **3** an elongated region of low barometric pressure. **4** a hollow between two wave crests. **5** the time of lowest economic performance etc. **6** a region around the minimum on a curve of variation of a quantity. **7** a low point or depression. [OE *trog* f. Gmc]

■ **2** see CHANNEL[1] 5a, 6. **5** see SLUMP *n.*

trounce /trownss/ *v.tr.* **1** defeat heavily. **2** beat, thrash. **3** punish severely. □□ **trouncer** *n.* **trouncing** *n.* [16th c., = afflict: orig. unkn.]

■ **1** see DEFEAT *v.* 1. **2** see BEAT *v.* 1. **3** see PUNISH 1. □□ **trouncing** see DEFEAT *n.*, *thrashing* (THRASH), PUNISHMENT 1, 2.

troupe /tro͞op/ *n.* a company of actors or acrobats etc. [F, = TROOP]

■ see COMPANY *n.* 4.

trouper /tro͞opər/ *n.* **1** a member of a theatrical troupe. **2** a staunch colleague.

■ **2** see STALWART *n.*

trousers /trówzərz/ *n.pl.* **1** an outer garment reaching from the waist usu. to the ankles, divided into two parts to cover the legs. **2** (**trouser**) (*attrib.*) designating parts of this (*trouser leg*). □ **trouser-clip** = *bicycle-clip*. **trouser suit** a woman's suit of trousers and jacket. **wear the trousers** be the dominant partner in a marriage. □□ **trousered** *adj.* **trouserless** *adj.* [archaic *trouse* (sing.) f. Ir. & Gael. *triubhas* TREWS: pl. form after *drawers*]

■ **1** slacks, (Oxford) bags, knickerbockers, flannels, bell-bottoms, flares, (blue) jeans, denims, cords, dungarees, *esp. Brit.* trews, *Sc.* breeks, *esp. US* knickers, *US* pants, *colloq.* breeches, *propr.* Levis, *Austral.* & *S. Afr. sl.* rammies.

trousseau /tro͞osō/ *n.* (*pl.* **trousseaus** or **trousseaux** /-sōz/) the clothes collected by a bride for her marriage. [F, lit. bundle, dimin. of *trousse* TRUSS]

trout /trowt/ *n.* (*pl.* same or **trouts**) **1** any of various freshwater fish of the genus *Salmo* of the northern hemisphere, valued as food. **2** a similar fish of the family Salmonidae (see also *salmon trout*). **3** *sl. derog.* a woman, esp. an old or ill-tempered one (usu. *old trout*). ▫▫ **troutlet** *n.* **troutling** *n.* **trouty** *adj.* [OE *truht* f. LL *tructa*]

trouvaille /tro͞ovīl/ *n.* a lucky find; a windfall. [F f. *trouver* find]

trouvère /tro͞ováir/ *n.* a medieval epic poet in Northern France in the 11th–14th c. [OF *trovere* f. *trover* find: cf. TROUBADOUR]
■ see MINSTREL.

trove /trōv/ *n.* = *treasure trove.* [AF *trové* f. *trover* find]

trover /trōvər/ *n. Law* **1** finding and keeping personal property. **2** common-law action to recover the value of personal property wrongfully taken etc. [OF *trover* find]

trow /trow, trō/ *v.tr. archaic* think, believe. [OE *trūwian, trēowian*, rel. to TRUCE]

trowel /trówəl/ *n.* & *v.* ● *n.* **1** a small hand-held tool with a flat pointed blade, used to apply and spread mortar etc. **2** a similar tool with a curved scoop for lifting plants or earth. ● *v.tr.* (**trowelled, trowelling**; *US* **troweled, troweling**) **1** apply (plaster etc.). **2** dress (a wall etc.) with a trowel. [ME f. OF *truele* f. med.L *truella* f. L *trulla* scoop, dimin. of *trua* ladle etc.]

troy /troy/ *n.* (in full **troy weight**) a system of weights used for precious metals and gems, with a pound of 12 ounces or 5,760 grains. [ME, prob. f. *Troyes* in France]

trs. *abbr.* transpose (letters or words etc.).

truant /tro͞oənt/ *n., adj.,* & *v.* ● *n.* **1** a child who stays away from school without leave or explanation. **2** a person missing from work etc. ● *adj.* (of a person, conduct, thoughts, etc.) shirking, idle, wandering. ● *v.intr.* (also **play truant**) stay away as a truant. ▫▫ **truancy** *n.* [ME f. OF, prob. ult. f. Celt.: cf. Welsh *truan*, Gael. *truaghan* wretched]
■ *n.* malingerer, runaway, absentee, dodger, shirker, idler, loafer, layabout, *Austral.* & *NZ sl.* bludger, *Brit. sl.* skiver, wag, *Brit. sl. esp. Mil.* scrimshanker. ● *adj.* malingering, runaway, absent, absentee, delinquent, shirking, loafing, *Brit. sl.* skiving. ● *v.* play truant, absent oneself, be absent, stay away, desert, malinger, *sl.* play hookey, *Austral.* & *NZ sl.* bludge, *Brit. sl.* skive, play the wag. ▫▫ **truancy** absenteeism, non-attendance, malingering, absence, *Brit. sl.* skiving (off).

truce /tro͞os/ *n.* **1** a temporary agreement to cease hostilities. **2** a suspension of private feuding or bickering. ▫▫ **truceless** *adj.* [ME *trew(e)s* (pl.) f. OE *trēow*, rel. to TRUE]
■ armistice, cease-fire, suspension of hostilities, lull, moratorium, respite, let-up.

truck[1] /truk/ *n.* & *v.* ● *n.* **1** *Brit.* an open railway wagon for carrying freight. **2** esp. *US* a vehicle for carrying heavy goods; a lorry. **3** a vehicle for transporting troops, supplies, etc. **4** a railway bogie. **5** a wheeled stand for transporting goods. **6 a** *Naut.* a wooden disc at the top of a mast with holes for halyards. **b** a small solid wheel. ● *v.* **1** *tr.* convey on or in a truck. **2** *intr. US* drive a truck. **3** *intr. US sl.* proceed; go, stroll. ▫▫ **truckage** *n.* [perh. short for TRUCKLE in sense 'wheel, pulley']

truck[2] /truk/ *n.* & *v.* ● *n.* **1** dealings; exchange, barter. **2** small wares. **3** *US* market-garden produce (*truck farm*). **4** *colloq.* odds and ends. **5** *hist.* the payment of workers in kind. ● *v.tr.* & *intr. archaic* barter, exchange. ▫ **have no truck with** avoid dealing with. [ME f. OF *troquer* (unrecorded) = *trocare*, of unkn. orig.]
■ *n.* **1** dealing(s), traffic, business, transaction, trade, commerce, barter, exchange, communication, contact, connection, (business *or* social) relations. **2, 4** merchandise, commodities, goods, stock, wares, stuff, bits and pieces, odds and ends, sundries.

trucker /trúkkər/ *n.* esp. *US* **1** a long-distance lorry-driver. **2** a firm dealing in long-distance carriage of goods.

truckie /trúkki/ *n. Austral. colloq.* a lorry-driver; a trucker.

trucking /trúkking/ *n.* esp. *US* conveyance of goods by lorry.

truckle /trúkk'l/ *n.* & *v.* ● *n.* **1** (in full **truckle-bed**) a low bed on wheels that can be stored under a larger bed. **2** orig. *dial.* a small barrel-shaped cheese. ● *v.intr.* (foll. by *to*) submit obsequiously. ▫▫ **truckler** *n.* [orig. = wheel, pulley, f. AF *trocle* f. L *trochlea* pulley]
■ *v.* kowtow, be obsequious, toady, fawn, bow, scrape, genuflect, salaam, drop to the ground, drop to one's knees, drop down on one's knees, submit, yield, cower, cringe, grovel, crawl, quail, lick a person's boots, *Austral.* & *NZ* smoodge, *colloq.* suck up, boot-lick; (*truckle to*) fawn on *or* upon, defer to, butter up. ▫▫ **truckler** see *flatterer* (FLATTER).

truculent /trúkyoolənt/ *adj.* **1** aggressively defiant. **2** aggressive, pugnacious. **3** fierce, savage. ▫▫ **truculence** *n.* **truculency** *n.* **truculently** *adv.* [L *truculentus* f. *trux trucis* fierce]
■ surly, sullen, bad-tempered, ill-tempered, unpleasant, nasty, obstreperous, defiant, rude, ferocious, fierce, savage, barbarous, harsh, scathing, virulent, combative, belligerent, antagonistic, aggressive, bellicose, hostile, contentious, warlike, violent, pugnacious, *Brit. colloq.* stroppy, *US sl.* feisty.

trudge /truj/ *v.* & *n.* ● *v.* **1** *intr.* go on foot esp. laboriously. **2** *tr.* traverse (a distance) in this way. ● *n.* a trudging walk. ▫▫ **trudger** *n.* [16th c.: orig. unkn.]
■ *v.* see TRAMP *v.* 1.

trudgen /trújən/ *n.* a swimming stroke like the crawl with a scissors movement of the legs. [J. *Trudgen*, 19th-c. English swimmer]

true /tro͞o/ *adj., adv.,* & *v.* ● *adj.* **1** in accordance with fact or reality (*a true story*). **2** genuine; rightly or strictly so called; not spurious or counterfeit (*a true friend*; *the true heir to the throne*). **3** (often foll. by *to*) loyal or faithful (*true to one's word*). **4** (foll. by *to*) accurately conforming (to a standard or expectation etc.) (*true to form*). **5** correctly positioned or balanced; upright, level. **6** exact, accurate (*a true aim*; *a true copy*). **7** (*absol.*) (also **it is true**) certainly, admittedly (*true, it would cost more*). **8** (of a note) exactly in tune. **9** *archaic* honest, upright (*twelve good men and true*). ● *adv.* **1** truly (*tell me true*). **2** accurately (*aim true*). **3** without variation (*breed true*). ● *v.tr.* (**trues, trued, truing** or **trueing**) bring (a tool, wheel, frame, etc.) into the exact position or form required. ▫ **come true** actually happen or be the case. **out of true** (or **the true**) not in the correct or exact position. **true bill** *US* & *hist.* a bill of indictment endorsed by a grand jury as being sustained by evidence. **true-blue** *adj.* extremely loyal or orthodox; Conservative. ● *n.* such a person, esp. a Conservative. **true-born** genuine (*a true-born Englishman*). **true-bred** of a genuine or good breed. **true-hearted** faithful, loyal. **true horizon** see HORIZON 1c. **true-love** a sweetheart. **true-love** (or **-lover's**) **knot** a kind of knot with interlacing bows on each side, symbolizing true love. **true north** etc. north etc. according to the earth's axis, not magnetic north. **true rib** a rib joined directly to the breastbone. **true to form** (or **type**) being or behaving etc. as expected. **true to life** accurately representing life. ▫▫ **trueish** *adj.* **trueness** *n.* [OE *trēowe, trȳwe*, f. the Gmc noun repr. by TRUCE]
■ *adj.* **1** accurate, correct, truthful, faithful, literal, authentic, actual, factual, realistic, genuine, right, valid, unelaborated, unvarnished, unadulterated, verified, verifiable, *formal* veracious. **2** genuine, authentic, bona fide, authorized, legitimate, rightful, legal, proper, real, veritable, *Austral.* & *NZ colloq.* dinkum. **3** staunch, faithful, devoted, dedicated, loyal, fast, firm, unswerving, steady, steadfast, trustworthy, dutiful, upright, honourable, constant, unwavering, stable, dependable, sincere, genuine, reliable, true-blue, true-hearted, *archaic* trusty. **5** square, parallel; see also LEVEL *adj.* 1. **6** proper, exact, accurate, unerring, correct, precise, right, *Brit. colloq.* spot on. **9** see HONEST *adj.* 1. ● *adv.* **1** truly, truthfully, honestly, accurately, candidly,

frankly, sincerely, straightforwardly. **2** exactly, correctly, precisely, accurately, unerringly. □ **come true** come to pass, occur, take place, happen, be realized, become a reality, be fulfilled. **true-blue** (*adj.*) see STAUNCH[1] 1, CONSERVATIVE *adj.* 1a. **true-hearted** see TRUE *adj.* 3 above. **true-love** see LOVE *n.* 4a, 5. **true to life** see LIFELIKE.

truffle /trúff'l/ *n.* **1** any strong-smelling underground fungus of the order Tuberales, used as a culinary delicacy and found esp. in France by trained dogs or pigs. **2** a usu. round sweet made of chocolate mixture covered with cocoa etc. [prob. f. Du. *truffel* f. obs. F *truffle* ult. f. L *tubera* pl. of TUBER]

trug /trug/ *n. Brit.* **1** a shallow oblong garden-basket usu. of wood strips. **2** *archaic* a wooden milk-pan. [perh. a dial. var. of TROUGH]

truism /tro͞o-iz'm/ *n.* **1** an obviously true or hackneyed statement. **2** a proposition that states nothing beyond what is implied in any of its terms. □□ **truistic** /-ístik/ *adj.*
■ **1** commonplace, platitude, bromide, axiom, cliché, maxim, saw.

trull /trul/ *n. archaic* a prostitute. [16th c.: cf. G *Trulle*, TROLLOP]

truly /tro͞oli/ *adv.* **1** sincerely, genuinely (*am truly grateful*). **2** really, indeed (*truly, I do not know*). **3** faithfully, loyally (*served them truly*). **4** accurately, truthfully (*is not truly depicted; has been truly stated*). **5** rightly, properly (*well and truly*). [OE *trēowlīce* (as TRUE, -LY[2])]
■ **1** truthfully, actually, really, honestly, in fact, in actuality, in reality, in all honesty, sincerely, genuinely, *literary* in truth. **2** definitely, really, actually, undoubtedly, indubitably, beyond (the shadow of) a doubt, beyond question, without a doubt, indeed, unquestionably, absolutely, positively, decidedly, certainly, surely, *archaic* (yea,) verily, *archaic or joc.* forsooth, *literary* in truth. **3** faithfully, loyally, devotedly, steadfastly, unswervingly, staunchly. **4** accurately, truthfully, correctly, faithfully, literally, factually, *formal* veraciously. **5** properly, rightly, rightfully, justly, legitimately, justifiably, duly, well and truly.

trumeau /tro͞omṓ/ *n.* (*pl.* **trumeaux** /-mṓz/) a section of wall or a pillar between two openings, e.g. a pillar dividing a large doorway. [F]

trump[1] /trump/ *n.* & *v.* ● *n.* **1** a playing-card of a suit ranking above the others. **2** an advantage esp. involving surprise. **3** *colloq.* **a** a helpful or admired person. **b** *Austral.* & *NZ* a person in authority. ● *v.* **1 a** *tr.* defeat (a card or its player) with a trump. **b** *intr.* play a trump card when another suit has been led. **2** *tr. colloq.* gain a surprising advantage over (a person, proposal, etc.). □ **trump card 1** a card belonging to, or turned up to determine, a trump suit. **2** *colloq.* **a** a valuable resource. **b** a surprise move to gain an advantage. **trump up** fabricate or invent (an accusation, excuse, etc.) (*on a trumped-up charge*). **turn up trumps** *Brit. colloq.* **1** turn out better than expected. **2** be greatly successful or helpful. [corrupt. of TRIUMPH in the same (now obs.) sense]
■ *n.* **3 a** see BRICK *n.* 4. **b** see BOSS[1] *n.* ● *v.* **2** see DISCOMFIT 1b, OUTDO. □ **trump up** see FABRICATE 2.

trump[2] /trump/ *n. archaic* a trumpet-blast. □ **the last trump** the trumpet-blast to wake the dead on Judgement Day. [ME f. OF *trompe* f. Frank.: prob. imit.]

trumpery /trúmpəri/ *n.* & *adj.* ● *n.* (*pl.* **-ies**) **1 a** worthless finery. **b** a worthless article. **2** rubbish. ● *adj.* **1** showy but worthless (*trumpery jewels*). **2** delusive, shallow (*trumpery arguments*). [ME f. OF *tromperie* f. *tromper* deceive]

trumpet /trúmpit/ *n.* & *v.* ● *n.* **1 a** a tubular or conical brass instrument with a flared bell and a bright penetrating tone. **b** its player. **c** an organ stop with a quality resembling a trumpet. **2 a** the tubular corona of a daffodil etc. **b** a trumpet-shaped thing (*ear-trumpet*). **3** a sound of or like a trumpet. ● *v.* (**trumpeted, trumpeting**) **1** *intr.* **a** blow a trumpet. **b** (of an enraged elephant etc.) make a loud sound as of a trumpet. **2** *tr.* proclaim loudly (a person's or thing's merit). □ **trumpet-call** an urgent summons to action. **trumpet major** the chief trumpeter of a cavalry regiment. □□ **trumpetless** *adj.* [ME f. OF *trompette* dimin. (as TRUMP[2])]
■ *v.* **2** see PROCLAIM 1.

trumpeter /trúmpitər/ *n.* **1** a person who plays or sounds a trumpet, esp. a cavalry soldier giving signals. **2** a bird making a trumpet-like sound, esp.: **a** a variety of domestic pigeon. **b** a large black S. American cranelike bird of the genus *Psophia.* □ **trumpeter swan** a large N. American wild swan, *Cygnus buccinator.*

truncal /trúngk'l/ *adj.* of or relating to the trunk of a body or a tree.

truncate *v.* & *adj.* ● *v.tr.* /trungkáyt, trúng-/ **1** cut the top or the end from (a tree, a body, a piece of writing, etc.). **2** *Crystallog.* replace (an edge or an angle) by a plane. ● *adj.* /trúngkayt/ *Bot.* & *Zool.* (of a leaf or feather etc.) ending abruptly as if cut off at the base or tip. □□ **truncately** /trúngkaytli/ *adv.* **truncation** /-káysh'n/ *n.* [L *truncare truncat-* maim]
■ *v.* **1** see CUT *v.* 3a, c.

truncheon /trúnchən/ *n.* **1** esp. *Brit.* a short club or cudgel, esp. carried by a policeman. **2** a staff or baton as a symbol of authority, esp. that of the Earl Marshal. [ME f. OF *tronchon* stump ult. f. L *truncus* trunk]

trundle /trúnd'l/ *v.tr.* & *intr.* roll or move heavily or noisily esp. on or as on wheels. □ **trundle-bed** = TRUCKLE *n.* 1. [var. of obs. or dial. *trendle, trindle*, f. OE *trendel* circle (as TREND)]
■ see ROLL *v.* 1, 3a.

trunk /trungk/ *n.* **1** the main stem of a tree as distinct from its branches and roots. **2** a person's or animal's body apart from the limbs and head. **3** the main part of any structure. **4** a large box with a hinged lid for transporting luggage, clothes, etc. **5** *US* the luggage compartment of a motor car. **6** an elephant's elongated prehensile nose. **7** (in *pl.*) men's close-fitting shorts worn for swimming, boxing, etc. **8** the main body of an artery, nerve, etc. **9** an enclosed shaft or conduit for cables, ventilation, etc. □ **trunk call** esp. *Brit.* a telephone call on a trunk line with charges made according to distance. **trunk line** a main line of a railway, telephone system, etc. **trunk road** esp. *Brit.* an important main road. □□ **trunkful** *n.* (*pl.* **-fuls**). **trunkless** *adj.* [ME f. OF *tronc* f. L *truncus*]
■ **1** main stem, stalk, stock, bole. **2** torso, body. **4** chest, locker, box, case, bin, coffer. **5** luggage compartment, *Brit.* boot. **6** snout, proboscis. **7** (*trunks*) see PANTS 1. □ **trunk call** long-distance *or* STD call, *US* toll call.

trunking /trúngking/ *n.* **1** a system of shafts or conduits for cables, ventilation, etc. **2** the use or arrangement of trunk lines.

trunnion /trúnyən/ *n.* **1** a supporting cylindrical projection on each side of a cannon or mortar. **2** a hollow gudgeon supporting a cylinder in a steam engine and giving passage to the steam. [F *trognon* core, tree-trunk, of unkn. orig.]

truss /truss/ *n.* & *v.* ● *n.* **1** a framework, e.g. of rafters and struts, supporting a roof or bridge etc. **2** a surgical appliance worn to support a hernia. **3** *Brit.* a bundle of old hay (56 lb.) or new hay (60 lb.) or straw (36 lb.). **4** a compact terminal cluster of flowers or fruit. **5** a large corbel supporting a monument etc. **6** *Naut.* a heavy iron ring securing the lower yards to a mast. ● *v.tr.* **1** tie up (a fowl) compactly for cooking. **2** (often foll. by *up*) tie (a person) up with the arms to the sides. **3** support (a roof or bridge etc.) with a truss or trusses. □□ **trusser** *n.* [ME f. OF *trusser* (v.), *trusse* (n.), of unkn. orig.]
■ *v.* **2** see TIE *v.* 1a.

trust /trust/ *n.* & *v.* ● *n.* **1 a** a firm belief in the reliability or truth or strength etc. of a person or thing. **b** the state of being relied on. **2** a confident expectation. **3 a** a thing or person committed to one's care. **b** the resulting obligation or responsibility (*am in a position of trust; have fulfilled my trust*). **4** a person or thing confided in (*is our sole trust*). **5** reliance on the truth of a statement etc. without examination. **6** commercial credit (*obtained goods on trust*). **7** *Law* **a**

confidence placed in a person by making that person the nominal owner of property to be used for another's benefit. **b** the right of the latter to benefit by such property. **c** the property so held. **d** the legal relation between the holder and the property so held. **8 a** a body of trustees. **b** an organization managed by trustees. **c** an organized association of several companies for the purpose of reducing or defeating competition etc., esp. one in which all or most of the stock is transferred to a central committee and shareholders lose their voting power although remaining entitled to profits. ● *v.* **1** *tr.* place trust in; believe in; rely on the character or behaviour of. **2** *tr.* (foll. by *with*) allow (a person) to have or use (a thing) from confidence in its proper use (*was reluctant to trust them with my books*). **3** *tr.* (often foll. by *that* + clause) have faith or confidence or hope that a thing will take place (*I trust you will not be late*; *I trust that she is recovering*). **4** *tr.* (foll. by *to*) consign (a thing) to (a person) with trust. **5** *tr.* (foll. by *for*) allow credit to (a customer) for (goods). **6** *intr.* (foll. by *in*) place reliance in (*we trust in you*). **7** *intr.* (foll. by *to*) place (esp. undue) reliance on (*shall have to trust to luck*). □ **in trust** *Law* held on the basis of trust (see sense 7 of *n.*). **on trust 1** on credit. **2** on the basis of trust or confidence. **take on trust** accept (an assertion, claim, etc.) without evidence or investigation. **trust company** a company formed to act as a trustee or to deal with trusts. **trust fund** a fund of money etc. held in trust. **trust territory** a territory under the trusteeship of the United Nations or of a State designated by them. □□ **trustable** *adj.* **truster** *n.* [ME *troste*, *truste* (n.) f. ON *traust* f. *traustr* strong: (v.) f. ON *treysta*, assim. to the noun]

■ *n.* **1, 5** confidence, reliance, faith, conviction, certitude, certainty, sureness, positiveness, assurance, belief, dependence, credence. **2** belief, conviction, expectation. **3 a** see RESPONSIBILITY 2. **b** see OBLIGATION 2. **6** credit, reliability, dependability, credibility, trustworthiness, *colloq.* tick. **7 d** custody, care, keeping, charge, guardianship, protection, safe keeping, trusteeship. **8 c** monopoly, cartel; group, corporation, conglomerate, syndicate. ● *v.* **1** rely on *or* upon, believe in, have faith *or* confidence in, confide in, depend *or* bank *or* count on *or* upon, pin one's faith *or* hopes on *or* upon. **2** (*trust with*) entrust *or* charge with, empower to. **3** see HOPE *v.* 1, 2. **4** entrust, commit, commend, give, delegate, make *or* turn *or* sign *or* hand over, depute, assign, consign. **6** (*trust in*) see TRUST *v.* 1 above. **7** (*trust to*) see TRUST *v.* 1 above. □ **on trust 1** on credit, *colloq.* on tick.

trustee /trustée/ *n.* **1** *Law* a person or member of a board given control or powers of administration of property in trust with a legal obligation to administer it solely for the purposes specified. **2** a State made responsible for the government of an area. □□ **trusteeship** *n.*

trustful /trústfŏŏl/ *adj.* **1** full of trust or confidence. **2** not feeling or showing suspicion. □□ **trustfully** *adv.* **trustfulness** *n.*

■ see TRUSTING.

trusting /trústing/ *adj.* having trust (esp. characteristically); trustful. □□ **trustingly** *adv.* **trustingness** *n.*

■ trustful, unsuspicious, confiding, confident, unsuspecting, unquestioning; naïve, innocent, gullible, incautious, credulous.

trustworthy /trústwurthi/ *adj.* deserving of trust; reliable. □□ **trustworthily** *adv.* **trustworthiness** *n.*

■ reliable, dependable, accurate; responsible, steady, steadfast, loyal, faithful, (tried and) true, honourable, honest, ethical, principled, moral, incorruptible, *archaic or joc.* trusty. □□ **trustworthiness** see LOYALTY, INTEGRITY 1.

trusty /trústi/ *adj.* & *n.* ● *adj.* (**trustier, trustiest**) **1** *archaic or joc.* trustworthy (*a trusty steed*). **2** *archaic* loyal (to a sovereign) (*my trusty subjects*). ● *n.* (*pl.* **-ies**) a prisoner who is given special privileges for good behaviour. □□ **trustily** *adv.* **trustiness** *n.*

■ *adj.* **1** see TRUSTWORTHY. **2** see LOYAL.

truth /trōōth/ *n.* (*pl.* **truths** /trōōthz, trōōths/) **1** the quality or a state of being true or truthful (*doubted the truth of the statement*; *there may be some truth in it*). **2 a** what is true (*tell us the whole truth*; *the truth is that I forgot*). **b** what is accepted as true (*one of the fundamental truths*). □ **in truth** *literary* truly, really. **to tell the truth** (or **truth to tell**) to be frank. **truth drug** any of various drugs supposedly able to induce a person to tell the truth. **truth table** a list indicating the truth or falsity of various propositions in logic etc. □□ **truthless** *adj.* [OE *trīewth*, *trēowth* (as TRUE)]

■ **1** veracity, truthfulness, verity, genuineness, correctness, accuracy, authenticity, factuality, fact. **2 a** fact(s), reality, actuality. **b** axiom, maxim, truism, rule, law, principle, given, gospel. □ **in truth** in fact, truly, actually, really, in reality, *archaic* verily, *archaic or joc.* forsooth.

truthful /trōōthfŏŏl/ *adj.* **1** habitually speaking the truth. **2** (of a story etc.) true. **3** (of a likeness etc.) corresponding to reality. □□ **truthfully** *adv.* **truthfulness** *n.*

■ **1** honest, reliable, faithful, trustworthy, straightforward, candid, frank, sincere, earnest, forthright, *formal* veracious. **2** true, accurate, factual, correct, true to life, honest, reliable, faithful, trustworthy, unvarnished, unembellished, unadulterated, unelaborated, *formal* veracious. **3** true, accurate, true to life, realistic, faithful. □□ **truthfully** see TRULY 1. **truthfulness** see HONESTY 2.

try /trī/ *v.* & *n.* ● *v.* (**-ies, -ied**) **1** *intr.* make an effort with a view to success (often foll. by *to* + infin.; *colloq.* foll. by *and* + infin.: *tried to be on time*; *try and be early*; *I shall try hard*). ¶ Use with *and* is uncommon in the past tense and in negative contexts (except in *imper.*). **2** *tr.* make an effort to achieve (*tried my best*; *had better try something easier*). **3** *tr.* **a** test (the quality of a thing) by use or experiment. **b** test the qualities of (a person or thing) (*try it before you buy*). **4** *tr.* make severe demands on (a person, quality, etc.) (*my patience has been sorely tried*). **5** *tr.* examine the effectiveness or usefulness of for a purpose (*try cold water*; *try the off-licence*; *have you tried kicking it?*). **6** *tr.* ascertain the state of fastening of (a door, window, etc.). **7** *tr.* **a** investigate and decide (a case or issue) judicially. **b** subject (a person) to trial (*will be tried for murder*). **8** *tr.* make an experiment in order to find out (*let us try which takes longest*). **9** *intr.* (foll. by *for*) **a** apply or compete for. **b** seek to reach or attain (*am going to try for a gold medal*). **10** *tr.* (often foll. by *out*) **a** extract (oil) from fat by heating. **b** treat (fat) in this way. **11** *tr.* (often foll. by *up*) smooth (roughly-planed wood) with a plane to give an accurately flat surface. ● *n.* (*pl.* **-ies**) **1** an effort to accomplish something; an attempt (*give it a try*). **2** *Rugby Football* the act of touching the ball down behind the opposing goal-line, scoring points and entitling the scoring side to a kick at goal. **3** *Amer. Football* an attempt to score an extra point in various ways after a touchdown. □ **tried and tested** (or **true**) proved reliable by experience; dependable. **try conclusions with** see CONCLUSION. **try a fall with** contend with. **try for size** try out or test for suitability. **try one's hand** see how skilful one is, esp. at the first attempt. **trying-plane** a plane used in trying (see sense 11 of *v.*). **try it on** *colloq.* **1** test another's patience. **2** attempt to outwit or deceive another person. **try on** put on (clothes etc.) to see if they fit or suit the wearer. **try-on** *n. Brit. colloq.* **1** an act of trying it on. **2** an attempt to fool or deceive. **try out 1** put to the test. **2** test thoroughly. **try-out** *n.* an experimental test of efficiency, popularity, etc. **try-sail** /trīs'l/ a small strong fore-and-aft sail set on the mainmast or other mast of a sailing-vessel in heavy weather. **try-square** a carpenter's square, usu. with one wooden and one metal limb. [ME, = separate, distinguish, etc., f. OF *trier* sift, of unkn. orig.]

■ *v.* **1, 2** attempt, endeavour, aim, undertake, venture, strive, struggle, make an effort, tackle, try one's hand (at), have a go (at), *archaic* seek, *colloq.* have a stab (at), take a shot *or* crack (at), *formal* essay, *sl.* have a whack (at). **3** test, try out, prove, evaluate, examine, inspect, investigate, sample, appraise, assay, look over, analyse, scrutinize, assess, judge, *US* check out. **4** test, strain, tax, *archaic* prove. **7** hear, sit on, adjudicate, judge, adjudge. ● *n.* **1** attempt, endeavour, undertaking, venture, struggle, effort, turn, go, fling, *colloq.* stab, shot, crack, whirl, *formal* essay, *sl.* whack. □ **tried and tested** (or **true**) see SAFE *adj.* 3. **try out** see TRY *v.* 3 above. **try-out** see TRIAL 2a–c.

trying /trī́-ing/ *adj.* annoying, vexatious; hard to endure. □□ **tryingly** *adv.*

■ irritating, exasperating, frustrating, annoying, irksome, infuriating, maddening, bothersome, tiresome, vexing, vexatious, troublesome, worrying, worrisome, distressing, disquieting, upsetting, dispiriting, taxing, demanding, tough, stressful, difficult, tiring, fatiguing, *Austral. sl.* on the nose.

trypanosome /trípənəsōm/ *n. Med.* any protozoan parasite of the genus *Trypanosoma* having a long trailing flagellum and infesting the blood etc. [Gk *trupanon* borer + -SOME[3]]

trypanosomiasis /trípənəsəmī́əsiss/ *n.* any of several diseases caused by a trypanosome including sleeping sickness and Chagas' disease.

trypsin /trípsin/ *n.* a digestive enzyme acting on proteins and present in the pancreatic juice. □□ **tryptic** *adj.* [Gk *tripsis* friction f. *tribō* rub (because it was first obtained by rubbing down the pancreas with glycerine)]

trypsinogen /tripsínnəjən/ *n.* a substance in the pancreas from which trypsin is formed.

tryptophan /tríptəfan/ *n. Biochem.* an amino acid essential in the diet of vertebrates. [as TRYPSIN + *-phan* f. Gk *phainō* appear]

tryst /trist/ *n.* & *v. archaic* ● *n.* **1** a time and place for a meeting, esp. of lovers. **2** such a meeting (*keep a tryst; break one's tryst*). ● *v.intr.* (foll. by *with*) make a tryst. □□ **tryster** *n.* [ME, = obs. *trist* (= TRUST) f. OF *triste* an appointed station in hunting]

■ *n.* see MEETING 1.

tsar /zaar/ *n.* (also **czar**) **1** *hist.* the title of the former emperor of Russia. **2** a person with great authority. □□ **tsardom** *n.* **tsarism** *n.* **tsarist** *n.* [Russ. *tsar'*, ult. f. L *Caesar*]

tsarevich /zaárivich/ *n.* (also **czarevich**) *hist.* the eldest son of an emperor of Russia. [Russ. *tsarevich* son of a tsar]

tsarina /zaareénə/ *n.* (also **czarina**) *hist.* the title of the former empress of Russia. [It. & Sp. *(c)zarina* f. G *Czarin, Zarin*, fem. of *Czar, Zar*]

tsetse /tsétsi, tétsi/ *n.* any fly of the genus *Glossina* native to Africa, that feeds on human and animal blood with a needle-like proboscis and transmits trypanosomiasis. [Setswana]

TSH *abbr.* **1** thyroid-stimulating hormone. **2** Their Serene Highnesses.

T-shirt /téeshurt/ *n.* (also **teeshirt**) a short-sleeved casual top, usu. of knitted cotton and having the form of a T when spread out.

tsp. *abbr.* (*pl.* **tsps.**) teaspoonful.

T-square /téeskwair/ *n.* a T-shaped instrument for drawing or testing right angles.

tsunami /tsoonaámi/ *n.* (*pl.* **tsunamis**) a long high sea wave caused by underwater earthquakes or other disturbances. [Jap. f. *tsu* harbour + *nami* wave]

Tswana /tswaánə/ *n.* (also **Setswana** /setswaánə/) **1** a southern African people living in Botswana and neighbouring areas. **2** a member of this people. **3** the Bantu language of this people. ¶ *Setswana* is now the preferred form for the language. [native name]

TT *abbr.* **1** Tourist Trophy. **2** tuberculin-tested. **3 a** teetotal. **b** teetotaller.

TU *abbr.* Trade Union.

Tu. *abbr.* Tuesday.

tuatara /tóōətaárə/ *n.* a large lizard-like reptile, *Sphenodon punctatus*, unique to certain small islands of New Zealand, having a crest of soft spines extending along its back, and a third eye on top of its head. [Maori f. *tua* on the back + *tara* spine]

tub /tub/ *n.* & *v.* ● *n.* **1** an open flat-bottomed usu. round container for various purposes. **2** a tub-shaped (usu. plastic) carton. **3** the amount a tub will hold. **4** *colloq.* a bath. **5 a** *colloq.* a clumsy slow boat. **b** a stout roomy boat for rowing practice. **6** (in mining) a container for conveying ore, coal, etc. ● *v.* (**tubbed, tubbing**) **1** *tr.* & *intr.* plant, bathe, or wash in a tub. **2** *tr.* enclose in a tub. **3** *tr.* line (a mine-shaft) with a wooden or iron casing. □ **tub chair** a chair with solid arms continuous with a usu. semicircular back. **tub-thumper** *colloq.* a ranting preacher or orator. **tub-thumping** *colloq.* ranting oratory. □□ **tubbable** *adj.* **tubbish** *adj.* **tubful** *n.* (*pl.* **-fuls**). [ME, prob. of LG or Du. orig.: cf. MLG, MDu. *tubbe*]

tuba /tyóōbə/ *n.* (*pl.* **tubas**) **1 a** a low-pitched brass wind instrument. **b** its player. **2** an organ stop with the quality of a tuba. [It. f. L, = trumpet]

tubal /tyóōb'l/ *adj. Anat.* of or relating to a tube, esp. the bronchial or Fallopian tubes.

tubby /túbbi/ *adj.* (**tubbier, tubbiest**) **1** (of a person) short and fat; tub-shaped. **2** (of a violin) dull-sounding, lacking resonance. □□ **tubbiness** *n.*

■ **1** see FAT *adj.* 1. □□ **tubbiness** see FAT *n.*

tube /tyoob/ *n.* & *v.* ● *n.* **1** a long hollow rigid or flexible cylinder, esp. for holding or carrying air, liquids, etc. **2** a soft metal or plastic cylinder sealed at one end and having a screw cap at the other, for holding a semi-liquid substance ready for use (*a tube of toothpaste*). **3** *Anat.* & *Zool.* a hollow cylindrical organ in the body (*bronchial tubes; Fallopian tubes*). **4** (often prec. by *the*) *colloq.* the London underground railway system (*went by tube*). **5 a** a cathode-ray tube esp. in a television set. **b** (prec. by *the*) esp. *US colloq.* television. **6** *US* a thermionic valve. **7** = *inner tube*. **8** the cylindrical body of a wind instrument. **9** *Austral. sl.* a can of beer. ● *v.tr.* **1** equip with tubes. **2** enclose in a tube. □□ **tubeless** *adj.* (esp. in sense 7 of *n.*). **tubelike** *adj.* [F *tube* or L *tubus*]

■ *n.* **1** see PIPE *n.* 1. **4** see UNDERGROUND *n.* 1. **5 b** (*the tube*) see TELEVISION 2, 3. **9** tin, can, *Austral. colloq.* stubby, *Austral. sl.* tinny.

tubectomy /tyoobéktəmi/ *n.* (*pl.* **-ies**) *Surgery* removal of a Fallopian tube.

tuber /tyóōbər/ *n.* **1 a** the short thick rounded part of a stem or rhizome, usu. found underground and covered with modified buds, e.g. in a potato. **b** the similar root of a dahlia etc. **2** *Anat.* a lump or swelling. [L, = hump, swelling]

tubercle /tyóōbərk'l/ *n.* **1** a small rounded protuberance esp. on a bone. **2** a small rounded swelling on the body or in an organ, esp. a nodular lesion characteristic of tuberculosis in the lungs etc. **3** a small tuber; a wartlike growth. □ **tubercle bacillus** a bacterium causing tuberculosis. □□ **tuberculate** /-bérkyoolət/ *adj.* **tuberculous** /-bérkyooləss/ *adj.* [L *tuberculum*, dimin. of *tuber*: see TUBER]

tubercular /tyoobérkyoolər/ *adj.* & *n.* ● *adj.* of or having tubercles or tuberculosis. ● *n.* a person with tuberculosis. [f. L *tuberculum* (as TUBERCLE)]

tuberculation /tyoobérkyooláysh'n/ *n.* **1** the formation of tubercles. **2** a growth of tubercles. [f. L *tuberculum* (as TUBERCLE)]

tuberculin /tyoobérkyoolin/ *n.* a sterile liquid from cultures of tubercle bacillus, used in the diagnosis and treatment of tuberculosis. □ **tuberculin test** a hypodermic injection of tuberculin to detect a tubercular infection. **tuberculin-tested** (of milk) from cows giving a negative response to a tuberculin test. [f. L *tuberculum* (as TUBERCLE)]

tuberculosis /tyoobérkyoolṓsiss/ *n.* an infectious disease caused by the bacillus *Mycobacterium tuberculosis*, characterized by tubercles, esp. in the lungs (see also *pulmonary tuberculosis*).

tuberose[1] /tyóōbərōss/ *adj.* **1** covered with tubers; knobby. **2** of or resembling a tuber. **3** bearing tubers. □□ **tuberosity** /-róssiti/ *n.* [L *tuberosus* f. TUBER]

tuberose[2] /tyóōbərōz/ *n.* a plant, *Polianthes tuberosa*, native to Mexico, having heavily scented white funnel-like flowers and strap-shaped leaves. [L *tuberosa* fem. (as TUBEROSE[1])]

tuberous /tyóōbərəss/ *adj.* = TUBEROSE[1]. □ **tuberous root** a thick and fleshy root like a tuber but without buds. [F *tubéreux* or L *tuberosus* f. TUBER]

tubifex /tyŏŏbifeks/ *n.* any red annelid worm of the genus *Tubifex*, found in mud at the bottom of rivers and lakes and used as food for aquarium fish. [mod.L f. L *tubus* tube + *-fex* f. *facere* make]

tubiform /tyŏŏbiform/ *adj.* tube-shaped.

tubing /tyŏŏbing/ *n.* **1** a length of tube. **2** a quantity of tubes.

tubular /tyŏŏbyoolər/ *adj.* **1** tube-shaped. **2** having or consisting of tubes. **3** (of furniture etc.) made of tubular pieces. □ **tubular bells** an orchestral instrument consisting of a row of vertically suspended brass tubes that are struck with a hammer.

tubule /tyŏŏbyōōl/ *n.* a small tube in a plant or an animal body. [L *tubulus*, dimin. of *tubus* tube]

tubulous /tyŏŏbyooləss/ *adj.* = TUBULAR.

TUC *abbr.* (in the UK) Trades Union Congress.

tuck /tuk/ *v.* & *n.* ● *v.* **1** *tr.* (often foll. by *in*, *up*) **a** draw, fold, or turn the outer or end parts of (cloth or clothes etc.) close together so as to be held; thrust in the edge of (a thing) so as to confine it (*tucked his shirt into his trousers*; *tucked the sheet under the mattress*). **b** thrust in the edges of bedclothes around (a person) (*came to tuck me in*). **2** *tr.* draw together into a small space (*tucked her legs under her*; *the bird tucked its head under its wing*). **3** *tr.* stow (a thing) away in a specified place or way (*tucked it in a corner*; *tucked it out of sight*). **4** *tr.* **a** make a stitched fold in (material, a garment, etc.). **b** shorten, tighten, or ornament with stitched folds. **5** *tr.* hit (a ball) to the desired place. ● *n.* **1** a flattened usu. stitched fold in material, a garment, etc., often one of several parallel folds for shortening, tightening, or ornament. **2** *Brit. colloq.* food, esp. cakes and sweets eaten by children (also *attrib.*: *tuck box*). **3** *Naut.* the part of a ship's hull where the planks meet under the stern. **4** (in full **tuck position**) (in diving, gymnastics, etc.) a position with the knees bent upwards into the chest and the hands clasped round the shins. □ **tuck in** *colloq.* eat food heartily. **tuck-in** *n. Brit. colloq.* a large meal. **tuck into** (or **away**) *colloq.* eat (food) heartily (*tucked into their dinner*; *could really tuck it away*). **tuck-net** (or **-seine**) a small net for taking caught fish from a larger net. **tuck shop** *Brit.* a small shop, esp. near or in a school, selling food to children. [ME *tukke*, *tokke*, f. MDu., MLG *tucken*, = OHG *zucchen* pull, rel. to TUG]
■ *n.* **2** see FOOD 1. □ **tuck in** see *dig in*.

tucker /túkkər/ *n.* & *v.* ● *n.* **1** a person or thing that tucks. **2** *hist.* a piece of lace or linen etc. in or on a woman's bodice. **3** *Austral. colloq.* food. ● *v.tr.* (esp. in *passive*; often foll. by *out*) *US colloq.* tire, exhaust. □ **best bib and tucker** see BIB[1]. **tucker-bag** (or **-box**) *Austral. colloq.* a container for food.

tucket /túkkit/ *n. archaic* a flourish on a trumpet. [ONF *toquer* beat (a drum)]

tucking /túkking/ *n.* a series of usu. stitched tucks in material or a garment.

-tude /tyōōd/ *suffix* forming abstract nouns (*altitude*; *attitude*; *solitude*). [from or after F *-tude* f. L *-tudo -tudinis*]

Tudor /tyŏŏdər/ *adj.* & *n. hist.* ● *adj.* **1** of, characteristic of, or associated with the royal family of England ruling 1485–1603 or this period. **2** of or relating to the architectural style of this period, esp. with half-timbering and elaborately decorated houses. ● *n.* a member of the Tudor royal family. □ **Tudor rose** (in late Perpendicular decoration) a conventional five-lobed figure of a rose esp. a red rose encircling a white one. [Owen *Tudor* of Wales, grandfather of Henry VII]

Tues. *abbr.* (also **Tue.**) Tuesday.

Tuesday /tyŏŏzday, -di/ *n.* & *adv.* ● *n.* the third day of the week, following Monday. ● *adv.* **1** *colloq.* on Tuesday. **2** (**Tuesdays**) on Tuesdays; each Tuesday. [OE *Tīwesdæg* f. *Tīw* the Gmc god identified with Roman Mars]

tufa /tyŏŏfə/ *n.* **1** a porous rock composed of calcium carbonate and formed round mineral springs. **2** = TUFF. □□ **tufaceous** /-fáyshəss/ *adj.* [It., var. of *tufo*: see TUFF]

tuff /tuf/ *n.* rock formed by the consolidation of volcanic ash. □□ **tuffaceous** /tufáyshəss/ *adj.* [F *tuf*, *tuffe* f. It. *tufo* f. LL *tofus*, L TOPHUS]

tuffet /túffit/ *n.* **1** = TUFT *n.* 1. **2** a low seat. [var. of TUFT]

tuft /tuft/ *n.* & *v.* ● *n.* **1** a bunch or collection of threads, grass, feathers, hair, etc., held or growing together at the base. **2** *Anat.* a bunch of small blood-vessels. ● *v.* **1** *tr.* provide with a tuft or tufts. **2** *tr.* make depressions at regular intervals in (a mattress etc.) by passing a thread through. **3** *intr.* grow in tufts. □□ **tufty** *adj.* [ME, prob. f. OF *tofe*, *toffe*, of unkn. orig.: for *-t* cf. GRAFT[1]]
■ *n.* **1** see WISP.

tufted /túftid/ *adj.* **1** having or growing in a tuft or tufts. **2** (of a bird) having a tuft of feathers on the head.

tug /tug/ *v.* & *n.* ● *v.* (**tugged**, **tugging**) **1** *tr.* & (foll. by *at*) *intr.* pull hard or violently; jerk (*tugged it from my grasp*; *tugged at my sleeve*). **2** *tr.* tow (a ship etc.) by means of a tugboat. ● *n.* **1** a hard, violent, or jerky pull (*gave a tug on the rope*). **2** a sudden strong emotional feeling (*felt a tug as I watched them go*). **3** a small powerful boat for towing larger boats and ships. **4** an aircraft towing a glider. **5** (of a horse's harness) a loop from a saddle supporting a shaft or trace. □ **tug of love** *colloq.* a dispute over the custody of a child. **tug of war** **1** a trial of strength between two sides pulling against each other on a rope. **2** a decisive or severe contest. □□ **tugger** *n.* [ME *togge*, *tugge*, intensive f. Gmc: see TOW[1]]
■ *v.* **1** pull, jerk, draw, drag, haul, lug, wrench, pluck, twitch, *colloq.* yank. **2** tow, pull, haul. ● *n.* **1** pull, tow, jerk, drag, haul, wrench, lug, *colloq.* yank. **2** wrench, pang.

tugboat /túgbōt/ *n.* = TUG *n.* 3.

tui /tōō-i/ *n. NZ* a large honey-eater, *Prosthemadura novaeseelandiae*, native to New Zealand and having a long protrusible bill and glossy bluish-black plumage with two white tufts at the throat. [Maori]

tuition /tyoo-ísh'n/ *n.* **1** teaching or instruction, esp. if paid for (*driving tuition*; *music tuition*). **2** a fee for this. □□ **tuitional** *adj.* [ME f. OF f. L *tuitio -onis* f. *tuēri tuit-* watch, guard]
■ **1** education, teaching, tutelage, training, schooling, instruction, guidance, preparation.

tularaemia /tōōlərēēmiə/ *n.* (*US* **tularemia**) a severe infectious disease of animals transmissible to man, caused by the bacterium *Pasteurella tularense* and characterized by ulcers at the site of infection, fever, and loss of weight. □□ **tularaemic** *adj.* [mod.L f. *Tulare* County in California, where it was first observed]

tulip /tyŏŏlip/ *n.* **1** any bulbous spring-flowering plant of the genus *Tulipa*, esp. one of the many cultivated forms with showy cup-shaped flowers of various colours and markings. **2** a flower of this plant. □ **tulip-root** a disease of oats etc. causing the base of the stem to swell. **tulip-tree** any of various trees esp. of the genus *Liriodendron*, producing tulip-like flowers. **tulip-wood** a fine-grained pale timber produced by the N. American tree *Liriodendron tulipifera*. [orig. *tulipa(n)* f. mod.L *tulipa* f. Turk. *tul(i)band* f. Pers. *dulband* TURBAN (from the shape of the expanded flower)]

tulle /tyōōl/ *n.* a soft fine silk etc. net for veils and dresses. [*Tulle* in SW France, where it was first made]

tum /tum/ *n. colloq.* stomach. [abbr. of TUMMY]

tumble /túmb'l/ *v.* & *n.* ● *v.* **1** *intr.* & *tr.* fall or cause to fall suddenly, clumsily, or headlong. **2** *intr.* fall rapidly in amount etc. (*prices tumbled*). **3** *intr.* (often foll. by *about*, *around*) roll or toss erratically or helplessly to and fro. **4** *intr.* move or rush in a headlong or blundering manner (*the children tumbled out of the car*). **5** *intr.* (often foll. by *to*) *colloq.* grasp the meaning or hidden implication of an idea, circumstance, etc. (*they quickly tumbled to our intentions*). **6** *tr.* overturn; fling or push roughly or carelessly. **7** *intr.* perform acrobatic feats, esp. somersaults. **8** *tr.* rumple or disarrange; pull about; disorder. **9** *tr.* dry (washing) in a tumble-drier. **10** *tr.* clean (castings, gemstones, etc.) in a tumbling-barrel. **11** *intr.* (of a pigeon) turn over backwards in flight. ● *n.* **1** a sudden or headlong fall. **2** a somersault or other acrobatic feat. **3** an untidy or confused state. □ **tumble-drier** *n.* a machine for drying washing in a heated rotating drum. **tumble-dry** *v.tr.* & *intr.* (**-dries, -dried**) dry in a tumble-drier. **tumbling-barrel** (or **-box** etc.) a revolving device containing an abrasive substance, in which castings, gemstones, etc., are cleaned by friction. **tumbling-bay 1** the outfall of a river, reservoir, etc. **2** a pool into which this flows. [ME *tumbel* f. MLG *tummelen*, OHG *tumalōn* frequent. of *tūmōn*: cf. OE *tumbian* dance]

■ *v.* **1** fall (down), pitch, turn end over end, turn head over heels, roll, drop, flop, collapse, topple, stumble, *sl.* come a cropper. **2** fall, drop, topple, nosedive, plummet, take a dive. **3** see ROLL *v.* 1. **5** see the light, *colloq.* get the message, catch on, twig, get wise, *esp. US colloq.* wise up; (*tumble to*) understand, apprehend, perceive, comprehend, realize, *colloq.* catch on to, twig (to), get wise to, *sl.* dig. **6** fling, throw, toss, drop, dump, push, shove; see also OVERTURN *v.* 1, 3. **8** rumple, disarrange, disorder, tousle, ruffle, mess up, jumble, pull about. ● *n.* **1** fall, slip, stumble, spill, *colloq.* header. **2** somersault, roll.

tumbledown /túmb'ldown/ *adj.* falling or fallen into ruin; dilapidated.

■ ramshackle, dilapidated, ruined, in ruins, decrepit, rickety, shaky, falling apart *or* to pieces, disintegrating, tottering, broken-down, crumbling, derelict, gone to rack and ruin.

tumbler /túmblər/ *n.* **1** a drinking-glass with no handle or foot (formerly with a rounded bottom so as not to stand upright). **2** an acrobat, esp. one performing somersaults. **3** (in full **tumbler-drier**) = *tumble-drier*. **4 a** a pivoted piece in a lock that holds the bolt until lifted by a key. **b** a notched pivoted plate in a gunlock. **5** a kind of pigeon that turns over backwards in flight. **6** an electrical switch worked by pushing a small sprung lever. **7** a toy figure that rocks when touched. **8** = *tumbling-barrel* (see TUMBLE). □□ **tumblerful** *n.* (*pl.* **-fuls**).

■ **1** see GLASS *n.* 2a.

tumbleweed /túmb'lweed/ *n. US* & *Austral.* a plant, *Amaranthus albus*, that forms a globular bush that breaks off in late summer and is tumbled about by the wind.

tumbrel /túmbrəl/ *n.* (also **tumbril** /-ril/) *hist.* **1** an open cart in which condemned persons were conveyed to their execution, esp. to the guillotine during the French Revolution. **2** a two-wheeled covered cart for carrying tools, ammunition, etc. **3** a cart that tips to empty its load, esp. one carrying dung. [ME f. OF *tumberel*, *tomberel* f. *tomber* fall]

tumefy /tyóomifī/ *v.* (**-ies, -ied**) **1** *intr.* swell, inflate; be inflated. **2** *tr.* cause to do this. □□ **tumefacient** /-fáysh'nt/ *adj.* **tumefaction** /-fáksh'n/ *n.* [F *tuméfier* f. L *tumefacere* f. *tumēre* swell]

tumescent /tyooméss'nt/ *adj.* **1** becoming tumid; swelling. **2** swelling as a response to sexual stimulation. □□ **tumescence** *n.* **tumescently** *adv.* [L *tumescere* (as TUMEFY)]

tumid /tyóomid/ *adj.* **1** (of parts of the body etc.) swollen, inflated. **2** (of a style etc.) inflated, bombastic. □□ **tumidity** /-midditi/ *n.* **tumidly** *adv.* **tumidness** *n.* [L *tumidus* f. *tumēre* swell]

tummy /túmmi/ *n.* (*pl.* **-ies**) *colloq.* the stomach. □ **tummy-ache** an abdominal pain; indigestion. **tummy-button** the navel. [childish pronunc. of STOMACH]

■ see STOMACH *n.* 2a.

tumour /tyóomər/ *n.* (*US* **tumor**) a swelling, esp. from an abnormal growth of tissue. □□ **tumorous** *adj.* [L *tumor* f. *tumēre* swell]

■ neoplasm, cancer, melanoma, sarcoma, malignancy, carcinoma, growth, lump, swelling, protuberance, excrescence.

tump /tump/ *n.* esp. *dial.* a hillock; a mound; a tumulus. [16th c.; orig. unkn.]

■ see HILL *n.* 1.

tumult /tyóomult/ *n.* **1** an uproar or din, esp. of a disorderly crowd. **2** an angry demonstration by a mob; a riot; a public disturbance. **3** a conflict of emotions in the mind. [ME f. OF *tumulte* or L *tumultus*]

■ **1, 2** commotion, disturbance, upset, uproar, din, riot, disorder, disquiet, insurrection, unrest, agitation, bedlam, chaos, brouhaha, fracas, hubbub, stir, pandemonium, hullabaloo, furore, brawl, Donnybrook, affray, mêlée, turbulence, ferment, ado, turmoil, confusion, rampage, frenzy, rage, excitement, *esp. US* ruckus, *colloq.* rumpus, row. **3** turmoil, confusion, upset, disquiet, agitation.

tumultuous /tyoomúltyooəss/ *adj.* **1** noisily vehement; uproarious; making a tumult (*a tumultuous welcome*). **2** disorderly. **3** agitated. □□ **tumultuously** *adv.* **tumultuousness** *n.* [OF *tumultuous* or L *tumultuosus* (as TUMULT)]

■ clamorous, noisy, boisterous, disorderly, turbulent, violent, vehement, uproarious, chaotic, frenzied, furious, excited, agitated, hectic, riotous, rowdy, unruly, unrestrained, fierce, savage, wild, hysterical, frantic, obstreperous, tempestuous, stormy, thunderous, *colloq.* rumbustious.

tumulus /tyóomyooləss/ *n.* (*pl.* **tumuli** /-lī/) an ancient burial mound or barrow. □□ **tumular** *adj.* [L f. *tumēre* swell]

tun /tun/ *n.* & *v.* ● *n.* **1** a large beer or wine cask. **2** a brewer's fermenting-vat. **3** a measure of capacity, equal to 252 wine gallons. ● *v.tr.* (**tunned, tunning**) store (wine etc.) in a tun. [OE *tunne* f. med.L *tunna*, prob. of Gaulish orig.]

tuna[1] /tyóonə/ *n.* (*pl.* same or **tunas**) **1** any marine fish of the family Scombridae native to tropical and warm waters, having a round body and pointed snout, and used for food. Also called TUNNY. **2** (in full **tuna-fish**) the flesh of the tuna or tunny, usu. tinned in oil or brine. [Amer. Sp., perh. f. Sp. *atún* tunny]

tuna[2] /tyóonə/ *n.* **1** a prickly pear, esp. *Opuntia tuna*. **2** the fruit of this. [Sp. f. Haitian]

tundish /túndish/ *n.* **1** a wooden funnel esp. in brewing. **2** an intermediate reservoir in metal-founding.

tundra /túndrə/ *n.* a vast level treeless Arctic region usu. with a marshy surface and underlying permafrost. [Lappish]

tune /tyoon/ *n.* & *v.* ● *n.* a melody with or without harmony. ● *v.* **1** *tr.* put (a musical instrument) in tune. **2 a** *tr.* adjust (a radio receiver etc.) to the particular frequency of the required signals. **b** *intr.* (foll. by *in*) adjust a radio receiver to the required signal (*tuned in to Radio 2*). **3** *tr.* adjust (an engine etc.) to run smoothly and efficiently. **4** *tr.* (foll. by *to*) adjust or adapt to a required or different purpose, situation, etc. **5** *intr.* (foll. by *with*) be in harmony with. □ **in tune 1** having the correct pitch or intonation (*sings in tune*). **2** (usu. foll. by *with*) harmonizing with one's company, surroundings, etc. **out of tune 1** not having the correct pitch or intonation (*always plays out of tune*). **2** (usu. foll. by *with*) clashing with one's company etc. **to the tune of** *colloq.* to the considerable sum or amount of. **tuned in 1** (of a radio etc.) adjusted to a particular frequency, station, etc. **2** (foll. by *on, to*) *sl.* in rapport or harmony with. **3** *colloq.* = *switched-on*. **tune up 1** (of an orchestra) bring the instruments to the proper or uniform pitch. **2** begin to play or sing. **3** bring to the most efficient condition. □□ **tunable** *adj.* (also **tuneable**). [ME: unexpl. var. of TONE]

■ *n.* melody, air, song, strain, motif, theme. ● *v.* **1** tune up, attune, adjust, modulate, temper. **3, 4** calibrate, adjust, regulate, coordinate, adapt, attune, align, set, fine-tune. □ **in tune, out of tune** see STEP *n.* 9a.

tuneful /tyóonfōōl/ *adj.* melodious, musical. □□ **tunefully** *adv.* **tunefulness** *n.*

■ melodic, musical, sweet-sounding, melodious, euphonious, dulcet, mellifluent, mellifluous, harmonic, catchy, mellow, smooth, rich, rhythmic, *colloq.* easy on the ear(s). □□ **tunefulness** see MELODY 4.

tuneless /tyōōnliss/ *adj.* **1** unmelodious, unmusical. **2** out of tune. ▫▫ **tunelessly** *adv.* **tunelessness** *n.*

tuner /tyōōnər/ *n.* **1** a person who tunes musical instruments, esp. pianos. **2** a device for tuning a radio receiver.

tung /tung/ *n.* (in full **tung-tree**) a tree, *Aleurites fordii*, native to China, bearing poisonous fruits containing seeds that yield oil. ▫ **tung oil** this oil used in paints and varnishes. [Chin. *tong*]

tungsten /túngstən/ *n. Chem.* a steel-grey dense metallic element with a very high melting-point, occurring naturally in scheelite and used for the filaments of electric lamps and for alloying steel etc. ¶ Symb.: **W**. ▫ **tungsten carbide** a very hard black substance used in making dies and cutting tools. ▫▫ **tungstate** /-stayt/ *n.* **tungstic** *adj.* **tungstous** *adj.* [Sw. f. *tung* heavy + *sten* stone]

tunic /tyōōnik/ *n.* **1 a** a close-fitting short coat of police or military etc. uniform. **b** a loose, often sleeveless garment usu. reaching to about the knees, as worn in ancient Greece and Rome. **c** any of various loose, pleated dresses gathered at the waist with a belt or cord. **d** a tunicle. **2** *Zool.* the rubbery outer coat of an ascidian etc. **3** *Bot.* **a** any of the concentric layers of a bulb. **b** the tough covering of a part of this. **4** *Anat.* a membrane enclosing or lining an organ. [F *tunique* or L *tunica*]

tunica /tyōōnikə/ *n.* (*pl.* **tunicae** /-kee/) *Bot.* & *Anat.* = TUNIC 3, 4. [L]

tunicate /tyōōnikət, -kayt/ *n.* & *adj.* ● *n.* any marine animal of the subphylum Urochordata having a rubbery or hard outer coat, including sea squirts. ● *adj.* **1** *Zool.* of or relating to this subphylum. **2 a** *Zool.* enclosed in a tunic. **b** *Bot.* having concentric layers. [L *tunicatus* past part. of *tunicare* clothe with a tunic (as TUNICA)]

tunicle /tyōōnik'l/ *n.* a short vestment worn by a bishop or subdeacon at the Eucharist etc. [ME f. OF *tunicle* or L *tunicula* dimin. of TUNICA]

tuning /tyōōning/ *n.* the process or a system of putting a musical instrument in tune. ▫ **tuning-fork** a two-pronged steel fork that gives a particular note when struck, used in tuning. **tuning-peg** (or **pin** etc.) a peg or pin etc. attached to the strings of a stringed instrument and turned to alter their tension in tuning.

tunnel /túnn'l/ *n.* & *v.* ● *n.* **1** an artificial underground passage through a hill or under a road or river etc., esp. for a railway or road to pass through, or in a mine. **2** an underground passage dug by a burrowing animal. **3** a prolonged period of difficulty or suffering (esp. in metaphors, e.g. *the end of the tunnel*). **4** a tube containing a propeller shaft etc. ● *v.* (**tunnelled, tunnelling**; *US* **tunneled, tunneling**) **1** *intr.* (foll. by *through*, *into*, etc.) make a tunnel through (a hill etc.). **2** *tr.* make (one's way) by tunnelling. **3** *intr. Physics* pass through a potential barrier. ▫ **tunnel diode** *Electronics* a two-terminal semiconductor diode using tunnelling electrons to perform high-speed switching operations. **tunnel-kiln** a kiln in which ceramic ware is carried on trucks along a continuously-heated passage. **tunnel-net** a fishing-net wide at the mouth and narrow at the other end. **tunnel vision 1** vision that is defective in not adequately including objects away from the centre of the field of view. **2** *colloq.* inability to grasp the wider implications of a situation. ▫▫ **tunneller** *n.* [ME f. OF *tonel* dimin. of *tonne* TUN]

■ *n.* **1** shaft, subway, (underground) passage(way), underpass. **2** burrow, hole, passage. ● *v.* **1** burrow, dig, hole, excavate, penetrate, mine, bore, drill.

tunny /túnni/ *n.* (*pl.* same or **-ies**) = TUNA[1]. [F *thon* f. Prov. *ton*, f. L *thunnus* f. Gk *thunnos*]

tup /tup/ *n.* & *v.* ● *n.* **1** esp. *Brit.* a male sheep; a ram. **2** the striking-head of a pile-driver, etc. ● *v.tr.* (**tupped, tupping**) esp. *Brit.* (of a ram) copulate with (a ewe). [ME *toje*, *tupe*, of unkn. orig.]

Tupamaro /tōōpəmaárō/ *n.* (*pl.* **-os**) a Marxist urban guerrilla in Uruguay. [*Tupac Amaru*, the names of two Inca leaders]

tupelo /tyōōpilō/ *n.* (*pl.* **-os**) **1** any of various Asian and N. American deciduous trees of the genus *Nyssa*, with colourful foliage and growing in swampy conditions. **2** the wood of this tree. [Creek f. *ito* tree + *opilwa* swamp]

Tupi /tōōpi/ *n.* & *adj.* ● *n.* (*pl.* same or **Tupis**) **1** a member of an American Indian people native to the Amazon valley. **2** the language of this people. ● *adj.* of or relating to this people or language. [native name]

tuppence /túppənss/ *n. Brit.* = TWOPENCE. [phonet. spelling]

tuppenny /túppəni/ *adj. Brit.* = TWOPENNY. [phonet. spelling]

Tupperware /túppərwair/ *n. propr.* a range of plastic containers for storing food. [*Tupper*, name of the US manufacturer, + WARE[1]]

tuque /tōōk/ *n.* a Canadian stocking cap. [Can. F form of TOQUE]

turaco /tóorəkō/ *n.* (also **touraco**) (*pl.* **-os**) any African bird of the family Musophagidae, with crimson and green plumage and a prominent crest. [F f. native W.Afr. name]

Turanian /tyooráyniən/ *n.* & *adj.* ● *n.* the group of Asian languages that are neither Semitic nor Indo-European, esp. the Ural-Altaic family. ● *adj.* of or relating to this group. [Pers. *Tūrān* region beyond the Oxus]

turban /túrb'n/ *n.* **1** a man's headdress of cotton or silk wound round a cap or the head, worn esp. by Muslims and Sikhs. **2** a woman's headdress or hat resembling this. ▫▫ **turbaned** *adj.* [16th c. (also *tulbant* etc.), ult. f. Turk. *tülbent* f. Pers. *dulband*: cf. TULIP]

turbary /túrbəri/ *n.* (*pl.* **-ies**) *Brit.* **1** the right of digging turf on common ground or on another's ground. **2** a place where turf or peat is dug. [ME f. AF *turberie*, OF *tourberie* f. *tourbe* TURF]

turbellarian /túrbiláiriən/ *n.* & *adj.* ● *n.* any usu. free-living flatworm of the class Turbellaria, having a ciliated surface. ● *adj.* of or relating to this class. [mod.L *Turbellaria* f. L *turbella* dimin. of *turba* crowd: see TURBID]

turbid /túrbid/ *adj.* **1** (of a liquid or colour) muddy, thick; not clear. **2** (of a style etc.) confused, disordered. ▫▫ **turbidity** /-bídditi/ *n.* **turbidly** *adv.* **turbidness** *n.* [L *turbidus* f. *turba* a crowd, a disturbance]

■ **1** see OPAQUE *adj.* 1, 2. **2** see INCOHERENT 2, DISORDERLY 1.

turbinate /túrbinət/ *adj.* **1** shaped like a spinning-top or inverted cone. **2** (of a shell) with whorls decreasing rapidly in size. **3** *Anat.* (esp. of some nasal bones) shaped like a scroll. ▫▫ **turbinal** *adj.* **turbination** /-náysh'n/ *n.* [L *turbinatus* (as TURBINE)]

turbine /túrbīn/ *n.* a rotary motor or engine driven by a flow of water, steam, gas, wind, etc., esp. to produce electrical power. [F f. L *turbo -binis* spinning-top, whirlwind]

turbit /túrbit/ *n.* a breed of domestic pigeon of stout build with a neck frill and short beak. [app. f. L *turbo* top, from its figure]

turbo /túrbō/ *n.* (*pl.* **-os**) = TURBOCHARGER.

turbo- /túrbō/ *comb. form* turbine.

turbocharger /túrbōchaarjər/ *n.* a supercharger driven by a turbine powered by the engine's exhaust gases.

turbofan /túrbōfan/ *n.* **1** a jet engine in which a turbine-driven fan provides additional thrust. **2** an aircraft powered by this.

turbojet /túrbōjet/ *n. Aeron.* **1** a jet engine in which the jet also operates a turbine-driven compressor for the air drawn into the engine. **2** an aircraft powered by this.

turboprop /túrbōprop/ *n. Aeron.* **1** a jet engine in which a turbine is used as in a turbojet and also to drive a propeller. **2** an aircraft powered by this.

turboshaft /túrbōshaaft/ *n.* a gas turbine that powers a shaft for driving heavy vehicles, generators, pumps, etc.

turbosupercharger /túrbōsōōpərchaarjər/ *n.* = TURBOCHARGER.

turbot /túrbət/ *n.* **1** a flatfish, *Scophthalmus maximus*, having large bony tubercles on the body and head and prized as food. **2** any of various similar fishes including halibut. [ME f. OF f. OSw. *törnbut* f. *törn* thorn + *but* BUTT[3]]

turbulence /túrbyooləns/ *n.* **1** an irregularly fluctuating flow of air or fluid. **2** *Meteorol.* stormy conditions as a result of atmospheric disturbance. **3** a disturbance, commotion, or tumult.
■ **3** see DISTURBANCE 1, 4; 2.

turbulent /túrbyoolənt/ *adj.* **1** disturbed; in commotion. **2** (of a flow of air etc.) varying irregularly; causing disturbance. **3** tumultuous. **4** insubordinate, riotous. □□ **turbulently** *adv.* [L *turbulentus* f. *turba* crowd]
■ **1, 3, 4** see DISORDERLY 2, TUMULTUOUS .

Turco /túrkō/ *n.* (*pl.* **-os**) *hist.* an Algerian soldier in the French army. [Sp., Port., & It., = TURK]

Turco- /túrkō/ *comb. form* (also **Turko-**) Turkish; Turkish and. [med.L (as TURK)]

Turcoman var. of TURKOMAN.

turd /turd/ *n. coarse sl.* **1** a lump of excrement. **2** a term of contempt for a person. ¶ Often considered a taboo word, esp. in sense 2. [OE *tord* f. Gmc]

turdoid /túrdoyd/ *adj.* thrushlike. [L *turdus* THRUSH[1]]

tureen /tyooreén, tə-/ *n.* a deep covered dish for serving soup etc. [earlier *terrine*, *-ene* f. F *terrine* large circular earthenware dish, fem. of OF *terrin* earthen ult. f. L *terra* earth]

turf /turf/ *n.* & *v.* ● *n.* (*pl.* **turfs** or **turves**) **1 a** a layer of grass etc. with earth and matted roots as the surface of grassland. **b** a piece of this cut from the ground. **2** a slab of peat for fuel. **3** (prec. by *the*) **a** horse-racing generally. **b** a general term for racecourses. **4** *sl.* a person's territory or sphere of influence. ● *v.tr.* **1** cover (ground) with turf. **2** (foll. by *out*) esp. *Brit. colloq.* expel or eject (a person or thing). □ **turf accountant** *Brit.* a bookmaker. [OE f. Gmc]
■ *n.* **1** sod, green, grass, lawn, *archaic or literary* greensward, *literary* sward. **3** (*the turf*) horse-racing, racing, the racing world, racecourse, racetrack. **4** territory, area, neighbourhood, backyard, stamping-ground, home ground, haunt, province, preserve, *colloq.* patch, *joc.* bailiwick; field, domain, sphere (of influence). ● *v.* **1** grass (over). **2** (*turf out*) eject, dismiss, expel, throw *or* toss *or* turn out, oust, banish, exile, boot *or* kick out, *colloq.* sack, give a person the boot *or* sack, chuck out, *sl.* bounce, fire.

turfman /túrfmən/ *n.* (*pl.* **-men**) esp. *US* a devotee of horse-racing.

turfy /túrfi/ *adj.* (**turfier, turfiest**) like turf; grassy.

turgescent /turjéss'nt/ *adj.* becoming turgid; swelling. □□ **turgescence** *n.*

turgid /túrjid/ *adj.* **1** swollen, inflated, enlarged. **2** (of language) pompous, bombastic. □□ **turgidity** /-jídditi/ *n.* **turgidly** *adv.* **turgidness** *n.* [L *turgidus* f. *turgēre* swell]
■ **1** see *swollen* (SWELL *v.* 6). **2** see POMPOUS 2. □□ **turgidity** see RANT *n.* 2.

turgor /túrgər/ *n. Bot.* the rigidity of cells due to the absorption of water. [LL (as TURGID)]

turion /tóoriən/ *n. Bot.* **1** a young shoot or sucker arising from an underground bud. **2** a bud formed by certain aquatic plants. [F f. L *turio -onis* shoot]

Turk /turk/ *n.* **1 a** a native or national of Turkey in SE Europe and Asia Minor. **b** a person of Turkish descent. **2** a member of a Central Asian people from whom the Ottomans derived, speaking Turkic languages. **3** *offens.* a ferocious, wild, or unmanageable person. □ **Turk's cap** a martagon lily or other plant with turban-like flowers. **Turk's head** a turban-like ornamental knot. [ME, = F *Turc*, It. etc. *Turco*, med.L *Turcus*, Pers. & Arab. *Turk*, of unkn. orig.]

turkey /túrki/ *n.* (*pl.* **-eys**) **1** a large mainly domesticated game-bird, *Meleagris gallopavo*, orig. of N. America, having dark plumage with a green or bronze sheen, prized as food esp. on festive occasions including Christmas and, in the US, Thanksgiving. **2** the flesh of the turkey as food. **3** *US sl.* **a** a theatrical failure; a flop. **b** a stupid or inept person. □ **talk turkey** *US colloq.* talk frankly and straightforwardly; get down to business. **turkey buzzard** (or **vulture**) an American vulture, *Cathartes aura.* [16th c.: short for *turkeycock* or *turkeyhen*, orig. applied to the guinea-fowl which was imported through Turkey, and then erron. to the Amer. bird]

Turkey carpet /túrki/ *n.* = *Turkish carpet.*

turkeycock /túrkikok/ *n.* **1** a male turkey. **2** a pompous or self-important person.

Turkey red /túrki/ *n.* **1** a scarlet pigment obtained from the madder or alizarin. **2** a cotton cloth dyed with this.

Turki /túrki/ *adj.* & *n.* ● *adj.* of or relating to a group of Ural-Altaic languages (including Turkish) and the peoples speaking them. ● *n.* the Turki group of languages. □□ **Turkic** *adj.* [Pers. *turkī* (as TURK)]

Turkish /túrkish/ *adj.* & *n.* ● *adj.* of or relating to Turkey in SE Europe and Asia Minor, or to the Turks or their language. ● *n.* this language. □ **Turkish bath 1** a hot-air or steam bath followed by washing, massage, etc. **2** (in *sing.* or *pl.*) a building for this. **Turkish carpet** a wool carpet with a thick pile and traditional bold design. **Turkish coffee** a strong black coffee. **Turkish delight** a sweet of lumps of flavoured gelatine coated in powdered sugar. **Turkish towel** a towel made of cotton terry.

Turko- var. of TURCO-.

Turkoman /túrkōmən/ *n.* (also **Turcoman**) (*pl.* **-mans**) **1** a member of any of various Turkic peoples in Turkmenistan in SW Middle Asia. **2** the language of these peoples. □ **Turkoman carpet** a traditional rich-coloured carpet with a soft long nap. [Pers. *Turkumān* (as TURK, *mānistan* resemble)]

turmeric /túrmərik/ *n.* **1** an E. Indian plant, *Curcuma longa*, of the ginger family, yielding aromatic rhizomes used as a spice and for yellow dye. **2** this powdered rhizome used as a spice esp. in curry-powder. [16th-c. forms *tarmaret* etc. perh. f. F *terre mérite* and mod.L *terra merita*, of unkn. orig.]

turmoil /túrmoyl/ *n.* **1** violent confusion; agitation. **2** din and bustle. [16th c.: orig. unkn.]
■ **1** see CONFUSION 2a. **2** see *excitement* (EXCITE).

turn /turn/ *v.* & *n.* ● *v.* **1** *tr.* & *intr.* move around a point or axis so that the point or axis remains in a central position; give a rotary motion to or receive a rotary motion (*turned the wheel*; *the wheel turns*; *the key turns in the lock*). **2** *tr.* & *intr.* change in position so that a different side, end, or part becomes outermost or uppermost etc.; invert or reverse or cause to be inverted or reversed (*turned inside out*; *turned it upside down*). **3 a** *tr.* give a new direction to (*turn your face this way*). **b** *intr.* take a new direction (*turn left here*; *my thoughts have often turned to you*). **4** *tr.* aim in a certain way (*turned the hose on them*). **5** *intr.* & *tr.* (foll. by *into*) change in nature, form, or condition to (*turned into a dragon*; *then turned him into a frog*; *turned the book into a play*). **6** *intr.* (foll. by *to*) **a** apply oneself to; set about (*turned to doing the ironing*). **b** have recourse to; begin to indulge in habitually (*turned to drink*; *turned to me for help*). **c** go on to consider next (*let us now turn to your report*). **7** *intr.* & *tr.* become or cause to become (*turned hostile*; *has turned informer*; *your comment turned them angry*). **8 a** *tr.* & *intr.* (foll. by *against*) make or become hostile to (*has turned them against us*). **b** *intr.* (foll. by *on*, *upon*) become hostile to; attack (*suddenly turned on them*). **9** *intr.* (of hair or leaves) change colour. **10** *intr.* (of milk) become sour. **11** *intr.* (of the stomach) be nauseated. **12** *intr.* (of the head) become giddy. **13** *tr.* cause (milk) to become sour, (the stomach) to be nauseated, or (the head) to become giddy. **14** *tr.* translate (*turn it into French*). **15** *tr.* move to the other side of; go round (*turned the corner*). **16** *tr.* pass the age or time of (*he has turned 40*; *it has now turned 4 o'clock*). **17** *intr.* (foll. by *on*) depend on; be determined by; concern (*it all turns on the weather tomorrow*; *the conversation turned on my motives*). **18** *tr.* send or put into a specified place or condition; cause to go (*was turned loose*; *turned the water out into a basin*). **19** *tr.* **a** perform (a somersault etc.) with rotary motion. **b** twist (an ankle) out of position; sprain. **20** *tr.* remake (a garment or, esp., a sheet) putting the worn outer side on the inside. **21** *tr.* make (a profit). **22** *tr.* (also foll. by *aside*) divert, deflect (something material or immaterial). **23** *tr.* blunt (the edge of a knife, slot of a screw-head, etc.). **24** *tr.* shape (an object) on a lathe. **25** *tr.* give an (esp. elegant) form to (*turn a compliment*). **26** *intr. Golf* begin the second half of a round. **27** *tr.* (esp. as **turned** *adj.*) *Printing* invert (type) to make it appear upside down (*a turned comma*). **28** *tr.* pass round (the flank etc. of an army) so as to attack it from the side or rear. **29** *intr.* (of the tide) change from flood to ebb or vice versa. ● *n.* **1** the act or process or an instance of turning; rotary motion (*a single turn of the handle*). **2 a** a changed or a change of direction or tendency (*took a sudden turn to the left*). **b** a deflection or deflected part (*full of twists and turns*). **3** a point at which a turning or change occurs. **4** a turning of a road. **5** a change of the tide from ebb to flow or from flow to ebb. **6** a change in the course of events. **7** a tendency or disposition (*is of a mechanical turn of mind*). **8** an opportunity or obligation etc. that comes successively to each of several persons etc. (*your turn will come*; *my turn to read*). **9** a short walk or ride (*shall take a turn in the garden*). **10** a short performance on stage or in a circus etc. **11** service of a specified kind (*did me a good turn*). **12** purpose (*served my turn*). **13** *colloq.* a momentary nervous shock or ill feeling (*gave me quite a turn*). **14** *Mus.* an ornament consisting of the principal note with those above and below it. **15** one round in a coil of rope etc. **16** *Printing* **a** inverted type as a temporary substitute for a missing letter. **b** a letter turned wrong side up. **17 a** *Brit.* the difference between the buying and selling price of stocks etc. **b** a profit made from this. □ **at every turn** continually; at each new stage etc. **by turns** in rotation of individuals or groups; alternately. **in turn** in succession; one by one. **in one's turn** when one's turn or opportunity comes. **not know which way** (or **where**) **to turn** be completely at a loss, unsure how to act, etc. **not turn a hair** see HAIR. **on the turn 1** changing. **2** (of milk) becoming sour. **3** at the turning-point. **out of turn 1** at a time when it is not one's turn. **2** inappropriately; inadvisedly or tactlessly (*did I speak out of turn?*). **take turns** (or **take it in turns**) act or work alternately or in succession. **to a turn** (esp. cooked) to exactly the right degree etc. **turn about** move so as to face in a new direction. **turn-about** *n.* **1** an act of turning about. **2** an abrupt change of policy etc. **turn and turn about** alternately. **turn around** esp. *US* = *turn round*. **turn aside** see TURN *v.* 22 above. **turn away 1** turn to face in another direction. **2** refuse to accept; reject. **3** send away. **turn back 1** begin or cause to retrace one's steps. **2** fold back. **turn one's back on** see BACK. **turn-bench** a watchmaker's portable lathe. **turn-buckle** a device for tightly connecting parts of a metal rod or wire. **turn-cap** a revolving chimney-top. **turn the corner 1** pass round it into another street. **2** pass the critical point in an illness, difficulty, etc. **turn a deaf ear** see DEAF. **turn down 1** reject (a proposal, application, etc.). **2** reduce the volume or strength of (sound, heat, etc.) by turning a knob etc. **3** fold down. **4** place downwards. **turn-down** *n.* a rejection, a refusal. *adj.* (of a collar) turned down. **turn one's hand to** see HAND. **turn a person's head** see HEAD. **turn an honest penny** see HONEST. **turn in 1** hand in or over; deliver. **2** achieve or register (a performance, score, etc.). **3** *colloq.* go to bed in the evening. **4** fold inwards. **5** incline inwards (*his toes turn in*). **6** *colloq.* abandon (a plan etc.). **turn in one's grave** see GRAVE[1]. **turn inside out** see INSIDE. **turn off 1 a** stop the flow or operation of (water, electricity, etc.) by means of a tap, switch, etc. **b** operate (a tap, switch, etc.) to achieve this. **2 a** enter a side-road. **b** (of a side-road) lead off from another road. **3** *colloq.* repel; cause to lose interest (*turned me right off with their complaining*). **4** dismiss from employment. **turn-off** *n.* **1** a turning off a main road. **2** *colloq.* something that repels or causes a loss of interest. **turn of speed** the ability to go fast when necessary. **turn on 1 a** start the flow or operation of (water, electricity, etc.) by means of a tap, switch, etc. **b** operate (a tap, switch, etc.) to achieve this. **2** *colloq.* excite; stimulate the interest of, esp. sexually. **3** *tr.* & *intr. colloq.* intoxicate or become intoxicated with drugs. **turn-on** *n. colloq.* a person or thing that causes (esp. sexual) arousal. **turn on a sixpence** see SIXPENCE. **turn on one's heel** see HEEL[1]. **turn out 1** expel. **2** extinguish (an electric light etc.). **3** dress or equip (*well turned out*). **4** produce (manufactured goods etc.). **5** empty or clean out (a room etc.). **6** empty (a pocket) to see the contents. **7** *colloq.* **a** get out of bed. **b** go out of doors. **8** *colloq.* assemble; attend a meeting etc. **9** (often foll. by *to* + infin. or *that* + clause) prove to be the case; result (*turned out to be true*; *we shall see how things turn out*). **10** *Mil.* call (a guard) from the guardroom. **turn over 1** reverse or cause to reverse vertical position; bring the under or reverse side into view (*turn over the page*). **2** upset; fall or cause to fall over. **3 a** cause (an engine) to run. **b** (of an engine) start running. **4** consider thoroughly. **5** (foll. by *to*) transfer the care or conduct of (a person or thing) to (a person) (*shall turn it all over to my deputy*; *turned him over to the authorities*). **6** do business to the amount of (*turns over £5000 a week*). **turn over a new leaf** improve one's conduct or performance. **turn round 1** turn so as to face in a new direction. **2 a** *Commerce* unload and reload (a ship, vehicle, etc.). **b** receive, process, and send out again; cause to progress through a system. **3** adopt new opinions or policy. **turn-round** *n.* **1 a** the process of loading and unloading. **b** the process of receiving, processing, and sending out again; progress through a system. **2** the reversal of an opinion or tendency. **turn the scales** see SCALE[2]. **turn the tables** see TABLE. **turn tail** turn one's back; run away. **turn the tide** reverse the trend of events. **turn to** set about one's work (*came home and immediately turned to*). **turn to account** see ACCOUNT. **turn turtle** see TURTLE. **turn up 1** increase the volume or strength of (sound, heat, etc.) by turning a knob etc. **2** place upwards. **3** discover or reveal. **4** be found, esp. by chance (*it turned up on a rubbish dump*). **5** happen or present itself; (of a person) put in an appearance (*a few people turned up late*). **6** *colloq.* cause to vomit (*the sight turned me up*). **7** shorten (a garment) by increasing the size of the hem. **turn-up** *n.* **1** *Brit.* the lower turned up end of a trouser leg. **2** *colloq.* an unexpected (esp. welcome) happening; a surprise. [OE *tyrnan*, *turnian* f. L *tornare* f. *tornus* lathe f. Gk *tornos* lathe, circular movement: prob. reinforced in ME f. OF *turner*, *torner*]

■ *v.* **1** rotate, revolve, spin, roll, reel, circle, gyrate, pirouette, whirl, wheel, go (a)round *or* about, pivot, orbit, swivel, spiral, twirl. **2** reverse, invert, turn upside down, turn inside out, turn *or* flip *or* roll over. **3 b** go *or* pass *or* move (a)round, veer, wheel, swing, swerve, corner, deviate, divert, shift, switch, move, face, head; twist, wind, snake, curve, bend, arc, coil, loop, meander, zigzag. **4** direct, aim, point. **5** alter, adapt, reorganize, remodel, modify, remake, refashion, reshape, reform, transform, make over, bring over; (*turn into*) become, change into *or* to, convert into *or* to, metamorphose into *or* to. **6** (*turn to*) **a** see *set about* 1 (SET[1]). **b** appeal to, apply to, resort to, have recourse to. **c** proceed to, go on to, refer to, pick *or* take up, *literary* advert to. **7** become, grow; make. **8 a** (*turn against*) defy, mutiny *or* rebel *or* revolt *or* rise (up) against. **b** (*turn on*) be hostile to, attack, assail, set upon, tear into. **10** go bad, spoil, curdle, sour, go off. **14** see TRANSLATE 1. **15** round, go *or* pass *or* move *or* veer (a)round. **17** (*turn on*) depend on *or* upon, be contingent on, hinge on *or* upon, hang on, be subject to; concern, revolve about *or* round, relate to. **19 b** twist, sprain, wrench. **22** turn aside *or* away, divert, block, avert, thwart, prevent, balk, parry, deflect, fend off, check. **25** form, make up, fashion, formulate, construct, cast, create, coin, concoct, express. ● *n.* **1** revolution, rotation, cycle, spin, whirl, circuit, round, roll, twirl; pirouette. **2** trend, direction, drift; deviation, turning, detour, shift, wind, deflection, change of direction *or* course *or* tendency. **3** turning-point, turning, crossroads, junction, watershed. **4** curve, bend, turning, corner, angle, sinuosity, dog-leg, hairpin bend *or* curve, irregularity, meander, twist, loop, zigzag. **6** change, alteration, shift, switch. **7** disposition, inclination, bent, bias, leaning, tendency. **8** opportunity, chance, say, round, spell, time, watch, shift, stint, tour (of duty), innings, move, trick, *colloq.* crack, shot, go, *sl.* whack. **9** airing, constitutional, ramble, saunter, stroll, walk, promenade, amble; drive, ride, *colloq.* spin. **10** see ACT *n.* 3a. **11** service, deed, act; (*bad turn*) disservice, harm, injury, wrong; (*good turn*) favour, good deed, (act of) kindness, courtesy, boon, mercy. **13** shock, fright, surprise, start, scare. **15** loop, coil, spiral, twist, round. □ **at every turn** everywhere, constantly, always, all the time, continually. **by turns** alternately, reciprocally, in rotation, successively, in succession. **in turn** sequentially, one after the other, in succession, successively, in (proper) order. **out of turn 1** out of sequence, out of order. **2** imprudently, indiscreetly, improperly, disobediently, inappropriately, inadvisedly, tactlessly. **take turns** (or **take it in turns**) alternate, vary, rotate, exchange. **turn-about** about-turn, volte-face, reversal, U-turn, turn-round, about-face. **turn away 2** see DISQUALIFY. **3** see *send off*. **turn back 1** go back, retrace one's steps, return; reverse, repulse, repel, rebuff, drive back, beat back. **turn down 1** refuse, reject, rebuff, spurn, decline, forgo, pass up, deny. **2** decrease *or* diminish *or* lessen *or* lower *or* soften the sound of, mute; decrease *or* lower *or* lessen the heat of. **turn-down** *n.* see *rejection* (REJECT). **turn in 1** hand in *or* over, turn over, deliver, give in, submit, offer, proffer, tender, give back, return, surrender, yield; deliver up, inform on, betray, *colloq.* rat on, tell on, *sl.* squeal on, *US sl.* finger. **3** go to bed *or* sleep, retire, withdraw, call it a day, *colloq.* hit the sack *or* hay. **turn off 1** stop, switch off, shut off, deactivate; extinguish; disconnect. **2** deviate, diverge, branch off. **3** disillusion, depress, cool (off), disenchant, disaffect, alienate, repel, repulse, bore, offend, put off, displease, sicken, nauseate, disgust. **4** see DISMISS 2. **turn-off 1** exit, side-road, feeder (road), auxiliary (road), *Brit.* slip-road. **2** damper. **turn on 1** start (up), switch on, energize, activate, set in motion, cause to function *or* operate. **2** excite, thrill, arouse, stimulate, titillate, work up, impassion. **3** see TRIP *v.* 7. **turn out 1** eject, evict, throw out, kick out, expel, oust, remove, dismiss, cashier, axe, *colloq.* sack, *esp. Brit. colloq.* turf out, *sl.* fire. **2** see EXTINGUISH 1. **3** dress, fit out, equip, rig out, accoutre. **4** make, form, shape, construct, build, fabricate, put together, assemble, manufacture, produce, put out, bring out. **8** come, arrive, appear, attend, assemble, meet, *colloq.* show (up), surface. **9** develop, evolve, happen, result, occur, arise, emerge, *formal* eventuate; prove, end up. **turn over 1** reverse, invert, turn upside down. **2** overturn, upset, knock *or* flip over; capsize, keel *or* fall *or* roll over, turn turtle. **3 b** rotate, revolve, spin, kick over. **4** consider, ruminate over *or* about, revolve, ponder (over), contemplate, reflect on, *literary* muse over *or* about. **6** sell. **turn over a new leaf** see REFORM *v.* 1. **turn-round 2** see *turn-about* above. **turn tail** turn one's back; run away, flee, bolt, take to one's heels, beat a hasty retreat, take off, *colloq.* scoot, scram, skedaddle, show a clean pair of heels, *sl.* cut and run, beat it, *Brit. sl.* do a bunk. **turn to** get to work, pitch in, buckle *or* knuckle down, get going *or* started, set to, *colloq.* get cracking. **turn up 1** increase *or* raise *or* amplify *or* intensify the sound of; raise *or* increase *or* intensify the heat of. **3** uncover, discover, find, unearth, come across, hit upon, dig up, expose, disclose, reveal, bring to light. **4** see *come to light* (LIGHT[1]). **5** come up, arise, happen, present itself, crop up, pop up; surface, appear, arrive, put in an appearance, show one's face, *colloq.* show (up).

turncoat /túrnkōt/ *n.* a person who changes sides in a conflict, dispute, etc.
■ renegade, traitor, betrayer, deserter, fifth-columnist, double agent, apostate, tergiversator, defector, backslider, snake in the grass.

turncock /túrnkok/ *n.* an official employed to turn on water for the mains supply etc.

turner /túrnər/ *n.* **1** a person or thing that turns. **2** a person who works with a lathe. [ME f. OF *tornere -eor* f. LL *tornator* (as TURN)]

turnery /túrnəri/ *n.* **1** objects made on a lathe. **2** work with a lathe.

turning /túrning/ *n.* **1 a** a road that branches off another. **b** a place where this occurs. **2 a** use of the lathe. **b** (in *pl.*) chips or shavings from a lathe. □ **turning-circle** the smallest circle in which a vehicle can turn without reversing. **turning-point** a point at which a decisive change occurs.

turnip /túrnip/ *n.* **1** a cruciferous plant, *Brassica rapa*, with a large white globular root and sprouting leaves. **2** this root used as a vegetable. **3** a large thick old-fashioned watch. □ **turnip-top** the leaves of the turnip eaten as a vegetable. □□ **turnipy** *adj.* [earlier *turnep(e)* f. *neep* f. L *napus*: first element of uncert. orig.]

turnkey /túrnkee/ *n.* & *adj.* ● *n.* (*pl.* **-eys**) *archaic* a jailer. ● *adj.* (of a contract etc.) providing for a supply of equipment in a state ready for operation.
■ see JAILER.

turnout /túrnowt/ *n.* **1** the number of people attending a meeting, voting at an election, etc. (*rain reduced the turnout*). **2** the quantity of goods produced in a given time. **3** a set or display of equipment, clothes, etc.
■ **1** assemblage, attendance, audience, crowd, gate, throng, gathering, *Austral. sl.* muster. **2** output, production, out-turn, volume; gross national product, GNP, gross domestic product, GDP. **3** gear, outfit, clothing, apparatus, equipment, trappings, fittings, equipage, *Brit. colloq.* rig-out, *formal* apparel.

turnover /túrnōvər/ *n.* **1** the act or an instance of turning over. **2** the amount of money taken in a business. **3** the number of people entering and leaving employment etc. **4** a small pie or tart made by folding a piece of pastry over a filling.
■ **2** (gross) revenue, (total) business, volume. **4** see TART[1] 2.

turnpike /túrnpīk/ *n.* **1** *hist.* a defensive frame of spikes. **2** *hist.* **a** a toll-gate. **b** a road on which a toll was collected at a toll-gate. **3** *US* a motorway on which a toll is charged.

turnsick /túrnsik/ *n.* = STURDY *n.*

turnside /túrnsīd/ *n.* giddiness in dogs and cattle.

turnsole /túrnsōl/ *n.* any of various plants supposed to turn with the sun. [OF *tournesole* f. Prov. *tournasol* f. L *tornare* TURN + *sol* sun]

turnspit /túrnspit/ *n. hist.* a person or small dog used to turn a spit.

turnstile /túrnstīl/ *n.* a gate for admission or exit, with revolving arms allowing people through singly.

turnstone /túrnstōn/ *n.* any wading bird of the genus *Arenaria*, related to the plover, that looks under stones for small animals to eat.

turntable /túrntayb'l/ *n.* **1** a circular revolving plate supporting a gramophone record that is being played. **2** a circular revolving platform for turning a railway locomotive or other vehicle.

turpentine /túrpəntīn/ *n.* & *v.* ● *n.* an oleo-resin secreted by several trees esp. of the genus *Pinus*, *Pistacia*, *Syncarpia*, or *Copaifera*, and used in various commercial preparations. ● *v.tr.* apply turpentine to. □ **Chian turpentine** the type of turpentine secreted by the terebinth. **oil of turpentine** a volatile pungent oil distilled from turpentine, used in mixing paints and varnishes, and in medicine. [ME f. OF *ter(e)bentine* f. L *ter(e)binthina* (*resina* resin) (as TEREBINTH)]

turpeth /túrpith/ *n.* (in full **turpeth root**) the root of an E. Indian plant, *Ipomoea turpethum*, used as a cathartic. [ME f. med.L *turbit(h)um* f. Arab. & Pers. *turbid*]

turpitude /túrpityōōd/ *n. formal* baseness, depravity, wickedness. [F *turpitude* or L *turpitudo* f. *turpis* disgraceful, base]
■ see EVIL *n.* 2.

turps /turps/ *n. colloq.* oil of turpentine. [abbr.]

turquoise /túrkwoyz, -kwaaz/ *n.* & *adj.* ● *n.* **1** a semiprecious stone, usu. opaque and greenish- or sky-blue, consisting of hydrated copper aluminium phosphate. **2** a greenish-blue colour. ● *adj.* of this colour. [ME *turkeis* etc. f. OF *turqueise* (later *-oise*) Turkish (stone)]

turret /túrrit/ *n.* **1** a small tower, usu. projecting from the wall of a building as a decorative addition. **2** a low flat usu. revolving armoured tower for a gun and gunners in a ship, aircraft, fort, or tank. **3** a rotating holder for tools in a lathe etc. □ **turret lathe** = *capstan lathe.* □□ **turreted** *adj.* [ME f. OF *to(u)rete* dimin. of *to(u)r* TOWER]

turtle /túrt'l/ *n.* **1** any of various marine or freshwater reptiles of the order Chelonia, encased in a shell of bony plates, and having flippers or webbed toes used in swimming. **2** the flesh of the turtle, esp. used for soup. **3** *Computing* a directional cursor in a computer graphics system which can be instructed to move around a screen. □ **turn turtle** capsize. **turtle-neck 1** a high close-fitting neck on a knitted garment. **2** *US* = *polo-neck.* [app. alt. of *tortue*: see TORTOISE]

■ □ **turn turtle** capsize, overturn, keel *or* turn over, upset, up-end, go bottom up.

turtle-dove /túrt'lduv/ *n.* any wild dove of the genus *Streptopelia*, esp. *S. turtur*, noted for its soft cooing and its affection for its mate and young. [archaic *turtle* (in the same sense) f. OE *turtla, turtle* f. L *turtur*, of imit. orig.]

turves *pl.* of TURF.

Tuscan /túskən/ *n.* & *adj.* ● *n.* **1** an inhabitant of Tuscany in central Italy. **2** the classical Italian language of Tuscany. ● *adj.* **1** of or relating to Tuscany or the Tuscans. **2** *Archit.* denoting the least ornamented of the classical orders. □ **Tuscan straw** fine yellow wheat-straw used for hats etc. [ME f. F f. L *Tuscanus* f. *Tuscus* Etruscan]

tush[1] /tush/ *int. archaic* expressing strong disapproval or scorn. [ME: imit.]

tush[2] /tush/ *n.* **1** a long pointed tooth, esp. a canine tooth of a horse. **2** an elephant's short tusk. [OE *tusc* TUSK]

tush[3] /tush/ *n.* esp. *US sl.* the buttocks. [20th c.: abbr. or dimin. of *tokus* f. Yiddish *tokhes*]

■ see *buttocks* (BUTTOCK).

tusk /tusk/ *n.* & *v.* ● *n.* **1** a long pointed tooth, esp. protruding from a closed mouth, as in the elephant, walrus, etc. **2** a tusklike tooth or other object. ● *v.tr.* gore, thrust at, or tear up with a tusk or tusks. □ **tusk shell 1** any of various molluscs of the class Scaphopoda. **2** its long tubular tusk-shaped shell. □□ **tusked** *adj.* (also in *comb.*). **tusky** *adj.* [ME alt. of OE *tux* var. of *tusc*: cf. TUSH[2]]

tusker /túskər/ *n.* an elephant or wild boar with well-developed tusks.

tussah *US* var. of TUSSORE.

tusser var. of TUSSORE.

tussive /tússiv/ *adj.* of or relating to a cough. [L *tussis* cough]

tussle /túss'l/ *n.* & *v.* ● *n.* a struggle or scuffle. ● *v.intr.* engage in a tussle. [orig. Sc. & N.Engl., perh. dimin. of *touse*: see TOUSLE]

■ *n.* see STRUGGLE *n.* 2.

tussock /tússək/ *n.* **1** a clump of grass etc. **2** (in full **tussock moth**) any moth of the genus *Orgyia* etc., with tufted larvae. □ **tussock grass** grass growing in tussocks, esp. *Poa flabellata* from Patagonia etc. □□ **tussocky** *adj.* [16th c.: perh. alt. f. dial. *tusk* tuft]

tussore /tússor, tússər/ *n.* (also **tusser**, *US* **tussah** /tússər/) **1** an Indian or Chinese silkworm, *Anthereae mylitta*, yielding strong but coarse brown silk. **2** (in full **tussore-silk**) silk from this and some other silkworms. [Urdu f. Hindi *tasar* f. Skr. *tasara* shuttle]

tut var. of TUT-TUT.

tutelage /tyóōtilij/ *n.* **1** guardianship. **2** the state or duration of being under this. **3** instruction, tuition. [L *tutela* f. *tuēri tuit-* or *tut-* watch]

■ **3** see TUITION.

tutelary /tyóōtiləri/ *adj.* (also **tutelar** /-tilər/) **1 a** serving as guardian. **b** relating to a guardian (*tutelary authority*). **2** giving protection (*tutelary saint*). [LL *tutelaris*, L *-arius* f. *tutela*: see TUTELAGE]

tutenag /tóōtinag/ *n.* **1** zinc imported from China and the E. Indies. **2** a white alloy like German silver. [Marathi *tuttināg* perh. f. Skr. *tuttha* copper sulphate + *nāga* tin, lead]

tutor /tyóōtər/ *n.* & *v.* ● *n.* **1** a private teacher, esp. in general charge of a person's education. **2** a university teacher supervising the studies or welfare of assigned undergraduates. **3** *Brit.* a book of instruction in a subject. ● *v.* **1** *tr.* act as a tutor to. **2** *intr.* work as a tutor. **3** *tr.* restrain, discipline. **4** *intr. US* receive tuition. □□ **tutorage** *n.* **tutorship** *n.* [ME f. AF, OF *tutour* or L *tutor* f. *tuēri tut-* watch]

■ *n.* **1, 2** teacher, instructor, instructress, educator, coach, mentor, guru. ● *v.* **1** teach, instruct, coach, educate, school, train, drill, enlighten, advise, direct, guide, prepare, ground, prime. **2** teach. **3** see DISCIPLINE *v.* 2.

tutorial /tyootóriəl/ *adj.* & *n.* ● *adj.* of or relating to a tutor or tuition. ● *n.* a period of individual tuition given by a tutor. □□ **tutorially** *adv.* [L *tutorius* (as TUTOR)]

tutsan /túts'n/ *n.* a species of St John's wort, *Hypericum androsaemum*, formerly used to heal wounds etc. [ME f. AF *tutsaine* all healthy]

tutti /tóōtti/ *adv.* & *n. Mus.* ● *adv.* with all voices or instruments together. ● *n.* (*pl.* **tuttis**) a passage to be performed in this way. [It., pl. of *tutto* all]

tutti-frutti /tóōtifróōti/ *n.* (*pl.* **-fruttis**) a confection, esp. ice-cream, of or flavoured with mixed fruits. [It., = all fruits]

tut-tut /tut-tút/ *int., n.,* & *v.* (also **tut** /tut/) ● *int.* expressing rebuke, impatience, or contempt. ● *n.* such an exclamation. ● *v.intr.* (**-tutted, -tutting**) exclaim this. [imit. of a click of the tongue against the teeth]

■ *v.* see OBJECT *v.*

tutty /tútti/ *n.* impure zinc oxide or carbonate used as a polishing powder. [ME f. OF *tutie* f. med.L *tutia* f. Arab. *tūtiyā*]

tutu[1] /tóōtōō/ *n.* a ballet dancer's short skirt of stiffened projecting frills. [F]

tutu[2] /tóōtōō/ *n. Bot.* a shrub, *Coriaria arborea*, native to New Zealand, bearing poisonous purplish-black berries. [Maori]

tu-whit, tu-whoo /tōōwit tōōwōō/ *n.* a representation of the cry of an owl. [imit.]

tux /tuks/ *n. US colloq.* = TUXEDO.

tuxedo /tukséedō/ *n.* (*pl.* **-os** or **-oes**) *US* **1** a dinner-jacket. **2** a suit of clothes including this. [after a country club at *Tuxedo* Park, New York]

tuyère /tweeyáir, tōō-/ *n.* (also **tuyere, twyer** /twīər/) a nozzle through which air is forced into a furnace etc. [F f. *tuyau* pipe]

TV *abbr.* television.

TVP *abbr. propr.* textured vegetable protein (in foods made from vegetable but given a meatlike texture).

twaddle /twódd'l/ *n.* & *v.* ● *n.* useless, senseless, or dull writing or talk. ● *v.intr.* indulge in this. □□ **twaddler** *n.* [alt. of earlier *twattle*, alt. of TATTLE]

■ *n.* see RUBBISH *n.* 3.

twain /twayn/ *adj.* & *n. archaic* two (usu. *in twain*). [OE *twegen*, masc. form of *twā* TWO]

twang /twang/ *n.* & *v.* ● *n.* **1** a strong ringing sound made by the plucked string of a musical instrument or bow. **2** the nasal quality of a voice compared to this. ● *v.* **1** *intr.* & *tr.* emit or cause to emit this sound. **2** *tr.* usu. *derog.* play (a tune or instrument) in this way. **3** *tr.* utter with a nasal twang. □□ **twangy** *adj.* [imit.]

'twas /twoz, twəz/ *archaic* it was. [contr.]

twat /twot/ *n. coarse sl.* ¶ Usually considered a taboo word. **1** the female genitals. **2** *Brit.* a term of contempt for a person. [17th c.: orig. unkn.]

twayblade /twáyblayd/ *n.* any orchid of the genus *Listera* etc., with green or purple flowers and a single pair of leaves. [*tway* var. of TWAIN + BLADE]

tweak /tweek/ *v.* & *n.* ● *v.tr.* **1** pinch and twist sharply; pull with a sharp jerk; twitch. **2** make fine adjustments to (a mechanism). ● *n.* an instance of tweaking. [prob. alt. of dial. *twick* & TWITCH]
■ *v.* **1** pinch, nip, twitch, squeeze, jerk, grip, pull. ● *n.* pinch, nip, twitch, squeeze, jerk, grip, pull.

twee /twee/ *adj.* (**tweer** /twéeər/; **tweest** /twée-ist/) *Brit.* usu. *derog.* affectedly dainty or quaint. ▫▫ **tweely** *adv.* **tweeness** *n.* [childish pronunc. of SWEET]
■ precious, sweet, sentimental, quaint, dainty, bijou, *esp. US colloq.* cute.

tweed /tweed/ *n.* **1** a rough-surfaced woollen cloth, usu. of mixed flecked colours, orig. produced in Scotland. **2** (in *pl.*) clothes made of tweed. [orig. a misreading of *tweel*, Sc. form of TWILL, infl. by assoc. with the river *Tweed*]

Tweedledum and Tweedledee /twéed'ldúm, twéed'ldée/ *n.* a pair of persons or things that are virtually indistinguishable. [after the stock names of rival musicians]

tweedy /twéedi/ *adj.* (**tweedier, tweediest**) **1** of or relating to tweed cloth. **2** characteristic of the country gentry, heartily informal. ▫▫ **tweedily** *adv.* **tweediness** *n.*

'tween /tween/ *prep. archaic* = BETWEEN. ▫ **'tween-decks** *Naut.* the space between decks. [contr.]

tweet /tweet/ *n.* & *v.* ● *n.* the chirp of a small bird. ● *v.intr.* make a chirping noise. [imit.]
■ *n.* see CHIRP *n.* ● *v.* see CHIRP *v.*

tweeter /twéetər/ *n.* a loudspeaker designed to reproduce high frequencies.

tweezers /twéezərz/ *n.pl.* a small pair of pincers for taking up small objects, plucking out hairs, etc. [extended form of *tweezes* (cf. *pincers* etc.) pl. of obs. *tweeze* case for small instruments, f. *etweese* = *étuis*, pl. of ÉTUI]

twelfth /twelfth/ *n.* & *adj.* ● *n.* **1** the position in a sequence corresponding to the number 12 in the sequence 1–12. **2** something occupying this position. **3** each of twelve equal parts of a thing. **4** *Mus.* **a** an interval or chord spanning an octave and a fifth in the diatonic scale. **b** a note separated from another by this interval. ● *adj.* that is the twelfth. ▫ **Twelfth Day** 6 Jan., the twelfth day after Christmas, the festival of the Epiphany. **twelfth man** a reserve member of a cricket team. **Twelfth Night** the evening of 5 Jan., the eve of the Epiphany. **twelfth part** = sense 3 of *n.* ▫▫ **twelfthly** *adv.* [OE *twelfta* (as TWELVE)]

twelve /twelv/ *n.* & *adj.* ● *n.* **1** one more than eleven; the product of two units and six units. **2** a symbol for this (12, xii, XII). **3** a size etc. denoted by twelve. **4** the time denoted by twelve o'clock (*is it twelve yet?*). **5** (**the Twelve**) the twelve apostles. **6** (**12**) *Brit.* (of films) classified as suitable for persons of 12 years and over. ● *adj.* that amount to twelve. ▫ **twelve-note** (or **-tone**) *Mus.* using the twelve chromatic notes of the octave on an equal basis without dependence on a key system. [OE *twelf(e)* f. Gmc, prob. rel. to TWO]

twelvefold /twélvfōld/ *adj.* & *adv.* **1** twelve times as much or as many. **2** consisting of twelve parts.

twelvemo /twélvmō/ *n.* = DUODECIMO.

twelvemonth /twélvmunth/ *n. archaic* a year; a period of twelve months.

twenty /twénti/ *n.* & *adj.* ● *n.* (*pl.* **-ies**) **1** the product of two and ten. **2** a symbol for this (20, xx, XX). **3** (in *pl.*) the numbers from 20 to 29, esp. the years of a century or of a person's life. **4** *colloq.* a large indefinite number (*have told you twenty times*). ● *adj.* that amount to twenty. ▫ **twenty-first, -second,** etc. the ordinal numbers between twentieth and thirtieth. **twenty-one, -two,** etc. the cardinal numbers between twenty and thirty. **twenty-twenty** (or **20/20**) **1** denoting vision of normal acuity. **2** *colloq.* denoting clear perception or hindsight. ▫▫ **twentieth** *adj.* & *n.* **twentyfold** *adj.* & *adv.* [OE *twentig* (perh. as TWO, -TY[2])]

■ *n.* **1** score. **4** see SCORE *n.* 3.

'twere /twer/ *archaic* it were. [contr.]

twerp /twerp/ *n.* (also **twirp**) *sl.* a stupid or objectionable person. [20th c.: orig. unkn.]
■ see FOOL[1] *n.* 1.

twibill /twībil/ *n.* a double-bladed battleaxe. [OE f. *twi-* double + BILL[3]]

twice /twīss/ *adv.* **1** two times (esp. of multiplication); on two occasions. **2** in double degree or quantity (*twice as good*). [ME *twiges* f. OE *twige* (as TWO, -S[3])]

twiddle /twídd'l/ *v.* & *n.* ● *v.* **1** *tr.* & (foll. by *with* etc.) *intr.* twirl, adjust, or play randomly or idly. **2** *intr.* move twirlingly. ● *n.* **1** an act of twiddling. **2** a twirled mark or sign. ▫ **twiddle one's thumbs 1** make them rotate round each other. **2** have nothing to do. ▫▫ **twiddler** *n.* **twiddly** *adj.* [app. imit., after *twirl, twist,* and *fiddle, piddle*]
■ *v.* **1** play with, twirl, fiddle (with), juggle, adjust, toy with, tinker with, fidget with, fool with, mess (about *or* around) with, monkey with, *colloq.* wiggle. ● *n.* **1** twirl, fiddle, jiggle, tinker, *colloq.* wiggle. ▫ **twiddle one's thumbs 2** do nothing, be idle, idle *or* while away (the) time, waste time.

twig[1] /twig/ *n.* **1** a small branch or shoot of a tree or shrub. **2** *Anat.* a small branch of an artery etc. ▫▫ **twigged** *adj.* (also in *comb.*). **twiggy** *adj.* [OE *twigge* f. a Gmc root *twi-* (unrecorded) as in TWICE, TWO]
■ **1** sprig, stem, shoot, offshoot, branchlet, stick, sucker, sprout, withe, tendril. ▫▫ **twiggy** see THIN *adj.* 4.

twig[2] /twig/ *v.tr.* (**twigged, twigging**) *colloq.* **1** (also *absol.*) understand; grasp the meaning or nature of. **2** perceive, observe. [18th c.: orig. unkn.]
■ **1** understand, grasp, fathom, get, comprehend, see, know, sense, divine, perceive, apprehend, *colloq.* catch on (to), be *or* get *or* become wise to, tumble to, *sl.* dig, *Brit. sl.* rumble.

twilight /twīlīt/ *n.* **1** the soft glowing light from the sky when the sun is below the horizon, esp. in the evening. **2** the period of this. **3** a faint light. **4** a state of imperfect knowledge or understanding. **5** a period of decline or destruction. **6** *attrib.* of, resembling, or occurring at twilight. ▫ **twilight sleep** *Med.* a state of partial narcosis, esp. to ease the pain of childbirth. **twilight zone 1** an urban area that is becoming dilapidated. **2** any physical or conceptual area which is undefined or intermediate. [ME f. OE *twi-* two (in uncert. sense) + LIGHT[1]]
■ **1, 2** dusk, sunset, sundown, half-light, *poet.* gloaming. **2** evening, nightfall, *archaic or poet.* eventide. **5** decline, wane, waning, ebb, downturn, down-swing, slump, decay, weakening, declination, diminution. **6** evening, crepuscular, dimming, twilit, darkening, darkish, shadowy, shady, dim, dark, obscure, sombre, gloomy, *poet.* darksome, darkling. ▫ **twilight zone 2** limbo.

twilit /twīlit/ *adj.* (also **twilighted** /-lītid/) dimly illuminated by or as by twilight. [past part. of *twilight* (v.) f. TWILIGHT]

twill /twil/ *n.* & *v.* ● *n.* a fabric so woven as to have a surface of diagonal parallel ridges. ● *v.tr.* (esp. as **twilled** *adj.*) weave (fabric) in this way. ▫▫ **twilled** *adj.* [N.Engl. var. of obs. *twilly*, OE *twili*, f. *twi-* double, after L *bilix* (as BI-, *licium* thread)]

'twill /twil/ *archaic* it will. [contr.]

twin /twin/ *n., adj.,* & *v.* ● *n.* **1** each of a closely related or associated pair, esp. of children or animals born at a birth. **2** the exact counterpart of a person or thing. **3** a compound crystal one part of which is in a reversed position with reference to the other. **4** (**the Twins**) the zodiacal sign or constellation Gemini. ● *adj.* **1** forming, or being one of, such a pair (*twin brothers*). **2** *Bot.* growing in pairs. **3** consisting of two closely connected and similar parts. ● *v.* (**twinned, twinning**) **1** *tr.* & *intr.* **a** join intimately together. **b** (foll. by *with*) pair. **2** *intr.* bear twins. **3** *intr.* grow as a twin crystal. **4** *intr.* & *tr. Brit.* link or cause (a town) to link with one in a different country, for the purposes of friendship and cultural exchange. ▫ **twin bed** each of a pair of single beds. **twin-engined** having two engines. **twin-screw** (of a ship) having two propellers on separate shafts with opposite twists. **twin set** esp. *Brit.* a woman's matching cardigan and jumper. **twin town** *Brit.* a town which is twinned with another. ▫▫ **twinning** *n.* [OE *twinn* double, f. *twi-* two: cf. ON *tvinnr*]

■ *n.* **2** double, clone, duplicate, look-alike, counterpart, *doppelgänger*, image, *colloq.* spitting image, *sl.* (dead) ringer. ● *adj.* **1, 3** identical, matching, matched, duplicate, corresponding, look-alike. ● *v.* **1, 4** pair, match, yoke, join, link, couple, combine, connect, associate.

twine /twīn/ *n.* & *v.* ● *n.* **1** a strong thread or string of two or more strands of hemp or cotton etc. twisted together. **2** a coil or twist. **3** a tangle; an interlacing. ● *v.* **1** *tr.* form (a string or thread etc.) by twisting strands together. **2** *tr.* form (a garland etc.) of interwoven material. **3** *tr.* (often foll. by *with*) garland (a brow etc.). **4** *intr.* (often foll. by *round, about*) coil or wind. **5** *intr.* & *refl.* (of a plant) grow in this way. ▫▫ **twiner** *n.* [OE *twīn, twigin* linen, ult. f. the stem of *twi-* two]

■ *n.* **1** cord, string, thread; rope, cable, yarn. ● *v.* entwine, braid, twist, intertwine, curl, wreathe, spiral, wind, coil, weave, interweave, interlace, encircle, wrap.

twinge /twinj/ *n.* & *v.* ● *n.* a sharp momentary local pain or pang (*a twinge of toothache*; *a twinge of conscience*). ● *v.intr.* & *tr.* experience or cause to experience a twinge. [*twinge* (v.) pinch, wring f. OE *twengan* f. Gmc]

■ *n.* stab, pang, cramp, spasm, pinch, stitch, (sharp) pain, prick, smart, bite, gripe. ● *v.* see HURT *v.* 3.

twinkle /twíngk'l/ *v.* & *n.* ● *v.* **1** *intr.* (of a star or light etc.) shine with rapidly intermittent gleams. **2** *intr.* (of the eyes) sparkle. **3** *intr.* (of the feet in dancing) move lightly and rapidly. **4** *tr.* emit (a light or signal) in quick gleams. **5** *tr.* blink or wink (one's eyes). ● *n.* **1 a** a sparkle or gleam of the eyes. **b** a blink or wink. **2** a slight flash of light; a glimmer. **3** a short rapid movement. ▫ **in a twinkle** (or **a twinkling** or **the twinkling of an eye**) in an instant. ▫▫ **twinkler** *n.* **twinkly** *adj.* [OE *twinclian*]

■ *v.* **1, 2, 4** scintillate, sparkle, coruscate, glitter, shimmer, wink, flicker, glisten, glint, flash, spark, dance, blink, shine, gleam. ● *n.* **1a, 2** twinkling, scintillation, scintillating, sparkle, sparkling, coruscation, coruscating, glitter, glittering, glimmer, glimmering, shimmer, shimmering, winking, flicker, flickering, glistening, glint, flash, flashing, spark, sparking, dancing, blinking, shine, shining, gleam, gleaming, dazzle, dazzling. ▫ **in a twinkle** (or **a twinkling** or **the twinkling of an eye**) in a (split) second, in a flash, in the wink of an eye, in a wink, in an instant, in a moment, in a trice, in two shakes (of a lamb's *or* dog's tail), *colloq.* in a jiffy, *esp. Brit. colloq.* in a tick, in two ticks.

twirl /twurl/ *v.* & *n.* ● *v.tr.* & *intr.* spin or swing or twist quickly and lightly round. ● *n.* **1** a twirling motion. **2** a form made by twirling, esp. a flourish made with a pen. ▫▫ **twirler** *n.* **twirly** *adj.* [16th c.: prob. alt. (after *whirl*) of obs. *tirl* TRILL]

■ *v.* spin, whirl, rotate, revolve, wheel, turn, gyrate, twist, pirouette, pivot, wind (about *or* around). ● *n.* **1** twirling, spin, spinning, whirl, whirling, turn, turning, revolution, pirouette. **2** whorl, winding, convolution, spiral, helix, coil, *Archit.* volute; flourish.

twirp var. of TWERP.

twist /twist/ *v.* & *n.* ● *v.* **1 a** *tr.* change the form of by rotating one end and not the other or the two ends in opposite directions. **b** *intr.* undergo such a change; take a twisted position (*twisted round in his seat*). **c** *tr.* wrench or pull out of shape with a twisting action (*twisted my ankle*). **2** *tr.* **a** wind (strands etc.) about each other. **b** form (a rope etc.) by winding the strands. **c** (foll. by *with, in with*) interweave. **d** form by interweaving or twining. **3 a** *tr.* give a spiral form to (a rod, column, cord, etc.) as by rotating the ends in opposite directions. **b** *intr.* take a spiral form. **4** *tr.* (foll. by *off*) break off or separate by twisting. **5** *tr.* distort or misrepresent the meaning of (words). **6 a** *intr.* take a curved course. **b** *tr.* make (one's way) in a winding manner. **7** *tr. Brit. colloq.* cheat (*twisted me out of £20*). **8** *tr.* cause (the ball, esp. in billiards) to rotate while following a curved path. **9** *tr.* (as **twisted** *adj.*) (of a person or mind) emotionally unbalanced. **10** *intr.* dance the twist. ● *n.* **1** the act or an instance of twisting. **2 a** a twisted state. **b** the manner or degree in which a thing is twisted. **3** a thing formed by or as by twisting, esp. a thread or rope etc. made by winding strands together. **4** the point at which a thing twists or bends. **5** usu. *derog.* a peculiar tendency of mind or character etc. **6 a** an unexpected development of events, esp. in a story etc. **b** an unusual interpretation or variation. **c** a distortion or bias. **7** a fine strong silk thread used by tailors etc. **8** a roll of bread, tobacco, etc., in the form of a twist. **9** *Brit.* a paper packet with screwed-up ends. **10** a curled piece of lemon etc. peel to flavour a drink. **11** a spinning motion given to a ball in cricket etc. to make it take a special curve. **12 a** a twisting strain. **b** the amount of twisting of a rod etc., or the angle showing this. **c** forward motion combined with rotation about an axis. **13** *Brit.* a drink made of two ingredients mixed together. **14** *Brit. colloq.* a swindle. **15** (prec. by *the*) a dance with a twisting movement of the body, popular in the 1960s. ▫ **round the twist** *Brit. sl.* crazy. **twist a person's arm** *colloq.* apply coercion, esp. by moral pressure. **twist round one's finger** see FINGER. ▫▫ **twistable** *adj.* **twisty** *adj.* (**twistier, twistiest**). [ME, rel. to TWIN, TWINE]

■ *v.* **1 a, b** contort, screw up, distort, buckle, warp; crumple. **c** wrench, turn, sprain, rick. **2** wind, plait, braid, weave, entwine, intertwine, twine, interweave, pleach, splice, wreathe, interlace, tangle, entangle. **3** see WIND[2] *v.* 4. **4** see WRENCH *v.* 1a. **5** distort, warp, contort, pervert, wrest, alter, change, slant, bias, colour, falsify, misquote, misstate, garble, misrepresent, violate; misinterpret, mistranslate, misunderstand, misconstrue. **6 a** wind, snake, meander, turn, zigzag, worm, bend, curve, kink, loop. **b** wriggle, worm, squirm, writhe, *colloq.* wiggle. **7** see FOOL[1] *v.* 1, 3. **9** (**twisted**) see UNSTABLE 2, 3. ● *n.* **1** rotation, turn, roll, twirl, spin, wind. **2** see TANGLE *n.* 1. **4** coil, spiral, corkscrew, helix, convolution, skew, zigzag, dog-leg, turn, curve, angle, bend, wind, bow, kink, loop, curl, meander. **5** quirk, kink, idiosyncrasy, crotchet, peculiarity, oddity, trick, eccentricity, incongruity, inconsistency, irregularity; weakness, flaw, fault, foible, failing. **6 b** interpretation, analysis, understanding, slant, angle, construction, construal; treatment, approach, version, variation. **c** distortion, misinterpretation, contortion, perversion, warping, alteration, change, departure, bias, colouring, falsification, misquotation, misstatement, garbling, misrepresentation; mistranslation, misunderstanding, misconstrual, misconstruction. **8, 9** roll, coil, *Brit.* screw. **12 a** wrench, turn, sprain, rick. **14** see SWINDLE *n.* 1, 3. ▫ **round the twist** mad, crazy, insane, eccentric, *colloq.* round the bend, *esp. Brit. colloq.* daft, *sl.* nuts, nutty, bonkers, cuckoo, batty, off one's rocker, *esp. Brit. sl.* barmy. **twist a person's arm** coerce *or* constrain *or* bully *or* pressurize *or* pressure a person, *colloq.* put the squeeze on, put the screws on.

twister /twístər/ *n.* **1** *Brit. colloq.* a swindler; a dishonest person. **2** a twisting ball in cricket or billiards. **3** *US* a tornado, waterspout, etc.

■ **1** cheat, confidence man, rogue, scoundrel, trickster, mountebank, deceiver, fraud, charlatan, impostor, *colloq.* crook, *esp. US colloq.* shyster, *sl.* con man, *Austral. sl.* magsman. **3** tornado, cyclone, typhoon, hurricane, whirlwind; waterspout.

twit[1] /twit/ *n.* esp. *Brit. sl.* a silly or foolish person. [orig. dial.: perh. f. TWIT[2]]

■ nincompoop, ass, ninny, fool, imbecile, blockhead, idiot, simpleton, *colloq.* nitwit, halfwit, chump, moron, silly billy, silly, *US colloq.* lame-brain, *sl.* dope, jerk, twerp, *Austral. sl.* galah, nong, bogan, *esp. US sl.* nerd.

twit[2] /twit/ *v.tr.* (**twitted, twitting**) reproach or taunt, usu. good-humouredly. [16th-c. *twite* f. *atwite* f. OE *ætwītan* reproach with f. *æt* at + *wītan* blame]
▪ tease, cajole, taunt, jeer (at), make fun of, banter, rag, gibe, chaff, ridicule, mock; blame, berate, deride, scorn, censure, revile, reproach, upbraid, *literary* contemn; pull a person's leg, *colloq.* kid.

twitch /twich/ *v.* & *n.* ● *v.* **1** *intr.* (of the features, muscles, limbs, etc.) move or contract spasmodically. **2** *tr.* give a short sharp pull at. ● *n.* **1** a sudden involuntary contraction or movement. **2** a sudden pull or jerk. **3** *colloq.* a state of nervousness. **4** a noose and stick for controlling a horse during a veterinary operation. ▫▫ **twitchy** *adj.* (**twitchier, twitchiest**) (in sense 3 of *n.*). [ME f. Gmc: cf. OE *twiccian*, dial. *twick*]
▪ *v.* **1** see JERK[1] *v.* 1. **2** see JERK[1] *v.* 2. ● *n.* **1, 2** see JERK[1] *n.* 1, 2.

twitcher /twíchər/ *n.* **1** *colloq.* a bird-watcher who tries to get sightings of rare birds. **2** a person or thing that twitches.

twitch grass /twich/ *n.* = COUCH[2]. [var. of QUITCH]

twite /twīt/ *n.* a moorland finch, *Carduelis flavirostris*, resembling the linnet. [imit. of its cry]

twitter /twíttər/ *v.* & *n.* ● *v.* **1** *intr.* (of or like a bird) emit a succession of light tremulous sounds. **2** *tr.* utter or express in this way. ● *n.* **1** the act or an instance of twittering. **2** *colloq.* a tremulously excited state. ▫▫ **twitterer** *n.* **twittery** *adj.* [ME, imit.: cf. -ER[4]]
▪ *v.* **1** peep, cheep, tweet, chirp, warble, trill, chirrup; chatter, prattle, gossip, giggle, prate, titter, snicker, snigger, simper. **2** chirp, warble, trill. ● *n.* **1** peep, peeping, cheep, cheeping, twittering, tweet, tweeting, chirrup, chirruping, chirp, chirping, warble, warbling, trill, trilling. **2** flutter, whirl, agitation, *colloq.* dither, stew, tizzy.

'twixt /twikst/ *prep. archaic* = BETWIXT. [contr.]

two /tōō/ *n.* & *adj.* ● *n.* **1** one more than one; the sum of one unit and another unit. **2** a symbol for this (2, ii, II). **3** a size etc. denoted by two. **4** the time of two o'clock (*is it ten yet?*). **5** a set of two. **6** a card with two pips. ● *adj.* that amount to two. ▫ **in two** in or into two pieces. **in two shakes** (or **ticks**) see SHAKE, TICK[1]. **or two** denoting several (*a thing or two* = several things). **put two and two together** make (esp. an obvious) inference from what is known or evident. **that makes two of us** *colloq.* that is true of me also. **two-bit** *US colloq.* cheap, petty. **two-by-four** a length of timber with a rectangular cross-section 2 in. by 4 in. **two by two** (or **two and two**) in pairs. **two can play at that game** *colloq.* another person's behaviour can be copied to that person's disadvantage. **two-dimensional 1** having or appearing to have length and breadth but no depth. **2** lacking depth or substance; superficial. **two-edged** double-edged. **two-faced 1** having two faces. **2** insincere; deceitful. **two-handed 1** having, using, or requiring the use of two hands. **2** (of a card-game) for two players. **two a penny** see PENNY. **two-piece** *adj.* (of a suit etc.) consisting of two matching items. ● *n.* a two-piece suit etc. **two-ply** *adj.* of two strands, webs, or thicknesses. ● *n.* **1** two-ply wool. **2** two-ply wood made by gluing together two layers with the grain in different directions. **two-seater 1** a vehicle or aircraft with two seats. **2** a sofa etc. for two people. **two-sided 1** having two sides. **2** having two aspects; controversial. **two-step** a round dance with a sliding step in march or polka time. **two-stroke** esp. *Brit.* (of an internal-combustion engine) having its power cycle completed in one up-and-down movement of the piston. **two-time** *colloq.* **1** deceive or be unfaithful to (esp. a partner or lover). **2** swindle, double-cross. **two-timer** *colloq.* a person who is deceitful or unfaithful. **two-tone** having two colours or sounds. **two-up** *Austral.* & *NZ* a gambling game with bets placed on a showing of two heads or two tails. **two-way 1** involving two ways or participants. **2** (of a switch) permitting a current to be switched on or off from either of two points. **3** (of a radio) capable of transmitting and receiving signals. **4** (of a tap etc.) permitting fluid etc. to flow in either of two channels or directions. **5** (of traffic etc.) moving in two esp. opposite directions. **two-way mirror** a panel of glass that can be seen through from one side and is a mirror on the other. **two-wheeler** a vehicle with two wheels. [OE *twā* (fem. & neut.), *tū* (neut.), with Gmc cognates and rel. to Skr. *dwau*, *dwe*, Gk & L *duo*]
▪ *n.* **5** set of two, couple, pair, brace, duo, duet, twosome. ● *adj.* a couple *or* pair *or* brace of. ▫ **put two and two together** see REASON *v.* 1. **two-bit** see CHEAP *adj.* 3. **two-dimensional 2** see SUPERFICIAL 1, 4. **two-faced 2** double-dealing, hypocritical, duplicitous, dissembling, deceitful, treacherous, dishonest, untrustworthy, insincere, disingenuous, scheming, designing, crafty, machiavellian, sly, perfidious, lying, mendacious. **two-time** see DECEIVE 1. **two-timer** see TRAITOR.

twofold /tōōfōld/ *adj.* & *adv.* **1** twice as much or as many. **2** consisting of two parts.
▪ *adj.* **1** double. **2** dual.

twopence /túppənss/ *n. Brit.* **1** the sum of two pence, esp. before decimalization. **2** *colloq.* (esp. with *neg.*) a thing of little value (*don't care twopence*).
▪ **2** see DAMN *n.* 2.

twopenny /túppəni/ *adj. Brit.* **1** costing two pence, esp. before decimalization. **2** *colloq.* cheap, worthless. ▫ **twopenny-halfpenny** /túpniháypni/ cheap, insignificant.
▪ **2** see CHEAP *adj.* 3.

twosome /tōōssəm/ *n.* **1** two persons together. **2** a game, dance, etc., for two persons.
▪ **1** couple, pair, duo.

'twould /twŏŏd/ *archaic* it would. [contr.]

twyer var. of TUYÈRE.

TX *abbr. US* Texas (in official postal use).

-ty[1] /ti/ *suffix* forming nouns denoting quality or condition (*cruelty*; *plenty*). [ME *-tie*, *-tee*, *-te* f. OF *-té*, *-tet* f. L *-tas -tatis*: cf. -ITY]

-ty[2] /ti/ *suffix* denoting tens (*twenty*; *thirty*; *ninety*). [OE *-tig*]

tychism /tīkiz'm/ *n. Philos.* the theory that chance controls the universe. [Gk *tukhē* chance]

tycoon /tīkōōn/ *n.* **1** a business magnate. **2** *hist.* a title applied by foreigners to the shogun of Japan 1854–68. [Jap. *taikun* great lord]
▪ **1** magnate, baron, financier, (multi)millionaire, billionaire, merchant prince, potentate, *colloq.* wheeler-dealer, mogul, big shot, (big-time) operator, bigwig, *sl.* big-timer, big cheese, big bug, *US sl.* honcho, big wheel.

tying *pres. part.* of TIE.

tyke /tīk/ *n.* (also **tike**) **1** esp. *Brit.* an unpleasant or coarse man. **2** a mongrel. **3** a small child. **4** *Brit. sl.* a Yorkshireman. **5** *Austral.* & *NZ sl. offens.* a Roman Catholic. [ME f. ON *tík* bitch: sense 5 assim. from TAIG]

tylopod /tīləpod/ *n.* & *adj. Zool.* ● *n.* any animal that bears its weight on the sole-pads of the feet rather than on the hoofs, esp. the camel. ● *adj.* (of an animal) bearing its weight in this way. ▫▫ **tylopodous** /-lóppədəss/ *adj.* [Gk *tulos* knob or *tulē* callus, cushion + *pous podos* foot]

tympan /tímpən/ *n.* **1** *Printing* an appliance in a printing-press used to equalize pressure between the platen etc. and a printing-sheet. **2** *Archit.* = TYMPANUM. [F *tympan* or L *tympanum*: see TYMPANUM]

tympana *pl.* of TYMPANUM.

tympani var. of TIMPANI.

tympanic /timpánnik/ *adj.* **1** *Anat.* of, relating to, or having a tympanum. **2** resembling or acting like a drumhead. ▫ **tympanic bone** *Anat.* the bone supporting the tympanic membrane. **tympanic membrane** *Anat.* the membrane separating the outer ear and middle ear and transmitting vibrations resulting from sound waves to the inner ear.

tympanites /tímpənīteez/ *n.* a swelling of the abdomen caused by gas in the intestine etc. ▫▫ **tympanitic** /-níttik/ *adj.* [LL f. Gk *tumpanitēs* of a drum (as TYMPANUM)]

tympanum /tímpənəm/ *n.* (*pl.* **tympanums** or **tympana** /-nə/) **1** *Anat.* **a** the middle ear. **b** the tympanic membrane. **2** *Zool.* the membrane covering the hearing organ on the leg of an insect. **3** *Archit.* **a** a vertical triangular space forming the centre of a pediment. **b** a similar space over a door between the lintel and the arch; a carving on this space. **4** a drum-wheel etc. for raising water from a stream. [L f. Gk *tumpanon* drum f. *tuptō* strike]

Tynwald /tínwold/ *n.* the parliament of the Isle of Man. [ON *thing-vǫllr* place of assembly f. *thing* assembly + *vǫllr* field]

type /tīp/ *n.* & *v.* ● *n.* **1 a** a class of things or persons having common characteristics. **b** a kind or sort (*would like a different type of car*). **2** a person, thing, or event serving as an illustration, symbol, or characteristic specimen of another, or of a class. **3** (in *comb.*) made of, resembling, or functioning as (*ceramic-type material*; *Cheddar-type cheese*). **4** *colloq.* a person, esp. of a specified character (*is rather a quiet type*; *is not really my type*). **5** an object, conception, or work of art serving as a model for subsequent artists. **6** *Printing* **a** a piece of metal etc. with a raised letter or character on its upper surface for use in printing. **b** a kind or size of such pieces (*printed in large type*). **c** a set or supply of these (*ran short of type*). **7** a device on either side of a medal or coin. **8** *Theol.* a foreshadowing in the Old Testament of a person or event of the Christian dispensation. **9** *Biol.* an organism having or chosen as having the essential characteristics of its group and giving its name to the next highest group. ● *v.* **1** *tr.* be a type or example of. **2** *tr.* & *intr.* write with a typewriter. **3** *tr.* esp. *Biol.* & *Med.* assign to a type; classify. **4** *tr.* = TYPECAST. □ **in type** *Printing* composed and ready for printing. **type-founder** a designer and maker of metal types. **type-foundry** a foundry where type is made. **type-metal** *Printing* an alloy of lead etc., used for casting printing-types. **type site** *Archaeol.* a site where objects regarded as defining the characteristics of a period etc. are found. **type specimen** *Biol.* the specimen used for naming and describing a new species. □□ **typal** *adj.* [ME f. F *type* or L *typus* f. Gk *tupos* impression, figure, type, f. *tuptō* strike]

■ *n.* **1** class, category, classification, kind, sort, genre, run, order, variety, breed, race, species, strain, group, genus, kidney, nature, *colloq. disp.* ilk; brand, make, marque, line, model, cast, form, version. **2** prototype, paradigm, archetype, epitome, embodiment, avatar, exemplar, model, specimen, illustration, example, symbol, pattern, personification, standard, quintessence, typification, typifier. **4** person, character, individual, *colloq.* sort. **6** *Printing* typeface, fount, font, print, printing, lettering, characters. ● *v.* **2** *formal* typewrite; key (in), keyboard; transcribe. **3** see CLASS *v.*

typecast /tīpkaast/ *v.tr.* (*past* and *past part.* **-cast**) assign (an actor or actress) repeatedly to the same type of role, esp. one in character.

typeface /tīpfayss/ *n. Printing* **1** a set of types or characters in a particular design. **2** the inked part of type, or the impression made by this.

■ see TYPE *n.* 6.

typescript /tīpskript/ *n.* a typewritten document.

typesetter /tīpsettər/ *n. Printing* **1** a person who composes type. **2** a composing-machine. □□ **typesetting** *n.*

typewrite /tīprīt/ *v.tr.* & *intr.* (*past* **-wrote**; *past part.* **-written**) *formal* = TYPE *v.* 2.

typewriter /tīprītər/ *n.* a machine with keys for producing printlike characters one at a time on paper inserted round a roller.

typewritten /tīpritt'n/ *adj.* produced with a typewriter.

typhlitis /tiflītiss/ *n.* inflammation of the caecum. □□ **typhlitic** /-líttik/ *adj.* [mod.L f. Gk *tuphlon* caecum or blind gut f. *tuphlos* blind + -ITIS]

typhoid /tīfoyd/ *n.* & *adj.* ● *n.* **1** (in full **typhoid fever**) an infectious bacterial fever with an eruption of red spots on the chest and abdomen and severe intestinal irritation. **2** a similar disease of animals. ● *adj.* like typhus. □ **typhoid condition** (or **state**) a state of depressed vitality occurring in many acute diseases. □□ **typhoidal** *adj.* [TYPHUS + -OID]

typhoon /tīfōōn/ *n.* a violent hurricane in E. Asian seas. □□ **typhonic** /-fónnik/ *adj.* [partly f. Port. *tufão* f. Arab. *ṭūfān* perh. f. Gk *tuphōn* whirlwind; partly f. Chin. dial. *tai fung* big wind]

■ see HURRICANE 1, 2.

typhus /tīfəss/ *n.* an infectious fever caused by rickettsiae, characterized by a purple rash, headaches, fever, and usu. delirium. □□ **typhous** *adj.* [mod.L f. Gk *tuphos* smoke, stupor f. *tuphō* to smoke]

typical /típpik'l/ *adj.* **1** serving as a characteristic example; representative. **2** characteristic of or serving to distinguish a type. **3** (often foll. by *of*) conforming to expected behaviour, attitudes, etc. (*is typical of them to forget*). **4** symbolic. □□ **typicality** /-kálliti/ *n.* **typically** *adv.* [med.L *typicalis* f. L *typicus* f. Gk *tupikos* (as TYPE)]

■ **1, 2** representative, characteristic, conventional, normal, standard, ordinary, average, regular, run-of-the-mill, orthodox, classic. **3** conventional, in character, in keeping, usual, commonplace, natural, customary, common, to be expected, proverbial, normal, ordinary. **4** see SYMBOLIC. □□ **typically** see *ordinarily* (ORDINARY).

typify /típpifī/ *v.tr.* (**-ies, -ied**) **1** be a representative example of; embody the characteristics of. **2** represent by a type or symbol; serve as a type, figure, or emblem of; symbolize. □□ **typification** /-fikáysh'n/ *n.* **typifier** *n.* [L *typus* TYPE + -FY]

■ **1** exemplify, instantiate, epitomize, personify, represent, characterize, embody, evince, symbolize. **2** represent, symbolize, characterize, stand for, suggest, emblematize, be emblematic of. □□ **typification** see SOUL 3, TYPE *n.* 2.

typist /tīpist/ *n.* a person who uses a typewriter, esp. professionally.

typo /tīpō/ *n.* (*pl.* **-os**) *colloq.* **1** a typographical error. **2** a typographer. [abbr.]

■ **1** see MISPRINT *n.*

typographer /tīpógrəfər/ *n.* a person skilled in typography.

typography /tīpógrəfi/ *n.* **1** printing as an art. **2** the style and appearance of printed matter. □□ **typographic** /-pəgráffik/ *adj.* **typographical** /-pəgráffik'l/ *adj.* **typographically** /-pəgráffikəli/ *adv.* [F *typographie* or mod.L *typographia* (as TYPE, -GRAPHY)]

typology /tīpólləji/ *n.* the study and interpretation of (esp. biblical) types. □□ **typological** /tīpəlójik'l/ *adj.* **typologist** *n.* [Gk *tupos* TYPE + -LOGY]

tyrannical /tiránnik'l/ *adj.* **1** acting like a tyrant; imperious, arbitrary. **2** given to or characteristic of tyranny. □□ **tyrannically** *adv.* [OF *tyrannique* f. L *tyrannicus* f. Gk *turannikos* (as TYRANT)]

■ tyrannous, oppressive, dictatorial, Fascistic, despotic, autocratic, absolute, authoritarian, arbitrary, imperious, peremptory, overbearing, exacting, unjust, high-handed, severe, harsh, heavy-handed. □□ **tyrannically** see *severely* (SEVERE), *arbitrarily* (ARBITRARY).

tyrannicide /tiránnisīd/ *n.* **1** the act or an instance of killing a tyrant. **2** the killer of a tyrant. □□ **tyrannicidal** /-sīd'l/ *adj.* [F f. L *tyrannicida, -cidium* (as TYRANT, -CIDE)]

tyrannize /tírrənīz/ *v.tr.* & (foll. by *over*) *intr.* (also **-ise**) behave like a tyrant towards; rule or treat despotically or cruelly. [F *tyranniser* (as TYRANT)]

■ domineer over, bully, subjugate, enthral, enslave, dominate, intimidate, dictate to, order about *or* around, ride roughshod over, browbeat, keep under one's thumb, oppress, persecute, subdue, suppress, keep down, grind down.

tyrannosaurus /tiránnəsáwrəss/ *n.* (also **tyrannosaur**) any bipedal flesh-eating dinosaur of the genus *Tyrannosaurus*, esp. *T. rex* having powerful hind legs, small clawlike front legs, and a long well-developed tail. [Gk *turannos* TYRANT, after *dinosaur*]

tyranny /tírrəni/ *n.* (*pl.* **-ies**) **1** the cruel and arbitrary use of authority. **2** a tyrannical act; tyrannical behaviour. **3 a** rule by a tyrant. **b** a period of this. **c** a State ruled by a tyrant. □□ **tyrannous** *adj.* **tyrannously** *adv.* [ME f. OF *tyrannie* f. med.L *tyrannia* f. Gk *turannia* (as TYRANT)]

■ **1–3b** autocracy, authoritarianism, absolutism, despotism, dictatorship; arbitrariness, oppression, suppression, subjugation, enslavement, enthralment, domination; Fascism; Nazism; Stalinism. □□ **tyrannous** see TYRANNICAL.

tyrant /tīrənt/ *n.* **1** an oppressive or cruel ruler. **2** a person exercising power arbitrarily or cruelly. **3** *Gk Hist.* an absolute ruler who seized power without the legal right. [ME *tyran, -ant,* f. OF *tiran, tyrant* f. L *tyrannus* f. Gk *turannos*]

■ **1, 2** dictator, despot, autocrat, martinet, Hitler, bully, oppressor, authoritarian, hard taskmaster, slave-driver, overlord.

tyre /tīr/ *n.* (*US* **tire**) a rubber covering, usu. inflated, placed round a wheel to form a soft contact with the road. □ **tyre-gauge** a portable device for measuring the air-pressure in a tyre. [var. of TIRE[2]]

Tyrian /tírriən/ *adj.* & *n.* ● *adj.* of or relating to ancient Tyre in Phoenicia. ● *n.* a native or citizen of Tyre. □ **Tyrian purple** see PURPLE *n.* 2. [L *Tyrius* f. *Tyrus* Tyre]

tyro var. of TIRO.

Tyrolean /tírrəleéən/ *adj.* of or characteristic of the Tyrol, an Alpine province of Austria. □□ **Tyrolese** *adj.* & *n.*

Tyrrhene /tíreen/ *adj.* & *n.* (also **Tyrrhenian** /tireéniən/) *archaic* or *poet.* = ETRUSCAN. [L *Tyrrhenus*]

tzatziki /tsatseéki/ *n.* a Greek side dish of yoghurt with cucumber. [mod. Gk]

tzigane /tsigaán/ *n.* **1** a Hungarian gypsy. **2** (*attrib.*) characteristic of the tziganes or (esp.) their music. [F f. Magyar *c(z)igány*]

Uu

U[1] /yo͞o/ *n.* (also **u**) (*pl.* **Us** or **U's**) **1** the twenty-first letter of the alphabet. **2** a U-shaped object or curve (esp. in *comb.*: *U-bolt*).

U[2] /yo͞o/ *adj.* esp. *Brit. colloq.* **1** upper class. **2** supposedly characteristic of the upper class. [abbr.]

U[3] /o͞o/ *adj.* a Burmese title of respect before a man's name. [Burmese]

U[4] *abbr.* (also **U.**) **1** *Brit.* universal (of films classified as suitable without restriction). **2** university.

U[5] *symb. Chem.* the element uranium.

u *prefix* = MU 2 (μ).

UAE *abbr.* United Arab Emirates.

ubiety /yoobī́əti/ *n.* the fact or condition of being in a definite place; local relation. [med.L *ubietas* f. L *ubi* where]

-ubility /yoobílliti/ *suffix* forming nouns from, or corresponding to, adjectives in *-uble* (*solubility*; *volubility*). [L *-ubilitas*: cf. -ITY]

ubiquitarian /yoobíkwitáiriən/ *adj.* & *n. Theol.* ● *adj.* relating to or believing in the doctrine of the omnipresence of Christ's body. ● *n.* a believer in this. ◻◻ **ubiquitarianism** *n.* [mod.L *ubiquitarius* (as UBIQUITOUS)]

ubiquitous /yoobíkwitəss/ *adj.* **1** present everywhere or in several places simultaneously. **2** often encountered. ◻◻ **ubiquitously** *adv.* **ubiquitousness** *n.* **ubiquity** *n.* [mod.L *ubiquitas* f. L *ubique* everywhere f. *ubi* where]
■ see PERVASIVE. ◻◻ **ubiquitously** see EVERYWHERE. **ubiquitousness, ubiquity** see *prevalence* (PREVALENT).

-uble /yoob'l/ *suffix* forming adjectives meaning 'that may or must be' (see -ABLE) (*soluble*; *voluble*). [F f. L *-ubilis*]

-ubly /yoobli/ *suffix* forming adverbs corresponding to adjectives in *-uble*.

U-boat /yo͞obōt/ *n. hist.* a German submarine. [G *U-boot* = *Unterseeboot* under-sea boat]

UC *abbr.* University College.

u.c. *abbr.* upper case.

UCATT *abbr.* (in the UK) Union of Construction, Allied Trades, and Technicians.

UCCA /úkkə/ *abbr.* (in the UK) Universities Central Council on Admissions.

UCW *abbr.* (in the UK) Union of Communication Workers.

UDA *abbr.* Ulster Defence Association (a Loyalist paramilitary organization).

udal /yo͞od'l/ *n.* (also **odal** /ōd'l/) the kind of freehold right based on uninterrupted possession prevailing in N. Europe before the feudal system and still in use in Orkney and Shetland. [ON *óthal* f. Gmc]

UDC *abbr. hist.* (in the UK) Urban District Council.

udder /úddər/ *n.* the mammary gland of cattle, sheep, etc., hanging as a baglike organ with several teats. ◻◻ **uddered** *adj.* (also in *comb.*). [OE *ūder* f. WG]

UDI *abbr.* unilateral declaration of independence.

udometer /yoodómmitər/ *n. formal* a rain-gauge. [F *udomètre* f. L *udus* damp]

UDR *abbr. hist.* Ulster Defence Regiment.

UEFA /yo͞o-éefə/ *abbr.* Union of European Football Associations.

uey /yo͞o-ee/ *n. Austral. colloq.* a U-turn.

UFO /yo͞o-eff-ṓ, yo͞ofō/ *n.* (also **ufo**) (*pl.* **UFOs** or **ufos**) unidentified flying object. [abbr.]

ufology /yooföllәji/ *n.* the study of UFOs. ◻◻ **ufologist** *n.*

ugh /əkh, ug, ukh/ *int.* **1** expressing disgust or horror. **2** the sound of a cough or grunt. [imit.]

Ugli /úgli/ *n.* (*pl.* **Uglis** or **Uglies**) *propr.* a mottled green and yellow citrus fruit, a hybrid of a grapefruit and tangerine. [UGLY]

uglify /úglifī/ *v.tr.* (**-ies, -ied**) make ugly. ◻◻ **uglification** /-fikáysh'n/ *n.*

ugly /úgli/ *adj.* (**uglier, ugliest**) **1** unpleasing or repulsive to see or hear (*an ugly scar*; *spoke with an ugly snarl*). **2** unpleasantly suggestive; discreditable (*ugly rumours are about*). **3** threatening, dangerous (*the sky has an ugly look*; *an ugly mood*). **4** morally repulsive; vile (*ugly vices*). ◻ **ugly customer** an unpleasantly formidable person. **ugly duckling** a person who turns out to be beautiful or talented etc. against all expectations (with ref. to a cygnet in a brood of ducks in a tale by Andersen). ◻◻ **uglily** *adv.* **ugliness** *n.* [ME f. ON *uggligr* to be dreaded f. *ugga* to dread]
■ **1** unattractive, unlovely, unbeautiful, unhandsome, unshapely, unprepossessing, unpleasing, unsightly, hideous, grotesque, gruesome, ghastly, offensive, horrible, horrid, repulsive, plain, plain-looking, plain-featured, bad-featured, ill-favoured, dreadful-looking, awful-looking, frightful-looking, *US* homely, *Austral. sl.* drack. **2** see *poisonous* (POISON). **3** unpleasant, disagreeable, surly, hostile, nasty, spiteful, bad-tempered, ill-tempered, currish, irascible, curmudgeonly, cantankerous, crabby, crabbed, crotchety, cross, mean, *esp. US* cranky; disquieting, uncomfortable, discomforting, forbidding, sinister, troublesome, awkward, disadvantageous, ominous, threatening, menacing, dangerous, perilous, hazardous. **4** objectionable, disagreeable, unpleasant, offensive, nasty, loathsome, repellent, repugnant, repulsive, nauseating, nauseous, revolting, sickening, disgusting, obnoxious, rotten, corrupt, filthy, vile, heinous, bad, sordid, evil, foul, perverted, immoral, depraved, degenerate, base, debased, detestable, hateful, abominable, execrable, despicable, odious, *literary* noisome.

Ugrian /o͞ogriən/ *adj.* & *n.* (also **Ugric** /o͞ogrik/) ● *adj.* of or relating to the eastern branch of Finnic peoples, esp. the Finns and Magyars. ● *n.* **1** a member of this people. **2** the language of this people. [Russ. *Ugry* name of a race dwelling E. of the Urals]

UHF *abbr.* ultra-high frequency.

uh-huh /úhú/ *int. colloq.* expressing assent. [imit.]

uhlan /o͞olaan, yo͞olən/ *n. hist.* a cavalryman armed with a lance in some European armies, esp. the former German army. [F & G f. Pol. (*h*)*ulan* f. Turk. *oğlan* youth, servant]

UHT *abbr.* ultra heat treated (esp. of milk, for long keeping).

Uitlander /áytlondər/ *n. S.Afr.* a foreigner or alien, esp. before the Boer War. [Afrik. f. Du. *uit* out + *land* land]

UK *abbr.* United Kingdom.

UKAEA *abbr.* United Kingdom Atomic Energy Authority.

ukase /yookáyz/ *n.* **1** an arbitrary command. **2** *hist.* an edict of the Tsarist Russian government. [Russ. *ukaz* ordinance, edict f. *ukazat'* show, decree]

Ukrainian /yookráyniən/ *n.* & *adj.* ● *n.* **1** a native of the Ukraine. **2** the language of the Ukraine. ● *adj.* of or relating to the Ukraine or its people or language. [*Ukraine* f. Russ. *ukraina* frontier region f. *u* at + *krai* edge]

ukulele /yo͞okəláyli/ *n.* a small four-stringed Hawaiian (orig. Portuguese) guitar. [Hawaiian, = jumping flea]

-ular /yoolər/ *suffix* forming adjectives, sometimes corresp. to nouns in *-ule* (*pustular*) but often without diminutive force (*angular*; *granular*). ▫▫ **-ularity** /-lárriti/ *suffix* forming nouns. [from or after L *-ularis* (as -ULE, -AR[1])]

ulcer /úlsər/ *n.* **1** an open sore on an external or internal surface of the body, often forming pus. **2 a** a moral blemish. **b** a corroding or corrupting influence etc. ▫▫ **ulcered** *adj.* **ulcerous** *adj.* [ME f. L *ulcus -eris*, rel. to Gk *helkos*]

■ **1** sore, lesion, abscess, ulceration, canker, chancre, boil, gumboil, eruption, carbuncle, inflammation, *Med.* furuncle. **2** cancer, canker, festering spot, blight, scourge, poison, disease, pestilence, curse, bane, plague. ▫▫ **ulcerous** ulcerative, cancerous, cankerous, festering, ulcerated, suppurating, suppurative, gangrenous, septic, *Med.* furuncular, furunculous, necrotic, necrosed.

ulcerate /úlsərayt/ *v.tr.* & *intr.* form into or affect with an ulcer. ▫▫ **ulcerable** *adj.* **ulceration** /-ráysh'n/ *n.* **ulcerative** /-rətiv/ *adj.* [ME f. L *ulcerare ulcerat-* (as ULCER)]

-ule /yo͞ol/ *suffix* forming diminutive nouns (*capsule*; *globule*). [from or after L *-ulus*, *-ula*, *-ulum*]

ulema /o͞olimə/ *n.* **1** a body of Muslim doctors of sacred law and theology. **2** a member of this. [Arab. *'ulamā* pl. of *'ālim* learned f. *'alama* know]

-ulent /yoolənt/ *suffix* forming adjectives meaning 'abounding in, full of' (*fraudulent*; *turbulent*). ▫▫ **-ulence** *suffix* forming nouns. [L *-ulentus*]

uliginose /yoolijinōss/ *adj.* (also **uliginous** /-nəss/) *Bot.* growing in wet or swampy places. [L *uliginosus* f. *uligo -ginis* moisture]

ullage /úllij/ *n.* **1** the amount by which a cask etc. falls short of being full. **2** loss by evaporation or leakage. [ME f. AF *ulliage*, OF *ouillage* f. *ouiller* fill up, ult. f. L *oculus* eye, with ref. to the bung-hole]

ulna /úlnə/ *n.* (*pl.* **ulnae** /-nee/) **1** the thinner and longer bone in the forearm, on the side opposite to the thumb (cf. RADIUS 3). **2** *Zool.* a corresponding bone in an animal's foreleg or a bird's wing. ▫▫ **ulnar** *adj.* [L, rel. to Gk *ōlenē* and ELL]

ulotrichan /yoolótrikən/ *adj.* & *n.* ● *adj.* (also **ulotrichous** /-kəss/) having tightly-curled hair, esp. denoting a human type. ● *n.* a person having such hair. [mod.L *Ulotrichi* f. Gk *oulos* woolly, crisp + *thrix trikhos* hair]

-ulous /yooləss/ *suffix* forming adjectives (*fabulous*; *populous*). [L *-ulosus*, *-ulus*]

ulster /úlstər/ *n.* a man's long loose overcoat of rough cloth. [*Ulster* in Ireland, where it was orig. sold]

Ulsterman /úlstərmən/ *n.* (*pl.* **-men**; *fem.* **Ulsterwoman**; *pl.* **-women**) a native of Ulster.

ult. *abbr.* ultimo.

ulterior /ulteériər/ *adj.* **1** existing in the background, or beyond what is evident or admitted; hidden, secret (esp. *ulterior motive*). **2** situated beyond. **3** more remote; not immediate; in the future. ▫▫ **ulteriorly** *adv.* [L, = further, more distant]

■ **1** hidden, concealed, covert, secret, unrevealed, undisclosed, unexpressed, private, personal, underlying, surreptitious, underhand(ed). **2** outside, beyond, further, farther, remote, more distant. **3** future, further, remote.

ultima /últimə/ *n.* the last syllable of a word. [L *ultima* (*syllaba*), fem. of *ultimus* last]

ultimata *pl.* of ULTIMATUM.

ultimate /últimət/ *adj.* & *n.* ● *adj.* **1** last, final. **2** beyond which no other exists or is possible (*the ultimate analysis*). **3** fundamental, primary, unanalysable (*ultimate truths*). **4** maximum (*ultimate tensile strength*). ● *n.* **1** (prec. by *the*) the best achievable or imaginable. **2** a final or fundamental fact or principle. ▫▫ **ultimately** *adj.* **ultimateness** *n.* [LL *ultimatus* past part. of *ultimare* come to an end]

■ *adj.* **1, 2** final, last, terminating, terminal, end, eventual, net, closing, conclusive, concluding, decisive, deciding, definitive; remotest, furthest, farthest, extreme, uttermost. **3** elemental, basic, fundamental, underlying, primary, root, essential, unanalysable, final. **4** final, maximum, highest, greatest, supreme, utmost, paramount. ▫▫ **ultimately** finally, at long last, in the final *or* last analysis, eventually, in the end, at the end of the day, when all is said and done, at (the) last, in the long run; fundamentally, essentially, basically, at bottom.

ultima Thule /últimə tho͞olee/ *n.* a far-away unknown region. [L, = furthest Thule, a remote northern region]

ultimatum /últimáytəm/ *n.* (*pl.* **ultimatums** or **ultimata** /-tə/) a final demand or statement of terms by one party, the rejection of which by another could cause a breakdown in relations, war, or an end of cooperation etc. [L neut. past part.: see ULTIMATE]

■ (final) demand(s), term(s), condition(s), stipulation(s), requirement(s).

ultimo /últimō/ *adj.* *Commerce* of last month (*the 28th ultimo*). [L *ultimo mense* in the last month]

ultimogeniture /últimōjénnichər/ *n.* a system in which the youngest son has the right of inheritance (cf. PRIMOGENITURE 2). [L *ultimus* last, after PRIMOGENITURE]

ultra /últrə/ *adj.* & *n.* ● *adj.* favouring extreme views or measures, esp. in religion or politics. ● *n.* an extremist. [orig. as abbr. of F *ultra-royaliste*: see ULTRA-]

■ *adj.* die-hard, rabid, unregenerate, unrepentant, unreformed, fundamentalist, extremist, prejudiced, opinionated, bigoted, *colloq.* hard-nosed. ● *n.* see EXTREMIST.

ultra- /últrə/ *comb. form* **1** beyond; on the other side of (opp. CIS-). **2** extreme(ly), excessive(ly) (*ultra-conservative*; *ultra-modern*). [L *ultra* beyond]

■ **1** beyond. **2** extreme(ly), immoderate(ly), excessive(ly), drastic(ally), radical(ly), fanatic, fanatical(ly), unmitigated(ly), outrageous(ly), unqualified, uncompromising(ly), sheer, blatant(ly), out and out, complete(ly), thorough(ly), thoroughgoing, dyed in the wool; arch-.

ultracentrifuge /últrəséntrifyo͞oj/ *n.* a high-speed centrifuge used to separate small particles and large molecules by their rate of sedimentation from sols.

ultra-high /últrəhī/ *adj.* (of a frequency) in the range 300 to 3000 megahertz.

ultraist /últrəist/ *n.* the holder of extreme positions in politics, religion, etc. ▫▫ **ultraism** *n.*

■ see EXTREMIST.

ultramarine /últrəməreén/ *n.* & *adj.* ● *n.* **1 a** a brilliant blue pigment orig. obtained from lapis lazuli. **b** an imitation of this from powdered fired clay, sodium carbonate, sulphur, and resin. **2** the colour of this. ● *adj.* **1** of this colour. **2** *archaic* situated beyond the sea. [obs. It. *oltramarino* & med.L *ultramarinus* beyond the sea (as ULTRA-, MARINE), because lapis lazuli was brought from beyond the sea]

ultramicroscope /últrəmīkrəskōp/ *n.* an optical microscope used to reveal very small particles by means of light scattered by them.

ultramicroscopic /últrəmīkrəskóppik/ *adj.* **1** too small to be seen by an ordinary optical microscope. **2** of or relating to an ultramicroscope.

ultramontane /últrəmóntayn/ *adj.* & *n.* ● *adj.* **1** situated on the other side of the Alps from the point of view of the speaker. **2** advocating supreme papal authority in matters of faith and discipline. ● *n.* **1** a person living on the other side of the Alps. **2** a person advocating supreme papal authority. [med.L *ultramontanus* (as ULTRA-, L *mons montis* mountain)]

ultramundane /últrəmúndayn/ *adj.* lying beyond the world or the solar system. [L *ultramundanus* (as ULTRA-, *mundanus* f. *mundus* world)]

ultrasonic /últrəsónnik/ *adj.* of or involving sound waves with a frequency above the upper limit of human hearing. □□ **ultrasonically** *adv.*

ultrasonics /últrəsónniks/ *n.pl.* (usu. treated as *sing.*) the science and application of ultrasonic waves.

ultrasound /últrəsownd/ *n.* **1** sound having an ultrasonic frequency. **2** ultrasonic waves. □ **ultrasound cardiography** = ECHOCARDIOGRAPHY.

ultrastructure /últrəstrukchər/ *n. Biol.* fine structure not visible with an optical microscope.

ultraviolet /últrəvī́ələt/ *adj. Physics* **1** having a wavelength (just) beyond the violet end of the visible spectrum. **2** of or using such radiation.

ultra vires /últrə vī́reez, o͞oltraa veérayz/ *adv.* & *predic.adj.* beyond one's legal power or authority. [L]

ululate /yo͞olyoolayt/ *v.intr.* howl, wail; make a hooting cry. □□ **ululant** *adj.* **ululation** /-láysh'n/ *n.* [L *ululare ululat-* (imit.)]

■ see HOWL *v.* 1. □□ **ululation** see HOWL *n.* 1.

um /um, əm/ *int.* expressing hesitation or a pause in speech. [imit.]

-um var. of -IUM 1.

umbel /úmb'l/ *n. Bot.* a flower-cluster in which stalks nearly equal in length spring from a common centre and form a flat or curved surface, as in parsley. □□ **umbellar** *adj.* **umbellate** /-bəlayt/ *adj.* **umbellule** /-bélyo͞ol/ *adj.* [obs. F *umbelle* or L *umbella* sunshade, dimin. of UMBRA]

umbellifer /umbéllifər/ *n.* any plant of the family Umbelliferae bearing umbels, including parsley and parsnip. □□ **umbelliferous** /-bəlíffərəss/ *adj.* [obs. F *umbellifère* f. L (as UMBEL, *-fer* bearing)]

umber /úmbər/ *n.* & *adj.* ● *n.* **1** a natural pigment like ochre but darker and browner. **2** the colour of this. ● *adj.* **1** of this colour. **2** dark, dusky. [F (*terre d'*)*ombre* or It. (*terra di*) *ombra* = shadow (earth), f. L UMBRA or *Umbra* fem. of *Umber* Umbrian]

umbilical /umbíllik'l, úmbilī́k'l/ *adj.* **1** of, situated near, or affecting the navel. **2** centrally placed. □ **umbilical cord 1** a flexible cordlike structure attaching a foetus to the placenta. **2** *Astronaut.* a supply cable linking a missile to its launcher, or an astronaut in space to a spacecraft. [obs. F *umbilical* or f. UMBILICUS]

umbilicate /umbíllikət/ *adj.* **1** shaped like a navel. **2** having an umbilicus.

umbilicus /umbíllikəss, úmbilī́kəss/ *n.* (*pl.* **umbilici** /-lisī, -lī́sī/ or **umbilicuses**) **1** *Anat.* the navel. **2** *Bot.* & *Zool.* a navel-like formation. **3** *Geom.* a point in a surface through which all cross-sections have the same curvature. [L, rel. to Gk *omphalos* and to NAVEL]

umbles /úmb'lz/ *n.pl.* the edible offal of deer etc. (cf. *humble pie*). [ME var. of NUMBLES]

umbo /úmbō/ *n.* (*pl.* **-os** or **umbones** /-bṓneez/) **1** the boss of a shield, esp. in the centre. **2** *Bot.* & *Zool.* a rounded knob or protuberance. □□ **umbonal** *adj.* **umbonate** /-bṓnət/ *adj.* [L *umbo -onis*]

umbra /úmbrə/ *n.* (*pl.* **umbras** or **umbrae** /-bree/) *Astron.* **1** a total shadow usu. cast on the earth by the moon during a solar eclipse. **2** the dark central part of a sunspot (cf. PENUMBRA). □□ **umbral** *adj.* [L, = shade]

umbrage /úmbrij/ *n.* **1** offence; a sense of slight or injury (esp. *give* or *take umbrage at*). **2** *archaic* **a** shade. **b** what gives shade. [ME f. OF ult. f. L *umbraticus* f. *umbra*: see UMBRA]

■ **1** (*take umbrage*) feel *or* be offended, take offence, be affronted, bridle, feel displeasure *or* annoyance *or* exasperation *or* indignation *or* vexation *or* bitterness *or* resentment, be piqued *or* displeased *or* annoyed *or* exasperated *or* indignant *or* vexed *or* resentful, take exception, harbour a grudge.

umbrella /umbréllə/ *n.* **1** a light portable device for protection against rain, strong sun, etc., consisting of a usu. circular canopy of cloth mounted by means of a collapsible metal frame on a central stick. **2** protection or patronage. **3** (often *attrib.*) a coordinating or unifying agency (*umbrella organization*). **4** a screen of fighter aircraft or a curtain of fire put up as a protection against enemy aircraft. **5** *Zool.* the gelatinous disc of a jellyfish etc., which it contracts and expands to move through the water. □ **umbrella bird** any S. American bird of the genus *Cephalopterus*, with a black radiating crest and long wattles. **umbrella pine 1** = *stone pine.* **2** a tall Japanese evergreen conifer, *Sciadopitys verticillata*, with leaves in umbrella-like whorls. **umbrella stand** a stand for holding closed upright umbrellas. **umbrella tree** a small magnolia, *Magnolia tripetala*, with leaves in a whorl like an umbrella. □□ **umbrellaed** /-ləd/ *adj.* **umbrella-like** *adj.* [It. *ombrella*, dimin. of *ombra* shade f. L *umbra*: see UMBRA]

■ **1** parasol, sunshade; *Brit. colloq.* gamp, brolly. **2** protection, cover, coverage, aegis, shield, screen, patronage. **3** (*attrib.*) catch-all, overall, blanket. **4** screen, shelter, shield, protection, cover, curtain.

Umbrian /úmbriən/ *adj.* & *n.* ● *adj.* of or relating to Umbria in central Italy. ● *n.* **1** the language of ancient Umbria, related to Latin. **2** an inhabitant of ancient Umbria. □ **Umbrian school** a Renaissance school of Italian painting, to which Raphael and Perugino belonged.

umbriferous /umbríffərəss/ *adj. formal* providing shade. [L *umbrifer* f. *umbra* shade: see -FEROUS]

umiak /o͞omiak/ *n.* an Eskimo skin-and-wood open boat propelled by women with paddles. [Eskimo]

umlaut /o͞omlowt/ *n.* & *v.* ● *n.* **1** a mark (̈) used over a vowel, esp. in Germanic languages, to indicate a vowel change. **2** such a vowel change, e.g. German *Mann*, *Männer*, English *man*, *men*, due to *i*, *j*, etc. (now usu. lost or altered) in the following syllable. ● *v.tr.* modify (a form or a sound) by an umlaut. [G f. *um* about + *Laut* sound]

umpire /úmpīr/ *n.* & *v.* ● *n.* **1** a person chosen to enforce the rules and settle disputes in various sports. **2** a person chosen to arbitrate between disputants, or to see fair play. ● *v.* **1** *intr.* (usu. foll. by *for*, *in*, etc.) act as umpire. **2** *tr.* act as umpire in (a game etc.). □□ **umpirage** /-pīrij/ *n.* **umpireship** *n.* [ME, later form of *noumpere* f. OF *nonper* not equal (as NON-, PEER[2]): for loss of *n-* cf. ADDER]

■ *n.* referee, arbiter, judge, moderator, go-between, adjudicator, arbitrator; official; *colloq.* ref. ● *v.* officiate; referee, arbitrate, judge, moderate, adjudicate.

umpteen /úmpteén/ *adj.* & *pron. sl.* ● *adj.* indefinitely many; a lot of. ● *pron.* indefinitely many. □□ **umpteenth** *adj.* **umpty** /úmpti/ *adj.* [joc. form. on -TEEN]

■ *adj.* a lot of, many, innumerable, unnumbered, countless, a huge number of, very many, numerous, *colloq.* hundreds of, thousands of, millions of, billions of, trillions of, zillions of, masses of.

umpty-doo /úmpti do͞o/ *adj. Austral. colloq.* drunk. [20th c.: prob. f. HUMPTY-DUMPTY]

■ see DRUNK *adj.* 1.

UN *abbr.* United Nations.

un-[1] /un/ *prefix* **1** added to adjectives and participles and their derivative nouns and adverbs, meaning: **a** not: denoting the absence of a quality or state (*unusable*; *uncalled-for*; *uneducated*; *unfailing*; *unofficially*; *unhappiness*). **b** the reverse of, usu. with an implication of approval or disapproval, or with some other special connotation (*unselfish*; *unsociable*; *unscientific*). ¶ Words formed in this way often have neutral counterparts in *non-* (see NON- 6) and counterparts in *in-* (see IN-[1]), e.g. *unadvisable*. **2** (less often) added to nouns, meaning 'a lack of' (*unrest*; *untruth*). ¶ The number of words that can be formed with this prefix (and similarly with *un-*[2]) is potentially as large as the number of adjectives in use; consequently only a selection, being considered the most current or semantically noteworthy, can be given here. [OE f. Gmc, rel. to L *in-*]

un-[2] /un/ *prefix* added to verbs and (less often) nouns, forming verbs denoting: **1** the reversal or cancellation of an action or state (*undress*; *unlock*; *unsettle*). **2** deprivation or separation (*unmask*). **3** release from (*unburden*; *uncage*). **4** causing to be no longer (*unman*). ¶ See the note at *un-*[1]. Both *un-*[1] and *un-*[2] can be understood in some forms in *-able*, *-ed* (especially), and *-ing*: for example, *undressed* can mean either 'not dressed' or 'no longer dressed'. [OE *un-*, *on-* f. Gmc]

'un /ən/ *pron. colloq.* one (*that's a good 'un*). [dial. var.]

UNA *abbr.* United Nations Association.

unabashed /únnəbásht/ *adj.* not abashed. □□ **unabashedly** /-shidli/ *adv.*

■ unashamed, unblushing, unembarrassed, brazen, barefaced, blatant, bold, undaunted, not abashed, undeterred, unawed, undismayed, unconcerned. □□ **unabashedly** see OPENLY.

unabated /únnəbáytid/ *adj.* not abated; undiminished. □□ **unabatedly** *adv.*

■ see RELENTLESS 2, UNMITIGATED 1.

unable /únnáyb'l/ *adj.* (usu. foll. by *to* + infin.) not able; lacking ability.

■ not able, powerless, unfit, unqualified, impotent, incompetent.

unabridged /únnəbríjd/ *adj.* (of a text etc.) complete; not abridged.

■ uncut, whole, full-length, entire, complete, intact, not abridged, uncondensed, unshortened; not bowdlerized, unexpurgated; extensive, thorough, comprehensive, full, exhaustive, all-encompassing, (all-)inclusive.

unabsorbed /únnəbzórbd, -sórbd/ *adj.* not absorbed.

unacademic /únnakədémmik/ *adj.* **1** not academic (esp. not scholarly or theoretical). **2** (of a person) not suited to academic study.

unaccented /únnakséntid/ *adj.* not accented; not emphasized.

■ unstressed, unemphasized, unaccentuated, weak.

unacceptable /únnəkséptəb'l/ *adj.* not acceptable. □□ **unacceptableness** *n.* **unacceptably** *adv.*

■ unsatisfactory, objectionable, exceptionable, wrong, bad, improper, unallowable, insupportable, intolerable, inadmissible, ineligible, undesirable, distasteful, disagreeable, unsuitable, inappropriate, alien, unpleasant, tasteless, beyond the pale, *colloq.* not on. □□ **unacceptably** see BADLY 1.

unacclaimed /únnəkláymd/ *adj.* not acclaimed.

unaccommodating /únnəkómmədayting/ *adj.* not accommodating; disobliging.

■ see DIFFICULT 2, INFLEXIBLE 2, 3.

unaccompanied /únnəkúmpənid/ *adj.* **1** not accompanied. **2** *Mus.* without accompaniment.

■ **1** alone, solo, lone, on one's own, by oneself, unescorted, unchaperoned, unattended, *archaic* sole. **2** solo, *Mus.* a cappella.

unaccomplished /únnəkúmplisht, -kómplisht/ *adj.* **1** not accomplished; uncompleted. **2** lacking accomplishments.

■ **1** see INCOMPLETE, UNDONE 1. **2** see UNREFINED, UNEDUCATED.

unaccountable /únnəkówntəb'l/ *adj.* **1** unable to be explained. **2** unpredictable or strange in behaviour. **3** not responsible. □□ **unaccountability** /-bílliti/ *n.* **unaccountableness** *n.* **unaccountably** *adv.*

■ **1, 2** unexplained, inexplicable, unexplainable, unaccounted for, mysterious, inscrutable, incomprehensible, unintelligible, enigmatic, strange, puzzling, baffling, mystifying, peculiar, odd, bizarre, unfathomable, unpredictable, weird, unheard-of, extraordinary, unusual, unorthodox, uncanny. **3** not answerable, not responsible.

unaccounted /únnəkówntid/ *adj.* of which no account is given. □ **unaccounted for** unexplained; not included in an account.

■ □ **unaccounted for** see UNACCOUNTABLE 1, 2.

unaccustomed /únnəkústəmd/ *adj.* **1** (usu. foll. by *to*) not accustomed. **2** not customary; unusual (*his unaccustomed silence*). □□ **unaccustomedly** *adv.*

■ **1** (*unaccustomed to*) unused to, inexperienced in *or* at, amateurish at, unpractised in *or* at, unfamiliar with, uninitiated in. **2** unfamiliar, unusual, rare, unwonted, unexpected, uncommon, unprecedented, unanticipated, curious, peculiar, atypical, untypical.

unachievable /únnəcheévəb'l/ *adj.* not achievable.

unacknowledged /únnəknóllijd/ *adj.* not acknowledged.

■ see THANKLESS 2, UNTHANKED.

unacquainted /únnəkwáyntid/ *adj.* (usu. foll. by *with*) not acquainted.

■ (*unaquainted with*) see UNFAMILIAR.

unadaptable /únnədáptəb'l/ *adj.* not adaptable.

■ see INFLEXIBLE 2, 3.

unadapted /únnədáptid/ *adj.* not adapted.

unaddressed /únnədrést/ *adj.* (esp. of a letter etc.) without an address.

unadjacent /únnəjáys'nt/ *adj.* not adjacent.

unadopted /únnədóptid/ *adj.* **1** not adopted. **2** *Brit.* (of a road) not taken over for maintenance by a local authority.

unadorned /únnədórnd/ *adj.* not adorned; plain.

■ plain, simple, unembellished, undecorated, unornamented, stark, bare, austere.

unadulterated /únnədúltəraytid/ *adj.* **1** not adulterated; pure; concentrated. **2** sheer, complete, utter (*unadulterated nonsense*).

■ **1** see PURE 1, 2. **2** see SHEER[1] *adj.* 1.

unadventurous /únnədvénchərəss/ *adj.* not adventurous. □□ **unadventurously** *adv.*

unadvertised /únnádvərtīzd/ *adj.* not advertised.

■ see UNHERALDED.

unadvisable /únnədvīzəb'l/ *adj.* **1** not open to advice. **2** (of a thing) inadvisable.

■ **2** see *ill-advised* 2.

unadvised /únnədvīzd/ *adj.* **1** indiscreet; rash. **2** not having had advice. □□ **unadvisedly** /-zidli/ *adv.* **unadvisedness** *n.*

■ **1** see *ill-advised* 2.

unaffected /únnəféktid/ *adj.* **1** (usu. foll. by *by*) not affected. **2** free from affectation; genuine; sincere. □□ **unaffectedly** *adv.* **unaffectedness** *n.*

■ **1** (*unaffected by*) impervious to, immune to, untouched by, unmoved by, unresponsive to, above, aloof to *or* from, uninfluenced by, unimpressed by, remote to *or* from, cool *or* cold to, unconcerned by, unstirred by, insensible to. **2** genuine, real, sincere, natural, simple, plain, unpretentious, unassuming, ingenuous, unsophisticated, unstudied, honest, guileless, artless, unartificial, unspoilt, straightforward, unfeigned. □□ **unaffectedly** see NATURALLY 1. **unaffectedness** see *sincerity* (SINCERE).

unaffiliated /únnəfilliaytid/ *adj.* not affiliated.

■ see NON-ALIGNED.

unafraid /únnəfráyd/ *adj.* not afraid.

■ see BRAVE *adj.* 1.

unaided /únnáydid/ *adj.* not aided; without help.

■ see *single-handed adj.*

unalienable /únnáyliənəb'l/ *adj. Law* = INALIENABLE.

unaligned /únnəlīnd/ *adj.* **1** = NON-ALIGNED. **2** not physically aligned.

unalike /únnəlík/ *adj.* not alike; different.

■ see DIFFERENT 1, 2.

unalive /únnəlív/ *adj.* **1** lacking in vitality. **2** (foll. by *to*) not fully susceptible or awake to.

unalleviated /únnəleéviaytid/ *adj.* not alleviated; relentless.

■ see RELENTLESS 2, UNMITIGATED 1.

unallied /únnəlīd/ *adj.* not allied; having no allies.

■ see NEUTRAL *adj.* 1, 2.

unallowable /únnəlówəb'l/ *adj.* not allowable.

■ see INADMISSIBLE.

unalloyed /únnəlóyd, únnál-/ *adj.* **1** not alloyed; pure. **2** complete; utter (*unalloyed joy*).

■ **1** see PURE 1, 2. **2** see PURE 8.

unalterable /únnáwltərəb'l, únnól-/ *adj.* not alterable. □□ **unalterableness** *n.* **unalterably** *adv.*
■ see INVARIABLE 1, CONSTANT *adj.* 3.

unaltered /únnáwltərd, únnól-/ *adj.* not altered; remaining the same.
■ see SAME *adj.* 2.

unamazed /únnəmáyzd/ *adj.* not amazed.

unambiguous /únnambígyooəss/ *adj.* not ambiguous; clear or definite in meaning. □□ **unambiguity** /-gyóō-iti/ *n.* **unambiguously** *adv.*
■ see CLEAR *adj.* 6b. □□ **unambiguously** see *expressly* (EXPRESS[2]).

unambitious /únnambíshəss/ *adj.* not ambitious; without ambition. □□ **unambitiously** *adv.* **unambitiousness** *n.*
■ see MEEK, SHIFTLESS.

unambivalent /únnambívvələnt/ *adj.* (of feelings etc.) not ambivalent; straightforward. □□ **unambivalently** *adv.*

un-American /únnəmérrikən/ *adj.* **1** not in accordance with American characteristics etc. **2** contrary to the interests of the US; (in the US) treasonable. □□ **un-Americanism** *n.*

unamiable /únnáymiəb'l/ *adj.* not amiable.
■ see UNSOCIAL.

unamplified /únnámplifīd/ *adj.* not amplified.

unamused /únnəmyóōzd/ *adj.* not amused.

unanalysable /únnánnəlīzəb'l/ *adj.* not able to be analysed.

unanalysed /únnánnəlīzd/ *adj.* not analysed.

unaneled /únnənéeld/ *adj.* *archaic* not having received extreme unction.

unanimous /yoonánniməss/ *adj.* **1** all in agreement (*the committee was unanimous*). **2** (of an opinion, vote, etc.) held or given by general consent (*the unanimous choice*). □□ **unanimity** /-nənímmiti/ *n.* **unanimously** *adv.* **unanimousness** *n.* [LL *unanimis*, L *unanimus* f. *unus* one + *animus* mind]
■ **1** see UNITED 3. □□ **unanimity** see ACCORD *n.* 1.

unannounced /únnənównst/ *adj.* not announced; without warning (of arrival etc.).
■ see UNHERALDED.

unanswerable /únnaánsərəb'l/ *adj.* **1** unable to be refuted (*has an unanswerable case*). **2** unable to be answered (*an unanswerable question*). □□ **unanswerableness** *n.* **unanswerably** *adv.*
■ **1** see INCONTROVERTIBLE.

unanswered /únnaánsərd/ *adj.* not answered.
■ see UNRESOLVED 2.

unanticipated /únnantíssipaytid/ *adj.* not anticipated.
■ see UNFORESEEN.

unapparent /únnəpárrənt/ *adj.* not apparent.

unappealable /únnəpéeləb'l/ *adj.* esp. *Law* not able to be appealed against.

unappealing /únnəpéeling/ *adj.* not appealing; unattractive. □□ **unappealingly** *adv.*
■ see UNINVITING.

unappeasable /únnəpéezəb'l/ *adj.* not appeasable.
■ see IMPLACABLE.

unappeased /únnəpéezd/ *adj.* not appeased.

unappetizing /únnáppitīzing/ *adj.* not appetizing. □□ **unappetizingly** *adv.*
■ see UNPALATABLE 1, UNINVITING.

unapplied /únnəplī́d/ *adj.* not applied.
■ see ABSTRACT *adj.* 1a.

unappreciated /únnəpréeshiaytid/ *adj.* not appreciated.
■ see THANKLESS 2, UNTHANKED.

unappreciative /únnəpréeshətiv/ *adj.* not appreciative.
■ see UNGRATEFUL.

unapproachable /únnəprṓchəb'l/ *adj.* **1** not approachable; remote, inaccessible. **2** (of a person) unfriendly. □□ **unapproachability** /-bílliti/ *n.* **unapproachableness** *n.* **unapproachably** *adv.*
■ **1** inaccessible, remote, unreachable, out of the way, out of reach, beyond reach. **2** distant, remote, aloof, reserved, standoffish, austere, withdrawn, unfriendly, unsociable, antisocial, forbidding, chilly, cool, cold, frigid.

unappropriated /únnəprṓpriaytid/ *adj.* **1** not allocated or assigned. **2** not taken into possession by anyone.

unapproved /únnəpróōvd/ *adj.* not approved or sanctioned.
■ see UNAUTHORIZED.

unapt /únnápt/ *adj.* **1** (usu. foll. by *for*) not suitable. **2** (usu. foll. by *to* + infin.) not apt. □□ **unaptly** *adv.* **unaptness** *n.*
■ **1** see INAPPROPRIATE. **2** see EXTRANEOUS 2b.

unarguable /únnaárgyooəb'l/ *adj.* not arguable; certain.
■ see CERTAIN *adj.* 1b.

unarm /únnaárm/ *v.tr.* deprive or free of arms or armour.
■ disarm, demilitarize.

unarmed /únnaármd/ *adj.* not armed; without weapons.
■ unprotected, defenceless, weaponless.

unarresting /únnərésting/ *adj.* uninteresting, dull. □□ **unarrestingly** *adv.*

unarticulated /únnaartíkyoolaytid/ *adj.* not articulated or distinct.

unartistic /únnaartístik/ *adj.* not artistic, esp. not concerned with art. □□ **unartistically** *adv.*
■ see MATTER-OF-FACT 1.

unascertainable /únnasərtáynəb'l/ *adj.* not ascertainable.
■ see UNCERTAIN 1.

unascertained /únnasərtáynd/ *adj.* not ascertained; unknown.
■ see UNCERTAIN 1.

unashamed /únnəsháymd/ *adj.* **1** feeling no guilt, shameless. **2** blatant; bold. □□ **unashamedly** /-midli/ *adv.* **unashamedness** /-midniss/ *n.*
■ **1** see SHAMELESS. **2** see BLATANT 1. □□ **unashamedly** see OPENLY 2.

unasked /únnaáskt/ *adj.* (often foll. by *for*) not asked, requested, or invited.
■ uninvited, unrequested, undemanded, unsolicited, unsought, unwanted, unprompted, gratuitous, volunteered, voluntary, unbidden, spontaneous, unwelcome, uncalled(-for).

unassailable /únnəsáyləb'l/ *adj.* unable to be attacked or questioned; impregnable. □□ **unassailability** /-bílliti/ *n.* **unassailableness** *n.* **unassailably** *adv.*
■ see INVINCIBLE, WATERTIGHT 2.

unassertive /únnəsértiv/ *adj.* (of a person) not assertive or forthcoming; reticent. □□ **unassertively** *adv.* **unassertiveness** *n.*
■ see PASSIVE 2. □□ **unassertiveness** see SUBMISSION 2.

unassignable /únnəsī́nəb'l/ *adj.* not assignable.

unassigned /únnəsī́nd/ *adj.* not assigned.

unassimilated /únnəsímmiláytid/ *adj.* not assimilated. □□ **unassimilable** *adj.*

unassisted /únnəsístid/ *adj.* not assisted.
■ see *single-handed adj.*

unassuaged /únnəswáyjd/ *adj.* not assuaged. □□ **unassuageable** *adj.*

unassuming /únnəsyóōming/ *adj.* not pretentious or arrogant; modest. □□ **unassumingly** *adv.* **unassumingness** *n.*
■ see MODEST 1, 2.

unatoned /únnətṓnd/ *adj.* not atoned for.

unattached /únnətácht/ *adj.* **1** (often foll. by *to*) not attached, esp. to a particular body, organization, etc. **2** not engaged or married.
■ **1** separate, unconnected, detached, independent, unaffiliated, self-governing, self-regulating, autonomous, self-reliant, self-sustaining, self-sustained; see also *detached* (DETACH 3). **2** single, unmarried, uncommitted, unengaged, on one's own, not spoken for.

unattackable /únnətákkəb'l/ *adj.* unable to be attacked or damaged.

unattainable /únnətáynəb'l/ *adj.* not attainable. □□ **unattainableness** *n.* **unattainably** *adv.*
■ see IMPOSSIBLE 1, UNAPPROACHABLE 1.

unattempted /únnətémptid/ *adj.* not attempted.

unattended /únnəténdid/ *adj.* **1** (usu. foll. by *to*) not attended. **2** (of a person, vehicle, etc.) not accompanied; alone; uncared for.
■ **2** see UNACCOMPANIED 1.

unattractive /únnətráktiv/ *adj.* not attractive. □□ **unattractively** *adv.* **unattractiveness** *n.*
■ see UGLY 1, UNINVITING.

unattributable /únnətríbyootəb'l/ *adj.* (esp. of information) that cannot or may not be attributed to a source etc. □□ **unattributably** *adv.*

unauthentic /únnawthéntik/ *adj.* not authentic. □□ **unauthentically** *adv.*
■ see FACTITIOUS.

unauthenticated /únnawthéntikaytid/ *adj.* not authenticated.

unauthorized /únnáwthərīzd/ *adj.* (also **unauthorised**) not authorized.
■ unsanctioned, unapproved, unofficial, unwarranted, unlawful, illegal, illicit, illegitimate.

unavailable /únnəváyləb'l/ *adj.* not available. □□ **unavailability** /-bílliti/ *n.* **unavailableness** *n.*
■ unobtainable, inaccessible; spoken for.

unavailing /únnəváyling/ *adj.* not availing; achieving nothing; ineffectual. □□ **unavailingly** *adv.*
■ see INEFFECTIVE 1, 3.

unavoidable /únnəvóydəb'l/ *adj.* not avoidable; inevitable. □□ **unavoidability** /-bílliti/ *n.* **unavoidableness** *n.* **unavoidably** *adv.*
■ inescapable, ineluctable, inevitable, irresistible, inexorable, necessary, compulsory, automatic, sure, certain, fated, destined, predestined, determined, predetermined, unchangeable, unalterable, settled, fixed, definite. □□ **unavoidability** inevitability, inevitableness, unavoidableness, necessity, ineluctability, inescapability, indispensability, indispensableness, inexorability. **unavoidably** see NECESSARILY.

unavowed /únnəvówd/ *adj.* not avowed.
■ see SECRET *adj.* 1.

unaware /únnəwáir/ *adj.* & *adv.* ● *adj.* **1** (usu. foll. by *of*, or *that* + clause) not aware; ignorant (*unaware of her presence*). **2** (of a person) insensitive; unperceptive. ● *adv.* = UNAWARES. □□ **unawareness** *n.*
■ *adj.* **1** ignorant, oblivious, unknowing, unsuspecting, unwitting, unconscious, uninformed, unenlightened, incognizant, inobservant, insensible, heedless, unwary, unmindful. **2** see THOUGHTLESS 1. □□ **unawareness** see IGNORANCE.

unawares /únnəwáirz/ *adv.* **1** unexpectedly (*met them unawares*). **2** inadvertently (*dropped it unawares*). [earlier *unware(s)* f. OE *unwær(es)*: see WARE[2]]
■ **1** unexpectedly, abruptly, by surprise, suddenly, off (one's) guard. **2** inadvertently, unconsciously, unintentionally, unknowingly, unwittingly, unaware, by mistake, mistakenly, by accident, accidentally, in an unguarded moment.

unbacked /únbákt/ *adj.* **1** not supported. **2** (of a horse etc.) having no backers. **3** (of a chair, picture, etc.) having no back or backing.

unbalance /únbállənss/ *v.* & *n.* ● *v.tr.* **1** upset the physical or mental balance of (*unbalanced by the blow*; *the shock unbalanced him*). **2** (as **unbalanced** *adj.*) **a** not balanced. **b** (of a mind or a person) unstable or deranged. ● *n.* lack of balance; instability, esp. mental.
■ *v.* **2** (**unbalanced**) **a** uneven, asymmetric(al), unsymmetric(al), lopsided, off-centre, unequal, overbalanced, unstable, wobbly, shaky, unsteady; one-sided, biased. **b** mad, demented, certifiable, crazy, insane, eccentric, *non compos (mentis)*, touched (in the head), unstable, unhinged, deranged, disturbed, of unsound mind, dizzy, *esp. Brit. colloq.* daft, *sl.* daffy, nuts, nutty, bananas, batty, bonkers, off one's head *or* rocker, loco, out of one's head, *Austral. sl.* not the full quid.

unban /únbán/ *v.tr.* (**unbanned, unbanning**) cease to ban; remove a ban from.

unbar /únbaár/ *v.tr.* (**unbarred, unbarring**) **1** remove a bar or bars from (a gate etc.). **2** unlock, open.

unbearable /únbáirəb'l/ *adj.* not bearable. □□ **unbearableness** *n.* **unbearably** *adv.*
■ intolerable, unsupportable, insupportable, unendurable, insufferable, unacceptable, oppressive, overwhelming, overpowering, *colloq.* too much.

unbeatable /únbeétəb'l/ *adj.* not beatable; excelling.
■ unsurpassable, undefeatable, unconquerable, invincible, excellent, unexcelled, incomparable, matchless, unrivalled, peerless, unparalleled, superlative, supreme, transcendent.

unbeaten /únbeét'n/ *adj.* **1** not beaten. **2** (of a record etc.) not surpassed. **3** *Cricket* (of a player) not out.

unbeautiful /únbyoótifool/ *adj.* not beautiful; ugly. □□ **unbeautifully** *adv.*
■ see UGLY 1.

unbecoming /únbikúmming/ *adj.* **1** (esp. of clothing) not flattering or suiting a person. **2** (usu. foll. by *to*, *for*) not fitting; indecorous or unsuitable. □□ **unbecomingly** *adv.* **unbecomingness** *n.*
■ **1** unflattering, unsuitable. **2** unbefitting, unfitting, unfit; indecorous, unseemly, indelicate, improper, ungentlemanly, unladylike, offensive, tasteless; unsuitable, inappropriate, unsuited, ill-suited, inapt, unapt, out of place.

unbefitting /únbifítting/ *adj.* not befitting; unsuitable. □□ **unbefittingly** *adv.* **unbefittingness** *n.*
■ see INAPPROPRIATE.

unbefriended /únbifréndid/ *adj.* not befriended.

unbegotten /únbigótt'n/ *adj.* not begotten.

unbeholden /únbihṓldən/ *predic.adj.* (usu. foll. by *to*) under no obligation.

unbeknown /únbinṓn/ *adj.* (also **unbeknownst** /-nṓnst/) (foll. by *to*) without the knowledge of (*was there all the time unbeknown to us*). [UN-[1] + *beknown* (archaic) = KNOWN]
■ (*unbeknown to*) see *unknown to*.

unbelief /únbileéf/ *n.* lack of belief, esp. in religious matters. □□ **unbeliever** *n.* **unbelieving** *adj.* **unbelievingly** *adv.* **unbelievingness** *n.*
■ see *scepticism* (SCEPTIC) □□ **unbeliever** see NON-BELIEVER. **unbelieving** incredulous, disbelieving, non-believing, doubting, mistrusting, distrusting, mistrustful, distrustful, suspicious, sceptical, unpersuaded, unconvinced; non-religious, faithless, unreligious.

unbelievable /únbileévəb'l/ *adj.* not believable; incredible. □□ **unbelievability** /-bílliti/ *n.* **unbelievableness** *n.* **unbelievably** *adv.*
■ incredible, preposterous, inconceivable, unimaginable, implausible, improbable, unthinkable, beyond belief; amazing, extraordinary, fantastic, astounding, staggering, fabulous, *colloq.* mind-boggling, *sl.* mind-blowing. □□ **unbelievably** see TERRIBLY 1.

unbeloved /únbilúvd/ *adj.* not beloved.

unbelt /únbélt/ *v.tr.* remove or undo the belt of (a garment etc.).

unbend /únbénd/ *v.* (*past* and *past part.* **unbent**) **1** *tr.* & *intr.* change from a bent position; straighten. **2** *intr.* relax from strain or severity; become affable. **3** *tr.* *Naut.* **a** unfasten (sails) from yards and stays. **b** cast (a cable) loose. **c** untie (a rope).
■ **2** see THAW *v.* 4, 6.

unbending /únbénding/ *adj.* **1** not bending; inflexible. **2** firm; austere (*unbending rectitude*). **3** relaxing from strain, activity, or formality. □□ **unbendingly** *adv.* **unbendingness** *n.*

■ **1** see INFLEXIBLE 1. **2** see INFLEXIBLE 2.

unbiased /únbīəst/ *adj.* (also **unbiassed**) not biased; impartial.

■ see IMPARTIAL.

unbiblical /únbíblik'l/ *adj.* **1** not in or authorized by the Bible. **2** contrary to the Bible.

unbiddable /únbíddəb'l/ *adj. Brit.* disobedient; not docile.

unbidden /únbídd'n/ *adj.* not commanded or invited (*arrived unbidden*).

■ see UNASKED.

unbind /únbīnd/ *v.tr.* (*past* and *past part.* **unbound**) release from bonds or binding.

unbirthday /únbúrthday/ *n.* (often *attrib.*) *joc.* any day but one's birthday (*an unbirthday party*).

unbleached /únbléecht/ *adj.* not bleached.

unblemished /únblémmisht/ *adj.* not blemished.

■ see *flawless* (FLAW[1]).

unblessed /únblést/ *adj.* (also **unblest**) not blessed.

■ see UNFORTUNATE *adj.* 1.

unblinking /únblíngking/ *adj.* **1** not blinking. **2** steadfast; not hesitating. **3** stolid; cool. ▫▫ **unblinkingly** *adv.*

■ **1, 3** see STEADY *adj.* 6. **2** see STEADFAST.

unblock /únblók/ *v.tr.* **1** remove an obstruction from (esp. a pipe, drain, etc.). **2** (also *absol.*) *Cards* allow the later unobstructed play of (a suit) by playing a high card.

■ **1** see CLEAR *v.* 2b.

unblown /únblṓn/ *adj.* **1** not blown. **2** *archaic* (of a flower) not yet in bloom.

unblushing /únblúshing/ *adj.* **1** not blushing. **2** unashamed; frank. ▫▫ **unblushingly** *adv.*

■ **2** see UNABASHED.

unbolt /únbṓlt/ *v.tr.* release (a door etc.) by drawing back the bolt.

unbolted /únbṓltid/ *adj.* **1** not bolted. **2** (of flour etc.) not sifted.

unbonnet /únbónnit/ *v.* (**unbonneted, unbonneting**) **1** *tr.* remove the bonnet from. **2** *intr. archaic* remove one's hat or bonnet esp. in respect.

unbookish /únbŏŏkkish/ *adj.* **1** not academic; not often inclined to read. **2** free from bookishness.

unboot /únbŏŏt/ *v.intr.* & *tr.* remove one's boots or the boots of (a person).

unborn /únbórn/ *adj.* **1** not yet born (*an unborn child*). **2** never to be brought into being (*unborn hopes*).

unbosom /únbŏŏzz'm/ *v.tr.* **1** disclose (thoughts, secrets, etc.). **2** (*refl.*) unburden (oneself) of one's thoughts, secrets, etc.

■ **1** see OPEN *v.* 9a.

unbothered /únbóthərd/ *adj.* not bothered; unconcerned.

unbound[1] /únbównd/ *adj.* **1** not bound or tied up. **2** unconstrained. **3 a** (of a book) not having a binding. **b** having paper covers. **4** (of a substance or particle) in a loose or free state.

■ **1** see LOOSE *adj.* 1.

unbound[2] *past* and *past part.* of UNBIND.

unbounded /únbówndid/ *adj.* not bounded; infinite (*unbounded optimism*). ▫▫ **unboundedly** *adv.* **unboundedness** *n.*

■ see LIMITLESS.

unbrace /únbráyss/ *v.tr.* **1** (also *absol.*) free from tension; relax (the nerves etc.). **2** remove a brace or braces from.

unbreachable /únbréechəb'l/ *adj.* not able to be breached.

unbreakable /únbráykəb'l/ *adj.* not breakable.

■ see INDESTRUCTIBLE.

unbreathable /únbréethəb'l/ *adj.* not able to be breathed.

unbribable /únbrībəb'l/ *adj.* not bribable.

unbridgeable /únbríjəb'l/ *adj.* unable to be bridged.

unbridle /únbrīd'l/ *v.tr.* **1** remove a bridle from (a horse). **2** remove constraints from (one's tongue, a person, etc.). **3** (as **unbridled** *adj.*) unconstrained (*unbridled insolence*).

■ **3** (**unbridled**) see UNINHIBITED.

unbroken /únbrṓkən/ *adj.* **1** not broken. **2** not tamed (*an unbroken horse*). **3** not interrupted (*unbroken sleep*). **4** not surpassed (*an unbroken record*). ▫▫ **unbrokenly** *adv.* **unbrokenness** /-ən-niss/ *n.*

■ **1** see INTACT 1. **2** see UNTAMED. **3** see CONTINUOUS.

unbruised /únbrŏŏzd/ *adj.* not bruised.

unbuckle /únbúkk'l/ *v.tr.* release the buckle of (a strap, shoe, etc.).

■ see UNDO 1.

unbuild /únbíld/ *v.tr.* (*past* and *past part.* **unbuilt**) **1** demolish or destroy (a building, theory, system, etc.). **2** (as **unbuilt** *adj.*) not yet built or (of land etc.) not yet built on.

unburden /únbúrd'n/ *v.tr.* **1** relieve of a burden. **2** (esp. *refl.*; often foll. by *to*) relieve (oneself, one's conscience, etc.) by confession etc. ▫▫ **unburdened** *adj.*

■ **1** (*unburden of*) see RELIEVE 6.

unburied /únbérrid/ *adj.* not buried.

unbury /únbérri/ *v.tr.* (**-ies, -ied**) **1** remove from the ground etc. after burial. **2** unearth (a secret etc.).

unbusinesslike /únbízníslīk/ *adj.* not businesslike.

unbutton /únbútt'n/ *v.tr.* **1 a** unfasten (a coat etc.) by taking the buttons out of the buttonholes. **b** unbutton the clothes of (a person). **2** (*absol.*) *colloq.* relax from tension or formality, become communicative. **3** (as **unbuttoned** *adj.*) **a** not buttoned. **b** *colloq.* communicative; informal.

■ **3 b** (**unbuttoned**) see INFORMAL.

uncage /únkáyj/ *v.tr.* **1** release from a cage. **2** release from constraint; liberate.

uncalled /únkáwld/ *adj.* not summoned or invited. ▫ **uncalled-for** (of an opinion, action, etc.) impertinent or unnecessary (*an uncalled-for remark*).

■ ▫ **uncalled-for** see UNWARRANTED 2.

uncandid /únkándid/ *adj.* not candid; disingenuous.

uncanny /únkánni/ *adj.* (**uncannier, uncanniest**) seemingly supernatural; mysterious. ▫▫ **uncannily** *adv.* **uncanniness** *n.* [(orig. Sc. & N.Engl.) f. UN-[1] + CANNY]

■ see EERIE.

uncanonical /únkənónnik'l/ *adj.* not canonical. ▫▫ **uncanonically** *adv.*

uncap /únkáp/ *v.tr.* (**uncapped, uncapping**) **1** remove the cap from (a jar, bottle, etc.). **2** remove a cap from (the head or another person).

uncared-for /únkáirdfor/ *adj.* disregarded; neglected.

uncaring /unkáiring/ *adj.* lacking compassion or concern for others.

uncase /únkáyss/ *v.tr.* remove from a cover or case.

uncashed /únkásht/ *adj.* not cashed.

uncaught /únkáwt/ *adj.* not caught.

unceasing /únséessing/ *adj.* not ceasing; continuous (*unceasing effort*). ▫▫ **unceasingly** *adv.*

■ see CONTINUOUS. ▫▫ **unceasingly** see NON-STOP *adv.*

uncensored /únsénsərd/ *adj.* not censored.

■ see ENTIRE *adj.* 1.

uncensured /únsénsyərd/ *adj.* not censured.

unceremonious /únserrimṓniəss/ *adj.* **1** lacking ceremony or formality. **2** abrupt; discourteous. ▫▫ **unceremoniously** *adv.* **unceremoniousness** *n.*

■ **1** see INFORMAL. **2** see CURT.

uncertain /únsért'n/ *adj.* **1** not certainly knowing or known (*uncertain what it means; the result is uncertain*). **2** unreliable (*his aim is uncertain*). **3** changeable, erratic (*uncertain weather*). ▫ **in no uncertain terms** clearly and forcefully. ▫▫ **uncertainly** *adv.*

■ **1** unsure, in two minds, vacillating, wavering, undecided, unclear, ambivalent, irresolute, indecisive, hesitant, hesitating, undetermined, shilly-shallying; indeterminate, (up) in the air, indefinite, unpredictable, undeterminable, indeterminable, unforeseeable, unascertainable, unascertained, unresolved, unsettled, in the balance, conjectural, unconjecturable, speculative, debatable, arguable, touch-and-go, unreliable, doubtful, dubious, questionable, vague, hazy, obscure, ambiguous, equivocal. **2** unreliable, unsure, unpredictable, haphazard, chance, arbitrary, random, aleatory, hit-or-miss, casual. **3** variable, changeable, inconstant, unfixed, unsettled, irregular, fickle, erratic, fitful, unsteady, wavering, unreliable, sporadic, occasional; unmethodical, unsystematic.

uncertainty /únsért'nti/ *n.* (*pl.* **-ies**) **1** the fact or condition of being uncertain. **2** an uncertain matter or circumstance. □ **uncertainty principle** (in full **Heisenberg uncertainty principle** after W. Heisenberg, Ger. physicist d. 1976) *Physics* the principle that the momentum and position of a particle cannot both be precisely determined at the same time.

■ **1** see DOUBT *n.* 1, AMBIGUITY 1a. **2** see QUESTION *n.* 4.

uncertified /únsértifīd/ *adj.* **1** not attested as certain. **2** not guaranteed by a certificate of competence etc. **3** not certified as insane.

unchain /únchāyn/ *v.tr.* **1** remove the chains from. **2** release; liberate.

■ **2** see RELEASE *v.* 1.

unchallengeable /únchállinjəb'l/ *adj.* not challengeable; unassailable. □□ **unchallengeably** *adv.*

■ see INALIENABLE.

unchallenged /únchállinjd/ *adj.* not challenged.

■ see UNDISPUTED.

unchangeable /únchāynjəb'l/ *adj.* not changeable; immutable, invariable. □□ **unchangeability** /-bílliti/ *n.* **unchangeableness** *n.* **unchangeably** *adv.*

■ see INVARIABLE 1.

unchanged /únchāynjd/ *adj.* not changed; unaltered.

■ see SAME *adj.* 2.

unchanging /únchāynjing/ *adj.* not changing; remaining the same. □□ **unchangingly** *adv.* **unchangingness** *n.*

■ see ABIDING.

unchaperoned /únsháppərōnd/ *adj.* without a chaperon.

■ see UNACCOMPANIED 1.

uncharacteristic /únkariktərístik/ *adj.* not characteristic. □□ **uncharacteristically** *adv.*

■ see UNNATURAL 1; (*uncharacteristic of*) see UNLIKE *adj.* 2.

uncharged /únchaárjd/ *adj.* not charged (esp. in senses 3, 7, 8 of CHARGE *v.*).

uncharitable /únchárritəb'l/ *adj.* censorious, severe in judgement. □□ **uncharitableness** *n.* **uncharitably** *adv.*

■ see UNKIND.

uncharted /únchaártid/ *adj.* not charted, mapped, or surveyed.

■ unmapped, unknown, unexplored, undiscovered, unfamiliar, strange, virgin, trackless.

unchartered /únchaártərd/ *adj.* **1** not furnished with a charter; not formally privileged or constituted. **2** unauthorized; illegal.

unchaste /únchāyst/ *adj.* not chaste. □□ **unchastely** *adv.* **unchasteness** *n.* **unchastity** /-chástiti/ *n.*

■ impure, wanton, immoral, unvirtuous, promiscuous, loose, dissolute, immodest, indecent, unclean, obscene, licentious, libertine, debased, lecherous, lewd, lascivious. □□ **unchastity** see IMPURITY 1.

unchecked /únchékt/ *adj.* **1** not checked. **2** freely allowed; unrestrained (*unchecked violence*).

■ see UNCONTROLLED, UNINHIBITED, UNIMPEDED.

unchivalrous /únshívvəlrəss/ *adj.* not chivalrous; rude. □□ **unchivalrously** *adv.*

unchosen /únchṓz'n/ *adj.* not chosen.

unchristian /únkrístyən/ *adj.* **1 a** contrary to Christian principles, esp. uncaring or selfish. **b** not Christian. **2** *colloq.* outrageous. □□ **unchristianly** *adv.*

■ **1 a** see UNKIND.

unchurch /únchúrch/ *v.tr.* **1** excommunicate. **2** deprive (a building) of its status as a church.

uncial /únsiəl, únsh'l/ *adj.* & *n.* ● *adj.* **1** of or written in majuscule writing with rounded unjoined letters found in manuscripts of the 4th–8th c., from which modern capitals are derived. **2** of or relating to an inch or an ounce. ● *n.* **1** an uncial letter. **2** an uncial style or MS. [L *uncialis* f. *uncia* inch: sense 1 in LL sense of *unciales litterae*, the orig. application of which is unclear]

unciform /únsiform/ *n.* = UNCINATE.

uncinate /únsinət/ *adj.* esp. *Anat.* hooked; crooked. [L *uncinatus* f. *uncinus* hook]

uncircumcised /únsúrkəmsīzd/ *adj.* **1** not circumcised. **2** spiritually impure; heathen. □□ **uncircumcision** /-sízh'n/ *n.*

uncivil /únsívvil/ *adj.* **1** ill-mannered; impolite. **2** not public-spirited. □□ **uncivilly** *adv.*

■ **1** see IMPOLITE.

uncivilized /únsívvilīzd/ *adj.* (also **uncivilised**) **1** not civilized. **2** rough; uncultured.

■ **1** barbarous, savage, wild, uncultivated, barbarian, barbaric, crude, primitive, brutish. **2** unrefined, uncultured, uncouth, loutish, coarse, uneducated, untutored, unpolished, churlish, boorish, philistine, provincial, rough, rude, unlearned, ill-mannered, unmannerly, unsophisticated, inelegant, gross, gauche.

unclad /únklád/ *adj.* not clad; naked.

■ see NAKED 1.

unclaimed /únkláymd/ *adj.* not claimed.

unclasp /únklaásp/ *v.tr.* **1** loosen the clasp or clasps of. **2** release the grip of (a hand etc.).

unclassifiable /únklássifīəb'l/ *adj.* not classifiable.

unclassified /únklássifīd/ *adj.* **1** not classified. **2** (of State information) not secret.

uncle /úngk'l/ *n.* **1 a** the brother of one's father or mother. **b** an aunt's husband. **2** *colloq.* a name given by children to a male family friend. **3** *sl.* esp. *hist.* a pawnbroker. □ **Uncle Sam** *colloq.* the federal government or citizens of the US (*will fight for Uncle Sam*). **Uncle Tom** *derog.* a Black man considered to be servile, cringing, etc. (from the hero of H. B. Stowe's *Uncle Tom's Cabin*, 1852). [ME f. AF *uncle*, OF *oncle* f. LL *aunculus* f. L *avunculus* maternal uncle: see AVUNCULAR]

-uncle /ungk'l/ *suffix* forming nouns, usu. diminutives (*carbuncle*). [OF *-uncle*, *-oncle* or L *-unculus*, *-la*, a special form of *-ulus* -ULE]

unclean /únkleén/ *adj.* **1** not clean. **2** unchaste. **3** unfit to be eaten; ceremonially impure. **4** *Bibl.* (of a spirit) wicked. □□ **uncleanly** *adv.* **uncleanly** /-klénli/ *adj.* **uncleanliness** /-klénliniss/ *n.* **uncleanness** *n.* [OE *unclǣne* (as UN-[1], CLEAN)]

■ **1** see DIRTY *adj.* 1. **2** see UNCHASTE. **3** profane, impure, adulterated, not kosher. □□ **uncleanness** see IMPURITY 1.

unclear /únkleér/ *adj.* **1** not clear or easy to understand; obscure, uncertain. **2** (of a person) doubtful, uncertain (*I'm unclear as to what you mean*). □□ **unclearly** *adv.* **unclearness** *n.*

■ **1** see OBSCURE *adj.* 1, 2, 4. **2** see UNCERTAIN 1.

unclench /únklénch/ *v.* **1** *tr.* release (clenched hands, features, teeth, etc.). **2** *intr.* (of clenched hands etc.) become relaxed or open.

unclinch /únklínch/ *v.tr.* & *intr.* release or become released from a clinch.

uncloak /únklṓk/ *v.tr.* **1** expose, reveal. **2** remove a cloak from.

unclog /únklóg/ *v.tr.* (**unclogged, unclogging**) unblock (a drain, pipe, etc.).

unclose /únklṓz/ *v.* **1** *tr.* & *intr.* open. **2** *tr.* reveal; disclose.

unclothe /únklṓth/ *v.tr.* **1** remove the clothes from. **2** strip of leaves or vegetation (*trees unclothed by the wind*). **3** expose, reveal. □□ **unclothed** *adj.*

■ **1** see STRIP[1] *v.* 1. □□ **unclothed** see NAKED 1.

unclouded /únklówdid/ *adj.* **1** not clouded; clear; bright. **2** untroubled (*unclouded serenity*).

■ **1** see CLEAR *adj.* 2, 3, 6c. **2** see SERENE *adj.*

uncluttered /únklúttərd/ *adj.* not cluttered; austere, simple.

■ see SIMPLE *adj.* 2, NEAT[1] 1.

unco /úngkō/ *adj.*, *adv.*, & *n.* *Sc.* ● *adj.* strange, unusual; notable. ● *adv.* remarkably; very. ● *n.* (*pl.* **-os**) **1** a stranger.

2 (in *pl.*) news. □ **the unco guid** /gid/ esp. *derog.* the rigidly religious. [ME, var. of UNCOUTH]

uncoil /únkóyl/ *v.tr.* & *intr.* unwind.

■ see *roll out*.

uncoloured /únkúllərd/ *adj.* (*US* **uncolored**) **1** having no colour. **2** not influenced; impartial. **3** not exaggerated.

■ **2** see OBJECTIVE *adj.* 2.

uncombed /únkṓmd/ *adj.* (of hair or a person) not combed.

■ see UNKEMPT 2.

uncome-at-able /únkumáttəb'l/ *adj. colloq.* inaccessible; unattainable. [UN-[1] + *come-at-able*: see COME]

■ unget-at-able; see also INACCESSIBLE 1.

uncomely /únkúmli/ *adj.* **1** improper; unseemly. **2** ugly.

uncomfortable /únkúmftəb'l/ *adj.* **1** not comfortable. **2** uneasy; causing or feeling disquiet (*an uncomfortable silence*). □□ **uncomfortableness** *n.* **uncomfortably** *adv.*

■ **1** see *cramped* (CRAMP), ROCKY *adj.* 1, 2, OPPRESSIVE 3. **2** see AWKWARD 3, 4.

uncommercial /únkəmérsh'l/ *adj.* **1** not commercial. **2** contrary to commercial principles.

uncommitted /únkəmíttid/ *adj.* **1** not committed. **2** unattached to any specific political cause or group.

■ see NEUTRAL *adj.* 1, 2, NON-ALIGNED.

uncommon /únkómmən/ *adj.* & *adv.* ● *adj.* **1** not common; unusual; remarkable. **2** remarkably great etc. (*an uncommon fear of spiders*). ● *adv. archaic* uncommonly (*he was uncommon fat*). □□ **uncommonly** *adv.* **uncommonness** /-mən-niss/ *n.*

■ *adj.* **1** see UNUSUAL. **2** see EXTREME *adj.* 1. □□ **uncommonly** see ESPECIALLY. **uncommonness** see RARITY 1, SINGULARITY 1.

uncommunicative /únkəmyóonikətiv/ *adj.* not wanting to communicate; taciturn. □□ **uncommunicatively** *adv.* **uncommunicativeness** *n.*

■ see TACITURN. □□ **uncommunicativeness** see SILENCE *n.* 2, 3.

uncompanionable /únkəmpányənəb'l/ *adj.* unsociable.

uncompensated /únkómpensaytid/ *adj.* not compensated.

uncompetitive /únkəmpéttitiv/ *adj.* not competitive.

uncomplaining /únkəmpláyning/ *adj.* not complaining; resigned. □□ **uncomplainingly** *adv.*

■ see SUBMISSIVE.

uncompleted /únkəmpléetid/ *adj.* not completed; incomplete.

■ see INCOMPLETE.

uncomplicated /únkómplikaytid/ *adj.* not complicated; simple; straightforward.

■ see SIMPLE *adj.* 1, 2.

uncomplimentary /únkompliméntəri/ *adj.* not complimentary; insulting.

■ see DEROGATORY.

uncompounded /únkəmpówndid/ *adj.* not compounded; unmixed.

uncomprehending /únkomprihénding/ *adj.* not comprehending. □□ **uncomprehendingly** *adv.* **uncomprehension** /-hénsh'n/ *n.*

■ see VACANT 2, *confused* (CONFUSE 4).

uncompromising /únkómprəmīzing/ *adj.* unwilling to compromise; stubborn; unyielding. □□ **uncompromisingly** *adv.* **uncompromisingness** *n.*

■ see RESOLUTE. □□ **uncompromisingly** see DOWNRIGHT *adv.*

unconcealed /únkənséeld/ *adj.* not concealed; obvious.

■ see OBVIOUS.

unconcern /únkənsérn/ *n.* lack of concern; indifference; apathy. □□ **unconcerned** *adj.* **unconcernedly** /-nidli/ *adv.*

■ see INDIFFERENCE 1, 2. □□ **unconcerned** see INDIFFERENT 4.

unconcluded /únkənklóodid/ *adj.* not concluded.

unconditional /únkəndíshən'l/ *adj.* not subject to conditions; complete (*unconditional surrender*). □□ **unconditionality** /-nálliti/ *n.* **unconditionally** *adv.*

■ see UNQUALIFIED 3, FULL[1] *adj.* 6.

unconditioned /únkəndísh'nd/ *adj.* **1** not subject to conditions or to an antecedent condition. **2** (of behaviour etc.) not determined by conditioning; natural. □ **unconditioned reflex** an instinctive response to a stimulus.

unconfined /únkənfínd/ *adj.* not confined; boundless.

■ see FREE *adj.* 3, LIMITLESS.

unconfirmed /únkənfúrmd/ *adj.* not confirmed.

■ see UNOFFICIAL 1.

unconformable /únkənfórməb'l/ *adj.* **1** not conformable or conforming. **2** (of rock strata) not having the same direction of stratification. **3** *hist.* not conforming to the provisions of the Act of Uniformity. □□ **unconformableness** *n.* **unconformably** *adv.* **unconformity** *n.*

uncongenial /únkənjéeniəl/ *adj.* not congenial.

■ see UNSOCIAL.

unconjecturable /únkənjékchərəb'l/ *adj.* not conjecturable.

■ see UNCERTAIN 1.

unconnected /únkənéktid/ *adj.* **1** not physically joined. **2** not connected or associated. **3** (of speech etc.) disconnected; not joined in order or sequence (*unconnected ideas*). **4** not related by family ties. □□ **unconnectedly** *adv.* **unconnectedness** *n.*

■ **1** see LOOSE *adj.* 2. **2** see UNRELATED, EXTRANEOUS 2b. **3** see DISCONNECTED 2.

unconquerable /únkóngkərəb'l/ *adj.* not conquerable. □□ **unconquerableness** *n.* **unconquerably** *adv.*

■ see IMPREGNABLE.

unconquered /únkóngkərd/ *adj.* not conquered or defeated.

unconscionable /únkónshənəb'l/ *adj.* **1 a** having no conscience. **b** contrary to conscience. **2 a** unreasonably excessive (*an unconscionable length of time*). **b** not right or reasonable. □□ **unconscionableness** *n.* **unconscionably** *adv.* [UN-[1] + obs. *conscionable* f. *conscions* obs. var. of CONSCIENCE]

■ **1** conscienceless, unscrupulous, amoral, unprincipled, immoral, unethical, evil, criminal, unjust, wicked, arrant. **2** excessive, extortionate, egregious, extreme, unwarranted, unreasonable, outrageous, inordinate, immoderate, exorbitant, indefensible, unpardonable, inexcusable, unforgivable.

unconscious /únkónshəss/ *adj.* & *n.* ● *adj.* not conscious (*unconscious of any change*; *fell unconscious on the floor*; *an unconscious prejudice*). ● *n.* that part of the mind which is inaccessible to the conscious mind but which affects behaviour, emotions, etc. (cf. *collective unconscious*). □□ **unconsciously** *adv.* **unconsciousness** *n.*

■ *adj.* insensible, knocked out, senseless, numb, stunned, comatose, blacked-out, *colloq.* out (cold), dead to the world; heedless, unheeding, unheedful, insensitive, mindless, unmindful, reflex, automatic, involuntary, mechanical, unintentional, instinctive, subliminal, unthinking, unpremeditated, subconscious, unwitting; blind, unaware, oblivious, deaf. ● *n.* see SUBCONSCIOUS *n.* □□ **unconsciously** see UNAWARES 2. **unconsciousness** see FAINT *n.*, STUPOR.

unconsecrated /únkónsikraytid/ *adj.* not consecrated.

unconsenting /únkənsénting/ *adj.* not consenting.

unconsidered /únkənsíddərd/ *adj.* **1** not considered; disregarded. **2** (of a response etc.) immediate; not premeditated.

■ **1** ignored, overlooked, disregarded. **2** see IMPULSIVE, UNTHINKING 1.

unconsolable /únkənsṓləb'l/ *adj.* unable to be consoled; inconsolable. □□ **unconsolably** *adv.*

■ see INCONSOLABLE.

unconstitutional /únkonstityóoshən'l/ *adj.* not in accordance with the political constitution or with procedural rules. □□ **unconstitutionality** /-nálliti/ *n.* **unconstitutionally** *adv.*

unconstrained /únkənstráynd/ *adj.* not constrained or compelled. □□ **unconstrainedly** /-nidli/ *adv.*

■ see FREE *adj.* 3, 6, NATURAL *adj.* 4. □□ **unconstrainedly** see *freely* (FREE).

unconstraint /únkənstráynt/ *n.* freedom from constraint.

■ see FREEDOM 5.
unconstricted /únkənstríktid/ *adj.* not constricted.
unconsumed /únkənsyóomd/ *adj.* not consumed.
■ left over, left, remaining, uneaten.
unconsummated /únkónsyoomaytid/ *adj.* not consummated.
uncontainable /únkəntáynəb'l/ *adj.* not containable.
■ see IRREPRESSIBLE.
uncontaminated /únkəntámminaytid/ *adj.* not contaminated.
■ see CLEAN *adj.* 1.
uncontested /únkəntéstid/ *adj.* not contested. □□ **uncontestedly** *adv.*
■ see UNDISPUTED.
uncontradicted /únkontrədíktid/ *adj.* not contradicted.
uncontrollable /únkəntrṓləb'l/ *adj.* not controllable. □□ **uncontrollableness** *n.* **uncontrollably** *adv.*
■ see INVOLUNTARY, IRREPRESSIBLE, UNRULY.
uncontrolled /únkəntrṓld/ *adj.* not controlled; unrestrained, unchecked.
■ unrestrained, ungoverned, unchecked, untrammelled, undisciplined, wild, unruly, boisterous, riotous, out of hand *or* control, rampant, frenzied, frantic; (going) berserk, running amok.
uncontroversial /únkontrəvérsh'l/ *adj.* not controversial. □□ **uncontroversially** *adv.*
uncontroverted /únkontrəvértid/ *adj.* not controverted. □□ **uncontrovertible** *adj.*
unconventional /únkənvénshən'l/ *adj.* not bound by convention or custom; unusual; unorthodox. □□ **unconventionalism** *n.* **unconventionality** /-nálliti/ *n.* **unconventionally** *adv.*
■ see UNORTHODOX.
unconverted /únkənvértid/ *adj.* not converted.
unconvinced /únkənvínst/ *adj.* not convinced.
■ see DOUBTFUL 1.
unconvincing /únkənvínsing/ *adj.* not convincing. □□ **unconvincingly** *adv.*
■ see *far-fetched*, WEAK 4.
uncooked /únkŏŏkt/ *adj.* not cooked; raw.
■ fresh, raw.
uncool /únkŏŏl/ *adj. sl.* **1** unrelaxed; unpleasant. **2** (of jazz) not cool.
uncooperative /únkō-óppərətiv/ *adj.* not cooperative. □□ **uncooperatively** *adv.*
■ see *resistant* (RESIST).
uncoordinated /únkō-órdinaytid/ *adj.* **1** not coordinated. **2** (of a person's movements etc.) clumsy.
■ **1** see INDISCRIMINATE 2. **2** see CLUMSY 1.
uncopiable /únkóppiəb'l/ *adj.* not able to be copied.
uncord /únkórd/ *v.tr.* remove the cord from.
uncordial /únkórdiəl/ *adj.* not congenial; unfriendly.
uncork /únkórk/ *v.tr.* **1** draw the cork from (a bottle). **2** allow (feelings etc.) to be vented.
uncorroborated /únkəróbbəraytid/ *adj.* (esp. of evidence etc.) not corroborated.
■ see *ill-founded*.
uncorrupted /únkərúptid/ *adj.* not corrupted.
■ see HONOURABLE 1a–c, INNOCENT *adj.* 1.
uncountable /únkówntəb'l/ *adj.* **1** inestimable, immense (*uncountable wealth*). **2** *Gram.* (of a noun) that cannot form a plural or be used with the indefinite article (e.g. *happiness*). □□ **uncountability** /-bílliti/ *n.* **uncountably** *adv.*
■ **1** see IMMEASURABLE.
uncounted /únkówntid/ *adj.* **1** not counted. **2** very many; innumerable.
■ **2** see NUMBERLESS.
uncouple /únkúpp'l/ *v.tr.* **1** release (wagons) from couplings. **2** release (dogs etc.) from couples. □□ **uncoupled** *adj.*
uncourtly /únkórtli/ *adj.* not courteous; ill-mannered.
uncouth /únkŏŏth/ *adj.* **1** (of a person, manners, appearance, etc.) lacking in ease and polish; uncultured, rough (*uncouth voices; behaviour was uncouth*). **2** *archaic* not known; desolate; wild; uncivilized (*an uncouth place*). □□ **uncouthly** *adv.* **uncouthness** *n.* [OE *uncūth* unknown (as UN-[1] + *cūth* past part. of *cunnan* know, CAN[1])]
■ **1** see ROUGH *adj.* 4a.
uncovenanted /únkúvvənəntid/ *adj.* **1** not bound by a covenant. **2** not promised by or based on a covenant, esp. God's covenant.
uncover /únkúvvər/ *v.* **1** *tr.* **a** remove a cover or covering from. **b** make known; disclose (*uncovered the truth at last*). **2** *intr. archaic* remove one's hat, cap, etc. **3** *tr.* (as **uncovered** *adj.*) **a** not covered by a roof, clothing, etc. **b** not wearing a hat.
■ **1 a** see BARE *v.* 1. **b** see BARE *v.* 2, DISCOVER 1a, b. **3 a** (**uncovered**) see BARE *adj.* 1, VULNERABLE 1.
uncreate /únkriáyt/ *v.tr. literary* annihilate.
uncreated /únkriáytid/ *adj.* existing without having been created; not created. [UN-[1] + obs. *create* f. L *creatus* past part. of *creare*: see CREATE]
uncreative /únkriáytiv/ *adj.* not creative.
uncritical /únkríttik'l/ *adj.* **1** not critical; complacently accepting. **2** not in accordance with the principles of criticism. □□ **uncritically** *adv.*
■ **1** see INDISCRIMINATE 1, PASSIVE 2.
uncropped /únkrópt/ *adj.* not cropped.
uncross /únkróss/ *v.tr.* **1** remove (the limbs, knives, etc.) from a crossed position. **2** (as **uncrossed** *adj.*) **a** *Brit.* (of a cheque) not crossed. **b** not thwarted or challenged. **c** not wearing a cross.
uncrown /únkrówn/ *v.tr.* **1** deprive (a monarch etc.) of a crown. **2** deprive (a person) of a position. **3** (as **uncrowned** *adj.*) **a** not crowned. **b** having the status but not the name of (*the uncrowned king of boxing*).
uncrushable /únkrúshəb'l/ *adj.* not crushable.
uncrushed /únkrúsht/ *adj.* not crushed.
UNCSTD *abbr.* United Nations Conference on Science and Technology for Development.
UNCTAD *abbr.* United Nations Conference on Trade and Development.
unction /úngksh'n/ *n.* **1 a** the act of anointing with oil etc. as a religious rite. **b** the oil etc. so used. **2 a** soothing words or thought. **b** excessive or insincere flattery. **3 a** the act of anointing for medical purposes. **b** an ointment so used. **4 a** a fervent or sympathetic quality in words or tone caused by or causing deep emotion. **b** a pretence of this. [ME f. L *unctio* f. *ung(u)ere unct-* anoint]
unctuous /úngktyooəss/ *adj.* **1** (of behaviour, speech, etc.) unpleasantly flattering; oily. **2** (esp. of minerals) having a greasy or soapy feel; oily. □□ **unctuously** *adv.* **unctuousness** *n.* [ME f. med.L *unctuosus* f. L *unctus* anointing (as UNCTION)]
■ **1** see OILY 3. **2** see OILY 1, 2. □□ **unctuousness** see *servility* (SERVILE).
unculled /únkúld/ *adj.* not culled.
uncultivated /únkúltivaytid/ *adj.* (esp. of land) not cultivated.
■ see WILD *adj.* 3.
uncultured /únkúlchərd/ *adj.* **1** not cultured, unrefined. **2** (of soil or plants) not cultivated.
■ **1** see UNREFINED.
uncurb /únkúrb/ *v.tr.* remove a curb or curbs from. □□ **uncurbed** *adj.*
■ □□ **uncurbed** see UNINHIBITED, LAVISH 3.
uncured /únkyóord/ *adj.* **1** not cured. **2** (of pork etc.) not salted or smoked.
uncurl /únkúrl/ *v.intr.* & *tr.* relax from a curled position, untwist.
■ see *roll out*.
uncurtailed /únkərtáyld/ *adj.* not curtailed.
uncurtained /únkúrt'nd/ *adj.* not curtained.
uncut /únkút/ *adj.* **1** not cut. **2** (of a book) with the pages not cut open or with untrimmed margins. **3** (of a book,

film, etc.) complete; uncensored. **4** (of a stone, esp. a diamond) not shaped by cutting. **5** (of fabric) having its pile-loops intact (*uncut moquette*).
■ **1** see INTACT 1. **3** see ENTIRE *adj*. 1.

undamaged /úndámmijd/ *adj*. not damaged; intact.
■ see INTACT 2.

undated /úndáytid/ *adj*. not provided or marked with a date.

undaunted /úndáwntid/ *adj*. not daunted. □□ **undauntedly** *adv*. **undauntedness** *n*.
■ see INDOMITABLE 2.

undecagon /undékkəgən/ *n*. = HENDECAGON. [L *undecim* eleven, after *decagon*]

undeceive /úndiseév/ *v.tr*. (often foll. by *of*) free (a person) from a misconception, deception, or error.

undecided /úndisīdid/ *adj*. **1** not settled or certain (*the question is undecided*). **2** hesitating; irresolute (*undecided about their relative merits*). □□ **undecidedly** *adv*.
■ **1** see UNRESOLVED 2. **2** see IRRESOLUTE 1.

undecipherable /úndisīfərəb'l/ *adj*. not decipherable.
■ see ILLEGIBLE, INCOMPREHENSIBLE.

undeclared /úndikláird/ *adj*. not declared.
■ see TACIT, *sneaking* (SNEAK *v*. 4a).

undefeated /úndifeétid/ *adj*. not defeated.
■ see TRIUMPHANT 1, INVINCIBLE.

undefended /úndiféndid/ *adj*. (esp. of a lawsuit) not defended.

undefiled /úndifīld/ *adj*. not defiled; pure.
■ see PURE 3, 4.

undefined /úndifīnd/ *adj*. **1** not defined. **2** not clearly marked; vague, indefinite. □□ **undefinable** *adj*. **undefinably** *adv*.
■ see INDEFINITE 1.

undelivered /úndilívvərd/ *adj*. **1** not delivered or handed over. **2** not set free or released. **3 a** (of a pregnant woman) not yet having given birth. **b** (of a child) not yet born.

undemanding /úndimaánding/ *adj*. not demanding; easily satisfied. □□ **undemandingness** *n*.
■ see EASY *adj*. 1, 3.

undemocratic /úndeməkráttik/ *adj*. not democratic. □□ **undemocratically** *adv*.
■ see TOTALITARIAN *adj*.

undemonstrated /úndémmənstraytid/ *adj*. not demonstrated.

undemonstrative /úndimónstrətiv/ *adj*. not expressing feelings etc. outwardly; reserved. □□ **undemonstratively** *adv*. **undemonstrativeness** *n*.
■ see RESERVED.

undeniable /úndinīəb'l/ *adj*. **1** unable to be denied or disputed; certain. **2** excellent (*was of undeniable character*). □□ **undeniableness** *n*. **undeniably** *adv*.
■ **1** see CERTAIN *adj*. 1b. □□ **undeniably** see *undoubtedly* (UNDOUBTED).

undenied /úndinīd/ *adj*. not denied.

undependable /úndipéndəb'l/ *adj*. not to be depended upon; unreliable.
■ see UNRELIABLE.

under /úndər/ *prep*., *adv*., & *adj*. ● *prep*. **1 a** in or to a position lower than; below; beneath (*fell under the table*; *under the left eye*). **b** within, on the inside of (a surface etc.) (*wore a vest under his shirt*). **2 a** inferior to; less than (*a captain is under a major*; *is under 18*). **b** at or for a lower cost than (*was under £20*). **3 a** subject or liable to; controlled or bound by (*lives under oppression*; *under pain of death*; *born under Saturn*; *the country prospered under him*). **b** undergoing (*is under repair*). **c** classified or subsumed in (*that book goes under biology*; *goes under many names*). **4** at the foot of or sheltered by (*hid under the wall*; *under the cliff*). **5** planted with (a crop). **6** powered by (sail, steam, etc.). **7** following (another player in a card game). **8** *archaic* attested by (esp. *under one's hand and seal* = signature). ● *adv*. **1** in or to a lower position or condition (*kept him under*). **2** *colloq*. in or into a state of unconsciousness (*put him under for the operation*). ● *adj*. lower (*the under jaw*). □ **under age** see AGE. **under one's arm** see ARM[1]. **under arms** see ARM[2]. **under one's belt** see BELT. **under one's breath** see BREATH. **under canvas** see CANVAS. **under a cloud** see CLOUD. **under control** see CONTROL. **under the counter** see COUNTER[1]. **under cover** see COVER *n*. 4. **under fire** see FIRE. **under foot** see FOOT. **under hatches** see HATCH[1]. **under a person's nose** see NOSE. **under the rose** see ROSE[1]. **under separate cover** in another envelope. **under the sun** anywhere in the world. **under water** in and covered by water. **under way** in motion; in progress. **under the weather** see WEATHER. □□ **undermost** *adj*. [OE f. Gmc]
■ *prep*. **1 a** beneath, below, underneath. **b** inside, within, covered by, beneath, underneath. **2 a** inferior to, second to, secondary to, subservient to, below, beneath, underneath, junior to, subordinate to, answerable to; less than. **b** less than, lower than. **3 a** subject to, liable to, at the beck and call of, at the mercy of, under the control of, directed *or* supervised *or* controlled *or* bound by; under the aegis *or* protection *or* eye *or* guardianship *or* care of. **c** included in *or* under, comprised in *or* under, subsumed under. **4** at the foot of, under the lee of, sheltered by. ● *adv*. **1** below, underneath, beneath, down, out of sight; underwater. ● *adj*. lower, inferior, *archaic* nether. □ **under water** underwater, undersea, submerged, inundated, flooded, immersed, sunken. **under way** proceeding, progressing, on the move, in motion, moving, advancing, going, begun, started, in progress, in the pipeline, operating, functioning, at work, *US* in work; *colloq*. in the works.

under- /úndər/ *prefix* in senses of UNDER: **1** below, beneath (*undercarriage*; *underground*). **2** lower in status; subordinate (*under-secretary*). **3** insufficiently, incompletely (*undercook*; *underdeveloped*). [OE (as UNDER)]

underachieve /úndərəcheév/ *v.intr*. do less well than might be expected (esp. scholastically). □□ **underachievement** *n*. **underachiever** *n*.

underact /úndərákt/ *v*. **1** *tr*. act (a part etc.) with insufficient force. **2** *intr*. act a part in this way.

underarm /úndəraarm/ *adj*. & *adv*. **1** *Sport*, esp. *Cricket* with the arm below shoulder-level. **2** under the arm. **3** in the armpit.

underbelly /úndərbelli/ *n*. (*pl*. **-ies**) the under surface of an animal, vehicle, etc., esp. as an area vulnerable to attack.

underbid *v*. & *n*. ● *v.tr*. /úndərbíd/ (**-bidding**; *past* and *past part*. **-bid**) **1** make a lower bid than (a person). **2** (also *absol*.) *Bridge* etc. bid less on (one's hand) than its strength warrants. ● *n*. /úndərbid/ **1** such a bid. **2** the act or an instance of underbidding.

underbidder /úndərbiddər/ *n*. **1** the person who makes the bid next below the highest. **2** *Bridge* etc. a player who underbids.

underbody /úndərboddi/ *n*. (*pl*. **-ies**) the under surface of the body of an animal, vehicle, etc.

underbred /úndərbréd/ *adj*. **1** ill-bred, vulgar. **2** not of pure breeding.

underbrush /úndərbrush/ *n*. *US* undergrowth in a forest.

undercarriage /úndərkarrij/ *n*. **1** a wheeled structure beneath an aircraft, usu. retracted when not in use, to receive the impact on landing and support the aircraft on the ground etc. **2** the supporting frame of a vehicle.

undercart /úndərkaart/ *n*. *Brit*. *colloq*. the undercarriage of an aircraft.

undercharge /úndərchaárj/ *v.tr*. **1** charge too little for (a thing) or to (a person). **2** give less than the proper charge to (a gun, an electric battery, etc.).
■ **1** see UNDERCUT *v*. 1.

underclass /úndərklaass/ *n*. a subordinate social class.

underclay /úndərklay/ *n*. a clay bed under a coal seam.

undercliff /úndərklif/ *n*. a terrace or lower cliff formed by a landslip.

underclothes /úndərklōthz, -klōz/ *n.pl.* clothes worn under others, esp. next to the skin.
■ underclothing, underwear, undergarments, lingerie, underlinen, *US* skivvies, *colloq.* underthings, undies, *Brit. colloq.* smalls, *joc.* unmentionables.

underclothing /úndərklōthing/ *n.* underclothes collectively.

undercoat /úndərkōt/ *n.* **1 a** a preliminary layer of paint under the finishing coat. **b** the paint used for this. **2** an animal's under layer of hair or down. **3** a coat worn under another. □□ **undercoating** *n.*

undercover /úndərkúvvər/ *adj.* (usu. *attrib.*) **1** surreptitious. **2** engaged in spying, esp. by working with or among those to be observed (*undercover agent*).
■ secret, private, clandestine, surreptitious, covert, confidential, spying, underground, stealthy.

undercroft /úndərkroft/ *n.* a crypt. [ME f. UNDER- + *croft* crypt f. MDu. *crofte* cave f. med.L *crupta* for L *crypta*: see CRYPT]

undercurrent /úndərkurrənt/ *n.* **1** a current below the surface. **2** an underlying often contrary feeling, activity, or influence (*an undercurrent of protest*).
■ **1** undertow, cross-current, rip tide, rip (current), underflow, *Naut.* underset. **2** undertone, subcurrent, trend, tendency, overtone, tenor, suggestion, trace, hint, murmur, buzz, implication, connotation, sense, feeling, aura, tinge, flavour, atmosphere, ambience; vibrations, *colloq.* vibes.

undercut *v.* & *n.* ● *v.tr.* /úndərkút/ (**-cutting**; *past* and *past part.* **-cut**) **1** sell or work at a lower price or lower wages than. **2** *Golf* strike (a ball) so as to make it rise high. **3 a** cut away the part below or under (a thing). **b** cut away material to show (a carved design etc.) in relief. **4** render unstable or less firm, undermine. ● *n.* /úndərkut/ **1** *Brit.* the underside of a sirloin. **2** *US* a notch cut in a tree-trunk to guide its fall when felled. **3** any space formed by the removal or absence of material from the lower part of something.
■ *v.* **1** underprice, undercharge, sell cheaply *or* at a loss, undersell. **3** undermine, excavate, hollow out, cut out *or* away, gouge out. **4** undermine, destabilize, weaken, debilitate, sabotage, subvert, impair, disable, damage.

underdeveloped /úndərdivélləpt/ *adj.* **1** not fully developed; immature. **2** (of a country etc.) below its potential economic level. **3** *Photog.* not developed sufficiently to give a normal image. □□ **underdevelopment** *n.*
■ **1** see IMMATURE 1, 3.

underdog /úndərdog/ *n.* **1** a dog, or usu. a person, losing a fight. **2** a person who is in a state of inferiority or subjection.
■ loser, scapegoat, victim; little fellow *or* guy, *sl.* fall guy.

underdone /úndərdún/ *adj.* **1** not thoroughly done. **2** (of food) lightly or insufficiently cooked.

underdress /úndərdréss/ *v.tr.* & *intr.* dress with too little formality or too lightly.

underemphasis /úndərémfəsiss/ *n.* (*pl.* **-emphases** /-seez/) an insufficient degree of emphasis. □□ **underemphasize** *v.tr.* (also **-ise**).

underemployed /úndərimplóyd/ *adj.* not fully employed. □□ **underemployment** *n.*

underestimate *v.* & *n.* ● *v.tr.* /úndəréstimayt/ form too low an estimate of. ● *n.* /úndəréstimət/ an estimate that is too low. □□ **underestimation** /-máysh'n/ *n.*
■ *v.* undervalue, underrate, discount, misjudge, miscalculate, minimize, depreciate, belittle, trivialize, not do justice to, fail to appreciate, set (too) little store by, think (too) little of, *literary* misprize.

underexpose /úndərikspṓz/ *v.tr. Photog.* expose (film) for too short a time or with insufficient light. □□ **underexposure** *n.*

underfed /úndərféd/ *adj.* insufficiently fed.
■ see THIN *adj.* 4.

underfelt /úndərfelt/ *n.* felt for laying under a carpet.

underfloor /úndərflor/ *attrib.adj.* situated or operating beneath the floor (*underfloor heating*).

underflow /úndərflō/ *n.* an undercurrent.
■ see UNDERCURRENT 1.

underfoot /úndərfŏŏt/ *adv.* **1** under one's feet. **2** on the ground. **3** in a state of subjection. **4** so as to obstruct or inconvenience.

undergarment /úndərgaarmənt/ *n.* a piece of underclothing.

undergird /úndərgúrd/ *v.tr.* **1** make secure underneath. **2** strengthen, support.

underglaze /úndərglayz/ *adj.* & *n.* ● *adj.* **1** (of painting on porcelain etc.) done before the glaze is applied. **2** (of colours) used in such painting. ● *n.* underglaze painting.

undergo /úndərgṓ/ *v.tr.* (*3rd sing. present* **-goes**; *past* **-went**; *past part.* **-gone**) be subjected to; suffer; endure. [OE *undergān* (as UNDER-, GO[1])]
■ suffer, bear, endure, experience, live *or* go through, be subjected to, subject oneself to, sustain, submit to, weather, put up with, stand, withstand.

undergrad /úndərgrád/ *n. colloq.* = UNDERGRADUATE. [abbr.]

undergraduate /úndərgrádyooət/ *n.* a student at a university who has not yet taken a first degree.

underground *adv.*, *adj.*, *n.*, & *v.* ● *adv.* /úndərgrównd/ **1** beneath the surface of the ground. **2** in or into secrecy or hiding. ● *adj.* /úndərgrownd/ **1** situated underground. **2** secret, hidden, esp. working secretly to subvert a ruling power. **3** unconventional, experimental (*underground press*). ● *n.* /úndərgrownd/ **1** an underground railway. **2** a secret group or activity, esp. aiming to subvert the established order. ● *v.tr.* /úndərgrownd/ lay (cables) below ground level.
■ *adv.* **1** see BENEATH *adv.* ● *adj.* **1** subterranean, buried, below-ground, sunken, covered. **2** secret, clandestine, concealed, hidden, covert, undercover, surreptitious, stealthy, private. **3** alternative, radical, experimental, avant-garde, nonconformist, unconventional, revolutionary. ● *n.* **1** metro, underground railway, *colloq.* tube, *esp. US* subway. **2** resistance, partisans, freedom fighters, Maquis, insurgents, insurrectionists, guerrillas, irregulars, extremists, revolutionaries; fifth-columnists, fifth column, saboteurs, subversives.

undergrowth /úndərgrōth/ *n.* a dense growth of shrubs etc., esp. under large trees.

underhand *adj.* & *adv.* ● *adj.* /úndərhand/ **1** secret, clandestine, not above-board. **2** deceptive, crafty. **3** *Sport*, esp. *Cricket* underarm. ● *adv.* /úndərhánd/ in an underhand manner. [OE (as UNDER-, HAND)]
■ **1, 2** see FURTIVE 1, 2, DISHONEST.

underhanded /úndərhándid/ *adj.* & *adv.* = UNDERHAND.

underhung /úndərhúng/ *adj.* **1** (of the lower jaw) projecting beyond the upper jaw. **2** having an underhung jaw.

underlay[1] *v.* & *n.* ● *v.tr.* /úndərláy/ (*past* and *past part.* **-laid**) lay something under (a thing) to support or raise it. ● *n.* /úndərlay/ a thing laid under another, esp. material laid under a carpet or mattress as protection or support. [OE *underlecgan* (as UNDER-, LAY[1])]

underlay[2] *past* of UNDERLIE.

underlease *n.* /úndərleess/ *v.tr.* /úndərleéss/ = SUBLEASE.

underlet /úndərlét/ *v.tr.* (**-letting**; *past* and *past part.* **-let**) **1** sublet. **2** let at less than the true value.

underlie /úndərlī́/ *v.tr.* (**-lying**; *past* **-lay**; *past part.* **-lain**) **1** (also *absol.*) lie or be situated under (a stratum etc.). **2** (also *absol.*) (esp. as **underlying** *adj.*) (of a principle, reason, etc.) be the basis of (a doctrine, law, conduct, etc.). **3** exist beneath the superficial aspect of. [OE *underlicgan* (as UNDER-, LIE[1])]
■ **2** (**underlying**) see BASIC *adj.* 2.

underline *v.* & *n.* ● *v.tr.* /úndərlī́n/ **1** draw a line under (a word etc.) to give emphasis or draw attention or indicate italic or other special type. **2** emphasize, stress. ● *n.* /úndərlīn/ **1** a line drawn under a word etc. **2** a caption below an illustration.
■ **1** underscore. **2** see EMPHASIZE.

underlinen /úndərlinnin/ *n.* underclothes esp. of linen.
■ see UNDERCLOTHES.

underling /úndərling/ *n.* usu. *derog.* a subordinate.
■ see SUBORDINATE *n.*

underlying *pres. part.* of UNDERLIE.

undermanned /úndərmánd/ *adj.* having too few people as crew or staff.
■ short-staffed, short-handed, understaffed.

undermentioned /úndərménsh'nd/ *adj. Brit.* mentioned at a later place in a book etc.

undermine /úndərmī́n/ *v.tr.* **1** injure (a person, reputation, influence, etc.) by secret or insidious means. **2** weaken, injure, or wear out (health etc.) imperceptibly or insidiously. **3** wear away the base or foundation of (*rivers undermine their banks*). **4** make a mine or excavation under. □□ **underminer** *n.* **underminingly** *adv.* [ME f. UNDER- + MINE[2]]
■ **1, 2** sap, drain, disable, weaken, debilitate, emasculate, enfeeble, undercut, wear away, erode, threaten, sabotage, subvert, damage, injure, hurt, harm, impair, ruin, dash, destroy, wreck, spoil, *sl.* queer. **3** wear away, wash away, erode. **4** undercut, excavate, mine *or* dig *or* tunnel *or* burrow under, cut out *or* away, hollow *or* gouge out.

underneath /úndərnéeth/ *prep., adv., n., & adj.* ● *prep.* **1** at or to a lower place than, below. **2** on the inside of, within. ● *adv.* **1** at or to a lower place. **2** inside. ● *n.* the lower surface or part. ● *adj.* lower. [OE *underneothan* (as UNDER + *neothan*: cf. BENEATH)]
■ *prep.* **1** see BELOW *prep.* 1, 2. ● *adv.* **1** see BELOW *adv.* 2a.

undernourished /úndərnúrrisht/ *adj.* insufficiently nourished. □□ **undernourishment** *n.*
■ see THIN *adj.* 4.

underpaid *past* and *past part.* of UNDERPAY.

underpants /úndərpants/ *n.pl.* an undergarment, esp. men's, covering the lower part of the body and part of the legs.
■ see PANTS 1.

under-part /úndərpaart/ *n.* **1** a lower part, esp. of an animal. **2** a subordinate part in a play etc.

underpass /úndərpaass/ *n.* **1** a road etc. passing under another. **2** a crossing of this form.
■ subway, tunnel.

underpay /úndərpáy/ *v.tr.* (*past* and *past part.* **-paid**) pay too little to (a person) or for (a thing). □□ **underpayment** *n.*

underpin /úndərpín/ *v.tr.* (**-pinned, -pinning**) **1** support from below with masonry etc. **2** support, strengthen.
■ **2** see SUSTAIN 2.

underpinning /úndərpinning/ *n.* **1** a physical or metaphorical foundation. **2** the action or process of supporting from below.

underplant /úndərplaánt/ *v.tr.* (usu. foll. by *with*) plant or cultivate the ground about (a tall plant) with smaller ones.

underplay /úndərpláy/ *v.* **1** *tr.* play down the importance of. **2** *intr.* & *tr. Theatr.* **a** perform with deliberate restraint. **b** underact.
■ **1** see TRIVIALIZE.

underplot /úndərplot/ *n.* a subordinate plot in a play etc.

underpopulated /úndərpópyooláytid/ *adj.* having an insufficient or very small population.

underprice /úndərprī́ss/ *v.tr.* price lower than what is usual or appropriate.
■ see UNDERCUT *v.* 1.

underprivileged /úndərprívvilijd/ *adj.* **1** less privileged than others. **2** not enjoying the normal standard of living or rights in a society.
■ see *deprived* (DEPRIVE 2).

underproduction /úndərprədúksh'n/ *n.* production of less than is usual or required.

underproof /úndərpro͞of/ *adj.* containing less alcohol than proof spirit does.

underprop /úndərpróp/ *v.tr.* (**-propped, -propping**) **1** support with a prop. **2** support, sustain.

underquote /úndərkwṓt/ *v.tr.* **1** quote a lower price than (a person). **2** quote a lower price than others for (goods etc.).

underrate /úndəráyt/ *v.tr.* have too low an opinion of.
■ see UNDERESTIMATE *v.*

underscore *v.* & *n.* ● *v.tr.* /úndərskór/ = UNDERLINE *v.* ● *n.* /úndərskor/ = UNDERLINE *n.* 1.

undersea /úndərsee/ *adj.* below the sea or the surface of the sea, submarine.
■ see UNDERWATER *adj.*

underseal /úndərseel/ *v.* & *n.* ● *v.tr.* seal the under-part of (esp. a motor vehicle against rust etc.). ● *n.* a protective coating for this.

under-secretary /úndərsékrətəri/ *n.* (*pl.* **-ies**) a subordinate official, esp. a junior minister or senior civil servant.

undersell /úndərsél/ *v.tr.* (*past* and *past part.* **-sold**) **1** sell at a lower price than (another seller). **2** sell at less than the true value.
■ see UNDERCUT *v.* 1.

underset *v.* & *n.* ● *v.tr.* /úndərsét/ (**-setting**; *past* and *past part.* **-set**) place something under (a thing). ● *n.* /úndərset/ *Naut.* an undercurrent.
■ *n.* see UNDERCURRENT 1.

undersexed /úndərsékst/ *adj.* having unusually weak sexual desires.

under-sheriff /úndərsherrif/ *n.* a deputy sheriff.

undershirt /úndərshurt/ *n.* esp. *US* an undergarment worn under a shirt; a vest.

undershoot *v.* & *n.* ● *v.tr.* /úndərsho͞ot/ (*past* and *past part.* **-shot**) **1** (of an aircraft) land short of (a runway etc.). **2** shoot short of or below. ● *n.* /úndərsho͞ot/ the act or an instance of undershooting.

undershorts /úndərshorts/ *n. US* short underpants; trunks.
■ see PANTS 1.

undershot /úndərshót/ *adj.* **1** (of a water-wheel) turned by water flowing under it. **2** = UNDERHUNG.

undershrub /úndərshrub/ *n.* = SUBSHRUB.

underside /úndərsīd/ *n.* the lower or under side or surface.
■ see REVERSE *n.* 5.

undersigned /úndərsī́nd/ *adj.* whose signature is appended (*we, the undersigned, wish to state. . .*).

undersized /úndərsī́zd,/ *adj.* of less than the usual size.
■ under-size, little, short, small, petite, tiny, diminutive, puny, elfin, bantam, slight; stunted, underdeveloped, runty, dwarf, dwarfish, dwarfed, pygmy, squat; underweight, undeveloped; midget, baby.

underskirt /úndərskurt/ *n.* a skirt worn under another; a petticoat.

underslung /úndərslúng/ *adj.* **1** supported from above. **2** (of a vehicle chassis) hanging lower than the axles.

undersold *past* and *past part.* of UNDERSELL.

undersow /úndərsṓ/ *v.tr.* (*past part.* **-sown**) **1** sow (a later-growing crop) on land already seeded with another crop. **2** (foll. by *with*) sow land already seeded with (a crop) with a later-growing crop.

underspend /úndərspénd/ *v.* (*past* and *past part.* **-spent**) **1** *tr.* spend less than (a specified amount). **2** *intr.* & *refl.* spend too little.

understaffed /úndərstaáft/ *adj.* having too few staff.
■ short-staffed, undermanned, short-handed.

understand /úndərstánd/ *v.* (*past* and *past part.* **-stood** /-sto͝od/) **1** *tr.* perceive the meaning of (words, a person, a language, etc.) (*does not understand what you say; understood you perfectly; cannot understand French*). **2** *tr.* perceive the significance or explanation or cause of (*do not understand why he came; could not understand what the noise was about; do not understand the point of his remark*). **3** *tr.* be sympathetically aware of the character or nature of, know how to deal with (*quite understand your difficulty; cannot understand him at all; could never understand algebra*). **4** *tr.* **a** (often foll. by *that* + clause) infer esp. from information received, take as implied, take for granted (*I understand that it begins at noon; I understand him to be a distant relation;*

am I to understand that you refuse?). **b** (*absol.*) believe or assume from knowledge or inference (*he is coming tomorrow, I understand*). **5** *tr.* supply (a word) mentally (*the verb may be either expressed or understood*). **6** *tr.* accept (terms, conditions, etc.) as part of an agreement. **7** *intr.* have understanding (in general or in particular). □ **understand each other 1** know each other's views or feelings. **2** be in agreement or collusion. □□ **understandable** *adj.* **understandably** *adv.* **understander** *n.* [OE *understandan* (as UNDER-, STAND)]

■ **1, 2** grasp, comprehend, see, perceive, discern, make out, make sense of, get the drift *or* hang *or* gist of, follow, appreciate, interpret, take cognizance of, recognize, be aware *or* conscious of, be conversant with, know, realize, conceive of, apprehend, penetrate, fathom, *colloq.* get, catch on to, get there, tumble to, cotton on to, twig, get a handle on, *sl.* dig, *Brit. sl.* suss. **3** sympathize *or* empathize with, be in sympathy with, show compassion for, commiserate with; accept, tolerate, allow, forgive, condone. **4** hear, gather, get wind, take it, be told *or* informed *or* advised, have found out *or* learnt, hear tell, be led to believe, infer, deduce, interpret, read, construe, surmise, assume, presume, suppose, believe, guess, conclude. **6** accept, agree (to), assent to; covenant. **7** be aware, *colloq.* get it, catch on, cotton on, twig, *Austral. sl.* jerry. □□ **understandable** see INTELLIGIBLE.

understanding /úndərstánding/ *n.* & *adj.* ● *n.* **1 a** the ability to understand or think; intelligence. **b** the power of apprehension; the power of abstract thought. **2** an individual's perception or judgement of a situation etc. **3** an agreement; a thing agreed upon, esp. informally (*had an understanding with the rival company*; *consented only on this understanding*). **4** harmony in opinion or feeling (*disturbed the good understanding between them*). **5** sympathetic awareness or tolerance. ● *adj.* **1** having understanding or insight or good judgement. **2** sympathetic to others' feelings. □□ **understandingly** *adv.* [OE (as UNDERSTAND)]

■ *n.* **1** intellect, intelligence, mind, brain, brainpower, sense, reason, reasoning power, wisdom, brains, acumen, penetration, insight, discernment, perception, perceptiveness, percipience, good sense, intuition, enlightenment, sagacity, sageness, *literary* sapience, *sl.* savvy; comprehension, apprehension, awareness, appreciation, cognizance, idea(s), knowledge; conception, grasp, command, mastery. **2** reading, interpretation, opinion, judgement, estimation, notion, view, perception, apperception, apprehension. **3** agreement, contract, arrangement, bargain, covenant, concession, pact, compact, accord, treaty, concordat, entente, alliance, truce, armistice, reconciliation, settlement. **4** harmony, agreement, sympathy, compatibility, rapport, entente, concord, accord, consensus, congeniality, closeness, affinity, unity. **5** sympathy, empathy, rapport, feeling, fellow-feeling, compassion, tolerance, sensitivity, sensitiveness. ● *adj.* **1** see JUDICIOUS. **2** see SYMPATHETIC *adj.* 1.

understate /úndərstáyt/ *v.tr.* (often as **understated** *adj.*) **1** express in greatly or unduly restrained terms. **2** represent as being less than it actually is. □□ **understatement** /úndərstáytmənt/ *n.* **understater** *n.*

■ (**understated**) **1** subtle, restrained, low-key, simple, basic, unembellished, unadorned.

understeer *n.* & *v.* ● *n.* /úndərsteer/ a tendency of a motor vehicle to turn less sharply than was intended. ● *v.intr.* /úndərsteér/ have such a tendency.

understood *past* and *past part.* of UNDERSTAND.

understorey /úndərstori/ *n.* (*pl.* **-eys**) **1** a layer of vegetation beneath the main canopy of a forest. **2** the plants forming this.

understudy /úndərstuddi/ *n.* & *v.* esp. *Theatr.* ● *n.* (*pl.* **-ies**) a person who studies another's role or duties in order to act at short notice in the absence of the other. ● *v.tr.* (**-ies, -ied**) **1** study (a role etc.) as an understudy. **2** act as an understudy to (a person).

■ *n.* second, substitute, stand-in, stand-by, backup, double, reserve, *esp. US* alternate, *US* pinch-hitter, *colloq.* sub. ● *v.* **2** substitute for, stand in for, back up, double for, second, replace.

undersubscribed /úndərsəbskríbd/ *adj.* without sufficient subscribers, participants, etc.

undersurface /úndərsurfiss/ *n.* the lower or under surface.

undertake /úndərtáyk/ *v.tr.* (*past* **-took**; *past part.* **-taken**) **1** bind oneself to perform, make oneself responsible for, engage in, enter upon (work, an enterprise, a responsibility). **2** (usu. foll. by *to* + infin.) accept an obligation, promise. **3** guarantee, affirm (*I will undertake that he has not heard a word*).

■ **1** assume, take on, take upon oneself, accept, take *or* assume *or* bear the responsibility for, enter upon, begin, start, set about, embark on, engage in, tackle, try, attempt. **2** promise, covenant, agree, consent, contract, pledge, vow, swear, warrant, guarantee, bargain, commit oneself. **3** see SWEAR *v.* 1a, 2.

undertaker /úndərtaykər/ *n.* **1** a person whose business is to make arrangements for funerals. **2** /also -táykər/ a person who undertakes to do something. **3** *hist.* an influential person in 17th-century England who undertook to procure particular legislation, esp. to obtain supplies from the House of Commons if the king would grant some concession.

■ **1** funeral director, *US* mortician.

undertaking /úndərtáyking/ *n.* **1** work etc. undertaken, an enterprise (*a serious undertaking*). **2** a pledge or promise. **3** /úndərtayking/ the management of funerals as a profession.

■ **1** enterprise, affair, business, project, task, operation, effort, endeavour, venture, mission, work, job, feat. **2** promise, pledge, commitment, assurance, contract, agreement, vow, guarantee, warranty.

undertenant /úndərtennənt/ *n.* a subtenant. □□ **undertenancy** *n.* (*pl.* **-ies**).

underthings /úndərthingz/ *n.pl. colloq.* underclothes.

■ see UNDERCLOTHES.

undertint /úndərtint/ *n.* a subdued tint.

undertone /úndərtōn/ *n.* **1** a subdued tone of sound or colour. **2** an underlying quality. **3** an undercurrent of feeling.

■ **1** see MURMUR *n.* 1, TINT *n.* 2. **2, 3** see UNDERCURRENT 2.

undertook *past* of UNDERTAKE.

undertow /úndərtō/ *n.* a current below the surface of the sea moving in the opposite direction to the surface current.

■ see UNDERCURRENT 1.

undertrick /úndərtrik/ *n. Bridge* a trick by which the declarer falls short of his or her contract.

undervalue /úndərvályoo/ *v.tr.* (**-values, -valued, -valuing**) **1** value insufficiently. **2** underestimate. □□ **undervaluation** /-vályoo-áysh'n/ *n.*

■ **2** see UNDERESTIMATE *v.*

undervest /úndərvest/ *n. Brit.* an undergarment worn on the upper part of the body; a vest.

underwater /úndərwáwtər/ *adj.* & *adv.* ● *adj.* situated or done under water. ● *adv.* under water.

■ *adj.* submarine, sub-aqua; see also SUNKEN 2.

underwear /úndərwair/ *n.* underclothes.

■ see UNDERCLOTHES.

underweight *adj.* & *n.* ● *adj.* /úndərwáyt/ weighing less than is normal or desirable. ● *n.* /úndərwayt/ insufficient weight.

■ *adj.* see LIGHT² *adj.* 2b, UNDERSIZED.

underwent *past* of UNDERGO.

underwhelm /úndərwélm/ *v.tr. joc.* fail to impress. [after OVERWHELM]

underwing /úndərwing/ *n.* a wing placed under or partly covered by another.

underwood /úndərwood/ *n.* undergrowth.

underwork /úndərwúrk/ *v.* **1** *tr.* impose too little work on. **2** *intr.* do too little work.

underworld /úndərwurld/ *n.* **1** the part of society comprising those who live by organized crime and immorality. **2** the

mythical abode of the dead under the earth. **3** the antipodes.
■ **1** organized crime, syndicate, Mafia, Cosa Nostra, criminals, criminal element, *colloq.* mob, gangland. **2** nether regions *or* world, lower regions *or* world, abode of the dead, infernal regions, Hades, hell.

underwrite /úndərīt/ *v.* (*past* **-wrote**; *past part.* **-written**) **1 a** *tr.* sign, and accept liability under (an insurance policy, esp. on shipping etc.). **b** *tr.* accept (liability) in this way. **c** *intr.* practise (marine) insurance. **2** *tr.* undertake to finance or support. **3** *tr.* engage to buy all the stock in (a company etc.) not bought by the public. **4** *tr.* write below (*the underwritten names*). □□ **underwriter** /ún-/ *n.*
■ **1 a, b** subscribe to, endorse, sign, countersign, consent to, agree to, confirm, accede to, sanction, ratify, approve, validate, *colloq.* OK, okay. **2** back (up), finance, support, invest in, subsidize, sponsor, uphold, approve, insure, guarantee.

undescended /úndiséndid/ *adj. Med.* (of a testicle) remaining in the abdomen instead of descending normally into the scrotum.

undeserved /úndizérvd/ *adj.* not deserved (as reward or punishment). □□ **undeservedly** /-vidli/ *adv.*
■ see UNWARRANTED 2.

undeserving /úndizérving/ *adj.* not deserving. □□ **undeservingly** *adv.*
■ see UNWORTHY 1.

undesigned /úndizīnd/ *adj.* unintentional. □□ **undesignedly** /-nidli/ *adv.*

undesirable /úndizīrəb'l/ *adj.* & *n.* ● *adj.* not desirable, objectionable, unpleasant. ● *n.* an undesirable person. □□ **undesirability** /-bílliti/ *n.* **undesirableness** *n.* **undesirably** *adv.*
■ *adj.* unwanted, objectionable, offensive, unacceptable, obnoxious, unsavoury, unwelcome, disliked, distasteful, repugnant, unfit, unbecoming, unsuitable, unpleasant. ● *n. persona non grata*, pariah, outcast, exile, reject, leper.

undesired /úndizīrd/ *adj.* not desired.
■ see UNWELCOME.

undesirous /úndizīrəss/ *adj.* not desirous.

undetectable /úndítéktəb'l/ *adj.* not detectable. □□ **undetectability** /-bílliti/ *n.* **undetectably** *adv.*
■ see IMPERCEPTIBLE 1.

undetected /úndítéktid/ *adj.* not detected.

undetermined /únditérmind/ *adj.* = UNDECIDED.

undeterred /únditérd/ *adj.* not deterred.
■ see INDOMITABLE 2, UNABASHED.

undeveloped /úndivéllәpt/ *adj.* not developed.
■ embryonic, premature, immature, rudimentary, seminal, primitive, crude, incipient, inchoate, potential, latent.

undeviating /úndeéviayting/ *adj.* not deviating; steady, constant. □□ **undeviatingly** *adv.*
■ see STEADY *adj.* 2, DIRECT *adj.* 1. □□ **undeviatingly** see DIRECTLY *adv.* 3.

undiagnosed /úndīəgnṓzd/ *adj.* not diagnosed.

undid *past* of UNDO.

undies /úndiz/ *n.pl. colloq.* (esp. women's) underclothes. [abbr.]
■ see UNDERCLOTHES.

undifferentiated /úndifərénshiaytid/ *adj.* not differentiated; amorphous.
■ see INDISTINGUISHABLE.

undigested /úndijéstid, úndī-/ *adj.* **1** not digested. **2** (esp. of information, facts, etc.) not properly arranged or considered.

undignified /úndígnifīd/ *adj.* lacking dignity.
■ see UNSEEMLY 2.

undiluted /úndīlyṓotid/ *adj.* not diluted.
■ pure, neat, straight, unmixed, uncut, unblended, unadulterated, unwatered, concentrated, unalloyed; see also UNMITIGATED.

undiminished /úndimínnisht/ *adj.* not diminished or lessened.
■ see UNMITIGATED 1.

undine /úndeen/ *n.* a female water-spirit. [mod.L *undina* (word invented by Paracelsus) f. L *unda* wave]

undiplomatic /úndipləmáttik/ *adj.* tactless. □□ **undiplomatically** *adv.*
■ see TACTLESS.

undischarged /úndischaárjd/ *adj.* (esp. of a bankrupt or a debt) not discharged.

undiscipline /úndíssiplin/ *n.* lack of discipline.

undisciplined /úndíssiplind/ *adj.* lacking discipline; not disciplined.
■ untrained, unschooled, unprepared, untutored, uneducated, untaught, unpractised, uncontrolled, disobedient, naughty, bad, wilful, wayward, unrestrained, erratic, unpredictable, disorderly, unruly, wild.

undisclosed /úndisklṓzd/ *adj.* not revealed or made known.
■ see PRIVATE *adj.* 3, 5.

undiscoverable /úndiskúvvərəb'l/ *adj.* that cannot be discovered.

undiscovered /úndiskúvvərd/ *adj.* not discovered.
■ see UNCHARTED, UNKNOWN *adj.*

undiscriminating /úndiskrímminayting/ *adj.* not showing good judgement.
■ see INDISCRIMINATE 1, BLIND *adj.* 3.

undisguised /úndisgīzd/ *adj.* not disguised. □□ **undisguisedly** /-zidli/ *adv.*
■ open, out and out, unmistakable, overt, unconcealed, barefaced, bald, unreserved, unrestrained, unfeigned, unpretended, obvious, evident, patent, manifest, clear, explicit, transparent, sincere, heartfelt, unalloyed, unmitigated.

undismayed /úndismáyd/ *adj.* not dismayed.
■ see UNABASHED.

undisputed /úndispyṓotid/ *adj.* not disputed or called in question.
■ unquestioned, unquestionable, beyond question, accepted, acknowledged, admitted, indisputable, indubitable, undoubted, certain, sure, unmistakable, definite, explicit, clear, (self-)evident, obvious, uncontested, unchallenged, incontestable, irrefutable, incontrovertible, undeniable, conclusive.

undissolved /úndizólvd/ *adj.* not dissolved.

undistinguishable /úndistínggwishəb'l/ *adj.* (often foll. by *from*) indistinguishable.

undistinguished /úndistínggwisht/ *adj.* not distinguished; mediocre.
■ ordinary, commonplace, common, everyday, run-of-the-mill, pedestrian, unexceptional, plain, homespun, simple, prosaic, unremarkable, nothing special *or* unusual *or* extraordinary; mediocre, middling, indifferent, so so, unexciting, unimpressive, unpretentious, homely, *colloq.* common or garden, no great shakes, no big deal, nothing to write home about.

undistributed /úndistríbyootid/ *adj.* not distributed. □ **undistributed middle** *Logic* a fallacy resulting from the failure of the middle term of a syllogism to refer to all the members of a class.

undisturbed /úndistúrbd/ *adj.* not disturbed or interfered with.
■ untouched; see also CALM *adj.* 1, 2.

undivided /úndivīdid/ *adj.* not divided or shared; whole, entire (*gave him my undivided attention*).
■ whole, entire, unbroken, uncut, intact, unseparated, unsplit; undiverted, devoted, wholehearted, concentrated, full, complete, exclusive, undistracted.

undo /úndṓo/ *v.tr.* (*3rd sing. present* **-does**; *past* **-did**; *past part.* **-done**) **1 a** unfasten or untie (a coat, button, parcel, etc.). **b** unfasten the clothing of (a person). **2** annul, cancel (*cannot undo the past*). **3** ruin the prospects, reputation, or morals of. [OE *undōn* (as UN-[2], DO[1])]
■ **1** loosen, loose, open, unfasten, unhook, unlace, unzip, unbutton, unbuckle, unclasp, unclip, untie, unknot, ungird, unpin; unlock, unbolt, unhasp, unhinge, unlash,

unlatch, unlink, unpeg; unwrap, uncover, unbind, unstrap; unpick, unravel; uncouple, detach, disconnect, disengage, release, free, unhitch, untether, unscrew, unplug, unrivet. **2** cancel, annul, rescind, nullify, void, declare null and void, reverse, invalidate. **3** see RUIN *v.* 1.

undock /úndók/ *v.tr.* **1** (also *absol.*) separate (a spacecraft) from another in space. **2** take (a ship) out of a dock.

undocumented /úndókyoomentid/ *adj.* **1** *US* not having the appropriate document. **2** not proved by or recorded in documents.
▪ **2** unrecorded; see also UNOFFICIAL 1.

undoing /úndŏŏing/ *n.* **1** ruin or a cause of ruin. **2** the process of reversing what has been done. **3** the action of opening or unfastening.
▪ **1** ruin, ruination, destruction, devastation, defeat, downfall, overthrow, fall, collapse, descent, debasement, degradation, abasement, mortification, humiliation, shame, disgrace; curse, misfortune, affliction, trouble, blight, *poet.* bane.

undomesticated /úndəméstikaytid/ *adj.* not domesticated.
▪ see UNTAMED.

undone /úndún/ *adj.* **1** not done; incomplete (*left the job undone*). **2** not fastened (*left the buttons undone*). **3** *archaic* ruined.
▪ **1** unaccomplished, uncompleted, incomplete, unfinished, omitted, neglected, left (out), skipped, missed, passed over, forgotten, unattended to. **2** open, loose, loosened, untied, unfastened, detached, unhooked, unlaced, unzipped, unsnapped, unbuttoned, unbuckled, unclipped, unclasped, unpinned, unstuck. **3** ruined, lost, wrecked, crushed, destroyed, devastated, shattered, brought to ruin, defeated, prostrated, overcome.

undoubtable /úndówtəb'l/ *adj.* that cannot be doubted; indubitable.

undoubted /úndówtid/ *adj.* certain, not questioned, not regarded as doubtful. ▫▫ **undoubtedly** *adv.*
▪ see UNDISPUTED, CERTAIN *adj.* 1b. ▫▫ **undoubtedly** indubitably, without (a) doubt, indisputably, unquestionably, beyond (a *or* the shadow of a) doubt, doubtless(ly), certainly, definitely, surely, assuredly, unmistakably, explicitly, clearly, obviously, of course, incontestably, irrefutably, incontrovertibly, undeniably.

undrained /úndráynd/ *adj.* not drained.

undraped /úndráypt/ *adj.* **1** not covered with drapery. **2** naked.

undreamed /úndreémd, úndrémt/ *adj.* (also **undreamt** /úndrémt/) (often foll. by *of*) not dreamed or thought of or imagined.
▪ (*undreamed of*) see UNFORESEEN, INCONCEIVABLE 1.

undress /úndréss/ *v.* & *n.* • *v.* **1** *intr.* take off one's clothes. **2** *tr.* take the clothes off (a person). • *n.* **1** ordinary dress as opposed to full dress or uniform. **2** casual or informal dress.
▪ *v.* see STRIP[1] *v.* 1, 2.

undressed /úndrést/ *adj.* **1** not or no longer dressed; partly or wholly naked. **2** (of leather etc.) not treated. **3** (of food) not having a dressing.
▪ **1** see NAKED 1.

undrinkable /úndríngkəb'l/ *adj.* unfit for drinking.

undue /úndyŏŏ/ *adj.* **1** excessive, disproportionate. **2** not suitable. **3** not owed. ▫ **undue influence** *Law* influence by which a person is induced to act otherwise than by his or her own free will, or without adequate attention to the consequences. ▫▫ **unduly** *adv.*
▪ **1** see EXCESSIVE. **2** see UNWARRANTED 2. ▫▫ **unduly** disproportionately, excessively, unnecessarily, inordinately, unreasonably, irrationally, unjustifiably, improperly, inappropriately, *esp. US* & *Sc.* overly; immoderately, lavishly, profusely, extravagantly.

undulant /úndyoolənt/ *adj.* moving like waves; fluctuating. ▫ **undulant fever** brucellosis in humans. [L *undulare* (as UNDULATE)]

undulate *v.* & *adj.* • *v.* /úndyoolayt/ *intr.* & *tr.* have or cause to have a wavy motion or look. • *adj.* /úndyoolət/ wavy, going alternately up and down or in and out (*leaves with undulate margins*). ▫▫ **undulately** *adv.* [LL *undulatus* f. L *unda* wave]
▪ *v.* see WAVE *v.* 2.

undulation /úndyooláysh'n/ *n.* **1** a wavy motion or form, a gentle rise and fall. **2** each wave of this. **3** a set of wavy lines.

undulatory /úndyoolətəri/ *adj.* **1** undulating, wavy. **2** of or due to undulation.

undutiful /úndyŏŏtifŏŏl/ *adj.* not dutiful. ▫▫ **undutifully** *adv.* **undutifulness** *n.*
▪ see DISOBEDIENT, REMISS.

undyed /úndī́d/ *adj.* not dyed.

undying /úndī́-ing/ *adj.* **1** immortal. **2** never-ending (*undying love*). ▫▫ **undyingly** *adv.*
▪ see IMMORTAL *adj.* 1a. ▫▫ **undyingly** see ALWAYS 4.

unearned /únnérnd/ *adj.* not earned. ▫ **unearned income** income from interest payments etc. as opposed to salary, wages, or fees. **unearned increment** an increase in the value of property not due to the owner's labour or outlay.

unearth /únnérth/ *v.tr.* **1 a** discover by searching or in the course of digging or rummaging. **b** dig out of the earth. **2** drive (a fox etc.) from its earth.
▪ **1** dig up, disinter, exhume; excavate, dredge up, mine, quarry, find, pull *or* root out, come across, discover, turn up, expose, uncover.

unearthly /únnérthli/ *adj.* **1** supernatural, mysterious. **2** *colloq.* absurdly early or inconvenient (*an unearthly hour*). **3** not earthly. ▫▫ **unearthliness** *n.*
▪ **1** supernatural, unnatural, preternatural, psychic(al), extrasensory, supersensory, out-of-(the)-body, incorporeal, metaphysical; weird, bizarre, macabre, nightmarish, uncanny, eerie, strange, mysterious, mystical, ghostly, spectral, unreal, *Sc.* eldritch, *colloq.* spooky, creepy. **2** strange, odd, peculiar, unusual, abnormal, absurd, out of the ordinary, extraordinary, outrageous; unheard-of, ridiculous, unreasonable, *colloq.* ungodly, *sl.* God-awful. **3** unworldly, other-worldly, extramundane, ultramundane, supramundane, extraterrestrial, sublime, celestial, heavenly, astral, divine, *esp. poet.* supernal.

unease /únneéz/ *n.* lack of ease, discomfort, distress.
▪ see MISGIVING.

uneasy /únneézi/ *adj.* (**uneasier**, **uneasiest**) **1** disturbed or uncomfortable in mind or body (*passed an uneasy night*). **2** disturbing (*had an uneasy suspicion*). ▫▫ **uneasily** *adv.* **uneasiness** *n.*
▪ **1** see ANXIOUS 1, RESTLESS 1, 2. **2** see *disturbing* (DISTURB).

uneatable /únneétəb'l/ *adj.* not able to be eaten, esp. because of its condition (cf. INEDIBLE).
▪ see UNPALATABLE.

uneaten /únneét'n/ *adj.* not eaten; left undevoured.
▪ see LEFTOVER *adj.*

uneconomic /únneekənómmik, únnek-/ *adj.* not economic; incapable of being profitably operated etc. ▫▫ **uneconomically** *adv.*
▪ see UNPROFITABLE, INEFFICIENT 1.

uneconomical /únneekənómmik'l, únnek-/ *adj.* not economical; wasteful.

unedifying /únnéddifī-ing/ *adj.* not edifying, esp. uninstructive or degrading. ▫▫ **unedifyingly** *adv.*

unedited /únnédditid/ *adj.* not edited.

uneducated /únnédyookaytid/ *adj.* not educated. ▫▫ **uneducable** /-kəb'l/ *adj.*
▪ unschooled, untaught, unlearned, uncultivated, unread, uncultured, unaccomplished, illiterate, unlettered, ignorant, unenlightened.

unelectable /únniléktəb'l/ *adj.* (of a candidate, party, etc.) associated with or holding views likely to bring defeat at an election.

unembellished /únnimbéllisht/ *adj.* not embellished or decorated.

■ see PLAIN[1] *adj.* 3.

unemotional /únnimṓshən'l/ *adj.* not emotional; lacking emotion. □□ **unemotionally** *adv.*

■ see COLD *adj.* 4, COOL *adj.* 3b.

unemphatic /únnimfáttik/ *adj.* not emphatic. □□ **unemphatically** *adv.*

unemployable /únnimplóyəb'l/ *adj.* & *n.* ● *adj.* unfitted for paid employment. ● *n.* an unemployable person. □□ **unemployability** /-bílliti/ *n.*

unemployed /únnimplóyd/ *adj.* **1** not having paid employment; out of work. **2** not in use.

■ **1** out of work, jobless, unwaged, idle, laid off, out of a job, workless, unoccupied, inactive, redundant, between engagements *or* assignments, at leisure, *Brit. colloq.* on the dole, *Brit. euphem.* resting, *US colloq.* on *or* collecting unemployment. **2** unused, not in use, idle, inactive, unoccupied.

unemployment /únnimplóymənt/ *n.* **1** the state of being unemployed. **2** the condition or extent of this in a country or region etc. (*the North has higher unemployment*). □ **unemployment benefit** a payment made by the State or (in the US) a trade union to an unemployed person.

unenclosed /únninklṓzd/ *adj.* not enclosed.

■ see OPEN *adj.* 1–4, 13, 20.

unencumbered /únninkúmbərd/ *adj.* **1** (of an estate) not having any liabilities (e.g. a mortgage) on it. **2** having no encumbrance; free.

■ **2** see FREE *adj.* 3a.

unending /únnénding/ *adj.* having or apparently having no end. □□ **unendingly** *adv.* **unendingness** *n.*

■ see ENDLESS 1. □□ **unendingly** see NON-STOP *adv.*, ALWAYS 4.

unendowed /únnindówd/ *adj.* not endowed.

unendurable /únnindyóorəb'l/ *adj.* that cannot be endured. □□ **unendurably** *adv.*

■ see UNBEARABLE.

unengaged /únningáyjd/ *adj.* not engaged; uncommitted.

un-English /únníngglish/ *adj.* **1** not characteristic of the English. **2** not English.

unenjoyable /únninjóyəb'l/ *adj.* not enjoyable.

unenlightened /únninlī́t'nd/ *adj.* not enlightened.

■ see IGNORANT 1a.

unenterprising /únnéntərprīzing/ *adj.* not enterprising.

■ see SHIFTLESS.

unenthusiastic /únninthyōōziástik, únninthōō-/ *adj.* not enthusiastic. □□ **unenthusiastically** *adv.*

■ lukewarm, half-hearted, cool, cold, uninterested, indifferent, blasé, unresponsive, apathetic, lackadaisical, listless, phlegmatic, nonchalant, tepid, unexcited, unimpressed.

unenviable /únnénviəb'l/ *adj.* not enviable. □□ **unenviably** *adv.*

■ uncoveted, undesirable, unwished for, unattractive.

unenvied /únnénvid/ *adj.* not envied.

unequal /únnéekwəl/ *adj.* **1** (often foll. by *to*) not equal. **2** of varying quality. **3** lacking equal advantage to both sides (*an unequal bargain*). □□ **unequally** *adv.*

■ **1** see UNLIKE *adj.* 3, LOPSIDED; (*unequal to*) see UNLIKE *adj.* 1, INCAPABLE 1a. **3** see UNREASONABLE 1.

unequalize /únnéekwəlīz/ *v.tr.* (also **-ise**) make unequal.

unequalled /únnéekwəld/ *adj.* superior to all others.

■ see *peerless* (PEER[2]).

unequipped /únnikwípt/ *adj.* not equipped.

■ see UNQUALIFIED 1, 2.

unequivocal /únnikwívvək'l/ *adj.* not ambiguous, plain, unmistakable. □□ **unequivocally** *adv.* **unequivocalness** *n.*

■ see PLAIN[1] *adj.* 1, 2, CATEGORICAL. □□ **unequivocally** see *expressly* (EXPRESS).

unerring /únnéring/ *adj.* not erring, failing, or missing the mark; true, certain. □□ **unerringly** *adv.* **unerringness** *n.*

■ see CERTAIN *adj.* 3, TRUE *adj.* 6. □□ **unerringly** see EXACTLY 1.

unescapable /únniskáypəb'l/ *adj.* inescapable.

UNESCO /yoonéskō/ *abbr.* (also **Unesco**) United Nations Educational, Scientific, and Cultural Organization.

unescorted /únniskórtid/ *adj.* not escorted.

■ see UNACCOMPANIED 1.

unessential /únnisénsh'l/ *adj.* & *n.* ● *adj.* **1** not essential (cf. INESSENTIAL). **2** not of the first importance. ● *n.* an unessential part or thing.

■ *adj.* see NON-ESSENTIAL.

unestablished /únnistáblisht/ *adj.* not established.

unethical /únnéthik'l/ *adj.* not ethical, esp. unscrupulous in business or professional conduct. □□ **unethically** *adv.*

■ see UNSCRUPULOUS, UNPROFESSIONAL 1.

unevangelical /únneevanjéllik'l/ *adj.* not evangelical.

uneven /únnéev'n/ *adj.* **1** not level or smooth. **2** not uniform or equable. **3** (of a contest) unequal. □□ **unevenly** *adv.* **unevenness** *n.* [OE *unefen* (as UN-[1], EVEN[1])]

■ **1, 2** see IRREGULAR *adj.* 1, 2. **3** see DISPROPORTIONATE. □□ **unevenness** see *irregularity* (IRREGULAR), DISPROPORTION.

uneventful /únnivéntfōōl/ *adj.* not eventful. □□ **uneventfully** *adv.* **uneventfulness** *n.*

■ see HUMDRUM *adj.*, SMOOTH *adj.* 6.

unexamined /únnigzámmind/ *adj.* not examined.

unexampled /únnigzáamp'ld/ *adj.* having no precedent or parallel.

unexceptionable /únniksépshənəb'l/ *adj.* with which no fault can be found; entirely satisfactory. □□ **unexceptionableness** *n.* **unexceptionably** *adv.*

■ see FAULTLESS.

unexceptional /únniksépshən'l/ *adj.* not out of the ordinary; usual, normal. □□ **unexceptionally** *adv.*

unexcitable /únniksī́təb'l/ *adj.* not easily excited. □□ **unexcitability** /-bílliti/ *n.*

■ see SERENE.

unexciting /únniksī́ting/ *adj.* not exciting; dull.

■ see TAME *adj.* 2.

unexecuted /únnéksikyōōtid/ *adj.* not carried out or put into effect.

unexhausted /únnigzáwstid/ *adj.* **1** not used up, expended, or brought to an end. **2** not emptied.

unexpected /únnikspéktid/ *adj.* not expected; surprising. □□ **unexpectedly** *adv.* **unexpectedness** *n.*

■ see UNFORESEEN. □□ **unexpectedly** see *suddenly* (SUDDEN).

unexpired /únnikspī́rd/ *adj.* that has not yet expired.

unexplainable /únnikspláynəb'l/ *adj.* inexplicable. □□ **unexplainably** *adv.*

■ see INEXPLICABLE.

unexplained /únnikspláynd/ *adj.* not explained.

■ see UNACCOUNTABLE 1, 2.

unexploited /únniksplóytid/ *adj.* (of resources etc.) not exploited.

unexplored /únniksplórd/ *adj.* not explored.

■ see UNCHARTED, UNKNOWN *adj.*

unexposed /únnikspṓzd/ *adj.* not exposed.

■ see SECURE *adj.* 1, 2.

unexpressed /únniksprést/ *adj.* not expressed or made known (*unexpressed fears*).

■ see TACIT.

unexpurgated /únnékspərgaytid/ *adj.* (esp. of a text etc.) not expurgated; complete.

■ see UNABRIDGED.

unfaceable /únfáysəb'l/ *adj.* that cannot be faced or confronted.

unfading /únfáyding/ *adj.* that never fades. □□ **unfadingly** *adv.*

■ see IMMORTAL *adj.* 2.

unfailing /únfáyling/ *adj.* **1** not failing. **2** not running short. **3** constant. **4** reliable. □□ **unfailingly** *adv.* **unfailingness** *n.*

■ **1** see CERTAIN *adj.* 3. **2** see INEXHAUSTIBLE 1. **3** see CONSTANT *adj.* 3. **4** see RELIABLE. ◻◻ **unfailingly** see *consistently* (CONSISTENT).

unfair /únfáir/ *adj.* **1** not equitable or honest (*obtained by unfair means*). **2** not impartial or according to the rules (*unfair play*). ◻◻ **unfairly** *adv.* **unfairness** *n.* [OE *unfæger* (as UN-[1], FAIR[1])]
■ **1** see DISHONEST. **2** see IRREGULAR *adj.* 3, *prejudiced* (PREJUDICE). ◻◻ **unfairly** see ILL *adv.* 1. **unfairness** see INJUSTICE 1.

unfaithful /únfáythfŏŏl/ *adj.* **1** not faithful, esp. adulterous. **2** not loyal. **3** treacherous. ◻◻ **unfaithfully** *adv.* **unfaithfulness** *n.*
■ see UNTRUE 2. ◻◻ **unfaithfulness** see INFIDELITY 1, PERFIDY.

unfaltering /únfáwltəring, únfól-/ *adj.* not faltering; steady, resolute. ◻◻ **unfalteringly** *adv.*
■ see STEADY *adj.* 6, RESOLUTE. ◻◻ **unfalteringly** see SURELY 3.

unfamiliar /únfəmílyər/ *adj.* not familiar. ◻◻ **unfamiliarity** /-liárriti/ *n.*
■ new, novel, unknown, unheard-of, unconventional, unusual, different, uncommon, alien, foreign, strange, odd, peculiar, bizarre, exotic; (*unfamiliar with*) unacquainted with, unaccustomed to, inexperienced in *or* with, unused to, unconversant with, uninformed about, ignorant of, unpractised in, unskilled in *or* at, uninitiated in, unversed in. ◻◻ **unfamiliarity** see IGNORANCE.

unfashionable /únfáshənəb'l/ *adj.* not fashionable. ◻◻ **unfashionableness** *n.* **unfashionably** *adv.*
■ see *old-fashioned.*

unfashioned /únfásh'nd/ *adj.* not made into its proper shape.

unfasten /únfaáss'n/ *v.* **1** *tr.* & *intr.* make or become loose. **2** *tr.* open the fastening(s) of. **3** *tr.* detach.
■ see LOOSEN, UNDO 1.

unfastened /únfaáss'nd/ *adj.* **1** that has not been fastened. **2** that has been loosened, opened, or detached.
■ see UNDONE 2.

unfathered /únfaáthərd/ *adj.* **1** having no known or acknowledged father; illegitimate. **2** of unknown origin (*unfathered rumours*).

unfatherly /únfaáthərli/ *adj.* not befitting a father. ◻◻ **unfatherliness** *n.*

unfathomable /únfáthəməb'l/ *adj.* incapable of being fathomed. ◻◻ **unfathomableness** *n.* **unfathomably** *adv.*
■ see INCOMPREHENSIBLE, IMMEASURABLE.

unfathomed /únfáthəmd/ *adj.* **1** of unascertained depth. **2** not fully explored or known.
■ **1** see BOTTOMLESS 1.

unfavourable /únfáyvərəb'l/ *adj.* (*US* **unfavorable**) not favourable; adverse, hostile. ◻◻ **unfavourableness** *n.* **unfavourably** *adv.*
■ see BAD *adj.* 2. ◻◻ **unfavourably** see ILL *adv.* 3.

unfavourite /únfáyvərit/ *adj.* (*US* **unfavorite**) *colloq.* least favourite; most disliked.

unfazed /únfáyzd/ *adj. colloq.* untroubled; not disconcerted.

unfeasible /únféezib'l/ *adj.* not feasible; impractical. ◻◻ **unfeasibility** /-bílliti/ *n.* **unfeasibly** *adv.*
■ see IMPOSSIBLE 1.

unfed /únféd/ *adj.* not fed.

unfeeling /únféeling/ *adj.* **1** unsympathetic, harsh, not caring about others' feelings. **2** lacking sensation or sensitivity. ◻◻ **unfeelingly** *adv.* **unfeelingness** *n.* [OE *unfelende* (as UN-[1], FEELING)]
■ **1** see UNSYMPATHETIC. **2** see DEAD *adj.* 3.

unfeigned /únfáynd/ *adj.* genuine, sincere. ◻◻ **unfeignedly** *adv.*
■ see SINCERE.

unfelt /únfélt/ *adj.* not felt.

unfeminine /únfémminin/ *adj.* not in accordance with, or appropriate to, female character. ◻◻ **unfemininity** /-nínniti/ *n.*

unfenced /únfénst/ *adj.* **1** not provided with fences. **2** unprotected.

unfermented /únfərméntid/ *adj.* not fermented.

unfertilized /únfértilīzd/ *adj.* (also **unfertilised**) not fertilized.

unfetter /únféttər/ *v.tr.* release from fetters.

unfettered /únféttərd/ *adj.* unrestrained, unrestricted.
■ see FREE *adj.* 3.

unfilial /únfílliəl/ *adj.* not befitting a son or daughter. ◻◻ **unfilially** *adv.*

unfilled /únfíld/ *adj.* not filled.
■ see EMPTY *adj.* 1, VACANT 1, OPEN *adj.* 12b.

unfiltered /únfíltərd/ *adj.* **1** not filtered. **2** (of a cigarette) not provided with a filter.

unfinancial /únfīnánsh'l/ *adj. Austral.* **1** insolvent. **2** not having paid a subscription (*some members are unfinancial*).
■ **1** see INSOLVENT 1.

unfinished /únfínnisht/ *adj.* not finished; incomplete.
■ see INCOMPLETE.

unfit /únfít/ *adj.* & *v.* ● *adj.* (often foll. by *for*, or *to* + infin.) not fit. ● *v.tr.* (**unfitted, unfitting**) (usu. foll. by *for*) make unsuitable. ◻◻ **unfitly** *adv.* **unfitness** *n.*
■ *adj.* out of condition *or* shape; see also INELIGIBLE, UNBECOMING 2; (*unfit for*) see UNWORTHY 1.

unfitted /únfíttid/ *adj.* **1** not fit. **2** not fitted or suited. **3** not provided with fittings.

unfitting /únfítting/ *adj.* not fitting or suitable, unbecoming. ◻◻ **unfittingly** *adv.*
■ see UNBECOMING 2.

unfix /únfíks/ *v.tr.* **1** release or loosen from a fixed state. **2** detach.

unfixed /únfíkst/ *adj.* not fixed.
■ see FLUID *adj.* 2.

unflagging /únflágging/ *adj.* tireless, persistent. ◻◻ **unflaggingly** *adv.*
■ see TIRELESS.

unflappable /únfláppəb'l/ *adj. colloq.* imperturbable; remaining calm in a crisis. ◻◻ **unflappability** /-bílliti/ *n.* **unflappably** *adv.*
■ see COOL *adj.* 3a. ◻◻ **unflappability** see SERENITY.

unflattering /únfláttəring/ *adj.* not flattering. ◻◻ **unflatteringly** *adv.*
■ uncomplimentary, insulting, unfavourable, depreciatory, disparaging, derogatory, slighting, pejorative; harsh, unsympathetic; realistic, stark, candid, *colloq.* warts and all.

unflavoured /únfláyvərd/ *adj.* not flavoured.

unfledged /únfléjd/ *adj.* **1** (of a person) inexperienced. **2** (of a bird) not yet fledged.
■ **1** inexperienced, immature, green, callow, raw, new, young, uninitiated. **2** undeveloped, immature, young.

unfleshed /únflésht/ *adj.* **1** not covered with flesh. **2** stripped of flesh.

unflinching /únflínching/ *adj.* not flinching. ◻◻ **unflinchingly** *adv.*
■ see STAUNCH[1] 1. ◻◻ **unflinchingly** see *intently* (INTENT).

unfocused /únfṓkəst/ *adj.* (also **unfocussed**) not focused.

unfold /únfṓld/ *v.* **1** *tr.* open the fold or folds of, spread out. **2** *tr.* reveal (thoughts etc.). **3** *intr.* become opened out. **4** *intr.* develop. ◻◻ **unfoldment** *n. US.* [OE *unfealdan* (as UN-[2], FOLD[1])]
■ **1, 3** open (out *or* up), spread (out), unfurl, stretch out, expand, extend, uncoil, unwind, straighten out. **2** see BARE *v.* 2. **4** develop, evolve, happen, take place, occur, be divulged, be disclosed *or* revealed.

unforced /únfórst/ *adj.* **1** not produced by effort; easy, natural. **2** not compelled or constrained. ◻◻ **unforcedly** *adv.*
■ **1** see SPONTANEOUS 4. **2** see OPTIONAL.

unfordable /únfórdəb'l/ *adj.* that cannot be forded.

unforeseeable /únforsééəb'l/ *adj.* not foreseeable.

■ see CHANCE *adj.*, UNCERTAIN 1.

unforeseen /únforseén/ *adj.* not foreseen.
■ unexpected, surprising, unanticipated, unpredicted, unlooked-for, unsought, unhoped for, undreamed of, unthought of, startling, surprise, chance, accidental, fortuitous.

unforetold /únfortṓld/ *adj.* not foretold; unpredicted.

unforgettable /únfərgéttəb'l/ *adj.* that cannot be forgotten; memorable, wonderful (*an unforgettable experience*). ▫▫ **unforgettably** *adv.*
■ see MEMORABLE.

unforgivable /únfərgívvəb'l/ *adj.* that cannot be forgiven. ▫▫ **unforgivably** *adv.*
■ see INEXCUSABLE, UNCONSCIONABLE 2.

unforgiven /únfərgívv'n/ *adj.* not forgiven.

unforgiving /únfərgívving/ *adj.* not forgiving. ▫▫ **unforgivingly** *adv.* **unforgivingness** *n.*
■ see IMPLACABLE.

unforgotten /únfərgótt'n/ *adj.* not forgotten.

unformed /únfórmd/ *adj.* **1** not formed. **2** shapeless. **3** not developed.
■ **1** see FLUID *adj.* 2. **2** see SHAPELESS. **3** see IMMATURE 1.

unformulated /únfórmyoolaytid/ *adj.* not formulated.

unforthcoming /únforthkúmming/ *adj.* not forthcoming.
■ see *tight-lipped* .

unfortified /únfórtifīd/ *adj.* not fortified.

unfortunate /únfórtyoonət, -fórchənət/ *adj.* & *n.* ● *adj.* **1** having bad fortune; unlucky. **2** unhappy. **3** regrettable. **4** disastrous. ● *n.* an unfortunate person.
■ *adj.* **1** unlucky, luckless, hapless; cursed, out of luck, unblessed, poor, doomed, ill-starred, ill-fated, *archaic* star-crossed, *colloq.* jinxed, down on one's luck. **2** miserable, wretched, woebegone, pathetic, dismal, unhappy, forlorn, pitiable, despondent, disconsolate, depressed, dejected. **3** deplorable, lamentable, regrettable, distressing, upsetting, disturbing. **4** catastrophic, disastrous, calamitous, tragic, grievous, ruinous, terrible, awful, dreadful, horrible, dire; inauspicious, untoward, unhappy. ● *n.* see WRETCH 1.

unfortunately /únfórtyoonətli, -fórchənətli/ *adv.* **1** (qualifying a whole sentence) it is unfortunate that. **2** in an unfortunate manner.
■ **1** see *sadly* (SAD).

unfounded /únfówndid/ *adj.* having no foundation (*unfounded hopes*; *unfounded rumour*). ▫▫ **unfoundedly** *adv.* **unfoundedness** *n.*
■ baseless, groundless, unwarranted, unjustified, unsupported, unsupportable, unsound, unjustifiable, unattested, unproven, unproved.

unframed /únfráymd/ *adj.* (esp. of a picture) not framed.

unfreeze /únfreéz/ *v.* (*past* **unfroze**; *past part.* **unfrozen**) **1** *tr.* cause to thaw. **2** *intr.* thaw. **3** *tr.* remove restrictions from, make (assets, credits, etc.) realizable.

unfrequented /únfrikwéntid/ *adj.* not frequented.
■ see ISOLATED 1.

unfriended /únfréndid/ *adj. literary* without friends.
■ see SOLITARY *adj.* 1.

unfriendly /únfréndli/ *adj.* (**unfriendlier, unfriendliest**) not friendly. ▫▫ **unfriendliness** *n.*
■ see UNSOCIAL. ▫▫ **unfriendliness** see CHILL *n.* 4, HOSTILITY 1.

unfrock /únfrók/ *v.tr.* = DEFROCK.

unfroze *past* of UNFREEZE.

unfrozen *past part.* of UNFREEZE.

unfruitful /únfrṓōtfŏŏl/ *adj.* **1** not producing good results, unprofitable. **2** not producing fruit or crops. ▫▫ **unfruitfully** *adv.* **unfruitfulness** *n.*
■ **1** see UNPROFITABLE.

unfulfilled /únfŏŏlfíld/ *adj.* not fulfilled. ▫▫ **unfulfillable** *adj.*
■ see *dissatisfied* (DISSATISFY).

unfunded /únfúndid/ *adj.* (of a debt) not funded.

unfunny /únfúnni/ *adj.* (**unfunnier, unfunniest**) not amusing (though meant to be). ▫▫ **unfunnily** *adv.* **unfunniness** *n.*

unfurl /únfúrl/ *v.* **1** *tr.* spread out (a sail, umbrella, etc.). **2** *intr.* become spread out.
■ **1** see SPREAD *v.* 1a. **2** see *roll out*.

unfurnished /únfúrnisht/ *adj.* **1** (usu. foll. by *with*) not supplied. **2** without furniture.

ungainly /úngáynli/ *adj.* (of a person, animal, or movement) awkward, clumsy. ▫▫ **ungainliness** *n.* [UN-[1] + obs. *gainly* graceful ult. f. ON *gegn* straight]
■ see AWKWARD 2.

ungallant /úngállənt/ *adj.* not gallant. ▫▫ **ungallantly** *adv.*

ungenerous /únjénnərəss/ *adj.* not generous; mean. ▫▫ **ungenerously** *adv.* **ungenerousness** *n.*
■ see MEAN[2] 1.

ungenial /únjeéniəl/ *adj.* not genial.

ungentle /únjént'l/ *adj.* not gentle. ▫▫ **ungentleness** *n.* **ungently** *adv.*

ungentlemanly /únjéntəlmənli/ *adj.* not gentlemanly. ▫▫ **ungentlemanliness** *n.*
■ see RUDE 1.

unget-at-able /úngetáttəb'l/ *adj. colloq.* inaccessible.
■ see INACCESSIBLE 1.

ungifted /úngíftid/ *adj.* not gifted or talented.

ungird /úngúrd/ *v.tr.* **1** release the girdle, belt, or girth of. **2** release or take off by undoing a belt or girth.
■ see UNDO 1.

unglazed /úngláyzd/ *adj.* not glazed.

ungloved /únglúvd/ *adj.* not wearing a glove or gloves.

ungodly /úngódli/ *adj.* **1** impious, wicked. **2** *colloq.* outrageous (*an ungodly hour to arrive*). ▫▫ **ungodliness** *n.*
■ **1** wicked, sinful, impious, blasphemous, heretical, irreligious, iconoclastic, atheist(ic), anti-religious, sacrilegious, irreverent, demonic, demoniac(al), diabolic(al), satanic, fiendish, hellish, infernal; depraved, godless, corrupt, immoral, evil, iniquitous, bad, villainous, heinous, flagitious, profane, vile. **2** awful, outrageous, indecent, monstrous, unseemly, objectionable, nasty, dreadful, terrible, appalling, frightful, shocking, *colloq.* unearthly, beastly, *sl.* God-awful. ▫▫ **ungodliness** see SIN[1] *n.* 1.

ungovernable /úngúvvərnəb'l/ *adj.* uncontrollable, violent. ▫▫ **ungovernability** /-bílliti/ *n.* **ungovernably** *adv.*
■ unruly, intractable, unmanageable, uncontrollable, rebellious, wild, disobedient, defiant, unrestrainable, obstreperous, refractory, recalcitrant, incorrigible, self-willed, violent.

ungraceful /úngráysfŏŏl/ *adj.* not graceful. ▫▫ **ungracefully** *adv.* **ungracefulness** *n.*
■ awkward, clumsy, ungainly, gauche, gawky, lubberly, uncoordinated, all thumbs, *colloq.* butter-fingered, *US sl.* klutzy; inelegant, graceless, coarse, crude, inartistic, vulgar, tasteless, unaesthetic, unrefined, barbarous, unlovely, ugly, unharmonious, inconsonant, unattractive, ill-proportioned, unsymmetrical, asymmetric(al).

ungracious /úngráyshəss/ *adj.* **1** not kindly or courteous; unkind. **2** unattractive. ▫▫ **ungraciously** *adv.* **ungraciousness** *n.*
■ **1** discourteous, overbearing, churlish, gauche, rude, uncivil, impolite, ill-bred, ill-mannered, bad-mannered, unmannerly, ungentlemanly, unladylike, unrefined, gruff, bluff, brusque, abrupt, surly, curmudgeonly; unkind, inconsiderate, insensitive.

ungrammatical /úngrəmáttik'l/ *adj.* contrary to the rules of grammar. ▫▫ **ungrammaticality** /-kálliti/ *n.* **ungrammatically** *adv.* **ungrammaticalness** *n.*

ungraspable /úngraáspəb'l/ *adj.* that cannot be grasped or comprehended.

ungrateful /úngráytfŏŏl/ *adj.* **1** not feeling or showing gratitude. **2** not pleasant or acceptable. □□ **ungratefully** *adv.* **ungratefulness** *n.*
■ **1** unthankful, unappreciative, rude; selfish, heedless. □□ **ungratefulness** see INGRATITUDE.

ungrounded /úngrówndid/ *adj.* **1** having no basis or justification; unfounded. **2** *Electr.* not earthed. **3** (foll. by *in* a subject) not properly instructed. **4** (of an aircraft, ship, etc.) no longer grounded.
■ **1** see GRATUITOUS 2, UNFOUNDED.

ungrudging /úngrújing/ *adj.* not grudging. □□ **ungrudgingly** *adv.*
■ see UNSELFISH. □□ **ungrudgingly** see *willingly* (WILLING).

ungual /únggwəl/ *adj.* of, like, or bearing a nail, hoof, or claw. [L UNGUIS]

unguard /úngaárd/ *v.tr. Cards* discard a low card that was protecting (a high card) from capture.

unguarded /úngaárdid/ *adj.* **1** incautious, thoughtless (*an unguarded remark*). **2** not guarded; without a guard. □ **in an unguarded moment** unawares. □□ **unguardedly** *adv.* **unguardedness** *n.*
■ **1** indiscreet, careless, imprudent, unwise, hasty, unthinking, thoughtless; guileless, incautious; inattentive, heedless, inobservant, inadvertent, unwary, unwatchful, unvigilant. **2** defenceless, unprotected, undefended, unfortified, unshielded, open, uncovered, exposed, vulnerable. □ **in an unguarded moment** see UNAWARES 2.

unguent /únggwənt/ *n.* a soft substance used as ointment or for lubrication. [L *unguentum* f. *unguere* anoint]
■ see OINTMENT.

unguessable /úngéssəb'l/ *adj.* that cannot be guessed or imagined.

unguiculate /unggwíkyoolət/ *adj.* **1** *Zool.* having one or more nails or claws. **2** *Bot.* (of petals) having an unguis. [mod.L *unguiculatus* f. *unguiculus* dimin. of UNGUIS]

unguided /úngī́did/ *adj.* not guided in a particular path or direction; left to take its own course.

unguis /únggwiss/ *n.* (*pl.* **ungues** /-weez/) **1** *Bot.* the narrow base of a petal. **2** *Zool.* a nail or claw. [L]

ungula /úngyoolə/ *n.* (*pl.* **ungulae** /-lee/) a hoof or claw. [L, dimin. of UNGUIS]

ungulate /úngyoolət, -layt/ *adj.* & *n.* ● *adj.* hoofed. ● *n.* a hoofed mammal. [LL *ungulatus* f. UNGULA]

unhallowed /únhállōd/ *adj.* **1** not consecrated. **2** not sacred; unholy, wicked.
■ **1** see PROFANE *adj.* 1.

unhampered /únhámpərd/ *adj.* not hampered.
■ see UNIMPEDED.

unhand /únhánd/ *v.tr. rhet.* or *joc.* **1** take one's hands off (a person). **2** release from one's grasp.

unhandsome /únhánsəm/ *adj.* not handsome.
■ see UGLY 1.

unhandy /únhándi/ *adj.* **1** not easy to handle or manage; awkward. **2** not skilful in using the hands. □□ **unhandily** *adv.* **unhandiness** *n.*

unhang /únháng/ *v.tr.* (*past* and *past part.* **unhung**) take down from a hanging position.

unhappy /únháppi/ *adj.* (**unhappier**, **unhappiest**) **1** not happy, miserable. **2** unsuccessful, unfortunate. **3** causing misfortune. **4** disastrous. **5** inauspicious. □□ **unhappily** *adv.* **unhappiness** *n.*
■ **1** sad, depressed, blue, dejected, melancholy, despondent, downcast, gloomy, dismal, downhearted, dispirited, disenchanted, heavy-hearted, long-faced, disconsolate, sorrowful, miserable, woebegone, woeful, crestfallen, cheerless, joyless, forlorn, wretched, low-spirited, glum, distressed, disgruntled, tearful, *colloq.* down, down in the mouth, *formal* lachrymose. **2** unlucky, unfortunate, unsuccessful, luckless, hapless, cursed, wretched, doomed, frustrated, disappointed, let down, *colloq.* jinxed. **4** see UNFORTUNATE *adj.* 4. **5** unpropitious, inauspicious, unlucky, unfortunate, unfavourable; ill-omened, ill-fated, ill-starred, *archaic* star-crossed; infelicitous, unfitting, inappropriate, unsuitable, unsuited, wrong, inexpedient, ill-advised, poor, bad, unsatisfactory. □□ **unhappily** see *sadly* (SAD). **unhappiness** see MISERY 1.

unharbour /únhaárbər/ *v.tr. Brit.* dislodge (a deer) from a covert.

unharmed /únhaármd/ *adj.* not harmed.
■ see INTACT 2.

unharmful /únhaármfŏŏl/ *adj.* not harmful.

unharmonious /únhaarmṓniəss/ *adj.* not harmonious.

unharness /únhaárniss/ *v.tr.* remove a harness from.

unhasp /únhaásp/ *v.tr.* free from a hasp or catch; unfasten.
■ see UNDO 1.

unhatched /únhácht/ *adj.* (of an egg etc.) not hatched.

unhealthful /únhélthfŏŏl/ *adj.* harmful to health, unwholesome. □□ **unhealthfulness** *n.*

unhealthy /únhélthi/ *adj.* (**unhealthier**, **unhealthiest**) **1** not in good health. **2 a** (of a place etc.) harmful to health. **b** unwholesome. **c** *sl.* dangerous to life. □□ **unhealthily** *adv.* **unhealthiness** *n.*
■ **1** ailing, unwell, ill, sickly, infirm, feeble, frail, debilitated, unsound, sick, peaky, in poor health *or* condition, in delicate health *or* condition, indisposed, invalid, valetudinarian, valetudinary. **2 a, b** unwholesome, harmful, sickly, noxious, detrimental, insalubrious, unhealthful, damaging, injurious, destructive, deleterious, malign. **c** risky, dangerous, perilous, life-threatening, touch-and-go.

unheard /únhérd/ *adj.* **1** not heard. **2** (usu. **unheard-of**) unprecedented, unknown.
■ **1** see UNNOTICED. **2** (**unheard-of**) unknown, unfamiliar, obscure, unidentified, nameless, unsung; unimaginable, undreamed of, unprecedented, unimagined, unbelievable, inconceivable, unusual; shocking, offensive, outrageous, disgraceful, extreme, unthinkable, outlandish.

unheated /únhéetid/ *adj.* not heated.

unheeded /únhéedid/ *adj.* not heeded; disregarded.

unheedful /únhéedfŏŏl/ *adj.* heedless; taking no notice.

unheeding /únhéeding/ *adj.* not giving heed; heedless. □□ **unheedingly** *adv.*
■ see UNCONSCIOUS *adj.*

unhelpful /únhélpfŏŏl/ *adj.* not helpful. □□ **unhelpfully** *adv.* **unhelpfulness** *n.*
■ see DIFFICULT 2, USELESS 1.

unheralded /únhérrəldid/ *adj.* not heralded; unannounced.
■ unannounced, unpublicized, unadvertised; unexpected, surprise, unanticipated, unforeseen, unpredicted.

unheroic /únhirṓ-ik/ *adj.* not heroic. □□ **unheroically** *adv.*

unhesitating /únhézzitayting/ *adj.* without hesitation. □□ **unhesitatingly** *adv.* **unhesitatingness** *n.*
■ swift, rapid, quick, immediate, instantaneous, prompt, ready, unhesitant; unfaltering, unwavering, wholehearted, unqualified, unswerving, undeviating, staunch, steadfast, implicit, resolute, decided. □□ **unhesitatingly** see IMMEDIATELY *adv.* 1.

unhindered /únhíndərd/ *adj.* not hindered.
■ see UNIMPEDED.

unhinge /únhínj/ *v.tr.* **1** take (a door etc.) off its hinges. **2** (esp. as **unhinged** *adj.*) unsettle or disorder (a person's mind etc.), make (a person) crazy.
■ **1** see UNDO 1. **2** (**unhinged**) see CRAZY 1.

unhip /únhíp/ *adj. sl.* unaware of current fashions.

unhistoric /únhistórrik/ *adj.* not historic or historical.

unhistorical /únhistórrik'l/ *adj.* not historical. □□ **unhistorically** *adv.*

unhitch /únhích/ *v.tr.* **1** release from a hitched state. **2** unhook, unfasten.
■ see DISCONNECT 1, UNDO 1.

unholy /únhṓli/ *adj.* (**unholier**, **unholiest**) **1** impious, profane, wicked. **2** *colloq.* dreadful, outrageous (*made an*

unholy row about it). **3** not holy. ▫▫ **unholiness** *n.* [OE *unhālig* (as UN-[1], HOLY)]
■ **1** see IMPIOUS. **2** see DREADFUL *adj.* 1.

unhonoured /ùnnónnərd/ *adj.* not honoured.

unhook /ùnhŏŏk/ *v.tr.* **1** remove from a hook or hooks. **2** unfasten by releasing a hook or hooks.
■ see DISCONNECT 1, UNDO 1.

unhoped /ùnhṓpt/ *adj.* (foll. by *for*) not hoped for or expected.
■ (*unhoped for*) see UNFORESEEN.

unhorse /ùnhórss/ *v.tr.* **1** throw or drag from a horse. **2** (of a horse) throw (a rider). **3** dislodge, overthrow.

unhouse /ùnhówz/ *v.tr.* deprive of shelter; turn out of a house.

unhuman /ùnhyŏŏmən/ *adj.* **1** not human. **2** superhuman. **3** inhuman, brutal.

unhung[1] /ùnhúng/ *adj.* **1** not (yet) executed by hanging. **2** not hung up (for exhibition).

unhung[2] *past* and *past part.* of UNHANG.

unhurried /ùnhúrrid/ *adj.* not hurried. ▫▫ **unhurriedly** *adv.*
■ leisurely, unrushed, easy, easygoing, relaxed, casual, gradual, deliberate, slow, steady, sedate, calm.
▫▫ **unhurriedly** at one's leisure *or* convenience, in one's own time, slowly, sedately, steadily, calmly, deliberately.

unhurt /ùnhúrt/ *adj.* not hurt.
■ see UNSCATHED.

unhusk /ùnhúsk/ *v.tr.* remove a husk or shell from.

unhygienic /ùnhījeénik/ *adj.* not hygienic. ▫▫ **unhygienically** *adv.*
■ see UNWHOLESOME 1.

unhyphenated /ùnhīfənaytid/ *adj.* not hyphenated.

uni /yŏŏni/ *n.* (*pl.* **unis**) esp. *Brit.*, *Austral.*, & *NZ colloq.* a university. [abbr.]

uni- /yŏŏni/ *comb. form* one; having or consisting of one. [L f. *unus* one]

Uniat /yŏŏniat/ *adj.* & *n.* (also **Uniate** /-ayt/) ● *adj.* of or relating to any community of Christians in E. Europe or the Near East that acknowledges papal supremacy but retains its own liturgy etc. ● *n.* a member of such a community. [Russ. *uniyat* f. *uniya* f. L *unio* UNION]

uniaxial /yŏŏniáksiəl/ *adj.* having a single axis. ▫▫ **uniaxially** *adv.*

unicameral /yŏŏnikámmərəl/ *adj.* with a single legislative chamber.

UNICEF /yŏŏnisef/ *abbr.* United Nations Children's (orig. International Children's Emergency) Fund.

unicellular /yŏŏnisélyoolər/ *adj.* (of an organism, organ, tissue, etc.) consisting of a single cell.

unicolour /yŏŏnikullər/ *adj.* (also **unicoloured**) of one colour.

unicorn /yŏŏnikorn/ *n.* **1 a** a fabulous animal with a horse's body and a single straight horn. **b** a heraldic representation of this, with a twisted horn, a deer's feet, a goat's beard, and a lion's tail. **c** used in old translations of the Old Testament for the Hebrew *r^eʾem*, a two-horned animal, probably a wild ox. **2 a** a pair of horses and a third horse in front. **b** an equipage with these. **3** (in full **unicorn whale** or **sea-unicorn**) the narwhal. [ME f. OF *unicorne* f. L *unicornis* f. UNI- + *cornu* horn, transl. Gk *monocerōs*]

unicuspid /yŏŏnikúspid/ *adj.* & *n.* ● *adj.* with one cusp. ● *n.* a unicuspid tooth.

unicycle /yŏŏnisīk'l/ *n.* a single-wheeled cycle, esp. as used by acrobats. ▫▫ **unicyclist** *n.*

unidea'd /ùnnīdeéəd/ *adj.* having no ideas.

unideal /ùnnīdeéəl/ *adj.* not ideal.

unidentifiable /ùnnīdéntifīəb'l/ *adj.* unable to be identified.
■ see NAMELESS 1, 3, 5.

unidentified /ùnnīdéntifīd/ *adj.* not identified.
■ nameless, anonymous, unknown, incognito, unmarked, unnamed, unfamiliar, unrecognized, mysterious, unspecified.

unidimensional /yŏŏnidīménshən'l/ *adj.* having (only) one dimension.

unidirectional /yŏŏnidirékshən'l, yŏŏnidī-/ *adj.* having only one direction of motion, operation, etc. ▫▫ **unidirectionality** /-nálliti/ *n.* **unidirectionally** *adv.*

unification /yŏŏnifikáysh'n/ *n.* the act or an instance of unifying; the state of being unified. ▫ **Unification Church** a religious organization founded in 1954 in Korea by Sun Myung Moon (cf. MOONIE). ▫▫ **unificatory** *adj.*
■ see UNION 1.

uniflow /yŏŏniflō/ *adj.* involving flow (esp. of steam or waste gases) in one direction only.

uniform /yŏŏniform/ *adj.*, *n.*, & *v.* ● *adj.* **1** not changing in form or character; the same, unvarying (*present a uniform appearance*; *all of uniform size and shape*). **2** conforming to the same standard, rules, or pattern. **3** constant in the course of time (*uniform acceleration*). **4** (of a tax, law, etc.) not varying with time or place. ● *n.* uniform distinctive clothing worn by members of the same body, e.g. by soldiers, police, and schoolchildren. ● *v.tr.* **1** clothe in uniform (*a uniformed officer*). **2** make uniform. ▫▫ **uniformly** *adv.* [F *uniforme* or L *uniformis* (as UNI-, FORM)]
■ *adj.* **1, 2** homogeneous, consistent, unvaried, unchanged, unaltered, constant; unvarying, unchanging; invariable, unchangeable, unalterable, regimented, standard; ordered, orderly, equal, like, identical, (the) same; alike; even, unbroken, smooth, regular, flat. **3** see EVEN[1] *adj.* 2a. ● *n.* livery, habit, regalia, costume, outfit; regimentals. ▫▫ **uniformly** see ALIKE *adv.*

uniformitarian /yŏŏnifórmitáiriən/ *adj.* & *n.* ● *adj.* of the theory that geological processes are always due to continuously and uniformly operating forces. ● *n.* a holder of this theory. ▫▫ **uniformitarianism** *n.*

uniformity /yŏŏnifórmiti/ *n.* (*pl.* **-ies**) **1** being uniform; sameness, consistency. **2** an instance of this. ▫ **Act of Uniformity** *hist.* any of four acts (esp. that of 1662) for securing uniformity in public worship and the use of a particular Book of Common Prayer. [ME f. OF *uniformité* or LL *uniformitas* (as UNIFORM)]
■ regularity, similarity, sameness, homogeneity, consistency, symmetry, evenness, invariability, unchangeability, unchangeableness, similitude, conformity, agreement, concord, accord, harmoniousness; harmony, concordance, accordance, conformance, correspondence; dullness, monotony, drabness, tedium, featurelessness, flatness, lack of variety, changelessness.

unify /yŏŏnifī/ *v.tr.* (also *absol.*) (**-ies, -ied**) reduce to unity or uniformity. ▫ **unified field theory** *Physics* a theory that seeks to explain all the field phenomena (e.g. gravitation and electromagnetism: see FIELD *n.* 9) formerly treated by separate theories. ▫▫ **unifier** *n.* [F *unifier* or LL *unificare* (as UNI-, -FY)]
■ consolidate, unite, combine, amalgamate, coalesce, bring together, fuse, join, weld, merge, confederate, incorporate, integrate.

unilateral /yŏŏniláttərəl/ *adj.* **1** performed by or affecting only one person or party (*unilateral disarmament*; *unilateral declaration of independence*). **2** one-sided. **3** (of the parking of vehicles) restricted to one side of the street. **4** (of leaves) all on the same side of the stem. **5** (of a line of descent) through ancestors of one sex only. ▫▫ **unilaterally** *adv.*
■ **1, 2** see *one-sided* 2.

unilateralism /yŏŏniláttərəliz'm/ *n.* **1** unilateral disarmament. **2** *US* the pursuit of a foreign policy without allies. ▫▫ **unilateralist** *n.* & *adj.*

unilingual /yŏŏnilínggwəl/ *adj.* of or in only one language. ▫▫ **unilingually** *adv.*

uniliteral /yŏŏnilíttərəl/ *adj.* consisting of one letter.

unilluminated /ùnnilŏŏminaytid, ùnnilyŏŏ-/ *adj.* not illuminated.
■ see DARK *adj.* 1.

unillustrated /ùnníllәstraytid/ *adj.* (esp. of a book) without illustrations.

unilocular /yoōnilókyoolər/ *adj. Bot. & Zool.* single-chambered.
unimaginable /únnimájinəb'l/ *adj.* impossible to imagine. □□ **unimaginably** *adv.*
■ see INCONCEIVABLE 1, UNTOLD 2.
unimaginative /únnimájinətiv/ *adj.* lacking imagination; stolid, dull. □□ **unimaginatively** *adv.* **unimaginativeness** *n.*
■ see PROSAIC.
unimpaired /únnimpáird/ *adj.* not impaired.
■ see *flawless* (FLAW[1]).
unimpassioned /únnimpásh'nd/ *adj.* not impassioned.
unimpeachable /únnimpeéchəb'l/ *adj.* giving no opportunity for censure; beyond reproach or question. □□ **unimpeachably** *adv.*
■ see IRREPROACHABLE.
unimpeded /únnimpeédid/ *adj.* not impeded. □□ **unimpededly** *adv.*
■ unblocked, unchecked, free, unconstrained, unrestrained, unhindered, unhampered, unencumbered, open, clear, untrammelled, unrestricted, unobstructed.
unimportance /únnimpórt'nss/ *n.* lack of importance.
■ see *triviality* (TRIVIAL).
unimportant /únnimpórt'nt/ *adj.* not important.
■ see INSIGNIFICANT 1.
unimposing /únnimpṓzing/ *adj.* unimpressive. □□ **unimposingly** *adv.*
■ unimpressive, nugatory, trivial, trifling, minor, unimportant, insignificant, puny, inconsiderable, negligible, ordinary, unexceptional, humble, modest.
unimpressed /únnimprést/ *adj.* not impressed.
■ see UNENTHUSIASTIC.
unimpressionable /únnimpréshənəb'l/ *adj.* not impressionable.
unimpressive /únnimpréssiv/ *adj.* not impressive. □□ **unimpressively** *adv.* **unimpressiveness** *n.*
■ see UNDISTINGUISHED.
unimproved /únnimproōvd/ *adj.* **1** not made better. **2** not made use of. **3** (of land) not used for agriculture or building; not developed.
unincorporated /únninkórpəraytid/ *adj.* **1** not incorporated or united. **2** not formed into a corporation.
uninfected /únninféktid/ *adj.* not infected.
uninflamed /únninfláymd/ *adj.* not inflamed.
uninflammable /únninflámməb'l/ *adj.* not inflammable.
uninflected /únninfléktid/ *adj.* **1** *Gram.* (of a language) not having inflections. **2** not changing or varying. **3** not bent or deflected.
uninfluenced /únninflooənst/ *adj.* (often foll. by *by*) not influenced.
■ (*uninfluenced by*) see UNAFFECTED 1.
uninfluential /únninfloo-énsh'l/ *adj.* having little or no influence.
uninformative /únninfórmətiv/ *adj.* not informative; giving little information.
uninformed /únninfórmd/ *adj.* **1** not informed or instructed. **2** ignorant, uneducated.
■ ignorant, unknowledgeable, unenlightened, uneducated, unschooled, untutored, untaught, uninstructed, unaware, incognizant, benighted, *literary* nescient.
uninhabitable /únninhábbitəb'l/ *adj.* that cannot be inhabited. □□ **uninhabitableness** *n.*
■ see INHOSPITABLE 2, DERELICT *adj.* 1, 2.
uninhabited /únninhábbitid/ *adj.* not inhabited.
■ desolate, empty, abandoned, deserted, unoccupied, vacant, vacated, tenantless, untenanted; desert, unpopulated, unpeopled, unlived-in, trackless, depopulated, waste, barren.
uninhibited /únninhíbbitid/ *adj.* not inhibited. □□ **uninhibitedly** *adv.* **uninhibitedness** *n.*
■ wild, unchecked, unbridled, uncurbed, rampant, intemperate, boisterous, unrepressed, unconstrained, unrestrained, abandoned, uncontrolled, unselfconscious, unreserved, relaxed, casual, easygoing, free (and easy), natural, spontaneous, open, frank, candid, outspoken, *colloq.* upfront.
uninitiated /únninishiaytid/ *adj.* not initiated; not admitted or instructed.
■ see *inexperienced* (INEXPERIENCE).
uninjured /únnínjərd/ *adj.* not injured.
■ see UNSCATHED.
uninspired /únninspīrd/ *adj.* **1** not inspired. **2** (of oratory etc.) commonplace.
■ **2** see PROSAIC.
uninspiring /únninspīring/ *adj.* not inspiring. □□ **uninspiringly** *adv.*
■ see PROSAIC.
uninstructed /únninstrúktid/ *adj.* not instructed or informed.
■ see UNINFORMED.
uninsurable /únninshoórəb'l/ *adj.* that cannot be insured.
uninsured /únninshoórd/ *adj.* not insured.
unintelligent /únnintéllijənt/ *adj.* not intelligent. □□ **unintelligently** *adv.*
■ see STUPID *adj.* 1, 5.
unintelligible /únnintéllijib'l/ *adj.* not intelligible. □□ **unintelligibility** /-bílliti/ *n.* **unintelligibleness** *n.* **unintelligibly** *adv.*
■ see INCOMPREHENSIBLE.
unintended /únninténdid/ *adj.* not intended.
■ see INADVERTENT 1, INVOLUNTARY.
unintentional /únninténshən'l/ *adj.* not intentional. □□ **unintentionally** *adv.*
■ see INADVERTENT 1, INVOLUNTARY. □□ **unintentionally** see UNAWARES 2.
uninterested /únníntrəstid, -tristid/ *adj.* **1** not interested. **2** unconcerned, indifferent. □□ **uninterestedly** *adv.* **uninterestedness** *n.*
■ see UNENTHUSIASTIC, see INDIFFERENT 4.
uninteresting /únníntrəsting, -tristing/ *adj.* not interesting. □□ **uninterestingly** *adv.* **uninterestingness** *n.*
■ see PROSAIC.
uninterpretable /únnintérpritəb'l/ *adj.* that cannot be interpreted.
uninterruptable /únnintərúptəb'l/ *adj.* that cannot be interrupted.
uninterrupted /únnintərúptid/ *adj.* not interrupted. □□ **uninterruptedly** *adv.* **uninterruptedness** *n.*
■ see NON-STOP *adj.*
uninucleate /yoōninyoōkliayt, -kliət/ *adj. Biol.* having a single nucleus.
uninventive /únninvéntiv/ *adj.* not inventive. □□ **uninventively** *adv.* **uninventiveness** *n.*
uninvestigated /únninvéstigaytid/ *adj.* not investigated.
uninvited /únninvītid/ *adj.* not invited. □□ **uninvitedly** *adv.*
■ see UNASKED.
uninviting /únninvīting/ *adj.* not inviting, unattractive, repellent. □□ **uninvitingly** *adv.*
■ repulsive, repellent, offensive, unappealing, unattractive, unpleasant, inhospitable, disagreeable, distasteful, unappetizing, unsavoury, sickening, revolting, nauseating, obnoxious, nasty, disgusting, *Brit.* off-putting.
uninvoked /únninvṓkt/ *adj.* not invoked.
uninvolved /únninvólvd/ *adj.* not involved.
■ see *detached* (DETACH 3a), SIMPLE *adj.* 1.
union /yoōnyən/ *n.* **1 a** the act or an instance of uniting; the state of being united. **b** (**the Union**) *hist.* the uniting of the English and Scottish crowns in 1603, of the English and Scottish parliaments in 1707, or of Great Britain and Ireland in 1801. **2 a** a whole resulting from the combination of parts or members. **b** a political unit formed in this way, esp. the US, the UK, or South Africa. **3** = *trade union.* **4** marriage, matrimony. **5** concord, agreement (*lived together in perfect union*). **6** (**Union**) **a** a general social club and

debating society at some universities and colleges. **b** the buildings or accommodation of such a society. **7** *Math.* the totality of the members of two or more sets. **8** *Brit. hist.* **a** two or more parishes consolidated for the administration of the poor laws. **b** (in full **union workhouse**) a workhouse erected by this. **9** *Brit.* an association of independent (esp. Congregational or Baptist) churches for purposes of cooperation. **10** a part of a flag with a device emblematic of union, normally occupying the upper corner next to the staff. **11** a joint or coupling for pipes etc. **12** a fabric of mixed materials, e.g. cotton with linen or silk. □ **union-bashing** *Brit. colloq.* active opposition to trade unions and their rights. **union catalogue** a catalogue of the combined holdings of several libraries. **union down** (of a flag) hoisted with the union below as a signal of distress. **Union Jack** (or **flag**) the national ensign of the United Kingdom formed by the union of the crosses of St George, St Andrew, and St Patrick. **union jack** (in the US) a jack consisting of the union from the national flag. **union shop** a shop, factory, trade, etc., in which employees must belong to a trade union or join one within an agreed time. **union suit** *US* a single undergarment for the body and legs; combinations. [ME f. OF *union* or eccl.L *unio* unity f. L *unus* one]

■ **1** unification, combination, junction, conjunction, alliance, association, coalition, amalgamation, fusion, bonding, bond, marriage, confederation, confederacy, synthesis, blending, blend, mixing, mixture, merger, federation, coherence, cohesion, togetherness. **2** alliance, association, organization, society, circle, fraternity, club, fellowship, team, ring, gang, syndicate, coalition, party, confederation, confederacy, federation, league, consortium, bloc, cartel, trust. **4** marriage, matrimony, wedlock, partnership. **5** agreement, accord, harmony, harmoniousness, concord, congruity, coherence, compatibility, unanimity, unity. **11** joint, seam, splice, junction, conjunction, weld; coupling; graft.

unionist /yŏŏnyənist/ *n.* **1 a** a member of a trade union. **b** an advocate of trade unions. **2** (usu. **Unionist**) an advocate of union, esp.: **a** a person opposed to the rupture of the parliamentary union between Great Britain and Northern Ireland (formerly between Great Britain and Ireland). **b** *hist.* a person who opposed secession during the American Civil War. □□ **unionism** *n.* **unionistic** /-nístik/ *adj.*

unionize /yŏŏnyənīz/ *v.tr.* & *intr.* (also **-ise**) bring or come under trade-union organization or rules. □□ **unionization** /-záysh'n/ *n.*

un-ionized /únnīənīzd/ *adj.* (also **-ised**) not ionized.

uniparous /yoonípparəss/ *adj.* **1** producing one offspring at a birth. **2** *Bot.* having one axis or branch.

uniped /yŏŏniped/ *n.* & *adj.* ● *n.* a person having only one foot or leg. ● *adj.* one-footed, one-legged. [UNI- + *pes pedis* foot]

unipersonal /yŏŏnipérsən'l/ *adj.* (of the Deity) existing only as one person.

uniplanar /yŏŏnipláynər/ *adj.* lying in one plane.

unipod /yŏŏnipod/ *n.* a one-legged support for a camera etc. [UNI-, after TRIPOD]

unipolar /yŏŏnipṓlər/ *adj.* **1** (esp. of an electric or magnetic apparatus) showing only one kind of polarity. **2** *Biol.* (of a nerve cell etc.) having only one pole. □□ **unipolarity** /-lárriti/ *n.*

unique /yooneék/ *adj.* & *n.* ● *adj.* **1** of which there is only one; unequalled; having no like, equal, or parallel (*his position was unique*; *this vase is considered unique*). **2** *disp.* unusual, remarkable (*the most unique man I ever met*). ● *n.* a unique thing or person. □□ **uniquely** *adv.* **uniqueness** *n.* [F f. L *unicus* f. *unus* one]

■ *adj.* **1** single, lone, (one and) only, solitary, one of a kind, *sui generis*, individual, distinctive, singular; unequalled, unparalleled, unrivalled, nonpareil, incomparable, inimitable, peerless, unmatched, unsurpassed, unexcelled, second to none, *colloq.* one-off. **2** see EXCEPTIONAL. □□ **uniqueness** see SINGULARITY 1.

unironed /únnīrnd/ *adj.* (esp. of clothing, linen, etc.) not ironed.

uniserial /yŏŏniseériəl/ *adj. Bot.* & *Zool.* arranged in one row.

unisex /yŏŏniseks/ *adj.* (of clothing, hairstyles, etc.) designed to be suitable for both sexes.

unisexual /yŏŏniséksyooəl, -sékshooəl/ *adj.* **1 a** of one sex. **b** *Bot.* having stamens or pistils but not both. **2** unisex. □□ **unisexuality** /-séksyoo-álliti, -sékshoo-álliti/ *n.* **unisexually** *adv.*

unison /yŏŏnis'n/ *n.* & *adj.* ● *n.* **1** *Mus.* **a** coincidence in pitch of sounds or notes. **b** this regarded as an interval. **2** *Mus.* a combination of voices or instruments at the same pitch or at pitches differing by one or more octaves (*sang in unison*). **3** agreement, concord (*acted in perfect unison*). ● *adj. Mus.* coinciding in pitch. □ **unison string** a string tuned in unison with another string and meant to be sounded with it. □□ **unisonant** /yoonissənənt/ *adj.* **unisonous** /yoonissənəss/ *adj.* [OF *unison* or LL *unisonus* (as UNI-, *sonus* SOUND[1])]

■ *n.* **3** see UNITY 2; (*in unison*) in harmony, together, as one, harmonious; (*in unison with*) corresponding exactly to *or* with, in (perfect) accord with, in consonance with, consonant with.

unissued /únnishŏŏd, -íssyŏŏd/ *adj.* not issued.

unit /yŏŏnit/ *n.* **1 a** an individual thing, person, or group regarded as single and complete, esp. for purposes of calculation. **b** each of the (smallest) separate individuals or groups into which a complex whole may be analysed (*the family as the unit of society*). **2** a quantity chosen as a standard in terms of which other quantities may be expressed (*unit of heat*; *SI unit*; *mass per unit volume*). **3** *Brit.* the smallest share in a unit trust. **4** a device with a specified function forming part of a complex mechanism. **5** a piece of furniture for fitting with others like it or made of complementary parts. **6** a group with a special function in an organization. **7** a group of buildings, wards, etc., in a hospital. **8** the number 'one'. □ **unit cell** *Crystallog.* the smallest repeating group of atoms, ions, or molecules in a crystal. **unit cost** the cost of producing one item of manufacture. **unit-holder** *Brit.* a person with a holding in a unit trust. **unit price** the price charged for each unit of goods supplied. **unit trust** *Brit.* an investment company investing combined contributions from many persons in various securities and paying them dividends in proportion to their holdings. [L *unus*, prob. after DIGIT]

■ **1, 4, 5** element, component, entity, part, item, constituent, piece, portion, segment, member, section, module. **6** see SQUAD, DIVISION 6.

Unitarian /yŏŏnitáiriən/ *n.* & *adj.* ● *n.* **1** a person who believes that God is not a Trinity but one person. **2** a member of a religious body maintaining this and advocating freedom from formal dogma or doctrine. ● *adj.* of or relating to the Unitarians. □□ **Unitarianism** *n.* [mod.L *unitarius* f. L *unitas* UNITY]

unitary /yŏŏnitəri, -tri/ *adj.* **1** of a unit or units. **2** marked by unity or uniformity. □□ **unitarily** *adv.* **unitarity** /-tárriti/ *n.*

unite /yoonīt/ *v.* **1** *tr.* & *intr.* join together; make or become one; combine. **2** *tr.* & *intr.* join together for a common purpose or action (*united in their struggle against injustice*). **3** *tr.* & *intr.* join in marriage. **4** *tr.* possess (qualities, features, etc.) in combination (*united anger with mercy*). **5** *intr.* & *tr.* form or cause to form a physical or chemical whole (*oil will not unite with water*). □□ **unitive** /yŏŏnitiv/ *adj.* **unitively** /yŏŏnitivli/ *adv.* [ME f. L *unire unit-* f. *unus* one]

■ **1, 5** bond, join *or* fuse *or* weld *or* solder *or* glue *or* stick *or* knit *or* splice *or* tie *or* bind *or* fasten *or* fix *or* fit (together); combine, integrate, incorporate, coalesce, compound, synthesize, blend, mix, intermix, amalgamate, consolidate, mingle, *literary* commingle. **2** combine, unify, merge, coalesce, amalgamate, consolidate, collaborate, ally, join forces, join (together), team up, band together, *colloq.* gang up. **3** join, unify, marry, link, connect, *colloq.* get spliced *or* hitched, *usu. formal or literary* wed. **4** combine, blend, compound, marry, mix, mingle.

united /yoonī́tid/ *adj.* **1** that has united or been united. **2 a** of or produced by two more persons or things in union; joint. **b** resulting from the union of two or more parts (esp. in the names of churches, societies, and football clubs). **3** in agreement, of like mind. □ **United Brethren** *Eccl.* the Moravians. **United Kingdom** Great Britain and Northern Ireland (until 1922, Great Britain and Ireland). **United Nations** (orig., in 1942) those united against the Axis powers in the war of 1939–45, (later) a supranational peace-seeking organization of these and many other States. **United Provinces** *hist.* **1** the seven provinces united in 1579 and forming the basis of the republic of the Netherlands. **2** an Indian administrative division formed by the union of Agra and Oudh and called Uttar Pradesh since 1950. **United Reformed Church** a Church formed in 1972 from the English Presbyterian and Congregational Churches. **United States** (in full **United States of America**) a federal republic of 50 States, mostly in N. America and including Alaska and Hawaii. □□ **unitedly** *adv.*

■ **1** merged, coalesced, unified, amalgamated, consolidated, combined, incorporated, connected, linked. **2 a** joint, common, communal, mutual, combined, allied, pooled, shared, collective; collaborative, cooperative, synergetic, synergistic, concerted, coordinated. **b** amalgamated, allied, unified, merged, combined, consolidated, incorporated. **3** agreed, unanimous, in agreement, of one mind, of like mind *or* opinion, like-minded, in accord, in harmony, harmonious.

unity /yóōniti/ *n.* (*pl.* **-ies**) **1** oneness; being one, single, or individual; being formed of parts that constitute a whole; due interconnection and coherence of parts (*disturbs the unity of the idea*; *the pictures lack unity*; *national unity*). **2** harmony or concord between persons etc. (*lived together in unity*). **3** a thing forming a complex whole (*a person regarded as a unity*). **4** *Math.* the number 'one', the factor that leaves unchanged the quantity on which it operates. **5** *Theatr.* each of the three dramatic principles requiring limitation of the supposed time of a drama to that occupied in acting it or to a single day (**unity of time**), use of one scene throughout (**unity of place**), and concentration on the development of a single plot (**unity of action**). [ME f. OF *unité* f. L *unitas -tatis* f. *unus* one]

■ **1** oneness, singularity, integrity, singleness, congruity, uniformity, congruence, homogeneity, identity, sameness, resemblance, likeness, similarity, similitude; coherence, cohesion, unification, union. **2** consistency, unanimity, constancy, uniformity, sameness, consensus, agreement, union, harmony, harmoniousness, concord, unison, concordance, consonance, accord, solidarity, compatibility, concurrence, continuity, rapport, sympathy, like-mindedness.

Univ. *abbr.* University.

univalent *adj.* & *n.* ● *adj.* **1** /yóōniváylənt/ *Chem.* having a valency of one. **2** /yoonívvələnt/ *Biol.* (of a chromosome) remaining unpaired during meiosis. ● *n.* /yoonívvələnt/ *Biol.* a univalent chromosome. [UNI- + *valent-* pres. part. stem (as VALENCE[1])]

univalve /yóōnivalv/ *adj.* & *n. Zool.* ● *adj.* having one valve. ● *n.* a univalve mollusc.

universal /yóōnivérs'l/ *adj.* & *n.* ● *adj.* **1** of, belonging to, or done etc. by all persons or things in the world or in the class concerned; applicable to all cases (*the feeling was universal*; *met with universal approval*). **2** *Logic* (of a proposition) in which something is asserted of all of a class (opp. PARTICULAR). ● *n.* **1** *Logic* a universal proposition. **2** *Philos.* **a** a term or concept of general application. **b** a nature or essence signified by a general term. □ **universal agent** an agent empowered to do all that can be delegated. **universal compass** a compass with legs that may be extended for large circles. **universal coupling** (or **joint**) a coupling or joint which can transmit rotary power by a shaft at any selected angle. **universal language** an artificial language intended for use by all nations. **universal proposition** *Logic* a proposition in which the predicate is affirmed or denied of all members of a class (opp. *particular proposition*). **universal suffrage** a suffrage extending to all adults with minor exceptions. **universal time** = GREENWICH MEAN TIME. □□ **universality** /-sálliti/ *n.* **universalize** *v.tr.* (also **-ise**). **universalization** /-līzáysh'n/ *n.* **universally** *adv.* [ME f. OF *universal* or L *universalis* (as UNIVERSE)]

■ *adj.* **1** prevalent, prevailing, general, global, worldwide, widespread, ubiquitous, omnipresent, common, pandemic, epidemic; cosmic, infinite, boundless, limitless, unlimited, measureless, endless, uncircumscribed, all-inclusive, all-embracing, all-encompassing, wide-ranging, comprehensive. □□ **universality** see *prevalence* (PREVALENT). **universally** in every case *or* instance, in all cases *or* instances, unexceptionally, without exception, uniformly, always, invariably, globally, extensively, widely, generally, everywhere.

universalist /yóōnivérsəlist/ *n. Theol.* **1** a person who holds that all mankind will eventually be saved. **2** a member of an organized body of Christians who hold this. □□ **universalism** *n.* **universalistic** /-lístik/ *adj.*

universe /yóōniverss/ *n.* **1 a** all existing things; the whole creation; the cosmos. **b** a sphere of existence, influence, activity, etc. **2** all mankind. **3** *Statistics* & *Logic* all the objects under consideration. □ **universe of discourse** *Logic* = sense 3. [F *univers* f. L *universum* neut. of *universus* combined into one, whole f. UNI- + *versus* past part. of *vertere* turn]

■ **1 a** cosmos, creation, macrocosm; world. **b** world, sphere, province, preserve, domain, circle, milieu, territory, corner, quarter, microcosm. **2** mankind, humanity, people, society, humankind, world, microcosm.

university /yóōnivérsiti/ *n.* (*pl.* **-ies**) **1** an educational institution designed for instruction, examination, or both, of students in many branches of advanced learning, conferring degrees in various faculties, and often embodying colleges and similar institutions. **2** the members of this collectively. **3** a team, crew, etc., representing a university. □ **at university** studying at a university. [ME f. OF *université* f. L *universitas -tatis* the whole (world), in LL college, guild (as UNIVERSE)]

univocal /yoonívvək'l, yóōnivṓk'l/ *adj.* & *n.* ● *adj.* (of a word etc.) having only one proper meaning. ● *n.* a univocal word. □□ **univocality** /yóōnivōkálliti/ *n.* **univocally** *adv.*

unjoin /únjóyn/ *v.tr.* detach from being joined; separate.

unjoined /únjóynd/ *adj.* not joined.

unjoint /únjóynt/ *v.tr.* **1** separate the joints of. **2** disunite.

unjust /únjúst/ *adj.* not just, contrary to justice or fairness. □□ **unjustly** *adv.* **unjustness** *n.*

■ see UNREASONABLE 1, *one-sided* 1. □□ **unjustly** see ILL *adv.* 1.

unjustifiable /únjústifīəb'l/ *adj.* not justifiable. □□ **unjustifiably** *adv.*

■ see UNTENABLE, UNREASONABLE 1. □□ **unjustifiably** see *unduly* (UNDUE).

unjustified /únjústifīd/ *adj.* not justified.

■ see UNWARRANTED 2.

unkempt /únkémpt/ *adj.* **1** untidy, of neglected appearance. **2** uncombed, dishevelled. □□ **unkemptly** *adv.* **unkemptness** *n.* [UN-[1] + archaic *kempt* past part. of *kemb* comb f. OE *cemban*]

■ **1** ungroomed, untidy, messy, messed-up, bedraggled, shaggy, rumpled, slovenly, sloppy, frowzy, blowzy, draggle-tailed, *colloq.* scruffy, *US colloq.* mussy, mussed(-up). **2** dishevelled, uncombed, tousled, disarranged, wind-blown, disordered, untidy, ungroomed, messy, messed-up, bedraggled, shaggy, blowzy, *colloq.* scruffy, *US colloq.* mussy, mussed(-up).

unkept /únképt/ *adj.* **1** (of a promise, law, etc.) not observed; disregarded. **2** not tended; neglected.

unkillable /únkílləb'l/ *adj.* that cannot be killed.

unkind /únkínd/ *adj.* **1** not kind. **2** harsh, cruel. **3** unpleasant. □□ **unkindly** *adv.* **unkindness** *n.*

■ inconsiderate, unthoughtful, thoughtless, unfeeling, unconcerned, insensitive, unfriendly, unsympathetic, uncharitable, unchristian, uncaring, hard-hearted, heartless, flinty, cold-hearted, hard, rigid, callous, tough, inflexible, unyielding, unbending, severe, harsh, stern, cruel, malicious, mean, hurtful, inhuman, unpleasant, brutal, *colloq.* beastly. □□ **unkindly** see ROUGHLY 1. **unkindness** see DISSERVICE.

unking /únkíng/ *v.tr.* **1** deprive of the position of king; dethrone. **2** deprive (a country) of a king.

unkink /únkíngk/ *v.* **1** *tr.* remove the kinks from; straighten. **2** *intr.* lose kinks; become straight.

unknit /ún-nít/ *v.tr.* (**unknitted, unknitting**) separate (things joined, knotted, or interlocked).

unknot /ún-nót/ *v.tr.* (**unknotted, unknotting**) release the knot or knots of, untie.

■ see UNDO 1.

unknowable /ún-nṓəb'l/ *adj.* & *n.* ● *adj.* that cannot be known. ● *n.* **1** an unknowable thing. **2** (**the Unknowable**) the postulated absolute or ultimate reality.

unknowing /ún-nṓing/ *adj.* & *n.* ● *adj.* (often foll. by *of*) not knowing; ignorant, unconscious. ● *n.* ignorance (*cloud of unknowing*). □□ **unknowingly** *adv.* **unknowingness** *n.*

■ *adj.* see UNAWARE *adj.* 1. □□ **unknowingly** see UNAWARES 2.

unknown /ún-nṓn/ *adj.* & *n.* ● *adj.* (often foll. by *to*) not known, unfamiliar (*his purpose was unknown to me*). ● *n.* **1** an unknown thing or person. **2** an unknown quantity (*equation in two unknowns*). □ **unknown country** see COUNTRY. **unknown quantity** a person or thing whose nature, significance, etc., cannot be determined. **Unknown Soldier** an unidentified representative member of a country's armed forces killed in war, given burial with special honours in a national memorial. **unknown to** without the knowledge of (*did it unknown to me*). **Unknown Warrior** = *Unknown Soldier*. □□ **unknownness** *n.*

■ *adj.* unrecognized, unfamiliar, strange, unnamed, anonymous, nameless, incognito, unidentified, unspecified; obscure, unheard-of, little-known, humble, undistinguished, unsung; unexplored, uninvestigated, unresearched, undiscovered, unrevealed, mysterious, uncharted, unmapped, untold, dark. ● *n.* **1** see NOBODY *n.* □ **unknown to** unbeknown(st) to.

unlabelled /únláyb'ld/ *adj.* (*US* **unlabeled**) not labelled; without a label.

unlaboured /únláybərd/ *adj.* (*US* **unlabored**) not laboured.

unlace /únláyss/ *v.tr.* **1** undo the lace or laces of. **2** unfasten or loosen in this way.

■ see UNDO 1.

unlade /únláyd/ *v.tr.* **1** take the cargo out of (a ship). **2** discharge (a cargo etc.) from a ship.

unladen /únláyd'n/ *adj.* not laden. □ **unladen weight** the weight of a vehicle etc. when not loaded with goods etc.

unladylike /únláydilīk/ *adj.* not ladylike.

■ see UNSEEMLY 2.

unlaid[1] /únláyd/ *adj.* not laid.

unlaid[2] *past* and *past part.* of UNLAY.

unlamented /únləméntid/ *adj.* not lamented.

■ unmissed, unmourned, unbemoaned, unbewailed, unloved.

unlash /únlásh/ *v.tr.* unfasten (a thing lashed down etc.).

■ see UNDO 1.

unlatch /únlách/ *v.* **1** *tr.* release the latch of. **2** *tr.* & *intr.* open or be opened in this way.

■ see UNDO 1.

unlawful /únláwfōōl/ *adj.* not lawful; illegal, not permissible. □□ **unlawfully** *adv.* **unlawfulness** *n.*

■ illegal, illicit, against the law, illegitimate, criminal, felonious, wrong; outlawed, banned, prohibited, forbidden, interdicted, disallowed, proscribed, *verboten*; unauthorized, unlicensed, unsanctioned, *colloq.* crooked, *Austral.* & *NZ sl.* sly.

unlay /únláy/ *v.tr.* (*past* and *past part.* **unlaid**) *Naut.* untwist (a rope). [UN-[2] + LAY[1]]

unleaded /únléddid/ *adj.* **1** (of petrol etc.) without added lead. **2** not covered, weighted, or framed with lead. **3** *Printing* not spaced with leads.

unlearn /únlérn/ *v.tr.* (*past* and *past part.* **unlearned** or **unlearnt**) **1** discard from one's memory. **2** rid oneself of (a habit, false information, etc.).

unlearned[1] /únlérnid/ *adj.* not well educated; untaught, ignorant. □□ **unlearnedly** *adv.*

unlearned[2] /únlérnd/ *adj.* (also **unlearnt** /-lérnt/) that has not been learnt.

unleash /únléesh/ *v.tr.* **1** release from a leash or restraint. **2** set free to engage in pursuit or attack.

■ **2** see RELEASE *v.* 1, LOOSE *v.* 5.

unleavened /únlévv'nd/ *adj.* not leavened; made without yeast or other raising agent.

unless /unléss, ənléss/ *conj.* if not; except when (*shall go unless I hear from you; always walked unless I had a bicycle*). [ON or IN + LESS, assim. to UN-[1]]

unlettered /únléttərd/ *adj.* **1** illiterate. **2** not well educated.

unliberated /únlíbbəraytid/ *adj.* not liberated.

unlicensed /únlī́s'nst/ *adj.* not licensed, esp. without a licence to sell alcoholic drink.

unlighted /únlī́tid/ *adj.* **1** not provided with light. **2** not set burning.

unlike /únlī́k/ *adj.* & *prep.* ● *adj.* **1** not like; different from (*is unlike both his parents*). **2** uncharacteristic of (*such behaviour is unlike him*). **3** dissimilar, different. ● *prep.* differently from (*acts quite unlike anyone else*). □ **unlike signs** *Math.* plus and minus. □□ **unlikeness** *n.* [perh. f. ON *úlíkr*, OE *ungelic*: see LIKE[1]]

■ *adj.* **1** different from, dissimilar to, distinct from, opposite from *or* to, contrasting with *or* to, contrastive with *or* to, separate from, divergent from, incompatible with, distinguishable from, far apart from, far from, distant from, ill-matched with, unequal to, unequivalent to. **2** atypical of, uncharacteristic of, untypical of. **3** unalike, different, dissimilar, distinct, disparate, opposite, contrasting, contrastive, divergent, diverse, varied, heterogeneous, distinguishable, separate, far apart, incompatible, ill-matched, unequal, unequivalent. ● *prep.* differently from, in contradistinction to, in contrast with *or* to, as opposed to. □□ **unlikeness** see DIFFERENCE *n.* 1.

unlikeable /únlī́kəb'l/ *adj.* (also **unlikable**) not easy to like; unpleasant.

■ see DISAGREEABLE 1.

unlikely /únlī́kli/ *adj.* (**unlikelier, unlikeliest**) **1** improbable (*unlikely tale*). **2** (foll. by *to* + infin.) not to be expected to do something (*he's unlikely to be available*). **3** unpromising (*an unlikely candidate*). □□ **unlikelihood** *n.* **unlikeliness** *n.*

■ **1** improbable, doubtful, dubious, remote, unthinkable, unimaginable, inconceivable, implausible, unbelievable, incredible, unconvincing, far-fetched. **3** unpropitious, unpromising, inauspicious.

unlimited /únlímmitid/ *adj.* without limit; unrestricted; very great in number or quantity (*has unlimited possibilities; an unlimited expanse of sea*). □□ **unlimitedly** *adv.* **unlimitedness** *n.*

■ unrestricted, unrestrained, limitless, unconstrained, unqualified, indefinite, full, absolute, unconditional, far-reaching, unchecked, uncontrolled; boundless, endless, vast, unbounded, immense, immeasurable, measureless, numberless, innumerable, inexhaustible, interminable, never-ending, infinite, extensive, *literary* myriad.

unlined[1] /únlīnd/ *adj.* **1** (of paper etc.) without lines. **2** (of a face etc.) without wrinkles.

unlined[2] /únlīnd/ *adj.* (of a garment etc.) without lining.

unlink /únlíngk/ *v.tr.* **1** undo the links of (a chain etc.). **2** detach or set free by undoing or unfastening a link or chain.
■ see UNDO 1.

unliquidated /únlíkwidaytid/ *adj.* not liquidated.

unlisted /únlístid/ *adj.* not included in a published list, esp. of Stock Exchange prices or of telephone numbers.

unlit /únlít/ *adj.* not lit.
■ see DARK *adj.* 1.

unlivable /únlívvəb'l/ *adj.* that cannot be lived or lived in.

unlived-in /únlívdin/ *adj.* **1** appearing to be uninhabited. **2** unused by the inhabitants.
■ **1** see UNINHABITED.

unload /únlṓd/ *v.tr.* **1** (also *absol.*) remove a load from (a vehicle etc.). **2** remove (a load) from a vehicle etc. **3** remove the charge from (a firearm etc.). **4** *colloq.* get rid of. **5** (often foll. by *on*) *colloq.* **a** divulge (information). **b** (also *absol.*) give vent to (feelings). ▫▫ **unloader** *n.*
■ **1, 2** empty, dump, unpack, offload, discharge; disburden, unburden. **4** see DUMP *v.* 2. **5 a** see DISCLOSE 1. **b** see FREE *v.* 2, VENT *v.* 2.

unlock /únlók/ *v.tr.* **1 a** release the lock of (a door, box, etc.). **b** release or disclose by unlocking. **2** release thoughts, feelings, etc., from (one's mind etc.).
■ **1 a** see OPEN *v.* 1–3, UNDO 1. **1b, 2** see RELEASE *v.* 1.

unlocked /únlókt/ *adj.* not locked.
■ see OPEN *adj.* 1–4, 13, 20.

unlooked-for /únlŏŏktfor/ *adj.* unexpected, unforeseen.
■ see UNFORESEEN.

unloose /únlōōss/ *v.tr.* (also **unloosen**) loose; set free.

unlovable /únlúvvəb'l/ *adj.* not lovable.

unloved /únlúvd/ *adj.* not loved.
■ see UNPOPULAR.

unlovely /únlúvli/ *adj.* not attractive; unpleasant, ugly. ▫▫ **unloveliness** *n.*
■ see UGLY 1.

unloving /únlúvving/ *adj.* not loving. ▫▫ **unlovingly** *adv.* **unlovingness** *n.*

unlucky /únlúkki/ *adj.* (**unluckier, unluckiest**) **1** not fortunate or successful. **2** wretched. **3** bringing bad luck. **4** ill-judged. ▫▫ **unluckily** *adv.* **unluckiness** *n.*
■ **1** see UNFORTUNATE *adj.* 1, UNSUCCESSFUL. **2** see TRAGIC. **3** see INAUSPICIOUS 1. **4** see *ill-advised* 2. ▫▫ **unluckily** see *sadly* (SAD).

unmade /únmáyd/ *adj.* **1** not made. **2** destroyed, annulled.

unmake /únmáyk/ *v.tr.* (*past* and *past part.* **unmade**) undo the making of; destroy, depose, annul.

unmalleable /únmálliəb'l/ *adj.* not malleable.

unman /únmán/ *v.tr.* (**unmanned, unmanning**) **1** deprive of supposed manly qualities (e.g. self-control, courage); cause to weep etc., discourage. **2** deprive (a ship etc.) of men.

unmanageable /únmánnijəb'l/ *adj.* not (easily) managed, manipulated, or controlled. ▫▫ **unmanageableness** *n.* **unmanageably** *adv.*
■ see DIFFICULT 2, UNWIELDY, WILD *adj.* 4.

unmanly /únmánli/ *adj.* not manly. ▫▫ **unmanliness** *n.*
■ see EFFEMINATE.

unmanned /únmánd/ *adj.* **1** not manned. **2** overcome by emotion etc.

unmannerly /únmánnərli/ *adj.* **1** without good manners. **2** (of actions, speech, etc.) showing a lack of good manners. ▫▫ **unmannerliness** *n.*
■ see RUDE 1.

unmarked /únmaárkt/ *adj.* **1** not marked. **2** not noticed.
■ **1** see UNIDENTIFIED, UNSCATHED. **2** see UNNOTICED.

unmarketable /únmaárkitəb'l/ *adj.* not marketable.

unmarried /únmárrid/ *adj.* not married; single.
■ single, unwed(ded), celibate, bachelor, spinster, old-maid, maiden, free.

unmask /únmaásk/ *v.* **1** *tr.* **a** remove the mask from. **b** expose the true character of. **2** *intr.* remove one's mask. ▫▫ **unmasker** *n.*
■ **1 b** see EXPOSE 5.

unmatchable /únmáchəb'l/ *adj.* that cannot be matched. ▫▫ **unmatchably** *adv.*

unmatched /únmácht/ *adj.* not matched or equalled.
■ see UNPARALLELED.

unmatured /únmətyóord/ *adj.* not yet matured.

unmeaning /únmeéning/ *adj.* having no meaning or significance; meaningless. ▫▫ **unmeaningly** *adv.* **unmeaningness** *n.*

unmeant /únmént/ *adj.* not meant or intended.

unmeasurable /únmézhərəb'l/ *adj.* that cannot be measured. ▫▫ **unmeasurably** *adv.*
■ see IMMEASURABLE.

unmeasured /únmézhərd/ *adj.* **1** not measured. **2** limitless.

unmelodious /únmilṓdiəss/ *adj.* not melodious; discordant. ▫▫ **unmelodiously** *adv.*

unmelted /únméltid/ *adj.* not melted.

unmemorable /únmémmərəb'l/ *adj.* not memorable. ▫▫ **unmemorably** *adv.*

unmentionable /únménshənəb'l/ *adj.* & *n.* ● *adj.* that cannot (properly) be mentioned. ● *n.* **1** (in *pl.*) *joc.* **a** undergarments. **b** *archaic* trousers. **2** a person or thing not to be mentioned. ▫▫ **unmentionability** /-bílliti/ *n.* **unmentionableness** *n.* **unmentionably** *adv.*
■ *adj.* unspeakable, unutterable, unprintable, ineffable, indescribable, nameless, taboo, scandalous, forbidden, interdicted, proscribed, prohibited; disgraceful, indecent, rude, immodest, shameful, shocking, appalling, dishonourable, obscene, filthy. ● *n.* **1 a** (*unmentionables*) underclothes, underclothing, underwear, undergarments, lingerie, *colloq.* underthings, undies, *Brit. colloq.* smalls, *US* skivvies.

unmentioned /únménsh'nd/ *adj.* not mentioned.

unmerchantable /únmérchəntəb'l/ *adj.* not merchantable.

unmerciful /únmérsifool/ *adj.* merciless. ▫▫ **unmercifully** *adv.* **unmercifulness** *n.*
■ merciless, pitiless, unsparing, unkind, relentless, unrelenting, inexorable, ruthless, unpitying, heartless, stony-hearted, hard-hearted, flinty, unfeeling, unsympathetic, unforgiving, inhuman, inhumane, harsh, mean, cruel, savage, brutal, brutish, vicious, barbarous. ▫▫ **unmercifully** see ROUGHLY 1, *endlessly* (ENDLESS).

unmerited /únmérritid/ *adj.* not merited.
■ see UNWARRANTED 2.

unmet /únmét/ *adj.* (of a quota, demand, goal, etc.) not achieved or fulfilled.

unmetalled /únmétt'ld/ *adj. Brit.* (of a road etc.) not made with road-metal.

unmethodical /únmithóddik'l/ *adj.* not methodical. ▫▫ **unmethodically** *adv.*
■ see *chaotic* (CHAOS), INDISCRIMINATE 2.

unmetrical /únmétrik'l/ *adj.* not metrical.

unmilitary /únmíllitəri, -tri/ *adj.* not military.

unmindful /únmīndfool/ *adj.* (often foll. by *of*) not mindful. ▫▫ **unmindfully** *adv.* **unmindfulness** *n.*
■ see UNAWARE *adj.* 1.

unmissable /únmíssəb'l/ *adj.* that cannot or should not be missed.

unmistakable /únmistáykəb'l/ *adj.* that cannot be mistaken or doubted, clear. ▫▫ **unmistakability** /-bílliti/ *n.* **unmistakableness** *n.* **unmistakably** *adv.*
■ see CLEAR *adj.* 6, OBVIOUS. ▫▫ **unmistakably** see *obviously* (OBVIOUS), EXPRESSLY, *undoubtedly* (UNDOUBTED).

unmistaken /únmistáykən/ *adj.* not mistaken; right, correct.

unmitigated /únmíttigaytid/ *adj.* **1** not mitigated or modified. **2** absolute, unqualified (*an unmitigated disaster*). □□ **unmitigatedly** *adv.*

■ **1** undiluted, unalloyed, unmixed, untempered, unmoderated, unmodified, unabated, unlessened, undiminished, unreduced, unrelieved, oppressive, immoderate, unalleviated, unmollified, unsoftened, relentless. **2** unqualified, out and out, thorough, thoroughgoing, outright, downright, categorical, absolute, sheer, complete, consummate, total, perfect, true, positive, pure, arrant, utter, plain. □□ **unmitigatedly** see DOWNRIGHT *adv.*

unmixed /únmíkst/ *adj.* not mixed. □ **unmixed blessing** a thing having advantages and no disadvantages.

■ see NEAT[1] 5, SEPARATE *adj.*

unmodified /únmóddifīd/ *adj.* not modified.

■ see SAME *adj.* 2, UNMITIGATED 1.

unmodulated /únmódyoolaytid/ *adj.* not modulated.

unmolested /únməléstid/ *adj.* not molested.

unmoor /únmoór, únmór/ *v.tr.* **1** (also *absol.*) release the moorings of (a vessel). **2** weigh all but one anchor of (a vessel).

unmoral /únmórrəl/ *adj.* not concerned with morality (cf. IMMORAL). □□ **unmorality** /únmərálliti/ *n.* **unmorally** *adv.*

unmotherly /únmúthərli/ *adj.* not motherly.

unmotivated /únmṓtivaytid/ *adj.* without motivation; without a motive.

■ see SHIFTLESS, WANTON 2.

unmounted /únmówntid/ *adj.* not mounted.

unmourned /únmórnd/ *adj.* not mourned.

■ see UNLAMENTED.

unmoved /únmōōvd/ *adj.* **1** not moved. **2** not changed in one's purpose. **3** not affected by emotion. □□ **unmovable** *adj.* (also **unmoveable**).

■ **2** see RELENTLESS 1. **3** cool, aloof, calm, collected, unaffected, untouched, unsympathetic, unstirred, undisturbed, apathetic, stoic(al), impassive, dispassionate, unemotional, unfeeling, unconcerned, indifferent, unreactive, unresponsive, stolid, stony, adamant, stony-hearted, hard-hearted. □□ **unmovable** see IMMOVABLE *adj.*

unmown /únmṓn/ *adj.* not mown.

unmuffle /únmúff'l/ *v.tr.* **1** remove a muffler from (a face, bell, etc.). **2** free of something that muffles or conceals.

unmurmuring /únmúrməring/ *adj.* not complaining. □□ **unmurmuringly** *adv.*

unmusical /únmyōōzik'l/ *adj.* **1** not pleasing to the ear. **2** unskilled in or indifferent to music. □□ **unmusicality** /-kálliti/ *n.* **unmusically** *adv.* **unmusicalness** *n.*

■ **1** see DISCORDANT 2.

unmutilated /únmyōōtilaytid/ *adj.* not mutilated.

unmuzzle /únmúzz'l/ *v.tr.* **1** remove a muzzle from. **2** relieve of an obligation to remain silent.

unnail /ún-náyl/ *v.tr.* unfasten by the removal of nails.

unnameable /ún-náyməb'l/ *adj.* that cannot be named, esp. too bad to be named.

unnamed /ún-náymd/ *adj.* not named.

■ see NAMELESS 1, 3, 5.

unnatural /ún-náchərəl/ *adj.* **1** contrary to nature or the usual course of nature; not normal. **2 a** lacking natural feelings. **b** extremely cruel or wicked. **3** artificial. **4** affected. □□ **unnaturally** *adv.* **unnaturalness** *n.*

■ **1** outlandish, weird, uncanny, peculiar, strange, odd, unaccountable, supernatural, preternatural, queer, grotesque, bizarre, extraordinary, eccentric, freakish; abnormal, unexpected, unusual, uncharacteristic, out of character. **2** abnormal, perverse, perverted, monstrous, aberrant, improper, unseemly; deviant, depraved, degenerate, bestial; unfeeling, callous, inhuman, inhumane, cruel, wicked, sadistic, warped, twisted, corrupted, *colloq.* kinky, *sl.* bent. **3** see ARTIFICIAL 1, 2. **4** laboured, forced, stilted, stiff, strained, restrained, artificial, false, insincere, sham, feigned, pretended, contrived, affected, mannered, self-conscious, theatrical, stagy, *colloq.* phoney. □□ **unnaturalness** see ODDITY 3.

unnavigable /ún-návvigəb'l/ *adj.* not navigable. □□ **unnavigability** /-bílliti/ *n.*

unnecessary /ún-néssəsəri/ *adj.* & *n.* ● *adj.* **1** not necessary. **2** more than is necessary (*with unnecessary care*). ● *n.* (*pl.* **-ies**) (usu. in *pl.*) an unnecessary thing. □□ **unnecessarily** *adv.* **unnecessariness** *n.*

■ *adj.* **1** unneeded, needless, unrequired, dispensable, disposable, expendable, unwanted, uncalled-for, inessential, unessential, non-essential. **2** surplus, superfluous, supererogatory, redundant, extra, *de trop*, undue, excessive. ● *n.* inessential, non-essential, supernumerary, extra. □□ **unnecessarily** see *unduly* (UNDUE).

unneeded /ún-néedid/ *adj.* not needed.

■ see NEEDLESS.

unneighbourly /ún-náybərli/ *adj.* not neighbourly. □□ **unneighbourliness** *n.*

unnerve /ún-nérv/ *v.tr.* deprive of strength or resolution. □□ **unnervingly** *adv.*

■ upset, agitate, perturb, ruffle, fluster, discomfit, discompose, unsettle, disconcert, dismay, intimidate, stun, stupefy, rock, shatter, *colloq.* shake (up), rattle, faze, throw.

unnoticeable /ún-nṓtisəb'l/ *adj.* not easily seen or noticed. □□ **unnoticeably** *adv.*

■ see INCONSPICUOUS, IMPERCEPTIBLE.

unnoticed /ún-nṓtist/ *adj.* not noticed.

■ unnoted, overlooked, unobserved, undiscovered, unremarked, unmarked, unperceived; unseen, unheard.

unnumbered /ún-númbərd/ *adj.* **1** not marked with a number. **2** not counted. **3** countless.

■ **3** see UMPTEEN *adj.*

UNO /yōōnō/ *abbr.* United Nations Organization.

unobjectionable /únnəbjékshənəb'l/ *adj.* not objectionable; acceptable. □□ **unobjectionableness** *n.* **unobjectionably** *adv.*

■ see INOFFENSIVE.

unobliging /únnəblījing/ *adj.* not obliging; unhelpful, uncooperative.

unobscured /únnəbskyoórd/ *adj.* not obscured.

■ see FULL[1] *adj.* 7b, DISTINCT 2.

unobservable /únnəbzérvəb'l/ *adj.* not observable; imperceptible.

unobservant /únnəbzérv'nt/ *adj.* not observant. □□ **unobservantly** *adv.*

■ see *heedless* (HEED).

unobserved /únnəbzérvd/ *adj.* not observed. □□ **unobservedly** /-vidli/ *adv.*

■ see UNNOTICED.

unobstructed /únnəbstrúktid/ *adj.* not obstructed.

■ see CLEAR *adj.* 10.

unobtainable /únnəbtáynəb'l/ *adj.* that cannot be obtained.

■ unavailable, inaccessible, unreachable; out of stock, sold out.

unobtrusive /únnəbtrōōssiv/ *adj.* not making oneself or itself noticed. □□ **unobtrusively** *adv.* **unobtrusiveness** *n.*

■ inconspicuous, unostentatious, low-key, retiring, modest, self-effacing, unpresuming, unpretentious, unassuming, quiet, humble, unassertive, non-assertive, subdued, reserved, reticent, suppressed, discreet, unnoticeable. □□ **unobtrusively** see *quietly* (QUIET).

unoccupied /únnókyoopīd/ *adj.* not occupied.

■ see IDLE *adj.* 2, VACANT 1.

unoffending /únnəfénding/ *adj.* not offending; harmless, innocent. □□ **unoffended** *adj.*

■ see INOFFENSIVE.

unofficial /únnəfísh'l/ *adj.* **1** not officially authorized or confirmed. **2** not characteristic of officials. □ **unofficial strike** a strike not formally approved by the strikers' trade union. □□ **unofficially** *adv.*

■ **1** informal, unauthorized, undocumented, unconfirmed, off the record, private, secret, unpublicized, unannounced. **2** see INFORMAL. □□ **unofficially** see *off the record* (RECORD).

unoiled /únnóyld/ *adj.* not oiled.

unopened /únnṓp'nd/ *adj.* not opened.
■ closed, shut.

unopposed /únnəpṓzd/ *adj.* not opposed.

unordained /únnordáynd/ *adj.* not ordained.

unordinary /únnórdinəri/ *adj.* not ordinary.

unorganized /únnórgənīzd/ *adj.* (also **-ised**) not organized (cf. DISORGANIZE).
■ see *chaotic* (CHAOS).

unoriginal /únnəríjin'l/ *adj.* lacking originality; derivative. □□ **unoriginality** /-nálliti/ *n.* **unoriginally** *adv.*
■ see TIRED 2, DERIVATIVE *adj.*

unornamental /únnornəmént'l/ *adj.* not ornamental; plain.

unornamented /únnórnəmentid/ *adj.* not ornamented.
■ see UNADORNED.

unorthodox /únnórthədoks/ *adj.* not orthodox. □□ **unorthodoxly** *adv.* **unorthodoxy** *n.*
■ irregular, unconventional, nonconformist, unconforming, nonconforming, non-standard, aberrant, aberrational, deviant, heretical, unsound, heteroclite, unusual, abnormal, uncustomary, uncommon, offbeat, *colloq.* way-out. □□ **unorthodoxy** see ORIGINALITY 1, 2.

unostentatious /únnostentáyshəss/ *adj.* not ostentatious. □□ **unostentatiously** *adv.* **unostentatiousness** *n.*
■ see MODEST 5.

unowned /únnṓnd/ *adj.* **1** unacknowledged. **2** having no owner.

unpack /únpák/ *v.tr.* **1** (also *absol.*) open and remove the contents of (a package, luggage, etc.). **2** take (a thing) out from a package etc. □□ **unpacker** *n.*
■ **1** see UNLOAD 1, 2.

unpaged /únpáyjd/ *adj.* with pages not numbered.

unpaid /únpáyd/ *adj.* (of a debt or a person) not paid.
■ payable, outstanding, owed, owing, due, unsettled; unsalaried, voluntary, volunteer, honorary.

unpainted /únpáyntid/ *adj.* not painted.

unpaired /únpáird/ *adj.* **1** not arranged in pairs. **2** not forming one of a pair.

unpalatable /únpállətəb'l/ *adj.* **1** not pleasant to taste. **2** (of an idea, suggestion, etc.) disagreeable, distasteful. □□ **unpalatability** /-bílliti/ *n.* **unpalatableness** *n.*
■ rancid, sour, off, turned, bitter, inedible, uneatable; distasteful, disagreeable, unpleasant, unsavoury, unappetizing, unattractive, repugnant, nasty, offensive, objectionable.

unparalleled /únpárrəleld/ *adj.* having no parallel or equal.
■ unequalled, incomparable, matchless, peerless, unrivalled, unmatched, nonpareil, inimitable, unexcelled, superior, supreme, superlative, unsurpassed, *hors concours*, surpassing, transcendent, unusual, special, singular, rare, unique, exceptional, consummate.

unpardonable /únpaárdənəb'l/ *adj.* that cannot be pardoned. □□ **unpardonableness** *n.* **unpardonably** *adv.*
■ see INEXCUSABLE.

unparliamentary /únpaarləméntəri/ *adj.* contrary to proper parliamentary usage. □ **unparliamentary language** oaths or abuse.

unpasteurized /únpaástyərīzd, -paáss-chərīzd, unpás-/ *adj.* not pasteurized.

unpatented /únpáyt'ntid, únpát-/ *adj.* not patented.

unpatriotic /únpatrióttik, únpay-/ *adj.* not patriotic. □□ **unpatriotically** *adv.*

unpaved /únpáyvd/ *adj.* not paved.

unpeeled /únpeéld/ *adj.* not peeled.

unpeg /únpég/ *v.tr.* (**unpegged, unpegging**) **1** unfasten by the removal of pegs. **2** cease to maintain or stabilize (prices etc.).
■ **1** see UNDO 1.

unpeople *v.* & *n.* ● *v.tr.* /únpeép'l/ depopulate. ● *n.pl.* /únpeep'l/ unpersons.

unperceived /únpərseévd/ *adj.* not perceived; unobserved.
■ see UNNOTICED.

unperceptive /únpərséptiv/ *adj.* not perceptive. □□ **unperceptively** *adv.* **unperceptiveness** *n.*
■ see BLIND *adj.* 2a.

unperfected /únpərféktid/ *adj.* not perfected.

unperforated /únpérfəraytid/ *adj.* not perforated.

unperformed /únpərfórmd/ *adj.* not performed.

unperfumed /únpérfyōōmd/ *adj.* not perfumed.
■ unscented, scentless, non-perfumed, plain, natural.

unperson /únpers'n/ *n.* a person whose name or existence is denied or ignored.

unpersuadable /únpərswáydəb'l/ *adj.* not able to be persuaded; obstinate.

unpersuaded /únpərswáydid/ *adj.* not persuaded.
■ see DOUBTFUL 1.

unpersuasive /únpərswáysiv/ *adj.* not persuasive. □□ **unpersuasively** *adv.*
■ see WEAK 4.

unperturbed /únpərtúrbd/ *adj.* not perturbed. □□ **unperturbedly** /-bidli/ *adv.*
■ see CALM *adj.* 2.

unphilosophical /únfiləsóffik'l/ *adj.* (also **unphilosophic**) **1** not according to philosophical principles. **2** lacking philosophy. □□ **unphilosophically** *adv.*

unphysiological /únfiziəlójik'l/ *adj.* (also **unphysiologic**) not in accordance with normal physiological functioning. □□ **unphysiologically** *adv.*

unpick /únpík/ *v.tr.* undo the sewing of (stitches, a garment, etc.).
■ see UNDO 1.

unpicked /únpíkt/ *adj.* **1** not selected. **2** (of a flower) not plucked.

unpicturesque /únpikchərésk/ *adj.* not picturesque.

unpin /únpín/ *v.tr.* (**unpinned, unpinning**) **1** unfasten or detach by removing a pin or pins. **2** *Chess* release (a piece that has been pinned).
■ **1** see UNDO 1.

unpitied /únpíttid/ *adj.* not pitied.

unpitying /únpítti-ing/ *adj.* not pitying. □□ **unpityingly** *adv.*
■ see UNSYMPATHETIC.

unplaceable /únpláysəb'l/ *adj.* that cannot be placed or classified (*his accent was unplaceable*).

unplaced /únpláyst/ *adj.* not placed, esp. not placed as one of the first three finishing in a race etc.

unplanned /únplánd/ *adj.* not planned.
■ see ACCIDENTAL *adj.* 1, IMPULSIVE, RAMBLING 2, 3.

unplanted /únplaántid/ *adj.* not planted.

unplausible /únpláwzib'l/ *adj.* not plausible.
■ see IMPLAUSIBLE.

unplayable /únpláyəb'l/ *adj.* **1** *Sport* (of a ball) that cannot be struck or returned. **2** that cannot be played. □□ **unplayably** *adv.*

unpleasant /únplézz'nt/ *adj.* not pleasant; displeasing; disagreeable. □□ **unpleasantly** *adv.* **unpleasantness** *n.*
■ see NASTY 1, 5a, b; 3. □□ **unpleasantly** see AWFULLY 1, *painfully* (PAINFUL). **unpleasantness** see TROUBLE *n.* 1.

unpleasing /únpleézing/ *adj.* not pleasing. □□ **unpleasingly** *adv.*
■ see DISAGREEABLE 1, UNWELCOME, UGLY 1.

unploughed /únplówd/ *adj.* not ploughed.

unplucked /únplúkt/ *adj.* not plucked.

unplug /únplúg/ *v.tr.* (**unplugged, unplugging**) **1** disconnect (an electrical device) by removing its plug from the socket. **2** unstop.
■ **1** see UNDO 1.

unplumbed /únplúmd/ *adj.* **1** not plumbed. **2** not fully explored or understood. □□ **unplumbable** *adj.*

unpoetic /únpō-éttik/ *adj.* (also **unpoetical**) not poetic.

unpointed /únpóyntid/ *adj.* **1** having no point or points. **2 a** not punctuated. **b** (of written Hebrew etc.) without vowel points. **3** (of masonry or brickwork) not pointed.

unpolished /únpóllisht/ *adj.* **1** not polished; rough. **2** without refinement; crude.
■ **2** see CRUDE *adj.* 1b.

unpolitic /únpóllitik/ *adj.* impolitic, unwise.

unpolitical /únpəlíttik'l/ *adj.* not concerned with politics. □□ **unpolitically** *adv.*

unpolled /únpōld/ *adj.* **1** not having voted at an election. **2** not included in an opinion poll.

unpolluted /únpəlo͞otid/ *adj.* not polluted.
■ see CLEAN *adj.* 1.

unpopular /únpópyoolər/ *adj.* not popular; not liked by the public or by people in general. □□ **unpopularity** /-lárriti/ *n.* **unpopularly** *adv.*
■ out of favour, in bad odour, unliked, disliked, shunned, avoided, snubbed, ignored, unsought after, unaccepted, unwanted, rejected, outcast, despised, unwelcome, undesirable; unloved, friendless.

unpopulated /únpópyoolaytid/ *adj.* not populated.
■ see UNINHABITED.

unpossessed /únpəzést/ *adj.* **1** (foll. by *of*) not in possession of. **2** not possessed.

unpractical /únpráktik'l/ *adj.* **1** not practical. **2** (of a person) not having practical skill. □□ **unpracticality** /-kálliti/ *n.* **unpractically** *adv.*
■ see IMPRACTICAL 1.

unpractised /únpráktist/ *adj.* (*US* **unpracticed**) **1** not experienced or skilled. **2** not put into practice.
■ **1** see *inexperienced* (INEXPERIENCE).

unprecedented /únpréssidentid/ *adj.* **1** having no precedent; unparalleled. **2** novel. □□ **unprecedentedly** *adv.*
■ **1** see EXTRAORDINARY 1, 2. **2** see ORIGINAL *adj.* 2.

unpredictable /únpridíktəb'l/ *adj.* that cannot be predicted. □□ **unpredictability** /-bílliti/ *n.* **unpredictableness** *n.* **unpredictably** *adv.*
■ see ARBITRARY 1, VARIABLE *adj.* 2. □□ **unpredictability** see VICISSITUDE, *inconstancy* (INCONSTANT).

unpredicted /únpridíktid/ *adj.* not predicted or foretold.
■ see UNFORESEEN.

unprejudiced /únpréjoodist/ *adj.* not prejudiced.
■ unbigoted, unbiased, impartial, not jaundiced, just, fair, objective, disinterested, neutral, fair-minded, non-partisan, liberal, open-minded, undogmatic.

unpremeditated /únpriméddititaytid/ *adj.* not previously thought over, not deliberately planned, unintentional. □□ **unpremeditatedly** *adv.*
■ unprepared, unplanned, unarranged, uncontrived, unstudied, unrehearsed, spontaneous, spur-of-the-moment, last-minute, impromptu, extemporaneous, extemporary, extempore, ad lib, improvised, offhand, casual, impulsive, natural, involuntary, automatic, unconscious, unintended, unintentional, *colloq.* off the cuff. □□ **unpremeditatedly** see *on the spur of the moment* (SPUR).

unprepared /únpripáird/ *adj.* not prepared (in advance); not ready. □□ **unpreparedly** *adv.* **unpreparedness** *n.*
■ (*of a person*) unready, ill-equipped, surprised, taken aback, unwarned, not forewarned, (caught) napping *or* off guard, dumbfounded, at sixes and sevens, *colloq.* (caught) with one's pants down, (caught) on the hop; (*of a thing*) unmade, not set up, unfinished, incomplete; (*of an action*) improvised, thrown together, *colloq.* done by the seat of one's pants; see also UNPREMEDITATED.

unprepossessing /únpreepəzéssing/ *adj.* not prepossessing; unattractive.
■ see ORDINARY *adj.*

unprescribed /únpriskrībd/ *adj.* (esp. of drugs) not prescribed.

unpresentable /únprizéntəb'l/ *adj.* not presentable.

unpressed /únprést/ *adj.* not pressed, esp. (of clothing) unironed.

unpresuming /únprizyo͞oming/ *adj.* not presuming; modest.

unpresumptuous /únprizúmptyooəss/ *adj.* not presumptuous.

unpretending /únpriténding/ *adj.* unpretentious. □□ **unpretendingly** *adv.* **unpretendingness** *n.*

unpretentious /únpriténshəss/ *adj.* not making a great display; simple, modest. □□ **unpretentiously** *adv.* **unpretentiousness** *n.*
■ see MODEST 1, 2, 5.

unpriced /únprīst/ *adj.* not having a price or prices fixed, marked, or stated.

unprimed /únprīmd/ *adj.* not primed.

unprincipled /únprínsip'ld/ *adj.* lacking or not based on good moral principles. □□ **unprincipledness** *n.*
■ see UNSCRUPULOUS.

unprintable /únpríntəb'l/ *adj.* that cannot be printed, esp. because too indecent or libellous or blasphemous. □□ **unprintably** *adv.*

unprinted /únpríntid/ *adj.* not printed.

unprivileged /únprívvilijd/ *adj.* not privileged.

unproblematic /únprobləmáttik/ *adj.* causing no difficulty. □□ **unproblematically** *adv.*

unproclaimed /únprōkláymd/ *adj.* not proclaimed.

unprocurable /únprəkyóorəb'l/ *adj.* that cannot be procured.

unproductive /únprədúktiv/ *adj.* not productive. □□ **unproductively** *adv.* **unproductiveness** *n.*
■ see FRUITLESS 1, 2.

unprofessional /únprəféshən'l/ *adj.* **1** contrary to professional standards of behaviour etc. **2** not belonging to a profession; amateur. □□ **unprofessionally** *adv.*
■ **1** unbecoming, improper, unethical, unprincipled, unseemly, undignified, unfitting, unbefitting, unworthy, unscholarly, negligent, lax; amateurish, inexpert, incompetent, unskilful, inferior, second-rate, inefficient, poor, shoddy, low-quality, sloppy. **2** amateur, non-professional, lay, unspecialized, non-specialist, inexpert, inexperienced, untrained, untutored, unschooled, unskilled. □□ **unprofessionally** see POORLY *adv.*

unprofitable /únpróffitəb'l/ *adj.* not profitable. □□ **unprofitableness** *n.* **unprofitably** *adv.*
■ profitless, ungainful, unremunerative, unfruitful, non-profit-making, uneconomic, uncommercial; breaking even; losing, loss-making; pointless, purposeless, unavailing, futile, fruitless, useless, unproductive, unrewarding, thankless, worthless, ineffective, inefficient, *archaic* bootless.

unprogressive /únprəgréssiv/ *adj.* not progressive.

unpromising /únprómmising/ *adj.* not likely to turn out well. □□ **unpromisingly** *adv.*
■ inauspicious, unpropitious, unfavourable, gloomy, ominous, adverse, portentous, baleful, hopeless.

unprompted /únprómptid/ *adj.* spontaneous.
■ see VOLUNTARY *adj.* 1.

unpronounceable /únprənównsəb'l/ *adj.* that cannot be pronounced. □□ **unpronounceably** *adv.*

unpropitious /únprəpíshəss/ *adj.* not propitious. □□ **unpropitiously** *adv.*
■ see INAUSPICIOUS 1. □□ **unpropitiously** inauspiciously, unluckily, regrettably.

unprosperous /únprósperəss/ *adj.* not prosperous. □□ **unprosperously** *adv.*

unprotected /únprətéktid/ *adj.* not protected. □□ **unprotectedness** *n.*
■ see *defenceless* (DEFENCE), OPEN *adj.* 1–4, 13, 20.

unprotesting /únprətésting/ *adj.* not protesting. □□ **unprotestingly** *adv.*

unprovable /únpro͞ovəb'l/ *adj.* that cannot be proved. □□ **unprovability** /-bílliti/ *n.* **unprovableness** *n.*

unproved /únpróovd/ *adj.* (also **unproven** /-v'n/) not proved.
■ see THEORETICAL 2.
unprovided /únprəvídid/ *adj.* (usu. foll. by *with*) not furnished, supplied, or equipped.
unprovoked /únprəvókt/ *adj.* (of a person or act) without provocation.
■ see UNWARRANTED 2, CALM *adj.* 2.
unpublished /únpúblisht/ *adj.* not published. □□ **unpublishable** *adj.*
unpunctual /únpúngktyooəl/ *adj.* not punctual. □□ **unpunctuality** /-tyoo-álliti/ *n.*
unpunctuated /únpúngktyoo-aytid/ *adj.* not punctuated.
unpunishable /únpúnnishəb'l/ *adj.* that cannot be punished.
unpunished /únpúnnisht/ *adj.* not punished.
unpurified /únpyóorifíd/ *adj.* not purified.
unputdownable /únpootdównəb'l/ *adj. colloq.* (of a book) so engrossing that one has to go on reading it.
unqualified /únkwóllifíd/ *adj.* **1** not competent (*unqualified to give an answer*). **2** not legally or officially qualified (*an unqualified practitioner*). **3** not modified or restricted; complete (*unqualified assent*; *unqualified success*).
■ **1** ineligible, unfit, incompetent, unable, ill-equipped, unsuited. **2** untrained, unequipped, unprepared, amateur. **3** unrestricted, unreserved, unconditional, categorical, outright, unmitigated, downright, out and out, wholehearted, pure (and simple), true, perfect, complete, utter, sheer, absolute, consummate.
unquenchable /únkwénchəb'l/ *adj.* that cannot be quenched. □□ **unquenchably** *adv.*
■ insatiable, unslakeable, unsatisfiable; inextinguishable, unsuppressible, irrepressible, indestructible.
unquenched /únkwéncht/ *adj.* not quenched.
unquestionable /únkwéss-chənəb'l/ *adj.* that cannot be disputed or doubted. □□ **unquestionability** /-billiti/ *n.* **unquestionableness** *n.* **unquestionably** *adv.*
■ unexceptionable, indubitable, undoubted, indisputable, incontestable, unimpeachable, undeniable, certain, sure, positive, irrefutable, manifest, obvious, patent, clear, definite, incontrovertible, unequivocal, unmistakable, conclusive, *Austral.* & *NZ* fair. □□ **unquestionably** see *undoubtedly* (UNDOUBTED).
unquestioned /únkwéss-chənd/ *adj.* **1** not disputed or doubted; definite, certain. **2** not interrogated.
■ see UNDISPUTED.
unquestioning /únkwéss-chəning/ *adj.* **1** asking no questions. **2** done etc. without asking questions. □□ **unquestioningly** *adv.*
■ **2** see IMPLICIT 3. □□ **unquestioningly** see *willingly* (WILLING), *implicitly* (IMPLICIT).
unquiet /únkwíət/ *adj.* **1** restless, agitated, stirring. **2** perturbed, anxious. □□ **unquietly** *adv.* **unquietness** *n.*
unquotable /únkwótəb'l/ *adj.* that cannot be quoted.
unquote /únkwót/ *v.tr.* (as *int.*) (in dictation, reading aloud, etc.) indicate the presence of closing quotation marks (cf. QUOTE *v.* 5 b).
unquoted /únkwótid/ *adj.* not quoted, esp. on the Stock Exchange.
unravel /únrávv'l/ *v.* (**unravelled**, **unravelling**; *US* **unraveled**, **unraveling**) **1** *tr.* cause to be no longer ravelled, tangled, or intertwined. **2** *tr.* probe and solve (a mystery etc.). **3** *tr.* undo (a fabric, esp. a knitted one). **4** *intr.* become disentangled or unknitted.
■ **1** untangle, disentangle, unsnarl, sort out. **2** see SOLVE. **3** see UNDO 1.
unreachable /únréechəb'l/ *adj.* that cannot be reached. □□ **unreachableness** *n.* **unreachably** *adv.*
■ see INACCESSIBLE 1, 2.
unread /únréd/ *adj.* **1** (of a book etc.) not read. **2** (of a person) not well-read.
■ **2** see UNEDUCATED.
unreadable /únréedəb'l/ *adj.* **1** too dull or too difficult to be worth reading. **2** illegible. □□ **unreadability** /-billiti/ *n.* **unreadably** *adv.*
■ **2** see ILLEGIBLE.
unready[1] /únréddi/ *adj.* **1** not ready. **2** not prompt in action. □□ **unreadily** *adv.* **unreadiness** *n.*
■ see UNPREPARED.
unready[2] /únréddi/ *adj. archaic* lacking good advice; rash (*Ethelred the Unready*). [UN-[1] + REDE, assim. to UNREADY[1]]
unreal /únreéəl/ *adj.* **1** not real. **2** imaginary, illusory. **3** *US* & *Austral. sl.* incredible, amazing. □□ **unreality** /-riálliti/ *n.* **unreally** *adv.*
■ **1** artificial, synthetic, synthesized, mock, false, fake(d), counterfeit, fraudulent, dummy, spurious, falsified, pretend(ed), sham, pseudo, make-believe. **2** imaginary, imagined, theoretical, hypothetical, mythical, made-up, invented, fictitious, fictional, fabulous, fantastic, chimeric(al), fanciful, fancied, illusory, make-believe, dreamlike, insubstantial, phantasmagoric(al), phantasmal, spectral, unrealistic, non-existent. **3** see INCREDIBLE. □□ **unreality** see FANCY *n.* 6.
unrealistic /únreeəlístik/ *adj.* not realistic. □□ **unrealistically** *adv.*
■ unreal, unlifelike, unnatural, unauthentic, non-representational, unrepresentative, inaccurate; impractical, illogical, unreasonable, unworkable, unrealizable, quixotic, idealistic, romantic, fanciful, far-fetched, visionary, delusional, delusive, delusory, *colloq.* starry-eyed.
unrealizable /únreéəlízəb'l/ *adj.* that cannot be realized.
■ see IMPOSSIBLE 1.
unrealized /únreéəlízd/ *adj.* not realized.
■ see POTENTIAL *adj.*
unreason /únreéz'n/ *n.* lack of reasonable thought or action. [ME, = injustice, f. UN-[1] + REASON]
unreasonable /únreézənəb'l/ *adj.* **1** going beyond the limits of what is reasonable or equitable (*unreasonable demands*). **2** not guided by or listening to reason. □□ **unreasonableness** *n.* **unreasonably** *adv.*
■ **1** excessive, outrageous, exorbitant, extravagant, immoderate, extortionate, inordinate, unconscionable, unjust, unwarranted, inequitable, unfair, unequal, improper, unjustified, unjustifiable, uncalled-for, *Austral.* & *NZ sl.* over the fence; inappropriate, unapt, inapt, unsuitable, unbefitting, impractical, unrealistic. **2** irrational, illogical, unthinking, absurd, foolish, senseless, nonsensical, mindless, brainless, thoughtless, silly, mad, crazy, insane, idiotic, moronic, imbecilic, stupid, fatuous, ridiculous, ludicrous, laughable, preposterous, far-fetched; unperceptive, undiscerning, short-sighted, myopic, blind. □□ **unreasonableness** see ABSURDITY 1, 2, FOLLY 1. **unreasonably** see *unduly* (UNDUE).
unreasoned /únreéz'nd/ *adj.* not reasoned.
■ see GROUNDLESS, ARBITRARY 1.
unreasoning /únreézəning/ *adj.* not reasoning. □□ **unreasoningly** *adv.*
■ see BLIND *adj.* 3.
unreceptive /únriséptiv/ *adj.* not receptive.
■ see CHILLY 3.
unreciprocated /únrisíprəkaytid/ *adj.* not reciprocated.
unreckoned /únrékkənd/ *adj.* not calculated or taken into account.
unreclaimed /únrikláymd/ *adj.* not reclaimed.
unrecognizable /únrékkəgnízəb'l/ *adj.* (also **-isable**) that cannot be recognized. □□ **unrecognizableness** *n.* **unrecognizably** *adv.*
■ see INDEFINITE 1, INCOGNITO *adj.* & *adv.*
unrecognized /únrékkəgnízd/ *adj.* (also **-ised**) not recognized.
■ see UNIDENTIFIED, THANKLESS 2.
unrecompensed /únrékkəmpenst/ *adj.* not recompensed.
unreconciled /únrékkənsíld/ *adj.* not reconciled.
unreconstructed /únreekənstrúktid/ *adj.* **1** not reconciled or converted to the current political orthodoxy. **2** not rebuilt.

unrecorded /únrikórdid/ *adj.* not recorded. □□ **unrecordable** *adj.*

unrectified /únréktifīd/ *adj.* not rectified.

unredeemable /únrideēməb'l/ *adj.* that cannot be redeemed. □□ **unredeemably** *adv.*

unredeemed /únrideēmd/ *adj.* not redeemed.

unredressed /únridrést/ *adj.* not redressed.

unreel /únreēl/ *v.tr.* & *intr.* unwind from a reel.

unreeve /únreēv/ *v.tr.* (*past* **unrove**) withdraw (a rope etc.) from being reeved.

unrefined /únrifīnd/ *adj.* not refined.

■ (*of a substance*) impure, unpurified, unclarified, raw, crude, coarse, untreated, unfinished, natural, unprocessed; (*of a person, behaviour, etc.*) coarse, rude, rough, unsophisticated, uncultured, uncivilized, uncultivated, unaccomplished, unpolished, inelegant, ill-bred, impolite, discourteous, unmannerly, ill-mannered, bad-mannered, ignoble, plebeian, undignified, unladylike, ungentlemanlike, ungentlemanly, uncourtly, ungracious, boorish, loutish, gross, vulgar, uncouth, cloddish, awkward, gauche.

unreflecting /únriflékting/ *adj.* not thoughtful. □□ **unreflectingly** *adv.* **unreflectingness** *n.*

unreformed /únrifórmd/ *adj.* not reformed.

unregarded /únrigaārdid/ *adj.* not regarded.

unregenerate /únrijénnərət/ *adj.* not regenerate; obstinately wrong or bad. □□ **unregeneracy** *n.* **unregenerately** *adv.*

unregistered /únréjistərd/ *adj.* not registered.

unregulated /únrégyoolaytid/ *adj.* not regulated.

■ see INDEPENDENT *adj.* 1a.

unrehearsed /únrihérst/ *adj.* not rehearsed.

■ see EXTEMPORANEOUS.

unrelated /únriláytid/ *adj.* not related. □□ **unrelatedness** *n.*

■ independent, separate, distinct, different, dissimilar, incompatible, inappropriate, irrelevant, extraneous, foreign, alien, unassociated, unaffiliated, unconnected, uncoupled, unlinked, unallied, uncoordinated.

unrelaxed /únrilákst/ *adj.* not relaxed.

■ see TENSE[1] *adj.*

unrelenting /únrilénting/ *adj.* **1** not relenting or yielding. **2** unmerciful. **3** not abating or relaxing. □□ **unrelentingly** *adv.* **unrelentingness** *n.*

■ **1, 2** see RELENTLESS 1. **3** see RELENTLESS 2.

unreliable /únrilīəb'l/ *adj.* not reliable; erratic. □□ **unreliability** /-bílliti/ *n.* **unreliableness** *n.* **unreliably** *adv.*

■ untrustworthy, undependable, irresponsible, uncertain, unpredictable, erratic, fickle, inconsistent, temperamental, unstable, unsound, treacherous, flimsy, weak, suspect, risky, chancy, *colloq.* dodgy, *sl.* dicey, *Austral. sl.* shonky, *Brit. sl.* dicky, iffy. □□ **unreliability** see *inconstancy* (INCONSTANT). **unreliably** see *by fits and starts* (FIT[2]).

unrelieved /únrileēvd/ *adj.* **1** lacking the relief given by contrast or variation. **2** not aided or assisted. □□ **unrelievedly** *adv.*

■ **1** see UNMITIGATED 1.

unreligious /únrilíjəss/ *adj.* **1** not concerned with religion. **2** irreligious.

■ see *unbelieving* (UNBELIEF).

unremarkable /únrimaārkəb'l/ *adj.* not remarkable; uninteresting. □□ **unremarkably** *adv.*

■ see ORDINARY *adj.*

unremembered /únrimémbərd/ *adj.* not remembered; forgotten.

unremitting /únrimítting/ *adj.* never relaxing or slackening, incessant. □□ **unremittingly** *adv.* **unremittingness** *n.*

■ see RELENTLESS 2.

unremorseful /únrimórsfōōl/ *adj.* lacking remorse. □□ **unremorsefully** *adv.*

■ see UNREPENTANT.

unremovable /únrimōōvəb'l/ *adj.* that cannot be removed.

unremunerative /únrimyōōnərətiv/ *adj.* bringing no, or not enough, profit or income. □□ **unremuneratively** *adv.* **unremunerativeness** *n.*

unrenewable /únrinyōōəb'l/ *adj.* that cannot be renewed. □□ **unrenewed** *adj.*

unrepealed /únripeēld/ *adj.* not repealed.

unrepeatable /únripeētəb'l/ *adj.* **1** that cannot be done, made, or said again. **2** too indecent to be said again. □□ **unrepeatability** /-bílliti/ *n.*

unrepentant /únripéntənt/ *adj.* not repentant, impenitent. □□ **unrepentantly** *adv.*

■ unrepenting, unremorseful, impenitent, unapologetic, unregretful, unashamed, unembarrassed, unselfconscious, remorseless, unreformed, unrehabilitated, unregenerate, unreformable, incorrigible, incurable, hardened, recidivist(ic).

unreported /únripórtid/ *adj.* not reported.

unrepresentative /únreprizéntətiv/ *adj.* not representative. □□ **unrepresentativeness** *n.*

■ see UNUSUAL 2.

unrepresented /únreprizéntid/ *adj.* not represented.

unreproved /únriprōōvd/ *adj.* not reproved.

unrequested /únrikwéstid/ *adj.* not requested or asked for.

■ see UNASKED.

unrequited /únrikwītid/ *adj.* (of love etc.) not returned. □□ **unrequitedly** *adv.* **unrequitedness** *n.*

■ see THANKLESS 2.

unreserve /únrizérv/ *n.* lack of reserve; frankness.

unreserved /únrizérvd/ *adj.* **1** not reserved (*unreserved seats*). **2** without reservations; absolute (*unreserved confidence*). **3** free from reserve (*an unreserved nature*). □□ **unreservedly** /-vidli/ *adv.* **unreservedness** *n.*

■ **1** see FREE *adj.* 8b. **2** see WHOLEHEARTED. **3** see OPEN *adj.* 8a. □□ **unreservedly** see ABSOLUTELY 1.

unresisted /únrizístid/ *adj.* not resisted. □□ **unresistedly** *adv.*

unresisting /únrizísting/ *adj.* not resisting. □□ **unresistingly** *adv.* **unresistingness** *n.*

■ see PASSIVE 2.

unresolvable /únrizólvəb'l/ *adj.* (of a problem, conflict, etc.) that cannot be resolved.

unresolved /únrizólvd/ *adj.* **1 a** uncertain how to act, irresolute. **b** uncertain in opinion, undecided. **2** (of questions etc.) undetermined, undecided, unsolved. **3** not broken up or dissolved. □□ **unresolvedly** /-vidli/ *adv.* **unresolvedness** *n.*

■ **1** undecided, uncertain, unsure, ambivalent, in two minds, wavering, vacillating, shilly-shallying, dithering, hesitant, irresolute. **2** unsettled, undetermined, undecided, open, up in the air, moot, pending, debatable, arguable, problematic(al), indefinite, vague, open to question, questionable, unanswered, unsolved.

unresponsive /únrispónsiv/ *adj.* not responsive. □□ **unresponsively** *adv.* **unresponsiveness** *n.*

■ see UNMOVED 3, SLOW *adj.* 5, INERT 1, 2.

unrest /únrést/ *n.* **1** lack of rest. **2** restlessness, disturbance, agitation.

■ **2** disquiet, uneasiness, restlessness, distress, anxiety, anxiousness, nervousness, anguish, unease, worry, concern, agony, agitation, ferment, turmoil, disturbance, turbulence, tumult, rioting, trouble, strife, *colloq.* ruction.

unrested /únréstid/ *adj.* not refreshed by rest.

unrestful /únréstfōōl/ *adj.* not restful. □□ **unrestfully** *adv.*

unresting /únrésting/ *adj.* not resting. □□ **unrestingly** *adv.*

unrestored /únristórd/ *adj.* not restored.

unrestrainable /únristráynəb'l/ *adj.* that cannot be restrained; irrepressible, ungovernable.

unrestrained /únristráynd/ *adj.* not restrained. □□ **unrestrainedly** /-nidli/ *adv.* **unrestrainedness** *n.*

■ see FREE *adj.* 3, UNCONTROLLED, LIMITLESS.
□□ **unrestrainedly** see *freely* (FREE).
unrestraint /únristráynt/ *n.* lack of restraint.
unrestricted /únristríktid/ *adj.* not restricted. □□ **unrestrictedly** *adv.* **unrestrictedness** *n.*
■ see ABSOLUTE *adj.* 2, FREE *adj.* 3a, LIMITLESS.
unreturned /únritúrnd/ *adj.* **1** not reciprocated or responded to. **2** not having returned or been returned.
unrevealed /únrivéeld/ *adj.* not revealed; secret.
■ see DORMANT 2b, UNTOLD 1.
unreversed /únrivérst/ *adj.* (esp. of a decision etc.) not reversed.
unrevised /únrivī́zd/ *adj.* not revised; in an original form.
unrevoked /únrivṓkt/ *adj.* not revoked or annulled; still in force.
unrewarded /únriwáwrdid/ *adj.* not rewarded.
unrewarding /únriwáwrding/ *adj.* not rewarding or satisfying.
■ see FRUITLESS 2, THANKLESS 2.
unrhymed /únrī́md/ *adj.* not rhymed.
unrhythmical /únríthmik'l/ *adj.* not rhythmical. □□ **unrhythmically** *adv.*
unridable /únrī́dəb'l/ *adj.* that cannot be ridden.
unridden /únrídd'n/ *adj.* not ridden.
unriddle /únrídd'l/ *v.tr.* solve or explain (a mystery etc.). □□ **unriddler** *n.*
unrig /únríg/ *v.tr.* (**unrigged, unrigging**) **1** remove the rigging from (a ship). **2** *dial.* undress.
unrighteous /únrī́chəss/ *adj.* not righteous; unjust, wicked, dishonest. □□ **unrighteously** *adv.* **unrighteousness** *n.* [OE *unrihtwīs* (as UN-[1], RIGHTEOUS)]
unrip /únríp/ *v.tr.* (**unripped, unripping**) open by ripping.
unripe /únrī́p/ *adj.* not ripe. □□ **unripeness** *n.*
■ see GREEN *adj.* 3.
unrisen /únrízz'n/ *adj.* that has not risen.
unrivalled /únrī́v'ld/ *adj.* (*US* **unrivaled**) having no equal; peerless.
■ see *peerless* (PEER[2]).
unrivet /únrívvit/ *v.tr.* (**unriveted, unriveting**) **1** undo, unfasten, or detach by the removal of rivets. **2** loosen, relax, undo, detach.
■ see UNDO 1.
unrobe /únrṓb/ *v.tr.* & *intr.* **1** disrobe. **2** undress.
unroll /únrṓl/ *v.tr.* & *intr.* **1** open out from a rolled-up state. **2** display or be displayed in this form.
■ see SPREAD *v.* 1a.
unromantic /únrəmántik/ *adj.* not romantic. □□ **unromantically** *adv.*
■ see PROSAIC.
unroof /únróof/ *v.tr.* remove the roof of.
unroofed /únróoft/ *adj.* not provided with a roof.
unroot /únróot/ *v.tr.* **1** uproot. **2** eradicate.
unrope /únrṓp/ *v.* **1** *tr.* detach by undoing a rope. **2** *intr.* *Mountaineering* detach oneself from a rope.
unrounded /únrówndid/ *adj.* not rounded.
unrove *past* of UNREEVE.
unroyal /únróyəl/ *adj.* not royal.
unruffled /únrúff'ld/ *adj.* **1** not agitated or disturbed; calm. **2** not physically ruffled.
■ **1** see CALM adj. 2. **2** see SMOOTH *adj.* 5.
unruled /únróold/ *adj.* **1** not ruled or governed. **2** not having ruled lines.
unruly /únróoli/ *adj.* (**unrulier, unruliest**) not easily controlled or disciplined, disorderly. □□ **unruliness** *n.* [ME f. UN-[1] + *ruly* f. RULE]
■ unmanageable, ungovernable, uncontrollable, uncontrolled, undisciplined, unregulated, lawless, disobedient, insubordinate, rebellious, mutinous, fractious, refractory, contumacious, obstreperous, wilful, headstrong, stubborn, recalcitrant, intractable, defiant, uncooperative, wayward, disorderly, turbulent, riotous, rowdy, tumultuous, wild, violent, stormy, tempestuous, *US colloq.* rambunctious.
UNRWA /únraa/ *abbr.* United Nations Relief and Works Agency.
unsaddle /únsádd'l/ *v.tr.* **1** remove the saddle from (a horse etc.). **2** dislodge from a saddle.
unsafe /únsáyf/ *adj.* not safe. □□ **unsafely** *adv.* **unsafeness** *n.*
■ see DANGEROUS, INSECURE 2a, b. □□ **unsafely** see *dangerously* (DANGEROUS).
unsaid[1] /únséd/ *adj.* not said or uttered.
■ see TACIT.
unsaid[2] *past* and *past part.* of UNSAY.
unsalaried /únsállərid/ *adj.* not salaried.
■ see UNPAID.
unsaleable /únsáyləb'l/ *adj.* not saleable. □□ **unsaleability** /-bílliti/ *n.*
unsalted /únsáwltid, únsólt-/ *adj.* not salted.
unsanctified /únsángktifīd/ *adj.* not sanctified.
unsanctioned /únsángksh'nd/ *adj.* not sanctioned.
■ see UNAUTHORIZED.
unsanitary /únsánnitəri, -tri/ *adj.* not sanitary.
■ see SORDID 1.
unsatisfactory /únsatisfáktəri, -tri/ *adj.* not satisfactory; poor, unacceptable. □□ **unsatisfactorily** *adv.* **unsatisfactoriness** *n.*
■ insufficient, inadequate, inferior, substandard, poor, unacceptable, displeasing, disappointing, dissatisfying, unsatisfying, unworthy, inappropriate, deficient, weak, wanting, lacking, unsuitable, imperfect, flawed, defective, faulty, not up to par *or* scratch.
□□ **unsatisfactorily** see POORLY *adv.*
unsatisfied /únsáttisfīd/ *adj.* not satisfied. □□ **unsatisfiedness** *n.*
■ see *dissatisfied* (DISSATISFY).
unsatisfying /únsáttisfī-ing/ *adj.* not satisfying. □□ **unsatisfyingly** *adv.*
■ see *disappointing* (DISAPPOINT), THIN *adj.* 6.
unsaturated /únsáchəraytid, -sátyooraytid/ *adj.* **1** *Chem.* (of a compound, esp. a fat or oil) having double or triple bonds in its molecule and therefore capable of further reaction. **2** not saturated. □□ **unsaturation** /-ráysh'n/ *n.*
unsaved /únsáyvd/ *adj.* not saved.
unsavoury /únsáyvəri/ *adj.* (*US* **unsavory**) **1** disagreeable to the taste, smell, or feelings; disgusting. **2** disagreeable, unpleasant (*an unsavoury character*). **3** morally offensive. □□ **unsavourily** *adv.* **unsavouriness** *n.*
■ unappetizing, unpalatable, inedible, uneatable; distasteful, objectionable, unpleasant, disagreeable, offensive, repugnant, obnoxious, repellent, nasty, repulsive, revolting, disgusting, nauseating, sickening, seamy, noxious, *literary* noisome.
unsay /únsáy/ *v.tr.* (*past* and *past part.* **unsaid**) retract (a statement).
unsayable /únsáyəb'l/ *adj.* that cannot be said.
unscalable /únskáyləb'l/ *adj.* that cannot be scaled.
unscarred /únskaárd/ *adj.* not scarred or damaged.
■ unblemished, clear; see also UNSCATHED.
unscathed /únskáythd/ *adj.* without suffering any injury.
■ unharmed, unhurt, uninjured, unmarked, untouched, undamaged, unscarred, unscratched, safe and sound, sound, in one piece, intact, whole, as new, *archaic* scatheless, *colloq.* like new.
unscented /únséntid/ *adj.* not scented.
■ see UNPERFUMED.
unscheduled /únshédyoold/ *adj.* not scheduled.
■ see ACCIDENTAL *adj.* 1, OPEN *adj.* 17.
unscholarly /únskóllərli/ *adj.* not scholarly. □□ **unscholarliness** *n.*
unschooled /únskóold/ *adj.* **1** uneducated, untaught. **2** not sent to school. **3** untrained, undisciplined. **4** not made artificial by education.

■ **1** see UNEDUCATED. **3** see *inexperienced* (INEXPERIENCE), UNDISCIPLINED.

unscientific /únsīəntíffik/ *adj.* **1** not in accordance with scientific principles. **2** not familiar with science. □□ **unscientifically** *adv.*

unscramble /únskrámb'l/ *v.tr.* restore from a scrambled state, esp. interpret (a scrambled transmission etc.). □□ **unscrambler** *n.*

■ see DECIPHER 2.

unscreened /únskreénd/ *adj.* **1 a** (esp. of coal) not passed through a screen or sieve. **b** not investigated or checked, esp. for security or medical problems. **2** not provided with a screen. **3** not shown on a screen.

unscrew /únskróō/ *v.* **1** *tr.* & *intr.* unfasten or be unfastened by turning or removing a screw or screws or by twisting like a screw. **2** *tr.* loosen (a screw).

■ see UNDO 1.

unscripted /únskríptid/ *adj.* (of a speech etc.) delivered without a prepared script.

■ see EXTEMPORANEOUS.

unscriptural /únskrípchərəl/ *adj.* against or not in accordance with Scripture. □□ **unscripturally** *adv.*

unscrupulous /únskróōpyooləss/ *adj.* having no scruples, unprincipled. □□ **unscrupulously** *adv.* **unscrupulousness** *n.*

■ unconscionable, conscienceless, unprincipled, amoral, unethical, immoral, dishonourable, corrupt, dishonest, deceitful, sly, cunning, artful, insidious, shady, sharp, sneaky, dirty, slippery, roguish, knavish, disingenuous, treacherous, perfidious, faithless, false, untrustworthy, wicked, evil, *colloq.* shifty, crooked.

unseal /únseél/ *v.tr.* break the seal of; open (a letter, receptacle, etc.).

unsealed /únseéld/ *adj.* not sealed.

■ see OPEN *adj.* 1–4, 13, 20.

unsearchable /únsérchəb'l/ *adj.* inscrutable. □□ **unsearchableness** *n.* **unsearchably** *adv.*

unsearched /únsércht/ *adj.* not searched.

unseasonable /únseézənəb'l/ *adj.* **1** not appropriate to the season. **2** untimely, inopportune. □□ **unseasonableness** *n.* **unseasonably** *adv.*

■ **2** unsuitable, inopportune, inappropriate, malapropos, untimely, ill-timed, inexpedient.

unseasoned /únseéz'nd/ *adj.* **1** not flavoured with salt, herbs, etc. **2** (esp. of timber) not matured. **3** not habituated.

■ **2** see GREEN *adj.* 3. **3** see *inexperienced* (INEXPERIENCE).

unseat /únseét/ *v.tr.* **1** remove from a seat, esp. in an election. **2** dislodge from a seat, esp. on horseback.

■ **1** see TOPPLE 1b.

unseaworthy /únseéwurthi/ *adj.* not seaworthy.

unsecured /únsikyoórd/ *adj.* not secured.

■ see LOOSE *adj.* 2.

unseeable /únseéəb'l/ *adj.* that cannot be seen.

■ see INVISIBLE 1, 2.

unseeded /únseédid/ *adj. Sport* (of a player) not seeded.

unseeing /únseéing/ *adj.* **1** unobservant. **2** blind. □□ **unseeingly** *adv.*

unseemly /únseémli/ *adj.* (**unseemlier**, **unseemliest**) **1** indecent. **2** unbecoming. □□ **unseemliness** *n.*

■ **1** improper, indecorous, indelicate, in poor *or* bad taste, risqué, naughty, indecent, shameful, offensive, lewd, lascivious, obscene, rude, coarse, *US* off colour. **2** unbecoming, unrefined, unladylike, ungentlemanly, undignified, unworthy, disreputable, discreditable, impolitic, unwise, imprudent, inapt, inappropriate, uncalled-for, unsuitable, improper, inadvisable, ill-advised, unbefitting, unfitting, out of place *or* keeping, awkward, inauspicious, inexpedient, unfortunate, ill-timed, untimely. □□ **unseemliness** see IMPROPRIETY 1.

unseen /únseén/ *adj.* & *n.* ● *adj.* **1** not seen. **2** invisible. **3** (of a translation) to be done without preparation. ● *n. Brit.* an unseen translation.

■ *adj.* **1** see UNNOTICED, BACKGROUND 2. **2** see INVISIBLE 1, 2.

unsegregated /únségrigaytid/ *adj.* not segregated.

unselect /únsilékt/ *adj.* not select.

unselective /únsiléktiv/ *adj.* not selective.

unselfconscious /únselfkónshəss/ *adj.* not self-conscious. □□ **unselfconsciously** *adv.* **unselfconsciousness** *n.*

■ see UNINHIBITED.

unselfish /únsélfish/ *adj.* mindful of others' interests. □□ **unselfishly** *adv.* **unselfishness** *n.*

■ generous, charitable, open-handed, ungrudging, unstinting, unsparing, free, liberal, giving, big-hearted, magnanimous, considerate, thoughtful, philanthropic, humanitarian, altruistic, public-spirited, selfless, self-sacrificing. □□ **unselfishness** see ALTRUISM.

unsensational /únsensáyshən'l/ *adj.* not sensational. □□ **unsensationally** *adv.*

unsentimental /únsentimént'l/ *adj.* not sentimental. □□ **unsentimentality** /-tálliti/ *n.* **unsentimentally** *adv.*

■ see HARD *adj.* 4, 7b, REALISTIC 2.

unseparated /únsépparaytid/ *adj.* not separated.

■ see UNDIVIDED.

unserviceable /únsérvisəb'l/ *adj.* not serviceable; unfit for use. □□ **unserviceability** /-bílliti/ *n.*

■ see *out of order* 1 (ORDER), USELESS.

unset /únsét/ *adj.* not set.

unsettle /únsétt'l/ *v.* **1** *tr.* disturb the settled state or arrangement of; discompose. **2** *tr.* derange. **3** *intr.* become unsettled. □□ **unsettlement** *n.* **unsettling** *adj.*

■ **1** upset, agitate, perturb, ruffle, fluster, discomfit, discompose, unnerve, disconcert, dismay, pull the rug from under, *colloq.* shake (up), rattle, faze, throw; see also DISORDER *v.* **2** see UPSET *v.* 3. □□ **unsettling** unnerving, upsetting, disturbing, perturbing, discomfiting, disconcerting, dismaying.

unsettled /únsétt'ld/ *adj.* **1** not (yet) settled. **2** liable or open to change or further discussion. **3** (of a bill etc.) unpaid. □□ **unsettledness** *n.*

■ **1** unfixed, unstable, changing, varying, variable, changeable, inconstant, ever-changing, protean, unpredictable, uncertain; disoriented, confused, mixed up, unorganized, disorganized, disorderly, disordered, tumultuous; disturbed, turbulent, agitated, disquieted, disconcerted, upset, perturbed, ruffled, flustered, restive, restless, unnerved, *colloq.* rattled, riled, *US* roiled. **2** see UNRESOLVED 2. **3** see UNPAID.

unsewn /únsṓn/ *adj.* not sewn. □ **unsewn binding** = *perfect binding.*

unsex /únséks/ *v.tr.* deprive (a person, esp. a woman) of the qualities of her or his sex.

unsexed /únsékst/ *adj.* having no sexual characteristics.

unshackle /únshákk'l/ *v.tr.* **1** release from shackles. **2** set free.

■ see RELEASE *v.* 1.

unshaded /únsháydid/ *adj.* not shaded.

unshakeable /únsháykəb'l/ *adj.* (also **unshakable**) that cannot be shaken; firm, obstinate. □□ **unshakeability** /-bílliti/ **unshakeably** *adv.*

■ see FIRM[1] *adj.* 2a, b.

unshaken /únsháykən/ *adj.* not shaken. □□ **unshakenly** *adv.*

unshapely /únsháypli/ *adj.* not shapely. □□ **unshapeliness** *n.*

■ see UGLY 1.

unshared /únsháird/ *adj.* not shared.

unsharp /únshaárp/ *adj. Photog.* not sharp. □□ **unsharpness** *n.*

unshaved /únsháyvd/ *adj.* not shaved.

unshaven /únsháyv'n/ *adj.* not shaved.

unsheathe /únsheéth/ *v.tr.* remove (a knife etc.) from a sheath.

■ see DRAW *v.* 7a.
unshed /únshéd/ *adj.* not shed.
unshell /únshél/ *v.tr.* (usu. as **unshelled** *adj.*) extract from its shell.
unsheltered /únshéltərd/ *adj.* not sheltered.
■ see OPEN *adj.*1–4, 13, 20.
unshielded /únsheeldid/ *adj.* not shielded or protected.
■ see VULNERABLE 1.
unship /únship/ *v.tr.* (**unshipped, unshipping**) **1** remove or discharge (a cargo or passenger) from a ship. **2** esp. *Naut.* remove (an object, esp. a mast or oar) from a fixed position.
unshockable /únshókkəb'l/ *adj.* that cannot be shocked. ▫▫ **unshockability** /-bílliti/ *n.* **unshockably** *adv.*
unshod /únshód/ *adj.* not wearing shoes.
unshorn /únshórn/ *adj.* not shorn.
■ see SHAGGY.
unshrinkable /únshríngkəb'l/ *adj.* (of fabric etc.) not liable to shrink. ▫▫ **unshrinkability** /-bílliti/ *n.*
unshrinking /únshríngking/ *adj.* unhesitating, fearless. ▫▫ **unshrinkingly** *adv.*
■ see OUTSPOKEN, STAUNCH[1] 1.
unsighted /únsítid/ *adj.* **1** not sighted or seen. **2** prevented from seeing, esp. by an obstruction.
unsightly /únsítli/ *adj.* unpleasant to look at, ugly. ▫▫ **unsightliness** *n.*
■ ugly, hideous, awful-looking, horrible, horrible-looking, frightful-looking, dreadful-looking, terrible-looking, grotesque, ghastly, offensive, unattractive, unprepossessing, unlovely, unpretty, plain, *US* homely.
unsigned /únsínd/ *adj.* not signed.
unsinkable /únsíngkəb'l/ *adj.* unable to be sunk. ▫▫ **unsinkability** /-bílliti/ *n.*
unsized[1] /únsízd/ *adj.* **1** not made to a size. **2** not sorted by size.
unsized[2] /únsízd/ *adj.* not treated with size.
unskilful /únskílfŏŏl/ *adj.* (*US* **unskillful**) not skilful. ▫▫ **unskilfully** *adv.* **unskilfulness** *n.*
■ see CLUMSY 1, AMATEUR *adj.* ▫▫ **unskilfully** see ROUGHLY 1.
unskilled /únskíld/ *adj.* lacking or not needing special skill or training.
■ see MENIAL *adj.*, AMATEUR *adj.*, *inexperienced* (INEXPERIENCE).
unskimmed /únskímd/ *adj.* (of milk) not skimmed.
unslakeable /únsláykəb'l/ *adj.* (also **unslakable**) that cannot be slaked or quenched.
■ see UNQUENCHABLE.
unsleeping /únsleeping/ *adj.* not or never sleeping. ▫▫ **unsleepingly** *adv.*
unsliced /únslíst/ *adj.* (esp. of a loaf of bread when it is bought) not having been cut into slices.
unsling /únslíng/ *v.tr.* (*past* and *past part.* **unslung**) free from being slung or suspended.
unsmiling /únsmíling/ *adj.* not smiling. ▫▫ **unsmilingly** *adv.* **unsmilingness** *n.*
■ see SOLEMN 4.
unsmoked /únsmőkt/ *adj.* **1** not cured by smoking (*unsmoked bacon*). **2** not consumed by smoking (*an unsmoked cigar*).
unsnarl /únsnaarl/ *v.tr.* disentangle. [UN-[2] + SNARL[2]]
unsociable /únsőshəb'l/ *adj.* not sociable, disliking the company of others. ▫▫ **unsociability** /-bílliti/ *n.* **unsociableness** *n.* **unsociably** *adv.*
■ see UNSOCIAL.
unsocial /únsősh'l/ *adj.* **1** not social; not suitable for, seeking, or conforming to society. **2** outside the normal working day (*unsocial hours*). **3** antisocial. ▫▫ **unsocially** *adv.*
■ **1, 3** unsociable, unfriendly, cool, cold, chilly, aloof, uncongenial, unamiable, unforthcoming, standoffish, inhospitable, withdrawn, reserved, solitary, retiring, private, distant, detached, reclusive, hermitic, eremitic(al), anchoritic, anchoretic; antisocial, misanthropic(al), hostile.
unsoiled /únsóyld/ *adj.* not soiled or dirtied.
■ see CLEAN *adj.* 1.
unsold /únsőld/ *adj.* not sold.
unsolder /únsőldər, unsól-/ *v.tr.* undo the soldering of.
unsoldierly /únsőljərli/ *adj.* not soldierly.
unsolicited /únsəlíssitid/ *adj.* not asked for; given or done voluntarily. ▫▫ **unsolicitedly** *adv.*
■ unlooked-for, unsought, not sought (after), unrequested, unasked for, uncalled-for, gratuitous, free, voluntary, uninvited, unbidden.
unsolvable /únsólvəb'l/ *adj.* that cannot be solved, insoluble. ▫▫ **unsolvability** /-bílliti/ *n.* **unsolvableness** *n.*
■ see IMPOSSIBLE 1, MYSTERIOUS.
unsolved /únsólvd/ *adj.* not solved.
■ see UNRESOLVED 2, MYSTERIOUS.
unsophisticated /únsəfístikaytid/ *adj.* **1** artless, simple, natural, ingenuous. **2** not adulterated or artificial. ▫▫ **unsophisticatedly** *adv.* **unsophisticatedness** *n.* **unsophistication** /-káysh'n/ *n.*
■ **1** naïve, inexperienced, callow, simple, childlike, unworldly, innocent, ingenuous, unaffected, artless, guileless, natural. **2** simple, plain, crude, undeveloped, primitive, rudimentary, uncomplicated, undetailed, uninvolved, unrefined, unadulterated, unembellished. ▫▫ **unsophisticatedness** see NAÏVETY, SIMPLICITY. **unsophistication** see INEXPERIENCE.
unsorted /únsórtid/ *adj.* not sorted.
unsought /únsáwt/ *adj.* **1** not searched out or sought for. **2** unasked; without being requested.
■ **1** see UNFORESEEN, GRATUITOUS 2. **2** see UNASKED.
unsound /únsównd/ *adj.* **1** unhealthy, diseased. **2** rotten, weak. **3 a** ill-founded, fallacious. **b** unorthodox, heretical. **4** unreliable. **5** wicked. ▫ **of unsound mind** insane. ▫▫ **unsoundly** *adv.* **unsoundness** *n.*
■ **1** unhealthy, diseased, ill, afflicted, in poor health, ailing, sickly, sick, unwell, delicate, injured, wounded. **2** weak, feeble, frail, flimsy, rickety, shaky, rocky, ramshackle, infirm, unstable, wobbly, tottering, teetering, unsteady, broken-down, crumbling, disintegrating, dilapidated, decrepit, defective, imperfect, faulty, decayed, rotten, *colloq.* manky, *Brit. sl.* wonky. **3 a** illogical, faulty, flawed, fallacious, untenable, invalid, groundless, unfounded, ill-founded, shaky, erroneous, defective, specious. **b** see UNORTHODOX. **4** see UNRELIABLE. ▫ **of unsound mind** mad, psychotic, unbalanced, unstable, unhinged, demented, deranged, lunatic, *colloq.* crazy, certifiable, mental, round the bend, not all there, *sl.* nuts, bats, bananas, bonkers; see also INSANE 1.
unsounded[1] /únsówndid/ *adj.* **1** not uttered or pronounced. **2** not made to sound.
unsounded[2] /únsówndid/ *adj.* unfathomed.
unsoured /únsówrd/ *adj.* not soured.
unsown /únsőn/ *adj.* not sown.
unsparing /únspáiring/ *adj.* **1** lavish, profuse. **2** merciless. ▫▫ **unsparingly** *adv.* **unsparingness** *n.*
■ **1** see LAVISH *adj.* 1, 2. **2** see MERCILESS.
unspeakable /únspeekəb'l/ *adj.* **1** that cannot be expressed in words. **2** indescribably bad or objectionable. ▫▫ **unspeakableness** *n.* **unspeakably** *adv.*
■ see INEXPRESSIBLE, OUTRAGEOUS 3. ▫▫ **unspeakably** see BADLY 1.
unspecialized /únspéshəlízd/ *adj.* not specialized.
■ see GENERAL *adj.* 6, UNPROFESSIONAL 2.
unspecified /únspéssifíd/ *adj.* not specified.
■ see VAGUE 1.
unspectacular /únspektákyoolər/ *adj.* not spectacular; dull. ▫▫ **unspectacularly** *adv.*
unspent /únspént/ *adj.* **1** not expended or used. **2** not exhausted or used up.
unspilled /únspíld/ *adj.* not spilt.
unspilt /únspílt/ *adj.* not spilt.

unspiritual /únspírrityooəl/ *adj.* not spiritual; earthly, worldly. ▫▫ **unspirituality** /-tyoo-álliti/ *n.* **unspiritually** *adv.* **unspiritualness** *n.*

unspoiled /únspóyld/ *adj.* **1** unspoilt. **2** not plundered.
■ **1** unspoilt, unsullied, pristine, perfect, virgin, whole, intact, unimpaired, undamaged, untainted, unstained, unblemished, immaculate, impeccable, uncorrupted, unpolluted, spotless, stainless, flawless, clean.

unspoilt /únspóylt/ *adj.* not spoilt.
■ see UNSPOILED.

unspoken /únspṓkən/ *adj.* **1** not expressed in speech. **2** not uttered as speech.
■ see TACIT.

unsporting /únspórting/ *adj.* not sportsmanlike; not fair or generous. ▫▫ **unsportingly** *adv.* **unsportingness** *n.*
■ see DIRTY *adj.* 5.

unsportsmanlike /únspórtsmənlīk/ *adj.* unsporting.
■ see DIRTY *adj.* 5.

unspotted /únspóttid/ *adj.* **1 a** not marked with a spot or spots. **b** morally pure. **2** unnoticed.

unsprung /únsprúng/ *adj.* not provided with a spring or springs; not resilient.

unstable /únstáyb'l/ *adj.* (**unstabler**, **unstablest**) **1** not stable. **2** changeable. **3** showing a tendency to sudden mental or emotional changes. ▫ **unstable equilibrium** a state in which a body when disturbed tends to move farther from equilibrium. ▫▫ **unstableness** *n.* **unstably** *adv.*
■ **1** see SHAKY. **2, 3** changeable, variable, unsteady, inconstant, inconsistent, insecure, capricious, fickle, irregular, unpredictable, unreliable, erratic, volatile, fluid, shifting, fluctuating, flighty, mercurial, moody, vacillating, tergiversating, indecisive, undecided, irresolute, unsteadfast, indefinite, unsettled, unbalanced, twisted.

unstained /únstáynd/ *adj.* not stained.
■ see CLEAN *adj.* 1, CHASTE 1.

unstamped /únstámpt/ *adj.* **1** not marked by stamping. **2** not having a stamp affixed.

unstarched /únstaárcht/ *adj.* not starched.

unstated /únstáytid/ *adj.* not stated or declared.
■ see TACIT.

unstatesmanlike /únstáytsmənlīk/ *adj.* not statesmanlike.

unstatutable /únstátyootəb'l/ *adj.* contrary to a statute or statutes. ▫▫ **unstatutably** *adv.*

unsteadfast /únstédfaast/ *adj.* not steadfast.
■ see UNSTABLE 2, 3.

unsteady /únstéddi/ *adj.* (**unsteadier**, **unsteadiest**) **1** not steady or firm. **2** changeable, fluctuating. **3** not uniform or regular. ▫▫ **unsteadily** *adv.* **unsteadiness** *n.*
■ **1** see SHAKY, *doddering* (DODDER[1]), FAINT *adj.* 2. **2** see VARIABLE *adj.* 2. ▫▫ **unsteadiness** see *fluctuation* (FLUCTUATE), *inconstancy* (INCONSTANT).

unstick *v.* & *n.* ● *v.* /únstík/ (*past* and *past part.* **unstuck**) **1** *tr.* separate (a thing stuck to another). **2** *Aeron. colloq.* **a** *intr.* take off. **b** *tr.* cause (an aircraft) to take off. ● *n.* /únstik/ *Aeron. colloq.* the moment of take-off. ▫ **come unstuck** *colloq.* come to grief, fail.

unstinted /únstíntid/ *adj.* not stinted. ▫▫ **unstintedly** *adv.*

unstinting /únstínting/ *adj.* ungrudging, lavish. ▫▫ **unstintingly** *adv.*
■ see GENEROUS 1, WHOLEHEARTED.

unstirred /únstúrd/ *adj.* not stirred.

unstitch /únstích/ *v.tr.* undo the stitches of.

unstop /únstóp/ *v.tr.* (**unstopped, unstopping**) **1** free from obstruction. **2** remove the stopper from.

unstoppable /únstóppəb'l/ *adj.* that cannot be stopped or prevented. ▫▫ **unstoppability** /-bílliti/ *n.* **unstoppably** *adv.*
■ see INDOMITABLE 1, RELENTLESS.

unstopper /únstóppər/ *v.tr.* remove the stopper from.

unstrained /únstráynd/ *adj.* **1** not subjected to straining or stretching. **2** not injured by overuse or excessive demands. **3** not forced or produced by effort. **4** not passed through a strainer.
■ **3** see EASY *adj.* 1, 3.

unstrap /únstráp/ *v.tr.* (**unstrapped**, **unstrapping**) undo the strap or straps of.
■ see UNDO 1.

unstreamed /únstreémd/ *adj. Brit.* (of schoolchildren) not arranged in streams.

unstressed /únstrést/ *adj.* **1** (of a word, syllable, etc.) not pronounced with stress. **2** not subjected to stress.
■ **1** see UNACCENTED.

unstring /únstríng/ *v.tr.* (*past* and *past part.* **unstrung**) **1** remove or relax the string or strings of (a bow, harp, etc.). **2** remove from a string. **3** (esp. as **unstrung** *adj.*) unnerve.

unstructured /únstrúkchərd/ *adj.* **1** not structured. **2** informal.
■ **1** see INCOHERENT 2, LOOSE *adj.* 6, 8, 9. **2** see INFORMAL.

unstuck *past* and *past part.* of UNSTICK.

unstudied /únstúddid/ *adj.* easy, natural, spontaneous. ▫▫ **unstudiedly** *adv.*
■ see NATURAL *adj.* 4.

unstuffed /únstúft/ *adj.* not stuffed.

unstuffy /únstúffi/ *adj.* **1** informal, casual. **2** not stuffy.

unsubdued /únsəbdyṓod/ *adj.* not subdued.

unsubjugated /únsúbjoogaytid/ *adj.* not subjugated.

unsubstantial /únsəbstánsh'l/ *adj.* having little or no solidity, reality, or factual basis. ▫▫ **unsubstantiality** /-shiálliti/ *n.* **unsubstantially** *adv.*
■ see INSUBSTANTIAL.

unsubstantiated /únsəbstánshiaytid/ *adj.* not substantiated.
■ see *ill-founded*, SHAKY.

unsuccess /únsəksés/ *n.* **1** lack of success; failure. **2** an instance of this.

unsuccessful /únsəksésfōol/ *adj.* not successful. ▫▫ **unsuccessfully** *adv.* **unsuccessfulness** *n.*
■ unfortunate, unavailing, vain, abortive, failed, useless, fruitless, unfruitful, unproductive, ineffective, ineffectual, inefficacious, worthless, unprofitable, sterile; unlucky, hapless, luckless, defeated, beaten, losing, cursed, foiled, frustrated, baulked, *archaic* bootless, *colloq.* jinxed. ▫▫ **unsuccessfully** see BADLY 1, *in vain* (VAIN).

unsugared /únshṓoggərd/ *adj.* not sugared.

unsuggestive /únsəjéstiv/ *adj.* not suggestive.

unsuitable /únsṓotəb'l, únsyṓo-/ *adj.* not suitable. ▫▫ **unsuitability** /-bílliti/ *n.* **unsuitableness** *n.* **unsuitably** *adv.*
■ see INAPPROPRIATE, UNACCEPTABLE, UNSATISFACTORY. ▫▫ **unsuitability** see IMPROPRIETY 4.

unsuited /únsṓotid, únsyṓo-/ *adj.* **1** (usu. foll. by *for*) not fit for a purpose. **2** (usu. foll. by *to*) not adapted.
■ see INAPPROPRIATE, UNQUALIFIED 1, INCOMPATIBLE 1, 3.

unsullied /únsúllid/ *adj.* not sullied.
■ see CLEAN *adj.* 1, INNOCENT *adj.* 1.

unsummoned /únsúmmənd/ *adj.* not summoned.

unsung /únsúng/ *adj.* **1** not celebrated in song; unknown. **2** not sung.
■ **1** uncelebrated, unrecognized, unglorified, unexalted, unpraised, unhonoured, unnoticed, disregarded, unknown, unheard-of, anonymous, unidentified, nameless, obscure, insignificant, inconspicuous.

unsupervised /únsṓopərvīzd, únsyṓo-/ *adj.* not supervised.

unsupportable /únsəpórtəb'l/ *adj.* **1** that cannot be endured. **2** indefensible. ▫▫ **unsupportably** *adv.*
■ **1** see UNBEARABLE. **2** see UNTENABLE.

unsupported /únsəpórtid/ *adj.* not supported. ▫▫ **unsupportedly** *adv.*
■ see GROUNDLESS, SHAKY.

unsure /únshóor, únshór/ *adj.* not sure. ▫▫ **unsurely** *adv.* **unsureness** *n.*

■ see UNCERTAIN 1, 2.
unsurpassable /únsərpaássəb'l/ *adj.* that cannot be surpassed. □□ **unsurpassably** *adv.*
■ see UNBEATABLE.
unsurpassed /únsərpaást/ *adj.* not surpassed.
■ see UNPARALLELED .
unsurprising /únsərpri̅zing/ *adj.* not surprising. □□ **unsurprisingly** *adv.*
unsusceptible /únsəséptib'l/ *adj.* not susceptible. □□ **unsusceptibility** /-bílliti/ *n.*
■ (*unsusceptible to*) see IMMUNE 2.
unsuspected /únsəspéktid/ *adj.* not suspected. □□ **unsuspectedly** *adv.*
unsuspecting /únsəspékting/ *adj.* not suspecting. □□ **unsuspectingly** *adv.* **unsuspectingness** *n.*
■ unsuspicious, unwary, unknowing, ignorant, unconscious, gullible, green, credulous, naïve, ingenuous, innocent, trusting; unaware, off guard.
unsuspicious /únsəspíshəss/ *adj.* not suspicious. □□ **unsuspiciously** *adv.* **unsuspiciousness** *n.*
unsustained /únsəstáynd/ *adj.* not sustained.
■ see SPASMODIC 2.
unswathe /únswáyth/ *v.tr.* free from being swathed.
unswayed /únswáyd/ *adj.* uninfluenced, unaffected.
unsweetened /únsweét'nd/ *adj.* not sweetened.
unswept /únswépt/ *adj.* not swept.
unswerving /únswérving/ *adj.* **1** steady, constant. **2** not turning aside. □□ **unswervingly** *adv.*
■ **1** see CONSTANT *adj.* 3. □□ **unswervingly** see *consistently* (CONSISTENT).
unsworn /únswórn/ *adj.* **1** (of a person) not subjected to or bound by an oath. **2** not confirmed by an oath.
unsymmetrical /únsimétrik'l/ *adj.* not symmetrical. □□ **unsymmetrically** *adv.*
■ see LOPSIDED.
unsympathetic /únsimpəthéttik/ *adj.* not sympathetic. □□ **unsympathetically** *adv.*
■ uncaring, unconcerned, callous, unfeeling, unaffected, untouched, unmoved, indifferent, unemotional, dispassionate, unreactive, unresponsive, impassive, stolid, cold, cool, aloof, unstirred, apathetic, insensitive, stoic(al), stony, adamant, hostile, stony-hearted, hard-hearted, heartless, uncharitable, unkind, unpitying, pitiless, unmerciful, merciless, ruthless. □□ **unsympathetically** see ROUGHLY 1.
unsystematic /únsistəmáttik/ *adj.* not systematic. □□ **unsystematically** *adv.*
■ see *chaotic* (CHAOS), RANDOM. □□ **unsystematically** see *at random* (RANDOM), HELTER-SKELTER *adv.*
untack /únták/ *v.tr.* detach, esp. by removing tacks.
untainted /úntáyntid/ *adj.* not tainted.
■ see PURE 1–4.
untalented /úntálləntid/ *adj.* not talented.
untameable /úntáyməb'l/ *adj.* that cannot be tamed.
untamed /úntáymd/ *adj.* not tamed, wild.
■ undomesticated, wild, unbroken, unsubdued, uncontrollable, savage, fierce, feral, ferocious, *Austral.* warrigal.
untangle /úntángg'l/ *v.tr.* **1** free from a tangled state. **2** free from entanglement.
■ **1, 2** see STRAIGHTEN, EXTRICATE.
untanned /úntánd/ *adj.* not tanned.
untapped /úntápt/ *adj.* not (yet) tapped or wired (*untapped resources*).
untarnished /úntaárnisht/ *adj.* not tarnished.
■ unsoiled, unsullied, immaculate, spotless, unspotted, unstained, unblemished, untainted, faultless, flawless, impeccable, uncorrupted, unfouled, chaste, clean, pure, lily-white, undefiled, virginal.
untasted /úntáystid/ *adj.* not tasted.
untaught /úntáwt/ *adj.* **1** not instructed by teaching; ignorant. **2** not acquired by teaching; natural, spontaneous.
■ **1** see UNEDUCATED. **2** see INBORN, NATURAL *adj.* 4.
untaxed /úntákst/ *adj.* not required to pay or not attracting taxes.
unteach /únteéch/ *v.tr.* (*past* and *past part.* **untaught**) **1** cause (a person) to forget or discard previous knowledge. **2** remove from the mind (something known or taught) by different teaching.
unteachable /únteéchəb'l/ *adj.* **1** incapable of being instructed. **2** that cannot be imparted by teaching.
untearable /úntáirəb'l/ *adj.* that cannot be torn.
untechnical /úntéknik'l/ *adj.* not technical. □□ **untechnically** *adv.*
untempered /úntémpərd/ *adj.* (of metal etc.) not brought to the proper hardness or consistency.
untenable /únténnəb'l/ *adj.* not tenable; that cannot be defended. □□ **untenability** /-bílliti/ *n.* **untenableness** *n.* **untenably** *adv.*
■ insupportable, unsupportable, indefensible, unsustainable, unmaintainable, unjustified, unjustifiable, baseless, groundless, unfounded, flawed, faulty, weak, illogical, specious, implausible, unreasonable, unsound, invalid.
untended /únténdid/ *adj.* not tended; neglected.
untested /úntéstid/ *adj.* not tested or proved.
■ see GREEN *adj.* 5, THEORETICAL 2, NOVEL[2].
untether /úntéthər/ *v.tr.* release (an animal) from a tether.
untethered /úntéthərd/ *adj.* not tethered.
unthanked /únthángkt/ *adj.* not thanked.
■ unacknowledged, unrecognized, unappreciated.
unthankful /únthángkfool/ *adj.* not thankful. □□ **unthankfully** *adv.* **unthankfulness** *n.*
■ see UNGRATEFUL.
unthinkable /únthíngkəb'l/ *adj.* **1** that cannot be imagined or grasped by the mind. **2** *colloq.* highly unlikely or undesirable. □□ **unthinkability** /-bílliti/ *n.* **unthinkableness** *n.* **unthinkably** *adv.*
■ **1** inconceivable, unbelievable, unimaginable, incredible, incomprehensible, extraordinary, *colloq.* mind-boggling, *sl.* mind-blowing. **2** unacceptable, unattractive, absurd, illogical, impossible, improbable, unlikely, out of the question, beyond belief, preposterous, ridiculous, laughable, ludicrous, *colloq.* not on.
unthinking /únthíngking/ *adj.* **1** thoughtless. **2** unintentional, inadvertent. □□ **unthinkingly** *adv.* **unthinkingness** *n.*
■ **1** thoughtless, inconsiderate, impolite, tactless, rude, undiplomatic, discourteous, uncivil, imprudent, unwise, indiscreet, neglectful, negligent, careless, mindless, heedless, undiscriminating, unconsidered, unreflecting, unthoughtful, irrational, unreasonable, illogical, unperceptive, unperceiving, undiscerning, witless, brainless, foolish, senseless, nonsensical, rash, impetuous, stupid, silly, mad, insane, idiotic, imbecilic, hasty, short-sighted, *colloq.* crazy, moronic. **2** see INADVERTENT 1. □□ **unthinkingly** see *blindly* (BLIND).
unthought /únthawt/ *adj.* (often foll. by *of*) not thought of.
■ (*unthought of*) see INCONCEIVABLE 1, UNFORESEEN.
unthoughtful /únthawtfool/ *adj.* unthinking, unmindful; thoughtless. □□ **unthoughtfully** *adv.* **unthoughtfulness** *n.*
■ see UNTHINKING 1.
unthread /únthréd/ *v.tr.* **1** take the thread out of (a needle etc.). **2** find one's way out of (a maze).
unthrifty /únthrífti/ *adj.* **1** wasteful, extravagant, prodigal. **2** not thriving or flourishing. □□ **unthriftily** *adv.* **unthriftiness** *n.*
■ **1** see WASTEFUL.
unthrone /únthrṓn/ *v.tr.* dethrone.
untidy /úntídi/ *adj.* (**untidier**, **untidiest**) not neat or orderly. □□ **untidily** *adv.* **untidiness** *n.*
■ disorderly, messy, dishevelled, unkempt, ungroomed, slovenly, slatternly, bedraggled, rumpled, tousled, frowzy, sloppy, shabby, draggle-tailed, *colloq.* scruffy,

tatty; littered, cluttered, chaotic, helter-skelter, jumbled, muddled, disorganized, disordered, disarranged, higgledy-piggledy, topsy-turvy, messed-up, *US colloq.* mussy, mussed-up. □□ **untidiness** see DISORDER *n.* 1.

untie /úntī́/ *v.tr.* (*pres. part.* **untying**) **1** undo (a knot etc.). **2** unfasten the cords etc. of (a package etc.). **3** release from bonds or attachment. [OE *untīgan* (as UN-[2], TIE)]
■ **1, 2** see UNDO 1. **3** see RELEASE *v.* 1.

untied /úntī́d/ *adj.* not tied.
■ see LOOSE *adj.* 1, 2, UNDONE 2.

until /əntíl, un-/ *prep.* & *conj.* = TILL[1]. ¶ Used esp. when beginning a sentence and in formal style, e.g. *until you told me, I had no idea; he resided there until his decease.* [orig. northern ME *untill* f. ON *und* as far as + TILL[1]]

untilled /úntíld/ *adj.* not tilled.

untimely /úntī́mli/ *adj.* & *adv.* ● *adj.* **1** inopportune. **2** (of death) premature. ● *adv. archaic* **1** inopportunely. **2** prematurely. □□ **untimeliness** *n.*
■ *adj.* **1** see INOPPORTUNE. **2** see PREMATURE 1.

untinged /úntínjd/ *adj.* not tinged.

untiring /úntī́ring/ *adj.* tireless. □□ **untiringly** *adv.*
■ unflagging, determined, indefatigable, dogged, persevering, persistent, assiduous, tireless, unwearying, unwearied, dedicated, unfailing, unfaltering, unwavering, steady. □□ **untiringly** see HARD *adv.* 1.

untitled /úntī́t'ld/ *adj.* having no title.

unto /úntoo, úntə/ *prep. archaic* = TO *prep.* (in all uses except as the sign of the infinitive); (*do unto others; faithful unto death; take unto oneself*). [ME f. UNTIL, with TO replacing northern TILL[1]]

untold /úntṓld/ *adj.* **1** not told. **2** not (able to be) counted or measured (*untold misery*). [OE *untēald* (as UN-[1], TOLD)]
■ **1** unrecounted, unnarrated, undescribed, unpublished, unrevealed, undisclosed, undivulged, unreported, private, hidden, secret. **2** countless, uncounted, uncountable, unnumbered, numberless, innumerable, incalculable, inestimable, *literary* myriad; immeasurable, measureless, unlimited; inexpressible, unutterable, indescribable, unimaginable, inconceivable, unthinkable, unspeakable.

untouchable /úntúchəb'l/ *adj.* & *n.* ● *adj.* that may not or cannot be touched. ● *n.* a member of a hereditary Hindu group held to defile members of higher castes on contact. ¶ Use of the term, and social restrictions accompanying it, were declared illegal under the Indian constitution in 1949. □□ **untouchability** /-bílliti/ *n.* **untouchableness** *n.*

untouched /úntúcht/ *adj.* **1** not touched. **2** not affected physically, not harmed, modified, used, or tasted. **3** not affected by emotion. **4** not discussed.
■ **2** see UNUSED 1b, UNSCATHED. **3** see UNMOVED 3.

untoward /úntəwáwrd, úntṓərd/ *adj.* **1** inconvenient, unlucky. **2** awkward. **3** perverse, refractory. **4** unseemly. □□ **untowardly** *adv.* **untowardness** *n.*
■ **1** adverse, unfavourable, unlucky, unpropitious, discouraging, inopportune, inconvenient, unpromising, inauspicious, bad, unfortunate. **4** unbecoming, unfitting, inappropriate, unapt, unsuitable, improper, impolite, rude, boorish, ungentlemanly, unladylike, indecorous, indelicate, unwarranted, uncalled-for, unrefined, unseemly, unwise, imprudent, undiplomatic, tactless, untactful; ill-conceived, silly, foolish, stupid, ill-timed.

untraceable /úntráysəb'l/ *adj.* that cannot be traced. □□ **untraceably** *adv.*

untraced /úntráyst/ *adj.* not traced.

untrained /úntráynd/ *adj.* not trained.
■ see AMATEUR *adj.*, *inexperienced* (INEXPERIENCE).

untrammelled /úntrámm'ld/ *adj.* not trammelled, unhampered.
■ see UNIMPEDED.

untransferable /úntransférəb'l, úntraans-/ *adj.* not transferable.
■ non-transferable, non-negotiable; see also *fixed* (FIX *v.* 20c).

untranslatable /úntranzláytəb'l, úntraanz-/ *adj.* that cannot be translated satisfactorily. □□ **untranslatability** /-bílliti/ *n.* **untranslatably** *adv.*

untransportable /úntranzpórtəb'l, úntraanz-/ *adj.* that cannot be transported.

untravelled /úntrávv'ld/ *adj.* (*US* **untraveled**) **1** that has not travelled. **2** that has not been travelled over or through.

untreatable /úntréetəb'l/ *adj.* (of a disease etc.) that cannot be treated.

untreated /úntréetid/ *adj.* not treated.

untried /úntrī́d/ *adj.* **1** not tried or tested. **2** inexperienced. **3** not yet tried by a judge.
■ **1** untested, unproved, unproven, new. **2** see RAW *adj.* 5.

untrodden /úntródd'n/ *adj.* not trodden, stepped on, or traversed.
■ see NEW *adj.* 6, TRACKLESS.

untroubled /úntrúbb'ld/ *adj.* not troubled; calm, tranquil.
■ see TRANQUIL.

untrue /úntrṓō/ *adj.* **1** not true, contrary to what is the fact. **2** (often foll. by *to*) not faithful or loyal. **3** deviating from an accepted standard. □□ **untruly** *adv.* [OE *untrēowe* etc. (as UN-[1], TRUE)]
■ **1** wrong, false, inaccurate, incorrect, erroneous, misleading, mistaken, distorted, invented, fictitious, made-up, fabricated, apocryphal. **2** unfaithful, faithless, disloyal, fickle, capricious, undependable, unreliable, dishonourable, untrustworthy, false, hypocritical, dishonest, insincere, two-faced, duplicitous, devious, deceitful, treacherous, traitorous, perfidious. **3** inexact, non-standard, substandard, imprecise, imperfect.

untruss /úntrúss/ *v.tr.* unfasten (a trussed fowl).

untrustworthy /úntrústwurthi/ *adj.* not trustworthy. □□ **untrustworthiness** *n.*
■ see DISHONEST, IRRESPONSIBLE 1.

untruth /úntrṓōth/ *n.* (*pl.* **untruths** /-trṓōthz, -trṓōths/) **1** the state of being untrue, falsehood. **2** a false statement (*told me an untruth*). [OE *untrēowth* etc. (as UN-[1], TRUTH)]
■ **2** see LIE[2] *n.*

untruthful /úntrṓōthfŏŏl/ *adj.* not truthful. □□ **untruthfully** *adv.* **untruthfulness** *n.*
■ see FALSE *adj.* 1, 2b, DECEITFUL. □□ **untruthfulness** see *falsity* (FALSE).

untuck /úntúk/ *v.tr.* free (bedclothes etc.) from being tucked in or up.

untunable /úntyṓōnəb'l/ *adj.* (of a piano etc.) that cannot be tuned.

untuned /úntyṓōnd/ *adj.* **1** not in tune, not made tuneful. **2** (of a radio receiver etc.) not tuned to any one frequency. **3** not in harmony or concord, disordered.

untuneful /úntyṓōnfŏŏl/ *adj.* not tuneful. □□ **untunefully** *adv.* **untunefulness** *n.*

unturned /úntúrnd/ *adj.* **1** not turned over, round, away, etc. **2** not shaped by turning.

untutored /úntyṓōtərd/ *adj.* uneducated, untaught.
■ see UNINFORMED.

untwine /úntwī́n/ *v.tr.* & *intr.* untwist, unwind.

untwist /úntwíst/ *v.tr.* & *intr.* open from a twisted or spiralled state.

untying *pres. part.* of UNTIE.

untypical /úntíppik'l/ *adj.* not typical, unusual.
■ see UNUSUAL 2.

unusable /únyṓōzəb'l/ *adj.* not usable.
■ see USELESS 1, DUD *adj.* 1.

unused *adj.* **1** /únyṓōzd/ **a** not in use. **b** never having been used. **2** /únyṓōst/ (foll. by *to*) not accustomed.
■ **1 a** disused, abandoned, derelict, neglected, given up, idle, vacant, empty, free. **b** (brand-)new, untouched, pristine, original, intact, virgin, fresh, firsthand; unconsumed, leftover, remaining, surplus, left. **2** (*unused to*) unaccustomed to, unfamiliar with, inexperienced in *or*

at, amateurish at, unpractised in *or* at, unversed in, uninitiated in.

unusual /únyóo͞zhooəl/ *adj.* **1** not usual. **2** exceptional, remarkable. □□ **unusually** *adv.* **unusualness** *n.*
■ **1** uncommon, rare, unexpected, surprising, unfamiliar, unaccustomed, unwonted, unprecedented, unconventional, unorthodox. **2** exceptional, atypical, untypical, different, singular, abnormal, irregular, out of the ordinary, extraordinary, odd, peculiar, curious, bizarre, strange, queer, remarkable, freakish, eccentric, weird, offbeat, *colloq.* way-out, *disp.* unique, *sl.* off-the-wall. □□ **unusually** see ESPECIALLY. **unusualness** see *eccentricity* (ECCENTRIC).

unutterable /ùnnúttərəb'l/ *adj.* inexpressible; beyond description (*unutterable torment; an unutterable fool*). □□ **unutterableness** *n.* **unutterably** *adv.*
■ see INEXPRESSIBLE.

unuttered /ùnnúttərd/ *adj.* not uttered or expressed.
■ see TACIT.

unvaccinated /ùnváksinaytid/ *adj.* not vaccinated.

unvalued /ùnvályo͞od/ *adj.* **1** not regarded as valuable. **2** not having been valued.

unvanquished /ùnvángkwisht/ *adj.* not vanquished.

unvaried /ùnváirid/ *adj.* not varied.
■ see UNIFORM *adj.* 1, 2, HUMDRUM.

unvarnished /ùnvaárnisht/ *adj.* **1** not varnished. **2** (of a statement or person) plain and straightforward (*the unvarnished truth*).
■ **1** see FLAT[1] *adj.* 8a. **2** plain, simple, pure, unembellished, straightforward, straight, direct, honest, unelaborated, naked, stark, sincere, frank, candid, outspoken.

unvarying /ùnváiri-ing/ *adj.* not varying. □□ **unvaryingly** *adv.* **unvaryingness** *n.*
■ see UNIFORM *adj.* 1, 2, HUMDRUM.

unveil /ùnváyl/ *v.* **1** *tr.* remove a veil from. **2** *tr.* remove a covering from (a statue, plaque, etc.) as part of the ceremony of the first public display. **3** *tr.* disclose, reveal, make publicly known. **4** *intr.* remove one's veil.
■ **1–3** reveal, expose, uncover, disclose, lay bare *or* open, bare; divulge, make known, bring to light.

unventilated /ùnvéntilaytid/ *adj.* **1** not provided with a means of ventilation. **2** not discussed.

unverifiable /ùnvérrifīəb'l/ *adj.* that cannot be verified.

unverified /ùnvérrifīd/ *adj.* not verified.

unversed /ùnvérst/ *adj.* (usu. foll. by *in*) not experienced or skilled.
■ (*unversed in*) see UNFAMILIAR.

unviable /ùnvīəb'l/ *adj.* not viable. □□ **unviability** /-bílliti/ *n.*

unviolated /ùnvīəlaytid/ *adj.* not violated.

unvisited /ùnvízzitid/ *adj.* not visited.

unvitiated /ùnvíshiaytid/ *adj.* not vitiated.

unvoiced /ùnvóyst/ *adj.* **1** not spoken. **2** *Phonet.* not voiced.
■ **1** see TACIT, *sneaking* (SNEAK *v.* 4a).

unwaged /ùnwáyjd/ *adj.* not receiving a wage; out of work.
■ see UNEMPLOYED 1.

unwanted /ùnwóntid/ *adj.* not wanted.
■ see REDUNDANT 1, UNWELCOME.

unwarlike /ùnwáwrlīk/ *adj.* not warlike.

unwarmed /ùnwáwrmd/ *adj.* not warmed.

unwarned /ùnwáwrnd/ *adj.* not warned or forewarned.
■ see UNPREPARED.

unwarrantable /ùnwórrəntəb'l/ *adj.* indefensible, unjustifiable. □□ **unwarrantableness** *n.* **unwarrantably** *adv.*

unwarranted /ùnwórrəntid/ *adj.* **1** unauthorized. **2** unjustified.
■ **1** see UNAUTHORIZED. **2** uncalled-for, unasked (for), unjustified, indefensible, unjust, unfair, unconscionable, unworthy, improper, inexcusable, gratuitous, unmerited, undeserved, unprovoked, outrageous, excessive, inordinate, unreasonable, unrestrained, intemperate, untempered, immoderate, undue, unnecessary.

unwary /ùnwáiri/ *adj.* **1** not cautious. **2** (often foll. by *of*) not aware of possible danger etc. □□ **unwarily** *adv.* **unwariness** *n.*
■ **1** heedless, careless, hasty, incautious, unguarded, unsuspecting, imprudent, rash, foolhardy, foolish, reckless, improvident, thoughtless, indiscreet, unthinking, mindless, unwise. **2** see UNAWARE *adj.* 1.

unwashed /ùnwósht/ *adj.* **1** not washed. **2** not usually washed or clean. □ **the great unwashed** *colloq.* the rabble.
■ dirty, uncleaned, unclean, uncleansed; filthy, grimy, begrimed, soiled. □ **the great unwashed** the rabble, the masses, the *hoi polloi*, people (at large *or* in general), the population, the man in the street, the working class(es), most people, the (silent) majority, Mr (& Mrs) Average, *colloq. usu. derog.* the plebs, *usu. derog.* the mob, the populace.

unwatched /ùnwócht/ *adj.* not watched.

unwatchful /ùnwóchfo͝ol/ *adj.* not watchful.

unwatered /ùnwáwtərd/ *adj.* not watered.

unwavering /ùnwáyvəring/ *adj.* not wavering. □□ **unwaveringly** *adv.*
■ see CONSTANT *adj.* 1, 3.

unweaned /ùnweénd/ *adj.* not weaned.

unwearable /ùnwáirəb'l/ *adj.* that cannot be worn.

unwearied /ùnweérid/ *adj.* **1** not wearied or tired. **2** never becoming weary, indefatigable. **3** unremitting. □□ **unweariedly** *adv.* **unweariedness** *n.*

unweary /ùnweéri/ *adj.* not weary.

unwearying /ùnweéri-ing/ *adj.* **1** persistent. **2** not causing or producing weariness. □□ **unwearyingly** *adv.*

unwed /ùnwéd/ *adj.* unmarried.
■ see UNMARRIED.

unwedded /ùnwéddid/ *adj.* unmarried. □□ **unweddedness** *n.*

unweeded /ùnweédid/ *adj.* not cleared of weeds.

unweighed /ùnwáyd/ *adj.* **1** not considered; hasty. **2** (of goods) not weighed.

unwelcome /ùnwélkəm/ *adj.* not welcome or acceptable. □□ **unwelcomely** *adv.* **unwelcomeness** *n.*
■ uninvited, unsought, unwished for, undesired, undesirable, displeasing, unpleasing, distasteful, unpleasant, unpopular, disagreeable, unacceptable; unwanted, *de trop*, rejected, unaccepted, excluded.

unwell /ùnwél/ *adj.* **1** not in good health; (somewhat) ill. **2** indisposed.
■ see ILL *adj.* 1.

unwept /ùnwépt/ *adj.* **1** not wept for. **2** (of tears) not wept.

unwetted /ùnwéttid/ *adj.* not wetted.

unwhipped /ùnwípt/ *adj.* **1** not punished by or as by whipping. **2** *Brit.* not subject to a party whip.

unwholesome /ùnhṓlsəm/ *adj.* **1** not promoting, or detrimental to, physical or moral health. **2** unhealthy, insalubrious. **3** unhealthy-looking. □□ **unwholesomely** *adv.* **unwholesomeness** *n.*
■ **1** unhealthy, unhealthful, detrimental, deleterious, pernicious, insalubrious, unhygienic, insanitary, harmful, noxious, toxic, injurious, destructive, damaging; corrupt, immoral, bad, wicked, evil, sinful, perverted; demoralizing, depraved, degrading, corrupting, perverting. **2** unhealthy, insalubrious. **3** ill, unhealthy, ailing, sickly, sick, pale, wan, anaemic, pallid, pasty, peaky.

unwieldy /ùnweéldi/ *adj.* (**unwieldier, unwieldiest**) cumbersome, clumsy, or hard to manage, owing to size, shape, or weight. □□ **unwieldily** *adv.* **unwieldiness** *n.* [ME f. UN-[1] + *wieldy* active (now dial.) f. WIELD]
■ awkward, clumsy, bulky, oversized, cumbersome, burdensome, ungainly, unmanageable, unhandy, inconvenient, unmanoeuvrable. □□ **unwieldiness** see INCONVENIENCE *n.* 1.

unwilling /ùnwílling/ *adj.* not willing or inclined; reluctant. □□ **unwillingly** *adv.* **unwillingness** *n.* [OE *unwillende* (as UN-[1], WILLING)]

■ see RELUCTANT. ▫▫ **unwillingly** see *under protest* (PROTEST).

unwind /únwī́nd/ *v.* (*past* and *past part.* **unwound**) **1 a** *tr.* draw out (a thing that has been wound). **b** *intr.* become drawn out after having been wound. **2** *intr.* & *tr. colloq.* relax.
■ **2** see RELAX 4.

unwinking /únwíngking/ *adj.* **1** not winking. **2** watchful, vigilant. ▫▫ **unwinkingly** *adv.*

unwinnable /únwínnəb'l/ *adj.* that cannot be won.

unwisdom /únwízdəm/ *n.* lack of wisdom, folly, imprudence. [OE *unwīsdōm* (as UN-¹, WISDOM)]

unwise /únwī́z/ *adj.* **1** foolish, imprudent. **2** injudicious. ▫▫ **unwisely** *adv.* [OE *unwīs* (as UN-¹, WISE¹)]
■ see IMPRUDENT.

unwished /únwísht/ *adj.* (usu. foll. by *for*) not wished for.
■ (*unwished for*) see UNWELCOME.

unwithered /únwíthərd/ *adj.* not withered; still vigorous or fresh.

unwitnessed /únwítnist/ *adj.* not witnessed.

unwitting /únwítting/ *adj.* **1** unaware of the state of the case (*an unwitting offender*). **2** unintentional. ▫▫ **unwittingly** *adv.* **unwittingness** *n.* [OE *unwitende* (as UN-¹, WIT²)]
■ **1** see UNAWARE *adj.* 1. **2** see INADVERTENT 1. ▫▫ **unwittingly** see UNAWARES 2.

unwomanly /únwŏŏmmənli/ *adj.* not womanly; not befitting a woman. ▫▫ **unwomanliness** *n.*

unwonted /únwṓntid/ *adj.* not customary or usual. ▫▫ **unwontedly** *adv.* **unwontedness** *n.*
■ infrequent, unusual, uncustomary, uncommon, unfamiliar, unprecedented, rare, singular, atypical, abnormal, peculiar, odd, strange, irregular, unconventional, unorthodox.

unwooded /únwŏŏddid/ *adj.* not wooded, treeless.

unworkable /únwúrkəb'l/ *adj.* not workable; impracticable. ▫▫ **unworkability** /-bílliti/ *n.* **unworkableness** *n.* **unworkably** *adv.*
■ see IMPOSSIBLE 1.

unworked /únwúrkt/ *adj.* **1** not wrought into shape. **2** not exploited or turned to account.

unworkmanlike /únwúrkmənlīk/ *adj.* badly done or made.

unworldly /únwúrldli/ *adj.* **1** spiritually-minded. **2** spiritual. ▫▫ **unworldliness** *n.*
■ see UNEARTHLY 3, SPIRITUAL *adj.*

unworn /únwórn/ *adj.* not worn or impaired by wear.

unworried /únwúrrid/ *adj.* not worried; calm.

unworthy /únwúrthi/ *adj.* (**unworthier, unworthiest**) **1** (often foll. by *of*) not worthy or befitting the character of a person etc. **2** discreditable, unseemly. **3** contemptible, base. ▫▫ **unworthily** *adv.* **unworthiness** *n.*
■ **1** unequal, meritless, unmerited, substandard, inferior, second-rate, menial, puny, petty, paltry, unprofessional, mediocre, unqualified, ineligible, undeserving, unbefitting; (*unworthy of*) unbecoming to, inappropriate to, unsuitable for, unfit for, out of character for, inconsistent with *or* for, out of place with *or* for, incongruous with *or* for, beneath, below. **2** dishonourable, ignoble, disreputable, discreditable, improper, unseemly, unbecoming, undignified, shameful, disgraceful. **3** see CONTEMPTIBLE.

unwound¹ /únwównd/ *adj.* not wound or wound up.

unwound² *past* and *past part.* of UNWIND.

unwounded /únwŏŏndid/ *adj.* not wounded, unhurt.

unwoven /únwṓv'n/ *adj.* not woven.

unwrap /únráp/ *v.* (**unwrapped, unwrapping**) **1** *tr.* remove the wrapping from. **2** *tr.* open or unfold. **3** *intr.* become unwrapped.
■ undo, open.

unwrinkled /únríngk'ld/ *adj.* free from wrinkles, smooth.

unwritable /únrī́təb'l/ *adj.* that cannot be written.

unwritten /únrítt'n/ *adj.* **1** not written. **2** (of a law etc.) resting originally on custom or judicial decision, not on statute.
■ **1** see VERBAL *adj.* 2.

unwrought /únráwt/ *adj.* (of metals) not hammered into shape or worked into a finished condition.

unyielding /únyeélding/ *adj.* **1** not yielding to pressure etc. **2** firm, obstinate. ▫▫ **unyieldingly** *adv.* **unyieldingness** *n.*
■ **1** see FIRM¹ *adj.* 1. **2** see FIRM¹ *adj.* 2a, b, OBSTINATE.

unyoke /únyṓk/ *v.* **1** *tr.* release from a yoke. **2** *intr.* cease work.

unzip /únzíp/ *v.tr.* (**unzipped, unzipping**) unfasten the zip of.
■ see UNDO 1.

up /up/ *adv., prep., adj., n., & v.* ● *adv.* **1** at, in, or towards a higher place or position (*jumped up in the air; what are they doing up there?*). **2** to or in a place regarded as higher, esp.: **a** northwards (*up in Scotland*). **b** *Brit.* towards a major city or a university (*went up to London*). **3** *colloq.* ahead etc. as indicated (*went up front*). **4 a** to or in an erect position or condition (*stood it up*). **b** to or in a prepared or required position (*wound up the watch*). **c** in or into a condition of efficiency, activity, or progress (*stirred up trouble; the house is up for sale; the hunt is up*). **5** *Brit.* in a stronger or winning position or condition (*our team was three goals up; am £10 up on the transaction*). **6** (of a computer) running and available for use. **7** to the place or time in question or where the speaker etc. is (*a child came up to me; went straight up to the door; has been fine up till now*). **8** at or to a higher price or value (*our costs are up; shares are up*). **9 a** completely or effectually (*burn up; eat up; tear up; use up*). **b** more loudly or clearly (*speak up*). **10** in a state of completion; denoting the end of availability, supply, etc. (*time is up*). **11** into a compact, accumulated, or secure state (*pack up; save up; tie up*). **12** out of bed (*are you up yet?*). **13** (of the sun etc.) having risen. **14** happening, esp. unusually or unexpectedly (*something is up*). **15** (usu. foll. by *on* or *in*) taught or informed (*is well up in French*). **16** (usu. foll. by *before*) appearing for trial etc. (*was up before the magistrate*). **17** (of a road etc.) being repaired. **18** (of a jockey) in the saddle. **19** towards the source of a river. **20** inland. **21** (of the points etc. in a game): **a** registered on the scoreboard. **b** forming the total score for the time being. **22** upstairs, esp. to bed (*are you going up yet?*). **23** (of a theatre-curtain) raised etc. to reveal the stage. **24** (as *int.*) get up. **25** (of a ship's helm) with rudder to leeward. **26** in rebellion. ● *prep.* **1** upwards along, through, or into (*climbed up the ladder*). **2** from the bottom to the top of. **3** along (*walked up the road*). **4 a** at or in a higher part of (*is situated up the street*). **b** towards the source of (a river). ● *adj.* **1** directed upwards (*up stroke*). **2** *Brit.* of travel towards a capital or centre (*the up train; the up platform*). **3** (of beer etc.) effervescent, frothy. ● *n.* a spell of good fortune. ● *v.* (**upped, upping**) **1** *intr. colloq.* start up; begin abruptly to say or do something (*upped and hit him*). **2** *intr.* (foll. by *with*) raise; pick up (*upped with his stick*). **3** *tr.* increase or raise, esp. abruptly (*upped all their prices*). ▫ **be all up with** be disastrous or hopeless for (a person). **on the up and up** *colloq.* **1** *Brit.* steadily improving. **2** esp. *US* honest(ly); on the level. **something is up** *colloq.* something unusual or undesirable is afoot or happening. **up against 1** close to. **2** in or into contact with. **3** *colloq.* confronted with (*up against a problem*). **up against it** *colloq.* in great difficulties. **up-anchor** *Naut.* weigh anchor. **up and about** (or **doing**) having risen from bed; active. **up-and-coming** *colloq.* (of a person) making good progress and likely to succeed. **up and down 1** to and fro (along). **2** in every direction. **3** *colloq.* in varying health or spirits. **up-and-over** (of a door) opened by being raised and pushed back into a horizontal position. **up draught** an upward draught, esp. in a chimney. **up for** available for or being considered for (office etc.). **up hill and down dale** up and down hills on an arduous journey. **up in arms** see ARM². **up-market** *adj.* & *adv.* towards or relating to the dearer or more affluent sector of the market.

up the pole see POLE[1]. **ups and downs 1** rises and falls. **2** alternate good and bad fortune. **up the spout** see SPOUT. **up stage** at or to the back of a theatre stage. **up sticks** see STICK[1]. **up-stroke** a stroke made or written upwards. **up to 1** until (*up to the present*). **2** not more than (*you can have up to five*). **3** less than or equal to (*sums up to £10*). **4** incumbent on (*it is up to you to say*). **5** capable of or fit for (*am not up to a long walk*). **6** occupied or busy with (*what have you been up to?*). **up to date** see DATE[1]. **up to the mark** see MARK[1]. **up to the minute** see MINUTE[1]. **up to snuff** see SNUFF[2]. **up to one's tricks** see TRICK. **up to a person's tricks** see TRICK. **up with** *int.* expressing support for a stated person or thing. **what's up?** *colloq.* **1** what is going on? **2** what is the matter? [OE *up(p)*, *uppe*, rel. to OHG *ūf*]

■ *adv.* **1** see ALOFT 1, 2. **15** see INFORMED 1. □ **on the up and up 1** improving, getting better. **2** see SINCERE, *above-board*. **up against it** see *in trouble* 1 (TROUBLE). **up and down 1, 2** see ABOUT *adv.* 3. **up-market** (*adj.*) see EXPENSIVE 1. **ups and downs 2** vicissitudes. **up to 5** (*be up to*) see *be equal to* (EQUAL).

up- /up/ *prefix* in senses of UP, added: **1** as an adverb to verbs and verbal derivations, = 'upwards' (*upcurved*; *update*). **2** as a preposition to nouns forming adverbs and adjectives (*up-country*; *uphill*). **3** as an adjective to nouns (*upland*; *up-stroke*). [OE *up(p)*-, = UP]

Upanishad /oopánnishad/ *n.* each of a series of philosophical compositions concluding the exposition of the Vedas. [Skr. f. *upa* near + *ni-ṣad* sit down]

upas /yoopəss/ *n.* **1** (in full **upas-tree**) **a** a Javanese tree, *Antiaris toxicaria*, yielding a milky sap used as arrow-poison. **b** *Mythol.* a Javanese tree thought to be fatal to whatever came near it. **c** a pernicious influence, practice, etc. **2** the poisonous sap of upas and other trees. [Malay *ūpas* poison]

upbeat /úpbeet/ *n.* & *adj.* ● *n.* an unaccented beat in music. ● *adj. colloq.* optimistic or cheerful.

■ *adj.* positive, optimistic, sanguine, favourable, cheerful, encouraging, heartening, buoyant, light-hearted.

upbraid /upbráyd/ *v.tr.* (often foll. by *with*, *for*) chide or reproach (a person). □□ **upbraiding** *n.* [OE *upbrēdan* (as UP-, *brēdan* = *bregdan* BRAID in obs. sense 'brandish')]

■ scold, rebuke, reprimand, reproach, berate, castigate, admonish, chastise, reprove, censure, take to task, give a person a piece of one's mind, call *or* haul a person over the coals, have a go at, *archaic or literary* chide, *colloq.* tell off, tick off, dress down, give a person a dressing-down, tell a person a thing or two, jump on, bawl out, *US colloq.* chew out. □□ **upbraiding** see REPRIMAND *n.*

upbringing /úpbringing/ *n.* the bringing up of a child; education. [obs. *upbring* to rear (as UP-, BRING)]

■ rearing, raising, bringing up, parenting, nurture, training, education, instruction, cultivation, breeding.

upcast *n.* & *v.* ● *n.* /úpkaast/ **1** the act of casting up; an upward throw. **2** *Mining* a shaft through which air leaves a mine. **3** *Geol.* = UPTHROW. ● *v.tr.* /úpkaast/ (*past* and *past part.* **upcast**) cast up.

upchuck /úpchuk/ *v.tr.* & *intr. US sl.* vomit.

upcoming /úpkúmming/ *adj.* esp. *US* forthcoming; about to happen.

■ see FORTHCOMING 1.

up-country /úpkúntri/ *adv.* & *adj.* inland; towards the interior of a country.

update *v.* & *n.* ● *v.tr.* /úpdáyt/ bring up to date. ● *n.* /úpdayt/ **1** the act or an instance of updating. **2** an updated version; a set of updated information. □□ **updater** *n.*

■ *v.* see MODERNIZE, REVISE *v.* 1. ● *n.* see REVISION.

up-end /úppénd/ *v.tr.* & *intr.* set or rise up on end.

■ see TIP[2] *v.* 2a, *turn over* 1.

upfield /úpfeeld/ *adv.* in or to a position nearer to the opponents' end of a football etc. field.

upfold /úpfōld/ *n. Geol.* an anticline.

upfront /úpfrúnt/ *adv.* & *adj. colloq.* ● *adv.* (usu. **up front**) **1** at the front; in front. **2** (of payments) in advance. ● *adj.* **1** honest, open, frank. **2** (of payments) made in advance. **3** at the front or most prominent.

■ *adj.* **1** open, straightforward, honest, direct, forthright, frank, candid. **3** see *in front* (FRONT).

upgrade *v.* & *n.* ● *v.tr.* /úpgráyd/ **1** raise in rank etc. **2** improve (equipment, machinery, etc.) esp. by replacing components. ● *n.* /úpgrayd/ **1** the act or an instance of upgrading. **2** an upgraded piece of equipment etc. **3** *US* an upward slope. □ **on the upgrade 1** improving in health etc. **2** advancing, progressing. □□ **upgrader** *n.*

■ *v.* **1** see PROMOTE 1. **2** see IMPROVE 1a. ● *n.* **1** see *promotion* (PROMOTE).

upgrowth /úpgrōth/ *n.* the process or result of growing upwards.

upheaval /upheév'l/ *n.* **1** a violent or sudden change or disruption. **2** *Geol.* an upward displacement of part of the earth's crust. **3** the act or an instance of heaving up.

■ **1** upset, unrest, commotion, change, revolution, cataclysm, turbulence, disruption, disturbance, disorder, confusion, chaos, havoc, uproar, furore. **2** uplift.

upheave /úpheév/ *v.* **1** *tr.* heave or lift up, esp. forcibly. **2** *intr.* rise up.

uphill *adv.*, *adj.*, & *n.* ● *adv.* /úphíl/ in an ascending direction up a hill, slope, etc. ● *adj.* /úphíl/ **1** sloping up; ascending. **2** arduous, difficult (*an uphill task*). ● *n.* /úphil/ an upward slope.

■ *adj.* **2** see LABORIOUS 1.

uphold /úphṓld/ *v.tr.* (*past* and *past part.* **upheld**) **1** confirm or maintain (a decision etc., esp. of another). **2** give support or countenance to (a person, practice, etc.). □□ **upholder** *n.*

■ **1** see CONFIRM 1, 2. **2** support, maintain, sustain, preserve, hold up, defend, protect, advocate, promote, espouse, embrace, endorse, back, champion, stand by *or* behind, stick up for. □□ **upholder** see PROPONENT *n.*

upholster /uphṓlstər/ *v.tr.* **1** provide (furniture) with upholstery. **2** furnish (a room etc.) with furniture, carpets, etc. □ **well-upholstered** *joc.* (of a person) fat. [back-form. f. UPHOLSTERER]

upholsterer /uphṓlstərər/ *n.* a person who upholsters furniture, esp. professionally. [obs. *upholster* (n.) f. UPHOLD (in obs. sense 'keep in repair') + -STER]

upholstery /uphṓlstəri/ *n.* **1** textile covering, padding, springs, etc., for furniture. **2** an upholsterer's work.

upkeep /úpkeep/ *n.* **1** maintenance in good condition. **2** the cost or means of this.

■ **1** maintenance, repair, support, preservation, conservation, running, operation. **2** (operating) costs, (running) expenses, outlay, expenditure, overheads, *Brit.* oncosts, *US* overhead.

upland /úplənd/ *n.* & *adj.* ● *n.* the higher or inland parts of a country. ● *adj.* of or relating to these parts.

■ *n.* see HILL *n.* 1, INTERIOR *n.* 2.

uplift *v.* & *n.* ● *v.tr.* /úplíft/ **1** raise; lift up. **2** elevate or stimulate morally or spiritually. ● *n.* /úplift/ **1** the act or an instance of being raised. **2** *Geol.* the raising of part of the earth's surface. **3** *colloq.* a morally or spiritually elevating influence. **4** support for the bust etc. from a garment. □□ **uplifter** /-líftər/ *n.* **uplifting** /-lífting/ *adj.* (esp. in sense 2 of *v.*).

■ *v.* **1** see RAISE *v.* 1. **2** see INSPIRE 1, 2. □□ **uplifting** see *exhilarating* (EXHILARATE).

upmost var. of UPPERMOST.

upon /əpón/ *prep.* = ON. ¶ *Upon* is sometimes more formal, and is preferred in *once upon a time* and *upon my word*, and in uses such as *row upon row of seats* and *Christmas is almost upon us*. [ME f. UP + ON *prep.*, after ON *upp á*]

upper[1] /úppər/ *adj.* & *n.* ● *adj.* **1 a** higher in place; situated above another part (*the upper atmosphere*; *the upper lip*). **b** *Geol.* designating a younger (and usually shallower) part of a stratigraphic division, or the period of its formation (*the Upper Jurassic*). **2** higher in rank or dignity etc. (*the upper class*). **3** situated on higher ground, further to the north, or further inland (*Upper Egypt*). ● *n.* the part of a boot or shoe above the sole. □ **on one's uppers** *colloq.* extremely short of money. **upper case** see CASE². **upper class** the highest class of society, esp. the aristocracy. **upper-class** *adj.* of the upper class. **the upper crust** *colloq.* the aristocracy. **upper-crust** *adj. colloq.* of the aristocracy. **upper-cut** *n.* an upward blow delivered with the arm bent. ● *v.tr.* hit with an upper-cut. **the upper hand** dominance or control. **Upper House** the higher house in a legislature, esp. the House of Lords. **the upper regions 1** the sky. **2** heaven. **upper works** the part of a ship that is above the water when fully laden. [ME f. UP + -ER²]

■ *adj.* **1 a** higher (up), loftier, topmost, more elevated, uppermost, superior. **b** later, more recent. **2** see SUPERIOR *adj.* 1. **3** higher, upland, more elevated; (more) northerly, northern; inland. □ **on one's uppers** poor, indigent, destitute, poverty-stricken, impoverished, penniless, penurious, insolvent, needy, down and out, *colloq.* strapped (for cash), flat broke, up against it, *Brit. sl.* skint, stony-broke; see also BROKE. **upper class** see *the upper crust* below. **upper-class** élite, aristocratic, blue-blooded, well-born, noble, high-born, patrician; high-class, elegant, genteel, fancy, luxurious, first-rate, de luxe, royal, regal, sumptuous, *colloq.* ritzy, posh, swanky, *esp. US colloq.* swank. **the upper crust** upper class, élite, aristocracy, aristocrats, gentility, nobility, nobles, the blue-blooded, *US* four hundred, *Brit. sl.* nobs. **upper-cut** see PUNCH¹ *n.* 1. **the upper hand** the whip hand, advantage, control, authority, power, sway, superiority, supremacy, command, dominance, ascendancy, the edge.

upper² /úppər/ *n. sl.* a stimulant drug, esp. an amphetamine. [UP *v.* + -ER¹]

uppermost /úppərmōst/ *adj.* & *adv.* ● *adj.* (also **upmost** /úpmōst/) **1** highest in place or rank. **2** predominant. ● *adv.* at or to the highest or most prominent position.

■ *adj.* **1** highest, topmost, loftiest, highest, top, supreme. **2** upmost, foremost, first, most important *or* prominent *or* influential *or* telling, principal, paramount, pre-eminent, predominant.

uppish /úppish/ *adj.* esp. *Brit. colloq.* self-assertive or arrogant. □□ **uppishly** *adv.* **uppishness** *n.*

■ affected, putting on airs, snobbish, conceited, overweening, self-important, self-assertive, arrogant, superior, supercilious, lofty, haughty, hoity-toity, *colloq.* uppity, snooty, high and mighty, highfalutin, stuck-up, on one's high horse, *sl.* snotty, *esp. Brit. sl.* toffee-nosed. □□ **uppishness** see *snobbery* (SNOB).

uppity /úppiti/ *adj. colloq.* uppish, snobbish. [fanciful f. UP]

■ see *snobbish* (SNOB).

upraise /úpráyz/ *v.tr.* raise to a higher level.

■ see RAISE *v.* 1, DIGNIFY.

upright /úprīt/ *adj., adv.* & *n.* ● *adj.* **1** erect, vertical (*an upright posture*; *stood upright*). **2** (of a piano) with vertical strings. **3** (of a person or behaviour) righteous; strictly honourable or honest. **4** (of a picture, book, etc.) greater in height than breadth. ● *adv.* in a vertical direction, vertically upwards; into an upright position. ● *n.* **1** a post or rod fixed upright esp. as a structural support. **2** an upright piano. □□ **uprightly** *adv.* **uprightness** *n.* [OE *upriht* (as UP, RIGHT)]

■ *adj.* **1** erect, perpendicular, vertical, on end, straight up and down, plumb, stand-up, standing (up), upstanding. **3** moral, principled, high-minded, ethical, virtuous, upstanding, righteous, straightforward, honourable, honest, just, trustworthy, unimpeachable, uncorrupted, incorruptible, scrupulous, decent, good, *colloq.* straight. ● *adv.* perpendicularly, vertically, upward(s), straight up (and down); right side up. ● *n.* **1** post, pole, column, pillar, stanchion, standard, vertical, perpendicular. □□ **uprightly** see UPRIGHT *adv.* above, HONESTLY 1. **uprightness** see RECTITUDE.

uprise /úpríz/ *v.intr.* (**uprose**, **uprisen**) rise (to a standing position, etc.).

uprising /úprīzing/ *n.* a rebellion or revolt.

■ rebellion, revolt, mutiny, revolution, insurrection, rising, putsch, coup, *coup d'état.*

uproar /úpror/ *n.* a tumult; a violent disturbance. [Du. *oproer* f. *op* up + *roer* confusion, assoc. with ROAR]

■ clamour, hubbub, disturbance, disorder, commotion, hullabaloo, brouhaha, din, racket, pandemonium, tumult, turmoil, turbulence, outcry, outburst, bedlam, chaos, confusion, agitation, frenzy, broil, fuss, to-do; affray, fracas, brawl; *colloq.* row, rumpus, *esp. Brit. colloq.* kerfuffle, *literary* pother, *sl.* hoo-ha, hoop-la.

uproarious /upróriəss/ *adj.* **1** very noisy; tumultuous. **2** provoking loud laughter. □□ **uproariously** *adv.* **uproariousness** *n.*

■ **1** clamorous, noisy, deafening, tumultuous, turbulent, tempestuous, excited, frenzied, rowdy, riotous, disorderly, wild. **2** hilarious, (screamingly) funny, side-splitting, too funny for words, *colloq.* hysterical, killing.

uproot /úproot/ *v.tr.* **1** pull (a plant etc.) up from the ground. **2** displace (a person) from an accustomed location. **3** eradicate, destroy. □□ **uprooter** *n.*

■ **1** pull up, root out, dig out *or* up, pluck out, tear out, grub up, weed out, *literary* deracinate. **2** transfer, transplant, move, displace; exile, banish. **3** extirpate, root out, dig out, pluck out, tear out, weed out; destroy, demolish, ruin, eradicate, eliminate, exterminate, annihilate, kill, ruin, devastate, ravage, *literary* deracinate.

uprose *past* of UPRISE.

uprush /úprush/ *n.* an upward rush, esp. *Psychol.* from the subconscious.

ups-a-daisy var. of UPSY-DAISY.

upset *v.*, *n.*, & *adj.* ● *v.* /úpsét/ (**upsetting**; *past* and *past part.* **upset**) **1 a** *tr.* & *intr.* overturn or be overturned. **b** *tr.* overcome, defeat. **2** *tr.* disturb the composure or digestion of (*was very upset by the news*; *ate something that upset me*). **3** *tr.* disrupt. **4** *tr.* shorten and thicken (metal, esp. a tire) by hammering or pressure. ● *n.* /úpset/ **1** a condition of upsetting or being upset (*a stomach upset*). **2** a surprising result in a game etc.; a giant-killing. ● *adj.* /úpsét/ disturbed (*an upset stomach*). □ **upset price** the lowest acceptable selling price of a property in an auction etc.; a reserve price. □□ **upsetter** /-séttər/ *n.* **upsettingly** /-séttingli/ *adv.*

■ *v.* **1 a** overturn, capsize, topple, up-end, upturn, tip over, knock over *or* down, invert, turn topsy-turvy *or* upside down, spill. **b** overthrow, topple, defeat, beat, worst, thrash, rout, conquer, overcome, win out over, get the better of, get *or* gain the advantage over, triumph over, be victorious over, *literary* vanquish. **2** disturb, agitate, distress, grieve, unsettle, put off, put out, offend, perturb, disquiet, fluster, ruffle, frighten, scare, disconcert, dismay, trouble, worry, bother, annoy, irritate, discompose, discomfit, make nervous, unnerve, *colloq.* rattle, *US joc.* discombobulate. **3** disturb, derange, disrupt, disarrange, disorder, unsettle, mess up, disorganize, snarl up, jumble, muddle, confuse; defeat, ruin, wreck, spoil, thwart, interfere with, destroy, demolish, *colloq.* gum up, *sl.* screw up, put the kibosh on. ● *n.* **1** disorder, ailment, malady; see also DISTURBANCE 1, 4; 2. **2** surprise, unexpected event *or* occurrence; giant-killing; defeat, conquest, overthrow, rout, thrashing; triumph, victory. ● *adj.* (*of digestion*) sick, queasy; (*of a person*) perturbed, disturbed, disquieted, disconcerted, agitated, distressed, worried, troubled, unnerved, distracted, apprehensive, nervous, frightened, scared, afraid; angry, irate, furious, beside oneself, mad, *colloq.* fit to be tied, freaked out.

upshot /úpshot/ *n.* the final or eventual outcome or conclusion.

■ result, end (result), outcome, ending, (end-)product, conclusion, termination, effect, after-effect, fallout, wake, backwash, repercussion, feedback, resolution, culmination, denouement, issue, *sl.* pay-off.

upside down /úpsīd dówn/ *adv.* & *adj.* ● *adv.* **1** with the upper part where the lower part should be; in an inverted position. **2** in or into total disorder (*everything was turned upside down*). ● *adj.* (also **upside-down** *attrib.*) that is positioned upside down; inverted. □ **upside-down cake** a sponge cake baked with fruit in a syrup at the bottom, and inverted for serving. [ME, orig. *up so down*, perh. = 'up as if down']
■ see TOPSY-TURVY.

upsides /úpsīdz/ *adv. Brit. colloq.* (foll. by *with*) equal with (a person) by revenge, retaliation, etc. [*upside* = top part]

upsilon /yoopsilon, upsīlən/ *n.* the twentieth letter of the Greek alphabet (*Υ, υ*). [Gk, = slender U f. *psilos* slender, with ref. to its later coincidence in sound with Gk *oi*]

upstage /úpstáyj/ *adj., adv.*, & *v.* ● *adj.* & *adv.* **1** nearer the back of a theatre stage. **2** snobbish(ly). ● *v.tr.* **1** (of an actor) move upstage to make (another actor) face away from the audience. **2** divert attention from (a person) to oneself; outshine.
■ *v.* **2** see TRANSCEND 2.

upstairs *adv., adj.*, & *n.* ● *adv.* /upstáirz/ to or on an upper floor. ● *adj.* /úpstairz/ (also **upstair**) situated upstairs. ● *n.* /upstáirz/ an upper floor.

upstanding /úpstánding/ *adj.* **1** standing up. **2** strong and healthy. **3** honest or straightforward.
■ **1** see UPRIGHT *adj.* 1. **3** see UPRIGHT *adj.* 3.

upstart /úpstaart/ *n.* & *adj.* ● *n.* a person who has risen suddenly to prominence, esp. one who behaves arrogantly. ● *adj.* **1** that is an upstart. **2** of or characteristic of an upstart.
■ *n.* parvenu(e), *arriviste, nouveau riche*, (social) climber, status-seeker, pretender, nobody, whippersnapper. ● *adj.* **2** parvenu(e), *nouveau riche*, social-climbing, status-seeking.

upstate /úpstáyt/ *n., adj.*, & *adv. US* ● *n.* part of a State remote from its large cities, esp. the northern part. ● *adj.* of or relating to this part. ● *adv.* in or to this part. □□ **upstater** *n.*

upstream /úpstreem/ *adv.* & *adj.* ● *adv.* against the flow of a stream etc. ● *adj.* moving upstream.

upsurge /úpsurj/ *n.* an upward surge; a rise (esp. in feelings etc.).
■ see REVIVAL 5, RISE *n.* 3.

upswept /úpswept/ *adj.* **1** (of the hair) combed to the top of the head. **2** curved or sloped upwards.

upswing /úpswing/ *n.* an upward movement or trend.
■ see REVIVAL 5, IMPROVEMENT 1, 2.

upsy-daisy /úpsidáyzi/ *int.* (also **ups-a-daisy**) expressing encouragement to a child who is being lifted or has fallen. [earlier *up-a-daisy*: cf. LACKADAISICAL]

uptake /úptayk/ *n.* **1** *colloq.* understanding; comprehension (esp. *quick* or *slow on the uptake*). **2** the act or an instance of taking up.
■ **1** comprehension, understanding, apprehension, grasp, perception, insight, perspicaciousness, perspicacity, perceptiveness, sensitivity.

upthrow /úpthrō/ *n.* **1** the act or an instance of throwing upwards. **2** *Geol.* an upward dislocation of strata.

upthrust /úpthrust/ *n.* **1** upward thrust, e.g. of a fluid on an immersed body. **2** *Geol.* = UPHEAVAL.

uptight /úptīt/ *adj. colloq.* **1** nervously tense or angry. **2** *US* rigidly conventional.

uptown /úptówn/ *adj., adv.*, & *n. US* ● *adj.* of or in the residential part of a town or city. ● *adv.* in or into this part. ● *n.* this part. □□ **uptowner** *n.*

upturn *n.* & *v.* ● *n.* /úpturn/ **1** an upward trend; an improvement. **2** an upheaval. ● *v.tr.* /úptúrn/ turn up or upside down.
■ *n.* **1** see REVIVAL 5, IMPROVEMENT 1, 2.

UPU *abbr.* Universal Postal Union.

upward /úpwərd/ *adv.* & *adj.* ● *adv.* (also **upwards**) towards what is higher, superior, larger in amount, more important, or earlier. ● *adj.* moving, extending, pointing, or leading upward. □ **upwards of** more than (*found upwards of forty specimens*). [OE *upweard(es)* (as UP, -WARD)]
■ □ **upwards of** see OVER *prep.* 10.

upwardly /úpwərdli/ *adv.* in an upward direction. □ **upwardly mobile** able or aspiring to advance socially or professionally.

upwarp /úpwawrp/ *n. Geol.* a broad surface elevation; an anticline.

upwind /úpwind/ *adj.* & *adv.* against the direction of the wind.

ur- /oor/ *comb. form* primitive, original, earliest. [G]

uracil /yoorəsil/ *n. Biochem.* a pyrimidine derivative found in living tissue as a component base of RNA. [UREA + ACETIC]

uraemia /yooreemiə/ *n.* (*US* **uremia**) *Med.* a morbid condition due to the presence in the blood of urinary matter normally eliminated by the kidneys. □□ **uraemic** *adj.* [Gk *ouron* urine + *haima* blood]

uraeus /yooreeəss/ *n.* the sacred serpent as an emblem of power represented on the head-dress of Egyptian divinities and sovereigns. [mod.L f. Gk *ouraios*, repr. the Egypt. word for 'cobra']

Ural-Altaic /yoorəlaltáyik/ *n.* & *adj.* ● *n. Philol.* a family of Finno-Ugric, Turkic, Mongolian, and other agglutinative languages of N. Europe and Asia. ● *adj.* **1** of or relating to this family of languages. **2** of or relating to the Ural and Altai mountains in central Asia.

uranium /yooráyniəm/ *n. Chem.* a radioactive grey dense metallic element occurring naturally in pitchblende, and capable of nuclear fission and therefore used as a source of nuclear energy. ¶ Symb.: **U.** □□ **uranic** /-ránnik/ *adj.* [mod.L, f. URANUS: cf. *tellurium*]

urano-[1] /yoorənō/ *comb. form* the heavens. [Gk *ouranos* heaven(s)]

urano-[2] /yoorənō/ *comb. form* uranium.

uranography /yoorənógrəfi/ *n.* the branch of astronomy concerned with describing and mapping the stars, planets, etc. □□ **uranographer** *n.* **uranographic** /-nəgráffik/ *adj.*

Uranus /yoorənəss, yooráynəss/ *n.* a planet discovered by Herschel in 1781, the outermost of the solar system except Neptune and Pluto. [L f. Gk *Ouranos* heaven, Uranus, in Gk Mythol. the son of Gaea (Earth) and father of Kronos (Saturn), the Titans, etc.]

urban /úrb'n/ *adj.* of, living in, or situated in a town or city (*an urban population*) (opp. RURAL). □ **urban district** *Brit. hist.* a group of urban communities governed by an elected council. **urban guerrilla** a terrorist operating in an urban area. **urban renewal** slum clearance and redevelopment in a city or town. **urban sprawl** the uncontrolled expansion of urban areas. [L *urbanus* f. *urbs urbis* city]

urbane /urbáyn/ *adj.* courteous; suave; elegant and refined in manner. □□ **urbanely** *adv.* **urbaneness** *n.* [F *urbain* or L *urbanus*: see URBAN]
■ see COURTEOUS, ELEGANT 1, 2.

urbanism /úrbəniz'm/ *n.* **1** urban character or way of life. **2** a study of urban life. □□ **urbanist** *n.*

urbanite /úrbənīt/ *n.* a dweller in a city or town.

urbanity /urbánniti/ *n.* **1** an urbane quality; refinement of manner. **2** urban life. [F *urbanité* or L *urbanitas* (as URBAN)]
■ **1** see REFINEMENT 3.

urbanize /úrbənīz/ *v.tr.* (also **-ise**) **1** make urban. **2** destroy the rural quality of (a district). □□ **urbanization** /-záysh'n/ *n.* [F *urbaniser* (as URBAN)]

urceolate /úrsiələt/ *adj. Bot.* having the shape of a pitcher, with a large body and small mouth. [L *urceolus* dimin. of *urceus* pitcher]

urchin /úrchin/ *n.* **1** a mischievous child, esp. young and raggedly dressed. **2** = *sea urchin*. **3** *archaic* **a** a hedgehog. **b** a goblin. [ME *hirchon, urcheon* f. ONF *herichon*, OF *heriçon* ult. f. L *(h)ericius* hedgehog]

■ **1** see RAGAMUFFIN.

Urdu /oŏrdōō, úr-/ *n.* a language related to Hindi but with many Persian words, an official language of Pakistan and also used in India. [Hind. (*zabān i*) *urdū* (language of the) camp, f. Pers. *urdū* f. Turki *ordū*: see HORDE]

-ure /yər/ *suffix* forming: **1** nouns of action or process (*censure*; *closure*; *seizure*). **2** nouns of result (*creature*; *scripture*). **3** collective nouns (*legislature*; *nature*). **4** nouns of function (*judicature*; *ligature*). [from or after OF *-ure* f. L *-ura*]

urea /yoŏriə, yooreéə/ *n. Biochem.* a soluble colourless crystalline nitrogenous compound contained esp. in the urine of mammals. □□ **ureal** *adj.* [mod.L f. F *urée* f. Gk *ouron* urine]

uremia *US* var. of URAEMIA.

ureter /yooreétər/ *n.* the duct by which urine passes from the kidney to the bladder or cloaca. □□ **ureteral** *adj.* **ureteric** /yóoritérrik/ *adj.* **ureteritis** /-rĭtiss/ *n.* [F *uretère* or mod.L *ureter* f. Gk *ourētēr* f. *oureō* urinate]

urethane /yooreéthayn, yoŏri-/ *n. Chem.* a crystalline amide, ethyl carbamate, used in plastics and paints. [F *uréthane* (as UREA, ETHANE)]

urethra /yooreéthrə/ *n.* (*pl.* **urethrae** /-ree/ or **urethras**) the duct by which urine is discharged from the bladder. □□ **urethral** *adj.* **urethritis** /-rithrĭtiss/ *n.* [LL f. Gk *ourēthra* (as URETER)]

urge /urj/ *v.* & *n.* ● *v.tr.* **1** (often foll. by *on*) drive forcibly; impel; hasten (*urged them on*; *urged the horses forward*). **2** (often foll. by *to* + infin. or *that* + clause) encourage or entreat earnestly or persistently (*urged them to go*; *urged them to action*; *urged that they should go*). **3** (often foll. by *on*, *upon*) advocate (an action or argument etc.) pressingly or emphatically (to a person). **4** adduce forcefully as a reason or justification (*urged the seriousness of the problem*). **5** ply (a person etc.) hard with argument or entreaty. ● *n.* **1** an urging impulse or tendency. **2** a strong desire. [L *urgēre* press, drive]

■ *v.* **1** press, push, drive, force, impel, speed, accelerate, hurry, rush, hustle, hasten, move, goad, prod, egg on, spur. **2** press, goad, prod, egg on, spur, prompt, induce, incite, constrain, exhort, encourage, demand, request, ask, plead (with), beseech, beg, entreat, implore, importune, coax, persuade, prevail (up)on, campaign (with), sway, influence, talk into, advise, suggest, counsel. **3** advocate, adduce, advise, argue. **4** argue, set forth, affirm, state, allege, assert, hold. ● *n.* **1** pressure, impetus, compulsion, impulse, drive. **2** desire, longing, yearning, hankering, fancy, itch, hunger, thirst, craving, wish, *colloq.* yen.

urgent /úrjənt/ *adj.* **1** requiring immediate action or attention (*an urgent need for help*). **2** importunate; earnest and persistent in demand. □□ **urgency** *n.* **urgently** *adv.* [ME f. F (as URGE)]

■ **1** immediate, instant, imperative, pressing, compelling, vital, life-and-death, life-or-death, important, serious, grave, desperate, necessary, exigent, rush, emergency, high-priority. **2** supplicant, begging, solicitous, earnest, importunate, insistent, persistent, loud, clamorous, active, energetic, pertinacious, tenacious, forceful, firm. □□ **urgency** imperativeness, pressure, stress, extremity, importance, seriousness, importunity, necessity, need, insistence, exigency, emergency. **urgently** see HARD *adv.* 1.

urger /úrjər/ *n.* **1** a person who urges or incites. **2** *Austral. sl.* a person who obtains money dishonestly, esp. as a racing tipster.

URI *abbr.* upper respiratory infection.

-uria /yoŏriə/ *comb. form* forming nouns denoting that a substance is (esp. excessively) present in the urine. [mod.L f. Gk *-ouria* (as URINE)]

uric /yoŏrik/ *adj.* of or relating to urine. □ **uric acid** a crystalline acid forming a constituent of urine. [F *urique* (as URINE)]

urinal /yoorĭn'l, yóorin'l/ *n.* **1** a sanitary fitting, usu. against a wall, for men to urinate into. **2** a place or receptacle for urination. [ME f. OF f. LL *urinal* neut. of *urinalis* (as URINE)]

urinalysis /yoŏrinállisiss/ *n.* (*pl.* **urinalyses** /-seez/) the chemical analysis of urine esp. for diagnostic purposes.

urinary /yóorinəri/ *adj.* **1** of or relating to urine. **2** affecting or occurring in the urinary system (*urinary diseases*).

urinate /yoŏrinayt/ *v.intr.* discharge urine. □□ **urination** /-náysh'n/ *n.* [med.L *urinare* (as URINE)]

■ pass *or* make water, void, excrete, relieve oneself; *colloq.* (have a) pee, tinkle, piddle, *Brit. colloq.* spend a penny, go to the loo, *US colloq.* take a pee, *euphem.* go to the men's *or* ladies' (room), go to the lavatory, excuse (oneself), wash (one's) hands, go to the bathroom, go to the powder-room, go to the little boys' *or* girls' room, *esp. Brit. sl.* (make *or* have a) wee, (go) wee-wee, *Brit. sl.* go for *or* have a slash. □□ **urination** passing water, voiding, excretion, *formal or Med.* micturition.

urine /yoŏrin/ *n.* a pale-yellow fluid secreted as waste from the blood by the kidneys, stored in the bladder, and discharged through the urethra. □□ **urinous** *adj.* [ME f. OF f. L *urina*]

urn /urn/ *n.* & *v.* ● *n.* **1** a vase with a foot and usu. a rounded body, esp. for storing the ashes of the cremated dead or as a vessel or measure. **2** a large vessel with a tap, in which tea or coffee etc. is made or kept hot. **3** *poet.* anything in which a dead body or its remains are preserved, e.g. a grave. ● *v.tr.* enclose in an urn. □□ **urnful** *n.* (*pl.* **-fuls**). [ME f. L *urna*, rel. to *urceus* pitcher]

uro-[1] /yoŏrō/ *comb. form* urine. [Gk *ouron* urine]

uro-[2] /yoŏrō/ *comb. form* tail. [Gk *oura* tail]

urochord /yoŏrōkord/ *n.* the notochord of a tunicate.

urodele /yoŏrōdeel/ *n.* any amphibian of the order Urodela, having a tail when in the adult form, including newts and salamanders. [URO-[2] + Gk *dēlos* evident]

urogenital /yoŏrəjénnit'l/ *adj.* of or relating to urinary and genital products or organs.

urology /yoorólləji/ *n.* the scientific study of the urinary system. □□ **urologic** /-rəlójik/ *adj.* **urologist** *n.*

uropygium /yoŏrōpíjiəm/ *n.* the rump of a bird. [med.L f. Gk *ouropugion*]

uroscopy /yooróskəpi/ *n. Med. hist.* the examination of urine, esp. in diagnosis.

Ursa Major /úrsə máyjər/ *n.* = *the Great Bear* (see BEAR[2]). [L, = greater bear]

Ursa Minor /úrsə mĭnər/ *n.* = *the Little Bear* (see BEAR[2]). [L, = lesser bear]

ursine /úrsīn/ *adj.* of or like a bear. [L *ursinus* f. *ursus* bear]

Ursuline /úrsyoolīn, -lin/ *n.* & *adj.* ● *n.* a nun of an order founded by St Angela in 1535 for nursing the sick and teaching girls. ● *adj.* of or relating to this order. [St *Ursula*, the founder's patron saint]

urticaria /úrtikáiriə/ *n. Med.* nettle-rash. [mod.L f. L *urtica* nettle f. *urere* burn]

urticate /úrtikayt/ *v.tr.* sting like a nettle. □□ **urtication** /-káysh'n/ *n.* [med.L *urticare* f. L *urtica*: see URTICARIA]

urus /yóorəss/ *n.* = AUROCHS. [L f. Gmc]

US *abbr.* **1** United States (of America). **2** Under-Secretary. **3** unserviceable.

us /uss, əss/ *pron.* **1** *objective case* of WE (*they saw us*). **2** *colloq.* = WE (*it's us again*). **3** *colloq.* = ME[1] (*give us a kiss*). [OE *ūs* f. Gmc]

USA *abbr.* **1** United States of America. **2** *US* United States Army.

usable /yōōzəb'l/ *adj.* that can be used. □□ **usability** /-bílliti/ *n.* **usableness** *n.*

■ see SERVICEABLE 1, 2, USEFUL.

USAF *abbr.* United States Air Force.

usage /yōōssij/ *n.* **1** a manner of using or treating; treatment (*damaged by rough usage*). **2** habitual or customary practice, esp. as creating a right, obligation, or standard. [ME f. OF f. *us* USE *n*.]

■ **1** treatment, use, management, handling, operation, manipulation, wear (and tear). **2** use (and wont), custom, habit, practice, routine, convention, form, tradition.

usance /yo͞oz'nss/ *n*. the time allowed by commercial usage for the payment of foreign bills of exchange. [ME f. OF (as USE)]

USDAW /úzdaw/ *abbr*. (in the UK) Union of Shop, Distributive, and Allied Workers.

use *v*. & *n*. ● *v.tr*. /yo͞oz/ **1 a** cause to act or serve for a purpose; bring into service; avail oneself of (*rarely uses the car*; *use your discretion*). **b** consume by eating or drinking; take (alcohol, a drug, etc.), esp. habitually. **2** treat (a person) in a specified manner (*they used him shamefully*). **3** exploit for one's own ends (*they are just using you*; *used his position*). **4** (in *past* /yo͞ost/; foll. by *to* + infin.) did or had in the past (but no longer) as a customary practice or state (*I used to be an archaeologist*; *it used not* (*or did not use*) *to rain so often*). **5** (as **used** *adj*.) second-hand. **6** (as **used** /yo͞ost/ *predic. adj*.) (foll. by *to*) familiar by habit; accustomed (*not used to hard work*). **7** apply (a name or title etc.) to oneself. ● *n*. /yo͞oss/ **1** the act of using or the state of being used; application to a purpose (*put it to good use*; *is in daily use*; *worn and polished with use*). **2** the right or power of using (*lost the use of my right arm*). **3 a** the ability to be used (*a torch would be of use*). **b** the purpose for which a thing can be used (*it's no use talking*). **4** custom or usage (*long use has reconciled me to it*). **5** the characteristic ritual and liturgy of a church or diocese etc. **6** *Law hist*. the benefit or profit of lands, esp. in the possession of another who holds them solely for the beneficiary. □ **could use** *colloq*. would be glad to have; would be improved by having. **have no use for 1** be unable to find a use for. **2** dislike or be impatient with. **make use of 1** employ, apply. **2** benefit from. **use and wont** established custom. **use a person's name** quote a person as an authority or reference etc. **use up 1** consume completely, use the whole of. **2** find a use for (something remaining). **3** exhaust or wear out e.g. with overwork. [ME f. OF *us*, *user*, ult. f. L *uti us-* use]

■ *v*. **1 a** employ, make use of, put into practice *or* operation, practise, operate, utilize, exercise, exert, apply, administer, wield, ply, work, bring into play, have recourse to, resort to, put *or* press into service, put to use, avail oneself of. **b** consume, eat, drink, smoke, take, partake of, ingest, inject, *sl*. do, shoot (up). **2** treat, handle, deal with, act *or* behave towards. **3** exploit, make use of, take advantage of, manipulate, manoeuvre, abuse, misuse; utilize, capitalize on, turn to account, profit by *or* from, play, work. **5** (**used**) second-hand, cast-off, old, worn, hand-me-down, reach-me-down. **6** (*used to*) accustomed to, habituated to, acclimatized *or US* acclimated to, adapted to, hardened to *or* against, toughened to *or* against, inured to *or* against, tempered to, tolerant of; familiar *or* acquainted with. **7** adopt, assume, take up. ● *n*. **1** usage, application, employment, utilization; using, handling; consumption. **2** usability, usefulness, utility, utilization, usage, function, functioning, service(s), serviceability, power. **3 a** utility, service. **b** advantage, benefit, good, service, interest, profit, avail; purpose, point, object, reason, basis, ground; demand, need, necessity, urgency, exigency. **4** see USAGE. □ **have no use for 2** execrate, detest, abhor, hate, despise, scorn, spurn, reject, dislike, *literary* contemn. **make use of 1** see USE *v*. 1a above. **2** see PROFIT *v*. 2, USE *v*. 3 above. **use up 1** consume, exhaust, expend, spend, run through, run out of, deplete; waste, squander, fritter away, pour down the drain, throw away, *sl*. blow. **3** see EXHAUST *v*. 2.

useful /yo͞osfo͝ol/ *adj*. **1 a** of use; serviceable. **b** producing or able to produce good results (*gave me some useful hints*). **2** *colloq*. highly creditable or efficient (*a useful performance*). □ **make oneself useful** perform useful services. **useful load** the load carried by an aircraft etc. in addition to its own weight. □□ **usefully** *adv*. **usefulness** *n*.

■ **1** utilitarian, functional, serviceable, practical, usable, of use, beneficial, salutary, advantageous, expedient, profitable, valuable, gainful, helpful, constructive, fruitful, productive, effective, worthwhile. □□ **usefulness** utility, applicability, practicability, purpose, purposefulness, use, point, practicality, good, benefit, advantage, expediency, profit, profitability, value, gain, help, fruitfulness, effectiveness, worth.

useless /yo͞osliss/ *adj*. **1** serving no purpose; unavailing (*the contents were made useless by damp*; *protest is useless*). **2** *colloq*. feeble or ineffectual (*am useless at swimming*; *a useless gadget*). □□ **uselessly** *adv*. **uselessness** *n*.

■ **1** ineffective, ineffectual, unserviceable, impractical, impracticable, unpractical, unavailing, vain, pointless, purposeless, idle, futile, unproductive, unprofitable, unsuccessful, impotent, sterile, barren, fruitless, abortive, unusable, worthless, *archaic* bootless. **2** inefficient, incompetent, unproductive, ineffectual, ineffective, no-good, hopeless, inept, feeble, *esp. US sl*. out to lunch; see also DUD *adj*. 1. □□ **uselessness** see *incompetence* (INCOMPETENT), VANITY 2a.

user /yo͞ozər/ *n*. **1** a person who uses (esp. a particular commodity or service, or a computer). **2** *colloq*. a drug addict. **3** *Law* the continued use or enjoyment of a right etc. □ **right of user** *Law* **1** a right to use. **2** a presumptive right arising from the user. **user-friendly** esp. *Computing* (of a machine or system) designed to be easy to use.

■ **1** consumer, owner; operator. **2** alcohol *or* drug *etc*. addict, alcohol *or* drug *or* substance *etc*. abuser. □ **user-friendly** simple, practicable, usable, explicit, accommodating, understandable, intelligible, comprehensible, accessible.

usher /úshər/ *n*. & *v*. ● *n*. **1** a person who shows people to their seats in a hall or theatre etc. **2** a doorkeeper at a court etc. **3** *Brit*. an officer walking before a person of rank. **4** *archaic* or *joc*. an assistant teacher. ● *v.tr*. **1** act as usher to. **2** (usu. foll. by *in*) announce or show in etc. (*ushered us into the room*; *ushered in a new era*). □□ **ushership** *n*. [ME f. AF *usser*, OF *uissier*, var. of *huissier* f. med.L *ustiarius* for L *ostiarius* f. *ostium* door]

■ *v*. see LEAD[1] *v*. 1.

usherette /úshərét/ *n*. a female usher esp. in a cinema.

USM *abbr*. *Stock Exch*. Unlisted Securities Market.

USN *abbr*. United States Navy.

usquebaugh /úskwibaw/ *n*. esp. *Ir*. & *Sc*. whisky. [Ir. & Sc. Gael. *uisge beatha* water of life: cf. WHISKY]

USS *abbr*. United States Ship.

USSR *abbr*. *hist*. Union of Soviet Socialist Republics.

usual /yo͞ozhooəl/ *adj*. **1** such as commonly occurs, or is observed or done; customary, habitual (*the usual formalities*; *it is usual to tip them*; *forgot my keys as usual*). **2** (prec. by *the*, *my*, etc.) *colloq*. a person's usual drink etc. □□ **usually** *adv*. **usualness** *n*. [ME f. OF *usual*, *usuel* or LL *usualis* (as USE)]

■ **1** same, customary, habitual, accustomed, familiar, well-known, common, everyday, established, traditional, set, time-honoured, old, conventional, standard, workaday, stock, wonted, regular, ordinary, normal, expected, routine, typical, run-of-the-mill, stereotypic(al), hackneyed, trite, prosaic, worn out, shop-worn, predictable, unexceptional, unoriginal, unremarkable, unimaginative. □□ **usually** customarily, as a rule, generally (speaking), in general, most of the time, for the most part, most often, mostly, almost always, inveterately, on the whole, normally, commonly, regularly, predominantly, chiefly, in the main, mainly, by and large, as usual, *colloq*. as per usual.

usucaption /yo͞ozyookápsh'n/ *n*. (also **usucapion** /-káypiən/) (in Roman and Scots law) the acquisition of a title or right to property by uninterrupted and undisputed possession for a prescribed term. [OF *usucap(t)ion* or L *usucap(t)io* f. *usucapere* acquire by prescription f. *usu* by use + *capere capt-* take]

usufruct /yo͞ozyoofrukt/ *n.* & *v.* ● *n.* (in Roman and Scots law) the right of enjoying the use and advantages of another's property short of the destruction or waste of its substance. ● *v.tr.* hold in usufruct. ▫▫ **usufructuary** /-frúktyoori/ *adj.* & *n.* [med.L *usufructus* f. L *usus (et) fructus* f. *usus* USE + *fructus* FRUIT]

usurer /yo͞ozhərər/ *n.* a person who practises usury. [ME f. AF *usurer*, OF *usureor* f. *usure* f. L *usura*: see USURY]

usurious /yoozhóoriəss/ *adj.* of, involving, or practising usury. ▫▫ **usuriously** *adv.*

usurp /yoozúrp/ *v.* **1** *tr.* seize or assume (a throne or power etc.) wrongfully. **2** *intr.* (foll. by *on*, *upon*) encroach. ▫▫ **usurpation** /yo͞ozərpáysh'n/ *n.* **usurper** *n.* [ME f. OF *usurper* f. L *usurpare* seize for use]

■ **1** see APPROPRIATE *v.* 1.

usury /yo͞ozhəri/ *n.* **1** the act or practice of lending money at interest, esp. *Law* at an exorbitant rate. **2** interest at this rate. ▫ **with usury** *rhet.* or *poet.* with increased force etc. [ME f. med.L *usuria* f. L *usura* (as USE)]

UT *abbr.* **1** universal time. **2** *US* Utah (in official postal use).

ute /yo͞ot/ *n. Austral.* & *NZ sl.* a utility truck. [abbr.]

utensil /yooténs'l/ *n.* an implement or vessel, esp. for domestic use (*cooking utensils*). [ME f. OF *utensile* f. med.L, neut. of L *utensilis* usable (as USE)]

uterine /yo͞otərīn, -rin/ *adj.* **1** of or relating to the uterus. **2** born of the same mother but not the same father (*sister uterine*). [ME f. LL *uterinus* (as UTERUS)]

uterus /yo͞otərəss/ *n.* (*pl.* **uteri** /-rī/) the womb. ▫▫ **uteritis** /-rītiss/ *n.* [L]

utile /yo͞otīl/ *adj.* useful; having utility. [ME f. OF f. L *utilis* f. *uti* use]

utilitarian /yo͞otilitáiriən/ *adj.* & *n.* ● *adj.* **1** designed to be useful for a purpose rather than attractive; severely practical. **2** of utilitarianism. ● *n.* an adherent of utilitarianism.

■ *adj.* **1** see PRACTICAL *adj.* 2.

utilitarianism /yo͞otilitáiriəniz'm/ *n.* **1** the doctrine that actions are right if they are useful or for the benefit of a majority. **2** the doctrine that the greatest happiness of the greatest number should be the guiding principle of conduct.

utility /yootílliti/ *n.* (*pl.* **-ies**) **1** the condition of being useful or profitable. **2** a useful thing. **3** = *public utility*. **4** (*attrib.*) **a** severely practical and standardized (*utility furniture*). **b** made or serving for utility. ▫ **utility room** a room equipped with appliances for washing, ironing, and other domestic work. **utility vehicle** (or **truck** etc.) a vehicle capable of serving various functions. [ME f. OF *utilité* f. L *utilitas -tatis* (as UTILE)]

■ **1** see *usefulness* (USEFUL).

utilize /yo͞otilīz/ *v.tr.* (also **-ise**) make practical use of; turn to account; use effectively. ▫▫ **utilizable** *adj.* **utilization** /-záysh'n/ *n.* **utilizer** *n.* [F *utiliser* f. It. *utilizzare* (as UTILE)]

■ see USE *v.* 1a. ▫▫ **utilization** see USE *n.* 1, 2.

-ution /yo͞osh'n, o͞osh'n/ *suffix* forming nouns, = -ATION (*solution*). [F f. L *-utio*]

utmost /útmōst/ *adj.* & *n.* ● *adj.* furthest, extreme, or greatest (*the utmost limits*; *showed the utmost reluctance*). ● *n.* (prec. by *the*) the utmost point or degree etc. ▫ **do one's utmost** do all that one can. [OE *ūt(e)mest* (as OUT, -MOST)]

■ *adj.* see MAXIMUM *adj.* ● *n.* see MAXIMUM *n.*

Utopia /yootṓpiə/ *n.* an imagined perfect place or state of things. [title of a book (1516) by Thomas More: mod.L f. Gk *ou* not + *topos* place]

■ paradise, heaven, seventh heaven, (Garden of) Eden, bliss, cloud-cuckoo-land, cloud-land, never-never land, Shangri-La, heaven on earth, perfection.

Utopian /yootṓpiən/ *adj.* & *n.* (also **utopian**) ● *adj.* characteristic of Utopia; idealistic. ● *n.* an idealistic reformer. ▫▫ **Utopianism** *n.*

utricle /yo͞otrik'l/ *n.* a small cell or sac in an animal or plant, esp. one in the inner ear. ▫▫ **utricular** /yootríkyoolər/ *adj.* [F *utricule* or L *utriculus* dimin. of *uter* leather bag]

utter[1] /úttər/ *attrib.adj.* complete, total, absolute (*utter misery*; *saw the utter absurdity of it*). ▫▫ **utterly** *adv.* **utterness** *n.* [OE *ūtera*, *ūttra*, compar. adj. f. *ūt* OUT: cf. OUTER]

■ see COMPLETE *adj.* 3, TOTAL *adj.* 2. ▫▫ **utterly** completely, perfectly, absolutely, thoroughly, fully, entirely, wholly, unreservedly, totally, unqualifiedly, out and out, altogether, downright, overwhelmingly, unequivocally, categorically, positively, definitely, (with) no holds barred, body and soul, head over heels; extremely, *colloq.* properly, *Brit. dial. or colloq.* proper.

utter[2] /úttər/ *v.tr.* **1** emit audibly (*uttered a startled cry*). **2** express in spoken or written words. **3** *Law* put (esp. forged money) into circulation. ▫▫ **utterable** *adj.* **utterer** *n.* [ME f. MDu. *ūteren* make known, assim. to UTTER[1]]

■ **1, 2** see VOICE *v.*

utterance /úttərənss/ *n.* **1** the act or an instance of uttering. **2** a thing spoken. **3 a** the power of speaking. **b** a manner of speaking. **4** *Linguistics* an uninterrupted chain of spoken or written words not necessarily corresponding to a single or complete grammatical unit.

■ **1** see EXPRESSION 1. **2** see STATEMENT 1–3, OBSERVATION 3.

uttermost /úttərmōst/ *adj.* furthest, extreme.

■ see MAXIMUM *adj.*

U-turn /yo͞oturn/ *n.* **1** the turning of a vehicle in a U-shaped course so as to face in the opposite direction. **2** a reversal of policy.

■ **2** see *reversal* (REVERSE).

UV *abbr.* ultraviolet.

uvea /yo͞oviə/ *n.* the pigmented layer of the eye, lying beneath the outer layer. [med.L f. L *uva* grape]

uvula /yo͞ovyoolə/ *n.* (*pl.* **uvulae** /-lee/) **1** a fleshy extension of the soft palate hanging above the throat. **2** a similar process in the bladder or cerebellum. [ME f. LL, dimin. of L *uva* grape]

uvular /yo͞ovyoolər/ *adj.* & *n.* ● *adj.* **1** of or relating to the uvula. **2** articulated with the back of the tongue and the uvula, as in *r* in French. ● *n.* a uvular consonant.

uxorial /uksóriəl/ *adj.* of or relating to a wife.

uxoricide /uksórrisīd/ *n.* **1** the killing of one's wife. **2** a person who does this. ▫▫ **uxoricidal** /-sīd'l/ *adj.* [L *uxor* wife + -CIDE]

uxorious /uksóriəss/ *adj.* **1** greatly or excessively fond of one's wife. **2** (of behaviour etc.) showing such fondness. ▫▫ **uxoriously** *adv.* **uxoriousness** *n.* [L *uxoriosus* f. *uxor* wife]

Uzbek /úzbek, o͞oz-/ *n.* (also **Uzbeg** /-beg/) **1** a member of a Turkic people living mainly in Uzbekistan. **2** the language of this people. [Uzbek]

Vv

V[1] /vee/ *n.* (also **v**) (*pl.* **Vs** or **V's**) **1** the twenty-second letter of the alphabet. **2** a V-shaped thing. **3** (as a Roman numeral) five.

V[2] *abbr.* (also **V.**) volt(s).

V[3] *symb. Chem.* the element vanadium.

v. *abbr.* **1** verse. **2** verso. **3** versus. **4** very. **5** *vide.*

VA *abbr.* **1** *US* Veterans' Administration. **2** Vicar Apostolic. **3** Vice Admiral. **4** *US* Virginia (in official postal use). **5** (in the UK) Order of Victoria and Albert.

Va. *abbr.* Virginia.

vac /vak/ *n. Brit. colloq.* vacation (esp. of universities). [abbr.]

vacancy /váykənsi/ *n.* (*pl.* **-ies**) **1 a** the state of being vacant or empty. **b** an instance of this; empty space. **2** an unoccupied post or job (*there are three vacancies for typists*). **3** an available room in a hotel etc. **4** emptiness of mind; idleness, listlessness.

■ **1** emptiness, voidness, blankness, hollowness; void, gap, lacuna, hiatus, blank, deficiency, opening, breach, space, vacuum. **2** (job) opening, slot, position, post, situation, place; (*vacancies*) sits vac, help wanted. **4** blankness, emptiness, vacuity, absent-mindedness, inanity, vacuousness, incomprehension, fatuity, unawareness; idleness, listlessness.

vacant /váykənt/ *adj.* **1** not filled or occupied; empty. **2** not mentally active; showing no interest (*had a vacant stare*). □ **vacant possession** *Brit.* ownership of a house etc. with any previous occupant having moved out. □□ **vacantly** *adv.* [ME f. OF *vacant* or L *vacare* (as VACATE)]

■ **1** free, unfilled, unused, unutilized, spare, extra, idle, unengaged, unspoken for; empty, void, hollow, unoccupied, untenanted, uninhabited, abandoned, deserted. **2** blank, expressionless, deadpan, empty, vacuous, dull, absent-minded, inane, uncomprehending, fatuous, unaware. □□ **vacantly** vaguely, blankly, vacuously, absently, absent-mindedly, idly, fatuously.

vacate /vəkáyt, vay-/ *v.tr.* **1** leave vacant or cease to occupy (a house, room, etc.). **2** give up tenure of (a post etc.). **3** *Law* annul (a judgement or contract etc.). □□ **vacatable** *adj.* [L *vacare vacat-* be empty]

■ **1** leave, depart (from), withdraw from, quit, evacuate, get *or* go out of; desert, abandon. **2** give up, relinquish, sacrifice, renounce, let go, resign, abdicate, cede, give up right *or* claim to, abandon. **3** annul, declare null and void, nullify, void, repudiate, override, overrule, rescind, revoke, recall, quash, set aside, invalidate.

vacation /vəkáysh'n/ *n.* & *v.* ● *n.* **1** a fixed period of cessation from work, esp. in universities and lawcourts. **2** *US* a holiday. **3** the act of vacating (a house or post etc.). ● *v.intr. US* take a holiday. □ **vacation land** *US* an area providing attractions for holidaymakers. □□ **vacationer** *n.* **vacationist** *n.* [ME f. OF *vacation* or L *vacatio* (as VACATE)]

■ *n.* **2** see HOLIDAY *n.* 1.

vaccinate /váksinayt/ *v.tr.* inoculate with a vaccine to procure immunity from a disease; immunize. □□ **vaccination** /-náysh'n/ *n.* **vaccinator** *n.*

■ □□ **vaccination** see JAB *n.* 2.

vaccine /vákseen/ *n.* & *adj.* ● *n.* **1** an antigenic preparation used to stimulate the production of antibodies and procure immunity from one or several diseases. **2** *hist.* the cowpox virus used in vaccination against smallpox. ● *adj.* of or relating to cowpox or vaccination. □□ **vaccinal** /-sin'l/ *adj.* [L *vaccinus* f. *vacca* cow]

vaccinia /vaksínniə/ *n. Med.* a virus used as a vaccine against smallpox. [mod.L (as VACCINE)]

vacillate /vássilayt/ *v.intr.* **1** fluctuate in opinion or resolution. **2** move from side to side; oscillate, waver. □□ **vacillation** /-láysh'n/ *n.* **vacillator** *n.* [L *vacillare vacillat-* sway]

■ see OSCILLATE. □□ **vacillation** see *fluctuation* (FLUCTUATE).

vacua *pl.* of VACUUM.

vacuole /vákyoo-ōl/ *n. Biol.* a tiny space within the cytoplasm of a cell containing air, fluid, food particles, etc. □□ **vacuolar** /vákyooələr/ *adj.* **vacuolation** /-láysh'n/ *n.* [F, dimin. of L *vacuus* empty]

vacuous /vákyooəss/ *adj.* **1** lacking expression (*a vacuous stare*). **2** unintelligent (*a vacuous remark*). **3** empty. □□ **vacuity** /vəkyo͞o-iti/ *n.* **vacuously** *adv.* **vacuousness** *n.* [L *vacuus* empty (as VACATE)]

■ **1** see BLANK *adj.* 3a. **2** see INANE 1. □□ **vacuousness** see VACANCY 4.

vacuum /vákyooəm/ *n.* & *v.* ● *n.* (*pl.* **vacuums** or **vacua** /-yooə/) **1** a space entirely devoid of matter. **2** a space or vessel from which the air has been completely or partly removed by a pump etc. **3 a** the absence of the normal or previous content of a place, environment, etc. **b** the absence of former circumstances, activities, etc. **4** (*pl.* **vacuums**) *colloq.* a vacuum cleaner. **5** a decrease of pressure below the normal atmospheric value. ● *v. colloq.* **1** *tr.* clean with a vacuum cleaner. **2** *intr.* use a vacuum cleaner. □ **vacuum brake** a brake in which pressure is caused by the exhaustion of air. **vacuum-clean** clean with a vacuum cleaner. **vacuum cleaner** an apparatus for removing dust etc. by suction. **vacuum flask** *Brit.* a vessel with a double wall enclosing a vacuum so that the liquid in the inner receptacle retains its temperature. **vacuum gauge** a gauge for testing the pressure after the production of a vacuum. **vacuum-packed** sealed after the partial removal of air. **vacuum pump** a pump for producing a vacuum. **vacuum tube** a tube with a near-vacuum for the free passage of electric current. [mod.L, neut. of L *vacuus* empty]

■ *n.* **3** see VOID *n.* 1.

VAD *abbr.* **1** Voluntary Aid Detachment. **2** a member of this.

vade-mecum /vaádimáykəm, váydimeékəm/ *n.* a handbook etc. carried constantly for use. [F f. mod.L, = go with me]

■ handbook, manual, companion, ready reference, book, guide.

vag /vag/ *n.* & *v. Austral.* & *US sl.* ● *n.* a vagrant. ● *v.tr.* charge with vagrancy. [abbr.]

vagabond /vággəbond/ *n., adj.,* & *v.* ● *n.* **1** a wanderer or vagrant, esp. an idle one. **2** *colloq.* a scamp or rascal. ● *adj.* having no fixed habitation; wandering. ● *v.intr.* wander about as a vagabond. □□ **vagabondage** *n.* [ME f. OF *vagabond* or L *vagabundus* f. *vagari* wander]

■ *n.* **1** gypsy, tramp, vagrant, wayfarer, rover, drifter, wanderer, itinerant, migrant, nomad, bird of passage, rolling stone, beachcomber, derelict, *Austral.* & *NZ* swagman, *US* hobo, *colloq.* knight of the road, *Austral. sl.* whaler, *US sl.* bum. **2** see RASCAL. ● *adj.* vagrant, wayfaring, roving, wandering, itinerant, migrant, derelict, nomadic, gypsy, rambling, roaming, drifting, peripatetic, transient, homeless, *archaic or joc.* peregrinating.

vagal see VAGUS.

vagary /váygəri/ *n.* (*pl.* **-ies**) a caprice; an eccentric idea or act (*the vagaries of Fortune*). □□ **vagarious** /vəgáiriəss/ *adj.* [L *vagari* wander]
■ see QUIRK 1.

vagi *pl.* of VAGUS.

vagina /vəjínə/ *n.* (*pl.* **vaginas** or **vaginae** /-nee/) **1** the canal between the uterus and vulva of a woman or other female mammal. **2** a sheath formed round a stem by the base of a leaf. □□ **vaginal** *adj.* **vaginitis** /vájinítiss/ *n.* [L, = sheath, scabbard]

vaginismus /vájinízməss/ *n.* a painful spasmodic contraction of the vagina, usu. in response to pressure. [mod.L (as VAGINA)]

vagrant /váygrənt/ *n.* & *adj.* ● *n.* **1** a person without a settled home or regular work. **2** a wanderer or vagabond. ● *adj.* **1** wandering or roving (*a vagrant musician*). **2** being a vagrant. □□ **vagrancy** *n.* **vagrantly** *adv.* [ME f. AF *vag(a)raunt*, perh. alt. f. AF *wakerant* etc. by assoc. with L *vagari* wander]
■ *n.* see TRAMP *n.* 1.

vague /vayg/ *adj.* **1** of uncertain or ill-defined meaning or character (*gave a vague answer*; *has some vague idea of emigrating*). **2** (of a person or mind) imprecise; inexact in thought, expression, or understanding. □□ **vaguely** *adv.* **vagueness** *n.* **vaguish** *adj.* [F *vague* or L *vagus* wandering, uncertain]
■ **1** indefinite, indistinct, imprecise, inexact, unclear, confused, woolly, loose, unspecified, non-specified, undetermined, indeterminate, unfixed, general, generalized, unspecific, non-specific, inexplicit, unexplicit, ambiguous, doubtful, in doubt, uncertain, equivocal; subliminal, subconscious, indefinable, unexplained; ill-defined, hazy, fuzzy, obscure, amorphous, shapeless, nebulous, blurred, blurry, filmy, dim, faint, shadowy, veiled, concealed, hidden, shrouded, bleary, foggy, misty, cloudy, clouded, hardly *or* barely distinguishable, hardly *or* barely discernible. **2** wishy-washy, imprecise, inexact, undecided, indecisive, irresolute, vacillating, wavering, inconstant, unsettled, uncertain; vacant, empty, blank, vacuous; see also ABSENT-MINDED. □□ **vaguely** ambiguously, imprecisely, inexactly, unclearly, confusedly, confusingly, hazily, fuzzily, nebulously, obscurely; distantly, remotely, indefinitely, dimly, subliminally, subconsciously, inexplicably; idly, vacantly, detachedly, absent-mindedly, dreamily, absently, distractedly. **vagueness** see *imprecision* (IMPRECISE).

vagus /váygəss/ *n.* (*pl.* **vagi** /-gī/) *Anat.* either of the tenth pair of cranial nerves with branches to the heart, lungs, and viscera. □□ **vagal** *adj.* [L: see VAGUE]

vail /vayl/ *v. archaic* **1** *tr.* lower or doff (one's plumes, pride, crown, etc.) esp. in token of submission. **2** *intr.* yield; give place; remove one's hat as a sign of respect etc. [ME f. obs. *avale* f. OF *avaler* to lower f. *a val* down, f. *val* VALE[1]]

vain /vayn/ *adj.* **1** excessively proud or conceited, esp. about one's own attributes. **2** empty, trivial, unsubstantial (*vain boasts*; *vain triumphs*). **3** useless; followed by no good result (*in the vain hope of dissuading them*). □ **in vain** without result or success (*it was in vain that we protested*). **take a person's name in vain** use it lightly or profanely. □□ **vainly** *adv.* **vainness** *n.* [ME f. OF f. L *vanus* empty, without substance]
■ **1** proud, conceited, haughty, arrogant, boastful, puffed up, egotistical, cocky, self-important, *Psychol.* narcissistic, *colloq.* big-headed, stuck-up, swollen-headed, *literary* vainglorious. **2** see EMPTY *adj.* 4a. **3** worthless, profitless, pointless, unsuccessful, futile, useless, unavailing, unproductive, fruitless, ineffective, *archaic* bootless; abortive. □ **in vain** vainly, futilely, unsuccessfully, fruitlessly, *archaic* bootlessly. **take a person's name in vain** use a person's name irreverently *or* blasphemously *or* disrespectfully *or* improperly *or* lightly *or* profanely. □□ **vainness** see VANITY.

vainglory /vaynglóri/ *n. literary* boastfulness; extreme vanity. □□ **vainglorious** *adj.* **vaingloriously** *adv.* **vaingloriousness** *n.* [ME, after OF *vaine gloire*, L *vana gloria*]
■ see VANITY 1. □□ **vainglorious** see BOASTFUL, VAIN 1.

vair /vair/ *n.* **1** *archaic* or *hist.* a squirrel-fur widely used for medieval linings and trimmings. **2** *Heraldry* fur represented by small shield-shaped or bell-shaped figures usu. alternately azure and argent. [ME f. OF f. L (as VARIOUS)]

Vaishnava /víshnaavaa/ *n. Hinduism* a devotee of Vishnu. [Skr. *vaiṣṇavá*]

Vaisya /vísyə/ *n.* **1** the third of the four great Hindu castes, comprising the merchants and agriculturalists. **2** a member of this caste. [Skr. *vaiśya* peasant, labourer]

valance /vállənss/ *n.* (also **valence**) a short curtain round the frame or canopy of a bedstead, above a window, or under a shelf. □□ **valanced** *adj.* [ME ult. f. OF *avaler* descend: see VAIL]
■ see FLOUNCE[2] *n.*

vale[1] /vayl/ *n. archaic* or *poet.* (except in place-names) a valley (*Vale of the White Horse*). □ **vale of tears** *literary* the world as a scene of life, trouble, etc. [ME f. OF *val* f. L *vallis*, *valles*]
■ see VALLEY.

vale[2] /vaalay/ *int.* & *n.* ● *int.* farewell. ● *n.* a farewell. [L, imper. of *valēre* be well or strong]

valediction /vállidíksh'n/ *n.* **1** the act or an instance of bidding farewell. **2** the words used in this. [L *valedicere valedict-* (as VALE[2], *dicere* say), after *benediction*]
■ **1** see FAREWELL *n.*

valedictorian /vállidiktóriən/ *n. US* a person who gives a valedictory, esp. the highest-ranking member of a graduating class.

valedictory /vállidíktəri/ *adj.* & *n.* ● *adj.* serving as a farewell. ● *n.* (*pl.* **-ies**) a farewell address.
■ *n.* see PARTING 1.

valence[1] /váylənss/ *n. Chem.* esp. *US* = VALENCY. □ **valence electron** an electron in the outermost shell of an atom involved in forming a chemical bond.

valence[2] var. of VALANCE.

Valenciennes /valónsi-én/ *n.* a rich kind of lace. [*Valenciennes* in NE France, where it was made in the 17th and 18th c.]

valency /váylənsi/ *n.* (*pl.* **-ies**) *Brit. Chem.* the combining power of an atom measured by the number of hydrogen atoms it can displace or combine with. [LL *valentia* power, competence f. *valēre* be well or strong]

valentine /vállәntīn/ *n.* **1** a card or gift sent, often anonymously, as a mark of love or affection on St Valentine's Day (14 Feb.). **2** a sweetheart chosen on this day. [ME f. OF *Valentin* f. L *Valentinus*, name of two saints]

valerian /vəléeriən/ *n.* **1** any of various flowering plants of the family Valerianaceae. **2** the root of any of these used as a medicinal sedative. □ **common valerian 1** a valerian, *Valeriana officinalis*, with pink or white flowers and a strong smell liked by cats: also called SETWALL. **2** the root of this used as a medicinal sedative. [ME f. OF *valeriane* f. med.L *valeriana (herba)*, app. fem. of *Valerianus* of Valerius]

valeric acid /vəlérrik, -léerik/ *n. Chem.* = PENTANOIC ACID. [VALERIAN + -IC]

valet /vállit, -lay/ *n.* & *v.* ● *n.* **1** a gentleman's personal attendant who looks after his clothes etc. **2** a hotel etc. employee with similar duties. ● *v.* (**valeted, valeting**) **1** *intr.* work as a valet. **2** *tr.* act as a valet to. **3** *tr.* clean or clean out (a car). [F, = OF *valet*, *vaslet*, VARLET: rel. to VASSAL]

■ *n.* **1** see MAN *n.* 4b.

valeta var. of VELETA.

valetudinarian /vállityōōdináiriən/ *n.* & *adj.* ● *n.* a person of poor health or unduly anxious about health. ● *adj.* **1** of or being a valetudinarian. **2** of poor health. **3** seeking to recover one's health. □□ **valetudinarianism** *n.* [L *valetudinarius* in ill health f. *valetudo -dinis* health f. *valēre* be well]

valetudinary /vállityōōdinəri/ *adj.* & *n.* (*pl.* **-ies**) = VALETUDINARIAN.

valgus /válgəss/ *n.* a deformity involving the outward displacement of the foot or hand from the midline. [L, = knock-kneed]

Valhalla /valhállə/ *n.* **1** (in Norse mythology) a palace in which the souls of slain heroes feasted for eternity. **2** a building used for honouring the illustrious. [mod.L f. ON *Valhöll* f. *valr* the slain + *höll* HALL]

valiant /vályənt/ *adj.* (of a person or conduct) brave, courageous. □□ **valiantly** *adv.* [ME f. AF *valiaunt*, OF *vailant* ult. f. L *valēre* be strong]

■ see BRAVE *adj.* 1.

valid /vállid/ *adj.* **1** (of a reason, objection, etc.) sound or defensible; well-grounded. **2 a** executed with the proper formalities (*a valid contract*). **b** legally acceptable (*a valid passport*). **c** not having reached its expiry date. □□ **validity** /vəlídditi/ *n.* **validly** *adv.* [F *valide* or L *validus* strong (as VALIANT)]

■ **1** see LEGITIMATE *adj.* 3. **2 a, b** see LEGITIMATE *adj.* 1, 2. **2 c** see *in force* (FORCE[1]). □□ **validity** legitimacy, soundness, truth, correctness, genuineness, authenticity; see also FORCE[1] *n.* 4.

validate /vállidayt/ *v.tr.* make valid; ratify, confirm. □□ **validation** /-dáysh'n/ *n.* [med.L *validare* f. L (as VALID)]

■ see RATIFY. □□ **validation** see SANCTION *n.* 2.

valine /váyleen/ *n. Biochem.* an amino acid that is an essential nutrient for vertebrates and a general constituent of proteins. [VALERIC (ACID) + -INE[4]]

valise /vəléez/ *n.* **1** a kitbag. **2** *US* a small portmanteau. [F f. It. *valigia* corresp. to med.L *valisia*, of unkn. orig.]

Valium /vállíəm/ *n. propr.* the drug diazepam used as a tranquillizer and relaxant. [20th c.: orig. uncert.]

Valkyrie /valkéeri, válkiri/ *n.* (in Norse mythology) each of Odin's twelve handmaidens who selected heroes destined to be slain in battle. [ON *Valkyrja*, lit. 'chooser of the slain' f. *valr* the slain + (unrecorded) *kur-*, *kuz-* rel. to CHOOSE]

vallecula /vəlékyoolə/ *n.* (*pl.* **valleculae** /-lee/) *Anat.* & *Bot.* a groove or furrow. □□ **vallecular** *adj.* **valleculate** /-layt/ *adj.* [LL, dimin. of L *vallis* valley]

valley /válli/ *n.* (*pl.* **-eys**) **1** a low area more or less enclosed by hills and usu. with a stream flowing through it. **2** any depression compared to this. **3** *Archit.* an internal angle formed by the intersecting planes of a roof. [ME f. AF *valey*, OF *valee* ult. f. L *vallis*, *valles*: cf. VALE[1]]

■ **1, 2** glen, dale, dell, dingle, hollow, basin, gorge, ravine, canyon, *Geog.* cwm, *Geol.* cirque, graben, *Austral.* & *NZ* gully, *Brit.* coomb, *Sc.* corrie, strath, *US* gulch, *archaic or poet.* vale.

vallum /vállәm/ *n. Rom. Antiq.* a rampart and stockade as a defence. [L, collect. f. *vallus* stake]

valonia /vəlṓniə/ *n.* acorn-cups of an evergreen oak, *Quercus macrolepis*, used in tanning, dyeing, and making ink. [It. *vallonia* ult. f. Gk *balanos* acorn]

valor *US* var. of VALOUR.

valorize /vállərīz/ *v.tr.* (also **-ise**) raise or fix the price of (a commodity etc.) by artificial means, esp. by government action. □□ **valorization** /-záysh'n/ *n.* [back-form. f. *valorization* f. F *valorisation* (as VALOUR)]

valour /vállər/ *n.* (*US* **valor**) personal courage, esp. in battle. □□ **valorous** *adj.* [ME f. OF f. LL *valor -oris* f. *valēre* be strong]

■ see COURAGE.

valse /vaalss, vawlss/ *n.* a waltz. [F f. G (as WALTZ)]

valuable /vályooəb'l/ *adj.* & *n.* ● *adj.* of great value, price, or worth (*a valuable property*; *valuable information*). ● *n.* (usu. in *pl.*) a valuable thing, esp. a small article of personal property. □□ **valuably** *adv.*

■ *adj.* see *advantageous* (ADVANTAGE), PRECIOUS *adj.* 1.

valuation /vályoo-áysh'n/ *n.* **1 a** an estimation (esp. by a professional valuer) of a thing's worth. **b** the worth estimated. **2** the price set on a thing. □□ **valuate** /vályoo-ayt/ *v.tr.* esp. *US.*

valuator /vályoo-aytər/ *n.* a person who makes valuations; a valuer.

value /vályōō/ *n.* & *v.* ● *n.* **1** the worth, desirability, or utility of a thing, or the qualities on which these depend (*the value of regular exercise*). **2** worth as estimated; valuation (*set a high value on my time*). **3** the amount of money or goods for which a thing can be exchanged in the open market; purchasing power. **4** the equivalent of a thing; what represents or is represented by or may be substituted for a thing (*paid them the value of their lost property*). **5** (in full **value for money**) something well worth the money spent. **6** the ability of a thing to serve a purpose or cause an effect (*news value*; *nuisance value*). **7** (in *pl.*) one's principles or standards; one's judgement of what is valuable or important in life. **8** *Mus.* the duration of the sound signified by a note. **9** *Math.* the amount denoted by an algebraic term or expression. **10** (foll. by *of*) **a** the meaning (of a word etc.). **b** the quality (of a spoken sound). **11** the relative rank or importance of a playing-card, chess-piece, etc., according to the rules of the game. **12** the relation of one part of a picture to others in respect of light and shade; the part being characterized by a particular tone. **13** *Physics* & *Chem.* the numerical measure of a quantity or a number denoting magnitude on some conventional scale (*the value of gravity at the equator*). ● *v.tr.* (**values, valued, valuing**) **1** estimate the value of; appraise (esp. professionally) (*valued the property at £200,000*). **2** have a high or specified opinion of; attach importance to (*a valued friend*). □ **value added tax** a tax on the amount by which the value of an article has been increased at each stage of its production. **value judgement** a subjective estimate of quality etc. **value received** money or its equivalent given for a bill of exchange. [ME f. OF, fem. past part. of *valoir* be worth f. L *valēre*]

■ *n.* **1** see *usefulness* (USEFUL). **3, 4** see PRICE *n.* 1. **7** (*values*) see PHILOSOPHY 2. ● *v.* **1** see ESTIMATE *v.* 2, 3. **2** see APPRECIATE 1a, b.

valueless /vályooliss/ *adj.* having no value. □□ **valuelessness** *n.*

■ see WORTHLESS.

valuer /vályooər/ *n.* a person who estimates or assesses values, esp. professionally.

valuta /vəlyṓōtə/ *n.* **1** the value of one currency with respect to another. **2** a currency considered in this way. [It., = VALUE]

valve /valv/ *n.* **1** a device for controlling the passage of fluid through a pipe etc., esp. an automatic device allowing movement in one direction only. **2** *Anat.* & *Zool.* a membranous part of an organ etc. allowing a flow of blood etc. in one direction only. **3** *Brit.* = *thermionic valve*. **4** a device to vary the effective length of the tube in a brass musical instrument. **5** each of the two shells of an oyster, mussel, etc. **6** *Bot.* each of the segments into which a capsule or dry fruit dehisces. **7** *archaic* a leaf of a folding door. □□ **valvate** /-vayt/ *adj.* **valved** *adj.* (also in *comb.*). **valveless** *adj.* **valvule** *n.* [ME f. L *valva* leaf of a folding door]

valvular /válvyoolər/ *adj.* **1** having a valve or valves. **2** having the form or function of a valve. [mod.L *valvula*, dimin. of L *valva*]

valvulitis /válvyoolítiss/ *n.* inflammation of the valves of the heart.

vambrace /vámbrayss/ *n. hist.* defensive armour for the forearm. [ME f. AF *vaunt-bras*, OF *avant-bras* f. *avant* before (see AVAUNT) + *bras* arm]

vamoose /vəmṓōss/ *v.intr. US* (esp. as *int.*) *sl.* depart hurriedly. [Sp. *vamos* let us go]

■ see LEAVE[1] *v.* 1b, 3, 4.

vamp[1] /vamp/ *n.* & *v.* ● *n.* **1** the upper front part of a boot or shoe. **2** a patched-up article. **3** an improvised musical accompaniment. ● *v.* **1** *tr.* (often foll. by *up*) repair or furbish. **2** *tr.* (foll. by *up*) make by patching or from odds and ends. **3 a** *tr.* & *intr.* improvise a musical accompaniment (to). **b** *tr.* improvise (a musical accompaniment). **4** *tr.* put a new vamp to (a boot or shoe). [ME f. OF *avantpié* f. *avant* before (see AVAUNT) + *pied* foot]

vamp[2] /vamp/ *n.* & *v. colloq.* ● *n.* **1** an unscrupulous flirt. **2** a woman who uses sexual attraction to exploit men. ● *v.* **1** *tr.* allure or exploit (a man). **2** *intr.* act as a vamp. [abbr. of VAMPIRE]

vampire /vámpīr/ *n.* **1** a ghost or reanimated corpse supposed to leave its grave at night to suck the blood of persons sleeping. **2** a person who preys ruthlessly on others. **3** (in full **vampire bat**) any tropical (esp. South American) bat of the family Desmodontidae, with incisors for piercing flesh and feeding on blood. **4** *Theatr.* a small spring trapdoor used for sudden disappearances. □□ **vampiric** /-pírrik/ *adj.* [F *vampire* or G *Vampir* f. Magyar *vampir* perh. f. Turk. *uber* witch]

vampirism /vámpīriz'm/ *n.* **1** belief in the existence of vampires. **2** the practices of a vampire.

vamplate /vámplayt/ *n. hist.* an iron plate on a lance protecting the hand when the lance was couched. [ME f. AF *vauntplate* (as VAMBRACE, PLATE)]

van[1] /van/ *n.* **1** a covered vehicle for conveying goods etc. **2** *Brit.* a railway carriage for luggage or for the use of the guard. **3** *Brit.* a gypsy caravan. [abbr. of CARAVAN]

van[2] /van/ *n.* **1** a vanguard. **2** the forefront (*in the van of progress*). [abbr. of VANGUARD]

■ **1** see SPEARHEAD *n.* **2** see FRONT *n.* 6; (*be in the van of*) see SPEARHEAD *v.*

van[3] /van/ *n.* **1** the testing of ore quality by washing on a shovel or by machine. **2** *archaic* a winnowing fan. **3** *archaic* or *poet.* a wing. [ME, southern & western var. of FAN[1], perh. partly f. OF *van* or L *vannus*]

van[4] /van/ *n. Brit. Tennis colloq.* = ADVANTAGE. [abbr.]

vanadium /vənáydiəm/ *n. Chem.* a hard grey metallic transition element occurring naturally in several ores and used in small quantities for strengthening some steels. ¶ Symb.: **V**. □□ **vanadate** /vánnədayt/ *n.* **vanadic** /-náddik/ *adj.* **vanadous** /vánnədəss/ *adj.* [mod.L f. ON *Vanadís* name of the Scand. goddess Freyja + -IUM]

Van Allen belt /van állən/ *n.* (also **Van Allen layer**) each of two regions of intense radiation partly surrounding the earth at heights of several thousand kilometres. [J. A. *Van Allen*, US physicist b. 1914]

V. & A. *abbr.* Victoria & Albert Museum (in London).

vandal /vánd'l/ *n.* & *adj.* ● *n.* **1** a person who wilfully or maliciously destroys or damages property. **2** (**Vandal**) a member of a Germanic people that ravaged Gaul, Spain, N. Africa, and Rome in the 4th–5th c., destroying many books and works of art. ● *adj.* of or relating to the Vandals. □□ **Vandalic** /-dállik/ *adj.* (in sense 2 of *n.*). [L *Vandalus* f. Gmc]

■ **1** hooligan, ruffian, tough, hoodlum, *Austral.* larrikin, *colloq.* hobbledehoy, *sl.* trog, *dial. sl.* roughie, *Brit. sl.* yob, yobbo, *esp. US sl.* lug.

vandalism /vándəliz'm/ *n.* wilful or malicious destruction or damage to works of art or other property. □□ **vandalistic** /-lístik/ *adj.* **vandalistically** /-lístikəli/ *adv.*

vandalize /vándəlīz/ *v.tr.* (also **-ise**) destroy or damage wilfully or maliciously.

■ see DAMAGE *v.* 1, MUTILATE 2.

van de Graaff generator /ván də graáf/ *n. Electr.* a machine devised to generate electrostatic charge by means of a vertical endless belt collecting charge from a voltage source and transferring it to a large insulated metal dome, where a high voltage is produced. [R. J. *van de Graaff*, US physicist d. 1967]

van der Waals forces /ván dər waálz/ *n.pl. Chem.* short-range attractive forces between uncharged molecules arising from the interaction of dipole moments. [J. *van der Waals*, Dutch physicist d. 1923]

vandyke /vandīk/ *n.* & *adj.* ● *n.* **1** each of a series of large points forming a border to lace or cloth etc. **2** a cape or collar etc. with these. ● *adj.* (**Vandyke**) in the style of dress, esp. with pointed borders, common in portraits by Van Dyck. □ **Vandyke beard** a neat pointed beard. **Vandyke brown** a deep rich brown. [Sir A. *Van Dyck*, Anglicized *Vandyke*, Flem. painter d. 1641]

vane /vayn/ *n.* **1** (in full **weather-vane**) a revolving pointer mounted on a church spire or other high place to show the direction of the wind (cf. WEATHERCOCK). **2** a blade of a screw propeller or a windmill etc. **3** the sight of surveying instruments, a quadrant, etc. **4** the flat part of a bird's feather formed by the barbs. □□ **vaned** *adj.* **vaneless** *adj.* [ME, southern & western var. of obs. *fane* f. OE *fana* banner f. Gmc]

vanessa /vənéssə/ *n.* any butterfly of the genus *Vanessa*, including the red admiral and the painted lady. [mod.L]

vang /vang/ *n. Naut.* each of two guy-ropes running from the end of a gaff to the deck. [earlier *fang* = gripping-device: OE f. ON *fang* grasp f. Gmc]

vanguard /vángaard/ *n.* **1** the foremost part of an army or fleet advancing or ready to advance. **2** the leaders of a movement or of opinion etc. [earlier *vandgard*, *(a)vantgard*, f. OF *avan(t)garde* f. *avant* before (see AVAUNT) + *garde* GUARD]

■ see SPEARHEAD *n.*

vanilla /vəníllə/ *n.* **1 a** any tropical climbing orchid of the genus *Vanilla*, esp. *V. planifolia*, with fragrant flowers. **b** (in full **vanilla-pod**) the fruit of these. **2** a substance obtained from the vanilla-pod or synthesized and used to flavour ice-cream, chocolate, etc. [Sp. *vainilla* pod, dimin. of *vaina* sheath, pod, f. L VAGINA]

vanillin /vəníllin/ *n.* the fragrant principle of vanilla.

vanish /vánnish/ *v.* **1** *intr.* **a** disappear suddenly. **b** disappear gradually; fade away. **2** *intr.* cease to exist. **3** *intr. Math.* become zero. **4** *tr.* cause to disappear. □ **vanishing cream** an ointment that leaves no visible trace when rubbed into the skin. **vanishing-point 1** the point at which receding parallel lines viewed in perspective appear to meet. **2** the state of complete disappearance of something. [ME f. OF *e(s)vaniss-* stem of *e(s)vanir* ult. f. L *evanescere* (as EX-[1], *vanus* empty)]

■ **1** see DISAPPEAR 1. **2** see DISAPPEAR 2.

Vanitory /vánnitəri/ *n.* (*pl.* **-ies**) *propr.* = *vanity unit*.

vanity /vánniti/ *n.* (*pl.* **-ies**) **1** conceit and desire for admiration of one's personal attainments or attractions. **2 a** futility or unsubstantiality (*the vanity of human achievement*). **b** an unreal thing. **3** ostentatious display. **4** *US* a dressing-table. □ **vanity bag** (or **case**) a bag or case carried by a woman and containing a small mirror, make-up, etc. **Vanity Fair** the world (allegorized in Bunyan's *Pilgrim's Progress*) as a scene of vanity. **vanity unit** a unit consisting of a wash-basin set into a flat top with cupboards beneath. [ME f. OF *vanité* f. L *vanitas -tatis* (as VAIN)]

■ **1** vainness, conceit, conceitedness, egotism, arrogance, cockiness, self-importance, haughtiness, pride, self-admiration, self-worship, *Psychol.* narcissism, *colloq.* big-headedness, *literary* vainglory. **2 a** vainness, emptiness, hollowness, worthlessness, futility, unreality, insubstantiality, unsubstantiality, pointlessness, idleness, uselessness, folly, vapidity, silliness, vacuousness, vacuity, foolishness, fatuity, frivolousness, *archaic* bootlessness. **3** see OSTENTATION.

vanquish /vángkwish/ *v.tr. literary* conquer or overcome. □□ **vanquishable** *adj.* **vanquisher** *n.* [ME *venkus*, *-quis*, etc., f. OF *vencus* past part. and *venquis* past tenses of *veintre* f. L *vincere*: assim. to -ISH[2]]

■ see OVERCOME 1.

vantage /vaántij/ *n.* **1** (also **vantage point** or **ground**) a place affording a good view or prospect. **2** *Tennis* =

ADVANTAGE. **3** *archaic* an advantage or gain. [ME f. AF f. OF *avantage* ADVANTAGE]
■ **1** see PERCH[1] *n.*

vapid /váppid/ *adj.* insipid; lacking interest; flat, dull (*vapid moralizing*). ▫▫ **vapidity** /vəpídditi/ *n.* **vapidly** *adv.* **vapidness** *n.* [L *vapidus*]
■ insipid, flavourless, tasteless, bland, watery, watered down, wishy-washy, jejune, colourless, unpalatable, flat, dull, dreary, tame, lifeless, boring, tedious, tiresome, uninteresting, trite, wearisome, wearying, humdrum, *colloq.* blah. ▫▫ **vapidity** see TEDIUM.

vapor *US* var. of VAPOUR.

vaporific /váypəríffik/ *adj.* concerned with or causing vapour or vaporization.

vaporimeter /váypərímmitər/ *n.* an instrument for measuring the amount of vapour.

vaporize /váypərīz/ *v.tr.* & *intr.* (also **-ise**) convert or be converted into vapour. ▫▫ **vaporizable** *adj.* (also **vaporable**). **vaporization** /-záysh'n/ *n.*
■ see EVAPORATE 1, 2. ▫▫ **vaporization** see *evaporation* (EVAPORATE).

vaporizer /váypərīzər/ *n.* a device that vaporizes substances, esp. for medicinal inhalation.
■ see SPRAY[1] *n.* 3.

vapour /váypər/ *n.* & *v.* (*US* **vapor**) ● *n.* **1** moisture or another substance diffused or suspended in air, e.g. mist or smoke. **2** *Physics* a gaseous form of a normally liquid or solid substance (cf. GAS). **3** a medicinal agent for inhaling. **4** (in *pl.*) *archaic* a state of depression or melancholy thought to be caused by exhalations of vapour from the stomach. ● *v.intr.* **1** rise as vapour. **2** make idle boasts or empty talk. ▫ **vapour density** the density of a gas or vapour relative to hydrogen etc. **vapour pressure** the pressure of a vapour in contact with its liquid or solid form. **vapour trail** a trail of condensed water from an aircraft or rocket at high altitude, seen as a white streak against the sky. ▫▫ **vaporous** *adj.* **vaporously** *adv.* **vaporousness** *n.* **vapourer** *n.* **vapouring** *n.* **vapourish** *adj.* **vapoury** *adj.* [ME f. OF *vapour* or L *vapor* steam, heat]
■ *n.* **1** mist, fog, haze, steam, cloud, smoke, smog, fumes, exhalation, *archaic* miasma. **3** inhalant, inhalation. **4** (*vapours*) morbidity, morbidness, melancholy, hypochondria, hysteria, nervousness, depression.

var. *abbr.* **1** variant. **2** variety.

varactor /vəráktər/ *n.* a semiconductor diode with a capacitance dependent on the applied voltage. [*var*ying re*actor*]

varec /várrek/ *n.* **1** seaweed. **2** = KELP. [F *varec(h)* f. ON: rel. to WRECK]

variable /váiriəb'l/ *adj.* & *n.* ● *adj.* **1 a** that can be varied or adapted (*a rod of variable length; the pressure is variable*). **b** (of a gear) designed to give varying speeds. **2** apt to vary; not constant; unsteady (*a variable mood; variable fortunes*). **3** *Math.* (of a quantity) indeterminate; able to assume different numerical values. **4** (of wind or currents) tending to change direction. **5** *Astron.* (of a star) periodically varying in brightness. **6** *Bot.* & *Zool.* (of a species) including individuals or groups that depart from the type. **7** *Biol.* (of an organism or part of it) tending to change in structure or function. ● *n.* **1** a variable thing or quantity. **2** *Math.* a variable quantity. **3** *Naut.* **a** a shifting wind. **b** (in *pl.*) the region between the NE and SE trade winds. ▫▫ **variability** /-bílliti/ *n.* **variableness** *n.* **variably** *adv.* [ME f. OF f. L *variabilis* (as VARY)]
■ *adj.* **1** adaptable, adjustable, alterable. **2** changeable, protean, changing, inconstant, fluid, varying, wavering, mercurial, fickle, capricious, erratic, fitful, unsteady, unfixed, unstable, uncertain, unreliable, undependable, unpredictable, inconsistent, fluctuating, vacillating, chameleonic, chameleon-like, *literary* mutable. ▫▫ **variability** see *inconstancy* (INCONSTANT).

variance /váiriənss/ *n.* **1** difference of opinion; dispute, disagreement; lack of harmony (*at variance among ourselves; a theory at variance with all known facts*). **2** *Law* a discrepancy between statements or documents. **3** *Statistics* a quantity equal to the square of the standard deviation. [ME f. OF f. L *variantia* difference (as VARY)]
■ **1** disagreement, misunderstanding, discord, difference (of opinion), dissension, contention, dispute, dissent, controversy, quarrel, conflict, argument, debate, lack of harmony, falling out, schism, rift; (*at variance*) in dispute, in disagreement, quarrelling, conflicting, clashing, disagreeing, in contention, in conflict, in opposition, at odds, at loggerheads, not in keeping, out of line. **2** variation, difference, disparity, discrepancy, disagreement, deviation, inconsistency, divergence, incongruity.

variant /váiriənt/ *adj.* & *n.* ● *adj.* **1** differing in form or details from the main one (*a variant spelling*). **2** having different forms (*forty variant types of pigeon*). **3** variable or changing. ● *n.* a variant form, spelling, type, reading, etc. [ME f. OF (as VARY)]
■ *adj.* **1** alternative, different, varying, deviant. **2** separate, distinct, different. **3** varying, variable, changing, altering, unstable, inconstant, fluctuating, deviant, deviating, different, differing. ● *n.* alternative, modification, variation, version.

variate /váiriət/ *n.* *Statistics* **1** a quantity having a numerical value for each member of a group. **2** a variable quantity, esp. one whose values occur according to a frequency distribution. [past part. of L *variare* (as VARY)]

variation /váiriáysh'n/ *n.* **1** the act or an instance of varying. **2** departure from a former or normal condition, action, or amount, or from a standard or type (*prices are subject to variation*). **3** the extent of this. **4** a thing that varies from a type. **5** *Mus.* a repetition (usu. one of several) of a theme in a changed or elaborated form. **6** *Astron.* a deviation of a heavenly body from its mean orbit or motion. **7** *Math.* a change in a function etc. due to small changes in the values of constants etc. **8** *Ballet* a solo dance. ▫▫ **variational** *adj.* [ME f. OF *variation* or L *variatio* (as VARY)]
■ **1** change, alteration, variety, modification, transformation, difference, diversification, diversity, modulation, fluctuation, conversion, permutation, mutation. **2, 3** variety, choice, novelty; diversity, inconsistency, departure (from the norm *or* usual), change of pace, divergence, deviation (from the norm). **4** see VARIANT *n.*

varicella /várrisélla/ *n.* *Med.* = CHICKENPOX. [mod.L, irreg. dimin. of VARIOLA]

varices *pl.* of VARIX.

varicocele /várrikəseel/ *n.* a mass of varicose veins in the spermatic cord. [formed as VARIX + -CELE]

varicoloured /váirikúllərd/ *adj.* (*US* **varicolored**) **1** variegated in colour. **2** of various or different colours. [L *varius* VARIOUS + COLOURED]
■ see VARIEGATE 1.

varicose /várrikōss/ *adj.* (esp. of the veins of the legs) affected by a condition causing them to become dilated and swollen. ▫▫ **varicosity** /-kóssiti/ *n.* [L *varicosus* f. VARIX]

varied /váirid/ *adj.* showing variety; diverse. ▫▫ **variedly** *adv.*
■ diverse, diversified, mixed, miscellaneous, assorted, heterogeneous; see also VARIOUS 1.

variegate /váirigayt, -riəgayt/ *v.tr.* **1** (often as **variegated** *adj.*) mark with irregular patches of different colours. **2** diversify in appearance, esp. in colour. **3** (as **variegated** *adj.*) *Bot.* (of plants) having leaves containing two or more colours. ▫▫ **variegation** /-gáysh'n/ *n.* [L *variegare variegat-* f. *varius* various]
■ **1, 3** (**variegated**) multicolour(ed), particolour(ed), varicoloured, many-coloured, versicoloured, motley, harlequin, pied, piebald, two-tone, brindle(d), mottled, marbled, polychrome, polychromatic; opalescent, opaline.

varietal /vərī́ət'l/ *adj.* **1** esp. *Bot.* & *Zool.* of, forming, or designating a variety. **2** (of wine) made from a single designated variety of grape. ▫▫ **varietally** *adv.*

varietist /vərī́ətist/ *n.* a person whose habits etc. differ from what is normal.

variety /vərī́əti/ *n.* (*pl.* **-ies**) **1** diversity; absence of uniformity; many-sidedness; the condition of being various (*not enough variety in our lives*). **2** a quantity or collection of different things (*for a variety of reasons*). **3 a** a class of things different in some common qualities from the rest of a larger class to which they belong. **b** a specimen or member of such a class. **4** (foll. by *of*) a different form of a thing, quality, etc. **5** *Biol.* **a** a subspecies. **b** a cultivar. **c** an individual or group usually fertile within the species to which it belongs but differing from the species type in some qualities capable of perpetuation. **6** a mixed sequence of dances, songs, comedy acts, etc. (usu. *attrib.*: *a variety show*). □ **variety store** *US* a shop selling many kinds of small items. [F *variété* or L *varietas* (as VARIOUS)]

■ **1** difference, heterogeneity, discrepancy, diversity, disparity, variation, contrast, many-sidedness, multifariousness. **2** diversity, multiplicity, number, range, array, assortment, medley, mixture, mix, blend, miscellany, selection, collection, combination. **3** sort, brand, make, mark, kind, class, category, breed, type, order, genre, species, genus, strain. **4** see VERSION 3. **6** *Brit.* music-hall, *esp. US* vaudeville.

varifocal /váirifṓk'l/ *adj.* & *n.* ● *adj.* having a focal length that can be varied, esp. of a lens that allows an infinite number of focusing distances for near, intermediate, and far vision. ● *n.* (in *pl.*) varifocal spectacles.

variform /váiriform/ *adj.* having various forms. [L *varius* + -FORM]

variola /vərī́ələ/ *n. Med.* smallpox. □□ **variolar** *adj.* **varioloid** /váiriəloyd/ *adj.* **variolous** *adj.* [med.L, = pustule, pock (as VARIOUS)]

variole /váiriōl/ *n.* **1** a shallow pit like a smallpox mark. **2** a small spherical mass in variolite. [med.L *variola*: see VARIOLA]

variolite /váiriəlīt/ *n.* a rock with embedded small spherical masses causing on its surface an appearance like smallpox pustules. □□ **variolitic** /-líttik/ *adj.* [as VARIOLE + -ITE[1]]

variometer /váiriómmitər/ *n.* **1** a device for varying the inductance in an electric circuit. **2** a device for indicating an aircraft's rate of change of altitude. [as VARIOUS + -METER]

variorum /váiriórəm/ *adj.* & *n.* ● *adj.* **1** (of an edition of a text) having notes by various editors or commentators. **2** (of an edition of an author's works) including variant readings. ● *n.* a variorum edition. [L f. *editio cum notis variorum* edition with notes by various (commentators): genit. pl. of *varius* VARIOUS]

various /váiriəss/ *adj.* **1** different, diverse (*too various to form a group*). **2** more than one, several (*for various reasons*). □□ **variously** *adv.* **variousness** *n.* [L *varius* changing, diverse]

■ **1** different, distinct, individual, diverse, varied, heterogeneous. **2** different, a number of, a variety of, diversified, diverse, several, many, numerous, sundry, multifarious, miscellaneous, assorted, *archaic or literary* divers, *literary* manifold.

varistor /vərístər/ *n.* a semiconductor diode with resistance dependent on the applied voltage. [*var*ying res*istor*]

varix /váiriks/ *n.* (*pl.* **varices** /várriseez/) **1** *Med.* **a** a permanent abnormal dilation of a vein or artery. **b** a vein etc. dilated in this way. **2** each of the ridges across the whorls of a univalve shell. [ME f. L *varix -icis*]

varlet /vaárlit/ *n.* **1** *archaic* or *joc.* a menial or rascal. **2** *hist.* a knight's attendant. □□ **varletry** *n.* [ME f. OF, var. of *vaslet*: see VALET]

■ **1** see WRETCH 2.

varmint /vaármint/ *n. US* or *dial.* a mischievous or discreditable person or animal, esp. a fox. [var. of *varmin*, VERMIN]

varna /vaárnə/ *n.* each of the four Hindu castes. [Skr., = colour, class]

varnish /vaárnish/ *n.* & *v.* ● *n.* **1** a resinous solution used to give a hard shiny transparent coating to wood, metal, paintings, etc. **2** any other preparation for a similar purpose (*nail varnish*). **3** external appearance or display without an underlying reality. **4** artificial or natural glossiness. **5** a superficial polish of manner. ● *v.tr.* **1** apply varnish to. **2** gloss over (a fact). □□ **varnisher** *n.* [ME f. OF *vernis* f. med.L *veronix* fragrant resin, sandarac or med.Gk *berenikē* prob. f. *Berenice* in Cyrenaica]

varsity /vaársiti/ *n.* (*pl.* **-ies**) **1** *Brit. colloq.* (esp. with ref. to sports) university. **2** *US* a university etc. first team in a sport. [abbr.]

varus /váirəss/ *n.* a deformity involving the inward displacement of the foot or hand from the midline. [L, = bent, crooked]

varve /vaarv/ *n.* annually deposited layers of clay and silt in a lake used to determine the chronology of glacial sediments. □□ **varved** *adj.* [Sw. *varv* layer]

vary /váiri/ *v.* (**-ies, -ied**) **1** *tr.* make different; modify, diversify (*seldom varies the routine*; *the style is not sufficiently varied*). **2** *intr.* **a** undergo change; become or be different (*the temperature varies from 30° to 70°*). **b** be of different kinds (*his mood varies*). **3** *intr.* (foll. by *as*) be in proportion to. □□ **varyingly** *adv.* [ME f. OF *varier* or L *variare* (as VARIOUS)]

■ **1** change, alter, diversify, transform, reshape, remodel, restyle, modify, adjust, reorganize. **2 a** change; depart, deviate, differ, diverge, shift, veer. **b** change, switch, alternate, fluctuate, vacillate, oscillate, see-saw, swing.

vas /vass/ *n.* (*pl.* **vasa** /váysə/) *Anat.* a vessel or duct. □ **vas deferens** /déffərenz/ (*pl.* **vasa deferentia** /défférénshiə/) *Anat.* the spermatic duct from the testicle to the urethra. □□ **vasal** /váys'l/ *adj.* [L, = vessel]

vascular /váskyoolər/ *adj.* of, made up of, or containing vessels for conveying blood or sap etc. (*vascular functions*; *vascular tissue*). □ **vascular plant** a plant with conducting tissue. □□ **vascularity** /-lárriti/ *n.* **vascularize** *v.tr.* (also **-ise**). **vascularly** *adv.* [mod.L *vascularis* f. L VASCULUM]

vasculum /váskyooləm/ *n.* (*pl.* **vascula** /-lə/) a botanist's (usu. metal) collecting-case with a lengthwise opening. [L, dimin. of VAS]

vase /vaaz/ *n.* a vessel, usu. tall and circular, used as an ornament or container, esp. for flowers. □□ **vaseful** *n.* (*pl.* **-fuls**). [F f. L VAS]

vasectomy /vəséktəmi/ *n.* (*pl.* **-ies**) the surgical removal of part of each vas deferens esp. as a means of sterilization. □□ **vasectomize** *v.tr.* (also **-ise**).

Vaseline /vássileén/ *n.* & *v.* ● *n. propr.* a type of petroleum jelly used as an ointment, lubricant, etc. ● *v.tr.* (**vaseline**) treat with Vaseline. [irreg. f. G *Wasser* + Gk *elaion* oil]

vasiform /váyziform/ *adj.* **1** duct-shaped. **2** vase-shaped. [L *vasi-* f. VAS + -FORM]

vaso- /váyzō/ *comb. form* a vessel, esp. a blood-vessel (*vasoconstrictive*). [L *vas*: see VAS]

vasoactive /váyzō-áktiv/ *adj.* = VASOMOTOR.

vasoconstrictive /váyzōkənstríktiv/ *adj.* causing constriction of blood-vessels.

vasodilating /váyzōdīláyting/ *adj.* causing dilatation of blood-vessels. □□ **vasodilation** *n.*

vasomotor /váyzōmṓtər/ *adj.* causing constriction or dilatation of blood-vessels.

vasopressin /váyzōpréssin/ *n.* a pituitary hormone acting to reduce diuresis and increase blood pressure. Also called ANTIDIURETIC HORMONE.

vassal /váss'l/ *n.* **1** *hist.* a holder of land by feudal tenure on conditions of homage and allegiance. **2** *rhet.* a humble dependant. □□ **vassalage** *n.* [ME f. OF f. med.L *vassallus* retainer, of Celt. orig.: the root *vassus* corresp. to Bret. *gwaz*, Welsh *gwas*, Ir. *foss*: cf. VAVASOUR]

■ **2** see SLAVE *n.* 1.

vast /vaast/ *adj.* & *n.* ● *adj.* **1** immense, huge; very great (*a vast expanse of water*; *a vast crowd*). **2** *colloq.* great, considerable (*makes a vast difference*). ● *n. poet.* or *rhet.* a vast space (*the vast of heaven*). ▫▫ **vastly** *adv.* **vastness** *n.* [L *vastus* void, immense]

▪ *adj.* **1** infinite, unlimited, boundless, limitless, unbounded, interminable, endless, never-ending, inexhaustible, indeterminate, immeasurable, incalculable, measureless, extensive; immense, enormous, huge, tremendous, great, prodigious, stupendous, gigantic, massive, voluminous, capacious, colossal, monumental, mammoth, elephantine, behemoth, Cyclopean, titanic, *colloq.* jumbo, *sl.* humongous, *Brit. sl.* ginormous. **2** big, large, considerable, sizeable, substantial, significant, great, goodly. ▫▫ **vastly** immensely, greatly, hugely, enormously, considerably, substantially, (almost) entirely, infinitely, exceedingly, extremely, profoundly, very (much). **vastness** see SIZE[1] *n.*

VAT /veé-aytee, vat/ *abbr.* (in the UK) value added tax.

vat /vat/ *n.* & *v.* ● *n.* **1** a large tank or other vessel, esp. for holding liquids or something in liquid in the process of brewing, tanning, dyeing, etc. **2** a dyeing liquor in which a textile is soaked to take up a colourless soluble dye afterwards coloured by oxidation in air. ● *v.tr.* (**vatted, vatting**) place or treat in a vat. ▫▫ **vatful** *n.* (*pl.* **-fuls**). [ME, southern & western var. of *fat*, OE *fæt* f. Gmc]

vatic /váttik/ *adj. formal* prophetic or inspired. [L *vates* prophet]

Vatican /váttikən/ *n.* **1** the palace and official residence of the Pope in Rome. **2** papal government. ▫ **Vatican City** an independent Papal State in Rome, instituted in 1929. **Vatican Council** an ecumenical council of the Roman Catholic Church, esp. that held in 1869–70 or that held in 1962–5. ▫▫ **Vaticanism** *n.* **Vaticanist** *n.* [F *Vatican* or L *Vaticanus* name of a hill in Rome]

vaticinate /vatíssinayt/ *v.tr.* & *intr. formal* prophesy. ▫▫ **vaticinal** *adj.* **vaticination** /-náysh'n/ *n.* **vaticinator** *n.* [L *vaticinari* f. *vates* prophet]

VATman /vátman/ *n.* (*pl.* **-men**) *colloq.* a customs and excise officer who administers VAT.

vaudeville /váwdəvil, vố-/ *n.* **1** esp. *US* variety entertainment. **2** a stage play on a trivial theme with interspersed songs. **3** a satirical or topical song with a refrain. ▫▫ **vaudevillian** /-víllian/ *adj.* & *n.* [F, orig. of convivial song esp. any of those composed by O. Basselin, 15th-c. poet born at *Vau de Vire* in Normandy]

Vaudois[1] /vốdwaa/ *n.* & *adj.* ● *n.* (*pl.* same) **1** a native of Vaud in W. Switzerland. **2** the French dialect spoken in Vaud. ● *adj.* of or relating to Vaud or its dialect. [F]

Vaudois[2] /vốdwaa/ *n.* & *adj.* ● *n.* (*pl.* same) a member of the Waldenses. ● *adj.* of or relating to the Waldenses. [F, repr. med.L *Valdensis*: see WALDENSES]

vault /vawlt, volt/ *n.* & *v.* ● *n.* **1 a** an arched roof. **b** a continuous arch. **c** a set or series of arches whose joints radiate from a central point or line. **2** a vaultlike covering (*the vault of heaven*). **3** an underground chamber: **a** as a place of storage (*bank vaults*). **b** as a place of interment beneath a church or in a cemetery etc. (*family vault*). **4** an act of vaulting. **5** *Anat.* the arched roof of a cavity. ● *v.* **1** *intr.* leap or spring, esp. while resting on one or both hands or with the help of a pole. **2** *tr.* spring over (a gate etc.) in this way. **3** *tr.* (esp. as **vaulted**) **a** make in the form of a vault. **b** provide with a vault or vaults. ▫▫ **vaulter** *n.* [OF *voute*, *vaute*, ult. f. L *volvere* roll]

▪ *v.* **1, 2** see LEAP *v.* 1, 2.

vaulting /váwlting, vólt-/ *n.* **1** arched work in a vaulted roof or ceiling. **2** a gymnastic or athletic exercise in which participants vault over obstacles. ▫ **vaulting-horse** a wooden block to be vaulted over by gymnasts.

vaunt /vawnt/ *v.* & *n. literary* ● *v.* **1** *intr.* boast, brag. **2** *tr.* boast of; extol boastfully. ● *n.* a boast. ▫▫ **vaunter** *n.* **vauntingly** *adv.* [ME f. AF *vaunter*, OF *vanter* f. LL *vantare* f. L *vanus* VAIN: partly obs. *avaunt* (v.) f. *avanter* f. *a-* intensive + *vanter*]

▪ *v.* **1** see BOAST *v.* 1. **2** see DISPLAY *v.* 2.

vavasory /vávvəsəri/ *n.* (*pl.* **-ies**) *hist.* the estate of a vavasour. [OF *vavasorie* or med.L *vavasoria* (as VAVASOUR)]

vavasour /vávvəsoor/ *n. hist.* a vassal owing allegiance to a great lord and having other vassals under him. [ME f. OF *vavas(s)our* f. med.L *vavassor*, perh. f. *vassus vassorum* VASSAL of vassals]

VC *abbr.* **1** Victoria Cross. **2** Vice-Chairman. **3** Vice-Chancellor. **4** Vice-Consul.

VCR *abbr.* video cassette recorder.

VD *abbr.* venereal disease.

VDU *abbr.* visual display unit.

VE *abbr.* Victory in Europe (in 1945). ▫ **VE day** 8 May, the day marking this.

've *abbr.* (chiefly after pronouns) = HAVE (*I've*; *they've*).

veal /veel/ *n.* calf's flesh as food. ▫▫ **vealy** *adj.* [ME f. AF *ve(e)l*, OF *veiaus veel* f. L *vitellus* dimin. of *vitulus* calf]

vector /véktər/ *n.* & *v.* ● *n.* **1** *Math.* & *Physics* a quantity having direction as well as magnitude, esp. as determining the position of one point in space relative to another (*radius vector*). **2** a carrier of disease. **3** a course to be taken by an aircraft. ● *v.tr.* direct (an aircraft in flight) to a desired point. ▫▫ **vectorial** /-tóriəl/ *adj.* **vectorize** *v.tr.* (also **-ise**) (in sense 1 of *n.*). **vectorization** /-tərīzáysh'n/ *n.* [L, = carrier, f. *vehere vect-* convey]

Veda /váydə, veé-/ *n.* (in *sing.* or *pl.*) the most ancient Hindu scriptures, esp. four collections called Rig-Veda, Sāma-Veda, Yajur-Veda, and Atharva-Veda. [Skr. *vēda*, lit. (sacred) knowledge]

Vedanta /vidántə, vedaán-/ *n.* **1** the Upanishads. **2** the Hindu philosophy based on these, esp. in its monistic form. ▫▫ **Vedantic** *adj.* **Vedantist** *n.* [Skr. *vedānta* (as VEDA, *anta* end)]

Vedda /véddə/ *n.* a Sri Lankan aboriginal. [Sinh. *veddā* hunter]

vedette /vidét/ *n.* a mounted sentry positioned beyond an army's outposts to observe the movements of the enemy. [F, = scout, f. It. *vedetta*, *veletta* f. Sp. *vela(r)* watch f. L *vigilare*]

Vedic /váydik, veé-/ *adj.* & *n.* ● *adj.* of or relating to the Veda or Vedas. ● *n.* the language of the Vedas, an older form of Sanskrit. [F *Védique* or G *Vedisch* (as VEDA)]

vee /vee/ *n.* **1** the letter V. **2** a thing shaped like a V. [name of the letter]

veer[1] /veer/ *v.* & *n.* ● *v.intr.* **1** change direction, esp. (of the wind) clockwise (cf. BACK *v.* 5). **2** change in course, opinion, conduct, emotions, etc. **3** *Naut.* = WEAR[2]. ● *n.* a change of course or direction. [F *virer* f. Rmc, perh. alt. f. L *gyrare* GYRATE]

▪ *v.* **1** see DEVIATE *v.*

veer[2] /veer/ *v.tr. Naut.* slacken or let out (a rope, cable, etc.). [ME f. MDu. *vieren*]

veg /vej/ *n. colloq.* a vegetable or vegetables. [abbr.]

Vega /veégə/ *n. Astron.* a brilliant blue star in the constellation of the Lyre. [Sp. or med.L *Vega* f. Arab., = the falling vulture]

vegan /veégən/ *n.* & *adj.* ● *n.* a person who does not eat or use animal products. ● *adj.* using or containing no animal products. [VEGETABLE + -AN]

Vegemite /véjəmīt/ *n. Austral. propr.* concentrated yeast extract, used as a spread in sandwiches and for flavouring. [blend of VEGETABLE and MARMITE]

vegetable /véjitəb'l, véjtəb'l/ *n.* & *adj.* ● *n.* **1** *Bot.* any of various plants, esp. a herbaceous plant used wholly or partly for food, e.g. a cabbage, potato, turnip, or bean. **2** *colloq.* **a** a person who is incapable of normal intellectual activity, esp. through brain injury etc. **b** a person lacking in animation or living a monotonous life. ● *adj.* **1** of, derived from, relating to, or comprising plants or plant life, esp. as distinct from animal life or mineral substances. **2** of or relating to vegetables as food. **3 a** unresponsive to stimulus (*vegetable behaviour*). **b** uneventful, monotonous (*a vegetable existence*). ▫ **vegetable butter** a vegetable fat with the consistency of butter. **vegetable ivory** see IVORY. **vegetable marrow** see MARROW 1. **vegetable oyster** = SALSIFY. **vegetable parchment** see PARCHMENT 2. **vegetable spaghetti 1** a variety of marrow with flesh resembling spaghetti. **2** its flesh. **vegetable sponge** = LOOFAH. **vegetable tallow** see TALLOW. **vegetable wax** an exudation of certain plants such as sumac. [ME f. OF *vegetable* or LL *vegetabilis* animating (as VEGETATE)]

vegetal /véjit'l/ *adj.* **1** of or having the nature of plants (*vegetal growth*). **2** vegetative. [med.L *vegetalis* f. L *vegetare* animate]

vegetarian /véjitáiriən/ *n.* & *adj.* ● *n.* a person who abstains from animal food, esp. that from slaughtered animals, though often not eggs and dairy products. ● *adj.* excluding animal food, esp. meat (*a vegetarian diet*). ▫▫ **vegetarianism** *n.* [irreg. f. VEGETABLE + -ARIAN]

vegetate /véjitayt/ *v.intr.* **1** live an uneventful or monotonous life. **2** grow as plants do; fulfil vegetal functions. [L *vegetare* animate f. *vegetus* f. *vegēre* be active]

■ **1** see STAGNATE.

vegetation /véjitáysh'n/ *n.* **1** plants collectively; plant life (*luxuriant vegetation*; *no sign of vegetation*). **2** the process of vegetating. ▫▫ **vegetational** *adj.* [med.L *vegetatio* growth (as VEGETATE)]

vegetative /véjitətiv/ *adj.* **1** concerned with growth and development as distinct from sexual reproduction. **2** of or relating to vegetation or plant life. ▫▫ **vegetatively** *adv.* **vegetativeness** *n.* [ME f. OF *vegetatif -ive* or med.L *vegetativus* (as VEGETATE)]

vegie /véji/ *n.* (also **veggie**) *colloq.* a vegetarian. [abbr.]

vehement /veéəmənt/ *adj.* showing or caused by strong feeling; forceful, ardent (*a vehement protest*; *vehement desire*). ▫▫ **vehemence** *n.* **vehemently** *adv.* [ME f. F *véhément* or L *vehemens -entis*, perh. f. *vemens* (unrecorded) deprived of mind, assoc. with *vehere* carry]

■ see IMPASSIONED. ▫▫ **vehemence** see FERVOUR 1. **vehemently** see *warmly* (WARM).

vehicle /veé-ik'l/ *n.* **1** any conveyance for transporting people, goods, etc., esp. on land. **2** a medium for thought, feeling, or action (*the stage is the best vehicle for their talents*). **3** a liquid etc. as a medium for suspending pigments, drugs, etc. **4** the literal meaning of a word or words used metaphorically (opp. TENOR 6). ▫▫ **vehicular** /vihíkyoolər/ *adj.* [F *véhicule* or L *vehiculum* f. *vehere* carry]

■ **1** conveyance. **2** medium, means, channel, mechanism, carrier, conduit, agency, instrument, agent, tool.

veil /vayl/ *n.* & *v.* ● *n.* **1** a piece of usu. more or less transparent fabric attached to a woman's hat etc., esp. to conceal the face or protect against the sun, dust, etc. **2** a piece of linen etc. as part of a nun's head-dress, resting on the head and shoulders. **3** a curtain, esp. that separating the sanctuary in the Jewish Temple. **4** a disguise; a pretext; a thing that conceals (*under the veil of friendship*; *a veil of mist*). **5** *Photog.* slight fogging. **6** huskiness of the voice. **7** = VELUM. ● *v.tr.* **1** cover with a veil. **2** (esp. as **veiled** *adj.*) partly conceal (*veiled threats*). ▫ **beyond the veil** in the unknown state of life after death. **draw a veil over** avoid discussing or calling attention to. **take the veil** become a nun. ▫▫ **veilless** *adj.* [ME f. AF *veil(e)*, OF *voil(e)* f. L *vela* pl. of VELUM]

■ *n.* **1** covering, yashmak. **4** covering, cover, screen, camouflage, cloak, mantle, curtain, cloud, mask, shroud; disguise, pretext. ● *v.* cover, conceal, hide, camouflage, cloak, mask, disguise, shroud, shield, obscure, *literary* enshroud; (**veiled**) concealed, hidden, masked, obscure, unrevealed, covert, disguised, secret, *sub rosa*, subtle.

veiling /váyling/ *n.* light fabric used for veils etc.

vein /vayn/ *n.* & *v.* ● *n.* **1 a** any of the tubes by which blood is conveyed to the heart (cf. ARTERY). **b** (in general use) any blood-vessel (*has royal blood in his veins*). **2** a nervure of an insect's wing. **3** a slender bundle of tissue forming a rib in the framework of a leaf. **4** a streak or stripe of a different colour in wood, marble, cheese, etc. **5** a fissure in rock filled with ore or other deposited material. **6** a source of a particular characteristic (*a rich vein of humour*). **7** a distinctive character or tendency; a cast of mind or disposition; a mood (*spoke in a sarcastic vein*). ● *v.tr.* fill or cover with or as with veins. ▫▫ **veinless** *n.* **veinlet** *n.* **veinlike** *adj.* **veiny** *adj.* (**veinier**, **veiniest**). [ME f. OF *veine* f. L *vena*]

■ *n.* **1** blood-vessel; *Anat.* venule. **2, 3** nervure, rib. **4** streak, seam, stripe, thread, strand, line, *Biol.* & *Geol.* striation, stria. **5** seam, lode, stratum, course, deposit, bed, pocket. **6** thread, hint, suggestion, touch, trace, streak, line, strain. **7** tendency, inclination, proclivity; mood, spirit, tone, note, tenor, feeling, attitude, disposition, cast of mind, humour, temper; way, manner, course, fashion, style, mode, pattern.

veining /váyning/ *n.* a pattern of streaks or veins.

veinstone /váynstōn/ *n.* = GANGUE.

vela *pl.* of VELUM.

velamen /viláymən/ *n.* (*pl.* **velamina** /-minə/) an enveloping membrane esp. of an aerial root of an orchid. [L f. *velare* cover]

velar /veélər/ *adj.* **1** of a veil or velum. **2** *Phonet.* (of a sound) pronounced with the back of the tongue near the soft palate. [L *velaris* f. *velum*: see VELUM]

Velcro /vélkrō/ *n. propr.* a fastener for clothes etc. consisting of two strips of nylon fabric, one looped and one burred, which adhere when pressed together. ▫▫ **Velcroed** *adj.* [F *velours croché* hooked velvet]

veld /velt/ *n.* (also **veldt**) *S.Afr.* open country; grassland. [Afrik. f. Du., = FIELD]

veldskoen /féltskōōn, féls-/ *n.* a strong suede or leather shoe or boot. [Afrik., = field-shoe]

veleta /vəleétə/ *n.* (also **valeta**) a ballroom dance in triple time. [Sp., = weather-vane]

velitation /véllitáysh'n/ *n.* *archaic* a slight skirmish or controversy. [L *velitatio* f. *velitari* skirmish f. *veles velitis* light-armed skirmisher]

velleity /veleé-iti/ *n.* *literary* **1** a low degree of volition not conducive to action. **2** a slight wish or inclination. [med.L *velleitas* f. L *velle* to wish]

vellum /vélləm/ *n.* **1 a** a fine parchment orig. from the skin of a calf. **b** a manuscript written on this. **2** smooth writing-paper imitating vellum. [ME f. OF *velin* (as VEAL)]

velocimeter /vélləsímmitər/ *n.* an instrument for measuring velocity.

velocipede /vilóssipeed/ *n.* **1** *hist.* an early form of bicycle propelled by pressure from the rider's feet on the ground. **2** *US* a child's tricycle. ▫▫ **velocipedist** *n.* [F *vélocipède* f. L *velox -ocis* swift + *pes pedis* foot]

velocity /vilóssiti/ *n.* (*pl.* **-ies**) **1** the measure of the rate of movement of a usu. inanimate object in a given direction. **2** speed in a given direction. **3** (in general use) speed. ▫ **velocity of escape** = *escape velocity*. [F *vélocité* or L *velocitas* f. *velox -ocis* swift]

■ **3** speed, swiftness, rapidity, quickness, briskness, alacrity, pace, rate of speed, miles per hour, m.p.h., kilometres per hour, km/hr, *archaic or literary* celerity, *poet. or literary* fleetness.

velodrome /vélləd rōm/ *n.* a special place or building with a track for cycle-racing. [F *vélodrome* f. *vélo* bicycle (as VELOCITY, -DROME)]

velour /vəlóor/ *n.* (also **velours**) **1** a plushlike woven fabric or felt. **2** *archaic* a hat of this felt . [F *velours* velvet f. OF *velour*, *velous* f. L *villosus* hairy f. *villus*: see VELVET]

velouté /vəlóotay/ *n.* a sauce made from a roux of butter and flour with white stock. [F, = velvety]

velum /veéləm/ *n.* (*pl.* **vela** /-lə/) a membrane, membranous covering, or flap. [L, = sail, curtain, covering, veil]

velutinous /vilóotinəss/ *adj.* covered with soft fine hairs. [perh. f. It. *vellutino* f. *velluto* VELVET]

velvet /vélvit/ *n.* & *adj.* ● *n.* **1** a closely woven fabric of silk, cotton, etc., with a thick short pile on one side. **2** the furry skin on a deer's growing antler. **3** anything smooth and soft like velvet. ● *adj.* of, like, or soft as velvet. ▫ **on** (or **in**) **velvet** in an advantageous or prosperous position. **velvet**

glove outward gentleness, esp. cloaking firmness or strength (cf. *iron hand*). □□ **velveted** *adj.* **velvety** *adj.* [ME f. OF *veluotte* f. *velu* velvety f. med.L *villutus* f. L *villus* tuft, down]
■ □□ **velvety** see SOFT *adj.* 2.

velveteen /vélvitéen/ *n.* **1** a cotton fabric with a pile like velvet. **2** (in *pl.*) trousers etc. made of this.

Ven. *abbr.* Venerable (as the title of an archdeacon).

vena cava /véenə káyvə/ *n.* (*pl.* **venae cavae** /-nee -vee/) each of usu. two veins carrying blood into the heart. [L, = hollow vein]

venal /véen'l/ *adj.* **1** (of a person) able to be bribed or corrupted. **2** (of conduct etc.) characteristic of a venal person. □□ **venality** /-nálliti/ *n.* **venally** *adv.* [L *venalis* f. *venum* thing for sale]
■ corruptible, bribable, buyable, purchasable, rapacious, avaricious, greedy, simoniacal, *sl.* bent; corrupt, mercenary, unprincipled, dishonourable, *colloq.* crooked. □□ **venality** see VICE[1] 1, 2.

venation /vináysh'n/ *n.* the arrangement of veins in a leaf or an insect's wing etc., or the system of venous blood vessels in an organism. □□ **venational** *adj.* [L *vena* vein]

vend /vend/ *v.tr.* **1** offer (small wares) for sale. **2** *Law* sell. □ **vending-machine** a machine that dispenses small articles for sale when a coin or token is inserted. □□ **vender** *n.* (usu. in *comb.*). **vendible** *adj.* [F *vendre* or L *vendere* sell (as VENAL, *dare* give)]

vendace /véndayss/ *n.* a small delicate fish, *Coregonus albula*, found in some British lakes. [OF *vendese*, *-oise* f. Gaulish]

vendee /vendée/ *n. Law* the buying party in a sale, esp. of property.

vendetta /vendéttə/ *n.* **1 a** a blood feud in which the family of a murdered person seeks vengeance on the murderer or the murderer's family. **b** this practice as prevalent in Corsica and Sicily. **2** a prolonged bitter quarrel. [It. f. L *vindicta*: see VINDICTIVE]
■ **1** (blood) feud. **2** quarrel, dispute, feud, conflict, rivalry; enmity, hostility, bitterness, hatred, ill will, bad blood.

vendeuse /vonDőz/ *n.* a saleswoman, esp. in a fashionable dress-shop. [F]

vendor /véndər, -dor/ *n.* **1** *Law* the seller in a sale, esp. of property. **2** = *vending-machine* (see VEND). [AF *vendour* (as VEND)]
■ **1** see SELLER.

vendue /vendyóo/ *n. US* a public auction. [Du. *vendu(e)* f. F *vendue* sale f. *vendre* VEND]

veneer /vinéer/ *n.* & *v.* ● *n.* **1 a** a thin covering of fine wood or other surface material applied to a coarser wood. **b** a layer in plywood. **2** (often foll. by *of*) a deceptive outward appearance of a good quality etc. ● *v.tr.* **1** apply a veneer to (wood, furniture, etc.). **2** disguise (an unattractive character etc.) with a more attractive manner etc. [earlier *fineer* f. G *furni(e)ren* f. OF *fournir* FURNISH]
■ *n.* **1** covering, coating, overlay, surface, exterior, finish, skin. **2** gloss, façade, exterior, pretence, cover, (false) front, (outward) show *or* display, appearance, semblance, mask, guise, face, aspect, surface. ● *v.* **1** see FACE *v.* 5a.

veneering /vinéering/ *n.* material used as veneer.

venepuncture /véenipungkchər/ *n.* (also **venipuncture**) *Med.* the puncture of a vein esp. with a hypodermic needle to withdraw blood or for an intravenous injection. [L *vena* vein + PUNCTURE]

venerable /vénnərəb'l/ *adj.* **1** entitled to veneration on account of character, age, associations, etc. (*a venerable priest*; *venerable relics*). **2** as the title of an archdeacon in the Church of England. **3** *RC Ch.* as the title of a deceased person who has attained a certain degree of sanctity but has not been fully beatified or canonized. □□ **venerability** /-bílliti/ *n.* **venerableness** *n.* **venerably** *adv.* [ME f. OF *venerable* or L *venerabilis* (as VENERATE)]
■ **1** respectable, honourable, estimable, respected, honoured, esteemed, august, dignified, impressive, revered, reverenced, venerated, worshipped; old, ancient, aged.

venerate /vénnərayt/ *v.tr.* **1** regard with deep respect. **2** revere on account of sanctity etc. □□ **veneration** /-ráysh'n/ *n.* **venerator** *n.* [L *venerari* adore, revere]
■ respect, honour, esteem, revere, reverence, worship, hallow, adore, admire, idolize, glorify, look up to, pay homage to. □□ **veneration** respect, honour, esteem, reverence, deference, homage, devotion, worship, admiration, adoration, idolization, awe.

venereal /vinéeriəl/ *adj.* **1** of or relating to sexual desire or intercourse. **2** relating to venereal disease. □ **venereal disease** any of various diseases contracted chiefly by sexual intercourse with a person already infected. □□ **venereally** *adv.* [ME f. L *venereus* f. *venus veneris* sexual love]
■ **1** see SEXUAL, EROTIC. **2** sexual; genital; sexually transmitted, gonorrhoeal, syphilitic.

venereology /vinéeriólləji/ *n.* the scientific study of venereal diseases. □□ **venereological** /-riəlójik'l/ *adj.* **venereologist** *n.*

venery[1] /vénnəri/ *n. archaic* sexual indulgence. [med.L *veneria* (as VENEREAL)]

venery[2] /vénnəri/ *n. archaic* hunting. [ME f. OF *venerie* f. *vener* to hunt ult. f. L *venari*]

venesection /véeniseksh'n/ *n.* (also **venisection**) phlebotomy. [med.L *venae sectio* cutting of a vein (as VEIN, SECTION)]

Venetian /vinéesh'n/ *n.* & *adj.* ● *n.* **1** a native or citizen of Venice in NE Italy. **2** the Italian dialect of Venice. **3** (**venetian**) = *venetian blind*. ● *adj.* of Venice. □ **venetian blind** a window-blind of adjustable horizontal slats to control the light. **Venetian glass** delicate glassware made at Murano near Venice. **Venetian red** a reddish pigment of ferric oxides. **Venetian window** a window with three separate openings, the central one being arched and highest. □□ **venetianed** *adj.* (in sense 3 of *n.*). [ME f. OF *Venicien*, assim. to med.L *Venetianus* f. *Venetia* Venice]

vengeance /vénjənss/ *n.* punishment inflicted or retribution exacted for wrong to oneself or to a person etc. whose cause one supports. □ **with a vengeance** in a higher degree than was expected or desired; in the fullest sense (*punctuality with a vengeance*). [ME f. OF f. *venger* avenge f. L (as VINDICATE)]
■ revenge, retaliation, retribution, requital, reprisal, settling *or* squaring of accounts. □ **with a vengeance** violently, fiercely, ferociously, wildly, vehemently, furiously, forcefully, energetically; to the fullest extent, to the utmost *or* fullest *or* limit, (with) no holds barred, enthusiastically, wholeheartedly.

vengeful /vénjfool/ *adj.* vindictive; seeking vengeance. □□ **vengefully** *adv.* **vengefulness** *n.* [obs. *venge* avenge (as VENGEANCE)]
■ see VINDICTIVE 1. □□ **vengefulness** see RANCOUR.

venial /véeniəl/ *adj.* (of a sin or fault) pardonable, excusable; not mortal. □□ **veniality** /-niálliti/ *n.* **venially** *adv.* **venialness** *n.* [ME f. OF f. LL *venialis* f. *venia* forgiveness]
■ forgivable, excusable, pardonable, tolerable, tolerated, minor, petty, insignificant, unimportant, remittable, remissible.

venipuncture var. of VENEPUNCTURE.

venisection var. of VENESECTION.

venison /vénnis'n, -z'n/ *n.* a deer's flesh as food. [ME f. OF *veneso(u)n* f. L *venatio -onis* hunting f. *venari* to hunt]

Venite /viníti/ *n.* **1** a canticle consisting of Psalm 95. **2** a musical setting of this. [ME f. L, = 'come ye', its first word]

Venn diagram /ven/ *n.* a diagram of usu. circular areas representing mathematical sets, the areas intersecting where they have elements in common. [J. *Venn*, Engl. logician d. 1923]

venom /vénnəm/ *n.* **1** a poisonous fluid secreted by snakes, scorpions, etc., usu. transmitted by a bite or sting. **2** malignity; virulence of feeling, language, or conduct. □□ **venomed** *adj.* [ME f. OF *venim*, var. of *venin* ult. f. L *venenum* poison]

■ **1** poison, toxin. **2** malice, maliciousness, malevolence, ill will, malignity, animosity, hate, hatred, hostility, antagonism, spite, spitefulness, spleen, rancour, bitterness, embitteredness, poison, poisonousness, virulence, *sl.* gall.

venomous /vénnəməss/ *adj.* **1 a** containing, secreting, or injecting venom. **b** (of a snake etc.) inflicting poisonous wounds by this means. **2** (of a person etc.) virulent, spiteful, malignant. ▫▫ **venomously** *adv.* **venomousness** *n.* [ME f. OF *venimeux* f. *venim*: see VENOM]

■ **1** poisonous, deadly, toxic, dangerous, life-threatening, lethal. **2** poisonous, virulent, malicious, malevolent, malign, malignant, savage, baleful, envenomed, hostile, antagonistic, spiteful, splenetic, acerbic, rancorous, bitter, embittered, mean, vicious. ▫▫ **venomousness** see *virulence* (VIRULENT).

venose /veénōz/ *adj.* having many or very marked veins. [L *venosus* f. *vena* vein]

venous /veénəss/ *adj.* of, full of, or contained in veins. ▫▫ **venosity** /vinóssiti/ *n.* **venously** *adv.* [L *venosus* VENOSE or L *vena* vein + -OUS]

vent[1] /vent/ *n.* & *v.* ● *n.* **1** (also **vent-hole**) a hole or opening allowing motion of air etc. out of or into a confined space. **2** an outlet; free passage or play (*gave vent to their indignation*). **3** the anus esp. of a lower animal, serving for both excretion and reproduction. **4** the venting of an otter, beaver, etc. **5** an aperture or outlet through which volcanic products are discharged at the earth's surface. **6** a touch-hole of a gun. **7** a finger-hole in a musical instrument. **8** a flue of a chimney. ● *v.* **1** *tr.* **a** make a vent in (a cask etc.). **b** provide (a machine) with a vent. **2** *tr.* give vent or free expression to (*vented my anger on the cat*). **3** *intr.* (of an otter or beaver) come to the surface for breath. **4** *tr.* & *intr.* discharge. ▫ **vent one's spleen on** scold or ill-treat without cause. ▫▫ **ventless** *adj.* [partly F *vent* f. L *ventus* wind, partly F *évent* f. *éventer* expose to air f. OF *esventer* ult. f. L *ventus* wind]

■ *n.* **1** opening, slit, slot, hole, aperture, air-hole, ventilator, blow-hole, vent-hole, orifice, outlet, inlet, funnel, duct, passage, pipe. **2** outlet, expression, free play *or* passage. **5** blow-hole, vent-hole, fumarole, mofette, fissure. **8** chimney, flue, smoke-duct, outlet, ventilator, vent-hole, funnel. ● *v.* **2** give vent to, express, verbalize, air, articulate, enunciate, declare, voice, announce, communicate, pronounce, proclaim, reveal, release, let go, let loose, allow to become known, make known, disclose, blurt out, make public, broadcast. **4** discharge, release, emit, eject, issue, empty, dump, expel, send out *or* forth, pour out *or* forth, throw out, *colloq.* unload.

vent[2] /vent/ *n.* a slit in a garment, esp. in the lower edge of the back of a coat. [ME, var. of *fent* f. OF *fente* slip ult. f. L *findere* cleave]

ventiduct /véntidukt/ *n. Archit.* an air-passage, esp. for ventilation. [L *ventus* wind + *ductus* DUCT]

ventifact /véntifakt/ *n.* a stone shaped by wind-blown sand. [L *ventus* wind + *factum* neut. past part. of *facere* make]

ventil /véntil/ *n. Mus.* **1** a valve in a wind instrument. **2** a shutter for regulating the air-flow in an organ. [G f. It. *ventile* f. med.L *ventile* sluice f. L *ventus* wind]

ventilate /véntilayt/ *v.tr.* **1** cause air to circulate freely in (a room etc.). **2** submit (a question, grievance, etc.) to public consideration and discussion. **3** *Med.* **a** oxygenate (the blood). **b** admit or force air into (the lungs). ▫▫ **ventilation** /-láysh'n/ *n.* **ventilative** /-láytiv/ *adj.* [L *ventilare ventilat-* blow, winnow, f. *ventus* wind]

■ **1** see AIR *v.* 2. **2** see AIR *v.* 3.

ventilator /véntilaytər/ *n.* **1** an appliance or aperture for ventilating a room etc. **2** *Med.* = RESPIRATOR 2.

ventral /véntrəl/ *adj.* **1** *Anat.* & *Zool.* of or on the abdomen (cf. DORSAL). **2** *Bot.* of the front or lower surface. ▫ **ventral fin** either of the ventrally placed fins on a fish. ▫▫ **ventrally** *adv.* [obs. *venter* abdomen f. L *venter ventr-*]

ventre à terre /vaántrə aa táir/ *adv.* at full speed. [F, lit. with belly to the ground]

ventricle /véntrik'l/ *n. Anat.* **1** a cavity in the body. **2** a hollow part of an organ, esp. in the brain or heart. ▫▫ **ventricular** /-tríkyoolər/ *adj.* [ME f. L *ventriculus* dimin. of *venter* belly]

ventricose /véntrikōz/ *adj.* **1** having a protruding belly. **2** *Bot.* distended, inflated. [irreg. f. VENTRICLE + -OSE[1]]

ventriloquism /ventrílləkwiz'm/ *n.* the skill of speaking or uttering sounds so that they seem to come from the speaker's dummy or a source other than the speaker. ▫▫ **ventriloquial** /véntrilṓkwiəl/ *adj.* **ventriloquist** *n.* **ventriloquize** *v.intr.* (also **-ise**). [ult. f. L *ventriloquus* ventriloquist f. *venter* belly + *loqui* speak]

ventriloquy /ventrílləkwi/ *n.* = VENTRILOQUISM.

venture /vénchər/ *n.* & *v.* ● *n.* **1 a** an undertaking of a risk. **b** a risky undertaking. **2** a commercial speculation. ● *v.* **1** *intr.* dare; not be afraid (*did not venture to stop them*). **2** *intr.* (usu. foll. by *out* etc.) dare to go (out), esp. outdoors. **3** *tr.* dare to put forward (an opinion, suggestion, etc.). **4 a** *tr.* expose to risk; stake (a bet etc.). **b** *intr.* take risks. **5** *intr.* (foll. by *on*, *upon*) dare to engage in etc. (*ventured on a longer journey*). ▫ **at a venture** at random; without previous consideration. **venture capital** = *risk capital.* **Venture Scout** *Brit.* a member of the Scout Association aged between 16 and 20. [*aventure* = ADVENTURE]

■ *n.* risk, chance, hazardous undertaking, enterprise, experiment, speculation, gamble, plunge, fling. ● *v.* **1** dare, make bold, be *or* make so bold as, presume, take the liberty, attempt, try, endeavour. **3** dare, risk, hazard, volunteer, tender, offer, broach, advance, proffer, put forward. **4 a** jeopardize, risk, endanger, hazard, imperil; gamble, bet, wager, stake, chance, plunge, put down.

venturer /vénchərər/ *n. hist.* a person who undertakes or shares in a trading venture.

venturesome /vénchərsəm/ *adj.* **1** disposed to take risks. **2** risky. ▫▫ **venturesomely** *adv.* **venturesomeness** *n.*

■ **1** daring, bold, intrepid, adventurous, courageous, plucky, adventuresome, audacious, daredevil, fearless, game, brave, spirited, sporting, *archaic or joc.* doughty. **2** risky, rash, reckless, daredevil, dangerous, perilous, hazardous.

venturi /ventyoóri/ *n.* (*pl.* **venturis**) a short piece of narrow tube between wider sections for measuring flow-rate or exerting suction. [G. B. *Venturi*, It. physicist d. 1822]

venue /vényoo/ *n.* **1 a** an appointed meeting-place esp. for a sports event, meeting, concert, etc. **b** a rendezvous. **2** *Law hist.* the county or other place within which a jury must be gathered and a cause tried (orig. the neighbourhood of the crime etc.). [F, = a coming, fem. past part. of *venir* come f. L *venire*]

■ **1 a** see LOCALE.

venule /vényool/ *n. Anat.* a small vein adjoining the capillaries. [L *venula* dimin. of *vena* vein]

Venus /veénəss/ *n.* (*pl.* **Venuses**) **1** the planet second from the sun in the solar system. **2** *poet.* **a** a beautiful woman. **b** sexual love; amorous influences or desires. ▫ **Venus** (or **Venus's**) **fly-trap** a flesh-consuming plant, *Dionaea muscipula*, with leaves that close on insects etc. **Venus's comb** = *shepherd's needle* (see SHEPHERD). **Venus's looking-glass** any of various plants of the genus *Legousia* with small blue flowers. ▫▫ **Venusian** /vinyoóziən/ *adj.* & *n.* [OE f. L *Venus Veneris*, the goddess of love]

veracious /vəráyshəss/ *adj. formal* **1** speaking or disposed to speak the truth. **2** (of a statement etc.) true or meant to be true. ▫▫ **veraciously** *adv.* **veraciousness** *n.* [L *verax veracis* f. *verus* true]

■ **1** see TRUTHFUL 1. **2** see TRUTHFUL 2.

veracity /vərássiti/ *n.* **1** truthfulness, honesty. **2** accuracy (of a statement etc.). [F *veracité* or med.L *veracitas* (as VERACIOUS)]

■ **1** see HONESTY 2. **2** see TRUTH 1.

veranda /vərándə/ *n.* (also **verandah**) **1** a portico or external gallery, usu. with a roof, along the side of a house. **2**

Austral. & *NZ* a roof over a pavement in front of a shop. [Hindi *varandā* f. Port. *varanda*]

veratrine /vérrətreen, -trin/ *n.* a poisonous compound obtained from sabadilla etc., and used esp. as a local irritant in the treatment of neuralgia and rheumatism. [F *vératrine* f. L *veratrum* hellebore]

verb /verb/ *n. Gram.* a word used to indicate an action, state, or occurrence, and forming the main part of the predicate of a sentence (e.g. *hear*, *become*, *happen*). [ME f. OF *verbe* or L *verbum* word, verb]

verbal /vérb'l/ *adj.*, *n.*, & *v.* ● *adj.* **1** of or concerned with words (*made a verbal distinction*; *verbal reasoning*). **2** oral, not written (*gave a verbal statement*). **3** *Gram.* of or in the nature of a verb (*verbal inflections*). **4** literal (*a verbal translation*). **5** talkative, articulate. ● *n.* **1** *Gram.* **a** a verbal noun. **b** a word or words functioning as a verb. **2** *sl.* a verbal statement, esp. one made to the police. **3** *sl.* an insult; abuse (*gave them the verbal*). ● *v.tr.* (**verballed, verballing**) *Brit. sl.* attribute a damaging statement to (a suspect). □ **verbal noun** *Gram.* a noun formed as an inflection of a verb and partly sharing its constructions (e.g. *smoking* in *smoking is forbidden*: see -ING[1]). □□ **verbally** *adv.* [ME f. F *verbal* or LL *verbalis* (as VERB)]
■ *adj.* **1** lexical; *attrib.* word, vocabulary. **2** spoken, oral, vocal, said, uttered, expressed, enunciated, articulated, colloquial, conversational, viva voce, word-of-mouth, unwritten. **4** word-for-word, verbatim, literal. ● *n.* **2** see STATEMENT 1–3.

verbalism /vérbəliz'm/ *n.* **1** minute attention to words: verbal criticism. **2** merely verbal expression. □□ **verbalist** *n.* **verbalistic** /-lístik/ *adj.*

verbalize /vérbəlīz/ *v.* (also **-ise**) **1** *tr.* express in words. **2** *intr.* be verbose. **3** *tr.* make (a noun etc.) into a verb. □□ **verbalizable** *adj.* **verbalization** /-záysh'n/ *n.* **verbalizer** *n.*
■ **1** see EXPRESS[1] 1, 2. □□ **verbalization** see EXPRESSION 1.

verbatim /verbáytim/ *adv.* & *adj.* in exactly the same words; word for word (*copied it verbatim*; *a verbatim report*). [ME f. med.L (adv.), f. L *verbum* word: cf. LITERATIM]
■ *adv.* word for word, verbatim et literatim, literally, exactly, precisely, accurately, faithfully, to the letter, strictly. ● *adj.* word for word, verbatim et literatim, literal, exact, precise, accurate, faithful, strict.

verbena /verbeénə/ *n.* any plant of the genus *Verbena*, bearing clusters of fragrant flowers. [L, = sacred bough of olive etc., in med.L vervain]

verbiage /vérbi-ij/ *n.* needless accumulation of words; verbosity. [F f. obs. *verbeier* chatter f. *verbe* word: see VERB]
■ see *hot air*.

verbose /verbṓss/ *adj.* using or expressed in more words than are needed. □□ **verbosely** *adv.* **verboseness** *n.* **verbosity** /-bóssiti/ *n.* [L *verbosus* f. *verbum* word]
■ see WORDY. □□ **verbosity** see RHETORIC 2.

verboten /ferbṓt'n/ *adj.* forbidden, esp. by an authority. [G]
■ see TABOO *adj.*

verb. sap. /verb sáp/ *int.* expressing the absence of the need for a further explicit statement. [abbr. of L *verbum sapienti sat est* a word is enough for the wise person]

verdant /vérd'nt/ *adj.* **1** (of grass etc.) green, fresh-coloured. **2** (of a field etc.) covered with green grass etc. **3** (of a person) unsophisticated, raw, green. □□ **verdancy** *n.* **verdantly** *adv.* [perh. f. OF *verdeant* part. of *verdoier* be green ult. f. L *viridis* green]
■ **1, 2** see LUSH[1] 1.

verd-antique /vérdanteék/ *n.* **1** ornamental usu. green serpentine. **2** a green incrustation on ancient bronze. **3** green porphyry. [obs. F, = antique green]

verderer /vérdərər/ *n. Brit.* a judicial officer of royal forests. [AF (earlier *verder*), OF *verdier* ult. f. L *viridis* green]

verdict /vérdikt/ *n.* **1** a decision on an issue of fact in a civil or criminal cause or an inquest. **2** a decision; a judgement. [ME f. AF *verdit*, OF *voirdit* f. *voir*, *veir* true f. L *verus* + *dit* f. L DICTUM saying]
■ see DECISION 2, 3.

verdigris /vérdigriss, -greess/ *n.* **1 a** a green crystallized substance formed on copper by the action of acetic acid. **b** this used as a medicine or pigment. **2** green rust on copper or brass. [ME f. OF *verte-gres*, *vert de Grece* green of Greece]

verdure /vérdyər/ *n.* **1** green vegetation. **2** the greenness of this. **3** *poet.* freshness. □□ **verdured** *adj.* **verdurous** *adj.* [ME f. OF f. *verd* green f. L *viridis*]

verge[1] /verj/ *n.* **1** an edge or border. **2** an extreme limit beyond which something happens (*on the verge of tears*). **3** *Brit.* a grass edging of a road, flower-bed, etc. **4** *Archit.* an edge of tiles projecting over a gable. **5** a wand or rod carried before a bishop, dean, etc., as an emblem of office. [ME f. OF f. L *virga* rod]
■ **1** edge, border, boundary, margin, brink, brim, bank, side, perimeter. **2** (*on the verge of*) about to, ready to, close to, near (to), on the brink of, on the (very) point of, on the threshold of; preparing to, soon to. **3** edging, border, edge. **5** see STAFF[1] *n.* 1a, b.

verge[2] /verj/ *v.intr.* **1** incline downwards or in a specified direction (*the now verging sun*; *verge to a close*). **2** (foll. by *on*) border on; approach closely (*verging on the ridiculous*). [L *vergere* bend, incline]
■ **1** incline, lean, tend, extend, stretch, turn; draw, move. **2** (*verge on*) border on, approach, come close to *or* near (to), be asymptotic to.

verger /vérjər/ *n.* (also **virger**) **1** an official in a church who acts as caretaker and attendant. **2** an officer who bears the staff before a bishop etc. □□ **vergership** *n.* [ME f. AF (as VERGE[1])]

verglas /váirglaa/ *n.* a thin coating of ice or frozen rain. [F]

veridical /viríddik'l/ *adj.* **1** *formal* truthful. **2** *Psychol.* (of visions etc.) coinciding with reality. □□ **veridicality** /-kálliti/ *n.* **veridically** *adv.* [L *veridicus* f. *verus* true + *dicere* say]

veriest /vérri-ist/ *adj.* (*superl.* of VERY). *archaic* real, extreme (*the veriest fool knows that*).

verification /vérrifikáysh'n/ *n.* **1** the process or an instance of establishing the truth or validity of something. **2** *Philos.* the establishment of the validity of a proposition empirically. **3** the process of verifying procedures laid down in weapons agreements.
■ **1** see PROOF *n.* 3.

verify /vérrifī/ *v.tr.* (**-ies, -ied**) **1** establish the truth or correctness of by examination or demonstration (*must verify the statement*; *verified my figures*). **2** (of an event etc.) bear out or fulfil (a prediction or promise). **3** *Law* append an affidavit to (pleadings); support (a statement) by testimony or proofs. □□ **verifiable** *adj.* **verifiably** *adv.* **verifier** *n.* [ME f. OF *verifier* f. med.L *verificare* f. *verus* true]
■ affirm, confirm, check over *or* out, testify to, attest (to), bear witness to, vouch for, corroborate, support, substantiate, uphold, prove, demonstrate, show, bear out, authenticate, validate, certify, guarantee, back up, warrant. □□ **verifiable** see DEMONSTRABLE.

verily /vérrili/ *adv. archaic* really, truly. [ME f. VERY + -LY[2], after OF & AF]
■ see TRULY 2.

verisimilitude /vérrisimíllityo͞od/ *n.* **1** the appearance or semblance of being true or real. **2** a statement etc. that seems true. □□ **verisimilar** /-símmilər/ *adj.* [L *verisimilitudo* f. *verisimilis* probable f. *veri* genit. of *verus* true + *similis* like]

verism /veériz'm/ *n.* realism in literature or art. □□ **verist** *n.* **veristic** /-rístik/ *adj.* [L *verus* or It. *vero* true + -ISM]

verismo /verízmō/ *n.* (esp. of opera) realism. [It. (as VERISM)]

veritable /vérritəb'l/ *adj.* real; rightly so called (*a veritable feast*). □□ **veritably** *adv.* [OF (as VERITY)]
■ real, true, genuine, proper, actual, legitimate, authentic. □□ **veritably** see FAIRLY 5.

verity /vérriti/ *n.* (*pl.* **-ies**) **1** a true statement, esp. one of fundamental import. **2** truth. **3** a really existent thing. [ME f. OF *verité*, *verté* f. L *veritas -tatis* f. *verus* true]

verjuice /vérjōōss/ *n.* **1** an acid liquor obtained from crab-apples, sour grapes, etc., and formerly used in cooking and medicine. **2** bitter feelings, thoughts, etc. [ME f. OF *vertjus* f. VERT green + *jus* JUICE]

verkrampte /fairkrámptə/ *adj.* & *n. S.Afr.* ● *adj.* politically or socially conservative or reactionary, esp. as regards apartheid. ● *n.* a person holding such views. [Afrik., lit. narrow, cramped]

verligte /fairlíkhtə/ *adj.* & *n. S.Afr.* ● *adj.* progressive or enlightened, esp. as regards apartheid. ● *n.* a person holding such views. [Afrik., = enlightened]

vermeil /vérmayl, -mil/ *n.* **1** silver gilt. **2** an orange-red garnet. **3** *poet.* vermilion. [ME f. OF: see VERMILION]

vermi- /vérmi/ *comb. form* worm. [L *vermis* worm]

vermian /vérmiən/ *adj.* of worms; wormlike. [L *vermis* worm]

vermicelli /vérmisélli, -chélli/ *n.* **1** pasta made in long slender threads. **2** shreds of chocolate used as cake decoration etc. [It., pl. of *vermicello* dimin. of *verme* f. L *vermis* worm]

vermicide /vérmisīd/ *n.* a substance that kills worms.

vermicular /vərmíkyoolər/ *adj.* **1** like a worm in form or movement; vermiform. **2** *Med.* of or caused by intestinal worms. **3** marked with close wavy lines. [med.L *vermicularis* f. L *vermiculus* dimin. of *vermis* worm]

vermiculate /vərmíkyoolət/ *adj.* **1** = VERMICULAR. **2** worm-eaten. [L *vermiculatus* past part. of *vermiculari* be full of worms (as VERMICULAR)]

vermiculation /vərmíkyooláysh'n/ *n.* **1** the state or process of being eaten or infested by or converted into worms. **2** a vermicular marking. **3** a wormeaten state. [L *vermiculatio* (as VERMICULATE)]

vermiculite /vərmíkyoolīt/ *n.* a hydrous silicate mineral usu. resulting from alteration of mica, and expandable into sponge by heating, used as an insulation material. [as VERMICULATE + -ITE[1]]

vermiform /vérmiform/ *adj.* worm-shaped. □ **vermiform appendix** see APPENDIX 1.

vermifuge /vérmifyōōj/ *adj.* & *n.* ● *adj.* that expels intestinal worms. ● *n.* a drug that does this.

vermilion /vərmílyən/ *n.* & *adj.* ● *n.* **1** cinnabar. **2 a** a brilliant red pigment made by grinding this or artificially. **b** the colour of this. ● *adj.* of this colour. [ME f. OF *vermeillon* f. *vermeil* f. L *vermiculus* dimin. of *vermis* worm]

vermin /vérmin/ *n.* (usu. treated as *pl.*) **1** mammals and birds injurious to game, crops, etc., e.g. foxes, rodents, and noxious insects. **2** parasitic worms or insects. **3** vile persons. □□ **verminous** *adj.* [ME f. OF *vermin*, *-ine* ult. f. L *vermis* worm]

■ **3** see RABBLE[1] 2.

verminate /vérminayt/ *v.intr.* **1** breed vermin. **2** become infested with parasites. □□ **vermination** /-náysh'n/ *n.* [L *verminare verminat-* f. *vermis* worm]

vermivorous /vermívvərəss/ *adj.* feeding on worms.

vermouth /vérməth, vərmōōth/ *n.* a wine flavoured with aromatic herbs. [F *vermout* f. G *Wermut* WORMWOOD]

vernacular /vərnákyoolər/ *n.* & *adj.* ● *n.* **1** the language or dialect of a particular country (*Latin gave place to the vernacular*). **2** the language of a particular clan or group. **3** homely speech. ● *adj.* **1** (of language) of one's native country; not of foreign origin or of learned formation. **2** (of architecture) concerned with ordinary rather than monumental buildings. □□ **vernacularism** *n.* **vernacularity** /-lárriti/ *n.* **vernacularize** *v.tr.* (also **-ise**). **vernacularly** *adv.* [L *vernaculus* domestic, native f. *verna* home-born slave]

■ *n.* **1** language, dialect, tongue. **2** jargon, patois, argot, vulgate, cant, idiom, phraseology, parlance, language, talk, speech, *colloq.* lingo. ● *adj.* **1** native, local, regional, indigenous, autochthonous; popular, informal, colloquial, conversational, ordinary, familiar, everyday, spoken, vulgar; plain, simple, straightforward, easy.

vernal /vérn'l/ *adj.* of, in, or appropriate to spring (*vernal equinox*; *vernal breezes*). □ **vernal grass** a sweet-scented European grass, *Anthoxanthum odoratum*, grown for hay. □□ **vernally** *adv.* [L *vernalis* f. *vernus* f. *ver* spring]

vernalization /vérnəlīzáysh'n/ *n.* (also **-isation**) the cooling of seed before planting, in order to accelerate flowering. □□ **vernalize** /vérnəlīz/ *v.tr.* (also **-ise**). [(transl. of Russ. *yarovizatsiya*) f. VERNAL]

vernation /vernáysh'n/ *n. Bot.* the arrangement of leaves in a leaf-bud (cf. AESTIVATION). [mod.L *vernatio* f. L *vernare* bloom (as VERNAL)]

vernicle /vérnik'l/ *n.* = VERONICA 2. [ME f. OF (earlier *ver(o)nique*), f. med.L VERONICA]

vernier /vérniər/ *n.* a small movable graduated scale for obtaining fractional parts of subdivisions on a fixed main scale of a barometer, sextant, etc. □ **vernier engine** an auxiliary engine for slight changes in the motion of a space rocket etc. [P. *Vernier*, Fr. mathematician d. 1637]

veronal /vérrən'l/ *n. propr.* a sedative drug, a derivative of barbituric acid. [G, f. *Verona* in Italy]

veronica /vərónnikə/ *n.* **1** any plant of the genus *Veronica* or *Hebe*, esp. speedwell. **2 a** a cloth supposedly impressed with an image of Christ's face. **b** any similar picture of Christ's face. **3** *Bullfighting* the movement of a matador's cape away from a charging bull. [med.L f. the name *Veronica*: in sense 2 from the association with St Veronica]

verruca /vərōōkə/ *n.* (*pl.* **verrucae** /-rōōssee/ or **verrucas**) a wart or similar growth. □□ **verrucose** /vérrookōz/ *adj.* **verrucous** /vérrookəss/ *adj.* [L]

versant /vérs'nt/ *n.* **1** the extent of land sloping in one direction. **2** the general slope of land. [F f. *verser* f. L *versare* frequent. of *vertere vers-* turn]

versatile /vérsətīl/ *adj.* **1** turning easily or readily from one subject or occupation to another; capable of dealing with many subjects (*a versatile mind*). **2** (of a device etc.) having many uses. **3** *Bot.* & *Zool.* moving freely about or up and down on a support (*versatile antenna*). **4** *archaic* changeable, inconstant. □□ **versatilely** *adv.* **versatility** /-tílliti/ *n.* [F *versatile* or L *versatilis* (as VERSANT)]

■ **1** adaptable, resourceful, all-round, multi-skilled, many-sided, multifaceted, flexible, protean, dexterous, handy, *US* all-around. **2** multi-purpose, all-purpose, handy, adjustable, flexible. **4** variable, changeable, protean, changing, flexible, fluctuating, inconstant. □□ **versatility** adaptability, flexibility, adjustability.

verse /verss/ *n.* & *v.* ● *n.* **1 a** metrical composition in general (*wrote pages of verse*). **b** a particular type of this (*English verse*). **2 a** a metrical line in accordance with the rules of prosody. **b** a group of a definite number of such lines. **c** a stanza of a poem or song with or without refrain. **3** each of the short numbered divisions of a chapter in the Bible or other scripture. **4 a** a versicle. **b** a passage (of an anthem etc.) for solo voice. ● *v.tr.* **1** express in verse. **2** (usu. *refl.*; foll. by *in*) instruct; make knowledgeable. □□ **verselet** *n.* [OE *fers* f. L *versus* a turn of the plough, a furrow, a line of writing f. *vertere vers-* turn: in ME reinforced by OF *vers* f. L *versus*]

■ *n.* **1** poetry, versification, *archaic* poesy; see also POEM.

versed[1] /verst/ *predic.adj.* (foll. by *in*) experienced or skilled in; knowledgeable about. [F *versé* or L *versatus* past part. of *versari* be engaged in (as VERSANT)]

■ (*versed in*) well-versed in, well-read in, (well-)informed in *or* about, (well-)trained in, (well-)grounded in, (well-)schooled in, (well-)educated in, (well-)tutored in, learned in, cultured in, lettered in, cultivated in, literate in, competent in, accomplished in, skilled in, (well) posted on, knowledgeable in *or* about, proficient in *or* at, experienced in *or* at, practised in *or* at, expert in *or* at, good in *or* at, conversant with, familiar with, (well-)acquainted with, *esp. Brit. colloq.* a dab hand at.

versed[2] /verst/ *adj. Math.* reversed. □ **versed sine** unity minus cosine. [mod.L (*sinus*) *versus* turned (sine), formed as VERSE]

verset /vérsit/ *n. Mus.* a short prelude or interlude for organ. [F: dimin. of *vers* VERSE]

versicle /vérsik'l/ *n.* each of the short sentences in a liturgy said or sung by a priest etc. and alternating with responses. ▫▫ **versicular** /-síkyoolər/ *adj.* [ME f. OF *versicule* or L *versiculus* dimin. of *versus*: see VERSE]

versicoloured /vérsikúllərd/ *adj.* **1** changing from one colour to another in different lights. **2** variegated. [L *versicolor* f. *versus* past part. of *vertere* turn + *color* colour]
▪ **2** see *variegated* (VARIEGATE).

versify /vérsifī/ *v.* (**-ies, -ied**) **1** *tr.* turn into or express in verse. **2** *intr.* compose verses. ▫▫ **versification** /-fikáysh'n/ *n.* **versifier** *n.* [ME f. OF *versifier* f. L *versificare* (as VERSE)]

versin /vérsīn/ *n.* (also **versine**) *Math.* = *versed sine* (see VERSED²).

version /vérsh'n/ *n.* **1** an account of a matter from a particular person's point of view (*told them my version of the incident*). **2** a book or work etc. in a particular edition or translation (*Authorized Version*). **3** a form or variant of a thing as performed, adapted, etc. **4** a piece of translation, esp. as a school exercise. **5** *Med.* the manual turning of a foetus in the womb to improve presentation. ▫▫ **versional** *adj.* [F *version* or med.L *versio* f. L *vertere vers-* turn]
▪ **1** story, account, report, description, rendering, rendition, translation, interpretation, reading, understanding, view, side. **2** edition, adaptation, translation, interpretation, rendering. **3** form, variant, variation, type, model, style, design, kind, variety, manifestation, portrayal, adaptation, rendition, interpretation, construct, construction, conception, idea.

vers libre /vair leébrə/ *n.* irregular or unrhymed verse in which the traditional rules of prosody are disregarded. [F, = free verse]

verso /vérsō/ *n.* (*pl.* **-os**) **1 a** the left-hand page of an open book. **b** the back of a printed leaf of paper or manuscript (opp. RECTO). **2** the reverse of a coin. [L *verso* (*folio*) on the turned (leaf)]

verst /verst/ *n.* a Russian measure of length, about 1.1 km (0.66 mile). [Russ. *versta*]

versus /vérsəss/ *prep.* against (esp. in legal and sports use). ¶ Abbr.: **v., vs.** [L, = towards, in med.L against]

vert /vert/ *n.* & (usu. placed after noun) *adj. Heraldry* green. [ME f. OF f. L *viridis* green]

vertebra /vértibrə/ *n.* (*pl.* **vertebrae** /-bree/) **1** each segment of the backbone. **2** (in *pl.*) the backbone. ▫▫ **vertebral** *adj.* [L f. *vertere* turn]
▪ **2** spine, backbone, spinal column.

vertebrate /vértibrət, -brayt/ *n.* & *adj.* ● *n.* any animal of the subphylum Vertebrata, having a spinal column, including mammals, birds, reptiles, amphibians, and fishes. ● *adj.* of or relating to the vertebrates. [L *vertebratus* jointed (as VERTEBRA)]

vertebration /vértibráysh'n/ *n.* division into vertebrae or similar segments.

vertex /vérteks/ *n.* (*pl.* **vertices** /-tiseez/ or **vertexes**) **1** the highest point; the top or apex. **2** *Geom.* **a** each angular point of a polygon, polyhedron, etc. **b** a meeting-point of two lines that form an angle. **c** the point at which an axis meets a curve or surface. **d** the point opposite the base of a figure. **3** *Anat.* the crown of the head. [L *vertex -ticis* whirlpool, crown of a head, vertex, f. *vertere* turn]
▪ **1** top, tip, extremity, zenith, meridian, apogee, peak, apex, acme, summit, pinnacle, crest, crown, cap, height(s).

vertical /vértik'l/ *adj.* & *n.* ● *adj.* **1** at right angles to a horizontal plane, perpendicular. **2** in a direction from top to bottom of a picture etc. **3** of or at the vertex or highest point. **4** at, or passing through, the zenith. **5** *Anat.* of or relating to the crown of the head. **6** involving all the levels in an organizational hierarchy or stages in the production of a class of goods (*vertical integration*). ● *n.* a vertical line or plane. ▫ **out of the vertical** not vertical. **vertical angles** *Math.* each pair of opposite angles made by two intersecting lines. **vertical fin** *Zool.* a dorsal, anal, or caudal fin. **vertical plane** a plane at right angles to the horizontal. **vertical take-off** the take-off of an aircraft directly upwards. ▫▫ **verticality** /-kálliti/ *n.* **verticalize** *v.tr.* (also **-ise**). **vertically** *adv.* [F *vertical* or LL *verticalis* (as VERTEX)]
▪ *adj.* **1, 2** see PERPENDICULAR *adj.* 2. ▫▫ **vertically** see UPRIGHT *adv.*

verticil /vértisil/ *n. Bot.* & *Zool.* a whorl; a set of parts arranged in a circle round an axis. ▫▫ **verticillate** /-tíssilət/ *adj.* [L *verticillus* whorl of a spindle, dimin. of VERTEX]

vertiginous /vərtijinəss/ *adj.* of or causing vertigo. ▫▫ **vertiginously** *adv.* [L *vertiginosus* (as VERTIGO)]
▪ see DIZZY *adj.* 1a, SHEER¹ 2, HIGH *adj.* 1a.

vertigo /vértigō/ *n.* a condition with a sensation of whirling and a tendency to lose balance; dizziness, giddiness. [L *vertigo -ginis* whirling f. *vertere* turn]
▪ dizziness, light-headedness, giddiness, muzziness, instability, unsteadiness, staggers, (*in sheep*) sturdy, *colloq.* wooziness.

vertu var. of VIRTU.

vervain /vérvayn/ *n. Bot.* any of various herbaceous plants of the genus *Verbena*, esp. *V. officinalis* with small blue, white, or purple flowers. [ME f. OF *verveine* f. L VERBENA]

verve /verv/ *n.* enthusiasm, vigour, spirit, esp. in artistic or literary work. [F, earlier = a form of expression, f. L *verba* words]
▪ spirit, vivacity, vivaciousness, vitality, life, liveliness, animation, sparkle, energy, vigour, exuberance, briskness, brio, *esprit*, *élan*, dash, flair, panache, flourish, enthusiasm, zeal, zest, gusto, zip, *colloq.* vim, get-up-and-go, pep, zing, *sl.* pizazz, oomph.

vervet /vérvit/ *n.* a small grey African monkey, *Cercopithecus aethiops*. [F]

very /vérri/ *adv.* & *adj.* ● *adv.* **1** in a high degree (*did it very easily*; *had a very bad cough*; *am very much better*). **2** in the fullest sense (foll. by *own* or superl. adj.: *at the very latest*; *do your very best*; *my very own room*). ● *adj.* **1** (usu. prec. by *the*, *this*, *his*, etc.) **a** real, true, actual; truly such (emphasizing identity, significance, or extreme degree: *the very thing we need*; *those were his very words*). **b** mere, sheer (*the very idea of it was horrible*). **2** *archaic* real, genuine (*very God*). ▫ **not very 1** in a low degree. **2** far from being. **very good** (or **well**) a formula of consent or approval. **very high frequency** (of radio frequency) in the range 30-300 megahertz. **Very Reverend** the title of a dean. **the very same** see SAME. [ME f. OF *verai* ult. f. L *verus* true]
▪ *adv.* **1** extremely, truly, really, to a great extent, exceedingly, greatly, highly, (very) much, most, profoundly, deeply, acutely, perfectly, thoroughly, unusually, extraordinarily, uncommonly, exceptionally, especially, particularly, remarkably, absolutely, completely, entirely, utterly, altogether, totally, quite, rather, hugely, enormously, vastly, *archaic* right, *colloq.* jolly, damn(ed), terribly, awfully, darned, *US sl.* plumb. ● *adj.* **1 a** exact, precise, perfect; same, selfsame, identical, particular; actual, real, true. **b** least, mere, merest, bare, barest, sheer, sheerest; utter, pure, simple. **2** real, true, genuine.

Very light /vérri, veéri/ *n.* a flare projected from a pistol for signalling or temporarily illuminating the surroundings. [E. W. *Very*, Amer. inventor d. 1910]

Very pistol /vérri, veéri/ *n.* a gun for firing a Very light.

vesica /véssikə/ *n.* **1** *Anat.* & *Zool.* a bladder, esp. the urinary bladder. **2** (in full **vesica piscis** or **piscium**) *Art* a pointed oval used as an aureole in medieval sculpture and painting. ▫▫ **vesical** *adj.* [L]

vesicate /véssikayt/ *v.tr.* raise blisters on. ▫▫ **vesicant** *adj.* & *n.* **vesication** /-káysh'n/ *n.* **vesicatory** /-káytəri/ *adj.* & *n.* [LL *vesicare vesicat-* (as VESICA)]

vesicle /véssik'l/ *n.* **1** *Anat.*, *Zool.*, & *Bot.* a small bladder, bubble, or hollow structure. **2** *Geol.* a small cavity in volcanic rock produced by gas bubbles. **3** *Med.* a blister. ▫▫ **vesicular** /visíkyoolər/ *adj.* **vesiculate** /visíkyoolət/ *adj.*

vesiculation /visíkyooláysh'n/ *n.* [F *vésicule* or L *vesicula* dimin. of VESICA]

vesper /véspər/ *n.* **1** Venus as the evening star. **2** *poet.* evening. **3** (in *pl.*) **a** the sixth of the canonical hours of prayer. **b** evensong. [L *vesper* evening (star): sense 3 partly f. OF *vespres* f. eccl.L *vesperas* f. L *vespera* evening]

vespertine /véspərtīn, -tin/ *adj.* **1** *Bot.* (of a flower) opening in the evening. **2** *Zool.* active in the evening. **3** *Astron.* setting near the time of sunset. **4** of or occurring in the evening. [L *vespertinus* f. *vesper* evening]

vespiary /véspiəri/ *n.* (*pl.* **-ies**) a nest of wasps. [irreg. f. L *vespa* wasp, after *apiary*]

vespine /véspīn/ *adj.* of or relating to wasps. [L *vespa* wasp]

vessel /véss'l/ *n.* **1** a hollow receptacle esp. for liquid, e.g. a cask, cup, pot, bottle, or dish. **2** a ship or boat, esp. a large one. **3 a** *Anat.* a duct or canal etc. holding or conveying blood or other fluid, esp. = *blood-vessel*. **b** *Bot.* a woody duct carrying or containing sap etc. **4** *Bibl.* or *joc.* a person regarded as the recipient or exponent of a quality (*a weak vessel*). [ME f. AF *vessel(e)*, OF *vaissel(le)* f. LL *vascellum* dimin. of *vas* vessel]

■ **1** container, receptacle, utensil, holder, repository. **2** craft, boat, ship, ark, *poet.* barque, bark, argosy. **3** duct, canal, tube; blood-vessel, vein, *Anat.* venule.

vest /vest/ *n.* & *v.* ● *n.* **1** an undergarment worn on the upper part of the body. **2** *US* & *Austral.* a waistcoat. **3** a usu. V-shaped piece of material to fill the opening at the neck of a woman's dress. ● *v.* **1** *tr.* (esp. in *passive*; foll. by *with*) bestow or confer (powers, authority, etc.) on (a person). **2** *tr.* (foll. by *in*) confer (property or power) on (a person) with an immediate fixed right of immediate or future possession. **3** *intr.* (foll. by *in*) (of property, a right, etc.) come into the possession of (a person). **4 a** *tr. poet.* clothe. **b** *intr. Eccl.* put on vestments. □ **vested interest 1** *Law* an interest (usu. in land or money held in trust) recognized as belonging to a person. **2** a personal interest in a state of affairs, usu. with an expectation of gain. [(n.) F *veste* f. It. *veste* f. L *vestis* garment: (v.) ME, orig. past part. f. OF *vestu* f. *vestir* f. L *vestire vestit-* clothe]

vesta /véstə/ *n. hist.* a short wooden or wax match. [*Vesta*, Roman goddess of the hearth and household]

vestal /vést'l/ *adj.* & *n.* ● *adj.* **1** chaste, pure. **2** of or relating to the Roman goddess Vesta. ● *n.* **1** a chaste woman, esp. a nun. **2** *Rom. Antiq.* a vestal virgin. □ **vestal virgin** *Rom. Antiq.* a virgin consecrated to Vesta and vowed to chastity, who shared the charge of maintaining the sacred fire burning on the goddess's altar. [ME f. L *vestalis* (adj. & n.) (as VESTA)]

■ *adj.* **1** see PURE 3, 4.

vestee /vesteé/ *n.* = VEST *n.* 3.

vestiary /véstiəri/ *n.* & *adj.* ● *n.* (*pl.* **-ies**) **1** a vestry. **2** a robing-room; a cloakroom. ● *adj.* of or relating to clothes or dress. [ME f. OF *vestiarie, vestiaire*: see VESTRY]

vestibule /véstibyoōl/ *n.* **1 a** an antechamber, hall, or lobby next to the outer door of a building. **b** a porch of a church etc. **2** *US* an enclosed entrance to a railway-carriage. **3** *Anat.* **a** a chamber or channel communicating with others. **b** part of the mouth outside the teeth. **c** the central cavity of the labyrinth of the inner ear. □□ **vestibular** /-stíbyoolər/ *adj.* [F *vestibule* or L *vestibulum* entrance-court]

■ **1 a** see HALL 1.

vestige /véstij/ *n.* **1** a trace or piece of evidence; a sign (*vestiges of an earlier civilization*; *found no vestige of their presence*). **2** a slight amount; a particle (*without a vestige of clothing*; *showed not a vestige of decency*). **3** *Biol.* a part or organ of an organism that is reduced or functionless but was well developed in its ancestors. [F f. L *vestigium* footprint]

■ **1** trace, suggestion, hint, inkling, sign, evidence, mark, token, scent; remnant, scrap, fragment, memorial, residue, relic, remains. **2** particle, trace, suggestion, soupçon, hint, glimmer, suspicion, whiff, tinge, taste, touch; iota, jot, speck, scrap, shred, bit, fragment.

vestigial /vestíjiəl, -jəl/ *adj.* **1** being a vestige or trace. **2** *Biol.* (of an organ) atrophied or functionless from the process of evolution (*a vestigial wing*). □□ **vestigially** *adv.*

■ **2** imperfect, undeveloped, underdeveloped, rudimentary, incomplete.

vestiture /véstichər/ *n.* **1** *Zool.* hair, scales, etc., covering a surface. **2** *archaic* **a** clothing. **b** investiture. [ME f. med.L *vestitura* f. L *vestire*: see VEST]

vestment /véstmənt/ *n.* **1** any of the official robes of clergy, choristers, etc., worn during divine service, esp. a chasuble. **2** a garment, esp. an official or state robe. [ME f. OF *vestiment, vestement* f. L *vestimentum* (as VEST)]

■ **2** (*vestments*) see ROBE *n.* 4.

vestry /véstri/ *n.* (*pl.* **-ies**) **1** a room or building attached to a church for keeping vestments in. **2** *hist.* **a** a meeting of parishioners usu. in a vestry for parochial business. **b** a body of parishioners meeting in this way. □□ **vestral** *adj.* [ME f. OF *vestiaire, vestiarie*, f. L *vestiarium* (as VEST)]

vestryman /véstrimən/ *n.* (*pl.* **-men**) a member of a vestry.

vesture /véss-chər/ *n.* & *v.* ● *n. poet.* **1** garments, dress. **2** a covering. ● *v.tr.* clothe. [ME f. OF f. med.L *vestitura* (as VEST)]

vet[1] /vet/ *n.* & *v.* ● *n. colloq.* a veterinary surgeon. ● *v.tr.* (**vetted, vetting**) **1** make a careful and critical examination of (a scheme, work, candidate, etc.). **2** examine or treat (an animal). [abbr.]

■ *n.* veterinary surgeon, veterinary, *US* veterinarian. ● *v.* **1** examine, review, investigate, scrutinize, inspect, check, look over, scan, screen; validate, authenticate; *US* check out, *colloq.* give a thing *or* person the once-over, size up, *Brit. sl.* suss out. **2** see TREAT *v.* 3.

vet[2] /vet/ *n. US colloq.* a veteran. [abbr.]

vetch /vech/ *n.* any plant of the genus *Vicia*, esp. *V. sativa*, largely used for silage or fodder. □□ **vetchy** *adj.* [ME f. AF & ONF *veche* f. L *vicia*]

vetchling /véchling/ *n.* any of various plants of the genus *Lathyrus*, related to vetch.

veteran /véttərən/ *n.* **1** a person who has grown old in or had long experience of esp. military service or an occupation (*a war veteran*; *a veteran of the theatre*; *a veteran marksman*). **2** *US* an ex-serviceman or servicewoman. **3** (*attrib.*) of or for veterans. □ **veteran car** *Brit.* a car made before 1916, or (strictly) before 1905. [F *vétéran* or L *veteranus* (adj. & n.) f. *vetus -eris* old]

■ **1** old hand, past master, trouper, *colloq.* warhorse, *US colloq.* old-timer. **2** ex-serviceman, ex-servicewoman, returned serviceman, returned servicewoman, returned soldier, *US colloq.* vet. **3** (*attrib.*) experienced, practised, seasoned, mature, long-serving, battle-scarred; old.

veterinarian /véttərináiriən/ *n. US* a veterinary surgeon. [L *veterinarius* (as VETERINARY)]

veterinary /véttərinəri/ *adj.* & *n.* ● *adj.* of or for diseases and injuries of farm and domestic animals, or their treatment. ● *n.* (*pl.* **-ies**) a veterinary surgeon. □ **veterinary surgeon** *Brit.* a person qualified to treat diseased or injured animals. [L *veterinarius* f. *veterinae* cattle]

vetiver /véttivər/ *n.* = CUSCUS[1]. [F *vétiver* f. Tamil *veṭṭivēru* f. *vēr* root]

veto /veétō/ *n.* & *v.* ● *n.* (*pl.* **-oes**) **1 a** a constitutional right to reject a legislative enactment. **b** the right of a permanent member of the UN Security Council to reject a resolution. **c** such a rejection. **d** an official message conveying this. **2** a prohibition (*put one's veto on a proposal*). ● *v.tr.* (**-oes, -oed**) **1** exercise a veto against (a measure etc.). **2** forbid authoritatively. □□ **vetoer** *n.* [L, = I forbid, with ref. to its use by Roman tribunes of the people in opposing measures of the Senate]

■ *n.* denial, ban, stoppage, block, embargo, turn-down, thumbs down, rejection, disallowance, quashing, prevention, prohibition, interdiction, taboo, proscription, preclusion. ● *v.* stop, block, deny, ban, turn down, say no to, reject, disallow, rule out, quash, prevent, prohibit, forbid, interdict, taboo, outlaw, proscribe, preclude, *colloq.* kill, *sl.* put the kibosh on, nix, put the mockers on.

vex /veks/ *v.tr.* **1** anger by a slight or a petty annoyance; irritate. **2** *archaic* grieve, afflict. ▫▫ **vexer** *n.* **vexing** *adj.* **vexingly** *adv.* [ME f. OF *vexer* f. L *vexare* shake, disturb]
■ **1** see ANGER *v.* ▫▫ **vexing** see IRKSOME.

vexation /veksáysh'n/ *n.* **1** the act or an instance of vexing; the state of being vexed. **2** an annoying or distressing thing. [ME f. OF *vexation* or L *vexatio -onis* (as VEX)]
■ **1** see ANGER *n.* **2** see PEST 1, WORRY *n.* 1.

vexatious /veksáyshəss/ *adj.* **1** such as to cause vexation. **2** *Law* not having sufficient grounds for action and seeking only to annoy the defendant. ▫▫ **vexatiously** *adv.* **vexatiousness** *n.*
■ **1** see IRKSOME.

vexed /vekst/ *adj.* **1** irritated, angered. **2** (of a problem, issue, etc.) difficult and much discussed; problematic. ▫▫ **vexedly** /véksidli/ *adv.*
■ **1** see ANGRY 1. **2** see DIFFICULT 1b.

vexillology /véksilólləji/ *n.* the study of flags. ▫▫ **vexillological** /-ləlójik'l/ *adj.* **vexillologist** *n.* [VEXILLUM + -LOGY]

vexillum /veksílləm/ *n.* (*pl.* **vexilla** /-lə/) **1** *Rom. Antiq.* **a** a military standard, esp. of a maniple. **b** a body of troops under this. **2** *Bot.* the large upper petal of a papilionaceous flower. **3** *Zool.* the vane of a feather. **4** *Eccl.* **a** a flag attached to a bishop's staff. **b** a processional banner or cross. [L = flag f. *vehere vect-* carry]

VG *abbr.* **1** very good. **2** Vicar-General.

VHF *abbr.* very high frequency.

VI *abbr.* Virgin Islands.

via /vī́ə/ *prep.* by way of; through (*London to Rome via Paris*; *send it via your secretary*). [L, ablat. of *via* way, road]
■ by way of, by means of; see also THROUGH *prep.* 4.

viable /vī́əb'l/ *adj.* **1** (of a plan etc.) feasible; practicable esp. from an economic standpoint. **2 a** (of a plant, animal, etc.) capable of living or existing in a particular climate etc. **b** (of a foetus or newborn child) capable of maintaining life. **3** (of a seed or spore) able to germinate. ▫▫ **viability** /-bílliti/ *n.* **viably** *adv.* [F f. *vie* life f. L *vita*]
■ **1** sustainable, supportable, sensible, reasonable, practical, practicable, applicable, workable, feasible, possible, achievable. ▫▫ **viability** see FEASIBILITY.

viaduct /vī́ədukt/ *n.* **1** a long bridgelike structure, esp. a series of arches, carrying a road or railway across a valley or dip in the ground. **2** such a road or railway. [L *via* way, after AQUEDUCT]

vial /vī́əl/ *n.* a small (usu. cylindrical glass) vessel esp. for holding liquid medicines. ▫▫ **vialful** *n.* (*pl.* **-fuls**). [ME, var. of *fiole* etc.: see PHIAL]

via media /vī́ə méédiə, vééə méddiə/ *n. literary* a middle way or compromise between extremes. [L]

viand /vī́ənd/ *n. formal* **1** an article of food. **2** (in *pl.*) provisions, victuals. [ME f. OF *viande* food, ult. f. L *vivenda*, neut. pl. gerundive of *vivere* to live]

viaticum /vīáttikəm/ *n.* (*pl.* **viatica** /-kə/) **1** the Eucharist as given to a person near or in danger of death. **2** provisions or an official allowance of money for a journey. [L, neut. of *viaticus* f. *via* road]

vibes /vībz/ *n.pl. colloq.* **1** vibrations, esp. in the sense of feelings or atmosphere communicated (*the house had bad vibes*). **2** = VIBRAPHONE. [abbr.]
■ **1** vibrations, feelings, sensations, resonance(s), rapport, empathy, sympathy.

vibraculum /vībrákyooləm/ *n.* (*pl.* **vibracula** /-lə/) *Zool.* a whiplike structure of bryozoans used to bring food within reach by lashing movements. ▫▫ **vibracular** *adj.* [mod.L (as VIBRATE)]

vibrant /vī́brənt/ *adj.* **1** vibrating. **2** (often foll. by *with*) (of a person or thing) thrilling, quivering (*vibrant with emotion*). **3** (of sound) resonant. **4** (of colour) bright and vivid. ▫▫ **vibrancy** *n.* **vibrantly** *adv.* [L *vibrare*: see VIBRATE]
■ **2** see ANIMATED 1. **4** see RICH 8.

vibraphone /vī́brəfōn/ *n.* a percussion instrument of tuned metal bars with motor-driven resonators and metal tubes giving a vibrato effect. ▫▫ **vibraphonist** *n.* [VIBRATO + -PHONE]

vibrate /vībráyt/ *v.* **1** *intr.* & *tr.* move or cause to move continuously and rapidly to and fro; oscillate. **2** *intr. Physics* move unceasingly to and fro, esp. rapidly. **3** *intr.* (of a sound) throb; continue to be heard. **4** *intr.* (foll. by *with*) quiver, thrill (*vibrating with passion*). **5** *intr.* (of a pendulum) swing to and fro. ▫▫ **vibrative** /-rətiv/ *adj.* [L *vibrare vibrat-* shake, swing]
■ **1, 2, 4** quiver, shiver, shudder, fluctuate, quake, shake, tremble, throb, pulsate, palpitate, oscillate, pulse. **3** throb, pulse, pulsate, quaver, quiver, shake, tremble, reverberate, resonate, *esp. Brit.* judder. **5** swing, oscillate.

vibratile /vī́brətīl/ *adj.* **1** capable of vibrating. **2** *Biol.* (of cilia etc.) used in vibratory motion. [VIBRATORY, after *pulsatile* etc.]

vibration /vībráysh'n/ *n.* **1** the act or an instance of vibrating; oscillation. **2** *Physics* (esp. rapid) motion to and fro esp. of the parts of a fluid or an elastic solid whose equilibrium has been disturbed or of an electromagnetic wave. **3** (in *pl.*) **a** a mental (esp. occult) influence. **b** a characteristic atmosphere or feeling in a place, regarded as communicable to people present in it. ▫▫ **vibrational** *adj.* [L *vibratio* (as VIBRATE)]

vibrato /vibraátō/ *n. Mus.* a rapid slight variation in pitch in singing or playing a stringed or wind instrument, producing a tremulous effect (cf. TREMOLO). [It., past part. of *vibrare* VIBRATE]

vibrator /vībráytər/ *n.* **1** a device that vibrates or causes vibration, esp. an electric or other instrument used in massage or for sexual stimulation. **2** *Mus.* a reed in a reed-organ.

vibratory /vī́brətəri, -bráytəri/ *adj.* causing vibration.

vibrissae /vībríssee/ *n.pl.* **1** stiff coarse hairs near the mouth of most mammals (e.g. a cat's whiskers) and in the human nostrils. **2** bristle-like feathers near the mouth of insect-eating birds. [L (as VIBRATE)]

viburnum /vībúrnəm, vi-/ *n. Bot.* any shrub of the genus *Viburnum*, usu. with white flowers, e.g. the guelder rose and wayfaring-tree. [L, = wayfaring-tree]

Vic. *abbr.* Victoria.

vicar /víkkər/ *n.* **1 a** (in the Church of England) an incumbent of a parish where tithes formerly passed to a chapter or religious house or layman (cf. RECTOR). **b** (in an Episcopal Church) a member of the clergy deputizing for another. **2** *RC Ch.* a representative or deputy of a bishop. **3** (in full **lay vicar** or **vicar choral**) a cleric or choir member appointed to sing certain parts of a cathedral service. ▫ **vicar apostolic** *RC Ch.* a Roman Catholic missionary or titular bishop. **vicar-general** (*pl.* **vicars-general**) **1** an Anglican official assisting or representing a bishop esp. in administrative matters. **2** *RC Ch.* a bishop's assistant in matters of jurisdiction etc. **Vicar of Christ** the Pope. ▫▫ **vicariate** /-káiriət/ *n.* **vicarship** *n.* [ME f. AF *viker(e)*, OF *vicaire* f. L *vicarius* substitute f. *vicis*: see VICE[3]]

vicarage /víkkərij/ *n.* the residence or benefice of a vicar.

vicarial /vikáiriəl/ *adj.* of or serving as a vicar.

vicarious /vikáiriəss/ *adj.* **1** experienced in the imagination through another person (*vicarious pleasure*). **2** acting or done for another (*vicarious suffering*). **3** deputed, delegated (*vicarious authority*). ▫▫ **vicariously** *adv.* **vicariousness** *n.* [L *vicarius*: see VICAR]
■ **1** indirect, second-hand. **2** substitute(d), surrogate. **3** delegated, deputed, commissioned, assigned.

vice[1] /vīss/ *n.* **1 a** evil or grossly immoral conduct. **b** a particular form of this, esp. involving prostitution, drugs, etc. **2 a** depravity, evil. **b** an evil habit; a particular form of depravity (*has the vice of gluttony*). **3** a defect of character or behaviour (*drunkenness was not among his vices*). **4** a fault or bad habit in a horse etc. ▫ **vice ring** a group of criminals involved in organizing illegal prostitution. **vice squad** a police department enforcing laws against prostitution, drug abuse, etc. □□ **viceless** *adj.* [ME f. OF f. L *vitium*]

■ **1, 2** immorality, corruption, evil, badness, depravity, degradation, degeneracy, iniquity, villainy, venality, evil-doing, wrongdoing, wickedness, profligacy, sin, sinning, sinfulness, transgression. **3** flaw, defect, fault, imperfection, blemish, shortcoming, failing, weakness, frailty, foible, infirmity, deficiency.

vice[2] /vīss/ *n.* & *v.* ● *n.* (*US* **vise**) an instrument, esp. attached to a workbench, with two movable jaws between which an object may be clamped so as to leave the hands free to work on it. ● *v.tr.* secure in a vice. □□ **vicelike** *adj.* [ME, = winding stair, screw, f. OF *vis* f. L *vitis* vine]

vice[3] /vī́si/ *prep.* in the place of; in succession to. [L, ablat. of *vix* (recorded in oblique forms in *vic-*) change]

vice[4] /vīss/ *n. colloq.* = VICE-PRESIDENT, VICE ADMIRAL, etc. [abbr.]

vice- /vīss/ *comb. form* forming nouns meaning: **1** acting as a substitute or deputy for (*vice-president*). **2** next in rank to (*vice admiral*). [as VICE[4]]

vice admiral /vī́ss ádmərəl/ *n.* a naval officer ranking below admiral and above rear admiral. □□ **vice-admiralty** *n.* (*pl.* **-ies**).

vice-chamberlain /vī́ss-cháymbərlin/ *n.* a deputy chamberlain, esp. the deputy of the Lord Chamberlain.

vice-chancellor /vī́ss-chaánsələr/ *n.* a deputy chancellor (esp. of a British university, discharging most of the administrative duties).

vicegerent /vī́ss-jérrənt/ *adj.* & *n.* ● *adj.* exercising delegated power. ● *n.* a vicegerent person; a deputy. □□ **vicegerency** *n.* (*pl.* **-ies**). [med.L *vicegerens* (as VICE[3], L *gerere* carry on)]

vicennial /vīsénniəl/ *adj.* lasting for or occurring every twenty years. [LL *vicennium* period of 20 years f. *vicies* 20 times f. *viginti* 20 + *annus* year]

vice-president /vī́ss-prézzid'nt/ *n.* an official ranking below and deputizing for a president. □□ **vice-presidency** *n.* (*pl.* **-ies**). **vice-presidential** /-dénsh'l/ *adj.*

viceregal /vī́ss-reég'l/ *adj.* of or relating to a viceroy. □□ **viceregally** *adv.*

vicereine /vī́srayn/ *n.* **1** the wife of a viceroy. **2** a woman viceroy. [F (as VICE-, *reine* queen)]

viceroy /vī́sroy/ *n.* a ruler exercising authority on behalf of a sovereign in a colony, province, etc. □□ **viceroyal** /-róyəl/ *adj.* **viceroyalty** /-róyəlti/ *n.* **viceroyship** *n.* [F (as VICE-, *roy* king)]

vicesimal /vīsézzim'l/ *adj.* = VIGESIMAL. [L *vicesimus* twentieth]

vice versa /vī́si vérsə, vīss vérsə/ *adv.* with the order of the terms or conditions changed; the other way round, conversely (*could go from left to right or vice versa*). [L, = the position being reversed (as VICE[3], *versa* ablat. fem. past part. of *vertere* turn)]

■ conversely, contrariwise, to *or* on the contrary, the reverse, the other way round *or* about *or* around.

vichyssoise /veésheeswaáz/ *n.* a creamy soup of leeks and potatoes, usu. served chilled. [F *vichyssois -oise* of Vichy (in France)]

Vichy water /veéshee/ *n.* an effervescent mineral water from Vichy in France.

vicinage /víssinij/ *n.* **1** a neighbourhood; a surrounding district. **2** relation in terms of nearness etc. to neighbours. [ME f. OF *vis(e)nage* ult. f. L *vicinus* neighbour]

vicinal /víssin'l, -sī́n'l/ *adj.* **1** neighbouring, adjacent. **2** of a neighbourhood; local. [F *vicinal* or L *vicinalis* f. *vicinus* neighbour]

vicinity /visínniti/ *n.* (*pl.* **-ies**) **1** a surrounding district. **2** (foll. by *to*) nearness or closeness of place or relationship. □ **in the vicinity** (often foll. by *of*) near (to). [L *vicinitas* (as VICINAL)]

■ **1** area, neighbourhood, locale, vicinage, environs, locality, precincts, purlieus, territory, district, region. **2** nearness, closeness, proximity, propinquity, contiguity. □ **in the vicinity** see NEARBY *adv.*

vicious /víshəss/ *adj.* **1** bad-tempered, spiteful (*a vicious dog*; *vicious remarks*). **2** violent, severe (*a vicious attack*). **3** of the nature of or addicted to vice. **4** (of language or reasoning etc.) faulty or unsound. □ **vicious circle** see CIRCLE *n.* 11. **vicious spiral** continual harmful interaction of causes and effects, esp. as causing repeated rises in both prices and wages. □□ **viciously** *adv.* **viciousness** *n.* [ME f. OF *vicious* or L *vitiosus* f. *vitium* VICE[1]]

■ **1** savage, wild, untamed, ferocious, fearful, bad-tempered, brutal, fierce, fiendish, bestial, feral, brutish, ravening, *poet. or rhet.* fell; malicious, spiteful, mean, nasty, hateful, malevolent, malignant, bitter, acrimonious, rancorous, venomous, vindictive, defamatory, slanderous, scandalous, *sl.* rotten, bitchy. **2** see SAVAGE *adj.* 1. **3** immoral, unprincipled, amoral, barbarous, corrupt, evil, bad, base, depraved, vile, atrocious, execrable, degraded, degrading, degenerate, venal, iniquitous, heinous, odious, perverted, nefarious, wicked, flagitious, devilish, diabolic(al), fiendish, monstrous, profligate, shameful, shameless, abominable, sinful. □□ **viciousness** see BARBARITY 1.

vicissitude /visíssityōōd, vī-/ *n.* **1** a change of circumstances, esp. variation of fortune. **2** *archaic* or *poet.* regular change; alternation. □□ **vicissitudinous** /-tyōōdinəss/ *adj.* [F *vicissitude* or L *vicissitudo -dinis* f. *vicissim* by turns (as VICE[3])]

■ change, mutation, alteration, changeability, mutability, variation, variability, variety, alternation, shift, contrast, flux, fluctuation, unpredictability, inconstancy, uncertainty, flukiness; (*vicissitudes*) ups and downs.

victim /víktim/ *n.* **1** a person injured or killed as a result of an event or circumstance (*a road victim*; *the victims of war*). **2** a person or thing injured or destroyed in pursuit of an object or in gratification of a passion etc. (*the victim of their ruthless ambition*). **3** a prey; a dupe (*fell victim to a confidence trick*). **4** a living creature sacrificed to a deity or in a religious rite. [L *victima*]

■ **1, 2** sufferer, casualty, fatality, injured party, martyr. **3** prey, quarry, target; dupe, gull, fool, butt, fair game, *colloq.* chump, *US colloq.* schlemiel, *sl.* sucker, sap, fall guy, *Austral. sl.* bunny, *Brit. sl.* mug, *esp. US sl.* patsy, *US sl.* schnook. **4** sacrifice, sacrificial lamb, scapegoat, offering.

victimize /víktimīz/ *v.tr.* (also **-ise**) **1** single out (a person) for punishment or unfair treatment, esp. dismissal from employment. **2** make (a person etc.) a victim. □□ **victimization** /-záysh'n/ *n.* **victimizer** *n.*

■ prey on, pursue, go after, pick on, bully, take advantage of, persecute, oppress, torment, exploit, use; cheat, swindle, defraud, dupe, hoodwink, deceive, gull, fool, trick, outwit, take (in), flimflam, screw, rook, *colloq.* outsmart, outfox, *US colloq.* shaft, suck in, *sl.* bilk. □□ **victimization** see PERSECUTION.

victor /víktər/ *n.* a winner in battle or in a contest. [ME f. AF *victo(u)r* or L *victor* f. *vincere vict-* conquer]

■ winner, champion, conqueror, prizewinner, *literary* vanquisher, *colloq.* top dog.

victoria /viktóriə/ *n.* **1** a low light four-wheeled carriage with a collapsible top, seats for two passengers, and a raised driver's seat. **2** a gigantic S. American water lily, *Victoria amazonica*. **3 a** a species of crowned pigeon. **b** a variety of domestic pigeon. **4** (also **victoria plum**) *Brit.* a large red luscious variety of plum. [Queen *Victoria*, d. 1901]

Victoria Cross /viktóriə/ *n.* a decoration awarded for conspicuous bravery in the armed services, instituted by Queen Victoria in 1856.

Victorian /viktóriən/ *adj.* & *n.* ● *adj.* **1** of or characteristic of the time of Queen Victoria. **2** associated with attitudes attributed to this time, esp. of prudery and moral strictness. ● *n.* a person, esp. a writer, of this time. □□ **Victorianism** *n.*

Victoriana /viktóriaánə/ *n.pl.* **1** articles, esp. collectors' items, of the Victorian period. **2** attitudes characteristic of this period.

Victoria sandwich /viktóriə/ *n.* (also **Victoria sponge**) a sponge cake consisting of two layers of sponge with a jam filling.

victorious /viktóriəss/ *adj.* **1** having won a victory; conquering, triumphant. **2** marked by victory (*victorious day*). □□ **victoriously** *adv.* **victoriousness** *n.* [ME f. AF *victorious*, OF *victorieux*, f. L *victoriosus* (as VICTORY)]
▪ **1** triumphant, successful, champion, conquering, prevailing, winning.

victor ludorum /víktər loodórəm/ *n.* the overall champion in a sports competition. [L, = victor of the games]

victory /víktəri/ *n.* (*pl.* **-ies**) **1** the process of defeating an enemy in battle or war or an opponent in a contest. **2** an instance of this; a triumph. [ME f. AF *victorie*, OF *victoire*, f. L *victoria* (as VICTOR)]
▪ **1** triumph, supremacy, superiority, success, overcoming, mastery, winning, quelling, crushing. **2** triumph, conquest, success, win, walk-over.

victual /vítt'l/ *n.* & *v.* ● *n.* (usu. in *pl.*) food, provisions, esp. as prepared for use. ● *v.* (**victualled, victualling**; *US* **victualed, victualing**) **1** *tr.* supply with victuals. **2** *intr.* obtain stores. **3** *intr.* eat victuals. □□ **victualless** *adj.* [ME f. OF *vitaille* f. LL *victualia*, neut. pl. of L *victualis* f. *victus* food, rel. to *vivere* live]
▪ *n.* (*victuals*) see FOOD 1.

victualler /vítlər/ *n.* (*US* **victualer**) **1 a** a person etc. who supplies victuals. **b** (in full **licensed victualler**) *Brit.* a publican etc. licensed to sell alcoholic liquor. **2** a ship carrying stores for other ships. [ME f. OF *vitaill(i)er*, *vitaillour* (as VICTUAL)]

vicuña /vikyóonə/ *n.* **1** a S. American mammal, *Vicugna vicugna*, related to the llama, with fine silky wool. **2 a** cloth made from its wool. **b** an imitation of this. [Sp. f. Quechua]

vide /vídday, veé-, vídi/ *v.tr.* (as an instruction in a reference to a passage in a book etc.) see, consult. [L, imper. of *vidēre* see]

videlicet /vidélliset/ *adv.* = VIZ. [ME f. L f. *vidēre* see + *licet* it is permissible]

video /víddiō/ *adj.*, *n.*, & *v.* ● *adj.* **1** relating to the recording, reproducing, or broadcasting of visual images on magnetic tape. **2** relating to the broadcasting of television pictures. ● *n.* (*pl.* **-os**) **1** the process of recording, reproducing, or broadcasting visual images on magnetic tape. **2** the visual element of television broadcasts. **3** *colloq.* = *video recorder*. **4** a film etc. recorded on a videotape. ● *v.tr.* (**-oes, -oed**) make a video recording of. □ **video cassette** a cassette of videotape. **video frequency** a frequency in the range used for video signals in television. **video game** a game played by electronically manipulating images produced by a computer program on a television screen. **video nasty** *colloq.* an explicitly horrific or pornographic video film. **video** (or **video cassette**) **recorder** an apparatus for recording and playing videotapes. **video signal** a signal containing information for producing a television image. [L *vidēre* see, after AUDIO]
▪ *n.* **4** see TAPE *n.* 4, FILM *n.* 3a. ● *v.* see TAPE *v.* 3, FILM *v.* 1.

videodisc /víddiōdisk/ *n.* a metal-coated disc on which visual material is recorded for reproduction on a television screen.

videophone /víddiōfōn/ *n.* a telephone device transmitting a visual image as well as sound.

videotape /víddiōtayp/ *n.* & *v.* ● *n.* magnetic tape for recording television pictures and sound. ● *v.tr.* make a recording of (broadcast material etc.) with this. □ **videotape recorder** = *video recorder*.
▪ *n.* see TAPE *n.* 4. ● *v.* see TAPE *v.* 3, FILM *v.* 1.

videotex /víddiōteks/ *n.* (also **videotext** /-tekst/) any electronic information system, esp. teletext or viewdata.

vidimus /vídiməss/ *n.* an inspection or certified copy of accounts etc. [L, = we have seen f. *vidēre* see]

vie /vī/ *v.intr.* (**vying**) (often foll. by *with*) compete; strive for superiority (*vied with each other for recognition*). [prob. f. ME (as ENVY)]
▪ compete, contend, struggle, strive.

vielle /vi-él/ *n.* a hurdy-gurdy. [F f. OF *viel(l)e*: see VIOL]

Vienna schnitzel see SCHNITZEL.

Viennese /veéəneéz/ *adj.* & *n.* ● *adj.* of, relating to, or associated with Vienna in Austria. ● *n.* (*pl.* same) a native or citizen of Vienna.

Vietnamese /vee-étnəmeéz/ *adj.* & *n.* ● *adj.* of or relating to Vietnam in SE Asia. ● *n.* (*pl.* same) **1** a native or national of Vietnam. **2** the language of Vietnam.

vieux jeu /vyö zhö/ *adj.* old-fashioned, hackneyed. [F, lit. old game]

view /vyōō/ *n.* & *v.* ● *n.* **1** range of vision; extent of visibility (*came into view; in full view of the crowd*). **2 a** what is seen from a particular point; a scene or prospect (*a fine view of the downs; a room with a view*). **b** a picture etc. representing this. **3** an inspection by the eye or mind; a visual or mental survey. **4** an opportunity for visual inspection; a viewing (*a private view of the exhibition*). **5 a** an opinion (*holds strong views on morality*). **b** a mental attitude (*took a favourable view of the matter*). **c** a manner of considering a thing (*took a long-term view of it*). ● *v.* **1** *tr.* look at; survey visually; inspect (*we are going to view the house*). **2** *tr.* examine; survey mentally (*different ways of viewing a subject*). **3** *tr.* form a mental impression or opinion of; consider (*does not view the matter in the same light*). **4** *intr.* watch television. **5** *tr.* see (a fox) break cover. □ **have in view 1** have as one's object. **2** bear (a circumstance) in mind in forming a judgement etc. **in view of** having regard to; considering. **on view** being shown (for observation or inspection); being exhibited. **view halloo** *Hunting* a shout on seeing a fox break cover. **with a view to 1** with the hope or intention of. **2** with the aim of attaining (*with a view to marriage*). □□ **viewable** *adj.* [ME f. AF *v(i)ewe*, OF *vēue* fem. past part. f. *vēoir* see f. L *vidēre*]
▪ *n.* **1** sight, vision. **2 a** outlook, aspect, prospect, scene, perspective, vista, panorama, spectacle; landscape, seascape, cityscape. **b** representation, projection, perspective, panorama, picture, tableau; landscape, seascape, cityscape. **3** inspection, survey, observation, scrutiny, examination, contemplation, study. **4** viewing, inspection. **5** opinion, point of view, angle, approach, position, judgement, belief, conviction, attitude, way of thinking, conception, understanding, impression, feeling, sentiment, notion. ● *v.* **1** look at *or* upon *or* over, see, take in, watch, observe, scrutinize, contemplate, gaze at, examine, inspect, survey, regard, witness, *literary* behold. **2** see SURVEY *v.* 1, 2. **3** regard, consider, think of, look on *or* upon, judge, believe, hold, estimate, rate, gauge, assess, *formal* deem. □ **in view of** in (the) light of, considering, in consideration of, having regard to, because of, on account of. **with a view to** with the aim *or* direction *or* intent *or* intention *or* purpose *or* objective *or* object *or* expectation *or* prospect *or* vision *or* hope *or* dream of. □□ **viewable** see PUBLIC *adj.* 3, OPEN *adj.* 9–11.

viewdata /vyóodaytə/ *n.* a news and information service from a computer source to which a television screen is connected by telephone link.

viewer /vyóoər/ *n.* **1** a person who views. **2** a person watching television. **3** a device for looking at film transparencies etc.

viewfinder /vyóofīndər/ *n.* a device on a camera showing the area covered by the lens in taking a photograph.

viewing /vyóoing/ *n.* **1** an opportunity or occasion to view; an exhibition. **2** the act or practice of watching television.

viewless /vyóoliss/ *adj.* **1** not having or affording a view. **2** lacking opinions.

viewpoint /vyóopoynt/ *n.* a point of view, a standpoint.
▪ standpoint, (point of) view, attitude, angle, slant, position, stance, vantage point, perspective, frame of reference, way of thinking, context.

vigesimal /vijéssim'l, vī-/ *adj.* **1** of twentieths or twenty. **2** reckoning or reckoned by twenties. □□ **vigesimally** *adv.* [L *vigesimus* f. *viginti* twenty]

vigil /víjil/ *n.* **1 a** keeping awake during the time usually given to sleep, esp. to keep watch or pray (*keep vigil*). **b** a period of this. **2** *Eccl.* the eve of a festival or holy day. **3** (in *pl.*) nocturnal devotions. [ME f. OF *vigile* f. L *vigilia* f. *vigil* awake]
■ **1** see WATCH *n.* 2, WAKE[1] *n.*

vigilance /víjiləns/ *n.* watchfulness, caution, circumspection. □ **vigilance committee** *US* a self-appointed body for the maintenance of order etc. [F *vigilance* or L *vigilantia* f. *vigilare* keep awake (as VIGIL)]
■ watchfulness, alertness, observance, guardedness, circumspection, attentiveness, caution, care.

vigilant /víjilənt/ *adj.* watchful against danger, difficulty, etc. □□ **vigilantly** *adv.* [L *vigilans -antis* (as VIGILANCE)]
■ watchful, alert, sharp, observant, guarded, circumspect, attentive, wakeful, awake, cautious, careful, wary, chary, on one's guard, on the alert, on the lookout, eagle-eyed, hawk-eyed, Argus-eyed, on the qui vive, on one's toes, with one's eyes open *or* skinned *or* peeled. □□ **vigilantly** see *attentively* (ATTENTIVE).

vigilante /víjilánti/ *n.* a member of a vigilance committee or similar body. [Sp., = vigilant]

vigneron /véenyəron/ *n.* a vine-grower. [F f. *vigne* VINE]

vignette /veenyét/ *n.* & *v.* ● *n.* **1** a short descriptive essay or character sketch. **2** an illustration or decorative design, esp. on the title-page of a book, not enclosed in a definite border. **3** a photograph or portrait showing only the head and shoulders with the background gradually shaded off. ● *v.tr.* **1** make a portrait of (a person) in vignette style. **2** shade off (a photograph or portrait). □□ **vignettist** *n.* [F, dimin. of *vigne* VINE]
■ *n.* **1** see PROFILE *n.* 2a.

vigor *US* var. of VIGOUR.

vigorish /víggərish/ *n. US sl.* the percentage deducted by the organizers of a game from a gambler's winnings; also, an excessive rate of interest on a loan. [prob. f. Yiddish f. Russ. *vȳigrȳsh* gain, winnings]

vigoro /víggərō/ *n. Austral.* a team ball game combining elements of cricket and baseball. [app. f. VIGOROUS]

vigorous /víggərəss/ *adj.* **1** strong and active; robust. **2** (of a plant) growing strongly. **3** forceful; acting or done with physical or mental vigour; energetic. **4** full of vigour; showing or requiring physical strength or activity. □□ **vigorously** *adv.* **vigorousness** *n.* [ME f. OF f. med.L *vigorosus* f. L *vigor* (as VIGOUR)]
■ **1, 3, 4** energetic, active, vivacious, dynamic, brisk, lively, spirited, forceful, zestful, robust, strong, strenuous, hardy, hale, hearty, vital, fit, lusty, stalwart, in good *or* fine fettle, spry, sprightly, resilient, *colloq.* peppy, full of pep, full of get-up-and-go, full of beans, zippy, snappy. **2** strong, robust, hardy, sturdy, flourishing, tough. □□ **vigorously** energetically, actively, vivaciously, animatedly, dynamically, briskly, spiritedly, robustly, strongly, forcefully, hardily, heartily, lustily, stalwartly, eagerly, with might and main, with a vengeance, strenuously, *colloq.* like mad, like crazy, hammer and tongs. **vigorousness** see STAMINA.

vigour /víggər/ *n.* (*US* **vigor**) **1** active physical strength or energy. **2** a flourishing physical condition. **3** healthy growth; vitality; vital force. **4 a** mental strength or activity shown in thought or speech or in literary style. **b** forcefulness; trenchancy, animation. □□ **vigourless** *adj.* [ME f. OF *vigour* f. L *vigor -oris* f. *vigēre* be lively]
■ **1** vitality, resilience, strength, power, potency, energy, forcefulness, force, stamina, endurance, mettle, mettlesomeness, pith, dynamism, spirit, liveliness, animation, *joie de vivre*, verve, vivacity, exuberance, brio, dash, briskness, zest, zeal, zealousness, enthusiasm, gusto, drive, eagerness, *colloq.* spunk, pep, vim, zing, get-up-and-go, *sl.* pizazz, oomph, zap. **3** see HEALTH 1.

vihara /vihaárə/ *n.* a Buddhist temple or monastery. [Skr.]

Viking /víking/ *n.* & *adj.* ● *n.* any of the Scandinavian seafaring pirates and traders who raided and settled in parts of NW Europe in the 8th–11th c. ● *adj.* of or relating to the Vikings or their time. [ON *víkingr*, perh. f. OE *wīcing* f. *wīc* camp]

vile /vīl/ *adj.* **1** disgusting. **2** morally base; depraved, shameful. **3** *colloq.* abominably bad (*vile weather*). **4** *archaic* worthless. □□ **vilely** *adv.* **vileness** *n.* [ME f. OF *vil vile* f. L *vilis* cheap, base]
■ **1** disgusting, nasty, sickening, nauseous, nauseating, foul, loathsome, offensive, noxious, obnoxious, objectionable, revolting, repulsive, repellent, repugnant. **2** base, abject, contemptible, debased, degenerate, depraved, bad, iniquitous, execrable, atrocious, sordid, immoral, amoral, wicked, evil, sinful, hellish, fiendish, ignoble, revolting, repulsive, despicable, odious, heinous, monstrous, horrid, horrible, dreadful, terrible, corrupt, mean, wretched, miserable, degrading, ignominious, disgraceful, shameful, shameless. **3** atrocious, foul, unpleasant, bad, wretched, woeful, miserable, *colloq.* abominable, abysmal, villainous, lousy, dreadful, horrible, horrid, terrible, awful, *sl.* rotten, stinking. □□ **vileness** see EVIL *n.* 2.

vilify /víllifī/ *v.tr.* (**-ies**, **-ied**) defame; speak evil of. □□ **vilification** /-fikáysh'n/ *n.* **vilifier** *n.* [ME in sense 'lower in value', f. LL *vilificare* (as VILE)]
■ depreciate, devalue, deprecate, debase, disparage, denigrate, diminish, discredit, traduce, defame, speak ill of, revile, slander, libel, abuse, defile, sully, smear, blacken, tarnish, malign, calumniate, asperse, run down, decry, *US* bad-mouth, *sl.* knock. □□ **vilification** see SLANDER *n.*

vill /vil/ *n. hist.* a feudal township. [AF f. OF *vile*, *ville* farm f. L (as VILLA)]

villa /víllə/ *n.* **1** *Rom. Antiq.* a large country house with an estate. **2** a country residence. **3** *Brit.* a detached or semi-detached house in a residential district. **4** a rented holiday home, esp. abroad. [It. & L]

village /víllij/ *n.* **1 a** a group of houses and associated buildings, larger than a hamlet and smaller than a town, esp. in a rural area. **b** the inhabitants of a village regarded as a community. **2** *Brit.* a self-contained district or community within a town or city, regarded as having features characteristic of village life. **3** *US* a small municipality with limited corporate powers. **4** *Austral.* a select suburban shopping centre. □□ **villager** *n.* **villagey** *adj.* [ME f. OF f. L *villa*]

villain /víllən/ *n.* **1** a person guilty or capable of great wickedness. **2** *colloq.* usu. *joc.* a rascal or rogue. **3** (also **villain of the piece**) (in a play etc.) a character whose evil actions or motives are important in the plot. **4** *Brit. colloq.* a professional criminal. **5** *archaic* a rustic; a boor. [ME f. OF *vilein*, *vilain* ult. f. L *villa*: see VILLA]
■ **1, 3** wretch, evil-doer, criminal, felon, lawbreaker, miscreant, blackguard, malefactor, wrongdoer, scoundrel, cur, viper, reptile, snake in the grass, *colloq.* crook, dog, baddy. **2** rogue, cad, knave, scallywag, scoundrel, *archaic or joc.* rapscallion, *colloq.* rat, scamp, *colloq. or joc.* bounder, *Brit. colloq.* blighter, *often joc.* rascal, *poet. or archaic* caitiff, *sl.* bastard, son of a bitch, *esp. Brit. sl.* rotter, *esp. US sl.* S.O.B.

villainous /víllənəss/ *adj.* **1** characteristic of a villain; wicked. **2** *colloq.* abominably bad; vile (*villainous weather*). □□ **villainously** *adv.* **villainousness** *n.*
■ **1** treacherous, perfidious, dishonest, unscrupulous, traitorous, corrupt, faithless, criminal, felonious, murderous; base, abject, contemptible, debased, degenerate, depraved, bad, iniquitous, execrable, atrocious, sordid, immoral, amoral, wicked, evil, sinful, hellish, fiendish, ignoble, revolting, despicable, rotten, horrid, horrible, dreadful, terrible, mean, wretched, miserable, degrading, ignominious, disgraceful, shameful, shameless, *colloq.* crooked, *sl.* bent. **2** see VILE 3. □□ **villainously** see BADLY 1.

villainy /vílləni/ *n.* (*pl.* **-ies**) **1** villainous behaviour. **2** a wicked act. [OF *vilenie* (as VILLAIN)]

■ **1** see DEVILRY. **2** see ATROCITY 1.

villanelle /villənél/ *n.* a usu. pastoral or lyrical poem of 19 lines, with only two rhymes throughout, and some lines repeated. [F f. It. *villanella* fem. of *villanello* rural, dimin. of *villano* (as VILLAIN)]

-ville /vil/ *comb. form colloq.* forming the names of fictitious places with ref. to a particular quality etc. (*dragsville*; *squaresville*). [F *ville* town, as in many US town-names]

villein /víllin/ *n. hist.* a feudal tenant entirely subject to a lord or attached to a manor. [ME, var. of VILLAIN]

villeinage /víllinij/ *n. hist.* the tenure or status of a villein.

villus /vílləss/ *n.* (*pl.* **villi** /-lī/) **1** *Anat.* each of the short finger-like processes on some membranes, esp. on the mucous membrane of the small intestine. **2** *Bot.* (in *pl.*) long soft hairs covering fruit, flowers, etc. ▫▫ **villiform** *adj.* **villose** *adj.* **villosity** /-lóssiti/ *n.* **villous** *adj.* [L, = shaggy hair]

vim /vim/ *n. colloq.* vigour. [perh. f. L, accus. of *vis* energy]
■ see VIGOUR 1.

vimineous /vimínniəss/ *adj. Bot.* of or producing twigs or shoots. [L *vimineus* f. *vimen viminis* osier]

vina /veénə/ *n.* an Indian four-stringed musical instrument with a fretted finger-board and a gourd at each end. [Skr. & Hindi *vīṇā*]

vinaceous /vīnáyshəss/ *adj.* wine-red. [L *vinaceus* f. *vinum* wine]

vinaigrette /vínnigrét/ *n.* **1** (in full **vinaigrette sauce**) a salad dressing of oil, wine vinegar, and seasoning. **2** a small ornamental bottle for holding smelling-salts. [F, dimin. of *vinaigre* VINEGAR]

vincible /vínsib'l/ *adj. literary* that can be overcome or conquered. ▫▫ **vincibility** /-bílliti/ *n.* [L *vincibilis* f. *vincere* overcome]

vinculum /víngkyooləm/ *n.* (*pl.* **vincula** /-lə/) **1** *Algebra* a horizontal line drawn over a group of terms to show they have a common relation to what follows or precedes (e.g. $a + \overline{b \times c} = ac + bc$, but $a + b \times c = a + bc$). **2** *Anat.* a ligament; a fraenum. [L, = bond, f. *vincire* bind]

vindicate /víndikayt/ *v.tr.* **1** clear of blame or suspicion. **2** establish the existence, merits, or justice of (one's courage, conduct, assertion, etc.). **3** justify (a person, oneself, etc.) by evidence or argument. ▫▫ **vindicable** /-kəb'l/ *adj.* **vindication** /-káysh'n/ *n.* **vindicative** /-kətiv/ *adj.* **vindicator** *n.* [L *vindicare* claim, avenge f. *vindex -dicis* claimant, avenger]
■ **1** clear, exonerate, absolve, acquit, excuse, *formal* exculpate. **2** justify, support, uphold, prove, defend. **3** justify, defend, bear out, back up. ▫▫ **vindication** see DEFENCE 4a.

vindicatory /víndikaytəri/ *adj.* **1** tending to vindicate. **2** (of laws) punitive.

vindictive /vindíktiv/ *adj.* **1** tending to seek revenge. **2** spiteful. ▫ **vindictive damages** *Law* damages exceeding simple compensation and awarded to punish the defendant. ▫▫ **vindictively** *adv.* **vindictiveness** *n.* [L *vindicta* vengeance (as VINDICATE)]
■ **1** avenging, vengeful, vindicatory, revengeful, retaliatory, retaliative, retributory, retributive, punitive. **2** spiteful, unforgiving, splenetic, malevolent, malicious, resentful, rancorous, implacable. ▫▫ **vindictiveness** see REVENGE *n.* 3, RANCOUR.

vine /vīn/ *n.* **1** any climbing or trailing woody-stemmed plant, esp. of the genus *Vitis*, bearing grapes. **2** a slender trailing or climbing stem. ▫ **vine-dresser** a person who prunes, trains, and cultivates vines. ▫▫ **viny** *adj.* [ME f. OF *vi(g)ne* f. L *vinea* vineyard f. *vinum* wine]

vinegar /vínnigər/ *n.* **1** a sour liquid obtained from wine, cider, etc., by fermentation and used as a condiment or for pickling. **2** sour behaviour or character. ▫▫ **vinegarish** *adj.* **vinegary** *adj.* [ME f. OF *vyn egre* ult. f. L *vinum* wine + *acer, acre* sour]
■ ▫▫ **vinegary** see SOUR *adj.* 1.

vinery /vī́nəri/ *n.* (*pl.* **-ies**) **1** a greenhouse for grapevines. **2** a vineyard.

vineyard /vínyaard, -yərd/ *n.* **1** a plantation of grapevines, esp. for wine-making. **2** *Bibl.* a sphere of action or labour (see Matt. 20:1). [ME f. VINE + YARD[2]]

vingt-et-un /vántayṓn/ *n.* = PONTOON[1]. [F, = twenty-one]

vini- /vínni/ *comb. form* wine. [L *vinum*]

viniculture /vínnikulchər/ *n.* the cultivation of grapevines. ▫▫ **vinicultural** /-kúlchərəl/ *adj.* **viniculturist** /-kúlchərist/ *n.*

vinification /vínnifikáysh'n/ *n.* the conversion of grape-juice etc. into wine.

vining /vī́ning/ *n.* the separation of leguminous crops from their vines and pods.

vino /veénō/ *n. sl.* wine, esp. of an inferior kind. [Sp. & It., = wine]

vin ordinaire /váN ordináir/ *n.* cheap (usu. red) wine as drunk in France mixed with water. [F, = ordinary wine]

vinous /vī́nəss/ *adj.* **1** of, like, or associated with wine. **2** addicted to wine. ▫▫ **vinosity** /-nóssiti/ *n.* [L *vinum* wine]

vin rosé /váN rōzáy/ *n.* = ROSÉ. [F]

vint[1] /vint/ *v.tr.* make (wine). [back-form. f. VINTAGE]

vint[2] /vint/ *n.* a Russian card-game like auction bridge. [Russ., = screw]

vintage /víntij/ *n.* & *adj.* ● *n.* **1 a** a season's produce of grapes. **b** the wine made from this. **2 a** the gathering of grapes for wine-making. **b** the season of this. **3** a wine of high quality from a single identified year and district. **4 a** the year etc. when a thing was made etc. **b** a thing made etc. in a particular year etc. **5** *poet.* or *rhet.* wine. ● *adj.* **1** of high quality, esp. from the past or characteristic of the best period of a person's work. **2** of a past season. ▫ **vintage car** *Brit.* a car made between 1917 and 1930. **vintage festival** a carnival to celebrate the beginning of the vintage. [alt. (after VINTNER) of ME *vendage*, *vindage* f. OF *vendange* f. L *vindemia* f. *vinum* wine + *demere* remove]
■ *n.* **1** year, crop, harvest. **2** harvest. **4** year, date, period, generation, origin. ● *adj.* **1** quality, choice, superior, better, good, high-quality, select, best, classic; aged, seasoned, mature(d), mellow(ed). **2** antiquated, old-fashioned, old-fogyish, antique, bygone, old-time, collector('s), *colloq.* over the hill.

vintager /víntijər/ *n.* a grape-gatherer.

vintner /víntnər/ *n.* a wine-merchant. [ME f. AL *vintenarius*, *vinetarius* f. AF *vineter*, OF *vinetier* f. med.L *vinetarius* f. L *vinetum* vineyard f. *vinum* wine]

viny see VINE.

vinyl /vī́nil/ *n.* any plastic made by polymerizing a compound containing the vinyl group, esp. polyvinyl chloride. ▫ **vinyl group** the organic radical or group CH_2CH. [L *vinum* wine + -YL]

viol /vī́əl/ *n.* a medieval stringed musical instrument, played with a bow and held vertically on the knees or between the legs. [ME *viel* etc. f. OF *viel(l)e*, alt. of *viole* f. Prov. *viola*, *viula*, prob. ult. f. L *vitulari* be joyful: cf. FIDDLE]

viola[1] /viṓlə/ *n.* **1 a** an instrument of the violin family, larger than the violin and of lower pitch. **b** a viola-player. **2** a viol. ▫ **viola da braccio** /də braáchō/ a viol corresponding to the modern viola. **viola da gamba** /də gámbə/ a viol held between the player's legs, esp. one corresponding to the modern cello. **viola d'amore** /damóray/ a sweet-toned tenor viol. [It. & Sp., prob. f. Prov.: see VIOL]

viola[2] /vī́ələ/ *n.* **1** any plant of the genus *Viola*, including the pansy and violet. **2** a cultivated hybrid of this genus. [L, = violet]

violaceous /vīəláyshəss/ *adj.* **1** of a violet colour. **2** *Bot.* of the violet family Violaceae. [L *violaceus* (as VIOLA[2])]

violate /vī́əlayt/ *v.tr.* **1** disregard; fail to comply with (an oath, treaty, law, etc.). **2** treat (a sanctuary etc.) profanely or with disrespect. **3** break in upon, disturb (a person's privacy etc.). **4** assault sexually; rape. ▫▫ **violable** *adj.*

violation /-láysh'n/ *n.* **violator** *n.* [ME f. L *violare* treat violently]

■ **1** break, breach, disobey, disregard, contravene, infringe, ignore. **2** dishonour, desecrate, profane, defile, degrade, debase, treat irreverently. **3** invade, disturb, abuse, intrude on, trespass on. **4** rape, debauch, deflower, ravish, ravage, molest, attack, assault (sexually), outrage. □□ **violation** infringement, breach, disregard, disobedience, contravention, abuse; profanation, sacrilege, desecration, defilement, degradation, dishonour, debasement; rape, ravishment, molestation, attack, outrage, assault.

violence /vī́ələnss/ *n.* **1** the quality of being violent. **2** violent conduct or treatment, outrage, injury. **3** *Law* **a** the unlawful exercise of physical force. **b** intimidation by the exhibition of this. □ **do violence to 1** act contrary to; outrage. **2** distort. [ME f. OF f. L *violentia* (as VIOLENT)]

■ **1** (brute *or* physical) force, might, power, strength, severity, intensity, energy, vehemence, ferocity, ferociousness, fierceness, fury, vigour; destructiveness, virulence; bestiality, brutality, barbarity, savagery, cruelty, bloodthirstiness, wildness, frenzy, passion, vehemence, murderousness. **2** see OUTRAGE *n.* 1. □ **do violence to 1** harm, damage, injure, outrage, offend, abuse, violate. **2** warp, twist, distort.

violent /vī́ələnt/ *adj.* **1** involving or using great physical force (*a violent person*; *a violent storm*; *came into violent collision*). **2 a** intense, vehement, passionate, furious (*a violent contrast*; *violent dislike*). **b** vivid (*violent colours*). **3** (of death) resulting from external force or from poison (cf. NATURAL *adj.* 2). **4** involving an unlawful exercise of force (*laid violent hands on him*). □□ **violently** *adv.* [ME f. OF f. L *violentus*]

■ **1** wild, physical, brutal, brutish, beastly, nasty, cruel, mean, barbarous, inhuman, savage, fierce, ferocious, furious, frenzied, vicious, uncontrollable, untamed, ungovernable, raging, raving, irrational, insane, crazed, hotheaded, *colloq.* fit to be tied; harmful, injurious, damaging, detrimental, destructive, deleterious, catastrophic, cataclysmic, ruinous, devastating. **2 a** acute, serious, severe, extreme, harsh, trenchant, virulent, intense, energetic, forceful, vehement, passionate, impassioned, impetuous, tempestuous, stormy, furious. **b** see VIVID 1. □□ **violently** see MADLY 2a, *fiercely* (FIERCE).

violet /vī́ələt/ *n.* & *adj.* ● *n.* **1 a** any plant of the genus *Viola*, esp. the sweet violet, with usu. purple, blue, or white flowers. **b** any of various plants resembling the sweet violet. **2** the bluish-purple colour seen at the end of the spectrum opposite red. **3 a** pigment of this colour. **b** clothes or material of this colour. ● *adj.* of this colour. [ME f. OF *violet(te)* dimin. of *viole* f. L VIOLA²]

violin /vī́əlín/ *n.* **1** a musical instrument with four strings of treble pitch played with a bow. **2** a violin-player. □□ **violinist** *n.* [It. *violino* dimin. of VIOLA¹]

■ fiddle.

violist /vī́əlist/ *n.* a viol- or viola-player.

violoncello /vī́ələnchéllō, véeə-/ *n.* (*pl.* **-os**) *formal* = CELLO. □□ **violoncellist** *n.* [It., dimin. of VIOLONE]

violone /viəlṓni/ *n.* a double-bass viol. [It., augment. of VIOLA¹]

VIP *abbr.* very important person.

■ see DIGNITARY.

viper /vī́pər/ *n.* **1** any venomous snake of the family Viperidae, esp. the common viper (see ADDER). **2** a malignant or treacherous person. □ **viper in one's bosom** a person who betrays those who have helped him or her. **viper's bugloss** a stiff bristly blue-flowered plant, *Echium vulgare*. **viper's grass** scorzonera. □□ **viperine** /-rīn/ *adj.* **viperish** *adj.* **viper-like** *adj.* **viperous** *adj.* [F *vipère* or L *vipera* f. *vivus* alive + *parere* bring forth]

■ **2** see SNAKE *n.* 2.

virago /viraágō, -ráygō/ *n.* (*pl.* **-os**) **1** a fierce or abusive woman. **2** *archaic* a woman of masculine strength or spirit. [OE f. L, = female warrior, f. *vir* man]

■ see FURY 5.

viral /vī́rəl/ *adj.* of or caused by a virus. □□ **virally** *adv.*

virelay /vírrilay/ *n.* a short (esp. old French) lyric poem with two rhymes to a stanza variously arranged. [ME f. OF *virelai*]

virement /vī́rmənt, véermoN/ *n.* the transfer of items from one financial account to another. [F f. *virer* turn: see VEER¹]

vireo /vírriō/ *n.* (*pl.* **-os**) any small American songbird of the family Vireonidae. [L, perh. = greenfinch]

virescence /viréss'nss/ *n.* **1** greenness. **2** *Bot.* abnormal greenness in petals etc. normally of some bright colour. □□ **virescent** *adj.* [L *virescere*, incept. of *virēre* be green]

virgate¹ /vúrgət/ *adj. Bot.* & *Zool.* slim, straight, and erect. [L *virgatus* f. *virga* rod]

virgate² /vúrgət/ *n. Brit. hist.* a varying measure of land, esp. 30 acres. [med.L *virgata* (rendering OE *gierd-land* yard-land) f. L *virga* rod]

virger var. of VERGER.

Virgilian /vurjílliən/ *adj.* of, or in the style of, the Roman poet Virgil (d. 19 BC). [L *Vergilianus* f. P. *Vergilius* Maro, Virgil]

virgin /vúrjin/ *n.* & *adj.* ● *n.* **1** a person (esp. a woman) who has never had sexual intercourse. **2 a** (**the Virgin**) Christ's mother the Blessed Virgin Mary. **b** a picture or statue of the Virgin. **3** (**the Virgin**) the zodiacal sign or constellation Virgo. **4** *colloq.* a naïve, innocent, or inexperienced person (*a political virgin*). **5** a member of any order of women under a vow to remain virgins. **6** a female insect producing eggs without impregnation. ● *adj.* **1** that is a virgin. **2** of or befitting a virgin (*virgin modesty*). **3** not yet used, penetrated, or tried (*virgin soil*). **4** undefiled, spotless. **5** (of clay) not fired. **6** (of metal) made from ore by smelting. **7** (of wool) not yet, or only once, spun or woven. **8** (of an insect) producing eggs without impregnation. □ **virgin birth 1** the doctrine of Christ's birth without a human father. **2** parthenogenesis. **virgin comb** a honeycomb that has been used only once for honey and never for brood. **virgin forest** a forest in its untouched natural state. **virgin honey** honey taken from a virgin comb, or drained from the comb without heat or pressure. **virgin queen** an unfertilized queen bee. **the Virgin Queen** Queen Elizabeth I of England. **virgin's bower** a clematis, *Clematis viticella*. □□ **virginhood** *n.* [ME f. AF & OF *virgine* f. L *virgo -ginis*]

■ *adj.* **1, 2** see PURE 3, 4. **3** see UNUSED 1b, UNCHARTED. **4** see UNSPOILED.

virginal /vúrjin'l/ *adj.* & *n.* ● *adj.* that is or befits or belongs to a virgin. ● *n.* (usu. in *pl.*) (in full **pair of virginals**) an early form of spinet in a box, used in the sixteenth and seventeenth centuries. □□ **virginalist** *n.* **virginally** *adv.* [ME f. OF *virginal* or L *virginalis* (as VIRGIN): name of the instrument perh. from its use by young women]

■ *adj.* see PURE 3, 4.

Virginia /vərjínniə/ *n.* **1** tobacco from Virginia. **2** a cigarette made of this. □ **Virginia creeper** a N. American vine, *Parthenocissus quinquefolia*, cultivated for ornament. **Virginia reel** *US* a country dance. **Virginia** (or **Virginian**) **stock** a cruciferous plant, *Malcolmia maritima*, with white or pink flowers. □□ **Virginian** *n.* & *adj.* [*Virginia* in US, orig. the first English settlement (1607), f. *Virgin Queen*]

virginity /vərjínniti/ *n.* the state of being a virgin. [OF *virginité* f. L *virginitas* (as VIRGIN)]

■ see VIRTUE 3.

Virgo /vúrgō/ *n.* (*pl.* **-os**) **1** a constellation, traditionally regarded as contained in the figure of a woman. **2 a** the sixth sign of the zodiac (the Virgin). **b** a person born when the sun is in this sign. □□ **Virgoan** *n.* & *adj.* [OE f. L, = virgin]

virgule /vúrgyool/ *n.* **1** a slanting line used to mark division of words or lines. **2** = SOLIDUS 1. [F, = comma, f. L *virgula* dimin. of *virga* rod]

viridescent /virridéss'nt/ *adj.* greenish, tending to become green. □□ **viridescence** *n.* [LL *viridescere* f. L *viridis*: see VIRIDIAN]

viridian /viríddiən/ *n.* & *adj.* ● *n.* **1** a bluish-green chromium oxide pigment. **2** the colour of this. ● *adj.* bluish-green. [L *viridis* green f. *virēre* be green]

viridity /virídditi/ *n. literary* greenness, verdancy. [ME f. OF *viridité* or L *viriditas* f. *viridis*: see VIRIDIAN]

virile /vírrīl/ *adj.* **1** of or characteristic of a man; having masculine (esp. sexual) vigour or strength. **2** of or having procreative power. **3** of a man as distinct from a woman or child. ▫▫ **virility** /virílliti/ *n.* [ME f. F *viril* or L *virilis* f. *vir* man]
■ **1** see MANLY 1. ▫▫ **virility** see MACHISMO.

virilism /vírriliz'm/ *n. Med.* the development of secondary male characteristics in a female or precociously in a male.

viroid /vīroyd/ *n.* an infectious entity affecting plants, similar to a virus but smaller and consisting only of nucleic acid without a protein coat.

virology /vīrólləji/ *n.* the scientific study of viruses. ▫▫ **virological** /-rəlójik'l/ *adj.* **virologically** /-rəlójikəli/ *adv.* **virologist** *n.*

virtu /vurtóo/ *n.* (also **vertu**) **1** a knowledge of or expertise in the fine arts. **2** virtuosity. ▫ **article** (or **object**) **of virtu** an article interesting because of its workmanship, antiquity, rarity, etc. [It. *virtù* VIRTUE, virtu]

virtual /vúrtyooəl/ *adj.* **1** that is such for practical purposes though not in name or according to strict definition (*is the virtual manager of the business; take this as a virtual promise*). **2** *Optics* relating to the points at which rays would meet if produced backwards (*virtual focus; virtual image*). **3** *Mech.* relating to an infinitesimal displacement of a point in a system. **4** *Computing* not physically existing as such but made by software to appear to do so (*virtual memory*). ▫ **virtual reality** the generation by computer software of an image or environment that appears real to the senses. ▫▫ **virtuality** /-tyoo-álliti/ *n.* **virtually** *adv.* [ME f. med.L *virtualis* f. L *virtus* after LL *virtuosus*]
■ **1** effective, essential; practical, understood, accepted. ▫▫ **virtually** essentially, effectively, practically, almost, to all intents and purposes, for all practical purposes, more or less, nearly, as good as, substantially, in effect, in essence.

virtue /vúrtyoo, -choo/ *n.* **1** moral excellence; uprightness, goodness. **2** a particular form of this (*patience is a virtue*). **3** chastity, esp. of a woman. **4** a good quality (*has the virtue of being adjustable*). **5** efficacy; inherent power (*no virtue in such drugs*). **6** an angelic being of the seventh order of the celestial hierarchy (see ORDER *n.* 19). ▫ **by** (or **in**) **virtue of** on the strength or ground of (*got the job by virtue of his experience*). **make a virtue of necessity** derive some credit or benefit from an unwelcome obligation. ▫▫ **virtueless** *adj.* [ME f. OF *vertu* f. L *virtus -tutis* f. *vir* man]
■ **1** morality, high-mindedness, honour, goodness, justness, righteousness, fairness, integrity, right-mindedness, honesty, probity, uprightness, rectitude, decency, worth, worthiness, nobility, character, respectability, virtuousness. **3** virginity, chastity, chasteness, honour, innocence, purity. **4** quality, credit, merit, strength, good point, strong point, advantage, asset. ▫ **by** (or **in**) **virtue of** by dint of, owing to, thanks to, by reason of, because of, on account of, on the strength of, on the grounds of.

virtuoso /vúrtyoo-ósō, -zō/ *n.* (*pl.* **virtuosi** /-see, -zee/ or **-os**) **1 a** a person highly skilled in the technique of a fine art, esp. music. **b** (*attrib.*) displaying the skills of a virtuoso. **2** a person with a special knowledge of or taste for works of art or virtu. ▫▫ **virtuosic** /-tyoo-óssik/ *adj.* **virtuosity** /-tyoo-óssiti/ *n.* **virtuosoship** *n.* [It., = learned, skilful, f. LL (as VIRTUOUS)]
■ **1 a** master, maestro, expert, genius, talent, prodigy, old hand, wizard, *colloq.* whiz, whiz-kid, *esp. Brit. colloq.* dab hand, *US colloq.* maven. **b** masterful, masterly, expert, talented, brilliant, dazzling, bravura, prodigious, excellent, superb, extraordinary, exceptional, superior, first-rate, superlative, matchless, peerless, sterling, marvellous, remarkable. ▫▫ **virtuosity** (technical) skill, technique, ability, expertise, mastery, virtu, excellence, brilliance, craftsmanship, craft, flair, dash, *élan*, éclat, panache, pyrotechnics, showmanship, show, staginess, *sl.* razzle-dazzle.

virtuous /vúrtyooəss, vúrchooəss/ *adj.* **1** possessing or showing moral rectitude. **2** chaste. ▫ **virtuous circle** a beneficial recurring cycle of cause and effect (cf. *vicious circle* (see CIRCLE *n.* 11)). ▫▫ **virtuously** *adv.* **virtuousness** *n.* [ME f. OF *vertuous* f. LL *virtuosus* f. *virtus* VIRTUE]
■ **1** moral, honourable, ethical, honest, good, upstanding, high-principled, upright, righteous, right, pure, uncorrupted, incorruptible, blameless, irreproachable, unimpeachable, just, fair, right-minded, fair-minded, high-minded, scrupulous, trustworthy. **2** chaste, innocent, virginal, virgin, pure; decent, proper, unsullied, faithful, true, uncorrupted. ▫▫ **virtuousness** see HONOUR *n.* 2, 3.

virulent /vírroolənt, vírryoo-/ *adj.* **1** strongly poisonous. **2** (of a disease) violent or malignant. **3** bitterly hostile (*virulent animosity; virulent abuse*). ▫▫ **virulence** *n.* **virulently** *adv.* [ME, orig. of a poisoned wound, f. L *virulentus* (as VIRUS)]
■ **1, 2** lethal, life-threatening, deadly, fatal, pernicious, septic, poisonous, toxic, baleful, noxious, dangerous, harmful, injurious, detrimental, deleterious, destructive, malignant, unhealthy, unwholesome. **3** vicious, venomous, bitter, spiteful, malignant, malign, malicious, malevolent, poisonous, splenetic, acrimonious, acerbic, acid, mordant, sarcastic, nasty, trenchant, caustic, antagonistic, hateful, hostile. ▫▫ **virulence** virulency, poisonousness, venomousness, toxicity, noxiousness, deadliness, perniciousness, injuriousness, destructiveness, malignity, malignancy, violence, balefulness; acrimony, acrimoniousness, bitterness, acerbity, rancour, spleen, poison, venom, malevolence, maliciousness, malice, spite, hostility, resentment, antagonism, hatred.

virus /vīrəss/ *n.* **1** a microscopic organism consisting mainly of nucleic acid in a protein coat, multiplying only in living cells and often causing diseases. **2** *Computing* = *computer virus*. **3** *archaic* a poison, a source of disease. **4** a harmful or corrupting influence. [L, = slimy liquid, poison]

Vis. *abbr.* Viscount.

visa /veezə/ *n.* & *v.* ● *n.* an endorsement on a passport etc. showing that it has been found correct, esp. as allowing the holder to enter or leave a country. ● *v.tr.* (**visas, visaed** /-zəd/ or **visa'd, visaing**) mark with a visa. [F f. L *visa* neut. pl. past part. of *vidēre* see]

visage /vizzij/ *n. literary* a face, a countenance. ▫▫ **visaged** *adj.* (also in *comb.*). [ME f. OF f. L *visus* sight (as VISA)]
■ see FACE *n.* 1.

vis-à-vis /veezaavee/ *prep., adv.,* & *n.* ● *prep.* **1** in relation to. **2** opposite to. ● *adv.* facing one another. ● *n.* (*pl.* same) **1** a person or thing facing another, esp. in some dances. **2** a person occupying a corresponding position in another group. **3** *US* a social partner. [F, = face to face, f. *vis* face f. L (as VISAGE)]
■ *prep.* **1** re, with reference to, regarding, with regard to. **2** see OPPOSITE *prep.* ● *adv.* see *face to face*.

Visc. *abbr.* Viscount.

viscacha /viskáchə/ *n.* (also **vizcacha** /viz-/) any S. American burrowing rodent of the genus *Lagidium*, having valuable fur. [Sp. f. Quechua (*h*)*uiscacha*]

viscera /víssərə/ *n.pl.* the interior organs in the great cavities of the body (e.g. brain, heart, liver), esp. in the abdomen (e.g. the intestines). [L, pl. of *viscus*: see VISCUS]

visceral /víssərəl/ *adj.* **1** of the viscera. **2** relating to inward feelings rather than conscious reasoning. ▫ **visceral nerve** a sympathetic nerve (see SYMPATHETIC *adj.* 9). ▫▫ **viscerally** *adv.*

viscid /víssid/ *adj.* **1** glutinous, sticky. **2** semifluid. ▫▫ **viscidity** /visídditi/ *n.* [LL *viscidus* f. L *viscum* birdlime]
■ **1** see STICKY *adj.* 2. **2** see THICK *adj.* 5a.

viscometer /viskómmitər/ *n.* an instrument for measuring the viscosity of liquids. ▫▫ **viscometric** /viskəmétrik/ *adj.*

viscometrically /vìskəmétrikəli/ *adv.* **viscometry** *n.* [var. of *viscosimeter* (as VISCOSITY)]

viscose /vískōz, -kōss/ *n.* **1** a form of cellulose in a highly viscous state suitable for drawing into yarn. **2** rayon made from this. [LL *viscosus* (as VISCOUS)]

viscosity /viskóssiti/ *n.* (*pl.* **-ies**) **1** the quality or degree of being viscous. **2** *Physics* **a** (of a fluid) internal friction, the resistance to flow. **b** a quantity expressing this. □ **dynamic viscosity** a quantity measuring the force needed to overcome internal friction. **kinematic viscosity** a quantity measuring the dynamic viscosity per unit density. □□ **viscosimeter** /-kəsímmitər/ *n.* [ME f. OF *viscosité* or med.L *viscositas* (as VISCOUS)]
■ **1** see BODY *n.* 8.

viscount /vī́kownt/ *n.* a British nobleman ranking between an earl and a baron. □□ **viscountcy** *n.* (*pl.* **-ies**). **viscountship** *n.* **viscounty** *n.* (*pl.* **-ies**). [ME f. AF *viscounte*, OF *vi(s)conte* f. med.L *vicecomes -mitis* (as VICE-, COUNT²)]

viscountess /vī́kowntiss/ *n.* **1** a viscount's wife or widow. **2** a woman holding the rank of viscount in her own right.

viscous /vískəss/ *adj.* **1** glutinous, sticky. **2** semifluid. **3** *Physics* having a high viscosity; not flowing freely. □□ **viscously** *adv.* **viscousness** *n.* [ME f. AF *viscous* or LL *viscosus* (as VISCID)]
■ **1** see STICKY *adj.* 2. **2** see THICK *adj.* 5a.

viscus /vískəss/ *n.* (*pl.* **viscera** /víssərə/) (usu. in *pl.*) any of the soft internal organs of the body. [L]

vise *US* var. of VICE².

Vishnu /víshnōō/ *n.* a Hindu god regarded by his worshippers as the supreme deity and saviour, by others as the second member of a triad with Brahma and Siva. □□ **Vishnuism** *n.* **Vishnuite** *n.* & *adj.* [Skr. *Vishṇu*]

visibility /vìzzibílliti/ *n.* **1** the state of being visible. **2** the range or possibility of vision as determined by the conditions of light and atmosphere (*visibility was down to 50 yards*). [F *visibilité* or LL *visibilitas* f. L *visibilis*: see VISIBLE]

visible /vízzib'l/ *adj.* **1 a** that can be seen by the eye. **b** (of light) within the range of wavelengths to which the eye is sensitive. **2** that can be perceived or ascertained; apparent, open (*has no visible means of support*; *spoke with visible impatience*). **3** (of exports etc.) consisting of actual goods (cf. *invisible exports*). □ **the Church visible** the whole body of professed Christian believers. **visible horizon** see HORIZON 1b. □□ **visibleness** *n.* **visibly** *adv.* [ME f. OF *visible* or L *visibilis* f. *vidēre vis-* see]
■ **1** seeable, perceivable, perceptible, discernible, detectable, discoverable, noticeable, unmistakable, clear, obvious, observable; visual. **2** obvious, conspicuous, evident, apparent, prominent, manifest, distinct, patent, well-defined, identifiable, overt, unconcealed, plain. □□ **visibly** see *outwardly* (OUTWARD).

Visigoth /vízzigoth/ *n.* a West Goth, a member of the branch of the Goths who settled in France and Spain in the 5th c. and ruled much of Spain until 711. [LL *Visigothus*]

vision /ví<u>zh</u>'n/ *n.* & *v.* ● *n.* **1** the act or faculty of seeing, sight (*has impaired his vision*). **2 a** a thing or person seen in a dream or trance. **b** a supernatural or prophetic apparition. **3** a thing or idea perceived vividly in the imagination (*the romantic visions of youth*; *had visions of warm sandy beaches*). **4** imaginative insight. **5** statesmanlike foresight; sagacity in planning. **6** a person etc. of unusual beauty. **7** what is seen on a television screen; television images collectively. ● *v.tr.* see or present in or as in a vision. □ **field of vision** all that comes into view when the eyes are turned in some direction. **vision-mixer** a person whose job is to switch from one image to another in television broadcasting or recording. □□ **visional** *adj.* **visionless** *adj.* [ME f. OF f. L *visio -onis* (as VISIBLE)]
■ *n.* **1** eyesight, perception, sight. **2** phantom, apparition, chimera, delusion, hallucination, mirage, spectre, eidolon, revenant, phantasm, materialization, illusion, ghost, wraith, *literary* shade, visitant. **3** view, perspective, perception, envisioning, visualization, envisaging, dream, idea, plan, scheme, conception, notion. **4, 5** far-sightedness, understanding, perception, imagination, foresight, foresightedness, insight, sagacity. **6** sight for sore eyes, (welcome) sight, dream, picture. **7** image(s), picture(s).

visionary /ví<u>zh</u>ənəri/ *adj.* & *n.* ● *adj.* **1** informed or inspired by visions; indulging in fanciful theories. **2** existing in or characteristic of a vision or the imagination. **3** not practicable. ● *n.* (*pl.* **-ies**) a visionary person. □□ **visionariness** *n.*
■ *adj.* **1** unpractical, dreamy, idealistic, unrealistic, romantic, quixotic, Utopian; see also IMAGINATIVE 2. **2** dreamy, dreamlike, speculative, fanciful, unreal; see also IMAGINARY. **3** unpractical, impractical, unrealistic, idealistic, unworkable, Utopian. ● *n.* dreamer, idealist, romantic, fantast, fantasist, wishful thinker, Don Quixote, Utopian.

visit /vízzit/ *v.* & *n.* ● *v.* (**visited, visiting**) **1 a** *tr.* (also *absol.*) go or come to see (a person, place, etc.) as an act of friendship or ceremony, on business or for a purpose, or from interest. **b** *tr.* go or come to see for the purpose of official inspection, supervision, consultation, or correction. **2** *tr.* reside temporarily with (a person) or at (a place). **3** *intr.* be a visitor. **4** *tr.* (of a disease, calamity, etc.) come upon, attack. **5** *tr. Bibl.* **a** (foll. by *with*) punish (a person). **b** (often foll. by *upon*) inflict punishment for (a sin). **6** *intr. US* **a** (foll. by *with*) go to see (a person) esp. socially. **b** (usu. foll. by *with*) converse, chat. **7** *tr. archaic* (often foll. by *with*) comfort, bless (with salvation etc.). ● *n.* **1 a** an act of visiting, a call on a person or at a place (*was on a visit to some friends*; *paid him a long visit*). **b** temporary residence with a person or at a place. **2** (foll. by *to*) an occasion of going to a doctor, dentist, etc. **3** a formal or official call for the purpose of inspection etc. **4** *US* a chat. □ **right of visit** = *right of visitation* (see VISITATION). □□ **visitable** *adj.* [ME f. OF *visiter* or L *visitare* go to see, frequent. of *visare* view f. *vidēre vis-* see: (n.) perh. f. F *visite*]
■ *v.* **1** (go *or* come to) see, call (in *or* on *or* upon), look in on, stop by, pop in *or* by, descend on, *US* stop in, *colloq.* drop by *or* in (on), look up, take in. **2** see STAY¹ *v.* 2. **4** afflict, attack, fall upon, come upon, assail, seize, scourge, descend upon, affect, *archaic or literary* smite, *poet.* befall. **5 b** see INFLICT. ● *n.* **1** stay, call, sojourn, stop, stopover. **3** visitation.

visitant /vízzit'nt/ *n.* & *adj.* ● *n.* **1** a visitor, esp. a supposedly supernatural one. **2** = VISITOR 2. ● *adj. archaic* or *poet.* visiting. [F *visitant* or L *visitare* (as VISIT)]
■ *n.* **1** see VISION *n.* 2.

visitation /vìzzitáysh'n/ *n.* **1** an official visit of inspection, esp. a bishop's examination of a church in his diocese. **2** trouble or difficulty regarded as a divine punishment. **3** (**Visitation**) **a** the visit of the Virgin Mary to Elizabeth related in Luke 1:39-56. **b** the festival commemorating this on 2 July. **4** *colloq.* an unduly protracted visit or social call. **5** the boarding of a vessel belonging to another State to learn its character and purpose. □ **right of visitation** the right to conduct a visitation of a vessel, not including the right of search. [ME f. OF *visitation* or LL *visitatio* (as VISIT)]
■ **1** visit, tour (of inspection). **2** affliction, ordeal, trial, punishment, disaster, catastrophe, cataclysm, calamity, tragedy, curse, scourge, blight, plague, pestilence.

visitatorial /vìzzitətóriəl/ *adj.* of an official visitor or visitation. [ult. f. L *visitare* (see VISIT)]

visiting /vízziting/ *n.* & *adj.* ● *n.* paying a visit or visits. ● *attrib.adj.* (of an academic) spending some time at another institution (*a visiting professor*). □ **visiting-card** a card with a person's name etc., sent or left in lieu of a formal visit. **visiting fireman** (*pl.* **-men**) *US sl.* a visitor given especially cordial treatment.

visitor /vízzitər/ *n.* **1** a person who visits a person or place. **2** a migratory bird present in a locality for part of the year (*winter visitor*). **3** *Brit.* (in a college etc.) an official with the right or duty of occasionally inspecting and reporting. □ **visitors' book** a book in which visitors to a hotel, church, embassy, etc., write their names and addresses and sometimes remarks. [ME f. AF *visitour*, OF *visiteur* (as VISIT)]

■ **1** caller, guest, company; tourist, sightseer, traveller, non-resident, foreigner, alien, migrant, visitant, *esp. Brit.* holiday-maker.

visitorial /vízzitóriəl/ *adj.* of an official visitor or visitation.

visor /vízər/ *n.* (also **vizor**) **1 a** a movable part of a helmet covering the face. **b** *hist.* a mask. **c** the projecting front part of a cap. **2** a shield (fixed or movable) to protect the eyes from unwanted light, esp. one at the top of a vehicle windscreen. ▫▫ **visored** *adj.* **visorless** *adj.* [ME f. AF *viser*, OF *visiere* f. *vis* face f. L *visus*: see VISAGE]

vista /vístə/ *n.* **1** a long narrow view as between rows of trees. **2** a mental view of a long succession of remembered or anticipated events (*opened up new vistas to his ambition*). ▫▫ **vistaed** *adj.* [It., = view, f. *visto* seen, past part. of *vedere* see f. L *vidēre*]

■ see VIEW *n.* 2a.

visual /vízyooəl, vízhooəl/ *adj.* & *n.* ● *adj.* of, concerned with, or used in seeing. ● *n.* (usu. in *pl.*) a visual image or display, a picture. ▫ **visual aid** a film, model, etc., as an aid to learning. **visual angle** the angle formed at the eye by rays from the extremities of an object viewed. **visual display unit** *Computing* a device displaying data as characters on a screen and usu. incorporating a keyboard. **visual field** field of vision. **visual purple** a light-sensitive pigment in the retina, rhodopsin. **visual ray** *Optics* a line extended from an object to the eye. ▫▫ **visuality** /vízyoo-álliti, vízhoo-alliti/ *n.* **visually** *adv.* [ME f. LL *visualis* f. L *visus* sight f. *vidēre* see]

■ *n.* see PICTURE *n.* 1a. ▫ **visual display unit** VDU, monitor.

visualize /vízyooəlīz, vízhooə-/ *v.tr.* (also **-ise**) **1** make visible esp. to one's mind (a thing not visible to the eye). **2** make visible to the eye. ▫▫ **visualizable** *adj.* **visualization** /-záysh'n/ *n.*

■ **1** see PICTURE *v.* 2.

vital /vít'l/ *adj.* & *n.* ● *adj.* **1** of, concerned with, or essential to organic life (*vital functions*). **2** essential to the existence of a thing or to the matter in hand (*a vital question*; *secrecy is vital*). **3** full of life or activity. **4** affecting life. **5** fatal to life or to success etc. (*a vital error*). **6** *disp.* important. ● *n.* (in *pl.*) the body's vital organs, e.g. the heart and brain. ▫ **vital capacity** the volume of air that can be expelled from the lungs after taking the deepest possible breath. **vital force 1** (in Bergson's philosophy) life-force. **2** any mysterious vital principle. **vital power** the power to sustain life. **vital statistics 1** the number of births, marriages, deaths, etc. **2** *colloq.* the measurements of a woman's bust, waist, and hips. ▫▫ **vitally** *adv.* [ME f. OF f. L *vitalis* f. *vita* life]

■ *adj.* **1** living, animate; life-giving, invigorating, quickening, animating, vitalizing, reviving, vivifying, revivifying, enlivening, rejuvenating. **2** imperative, essential, necessary, needed, requisite, required, indispensable, mandatory, compulsory, cardinal, fundamental, basic, critical, crucial, central, pivotal, life-and-death, key, paramount, main. **3** lively, full of life, vivacious, spirited, vigorous, dynamic, alive, animated, brisk, energetic, sprightly. **5** fatal, grave, serious. **6** see IMPORTANT 1. ● *n.* (*vitals*) see GUT *n.* 1, 2.

vitalism /vítəliz'm/ *n. Biol.* the doctrine that life originates in a vital principle distinct from chemical and other physical forces. ▫▫ **vitalist** *n.* **vitalistic** /-lístik/ *adj.* [F *vitalisme* or f. VITAL]

vitality /vītálliti/ *n.* **1** liveliness, animation. **2** the ability to sustain life, vital power. **3** (of an institution, language, etc.) the ability to endure and to perform its functions. [L *vitalitas* (as VITAL)]

■ **1** energy, vigour, power, intensity, force, liveliness, vivacity, vivaciousness, verve, animation, sparkle, spiritedness, *joie de vivre*, exuberance, go, zip, *colloq.* zing, pep, get-up-and-go, vim, *sl.* pizazz, oomph. **2** life, life-force, vigour, vital force, vital power. **3** stamina, hardiness, endurance, energy, strength, robustness.

vitalize /vítəlīz/ *v.tr.* (also **-ise**) **1** endow with life. **2** infuse with vigour. ▫▫ **vitalization** /-záysh'n/ *n.*

■ stimulate, activate, arouse, vivify, animate, awaken, inspirit, invigorate, enliven, inspire, revive, rejuvenate, energize, fortify, reinvigorate, renew, refresh, charge (up), perk up, *colloq.* pep up.

vitally /vítəli/ *adv.* essentially, indispensably.

vitamin /víttəmin, ví-/ *n.* any of a group of organic compounds essential in small amounts for many living organisms to maintain normal health and development. ▫ **vitamin A** = RETINOL. **vitamin B complex** (or **B vitamins**) any of a group of vitamins which, although not chemically related, are often found together in the same foods. **vitamin B_1** = THIAMINE. **vitamin B_2** = RIBOFLAVIN. **vitamin B_6** = PYRIDOXINE. **vitamin B_{12}** = CYANOCOBALAMIN. **vitamin C** = ASCORBIC ACID. **vitamin D** any of a group of vitamins found in liver and fish oils, essential for the absorption of calcium and the prevention of rickets in children and osteomalacia in adults. **vitamin D_2** = CALCIFEROL. **vitamin D_3** = CHOLECALCIFEROL. **vitamin E** = TOCOPHEROL. **vitamin K** any of a group of vitamins found mainly in green leaves and essential for the blood-clotting process. **vitamin K_1** = PHYLLOQUINONE. **vitamin K_2** = MENAQUINONE. **vitamin M** esp. *US* = FOLIC ACID. [orig. *vitamine* f. L *vita* life + AMINE, because orig. thought to contain an amino acid]

vitaminize /víttəminīz, ví-/ *v.tr.* (also **-ise**) add vitamins to.

vitellary /vitéllәri, vī-/ *adj.* of or relating to the vitellus.

vitelli *pl.* of VITELLUS.

vitellin /vitéllin, vī-/ *n. Chem.* the chief protein constituent of the yolk of egg. [VITELLUS + -IN]

vitelline /vitéllīn, vī-, -lin/ *adj.* of the vitellus. ▫ **vitelline membrane** the yolk-sac. [med.L *vitellinus* (as VITELLUS)]

vitellus /vitélləss, vī-/ *n.* (*pl.* **vitelli** /-lī/) **1** the yolk of an egg. **2** the contents of the ovum. [L, = yolk]

vitiate /víshiayt/ *v.tr.* **1** impair the quality or efficiency of; corrupt, debase, contaminate. **2** make invalid or ineffectual. ▫▫ **vitiation** /-shiáysh'n/ *n.* **vitiator** *n.* [L *vitiare* f. *vitium* VICE[1]]

■ **1** spoil, ruin, harm, impair, mar, sully, contaminate, adulterate, weaken, degrade, downgrade, depreciate, diminish, depress, vulgarize, lower, reduce, undermine; debase, deprave, pervert, corrupt, defile, *archaic* demoralize. **2** invalidate, destroy, delete, cancel, nullify, annul, revoke, void, abrogate, abolish, withdraw, quash, suppress. ▫▫ **vitiation** see *impairment* (IMPAIR).

viticulture /víttikulchər/ *n.* the cultivation of grapevines; the science or study of this. ▫▫ **viticultural** /-kúlchərəl/ *adj.* **viticulturist** /-kúlchərist/ *n.* [L *vitis* vine + CULTURE]

vitreous /vítriəss/ *adj.* **1** of, or of the nature of, glass. **2** like glass in hardness, brittleness, transparency, structure, etc. (*vitreous enamel*). ▫ **vitreous humour** (or **body**) *Anat.* a transparent jelly-like tissue filling the eyeball. ▫▫ **vitreousness** *n.* [L *vitreus* f. *vitrum* glass]

vitrescent /vitréss'nt/ *adj.* tending to become glass. ▫▫ **vitrescence** *n.*

vitriform /vítriform/ *adj.* having the form or appearance of glass.

vitrify /vítrifī/ *v.tr.* & *intr.* (**-ies**, **-ied**) convert or be converted into glass or a glasslike substance esp. by heat. ▫▫ **vitrifaction** /-fáksh'n/ *n.* **vitrifiable** *adj.* **vitrification** /-fikáysh'n/ *n.* [F *vitrifier* or med.L *vitrificare* (as VITREOUS)]

vitriol /vítriəl/ *n.* **1** sulphuric acid or a sulphate, orig. one of glassy appearance. **2** caustic or hostile speech, criticism, or feeling. ▫ **copper vitriol** copper sulphate. **oil of vitriol** concentrated sulphuric acid. [ME f. OF *vitriol* or med.L *vitriolum* f. L *vitrum* glass]

■ **2** see GALL[1] 1, 2.

vitriolic /vítriόllik/ *adj.* (of speech or criticism) caustic or hostile.

■ see *scathing* (SCATHE *v.* 2).

vitta /víttə/ *n.* (*pl.* **vittae** /víttee/) **1** *Bot.* an oil-tube in the fruit of some plants. **2** *Zool.* a stripe of colour. ▫▫ **vittate** *adj.* [L, = band, chaplet]

vituperate /vityóopərayt, vī-/ *v.tr.* & *intr.* revile, abuse. ▫▫ **vituperation** /-ráysh'n/ *n.* **vituperative** /-rətiv/ *adj.* **vituperator** *n.* [L *vituperare* f. *vitium* VICE[1]]

■ berate, rate, reproach, revile, vilify, execrate, abuse, denounce, decry, deprecate, disparage, devalue, diminish, put down, run down, devaluate, depreciate, blame, inculpate, censure, find fault with, criticize, attack, assail, castigate, scold, reprimand, upbraid, rebuke, chasten, *archaic or literary* chide, *sl.* knock. ▫▫ **vituperation** see ABUSE *n.* 2. **vituperative** abusive, calumniatory, calumnious, scurrilous, derogatory, belittling, depreciatory, depreciative, detractory, contemptuous, damning, denunciatory, denigrating, deprecatory, censorious, aspersive, defamatory, slanderous, libellous, castigatory, condemnatory, malign, scornful, withering, harsh, sardonic, sarcastic, biting, acid, contumelious, opprobrious, insulting.

viva[1] /vívə/ *n.* & *v.* *Brit. colloq.* ● *n.* = VIVA VOCE *n.* ● *v.tr.* (**vivas, vivaed** /-vəd/ or **viva'd, vivaing**) = VIVA VOCE *v.* [abbr.]

viva[2] /véevə/ *int.* & *n.* ● *int.* long live. ● *n.* a cry of this as a salute etc. [It., 3rd sing. pres. subj. of *vivere* live f. L]

vivace /viváachi/ *adv.* *Mus.* in a lively brisk manner. [It. f. L (as VIVACIOUS)]

vivacious /viváyshəss/ *adj.* lively, sprightly, animated. ▫▫ **vivaciously** *adv.* **vivaciousness** *n.* **vivacity** /vivássiti/ *n.* [L *vivax -acis* f. *vivere* live]

■ lively, spirited, sprightly, spry, energetic, animated, brisk, ebullient, effervescent, bubbly, gay, cheerful, happy, perky, jaunty, bouncy, light-hearted, sunny, merry, high-spirited, buoyant, *colloq.* peppy, full of pep, full of beans, zippy, *esp. US colloq.* chipper, *poet.* blithe. ▫▫ **vivaciousness, vivacity** see VITALITY 1.

vivarium /vīváiriəm, vi-/ *n.* (*pl.* **vivaria** /-riə/) a place artificially prepared for keeping animals in (nearly) their natural state. [L, = warren, fishpond, f. *vivus* living f. *vivere* live]

vivat /vívat, véevat/ *int.* & *n.* = VIVA[2]. [L, 3rd sing. pres. subj. of *vivere* live]

viva voce /vívə vóchi, vósi/ *adj.*, *adv.*, *n.*, & *v.* ● *adj.* oral. ● *adv.* orally. ● *n.* an oral examination for an academic qualification. ● *v.tr.* (**viva-voce**) (**-vocees, -voceed, -voceing**) examine orally. [med.L, = with the living voice]

■ *adj.* see ORAL *adj.*

viverrid /vivérrid, vī-/ *n.* & *adj.* ● *n.* any mammal of the family Viverridae, including civets, mongooses, and genets. ● *adj.* of or relating to this family. [L *viverra* ferret + -ID[3]]

vivers /vívərz/ *n.pl.* *Sc.* food, victuals. [F *vivres* f. *vivre* live f. L *vivere*]

vivid /vívvid/ *adj.* **1** (of light or colour) strong, intense, glaring (*a vivid flash of lightning*; *of a vivid green*). **2** (of a mental faculty, impression, or description) clear, lively, graphic (*has a vivid imagination*; *have a vivid recollection of the scene*). **3** (of a person) lively, vigorous. ▫▫ **vividly** *adv.* **vividness** *n.* [L *vividus* f. *vivere* live]

■ **1** intense, strong, brilliant, fresh, bright, dazzling, rich, clear, colourful, bold, violent, glowing, lurid, glaring, *poet.* lucid. **2** clear, detailed, sharp, realistic, graphic, expressive, true to life, lifelike, distinct, powerful, strong, memorable, dramatic, striking; lively, prolific, fruitful, fertile, fecund, inventive, creative, active.

vivify /vívvifī/ *v.tr.* (**-ies, -ied**) enliven, animate, make lively or living. ▫▫ **vivification** /-fikáysh'n/ *n.* [F *vivifier* f. LL *vivificare* f. L *vivus* living f. *vivere* live]

■ see ENLIVEN 1.

viviparous /vivíppərəss, vī-/ *adj.* **1** *Zool.* bringing forth young alive, not hatching them by means of eggs (cf. OVIPAROUS). **2** *Bot.* producing bulbs or seeds that germinate while still attached to the parent plant. ▫▫ **viviparity** /vívvipárriti/ *n.* **viviparously** *adv.* **viviparousness** *n.* [L *viviparus* f. *vivus*: see VIVIFY]

vivisect /vívvisekt/ *v.tr.* perform vivisection on. [back-form. f. VIVISECTION]

vivisection /vívvisékshʼn/ *n.* **1** dissection or other painful treatment of living animals for purposes of scientific research. **2** unduly detailed or ruthless criticism. ▫▫ **vivisectional** *adj.* **vivisectionist** *n.* **vivisector** /vívvisektər/ *n.* [L *vivus* living (see VIVIFY), after DISSECTION (as DISSECT)]

vixen /víks'n/ *n.* **1** a female fox. **2** a spiteful or quarrelsome woman. ▫▫ **vixenish** *adj.* **vixenly** *adj.* [ME *fixen* f. OE, fem. of FOX]

■ **2** see SHREW.

viz. /viz, or by substitution náymli/ *adv.* (usu. introducing a gloss or explanation) namely; that is to say; in other words (*came to a firm conclusion, viz. that we were right*). [abbr. of VIDELICET, *z* being med.L symbol for abbr. of *-et*]

■ see NAMELY.

vizard /vízzərd/ *n.* *archaic* a mask or disguise. [VISOR + -ARD]

vizcacha var. of VISCACHA.

vizier /vizéer, vízziər/ *n.* *hist.* a high official in some Muslim countries, esp. in Turkey under Ottoman rule. ▫▫ **vizierate** /-rət/ *n.* **vizierial** /vizéeriəl/ *adj.* **viziership** *n.* [ult. f. Arab. *wazīr* caliph's chief counsellor]

vizor var. of VISOR.

Vlach /vlak/ *n.* & *adj.* ● *n.* a member of a people chiefly inhabiting Romania and Moldova. ● *adj.* of or relating to this people. [Bulg. f. OSlav. *Vlachŭ* Romanian etc. f. Gmc, = foreigner]

vlei /flay/ *n.* *S.Afr.* a hollow in which water collects during the rainy season. [Du. dial. f. Du. *vallei* valley]

V-neck /véenék/ *n.* (often *attrib.*) **1** a neck of a pullover etc. with straight sides meeting at an angle in the front to form a V. **2** a garment with this.

VO *abbr.* (in the UK) Royal Victorian Order.

vocable /vókəb'l/ *n.* a word, esp. with reference to form rather than meaning. [F *vocable* or L *vocabulum* f. *vocare* call]

vocabulary /vəkábyooləri/ *n.* (*pl.* **-ies**) **1** the (principal) words used in a language or a particular book or branch of science etc. or by a particular author (*scientific vocabulary*; *the vocabulary of Shakespeare*). **2** a list of these, arranged alphabetically with definitions or translations. **3** the range of words known to an individual (*his vocabulary is limited*). **4** a set of artistic or stylistic forms or techniques, esp. a range of set movements in ballet etc. [med.L *vocabularius*, *-um* (as VOCABLE)]

■ **1** see TERMINOLOGY.

vocal /vók'l/ *adj.* & *n.* ● *adj.* **1** of or concerned with or uttered by the voice (*a vocal communication*). **2** expressing one's feelings freely in speech (*was very vocal about his rights*). **3** *Phonet.* voiced. **4** *poet.* (of trees, water, etc.) endowed with a voice or a similar faculty. **5** (of music) written for or produced by the voice with or without accompaniment (cf. INSTRUMENTAL). ● *n.* **1** (in *sing.* or *pl.*) the sung part of a musical composition. **2** a musical performance with singing. ▫ **vocal cords** folds of the lining membrane of the larynx near the opening of the glottis, with edges vibrating in the air-stream to produce the voice. **vocal score** a musical score showing the voice parts in full. ▫▫ **vocality** /vəkálliti/ *n.* **vocally** *adv.* [ME f. L *vocalis* (as VOICE)]

■ *adj.* **1** see ORAL *adj.*

vocalic /vəkállik/ *adj.* of or consisting of a vowel or vowels.

vocalism /vókəliz'm/ *n.* **1** the use of the voice in speaking or singing. **2** a vowel sound or system.

vocalist /vókəlist/ *n.* a singer, esp. of jazz or popular songs.

■ singer, soloist, choirboy, choir girl, choir member, chorus boy, chorus girl, chorus member, chorister, caroller, songster, minstrel, *US* chorine; diva, prima donna, *chanteuse*; cantor, crooner.

vocalize /vṓkəlīz/ *v.* (also **-ise**) **1** *tr.* **a** form (a sound) or utter (a word) with the voice. **b** make sonant (*f is vocalized into v*). **2** *intr.* utter a vocal sound. **3** *tr.* write (Hebrew etc.) with vowel points. **4** *intr. Mus.* sing with several notes to one vowel. ▫▫ **vocalization** /-záysh'n/ *n.* **vocalizer** *n.*
■ **1a, 2** see ENUNCIATE 1.

vocation /vəkáysh'n/ *n.* **1** a strong feeling of fitness for a particular career or occupation (in religious contexts regarded as a divine call). **2 a** a person's employment, esp. regarded as requiring dedication. **b** a trade or profession. [ME f. OF *vocation* or L *vocatio* f. *vocare* call]
■ **1** call, calling. **2** calling, mission, trade, *métier*, business, profession, occupation, career, employment, job, pursuit, life's-work, work, line (of work), *colloq.* thing, *sl.* bag.

vocational /vəkáyshən'l/ *adj.* **1** of or relating to an occupation or employment. **2** (of education or training) directed at a particular occupation and its skills. ▫▫ **vocationalism** *n.* **vocationalize** *v.tr.* (also **-ise**). **vocationally** *adv.*

vocative /vókkətiv/ *n.* & *adj. Gram.* ● *n.* the case of nouns, pronouns, and adjectives used in addressing or invoking a person or thing. ● *adj.* of or in this case. [ME f. OF *vocatif -ive* or L *vocativus* f. *vocare* call]

vociferate /vəsíffərayt/ *v.* **1** *tr.* utter (words etc.) noisily. **2** *intr.* shout, bawl. ▫▫ **vociferance** *n.* **vociferant** *adj.* & *n.* **vociferation** /-ráysh'n/ *n.* **vociferator** *n.* [L *vociferari* f. *vox* voice + *ferre* bear]
■ see BAWL 1, SHOUT *v.*

vociferous /vəsíffərəss/ *adj.* **1** (of a person, speech, etc.) noisy, clamorous. **2** insistently and forcibly expressing one's views. ▫▫ **vociferously** *adv.* **vociferousness** *n.*
■ **1** see OBSTREPEROUS. **2** see INSISTENT 2. ▫▫ **vociferously** see *warmly* (WARM).

vocoder /vōkṓdər/ *n.* a synthesizer that produces sounds from an analysis of speech input. [VOICE + CODE]

vodka /vódkə/ *n.* an alcoholic spirit made esp. in Russia by distillation of rye etc. [Russ., dimin. of *voda* water]

voe /vō/ *n.* a small bay or creek in Orkney or Shetland. [Norw. *våg*, ON *vágr*]

vogue /vōg/ *n.* **1** (prec. by *the*) the prevailing fashion. **2** popular use or currency (*has had a great vogue*). ▫ **in vogue** in fashion, generally current. **vogue-word** a word currently fashionable. ▫▫ **voguish** *adj.* [F f. It. *voga* rowing, fashion f. *vogare* row, go well]
■ **1** fashion, mode, style, look, trend, rage, craze, last word, *dernier cri*, (latest) thing, fad, latest. **2** popularity, favour, preference, acceptance, currency, prevalence, fashionableness. ▫ **in vogue** see FASHIONABLE.

voice /voyss/ *n.* & *v.* ● *n.* **1 a** sound formed in the larynx etc. and uttered by the mouth, esp. human utterance in speaking, shouting, singing, etc. (*heard a voice; spoke in a low voice*). **b** the ability to produce this (*has lost her voice*). **2 a** the use of the voice; utterance, esp. in spoken or written words (esp. *give voice*). **b** an opinion so expressed. **c** the right to express an opinion (*I have no voice in the matter*). **d** an agency by which an opinion is expressed. **3** *Gram.* a form or set of forms of a verb showing the relation of the subject to the action (*active voice; passive voice*). **4** *Mus.* **a** a vocal part in a composition. **b** a constituent part in a fugue. **5** *Phonet.* sound uttered with resonance of the vocal cords, not with mere breath. **6** (usu. in *pl.*) the supposed utterance of an invisible guiding or directing spirit. ● *v.tr.* **1** give utterance to; express (*the letter voices our opinion*). **2** (esp. as **voiced** *adj.*) *Phonet.* utter with vibration of the vocal cords (e.g. *b, d, g, v, z*). **3** *Mus.* regulate the tone-quality of (organ-pipes). ▫ **in voice** (or **good voice**) in proper vocal condition for singing or speaking. **voice-box** the larynx. **the voice of God** the expression of God's will, wrath, etc. **voice-over** narration in a film etc. not accompanied by a picture of the speaker. **voice-print** a visual record of speech, analysed with respect to frequency, duration, and amplitude. **voice vote** *US* a vote taken by noting the relative strength of calls of *aye* and *no*. **with one voice** unanimously. ▫▫ **-voiced** *adj.* **voicer** *n.* (in sense 3 of v.). [ME f. AF *voiz*, OF *vois* f. L *vox vocis*]
■ *n.* **2 a** speech, utterance, articulation, words, expression. **c** share, part, vote, participation, say, decision, option, turn. **d** spokesman, spokeswoman, spokesperson, representative, agent, agency, instrument; organ, medium, vehicle, forum, publication. ● *v.* **1** express, utter, articulate, enunciate, present, verbalize, put into words, give utterance *or* voice *or* expression *or* tongue *or* vent to, vocalize, communicate, convey, declare, state, assert, make known, reveal, disclose, raise, bring up, air, ventilate. ▫ **voice-over** see *narration* (NARRATE).

voiceful /vóysfōōl/ *adj. poet.* or *rhet.* **1** vocal. **2** sonorous.

voiceless /vóysliss/ *adj.* **1** dumb, mute, speechless. **2** *Phonet.* uttered without vibration of the vocal cords (e.g. *f, k, p, s, t*). ▫▫ **voicelessly** *adv.* **voicelessness** *n.*
■ **1** see DUMB 1, 2.

void /voyd/ *adj., n.,* & *v.* ● *adj.* **1 a** empty, vacant. **b** (foll. by *of*) lacking; free from (*a style void of affectation*). **2** esp. *Law* (of a contract, deed, promise, etc.) invalid, not binding (*null and void*). **3** useless, ineffectual. **4** (often foll. by *in*) *Cards* (of a hand) having no cards in a given suit. **5** (of an office) vacant (esp. *fall void*). ● *n.* **1** an empty space, a vacuum (*vanished into the void; cannot fill the void made by death*). **2** an unfilled space in a wall or building. **3** (often foll. by *in*) *Cards* the absence of cards in a particular suit. ● *v.tr.* **1** render invalid. **2** (also *absol.*) excrete. ▫▫ **voidable** *adj.* **voidness** *n.* [ME f. OF dial. *voide*, OF *vuide, vuit*, rel. to L *vacare* VACATE: v. partly f. AVOID, partly f. OF *voider*]
■ *adj.* **1 a** empty, vacant, unused, unutilized, blank, clear; bare, deserted. **b** (*void of*) devoid of, without, lacking, free from; destitute of, bereft of. **2** null and void, invalid, not (legally) binding, inoperative, unenforceable. **3** ineffectual, futile, ineffective, vain, unavailing, idle, useless, pointless, *archaic* bootless. **5** vacant, unoccupied, unfilled. ● *n.* **1** emptiness, vacantness, vacuum, blankness, nothingness, voidness, vacuity, hollowness; hole, space, niche, slot, opening, place, vacancy, gap. **2** gap, space, opening. ● *v.* **1** nullify, annul, cancel, delete, declare *or* render null and void, invalidate, quash, abandon, disestablish, neutralize, disenact, set *or* put aside, rescind, reverse, abnegate, abrogate, *Law* vacate, discharge. **2** evacuate, discharge, expel, emit, purge, clear, empty, drain, eject; excrete, urinate, defecate.

voidance /vóyd'nss/ *n.* **1** *Eccl.* a vacancy in a benefice. **2** the act or an instance of voiding; the state of being voided. [ME f. OF (as VOID)]

voided /vóydid/ *adj. Heraldry* (of a bearing) having the central area cut away so as to show the field.

voile /voyl, vwaal/ *n.* a thin semi-transparent dress-material of cotton, wool, or silk. [F, = VEIL]

vol. *abbr.* volume.

volant /vṓlənt/ *adj.* **1** *Zool.* flying, able to fly. **2** *Heraldry* represented as flying. **3** *literary* nimble, rapid. [F f. *voler* f. L *volare* fly]

volar /vṓlər/ *adj. Anat.* of the palm or sole. [L *vola* hollow of hand or foot]

volatile /vóllətīl/ *adj.* & *n.* ● *adj.* **1** evaporating rapidly (*volatile salts*). **2** changeable, fickle. **3** lively, light-hearted. **4** apt to break out into violence. **5** transient. ● *n.* a volatile substance. ▫ **volatile oil** = *essential oil*. ▫▫ **volatileness** *n.* **volatility** /-tílliti/ *n.* [OF *volatil* or L *volatilis* f. *volare volat-* fly]
■ *adj.* **1** vaporizing, evaporable, evaporative. **2** changeable, fickle, flighty, inconstant, erratic, restless, unstable, variable, mercurial, capricious, unpredictable, temperamental. **4** explosive, hair-trigger, sensitive, charged, eruptive, tense, tension-ridden. **5** see TRANSIENT *adj.* ▫▫ **volatileness, volatility** see *inconstancy* (INCONSTANT).

volatilize /vəláttilīz/ *v.* (also **-ise**) **1** *tr.* cause to evaporate. **2** *intr.* evaporate. ▫▫ **volatilizable** *adj.* **volatilization** /-záysh'n/ *n.*

vol-au-vent /vóllōvon/ *n.* a (usu. small) round case of puff pastry filled with meat, fish, etc., and sauce. [F, lit. 'flight in the wind']

volcanic /volkánnik/ *adj.* (also **vulcanic** /vul-/) of, like, or produced by a volcano. □ **volcanic bomb** a mass of ejected lava usu. rounded and sometimes hollow. **volcanic glass** obsidian. □□ **volcanically** *adv.* **volcanicity** /vólkənissiti/ *n.* [F *volcanique* f. *volcan* VOLCANO]

volcano /volkáynō/ *n.* (*pl.* **-oes**) **1** a mountain or hill having an opening or openings in the earth's crust through which lava, cinders, steam, gases, etc., are or have been expelled continuously or at intervals. **2 a** a state of things likely to cause a violent outburst. **b** a violent esp. suppressed feeling. [It. f. L *Volcanus* Vulcan, Roman god of fire]

volcanology var. of VULCANOLOGY.

vole[1] /vōl/ *n.* any small ratlike or mouselike plant-eating rodent of the family Cricetidae. [orig. *vole-mouse* f. Norw. f. *voll* field + *mus* mouse]

vole[2] /vōl/ *n.* *archaic* the winning of all tricks at cards. [F f. *voler* fly f. L *volare*]

volet /vóllay/ *n.* a panel or wing of a triptych. [F f. *voler* fly f. L *volare*]

volitant /vóllit'nt/ *adj.* *Zool.* volant. [L *volitare* frequent. of *volare* fly]

volition /vəlísh'n/ *n.* **1** the exercise of the will. **2** the power of willing. □ **of** (or **by**) **one's own volition** voluntarily. □□ **volitional** *adj.* **volitionally** *adv.* **volitive** /vóllitiv/ *adj.* [F *volition* or med.L *volitio* f. *volo* I wish]

■ **1** (free) will, choice, option, choosing, choice, discretion, preference. □ **of** (or **by**) **one's own volition** see *voluntarily* (VOLUNTARY). □□ **volitional** see VOLUNTARY *adj.* 1, 7.

Völkerwanderung /fṓlkərvaandəróóng/ *n.* a migration of peoples, esp. that of Germanic and Slavic peoples in Europe from the second to the eleventh centuries. [G]

volley /vólli/ *n.* & *v.* ● *n.* (*pl.* **-eys**) **1 a** the simultaneous discharge of a number of weapons. **b** the bullets etc. discharged in a volley. **2** (usu. foll. by *of*) a noisy emission of oaths etc. in quick succession. **3** *Tennis* the return of a ball in play before it touches the ground. **4** *Football* the kicking of a ball in play before it touches the ground. **5** *Cricket* **a** a ball pitched right up to the batsman or the stumps without bouncing. **b** the pitching of the ball in this way. ● *v.* (**-eys, -eyed**) **1** *tr.* (also *absol.*) *Tennis* & *Football* return or send (a ball) by a volley. **2** *tr.* & *absol.* discharge (bullets, abuse, etc.) in a volley. **3** *intr.* (of bullets etc.) fly in a volley. **4** *intr.* (of guns etc.) sound together. **5** *intr.* make a sound like a volley of artillery. □□ **volleyer** *n.* [F *volée* ult. f. L *volare* fly]

■ *n.* **1** salvo, bombardment, barrage, cannonade, fusillade, discharge, hail, shower. **2** outpouring, torrent, flood, deluge, inundation, burst, storm, outbreak. ● *v.* **3** see HAIL[1] *v.* 2.

volleyball /vóllibawl/ *n.* a game for two teams of six hitting a large ball by hand over a net.

volplane /vólplayn/ *n.* & *v.* *Aeron.* ● *n.* a glide. ● *v.intr.* glide. [F *vol plané* f. *vol* flight + *plané* past part. of *planer* hover, rel. to PLANE[1]]

vols. *abbr.* volumes.

volt[1] /vōlt/ *n.* the SI unit of electromotive force, the difference of potential that would carry one ampere of current against one ohm resistance. ¶ Abbr.: **V.** [A. *Volta*, It. physicist d. 1827]

volt[2] /volt, vōlt/ *v.* & *n.* ● *v.intr.* *Fencing* make a volte. ● *n.* var. of VOLTE. [F *volter* (as VOLTE)]

voltage /vṓltij/ *n.* electromotive force or potential difference expressed in volts.

voltaic /voltáyik/ *adj.* *archaic* of electricity from a primary battery; galvanic (*voltaic battery*).

voltameter /voltámmitər/ *n.* an instrument for measuring an electric charge.

volte /volt, vōlt/ *n.* (also **volt**) **1** *Fencing* a quick movement to escape a thrust. **2** a sideways circular movement of a horse. [F f. It. *volta* turn, fem. past part. of *volgere* turn f. L *volvere* roll]

volte-face /voltfaáss/ *n.* **1** a complete reversal of position in argument or opinion. **2** the act or an instance of turning round. [F f. It. *voltafaccia*, ult. f. L *volvere* roll + *facies* appearance, face]

■ see *reversal* (REVERSE).

voltmeter /vṓltmeetər/ *n.* an instrument for measuring electric potential in volts.

voluble /vólyoob'l/ *adj.* **1** speaking or spoken vehemently, incessantly, or fluently (*voluble spokesman*; *voluble excuses*). **2** *Bot.* twisting round a support, twining. □□ **volubility** /-bílliti/ *n.* **volubleness** *n.* **volubly** *adv.* [F *voluble* or L *volubilis* f. *volvere* roll]

■ **1** talkative, glib, fluent, loquacious, garrulous, chatty, profuse, gossipy, exuberant, long-winded, bombastic, windy, wordy, *colloq.* blessed with the gift of the gab.

volume /vólyōōm/ *n.* **1 a** a set of sheets of paper, usu. printed, bound together and forming part or the whole of a work or comprising several works (*issued in three volumes*; *a library of 12,000 volumes*). **b** *hist.* a scroll of papyrus etc., an ancient form of book. **2 a** solid content, bulk. **b** the space occupied by a gas or liquid. **c** (foll. by *of*) an amount or quantity (*large volume of business*). **3 a** quantity or power of sound. **b** fullness of tone. **4** (foll. by *of*) **a** a moving mass of water etc. **b** (usu. in *pl.*) a wreath or coil or rounded mass of smoke etc. □□ **volumed** *adj.* (also in *comb.*). [ME f. OF *volum(e)* f. L *volumen -minis* roll f. *volvere* to roll]

■ **1** book, tome. **2 a** mass, bulk, content. **b** capacity, size, dimensions, measure. **c** amount, quantity, supply, abundance, sum total, aggregate. **3** loudness.

volumetric /vólyoométrik/ *adj.* of or relating to measurement by volume. □□ **volumetrically** *adv.* [VOLUME + METRIC]

voluminous /vəlyōōminəss, vəlōō-/ *adj.* **1** large in volume; bulky. **2** (of drapery etc.) loose and ample. **3** consisting of many volumes. **4** (of a writer) producing many books. □□ **voluminosity** /-nóssiti/ *n.* **voluminously** *adv.* **voluminousness** *n.* [LL *voluminosus* (as VOLUME)]

■ **1** large, extensive, great, spacious, capacious, expansive, roomy, big, bulky, cavernous, oversize(d), outsize, massive, huge, immense, substantial, tremendous, enormous, gigantic, mammoth, vast. **2** ample, billowing, full, loose. **4** copious, prolific, productive.

voluntarism /vólləntəriz'm/ *n.* **1** the principle of relying on voluntary action rather than compulsion. **2** *Philos.* the doctrine that the will is a fundamental or dominant factor in the individual or the universe. **3** *hist.* the doctrine that the Church or schools should be independent of the State and supported by voluntary contributions. □□ **voluntarist** *n.* [irreg. f. VOLUNTARY]

voluntary /vóllənteri, -tri/ *adj.* & *n.* ● *adj.* **1** done, acting, or able to act of one's own free will; not constrained or compulsory, intentional (*a voluntary gift*). **2** unpaid (*voluntary work*). **3** (of an institution) supported by voluntary contributions. **4** *Brit.* (of a school) built by a voluntary institution but maintained by a local education authority. **5** brought about, produced, etc., by voluntary action. **6** (of a movement, muscle, or limb) controlled by the will. **7** (of a confession by a criminal) not prompted by a promise or threat. **8** *Law* (of a conveyance or disposition) made without return in money or other consideration. ● *n.* (*pl.* **-ies**) **1 a** an organ solo played before, during, or after a church service. **b** the music for this. **c** *archaic* an extempore performance esp. as a prelude to other music. **2** (in competitions) a special performance left to the performer's choice. **3** *hist.* a person who holds that the Church or schools should be independent of the State and supported by voluntary contributions. □ **Voluntary Aid Detachment** (in the UK) a group of organized voluntary first-aid and nursing workers. **Voluntary Service Overseas** a British organization promoting voluntary work in underdeveloped countries. □□ **voluntarily** *adv.* **voluntariness** *n.* [ME f. OF *volontaire* or L *voluntarius* f. *voluntas* will]

■ *adj.* **1** free, elective, willing, spontaneous, unsolicited, unbidden, unasked, unprompted. **2** see UNPAID. **7** discretionary, discretional, unconstrained, intentional, wilful, deliberate, conscious, intended, premeditated, planned, volitional, optional. □□ **voluntarily** freely, willingly, spontaneously, of *or* by one's own volition, of one's own accord *or* free will, on one's own (initiative *or* recognizance *or* responsibility), off one's own bat, without prompting, without being prompted *or* asked, gratis, gratuitously; by choice, intentionally, purposely, on purpose, deliberately.

voluntaryism /vóllәntәri-iz'm/ *n. hist.* = VOLUNTARISM 1, 3. □□ **voluntaryist** *n.*

volunteer /vóllәnteér/ *n.* & *v.* ● *n.* **1** a person who voluntarily undertakes a task or enters military or other service, esp. *Mil. hist.* a member of any of the corps of voluntary soldiers formerly organized in the UK and provided with instructors, arms, etc., by the State. **2** (usu. *attrib.*) a self-sown plant. ● *v.* **1** *tr.* (often foll. by *to* + infin.) undertake or offer (one's services, a remark or explanation, etc.) voluntarily. **2** *intr.* (often foll. by *for*) make a voluntary offer of one's services; be a volunteer. [F *volontaire* (as VOLUNTARY), assim. to -EER]
■ *v.* see OFFER *v.* 2, ENROL 1.

voluptuary /vәlúptyoori/ *n.* & *adj.* ● *n.* (*pl.* **-ies**) a person given up to luxury and sensual pleasure. ● *adj.* concerned with luxury and sensual pleasure. [L *volupt(u)arius* (as VOLUPTUOUS)]

voluptuous /vәlúptyooәss/ *adj.* **1** of, tending to, occupied with, or derived from, sensuous or sensual pleasure. **2** full of sexual promise, esp. through shapeliness or fullness. □□ **voluptuously** *adv.* **voluptuousness** *n.* [ME f. OF *voluptueux* or L *voluptuosus* f. *voluptas* pleasure]
■ **1** sensual, sensualistic, sensuous, luxurious, voluptuary, sybaritic(al), hedonist(ic), pleasure-seeking, pleasure-loving, luxury-loving, (self-)indulgent. **2** seductive, erotic, sexy, attractive, desirable, beautiful, tempting, inviting, appealing, enticing, alluring, ravishing, luscious, ripe, delicious, gorgeous; shapely, buxom, busty, well-proportioned, well-built, *colloq.* well-endowed, curvaceous. □□ **voluptuousness** see LUXURY 1.

volute /vәlyoót/ *n.* & *adj.* ● *n.* **1** *Archit.* a spiral scroll characteristic of Ionic capitals and also used in Corinthian and composite capitals. **2 a** any marine gastropod mollusc of the genus *Voluta*. **b** the spiral shell of this. ● *adj.* esp. *Bot.* rolled up. □□ **voluted** *adj.* [F *volute* or L *voluta* fem. past part. of *volvere* roll]

volution /vәlóosh'n, vәlyoó-/ *n.* **1** a rolling motion. **2** a spiral turn. **3** a whorl of a spiral shell. **4** *Anat.* a convolution. [as VOLUTE, after REVOLUTION etc.]

vomer /vṓmәr/ *n. Anat.* the small thin bone separating the nostrils in man and most vertebrates. [L, = ploughshare]

vomit /vómmit/ *v.* & *n.* ● *v.tr.* (**vomited, vomiting**) **1** (also *absol.*) eject (matter) from the stomach through the mouth. **2** (of a volcano, chimney, etc.) eject violently, belch (forth). ● *n.* **1** matter vomited from the stomach. **2** *archaic* an emetic. □□ **vomiter** *n.* [ME ult. f. L *vomere vomit-* or frequent. L *vomitare*]
■ *v.* **1** spew, bring up; regurgitate, gag, retch, heave, *colloq.* throw up, return (food), *Brit. colloq.* sick up, *sl.* puke, barf, *Austral. sl.* chunder, *US sl.* upchuck. **2** eject, spew out *or* up, spit up, belch forth. ● *n.* **1** *Brit. colloq.* sick, *Austral. sl.* chunder.

vomitorium /vómmitóriәm/ *n.* (*pl.* **vomitoria** /-riә/) *Rom. Antiq.* a vomitory. [L; see VOMITORY]

vomitory /vómmitәri/ *adj.* & *n.* ● *adj.* emetic. ● *n.* (*pl.* **-ies**) *Rom. Antiq.* each of a series of passages for entrance and exit in an amphitheatre or theatre. [L *vomitorius* (adj.), *-um* (n.) (as VOMIT)]

V-1 /veéwún/ *n. hist.* a type of German flying bomb used in the war of 1939–45. [abbr. of G *Vergeltungswaffe* reprisal weapon]

voodoo /voódoo/ *n.* & *v.* ● *n.* **1** use of or belief in religious witchcraft as practised among Blacks esp. in the W. Indies. **2** a person skilled in this. **3** a voodoo spell. ● *v.tr.* (**voodoos, voodooed**) affect by voodoo; bewitch. □□ **voodooism** *n.* **voodooist** *n.* [Dahomey *vodu*]

voracious /vәráyshәss/ *adj.* **1** greedy in eating, ravenous. **2** very eager in some activity (*a voracious reader*). □□ **voraciously** *adv.* **voraciousness** *n.* **voracity** /vәrássiti/ *n.* [L *vorax* f. *vorare* devour]
■ **1** insatiable, gluttonous, ravenous, ravening, rapacious, piggish, hoggish, predacious, devouring, greedy, avaricious, uncontrollable, uncontrolled, unquenchable, enormous, prodigious, *archaic or joc.* esurient, *literary or joc.* edacious. **2** thirsty, hungry, desirous, avid, eager, zealous, enthusiastic, fervent, fervid, ardent, earnest, passionate, devoted.

-vorous /vәrәss/ *comb. form* forming adjectives meaning 'feeding on' (*carnivorous*). □□ **-vora** /vәrә/ *comb. form* forming names of groups. **-vore** /vor/ *comb. form* forming names of individuals. [L *-vorus* f. *vorare* devour]

vortex /vórteks/ *n.* (*pl.* **vortexes** or **vortices** /-tiseez/) **1** a mass of whirling fluid, esp. a whirlpool or whirlwind. **2** any whirling motion or mass. **3** a system, occupation, pursuit, etc., viewed as swallowing up or engrossing those who approach it (*the vortex of society*). **4** *Physics* a portion of fluid whose particles have rotatory motion. □ **vortex-ring** a vortex whose axis is a closed curve, e.g. a smoke-ring. □□ **vortical** *adj.* **vortically** *adv.* **vorticity** /vortíssiti/ *n.* **vorticose** *adj.* **vorticular** /vortíkyoolәr/ *adj.* [L *vortex -icis* eddy, var. of VERTEX]
■ **1–3** see EDDY *n.*

vorticella /vórtisélla/ *n.* any sedentary protozoan of the family Vorticellidae, consisting of a tubular stalk with a bell-shaped ciliated opening. [mod.L, dimin. of VORTEX]

vorticist /vórtisist/ *n.* **1** *Art* a painter, writer, etc., of a school influenced by futurism and using the 'vortices' of modern civilization as a basis. **2** *Metaphysics* a person regarding the universe, with Descartes, as a plenum in which motion propagates itself in circles. □□ **vorticism** *n.*

votary /vṓtәri/ *n.* (*pl.* **-ies**; *fem.* **votaress**) (usu. foll. by *of*) **1** a person vowed to the service of God or a god or cult. **2** a devoted follower, adherent, or advocate of a person, system, occupation, etc. □□ **votarist** *n.* [L *vot-*: see VOTE]

vote /vōt/ *n.* & *v.* ● *n.* **1** a formal expression of choice or opinion by means of a ballot, show of hands, etc., concerning a choice of candidate, approval of a motion or resolution, etc. (*let us take a vote on it*; *gave my vote to the independent candidate*). **2** (usu. prec. by *the*) the right to vote, esp. in a State election. **3 a** an opinion expressed by a majority of votes. **b** *Brit.* money granted by a majority of votes. **4** the collective votes that are or may be given by or for a particular group (*will lose the Welsh vote*; *the Conservative vote increased*). **5** a ticket etc. used for recording a vote. ● *v.* **1** *intr.* (often foll. by *for*, *against*, or *to* + infin.) give a vote. **2** *tr.* **a** (often foll. by *that* + clause) enact or resolve by a majority of votes. **b** grant (a sum of money) by a majority of votes. **c** cause to be in a specified position by a majority of votes (*was voted off the committee*). **3** *tr. colloq.* pronounce or declare by general consent (*was voted a failure*). **4** *tr.* (often foll. by *that* + clause) *colloq.* announce one's proposal (*I vote that we all go home*). □ **put to a** (or **the**) **vote** submit to a decision by voting. **vote down** defeat (a proposal etc.) in a vote. **vote in** elect by votes. **vote of censure** = *vote of no confidence*. **vote of confidence** (or **no confidence**) a vote showing that the majority support (or do not support) the policy of the governing body etc. **vote with one's feet** *colloq.* indicate an opinion by one's presence or absence. **voting-machine** (esp. in the US) a machine for the automatic registering of votes. **voting-paper** a paper used in voting by ballot. **voting stock** stock entitling the holder to a vote. □□ **votable** *adj.* **voteless** *adj.* [ME f. past part. stem *vot-* of L *vovēre* vow]

■ *n.* **1** ballot, election, poll, show of hands, referendum, plebiscite. **2** suffrage, franchise, right to vote; voice, say. **3 a** opinion, preference, selection, choice. **4** voter(s), elector(s). **5** ticket, voting card *or* slip *or* paper. ● *v.* **1** cast one's vote, ballot, express *or* signify one's opinion, express *or* signify one's preference, express *or* signify one's desire; (*vote for*) choose, elect, select, pick, opt for, plump for, settle on, come out for, return; (*vote against*) come out against, veto, reject. **2 a** resolve, decide, pass, enact. **3** declare, pronounce, proclaim.

voter /vṓtər/ *n.* **1** a person with the right to vote at an election. **2** a person voting.

votive /vṓtiv/ *adj.* offered or consecrated in fulfilment of a vow (*votive offering*; *votive picture*). □ **votive mass** *Eccl.* a mass celebrated for a special purpose or occasion. [L *votivus* (as VOTE)]

vouch /vowch/ *v.* **1** *intr.* (foll. by *for*) answer for, be surety for (*will vouch for the truth of this*; *can vouch for him*; *could not vouch for his honesty*). **2** *tr. archaic* cite as an authority. **3** *tr. archaic* confirm or uphold (a statement) by evidence or assertion. [ME f. OF *vo(u)cher* summon etc., ult. f. L *vocare* call]

■ **1** (*vouch for*) support, guarantee, be surety for, answer for, back (up), endorse, certify; uphold, sponsor, bear witness to, attest to.

voucher /vówchər/ *n.* **1** a document which can be exchanged for goods or services as a token of payment made or promised by the holder or another. **2** a document establishing the payment of money or the truth of accounts. **3** a person who vouches for a person, statement, etc. [AF *voucher* (as VOUCH) or f. VOUCH]

■ **1, 2** token, coupon; see also CHECK[1] *n.* 5.

vouchsafe /vówchsáyf/ *v.tr. formal* **1** condescend to give or grant (*vouchsafed me no answer*). **2** (foll. by *to* + infin.) condescend. [ME f. VOUCH in sense 'warrant' + SAFE]

■ **1** offer, give (up), yield, accord, supply, grant, impart, bestow, condescend to give, permit, allow, *archaic* deign to give, suffer. **2** see GRANT *v.* 1b.

voussoir /vóoswaar/ *n.* each of the wedge-shaped or tapered stones forming an arch. [OF *vossoir* etc. f. pop.L *volsorium* ult. f. L *volvere* roll]

vow /vow/ *n.* & *v.* ● *n.* **1** *Relig.* a solemn promise esp. in the form of an oath to God or another deity or to a saint. **2** (in *pl.*) the promises by which a monk or nun is bound to poverty, chastity, and obedience. **3** a promise of fidelity (*lovers' vows*; *marriage vows*). **4** (usu. as **baptismal vows**) the promises given at baptism by the baptized person or by sponsors. ● *v.tr.* **1** promise solemnly (*vowed obedience*). **2** dedicate to a deity. **3** (also *absol.*) *archaic* declare solemnly. □ **under a vow** having made a vow. [ME f. AF *v(o)u*, OF *vo(u)*, f. L (as VOTE): (v.) f. OF *vouer*, in sense 2 partly f. AVOW]

■ *n.* oath, pledge, promise, agreement; (solemn) word (of honour). ● *v.* **1** swear, pledge, promise, assure, state, declare, give (one's) (solemn) word (of honour), *archaic* plight one's troth.

vowel /vówəl/ *n.* **1** a speech-sound made with vibration of the vocal cords but without audible friction, more open than a consonant and capable of forming a syllable. **2** a letter or letters representing this, as *a*, *e*, *i*, *o*, *u*, *aw*, *ah*. □ **vowel gradation** = ABLAUT. **vowel mutation** = UMLAUT 2. **vowel-point** each of a set of marks indicating vowels in Hebrew etc. □□ **vowelled** *adj.* (also in *comb.*). **vowelless** *adj.* **vowelly** *adj.* [ME f. OF *vouel*, *voiel* f. L *vocalis* (*littera*) VOCAL (letter)]

vowelize /vówəlīz/ *v.tr.* (also **-ise**) insert the vowels in (shorthand, Hebrew, etc.).

vox angelica /vóks anjéllikə/ *n.* an organ-stop with a soft tremulous tone. [LL, = angelic voice]

vox humana /vóks hyoomaánə/ *n.* an organ-stop with a tone supposed to resemble a human voice. [L, = human voice]

vox pop /vóks póp/ *n. Broadcasting colloq.* popular opinion as represented by informal comments from members of the public; statements or interviews of this kind. [abbr. of VOX POPULI]

vox populi /vóks pópyoolee, -lī/ *n.* public opinion, the general verdict, popular belief or rumour. [L, = the people's voice]

voyage /vóyij/ *n.* & *v.* ● *n.* **1** a journey, esp. a long one by water, air, or in space. **2** an account of this. ● *v.* **1** *intr.* make a voyage. **2** *tr.* traverse, esp. by water or air. □□ **voyageable** *adj.* **voyager** *n.* [ME f. AF & OF *veiage*, *voiage* f. L *viaticum*]

■ *n.* **1** see JOURNEY *n.* ● *v.* **1** see JOURNEY *v.* **2** see TRAVERSE *v.* 1. □□ **voyager** see TRAVELLER 1.

voyageur /vwaáyaazhṓr/ *n.* a Canadian boatman, esp. *hist.* one employed in transporting goods and passengers between trading posts. [F, = voyager (as VOYAGE)]

voyeur /vwaayṓr/ *n.* a person who obtains sexual gratification from observing others' sexual actions or organs. □□ **voyeurism** *n.* **voyeuristic** /-rístik/ *adj.* **voyeuristically** /-rístikəli/ *adj.* [F f. *voir* see]

VP *abbr.* Vice-President.

VR *abbr.* **1** Queen Victoria. **2** variant reading. [sense 1 f. L *Victoria Regina*]

VS *abbr.* Veterinary Surgeon.

vs. *abbr.* versus.

V-sign /veé-sīn/ *n.* **1** *Brit.* a sign of the letter V made with the first two fingers pointing up and the back of the hand facing outwards, as a gesture of abuse, contempt, etc. **2** a similar sign made with the palm of the hand facing outwards, as a symbol of victory.

VSO *abbr.* Voluntary Service Overseas.

VSOP *abbr.* Very Special Old Pale (brandy).

VT *abbr. US* Vermont (in official postal use).

Vt. *abbr.* Vermont.

VTO *abbr.* vertical take-off.

VTOL /veétol/ *abbr.* vertical take-off and landing.

V-2 /veétóo/ *n.* a type of German rocket-powered missile used in the war of 1939–45. [abbr. of G *Vergeltungswaffe* reprisal weapon]

vug /vug/ *n.* a rock-cavity lined with crystals. □□ **vuggy** *adj.* **vugular** *adj.* [Corn. *vooga*]

vulcanic var. of VOLCANIC.

vulcanite /vúlkənīt/ *n.* a hard black vulcanized rubber, ebonite. [as VULCANIZE]

vulcanize /vúlkənīz/ *v.tr.* (also **-ise**) treat (rubber or rubberlike material) with sulphur etc. esp. at a high temperature to increase its strength. □□ **vulcanizable** *adj.* **vulcanization** /-záysh'n/ *n.* **vulcanizer** *n.* [*Vulcan*, Roman god of fire and metal-working]

vulcanology /vúlkənólləji/ *n.* (also **volcanology** /vól-/) the scientific study of volcanoes. □□ **vulcanological** /-nəlójik'l/ *adj.* **vulcanologist** *n.*

vulgar /vúlgər/ *adj.* **1 a** of or characteristic of the common people, plebeian. **b** coarse in manners; low (*vulgar expressions*; *vulgar tastes*). **2** in common use; generally prevalent (*vulgar errors*). □ **vulgar fraction** a fraction expressed by numerator and denominator, not decimally. **vulgar Latin** informal Latin of classical times. **the vulgar tongue** the national or vernacular language, esp. formerly as opposed to Latin. □□ **vulgarly** *adv.* [ME f. L *vulgaris* f. *vulgus* common people]

■ **1 a** common, plebeian, uncultured, uncultivated, unrefined, low, lowbrow, low-class. **b** indelicate, boorish, inelegant, unladylike, ungentlemanly, gauche, uncouth, ill-bred, ill-mannered, uncivilized, barbarian, coarse, tasteless, ostentatious, ignoble; indecent, rude, crude, naughty, dirty, improper, impolite, off colour, risqué, ribald, blue, low, indecorous, nasty, offensive, gross, lustful, obscene, lewd, lascivious, licentious, smutty, salacious, scatological, filthy, pornographic, *colloq.* tarty, flash, raunchy. **2** popular, vernacular, ordinary, everyday, general, homespun, common, commonplace, household, average.

vulgarian /vulgáiriən/ *n.* a vulgar (esp. rich) person.

vulgarism /vúlgəriz'm/ *n.* **1** a word or expression in coarse or uneducated use. **2** an instance of coarse or uneducated behaviour.

vulgarity /vulgárriti/ *n.* (*pl.* **-ies**) **1** the quality of being vulgar. **2** an instance of this.
■ **1** coarseness, lack of refinement *or* sophistication, crudeness, rudeness, indelicacy, tawdriness, baseness, unsophistication, gaucherie, gaucheness, ignobility; impropriety, ribaldry, lewdness, grossness, foulness, vileness, filthiness, obscenity, *colloq.* raunchiness.

vulgarize /vúlgərīz/ *v.tr.* (also **-ise**) **1** make (a person, manners, etc.) vulgar, infect with vulgarity. **2** spoil (a scene, sentiment, etc.) by making it too common, frequented, or well known. **3** popularize. ▫▫ **vulgarization** /-záysh'n/ *n.*
■ **1** see VITIATE 1.

Vulgate /vúlgayt, -gət/ *n.* **1 a** the Latin version of the Bible prepared mainly by St Jerome in the late fourth century. **b** the official Roman Catholic Latin text as revised in 1592. **2** (**vulgate**) the traditionally accepted text of any author. **3** (**vulgate**) common or colloquial speech. [L *vulgata* (*editio* edition), fem. past part. of *vulgare* make public f. *vulgus*: see VULGAR]

vulnerable /vúlnərəb'l, *disp.* vúnn-/ *adj.* **1** that may be wounded or harmed. **2** (foll. by *to*) exposed to damage by a weapon, criticism, etc. **3** *Bridge* having won one game towards rubber and therefore liable to higher penalties. ▫▫ **vulnerability** /-bílliti/ *n.* **vulnerableness** *n.* **vulnerably** *adv.* [LL *vulnerabilis* f. L *vulnerare* to wound f. *vulnus -eris* wound]
■ **1** exposed, defenceless, weak, sensitive, unprotected, unguarded, unshielded, helpless, powerless, insecure. **2** (*vulnerable to*) see SUSCEPTIBLE 2a. ▫▫ **vulnerability, vulnerableness** see FRAILTY 1, 2.

vulnerary /vúlnərəri/ *adj.* & *n.* ● *adj.* useful or used for the healing of wounds. ● *n.* (*pl.* **-ies**) a vulnerary drug, plant, etc. [L *vulnerarius* f. *vulnus*: see VULNERABLE]

vulpine /vúlpīn/ *adj.* **1** of or like a fox. **2** crafty, cunning. [L *vulpinus* f. *vulpes* fox]

vulture /vúlchər/ *n.* **1** any of various large birds of prey of the family Cathartidae or Accipitridae, with the head and neck more or less bare of feathers, feeding chiefly on carrion and reputed to gather with others in anticipation of a death. **2** a rapacious person. ▫▫ **vulturine** /-rīn/ *adj.* **vulturish** *adj.* **vulturous** *adj.* [ME f. AF *vultur*, OF *voltour* etc., f. L *vulturius*]

vulva /vúlvə/ *n.* (*pl.* **vulvas**) *Anat.* the external female genitals, esp. the external opening of the vagina. ▫▫ **vulvar** *adj.* **vulvitis** /-vītiss/ *n.* [L, = womb]

vv. *abbr.* **1** verses. **2** volumes.

vying *pres. part.* of VIE.

Ww

W[1] /dúbb'lyōō/ *n.* (also **w**) (*pl.* **Ws** or **W's**) the twenty-third letter of the alphabet.

W[2] *abbr.* (also **W.**) **1** watt(s). **2** West; Western. **3** women's (size). **4** Welsh.

W[3] *symb. Chem.* the element tungsten.

w. *abbr.* **1** wicket(s). **2** wide(s). **3** with. **4** wife.

WA *abbr.* **1** Western Australia. **2** *US* Washington (State) (in official postal use).

Waac /wak/ *n. hist.* a member of the Women's Army Auxiliary Corps (*Brit.* 1917-19 or *US* 1942-8). [initials *WAAC*]

Waaf /waf/ *n. Brit. hist.* a member of the Women's Auxiliary Air Force (1939-48). [initials *WAAF*]

WAC *abbr.* (in the US) Women's Army Corps.

wack[1] /wak/ *n.* esp. *US sl.* a crazy person. [prob. back-form. f. WACKY]

wack[2] /wak/ *n. dial.* a familiar term of address. [perh. f. *wacker* Liverpudlian]

wacke /wákkə/ *n. hist.* a greyish-green or brownish rock resulting from the decomposition of basaltic rock. [G f. MHG *wacke* large stone, OHG *wacko* pebble]

wacko /wákkō/ *adj.* & *n. US sl.* ● *adj.* crazy. ● *n.* (*pl.* **-os** or **-oes**) a crazy person. [WACKY + -O]

wacky /wákki/ *adj.* & *n.* (also **whacky**) *sl.* ● *adj.* (**-ier**, **-iest**) crazy. ● *n.* (*pl.* **-ies**) a crazy person. □□ **wackily** *adv.* **wackiness** *n.* [orig. dial., = left-handed, f. WHACK]
■ *adj.* see CRAZY 1.

wad /wod/ *n.* & *v.* ● *n.* **1** a lump or bundle of soft material used esp. to keep things apart or in place or to stuff up an opening. **2** a disc of felt etc. keeping powder or shot in place in a gun. **3** a number of banknotes or documents placed together. **4** *Brit. sl.* a bun, sandwich, etc. **5** (in *sing.* or *pl.*) a large quantity esp. of money. ● *v.tr.* (**wadded**, **wadding**) **1** stop up (an aperture or a gun-barrel) with a wad. **2** keep (powder etc.) in place with a wad. **3** line or stuff (a garment or coverlet) with wadding. **4** protect (a person, walls, etc.) with wadding. **5** press (cotton etc.) into a wad or wadding. [perh. rel. to Du. *watten*, F *ouate* padding, cotton wool]
■ *n.* **1** pad, mass, lump, clod, ball, plug, chunk, hunk, block, pack, *Brit. colloq.* wodge. **3** roll, bundle, pocketful, heap, quantity, load, *US* bankroll. **5** see MINT[2] *n.* 2 ● *v.* **1** see STOP *v.* 7. **3** see PAD *v.* 1.

wadding /wódding/ *n.* **1** soft pliable material of cotton or wool etc. used to line or stuff garments, quilts, etc., or to pack fragile articles. **2** any material from which gun-wads are made.
■ **1** padding, filling, stuffing.

waddle /wódd'l/ *v.* & *n.* ● *v.intr.* walk with short steps and a swaying motion, like a stout short-legged person or a bird with short legs set far apart (e.g. a duck or goose). ● *n.* a waddling gait. □□ **waddler** *n.* [perh. frequent. of WADE]
■ *v.* toddle, shuffle, wobble, totter, pad, duck-walk, *colloq.* waggle.

waddy /wóddi/ *n.* (*pl.* **-ies**) **1** an Australian Aboriginal's war-club. **2** *Austral.* & *NZ* any club or stick. [Aboriginal, perh. f. WOOD]
■ **2** see CLUB *n.* 1.

wade /wayd/ *v.* & *n.* ● *v.* **1** *intr.* walk through water or some impeding medium e.g. snow, mud, or sand. **2** *intr.* make one's way with difficulty or by force. **3** *intr.* (foll. by *through*) read (a book etc.) in spite of its dullness etc. **4** *intr.* (foll. by *into*) *colloq.* attack (a person or task) vigorously. **5** *tr.* ford (a stream etc.) on foot. ● *n.* a spell of wading. □ **wade in** *colloq.* make a vigorous attack or intervention. **wading bird** any long-legged water-bird that wades. □□ **wadable** *adj.* (also **wadeable**). [OE *wadan* f. Gmc, = go (through)]
■ *v.* **1** paddle, splash, plod, trudge, squelch. **2** make one's way, trek, trudge, plough. **3** (*wade through*) plough through, work one's way through, plod through, hammer *or* pound away at, peg away at. **4** (*wade into*) attack, approach, get *or* set to work on, plunge *or* dive into, *sl.* get stuck into; lunge at. **5** ford, cross, traverse, walk across, make one's way across. □ **wade in** enter, get in, join in, attack, get *or* set to work, plunge in, dive in, *sl.* get stuck in.

wader /wáydər/ *n.* **1 a** a person who wades. **b** a wading bird, esp. any of various birds of the order Charadriiformes. **2** (in *pl.*) high waterproof boots, or a waterproof garment for the legs and body, worn in fishing etc.

wadgula /wádyoolaa/ *n. Austral.* (in Aboriginal English) a white person. [alt. of *white fellow*]

wadi /wóddi, waádi/ *n.* (also **wady**) (*pl.* **wadis** or **wadies**) a rocky watercourse in N. Africa etc., dry except in the rainy season. [Arab. *wādī*]

WAF *abbr.* (in the US) Women in the Air Force.

w.a.f. *abbr.* with all faults.

wafer /wáyfər/ *n.* & *v.* ● *n.* **1** a very thin light crisp sweet biscuit, esp. of a kind eaten with ice-cream. **2** a thin disc of unleavened bread used in the Eucharist. **3** a disc of red paper stuck on a legal document instead of a seal. **4** *Electronics* a very thin slice of a semiconductor crystal used as the substrate for solid-state circuitry. **5** *hist.* a small disc of dried paste formerly used for fastening letters, holding papers together, etc. ● *v.tr.* fasten or seal with a wafer. □ **wafer-thin** very thin. □□ **wafery** *adj.* [ME f. AF *wafre*, ONF *waufre*, OF *gaufre* (cf. GOFFER) f. MLG *wāfel* waffle: cf. WAFFLE[2]]

waffle[1] /wóff'l/ *n.* & *v.* esp. *Brit. colloq.* ● *n.* verbose but aimless, misleading, or ignorant talk or writing. ● *v.intr.* indulge in waffle. □□ **waffler** *n.* **waffly** *adj.* [orig. dial., frequent. of *waff* = yelp, yap (imit.)]
■ *n.* talk, palaver, verbiage, prattle, twaddle, blather, prolixity, wordiness, jabber, prevarication, evasiveness, *sl.* hot air. ● *v.* carry on, jabber (on), prattle (on), prate, blather (on *or* away), run on; equivocate, hedge, quibble, shuffle, tergiversate, hem and haw, prevaricate, beat about the bush; *colloq.* witter (on), natter (on); *Brit. colloq.* rabbit on.

waffle[2] /wóff'l/ *n.* esp. *US* a small crisp batter cake. □ **waffle-iron** a utensil, usu. of two shallow metal pans hinged together, for baking waffles. [Du. *wafel*, *waefel* f. MLG *wāfel*: cf. WAFER]

waft /woft, waaft/ *v.* & *n.* ● *v.tr.* & *intr.* convey or travel easily as through air or over water; sweep smoothly and lightly along. ● *n.* **1** (usu. foll. by *of*) a whiff or scent. **2** a transient sensation of peace, joy, etc. **3** (also **weft** /weft/) *Naut.* a distress signal, e.g. an ensign rolled or knotted or a garment flown in the rigging. [orig. 'convoy (ship etc.)', back-form. f. obs. *waughter*, *wafter* armed convoy-ship, f. Du. or LG *wachter* f. *wachten* to guard]

■ *v.* drift, float, blow, whiff, be borne *or* carried *or* conveyed *or* transported. ● *n.* **1** breath, suggestion, puff, whiff, scent, hint.

wag[1] /wag/ *v.* & *n.* ● *v.* (**wagged, wagging**) **1** *tr.* & *intr.* shake or wave rapidly or energetically to and fro. **2** *intr. archaic* (of the world, times, etc.) go along with varied fortune or characteristics. ● *n.* a single wagging motion (*with a wag of his tail*). □ **the tail wags the dog** the less or least important member of a society, section of a party, or part of a structure has control. **tongues** (or **beards** or **chins** or **jaws**) **wag** there is talk. [ME *waggen* f. root of OE *wagian* sway]

■ *v.* **1** wave, oscillate, fluctuate, sway, undulate, flutter, flap, flip, flicker, shake, vibrate, quiver, wiggle, nod, rock, dance, wobble, bob, waver, *colloq.* waggle. ● *n.* wave, oscillation, fluctuation, sway, undulation, flutter, flap, flip, flicker, shake, vibration, quiver, wiggle, nod, wobble, waver, *colloq.* waggle.

wag[2] /wag/ *n.* **1** a facetious person, a joker. **2** *Brit. sl.* a truant (*play the wag*). [prob. f. obs. *waghalter* one likely to be hanged (as WAG[1], HALTER)]

■ **1** comedian, wit, punster, pundit, joker, jester, comic, jokester, droll, merry andrew, clown, *colloq.* card. **2** truant, absentee, *Brit. sl.* skiver.

wage /wayj/ *n.* & *v.* ● *n.* **1** (in *sing.* or *pl.*) a fixed regular payment, usu. daily or weekly, made by an employer to an employee, esp. to a manual or unskilled worker (cf. SALARY). **2** (in *sing.* or *pl.*) requital (*the wages of sin is death*). **3** (in *pl.*) *Econ.* the part of total production that rewards labour rather than remunerating capital. ● *v.tr.* carry on (a war, conflict, or contest). □ **living wage** a wage that affords the means of normal subsistence. **wage-claim** = *pay-claim* (see PAY[1]). **wage-earner** a person who works for wages. **wages council** a board of workers' and employers' representatives determining wages where there is no collective bargaining. **wage slave** a person dependent on income from labour in conditions like slavery. [ME f. AF & ONF *wage*, OF *g(u)age*, f. Gmc, rel. to GAGE[1], WED]

■ *n.* **1** pay, compensation, emolument, remuneration, payment, fee, salary, stipend, recompense, reward, earnings, income; honorarium. **2** requital, return, reward, recompense. ● *v.* carry on, pursue, conduct, engage in, practise, prosecute, proceed with.

wager /wáyjər/ *n.* & *v.tr.* & *intr.* = BET. □ **wager of battle** *hist.* an ancient form of trial by personal combat between the parties or their champions. **wager of law** *hist.* a form of trial in which the defendant was required to produce witnesses who would swear to his or her innocence. [ME f. AF *wageure* f. *wager* (as WAGE)]

waggery /wággəri/ *n.* (*pl.* **-ies**) **1** waggish behaviour, joking. **2** a waggish action or remark, a joke.

waggish /wággish/ *adj.* playful, facetious. □□ **waggishly** *adv.* **waggishness** *n.*

■ see COMIC *adj.* □□ **waggishness** see HUMOUR *n.* 1a.

waggle /wágg'l/ *v.* & *n. colloq.* ● *v.* **1** *intr.* & *tr.* wag. **2** *intr. Golf* swing the club-head to and fro over the ball before playing a shot. ● *n.* a waggling motion. [WAG[1] + -LE[4]]

■ *v.* **1** see WAG[1] *v.* ● *n.* see WAG[1] *n.*

waggly /wágli/ *adj.* unsteady.

Wagnerian /vaagnéeriən/ *adj.* & *n.* ● *adj.* of, relating to, or characteristic of the music dramas of Richard Wagner, German composer d. 1883, esp. with reference to their large scale. ● *n.* an admirer of Wagner or his music.

wagon /wággən/ *n.* (also *Brit.* **waggon**) **1 a** a four-wheeled vehicle for heavy loads, often with a removable tilt or cover. **b** a lorry or truck. **2** *Brit.* a railway vehicle for goods, esp. an open truck. **3** a trolley for conveying tea etc. **4** (in full **water-wagon**) a vehicle for carrying water. **5** *US* a light horse-drawn vehicle. **6** *colloq.* a motor car, esp. an estate car. □ **on the wagon** (or **water-wagon**) *sl.* teetotal. **wagon-roof** (or **-vault**) = *barrel vault*. [earlier *wagon*, *wag(h)en*, f. Du. *wag(h)en*, rel. to OE *wægn* WAIN]

wagoner /wággənər/ *n.* (also *Brit.* **waggoner**) the driver of a wagon. [Du. *wagenaar* (as WAGON)]

wagonette /wággənét/ *n.* (also *Brit.* **waggonette**) a four-wheeled horse-drawn pleasure vehicle, usu. open, with facing side-seats.

wagon-lit /vággonlée/ *n.* (*pl.* **wagons-lits** *pronunc.* same) a sleeping-car on a Continental railway. [F]

wagtail /wágtayl/ *n.* any small bird of the genus *Motacilla* with a long tail in frequent motion.

Wahabi /wəhaábi/ *n.* (also **Wahhabi**) (*pl.* **-is**) a member of a sect of Muslim puritans following strictly the original words of the Koran. [Muhammad ibn Abd-el-*Wahhab*, founder in the 18th c.]

wahine /waahéeni/ *n. NZ* a woman or wife. [Maori]

wah-wah /waáwaa/ *n.* (also **wa-wa**) *Mus.* an effect achieved on brass instruments by alternately applying and removing a mute and on an electric guitar by controlling the output from the amplifier with a pedal. [imit.]

waif /wayf/ *n.* **1** a homeless and helpless person, esp. an abandoned child. **2** an ownerless object or animal, a thing cast up by or drifting in the sea or brought by an unknown agency. □ **waifs and strays 1** homeless or neglected children. **2** odds and ends. □□ **waifish** *adj.* [ME f. AF *waif*, *weif*, ONF *gaif*, prob. of Scand. orig.]

■ see FOUNDLING.

wail /wayl/ *n.* & *v.* ● *n.* **1** a prolonged and plaintive loud high-pitched cry of pain, grief, etc. **2** a sound like or suggestive of this. ● *v.* **1** *intr.* utter a wail. **2** *intr.* lament or complain persistently or bitterly. **3** *intr.* (of the wind etc.) make a sound like a person wailing. **4** *tr. poet.* or *rhet.* bewail; wail over. □ **Wailing Wall** a high wall in Jerusalem said to stand on the site of Herod's temple, where Jews traditionally pray and lament on Fridays. □□ **wailer** *n.* **wailful** *adj. poet.* **wailingly** *adv.* [ME f. ON, rel. to WOE]

■ *n.* **1, 2** see CRY *n.* ● *v.* **1** see CRY *v.* 2a. **2** see COMPLAIN 1, LAMENT *v.* **3** howl, moan.

wain /wayn/ *n. archaic* **1** a wagon. **2** (prec. by *the*) = CHARLES'S WAIN. [OE *wæg(e)n*, *wǣn*, f. Gmc, rel. to WAY, WEIGH[1]]

wainscot /wáynskət/ *n.* & *v.* ● *n.* **1** boarding or wooden panelling on the lower part of a room-wall. **2** *Brit. hist.* imported oak of fine quality. ● *v.tr.* (**wainscoted, wainscoting**) line with wainscot. [ME f. MLG *wagenschot*, app. f. *wagen* WAGON + *schot* of uncert. meaning]

wainscoting /wáynskəting/ *n.* **1** a wainscot. **2** material for this.

wainwright /wáynrīt/ *n.* a wagon-builder.

waist /wayst/ *n.* **1 a** the part of the human body below the ribs and above the hips, usu. of smaller circumference than these; the narrower middle part of the normal human figure. **b** the circumference of this. **2** a similar narrow part in the middle of a violin, hourglass, wasp, etc. **3 a** the part of a garment encircling or covering the waist. **b** the narrow middle part of a woman's dress etc. **c** *US* a blouse or bodice. **4** the middle part of a ship, between the forecastle and the quarterdeck. □ **waist-cloth** a loincloth. **waist-deep** (or **-high**) up to the waist (*waist-deep in water*). □□ **waisted** *adj.* (also in *comb.*). **waistless** *adj.* [ME *wast*, perh. f. OE f. the root of WAX[2]]

■ **1** see MIDDLE *n.* 2.

waistband /wáystband/ *n.* a strip of cloth forming the waist of a garment.

waistcoat /wáyskōt, wáystkōt, wéskət/ *n. Brit.* a close-fitting waist-length garment, without sleeves or collar but usu. buttoned, worn usu. by men over a shirt and under a jacket.

waistline /wáystlīn/ *n.* the outline or the size of a person's body at the waist.

wait /wayt/ *v.* & *n.* ● *v.* **1** *intr.* **a** defer action or departure for a specified time or until some expected event occurs (*wait a minute*; *wait till I come*; *wait for a fine day*). **b** be expectant or on the watch (*waited to see what would happen*). **c** (foll. by *for*) refrain from going so fast that (a person) is left behind (*wait for me!*). **2** *tr.* await (an opportunity, one's turn, etc.). **3** *tr.* defer (an activity) until a person's arrival or until some expected event occurs. **4** *intr.* (usu. as **waiting** *n.*) park a vehicle for a short time at the side of a road etc. (*no waiting*). **5** *intr.* **a** (in full **wait at** or *US* **on table**) act as a waiter or as a servant with similar functions. **b** act as an attendant. **6** *intr.* (foll. by *on, upon*) **a** await the convenience of. **b** serve as an attendant to. **c** pay a respectful visit to. ● *n.* **1** a period of waiting (*had a long wait for the train*). **2** (usu. foll. by *for*) watching for an enemy; ambush (*lie in wait*; *lay wait*). **3** (in *pl.*) *Brit.* **a** *archaic* street singers of Christmas carols. **b** *hist.* official bands of musicians maintained by a city or town. □ **cannot wait 1** is impatient. **2** needs to be dealt with immediately. **can wait** need not be dealt with immediately. **wait-a-bit** a plant with hooked thorns etc. that catch the clothing. **wait and see** await the progress of events. **wait for it!** *colloq.* **1** do not begin before the proper moment. **2** used to create an interval of suspense before saying something unexpected or amusing. **wait on** *Austral., NZ, & N.Engl.* be patient, wait. **wait up** (often foll. by *for*) not go to bed until a person arrives or an event happens. **you wait!** used to imply a threat, warning, or promise. [ME f. ONF *waitier* f. Gmc, rel. to WAKE[1]]

■ *v.* **1 a** linger, hold on, stay, stop, remain, rest, pause, bide one's time, mark time, stand by, hang about *or* around, dally, cool one's heels, *archaic or literary* tarry, *colloq.* stick around, sit tight, stay put, hang on. **b** see *watch out* 1. **2** await, wait for. **3** defer, delay, postpone, shelve, put off, *colloq.* put on ice *or* the back burner. **6 b** (*wait on* or *upon*) serve, attend, minister to. ● *n.* **1** delay, pause, stay, hold-up, interval, halt, stop, stoppage, break, hiatus, lacuna, gap, respite, rest (period), intermission, discontinuation, postponement, moratorium, recess.

waiter /wáytər/ *n.* **1** a man who serves at table in a hotel or restaurant etc. **2** a person who waits for a time, event, or opportunity. **3** a tray or salver.

■ **1** boy, *garçon*, steward, attendant, *US usu. derog.* flunkey; head waiter, *maître d'hôtel*, host; *sommelier (des vins)*, wine steward, wine waiter, cupbearer; *US colloq.* carhop.

waiting /wáyting/ *n.* **1** in senses of WAIT *v.* **2 a** official attendance at court. **b** one's period of this. □ **waiting game** abstention from early action in a contest etc. so as to act more effectively later. **waiting-list** a list of people waiting for a thing not immediately available. **waiting-room** a room provided for people to wait in, esp. by a doctor, dentist, etc., or at a railway or bus station.

waitress /wáytriss/ *n.* a woman who serves at table in a hotel or restaurant etc.

■ hostess, stewardess; bunny (girl).

waive /wayv/ *v.tr.* refrain from insisting on or using (a right, claim, opportunity, legitimate plea, rule, etc.). [ME f. AF *weyver*, OF *gaiver* allow to become a WAIF, abandon]

■ give up, relinquish, renounce, resign, forsake, forgo, cede, sign away, surrender, abandon, disclaim, yield, dispense with, set *or* put aside; ignore, disregard, overlook.

waiver /wáyvər/ *n. Law* the act or an instance of waiving. [as WAIVE]

■ renunciation, relinquishment, cession, resignation, surrender, abandonment, deferral, remission.

wake[1] /wayk/ *v.* & *n.* ● *v.* (*past* **woke** /wōk/ or **waked**; *past part.* **woken** /wōkən/ or **waked**) **1** *intr.* & *tr.* (often foll. by *up*) cease or cause to cease to sleep. **2** *intr.* & *tr.* (often foll. by *up*) become or cause to become alert, attentive, or active (*needs something to wake him up*). **3** *intr.* (*archaic* except as **waking** *adj.* & *n.*) be awake (*in her waking hours*; *waking or sleeping*). **4** *tr.* disturb (silence or a place) with noise; make re-echo. **5** *tr.* evoke (an echo). **6** *intr.* & *tr.* rise or raise from the dead. ● *n.* **1** a watch beside a corpse before burial; lamentation and (less often) merrymaking in connection with this. **2** (usu. in *pl.*) an annual holiday in (industrial) northern England. **3** *hist.* **a** a vigil commemorating the dedication of a church. **b** a fair or merrymaking on this occasion. □ **be a wake-up** (often foll. by *to*) *Austral. sl.* be alert or aware. **wake-robin 1** *Brit.* an arum, esp. the cuckoo-pint. **2** *US* any plant of the genus *Trillium.* □□ **waker** *n.* [OE *wacan* (recorded only in past *woc*), *wacian* (weak form), rel. to WATCH: sense 'vigil' perh. f. ON]

■ *v.* **1** awaken, awake, rouse, waken, bring round; stir, bestir oneself, become conscious, get up, rise, come to, get going. **2** awake, waken, awaken, reawaken, animate, stimulate, enliven, galvanize, fire, quicken, inspirit, inspire, activate, liven up, vivify, kindle, vitalize, stir, arouse, get a person going, bring to life. **5** see *call forth.* ● *n.* **1** vigil, watch.

wake[2] /wayk/ *n.* **1** the track left on the water's surface by a moving ship. **2** turbulent air left behind a moving aircraft etc. □ **in the wake of** behind, following, as a result of, in imitation of. [prob. f. MLG f. ON *vök* hole or opening in ice]

■ **1** track, trail, aftermath, path, backwash, wash, bow wave. **2** turbulence, track, trail, path. □ **in the wake of** following (on *or* upon), behind, after, subsequent to; as a result *or* consequence of, on account of, because of, owing to, by virtue of; in imitation of.

wakeful /wáykfŏŏl/ *adj.* **1** unable to sleep. **2** (of a night etc.) passed with little or no sleep. **3** vigilant. □□ **wakefully** *adv.* **wakefulness** *n.*

■ **1** awake, sleepless, waking, unsleeping, restless, restive, insomniac. **2** sleepless, disturbed, restless. **3** watchful, (on the) alert, on the qui vive, sharp, attentive, vigilant, wary, cautious, observant, heedful, on the lookout.

waken /wáykən/ *v.tr.* & *intr.* make or become awake. [ON *vakna* f. Gmc, rel. to WAKE[1]]

■ see WAKE[1] *v.* 1, 2.

Walachian var. of WALLACHIAN.

Waldenses /woldénseez/ *n.pl.* a puritan religious sect orig. in S. France, now chiefly in Italy and America, founded *c.*1170 and much persecuted. □□ **Waldensian** *adj.* & *n.* [med.L f. Peter *Waldo* of Lyons, founder]

wale /wayl/ *n.* & *v.* ● *n.* **1** = WEAL[1]. **2** a ridge on a woven fabric, e.g. corduroy. **3** *Naut.* a broad thick timber along a ship's side. **4** a specially woven strong band round a woven basket. ● *v.tr.* provide or mark with wales; thrash, whip. □ **wale-knot** a knot made at the end of a rope by intertwining strands to prevent unravelling or act as a stopper. [OE *walu* stripe, ridge]

walk /wawk/ *v.* & *n.* ● *v.* **1** *intr.* **a** (of a person or other biped) progress by lifting and setting down each foot in turn, never having both feet off the ground at once. **b** progress with similar movements (*walked on his hands*). **c** go with the gait usual except when speed is desired. **d** (of a quadruped) go with the slowest gait, always having at least two feet on the ground at once. **2** *intr.* **a** travel or go on foot. **b** take exercise in this way (*walks for two hours each day*). **3** *tr.* **a** perambulate, traverse on foot at walking speed, tread the floor or surface of. **b** traverse or cover (a specified distance) on foot (*walks five miles a day*). **4** *tr.* **a** cause to walk with one. **b** accompany in walking. **c** ride or lead (a horse, dog, etc.) at walking pace. **d** take charge of (a puppy) at walk (see sense 4 of *n.*). **5** *intr.* (of a ghost) appear. **6** *intr. Cricket* leave the wicket on being out. **7** *Baseball* **a** *intr.* reach first base on balls. **b** *tr.* allow to do this. **8** *intr. archaic* live in a specified manner, conduct oneself (*walk humbly*; *walk with God*). **9** *intr. US sl.* be released from suspicion or from a charge. ● *n.* **1 a** an act of walking, the ordinary human gait (*go at a walk*). **b** the slowest gait of an animal. **c** a person's manner of walking (*know him by his walk*). **2 a** taking a (usu. specified) time to walk a distance (*is only ten minutes' walk from here*; *it's quite a walk to the bus-stop*). **b** an excursion on foot, a stroll or constitutional (*go for a walk*). **c** a journey on foot completed to earn money promised for a charity etc. **3 a** a place, track, or route intended or suitable for walking; a promenade, colonnade, or footpath. **b** a person's favourite place or route for walking. **c** the round of a postman, hawker, etc. **4** a farm etc.

where a hound-puppy is sent to accustom it to various surroundings. **5** the place where a gamecock is kept. **6** a part of a forest under one keeper. □ **in a walk** without effort (*won in a walk*). **walk about** stroll. **walk all over** *colloq.* **1** defeat easily. **2** take advantage of. **walk away from 1** easily outdistance. **2** refuse to become involved with; fail to deal with. **3** survive (an accident etc.) without serious injury. **walk away with** *colloq.* = *walk off with.* **walk the boards** be an actor. **walk the hospitals** = *walk the wards.* **walk in** (often foll. by *on*) enter or arrive, esp. unexpectedly or easily. **walk into 1** *colloq.* encounter through unwariness (*walked into the trap*). **2** *sl. archaic* attack forcefully. **3** *sl. archaic* eat heartily. **walk it 1** make a journey on foot, not ride. **2** *colloq.* achieve something (esp. a victory) easily. **walk Matilda** see MATILDA. **walk off 1** depart (esp. abruptly). **2** get rid of the effects of (a meal, ailment, etc.) by walking (*walked off his anger*). **walk a person off his** or **her feet** (or **legs**) exhaust a person with walking. **walk off with** *colloq.* **1** steal. **2** win easily. **walk of life** an occupation, profession, or calling. **walk-on 1** (in full **walk-on part**) = *walking-on part.* **2** the player of this. **walk on air** see AIR. **walk out 1** depart suddenly or angrily. **2** (usu. foll. by *with*) *Brit. archaic* go for walks in courtship. **3** cease work, esp. to go on strike. **walk-out** *n.* a sudden angry departure, esp. as a protest or strike. **walk out on** desert, abandon. **walk over 1** *colloq.* = *walk all over.* **2** (often *absol.*) traverse (a racecourse) without needing to hurry, because one has no opponents or only inferior ones. **walk-over** *n.* an easy victory or achievement. **walk the plank** see PLANK. **walk the streets 1** be a prostitute. **2** traverse the streets esp. in search of work etc. **walk tall** *colloq.* feel justifiable pride. **walk up!** a showman's invitation to a circus etc. **walk-up** *US adj.* (of a building) allowing access to the upper floors only by stairs. ● *n.* a walk-up building. **walk up to** approach (a person) for a talk etc. **walk the wards** be a medical student. □□ **walkable** *adj.* [OE *wealcan* roll, toss, wander, f. Gmc]

■ *v.* **1, 2** advance, proceed, move, go, go *or* make one's way on foot, travel on foot, tread, step, perambulate, stalk, stride, tramp, stroll, amble, ramble, shamble, pad, shuffle, saunter, trudge, trek, wade, plod, slog, footslog, foot it, hike, parade, promenade, strut, swagger, prance, march, goose-step, pace, trip, sidle, tiptoe, flounce, stagger, lurch, limp, waddle, stamp, mince, slink, steal, prowl, skulk, sneak, creep, pussyfoot, go by shanks's mare *or* pony, ride by shanks's mare *or* pony, *colloq. or dial.* traipse, *esp. US colloq.* sashay, *literary or archaic* wend, *Brit. sl.* yomp; *sl.* hoof it. **3 a** patrol, trace out, stalk, cover, traverse, prowl, wander, roam, rove, range about in *or* on, frequent. **b** see WALK *v.* 1, 2 above. **4** take, convoy, accompany, escort, go with; conduct, lead. ● *n.* **1** gait, step, pace, stride. **2 b** constitutional, stroll, perambulation, promenade, amble, ramble, saunter, turn, walkabout, wander; slog, footslog, tramp, trek, hike. **3 a** path, lane, pathway, walkway, alley, arcade, track, route, trail, pavement, footpath, promenade, esplanade, footway, *US* boardwalk, sidewalk. **c** round, beat, circuit, route. □ **walk all over 1** see ROUT *v.* **walk off with 1** see STEAL *v.* 1. **2** see WIN *v.* 1. **walk of life** see SPHERE *n.* 4b. **walk out 1, 3** leave, depart, storm out; strike, go (out) on strike, walk off the job, protest, take industrial action, *colloq.* down tools. **2** see *go out* 4 (GO[1]). **walk-out** see STRIKE *n.* 2. **walk out on** see DESERT[1] *v.* 2. **walk-over** see PUSHOVER.

walkabout /wáwkəbowt/ *n.* **1** an informal stroll among a crowd by a visiting dignitary. **2** a period of wandering in the bush by an Australian Aboriginal.

walkathon /wáwkəthon/ *n.* an organized fund-raising walk. [WALK, after MARATHON]

walker /wáwkər/ *n.* **1** a person or animal that walks. **2 a** a wheeled or footed framework in which a baby can learn to walk. **b** = *walking frame.*

■ **1** see PEDESTRIAN *n.* 1.

walkie-talkie /wáwkitáwki/ *n.* a two-way radio carried on the person, esp. by policemen etc.

walking /wáwking/ *n.* & *adj.* in senses of WALK *n.* □ **walking delegate** a trade-union official who visits members and their employers for discussions. **walking dictionary** (or **encyclopedia**) *colloq.* a person having a wide general knowledge. **walking fern** any American evergreen fern of the genus *Camptosorus*, with fronds that root at the ends. **walking frame** a usu. tubular metal frame with rubberized ferrules, used by disabled or old people to help them walk. **walking gentleman** (or **lady**) *Theatr.* a non-speaking extra; a supernumerary. **walking leaf** = *walking fern.* **walking-on part** a non-speaking dramatic role. **walking papers** *colloq.* dismissal (*gave him his walking papers*). **walking-stick 1** a stick carried when walking, esp. for extra support. **2** *US* = *stick insect* (see STICK[1]). **walking-tour** a holiday journey on foot, esp. of several days. **walking wounded 1** (of soldiers etc.) able to walk despite injuries; not bedridden. **2** *colloq.* a person or people having esp. mental or emotional difficulties.

■ □ **walking dictionary** (or **encyclopedia**) see PRODIGY 1. **walking-on part** extra, supernumary, walk-on (part), *Theatr.* super. **walking papers** see *dismissal* (DISMISS).

Walkman /wáwkmən/ *n.* (*pl.* **-mans**) *propr.* a type of personal stereo equipment.

walkway /wáwkway/ *n.* a passage or path for walking along, esp.: **1** a raised passageway connecting different sections of a building. **2** a wide path in a garden etc.

■ see PATH 1.

wall /wawl/ *n.* & *v.* ● *n.* **1 a** a continuous and usu. vertical structure of usu. brick or stone, having little width in proportion to its length and height and esp. enclosing, protecting, or dividing a space or supporting a roof. **b** the surface of a wall, esp. inside a room (*hung the picture on the wall*). **2** anything like a wall in appearance or effect, esp.: **a** the steep side of a mountain. **b** a protection or obstacle (*a wall of steel bayonets*; *a wall of indifference*). **c** *Anat.* the outermost layer or enclosing membrane etc. of an organ, structure, etc. **d** the outermost part of a hollow structure (*stomach wall*). **e** *Mining* rock enclosing a lode or seam. ● *v.tr.* **1** (esp. as **walled** *adj.*) surround or protect with a wall (*walled garden*). **2 a** (usu. foll. by *up*, *off*) block or seal (a space etc.) with a wall. **b** (foll. by *up*) enclose (a person) within a sealed space (*walled them up in the dungeon*). □ **drive a person up the wall** *colloq.* **1** make a person angry; infuriate. **2** drive a person mad. **go to the wall** be defeated or ruined. **off the wall** *sl.* unorthodox, unconventional; crazy, outlandish. **up the wall** *colloq.* crazy or furious (*went up the wall when he heard*). **wall bar** one of a set of parallel bars, attached to the wall of a gymnasium, on which exercises are performed. **wall-barley** wild barley as a weed. **wall-board** a type of wall-covering made from wood pulp etc. **wall cress** = ARABIS. **wall-fern** an evergreen polypody, *Polypodium vulgare*, with very large leaves. **wall-fruit** fruit grown on trees trained against a wall for protection and warmth. **wall game** *Brit.* a form of football played at Eton. **wall-knot** = *wale-knot.* **wall-painting** a mural or fresco. **wall pepper** a succulent stonecrop, *Sedum acre*, with a pungent taste. **wall-plate** timber laid in or on a wall to distribute the pressure of a girder etc. **wall rocket** see ROCKET[2]. **wall rue** a small fern, *Asplenium ruta-muraria*, with leaves like rue, growing on walls and rocks. **walls have ears** it is unsafe to speak openly, as there may be eavesdroppers. **wall-to-wall 1** (of a carpet) fitted to cover a whole room etc. **2** *colloq.* profuse, ubiquitous (*wall-to-wall pop music*). □□ **walling** *n.* **wall-less** *adj.* [OE f. L *vallum* rampart f. *vallus* stake]

■ *n.* **1** barricade, fortification, bulwark, breastwork, parapet, embankment, dyke, rampart, palisade, stockade. **2** screen, partition, divider, enclosure, separator, bulkhead, barrier, obstruction, obstacle, impediment, block, fence, protection, defence. ● *v.* **2 a** block, seal, close, brick, enclose, fence, screen, partition. **b** (*wall up*) immure, imprison, shut up, lock up, confine. □ **drive a person up the wall 1** see IRRITATE 1. **2** drive a person crazy *or* insane *or* mad, madden, unhinge, dement, derange. **go to the wall** fail, collapse, be ruined, face ruin, go bankrupt, go under, lose everything, *colloq.* go broke, fold (up), go bust. **off the wall** see OFFBEAT *adj.* **up the wall** insane, mad, frantic, furious, out of one's mind, *colloq.* crazy, livid, round the bend, *sl.* off one's rocker *or* nut, *Brit. sl.* round the twist, off one's chump; see also INSANE 1.

wallaby /wóllәbi/ *n.* (*pl.* **-ies**) **1** any of various marsupials of the family Macropodidae, smaller than kangaroos, and having large hind feet and long tails. **2** (**Wallabies**) *colloq.* the Australian international Rugby Union team. □ **on the wallaby** (or **wallaby track**) *Austral.* vagrant; unemployed. [Aboriginal *wolabā*]

Wallachian /woláykiәn/ *adj.* & *n.* (also **Walachian**) ● *adj.* of the former Principality of Wallachia, now part of Romania. ● *n.* a native of Wallachia. [*Wallachia* (as VLACH)]

wallah /wóllә/ *n.* orig. *Anglo-Ind.*, now *sl.* **1** a person concerned with or in charge of a usu. specified thing, business, etc. (*asked the ticket wallah*). **2** a person doing a routine administrative job; a bureaucrat. [Hindi *-wālā* suffix = -ER[1]]

wallaroo /wóllәroó/ *n.* a large brownish-black kangaroo, *Macropus robustus.* [Aboriginal *wolarū*]

wallet /wóllit/ *n.* **1** a small flat esp. leather case for holding banknotes etc. **2** *archaic* a bag for carrying food etc. on a journey, esp. as used by a pilgrim or beggar. [ME *walet*, prob. f. AF *walet* (unrecorded), perh. f. Gmc]

▪ purse, pocketbook, notecase, *US* billfold.

wall-eye /wáwlī/ *n.* **1 a** an eye with a streaked or opaque white iris. **b** an eye squinting outwards. **2** an American perch, *Stizostedion vitreum*, with large prominent eyes. □□ **wall-eyed** *adj.* [back-form. f. *wall-eyed*: ME f. ON *vagleygr* f. *vagl* (unrecorded: cf. Icel. *vagl* film over the eye) + *auga* EYE]

wallflower /wáwlflowr/ *n.* **1 a** a fragrant spring garden-plant, *Cheiranthus cheiri*, with esp. brown, yellow, or dark-red clustered flowers. **b** any of various flowering plants of the genus *Cheiranthus* or *Erysimum*, growing wild on old walls. **2** *colloq.* a neglected or socially awkward person, esp. a woman sitting out at a dance for lack of partners.

Walloon /wolóon/ *n.* & *adj.* ● *n.* **1** a member of a French-speaking people inhabiting S. and E. Belgium and neighbouring France (see also FLEMING). **2** the French dialect spoken by this people. ● *adj.* of or concerning the Walloons or their language. [F *Wallon* f. med.L *Wallo -onis* f. Gmc: cf. WELSH]

wallop /wóllәp/ *v.* & *n. sl.* ● *v.tr.* (**walloped, walloping**) **1 a** thrash; beat. **b** hit hard. **2** (as **walloping** *adj.*) big; strapping; thumping (*a walloping profit*). ● *n.* **1** a heavy blow; a thump. **2** *Brit.* beer or any alcoholic drink. □□ **walloping** *n.* [earlier senses 'gallop', 'boil', f. ONF (*walop* n. f.) *waloper*, OF *galoper*: cf. GALLOP]

▪ *v.* **1** see BEAT *v.* 1. **2** (**walloping**) see THUMPING. ● *n.* **1** see BLOW[2] 1.

walloper /wóllәpәr/ *n.* **1** a person or thing that wallops. **2** *Austral. sl.* a policeman.

▪ **2** see *police officer.*

wallow /wóllō/ *v.* & *n.* ● *v.intr.* **1** (esp. of an animal) roll about in mud, sand, water, etc. **2** (usu. foll. by *in*) indulge in unrestrained sensuality, pleasure, misery, etc. (*wallows in nostalgia*). ● *n.* **1** the act or an instance of wallowing. **2 a** a place used by buffalo etc. for wallowing. **b** the depression in the ground caused by this. □□ **wallower** *n.* [OE *walwian* roll f. Gmc]

▪ *v.* **1** roll about *or* around, loll about *or* around, welter, writhe, tumble, splash, plash. **2** (*wallow in*) luxuriate in, bask in, revel in, glory in, indulge (oneself) in, give oneself up to, succumb to, take to, appreciate, fancy, enjoy, like, love, savour, *colloq.* get a kick from *or* out of; *sl.* get a buzz from *or* out of, *US sl.* get a bang from.

wallpaper /wáwlpaypәr/ *n.* & *v.* ● *n.* **1** paper sold in rolls for pasting on to interior walls as decoration. **2** an unobtrusive background, esp. (usu. *derog.*) with ref. to sound, music, etc. ● *v.tr.* (often *absol.*) decorate with wallpaper.

Wall Street *n.* the American financial world or money market. [street in New York City where banks, the Stock Exchange, etc. are situated]

wally /wólli/ *n.* (*pl.* **-ies**) *Brit. sl.* a foolish or inept person. [orig. uncert., perh. shortened form of *Walter*]

walnut /wáwlnut/ *n.* **1** any tree of the genus *Juglans*, having aromatic leaves and drooping catkins. **2** the nut of this tree containing an edible kernel in two half shells shaped like boats. **3** the timber of the walnut-tree used in cabinet-making. [OE *walh-hnutu* f. Gmc NUT]

Walpurgis night /valpoórgiss/ *n.* the eve of 1 May when witches are alleged to meet on the Brocken mountain in Germany and hold revels with the Devil. [G *Walpurgisnacht* f. *Walpurgis* genit. of *Walpurga* Engl. woman saint (8th c.) + *Nacht* NIGHT]

walrus /wáwlrәss, wól-/ *n.* a large amphibious long-tusked arctic mammal, *Odobenus rosmarus*, related to the seal and sea lion. □ **walrus moustache** a long thick drooping moustache. [prob. f. Du. *walrus*, *-ros*, perh. by metath. after *walvisch* 'whale-fish' f. word repr. by OE *horschwæl* 'horse-whale']

waltz /wawlss, wawlts, wolts/ *n.* & *v.* ● *n.* **1** a dance in triple time performed by couples who rotate and progress round the floor. **2** the usu. flowing and melodious music for this. ● *v.* **1** *intr.* dance a waltz. **2** *intr.* (often foll. by *in*, *out*, *round*, etc.) *colloq.* move lightly, casually, with deceptive ease, etc. (*waltzed in and took first prize*). **3** *tr.* move (a person) in or as if in a waltz, with ease (*was waltzed off to Paris*). □ **waltz Matilda** see MATILDA. □□ **waltzer** *n.* [G *Walzer* f. *walzen* revolve]

wampum /wómpәm/ *n.* beads made from shells and strung together for use as money, decoration, or as aids to memory by N. American Indians. [Algonquian *wampumpeag* f. *wap* white + *umpe* string + *-ag* pl. suffix]

wan /won/ *adj.* **1** (of a person's complexion or appearance) pale; exhausted, weak; worn. **2** (of a star etc. or its light) partly obscured; faint. **3** *archaic* (of night, water, etc.) dark, black. □□ **wanly** *adv.* **wanness** *n.* [OE *wann* dark, black, of unkn. orig.]

▪ **1** white, sickly, pale, pallid, livid, pasty, peaky, ashen, bloodless, waxen, whey-faced, washed-out, sallow, colourless, deathly, ghostly, ghastly, cadaverous, exhausted, worn, weary, drawn, weak, feeble, faint, frail. **2** weak, feeble, faint.

wand /wond/ *n.* **1 a** a supposedly magic stick used in casting spells by a fairy, magician, etc. **b** a stick used by a conjuror for effect. **2** a slender rod carried or used as a marker in the ground. **3** a staff symbolizing some officials' authority. **4** *colloq.* a conductor's baton. **5** a hand-held electronic device which can be passed over a bar-code to read the data this represents. [ME prob. f. Gmc: cf. WEND, WIND[2]]

▪ **1–4** baton, stick, staff, rod.

wander /wóndәr/ *v.* & *n.* ● *v.* **1** *intr.* (often foll. by *in*, *off*, etc.) go about from place to place aimlessly. **2** *intr.* **a** (of a person, river, road, etc.) wind about; diverge; meander. **b** (of esp. a person) get lost; leave home; stray from a path etc. **3** *intr.* talk or think incoherently; be inattentive or delirious. **4** *tr.* cover while wandering (*wanders the world*). ● *n.* the act or an instance of wandering (*went for a wander round the garden*). □ **wandering Jew 1 a** a legendary person said to have been condemned by Christ to wander the earth until the second advent. **b** a person who never settles down. **2 a** a climbing plant, *Tradescantia albiflora*, with stemless variegated leaves. **b** a trailing plant, *Zebrina pendula*, with pink flowers. **wandering sailor** the moneywort. **wander-plug** a plug that can be fitted into any of various sockets in an electrical device. □□ **wanderer** *n.* **wandering** *n.* (esp. in *pl.*). [OE *wandrian* (as WEND)]

▪ *v.* **1** walk, go, roam, rove, range, stray, ramble, stroll, saunter, knock about *or* around, travel, meander, drift, cruise, prowl, *colloq.* mooch, tootle; *sl.* mosey. **2 a** wind, meander, snake, zigzag, turn this way and that; diverge.

3 deviate, digress, turn, stray, drift, depart, go off at a tangent, lose one's train of thought, lapse, lose the thread; go off, become absent-minded, go wool-gathering, lose concentration *or* focus; *literary* divagate. ● *n.* see STROLL *n.* ▫▫ **wanderer** see ROVER[1]. **wandering** see TRAVEL *n.* 1b.

wanderlust /wóndərlust, vándərlo͝ost/ *n.* an eagerness for travelling or wandering. [G]

wanderoo /wondəro͞o/ *n.* a langur, *Semnopithecus vetulus*, of Sri Lanka. [Sinh. *wanderu* monkey]

wane /wayn/ *v.* & *n.* ● *v.intr.* **1** (of the moon) decrease in apparent size after the full moon (cf. WAX[2]). **2** decrease in power, vigour, importance, brilliance, size, etc.; decline. ● *n.* **1** the process of waning. **2** a defect of a plank etc. that lacks square corners. ▫ **on the wane** waning; declining. ▫▫ **waney** *adj.* (in sense 2 of *n.*). [OE *wanian* lessen f. Gmc]
■ *v.* decrease, diminish, grow less, lessen, dwindle, shrink, decline, die out, abate, ebb, subside, fade (away), dim, taper off, peter out, draw to a close, wind down, weaken. ● *n.* **1** decrease, diminution, lessening, dwindling, decline, abatement, ebb, subsidence, fading, tapering off, petering out, winding down, weakening, deterioration, degeneration. ▫ **on the wane** on the decrease *or* decline *or* ebb, diminishing, decreasing, declining, waning, abating, subsiding, fading, tapering off, petering out, winding down, weakening, deteriorating, degenerating.

wangle /wángg'l/ *v.* & *n. colloq.* ● *v.tr.* **1** (often *refl.*) to obtain (a favour etc.) by scheming etc. (*wangled himself a free trip*). **2** alter or fake (a report etc.) to appear more favourable. ● *n.* the act or an instance of wangling. ▫▫ **wangler** *n.* [19th-c. printers' sl.: orig. unkn.]
■ *v.* **1** scheme, plot, work out, contrive, manoeuvre, engineer, manage, pull off, *colloq.* fix, work, finagle, swing, *sl.* fiddle. **2** see FIDDLE *v.* 2b.

wank /wangk/ *v.* & *n. coarse sl.* ¶ Usually considered a taboo word. ● *v.intr.* & *tr.* masturbate. ● *n.* an act of masturbating. [20th c.: orig. unkn.]

Wankel engine /wángk'l, váng-/ *n.* a rotary internal-combustion engine with a continuously rotated and eccentrically pivoted nearly triangular shaft. [F. *Wankel*, Ger. engineer d. 1988]

wanker /wángkər/ *n. coarse sl.* ¶ Usually considered a taboo word. **1** a contemptible or ineffectual person. **2** a person who masturbates.

wannabe /wónnəbi/ *n. sl.* an avid fan who tries to emulate the person he or she admires; also, anyone who would like to be someone else.

want /wont/ *v.* & *n.* ● *v.* **1** *tr.* **a** (often foll. by *to* + infin.) desire; wish for possession of; need (*wants a toy train*; *wants it done immediately*; *wanted to leave*; *wanted him to leave*). **b** need or desire (a person, esp. sexually). **c** esp. *Brit.* require to be attended to in esp. a specified way (*the garden wants weeding*). **d** (foll. by *to* + infin.) *colloq.* ought; should; need (*you want to pull yourself together*; *you don't want to overdo it*). **2** *intr.* (usu. foll. by *for*) lack; be deficient (*wants for nothing*). **3** *tr.* be without or fall short by (esp. a specified amount or thing) (*the drawer wants a handle*). **4** *intr.* (foll. by *in*, *out*) esp. *US colloq.* desire to be in, out, etc. (*wants in on the deal*). **5** *tr.* (as **wanted** *adj.*) (of a suspected criminal etc.) sought by the police. ● *n.* **1** (often foll. by *of*) **a** a lack, absence, or deficiency (*could not go for want of time*; *shows great want of judgement*). **b** poverty; need (*living in great want*; *in want of necessities*). **2 a** a desire for a thing etc. (*meets a long-felt want*). **b** a thing so desired (*can supply your wants*). ▫ **do not want to** am unwilling to. **want ad** *US* a classified newspaper advertisement for something sought. ▫▫ **wanter** *n.* [ME f. ON *vant* neut. of *vanr* lacking = OE *wana*, formed as WANE]
■ *v.* **1 a** desire, crave, wish (for), long for, pine for, hope (for), fancy, covet, hanker after, lust after, hunger for *or* after, thirst for *or* after, yearn for, *colloq.* have a yen for. **c** need, require, call for, demand, be in want *or* need of, stand in want *or* need of. **d** ought, should, need, must. **2, 3** need, lack, miss, require, call for, demand, be deficient in, be in want *or* need of, stand in want *or* need of; be *or* fall short of. ● *n.* **1 a** need, lack, shortage, deficiency, dearth, scarcity, scarceness, insufficiency, scantiness, inadequacy, paucity; absence. **b** poverty, need, indigence, destitution, privation, pauperism, penury, neediness, impecuniousness. **2 a** appetite, hunger, thirst, craving, desire, fancy, wish, aspiration, longing, yearning, hankering, demand, *colloq.* yen. **b** desire, fancy, wish, necessity, requirement, requisite, prerequisite.

wanting /wónting/ *adj.* **1** lacking (in quality or quantity); deficient, not equal to requirements (*wanting in judgement*; *the standard is sadly wanting*). **2** absent, not supplied or provided. ▫ **be found wanting** fail to meet requirements.
■ **1** lacking, deficient, inadequate, not up to par *or* scratch *or* expectations, insufficient, leaving much to be desired, unsatisfactory, unsatisfying, disappointing, second-rate, inferior, poor, shabby, shoddy, flawed, faulty, imperfect, incomplete, unfinished, defective, patchy, impaired, unsound. **2** absent, missing, lacking, short (of), *colloq.* shy (of). ▫ **be found wanting** see FAIL *v.* 1, 2a.

wanton /wóntən/ *adj.*, *n.*, & *v.* ● *adj.* **1** licentious; lewd; sexually promiscuous. **2** capricious; random; arbitrary; motiveless (*wanton destruction*; *wanton wind*). **3** luxuriant; unrestrained; unruly (*wanton extravagance*; *wanton behaviour*). **4** *archaic* playful; sportive (*a wanton child*). ● *n. literary* an immoral or licentious person, esp. a woman. ● *v.intr. literary* **1** gambol; sport; move capriciously. **2** (foll. by *with*) behave licentiously. ▫▫ **wantonly** *adv.* **wantonness** *n.* [ME *wantowen* (*wan-* UN-[1] + *towen* f. OE *togen* past part. of *tēon* discipline, rel. to TEAM)]
■ *adj.* **1** immoral, dissolute, profligate, dissipated, depraved, loose, promiscuous, shameless, lustful, licentious, lecherous, wild, fast, libidinous, lewd, lascivious, unchaste. **2** capricious, random, indiscriminate, whimsical, unjustified, unprovoked, uncalled-for, purposeless, aimless, groundless, motiveless, unmotivated, unjustifiable, arbitrary, gratuitous; reckless, rash, heedless, irresponsible, careless. **3** lavish, extravagant, luxuriant, luxurious; abandoned, unrestrained, undisciplined, ungoverned, ungovernable, unmanageable, outrageous, immoderate, intemperate, untempered. ● *n.* loose woman, prostitute, voluptuary, trollop, Jezebel, call-girl, *archaic* harlot, *archaic or rhet.* strumpet, *colloq.* vamp, *derog.* whore, slut, *sl.* tart, hooker, *sl. derog.* slag, *US sl.* working girl; see also TART[2] *n.* ● *v.* **1** see SPORT *v.* 1. **2** (*wanton with*) see TRIFLE *v.* 2. ▫▫ **wantonly** see FAST[1] *adv.* 5. **wantonness** see DISSIPATION 1.

wapentake /wóppəntayk, wáp-/ *n. Brit. hist.* (in areas of England with a large Danish population) a division of a shire; a hundred. [OE *wǣpen(ge)tæc* f. ON *vápnatak* f. *vápn* weapon + *tak* taking f. *taka* TAKE: perh. with ref. to voting in assembly by show of weapons]

wapiti /wóppiti/ *n.* (*pl.* **wapitis**) a N. American deer, *Cervus canadensis*. [Cree *wapitik* white deer]

War. *abbr.* Warwickshire.

war /wawr/ *n.* & *v.* ● *n.* **1 a** armed hostilities between esp. nations; conflict (*war broke out*; *war zone*). **b** a specific conflict or the period of time during which such conflict exists (*was before the war*). **c** the suspension of international law etc. during such a conflict. **2** (as **the War**) a war in progress or recently ended; the most recent major war. **3 a** hostility or contention between people, groups, etc. (*war of words*). **b** (often foll. by *on*) a sustained campaign against crime, disease, poverty, etc. ● *v.intr.* (**warred, warring**) **1** (as **warring** *adj.*) **a** rival; fighting (*warring factions*). **b** conflicting (*warring principles*). **2** make war. ▫ **art of war** strategy and tactics. **at war** (often foll. by *with*) engaged in a war. **go to war** declare or begin a war. **go to the wars** *archaic* serve as a soldier. **have been in the wars** *colloq.* appear injured, bruised, unkempt, etc. **war baby** a child, esp. illegitimate, born in wartime. **war bride** a woman who marries a serviceman met during a war. **war chest**

funds for a war or any other campaign. **war-cloud** a threatening international situation. **war correspondent** a correspondent reporting from a scene of war. **war crime** a crime violating the international laws of war. **war criminal** a person committing or sentenced for such crimes. **war cry 1** a phrase or name shouted to rally one's troops. **2** a party slogan etc. **war damage** damage to property etc. caused by bombing, shelling, etc. **war dance** a dance performed by primitive peoples etc. before a battle or to celebrate victory. **war department** the State office in charge of the army etc. **war-game 1** a military exercise testing or improving tactical knowledge etc. **2** a battle etc. conducted with toy soldiers. **war-gaming** the playing of war-games. **war grave** the grave of a serviceman who died on active service, esp. one in a special cemetery etc. **war loan** stock issued by the British Government to raise funds in wartime. **war memorial** a monument etc. commemorating those killed in a war. **war of attrition** a war in which each side seeks to wear out the other over a long period. **war of the elements** *poet.* storms or natural catastrophes. **War Office** *hist.* the British State department in charge of the army. **war of nerves** an attempt to wear down an opponent by psychological means. **war-plane** a military aircraft. **war poet** a poet writing on war themes, esp. of the two world wars. **Wars of the Roses** *hist.* the 15th-c. civil wars between the houses of York and Lancaster, represented by white and red roses. **war-weary** (esp. of a population) exhausted and dispirited by war. **war widow** a woman whose husband has been killed in war. **war-worn** = *war-weary*. **war zone** an area in which a war takes place. [ME *werre* f. AF, ONF var. of OF *guerre*: cf. WORSE]

■ *n.* **1** warfare, combat, conflict, fighting, clash, hostilities, battle, action, struggle, engagement, encounter, strife, contention. **3 b** campaign, drive, crusade, battle, fight, attack, offensive, struggle. ● *v.* **1** (**warring**) see HOSTILE 1. **2** do battle, fight, struggle, (engage in) combat, make *or* wage war, take up arms, strive, campaign, tilt, cross swords, contend, *hist.* joust. □ **at war** fighting, battling, in combat, in conflict; in disagreement, in dispute, in contention, struggling, antagonistic, at daggers drawn. **war cry** see SLOGAN. **war-game 1** see MANOEUVRE *n.* 2.

waratah /wórrətə/ *n.* an Australian crimson-flowered shrub, *Telopea speciosissima*. [Aboriginal]

warb /wawrb/ *n. Austral. sl.* an idle, unkempt, or disreputable person. [20th c.: orig. unkn.]

■ see IDLER.

warble[1] /wáwrb'l/ *v.* & *n.* ● *v.* **1** *intr.* & *tr.* sing in a gentle trilling manner. **2** *tr.* **a** speak or utter in a warbling manner. **b** express in a song or verse (*warbled his love*). ● *n.* a warbled song or utterance. [ME f. ONF *werble(r)* f. Frank. *hwirbilōn* whirl, trill]

■ *v.* see SING *v.* 1, 2.

warble[2] /wáwrb'l/ *n.* **1** a hard lump on a horse's back caused by the galling of a saddle. **2 a** the larva of a warble fly beneath the skin of cattle etc. **b** a tumour produced by this. □ **warble fly** any of various flies of the genus *Hypoderma*, infesting the skin of cattle and horses. [16th c.: orig. uncert.]

warbler /wáwrblər/ *n.* **1** a person, bird, etc. that warbles. **2** any small insect-eating bird of the family Sylviidae or, in N. America, Parulidae, including the blackcap, whitethroat, and chiff-chaff, not always remarkable for their song.

warby /wáwrbi/ *adj. Austral. sl.* shabby, decrepit. [f. WARB]

ward /wawrd/ *n.* & *v.* ● *n.* **1** a separate room or division of a hospital, prison, etc. (*men's surgical ward*). **2 a** *Brit.* an administrative division of a constituency, usu. electing a councillor or councillors etc. **b** esp. *US* a similar administrative division. **3 a** a minor under the care of a guardian appointed by the parents or a court. **b** (in full **ward of court**) a minor or mentally deficient person placed under the protection of a court. **4** (in *pl.*) the corresponding notches and projections in a key and a lock. **5** *archaic* **a** the act of guarding or defending a place etc. **b** the bailey of a castle. **c** a guardian's control; confinement; custody. ● *v.tr.* *archaic* guard; protect. □ **ward-heeler** *US* a party worker in elections etc. **ward off 1** parry (a blow). **2** avert (danger, poverty, etc.). [OE *weard, weardian* f. Gmc: cf. GUARD]

■ *n.* **2** district, division, precinct, section, zone, quarter. **3** minor, dependant, charge, protégé(e). □ **ward off** parry, fend off, repel, avert, avoid, block, thwart, keep away *or* off, keep at bay *or* arm's length, stave off, check, repulse, chase away *or* off, forestall.

-ward /wərd/ *suffix* (also **-wards**) added to nouns of place or destination and to adverbs of direction and forming: **1** adverbs (usu. **-wards**) meaning 'towards the place etc.' (*moving backwards*; *set off homewards*). **2** adjectives (usu. **-ward**) meaning 'turned or tending towards' (*a downward look*; *an onward rush*). **3** (less commonly) nouns meaning 'the region towards or about' (*look to the eastward*). [from or after OE *-weard* f. a Gmc root meaning 'turn']

warden /wáwrd'n/ *n.* **1** (usu. in *comb.*) a supervising official (*churchwarden*; *traffic warden*). **2 a** *Brit.* a president or governor of a college, school, hospital, youth hostel, etc. **b** esp. *US* a prison governor. □□ **wardenship** *n.* [ME f. AF & ONF *wardein* var. of OF *g(u)arden* GUARDIAN]

■ **1** see KEEPER.

warder /wáwrdər/ *n.* **1** *Brit.* (*fem.* **wardress**) a prison officer. **2** a guard. [ME f. AF *wardere, -our* f. ONF *warder*, OF *garder* to GUARD]

■ **1** see JAILER. **2** see GUARD *n.* 2.

wardrobe /wáwrdrōb/ *n.* **1** a large movable or built-in cupboard with rails, shelves, hooks, etc., for storing clothes. **2** a person's entire stock of clothes. **3** the costume department or costumes of a theatre, a film company, etc. **4** a department of a royal household in charge of clothing. □ **wardrobe mistress** (or **master**) a person in charge of a theatrical or film wardrobe. **wardrobe trunk** a trunk fitted with rails, shelves, etc. for use as a travelling wardrobe. [ME f. ONF *warderobe*, OF *garderobe* (as GUARD, ROBE)]

■ **1** closet, clothes-cupboard. **2** (collection *or* stock of) clothing *or* clothes *or formal* attire *or* apparel.

wardroom /wáwrdrōōm, -rŏŏm/ *n.* a room in a warship for the use of commissioned officers.

-wards var. of -WARD.

wardship /wáwrdship/ *n.* **1** a guardian's care or tutelage (*under his wardship*). **2** the condition of being a ward.

■ **1** see CHARGE *n.* 3b.

ware[1] /wair/ *n.* **1** (esp. in *comb.*) things of the same kind, esp. ceramics, made usu. for sale (*chinaware*; *hardware*). **2** (usu. in *pl.*) **a** articles for sale (*displayed his wares*). **b** a person's skills, talents, etc. **3** ceramics etc. of a specified material, factory, or kind (*Wedgwood ware*; *Delft ware*). [OE *waru* f. Gmc, perh. orig. = 'object of care', rel. to WARE[3]]

■ **2 a** merchandise, goods, commodities, manufactures, produce, stock(-in-trade), supplies, lines, truck.

ware[2] /wair/ *v.tr.* (also **'ware**) (esp. in hunting) look out for; avoid (usu. in *imper.*: *ware hounds!*). [OE *warian* f. Gmc (as WARE[3]), & f. ONF *warer*]

ware[3] /wair/ *predic.adj. poet.* aware. [OE *wær* f. Gmc: cf. WARD]

warehouse /wáirhowss/ *n.* & *v.* ● *n.* **1** a building in which esp. retail goods are stored; a repository. **2** esp. *Brit.* a wholesale or large retail store. ● *v.tr.* /also -howz/ store (esp. furniture or bonded goods) temporarily in a repository. □□ **warehouseman** *n.* (*pl.* **-men**).

■ *n.* **1** storehouse, store, storeroom, depository, repository, stockroom, depot, entrepôt, godown.

warfare /wáwrfair/ *n.* a state of war; campaigning, engaging in war (*chemical warfare*).

■ see WAR *n.* 1.

warfarin /wáwrfərin/ *n.* a water-soluble anticoagulant used esp. as a rat poison. [*W*isconsin *A*lumni *R*esearch *F*oundation + *-arin*, after COUMARIN]

warhead /wáwrhed/ *n.* the explosive head of a missile, torpedo, or similar weapon.

warhorse /wáwrhorss/ *n.* **1** *hist.* a knight's or trooper's powerful horse. **2** *colloq.* a veteran soldier, politician, etc.; a reliable hack.
■ **2** see VETERAN 1.

warlike /wáwrlīk/ *adj.* **1** threatening war; hostile. **2** martial; soldierly. **3** of or for war; military (*warlike preparations*).
■ **1** combative, militant, belligerent, bellicose, aggressive, pugnacious, hostile, bloodthirsty; hawkish, militaristic, jingoistic, warmongering. **2** see MARTIAL 2. **3** military, martial.

warlock /wáwrlok/ *n. archaic* a sorcerer or wizard. [OE *wǣr-loga* traitor f. *wǣr* covenant: *loga* rel. to LIE[2]]
■ see SORCERER.

warlord /wáwrlord/ *n.* a military commander or commander-in-chief.

warm /wawrm/ *adj.*, *v.*, & *n.* ● *adj.* **1** of or at a fairly or comfortably high temperature. **2** (of clothes etc.) affording warmth (*needs warm gloves*). **3 a** (of a person, action, feelings, etc.) sympathetic; cordial; friendly; loving (*a warm welcome*; *has a warm heart*). **b** enthusiastic; hearty (*was warm in her praise*). **4** animated, heated, excited; indignant (*the dispute grew warm*). **5** *colloq. iron.* dangerous, difficult, or hostile (*met a warm reception*). **6** *colloq.* **a** (of a participant in esp. a children's game of seeking) close to the object etc. sought. **b** near to guessing or finding out a secret. **7** (of a colour, light, etc.) reddish, pink, or yellowish, etc., suggestive of warmth. **8** *Hunting* (of a scent) fresh and strong. **9 a** (of a person's temperament) amorous; sexually demanding. **b** erotic; arousing. ● *v.* **1** *tr.* **a** make warm (*fire warms the room*). **b** excite; make cheerful (*warms the heart*). **2** *intr.* **a** (often foll. by *up*) warm oneself at a fire etc. (*warmed himself up*). **b** (often foll. by *to*) become animated, enthusiastic, or sympathetic (*warmed to his subject*). ● *n.* **1** the act of warming; the state of being warmed (*gave it a warm*; *had a nice warm by the fire*). **2** the warmth of the atmosphere etc. **3** *Brit. archaic* a warm garment, esp. an army greatcoat. □ **warmed-up** (*US* **-over**) **1** (of food etc.) reheated or stale. **2** stale; second-hand. **warm front** an advancing mass of warm air. **warming-pan** *hist.* a usu. brass container for live coals with a flat body and a long handle, used for warming a bed. **warm up 1** (of an athlete, performer, etc.) prepare for a contest, performance, etc. by practising. **2** (of a room etc.) become warmer. **3** (of a person) become enthusiastic etc. **4** (of a radio, engine, etc.) reach a temperature for efficient working. **5** reheat (food). **warm-up** *n.* a period of preparatory exercise for a contest or performance. **warm work 1** work etc. that makes one warm through exertion. **2** dangerous conflict etc. □□ **warmer** *n.* (also in *comb.*). **warmish** *adj.* **warmly** *adv.* **warmness** *n.* **warmth** *n.* [OE *wearm* f. Gmc]
■ *adj.* **1** heated, tepid, lukewarm, warmish, cosy, comfortable, not uncomfortable, balmy. **3 a** amiable, friendly, cordial, affable, sympathetic, pleasant, genial, cheerful, kindly, hospitable; affectionate, tender, mellow, loving, amorous. **b** ardent, enthusiastic, hearty, wholehearted, earnest, eager, sincere. **4** passionate, impassioned, excited, animated, fervent, fervid, spirited, ardent, zealous, keen, eager, emotional, heated, intense, furious, stormy, turbulent, vigorous, violent, *joc.* lively; indignant, irritated, annoyed, vexed, angry, irate, testy, short-tempered, touchy, quick-tempered, irascible, irritable, hot under the collar, *colloq.* worked up, steamed up. **5** uncomfortable, awkward, difficult, unpleasant, strained, tense, dangerous; hostile, unfriendly, unsympathetic. **6** close *or* near (to making a discovery), about to make *or* on the brink of a discovery. ● *v.* **1 a** heat (up), warm up *or* over. **b** stir, move, excite, please, delight, gladden, make a person feel good, cheer (up), encourage, brighten. **2 b** (*warm to*) become less antagonistic *or* hostile to *or* toward(s), become enthusiastic *or* supportive of, become excited *or* animated about *or* over, be attracted *or* sympathetic to *or* toward(s), come to like *or* feel affection for. □ **warmed-up** (*US* **-over**) **2** see STALE *adj.*[1] 2. **warm up 1** see EXERCISE *v.* 3. **5** reheat, heat up, *US* warm over, *Brit. colloq.* hot up. **warm-up** see EXERCISE *n.* 3. □□ **warmish** tepid, lukewarm. **warmly** cordially, amiably, amicably, solicitously, warm-heartedly; affectionately, tenderly, fondly, lovingly; well, kindly; vigorously, intensely, fiercely, intensively, intently, energetically, doggedly, persistently, zealously, fervently, fervidly, hotly, ardently, enthusiastically, earnestly, eagerly, heartily; heatedly, vehemently, vociferously, forcefully, feverishly, frantically, furiously, angrily, violently. **warmth** heat, warmness, hotness, torridness, torridity, fieriness, warm; cordiality, heartiness, friendliness, geniality, amiableness, kindliness, tenderness, affability, love; ardour, effusiveness, enthusiasm, zeal, excitedness, fervour, vehemence, vigour, ebullience, passion; irritation, indignation, annoyance.

warm-blooded /wáwrmblúddid/ *adj.* **1** (of an organism) having warm blood; mammalian (see HOMOEOTHERM). **2** ardent, passionate. □□ **warm-bloodedness** *n.*
■ **1** homoeothermic, homoeothermal. **2** passionate, ardent, fervid, hot-blooded, impetuous, randy.

warm-hearted /wáwrmhaártid/ *adj.* having a warm heart; kind, friendly. □□ **warm-heartedly** *adv.* **warm-heartedness** *n.*
■ see KIND[2]. □□ **warm-heartedly** see *warmly* (WARM). **warm-heartedness** see KINDNESS 1.

warmonger /wáwrmunggər/ *n.* a person who seeks to bring about or promote war. □□ **warmongering** *n.* & *adj.*
■ see AGGRESSOR. □□ **warmongering** (*adj.*) see BELLIGERENT *adj.* 1. (*n.*) see *jingoism* (JINGO).

warn /wawrn/ *v.tr.* **1** (also *absol.*) **a** (often foll. by *of*, or *that* + clause, or *to* + infin.) inform of danger, unknown circumstances, etc. (*warned them of the danger*; *warned her that she was being watched*; *warned him to expect a visit*). **b** (often foll. by *against*) inform (a person etc.) about a specific danger, hostile person, etc. (*warned her against trusting him*). **2** (usu. with *neg.*) admonish; tell forcefully (*has been warned not to go*). **3** give (a person) cautionary notice regarding conduct etc. (*shall not warn you again*). □ **warn off 1** tell (a person) to keep away (from). **2** prohibit from attending races, esp. at a specified course. □□ **warner** *n.* [OE *war(e)nian*, *wearnian* ult. f. Gmc: cf. WARE[3]]
■ **1, 2** caution, admonish, advise, notify, apprise, inform, give (fair) warning, alert, give (prior) notice, put a person on notice *or* guard *or* the alert, make a person aware (of), forewarn, tip off, counsel.

warning /wáwrning/ *n.* **1** in senses of WARN *v.* **2** anything that serves to warn; a hint or indication of difficulty, danger, etc. **3** *archaic* = NOTICE *n.* 3b. □ **warning coloration** *Biol.* conspicuous colouring that warns a predator etc. against attacking. □□ **warningly** *adv.* [OE *war(e)nung* etc. (as WARN, -ING[1])]
■ **1** caution, admonition, advice, counsel, caveat, word (to the wise), tip, notification, notice, tip-off; threat. **2** lesson, example; omen, sign, signal, indication, hint, augury, foretoken, portent, presage, premonition, foreshadowing, forewarning, prophecy, knell.

warp /wawrp/ *v.* & *n.* ● *v.* **1** *tr.* & *intr.* **a** make or become bent or twisted out of shape, esp. by the action of heat, damp, etc. **b** make or become perverted, bitter, or strange (*a warped sense of humour*). **2 a** *tr.* haul (a ship) by a rope attached to a fixed point. **b** *intr.* progress in this way. **3** *tr.* fertilize by flooding with warp. **4** *tr.* (foll. by *up*) choke (a channel) with an alluvial deposit etc. **5** *tr.* arrange (threads) as a warp. ● *n.* **1 a** a state of being warped, esp. of shrunken or expanded timber. **b** perversion, bitterness, etc. of the mind or character. **2** the threads stretched lengthwise in a loom to be crossed by the weft. **3** a rope used in towing or warping, or attached to a trawl-net. **4** sediment etc. left esp. on poor land by standing water. □□ **warpage** *n.* (esp. in sense 1a of *v.*). **warper** *n.* (in sense 5 of *v.*). [OE *weorpan* throw, *wearp* f. Gmc]

■ *v.* **1 a** twist, contort, distort, deform, bend out of shape, buckle, kink, curve, wrench, misshape. **b** pervert, corrupt, twist, distort. ● *n.* **1** twist, contortion, distortion, bias, deformity, deformation, bend, wrench, perversion, kink, idiosyncrasy, quirk, deviation.

warpaint /wáwrpaynt/ *n.* **1** paint used to adorn the body before battle, esp. by N. American Indians. **2** *colloq.* elaborate make-up.

warpath /wáwrpaath/ *n.* **1** a warlike expedition of N. American Indians. **2** *colloq.* any hostile course or attitude (*is on the warpath again*).

warragal var. of WARRIGAL.

warrant /wórrənt/ *n.* & *v.* ● *n.* **1 a** anything that authorizes a person or an action (*have no warrant for this*). **b** a person so authorizing (*I will be your warrant*). **2 a** a written authorization, money voucher, travel document, etc. (*a dividend warrant*). **b** a written authorization allowing police to search premises, arrest a suspect, etc. **3** a document authorizing counsel to represent the principal in a lawsuit (*warrant of attorney*). **4** a certificate of service rank held by a warrant-officer. ● *v.tr.* **1** serve as a warrant for; justify (*nothing can warrant his behaviour*). **2** guarantee or attest to esp. the genuineness of an article, the worth of a person, etc. □ **I** (or **I'll**) **warrant** I am certain; no doubt (*he'll be sorry, I'll warrant*). **warrant-officer** an officer ranking between commissioned officers and NCOs. □□ **warranter** *n.* **warrantor** *n.* [ME f. ONF *warant*, var. of OF *guarant*, *-and* f. Frank. *werēnd* (unrecorded) f. *giwerēn* be surety for]

■ *n.* **1 a** authorization, sanction, reason, justification, approval, validation, licence, right, certification, entitlement, grounds, cause, rationale, basis, assurance, *carte blanche*, guarantee, pledge, security, charter, warranty. **2** writ, order, affidavit, paper, document, credential, authority, entitlement, licence, permit, voucher, summons, subpoena, mandate, decree, fiat, edict, ukase. ● *v.* **1** authorize, sanction, justify, explain, approve, verify, validate, permit, allow, provide *or* offer grounds for, provide *or* offer justification for, provide *or* offer cause for, provide *or* offer reason for, call for, necessitate, entitle, empower, excuse, license. **2** guarantee, attest to, promise, assure, ensure, insure, answer for, be answerable for, certify, vouch for, underwrite, back up, uphold, stand by *or* behind.

warrantable /wórrəntəb'l/ *adj.* **1** able to be warranted. **2** (of a stag) old enough to be hunted (5 or 6 years). □□ **warrantableness** *n.* **warrantably** *adv.*

warrantee /wórrəntée/ *n.* a person to whom a warranty is given.

warranty /wórrənti/ *n.* (*pl.* **-ies**) **1** an undertaking as to the ownership or quality of a thing sold, hired, etc., often accepting responsibility for defects or liability for repairs needed over a specified period. **2** (usu. foll. by *for* + verbal noun) an authority or justification. **3** an undertaking by an insured person of the truth of a statement or fulfilment of a condition. [ME f. AF *warantie*, var. of *garantie* (as WARRANT)]

■ **1** guarantee, assurance, promise, commitment, covenant, undertaking, agreement, pledge, bond. **2** see WARRANT *n.* 1a.

warren /wórrən/ *n.* **1 a** a network of interconnecting rabbit burrows. **b** a piece of ground occupied by this. **2** a densely populated or labyrinthine building or district. **3** *hist.* a piece of ground on which game is preserved. [ME f. AF & ONF *warenne*, OF *garenne* game-park f. Gmc]

warrigal /wórrig'l/ *n.* & *adj.* (also **warragal**) *Austral.* ● *n.* **1** a dingo dog. **2** an untamed horse. **3** a wild Aboriginal. ● *adj.* wild, untamed. [Aboriginal]

■ *adj.* see UNTAMED.

warring /wáwring/ *adj.* rival, antagonistic.

■ rival, antagonistic, competing, battling, contending; see also HOSTILE 1.

warrior /wórriər/ *n.* **1** a person experienced or distinguished in fighting. **2** a fighting man, esp. of primitive peoples. **3** (*attrib.*) martial (*a warrior nation*). [ME f. ONF *werreior* etc., OF *guerreior* etc. f. *werreier*, *guerreier* make WAR]

warship /wáwrship/ *n.* an armoured ship used in war.

wart /wawrt/ *n.* **1** a small hardish roundish growth on the skin caused by a virus-induced abnormal growth of papillae and thickening of the epidermis. **2** a protuberance on the skin of an animal, surface of a plant, etc. **3** *colloq.* an objectionable person. □ **wart-hog** an African wild pig of the genus *Phacochoerus*, with a large head and warty lumps on its face, and large curved tusks. **warts and all** *colloq.* with no attempt to conceal blemishes or inadequacies. □□ **warty** *adj.* [OE *wearte* f. Gmc]

wartime /wáwrtīm/ *n.* the period during which a war is waged.

wary /wáiri/ *adj.* (**warier**, **wariest**) **1** on one's guard; given to caution; circumspect. **2** (foll. by *of*) cautious, suspicious (*am wary of using lifts*). **3** showing or done with caution or suspicion (*a wary expression*). □□ **warily** *adv.* **wariness** *n.* [WARE[2] + -Y[1]]

■ cautious, careful, on (one's) guard, circumspect, guarded, prudent, apprehensive, chary, suspicious, distrustful, watchful, vigilant, on the qui vive, heedful, observant, on one's toes, *colloq.* cagey, wide awake; *sl.* leery. □□ **warily** see GINGERLY *adv.* **wariness** see SUSPICION 1.

was *1st* & *3rd sing. past* of BE.

Wash. *abbr.* Washington.

wash /wosh/ *v.* & *n.* ● *v.* **1** *tr.* cleanse (oneself or a part of oneself, clothes, etc.) with liquid, esp. water. **2** *tr.* (foll. by *out*, *off*, *away*, etc.) remove (a stain or dirt, a surface, or some physical feature of the surface) in this way; eradicate all traces of. **3** *intr.* wash oneself or esp. one's hands and face. **4** *intr.* wash clothes etc. **5** *intr.* (of fabric or dye) bear washing without damage. **6** *intr.* (foll. by *off*, *out*) (of a stain etc.) be removed by washing. **7** *tr. poet.* moisten, water (*tear-washed eyes*; *a rose washed with dew*). **8** *tr.* (of a river, sea, etc.) touch (a country, coast, etc.) with its waters. **9** *tr.* (of moving liquid) carry along in a specified direction (*a wave washed him overboard*; *was washed up on the shore*). **10** *tr.* (also foll. by *away*, *out*) **a** scoop out (*the water had washed a channel*). **b** erode, denude (*sea-washed cliffs*). **11** *intr.* (foll. by *over*, *along*, etc.) sweep, move, or splash. **12** *tr.* sift (ore) by the action of water. **13** *tr.* **a** brush a thin coat of watery paint or ink over (paper in water-colour painting etc., or a wall). **b** (foll. by *with*) coat (inferior metal) with gold etc. ● *n.* **1 a** the act or an instance of washing; the process of being washed (*give them a good wash*; *only needed one wash*). **b** (prec. by *the*) treatment at a laundry etc. (*sent them to the wash*). **2** a quantity of clothes for washing or just washed. **3** the visible or audible motion of agitated water or air, esp. due to the passage of a ship etc. or aircraft. **4 a** soil swept off by water; alluvium. **b** a sandbank exposed only at low tide. **5** kitchen slops and scraps given to pigs. **6 a** thin, weak, or inferior liquid food. **b** liquid food for animals. **7** a liquid to spread over a surface to cleanse, heal, or colour. **8** a thin coating of water-colour, wall-colouring, or metal. **9** malt etc. fermenting before distillation. **10** a lotion or cosmetic. □ **come out in the wash** *colloq.* be clarified, or (of contingent difficulties) be resolved or removed, in the course of time. **wash-and-wear** *adj.* (of a fabric or garment) easily and quickly laundered. **wash-basin** a basin for washing one's hands, face, etc. **wash one's dirty linen in public** see LINEN. **wash down** **1** wash completely (esp. a large surface or object). **2** (usu. foll. by *with*) accompany or follow (food) with a drink. **washed out** **1** faded by washing. **2** pale. **3** *colloq.* limp, enfeebled. **washed up** esp. *US sl.* defeated, having failed. **wash one's hands** *euphem.* go to the lavatory. **wash one's hands of** renounce responsibility for. **wash-hand stand** = WASHSTAND. **wash-house** a building where clothes are washed. **wash-leather** chamois or similar leather for washing windows etc. **wash out** **1** clean the inside of (a thing) by washing. **2** clean (a garment etc.) by brief washing. **3 a** rain off (an event etc.). **b** *colloq.* cancel. **4** (of a flood, downpour, etc.) make a breach in (a road etc.). **wash-out** *n.* **1** *colloq.* a fiasco; a complete failure. **2** a breach in a road, railway track, etc., caused by flooding (see also WASHOUT). **wash up 1** *tr.* (also *absol.*) esp. *Brit.* wash (crockery and cutlery) after use. **2** *US* wash one's face and hands. **won't wash** esp. *Brit. colloq.* (of an argument etc.) will not be believed or accepted. [OE *wæscan* etc. f. Gmc, rel. to WATER]

▪ *v.* **1, 3** wash up, clean (up), bathe, shower, douche, douse, scrub (up), shampoo, soap up, lather, launder, scour, wash down, soak, rinse, flush, wet, wash out, irrigate, drench, sponge (off), *Brit.* bath, *colloq.* perform one's ablutions, *usu. formal* cleanse, *literary* lave. **2** scrub off, clean off, rinse off, soak out, sponge off; wear away, remove, delete, erase, expunge, destroy, eradicate, obliterate, extinguish, blot out, wipe off *or* out. **9** remove, move, transport, carry, bear, convey, deliver, deposit, drive, sweep. **10 a** erode, cut *or* dig *or* wear *or* eat *or* dredge (away *or* out), excavate, scoop out, channel. **b** erode, denude, undermine, wear away. **11** splash, spatter, splatter, plash, dash, beat, pound, thrash, break, toss, surge, undulate, rush, run, lap, ripple, roll, flow, sweep. **12** decontaminate, purify, sift, filter, depurate. **13** overlay, film, coat, paint, glaze; plate. ● *n.* **1** clean, scrub, scour, shampoo, bath, shower, sponge, sponge bath; laundering; *colloq.* ablutions, tub. **2** washing, laundry. **3** wave, wake, surge, backwash; flow, swell, welling, sweep, ebb and flow, undulation, rise and fall. **5** swill, pigswill, hogwash, pigwash, slop(s). **7, 10** lotion, rinse, liniment, salve, embrocation, emulsion; mouthwash, gargle; eyewash, collyrium. **8** coat, coating, film, overlay, glaze; plating. □ **wash-basin** see SINK *n.* 1. **wash down 1** see WASH *v.* 1, 3 above. **washed out 1** faded, bleached. **2** wan, pale, pallid, peaky, colourless, faded, lacklustre, flat; blanched, bleached, etiolated. **3** exhausted, spent, tired, tired out, weary, worn out, fatigued, drained, enfeebled, enervated, knocked up, *colloq.* fagged (out), bone-tired, done in, all in, knocked out, *US colloq.* bushed, tuckered out, pooped, *sl.* beat, *Brit. sl.* knackered. **washed up** finished, through, failed, defeated, done for, played out, over (and done with), *sl.* kaput. **wash one's hands of** stay *or* keep away from, disown, repudiate, turn one's back on, have nothing more *or* further to do with, get rid of, rid oneself of, desert, abandon, leave. **wash out 1, 2** see WASH *v.* 1, 3 above. **3 a** rain off, *US* rain out. **wash-out 1** failure, disaster, débâcle, (total) loss, fiasco, disappointment, damp squib, *US colloq.* lead balloon, *sl.* flop, dud, *Austral. sl.* shicer. **won't wash** won't hold up, won't stand up, won't stand the test of time, won't carry weight, won't bear scrutiny, won't prove true, won't make sense, won't be believable *or* credible, won't hold water.

washable /wóshəb'l/ *adj.* that can be washed, esp. without damage. □□ **washability** /-bílliti/ *n.*

washboard /wóshbord/ *n.* **1** a board of ribbed wood or a sheet of corrugated zinc on which clothes are scrubbed in washing. **2** this used as a percussion instrument, played with the fingers.

washday /wóshday/ *n.* a day on which clothes etc. are washed.

washer /wóshər/ *n.* **1 a** a person or thing that washes. **b** a washing-machine. **2** a flat ring of rubber, metal, leather, etc., inserted at a joint to tighten it and prevent leakage. **3** a similar ring placed under the head of a screw, bolt, etc., or under a nut, to disperse its pressure. **4** *Austral.* a cloth for washing the face. □ **washer-up** (*pl.* **washers-up**) a person who washes up dishes etc.

washerwoman /wóshərwŏŏmmən/ *n.* (*pl.* **-women**) a woman whose occupation is washing clothes; a laundress.

washeteria /wóshətéeriə/ *n.* = LAUNDERETTE.

washing /wóshing/ *n.* a quantity of clothes for washing or just washed. □ **washing-machine** a machine for washing clothes and linen etc. **washing-powder** powder of soap or detergent for washing clothes. **washing-soda** sodium carbonate, used dissolved in water for washing and cleaning. **washing-up** *Brit.* **1** the process of washing dishes etc. after use. **2** used dishes etc. for washing.

▪ laundry, clothes.

washland /wóshland/ *n.* land periodically flooded by a stream.

washout /wóshowt/ *n. Geol.* a narrow river-channel that cuts into pre-existing sediments (see also *wash-out*).

washroom /wóshrōōm, -rŏŏm/ *n. US* a room with washing and toilet facilities.

▪ see TOILET 1.

washstand /wóshstand/ *n.* a piece of furniture to hold a basin, jug, soap, etc.

washtub /wóshtub/ *n.* a tub or vessel for washing clothes etc.

washy /wóshi/ *adj.* (**washier, washiest**) **1** (of liquid food) too watery or weak; insipid. **2** (of colour) faded-looking, thin, faint. **3** (of a style, sentiment, etc.) lacking vigour or intensity. □□ **washily** *adv.* **washiness** *n.*

wasn't /wózz'nt/ *contr.* was not.

Wasp /wosp/ *n.* (also **WASP**) *US* usu. *derog.* a middle-class American White Protestant descended from early European settlers. □□ **Waspy** *adj.* (also **WASPy**). [*W*hite *A*nglo-*S*axon *P*rotestant]

wasp /wosp/ *n.* **1** a stinging often flesh-eating insect of the order Hymenoptera, esp. the common social wasp *Vespa vulgaris*, with black and yellow stripes and a very thin waist. **2** (in *comb.*) any of various insects resembling a wasp in some way (*wasp-beetle*). □ **wasp-waist** a very slender waist. **wasp-waisted** having a very slender waist. □□ **wasplike** *adj.* [OE *wæfs*, *wæps*, *wæsp*, f. WG: perh. rel. to WEAVE[1] (from the weblike form of its nest)]

waspish /wóspish/ *adj.* irritable, petulant; sharp in retort. □□ **waspishly** *adv.* **waspishness** *n.*

▪ irascible, irritable, bad-tempered, foul-tempered, temperamental, testy, grouchy, sensitive, volatile, querulous, edgy, petulant, spiteful, peevish, cantankerous, curmudgeonly, cross, crabby, crabbed, crotchety, splenetic, grumpy, captious, crusty; *esp. US* cranky.

wassail /wóssayl, wóss'l/ *n.* & *v. archaic* ● *n.* **1** a festive occasion; a drinking-bout. **2** a kind of liquor drunk on such an occasion. ● *v.intr.* make merry; celebrate with drinking etc. □ **wassail-bowl** (or **-cup**) a bowl or cup from which healths were drunk, esp. on Christmas Eve and Twelfth Night. □□ **wassailer** *n.* [ME *wæs hæil* etc. f. ON *ves heill*, corresp. to OE *wes hāl* 'be in health', a form of salutation: cf. HALE[1]]

Wassermann test /vaássərmən/ *n.* a test for syphilis using the reaction of the patient's blood serum. [A. von *Wassermann*, Ger. pathologist d. 1925]

wast /wost, wəst/ *archaic* or *dial. 2nd sing. past* of BE.

wastage /wáystij/ *n.* **1** an amount wasted. **2** loss by use, wear, or leakage. **3** *Commerce* loss of employees other than by redundancy.

▪ **1, 2** see LOSS 2.

waste /wayst/ *v.*, *adj.*, & *n.* ● *v.* **1** *tr.* use to no purpose or for inadequate result or extravagantly (*waste time*). **2** *tr.* fail to use (esp. an opportunity). **3** *tr.* (often foll. by *on*) give (advice etc.), utter (words etc.), without effect. **4** *tr.* & *intr.* wear gradually away; make or become weak; wither. **5** *tr.* **a** ravage, devastate. **b** *US sl.* murder, kill. **6** *tr.* treat as wasted or valueless. **7** *intr.* be expended without useful effect. ● *adj.* **1** superfluous; no longer serving a purpose. **2** (of a district etc.) not inhabited or cultivated; desolate (*waste ground*). **3** presenting no features of interest. ● *n.* **1** the act or an instance of wasting; extravagant or ineffectual use of an asset, of time, etc. **2** waste material or food; refuse; useless remains or by-products. **3** a waste region; a desert etc. **4** the state of being used up; diminution by wear and tear. **5** *Law* damage to an estate caused by an act or by neglect, esp. by a life-tenant. **6** = *waste pipe*. □ **go** (or run) **to waste** be wasted. **lay waste** ravage, devastate. **waste-basket** esp. *US* = *waste-paper basket*. **waste one's breath** see BREATH. **waste not, want not** extravagance leads to poverty. **waste paper** spoiled or valueless paper. **waste-paper basket** esp. *Brit.* a receptacle for waste paper. **waste pipe** a pipe to carry off waste material, e.g. from a sink. **waste products** useless by-products of manufacture or of an organism or organisms. **waste words** see WORD. ▫▫ **wastable** *adj.* **wasteless** *adj.* [ME f. ONF *wast(e)*, var. of OF *g(u)ast(e)*, f. L *vastus*]

■ *v.* **1** squander, misuse, throw away, fritter away, misspend, dissipate, *colloq.* splurge; *sl.* blow; *Austral.* & *NZ sl.* knock down. **2** see LOSE 9. **4** enervate, enfeeble, emaciate, gnaw, destroy, consume, debilitate, exhaust, disable; diminish, deteriorate, dwindle, decline, decay, atrophy, wither, shrink, weaken, become debilitated, fade, peak, become enervated *or* enfeebled *or* emaciated, regress, ebb, sink. **5 a** see DEVASTATE 1. **b** assassinate, murder, kill, *colloq.* do away with, *sl.* put away, *esp. US sl.* rub out, ice; see also KILL[1] *v.* 1. ● *adj.* **1** extra, leftover, unused, superfluous; worthless, useless, unproductive, unusable, unsalvageable, unrecyclable, unprofitable. **2** barren, empty, uninhabited, unpopulated, uncultivated, unproductive, desert, desolate, wild. ● *n.* **1** extravagance, prodigality, wastefulness, squandering, indulgence, lavishness, profligacy, dissoluteness, improvidence, overindulgence; misuse, misapplication, dissipation, misemployment, abuse, neglect. **2** refuse, rubbish, garbage, dregs, debris, dross, leavings, scrap, sweepings, litter, slag, *Austral. or dial.* mullock, *esp. US* trash. **3** wasteland, desert, wilderness, barrens, wilds, emptiness, vastness. ▫ **lay waste** devastate, destroy, demolish, ruin, wreck, ravage, pillage, sack, plunder, loot, rob, strip, spoil, gut, ransack, wreak havoc (up)on, crush, raze, annihilate, *literary* despoil.

wasteful /wáystfōōl/ *adj.* **1** extravagant. **2** causing or showing waste. ▫▫ **wastefully** *adj.* **wastefulness** *n.*

■ extravagant, spendthrift, profligate, prodigal, lavish, improvident, unthrifty, uneconomical, thriftless, penny wise and pound foolish. ▫▫ **wastefully** see *like water* (WATER). **wastefulness** see WASTE *n.* 1.

wasteland /wáystland/ *n.* **1** an unproductive or useless area of land. **2** a place or time considered spiritually or intellectually barren.

■ **1** rough ground, scrub, badlands, bomb site; see also WILD *n.*

waster /wáystər/ *n.* **1** a wasteful person. **2** *colloq.* a wastrel.

■ **2** see LOAFER.

wastrel /wáystrəl/ *n.* **1** a wasteful or good-for-nothing person. **2** a waif; a neglected child.

■ **1** spendthrift, profligate, waster, prodigal, big spender, squanderer; idler, layabout, malingerer, loafer, shirker, good-for-nothing, ne'er-do-well, drone, *colloq.* lazybones, *Brit. sl.* skiver.

watch /woch/ *v.* & *n.* ● *v.* **1** *tr.* keep the eyes fixed on; look at attentively. **2** *tr.* **a** keep under observation; follow observantly. **b** monitor or consider carefully; pay attention to (*have to watch my weight*; *watched their progress with interest*). **3** *intr.* (often foll. by *for*) be in an alert state; be vigilant; take heed (*watch for the holes in the road*; *watch for an opportunity*). **4** *intr.* (foll. by *over*) look after; take care of. **5** *intr. archaic* remain awake for devotions etc. ● *n.* **1** a small portable timepiece for carrying on one's person. **2** a state of alert or constant observation or attention. **3** *Naut.* **a** a four-hour spell of duty. **b** (in full **starboard** or **port watch**) each of the halves, divided according to the position of the bunks, into which a ship's crew is divided to take alternate watches. **4** *hist.* a watchman or group of watchmen, esp. patrolling the streets at night. **5** a former division of the night. **6** a period of wakefulness at night. **7** *hist.* irregular Highland troops in the 18th c. ▫ **on the watch** waiting for an expected or feared occurrence. **set the watch** *Naut.* station sentinels etc. **watch-case** the outer metal case enclosing the works of a watch. **watch-chain** a metal chain for securing a pocket-watch. **Watch Committee** *hist.* (in the UK) the committee of a county borough council dealing with policing etc. **watch-glass 1** a glass disc covering the dial of a watch. **2** a similar disc used in a laboratory etc. to hold material for use in experiments. **watching brief** see BRIEF. **watch it** (or **oneself**) *colloq.* be careful. **watch-night 1** the last night of the year. **2** a religious service held on this night. **watch out 1** (often foll. by *for*) be on one's guard. **2** as a warning of immediate danger. **watch-spring** the mainspring of a watch. **watch one's step** proceed cautiously. **watch-strap** esp. *Brit.* a strap for fastening a watch on the wrist. **watch-tower** a tower from which observation can be kept. ▫▫ **watchable** *adj.* **watcher** *n.* (also in *comb.*). [OE *wæcce* (n.), rel. to WAKE[1]]

■ *v.* **1** observe, regard, look at, gaze at *or* on, take in, contemplate, eye, peer at; ogle, make eyes at. **2 a, 4** look after, tend, mind, keep an eye on, watch over, guard, care for, take care of, safeguard, protect, shield, keep safe, supervise, superintend; chaperon, accompany, attend; babysit, sit (with). **b** observe, note, notice, make *or* take note of, see, pay attention to, attend (to), follow, heed, take heed of, monitor, examine, inspect, scrutinize, pore over. **3** see *watch out* below; (*watch for*) watch out for, look for, be on the watch *or* lookout *or* alert for, guard against, keep an eye open for, be watchful for, note, take note *or* notice of, take heed of, be vigilant for *or* of, keep one's eyes open *or* peeled *or* skinned for, keep a (sharp) lookout for, be prepared *or* ready for, be careful of, await, wait for, keep a *or* one's weather eye open for, *disp.* anticipate. ● *n.* **1** clock, timepiece, pocket watch, wrist-watch; chronometer. **2** vigil, surveillance, observation, lookout. **4** sentry, sentinel, (security) guard, lookout, (night-)watchman, caretaker. ▫ **on the watch** on the alert, on the lookout, on (one's) guard, on the qui vive, alert, awake, observant, watchful, cautious, wary, vigilant, circumspect. **watch out 1** watch, look, look out, be on the watch *or* lookout *or* alert *or* qui vive, be on (one's) guard, keep an eye open, be watchful, take note *or* notice, take heed, be vigilant, keep one's eyes open *or* peeled *or* skinned, keep a (sharp) lookout, be prepared *or* ready, be careful, wait, keep a *or* one's weather eye open. **watch one's step** see *mind one's step* (STEP). ▫▫ **watcher** see OBSERVER.

watchband /wóchband/ *n. US* = *watch-strap*.

watchdog /wóchdog/ *n.* & *v.* ● *n.* **1** a dog kept to guard property etc. **2** a person or body monitoring others' rights, behaviour, etc. ● *v.tr.* (**-dogged**, **-dogging**) maintain surveillance over.

■ *n.* **1** guard dog. **2** see MONITOR *n.* 1.

watchful /wóchfōōl/ *adj.* **1** accustomed to watching. **2** on the watch. **3** showing vigilance. **4** *archaic* wakeful. ▫▫ **watchfully** *adv.* **watchfulness** *n.*

■ **2, 3** see VIGILANT. ▫▫ **watchfulness** see VIGILANCE.

watchmaker /wóchmaykər/ *n.* a person who makes and repairs watches and clocks. ▫▫ **watchmaking** *n.*

watchman /wóchmən/ *n.* (*pl.* **-men**) **1** a man employed to look after an empty building etc. at night. **2** *archaic* or *hist.* a member of a night-watch.

■ (security) guard, sentinel, sentry, lookout, watch, night-watchman, custodian, caretaker.

watchword /wóchwurd/ *n.* **1** a phrase summarizing a guiding principle; a slogan. **2** *hist.* a military password.

■ see SLOGAN 1–3.

water /wáwtər/ *n.* & *v.* ● *n.* **1** a colourless transparent odourless tasteless liquid compound of oxygen and hydrogen. ¶ Chem. formula: H_2O. **2** a liquid consisting chiefly of this and found in seas, lakes, and rivers, in rain, and in secretions of organisms. **3** an expanse of water; a sea, lake, river, etc. **4** (in *pl.*) part of a sea or river (*in Icelandic waters*). **5** (often as **the waters**) mineral water at a spa etc. **6** the state of a tide (*high water*). **7** a solution of a specified substance in water (*lavender-water*). **8** the quality of the transparency and brilliance of a gem, esp. a diamond. **9**

Finance an amount of nominal capital added by watering (see sense 10 of *v.*). **10** (*attrib.*) **a** found in or near water. **b** of, for, or worked by water. **c** involving, using, or yielding water. ● *v.* **1** *tr.* sprinkle or soak with water. **2** *tr.* supply (a plant) with water. **3** *tr.* give water to (an animal) to drink. **4** *intr.* (of the mouth or eyes) secrete water as saliva or tears. **5** *tr.* (as **watered** *adj.*) (of silk etc.) having irregular wavy glossy markings. **6** *tr.* adulterate (milk, beer, etc.) with water. **7** *tr.* (of a river etc.) supply (a place) with water. **8** *intr.* (of an animal) go to a pool etc. to drink. **9** *intr.* (of a ship, engine, etc., or the person in charge of it) take in a supply of water. **10** *tr. Finance* increase (a company's debt, or nominal capital) by the issue of new shares without a corresponding addition to assets. □ **by water** using a ship etc. for travel or transport. **cast one's bread upon the waters** see BREAD. **like water** lavishly, profusely. **like water off a duck's back** see DUCK[1]. **make one's mouth water** cause one's saliva to flow, stimulate one's appetite or anticipation. **of the first water 1** (of a diamond) of the greatest brilliance and transparency. **2** of the finest quality or extreme degree. **on the water** on a ship etc. **on the water-wagon** see WAGON. **water-bag** a bag of leather, canvas, etc., for holding water. **water bailiff 1** an official enforcing fishing laws. **2** *hist.* a custom-house officer at a port. **water bear** = TARDIGRADE *n.* **water-bed** a mattress of rubber or plastic etc. filled with water. **water-biscuit** a thin crisp unsweetened biscuit made from flour and water. **water blister** a blister containing a colourless fluid, not blood or pus. **water-boatman** any aquatic bug of the family Notonectidae or Corixidae, swimming with oarlike hind legs. **water-borne 1** (of goods etc.) conveyed by or travelling on water. **2** (of a disease) communicated or propagated by contaminated water. **water-buck** any of various African antelopes of the genus *Kobus*, frequenting river-banks. **water-buffalo** the common domestic Indian buffalo, *Bubalus arnee*. **water bus** a boat carrying passengers on a regular run on a river, lake, etc. **water-butt** a barrel used to catch rainwater. **water-cannon** a device giving a powerful jet of water to disperse a crowd etc. **the Water-carrier** (or **-bearer**) the zodiacal sign or constellation Aquarius. **water chestnut 1** an aquatic plant, *Trapa natans*, bearing an edible seed. **2 a** (in full **Chinese water chestnut**) a sedge, *Eleocharis tuberosa*, with rushlike leaves arising from a corm. **b** this corm used as food. **water-clock** a clock measuring time by the flow of water. **water-closet 1** a lavatory with the means for flushing the pan with water. **2** a room containing this. **water-colour** (*US* **-color**) **1** artists' paint made of pigment to be diluted with water and not oil. **2** a picture painted with this. **3** the art of painting with water-colours. **water-colourist** (*US* **-colorist**) a painter in water-colours. **water-cooled** cooled by the circulation of water. **water-cooler** a tank of cooled drinking-water. **water cure** = HYDROPATHY. **water-diviner** *Brit.* a person who dowses (see DOWSE[1]) for water. **water down 1** dilute with water. **2** make less vivid, forceful, or horrifying. **water gauge 1** a glass tube etc. indicating the height of water in a reservoir, boiler, etc. **2** pressure expressed in terms of a head of water. **water-glass 1** a solution of sodium or potassium silicate used for preserving eggs, as a vehicle for fresco-painting, and for hardening artificial stone. **2** a tube with a glass bottom enabling objects under water to be observed. **water-hammer** a knocking noise in a water-pipe when a tap is suddenly turned off. **water-heater** a device for heating (esp. domestic) water. **water hemlock** a poisonous plant, *Cicuta maculata*, found in marshes etc.: also called COWBANE. **water-hole** a shallow depression in which water collects (esp. in the bed of a river otherwise dry). **water hyacinth** a tropical river-weed, *Eichhornia crassipes*. **water-ice** a confection of flavoured and frozen water and sugar etc.; a sorbet. **water jump** a place where a horse in a steeplechase etc. must jump over water. **water-level 1 a** the surface of the water in a reservoir etc. **b** the height of this. **2** a level below which the ground is saturated with water. **3** a level using water to determine the horizontal. **water lily** any aquatic plant of the family Nymphaeaceae, with broad flat floating leaves and large usu. cup-shaped floating flowers. **water-line 1** the line along which the surface of water touches a ship's side (marked on a ship for use in loading). **2** a linear watermark. **water main** the main pipe in a water-supply system. **water-meadow** a meadow periodically flooded by a stream. **water melon** a large smooth green melon, *Citrullus lanatus*, with red pulp and watery juice. **water meter** a device for measuring and recording the amount of water supplied to a house etc. **water-mill** a mill worked by a water-wheel. **water-nymph** a nymph regarded as inhabiting or presiding over water. **water of crystallization** water forming an essential part of the structure of some crystals. **water of life** *rhet.* spiritual enlightenment. **water ouzel** = DIPPER 1. **water-pepper** an aquatic herb, *Polygonum hydropiper*: also called SMARTWEED. **water-pipe 1** a pipe for conveying water. **2** a hookah. **water-pistol** a toy pistol shooting a jet of water. **water plantain** any ditch-plant of the genus *Alisma*, with plantain-like leaves. **water polo** a game played by swimmers, with a ball like a football. **water-power 1** mechanical force derived from the weight or motion of water. **2** a fall in the level of a river, as a source of this force. **water purslane** a creeping plant, *Lythrum portula*, growing in damp places. **water rail** a wading bird, *Rallus aquaticus*, frequenting marshes etc. **water-rat** = *water-vole*. **water-rate** a charge made for the use of the public water-supply. **water-repellent** not easily penetrated by water. **water-scorpion** any aquatic bug of the family Nepidae, living submerged and breathing through a bristle-like tubular tail. **water-softener** an apparatus or substance for softening hard water. **water-soluble** soluble in water. **water-splash** part of a road submerged by a stream or pool. **water starwort** any plant of the genus *Callitriche*, growing in water. **water-supply** the provision and storage of water, or the amount of water stored, for the use of a town, house, etc. **water-table** = *water-level* 2. **water torture** a form of torture in which the victim is exposed to the incessant dripping of water on the head, or the sound of dripping. **water-tower** a tower with an elevated tank to give pressure for distributing water. **water under the bridge** past events accepted as past and irrevocable. **water-vole** an aquatic vole, esp. *Arvicola amphibius*. **water-weed** any of various aquatic plants. **water-wheel** a wheel driven by water to work machinery, or to raise water. **water-wings** inflated floats fixed on the arms of a person learning to swim. □□ **waterer** *n.* **waterless** *adj.* [OE *wæter* f. Gmc, rel. to WET]

■ *n.* **1, 2** H_2O, Adam's ale; distilled water, tap water, drinking-water, rainwater, bottled water, spa water, still water, soda (water), effervescent water, fizzy water, mineral water; sea water, brine, salt water; ditch-water, dishwater, bath-water, heavy water, deuterium oxide. ● *v.* **1** inundate, flood, drench, saturate, soak, douse, irrigate, besprinkle, hose, wet, shower, splash, spray, sprinkle, moisten, damp, dampen, bedew. **4** run, stream. **6** see *water down* 1 below. □ **like water** lavishly, extravagantly, freely, wastefully, profligately, open-handedly, liberally, excessively, copiously, profusely, unstintingly, unreservedly. **of the first water 2** of superior quality *or* grade, of excellent quality *or* grade, of first quality *or* grade, of top quality *or* grade, of A1 quality *or* grade, of the finest quality *or* grade, of the highest quality *or* grade, of the best quality *or* grade; first-grade, top-grade; of the worst *or* lowest *or* basest kind. **water-closet** see TOILET 1. **water-colour 2** aquarelle. **water down 1** dilute, weaken, water, thin out, adulterate, *US* cut, *colloq.* doctor. **2** mollify, modify, soften, tone down, qualify, moderate, soft-pedal. **water-hole** watering-hole, watering-place, *Austral.* gnamma, clay-pan. **water main** see MAIN *n.*[1] 1. **water-pipe 1** see PIPE *n.* 1. **water-splash** ford. □□ **waterless** see DRY *adj.* 1.

waterbrash /wáwtərbrash/ *n.* pyrosis. [WATER + BRASH[3]]

watercourse /wáwtərkorss/ *n.* **1** a brook, stream, or artificial water-channel. **2** the bed along which this flows.
■ **1** see STREAM *n.* 1.

watercress /wáwtərkress/ *n.* a hardy perennial cress, *Nasturtium officinale*, growing in running water, with pungent leaves used in salad.

waterfall /wáwtərfawl/ *n.* a stream or river flowing over a precipice or down a steep hillside.
■ cascade, cataract, fall(s), *N.Engl.* force; *Sc.* linn.

Waterford glass /wáwtərfərd/ *n.* a clear colourless flint glass. [*Waterford* in Ireland]

waterfowl /wáwtərfowl/ *n.* (usu. collect. as *pl.*) birds frequenting water, esp. swimming game-birds.

waterfront /wáwtərfrunt/ *n.* the part of a town adjoining a river, lake, harbour, etc.

Watergate /wáwtərgayt/ *n.* a political or commercial scandal on a large scale. [a building in Washington, DC, USA and the national headquarters of the Democratic Party, the bugging and burglary of which in 1972 by people connected with the Republican administration led to a national scandal and the resignation of President R. M. Nixon]

watergate /wáwtərgayt/ *n.* **1** a floodgate. **2** a gate giving access to a river etc.

watering /wáwtəring/ *n.* the act or an instance of supplying water or (of an animal) obtaining water. □ **watering-can** a portable container with a long spout usu. ending in a perforated sprinkler, for watering plants. **watering-hole 1** a pool of water from which animals regularly drink; = *water-hole*. **2** *sl.* a bar. **watering-place 1** = *watering-hole*. **2** a spa or seaside resort. **3** a place where water is obtained. [OE *wæterung* (as WATER, -ING[1])]
■ □ **watering hole** see PUB 2.

waterlogged /wáwtərlogd/ *adj.* **1** saturated with water. **2** (of a boat etc.) hardly able to float from being saturated or filled with water. **3** (of ground) made useless by being saturated with water. [*waterlog* (v.), f. WATER + LOG[1], prob. orig. = 'reduce (a ship) to the condition of a log']
■ **1, 3** see *soaking n.* (SOAK).

Waterloo /wáwtərlóo/ *n.* a decisive defeat or contest (*meet one's Waterloo*). [*Waterloo* in Belgium, where Napoleon was finally defeated in 1815]

waterman /wáwtərmən/ *n.* (*pl.* **-men**) **1** a boatman plying for hire. **2** an oarsman as regards skill in keeping the boat balanced.

watermark /wáwtərmaark/ *n.* & *v.* ● *n.* a faint design made in some paper during manufacture, visible when held against the light, identifying the maker etc. ● *v.tr.* mark with this.

waterproof /wáwtərproof/ *adj.*, *n.*, & *v.* ● *adj.* impervious to water. ● *n.* a waterproof garment or material. ● *v.tr.* make waterproof.
■ *adj.* watertight, sealed.

watershed /wáwtərshed/ *n.* **1** a line of separation between waters flowing to different rivers, basins, or seas. **2** a turning-point in affairs. [WATER + *shed* ridge of high ground (rel. to SHED[2]), after G *Wasserscheide*]
■ **2** see LANDMARK 2.

waterside /wáwtərsīd/ *n.* the margin of a sea, lake, or river.

water-ski /wáwtərskee/ *n.* & *v.* ● *n.* (*pl.* **-skis**) each of a pair of skis for skimming the surface of the water when towed by a motor boat. ● *v.intr.* (**-skis, -ski'd** or **-skied** /-skeed/; **-skiing**) travel on water-skis. □□ **water-skier** *n.*

waterspout /wáwtərspowt/ *n.* a gyrating column of water and spray formed by a whirlwind between sea and cloud.

watertight /wáwtərtīt/ *adj.* **1** (of a joint, container, vessel, etc.) closely fastened or fitted or made so as to prevent the passage of water. **2** (of an argument etc.) unassailable.
■ **1** sealed, waterproof. **2** unassailable, impregnable, solid, airtight, flawless, faultless, incontrovertible; without loopholes.

waterway /wáwtərway/ *n.* **1** a navigable channel. **2** a route for travel by water. **3** a thick plank at the outer edge of a deck along which a channel is hollowed for water to run off by.

waterworks /wáwtərwurks/ *n.* **1** an establishment for managing a water-supply. **2** *colloq.* the shedding of tears. **3** *Brit. colloq.* the urinary system.

watery /wáwtəri/ *adj.* **1** containing too much water. **2** too thin in consistency. **3** of or consisting of water. **4** (of the eyes) suffused or running with water. **5** (of conversation, style, etc.) vapid, uninteresting. **6** (of colour) pale. **7** (of the sun, moon, or sky) rainy-looking. □ **watery grave** the bottom of the sea as a place where a person lies drowned. □□ **wateriness** *n.* [OE *wæterig* (as WATER, -Y[1])]
■ **1** wet, swampy, boggy, marshy, aqueous, squelchy, squashy, squishy; soggy, moist, damp, humid; *colloq.* squidgy. **2** weak, dilute(d), watered down, thin, liquid, runny, sloppy, wishy-washy. **4** weeping, teary, tearful, bleary, running, streaming, damp, moist, weepy, rheumy, *formal* lachrymose. **5** vapid, uninteresting, insipid, jejune, flat, dull, bland, tame. **6** pale, anaemic, pallid, weak, feeble, washed-out, wishy-washy, colourless.

watjin /waadyín/ *n.* (also **waatgin, wijen, wodgin**) *Austral.* (in Aboriginal English) a white woman. [alt. of *white gin*: see GIN[3]]

watt /wot/ *n.* the SI unit of power, equivalent to one joule per second, corresponding to the rate of energy in an electric circuit where the potential difference is one volt and the current one ampere. ¶ Symb.: **W**. □ **watt-hour** the energy used when one watt is applied for one hour. [J. *Watt*, Sc. engineer d. 1819]

wattage /wóttij/ *n.* an amount of electrical power expressed in watts.

wattle[1] /wótt'l/ *n.* & *v.* ● *n.* **1 a** interlaced rods and split rods as a material for making fences, walls, etc. **b** (in *sing.* or *pl.*) rods and twigs for this use. **2** an Australian acacia with long pliant branches, with bark used in tanning and golden flowers used as the national emblem. **3** *dial.* a wicker hurdle. ● *v.tr.* **1** make of wattle. **2** enclose or fill up with wattles. □ **wattle and daub** a network of rods and twigs plastered with mud or clay as a building material. [OE *watul*, of unkn. orig.]

wattle[2] /wótt'l/ *n.* **1** a loose fleshy appendage on the head or throat of a turkey or other birds. **2** = BARB *n.* 3. □□ **wattled** *adj.* [16th c.: orig. unkn.]

wattmeter /wótmeetər/ *n.* a meter for measuring the amount of electricity in watts.

waul /wawl/ *v.intr.* (also **wawl**) give a loud plaintive cry like a cat. [imit.]

wave /wayv/ *v.* & *n.* ● *v.* **1 a** *intr.* (often foll. by *to*) move a hand etc. to and fro in greeting or as a signal (*waved to me across the street*). **b** *tr.* move (a hand etc.) in this way. **2 a** *intr.* show a sinuous or sweeping motion as of a flag, tree, or a cornfield in the wind; flutter, undulate. **b** *tr.* impart a waving motion to. **3** *tr.* brandish (a sword etc.) as an encouragement to followers etc. **4** *tr.* tell or direct (a person) by waving (*waved them away*; *waved them to follow*). **5** *tr.* express (a greeting etc.) by waving (*waved goodbye to them*). **6** *tr.* give an undulating form to (hair, drawn lines, etc.); make wavy. **7** *intr.* (of hair etc.) have such a form; be wavy. ● *n.* **1** a ridge of water between two depressions. **2** a long body of water curling into an arched form and breaking on the shore. **3** a thing compared to this, e.g. a body of persons in one of successive advancing groups. **4** a gesture of waving. **5 a** the process of waving the hair. **b** an undulating form produced in the hair by waving. **6 a** a temporary occurrence or increase of a condition, emotion, or influence (*a wave of enthusiasm*). **b** a specified period of widespread weather (*heat wave*). **7** *Physics* **a** the disturbance of the particles of a fluid medium to form ridges and troughs for the propagation or direction of motion, heat, light, sound, etc., without the advance of the particles. **b** a single curve in the course of this motion (see also *standing wave*, *travelling wave* (see TRAVEL)). **8** *Electr.* a similar variation of an electromagnetic field in the propagation of radiation through a medium or vacuum. **9** (in *pl.*; prec. by *the*) *poet.* the sea; water. □ **make waves** *colloq.* cause trouble. **wave aside** dismiss as intrusive or irrelevant. **wave down** wave to (a vehicle or its driver) as a signal to stop. **wave equation** a differential equation expressing the properties of motion in waves. **wave-form** *Physics* a curve showing the shape of a wave at a given time. **wave-front** *Physics* a surface containing points affected in the same way by a wave at a given time. **wave function** a function satisfying a wave equation and describing the properties of a wave. **wave mechanics** a method of analysis of the behaviour esp. of atomic phenomena with particles represented by wave equations (see *quantum mechanics*). **wave number** *Physics* the number of waves in a unit distance. **wave theory** *hist.* the theory that light is propagated through the ether by a wave-motion imparted to the ether by the molecular vibrations of the radiant body. □□ **waveless** *adj.* **wavelike** *adj.* & *adv.* [OE *wafian* (v.) f. Gmc: (n.) also alt. of ME *wawe, wage*]

■ *v.* **1 a** signal, sign, gesture, gesticulate. **2** undulate, billow, move to and fro, flap, flutter, quiver, flip-flop, swing, sway, ripple, oscillate, zigzag, fluctuate, shake; wag, whiffle, brandish, *colloq.* wigwag, wiggle, waggle. **3** see FLOURISH *v.* 4. **5** signal, sign, indicate, signify; gesture, gesticulate. ● *n.* **1, 2** swell, undulation, billow, sea, heave, roller, whitecap, white horse; ripple, wavelet, breaker, comber, boomer, *Austral.* & *NZ* dumper. **4** signal, sign, gesticulation, gesture. **6 a** surge, swell, welling up, ground swell, movement, flood, spurt, upsurge, uprising, current, tide. **b** spell. □ **wave aside** see DISMISS 4.

waveband /wáyvband/ *n.* a range of (esp. radio) wavelengths between certain limits.

waveguide /wáyvgīd/ *n. Electr.* a metal tube etc. confining and conveying microwaves.

wavelength /wáyvlength, -lengkth/ *n.* **1** the distance between successive crests of a wave, esp. points in a sound wave or electromagnetic wave. ¶ Symb.: λ. **2** this as a distinctive feature of radio waves from a transmitter. **3** *colloq.* a particular mode or range of thinking and communicating (*we don't seem to be on the same wavelength*).

■ **3** (*be on the same wavelength with*) see SYMPATHIZE 1.

wavelet /wáyvlit/ *n.* a small wave on water.

■ see RIPPLE *n.*[1] 1.

waver /wáyvər/ *v.intr.* **1** be or become unsteady; falter; begin to give way. **2** be irresolute or undecided between different courses or opinions; be shaken in resolution or belief. **3** (of a light) flicker. □□ **waverer** *n.* **waveringly** *adv.* [ME f. ON *vafra* flicker f. Gmc, rel. to WAVE]

■ **1** see TEETER 1, FLUCTUATE . **2** see DOUBT *v.* 2, 3.

wavy /wáyvi/ *adj.* (**wavier, waviest**) (of a line or surface) having waves or alternate contrary curves (*wavy hair*). □□ **wavily** *adv.* **waviness** *n.*

wa-wa var. of WAH-WAH.

wawl var. of WAUL.

wax[1] /waks/ *n.* & *v.* ● *n.* **1** a sticky plastic yellowish substance secreted by bees as the material of honeycomb cells; beeswax. **2** a white translucent material obtained from this by bleaching and purifying and used for candles, in modelling, as a basis of polishes, and for other purposes. **3** any similar substance, e.g. earwax. **4** *colloq.* **a** a gramophone record. **b** material for the manufacture of this. **5** (*attrib.*) made of wax. ● *v.tr.* **1** cover or treat with wax. **2** *colloq.* record for the gramophone. □ **be wax in a person's hands** be entirely subservient to a person. **lost wax** = CIRE PERDUE. **wax-light** a taper or candle of wax. **wax-myrtle** a tree, *Myrtus cerifera*, yielding wax and oil used for candles. **wax-painting** = ENCAUSTIC. **wax palm 1** a South American palm, *Ceroxylon alpinum*, with its stem coated in a mixture of resin and wax. **2** a carnauba. **wax paper** paper waterproofed with a layer of wax. **wax-pod** a yellow-podded bean. **wax-tree** an Asian tree, *Rhus succedanea*, having white berries which yield wax. □□ **waxer** *n.* [OE *wæx, weax* f. Gmc]

wax[2] /waks/ *v.intr.* **1** (of the moon between new and full) have a progressively larger part of its visible surface illuminated, increasing in apparent size. **2** become larger or stronger. **3** pass into a specified state or mood (*wax lyrical*). □ **wax and wane** undergo alternate increases and decreases. [OE *weaxan* f. Gmc]

■ **2** see GROW 1. **3** see BECOME 1.

wax[3] /waks/ *n. sl.* a fit of anger. [19th c.: orig. uncert.: perh. f. WAX[2] *wroth* etc.]

waxberry /wáksbəri/ *n.* (*pl.* **-ies**) **1** a wax-myrtle. **2** the fruit of this.

waxbill /wáksbil/ *n.* any of various birds esp. of the family Estrildidae, with usu. red bills resembling the colour of sealing wax.

waxcloth /wákskloth/ *n.* oilcloth.

waxen /wáks'n/ *adj.* **1** having a smooth pale translucent surface as of wax. **2** able to receive impressions like wax; plastic. **3** *archaic* made of wax.

waxwing /wákswing/ *n.* any bird of the genus *Bombycilla*, with small tips like red sealing-wax to some wing-feathers.

waxwork /wákswurk/ *n.* **1 a** an object, esp. a lifelike dummy, modelled in wax. **b** the making of waxworks. **2** (in *pl.*) an exhibition of wax dummies.

waxy[1] /wáksi/ *adj.* (**waxier, waxiest**) resembling wax in consistency or in its surface. □□ **waxily** *adv.* **waxiness** *n.* [WAX[1] + -Y[1]]

■ see GREASY 1, PLASTIC *adj.* 1a.

waxy[2] /wáksi/ *adj.* (**waxier, waxiest**) *Brit. sl.* angry, quick-tempered. [WAX[3] + -Y[1]]

way /way/ *n.* & *adv.* ● *n.* **1** a road, track, path, etc., for passing along. **2** a course or route for reaching a place, esp. the best one (*asked the way to London*). **3** a place of passage into a building, through a door, etc. (*could not find the way out*). **4 a** a method or plan for attaining an object (*that is not the way to do it*). **b** the ability to obtain one's object (*has a way with him*). **5 a** a person's desired or chosen course of action. **b** a custom or manner of behaving; a personal peculiarity (*has a way of forgetting things*; *things had a way of going badly*). **6** a specific manner of life or procedure (*soon got into the way of it*). **7** the normal course of events (*that is always the way*). **8** a travelling distance; a length traversed or to be traversed (*is a long way away*). **9 a** an unimpeded opportunity of advance. **b** a space free of obstacles. **10** a region or ground over which advance is desired or natural. **11** advance in some direction; impetus, progress (*pushed my way through*). **12** movement of a ship etc. (*gather way*; *lose way*). **13** the state of being engaged in movement from place to place; time spent in this (*met them on the way home*; *with songs to cheer the way*). **14** a specified direction (*step this way*; *which way are you going?*). **15** (in *pl.*) parts into which a thing is divided (*split it three ways*). **16** *colloq.* the scope or range of something (*want a few things in the stationery way*). **17** a person's line of occupation or business. **18** a specified condition or state (*things are in a bad way*). **19** a respect (*is useful in some ways*). **20 a** (in *pl.*) a structure of timber etc. down which a new ship is launched. **b** parallel rails etc. as a track for the movement of a machine. ● *adv. colloq.* to a considerable extent; far (*you're way off the mark*). □ **across** (or **over**) **the way** opposite. **any way** = ANYWAY. **be on one's way** set off; depart. **by the way 1** incidentally; as a more or less irrelevant comment. **2** during a journey. **by way of 1** through; by means of. **2** as a substitute for or as a form of (*did it by way of apology*). **3** with the intention of (*asked by way of discovering the truth*). **come one's way** become available to one; become one's lot. **find a way** discover a means of obtaining one's object. **get** (or **have**) **one's way** (or **have it one's own way** etc.) get what one wants; ensure one's wishes are met. **give way 1 a** make concessions. **b** fail to resist; yield. **2** (often foll. by *to*) concede precedence (to). **3** (of a structure etc.) be dislodged or broken under a load; collapse. **4** (foll. by *to*) be superseded by. **5** (foll. by *to*) be overcome by (an emotion etc.). **6** (of rowers) row hard. **go out of one's way** (often foll. by *to* + infin.) make a special effort; act gratuitously or without compulsion (*went out of their way to help*). **go one's own way** act independently, esp. against contrary advice. **go one's way 1** leave, depart. **2** (of events, circumstances, etc.) be favourable to one. **go a person's way** accompany a person (*are you going my way?*). **have it both ways** see BOTH. **in its way** if regarded from a particular standpoint appropriate to it. **in no way** not at all; by no means. **in a way** in a certain respect but not altogether or completely. **in the** (or **one's**) **way** forming an obstacle or hindrance. **lead the way 1** act as guide or leader. **2** show how to do something. **look the other way 1** ignore what one should notice. **2** disregard an acquaintance etc. whom one sees. **one way and another** taking various considerations into account. **one way or another** by some means. **on the** (or **one's**) **way 1** in the course of a journey etc. **2** having progressed (*is well on the way to completion*); in the pipeline. **3** *colloq.* (of a child) conceived but not yet born. **on the way out** *colloq.* going down in status, estimation, or favour; going out of fashion. **the other way about** (or **round**) in an inverted or reversed position or direction. **out of the way 1** no longer an obstacle or hindrance. **2** disposed of; settled. **3** (of a person) imprisoned or killed. **4** uncommon, remarkable; seldom met with (*nothing out of the way*). **5** (of a place) remote, inaccessible. **out of one's way** not on one's intended route. **put a person in the way of** give a person the opportunity of. **way back** *colloq.* long ago. **way-leave** a right of way rented to another. **the way of the Cross** a series of paintings or representations of the events in Christ's passion, esp. in a church. **way of life** the principles or habits governing all one's actions etc. **way of thinking** one's customary opinion of matters. **way of the world** conduct no worse than is customary. **way-out** *colloq.* **1** unusual, eccentric. **2** avant-garde, progressive. **3** excellent, exciting. **ways and means 1** methods of achieving something. **2** methods of raising government revenue. **way station** *US* **1** a minor station on a railway. **2** a point marking progress in a certain course of action etc. **way-worn** tired with travel. [OE *weg* f. Gmc: (adv.) f. AWAY]

■ *n.* **1, 2** path, road, street, avenue, course, route, track, trail, channel, direction. **4 a** manner, method, mode, fashion, means, system, course (of action), strategy, plan, policy, procedure, approach, scheme, technique, practice, *modus operandi*, m.o. **b** knack, skill, ability, facility, art. **5 b** habit, custom, knack, behaviour pattern, manner, approach, style, conduct, technique, nature, mores; idiosyncrasy, peculiarity, eccentricity, oddity, characteristic, personality, temperament, disposition, habit. **6** way of life, lifestyle, *modus vivendi*; see also ROUTINE *n.* 1. **8** distance, haul. **9** clearance, pathway, opening, space, room, avenue, scope, freedom, opportunity. **11** progress, passage, advance, headway. **12** speed, velocity, motion, (forward) movement, impetus, momentum. **13** see JOURNEY *n.* **18** condition, situation, state. **19** aspect, respect, particular, detail, point, sense, feature. □ **by the way 1** incidentally, by the by, parenthetically, in passing, *en passant*, apropos. **by way of 1** via, through, by means of. **2** (functioning) as, in (the) way of, in the capacity of, equivalent to, more or less, as a substitute for, as a form of, instead of, something like. **give way 1** yield, surrender, retreat, concede, withdraw, accede, defer, make concessions, acquiesce. **3** give, collapse, break (down), fail, cave in, fall (down), crumble, crumple, snap, disintegrate, go to pieces. **go out of one's way** see *make a point of* (POINT). **go one's way 1** see LEAVE[1] *v.* 1b, 3, 4. **lead the way 1** see GUIDE *v.* 1, 3. **2** see TEACH 1. **look the other way 1** turn a blind eye, turn a deaf ear, pay no attention, take no notice, turn one's back. **one way or another** see SOMEHOW. **on the** (or **one's**) **way 1** see *on the move* 2 (MOVE). **2** see *in the pipeline* (PIPELINE). **on the way out** see OBSOLESCENT. **the other way about** (or **round**) see VICE VERSA. **out of the way 2** disposed of, dealt with, settled, finished with, finalized. **4** see PECULIAR 1. **5** untravelled, unfrequented, isolated, outlying, secluded, inaccessible, distant, far-flung. **way back** see FORMERLY. **way of life** see CULTURE *n.* 2, CUSTOM 1. **way of thinking** see OPINION 1, 3. **way-out 1** bizarre, mad, weird, crazy, strange, odd, peculiar, freakish, freaky, unusual, eccentric, queer, abnormal, offbeat, outrageous, wild, exotic, esoteric, far-out, *colloq.* kinky, *sl.* kooky, screwy, nutty, batty, *esp. US sl.* flaky, screwball, off-the-wall. **2** avant-garde, advanced, original, innovative, unorthodox, unconventional, experimental, precedent-setting, progressive, exploratory, ground-breaking, trail-blazing, far-out. **3** see SPLENDID 3.

-way /way/ *suffix* = -WAYS.

wayback /wáybak/ *n.* esp. *Austral.* = OUTBACK.

waybill /wáybil/ *n.* a list of passengers or parcels on a vehicle.

waybread /wáybred/ *n. Brit. archaic* a broad-leaved plantain (see PLANTAIN[1]). [OE *wegbrǣde* (as WAY, BROAD)]

wayfarer /wáyfairər/ *n.* a traveller, esp. on foot.
■ see TRAVELLER 1.

wayfaring /wáyfairing/ *n.* travelling, esp. on foot. □ **wayfaring-tree** a white-flowered European and Asian shrub, *Viburnum lantana*, common along roadsides, with berries turning from green through red to black.

waylay /wayláy/ *v.tr.* (*past* and *past part.* **waylaid**) **1** lie in wait for. **2** stop to rob or interview. □□ **waylayer** *n.*
■ **1** ambush, lie in wait for, await, *US* bushwhack. **2** hold up, detain, intercept, pounce upon *or* on, swoop down on *or* upon, set upon, attack, mug, seize, assault, assail, accost, *Austral.* & *NZ* bail up, *colloq.* buttonhole.

waymark /wáymaark/ *n.* a natural or artificial object as a guide to travellers, esp. walkers.

-ways /wayz/ *suffix* forming adjectives and adverbs of direction or manner (*sideways*) (cf. -WISE). [WAY + -'S]

wayside /wáysīd/ *n.* **1** the side or margin of a road. **2** the land at the side of a road. □ **fall by the wayside** fail to continue in an endeavour or undertaking (after Luke 8:5).

wayward /wáywərd/ *adj.* **1** childishly self-willed or perverse; capricious. **2** unaccountable or freakish. □□ **waywardly** *adv.* **waywardness** *n.* [ME f. obs. *awayward* turned away f. AWAY + -WARD: cf. FROWARD]
■ see CAPRICIOUS, PERVERSE 2.

wayzgoose /wáyzgōōss/ *n.* (*pl.* **-gooses**) an annual summer dinner or outing held by a printing-house for its employees. [17th c. (earlier *waygoose*): orig. unkn.]

Wb *abbr.* weber(s).

WC *abbr.* **1** water-closet. **2** West Central.
■ **1** see TOILET 1.

WCC *abbr.* World Council of Churches.

W/Cdr. *abbr.* Wing Commander.

WD *abbr.* **1** War Department. **2** Works Department.

we /wee, wi/ *pron.* (*obj.* **us**; *poss.* **our, ours**) **1** (*pl.* of I[2]) used by and with reference to more than one person speaking or writing, or one such person and one or more associated persons. **2** used for or by a royal person in a proclamation etc. and by a writer or editor in a formal context. **3** people in general (cf. ONE *pron.* 2). **4** *colloq.* = I[2] (*give us a chance*). **5** *colloq.* (often implying condescension) you (*how are we feeling today?*). [OE f. Gmc]

WEA *abbr.* (in the UK) Workers' Educational Association.

weak /week/ *adj.* **1** deficient in strength, power, or number; fragile; easily broken or bent or defeated. **2** deficient in vigour; sickly, feeble (*weak health*; *a weak imagination*). **3 a** deficient in resolution; easily led (*a weak character*). **b** (of an action or features) indicating a lack of resolution (*a weak surrender*; *a weak chin*). **4** unconvincing or logically deficient (*weak evidence*; *a weak argument*). **5** (of a mixed liquid or solution) watery, thin, dilute (*weak tea*). **6** (of a style etc.) not vigorous or well-knit; diffuse, slipshod. **7** (of a crew) short-handed. **8** (of a syllable etc.) unstressed. **9** *Gram.* in Germanic languages: **a** (of a verb) forming inflections by the addition of a suffix to the stem. **b** (of a noun or adjective) belonging to a declension in which the stem originally ended in *-n* (opp. STRONG *adj.* 22). □ **weak ending** an unstressed syllable in a normally stressed place at the end of a verse-line. **the weaker sex** *derog.* women. **weak grade** *Gram.* an unstressed ablaut-form. **weak interaction** *Physics* the weakest form of interaction between elementary particles. **weak-kneed** *colloq.* lacking resolution. **weak-minded 1** mentally deficient. **2** lacking in resolution. **weak-mindedness** the state of being weak-minded. **weak moment** a time when one is unusually compliant or temptable. **weak point** (or **spot**) **1** a place where defences are assailable. **2** a flaw in an argument or character or in resistance to temptation. □□ **weakish** *adj.* [ME f. ON *veikr* f. Gmc]

■ **1** feeble, frail, fragile, unsubstantial, insubstantial, flimsy, breakable, frangible, delicate, rickety, unsteady, unsound, decrepit, shaky, infirm; powerless, helpless, defenceless, unprotected, unguarded, unshielded, vulnerable, exposed; (*of visible or audible things*) faint, subdued, indistinct, wavering, faltering, unclear, muted; (*of visible things*) dim, poor, dull, pale, faded, vague, hazy, imperceptible, indiscernible, blurred, blurry, muzzy, ill-defined, flickering; (*of audible things*) low, soft, hushed, muffled, almost inaudible, stifled. **2** frail, feeble, infirm, debilitated, enervated, incapacitated, weedy, delicate, sickly, anaemic, wasted, decrepit, puny, effete, worn out, tired, exhausted. **3 a** unassertive, retiring, namby-pamby, spineless, irresolute, impotent, powerless, ineffectual, ineffective, incompetent, feckless, inept, wishy-washy, weak-minded, timid, meek, craven, timorous, cowardly, pusillanimous, lily-livered, chicken-hearted, faint-hearted, *colloq.* chicken, weak-kneed, yellow. **4** feeble, lame, half-baked, poor, miserable, unconvincing, unpersuasive, empty, shallow, hollow, flimsy, tenuous, pathetic, pitiful, unbelievable, untenable. **5** see WATERY 2. **8** see UNACCENTED.
□ **weak-kneed** see WEAK 3a above. **weak-minded 1** dim-witted, dull-witted, slow-witted, foolish, feeble-minded, simple, simple-minded, soft-headed, stupid, dull, moronic, imbecilic, *esp. US colloq.* dumb. **2** see WEAK 3a above. **weak-mindedness** see *stupidity* (STUPID). **weak point** (or **spot**) **2** see WEAKNESS 2.

weaken /weékən/ *v.* **1** *tr.* & *intr.* make or become weak or weaker. **2** *intr.* relent, give way; succumb to temptation etc. □□ **weakener** *n.*

■ **1** debilitate, enfeeble, enervate, emasculate, mitigate, moderate, deplete, diminish, lessen, depress, lower, reduce, sap, undermine, vitiate, erode, drain, exhaust, impoverish, impair, cripple, water (down), dilute, thin (out); fade, dwindle, decline, tire, droop, sink, sag, fail, give way, crumble, flag, abate, wane, ebb, subside. **2** give in, relent, acquiesce, give way, yield, accede, consent, agree, assent; soften, bend, ease up, let up, ease off, relax; succumb (to temptation), fall.

weakfish /weékfish/ *n.* (*pl.* same or **-fishes**) *US* a marine fish of the genus *Cynoscion*, used as food. [obs. Du. *weekvisch* f. *week* soft (formed as WEAK) + *visch* FISH[1]]

weakling /weékling/ *n.* a feeble person or animal.

■ weed, runt, milksop, baby, mollycoddle, lightweight, namby-pamby, *colloq.* cream puff, sissy, loser, jellyfish, pushover, softie, wimp, *US colloq.* schlemiel, *sl.* twerp, *US sl.* schnook.

weakly /weékli/ *adv.* & *adj.* ● *adv.* in a weak manner. ● *adj.* (**weaklier, weakliest**) sickly, not robust. □□ **weakliness** *n.*

■ *adj.* see PUNY 1, 2, UNHEALTHY 1.

weakness /weékniss/ *n.* **1** the state or condition of being weak. **2** a weak point; a defect. **3** the inability to resist a particular temptation. **4** (foll. by *for*) a self-indulgent liking (*have a weakness for chocolate*).

■ **1** feebleness, frailty, fragility, delicacy, delicateness, flimsiness, vulnerability, infirmity, debility, decrepitude, puniness. **2** weak point *or* spot, foible, failing, fault, shortcoming, deficiency, flaw, Achilles heel, defect, imperfection, liability. **3** incapacity, irresolution, irresoluteness, impotence, powerlessness. **4** soft spot, fondness, affection, liking, preference, bent, leaning, inclination, fancy, penchant, predilection, proclivity, predisposition, partiality, appreciation, appetite, sweet tooth, taste, eye.

weal[1] /weel/ *n.* & *v.* ● *n.* a ridge raised on the flesh by a stroke of a rod or whip. ● *v.tr.* mark with a weal. [var. of WALE, infl. by obs. *wheal* suppurate]

■ *n.* see WELT *n.* 2.

weal[2] /weel/ *n. literary* welfare, prosperity; good fortune. [OE *wela* f. WG (as WELL[1])]

Weald /weeld/ *n.* (also **weald**) (prec. by *the*) *Brit.* a formerly wooded district including parts of Kent, Surrey, and East Sussex. □ **weald-clay** beds of clay, sandstone, limestone, and ironstone, forming the top of Wealden strata, with abundant fossil remains. [OE, = *wald* WOLD]

Wealden /weéldən/ *adj.* & *n. Brit.* ● *adj.* **1** of the Weald. **2** resembling the Weald geologically. ● *n.* a series of Lower Cretaceous freshwater deposits above Jurassic strata and below chalk, best exemplified in the Weald.

wealth /welth/ *n.* **1** riches; abundant possessions; opulence. **2** the state of being rich. **3** (foll. by *of*) an abundance or profusion (*a wealth of new material*). **4** *archaic* welfare or prosperity. □ **wealth tax** a tax on personal capital. [ME *welthe*, f. WELL[1] or WEAL[2] + -TH[2], after *health*]

■ **1** affluence, riches, money, opulence, prosperity, property, possessions, holdings, substance, capital, assets, fortune, *colloq.* wherewithal, cash. **2** affluence, prosperity, opulence. **3** profusion, abundance, bounty, copiousness, fullness, store, cornucopia, richness, *literary* plenitude, *poet.* bounteousness, plenteousness.

wealthy /wélthi/ *adj.* (**wealthier, wealthiest**) having an abundance esp. of money. □□ **wealthily** *adv.* **wealthiness** *n.*

■ rich, affluent, well off, prosperous, well-to-do, opulent, comfortable, moneyed, in clover, *colloq.* in the money, on Easy Street, flush, filthy rich, rolling in it, well-heeled, *sl.* loaded, stinking (rich), quids in, *Austral.* & *NZ sl.* financial.

wean[1] /ween/ *v.tr.* **1** accustom (an infant or other young mammal) to food other than (esp. its mother's) milk. **2** (often foll. by *from*, *away from*) disengage (from a habit etc.) by enforced discontinuance. [OE *wenian* accustom f. Gmc: cf. WONT]

wean[2] /ween/ *n. Sc.* a young child. [contr. of *wee ane* little one]

weaner /weénər/ *n.* a young animal recently weaned.

weanling /weénling/ *n.* a newly-weaned child etc.

weapon /wépp'n/ *n.* **1** a thing designed or used or usable for inflicting bodily harm (e.g. a gun or cosh). **2** a means employed for trying to gain the advantage in a conflict (*irony is a double-edged weapon*). □□ **weaponed** *adj.* (also in *comb.*). **weaponless** *adj.* [OE *wǣp(e)n* f. Gmc]

■ **2** see DEVICE 2, TOOL *n.* 2. □□ **weaponless** unarmed, unprotected, defenceless.

weaponry /wéppənri/ *n.* weapons collectively.

wear[1] /wair/ *v.* & *n.* ● *v.* (*past* **wore** /wor/; *past part.* **worn** /worn/) **1** *tr.* have on one's person as clothing or an ornament etc. (*is wearing shorts*; *wears earrings*). **2** *tr.* be dressed habitually in (*wears green*). **3** *tr.* exhibit or present (a facial expression or appearance) (*wore a frown*; *the day wore a different aspect*). **4** *tr. Brit. colloq.* (usu. with *neg.*) tolerate, accept (*they won't wear that excuse*). **5** (often foll. by *away*) **a** *tr.* injure the surface of, or partly obliterate or alter, by rubbing, stress, or use. **b** *intr.* undergo such injury or change. **6** *tr.* & *intr.* (foll. by *off*, *away*) rub or be rubbed off. **7** *tr.* make (a hole etc.) by constant rubbing or dripping etc. **8** *tr.* & *intr.* (often foll. by *out*) exhaust, tire or be tired. **9** *tr.* (foll. by *down*) overcome by persistence. **10** *intr.* **a** remain for a specified time in working order or a presentable state; last long. **b** (foll. by *well*, *badly*, etc.) endure continued use or life. **11 a** *intr.* (of time) pass, esp. tediously. **b** *tr.* pass (time) gradually away. **12** *tr.* (of a ship) fly (a flag). ● *n.* **1** the act of wearing or the state of being worn (*suitable for informal wear*). **2** things worn; fashionable or suitable clothing (*sportswear*; *footwear*). **3** (in full **wear and tear**) damage sustained from continuous use. **4** the capacity for resisting wear and tear (*still a great deal of wear left in it*). □ **in wear** being regularly worn. **wear one's heart on one's sleeve** see HEART. **wear off** lose effectiveness or intensity. **wear out 1** use or be used until no longer usable. **2** tire or be tired out. **wear thin** (of patience, excuses, etc.) begin to fail. **wear the trousers** see TROUSERS. **wear** (or **wear one's years**) **well** *colloq.* remain young-looking. □□ **wearable** *adj.* **wearability** /wáirəbilliti/ *n.* **wearer** *n.* **wearing** *adj.* **wearingly** *adv.* [OE *werian* f. Gmc]

■ *v.* **1, 2** be dressed *or* clothed in, dress in, be in, have on, sport. **3** display, show, exhibit, present, have, sport, adopt, assume. **4** see TOLERATE 1, 3, 6. **5** wear down *or* away, damage, impair, harm, fray, chafe, rub, erode, abrade, corrode. **8** tire, fatigue, exhaust, debilitate, weary, enervate, drain, burden. **9** (*wear down*) see GRIND *v.* 3. **10** last, endure, survive, hold up, bear up, stand up. **11 a** drag, pass slowly, creep by *or* along, go by gradually *or* tediously. ● *n.* **1** wearing, use, utilization. **2** garb, clothing, clothes, dress, *Austral.* & *NZ* mocker, *colloq.* gear, *formal* attire, apparel. **3** wear and tear, attrition, deterioration, damage, fraying, chafing, abrasion, erosion, corrosion. □ **wear off** see SUBSIDE 1. **wear out 2** see WEAR *v.* 8 above. □□ **wearing** tiring, exhausting, wearying, enervating, taxing, strenuous, burdensome, wearisome; irksome, tedious, vexing, annoying, irritating, exasperating.

wear[2] /wair/ *v.* (*past* and *past part.* **wore** /wor/) **1** *tr.* bring (a ship) about by turning its head away from the wind. **2** *intr.* (of a ship) come about in this way (cf. TACK[1] *v.* 4a). [17th c.: orig. unkn.]

wearisome /wéérisəm/ *adj.* tedious; tiring by monotony or length. □□ **wearisomely** *adv.* **wearisomeness** *n.*

■ see TEDIOUS.

weary /wééri/ *adj.* & *v.* ● *adj.* (**wearier, weariest**) **1** unequal to or disinclined for further exertion or endurance; tired. **2** (foll. by *of*) dismayed at the continuing of; impatient of. **3** tiring or tedious. ● *v.* (**-ies, -ied**) **1** *tr.* & *intr.* make or grow weary. **2** *intr.* esp. *Sc.* long. □□ **weariless** *adj.* **wearily** *adv.* **weariness** *n.* **wearyingly** *adv.* [OE *wērig*, *wǣrig* f. WG]

■ *adj.* **1** tired, fatigued, exhausted, worn out, drained, spent, ready to drop, dog-tired, knocked up, *colloq.* fagged (out), all in, done in, dead (on one's feet), frazzled, dead beat, knocked out, shot; *esp. Brit. colloq.* whacked; *US colloq.* pooped, bushed, tuckered out; *sl.* zonked (out); *Brit. sl.* knackered. **2** bored, impatient, jaded, blasé, fed up, *colloq.* sick and tired, sick to death, *sl.* browned off. **3** boring, irksome, irritating, tedious, vexing, annoying, exasperating, burdensome, wearying, tiring, fatiguing, draining, taxing, wearisome. ● *v.* **1** exhaust, enervate, fatigue, tire, debilitate, drain, tax, wear *or* tire out; tire (of), be *or* become bored (with *or* by), be *or* become impatient (with), be *or* become jaded (with *or* by), be *or* become fed up (with), *colloq.* be *or* become sick and tired (of) *or* sick to death (of). □□ **weariness** see LETHARGY 2.

weasel /wééz'l/ *n.* & *v.* ● *n.* **1** a small reddish-brown flesh-eating mammal, *Mustela nivalis*, with a slender body, related to the stoat and ferret. **2** a stoat. **3** *colloq.* a deceitful or treacherous person. ● *v.intr.* (**weaselled, weaselling**; *US* **weaseled, weaseling**) **1** esp. *US* equivocate or quibble. **2** (foll. by *on, out*) default on an obligation. □ **weasel-faced** having thin sharp features. **weasel word** (usu. in *pl.*) a word that is intentionally ambiguous or misleading. □□ **weaselly** *adj.* [OE *wesle*, *wesule* f. WG]

■ *v.* **1** see EQUIVOCATE. **2** (*weasel out of*) see EVADE 1, 2. □ **weasel word** (*weasel words*) see FLANNEL *n.* 3.

weather /wéthər/ *n.* & *v.* ● *n.* **1** the state of the atmosphere at a place and time as regards heat, cloudiness, dryness, sunshine, wind, and rain etc. **2** (*attrib.*) *Naut.* windward (*on the weather side*). ● *v.* **1** *tr.* expose to or affect by atmospheric changes, esp. deliberately to dry, season, etc. (*weathered timber*). **2 a** *tr.* (usu. in *passive*) discolour or partly disintegrate (rock or stones) by exposure to air. **b** *intr.* be discoloured or worn in this way. **3** *tr.* make (boards or tiles) overlap downwards to keep out rain etc. **4** *tr.* **a** come safely through (a storm). **b** survive (a difficult period etc.). **5** *tr.* (of a ship or its crew) get to the windward of (a cape etc.). □ **keep a** (or **one's**) **weather eye open** be watchful. **make good** (or **bad**) **weather of it** *Naut.* (of a ship) behave well (or badly) in a storm. **make heavy weather of** *colloq.* exaggerate the difficulty or burden presented by (a problem, course of action, etc.). **under the weather** *colloq.* indisposed or out of sorts; drunk. **weather-beaten** affected by exposure to the weather. **weather-bound** unable to proceed owing to bad weather. **weather-chart** (or **-map**) a diagram showing the state of the weather over a large area. **weather forecast** an analysis of the state of the weather with an assessment of likely developments over a certain time. **weather-glass** a barometer. **weather side** the side from which the wind is blowing (opp. *lee side*). **weather station** an observation post for recording meteorological data. **weather-strip** a piece of material used to make a door or window proof against rain or wind. **weather-tiles** tiles arranged to overlap like weatherboards. **weather-vane** see VANE. **weather-worn** damaged by storms etc. [OE *weder* f. Gmc]

■ *n.* **1** (meteorological) condition(s), climate, the elements. ● *v.* **4** stand, survive, suffer, bear up against, endure, withstand, rise above, ride out, live through, come through, brave. □ **keep a** (or **one's**) **weather eye open** see *watch out*. **under the weather** ailing, ill, sickly, unwell, indisposed, out of sorts, off colour, sick, poorly, *colloq.* seedy; see also DRUNK *adj.* 1. **weather-beaten** dry, craggy, rugged, rough; tanned, brown, bronzed, sunburnt, suntanned.

weatherboard /wéthərbord/ *n.* & *v.* ● *n.* **1** a sloping board attached to the bottom of an outside door to keep out the rain etc. **2** each of a series of horizontal boards with edges overlapping to keep out the rain etc. ● *v.tr.* fit or supply with weatherboards. □□ **weatherboarding** *n.* (in sense 2 of *n.*).

weathercock /wéthərkok/ *n.* **1** a weather-vane (see VANE) in the form of a cock. **2** an inconstant person.

weathering /wéthəring/ *n.* **1** the action of the weather on materials etc. exposed to it. **2** exposure to adverse weather conditions (see WEATHER *v.* 1).

■ **1** see EROSION .

weatherly /wéthərli/ *adj. Naut.* **1** (of a ship) making little leeway. **2** capable of keeping close to the wind. □□ **weatherliness** *n.*

weatherman /wéthərman/ *n.* (*pl.* **-men**) a meteorologist, esp. one who broadcasts a weather forecast.

weatherproof /wéthərproof/ *adj.* & *v.* ● *adj.* resistant to the effects of bad weather, esp. rain. ● *v.tr.* make weatherproof. □□ **weatherproofed** *adj.*

weave[1] /weev/ *v.* & *n.* ● *v.* (*past* **wove** /wōv/; *past part.* **woven** /wōv'n/ or **wove**) **1** *tr.* **a** form (fabric) by interlacing long threads in two directions. **b** form (thread) into fabric in this way. **2** *intr.* **a** make fabric in this way. **b** work at a loom. **3** *tr.* make (a basket or wreath etc.) by interlacing rods or flowers etc. **4** *tr.* **a** (foll. by *into*) make (facts etc.) into a story or connected whole. **b** make (a story) in this way. ● *n.* a style of weaving. [OE *wefan* f. Gmc]

■ *v.* **1 b** braid, plait, entwine, intertwine, interlace, interweave, criss-cross, knit (together). **4 a** blend, combine, fuse, merge, unite, intermingle, mesh, splice, dovetail, join. **b** construct, make, contrive, build, create, fabricate, compose, spin, design.

weave[2] /weev/ *v.intr.* **1** move repeatedly from side to side; take an intricate course to avoid obstructions. **2** *colloq.* manoeuvre an aircraft in this way; take evasive action. □ **get weaving** *sl.* begin action; hurry. [prob. f. ME *weve*, var. of *waive* f. ON *veifa* WAVE]

■ **1** zigzag, criss-cross, make one's way, wind, dodge, bob and weave, shift, *literary or archaic* wend one's way. □ **get weaving** get started, get a move on, hurry (up), start, shake a leg, *colloq.* get cracking, *sl.* get *or* pull one's finger out, *esp. US sl.* get a wiggle on.

weaver /wéevər/ *n.* **1** a person whose occupation is weaving. **2** (in full **weaver-bird**) any tropical bird of the family Ploceidae, building elaborately woven nests. □ **weaver's knot** a sheet bend (see SHEET[2]) used in weaving.

web /web/ *n.* & *v.* ● *n.* **1 a** a woven fabric. **b** an amount woven in one piece. **2** a complete structure or connected series (*a web of lies*). **3** a cobweb, gossamer, or a similar product of a spinning creature. **4 a** a membrane between the toes of a swimming animal or bird. **b** the vane of a bird's feather. **5 a** a large roll of paper used in a continuous printing process. **b** an endless wire mesh on rollers, on which this is made. **6** a thin flat part connecting thicker or more solid parts in machinery etc. ● *v.* (**webbed, webbing**) **1** *tr.* weave a web on. **2** *intr.* weave a web. □ **web-footed** having the toes connected by webs. **web offset** offset printing on a web of paper. **web-wheel** a wheel having a plate or web instead of spokes, or with rim, spokes, and centre in one piece as in watch-wheels. **web-worm** *US* a gregarious caterpillar spinning a large web in which to sleep or to feed on enclosed foliage. □□ **webbed** *adj.* [OE *web, webb* f. Gmc]

■ *n.* **2** net, network, mesh, entanglement, tangle, tissue, series. **3** spider's web, cobweb, gossamer; snare, trap.

webbing /wébbing/ *n.* strong narrow closely-woven fabric used for supporting upholstery, for belts, etc.

weber /váybər/ *n.* the SI unit of magnetic flux, causing the electromotive force of one volt in a circuit of one turn when generated or removed in one second. ¶ Abbr.: **Wb.** [W. E. *Weber*, Ger. physicist d. 1891]

Wed. *abbr.* Wednesday.

wed /wed/ *v.* (**wedding**; *past* and *past part.* **wedded** or **wed**) **1** usu. *formal* or *literary* **a** *tr.* & *intr.* marry. **b** *tr.* join in marriage. **2** *tr.* unite (*wed efficiency to economy*). **3** *tr.* (as **wedded** *adj.*) of or in marriage (*wedded bliss*). **4** *tr.* (as **wedded** *adj.*) (foll. by *to*) obstinately attached or devoted (to a pursuit etc.). [OE *weddian* to pledge f. Gmc]

■ **1** marry, get married, become husband and wife, say *or* take (one's) (marriage) vows, join in marriage, join *or* unite in holy wedlock, join *or* unite in holy matrimony, *archaic* espouse; lead down the aisle, lead to the altar, *archaic* wive; *colloq.* tie the knot, get hitched, get spliced. **2** combine, unite, ally, marry, blend, merge, join, mingle, intermingle, mix, intermix, amalgamate, compound, alloy, fuse, *literary* commingle. **3** (**wedded**) see *matrimonial* (MATRIMONY). **4** (*wedded to*) intimately attached *or* connected to, obstinately attached *or* connected to, enamoured of, devoted to.

we'd /weed, wid/ *contr.* **1** we had. **2** we should; we would.

wedding /wédding/ *n.* a marriage ceremony (considered by itself or with the associated celebrations). □ **wedding breakfast** a meal etc. usually served between a wedding and the departure for the honeymoon. **wedding cake** a rich iced cake served at a wedding reception. **wedding day** the day or anniversary of a wedding. **wedding march** a march played at the entrance of the bride or the exit of the couple at a wedding. **wedding night** the night after a wedding (esp. with ref. to its consummation). **wedding ring** a ring worn by a married person. [OE *weddung* (as WED, -ING[1])]

■ marriage (ceremony), wedding ceremony, nuptials.

wedge[1] /wej/ *n.* & *v.* ● *n.* **1** a piece of wood or metal etc. tapering to a sharp edge, that is driven between two objects or parts of an object to secure or separate them; a thing separating two people or groups of people. **2** anything resembling a wedge (*a wedge of cheese*; *troops formed a wedge*). **3** a golf club with a wedge-shaped head. **4 a** a wedge-shaped heel. **b** a shoe with this. ● *v.tr.* **1** tighten, secure, or fasten by means of a wedge (*wedged the door open*). **2** force open or apart with a wedge. **3** (foll. by *in, into*) pack or thrust (a thing or oneself) tightly in or into. □ **thin end of the wedge** *colloq.* an action or procedure of little importance in itself, but likely to lead to more serious developments. **wedge-shaped 1** shaped like a solid wedge. **2** V-shaped. □□ **wedgelike** *adj.* **wedgewise** *adv.* [OE *wecg* f. Gmc]

■ *n.* **1** block, chock, cleat; separation, separator, division, partition, split, fissure, cleavage. **2** see SLAB *n.* **4 b** *colloq.* wedgie. ● *v.* **3** ram, jam, stuff, cram, crowd, force, squeeze, sandwich, pack, thrust.

wedge[2] /wej/ *v.tr. Pottery* prepare (clay) for use by cutting, kneading, and throwing down. [17th c.: orig. uncert.]

wedgie /wéji/ *n. colloq.* a shoe with an extended wedge-shaped heel.

Wedgwood /wéjwŏŏd/ *n. propr.* **1** ceramic ware made by J. Wedgwood, Engl. potter d. 1795, and his successors, esp. a kind of fine stoneware usu. with a white cameo design. **2** the characteristic blue colour of this stoneware.

wedlock /wédlok/ *n.* the married state. □ **born in** (or **out of**) **wedlock** born of married (or unmarried) parents. [OE *wedlāc* marriage vow f. *wed* pledge (rel. to WED) + *-lāc* suffix denoting action]

■ marriage, matrimony.

Wednesday /wénzday, -di/ *n.* & *adv.* ● *n.* the fourth day of the week, following Tuesday. ● *adv. colloq.* **1** on Wednesday. **2** (**Wednesdays**) on Wednesdays; each Wednesday. [ME *wednesdei*, OE *wōdnesdæg* day of (the god) Odin]

Weds. *abbr.* Wednesday.

wee[1] /wee/ *adj.* (**weer** /wéeər/; **weest** /wée-ist/) **1** esp. *Sc.* little; very small. **2** *colloq.* tiny; extremely small (*a wee bit*). [orig. Sc. noun, f. north.ME *wei* (small) quantity f. Anglian *wēg*: cf. WEY]

■ tiny, small, diminutive, little, minuscule, midget, minute, miniature, lilliputian, microscopic; unimportant, insignificant, trivial, puny; *colloq.* teeny(-weeny), teensy(-weensy); *colloq. usu. derog.* itty-bitty, itsy-bitsy.

wee[2] /wee/ *n.* esp. *Brit. sl.* = WEE-WEE.

weed /weed/ *n.* & *v.* ● *n.* **1** a wild plant growing where it is not wanted. **2** a thin weak-looking person or horse. **3** (prec. by *the*) *sl.* **a** marijuana. **b** tobacco. ● *v.* **1** *tr.* **a** clear (an area) of weeds. **b** remove unwanted parts from. **2** *tr.* (foll. by *out*) **a** sort out (inferior or unwanted parts etc.) for removal. **b** rid (a quantity or company) of inferior or unwanted members etc. **3** *intr.* cut off or uproot weeds. □ **weed-grown** overgrown with weeds. **weed-killer** a substance used to destroy weeds. □□ **weeder** *n.* **weedless** *adj.* [OE *wēod*, of unkn. orig.]

■ *n.* **2** see DRIP *n.* 2, WEAKLING. ● *v.* **2** (*weed out*) exclude, eliminate, remove, rout out, root out; screen, sift, winnow, clarify, refine, purify, clean, purge, *usu. formal* cleanse.

weeds /weedz/ *n.pl.* (in full **widow's weeds**) *archaic* deep mourning worn by a widow. [OE *wǣd(e)* garment f. Gmc]

weedy /wéedi/ *adj.* (**weedier, weediest**) **1** having many weeds. **2** (esp. of a person) weak, feeble; of poor stature. □□ **weediness** *n.*

week /week/ *n.* **1** a period of seven days reckoned usu. from and to midnight on Saturday–Sunday. **2** a period of seven days reckoned from any point (*would like to stay for a week*). **3** the six days between Sundays. **4 a** the five days Monday to Friday. **b** a normal amount of work done in this period (*a 35-hour week*). **5** (in *pl.*) a long time; several weeks (*have not seen you for weeks*; *did it weeks ago*). **6** (prec. by a specified day) a week after (that day) (*Tuesday week*; *tomorrow week*). [OE *wice* f. Gmc, prob. orig. = sequence]

weekday /wéekday/ *n.* a day other than Sunday or other than at a weekend (often *attrib.*: *a weekday afternoon*).

weekend /wéekénd/ *n.* & *v.* ● *n.* **1** Sunday and Saturday or part of Saturday. **2** this period extended slightly esp. for a holiday or visit etc. (*going away for the weekend*; *a weekend cottage*). ● *v.intr.* spend a weekend (*decided to weekend in the country*).

weekender /wéekéndər/ *n.* **1** a person who spends weekends away from home. **2** *Austral. colloq.* a holiday cottage.

weeklong /wéeklóng/ *adj.* lasting for a week.

weekly /wéekli/ *adj.*, *adv.*, & *n.* ● *adj.* done, produced, or occurring once a week. ● *adv.* once a week; from week to week. ● *n.* (*pl.* **-ies**) a weekly newspaper or periodical.

ween /ween/ *v.tr. archaic* be of the opinion; think, suppose. [OE *wēnan* f. Gmc]

weeny /wéeni/ *adj.* (**weenier, weeniest**) *colloq.* tiny. □ **weeny-bopper** a girl like a teeny-bopper but younger. [WEE[1] after *tiny*, *teeny*]

weep /weep/ *v.* & *n.* ● *v.* (*past* and *past part.* **wept** /wept/) **1** *intr.* shed tears. **2 a** *tr.* & (foll. by *for*) *intr.* shed tears for; bewail, lament over. **b** *tr.* utter or express with tears (*'Don't go,' he wept*; *wept her thanks*). **3 a** *intr.* be covered with or send forth drops. **b** *intr.* & *tr.* come or send forth in drops; exude liquid (*weeping sore*). **4** *intr.* (as **weeping** *adj.*) (of a tree) having drooping branches (*weeping willow*). ● *n.* a fit or spell of weeping. □ **weep out** utter with tears. □□ **weepingly** *adv.* [OE *wēpan* f. Gmc (prob. imit.)]

■ *v.* **1, 2** cry, shed tears, bawl, blubber, sob, wail, keen, lament, mourn, moan, grieve, whine, whimper, mewl, snivel, *colloq.* whinge, *Brit. colloq.* grizzle, *literary* pule, *sl.* blub; (*weep for* or *over*) bemoan, bewail. **3** ooze, seep, exude, drip.

weeper /wéepər/ *n.* **1** a person who weeps, esp. *hist.* a hired mourner at a funeral. **2** a small image of a mourner on a monument. **3** (in *pl.*) *hist.* **a** a man's crape hatband for funerals. **b** a widow's black crape veil or white cuffs.

weepie /wéepi/ *n.* (also **weepy**) (*pl.* **-ies**) *colloq.* a sentimental or emotional film, play, etc.

weepy /wéepi/ *adj.* (**weepier, weepiest**) *colloq.* inclined to weep; tearful. □□ **weepily** *adv.* **weepiness** *n.*

■ see TEARFUL 1.

weever /wéevər/ *n.* any marine fish of the genus *Trachinus*, with sharp venomous dorsal spines. [perh. f. OF *wivre*, *guivre*, serpent, dragon, f. L *vipera* VIPER]

weevil /wéevil/ *n.* **1** any destructive beetle of the family Curculionidae, with its head extended into a beak or rostrum and feeding esp. on grain. **2** any insect damaging stored grain. □□ **weevily** *adj.* [ME f. MLG *wevel* f. Gmc]

wee-wee /wéewee/ *n.* & *v.* esp. *Brit. sl.* ● *n.* **1** the act or an instance of urinating. **2** urine. ● *v.intr.* (**-wees, -weed**) urinate. [20th c.: orig. unkn.]

■ *v.* see URINATE.

w.e.f. *abbr.* with effect from.

weft[1] /weft/ *n.* **1 a** the threads woven across a warp to make fabric. **b** yarn for these. **c** a thing woven. **2** filling-strips in basket-weaving. [OE *weft(a)* f. Gmc: rel. to WEAVE[1]]

weft[2] var. of WAFT *n.* 3.

Wehrmacht /váirmaakht/ *n. hist.* the German armed forces, esp. the army, from 1921 to 1945. [G, = defensive force]

weigh[1] /way/ *v.* **1** *tr.* find the weight of. **2** *tr.* balance in the hands to guess or as if to guess the weight of. **3** *tr.* (often foll. by *out*) **a** take a definite weight of; take a specified weight from a larger quantity. **b** distribute in exact amounts by weight. **4** *tr.* **a** estimate the relative value, importance, or desirability of; consider with a view to choice, rejection, or preference (*weighed the consequences*; *weighed the merits of the candidates*). **b** (foll. by *with*, *against*) compare (one consideration with another). **5** *tr.* be equal to (a specified weight) (*weighs three kilos*; *weighs very little*). **6** *intr.* **a** have (esp. a specified) importance; exert an influence. **b** (foll. by *with*) be regarded as important by (*the point that weighs with me*). **7** *intr.* (often foll. by *on*) be heavy or burdensome (to); be depressing (to). □ **weigh anchor** see ANCHOR. **weigh down 1** bring or keep down by exerting weight. **2** be oppressive or burdensome to (*weighed down with worries*). **weigh in** (of a boxer before a contest, or a jockey after a race) be weighed. **weigh-in** *n.* the weighing of a boxer before a fight. **weighing-machine** a machine for weighing persons or large weights. **weigh into** *colloq.* attack (physically or verbally). **weigh in with** *colloq.* advance (an argument etc.) assertively or boldly. **weigh out** (of a jockey) be weighed before a race. **weigh up** *colloq.* form an estimate of; consider carefully. **weigh one's words** carefully choose the way one expresses something. □□ **weighable** *adj.* **weigher** *n.* [OE *wegan* f. Gmc, rel. to WAY]

■ **3** see MEASURE *v.* 6. **4 a** judge, estimate, assess, evaluate, value, gauge, determine; consider, ponder, contemplate, think over *or* about, mull over, turn over in the *or* one's mind, ruminate over *or* on, chew over, reflect on *or* upon, brood over, pore over, study, examine, *archaic* think on, *colloq.* weigh up. **b** see COMPARE *v.* 2. **5** weigh in at *or* out at, tip *or* turn the scales at. **6** matter, count, have (an) effect *or* influence, carry weight, be of value *or* account, *sl.* cut any ice. **7** (*weigh on*) lie heavy on, burden, depress, prey on, preoccupy, oppress, disturb, perturb, upset. □ **weigh down 1** see WEIGHT *v.* **2** burden, overburden, load, overload, encumber, tax, overtax, strain, trouble, afflict, worry, depress, oppress. **weigh into** see ATTACK *v.* 1, 3. **weigh up** see WEIGH[1] 4a above.

weigh[2] /way/ *n.* □ **under weigh** *disp.* = *under way*. [18th c.: from an erron. assoc. with *weigh anchor*]

weighbridge /wáybrij/ *n.* a weighing-machine for vehicles, usu. having a plate set into the road for vehicles to drive on to.

weight /wayt/ *n.* & *v.* ● *n.* **1** *Physics* **a** the force experienced by a body as a result of the earth's gravitation (cf. MASS[1] *n.* 8). **b** any similar force with which a body tends to a centre of attraction. **2** the heaviness of a body regarded as a property of it; its relative mass or the quantity of matter contained by it giving rise to a downward force (*is twice your weight*; *kept in position by its weight*). **3 a** the quantitative expression of a body's weight (*has a weight of three pounds*). **b** a scale of such weights (*troy weight*). **4** a body of a known weight for use in weighing. **5** a heavy body esp. used in a mechanism etc. (*a clock worked by weights*). **6** a load or burden (*a weight off my mind*). **7 a** influence, importance (*carried weight with the public*). **b** preponderance (*the weight of evidence was against them*). **8** a heavy object thrown as an athletic exercise; = SHOT[1] 7. **9** the surface density of cloth etc. as a measure of its suitability. ● *v.tr.* **1 a** attach a weight to. **b** hold down with a weight or weights. **2** (foll. by *with*) impede or burden. **3** *Statistics* multiply the components of (an average) by factors to take account of their importance. **4** assign a handicap weight to (a horse). **5** treat (a fabric) with a mineral etc. to make it seem stouter. □ **put on weight 1** increase one's weight. **2** get fat. **throw one's weight about** (or **around**) *colloq.* be unpleasantly self-assertive. **worth one's weight in gold** (of a person) exceedingly useful or helpful. [OE *(ge)wiht* f. Gmc: cf. WEIGH[1]]

■ *n.* **2, 3** heaviness, mass, tonnage, *dial. or US* heft. **6** burden, load, millstone, onus, pressure, strain, encumbrance, albatross, cross. **7 a** influence, authority, power, substance, force, moment, importance, consequence, impact, persuasiveness, value, worth, *colloq.* clout. **b** mass, preponderance, bulk, *disp.* majority. ● *v.* **1** load, charge, ballast, weigh down, weight down.

weighting /wáyting/ *n.* an extra allowance paid in special cases, esp. to allow for a higher cost of living (*London weighting*).

weightless /wáytliss/ *adj.* (of a body, esp. in an orbiting spacecraft etc.) not apparently acted on by gravity. □□ **weightlessly** *adv.* **weightlessness** *n.*

weightlifting /wáytlifting/ *n.* the sport or exercise of lifting a heavy weight, esp. a barbell. □□ **weightlifter** *n.*

weighty /wáyti/ *adj.* (**weightier, weightiest**) **1** weighing much; heavy. **2** momentous, important. **3** (of utterances etc.) deserving consideration; careful and serious. **4** influential, authoritative. □□ **weightily** *adv.* **weightiness** *n.*

■ **1** heavy, ponderous; massive, huge, bulky, substantial, ample, large, mammoth, colossal, immense, enormous, gigantic, prodigious; corpulent, fat, obese, adipose, hefty. **2** important, consequential, significant, momentous, grave, serious, crucial, portentous, thought-provoking, provocative. **3, 4** influential, convincing, persuasive, authoritative, impressive, telling, powerful, potent, leading; forceful. □□ **weightiness** see GRAVITY 3a.

Weimaraner /wī́mərāánə, vī́-/ *n.* a usu. grey dog of a variety of pointer used as a gun dog. [G, f. *Weimar* in Germany, where it was developed]

weir /weer/ *n.* **1** a dam built across a river to raise the level of water upstream or regulate its flow. **2** an enclosure of stakes etc. set in a stream as a trap for fish. [OE *wer* f. *werian* dam up]

weird /weerd/ *adj.* & *n.* ● *adj.* **1** uncanny, supernatural. **2** *colloq.* strange, queer, incomprehensible. **3** *archaic* connected with fate. ● *n.* esp. *Sc. archaic* fate, destiny. □ **the weird sisters 1** the Fates. **2** witches. □□ **weirdly** *adv.* **weirdness** *n.* [(earlier as noun) f. OE *wyrd* destiny f. Gmc]
■ *adj.* **1, 2** strange, odd, peculiar, bizarre, curious, incomprehensible, abnormal, unnatural, eerie, queer, grotesque, freakish, freaky, outlandish, far-out, uncanny, unearthly, other-worldly, supernatural, preternatural, *colloq.* spooky, kinky, way-out, *Sc.* eldritch.
□□ **weirdness** see ODDITY 3.

weirdie /weérdi/ *n.* (also **weirdy**) (*pl.* **-ies**) *colloq.* = WEIRDO.

weirdo /weérdō/ *n.* (*pl.* **-os**) *colloq.* an odd or eccentric person.
■ eccentric, madman, madwoman, lunatic, psychotic, crank, *colloq.* crazy, weirdie, oddball, queer fish, freak, psycho, *sl.* nutcase, nut, crackpot, loony, *Brit. sl.* nutter, *US sl.* screwball, kook.

Weismannism /vī́smənìz'm/ *n.* the theory of heredity assuming continuity of germ-plasm and non-transmission of acquired characteristics. [A. *Weismann*, Ger. biologist d. 1914]

weka /wékkə/ *n.* any flightless New Zealand rail of the genus *Gallirallus*. [Maori: imit. of its cry]

Welch /welsh/ var. of WELSH (now only in *Royal Welch Fusiliers*).

welch var. of WELSH.

welcome /wélkəm/ *n.*, *int.*, *v.*, & *adj.* ● *n.* the act or an instance of greeting or receiving (a person, idea, etc.) gladly; a kind or glad reception (*gave them a warm welcome*). ● *int.* expressing such a greeting (*welcome!*; *welcome home!*). ● *v.tr.* receive with a welcome (*welcomed them home*; *would welcome the opportunity*). ● *adj.* **1** that one receives with pleasure (*a welcome guest*; *welcome news*). **2** (foll. by *to*, or *to* + infin.) **a** cordially allowed or invited; released of obligation (*you are welcome to use my car*). **b** *iron.* gladly given (an unwelcome task, thing, etc.) (*here's my work and you are welcome to it*). □ **make welcome** receive hospitably. **outstay one's welcome** stay too long as a visitor etc. **you are welcome** there is no need for thanks. □□ **welcomely** *adv.* **welcomeness** *n.* **welcomer** *n.* **welcomingly** *adv.* [orig. OE *wilcuma* one whose coming is pleasing f. *wil-* desire, pleasure + *cuma* comer, with later change to *wel-* WELL[1] after OF *bien venu* or ON *velkominn*]
■ *n.* reception, greeting, salutation, glad hand. ● *v.* greet, hail, meet, receive, accept, make welcome, offer hospitality to. ● *adj.* **1** accepted, acceptable, well-received, desirable, agreeable, gratifying, appreciated. **2 a** freely permitted *or* allowed, invited, entitled, suffered; (*be welcome*) may.

weld[1] /weld/ *v.* & *n.* ● *v.tr.* **1 a** hammer or press (pieces of iron or other metal usu. heated but not melted) into one piece. **b** join by fusion with an electric arc etc. **c** form by welding into some article. **2** fashion (arguments, members of a group, etc.) into an effectual or homogeneous whole. ● *n.* a welded joint. □□ **weldable** *adj.* **weldability** /wéldəbílliti/ *n.* **welder** *n.* [alt. of WELL[2] *v.* in obs. sense 'melt or weld (heated metal)', prob. infl. by past part.]
■ *v.* **1** fuse, attach, connect, link, join; solder, braze, cement, bond. **2** unite, combine, merge, fuse, connect, link, join, cement, bond, weave. ● *n.* seam, joint, juncture, union, commissure.

weld[2] /weld/ *n.* **1** a plant, *Reseda luteola*, yielding a yellow dye. **2** *hist.* this dye. [ME f. OE *w(e)alde* (unrecorded): cf. MDu. *woude*, MLG *walde*]

welfare /wélfair/ *n.* **1** well-being, happiness; health and prosperity (of a person or a community etc.). **2** (**Welfare**) **a** the maintenance of persons in such a condition esp. by statutory procedure or social effort. **b** financial support given for this purpose. □ **welfare state 1** a system whereby the State undertakes to protect the health and well-being of its citizens, esp. those in financial or social need, by means of grants, pensions, etc. **2** a country practising this system. **welfare work** organized effort for the welfare of the poor, disabled, etc. [ME f. WELL[1] + FARE]
■ **1** benefit, good, advantage, well-being, prosperity, (good) fortune, profit, interest, (good) health, happiness, felicity. **2 b** see CHARITY 1b.

welfarism /wélfairiz'm/ *n.* principles characteristic of a welfare state. □□ **welfarist** *n.*

welkin /wélkin/ *n. poet.* sky; the upper air. [OE *wolcen* cloud, sky]

well[1] /wel/ *adv.*, *adj.*, & *int.* ● *adv.* (**better**, **best**) **1** in a satisfactory way (*you have worked well*). **2** in the right way (*well said*; *you did well to tell me*). **3** with some talent or distinction (*plays the piano well*). **4** in a kind way (*treated me well*). **5 a** thoroughly, carefully (*polish it well*). **b** intimately, closely (*knew them well*). **6** with heartiness or approval; favourably (*speak well of*; *the book was well reviewed*). **7** probably, reasonably, advisably (*you may well be right*; *you may well ask*; *we might well take the risk*). **8** to a considerable extent (*is well over forty*). **9** successfully, fortunately (*it turned out well*). **10** luckily, opportunely (*well met!*). **11** with a fortunate outcome; without disaster (*were well rid of them*). **12** profitably (*did well for themselves*). **13** comfortably, abundantly, liberally (*we live well here*; *the job pays well*). ● *adj.* (**better**, **best**) **1** (usu. *predic.*) in good health (*are you well?*; *was not a well person*). **2** (*predic.*) **a** in a satisfactory state or position (*all is well*). **b** advisable (*it would be well to enquire*). ● *int.* expressing surprise, resignation, insistence, etc., or resumption or continuation of talk, used esp. after a pause in speaking (*well I never!*; *well, I suppose so*; *well, who was it?*). □ **as well 1** in addition; to an equal extent. **2** (also **just as well**) with equal reason; with no loss of advantage or need for regret (*may as well give up*; *it would be just as well to stop now*). **as well as** in addition to. **leave** (or **let**) **well alone** avoid needless change or disturbance. **take well** react calmly to (a thing, esp. bad news). **well-acquainted** (usu. foll. by *with*) familiar. **well-adjusted 1** in a good state of adjustment. **2** *Psychol.* mentally and emotionally stable. **well-advised** (usu. foll. by *to* + infin.) (of a person) prudent (*would be well-advised to wait*). **well-affected** (often foll. by *to*, *towards*) favourably disposed. **well and good** expressing dispassionate acceptance of a decision etc. **well and truly** decisively, completely. **well-appointed** having all the necessary equipment. **well aware** certainly aware (*well aware of the danger*). **well away 1** having made considerable progress. **2** *colloq.* fast asleep or drunk. **well-balanced 1** sane, sensible. **2** equally matched. **3** having a symmetrical or orderly arrangement of parts. **well-behaved** see BEHAVE. **well-being** a state of being well, healthy, contented, etc. **well-beloved** *adj.* dearly loved. ● *n.* (*pl.* same) a dearly loved person. **well-born** of noble family. **well-bred** having or showing good breeding or manners. **well-built 1** of good construction. **2** (of a person) big and strong and well-proportioned. **well-chosen** (of words etc.) carefully selected for effect. **well-conditioned** in good physical or moral condition. **well-conducted** (of a meeting etc.) properly organized and controlled. **well-connected** see CONNECTED. **well-covered** *colloq.* plump, corpulent. **well-defined** clearly indicated or determined. **well-deserved** rightfully merited or earned. **well-disposed** (often foll. by *towards*) having a good disposition or friendly feeling (for). **well done 1** (of meat etc.) thoroughly cooked. **2** (of a task etc.) performed well (also as *int.*). **well-dressed** fashionably smart. **well-earned** fully deserved. **well-endowed 1** well provided with talent etc. **2** *colloq.* sexually potent or attractive; having large sexual organs. **well-established** long-standing, familiar, traditional. **well-favoured** good-looking. **well-fed** having or having had plenty to eat. **well-found** = *well-appointed.* **well-founded** (of suspicions etc.) based on good evidence; having a foundation in fact or reason. **well-groomed** (of a person) with carefully tended hair, clothes, etc. **well-grounded 1** = *well-founded.* **2** having a good training in or knowledge of the groundwork of a subject. **well-heeled** *colloq.* wealthy. **well-hung** *colloq.* (of a man) having large genitals. **well-informed** having much knowledge or information about a subject. **well-intentioned** having or showing good intentions. **well-judged** opportunely, skilfully, or discreetly done. **well-kept** kept in good order or condition. **well-knit** (esp. of a person) compact; not loose-jointed or sprawling. **well-known 1** known to many. **2** known thoroughly. **well-made 1** strongly or skilfully manufactured. **2** (of a person or animal) having a good build. **well-mannered** having good manners. **well-marked** distinct; easy to detect. **well-matched** see MATCH[1]. **well-meaning** (or **-meant**) well-intentioned (but ineffective or unwise). **well off 1** having plenty of money. **2** in a fortunate situation or circumstances. **well-oiled** *colloq.* **1** drunk. **2** (of a compliment etc.) easily expressed through habitual use. **well-ordered** arranged in an orderly manner. **well-paid 1** (of a job) that pays well. **2** (of a person) amply rewarded for a job. **well-pleased** highly gratified or satisfied. **well-preserved** see PRESERVE. **well-read** knowledgeable through much reading. **well-received** welcomed; favourably received. **well-rounded 1** complete and symmetrical. **2** (of a phrase etc.) complete and well expressed. **3** (of a person) having or showing a fully developed personality, ability, etc. **4** fleshy, plump. **well-spent** (esp. of money or time) used profitably. **well-spoken** articulate or refined in speech. **well-thought-of** having a good reputation; esteemed, respected. **well-thought-out** carefully devised. **well-thumbed** bearing marks of frequent handling. **well-timed** opportune, timely. **well-to-do** prosperous. **well-tried** often tested with good results. **well-trodden** much frequented. **well-turned 1** (of a compliment, phrase, or verse) elegantly expressed. **2** (of a leg, ankle, etc.) elegantly shaped or displayed. **well-upholstered** see UPHOLSTER. **well-wisher** a person who wishes one well. **well-woman** a woman who has undergone satisfactory gynaecological tests (often *attrib.*: *well-woman clinic*). **well-worn 1** much worn by use. **2** (of a phrase etc.) trite, hackneyed. **well worth** certainly worth (*well worth a visit*; *well worth visiting*). ¶ A hyphen is normally used in combinations of *well-* when used attributively, but not when used predicatively, e.g. *a well-made coat* but *the coat is well made.* □□ **wellness** *n.* [OE *wel, well* prob. f. the same stem as WILL[1]]

■ *adv.* **1** satisfactorily, sufficiently, adequately, agreeably, nicely, (well) enough, *colloq.* OK, okay. **2** appropriately, correctly, accurately, properly, proficiently, effectively. **3** skilfully, expertly, adeptly, proficiently, ably. **4** kindly, graciously, thoughtfully, considerately, hospitably, cordially, genially, humanely. **5 a** thoroughly, extensively, exhaustively, intensively, completely, through and through, carefully, painstakingly, sedulously, assiduously, scrupulously, meticulously. **b** intimately, closely, familiarly, personally; thoroughly, profoundly, soundly, fully, in detail, through and through, completely. **6** graciously, kindly, highly, favourably, glowingly, approvingly, warmly, genially, cordially, amiably, kind-heartedly, warm-heartedly, affectionately, lovingly. **7** likely, probably, in all probability, doubtless(ly), without doubt, not unexpectedly, indeed; reasonably, justifiably, rightly, justly, properly, understandably, advisably, advisedly. **8** far, by a long way, immeasurably, considerably, (very) much; far and away, definitely, positively, obviously, clearly, plainly, manifestly, evidently, unquestionably, decidedly, beyond (the shadow of a) doubt, indubitably, *Brit.* by a long chalk. **9** successfully, fortunately, happily, smoothly, famously, marvellously, wonderfully, fabulously, incredibly, splendidly, admirably, spectacularly, excellently, superbly, swimmingly. **10** luckily, opportunely, propitiously. **12** profitably, advantageously, favourably. **13** comfortably, luxuriously, prosperously, extravagantly, showily, pretentiously, ostentatiously, sumptuously, grandly, opulently; fairly, justly, suitably, properly, adequately, reasonably, fully, abundantly, generously, liberally, amply. ● *adj.* **1** healthy, fit, hale (and hearty), robust, vigorous, hearty, in good health, in fine *or* good fettle, in good shape, *colloq.* in the pink. **2 a** satisfactory, pleasing, agreeable, good, right, all right, fine, proper, in order, *colloq.* OK, okay. **b** see ADVISABLE. □ **as well 1** see *in addition* (ADDITION). **as well as** see *in addition to* (ADDITION). **take well** accept, resign oneself to, react good-naturedly *or* equably *or* coolly *or* serenely *or* calmly *or* soberly *or* unexcitedly *or* sedately to, receive *or* take good-naturedly *or* equably *or* coolly *or* serenely *or* calmly *or* soberly *or* unexcitedly *or* sedately. **well-acquainted** see FAMILIAR *adj.* 3; (*well-acquainted with*) see FAMILIAR *adj.* 2. **well-adjusted 2** see *well-balanced* 1 below. **well-advised** prudent, wise, sensible, intelligent, smart. **well and truly** see TRULY 5. **well-balanced 1** rational, sane, sensible, reasonable, level-headed, sober, sound, well-adjusted, stable, cool(-headed), *colloq.* together. **2** evenly matched *or* balanced, equally matched *or* balanced, equal. **3** even, symmetric(al), harmonious, well-proportioned, orderly, well-ordered, well-disposed. **well-being** see WELFARE *n.* 1. **well-born** see *upper-class* (UPPER[1]). **well-bred** well brought up, well-mannered, polite, decorous, mannerly, refined, courteous, cultivated, polished, cultured, gentlemanly, ladylike, elegant, suave, urbane, sophisticated, gracious, courtly, genteel, gallant, chivalrous. **well-built 1** see STRONG *adj.* 1. **2** see STURDY *adj.* 1. **well-chosen** see APPROPRIATE *adj.* **well-covered** see PLUMP[1] *adj.* **well-defined** see DISTINCT 2. **well-deserved** see JUST *adj.* 2. **well-disposed** (*well-disposed to*) see SYMPATHETIC *adj.* 5. **well done 1** thoroughly cooked, cooked through and through, completely cooked. **2** properly done, first-class, first-rate, *colloq.* top-notch, tiptop, *Anglo-Ind.* pukka. **well-dressed** see DAPPER 1. **well-earned** see DUE *adj.* 2, 3. **well-endowed 2** see VOLUPTUOUS 2. **well-established** long-standing, traditional, set, venerable, well-known, accepted, familiar, well-founded. **well-fed** plump, chunky, thickset, chubby, (well-)rounded, rotund, portly, stout, fleshy, overweight, adipose, fat, obese, gross, podgy, *colloq.* pudgy. **well-founded** see SOLID *adj.* 6a. **well-groomed** neat, dapper, fastidious, tidy, trim, smart, chic, *soigné(e)*, clean-cut, spruce, well-dressed, *archaic sl.* spiffing, *colloq.* natty, nifty, *esp. US sl.* spiffy. **well-grounded 2** (*well-grounded in*) see VERSED. **well-heeled** see WEALTHY. **well-informed** knowledgeable, learned, well-read, well-versed, well up, well-educated, lettered, literate, educated, enlightened, *au courant*, *au fait*, apprised, aware, *colloq.* in the know, *US colloq.* wise, *sl.* hip. **well-intentioned** see KIND[2]. **well-kept** see TIDY *adj.* 1. **well-knit** well-proportioned, compact; see ROBUST 1. **well-known 1** famous, noted, notable, celebrated, renowned, illustrious, legendary, famed, public, prominent, eminent, pre-eminent. **2** known, familiar, (well-)established, acknowledged, proverbial, customary, everyday. **well-made 1** see SOLID *adj.* 4, EXQUISITE *adj.* 1. **2** see STURDY *adj.* 1. **well-mannered** see COURTEOUS. **well-meaning** see KIND[2]. **well off 1** comfortable, wealthy, rich, affluent, prosperous, opulent, moneyed, well-to-do, *colloq.* flush, well-heeled, *sl.* loaded. **2** fortunate, lucky, blessed. **well-ordered** see SYSTEMATIC 1. **well-paid 1** see PROFITABLE 1. **well-pleased** see PROUD 1. **well-read** see KNOWLEDGEABLE. **well-received** popular, successful, celebrated, well-liked, favourite, favoured; see also FASHIONABLE, WELCOME *adj.* 1. **well-rounded 4** see FULL[1] *adj.* 8. **well-spent** see FRUITFUL 2. **well-spoken** see ELOQUENT 1. **well-thought-of** admired, highly regarded, respected, reputable, venerated, esteemed, revered, looked-up-to, valued. **well-timed** timely, seasonable, opportune, auspicious, favourable, propitious, advantageous, beneficial. **well-to-do** see *well off* (WELL[1]) above. **well-worn** see *time-worn.*

well[2] /wel/ *n.* & *v.* ● *n.* **1** a shaft sunk into the ground to obtain water, oil, etc. **2** an enclosed space like a well-shaft, e.g. in the middle of a building for stairs or a lift, or for light or ventilation. **3** (foll. by *of*) a source, esp. a copious one (*a well of information*). **4 a** a mineral spring. **b** (in *pl.*) a spa. **5** = *ink-well.* **6** *archaic* a water-spring or fountain. **7** *Brit.* a railed space for solicitors etc. in a lawcourt. **8** a depression for gravy etc. in a dish or tray, or for a mat in the floor. **9** *Physics* a region of minimum potential etc. ● *v.intr.* (foll. by *out, up*) spring as from a fountain; flow copiously. □ **well-head** (or **-spring**) a source. [OE *wella* (= OHG *wella* wave, ON *vella* boiling heat), *wellan* boil, melt f. Gmc]

■ *n.* **1** shaft, bore, borehole; gusher. **3** source, spring, well-spring, fountain, mine, reservoir, supply, *poet.* fount. **4a, 6** well-spring, spring, fountain, well-head, fountain-head, source, reservoir, *poet.* fount. ● *v.* flow, spring, surge, rise, stream, brim over, swell, start; gush, spurt, jet, spout. □ **well-head** (or **-spring**) see SOURCE *n.* 1.

we'll /weel, wil/ *contr.* we shall; we will.

wellies /wéliz/ *n.pl. Brit. colloq.* wellingtons. [abbr.]

wellington /wéllingtən/ *n.* (in full **wellington boot**) *Brit.* a waterproof rubber or plastic boot usu. reaching the knee. [after the 1st Duke of *Wellington*, Brit. general and statesman d. 1852]

wellnigh /wélnī/ *adv. archaic* or *rhet.* almost (*wellnigh impossible*).

■ see ALMOST.

Welsh /welsh/ *adj.* & *n.* ● *adj.* of or relating to Wales or its people or language. ● *n.* **1** the Celtic language of Wales. **2** (prec. by *the*; treated as *pl.*) the people of Wales. □ **Welsh corgi** see CORGI. **Welsh dresser** a type of dresser with open shelves above a cupboard. **Welsh harp** a harp with three rows of strings. **Welsh onion** a species of onion, *Allium fistulosum*, forming clusters of bulbs. **Welsh rabbit** (or **rarebit** by folk etymology) a dish of melted cheese etc. on toast. [OE *Welisc, Wælisc*, etc., f. Gmc f. L *Volcae*, the name of a Celtic people]

welsh /welsh/ *v.intr.* (also **welch** /welch/) **1** (of a loser of a bet, esp. a bookmaker) decamp without paying. **2** evade an obligation. **3** (foll. by *on*) **a** fail to carry out a promise to (a person). **b** fail to honour (an obligation). □□ **welsher** *n.* [19th c.: orig. unkn.]

■ **3 b** (*welsh on*) see *go back on* (BACK). □□ **welsher** non-payer, cheat, cheater, swindler, *US sl.* dead-beat.

Welshman /wélshmən/ *n.* (*pl.* **-men**) a man who is Welsh by birth or descent.

Welshwoman /wélshwŏŏmmən/ *n.* (*pl.* **-women**) a woman who is Welsh by birth or descent.

welt /welt/ *n.* & *v.* ● *n.* **1** a leather rim sewn round the edge of a shoe-upper for the sole to be attached to. **2** = WEAL[1]. **3** a ribbed or reinforced border of a garment; a trimming. **4** a heavy blow. ● *v.tr.* **1** provide with a welt. **2** rain welts on; thrash. [ME *welte, walt*, of unkn. orig.]

■ *n.* **2** bruise, contusion, bump, lump, ridge, scar, weal. **3** bead, ridge, seam, edge, wale, stripe, binding, trimming. ● *v.* **2** see BEAT *v.* 1.

Weltanschauung /véltaanshówŏŏng/ *n.* a particular philosophy or view of life; a conception of the world. [G f. *Welt* world + *Anschauung* perception]

welter[1] /wéltər/ *v.* & *n.* ● *v.intr.* **1** roll, wallow; be washed about. **2** (foll. by *in*) lie prostrate or be soaked or steeped in blood etc. ● *n.* **1** a state of general confusion. **2** (foll. by *of*) a disorderly mixture or contrast of beliefs, policies, etc. [ME f. MDu., MLG *welteren*]

■ *v.* **1** roll (about), flounder, wallow. **2** (*welter in*) be soaked in, lie prostrate in; be sunk *or* involved in, be bogged down in, be entangled *or* ensnarled in. ● *n.* **2** mass, mess, jumble, tangle, confusion, mishmash, muddle, clutter, hotchpotch, hodgepodge.

welter[2] /wéltər/ *n.* **1** a heavy rider or boxer. **2** *colloq.* a heavy blow. **3** *colloq.* a big person or thing. [19th c.: orig. unkn.]

welterweight /wéltərwayt/ *n.* **1** a weight in certain sports intermediate between lightweight and middleweight, in the amateur boxing scale 63.5-67 kg but differing for professionals, wrestlers, and weightlifters. **2** a sportsman of this weight. □ **junior welterweight 1** a weight in professional boxing of 61.2-63.5 kg. **2** a professional boxer of this weight. **light welterweight 1** a weight in amateur boxing of 60-63.5 kg. **2** an amateur boxer of this weight.

Weltschmerz /véltshmairts/ *n.* a feeling of pessimism; an apathetic or vaguely yearning outlook on life. [G f. *Welt* world + *Schmerz* pain]

wen[1] /wen/ *n.* **1** a benign tumour on the skin esp. of the scalp. **2** an outstandingly large or congested city. □ **the great wen** London. [OE *wen, wenn*, of unkn. orig.: cf. Du. *wen*, MLG *wene*, LG *wehne* tumour, wart]

wen[2] /wen/ *n.* (also **wyn** /win/) a runic letter in Old and Middle English, later replaced by *w.* [OE, var. of *wyn* joy (see WINSOME), used because it begins with this letter: cf. THORN 3]

wench /wench/ *n.* & *v.* ● *n.* **1** *joc.* a girl or young woman. **2** *archaic* a prostitute. ● *v.intr. archaic* (of a man) consort with prostitutes. □□ **wencher** *n.* [ME *wenche, wenchel* f. OE *wencel* child: cf. OE *wancol* weak, tottering]

■ *n.* **1** see GIRL 2.

Wend /wend/ *n.* a member of a Slavic people of N. Germany, now inhabiting E. Saxony. □□ **Wendic** *adj.* **Wendish** *adj.* [G *Wende* f. OHG *Winida*, of unkn. orig.]

wend /wend/ *v.tr.* & *intr. literary* or *archaic* go. □ **wend one's way** make one's way. [OE *wendan* turn f. Gmc, rel. to WIND[2]]

Wendy house /wéndi/ *n.* a children's small houselike tent or structure for playing in. [after the house built around *Wendy* in Barrie's *Peter Pan*]

Wensleydale /wénzlidayl/ *n.* **1** a variety of white or blue cheese. **2 a** a sheep of a breed with long wool. **b** this breed. [*Wensleydale* in Yorkshire]

went *past* of GO[1].

wentletrap /wént'ltrap/ *n.* any marine snail of the genus *Clathrus*, with a spiral shell of many whorls. [Du. *wenteltrap* winding stair, spiral shell]

wept *past* of WEEP.

were *2nd sing. past, pl. past, and past subj.* of BE.

we're /weer/ *contr.* we are.

weren't /wernt/ *contr.* were not.

werewolf /wéerwŏŏlf, wáir-/ *n.* (also **werwolf** /wer-/) (*pl.* **-wolves**) a mythical being who at times changes from a person to a wolf. [OE *werewulf*: first element perh. f. OE *wer* man = L *vir*]

wert *archaic 2nd sing. past* of BE.

Wesleyan /wézliən/ *adj.* & *n.* ● *adj.* of or relating to a Protestant denomination founded by the English evangelist John Wesley (d. 1791) (cf. METHODIST). ● *n.* a member of this denomination. □□ **Wesleyanism** *n.*

west /west/ *n., adj.,* & *adv.* ● *n.* **1 a** the point of the horizon where the sun sets at the equinoxes (cardinal point 90° to the left of north). **b** the compass point corresponding to this. **c** the direction in which this lies. **2** (usu. **the West**) **a** European in contrast to Oriental civilization. **b** the non-Communist States of Europe and N. America. **c** the western part of the late Roman Empire. **d** the western part of a country, town, etc. **3** *Bridge* a player occupying the position designated 'west'. ● *adj.* **1** towards, at, near, or facing west. **2** coming from the west (*west wind*). ● *adv.* **1** towards, at, or near the west. **2** (foll. by *of*) further west than. □ **go west** *sl.* be killed or destroyed etc. **West Bank** a region west of the River Jordan assigned to Jordan in 1948 and occupied by Israel since 1967. **West Country** the south-western counties of England. **West End** the entertainment and shopping area of London to the west of the

City. **West Indian 1** a native or national of any island of the West Indies. **2** a person of West Indian descent. **West Indies** the islands of Central America, including Cuba and the Bahamas. **west-north-** (or **south-**) **west** the direction or compass-point midway between west and north-west (or south-west). **West Side** *US* the western part of Manhattan. [OE f. Gmc]

westbound /wéstbownd/ *adj.* travelling or leading westwards.

westering /wéstəring/ *adj.* (of the sun) nearing the west. [*wester* (v.) ME f. WEST]

westerly /wéstərli/ *adj.*, *adv.*, & *n.* ● *adj.* & *adv.* **1** in a western position or direction. **2** (of a wind) blowing from the west. ● *n.* (*pl.* **-ies**) a wind blowing from the west. [*wester* (adj.) f. OE *westra* f. WEST]

western /wéstərn/ *adj.* & *n.* ● *adj.* **1** of or in the west; inhabiting the west. **2** lying or directed towards the west. **3** (**Western**) of or relating to the West (see WEST *n.* 2). ● *n.* a film or novel about cowboys in western North America. □ **Western Church** the part of Christendom that has continued to derive its authority, doctrine, and ritual from the popes in Rome. **Western hemisphere** the half of the earth containing the Americas. **Western roll** a technique of turning the body over the bar in high jump. □□ **westernmost** *adj.* [OE *westerne* (as WEST, -ERN)]

westerner /wéstərnər/ *n.* a native or inhabitant of the west.

westernize /wéstərnīz/ *v.tr.* (also **Westernize**, **-ise**) influence with or convert to the ideas and customs etc. of the West. □□ **westernization** /-záysh'n/ *n.* **westernizer** *n.*

westing /wésting/ *n. Naut.* the distance travelled or the angle of longitude measured westward from either a defined north–south grid line or a meridian.

Westminster /wéstminstər/ *n.* the Parliament at Westminster in London.
■ see PARLIAMENT 1a.

westward /wéstwərd/ *adj.*, *adv.*, & *n.* ● *adj.* & *adv.* (also **westwards**) towards the west. ● *n.* a westward direction or region.

wet /wet/ *adj.*, *v.*, & *n.* ● *adj.* (**wetter**, **wettest**) **1** soaked, covered, or dampened with water or other liquid (*a wet sponge*; *a wet surface*; *got my feet wet*). **2** (of the weather etc.) rainy (*a wet day*). **3** (of paint, ink, etc.) not yet dried. **4** used with water (*wet shampoo*). **5** *Brit. colloq.* feeble, inept. **6** *Brit. Polit. colloq.* Conservative with liberal tendencies, esp. as regarded by right-wing Conservatives. **7** *sl.* (of a country, of legislation, etc.) allowing the free sale of alcoholic drink. **8** (of a baby or young child) incontinent (*is still wet at night*). ● *v.tr.* (**wetting**; *past* and *past part.* **wet** or **wetted**) **1** make wet. **2 a** urinate in or on (*wet the bed*). **b** *refl.* urinate involuntarily. ● *n.* **1** moisture; liquid that wets something. **2** rainy weather; a time of rain. **3** *Brit. colloq.* a feeble or inept person. **4** *Brit. Polit. colloq.* a Conservative with liberal tendencies (see sense 6 of *adj.*). **5** *colloq.* a drink. □ **wet the baby's head** *colloq.* celebrate its birth with a (usu. alcoholic) drink. **wet behind the ears** immature, inexperienced. **wet blanket** see BLANKET. **wet dock** a dock in which a ship can float. **wet dream** an erotic dream with involuntary ejaculation of semen. **wet fly** an artificial fly used under water by an angler. **wet look** a shiny surface given to clothing materials. **wet-nurse** *n.* a woman employed to suckle another's child. ● *v.tr.* **1** act as a wet-nurse to. **2** *colloq.* treat as if helpless. **wet pack** the therapeutic wrapping of the body in wet cloths etc. **wet suit** a close-fitting rubber garment worn by skin-divers etc. to keep warm. **wet through** (or **to the skin**) with one's clothes soaked. **wetting agent** a substance that helps water etc. to spread or penetrate. **wet one's whistle** *colloq.* drink. □□ **wetly** *adv.* **wetness** *n.* **wettable** *adj.* **wetting** *n.* **wettish** *adj.* [OE *wǣt* (adj. & n.), *wǣtan* (v.), rel. to WATER: in ME replaced by past part. of the verb]
■ *adj.* **1** moist, moistened, damp, dampened, soaked, soaking, sopping, wringing, dripping, sodden, soggy, soppy, saturated, drenched, awash, waterlogged, watery; clammy, humid, dank. **2** rainy, raining, teeming, pouring, drizzling, showery. **3** tacky, sticky. **5** feeble, weak, irresolute, effete, namby-pamby, foolish, ineffectual, ineffective, weedy, inept, spineless, timorous, cowardly. ● *v.* **1** dampen, damp, moisten, saturate, drench, souse, douse, steep, immerse, submerge, dip, soak, water. ● *n.* **1** moisture, water, wetness, dampness, damp, humidity, liquid. **2** rain, wetness, drizzle, damp. **3** milksop, lightweight, weed, *colloq.* drip, loser, sissy, softie, wimp; *US sl.* schnook. □ **wet behind the ears** see *inexperienced* (INEXPERIENCE). **wet-nurse 1** see NURSE *v.* 2. **wet one's whistle** see DRINK *v.* 1. □□ **wetness** see PERSPIRATION, WET *n.* 1, 2 above.

wetback /wétbak/ *n. US colloq.* an illegal immigrant from Mexico to the US. [WET + BACK: from the practice of swimming the Rio Grande to reach the US]

wether /wéthər/ *n.* a castrated ram. [OE f. Gmc]

wetlands /wétləndz/ *n.pl.* swamps and other damp areas of land.

we've /weev/ *contr.* we have.

wey /way/ *n.* a former unit of weight or volume varying with different kinds of goods, e.g. 3 cwt. of cheese. [OE *wǣg(e)* balance, weight f. Gmc, rel. to WEIGH[1]]

w.f. *abbr. Printing* wrong fount.

WFTU *abbr.* World Federation of Trade Unions.

Wg. Cdr. *abbr.* Wing Commander.

whack /wak/ *v.* & *n. colloq.* ● *v.tr.* **1** strike or beat forcefully with a sharp blow. **2** (as **whacked** *adj.*) esp. *Brit.* tired out; exhausted. ● *n.* **1** a sharp or resounding blow. **2** *sl.* a share. □ **have a whack at** *sl.* attempt. **out of whack** esp. *US sl.* out of order; malfunctioning. □□ **whacker** *n.* **whacking** *n.* [imit., or alt. of THWACK]
■ *v.* **1** see BEAT *v.* 1. **2** (**whacked**) see TIRED 1. ● *n.* **1** see BLOW[2] 1. **2** see STINT *n.* 2. □ **out of whack** see *out of order* 1 (ORDER).

whacking /wákking/ *adj.* & *adv. colloq.* ● *adj.* very large. ● *adv.* very (*a whacking great skyscraper*).

whacko /wákkō/ *int. sl.* expressing delight or enjoyment.

whacky var. of WACKY.

whale[1] /wayl/ *n.* (*pl.* same or **whales**) any of the larger marine mammals of the order Cetacea, having a streamlined body and horizontal tail, and breathing through a blowhole on the head. □ **a whale of a** *colloq.* an exceedingly good or fine etc. **whale-oil** oil from the blubber of whales. **whale shark** a large tropical whalelike shark, *Rhincodon typus*, feeding close to the surface. [OE *hwæl*]

whale[2] /wayl/ *v.tr.* esp. *US colloq.* beat, thrash. [var. of WALE]

whaleback /wáylbak/ *n.* anything shaped like a whale's back.

whaleboat /wáylbōt/ *n.* a double-bowed boat of a kind used in whaling.

whalebone /wáylbōn/ *n.* an elastic horny substance growing in thin parallel plates in the upper jaw of some whales, used as stiffening etc. □ **whalebone whale** a baleen whale.

whaler /wáylər/ *n.* **1** a whaling ship or a seaman engaged in whaling. **2** an Australian shark of the genus *Carcharhinus*. **3** *Austral. sl.* a tramp.
■ **3** see TRAMP *n.* 1.

whaling /wáyling/ *n.* the practice or industry of hunting and killing whales, esp. for their oil or whalebone. □ **whaling-master** the captain of a whaler.

wham /wam/ *int.*, *n.*, & *v. colloq.* ● *int.* expressing the sound of a forcible impact. ● *n.* such a sound. ● *v.* (**whammed**, **whamming**) **1** *intr.* make such a sound or impact. **2** *tr.* strike forcibly. [imit.]
■ *int.* & *n.* see THUD *n.*

whammy /wámmi/ *n.* (*pl.* **-ies**) *US colloq.* an evil or unlucky influence. [20th c.: orig. unkn.]

whang /wang/ *v.* & *n. colloq.* ● *v.* **1** *tr.* strike heavily and loudly; whack. **2** *intr.* (of a drum etc.) sound under or as under a blow. ● *n.* a whanging sound or blow. [imit.]

whangee /wanggeé/ *n.* **1** a Chinese or Japanese bamboo of the genus *Phyllostachys*. **2** a cane made from this. [Chin. *huang* old bamboo-sprouts]

whare /wórri/ *n.* a Maori hut or house. [Maori]

wharf /wawrf/ *n.* & *v.* ● *n.* (*pl.* **wharves** /wawrvz/ or **wharfs**) a level quayside area to which a ship may be moved to load and unload. ● *v.tr.* **1** moor (a ship) at a wharf. **2** store (goods) on a wharf. [OE *hwearf*]

wharfage /wáwrfij/ *n.* **1** accommodation at a wharf. **2** a fee for this.

wharfie /wáwrfi/ *n. Austral.* & *NZ colloq.* a waterside worker; a wharf-labourer.

wharfinger /wáwrfinjər/ *n.* an owner or keeper of a wharf. [prob. ult. f. WHARFAGE]

wharves *pl.* of WHARF.

what /wot/ *adj.*, *pron.*, & *adv.* ● *interrog.adj.* **1** asking for a choice from an indefinite number or for a statement of amount, number, or kind (*what books have you read?*; *what news have you?*). **2** *colloq.* = WHICH *interrog.adj.* (*what book have you chosen?*). ● *adj.* (usu. in exclam.) how great or remarkable (*what luck!*). ● *rel.adj.* the or any . . . that (*will give you what help I can*). ● *pron.* (corresp. to the functions of the *adj.*) **1** what thing or things? (*what is your name?*; *I don't know what you mean*). **2** (asking for a remark to be repeated) = what did you say? **3** asking for confirmation or agreement of something not completely understood (*you did what?*; *what, you really mean it?*). **4** how much (*what you must have suffered!*). **5** (as *rel.pron.*) that or those which; a or the or any thing which (*what followed was worse*; *tell me what you think*). ● *adv.* to what extent (*what does it matter?*). □ **what about** what is the news or position or your opinion of (*what about me?*; *what about a game of tennis?*). **what-d'you-call-it** (or **whatchamacallit** or **what's-its-name**) *colloq.* a substitute for a name not recalled. **what ever** what at all or in any way (*what ever do you mean?*) (see also WHATEVER). **what for** *colloq.* **1** for what reason? **2** a severe reprimand (esp. *give a person what for*). **what have you** *colloq.* (prec. by *or*) anything else similar. **what if?** **1** what would result etc. if. **2** what would it matter if. **what is more** and as an additional point; moreover. **what next?** *colloq.* what more absurd, shocking, or surprising thing is possible? **what not** (prec. by *and*) other similar things. **what of?** what is the news concerning? **what of it?** why should that be considered significant? **what's-his** (or **-its**) **-name** = *what-d'you-call-it*. **what's what** *colloq.* what is useful or important etc. **what with** *colloq.* because of (usu. several things). [OE *hwæt* f. Gmc]

■ □ **what for 2** see *piece of one's mind*. **what is more** see MOREOVER. **what's what** see ROPE *n.* 3a.

whate'er /wotáir/ *poet.* var. of WHATEVER.

whatever /wotévvər/ *adj.* & *pron.* **1** = WHAT (in relative uses) with the emphasis on indefiniteness (*lend me whatever you can*; *whatever money you have*). **2** though anything (*we are safe whatever happens*). **3** (with *neg.* or *interrog.*) at all; of any kind (*there is no doubt whatever*). **4** *colloq.* = *what ever*. □ **or whatever** *colloq.* or anything similar.

whatnot /wótnot/ *n.* **1** an indefinite or trivial thing. **2** a stand with shelves for small objects.

whatsit /wótsit/ *n. colloq.* a person or thing whose name one cannot recall or does not know.

whatso /wótsō/ *adj.* & *pron. archaic* = WHATEVER 1, 2. [ME, = WHAT + SO, f. OE *swā hwæt swā*]

whatsoe'er /wótsō-áir/ *poet.* var. of WHATSOEVER.

whatsoever /wótsō-évvər/ *adj.* & *pron.* = WHATEVER 1–3.

whaup /wawp/ *n.* esp. *Sc.* a curlew. [imit. of its cry]

wheal var. of WEAL[1].

wheat /weet/ *n.* **1** any cereal plant of the genus *Triticum*, bearing dense four-sided seed-spikes. **2** its grain, used in making flour etc. □ **separate the wheat from the chaff** see CHAFF. **wheat-belt** a region where wheat is the chief agricultural product. **wheat germ** the embryo of the wheat grain, extracted as a source of vitamins. **wheat-grass** = *couch grass* (see COUCH[2]). [OE *hwǣte* f. Gmc, rel. to WHITE]

wheatear /weéteer/ *n.* any small migratory bird of the genus *Oenanthe*, esp. with a white belly and rump. [app. f. *wheatears* (as WHITE, ARSE)]

wheaten /weét'n/ *adj.* made of wheat.

wheatmeal /weétmeel/ *n.* flour made from wheat with some of the bran and germ removed.

Wheatstone bridge /weétstōn/ *n.* an apparatus for measuring electrical resistances by equalizing the potential at two points of a circuit. [C. *Wheatstone*, Engl. physicist d. 1875]

whee /wee/ *int.* expressing delight or excitement. [imit.]

wheedle /weéd'l/ *v.tr.* **1** coax by flattery or endearments. **2** (foll. by *out*) **a** get (a thing) out of a person by wheedling. **b** cheat (a person) out of a thing by wheedling. □□ **wheedler** *n.* **wheedling** *adj.* **wheedlingly** *adv.* [perh. f. G *wedeln* fawn, cringe f. *Wedel* tail]

■ **1** coax, cajole, inveigle, charm, beguile, persuade, induce, talk round, *colloq.* butter up, sweet-talk, *sl.* con.

wheel /weel/ *n.* & *v.* ● *n.* **1** a circular frame or disc arranged to revolve on an axle and used to facilitate the motion of a vehicle or for various mechanical purposes. **2** a wheel-like thing (*Catherine wheel*; *potter's wheel*; *steering wheel*). **3** motion as of a wheel, esp. the movement of a line of people with one end as a pivot. **4** a machine etc. of which a wheel is an essential part. **5** (in *pl.*) *sl.* a car. **6** *US sl.* = *big wheel* 2. **7** a set of short lines concluding a stanza. ● *v.* **1** *intr.* & *tr.* **a** turn on an axis or pivot. **b** swing round in line with one end as a pivot. **2 a** *intr.* (often foll. by *about*, *round*) change direction or face another way. **b** *tr.* cause to do this. **3** *tr.* push or pull (a wheeled thing esp. a barrow, bicycle, or pram, or its load or occupant). **4** *intr.* go in circles or curves (*seagulls wheeling overhead*). □ **at the wheel 1** driving a vehicle. **2** directing a ship. **3** in control of affairs. **on wheels** (or **oiled wheels**) smoothly. **wheel and deal** engage in political or commercial scheming. **wheel-back** *adj.* (of a chair) with a back shaped like or containing the design of a wheel. **wheel clamp** a clamp for locking the wheel of an illegally parked motor vehicle so as to immobilize it until the appropriate parking fine has been paid. **wheel-house** a steersman's shelter. **wheel-lock 1** an old kind of gunlock having a steel wheel to rub against flint etc. **2** a gun with this. **wheel of Fortune** luck. **wheel-spin** rotation of a vehicle's wheels without traction. **wheels within wheels 1** intricate machinery. **2** *colloq.* indirect or secret agencies. □□ **wheeled** *adj.* (also in *comb.*). **wheelless** *adj.* [OE *hwēol*, *hwēogol* f. Gmc]

■ *n.* **1** disc, ring, circle, hoop, *esp. Math.* & *Biol.* annulus. **3** see REVOLUTION 3, 4. **5** (*wheels*) see CAR 1. ● *v.* **1** see REVOLVE 1, 2. **2** spin, turn, veer, swivel, pivot, swing, whirl. **4** circle, go round, gyrate. □ **at the wheel 3** in control, in charge, in command, at the helm, in the driver's seat, in the saddle; (*be at the wheel*) be in charge *or* control *or* command, have the whip hand, wear the trousers.

wheelbarrow /weélbarrō/ *n.* a small cart with one wheel and two shafts for carrying garden loads etc.

wheelbase /weélbayss/ *n.* the distance between the front and rear axles of a vehicle.

wheelchair /weélchair/ *n.* a chair on wheels for an invalid or disabled person.

wheeler /weélər/ *n.* **1** (in *comb.*) a vehicle having a specified number of wheels. **2** a wheelwright. **3** a horse harnessed next to the wheels and behind another. □ **wheeler-dealer** *colloq.* a person who wheels and deals.

wheelie /weéli/ *n. sl.* the stunt of riding a bicycle or motor cycle for a short distance with the front wheel off the ground.

wheelman *n.* esp. *US* **1** a driver of a wheeled vehicle. **2** a helmsman.

wheelsman /weélzmən/ *n.* (*pl.* **-men**) *US* a steersman.

wheelwright /weélrīt/ *n.* a person who makes or repairs esp. wooden wheels.

wheeze /weez/ *v.* & *n.* ● *v.* **1** *intr.* breathe with an audible chesty whistling sound. **2** *tr.* (often foll. by *out*) utter in this way. ● *n.* **1** a sound of wheezing. **2** *colloq.* **a** *Brit.* a clever scheme. **b** an actor's interpolated joke etc. **c** a catch-phrase. □□ **wheezer** *n.* **wheezingly** *adv.* **wheezy** *adj.* (**wheezier, wheeziest**). **wheezily** *adv.* **wheeziness** *n.* [prob. f. ON *hvæsa* to hiss]

■ *n.* **2 a** see DODGE *n.*

whelk[1] /welk/ *n.* any predatory marine gastropod mollusc of the family Buccinidae, esp. the edible kind of the genus *Baccinum*, having a spiral shell. [OE *wioloc, weoloc*, of unkn. orig.: perh. infl. by WHELK[2]]

whelk[2] /welk/ *n.* a pimple. [OE *hwylca* f. *hwelian* suppurate]

whelm /welm/ *v.tr. poet.* **1** engulf, submerge. **2** crush with weight, overwhelm. [OE *hwelman* (unrecorded) = *hwylfan* overturn]

whelp /welp/ *n.* & *v.* ● *n.* **1** a young dog; a puppy. **2** *archaic* a cub. **3** an ill-mannered child or youth. **4** (esp. in *pl.*) a projection on the barrel of a capstan or windlass. ● *v.tr.* (also *absol.*) **1** bring forth (a whelp or whelps). **2** *derog.* (of a human mother) give birth to. **3** originate (an evil scheme etc.). [OE *hwelp*]

■ *n.* **1** pup, puppy. **3** see PUP *n.* 3.

when /wen/ *adv.*, *conj.*, *pron.*, & *n.* ● *interrog.adv.* **1** at what time? **2** on what occasion? **3** how soon? **4** how long ago? ● *rel.adv.* (prec. by *time* etc.) at or on which (*there are times when I could cry*). ● *conj.* **1** at the or any time that; as soon as (*come when you like*; *come when ready*; *when I was your age*). **2** although; considering that (*why stand up when you could sit down?*). **3** after which; and then; but just then (*was nearly asleep when the bell rang*). ● *pron.* what time? (*till when can you stay?*; *since when it has been better*). ● *n.* time, occasion, date (*fixed the where and when*). [OE *hwanne, hwenne*]

whence /wenss/ *adv.* & *conj. formal* ● *adv.* from what place? (*whence did they come?*). ● *conj.* **1** to the place from which (*return whence you came*). **2** (often prec. by *place* etc.) from which (*the source whence these errors arise*). **3** and thence (*whence it follows that*). ¶ Use of *from whence* as in *the place from whence they came*, though common, is generally considered incorrect. [ME *whannes, whennes* f. *whanne, whenne* f. OE *hwanon(e)* whence, formed as WHEN + -s[3]: cf. THENCE]

whencesoever /wénss-sō-évvər/ *adv.* & *conj. formal* from whatever place or source.

whene'er /wenáir/ *poet.* var. of WHENEVER.

whenever /wenévvər/ *conj.* & *adv.* **1** at whatever time; on whatever occasion. **2** every time that. □ **or whenever** *colloq.* or at any similar time.

whensoe'er /wénsō-áir/ *poet.* var. of WHENSOEVER.

whensoever /wénsō-évvər/ *conj.* & *adv. formal* = WHENEVER.

where /wair/ *adv.*, *conj.*, *pron.*, & *n.* ● *interrog.adv.* **1** in or to what place or position? (*where is the milk?*; *where are you going?*). **2** in what direction or respect? (*where does the argument lead?*; *where does it concern us?*). **3** in what book etc.?; from whom? (*where did you read that?*; *where did you hear that?*). **4** in what situation or condition? (*where does that leave us?*). ● *rel.adv.* (prec. by *place* etc.) in or to which (*places where they meet*). ● *conj.* **1** in or to the or any place, direction, or respect in which (*go where you like*; *that is where you are wrong*; *delete where applicable*). **2** and there (*reached Crewe, where the car broke down*). ● *pron.* what place? (*where do you come from?*; *where are you going to?*). ● *n.* place; scene of something (see WHEN *n.*). [OE *hwǣr, hwār*]

whereabouts *adv.* & *n.* ● *adv.* /wáirəbówts/ where or approximately where? (*whereabouts are they?*; *show me whereabouts to look*). ● *n.* /wáirəbowts/ (as *sing.* or *pl.*) a person's or thing's location roughly defined.

■ *adv.* where, in *or* at *or* to what place, *archaic* whither. ● *n.* location, position, place, site, situation, address, locale.

whereafter /wairáaftər/ *conj. formal* after which.

whereas /wairáz/ *conj.* **1** in contrast or comparison with the fact that. **2** (esp. in legal preambles) taking into consideration the fact that.

■ **2** see SEEING *conj.*

whereat /wairát/ *conj. archaic* **1** at which place or point. **2** for which reason.

whereby /wairbī́/ *conj.* by what or which means.

where'er /wairáir/ *poet.* var. of WHEREVER.

wherefore /wáirfor/ *adv.* & *n.* ● *adv. archaic* **1** for what reason? **2** for which reason. ● *n.* a reason (*the whys and wherefores*).

■ *adv.* **2** see THEREFORE.

wherefrom /wairfróm/ *conj. archaic* from which, from where.

wherein /wairín/ *conj.* & *adv. formal* ● *conj.* in what or which place or respect. ● *adv.* in what place or respect?

whereof /wairóv/ *conj.* & *adv. formal* ● *conj.* of what or which (*the means whereof*). ● *adv.* of what?

whereon /wairón/ *conj.* & *adv. archaic* ● *conj.* on what or which. ● *adv.* on what?

wheresoe'er /wáirsōáir/ *poet.* var. of WHERESOEVER.

wheresoever /wáirsō-évvər/ *conj.* & *adv. formal* or *literary* = WHEREVER.

whereto /wairto͞o/ *conj.* & *adv. formal* ● *conj.* to what or which. ● *adv.* to what?

whereupon /wáirəpón/ *conj.* immediately after which.

wherever /wairévvər/ *adv.* & *conj.* ● *adv.* in or to whatever place. ● *conj.* in every place that. □ **or wherever** *colloq.* or in any similar place.

wherewithal /wáirwi<u>th</u>awl/ *n. colloq.* money etc. needed for a purpose (*has not the wherewithal to do it*).

■ see MONEY 3.

wherry /wérri/ *n.* (*pl.* **-ies**) **1** a light rowing-boat usu. for carrying passengers. **2** a large light barge. [ME: orig. unkn.]

wherryman /wérrimən/ *n.* (*pl.* **-men**) a man employed on a wherry.

whet /wet/ *v.* & *n.* ● *v.tr.* (**whetted, whetting**) **1** sharpen (a scythe or other tool) by grinding. **2** stimulate (the appetite or a desire, interest, etc.). ● *n.* **1** the act or an instance of whetting. **2** a small quantity stimulating one's appetite for more. □□ **whetter** *n.* (also in *comb.*). [OE *hwettan* f. Gmc]

■ *v.* **1** sharpen, hone, grind, file, put an edge on, strop. **2** pique, sharpen, awaken, arouse, stimulate, kindle, fire, increase, excite, enhance.

whether /wé<u>th</u>ər/ *conj.* introducing the first or both of alternative possibilities (*I doubt whether it matters*; *I do not know whether they have arrived or not*). □ **whether or no** see NO[2]. [OE *hwæther, hwether* f. Gmc]

whetstone /wétstōn/ *n.* **1** a tapered stone used with water to sharpen curved tools, e.g. sickles, hooks (cf. OILSTONE). **2** a thing that sharpens the senses etc.

whew /hwyo͞o/ *int.* expressing surprise, consternation, or relief. [imit.: cf. PHEW]

whey /way/ *n.* the watery liquid left when milk forms curds. □ **whey-faced** pale esp. with fear. [OE *hwæg, hweg* f. LG]

which /wich/ *adj.* & *pron.* ● *interrog.adj.* asking for choice from a definite set of alternatives (*which John do you mean?*; *say which book you prefer*; *which way shall we go?*). ● *rel.adj.* being the one just referred to; and this or these (*ten years, during which time they admitted nothing*; *a word of advice, which action is within your power, will set things straight*). ● *interrog.pron.* **1** which person or persons (*which of you is responsible?*). **2** which thing or things (*say which you prefer*). ● *rel.pron.* (*poss.* **of which, whose** /hooz/) **1** which thing or things, usu. introducing a clause not essential for identification (cf. THAT *pron.* 7) (*the house, which is empty, has been damaged*). **2** used in place of *that* after *in* or *that* (*there is the house in which I was born*; *that which you have just seen*). □ **which is which** a phrase used when two or more persons or things are difficult to distinguish from each other. [OE *hwilc* f. Gmc]

whichever /wichévvər/ *adj.* & *pron.* **1** any which (*take whichever you like*; *whichever one you like*). **2** no matter which (*whichever one wins, they both get a prize*).

whichsoever/wíchsō-évvər/ *adj.* & *pron. archaic* = WHICHEVER.

whidah var. of WHYDAH.

whiff /wif/ *n.* & *v.* ● *n.* **1** a puff or breath of air, smoke, etc. (*went outside for a whiff of fresh air*). **2** a smell (*caught the whiff of a cigar*). **3** (foll. by *of*) a trace or suggestion of scandal etc. **4** a small cigar. **5** a minor discharge (of grapeshot etc.). **6** a light narrow outrigged sculling-boat. ● *v.* **1** *tr.* & *intr.* blow or puff lightly. **2** *intr. Brit.* smell (esp. unpleasant). **3** *tr.* get a slight smell of. [imit.]

■ *n.* **1** see BREATH 2a. **2** see SMELL *n.* 2. **3** see HINT *n.* 3.

whiffle /wíff'l/ *v.* & *n.* ● *v.* **1** *intr.* & *tr.* (of the wind) blow lightly, shift about. **2** *intr.* be variable or evasive. **3** *intr.* (of a flame, leaves, etc.) flicker, flutter. **4** *intr.* make the sound of a light wind in breathing etc. ● *n.* a slight movement of air. ▫▫ **whiffler** *n.* [WHIFF + -LE[4]]

whiffletree /wíff'ltree/ *n. US* = SWINGLETREE. [var. of WHIPPLETREE]

whiffy /wíffi/ *adj. colloq.* (**whiffier, whiffiest**) having an unpleasant smell.

■ see SMELLY.

Whig /wig/ *n. hist.* **1** *Polit.* a member of the British reforming and constitutional party that after 1688 sought the supremacy of Parliament and was eventually succeeded in the 19th c. by the Liberal Party (opp. TORY *n.* 2). **2** a 17th-c. Scottish Presbyterian. **3** *US* **a** a supporter of the American Revolution. **b** a member of an American political party in the 19th c., succeeded by the Republicans. ▫▫ **Whiggery** *n.* **Whiggish** *adj.* **Whiggism** *n.* [prob. a shortening of Sc. *whiggamer, -more*, nickname of 17th-c. Sc. rebels, f. *whig* to drive + MARE[1]]

while /wīl/ *n.*, *conj.*, *v.*, & *adv.* ● *n.* **1** a space of time, time spent in some action (*a long while ago*; *waited a while*; *all this while*). **2** (prec. by *the*) **a** during some other process. **b** *poet.* during the time that. **3** (prec. by *a*) for some time (*have not seen you a while*). ● *conj.* **1** during the time that; for as long as; at the same time as (*while I was away, the house was burgled*; *fell asleep while reading*). **2** in spite of the fact that; although, whereas (*while I want to believe it, I cannot*). **3** *N.Engl.* until (*wait while Monday*). ● *v.tr.* (foll. by *away*) pass (time etc.) in a leisurely or interesting manner. ● *rel.adv.* (prec. by *time* etc.) during which (*the summer while I was abroad*). ▫ **all the while** during the whole time (that). **for a long while** for a long time past. **for a while** for some time. **a good** (or **great**) **while** a considerable time. **in a while** (or **little while**) soon, shortly. **worth while** (or **one's while**) worth the time or effort spent. [OE *hwīl* f. Gmc: (conj.) abbr. of OE *thā hwīle the*, ME *the while that*]

■ *n.* **1** see TIME *n.* 4, 6. ● *conj.* **2** see THOUGH *conj.* 1. ● *v.* (*while away*) see PASS[1] *v.* 12. ▫ **for a while** see *temporarily* (TEMPORARY). **in a while** (or **little while**) see SHORTLY 1.

whiles /wīlz/ *conj. archaic* = WHILE. [orig. in the adverbs *somewhiles, otherwhiles*]

whilom /wīləm/ *adv.* & *adj. archaic* ● *adv.* formerly, once. ● *adj.* former, erstwhile (*my whilom friend*). [OE *hwīlum* dative pl. of *hwīl* WHILE]

whilst /wīlst/ *adv.* & *conj.* esp. *Brit.* while. [ME f. WHILES: cf. AGAINST]

whim /wim/ *n.* **1 a** a sudden fancy; a caprice. **b** capriciousness. **2** *archaic* a kind of windlass for raising ore or water from a mine. [17th c.: orig. unkn.]

■ **1 a** see FANCY *n.* 2.

whimbrel /wímbril/ *n.* a small curlew, esp. *Numenius phaeopus*. [WHIMPER (imit.): cf. *dotterel*]

whimper /wímpər/ *v.* & *n.* ● *v.* **1** *intr.* make feeble, querulous, or frightened sounds; cry and whine softly. **2** *tr.* utter whimperingly. ● *n.* **1** a whimpering sound. **2** a feeble note or tone (*the conference ended on a whimper*). ▫▫ **whimperer** *n.* **whimperingly** *adv.* [imit., f. dial. *whimp*]

■ *v.* **1, 2** see CRY *v.* 2a, WEEP *v.* 1, 2. ● *n.* **1** see GROAN *n.*

whimsical /wímzik'l/ *adj.* **1** capricious. **2** fantastic. **3** odd or quaint; fanciful, humorous. ▫▫ **whimsicality** /-kálliti/ *n.* **whimsically** *adv.* **whimsicalness** *n.*

■ **1** capricious, erratic, eccentric, wavering, flighty, unsettled, fickle, mercurial, wavering, fluctuating, unpredictable, inconsistent, volatile, unsteady. **2, 3** quaint, fey, fanciful, odd, curious, unusual, chimeric(al), queer, singular, peculiar, funny, humorous, fantastic(al), pixyish, playful, puckish, absurd, preposterous, offbeat.

whimsy /wímzi/ *n.* (also **whimsey**) (*pl.* **-ies** or **-eys**) **1** a whim; a capricious notion or fancy. **2** capricious or quaint humour. [rel. to WHIM-WHAM: cf. *flimsy*]

■ **1** see FANCY *n.* 2.

whim-wham /wímwam/ *n. archaic* **1** a toy or plaything. **2** = WHIM 1. [redupl.: orig. uncert.]

whin[1] /win/ *n.* (in *sing.* or *pl.*) furze, gorse. [prob. Scand.: cf. Norw. *hvine*, Sw. *hven*]

whin[2] /win/ *n.* **1** hard dark esp. basaltic rock or stone. **2** a piece of this. [ME: orig. unkn.]

whinchat /wínchat/ *n.* a small brownish songbird, *Saxicola rubetra*. [WHIN[1] + CHAT[2]]

whine /wīn/ *n.* & *v.* ● *n.* **1** a complaining long-drawn wail as of a dog. **2** a similar shrill prolonged sound. **3 a** a querulous tone. **b** an instance of feeble or undignified complaining. ● *v.* **1** *intr.* emit or utter a whine. **2** *intr.* complain in a querulous tone or in a feeble or undignified way. **3** *tr.* utter in a whining tone. ▫▫ **whiner** *n.* **whiningly** *adv.* **whiny** *adj.* (**whinier, whiniest**). [OE *hwīnan*]

■ *n.* **1, 2** see HOWL *n.* 1. **3 b** see GRIPE *n.* 2. ● *v.* **1** see HOWL *v.* 1. **2** see MOAN *v.*

whinge /winj/ *v.* & *n. colloq.* ● *v.intr.* whine; grumble peevishly. ● *n.* a whining complaint; a peevish grumbling. ▫▫ **whinger** *n.* **whingingly** *adv.* **whingy** *adj.* [OE *hwinsian* f. Gmc]

■ *v.* see GRIPE *v.* 1. ● *n.* see GRIPE *n.* 2.

whinny /wínni/ *n.* & *v.* ● *n.* (*pl.* **-ies**) a gentle or joyful neigh. ● *v.intr.* (**-ies, -ied**) give a whinny. [imit.: cf. WHINE]

whinstone /wínstōn/ *n.* = WHIN[2].

whip /wip/ *n.* & *v.* ● *n.* **1** a lash attached to a stick for urging on animals or punishing etc. **2 a** a member of a political party in Parliament appointed to control its parliamentary discipline and tactics, esp. ensuring attendance and voting in debates. **b** *Brit.* the whips' written notice requesting or requiring attendance for voting at a division etc., variously underlined according to the degree of urgency (*three-line whip*). **c** (prec. by *the*) party discipline and instructions (*asked for the Labour whip*). **3** a dessert made with whipped cream etc. **4** the action of beating cream, eggs, etc., into a froth. **5** = WHIPPER-IN. **6** a rope-and-pulley hoisting apparatus. ● *v.* (**whipped, whipping**) **1** *tr.* beat or urge on with a whip. **2** *tr.* beat (cream or eggs etc.) into a froth. **3** *tr.* & *intr.* take or move suddenly, unexpectedly, or rapidly (*whipped away the tablecloth*; *whipped out a knife*; *whip off your coat*; *whipped behind the door*). **4** *tr. Brit. sl.* steal (*who's whipped my pen?*). **5** *tr. sl.* **a** excel. **b** defeat. **6** *tr.* bind with spirally wound twine. **7** *tr.* sew with overcast stitches. ▫ **whip-bird** any Australian bird of the genus *Psophodes* with a cry like the crack of a whip. **whip-crane** a light derrick with tackle for hoisting. **whip-graft** *Hort.* a graft with the tongue of the scion in a slot in the stock and vice versa. **whip hand 1** a hand that holds the whip (in riding etc.). **2** (usu. prec. by *the*) the advantage or control in any situation. **whip in** bring (hounds) together. **whip on** urge into action. **whip-round** esp. *Brit. colloq.* an informal collection of money from a group of people. **whip scorpion** any arachnid of the order Uropygi, with a long slender tail-like appendage, which secretes an irritating vapour. **whip snake** any of various long slender snakes of the family Colubridae. **whip-stitch** a stitch made by whipping. **whip up 1** excite or stir up (feeling etc.). **2** gather, summon up. **3** prepare (a meal etc.) hurriedly. □□ **whipless** *adj.* **whiplike** *adj.* **whipper** *n.* [ME *(h)wippen* (v.), prob. f. MLG & MDu. *wippen* swing, leap, dance]

■ *n.* **1** scourge, lash, rawhide, quirt, horsewhip, bull-whip, cane, birch, switch, thong, (riding-)crop, kourbash, sjambok, *Bibl.* scorpion, *Austral.* pizzle, *hist.* cat-o'-nine-tails, rope's end, cat, knout. ● *v.* **1** beat, thrash, lash, flog, horsewhip, scourge, switch, cane, birch, flagellate, leather, wale, spank, strap, *colloq.* lambaste, *sl.* tan; castigate, chastise, punish, discipline. **2** beat, whisk, fluff up. **3** whisk, pull, jerk, snatch, *colloq.* yank; run, scamper, scoot, race, scurry, scramble, hurry, flit, rush, dash, dart, flash, zip, zoom, *colloq.* skedaddle. **4** see SWIPE *v.* 2. **5** **a** see EXCEL 1. **b** trounce, defeat, beat, conquer, overwhelm, rout, overcome, overpower, thwart, check, worst, drub, batter, stop, outdo, destroy, smash, *colloq.* lick, best, murder, slaughter, kill, wipe the floor with, pulverize, *US colloq.* cream, *sl.* clobber, ruin, squash. **6** bind, fasten, tie, *Naut.* seize. **7** overcast. □ **whip hand** see *predominance* (PREDOMINANT). **whip-round** collection. **whip up 1** stir up, agitate, arouse, rouse, work up, kindle, fuel, inflame, excite, incite. **2** see *summon up*. **3** improvise, put together quickly *or* hurriedly, assemble quickly *or* hurriedly, prepare quickly *or* hurriedly, knock together, knock up, slap *or* throw together.

whipcord /wípkord/ *n.* **1** a tightly twisted cord such as is used for making whiplashes. **2** a close-woven worsted fabric.

whiplash /wíplash/ *n.* **1** the flexible end of a whip. **2** a blow with a whip. □ **whiplash injury** an injury to the neck caused by a jerk of the head, esp. as in a motor accident.

whipper-in /wippərin/ *n.* a huntsman's assistant who manages the hounds.

whippersnapper /wippərsnappər/ *n.* **1** a small child. **2** an insignificant but presumptuous or intrusive (esp. young) person. [perh. for *whipsnapper*, implying noise and unimportance]

■ **1** see CHILD 1a. **2** see PUP *n.* 3.

whippet /wíppit/ *n.* a cross-bred dog of the greyhound type used for racing. [prob. f. obs. *whippet* move briskly, f. *whip it*]

whipping /wípping/ *n.* **1** a beating, esp. with a whip. **2** cord wound round in binding. □ **whipping-boy 1** a scapegoat. **2** *hist.* a boy educated with a young prince and punished instead of him. **whipping-cream** cream suitable for whipping. **whipping-post** *hist.* a post used for public whippings. **whipping-top** a top kept spinning by blows of a lash.

■ **1** beating, thrashing, lashing, flogging, horsewhipping, drubbing, scourging, switching, caning, birching, flagellation, spanking. **2** binding, tying, winding, fastening, *Naut.* seizing. □ **whipping-boy 1** see SCAPEGOAT *n.*

whippletree /wipp'ltree/ *n.* = SWINGLETREE. [app. f. WHIP + TREE]

whippoorwill /wíppoorwil/ *n.* an American nightjar, *Caprimulgus vociferus.* [imit. of its cry]

whippy /wíppi/ *adj.* (**whippier**, **whippiest**) flexible, springy. □□ **whippiness** *n.*

whipsaw /wípsaw/ *n.* & *v.* ● *n.* a saw with a narrow blade held at each end by a frame. ● *v.* (*past part.* **-sawn** or **-sawed**) **1** *tr.* cut with a whipsaw. **2** *US sl.* **a** *tr.* cheat by joint action on two others. **b** *intr.* be cheated in this way.

whipstock /wípstok/ *n.* the handle of a whip.

whir var. of WHIRR.

whirl /wurl/ *v.* & *n.* ● *v.* **1** *tr.* & *intr.* swing round and round; revolve rapidly. **2** *tr.* & *intr.* (foll. by *away*) convey or go rapidly in a vehicle etc. **3** *tr.* & *intr.* send or travel swiftly in an orbit or a curve. **4** *intr.* **a** (of the brain, senses, etc.) seem to spin round. **b** (of thoughts etc.) be confused; follow each other in bewildering succession. ● *n.* **1** a whirling movement (*vanished in a whirl of dust*). **2** a state of intense activity (*the social whirl*). **3** a state of confusion (*my mind is in a whirl*). **4** *colloq.* an attempt (*give it a whirl*). □ **whirling dervish** see DERVISH. □□ **whirler** *n.* **whirlingly** *adv.* [ME: (v.) f. ON *hvirfla*: (n.) f. MLG & MDu. *wervel* spindle & ON *hvirfill* circle f. Gmc]

■ *v.* **1** see REVOLVE 1, 2. **4** see SWIRL *v.* ● *n.* **1** swirl, twist, roll, curl, twirl, spiral; see also EDDY *n.*, SPIN *n.* 1, 3. **2** see FLURRY *n.* 3. **3** see MUDDLE *n.* **4** see GO *n.*[1] 5.

whirligig /wúrligig/ *n.* **1** a spinning or whirling toy. **2** a merry-go-round. **3** a revolving motion. **4** anything regarded as hectic or constantly changing (*the whirligig of time*). **5** any freshwater beetle of the family Gyrinidae that circles about on the surface. [ME f. WHIRL + obs. *gig* whipping-top]

whirlpool /wúrlpōōl/ *n.* a powerful circular eddy in the sea etc. often causing suction to its centre.

■ maelstrom, vortex, eddy, whirl, swirl; waterspout.

whirlwind /wúrlwind/ *n.* **1** a mass or column of air whirling rapidly round and round in a cylindrical or funnel shape over land or water. **2** a confused tumultuous process. **3** (*attrib.*) very rapid (*a whirlwind romance*). □ **reap the whirlwind** suffer worse results of a bad action.

■ **1** vortex, cyclone, typhoon, hurricane, tornado, *Austral.* willy-willy, *S.Afr.* dust devil, *US* twister; waterspout. **2** confusion, tumult, turmoil, pandemonium, whirl, disorder, bedlam, chaos. **3** (*attrib.*) speedy, quick, swift, rapid, sudden, precipitous, precipitate, lightning, headlong, hasty, rash, impetuous.

whirlybird /wúrliburd/ *n. colloq.* a helicopter.

whirr /wur/ *n.* & *v.* (also **whir**) ● *n.* a continuous rapid buzzing or softly clicking sound as of a bird's wings or of cog-wheels in constant motion. ● *v.intr.* (**whirred**, **whirring**) make this sound. [ME, prob. Scand.: cf. Da. *hvirre*, Norw. *kvirra*, perh. rel. to WHIRL]

■ *v.* see HUM[1] *v.* 1.

whisht /hwisht/ *v.* (also **whist** /hwist/) esp. *Sc.* & *Ir. dial.* **1** *intr.* (esp. as *int.*) be quiet; hush. **2** *tr.* quieten. [imit.]

whisk /wisk/ *v.* & *n.* ● *v.* **1** *tr.* (foll. by *away*, *off*) **a** brush with a sweeping movement. **b** take with a sudden motion (*whisked the plate away*). **2** *tr.* whip (cream, eggs, etc.). **3** *tr.* & *intr.* convey or go (esp. out of sight) lightly or quickly (*whisked me off to the doctor*; *the mouse whisked into its hole*). **4** *tr.* wave or lightly brandish. ● *n.* **1** a whisking action or motion. **2** a utensil for whisking eggs or cream etc. **3** a bunch of grass, twigs, bristles, etc., for removing dust or flies. [ME *wisk*, prob. Scand.: cf. ON *visk* wisp]

■ *v.* **1** sweep, brush. **2** whip, beat, fluff up, stir. **3** speed, rush, carry, whip, hasten, hustle, hurry; dart, flit, sweep. ● *n.* **1** sweep, wave, brush, flick. **2** beater, whip. **3** brush, fly-whisk.

whisker /wískər/ *n.* **1** (usu. in *pl.*) the hair growing on a man's face, esp. on the cheek. **2** each of the bristles on the face of a cat etc. **3** *colloq.* a small distance (*within a whisker of*; *won by a whisker*). **4** a strong hairlike crystal of metal etc. □ **have** (or **have grown**) **whiskers** *colloq.* (esp. of a story etc.) be very old. □□ **whiskered** *adj.* **whiskery** *adj.* [WHISK + -ER[1]]

whisky /wíski/ *n.* (*Ir.*, *US* **whiskey**) (*pl.* **-ies** or **-eys**) **1** a spirit distilled esp. from malted barley, other grains, or potatoes, etc. **2** a drink of this. [abbr. of obs. *whiskybae*, var. of USQUEBAUGH]

■ **1** Scotch, rye, *esp. Ir.* & *Sc.* usquebaugh, *US* bourbon, *colloq.* malt, fire-water, *US colloq.* hooch, *sl.* hard stuff, *US sl.* red-eye; *propr.* Drambuie.

whisper /wíspər/ *v.* & *n.* ● *v.* **1** **a** *intr.* speak very softly without vibration of the vocal cords. **b** *intr.* & *tr.* talk or say in a barely audible tone or in a secret or confidential way. **2** *intr.* speak privately or conspiratorially. **3** *intr.* (of leaves, wind, or water) rustle or murmur. ● *n.* **1** whispering speech (*talking in whispers*). **2** a whispering sound. **3** a thing whispered. **4** a rumour or piece of gossip. **5** a brief mention; a hint or suggestion. □ **it is whispered** there is a rumour. **whispering-gallery** a gallery esp. under a dome with acoustic properties such that a whisper may be heard round its entire circumference. ▫▫ **whisperer** *n.* **whispering** *n.* [OE *hwisprian* f. Gmc]

■ *v.* **1** breathe, murmur, mutter, mumble, hiss, speak *or* say softly, speak *or* say under one's breath, sigh. **2** gossip, bruit about, noise abroad, murmur, insinuate, hint, rumour, disclose, divulge, reveal, breathe a word. **3** rustle, swish, sibilate, swoosh, whoosh, hiss, whisk. ● *n.* **1** murmur, undertone, hushed tone(s), *literary* susurration, susurrus. **2** swoosh, whoosh, whisk; see also RUSTLE *n.* **4** rumour, hearsay, gossip. **5** hint, suggestion, inkling, soupçon, suspicion. ▫▫ **whispering** see MURMUR *n.* 1.

whist[1] /wist/ *n.* a card-game usu. for four players, with the winning of tricks. ▫ **whist drive** a social occasion with the playing of progressive whist. [earlier *whisk*, perh. f. WHISK (with ref. to whisking away the tricks): perh. assoc. with WHIST[2]]

whist[2] var. of WHISHT.

whistle /wiss'l/ *n.* & *v.* ● *n.* **1** a clear shrill sound made by forcing breath through a small hole between nearly closed lips. **2** a similar sound made by a bird, the wind, a missile, etc. **3** an instrument used to produce such a sound. ● *v.* **1** *intr.* emit a whistle. **2 a** *intr.* give a signal or express surprise or derision by whistling. **b** *tr.* (often foll. by *up*) summon or give a signal to (a dog etc.) by whistling. **3** *tr.* (also *absol.*) produce (a tune) by whistling. **4** *intr.* (foll. by *for*) vainly seek or desire. ▫ **as clean** (or **clear** or **dry**) **as a whistle** very clean or clear or dry. **blow the whistle on** *colloq.* bring (an activity) to an end; inform on (those responsible). **whistle down the wind 1** let go, abandon. **2** turn (a hawk) loose. **whistle in the dark** pretend to be unafraid. **whistle-stop 1** *US* a small unimportant town on a railway. **2** a politician's brief pause for an electioneering speech on tour. **3** (*attrib.*) with brief pauses (*a whistle-stop tour*). **whistling kettle** a kettle fitted with a whistle sounded by steam when the kettle is boiling. [OE *(h)wistlian* (v.), *(h)wistle* (n.) of imit. orig.: cf. ON *hvísla* whisper, MSw. *hvisla* whistle]

whistler /wislər/ *n.* **1** any bird of the genus *Pachycephala*, with a whistling cry. **2** a kind of marmot.

Whit /wit/ *adj.* connected with, belonging to, or following Whit Sunday (*Whit Monday*; *Whit weekend*). ▫ **Whit Sunday** the seventh Sunday after Easter, commemorating the descent of the Holy Spirit at Pentecost (Acts 2). [OE *Hwīta Sunnandæg*, lit. white Sunday, prob. f. the white robes of the newly-baptized at Pentecost]

whit /wit/ *n.* a particle; a least possible amount (*not a whit better*). ▫ **every whit** the whole; wholly. **no** (or **never a** or **not a**) **whit** not at all. [earlier *w(h)yt* app. alt. f. WIGHT in phr. *no wight* etc.]

■ see PARTICLE 2.

white /wīt/ *adj.*, *n.*, & *v.* ● *adj.* **1** resembling a surface reflecting sunlight without absorbing any of the visible rays; of the colour of milk or fresh snow. **2** approaching such a colour; pale esp. in the face (*turned as white as a sheet*). **3** less dark than other things of the same kind. **4** (**White**) **a** of the human group having light-coloured skin. **b** of or relating to White people. **5** albino (*white mouse*). **6 a** (of hair) having lost its colour esp. in old age. **b** (of a person) white-haired. **7** *colloq.* innocent, untainted. **8** (in *comb.*) (of esp. animals) having some white on the body (*white-throated*). **9 a** (of a plant) having white flowers or pale-coloured fruit etc. (*white hyacinth*; *white cauliflower*). **b** (of a tree) having light-coloured bark etc. (*white ash*; *white poplar*). **10** (of wine) made from white grapes or dark grapes with the skins removed. **11** (of coffee) with milk or cream added. **12** transparent, colourless (*white glass*). **13** *hist.* counter-revolutionary or reactionary (*white guard*; *white army*). ● *n.* **1** a white colour or pigment. **2 a** white clothes or material (*dressed in white*). **b** (in *pl.*) white garments as worn in cricket, tennis, etc. **3 a** (in a game or sport) a white piece, ball, etc. **b** the player using such pieces. **4** the white part or albumen round the yolk of an egg. **5** the visible part of the eyeball round the iris. **6** (**White**) a member of a light-skinned race. **7** a white butterfly. **8** a blank space in printing. ● *v.tr. archaic* make white. ▫ **bleed white** drain (a person, country, etc.) of wealth etc. **white admiral** a butterfly, *Limenitis camilla*, with a white band across its wings. **white ant** a termite. **white cell** (or **corpuscle**) a leucocyte. **white Christmas** Christmas with snow on the ground. **white coal** water as a source of power. **white-collar** (of a worker) engaged in clerical or administrative rather than manual work. **white currant** a cultivar of redcurrant with pale edible berries. **whited sepulchre** see SEPULCHRE. **white dwarf** a small very dense star. **white elephant** a useless and troublesome possession or thing. **white ensign** see ENSIGN. **white feather** a symbol of cowardice (a white feather in the tail of a game-bird being a mark of bad breeding). **white fish** fish with pale flesh, e.g. plaice, cod, etc. **white flag** a symbol of surrender or a period of truce. **White Friar** a Carmelite. **white frost** see FROST. **white goods 1** domestic linen. **2** large domestic electrical equipment. **white heat 1** the temperature at which metal emits white light. **2** a state of intense passion or activity. **white hope** a person expected to achieve much for a group, organization, etc. **white horses** white-crested waves at sea. **white-hot** at white heat. **White House** the official residence of the US President in Washington. **white lead** a mixture of lead carbonate and hydrated lead oxide used as pigment. **white lie** a harmless or trivial untruth. **white light** colourless light, e.g. ordinary daylight. **white lime** lime mixed with water as a coating for walls; whitewash. **white magic** magic used only for beneficent purposes. **white matter** the part of the brain and spinal cord consisting mainly of nerve fibres (see also *grey matter*). **white meat** poultry, veal, rabbit, and pork. **white metal** a white or silvery alloy. **white monk** a Cistercian. **white night** a sleepless night. **white noise** noise containing many frequencies with equal intensities. **white-out** a dense blizzard esp. in polar regions. **white ox-eye** = *ox-eye daisy*. **White Paper** (in the UK) a Government report giving information or proposals on an issue. **white pepper** see PEPPER. **white poplar** = ABELE. **white rose** the emblem of Yorkshire or the House of York. **White Russian** a Belorussian. **white sale** a sale of household linen. **white sauce** a sauce of flour, melted butter, and milk or cream. **White slave** a woman tricked or forced into prostitution, usu. abroad. **White slavery** traffic in White slaves. **white sock** = STOCKING 3. **white spirit** light petroleum as a solvent. **white sugar** purified sugar. **white tie** a man's white bow-tie as part of full evening dress. **white vitriol** *Chem.* zinc sulphate. **white water** a shallow or foamy stretch of water. **white wedding** a wedding at which the bride wears a formal white wedding dress. **white whale** a northern cetacean, *Delphinapterus leucas*, white when adult: also called BELUGA. ▫▫ **whitely** *adv.* **whiteness** *n.* **whitish** *adj.* [OE *hwīt* f. Gmc]

■ *adj.* **1** snow-white, snowy, chalk-white, chalky, ivory, creamy, milky, whitish, milk-white, oyster-white, off-white, lily-white; silver, hoary. **2** pale, pallid, pasty, wan, whey-faced, ashen, bloodless, drained, washed out, whitish, waxen, ghastly, ghostly, anaemic, dead white, deathly white, cadaverous, corpse-like. **4** Caucasian, Caucasoid, light-skinned, fair-skinned, pale-complexioned. **7** innocent, pure, unsullied, untainted, stainless, unblemished, spotless, immaculate, virginal, virtuous, undefiled, chaste. **12** colourless, transparent, see-through, clear, pellucid. ▫ **white-collar** see CLERICAL 2. **white elephant** see LUMBER[2] *n.* 1, 2. **white horses** see WAVE *n.* 1, 2. **white-hot** see HOT *adj.* 1. **white lie** see FIB *n.* **white magic** see MAGIC *n.* 1. ▫▫ **whitish** see WHITE *adj.* 2 above.

whitebait /wītbayt/ *n.* (*pl.* same) **1** (usu. *pl.*) the small silvery-white young of herrings and sprats esp. as food. **2** *NZ* a young inanga.

whitebeam /wītbeem/ *n.* a rosaceous tree, *Sorbus aria*, having red berries and leaves with a white downy under-side.

whiteface /wītfayss/ *n.* the white make-up of an actor etc.

whitefish /wī́tfish/ *n.* (*pl.* same or **-fishes**) any freshwater fish of the genus *Coregonus* etc., of the trout family, and used esp. for food.

whitefly /wī́tflī/ *n.* (*pl.* **-flies**) any small insect of the family Aleyrodidae, having wings covered with white powder and feeding on the sap of shrubs, crops, etc.

Whitehall /wī́t-hawl/ *n.* **1** the British Government. **2** its offices or policy. [a street in London in which Government offices are situated]

whitehead /wī́t-hed/ *n. colloq.* a white or white-topped skin-pustule.

■ see PIMPLE.

whiten /wī́t'n/ *v.tr.* & *intr.* make or become white. □□ **whitener** *n.* **whitening** *n.*

■ see BLEACH *v.*

whitesmith /wī́tsmith/ *n.* **1** a worker in tin. **2** a polisher or finisher of metal goods.

whitethorn /wī́t-thorn/ *n.* the hawthorn.

whitethroat /wī́t-thrōt/ *n.* a warbler, *Sylvia communis*, with a white patch on the throat.

whitewash /wī́twosh/ *n.* & *v.* ● *n.* **1** a solution of quicklime or of whiting and size for whitening walls etc. **2** a means employed to conceal mistakes or faults in order to clear a person or institution of imputations. ● *v.tr.* **1** cover with whitewash. **2** attempt by concealment to clear the reputation of. **3** (in *passive*) (of an insolvent) get a fresh start by passage through a bankruptcy court. **4** *US* defeat (an opponent) without allowing any opposing score. □□ **whitewasher** *n.*

■ *v.* **2** gloss over, cover up, sugar-coat, hide, camouflage, conceal, qualify, minimize, extenuate, diminish, play down, downplay, make light of, rationalize, excuse. **4** see SLAUGHTER *v.* 3.

whitewood /wī́twŏŏd/ *n.* a light-coloured wood esp. prepared for staining etc.

Whitey /wī́ti/ *n.* (*pl.* **-eys**) *sl. offens.* **1** a White person. **2** White people collectively.

whither /wíthər/ *adv.* & *conj. archaic* ● *adv.* **1** to what place, position, or state? **2** (prec. by *place* etc.) to which (*the house whither we were walking*). ● *conj.* **1** to the or any place to which (*go whither you will*). **2** and thither (*we saw a house, whither we walked*). [OE *hwider* f. Gmc: cf. WHICH, HITHER, THITHER]

■ *adv.* **1** see WHEREABOUTS *adv.*

whithersoever /wíthərsō-évvər/ *adj.* & *conj. archaic* to any place to which.

whiting[1] /wī́ting/ *n.* a small white-fleshed fish, *Merlangus merlangus*, used as food. [ME f. MDu. *wijting*, app. formed as WHITE + -ING[3]]

whiting[2] /wī́ting/ *n.* ground chalk used in whitewashing, plate-cleaning, etc.

whitleather /wítlethər/ *n.* tawed leather. [ME f. WHITE + LEATHER]

whitlow /wítlō/ *n.* an inflammation near a fingernail or toenail. [ME *whitflaw*, *-flow*, app. = WHITE + FLAW[1] in the sense 'crack', but perh. of LG orig.: cf. Du. *fijt*, LG *fīt* whitlow]

Whitsun /wíts'n/ *n.* & *adj.* ● *n.* = WHITSUNTIDE. ● *adj.* = WHIT. [ME, f. *Whitsun Day* = Whit Sunday]

Whitsuntide /wíts'ntīd/ *n.* the weekend or week including Whit Sunday.

whittle /wítt'l/ *v.* **1** *tr.* & (foll. by *at*) *intr.* pare (wood etc.) with repeated slicing with a knife. **2** *tr.* (often foll. by *away*, *down*) reduce by repeated subtractions. [var. of ME *thwitel* long knife f. OE *thwītan* to cut off]

■ **1** pare (down *or* away), shave, trim, cut, carve, hew, shape. **2** pare, shave, cut, trim, reduce, diminish, erode, eat away at.

whity /wī́ti/ *adj.* whitish; rather white (usu. in *comb.*: *whity-brown*) (cf. WHITEY).

whiz /wiz/ *n.* & *v.* (also **whizz**) *colloq.* ● *n.* **1** the sound made by the friction of a body moving through the air at great speed. **2** (also **wiz**) *colloq.* a person who is remarkable or skilful in some respect (*is a whiz at chess*). ● *v.intr.* (**whizzed**, **whizzing**) move with or make a whiz. □ **whiz-bang** *colloq.* **1** a high-velocity shell from a small-calibre gun, whose passage is heard before the gun's report. **2** a jumping kind of firework. **whiz-kid** *colloq.* a brilliant or highly successful young person. [imit.: in sense 2 infl. by WIZARD]

■ *n.* **1** whoosh, swish, whistle. **2** see EXPERT *n.* ● *v.* see FLASH *v.* 4b. □ **whiz-kid** see VIRTUOSO 1a.

WHO *abbr.* World Health Organization.

who /hōō/ *pron.* (*obj.* **whom** /hōōm/ or *colloq.* **who**; *poss.* **whose** /hōōz/) **1 a** what or which person or persons? (*who called?*; *you know who it was*; *whom* or *who did you see?*). ¶ In the last example *whom* is correct but *who* is common in less formal contexts. **b** what sort of person or persons? (*who am I to object?*). **2** (a person) that (*anyone who wishes can come*; *the woman whom you met*; *the man who you saw*). ¶ In the last two examples *whom* is correct but *who* is common in less formal contexts. **3** and or but he, she, they, etc. (*gave it to Tom, who sold it to Jim*). **4** *archaic* the or any person or persons that (*whom the gods love die young*). □ **as who should say** like a person who said; as though one said. **who-does-what** (of a dispute etc.) about which group of workers should do a particular job. **who goes there?** see GO[1]. **who's who 1** who or what each person is (*know who's who*). **2** a list or directory with facts about notable persons. [OE *hwā* f. Gmc: *whom* f. OE dative *hwām*, *hwǣm*: *whose* f. genit. *hwæs*]

whoa /wō/ *int.* used as a command to stop or slow a horse etc. [var. of HO]

who'd /hōōd/ *contr.* **1** who had. **2** who would.

whodunit /hōōdúnnit/ *n.* (also **whodunnit**) *colloq.* a story or play about the detection of a crime etc., esp. murder. [= *who done* (illiterate for *did*) *it?*]

■ see MYSTERY[1] 5.

whoe'er /hōō-áir/ *poet.* var. of WHOEVER.

whoever /hōō-évvər/ *pron.* (*obj.* **whomever** /hōōm-/ or *colloq.* **whoever**; *poss.* **whosever** /hōōz-/) **1** the or any person or persons who (*whoever comes is welcome*). **2** though anyone (*whoever else objects, I do not*; *whosever it is, I want it*). **3** *colloq.* (as an intensive) who ever; who at all (*whoever heard of such a thing?*).

whole /hōl/ *adj.* & *n.* ● *adj.* **1** in an uninjured, unbroken, intact, or undiminished state (*swallowed it whole*; *there is not a plate left whole*). **2** not less than; all there is of; entire, complete (*waited a whole year*; *tell the whole truth*; *the whole school knows*). **3** (of blood or milk etc.) with no part removed. **4** (of a person) healthy, recovered from illness or injury. ● *n.* **1** a thing complete in itself. **2** all there is of a thing (*spent the whole of the summer by the sea*). **3** (foll. by *of*) all members, inhabitants, etc., of (*the whole of London knows it*). □ **as a whole** as a unity; not as separate parts. **go the whole hog** see HOG. **on the whole** taking everything relevant into account; in general (*it was, on the whole, a good report*; *they behaved well on the whole*). **whole cloth** cloth of full size as manufactured. **whole holiday** a whole day taken as a holiday (cf. *half holiday*). **whole-life insurance** life insurance for which premiums are payable throughout the remaining life of the person insured. **whole lot** see LOT. **whole note** esp. *US Mus.* = SEMIBREVE. **whole number** a number without fractions; an integer. **whole-tone scale** *Mus.* a scale consisting entirely of tones, with no semitones. □□ **wholeness** *n.* [OE *hāl* f. Gmc]

■ *adj.* **1** entire, complete, full, total, intact, uncut, unbroken, undiminished, unabridged, unabbreviated, undivided; in one piece, unharmed, undamaged, unscathed, unimpaired, unhurt, uninjured. **2** complete, entire, full, total. **4** well, healthy, sound, fit, strong, recovered, healed. ● *n.* **1** ensemble, aggregate, composite; everything; *sl.* whole kit and caboodle. **2** all, entirety, (sum) total, totality, lot. □ **as a whole** see *at large* (LARGE *n.* 2). **on the whole** largely, mostly, usually, more often than not, for the most part, in general, generally, by and large, with few exceptions, all things considered, all in all, altogether, as a rule, chiefly, mainly, in the main, predominantly. ▫▫ **wholeness** see ENTIRETY 1.

wholefood /hṓlfōōd/ *n.* food which has not been unnecessarily processed or refined.

wholegrain /hṓlgrayn/ *adj.* made with or containing whole grains (*wholegrain bread*).

wholehearted /hṓlhaártid/ *adj.* **1** (of a person) completely devoted or committed. **2** (of an action etc.) done with all possible effort, attention, or sincerity; thorough. ▫▫ **wholeheartedly** *adv.* **wholeheartedness** *n.*

▪ devoted, dedicated, committed, earnest, sincere, real, true, genuine, hearty, serious, enthusiastic, zealous, warm, fervent, ardent, spirited, eager, energetic; (*only of an action etc.*) unqualified, unmitigated, unreserved, unequivocal, unconditional, complete, entire, thorough, unstinting, heartfelt. ▫▫ **wholeheartedly** see SINCERELY. **wholeheartedness** see DEDICATION 1.

wholemeal /hṓlmeel/ *n.* (usu. *attrib.*) *Brit.* meal of wheat or other cereals with none of the bran or germ removed.

wholesale /hṓlsayl/ *n.*, *adj.*, *adv.*, & *v.* ● *n.* the selling of things in large quantities to be retailed by others (cf. RETAIL). ● *adj.* & *adv.* **1** by wholesale; at a wholesale price (*can get it for you wholesale*). **2** on a large scale (*wholesale destruction occurred*; *was handing out samples wholesale*). ● *v.tr.* sell wholesale. ▫▫ **wholesaler** *n.* [ME: orig. *by whole sale*]

▪ *adj.* **2** see SWEEPING *adj.* 1.

wholesome /hṓlsəm/ *adj.* **1** promoting or indicating physical, mental, or moral health (*wholesome pursuits*; *a wholesome appearance*). **2** prudent (*wholesome respect*). ▫▫ **wholesomely** *adv.* **wholesomeness** *n.* [ME, prob. f. OE (unrecorded) *hālsum* (as WHOLE, -SOME[1])]

▪ **1** healthful, healthy, health-giving, nutritious, nourishing, beneficial, tonic, salubrious, strengthening, bracing, stimulating; moral, ethical, righteous, upright, honourable, decent, principled, proper, fit, *archaic* meet, salutary. **2** see SOUND[2] *adj.* 3.

wholewheat /hṓlweet/ *n.* (usu. *attrib.*) wheat with none of the bran or germ removed; wholemeal.

wholism var. of HOLISM.

wholly /hṓl-li/ *adv.* **1** entirely; without limitation or diminution (*I am wholly at a loss*). **2** purely, exclusively (*a wholly bad example*). [ME, f. OE (unrecorded) *hāllīce* (as WHOLE, -LY[2])]

▪ **1** altogether, entirely, absolutely, quite, totally, thoroughly, completely, *in toto*, fully, in all respects, in every way, all in all, utterly, unqualifiedly, every inch, a *or* one hundred per cent; lock, stock, and barrel; root and branch; bag and baggage; hook, line, and sinker; to the nth degree, *colloq.* (the) whole hog. **2** only, exclusively, solely, purely, categorically, unequivocally, unambiguously, explicitly.

whom *objective case* of WHO.

whomever *objective case* of WHOEVER.

whomso *archaic objective case* of WHOSO.

whomsoever *objective case* of WHOSOEVER.

whoop /hōōp, wōōp/ *n.* & *v.* (also **hoop**) ● *n.* **1** a loud cry of or as of excitement etc. **2** a long rasping indrawn breath in whooping cough. ● *v.intr.* utter a whoop. ▫ **whooping cough** an infectious bacterial disease, esp. of children, with a series of short violent coughs followed by a whoop. **whooping swan** a swan, *Cygnus cygnus*, with a characteristic whooping sound in flight. **whoop it up** *colloq.* **1** engage in revelry. **2** *US* make a stir. [ME: imit.]

▪ *n.* **1** shout, shriek, yell, roar, bellow, hoot, (battle *or* war) cry, war-whoop, outcry, scream, screech, squeal, yelp, yowl, howl, bark; cheer, hurrah, hurray; *US colloq.* holler. ● *v.* shout, shriek, yell, roar, bellow, hoot, cry (out), scream, screech, squeal, yelp, yowl, howl, bark, *US colloq.* holler; cheer, hurrah. ▫ **whoop it up 1** see REVEL *v.* 1.

whoopee *int.* & *n.* *colloq.* ● *int.* /wŏŏpeé/ expressing exuberant joy. ● *n.* /wŏŏppi/ exuberant enjoyment or revelry. ▫ **make whoopee** *colloq.* rejoice noisily or hilariously. **whoopee cushion** a rubber cushion that when sat on makes a sound like the breaking of wind.

whooper /hōōpər/ *n.* a whooping swan.

whoops /wŏŏps/ *int.* *colloq.* expressing surprise or apology, esp. on making an obvious mistake. [var. of OOPS]

whoosh /wŏŏsh/ *v.*, *n.*, & *int.* (also **woosh**) ● *v.intr.* & *tr.* move or cause to move with a rushing sound. ● *n.* a sudden movement accompanied by a rushing sound. ● *int.* an exclamation imitating this. [imit.]

▪ *v.* see SWISH *v.* ● *n.* see SWISH *n.*

whop /wop/ *v.tr.* (**whopped**, **whopping**) *sl.* **1** thrash. **2** defeat, overcome. [ME: var. of dial. *wap*, of unkn. orig.]

whopper /wóppər/ *n.* *sl.* **1** something big of its kind. **2** a great lie.

whopping /wópping/ *adj.* *sl.* very big (*a whopping lie*; *a whopping fish*).

▪ huge, great, enormous, colossal, gigantic, immense, tremendous, prodigious, monstrous, mammoth, massive; outrageous, extravagant, *colloq.* thumping, terrible, awful.

whore /hor/ *n.* & *v.* ● *n.* **1** a prostitute. **2** *derog.* a promiscuous woman. ● *v.intr.* **1** (of a man) seek or chase after whores. **2** *archaic* (foll. by *after*) commit idolatry or iniquity. ▫ **whore-house** a brothel. ▫▫ **whoredom** *n.* **whorer** *n.* [OE *hōre* f. Gmc]

▪ *n.* **1** see PROSTITUTE *n.* 1a. **2** slattern, sloven, trollop, *derog.* slut, jade, hussy, *sl.* slag. ▫ **whore-house** see BROTHEL.

whoremaster /hórmaastər/ *n.* *archaic* = WHOREMONGER.

whoremonger /hórmunggər/ *n.* *archaic* a sexually promiscuous man; a lecher.

whoreson /hórs'n/ *n.* *archaic* **1** a disliked person. **2** (*attrib.*) (of a person or thing) vile.

whorish /hórish/ *adj.* of or like a whore. ▫▫ **whorishly** *adv.* **whorishness** *n.*

whorl /worl, wurl/ *n.* **1** a ring of leaves or other organs round a stem of a plant. **2** one turn of a spiral, esp. on a shell. **3** a complete circle in a fingerprint. **4** *archaic* a small wheel on a spindle steadying its motion. ▫▫ **whorled** *adj.* [ME *wharwyl*, *whorwil*, app. var. of WHIRL: infl. by *wharve* (n.) = whorl of a spindle]

whortleberry /wúrt'lberri/ *n.* (*pl.* **-ies**) a bilberry. [16th c.: dial. form of *hurtleberry*, ME, of unkn. orig.]

whose /hōōz/ *pron.* & *adj.* ● *pron.* of or belonging to which person (*whose is this book?*). ● *adj.* of whom or which (*whose book is this?*; *the man, whose name was Tim*; *the house whose roof was damaged*).

whoseso *archaic poss.* of WHOSO.

whosesoever *poss.* of WHOSOEVER.

whosever /hōōzévvər/ *poss.* of WHOEVER.

whoso /hōōssō/ *pron.* (*obj.* **whomso** /hōōm-/; *poss.* **whoseso** /hōōz-/) *archaic* = WHOEVER. [ME, = WHO + SO[1], f. OE *swā hwā swā*]

whosoever /hōōssō-évvər/ *pron.* (*obj.* **whomsoever** /hōōm-/; *poss.* **whosesoever** /hōōz-/) *archaic* = WHOEVER.

why /wī/ *adv.*, *int.*, & *n.* ● *adv.* **1 a** for what reason or purpose (*why did you do it?*; *I do not know why you came*). **b** on what grounds (*why do you say that?*). **2** (prec. by *reason* etc.) for which (*the reasons why I did it*). ● *int.* expressing: **1** surprised discovery or recognition (*why, it's you!*). **2** impatience (*why, of course I do!*). **3** reflection (*why, yes, I think so*). **4** objection (*why, what is wrong with it?*). ● *n.* (*pl.* **whys**) a reason or explanation (esp. *whys and wherefores*). ▫ **why so?** on what grounds?; for what reason or purpose? [OE *hwī*, *hwȳ* instr. of *hwæt* WHAT f. Gmc]

whydah /weédə/ *n.* (also **whidah**) any small African weaver-bird of the genus *Vidua*, the male having mainly black plumage and tail-feathers of great length. [orig. *widow-bird*, altered f. assoc. with *Whidah* (now Ouidah) in Benin]

WI *abbr.* **1** West Indies. **2** *Brit.* Women's Institute. **3** *US* Wisconsin (in official postal use).

wich- var. of WYCH-.

wick[1] /wik/ *n.* **1** a strip or thread of fibrous or spongy material feeding a flame with fuel in a candle, lamp, etc. **2** *Surgery* a gauze strip inserted in a wound to drain it. □ **dip one's wick** *coarse sl.* (of a man) have sexual intercourse. **get on a person's wick** *Brit. colloq.* annoy a person. [OE *wēoce*, *-wēoc* (cf. MDu. *wiecke*, MLG *wēke*), of unkn. orig.]

wick[2] /wik/ *n. dial.* exc. in compounds e.g. *bailiwick*, and in place-names e.g. *Hampton Wick*, *Warwick* **1** a town, hamlet, or district. **2** a dairy farm. [OE *wīc*, prob. f. Gmc f. L *vicus* street, village]

wicked /wíkkid/ *adj.* (**wickeder**, **wickedest**) **1** sinful, iniquitous, given to or involving immorality. **2** spiteful, ill-tempered; intending or intended to give pain. **3** playfully malicious. **4** *colloq.* foul; very bad; formidable (*wicked weather*; *a wicked cough*). **5** *sl.* excellent, remarkable. □ **Wicked Bible** an edition of 1631, with the misprinted commandment 'thou shalt commit adultery'. □□ **wickedly** *adv.* **wickedness** *n.* [ME f. obs. *wick* (perh. adj. use of OE *wicca* wizard) + -ED[1] as in *wretched*]

■ **1** evil, bad, immoral, amoral, unprincipled, sinful, impious, irreligious, blasphemous, profane, sacrilegious, ungodly, godless, diabolic(al), satanic, Mephistophelian, demonic, demoniac(al), hellish, infernal, accursed, damnable, fiendish, ghoulish; depraved, dissolute, villainous, black-hearted, iniquitous, nefarious, horrible, horrid, hideous, heinous, beastly, base, low, vile, debased, degenerate, perverse, perverted, corrupt, foul, offensive, abominable, disgraceful, shameful, scandalous, dreadful, awful, gross, gruesome, grim, appalling, grisly, loathsome, lawless, unrepentant, unregenerate, incorrigible, criminal, felonious, knavish, terrible, egregious, execrable; dirty, pornographic, filthy, erotic, obscene, lewd, offensive, indecent, prurient, smutty, rude, taboo, blue, coarse, bawdy, vulgar, salacious, licentious, nasty, *colloq.* raunchy, *often joc.* rascally. **2** vicious, beastly, savage, cruel, nasty, bad, violent, mean, spiteful, ill-tempered, malicious, malignant, malevolent, vindictive. **3** naughty, mischievous, impish, sly, devilish, roguish, scampish, knavish, puckish, *often joc.* rascally; vexatious, exasperating, annoying, irritating, irksome, trying, galling, bothersome. **4** foul, offensive, pernicious, baleful, baneful, mephitic, disgusting, revolting, sickening, repulsive, repellent, objectionable, nauseous, nauseating, repugnant, rotten, pestilential, noxious, formidable, *sl.* stinking, dreadful. **5** expert, ingenious, superior, superb, superlative, excellent, outstanding, remarkable, masterful, masterly, skilful, deft, adept, *esp. US sl.* bad. □□ **wickedly** see BADLY 1. **wickedness** see EVIL *n.* 2.

wicker /wíkkər/ *n.* plaited twigs or osiers etc. as material for chairs, baskets, mats, etc. [ME, f. E.Scand.: cf. Sw. *viker* willow, rel. to *vika* bend]

wickerwork /wíkkərwurk/ *n.* **1** wicker. **2** things made of wicker.

wicket /wíkit/ *n.* **1** *Cricket* **a** a set of three stumps with the bails in position defended by a batsman. **b** the ground between two wickets. **c** the state of this (*a slow wicket*). **d** an instance of a batsman being got out (*bowler has taken four wickets*). **e** a pair of batsmen batting at the same time (*a third-wicket partnership*). **2** (in full **wicket-door** or **-gate**) a small door or gate esp. beside or in a larger one or closing the lower part only of a doorway. **3** *US* an aperture in a door or wall usu. closed with a sliding panel. **4** *US* a croquet hoop. □ **at the wicket** *Cricket* **1** batting. **2** by the wicket-keeper (*caught at the wicket*). **keep wicket** *Cricket* be a wicket-keeper. **on a good** (or **sticky**) **wicket** *colloq.* in a favourable (or unfavourable) position. **wicket-keeper** *Cricket* the fielder stationed close behind a batsman's wicket. [ME f. AF & ONF *wiket*, OF *guichet*, of uncert. orig.]

wickiup /wíkkiup/ *n.* an American Indian hut of a frame covered with grass etc. [Fox *wikiyap*]

widdershins var. of WITHERSHINS.

wide /wīd/ *adj.*, *adv.*, & *n.* ● *adj.* **1 a** measuring much or more than other things of the same kind across or from side to side. **b** considerable; more than is needed (*a wide margin*). **2** (following a measurement) in width (*a metre wide*). **3** extending far; embracing much; of great extent (*has a wide range*; *has wide experience*; *reached a wide public*). **4** not tight or close or restricted; loose. **5 a** free, liberal; unprejudiced (*takes wide views*). **b** not specialized; general. **6** open to the full extent (*staring with wide eyes*). **7 a** (foll. by *of*) not within a reasonable distance of. **b** at a considerable distance from a point or mark. **8** *Brit. sl.* shrewd; skilled in sharp practice (*wide boy*). **9** (in *comb.*) extending over the whole of (*nationwide*). ● *adv.* **1** widely. **2** to the full extent (*wide awake*). **3** far from the target etc. (*is shooting wide*). ● *n.* **1** *Cricket* a ball judged to pass the wicket beyond the batsman's reach and so scoring a run. **2** (prec. by *the*) the wide world. □ **give a wide berth to** see BERTH. **wide-angle** (of a lens) having a short focal length and hence a field covering a wide angle. **wide awake 1** fully awake. **2** *colloq.* wary, knowing. **wide ball** *Cricket* (sense 1 of *n.*). **wide-eyed** surprised or naïve. **wide of the mark** see MARK[1]. **wide open** (often foll. by *to*) exposed or vulnerable (to attack etc.). **wide-ranging** covering an extensive range. **the wide world** all the world great as it is. □□ **wideness** *n.* **widish** *adj.* [OE *wīd* (adj.), *wīde* (adv.) f. Gmc]

■ *adj.* **1 a** spacious, roomy, ample, extensive, expansive, broad, vast. **b** considerable, substantial, sizeable, major, big, large, extreme. **3** broad, extensive, comprehensive, encyclopedic, (all-)inclusive, all-embracing, all-encompassing, far-reaching, wide-ranging, widespread, sweeping. **4** full, ample, generous; see also LOOSE *adj.* 3–5. **5 a** broad, broad-minded, free, liberal, tolerant, unprejudiced, latitudinarian. **b** general, non-specialized, non-specific, global, overall, universal, generalized. ● *adv.* **1** widely, far apart, stretched out. **2** all the way, as much as possible, fully, completely, to the utmost. **3** astray, afield, wide of the mark, off the mark, off (the) target, off course, not on target, to one side. □ **wide awake 1** see AWAKE *adj.* 1a. **2** see ALERT *adj.* 1. **wide-eyed** see *goggle-eyed*, GULLIBLE. **wide open** open, exposed, unprotected, undefended, unguarded, vulnerable. **wide-ranging** see EXTENSIVE 2. □□ **wideness** see WIDTH 1.

wideawake /wī́dəwáyk/ *n.* a soft felt hat with a low crown and wide brim.

widely /wī́dli/ *adv.* **1** to a wide extent; far apart. **2** extensively (*widely read*; *widely distributed*). **3** by many people (*it is widely thought that*). **4** considerably; to a large degree (*holds a widely different view*).

■ **2** see *far and wide*. **3** extensively, thoroughly, universally, everywhere, generally, popularly, by many. **4** to a large *or* great extent, greatly, largely, very much, extremely, considerably, substantially.

widen /wī́d'n/ *v.tr.* & *intr.* make or become wider. □□ **widener** *n.*

■ distend, dilate, open out, spread, stretch, enlarge, increase, expand; extend, broaden, supplement, add to, augment.

widespread /wī́dspréd/ *adj.* widely distributed or disseminated.

■ see EXTENSIVE 2.

widgeon /wíjən/ *n.* (also **wigeon**) a species of dabbling duck, esp. *Anas penelope* or *Anas americana*. [16th c.: orig. uncert.]

widget /wíjit/ *n. colloq.* any gadget or device. [perh. alt. of GADGET]

■ see GADGET.

widgie /wíji/ *n. Austral. colloq.* the female counterpart of a bodgie (see BODGIE 1). [20th c.: orig. unkn.]

widow /wíddō/ *n.* & *v.* ● *n.* **1** a woman who has lost her husband by death and has not married again. **2** a woman whose husband is often away on a specified activity (*golf widow*). **3** extra cards dealt separately and taken by the highest bidder. **4** *Printing* the short last line of a paragraph at the top of a page or column. ● *v.tr.* **1** make into a widow or widower. **2** (as **widowed** *adj.*) bereft by the death of a spouse (*my widowed mother*). **3** (foll. by *of*) deprive of. ▫ **widow-bird** a whydah. **widow's cruse** an apparently small supply that proves or seems inexhaustible (see 1 Kgs. 17:10–16). **widow's mite** a small money contribution (see Mark 12:42). **widow's peak** a V-shaped growth of hair towards the centre of the forehead. **widow's weeds** see WEEDS. [OE *widewe*, rel. to OHG *wituwa*, Skr. *vidhávā*, L *viduus* bereft, widowed, Gk *ēitheos* unmarried man]

widower /wíddōər/ *n.* a man who has lost his wife by death and has not married again.

widowhood /wíddōhŏŏd/ *n.* the state or period of being a widow.

width /witth, width/ *n.* **1** measurement or distance from side to side. **2** a large extent. **3** breadth or liberality of thought, views, etc. **4** a strip of material of full width as woven. ▫▫ **widthways** *adv.* **widthwise** *adv.* [17th c. (as WIDE, -TH[2]) replacing *wideness*]

▪ **1** breadth, wideness, compass, broadness, span; diameter, calibre, bore; measure; *Naut.* beam. **2** reach, scope, range, breadth, extent, extensiveness. **3** see BREADTH 4.

wield /weeld/ *v.tr.* **1** hold and use (a weapon or tool). **2** exert or command (power or authority etc.). ▫▫ **wielder** *n.* [OE *wealdan*, *wieldan* f. Gmc]

▪ **1** flourish, swing, brandish, wave, handle, ply, use, employ. **2** exercise, employ, exert, command, use, utilize.

wieldy /wéeldi/ *adj.* (**wieldier**, **wieldiest**) easily wielded, controlled, or handled.

Wiener schnitzel /véenər shníts'l/ *n.* a veal escalope breaded, fried, and garnished. [G, = Viennese slice]

wife /wīf/ *n.* (*pl.* **wives** /wīvz/) **1** a married woman esp. in relation to her husband. **2** *archaic* a woman, esp. an old or uneducated one. **3** (in *comb.*) a woman engaged in a specified activity (*fishwife*; *housewife*; *midwife*). ▫ **have** (or **take**) **to wife** *archaic* marry (a woman). **wife-swapping** *colloq.* exchanging wives for sexual relations. ▫▫ **wifehood** *n.* **wifeless** *adj.* **wifelike** *adj.* **wifely** *adj.* **wifeliness** *n.* **wifish** *adj.* [OE *wīf* woman: ult. orig. unkn.]

▪ **1** mate, helpmate, spouse, bride, partner, *colloq.* better half, old lady *or* woman, *colloq. or joc.* her indoors, *colloq. often derog.* little woman, *joc.* lady wife, *rhyming sl.* trouble and strife; *sl. or joc.* the missis.

wig[1] /wig/ *n.* an artificial head of hair esp. to conceal baldness or as a disguise, or worn by a judge or barrister or as period dress. ▫▫ **wigged** *adj.* (also in *comb.*). **wigless** *adj.* [abbr. of PERIWIG: cf. WINKLE]

wig[2] /wig/ *v.tr.* (**wigged**, **wigging**) *colloq.* rebuke sharply; rate. [app. f. WIG[1] in sl. or colloq. sense 'rebuke' (19th c.)]

▪ see REBUKE *v.*

wigeon var. of WIDGEON.

wigging /wígging/ *n. colloq.* a reprimand.

▪ see REPRIMAND *n.*

wiggle /wígg'l/ *v.* & *n. colloq.* ● *v.intr.* & *tr.* move or cause to move quickly from side to side etc. ● *n.* an act of wiggling. ▫ **get a wiggle on** esp. *US sl.* hurry up. ▫▫ **wiggler** *n.* [ME f. MLG & MDu. *wiggelen*: cf. WAG[1], WAGGLE]

▪ *v.* see WAG[1] *v.* 1. ● *n.* see WAG[1] *n.*

wiggly /wígli/ *adj.* (**wigglier**, **wiggliest**) *colloq.* **1** showing wiggles. **2** having small irregular undulations.

wight /wīt/ *n. archaic* a person (*wretched wight*). [OE *wiht* = thing, creature, of unkn. orig.]

wigwag /wígwag/ *v.intr.* (**wigwagged**, **wigwagging**) *colloq.* **1** move lightly to and fro. **2** wave flags in this way in signalling. [redupl. f. WAG[1]]

wigwam /wígwam/ *n.* **1** a N. American Indian's hut or tent of skins, mats, or bark on poles. **2** a similar structure for children etc. [Ojibwa *wigwaum*, Algonquian *wikiwam* their house]

wilco /wílkō/ *int. colloq.* expressing compliance or agreement, esp. acceptance of instructions received by radio. [abbr. of *will comply*]

wild /wīld/ *adj.*, *adv.*, & *n.* ● *adj.* **1** (of an animal or plant) in its original natural state; not domesticated or cultivated (esp. of species or varieties allied to others that are not wild). **2** not civilized; barbarous. **3** (of scenery etc.) having a conspicuously desolate appearance. **4** unrestrained, disorderly, uncontrolled (*a wild youth*; *wild hair*). **5** tempestuous, violent (*a wild night*). **6 a** intensely eager; excited, frantic (*wild with excitement*; *wild delight*). **b** (of looks, appearance, etc.) indicating distraction. **c** (foll. by *about*) *colloq.* enthusiastically devoted to (a person or subject). **7** *colloq.* infuriated, angry (*makes me wild*). **8** haphazard, ill-aimed, rash (*a wild guess*; *a wild shot*; *a wild venture*). **9** (of a horse, game-bird, etc.) shy; easily startled. **10** *colloq.* exciting, delightful. **11** (of a card) having any rank chosen by the player holding it (*the joker is wild*). ● *adv.* in a wild manner (*shooting wild*). ● *n.* **1** a wild tract. **2** a desert. ▫ **in the wild** in an uncultivated etc. state. **in** (or **out in**) **the wilds** *colloq.* far from normal habitation. **run wild** grow or stray unchecked or undisciplined. **sow one's wild oats** see OAT. **wild and woolly** uncouth; lacking refinement. **wild boar** see BOAR. **wild card 1** see sense 11 of *adj.* **2** *Computing* a character that will match any character or sequence of characters in a file name etc. **3** *Sport* an extra player or team chosen to enter a competition at the selectors' discretion. **wild cat** any of various smallish cats, esp. the European *Felis sylvestris* (cf. WILDCAT). **wild-goose chase** a foolish or hopeless and unproductive quest. **wild horse 1** a horse not domesticated or broken in. **2** (in *pl.*) *colloq.* even the most powerful influence etc. (*wild horses would not drag the secret from me*). **wild hyacinth** = BLUEBELL 1. **wild man of the woods** *colloq.* an orang-utan. **wild rice** any tall grass of the genus *Zizania*, yielding edible grains. **wild silk 1** silk from wild silkworms. **2** an imitation of this from short silk fibres. **Wild West** the western US in a time of lawlessness in its early history. ▫▫ **wildish** *adj.* **wildly** *adv.* **wildness** *n.* [OE *wilde* f. Gmc]

▪ *adj.* **1** undomesticated, untamed, unbroken, savage, feral; natural, uncultivated. **2** savage, uncivilized, barbarous, primitive, rude, uncultured, uncultivated, brutish, barbaric, fierce, ferocious. **3** uncultivated, uninhabited, waste, desert, deserted, desolate, virgin, unpopulated, empty, trackless, barren, lifeless; rugged, rough. **4** uncontrolled, unrestricted, unrestrained, untrammelled, unbridled, unfettered, unshackled, free, unchecked, uninhibited, impetuous, unconventional, undisciplined, disobedient, insubordinate, obstreperous, self-willed, wayward, mutinous, rowdy(ish), boisterous, tumultuous, unruly, uproarious, chaotic; uncontrollable, unmanageable, ungovernable, intractable, unrestrainable; disordered, disorderly, dishevelled, unkempt, untidy, tousled, wind-blown, messed-up, *US colloq.* mussed-up. **5** tempestuous, turbulent, violent; see also STORMY 1, 2. **6 a, b** excited, eager, vehement, passionate, mad, maniac(al), crazed, crazy, frenzied, frantic, distracted, distraught, hysterical, raving, raging, demented, delirious, berserk. **c** enthusiastic, avid, eager, mad, excited, infatuated, passionate, *colloq.* crazy, dotty, nuts, *esp. Brit. colloq.* daft, *sl.* nutty, *Brit. sl.* potty. **7** see FURIOUS 1, 2. **8** haphazard, random, ill-aimed, absurd, crazy, irrational, unreasonable, unthinking, extravagant, fantastic, imprudent, foolish, foolhardy, ill-conceived, impractical, impracticable, unpractical, unworkable, ridiculous, reckless, rash, silly, giddy, flighty, madcap, outrageous, preposterous, offbeat, *colloq.* cock-eyed. **10** see *thrilling* (THRILL). ● *n.* waste, wasteland, wilderness, desert; vastness, emptiness. ▫ **in** (or **out in**) **the wilds** in the back of beyond, in the backwoods, in the bush, *esp. Austral.* in the outback, *colloq.* in the middle of nowhere, in the sticks, *Austral.* & *NZ sl.* in Woop Woop, *US sl.* in the boondocks. **wild horse 1** bronco, *Austral.* brumby. ▫▫ **wildly** see MADLY 2. **wildness** see NATURE 6, VIOLENCE 1.

wildcat /wīldkat/ *n.* & *adj.* ● *n.* **1** a hot-tempered or violent person. **2** *US* a bobcat see *wild cat.* **3** an exploratory oil

well. ● *adj.* (*attrib.*) **1** esp. *US* reckless; financially unsound. **2** (of a strike) sudden and unofficial.
■ *adj.* **1** see RECKLESS.

wildebeest /wíldəbeest, víl-/ *n.* = GNU. [Afrik. (as WILD, BEAST)]

wilder /wíldər/ *v.tr. archaic* **1** lead astray. **2** bewilder. [perh. based on WILDERNESS]

wilderness /wíldərniss/ *n.* **1** a desert; an uncultivated and uninhabited region. **2** part of a garden left with an uncultivated appearance. **3** (foll. by *of*) a confused assemblage of things. □ **in the wilderness** out of political office. **voice in the wilderness** an unheeded advocate of reform (see Matt. 3:3 etc.). [OE *wildēornes* f. *wild dēor* wild deer]
■ **1** see DESERT[2] *n.* **2** jungle.

wildfire /wīldfīr/ *n. hist.* **1** a combustible liquid, esp. Greek fire, formerly used in warfare. **2** = WILL-O'-THE-WISP. □ **spread like wildfire** spread with great speed.

wildfowl /wīldfowl/ *n.* (*pl.* same) a game-bird, esp. an aquatic one.

wilding /wīlding/ *n.* (also **wildling** /-ling/) **1** a plant sown by natural agency, esp. a wild crab-apple. **2** the fruit of such a plant. [WILD + -ING[3]]

wildlife /wīldlīf/ *n.* wild animals collectively.

wildwood /wīldwŏŏd/ *n. poet.* uncultivated or unfrequented woodland.

wile /wīl/ *n.* & *v.* ● *n.* (usu. in *pl.*) a stratagem; a trick or cunning procedure. ● *v.tr.* (foll. by *away*, *into*, etc.) lure or entice. [ME *wīl*, perh. f. Scand. (ON *vél* craft)]
■ *n.* trick, stratagem, ruse, artifice, subterfuge, dodge, trap, snare, manoeuvre, contrivance, move, gambit, plot, scheme, machination, (little) game, *colloq.* ploy. ● *v.* see ENTICE.

wilful /wílfŏŏl/ *adj.* (*US* **willful**) **1** (of an action or state) intentional, deliberate (*wilful murder*; *wilful neglect*; *wilful disobedience*). **2** (of a person) obstinate, headstrong. □□ **wilfully** *adv.* **wilfulness** *n.* [ME f. WILL[2] + -FUL]
■ **1** intentional, deliberate, voluntary, conscious, intended, purposeful, premeditated. **2** stubborn, headstrong, pigheaded, obstinate, mulish, inflexible, adamant, obdurate, intransigent, unyielding, self-willed, ungovernable, recalcitrant, unruly, immovable, intractable, dogged, determined, refractory, uncompromising, wayward, perverse, contrary. □□ **wilfully** see *deliberately* (DELIBERATE). **wilfulness** see *obstinacy* (OBSTINATE).

wilga /wílgə/ *n. Austral.* a small tree of the genus *Geijera*, with white flowers. [Aboriginal]

wiliness see WILY.

will[1] /wil/ *v.aux.* & *tr.* (*3rd sing. present* **will**; *past* **would** /wŏŏd/) (foll. by infin. without *to*, or *absol.*; present and past only in use) **1** (in the 2nd and 3rd persons, and often in the 1st: see SHALL) expressing the future tense in statements, commands, or questions (*you will regret this*; *they will leave at once*; *will you go to the party?*). **2** (in the 1st person) expressing a wish or intention (*I will return soon*). ¶ For the other persons in senses 1, 2, see SHALL. **3** expressing desire, consent, or inclination (*will you have a sandwich?*; *come when you will*; *the door will not open*). **4** expressing ability or capacity (*the jar will hold a kilo*). **5** expressing habitual or inevitable tendency (*accidents will happen*; *will sit there for hours*). **6** expressing probability or expectation (*that will be my wife*). □ **will do** *colloq.* expressing willingness to carry out a request. [OE *wyllan*, (unrecorded) *willan* f. Gmc: rel. to L *volo*]

will[2] /wil/ *n.* & *v.* ● *n.* **1** the faculty by which a person decides or is regarded as deciding on and initiating action (*the mind consists of the understanding and the will*). **2** (also **will-power**) control exercised by deliberate purpose over impulse; self-control (*has a strong will*; *overcame his shyness by will-power*). **3** a deliberate or fixed desire or intention (*a will to live*). **4** energy of intention; the power of effecting one's intentions or dominating others. **5** directions (usu. written) in legal form for the disposition of one's property after death (*make one's will*). **6** disposition towards others (*good will*). **7** *archaic* what one desires or ordains (*thy will be done*). ● *v.tr.* **1** have as the object of one's will; intend unconditionally (*what God wills*; *willed that we should succeed*). **2** (*absol.*) exercise will-power. **3** instigate or impel or compel by the exercise of will-power (*you can will yourself into contentment*). **4** bequeath by the terms of a will (*shall will my money to charity*). □ **at will 1** whenever one pleases. **2** *Law* able to be evicted without notice (*tenant at will*). **have one's will** obtain what one wants. **what is your will?** what do you wish done? **where there's a will there's a way** determination will overcome any obstacle. **a will of one's own** obstinacy; wilfulness of character. **with the best will in the world** however good one's intentions. **with a will** energetically or resolutely. □□ **willed** *adj.* (also in *comb.*). **willer** *n.* **will-less** *adj.* [OE *willa* f. Gmc]
■ *n.* **2** will-power, self-control, resolve, commitment, resolution, determination, volition, fortitude, *colloq.* guts. **3** desire, wish, longing, liking, inclination, disposition, intent, intention, resolve, commitment, resolution, determination. **4** drive, purposefulness, purpose, intent, intention, motivation. **5** (last will and) testament, last wishes. **6** disposition, attitude, feeling(s), intentions. **7** choice, wishes, desire, inclination. ● *v.* **1** want, desire, wish, choose, intend, command, order, ordain, require, see fit. **3** make, compel, force, instigate, impel. **4** leave, bequeath, hand down *or* on, pass on, transfer; *Law* devise. □ **at will 1** as *or* when one pleases, as *or* when one wishes, as *or* when one thinks fit(ting), at one's desire *or* whim *or* discretion, *formal* at one's pleasure.

willet /wíllit/ *n.* (*pl.* same) a large N. American wader, *Catoptrophorus semipalmatus*. [*pill-will-willet*, imit. of its cry]

willful *US* var. of WILFUL.

willie var. of WILLY.

willies /wíliz/ *n.pl. colloq.* nervous discomfort (esp. *give* or *get the willies*). [19th c.: orig. unkn.]
■ see JITTER *n.*

willing /wílling/ *adj.* & *n.* ● *adj.* **1** ready to consent or undertake (*a willing ally*; *am willing to do it*). **2** given or done etc. by a willing person (*willing hands*; *willing help*). ● *n.* cheerful intention (*show willing*). □□ **willingly** *adv.* **willingness** *n.*
■ *adj.* **1** agreeable, acquiescent, compliant, amenable, consenting, assenting, complaisant, ready, well-disposed, inclined, prepared, happy, content, pleased, delighted, enthusiastic, avid, eager, zealous, keen, game. □□ **willingly** readily, happily, contentedly, gladly, cheerfully, amenably, agreeably, freely, of one's own accord *or* free will, on one's own, ungrudgingly, by choice, voluntarily, unhesitatingly, nothing loath, eagerly, enthusiastically, zealously, avidly, at the drop of a hat.

will-o'-the-wisp /wíllə<u>th</u>əwisp/ *n.* **1** a phosphorescent light seen on marshy ground, perhaps resulting from the combustion of gases. **2** an elusive person. **3** a delusive hope or plan. [orig. *Will with the wisp*: *wisp* = handful of (lighted) hay etc.]
■ **3** see ILLUSION 4.

willow /wíllō/ *n.* **1** a tree or shrub of the genus *Salix*, growing usu. near water in temperate climates, with small flowers borne on catkins, and pliant branches yielding osiers and timber for cricket-bats, baskets, etc. **2** a cricket-bat. □ **willow grouse** a common European grouse, *Lagopus lagopus*, with brown breeding plumage and white winter plumage. **willow-herb** any plant of the genus *Epilobium* etc., esp. one with leaves like a willow and pale purple flowers. **willow-pattern** a conventional design representing a Chinese scene, often with a willow tree, of blue on white porcelain, stoneware, or earthenware. **willow-warbler** (or **-wren**) a small woodland bird, *Phylloscopus trochilus*, with a tuneful song. [OE *welig*]

willowy /wíllō-i/ *adj.* **1** having or bordered by willows. **2** lithe and slender.
■ **2** lissom, pliant, lithe, flexible, supple, limber, loose-limbed; slim, slender, graceful, sylphlike, svelte, thin, long-limbed, clean(-limbed).

willy /wílli/ *n.* (also **willie**) (*pl.* **-ies**) *Brit. sl.* the penis.

willy-nilly /willinílli/ *adv.* & *adj.* ● *adv.* whether one likes it or not. ● *adj.* existing or occurring willy-nilly. [later spelling of *will I, nill I* I am willing, I am unwilling]
■ *adv.* whether one likes it or not, inevitably, necessarily, of necessity, one way or the other, *archaic* perforce, *colloq.* like it or not, so there, *literary nolens volens* . ● *adj.* necessary, unavoidable, inevitable, involuntary.

willy-willy /williwilli/ *n.* (*pl.* **-ies**) *Austral.* a cyclone or dust-storm. [Aboriginal]

wilt[1] /wilt/ *v.* & *n.* ● *v.* **1** *intr.* (of a plant, leaf, or flower) wither, droop. **2** *intr.* (of a person) lose one's energy, flag, tire, droop. **3** *tr.* cause to wilt. ● *n.* a plant-disease causing wilting. [orig. dial.: perh. alt. f. *wilk, welk,* of LG or Du. orig.]
■ *v.* **1** sag, droop, wither, shrink, shrivel (up *or* away), flop, diminish. **2** sag, droop, bow, weaken, sink, wane, wither, lose courage *or* nerve, flag, dwindle, languish, tire.

wilt[2] /wilt/ *archaic 2nd person sing.* of WILL[1].

Wilton /wíltən/ *n.* a kind of woven carpet with a thick pile. [*Wilton* in S. England]

Wilts. /wilts/ *abbr.* Wiltshire.

wily /wīli/ *adj.* (**wilier, wiliest**) full of wiles; crafty, cunning. □□ **wilily** *adv.* **wiliness** *n.*
■ shrewd, cunning, crafty, sly, artful, guileful, clever, foxy, vulpine, disingenuous, scheming, plotting, calculating, designing, sharp, canny, deceitful, deceiving, deceptive, treacherous, perfidious, false, double-dealing, dishonest, underhand(ed), tricky, smooth, slick, slippery, oily, unctuous, *colloq.* cagey, shifty, crooked, two-timing, *Brit. sl.* fly, *Sc.* & *dial.* pawky.

wimp /wimp/ *n. colloq.* a feeble or ineffectual person. □□ **wimpish** *adj.* **wimpishly** *adv.* **wimpishness** *n.* **wimpy** *adj.* [20th c.: orig. uncert.]
■ see DRIP *n.* 2.

wimple /wímp'l/ *n.* & *v.* ● *n.* a linen or silk head-dress covering the neck and the sides of the face, formerly worn by women and still worn by some nuns. ● *v.tr.* & *intr.* arrange or fall in folds. [OE *wimpel*]

Wimpy /wímpi/ *n.* (*pl.* **-ies**) *propr.* a hamburger served in a plain bun.

Wimshurst machine /wímzhurst/ *n.* a device for generating an electric charge by turning glass discs in opposite directions. [J. *Wimshurst*, Engl. engineer d. 1903]

win /win/ *v.* & *n.* ● *v.* (**winning**; *past* and *past part.* **won** /wun/) **1** *tr.* acquire or secure as a result of a fight, contest, bet, litigation, or some other effort (*won some money*; *won my admiration*). **2** *tr.* be victorious in (a fight, game, race, etc.). **3** *intr.* **a** be the victor; win a race or contest etc. (*who won?*; *persevere, and you will win*). **b** (foll. by *through, free,* etc.) make one's way or become by successful effort. **4** *tr.* reach by effort (*win the summit*; *win the shore*). **5** *tr.* obtain (ore) from a mine. **6** *tr.* dry (hay etc.) by exposure to the air. ● *n.* victory in a game or bet etc. □ **win the day** be victorious in battle, argument, etc. **win over** persuade, gain the support of. **win one's spurs 1** *colloq.* gain distinction or fame. **2** *hist.* gain a knighthood. **win through** (or **out**) overcome obstacles. **you can't win** *colloq.* there is no way to succeed. **you can't win them all** *colloq.* a resigned expression of consolation on failure. □□ **winnable** *adj.* [OE *winnan* toil, endure: cf. OHG *winnan*, ON *vinna*]
■ *v.* **1** gain, carry off *or* away, bear off *or* away, attain, acquire, get, obtain, secure, procure, receive, collect, net, earn, achieve, realize, pick up, glean, *colloq.* bag, walk off *or* away with. **2** finish first in, achieve first place in, triumph in, be victorious in, be the victor in, gain a victory in, prevail in, succeed in, carry off, take first prize in. **3 a** come (in *or* out) first, finish first, achieve first place, carry the day, carry off the palm, win the day, conquer, overcome, triumph, be victorious, be the victor, gain a victory, prevail, succeed, take first prize, *colloq.* bring home the bacon. **4** reach, attain, arrive at, get to, *colloq.* make it to. ● *n.* victory, conquest, triumph, success. □ **win over** influence, sway, incline, persuade, charm, prevail upon, convert, induce, bring round, gain the support of, convince.

wince[1] /winss/ *n.* & *v.* ● *n.* a start or involuntary shrinking movement showing pain or distress. ● *v.intr.* give a wince. □□ **wincer** *n.* **wincingly** *adv.* [ME f. OF *guenchir* turn aside: cf. WINCH, WINK]
■ *v.* see CRINGE *v.* 1.

wince[2] /winss/ *n.* a roller for moving textile fabric through a dyeing-vat. [var. of WINCH]

wincey /wínsi/ *n.* (*pl.* **winceys**) a strong lightweight fabric of wool and cotton or linen. [orig. Sc.: app. f. *woolsey* in LINSEY-WOOLSEY]

winceyette /winsi-ét/ *n. Brit.* a lightweight napped flannelette used esp. for nightclothes.

winch /winch/ *n.* & *v.* ● *n.* **1** the crank of a wheel or axle. **2** a windlass. **3** the reel of a fishing-rod. **4** = WINCE[2]. ● *v.tr.* lift with a winch. □□ **wincher** *n.* [OE *wince* f. Gmc: cf. WINCE[1]]

Winchester /wínchistər/ *n.* **1** *propr.* a breech-loading repeating rifle. **2** (in full **Winchester disk**) *Computing* a hermetically sealed data-storage device with high capacity (so called because its original numerical designation corresponded to that of the rifle's calibre). [O. F. *Winchester* d. 1880, US manufacturer of the rifle]

wind[1] /wind/ *n.* & *v.* ● *n.* **1 a** air in more or less rapid natural motion, esp. from an area of high pressure to one of low pressure. **b** a current of wind blowing from a specified direction or otherwise defined (*north wind*; *contrary wind*). **2 a** breath as needed in physical exertion or in speech. **b** the power of breathing without difficulty while running or making a similar continuous effort (*let me recover my wind*). **c** a spot below the centre of the chest where a blow temporarily paralyses breathing. **3** mere empty words; meaningless rhetoric. **4** gas generated in the bowels etc. by indigestion; flatulence. **5 a** an artifically produced current of air, esp. for sounding an organ or other wind instrument. **b** air stored for use or used as a current. **c** the wind instruments of an orchestra collectively (*poor balance between wind and strings*). **6** a scent carried by the wind, indicating the presence or proximity of an animal etc. ● *v.tr.* **1** exhaust the wind of by exertion or a blow. **2** renew the wind of by rest (*stopped to wind the horses*). **3** make breathe quickly and deeply by exercise. **4** make (a baby) bring up wind after feeding. **5** detect the presence of by a scent. **6** /wīnd/ (*past* and *past part.* **winded** or **wound** /wownd/) *poet.* sound (a bugle or call) by blowing. □ **before the wind** helped by the wind's force. **between wind and water** at a vulnerable point. **close to** (or **near**) **the wind 1** sailing as nearly against the wind as is consistent with using its force. **2** *colloq.* verging on indecency or dishonesty. **get wind of 1** smell out. **2** begin to suspect; hear a rumour of. **get** (or **have**) **the wind up** *colloq.* be alarmed or frightened. **how** (or **which way**) **the wind blows** (or **lies**) **1** what is the state of opinion. **2** what developments are likely. **in the wind** happening or about to happen. **in the wind's eye** directly against the wind. **like the wind** swiftly. **off the wind** *Naut.* with the wind on the quarter. **on a wind** *Naut.* against a wind on either bow. **on the wind** (of a sound or scent) carried by the wind. **put the wind up** *colloq.* alarm or frighten. **take wind** be rumoured; become known. **take the wind out of a person's sails** frustrate a person by anticipating an action or remark etc. **throw caution to the winds** not worry about taking risks; be reckless. **to the winds** (or **four winds**) **1** in all directions. **2** into a state of abandonment or neglect. **wind and weather** exposure to the effects of the elements. **wind band** a group of wind instruments as a band or section of an orchestra. **wind-break** a row of trees or a fence or wall etc. serving to break the force of the wind. **wind-blown** exposed to or blown about by the wind. **wind-chill** the cooling effect of wind blowing on a surface. **wind-cone** = *wind-sock*. **wind-force** the force of the wind esp. as measured on the Beaufort etc. scale. **wind-gap** a dried-up former river valley through ridges or hills. **wind-gauge 1** an anemometer. **2** an apparatus attached to the sights of a gun enabling allowance to be made for the wind in shooting. **3** a device showing the amount of wind in an organ. **wind instrument** a musical instrument in which sound is produced by a current of air, esp. the breath. **wind-jammer** a merchant sailing-ship. **wind machine** a device for producing a blast of air or the sound of wind. **wind** (or **winds**) **of change** a force or influence for reform. **wind-rose** a diagram of the relative frequency of wind directions at a place. **wind-row** a line of raked hay, corn-sheaves, peats, etc., for drying by the wind. **wind-sail** a canvas funnel conveying air to the lower parts of a ship. **wind shear** a variation in wind velocity at right angles to the wind's direction. **wind-sleeve** = *wind-sock*. **wind-sock** a canvas cylinder or cone on a mast to show the direction of the wind at an airfield etc. **wind-tunnel** a tunnel-like device to produce an air-stream past models of aircraft etc. for the study of wind effects on them. □□ **windless** *adj*. [OE f. Gmc]

■ *n*. **1** breeze, *literary* zephyr; puff, gust, blast, squall, breath, draught, current (of air). **2a, b** breath, air, puff. **3** puffery, bombast, rodomontade, rhetoric, bluster, boasting, braggadocio, vain speech, blather, (idle *or* empty) talk, fustian, nonsense, twaddle, humbug, babble, gibberish, claptrap, *colloq*. gab, hogwash, *esp. Brit. colloq*. waffle, *sl*. hot air, hooey, rot, boloney, *Brit. sl*. (load of (old)) cobblers. **4** gas, flatulence, windiness, flatus, borborygmus. **6** whiff, scent, smell, trace. ● *v*. **4** bring up the wind of, *colloq*. burp. □ **before the wind** downwind, *Naut*. off the wind. **get wind of 1** see SMELL *v*. 1. **2** hear of, learn of, come to know, pick up, be made *or* become aware of, gather, understand, hear tell of, *colloq*. hear on the grapevine. **get** (or **have**) **the wind up** take fright, become alarmed *or* frightened *or* afraid *or* apprehensive, panic. **in the wind** around, about, rumoured, in the air, detectable, discernible, discoverable, imminent, impending, approaching, close (at hand), about to happen *or* take place *or* occur, afoot, in the offing, near, on the way, on *or US* in the cards. **like the wind** see *swiftly* (SWIFT). **off the wind** before the wind, downwind. **on a wind** upwind, windward, *Naut*. to the wind, into (the teeth *or* eye of) the wind, in the wind's eye; close to *or* near the wind. **put the wind up** scare, frighten, alarm, unnerve, *colloq*. scare the pants off. **take the wind out of a person's sails** deflate *or* disconcert a person, destroy a person's advantage, ruin a person's superiority *or* supremacy *or* ascendancy. **wind-sock** wind-sleeeve, wind-cone, *Aeronaut*. drogue. □□ **windless** see CALM *adj*. 1.

wind[2] /wīnd/ *v*. & *n*. ● *v*. (*past* and *past part*. **wound** /wownd/) **1** *intr*. go in a circular, spiral, curved, or crooked course (*a winding staircase*; *the path winds up the hill*). **2** *tr*. make (one's way) by such a course (*wind your way up to bed*; *wound their way into our affections*). **3** *tr*. wrap closely; surround with or as with a coil (*wound the blanket round me*; *wound my arms round the child*; *wound the child in my arms*). **4 a** *tr*. coil; provide with a coiled thread etc. (*wind the ribbon on to the card*; *wound cotton on a reel*; *winding wool into a ball*). **b** *intr*. coil; (of wool etc.) coil into a ball (*the creeper winds round the pole*; *the wool wound into a ball*). **5** *tr*. wind up (a clock etc.). **6** *tr*. hoist or draw with a windlass etc. (*wound the cable-car up the mountain*). ● *n*. **1** a bend or turn in a course. **2** a single turn when winding. □ **wind down 1** lower by winding. **2** (of a mechanism) unwind. **3** (of a person) relax. **4** draw gradually to a close. **wind-down** *n. colloq*. a gradual lessening of excitement or reduction of activity. **wind off** unwind (string, wool, etc.). **wind round one's finger** see FINGER. **wind up 1** coil the whole of (a piece of string etc.). **2** tighten the coiling or coiled spring of (esp. a clock etc.). **3 a** *colloq*. increase the tension or intensity of (*wound myself up to fever pitch*). **b** irritate or provoke (a person) to the point of anger. **4** bring to a conclusion; end (*wound up his speech*). **5** *Commerce* **a** arrange the affairs of and dissolve (a company). **b** (of a company) cease business and go into liquidation. **6** *colloq*. arrive finally; end in a specified state or circumstance (*you'll wind up in prison*; *wound up owing £100*). **wind-up** *n*. **1** a conclusion; a finish. **2** a state of anxiety; the provocation of this. **wound up** *adj*. (of a person) excited or tense or angry. [OE *windan* f. Gmc, rel. to WANDER, WEND]

■ *v*. **1** turn, bend, twist, spiral, circle, snake, worm, twine, zigzag, slew, swerve, loop, coil, curve, meander, wander, ramble, veer. **3** wrap, fold, enfold, encircle, envelop. **4** reel, roll, spiral, turn, twist, curl, coil, wrap, twine, wreathe, twirl. **5** crank (up), wind up. ● *n*. **1** see TURN *n*. 2. **2** turn, revolution, rotation, twist, coil. □ **wind down 3** relax, become calm *or* tranquil, calm down, cool off *or* down, regain one's equilibrium *or* composure, ease up *or* off, take it easy, *colloq*. unwind, let one's hair down. **4** taper off, slow down, diminish, reduce, close down, slacken *or* slack off (on), ease (up on), decrease, cut back *or* down (on); wind up, *US* close out. **wind up 3 a** excite, energize, stimulate, inspire, arouse, invigorate, stir up. **b** agitate, fluster, disconcert, ruffle, irritate, exasperate, annoy, anger, provoke, nettle, madden, *colloq*. rile, needle. **4** end, close, conclude, terminate, finish, bring to an end *or* a close *or* conclusion, wrap up. **5** close (down *or* up), finish (up), wrap up; dissolve, liquidate, settle. **6** end up, finish (up), land (up), land oneself, find oneself. **wound up** see TENSE[1] *adj*. 1.

windage /wíndij/ *n*. **1** the friction of air against the moving part of a machine. **2 a** the effect of the wind in deflecting a missile. **b** an allowance for this. **3** the difference between the diameter of a gun's bore and its projectile, allowing the escape of gas.

windbag /wíndbag/ *n. colloq*. a person who talks a lot but says little of any value.

■ see *talker* (TALK).

windbound /wíndbownd/ *adj*. unable to sail because of contrary winds.

windbreaker /wíndbraykər/ *n. US* = WINDCHEATER.

windburn /wíndburn/ *n*. inflammation of the skin caused by exposure to the wind.

windcheater /wíndcheetər/ *n*. a kind of wind-resistant outer jacket with close-fitting neck, cuffs, and lower edge.

winder /wī́ndər/ *n*. a winding mechanism esp. of a clock or watch.

windfall /wíndfawl/ *n*. **1** an apple or other fruit blown to the ground by the wind. **2** a piece of unexpected good fortune, esp. a legacy.

■ **2** bonanza, godsend, stroke of (good) fortune, serendipitous find, boon, piece of (good) luck, jackpot, (lucky) strike.

windflower /wíndflowr/ *n*. an anemone.

windhover /wíndhovvər/ *n. Brit*. a kestrel.

winding /wī́nding/ *n*. **1** in senses of WIND[2] *v*. **2** curved or sinuous motion or movement. **3 a** a thing that is wound round or coiled. **b** *Electr*. coils of wire as a conductor round an armature etc. □ **winding-engine** a machine for hoisting. **winding-sheet** a sheet in which a corpse is wrapped for burial.

■ □ **winding-sheet** see SHROUD *n*. 1.

windlass /wíndləss/ *n*. & *v*. ● *n*. a machine with a horizontal axle for hauling or hoisting. ● *v.tr*. hoist or haul with a windlass. [alt. (perh. by assoc. with dial. *windle* to wind) of obs. *windas* f. OF *guindas* f. ON *vindáss* f. *vinda* WIND[2] + *áss* pole]

windlestraw /wind'lstraw/ *n. archaic* an old dry stalk of grass. [OE *windelstrēaw* grass for plaiting f. *windel* basket (as WIND[2], -LE[1]) + *strēaw* STRAW]

windmill /wíndmil/ *n*. **1** a mill worked by the action of the wind on its sails. **2** esp. *Brit*. a toy consisting of a stick with curved vanes attached that revolve in a wind. □ **throw one's cap** (or **bonnet**) **over the windmill** act recklessly or unconventionally. **tilt at** (or **fight**) **windmills** attack an imaginary enemy or grievance.

window /wíndō/ *n.* **1 a** an opening in a wall, roof, or vehicle etc., usu. with glass in fixed, sliding, or hinged frames, to admit light or air etc. and allow the occupants to see out. **b** the glass filling this opening (*have broken the window*). **2** a space for display behind the front window of a shop. **3** an aperture in a wall etc. through which customers are served in a bank, ticket office, etc. **4** an opportunity to observe or learn. **5** an opening or transparent part in an envelope to show an address. **6** a part of a VDU display selected to show a particular category or part of the data. **7 a** an interval during which atmospheric and astronomical circumstances are suitable for the launch of a spacecraft. **b** any interval or opportunity for action. **8** strips of metal foil dispersed in the air to obstruct radar detection. **9** a range of electromagnetic wavelengths for which a medium is transparent. □ **out of the window** *colloq.* no longer taken into account. **window-box** a box placed on an outside window-sill for growing flowers. **window-cleaner** a person who is employed to clean windows. **window-dressing 1** the art of arranging a display in a shop-window etc. **2** an adroit presentation of facts etc. to give a deceptively favourable impression. **window-ledge** = *window-sill.* **window-pane** a pane of glass in a window. **window-seat 1** a seat below a window, esp. in a bay or alcove. **2** a seat next to a window in an aircraft, train, etc. **window-shop** (**-shopped, -shopping**) look at goods displayed in shop-windows, usu. without buying anything. **window-shopper** a person who window-shops. **window-sill** a sill below a window. **window tax** *Brit. hist.* a tax on windows or similar openings (abolished in 1851). □□ **windowed** *adj.* (also in *comb.*). **windowless** *adj.* [ME f. ON *vindauga* (as WIND[1], EYE)]

windowing /wíndō-ing/ *n. Computing* the selection of part of a stored image for display or enlargement.

windpipe /wíndpīp/ *n.* the air-passage from the throat to the lungs; the trachea.

windscreen /wíndskreen/ *n. Brit.* a screen of glass at the front of a motor vehicle. □ **windscreen wiper** a device consisting of a rubber blade on an arm, moving in an arc, for keeping a windscreen clear of rain etc.

windshield /wíndsheeld/ *n. US* = WINDSCREEN.

Windsor /wínzər/ *n.* (usu. *attrib.*) denoting or relating to the British Royal Family since 1917. [*Windsor* in S. England, site of the royal residence at Windsor Castle]

Windsor chair *n.* a wooden dining chair with a semicircular back supported by upright rods.

windsurfing /wíndsurfing/ *n.* the sport of riding on water on a sailboard. □□ **windsurf** *v.intr.* **windsurfer** *n.*

windswept /wíndswept/ *adj.* exposed to or swept back by the wind.

■ disordered, disorderly, dishevelled, unkempt, untidy, tousled, wind-blown, messed-up, *US colloq.* mussed-up; see also BLEAK[1] 1.

windward /wíndwərd/ *adj., adv., & n.* ● *adj. & adv.* on the side from which the wind is blowing (opp. LEEWARD). ● *n.* the windward region, side, or direction (*to windward; on the windward of*). □ **get to windward of 1** place oneself there to avoid the smell of. **2** gain an advantage over.

windy /wíndi/ *adj.* (**windier, windiest**) **1** stormy with wind (*a windy night*). **2** exposed to the wind; windswept (*a windy plain*). **3** generating or characterized by flatulence. **4** *colloq.* wordy, verbose, empty (*a windy speech*). **5** *colloq.* nervous, frightened. □□ **windily** *adv.* **windiness** *n.* [OE *windig* (as WIND[1], -Y[1])]

■ **1** blustery, blowing, blowy, breezy, gusting, gusty, wild, boisterous, rough, squally, stormy, tempestuous. **2** windswept, exposed, unprotected, bleak. **3** flatulent. **4** talkative, long-winded, garrulous, wordy, verbose, prolix, loquacious, rambling, voluble, fluent, effusive, glib, turgid, bombastic, pompous.

wine /wīn/ *n. & v.* ● *n.* **1** fermented grape-juice as an alcoholic drink. **2** a fermented drink resembling this made from other fruits etc. as specified (*elderberry wine; ginger wine*). **3** the dark-red colour of red wine. ● *v.* **1** *intr.* drink wine. **2** *tr.* entertain to wine. □ **wine and dine** entertain to or have a meal with wine. **wine bar** a bar or small restaurant where wine is the main drink available. **wine bottle** a glass bottle for wine, the standard size holding 75 cl or 26 ⅔ fl. oz. **wine box** a square carton of wine with a dispensing tap. **wine cellar 1** a cellar for storing wine. **2** the contents of this. **wine-grower** a cultivator of grapes for wine. **wine list** a list of wines available in a restaurant etc. **wine-tasting 1** judging the quality of wine by tasting it. **2** an occasion for this. **wine vinegar** vinegar made from wine as distinct from malt. **wine waiter** a waiter responsible for serving wine. □□ **wineless** *adj.* [OE *wīn* f. Gmc f. L *vinum*]

wineberry /wīnbəri/ *n.* (*pl.* **-ies**) **1 a** a deciduous bristly shrub, *Rubus phoenicolasius*, from China and Japan, producing scarlet berries used in cookery. **b** this berry. **2** = MAKO[2].

winebibber /wīnbibbər/ *n.* a tippler or drunkard. □□ **winebibbing** *n. & adj.* [WINE + *bib* to tipple]

wineglass /wīnglaass/ *n.* **1** a glass for wine, usu. with a stem and foot. **2** the contents of this, a wineglassful.

wineglassful /wīnglaasfŏŏl/ *n.* (*pl.* **-fuls**) **1** the capacity of a wineglass, esp. of the size used for sherry, as a measure of liquid, about four tablespoons. **2** the contents of a wineglass.

winepress /wīnpress/ *n.* a press in which grapes are squeezed in making wine.

winery /wīnəri/ *n.* (*pl.* **-ies**) esp. *US* an establishment where wine is made.

wineskin /wīnskin/ *n.* a whole skin of a goat etc. sown up and used to hold wine.

wing /wing/ *n. & v.* ● *n.* **1** each of the limbs or organs by which a bird, bat, or insect is able to fly. **2** a rigid horizontal winglike structure forming a supporting part of an aircraft. **3** part of a building etc. which projects or is extended in a certain direction (*lived in the north wing*). **4 a** a forward player at either end of a line in football, hockey, etc. **b** the side part of a playing-area. **5** (in *pl.*) the sides of a theatre stage out of view of the audience. **6** a section of a political party in terms of the extremity of its views. **7** a flank of a battle array (*the cavalry were massed on the left wing*). **8** *Brit.* the part of a motor vehicle covering a wheel. **9 a** an air-force unit of several squadrons or groups. **b** (in *pl.*) a pilot's badge in the RAF etc. (*get one's wings*). **10** *Anat. & Bot.* a lateral part or projection of an organ or structure. ● *v.* **1** *intr. & tr.* travel or traverse on wings or in an aircraft (*winging through the air; am winging my way home*). **2** *tr.* wound in a wing or an arm. **3** *tr.* equip with wings. **4** *tr.* enable to fly; send in flight (*fear winged my steps; winged an arrow towards them*). □ **give** (or **lend**) **wings to** speed up (a person or a thing). **on the wing** flying or in flight. **on a wing and a prayer** with only the slightest chance of success. **spread** (or **stretch**) **one's wings** develop one's powers fully. **take under one's wing** treat as a protégé. **take wing** fly away; soar. **waiting in the wings** holding oneself in readiness. **wing-beat** one complete set of motions with a wing in flying. **wing-case** the horny cover of an insect's wing. **wing-chair** a chair with side-pieces projecting forwards at the top of a high back. **wing-collar** a man's high stiff collar with turned-down corners. **wing commander** an RAF officer next below group captain. **winged words** highly apposite or significant words. **wing-game** game-birds. **wing-nut** a nut with projections for the fingers to turn it on a screw. **wing-span** (or **-spread**) measurement right across the wings of a bird or aircraft. **wing-stroke** = *wing-beat.* **wing-tip** the outer end of an aircraft's or a bird's wing. □□ **winged** *adj.* (also in *comb.*). **wingless** *adj.* **winglet** *n.* **winglike** *adj.* [ME pl. *wenge, -en, -es* f. ON *vængir*, pl. of *vængr*]

■ *n.* **6** faction, group, fringe movement, lobby. ● *v.* **1** see FLY[1] *v.* 1. **2** see WOUND[1] *v.* □ **take under one's wing** see PROVIDE 2b. **take wing** see FLY[1] *v.* 1.

wingding /wíngding/ *n. sl.* **1** esp. *US* a wild party. **2** *US* a drug addict's real or feigned seizure. [20th c.: orig. unkn.]

winger /wíngər/ *n.* **1** a player on a wing in football, hockey, etc. **2** (in *comb.*) a member of a specified political wing (*left-winger*).

wink /wingk/ *v.* & *n.* ● *v.* **1 a** *tr.* close and open (one eye or both eyes) quickly. **b** *intr.* close and open an eye. **2** *intr.* (often foll. by *at*) wink one eye as a signal of friendship or greeting or to convey a message to a person. **3** *intr.* (of a light etc.) twinkle; shine or flash intermittently. ● *n.* **1** the act or an instance of winking, esp. as a signal etc. **2** *colloq.* a brief moment of sleep (*didn't sleep a wink*). □ **as easy as winking** *colloq.* very easy. **in a wink** very quickly. **wink at 1** purposely avoid seeing; pretend not to notice. **2** connive at (a wrongdoing etc.). [OE *wincian* f. Gmc: cf. WINCE[1], WINCH]

■ *v.* **3** see TWINKLE *v.* □ **in a wink** see *rapidly* (RAPID). **wink at** see OVERLOOK *v.* 1.

winker /wíngkər/ *n.* **1** *colloq.* a flashing indicator light on a motor vehicle. **2** (usu. in *pl.*) a horse's blinker.

winkle /wíngk'l/ *n.* & *v.* ● *n.* any edible marine gastropod mollusc of the genus *Littorina*; a periwinkle. ● *v.tr.* (foll. by *out*) esp. *Brit.* extract or eject (*winkled the information out of them*). □ **winkle-picker** *sl.* a shoe with a long pointed toe. □□ **winkler** *n.* [abbr. of PERIWINKLE[2]: cf. WIG[1]]

■ *v.* (*winkle out*) see EXTRACT *v.* 2.

winner /wínnər/ *n.* **1** a person, racehorse, etc. that wins. **2** *colloq.* a successful or highly promising idea, enterprise, etc. (*the new scheme seemed a winner*).

■ **1** victor, champion, prizewinner, title-holder, victor ludorum, conqueror, conquering hero, *colloq.* top dog, *literary* vanquisher, *sl.* champ. **2** see KNOCKOUT 4.

winning /wínning/ *adj.* & *n.* ● *adj.* **1** having or bringing victory or an advantage (*the winning entry*; *a winning stroke*). **2** attractive, persuasive (*a winning smile*; *winning ways*). ● *n.* (in *pl.*) money won esp. in betting etc. □ **winning-post** a post marking the end of a race. □□ **winningly** *adv.* **winningness** *n.*

■ *adj.* **1** triumphant, conquering, victorious, successful. **2** engaging, attractive, appealing, alluring, captivating, endearing, prepossessing, winsome, bewitching, fetching, taking, persuasive, seductive, enchanting, pleasing, delightful, charming, amiable, friendly, pleasant, sweet. ● *n.* (*winnings*) see PRIZE[1] *n.* 2.

winnow /wínnō/ *v.tr.* **1** blow (grain) free of chaff etc. by an air-current. **2** (foll. by *out*, *away*, *from*, etc.) get rid of (chaff etc.) from grain. **3 a** sift, separate; clear of refuse or inferior specimens. **b** sift or examine (evidence for falsehood etc.). **c** clear, sort, or weed out (rubbish etc.). **4** *poet.* **a** fan (the air with wings). **b** flap (wings). **c** stir (the hair etc.). □□ **winnower** *n.* (in senses 1, 2). [OE *windwian* (as WIND[1])]

wino /wīnō/ *n.* (*pl.* **-os**) *sl.* a habitual excessive drinker of cheap wine; an alcoholic.

■ see ALCOHOLIC *n.*

winsome /wínsəm/ *adj.* (of a person, looks, or manner) winning, attractive, engaging. □□ **winsomely** *adv.* **winsomeness** *n.* [OE *wynsum* f. *wyn* JOY + -SOME[1]]

■ see WINNING *adj.* 2.

winter /wíntər/ *n.* & *v.* ● *n.* **1** the coldest season of the year, in the N. hemisphere from December to February and in the S. hemisphere from June to August. **2** *Astron.* the period from the winter solstice to the vernal equinox. **3** a bleak or lifeless period or region etc. (*nuclear winter*). **4** *poet.* a year (esp. of a person's age) (*a man of fifty winters*). **5** (*attrib.*) **a** characteristic of or suitable for winter (*winter light*; *winter clothes*). **b** (of fruit) ripening late or keeping until or during winter. **c** (of wheat or other crops) sown in autumn for harvesting the following year. ● *v.* **1** *intr.* (usu. foll. by *at*, *in*) pass the winter (*likes to winter in the Canaries*). **2** *tr.* keep or feed (plants, cattle) during winter. □ **winter aconite** see ACONITE 2. **winter cress** any bitter-tasting cress of the genus *Barbarea*, esp. *B. vulgaris*. **winter garden** a garden or conservatory of plants flourishing in winter. **winter jasmine** a jasmine, *Jasminum nudiflorum*, with yellow flowers. **winter quarters** a place where soldiers spend the winter. **winter sleep** hibernation. **winter solstice** see SOLSTICE. **winter sports** sports performed on snow or ice esp. in winter (e.g. skiing and ice-skating). **winter-tide** *poet.* = WINTERTIME. □□ **winterer** *n.* **winterless** *adj.* **winterly** *adj.* [OE f. Gmc, prob. rel. to WET]

wintergreen /wíntərgreen/ *n.* any of several plants esp. of the genus *Pyrola* or *Gaultheria* remaining green through the winter.

winterize /wíntərīz/ *v.tr.* (also **-ise**) esp. *US* adapt for operation or use in cold weather. □□ **winterization** /-zāysh'n/ *n.*

wintertime /wíntərtīm/ *n.* the season of winter.

wintry /wíntri/ *adj.* (also **wintery**) (/-təri/; **wintrier, wintriest**) **1** characteristic of winter (*wintry weather*; *a wintry sun*; *a wintry landscape*). **2** (of a smile, greeting, etc.) lacking warmth or enthusiasm. □□ **wintrily** *adv.* **wintriness** *n.* [OE *wintrig*, or f. WINTER]

■ **1** icy, snowy, freezing, frozen, frosty, cold, frigid, bitter (cold), chilly, chilling, piercing, cutting, glacial, hyperborean, *colloq.* arctic, nippy, *Brit. colloq.* parky, *literary* chill. **2** cold, frigid, chilly, cool, chilling, icy, frosty, glacial; forbidding, bleak, dismal, cheerless, dreary, harsh, unfriendly, ugly, menacing, ominous, threatening, dark, uninviting.

winy /wīni/ *adj.* (**winier, winiest**) resembling wine in taste or appearance. □□ **wininess** *n.*

wipe /wīp/ *v.* & *n.* ● *v.tr.* **1** clean or dry the surface of by rubbing with the hands or a cloth etc. **2** rub (a cloth) over a surface. **3** spread (a liquid etc.) over a surface by rubbing. **4** (often foll. by *away*, *off*, etc.) **a** clear or remove by wiping (*wiped the mess off the table*; *wipe away your tears*). **b** remove or eliminate completely (*the village was wiped off the map*). **5 a** erase (data, a recording, etc., from a magnetic medium). **b** erase data from (the medium). **6** *Austral.* & *NZ sl.* reject or dismiss (a person or idea). ● *n.* **1** an act of wiping (*give the floor a wipe*). **2** a piece of disposable absorbent cloth, usu. treated with a cleansing agent, for wiping something clean (*antiseptic wipes*). □ **wipe down** clean (esp. a vertical surface) by wiping. **wipe a person's eye** *colloq.* get the better of a person. **wipe the floor with** *colloq.* inflict a humiliating defeat on. **wipe off** annul (a debt etc.). **wipe out 1 a** destroy, annihilate (*the whole population was wiped out*). **b** obliterate (*wiped it out of my memory*). **2** *sl.* murder. **3** clean the inside of. **4** avenge (an insult etc.). **wipe-out** *n.* **1** the obliteration of one radio signal by another. **2** an instance of destruction or annihilation. **3** *sl.* a fall from a surfboard. **wiped out** *adj. sl.* tired out, exhausted. **wipe the slate clean** see SLATE. **wipe up 1** *Brit.* dry (dishes etc.). **2** take up (a liquid etc.) by wiping. □□ **wipeable** *adj.* [OE *wīpian*: cf. OHG *wīfan* wind round, Goth. *weipan* crown: rel. to WHIP]

■ *v.* **1** wipe off *or* out *or* up, rub, clean (off *or* out *or* up), *usu. formal* cleanse; dry (off *or* out *or* up), dust (off), polish, mop (up), blot, swab, sponge (off *or* up). **3** spread, smear, rub, apply. **4 a** remove, clear, take off *or* away, get rid of. **b** remove, eliminate, get rid of. **5** see ERASE 1. **6** see DISMISS 2, 4, REJECT *v.* 3. ● *n.* **1** rub, clean, dust, mop, sponge, brush, sweep, polish. □ **wipe the floor with** see ROUT[1] *v.* **wipe off** annul, cancel, remove, erase, get rid of, write off. **wipe out 1 a** annihilate, destroy, massacre, kill (off), eradicate, exterminate, extirpate, root out, stamp out, dispose of, wipe off the face of the earth. **b** obliterate, remove, get rid of, efface, erase, delete, blot out, extinguish, expunge, eradicate, *literary* deracinate. **2** murder, kill (off), annihilate, massacre, dispose of, eliminate, exterminate, get rid of, wipe off the face of the earth, *colloq.* do away with, finish (off).

wiper /wīpər/ *n.* **1** = *windscreen wiper*. **2** *Electr.* a moving contact. **3** a cam or tappet.

WIPO *abbr.* World Intellectual Property Organization.

wire /wīr/ *n.* & *v.* ● *n.* **1 a** metal drawn out into the form of a thread or thin flexible rod. **b** a piece of this. **c** (*attrib.*)

made of wire. **2** a length or quantity of wire used for fencing or to carry an electric current etc. **3** esp. *US colloq.* a telegram or cablegram. ● *v.tr.* **1** provide, fasten, strengthen, etc., with wire. **2** (often foll. by *up*) *Electr.* install electrical circuits in (a building, piece of equipment, etc.). **3** esp. *US colloq.* telegraph (*wired me that they were coming*). **4** snare (an animal etc.) with wire. **5** (usu. in *passive*) *Croquet* obstruct (a ball, shot, or player) by a hoop. □ **by wire** by telegraph. **get one's wires crossed** become confused and misunderstood. **wire brush 1** a brush with tough wire bristles for cleaning hard surfaces, esp. metal. **2** a brush with wire strands brushed against cymbals to produce a soft metallic sound. **wire cloth** cloth woven from wire. **wire-cutter** a tool for cutting wire. **wire gauge 1** a gauge for measuring the diameter of wire etc. **2** a standard series of sizes in which wire etc. is made. **wire gauze** a stiff gauze woven from wire. **wire grass** any of various grasses with tough wiry stems. **wire-haired** (esp. of a dog) having stiff or wiry hair. **wire mattress** a mattress supported by wires stretched in a frame. **wire netting** netting of wire twisted into meshes. **wire rope** rope made by twisting wires together as strands. **wire-tapper** a person who indulges in wire-tapping. **wire-tapping** the practice of tapping (see TAP[1] *v.* 4) a telephone or telegraph line to eavesdrop. **wire-walker** an acrobat performing feats on a wire rope. **wire wheel** a vehicle-wheel with spokes of wire. **wire wool** a mass of fine wire for cleaning. □□ **wirer** *n.* [OE *wīr*]

■ *n.* **2** see CABLE *n.* 1. **3** see TELEGRAM. ● *v.* **3** see CABLE *v.* 3.

wiredraw /wī́rdraw/ *v.tr.* (*past* **-drew** /-dro͞o/; *past part.* **-drawn** /-drawn/) **1** draw (metal) out into wire. **2** elongate; protract unduly. **3** (esp. as **wiredrawn** *adj.*) refine or apply or press (an argument etc.) with idle or excessive subtlety.

wireless /wī́rliss/ *n.* & *adj.* ● *n.* **1** esp. *Brit.* **a** (in full **wireless set**) a radio receiving set. **b** the transmission and reception of radio signals. ¶ Now old-fashioned, esp. with ref. to broadcasting, and superseded by *radio*. **2** = *wireless telegraphy*. ● *adj.* lacking or not requiring wires. □ **wireless telegraphy** = RADIO-TELEGRAPHY.

■ *n.* **1 a** see RADIO *n.*

wireman /wī́rmən/ *n.* (*pl.* **-men**) **1** esp. *US* an installer or repairer of electric wires. **2** a journalist working for a telegraphic news agency.

wirepuller /wī́rpo͝ollər/ *n.* esp. *US* a politician etc. who exerts a hidden influence. □□ **wirepulling** *n.*

wireworm /wī́rwurm/ *n.* the larva of the click beetle causing damage to crop plants.

wiring /wī́ring/ *n.* **1** a system of wires providing electrical circuits. **2** the installation of this (*came to do the wiring*).

wiry /wī́ri/ *adj.* (**wirier, wiriest**) **1** tough and flexible as wire. **2** (of a person) thin and sinewy; untiring. **3** made of wire. □□ **wirily** *adv.* **wiriness** *n.*

■ **1** tough, flexible. **2** muscular, sinewy, lean, lank, spare, skinny, thin, strong, tough; untiring, tireless.

Wis. *abbr.* Wisconsin.

wis /wiss/ *v.intr. archaic* know well. [orig. *I wis* = obs. *iwis* 'certainly' f. OE *gewis*, erron. taken as 'I know' and as pres. tense of *wist* (WIT[2])]

Wisd. *abbr.* Wisdom of Solomon (Apocrypha).

wisdom /wízdəm/ *n.* **1** the state of being wise. **2** experience and knowledge together with the power of applying them critically or practically. **3** sagacity, prudence; common sense. **4** wise sayings, thoughts, etc., regarded collectively. □ **in his** (or **her** etc.) **wisdom** usu. *iron.* thinking it would be best (*the committee in its wisdom decided to abandon the project*). **wisdom tooth** each of four hindmost molars not usu. cut before 20 years of age. [OE *wīsdōm* (as WISE[1], -DOM)]

■ **2, 3** sagacity, sageness, judgement, discernment, reason, prudence, judiciousness, (common) sense, insight, penetration, sapience, understanding, rationality, clear-sightedness, clear-headedness, perspicacity, perspicuity, percipience, perception, perceptiveness, intelligence, acuteness, acumen, astuteness, sharpness, shrewdness, long-headedness, *colloq.* nous. **4** knowledge, learning, erudition, lore, scholarship, enlightenment.

wise[1] /wīz/ *adj.* & *v.* ● *adj.* **1 a** having experience and knowledge and judiciously applying them. **b** (of an action, behaviour, etc.) determined by or showing or in harmony with such experience and knowledge. **2** sagacious, prudent, sensible, discreet. **3** having knowledge. **4** suggestive of wisdom (*with a wise nod of the head*). **5** *US colloq.* **a** alert, crafty. **b** (often foll. by *to*) having (usu. confidential) information (about). ● *v.tr.* & *intr.* (foll. by *up*) esp. *US colloq.* put or get wise. □ **be** (or **get**) **wise to** *colloq.* become aware of. **no** (or **none the** or **not much**) **wiser** knowing no more than before. **put a person wise** (often foll. by *to*) *colloq.* inform a person (about). **wise after the event** able to understand and assess an event or circumstance after its implications have become obvious. **wise guy** *colloq.* a know-all. **wise man** a wizard, esp. one of the Magi. **wise saw** a proverbial saying. **without anyone's being the wiser** undetected. □□ **wisely** *adv.* [OE *wīs* f. Gmc: see WIT[2]]

■ *adj.* **1** sage, sagacious, judicious, reasonable, commonsensical, prudent, sensible, insightful, understanding, rational, sound, clear-sighted, clear-headed, discerning, perspicacious, perspicuous, percipient, perceptive, intelligent, acute, astute, sharp, shrewd, crafty, clever, bright, quick-witted, smart, brilliant, long-headed, brainy, *literary* sapient. **2** well-advised, advisable, judicious, sensible, sagacious, expedient, reasonable, sound, strategic, tactful, tactical, prudent, politic, discreet, diplomatic, well-thought-out, well-considered, proper, fitting, appropriate, *archaic* meet. **3** knowledgeable, learned, enlightened, informed, erudite; (well-)educated, knowing, well-read, well-versed, well-informed, lettered, scholarly. **4** knowing, shrewd, perceptive, understanding. **5 a** see FOXY 2, ALERT *adj.* 1. **b** aware, knowledgeable, informed, awake, *colloq.* in the know. ● *v.* see *be (or get) wise to*, *put a person wise* below. □ **be** (or **get**) **wise to** be *or* become aware of, be *or* become knowledgeable of *or* about, be *or* become informed of *or* about, be *or* become sensitive to, be on to, be *or* become awake to, wake up to, *colloq.* be in the know about, *esp. US colloq.* wise up about. **put a person wise** inform *or* advise *or* warn a person, put in the picture, *esp. US colloq.* wise up. **wise guy** wiseacre, *archaic usu. derog.* witling; *colloq.* know-(it)-all, smart alec, smarty-pants, smarty-boots, smarty, clever Dick, clever clogs, *sl.* smart-arse, *US sl.* smart-ass.

wise[2] /wīz/ *n. archaic* way, manner, or degree (*in solemn wise*; *on this wise*). □ **in no wise** not at all. [OE *wīse* f. Gmc f. WIT[2]]

-wise /wīz/ *suffix* forming adjectives and adverbs of manner (*crosswise*; *clockwise*; *lengthwise*) or respect (*moneywise*) (cf. -WAYS). ¶ More fanciful phrase-based combinations, such as *employment-wise* (= as regards employment) are *colloq.*, and restricted to informal contexts. [as WISE[2]]

wiseacre /wī́zaykər/ *n.* a person who affects a wise manner. [MDu. *wijsseggher* soothsayer, prob. f. OHG *wīssago*, *wīzago*, assim. to WISE[1], ACRE]

■ see *wise guy* (WISE[1]).

wisecrack /wī́zkrak/ *n.* & *v. colloq.* ● *n.* a smart pithy remark. ● *v.intr.* make a wisecrack. □□ **wisecracker** *n.*

■ *n.* joke, quip, rejoinder, witticism, pun, barb, jest, gag, gibe, *colloq.* dig. ● *v.* joke, quip, pun, gibe.

wisent /weéz'nt/ *n.* the European bison, *Bison bonasus*. [G: cf. BISON]

wish /wish/ *v.* & *n.* ● *v.* **1** *intr.* (often foll. by *for*) have or express a desire or aspiration for (*wish for happiness*). **2** *tr.* (often foll. by *that* + clause, usu. with *that* omitted) have as a desire or aspiration (*I wish I could sing*; *I wished that I was dead*). **3** *tr.* want or demand, usu. so as to bring about what is wanted (*I wish to go*; *I wish you to do it*; *I wish it done*). **4** *tr.* express one's hopes for (*we wish you well*; *wish them no harm*; *wished us a pleasant journey*). **5** *tr.* (foll. by *on*, *upon*) *colloq.* foist on a person. ● *n.* **1 a** a desire, request, or aspiration. **b** an expression of this. **2** a thing desired (*got my wish*). □ **best** (or **good**) **wishes** hopes felt or expressed for another's happiness etc. **wish-fulfilment** a tendency for subconscious desire to be satisfied in fantasy. **wishing-well** a well into which coins are dropped and a wish is made. **the wish is father to the thought** we believe a thing because we wish it true. □□ **wisher** *n.* (in sense 4 of *v.*); (also in *comb.*). [OE *wȳscan*, OHG *wunsken* f. Gmc, ult. rel. to WEEN, WONT]

■ *v.* **1** yearn, long, hope, aspire, hanker, have a mind, (have a) fancy, care; (*wish for*) desire, want, crave, choose. **3** require, request, want, demand, order. **5** (*wish on*) foist *or* force *or* thrust *or* impose on, fob *or* palm off on. ● *n.* **1** desire, request, whim, want, need, aspiration, craving, longing, hankering, yearning, thirst, appetite, hunger, urge, itch, liking, passion, fondness, fancy, preference, predisposition, disposition, inclination, *colloq.* yen.

wishbone /wíshbōn/ *n.* **1** a forked bone between the neck and breast of a cooked bird: when broken between two people the longer portion entitles the holder to make a wish. **2** an object of similar shape.

wishful /wíshfŏŏl/ *adj.* **1** (often foll. by *to* + infin.) desiring, wishing. **2** having or expressing a wish. □ **wishful thinking** belief founded on wishes rather than facts. □□ **wishfully** *adv.* **wishfulness** *n.*

■ see DESIROUS 2.

wish-wash /wishwosh/ *n.* **1** a weak or watery drink. **2** insipid talk or writing. [redupl. of WASH]

wishy-washy /wíshiwóshi/ *adj.* **1** feeble, insipid, or indecisive in quality or character. **2** (of tea, soup, etc.) weak, watery, sloppy. [redupl. of WASHY]

■ **1** neither here nor there, undecided, indecisive, irresolute, insipid, feeble, vapid, half-hearted, lukewarm, namby-pamby, shilly-shallying, tergiversating, vacillating, uncertain, of *or* having mixed feelings, in two minds. **2** feeble, weak, watery, watered down, thin, vapid, flat, bland, runny, sloppy, diluted, tasteless, insipid, flavourless, stale.

wisp /wisp/ *n.* **1** a small bundle or twist of straw etc. **2** a small separate quantity of smoke, hair, etc. **3** a small thin person etc. **4** a flock (of snipe). □□ **wispy** *adj.* (**wispier**, **wispiest**). **wispily** *adv.* **wispiness** *n.* [ME: orig. uncert.: cf. WFris. *wisp*, and WHISK]

■ **2** streak, shred, scrap, strand, thread, snippet, tuft, lock. □ **wispy** thin, streaky, flimsy, insubstantial, gossamer.

wist *past* and *past part.* of WIT².

wisteria /wisteéria/ *n.* (also **wistaria** /-stáiria/) any climbing plant of the genus *Wisteria*, with hanging racemes of blue, purple, or white flowers. [C. *Wistar* (or *Wister*), Amer. anatomist d. 1818]

wistful /wístfŏŏl/ *adj.* (of a person, looks, etc.) yearningly or mournfully expectant, thoughtful, or wishful. □□ **wistfully** *adv.* **wistfulness** *n.* [app. assim. of obs. *wistly* (adv.) intently (cf. WHISHT) to *wishful*, with corresp. change of sense]

■ melancholy, mournful, sad, morose, sorrowful, disconsolate, heartsick, forlorn, woeful, woebegone, doleful, desirous, longing, yearning; thoughtful, contemplative, pensive, absent-minded, detached, absorbed, in a brown study, preoccupied, meditating, meditative, reflective, ruminating, ruminative, dreamy, dreaming, day-dreaming, musing.

wit¹ /wit/ *n.* **1** (in *sing.* or *pl.*) intelligence; quick understanding (*has quick wits*; *a nimble wit*). **2 a** the unexpected, quick, and humorous combining or contrasting of ideas or expressions (*conversation sparkling with wit*). **b** the power of giving intellectual pleasure by this. **3** a person possessing such a power, esp. a cleverly humorous person. □ **at one's wit's** (or **wits'**) **end** utterly at a loss or in despair. **have** (or **keep**) **one's wits about one** be alert or vigilant or of lively intelligence. **live by one's wits** live by ingenious or crafty expedients, without a settled occupation. **out of one's wits** mad, distracted. **set one's wits to** argue with. □□ **witted** *adj.* (in sense 1); (also in *comb.*). [OE *wit(t)*, *gewit(t)* f. Gmc]

■ **1** intelligence, brains, mind, (common) sense, judgement, understanding, discernment, wisdom, sagacity, insight, astuteness, cleverness, *colloq.* nous, *sl.* savvy. **2** humour, drollery, levity, joking, repartee, raillery, facetiousness, waggishness, *badinage*, banter, jocularity, wordplay, paronomasia; amusement, entertainment. **3** comedian, comedienne, humorist, comic, wag, joker, jester, *farceur*, *farceuse*, punster, madcap, zany; parodist, satirist, caricaturist; *colloq.* card, character; *archaic usu. derog.* witling. □ **at one's wit's** (or **wits'**) **end** see FRANTIC 2.

wit² /wit/ *v.tr.* & *intr.* (*1st* & *3rd sing. present* **wot** /wot/; *past* and *past part.* **wist**) (often foll. by *of*) *archaic* know. □ **to wit** that is to say; namely. [OE *witan* f. Gmc]

witch /wich/ *n.* & *v.* ● *n.* **1** a sorceress, esp. a woman supposed to have dealings with the devil or evil spirits. **2** an ugly old woman; a hag. **3** a fascinating girl or woman. **4** a flat-fish, *Pleuronectes cynoglossus*, resembling the lemon sole. ● *v.tr. archaic* **1** bewitch. **2** fascinate, charm, lure. □ **witch-doctor** a tribal magician of primitive people. **witches' sabbath** see SABBATH 3. **witch-hunt 1** *hist.* a search for and persecution of supposed witches. **2** a campaign directed against a particular group of those holding unpopular or unorthodox views, esp. communists. **the witching hour** midnight, when witches are supposedly active (after Shakesp. *Hamlet* III. ii. 377 *the witching time of night*). □□ **witching** *adj.* **witchlike** *adj.* [OE *wicca* (masc.), *wicce* (fem.), rel. to *wiccian* (v.) practise magic arts]

■ *n.* **1** sorceress, enchantress, sibyl, pythoness. **2** hag, fury, crone, gorgon, ogress, Xanthippe, shrew, virago, harridan, fishwife, termagant, *archaic* beldam, *colloq.* battleaxe, *sl. derog.* old bag, *sl. offens.* bitch. ● *v.* **1, 2** see BEWITCH. □ **witch-doctor** see SORCERER.

witch- var. of WYCH-.

witchcraft /wichkraaft/ *n.* the use of magic; sorcery.

■ see *sorcery* (SORCERER).

witchery /wíchəri/ *n.* **1** witchcraft. **2** power exercised by beauty or eloquence or the like.

■ **1** see *sorcery* (SORCERER). **2** see MAGIC *n.* 4.

witchetty /wíchəti/ *n.* (*pl.* **-ies**) *Austral.* a large white larva of a beetle or moth, eaten as food by Aborigines. [Aboriginal]

witch-hazel /wích-hayz'l/ *n.* (also **wych-hazel**) **1** any American shrub of the genus *Hamamelis*, with bark yielding an astringent lotion. **2** this lotion, esp. from the leaves of *H. virginiana*.

witenagemot /wíttənəgəmōt/ *n. hist.* an Anglo-Saxon national council or parliament. [OE f. *witena* genit. pl. of *wita* wise man (as WIT²) + *gemōt* meeting: cf. MOOT]

with /wi*th*/ *prep.* expressing: **1** an instrument or means used (*cut with a knife*; *can walk with assistance*). **2** association or company (*lives with his mother*; *works with Shell*; *lamb with mint sauce*). **3** cause or origin (*shiver with fear*; *in bed with measles*). **4** possession, attribution (*the man with dark hair*; *a vase with handles*). **5** circumstances; accompanying conditions (*sleep with the window open*; *a holiday with all expenses paid*). **6** manner adopted or displayed (*behaved with dignity*; *spoke with vehemence*; *handle with care*; *won with ease*). **7** agreement or harmony (*sympathize with*; *I believe with you that it can be done*). **8** disagreement, antagonism, competition (*incompatible with*; *stop arguing with me*). **9** responsibility or care for (*the decision rests with you*; *leave the child with me*). **10** material (*made with gold*). **11** addition or supply; possession of as a material, attribute, circumstance, etc. (*fill it with water*; *threaten with dismissal*; *decorate with holly*). **12** reference or regard (*be patient with them*; *how are things with you?*; *what do you want with me?*; *there's nothing wrong with expressing one's opinion*). **13** relation or causative association (*changes with the weather*; *keeps pace with the cost of living*). **14** an accepted circumstance or consideration (*with all your faults, we like you*). □ **away** (or **in** or **out** etc.) **with** (as *int.*) take, send, or put (a person or thing) away, in, out, etc. **be with a person 1** agree with and support a person. **2** *colloq.* follow a person's meaning (*are you with me?*). **one with** part of the same whole as. **with child** (or

young) *literary* pregnant. **with it** *colloq.* **1** up to date; conversant with modern ideas etc. **2** alert and comprehending. **with-it** *adj. colloq.* (of clothes etc.) fashionable. **with that** thereupon. [OE, prob. shortened f. a Gmc prep. corresp. to OE *wither*, OHG *widar* against]
■ **2** BESIDE 1. □ **with it 1** see MODERN *adj.* **2** see ALERT *adj.*

withal /wit͟hάwl/ *adv.* & *prep. archaic* ● *adv.* moreover; as well; at the same time. ● *prep.* (placed after its expressed or omitted object) with (*what shall he fill his belly withal?*). [ME f. WITH + ALL]
■ see *in addition* (ADDITION).

withdraw /wit͟hdráw/ *v.* (*past* **withdrew** /-dróo/; *past part.* **withdrawn** /-dráwn/) **1** *tr.* pull or take aside or back (*withdrew my hand*). **2** *tr.* discontinue, cancel, retract (*withdrew my support; the promise was later withdrawn*). **3** *tr.* remove; take away (*withdrew the child from school; withdrew their troops*). **4** *tr.* take (money) out of an account. **5** *intr.* retire or go away; move away or back. **6** *intr.* (as **withdrawn** *adj.*) abnormally shy and unsociable; mentally detached. □ **withdrawing-room** *archaic* = DRAWING-ROOM 1. □□ **withdrawer** *n.* [ME f. *with-* away (as WITH) + DRAW]
■ **1** draw back, retract, pull back *or* aside *or* away, take back *or* aside. **2** retract, recall, take back, cancel, discontinue, rescind, recant, disavow, disclaim, abjure, void, annul, go back on, back down (on). **3** remove, extract, take away *or* out, pull out; recall. **4** remove, take *or* get (out). **5** retire, retreat, go (away), repair, leave, depart, secede, absent oneself, beat a retreat, *colloq.* drop out, make oneself scarce; move away *or* back, back away *or* out, pull back *or* out, draw back, recoil, shrink back. **6** (**withdrawn**) reserved, detached, distant, remote, standoffish, aloof, shy, unsociable, antisocial, reclusive, diffident, bashful, timid, timorous, introverted, taciturn, reticent, silent, quiet, retiring, shrinking.

withdrawal /wit͟hdráwəl/ *n.* **1** the act or an instance of withdrawing or being withdrawn. **2** a process of ceasing to take addictive drugs, often with an unpleasant physical reaction (*withdrawal symptoms*). **3** = *coitus interruptus*.
■ **1** extraction, removal; see also RETREAT *n.* 1a, 2, CANCELLATION, DENIAL 2.

withe /with, wit͟h, wīt͟h/ (also **withy** /wít͟hi/) (*pl.* **withes** or **-ies**) *n.* a tough flexible shoot esp. of willow or osier used for tying a bundle of wood etc. [OE *withthe, withig* f. Gmc, rel. to WIRE]

wither /wít͟hər/ *v.* **1** *tr.* & *intr.* (often foll. by *up*) make or become dry and shrivelled (*withered flowers*). **2** *tr.* & *intr.* (often foll. by *away*) deprive of or lose vigour, vitality, freshness, or importance. **3** *intr.* decay, decline. **4** *tr.* **a** blight with scorn etc. **b** (as **withering** *adj.*) scornful (*a withering look*). □□ **witheringly** *adv.* [ME, app. var. of WEATHER differentiated for certain senses]
■ **1** see SHRIVEL. **2, 3** see WASTE *v.* 4. **4 b** (**withering**) see SCORNFUL.

withers /wít͟hərz/ *n.pl.* the ridge between a horse's shoulder-blades. [shortening of (16th-c.) *widersome* (or *-sone*) f. *wider-*, *wither-* against (cf. WITH), as the part that resists the strain of the collar: second element obscure]

withershins /wít͟hərshinz/ *adv.* (also **widdershins** /wid-/) esp. *Sc.* **1** in a direction contrary to the sun's course (considered as unlucky). **2** anticlockwise. [MLG *weddersins* f. MHG *widdersinnes* f. *wider* against + *sin* direction]

withhold /wit͟h-hṓld/ *v.tr.* (*past* and *past part.* **-held** /-héld/) **1** (often foll. by *from*) hold back; restrain. **2** refuse to give, grant, or allow (*withhold one's consent; withhold the truth*). □□ **withholder** *n.* [ME f. *with-* away (as WITH) + HOLD[1]]
■ **1** hold *or* keep back, deduct, retain, reserve; restrain, control, repress, suppress, check, hide, conceal. **2** refuse, deny, deprive (of), disallow.

within /wit͟hín/ *adv.* & *prep.* ● *adv. archaic* or *literary* **1** inside; to, at, or on the inside; internally. **2** indoors (*is anyone within?*). **3** in spirit (*make me pure within*). **4** inside the city walls (*Bishopsgate within*). ● *prep.* **1** inside; enclosed or contained by. **2 a** not beyond or exceeding (*within one's means*). **b** not transgressing (*within the law; within reason*). **3** not further off than (*within three miles of a station; within shouting distance; within ten days*). □ **within doors** in or into a house. **within one's grasp** see GRASP. **within reach** (or **sight**) **of** near enough to be reached or seen. [OE *withinnan* on the inside (as WITH, *innan* (adv. & prep.) within, formed as IN)]
■ *adv.* **1–3** see INSIDE *adv.* 1.

without /wit͟hówt/ *prep.* & *adv.* ● *prep.* **1** not having, feeling, or showing (*came without any money; without hesitation; without any emotion*). **2** with freedom from (*without fear; without embarrassment*). **3** in the absence of (*cannot live without you; the train left without us*). **4** with neglect or avoidance of (*do not leave without telling me*). ¶ Use as a *conj.*, as in *do not leave without you tell me*, is non-standard. **5** *archaic* outside (*without the city wall*). ● *adv. archaic* or *literary* **1** outside (*seen from without*). **2** out of doors (*remained shivering without*). **3** in outward appearance (*rough without but kind within*). **4** outside the city walls (*Bishopsgate without*). □ **without end** infinite, eternal. [OE *withūtan* (as WITH, *ūtan* from outside, formed as OUT)]
■ *prep.* **1** see EMPTY *adj.* 6. **2** see FREE *adj.* 4. ● *adv.* **1–3** see OUTSIDE *adv.*

withstand /wit͟hstánd/ *v.* (*past* and *past part.* **-stood** /-stóod/) **1** *tr.* oppose, resist, hold out against (a person, force, etc.). **2** *intr.* make opposition; offer resistance. □□ **withstander** *n.* [OE *withstandan* f. *with-* against (as WITH) + STAND]
■ **1** resist, oppose, stand (up to), face, defy, confront, combat, grapple with, fight against, cope with, hold out against, bear up against, weather, suffer, survive, tolerate, take, bear, last through, endure, support, brave, *colloq.* stick.

withy /wít͟hi/ *n.* (*pl.* **-ies**) **1** a willow of any species. **2** var. of WITHE.

witless /wítliss/ *adj.* **1** lacking wits; foolish, stupid. **2** crazy. □□ **witlessly** *adv.* **witlessness** *n.* [OE *witlēas* (as WIT[1], -LESS)]
■ see FOOLISH.

witling /wítling/ *n. archaic* usu. *derog.* a person who fancies himself or herself as a wit.

witness /wítniss/ *n.* & *v.* ● *n.* **1** a person present at some event and able to give information about it (cf. EYEWITNESS). **2 a** a person giving sworn testimony. **b** a person attesting another's signature to a document. **3** (foll. by *to, of*) a person or thing whose existence, condition, etc., attests or proves something (*is a living witness to their generosity*). **4** testimony, evidence, confirmation. ● *v.* **1** *tr.* be a witness of (an event etc.) (*did you witness the accident?*). **2** *tr.* be witness to the authenticity of (a document or signature). **3** *tr.* serve as evidence or an indication of. **4** *intr.* (foll. by *against, for, to*) give or serve as evidence. □ **bear witness to** (or **of**) **1** attest the truth of. **2** state one's belief in. **call to witness** appeal to for confirmation etc. **witness-box** (*US* **-stand**) an enclosure in a lawcourt from which witnesses give evidence. [OE *witnes* (as WIT[1], -NESS)]
■ *n.* **1** observer, onlooker, spectator, viewer, eyewitness, bystander, watcher, looker-on. **2** *Law* deponent, testifier, corroborating witness, corroborator. **3** see MONUMENT 4. **4** see TESTIMONY 1, 2. ● *v.* **1** see, observe, watch, look on *or* at, view, mark, note, notice, take in, catch, *colloq.* spot, *literary* behold. **2** countersign, sign, certify, endorse, substantiate, validate, document, certificate, *US* notarize. **3, 4** see *bear witness to* below. □ **bear witness to** (or **of**) **1** testify (to), attest (to), witness (to), be *or* give *or* provide *or* furnish *or* constitute evidence of *or* to, be *or* give *or* provide *or* furnish *or* constitute proof of *or* to, be *or* give *or* provide *or* furnish *or* constitute testimony of *or* to, verify, confirm, corroborate, show, prove, bear out. **2** avow, asseverate, confess, profess, declare, affirm, *archaic or rhet.* avouch, *formal* aver.

witter /wíttər/ *v.intr.* (often foll. by *on*) *colloq.* speak tediously on trivial matters. [20th c.: prob. imit.]

■ see PRATTLE *v.*

witticism /wíttisiz'm/ *n.* a witty remark. [coined by Dryden (1677) f. WITTY, after *criticism*]

■ pun, quip, play on words, paronomasia, *bon mot*, *mot*, jest, joke, epigram, clever remark, sally, gag, *colloq.* wisecrack, one-liner, *literary* conceit.

witting /wítting/ *adj.* **1** aware. **2** intentional. □□ **wittingly** *adv.* [ME f. WIT[2] + -ING[2]]

■ □□ **wittingly** see *deliberately* (DELIBERATE).

witty /wítti/ *adj.* (**wittier, wittiest**) **1** showing verbal wit. **2** characterized by wit or humour. □□ **wittily** *adv.* **wittiness** *n.* [OE *witig*, *wittig* (as WIT[1], -Y[1])]

■ ingenious, subtle, clever, quick-witted, sharp-witted, humorous, sarcastic, sardonic, piquant, epigrammatic, humorous, comic(al), facetious, amusing, jocular, waggish, droll, funny.

wivern var. of WYVERN.

wives *pl.* of WIFE.

wiz var. of WHIZ *n.* 2.

wizard /wízzərd/ *n.* & *adj.* ● *n.* **1** a sorcerer; a magician. **2** a person of remarkable powers, a genius. **3** a conjuror. ● *adj. sl.* esp. *Brit.* wonderful, excellent. □□ **wizardly** *adj.* **wizardry** *n.* [ME f. WISE[1] + -ARD]

■ *n.* **1, 3** see MAGICIAN 1. **2** see VIRTUOSO 1a. □□ **wizardry** see MAGIC *n.* 1, 2.

wizened /wízz'nd/ *adj.* (also **wizen**) (of a person or face etc.) shrivelled-looking. [past part. of *wizen* shrivel f. OE *wisnian* f. Gmc]

■ wrinkled, shrunken, shrivelled (up), withered, gnarled, dried up, wilted, faded, wasted.

wk. *abbr.* **1** week. **2** work. **3** weak.

wks. *abbr.* weeks.

Wm. *abbr.* William.

WMO *abbr.* World Meteorological Organization.

WNW *abbr.* west-north-west.

WO *abbr.* Warrant Officer.

wo /wō/ *int.* = WHOA. [var. of *who* (int.), HO]

w.o. *abbr.* walk-over.

woad /wōd/ *n. hist.* **1** a cruciferous plant, *Isatis tinctoria*, yielding a blue dye now superseded by indigo. **2** the dye obtained from this. [OE *wād* f. Gmc]

wobbegong /wóbbigong/ *n.* an Australian brown shark, *Orectolobus maculatus*, with buff patterned markings. [Aboriginal]

wobble /wóbb'l/ *v.* & *n.* ● *v.* **1 a** *intr.* sway or vibrate unsteadily from side to side. **b** *tr.* cause to do this. **2** *intr.* stand or go unsteadily; stagger. **3** *intr.* waver, vacillate; act inconsistently. **4** *intr.* (of the voice or sound) quaver, pulsate. ● *n.* **1** a wobbling movement. **2** an instance of vacillation or pulsation. □ **wobble-board** *Austral.* a piece of fibreboard used as a musical instrument with a low booming sound. □□ **wobbler** *n.* [earlier *wabble*, corresp. to LG *wabbeln*, ON *vafla* waver f. Gmc: cf. WAVE, WAVER, -LE[4]]

■ *v.* **1** see SHAKE *v.* 1, 2, 5. **2** see STAGGER *v.* 1a. **4** see QUIVER[1] *v.* ● *n.* see SHAKE *n.* 1.

wobbly /wóbli/ *adj.* (**wobblier, wobbliest**) **1** wobbling or tending to wobble. **2** wavy, undulating (*a wobbly line*). **3** unsteady; weak after illness (*feeling wobbly*). **4** wavering, vacillating, insecure (*the economy was wobbly*). □ **throw a wobbly** *sl.* have a fit of nerves. □□ **wobbliness** *n.*

■ see SHAKY. □ **throw a wobbly** see RAGE *v.*

wodge /woj/ *n. Brit. colloq.* a chunk or lump. [alt. of WEDGE[1]]

■ see SLAB *n.*

woe /wō/ *n. archaic* or *literary* **1** affliction; bitter grief; distress. **2** (in *pl.*) calamities, troubles. **3** *joc.* problems (*told me a tale of woe*). □ **woe betide** there will be unfortunate consequences for (*woe betide you if you are late*). **woe is me** an exclamation of distress. [OE *wā*, *wǣ* f. Gmc, a natural exclam. of lament]

■ **1** trouble, hardship, adversity, misery, anguish, tribulation, calamity, wretchedness, grief, unhappiness, desolation, melancholy, gloom, depression, sadness, disconsolateness, misfortune, affliction, sorrow, distress, suffering, *literary* dolour. **2** (*woes*) troubles, calamities, hardships, trials, tribulations, adversities, misfortunes, afflictions, problems.

woebegone /wṓbigon/ *adj.* dismal-looking. [WOE + *begone* = surrounded f. OE *begān* (as BE-, GO[1])]

■ troubled, miserable, anguished, wretched, grief-stricken, unhappy, desolate, doleful, melancholy, melancholic, gloomy, mournful, sorrowful, depressed, dejected, sad, glum, crestfallen, chap-fallen, lugubrious, downcast, disconsolate, dismal, unfortunate, afflicted, distressed, woeful, forlorn, downhearted, broken-hearted, heartbroken, disheartened, *archaic* star-crossed, *literary* or *joc.* dolorous.

woeful /wṓfōōl/ *adj.* **1** sorrowful; afflicted with distress (*a woeful expression*). **2** causing sorrow or affliction. **3** very bad; wretched (*woeful ignorance*). □□ **woefully** *adv.* **woefulness** *n.*

■ **1** see SORROWFUL 1. **2** see PATHETIC 1. **3** see AWFUL 1a, b. □□ **woefully** see *painfully* (PAINFUL).

wog[1] /wog/ *n. sl. offens.* a foreigner, esp. a non-White one. [20th c.: orig. unkn.]

wog[2] /wog/ *n. Austral. sl.* an illness or infection. [20th c.: orig. unkn.]

woggle /wógg'l/ *n.* a leather etc. ring through which the ends of a Scout's neckerchief are passed at the neck. [20th c.: orig. unkn.]

wok /wok/ *n.* a bowl-shaped frying-pan used in esp. Chinese cookery. [Cantonese]

woke *past* of WAKE[1].

woken *past part.* of WAKE[1].

wold /wōld/ *n.* a piece of high open uncultivated land or moor. [OE *wald* f. Gmc, perh. rel. to WILD: cf. WEALD]

wolf /wŏŏlf/ *n.* & *v.* ● *n.* (*pl.* **wolves** /wŏŏlvz/) **1** a wild flesh-eating tawny-grey mammal related to the dog, esp. *Canis lupus*, preying on sheep etc. and hunting in packs. **2** *sl.* a man given to seducing women. **3** a rapacious or greedy person. **4** *Mus.* **a** a jarring sound from some notes in a bowed instrument. **b** an out-of-tune effect when playing certain chords on old organs (before the present 'equal temperament' was in use). ● *v.tr.* (often foll. by *down*) devour (food) greedily. □ **cry wolf** raise repeated false alarms (so that a genuine one is disregarded). **have** (or **hold**) **a wolf by the ears** be in a precarious position. **keep the wolf from the door** avert hunger or starvation. **lone wolf** a person who prefers to act alone. **throw to the wolves** sacrifice without compunction. **wolf-cub 1** a young wolf. **2** *Brit.* the former name for a Cub Scout. **wolf-fish** any large voracious blenny of the genus *Anarrhichas*. **wolf in sheep's clothing** a hostile person who pretends friendship. **wolf-pack** an attacking group of submarines or aircraft. **wolf's-milk** spurge. **wolf-spider** any ground-dwelling spider of the family Lycosidae, hunting instead of trapping its prey. **wolf-whistle** *n.* a sexually admiring whistle by a man to a woman. ● *v.intr.* make a wolf-whistle. □□ **wolfish** *adj.* **wolfishly** *adv.* **wolflike** *adj.* & *adv.* [OE *wulf* f. Gmc]

■ *v.* see DEVOUR 1.

wolfhound /wŏŏlfhownd/ *n.* a borzoi or other dog of a kind used orig. to hunt wolves.

wolfram /wŏŏlfrəm/ *n.* **1** tungsten. **2** tungsten ore; a native tungstate of iron and manganese. [G: perh. f. *Wolf* WOLF + *Rahm* cream, or MHG *rām* dirt, soot]

wolframite /wŏŏlfrəmīt/ *n.* = WOLFRAM 2.

wolfsbane /wŏŏlfsbayn/ *n.* an aconite, esp. *Aconitum lycoctonum*.

wolfskin /wŏŏlfskin/ *n.* **1** the skin of a wolf. **2** a mat, cloak, etc., made from this.

wolverine /wŏŏlvəreen/ *n.* (also **wolverene**) = GLUTTON 3. [16th-c. *wolvering*, somehow derived f. *wolv-*, stem of WOLF]

wolves *pl.* of WOLF.

woman /wŏŏmmən/ *n.* (*pl.* **women** /wímmin/) **1** an adult human female. **2** the female sex; any or an average woman (*how does woman differ from man?*). **3** a wife or female sexual partner. **4** (prec. by *the*) emotions or characteristics traditionally associated with women (*brought out the woman in him*). **5** a man with characteristics traditionally associated with women. **6** (*attrib.*) female (*woman driver; women friends*). **7** (as second element in *comb.*) a woman of a specified nationality, profession, skill, etc. (*Englishwoman; horsewoman*). **8** *colloq.* a female domestic help. **9** *archaic* or *hist.* a queen's etc. female attendant ranking below lady (*woman of the bedchamber*). □ **woman of the streets** a prostitute. **Women's Institute** an organization of women in rural areas to meet regularly and participate in crafts, cultural activities, etc. **women's lib** *colloq.* = *women's liberation.* **women's libber** *colloq.* a supporter of women's liberation. **women's liberation** the liberation of women from inequalities and subservient status in relation to men, and from attitudes causing these. **Women's Liberation** (or **Movement**) a movement campaigning for women's liberation. **women's rights** rights that promote a position of legal and social equality of women with men. □□ **womanless** *adj.* **womanlike** *adj.* [OE *wīfmon, -man* (as WIFE, MAN), a formation peculiar to English, the ancient word being WIFE]

■ **1** female, lady, miss, *esp. Sc. & N.Engl. or poet.* lass, *archaic* gentlewoman, *archaic or literary* damsel, *archaic or poet.* maid, maiden, *archaic or US sl.* dame, *colloq.* girl; *colloq.* popsy, lassie, *joc. or derog.* baggage, *sl.* chick, gal, moll, *sl. derog.* piece, piece of goods, heifer, *sl. offens.* (bit *or* piece of) skirt, bit of fluff, *Austral. & NZ sl.* sheila, *Brit. sl.* bird, *US sl.* broad. **2** womankind, womenkind, womenfolk, the fair sex, *derog.* the weaker sex. **3** wife, spouse, bride, lady-love, sweetheart, lady, girl, girlfriend, mistress, concubine, mate, helpmate, partner, lover, inamorata, paramour, *archaic* leman, *colloq.* sweetie, better half, old lady *or* woman, *colloq. often derog.* little woman, *joc.* lady wife, *rhyming sl.* trouble and strife, *sl. or joc.* the missis. **8** domestic, (domestic) help, housekeeper, maid, cleaning woman *or* lady, cleaner, maidservant, chambermaid, charwoman, *archaic* handmaid(en), *Brit. colloq.* char, daily. **9** attendant, lady-in-waiting. □□ **womanlike** see FEMININE *adj.* 1.

womanhood /wŏŏmmənhŏŏd/ *n.* **1** female maturity. **2** womanly instinct. **3** womankind.

womanish /wŏŏmmənish/ *adj.* usu. *derog.* **1** (of a man) effeminate, unmanly. **2** suitable to or characteristic of a woman. □□ **womanishly** *adv.* **womanishness** *n.*

■ **1** see EFFEMINATE. **2** see FEMININE *adj.* 1.

womanize /wŏŏmmənīz/ *v.* (also **-ise**) **1** *intr.* chase after women; philander. **2** *tr.* make womanish. □□ **womanizer** *n.*

■ **1** see PHILANDER. □□ **womanizer** see *philanderer* (PHILANDER).

womankind /wŏŏmmənkīnd/ *n.* (also **womenkind** /wimmin-/) women in general.

womanly /wŏŏmmənli/ *adj.* (of a woman) having or showing qualities traditionally associated with women; not masculine or girlish. □□ **womanliness** *n.*

■ see FEMININE *adj.* 1.

womb /wōōm/ *n.* **1** the organ of conception and gestation in a woman and other female mammals; the uterus. **2** a place of origination and development. □□ **womblike** *adj.* [OE *wamb, womb*]

wombat /wómbat/ *n.* any burrowing plant-eating Australian marsupial of the family Vombatidae, resembling a small bear, with short legs. [Aboriginal]

women *pl.* of WOMAN.

womenfolk /wímminfōk/ *n.* **1** women in general. **2** the women in a family.

womenkind var. of WOMANKIND.

won *past* and *past part.* of WIN.

wonder /wúndər/ *n.* & *v.* ● *n.* **1** an emotion excited by what is unexpected, unfamiliar, or inexplicable, esp. surprise mingled with admiration or curiosity etc. **2** a strange or remarkable person or thing, specimen, event, etc. **3** (*attrib.*) having marvellous or amazing properties etc. (*a wonder drug*). **4** a surprising thing (*it is a wonder you were not hurt*). ● *v.* **1** *intr.* (often foll. by *at*, or *to* + infin.) be filled with wonder or great surprise. **2** *tr.* (foll. by *that* + clause) be surprised to find. **3** *tr.* desire or be curious to know (*I wonder what the time is*). **4** *tr.* expressing a tentative enquiry (*I wonder whether you would mind?*). **5** *intr.* (foll. by *about*) ask oneself with puzzlement or doubt about; question (*wondered about the sense of the decision*). □ **I shouldn't wonder** *colloq.* I think it likely. **I wonder** I very much doubt it. **no** (or **small**) **wonder** (often foll. by *that* + clause) one cannot be surprised; one might have guessed; it is natural. **the seven wonders of the world** seven buildings and monuments regarded in antiquity as specially remarkable. **wonder-struck** (or **-stricken**) reduced to silence by wonder. **wonders will never cease** an exclamation of extreme (usu. agreeable) surprise. **wonder-worker** a person who performs wonders. **work** (or **do**) **wonders 1** do miracles. **2** succeed remarkably. □□ **wonderer** *n.* [OE *wundor, wundrian*, of unkn. orig.]

■ *n.* **1** awe, astonishment, admiration, amazement, wonderment, surprise, stupefaction, fascination, curiosity. **2** prodigy, phenomenon, spectacle, rarity, sight, curiosity, miracle, *colloq.* knockout, stunner. ● *v.* **1** marvel, goggle, gawk, gape, stare, be awed, be thunderstruck, be amazed, be astonished, be surprised. **3** ponder, meditate, think, theorize, conjecture, puzzle, query, question, inquire, be inquisitive, be curious, ask oneself, speculate, cudgel one's brains, *literary* marvel, muse. **5** (*wonder about*) ask oneself about, question, doubt, puzzle over *or* about; question *or* doubt the sanity *or* reason *or* reasonableness of.

wonderful /wúndərfŏŏl/ *adj.* **1** very remarkable or admirable. **2** arousing wonder. □□ **wonderfully** *adv.* **wonderfulness** *n.* [OE *wunderfull* (as WONDER, -FUL)]

■ **1** see TERRIFIC 1b. **2** see STUNNING. □□ **wonderfully** see *beautifully* (BEAUTIFUL), WELL[1] *adv.* 9.

wondering /wúndəring/ *adj.* filled with wonder; marvelling (*their wondering gaze*). □□ **wonderingly** *adv.*

wonderland /wúndərland/ *n.* **1** a fairyland. **2** a land of surprises or marvels.

wonderment /wúndərmənt/ *n.* surprise, awe.

■ see WONDER *n.* 1.

wondrous /wúndrəss/ *adj.* & *adv. poet.* ● *adj.* wonderful. ● *adv.* wonderfully (*wondrous kind*). □□ **wondrously** *adv.* **wondrousness** *n.* [alt. of obs. *wonders* (adj. & adv.), = genit. of WONDER (cf. -S[3]) after *marvellous*]

wonky /wóngki/ *adj.* (**wonkier, wonkiest**) *Brit. sl.* **1** crooked. **2** loose, unsteady. **3** unreliable. □□ **wonkily** *adv.* **wonkiness** *n.* [fanciful formation]

■ **1** see CROOKED 1. **2** see SHAKY.

wont /wōnt/ *adj., n.,* & *v.* ● *predic.adj. archaic* or *literary* (foll. by *to* + infin.) accustomed (*as we were wont to say*). ● *n. formal* or *joc.* what is customary, one's habit (*as is my wont*). ● *v.tr.* & *intr.* (*3rd sing. present* **wonts** or **wont**; *past* **wont** or **wonted**) *archaic* make or become accustomed. [OE *gewunod* past part. of *gewunian* f. *wunian* dwell]

■ *n.* see CUSTOM 1a.

won't /wōnt/ *contr.* will not.

wonted /wṓntid/ *attrib.adj.* habitual, accustomed, usual.

woo /wōō/ *v.tr.* (**woos, wooed**) **1** court; seek the hand or love of (a woman). **2** try to win (fame, fortune, etc.). **3** seek the favour or support of. **4** coax or importune. □□ **wooable** *adj.* **wooer** *n.* [OE *wōgian* (intr.), *āwōgian* (tr.), of unkn. orig.]

■ **1** see COURT *v.* 1b. **2** chase, follow, pursue, seek. **3** make advances to, ingratiate oneself with, pay court to, curry favour with, *sl.* suck up to, butter up, *US* shine up to.

wood /wŏŏd/ *n.* **1 a** a hard fibrous material that forms the main substance of the trunk or branches of a tree or shrub. **b** this cut for timber or for fuel, or for use in crafts, manufacture, etc. **2** (in *sing.* or *pl.*) growing trees densely occupying a tract of land. **3** (prec. by *the*) wooden storage, esp. a cask, for wine etc. (*poured straight from the wood*). **4** a wooden-headed golf club. **5** = BOWL[2] *n.* 1. □ **not see the wood for the trees** fail to grasp the main issue from over-attention to details. **out of the wood** (or **woods**) out of danger or difficulty. **wood alcohol** methanol. **wood anemone** a wild spring-flowering anemone, *Anemone nemorosa*. **wood-engraver** a maker of wood-engravings. **wood-engraving 1** a relief cut on a block of wood sawn across the grain. **2** a print made from this. **3** the technique of making such reliefs and prints. **wood-fibre** fibre obtained from wood esp. as material for paper. **wood hyacinth** = BLUEBELL 1 . **wood nymph** a dryad or hamadryad. **wood pulp** wood-fibre reduced chemically or mechanically to pulp as raw material for paper. **wood-screw** a metal male screw with a slotted head and sharp point. **wood sorrel** a small plant, *Oxalis acetosella*, with trifoliate leaves and white flowers streaked with purple. **wood spirit** crude methanol obtained from wood. **wood warbler 1** a European woodland bird, *Phylloscopus sibilatrix*, with a trilling song. **2** any American warbler of the family Parulidae. **wood wool** fine pine etc. shavings used as a surgical dressing or for packing. □□ **woodless** *adj.* [OE *wudu*, *wi(o)du* f. Gmc]

■ **1 b** see TIMBER 1. **2** (*wood* or *woods*) woodland, forest, copse, brake, grove, covert, thicket, *Brit.* spinney, *esp. US* & *Austral.* brush; timber, trees.

woodbind /wŏŏdbīnd/ *n.* = WOODBINE.

woodbine /wŏŏdbīn/ *n.* **1** wild honeysuckle. **2** *US* Virginia creeper.

woodblock /wŏŏdblok/ *n.* a block from which woodcuts are made.

woodchuck /wŏŏdchuk/ *n.* a reddish-brown and grey N. American marmot, *Marmota monax*. Also called *groundhog*. [Amer. Ind. name: cf. Cree *wuchak*, *otchock*]

woodcock /wŏŏdkok/ *n.* (*pl.* same) any game-bird of the genus *Scolopax*, inhabiting woodland.

woodcraft /wŏŏdkraaft/ *n.* esp. *US* **1** skill in woodwork. **2** knowledge of woodland esp. in camping, scouting, etc.

woodcut /wŏŏdkut/ *n.* **1** a relief cut on a block of wood sawn along the grain. **2** a print made from this, esp. as an illustration in a book. **3** the technique of making such reliefs and prints.

woodcutter /wŏŏdkuttər/ *n.* **1** a person who cuts wood. **2** a maker of woodcuts.

wooded /wŏŏddid/ *adj.* having woods or many trees.

■ sylvan, forested, afforested, tree-covered, woody, timbered, *literary* bosky.

wooden /wŏŏdd'n/ *adj.* **1** made of wood. **2** like wood. **3 a** stiff, clumsy, or stilted; without animation or flexibility (*wooden movements*; *a wooden performance*). **b** expressionless (*a wooden stare*). □ **wooden-head** *colloq.* a stupid person. **wooden-headed** *colloq.* stupid. **wooden-headedness** *colloq.* stupidity. **wooden horse** = *Trojan Horse*. **wooden spoon** a booby prize (orig. a spoon given to the candidate coming last in the Cambridge mathematical tripos). □□ **woodenly** *adv.* **woodenness** *n.*

■ **1** wood, woody, ligneous. **3 a** stiff, rigid, inflexible, artificial, clumsy, stilted, unnatural, awkward, ungainly, spiritless, unanimated, dead, lifeless, dry, passionless, unimpassioned, colourless, deadpan. **b** vacant, empty, expressionless, impassive, deadpan, poker-faced. □ **wooden-headed** unintelligent, blockheaded, stupid, dull, insensitive, slow-witted, dull-witted, obtuse, oafish, doltish, tiny-minded, dim-witted, dunderheaded, *colloq.* thick.

woodgrouse /wŏŏdgrowss/ *n.* = CAPERCAILLIE.

woodland /wŏŏdlənd/ *n.* wooded country, woods (often *attrib.*: *woodland scenery*). □□ **woodlander** *n.*

woodlark /wŏŏdlaark/ *n.* a lark, *Lullula arborea*.

woodlouse /wŏŏdlowss/ *n.* (*pl.* **-lice** /-līss/) any small terrestrial isopod crustacean of the genus *Oniscus* etc. feeding on rotten wood etc. and often able to roll into a ball.

woodman /wŏŏdmən/ *n.* (*pl.* **-men**) **1** a forester. **2** a woodcutter.

woodmouse /wŏŏdmowss/ *n.* (*pl.* **-mice** /-mīss/) a fieldmouse.

woodnote /wŏŏdnōt/ *n.* (often in *pl.*) a natural or spontaneous note of a bird etc.

woodpecker /wŏŏdpekkər/ *n.* any bird of the family Picidae that climbs and taps tree-trunks in search of insects.

woodpie /wŏŏdpī/ *n.* a greater spotted woodpecker.

woodpigeon /wŏŏdpijən/ *n.* a dove, *Columba palumbus*, having white patches like a ring round its neck. Also called *ring-dove* (see RING[1]).

woodpile /wŏŏdpīl/ *n.* a pile of wood, esp. for fuel.

woodruff /wŏŏdruf/ *n.* a white-flowered plant of the genus *Galium*, esp. *G. odoratum* grown for the fragrance of its whorled leaves when dried or crushed.

woodrush /wŏŏdrush/ *n.* any grassy herbaceous plant of the genus *Luzula*.

woodshed /wŏŏdshed/ *n.* a shed where wood for fuel is stored. □ **something nasty in the woodshed** *colloq.* a shocking or distasteful thing kept secret.

woodsman /wŏŏdzmən/ *n.* (*pl.* **-men**) **1** a person who lives in or is familiar with woodland. **2** a person skilled in woodcraft.

woodsy /wŏŏdzi/ *adj.* *US* like or characteristic of woods. [irreg. f. WOOD + -Y[1]]

woodwasp /wŏŏdwosp/ *n.* any sawfly of the family Siricidae, esp. *Urocerus gigas*, that hangs its nest in trees and inserts its eggs into the wood of conifers where the larvae bore damaging tunnels.

woodwind /wŏŏdwind/ *n.* (often *attrib.*) **1** (*collect.*) the wind instruments of the orchestra that were (mostly) orig. made of wood, e.g. the flute and clarinet. **2** (usu. in *pl.*) an individual instrument of this kind or its player (*the woodwinds are out of tune*).

woodwork /wŏŏdwurk/ *n.* **1** the making of things in wood. **2** things made of wood, esp. the wooden parts of a building. □ **crawl** (or **come**) **out of the woodwork** *colloq.* (of something unwelcome) appear; become known. □□ **woodworker** *n.* **woodworking** *n.*

woodworm /wŏŏdwurm/ *n.* **1** the wood-boring larva of the furniture beetle. **2** the damaged condition of wood affected by this.

woody /wŏŏddi/ *adj.* (**woodier**, **woodiest**) **1** (of a region) wooded; abounding in woods. **2** like or of wood (*woody tissue*). □ **woody nightshade** see NIGHTSHADE. □□ **woodiness** *n.*

■ **1** see WOODED.

woodyard /wŏŏdyaard/ *n.* a yard where wood is used or stored.

woof[1] /wŏŏf/ *n.* & *v.* ● *n.* the gruff bark of a dog. ● *v.intr.* give a woof. [imit.]

woof[2] /wŏŏf/ *n.* = WEFT[1]. [OE *ōwef*, alt. of *ōwebb* (after *wefan* WEAVE[1]), formed as A-[2], WEB: infl. by *warp*]

woofer /wŏŏfər/ *n.* a loudspeaker designed to reproduce low frequencies (cf. TWEETER). [WOOF[1] + -ER[1]]

wool /wŏŏl/ *n.* **1** fine soft wavy hair from the fleece of sheep, goats, etc. **2 a** yarn produced from this hair. **b** cloth or clothing made from it. **3** any of various wool-like substances (*steel wool*). **4** soft short under-fur or down. **5** *colloq.* a person's hair, esp. when short and curly. □ **pull the wool over a person's eyes** deceive a person. **wool-fat** lanolin. **wool-fell** *Brit.* the skin of a sheep etc. with the fleece still on. **wool-gathering** absent-mindedness; dreamy inattention. **wool-grower** a breeder of sheep for wool. **wool-oil** suint. **wool-pack 1** a fleecy cumulus cloud. **2** *hist.* a bale of wool. **wool-skin** = *wool-fell*. **wool-sorters' disease** anthrax. **wool-stapler** a person who grades wool. □□ **wool-like** *adj.* [OE *wull* f. Gmc]

woollen /wŏŏllən/ *adj.* & *n.* (*US* **woolen**) ● *adj.* made wholly or partly of wool, esp. from short fibres. ● *n.* **1** a fabric produced from wool. **2** (in *pl.*) woollen garments. [OE *wullen* (as WOOL, -EN[2])]

woolly /wŏŏlli/ *adj.* & *n.* ● *adj.* (**woollier, woolliest**) **1** bearing or naturally covered with wool or wool-like hair. **2** resembling or suggesting wool (*woolly clouds*). **3** (of a sound) indistinct. **4** (of thought) vague or confused. **5** *Bot.* downy. **6** lacking in definition, luminosity, or incisiveness. ● *n.* (*pl.* **-ies**) *colloq.* a woollen garment, esp. a knitted pullover. □ **woolly-bear** a large hairy caterpillar, esp. of the tiger moth. □□ **woolliness** *n.*

■ *adj.* **1** fleecy, woollen, wool-bearing, laniferous, lanigerous, downy, fuzzy, furry, fluffy, shaggy, hairy, flocculent, flocky. **2** fleecy, fluffy, flocculent, flocky. **3, 4, 6** hazy, fuzzy, unclear, obscure(d), foggy, indistinct, confused, vague, cloudy, clouded, nebulous, ill-defined, imprecise.

Woolsack /wŏŏlsak/ *n.* **1** (in the UK) the Lord Chancellor's wool-stuffed seat in the House of Lords. **2** the position of Lord Chancellor.

woolshed /wŏŏlshed/ *n. Austral.* & *NZ* a large shed for shearing and baling wool.

woomera /wŏŏmmərə/ *n. Austral.* **1** an Aboriginal stick for throwing a dart or spear more forcibly. **2** a club used as a missile. [Aboriginal]

woop woop /wŏŏp wŏŏp/ *n. Austral.* & *NZ sl.* **1** a jocular name for a remote outback town or district. **2** (**Woop Woop**) an imaginary remote place. [mock Aboriginal]

woosh var. of WHOOSH.

woozy /wŏŏzi/ *adj.* (**woozier, wooziest**) *colloq.* **1** dizzy or unsteady. **2** dazed or slightly drunk. **3** vague. □□ **woozily** *adv.* **wooziness** *n.* [19th c.: orig. unkn.]

■ **1** see DIZZY *adj.* 1a. **2** see TIGHT *adj.* 6.

wop /wop/ *n. sl. offens.* an Italian or other S. European. [20th c.: orig. uncert.: perh. f. It. *guappo* bold, showy, f. Sp. *guapo* dandy]

Worcester sauce /wŏŏstər/ *n.* a pungent sauce first made in Worcester. [*Worcester* in S. England]

Worcs. *abbr.* Worcestershire.

word /wurd/ *n.* & *v.* ● *n.* **1** a sound or combination of sounds forming a meaningful element of speech, usu. shown with a space on either side of it when written or printed, used as part (or occas. as the whole) of a sentence. **2** speech, esp. as distinct from action (*bold in word only*). **3** one's promise or assurance (*gave us their word*). **4** (in *sing.* or *pl.*) a thing said, a remark or conversation. **5** (in *pl.*) the text of a song or an actor's part. **6** (in *pl.*) angry talk (*they had words*). **7** news, intelligence; a message. **8** a command, password, or motto (*gave the word to begin*). **9** a basic unit of the expression of data in a computer. ● *v.tr.* put into words; select words to express (*how shall we word that?*). □ **at a word** as soon as requested. **be as good as** (or **better than**) **one's word** fulfil (or exceed) what one has promised. **break one's word** fail to do what one has promised. **have no words for** be unable to express. **have a word** (often foll. by *with*) speak briefly (to). **in other words** expressing the same thing differently. **in so many words** explicitly or bluntly. **in a** (or **one**) **word** briefly. **keep one's word** do what one has promised. **my** (or **upon my**) **word** an exclamation of surprise or consternation. **not the word for it** not an adequate or appropriate description. **of few words** taciturn. **of one's word** reliable in keeping promises (*a woman of her word*). **on** (or **upon**) **my word** a form of asseveration. **put into words** express in speech or writing. **take a person at his** or **her word** interpret a person's words literally or exactly. **take a person's word for it** believe a person's statement without investigation etc. **too ... for words** too ... to be adequately described (*was too funny for words*). **waste words** talk in vain. **the Word** (or **Word of God**) the Bible. **word-blind** incapable of identifying written or printed words owing to a brain defect. **word-blindness** this condition. **word-deaf** incapable of identifying spoken words owing to a brain defect. **word-deafness** this condition. **word for word** in exactly the same or (of translation) corresponding words. **word-game** a game involving the making or selection etc. of words. **word of honour** an assurance given upon one's honour. **word of mouth** speech (only). **word-of-mouth** verbal, unwritten. **word order** the sequence of words in a sentence, esp. affecting meaning etc. **word-painting** a vivid description in writing. **word-perfect** knowing one's part etc. by heart. **word-picture** a piece of word-painting. **word processor** a purpose-built computer system for electronically storing text entered from a keyboard, incorporating corrections, and providing a printout. **words fail me** an expression of disbelief, dismay, etc. **word-square** a set of words of equal length written one under another to read the same down as across (e.g. *too old ode*). **a word to the wise** = VERB. SAP. □□ **wordage** *n.* **wordless** *adj.* **wordlessly** *adv.* **wordlessness** *n.* [OE f. Gmc]

■ *n.* **1** name, term, designation, locution, expression, phrase, *formal* appellation. **3** promise, pledge, vow, oath, (solemn) word of honour, undertaking, parole, assurance, warrant, guarantee, warranty. **4** utterance, expression, declaration, statement, remark, comment, observation; (little) talk, (brief) conversation, chat, discussion, consultation, dialogue, huddle, parley, tête-à-tête, confabulation, conference, interview, powwow, *colloq.* chit-chat, confab. **5** (*words*) lyrics, book, libretto, text, script, lines. **6** (*words*) quarrel, dispute, argument. **7** news, intelligence, information, facts, data, report, story, account, communiqué, bulletin, dispatch, advice, message, notice, notification, *colloq.* low-down, info, *literary* tidings, *sl.* dope, *Brit. sl.* gen, *esp. US sl.* poop. **8** command, order, decree, signal, direction, instruction, password, motto, *US colloq.* high sign. ● *v.* **1** put (forth), say, couch, express, phrase, utter, state, term, style, set forth. □ **break one's word** see RENEGE 1a. **have a word** speak, communicate, chat, converse, talk. **in a** (or **one**) **word** succinctly, briefly, in brief, in a few words, concisely, in short, in fine, in summary, in sum, in a nutshell, not to mince words, to make a long story short, when all is said and done, when it's all boiled down, in the final analysis, not to beat about the bush. **put into words** see EXPRESS[1] 1, 2. **the Word** (or **Word of God**) see SCRIPTURE 2a. **word for word** see VERBATIM. **word-of-mouth** see VERBAL *adj.* 2. □□ **wordless** see MUTE *adj.* 1–3. **wordlessly** see *silently* (SILENT).

wordbook /wúrdbŏŏk/ *n.* a book with lists of words; a vocabulary or dictionary.

wordfinder /wúrdfīndər/ *n.* (also **word-finder**; *US propr.* **Word finder**) a lexical reference tool designed to help the user select a suitable word for a given context; a thesaurus.

wording /wúrding/ *n.* **1** a form of words used. **2** the way in which something is expressed.

■ phraseology, language, phrasing, expression, diction, terminology, choice of words, word choice.

wordplay /wúrdplay/ *n.* use of words to witty effect, esp. by punning.

■ see WIT[1] 2.

wordsmith /wúrdsmith/ *n.* a skilled user or maker of words.

■ see WRITER 1.

wordy /wúrdi/ *adj.* (**wordier, wordiest**) **1** using or expressed in many or too many words; verbose. **2** consisting of words. □□ **wordily** *adv.* **wordiness** *n.* [OE *wordig* (as WORD, -Y[1])]

■ **1** verbose, prolix, rambling, long-winded, ponderous; pleonastic, redundant, repetitious; garrulous, windy, talkative, loquacious. □□ **wordiness** see RHETORIC 2.

wore[1] *past* of WEAR[1].

wore[2] *past* and *past part.* of WEAR[2].

work /wurk/ *n.* & *v.* ● *n.* **1** the application of mental or physical effort to a purpose; the use of energy. **2 a** a task to be undertaken. **b** the materials for this. **c** (prec. by *the*; foll. by *of*) a task occupying (no more than) a specified time (*the work of a moment*). **3** a thing done or made by work; the result of an action; an achievement; a thing made. **4** a person's employment or occupation etc., esp. as a means of earning income (*looked for work*; *is out of work*). **5 a** a literary or musical composition. **b** (in *pl.*) all such by an author or composer etc. **6** actions or experiences of a specified kind (*good work!*; *this is thirsty work*). **7 a** (in *comb.*) things or parts made of a specified material or with specified tools etc. (*ironwork*; *needlework*). **b** *archaic* needlework. **8** (in *pl.*) the operative part of a clock or machine. **9** *Physics* the exertion of force overcoming resistance or producing molecular change (*convert heat into work*). **10** (in *pl.*) *colloq.* all that is available; everything needed. **11** (in *pl.*) operations of building or repair (*road works*). **12** (in *pl.*; often treated as *sing.*) a place where manufacture is carried on. **13** (usu. in *pl.*) *Theol.* a meritorious act. **14** (usu. in *pl.* or in *comb.*) a defensive structure (*earthworks*). **15** (in *comb.*) **a** ornamentation of a specified kind (*poker-work*). **b** articles having this. ● *v.* (*past* and *past part.* **worked** or (esp. as *adj.*) **wrought**) **1** *intr.* (often foll. by *at*, *on*) do work; be engaged in bodily or mental activity. **2** *intr.* **a** be employed in certain work (*works in industry*; *works as a secretary*). **b** (foll. by *with*) be the workmate of (a person). **3** *intr.* (often foll. by *for*) make efforts; conduct a campaign (*works for peace*). **4** *intr.* (foll. by *in*) be a craftsman (in a material). **5** *intr.* operate or function, esp. effectively (*how does this machine work?*; *your idea will not work*). **6** *intr.* (of a part of a machine) run, revolve; go through regular motions. **7** *tr.* carry on, manage, or control (*cannot work the machine*). **8** *tr.* **a** put or keep in operation or at work; cause to toil (*this mine is no longer worked*; *works the staff very hard*). **b** cultivate (land). **9** *tr.* bring about; produce as a result (*worked miracles*). **10** *tr.* knead, hammer; bring to a desired shape or consistency. **11** *tr.* do, or make by, needlework etc. **12** *tr.* & *intr.* (cause to) progress or penetrate, or make (one's way), gradually or with difficulty in a specified way (*worked our way through the crowd*; *worked the peg into the hole*). **13** *intr.* (foll. by *loose* etc.) gradually become (loose etc.) by constant movement. **14** *tr.* artificially excite (*worked themselves into a rage*). **15** *tr.* solve (a sum) by mathematics. **16** *tr.* **a** purchase with one's labour instead of money (*work one's passage*). **b** obtain by labour the money for (one's way through university etc.). **17** *intr.* (foll. by *on*, *upon*) have influence. **18** *intr.* be in motion or agitated; cause agitation, ferment (*his features worked violently*; *the yeast began to work*). **19** *intr.* *Naut.* sail against the wind. □ **at work** in action or engaged in work. **give a person the works 1** *colloq.* give or tell a person everything. **2** *colloq.* treat a person harshly. **3** *sl.* kill a person. **have one's work cut out** be faced with a hard task. **in the works** *colloq.* in progress, in the pipeline. **in work 1** having a job. **2** *US* = *in the works* above. **out of work** unemployed. **set to work** begin or cause to begin operations. **work away** (or **on**) continue to work. **work-basket** (or **-bag** etc.) a basket or bag etc. containing sewing materials. **work camp** a camp at which community work is done esp. by young volunteers. **work one's fingers to the bone** see BONE. **work in** find a place for. **work it** *colloq.* bring it about; achieve a desired result. **work of art** a fine picture, poem, or building etc. **work off** get rid of by work or activity. **work out 1** solve (a sum) or find out (an amount) by calculation; resolve (a problem etc.). **2** (foll. by *at*) be calculated (*the total works out at 230*). **3** give a definite result (*this sum will not work out*). **4** have a specified or satisfactory result (*the plan worked out well*; *glad the arrangement worked out*). **5** provide for the details of (*has worked out a scheme*). **6** accomplish or attain with difficulty (*work out one's salvation*). **7** exhaust with work (*the mine is worked out*). **8** engage in physical exercise or training. **work over 1** examine thoroughly. **2** *colloq.* treat with violence. **works council** esp. *Brit.* a group of employees representing those employed in a works etc. in discussions with their employers. **work-shy** disinclined to work. **works of supererogation** see SUPEREROGATION. **work study** a system of assessing methods of working so as to achieve the maximum output and efficiency. **work table** a table for working at, esp. with a sewing-machine. **work to rule** (esp. as a form of industrial action) follow official working rules exactly in order to reduce output and efficiency. **work-to-rule** the act or an instance of working to rule. **work up 1** bring gradually to an efficient state. **2** (foll. by *to*) advance gradually to a climax. **3** elaborate or excite by degrees; bring to a state of agitation. **4** mingle (ingredients) into a whole. **5** learn (a subject) by study. **work one's will** (foll. by *on*, *upon*) *archaic* accomplish one's purpose on (a person or thing). **work wonders** see WONDER. □□ **workless** *adj.* [OE *weorc* etc. f. Gmc]

■ *n.* **1** labour, toil, effort, drudgery, exertion, industry, slog, *colloq.* grind, sweat, elbow-grease, *esp. Brit. colloq.* fag, *literary* travail, *sl.* graft, *Austral. sl.* yakka. **2** task, function, duty, service, assignment, job, project, charge, responsibility, chore, commission, undertaking, stint. **3** feat, achievement, creation, accomplishment, handiwork, workmanship, output, result, product, end-product, production. **4** employment, business, occupation, vocation, calling, profession, trade, line, *métier*, career, livelihood, job, post, position, situation. **5** opus, *oeuvre*, production; composition, creation, piece, writing(s), master-work, masterpiece, *chef-d'œuvre*, *magnum opus*. **8** (*works*) mechanism, machinery, action, workings, (moving *or* working) parts, guts, *colloq.* innards, insides; clockwork. **10** (*the works*) everything, the lot, everything but the kitchen sink, *colloq.* the whole shooting match, *sl.* the whole (kit and) caboodle, *US sl.* the whole shebang. **12** (*works*) plant, factory, workshop, shop, mill. ● *v.* **1** labour, toil, exert oneself, sweat, slave (away), peg away, slog (away), grind (away), fag, *archaic* moil, *colloq.* beaver, plug (away), *sl.* graft. **2 a** have a job, hold (down) a post *or* position, earn a living, be employed. **3** see STRIVE 1. **5** function, operate, run, go, perform; be effective, succeed. **7** control, manage, manipulate, manoeuvre, wield, ply, handle, operate, use, make use of, utilize, exploit, deal with, bring into play. **8 a** operate, use, employ, put to (good *or* effective) use; drive, exploit. **b** till, plough, farm, cultivate. **9** bring about, effect, accomplish, carry out *or* off, make, produce, achieve, engender, create, do, put through, execute, effectuate, implement, realize, *literary* beget. **10** knead, hammer, mould, form, fashion, shape; mix, stir, incorporate. **12** wade, plod, plough; manoeuvre, manipulate, guide, direct. **17** (*work on*) importune, press, pressurize, pressure; influence, persuade, wheedle, coax, act on, prevail upon, induce, dispose, urge. **18** see FERMENT *v.* 1, TWIST *v.* 1a, b. □ **give a person the works 2** give a person a thrashing *or* beating *or* drubbing *or* battering *or* flogging *or* lambasting, beat, thrash, *sl.* wallop. **in the works** in production, under way, being done, being planned, in the pipeline, in the planning stage(s), *US* in work. **out of work** unemployed, idle, jobless, between engagements, unwaged, available, free, redundant, *Brit. colloq.* on the dole, *US colloq.* on *or* collecting unemployment, *Brit. euphem.* resting. **work in** find time *or* space for, find a place for, include, insert, introduce, fit in, squeeze in, accommodate. **work of art** see MASTERPIECE 1. **work out 1** see SOLVE. **2** (*work out at*) equal, total (up to), tot up to, result in, amount to, come to. **4** go, develop, turn out, pan out, evolve; succeed, prosper, come out all right, prove satisfactory, go well, be effective. **5** formulate, work up, contrive, draw up, detail, plan, develop, devise, put together, elaborate, expand, enlarge (on). **8** exercise, do callisthenics, do aerobics, warm up, do setting-up exercises, jog, lift weights, train, *Brit. colloq.* do one's daily dozen. **work over 2** see POUND[2] 1a, b. **work-to-rule** slow-down, *Brit.* go-slow, industrial action. **work up 1** prepare, (make *or* get) ready, whip into shape, develop, come up with, write up, put together, produce, turn out. **2** advance, ascend, rise (in a crescendo), move up *or* ahead *or* on. **3** excite, make excited, agitate, inflame, arouse, rouse, foment, stir, move, animate, incite, spur, fire (up), *colloq.* get a person (all) steamed *or* het up, *literary* enkindle. □□ **workless** see *out of work* above.

workable /wúrkəb'l/ *adj.* **1** that can be worked or will work. **2** that is worth working; practicable, feasible (*a workable*

quarry; a workable scheme). □□ **workability** (/-bílliti/) *n.* **workableness** *n.* **workably** *adv.*
■ **1** see OPERABLE. **2** see FEASIBLE 1.

workaday /wúrkəday/ *adj.* **1** ordinary, everyday, practical. **2** fit for, used, or seen on workdays.
■ **1** see ORDINARY *adj.*

workaholic /wúrkəhóllik/ *n.* & *adj. colloq.* (a person) addicted to working.

workbench /wúrkbench/ *n.* a bench for doing mechanical or practical work, esp. carpentry.

workbox /wúrkboks/ *n.* a box for holding tools, materials for sewing, etc.

workday /wúrkday/ *n.* esp. *US* a day on which work is usually done.

worker /wúrkər/ *n.* **1** a person who works, esp. a manual or industrial employee. **2** a neuter or undeveloped female of various social insects, esp. a bee or ant, that does the basic work of its colony. □ **worker priest** a French Roman Catholic or an Anglican priest who engages part-time in secular work.
■ **1** labourer, working man *or* woman, workman, hand, operative, operator, employee; artisan, craftsman, tradesman, mechanic; drudge, journeyman, white-collar worker, blue-collar worker, proletarian, breadwinner, wage-earner.

workforce /wúrkforss/ *n.* **1** the workers engaged or available in an industry etc. **2** the number of such workers.
■ see STAFF[1] *n.* 2.

workhorse /wúrk-horss/ *n.* a horse, person, or machine that performs hard work.
■ see SLAVE *n.* 2.

workhouse /wúrk-howss/ *n.* **1** *Brit. hist.* a public institution in which the destitute of a parish received board and lodging in return for work done. **2** *US* a house of correction for petty offenders.

working /wúrking/ *adj.* & *n.* ● *adj.* **1** engaged in work, esp. in manual or industrial labour. **2** functioning or able to function. ● *n.* **1** the activity of work. **2** the act or manner of functioning of a thing. **3 a** a mine or quarry. **b** the part of this in which work is being or has been done (*a disused working*). □ **working capital** the capital actually used in a business. **working class** the class of people who are employed for wages, esp. in manual or industrial work. **working-class** *adj.* of the working class. **working day** esp. *Brit.* **1** a workday. **2** the part of the day devoted to work. **working drawing** a drawing to scale, serving as a guide for construction or manufacture. **working girl** *US sl.* a prostitute. **working hours** hours normally devoted to work. **working hypothesis** a hypothesis used as a basis for action. **working knowledge** knowledge adequate to work with. **working lunch** etc. a meal at which business is conducted. **working order** the condition in which a machine works (satisfactorily or as specified). **working-out 1** the calculation of results. **2** the elaboration of details. **working party** a group of people appointed to study a particular problem or advise on some question.
■ *adj.* **1** see BUSY *adj.* 3. **2** see FUNCTIONAL 1, ACTIVE *adj.* 2, 3. ● *n.* **3** see PIT[1] *n.* 1. □ **working-class** (*adj.*) see PLEBEIAN *adj.* 1.

workload /wúrklōd/ *n.* the amount of work to be done by an individual etc.

workman /wúrkmən/ *n.* (*pl.* **-men**) **1** a man employed to do manual labour. **2** a person considered with regard to skill in a job (*a good workman*).
■ see WORKER.

workmanlike /wúrkmənlīk/ *adj.* characteristic of a good workman; showing practised skill.
■ see YEOMANLY.

workmanship /wúrkmənship/ *n.* **1** the degree of skill in doing a task or of finish in the product made. **2** a thing made or created by a specified person etc.
■ **1** craft, craftsmanship, artistry, art, technique, handiwork, skill, skilfulness, mastery, artisanship.

workmate /wúrkmayt/ *n.* a person engaged in the same work as another.

workout /wúrkowt/ *n.* a session of physical exercise or training.
■ see EXERCISE *n.* 3.

workpeople /wúrkpeep'l/ *n.pl.* people in paid employment.

workpiece /wúrkpeess/ *n.* a thing worked on with a tool or machine.

workplace /wúrkplayss/ *n.* a place at which a person works; an office, factory, etc.

workroom /wúrkrōōm, -rŏŏm/ *n.* a room for working in, esp. one equipped for a certain kind of work.

worksheet /wúrksheet/ *n.* **1** a paper for recording work done or in progress. **2** a paper listing questions or activities for students etc. to work through.

workshop /wúrkshop/ *n.* **1** a room or building in which goods are manufactured. **2 a** a meeting for concerted discussion or activity (*a dance workshop*). **b** the members of such a meeting.

workstation /wúrkstaysh'n/ *n.* **1** the location of a stage in a manufacturing process. **2** a computer terminal or the desk etc. where this is located.

worktop /wúrktop/ *n.* a flat surface for working on, esp. in a kitchen.

workwoman /wúrkwŏŏmmən/ *n.* (*pl.* **-women**) a female worker or operative.

world /wurld/ *n.* **1 a** the earth, or a planetary body like it. **b** its countries and their inhabitants. **c** all people; the earth as known or in some particular respect. **2 a** the universe or all that exists; everything. **b** everything that exists outside oneself (*dead to the world*). **3 a** the time, state, or scene of human existence. **b** (prec. by *the, this*) mortal life. **4** secular interests and affairs. **5** human affairs; their course and conditions; active life (*how goes the world with you?*). **6** average, respectable, or fashionable people or their customs or opinions. **7** all that concerns or all who belong to a specified class, time, domain, or sphere of activity (*the medieval world; the world of sport*). **8** (foll. by *of*) a vast amount (*that makes a world of difference*). **9** (*attrib.*) affecting many nations, of all nations (*world politics; a world champion*). □ **all the world and his wife 1** any large mixed gathering of people. **2** all with pretensions to fashion. **be worlds apart** differ greatly, esp. in nature or opinion. **bring into the world** give birth to or attend at the birth of. **carry the world before one** have rapid and complete success. **come into the world** be born. **for all the world** (foll. by *like, as if*) precisely (*looked for all the world as if they were real*). **get the best of both worlds** benefit from two incompatible sets of ideas, circumstances, etc. **in the world** of all; at all (used as an intensifier in questions) (*what in the world is it?*). **man** (or **woman**) **of the world** a person experienced and practical in human affairs. **the next** (or **other**) **world** a supposed life after death. **out of this world** *colloq.* extremely good etc. (*the food was out of this world*). **see the world** travel widely; gain wide experience. **think the world of** have a very high regard for. **World Bank** *colloq.* the International Bank for Reconstruction and Development, an organization administering economic aid between member nations. **world-beater** a person or thing surpassing all others. **world-class** of a quality or standard regarded as high throughout the world. **World Cup** a competition between football or other sporting teams from various countries. **world-famous** known throughout the world. **the world, the flesh, and the devil** the various kinds of temptation. **world language 1** an artificial language for international use. **2** a language spoken in many countries. **world-line** *Physics* a curve in space-time joining the positions of a particle throughout its existence. **the** (or **all the**) **world over** throughout the world. **world power** a nation having power and influence in world affairs. **the world's end** the farthest attainable point of travel. **World**

Series the US championship for baseball teams. **world-shaking** of supreme importance. **the world to come** supposed life after death. **world-view** = WELTANSCHAUUNG. **world war** a war involving many important nations (*First World War* of 1914-18; *Second World War* of 1939-45). **world-weariness** being world-weary. **world-weary** weary of the world and life on it. **world without end** for ever. [OE *w(e)orold, world* f. a Gmc root meaning 'age': rel. to OLD]

■ **1 a** earth, planet, sphere, globe. **c** humanity, mankind, people, the human race, society, the public, men, humankind, everybody, everyone, the world at large. **2 a** universe, cosmos, existence, creation, life; everything. **5** affairs, things, circumstances, events, life. **7** period, time, age, era, epoch, time(s); area, sphere, domain, community, clique, crowd, circle, fraternity, faction, set, coterie. □ **bring into the world** deliver, have, bear, give birth to, *US colloq.* birth, *literary* beget. **for all the world** precisely, exactly, in all respects, in every respect, in every way, just. **out of this world** marvellous, wonderful, exceptional, unbelievable, incredible, excellent, superb, far-out, *colloq.* great, smashing, fantastic, fabulous, out of sight, magic; see also EXCELLENT.

worldling /wúrldling/ *n.* a worldly person.

worldly /wúrldli/ *adj.* (**worldlier, worldliest**) **1** temporal or earthly (*worldly goods*). **2** engrossed in temporal affairs, esp. the pursuit of wealth and pleasure. □ **worldly-minded** intent on worldly things. **worldly wisdom** prudence as regards one's own interests. **worldly-wise** having worldly wisdom. □□ **worldliness** *n.* [OE *woruldlic* (as WORLD, -LY[1])]

■ **1** mundane, earthly, terrestrial, temporal, physical, carnal, fleshly, corporeal, human, material; lay, non-spiritual, non-religious, civic, secular, profane. **2** urbane, suave, sophisticated, cosmopolitan, worldly-wise, *colloq.* with it, *sl.* hip, hep, cool.

worldwide /wúrldwīd/ *adj.* & *adv.* ● *adj.* affecting, occurring in, or known in all parts of the world. ● *adv.* throughout the world.

■ *adj.* see GLOBAL 1.

worm /wurm/ *n.* & *v.* ● *n.* **1** any of various types of creeping or burrowing invertebrate animals with long slender bodies and no limbs, esp. segmented in rings or parasitic in the intestines or tissues. **2** the long slender larva of an insect, esp. in fruit or wood. **3** (in *pl.*) intestinal or other internal parasites. **4** a blindworm or slow-worm. **5** a maggot supposed to eat dead bodies in the grave. **6** an insignificant or contemptible person. **7 a** the spiral part of a screw. **b** a short screw working in a worm-gear. **8** the spiral pipe of a still in which the vapour is cooled and condensed. **9** the ligament under a dog's tongue. ● *v.* **1** *intr.* & *tr.* (often *refl.*) move with a crawling motion (*wormed through the bushes*; *wormed our way through the bushes*). **2** *intr.* & *refl.* (foll. by *into*) insinuate oneself into a person's favour, confidence, etc. **3** *tr.* (foll. by *out*) obtain (a secret etc.) by cunning persistence (*managed to worm the truth out of them*). **4** *tr.* cut the worm of (a dog's tongue). **5** *tr.* rid (a plant or dog etc.) of worms. **6** *tr. Naut.* make (a rope etc.) smooth by winding thread between the strands. □ **food for worms** a dead person. **worm-cast** a convoluted mass of earth left on the surface by a burrowing earthworm. **worm-fishing** fishing with worms for bait. **worm-gear** an arrangement of a toothed wheel worked by a revolving spiral. **worm-hole** a hole left by the passage of a worm. **worm-seed 1** seed used to expel intestinal worms. **2** a plant e.g. santonica bearing this seed. **worm's-eye view** a view as seen from below or from a humble position. **worm-wheel** the wheel of a worm-gear. **a** (or **even a**) **worm will turn** the meekest will resist or retaliate if pushed too far. □□ **wormer** *n.* **wormlike** *adj.* [OE *wyrm* f. Gmc]

■ *n.* **6** see WRETCH 2. ● *v.* **1** see SLITHER *v.* **2** (*worm oneself*) see INSINUATE 2a, b. **3** (*worm out*) see EXTRACT *v.* 2.

wormeaten /wúrmeet'n/ *adj.* **1 a** eaten into by worms. **b** rotten, decayed. **2** old and dilapidated.

wormwood /wúrmwŏŏd/ *n.* **1** any woody shrub of the genus *Artemisia*, with a bitter aromatic taste, used in the preparation of vermouth and absinthe and in medicine. **2** bitter mortification or a source of this. [ME, alt. f. obs. *wormod* f. OE *wormōd, wermōd*, after *worm, wood*: cf. VERMOUTH]

wormy /wúrmi/ *adj.* (**wormier, wormiest**) **1** full of worms. **2** wormeaten. □□ **worminess** *n.*

worn /worn/ *past part.* of WEAR[1]. ● *adj.* **1** damaged by use or wear. **2** looking tired and exhausted. **3** (in full **well-worn**) (of a joke etc.) stale; often heard.

■ *adj.* **1** shabby, threadbare, tatty, tattered, ragged, frayed, dilapidated, *Austral. sl.* warby. **2** worn out, tired, fatigued, exhausted, spent, jaded, played out, haggard, drawn, shattered, the worse for wear, dog-tired, *colloq.* fagged (out), dead (on one's feet), frazzled, all in, done in, *esp. Brit. colloq.* whacked, *US colloq.* pooped, *sl.* beat, *Brit. sl.* knackered. **3** see BANAL.

worriment /wúrrimənt/ *n.* esp. *US* **1** the act of worrying or state of being worried. **2** a cause of worry.

worrisome /wúrrisəm/ *adj.* causing or apt to cause worry or distress. □□ **worrisomely** *adv.*

■ see TROUBLESOME 2.

worrit /wúrrit/ *n. colloq.* = WORRY. [orig. alt. in general use of WORRY]

worry /wúrri/ *v.* & *n.* ● *v.* (**-ies, -ied**) **1** *intr.* give way to anxiety or unease; allow one's mind to dwell on difficulty or troubles. **2** *tr.* harass, importune; be a trouble or anxiety to. **3** *tr.* **a** (of a dog etc.) shake or pull about with the teeth. **b** attack repeatedly. **4** (as **worried** *adj.*) **a** uneasy, troubled in the mind. **b** suggesting worry (*a worried look*). ● *n.* (*pl.* **-ies**) **1** a thing that causes anxiety or disturbs a person's tranquillity. **2** a disturbed state of mind; anxiety; a worried state. **3** a dog's worrying of its quarry. □ **not to worry** *colloq.* there is no need to worry. **worry along** (or **through**) manage to advance by persistence in spite of obstacles. **worry beads** a string of beads manipulated with the fingers to occupy or calm oneself. **worry-guts** (or **-wart**) *colloq.* a person who habitually worries unduly. **worry oneself** (usu. in *neg.*) take needless trouble. **worry out** obtain (the solution to a problem etc.) by dogged effort. □□ **worriedly** *adv.* **worrier** *n.* **worryingly** *adv.* [OE *wyrgan* strangle f. WG]

■ *v.* **1** be anxious, be fearful, be apprehensive, be nervous *or* a bundle of nerves, be concerned, fret, brood, agonize, be distressed, be vexed, *colloq.* stew, bite *or* chew one's nails, go *or* get grey, get grey hair, sweat blood. **2** annoy, irk, pester, nettle, harry, harass, irritate, tease, bother, torment, trouble, perturb, vex, plague, provoke, importune, hector, badger, gall, get on a person's nerves, get *or* put a person's back up, *colloq.* peeve, hassle, needle. **4** (**worried**) fearful, apprehensive, anxious, distressed, nervous, uneasy, anguished, disquieted, agonized, agonizing, distraught, on edge, on tenterhooks, ill at ease, troubled, fretful, agitated, perturbed, upset, suffering. ● *n.* **1** concern, care, responsibility; problem, bother, burden, trouble, tribulation, affliction, irritation, annoyance, vexation. **2** anguish, anxiety, uneasiness, unease, nervousness, distress, apprehension, disquiet, perturbation, agitation, upset, misgiving, *colloq.* worrit.

worse /wurss/ *adj.*, *adv.*, & *n.* ● *adj.* **1** more bad. **2** (*predic.*) in or into worse health or a worse condition (*is getting worse*; *is none the worse for it*). ● *adv.* more badly or more ill. ● *n.* **1** a worse thing or things (*you might do worse than accept*). **2** (prec. by *the*) a worse condition (*a change for the worse*). □ **none the worse** (often foll. by *for*) not adversely affected (by). **or worse** or as an even worse alternative. **the worse for drink** fairly drunk. **the worse for wear 1** damaged by use. **2** injured. **3** *joc.* drunk. **worse luck** see LUCK. **worse off** in a worse (esp. financial) position. [OE *wyrsa, wiersa* f. Gmc]

worsen /wúrs'n/ *v.tr.* & *intr.* make or become worse.

■ exacerbate, aggravate; weaken, deteriorate, decline, degenerate, decay, slip, sink, slide, fail, disintegrate, take a turn for the worse, get worse, go from bad to worse, *colloq.* go downhill.

worship /wúrship/ *n.* & *v.* ● *n.* **1 a** homage or reverence paid to a deity, esp. in a formal service. **b** the acts, rites, or ceremonies of worship. **2** adoration or devotion comparable to religious homage shown towards a person or principle (*the worship of wealth*; *regarded them with worship in their eyes*). **3** *archaic* worthiness, merit; recognition given or due to these; honour and respect. ● *v.* (**worshipped, worshipping**; *US* **worshiped, worshiping**) **1** *tr.* adore as divine; honour with religious rites. **2** *tr.* idolize or regard with adoration (*worships the ground she walks on*). **3** *intr.* attend public worship. **4** *intr.* be full of adoration. □ **Your** (or **His** or **Her**) **Worship** esp. *Brit.* a title of respect used to or of a mayor, certain magistrates, etc. □□ **worshipper** *n.* (*US* **worshiper**). [OE *weorthscipe* (as WORTH, -SHIP)]
■ *n.* **1, 2** veneration, reverence, adoration, devotion, homage, honour, respect, esteem, exaltation, praise, admiration, adulation, glorification, deification, idolatry. ● *v.* **1, 2** venerate, revere, reverence, extol, honour, hallow, exalt, praise, admire, adore, adulate, glorify, deify, idolize, be devoted to, pay homage to, bow down before, kneel before, put on a pedestal, *archaic* magnify.

worshipful /wúrshipfŏŏl/ *adj.* **1** (usu. **Worshipful**) *Brit.* a title given to justices of the peace and to certain old companies or their officers etc. **2** *archaic* entitled to honour or respect. **3** *archaic* imbued with a spirit of veneration. □□ **worshipfully** *adv.* **worshipfulness** *n.*

worst /wurst/ *adj., adv., n.,* & *v.* ● *adj.* most bad. ● *adv.* most badly. ● *n.* the worst part, event, circumstance, or possibility (*the worst of the storm is over*; *prepare for the worst*). ● *v.tr.* get the better of; defeat, outdo. □ **at its** etc. **worst** in the worst state. **at worst** (or **the worst**) in the worst possible case. **do your worst** an expression of defiance. **get** (or **have**) **the worst of it** be defeated. **if the worst comes to the worst** if the worst happens. [OE *wierresta, wyrresta* (adj.), *wyrst, wyrrest* (adv.), f. Gmc]
■ *v.* see BEAT *v.* 3a.

worsted /wŏŏstid/ *n.* **1** a fine smooth yarn spun from combed long staple wool. **2** fabric made from this. [*Worste(a)d* in S. England]

wort /wurt/ *n.* **1** *archaic* (except in names) a plant or herb (*liverwort*; *St John's wort*). **2** the infusion of malt which after fermentation becomes beer. [OE *wyrt*: rel. to ROOT[1]]

worth /wurth/ *adj.* & *n.* ● *predic.adj.* (governing a noun like a preposition) **1** of a value equivalent to (*is worth £50*; *is worth very little*). **2** such as to justify or repay; deserving; bringing compensation for (*worth doing*; *not worth the trouble*). **3** possessing or having property amounting to (*is worth a million pounds*). ● *n.* **1** what a person or thing is worth; the (usu. specified) merit of (*of great worth*; *persons of worth*). **2** the equivalent of money in a commodity (*ten pounds' worth of petrol*). □ **for all one is worth** *colloq.* with one's utmost efforts; without reserve. **for what it is worth** without a guarantee of its truth or value. **worth it** *colloq.* worth the time or effort spent. **worth one's salt** see SALT. **worth while** (or **one's while**) see WHILE. [OE *w(e)orth*]
■ *n.* **1** quality, merit, value, advantage, benefit, good, importance, significance, usefulness.

worthless /wúrthliss/ *adj.* without value or merit. □□ **worthlessly** *adv.* **worthlessness** *n.*
■ valueless, unimportant, insignificant, inessential, unessential, dispensable, disposable, meaningless, paltry, trifling; pointless, silly, inane, vain, unavailing, useless, futile, fruitless, unproductive, unprofitable, *archaic* bootless; cheap, tawdry, poor, trashy, rubbishy, shabby, wretched, tinny, chintzy, *sl.* cheesy.

worthwhile /wúrthwīl/ *adj.* that is worth the time or effort spent; of value or importance. □□ **worthwhileness** *n.*
■ profitable, justifiable, productive, gainful, rewarding, fruitful, cost-effective, remunerative, beneficial, helpful, advantageous; useful, valuable, invaluable, important, good, worthy, desirable.

worthy /wúrthi/ *adj.* & *n.* ● *adj.* (**worthier, worthiest**) **1** estimable; having some moral worth; deserving respect (*lived a worthy life*). **2** (of a person) entitled to (esp. condescending) recognition (*a worthy old couple*). **3 a** (foll. by *of* or *to* + infin.) deserving (*worthy of a mention*; *worthy to be remembered*). **b** (foll. by *of*) adequate or suitable to the dignity etc. of (*in words worthy of the occasion*). ● *n.* (*pl.* **-ies**) **1** a worthy person. **2** a person of some distinction. **3** *joc.* a person. □□ **worthily** *adv.* **worthiness** *n.* [ME *wurthi* etc. f. WORTH]
■ *adj.* **1** worthwhile, meritorious, praiseworthy, good, estimable, exemplary, creditable, commendable, laudable, honourable, upright, sterling, irreproachable, respectable. **3 a** deserving, meriting, qualified, fit. ● *n.* **2** dignitary, personage, notable, eminence, celebrity, luminary.

-worthy /wurthi/ *comb. form* forming adjectives meaning: **1** deserving of (*blameworthy*; *noteworthy*). **2** suitable or fit for (*newsworthy*; *roadworthy*).

wot see WIT[2].

wotcher /wóchər/ *int. Brit. sl.* a form of casual greeting. [corrupt. of *what cheer*]

would /wŏŏd, wəd/ *v.aux.* (*3rd sing.* **would**) *past* of WILL[1], used esp.: **1** (in the 2nd and 3rd persons, and often in the 1st: see SHOULD). **a** in reported speech (*he said he would be home by evening*). **b** to express the conditional mood (*they would have been killed if they had gone*). **2** to express habitual action (*would wait for her every evening*). **3** to express a question or polite request (*would they like it?*; *would you come in, please?*). **4** to express probability (*I guess she would be over fifty by now*). **5** (foll. by *that* + clause) *literary* to express a wish (*would that you were here*). **6** to express consent (*they would not help*). □ **would-be** often *derog.* desiring or aspiring to be (*a would-be politician*). [OE *wolde*, past of *wyllan*: see WILL[1]]
■ □ **would-be** professed; see also SELF-STYLED.

wouldn't /wŏŏdd'nt/ *contr.* would not. □ **I wouldn't know** *colloq.* (as is to be expected) I do not know. **wouldn't it!** esp. *Austral.* & *NZ sl.* an interjection expressing dismay or disgust.

wouldst /wŏŏdst/ *archaic 2nd sing. past* of WOULD.

Woulfe bottle /wŏŏlf/ *n. Chem.* a jar with more than one neck, used for passing a gas through a liquid etc. [P. *Woulfe*, Engl. chemist d. 1803]

wound[1] /wŏŏnd/ *n.* & *v.* ● *n.* **1** an injury done to living tissue by a cut or blow etc., esp. beyond the cutting or piercing of the skin. **2** an injury to a person's reputation or a pain inflicted on a person's feelings. **3** *poet.* the pangs of love. ● *v.tr.* inflict a wound on (*wounded soldiers*; *wounded feelings*). □□ **woundingly** *adv.* **woundless** *adj.* [OE *wund* (n.), *wundian* (v.)]
■ *n.* **1** damage, hurt, injury, trauma, traumatism; laceration, puncture, cut, gash, slash, lesion, bruise, contusion. **2** slight, damage, injury, harm, blow, distress, mortification, torment, torture, anguish, pain, insult. ● *v.* harm, injure, hurt, traumatize, maim; cut, slash, gash, lacerate, slit, stab, shoot, wing; slight, distress, damage, mortify, insult, pain, grieve, offend, wrong.

wound[2] *past* and *past part.* of WIND[2] (cf. WIND[1] *v.* 6).

woundwort /wŏŏndwurt/ *n.* any of various plants esp. of the genus *Stachys*, formerly supposed to have healing properties.

wove[1] *past* of WEAVE[1].

wove[2] /wōv/ *adj.* (of paper) made on a wire-gauze mesh and so having a uniform unlined surface. [var. of *woven*, past part. of WEAVE[1]]

woven *past part.* of WEAVE[1].

wow[1] /wow/ *int., n.,* & *v.* ● *int.* expressing astonishment or admiration. ● *n. sl.* a sensational success. ● *v.tr. sl.* impress or excite greatly. [orig. Sc.: imit.]

wow[2] /wow/ *n.* a slow pitch-fluctuation in sound-reproduction, perceptible in long notes. [imit.]

wowser /wówzər/ *n. Austral. sl.* **1** a puritanical fanatic. **2** a spoilsport. **3** a teetotaller. [20th c.: orig. uncert.]

■ **1** see PURITAN *n.* 3. **2** see SPOILSPORT.

WP *abbr.* word processor or processing.

w.p. *abbr.* weather permitting.

w.p.b. *abbr.* waste-paper basket.

WPC *abbr.* (in the UK) woman police constable.

w.p.m. *abbr.* words per minute.

WRAC *abbr.* (in the UK) Women's Royal Army Corps.

wrack /rak/ *n.* **1** seaweed cast up or growing on the shore. **2** destruction. **3** a wreck or wreckage. **4** = RACK[2]. **5** = RACK[5]. [ME f. MDu. *wrak* or MLG *wra(c)k*, a parallel formation to OE *wræc*, rel. to *wrecan* WREAK: cf. WRECK, RACK[5]]

WRAF *abbr.* (in the UK) Women's Royal Air Force.

wraggle-taggle var. of RAGGLE-TAGGLE.

wraith /rayth/ *n.* **1** a ghost or apparition. **2** the spectral appearance of a living person supposed to portend that person's death. □□ **wraithlike** *adj.* [16th-c. Sc.: orig. unkn.]
■ see GHOST *n.* 1. □□ **wraithlike** see GHOSTLY.

wrangle /rángg'l/ *n.* & *v.* ● *n.* a noisy argument, altercation, or dispute. ● *v.* **1** *intr.* engage in a wrangle. **2** *tr. US* herd (cattle). [ME, prob. f. LG or Du.: cf. LG *wrangelen*, frequent. of *wrangen* to struggle, rel. to WRING]
■ *n.* see ARGUMENT 1. ● *v.* **1** see ARGUE 1.

wrangler /rángglər/ *n.* **1** a person who wrangles. **2** *US* a cowboy. **3** (at Cambridge University) a person placed in the first class of the mathematical tripos.

wrap /rap/ *v.* & *n.* ● *v.tr.* (**wrapped**, **wrapping**) **1** (often foll. by *up*) envelop in folded or soft encircling material (*wrap it up in paper*; *wrap up a parcel*). **2** (foll. by *round, about*) arrange or draw (a pliant covering) round (a person) (*wrapped the scarf closer around me*). **3** (foll. by *round*) *sl.* crash (a vehicle) into a stationary object. ● *n.* **1** a shawl or scarf or other such addition to clothing; a wrapper. **2** esp. *US* material used for wrapping. □ **take the wraps off** disclose. **under wraps** in secrecy. **wrap-over** *adj.* (*attrib.*) (of a garment) having no seam at one side but wrapped around the body and fastened. ● *n.* such a garment. **wrapped up in** engrossed or absorbed in. **wrap up 1** finish off, bring to completion (*wrapped up the deal in two days*). **2** put on warm clothes (*mind you wrap up well*). **3** (in *imper.*) *sl.* be quiet. [ME: orig. unkn.]
■ *v.* **1** swathe, swaddle, bind, cover, envelop, surround, shroud, enfold, fold, muffle, enclose, lag, sheathe, cocoon, encase, *literary* enshroud, enwrap; pack, package, do up, gift-wrap. **2** twine, wind, entwine, coil. ● *n.* **1** stole, shawl, scarf, mantle, poncho, serape, wrapper, cloak, cape, coat. **2** wrapping, packaging, covering. □ **under wraps** see SECRET *adj.* 1. **wrapped up in** immersed in, submerged in, buried in, absorbed in, engrossed in, bound up in, involved in, occupied with *or* by *or* in, engaged in, dedicated to, devoted to. **wrap up 1** complete, conclude, finish, end, bring to a close, terminate, finalize, wind up, settle, tidy up. **3** be silent, be quiet, stop talking, *colloq.* hold your tongue, shut up, *sl.* shut your face, shut your head, shut your trap, shut your mouth, *Brit. sl.* put a sock in it, belt up.

wraparound /ráppərownd/ *adj.* & *n.* (also **wrapround** /ráprownd/) ● *adj.* **1** (esp. of clothing) designed to wrap round. **2** curving or extending round at the edges. ● *n.* anything that wraps round.

wrappage /ráppij/ *n.* a wrapping or wrappings.

wrapper /ráppər/ *n.* **1** a cover for a sweet, chocolate, etc. **2** a cover enclosing a newspaper or similar packet for posting. **3** a paper cover of a book, usu. detachable. **4** a loose enveloping robe or gown. **5** a tobacco-leaf of superior quality enclosing a cigar.
■ **1, 2** envelope, package, packing, wrapping, covering, jacket, case, casing, container. **3** cover, jacket, dust cover, dust-jacket, sleeve, dust-wrapper. **4** housecoat, robe, dressing-gown, bathrobe, kimono, happi(-coat), negligee, lounging robe, peignoir.

wrapping /rápping/ *n.* (esp. in *pl.*) material used to wrap; wraps, wrappers. □ **wrapping paper** strong or decorative paper for wrapping parcels.
■ see WRAPPER 1, 2.

wrapround var. of WRAPAROUND.

wrasse /rass/ *n.* any bright-coloured marine fish of the family Labridae with thick lips and strong teeth. [Corn. *wrach*, var. of *gwrach*, = Welsh *gwrach*, lit. 'old woman']

wrath /roth, rawth/ *n. literary* extreme anger. [OE *wrǣththu* f. *wrāth* WROTH]
■ see ANGER *n.*

wrathful /róthfŏŏl, ráwth-/ *adj. literary* extremely angry. □□ **wrathfully** *adv.* **wrathfulness** *n.*
■ see ANGRY 1.

wrathy /ráwthi/ *adj. US* = WRATHFUL.

wreak /reek/ *v.tr.* **1** (usu. foll. by *upon*) give play or satisfaction to; put in operation (vengeance or one's anger etc.). **2** cause (damage etc.) (*the hurricane wreaked havoc on the crops*). **3** *archaic* avenge (a wrong or wronged person). □□ **wreaker** *n.* [OE *wrecan* drive, avenge, etc., f. Gmc: cf. WRACK, WRECK, WRETCH]
■ **1** inflict, exercise, exert, carry out, bring (to bear), visit, effect, work, unleash, execute, impose, force, vent, let loose, loose.

wreath /reeth/ *n.* (*pl.* **wreaths** /reethz, reeths/) **1** flowers or leaves fastened in a ring esp. as an ornament for a person's head or a building or for laying on a grave etc. as a mark of honour or respect. **2 a** a similar ring of soft twisted material such as silk. **b** *Heraldry* a representation of this below a crest. **3** a carved representation of a wreath. **4** (foll. by *of*) a curl or ring of smoke or cloud. **5** a light drifting mass of snow etc. [OE *writha* f. weak grade of *wrīthan* WRITHE]
■ **1** see GARLAND *n.* 1.

wreathe /reeth/ *v.* **1** *tr.* encircle as, with, or like a wreath. **2** *tr.* (foll. by *round*) put (one's arms etc.) round (a person etc.). **3** *intr.* (of smoke etc.) move in the shape of wreaths. **4** *tr.* form (flowers, silk, etc.) into a wreath. **5** *tr.* make (a garland). [partly back-form. f. archaic *wrethen* past part. of WRITHE; partly f. WREATH]
■ **1** see CIRCLE *v.* 2. **3** see TWINE *v.*

wreck /rek/ *n.* & *v.* ● *n.* **1** the destruction or disablement esp. of a ship. **2** a ship that has suffered a wreck (*the shores are strewn with wrecks*). **3** a greatly damaged or disabled building, thing, or person (*had become a physical and mental wreck*). **4** (foll. by *of*) a wretched remnant or disorganized set of remains. **5** *Law* goods etc. cast up by the sea. ● *v.* **1** *tr.* cause the wreck of (a ship etc.). **2** *tr.* completely ruin (hopes, chances, etc.). **3** *intr.* suffer a wreck. **4** *tr.* (as **wrecked** *adj.*) involved in a shipwreck (*wrecked sailors*). **5** *intr. US* deal with wrecked vehicles etc. □ **wreck-master** an officer appointed to take charge of goods etc. cast up from a wrecked ship. [ME f. AF *wrec* etc. (cf. VAREC) f. a Gmc root meaning 'to drive': cf. WREAK]
■ *n.* **1** destruction, loss, sinking, devastation, foundering, grounding, capsizal, capsizing, disabling, disablement, wreckage, wrecking; demolition, demolishing, levelling, tearing down, razing, pulling down, obliteration, ruin, ruining. **2** hulk, shipwreck, ruins. **3** mess, disaster, ruin(s); wrack. **4** remnant, remains, remainder, wreckage. **5** flotsam, jetsam. ● *v.* **1** sink, scuttle, shipwreck, run aground, founder, capsize; destroy, ruin, devastate, demolish, smash, shatter, spoil, dash (to pieces), reduce to nothing, annihilate, *Brit. sl.* scupper. **2** ruin, destroy, demolish, devastate, shatter, dash, spoil, annihilate, undermine, sabotage, *Austral.* euchre, *Brit. sl.* scupper.

wreckage /rékkij/ *n.* **1** wrecked material. **2** the remnants of a wreck. **3** the action or process of wrecking.
■ **1, 2** debris, fragments, pieces, remains, flotsam, rubble, ruin(s), wrack. **3** see WRECK *n.* 1.

wrecker /rékkər/ *n.* **1** a person or thing that wrecks or destroys. **2** esp. *hist.* a person on the shore who tries to bring about a shipwreck in order to plunder or profit by the wreckage. **3** esp. *US* a person employed in demolition, or in recovering a wrecked ship or its contents. **4** *US* a person who breaks up damaged vehicles for spares and scrap. **5** *US* a vehicle or train used in recovering a damaged one.

Wren /ren/ *n.* (in the UK) a member of the Women's Royal Naval Service. [orig. in pl., f. abbr. WRNS]

wren /ren/ *n.* any small usu. brown short-winged songbird of the family Troglodytidae, esp. *Troglodytes troglodytes* of Europe, having an erect tail. [OE *wrenna*, rel. to OHG *wrendo, wrendilo*, Icel. *rindill*]

wrench /rench/ *n.* & *v.* ● *n.* **1** a violent twist or oblique pull or act of tearing off. **2** an adjustable tool like a spanner for gripping and turning nuts etc. **3** an instance of painful uprooting or parting (*leaving home was a great wrench*). **4** *Physics* a combination of a couple with the force along its axis. ● *v.tr.* **1 a** a twist or pull violently round or sideways. **b** injure (a limb etc.) by undue straining; sprain. **2** (often foll. by *off*, *away*, etc.) pull off with a wrench. **3** seize or take forcibly. **4** distort (facts) to suit a theory etc. [(earlier as verb:) OE *wrencan* twist]

■ *n.* **1** twist, jerk, pull, tug, rip, *colloq.* yank. **2** monkey wrench, *Brit.* spanner, adjustable spanner. ● *v.* **1 a** twist, jerk, force, pull, tug, tear, wring, rip, wrest, *colloq.* yank. **b** strain, sprain, overstrain, rick, rack. **3** extract, wrest, wring, force, prise, *US* pry. **4** distort, twist, pervert, slant, warp.

wrest /rest/ *v.* & *n.* ● *v.tr.* **1** force or wrench away from a person's grasp. **2** (foll. by *from*) obtain by effort or with difficulty. **3** distort into accordance with one's interests or views (*wrest the law to suit themselves*). ● *n. archaic* a key for tuning a harp or piano etc. □ **wrest-block** (or **-plank**) the part of a piano or harpsichord holding the wrest-pins. **wrest-pin** each of the pins to which the strings of a piano or harpsichord are attached. [OE *wrǣstan* f. Gmc, rel. to WRIST]

■ *v.* **1** see WRENCH *v.* 1a, 3, SNATCH *v.* 1, 3. **2** see EXTRACT *v.* 2.

wrestle /réss'l/ *n.* & *v.* ● *n.* **1** a contest in which two opponents grapple and try to throw each other to the ground esp. as an athletic sport under a code of rules. **2** a hard struggle. ● *v.* **1** *intr.* (often foll. by *with*) take part in a wrestle. **2** *tr.* fight (a person) in a wrestle (*wrestled his opponent to the ground*). **3** *intr.* **a** (foll. by *with*, *against*) struggle, contend. **b** (foll. by *with*) do one's utmost to deal with (a task, difficulty, etc.). **4** *tr.* move with efforts as if wrestling. □□ **wrestler** *n.* **wrestling** *n.* [OE (unrecorded) *wrǣstlian*: cf. MLG *wrostelen*, OE *wraxlian*]

■ *n.* **1** see STRUGGLE *n.* 2. **2** fight, battle, tussle, effort, strain, struggle; see also LABOUR *n.* 1. ● *v.* **1, 3** battle, fight, contend, tussle, struggle, grapple, strive, do battle.

wretch /rech/ *n.* **1** an unfortunate or pitiable person. **2** (often as a playful term of depreciation) a reprehensible or contemptible person. [OE *wrecca* f. Gmc]

■ **1** unfortunate, miserable creature, down-and-out, *colloq.* poor fellow *or* chap *or* beggar, poor devil, *US colloq.* sad sack, *sl.* poor bastard *or* son of a bitch. **2** scoundrel, blackguard, worm, villain, cur, rogue, good-for-nothing, knave, scallywag, *archaic* whoreson, *archaic or joc.* varlet, rapscallion, *often joc.* rascal, *poet. or archaic* caitiff, *colloq.* beast, dog, rat, swine, *colloq. or joc.* bounder, *Brit. colloq.* blighter, *sl.* bastard, stinker, louse, scumbag, creep, *esp. Brit. sl.* rotter, *US sl.* bum.

wretched /réchid/ *adj.* (**wretcheder**, **wretchedest**) **1** unhappy or miserable. **2** of bad quality or no merit; contemptible. **3** unsatisfactory or displeasing. □ **feel wretched 1** be unwell. **2** be much embarrassed. □□ **wretchedly** *adv.* **wretchedness** *n.* [ME, irreg. f. WRETCH + -ED[1]: cf. WICKED]

■ **1** unhappy, sad, miserable, woebegone, woeful, dismal, downhearted, heartbroken, broken-hearted, heartsick, dejected, depressed, melancholic, melancholy, mournful, disconsolate, inconsolable, doleful, cheerless, crestfallen, joyless, desolate; pitiable, pathetic, sorry, pitiful, hapless, hopeless, unfortunate. **2** worthless, inferior, shabby, tawdry, trashy, rubbishy, poor, cheap; vile, shameful, scurvy, underhand(ed), treacherous, contemptible, despicable, base, low, mean, paltry, mean-spirited, detestable. **3** unsatisfactory, displeasing, miserable, atrocious, deplorable, unpleasant, disagreeable, *colloq.* awful, dreadful, lousy, terrible, *sl.* rotten; see also BAD *adj.* 1, REPULSIVE.

wrick *Brit.* var. of RICK[2].

wriggle /rigg'l/ *v.* & *n.* ● *v.* **1** *intr.* (of a worm etc.) twist or turn its body with short writhing movements. **2** *intr.* (of a person or animal) make wriggling motions. **3** *tr.* & *intr.* (foll. by *along* etc.) move or go in this way (*wriggled into the corner*; *wriggled his hand into the hole*). **4** *tr.* make (one's way) by wriggling. **5** *intr.* practise evasion. ● *n.* an act of wriggling. □ **wriggle out of** *colloq.* avoid on a contrived pretext. □□ **wriggler** *n.* **wriggly** *adj.* [ME f. MLG *wriggelen* frequent. of *wriggen*]

■ *v.* **1–3** twist, squirm, snake, worm, writhe, slither, crawl; wobble, shake, tremble, quiver, jiggle, fidget, *colloq.* wiggle, waggle. ● *n.* wriggling, writhing, squirm, squirming, slither, slithering, shaking, trembling, quiver, quivering, shimmying, twisting, twist, *colloq.* wiggle, wiggling, waggle, waggling. □ **wriggle out of** get out of, escape, evade, avoid, back out of, weasel out of, *colloq.* duck (out of).

wright /rīt/ *n.* a maker or builder (usu. in *comb.*: *playwright*; *shipwright*). [OE *wryhta*, *wyrhta* f. WG: cf. WORK]

wring /ring/ *v.* & *n.* ● *v.tr.* (*past* and *past part.* **wrung** /rung/) **1 a** squeeze tightly. **b** (often foll. by *out*) squeeze and twist esp. to remove liquid. **2** twist forcibly; break by twisting. **3** distress or torture. **4** extract by squeezing. **5** (foll. by *out*, *from*) obtain by pressure or importunity; extort. ● *n.* an act of wringing; a squeeze. □ **wring a person's hand** clasp it forcibly or press it with emotion. **wring one's hands** clasp them as a gesture of great distress. **wring the neck of** kill (a chicken etc.) by twisting its neck. [OE *wringan*, rel. to WRONG]

■ *v.* **5** see EXTORT.

wringer /ríngər/ *n.* a device for wringing water from washed clothes etc.

wringing /ríngiŋ/ *adj.* (in full **wringing wet**) so wet that water can be wrung out.

■ see WET *adj.* 1.

wrinkle /ríngk'l/ *n.* & *v.* ● *n.* **1** a slight crease or depression in the skin such as is produced by age. **2** a similar mark in another flexible surface. **3** *colloq.* a useful tip or clever expedient. ● *v.* **1** *tr.* make wrinkles in. **2** *intr.* form wrinkles; become marked with wrinkles. [orig. repr. OE *gewrinclod* sinuous]

■ *n.* **1** crow's-foot, dimple, crease, fold, line, furrow, crinkle, depression, corrugation, pucker, ridge. **2** crease, fold, line, furrow, crinkle, depression, corrugation, pucker, ridge. **3** dodge, device, ruse, scheme, tip, trick, expedient, idea, plan, plot, stunt, way, approach, technique, method, *colloq.* gimmick, ploy, *Brit. colloq.* wheeze. ● *v.* **1** crease, fold, line, furrow, crinkle, corrugate, pucker, gather, ruck (up), crimp, screw up, rumple, crumple. **2** crease, fold, furrow, crinkle, pucker, ruck up, rumple, crumple.

wrinkly /ríngkli/ *adj.* & *n.* ● *adj.* (**wrinklier**, **wrinkliest**) having many wrinkles. ● *n.* (also **wrinklie**) (*pl.* **-ies**) *sl. offens.* an old or middle-aged person.

wrist /rist/ *n.* **1** the part connecting the hand with the forearm. **2** the corresponding part in an animal. **3** the part of a garment covering the wrist. **4 a** (in full **wrist-work**) the act or practice of working the hand without moving the arm. **b** the effect got in fencing, ball games, sleight of hand, etc., by this. **5** (in full **wrist-pin**) *Mech.* a stud projecting from a crank etc. as an attachment for a connecting-rod. □ **wrist-drop** the inability to extend the hand through paralysis of the forearm muscles. **wrist-watch** a small watch worn on a strap round the wrist. [OE f. Gmc, prob. f. a root rel. to WRITHE]

wristband /ristband/ *n.* a band forming or concealing the end of a shirt-sleeve; a cuff.

wristlet /rístlit/ *n.* a band or ring worn on the wrist to strengthen or guard it or as an ornament, bracelet, handcuff, etc.

wristy /rísti/ *adj.* (esp. of a shot in cricket, tennis, etc.) involving or characterized by movement of the wrist.

writ[1] /rit/ *n.* **1** a form of written command in the name of a sovereign, court, State, etc., to act or abstain from acting in some way. **2** a Crown document summoning a peer to Parliament or ordering the election of a member or members of Parliament. □ **serve a writ on** deliver a writ to (a person). **one's writ runs** one has authority (as specified). [OE (as WRITE)]
■ see WARRANT *n.* 2.

writ[2] /rit/ *archaic past part.* of WRITE. □ **writ large** in magnified or emphasized form.

write /rīt/ *v.* (*past* **wrote** /rōt/; *past part.* **written** /rítt'n/) **1** *intr.* mark paper or some other surface by means of a pen, pencil, etc., with symbols, letters, or words. **2** *tr.* form or mark (such symbols etc.). **3** *tr.* form or mark the symbols that represent or constitute (a word or sentence, or a document etc.). **4** *tr.* fill or complete (a sheet, cheque, etc.) with writing. **5** *tr.* put (data) into a computer store. **6** *tr.* (esp. in *passive*) indicate (a quality or condition) by one's or its appearance (*guilt was written on his face*). **7** *tr.* compose (a text, article, novel, etc.) for written or printed reproduction or publication; put into literary etc. form and set down in writing. **8** *intr.* be engaged in composing a text, article, etc. (*writes for the local newspaper*). **9** *intr.* (foll. by *to*) write and send a letter (to a recipient). **10** *tr. US* or *colloq.* write and send a letter to (a person) (*wrote him last week*). **11** *tr.* convey (news, information, etc.) by letter (*wrote that they would arrive next Friday*). **12** *tr.* state in written or printed form (*it is written that*). **13** *tr.* cause to be recorded. **14** *tr.* underwrite (an insurance policy). **15** *tr.* (foll. by *into*, *out of*) include or exclude (a character or episode) in a story by suitable changes of the text. **16** *tr. archaic* describe in writing. □ **nothing to write home about** *colloq.* of little interest or value. **write down 1** record or take note of in writing. **2** write as if for those considered inferior. **3** disparage in writing. **4** reduce the nominal value of (stock, goods, etc.). **write in 1** send a suggestion, query, etc., in writing to an organization, esp. a broadcasting station. **2** *US* add (an extra name) on a list of candidates when voting. **write-in** *n. US* an instance of writing in (see *write in* 2). **write off 1** write and send a letter. **2** cancel the record of (a bad debt etc.); acknowledge the loss of or failure to recover (an asset). **3** damage (a vehicle etc.) so badly that it cannot be repaired. **4** compose with facility. **5** dismiss as insignificant. **write-off** *n.* a thing written off, esp. a vehicle too badly damaged to be repaired. **write out 1** write in full or in finished form. **2** exhaust (oneself) by writing (*have written myself out*). **write up 1** write a full account of. **2** praise in writing. **3** make entries to bring (a diary etc.) up to date. **write-up** *n. colloq.* a written or published account, a review. □□ **writable** *adj.* [OE *wrītan* scratch, score, write, f. Gmc: orig. used of symbols inscribed with sharp tools on stone or wood]
■ **2** inscribe, pen, pencil, scribble, scrawl. **3, 4** pen, scribble, get off, dash off; inscribe, make out, draw up, draft, *formal or joc.* indite. **5** input, load. **7** compose, create, make up, compile, *disp.* author. **9** (*write to*) correspond with, send a letter *or* note *or* postcard *or US also* postal card to, communicate with. **10** see sense 9 above. □ **nothing to write home about** see UNDISTINGUISHED. **write down 1** register, list, catalogue, note, make a note *or* notation of, record, transcribe, document, chronicle, report, set *or* jot *or* take down, note, put in writing, put in black and white. **3** decry, disparage, put down, minimize, make little of, play down, detract, belittle, *formal* derogate. **write off 2** delete, cancel, disregard, ignore, forgive, forget (about), annul, eradicate, erase. **write-up** see REPORT *n.* 2.

writer /rītər/ *n.* **1** a person who writes or has written something. **2** a person who writes books; an author. **3** a clerk, esp. in the Navy or in government offices. **4** a scribe. □ **writer's cramp** a muscular spasm due to excessive writing. **Writer to the Signet** a Scottish solicitor conducting cases in the Court of Session. [OE *wrītere* (as WRITE)]
■ **1** author, wordsmith, penny-a-liner, hack, journalist, newsman, reporter, correspondent, (gossip) columnist, ghost-writer, *colloq.* stringer, *colloq. derog.* pen-pusher, pencil-pusher, *Austral. colloq.* journo, *US colloq.* scribe, *often derog.* scribbler, *joc.* member of the fourth estate. **2** author, novelist, littérateur, man of letters, penman; essayist, poet, dramatist. **3, 4** scribe, copyist, scrivener, clerk, amanuensis, secretary.

writhe /rī*th*/ *v.* & *n.* ● *v.* **1** *intr.* twist or roll oneself about in or as if in acute pain. **2** *intr.* suffer severe mental discomfort or embarrassment (*writhed with shame*; *writhed at the thought of it*). **3** *tr.* twist (one's body etc.) about. ● *n.* an act of writhing. [OE *wrīthan*, rel. to WREATHE]
■ *v.* **1, 3** wriggle, worm, squirm, wiggle, twist, flounder, fidget, shift. **2** see SQUIRM *v.* 2, SWEAT *v.* 2.

writing /rīting/ *n.* **1** a group or sequence of letters or symbols. **2** = HANDWRITING. **3** the art or profession of literary composition. **4** (usu. in *pl.*) a piece of literary work done; a book, article, etc. **5** (**Writings**) the Hagiographa. □ **in writing** in written form. **writing-desk** a desk for writing at, esp. with compartments for papers etc. **the writing on the wall** an ominously significant event etc. (see Dan. 5:5, 25-8). **writing-pad** a pad (see PAD[1] *n.* 2) of paper for writing on. **writing-paper** paper for writing (esp. letters) on.
■ **1** notation, letters, characters, symbols, hieroglyphs, runes. **2** handwriting, longhand, penmanship, printing, script, calligraphy, chirography, *derog.* scrawl, scribble, *sl.* fist. **3** literature, belles-lettres, letters, creative writing. **4** (literary) work(s) *or* text(s), composition(s), publication(s); prose, poetry, non-fiction, fiction; book, article, piece, critique, criticism, review, editorial, column, exposé, essay, poem, novel, novelette, drama, play, document, letter, correspondence, leading article, *Brit.* leader.

written *past part.* of WRITE.

WRNS *abbr.* (in the UK) Women's Royal Naval Service.

wrong /rong/ *adj.*, *adv.*, *n.*, & *v.* ● *adj.* **1** mistaken; not true; in error (*gave a wrong answer*; *we were wrong to think that*). **2** unsuitable; less or least desirable (*the wrong road*; *a wrong decision*). **3** contrary to law or morality (*it is wrong to steal*). **4** amiss; out of order, in or into a bad or abnormal condition (*something wrong with my heart*; *my watch has gone wrong*). ● *adv.* (usually placed last) in a wrong manner or direction; with an incorrect result (*guessed wrong*; *told them wrong*). ● *n.* **1** what is morally wrong; a wrong action. **2** injustice; unjust action or treatment (*suffer wrong*). ● *v.tr.* **1** treat unjustly; do wrong to. **2** mistakenly attribute bad motives to; discredit. □ **do wrong** commit sin; transgress, offend. **do wrong to** malign or mistreat (a person). **get in wrong with** incur the dislike or disapproval of (a person). **get on the wrong side of** fall into disfavour with. **get wrong 1** misunderstand (a person, statement, etc.). **2** obtain an incorrect answer to. **get** (or **get hold of**) **the wrong end of the stick** misunderstand completely. **go down the wrong way** (of food) enter the windpipe instead of the gullet. **go wrong 1** take the wrong path. **2** stop functioning properly. **3** depart from virtuous or suitable behaviour. **in the wrong** responsible for a quarrel, mistake, or offence. **on the wrong side of 1** out of favour with (a person). **2** somewhat more than (a stated age). **wrong-foot** *colloq.* **1** (in tennis, football, etc.) play so as to catch (an opponent) off balance. **2** disconcert; catch unprepared. **wrong-headed** perverse and obstinate. **wrong-headedly** in a wrong-headed manner. **wrong-headedness** the state of being wrong-headed. **wrong side** the worse or undesired or unusable side of something, esp. fabric. **wrong side out** inside out. **wrong way round** in the opposite or reverse of the normal or desirable orientation or sequence etc. □□ **wronger** *n.* **wrongly** *adv.* **wrongness** *n.* [OE *wrang* f. ON *rangr* awry, unjust, rel. to WRING]

■ *adj.* **1** mistaken, in error, erroneous, incorrect, inaccurate, imprecise, inexact, fallacious, untrue, askew, false, wide of the mark, *colloq.* off target, off beam, *US colloq.* off the target, off the beam. **2** incorrect, improper, unsuitable, inappropriate, inapt, unfitting, unacceptable, undesirable, incongruous, out of place; ill-considered, wrong-headed, imprudent, misguided, inexpedient, impolitic, injudicious, infelicitous. **3** improper, unjust, unfair, unethical, terrible, foul, awful, bad, immoral, sinful, evil, iniquitous, villainous, wicked, vile, diabolic(al), infernal, fiendish, corrupt, dishonest, reprehensible, abominable, dreadful, dishonourable, blameworthy, shameful, disgraceful, criminal, felonious, illegal, illicit, unlawful, illegitimate, indecorous, unseemly, unbecoming, out of order, out of line, *archaic* naughty, *colloq.* crooked, *sl.* bent. **4** out of order, not working, faulty, abnormal, awry, amiss, defective, imperfect, unsound, flawed, deficient, *colloq.* out of sync. ● *adv.* awry, imperfectly, incorrectly, improperly, inappropriately, amiss, badly, wrongly, *Sc.* agley. ● *n.* **1** see SIN¹ *n.* 1. **2** see GRIEVANCE. ● *v.* **1** abuse, mistreat, injure, misuse, maltreat, ill-use, ill-treat, impose upon, take advantage of, harm, damage, oppress. **2** discredit, asperse, malign, vilify, (be)smirch, (be)smear, sully, calumniate, slander, libel, dishonour. □ **do wrong** see TRANSGRESS. **do wrong to** see *ill-treat.* **get wrong 1** see MISUNDERSTAND. **get** (or **get hold of**) **the wrong end of the stick** see MISUNDERSTAND. **go wrong 2** fail, malfunction, break down, miscarry, backfire, fall through, come to grief, *colloq.* go phut, go bust, *sl.* flop, go kaput, *Austral.* & *NZ sl.* go bung. **3** go astray, falter, fail, lapse, err, fall from grace, go to the bad, deteriorate, go downhill, backslide, regress, retrogress, *sl.* go to the dogs. **in the wrong** see *at fault* (FAULT).**wrong-headed** see PERVERSE 2, 3. **wrong side** see REVERSE *n.* 5. **wrong side out** see *inside out.* □□ **wrongly** see ILL *adv.* 1.

wrongdoer /róngdōōər/ *n.* a person who behaves immorally or illegally. □□ **wrongdoing** *n.*
■ see *transgressor* (TRANSGRESS). □□ **wrongdoing** see *transgression* (TRANSGRESS).

wrongful /róngfōōl/ *adj.* **1** characterized by unfairness or injustice. **2** contrary to law. **3** (of a person) not entitled to the position etc. occupied. □□ **wrongfully** *adv.* **wrongfulness** *n.*
■ **1** see GRIEVOUS 2, 3. **2** see ILLEGAL 2. □□ **wrongfully** see ILL *adv.* 1. **wrongfulness** see SIN¹ *n.* 1.

wrong'un /róngən/ *n. colloq.* a person of bad character. [contr. of *wrong one*]

wrote *past* of WRITE.

wroth /rōth, roth/ *predic.adj. archaic* angry. [OE *wrāth* f. Gmc]
■ see ANGRY 1.

wrought /rawt/ *archaic past* and *past part.* of WORK. ● *adj.* (of metals) beaten out or shaped by hammering. □ **wrought iron** a tough malleable form of iron suitable for forging or rolling, not cast.

wrung *past* and *past part.* of WRING.

WRVS *abbr.* (in the UK) Women's Royal Voluntary Service.

wry /rī/ *adj.* (**wryer, wryest** or **wrier, wriest**) **1** distorted or turned to one side. **2** (of a face or smile etc.) contorted in disgust, disappointment, or mockery. **3** (of humour) dry and mocking. □□ **wryly** *adv.* **wryness** *n.* [*wry* (v.) f. OE *wrīgian* tend, incline, in ME deviate, swerve, contort]
■ **1** distorted, contorted, twisted, lopsided, deformed, crooked, one-sided, askew, awry, bent, tilted, off-centre. **2** contorted, distorted, twisted. **3** dry, droll, witty, sardonic, sarcastic, ironic(al), mocking, amusing; perverse, fey, *Sc.* & *dial.* pawky.

wryneck /rīnek/ *n.* **1** = TORTICOLLIS. **2** any bird of the genus *Jynx* of the woodpecker family, able to turn its head over its shoulder.

WSW *abbr.* west-south-west.

wt. *abbr.* weight.

Wu /wōō/ *n.* a dialect of Chinese spoken in the Kiangsu and Chekiang Provinces. [Chin.]

wunderkind /vōōndərkint/ *n. colloq.* a person who achieves great success while relatively young. [G f. *Wunder* wonder + *Kind* child]

wurst /voorst, vurst/ *n.* German or Austrian sausage. [G]

WV *abbr. US* West Virginia (in official postal use).

W.Va. *abbr.* West Virginia.

WW *abbr. US* World War (I, II).

WX *abbr.* women's extra-large size.

WY *abbr. US* Wyoming (in official postal use).

wych- /wich/ *comb. form* (also **wich-, witch-**) in names of trees with pliant branches. [OE *wic(e)* app. f. a Gmc root meaning 'bend': rel. to WEAK]

wych-alder /wíchawldər/ *n.* an American plant, *Fothergilla gardenii*, with alder-like leaves.

wych-elm /wíchelm/ *n.* a species of elm, *Ulmus glabra.*

wych-hazel /wích-hayz'l/ *n.* **1** var. of WITCH-HAZEL. **2** = WYCH-ELM.

Wykehamist /wíkkəmist/ *adj.* & *n.* ● *adj.* of or concerning Winchester College. ● *n.* a past or present member of Winchester College. [mod.L *Wykehamista* f. William of *Wykeham*, bishop of Winchester and founder of the college (d. 1404)]

wyn var. of WEN².

wynd /wīnd/ *n. Sc.* a narrow street or alley. [ME, app. f. the stem of WIND²]

Wyo. *abbr.* Wyoming.

WYSIWYG /wízziwig/ *adj.* (also **wysiwyg**) *Computing* denoting the representation of text onscreen in a form exactly corresponding to its appearance on a printout. [acronym of *what you see is what you get*]

wyvern /wīvərn/ *n.* (also **wivern**) *Heraldry* a winged two-legged dragon with a barbed tail. [ME *wyver* f. OF *wivre, guivre* f. L *vipera*: for *-n* cf. BITTERN]

Xx

X[1] /eks/ *n.* (also **x**) (*pl.* **Xs** or **X's**) **1** the twenty-fourth letter of the alphabet. **2** (as a Roman numeral) ten. **3** (usu. **x**) *Algebra* the first unknown quantity. **4** *Geom.* the first coordinate. **5** an unknown or unspecified number or person etc. **6** a cross-shaped symbol esp. used to indicate position (*X marks the spot*) or incorrectness or to symbolize a kiss or a vote, or as the signature of a person who cannot write.

X[2] *symb.* (of films) classified as suitable for adults only. ¶ Formerly used in the UK to indicate that persons under 18 would not be admitted; it was replaced in 1983 by *18*, but is still used in the US.
■ see BLUE[1] *adj.* 3.

-x /z/ *suffix* forming the plural of many nouns in *-u* taken from French (*beaux*; *tableaux*). [F]

xanthate /zánthayt/ *n.* any salt or ester of xanthic acid.

xanthic /zánthik/ *adj.* yellowish. □ **xanthic acid** any colourless unstable acid containing the $-OCS_2H$ group. [Gk *xanthos* yellow]

Xanthippe /zanthíppi/ *n.* (also **Xantippe** /-típpi/) a shrewish or ill-tempered woman or wife. [name of Socrates' wife]
■ see SHREW 2.

xanthoma /zanthṓmə/ *n.* (*pl.* **xanthomas** or **xanthomata** /-mətə/) *Med.* **1** a skin disease characterized by irregular yellow patches. **2** such a patch. [as XANTHIC + -OMA]

xanthophyll /zánthəfil/ *n.* any of various oxygen-containing carotenoids associated with chlorophyll, some of which cause the yellow colour of leaves in the autumn. [as XANTHIC + Gk *phullon* leaf]

X-chromosome /éks-krṓməsōm/ *n.* a sex chromosome of which the number in female cells is twice that in male cells. [*X* as an arbitrary label + CHROMOSOME]

x.d. *abbr.* ex dividend.

Xe *symb. Chem.* the element xenon.

xebec /zéebek/ *n.* (also **zebec, zebeck**) a small three-masted Mediterranean vessel with lateen and usu. some square sails. [alt. (after Sp. *xabeque*) of F *chebec* f. It. *sciabecco* f. Arab. *šabāk*]

xeno- /zénnō/ *comb. form* **1 a** foreign. **b** a foreigner. **2** other. [Gk *xenos* strange, foreign, stranger]

xenogamy /zenóggəmi/ *n. Bot.* cross-fertilization. □□ **xenogamous** *adj.*

xenolith /zénnəlith/ *n. Geol.* an inclusion within an igneous rock mass, usu. derived from the immediately surrounding rock.

xenon /zénnon/ *n. Chem.* a heavy colourless odourless inert gaseous element occurring in traces in the atmosphere and used in fluorescent lamps. ¶ Symb.: **Xe**. [Gk, neut. of *xenos* strange]

xenophobe /zénnəfōb/ *n.* a person given to xenophobia.

xenophobia /zénnəfṓbiə/ *n.* a deep dislike of foreigners. □□ **xenophobic** *adj.*
■ see *intolerance* (INTOLERANT). □□ **xenophobic** see INHOSPITABLE 1.

xeranthemum /zeeránthiməm/ *n.* a composite plant of the genus *Xeranthemum*, with dry everlasting composite flowers. [mod.L f. Gk *xēros* dry + *anthemon* flower]

xeric /zéerik/ *adj. Ecol.* having or characterized by dry conditions. [as XERO- + -IC]

xero- /zéerō, zérrō/ *comb. form* dry. [Gk *xēros* dry]

xeroderma /zéerədérmə/ *n.* any of various diseases characterized by extreme dryness of the skin, esp. ichthyosis. [mod.L (as XERO-, Gk *derma* skin)]

xerograph /zéerəgraaf, zérrə-/ *n.* a copy produced by xerography.

xerography /zeerógrəfi, ze-/ *n.* a dry copying process in which black or coloured powder adheres to parts of a surface remaining electrically charged after exposure of the surface to light from an image of the document to be copied. □□ **xerographic** /-rəgráffik/ *adj.* **xerographically** /-rəgráffikəli/ *adv.*

xerophilous /zeeróffiləss, ze-/ *adj.* (of a plant) adapted to extremely dry conditions.

xerophyte /zéerəfīt, zérrə-/ *n.* (also **xerophile** /-fīl/) a plant able to grow in very dry conditions, e.g. in a desert.

Xerox /zéeroks, zérroks/ *n.* & *v.* ● *n. propr.* **1** a machine for copying by xerography. **2** a copy made using this machine. ● *v.tr.* (**xerox**) reproduce by this process. [invented f. XEROGRAPHY]
■ *n.* **2** see DUPLICATE *n.* ● *v.* see DUPLICATE *v.*

Xhosa /kṓsə, káw-/ *n.* & *adj.* ● *n.* **1** (*pl.* same or **Xhosas**) a member of a Bantu people of Cape Province, South Africa. **2** the Bantu language of this people, similar to Zulu. ● *adj.* of or relating to this people or language. [native name]

xi /sī, gzī, zī/ *n.* the fourteenth letter of the Greek alphabet (*Ξ*, *ξ*). [Gk]

-xion /ksh'n/ *suffix* forming nouns (see -ION) from Latin participial stems in *-x-* (*fluxion*).

xiphisternum /zíffistérnəm/ *n. Anat.* = *xiphoid process*. [as XIPHOID + STERNUM]

xiphoid /zíffoyd/ *adj. Biol.* sword-shaped. □ **xiphoid process** the cartilaginous process at the lower end of the sternum. [Gk *xiphoeidēs* f. *xiphos* sword]

Xmas /krísməss, éksməss/ *n. colloq.* = CHRISTMAS. [abbr., with X for the initial chi of Gk *Khristos* Christ]

xoanon /zṓənon/ *n.* (*pl.* **xoana** /-nə/) *Gk Antiq.* a primitive usu. wooden image of a deity supposed to have fallen from heaven. [Gk f. *xeō* carve]

X-ray /éksray/ *n.* & *v.* (also **x-ray**) ● *n.* **1** (in *pl.*) electromagnetic radiation of short wavelength, able to pass through opaque bodies. **2** an image made by the effect of X-rays on a photographic plate, esp. showing the position of bones etc. by their greater absorption of the rays. ● *v.tr.* photograph, examine, or treat with X-rays. □ **X-ray astronomy** the branch of astronomy concerned with the X-ray emissions of celestial bodies. **X-ray crystallography** the study of crystals and their structure by means of the diffraction of X-rays by the regularly spaced atoms of a crystalline material. **X-ray tube** a device for generating X-rays by accelerating electrons to high energies and causing them to strike a metal target from which the X-rays are emitted. [transl. of G *x-Strahlen* (pl.) f. *Strahl* ray, so called because when discovered in 1895 the nature of the rays was unknown]

xylem /zīlem/ *n. Bot.* woody tissue (cf. PHLOEM). [Gk *xulon* wood]

xylene /zíleen/ *n. Chem.* one of three isomeric hydrocarbons formed from benzene by the substitution of two methyl groups, obtained from wood etc. [formed as XYLEM + -ENE]

xylo- /zílō/ *comb. form* wood. [Gk *xulon* wood]

xylocarp /zíləkaarp/ *n.* a hard woody fruit. □□ **xylocarpous** /-kaárpəss/ *adj.*

xylograph /zíləgraaf/ *n.* a woodcut or wood-engraving (esp. an early one).

xylography /zīlógrəfi/ *n.* **1** the (esp. early or primitive) practice of making woodcuts or wood-engravings. **2** the use of wood blocks in printing.

Xylonite /zílənīt/ *n. propr.* a kind of celluloid. [irreg. f. *xyloidin* (as XYLO-) + -ITE^1]

xylophagous /zīlóffəgəss/ *adj.* (of an insect or mollusc) eating, or boring into, wood.

xylophone /zíləfōn/ *n.* a musical instrument of wooden or metal bars graduated in length and struck with a small wooden hammer or hammers. □□ **xylophonic** /-fónnik/ *adj.* **xylophonist** *n.* [Gk *xulon* wood + -PHONE]

xystus /zistəss/ *n.* (*pl.* **xysti** /-tī/) **1** a covered portico used by athletes in ancient Greece for exercise. **2** *Rom. Antiq.* a garden walk or terrace. [L f. Gk *xustos* smooth f. *xuō* scrape]

Yy

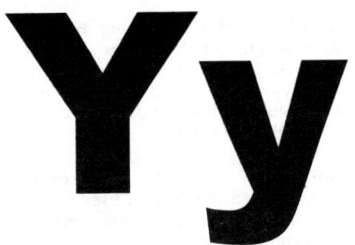

Y[1] /wī/ *n.* (also **y**) (*pl.* **Ys** or **Y's**) **1** the twenty-fifth letter of the alphabet. **2** (usu. **y**) *Algebra* the second unknown quantity. **3** *Geom.* the second coordinate. **4 a** a Y-shaped thing, esp. an arrangement of lines, piping, roads, etc. **b** a forked clamp or support.

Y[2] *abbr.* (also **Y.**) **1** yen. **2** Yeomanry. **3** *US* = YMCA, YWCA.

Y[3] *symb. Chem.* the element yttrium.

y. *abbr.* year(s).

y- /i/ *prefix archaic* forming past participles, collective nouns, etc. (*yclept*). [OE *ge-* f. Gmc]

-y[1] /i/ *suffix* forming adjectives: **1** from nouns and adjectives, meaning: **a** full of; having the quality of (*messy*; *icy*; *horsy*). **b** addicted to (*boozy*). **2** from verbs, meaning 'inclined to', 'apt to' (*runny*; *sticky*). [from or after OE *-ig* f. Gmc]

-y[2] /i/ *suffix* (also **-ey, -ie**) forming diminutive nouns, pet names, etc. (*granny*; *Sally*; *nightie*; *Mickey*). [ME (orig. Sc.)]

-y[3] /i/ *suffix* forming nouns denoting: **1** state, condition, or quality (*courtesy*; *orthodoxy*; *modesty*). **2** an action or its result (*colloquy*; *remedy*; *subsidy*). [from or after F *-ie* f. L *-ia*, *-ium*, Gk *-eia*, *-ia*: cf. -ACY, -ERY, -GRAPHY, and others]

yabber /yábbər/ *v.* & *n. Austral.* & *NZ colloq.* ● *v.intr.* & *tr.* talk. ● *n.* talk, conversation, language. □ **yabber stick** = *message stick*. [perh. f. an Aboriginal language]
■ *v.* see TALK *v.* 1, 3a. ● *n.* see TALK *n.* 1.

yabby /yábbi/ *n.* (also **yabbie**) (*pl.* **-ies**) *Austral.* **1** a small freshwater crayfish, esp. of the genus *Cherax*. **2** a marine prawn, *Callianassa australiensis*, often used as bait. [Aboriginal]

yacht /yot/ *n.* & *v.* ● *n.* **1** a light sailing-vessel, esp. equipped for racing. **2** a larger usu. power-driven vessel equipped for cruising. **3** a light vessel for travel on sand or ice. ● *v.intr.* race or cruise in a yacht. □ **yacht-club** a club esp. for yacht-racing. □□ **yachting** *n.* [early mod.Du. *jaghte* = *jaghtschip* fast pirate-ship f. *jag(h)t* chase f. *jagen* to hunt + *schip* SHIP]
■ *n.* **1** see BOAT *n.* ● *v.* see CRUISE *v.*

yachtsman /yótsmən/ *n.* (*pl.* **-men**; *fem.* **yachtswoman**, *pl.* **-women**) a person who sails yachts.

yack /yak/ *n.* & *v.* (also **yackety-yack** /yákətiyák/) *sl. derog.* ● *n.* trivial or unduly persistent conversation. ● *v.intr.* engage in this. [imit.]
■ *n.* see JABBER *n.* ● *v.* see JABBER *v.* 1.

yacka (also **yacker**) var. of YAKKA.

yaffle /yáff'l/ *n. dial.* a green woodpecker, *Picus viridus*. [imit. of its laughing cry]

yager var. of JAEGER.

yah /yaa/ *int.* expressing derision or defiance. [imit.]

yahoo /yaáhōō/ *n.* a coarse bestial person. [name of an imaginary race of brutish creatures in Swift's *Gulliver's Travels* (1726)]
■ see BARBARIAN *n.* 1.

Yahweh /yaáway/ *n.* (also **Yahveh** /-vay/) the Hebrew name of God in the Old Testament. [Heb. *YHVH* with added vowels: see JEHOVAH]

Yahwist /yaáwist/ *n.* (also **Yahvist** /-vist/) the postulated author or authors of parts of the Hexateuch in which God is regularly named *Yahweh*.

yak /yak/ *n.* a long-haired humped Tibetan ox, *Bos grunniens*. [Tibetan *gyag*]

yakka /yákkə/ *n.* (also **yacka, yacker**) *Austral. sl.* work. [Aboriginal]

Yale lock /yayl/ *n. propr.* a type of lock for doors etc. with a cylindrical barrel turned by a flat key with a serrated edge. [L. *Yale*, Amer. inventor d. 1868]

yam /yam/ *n.* **1 a** any tropical or subtropical climbing plant of the genus *Dioscorea*. **b** the edible starchy tuber of this. **2** *US* a sweet potato. [Port. *inhame* or Sp. *iñame*, of unkn. orig.]

yammer /yámmər/ *n.* & *v. colloq.* or *dial.* ● *n.* **1** a lament, wail, or grumble. **2** voluble talk. ● *v.intr.* **1** utter a yammer. **2** talk volubly. □□ **yammerer** *n.* [OE *geōmrian* f. *geōmor* sorrowful]
■ *v.* **1** see MOAN *v.* 2. **2** see YAP *v.* 2.

yandy /yándi/ *v.* & *n. Austral.* ● *v.tr.* (**-ies, -ied**) separate (grass seed) from refuse by special shaking. ● *n.* (*pl.* **-ies**) a shallow dish used for this. [Aboriginal]

yang /yang/ *n.* (in Chinese philosophy) the active male principle of the universe (cf. YIN). [Chin.]

Yank /yangk/ *n. colloq.* often *derog.* an inhabitant of the US; an American. [abbr.]

yank /yangk/ *v.* & *n. colloq.* ● *v.tr.* pull with a jerk. ● *n.* a sudden hard pull. [19th c.: orig. unkn.]
■ *v.* & *n.* jerk, jolt, tug, wrench, snatch, hitch.

Yankee /yángki/ *n. colloq.* **1** often *derog.* = YANK. **2** *US* an inhabitant of New England or one of the northern States. **3** *hist.* a Federal soldier in the Civil War. **4** a type of bet on four or more horses to win (or be placed) in different races. **5** (*attrib.*) of or as of the Yankees. □ **Yankee Doodle 1** an American tune and song regarded as a national air. **2** = YANKEE. [18th c.: orig. uncert.: perh. f. Du. *Janke* dimin. of *Jan* John attested (17th c.) as a nickname]

yap /yap/ *v.* & *n.* ● *v.intr.* (**yapped, yapping**) **1** bark shrilly or fussily. **2** *colloq.* talk noisily, foolishly, or complainingly. ● *n.* **1** a sound of yapping. **2** *US sl.* the mouth. □□ **yapper** *n.* [imit.]
■ *v.* **1** bark, yelp. **2** gabble, babble, blather, chatter, jabber, tattle, prattle, prate, run on, *colloq.* witter (on), natter, jaw, *colloq. or dial.* yammer, yatter (on), *Brit. colloq.* rabbit (on). ● *n.* **1** bark, yelp. **2** mouth, *sl.* trap, *esp. Brit. sl.* gob.

yapok /yáppok/ *n.* = POSSUM 2. [*Oyapok*, *Oiapoque*, N. Brazilian river]

yapp /yap/ *n. Brit.* a form of bookbinding with a limp leather cover projecting to fold over the edges of the leaves. [name of a London bookseller *c.*1860, for whom it was first made]

yarborough /yaárbərə/ *n.* a whist or bridge hand with no card above a 9. [Earl of *Yarborough* (d. 1897), said to have betted against its occurrence]

yard[1] /yaard/ *n.* **1** a unit of linear measure equal to 3 feet (0.9144 metre). **2** this length of material (*a yard and a half of cloth*). **3** a square or cubic yard esp. (in building) of sand etc. **4** a cylindrical spar tapering to each end slung across a

mast for a sail to hang from. **5** (in *pl.*; foll. by *of*) *colloq.* a great length (*yards of spare wallpaper*). □ **by the yard** at great length. **yard-arm** the outer extremity of a ship's yard. **yard of ale** *Brit.* **1** a deep slender beer glass, about a yard long and holding two to three pints. **2** the contents of this. [OE *gerd* f. WG]
■ **4** see SPAR[1].

yard[2] /yaard/ *n.* & *v.* ● *n.* **1** a piece of enclosed ground esp. attached to a building or used for a particular purpose. **2** *US* the garden of a house. ● *v.tr.* put (cattle) into a stockyard. □ **the Yard** *Brit. colloq.* = SCOTLAND YARD. **yard-man** **1** a person working in a railway-yard or timber-yard. **2** *US* a gardener or a person who does various outdoor jobs. **yard-master** the manager of a railway-yard. [OE *geard* enclosure, region, f. Gmc: cf. GARDEN]
■ *n.* **1** see ENCLOSURE 2. **2** garden, backyard.

yardage /yaárdij/ *n.* **1** a number of yards of material etc. **2 a** the use of a stockyard etc. **b** payment for this.
■ **1** see MEASUREMENT 2.

yardbird /yaárdburd/ *n. US sl.* **1** a new military recruit. **2** a convict.

yardstick /yaárdstik/ *n.* **1** a standard used for comparison. **2** a measuring rod a yard long, usu. divided into inches etc.
■ **1** measure, benchmark, criterion, standard, norm, gauge, basis, touchstone, scale, exemplar.

yarmulke /yaármәlkә/ *n.* (also **yarmulka**) a skullcap worn by Jewish men. [Yiddish]

yarn /yaarn/ *n.* & *v.* ● *n.* **1** any spun thread, esp. for knitting, weaving, rope-making, etc. **2** *colloq.* a long or rambling story or discourse. ● *v.intr. colloq.* tell yarns. [OE *gearn*]
■ *n.* **1** thread, fibre, strand. **2** tale, story, account, narrative, anecdote; tall tale, fable, fabrication, fiction, cock-and-bull story, *Brit. colloq.* fishing story, *sl.* whopper.

yarran /yárrәn/ *n.* any of several Australian acacias, esp. *Acacia homalophylla*, a small tree with scented wood used for fencing, fuel, etc. [Aboriginal]

yarrow /yárrō/ *n.* any perennial herb of the genus *Achillea*, esp. milfoil. [OE *gearwe*, of unkn. orig.]

yashmak /yáshmak/ *n.* a veil concealing the face except the eyes, worn by some Muslim women when in public. [Arab. *yašmaķ*, Turk. *yaşmak*]

yataghan /yáttәgan/ *n.* a sword without a guard and often with a double-curved blade, used in Muslim countries. [Turk. *yātāğan*]

yatter /yáttәr/ *v.* & *n. colloq.* or *dial.* ● *v.intr.* (often foll. by *on*) talk idly or incessantly; chatter. ● *n.* idle talk; incessant chatter. □□ **yattering** *n.* & *adj.*

yaw /yaw/ *v.* & *n.* ● *v.intr.* (of a ship or aircraft etc.) fail to hold a straight course; fall off; go unsteadily (esp. turning from side to side). ● *n.* the yawing of a ship etc. from its course. [16th c.: orig. unkn.]
■ *v.* see TOSS *v.* 2.

yawl /yawl/ *n.* **1** a two-masted fore-and-aft sailing-boat with the mizen-mast stepped far aft. **2** a small kind of fishing-boat. **3** *hist.* a ship's jolly boat with four or six oars. [MLG *jolle* or Du. *jol*, of unkn. orig.: cf. JOLLY[2]]

yawn /yawn/ *v.* & *n.* ● *v.* **1** *intr.* (as a reflex) open the mouth wide and inhale esp. when sleepy or bored. **2** *intr.* (of a chasm etc.) gape, be wide open. **3** *tr.* utter or say with a yawn. ● *n.* **1** an act of yawning. **2** *colloq.* a boring or tedious idea, activity, etc. □□ **yawner** *n.* **yawningly** *adv.* [OE *ginian*, *geonian*]

yawp /yawp/ *n.* & *v. US* ● *n.* **1** a harsh or hoarse cry. **2** foolish talk. ● *v.intr.* utter these. □□ **yawper** *n.* [ME (imit.)]

yaws /yawz/ *n.pl.* (usu. treated as *sing.*) a contagious tropical skin-disease with large red swellings. [17th c.: orig. unkn.]

Yb *symb. Chem.* the element ytterbium.

Y-chromosome /wī́-krṓmәsōm/ *n.* a sex chromosome occurring only in male cells. [*Y* as an arbitrary label + CHROMOSOME]

yclept /iklépt/ *adj. archaic* or *joc.* called (by the name of). [OE *gecleopod* past part. of *cleopian* call f. Gmc]

yd. *abbr.* yard (measure).

yds. *abbr.* yards (measure).

ye[1] /yee/ *pron. archaic pl.* of THOU[1]. □ **ye gods!** *joc.* an exclamation of astonishment. [OE *ge* f. Gmc]

ye[2] /yee/ *adj. pseudo-archaic* = THE (*ye olde tea-shoppe*). [var. spelling f. the *y*-shaped letter THORN (representing *th*) in the 14th c.]

yea /yay/ *adv.* & *n. archaic* ● *adv.* **1** yes. **2** indeed, nay (*ready, yea eager*). ● *n.* the word 'yea'. □ **yea and nay** shilly-shally. **yeas and nays** affirmative and negative votes. [OE *gea*, *ge* f. Gmc]

yeah /yeә/ *adv. colloq.* yes. □ **oh yeah?** expressing incredulity. [casual pronunc. of YES]

yean /yeen/ *v.tr.* & *intr. archaic* bring forth (a lamb or kid). [perh. f. OE *geēanian* (unrecorded, as Y-, *ēanian* to lamb)]

yeanling /yeénling/ *n. archaic* a young lamb or kid.

year /yeer, yer/ *n.* **1** (also **astronomical year, equinoctial year, natural year, solar year, tropical year**) the time occupied by the earth in one revolution round the sun, 365 days, 5 hours, 48 minutes, and 46 seconds in length (cf. *sidereal year*). **2** (also **calendar year, civil year**) the period of 365 days (**common year**) or 366 days (see *leap year*) from 1 Jan. to 31 Dec., used for reckoning time in ordinary affairs. **3 a** a period of the same length as this starting at any point (*four years ago*). **b** such a period in terms of a particular activity etc. occupying its duration (*school year*; *tax year*). **4** (in *pl.*) age or time of life (*young for his years*). **5** (usu. in *pl.*) *colloq.* a very long time (*it took years to get served*). **6** a group of students entering college etc. in the same academic year. □ **in the year of Our Lord** (foll. by the year) in a specified year AD. **of the year** chosen as outstanding in a particular year (*sportsman of the year*). **a year and a day** the period specified in some legal matters to ensure the completion of a full year. **the year dot** see DOT[1]. **year in, year out** continually over a period of years. **year-long** lasting a year or the whole year. **year of grace** the year AD. **year-round** existing etc. throughout the year. [OE *gē(a)r* f. Gmc]
■ **5** (*years*) see AGE *n.* 2a. **6** class, form, *US* grade.

yearbook /yeérbŏŏk, yér-/ *n.* an annual publication dealing with events or aspects of the (usu. preceding) year.
■ annual, annal, almanac.

yearling /yeérling, yér-/ *n.* & *adj.* ● *n.* **1** an animal between one and two years old. **2** a racehorse in the calendar year after the year of foaling. ● *adj.* **1** a year old; having existed or been such for a year (*a yearling heifer*). **2** intended to terminate after one year (*yearling bonds*).

yearly /yeérli, yér-/ *adj.* & *adv.* ● *adj.* **1** done, produced, or occurring once a year. **2** of or lasting a year. ● *adv.* once a year; from year to year. [OE *gēarlic*, *-lice* (as YEAR)]
■ *adj.* **1** annual, once-a-year. ● *adv.* annually, once a year, per year, per annum, by the year, each year; perennially, every year, year after year, year in (and) year out, regularly.

yearn /yern/ *v.intr.* **1** (usu. foll. by *for*, *after*, or *to* + infin.) have a strong emotional longing. **2** (usu. foll. by *to*, *towards*) be filled with compassion or tenderness. □□ **yearner** *n.* **yearning** *n.* & *adj.* **yearningly** *adv.* [OE *giernan* f. a Gmc root meaning 'eager']
■ **1** long, pine, ache, hanker, itch, hunger, thirst, crave, have a craving, desire, wish, want, fancy, prefer. □□ **yearning** (*n.*) see LONGING *n.* (*adj.*) see DESIROUS 2.

yeast /yeest/ *n.* **1** a greyish-yellow fungous substance obtained esp. from fermenting malt liquors and used as a fermenting agent, to raise bread, etc. **2** any of various unicellular fungi in which vegetative reproduction takes place by budding or fission. □□ **yeastless** *adj.* **yeastlike** *adj.* [OE *gist*, *giest* (unrecorded): cf. MDu. *ghist*, MHG *jist*, ON *jöstr*]

yeasty /yeésti/ *adj.* (**yeastier, yeastiest**) **1** frothy or tasting like yeast. **2** in a ferment. **3** working like yeast. **4** (of talk etc.) light and superficial. □□ **yeastily** *adv.* **yeastiness** *n.*

yegg /yeg/ *n. US sl.* a travelling burglar or safe-breaker. [20th c.: perh. a surname]

yell /yel/ *n. & v.* ● *n.* **1** a loud sharp cry of pain, anger, fright, encouragement, delight, etc. **2** a shout. **3** *US* an organized cry, used esp. to support a sports team. **4** *sl.* an amusing person or thing. ● *v.tr. & intr.* utter with or make a yell. [OE *g(i)ellan* f. Gmc]
■ *n.* **1, 2** shout, scream, cry, bellow, bawl, howl, screech, yowl, roar, caterwaul, squall, yelp, *US colloq.* holler. **4** see SCREAM *n.* 3.

yellow /yéllō/ *adj., n., & v.* ● *adj.* **1** of the colour between green and orange in the spectrum, of buttercups, lemons, egg-yolks, or gold. **2** of the colour of faded leaves, ripe wheat, etc. **3** having a yellow skin or complexion. **4** *colloq.* cowardly. **5** (of looks, feelings, etc.) jealous, envious, or suspicious. **6** (of newspapers etc.) unscrupulously sensational. ● *n.* **1** a yellow colour or pigment. **2** yellow clothes or material (*dressed in yellow*). **3 a** a yellow ball, piece, etc., in a game or sport. **b** the player using such pieces. **4** (usu. in *comb.*) a yellow moth or butterfly. **5** (in *pl.*) jaundice of horses etc. **6** *US* a peach-disease with yellowed leaves. ● *v.tr. & intr.* make or become yellow. □ **yellow arsenic** = ORPIMENT. **yellow-bellied 1** *colloq.* cowardly. **2** (of a fish) having yellow underparts. **yellow-belly 1** *colloq.* a coward. **2** any of various fish with yellow underparts. **yellow card** *Football* a card shown by the referee to a player being cautioned. **yellow fever** a tropical virus disease with fever and jaundice. **yellow flag 1** a flag displayed by a ship in quarantine. **2** an iridaceous plant, *Iris pseudacorus*, with slender sword-shaped leaves and yellow flowers. **yellow jack 1** = *yellow fever*. **2** = *yellow flag*. **yellow line** (in the UK) a line painted along the side of the road in yellow either singly or in pairs to denote parking restrictions. **yellow metal** brass of 60 parts copper and 40 parts zinc. **Yellow Pages** *propr.* a section of a telephone directory on yellow paper and listing business subscribers according to the goods or services they offer. **the yellow peril** the political or military threat regarded as emanating from Asian peoples, esp. the Chinese. **yellow rattle** a yellow-flowered plant of the genus *Rhinanthus*. **yellow rocket** see ROCKET². **yellow spot** the point of acutest vision in the retina. **yellow streak** *colloq.* a trait of cowardice. □□ **yellowish** *adj.* **yellowly** *adv.* **yellowness** *n.* **yellowy** *adj.* [OE *geolu, geolo* f. WG, rel. to GOLD]
■ *adj.* **4** see COWARDLY *adj.* □ **yellow-belly 1** see COWARD *n.* □□ **yellowish** see GOLDEN 2.

yellowback /yéllōbak/ *n.* a cheap novel etc. in a yellow cover.

yellowhammer /yéllōhammər/ *n.* a bunting, *Emberiza citrinella*, of which the male has a yellow head, neck, and breast. [16th c.: orig. of *hammer* uncert.]

yelp /yelp/ *n. & v.* ● *n.* a sharp shrill cry of or as of a dog in pain or excitement. ● *v.intr.* utter a yelp. □□ **yelper** *n.* [OE *gielp(an)* boast (imit.): cf. YAWP]
■ *n.* see HOWL *n.* 1. ● *v.* see HOWL *v.* 1.

yen¹ /yen/ *n.* (*pl.* same) the chief monetary unit of Japan. [Jap. f. Chin. *yuan* round, dollar]

yen² /yen/ *n. & v. colloq.* ● *n.* a longing or yearning. ● *v.intr.* (**yenned, yenning**) feel a longing. [Chin. dial.]
■ *n.* see LONGING *n.*

yeoman /yṓmən/ *n.* (*pl.* **-men**) **1** esp. *hist.* a man holding and cultivating a small landed estate. **2** *hist.* a person qualified by possessing free land of an annual value of 40 shillings to serve on juries, vote for the knight of the shire, etc. **3** *Brit.* a member of the yeomanry force. **4** *hist.* a servant in a royal or noble household. **5** (in full **yeoman of signals**) a petty officer in the Navy, concerned with visual signalling. **6** *US* a petty officer performing clerical duties on board ship. □ **Yeoman of the Guard 1** a member of the British sovereign's bodyguard. **2** (in general use) a warder in the Tower of London. **yeoman** (or **yeoman's**) **service** efficient or useful help in need. **Yeoman Usher** *Brit.* the deputy of Black Rod. [ME *yoman, yeman*, etc., prob. f. YOUNG + MAN]
■ **1** see FARMER.

yeomanly /yṓmənli/ *adj.* **1** of the rank of yeoman. **2** characteristic of or befitting a yeoman; sturdy, reliable.
■ **2** workmanlike, useful, staunch, courageous, loyal, dedicated, faithful, steadfast, unswerving, unwavering, firm, sturdy, reliable, solid.

yeomanry /yṓmənri/ *n.* (*pl.* **-ies**) **1** a body of yeomen. **2** *Brit. hist.* a volunteer cavalry force raised from the yeoman class (1794–1908).

yep /yep/ *adv. & n.* (also **yup** /yup/) *US colloq.* = YES. [corrupt.]

-yer /yər/ *suffix* var. of -IER esp. after *w* (*bowyer*; *lawyer*).

yerba maté /yérbə máttay/ *n.* = MATÉ. [Sp., = herb maté]

yes /yess/ *adv. & n.* ● *adv.* **1** equivalent to an affirmative sentence: the answer to your question is affirmative, it is as you say or as I have said, the statement etc. made is correct, the request or command will be complied with, the negative statement etc. made is not correct. **2** (in answer to a summons or address) an acknowledgement of one's presence. ● *n.* an utterance of the word *yes*. □ **say yes** grant a request or confirm a statement. **yes? 1** indeed? is that so? **2** what do you want? **yes and** a form for introducing a stronger phrase (*he came home drunk — yes, and was sick*). **yes and no** that is partly true and partly untrue. **yes-man** (*pl.* **-men**) *colloq.* a weakly acquiescent person. [OE *gēse, gīse*, prob. f. *gīa sīe* may it be (*gīa* is unrecorded)]
■ *adv.* **1** *archaic* yea, *archaic or dial.* aye. **2** here, present, *colloq.* yeah, *US colloq.* yep. □ **yes-man** toady, sycophant, time-server, hanger-on, lickspittle, truckler, courtier, spaniel, lap-dog, *archaic* toad-eater, *colloq.* bootlicker, jackal, *usu. derog.* flunkey.

yester- /yéstər/ *comb. form poet.* or *archaic* of yesterday; that is the last past (*yester-eve*). [OE *geostran*]

yesterday /yéstərday/ *adv. & n.* ● *adv.* **1** on the day before today. **2** in the recent past. ● *n.* **1** the day before today. **2** the recent past. □ **yesterday morning** (or **afternoon** etc.) in the morning (or afternoon etc.) of yesterday. [OE *giestran dæg* (as YESTER-, DAY)]
■ *n.* **2** see PAST *n.* 1.

yesteryear /yéstəryeer/ *n. literary* **1** last year. **2** the recent past.
■ **2** see PAST *n.* 1.

yet /yet/ *adv. & conj.* ● *adv.* **1** as late as, or until, now or then (*there is yet time; your best work yet*). **2** (with *neg.* or *interrog.*) so soon as, or by, now or then (*it is not time yet; have you finished yet?*). **3** again; in addition (*more and yet more*). **4** in the remaining time available; before all is over (*I will do it yet*). **5** (foll. by *compar.*) even (*a yet more difficult task*). **6** nevertheless; and in spite of that; but for all that (*it is strange, and yet it is true*). ● *conj.* but at the same time; but nevertheless (*I won, yet what good has it done?*). □ **nor yet** and also not (*won't listen to me nor yet to you*). [OE *gīet(a)*, = OFris. *īēta*, of unkn. orig.]
■ *adv.* **1** still, even now, up to this time, up to now, till *or* until now, to this day. **2** as yet, (up) till *or* until now, up to now, so far, hitherto, to the present (time), *formal* thus far. **3, 5** even, still. **4** in the future, in time to come, later, eventually. **6** still, notwithstanding, anyway, anyhow, nonetheless, nevertheless, in spite of *or* despite everything, just *or* all the same, even so, after all, *colloq.* still and all. ● *conj.* still, but.

yeti /yétti/ *n.* = *Abominable Snowman*. [Tibetan]

yew /yōō/ *n.* **1** any dark-leaved evergreen coniferous tree of the genus *Taxus*, having seeds enclosed in a fleshy red aril, and often planted in churchyards. **2** its wood, used formerly as a material for bows and still in cabinet-making. [OE *īw, ēow* f. Gmc]

Y-fronts /wī́frunts/ *n. propr.* men's or boys' briefs with a Y-shaped seam at the front.
■ see PANTS 1.

Yggdrasil /ígdrəsil/ *n.* (in Scandinavian mythology) an ash-tree whose roots and branches join heaven, earth, and hell. [ON *yg(g)drasill* f. *Yggr* Odin + *drasill* horse]

YHA *abbr.* (in the UK) Youth Hostels Association.

Yid /yid/ *n. sl. offens.* a Jew. [back-form. f. YIDDISH]

Yiddish /yíddish/ *n.* & *adj.* ● *n.* a vernacular used by Jews in or from central and eastern Europe, orig. a German dialect with words from Hebrew and several modern languages. ● *adj.* of or relating to this language. [G *jüdisch* Jewish]

Yiddisher /yíddishər/ *n.* & *adj.* ● *n.* a person speaking Yiddish. ● *adj.* Yiddish-speaking.

yield /yeeld/ *v.* & *n.* ● *v.* **1** *tr.* (also *absol.*) produce or return as a fruit, profit, or result (*the land yields crops; the land yields poorly; the investment yields 15%*). **2** *tr.* give up; surrender, concede; comply with a demand for (*yielded the fortress; yielded themselves prisoners*). **3** *intr.* (often foll. by *to*) **a** surrender; make submission. **b** give consent or change one's course of action in deference to; respond as required to (*yielded to persuasion*). **4** *intr.* (foll. by *to*) be inferior or confess inferiority to (*I yield to none in understanding the problem*). **5** *intr.* (foll. by *to*) give right of way to other traffic. **6** *intr. US* allow another the right to speak in a debate etc. ● *n.* an amount yielded or produced; an output or return. □ **yield point** *Physics* the stress beyond which a material becomes plastic. □□ **yielder** *n.* [OE *g(i)eldan* pay f. Gmc]

■ *v.* **1** produce, bear, supply, bring forth; earn, return, pay, bring in, generate, net. **2** give up, surrender, give over, hand in *or* over, abandon, relinquish, concede, renounce, cede. **3 a** surrender, give up (the fight *or* struggle), give in, knuckle under, submit, cede, cry quits, throw in the towel *or* the sponge, capitulate, succumb, raise the white flag. **b** agree, consent, comply, concede, relent, assent, give way, accede, concur. ● *n.* crop, harvest, production, product; return, output, revenue, takings, gate, earnings, income, proceeds, profit, gain.

yielding /yeélding/ *adj.* **1** compliant, submissive. **2** (of a substance) able to bend; not stiff or rigid. □□ **yieldingly** *adv.* **yieldingness** *n.*

■ **1** accommodating, docile, submissive, amenable, tractable, compliant, obedient, flexible, acquiescent, agreeable, obliging, manageable, manipulable. **2** pliant, flexible, pliable, soft, plastic, elastic, resilient, supple, springy, bouncy, spongy, rubbery, *archaic* flexile.

yin /yin/ *n.* (in Chinese philosophy) the passive female principle of the universe (cf. YANG). [Chin.]

yip /yip/ *v.* & *n. US* ● *v.intr.* (**yipped, yipping**) = YELP *v.* ● *n.* = YELP *n.* [imit.]

yippee /yíppee, -peé/ *int.* expressing delight or excitement. [natural excl.]

-yl /il/ *suffix Chem.* forming nouns denoting a radical (*ethyl; hydroxyl; phenyl*).

ylang-ylang /eélangeélang/ *n.* (also **ilang-ilang**) **1** a Malayan tree, *Cananga odorata*, from the fragrant yellow flowers of which a perfume is distilled. **2** the perfume itself. [Tagalog *álang-ilang*]

YMCA *abbr.* Young Men's Christian Association.

-yne /īn/ *suffix Chem.* forming names of unsaturated compounds containing a triple bond (*ethyne* = acetylene).

yob /yob/ *n. Brit. sl.* a lout or hooligan. □□ **yobbish** *adj.* **yobbishly** *adv.* **yobbishness** *n.* [back sl. for BOY]

■ see HOODLUM 1.

yobbo /yóbbō/ *n.* (*pl.* **-os**) *Brit. sl.* = YOB.

yod /yod/ *n.* **1** the tenth and smallest letter of the Hebrew alphabet. **2** its semivowel sound /y/. [Heb. *yōḏ* f. *yaḏ* hand]

yodel /yṓd'l/ *v.* & *n.* ● *v.tr.* & *intr.* (**yodelled, yodelling;** *US* **yodeled, yodeling**) sing with melodious inarticulate sounds and frequent changes between falsetto and the normal voice in the manner of the Swiss mountain-dwellers. ● *n.* a yodelling cry. □□ **yodeller** *n.* [G *jodeln*]

■ *v.* see SING *v.* 1, 2.

yoga /yṓgə/ *n.* **1** a Hindu system of philosophic meditation and asceticism designed to effect reunion with the universal spirit. **2** = HATHA YOGA. □□ **yogic** /yṓgik/ *adj.* [Hind. f. Skr., = union]

yogh /yog/ *n.* a Middle English letter used for certain values of *g* and *y*. [ME]

yoghurt /yóggərt/ *n.* (also **yogurt**) a semi-solid sourish food prepared from milk fermented by added bacteria. [Turk. *yoğurt*]

yogi /yṓgi/ *n.* a person proficient in yoga. □□ **yogism** *n.* [Hind. f. YOGA]

yo-heave-ho /yṓheevhṓ/ *int.* & *n.* = *heave-ho.*

yohi /yṓ-wī/ *n.* (also **youi**) *Austral.* (in Aboriginal English) an affirmative reply, 'yes'. [Yagara *yaway*]

yo-ho /yōhṓ/ *int.* (also **yo-ho-ho** /yṓhōhṓ/) **1** used to attract attention. **2** = YO-HEAVE-HO. [cf. YO-HEAVE-HO & HO]

yoicks /yoyks/ *int.* (also **hoicks** /hoyks/) a cry used by fox-hunters to urge on the hounds. [orig. unkn.: cf. *hyke* call to hounds, HEY[1]]

yoke /yōk/ *n.* & *v.* ● *n.* **1** a wooden crosspiece fastened over the necks of two oxen etc. and attached to the plough or wagon to be drawn. **2** (*pl.* same or **yokes**) a pair (of oxen etc.). **3** an object like a yoke in form or function, e.g. a wooden shoulder-piece for carrying a pair of pails, the top section of a dress or skirt etc. from which the rest hangs. **4** sway, dominion, or servitude, esp. when oppressive. **5** a bond of union, esp. that of marriage. **6** *Rom.Hist.* an uplifted yoke, or an arch of three spears symbolizing it, under which a defeated army was made to march. **7** *archaic* the amount of land that one yoke of oxen could plough in a day. **8** a crossbar on which a bell swings. **9** the crossbar of a rudder to whose ends ropes are fastened. **10** a bar of soft iron between the poles of an electromagnet. ● *v.* **1** *tr.* put a yoke on. **2** *tr.* couple or unite (a pair). **3** *tr.* (foll. by *to*) link (one thing) to (another). **4** *intr.* match or work together. [OE *geoc* f. Gmc]

■ *n.* **2** see TEAM *n.* 2. **4** see SLAVERY 1. **5** bond, union, tie, link. ● *v.* **2** see COUPLE *v.* 1. **4** see TWIN *v.*

yokel /yṓk'l/ *n.* a rustic; a country bumpkin. [perh. f. dial. *yokel* green woodpecker]

■ see RUSTIC *n.*

yolk[1] /yōk/ *n.* **1** the yellow internal part of an egg that nourishes the young before it hatches. **2** *Biol.* the corresponding part of any animal ovum. □ **yolk-bag** (or **-sac**) a membrane enclosing the yolk of an egg. □□ **yolked** *adj.* (also in *comb.*). **yolkless** *adj.* **yolky** *adj.* [OE *geol(o)ca* f. *geolu* YELLOW]

yolk[2] /yōk/ *n.* = SUINT. [OE *eowoca* (unrecorded)]

Yom Kippur /yom kíppər/ *n.* = *Day of Atonement* (see ATONEMENT). [Heb.]

yomp /yomp/ *v.intr. Brit. sl.* march with heavy equipment over difficult terrain. [20th c.: orig. unkn.]

yon /yon/ *adj., adv.,* & *pron. literary* & *dial.* ● *adj.* & *adv.* yonder. ● *pron.* yonder person or thing. [OE *geon*]

yonder /yóndər/ *adv.* & *adj.* ● *adv.* over there; at some distance in that direction; in the place indicated by pointing etc. ● *adj.* situated yonder. [ME: cf. OS *gendra*, Goth. *jaindrē*]

yoni /yṓni/ *n.* a symbol of the female genitals venerated by Hindus etc. [Skr., = source, womb, female genitals]

yonks /yongks/ *n.pl. sl.* a long time (*haven't seen them for yonks*). [20th c.: orig. unkn.]

yoo-hoo /yṓōhṓō/ *int.* used to attract a person's attention. [natural excl.]

yore /yor/ *n. literary* □ **of yore** formerly; in or of old days. [OE *geāra, geāre*, etc., adv. forms of uncert. orig.]

york /york/ *v.tr. Cricket* bowl with a yorker. [back-form. f. YORKER]

yorker /yórkər/ *n. Cricket* a ball bowled so that it pitches immediately under the bat. [prob. f. *York*, as having been introduced by Yorkshire players]

Yorkist /yórkist/ *n.* & *adj.* ● *n. hist.* a follower of the House of York or of the White Rose party supporting it in the Wars of the Roses (cf. LANCASTRIAN). ● *adj.* of or concerning the House of York.

Yorks. *abbr.* Yorkshire.

Yorkshire fog /yórkshər/ *n.* a fodder-grass, *Holcus lanatus.*

Yorkshireman /yórkshərmən/ *n.* (*pl.* **-men**; *fem.* **Yorkshirewoman**, *pl.* **-women**) a native of Yorkshire in N. England.

Yorkshire pudding /yórkshər/ *n.* a baked batter pudding usu. eaten with roast beef. [*Yorkshire* in N. England]

Yorkshire terrier /yórkshər/ *n.* a small long-haired blue-grey and tan kind of terrier.

Yoruba /yórroobə/ *n.* **1** a member of a Black African people inhabiting the west coast, esp. Nigeria. **2** the language of this people. [native name]

you /yōō/ *pron.* (*obj.* **you**; *poss.* **your, yours**) **1** used with reference to the person or persons addressed or one such person and one or more associated persons. **2** (as *int.* with a noun) in an exclamatory statement (*you fools!*). **3** (in general statements) one, a person, anyone, or everyone (*it's bad at first, but you get used to it*). □ **you-all** *US colloq.* you (usu. more than one person). **you and yours** you together with your family, property, etc. **you-know-what** (or **-who**) something or someone unspecified but understood. [OE *ēow* accus. & dative of *gē* YE[1] f. WG: supplanting *ye* because of the more frequent use of the obj. case, and *thou* and *thee* as the more courteous form]

you'd /yōōd, yŏŏd/ *contr.* **1** you had. **2** you would.

youi var. of YOHI.

you'll /yōōl, yŏŏl, yawl/ *contr.* you will; you shall.

young /yung/ *adj.* & *n.* ● *adj.* (**younger** /yúnggər/; **youngest** /yúnggist/) **1** not far advanced in life, development, or existence; not yet old. **2** immature or inexperienced. **3** felt in or characteristic of youth (*young love*; *young ambition*). **4** representing young people (*Young Conservatives*; *Young England*). **5** distinguishing a son from his father (*young Jones*). **6** (**younger**) **a** distinguishing one person from another of the same name (*the younger Pitt*). **b** *Sc.* the heir of a landed commoner. ● *n.* (*collect.*) offspring, esp. of animals before or soon after birth. □ **with young** (of an animal) pregnant. **young blood** see BLOOD. **younger hand** *Cards* the second player of two. **young fustic** see FUSTIC. **young hopeful** see HOPEFUL. **young idea** the child's mind. **young lady** *colloq.* a girlfriend or sweetheart. **young man** a boyfriend or sweetheart. **young person** *Law* (in the UK) a person generally between 14 and 17 years of age. **Young Pretender** Charles Stuart (1720–80), grandson of James II and claimant to the British throne. **young thing** *archaic* or *colloq.* an indulgent term for a young person. **Young Turk 1** a member of a revolutionary party in Turkey in 1908. **2** a young person eager for radical change to the established order. **young turk** *offens.* a violent child or youth. **young 'un** *colloq.* a youngster. **young woman** *colloq.* a girlfriend or sweetheart. □□ **youngish** *adj.* **youngling** *n.* [OE *g(e)ong* f. Gmc]
■ *adj.* **1** youthful, teenage(d), adolescent, prepubescent, pubescent, juvenile, minor, junior, under age; new, developing, undeveloped. **2** immature, callow, green, inexperienced, unfledged, uninitiated, unsophisticated, childlike, innocent, naïve. **3** childish, boyish, girlish, puerile, infantile, babyish, *US* sophomoric. ● *n.* offspring, babies, little ones, progeny, litter, brood; children, small fry. □ **young lady, young man** see LOVE *n.* 4a, 5.

youngster /yúngstər/ *n.* a child or young person.
■ see YOUTH 4.

younker /yúngkər/ *n. archaic* = YOUNGSTER. [MDu. *jonckher* f. *jonc* YOUNG + *hēre* lord: cf. JUNKER]

your /yor, yoor/ *poss.pron.* (*attrib.*) **1** of or belonging to you or yourself or yourselves (*your house*; *your own business*). **2** *colloq.* usu. *derog.* much talked of; well known (*none so fallible as your self-styled expert*). [OE *ēower* genit. of *gē* YE[1]]

you're /yoor, yər, yor/ *contr.* you are.

yours /yorz, yoorz/ *poss.pron.* **1** the one or ones belonging to or associated with you (*it is yours*; *yours are over there*). **2** your letter (*yours of the 10th*). **3** introducing a formula ending a letter (*yours ever*; *yours truly*). □ **of yours** of or belonging to you (*a friend of yours*).

yourself /yorsélf, yoor-/ *pron.* (*pl.* **yourselves** /-sélvz/) **1 a** *emphat. form* of YOU. **b** *refl. form* of YOU. **2** in your normal state of body or mind (*are quite yourself again*). □ **be yourself** act in your normal, unconstrained manner. **how's yourself?** *sl.* how are you? (esp. after answering a similar enquiry).

youth /yōōth/ *n.* (*pl.* **youths** /yōōthz/) **1** the state of being young; the period between childhood and adult age. **2** the vigour or enthusiasm, inexperience, or other characteristic of this period. **3** an early stage of development etc. **4** a young person (esp. male). **5** (*pl.*) young people collectively (*the youth of the country*). □ **youth club** (or **centre**) a place or organization provided for young people's leisure activities. **youth hostel** a place where (esp. young) holiday-makers can put up cheaply for the night. **youth hosteller** a user of a youth hostel. [OE *geoguth* f. Gmc, rel. to YOUNG]
■ **1** childhood, boyhood, girlhood, young manhood, young womanhood, prepubescence, pubescence, adolescence, teens, salad days; minority, immaturity. **3** infancy, beginning, start, emergence, dawn. **4** child, youngster, schoolchild, teenager, teen, minor, juvenile, adolescent, *colloq.* young 'un, kid, sprog; boy, schoolboy, stripling, young boy *or* man, lad, whippersnapper; *colloq.* (little) shaver, laddie; *esp. Sc.* & *N.Engl. or poet.* lass, *colloq.* lassie. **5** children, youngsters, juveniles, adolescents, young people, young, *colloq.* kids.

youthful /yōōthfŏŏl/ *adj.* **1** young, esp. in appearance or manner. **2** having the characteristics of youth (*youthful impatience*). **3** having the freshness or vigour of youth (*a youthful complexion*). □□ **youthfully** *adv.* **youthfulness** *n.*
■ **1** see YOUNG *adj.* 1. **2** see CHILDLIKE

you've /yōōv, yŏŏv/ *contr.* you have.

yowl /yowl/ *n.* & *v.* ● *n.* a loud wailing cry of or as of a cat or dog in pain or distress. ● *v.intr.* utter a yowl. [imit.]
■ *n.* see HOWL *n.* 1. ● *v.* see HOWL *v.* 1.

yo-yo /yṓyō/ *n.* & *v.* ● *n.* (*pl.* **yo-yos**) *propr.* **1** a toy consisting of a pair of discs with a deep groove between them in which string is attached and wound, and which can be spun alternately downward and upward by its weight and momentum as the string unwinds and rewinds. **2** a thing that repeatedly falls and rises again. ● *v.intr.* (**yo-yoes, yo-yoed**) **1** play with a yo-yo. **2** move up and down; fluctuate. [20th c.: orig. unkn.]
■ *v.* **2** see FLUCTUATE.

yr. *abbr.* **1** year(s). **2** younger. **3** your.

yrs. *abbr.* **1** years. **2** yours.

ytterbium /itérbiəm/ *n. Chem.* a silvery metallic element of the lanthanide series occurring naturally as various isotopes. ¶ Symb.: **Yb**. [mod.L f. *Ytterby* in Sweden]

yttrium /ítriəm/ *n. Chem.* a greyish metallic element resembling the lanthanides, occurring naturally in uranium ores and used in making superconductors. ¶ Symb.: **Y**. [formed as YTTERBIUM]

yuan /yoo-áan/ *n.* (*pl.* same) the chief monetary unit of China. [Chin.: see YEN[1]]

yucca /yúkkə/ *n.* any American white-flowered liliaceous plant of the genus *Yucca*, with swordlike leaves. [Carib]

yuck /yuk/ *int.* & *n.* (also **yuk**) *sl.* ● *int.* an expression of strong distaste or disgust. ● *n.* something messy or repellent. [imit.]

yucky /yúkki/ *adj.* (also **yukky**) (**-ier, -iest**) *sl.* **1** messy, repellent. **2** sickly, sentimental.
■ **1** disgusting, repugnant, repellent, unappetizing, vomit-provoking, sickening, nauseous, nauseating, revolting, foul, mucky, messy, beastly, awful, *colloq.* sick-making, *Brit. sl.* grotty. **2** see SENTIMENTAL.

Yugoslav /yōōgəslaav/ *n.* & *adj.* (also **Jugoslav**) *hist.* ● *n.* **1** a native or national of Yugoslavia. **2** a person of Yugoslav descent. ● *adj.* of or relating to Yugoslavia or its people. □□ **Yugoslavian** *adj.* & *n.* [Austrian G *Jugoslav* f. Serb. *jugo-* f. *jug* south + SLAV]

yuk var. of YUCK.

yukky var. of YUCKY.

yule /yo͞ol/ *n.* (in full **yule-tide**) *archaic* the Christmas festival. □ **yule-log 1** a large log burnt in the hearth on Christmas Eve. **2** a log-shaped chocolate cake eaten at Christmas. [OE *gēol*(*a*): cf. ON *jól*]

yummy /yúmmi/ *adj.* (**yummier, yummiest**) *colloq.* tasty, delicious. [YUM-YUM + -Y[1]]

▪ delicious, mouth-watering, luscious, appetizing, tasty, toothsome, savoury, ambrosial, *colloq.* scrumptious, *literary* delectable.

yum-yum /yúmyúm/ *int.* expressing pleasure from eating or the prospect of eating. [natural excl.]

yup var. of YEP.

yuppie /yúppi/ *n.* & *adj.* (also **yuppy**; *pl.* **-ies**) *colloq.*, usu. *derog.* ● *n.* a young middle-class professional person working in a city. ● *adj.* characteristic of a yuppie or yuppies. [*y*oung *u*rban *p*rofessional]

YWCA *abbr.* Young Women's Christian Association.

Zz

Z /zed/ *n.* (also **z**) (*pl.* **Zs** or **Z's**) **1** the twenty-sixth letter of the alphabet. **2** (usu. **z**) *Algebra* the third unknown quantity. **3** *Geom.* the third coordinate. **4** *Chem.* atomic number.

zabaglione /zaabaalyṓnay/ *n.* an Italian sweet of whipped and heated egg yolks, sugar, and (esp. Marsala) wine. [It.]

zaffre /záffər/ *n.* (*US* **zaffer**) an impure cobalt oxide used as a blue pigment. [It. *zaffera* or F *safre*]

zag /zag/ *n.* a sharp change of direction in a zigzag course. [ZIGZAG]

ZANU /za'anoo/ *abbr.* Zimbabwe African National Union.

zany /záyni/ *adj.* & *n.* ● *adj.* (**zanier**, **zaniest**) comically idiotic; crazily ridiculous. ● *n.* **1** a buffoon or jester. **2** *hist.* an attendant clown awkwardly mimicking a chief clown in shows; a merry andrew. ▫▫ **zanily** *adv.* **zaniness** *n.* [F *zani* or It. *zan(n)i*, Venetian form of *Gianni*, *Giovanni* John]

■ *adj.* **1** clownish, mad, wild, frolicsome, sportive, playful, gay, merry, slapstick, funny, comic(al), amusing, hilarious, absurd, nonsensical, ludicrous, ridiculous, silly, foolish, inane, madcap, idiotic, eccentric, *colloq.* crazy, *sl.* goofy, wacky, loony, crackpot, nutty, kooky. ● *n.* clown, comic, jester, fool, joker, buffoon, wag, comedian, merry andrew, laughing-stock, *sl.* nut, *US sl.* screwball.

zap /zap/ *v.*, *n.*, & *int. sl.* ● *v.* (**zapped**, **zapping**) **1** *tr.* **a** kill or destroy; deal a sudden blow to. **b** hit forcibly (*zapped the ball over the net*). **2** *intr.* move quickly and vigorously. **3** *tr.* overwhelm emotionally. **4** *tr. Computing* erase or change (an item in a program). **5** *intr.* (foll. by *through*) fast-wind a videotape to skip a section. ● *n.* **1** energy, vigour. **2** a strong emotional effect. ● *int.* expressing the sound or impact of a bullet, ray gun, etc., or any sudden event. [imit.]

■ *v.* **1 a** destroy, kill, slaughter, annihilate, murder, assassinate, liquidate, erase, snuff out, shoot, electrocute, *colloq.* do away with, finish (off), *literary or joc.* slay, *sl.* knock off, bump off, *esp. US sl.* rub out, hit, *US sl.* ice. **b** see HIT *v.* 1a. **2** see RUSH[1] *v.* 1. ● *n.* **1** see VIGOUR 1.

zapateado /za'apətiaádō/ *n.* (*pl.* **-os**) **1** a flamenco dance with rhythmic stamping of the feet. **2** this technique or action. [Sp. f. *zapato* shoe]

zappy /záppi/ *adj.* (**zappier**, **zappiest**) *colloq.* **1** lively, energetic. **2** striking.

ZAPU /za'apoo/ *abbr.* Zimbabwe African People's Union.

zarape var. of SERAPE.

Zarathustrian var. of ZOROASTRIAN.

zariba /zəre'ebə/ *n.* (also **zareba**) **1** a hedged or palisaded enclosure for the protection of a camp or village in the Sudan etc. **2** a restricting or confining influence. [Arab. *zarība* cattle-pen]

zarzuela /thaarthwáylə/ *n.* a Spanish traditional form of musical comedy. [Sp.: app. f. a place-name]

zax var. of SAX[2].

zeal /zeel/ *n.* **1** earnestness or fervour in advancing a cause or rendering service. **2** hearty and persistent endeavour. [ME *zele* f. eccl.L *zelus* f. Gk *zēlos*]

■ **1** see ENTHUSIASM 1. **2** diligence, persistence, sedulousness, sedulity, tirelessness, indefatigability, perseverance.

zealot /zéllət/ *n.* **1** an uncompromising or extreme partisan; a fanatic. **2** (**Zealot**) *hist.* a member of an ancient Jewish sect aiming at a world Jewish theocracy and resisting the Romans until AD 70. ▫▫ **zealotry** *n.* [eccl.L *zelotes* f. Gk *zēlōtēs* (as ZEAL)]

■ **1** fanatic, extremist, partisan, radical, bigot, maniac, crank, militant. ▫▫ **zealotry** fanaticism, extremism, radicalism, bigotry, militantism, militancy; single-mindedness, monomania, fervour, frenzy, hysteria, obsession, obsessiveness.

zealous /zélləss/ *adj.* full of zeal; enthusiastic. ▫▫ **zealously** *adv.* **zealousness** *n.*

■ see ENTHUSIASTIC.

zebec (also **zebeck**) var. of XEBEC.

zebra /zébrə, zée-/ *n.* **1** any of various African quadrupeds, esp. *Equus burchelli*, related to the ass and horse, with black and white stripes. **2** (*attrib.*) with alternate dark and pale stripes. ▫ **zebra crossing** *Brit.* a striped street-crossing where pedestrians have precedence over vehicles. ▫▫ **zebrine** /-brīn/ *adj.* [It. or Port. f. Congolese]

zebu /zéeboo/ *n.* a humped ox, *Bos indicus*, of India, E. Asia, and Africa. [F *zébu*, of unkn. orig.]

Zech. *abbr.* Zechariah (Old Testament).

zed /zed/ *n. Brit.* the letter Z. [F *zède* f. LL *zeta* f. Gk ZETA]

zedoary /zéddōəri/ *n.* an aromatic ginger-like substance made from the rootstock of E. Indian plants of the genus *Curcuma* and used in medicine, perfumery, and dyeing. [ME f. med.L *zedoarium* f. Pers. *zidwār*]

zee /zee/ *n. US* the letter Z. [17th c.: var. of ZED]

Zeeman effect /záymən/ *n. Physics* the splitting of the spectrum line into several components by a magnetic field. [P. *Zeeman*, Du. physicist d. 1943]

zein /zée-in/ *n. Biochem.* the principal protein of maize. [*Zea* the generic name of maize + -IN]

Zeitgeist /tsītgīst/ *n.* **1** the spirit of the times. **2** the trend of thought and feeling in a period. [G f. *Zeit* time + *Geist* spirit]

Zen /zen/ *n.* a form of Mahayana Buddhism emphasizing the value of meditation and intuition. ▫▫ **Zenist** *n.* (also **Zennist**). [Jap., = meditation]

zenana /zinaanə/ *n.* the part of a house for the seclusion of women of high-caste families in India and Iran. [Hind. *zenāna* f. Pers. *zanāna* f. *zan* woman]

Zend /zend/ *n.* an interpretation of the Avesta, each Zend being part of the Zend-Avesta. ▫ **Zend-Avesta** the Zoroastrian sacred writings of the Avesta or text and Zend or commentary. [Pers. *zand* interpretation]

Zener cards /zéenər/ *n.* a set of 25 cards each with one of five different symbols, used in ESP research. [K. E. *Zener*, Amer. psychologist b. 1903]

zenith /zénnith, zée-/ *n.* **1** the part of the celestial sphere directly above an observer (opp. NADIR). **2** the highest point in one's fortunes; a time of great prosperity etc. ▫ **zenith distance** an arc intercepted between a celestial body and its zenith; the complement of a body's altitude. [ME f. OF *cenit* or med.L *cenit* ult. f. Arab. *samt* (*ar-ra's*) path (over the head)]

■ **2** meridian, summit, acme, apex, vertex, apogee, high point, top, peak, pinnacle.

zenithal /zénnithəl, zeé-/ *adj.* of or relating to a zenith. □ **zenithal projection** a projection of part of a globe on to a plane tangential to the centre of the part, showing the correct directions of all points from the centre.

zeolite /zeéəlīt/ *n.* each of a number of minerals consisting mainly of hydrous silicates of calcium, sodium, and aluminium, able to act as cation exchangers. □□ **zeolitic** /-líttik/ *adj.* [Sw. & G *zeolit* f. Gk *zeō* boil + -LITE (from their characteristic swelling and fusing under the blowpipe)]

Zeph. *abbr.* Zephaniah (Old Testament).

zephyr /zéffər/ *n.* **1** *literary* a mild gentle wind or breeze. **2** a fine cotton fabric. **3** an athlete's thin gauzy jersey. [F *zéphyr* or L *zephyrus* f. Gk *zephuros* (god of the) west wind]
■ **1** see BREEZE[1] *n.* 1.

Zeppelin /zéppəlin/ *n. hist.* a German large dirigible airship of the early 20th c., orig. for military use. [Count F. von *Zeppelin*, Ger. airman d. 1917, its first constructor]

zero /zeérō/ *n.* & *v.* ● *n.* (*pl.* **-os**) **1 a** the figure 0; nought. **b** no quantity or number; nil. **2** a point on the scale of an instrument from which a positive or negative quantity is reckoned. **3** (*attrib.*) having a value of zero; no, not any (*zero population growth*). **4** (in full **zero-hour**) **a** the hour at which a planned, esp. military, operation is timed to begin. **b** a crucial moment. **5** the lowest point; a nullity or nonentity. ● *v.tr.* (**-oes, -oed**) **1** adjust (an instrument etc.) to zero point. **2** set the sights of (a gun) for firing. □ **zero in on 1** take aim at. **2** focus one's attention on. **zero option** a disarmament proposal for the total removal of certain types of weapons on both sides. **zero-rated** on which no value added tax is charged. **zero-sum** (of a game, political situation, etc.) in which whatever is gained by one side is lost by the other so that the net change is always zero. [F *zéro* or It. *zero* f. OSp. f. Arab. *ṣifr* CIPHER]
■ *n.* **1** nil, null, nothing, nought, cipher, duck's-egg, *Cricket* duck, *archaic* aught, *US* goose-egg, *archaic or literary or US* naught, *sl.* nix, *Brit sl.* (sweet) Fanny Adams *or* FA, *esp. US sl.* zilch. **5** (rock) bottom, nadir; nobody, nothing, nonentity, nullity, *colloq.* nebbish. □ **zero in on 2** focus on, pinpoint, fix on, home in on, concentrate on, bring to bear on.

zeroth /zeérōth/ *adj.* immediately preceding what is regarded as 'first' in a series.

zest /zest/ *n.* **1** piquancy; a stimulating flavour or quality. **2 a** keen enjoyment or interest. **b** (often foll. by *for*) relish. **c** gusto (*entered into it with zest*). **3** a scraping of orange or lemon peel as flavouring. □□ **zestful** *adj.* **zestfully** *adv.* **zestfulness** *n.* **zestiness** *n.* **zesty** *adj.* (**zestier, zestiest**). [F *zeste* orange or lemon peel, of unkn. orig.]
■ **1** spice, relish, tang, pepper, ginger, piquancy, pungency, edge, bite, flavour, zip, *colloq.* zing, *sl.* pizazz. **2** eagerness, zestfulness, exuberance, enjoyment, gusto, appetite, interest, enthusiasm, zeal, relish, hunger, thirst. **3** peel, rind. □□ **zestful** see ENERGETIC 1, 2, SPICY 1.

zeta /zeétə/ *n.* the sixth letter of the Greek alphabet (*Z*, *ζ*). [Gk *zēta*]

zetetic /zeetéttik/ *adj.* proceeding by inquiry. [Gk *zētētikos* f. *zēteō* seek]

zeugma /zyóogmə/ *n.* a figure of speech using a verb or adjective with two nouns, to one of which it is strictly applicable while the word appropriate to the other is not used (e.g. *with weeping eyes and* [sc. *grieving*] *hearts*) (cf. SYLLEPSIS). □□ **zeugmatic** /-máttik/ *adj.* [L f. Gk *zeugma* -*atos* f. *zeugnumi* to yoke, *zugon* yoke]

zho var. of DZHO.

zibet /zíbbit/ *n.* (*US* **zibeth**) **1** an Asian or Indian civet, *Viverra zibetha*. **2** its scent. [med.L *zibethum*: see CIVET]

zidovudine /zīdōvyóodeen/ *n.* = AZT. [chem. name *azidothymidine*]

ziff /zif/ *n. Austral. sl.* a beard. [20th c.: orig. unkn.]

ziggurat /zíggərat/ *n.* a rectangular stepped tower in ancient Mesopotamia, surmounted by a temple. [Assyr. *ziqquratu* pinnacle]

zigzag /zígzag/ *n.*, *adj.*, *adv.*, & *v.* ● *n.* **1** a line or course having abrupt alternate right and left turns. **2** (often in *pl.*) each of these turns. ● *adj.* having the form of a zigzag; alternating right and left. ● *adv.* with a zigzag course. ● *v.intr.* (**zigzagged, zigzagging**) move in a zigzag course. □□ **zigzaggedly** *adv.* [F f. G *zickzack*]
■ *n.* **2** see TWIST *n.* 4. ● *adj.* see TORTUOUS 1. ● *v.* see WIND[2] *v.* 1.

zilch /zilch/ *n.* esp. *US sl.* nothing. [20th c.: orig. uncert.]
■ see ZERO *n.* 1.

zillah /zíllə/ *n.* an administrative district in India, containing several parganas. [Hind. *ḍilah* division]

zillion /zílyən/ *n. colloq.* an indefinite large number. □□ **zillionth** *adj.* & *n.* [Z (perh. = unknown quantity) + MILLION]
■ (*zillions*) see LOT *n.* 1.

zinc /zingk/ *n. Chem.* a white metallic element occurring naturally as zinc blende, and used as a component of brass, in galvanizing sheet iron, in electric batteries, and in printing-plates. ¶ Symb.: **Zn.** □ **flowers of zinc** = *zinc oxide*. **zinc blende** see BLENDE. **zinc chloride** a white crystalline deliquescent solid used as a preservative and flux. **zinc cream** esp. *Austral.* a heavy cream used as a preventative against sunburn. **zinc oxide** a powder used as a white pigment and in medicinal ointments. **zinc sulphate** a white water-soluble compound used as a mordant. □□ **zinced** *adj.* [G *Zink*, of unkn. orig.]

zinco /zíngkō/ *n.* & *v.* ● *n.* (*pl.* **-os**) = ZINCOGRAPH. ● *v.tr.* & *intr.* (**-oes, -oed**) = ZINCOGRAPH. [abbr.]

zincograph /zíngkəgraaf/ *n.* & *v.* ● *n.* **1** a zinc plate with a design etched in relief on it for printing from. **2** a print taken from this. ● *v.* **1** *tr.* & *intr.* etch on zinc. **2** *tr.* reproduce (a design) in this way. □□ **zincography** /-kógrəfi/ *n.*

zincotype /zíngkətīp/ *n.* = ZINCOGRAPH.

zing /zing/ *n.* & *v. colloq.* ● *n.* vigour, energy. ● *v.intr.* move swiftly or with a shrill sound. □□ **zingy** *adj.* (**zingier, zingiest**). [imit.]
■ *n.* see VIGOUR 1.

Zingaro /zínggərō/ *n.* (*pl.* **Zingari** /-ree/) a gypsy. [It.]

zinger /zíngər/ *n. US sl.* an outstanding person or thing.

zinnia /zínniə/ *n.* a composite plant of the genus *Zinnia*, with showy rayed flowers of deep red and other colours. [J. G. *Zinn*, Ger. physician and botanist d. 1759]

Zion /zīən/ *n.* (also **Sion** /sīən/) **1** the hill of Jerusalem on which the city of David was built. **2 a** the Jewish people or religion. **b** the Christian Church. **3** (in Christian thought) the Kingdom of God in Heaven. [OE f. eccl.L *Sion* f. Heb. *ṣīyôn*]

Zionism /zīəniz'm/ *n.* a movement (orig.) for the re-establishment and (now) the development of a Jewish nation in what is now Israel. □□ **Zionist** *n.*

zip /zip/ *n.* & *v.* ● *n.* **1** a light fast sound, as of a bullet passing through air. **2** energy, vigour. **3** esp. *Brit.* **a** (in full **zip-fastener**) a fastening device of two flexible strips with interlocking projections closed or opened by pulling a slide along them. **b** (*attrib.*) having a zip-fastener (*zip bag*). ● *v.* (**zipped, zipping**) **1** *tr.* & *intr.* (often foll. by *up*) fasten with a zip-fastener. **2** *intr.* move with zip or at high speed. [imit.]
■ *n.* **2** see ENERGY 1. ● *v.* **2** see STREAK *v.* 2.

Zip code /zip/ *n. US* a system of postal codes consisting of five-digit numbers. [*z*one *i*mprovement *p*lan]

zipper /zíppər/ *n.* & *v.* esp. *US* ● *n.* a zip-fastener. ● *v.tr.* (often foll. by *up*) fasten with a zipper. □□ **zippered** *adj.*

zippy /zíppi/ *adj.* (**zippier, zippiest**) *colloq.* **1** bright, fresh, lively. **2** fast, speedy. □□ **zippily** *adv.* **zippiness** *n.*
■ **1** see ENERGETIC 1, 2. **2** fast, quick, speedy.

zircon /zúrkən/ *n.* a zirconium silicate of which some translucent varieties are cut into gems (see HYACINTH 4, JARGON[2]). [G *Zirkon*: cf. JARGON[2]]

zirconium /zərkṓniəm/ *n. Chem.* a grey metallic element occurring naturally in zircon and used in various industrial applications. ¶ Symb.: **Zr.** [mod.L f. ZIRCON + -IUM]

zit /zit/ *n.* esp. *US sl.* a pimple. [20th c.: orig. unkn.]

zither /zíthər/ *n.* a musical instrument consisting of a flat wooden soundbox with numerous strings stretched across it, placed horizontally and played with the fingers and a plectrum. □□ **zitherist** *n.* [G (as CITTERN)]

zizz /ziz/ *n.* & *v. colloq.* ● *n.* **1** a whizzing or buzzing sound. **2** a short sleep. ● *v.intr.* **1** make a whizzing sound. **2** doze or sleep. [imit.]

■ *n.* **2** see SLEEP *n.* 2. ● *v.* **2** see DOZE *v.*

zloty /zlótti/ *n.* (*pl.* same or **zlotys**) the chief monetary unit of Poland. [Pol., lit. 'golden']

Zn *symb. Chem.* the element zinc.

zodiac /zṓdiak/ *n.* **1 a** a belt of the heavens limited by lines about 8° from the ecliptic on each side, including all apparent positions of the sun, moon, and planets as known to ancient astronomers, and divided into twelve equal parts (**signs of the zodiac**), each formerly containing the similarly named constellation but now by precession of the equinoxes coinciding with the constellation that bears the name of the preceding sign: Aries, Taurus, Gemini, Cancer, Leo, Virgo, Libra, Scorpio, Sagittarius, Capricorn(us), Aquarius, Pisces. **b** a diagram of these signs. **2** a complete cycle, circuit, or compass. [ME f. OF *zodiaque* f. L *zodiacus* f. Gk *zōidiakos* f. *zōidion* sculptured animal-figure, dimin. of *zōion* animal]

zodiacal /zədī́ək'l/ *adj.* of or in the zodiac. □ **zodiacal light** a luminous area of sky shaped like a tall triangle occasionally seen in the east before sunrise or in the west after sunset, esp. in the Tropics. [F (as ZODIAC)]

zoetrope /zṓ-itrōp/ *n. hist.* an optical toy in the form of a cylinder with a series of pictures on the inner surface which give an impression of continuous motion when viewed through slits with the cylinder rotating. [irreg. f. Gk *zōē* life + *-tropos* turning]

zoic /zṓ-ik/ *adj.* **1** of or relating to animals. **2** *Geol.* (of rock etc.) containing fossils; with traces of animal or plant life. [prob. back-form. f. AZOIC]

Zöllner's lines /tsṓlnərz/ *n.* parallel lines made to appear not parallel by short oblique intersecting lines. [J. K. F. *Zöllner*, Ger. physicist d. 1882]

zollverein /tsólfərīn/ *n. hist.* a customs union, esp. of German States in the 19th c. [G]

zombie /zómbi/ *n.* **1** *colloq.* a dull or apathetic person. **2** a corpse said to be revived by witchcraft. [W.Afr. *zumbi* fetish]

zonation /zōnáysh'n/ *n.* distribution in zones, esp. (*Ecol.*) of plants into zones characterized by the dominant species.

zonda /zóndə/ *n.* a hot dusty north wind in Argentina. [Amer. Sp.]

zone /zōn/ *n.* & *v.* ● *n.* **1** an area having particular features, properties, purpose, or use (*danger zone*; *erogenous zone*; *smokeless zone*). **2** any well-defined region of more or less beltlike form. **3 a** an area between two exact or approximate concentric circles. **b** a part of the surface of a sphere enclosed between two parallel planes, or of a cone or cylinder etc., between such planes cutting it perpendicularly to the axis. **4** (in full **time zone**) a range of longitudes where a common standard time is used. **5** *Geol.* etc. a range between specified limits of depth, height, etc., esp. a section of strata distinguished by characteristic fossils. **6** *Geog.* any of five divisions of the earth bounded by circles parallel to the equator (see FRIGID, TEMPERATE, TORRID). **7** an encircling band or stripe distinguishable in colour, texture, or character from the rest of the object encircled. **8** *archaic* a belt or girdle worn round the body. ● *v.tr.* **1** encircle as or with a zone. **2** arrange or distribute by zones. **3** assign as or to a particular area. □□ **zonal** *adj.* **zoning** *n.* (in sense 3 of *v.*). [F *zone* or L *zona* girdle f. Gk *zōnē*]

■ *n.* **1, 2** area, quarter, district, region, sector, section, sphere, belt, territory, province, realm, domain, precinct, department, terrain, tract, stretch, circle, locality, locale, *joc.* bailiwick.

zonk /zongk/ *v.* & *n. sl.* ● *v.* **1** *tr.* hit or strike. **2** (foll. by *out*) **a** *tr.* overcome with sleep; intoxicate. **b** *intr.* fall heavily asleep. ● *n.* (often as *int.*) the sound of a blow or heavy impact. [imit.]

zonked /zongkt/ *adj. sl.* (often foll by *out*) exhausted; intoxicated.

■ see WEARY *adj.* 1.

zoo /zōō/ *n.* a zoological garden. [abbr.]

■ zoological garden(s), menagerie, (safari *or* wildlife) park.

zoo- /zṓə/ *comb. form* of animals or animal life. [Gk *zōio-* f. *zōion* animal]

zoogeography /zṓəjiógrəfi/ *n.* the branch of zoology dealing with the geographical distribution of animals. □□ **zoogeographic** /-jéeəgráffik/ *adj.* **zoogeographical** /-jéeəgráffik'l/ *adj.* **zoogeographically** /-jéeəgráffikəli/ *adv.*

zoography /zō-ógrəfi/ *n.* descriptive zoology.

zooid /zṓ-oyd/ *n.* **1** a more or less independent invertebrate organism arising by budding or fission. **2** a distinct member of an invertebrate colony. □□ **zooidal** /-óyd'l/ *adj.* [formed as ZOO- + -OID]

zoolatry /zō-óllətri/ *n.* the worship of animals.

zoological /zṓəlójik'l, *disp.* zṓōə-/ *adj.* of or relating to zoology. □ **zoological garden** (or **gardens**) a public garden or park with a collection of animals for exhibition and study. □□ **zoologically** *adv.*

zoology /zō-ólləji, *disp.* zōō-ól-/ *n.* the scientific study of animals, esp. with reference to their structure, physiology, classification, and distribution. □□ **zoologist** *n.* [mod.L *zoologia* (as ZOO-, -LOGY)]

zoom /zōōm/ *v.* & *n.* ● *v.* **1** *intr.* move quickly, esp. with a buzzing sound. **2 a** *intr.* cause an aeroplane to mount at high speed and a steep angle. **b** *tr.* cause (an aeroplane) to do this. **3 a** *intr.* (of a camera) close up rapidly from a long shot to a close-up. **b** *tr.* cause (a lens or camera) to do this. ● *n.* **1** an aeroplane's steep climb. **2** a zooming camera shot. □ **zoom lens** a lens allowing a camera to zoom by varying the focal length. [imit.]

■ *v.* **1** see SPEED *v.* 1.

zoomancy /zṓəmansi/ *n.* divination from the appearances or behaviour of animals.

zoomorphic /zṓəmórfik/ *adj.* **1** dealing with or represented in animal forms. **2** having gods of animal form. □□ **zoomorphism** *n.*

zoonosis /zṓənṓsiss/ *n.* any of various diseases which can be transmitted to humans from animals. [ZOO- + Gk *nosos* disease]

zoophyte /zṓəfīt/ *n.* a plantlike animal, esp. a coral, sea anemone, or sponge. □□ **zoophytic** /-fíttik/ *adj.* [Gk *zōophuton* (as ZOO-, -PHYTE)]

zooplankton /zṓəplángktən/ *n.* plankton consisting of animals.

zoospore /zṓəspor/ *n.* a spore of fungi, algae, etc. capable of motion. □□ **zoosporic** /-spórik/ *adj.*

zootomy /zō-óttəmi/ *n.* the dissection or anatomy of animals.

zoot suit /zōōt/ *n. colloq.* a man's suit with a long loose jacket and high-waisted tapering trousers. [rhyming on SUIT]

zori /zórri/ *n.* (*pl.* **zoris**) a Japanese straw or rubber etc. sandal. [Jap.]

zoril /zórril/ *n.* (also **zorille**) a flesh-eating African mammal, *Ictonyx striatus*, of the skunk and the weasel family. [F *zorille* f. Sp. *zorrilla* dimin. of *zorro* fox]

Zoroastrian /zórrō-ástriən/ *adj.* & *n.* (also **Zarathustrian** /zárrəthōōstriən/) ● *adj.* of or relating to Zoroaster (or Zarathustra) or the dualistic religious system taught by him or his followers in the Zend-Avesta, based on the concept of a conflict between a spirit of light and good and a spirit of darkness and evil. ● *n.* a follower of Zoroaster. □□ **Zoroastrianism** *n.* [L *Zoroastres* f. Gk *Zōroastrēs* f.

Avestan *Zarathustra*, Persian founder of the religion in the 6th c. BC]

Zouave /zōō-aáv, zwaav/ *n.* a member of a French light-infantry corps originally formed of Algerians and retaining their oriental uniform. [F f. *Zouaoua*, name of a tribe]

zounds /zowndz/ *int. archaic* expressing surprise or indignation. [(*God*)'*s wounds* (i.e. those of Christ on the Cross)]

ZPG *abbr.* zero population growth.

Zr *symb. Chem.* the element zirconium.

zucchetto /tsookéttō/ *n.* (*pl.* **-os**) a Roman Catholic ecclesiastic's skullcap, black for a priest, purple for a bishop, red for a cardinal, and white for a pope. [It. *zucchetta* dimin. of *zucca* gourd, head]

zucchini /zookeéni/ *n.* (*pl.* same or **zucchinis**) esp. *US* & *Austral.* a courgette. [It., pl. of *zucchino* dimin. of *zucca* gourd]

zugzwang /tsoŏktsvaang/ *n. Chess* an obligation to move in one's turn even when this must be disadvantageous. [G f. *Zug* move + *Zwang* compulsion]

Zulu /zōōlōō/ *n.* & *adj.* • *n.* **1** a member of a Black South African people orig. inhabiting Zululand and Natal. **2** the language of this people. • *adj.* of or relating to this people or language. [native name]

zwieback /zweébak, tsveébaak/ *n.* a kind of biscuit rusk or sweet cake toasted in slices. [G, = twice baked]

Zwinglian /zwíngglian, tsvíng-/ *n.* & *adj.* • *n.* a follower of the Swiss religious reformer U. Zwingli (d. 1531). • *adj.* of or relating to Zwingli or his reforms.

zwitterion /zwíttərīən, tsvít-/ *n.* a molecule or ion having separate positively and negatively charged groups. [G f. *Zwitter* a hybrid]

zygo- /zī́gō, zíggō/ *comb. form* joining, pairing. [Gk *zugo-* f. *zugon* yoke]

zygodactyl /zī́gōdáktil, zíggə-/ *adj.* & *n.* • *adj.* (of a bird) having two toes pointing forward and two backward. • *n.* such a bird. □□ **zygodactylous** *adj.*

zygoma /zīgṓmə, zi-/ *n.* (*pl.* **zygomata** /-tə/) the bony arch of the cheek formed by connection of the zygomatic and temporal bones. [Gk *zugōma -atos* f. *zugon* yoke]

zygomatic /zī́gəmáttik, zíggə-/ *adj.* of or relating to the zygoma. □ **zygomatic arch** = ZYGOMA. **zygomatic bone** the bone that forms the prominent part of the cheek.

zygomorphic /zī́gəmórfik, zìggə-/ *adj.* (also **zygomorphous** /-mórfəss/) (of a flower) divisible into similar halves only by one plane of symmetry.

zygospore /zī́gəspor, zíggə-/ *n.* a thick-walled spore formed by certain fungi.

zygote /zī́gōt, zíg-/ *n. Biol.* a cell formed by the union of two gametes. □□ **zygotic** /-góttik/ *adj.* **zygotically** /-góttikəli/ *adv.* [Gk *zugōtos* yoked f. *zugoō* to yoke]

zymase /zī́mayss/ *n.* the enzyme fraction in yeast which catalyses the alcoholic fermentation of glucose. [F f. Gk *zumē* leaven]

zymology /zīmólləji/ *n. Chem.* the scientific study of fermentation. □□ **zymological** /-məlójik'l/ *adj.* **zymologist** *n.* [as ZYMASE + -LOGY]

zymosis /zīmṓsiss, zi-/ *n. archaic* fermentation. [mod.L f. Gk *zumōsis* (as ZYMASE)]

zymotic /zīmóttik, zi-/ *adj. archaic* of or relating to fermentation. □ **zymotic disease** *archaic* an epidemic, endemic, contagious, infectious, or sporadic disease regarded as caused by the multiplication of germs introduced from outside. [Gk *zumōtikos* (as ZYMOSIS)]

zymurgy /zī́murji, zím-/ *n.* the branch of applied chemistry dealing with the use of fermentation in brewing etc. [Gk *zumē* leaven, after *metallurgy*]

Appendices

Appendix 1 The History of English

1. Fifteen centuries of English cannot easily be summarized in about the same number of paragraphs, and this account is intended to pick out features on the landscape of language rather than to describe the scene in detail. This may afford some perspective to the information given in the dictionary, and help to make more sense of the strange and often unpredictable ways in which words seem to behave.

Origins

2.1 English belongs to the Indo-European family of languages, a vast group with many branches, thought to be derived from a common ancestor-language called Proto-Indo-European. The words we use in English are derived from a wide range of sources, mostly within this family. The earliest sources are Germanic, Norse, and Romanic; later, they are the languages of Europe more generally; and most recently, with the growth and decline of the British Empire and the rapid development of communications, they have been worldwide.

2.2 It is difficult to be sure exactly what we mean by an 'English' word. Most obviously, words are English if they can be traced back to the Anglo-Saxons, Germanic peoples who settled in Britain from the fifth century and eventually established several kingdoms together corresponding roughly to present-day England. From this time are derived many common words such as *eat, drink, speak, work, house, door, man, woman, husband, wife*. They displaced the Celtic peoples, whose speech survives in Scottish and Irish Gaelic, in Welsh, and in the local languages of two extremities of the British Isles, Manx (in the Isle of Man) and Cornish. Little Celtic influence remains in English, except in names of places such as *Brecon, Carlisle*, and *London*, and in many river names, such as *Avon, Thames*, and *Trent*. This fact may be attributed to a lack of cultural interaction, the Celts being forced back into the fringes of the British Isles by the Anglo-Saxon invaders, although there must have been some social integration.

3. Anglo-Saxon Britain continued to have contact with the Roman Empire, of which Britain had formerly been a part, and with Latin, which was the official language throughout the Empire and survived as a language of ritual (and for a time also of learning and communication) in the Western Christian Church. Christianity was brought to England with the mission of St Augustine in AD 597. The Christianized Anglo-Saxons built churches and monasteries, and there were considerable advances in art and learning. At this time English was enriched by many words from Latin, some of which are still in use, such as *angel, disciple, martyr*, and *shrine*. Other words were derived from Latin via the Germanic languages, for example *copper, mint* (in the sense of coinage), *pound, sack*, and *tile*, and others were ultimately of oriental origin, for example *camel* and *pepper*.

4.1 The next important influence on the vocabulary of English came from the Danish and other Scandinavian invaders of the ninth and tenth centuries, collectively called Vikings. They occupied much of the east side of England, and under Cnut (Canute) ruled the whole country for a time. The Danes had much more contact with the Anglo-Saxons than did the Celts, and their period of occupation has left its mark in the number of Scandinavian (Old Norse) words taken into English. Because Old Norse was also a Germanic language (of a different branch from English) many words were similar to the Anglo-Saxon ones, and it is difficult to establish the extent of the Old Norse influence. However, a number of Norse words are identifiable and are still in use, such as *call, take*, and *law*, names of parts of the body such as *leg*, and other basic words such as *egg, root*, and *window*. Many more Norse words are preserved in some dialects of the east side of England, in place-names such as those ending in *-thwaite* and *-thorpe* (both meaning 'settlement') and in *-by* (*Grimsby, Rugby, Whitby*, and so on), and in street-names ending in *-gate* (from the Old Norse *gata* meaning 'street') such as *Coppergate* in York.

4.2 In the Saxon kingdom of Wessex, King Alfred (871–99) and his successors did much to keep English alive by using it (rather than Latin) as the language of education and learning; by the tenth century there was a considerable amount of English prose and verse literature. Saxon and Danish kingdoms existed side by side for several generations, and there was much linguistic interaction. One very important effect on English was the gradual disappearance of many word-endings, or inflections, leading to a simpler grammar. This was partly because the stems of English and Norse words were often very close in form (for example, *stān* and *steinn*, meaning 'stone'), and only the inflections differed as an impediment to mutual understanding. So forms such as *stāne, stānes*, etc., began to be simplified and, eventually, eliminated. The process continued for hundreds of years into Middle English (see below).

The Norman Conquest

5. In 1066 William of Normandy defeated the English king, Harold, at the Battle of Hastings; he was crowned King of England on Christmas Day. The arrival of the French-speaking Normans as a ruling nobility brought a transforming Romance influence on the language. The Romance languages (chiefly French, Italian, Spanish, Portuguese, and Romanian) have their roots in the spoken or 'vulgar' Latin that continued in use until about AD 600. For two hundred years after the Norman Conquest, French (in its regional Norman form) was the language of the aristocracy, the lawcourts, and the Church hierarchy in England. Gradually the Normans were integrated into English society (for example, by inter-marriage), and by the reign of Henry II (1154–89) many of the aristocracy spoke English. During these years many French words were adopted into English. Some were connected with law and government, such as *justice, council*, and *tax*, and some were abstract terms such as *liberty, charity*, and *conflict*. The Normans also had an important effect on the spelling of English words. The combination of letters *cw-*, for example, was standardized in the Norman manner to *qu-*, so that *cwēn* became *queen* and *cwic* became *quik* (later *quick*).

6. This mixture of conquering peoples and their languages—Germanic, Scandinavian, and Romance—has had a decisive effect on the forms of words in modern English. The three elements make up the basic stock of English vocabulary, and different practices of putting sounds into writing are reflected in each. The different grammatical characteristics of each element can be seen in the structure and endings of many words. Many of the variable endings such as *-ant* and *-ent, -er* and *-or, -able* and *-ible* exist because the Latin words on which they are based belonged to different classes of verbs and nouns, each of which had a different ending. For example, *important* comes from the Latin verb *portare*, meaning 'to carry' (which belongs to one class or conjugation) while *repellent* comes from the Latin verb *pellere*, meaning 'to drive' (which belongs to another). *Capable* comes from a Latin word ending in *-abilis*, while *sensible* comes from one ending in *-ibilis*, and so on.

Middle English

7. Middle English, as the English of *c.*1100–1500 is called, emerged as the spoken and written form of the language under these influences. The use of French diminished, especially after King John (1199–1216) lost possession of Normandy in 1204, severing an important Anglo-French link. Many Anglo-Saxon words continued in use, while others disappeared altogether: for example, *niman* was replaced by the Old Norse (Scandinavian) *taka* (meaning 'take'), and the Old English *sige* was replaced by a word derived from Old French, *victory*. Other Old English words that disappeared are *ādl* (disease), *lof* (praise), and *lyft* (air: compare German *Luft*).

Sometimes new and old words continued in use side by side, in some cases on a roughly equal footing, and in others with a distinction in meaning (as with *doom* and *judgement*, and *stench* and *smell*). This has produced pairs of words which are both in use today, such as *shut* and *close*, and *buy* and *purchase*, in which the second word of each pair is Romance in origin. Sometimes an even larger overlap was produced, as when *commence* (from the French) was added to the existing Old English *begin* and *start*. (The original meaning of *start* was 'leap', 'move suddenly', which is still current though no longer the main sense.)

8. Hundreds of the Romance words were short simple words that would now be distinguished with difficulty from Old English words if their origin were not known: for example, *bar, cry, fool, mean, pity, stuff, touch,* and *tender*. Others, such as *commence* and *purchase*, have more formal connotations. The result was a mixture of types of words, which is a feature especially of modern English. For many meanings we now have a choice of less and more formal words, and the more formal ones in some cases are used only in very specific circumstances. For example, the word *vendor* is used instead of *seller* only in the context of buying or selling property. Many technical words derived from or ultimately from Latin, such as *estop* and *usucaption*, survive only in legal contexts, to the great confusion of the layman. These levels of formality are reflected in the dictionary's identification of usage level in particular cases as colloquial, formal, and so on, more fully explained in the *Detailed explanations of defining sections* (A9 on p. xiv).

Printing

9. There was much regional variation in the spelling and pronunciation of Middle English, although a good measure of uniformity was imposed by the development of printing from the fifteenth century. This uniformity was based as much on practical considerations of the printing process as on what seemed most 'correct' or suitable. It became common practice, for example, to add a final *e* to words to fill a line of print. The printers—many of whom were foreign—used rules from their own languages, especially Dutch and Flemish, when setting English into type. William Caxton, the first English printer (1422–91), exercised an important but not always beneficial influence. The unnecessary insertion of *h* in *ghost*, for example, is due to Caxton (who learned the business of printing on the Continent), and the change had its effect on other words such as *ghastly* and (perhaps) *ghetto*. In general, Caxton used the form of English prevalent in the south-east of England, although the East Midland dialect was the more extensive. This choice, together with the growing importance of London as the English capital, gave the dialect of the South-East a special importance that survives to the present day.

Pronunciation

10. At roughly the same time as the early development of printing, the pronunciation of English was also undergoing major changes. The main change, which began in the fourteenth century during the lifetime of the poet Chaucer, was in the pronunciation of vowel sounds. The so-called 'great vowel shift' resulted in the reduction of the number of long vowels (for example, in *deed* as distinct from *dead*) from seven to the five which we know today (discernible in the words *bean, barn, born, boon,* and *burn*). It also affected the pronunciation of other vowels: the word *life*, for example, was once pronounced as we now pronounce *leaf*, and *name* was pronounced as two syllables to rhyme with *farmer*. In many cases, as with *name*, the form of the word did not change; and this accounts for many of the 'silent' vowels at the ends of words. The result of these developments was a growing difference between what was spoken and what was written.

The Renaissance

11. The rediscovery in Europe of the culture and history of the ancient Greek and Roman worlds exercised a further Romanizing influence on English. This began at the end of the Middle Ages and blossomed in the European Renaissance of the fifteenth to seventeenth centuries. Scholarship flourished, and the language used by scholars and writers was Latin. During the Renaissance words such as *arena, dexterity, excision, genius, habitual, malignant, specimen,* and *stimulus* came into use in English. They are familiar and useful words but their Latin origins sometimes make them awkward to handle, as, for example, when we use *arena, genius,* and *stimulus* in the plural. There was also a tendency in the Renaissance to try to emphasize the Greek or Latin origins of words when writing them. This accounts for the *b* in *debt* (the earlier English word was *det*; in Latin it is *debitum*), the *l* in *fault* (earlier *faut*; the Latin source is *fallere* fail), the *s* in *isle* (earlier *ile*; *insula* in Latin) and the *p* in *receipt* (earlier *receit*; *recepta* in Latin). Some words that had gone out of use were reintroduced, usually with changed meanings, for example *artificial, disc* (originally the same as *dish*), and *fastidious*.

Later influences

12. The development of machines and technology in Britain from the eighteenth century onwards, followed by the electronic revolution of our own times, has also played a part in continuing the influence of Latin. New technical terms have come into use, and they have often been formed on Latin or Greek source-words because these can convey precise ideas in easily combinable forms, for example *bacteriology, microscope, radioactive,* and *semiconductor*. Combinations of Germanic elements are also used, as in *software, splashdown,* and *take-off*. This process has sometimes produced odd mixtures, such as *television*, which is half Greek and half Latin, and *microchip*, which is half Greek and half Germanic.

13.1 In recent times English speakers have come into contact with people from other parts of the world, through trade, the growth of the British Empire, and improved communications generally. This contact has produced a rich supply of new words that are often strange in form. India, where the British first had major dealings in the seventeenth century, is the source of words such as *bungalow, jodhpurs,* and *khaki*. Usually these words have been altered or assimilated to make them look more natural in English (e.g. *bungalow* from Gujarati *bangalo*). Examples from other parts of the world are *harem* and *mufti* (from Arabic), *bazaar* (from Persian), *kiosk* (from Turkish), and *anorak* (from Eskimo). From European countries we have acquired *balcony* (from Italian), *envelope* (from French), and *yacht* (from Dutch).

13.2 Thousands of such words, though not English in the Germanic sense, are regarded as fully absorbed into English. In addition, there are many unnaturalized words and phrases that are used in English contexts but are generally regarded as 'foreign', and are conventionally printed in italics to distinguish them when used in an English context. Very many of these are French, for example *accouchement* (childbirth), *bagarre* (a scuffle), *bonhomie* (geniality), *flânerie* (idleness), and *rangé* (domesticated), but other languages are represented, as with *echt* (genuine) and *macht-politik* (power politics) from German, and *mañana* (tomorrow) from Spanish.

14.1 Usage often recognizes the difficulties of absorbing words from various sources by assimilating them into forms that are already familiar. The word *picturesque*, which came into use in the eighteenth century, is a compromise between its French source *pittoresque* and the existing Middle English word *picture*, to which it is obviously related. The English word *cockroach* is a conversion of its Spanish source-word *cucaracha* into a pair of familiar words *cock* (a bird) and *roach* (a fish). Cockroaches have nothing to do with cocks or roaches, and the association is simply a matter of linguistic convenience.

14.2 Problems of inflection arise with words taken from other languages. The ending *-i* in particular is very unnatural in English, and usage varies between *-is* and *-ies* in the plural. A similar difficulty occurs with the many adopted nouns ending in *-o*, some of which come from the Italian (*solo*), some from Spanish (*armadillo*), and some from Latin (*hero*); here usage varies between *-os* and *-oes*. Verbs often need special treatment, as for example *bivouac* (from French, and before that probably from Swiss German) which needs a *k* in the past tense (*bivouacked*, not *bivouaced* which might be mispronounced), and *ski* (from Norwegian) where usage allows both *ski'd* and *skied* as past forms (though neither is satisfactory). In this dictionary extensive help is given with these and other difficulties of inflection.

Dictionaries

15.1 One obvious consequence of the development of printing in the fifteenth century was that it allowed the language to be recorded in glossaries and dictionaries, and this might be expected to have had a considerable effect on the way words were used and spelt. However, listing all the words in the language systematically in alphabetical order with their spellings and meanings is a relatively recent idea. There was nothing of the sort in Shakespeare's time, for example. In 1580, when Shakespeare was sixteen, a schoolmaster named William Bullokar published a manual for the 'ease, speed, and perfect reading and writing of English', and he called for the writing of an English dictionary. Such a dictionary, the work of Robert Cawdrey (another schoolmaster), was not published until 1604. Like the dictionaries that followed in quick succession (including Bullokar's own *English Expositor*), its purpose was described as being for the understanding of 'hard words'. It was not until the eighteenth century that dictionaries systematically listed all the words in general use at the time regardless of how 'easy' or 'hard' they were; the most notable of these were compiled by Nathaniel Bailey (1721) and, especially, Samuel Johnson (1755). They were partly a response to a call, expressed by Swift, Pope, Addison, and other writers, for the language to be fixed and stabilized, and for the establishment of an English Academy to monitor it. None of these hopes as such were realized, but the dictionaries played an important role in settling the form and senses of English words.

15.2 The systematic investigation and recording of words in all their aspects and on a historical basis is first and exclusively represented in the *Oxford English Dictionary*, begun by the Scottish schoolmaster James A. H. Murray in 1879. This describes historically the spelling, inflection, origin, and meaning of words, and is supported by citations from printed literature and other sources as evidence from Old English to the present day. To take account of more recent changes and developments in the language, a four-volume *Supplement* was added to the work from 1972 to 1986, and a new edition integrating the original dictionary and its *Supplement* appeared in 1989. Because of its depth of scholarship, the *Oxford English Dictionary* forms a major basis of all English dictionaries produced since. Smaller concise and other household dictionaries that aim at recording the main vocabulary in current use began to appear early this century and in recent years the number has grown remarkably.

15.3 Dictionaries of current English, as distinct from historical dictionaries, generally record the language as it is being used at the time, and with usage constantly changing the distinction between 'right' and 'wrong' is sometimes difficult to establish. Unlike French, which is guided by the rulings of the *Académie Française*, English is not monitored by any single authority; established usage is the principal criterion. One result of this is that English tolerates many more alternative spellings than other languages. The alternatives are based on certain patterns of word formation and variation in the different languages through which they have passed before reaching ours.

15.4 It should also be remembered that the smaller dictionaries, such as this one, provide a selection, based on currency, of a recorded stock of over half a million words; that is to say, they represent about 15–20 per cent of what is attested to exist by printed sources and other materials. Dictionaries therefore differ in the selection they make, beyond the core of vocabulary and idiom that can be expected to be found in any dictionary.

Dialect

16. Within the British Isles, regional forms and dialects, with varying accents and usage, have continued to exist since the Middle Ages, although in recent times, especially with the emergence of mass communications, they have been in decline. A special feature of a dialect is its vocabulary of words (often for everyday things) that are understood only locally. It is not possible in a small dictionary to treat this kind of vocabulary in any detail, but its influence can be seen in the origins of words that have achieved a more general currency, for example *boss-eyed* (from a dialect word *boss* meaning 'miss', 'bungle'), *fad*, *scrounge* (from dialect *scrunge* meaning 'steal'), and *shoddy*. Far more information on dialect words is available in *The English Dialect Dictionary* (ed. J. Wright, London, 1898–1905), in the *Oxford English Dictionary*, and in numerous glossaries published by dialect societies.

English Worldwide

17.1 Usage in modern times is greatly influenced by rapid worldwide communications, by newspapers and, in particular, by television and radio. Speakers of British English are brought into daily contact with alternative forms of the language, especially American English. This influence is often regarded as unsettling or harmful but it has had a considerable effect on the vocabulary, idiom, and spelling of British English, and continues to do so. Among the many words and idioms in use in British English, usually without any awareness of or concern about their American origin, are *OK*, *to fall for*, *to fly off the handle*, *round trip*, and *to snoop*. American English often has more regular spellings, for example the substitution of *-er* for *-re* in words such as *theatre*, the standardization of *-or* and *-our* to *-or* in words such as *harbour*, and the use of *-se* in forms such as *defense* and *license*, where British English either has *-ce* only or both forms (for example, a *practice* but to *practise*).

17.2 English is now used all over the world; as a result, there are many varieties of English, with varying accents, vocabulary, and usage. In addition to British and American English there are varieties in use in Southern Africa, India, Australia, New Zealand, Canada, and elsewhere. These varieties have an equal claim to be regarded as 'English' and, although learners of English may look to British English as the centre of an English-speaking world, or British and American English as the two poles of such a world, it is very important that dictionaries should take account of English overseas, especially as it affects that in use in Britain. The process is a strengthening and enriching one, and is the mark of a living and flourishing language.

Further reading

18. This survey has had to be brief, and restricted to those aspects of English that are of immediate concern to the users of a dictionary. Those who are interested in exploring further will find a host of books on the history and development of English. Good general accounts are A. C. Baugh and T. Cable, *A History of the English Language* (3rd edn., New Jersey and

London, 1978) and B. M. H. Strang, *A History of English* (London, 1970). At a more popular level, and more up to date on recent trends, are R. W. Burchfield, *The English Language* (Oxford, 1985) and R. McCrum *et al.*, *The Story of English* (London, 1986). *The Oxford Companion to the English Language* (ed. T. McArthur, Oxford, 1992) contains much that will interest those who want to know more about the English of today and its place among the languages of the world.

A chronology of English

A selection of dates associated with the history and spread of the English language from Roman times to 1990.

55 BC Roman military expedition to Britain by Julius Caesar.

AD 43 Roman invasion of Britain under the Emperor Claudius, beginning 400 years of control over much of the island.

150 From around this date, with Roman permission, small numbers of settlers arrive from the coastlands of Germany, speaking dialects ancestral to English.

297 First mention of the Picts of Caledonia, tribes beyond Roman control, well to the north of Hadrian's Wall.

410 The Goths sack Rome.

436 The end of a period of gradual Roman withdrawal. Britons south of the Wall are attacked by the Picts and by Scots from Ireland. Angles, Saxons, and other Germanic settlers come first as mercenaries to help the Britons, then take over more and more territory.

449 The traditional date for the beginning of the Anglo-Saxon settlements.

450–80 The first surviving Old English inscriptions, in runic letters.

495 The Saxon kingdom of Wessex established.

500 The kingdom of Dalriada established in Argyll by Scots from Ireland.

527 The Saxon kingdoms of Essex and Middlesex established.

550 The Angle kingdoms of Mercia, East Anglia, and Northumbria established.

557 At the Battle of Deorham, the West Saxons drive a wedge between the Britons of Wales and Cornwall.

597 Aethelberht, king of Kent, welcomes Augustine and the conversion of the Anglo-Saxons to Christianity begins.

613 At the Battle of Chester, the Angles of Northumbria drive a wedge between the Britons of Wales and Cumbria.

638 Edwin of Northumbria takes Lothian from the Britons.

700 The first manuscript records of Old English from about this time.

792 Scandinavians begin to raid and settle in Britain, Ireland, and France. In 793, they sack the monastery of Lindisfarne, the centre of Northumbrian scholarship.

795 The Danes settle in parts of Ireland.

815 Egbert of Wessex defeats the south-western Britons of Cornwall and incorporates Cornwall into his kingdom.

828 Egbert of Wessex is hailed as *bretwalda* (lord of Britain), overlord of the Seven Kingdoms of the Angles and Saxons (the Heptarchy). England begins to emerge.

834 The Danes raid England.

843 Kenneth MacAlpin, King of Scots, gains the throne of Pictland.

865 The Danes occupy Northumbria and establish a kingdom at York. Danish begins to influence English.

871 Alfred becomes king of Wessex, translates works of Latin into English, and establishes the writing of prose in English.

886 The boundaries of the Danelaw are settled.

911 Charles II of France grants lands on the lower Seine to the Viking chief Hrolf the Ganger (Rollo the Rover). The beginnings of Normandy and Norman French.

954 The expulsion of Eric Blood-Axe, last Danish king of York.

965 The English invade the northern Welsh kingdom of Gwynedd.

973 Edgar of England cedes Lothian to Kenneth II, King of Scots. Scotland multilingual: Gaelic dominant, Norse in the north, Cumbric in the south-west, English in the south-east, Latin for church and law.

992 A treaty between Ethelred of England and the Normans.

1000 The approximate date of the only surviving manuscript of the Old English epic poem *Beowulf.*

1007 Ethelred the Unready pays *danegeld* to stop the Danes attacking England. In 1013, however, they take the country and Ethelred flees to Normandy.

1014 The end of Danish rule in Ireland.

1016–42 The reigns of Canute/Cnut and his sons over Denmark, Norway, and England.

1051 Edward the Confessor, King of England, impressed by the Normans and with French-speaking counsellors at his court, names as his heir William, Duke of Normandy, but reneges on his promise before his death.

1066 The Norman Conquest. William defeats King Harold at Hastings, and sets in train the Normanization of the upper classes of the British Isles. England multilingual: English the majority language, Danish in the north, Cornish in the far south-west, Welsh on the border with Wales, Norman French at court and in the courts, and Latin in church and school.

1150 The first surviving texts of Middle English.

1167 The closure of the University of Paris to students from England accelerates the development of a university at Oxford.

1171 Henry II invades Ireland and declares himself its overlord, introducing Norman French and English into the island.

1204 King John loses the Duchy of Normandy to France.

1209 The exodus of a number of students from Oxford leads to the establishment of a second university in Cambridge.

1272–1307 The reign of Edward I, who consolidates royal authority in England, and extends it permanently to Wales and temporarily to Scotland.

1282 Death of Llewelyn, last native prince of Wales. In 1301, Edward of England's son and heir is invested as Prince of Wales.

1284 The Statute of Rhuddlan establishes the law of England in Wales (in French and Latin), but retains the legal use of Welsh.

1314 Robert Bruce reasserts Scottish independence by defeating Edward II at Bannockburn, an achievement later celebrated in an epic written in Scots.

1337 The outbreak of the Hundred Years War between England and France, which ends with the loss of all England's French possessions save the Channel Islands.

1343?–1400 The life of Geoffrey Chaucer.

1348 (1) English replaces Latin as medium of instruction in schools, but not at Oxford and Cambridge. (2) The worst year of the Black Death.

1362 (1) Through the Statute of Pleading, written in French, English replaces French as the language of law in England, but the records continue to be kept in Latin. (2) English is used for the first time in Parliament.

1384 The publication of John Wycliffe's English translation of the Latin Bible.

1385 The scholar John of Trevisa notes that 'in all the gramere scoles of Engelond, children leveth Frensche and construeth and lerneth in Englische'.

1400 By this date the Great Vowel Shift has begun.

1450 Printing by movable type invented in the Rhineland.

1476 (1) The first English book printed: *The Recuyell of the Historyes of Troye*, translated from French by William Caxton, who printed it at Bruges in Flanders. (2) Caxton sets up the first printing press in England, at Westminster. In 1478, he publishes Chaucer's *Canterbury Tales*.

1485 The Battle of Bosworth, after which the part-Welsh Henry Tudor becomes King of England. Welsh nobles follow him to London.

1492 Christopher Columbus discovers the New World.

1497 Giovanni Caboto (Anglicized as 'John Cabot'), in a ship from Bristol, lands on the Atlantic coast of North America.

1499 The publication of *Thesaurus linguae romanae et britannicae* (Treasury of the Roman and British Tongues), the first English-to-Latin wordbook, the work of Galfridus Grammaticus (Geoffrey the Grammarian).

1504 The settlement of St John's on Newfoundland as a shore base for English fisheries.

1507 The German geographer Martin Waldseemüller puts the name *America* on his map of the world.

1525 The publication of William Tyndale's translation of the New Testament of the Bible.

1534 Jacques Cartier lands on the Gaspé Peninsula in North America and claims it for France.

1536 and **1542** The Statute of Wales (Acts of Union) unites England and Wales, excluding Welsh from official use.

1542 Henry VIII of England proclaims himself King of Ireland.

1549 The publication of the first version of the Book of Common Prayer of the Church of England, the work in the main of Thomas Cranmer.

1558–1603 The reign of Elizabeth I.

1560–1620 The plantation of Ireland, first by English settlers and after 1603 also by Scots, establishing English throughout the island and Scots in Ulster.

1564–1616 The life of William Shakespeare.

1583 Sir Humphrey Gilbert establishes Newfoundland as England's first colony beyond the British Isles.

1584 The settlement on Roanoke Island by colonists led by Sir Walter Raleigh. In 1587, Virginia Dare born at Roanoke, first child of English parents in North America. In 1590, the settlers of Roanoke disappear without trace.

1588 The publication of Bishop Morgan's translation of the Bible into Welsh, serving as a focus for the survival of the language.

1600 English traders establish the East India Company.

1603 The Union of the Crowns under James VI of Scotland, I of England.

1604 The publication of Robert Cawdrey's *Table Alphabeticall*, the first dictionary of English.

1606 The Dutch explore northern New Holland (Terra Australis).

1607 The Jamestown colony in Virginia, the first permanent English settlement and the first representative assembly in the New World.

1608 Samuel Champlain founds the city of Quebec in New France.

1611 The publication of the Authorized or King James Version of the Bible, intended for use in the Protestant services of England, Scotland, and Ireland. A major influence on the written language and in adapting Scots towards English.

1612 (1) Bermuda colonized under the charter of the Virginia Company. (2) Traders of the East India Company establish themselves in Gujarat, India.

1614 King James writes in English to the Moghul Emperor Jehangir, in order to encourage trade with 'the Orientall Indies'.

1619 At the Jamestown colony in America, the first African slaves arrive on a Dutch ship.

1620 The *Mayflower* arrives in the New World and the Pilgrim Fathers set up Plimoth Plantation in Massachusetts. English is now in competition as a colonial language in the Americas with Dutch, French, Spanish, and Portuguese.

1622 Publication in London of the first English newspaper, *Weekly News*.

1623 Publication in London of the First Folio of Shakespeare's plays.

1627 An English colony established on Barbados in the Caribbean.

1637 (1) English traders arrive on the coast of China. (2) The Académie française founded

1640 An English trading factory established at Madras.

1647 The Bahamas colonized by settlers from Bermuda.

1652 The first Dutch settlers arrive in southern Africa.

1655 England acquires Jamaica from Spain.

1659 The East India Company annexes St Helena in the south Atlantic.

1660 John Dryden expresses his admiration for the Académie française and its work in 'fixing' French and wishes for something similar to serve English.

1662 The Royal Society of London receives its charter from Charles II. In 1664, it appoints a committee to consider ways of improving English as a language of science.

1670 The Hudson's Bay Company founded for fur trading in northern America.

1674 Charles II receives Bombay from the Portuguese in the dowry of Catherine of Braganza and gives it to the East India Company.

1687 Isaac Newton writes *Principia Mathematica* in Latin: see 1704.

1688 The publication of *Oronooko, or the History of the Royal Slave*, by Aphra Behn: one of the first novels in English, by the first woman novelist in English, based on personal experience of a slave revolt in Surinam.

1690 A trading factory established at Calcutta in Bengal.

1696 British and French colonists in North America in open conflict.

1697 The Boston clergyman Cotton Mather applies the term *American* to English-speaking settlers in the New World.

1702 Publication in London of the first regular daily newspaper in English, *The Daily Courant*.

1704 Isaac Newton writes his second major work, *Opticks*, in English: see 1687.

1707 The Act of Union, uniting the Parliaments of England and Scotland, creating the United Kingdom of Great Britain, but keeping separate the state religions, educational systems, and laws of the two kingdoms.

1712 (1) Jonathan Swift in Dublin proposes an English Academy to 'fix' the language and compete adequately with French. (2) In India, the Moghul Empire begins to decline.

1713 (1) At the Treaty of Utrecht, France surrenders Hudson's Bay, Acadia, and Newfoundland to the British. (2) Gibraltar is ceded to Britain by Spain.

1726 Ephraim Chambers publishes his *Cyclopaedia*, the first encyclopedia.

1731 The abolition of Law French in England.

1746 The Wales and Berwick Act, by which England is deemed to include Wales and the Scottish town of Berwick is incorporated into England.

1755 The publication of Samuel Johnson's *Dictionary of the English Language*.

1757 The East India Company becomes the power behind the government of Bengal.

1759 General James Wolfe takes Quebec for the British.

1759–96 The life of Robert Burns.

1762 The publication of Robert Lowth's *Short Introduction to English Grammar*.

1763 The French cede New France to Britain, retaining only St Pierre and Miquelon (islands off Newfoundland).

1768–71 The partwork publication in Edinburgh of *The Encyclopaedia Britannica*.

1770 Captain James Cook takes possession of the Australian continent for Britain.

1770–1850 The life of William Wordsworth.

1771–1832 The life of Sir Walter Scott.

1774 (1) The Quebec Act creates the British province of Quebec, extending to the Ohio and Mississippi. (2) The Regulating Act places Bombay and Madras under the control of Bengal and the East India Company becomes a kind of state.

1776 The Declaration of Independence by thirteen British colonies in North America and the start of the American War of Independence (1776–83) which created the United States of America, the first nation outside the British Isles with English as its principal language.

1778 Captain James Cook visits and names the Sandwich Islands (Hawaii).

1780–1800 British Empire loyalists move from the US to Canada.

1785 In London, the newspaper *The Daily Universal Register* founded. Renamed *The Times* in 1788.

1786 (1) Lord Cornwallis is appointed first Governor-General of British India. (2) A British penal colony is established at Botany Bay in Australia. In 1788, the first convicts arrive there.

1791 (1) The British colonies of Upper Canada (Ontario) and Lower Canada (Quebec) are established. (2) In London, the newspaper *The Observer* is founded, the oldest national Sunday newspaper in Britain.

1792 The first Europeans settle in New Zealand.

1794 The publication of Lindley Murray's *English Grammar*.

1802 The establishment of the British colonies of Ceylon and Trinidad.

1803 (1) The Act of Union incorporating Ireland into Britain, as the United Kingdom of Great Britain and Ireland. (2) The Louisiana Purchase, by which the US buys from France its remaining North American territories, and doubles its size.

1806 The British take control of Cape Colony in southern Africa.

1808 The establishment of the British colony of Sierra Leone.

1814 (1) The British annex Cape Colony. (2) France cedes to Britain Malta, Mauritius, St Lucia, and Tobago.

1816 The establishment of the British colony of Bathurst (the Gambia).

1819 (1) The establishment of the British colony of Singapore. (2) The US purchases Florida from Spain.

1820 Christian missionaries from the US visit Hawaii.

1821 American settlers arrive in the Mexican territory of Texas.

1828 The publication of Noah Webster's *American Dictionary of the English Language*.

1829 Australia becomes a British dependency.

1831 The establishment of the colony of British Guiana.

1833 (1) The abolition of slavery in the British Empire. (2) St Helena becomes a British colony.

1835 Thomas Macaulay writes the Minute on Education whereby the British rulers of India endorse English as a language of education for Indians.

1835–1910 The life of Sam Clemens (Mark Twain).

1836 Texas declares its independence from Mexico.

1839 The first Boer Republic is established in Natal, South Africa, after the Great Trek from the Cape.

1840 (1) The Treaty of Waitangi, by which the Maori of New Zealand cede all rights and powers of government to Britain. (2) The transportation of convicts to Eastern Australia is ended.

1841 (1) Upper and Lower Canada are brought together as British North America. (2) New Zealand becomes a British colony. (3) In London, the founding of the weekly magazine *Punch*.

1842 (1) The opening of Chinese ports other than Canton to Western traders, after the defeat of China in the Opium War. Hong Kong is ceded by China to Britain as a Crown Colony. (2) The Philological Society is formed in London.

1844 The first telegraph message transmitted, between Washington and Baltimore.

1845 Texas becomes a state of the United States.

1846 The British annex Natal but recognize the Transvaal and the Orange Free State as autonomous Boer republics.

1848 In the Treaty of Guadalupe Hidalgo, Mexico cedes vast western territories to the US.

1850 (1) Britain takes control of the Bay Islands of Honduras, an English-speaking enclave in Central America. (2) Legislative councils are established in Australia by British Act of Parliament.

1852 The publication of *Roget's Thesaurus*.

1853 (1) Japan is forced by Commander Matthew Perry of the US Navy to open its harbours to Western trade. (2) The transportation of convicts to Tasmania is ended.

1855 The government of the colony of New South Wales is established.

1856 The governments of the colonies of Tasmania and Victoria are established.

1856–1950 The life of George Bernard Shaw.

1857 The Sepoy Rebellion (War of Independence, Indian Mutiny) in India leads to the transfer of British India from the East India Company to the Crown.

1858 (1) The Philological Society passes a resolution calling for a new dictionary of English on historical principles. (2) Britain cedes the Bay Islands to Honduras.

1861 The establishment of the British colony of Lagos (Nigeria).

1862 The establishment of the colony of British Honduras.

1863 The establishment of the Cambridge Overseas Examinations.

1865 The abolition of slavery in the US, at the end of the Civil War. At the outbreak of the war there were over 4m slaves.

1867 (1) The Dominion of Canada is created, consisting of Quebec, Ontario, Nova Scotia, and New Brunswick. (2) Alaska is purchased from Russia by the US.

1868 (1) Transportation of convicts to Western Australia is ended. (2) In the US, Christopher Latham Sholes and colleagues patent the first successful typewriter.

1869 (1) Rupert's Land and the Northwest Territories are bought by Canada from the Hudson's Bay Company. (2) Basutoland becomes a British protectorate.

1870 Manitoba becomes a province of Canada.

1871 British Columbia becomes a province of Canada.

1873 (1) The formation of the English Dialect Society (dissolved in 1896). (2) Prince Edward Island becomes a province of Canada.

1874 The establishment of the British colony of the Gold Coast in West Africa.

1879 James A. H. Murray begins editing the Philological Society's *New English Dictionary on Historical Principles.*

1882–1941 The life of James Joyce.

1884 (1) The Berlin Conference, in which European powers begin 'the scramble for Africa'. (2) Britain declares a protectorate over South East New Guinea. (3) The French, Germans, and British attempt to annex what shortly becomes the German colony of Kamerun. (4) Publication of the first fascicle, *A-Ant*, of Murray's dictionary (the *OED*).

1886 The annexation of Burma into British India and the abolition of the Burmese monarchy.

1888–94 The establishment of British protectorates in Kenya, Uganda, and Zanzibar.

1889 The formation of the American Dialect Society.

1895 The establishment of the British East African Protectorate, open to white settlers.

1898 (1) The annexation of Hawaii by the US. In 1900, it becomes a US territory. (2) Spain cedes the Philippines and Puerto Rico to the US. (3) Yukon Territory comes under Canadian government control.

1901 (1) The establishment of the Commonwealth of Australia as a dominion of the British Empire. (2) The first wireless telegraphy messages sent across the Atlantic by Guglielmo Marconi (Cornwall to Newfoundland). (3) The first film-show, in an arcade opened in Los Angeles, California.

1903 (1) A message from US President Theodore Roosevelt circles the world in less than 10 minutes by Pacific Cable.

1903–50 The life of George Orwell.

1905 (1) Alberta and Saskatchewan become provinces of Canada. (2) The first cartoon strip, 'Little Nemo', appears in the *New York Herald.*

1906 (1) The formation of the English Association. (2) The first full-length motion picture, *The Story of the Kelly Gang.* (3) the publication of the Fowler brothers' *The King's English.*

1907 (1) The establishment of New Zealand as a dominion of the British Empire. (2) The first regular studio-based radio broadcasts by the De Forest Radio Telephone Company in the US. (3) The foundation of Hollywood as a film-making centre.

1910 (1) The establishment of the Union of South Africa as a dominion of the British Empire. (2) The first radio receivers made in kit form for sale in the US.

1911 The publication of the Fowler brothers' *Concise Oxford Dictionary.*

1913 (1) The formation of the Society for Pure English. (2) The first crossword puzzle published, in the *New York World.*

1914 (1) A third Home Rule Bill for Ireland passed by the British Parliament, but prevented from coming into operation by the outbreak of the First World War. (2) The German colony of Kamerun invaded by the French and British.

1915 The death of Sir James A. H. Murray, aged 78, having finished the section *Trink–Turndown* in the *OED.*

1916 (1) The Easter Rising in Dublin, an unsuccessful armed rebellion against the British, during which an Irish Republic is proclaimed. (2) The Technicolor process is first used in the film *The Gulf Between*, in the US.

1917 The publication of Daniel Jones's *English Pronouncing Dictionary.*

1918 (1) The formation of the English-Speaking Union. (2) The US War Industries Board declares moving pictures an essential industry.

1919 (1) The German colony of Tanganyika ceded to Britain. (2) The German colony of Kamerun divided between France (Cameroun) and Britain (Cameroon). (3) The publication of H. L. Mencken's *The American Language.*

1920 (1) The Partition of Ireland. (2) Kenya becomes a British colony. (3) The first public radio station set up by Marconi in the US.

1921 (1) A treaty between the United Kingdom and the Irish Free State, which accepts dominion status within the British Empire. (2) The first full-length 'talkie' *Dream Street* produced by United Artists, in the US.

1922 (1) The establishment of the British Broadcasting Company, renamed in 1927 the British Broadcasting Corporation (BBC). (2) The founding in the US of the monthly magazine *The Reader's Digest.*

1923 The founding of *Time* magazine in the US.

1925 (1) The borders of the Republic of Ireland and Northern Ireland established. (2) Afrikaans gains official status in South Africa. (3) The founding of the weekly magazine *The New Yorker.*

1926 The publication of Henry W. Fowler's *Dictionary of Modern English Usage.*

1927 (1) Fox's Movietone News, the first sound newsfilm, released in the US. (2) The first film with dialogue, *They're Coming to Get Me*, released in the US.

1928 The publication of Murray's Dictionary as *The Oxford English Dictionary*, 70 years after Trench's proposal to the Philological Society.

1930 (1) C. K. Ogden launches Basic English. (2) The first television programme with synchronized sight and sound broadcast by the BBC.

1931 (1) The British Commonwealth of Nations formed. (2) South Africa becomes a dominion of the British Empire. (3) The Cambridge Proficiency Examination held outside Britain for the first time.

1933 The publication of a supplement to *The Oxford English Dictionary.*

1934 The British Council created as an arm of British cultural diplomacy and a focus for teaching English as a foreign language.

1935 (1) The Philippines become a self-governing Commonwealth in association with the US. (2) The publication of the first ten Penguin paperback titles.

1936 The Republic of Ireland severs all constitutional links with Great Britain.

1937 (1) Burma is separated from British India and granted a constitution and limited self-rule. (2) In Wales, a new constitution for the National Eisteddfod makes Welsh its official language.

1938 Photocopying invented.

1942 The publication in Japan of the *Idiomatic and Syntactic English Dictionary*, prepared before the war by A. S. Hornby, E. V. Gatenby, and H. Wakefield.

1945 Japan is occupied by the Americans on behalf of the Allies.

1946 (1) The Philippines gain their independence from the US. (2) The French colony of Cameroun and the British colony of Cameroon become United Nations trusteeships.

1947 (1) British India is partitioned and India and Pakistan become independent states. (2) New Zealand gains its independence from Britain.

1948 (1) Burma and Ceylon gain their independence from Britain. (2) The dictionary of Hornby *et al.* is brought out by Oxford University Press as *A Learner's Dictionary of Current English.*

1949 (1) Newfoundland becomes a province of Canada. (2) Two New Guinea territories are combined by the United Nations as an Australian mandate: the United Nations Trust Territory of Papua and New Guinea.

1951 The launch of the first two working business computers: the LED in the UK and the UNIVAC in the US.

1952 Puerto Rico becomes a Commonwealth in association with the US.

1957 (1) The Gold Coast becomes independent from Britain as the Republic of Ghana. (2) Robert W. Burchfield is appointed editor of a new Supplement to *The Oxford English Dictionary*.

1957–63 The British colonies of Malaya and Borneo become independent and unite as Malaysia.

1959 Alaska and Hawaii become states of the US.

1960 Nigeria and French Cameroun become independent.

1961 (1) South Africa becomes a republic, leaves the Commonwealth, and adopts Afrikaans and English as its two official languages. (2) The British colony of Cameroon divides, part joining Nigeria, part joining the ex-French colony to become the Republic of Cameroon. (3) Sierra Leone and Cyprus gain their independence from Britain. (4) The publication of *Webster's Third International Dictionary*.

1962 Jamaica, Trinidad and Tobago, and Uganda gain their independence from Britain.

1963 (1) Kenya gains its independence from Britain. (2) The first protests in Wales by the Cymdeithas yr Iaith Gymraeg/Welsh Language Society, aimed at achieving fuller use of Welsh.

1964 (1) Malta, Nyasaland (as Malawi), Tanganyika and Zanzibar (as Tanzania), and Northern Rhodesia (as Zambia) gain their independence from Britain. (2) The publication in Paris of René Etiemble's *Parlez-vous franglais?*

1965 Gambia and Singapore gain their independence from Britain.

1966 Barbados, Basutoland (as Lesotho), Bechuanaland (as Botswana), and British Guiana (as Guyana) gain their independence from Britain.

1967 The Welsh Language Act gives Welsh equal validity with English in Wales, and Wales is no longer deemed to be a part of England.

1968 Mauritius, Swaziland, and Nauru gain their independence from Britain.

1969 Canada becomes officially bilingual, with a commitment to federal services in English and French.

1971 The invention of the microprocessor, a revolutionary development in computing.

1972 (1) East Pakistan secedes and becomes the Republic of Bangladesh. (2) Two feminist magazines launched: *Ms* in the US and *Spare Rib* in the UK.

1973 The Bahamas gain their independence.

1974 Cyngor yr Iaith Gymraeg/Council for the Welsh Language set up to advise the Secretary of State for Wales on matters concerning the language.

1975 (1) Papua New Guinea gains its independence from Australia. (2) The Bas-Lauriol law is passed in France, requiring the use of the French language alone in advertising and commerce.

1977 (1) The spacecraft *Voyager* travels into deep space, carrying a message in English to any extra-terrestrials. (2) In Quebec, Loi 101/Bill 101 is passed, making French the sole official language of the province, limiting access to English-medium schools, and banning public signs in languages other than French.

1978 The government of Northern Territory in Australia is established.

1980 The British government averts a fast to the death by Gwynfor Evans, leader of Plaid Cymru (Welsh National Party), by honouring election pledges to provide a fourth television channel using both Welsh and English.

1981 British Honduras gains its independence as Belize.

1982 The patriation of Canada's constitution. The Canada Act is the last act of the British Parliament concerning Canadian affairs.

1983 The publication of *The New Testament in Scots*, a translation by William L. Lorimer.

1984 The launch of the Apple Macintosh personal (desktop) computer.

1985 (1) The publication by Longman of *A Comprehensive Grammar of the English Language*. (2) The publication by Belknap Press of the first volume of the *Dictionary of American Regional English*. (3) The launch by Cambridge University Press of the quarterly magazine-cum-journal *English Today: The International Review of the English Language*.

1986 Showing by the BBC in the UK and public television in the US of *The Story of English*, a television series with both British and American backers, accompanied by a book, and followed by a radio version on BBC World Service.

1989 The publication of the 2nd edition of *The Oxford English Dictionary*, blending the first edition and its supplements.

Appendix 2 Some Points of English Usage

1 Meanings

The following words are often used wrongly or carelessly, or confused with other similar words.

affect/effect

Both these words are both verbs and nouns, but only **effect** is common as a noun, usually meaning 'a result, consequence, impression, etc.', e.g. *My father's strictness had no effect on my desire to learn.* As verbs they are used differently. **Affect** means 'to produce an effect upon', e.g. *Smoking during pregnancy can affect a baby's development.* **Effect** means 'to bring about', e.g. *Alterations were effected with some sympathy for the existing fabric.*

aggravate

This word is commonly used in informal contexts to mean 'to annoy or exasperate', rather than 'to make worse or more serious'; this is considered incorrect by many people. An example of correct usage is *The psychological stress aggravates the horse's physical stress.*

alibi

The chief meaning of this word is 'evidence that when something took place one was elsewhere', e.g. *He has no alibi for Wednesday afternoon.* It is also sometimes used informally to mean 'an excuse, pretext, or justification'; this is considered incorrect by many people.

all right/alright

Although found widely, **alright** remains non-standard, even where standard spelling is somewhat cumbersome, e.g. *I wanted to make sure it was all all right.*

all together/altogether

These variants are used in different contexts. **All together** means 'all at once' or 'all in one place or in one group', e.g. *They came all together*; *We managed to get three bedrooms all together* (i.e. near each other). **Altogether** means 'in total', e.g. *The hotel has twenty rooms altogether.*

alternate/alternative

These words should not be confused. In British English **alternate** means 'every other', e.g. *There will be a dance on alternate Saturdays*, whereas **alternative** means 'available as another choice', e.g. *an alternative route.* In American usage, however, **alternate** can be used to mean 'available as another choice'.

altogether see all together

amend/emend

Amend, meaning 'to make improvements or corrections in', is often confused with **emend**, a more technical word used in the context of textual correction. Examples of each are: *The policy, in popular and amended form, was offered to the electorate in early 1929*; *The poems have been collected, arranged, and emended.*

anticipate

Anticipate in the sense 'expect, foresee' is well-established in informal use (e.g. *He anticipated a restless night*), but is regarded as incorrect by some people. The formal sense, 'deal with or use before the proper time', is illustrated by the sentence *The specialist would find that the thesis he had been planning had already been anticipated.*

antisocial/unsociable/unsocial

These words are often confused. There is some overlap in meaning but, in general, **antisocial** is used to describe behaviour which harms society, **unsociable** refers to a person who dislikes being in the company of others, and **unsocial** is used in the phrase *unsocial hours* meaning 'hours outside normal working hours'. **Unsociable** can also be used in the phrase *unsociable hours*, but *unsocial hours* is preferable.

anyone/any one

Anyone is written as two words only to emphasize a numerical sense, e.g. *Any one of us can do it.* Otherwise it is written as one word, e.g. *Anyone who wants to can come.*

Arab/Arabian

Arab is now the usual term for a native of Arabia. **Arabian** is generally used as an adjective, especially in geographical contexts (e.g. *Arabian peninsula*).

baluster/banister

These words are sometimes confused. A **baluster** is usually part of a balustrade, whereas a **banister** supports the handrail of a staircase.

beg the question

This phrase is often used to mean (1) to evade a difficulty, or (2) to pose or invite the question (that ...), instead of (3) to assume the truth of an argument or proposition to be proved. (1) and (2) are considered incorrect by many people.

born/borne

Born is used with reference to birth (e.g. *was born in Dublin*), except for *borne by* followed by the name of the mother (e.g. *was borne by Mary*). **Borne** is used in other senses (e.g. *a litter borne by four slaves*).

censor/censure

Both these words are both verbs and nouns, but **censor** is used to mean 'to cut unacceptable parts out of a book, film, etc.' or 'a person who does this', while **censure** means 'to criticize harshly' or 'harsh criticism'.

chronic

This word is sometimes used to mean 'very bad', e.g. *the film was chronic*, or 'habitual, inveterate', e.g. *a chronic liar.* The former use is extremely informal whereas the latter is considered to be incorrect by some people. The correct meaning of this word is 'persisting for a long time' and it is used chiefly of illnesses or other problems e.g. *Over one million people in the UK have chronic bronchitis.*

complacent/complaisant

Complacent means 'smugly self-satisfied', e.g. *The British are still largely complacent about their eating habits*, while **complaisant**, a much rarer word, means 'deferential, willing to please', e.g. in *When unharnessed, the dogs are very peaceful and complaisant.*

compose/comprise

Both these words can be used to mean 'to constitute or make up' but **compose** is preferred in this sense, e.g. *Citizens act as witnesses in the courts and finally may compose the jury.* **Comprise** is correctly used to mean 'to be composed of, consist of', e.g. *Each crew comprises a commander, a gunner, and a driver.*

condole/console

Condole is sometimes confused with **console** but is much rarer. It is usually used with *with* and means 'to express sympathy with', e.g. *Her friends came to condole with her.* **Console** means 'to comfort in grief or disappointment', e.g. *They consoled themselves with the thought that they wouldn't have enjoyed the concert anyway.*

continual/continuous

Continual is used of something that happens very frequently, e.g. *There were continual interruptions*, whereas **continuous** is used of something that happens without pause, e.g. *There was a dull, continuous background noise.*

credible/credulous

The adjective **credible** means 'believable' or 'convincing' and can be applied to a situation, statement, policy, or threat to a person. **Credulous** means 'too ready to believe, gullible' and is usually used to describe a person.

crucial

Crucial is used in formal contexts to mean 'decisive, critical', e.g. *The first five years of a child's life are crucial.* Its use to mean 'very important', as in *It is crucial not to forget your passport*, should be restricted to informal contexts.

decimate

The usual sense of this word is now 'destroy a large proportion of'. This use is considered inappropriate by some people because the original and literal sense is 'to kill or remove one in ten of'. In any case, this word should not be used to mean 'to defeat utterly'.

definite/definitive

Definitive in the sense '(of an answer, verdict, etc.) decisive, unconditional, final' is sometimes confused with **definite**. However, **definite** does not have the connotations of authority: *a definite no* is simply a firm refusal, whereas *a definitive no* is an authoritative judgement or decision that something is not the case.

deprecate/depreciate

Deprecate means 'to express disapproval of, to deplore', e.g. *The establishment magazines began by deprecating the film's free and easy attitudes to drugs and sex*, while **depreciate** (apart from its financial senses) means 'to disparage or belittle', e.g. *Writing to her sister soon after the auction, Virginia was already depreciating her own aesthetic taste.*

dilemma

This word should be used with regard to situations in which a difficult choice has to be made between undesirable alternatives, as in *You see his dilemma? Whatever he did next, his wife would find out, divorce him, and get custody of the child.* Its use to mean simply 'a difficult situation' is considered incorrect by some people.

disinterested/uninterested

Disinterested is sometimes used in informal contexts to mean 'not interested or uninterested', but this is widely regarded as incorrect. The proper meaning is 'impartial', e.g. *I for one am making a disinterested search for information.* The use of the noun **disinterest** to mean 'a lack of interest' is also objected to, but it is rarely used in any other sense and the alternative **uninterest** is rare.

effect see affect

emend see amend

emotional/emotive

Although the senses of these two words overlap, **emotive** is more common in the sense 'arousing emotion', e.g. *Drug use is an emotive issue*, and is not used at all to describe a person as being liable to excessive emotion.

enormity

This word is commonly used to mean 'great size', e.g. *wilting under the enormity of the work*, but this is regarded as incorrect by some people. The original and preferred meaning is 'extreme wickedness', as in *the enormity of the crime.*

exceptionable/exceptional

Exceptionable means 'open to objection', e.g. *There was nothing exceptionable in her behaviour*, and is usually found in negative contexts. It is sometimes confused with the much commoner word **exceptional** meaning 'unusual, outstanding'.

feasible

The correct meaning of this word is 'practicable' or 'possible', e.g. *Walking all night was not feasible without the aid of moon or torch.* It should not be used to mean 'likely' or 'probable'.

flammable see inflammable

flaunt/flout

These words are often confused because both suggest an element of arrogance or showing off. However, **flaunt** means 'to display ostentatiously', e.g. *He liked to flaunt his wealth*, while **flout** means 'to express contempt for or disobey (laws, convention, etc.)', e.g. *The fine is too low for those who flout the law continuously.*

-fuls/-s full

The combining form -**ful** is used to form nouns meaning 'the amount needed to fill', e.g. *cupful, spoonful*. The plural form of such words is -s, (*cupfuls, spoonfuls*, etc.). *Three cups full* would denote the individual cups rather than a quantity regarded in terms of a cup used as a measure, and would be used in contexts such as *They brought us three cups full of water.*

fulsome

This word means 'excessive, cloying, or insincere', but is sometimes misunderstood as meaning 'generous' in the phrase *fulsome praise.*

hoi polloi

This phrase is usually preceded by *the*, e.g. *The hoi polloi grew weary and sat on the floor.* Strictly speaking, the *the* is unnecessary because *hoi* means 'the' (in Greek).

hopefully

Strictly speaking, this word should be used only to mean 'in a hopeful manner', e.g. *Robert peered hopefully into the fridge.* However, it is also very commonly used to mean 'it is to be hoped', e.g. *Hopefully, all the details will be in this evening's newspapers.* This usage is considered incorrect by some people.

impedance/impediment

Impedance is a specialized electrical term, while **impediment** is an everyday term meaning 'a hindrance or obstruction', e.g. *He would have to write by hand but that was no impediment.*

imply see infer

inchoate

This word means 'just begun' or 'rudimentary, undeveloped' e.g. *All was as yet in an inchoate state*, but it is often used incorrectly to mean 'chaotic' or 'incoherent'.

infer/imply

Infer should be used to mean 'to deduce or conclude', as in *We can infer from these studies that....* Its use to mean 'to imply or suggest' is widely considered incorrect.

inflammable/flammable/non-flammable

Both **inflammable** and **flammable** mean 'easily set on fire or excited'. The opposite is **non-flammable**. Where there is a danger of **inflammable** being understood to mean the opposite, i.e. 'not easily set on fire', **flammable** can be used to avoid confusion.

ingenious/ingenuous

These words are sometimes confused. **Ingenious** means 'clever, skilful, or resourceful', e.g. *an ingenious device*, while **ingenuous** means 'artless' or 'frank', e.g. *She is both ingenuous and sophisticated by turns.*

intense/intensive

Intense is sometimes wrongly used instead of **intensive** to describe a course of study which consists in covering a large amount of material in a short space of time.

interface

The use of **interface** to mean 'a place or means of interaction', e.g. *Experts looked at the crucial interface between broadcasters and independents*, or as a verb meaning 'to interact', e.g. *courses where business executives interface with nature at great expense*, is deplored by some people.

interment/internment

Interment means 'the burial of a corpse', while **internment** means 'the confining of a prisoner etc.'.

latter

This word means 'the second-mentioned of two'. Its use to mean 'the last-mentioned of three or more' is common, but considered incorrect by some people since *latter* means 'later' rather than 'latest'. **Last** or **last-mentioned** is to be preferred where three or more things are involved.

laudable/laudatory

These words are sometimes confused. **Laudable** is the more common and means 'commendable' or 'praiseworthy', e.g. *The Orthodox Palestinian Society pursued a laudable charitable programme which involved the foundation and maintenance of schools and hospitals.* **Laudatory** means 'expressing praise', e.g. *The new manifesto enjoyed a good reception—including a laudatory front-page endorsement from London's only daily newspaper.*

lay/lie

In standard English **lay** is a transitive verb and **lie** intransitive. The intransitive use of **lay**, as in *It gave him the opportunity of laying on the grass at lunchtime*, is incorrect. Similarly, the transitive use of **lie**, as in *Lie it on the table* is also incorrect. In the first example *laying* should be *lying* and in the second *lie* should be *lay*. The noun meaning 'a prolonged stay in bed in the morning' is **lie-in**; **lay-in** is incorrect.

leading question

This phrase means 'a question that prompts the answer wanted' and was originally a legal term. In weakened use it tends to mean 'an awkward, pointed, or loaded question', or even 'principal question', but these usages are considered incorrect by some people.

liable

This word is commonly used with *to* to mean 'likely to do something undesirable', e.g. *Without his glasses he's liable to smash into a tree.* This usage is considered incorrect by some people. Correct usage is exemplified by the sentence *You could be liable for a heavy fine if you are caught out.*

lie see lay

like

The use of **like** as a conjunction meaning 'as' or 'as if', e.g. *I don't have a posh set of in-laws like you do; They sit up like they're begging for food*, is considered incorrect by some people.

locate

In standard English it is not acceptable to use **locate** to mean merely 'find', e.g. *It drives him out of his mind when he can't locate something.* **Locate** should be used more precisely to mean 'discover the exact place or position of', e.g. *One club member was proposing to use an echo sounder to help locate fish in the lake.*

luxuriant/luxurious

These words are sometimes confused. **Luxuriant** means 'lush, profuse, or prolific', e.g. *forests of dark luxuriant foliage; luxuriant black eyelashes.* **Luxurious**, a much commoner word, means 'supplied with luxuries, extremely comfortable', e.g. *a luxurious hotel.*

masterful/masterly

These words overlap in meaning and are sometimes confused. Apart from meaning 'domineering', **masterful** also means 'masterly' or 'very skilful'. However, **masterful** is generally used in this sense to describe a person, e.g. *He's just got a marginal talent he's masterful at exploiting*, while **masterly** usually describes an achievement or action, e.g. *This was a masterly realization of the score.*

militate/mitigate

These words are often confused but have quite different meanings. **Militate** means 'to have force or effect' and is usually used with *against*, e.g. *The rules militated against the weak, the infirm, or even the well-mannered.* **Mitigate**, on the other hand, means 'to make milder or less severe', e.g. *His disappointment was mitigated by the generous offer of a free holiday.*

mutual

This word is sometimes used with no sense of reciprocity, simply to mean 'common to two or more people', as in *a mutual friend; a mutual interest.* Such use is considered incorrect by some people, for whom **common** is preferable.

non-flammable see inflammable

off/off of

The use of **off of** to mean **off**, e.g. *He took the cup off of the table*, is non-standard and to be avoided.

perquisite/prerequisite

These words are sometimes confused. **Perquisite** usually means 'an extra benefit or privilege', e.g. *There were no perquisites attached to their offices, apart from one or two special privileges.* **Prerequisite** means 'something required as a precondition', e.g. *A general education in the sciences is a prerequisite of professional medical training.*

plus

The use of **plus** as a conjunction meaning 'and furthermore', e.g. *plus we will be pleased to give you personal financial advice*, is considered incorrect by many people.

prerequisite see perquisite

prescribe/proscribe

These words are sometimes confused, but they are opposite in meaning. **Prescribe** means 'to advise the use of' or 'impose authoritatively', whereas **proscribe** means 'to reject, denounce, or ban'. Examples of each are as follows:

The teachers would prescribe topics to be dealt with.

She proscribed all religious, philosophical, or psychological books for village libraries.

A regime which both prescribes and proscribes literature.

prevaricate/procrastinate

Prevaricate means 'to act or speak evasively', e.g. *When I was asked what subject I was reading, I knew I would have to prevaricate or face problems.* It is sometimes confused with **procrastinate** which means 'to postpone or put off an action', e.g. *He hesitates and procrastinates until the time for action is over.*

proscribe see prescribe

protagonist

The correct meaning of this word is 'chief or leading person', e.g. *The choreographer must create movements which display each protagonist's particular behaviour and reactions.* However, it is also used, usually with *of* or *for*, to mean 'an advocate or champion of a cause etc.', e.g. *... the flawed economics of the nuclear protagonists' case.*

proved/proven

The usual past participle of *prove* is **proved**. **Proven** is uncommon except in certain expressions such as *of proven ability, proven reliability*, and *proven success*. It is, however, standard in Scots and American English.

refute/repudiate

Strictly speaking, **refute** means 'to prove (a person or statement) to be wrong', e.g. *No amount of empirical research can either confirm or refute it.* However, it is also sometimes used to mean 'to deny or repudiate'. This usage is considered incorrect by some people.

scenario

The proper meaning of this word is 'an outline of a plot' or 'a postulated sequence of events'. It should not be used in standard English to mean 'situation', e.g. *a nightmare scenario.*

Scotch/Scots/Scottish

In Scotland the terms **Scots** and **Scottish** are preferred to **Scotch** and they mean the same (e.g. *a Scots/Scottish accent, miner, farmer*, etc.). **Scotch** is used in various compound nouns such as *Scotch broth, egg, fir, mist, terrier*, and *whisky*. Similarly, **Scotsman** and **Scotswoman** are preferred to **Scotchman** and **Scotchwoman**.

seasonable/seasonal

Seasonable means 'usual or suitable for the season' or 'opportune', e.g. *Although seasonable, the weather was not suitable for picnics.* **Seasonal** means 'of, depending on, or varying with the season', e.g. *Seasonal changes posed problems for mills situated on larger rivers.*

sensual/sensuous

These two words are of similar meaning and are often, therefore, confused. Both mean 'of the senses', but **sensual** means 'of the senses as opposed to the intellect or spirit' and has sexual overtones while **sensuous** is used with regard to the senses aesthetically rather than physically. Examples illustrate this difference:

The smoke-filled room was invaded by sexy, sensual snarls of guitars and harmonicas.

The shadowy interior is a sensuous baroque mix of gilt and candle wax.

thankfully

The most common use of this word is in the sense 'fortunately, let us be thankful', e.g. *Thankfully, the damage was minimal.* This usage is still considered incorrect by some people (cf. **hopefully**). The strict sense of this word is 'in a thankful or grateful manner', e.g. *He heaped a plate for him and Cameron took it thankfully.*

'til/till see until

tortuous/torturous

These words sound similar but have different meanings. **Tortuous** means 'full of twists and turns' or 'devious, circuitous', e.g. *Both paths have proved tortuous and are strewn with awkward boulders* or *He got into a tortuous discussion about the cubic capacity of the engine of the car.*

Torturous is the adjective which relates to *torture* and means 'involving torture, excruciating', e.g. *The experience had become pure music, each note torturous yet unbearably sweet.*

triumphal/triumphant

These words are sometimes confused. The more common, **triumphant**, means 'victorious' or 'exultant', e.g. *She had chaired a difficult meeting through to its triumphant conclusion*, or *Rosie returned triumphant with the file and the man went away.*

Triumphal means 'used in or celebrating a triumph', e.g. *The last element to be added was the magnificent triumphal arch*, or *Any prospect of retaking the Falklands as an uninterrupted triumphal procession was illusory.*

turbid/turgid

Turbid is used of a liquid or colour to mean 'muddy, not clear', or of literary style etc. to mean 'confused', e.g. *the turbid utterances and twisted language of Carlyle.*

Turgid means 'swollen, inflated, or enlarged' but is also often used to describe literary style which is pompous or bombastic, e.g. *Communications arriving at the orderly room were largely turgid documents in 'Whitehallese' from the War Office.*

unexceptionable see exceptionable

unsociable/unsocial see antisocial

until/till/'til

Until is more formal than 'till', and is more usual at the beginning of a sentence, e.g. *Until 1921 some elements among the peasantry had kept a certain independence of outlook.*

Til is considered incorrect in standard English and should be avoided.

venal/venial

These words are sometimes confused. **Venal** means 'corrupt, able to be bribed, or involving bribery', e.g. *The lawcourts are venal and can take decades to decide a case.*

Venial is used among Christians to describe a certain type of sin and means 'pardonable, excusable, not mortal', e.g. *The Reformation had renounced purgatory as an intermediate stage, in which those who had committed venial sins might work their passage to a better world.*

worth while/worthwhile

Worth while (two words) is used only predicatively, e.g. *Nobody had thought it worth while to ring the police*, and means 'worth the time or effort spent'.

Worthwhile (one word) also has this meaning but can be used both predicatively and attributively, e.g. *Only in unusual circumstances would investment be worthwhile* (predicative), or *He was a worthwhile subject for the 'cure'* (attributive). In addition, **worthwhile** has the sense 'of value or importance', e.g. *It's great to be doing such a worthwhile job.*

2 Plurals

The most common mistake with regard to the following words is the use of the plural form as if it were the singular.

bacterium (plural bacteria)

Bacteria is often used incorrectly instead of **bacterium** for the singular form. Correct usage is as follows:

A close relative of E. coli is salmonella, a bacterium whose primary habitat is the intestines of birds (singular); *New close-up filming techniques reveal lice, mites, and bacteria stalking the landscape of the human body* (plural).

criterion (plural criteria)

Many people use **criteria** as if it were the singular form. Examples of correct usage are:

Many borrowers choose an appealing discount deal as the sole criterion when they take out a loan (singular); *Aesthetic criteria are also clearly important* (plural).

datum (plural data)

In general, the singular form is **datum**, not **data**, as shown by the following examples:

The object under scrutiny is compared with an observed or preconceived datum (singular); *The data support a trend that has so far been supported only by anecdotal evidence* (plural).

In the context of computers, **data** is now often used as if it were a singular collective noun (like 'information'), e.g. *You can guarantee that the data is accurate and charges reach you faster than they normally would on the paper system.* This use is acceptable.

In other contexts, **data** should be used (like 'facts') with a plural verb, e.g. *These data do lend some support to the prevailing public opinion.*

die/dice

The form **dice** is now standard for both the singular and plural in the sense 'a cube used in games', e.g. *There was a furry dice hanging from the mirror; The dice are loaded against the Gorbachev reforms.*

Die (plural **dies**) means 'a device for stamping, cutting or moulding', e.g. *The dies used to make Roman bronze medallions might last for ten years.*

Die (plural **dice**) is an architectural term meaning 'the cubical part of a pedestal between the base and the cornice'.

-fuls/-s full

See Section 1 (**Meanings**)

graffito (plural graffiti)

Strictly speaking, **graffiti** should be used only with a plural construction, e.g. *The graffiti were aggressive and insulting.* The singular and collective use is considered incorrect by many people, but is often found, e.g. *The most common graffiti is 'Vive le Roi'.* **Graffito** is the correct singular form, e.g. *The meanest graffito, if fully understood, can be a treasure of human expressiveness.*

medium (plural media)

A very common mistake is the use of **media** as a collective noun with a singular verb, especially in the sense 'a means of communication'. Correct usage is as follows: *Loads of my friends are miserable over the way they look, and the media are basically* *saying, 'Yes you're right to be miserable'.* INCORRECT usage is shown by the example *I have always found councillors very approachable—very different from the image the media gives them.* In the second example, *gives* should be *give*.

An example of the correct use of the singular is as follows:

Television is the most important medium for getting known by the general public.

phenomenon (plural phenomena)

Phenomena is often used wrongly, as if it were the singular form rather than the plural. The following examples illustrate correct usage:

This phenomenon can best be observed in Santander, that most elegant of ferry ports.

Men began to regard these phenomena with more composure.

stratum (plural strata)

Strata is often used wrongly, as if it were the singular form rather than the plural. Examples of correct usage are as follows:

Very occasionally a coin can be dated from the other objects in the same stratum.

Below all these strata lay the immemorial peasant base of straight barter.

See the paragraphs headed **f to v** and **plural formation** in Section 4 (**Word Formation**).

3 Grammar

as

In the following sentences, formal usage requires the *subjective* case (*I, he, she, we, they*) because the pronoun would be the subject if a verb were supplied:

You are just as intelligent as he (in full, *as he is*)

He . . . might not have heard the motif so often as I (in full, *as I had*)

Informal usage permits *You are just as intelligent as* him.

Formal English uses the *objective* case (*me, him, her, us, them*) only when the pronoun would be the object if a verb were supplied:

I thought you preferred John to Mary, but I see that you like her just as much as him (which means . . . *just as much as you like him*).

collective nouns

Collective nouns are singular words that denote many individuals, e.g. *audience, government, orchestra, the clergy, the public.*

It is normal for collective nouns, being singular, to be followed by singular verbs and pronouns (*is, has, consists,* and *it* in the examples below):

The Government is *determined to beat inflation, as* it has *promised*

Their family is *huge:* it consists *of five boys and three girls*

The bourgeoisie is *despised for not being proletarian*

The singular verb and pronouns are preferable unless the collective is clearly and unmistakably used to refer to separate individuals rather than to a united body, e.g.

The Cabinet has made its *decision,* but

The Cabinet are *resuming* their *places around the table at Number 10 Downing Street*

The singular should always be used if the collective noun is qualified by a singular word like *this, that, every,* etc.:

This family is *divided*

Every team has its *chance to win*

- Do not mix singular and plural, as (wrongly) in

The congregation were *now dispersing.* It *tended to form knots and groups*

comparison of adjectives and adverbs

Whether to use *-er, -est* or *more, most.*

The two ways of forming the comparative and superlative of adjectives and adverbs are:

(*a*) The addition of the comparative and superlative suffixes *-er* and *-est.* Monosyllabic adjectives and adverbs almost always require these suffixes, e.g. *big* (*bigger, biggest*), *soon* (*sooner, soonest*), and so normally do many adjectives of two syllables, e.g. *narrow* (*narrower, narrowest*), *silly* (*sillier, silliest*).

(*b*) The placing of the comparative and superlative adverbs *more* and *most* before the adjective or adverb. These are used with adjectives of three syllables or more (e.g. *difficult, memorable*), participles (e.g. *bored, boring*), many adjectives of two syllables (e.g. *afraid, awful, childish, harmless, static*), and adverbs ending in *-ly* (e.g. *highly, slowly*).

Adjectives with two syllables vary between the use of the suffixes and of the adverbs.

There are many which never take the suffixes, e.g.

antique	*breathless*	*futile*
bizarre	*constant*	*steadfast*

There is also a large class which is acceptable with either, e.g.

clever	*handsome*	*polite*
common	*honest*	*solemn*
cruel	*pleasant*	*tranquil*
extreme		

The choice is largely a matter of style.

group possessive

The group possessive is the construction by which the ending *-'s* of the possessive case can be added to the last word of a noun phrase, which is regarded as a single unit, e.g.

The king of Spain's daughter

John and Mary's baby

Somebody else's umbrella

A quarter of an hour's drive

Expressions like these are natural and acceptable.

Informal language, however, permits the extension of the construction to long and complicated phrases:

The people in the house opposite's geraniums

The man who called last week's umbrella is still in the hall

In these, the connection between the words forming the group possessive is much looser and more complicated than in the earlier examples. The effect is often somewhat ludicrous.

- Expressions of this sort should not be used in serious prose. Substitute:

The geraniums of the people in the house opposite

The umbrella of the man who called last week is still in the hall

-ics, nouns in

Nouns ending in *-ics* denoting subjects or disciplines are sometimes treated as singular and sometimes as plural. Examples are:

apologetics	*genetics*	*optics*
classics (as a study)	*linguistics*	*phonetics*
	mathematics	*physics*
dynamics	*mechanics*	*politics*
economics	*metaphysics*	*statistics*
electronics	*obstetrics*	*tactics*
ethics		

When used strictly as the name of a discipline they are treated as singular:

Psychometrics is *unable to investigate the nature of intelligence*

So also when the complement is singular:

Mathematics is *his strong point*

When used more loosely, to denote a manifestation of qualities, often accompanied by a possessive, they are treated as plural:

His politics were *a mixture of fear, greed, and envy*

I don't understand the mathematics of it, which are *complicated*

The acoustics in this hall are *dreadful*

So also when they denote a set of activities or pattern of behaviour, as commonly with words like:

acrobatics	*dramatics*	*heroics*
athletics	*gymnastics*	*hysterics*

E.g. *The mental gymnastics required to believe this* are *beyond me.*

I or *me*, *we* or *us*, etc.

There is often confusion about which case of a personal pronoun to use when the pronoun stands alone or follows the verb *to be.*

1. When the personal pronoun stands alone, as when it forms the answer to a question, formal usage requires it to have the case it would have if the verb were supplied:

Who killed Cock Robin?—I (in full, *I killed him*)

Which of you did he approach?—Me (in full, *he approached me*)

Informal usage permits the objective case in both kinds of sentence, but this is not acceptable in formal style. It so happens that the subjective case often sounds stilted. It is then best to avoid the problem by providing the substitute verb *do*, or, if the preceding sentence contains an auxiliary, by repeating the auxiliary, e.g.

Who likes cooking?—I do

Who can cook?—I can

2. When a personal pronoun follows *it is, it was, it may be, it could have been*, etc., it should always have the subjective case:

Nobody could suspect that it was she

We are given no clues as to what it must have felt like to be he

Informal usage favours the objective case:

I thought it might have been him *at the door*

Don't tell me it's them *again!*

• This is not acceptable in formal usage.

When *who* or *whom* follows, the subjective case is obligatory in formal usage and quite usual informally:

It was I *who painted the back door purple*

The informal use of the objective case often sounds substandard:

It was her *who would get into trouble*

(For agreement between the personal pronoun antecedent and the verb in *It is I who* etc., see ***I who, you who,*** etc.)

In constructions which have the form *I am* + noun or noun phrase + *who*, the verb following *who* agrees with the noun (the antecedent of *who*) and is therefore always in the third person (singular or plural)

I am the sort of person who likes *peace and quiet*

You are the fourth of my colleagues who's *told me that* ('s = has, agreeing with *the fourth*)

I should or *I would*

There is often uncertainty whether to use *should* or *would* in the first person singular and plural before verbs such as *like* or *think* and before the adverbs *rather* and *sooner.*

1. *Should* is correct before verbs of liking, e.g. *be glad, be inclined, care, like*, and *prefer.*

Would you like a beer?—I should prefer *a cup of coffee, if you don't mind*

2. *Should* is correct in tentative statements of opinion, with verbs such as *guess, imagine, say*, and *think.*

I should imagine *that you are right*

I shouldn't have thought *it was difficult*

3. *Would* is correct before the adverbs *rather* and *sooner*, e.g.

I would *truly* rather *be in the middle of this than sitting in that church in a tight collar*

Would is always correct with persons other than the first person singular and plural.

I who, you who, etc.

The verb following a personal pronoun (*I, you, he*, etc.) + *who* should agree with the pronoun and should not be in the third person singular unless the third person singular pronoun precedes *who:*

I, who have *no savings to speak of, had to pay for the work*

This remains so even if the personal pronoun is in the objective case:

They made me, who have *no savings at all, pay for the work* (not *who has*)

When *it is* (*it was*, etc.) precedes *I who*, etc., the same rule applies: the verb agrees with the personal pronoun:

It's I who have *done it*

It could have been we who were *mistaken*

Informal usage sometimes permits the third person to be used (especially when the verb *to be* follows *who*):

You who's *supposed to be so practical!*

Is it me who's *supposed to be keeping an eye on you?*

• This is not acceptable in formal usage.

may or *might*

There is sometimes confusion about whether to use *may* or *might* with the perfect infinitive referring to a past event, e.g. *He may have done* or *He might have done.*

1. If uncertainty about the action or state denoted by the perfect infinitive remains, i.e. at the time of speaking or writing the truth of the event is still unknown, then either *may* or *might* is acceptable:

As they all wore so many different clothes of identically the same kind . . . there may *have been several more or several less*

For all we knew we were both bastards, although of course there might *have been a ceremony*

2. If there is no longer uncertainty about the event, or the matter was never put to the test, and therefore the event did not in fact occur, use *might:*

If that had come ten days ago my whole life might *have been different*

You should not have let him come home alone; he might *have got lost*

• It is a common error to use *may* instead of *might* in these circumstances:

If he (President Galtieri) *had not invaded, then eventually the islands* may *have fallen into their lap*

I am grateful for his intervention without which they may *have remained in the refugee camp indefinitely*

Schoenberg may *never have gone atonal but for the break-up of his marriage*

(These are all from recent newspaper articles. *Might* should be substituted for *may* in each.)

none (pronoun)

The pronoun *none* can be followed either by singular verb and singular pronouns, or by plural ones. Either is acceptable, although the plural tends to be more common.

Singular: *None of them* was *allowed to forget for a moment*
Plural: *None of the fountains ever* play
None of the authors expected their *books to become best sellers*

ought

Oughtn't or *didn't ought?*

The standard form of the negative of *ought* is *ought not* or *oughtn't:*

A look from Claudia showed me I ought not *to have begun it*

Being an auxiliary verb, *ought* can precede *not* and does not require the verb *do*. It is non-standard to form the negative with *do* (*didn't ought*):

I hope that none here will say I did anything I didn't ought. *For I only done my duty*

When the negative is used to reinforce a question in a short extra clause or 'question tag', the negative should be formed according to the rule above:

You ought to be pleased, oughtn't you? (not *didn't you?*)

In the same way *do* should not be used as a substitute verb for *ought*, e.g.

Ought he to go?—Yes, he ought (not *he did*)

You ought not to be pleased, ought *you?* (not *did you?*)

shall and *will*

'The horror of that moment,' the King went on, 'I shall never, never forget!' 'You will, though,' the Queen said, 'if you don't make a memorandum of it.'

There is considerable confusion about when to use *shall* and *will*. Put simply, the traditional rule in standard British English is:

1. In the first person, singular and plural.

(*a*) *I shall, we shall* express the simple future, e.g.

I am not a manual worker and please God I never shall *be one*

In the following pages we shall *see good words ... losing their edge*

(*b*) *I will, we will* express intention or determination on the part of the speaker (especially a promise made by him or her), e.g.

I will *take you to see her tomorrow morning*

I will *no longer accept responsibility for the fruitless loss of life*

'I don't think we will *ask Mr. Fraser's opinion,' she said coldly*

2. For the second and third persons, singular and plural, the rule is exactly the converse.

(*a*) *You, he, she, it,* or *they will* express the simple future, e.g.

Will *it disturb you if I keep the lamp on for a bit?*

Serapina will *last much longer than a car. She'll probably last longer than you* will

(*b*) *You, he, she, it,* or *they shall* express intention or determination on the part of the speaker or someone other than the actual subject of the verb, especially a promise made by the speaker to or about the subject, e.g.

Today you shall *be with me in Paradise*

One day you shall *know my full story*

Shall *the common man be pushed back into the mud, or* shall *he not?*

The two uses of *will*, and one of those of *shall*, are well illustrated by:

'I will *follow you to the ends of the earth,' replied Susan, passionately. 'It* will *not be necessary,' said George. 'I am only going down to the coal-cellar. I* shall *spend the next half-hour or so there.'*

In informal usage *I will* and *we will* are quite often used for the simple future, e.g.

I will *be a different person when I live in England*

More often the distinction is covered up by the contracted form *'ll*, e.g.

I don't quite know when I'll *get the time to write again*

• The use of *will* for *shall* in the first person is not regarded as fully acceptable in formal usage.

singular or plural

1. When subject and complement are different in number (i.e. one is singular, the other plural), the verb normally agrees with the subject, e.g.

(Plural subject)

Their wages were *a mere pittance*

Liqueur chocolates are *our speciality*

The Biblical *The wages of sin is death* reflects an obsolete idiom by which *wages* took a singular verb.

(Singular subject)

What we need is *customers*

Our speciality is *liqueur chocolates*

2. A plural word or phrase used as a name, title, or quotation counts as singular, e.g.

Sons and Lovers has *always been one of Lawrence's most popular novels*

3. A singular phrase that happens to end with a plural word should nevertheless be followed by a singular verb, e.g.

Everyone except the French wants (not *want*) *Britain to join*

One in six has (not *have*) *this problem*

See also **ics, -s plural or singular**

-s plural or singular

Some nouns, though they have the plural ending *-s*, are nevertheless usually treated as singulars, taking singular verbs and pronouns referring back to them.

1. *News*

2. Diseases:

measles *mumps* *rickets* *shingles*

Measles and *rickets* can also be treated as ordinary plural nouns.

3. Games:

billiards	*dominoes*	*ninepins*
bowls	*draughts*	*skittles*
darts	*fives*	

4. Countries:

the Bahamas	*the Philippines*
the Netherlands	*the United States*

These are treated as singular when considered as a unit, which they commonly are in a political context, or when the complement is singular, e.g.

The Philippines is *a predominantly agricultural country*

The United States has *withdrawn its ambassador*

The Bahamas and *the Philippines* are also the geographical names of the groups of islands which the two nations comprise, and in this use can be treated as plurals, e.g.

The Bahamas were *settled by British subjects*

See also *-ics*.

used to

The negative and interrogative of *used to* can be formed in two ways:

(i) Negative: *used not to*
Interrogative: *used X to?*

This formation follows the pattern of the other auxiliary verbs.

Examples:

Used you to beat your mother?

You used not to have a moustache, used you?

(ii) Negative: *did not use to, didn't use to*
Interrogative: *did X use to?*

This formation is the same as that used with regular verbs.

Examples:

She didn't use to find sex revolting
Did you use to be a flirt?

□ Either form is acceptable. On the whole *used you to, used he to,* etc. tend to sound rather stilted.

• The correct spellings of the negative forms are:

usedn't to and *didn't use to*

not:

usen't to and *didn't used to*

we (with phrase following)

Expressions consisting of *we* or *us* followed by a qualifying word or phrase, e.g. *we English, us English*, are often misused with the wrong case of the first person plural pronoun. In fact the rules are exactly the same as for *we* or *us* standing alone.

If the expression is the subject, *we* should be used:

(Correct) *Not always laughing as heartily as* we English *are supposed to do*

(Incorrect) *We all make mistakes, even* us anarchists (substitute *we anarchists*)

If the expression is the object or the complement of a preposition, *us* should be used:

(Correct) *To* us English, *Europe is not a very vivid conception*

(Incorrect) *The Manchester Guardian has said some nice things about* we in the North-East

you and I or *you and me*

When a personal pronoun is linked by *and* or *or* to a noun or another pronoun there is often confusion about which case to put the pronoun in. In fact the rule is exactly as it would be for the pronoun standing alone.

1. If the two words linked by *and* or *or* constitute the subject, the pronoun should be in the subjective case, e.g.

Only she *and her mother cared for the old house*

That's what we would do, that is, John and I

Who could go?—Either you or he

The use of the objective case is quite common in informal speech, but it is non-standard, e.g. (examples from the speech of characters in novels)

Perhaps only her *and Mrs Natwick had stuck to the christened name*

That's how we look at it, me *and Martha*

Either Mary had to leave or me

2. If the two words linked by *and* or *or* constitute the object of the verb, or the complement of a preposition, the objective case must be used:

The afternoon would suit her *and John better*

It was time for Sebastian and me *to go down to the drawing-room*

The use of the subjective case is very common informally. It probably arises from an exaggerated fear of the error indicated under 1 above.

- It remains, however, non-standard, e.g.

It was this that set Charles and I *talking of old times*

Why is it that people like you and I *are so unpopular?*

Between you and I

This last expression is very commonly heard. *Between you and me* should always be substituted.

4 Word Formation

-able and *-ible*

Words ending in *-able* generally owe their form to the Latin termination *-abilis* or the Old French *-able* (or both), and words in *-ible* to the Latin *-ibilis*. The suffix *-able* is also added to words of distinctly French or English origin, and as a living element to English roots.

A. Words ending in *-able*. The following alterations are made to the stem:

1. Silent *-e* is dropped, e.g. *adorable, imaginable*.

Exceptions: words whose stem ends in *-ce, -ee, -ge, -le*, and the following:

blameable	*dyeable*
giveable (but *forgivable*)	*ropeable*
hireable	*saleable*
holeable	*shareable*
likeable	*sizeable*
liveable	*tameable*
nameable	*tuneable*
rateable	*unshakeable*

- American spelling tends to omit *-e-* in the words above.

2. Final *-y* becomes *-i-* (see **y to i B**).

Exception: *flyable*.

3. A final consonant may be doubled, e.g. *clubbable*.

Exceptions:

inferable	*referable*
preferable (but *conferrable*)	*transferable*

4. Most verbs of more than two syllables ending in *-ate* drop this ending when forming adjectives in *-able*, e.g. *alienable, calculable, demonstrable*, etc. Verbs of two syllables ending in *-ate* form adjectives in *-able* regularly, e.g. *creatable, debatable, dictatable*, etc.

B. Words ending in *-ible*. These are fewer, since *-ible* is not a living suffix. Below is a list of the commonest. Almost all form their negative in *in-, il-*, etc., so that the negative form can be inferred from the positive in the list below; the exceptions are indicated by (*un*).

accessible	*edible*	*perfectible*
adducible	*eligible*	*permissible*
admissible	*exhaustible*	*persuasible*
audible	*expressible*	*plausible*
avertible	*extensible*	*possible*
collapsible	*fallible*	*reducible*
combustible	(*un*)*feasible*	*repressible*
compatible	*flexible*	*reproducible*
comprehensible	*forcible*	*resistible*
contemptible	*fusible*	*responsible*
corrigible	*gullible*	*reversible*
corruptible	*indelible*	*risible*
credible	(*un*)*intelligible*	*sensible*
defensible	*irascible*	(*un*)*susceptible*
destructible	*legible*	*tangible*
digestible	*negligible*	*vendible*
dirigible	*ostensible*	*vincible*
discernible	*perceptible*	*visible*
divisible		

-ant or *-ent*

-ant is the noun ending, *-ent* the adjective ending in the following:

dependant	*dependent*
descendant	*descendent*
pendant	*pendent*
propellant	*propellent*

independent is both adjective and noun; *dependence, independence* are the abstract nouns.

The following are correct spellings:

ascendant, -nce, -ncy	*relevant, -nce*
attendant, -nce	*repellent*
expellent	*superintendent, -ncy*
impellent	*tendency*
intendent, -ncy	*transcendent, -nce*

-ative or *-ive*

Correct are:

(*a*) *authoritative*	*qualitative*
interpretative	*quantitative*
(*b*) *assertive*	*preventive*
exploitive	

c and *ck*

Words ending in *-c* interpose *k* before suffixes which otherwise would indicate a soft *c*, chiefly *-ed, -er, -ing, -y*, e.g.:

bivouacker, -ing	*colicky*

frolicked, -ing	*picnicked, -er, -ing*
mimicked, -ing	*plasticky*
panicky	*trafficked, -ing*

Exceptions: *arced, -ing, zinced, zincify, zincing.*

Before *-ism, -ist, -ity,* and *-ize c* (chiefly occurring in the suffix *-ic*) remains and is pronounced soft, e.g. *Anglicism, physicist, domesticity, italicize.*

-cede or -ceed

Exceed, proceed, succeed; the other verbs similarly formed have *-cede*, e.g. *concede, intercede, recede.* Note also *supersede.*

-ce or -se

Advice, device, licence, and *practice* are nouns; the related verbs are spelt with *-se*: *advise, devise, license, practise.* Similarly *prophecy* (noun), *prophesy* (verb).

• American spelling favours *licence, practice* for both noun and verb; but the nouns *defence, offence, pretence* are spelt with *c* in Britain, *s* in America.

en- or in-

The following pairs of words can give trouble:

encrust (verb)	*incrustation*
engrain (verb) to dye in the raw state	*ingrain* (adjective) dyed in the yarn; *ingrained* deeply rooted
enquire ask	*inquire* undertake a formal investigation
enquiry question	*inquiry* official investigation
ensure make sure	*insure* take out insurance (against risk: note *assurance* of life)

-erous or -rous

The ending *-erous* is normal in adjectives related to nouns ending in *-er*, e.g. *murderous, slanderous, thunderous.* The exceptions are:

ambidextrous	*disastrous*	*monstrous*
cumbrous	*leprous*	*slumbrous*
dextrous	*meandrous*	*wondrous*

for- and fore-

The prefix *for-* means 'away, out, completely', or implies prohibition or abstention. *Fore-* is the same as the ordinary word so spelt, = 'beforehand, in front'.

Note especially:

forbear refrain	*forebear* ancestor
forgather	*foreclose*
forgo abstain from	*forego* (esp. in *foregoing (list), foregone (conclusion)*)
forfeit	

f to v

Certain nouns that end in *f* or *f* followed by silent *e* change this *f* to *v* in some derivatives. Most are familiar, but with a few derivatives there is variation between *f* and *v* or uncertainty about which consonant is correct; only these are dealt with below.

beef: plural *beeves* oxen, *beefs* kinds of beef.
calf (young bovine animal): *calfish* calflike; *calves-foot jelly.*
calf (of leg): *(enormously) calved* having (enormous) calves.
corf (basket): plural *corves.*
dwarf: plural usually *dwarfs*, but *dwarves* is commonly found.
elf: *elfish* and *elvish* are both acceptable; *elfin* but *elven.*
handkerchief: plural usually *handkerchiefs*, but *handkerchieves* is commonly found.
hoof: plural usually *hoofs*, but *hooves* is commonly found; adjective *hoofed* or *hooved.*
knife: verb *knife.*
leaf: *leaved* having leaves (*broad-leaved*, etc.) but *leafed* as past of *leaf (through a book*, etc.).
life: *lifelong* lasting a lifetime; *livelong* (*day*, etc., poetic: the *i* is short); the plural of *still life* is *still lifes.*
oaf: plural *oafs.*
roof: plural *roofs.* • *Rooves* is commonly heard and sometimes written. Its written use should be avoided.
scarf (garment): plural usually *scarves*, but *scarfs* is commonly found.
scarf (joint): plural and verb keep *f.*
sheaf: plural *sheaves*; verb *sheaf* or *sheave*; *sheaved* made into a sheaf.
shelf: plural *shelves*; *shelvy* having sandbanks.
staff: plural *staffs* but archaic and musical *staves.*
turf: plural *turfs* or *turves*; verb *turf*; *turfy.*
wharf: plural *wharfs* or *wharves.*
wolf: *wolfish* of a wolf.

-ize and -ise

-ize should be preferred to *-ise* as a verbal ending in words in which both are in use.

1. The choice arises only where the ending is pronounced *eyes*, not where it is *ice, iss* or *eez.* So: *precise, promise, expertise, remise.*

2. The choice applies only to the verbal suffix (of Greek origin), added to nouns and adjectives with the sense 'make into, treat with, or act in the way of (that which is indicated by the stem word)'.

Hence are eliminated

(*a*) nouns in *-ise*:

compromise	*exercise*	*revise*
demise	*franchise*	*surmise*
disguise	*merchandise*	*surprise*
enterprise		

(*b*) verbs corresponding to a noun which has *-is-* as a part of the stem (e.g. in the syllables *-vis-, -cis-, -mis-*), or identical with a noun in *-ise.* Some of the more common verbs in *-ise* are:

advertise	*despise*	*incise*
advise	*devise*	*merchandise*
apprise	*disguise*	*premise*
arise	*emprise*	*prise* (open)
chastise	*enfranchise*	*revise*
circumcise	*enterprise*	*supervise*
comprise	*excise*	*surmise*
compromise	*exercise*	*surprise*
demise	*improvise*	*televise*

3. In most cases, *-ize* verbs are formed on familiar English stems, e.g. *authorize, familiarize, symbolize*; or with a slight alteration to the stem, e.g. *agonize, dogmatize, sterilize.* A few words have no such immediate stem; *aggrandize* (cf. *aggrandizement*), *appetize* (cf. *appetite*), *baptize* (cf. *baptism*), *catechize* (cf. *catechism*), *recognize* (cf. *recognition*); and *capsize.*

-or and -er

These two suffixes, denoting 'one who or that which performs (the action of the verb)' are from Latin (through French) and Old English respectively, but their origin is not a sure guide to their distribution.

1. *-er* is the living suffix, forming most newly-coined agent nouns; but *-or* is frequently used with words of Latin origin to coin technical terms.

2. *-er* is usual after doubled consonants (except *-ss-*), after soft *c* and g, after *-i-*, after *ch* and *sh*, and after *-er, -graph, -ion,* and *-iz-*, e.g.

chopper, producer, avenger, qualifier, launcher, furnisher, discoverer, photographer, executioner, organizer.

Principal exceptions: *counsellor, carburettor, conqueror.*

3. *-or* follows *-at-* to form a suffix *-ator*, often but not always in words related to verbs in *-ate*, e.g. *duplicator, incubator.*

Exception: *debater.*

Note: nouns in *-olater*, as *idolater*, do not contain the agent suffix.

4. No rule can predict whether a given word having *-s-, -ss-,* or *-t-* (apart from *-at-*) before the suffix requires *-or* or *-er.* So *supervisor, compressor, prospector*, but *adviser, presser, perfecter. -tor* usually follows *-c*, unstressed *i*, and *u*, e.g. *actor, compositor, executor*; *-ter* usually follows *f, gh, l, r*, and *s*, e.g. *drifter, fighter, defaulter, exporter, protester*; but there are numerous exceptions.

5. A functional distinction is made between *-or* and *-er* in the following:

accepter one who accepts	*acceptor* (in scientific use)
adapter one who adapts	*adaptor* electrical device
caster one who casts, casting machine	*castor* beaver; plant giving oil; sugar (sprinkler); wheel
censer vessel for incense	*censor* official
conveyer one who conveys	*conveyor* device
resister one who resists	*resistor* electrical device
sailer ship of specified power	*sailor* seaman

6. A number of words have *-er* in normal use but *-or* in Law:

abetter	*mortgager (mortgagor)*
accepter	*settler*
granter	

-our or -or

1. In agent nouns, only *-or* occurs as the ending (cf. **-or and -er**), e.g. *actor, counsellor.*

Exception: *saviour.*

2. In abstract nouns, *-our* is usual, e.g. *colour, favour, humour.* Only the following end in *-or*:

error	*pallor*	*terror*
horror	*squalor*	*torpor*
languor	*stupor*	*tremor*
liquor		

● In American English *-or* is usual in nearly all words in which British English has *-our* (*glamour* and *saviour* are the main exceptions).

3. Nouns in *-our* change this to *-or* before the suffixes *-ation, -iferous, -ific, -ize,* and *-ous,* e.g.

coloration, humorous, odoriferous, soporific, vaporize, vigorous.

But *-our* keeps the *u* before *-able, -er, -ful, -ism, ist, -ite,* and *-less,* e.g.

armourer, behaviourism, colourful, favourite, honourable, labourite, odourless, rigourist.

plural formation

Most nouns simply add *-s,* e.g. *cats, dogs, horses, cameras.*

A. The regular plural suffix *-s* is preceded by *-e-*:

1. After sibilant consonants, where ease of pronunciation requires a separating vowel, i.e. after

ch: e.g. *branches, coaches, matches* (but not *conchs, lochs, stomachs* where the *ch* has a different sound)
s: e.g. *buses, gases, pluses, yeses* (note that single *s* is not doubled)
sh: e.g. *ashes, bushes*
ss: e.g. *grasses, successes*
x: e.g. *boxes, sphinxes*
z: e.g. *buzzes, waltzes* (note *quizzes* with doubling of *z*)

Proper names follow the same rule, e.g. *the Joneses, the Rogerses, the two Charleses.*

● *-es* should not be replaced by an apostrophe, as *the Jones'.*

2. After *-y* (not preceded by a vowel), which changes to *i,* e.g. *ladies, soliloquies, spies.*

Exceptions: proper names, e.g. *the Willoughbys, the three Marys;* also *trilbys, lay-bys, standbys, zlotys* (Polish currency).

3. After *-o* in certain words:

buffaloes	*haloes*	*stuccoes*
calicoes	*heroes*	*tomatoes*
dingoes	*mosquitoes*	*tornadoes*
dominoes	*mottoes*	*torpedoes*
echoes	*Negroes*	*vetoes*
embargoes	*noes*	*volcanoes*
goes	*potatoes*	

Words not in this list add only *-s.* Some words (e.g. *cargo, grotto, innuendo, mango, memento, peccadillo,* and *portico*) are found with either plural form.

It is helpful to remember that *-e-* is never inserted:

(*a*) when the *o* is preceded by another vowel, e.g. *cuckoos, embryos, ratios.*
(*b*) when the word is an abbreviation, e.g. *hippos, kilos.*
(*c*) with proper names, e.g. *Lotharios, Figaros, the Munros.*

4. With words which change final *f* to *v* (see **f to v**), e.g. *calves, scarves.*

B. Plural of compound nouns.

1. Compounds made up of a noun followed by an adjective, a prepositional phrase, or an adverb attach *-s* to the noun, e.g.

(*a*) *courts martial* — *heirs presumptive*
cousins-german — *poets laureate*

But *brigadier-generals, lieutenant-colonels, sergeant-majors.*

(*b*) *men-of-war* — *tugs of war*
sons-in-law

(*c*) *hangers-on* — *whippers-in*
runners-up

Note: In informal usage *-s* is not infrequently transferred to the second element of compounds of type (*a*).

2. Compounds which contain no noun, or in which the noun element is now disguised, add *-s* at the end. So also do nouns formed from phrasal verbs and compounds ending in *-ful,* e.g.

(*a*) *ne'er-do-wells* — *will-o'-the-wisps*
forget-me-nots

(*b*) *pullovers* — *set-ups*
run-throughs

(*c*) *handfuls* — *spoonfuls*

(See also **-ful/-s full** in Section 1 **Meanings**)

3. Compounds containing *man* or *woman* make both elements plural, as usually do those made up of two words linked by *and,* e.g.

(*a*) *gentlemen ushers* — *women doctors*
menservants

(*b*) *pros and cons* — *ups and downs*

C. The plural of the following nouns with a singular in *-s* is unchanged:

biceps	*means*	*species*
congeries	*mews*	*superficies*
forceps	*series*	*thrips*
innings		

The following are mass nouns, not plurals:

bona fides (= 'good faith'), *kudos*

● The singulars *bona fide* (as a noun; there is an adjective *bona-fide*), *congery, kudo,* sometimes seen, are erroneous.

D. Plural of nouns of foreign origin. The terminations that may form their plurals according to a foreign pattern are given in alphabetical order below; to each is added a list of the words that normally follow this pattern, although some of these (marked *) are found with *-s* or *-es* if they are considered to be sufficiently assimilated into English. It is recommended that the regular plural (in *-s*) should be used for all the other words with these terminations, even though some are found with either type of plural.

1. *-a* (Latin and Greek) becomes *-ae* (or * *-as*):

alga	*lamina*	*nebula**
alumna	*larva*	*papilla*

Note: *formula* has *-ae* in mathematical and scientific use.

2. *-eau, -eu* (French) add *-x* (or *-s*):

*beau**	*château*	*plateau**
*bureau**	*milieu**	*tableau*

3. *-ex, -ix* (Latin) become *-ices*:

appendix	*cortex*	*matrix*
calix	*helix*	*radix*

Note: *index, vortex* have *-ices* in mathematical and scientific use (otherwise regular).

4. *-is* (Greek and Latin) becomes *-es* (pronounced *eez*):

amanuensis	*axis*	*ellipsis*
analysis	*basis*	*hypothesis*
antithesis	*crisis*	*metamorphosis*

oasis *synopsis* *thesis* *parenthesis*

5. *-o* (Italian) becomes *-i* (or **-os*):

*concerto grosso** (*concerti grossi*) *graffito* *ripieno** *maestro** *virtuoso**

Note: *solo* and *soprano* sometimes have *-i* in technical contexts (otherwise regular).

6. *-on* (Greek) becomes *-a*:

criterion *parhelion* *phenomenon*

Note: The plural of *automaton* is in *-a* when used collectively (otherwise regular).

7. *-s* (French) is unchanged in the plural (note: it is silent in the singular, but pronounced *-z* in the plural):

chamois *corps* *fracas* *chassis* *faux pas* *patois*

Also (not a noun in French): *rendezvous*.

8. *-um* (Latin) becomes *-a* (or **-ums*):

addendum *datum* *maximum* *bacterium* *desideratum* *minimum* *candelabrum* *dictum** *quantum* *compendium** *effluvium* *scholium* *corrigendum* *emporium** *spectrum* *cranium** *epithalamium** *speculum* *crematorium** *erratum* *stratum* *curriculum*

Note: *medium* in scientific use, and in the sense 'a means of communication' (as *mass medium*) has plural in *-a*; the collective plural of *memorandum* 'things to be noted' is in *-a*; *rostrum* has *-a* in technical use; otherwise these words are regular. In the technical sense 'starting-point' *datum* has a regular plural.

9. *-us* (Latin) becomes *-i* (or **-uses*):

alumnus *fungus** *nucleus* *bacillus* *gladiolus** *radius** *bronchus* *locus* *stimulus* *cactus** *narcissus** *terminus** *calculus**

Note: *focus* has plural in *-i* in scientific use, but otherwise is regular; *genius* has plura *genii* when used to mean 'guardian spirit', but in its usual sense is regular; *genus* becomes *genera*, while *corpus* becomes *corpora* or *corpuses*, and *opus* becomes *opera* or *opuses*.

• The following words of foreign origin are plural nouns; they should normally not be construed as singulars (see also Section 2, *Plurals*, where some of these are treated as separate entries).

bacteria *graffiti* *phenomena* *candelabra* *insignia* *regalia* *criteria* *media* *strata* *data*

E. There is no need to use an apostrophe before *-s*:

1. After figures: *the 1890s*.
2. After abbreviations: *MPs*, *SOSs*.

But it is needed in: *dot the i's and cross the t's*.

possessive case

To form the possessive:

1. Normally, add *-'s* in the singular and *-s'* (i.e. apostrophe following the plural suffix *-s*) in the plural, e.g.

Bill's book *the Johnsons' dog* *his master's voice* *a girls' school*

Nouns that do not form plural in *-s* add *-'s* to the plural form, e.g.

children's books *women's liberation*

2. Nouns ending in *s* add *'s* for the singular possessive, e.g.

boss's *Charles's* *Burns's* *Father Christmas's* *Hicks's* *Tess's* *St James's Square* *Thomas's*

To form the plural possessive, they add an apostrophe to the *s* of the plural in the normal way, e.g.

bosses' *the octopuses' tentacles* *the Joneses' dog* *the Thomases' dog*

French names ending in silent *s* or *x* add *-'s*, which is pronounced as *z*, e.g.

Dumas's (= Dumah's) *Crémieux's*

Names ending in *-es* pronounced *iz* are treated like plurals and take only an apostrophe (following the pronunciation, which is *iz*, not *iziz*), e.g.

Bridges' *Moses'* *Hodges'* *Riches'*

Polysyllables not accented on the last or second last syllable can take the apostrophe alone, but the form with *-'s* is equally acceptable, e.g.

Barnabas' or *Barnabas's*
Nicholas' or *Nicholas's*

It is the custom in classical works to use the apostrophe only, irrespective of pronunciation, for ancient classical names ending in *-s*, e.g.

Ceres' *Herodotus'* *Venus'* *Demosthenes'* *Mars'* *Xerxes'*

Jesus' is an accepted liturgical archaism. But in non-liturgical use, *Jesus's* is acceptable.

With the possessive preceding the word *sake*, be guided by the pronunciation, e.g.

for goodness' sake but *for God's sake*
for conscience' sake (!) *for Charles's sake*

After *-x* and *-z*, use *-'s*, e.g. *Ajax's*, *Berlioz's music*, *Leibniz's law*, *Lenz's law*.

3. Expressions such as:

a fortnight's holiday *two weeks' holiday* *a pound's worth* *two pounds' worth* *your money's worth*

contain possessives and should have apostrophes correctly placed, as in the examples above.

4. In *I'm going to the butcher's*, *grocer's*, etc. there is a possessive with ellipsis of the word 'shop'. The same construction is used in *I'm going to Brown's*, *Green's*, etc., so that properly an apostrophe is called for. Where a business calls itself *Brown*, *Green*, or the like (e.g. *Marks and Spencer*, *J. Sainsbury*) the apostrophe would be expected before *-s*. But many businesses use the title *Browns*, *Greens*, etc., without an apostrophe (e.g. *Debenhams*, *Barclays Bank*). No apostrophe is necessary in *a Debenhams store* or in (*go to* or *take to*) *the cleaners*.

5. The apostrophe must not be used:

(*a*) with the plural non-possessive *-s*: notices such as *TEA'S* are often seen, but are wrong.
(*b*) with the possessive of pronouns: *hers*, *its*, *ours*, *theirs*, *yours*; the possessive of *who* is *whose*.

• *it's* = *it is*; *who's* = *who is*.

• There are no words *her's*, *our's*, *their's*, *your's*.

-re or -er

The principal words in which the ending *-re* (with the unstressed ə sound—there are others with the sound *rə*, e.g. *macabre*, or *ray*, e.g. *padre*) is found are:

accoutre *fibre* **massacre* **acre* *goitre* **meagre* *amphitheatre* *litre* **mediocre* **cadre* *louvre* *metre* (note *meter* the measuring device) *calibre* **lucre* *mitre* *centre* *lustre* **euchre* *manœuvre*

nitre	*sabre*	*spectre*
ochre	*sceptre*	*theatre*
* *ogre*	*sepulchre*	*titre*
philtre	*sombre*	* *wiseacre*
reconnoitre		

• All but those marked * are spelt with *-er* in American English.

re- prefix

This prefix is followed by a hyphen:

1. Before another *e*, e.g. *re-echo, re-entry*.

2. So as to distinguish the compound so formed from the more familiar identically spelt word written solid, e.g.

re-cover (put new cover on): *recover*
re-form (form again): *reform*
re-sign (sign again): *resign*

-s suffix

A. As the inflexion of the plural of nouns: see **plural formation**.

B. As the inflexion of the third person singular present indicative of verbs, it requires the same changes in the stem as the plural ending, namely the insertion of *-e-*:

1. After sibilants (*ch, s, sh, x, z*), e.g. *catches, tosses, pushes, fixes, buzzes*; note that single *s* and *z* are subject to doubling of final consonant, though the forms in which they occur are rare, e.g. *gasses, nonplusses, quizzes, whizzes*.

2. After *y*, which is subject to the change of *y* to *i*, e.g. *cries, flies, carries, copies*.

3. After *o*: *echo, go, torpedo, veto*, like the corresponding nouns, insert *-e-* before *-s*.

-xion or -ction

Complexion, crucifixion, effluxion, fluxion, genuflexion, inflexion all have *-x-*; *connection, reflection* (which formerly sometimes had *-x-*) have *-ct-*; *deflexion* is increasingly being replaced by *deflection*.

• In American spelling *-ction* is more usual in *connection, deflection, genuflection, inflection, reflection*.

-y or -ey adjectives

When *-y* is added to a word to form an adjective, the following changes in spelling occur:

1. Doubling of final consonant, e.g. *shrubby*.

2. Dropping of silent *-e*, e.g. *bony, chancy, mousy*.

Exceptions:

(*a*) After *u*:

bluey *gluey* *tissuey*

(*b*) In words that are not well established in the written language, where the retention of *-e* helps to clarify the sense:

cottagey *dicey*
pacey *villagey*

Note also *holey* (distinguished from *holy*); *phoney* (of unknown origin).

3. *Insertion of -e-* when *-y* is also the final letter of the stem:

clayey *skyey* *sprayey* *wheyey*

Also in *gooey*.

4. Adjectives ending in unstressed *-ey* (2 (*a*) and (*b*) and 3 above) change this *-ey* to *-i-* before the comparative and superlative suffixes *-er* and *-est* and the adverbial suffix *-ly*, e.g.

dicey: *dicier* *gooey*: *gooier* *pacey*: *pacier*
phoney: *phonily*

Before *-ness* there is variation, e.g.

clayey: *clayeyness* *phoney*: *phoniness* *wheyey*: *wheyiness*

y or i

There is often uncertainty about whether *y* or *i* should be written in the following words:

Write *i* in:	Write *y* in:
cider	*dyke* (*dike* is also found)
cipher (*cypher* is also found)	*Gypsy* (*Gipsy* is also found)
Libya	*lyke-wake*
lich-gate (*lych-* is also found)	*lynch law*
linchpin	*pygmy* (*pigmy* is also found)
sibyl (classical)	*style* (manner)
silvan	*stylus*
siphon (*syphon* is also found)	*stymie* (*stimy* is also found)
siren	*Sybil* (frequently as Christian name)
stile (in fence)	*syllabub* (*sillabub* is also found)
timpani (drums; *tympani* is also found)	*syrup*
tiro (*tyro* is also found)	*tyke* (*tike* is also found)
witch-hazel (*wych-hazel* is also found)	*tympanum* (ear-drum)
	tyre (of wheel)
	wych-elm

-yse or -yze

This verbal ending (e.g. in *analyse, catalyse, paralyse*) is not a suffix but part of the Greek stem *-lyse*. It should not be written with *z* (though *z* is normally used in such words in America).

y to i

Words that end in *-y* change this to *-i-* before certain suffixes. The conditions are:

A. When the *-y* is not preceded by a vowel (except *-u-* in *-guy, -quy*).

-y does not change to *-i-* when preceded by a vowel (other than *u* in *-guy, -quy*). So *enjoyable, conveyed, parleyed, gayer, gayest, donkeys, buys, employer, joyful, coyly, enjoyment, greyness*.

Exceptions: *daily, gaily*, and adjectives ending in unstressed *-ey*.

B. When the suffix is:

1. *-able*, e.g. *deniable, justifiable, variable*.

Exception: *flyable*.

2. *-ed* (the past tense and past participle), e.g. *carried, denied, tried*.

3. *-er* (agent-noun suffix), e.g. *carrier, crier, supplier*.

Exceptions: *flyer, fryer, shyer* (one who, a horse which, shies), *skyer* (in cricket). Note that *drier, prier, trier* (one who tries) are regular.

4. *-er, -est* (comparative and superlative); e.g. *drier, driest; happier, happiest*.

5. *-es* (noun plural and third person singular present indicative), e.g. *ladies, soliloquies, spies; carries, denies, tries*.

Exceptions: see **plural formation** A2.

6. *-ful* (adjectives), e.g. *beautiful, fanciful*. (*Bellyful* is a noun, not an adjective.)

7. *-less* (adjectives), e.g. *merciless, remediless*.

Exceptions: some rare compounds, e.g. *countryless, hobbyless, partyless*.

8. *-ly* (adverbs), e.g. *drily, happily, plaguily*.

Exceptions: *shyly, slyly, spryly, wryly*.

9. *-ment* (nouns), e.g. *embodiment, merriment*.

10. *-ness* (nouns), e.g. *happiness, cliquiness*.

Exceptions: *dryness, flyness, shyness, slyness, spryness, wryness; busyness* (distinguished from *business*).

5 Pronunciation

The following words are often mispronounced:

comparable	/kómpərəb'l/	*is preferred to*	/kompárrəb'l/
contribute	/kəntríbyoot/	„	/kóntribyo͞ot/
controversy	/kóntrəversi/	„	/kəntróvvərsi/
decade	/dékkayd/	„	/dikáyd/
deity	/dée-iti/	„	/dáyiti/
diphtheria	/difthéeriə/	„	/diptheériə/
dispute	/dispyó͞ot/	„	/díspyo͞ot/
distribute	/distríbyoot/	„	/dístribyo͞ot/
exquisite	/ékskwizit/	„	/ikskwízzit/
formidable	/fórmidəb'l/	„	/formíddəb'l/
harass(ment)	/hárrəss(mənt)/	„	/hərάss(mənt)/
integral *adj.*	/íntigr'l/	„	/intégr'l/
irreparable	/iréppərəb'l/	„	/irripárrəb'l/
irrevocable	/irévvəkəb'l/	„	/irrivōkəb'l/
kilometre	/kílləmeetər/	„	/kilómmitər/
lamentable	/lámməntəb'l/	*is preferred to*	/ləméntəb'l/
length	/length/	„	/lengkth/
preferable	/préffərəb'l/	„	/priférəb'l/
primarily	/prī́mərili/	„	/prīmaírili/
reputable	/répyootəb'l/	„	/ripyó͞otəb'l/
research	/risérch/	„	/réeserch/
romance	/rōmánss/	„	/rṓmanss/
secretary	/sékritəri/ or /sékrətri/	„	/sékkitairi/
strength	/strength/	„	/strengkth/
surveillance	/survάylənss/	„	/səvάy-yənss/
temporarily	/témpərərili/	„	/tempəraírili/
trait	/tray/	„	/trayt/
vulnerable	/vúlnərəb'l/	„	/vúnnərəb'l/
zoology	/zō-óllәji/	„	/zo͞o-ólləji/

Appendix 3 Punctuation Marks

Punctuation is a complicated subject, and only the main principles can be discussed here. The explanations are based on practice in British English; usage in American English differs in some instances. The main headings are as follows:

1 General remarks
2 Capital letter
3 Full stop
4 Semicolon
5 Comma
6 Colon
7 Question mark
8 Exclamation mark
9 Apostrophe
10 Quotation marks
11 Brackets
12 Dash
13 Hyphen

1 General remarks

The purpose of punctuation is to mark out strings of words into manageable groups and help clarify their meaning (or in some cases to prevent a wrong meaning being deduced). The marks most commonly used to divide a piece of prose or other writing are the full stop, the semicolon, and the comma, with the strength of the dividing or separating role diminishing from the full stop to the comma. The full stop therefore marks the main division into sentences; the semicolon joins sentences (as in this sentence); and the comma (which is the most flexible in use and causes most problems) separates smaller elements with the least loss of continuity. Brackets and dashes also serve as separators—often more strikingly than commas, as in this sentence.

2 Capital letter A

1.1 This is used for the first letter of the word beginning a sentence in most cases:

He decided not to come. Later he changed his mind.

1.2 A sentence or clause contained in a subordinate or parenthetic role within a larger one does not normally begin with a capital letter:

I have written several letters (there are many to be written) and hope to finish them tomorrow.

1.3 In the following, however, the sentence is a separate one and therefore does begin with a capital letter:

There is more than one possibility. (I have said this often before.) So we should think carefully before acting.

1.4 A capital letter also begins sentences that form quoted speech:

The assistant turned and replied, 'There are no more left.'

2 It is used in proper names (*Paris*, *John Smith*), names of people and languages and related adjectives (*Englishman*, *Austrian*, *French*), names of institutions and institutional groups (*the British Museum*, *Protestants*, *Conservatives*), and names of days and months (*Tuesday*, *March*) and related words (*Easter Sunday*). It is also used by convention in names that are trade marks (*Biro*, *Jacuzzi*).

3 It is used in titles of books, newspapers, plays, films, television programmes, etc., and in headings and captions.

4 It is used in designations of rank or relationship when used as titles (*King John*, *Aunt Mabel*, *Pope Gregory*), and to designate divinity (*God*, *the Almighty*, etc.).

5 Lines of verse often begin with a capital letter.

6. Many abbreviations consist partly or entirely of the initial letters of words in capital letters (with or without a full stop): *BBC*, *DoE*, *M.Litt.*

3 Full stop .

1 This is used to mark the end of a sentence when it is a statement (and not a question or exclamation). In prose, sentences marked by full stops normally represent a discrete or distinct statement; more closely connected or complementary statements are joined by a semicolon (as here).

2.1 Full stops are used to mark many abbreviations (*Weds.*, *Gen.*, *p.m.*). They are often omitted in abbreviations that are familiar or very common (*Dr*, *Mr*, *Mrs*, etc.), in abbreviations that consist entirely of capital letters (*BBC*, *GMT*, etc.), and in acronyms that are pronounced as a word rather than a sequence of letters (*Nato*, *Ernie*, etc.).

2.2 If an abbreviation with a full stop comes at the end of a sentence, another full stop is not added when the full stop of the abbreviation is the last character:

They have a collection of many animals, including dogs, cats, tortoises, snakes, etc.

but

They have a collection of many animals (dogs, cats, tortoises, snakes, etc.).

3 A sequence of three full stops is used to mark an ellipsis or omission in a sequence of words, especially when forming an incomplete quotation. When the omission occurs at the end of a sentence, a fourth point is added as the full stop of the whole sentence:

He left the room, banged the door, . . . and went out.
The report said: 'There are many issues to be considered, of which the chief are money, time, and personnel. . . . Let us consider personnel first.'

4 A full stop is used as a decimal point (*10.5 per cent*; *£1.65*), and to divide hours and minutes in giving time (*6.15 p.m.*), although a colon is usual in American use (*6:15 p.m.*).

4 Semicolon ;

1.1 The main role of the semicolon is to unite sentences that are closely associated or that complement or parallel each other in some way, as in the following:

In the north of the city there is a large industrial area with little private housing; further east is the university.
To err is human; to forgive, divine.

1.2 It is often used as a stronger division in a sentence that already includes divisions by means of commas:

He came out of the house, which lay back from the road, and saw her at the end of the path; but instead of continuing towards her, he hid until she had gone.

2 It is used in a similar way in lists of names or other items, to indicate a stronger division:

I should like to thank the managing director, Stephen Jones; my secretary, Mary Cartwright; and my assistant, Kenneth Sloane.

5 Comma ,

1 Use of the comma is more difficult to describe than other punctuation marks, and there is much variation in practice. Essentially, its role is to give detail to the structure of sentences, especially longer ones, and make their meaning clear. Too many commas can be distracting; too few can make a piece of writing difficult to read or, worse, difficult to understand.

2.1 The comma is widely used to separate the main clauses of a compound sentence when they are not sufficiently close in meaning or content to form a continuous unpunctuated sentence, and are not distinct enough to warrant a semicolon. A conjunction such as *and*, *but*, *yet*, etc., is normally used:

The road runs through a beautiful wooded valley, and the railway line follows it closely.

2.2 It is considered incorrect to join the clauses of a compound sentence without a conjunction. In the following sentence, the comma should either be replaced by a semicolon, or be retained and followed by *and*:

I like swimming very much, I go to the pool every week.

2.3 It is also considered incorrect to separate a subject from its verb with a comma:

Those with the smallest incomes and no other means, should get most support.

3.1 Commas are usually inserted between adjectives coming before a noun:

An enterprising, ambitious person.
A cold, damp, badly heated room.

3.2 But the comma is omitted when the last adjective has a closer relation to the noun than the others:

A distinguished foreign politician.
A little old lady.

4 An important role of the comma is to prevent ambiguity or (momentary) misunderstanding, especially after a verb used intransitively where it might otherwise be taken to be transitive:

With the police pursuing, the people shouted loudly.

Other examples follow:

He did not want to leave, from a feeling of loyalty.
In the valley below, the houses appeared very small.
However, much as I should like to I cannot agree.
(compare *However much I should like to I cannot agree.*)

5.1 The comma is used in pairs to separate elements in a sentence that are not part of the main statement:

I should like you all, ladies and gentlemen, to raise your glasses.
There is no sense, as far as I can see, in this suggestion.
It appears, however, that we were wrong.

5.2 It is also used to separate a relative clause from its antecedent when the clause is not serving an identifying function:

The book, which was on the table, was a present.

In the above sentence, the information in the *which* clause is incidental to the main statement; without the comma, it would form an essential part of it in identifying which book is being referred to (and could be replaced by *that*):

The book which/that was on the table was a present.

6.1 Commas are used to separate items in a list or sequence. Usage varies as to the inclusion of a comma before *and* in the last item; the practice in this dictionary is to include it:

The following will report at 9.30 sharp: Jones, Smith, Thompson, and Williams.

6.2 A final comma before *and*, when used regularly and consistently, has the advantage of clarifying the grouping at a composite name occurring at the end of a list:

We shall go to Smiths, Boots, Woolworths, and Marks and Spencer.

7 A comma is used in numbers of four or more figures, to separate each group of three consecutive figures starting from the right (e.g. *10,135,793*).

6 Colon :

1 The main role of the colon is to separate main clauses when there is a step forward from the first to the second, especially from introduction to main point, from general statement to example, from cause to effect, and from premiss to conclusion:

There is something I want to say: I should like you all to know how grateful I am to you.
It was not easy: to begin with I had to find the right house.
The weather was bad: so we decided to stay at home.
(In this example, a comma could be used, but the emphasis on cause and effect would be much reduced.)

2 It also introduces a list of items. In this use a dash should not be added:

The following will be needed: a pen, pencil, rubber, piece of paper, and ruler.

3 It is used to introduce, more formally and emphatically than a comma would, speech or quoted material:

I told them last week: 'Do not in any circumstances open this door.'

7 Question mark ?

1.1 This is used in place of the full stop to show that the preceding sentence is a question:

Do you want another piece of cake?
He really is her husband?

1.2 It is not used when the question is implied by indirect speech:

I asked you whether you wanted another piece of cake.

2 It is used (often in brackets) to express doubt or uncertainty about a word or phrase immediately following or preceding it:

Julius Caesar, born (?) 100 BC.
They were then seen boarding a bus (to London?).

8 Exclamation mark !

This is used after an exclamatory word, phrase, or sentence expressing any of the following:

1 Absurdity:	*What an idea!*
2 Command or warning:	*Go to your room!* *Be careful!*
3 Contempt or disgust:	*They are revolting!*
4 Emotion or pain:	*I hate you!* *That really hurts!* *Ouch!*
5 Enthusiasm:	*I'd love to come!*
6 Wish or regret:	*Let me come!* *If only I could swim!*
7 Wonder, admiration, or surprise:	*What a good idea!* *Aren't they beautiful!*

9 Apostrophe '

1.1 The main use is to indicate the possessive case, as in *John's book, the girls' mother*, etc. It comes before the *s* in singular and plural nouns not ending in *s*, as in *the boy's games* and *the women's games*. It comes after the *s* in plural nouns ending in *s*, as in *the boys' games*.

1.2 In singular nouns ending in *s* practice differs between (for example) *Charles'* and *Charles's*; in some cases the shorter form is preferable for reasons of sound, as in *Xerxes' fleet*.

1.3 It is also used to indicate a place or business, e.g. *the butcher's*. In this use it is often omitted in some names, e.g. *Smiths, Lloyds Bank*.

2 It is used to indicate a contraction, e.g. *he's, wouldn't, Bo's'un, o'clock*.

3 It is sometimes used to form a plural of individual letters or numbers, although this use is diminishing. It is helpful in *cross your t's* but unnecessary in *MPs* and *1940s*.

4 For its use as a quotation mark, see section 10.

10 Quotation marks ' '

1 The main use is to indicate direct speech and quotations. A single turned comma (') is normally used at the beginning, and a single apostrophe (') at the end of the quoted matter:

She said, 'I have something to ask you.'

2 The closing quotation mark should come after any punctuation mark which is part of the quoted matter, but before any mark which is not:

They shouted, 'Watch out!'
They were described as 'an unruly bunch'.
Did I hear you say 'go away!'?

3 Punctuation dividing a sentence of reported speech is put inside the quotation marks:

'Go away,' he said, 'and don't ever come back.'

4 Quotation marks are also used for cited words and phrases:

What does 'integrated circuit' mean?

5 A quotation within a quotation is put in double quotation marks:

'Have you any idea,' he said, 'what "integrated circuit" means?'

11 Brackets ([ ])

1 The types of brackets used in normal punctuation are round brackets () and square brackets [].

2 The main use of round brackets is to enclose explanations and extra information or comment:

He is (as he always was) a rebel.
Zimbabwe (formerly Rhodesia).
They talked about Machtpolitik (*power politics*).

3 They are used to give references and citations:

Thomas Carlyle (1795–1881).
A discussion of integrated circuits (see p. 38).

4 They are used to enclose reference letters or figures, e.g. *(1) (a)*.

5 They are used to enclose optional words:

There are many (apparent) difficulties.
(In this example, the difficulties may or may not be only apparent.)

6.1 Square brackets are used less often. The main use is to enclose extra information attributable to someone (normally an editor) other than the writer of the surrounding text:

The man walked in, and his sister [Sarah] greeted him.

6.2 They are used in some contexts to convey special kinds of information, especially when round brackets are also used for other purposes: for example, in this dictionary they are used to give the etymologies at the end of entries.

12 Dash —

1 A single dash is used to indicate a pause, whether a hesitation in speech or to introduce an explanation or expansion of what comes before it:

'I think you should have—told me,' he replied.
We then saw the reptiles—snakes, crocodiles, that sort of thing.

2 A pair of dashes is used to indicate asides and parentheses, like the use of commas as explained at 5.5.1 above, but forming a more distinct break:

People in the north are more friendly—and helpful—than those in the south.
There is nothing to be gained—unless you want a more active social life—in moving to the city.

3 It is sometimes used to indicate an omitted word, for example a coarse word in reported speech:

'—you all,' he said.

13 Hyphen -

1 The hyphen has two main functions: to link words or elements of words into longer words and compounds, and to mark the division of a word at the end of a line in print or writing.

2.1 The use of the hyphen to connect words to form compound words is diminishing in English, especially when the elements are of one syllable as in *birdsong, eardrum,* and *playgroup,* and also in some longer formations such as *figurehead* and *nationwide.* The hyphen is used more often in routine and occasional couplings, especially when reference to the senses of the separate elements is considered important or unavoidable, as in *boiler-room.* It is often retained to avoid awkward collisions of letters, as in *breast-stroke.*

2.2 The hyphen serves to connect words that have a syntactic link, as in *hard-covered books* and *French-speaking people,* where the reference is to books with hard covers and people who speak French, rather than hard books with covers and French people who can speak (which would be the senses conveyed if the hyphens were omitted). It is also used to avoid more extreme kinds of ambiguity, as in *twenty-odd people.*

2.3 A particularly important use of the hyphen is to link compounds and phrases used attributively, as in *a well-known man* (but *the man is well known*), and *Christmas-tree lights* (but *the lights on the Christmas tree*).

2.4 It is also used to connect elements to form words in cases such as *re-enact* (where the collision of two *es* would be awkward), *re-form* (= to form again, to distinguish it from *reform*), and some other prefixed words such as those in *anti-, non-, over-,* and *post-.* Usage varies in this regard, and much depends on how well established and clearly recognizable the resulting formation is. When the second element is a name, a hyphen is usual (as in *anti-Darwinian*).

2.5 It is used to indicate a common second element in all but the last of a list, e.g. *two-, three-,* or *fourfold.*

3 The hyphen used to divide a word at the end of a line is a different matter, because it is not a permanent feature of the spelling. It is more common in print, where the text has to be accurately spaced and the margin justified; in handwritten and typed or word-processed material it can be avoided altogether. In print, words need to be divided carefully and consistently, taking account of the appearance and structure of the word. Detailed guidance on word-division may be found in the *Oxford Spelling Dictionary* (1986).

Appendix 4 Terms for Groups of Animals etc.

Terms marked † belong to 15th-c. lists of 'proper terms', notably that in the *Book of St Albans* attributed to Dame Juliana Barnes (1486). Many of these are fanciful or humorous terms which probably never had any real currency, but have been taken up by Joseph Strutt in *Sports and Pastimes of England* (1801) and by other antiquarian writers.

a †shrewdness of apes
a herd or †pace of asses
a †cete of badgers
a †sloth or †sleuth of bears
a hive of bees; a swarm, drift, or bike of bees
a flock, flight, (*dial.*) parcel, pod (= small flock), †fleet, or †dissimulation of (small) birds; a volary of birds in an aviary
a sounder of wild boar
a †blush of boys
a herd or gang of buffalo
a †clowder or †glaring of cats; a †dowt (= ?do-out) or †destruction of wild cats
a herd, drove, (*dial.*) drift, or (*US* & *Austral.*) mob of cattle
a brood, (*dial.*) cletch or clutch, or †peep of chickens
a †chattering or †clattering of choughs
a †drunkship of cobblers
a †rag or †rake of colts
a †hastiness of cooks
a †covert of coots
a herd of cranes
a litter of cubs
a herd of curlew
a †cowardice of curs
a herd or mob of deer
a pack or kennel of dogs
a trip of dotterel
a flight, †dole, or †piteousness of doves
a raft, bunch, or †paddling of ducks on water; a team of wild ducks in flight
a fling of dunlins
a herd of elephants
a herd or (*US*) gang of elk
a †business of ferrets
a charm or †chirm of finches
a shoal of fish; a run of fish in motion
a cloud of flies
a †stalk of foresters
a †skulk of foxes
a gaggle or (in the air) a skein, team, or wedge of geese
a herd of giraffes
a flock, herd, or (*dial.*) trip of goats
a pack or covey of grouse
a †husk or †down of hares
a cast of hawks let fly
an †observance of hermits
a †siege of herons
a stud or †haras of (breeding) horses; (*dial.*) a team of horses
a kennel, pack, cry, or †mute of hounds
a flight or swarm of insects
a mob or troop of kangaroos
a kindle of kittens
a bevy of ladies
a †desert of lapwing
an †exaltation or bevy of larks
a †leap of leopards
a pride of lions
a †tiding of magpies
a †sord or †sute (= suit) of mallard
a †richesse of martens
a †faith of merchants
a †labour of moles
a troop of monkeys
a †barren of mules
a †watch of nightingales
a †superfluity of nuns
a covey of partridges
a †muster of peacocks
a †malapertness (= impertinence) of pedlars
a rookery of penguins
a head or (*dial.*) nye of pheasants
a kit of pigeons flying together
a herd of pigs
a stand, wing, or †congregation of plovers
a rush or flight of pochards
a herd, pod, or school of porpoises
a †pity of prisoners
a covey of ptarmigan
a litter of pups
a bevy or drift of quail
a string of racehorses
an †unkindness of ravens
a bevy of roes
a parliament or †building of rooks
a hill of ruffs
a herd or rookery of seals; a pod (= small herd) of seals
a flock, herd, (*dial.*) drift or trip, or (*Austral.*) mob of sheep
a †dopping of sheldrake
a wisp or †walk of snipe
a †host of sparrows
a †murmuration of starlings
a flight of swallows
a game or herd of swans; a wedge of swans in the air
a herd of swine; a †sounder of tame swine, a †drift of wild swine
a †glozing (= fawning) of taverners
a †spring of teal
a bunch or knob of waterfowl
a school, herd, or gam of whales; a pod (= small school) of whales; a grind of bottle-nosed whales
a company or trip of widgeon
a bunch, trip, or plump of wildfowl; a knob (less than 30) of wildfowl
a pack or †rout of wolves
a gaggle of women (*derisive*)
a †fall of woodcock
a herd of wrens

Appendix 5 Names for Collectors

arctophile, arctophilist
lover or collector of teddy-bears

aurelian
collector of butterflies and moths

bibliophile
collector or connoisseur of books

cartophilist
collector of cigarette cards etc.

conchologist
expert in or collector of shells

copoclephile
collector of key-rings

deltiologist
collector of postcards

discophile
collector of gramophone records

exlibrist
collector of bookplates

iconophile
connoisseur or collector of book illustrations, engravings, etc.

lepidopterist
expert in or collector of butterflies and moths

notaphilist
collector of banknotes

numismatist
expert in or collector of coins

oologist
expert in or collector of birds' eggs

paroemiographer
writer or collector of proverbs

philatelist
collector of postage stamps

phillumenist
collector of matches, matchboxes, and books of matches

porcelainist
connoisseur or collector of porcelain

tegestologist
collector of beermats

virtuoso
connoisseur or collector of works of art or curios

Appendix 6 Selected English Proverbs

A

ABSENCE makes the heart grow fonder

He who is **ABSENT** is always in the wrong

ACCIDENTS will happen (in the best-regulated families)

There is no **ACCOUNTING** for tastes

ACTIONS speak louder than words

When **ADAM** delved and Eve span, who was then the gentleman?

As good be an **ADDLED** egg as an idle bird

ADVENTURES are to the adventurous

ADVERSITY makes strange bedfellows

AFTER a storm comes a calm

AFTER dinner rest a while, after supper walk a mile

ALL good things must come to an end

It takes **ALL** sorts to make a world

ALL things are possible with God

ALL things come to those who wait

Good **AMERICANS** when they die go to Paris

ANY port in a storm

If **ANYTHING** can go wrong, it will

An **APE**'s an ape, a varlet's a varlet, though they be clad in silk or scarlet

APPEARANCES are deceptive

APPETITE comes with eating

An **APPLE** a day keeps the doctor away

The **APPLE** never falls far from the tree

APRIL showers bring forth May flowers

An **ARMY** marches on its stomach

ART is long and life is short

ASK a silly question and you get a silly answer

ASK no questions and hear no lies

ATTACK is the best form of defence

B

A **BAD** excuse is better than none

BAD money drives out good

BAD news travels fast

A **BAD** penny always turns up .

A **BAD** workman blames his tools

As you **BAKE**, so shall you brew

A **BARKING** dog never bites

BARNABY bright, Barnaby bright, the longest day and the shortest night

BE what you would seem to be

BEAR and forbear

If you can't **BEAT** them, join them

BEAUTY draws with a single hair

BEAUTY is in the eye of the beholder

BEAUTY is only skin-deep

Where **BEES** are, there is honey

Set a **BEGGAR** on horseback, and he'll ride to the Devil

BEGGARS can't be choosers

BELIEVE nothing of what you hear, and only half of what you see

A **BELLOWING** cow soon forgets her calf

All's for the **BEST** in the best of all possible worlds

The **BEST** is the enemy of the good

The **BEST**-laid schemes of mice and men gang aft agley

The **BEST** of friends must part

The **BEST** of men are but men at best

The **BEST** things come in small packages

The **BEST** things in life are free

It is **BEST** to be on the safe side

BETTER a dinner of herbs than a stalled ox where hate is

BETTER a good cow than a cow of a good kind

BETTER be an old man's darling, than a young man's slave

BETTER be envied than pitied

BETTER be out of the world than out of the fashion

BETTER be safe than sorry

BETTER late than never

BETTER one house spoiled than two

The **BETTER** the day, the better the deed

BETTER the devil you know than the devil you don't know

It is **BETTER** to be born lucky than rich

It is **BETTER** to give than to receive

'Tis **BETTER** to have loved and lost, than never to have loved at all

It is **BETTER** to travel hopefully than to arrive

BETTER to wear out than to rust out

BETTER wed over the mixen than over the moor

BETWEEN two stools one falls to the ground

BIG fish eat little fish

BIG fleas have little fleas upon their backs to bite them, and little fleas have lesser fleas, and so *ad infinitum*

The **BIGGER** they are, the harder they fall

A **BIRD** in the hand is worth two in the bush

A **BIRD** never flew on one wing

There are no **BIRDS** in last year's nest

BIRDS in their little nests agree

BIRDS of a feather flock together

Little **BIRDS** that can sing and won't sing must be made to sing

A **BLEATING** sheep loses a bite

BLESSED is he who expects nothing, for he shall never be disappointed

BLESSINGS brighten as they take their flight

There's none so **BLIND** as those who will not see

When the **BLIND** lead the blind, both shall fall into the ditch

A **BLIND** man's wife needs no paint

You cannot get **BLOOD** from a stone

BLOOD is thicker than water

The **BLOOD** of the martyrs is the seed of the Church

BLOOD will have blood

BLOOD will tell

BLUE are the hills that are far away

You can't tell a **BOOK** by its cover

If you're **BORN** to be hanged then you'll never be drowned

You can take the **BOY** out of the country but you can't take the country out of the boy

Never send a **BOY** to do a man's job

Two **BOYS** are half a boy, and three boys are no boy at all

BOYS will be boys

BRAG is a good dog, but Holdfast is better

None but the **BRAVE** deserves the fair
BRAVE men lived before Agamemnon
The **BREAD** never falls but on its buttered side
What's **BRED** in the bone will come out in the flesh
BREVITY is the soul of wit
As you **BREW**, so shall you bake
You cannot make **BRICKS** without straw
Happy is the **BRIDE** that the sun shines on
Always a **BRIDESMAID**, never a bride
It is good to make a **BRIDGE** of gold to a flying enemy
If it ain't **BROKE**, don't fix it
Every **BULLET** has its billet
A **BULLY** is always a coward
A **BURNT** child dreads the fire
The **BUSIEST** men have the most leisure
BUSINESS before pleasure
BUY in the cheapest market and sell in the dearest
You **BUY** land, you buy stones; you buy meat, you buy bones
Let the **BUYER** beware
The **BUYER** has need of a hundred eyes, the seller of but one

C

CAESAR's wife must be above suspicion
He who **CAN**, does; he who cannot, teaches
If **CANDLEMAS** day be sunny and bright, winter will have another flight; if Candlemas day be cloudy with rain, winter is gone, and won't come again
CANDLEMAS day, put beans in the clay; put candles and candlesticks away
If the **CAP** fits, wear it
Where the **CARCASE** is, there shall the eagles be gathered together
CARE killed the cat
A **CARPENTER** is known by his chips
Ne'er **CAST** a clout till May be out
A **CAT** in gloves catches no mice
A **CAT** may look at a king
When the **CAT**'s away, the mice will play
The **CAT**, the rat, and Lovell the dog, rule all England under the hog
The **CAT** would eat fish, but would not wet her feet
You cannot **CATCH** old birds with chaff
CATCHING's before hanging
All **CATS** are grey in the dark
A **CHAIN** is no stronger than its weakest link
Don't **CHANGE** horses in mid-stream
A **CHANGE** is as good as a rest
CHARITY begins at home
CHARITY covers a multitude of sins
It is as **CHEAP** sitting as standing
CHEATS never prosper
A **CHERRY** year, a merry year; a plum year, a dumb year
Monday's **CHILD** is fair of face
The **CHILD** is the father of the man
CHILDREN and fools tell the truth
CHILDREN are certain cares, but uncertain comforts
CHILDREN should be seen and not heard
Never **CHOOSE** your women or your linen by candlelight
The **CHURCH** is an anvil which has worn out many hammers
CIRCUMSTANCES alter cases
A **CIVIL** question deserves a civil answer
CIVILITY costs nothing
CLEANLINESS is next to godliness
CLERGYMEN's sons always turn out badly
Hasty **CLIMBERS** have sudden falls
From **CLOGS** to clogs is only three generations
CLOTHES make the man
Every **CLOUD** has a silver lining
Let the **COBBLER** stick to his last
The **COBBLER** to his last and the gunner to his linstock
Every **COCK** will crow upon his own dunghill
COLD hands, warm heart
COMING events cast their shadows before
COMMON fame is seldom to blame
A man is known by the **COMPANY** he keeps
The **COMPANY** makes the feast
COMPARISONS are odious
He that **COMPLIES** against his will is of his own opinion still
CONFESS and be hanged
CONFESSION is good for the soul
CONSCIENCE makes cowards of us all
CONSTANT dropping wears away a stone
CORPORATIONS have neither bodies to be punished nor souls to be damned
COUNCILS of war never fight
Don't **COUNT** your chickens before they are hatched
In the **COUNTRY** of the blind, the one-eyed man is king
Happy is the **COUNTRY** which has no history
The **COURSE** of true love never did run smooth
Why buy a **COW** when milk is so cheap?
COWARDS die many times before their death
The **COWL** does not make the monk
A **CREAKING** door hangs longest
Give **CREDIT** where credit is due
Don't **CROSS** the bridge till you come to it
CROSSES are ladders that lead to heaven
Don't **CRY** before you're hurt
It is no use **CRYING** over spilt milk
He that will to **CUPAR** maun to Cupar
What can't be **CURED** must be endured
CURIOSITY killed the cat
CURSES, like chickens, come home to roost
The **CUSTOMER** is always right
Don't **CUT** off your nose to spite your face
CUT your coat according to your cloth

D

They that **DANCE** must pay the fiddler
The **DARKEST** hour is just before the dawn
As the **DAY** lengthens, so the cold strengthens

Be the **DAY** weary or be the day long, at last it ringeth to evensong

Let the **DEAD** bury the dead

DEAD men don't bite

DEAD men tell no tales

Blessed are the **DEAD** that the rain rains on

There's none so **DEAF** as those who will not hear

A **DEAF** husband and a blind wife are always a happy couple

DEATH is the great leveller

DEATH pays all debts

DELAYS are dangerous

DESPERATE diseases must have desperate remedies

The **DEVIL** can quote Scripture for his own ends

The **DEVIL** finds work for idle hands to do

Why should the **DEVIL** have all the best tunes?

The **DEVIL** is not so black as he is painted

The **DEVIL** looks after his own

The **DEVIL** makes his Christmas pies of lawyers' tongues and clerks' fingers

The **DEVIL**'s children have the Devil's luck

DEVIL take the hindmost

The **DEVIL** was sick, the Devil a saint would be; the Devil was well, the devil a saint was he!

DIAMOND cuts diamond

You can only **DIE** once

DIFFERENT strokes for different folks

The **DIFFICULT** is done at once, the impossible takes a little longer

DILIGENCE is the mother of good luck

Throw **DIRT** enough, and some will stick

DIRTY water will quench fire

DISCRETION is the better part of valour

DISTANCE lends enchantment to the view

DIVIDE and rule

DO as I say, not as I do

DO as you would be done by

DO right and fear no man

DO unto others as you would they should do unto you

The best **DOCTORS** are Dr Diet, Dr Quiet, and Dr Merryman

Give a **DOG** a bad name and hang him

DOG does not eat dog

Every **DOG** has his day

Every **DOG** is allowed one bite

The **DOG** returns to its vomit

A **DOG** that will fetch a bone will carry a bone

It's **DOGGED** as does it

DOGS bark, but the caravan goes on

What's **DONE** cannot be undone

A **DOOR** must either be shut or open

When in **DOUBT**, do nowt

Whosoever **DRAWS** his sword against the prince must throw the scabbard away

DREAM of a funeral and you hear of a marriage

DREAMS go by contraries

He that **DRINKS** beer, thinks beer

A **DRIPPING** June sets all in tune

DRIVE gently over the stones

You can **DRIVE** out Nature with a pitchfork, but she keeps on coming back

A **DROWNING** man will clutch at a straw

E

EAGLES don't catch flies

The **EARLY** bird catches the worm

The **EARLY** man never borrows from the late man

EARLY to bed and early to rise, makes a man healthy, wealthy, and wise

EAST, west, home's best

EASY come, easy go

EASY does it

You are what you **EAT**

We must **EAT** a peck of dirt before we die

He that would **EAT** the fruit must climb the tree

EAT to live, not live to eat

Don't put all your **EGGS** in one basket

Every **ELM** has its man

EMPTY sacks will never stand upright

EMPTY vessels make the most sound

The **END** crowns the work

The **END** justifies the means

ENGLAND is the paradise of women, the hell of horses, and the purgatory of servants

ENGLAND's difficulty is Ireland's opportunity

The **ENGLISH** are a nation of shop-keepers

One **ENGLISHMAN** can beat three Frenchmen

An **ENGLISHMAN**'s home is his castle

An **ENGLISHMAN**'s word is his bond

ENOUGH is as good as a feast

To **ERR** is human (to forgive divine)

EVERY little helps

EVERY man for himself

EVERY man for himself, and God for us all

EVERY man for himself, and the Devil take the hindmost

EVERY man has his price

EVERY man is the architect of his own fortune

EVERY man to his taste

EVERY man to his trade

EVERYBODY loves a lord

What **EVERYBODY** says must be true

EVERYBODY's business is nobody's business

EVERYTHING has an end

EVIL communications corrupt good manners

Never do **EVIL** that good may come of it

EVIL doers are evil dreaders

Of two **EVILS** choose the less

EXAMPLE is better than precept

The **EXCEPTION** proves the rule

There is an **EXCEPTION** to every rule

A fair **EXCHANGE** is no robbery

He who **EXCUSES**, accuses himself

What can you **EXPECT** from a pig but a grunt?

EXPERIENCE is the best teacher

EXPERIENCE is the father of wisdom

EXPERIENCE keeps a dear school

EXTREMES meet

What the **EYE** doesn't see, the heart doesn't grieve over

The **EYE** of a master does more work than both his hands

The **EYES** are the window of the soul

F

FACT is stranger than fiction

FACTS are stubborn things

FAINT heart never won fair lady

FAIR and softly goes far in a day

All's **FAIR** in love and war

FAIR play's a jewel

FAITH will move mountains

FAMILIARITY breeds contempt

The **FAMILY** that prays together stays together

FAR-FETCHED and dear-bought is good for ladies

Like **FATHER**, like son

A **FAULT** confessed is half redressed

FEAR the Greeks bearing gifts

FEBRUARY fill dyke, be it black or be it white

If in **FEBRUARY** there be no rain, 'tis neither good for hay nor grain

FEED a cold and starve a fever

The **FEMALE** of the species is more deadly than the male

FIELDS have eyes, and woods have ears

FIGHT fire with fire

He who **FIGHTS** and runs away, may live to fight another day

FINDERS keepers (losers weepers)

FINDINGS keepings

FINE feathers make fine birds

FINE words butter no parsnips

FINGERS were made before forks

FIRE is a good servant but a bad master

FIRST catch your hare

FIRST come, first served

The **FIRST** duty of a soldier is obedience

FIRST impressions are the most lasting

On the **FIRST** of March, the crows begin to search

It is the **FIRST** step that is difficult

FIRST things first

There is always a **FIRST** time

The **FISH** always stinks from the head downwards

FISH and guests stink after three days

There are as good **FISH** in the sea as ever came out of it

All is **FISH** that comes to the net

He that **FOLLOWS** freits, freits will follow him

A **FOOL** and his money are soon parted

A **FOOL** at forty is a fool indeed

There's no **FOOL** like an old fool

A **FOOL** may give a wise man counsel

FOOLS and bairns should never see half-done work

FOOLS ask questions that wise men cannot answer

FOOLS build houses and wise men live in them

FOOLS for luck

FOOLS rush in where angels fear to tread

FOREWARNED is forearmed

FORTUNE favours fools

FORTUNE favours the brave

FOUR eyes see more than two

There's no such thing as a **FREE** lunch

A **FRIEND** in need is a friend indeed

When all **FRUIT** fails, welcome haws

FULL cup, steady hand

It's ill speaking between a **FULL** man and a fasting

Out of the **FULLNESS** of the heart the mouth speaks

One **FUNERAL** makes many

When the **FURZE** is in bloom, my love's in tune

G

GARBAGE in, garbage out

It takes three **GENERATIONS** to make a gentleman

GENIUS is an infinite capacity for taking pains

Never look a **GIFT** horse in the mouth

GIVE and take is fair play

GIVE a thing, and take a thing, to wear the Devil's gold ring

GIVE the Devil his due

He **GIVES** twice who gives quickly

Those who live in **GLASS** houses shouldn't throw stones

All that **GLITTERS** is not gold

GO abroad and you'll hear news of home

GO further and fare worse

You cannot serve **GOD** and Mammon

Where **GOD** builds a church, the Devil will build a chapel

GOD helps them that help themselves

GOD made the country, and man made the town

GOD makes the back to the burden

GOD never sends mouths but He sends meat

GOD sends meat, but the Devil sends cooks

GOD's in his heaven; all's right with the world

GOD tempers the wind to the shorn lamb

Whom the **GODS** love die young

The **GODS** send nuts to those who have no teeth

Whom the **GODS** would destroy, they first make mad

He that **GOES** a-borrowing, goes a-sorrowing

What **GOES** around comes around

When the **GOING** gets tough, the tough get going

GOLD may be bought too dear

A **GOLDEN** key can open any door

If you can't be **GOOD**, be careful

A **GOOD** beginning makes a good ending

There's many a **GOOD** cock come out of a tattered bag

The **GOOD** die young

He is a **GOOD** dog who goes to church

GOOD fences make good neighbours

A **GOOD** horse cannot be of a bad colour

The **GOOD** is the enemy of the best

A **GOOD** Jack makes a good Jill

GOOD men are scarce

There's many a **GOOD** tune played on an old fiddle

One **GOOD** turn deserves another

GOOD wine needs no bush

When the **GORSE** is out of bloom, kissing's out of fashion

What is **GOT** over the Devil's back is spent under his belly

While the **GRASS** grows, the steed starves

The **GRASS** is always greener on the other side of the fence

A **GREAT** book is a great evil

GREAT minds think alike

GREAT oaks from little acorns grow

The **GREATER** the sinner, the greater the saint

The **GREATER** the truth, the greater the libel

When **GREEK** meets Greek, then comes the tug of war

A **GREEN** Yule makes a fat churchyard

The **GREY** mare is the better horse

All is **GRIST** that comes to the mill

A **GUILTY** conscience needs no accuser

H

What you've never **HAD** you never miss

HALF a loaf is better than no bread

The **HALF** is better than the whole

One **HALF** of the world does not know how the other half lives

HALF the truth is often a whole lie

Don't **HALLOO** till you are out of the wood

When all you have is a **HAMMER**, everything looks like a nail

One **HAND** for oneself and one for the ship

The **HAND** that rocks the cradle rules the world

One **HAND** washes the other

HANDSOME is as handsome does

HANG a thief when he's young, and he'll no' steal when he's old

One might as well be **HANGED** for a sheep as a lamb

HANGING and wiving go by destiny

If you would be **HAPPY** for a week take a wife; if you would be happy for a month kill a pig; but if you would be happy all your life plant a garden

Call no man **HAPPY** till he dies

HARD cases make bad law

HARD words break no bones

HASTE is from the Devil

More **HASTE**, less speed

HASTE makes waste

Make **HASTE** slowly

What you **HAVE**, hold

You cannot **HAVE** your cake and eat it

HAWKS will not pick out hawks' eyes

HEAR all, see all, say nowt, tak' all, keep all, gie nowt, and if tha ever does owt for nowt do it for thysen

If you don't like the **HEAT**, get out of the kitchen

HEAVEN protects children, sailors, and drunken men

HELL hath no fury like a woman scorned

Every **HERRING** must hang by its own gill

He who **HESITATES** is lost

Those who **HIDE** can find

The **HIGHER** the monkey climbs the more he shows his tail

HISTORY repeats itself

HOME is home, as the Devil said when he found himself in the Court of Session

HOME is home though it's never so homely

HOME is where the heart is

HOMER sometimes nods

HONESTY is the best policy

HONEY catches more flies than vinegar

There is **HONOUR** among thieves

The post of **HONOUR** is the post of danger

HOPE deferred makes the heart sick

HOPE for the best and prepare for the worst

HOPE is a good breakfast but a bad supper

HOPE springs eternal

If it were not for **HOPE**, the heart would break

You can take a **HORSE** to the water, but you can't make him drink

HORSES for courses

One **HOUR**'s sleep before midnight is worth two after

When **HOUSE** and land are gone and spent, then learning is most excellent

A **HOUSE** divided cannot stand

HUNGER drives the wolf out of the wood

HUNGER is the best sauce

A **HUNGRY** man is an angry man

HURRY no man's cattle

The **HUSBAND** is always the last to know

I

An **IDLE** brain is the Devil's workshop

IDLE people have the least leisure

IDLENESS is the root of all evil

If **IFS** and ands were pots and pans, there'd be no work for tinkers' hands

Where **IGNORANCE** is bliss, 'tis folly to be wise

IGNORANCE of the law is no excuse for breaking it

It's an **ILL** bird that fouls its own nest

ILL gotten goods never thrive

He that has an **ILL** name is half hanged

It's **ILL** waiting for dead men's shoes

ILL weeds grow apace

It's an **ILL** wind that blows nobody any good

IMITATION is the sincerest form of flattery

IN for a penny, in for a pound

J

Every **JACK** has his Jill

JACK is as good as his master

JAM tomorrow and jam yesterday, but never jam today

JOUK and let the jaw go by

JOVE but laughs at lovers' perjury

No one should be **JUDGE** in his own cause

JUDGE not, that ye be not judged

Be **JUST** before you're generous

K

Why **KEEP** a dog and bark yourself?

KEEP a thing seven years and you'll always find a use for it

KEEP no more cats than will catch mice

KEEP your own fish-guts for your own sea-maws

KEEP your shop and your shop will keep you

KILLING no murder

The **KING** can do no wrong

A **KING**'s chaff is worth more than other men's corn

KINGS have long arms

KISSING goes by favour

To **KNOW** all is to forgive all

You should **KNOW** a man seven years before you stir his fire

What you don't **KNOW** can't hurt you

KNOW thyself

You never **KNOW** what you can do till you try

KNOWLEDGE is power

L

The **LABOURER** is worthy of his hire

Every **LAND** has its own law

The **LAST** drop makes the cup run over

It is the **LAST** straw that breaks the camel's back

LAUGH and the world laughs with you; weep and you weep alone

Let them **LAUGH** that win

He **LAUGHS** best who laughs last

He who **LAUGHS** last, laughs longest

One **LAW** for the rich and another for the poor

A man who is his own **LAWYER** has a fool for his client

LAY-OVERS for meddlers

LEARNING is better than house and land

LEAST said, soonest mended

There is nothing like **LEATHER**

LEND your money and lose your friend

LENGTH begets loathing

The **LEOPARD** does not change his spots

LESS is more

LET well alone

A **LIAR** ought to have a good memory

If you **LIE** down with dogs, you will get up with fleas

LIFE begins at forty

LIFE isn't all beer and skittles

While there's **LIFE** there's hope

LIGHT come, light go

LIGHTNING never strikes the same place twice

LIKE breeds like

LIKE will to like

LISTENERS never hear any good of themselves

There is no **LITTLE** enemy

LITTLE fish are sweet

A **LITTLE** knowledge is a dangerous thing

LITTLE leaks sink the ship

LITTLE pitchers have large ears

A **LITTLE** pot is soon hot

LITTLE strokes fell great oaks

LITTLE thieves are hanged, but great ones escape

LITTLE things please little minds

LIVE and learn

LIVE and let live

If you want to **LIVE** and thrive, let the spider run alive

A **LIVE** dog is better than a dead lion

They that **LIVE** longest, see most

Come **LIVE** with me and you'll know me

He who **LIVES** by the sword dies by the sword

He that **LIVES** in hope dances to an ill tune

He **LIVES** long who lives well

LONG and lazy, little and loud; fat and fulsome, pretty and proud

LONG foretold, long last; short notice, soon past

It is a **LONG** lane that has no turning

The **LONGEST** way round is the shortest way home

LOOK before you leap

LOOKERS-ON see most of the game

What you **LOSE** on the swings you gain on the roundabouts

You cannot **LOSE** what you never had

One man's **LOSS** is another man's gain

There's no great **LOSS** without some gain

LOVE and a cough cannot be hid

One cannot **LOVE** and be wise

LOVE begets love

LOVE is blind

LOVE laughs at locksmiths

LOVE makes the world go round

LOVE me little, love me long

LOVE me, love my dog

LOVE will find a way

There is **LUCK** in leisure

There is **LUCK** in odd numbers

LUCKY at cards, unlucky in love

M

Where **MACGREGOR** sits is the head of the table

Dont' get **MAD**, get even

MAKE hay while the sun shines

As you **MAKE** your bed, so you must lie upon it

MAN cannot live by bread alone

Whatever **MAN** has done, man may do

A **MAN** is as old as he feels, and a woman as old as she looks

MAN is the measure of all things

MAN proposes, God disposes

MAN's extremity is God's opportunity

The **MAN** who is born in a stable is not a horse

What **MANCHESTER** says today, the rest of England says tomorrow

MANNERS maketh man

MANY a little makes a mickle

MANY a mickle makes a muckle

There's **MANY** a slip 'twixt cup and lip

MANY are called but few are chosen

MANY hands make light work

MARCH comes in like a lion, and goes out like a lamb

MARRIAGE is a lottery

There goes more to **MARRIAGE** than four bare legs in a bed

MARRIAGES are made in heaven

Never **MARRY** for money, but marry where money is

MARRY in haste and repent at leisure

MARRY in May, rue for aye

Like **MASTER**, like man

MAY chickens come cheeping

There is **MEASURE** in all things

MEAT and mass never hindered man

One man's **MEAT** is another man's poison

Do not **MEET** troubles half-way

So many **MEN**, so many opinions

It is **MERRY** in hall when beards wag all

MIGHT is right

The **MILL** cannot grind with the water that is past

The **MILLS** of God grind slowly, yet they grind exceeding small

The age of **MIRACLES** is past

MISERY loves company

MISFORTUNES never come singly

A **MISS** is as good as a mile

You never **MISS** the water till the well runs dry

If you don't make **MISTAKES** you don't make anything

So many **MISTS** in March, so many frosts in May

MODERATION in all things

MONEY has no smell

MONEY isn't everything

MONEY is power

MONEY is the root of all evil

MONEY makes a man

MONEY makes money

MONEY makes the mare to go

MONEY talks

A **MONEYLESS** man goes fast through the market

MORE people know Tom Fool than Tom Fool knows

The **MORE** the merrier

The **MORE** you get, the more you want

MORNING dreams come true

Like **MOTHER**, like daughter

The **MOTHER** of mischief is no bigger than a midge's wing

If the **MOUNTAIN** will not come to Mahomet, Mahomet must go to the mountain

A **MOUSE** may help a lion

Out of the **MOUTHS** of babes—

MUCH cry and little wool

MUCH would have more

Where there's **MUCK** there's brass

MURDER will out

What **MUST** be, must be

N

NATURE abhors a vacuum

NEAR is my kirtle, but nearer is my smock

NEAR is my shirt, but nearer is my skin

The **NEARER** the bone, the sweeter the meat

The **NEARER** the church, the farther from God

NECESSITY is the mother of invention

NECESSITY knows no law

NEEDS must when the Devil drives

What a **NEIGHBOUR** gets is not lost

In vain the **NET** is spread in the sight of the bird

If you gently touch a **NETTLE** it'll sting you for your pains; grasp it like a lad of mettle, an' as soft as silk remains

NEVER is a long time

It is **NEVER** too late to learn

It is **NEVER** too late to mend

NEVER too old to learn

NEW brooms sweep clean

What is **NEW** cannot be true

NEW lords, new laws

You can't put **NEW** wine in old bottles

NIGHT brings counsel

NINE tailors make a man

NO cure, no pay

NO man can serve two masters

NO man is a hero to his valet

NO moon, no man

NO names, no pack-drill

NO news is good news

NO pain, no gain

NO penny, no paternoster

A **NOD**'s as good as a wink to a blind horse

NOTHING comes of nothing

NOTHING for nothing

NOTHING is certain but death and taxes

NOTHING is certain but the unforeseen

There is **NOTHING** lost by civility

There is **NOTHING** new under the sun

NOTHING should be done in haste but gripping a flea

NOTHING so bad but it might have been worse

NOTHING so bold as a blind mare

There is **NOTHING** so good for the inside of a man as the outside of a horse

NOTHING succeeds like success

NOTHING venture, nothing gain

NOTHING venture, nothing have

There's **NOWT** so queer as folk

O

When the **OAK** is before the ash, then you will only get a splash; when the ash is before the oak, then you may expect a soak

Beware of an **OAK**, it draws the stroke; avoid an ash, it counts the flash; creep under the thorn, it can save you from harm

He that cannot **OBEY** cannot command

OBEY orders, if you break owners

It is best to be **OFF** with the old love before you are on with the new

OFFENDERS never pardon

OLD habits die hard

You cannot put an **OLD** head on young shoulders

OLD sins cast long shadows

OLD soldiers never die

You cannot make an **OMELETTE** without breaking eggs

ONCE a —, always a —

ONCE a priest, always a priest

ONCE a whore, always a whore

ONCE bitten, twice shy

When **ONE** door shuts, another opens

ONE for sorrow, two for mirth; three for a wedding, four for a birth

ONE for the mouse, one for the crow, one to rot, one to grow

ONE nail drives out another

ONE year's seeding makes seven years' weeding

The **OPERA** isn't over till the fat lady sings

OPPORTUNITY makes a thief

OPPORTUNITY never knocks twice at any man's door

OTHER times, other manners

An **OUNCE** of practice is worth a pound of precept

OUT of debt, out of danger

OUT of sight, out of mind

P

It is the **PACE** that kills

PARSLEY seed goes nine times to the Devil

Things **PAST** cannot be recalled

PATIENCE is a virtue

PAY beforehand was never well served

He that cannot **PAY**, let him pray

If you **PAY** peanuts, you get monkeys

He who **PAYS** the piper calls the tune

You **PAYS** your money and you takes your choice

If you want **PEACE**, you must prepare for war

Do not throw **PEARLS** to swine

A **PECK** of March dust is worth a king's ransom

The **PEN** is mightier than the sword

Take care of the **PENCE** and the pounds will take care of themselves

A **PENNY** saved is a penny earned

PENNY wise and pound foolish

Like **PEOPLE**, like priest

PHYSICIAN, heal thyself

One **PICTURE** is worth ten thousand words

Every **PICTURE** tells a story

See a **PIN** and pick it up, all the day you'll have good luck; see a pin and let it lie, bad luck you'll have all the day

The **PITCHER** will go to the well once too often

PITY is akin to love

A **PLACE** for everything, and everything in its place

There's no **PLACE** like home

Those who **PLAY** at bowls must look out for rubbers

If you **PLAY** with fire you get burnt

You can't **PLEASE** everyone

PLEASE your eye and plague your heart

An old **POACHER** makes the best gamekeeper

POLITICS makes strange bedfellows

It is a **POOR** dog that's not worth whistling for

It is a **POOR** heart that never rejoices

POSSESSION is nine points of the law

A **POSTERN** door makes a thief

When **POVERTY** comes in at the door, love flies out of the window

POVERTY is no disgrace, but it is a great inconvenience

POVERTY is not a crime

POWER corrupts

PRACTICE makes perfect

PRACTISE what you preach

PRAISE the child, and you make love to the mother

PREVENTION is better than cure

PRIDE feels no pain

PRIDE goes before a fall

PROCRASTINATION is the thief of time

PROMISES, like pie-crust, are made to be broken

The **PROOF** of the pudding is in the eating

A **PROPHET** is not without honour save in his own country

PROVIDENCE is always on the side of the big battalions

Any **PUBLICITY** is good publicity

It is easier to **PULL** down than to build up

PUNCTUALITY is the politeness of princes

PUNCTUALITY is the soul of business

To the **PURE** all things are pure

Never **PUT** off till tomorrow what you can do today

Q

The **QUARREL** of lovers is the renewal of love

You cannot get a **QUART** into a pint pot

QUICKLY come, quickly go

R

The **RACE** is not to the swift, nor the battle to the strong

RAIN before seven, fine before eleven

It never **RAINS** but it pours

It is easier to **RAISE** the Devil than to lay him

There is **REASON** in the roasting of eggs

If there were no **RECEIVERS**, there would be no thieves

RED sky at night, shepherd's delight; red sky in the morning, shepherd's warning

A **REED** before the wind lives on, while mighty oaks do fall

There is a **REMEDY** for everything except death

REVENGE is a dish that can be eaten cold

REVENGE is sweet

REVOLUTIONS are not made with rose-water

The **RICH** man has his ice in the summer and the poor man gets his in the winter

If you can't **RIDE** two horses at once, you shouldn't be in the circus

He who **RIDES** a tiger is afraid to dismount

A **RISING** tide lifts all boats

The **ROAD** to hell is paved with good intentions

All **ROADS** lead to Rome

The **ROBIN** and the wren are God's cock and hen; the martin and the swallow are God's mate and marrow

ROBIN Hood could brave all weathers but a thaw wind

A **ROLLING** stone gathers no moss

When in **ROME**, do as the Romans do

ROME was not built in a day

There is always **ROOM** at the top

Give a man **ROPE** enough and he will hang himself

Never mention **ROPE** in the house of a man who has been hanged

The **ROTTEN** apple injures its neighbour

There is no **ROYAL** road to learning

Who won't be **RULED** by the rudder must be ruled by the rock

If you **RUN** after two hares you will catch neither

You cannot **RUN** with the hare and hunt with the hounds

S

SAFE bind, safe find

There is **SAFETY** in numbers

If **SAINT** Paul's day be fair and clear, it will betide a happy year

SAINT Swithun's day, if thou be fair, for forty days it will remain; Saint Swithun's day, if thou bring rain, for forty days it will remain

On **SAINT** Thomas the Divine kill all turkeys, geese, and swine.

Help you to **SALT**, help you to sorrow

What's **SAUCE** for the goose is sauce for the gander

SAVE us from our friends

Who **SAYS** A must say B

SCRATCH a Russian and you find a Tartar

He that would go to **SEA** for pleasure, would go to hell for a pastime

The **SEA** refuses no river

SECOND thoughts are best

What you **SEE** is what you get

SEE no evil, hear no evil, speak no evil

Good **SEED** makes a good crop

SEEING is believing

SEEK and ye shall find

SELF-praise is no recommendation

SELF-preservation is the first law of nature

SEPTEMBER blow soft, till the fruit's in the loft

If you would be well **SERVED**, serve yourself

The **SHARPER** the storm, the sooner it's over

You cannot **SHIFT** an old tree without it dying

Do not spoil the **SHIP** for a ha'porth of tar

From **SHIRTSLEEVES** to shirtsleeves in three generations

If the **SHOE** fits, wear it

The **SHOEMAKER**'s son always goes barefoot

A **SHORT** horse is soon curried

SHORT reckonings make long friends

SHROUDS have no pockets

A **SHUT** mouth catches no flies

SILENCE is a woman's best garment

SILENCE is golden

SILENCE means consent

You can't make a **SILK** purse out of a sow's ear

It's a **SIN** to steal a pin

SING before breakfast, cry before night

It is ill **SITTING** at Rome and striving with the Pope

SIX hours' sleep for a man, seven for a woman, and eight for a fool

If the **SKY** falls we shall catch larks

Let **SLEEPING** dogs lie

A **SLICE** off a cut loaf isn't missed

SLOW but sure

SMALL choice in rotten apples

SMALL is beautiful

No **SMOKE** without fire

A **SOFT** answer turneth away wrath

SOFTLY, softly, catchee monkey

What the **SOLDIER** said isn't evidence

If you're not part of the **SOLUTION**, you're part of the problem

You don't get **SOMETHING** for nothing

SOMETHING is better than nothing

My **SON** is my son till he gets him a wife, but my daughter's my daugher all the days of her life

SOON ripe, soon rotten

The **SOONER** begun, the sooner done

SOW dry and set wet

A **SOW** may whistle, though it has an ill mouth for it

As you **SOW**, so you reap

They that **SOW** the wind shall reap the whirlwind

SPARE at the spigot, and let out at the bung-hole

SPARE the rod and spoil the child

SPARE well and have to spend

Never **SPEAK** ill of the dead

SPEAK not of my debts unless you mean to pay them

Everyone **SPEAKS** well of the bridge which carries him over

If you don't **SPECULATE**, you can't accumulate

SPEECH is silver, but silence is golden

What you **SPEND**, you have

It is not **SPRING** until you can plant your foot upon twelve daisies

The **SQUEAKING** wheel gets the grease

It is too late to shut the **STABLE**-door after the horse has bolted

One man may **STEAL** a horse, while another may not look over a hedge

One **STEP** at a time

A **STERN** chase is a long chase

It is easy to find a **STICK** to beat a dog

STICKS and stones may break my bones, but words will never hurt me

A **STILL** tongue makes a wise head

STILL waters run deep

The more you **STIR** it the worse it stinks

A **STITCH** in time saves nine

STOLEN fruit is sweet

STOLEN waters are sweet

STONE-dead hath no fellow

One **STORY** is good till another is told

Put a **STOUT** heart to a stey brae

STRAWS tell which way the wind blows

A **STREAM** cannot rise above its source

STRETCH your arm no further than your sleeve will reach

Everyone **STRETCHES** his legs according to the length of his coverlet

STRIKE while the iron is hot

The **STYLE** is the man

From the **SUBLIME** to the ridiculous is only a step

If at first you don't **SUCCEED**, try, try, try again

SUCCESS has many fathers, while failure is an orphan

Never give a **SUCKER** an even break

SUE a beggar and catch a louse

SUFFICIENT unto the day is the evil thereof

Never let the **SUN** go down on your anger

The **SUN** loses nothing by shining into a puddle

He who **SUPS** with the Devil should have a long spoon

SUSSEX won't be druv

One **SWALLOW** does not make a summer

It is idle to **SWALLOW** the cow and choke on the tail

A **SWARM** in May is worth a load of hay; a swarm in June is worth a silver spoon; but a swarm in July is not worth a fly

If every man would **SWEEP** his own door-step the city would soon be clean

From the **SWEETEST** wine, the tartest vinegar

T

TAKE the goods the gods provide

A **TALE** never loses in the telling

Never tell **TALES** out of school

TALK is cheap

TALK of the Devil, and he is bound to appear

TASTES differ

You can't **TEACH** an old dog new tricks

Don't **TEACH** your grandmother to suck eggs

TELL the truth and shame the Devil

Set a **THIEF** to catch a thief

When **THIEVES** fall out, honest men come by their own

If a **THING**'s worth doing, it's worth doing well

When **THINGS** are at the worst they begin to mend

THINK first and speak afterwards

THIRD time lucky

The **THIRD** time pays for all

THOUGHT is free

THREATENED men live long

THREE may keep a secret, if two of them are dead

THREE removals are as bad as a fire

THREE things are not to be trusted: a cow's horn, a dog's tooth, and a horse's hoof

THRIFT is a great revenue

He that will **THRIVE** must first ask his wife

Don't **THROW** out your dirty water until you get in fresh

Don't **THROW** the baby out with the bathwater

There is a **TIME** and place for everything

TIME and tide wait for no man

TIME flies

There is a **TIME** for everything

TIME is a great healer

TIME is money

No **TIME** like the present

TIME will tell

TIME works wonders

TIMES change and we with time

TODAY you; tomorrow me

TOMORROW is another day

TOMORROW never comes

The **TONGUE** always returns to the sore tooth

TOO many cooks spoil the broth

You can have **TOO** much of a good thing

He that **TOUCHES** pitch shall be defiled

TRADE follows the flag

TRAVEL broadens the mind

He **TRAVELS** fastest who travels alone

As a **TREE** falls, so shall it lie

The **TREE** is known by its fruit

There are **TRICKS** in every trade

A **TROUBLE** shared is a trouble halved

Never **TROUBLE** trouble till trouble troubles you

Many a **TRUE** word is spoken in jest

Put your **TRUST** in God, and keep your powder dry

There is **TRUTH** in wine

TRUTH is stranger than fiction

TRUTH lies at the bottom of a well

TRUTH will out

Every **TUB** must stand on its own bottom

TURKEY, heresy, hops, and beer came into England all in one year

TURN about is fair play

As the **TWIG** is bent, so is the tree inclined

TWO blacks don't make a white

While **TWO** dogs are fighting for a bone, a third runs away with it

TWO heads are better than one

TWO is company, but three is none

TWO of a trade never agree

If **TWO** ride on a horse, one must ride behind

There are **TWO** sides to every question

It takes **TWO** to make a bargain

It takes **TWO** to make a quarrel

It takes **TWO** to tango

TWO wrongs don't make a right

U

The **UNEXPECTED** always happens

UNION is strength

UNITED we stand, divided we fall

What goes **UP** must come down

V

VARIETY is the spice of life

VIRTUE is its own reward

The **VOICE** of the people is the voice of God

One **VOLUNTEER** is worth two pressed men

W

We must learn to **WALK** before we can run

WALLS have ears

WALNUTS and pears you plant for your heirs

If you **WANT** a thing done well, do it yourself

For **WANT** of a nail the shoe was lost; for want of a shoe the horse was lost; and for want of a horse the man was lost

WANTON kittens make sober cats

One does not **WASH** one's dirty linen in public

WASTE not, want not

A **WATCHED** pot never boils

Don't go near the **WATER** until you learn how to swim

The **WAY** to a man's heart is through his stomach

There are more **WAYS** of killing a cat than choking it with cream

There are more **WAYS** of killing a dog than choking it with butter

There are more **WAYS** of killing a dog than hanging it

The **WEAKEST** go to the wall

One **WEDDING** brings another

WEDLOCK is a padlock

WELL begun is half done

All's **WELL** that ends well

A **WHISTLING** woman and a crowing hen are neither fit for God nor men

One **WHITE** foot, buy him; two white feet, try him; three white feet, look well about him; four white feet, go without him

A **WILFUL** man must have his way

WILFUL waste makes woeful want

He that **WILL** not when he may, when he will he shall have nay

Where there's a **WILL**, there's a way

He who **WILLS** the end, wills the means

You **WIN** a few, you lose a few

You can't **WIN** them all

When the **WIND** is in the east, 'tis neither good for man nor beast

When the **WINE** is in, the wit is out

WINTER never rots in the sky

It is easy to be **WISE** after the event

It is a **WISE** child that knows its own father

The **WISH** is father to the thought

If **WISHES** were horses, beggars would ride

A **WOMAN**, a dog, and a walnut tree, the more you beat them the better they be

A **WOMAN** and a ship ever want mending

A **WOMAN**'s place is in the home

A **WOMAN**'s work is never done

WONDERS will never cease

Happy's the **WOOING** that is not long a-doing

Many go out for **WOOL** and come home shorn

A **WORD** to the wise is enough

All **WORK** and no play makes Jack a dull boy

WORK expands so as to fill the time available

It is not **WORK** that kills, but worry

If you won't **WORK** you shan't eat

Even a **WORM** will turn

The **WORTH** of a thing is what it will bring

Y

YORKSHIRE born and Yorkshire bred, strong in the arm and weak in the head

YOUNG folks think old folks to be fools, but old folks know young folks to be fools

A **YOUNG** man married is a young man marred

YOUNG men may die, but old men must die

YOUNG saint, old devil

YOUTH must be served

Fossil history

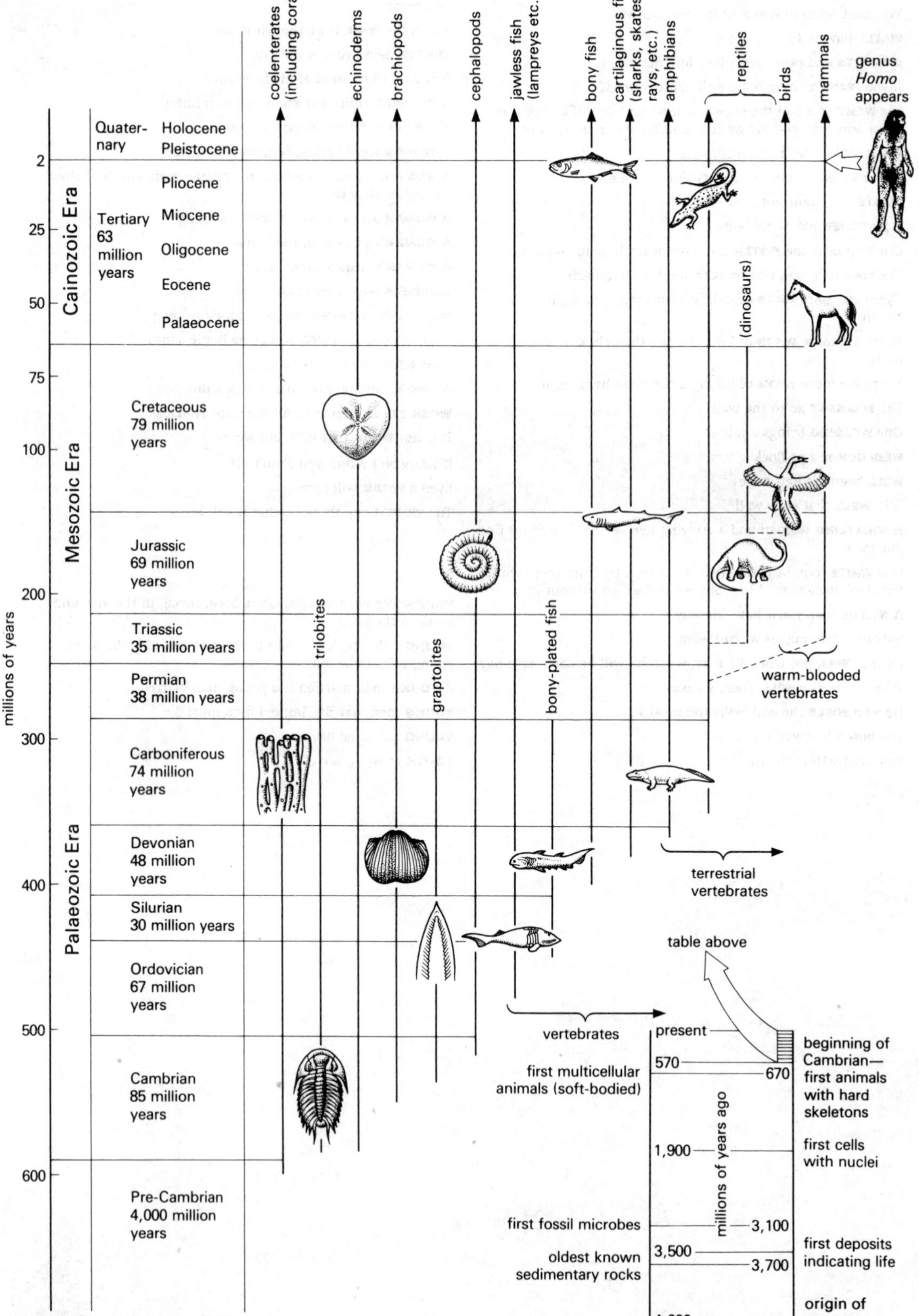

(note: all figures are approximate and are based on present evidence)

Time-scale of events in the Earth's history

Appendix 8 Weights, Measures, and Notations

Note. The conversion factors are not exact unless so marked. They are given only to the accuracy likely to be needed in everyday calculations.

1. British and American, with metric equivalents

Linear measure

1 inch	= 25.4 millimetres exactly
1 foot = 12 inches	= 0.3048 metre exactly
1 yard = 3 feet	= 0.9144 metre exactly
1 (statute) mile = 1,760 yards	= 1.609 kilometres

Square measure

1 square inch	= 6.45 sq. centimetres
1 square foot = 144 sq. in.	= 9.29 sq. decimetres
1 square yard = 9 sq. ft.	= 0.836 sq. metre
1 acre = 4,840 sq. yd.	= 0.405 hectare
1 square mile = 640 acres	= 259 hectares

Cubic measure

1 cubic inch	= 16.4 cu. centimetres
1 cubic foot = 1,728 cu. in.	= 0.0283 cu. metre
1 cubic yard = 27 cu. ft.	= 0.765 cu. metre

Capacity measure

British

1 pint = 20 fluid oz. = 34.68 cu. in.	= 0.568 litre
1 quart = 2 pints	= 1.136 litres
1 gallon = 4 quarts	= 4.546 litres
1 peck = 2 gallons	= 9.092 litres
1 bushel = 4 pecks	= 36.4 litres
1 quarter = 8 bushels	= 2.91 hectolitres

American dry

1 pint = 33.60 cu. in.	= 0.550 litre
1 quart = 2 pints	= 1.101 litres
1 peck = 8 quarts	= 8.81 litres
1 bushel = 4 pecks	= 35.3 litres

American liquid

1 pint = 16 fluid oz. = 28.88 cu. in.	= 0.473 litre
1 quart = 2 pints	= 0.946 litre
1 gallon = 4 quarts	= 3.785 litres

Avoirdupois weight

1 grain	= 0.065 gram
1 dram	= 1.772 grams
1 ounce = 16 drams	= 28.35 grams
1 pound = 16 ounces = 7,000 grains	= 0.4536 kilogram (0.45359237 exactly)
1 stone = 14 pounds	= 6.35 kilograms
1 quarter = 2 stones	= 12.70 kilograms
1 hundredweight = 4 quarters	= 50.80 kilograms
1 (long) ton = 20 hundredweight	= 1.016 tonnes
1 short ton = 2,000 pounds	= 0.907 tonne

2. Metric, with British equivalents

Linear measure

1 millimetre	= 0.039 inch
1 centimetre = 10 mm	= 0.394 inch
1 decimetre = 10 cm	= 3.94 inches
1 metre = 10 dm	= 1.094 yards
1 decametre = 10 m	= 10.94 yards
1 hectometre = 100 m	= 109.4 yards
1 kilometre = 1,000 m	= 0.6214 mile

Square measure

1 square centimetre	= 0.155 sq. inch
1 square metre = 10,000 sq. cm	= 1.196 sq. yards
1 are = 100 sq. metres	= 119.6 sq. yards
1 hectare = 100 ares	= 2.471 acres
1 square kilometre = 100 hectares	= 0.386 sq. mile

Cubic measure

1 cubic centimetre	= 0.061 cu. inch
1 cubic metre = 1,000,000 cu. cm	= 1.308 cu. yards

Capacity measure

1 millilitre	= 0.002 pint (British)
1 centilitre = 10 ml	= 0.018 pint
1 decilitre = 10 cl	= 0.176 pint
1 litre = 10 dl	= 1.76 pints
1 decalitre = 10 l	= 2.20 gallons
1 hectolitre = 100 l	= 2.75 bushels
1 kilolitre = 1,000 l	= 3.44 quarters

Weight

1 milligram	= 0.015 grain
1 centigram = 10 mg	= 0.154 grain
1 decigram = 10 cg	= 1.543 grain
1 gram = 10 dg	= 15.43 grain
1 decagram = 10 g	= 5.64 drams
1 hectogram = 100 g	= 3.527 ounces
1 kilogram = 1,000 g	= 2.205 pounds
1 tonne (metric ton) = 1,000 kg	= 0.984 (long) ton

3. Power notation

This expresses concisely any power of ten (any number that is composed of factors 10), and is sometimes used in the dictionary. 10^2 or ten squared = 10×10 = 100; 10^3 or ten cubed = $10 \times 10 \times 10$ = 1,000. Similarly, 10^4 = 10,000 and 10^{10} = 1 followed by ten noughts = 10,000,000,000. Proceeding in the opposite direction, dividing by ten and subtracting one from the index, we have $10^2 = 100$, $10^1 = 10$, $10^0 = 1$, $10^{-1} = \frac{1}{10}$, $10^{-2} = \frac{1}{100}$, and so on; $10^{-10} = 1/10^{10}$ = 1/10,000,000,000.

4. Temperature

Fahrenheit: Water boils (under standard conditions) at 212° and freezes at 32°.
Celsius or Centigrade: Water boils at 100° and freezes at 0°.
Kelvin: Water boils at 373.15 K and freezes at 273.15 K.

Celsius	*Fahrenheit*
−17. 8°	0°
−10°	14°
0°	32°
10°	50°
20°	68°
30°	86°
40°	104°
50°	122°
60°	140°
70°	158°
80°	176°
90°	194°
100°	212°

To convert Celsius into Fahrenheit: multiply by 9, divide by 5, and add 32.
To convert Fahrenheit into Celsius: subtract 32, multiply by 5, and divide by 9.

5. Metric prefixes

	Abbreviation or Symbol	*Factor*
deca-	da	10
hecto-	h	10^{2}
kilo-	k	10^{3}
mega-	M	10^{6}
giga-	G	10^{9}
tera-	T	10^{12}
peta-	P	10^{15}
exa-	E	10^{18}
deci-	d	10^{-1}
centi-	c	10^{-2}
milli-	m	10^{-3}
micro-	μ	10^{-6}
nano-	n	10^{-9}
pico-	p	10^{-12}
femto-	f	10^{-15}
atto-	a	10^{-18}

Pronunciations and derivations of these are given at their alphabetical places in the dictionary. They may be applied to any units of the metric system: hectogram (abbr. hg) = 100 grams; kilowatt (abbr. kW) = 1,000 watts; megahertz (MHz) = 1 million hertz; centimetre (cm) = $\frac{1}{100}$ metre; microvolt (μV) = one millionth of a volt; picofarad (pF) = 10^{-12} farad, and are sometimes applied to other units (megabit, microinch).

6. Chemical notation

The symbol for a molecule (such as H_2O, CH_4, H_2SO_4) shows the symbols for the elements contained in it (C = carbon, H = hydrogen, etc.), followed by a subscript numeral denoting the number of atoms of each element in the molecule where this number is more than one. For example, the water molecule (H_2O) contains two atoms of hydrogen and one of oxygen.

7. SI units

Base units

Physical quantity	*Name*	*Abbreviation or Symbol*
length	metre	m
mass	kilogram	kg
time	second	s
electric current	ampere	A
temperature	kelvin	K
amount of substance	mole	mol
luminous intensity	candela	cd

Supplementary units

Physical quantity	*Name*	*Abbreviation or Symbol*
plane angle	radian	rad
solid angle	steradian	sr

Derived units with special names

Physical quantity	*Name*	*Abbreviation or Symbol*
frequency	hertz	Hz
energy	joule	J
force	newton	N
power	watt	W
pressure	pascal	Pa
electric charge	coulomb	C
electromotive force	volt	V
electric resistance	ohm	Ω
electric conductance	siemens	S
electric capacitance	farad	F
magnetic flux	weber	Wb
inductance	henry	H
magnetic flux density	tesla	T
luminous flux	lumen	lm
illumination	lux	lx

8. Binary system

Only two units (0 and 1) are used, and the position of each unit indicates a power of two.

One to ten written in binary form:

	eights (2^3)	*fours* (2^2)	*twos* (2^1)	*one*
1				1
2			1	0
3			1	1
4		1	0	0
5		1	0	1
6		1	1	0
7		1	1	1
8	1	0	0	0
9	1	0	0	1
10	1	0	1	0

i.e. ten is written as 1010 (2^3+0+2^1+0); one hundred is written as 1100100 ($2^6+2^5+0+0+2^2+0+0$)

Appendix 9 Shapes and Forms in Mathematics

Circles and cones

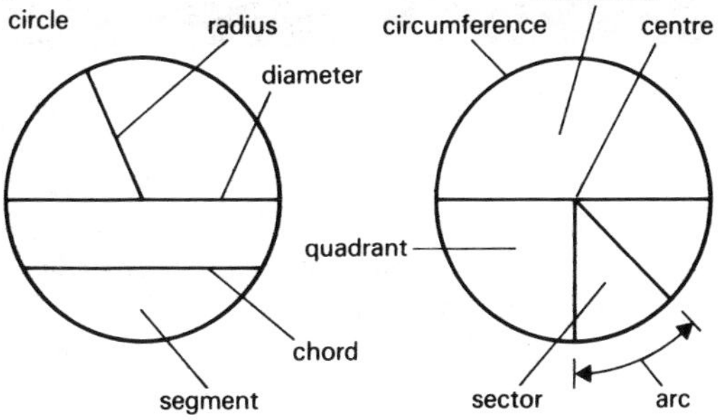

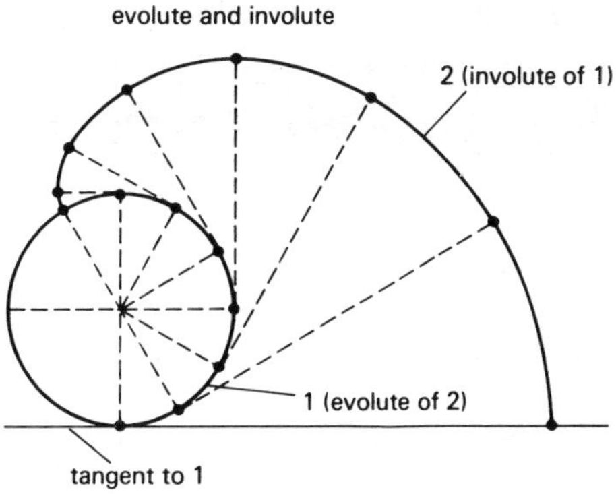

conic sections

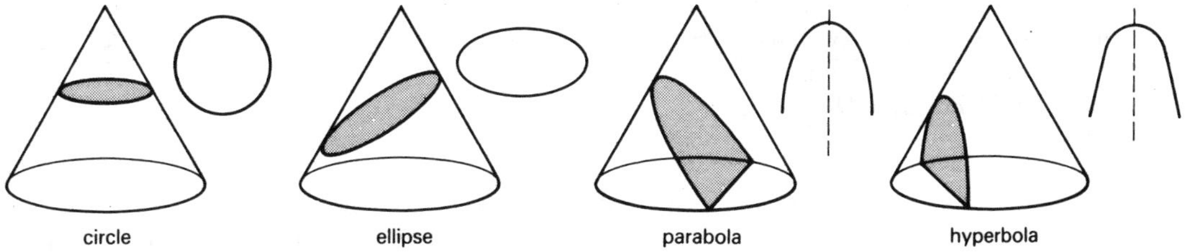

Plane figures

triangles

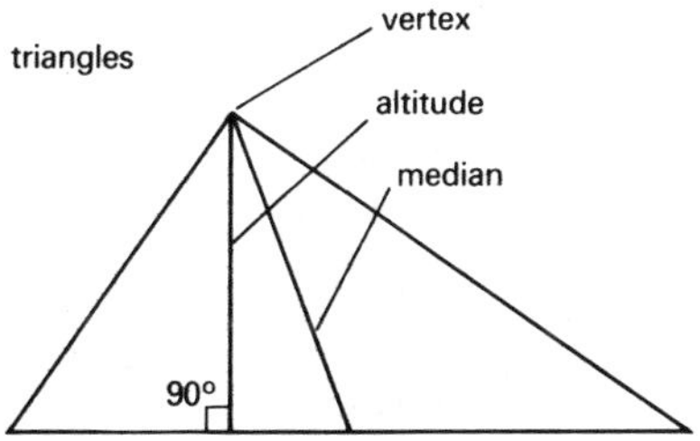

trigonometrical ratios

a/b = sine x b/c = secant x
c/b = cosine x b/a = cosecant x
a/c = tangent x c/a = cotangent x

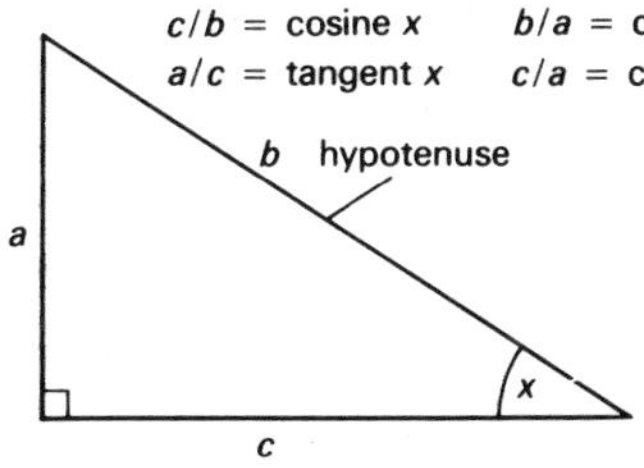

Solids

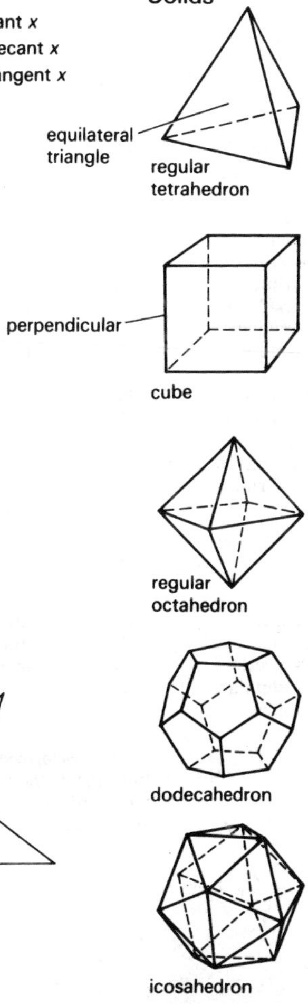

quadrilaterals

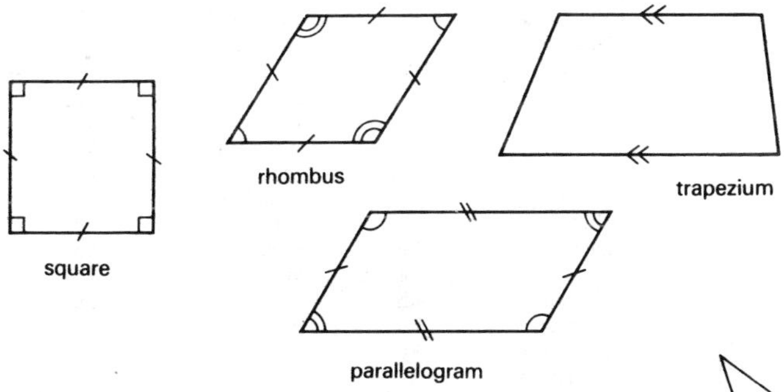

pentagons

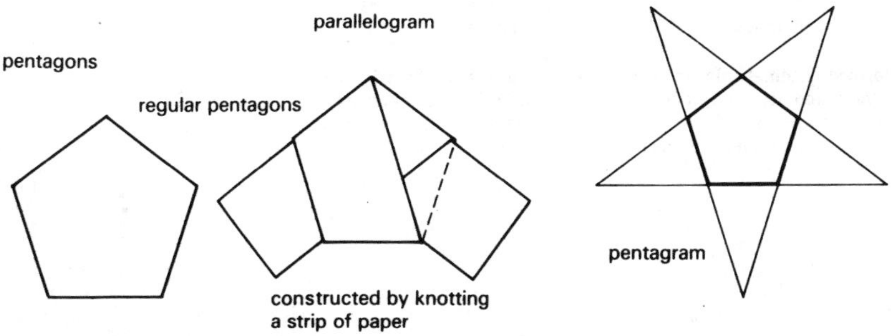

Appendix 10 Chemical Elements

Periodic Table of the Elements

IA	IIA	IIIB	IVB	VB	VIB	VIIB	VIII			IB	IIB	IIIA	IVA	VA	VIA	VIIA	O
1 H																	2 He
3 Li	4 Be											5 B	6 C	7 N	8 O	9 F	10 Ne
11 Na	12 Mg	Transitional metals										13 Al	14 Si	15 P	16 S	17 Cl	18 Ar
19 K	20 Ca	21 Sc	22 Ti	23 V	24 Cr	25 Mn	26 Fe	27 Co	28 Ni	29 Cu	30 Zn	31 Ga	32 Ge	33 As	34 Se	35 Br	36 Kr
37 Rb	38 Sr	39 Y	40 Zr	41 Nb	42 Mo	43 Tc	44 Ru	45 Rh	46 Pd	47 Ag	48 Cd	49 In	50 Sn	51 Sb	52 Te	53 I	54 Xe
55 Cs	56 Ba	*57 La	72 Hf	73 Ta	74 W	75 Re	76 Os	77 Ir	78 Pt	79 Au	80 Hg	81 Ti	82 Pb	83 Bi	84 Po	85 At	86 Rn
87 Fr	88 Ra	†89 Ac	104 Unq	105 Unp	106 Unh	107 Uns											

* Lanthanides	57 La	58 Ce	59 Pr	60 Nd	61 Pm	62 Sm	63 Eu	64 Gd	65 Tb	66 Dy	67 Ho	68 Er	69 Tm	70 Yb	71 Lu
† Actinides	89 Ac	90 Th	91 Pa	92 U	93 Np	94 Pu	95 Am	96 Cm	97 Bk	98 Cf	99 Es	100 Fm	101 Md	102 No	103 Lr

Element	*Symbol*	*Element*	*Symbol*	*Element*	*Symbol*	*Element*	*Symbol*
actinium	Ac	europium	Eu	mercury	Hg	samarium	Sm
aluminium	Al	fermium	Fm	molybdenum	Mo	scandium	Sc
americium	Am	fluorine	F	neodymium	Nd	selenium	Se
antimony	Sb	francium	Fr	neon	Ne	silicon	Si
argon	Ar	gadolinium	Gd	neptunium	Np	silver	Ag
arsenic	As	gallium	Ga	nickel	Ni	sodium	Na
astatine	At	germanium	Ge	niobium	Nb	strontium	Sr
barium	Ba	gold	Au	nitrogen	N	sulphur	S
berkelium	Bk	hafnium	Hf	nobelium	No	tantalum	Ta
beryllium	Be	hahnium[1]	Ha	osmium	Os	technetium	Tc
bismuth	Bi	helium	He	oxygen	O	tellurium	Te
boron	B	holmium	Ho	palladium	Pd	terbium	Tb
bromine	Br	hydrogen	H	phosphorus	P	thallium	Tl
cadmium	Cd	indium	In	platinum	Pt	thorium	Th
caesium	Cs	iodine	I	plutonium	Pu	thulium	Tm
calcium	Ca	iridium	Ir	polonium	Po	tin	Sn
californium	Cf	iron	Fe	potassium	K	titanium	Ti
carbon	C	krypton	Kr	praseodymium	Pr	tungsten	W
cerium	Ce	kurchatovium[1]	Ku	promethium	Pm	uranium	U
chlorine	Cl	lanthanum	La	protactinium	Pa	vanadium	V
chromium	Cr	lawrencium	Lr	radium	Ra	xenon	Xe
cobalt	Co	lead	Pb	radon	Rn	ytterbium	Yb
copper	Cu	lithium	Li	rhenium	Re	yttrium	Y
curium	Cm	lutetium	Lu	rhodium	Rh	zinc	Zn
dysprosium	Dy	magnesium	Mg	rubidium	Rb	zirconium	Zr
einsteinium	Es	manganese	Mn	ruthenium	Ru		
erbium	Er	mendelevium	Md	rutherfordium[1]	Rf		

[1] Names formed systematically and without attribution are preferred by IUPAC for numbers from 104 onward, and are used exclusively for numbers from 106 onward. Names based on the atomic number are formed on the numerical roots *nil* (= 0), *un* (= 1), *bi* (= 2), etc. (e.g. *unnilquadium* = 104, *ununbium* = 112, etc.)

Appendix 11 Weather

Winds and pressure systems

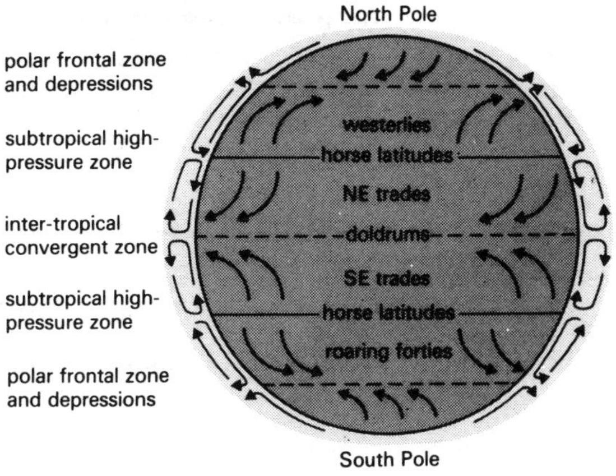

The atmosphere

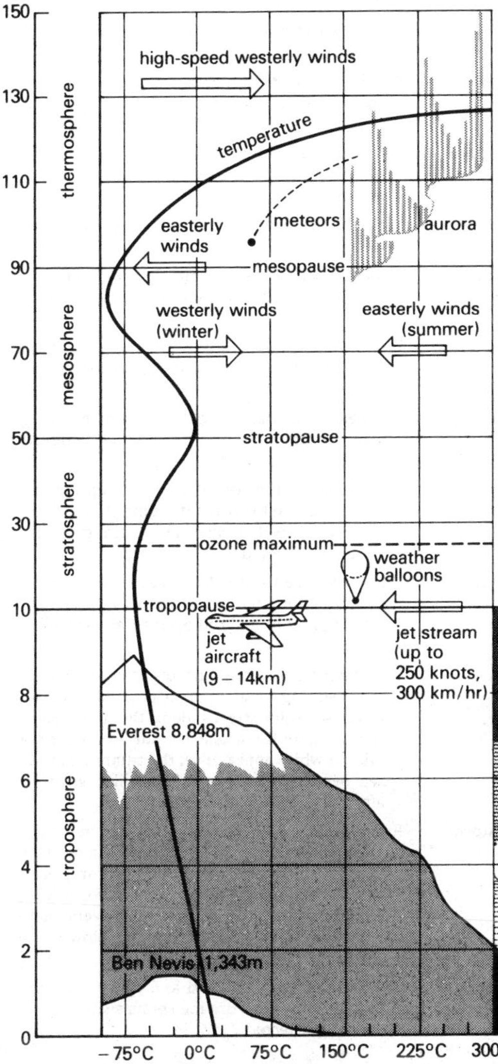

temperature in the atmosphere in a temperate zone, varying with altitude (°C)

Clouds

high level (5 – 13km)
- Cs cirrostratus
- Cc cirrocumulus
- Ci cirrus

middle level (2 – 7km)
- Cb cumulonimbus
- Ac altocumulus
- As altostratus

low level (0 – 3km)
- St stratus
- Ns nimbo-stratus
- Cu cumulus
- Sc stratocumulus

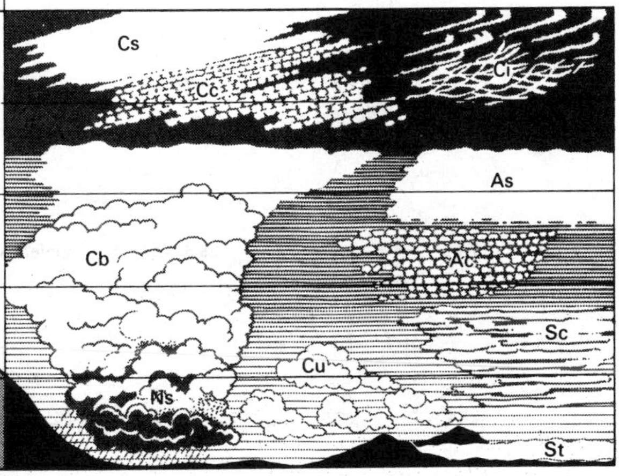

Thunderstorms

When the upper part of the cloud becomes positively charged and the lower part negatively charged to a sufficient extent, a giant spark of lightning occurs and the air expands rapidly, producing a thunderclap. Rain is typically (but not essentially) present.

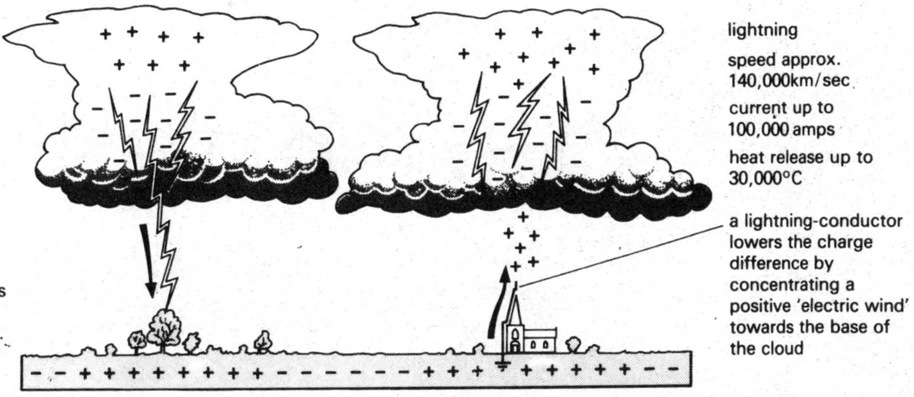

Appendix 12 The Beaufort Scale of Wind Force

Beaufort Number	*Knots*	*Miles per hour*	*Metres per second*	*Description of wind*	*Specifications for use at sea*
	Equivalent speed at 10 m above ground				
0	<1	<1	0.0–0.2	Calm	Sea like a mirror
1	1–3	1–3	0.3–1.5	Light air	Ripples with the appearance of scales formed but without foam crests
2	4–6	4–7	1.6–3.3	Light breeze	Small wavelets, still short but more pronounced; crests have a glassy appearance and do not break
3	7–10	8–12	3.4–5.4	Gentle breeze	Large wavelets; crests begin to break; foam of glassy appearance; perhaps scattered white horses
4	11–16	13–18	5.5–7.9	Moderate breeze	Small waves, becoming longer; fairly frequent white horses
5	17–21	19–24	8.0–10.7	Fresh breeze	Moderate waves, taking a more pronounced long form; many white horses are formed; chance of some spray
6	22–27	25–31	10.8–13.8	Strong breeze	Large waves begin to form; the white foam crests are more extensive everywhere; probably some spray
7	28–33	32–38	13.9–17.1	Near gale	Sea heaps up and white foam from breaking waves begins to be blown in streaks along the direction of the wind
8	34–40	39–46	17.2–20.7	Gale	Moderately high waves of greater length; edges of crests begin to break into spindrift; the foam is blown in well-marked streaks along the direction of the wind
9	41–47	47–54	20.8–24.4	Strong gale	High waves; dense streaks of foam along the direction of the wind; crests of waves begin to topple, tumble, and roll over; spray may affect visibility
10	48–55	55–63	24.5–28.4	Storm	Very high waves with long overhanging crests; the resulting foam, in great patches, is blown in dense white streaks along the direction of the wind; on the whole, the surface of the sea takes a white appearance; the tumbling of the sea becomes heavy and shock-like; visibility affected
11	56–63	64–72	28.5–32.6	Violent storm	Exceptionally high waves (small and medium-sized ships might be for a time lost to view behind the waves); the sea is completely covered with long white patches of foam lying along the direction of the wind; everywhere the edges of the wave crests are blown into froth; visibility affected
12	⩾64	⩾73	⩾32.7	Hurricane	The air is filled with foam and spray; sea completely white with driving spray; visibility very seriously affected

Appendix 13 Electronics

Some symbols and components

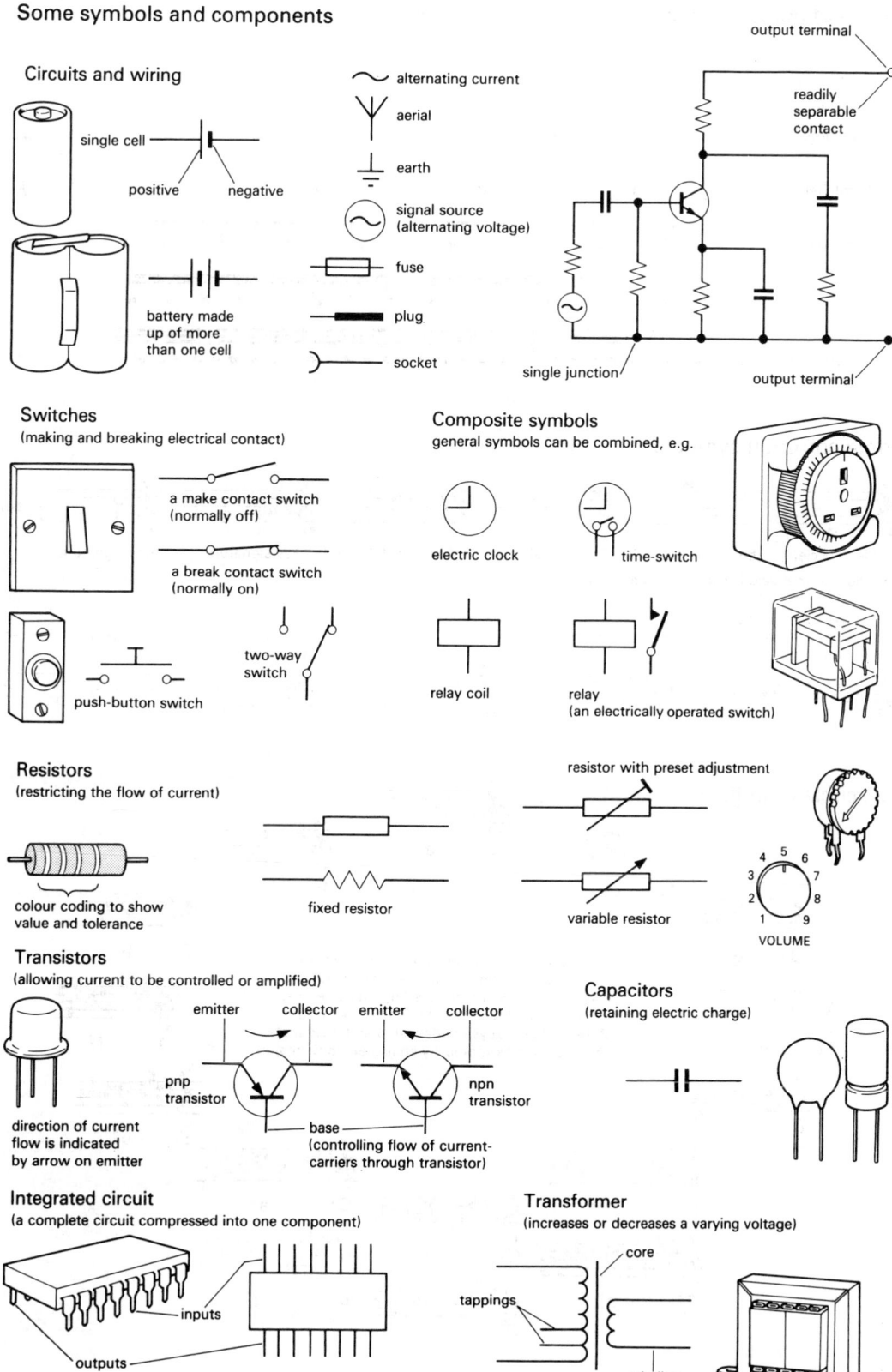

Circuits and wiring

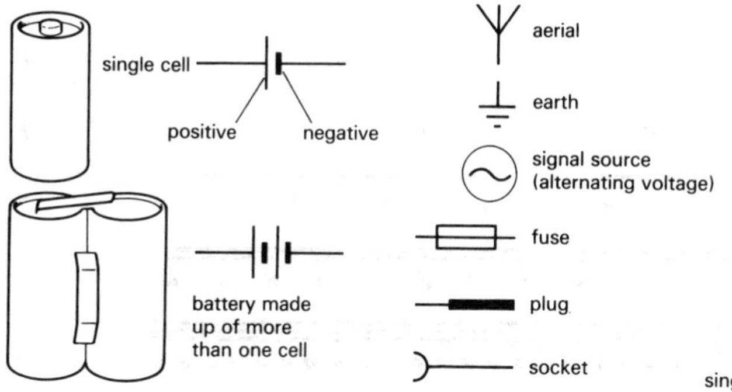

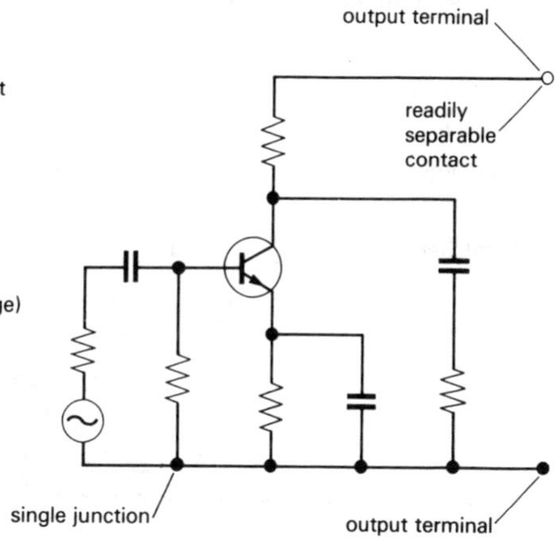

Switches
(making and breaking electrical contact)

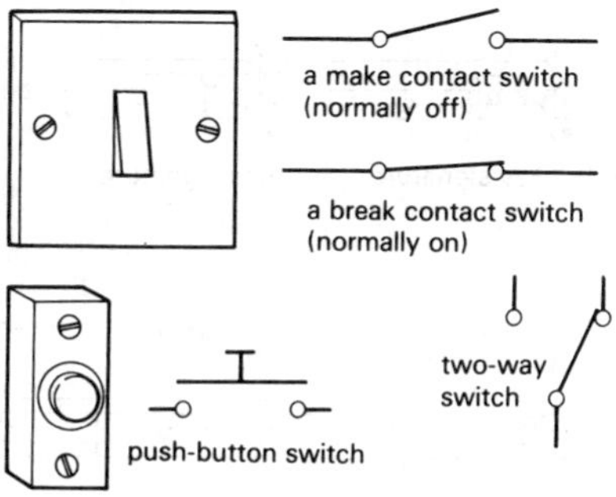

Composite symbols
general symbols can be combined, e.g.

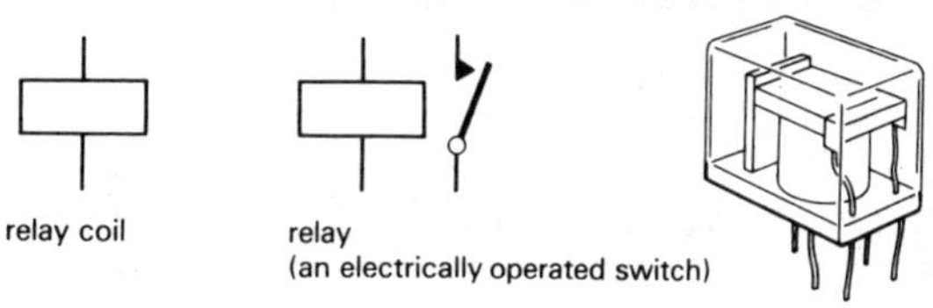

Resistors
(restricting the flow of current)

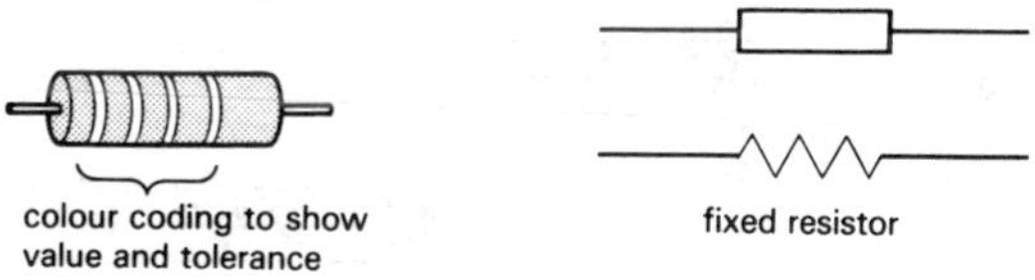

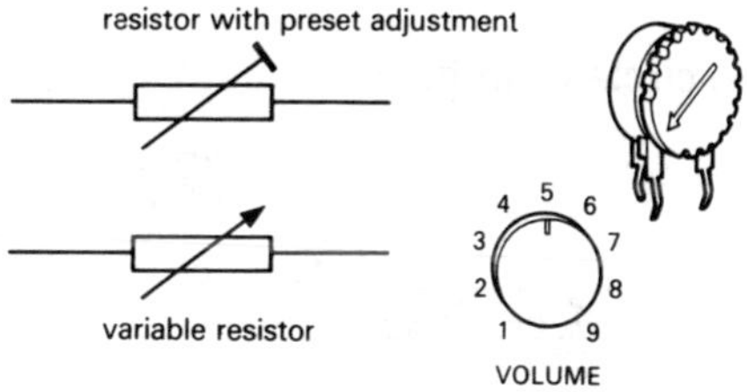

Transistors
(allowing current to be controlled or amplified)

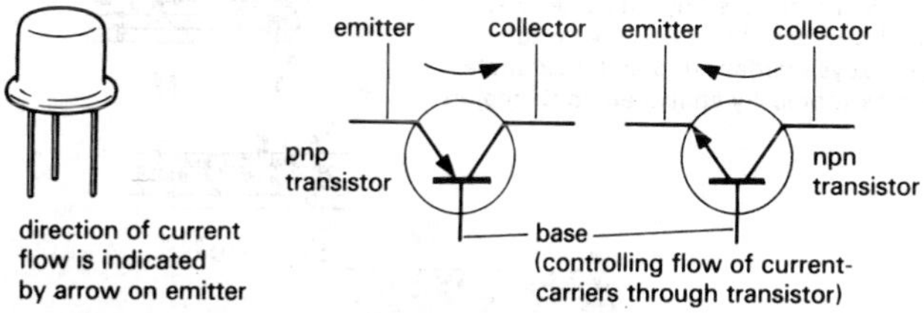

Capacitors
(retaining electric charge)

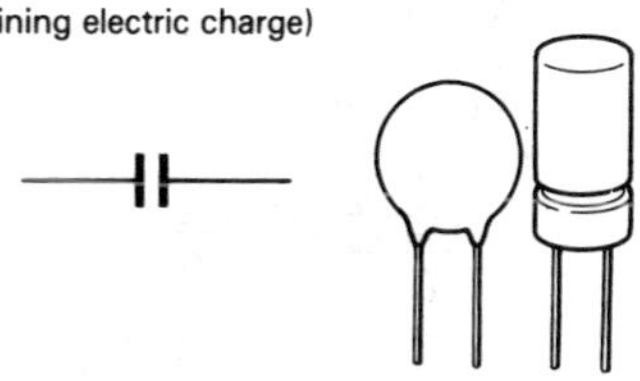

Integrated circuit
(a complete circuit compressed into one component)

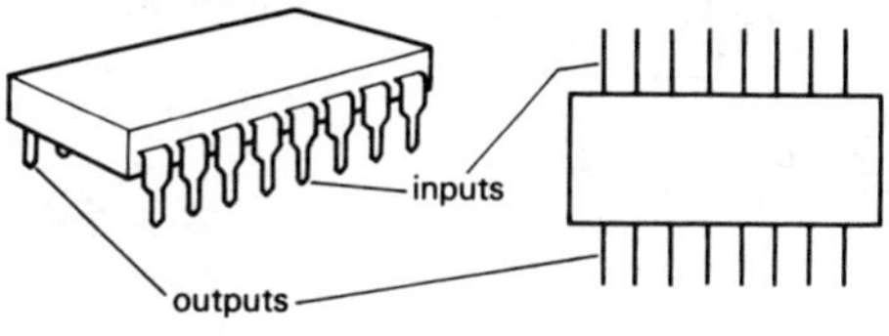

Transformer
(increases or decreases a varying voltage)

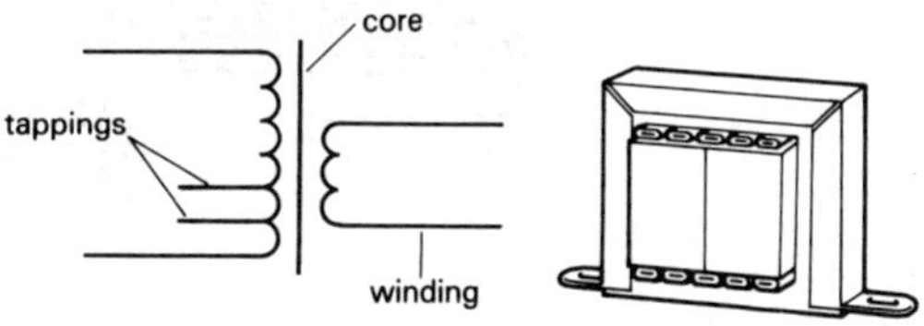

Appendix 14 Musical Notation and the Orchestra

Values of notes and rests

Some common symbols

The circle of fifths

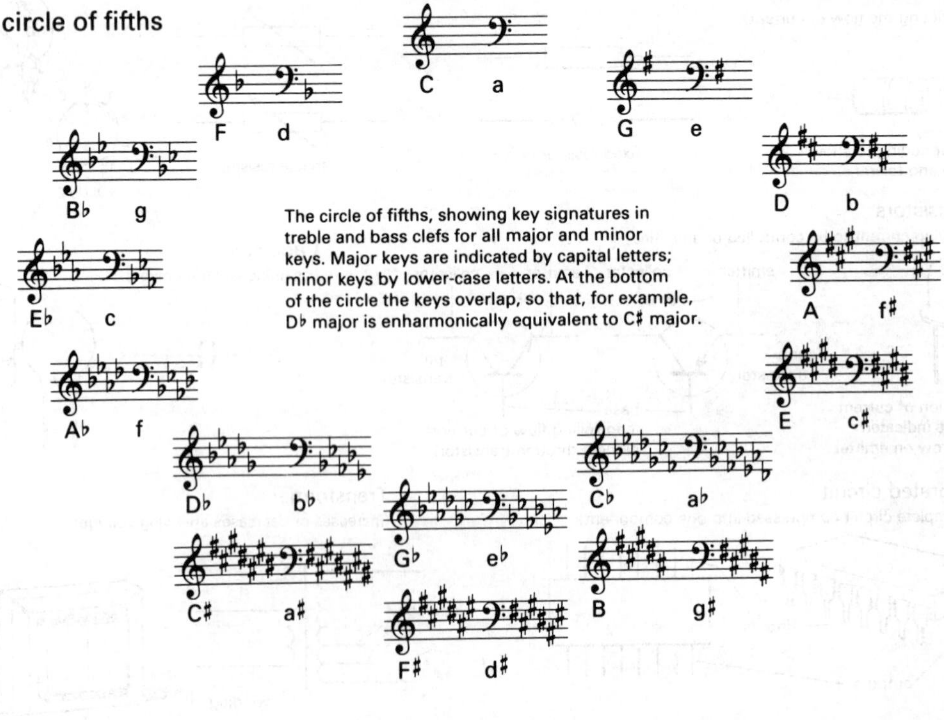

The circle of fifths, showing key signatures in treble and bass clefs for all major and minor keys. Major keys are indicated by capital letters; minor keys by lower-case letters. At the bottom of the circle the keys overlap, so that, for example, D♭ major is enharmonically equivalent to C♯ major.

Orchestral layout

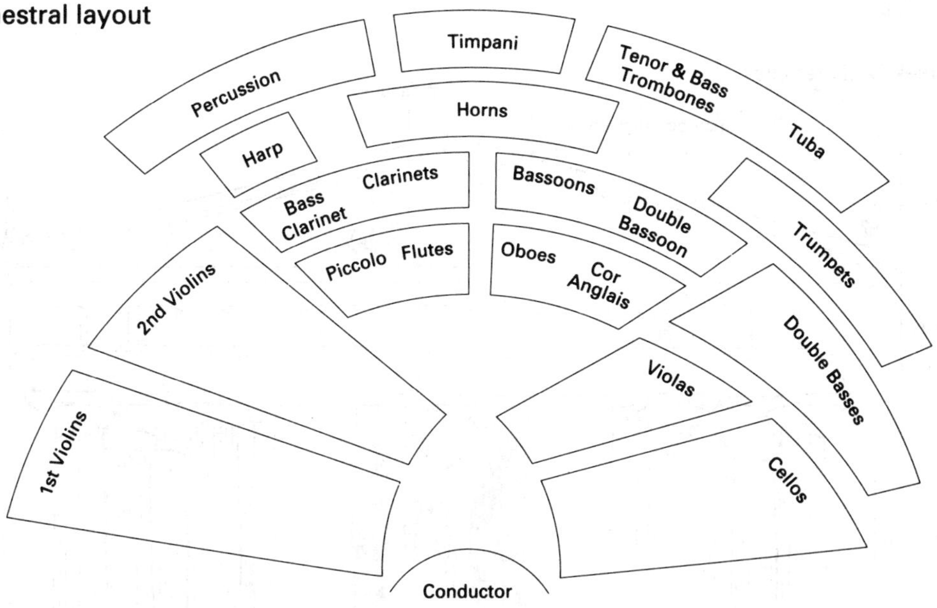

Dynamics

<	*crescendo*	get louder
>	*diminuendo*	get quieter
ppp		very, very quiet
pp	*pianissimo*	very quiet
p	*piano*	quiet
mp	*mezzopiano*	quite quiet
mf	*mezzoforte*	quite loud
f	*forte*	loud
ff	*fortissimo*	very loud
fff		very, very loud
sf	*sforzando*	suddenly very loud

Tempo indicators

adagio	slow
largo	slow and dignified
andante	flowing, at a walking pace
allegro	quick and bright
allegretto	not as quick as allegro
vivace	fast and lively
presto	very quick
accelerando	getting faster
ritenuto (rit.)	holding back
rallentando (rall.)	getting slower
rubato	flexible tempo

Interpretive indicators

cantabile	singing style
dolce	soft and sweet
espressivo	expressively
legato	smooth
staccato	detached

Appendix 15 Architecture

Classical

A Greek Doric temple

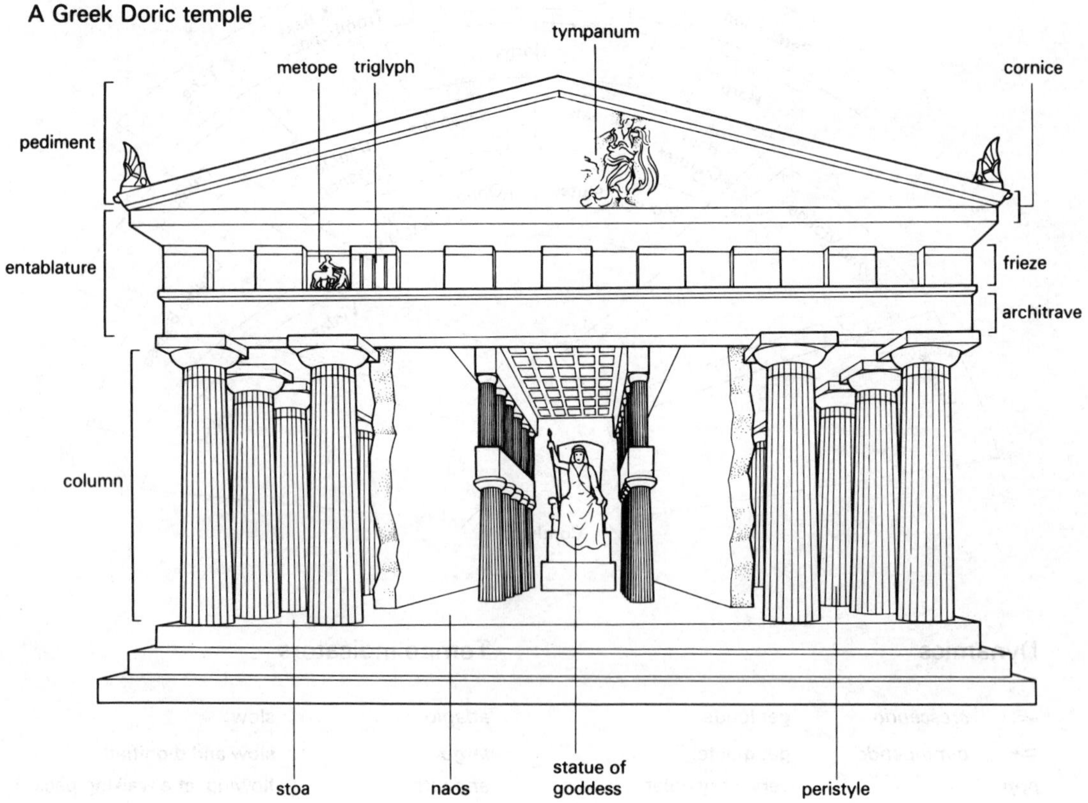

Orders of architecture: Greek origin

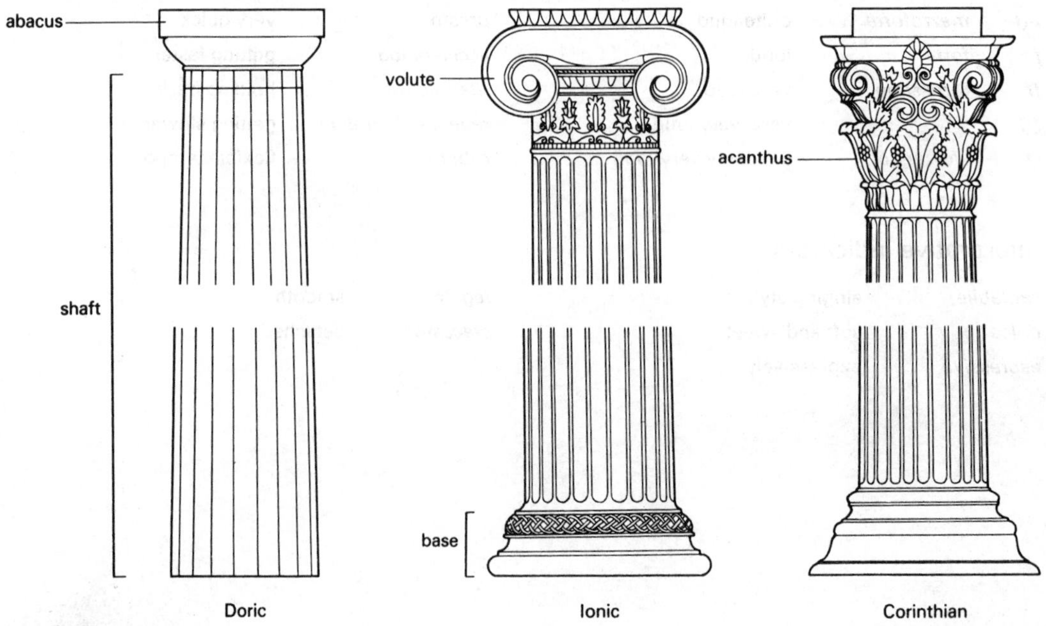

Structure

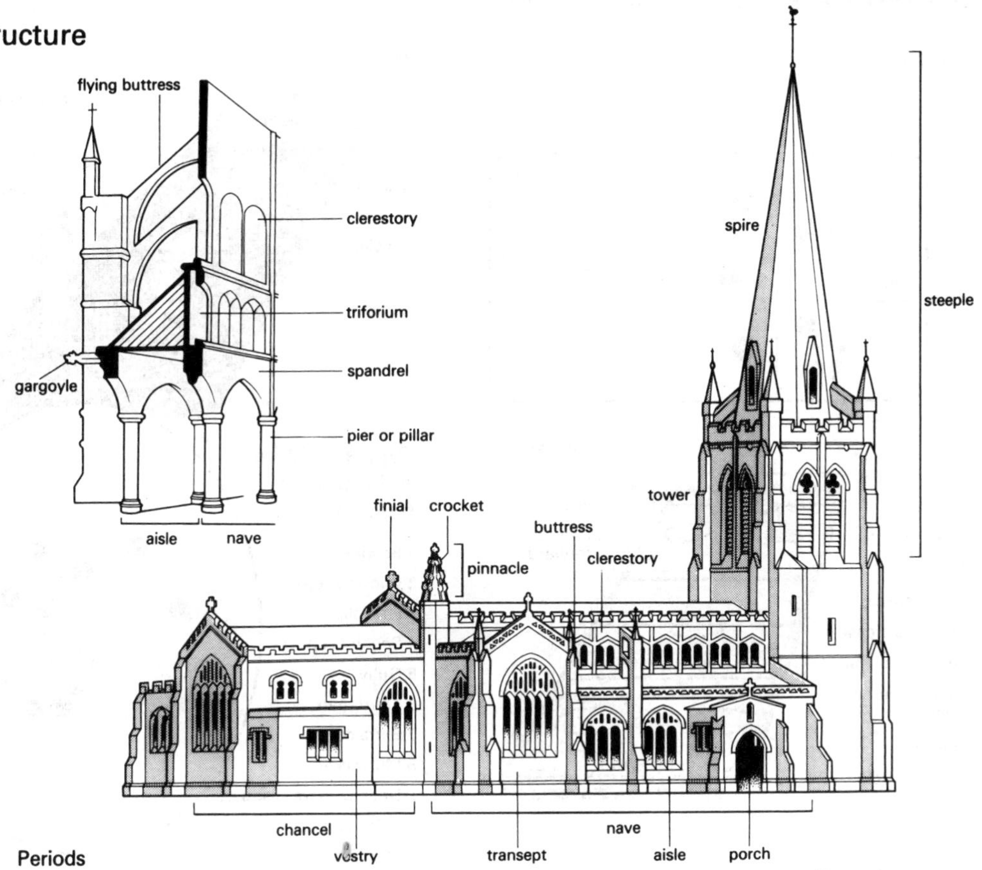

Periods

(note: some churches include architectural details which are earlier or later than the main periods which they illustrate)

Windows

Norman, 12th c.

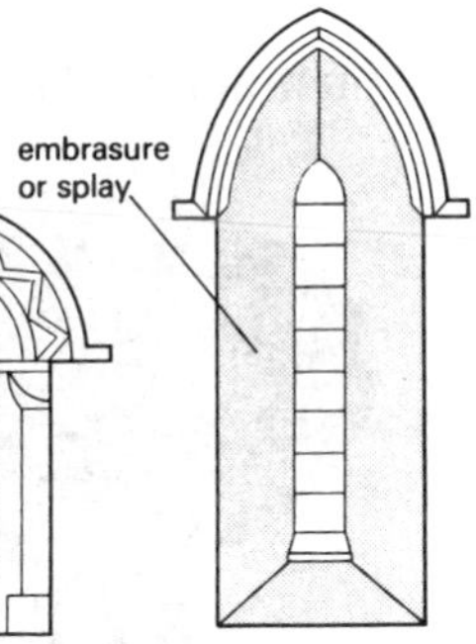

lancet, early 13th c.
(interior)

geometric bar tracery,
late 13th c.

Decorated curvilinear
tracery with ogee arch,
14th c.

Perpendicular
tracery, 15th c.

Vaults

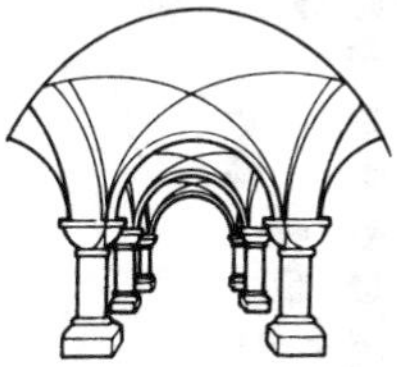

groined vault

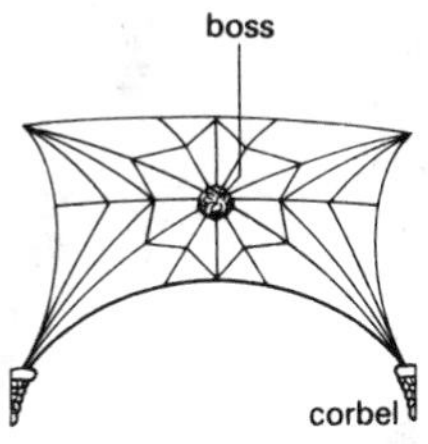

ribbed vault

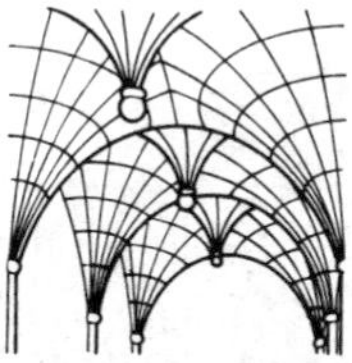

fan vault

Hammer-beam roof

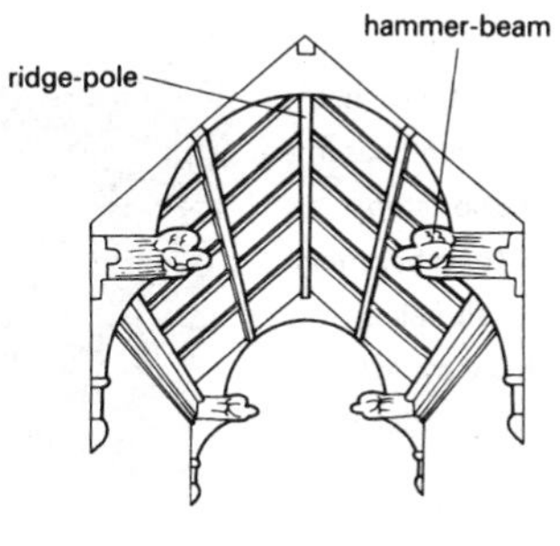

Appendix 16 Sports and Games

Ice hockey

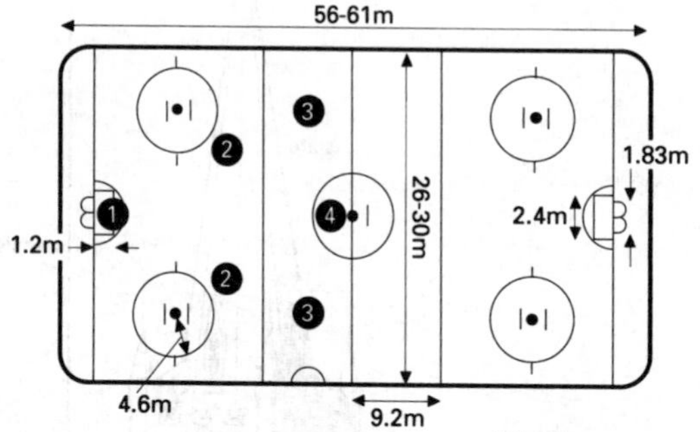

1 Goalkeeper
2 Defenceman
3 Winger
4 Centre forward

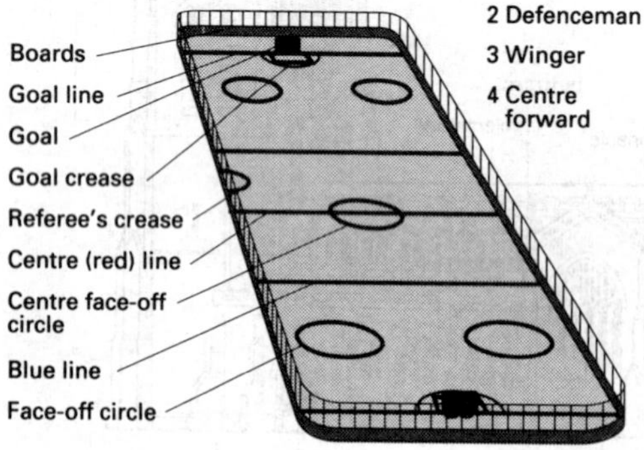

Cricket

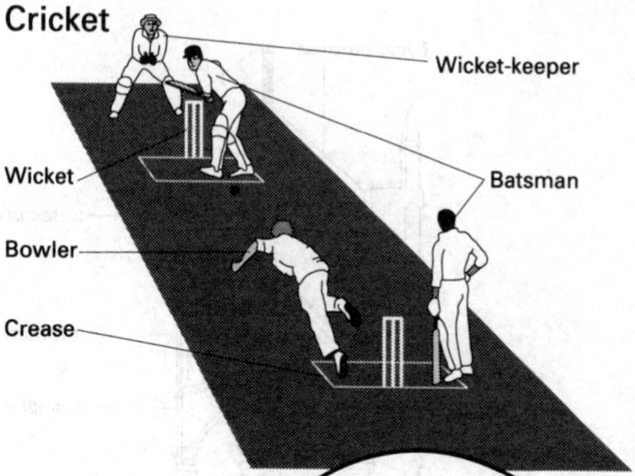

Typical field for right-handed batsman (B1)

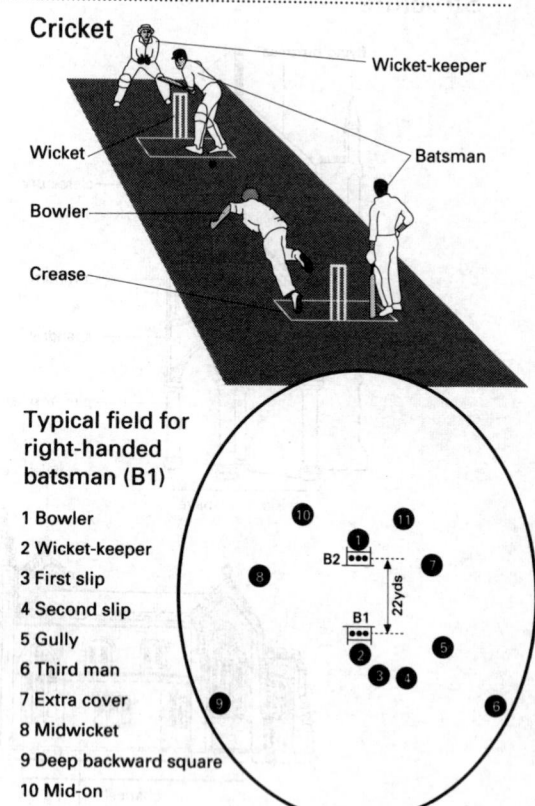

1 Bowler
2 Wicket-keeper
3 First slip
4 Second slip
5 Gully
6 Third man
7 Extra cover
8 Midwicket
9 Deep backward square
10 Mid-on
11 Mid-off

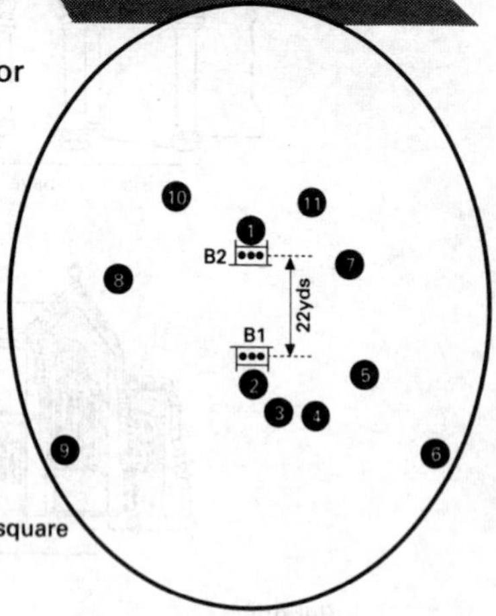

Baseball

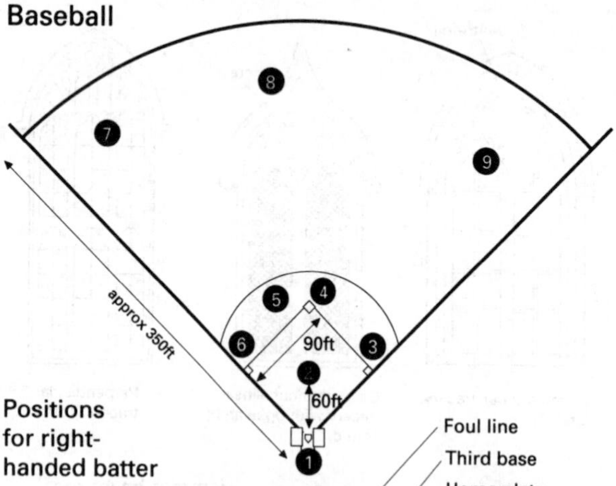

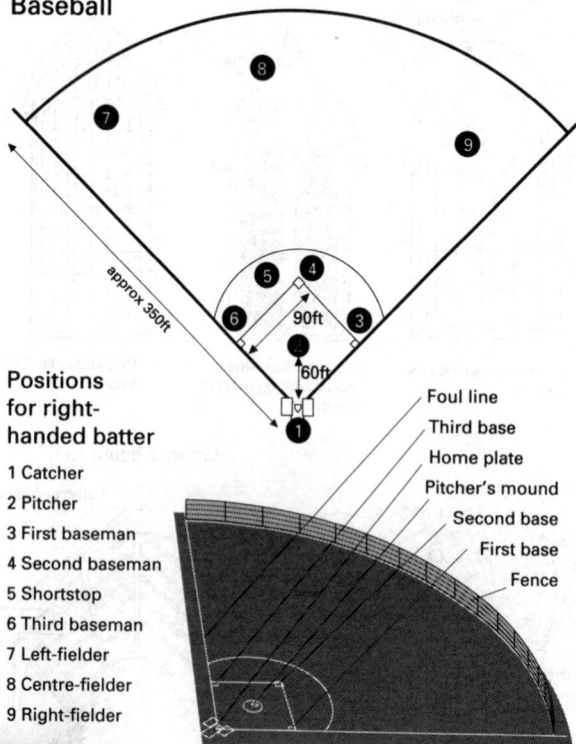

Positions for right-handed batter

1 Catcher
2 Pitcher
3 First baseman
4 Second baseman
5 Shortstop
6 Third baseman
7 Left-fielder
8 Centre-fielder
9 Right-fielder

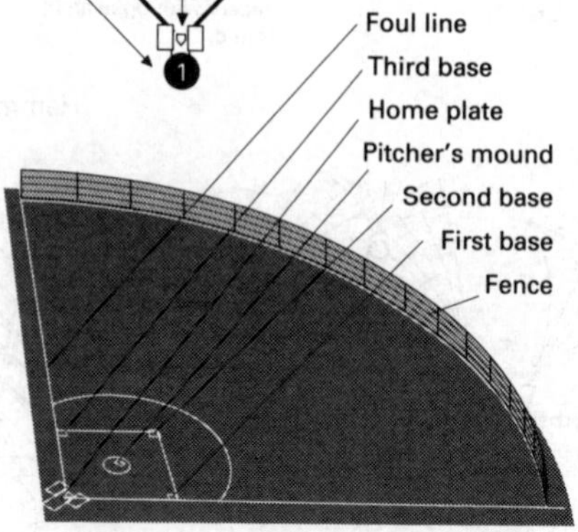

Australian rules football

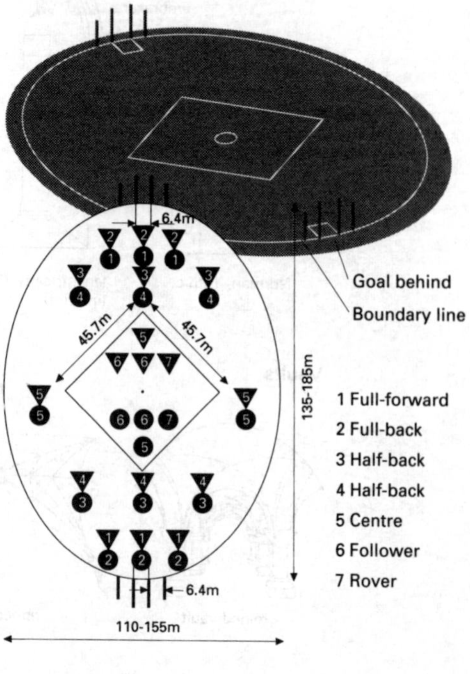

1 Full-forward
2 Full-back
3 Half-back
4 Half-back
5 Centre
6 Follower
7 Rover

Association Football

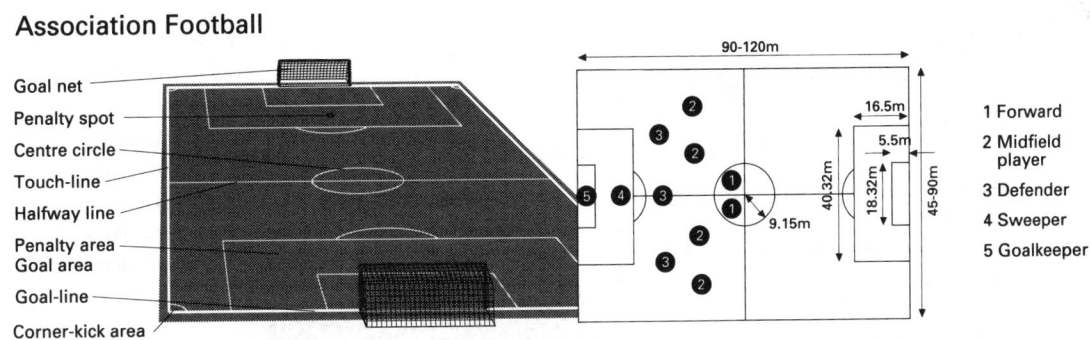

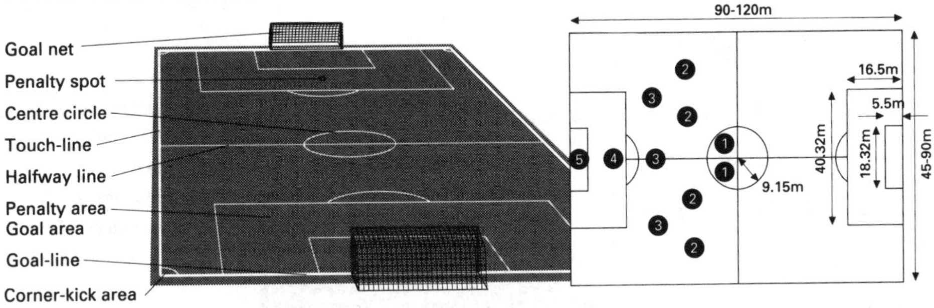

1 Forward
2 Midfield player
3 Defender
4 Sweeper
5 Goalkeeper

Rugby Union

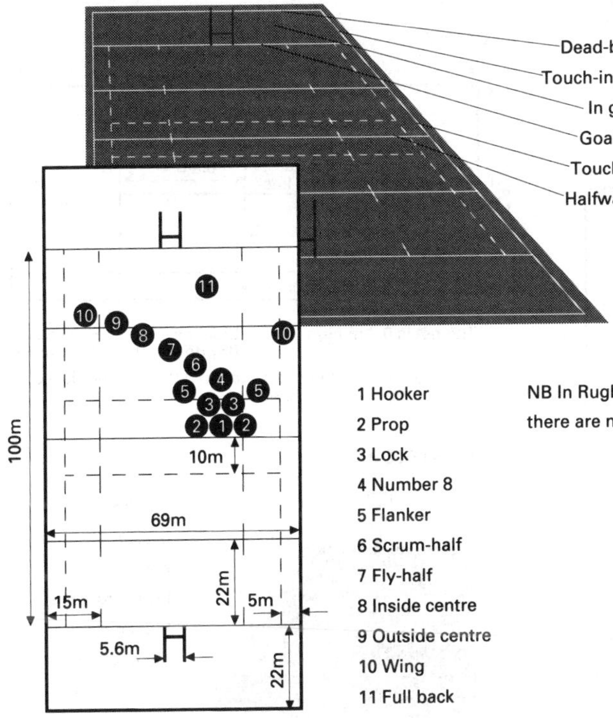

1 Hooker
2 Prop
3 Lock
4 Number 8
5 Flanker
6 Scrum-half
7 Fly-half
8 Inside centre
9 Outside centre
10 Wing
11 Full back

NB In Rugby League there are no flankers

Rugby League

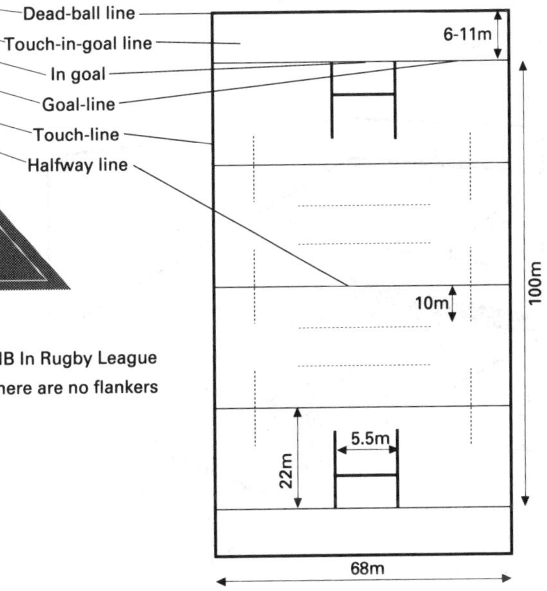

American Football

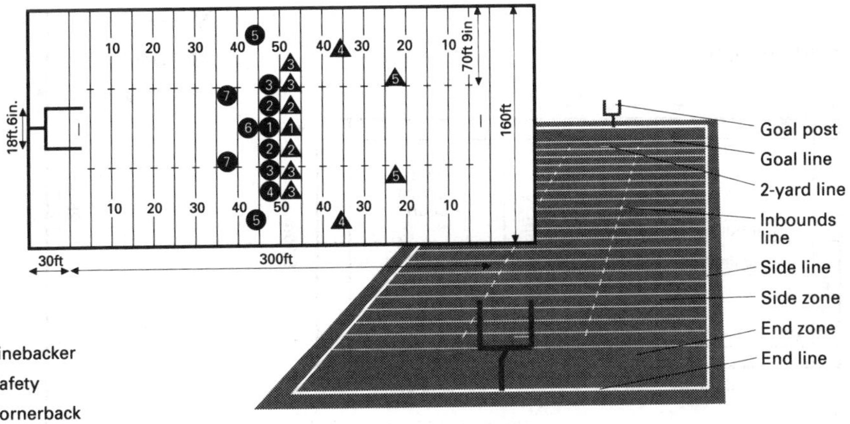

Offense ●

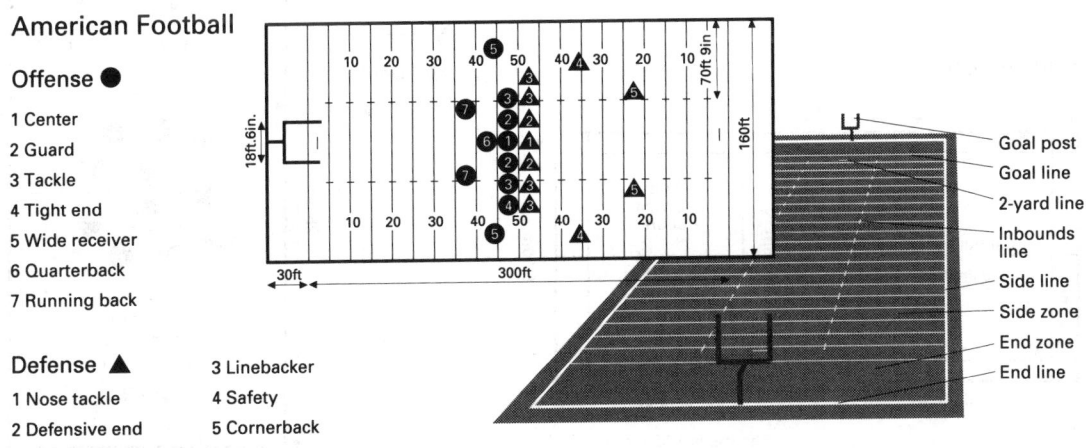

1 Center
2 Guard
3 Tackle
4 Tight end
5 Wide receiver
6 Quarterback
7 Running back

Defense ▲

1 Nose tackle
2 Defensive end
3 Linebacker
4 Safety
5 Cornerback

Hockey

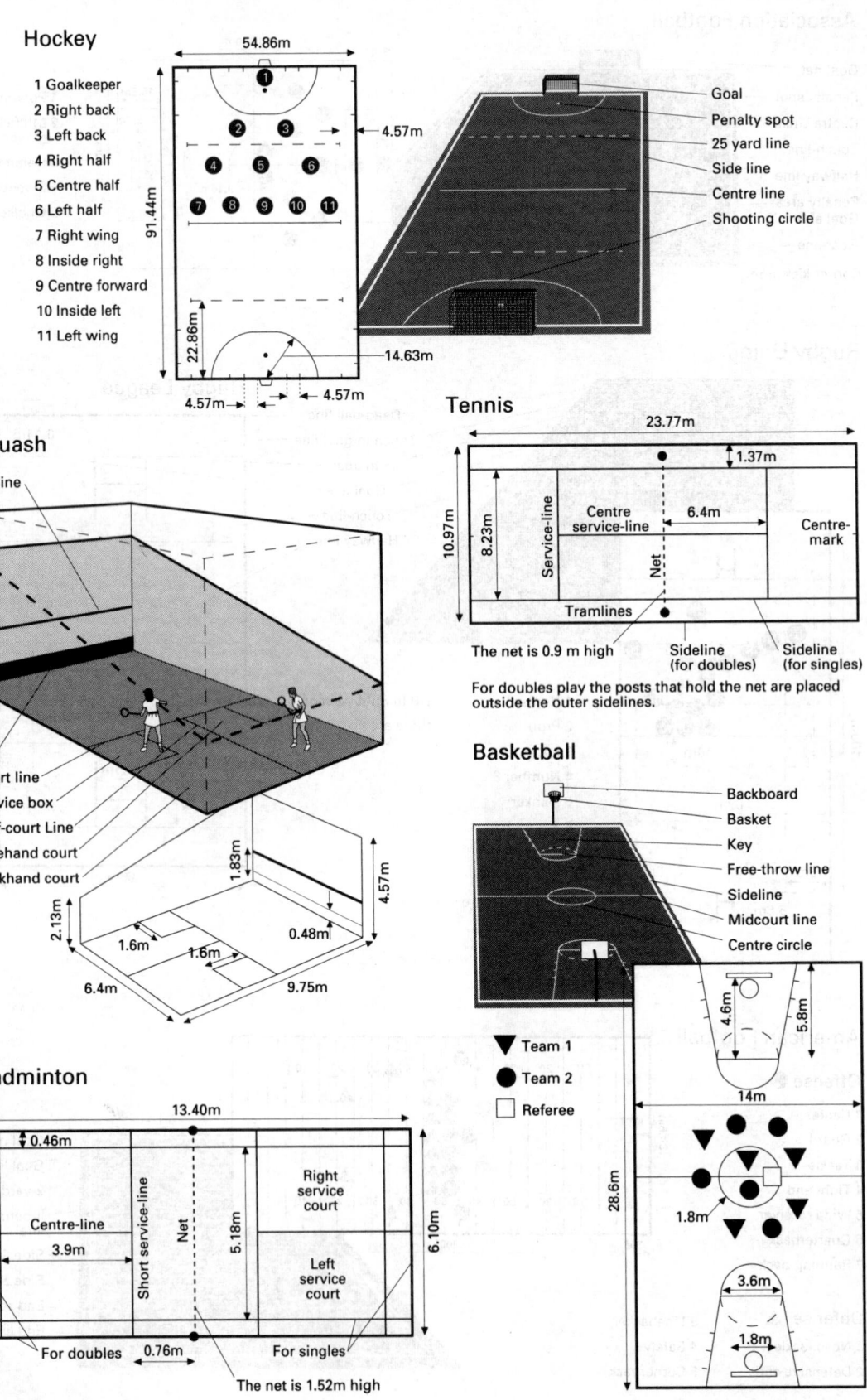

1 Goalkeeper
2 Right back
3 Left back
4 Right half
5 Centre half
6 Left half
7 Right wing
8 Inside right
9 Centre forward
10 Inside left
11 Left wing

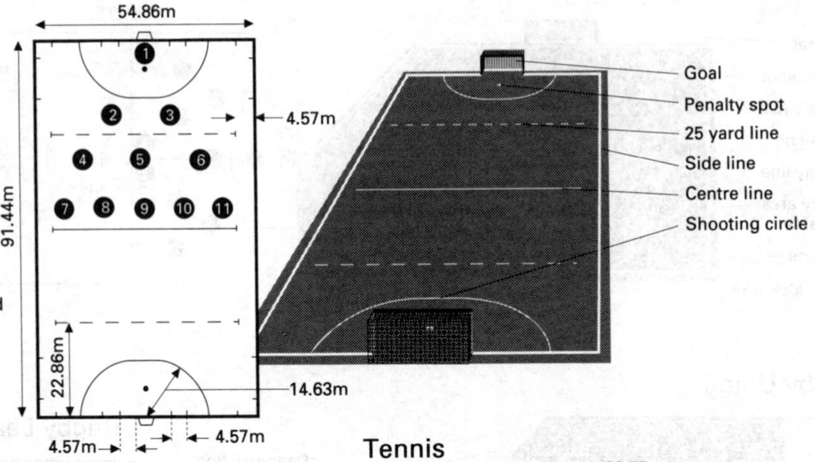

Squash

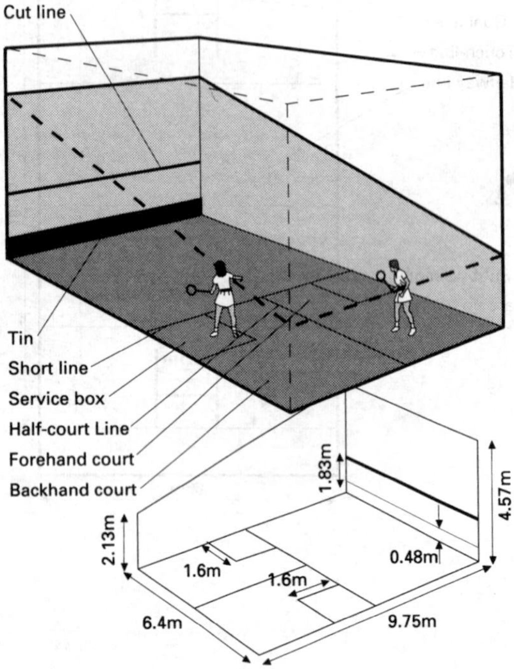

Tennis

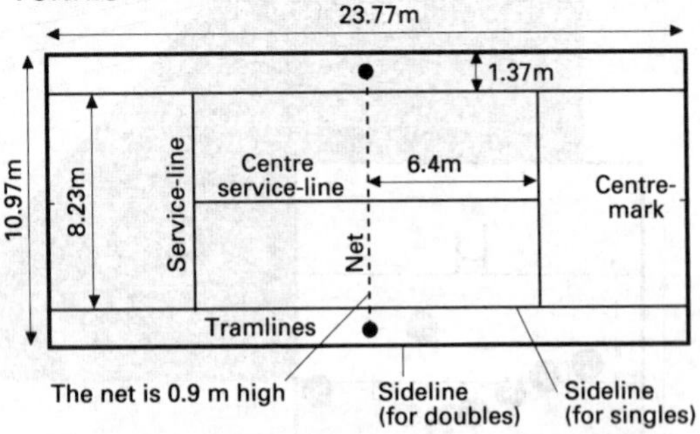

For doubles play the posts that hold the net are placed outside the outer sidelines.

Basketball

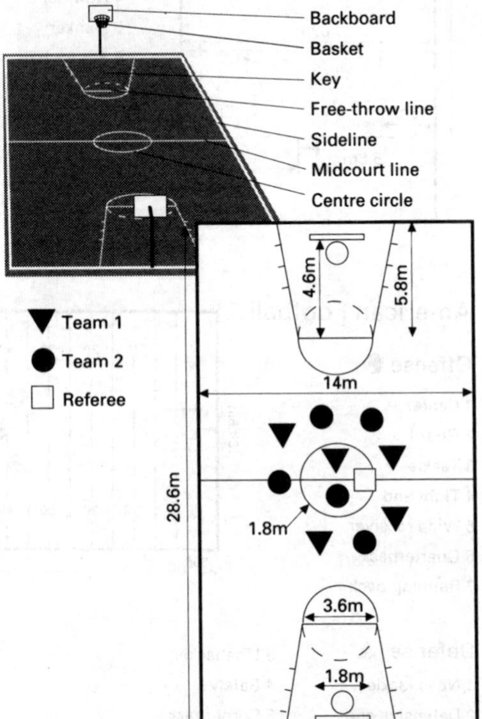

Badminton

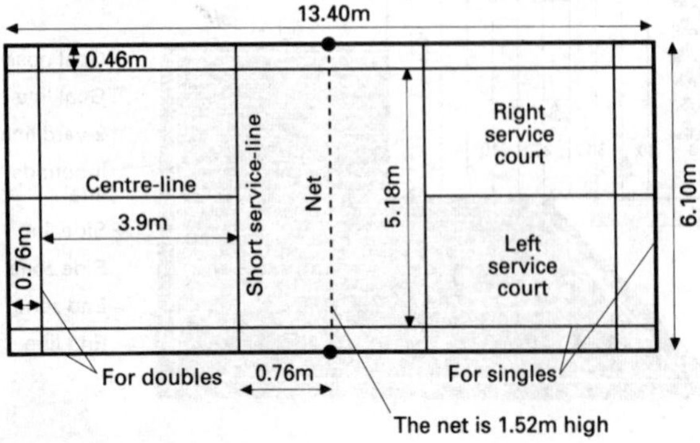

Appendix 17 Hallmarks

A hallmark

All marks shown relate to silver except where otherwise indicated

Maker's mark (from 1363)

originally symbols, now initials

symbol

symbol and initials

initials

Assay Office mark (from 1300)

now only London, Birmingham, Sheffield, and Edinburgh

London

gold and silver (leopard's head uncrowned from 1821; mark includes platinum from 1975)

Britannia silver (prior to 1975)

Edinburgh

gold and silver (also platinum from 1975)

Birmingham

gold (also platinum from 1975)

silver

Sheffield

silver (prior to 1975)

gold (also silver and platinum from 1975)

Some earlier Assay Office marks (with dates of closure)

Norwich (1702)

York (1856)

Exeter (1883)

Newcastle (1884)

Chester (1962)

Glasgow (1964)

Standard mark (from 1544)

Marks guaranteeing pure metal content of the percentage shown

sterling silver 92.5%

marked in England

marked in Scotland (from 1975)

marked in Scotland (prior to 1975)

Britannia standard silver (1697–1720, also occasional use since) 95.8%

gold (crown followed by millesimal figure of the standard)

750 i.e. 18 carat 75%

916 22 carat 91.6%

585 14 carat 58.5%

375 9 carat 37.5%

(prior to 1975 marks incorporated the carat figure, and Scottish 18 and 22 carat gold bore a thistle mark instead of the crown)

Date letter (from 1478)

one letter per year before changing to next style of letter and/or shield cycles vary between Assay Offices

London date letters (A-U used, excluding J) showing style of first letter and years of cycle

a	1498–1518[1]	A	1598–1618	a	1697[3]–1716	A	1796–1816	a	1896–1916
A	1518–1538	a	1618–1638	A	1716–1736	a	1816–1836	a	1916–1936
A	1538–1558	a	1638–1658	a	1736–1756	A	1836–1856	A	1936–1956
a	1558–1578	A	1658–1678	A	1756–1776	A	1856–1876	a	1956–1974[2]
A	1578–1598	a	1678–1697[2]	a	1776–1796	A	1876–1896	A	1975[4]–

Notes 1. Letter changed on 19 May until 1697 2. No U used in these cycles
3. A from 27 March–28 May 1697; year letters then changed on 29 May until 1975
4. Year letter changed with each calendar year; from 1975 all UK Offices use the same date letters and shield shape

Appendix 18 Countries of the World

(Countries are given for linguistic information on the names in use; some dependent territories are included.)

country	**person** (*name in general use*)	**related adjective** (*in general use*)
Afghanistan	Afghan	Afghan
Albania	Albanian	Albanian
Algeria	Algerian	Algerian
America *see* United States of America		
Andorra	Andorran	Andorran
Angola	Angolan	Angolan
Anguilla	Anguillan	Anguillan *or* Anguilla
Antigua and Barbuda	Citizen of Antigua and Barbuda	Antiguan, Barbudan *or* Antigua and Barbuda
Argentina	Argentinian	Argentine *or* Argentinian
Armenia	Armenian	Armenian
Australia	Australian	Australian
Austria	Austrian	Austrian
Azerbaijan	Azerbaijani	Azerbaijani
the Bahamas	Bahamian	Bahamian
Bahrain	Bahraini	Bahraini *or* Bahrain
Bangladesh	Bangladeshi	Bangladeshi
Barbados	Barbadian	Barbadian
Belgium	Belgian	Belgian
Belize	Belizean	Belizean
Belarus	Belorussian	Belorussian
Benin	Beninese	Beninese
Bermuda (*dependent territory*)	Bermudan	Bermudan
Bhutan	Bhutanese	Bhutanese
Bolivia	Bolivian	Bolivian
Bosnia-Hercegovina	Citizen of Bosnia-Hercegovina	Bosnian *or* Bosnian and Hercegovinian
Botswana *see also* TSWANA in the dictionary		
Brazil	Brazilian	Brazilian
Britain *see* Great Britain		
Brunei	Citizen of Brunei	Bruneian *or* Brunei
Bulgaria	Bulgarian	Bulgarian
Burkina	Burkinan	Burkinan *or* Burkina
Burma (*now officially called* Myanmar)	Burmese	Burmese
Burundi	Citizen of Burundi	Burundi
Cambodia (*also called* Kampuchea)	Cambodian	Cambodian
Cameroon	Cameroonian	Cameroonian
Canada	Canadian	Canadian
Cape Verde Islands	Cape Verdean	Cape Verdean
Cayman Islands (*dependent territory*)	Cayman Islander *or* Caymanian	Cayman Islands
Central African Republic	Citizen of Central African Republic	Central African Republic
Chad	Chadian	Chadian
Chile	Chilean	Chilean
China	Chinese	Chinese
Colombia	Colombian	Colombian
Comoros	Comoran	Comoran
Congo	Congolese	Congolese
Costa Rica	Costa Rican	Costa Rican
Croatia	Croat	Croatian
Cuba	Cuban	Cuban
Cyprus	Cypriot	Cypriot *or* Cyprus
Czech Republic	Czech	Czech
Denmark	Dane	Danish
Djibouti	Djiboutian	Djiboutian
Dominica	Dominican	Dominican
Dominican Republic	Citizen of Dominican Republic	Dominican Republic
Ecuador	Ecuadorean	Ecuadorean
Egypt	Egyptian	Egyptian
El Salvador	Salvadorean	Salvadorean
England	Englishman, Englishwoman	English
Equatorial Guinea	Equatorial Guinean	of Equatorial Guinea
Estonia	Estonian	Estonian
Ethiopia	Ethiopian	Ethiopian
Falkland Islands (*dependent territory*)	Falkland Islander	Falkland Islands
Fiji	Citizen of Fiji	Fiji
Finland	Finn	Finnish
France	Frenchman, Frenchwoman	French
Gabon	Gabonese	Gabonese
Gambia	Gambian	Gambian
Georgia	Georgian	Georgian
Germany	German	German
Ghana	Ghanaian	Ghanaian *or* Ghana
Gibraltar (*dependent territory*)	Gibraltarian	Gibraltarian *or* Gibraltar
Great Britain	Briton	British
Greece	Greek	Greek
Grenada	Grenadian	Grenadian
Guatemala	Guatemalan	Guatemalan
Guinea	Guinean	Guinean
Guinea-Bissau	Citizen of Guinea-Bissau	Guinea-Bissau
Guyana	Guyanese	Guyanese
Haiti	Haitian	Haitian
Holland *see* Netherlands		
Honduras	Honduran	Honduran
Hong Kong (*dependent territory*)	inhabitant of Hong Kong	Hong Kong
Hungary	Hungarian	Hungarian
Iceland	Icelander	Icelandic
India	Indian	Indian
Indonesia	Indonesian	Indonesian
Iran	Iranian	Iranian
Iraq	Iraqi	Iraqi *or* Iraq
Ireland, Republic of	Irishman, Irishwoman	Irish
Israel	Israeli	Israeli *or* Israel
Italy	Italian	Italian
Ivory Coast	Citizen of Ivory Coast	Ivory Coast *or* Ivorian
Jamaica	Jamaican	Jamaican
Japan	Japanese	Japanese
Jordan	Jordanian	Jordanian
Kampuchea *see* Cambodia		
Kazakhstan	Kazakh	Kazakh
Kenya	Kenyan	Kenyan
Kiribati		Kiribati

country	person (*name in general use*)	related adjective (*in general use*)
Korea, North	North Korean	North Korean
Korea, South	South Korean	South Korean
Kuwait	Kuwaiti	Kuwaiti
Kyrgyzstan	Kyrgyz	Kyrgyz
Laos	Laotian	Laotian
Latvia	Latvian	Latvian
Lebanon	Lebanese	Lebanese
Lesotho	Mosotho, *pl.* Basotho	
Liberia	Liberian	Liberian
Libya	Libyan	Libyan
Liechtenstein	Liechtensteiner	Liechtenstein
Lithuania	Lithuanian	Lithuanian
Luxemburg	Luxemburger	Luxemburg
Macedonia	Macedonian	Macedonian
Madagascar	Citizen of Madagascar	Malagasy
Malawi	Malawian	Malawian
Malayasia	Citizen of Malaysia	Malaysian
Maldives, the	Maldivian	Maldivian
Mali	Malian	Malian
Malta	Maltese	Maltese
Marshall Islands	Marshall Islander	Marshall Islands
Mauritanian	Mauritanian	Mauritanian
Mauritius	Mauritian	Mauritian
Mexico	Mexican	Mexican
Micronesia	Micronesian	Micronesian
Moldova	Moldavian	Moldavian
Monaco	Monegasque	Monegasque
Mongolia	Mongolian	Mongolian
Montenegro	Montenegrin	Montenegrin
Montserrat (*dependent territory*)	Montserratian	Monserrat
Morocco	Moroccan	Moroccan
Mozambique	Mozambican	Mozambican *or* Mozambique
Myanmar *see* Burma		
Namibia	Namibian	Namibian
Nauru	Nauruan	Nauruan
Nepal	Nepalese	Nepalese
Netherlands	Dutchman *or* Dutchwoman *or* Netherlander	Dutch *or* Netherlands
New Zealand	New Zealander	New Zealand
Nicaragua	Nicaraguan	Nicaraguan
Niger	Citizen of Niger	Niger
Nigeria	Nigerian	Nigerian
Northern Ireland	Ulsterman, Ulsterwoman	Northern Irish *or* Northern Ireland *or* Ulster
Norway	Norwegian	Norwegian
Oman	Omani	Omani *or* Oman
Pakistan	Pakistani	Pakistani
Panama	Panamanian	Panamanian
Papua New Guinea	Papua New Guinean	Papua New Guinean
Paraguay	Paraguayan	Paraguayan
Peru	Peruvian	Peruvian
Philippines	Filipino, Filipina	Philippine
Pitcairn Islands (*dependent territory*)	Pitcairn Islander	Pitcairn
Poland	Pole	Polish
Portugal	Portugese	Portuguese
Puerto Rico	Puerto Rican	Puerto Rican
Qatar	Qatari	Qatari *or* Qatar
Romania	Romanian	Romanian
Russia	Russian	Russian
Rwanda	Rwanadan	Rwandan
St Helena (*dependent territory*)	St Helenian	St Helenian or St Helena
St Kitts and Nevis	Citizen of St Kitts and Nevis	Kittitian, Nevisian, or St Kitts and Nevis
St Lucia	St Lucian	St Lucian *or* St Lucia
St Vincent	Vincentian	St Vincent
San Marino	Citizen of San Marino	San Marino
São Tomé and Principe	Citizen of São Tomé and Principe	of São Tomé and Principe
Saudi Arabia	Saudi Arabian *or* Saudi	Saudi Arabian *or* Saudi
Scotland	Scot, Scotsman, Scotswoman	Scottish *or* Scots *or* Scotch (*see* SCOTCH in the dictionary)
Senegal	Senegalese	Senegalese
Serbia	Serb	Serbian
Seychelles	Seychelles	Seychelles
Sierra Leone	Sierra Leone	Sierra Leone
Singapore	Singaporean	Singaporean
Slovakia	Slovak	Slovak
Slovenia	Slovene	Slovenian
Solomon Islands	Solomon Islander	Solomon Islands
Somalia	Somali	Somali
South Africa	South African	South African
Spain	Spaniard	Spanish
Sri Lanka	Citizen of Sri Lanka	Sri Lankan *or* Sri Lanka
Sudan	Sudanese	Sudanese
Suriname	Surinamer	Surinamese
Swaziland	Swazi	Swazi
Sweden	Swede	Swedish
Switzerland	Swiss	Swiss
Syria	Syrian	Syrian
Taiwan	Taiwanese	Taiwanese
Tajikistan	Tajik	Tajik
Tanzania	Tanzanian	Tanzanian
Thailand	Thai	Thai
Togo	Togolese	Togolese
Tonga	Tongan	Tongan
Trinidad and Tobago	Trinidadian and Tobagan *or* Tobagonian *or* Trinidad and Tobago citizen	Trinidadian and Tobagan *or* Tobagonian
Tunisia	Tunisian	Tunisian
Turkey	Turk	Turkish
Turkmenistan	Turkmen	Turkmen
Tuvalu	Tuvaluan	Tuvaluan
Uganda	Ugandan	Ugandan *or* Uganda
Ukraine	Ukrainian	Ukrainian
United Arab Emirates	Citizen of the United Arab Emirates	of the United Arab Emirates
United Kingdom	Briton	British
United States of America	United States citizen	United States
Uruguay	Uruguayan	Uruguayan
Uzbekistan	Uzbek	Uzbek
Vanuatu	Citizen of Vanuatu	Vanuatu

Appendix 18

country	person (*name in general use*)	related adjective (*in general use*)
Vatican City	Vatican citizen	Vatican
Venezuela	Venezuelan	Venezuelan
Vietnam	Vietnamese	Vietnamese
Virgin Islands	Virgin Islander	Virgin Islands
Wales	Welshman, Welshwoman	Welsh
Western Samoa	Western Samoan	Western Samoan
Yemen Arab Republic	Yemeni	Yemeni
Yemen, People's Democratic Republic of	South Yemeni	South Yemeni
Yugoslavia	Yugoslav	Yugoslav
Zaire	Zairean	Zairean
Zambia	Zambian	Zambian
Zimbabwe	Zimbabwean	Zimbabwean *or* Zimbabwe

Appendix 19 States of the United States of America

State (with official and postal abbreviations)	*Capital*	*Popular name*
Alabama (Ala., AL)	Montgomery	Yellowhammer State, Heart of Dixie, Cotton State
Alaska (Alas., AK)	Juneau	Great Land
Arizona (Ariz., AZ)	Phoenix	Grand Canyon State
Arkansas (Ark., AR)	Little Rock	Land of Opportunity
California (Calif., CA)	Sacramento	Golden State
Colorado (Col., CO)	Denver	Centennial State
Connecticut (Conn., CT)	Hartford	Constitution State, Nutmeg State
Delaware (Del., DE)	Dover	First State, Diamond State
Florida (Fla., FL)	Tallahassee	Sunshine State
Georgia (Ga., GA)	Atlanta	Empire State of the South, Peach State
Hawaii (HI)	Honolulu	The Aloha State
Idaho (ID)	Boise	Gem State
Illinois (Ill., IL)	Springfield	Prairie State
Indiana (Ind., IN)	Indianapolis	Hoosier State
Iowa (Ia., IA)	Des Moines	Hawkeye State
Kansas (Kan., KS)	Topeka	Sunflower State
Kentucky (Ky., KY)	Frankfort	Bluegrass State
Louisiana (La., LA)	Baton Rouge	Pelican State
Maine (Me., ME)	Augusta	Pine Tree State
Maryland (Md., MD)	Annapolis	Old Line State, Free State
Massachusetts (Mass., MA)	Boston	Bay State, Old Colony
Michigan (Mich., MI)	Lansing	Great Lake State, Wolverine State
Minnesota (Minn., MN)	St Paul	North Star State, Gopher State
Mississippi (Miss., MS)	Jackson	Magnolia State
Missouri (Mo., MO)	Jefferson City	Show Me State
Montana (Mont., MT)	Helena	Treasure State
Nebraska (Nebr., NB)	Lincoln	Cornhusker State
Nevada (Nev., NV)	Carson City	Sagebrush State, Battleborn State, Silver State
New Hampshire (NH)	Concord	Granite State
New Jersey (NJ)	Trenton	Garden State
New Mexico (N. Mex., NM)	Santa Fe	Land of Enchantment
New York (NY)	Albany	Empire State
North Carolina (NC)	Raleigh	Tar Heel State, Old North State
North Dakota (N. Dak., ND)	Bismarck	Peace Garden State
Ohio (OH)	Columbus	Buckeye State
Oklahoma (Okla., OK)	Oklahoma City	Sooner State
Oregon (Oreg., OR)	Salem	Beaver State
Pennsylvania (Pa., PA)	Harrisburg	Keystone State
Rhode Island (RI)	Providence	Little Rhody, Ocean State
South Carolina (SC)	Columbia	Palmetto State
South Dakota (S. Dak., SD)	Pierre	Coyote State, Sunshine State
Tennessee (Tenn., TN)	Nashville	Volunteer State
Texas (Tex., TX)	Austin	Lone Star State
Utah (UT)	Salt Lake City	Beehive State
Vermont (Vt., VT)	Montpelier	Green Mountain State
Virginia (Va., VA)	Richmond	Old Dominion
Washington (Wash., WA)	Olympia	Evergreen State
West Virginia (W. Va., WV)	Charleston	Mountain State
Wisconsin (Wis., WI)	Madison	Badger State
Wyoming (Wyo., WY)	Cheyenne	Equality State

Appendix 20 Alphabets

Alphabets for the deaf, and for the blind

finger spelling

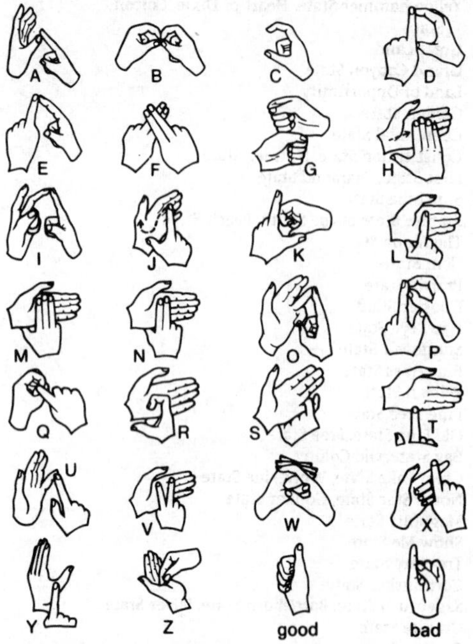

Braille

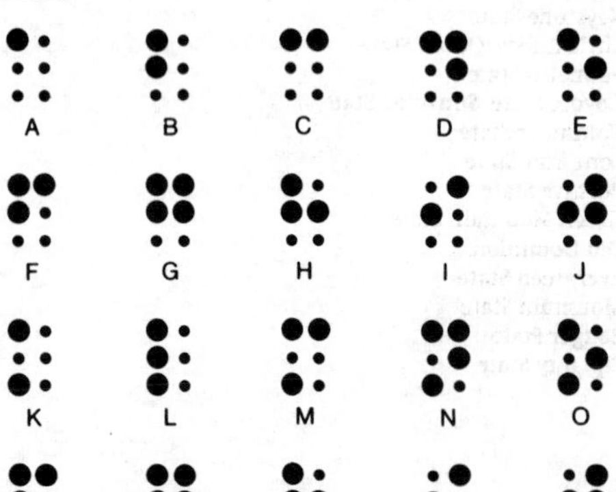

Alphabets for signalling

Morse code

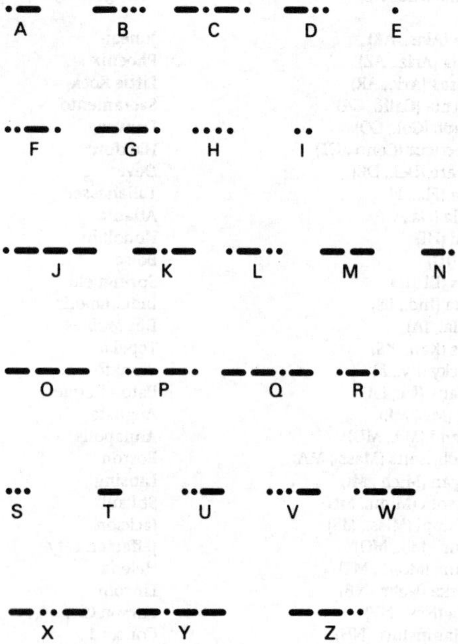

semaphore

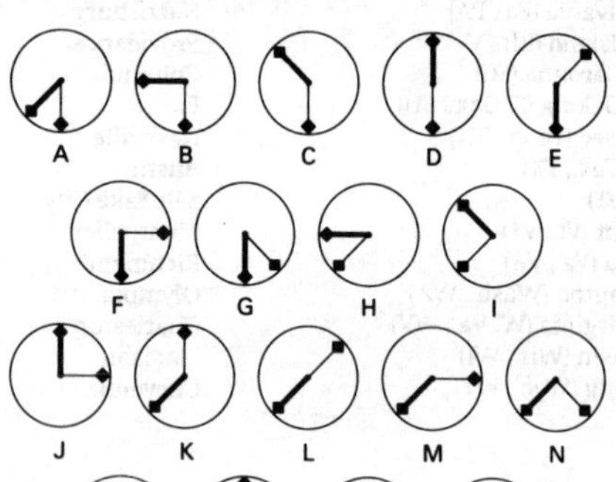

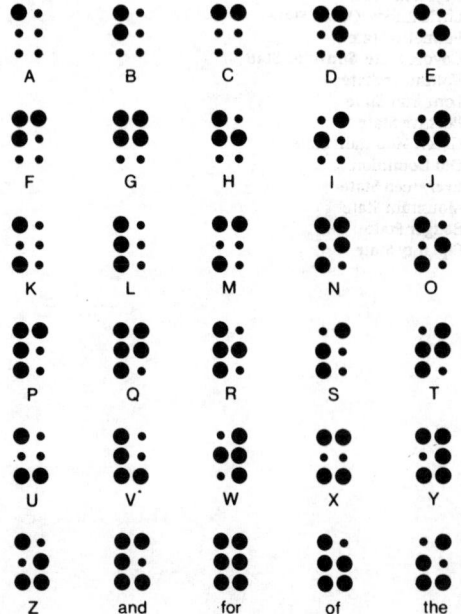

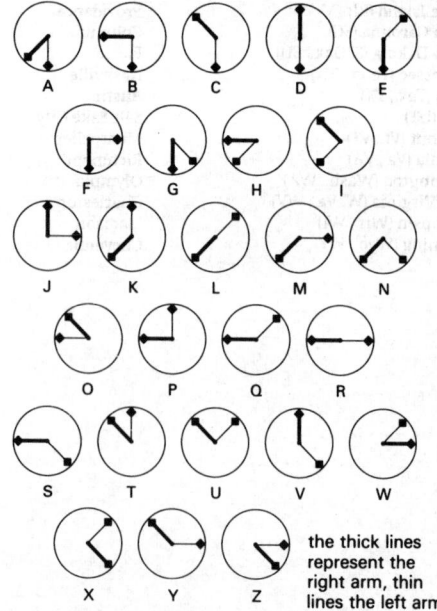

the thick lines represent the right arm, thin lines the left arm

Arabic

ا	ـا			'alif	'
ب	ـب	ـبـ	بـ	bā'	b
ت	ـت	ـتـ	تـ	tā'	t
ث	ـث	ـثـ	ثـ	thā'	th
ج	ـج	ـجـ	جـ	jīm	j
ح	ـح	ـحـ	حـ	ḥā'	ḥ
خ	ـخ	ـخـ	خـ	khā'	kh
د	ـد			dāl	d
ذ	ـذ			dhāl	dh
ر	ـر			rā'	r
ز	ـز			zay	z
س	ـس	ـسـ	سـ	sīn	s
ش	ـش	ـشـ	شـ	shīn	sh
ص	ـص	ـصـ	صـ	ṣād	ṣ
ض	ـض	ـضـ	ضـ	ḍād	ḍ
ط	ـط	ـطـ	طـ	ṭā'	ṭ
ظ	ـظ	ـظـ	ظـ	ẓā'	ẓ
ع	ـع	ـعـ	عـ	'ayn	'
غ	ـغ	ـغـ	غـ	ghayn	gh
ف	ـف	ـفـ	فـ	fā'	f
ق	ـق	ـقـ	قـ	qāf	q
ك	ـك	ـكـ	كـ	kāf	k
ل	ـل	ـلـ	لـ	lām	l
م	ـم	ـمـ	مـ	mīm	m
ن	ـن	ـنـ	نـ	nūn	n
ه	ـه	ـهـ	هـ	hā'	h
و	ـو			wāw	w
ى	ـى	ـيـ	يـ	yā'	y

Hebrew

א	aleph	'
ב	beth	b, bh
ג	gimel	g, gh
ד	daleth	d, dh
ה	he	h
ו	waw	w
ז	zayin	z
ח	ḥeth	ḥ
ט	ṭeth	ṭ
י	yodh	y
כ ך	kaph	k, kh
ל	lamedh	l
מ ם	mem	m
נ ן	nun	n
ס	samekh	s
ע	'ayin	'
פ ף	pe	p, ph
צ ץ	ṣadhe	ṣ
ק	qoph	q
ר	resh	r
שׂ	śin	ś
שׁ	shin	sh
ת	taw	t, th

Greek

Α α	alpha	a
Β β	beta	b
Γ γ	gamma	g
Δ δ	delta	d
Ε ϵ	epsilon	e
Ζ ζ	zeta	z
Η η	eta	ē
Θ θ	theta	th
Ι ι	iota	i
Κ κ	kappa	k
Λ λ	lambda	l
Μ μ	mu	m
Ν ν	nu	n
Ξ ξ	xi	x
Ο ο	omicron	o
Π π	pi	p
Ρ ρ	rho	r, rh
Σ σ ς	sigma	s
Τ τ	tau	t
Υ υ	upsilon	u
Φ φ	phi	ph
Χ χ	chi	kh
Ψ ψ	psi	ps
Ω ω	omega	ō

Russian

А а	a
Б б	b
В в	v
Г г	g
Д д	d
Е е	e
Ё ё	ë
Ж ж	zh
З з	z
И и	i
Й й	ĭ
К к	k
Л л	l
М м	m
Н н	n
О о	o
П п	p
Р р	r
С с	s
Т т	t
У у	u
Ф ф	f
Х х	kh
Ц ц	ts
Ч ч	ch
Ш ш	sh
Щ щ	shch
Ъ ъ	" ('hard sign')
Ы ы	y
Ь ь	' ('soft sign')
Э э	é
Ю ю	yu
Я я	ya

Appendix 21 Indo-European Languages

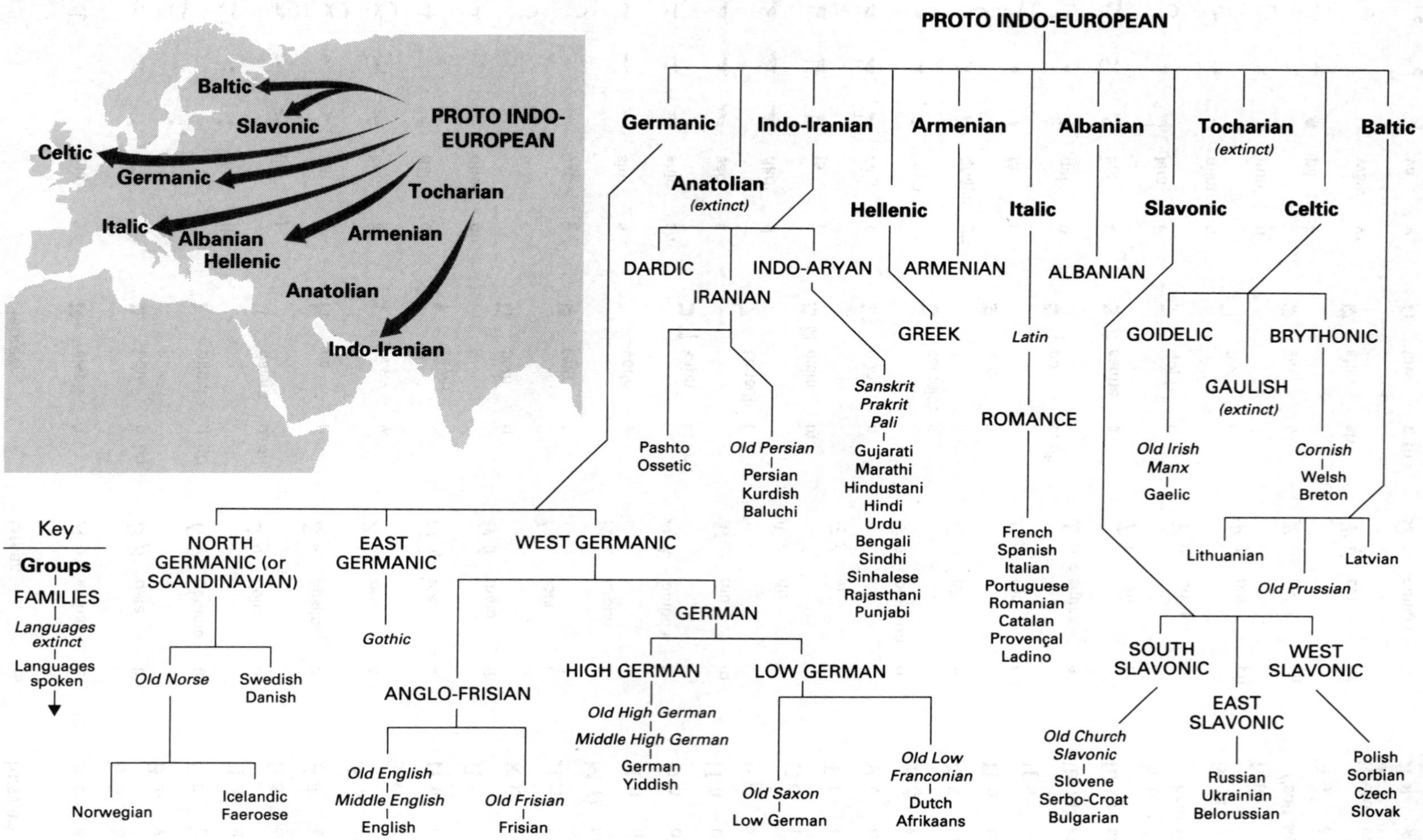

Appendix 22 Books of the Bible

Old Testament

Genesis (Gen.)
Exodus (Exod.)
Leviticus (Lev.)
Numbers (Num.)
Deuteronomy (Deut.)
Joshua (Josh.)
Judges (Judg.)
Ruth
First Book of Samuel (1 Sam.)
Second Book of Samuel (2 Sam.)
First Book of Kings (1 Kgs.)
Second Book of Kings (2 Kgs.)
First Book of Chronicles (1 Chr.)
Second Book of Chronicles (2 Chr.)
Ezra
Nehemiah (Neh.)
Esther
Job
Psalms (Ps.)
Proverbs (Prov.)
Ecclesiastes (Eccles.)
Song of Songs, Song of Solomon, Canticles (S. of S., Cant.)
Isaiah (Isa.)
Jeremiah (Jer.)
Lamentations (Lam.)
Ezekiel (Ezek.)
Daniel (Dan.)
Hosea (Hos.)
Joel
Amos
Obadiah (Obad.)
Jonah
Micah (Mic.)
Nahum (Nah.)
Habakkuk (Hab.)
Zephaniah (Zeph.)
Haggai (Hag.)
Zechariah (Zech.)
Malachi (Mal.)

Apocrypha

First Book of Esdras (1 Esd.)
Second Book of Esdras (2 Esd.)
Tobit
Judith
Rest of Esther (Rest of Esth.)
Wisdom of Solomon (Wisd.)
Ecclesiasticus, Wisdom of Jesus the Son of Sirach (Ecclus., Sir.)
Baruch
Song of the Three Children (S. of III Ch.)
Susanna (Sus.)
Bel and the Dragon (Bel & Dr.)
Prayer of Manasses (Pr. of Man.)
First Book of Maccabees (1 Macc.)
Second Book of Maccabees (2 Macc.)

New Testament

Gospel according to St Matthew (Matt.)
Gospel according to St Mark (Mark)
Gospel according to St Luke (Luke)
Gospel according to St John (John)
Acts of the Apostles (Acts)
Epistle to the Romans (Rom.)
First Epistle to the Corinthians (1 Cor.)
Second Epistle to the Corinthians (2 Cor.)
Epistle to the Galatians (Gal.)
Epistle to the Ephesians (Eph.)
Epistle to the Philippians (Phil.)
Epistle to the Colossians (Col.)
First Epistle to the Thessalonians (1 Thess.)
Second Epistle to the Thessalonians (2 Thess.)
First Epistle to Timothy (1 Tim.)
Second Epistle to Timothy (2 Tim.)
Epistle to Titus (Tit.)
Epistle to Philemon (Philem.)
Epistle to the Hebrews (Heb.)
Epistle of James (Jas.)
First Epistle of Peter (1 Pet.)
Second Epistle of Peter (2 Pet.)
First Epistle of John (1 John)
Second Epistle of John (2 John)
Third Epistle of John (3 John)
Epistle of Jude (Jude)
Revelation, Apocalypse (Rev., Apoc.)

Appendix 23 Leaders and Rulers

aga high-ranking official of the Ottoman Empire

Asantehene paramount chief of the Ashanti people of West Africa

ataman/hetman Cossack chief

ayatollah highest ranking religious leader of the Shiite branch of Islam

bey/beg provincial governor or other high official in the Ottoman Empire

cacique chief of an American Indian tribe in Latin America; local political boss in Latin America

Caesar Roman emperor; any powerful or dictatorial leader

caliph ruler of a Muslim state

capo divisional leader in the Mafia

caudillo Spanish military dictator

Chogyal ruler of Sikkim

collector chief administrative officer of a district of India during British rule

consul chief official or magistrate in the ancient Roman Republic, ruling in a pair

Dalai Lama leader of Tibetan Buddhists

dey Turkish governor or commander in Algeria in former times

doge chief magistrate of the old republics of Venice and of Genoa

duce leader or ruler in Italy

emir Muslim prince, chieftain, or governor in the Middle East

fugleman political leader; formerly, a leader or demonstrator in military drill

Führer leader or dictator in Germany

Gauleiter district governor in Nazi Germany

kabaka former ruler of the Baganda people of Uganda

Kaiser Holy Roman emperor, Austro-Hungarian emperor, or German emperor

khan/cham medieval emperor or ruler in China or central Asia

khedive viceroy in Egypt during the period of Ottoman control

mandarin senior civil servant in imperial China; any powerful and relatively independent official

mikado, Tenno emperor of Japan

nawab Muslim prince or ruler in India in former times

nizam former ruler of Hyderabad

pasha former provincial governor in the Ottoman Empire

sachem, sagamore North American Indian tribal chief

satrap provincial governor in ancient Persia; any dictatorial minor ruler

sheikh leader of an Arab tribe or village; Muslim religious leader

shogun Japanese military commander, especially any of those who effectively ruled Japan in former times

stadholder chief magistrate or provincial governor in the Netherlands in former times

sultan ruler of a Muslim state, especially under the Ottoman Empire

suzerain feudal lord

Taoiseach prime minister of the Irish Republic

tetrarch any of four joint rulers, or ruler of a quarter of a region; prince enjoying limited power in the Roman Empire

tsar emperor of Russia in former times

tuchun military governor of a Chinese province in former times

viceroy governor of a country, colony, or the like, ruling in the name of his sovereign or government

vizier high-ranking official, such as provincial governor or chief minister, in Muslim countries, especially under the Ottoman Empire

40-343-5